EDUCATION   AT SE

The Penguin English Dictionary

THE
PENGUIN
ENGLISH DICTIONARY

Consultant Editor
Robert Allen

PENGUIN BOOKS

PENGUIN BOOKS

Published by the Penguin Group
Penguin Books Ltd, 80 Strand, London WC2R 0RL, England
Penguin Putnam Inc., 375 Hudson Street, New York, New York 10014, USA
Penguin Books Australia Ltd, 250 Camberwell Road, Camberwell, Victoria 3124, Australia
Penguin Books Canada Ltd, 10 Alcorn Avenue, Toronto, Ontario, Canada M4V 3B2
Penguin Books India (P) Ltd, 11, Community Centre, Panchsheel Park, New Delhi – 110 017, India
Penguin Books (NZ) Ltd, Cnr Rosedale and Airborne Roads, Albany, Auckland, New Zealand
Penguin Books (South Africa) (Pty) Ltd, 24 Sturdee Avenue, Rosebank 2196, South Africa

Penguin Books Ltd, Registered Offices: 80 Strand, London WC2R 0RL, England

www.penguin.com

First published as a Penguin hardback 2000
Published in Penguin Books 2001
This revised edition published 2003
1

Original material copyright © Merriam-Webster Inc. and Longman Group Ltd, 1986
Revisions, updating and new material copyright © Penguin Books, 2000, 2003
All rights reserved

ISBN (HARDBACK EDITION) 014051533X

Typeset in ITC Stone
Printed in Finland by WS Bookwell

The English language is used by over a billion people, or a quarter of the world's population, a figure that is higher than for any other language and is still growing. Of these, about 400 million people speak English as their first language. It makes English the most universally used language since Latin spread through the western world under Roman rule; and like Latin, English has spread in the wake of political power, first British and later American.

English is constantly changing, acquiring new words and meanings and new patterns of grammar and usage. We are all aware of new words and meanings coming into use; electronic communication, to take just one area of human activity, has given us *email, e-commerce, dotcoms, viruses, smart cards,* and *virtual reality.* But changes closer to the core of English are taking place less noticeably. As well as telling people to *turn round* and *make up,* we now speak about them *chilling out, dumbing down,* and being *spaced out,* phrases that were hardly known as little as ten years ago and build in seemingly unlimited ways on the most basic words of English vocabulary. Increased sensitivities about the ways in which we refer to gender, ethnic origin, religions, and social minorities are continuing to have a major impact on the way we use language and on the language itself.

In this new dictionary we do a great deal more than list words and explain how to spell them and what they mean, important though these things are. Users of dictionaries want to know more about the different uses of English as spoken and written today, about the origins of words and phrases, about the concepts that lie behind words, and about uses from the past which, while no longer forming a part of everyday communication, are encountered in reading and broadcasting, in the arts, and in other areas of human activity and learning.

All these aspects of language are dealt with in special features of the dictionary entries. Many of the illustrative examples are taken from real usage in literature ranging from Shakespeare to the present day. The accounts of word origins (etymologies) include extra historical information on words of special interest (such as *assassin, cabal, codswallop, juggernaut, marathon,* and *silhouette*) and, uniquely in a dictionary of this size, include phrases and idioms (such as *carry the can* and *go by the board*) as well as single words, many of them colourful and surprising in their diversity. To go behind the facts of words' meanings to explore the concepts behind them, we have invited a range of distinguished writers and academics to write miniature essays on topics that relate to their work.

The result of all these extra features is a dictionary that is not just a word list but a guide to the living language of today and its roots in the past.

REA
June 2000

The world has changed in the three years since this dictionary was first published, and the English language, one of the greatest organs of communication the world has seen, has moved on with it. Every aspect of technological progress seems to entail the vocabulary of menace. The Internet, while still a resource of ever-increasing richness, has taken on sinister aspects reflected in *cyberstalking* and *grooming,* and our high street technology has given rise to the risk of *identity theft* and *shoulder surfing.* Overcrowded cities face *congestion charging.* The language of war and terror attests to the heightened awareness of global horrors, with *wake-up calls, WMDs, bioterrorism, dirty bombs, standoff weapons,* and other terms whose linguistic simplicity belies a savagery that is hard to comprehend. Meanwhile the language of everyday life continues undaunted and apace: *chick-lit* has been joined by *lad-lit, text messaging* by *photo, picture,* and *multimedia messaging,* and *web pages* by *weblogs* for *Netizens* to find and communicate with one another. So the language of social interaction affords us grounds for consolation and optimism.

This updated edition of a highly acclaimed dictionary keeps pace with all these developments, and continues to be a rich resource for understanding the use of English throughout a much-altered world.

REA
March 2003

Acknowledgments

Consultant Editor
Robert Allen

Publishing Director
Nigel Wilcockson

Publisher
Martin Toseland

Lexicographers
Stephen Curtis, George Davidson, Andrew Delahunty,
Jessica Feinstein, Rosalind Fergusson, Alice Grandison,
Patricia Marshall, Howard Sargeant, Anne Seaton

Phonetics Editor
Jock Graham

Etymologies Editor
Fred McDonald

Usage Editors
Stephen Curtis
Martin Manser

Editorial Checking
Richard Duguid, Colin Hope, Helen Kemp, Helen Liebeck,
Jenny Rayner, Ellie Smith

Database Editor
Rachael Arthur

Proof-readers
Audrey Aitken, Anne Cook, David Cumming, David
Duguid, John English, Guy Holland, Anthony John,
Henrietta Llewelyn-Davies, Michael Page, Stephen Perkin,
Anne Hendrie Williams, Norman Woods

Designer
Richard Marston

Database Systems
Librios Ltd

Typesetting
Gem Graphics

Specialist Advisers and Contributors

Peter Atkins
*Professor of Chemistry, University of Oxford, and Fellow of
Lincoln College*

Paul Bahn
Archaeologist and freelance writer

Jill Bailey
Biologist and freelance writer

Catherine Belsey
*Chair of Centre for Critical and Cultural Theory,
University of Wales, Cardiff*

Dr Susan Blackmore
Reader in Psychology, University of West of England

David Blatner
Freelance writer

Vernon Bogdanor
Professor of Government and Politics, University of Oxford

Malcolm Bradbury
Professor of American Studies, University of East Anglia

Simon Bradley
Assistant Editor, Buildings of England

Bridget Cherry
Editor, Buildings of England

Peter Clarke
Professor of Modern British History, University of Cambridge

Andrew Clements
Chief music critic of the Guardian

Michael Clugston
Teacher and science writer

Richard Cook
Writer on jazz

Dr John Cormack
Medical writer and broadcaster

David Crystal
Honorary Professor of Linguistics, University of Wales

Dr Andrew Dalby
Linguist and historian

Jonathan Dancy
Professor of Philosophy, University of Reading

Evan Davis
BBC Economics correspondent

Richard Dawkins
*Simonyi Professor of the Public Understanding of Science,
University of Oxford*

Michael Freeden
Professor of Politics, University of Oxford

Martin Gayford
Art critic of the Spectator and Daily Telegraph

Dr A C Grayling
*Reader in Philosophy, Birkbeck College, University of
London*

Jonathon Green
Slang lexicographer, writer, and broadcaster

Richard Gregory
Professor of Neuropsychology, University of Bristol

Amanda Holden
*Librettist, opera translator, and founder-editor of the
Penguin Opera Guides*

Christopher Hookway
Professor of Philosophy, University of Sheffield

Helena Kennedy, QC
Chair of the British Council

Professor Leszek Kołakowski
*Emeritus Professor, Committee of Social Thought,
University of Chicago*

Donald S Lopez, Jr
*Carl W Belser Professor of Buddhist and Tibetan Studies,
University of Michigan*

Thomas Mautner
*Senior Lecturer, Department of Philosophy, Australian
National University*

Dr Jacqueline Mitton
Writer on astronomy

David Nelson
*Lecturer in Education (Mathematics), University of
Manchester*

Jill Norman
Writer on food and wine

Charles O'Brien
Research Assistant, Buildings of England

Dick Pountain
*Technical author, magazine editor, and director of
Dennis Publishing*

Dr Mark Ridley
*Research Associate, Department of Zoology,
Oxford University*

Geoffrey Robertson, QC
Head of Doughty Street Chambers

John Rogerson
Emeritus Professor of Biblical Studies, University of Sheffield

Adrian Room
Specialist lexicographer

Steven Rose
*Professor of Biology and Director of the Brain and Behaviour
Research Group, Open University*

Michael Thain
Member of the Department of Biology, Harrow School

Ben Thompson
Freelance writer and critic

Dr Mel Thompson
*Consultant Editor, Oneworld Publications, Oxford, and
freelance writer*

David Thomson
Film writer

Dr Maria Tippett
*Member of the Faculty of History and Fellow of Churchill
College, University of Cambridge*

Martin Tolley
Freelance writer

Dr John Whittow
Senior Lecturer (retired), University of Reading

Guide to the Dictionary

The text of the dictionary has been organized in a way that calls for the minimum of additional explanation. The display below shows the main features of a dictionary entry, and this is followed by notes on special points of interest and an explanation of the pronunciation system.

headword

darter /'dahtə/ *noun* **1** a fish-eating bird that has a long slender neck and flies with darting movements: genus *Anhinga*. **2** either of two genera of small, brightly coloured freshwater fishes of N America: genera *Etheostoma* and *Percina*. **3** any of several species of dragonflies with a wide body that catch prey by darting out from a perch: family Libellulidae and related families.

pronunciation

Dartmoor pony /'dahtmaw/ *noun* an animal of an old breed of small shaggy English ponies. [named after *Dartmoor*, region of SW England where the breed originated]

part of speech

darts /dahts/ *pl noun* (*usu treated as sing.*) an indoor game in which darts are thrown at a dartboard to score points.

Darwinism /'dahwiniz(ə)m/ *noun* a theory of evolution developed by Charles Darwin. It asserts that widely divergent groups of plants and animals have arisen from common ancestors as a result of natural selection of offspring which develop slight variations that make them better adapted to their environment.

editorial note

Editorial note
A term used for evolution itself (which Darwin did most to establish) and for Darwin's theory of its mechanism – natural selection. Darwin himself recognized other causes of evolution, but only natural selection accounts for the apparent 'design' of organisms. Neo-Darwinism unites Darwinism with Mendelism: particulate genes have a frequency in the gene pool, which is biased over the generations by non-random selection — Professor Richard Dawkins.

⯈⯈ **Darwinian** /dah'wini·ən/ *noun and adj*, **Darwinist** *noun and adj*. [Charles *Darwin* d.1882, English naturalist]

definition

dash[1] /dash/ *verb intrans* **1** to move with speed or haste. **2** to smash against something. ⯈ *verb trans* **1a** to hurl or fling (something) with great force. **b** to strike or knock (something) violently. **2** to destroy or ruin (a hope or plan). [Middle English *dasshen*, prob of imitative origin]

word origin (etymology)

dash[2] *noun* **1** a punctuation mark (—) used to indicate a break in the structure of a sentence, or to stand for missing words or letters. **2** in Morse code, a signal, e.g. a flash or audible tone, of relatively long duration: compare DOT[1] (5). **3** in music, a vertical line written above or below a note, showing that it is to be played staccato. **4a** a speedy or hasty movement or journey. **b** *chiefly NAmer* a sprint. **5** a small amount of a substance: *a dash of salt*. **6** liveliness of style and action; panache. **7** = DASHBOARD.

regional label

dash[3] *interj Brit, informal, dated* used to express annoyance.

dashboard *noun* a panel containing dials and controls in a car or other vehicle.

word history

Word history
DASH[1], in an obsolete sense 'to splash, splatter', + BOARD[1]. A dashboard was orig a board or panel that protected the driver of a carriage from being splattered with mud.

usage label

dashed /dasht/ *adj Brit, informal, dated* used for emphasis: *a dashed pity*.

dashiki /də'sheeki/ *noun* (*pl* **dashikis**) a loose brightly coloured shirt without buttons, traditionally worn by men in W Africa. [alteration of Yoruba *danshiki*]

dashing *adj* **1** marked by vigorous action; spirited. **2** smart and stylish in dress and manners. >> **dashingly** *adv.*

dash off *verb trans* to complete or execute (e.g. writing or drawing) hastily.

dashpot *noun* a device for cushioning or damping a movement, e.g. of a mechanical part, to avoid shock.

dassie /'dahsi/ *noun* any of several species of hyraxes of Africa and SW Asia, *esp* the rock hyrax: family Procaviidae. [Afrikaans *dassie* from Dutch *das* badger]

dastard /'dastəd/ *noun archaic* a coward, *esp* one who commits malicious acts. [Middle English, perhaps from Old Norse *dæstr* exhausted]

dastardly *adj dated* despicably malicious or cowardly: *One could do a dastardly thing if one chose, but it was contemptible to regret it afterwards* — Somerset Maugham. >> **dastardliness** *noun.*

illustrative example of usage

dasyure /'dasiyooə/ *noun* any of a genus of tree-dwelling flesh-eating marsupial mammals of Australia and Tasmania resembling large weasels: genus *Dasyurus*. Also called QUOLL. [Greek *dasys* thick with hair + *oura* tail]

DAT /dat/ *abbr* digital audiotape.

dat. *abbr* dative.

data /'daytə/ *pl noun* (*treated as sing. or pl*) **1** factual information, e.g. measurements or statistics, used as a basis for reasoning, discussion, or calculation. **2** in computing, the numbers, characters, etc on which a computer operates. [pl of DATUM]

Usage note
Data is, strictly speaking, a plural noun with a comparatively rare singular form *datum*. With the advent of computers and data processing, *data* has come increasingly to be seen and used as a singular mass noun like *information* or *news*: *The data is currently being processed.* Traditionalists insist however that this should be: *The data are currently being processed.*

usage note on points of grammar and language sensitivity

databank *noun* a collection of computer data organized for rapid search and retrieval, e.g. by computer.

database *noun* a set of data held in structured form by a computer.

database management system *noun* a software system that organizes and arranges the structure of data in a database and controls access to, input to, and output of that data.

datable or **dateable** /'daytəbl/ *adj* able to be given a particular date.

alternative spelling

data capture *noun* in computing, the act of collecting data and converting it into a form that a computer can use, or a method of doing this.

data compression *noun* in computing, the reorganization or restructuring of data so that it takes up less storage space.

dataglove *noun* a glove fitted with sensors that transmits the hand movements of the person wearing it to a virtual-reality system.

data mining *noun* in marketing, counterespionage, etc: the computer analysis of large databases for the purpose of extracting from them useful but previously undiscovered information.

data processing *noun* the entering, storing, maintaining, and arranging of data, *esp* by a computer. >> **data processor** *noun.*

derived word with meaning deducible from the headword

data protection *noun Brit* legal protection of the privacy and security of information stored in computers.

datcha /'dahchə/ *noun* see DACHA.

cross-reference to another entry

date[1] /dayt/ *noun* **1** a particular day of the month or year, identified by a number or phrase. **2a** the time at which a particular event has occurred or will occur. **b** the period of time to which something belongs. **c** (*in pl*) the two dates marking the beginning and end of something, *esp* the dates of somebody's birth and death. **3** *informal* **a** an appointment, *esp* a romantic or social engagement. **b** a person with whom one has arranged such an appointment. **4** a show or concert, *esp* one that is part of a series being performed in different venues. * **to date** until the present moment. [Middle English via French from Latin *data*, as in *data Romae* (letter) given at Rome, fem past part. of *dare* to give]

idiom or phrase

date[2] *verb trans* **1** to determine the date of (something). **2** to mark (a document, letter, etc) with a date. **3** to make (somebody) appear old-fashioned: *His record collection dates him.* **4** *informal* to go on a date with (somebody). >> *verb intrans* **1** (*usu* + from) to have been in existence for a specified time: *coins dating from Anglo-*

grammatical information showing how a word is used in context

inflected form when irregular or noteworthy

Alternative spellings

Some words in English can be correctly spelt in more than one way (such as **judgment** and **judgement**). In these cases the alternative forms are given after the headword or at an appropriate place in the entry if they apply to a particular meaning:

aboulia or **abulia** /ay'boohli·ə/ *noun* in psychiatry, a pathological loss of willpower...

bourbon /'buhbən, 'booəbən (*French* burbɔ̃)/ *noun* **1** (**Bourbon**) a member of a royal dynasty who ruled in France, Spain, etc. **2** (*often* **Bourbon**) *chiefly NAmer* an extreme political reactionary...

Spellings that are used in American English are shown with the label *NAmer*:

colour[1] (*NAmer* **color**) /'kulə/ *noun* **1 a** a visual sensation, e.g. of redness, blueness, etc, caused by the wavelength of perceived light. **b** the property of objects and light sources that enables...

The distinction implied here is not absolute, since usage varies considerably within North America. Spellings labelled as American are sometimes also found in British English and in other varieties of English; conversely British spellings are also sometimes found in American English and in other varieties. Information of this kind indicates what is typical rather than what is invariable.

Inflections

Inflections, or changes in the endings of words (mainly nouns, verbs, and adjectives), are given when they are irregular or, though regular, cause users difficulty.

The following inflections are regarded as regular and are not routinely given:

- third person singular present tenses of verbs formed by adding *-s* to the stem, or *-es* to stems ending in *-s*, *-x*, *-z*, *-sh*, or soft *-ch*, e.g. **look**, **looks**; **stare**, **stares**; **mash**, **mashes**, **crunch**, **crunches**.

- past tense and past participles of verbs formed by adding *-ed* to the stem, verbs ending in a silent *-e* dropping this *e*: e.g. **look**, **looked**; **stare**, **stared**.

- present participles of verbs formed by adding *-ing* to the stem, verbs ending in a silent *-e* dropping this *e*: e.g. **look**, **looking**; **stare**, **staring**.

- plurals of nouns formed by adding *-s* to the stem, or *-es* to stems ending in *-s*, *-x*, *-z*, *-sh*, or soft *-ch*: **bat**, **bats**; **fox**, **foxes**; **sash**, **sashes**; **church**, **churches**.

Other types of inflection are shown after the headword:

brag[1] /brag/ *verb intrans* (**bragged**, **bragging**) to talk boastfully...

query[2] *verb trans* (**queries**, **queried**, **querying**) **1 a** to question the accuracy of (e.g. a statement)...

go[1] /goh/ *verb* (*past tense* **went** /went/, *past part.* **gone** /gon/) ➤ *verb intrans* **1** to proceed on a course; to travel...

Comparative and superlative forms of adjectives and adverbs are shown when these involve modification of the stem, principally doubling of a final consonant or changing a final *y* to *i*:

hot[1] /hot/ *adj* (**hotter**, **hottest**) **1** having a relatively high temperature...

dry[1] /drie/ *adj* (**drier** *or* **dryer**, **driest** *or* **dryest**) **1 a** free from moisture or liquid, *esp* water...

Comparative and superlative forms are also shown for adjectives and adverbs of more than one syllable that have such forms: principally adjectives ending in *-y* (**happier**, **happiest**) and their negative forms (**unhappier**, **unhappi-**

est) and a few others such as **commoner**, **commonest** and **pleasanter**, **pleasantest**. Others have to be formed with *more* and *most* (such as **more hostile**, **most hostile**).

Grammar

The traditional names are used to identify wordclasses or parts of speech. These are *noun*, *verb*, *adj* (= adjective), *adv* (= adverb), *pronoun*, *conj* (= conjunction), *prep* (= preposition), and *interj* (= interjection or exclamation).

The words used to link words (especially verbs) to other words in sentences, known as collocations, are shown in round brackets:

aware /ə'weə/ *adj* **1** (*often* + of) having or showing realization; conscious of something: *I was not aware of her presence till she spoke...*

Typical objects of transitive verbs are shown by means of round brackets:

confuse /kən'fyoohz/ *verb trans* **1** to bewilder or perplex (somebody). **2** *archaic* to embarrass or abash (somebody). **3** to muddle or befuddle (a person or their mind, etc); *He had not drunk enough wine to confuse his wits...*

Other labels used to show grammatical information are:

VERBS

in passive: shows that the verb is used in the passive voice in the meaning being given:

reincarnate /reein'kahnayt/ *verb trans* (*usu in passive*) to cause (a person or his or her soul) to be reborn in another body after death...

NOUNS

in pl: shows that the noun is used in the plural form in the meaning being given:

ablution /ə'bloohsh(ə)n/ *noun* **1** (*usu in pl*) the washing of the body. **2** the washing of the hands, sacred vessels, etc in a ritual purification...

treated as sing.: shows that the noun is used in the plural but takes a singular form of verb:

Chinese chequers (*NAmer* **Chinese checkers**) *pl noun* (*treated as sing.*) a board game for two to six players...

These labels are sometimes qualified by the word *usu* (= usually), which shows that the word is mostly, but not always, used in the way indicated.

Idioms and phrases

These are put in a single alphabetical sequence at the end of the entry:

better /'betə/ *adj* **1** of a higher quality or more excellent type. **2** more appropriate or advisable: *It would be better to take them with you.* **3** improved in health; partly or wholly recovered from an illness or injury: *Is she at all better yet?* ✳ **better off** enjoying better circumstances, *esp* financially. **go one better** to improve slightly on what somebody else has achieved. **the better part of** most or nearly all of something: *We waited for the better part of an hour...*

Multi-word items that are noun-equivalents (such as **man of God**) and unvariable are usually entered as main entries in their own right.

Phrasal verbs consisting of a verb and an adverb (e.g. **come off**, **take in**) are entered as main entries.

Usage labels and notes

Levels of formality with which words are associated are shown by the following labels:

formal	shows that the word is normally confined to written and printed documents
literary	shows that the word is normally found in literature

archaic	shows that the word is mainly found in older usage and has a dated or old-fashioned effect in modern contexts
non-standard	shows that the word is not regarded as standard (e.g. *ain't*) either in writing or in speech
dated	shows that the word is no longer in general use but is occasionally heard or seen in print
humorous	shows that the word is normally intended to sound amusing or witty
dialect	shows that the word is not part of standard English but is used locally in parts of the English-speaking world
informal	shows that the word is normally confined to conversation and informal writing
slang	shows that the word is highly informal and is mainly used by particular groups (e.g. young people)
coarse slang	used for slang words that are regarded as vulgar or offensive
derog (= derogatory)	shows that the word is normally used in a depreciatory or disapproving way
offensive	shows that the word normally causes offence
taboo	shows that the word is normally regarded as socially unacceptable
euphem (= euphemistic)	shows that the word is normally used as a euphemism, i.e. as a more pleasant-sounding alternative for an unpleasant word or concept

Special notes are given at some entries to alert the user to usage that is controversial or disputed:

Usage note

Feasible means 'able to be done or capable of being dealt with': *a feasible project*. Its use to mean 'likely' or 'probable' (*a feasible explanation of the events*) is best avoided in formal contexts.

Regional labels

Words and meanings that are chiefly used in certain regional varieties of English are marked accordingly:

bagman *noun* (*pl* **bagmen**) **1** *chiefly Brit, dated* a sales representative; a travelling salesman. **2** *chiefly NAmer* a person who collects or distributes dishonestly or illegally gained money, on behalf of another. **3** *Aus* a tramp; a swagman.

Again distinctions are not always clear-cut. For example, many uses identified as North American or as British are also used in other parts of the English-speaking world, such as Australia and New Zealand, and uses identified as Australian may also have filtered into North American use and even into occasional British use.

Cross-references

These are shown in small capital letters:

abduct /əb'dukt/ *verb trans* **1** to carry (somebody) off secretly or by force: compare KIDNAP. **2** said of a muscle: to draw away (a limb etc) from a position near or parallel to the main part of the body: compare ADDUCT¹...

Sometimes it is necessary in explaining technical terms to refer to other technical terms. In these cases we have added a short gloss or explanation, so that the definition is self-contained but still links the information to related terms that users can look up if they wish to:

jurat /'jooərat/ *noun* **1** a certificate added to an AFFIDAVIT (sworn declaration in writing) stating when, before whom, and where it was made...

Word origins

Word origins, or etymologies, are shown in square brackets at the end of entries. The immediate source language is given first, followed by earlier languages leading back to the ultimate source, or the earliest known source:

assess /ə'ses/ *verb trans* **1** to determine the rate or amount of (a tax, claim for damages, etc)... [Middle English *assessen*, prob from medieval Latin *assess-*, past part. stem of *assidēre* to sit beside, assist in the office of a judge, from AS- + *sedēre* to sit]

In some cases the source is an earlier form of English, either Old English (or Anglo-Saxon, the form in use from the 7th century to the Norman Conquest) or Middle English (the form that developed under French influence after the Norman Conquest, from the 12th century to the late 15th century).

In some entries, additional historical information has been added where this is of special interest.

junket¹ /'jungkit/ *noun* **1** a dessert of sweetened flavoured milk curdled with rennet. **2** *chiefly informal* a trip made by an official, business person, etc at public or a firm's expense.

Word history

Middle English *ioncate* rush basket, ultimately from Latin *juncus* rush. In the 15th cent. the word referred to a kind of cream cheese made in a rush basket or served on a rush mat, later to other dishes made with cream; (sense 2) from a 16th-cent. sense 'feast, banquet'.

Word elements (such as *in-*, *re-*, *un-*, etc) are given in the form of cross-references when there are separate entries for them. This is done regardless of whether the element originated in a source language (as with IN- in *indifferent* and RE- in *recapitulate*) or in English (as with IN- in *inexact* and RE- in *recapture*).

Pronunciation

Pronunciations are shown within slashes / / after headwords or other word forms. Pronunciations vary within the British Isles and throughout the English-speaking world. The system followed here is the so-called 'Received Pronunciation' characteristic of educated speech in southeast England and conventionally used as a model in the teaching of English.

The following characters are used to represent sounds in English:

CONSONANTS

b, d, f, h, k, l, m, n, p, r, s, t, v, w, and z have their normal values.

ch	stands for the sound as in	cheer
dh	stands for the sound as in	they
g	stands for the sound as in	get
j	stands for the sound as in	jump
kh	stands for the sound as in	loch
ng	stands for the sound as in	sing
nh	stands for the sound as in	restaurant
sh	stands for the sound as in	ship
th	stands for the sound as in	thing
y	stands for the sound as in	yell
z	stands for the sound as in	zero

VOWELS

short vowels:

a	stands for the sound as in	hat
e	stands for the sound as in	bed
i	stands for the sound as in	sit, happy
o	stands for the sound as in	pot, cough
u	stands for the sound as in	mud, tough
ə	stands for the sound as in	alike, porter

The symbol (ə), with round brackets, indicates that the following consonant (normally l, m, or n) has a syllabic value, as in *garden*.

long vowels:

ah	stands for the sound as in	father
aw	stands for the sound as in	horn, awful
ee	stands for the sound as in	sheep, team

ie	stands for the sound as in	bite, fight
oh	stands for the sound as in	bone, loan
oo	stands for the sound as in	book, put
ooh	stands for the sound as in	boot, lute
uh	stands for the sound as in	bird, absurd

A vowel sound is called 'strong' when the syllable is pronounced with special emphasis, as in *I'll **be*** (= /bee/) *there* as distinct from *I'll be* (= /bi/) ***there***.

diphthongs (vowels made up of two sounds) and triphthongs (vowels made up of three sounds):

ay	stands for the sound as in	day
eə	stands for the sound as in	hair, there
ie·ə	stands for the sound as in	fire
iə	stands for the sound as in	beer, here
ooə	stands for the sound as in	cure, jury
ow	stands for the sound as in	now, rout
owə	stands for the sound as in	sour, power
oy	stands for the sound as in	boy, loiter

The main stress in a word, i.e. the syllable that receives the main emphasis, is shown by the raised symbol ', as in

father /'fahdhə/

A secondary stress, if any, is shown by the inferior symbol ,, as in

annunciation /ə,nunsi'aysh(ə)n/

Words and phrases that are borrowed from other languages (such as French *amour propre* and German *Bildungsroman*) tend to develop an anglicized pronunciation, and this is the form normally given for these items. For less fully assimilated French and German words a pronunciation reflecting that of the original language is also given. Because the letters of the English alphabet are inadequate for this purpose, special symbols of the International Phonetic Alphabet are used. A table of these is given below.

Symbol	as in:		Nearest English Equivalent
	French	German	
i	nid	Inhalt	heat
iː	—	riechen	feed
iə	—	Bier	beer
e	été	Medikament	day
eː	—	mehr	fair
ε	sept	Kette	pet
εː	mère	Rätsel	fair
eə	—	Wiedersehen	fair
a	patte	Album	cart
aː	tard	—	card
aɪ	—	Fräulein	tie
aʊ	—	auf	cow
ɑ	bas	Ahnung	card
ɑː	sable	—	card
ɔ	tonne	Post	hot
ɔː	mors	—	sort
ɔɪ	—	Fräulein	toy
o	chaud	Tomate	coat
oː	rose	Kohle	code
ʊ	—	unter	put
u	coup	—	cool
uː	rouge	Uhr	cool
y	cru	Führer	crude
yː	buche	physisch	crude
ø	bleu	öffnen	early
øː	jeune	böse	early
œ	seul	—	early
œ̃	peur	—	early
ə	le	genug	ado
ɛ̃	vin	—	—
ɑ̃	blanc	—	restaurant

5̃	non	—	—
ŵ	jeune	—	—
ɥ	nuit	—	wheat
ç	—	ich	—
x	—	nach	loch
ɲ	pagne	—	new
ŋ	—	ringen	pang
ʒ	journal	Genie	pleasure
ʃ	chat	Strasse	show
tʃ	(tcheque)	—	cheat
j	mieux	Jahr	you

List of Abbreviations

Abbreviations in general use (such as AD and i.e.) are given in the main text.

Special abbreviations are as follows:

abbr	abbreviation
adj	adjective
adv	adverb
attrib	attributive(ly)
Aus	Australian
aux	auxiliary (verb)
b.	born
Brit	British
c.	circa
Can	Canadian
cent.	century
cents	centuries
comb. form	combining form
compar	comparative
conj	conjunction
d.	died
derog	derogatory
dimin.	diminutive
esp	especially
euphem	euphemistic
fem	feminine
fl	floruit
interj	interjection
intrans	intransitive
irreg	irregular(ly)
masc	masculine
NAmer	North American
N Eng	Northern English
NZ	New Zealand
orig	originally
part.	participle
pers	person
pl	plural
prep	preposition
pres part.	present participle
prob	probably
SAfr	South Africa(n)
Scot	Scottish
sing.	singular
specif	specifically
superl	superlative
trans	transitive
usu	usually
verb aux	auxiliary verb
verb intrans	intransitive verb
verb trans	transitive verb

Trademarks

Words included in the dictionary that the publishers have reason to believe are trademarks are labelled as such purely as a matter of courtesy.

The Dictionary

A¹ *or* **a** *noun* (*pl* **A's** *or* **As** *or* **a's**) **1a** the first letter of the English alphabet. **b** a written character or design denoting this letter. **c** the sound represented by this letter, one of the English vowels. **2** an item designated as A, *esp* the first in a series. **3** a mark or grade rating a student's work as excellent. **4** in music, the sixth note of the diatonic scale of C major. ✳ **from A to Z** from beginning to end.

A² *abbr* **1** ampere. **2** answer. **3** Austria (international vehicle registration). **4** a blood type of the ABO system, containing the A antigen.

Å *symbol* angstrom.

a¹ /ə; *strong* ay/ *or* **an** /ən; *strong* an/ *indefinite article* **1** used before a singular noun to denote a person or thing not previously specified: *a book about birds*. **2** one single: *a quarter of an hour*. **3** used before a verbal noun or a noun formed from a verb to denote an instance of an activity: *We heard a crashing of gears; He had a little grumble*. **4a** used before a proper name to denote a member of a class or type: *His sister-in-law is a Campbell; a Daniel come to judgment*. **b** a person named but not otherwise known: *A Mrs Jones is on the phone*. **5** every; per: *once a week*. [Old English *ān* ONE¹]

Usage note

a *or* an? The rule is that *an* should be used instead of *a* in front of all words beginning with a vowel sound. These include all words whose first letter is *a* or *i*, most words beginning with *e*, *o*, and *u*, and a few beginning with *h*: *an ace; an interesting evening*. The exceptions among words spelt with an initial vowel are as follows. When *u* is pronounced *yoo*, it is preceded by *a*: *a unit; a useful tool*. Words beginning with *eu* (also pronounced *yoo*) take *a*: *a eucalyptus tree; a European*. One and words beginning with the same sound take *a*: *a one-off; a once mighty empire*. Words spelt with an initial *h* that is not pronounced take *an*: *an hour; an honour*. Most modern authorities recommend that other words beginning with *h* should be preceded by *a*: *a hacker, a horse, a historian, a hotel*. It is not strictly incorrect, however, to write *an hotel* or *an heroic achievement*, and in speaking it may seem less awkward to say *an (h)otel* than *a hotel*.

a² *abbr* **1** acceleration. **2** acre. **3** are (unit of area). **4** arrives (used in timetables). **5** atto-.

a-¹ *prefix* forming adjectives and adverbs, with the meanings: **1** on; in; at; to: *abed; ajar*. **2** in the specified state or manner: *ablaze; aloud*. **3** in the specified act or process: *gone a-hunting; atingle*. [Old English]

a-² *or* **an-** *prefix* forming words, with the meaning: not; without: *asexual; anaesthetic*. [via Latin from Greek]

a-³ *prefix* see AD-.

-a- *comb. form* forming words, with the meaning: replacing carbon, *esp* in a ring: *aza-*.

-a *suffix* forming nouns, denoting: oxide: *thoria; alumina*. [scientific Latin, from *-a* as in MAGNESIA]

A1 *adj* **1** said of a ship: having the highest classification of seaworthiness for insurance purposes. **2** *informal* of the finest quality; first-rate.

A3 *noun* a size of paper 297 × 420mm (about 11¾ × 16½in.).

A4 *noun* a size of paper 297 × 210mm (about 11¾ × 8¼in.).

A5 *noun* a size of paper 210 × 148mm (about 8¼ × 5⅞in.).

AA *abbr* **1** Alcoholics Anonymous. **2** anti-aircraft. **3** Automobile Association.

AAA *abbr* **1** Amateur Athletic Association. **2** American Automobile Association.

AAAS *abbr* American Association for the Advancement of Science.

AAM *abbr* air-to-air missile.

A and E *abbr* accident and emergency (hospital department).

A and M *abbr* ancient and modern (hymns).

A and R *abbr* artists and repertoire, a division of a recording company responsible for discovering and recruiting new musical talent.

aardvark /'ahdvahk/ *noun* a large burrowing nocturnal African mammal that has a long extendable tongue, large ears, and a heavy tail and feeds on ants and termites: *Orycteropus afer*. [obsolete Afrikaans *aardvark*, from *aard* earth + *vark* pig]

aardwolf /'ahdwoolf/ *noun* (*pl* **aardwolves** /'ahdwoolvz/) a striped African mammal that resembles the hyenas and eats chiefly carrion and insects: *Proteles cristatus*. [Afrikaans *aardwolf*, from *aard* earth + *wolf* wolf]

Aaron's beard /'eərənz/ *noun* any of various plants having flower parts or other structures resembling hair, *esp* the rose of Sharon or Saint John's wort. [from the reference to the beard of Aaron, brother of Moses, in Psalms 133:2]

Aaron's rod *noun* a plant of the foxglove family with long tall stems and spikes of yellow flowers: *Verbascum thapsus*. [from the rod belonging to Aaron which miraculously blossomed (Numbers 17:1–8)]

AB *abbr* **1** able seaman. **2** Alberta (Canadian postal abbreviation). **3** *NAmer* Bachelor of Arts. **4** a blood type of the ABO system, containing the A and B antigens. [(sense 3) from Latin *artium baccalaureus*]

ab- *prefix* forming words, with the meaning: from; away; off: *abaxial; abduct*. [Middle English via Old French from Latin *ab-, abs-*]

ABA *abbr* **1** Amateur Boxing Association. **2** American Bar Association.

aba /ə'bah, ah'bah/ *noun* a loose sleeveless outer garment worn by Arabs. [Arabic *'abā*]

abaca /abə'kah/ *noun* **1** a banana plant native to the Philippines that is the source of Manila hemp: *Musa textilis*. **2** = MANILA (1). [Spanish *abacá* from Tagalog *abaká*]

abaci /'abakie, -sie/ *noun* pl of ABACUS.

aback /ə'bak/ *adv* said of a sail: in a position to catch the wind on what is normally the leeward side. ✳ **taken aback** surprised or shocked [orig said of a ship whose sails had been blown back against the mast, stopping it or blowing backwards]. [Middle English *abak* back, backwards, from Old English *on* ON[1] + *bæc* BACK[1]]

abacus /'abəkəs/ *noun* (*pl* **abaci** /-kie, -sie/ *or* **abacuses**) **1** an instrument for performing calculations by sliding beads as counters along rods or in grooves. **2** in architecture, a slab that forms the uppermost part of the capital of a column.

Word history
via Latin from Greek *abak-, abax* slab. The original abacus was a slab of wood strewn with dust on which to write or add up figures.

abaft[1] /ə'bahft/ *adv* towards or at the stern of a ship. [A-[1] + archaic *baft* aft]

abaft[2] *prep* in a ship, nearer the stern than (a given position): *The wind was abaft the beam.*

abalone /abə'lohni/ *noun* an edible rock-clinging invertebrate animal related to the snails and limpets that has a flattened ear-shaped shell lined with a type of mother-of-pearl used in jewellery: genus *Haliotis*. [American Spanish *abulón*]

abandon[1] /ə'band(ə)n/ *verb trans* (**abandoned, abandoning**) **1** to give (something) up completely, *esp* with the intention of never resuming or reclaiming it: *He abandoned his studies.* **2** to leave (a vehicle or place) or desert, often in the face of danger: *to abandon ship.* **3** to forsake or desert (somebody), *esp* in spite of an allegiance, duty, or responsibility: *Was she now to endure the ignominy of his abandoning her?* — D H Lawrence. **4** (+ to) to give (oneself) over unrestrainedly to a feeling or emotion: *They abandoned themselves to their grief.* ➤➤ **abandonment** *noun*. [Middle English *abandounen* to control, to leave to somebody else's control, from early French *abandoner*, from *a bandon* in one's power]

abandon[2] *noun* freedom from constraint or inhibitions: *They danced with gay abandon.*

abandoned *adj* **1** forsaken or deserted: *an abandoned car.* **2** wholly free from restraint: *The dancing became more abandoned.*

abase /ə'bays/ *verb trans* to bring (*esp* oneself) to a position lower in rank, office, prestige, or esteem: *He would atone for his sins … and abase himself like a worm before the injured damsel* — Louisa M Alcott. ➤➤ **abasement** *noun*. [Middle English *abassen* from early French *abaisser*, from AD- + (assumed) vulgar Latin *bassiare* to lower]

abash /ə'bash/ *verb trans* (*usu in passive*) to destroy the self-possession or self-confidence of (somebody); to disconcert (somebody). ➤➤ **abashment** *noun*. [Middle English *abaishen* from early French *esbair*, from EX-[1] + *baer* to yawn, from medieval Latin *batare*]

abate /ə'bayt/ *verb intrans* to decrease in force or intensity: *The wind has abated.* ➤ *verb trans* **1** in law, to put an end to or abolish (a nuisance). **2** to reduce (something) in amount, intensity, or degree; to moderate (something): *abate a tax.* ➤➤ **abatement** *noun*. [Middle English *abaten* from Old French *abattre* to beat down, slaughter]

abatis *or* **abattis** /'abətis/ *noun* (*pl* **abatis** *or* **abatises** *or* **abattis** *or* **abattises**) a defensive obstacle made of barbed wire or, in former times, of felled trees with sharpened branches positioned facing the enemy. [French *abatis* from *abattre*: see ABATE]

abattoir /'abətwah/ *noun* = SLAUGHTERHOUSE. [French *abattoir* from *abattre*: see ABATE]

abaxial /ab'aksi·əl/ *adj* situated outside or directed away from the axis of an organ, plant part, or organism: compare ADAXIAL.

Abba /'abə/ *noun* **1** in the New Testament, God the father. **2** in the Syrian, Coptic, and Ethiopian Churches, a title given to bishops and patriarchs.

abbacy /'abəsee/ *noun* (*pl* **abbacies**) the office, jurisdiction, or tenure of an abbot or abbess. [Middle English *abbatie* from late Latin *abbatia*: see ABBEY]

abbatial /ə'baysh(ə)l/ *adj* relating to an abbey, abbess, or abbot.

abbé /'abay/ *noun* often used as a title: a member of the French secular clergy in major or minor orders. [French *abbé* from late Latin *abbat-, abbas*: see ABBOT]

abbess /'abes/ *noun* the superior of an abbey of nuns. [Middle English *abbesse* via Old French from late Latin *abbatissa*, fem of *abbat-, abbas*: see ABBOT]

Abbevillian /ab(ə)'vilyən/ *adj* of the earliest Palaeolithic culture in Europe, characterized *esp* by crudely chipped stone axes. [*Abbeville*, town in France where remains of this culture were discovered]

abbey /'abi/ *noun* (*pl* **abbeys**) **1** a religious community governed by an abbot or abbess. **2** the buildings, *esp* the church, of a monastery or a former monastery: *Westminster Abbey.* [Middle English via Old French from late Latin *abbatia*, from *abbat-, abbas*: see ABBOT]

abbot /'abət/ *noun* the superior of an abbey of monks. [Middle English *abbod* from late Latin *abbat-, abbas*, ultimately from Aramaic *abbā* father]

abbreviate /ə'breeviayt/ *verb trans* to make (something) briefer, *esp* to reduce (a written word or phrase) to a shorter form intended to stand for the whole. [Middle English *abbreviaten* from late Latin *abbreviatus*, past part. of *abbreviare*: see ABRIDGE]

abbreviation /ə,breevi'aysh(ə)n/ *noun* a shortened form of a written word or phrase, e.g. *dept* for *department* and *Tues.* for *Tuesday.*

Usage note
Practice differs greatly with regard to the use of full stops in abbreviations: the general trend, however, is to use full stops less and less. In abbreviations made up of the initial letters of a number of words the usual modern practice is to omit them: *BBC, UN, USA.* It is not incorrect to write *B.B.C.* etc., but it is not necessary to do so. In an acronym, a string of initial letters that is pronounced as a word (*BUPA, NATO, Aids*), the use of full stops is even less necessary. In British English, it is becoming increasingly common to omit the full stop after an abbreviation containing the first and last letters of a word (*Dr, Ltd, St*). In American English, however, the full stops after such abbreviations are more likely to be retained.

ABC[1] *noun* (*pl* **ABC's** *or* **ABCs**) **1** the alphabet: *She's learning her ABC.* **2** the rudiments of a subject: *the ABC of photography.* **3** an alphabetical guide or manual: *the ABC of allergies.*

ABC[2] *abbr* **1** American Broadcasting Company. **2** Australian Broadcasting Corporation.

abdicate /'abdikayt/ *verb intrans* said of a monarch: to renounce a throne. ➤ *verb trans* **1** to relinquish (sovereign power) formally: *The king abdicated the throne.* **2** to renounce (a responsibility or right). ➤➤ **abdication** /-'kaysh(ə)n/ *noun*, **abdicator** *noun*. [Latin *abdicatus*, past part. of *abdicare*, from AB- + *dicare* to proclaim]

abdomen /'abdəmən, əb'dohmən/ *noun* **1** the part of the body between the thorax and the pelvis, or the cavity of this part containing the liver, gut, etc. **2** in an insect or other arthropod, the rear part of the body behind the thorax. ➤➤ **abdominal** /əb'domin(ə)l, ab-/ *adj*. [early French *abdomen* from Latin]

abdominals /əb'domin(ə)lz/ *pl noun* abdominal muscles.

abduct /əb'dukt/ *verb trans* **1** to carry (somebody) off secretly or by force: compare KIDNAP. **2** said of a muscle: to draw away (a limb etc.) from a position near or parallel to the main part of the body: compare ADDUCT[1]. ➤➤ **abduction** *noun*, **abductor** *noun*. [Latin *abductus*, past part. of *abducere* to lead away, from AB- + *ducere* to lead]

abeam /ə'beem/ *adv and adj* on a line at right angles to the length of a ship or aircraft. [A-[1] + BEAM[1]]

abed /ə'bed/ *adv and adj archaic* in bed: *She meant to lie abed tomorrow morning for a good long rest* — Dickens.

Aberdeen Angus /,abədeen 'anggəs/ *noun* an animal of a breed of black hornless beef cattle, originating in Scotland. [named after *Aberdeen* and *Angus*, former counties in Scotland where the breed originated]

Aberdonian /abə'dohni·ən/ *noun* a native or inhabitant of Aberdeen, in NE Scotland. ➤➤ **Aberdonian** *adj*. [medieval Latin *Aberdonia* Aberdeen]

aberrant /ə'berənt/ *adj* **1** said of behaviour: deviating from the right or usual way. **2** diverging from the usual or natural type. ➤➤ **aberrance** *noun*, **aberrancy** *noun*. [Latin *aberrant-, aberrans*, present part. of *aberrare* to go astray, from AB- + *errare* to wander, ERR]

aberration /abə'raysh(ə)n/ *noun* **1a** a departure from a normal state or moral standard. **b** something unusual or deviating from normal. **2** unsoundness or disorder of the mind, or an instance of this. **3** the failure of a mirror, lens, etc to produce an exact correspondence between an object and its image. **4** in astronomy, a small periodic change of apparent position in celestial bodies due to the combined effect of the speed of light and the motion of the observer. [Latin *aberratus*, past part. of *aberrare*: see ABERRANT]

abet /ə'bet/ *verb trans* (**abetted, abetting**) to give active encouragement or approval to (somebody): *He was aided and abetted in the crime by his wife.* ➤➤ **abetment** *noun*, **abetter** *noun*, **abettor** *noun*. [Middle English *abetten* from early French *abeter*, from AD- + *beter* to bait, of Germanic origin]

abeyance /ə'bayəns/ ✳ **in abeyance** temporarily suspended or out of use; in law, denoting a property or title lacking a legal holder or claimant. [early French *abeance* expectation, from *abaer* to desire, from *a-* to, towards + *baer* to yawn, from medieval Latin *batare*]

ABH *abbr* actual bodily harm.

abhor /əb'(h)aw/ *verb trans* (**abhorred, abhorring**) to regard (something or somebody) with extreme repugnance; to loathe. ➤➤ **abhorrer** *noun*. [Middle English *abhorren* from Latin *abhorrēre*, from AB- + *horrēre* to shudder]

abhorrent /əb'(h)orənt/ *adj* 1 causing horror; repugnant: *These acts are abhorrent to every right-minded person.* 2 (+ to) opposed or contrary to (something). ➤➤ **abhorrence** *noun*. [Latin *abhorrent-, abhorrens,* present part. of *abhorrēre*: see ABHOR]

abide /ə'bied/ *verb* (**abided** or **abode** /ə'bohd/, **abiding**) ➤ *verb trans* (*usu* **cannot abide** or **could not abide**) to bear (somebody or something) patiently; to tolerate: *Don't be a booby, boy! I cannot abide a booby* — Will Self. ➤ *verb intrans* 1 to remain stable or fixed in a state: *The uncertainty remains, the mystery abides* — Mark Twain. 2 *archaic* to live or dwell: *He was … grateful for the shelter of Mr Evarts's house … where he abode in safety and content till he found rooms* — Henry Adams. ✳ **abide by 1** to comply with (a rule or law). 2 to remain true to (one's word or a decision). ➤➤ **abidance** *noun*, **abider** *noun*. [Old English *ābīdan*, from A-¹ + *bīdan* BIDE]

abiding *adj* enduring for a long time: *an abiding interest in nature.* ➤➤ **abidingly** *adv*.

ability /ə'biliti/ *noun* (*pl* **abilities**) **1a** being able, *esp* the physical, mental, or legal power to do something: *I doubted their ability to walk so far.* **b** natural or acquired competence in doing something; skill: *a man of great ability.* **2** (*usu in pl*) a natural talent; aptitude: *The team needs a player of your abilities.* [Middle English *abilite* via French from Latin *habilitat-, habilitas,* from *habilis*: see ABLE]

-ability or **-ibility** *suffix* forming nouns from verbs, denoting: capacity, suitability, or tendency to act or be acted on in the specified way: *readability; credibility.* [Middle English *-abilite, -ibilite* via French from Latin *-abilitas, -ibilitas,* from *-abilis, -ibilis* (see -ABLE) + *-tas* -ty]

ab initio /ab i'nishioh/ *adv* from the beginning. [Latin *ab initio*]

abiogenesis /,aybieoh'jenisis/ *noun* the supposed spontaneous origination of living organisms directly from lifeless matter. Also called SPONTANEOUS GENERATION. ➤➤ **abiogenic** *adj*. [scientific Latin *abiogenesis*, from A-² + BIO- + Latin *genesis*: see GENESIS]

abiotic /aybie'otik/ *adj* not involving or produced by living organisms.

abject /'abjekt/ *adj* 1 showing utter hopelessness; wretched; miserable: *abject poverty.* 2 despicable; degraded: *an abject coward.* 3 humble and undignified: *an abject apology.* ➤➤ **abjection** /əb'jeksh(ə)n/ *noun*, **abjectly** *adv*, **abjectness** *noun*. [Middle English from Latin *abjectus*, past part. of *abicere* to cast off, from AB- + *jacere* to throw]

abjure /əb'jooə/ *verb trans* to renounce (*esp* a claim, opinion, or allegiance) on oath, solemnly, or formally: *As solemnly as I took his name, I now abjure it* — Mary Wollstonecraft. ➤➤ **abjuration** /abjə'raysh(ə)n/ *noun*, **abjurer** *noun*. [Middle English *abjuren* via French from Latin *abjurare*, from AB- + *jurare*: see JURY¹]

abl. *abbr* ablative.

ablate /ə'blayt/ *verb trans* to remove (something) by ablation. ➤ *verb intrans* to be removed by ablation. [Latin *ablatus*, past part. of *auferre* to remove, from *au-* away + *ferre* to carry]

ablation /ə'blaysh(ə)n/ *noun* 1 the surgical removal of a body part or tissue. 2 the wearing away of something, *esp*: **a** the outside of the nose cone of a rocket, by melting or vaporization. **b** rock, by abrasion or erosion. **c** snow, ice, or water from a glacier.

ablative¹ /'ablətiv/ *adj* denoting a grammatical case typically expressing separation, source, cause, or instrument. [Middle English via French from Latin *ablativus*, from *ablatus*: see ABLATE]

ablative² *noun* the ablative case or a word in this case.

ablative absolute *noun* a grammatical construction in Latin in which a noun or pronoun and a participle or adjective, both in the ablative case, together form an adverbial phrase.

ablaut /'ablowt/ *noun* a systematic variation of vowels in the same root, *esp* in the Indo-European languages, usu accompanied by differences in use or meaning, e.g. in *sing, sang, sung, song.* [German *Ablaut*, from *ab* away from + *Laut* sound]

ablaze /ə'blayz/ *adj and adv* 1 burning strongly. 2 radiant with light or bright colour. 3 (*often* + with) showing strong emotion: *His eyes were ablaze with anger.*

able /'aybl/ *adj* (**abler, ablest**) 1 (+ to) having sufficient power, skill, or means to do something: *With more money I would be better able to help.* 2 having adequate skill or competence. ➤➤ **ably** *adv*. [Middle English via French from Latin *habilis* apt, from *habēre* to have]

-able or **-ible** *suffix* 1 forming adjectives from verbs, with the meaning: fit for, able to, liable to, or worthy to act or be acted on in the specified way: *breakable; reliable; credible; get-at-able.* 2 forming adjectives from nouns, with the meaning: marked by, providing, or possessing the quality or attribute specified: *knowledgeable; comfortable.* ➤➤ **-ably** *suffix*. [Middle English via Old French from Latin *-abilis, -ibilis,* from *-bilis* capable or worthy of]

able-bodied *adj* physically strong and healthy; fit.

abled /'aybld/ *adj* 1 having unimpaired physical and mental abilities; able-bodied. 2 having physical or mental abilities as specified: *differently abled.*

ableism /'aybliz(ə)m/ *noun* discrimination against disabled people. ➤➤ **ableist** *adj*.

able seaman *noun* a seaman ranking above ordinary seaman and below leading seaman in the Royal Navy.

abloom /ə'bloohm/ *adj literary* in flower.

ablution /ə'bloohsh(ə)n/ *noun* 1 (*usu in pl*) the washing of the body. 2 the washing of the hands, sacred vessels, etc in a ritual purification. 3 *informal* (*in pl*) a place with washing and toilet facilities. ➤➤ **ablutionary** /-(ə)ri/ *adj*. [Middle English via French from Latin *ablution-, ablutio* from *abluere* to wash away, from AB- + *lavere* to wash]

-ably *suffix* see -ABLE.

ABM *abbr* antiballistic missile.

abnegate /'abnigayt/ *verb trans* to relinquish or renounce (something), *esp* as an act of self-denial. ➤➤ **abnegation** /-'gaysh(ə)n/ *noun*, **abnegator** *noun*. [back-formation from *abnegation*, from late Latin *abnegation-, abnegatio* from Latin *abnegare* to refute, from AB- + *negare*: see NEGATE]

abnormal /ab'nawməl, əb-/ *adj* deviating significantly from the normal or average. ➤➤ **abnormality** /-'maliti/ *noun*, **abnormally** *adv*. [alteration of earlier *anormal* via French from medieval Latin *anormalis*, from A-² + late Latin *normalis*: see NORMAL¹]

abnormal psychology *noun* the psychology of mental disorder.

Abo /'aboh/ *noun* (*pl* **Abos**) *Aus, usu derog* an Australian Aborigine. ➤➤ **Abo** *adj*. [by shortening]

aboard /ə'bawd/ *prep and adv* on, onto, or within (a ship, aircraft, train, or road vehicle): *climb aboard; aboard a plane bound for Rome.* [Middle English *abord*, from A-¹ + *bord*: see BOARD¹]

abode¹ /ə'bohd/ *noun formal* a home or residence. [Middle English *abod* from *abiden*: see ABIDE]

abode² *verb* past tense of ABIDE.

abolish /ə'bolish/ *verb trans* to do away with (something, e.g. a law or custom) wholly; to annul (it). ➤➤ **abolishable** *adj*, **abolisher** *noun*, **abolishment** *noun*, **abolition** /abə'lish(ə)n/ *noun*. [Middle English *abolisshen* via French from Latin *abolēre*, prob back-formation from *abolescere* to disappear, from AB- + *-olescere*: see ADULT¹]

abolitionist *noun* a person who advocates the abolishing of something, e.g. capital punishment or (formerly) slavery. ➤➤ **abolitionism** *noun*.

abomasum /abə'mays(ə)m/ *noun* (*pl* **abomasa** /-sə/) the fourth or true digestive stomach of a ruminant mammal. [scientific Latin *abomasum*, from AB- + Latin *omasum* tripe of a bullock]

A-bomb *noun* = ATOM BOMB.

abominable /ə'bominəbl/ *adj* 1 worthy of or causing disgust or hatred; detestable. 2 *informal* very disagreeable or unpleasant: *What abominable weather!* ➤➤ **abominably** *adv*.

Word history
Middle English via French from Latin *abominabilis* from *abominari*, literally 'to deprecate as an ill-omen', from AB- + *omin-*, *omen* OMEN[1]. It is a very old etymological misconception that this word derives from Latin *ab homine* (literally 'from the man', suggesting 'inhuman, unnatural'). This notion produced the form *abhominable* in early French, which was borrowed into English in the 14th cent. and was the normal spelling until the 17th cent.

abominable snowman *noun* (*often* **Abominable Snowman**) a large hairy manlike animal reported as existing high in the Himalayas. Also called YETI.

abominate /ə'bominayt/ *verb trans* to hate or loathe (something or somebody) intensely and unremittingly; to abhor: *There is nothing I so abominate for young people as a long engagement* — Jane Austen. ➤➤ **abominator** *noun*. [Latin *abominatus*, past part. of *abominari*: see ABOMINABLE]

abomination /ə,bomi'naysh(ə)n/ *noun* **1** something or somebody abominable, *esp* a detestable or shameful action. **2** extreme disgust and hatred; loathing. [Middle English *abominacioun* via French from late Latin *abomination-*, *abominatio*, from Latin *abominari*: see ABOMINABLE]

aboriginal[1] /abə'rijin(ə)l/ *adj* **1** originating, growing, or living naturally in a particular region or environment. **2** (**Aboriginal**) of Australian Aborigines. ➤➤ **aboriginally** *adv*.

aboriginal[2] *noun* **1** an aboriginal person, animal, or plant. **2** (**Aboriginal**) = ABORIGINE (2).
Usage note
Aboriginal *or* Aborigine? It is correct to refer to the indigenous people of Australia either as *Aborigines* or as *Aboriginals*. *Aboriginals* is slightly more formal. The singular form *Aborigine* is standard.

aborigine /abə'rijinee/ *noun* **1** an indigenous inhabitant, *esp* as contrasted with colonists. **2** (**Aborigine**). **a** a member of the indigenous people of Australia. Also called ABORIGINAL[2]. **b** any of the languages of this people. Also called ABORIGINAL[2]. **3** (*in pl*) the original fauna and flora of an area. [Latin *aborigines* (pl), from *ab origine* from the beginning]
Usage note
Aborigine *or* Aboriginal? See note at ABORIGINAL[2].

abort[1] /ə'bawt/ *verb trans* **1** to induce the abortion of (a foetus). **2** to end (an enterprise) prematurely. ➤ *verb intrans* **1** to fail to develop completely; to shrink away. **2** to expel a premature nonviable foetus. [Latin *abortare* from *abortus*, past part. of *aboriri* to miscarry, from AB- + *oriri* to rise, be born]

abort[2] *noun* the premature termination of a mission or procedure, *esp* one involving a military aircraft or spacecraft.

abortifacient[1] /ə,bawti'faysh(ə)nt/ *adj* inducing abortion.

abortifacient[2] *noun* a drug or other agent that induces abortion.

abortion /ə'bawsh(ə)n/ *noun* **1a** the induced expulsion of a foetus for the purpose of terminating a pregnancy. **b** the spontaneous expulsion of a nonviable foetus. **2** in biology, an arrest of development of a part, process, etc, or the result of this. **3** the failure or abandonment of an enterprise. **4** *informal* a monstrosity. ➤➤ **abortionist** *noun*.

abortive /ə'bawtiv/ *adj* **1** fruitless; unsuccessful: *an abortive attempt*. **2** said of an organ or organism: imperfectly formed or developed. ➤➤ **abortively** *adv*.

ABO system *noun* the system of classifying human blood into four blood groups, A, B, AB, or O, on the basis of the presence or absence of either or both of two antigens.

aboulia *or* **abulia** /ay'boohli·ə/ *noun* in psychiatry, a pathological loss of willpower. [scientific Latin *aboulia*, from A-[2] + Greek *boulē* will]

abound /ə'bownd/ *verb intrans* **1** to be present in large numbers or in great quantity: *Wild animals abound in the forest*. **2** (+ in/with) to have a large number or amount of (something): *The old edition abounded in coloured pictures*. [Middle English *abounden* via early French *abonder* from Latin *abundare*, from AB- + *unda* wave]

about[1] /ə'bowt/ *adv* **1a** on or to all sides; round. **b** here and there: *running about*. **2** in succession or rotation; alternately: *turn and turn about*. **3** approximately: *The wine cost about £5*. **4** almost: *I'm about ready*. **5** in the vicinity: *There was nobody about*. ✳ **about to 1** on the verge of: *about to join the army*. **2** used in the negative to express intention or determination: *The prime minister is not about to quit*. [Old English *abūtan*, from A-[1] + *būtan* outside]

Usage note
about, around, *or* **round**? See note at AROUND[1].

about[2] *prep* **1** with regard to or concerning (something or somebody): *a story about rabbits*. **2** carried by or associated with (a person): *There's a genuine charm about her*. **3** in different parts of (a place): *lying about the house*. **4** surrounding (a place). ✳ **know what one is about** *informal* to act sensibly and wisely.

about-turn[1] (*NAmer* **about-face**) *noun* **1** a 180° turn to the right, *esp* as a military drill movement. **2** a reversal of direction, policy, or opinion: *a massive about-turn on the Stock Exchange* — Daily Mirror. [from the military command *about turn*]

about-turn[2] (*NAmer* **about-face**) *verb intrans* to make an about-turn.

above[1] /ə'buv/ *adv* **1** in or to a higher place. **2** higher on the same or an earlier page: *see above*. **3** in or to a higher rank or number: *30 and above*. [Old English *abufan*, from A-[1] + *bufan* above, from BE- + *ufan* above]

above[2] *prep* **1** higher than the level of (something or somebody): *rise above the clouds*; *shout above the noise*. **2** more than (something): *She values safety above excitement*; *nothing above £5*. **3a** beyond or transcending (something or somebody): *above criticism*. **b** too difficult for (somebody) to understand: *The lecture was above me*. **4a** superior to (somebody), e.g. in rank. **b** too proud or honourable to stoop to (doing something): *He is not above fiddling his taxes*. **5** upstream from (a place). ✳ **above all** before every other consideration; especially. **get above oneself** to become excessively self-satisfied.

aboveboard *or* **above board** *adj and adv* free from all traces of deceit or dishonesty. [from the difficulty of cheating at cards when the hands are above the table]

Abp *abbr* archbishop.

abracadabra /,abrəkə'dabrə/ *noun* used as an exclamation to accompany conjuring tricks: a magical charm or incantation. [late Latin *abracadabra*, a mystical word thought to ward off the plague]

abrade /ə'brayd/ *verb trans* to roughen or wear away (something), *esp* by friction. ➤➤ **abrader** *noun*. [Latin *abradere* to scrape off, from AB- + *radere* to scrape]

abrasion /ə'brayzh(ə)n/ *noun* **1** a process of wearing, grinding, or rubbing away by friction. **2** an abraded area, *esp* of the skin. [medieval Latin *abrasion-*, *abrasio* from Latin *abrasus*, past part. of *abradere*: see ABRADE]

abrasive[1] /ə'braysiv, -ziv/ *adj* **1** denoting a substance that may be used for grinding away, smoothing, cleaning, or polishing; rough. **2** causing irritation; rude or unpleasant: *an abrasive personality*.

abrasive[2] *noun* a substance, e.g. emery, that is used for cleaning or smoothing a surface by rubbing or grinding it.

abreaction /abri'aksh(ə)n/ *noun* in psychoanalysis, the release of tension due to a repressed emotion by reliving the situation in which it first occurred. [part translation of German *Abreagierung*, from *ab* away from + *Reagierung* reaction]

abreast /ə'brest/ *adj and adv* **1** side by side and facing in the same direction: *columns of men five abreast*. **2** (+ of) up-to-date with (trends, developments, news, etc). [Middle English *abrest*, from A-[1] + *brest* BREAST[1]]

abridge /ə'brij/ *verb trans* **1** to shorten (a book or other piece of writing) by reducing the number of words used; to condense. **2** to reduce or curtail (a right or privilege): *attempts to abridge the right of free speech*. ➤➤ **abridgeable** *adj*, **abridger** *noun*. [Middle English *abregen* via French from late Latin *abbreviare*, from AD- + Latin *brevis* BRIEF[1]]

abridgment *or* **abridgement** *noun* a shortened form of a book or other piece of writing retaining the sense and unity of the original.

abroad /ə'brawd/ *adv and adj* **1** beyond the boundaries of one's country: *We're going abroad on holiday*. **2** over a wide area; widely: *scattered abroad*. **3** in wide circulation; about: *The idea has got abroad*. **4** dated away from one's home; out of doors: *There are few people abroad at this hour*. [Middle English *abrood*, from A-[1] + *brood* BROAD[1]]

abrogate /'abrəgayt/ *verb trans* to abolish (a law or agreement) by authoritative action; to annul or repeal. ➤➤ **abrogation** /-'gaysh(ə)n/ *noun*. [Latin *abrogatus*, past part. of *abrogare*, from AB- + *rogare* to ask, propose a law]

Usage note
abrogate or **arrogate**? These two formal verbs are sometimes confused. To *abrogate* something such as a treaty or a right is to 'annul' or 'abolish' it. To *arrogate* is to 'claim or seize something without justification' – it is related to *arrogant* and usually occurs in the form *arrogate something to oneself*: *She has recently arrogated to herself the role of decision-maker for the whole group.*

abrupt /ə'brupt/ *adj* **1a** occurring without warning; unexpected: *an abrupt change in the weather.* **b** unceremoniously curt. **2** rising or dropping sharply; steep. **3** in botany, ending as if sharply cut off; truncated. ⟫ **abruptly** *adv*, **abruptness** *noun*. [Latin *abruptus*, past part. of *abrumpere* to break off, from AB- + *rumpere* to break]

abs /abz/ *pl noun informal* abdominal muscles.

ABS *abbr* anti-lock braking system.

abscess /'abses, -sis/ *noun* an accumulation of pus surrounded by inflamed tissue. ⟫ **abscessed** *adj*. [Latin *abscessus*, literally 'act of going away', from *abscedere* to go away, from AB- + *cedere* to go, CEDE]

abscisic acid /ab'sisik, ab'sizik/ *noun* a plant hormone that typically promotes ABSCISSION (natural separation) of dead leaves and dormancy of seeds and buds. [*abscision* (variant of ABSCISSION) + -IC[1]]

abscissa /ab'sisə, ab-/ *noun* (*pl* **abscissas** or **abscissae** /-see/) in mathematics, the coordinate of a point in a Cartesian coordinate system obtained by measuring the distance from the y-axis parallel to the x-axis: compare ORDINATE. [scientific Latin *abscissa* from Latin, fem of *abscissus*, past part. of *abscindere* to cut off, from AB- + *scindere* to cut]

abscission /ab'sish(ə)n, əb-/ *noun* the natural separation of flowers, leaves, etc from plants. [Latin *abscission-*, *abscissio* from *abscissus*: see ABSCISSA]

abscond /əb'skond/ *verb intrans* to leave secretly or hurriedly, *esp* to avoid discovery or arrest. ⟫ **absconder** *noun*. [Latin *abscondere* to hide away, from AB- + *condere* to store up, conceal]

abseil /'absayl/ *verb intrans* to descend a vertical surface by sliding down a rope secured from above and wound round the body. [German *abseilen*, from *ab-* down + *Seil* rope]

absence /'absəns/ *noun* **1** the state of being absent. **2** the period of time that somebody or something is absent. **3** (+ of) a lack of (something): *an absence of detail.*

absent[1] /'abs(ə)nt/ *adj* **1** not present or attending; missing. **2** not existing; lacking. **3** not paying attention; preoccupied. ⟫ **absently** *adv*. [Middle English via French from Latin *absent-*, *absens*, present part. of *abesse* to be away, from AB- + *esse* to be]

absent[2] /əb'sent/ *verb trans* (*often* + from) to take or keep (oneself) away.

absentee /abs(ə)n'tee/ *noun* **1** somebody who is absent. **2** (*used before a noun*) not personally living in a place: *an absentee landlord.*

absenteeism *noun* persistent and deliberate absence from work, school, duty, etc.

absentminded *adj* lost in thought and unaware of one's surroundings or actions; forgetful, *esp* habitually. ⟫ **absentmindedly** *adv*, **absentmindedness** *noun*.

absinthe or **absinth** /'absinth (*French* absɛ̃t)/ *noun* **1** = WORMWOOD (1). **2** a green liqueur flavoured with wormwood or a substitute, aniseed, and other aromatics. [French *absinthe* via Latin from Greek *apsinthion*]

absolute[1] /'absəlooht/ *adj* **1** complete or perfect; outright: *absolute bliss; an absolute lie.* **2** free from restraint or limitation: *an absolute monarch; absolute ownership.* **3** in grammar, standing apart from a usual syntactic relation with other words or sentence elements: *an absolute construction.* **4** free of external references or relationships: *an absolute term in logic.* ⟫ **absoluteness** *noun*. [Middle English *absolut* from Latin *absolutus*, past part. of *absolvere*: see ABSOLVE]

absolute[2] *noun* **1** something that is absolute, *esp* something independent of human perception or valuation: *talking in absolutes.* **2** (*usu* **Absolute**) the transcendent or underlying unity of spirit and matter.

absolutely /absə'loohtli/ *adv* **1** often used alone to express emphatic agreement: totally, completely: *I'm absolutely exhausted.* **2** in an absolute manner: *The president ruled absolutely for ten years.*

absolute magnitude *noun* the intrinsic brightness of a star or other celestial body.

absolute majority *noun* a number of votes greater than half the total cast or exceeding the total of votes for all other candidates.

absolute pitch *noun* **1** the pitch of a note determined by its rate of vibration. **2** the ability to recognize the pitch of a note or to produce a note of a given pitch.

absolute temperature *noun* temperature measured on a scale that has absolute zero as its lower reference point.

absolute value *noun* in mathematics, the numerical magnitude of a real number irrespective of its sign, indicated by a vertical line on each side of the number.

absolute zero *noun* the lowest temperature theoretically possible, equivalent to about -273.15°C or 0°K, at which the particles whose motion constitutes heat are at rest.

absolution /absə'loohsh(ə)n/ *noun* the act of absolving; *specif* a declaration of forgiveness of sins pronounced by a priest.

absolutism *noun* government by an absolute ruler or authority, or the theory favouring this. ⟫ **absolutist** *noun and adj*.

absolve /əb'zolv/ *verb trans* **1** (*often* + of/from) to set (somebody) free from an obligation or the consequences of guilt: *that these United Colonies … are absolved from all allegiance to the British Crown* — Thomas Jefferson. **2a** to declare (somebody) forgiven for a sin by absolution. **b** to declare (a sin) forgiven by absolution. ⟫ **absolver** *noun*. [Middle English *absolven* from Latin *absolvere*, from AB- + *solvere*: see SOLVE]

absorb /əb'zawb, əb'sawb/ *verb trans* **1a** to soak or take in (a liquid or other substance). **b** to learn (information, ideas, etc). **2** to take in (something or somebody) and make them part of an existing whole; to incorporate: *absorb new entrants easily into school life* — H C Dent. **3** to engage or occupy (somebody) wholly. **4** to receive and transform (sound, radiant energy, etc) without reflecting or transmitting it. ⟫ **absorbability** /-'biliti/ *noun*, **absorbable** *adj*, **absorber** *noun*. [early French *absorber* from Latin *absorbēre*, from AB- + *sorbēre* to suck up]

absorbance /əb'zawb(ə)ns/ *noun* in physics, the ability of a substance to absorb radiation.

absorbed *adj* engrossed or preoccupied in an activity.

absorbent[1] *adj* able to absorb a liquid, gas, etc. ⟫ **absorbency** *noun*. [Latin *absorbent-*, *absorbens*, present part. of *absorbēre*: see ABSORB]

absorbent[2] *noun* an absorbent substance.

absorbing *adj* engaging one's full attention; engrossing. ⟫ **absorbingly** *adv*.

absorption /əb'zawpsh(ə)n, əb'sawpsh(ə)n/ *noun* **1** the process of absorbing or being absorbed: compare ADSORPTION. **2** total involvement of the mind: *Their absorption in their work is remarkable.* ⟫ **absorptive** *adj*. [French *absorption* from Latin *absorption-*, *absorptio*, from *absorbēre*: see ABSORB]

absorption costing *noun* a method of costing a product or undertaking that allows full recovery of overheads.

abstain /əb'stayn/ *verb intrans* **1** (+ from) to refrain deliberately, and often with an effort of self-denial, from something: *He resolved to abstain from intoxicating liquor.* **2** to refrain from casting a vote. ⟫ **abstainer** *noun*. [Middle English *absteinen* via early French *abstenir* from Latin *abstinēre*, from AB- + *tenēre* to hold]

abstemious /əb'steemi·əs/ *adj* sparing, *esp* in eating or drinking; marked by abstinence. ⟫ **abstemiously** *adv*, **abstemiousness** *noun*. [Latin *abstemius*, from AB- + *temetum* mead, strong drink]

abstention /əb'stensh(ə)n/ *noun* **1** (*often* + from) abstaining: *abstention from smoking.* **2** an instance of abstaining from voting. [late Latin *abstention-*, *abstentio* from *abstinēre*: see ABSTAIN]

abstinence /'abstinəns/ *noun* **1** (*often* + from) voluntary forbearance, *esp* from indulgence of appetite or from eating some foods. **2** habitual abstaining from alcoholic drinks: *total abstinence.* ⟫ **abstinent** *adj*, **abstinently** *adv*. [Middle English via French from Latin *abstinens*, present part. of *abstinēre*: see ABSTAIN]

abstract[1] /'abstrakt/ *adj* **1** theoretical rather than practical: *an abstract science.* **2** said of art: having little or no element of pictorial representation. **3** said of a noun: naming a quality, state, or action rather than a thing; not concrete. **4** detached from any specific instance or object: *an abstract entity.*

Editorial note
Abstraction has been a prominent mode in 20th-cent. art, in various diverse forms – splashily painterly, tightly geometric, and so forth. But it is disputable how abstract that abstraction actually is. Within the most resolutely

non-objective images some reference to landscape or figure often lurks. It may be impossible to construct a work of art which does not echo some aspect of the world — Martin Gayford.

⋙ **abstractly** *adv*, **abstractness** *noun*. [medieval Latin *abstractus* from Latin, past part. of *abstrahere* to draw away, from AB- + *trahere* to draw]

abstract² *noun* **1** a summary of the main points, e.g. of a piece of writing; an epitome: *Let them [the players] be well us'd; for they are the abstract and brief chronicles of our time* — Shakespeare. **2** an abstract concept or state. **3** an abstract composition or creation. *** in the abstract** in general; without being specific. [Middle English from Latin *abstractus*: see ABSTRACT¹]

abstract³ /əb'strakt/ *verb trans* **1** (*often* + from) to remove, separate, or extract (something). **2** to consider (something) in the abstract. **3** to summarize (a piece of writing). **4** *euphem* to steal or purloin (something): *John Homer, a plumber, was accused of having abstracted it from the lady's jewel-case* — Conan Doyle. ⋙ **abstractor** *noun*.

abstracted /əb'straktid/ *adj* preoccupied or absentminded. ⋙ **abstractedly** *adv*.

abstract expressionism *noun* art in which the artist attempts to express attitudes and emotions spontaneously through non-representational means.

abstraction /əb'straksh(ə)n/ *noun* **1** an abstract idea or term without its concrete manifestations. **2a** the act or process of abstracting something. **b** the quality of being abstract. **3** preoccupation or absentmindedness. **4** an abstract composition or creation. ⋙ **abstractive** *adj*.

abstractionism *noun* the principles or practice of creating abstract art. ⋙ **abstractionist** *noun and adj*.

abstract of title *noun* a statement summarizing the events and facts, e.g. successive conveyances, on which a person's legal title to a piece of land rests.

abstruse /əb'stroohs/ *adj* difficult to understand; recondite. ⋙ **abstrusely** *adv*, **abstruseness** *noun*. [Latin *abstrusus*, past part. of *abstrudere* to conceal, from AB- + *trudere* to push]

absurd /əb'suhd/ *adj* **1** blatantly or ridiculously unreasonable or incongruous; silly. **2** lacking order or value; meaningless. ⋙ **absurdity** *noun*, **absurdly** *adv*, **absurdness** *noun*. [early French *absurde* from Latin *absurdus*, literally 'out of tune', from AB- + *surdus* deaf, stupid]

absurdism *noun* the belief, *esp* in 20th-cent. thought, that human beings exist in an irrational and meaningless universe, in which life has no significance beyond itself. ⋙ **absurdist** *noun and adj*.

ABTA /'abtə/ *abbr* Association of British Travel Agents.

abulia /ay'boohli-ə/ *noun* see ABOULIA.

abundance /ə'bund(ə)ns/ *noun* **1** a large quantity of something; a profusion. **2** wealth or prosperity. **3** the relative plentifulness of a living organism, substance, etc in an area or sample. **4** in solo whist, a bid to win at least nine tricks.

abundant /ə'bund(ə)nt/ *adj* **1** having or providing plenty of something, *esp* resources. **2** (+ in) amply supplied with or abounding in (something). ⋙ **abundantly** *adv*. [Middle English via French from Latin *abundant-*, *abundans*, present part. of *abundare*: see ABOUND]

abuse¹ /ə'byoohz/ *verb trans* **1** to put (something) to a wrong or improper use: *You must not abuse the privilege of your position.* **2** to attack (somebody) in words; to revile. **3** to harm or injure (a person or animal) by wrong or cruel treatment; to maltreat: *This dog was abused by its previous owner.* ⋙ **abuser** *noun*. [Middle English *abusen* via French from Latin *abusus*, past part. of *abuti*, from AB- + *uti* to use]

Usage note

abuse *or* **misuse**? There is a subtle distinction between these two words, which are generally similar in meaning both as nouns and as verbs. *Abuse* usually suggests morally improper treatment, often involving a breach of trust: *to abuse somebody's hospitality*; *child abuse*. *Misuse*, on the other hand, may refer simply to incorrect use (*to misuse a word*), though often with suggestions of moral disapproval as well: *a misuse of taxpayers' money*. Unlike *abuse*, *misuse* does not normally refer to the treatment of people.

abuse² /ə'byoohs/ *noun* **1** improper use or treatment; misuse or an instance of misuse: *drug abuse*. **2** vehemently expressed condemnation or disapproval: *He greeted them with a torrent of abuse.* **3** physical maltreatment, *esp* sexual assault of a person: *child abuse*. **4** a corrupt practice or custom.

abusive /ə'byoohsiv, -ziv/ *adj* **1a** involving verbal abuse; insulting. **b** involving or inflicting physical abuse. **2** characterized by wrong or improper use or action; corrupt: *abusive financial practices*. ⋙ **abusively** *adv*, **abusiveness** *noun*.

abut /ə'but/ *verb* (**abutted, abutting**) ⋙ *verb intrans* **1** (+ on/upon) said of an area: to touch (another area) along a boundary; to border: *Our land abuts on theirs.* **2a** (+ on/against) to terminate at a point of contact with (something); to be adjacent to: *The town hall abuts on the church.* **b** (+ on/upon) to lean on (something) for support: *Their shed abuts on our wall.* ⋙ *verb trans* to abut on or against (something). ⋙ **abutter** *noun*. [Middle English *abutten*; partly from Old French *aboter* to border on, from AD- + *bout* blow, end, from *boter* to strike; partly from Old French *abuter* to come to an end, from AD- + *but* end, aim, both of Germanic origin]

abutment /ə'butmənt/ *noun* **1** the place at which two things abut on each other. **2** the part of a structure that directly receives thrust or pressure, e.g. from an arch.

abuzz /ə'buz/ *adj* (*usu* + with) said of a place: filled with excitement, conversation, or activity: *abuzz with rumours*.

abysm /ə'bizəm/ *noun literary* an abyss. [Middle English from Old French *abisme*, modification of late Latin *abyssus*: see ABYSS]

abysmal /ə'bizməl/ *adj* **1** deplorably bad: *abysmal ignorance*. **2** *literary* immeasurably deep. ⋙ **abysmally** *adv*.

abyss /ə'bis/ *noun* **1** an immeasurably deep chasm or void. **2** (**the abyss**) a catastrophic situation seen as imminent or unavoidable. [Middle English *abissus* via late Latin *abyssus* from Greek *abyssos*, literally 'bottomless', from A-² + *byssos* depth]

abyssal /ə'bis(ə)l/ *adj* at or of the bottom or deepest part of the ocean.

Abyssinian /abi'sini-ən/ *noun* **1** in former times, a native or inhabitant of Abyssinia. **2** (*also* **Abyssinian cat**) a small slender cat of a breed originating in Africa, having short brownish hair flecked with darker colouring. ⋙ **Abyssinian** *adj*. [*Abyssinia*, the former name for Ethiopia]

AC *abbr* **1** air conditioning. **2** alternating current. **3** appellation contrôlée. **4** athletic club. **5** before Christ. **6** Companion of the Order of Australia. [(sense 4) from Latin *ante Christum*]

Ac *abbr* the chemical symbol for actinium.

a/c *abbr* account.

ac- *prefix* see AD-.

-ac *suffix* **1** forming nouns, denoting: a person affected with something: *maniac*; *haemophiliac*. **2** forming adjectives, with the meaning: of or relating to the thing specified: *cardiac*; *iliac*. [scientific Latin *-acus* of or relating to, from Greek *-akos*]

acacia /ə'kaysh(y)ə/ *noun* any of a genus of woody plants of the pea family, of warm regions, with white or yellow flowers: genus *Acacia*. [from the Latin genus name, ultimately from Greek *akakia*, a tree]

academia /akə'deemi-ə/ *or* **academe** /'akədeem/ *noun* the academic environment, *esp* of colleges and universities, or an academic community. [Latin *academia*: see ACADEMY]

academic¹ /akə'demik/ *adj* **1** relating to formal study or education; scholarly. **2a** theoretical with no practical or useful bearing: *an academic question*. **b** very learned and unconcerned or inexperienced in practical matters. **3** *chiefly NAmer* relating to liberal rather than technical or vocational studies. ⋙ **academically** *adv*.

academic² *noun* a member of the teaching staff or a research student at an institution of higher learning.

academicals /akə'demiklz/ *pl noun* the cap and gown worn as formal academic dress.

academician /ə,kadə'mish(ə)n/ *noun* a member of an academy for the advancement of the arts or sciences.

academicism /akə'demisiz(ə)m/ *noun* purely speculative thought and attitudes.

academy /ə'kadəmi/ *noun* (*pl* **academies**) **1a** a college in which special subjects or skills are taught: *an academy of music*. **b** used in names: a secondary school, *esp* a private high school. **2** a society of learned people organized to promote the arts or sciences. **3** (**Academy**) the school of philosophy founded by Plato.

Word history

Latin *academia* from Greek *Akadēmeia*, name of the gymnasium where Plato taught, from *Akadēmos* Attic mythological hero; (senses 1 and 2) largely via French *académie* university. Plato's gymnasium was on land formerly dedicated to Akadēmos.

Academy Award *noun* = OSCAR.

Acadian /ə'kaydi·ən/ *noun* **1** an inhabitant of Acadia, a former French colony on the NE seaboard of N America. **2** a French-speaking descendant of the early Acadians. ⟫ **Acadian** *adj*. [*Acadia*, from French *Acidie*]

acanthus /ə'kanthəs/ *noun* (*pl* **acanthuses** *or* **acanthi** /-thie/) **1** any of a genus of large prickly plants or shrubs, *esp* of the Mediterranean region, with spiny leaves and white or purple flower spikes: genus *Acanthus*. **2** an ornamental device representing the leaves of the acanthus, e.g. on a Corinthian column. [from the Latin genus name, from Greek *akanthos*, a hellebore, from *akantha* thorn]

a cappella *or* **a capella** /,ah kə'pelə/ *adj and adv* said of a piece of music, *esp* sacred choral music: to be performed without instrumental accompaniment. [Italian *a cappella* in chapel style]

acariasis /akə'rie·əsis/ *noun* infestation with or disease caused by mites. [scientific Latin *acariasis*, from *Acarus*: see ACARID]

acaricide /ə'karisied/ *noun* a substance, e.g. a dust or spray, used to control or kill mites, ticks, etc. [Greek *akari* mite + -CIDE]

acarid /'akərid/ *noun* any of an order of invertebrate animals related to the spiders and scorpions, including the mites and ticks: order Acarina. [scientific Latin *Acarida* from *Acarus*, genus name, from Greek *akari* mite]

ACAS /'aykas/ *abbr* Advisory, Conciliation, and Arbitration Service.

acausal /'aykawzl/ *adj* not governed by the laws of cause and effect.

acc. *abbr* **1** according to. **2** account. **3** accusative.

accede /ək'seed/ *verb intrans* (*usu* + to) **1** (*usu* + to) to express approval of or give consent to (something), often in response to urging: *She acceded to the suggestion of bouillon* — Kate Chopin. **2** (*usu* + to) to enter on (an office or position, *esp* the monarchy): *accede to the throne*. **3** (*usu* + to) to become a party to (something, e.g. a treaty). [Middle English *acceden* to approach, from Latin *accedere* to go to, be added, from AD- + *cedere* to go, CEDE]

accelerando /ək,selə'randoh/ *adj and adv* said of a piece of music: to be performed with increasing speed. [Italian *accelerando*, literally 'accelerating', from Latin *accelerandum*, verbal noun from *accelerare*: see ACCELERATE]

accelerant /ək'selərənt/ *noun* = ACCELERATOR (2).

accelerate /ək'selərayt/ *verb intrans* **1** to move faster; to gain speed. **2** to increase more rapidly. ⟩ *verb trans* **1** to cause (something) to happen at an earlier time. **2** to increase the speed of (something). **3** to hasten the progress or development of (something). ⟫ **accelerative** /-rətiv/ *adj*. [Latin *acceleratus*, past part. of *accelerare*, from AD- + *celer* swift]

acceleration /ək,selə'raysh(ə)n/ *noun* increase in speed or velocity; the rate of this change.

accelerator /ək'seləraytə/ *noun* **1** a pedal in a motor vehicle that controls the speed of the engine. **2** a substance that speeds up a chemical reaction. Also called ACCELERANT. **3** in physics, an apparatus for giving high velocities to charged particles, e.g. electrons.

accelerometer /ək,selə'romitə/ *noun* an instrument for measuring acceleration. [ACCELERATION + -O- + -METER²]

accent¹ /'aksənt/ *noun* **1** a distinctive manner of expression; *specif* a distinctive pattern of pronunciation and intonation that is characteristic of a geographical area or social class. **2a** prominence given to one syllable over others by stress or a change in pitch. **b** greater stress given to one musical note. **c** rhythmically significant stress on certain syllables of a verse. **3a** a mark added to a letter, e.g. in *à, ñ, ç*, to indicate how it should be pronounced. **b** a symbol used to indicate musical stress. **4** special concern or attention; emphasis: *The accent this year is on youth*. [early French *accent* from Latin *accentus*, from AD- + *cantus* song, from *canere* to sing, CHANT¹]

accent² /ək'sent/ *verb trans* **1a** to stress (a vowel, syllable, or word). **b** to mark (a word or letter) with a written or printed accent. **2** to make (something) more prominent or emphasize it.

accented /ak'sentid/ *adj* spoken or pronounced with an accent, *esp* a regional or foreign accent.

accentor /ək'sentaw, -tə/ *noun* any of several species of birds with drab plumage resembling sparrows, e.g. the dunnock: genus *Prunella*. [scientific Latin *accentor* from medieval Latin, one who sings with another, from Latin AD- + *cantor* singer, from *canere*: see ACCENT¹]

accentual /ak'sentyoo·əl, -choo·əl/ *adj* **1** of or characterized by accent. **2** said of metre in poetry: based on the stress patterns of

syllables rather than their length: compare QUANTITATIVE. ⟫ **accentually** *adv*. [Latin *accentus*: see ACCENT¹]

accentuate /ək'sentyooayt, -chooayt/ *verb trans* to accent or emphasize (something): *Brilliant rays penetrated to earth, but ... they only served to accentuate the Stygian blackness of the jungle's depths* — Edgar Rice Burroughs. ⟫ **accentuation** /-'aysh(ə)n/ *noun*. [medieval Latin *accentuatus*, past part. of *accentuare*, from Latin *accentus*: see ACCENT¹]

accept /ək'sept/ *verb trans* **1a** to agree to receive (something offered). **b** to agree to (something): *They accepted her invitation*. **c** to be able or be designed to take or hold (something applied or inserted): *The machine accepts only coins*. **2** to give admittance or approval to (somebody): *They accepted her as one of the group*. **3a** to endure (something) without protest; to accommodate oneself to (it): *They have to accept poor living conditions*. **b** to regard (something) as proper, normal, or inevitable. **c** to recognize (something) as true, factual, or adequate: *He refused to accept my explanation*. **4** to undertake (an obligation or responsibility). [Middle English *accepten* via early French from Latin *acceptare*, from *accipere* to receive, from AD- + *capere* to take]

acceptable /ak'septəbl/ *adj* **1** capable or worthy of being accepted; satisfactory. **2** welcome or pleasing to the receiver: *Compliments are always acceptable*. **3** tolerable. ⟫ **acceptability** /-'biliti/ *noun*, **acceptableness** *noun*, **acceptably** *adv*.

acceptance /ək'sept(ə)ns/ *noun* **1** the act of accepting or being accepted. **2** favourable reception; approval.

acceptation /aksep'taysh(ə)n/ *noun* the accepted meaning of a word or concept.

accepted *adj* generally approved or used; customary.

acceptor *noun* **1** somebody who accepts something. **2** in electronics, an impurity that is added to a semiconductor to change its conduction properties.

access¹ /'akses/ *noun* **1a** freedom to approach, reach, or make use of something: *access to classified information*. **b** a means of access, e.g. a doorway or channel. **c** the state of being readily reached or obtained: *The building is not easy of access*. **2** (+ of) a fit of tense feeling; an outburst: *an access of rage*. **3** (*used before a noun*) devised by or intended for the general public and not specially qualified people: *an access course in computing*. [Middle English via French from Latin *accessus* approach, from *accedere*: see ACCEDE]

access² *verb trans* to gain access to (something, *esp* data).

accessary¹ /ək'ses(ə)ri/ *noun* see ACCESSORY¹.

accessary² *adj* see ACCESSORY².

accessible /ək'sesəbl/ *adj* **1** said of a place: capable of being reached: *The town is accessible by rail*. **2** (*often* + to) of or in a form that can be readily grasped intellectually: *making opera accessible to a wide audience*. **3** (+ to) able to be influenced by (something): *accessible to persuasion*. ⟫ **accessibility** /-'biliti/ *noun*, **accessibly** *adv*.

accession¹ /ək'sesh(ə)n/ *noun* **1** the act of entering on a high office: *her accession to the throne*. **2** something acquired or added; *specif* a book added to a library. **3** the act by which a nation becomes party to an agreement already in force. **4a** an increase due to something added. **b** acquisition of property by addition to existing property. **5** *formal* assent or agreement. ⟫ **accessional** *adj*.

accession² *verb trans* to record (e.g. books) in order of acquisition.

accessorize *or* **accessorise** /ək'sesəriez/ *verb trans* to furnish (e.g. an outfit or a room) with accessories.

accessory¹ /ək'sesəri/ *or* **accessary** *noun* (*pl* **accessories** *or* **accessaries**) **1** an inessential object or device that adds to the attractiveness, convenience, or effectiveness of something else: *a fashion accessory*. **2** a person involved in or privy to a crime, but not present when it is committed. ⟫ **accessorial** /akse'sawri·əl/ *adj*. [Middle English from late Latin *accessorius* additional thing, from Latin *access-, accedere*: see ACCEDE]

accessory² *or* **accessary** *adj* **1** aiding or contributing in a secondary way; supplementary or subordinate. **2** involved in or privy to a crime, but not present when it is committed.

access road *noun* a road that provides access to a particular area.

access time *noun* the time lag between the request for and delivery of stored information, e.g. in a computer.

acciaccatura /ə,chakə'tooarə/ *noun* a GRACE NOTE (musical note added as ornament) sounded with or immediately before a principal note or chord and quickly released: compare APPOGGIATURA. [Italian *acciaccatura* crushing, from *acciaccare* to crush]

accidence /'aksid(ə)ns/ *noun* the part of grammar that deals with the changes in form that words undergo to mark distinctions in tense, person, number, gender, etc. [Latin *accidentia* inflections of words, non-essential qualities, pl of *accident-*, *accidens*: see ACCIDENT]

accident /'aksid(ə)nt/ *noun* **1a** an event, usu of an unfortunate nature, occurring by chance or arising from unknown causes. **b** lack of intention or necessity; chance: *We met by accident rather than by design.* **2** an unexpected happening causing loss or injury. **3** a non-essential property or condition of something. **4** an irregularity of a surface, e.g. of the moon. [Middle English via French from Latin *accident-*, *accidens* non-essential quality, chance, present part. of *accidere* to happen, from AD- +*cadere* to fall]

accidental[1] /aksi'dentl/ *adj* **1a** occurring unexpectedly or by chance. **b** happening without intent or through carelessness and often with unfortunate results. **2** arising incidentally; non-essential. ➤➤ **accidentally** *adv.*

accidental[2] *noun* **1a** in music, a sharp, flat, or natural sign placed before a note that is not in the key indicated by a key signature. **b** a note altered in this way. **2** a non-essential property or condition of something.

accident-prone *adj* tending to have more accidents than is usual.

accidie /'aksidi/ *noun* a condition of hopeless listlessness; spiritual apathy: *There is nothing before you but sloth and apathy, accidie, which is a lingering suicide* — H G Wells. [Middle English via Old French from Middle Latin *accidia*, alteration of late Latin *acedia*: see ACEDIA]

accipiter /ək'sipitə/ *noun* any of a genus of medium-sized hawks that have short wings and long legs, e.g. the sparrow hawk: genus *Accipiter*. ➤➤ **accipitrine** /-treen/ *adj.* [from the Latin genus name, from Latin *accipiter* hawk]

acclaim[1] /ə'klaym/ *verb trans* **1** to applaud or praise (somebody or something). **2** to hail (somebody as something) by acclamation: *They acclaimed her queen.* ➤➤ **acclaimer** *noun.* [Latin *acclamare* to shout at, from AD- + *clamare* to shout]

acclaim[2] *noun* = ACCLAMATION (1).

acclamation /aklə'maysh(ə)n/ *noun* **1** a loud expression of praise, goodwill, or assent. **2** an overwhelming affirmative vote by cheers or applause rather than by ballot: *The motion was carried by acclamation.* [Latin *acclamation-*, *acclamatio*, from *acclamare*: see ACCLAIM[1]]

acclimate /'aklimayt, ə'kliemət/ *verb trans NAmer* to acclimatize (somebody or oneself). ➤➤ **acclimation** /akli'maysh(ə)n/ *noun.* [French *acclimater*, from AD- + *climat*: see CLIMATE]

acclimatize *or* **acclimatise** /ə'kliemətiez/ *verb trans* (*often* + to) to cause (somebody or oneself) to adapt to a new climate or situation: *It took me a while to become acclimatized to the heat in Spain.* ➤ *verb intrans* to adapt to a new climate or situation. ➤➤ **acclimatization** /-'zaysh(ə)n/ *noun.*

acclivity /ə'kliviti/ *noun* (*pl* **acclivities**) an ascending slope: *I pushed up the acclivity and soon gained its summit* — Herman Melville. ➤➤ **acclivitous** *adj.* [Latin *acclivitas* from *acclivis* ascending, from AD- + *clivus* slope]

accolade /'akəlayd/ *noun* **1a** a mark of acknowledgment or honour; an award. **b** an expression of strong praise. **2** a ceremony marking the conferral of knighthood, in which each of the candidate's shoulders is touched with a sword.

Word history
French *accolade* from *accoler* to embrace, ultimately from AD- + Latin *collum* neck. Knighthoods were orig conferred with an embrace.

accommodate /ə'komədayt/ *verb trans* **1a** to have or make adequate room for (somebody or something). **b** to provide (somebody) with lodgings; to house (somebody). **2** to bring (people or things) into agreement or concord; to reconcile. **3** (+ to) to make (something or somebody) fit, suitable for, or appropriate to (something or somebody else): *We must accommodate ourselves to changing circumstances.* **4** to oblige or give help to (somebody). **5** to give consideration to (somebody or something); to allow for. [Latin *accommodatus*, past part. of *accommodare*, from AD- + *commodare* to make fit, from *commodus*: see COMMODE]

accommodating /ə'komədayting/ *adj* helpful or obliging. ➤➤ **accommodatingly** *adv.*

accommodation /ə,komə'daysh(ə)n/ *noun* **1** a building or space in which a person or group of people may live or carry on business.

2a an adaptation or adjustment, *esp* to new circumstances. **b** a settlement or agreement. **c** the automatic adjustment of the eye, *esp* by changes in the amount by which the lens bends light, for seeing at different distances, or the range of this. **3** something needed or desired for convenience; a facility. **4** the endorsement of a bank loan or bill of exchange.

Usage note
Accommodation is often misspelt. It has two *c*'s and two *m*'s.

accommodation address *noun* an address to which letters may be sent to somebody who does not have or does not wish to give a permanent address.

accommodation ladder *noun* a ladder hung over the side of a ship to provide access from and to small boats.

accompaniment /ə'kump(ə)nimənt/ *noun* **1** a subordinate instrumental or vocal part supporting or complementing a principal voice or instrument. **2** an addition intended to complete something; a complement.

accompanist /ə'kumpənist/ *noun* a player of a musical accompaniment, e.g. on a piano.

accompany /ə'kump(ə)ni/ *verb* (**accompanies, accompanied, accompanying**) ➤ *verb trans* **1** to go with (somebody) as an escort or companion. **2** to perform an accompaniment for (a singer or musician). **3a** (+ with) to supplement (one thing) with another: *He accompanied his advice with a warning.* **b** to happen or exist with (something): *the pictures that accompany the text.* ➤ *verb intrans* to perform a musical accompaniment. [Middle English *accompanien* from early French *acompaignier*, from AD- + *compaing* companion, from late Latin *companio*: see COMPANION[1]]

accomplice /ə'kumplis, ə'kom-/ *noun* somebody who collaborates with another, *esp* in wrongdoing. [alteration (by incorrect division of *a complice*) of archaic *complice* associate, via Middle English and French from late Latin *complic-*, *complex*, from COM- + Latin *plicare* to fold]

accomplish /ə'kumplish, ə'kom-/ *verb trans* **1** to bring (something) to a successful conclusion; to achieve. **2** to manage to complete (an undertaking). [Middle English *accomplisshen* from early French *acompliss-*, stem of *acomplir*, ultimately from AD- + Latin *complēre*: see COMPLETE[1]]

accomplished *adj* **1** fully effected; completed: *an accomplished fact.* **2a** skilled or proficient: *an accomplished dancer.* **b** having many social accomplishments.

accomplishment *noun* **1** completion; fulfilment. **2** an achievement. **3** an acquired ability or social skill.

accord[1] /ə'kawd/ *verb trans* **1** to grant or concede (something) to somebody: *The council accorded them permission to proceed with their plans.* **2** to give or award (something) to somebody: *The audience accorded her a warm welcome.* ➤ *verb intrans* (+ with) to be consistent with something: *His actions do not accord with his socialist principles.* [Middle English *accorden* to reconcile, agree, from Old French *acorder*, ultimately from AD- + Latin *cord-*, *cor* heart]

accord[2] *noun* **1a** agreement; conformity. **b** a formal treaty of agreement: *a peace accord.* **2** balanced interrelationship, e.g. of colours or sounds; harmony. ✳ **of one's own accord** on one's own initiative; voluntarily. **with one accord** with everyone's agreement or involvement. [Middle English from Old French *acort*, from *acorder*: see ACCORD[1]]

accordance /ə'kawd(ə)ns/ *noun* agreement or conformity: *in accordance with a rule.*

accordant /ə'kawd(ə)nt/ *adj* (*often* + with) in agreement or conformity.

according /ə'kawding/ ✳ **according as** depending on how or whether: *Everyone contributed according as they were able.* **according to** in a way corresponding to, determined by, or in proportion to: *according to the rules; according to this book.*

accordingly *adv* **1** in an appropriate or corresponding way. **2** consequently; so.

accordion /ə'kawdi·ən/ *noun* a portable musical instrument of the reed organ family in which wind is forced past free steel reeds by means of a hand-operated bellows and notes are produced by pressing keys or buttons. ➤➤ **accordionist** *noun.* [German *Akkordion* from *Akkord* chord, from French *accord*, from Old French *acort*: see ACCORD[2]]

accost /ə'kost/ *verb trans* **1** to approach and speak to (somebody, *esp* a stranger), usu boldly or challengingly. **2** said of a prostitute:

to solicit (a prospective client). [early French *accoster* to lie or go alongside, ultimately from AD- + Latin *costa* rib, side]

accouchement /ə'koohshmənt, -monh (*French* akushmā)/ *noun* archaic confinement for childbirth or the act of giving birth: *She heard Madame Ratignolle relating … the harrowing story of one of her accouchements, withholding no intimate detail* — Kate Chopin. [French *accouchement* from *accoucher* to deliver a child, from Old French *accouchier* to lie down]

accoucheur /əkooh'shuh (*French* akuʃœ:r)/ *or* **accoucheuse** /-'shuhz (*French* akuʃœ:z)/ *noun* a man or woman who assists at a birth. [French *accoucheur* from *accoucher*: see ACCOUCHEMENT]

account¹ /ə'kownt/ *noun* **1** a statement or description of facts or events: *a newspaper account*. **2a** a record of debits and credits relating to a particular item, person, or concern. **b** (*usu in pl*) a list of items of expenditure to be balanced against income: *She is doing her monthly accounts*. **c** a facility whereby customers may purchase goods on credit subject to payment of bills presented periodically: *an account with a mail-order company*. **d** a statement listing purchases made on such an account and sums due. **3** a business arrangement whereby money is deposited in, and may be withdrawn from, a bank or other financial institution. **4** business or patronage, *esp* a commission to carry out a particular business operation, e.g. an advertising campaign, given by one company to another. **5a** value or importance: *a person of no account*. **b** profit or advantage: *He turned his wit to good account*. **6** careful thought; consideration: *They left nothing out of account*. **7** a version or rendering: *the pianist's sensitive account of the sonata*. ✳ **by all accounts** according to what one hears or is told. **give a good account of (oneself)** to acquit (oneself) well. **on account of** due to; because of. **on no account/not on any account** under no circumstances. **on one's own account 1** on one's own behalf. **2** at one's own risk. **on somebody's account** for somebody's sake: *Please don't go on my account*. **take something into account/take account of something** to make allowances for something; to consider it as a factor, e.g. when making a decision: *The judge took the boy's circumstances into account when passing sentence*.

account² *verb trans* to consider or think of (somebody or something) in a certain way: *He accounts himself lucky*. ✳ **account for 1** to give an explanation or reason for (something). **2** to be the sole or primary explanation for (something). **3** to bring about the defeat, death, or destruction of (somebody). [Middle English *accounten* from early French *acompter*, from AD- + *compter*: see COUNT¹]

accountable *adj* **1** (*often* + to/for) responsible; answerable. **2** able to be explained; explicable. ➤➤ **accountability** /-'biliti/ *noun*, **accountably** *adv*.

accountancy /ə'kownt(ə)nsi/ *noun* the profession or practice of accounting.

accountant /ə'kownt(ə)nt/ *noun* a person who practises accounting.

accounting /ə'kownting/ *noun* the recording, analysis, and verification of business and financial transactions.

accoutre (*NAmer* **accouter**) /ə'koohtə/ *verb trans* to provide (somebody) with equipment, *esp* in the form of military costume and trappings; to fit out: *Fergus was attended … by about three hundred of his clan, well armed, and accoutred in their best fashion* — Scott. [French *accoutrer* from early French *acoustrer*, from AD- + *cousture*: see COUTURE]

accoutrement /ə'koohtrəmənt/ (*NAmer* **accouterment** /-təmənt/) *noun* **1** (*usu in pl*) an item of equipment, dress, etc. **2** (*also in pl*) a soldier's outfit excluding clothes and weapons. [early French *accoutrement*, from *accoutrer*: see ACCOUTRE]

accredit /ə'kredit/ *verb trans* (**accredited, accrediting**) **1a** to give official authorization to or approval of (somebody or something): *an accredited practitioner*. **b** to send (somebody, *esp* an envoy) somewhere with credentials. **c** to recognize or vouch for (something or somebody) as conforming to a standard: *an accredited dairy herd*. **2a** (+ with) to credit (somebody) with something, *esp* a saying. **b** (+ to) to attribute (something, *esp* a saying) to somebody. **3** *NZ* to pass (somebody) for university entrance without examination. ➤➤ **accreditation** /-'taysh(ə)n/ *noun*. [French *accréditer*, from AD- + *crédit*: see CREDIT¹]

accrete /ə'kreet/ *verb intrans* to grow or become attached by accretion. ➤ *verb trans* to cause (parts or things) to accrete. [back-formation from ACCRETION]

accretion /ə'kreesh(ə)n/ *noun* **1a** an increase in size caused by natural growth or the external adhesion or addition of matter. **b** something added or stuck on extraneously. **2** the growth of separate particles or parts, e.g. of a plant, into one; concretion. ➤➤ **accretive** /-tiv/ *adj*. [Latin *accretion-, accretio*, from *accrescere*: see ACCRUE]

accrue /ə'krooh/ *verb* (**accrues, accrued, accruing**) ➤ *verb intrans* **1** (*often* + to) to come as an increase or addition; to arise as a growth or result: *advantages that have accrued to society from the freedom of the press*. **2** to be periodically accumulated: *Interest has accrued over the year*. ➤ *verb trans* to collect or accumulate (something). ➤➤ **accrual** *noun*. [Middle English *acreuen*, prob from early French *acreue* increase, from *acreistre* to increase, from Latin *accrescere*, from AD- + *crescere* to grow]

acct *abbr* account.

acculturate /ə'kulchərayt/ *verb trans and intrans* to assimilate to or adopt the values of a different culture. ➤➤ **acculturation** /-'raysh(ə)n/ *noun*. [AD- + CULTURE¹ + -ATE⁴]

accumulate /ə'kyoohmyoolayt/ *verb trans* to collect (things) together gradually; to amass. ➤ *verb intrans* to increase in quantity or number. [Latin *accumulatus*, past part. of *accumulare*, from AD- + *cumulare* to heap up, from *cumulus* mass]

accumulation /ə,kyoohmyoo'laysh(ə)n/ *noun* **1** increase or growth caused *esp* by repeated or continuous addition. **2** something that has accumulated: *an accumulation of tartar on the teeth*.

accumulative /ə'kyoohmyoolətiv/ *adj* increasing by successive additions; cumulative. ➤➤ **accumulatively** *adv*.

accumulator *noun* **1** the part of a computer where numbers are added or stored. **2** *Brit* a rechargeable secondary electric cell, or a connected set of these. **3** *Brit* a bet whereby the winnings from one of a series of events are staked on the next event.

accurate /'akyoorət/ *adj* **1** free from error, *esp* as the result of care: *an accurate estimate*. **2** conforming precisely to truth or a measurable standard; exact: *accurate instruments*. ➤➤ **accuracy** /-si/ *noun*, **accurately** *adv*. [Latin *accuratus*, past part. of *accurare* to take care of, from AD- + *cura* care]

accursed /ə'kuhst, ə'kuhsid/ *or* **accurst** /ə'kuhst/ *adj* **1** *literary* under a curse; ill-fated. **2** *informal* detestable; irritating. ➤➤ **accursedly** /-sidli/ *adv*, **accursedness** /-sidnis/ *noun*. [Middle English *acursed*, from past part. of *acursen* to consign to destruction with a curse, from A-¹ + *cursen* to CURSE¹]

accusation /akyoo'zaysh(ə)n/ *noun* **1** a charge of wrongdoing; an allegation. **2** accusing or being accused.

accusative¹ /ə'kyoohzətiv/ *adj* denoting a grammatical case expressing the direct object of a verb or of some prepositions. [Middle English via French from Latin *accusativus*, from *accusare*: see ACCUSE]

accusative² *noun* the accusative case or a word in this case, e.g. *me*.

accusatorial /ə,kyoohzə'tawri·əl/ *adj* **1** containing an accusation or expressing accusation; accusatory. **2** said of a system of criminal procedure: in which the judge is impartial and there is also a prosecutor: compare INQUISITORIAL.

accusatory /ə'kyoohzət(ə)ri/ *adj* containing an accusation or expressing accusation.

accuse /ə'kyoohz/ *verb trans* (*often* + of) to charge (somebody) with a fault or crime; to blame. ➤➤ **accuser** *noun*, **accusing** *adj*, **accusingly** *adv*. [Middle English *accusen* via Old French from Latin *accusare* to call to account, from AD- + *causa* lawsuit, CAUSE¹]

accused *noun* (**the accused**) the defendant or defendants in a criminal case.

accustom /ə'kust(ə)m/ *verb trans* (**accustomed, accustoming**) (+ to) to make (oneself, somebody else, or something) used to (something) through use or experience; to habituate: *Her eyes gradually became accustomed to the dark*. [Middle English *accustomen* from early French *acostumer*, from AD- + *costume*: see COSTUME¹]

accustomed *adj* **1** customary or habitual: *in their accustomed manner*. **2** (+ to) in the habit of or used to (doing something): *accustomed to making decisions*.

AC/DC *abbr* **1** alternating current/direct current. **2** *informal* = BISEXUAL¹ (1B).

ace¹ /ays/ *noun* **1a** a playing card, face of a dice, or domino marked with one spot or pip. **b** the single spot or pip on any of these. **2a** a shot, *esp* a service in tennis, that an opponent fails to reach. **b** a point scored by such a shot. **3a** *informal* an expert or leading performer in a specified field. **b** a combat pilot who has brought down five or more enemy aircraft. **4** *chiefly NAmer* in golf, a hole in one (see HOLE¹). **⁎ ace in the hole** *NAmer* an effective argument or resource held in reserve [a term in stud poker for an ace dealt face down so that its value is concealed]. **ace up one's sleeve** an effective argument or resource held in reserve. **hold all the aces** to have all the advantages or initiative. **within an ace of** on the point of; very near to: *They came within an ace of winning.* [Middle English *as* via Old French from Latin *as* a unit, a copper coin]

ace² *adj informal* excellent.

-acea *suffix* forming nouns, denoting: members of a class or order of animals: *Crustacea.* [scientific Latin *-acea* from Latin, neuter pl of *-aceus* -ACEOUS]

-aceae *suffix* forming nouns, denoting: members of a plant family: *Rosaceae.* [scientific Latin *-aceae* from Latin, fem pl of *-aceus* -ACEOUS]

acedia /ə'seedyə/ *noun* = ACCIDIE. [late Latin *acedia* from Greek *akēdeia*, from A-² + *kēdos* care, grief]

-aceous *suffix* forming adjectives, denoting: **1** characteristics or content: *herbaceous; farinaceous.* **2** a group of animals characterized by the form or feature specified: *cetaceous.* **3** a specified plant family: *rosaceous.* [Latin *-aceus*]

acephalous /ə'sefələs, ay-/ *adj* lacking a head or having the head reduced. [Greek *akephalos*, from A-² + *kephalē* head]

acer /'aysə/ *noun* any of a genus of trees or shrubs that have brightly coloured leaves with five pointed lobes; an ornamental maple: genus *Acer.* [from the Latin genus name, from Latin *acer* maple]

acerbic /ə'suhbik/ *adj* **1** bitter or sour in taste. **2** sharp or vitriolic in speech, temper, or manner: *acerbic wit.* **➤➤ acerbically** *adv,* **acerbity** *noun.* [French *acerbe* from Latin *acerbus* from *acer* sharp]

acet- *comb. form* see ACETO-.

acetabulum /asi'tabyoolǝm/ *noun* (pl **acetabulums** or **acetabula** /-lǝ/) **1** the cup-shaped socket in the hipbone into which the head of the thighbone fits. **2** a round sucker of a leech or other invertebrate animal. [Latin *acetabulum*, literally 'vinegar cup', from *acetum*: see ACETO-]

acetal /'asital/ *noun* any of various chemical compounds containing the group $C(OR)_2$, formed by adding alcohol to an aldehyde or a ketone. [German *Azetal*, from *Azet-* acetic + *Alkohol* alcohol]

acetaldehyde /asi'taldihied/ *noun* a colourless volatile liquid ALDEHYDE (chemical compound) used chiefly in the synthesis of other organic chemical compounds: formula CH_3CHO. [ACETIC + ALDEHYDE]

acetanilide /asi'tanilied/ *noun* a chemical compound derived from aniline that is used in the synthesis of other chemical compounds: formula $C_6H_5NHCOCH_3$. [ACETIC + ANILINE + -IDE]

acetate /'asitayt/ *noun* **1** *no longer in technical use* a salt or ester of acetic acid. **2a** = CELLULOSE ACETATE. **b** a textile fibre made from cellulose acetate. **c** an audio recording disc coated with cellulose acetate.

acetic /ə'seetik, ə'setik/ *adj no longer in technical use* of or producing acetic acid or vinegar. [prob via French *acétique* from Latin *acetum*: see ACETO-]

acetic acid *noun no longer in technical use* a pungent liquid acid that is the major acid in vinegar: formula CH_3COOH.

acetify /ə'seetifie, ə'set-/ *verb trans and intrans* (**acetifies, acetified, acetifying**) to form or turn into acetic acid or vinegar. **➤➤ acetification** /-fi'kaysh(ə)n/ *noun.*

aceto- or **acet-** *comb. form* forming words, denoting: acetic acid: *acetyl.* [via French *acét-* from Latin *acet-* from *acetum* vinegar, from *acēre* to be sour, from *acer* sharp]

acetone /'asitohn/ *noun no longer in technical use* a volatile fragrant liquid KETONE (organic chemical compound) used as a solvent, e.g. in varnishes, and in organic chemical synthesis: formula CH_3COCH_3. [German *Azeton* from Latin *acetum*: see ACETO-]

acetous /'asitəs/ *adj* **1** of or producing acetic acid or vinegar. **2** sour or vinegary.

acetyl /'asitil, -tiel/ *noun* the chemical group that is characteristic of acetic acid: formula CH_3CO.

acetylcholine /ˌasitil'kohleen, -lin/ *noun* a chemical compound that is released at many nerve endings and transmits nerve impulses. [ACETYL + *choline*, ultimately from Greek *cholē* bile]

acetylene /ə'setileen, -lin/ *noun* a colourless inflammable gas used *esp* as a fuel, e.g. in oxyacetylene torches, and in the synthesis of organic chemical compounds: formula C_2H_2.

acetylsalicylic acid /ˌasitil,sali'silik/ *noun* the chemical name for aspirin. [ACETYL + *salicylic* (from French *salicyle* the radical of the acid) + ACID²]

Achaean /ə'keeən/ *noun* **1** a native or inhabitant of Achaea in ancient Greece. **2** *literary* an ancient Greek. **➤➤ Achaean** *adj.* [Latin *Achaeus*, from Greek *Akhaios*]

ache¹ /ayk/ *verb intrans* **1a** to suffer a dull persistent pain. **b** (*often + for*) to feel anguish or distress: *His heart ached for her.* **2** to yearn or long to do something: *I ached to go home.* **➤➤ aching** *adj,* **achingly** *adv.* [Old English *acan*]

ache² *noun* a dull persistent pain.

achene /ə'keen/ *noun* a small dry one-seeded fruit that does not split open at maturity. [scientific Latin *achaenium*, from A-² + Greek *chainein* to yawn]

Acheulian or **Acheulean** /ə'shoohli·ən/ *adj* of a Lower Palaeolithic culture that followed the Abbevillian in Europe and was characterized by two-faced tools with round cutting edges. [French *Acheuléen*, from St *Acheul*, near Amiens in France, where objects from this culture were found]

achieve /ə'cheev/ *verb trans* **1** to accomplish (something) successfully. **2** to obtain (something) by effort; to win. **➤➤ achievable** *adj,* **achiever** *noun.* [Middle English *acheven* from early French *achever* to finish, from AD- + *chief*: see CHIEF¹]

achievement *noun* **1** something accomplished, *esp* by resolve, persistence, or courage; a feat. **2** successful completion or accomplishment. **3** performance in a test or academic course. **4** in heraldry, a coat of arms with its formal accompaniments, e.g. helm, crest, and supporters.

Achilles' heel /ə'kileez/ *noun* a single weak or vulnerable point.

Word history
Achilles, legendary Greek warrior, reputedly vulnerable only in the heel. As a child he was dipped in the River Styx by his mother to make him invulnerable, but the heel by which she held him did not touch the water.

Achilles tendon *noun* the strong tendon joining the muscles in the calf to the heelbone.

achlorhydria /ayklaw'hiedri·ə/ *noun* abnormal absence of hydrochloric acid from the digestive liquid in the stomach. [A-² + CHLORINE + HYDROGEN]

achondroplasia /ay,kondrə'playzi·ə/ *noun* the failure of normal development of cartilage in humans, resulting in dwarfism. **➤➤ achondroplastic** /-'plastik/ *adj.* [A-² + Greek *chondros* cartilage + -PLASIA]

achromat /'akrohmat/ *noun* an achromatic lens.

achromatic /akroh'matik, akrə-/ *adj* **1** transmitting light without dispersing it into its constituent colours: *an achromatic lens.* **2** possessing no hue; neutral: *Grey is an achromatic colour.* **3** in music, having no sharps or flats. **➤➤ achromatically** *adv,* **achromaticity** /ə,krohmə'tisiti/ *noun,* **achromatism** /ə'krohmətiz(ə)m/ *noun.* [French *achromatique* from Greek *achromatos*, from A-² + *chromat-, chroma* colour]

achy /'ayki/ *adj* (**achier, achiest**) suffering from aches.

acid¹ /'asid/ *adj* **1a** sour or sharp to the taste. **b** sharp, biting, or sour in speech, manner, or disposition; caustic: *an acid wit.* **2** of, containing, or being an acid: *acid soil.* **3** said of substances: having a pH of less than seven. **4** said of rock: rich in quartz. **5** said of a colour: piercingly intense: *acid yellow.* **➤➤ acidity** /ə'siditi/ *noun,* **acidly** *adv,* **acidness** *noun.* [French *acide* from Latin *acidus* from *acēre* to be sour, from *acer* sharp]

acid² *noun* **1a** any of various sour typically water-soluble compounds that have a pH of less than seven, turn litmus paper red, and are capable of reacting with an alkali or other chemical base to form a salt: compare ALKALI, BASE¹ (7). **b** any sour substance. **2** *slang* the hallucinogenic drug LSD. **3** = ACID HOUSE. **➤➤ acidic** /ə'sidik/ *adj.*

acid drop *noun* a hard sharp-tasting sweet made with sugar and tartaric acid.

acid house *noun* a style of very fast dance music with a lively beat that originated in the late 1980s. [prob from ACID² (2) + HOUSE MUSIC]

acidify /ə'sidifie/ *verb trans and intrans* (**acidifies, acidified, acidifying**) to form or convert (something) into an acidic solution. >> **acidification** /ə,sidifi'kaysh(ə)n/ *noun*.

acid jazz *noun* a kind of dance music containing features of jazz and soul music.

acidophilic /,asidoh'filik/ *adj* **1** said of a cell: staining readily with acid dyes. **2** said of a plant: preferring or thriving in an acid environment.

acidophilus /asi'dofiləs/ *noun* a bacterium used to make yogurt that has a beneficial effect on the digestive system: *Lactobacillus acidophilus*. [Latin *acidophilus* acidophilic]

acidosis /asi'dohsis/ *noun* a disorder in which the blood, tissues, etc are unusually acid. >> **acidotic** /-'dotik/ *adj*.

acid peel *noun* a beauty treatment involving exfoliation of the skin by means of any of a number of mild acids such as lactic acid or glycolic acid: compare PEEL² (2).

acid rain *noun* rain containing high levels of acid, *esp* sulphuric and nitric acid, caused by the release of pollution from burning fuel into the atmosphere

acid rock *noun* rock music marked by long passages of electronic musical effects intended to convey the atmosphere of drug-induced hallucinations.

acid test *noun* a severe or crucial test, e.g. of value or suitability. [from use of nitric acid to test for gold]

acidulate /ə'sidyoolayt/ *verb trans no longer in technical use* to make (something) slightly acid. >> **acidulation** /-'laysh(ə)n/ *noun*. [Latin *acidulus*: see ACIDULOUS]

acidulous /ə'sidyooləs/ *adj* somewhat acid in taste or manner; caustic: *The acidulous humour with which the American treated the Church of England disconcerted him* — Somerset Maugham. >> **acidulosity** /-'lositi/ *noun*. [Latin *acidulus* sourish, from *acidus*: see ACID¹]

acinus /'asinəs/ *noun* (*pl* **acini** /'asini/) **1** any of the small sacs lined with secreting cells found in certain glands, e.g. the pancreas. **2** any of the small individual fruits that make up a raspberry, blackberry, etc. >> **acinous** *adj*. [scientific Latin *acinus* from Latin, berry, berry seed]

ack-ack /'akak/ *adj* anti-aircraft. [signallers' terms for *AA* from *anti-aircraft*]

ackee /'akee, a'kee/ *noun* **1** a tropical tree bearing a red fruit: *Blighia sapida*. **2** the fruit of this tree, which is edible when fully ripe and cooked. [Kru *ā-kee*]

acknowledge /ək'nolij/ *verb trans* **1** to admit knowledge of (something); to concede (something) to be true, valid, or real. **2a** to express gratitude or obligation for (a service or kindness). **b** to show recognition of (somebody or their presence), e.g. by smiling or nodding. **c** to confirm receipt of (a letter). **3** to recognize the status or claims of (somebody). >> **acknowledgeable** *adj*. [ultimately from AD- + KNOWLEDGE]

acknowledgment *or* **acknowledgement** *noun* **1** acknowledging or being acknowledged. **2** something done or given in recognition of something received. **3** a declaration or avowal of a fact. **4** (*usu in pl*) a list of people to whom an author is indebted, usu appearing at the front of a book.

aclinic line /ə'klinik/ *noun* = MAGNETIC EQUATOR. [A-² + -CLINE]

acme /'akmi/ *noun* the highest point or stage, *esp* a perfect representative of a specified class or thing: *He was the acme of courtesy*. [Greek *akmē* point, highest point]

acne /'akni/ *noun* a skin disorder characterized by inflammation of the skin glands and hair follicles and causing red pustules, *esp* on the face and neck. >> **acned** *adj*. [Greek *aknē* eruption of the face, a misreading of *akmē* highest point]

acolyte /'akəliet/ *noun* **1** somebody who attends or assists another; a follower. **2** an assistant performing minor duties in a service of worship. [Middle English *acolite* via Old French and medieval Latin from Greek *akolouthos* follower, from *a-, ha-* (related to Greek *homos* same) + *keleuthos* path]

aconite /'akəniet/ *noun* **1** any of a genus of poisonous plants of the buttercup family bearing spikes of usu white, bluish, or purplish flowers, e.g. monkshood: genus *Aconitum*. **2** the dried tuberous root of monkshood or a related plant that yields a drug formerly used to reduce fever. **3** = WINTER ACONITE. >> **aconitic** /-'nitik/ *adj*. [French *aconite* via Latin from Greek *akoniton*]

acorn /'aykawn/ *noun* the nut of the oak, a smooth hard oval fruit in a cuplike base. [Old English *æcern*]

acorn barnacle *noun* a marine barnacle that forms an incrustation on coastal rocks: *Balanus balanoides*.

acorn worm *noun* a burrowing wormlike marine animal with an acorn-shaped proboscis: class Enteropneusta.

acoustic /ə'koohstik/ *or* **acoustical** /-kl/ *adj* **1** of sound, the sense of hearing, or acoustics. **2** denoting a musical instrument having sound that is not electronically amplified. **3** deadening or absorbing sound: *acoustic panelling*. >> **acoustically** *adv*. [Greek *akoustikos* of hearing, from *akouein* to hear]

acoustic impedance *noun* = IMPEDANCE (2).

acoustics *pl noun* **1** (*treated as sing. or pl*) the science of sound: *Acoustics is a branch of physics*. **2** the properties of a room, hall, etc that govern the quality of sound heard: *The room has good acoustics*. >> **acoustician** /akooh'stish(ə)n/ *noun*.

acquaint /ə'kwaynt/ *verb trans* (+ with) to cause (oneself or somebody else) to know something; to make (somebody) familiar with something: *I went out ... every day ... to acquaint myself with what the island produced* — Defoe. [Middle English *aquainten* via Old French *acointier* from medieval Latin *accognitare* from late Latin *accognoscere* to know perfectly, from AD- + Latin *cognoscere* to know]

acquaintance /ə'kwaynt(ə)ns/ *noun* **1** (*often* + with) personal knowledge; familiarity. **2a** somebody one knows but who is not a particularly close friend. **b** (*treated as sing. or pl*) the people with whom one is acquainted. * **make the acquaintance of** to meet or come to know (somebody). >> **acquaintanceship** *noun*.

acquaintance rape *noun* rape committed by a person known to the victim.

acquainted *adj* (*often* + with) said of people: having met one another socially; on familiar but not intimate terms.

acquiesce /akwee'es/ *verb intrans* (*often* + in) to submit or comply tacitly or passively: *Mr Trotter acquiesced in this agreeable proposal* — Dickens. >> **acquiescence** *noun*, **acquiescent** *adj*. [French *acquiescer* from Latin *acquiescere*, from AD- + *quiescere* to be quiet, from *quies* quiet, rest]

acquire /ə'kwie·ə/ *verb trans* **1** to gain or come into possession of (something), often by unspecified means. **2** to gain (something) as a new characteristic or ability. * **acquired taste** something one likes increasingly over time. >> **acquirable** *adj*, **acquirement** *noun*, **acquirer** *noun*. [Middle English *aqueren* via French from Latin *acquirere*, from AD- + *quaerere* to seek, obtain]

acquired characteristic *noun* a characteristic of an organism that is caused by the environment.

acquired immune deficiency syndrome *noun* see AIDS.

acquisition /akwi'zish(ə)n/ *noun* **1** acquiring or gaining possession. **2** something or somebody acquired, *esp* to the advantage of the acquirer. [Middle English *acquisicioun* via French from Latin *acquisition-, acquisitio*, from *acquirere*: see ACQUIRE]

acquisitive /ə'kwizətiv/ *adj* keen or tending to acquire and own material possessions. >> **acquisitively** *adv*, **acquisitiveness** *noun*.

acquit /ə'kwit/ *verb trans* (**acquitted, acquitting**) **1** (*often* + of) to free (somebody) from responsibility or obligation; *specif* to declare (an accused person) not guilty. **2** to conduct (oneself) in a specified, usu favourable, manner: *She acquitted herself well in the exam*. >> **acquitter** *noun*. [Middle English *aquiten* from Old French *aquiter*, from AD- + *quite*: see QUIT¹]

acquittal /ə'kwitl/ *noun* a judicial release from a criminal charge.

acquittance /ə'kwit(ə)ns/ *noun* a settlement of a debt, or a document certifying this.

acr- *comb. form* see ACRO-.

acre /'aykə/ *noun* **1** a unit of area equal to 4840yd² (about 0.405ha). **2** (*in pl*) lands; fields. **3** *informal* (*in pl*, + of) great quantities: *She was showing acres of flesh*. [Old English *æcer*]

acreage /'ayk(ə)rij/ *noun* an area of land in acres.

acrid /'akrid/ *adj* **1** unpleasantly pungent: *an acrid smell*. **2** violently bitter in manner or language; acrimonious. >> **acridity** /ə'kriditi/ *noun*, **acridly** *adv*. [modification of Latin *acr-, acer* sharp]

acridine /'akrideen/ *noun* a colourless solid chemical compound that occurs in coal tar and is used in the manufacture of dyes and antiseptics: formula $C_{13}H_9N$.

acriflavine /akri'flayveen, -vin/ *noun* a red or orange dye used as a skin disinfectant and antiseptic. [ACRIDINE + *flavine* from Latin *flavus* yellow]

acrimony /'akriməni/ *noun* caustic sharpness of manner or language resulting from anger or ill nature. ⟫⟫ **acrimonious** /akri'mohnyəs/ *adj,* **acrimoniously** *adv.* [early French *acrimonie* from Latin *acrimonia,* from *acr-, acer* sharp]

acro- *or* **acr-** *comb. form* forming words, denoting: **1** a beginning or end: *acronym; acrostic.* **2** a peak or height: *acropolis; acrophobia.* [early French *acro-* from Greek *akr-, akro-,* from *akros* topmost, extreme]

acrobat /'akrəbat/ *noun* somebody who performs gymnastic feats requiring skilful control of the body. ⟫⟫ **acrobatic** /-'batik/ *adj,* **acrobatically** /-'batikli/ *adv.* [French *acrobate* from Greek *akrobatēs* from *akrobatos* walking on tiptoe, from *akros* topmost + *bainein* to go]

acrobatics *pl noun* **1** (*treated as sing. or pl*) the art or performance of an acrobat. **2** a spectacular performance involving great agility: *vocal acrobatics.*

acromegaly /akroh'megəli, akrə-/ *noun* abnormal enlargement of the hands, feet, and face caused by excessive production of growth hormone by the pituitary gland. ⟫⟫ **acromegalic** /-mə'galik/ *adj and noun.* [French *acromégalie,* from ACRO- + Greek *megal-, megas* large]

acronym /'akrənim/ *noun* a word formed from the initial letters of other words, e.g. *Aids* from *acquired immune deficiency syndrome.* [ACRO- + *-onym* as in HOMONYM]

Usage note
See note at ABBREVIATION.

acrophobia /akrə'fohbi·ə/ *noun* abnormal dread of being at a great height. ⟫⟫ **acrophobic** *adj and noun.*

acropolis /ə'kropəlis/ *noun* the citadel of an ancient Greek city. [Greek *akropolis,* from ACRO- + *polis* city]

across[1] /ə'kros/ *adv* **1** from one side to the other: *Pull the curtain across.* **2** to or on the opposite side: *I swam across to the far bank of the river.* **3** so as to be understandable, acceptable, or successful: *We need to get the message across.* [Middle English *acros* from Anglo-French *an crois,* from Latin *in* in + *crux* cross]

across[2] *prep* **1a** from one side to the other of (something): *He walked across the lawn.* **b** on the opposite side of (something): *She lives across the street.* **2** so as to intersect (something) at an angle: *sawing across the grain of the wood.*

across the board *adv* so as to embrace all classes or categories: *The pay rise will be applied across the board.*

across-the-board *adj* embracing all classes or categories: *an across-the-board pay rise.*

acrostic /ə'krostik/ *noun* **1** a composition, usu in verse, in which sets of letters, e.g. the first of each line, form a word or phrase: *I had an acrostic once sent to me upon my name, which I was not at all pleased with* — Jane Austen. **2** a series of words of equal length arranged to read the same horizontally or vertically. [early French *acrostiche* from Greek *akrostichis,* from ACRO- + *stichos* line of verse]

acrylamide /ə'krilləmied/ *noun* the amide of acrylic acid, a white, odourless, water-soluble, combustible substance with possible carcinogenic, genotoxic and neurotoxic effects: formula C_3H_5NO. It is used in many industrial processes, such as water purification, and is found in food that has been cooked or processed at a high temperature.

acrylic[1] /ə'krilik/ *adj* of acrylic acid or its derivatives: *acrylic polymers.* [from *acrolein* a liquid aldehyde, from Latin *acr-, acer* sharp + *olēre* to smell]

acrylic[2] *noun* **1a** = ACRYLIC RESIN. **b** a paint containing an acrylic resin. **c** a painting done in this paint. **2** = ACRYLIC FIBRE.

acrylic acid *noun no longer in technical use* an unsaturated liquid acid used in the manufacture of acrylic resins and other plastics: formula $CH_2:CHCOOH$.

acrylic fibre *noun* a synthetic textile fibre made from the chemical compound acrylonitrile and usu other polymers.

acrylic resin *noun* a glasslike plastic made by causing acrylic acid or one of its derivatives to react to form a polymer.

ACT *abbr* **1** advance corporation tax. **2** Australian Capital Territory.

act[1] /akt/ *noun* **1a** a thing done. **b** the process of doing something: *He was in the act of opening the door.* **2** (*often* **Act**). **a** a formal record of something done or transacted. **b** = STATUTE (1). **c** a decree or edict. **3a** any of the principal divisions of a play or opera. **b** any of the successive parts or performances in an entertainment, e.g. a circus. **4a** a display of affected behaviour; a pretence: *Her show of concern was just an act.* **b** a particular kind of behaviour: *He was doing his Robin Hood act.* ✳ **be/get in on the act** to be or become involved in a situation or undertaking, *esp* for one's own advantage. **get one's act together** *informal* to organize one's affairs and become more efficient. [Middle English; partly from Latin *actus* doing, act, from *agere* to drive, do; partly from Latin *actum* thing done, record, neuter of *actus*]

act[2] *verb intrans* **1a** to take action; to do something. **b** to function or behave in a specified manner: *She acted for the best.* **2** (+ as) to perform a specified function; to serve as something specified: *The threat acts as a deterrent.* **3** (+ for) to be a substitute or representative, especially in a legal case: *acting for the defendant.* **4** (*often* + on) to produce an effect: *The drug acts on the nervous system.* **5** (+ on) to do something in accordance with advice or instructions: *The police were acting on information received from the public.* **6a** to perform on the stage; to engage in acting. **b** to behave insincerely: *He appeared sympathetic, but he was only acting.* ⟩ *verb trans* **1** to represent (a part) by action, *esp* on the stage. **2** to feign or simulate (a feeling). **3** to play the part of (somebody or something) in or as if in a play: *He always wanted to act Hamlet; Don't act the fool.* **4** to behave in a manner suitable to (e.g. one's age). ⟫⟫ **actability** /-'biliti/ *noun,* **actable** *adj.*

ACTH *abbr* adrenocorticotrophic hormone.

actin /'aktin/ *noun* a protein found in muscle and other cells that combines with myosin in producing muscular contraction. [Latin *actus*: see ACT[1]]

actin- *or* **actino-** *comb. form* forming words, denoting: **1** a radiate form: *actinomorphic.* **2** radiation: *actinometer.* [scientific Latin *actin-, actino-* from Greek *aktin-, aktino-,* from *aktin-, aktis* ray]

acting[1] /'akting/ *adj* holding a temporary rank or position: *the acting president.*

acting[2] *noun* the art or practice of representing a character in a dramatic production.

actinia /ak'tiniə/ *noun* a sea anemone found in rock pools: genus *Actinia.* [from the Latin genus name, from ACTIN- + -IA[1]]

actinic /ak'tinik/ *adj* said of radiant energy, *esp* visible and ultraviolet light: having the property by which chemical changes are produced. ⟫⟫ **actinism** /'aktiniz(ə)m/ *noun.*

actinide /'aktinied/ *noun* any of a series of 15 radioactive elements from actinium (atomic number 89) to lawrencium (atomic number 103). [ACTINIUM + -IDE]

actinium /ak'tini·əm/ *noun* a radioactive metallic chemical element found *esp* in pitchblende: symbol Ac, atomic number 89. [scientific Latin *actinium* from Greek *aktin-, aktis* ray]

actino- *comb. form* see ACTIN-.

actinoid /'aktinoyd/ *adj* having a radiate form.

actinometer /akti'nomitə/ *noun* an instrument for measuring the intensity of radiation, *esp* solar radiation.

actinomorphic /,aktinoh'mawfik/ *adj* said of an organism or part: radially symmetrical. [ACTIN- + Greek *morphē* form, shape]

actinomycete /,aktinoh'mieseet/ *noun* any of an order of threadlike or rod-shaped bacteria: order Actinomycetales. [ACTIN- + Greek *mykēt-, mykēs* fungus]

actinozoan /,aktinoh'zoh·ən/ *noun* = ANTHOZOAN. ⟫⟫ **actinozoan** *adj.* [ACTIN- + Greek *zōion* animal]

action[1] /'aksh(ə)n/ *noun* **1a** practical activity usu directed towards a particular aim. **b** the state of functioning actively: *while the machine is in action.* **c** energetic activity, initiative, or enterprise: *a man of action.* **2** the process of acting or working, *esp* to produce alteration by force or through a natural agency. **3** a voluntary act; a deed. **4** the events in a play or work of fiction. **5** armed combat in war, or an occurrence of this: *killed in action.* **6a** the operating part of a mechanism or device. **b** the manner in which it operates. **c** a movement of the body, or the manner of this. **7** a civil legal proceeding. **8** (**the action**) *informal* lively or productive activity: *We go where the action is.* ✳ **out of action** not working or functioning actively. **take action 1** to begin to act; to do something. **2** to begin legal proceedings. [Middle English *accioun* via French from Latin *action-, actio,* from *agere* to drive, do]

action[2] *verb trans* to take action on (a plan, proposal, etc.).

actionable *adj* giving grounds for an action at law. ➤➤ **actionably** *adv*.

action painting *noun* abstract art in which spontaneous techniques, e.g. throwing, dripping, or smearing, are used to apply paint.

action replay *noun* a recording of a televised incident, *esp* in a sporting event, usu played back in slow motion.

action stations *pl noun* **1** the positions taken up by members of the armed forces preparing for military action. **2** a state of readiness.

activate /'aktivayt/ *verb trans* **1** to cause (something) to start operating. **2** to make (something) active or reactive, or more so, *esp* in chemical or physical properties, e.g.. **a** to make (a substance) radioactive. **b** to increase the rate of (a chemical reaction). **3** *NAmer* to put (troops) on active duty. ➤➤ **activation** /-'vaysh(ə)n/ *noun*, **activator** *noun*.

activated carbon or **activated charcoal** *noun* powdered or granular carbon that has been chemically treated to increase its adsorptive properties and is used chiefly for removing impurities, e.g. from alcohol, by adsorption.

activated sludge *noun* sewage aerated to favour the growth of organisms that decompose organic matter.

active[1] /'aktiv/ *adj* **1** moving, working, or operating, not at rest. **2a** quick in physical movement; lively. **b** marked by or requiring vigorous activity: *active sports*. **c** full of activity; busy: *an active life*. **3** characterized by practical action rather than by contemplation or speculation: *an active interest in politics*. **4** having practical results; effective: *an active ingredient*. **5** said of a volcano: liable to erupt; not extinct. **6a** in grammar, said of a verb form or voice: having as the subject the person or thing doing the action. **b** said of a sentence: containing an active verb form. **7** relating to full-time service, *esp* in the armed forces. **8** said of a substance: capable of acting or reacting; activated. **9** said of an electronic device, a transistor or valve: using electrical power for amplifying or controlling an electrical signal. ➤➤ **actively** *adv*, **activeness** *noun*. [Middle English via French from Latin *activus*, from *agere* to drive, do]

active[2] *noun* **1** an active form of a verb. **2** the active voice of a language.

active list *noun* a list of officers in the armed forces who are available for duty.

active transport *noun* the movement of a chemical substance across a cell membrane in living tissue by the expenditure of energy.

activism /'aktiviz(ə)m/ *noun* a doctrine or practice that emphasizes direct vigorous or militant action, e.g. the use of mass demonstrations, in support of or opposition to a controversial, *esp* political, cause. ➤➤ **activist** *noun*.

activity /ak'tiviti/ *noun* (*pl* **activities**) **1** the quality or state of being active. **2** vigorous or energetic action; liveliness. **3** a pursuit in which a person takes part for business, recreation, etc. **4** in chemistry, the capacity of a substance to react.

act of God *noun* a sudden event, *esp* a catastrophe, brought about by uncontrollable natural forces.

actor /'aktə/ *noun* a man or woman who represents a character in a dramatic production; *esp* one whose profession is acting.

act out *verb trans* to represent (ideas, feelings, beliefs, etc) by actions: *Children act out what they read*.

actress /'aktris/ *noun* a female actor.

actual /'aktyoo(ə)l, 'akchoo(ə)l/ *adj* existing or happening in fact or at the time. [Middle English *actuel* via French from late Latin *actualis*, from Latin *actus*: see ACT[1]]

actual bodily harm *noun* physical harm, less serious than grievous bodily harm, deliberately inflicted by one person on another.

actualise *verb trans* see ACTUALIZE.

actuality /aktyoo'aliti, akchoo-/ *noun* (*pl* **actualities**) **1** the quality or state of being actual; reality. **2** (*often in pl*) an existing circumstance; a real fact: *possible risks which have been seized upon as actualities* — T S Eliot.

actualize or **actualise** *verb trans* to make (an idea, hope, etc) actual or real. ➤➤ **actualization** /-'zaysh(ə)n/ *noun*.

actually *adv* **1** really; in fact. **2** at the present moment: *the party actually in power*. **3** strange as it may seem; even: *She actually spoke Latin*.

Usage note

In the first sense *actually*, like *really*, is a useful word, especially in speech. It is used to reinforce or emphasize a point and can enhance the continuity and balance of a sentence: *'I told you.' 'Actually, I don't think you did.'* (Here, *actually* softens the contradiction.) But with frequent use it can become irritating, especially in writing and when it is clearly redundant, i.e. when the sentence would mean exactly the same without it and it hardly improves the flow: *It's actually quite cold. Did you actually mean that? Actually, I think I'll stay here.*

actuary /'aktyoo(ə)ri, 'akchoo-/ *noun* (*pl* **actuaries**) a statistician who calculates insurance risks and premiums. ➤➤ **actuarial** /aktyoo'eəri·əl, akchoo-/ *adj*, **actuarially** *adv*. [Latin *actuarius* shorthand writer, accountant, from *actum*: see ACT[1]]

actuate /'aktyooayt, 'akchooayt/ *verb trans* **1** to put (a device or machine) into action or motion. **2** to incite (somebody) to action; to motivate (somebody): *They were actuated by greed*. ➤➤ **actuation** /-'aysh(ə)n/ *noun*, **actuator** *noun*. [medieval Latin *actuatus*, past part. of *actuare*, from Latin *actus*: see ACT[1]]

act up *verb intrans informal* to behave badly or perform erratically.

acuity /ə'kyooh·iti/ *noun formal* keenness of mental or physical perception. [early French *acuité*, ultimately from Latin *acutus*: see ACUTE[1]]

aculeate /ə'kyoohli·ət/ *adj* **1** said of an insect: having a sting. **2** said of a plant: having thorns or prickles. [Latin *aculeatus* having stings, from *aculeus*, dimin. of *acus* needle]

acumen /'akyoomən/ *noun* keenness and depth of discernment or discrimination, *esp* in practical matters; shrewdness. [Latin *acumin-, acumen* point, from *acuere*: see ACUTE[1]]

acuminate /ə'kyoohminət/ *adj* said e.g. of a leaf: tapering to a slender point. [Latin *acumin-, acumen* (see ACUMEN) + -ATE[3]]

acupoint /'akyoopoynt/ *noun* any of the points on the body at which acupuncture or acupressure is applied. [ACUPUNCTURE + POINT[1]]

acupressure /'ak(y)oopreshə/ *noun* the application of controlled pressure to the body at particular points, usu with the fingers, for therapeutic purposes, e.g. to relieve pain. Also called SHIATSU. [ACUPUNCTURE + PRESSURE[1]]

acupuncture /'ak(y)oopungkchə/ *noun* the practice, Chinese in origin, of puncturing the body at particular points with needles to cure disease, relieve pain, produce anaesthesia, etc. ➤➤ **acupuncturist** *noun*. [Latin *acus* needle + PUNCTURE[1]]

acute[1] /ə'kyooht/ *adj* **1a** marked by keen discernment or intellectual perception, *esp* of subtle distinctions: *an acute thinker*. **b** highly responsive to impressions or stimuli: *acute eyesight*. **2** intensely felt or perceived: *acute pain*. **3** said of an illness: having a sudden severe onset and short course: compare CHRONIC. **4** demanding urgent attention; severe: *an acute housing shortage*. **5a** said of an angle: measuring less than 90°. **b** composed of acute angles: *an acute triangle*. **6** marked with or being an acute accent: *e acute*. ➤➤ **acutely** *adv*, **acuteness** *noun*. [Latin *acutus*, past part. of *acuere* to sharpen, from *acus* needle]

acute[2] *noun* = ACUTE ACCENT.

acute accent *noun* a mark (´) placed over certain vowels in some languages, e.g. over *e* in French, to show a particular vowel quality or stress.

ACW *abbr* aircraftwoman.

acyclovir /ay'siekləvieə/ *noun* an antiviral drug used in the treatment of herpes and HIV infections. [A-[2] + CYCLIC + VIRAL]

acyl /'as(i)l, 'asiel/ *noun* a chemical group derived from an organic chemical acid by removal of the hydroxyl group. [ACID[1] + -YL]

AD *abbr* anno Domini, used to indicate that a year or century comes within the Christian era.

Usage note

AD and BC. AD is traditionally written before a number signifying a year: *AD 1625*. This is because the abbreviation *AD* means *Anno Domini* (in the year of our Lord), and if the phrase were written out in full it would make better sense before the date than after it. This practice is by no means universally adhered to with year numbers, however, and when referring to centuries it is necessary to place *AD* at the end of the phrase: *in the third century AD*. *BC* always follows a date: *440 BC; the seventh century BC*. In printed text these abbreviations are often written in small capitals: AD and BC.

ad /ad/ *noun informal* an advertisement.

ad- *or* **a-** *or* **ac-** *or* **af-** *or* **ag-** *or* **al-** *or* **ap-** *or* **ar-** *or* **as-** *or* **at-** *prefix* (a- before sc, sp, st; ac- before c, k, q; af- before f; ag- before g; al- before l; ap- before p; as- before s; at- before t) forming words, denoting: **1** movement or direction: *advance*; *aggression*. **2** proximity: *adrenal*. [Middle English via Old French, from Latin *ad*]

adage /'adij/ *noun* a maxim or proverb that embodies a commonly accepted observation: *Talk of the devil – excuse the adage!* — Henry James. [French *adage* from Latin *adagium*, from AD- + *-agium* (related to *aio* I say)]

adagio /ə'dahjioh/ *adj and adv* said of a piece of music: to be performed in a slow gentle tempo. ⟫ **adagio** *noun*. [Italian *adagio*, from *ad* at, to + *agio* ease]

adamant¹ /'adəmənt/ *adj* refusing to change one's mind; determined; unyielding. ⟫ **adamance** *noun*, **adamantly** *adv*.

adamant² *noun* a legendary stone said to be of impenetrable hardness and sometimes identified with the diamond.

adamantine /adə'mantien/ *adj* made of or like adamant; impenetrably hard or unbreakable: *to bottomless perdition, there to dwell in adamantine chains and penal fire* — Milton.

Adam's apple *noun* the projection in the front of the neck, more prominent in men, formed by the largest cartilage of the larynx. [from the legend that when Adam, the first man according to the Bible, ate the forbidden fruit, a piece of it stuck in his throat]

adapt /ə'dapt/ *verb trans and intrans* (*often* + to) to make (a person or thing) or become suited to different circumstances, etc, often by modification. ⟫ **adaptability** /-'biliti/ *noun*, **adaptable** *adj*, **adaptive** *adj*. [French *adapter* from Latin *adaptare*, from AD- + *aptare* to fit, from *aptus* apt, fit]

adaptation /adap'taysh(ə)n/ *noun* **1** adapting or being adapted; adjustment to prevailing or changing conditions. **2a** adjustment of a sense organ to the intensity or quality of stimulation. **b** modification of an organism or its parts, fitting it better for existence and successful breeding under the conditions of its environment. **3** a composition rewritten in a new form or for a different medium, *esp* a play or film.

adapter *or* **adaptor** /ə'daptə/ *noun* **1** somebody who adapts something; *specif* the writer of an adaptation. **2a** a device for connecting two pieces of apparatus not orig intended to be joined. **b** a device for converting a tool or piece of apparatus to some new use. **c** a device for connecting several pieces of electrical apparatus to a single power point, or connecting a plug of one type to a socket of a different type.

adaxial /ad'aksi·əl/ *adj* situated on the same side as or facing the axis of an organ, plant part, or organism; compare ABAXIAL.

ADC *abbr* **1** aide-de-camp. **2** analogue-to-digital converter.

add /ad/ *verb trans* **1** to join (something to something else) so as to bring about an increase or improvement: *Wine adds a creative touch to cooking*. **2** to say or write (something) further: *She added that she might be late*. **3** (*often* + up) to combine (numbers) into a single number. ⟫ *verb intrans* **1** to add up numbers: *The children are learning to add*. **2** (+ to) to make or serve as an addition to something: *Being robbed just added to his misery*. [Middle English *adden* from Latin *addere*, from AD- + *-dere* to put]

addax /'adaks/ *noun* a large antelope with spiral horns and a light-coloured coat that lives in the deserts of N Africa: *Addax nasomaculatus*. [from an ancient African word]

addend /'adend, ə'dend/ *noun* a number to be added to another. [short for ADDENDUM]

addendum /ə'dendəm/ *noun* (*pl* **addenda** /-də/) **1** something added; an addition. **2** (*often in pl*) an extra item at the end of a book. [Latin *addendum*, neuter of *addendus*, gerundive of *addere*: see ADD]

adder /'adə/ *noun* **1** a common European venomous viper that has a dark zigzag pattern along the back: *Vipera berus*. **2** any of various similar or related snakes.

Word history

Middle English, alteration (by incorrect division of *a naddre*) of *naddre*, from Old English *nædre*. This word has lost its original initial *n* through a process that also affected *apron* and *umpire* in the 14th and 15th cents. When it was preceded by the indefinite article, the two words were misinterpreted: *a nadder* was taken as *an adder*, and likewise *a napron* as *an apron* and *a numpire* as *an umpire*. The form *nether*, preserving the initial *n*, still exists dialectally. For the opposite process, by which a word has gained an initial *n*, see note at NEWT.

adder's-tongue *noun* a fern with a spore-bearing spike that resembles a snake's tongue: genus *Ophioglossum*.

addict¹ /ə'dikt/ *verb trans* (*usu in passive*) **1** to cause (somebody) to become dependent on a habit-forming drug: *She was addicted to tranquillizers*. **2** to cause (somebody) to indulge habitually or obsessively in (an activity): *He is addicted to computer games*. ⟫ **addiction** *noun*, **addictive** *adj*. [Latin *addictus*, past part. of *addicere* to favour, from AD- + *dicere* to say]

addict² /'adikt/ *noun* **1** somebody who is addicted to a drug: *a heroin addict*. **2** an enthusiast or devotee: *a detective-novel addict*.

Addison's disease /'adis(ə)nz/ *noun* a disease marked by deficient secretion of the hormones of the outer region of the adrenal gland and characterized by extreme weakness, loss of weight, and brownish pigmentation of the skin. [named after Thomas *Addison* d.1860, English physician]

addition /ə'dish(ə)n/ *noun* **1** the act or process of adding, *esp* adding numbers. **2** something or somebody added: *They say the lady is fair … and wise, but for loving me – by my troth, it is no addition to her wit* — Shakespeare. ✳ **in addition** (*often* + to) also; as well. [Middle English via French from Latin *addition-*, *additio*, from *addere*: see ADD]

additional *adj* added, extra, or supplementary. ⟫ **additionally** *adv*.

additional member system *noun* a system of proportional representation in which electors vote separately for the party of their choice and a candidate representing that party.

additive¹ /'adətiv/ *noun* a substance added to another in relatively small amounts to impart desirable properties or suppress undesirable ones.

additive² *adj* of, characterized by, or produced by addition.

addle¹ /'adl/ *adj* **1** (*used in combinations*) confused or muddled: *addle-headed*. **2** *archaic* said of an egg: rotten. [Old English *adela* filth]

addle² *verb trans and intrans* **1** to confuse or muddle (somebody), or to become muddled. **2** said of an egg: to become rotten.

add-on¹ *noun* **1** an additional piece of equipment connected to an electronic device, e.g. a computer, to supply auxiliary functions; a peripheral. **2** an accessory or extension.

add-on² *adj* of or being an add-on: *an add-on feature*.

address¹ /ə'dres/ *verb trans* **1** to mark directions for delivery on (e.g. a letter or package). **2a** to speak or write directly to (somebody). **b** to deliver a formal speech to (a group of people). **c** (+ to) to communicate (something) directly to somebody: *Address your thanks to your host*. **3** (+ as) to greet (somebody) by a prescribed form: *They addressed him as 'My Lord'*. **4a** (+ to) to direct the efforts or attention of (oneself) to something: *He addressed himself to the problem*. **b** to deal with, apply oneself to, or tackle (e.g. a problem). **5** in golf etc, to take one's stance and adjust the club before hitting (the ball). ⟫ **addressee** /adre'see/ *noun*, **addresser** *noun*. [Middle English *adressen* from early French *adresser*, from AD- + *dresser* to arrange: see DRESS¹]

address² *noun* **1a** a place, *esp* of residence, where a person or organization may be reached by a communication. **b** a description of such a location in conventional form, e.g. written on an envelope. **2a** a location, e.g. in the memory of a computer, where particular information is stored. **b** the digits that identify such a location. **3** a prepared speech delivered to an audience. **4** *dated* (*usu in pl*) dutiful and courteous attention, *esp* in courtship: *He paid his addresses to her*.

addressable *adj* in computing, denoting a location in memory that can be separately accessed by a program.

adduce /ə'dyoohs/ *verb trans formal* to offer (something) as example, reason, or proof in discussion or analysis: *Many analogous cases could be adduced* — Darwin. ⟫ **adducible** *adj*, **adduction** /ə'duksh(ə)n/ *noun*. [Latin *adducere* to lead to, from AD- + *ducere* to lead]

adduct¹ /ə'dukt/ *verb trans* said of a muscle: to draw (e.g. a limb) towards the main part of the body: compare ABDUCT. ⟫ **adduction** *noun*, **adductor** *noun*. [Latin *adductus*, past part. of *adducere*: see ADDUCE]

adduct² /'adukt/ *noun* a chemical compound, molecule, etc formed by direct combination of two or more compounds, molecules, or elements. [ADDITION + PRODUCT]

add up *verb intrans* **1a** to come to the expected total. **b** *informal* to be internally consistent; to make sense: *His version of events just doesn't add up.* **2** (+ to) to amount to something in total or substance: *It all adds up to a great experience.*

-ade *suffix* forming nouns, denoting: **1a** an act or action: *blockade; escapade.* **b** an individual or group of people involved in an action: *cavalcade; renegade.* **2** a product, *esp* a sweet drink made from a specified fruit: *limeade.* [Middle English via French from Old Provençal *-ada* from late Latin *-ata*, from Latin, fem of *-atus* -ATE²]

aden- *or* **adeno-** *comb. form* forming words, denoting: gland: *adenoid.* [scientific Latin *aden-, adeno-* from Greek, from *aden-, adēn* gland]

adenine /'adəneen, -nin/ *noun* a PURINE (chemical compound) that is one of the four bases whose order in a DNA or RNA chain codes genetic information: compare CYTOSINE, GUANINE, THYMINE, URACIL. [ADEN- + -INE²: from its presence in glandular tissue]

adeno- *comb. form* see ADEN-.

adenoid /'adinoyd/ *noun* (*usu in pl*) a mass of glandular tissue at the back of the pharynx that characteristically obstructs breathing when enlarged. [Greek *adenoeidēs* glandular, from *adēn* gland]

adenoidal /adə'noydl/ *adj* **1** of the adenoids. **2** of or characteristic of somebody with enlarged adenoids: *an adenoidal voice.*

adenoma /adə'nohmə/ *noun* (*pl* **adenomas** *or* **adenomata** /-'mahtə/) a benign tumour of a glandular structure or of glandular origin. [scientific Latin *adenomat-, adenoma*, from Greek *ādēn* gland]

adenosine /ə'denəseen, -sin/ *noun* a NUCLEOSIDE (chemical compound) containing adenine and ribose that forms part of RNA. [ADENINE + RIBOSE]

adenosine diphosphate *noun* see ADP¹.

adenosine monophosphate *noun* see AMP.

adenosine triphosphate *noun* see ATP¹.

adept¹ /'adept, ə'dept/ *adj* (*often* + at) highly skilled or proficient: *adept at changing the subject.* ▶▶ **adeptly** /ə'deptli/ *adv*, **adeptness** /ə'deptnis/ *noun*. [Latin *adeptus* alchemist who has discovered how to change base metals into gold, from *adipisci* to attain, from AD- + *apisci* to reach]

adept² /'adept/ *noun* a highly skilled person: *an adept at negotiating.*

adequate /'adikwət/ *adj* **1** sufficient for a specific requirement: *adequate grounds for divorce.* **2** barely sufficient or satisfactory. ▶▶ **adequacy** /-si/ *noun*, **adequately** *adv*. [Latin *adaequatus*, past part. of *adaequare* to make equal, from AD- + *aequare* to equal]

à deux /ah 'duh (*French* a dø)/ *adj* of, for, or involving only two people: *a cosy evening à deux.* [French *à deux*]

ADF *abbr* automatic direction-finder.

ADH *abbr* antidiuretic hormone.

ADHD *abbr* attention deficit hyperactivity disorder, a condition occurring mainly in children, characterized by impaired concentration, hyperactivity, and learning and behavioural difficulties.

adhere /əd'(h)iə/ *verb intrans* **1** (*usu* + to) to stick or hold fast by or as if by gluing, suction, grasping, etc. **2a** (+ to) to give continued support or loyalty to (e.g. a political party or religion). **b** (+ to) to observe or follow (something) exactly: *adhere to the rules.* ▶▶ **adherence** *noun*. [French *adhérer* from Latin *adhaerēre*, from AD- + *haerēre* to stick]

adherent¹ /əd'(h)iərənt/ *noun* a supporter of a leader, cause, etc. [Middle English via French from Latin *adhaerent-, adhaerens*, present part. of *adhaerēre*: see ADHERE]

adherent² *adj* sticking or holding fast; adhering.

adhesion /əd'(h)eezh(ə)n, ad'heezh(ə)n/ *noun* **1** the action or state of adhering. **2a** in medicine, an abnormal union of tissues that are usu separated in the body. **b** the tissues united by this process. [French *adhésion* from Latin *adhaesion-, adhaesio*, from *adhaerēre*: see ADHERE]

adhesive¹ /əd'(h)eeziv, -siv/ *adj* causing adherence or prepared for adhering; sticky. ▶▶ **adhesively** *adv*, **adhesiveness** *noun*.

adhesive² *noun* an adhesive substance, e.g. glue.

ad hoc /ad 'hok/ *adj and adv* for the particular purpose at hand and without consideration of wider applications: *an ad hoc investigation.* [Latin *ad hoc* for this]

ad hominem /ad 'hominem/ *adj and adv* **1** based on personal rather than intellectual grounds: *an ad hominem argument.* **2**

associated with a particular person: *an ad hominem appointment.* [Latin *ad hominem*, literally 'to the man']

adiabatic /,adi-ə'batik/ *adj* said of a thermodynamic process: occurring without loss or gain of heat. ▶▶ **adiabatically** *adv*. [Greek *adiabatos* impassable, from A-¹ + *diabatos* passable, from *diabainein* to go across, from DIA- + *bainein* to go]

adieu /ə'dyooh, ə'dyuh (*French* adjø)/ *interj and noun* (*pl* **adieus** *or* **adieux** /ə'dyooh(z), ə'dyuh(z) (*French* adjø)/) *chiefly literary* goodbye. [Middle English from early French *a Dieu* to God, from Latin *Deus*]

ad infinitum /,ad infi'nietəm/ *adv* without end or limit; indefinitely. [Latin *ad infinitum* to an infinite extent]

ad interim *adj and adv* in the meantime. [Latin *ad interim*]

adipocere /adipoh'siə/ *noun* a fatty substance resembling wax that sometimes forms in dead bodies during decomposition. [Latin *adip-, adeps* fat + French *cire* wax]

adipose /'adipohs, -pohz/ *adj* of or containing animal fat; fatty: *adipose tissue.* ▶▶ **adiposity** /-'positi/ *noun*. [scientific Latin *adiposus*, from Latin *adip-, adeps* fat, from Greek *aleipha*]

adit /'adit/ *noun* a nearly horizontal passage from the surface into a mine for access or drainage. [Latin *aditus* an approach, past part. of *adire* to go to, from AD- + *ire* to go]

adj. *abbr* **1** adjective. **2** adjutant.

adjacent /ə'jays(ə)nt/ *adj* **1** (*often* + to) having a common boundary or border: *the video shop adjacent to the post office.* **2** neighbouring or nearby: *the town and adjacent villages.* **3** said of two angles: having the point from which the lines diverge and one side in common. ▶▶ **adjacency** *noun*, **adjacently** *adv*. [Middle English via French from Latin *adjacent-, adjacens*, present part. of *adjacēre* to lie near, from AD- + *jacēre* to lie]

adjective /'ajiktiv/ *noun* **1** a word that modifies a noun or pronoun by describing a particular characteristic of it. **2** (*used before a noun*) functioning as an adjective: *an adjective phrase.* ▶▶ **adjectival** /-'tievl/ *adj*, **adjectivally** /-'tievəli/ *adv*. [Middle English via French from late Latin *adjectivus* from Latin *adjicere* to throw to, from AD- + *jacere* to throw]

adjoin /ə'joyn/ *verb trans* said of e.g. a building, room, or piece of land: to be next to, in contact with, or joined to (another). ▶▶ **adjoining** *adj*. [Middle English *adjoinen* via early French *adjoindre* from Latin *adjungere*, from AD- + *jungere* to join]

adjourn /ə'juhn/ *verb trans* **1** to suspend (e.g. a session or meeting) until a later usu stated time. **2** to defer (something) for later consideration or resolution. ▶ *verb intrans* **1** to suspend a session, meeting, etc. **2** *informal* to move to another place: *We adjourned to one of those pretty cafes and took supper* — Mark Twain. ▶▶ **adjournment** *noun*. [Middle English *ajournen* from early French *ajourner*, from AD- + *jour* day]

adjudge /ə'juj/ *verb trans* **1a** to adjudicate (a matter). **b** to declare or judge (somebody) formally to be as specified: *He was adjudged guilty.* **c** to award or grant (e.g. costs) judicially. **2** to hold or declare (something) to be as specified: *The critics adjudge the book a success.* [Middle English *ajugen* via French from Latin *adjudicare*, from AD- + *judicare*: see JUDGE¹]

adjudicate /ə'joohdikayt/ *verb trans* to make a judicial decision on (a matter). ▶ *verb intrans* to act as judge, e.g. in a competition. ▶▶ **adjudication** /-'kaysh(ə)n/ *noun*, **adjudicative** *adj*, **adjudicator** *noun*. [Latin *adjudicatus*, past part. of *adjudicare*: see ADJUDGE]

adjunct¹ /'ajungkt/ *noun* **1** (*often* + to/of) something added or joined to another thing as an incidental accompaniment rather than an essential part: *Hitherto galleries had been living-rooms presenting pictures as adjuncts to polite living* — Daily Telegraph. **2** in grammar, a word or group of words, e.g. an adverb or prepositional phrase, that is not one of the principal structural elements in a sentence. **3** a person, usu in a subordinate or temporary capacity, assisting another to perform some duty or service: *Walpole was a minister given by the King to the people: Pitt was a minister given by the people to the King, – as an adjunct* — Dr Johnson. ▶▶ **adjunctive** /ə'jungktiv/ *adj*. [Latin *adjunctum*, neuter of *adjunctus*, past part. of *adjungere*: see ADJOIN]

adjunct² *adj* attached in a subordinate or temporary capacity; auxiliary: *an adjunct psychiatrist.*

adjure /ə'jooə/ *verb trans formal* **1** to charge or command (somebody) solemnly, *esp* under oath or penalty of a curse, to do something: *The woman was adjured by the priest to swear whether she were false or no* — Milton. **2** to entreat or advise (somebody) earnestly to do something: *I was adjuring him to bring the corkscrew, that I might open another bottle of wine* — Dickens. ➤➤ **adjuration** /ˌajooˈraysh(ə)n/ *noun*, **adjuratory** /-rət(ə)ri/ *adj*. [Middle English *adjuren* via early French *ajurer* from Latin *adjurare*, from AD- + *jurare* to swear, from *jur-*, *jus* JUST¹]

adjust /əˈjust/ *verb trans* **1** to bring (something) to a more satisfactory or correct state by minor change or adaptation; to regulate, correct, or modify (something): *You will have to adjust your lifestyle to suit your income.* **2** to determine the amount to be paid under an insurance policy in settlement of (a loss). ➤ *verb intrans* (often + to) to adapt or conform oneself, e.g. to a new environment or different conditions. ➤➤ **adjustability** /-ˈbiliti/ *noun*, **adjustable** *adj*, **adjuster** *noun*. [French *ajuster*, from AD- + *juste* exact, just, from Latin *jur-*, *jus* JUST¹]

adjustment /əˈjustmənt/ *noun* **1a** adjusting or being adjusted. **b** a minor change or improvement. **2** a means, e.g. a mechanism, by which things are adjusted. **3** a settlement of a disputed claim or debt.

adjutant /ˈajoot(ə)nt/ *noun* a military officer who assists a commanding officer and is responsible for correspondence and other administrative matters. ➤➤ **adjutancy** /-si/ *noun*. [Latin *adjutant-*, *adjutans*, present part. of *adjutare* to help]

adjutant bird *noun* either of two large Indian storks that have black and white plumage and a large bill and feed on carrion: genus *Leptoptilos*.

adjutant general *noun* (*pl* **adjutants general**) the chief administrative officer of an army, responsible for personnel records, welfare, training, etc.

adjutant stork *noun* = ADJUTANT BIRD.

adjuvant¹ /ˈajoov(ə)nt/ *adj* **1** serving to assist or contribute. **2** said of therapy: serving to enhance the effectiveness of medical treatment. [French *adjuvant* auxiliary, from Latin *adjuvant-*, *adjuvans*, present part. of *adjuvare* to aid, from AD- + *juvare* to help]

adjuvant² *noun* something that helps, *esp* something that makes medical treatment more effective.

ad lib /ˌad ˈlib/ *adv* **1** without restraint or limit; as desired. **2** without preparation; spontaneously: *The guest spoke ad lib to the group.* [Latin *ad libitum* in accordance with desire]

ad-lib¹ *adj* spoken, composed, or performed without preparation; impromptu: *an ad-lib speech.*

ad-lib² *verb* (**ad-libbed, ad-libbing**) ➤ *verb intrans* to say lines or a speech spontaneously and without preparation; to improvise. ➤ *verb trans* to improvise (lines or a speech).

ad-lib³ *noun* an improvised speech, line, or performance.

ad libitum /ˌad ˈlibitəm/ *adj and adv* **1** without restraint or limit. **2** without preparation; impromptu. **3** said of a piece of music: to be performed if desired.

Adm. *abbr* Admiral.

adman /ˈadman/ *noun* (*pl* **admen**) *informal* a member of the advertising profession.

admass /ˈadmas/ *noun chiefly Brit* the section of society readily influenced by mass-media advertising.

admeasure /adˈmezhə/ *verb trans formal* to assign (something) in shares; to apportion. [Middle English *amesuren* from early French *amesurer*, from AD- + *mesurer* to measure]

admin /ˈadmin/ *noun chiefly Brit, informal* administration.

administer /ədˈministə/ *verb trans* (**administered, administering**) **1** to manage or supervise (a country, organization, etc). **2a** to mete out or dispense (e.g. punishment or justice). **b** to give or perform (something) ritually: *The priest administered the last rites.* **c** to give (a drug, medicine, etc) as a remedy. **3** in law, to supervise or direct the taking of (an oath). ➤➤ **administrable** /-strəbl/ *adj*. [Middle English *administren* via French from Latin *administrare*, from AD- + *ministrare* to serve, from *minister* servant]

administrate /ədˈministrayt/ *verb intrans and trans* to perform the office of administrator; to manage (affairs).

administration /ədˌminiˈstraysh(ə)n/ *noun* **1** the act or process of administering. **2** performance of executive duties; management. **3** the execution of public affairs as distinguished from the making of policy. **4a** (*treated as sing. or pl*) a body of people who administer. **b** *chiefly NAmer* the term of office of a leader or government: *the Kennedy administration.* **c** *chiefly NAmer* a governmental agency or board. **5** in law, the management of the estate of a deceased person.

[Middle English *administracioun* via French from Latin *administration-*, *administratio*, from *administrare*: see ADMINISTER]

administration order *noun* a court order appointing an administrator to manage the affairs of a company that is in financial difficulties.

administrative /ədˈministrətiv/ *adj* of administration; executive. ➤➤ **administratively** *adv*.

administrator /ədˈministraytə/ *noun* **1** somebody who administers the affairs of a government, business, or other institution. **2** in law, an officer appointed to manage the estate of a deceased person or the property of an individual or company that is in financial difficulties.

administratrix /ədˈministrətriks/ *noun* (*pl* **administratrices** /-ˈstraytrəseez/) a female administrator, *esp* of an estate.

admirable /ˈadmərəbl/ *adj* deserving the highest respect; excellent. ➤➤ **admirably** *adv*.

admiral /ˈadmərəl/ *noun* **1** the commander-in-chief of a fleet or navy. **2** an officer in the Royal Navy or US Navy ranking below an admiral of the fleet or fleet admiral. **3** a senior naval officer of the rank of rear admiral or above. ➤➤ **admiralship** *noun*.

Word history
Middle English via French and medieval Latin from Arabic *amīr-al-* commander of the (as in *amīr-al-baḥr* commander of the sea). Early Christian writers understood *amīr-al* as one word meaning 'commander'; the original title of an admiral was *admiral of the sea* or *of the navy*.

admiral of the fleet *noun* an officer of the highest rank in the Royal Navy.

admiralty *noun* (*pl* **admiralties**) **1** (**Admiralty**) (*treated as sing. or pl*) in Britain, the executive department formerly having authority over naval affairs. **2a** the courts of law having jurisdiction over maritime affairs. **b** the jurisdiction of these courts.

admiration /adməˈraysh(ə)n/ *noun* **1** (*often* + for) a feeling of great respect or approval: *I have the greatest admiration for my predecessor.* **2** somebody or something that is greatly admired. **3** *archaic* astonishment; amazement: *Season your admiration ... till I may deliver, upon the witness of these gentlemen, this marvel to you* — Shakespeare.

admire /ədˈmie-ə/ *verb trans* to admire or think highly of (somebody or something). ➤➤ **admiring** *adj*, **admiringly** *adv*. [early French *admirer* to wonder at, from Latin *admirari*, from AD- + *mirari* to wonder]

admirer /ədˈmie-ərə/ *noun* a person who admires somebody or something; *specif* a woman's suitor.

admissible /ədˈmisəbl/ *adj* **1** capable of being allowed or accepted; permissible. **2** acceptable as legal evidence. **3** entitled or worthy to be allowed to enter. ➤➤ **admissibility** /-ˈbiliti/ *noun*. [French *admissible* from medieval Latin *admissibilis* from Latin *admittere*: see ADMIT]

admission /ədˈmish(ə)n/ *noun* **1** acknowledgment that a fact or allegation is true: *an admission of guilt.* **2** (*often* + to) the right of being allowed to enter a place or become a member of a group: *free admission to the museum.* ➤➤ **admissive** /-siv/ *adj*.

admit /ədˈmit/ *verb* (**admitted, admitting**) ➤ *verb trans* **1a** to concede (something) as true or valid. **b** to allow scope for or permit (something). **2** to allow (somebody) to enter a place or become a member of a group. ➤ *verb intrans* **1** (+ of) to allow or permit something: *The plan does not admit of variations.* **2** (+ to) to make an acknowledgment of something: *He admitted to smoking occasionally.* [Middle English *admitten* from Latin *admittere*, from AD- + *mittere* to send]

admittance /ədˈmit(ə)ns/ *noun* **1** permission to enter a place. **2** access or entrance. **3** the ease with which an alternating current can pass through an electrical circuit; the reciprocal of the impedance.

admittedly /ədˈmitidli/ *adv* as must reluctantly be admitted: *Admittedly, it was a clever hoax.*

admix /ədˈmiks/ *verb trans* to mix or blend (something). [back-formation from obsolete *admixt* mingled, from Latin *admixtus*: see ADMIXTURE]

admixture /ədˈmikschə/ *noun* **1** mixing or being mixed. **2** an ingredient added by mixing, or the resulting mixture. [Latin *admixtus*, past part. of *admiscēre* to mix with, from AD- + *miscēre* to MIX¹]

admonish /ədˈmonish/ *verb trans* **1** (*often* + for) to reprove (somebody) for remissness or error, *esp* gently. **2** to advise, urge, or warn (somebody): *She admonished us to be careful.* ➤➤ **admonishment**

noun. [Middle English *admonesten* from early French *admonester*, ultimately from Latin *admonēre* to warn, from AD- + *monēre* to warn]

admonition /admə'nish(ə)n/ *noun* a gentle friendly reproof, counsel, or warning. [Middle English *amonicioun* via French from Latin *admonition-, admonitio*, from *admonēre*: see ADMONISH]

admonitory /əd'monit(ə)ri/ *adj* expressing admonition; warning. ⮞ **admonitorily** *adv.*

ad nauseam /ad 'nawziam/ *adv* to a tediously excessive degree. [Latin *ad nauseam* to sickness]

ado /ə'dooh/ *noun* fussy bustling excitement, *esp* over trivia; a to-do. ✱ **without more/further ado** without any further delay. [Middle English, from *at do* to do]

adobe /ə'dohbi/ *noun* **1** a building brick of sun-dried earth and straw. **2** a heavy clay used in making adobe bricks. [Spanish *adobe* via Arabic *aṭ-ṭub* the brick, from Coptic *tōbe* brick]

adolescent[1] /adə'les(ə)nt/ *adj* **1** of or in the period of life between puberty and maturity: *adolescent girls.* **2** immature or puerile: *adolescent behaviour.* ⮞ **adolescence** *noun.* [French *adolescent* from Latin *adolescent-, adolescens, present part. of adolescere*: see ADULT[1]]

adolescent[2] *noun* somebody in the period of life between puberty and maturity.

Adonai /adə'nie, -'nay-e/ *noun* a name used as the sacred title of the God of the Jews, only to be pronounced in solemn prayer and with the head covered. [Hebrew *ădhōnāy*]

Adonis /ə'dohnis/ *noun* a strikingly handsome young man. [*Adonis*, a handsome youth in Greek mythology loved by Aphrodite. He was killed by a wild boar and restored to Aphrodite from Hades]

adopt /ə'dopt/ *verb trans* **1** to bring up (a child of other parents) as one's own child after undergoing certain legal formalities. **2** to take up and begin to use (e.g. a strategy): *Try to adopt a less dogmatic tone.* **3** to take over (e.g. a belief) from somebody else and use it as one's own: *adopt the customs of another country.* **4** to vote to accept (something): *adopt a constitutional amendment.* **5** said of a constituency: to nominate (somebody) as a Parliamentary candidate. **6** *Brit* said of a local authority: to assume responsibility for the maintenance of (e.g. a road). ⮞ **adoptable** *adj,* **adoptee** /adop'tee/ *noun,* **adopter** *noun,* **adoption** *noun.* [French *adopter*, or its source, Latin *adoptare*, from AD- + *optare* to choose]

adoptive /ə'doptiv/ *adj* adopting or acquired by adoption: *the adoptive father.* ⮞ **adoptively** *adv.*

adorable /ə'dawrəbl/ *adj* sweetly lovable; charming. ⮞ **adorably** *adv.*

adore /ə'daw/ *verb trans* **1** to regard (somebody) with reverent admiration and devotion; to love (somebody) greatly. **2** to worship or honour (somebody) as a deity. **3** *informal* to like (something) very much: *I adore his accent.* ⮞ **adoration** /adə'raysh(ə)n/ *noun,* **adorer** *noun,* **adoring** *adj,* **adoringly** *adv.* [French *adorer* from Latin *adorare*, from AD- + *orare* to speak, pray]

adorn /ə'dawn/ *verb trans* **1** to decorate (something or somebody), *esp* with ornaments. **2** to add to the pleasantness or attractiveness of (something). ⮞ **adornment** *noun.* [Middle English *adornen* via French from Latin *adornare*, from AD- + *ornare* to furnish, embellish]

ADP[1] *noun* adenosine diphosphate, a derivative of adenine that is reversibly converted from and to ATP for the release and storage of energy in living cells.

ADP[2] *abbr* automatic data processing.

ad rem /ad 'rem/ *adv and adj* to the point or purpose. [Latin *ad rem* to the matter]

adren- *or* **adreno-** *comb. form* forming words, with the meaning: adrenal: *adrenocorticotrophic.*

adrenal[1] /ə'dreenl/ *adj* **1** relating to or in the region of the kidneys. **2** of or derived from the adrenal glands. ⮞ **adrenally** *adv.* [AD- + RENAL]

adrenal[2] *noun* = ADRENAL GLAND.

adrenal gland *noun* an endocrine gland near the front of each kidney with a CORTEX (outer region) that secretes steroid hormones and a MEDULLA (inner region) that secretes adrenalin.

adrenalin *or* **adrenaline** /ə'drenəlin/ *noun* a hormone produced by the adrenal gland, often in response to stress or excitement, that increases the heart rate and blood pressure. It occurs as a neurotransmitter in the sympathetic nervous system and may be admin-

istered medically to stimulate the heart and cause constriction of blood vessels and relaxation of smooth muscle.

adreno- *comb. form* see ADREN-.

adrenocorticotrophic /ə,dreenoh,kawtikoh'trohfik/ *or* **adrenocorticotropic** /-'trohpik, -'tropik/ *adj* acting on or stimulating the adrenal cortex.

adrenocorticotrophic hormone *noun* a hormone of the front lobe of the pituitary gland that stimulates the adrenal cortex. Also called CORTICOTROPHIN.

adrenocorticotrophin /ə,dreenoh,kawtikoh'trohfin/ *noun* = ADRENOCORTICOTROPHIC HORMONE.

adrenocorticotropic /ə,dreenoh,kawtikoh'trohpik, -'tropik/ *adj* see ADRENOCORTICOTROPHIC.

adrift /ə'drift/ *adv and adj* **1** said of a boat: afloat without power, steerage, or mooring and at the mercy of winds and currents. **2** drifting or aimless: *adrift in the big city.* **3** *informal* astray: *His reasoning's gone completely adrift.* ✱ **come adrift** to become unfastened or unstuck. [A-[1] + DRIFT[1]]

adroit /ə'droyt/ *adj* **1** dexterous, nimble, or skilful. **2** shrewd or resourceful in coping with difficulty or danger. ⮞ **adroitly** *adv,* **adroitness** *noun.* [French *adroit* from *à droit* properly, from *à* to, at + *droit* right]

ADSL *abbr* asymmetric (or asynchronous) digital subscriber line, a high-speed always-on Internet connection that does not require a dedicated telephone line.

adsorb /əd'zawb/ *verb trans* to take up and hold (molecules of gases, liquids, etc) by adsorption. ⮞ *verb intrans* to become adsorbed. ⮞ **adsorbable** *adj,* **adsorbent** *adj and noun.* [AD- + -*sorb* as in ABSORB]

adsorbate /əd'zawbayt/ *noun* an adsorbed substance.

adsorption /əd'zawpsh(ə)n/ *noun* the adhesion of an extremely thin layer of molecules of gases, liquids, etc to the surface of solids or liquids: compare ABSORPTION. ⮞ **adsorptive** *adj.*

ADT *abbr* Atlantic daylight time (time zone).

aduki /ə'doohki/ *or* **aduki bean** *noun* see ADZUKI.

adulate /'adyoolayt/ *verb trans* to flatter or admire (somebody) excessively or slavishly. ⮞ **adulation** /-'laysh(ə)n/ *noun,* **adulator, adulatory** /-lət(ə)ri/ *adj.* [back-formation from *adulation* from Middle English via French from Latin *adulation-, adulatio*, from *adulari* to flatter]

adult[1] /'adult, ə'dult/ *adj* **1** fully developed and mature; grown-up. **2** typical of or appropriate to adults: *an adult approach to a problem.* **3** considered suitable only for adults, usu because of pornographic content: *adult magazines.* ⮞ **adulthood** *noun,* **adultness** *noun.* [Latin *adultus, past part. of adolescere* to grow up, from AD- + *alescere* to grow]

adult[2] *noun* a grown-up person or animal; *esp* a human being of or past an age specified by law (in Britain, 18).

adulterate[1] /ə'dultərayt/ *verb trans* to corrupt (a substance) or make it impure by the addition of a foreign or inferior substance. ⮞ **adulterant** *noun and adj,* **adulteration** /-'raysh(ə)n/ *noun,* **adulterator** *noun.* [Latin *adulteratus, past part. of adulterare*, from AD- + *alter* other]

adulterate[2] /ə'dultərət/ *adj* adulterated, debased, or impure.

adulterer /ə'dultərə/ *or* **adulteress** /-ris/ *noun* a man or woman who commits adultery.

adultery /ə'dultəri/ *noun* (*pl* **adulteries**) **1** voluntary sexual intercourse between a married person and somebody other than his or her spouse. **2** an act of adultery. ⮞ **adulterous** *adj,* **adulterously** *adv.* [Middle English, alteration of *avoutrie* from French from Latin *adulter* adulterer, back-formation from *adulterare*: see ADULTERATE[1]]

adumbrate /'adəmbrayt/ *verb trans formal* **1** to outline (something) broadly without details. **2** to foreshadow (a future event) vaguely. **3** to cast a shadow over or obscure (something). ⮞ **adumbration** /-'braysh(ə)n/ *noun,* **adumbrative** /ə'dumbrətiv/ *adj.* [Latin *adumbratus, past part. of adumbrare*, from AD- + *umbra* shadow]

adv. *abbr* **1** adverb. **2** adverbial. **3** against. [(in sense 3) Latin *adversus*: see ADVERSE]

ad valorem /ad va'lawrəm/ *adj and adv* said of a tax: imposed at a rate proportional to the stated value: compare SPECIFIC[1] (6). [Latin *ad valorem* according to the value]

advance¹ /əd'vahns/ *verb trans* **1** to bring or move (something) forward in position or time: *We had better advance the date of the meeting.* **2** to accelerate the growth or progress of (something); to further (something): *This will not advance our cause.* **3** to raise (somebody) in rank; to promote (somebody). **4** to supply (money or goods) ahead of time or as a loan. **5** to bring (an opinion or argument) forward for notice; to propose (something). ➤ *verb intrans* **1a** to go forward; to proceed. **b** (+ on) to approach in a threatening manner. **2** to develop or make progress. **3** to rise in rank, position, or importance. ➤➤ **advancer** *noun.* [Middle English *advauncen* via Old French from Latin *abante* before, from AB- + *ante* before]

advance² *noun* **1a** a forward movement. **b** a signal for forward movement of troops. **2a** progress in development; an improvement: *an advance in medical technique.* **b** = ADVANCEMENT (1A). **3** (*usu in pl*) a friendly or amorous approach: *Her attitude discouraged all advances.* **4** money or goods supplied ahead of time or before a return is received. ✳ **in advance** beforehand.

advance³ *adj* **1** made, sent, or provided ahead of time: *advance warning.* **2** going or situated ahead of others: *an advance party of soldiers.*

advanced *adj* **1** far on in time or course: *a man advanced in years.* **2** beyond the elementary; more developed: *advanced chemistry.*

advanced gas-cooled reactor *noun* a type of nuclear reactor that uses carbon dioxide as the coolant, graphite as the moderator, and uranium oxide cased in steel as the fuel.

Advanced level *noun* = A LEVEL.

advancement *noun* **1a** promotion or elevation to a higher rank or position. **b** furtherance towards perfection or completeness: *the advancement of knowledge.* **2** forward movement or progress.

advantage /əd'vahntij/ *noun* **1** (*often* + of/over) superiority of position or condition: *Higher ground gave the enemy the advantage.* **2** a factor or circumstance that makes something or somebody superior to others: *the advantages of a computerized system.* **3** a benefit or gain, *esp* one resulting from some course of action: *a mistake that turned out to our advantage.* **4** the first point won in tennis after deuce. ✳ **have the advantage of somebody** to have superiority over somebody; *specif* to have personal unreciprocated knowledge of somebody: *I'm afraid you have the advantage of me.* **take advantage of somebody or something** to use something to one's advantage or benefit; to profit by it. **2** to impose on or exploit somebody, or their good nature. **to advantage** in a way that produces a favourable impression or effect: *Wore my sprigged muslin robe with blue trimmings – plain black shoes – appeared to much advantage —* Jane Austen. [Middle English *avantage* via French from Latin *abante*; see ADVANCE¹]

advantageous /adv(ə)n'tayjəs/ *adj* providing an advantage; favourable. ➤➤ **advantageously** *adv.*

advection /əd'veksh(ə)n/ *noun* the usu horizontal movement of a mass of air causing changes in its temperature and other physical properties. ➤➤ **advective** /-tiv/ *adj.* [Latin *advection-, advectio* act of bringing, from *advehere* to carry to, from AD- + *vehere* to carry]

Advent /'advent, -vənt/ *noun* **1** the period of approximately four weeks beginning on the fourth Sunday before Christmas and ending at Christmas itself: *the second Sunday in Advent.* **2** the coming of Christ to earth as a human being: compare INCARNATION (3). **3** (**advent**) a coming into being; an arrival: *the advent of spring.* [Middle English via medieval Latin from Latin *adventus*: see ADVENTURE¹]

Advent calendar *noun* a large card representing a Christmas or winter scene with 24 numbered windows to be opened, one each day of December up to Christmas Eve, revealing a small picture or gift.

Adventism /'adventiz(ə)m, 'advən-/ *noun* the doctrine that the second coming of Christ and the end of the world are near at hand. ➤➤ **Adventist** *adj and noun.*

adventitious /advən'tishəs, adven-/ *adj* **1** coming accidentally or unexpectedly from another source; extraneous: *And if there be any original defects, or adventitious ones introduced by time or corruption, it is not an easy thing to get them changed —* John Locke. **2** said of part of a plant or animal: occurring sporadically or in an unusual place: *adventitious buds.* ➤➤ **adventitiously** *adv,* **adventitiousness** *noun.* [Latin *adventicius* coming from outside, from *adventus*: see ADVENTURE¹]

adventure¹ /əd'venchə/ *noun* **1a** an undertaking involving danger, risks, and uncertainty of outcome. **b** an exciting or remarkable experience. **2** an enterprise involving financial risk. ➤➤ **adventuresome** /-s(ə)m/ *adj.* [Middle English *aventure* via Old French from Latin *adventus*, past part. of *advenire* to arrive, from AD- + *venire* to come]

adventure² *verb trans* to venture or risk (something). ➤ *verb intrans* **1** (*usu* + into/on/upon) to dare to go, undertake, or enter. **2** to take a risk.

adventure playground *noun* a children's playground with interesting or exciting equipment for climbing, building, and other activities.

adventurer *or* **adventuress** *noun* **1a** somebody who enjoys taking part in adventures. **b** = SOLDIER OF FORTUNE. **c** somebody who engages in risky commercial enterprises for profit. **2** somebody who seeks wealth or position by unscrupulous means.

adventurism *noun* risky involvement or intervention, *esp* in politics. ➤➤ **adventurist** *noun.*

adventurous /əd'venchərəs/ *adj* prepared to take risks or try new experiences. ➤➤ **adventurously** *adv,* **adventurousness** *noun.*

adverb /'advuhb/ *noun* a word that modifies a verb, an adjective, another adverb, or a sentence, and that answers such questions as *how?, when?, where?,* etc. [early French *adverbe* from Latin *adverbium,* from AD- + *verbum* word]

adverbial¹ /əd'vuhbi·əl/ *adj* functioning as an adverb. ➤➤ **adverbially** *adv.*

adverbial² *noun* a word or phrase that functions as an adverb.

adversarial /advə'seəri·əl/ *adj* involving opposition, hostility, or conflict; antagonistic: *adversarial party politics.*

adversary /'advəs(ə)ri/ *noun* (*pl* **adversaries**) **1** an enemy, opponent, or opposing faction. **2** (**the Adversary**) *archaic* the Devil; Satan: *Or shall the Adversary thus obtain His end? —* Milton.

adversative /əd'vuhsətiv/ *adj* said of a word or phrase: expressing contrast, opposition, or adverse circumstance: *the adversative conjunction 'but'.* ➤➤ **adversatively** *adv.*

adverse /'advuhs, əd'vuhs/ *adj* **1** acting against or in a contrary direction: *We were hindered by adverse winds.* **2** unfavourable: *adverse criticism.* ➤➤ **adversely** *adv,* **adverseness** *noun.* [Middle English via French from Latin *adversus,* past part. of *advertere:* see ADVERT²]

Usage note ━━━━━━━━━━━━━━━━━━
adverse or **averse**? These two words are sometimes confused. *Adverse* means 'acting against' or 'unfavourable' and is almost always used before a noun: *adverse criticism; adverse weather conditions. Averse* means 'strongly opposed to or disliking', usually comes after a verb, and is followed by the preposition *to: I wouldn't be averse to giving it another try.*

adversity /əd'vuhsiti/ *noun* (*pl* **adversities**) a condition of suffering, affliction, or hardship.

advert¹ /'advuht/ *noun chiefly Brit, informal* an advertisement.

advert² /əd'vuht/ *verb intrans formal* (+ to) to make a glancing or casual reference in speech or writing. [Middle English *adverten* via early French *advertir* from Latin *advertere,* from AD- + *vertere* to turn]

advertise /'advətiez/ *verb trans* **1** to announce or publish an article for sale, a vacancy, or forthcoming event) publicly, *esp* in the press. **2** to encourage sales or patronage of (e.g. a product or service), *esp* by emphasizing desirable qualities. **3** to draw attention to (something): *the swallowing of mugs of beer to advertise what one could 'stand' —* Henry James. **4** *archaic* to inform (somebody) about something: *I thought it convenient to advertise the reader that … there was one alteration —* John Locke. ➤ *verb intrans* **1** to describe and praise something, *esp* in the mass media, in order to encourage sales or patronage. **2** (+ for) to seek by means of advertising: *They are advertising for a sales manager.* ➤➤ **advertiser** *noun.* [Middle English *advertisen* from early French *advertiss-,* stem of *advertir:* see ADVERT²]

advertisement /əd'vuhtismənt, -tizmənt/ *noun* a public notice; *esp* one published, broadcast, or displayed publicly to advertise a product, service, etc.

advertising /'advətiezing/ *noun* **1** the action of calling something to the attention of the public, *esp* by displaying, broadcasting, or publishing announcements. **2** advertisements: *The magazine contains too much advertising.* **3** the profession of preparing advertisements for publication, broadcast, or display.

advertorial /advə'tawri·əl/ *noun* an advertisement in a magazine or newspaper that is designed to look like an editorial feature and may be produced partly by the staff of the journal. [blend of ADVERTISEMENT + EDITORIAL²]

advice /əd'vies/ *noun* **1** recommendation regarding a decision or course of conduct: *She followed my advice.* **2** an official notice concerning a business transaction: *a remittance advice.* **3** *archaic (usu in pl)* communication, *esp* from a distance.
Word history
Middle English from Old French *avis* opinion. The origin of the French word probably lies in the phrase *ce m'est à vis* that appears to me, part translation of Latin *mihi visum est* it seemed so to me, I decided.

advisable /əd'viezəbl/ *adj* worthy of being recommended or done; prudent: *It is advisable to take out travel insurance.* ⟫⟫ **advisability** /-'biliti/ *noun,* **advisably** *adv.*

advise /əd'viez/ *verb trans* **1a** to give advice to (somebody): *I advised her to try a different shampoo.* **b** to caution or warn (somebody): *They advised him against going.* **2** to give information or notice to (somebody); to inform (somebody): *You must advise us of your intentions.* ⟫ *verb intrans* to give advice. [early French *advisen* from Old French *aviser* from *avis:* see ADVICE]

advised *adj* thought out; considered: compare ILL-ADVISED, UNADVISED, WELL-ADVISED. ✳ **keep somebody advised** to keep somebody informed about facts or events. ⟫⟫ **advisedly** /-zidli/ *adv.*

advisement /əd'viezmənt/ *noun NAmer* careful consideration. ✳ **take something under advisement** to give a matter careful consideration, often involving consultation.

adviser *or* **advisor** *noun* somebody who gives advice, *esp* professionally in a specialized field: *the medical adviser to the Queen.*

advisory /əd'viez(ə)ri/ *adj* **1** having or exercising power to advise: *in an advisory capacity.* **2** containing or giving advice.

advocaat /'advəkah/ *noun* a sweet liqueur consisting chiefly of brandy and eggs. [Dutch *advocaat,* short for *advocatenborrel* lawyer's drink. The drink was orig favoured by lawyers]

advocacy /'advəkəsi/ *noun (pl* **advocacies)** **1** active support or pleading: *her advocacy of reform.* **2** the function of an advocate.

advocate[1] /'advəkət/ *noun* **1a** somebody who pleads the cause of another before a tribunal or court. **b** *Scot* = BARRISTER. **2** somebody who defends or supports a cause or proposal. [Middle English *advocat* via French from Latin *advocatus,* past part. of *advocare* to summon, from AD- + *vocare* to call. More at VOICE[1]]

advocate[2] /'advəkayt/ *verb trans* to recommend or plead in favour of (e.g. a cause or proposal).

advowson /əd'vowz(ə)n/ *noun* the right of presenting a nominee to a vacant benefice in the Church of England. [Middle English via Old French from medieval Latin *advocation-, advocatio* act of calling, from Latin *advocare:* see ADVOCATE[1]]

advt *abbr* advertisement.

adytum /'aditəm/ *noun (pl* **adyta** /-tə/) the innermost sanctuary in an ancient temple; the sanctum. [Latin *adytum* from Greek *adyton,* neuter of *adytos* not to be entered, from A-[1] + *dyein* to enter]

adze (*NAmer* **adz**) /adz/ *noun* a tool with a blade attached at right angles to a handle, used for cutting or shaping wood. [Old English *adese*]

adzuki /əd'zoohki/ *or* **aduki** /ə'doohki/ *noun (pl* **adzukis** *or* **adukis)** **1** a plant of the pea family that is widely cultivated in Japan and China as a food crop: *Phaseolus angularis.* **2** (*also* **adzuki bean** *or* **aduki bean**) the small round edible dark red seed of the adzuki plant. [Japanese *azuki*]

ae /ay/ *adj chiefly Scot* one. [Middle English (northern) *a,* alteration of AN[1]]

-ae *suffix* **1** forming pl nouns, denoting: members of some plant and animal families and subfamilies: *Compositae.* **2** forming the pl of some nouns of Latin and Greek origin ending in -*a: formulae; larvae.* [Latin -*ae,* pl of -*a,* ending of fem nouns and adjectives]

AEA *abbr Brit* Atomic Energy Authority.

AEC *abbr NAmer* formerly, Atomic Energy Commission.

aedile /'eediel/ *noun* an ancient Roman official in charge of public works, the grain supply, etc. [Latin *aedilis,* from *aedes* temple]

AEEU *abbr* Amalgamated Engineering and Electrical Union.

aegis /'eejis/ *noun* auspices, patronage, or sponsorship: *under the aegis of the education department.* [via Latin from Greek *aigis* goatskin, shield of Zeus]

aegrotat /'iegrətat/ *noun* **1** an unclassified degree awarded in British universities to students prevented by illness from taking their examinations. **2** a certificate stating that a student is too ill

to take an examination. [Latin *aegrotat* he or she is ill, from *aegrotare* to be ill, from *aegr-, aeger* ill]

-aemia *or* **-haemia** (*NAmer* **-emia** *or* **-hemia**) *comb. form* forming nouns, denoting: **1** the condition of having the specified type or abnormality of blood: *leukaemia.* **2** the condition of having the specified thing in the blood, usu abnormally or to excess: *uraemia.* [scientific Latin from Greek -*aimia,* from *haima* blood]

aeolian (*NAmer* **eolian**) /ee'ohli-ən/ *adj* carried, deposited, or produced by the wind. [Latin *Aeolus,* god of the winds, from Greek *Aiolos*]

aeolian harp *noun* a stringed musical instrument on which the wind produces varying harmonics over the same fundamental tone.

aeolotropic /,ee-əloh'tropik/ *adj* = ANISOTROPIC. ⟫⟫ **aeolotropy** /-'lotrəpi/ *noun.* [Greek *aiolos* variegated]

aeon *or* **eon** /'ee-ən, 'eeon/ *noun* **1** an immeasurably or indefinitely long period of time. **2** in astronomy, a period of 1000 million years. **3** a division of geological time that may be subdivided into eras. [Latin *aeon* from Greek *aiōn* age]

aer- *or* **aero-** *comb. form* forming words, denoting: **1** air; atmosphere: *aerate; aerobiology.* **2** gas: *aerosol.* **3** aircraft: *aerodrome.* [Middle English *aero-* via French and Latin from Greek *aer-, aero-* from *aēr* AIR[1]]

aerate /'eərayt, eə'rayt/ *verb trans* **1** to combine, supply, charge, or impregnate (something) with a gas, *esp* air, oxygen, or carbon dioxide. **2** to make (a liquid) effervescent: *aerated drinks.* ⟫⟫ **aeration** /eə'raysh(ə)n/ *noun,* **aerator** *noun.*

aerated /'eər(i)aytid/ *adj Brit, informal* highly excited or upset.

aerial[1] /'eəri-əl/ *adj* **1a** of or occurring in the air or atmosphere. **b** consisting of air. **c** growing in the air rather than in the ground or water: *aerial roots.* **d** operating overhead on elevated cables or rails: *an aerial railway.* **2a** of or involving aircraft: *aerial navigation.* **b** by or from an aircraft: *aerial photo.* **3** lacking substance; thin. **4** *literary* lofty: *aerial spires.* ⟫⟫ **aerially** *adv.* [Latin *aerius* from Greek *aerios* from *aēr* AIR[1]]

aerial[2] *noun* a conductor, usu a metal rod or wire, designed to radiate or receive radio waves, e.g. in a television system or in mobile telecommunications.

aerialist *noun* somebody who performs on a tightrope or trapeze.

aerie /'eəri, 'iəri/ *noun* see EYRIE.

aero /'eəroh/ *adj* relating to aircraft or aeronautics: *an aero engine.*

aero- *comb. form* see AER-.

aerobatics /,eərə'batiks/ *pl noun* (*treated as sing. or pl*) the performance of stunts in an aircraft, usu for the entertainment of spectators. ⟫⟫ **aerobatic** *adj.* [blend of AER- and ACROBATICS]

aerobe /'eərohb/ *noun* a bacterium or other organism that lives only in the presence of oxygen. [French *aérobie,* from *aér-* AER- + -*bie* from Greek *bios* life]

aerobic /eə'rohbik/ *adj* **1** to do with aerobics: *aerobic exercises.* **2** living, active, or occurring only in the presence of oxygen: *aerobic respiration.* **3** of or induced by aerobes: *aerobic fermentation.*

aerobics *pl noun* (*treated as sing. or pl*) a system of physical exercises designed to improve respiration and circulation, usu done to music and resembling a dance routine.

aerodrome /'eərədrohm/ *noun chiefly Brit* a small airport or airfield.

aerodynamics /,eərohdie'namiks, -di'namiks/ *pl noun* **1** (*treated as sing. or pl*) the dynamics of the motion of gases, e.g. air, and solid bodies moving through them. **2** the particular properties of a solid body that determine how fast and efficiently it can move through the air. ⟫⟫ **aerodynamic** *adj,* **aerodynamically** *adv,* **aerodynamicist** /-die'namisist, -di'namisist/ *noun.*

aerofoil /'eərəfoyl, 'eəroh-/ *noun chiefly Brit* a structure on an aircraft, car, etc designed to provide lift or steerage as the vehicle moves through the air.

aerogram *or* **aerogramme** /'eərəgram/ *noun* a sheet of airmail stationery that can be folded and sealed with the message inside and the address outside.

aerolite /'eərəliet/ *noun* a stony meteorite. ⟫⟫ **aerolitic** /-'litik/ *adj.* [from AER- + -*ite* as in *meteorite*]

aerology /eə'roləji/ *noun* a branch of meteorology dealing with the upper atmosphere. ⟫⟫ **aerological** /,eərə'lojikl/ *adj,* **aerologist** *noun.*

aeronaut /'eərənawt/ *noun* somebody who operates or travels in an airship or balloon. [French *aéronaute*, from *aér-* AER- + Greek *nautēs* sailor]

aeronautics /eərə'nawtiks/ *pl noun* (*treated as sing. or pl*) the science or practice of flight. ➤➤ **aeronautic** *adj*, **aeronautical** *adj*, **aeronautically** *adv*.

aeroplane /'eərəplayn/ *noun* an aircraft that is heavier than air, has fixed wings from which it derives its lift, and is mechanically propelled, e.g. by a propeller or jet engine. [French *aéroplane*, from AER- + Greek *planos* wandering, from *planasthai* to wander]

aerosol /'eərəsol/ *noun* 1 a suspension of fine solid or liquid particles in gas. 2 a substance dispersed from a pressurized container as an aerosol. 3 a metal container for substances in aerosol form. [AER- + SOL³]

aerospace /'eərohspays/ *noun* 1a the earth's atmosphere and the space beyond. b the branch of physical science dealing with aerospace. 2 the industry or technology involved in travel in aerospace. 3 (*used before a noun*) relating to aerospace or to travel in aerospace: *aerospace research*; *aerospace medicine*.

aerostat /'eərəstat/ *noun* a balloon or other aircraft that is lighter than the surrounding air. [French *aérostat*, from AER- + -STAT from Greek *statēs*, from *histanai* to cause to stand]

Aesculapian /eskyoo'laypi·ən/ *adj* relating to the healing art; medical. [Latin *Aesculapius*, Greco-Roman god of medicine, from Greek *Asklēpios*]

aesthesia (*NAmer* **esthesia**) /ees'theezyə, -zhə/ *noun* the capacity for sensation and feeling. [back-formation from *anaesthesia*]

aesthete (*NAmer* **esthete**) /'eestheet/ *noun* 1 somebody who has or professes a developed sensitivity to the beautiful in art or nature: *The aesthetes touched the last insane limits of language in their eulogy on lovely things* — G K Chesterton. 2 somebody who affects concern for the arts and indifference to practical affairs. [back-formation from *aesthetic*]

aesthetic /ees'thetik/ *or* **aesthetical** (*NAmer* **esthetic** *or* **esthetical**) *adj* 1a to do with aesthetics, beauty, or the appreciation of the beautiful: *aesthetic theories*. b artistic: *a work of aesthetic value*. 2 having a developed sense of beauty. ➤➤ **aesthetically** *adv*. [German *ästhetisch* via Latin from Greek *aisthētikos* of sense perception, from *aisthanesthai* to perceive]

aestheticism /ees'thetisiz(ə)m/ (*NAmer* **estheticism** /ees-, es-/) *noun* 1 the doctrine that the principles of beauty are of greater importance than moral and other principles. 2 devotion to or emphasis on beauty or the cultivation of the arts.

aesthetics /ees'thetiks/ (*NAmer* **esthetics** /ees-, es-/) *pl noun* 1 (*treated as sing. or pl*) a branch of philosophy dealing with the nature of beauty and aesthetic taste. 2 the principles concerning the nature and understanding of beauty. ➤➤ **aesthetician** /-thə'tish(ə)n/ *noun*.

aestival (*NAmer* **estival**) /ee'stievl, 'eestivl/ *adj formal* relating to the summer. [Middle English *estival* via French or Latin from Latin *aestivas*: see AESTIVATE]

aestivate (*NAmer* **estivate**) /'eestivayt/ *verb intrans* 1 said of animals, *esp* insects: to pass the summer in a state of torpor: compare HIBERNATE. 2 *formal* to spend the summer. [Latin *aestivatus*, past part. of *aestivare* to spend the summer, from *aestas* summer]

aestivation (*NAmer* **estivation**) /eesti'vaysh(ə)n/ *noun* 1 the act or state of aestivating. 2 the arrangement of floral parts in a bud: compare VERNATION.

aet. *or* **aetat.** *abbr* of the specified age; aged. [Latin *aetatis*]

aether /'eethə/ *noun* see ETHER (2), (3).

aetiology (*NAmer* **etiology**) /eeti'oləji/ *noun* (*pl* **aetiologies**, *NAmer* **etiologies**) 1 the cause or origin of something, *esp* a disease or abnormal condition. 2 the study of all the causes of something, *esp* a disease. ➤➤ **aetiologic** /,eeti-ə'lojik/ *adj*, **aetiological** /-'lojikl/ *adj*, **aetiologically** /-'lojikli/ *adv*. [via medieval Latin from Greek *aitiologia* statement of causes, from *aitia* cause]

AF *abbr* 1 Anglo-French. 2 audio frequency. 3 autofocus.

af- *prefix* see AD-.

afar /ə'fah/ *adv* from, to, or at a great distance: *I saw her afar off*. ✳ **from afar** from a great distance: *We saw him from afar*. [Middle English *afer*, from *on fer* at a distance and *of fer* from a distance]

AFC *abbr* 1 Air Force Cross. 2 Association Football Club. 3 automatic frequency control.

affable /'afəbl/ *adj* 1 pleasant and relaxed in talking to others: *an affable fellow*. 2 characterized by ease and friendliness: *He had lost his affable smile and wore a look of almost military resolution* — Henry James. ➤➤ **affability** /-'biliti/ *noun*, **affably** *adv*. [early French from Latin *affabilis* from *affari* to speak to, from AD- + *fari* to speak]

affair /ə'feə/ *noun* 1a a particular or personal concern: *That's my affair, not yours*. b (*in pl*) commercial, professional, or public business or matters: *world affairs*. 2a a procedure, action, or occasion vaguely specified: *I slept through the whole affair*. b a social event; a party. 3 a love affair. 4 a matter causing public anxiety, controversy, or scandal: *the Dreyfus affair*. 5 *informal* an object or collection of objects vaguely specified: *The house was a two-storey affair*. [Middle English *affaire* from early French, from *a faire* to do]

affaire /ə'feə (*French* afɛːr)/ *noun* a romantic or sexual relationship between two people who are not married to each other.

affect¹ /ə'fekt/ *verb trans* 1 to have a material effect on (something) or produce an alteration in it: *Paralysis affected his limbs*. 2 to act on (somebody or their feelings) so as to bring about a response: *She was deeply affected by the news*. [French *affecter* or its source, Latin *affectare* from *afficere* to influence, from AD- + *facere* to do]

Usage note

affect *or* effect? These two words, which are pronounced the same, are sometimes confused. *Affect* is a verb that means 'to influence or change': *How will this affect my pension prospects? Effect* is most commonly used as a noun: *What effect will this have on my pension prospects? Effect* can also be used, slightly formally, as a verb. In this case its meaning is to 'bring about' or to 'carry out': *The police effected an entry into the premises; Frederick here! O joy, O rapture! Summon your men and effect their capture!* — W S Gilbert.

affect² /ə'fekt/ *verb trans* 1a to pretend to feel or show (a quality): *to affect indifference*. b to assume the character or attitude of (a particular type of person): *to affect the experienced traveller*. 2 to wear or use (e.g. clothes) ostentatiously. 3 *archaic* to be fond of (somebody or something): *Dost thou affect her, Claudio?* — Shakespeare. [Middle English via Old French from Latin *affectare*, frequentative of *afficere*: see AFFECT¹]

affect³ /'afekt/ *noun* the conscious subjective aspect of an emotion considered as affecting behaviour. [German *Affekt* from Latin *affectus* disposition, past part. of *afficere*: see AFFECT¹]

affectation /afek'taysh(ə)n/ *noun* 1 an insincere display of a quality not really possessed: *the affectation of righteous indignation*. 2 a deliberately assumed peculiarity of speech or conduct; an artificiality.

affected /ə'fektid/ *adj* 1 given to affectation; insincere or pretentious. 2 assumed artificially or falsely; pretended: *an affected interest in art*. ➤➤ **affectedly** *adv*, **affectedness** *noun*.

affecting /ə'fekting/ *adj* evoking a strong emotional response; moving. ➤➤ **affectingly** *adv*.

affection /ə'feksh(ə)n/ *noun* 1 tender and lasting attachment; fondness: *She had a deep affection for her parents*. 2 (*also in pl*) emotion or feeling as compared with reason: *He had been toying with my affections*. 3 a disease or other abnormal condition. ➤➤ **affectional** *adj*. [Middle English via French from Latin *affection-, affectio*, from *afficere*: see AFFECT¹]

affectionate /ə'feksh(ə)nət/ *adj* 1 having or feeling affection or warm regard; loving: *an affectionate child*. 2 showing or resulting from affection; tender: *affectionate care*. ➤➤ **affectionately** *adv*.

affective /ə'fektiv/ *adj* 1 expressing or to do with emotion: *affective language*. 2 arising from or influencing the conscious subjective aspect of emotion: *affective disorders*. ➤➤ **affectively** *adv*, **affectivity** /afek'tiv-/ *noun*.

afferent /'afərənt/ *adj* bearing or conducting something inwards, e.g. nervous impulses towards the brain: compare EFFERENT¹. ➤➤ **afferently** *adv*. [Latin *afferent-, afferens*, present part. of *afferre* to bring to, from AD- + *ferre* to bear]

affiance /ə'fie·əns/ *verb trans* to promise (oneself or another) solemnly in marriage: *He was affianced to a fair and winning girl* — Hardy. [early French *afiancer* via medieval Latin *affidare* to pledge, from AD- + *fidare* to trust]

affidavit /afi'dayvit/ *noun* a sworn written statement for use as judicial proof. [medieval Latin *affidavit*, he or she has made an oath, from *affidare*: see AFFIANCE]

affiliate¹ /ə'filiayt/ *verb trans* (+ to/with) to attach (e.g. an organization) as a member or branch: *The union is affiliated to the TUC*. ➤ *verb intrans* (+ with) to connect or associate oneself with another, often in a dependent or subordinate position.

➤➤ **affiliation** /-'aysh(ə)n/ *noun.* [medieval Latin *affiliatus*, past part. of *affiliare* to adopt as a son, from Latin AD- + *filius* son]

affiliate² /ə'filiət/ *noun* an affiliated person or organization.

affiliation order *noun* a legal order that the father of an illegitimate child must pay towards its maintenance.

affine¹ /ə'fien, a-/ *noun* in anthropology, a person related by marriage. ➤➤ **affinal** *adj.* [early French *affin* from Latin *affins* related]

affine² *adj* relating to a mathematical transformation that preserves straightness and parallelism of lines but may alter distances between points and angles between lines: *affine geometry*.

affinity /ə'finiti/ *noun* (*pl* **affinities**) **1a** a natural liking for somebody or an inclination to think and feel alike: *this mysterious affinity between us.* **b** an attraction to or taste for something. **2** relationship by marriage. **3** resemblance based on relationship or causal connection. **4** a chemical attraction between substances, causing them to combine. **5** a relation between biological groups with similar structure and common ancestry. [Middle English *affinite* via French from Latin *affinis* bordering on, related by marriage, from AD- + *finis* end, border]

affinity card *noun Brit* a credit card or bank card issued with an undertaking that a percentage of the money spent by the user will be donated to a specified charity.

affirm /ə'fuhm/ *verb trans* **1a** to validate or confirm (something). **b** to state (something) positively. **2** to assert (e.g. a judgment of a lower court) as valid. ➤ *verb intrans* **1** to testify by affirmation. **2** to uphold a judgment or decree of a lower court. ➤➤ **affirmable** *adj*, **affirmer** *noun*. [Middle English *affermen* via French from Latin *affirmare*, from AD- + *firmare* to make firm, from *firmus* FIRM¹]

affirmation /afə'maysh(ə)n/ *noun* **1** something affirmed; a positive assertion. **2** a solemn declaration made by somebody who conscientiously declines taking an oath.

affirmative¹ /ə'fuhmətiv/ *adj* **1** asserting or answering that something is true or correct: *He gave an affirmative nod.* **2** favouring or supporting a proposition or motion: *an affirmative vote.* ➤➤ **affirmatively** *adv.*

affirmative² *noun* a word, phrase, or statement expressing agreement or assent: *She answered in the affirmative.*

affirmative action *noun NAmer* = POSITIVE DISCRIMINATION.

affix¹ /ə'fiks/ *verb trans* **1** to attach (something) physically: *affix a stamp to a letter.* **2** to add (something) in writing: *affix a signature.* ➤➤ **affixable** *adj*, **affixation** /afik'saysh(ə)n/ *noun.* [medieval Latin *affixare*, from Latin *affixus*, past part. of *affigere* to fasten to, from AD- + *figere* to fasten]

affix² /'afiks/ *noun* **1** an addition to a word or root, usu at the beginning or end, producing a derivative or inflectional form or a word with a related meaning; a prefix, suffix, or infix. **2** an appendage.

afflatus /ə'flaytəs/ *noun* divine imparting of knowledge or mental power; inspiration. [Latin *afflatus*, act of blowing or breathing on, past part. of *afflare* to blow on, from AD- + *flare* to blow]

afflict /ə'flikt/ *verb trans* **1** to distress (somebody) very severely, causing great suffering. **2** to cause serious problems or trouble to (somebody or something): *afflicted with shyness; an industry afflicted by strikes.* ➤➤ **afflictive** *adj.* [Middle English *afflicten* to overthrow, from Latin *afflictus*, past part. of *affligere* to cast down, from AD- + *fligere* to strike]

affliction /ə'fliksh(ə)n/ *noun* **1** great suffering. **2** a cause of persistent pain or distress.

affluent¹ /'afloo·ənt/ *adj* **1** having an abundant supply of material possessions; wealthy: *our affluent society.* **2** flowing in abundance. ➤➤ **affluence** *noun*, **affluently** *adv.* [Middle English via French from Latin *affluent-, affluens*, present part. of *affluere* to flow to, flow abundantly, from AD- + *fluere* to flow]

affluent² *noun* a tributary stream.

affluenza /afloo'enzə/ *noun* a psychological disorder supposedly affecting affluent young people, characterized by feelings of guilt and self-doubt. [*affluence* and INFLUENZA]

afflux /'aflucks/ *noun* a flow to or towards a point. [via French from Latin *affluxus*, from *affluere* to flow to]

afford /ə'fawd/ *verb trans* **1** (*usu* + can/could/able to). **a** to be able to bear the cost of (something): *He couldn't afford a new coat.* **b** to be able to do (something) without serious harm: *You can't afford to neglect your health.* **c** to be able to spare (something): *Don't give more than you are able to afford.* **2** to provide or supply (something): *Her letters afford no clue to her intentions.* ➤➤ **affordability** /-'biliti/

noun, **affordable** *adj.* [Old English *geforthian* to carry out, ultimately from FORTH]

afforest /a'forist/ *verb trans* to establish a forest on (an area of land); to plant (land) with trees. ➤➤ **afforestation** /-'staysh(ə)n/ *noun.* [medieval Latin *afforestare*, from AD- + *forestis*: see FOREST¹]

affranchise /ə'franchiez/ *verb trans* to set (somebody) free from servitude or obligation. [modification of early French *afranchiss-*, stem of *afranchir*, from AD- + *franchir*: see FRANCHISE¹]

affray /ə'fray/ *noun* a brawl in a public place. [Middle English from early French, from *affreer* to startle, of Germanic origin]

affricate /'afrikət/ *noun* a composite speech sound consisting of a stop immediately followed by a fricative, e.g. the /t/ and /sh/ that make up the /tsh/ in *choose*. [prob via German *affrikata* from Latin *affricata*, fem past part. of *affricare* to rub against, from AD- + *fricare* to rub]

affright¹ /ə'friet/ *verb trans archaic* to frighten or alarm (somebody): *a strange wild country, that began a little to affright us* — Defoe. [Old English *afyrht*]

affright² *noun archaic* sudden terror.

affront /ə'frunt/ *verb trans* to insult (somebody) by openly insolent or disrespectful behaviour or language; to give offence to (somebody). ➤➤ **affront** *noun.* [Middle English *afronten* from early French, ultimately from Latin AD- + *front-, frons* forehead]

AFG *abbr* Afghanistan (international vehicle registration).

Afghan /'afgan/ *noun* **1** a native or inhabitant of Afghanistan. **2** = PASHTO. **3** (**afghan**). **a** a blanket or shawl of coloured wool knitted or crocheted in strips or squares. **b** an embroidered sheepskin coat with a long shaggy pile on the inside. **4** (*also* **Afghan hound**) a tall hunting dog of a breed with silky thick hair. ➤➤ **Afghan** *adj.* [Pashto *afghānī*]

afghani /af'gahni/ *noun* (*pl* **afghanis**) the basic monetary unit of Afghanistan, divided into 100 puls. [Pashto *afghānī* 'Afghan']

aficionado /ə,fishyə'nahdoh/ *noun* (*pl* **aficionados**) a devotee or fan: *aficionados of wrestling.*

Word history

Spanish *aficionado* from past part. of *aficionar* to inspire affection, from *afición* affection, from Latin *affection-, affectio*: see AFFECTION. The term was orig applied to devotees of bullfighting.

afield /ə'feeld/ *adv* **1** away from home; abroad: *She had travelled far afield.* **2** out of the way; astray: *irrelevant remarks that carried us far afield.* **3** to, in, or on the field. [Old English *on felda*, from ON¹ + *feld* FIELD¹]

afire /ə'fie·ə/ *adj and adv* **1** on fire. **2** intensely or passionately aroused: *afire with enthusiasm.*

AFL *abbr* Australian Football League.

aflame /ə'flaym/ *adj and adv* = AFIRE.

aflatoxin /aflə'toksin/ *noun* any of several poisons that are produced by moulds, e.g. in badly stored peanuts, and cause liver cancers and other diseases. [scientific Latin *Aspergillus flavus*, species of mould + TOXIN]

AFL-CIO *abbr* American Federation of Labor and Congress of Industrial Organizations.

afloat /ə'floht/ *adj and adv* **1a** floating on the water or in the air. **b** on a boat or ship; at sea. **2** free of debt. **3** flooded with or submerged under water. [Old English *on flot*, from ON¹ + *flot* deep water, sea]

aflutter /ə'flutə/ *adj and adv* **1** fluttering: *with its wings aflutter.* **2** nervously excited: *I was all aflutter.*

AFM *abbr* Air Force Medal.

afoot /ə'foot/ *adv and adj* **1** happening; astir: *There's trouble afoot.* **2** on foot: *many mile a day afoot* — Dickens.

afore /ə'faw/ *adv, conj, and prep chiefly dialect* before. [Old English *onforan*, from ON¹ + *foran* before]

aforementioned /ə'fawmensh(ə)nd/ *adj* mentioned previously.

aforesaid /ə'fawsed/ *adj* = AFOREMENTIONED.

aforethought /ə'fawthawt/ *adj formal* premeditated or deliberate: *with malice aforethought.*

a fortiori /ay fawti'awri/ *adv* with still greater reason or certainty: *If he can afford a house, a fortiori, he can afford a tent.* [Latin *a fortiori*, literally 'from the stronger (argument)']

Afr. *abbr* **1** Africa. **2** African.

Afr- *comb. form* see AFRO-.

afraid /ə'frayd/ *adj* **1** (*often* + of/to) filled with fear or apprehension: *afraid of machines*; *afraid to leave the house.* **2** regretfully of the opinion: *I'm afraid I won't be able to go.* [Middle English *affraied*, past part. of *affraien* to frighten, from French *affreer*: see AFFRAY]

afreet /'afreet, ə'freet/ *or* **afrit** /ə'frit/ *noun* a powerful evil spirit or monster in Arabic mythology. [Arabic *'ifrit*]

afresh /ə'fresh/ *adv* anew or again: *We'll start afresh.*

African /'afrikən/ *noun* **1** a native or inhabitant of Africa. **2** a person of African descent, *esp* a black person. ➤➤ **African** *adj.* [Middle English from Latin *Africanus*, from *Africa*]

Africana /afri'kahnə/ *noun* a collection of materials concerning or characteristic of Africa.

African-American *noun* an American of black African descent. ➤➤ **African-American** *adj.*

Africander *or* **Afrikander** /afri'kandə/ *noun* an animal of a breed of tall red southern African cattle with large horns. [Afrikaans *Afrikaner*, *Afrikaander*: see AFRIKANER]

Africanise /'afrikəniez/ *verb trans* see AFRICANIZE.

Africanism *noun* **1** a characteristic feature of African culture or language. **2** allegiance to the traditions, interests, or ideals of Africa.

Africanist *noun* a specialist in African cultures or languages.

Africanize *or* **Africanise** /'afrikəniez/ *verb trans* to make (something) African or to bring it under African control. ➤➤ **Africanization** /-'zaysh(ə)n/ *noun.*

African violet *noun* any of several species of tropical African plants grown as houseplants for their velvety leaves and showy purple, pink, or white flowers: genus *Saintpaulia.*

Afrikaans /afri'kahns, -'kahnz/ *noun* a language of S Africa developed from 17th-cent. Dutch.

Word history
Afrikaans *afrikaans* African, ultimately from Latin *africanus*. Words from Afrikaans that have passed into worldwide English include *apartheid, commandeer, commando, spoor,* and *trek,* as well as several – such as *aardvark, springbok, veld,* and *wildebeest* – describing regional flora, fauna, and natural features.

Afrikander /afri'kandə/ *noun* see AFRICANDER.

Afrikaner /afri'kahnə/ *noun* an Afrikaans-speaking S African of European, *esp* Dutch, descent. [Afrikaans *Afrikaner*, literally 'African', from Latin *africanus*]

afrit /ə'frit/ *noun* see AFREET.

Afro[1] /'afroh/ *adj* said of a hairstyle: shaped into a round curly bushy mass. [prob from AFRO-AMERICAN]

Afro[2] *noun* (*pl* **Afros**) an Afro hairstyle worn by a man or woman.

Afro- *or* **Afr-** *comb. form* forming words, with the meanings: **1** African: *Afro-American.* **2** African and: *Afro-Asiatic.* [Latin *Afr-, Afer*]

Afro-American *noun* = AFRICAN-AMERICAN. ➤➤ **Afro-American** *adj.*

Afro-Asiatic *adj* of or constituting a family of languages comprising Semitic, Egyptian, Berber, Cushitic, and Chadic.

Afro-Caribbean *noun* a West Indian person of black African descent. ➤➤ **Afro-Caribbean** *adj.*

afrormosia /afraw'mohzyə, -zh(y)ə/ *noun* **1** an African tree of the pea family: genus *Pericopsis* (formerly genus *Afrormosia*). **2** the dark hard wood of this tree, which resembles teak and is used for furniture. [scientific Latin *Afrormosia*, genus name, from AFR- + *Ormosia*, a genus of trees, from Greek *hormos* chain, necklace]

aft /ahft/ *adv and adj* near, towards, or in the stern of a ship or the tail of an aircraft: *go aft; the aft cabin.* [Old English *æftan* from behind, behind]

after[1] /'ahftə/ *prep* **1** behind (somebody or something) in place or order: *Shut the door after you.* **2a** following (something) in time; later than (something): *after breakfast.* **b** continuously succeeding (one another): *day after day.* **c** in view of or in spite of (something preceding): *after all our advice.* **3** in search or pursuit of (something or somebody): *go after gold.* **4** about or concerning (something or somebody): *I asked after his health.* **5** next in importance to (something): *They put quantity after quality.* **6a** in accordance with (something): *a woman after my own heart.* **b** in allusion to the name of (an inventor, relative, etc): *named after her grandmother.* **c** in the characteristic manner of (something or somebody): *after the current fashion.* **d** in imitation of (an artist, composer, etc): *a painting after Titian.* ✳ **after you** a formula used in asking for the next turn or in yielding precedence: *After you with the scissors; After you!* [Old English *æfter*]

after[2] *adv* **1** in the rear; behind. **2** afterwards.

after[3] *conj* later than the time when.

after[4] *adj* **1** *archaic* later or subsequent: *in after years.* **2** located towards the rear of a ship, aircraft, etc: *the after decks.*

after all *adv* **1** in spite of everything. **2** it must be remembered: *After all, he's only a beginner.*

afterbirth *noun* the placenta and foetal membranes expelled after delivery of a baby, young animal, etc.

afterburner *noun* a device in a jet engine for providing extra power.

aftercare *noun* **1** the care, treatment, etc given to people discharged from a hospital, prison, or other institution. **2** care, maintenance, or support provided after purchase of a product, use of a service, etc.

afterdamp *noun* a poisonous gas mixture remaining after an explosion of firedamp in a mine.

aftereffect *noun* an effect that follows its cause after an interval of time.

afterglow *noun* **1** a glow remaining where a light source has disappeared, e.g. in the sky after sunset. **2** a vestige of past splendour, success, or happy emotion.

after-hours *adj and adv* after closing time: *after-hours drinking in the pub.*

afterimage *noun* a sensation remaining after stimulation has ceased, *esp* a visual sensation.

afterlife *noun* **1** an existence after death. **2** a later period in one's life.

aftermath /'ahftəmahth, -math/ *noun* **1** the period immediately following an unpleasant or ruinous event: *in the aftermath of the war.* **2** a consequence or result of something unpleasant or undesirable. **3** a second growth of forage after the harvest of an earlier crop. [AFTER[4] + dialect *math* mowing, crop]

aftermost *adj* farthest aft.

afternoon *noun* **1** the time between noon and evening, or between lunchtime and the end of the normal working day. **2** a relatively late period: *in the afternoon of his life.* **3** (*used before a noun*) done or happening in the afternoon: *an afternoon performance.*

afternoons *adv chiefly NAmer* in the afternoon repeatedly; on any afternoon: *Afternoons he usually slept.*

afterpains *pl noun* cramping pains that follow childbirth, caused by contraction of the womb.

afters *pl noun Brit, informal* (*treated as sing. or pl*) a dessert.

aftershave *noun* a scented lotion for use on the face after shaving.

aftershock *noun* a smaller shock occurring after the main shock of an earthquake.

aftertaste *noun* **1** persistence of a flavour after eating or drinking. **2** persistence of an impression: *the bitter aftertaste of a quarrel.*

afterthought *noun* **1** an idea occurring later: *The introduction of a he-goat from a neighbouring orchard was a brilliant afterthought —* Saki. **2** something added later.

afterwards /'ahftəwədz/ *or* **afterward** /-wəd/ *adv* after that; subsequently, thereafter: *for years afterwards.*

afterword *noun* = EPILOGUE (1).

AG *abbr* **1** adjutant general. **2** attorney general. **3** joint-stock company. [(in sense 3) abbr of German *Aktiengesellschaft*]

Ag *abbr* the chemical symbol for silver. [Latin *argentum*]

ag- *prefix* see AD-.

Aga /'ahgə/ *noun trademark* a large solid metal kitchen stove. [acronym from Swedish (*Svenska*) *Aktiebulager Gasackumulator* (Swedish) Gas Accumulator Company, its original manufacturer]

aga /'ahgə/ *noun* a title of respect for a leader or elder in some Muslim countries, *esp* in the Ottoman Empire. [Turkish *ağa* lord, master]

again /ə'gayn, ə'gen/ *adv* **1** another time; once more. **2** so as to be as before: *Put it back again.* **3** on the other hand: *He might go, and again he might not.* **4** further; in addition: *I could eat as much again.* ✳ **again and again** often; repeatedly. [Old English *ongēan* opposite, back, from ON[1] + *gēn, gēan* still, again]

against[1] /ə'gaynst, ə'genst/ *prep* **1a** in opposition or hostility to (something): *the rule against smoking.* **b** unfavourable to (somebody): *His appearance is against him.* **c** as a defence or protection from (something): *She warned them against opening the box.* **2** contrasted with (something): *silhouetted against the sky.* **3** in the direction of and in contact with (something): *Rain beat against the windows.* **4** in a direction opposite to the motion or course of (something): *We swam against the tide.* **5a** in preparation or provision for (something): *saving against his retirement.* **b** with respect to (something): *customs that had the force of law against both parties.* **6** in exchange for (something). ✱ **as against** compared with (something else). **have something against** to have a reason for disliking (somebody). [Middle English, alteration of *againes*, from AGAIN]

against[2] *adj* **1** opposed to a motion or measure: *162 for and 238 against.* **2** unfavourable to a specified degree; *esp* unfavourable to a win: *The odds are two to one against.*

Aga Khan /ˌahgə 'kahn/ *noun* the leader of a Shiite sect of Muslims.

agamic /ay'gamik, ə-/ *adj* reproducing without fertilization; asexual or parthenogenetic. ⪢ **agamically** *adv.* [Greek *agamos* unmarried, from A-[2] + *gamos* marriage]

agapanthus /agə'panthəs/ *noun* (*pl* **agapanthuses**) an African plant of the lily family with clusters of showy blue or purple flowers: genus *Agapanthus.* [scientific Latin *Agapanthus,* genus name, from Greek *agapē* (see AGAPE[2]) + *anthos* flower]

agape[1] /ə'gayp/ *adj* **1** wide open; gaping: *with mouths agape.* **2** in a state of wonder: *agape with expectation.*

agape[2] /'agəpi, ə'gapay/ *noun* **1** = LOVE FEAST. **2** Christian love. ⪢ **agapeic** /agə'payik/ *adj.* [late Latin from Greek *agapē* love, from *agapan* to welcome, love]

agar or **agar jelly** /'aygah/ *noun* = AGAR-AGAR.

agar-agar /aygahr 'aygah/ *noun* a gelatinous extract from any of various red algae, used in culture media, as a thickening agent in foods, etc. [Malay *agar*]

agaric /'agərik, ə'garik/ *noun* any of a family of fungi, e.g. the common edible mushroom, that has an umbrella-shaped cap with radiating gills on the underside: family Agaricaceae. [Latin *agaricum* a fungus, from Greek *agarikon*]

agate /'agət, 'agayt/ *noun* a mineral used as a gem composed of quartz of various colours, often arranged in bands. [French *agate* via Latin from Greek *achatēs*]

agave /ə'gayvi/ *noun* any of a genus of N or S American plants of the daffodil family with spiny leaves and flowers in tall spreading flat clusters: genus *Agave.* [scientific Latin *Agave*, genus name, from the Latin name of a daughter of Cadmus in mythology, from Greek *Agauē*]

age[1] /ayj/ *noun* **1a** the length of time a person has lived or a thing existed: *ten years of age.* **b** the time of life at which some particular qualification, power, or capacity arises: *The voting age is 18.* **c** a stage of life: *the seven ages of man.* **2** a generation: *the ages to come.* **3a** a period of past time dominated by a central figure or prominent feature: *the age of Elizabeth I; the steam age.* **b** a cultural period marked by the prominence of a specified item: *the space age.* **c** a division of geological time, shorter than an epoch. **4** a person's development in terms of the years required by an average individual for similar development: *a mental age of six.* **5** *informal* (*usu in pl*) a long time: *I have been waiting for you at least this age! — Jane Austen; I haven't seen her for ages.* ✱ **act one's age** to behave appropriately for one's age. **come of age** to reach legal adult status. **of an age** of a similar age: *My cousin and I are of an age.* [Middle English via Old French from Latin *aetat-, aetas,* from *aevum* lifetime]

age[2] *verb* (**ageing** or **aging**) ➤ *verb intrans* **1** to become old; to show the effects of increasing age: *He's aged terribly since you last saw him.* **2** to become mellow or mature; to ripen: *This cheese has aged for nearly two years.* ➤ *verb trans* **1** to cause (somebody) to seem old, *esp* prematurely: *Illness has aged her.* **2** to bring (something) to a state fit for use or to maturity: *The wine is aged in oak casks.*

-age *suffix* forming nouns, denoting: **1** an aggregate or collection: *baggage; acreage.* **2a** an action or process: *haulage.* **b** a cumulative result: *breakage; spillage.* **c** a rate or amount: *dosage.* **3** a house or place: *orphanage.* **4** a condition or rank: *bondage; peerage.* **5** a fee or charge: *postage; wharfage.* [Middle English via Old French from Latin *-aticum*]

aged /'ayjid/ *adj* **1** of an advanced age. **2** typical of old age: *his aged steps.* **3** /ayjd/ having attained a specified age: *a girl aged five.* ⪢ **agedness** *noun.*

age group *noun* the part of a population that is of approximately the same age or within a specified range of ages.

ageing[1] or **aging** /'ayjing/ *noun* **1** the process of growing old. **2** the process of becoming mellow or mature.

ageing[2] or **aging** *adj* becoming old, often with an implied loss of usefulness, reliability, etc: *a manuscript produced on an ageing typewriter.*

ageism or **agism** /'ayjiz(ə)m/ *noun* discrimination on grounds of age, *esp* of advanced age. ⪢ **ageist** *adj and noun.*

ageless /'ayjlis/ *adj* **1** never growing old or showing the effects of age. **2** timeless or eternal: *ageless truths.*

agency /'ayjənsi/ *noun* (*pl* **agencies**) **1** an establishment that does a particular type of business, usu on behalf of another: *an advertising agency.* **2** the function or place of business of an agent or representative. **3** intervention or instrumentality: *He acted through the agency of his ambassador.* **4** the power or force behind a certain phenomenon or effect: *that invisible agency by which all the component parts of the immense machine of the universe have influence upon each other* — Thomas Paine.

agenda /ə'jendə/ *noun* **1** a list of items to be discussed or business to be transacted, e.g. at a meeting: *the next item on the agenda.* **2** a plan of procedure; a programme: *at the top of my agenda.* [Latin *agenda,* pl of *agendum,* neuter of *agendus,* gerundive of *agere* to act, do]

Usage note ⸻

Although *agenda* was originally a plural noun, it is now always treated as a singular and has its own plural *agendas: draw up an agenda; Today's agenda includes a discussion of the financial subcommittee's report.* There is a singular form *agendum* ('an item to be dealt with'), but it is very rare and best replaced with *item on the agenda.*

agent /'ayjənt/ *noun* **1a** a person who is authorized to act for or in the place of another, e.g. a business representative: *my literary agent.* **b** somebody employed by or controlling an agency: *an estate agent.* **2a** a representative of a government. **b** a spy. **3a** something or somebody that produces an effect or exerts power. **b** a chemically, physically, or biologically active substance. [Middle English from Latin *agent-, agens,* present part. of *agere* to drive, lead, act, do]

agent-general *noun* (*pl* **agents-general**) a representative in Britain of an Australian state or a Canadian province.

agent provocateur /ˌahzhonh prəˌvokə'tuh (French ajã provokatœːr)/ *noun* (*pl* **agents provocateurs** /ˌahzhonh prəˌvokə'tuh/) a person employed to incite suspected people to some open action that will make them liable to punishment. [French *agent provocateur,* literally 'provoking agent']

age of consent *noun* the age at which one is legally competent to give consent; *specif* that at which a person may consent to sexual intercourse.

age of reason *noun* **1** (*often* **Age of Reason**) a period characterized by the repudiation of religious, social, and philosophical beliefs not founded on reason; *esp* the 18th cent. in Europe. **2** the time of life when one begins to be able to distinguish right from wrong.

age-old *adj* having existed for a long time; ancient.

agglomerate[1] /ə'glomərayt/ *verb intrans* to gather into a cluster or disorderly mass. ➤ *verb trans* to cause (things) to gather in such a mass. [Latin *agglomeratus,* past part. of *agglomerare* to heap up, join, from AD- + *glomer-, glomus* ball]

agglomerate[2] /ə'glomərət/ *adj* gathered into a ball, mass, or cluster.

agglomerate[3] /ə'glomərət/ *noun* **1** a disorderly mass or collection. **2** a rock composed of irregular volcanic fragments.

agglomeration /əˌglomə'raysh(ə)n/ *noun* **1** a mass or cluster of disparate elements. **2** the action or process of agglomerating. ⪢ **agglomerative** /ə'glomərətiv/ *adj.*

agglutinate /ə'gloohtinayt/ *verb trans* **1** to cause (things) to stick together; to fasten (things) together as if with glue. **2** to combine (words) into a compound; to attach (word elements, e.g. affixes and roots) together to form words. **3** to cause (e.g. red blood cells) to undergo agglutination. ➤ *verb intrans* to form words by agglutination. [Latin *agglutinatus,* past part. of *agglutinare* to glue to, from AD- + *glutin-, gluten* glue]

agglutination /əˌgloohti'naysh(ə)n/ *noun* **1** the formation of compound words by combining other words or word elements that already have a single definite meaning. **2** the collection of red blood cells or other minute suspended particles into clumps, *esp* as a response to a specific antibody. ➤➤ **agglutinative** /ə'glooh-tinativ/ *adj*.

agglutinin /ə'gloohtinin/ *noun* a substance producing biological agglutination. [AGGLUTINATION + -IN¹]

aggrandize *or* **aggrandise** /ə'grandiez/ *verb trans* **1** to enhance the power, wealth, position, or reputation of (somebody or something). **2** to give a false air of greatness to (something or somebody); to praise (something or somebody) too highly: *He had the fault of aggrandizing the one and disparaging the other.* ➤➤ **aggrandizement** /ə'grandizmənt/ *noun*, **aggrandizer** /'agrəndiezə/ *noun*. [French *agrandiss-*, stem of *agrandir*, from AD- + *grandir* to increase from Latin *grandire*, from *grandis* great, GRAND¹]

aggravate /'agrəvayt/ *verb trans* **1** to make (something, e.g. an illness) worse or more severe. **2** *informal* to annoy or irritate (somebody). ➤➤ **aggravating** *adj*, **aggravation** /-'vaysh(ə)n/ *noun*. [Latin *aggravatus*, past part. of *aggravare* to make heavier, from AD- + *gravare* to burden, from *gravis* heavy]

Usage note
Aggravate is related etymologically to the word *grave* ('serious'). Its oldest surviving meaning is 'to make worse or more serious': *We ought not to do anything that might aggravate the situation.* Some traditionalists contend that this is its only true meaning and disapprove of the use of *aggravate* to mean 'annoy'. This other meaning has, however, been well established for centuries.

aggravated *adj* said of an offence: made more serious, e.g. by violence: *aggravated burglary*.

aggregate¹ /'agrigət/ *adj* **1a** formed by the collection of units or particles into a body, mass, or amount. **b** taking all units as a whole; total: *aggregate earnings; aggregate sales.* **2a** said of a flower: clustered in a dense mass or head. **b** said of a fruit: formed from the several ovaries of a single flower. [Middle English *aggregat* from Latin *aggregatus*, past part. of *aggregare* to add to, from AD- + *greg-*, *grex* flock]

aggregate² /'agrigayt/ *verb trans* **1** to bring (units or particles) together into a mass or whole. **2** to amount to (a specified total). ➤➤ **aggregation** /-'gaysh(ə)n/ *noun*, **aggregational** *adj*, **aggregative** *adj*.

aggregate³ /'agrigət/ *noun* **1** a mass of loosely associated parts. **2** the whole amount; the sum total. **3a** a rock composed of closely packed mineral crystals of one or more kinds or of mineral rock fragments. **b** sand, gravel, etc for mixing with cement to make concrete. **c** a clustered mass of individual particles of various shapes and sizes that is considered to be the basic structural unit of soil. ✳ **in the aggregate** considered as a whole; collectively.

aggression /ə'gresh(ə)n/ *noun* **1** attack, violent hostility, or encroachment; *esp* unprovoked violation by one country of the territory of another. **2** a hostile attack; *esp* one made without just cause. **3** hostile, injurious, or destructive behaviour or outlook. ➤➤ **aggressor** *noun*. [Latin *aggression-*, *aggressio* from *aggredi* to attack, from AD- + *gradi* to step, go]

aggressive /ə'gresiv/ *adj* **1a** showing, tending towards, or practising aggression: *an aggressive foreign policy.* **b** ready to attack: *an aggressive fighter.* **2** forceful, dynamic, or self-assertive: *an aggressive salesman.* ➤➤ **aggressively** *adv*, **aggressiveness** *noun*.

aggrieve /ə'greev/ *verb trans* to give pain or trouble to (somebody); to distress (somebody). [Middle English *agreven* via French from Latin *aggravare*: see AGGRAVATE]

aggrieved *adj* **1** showing or expressing resentment; hurt. **2** treated unfairly or unjustly. ➤➤ **aggrievedly** /-vidli/ *adv*.

aggro /'agroh/ *noun chiefly Brit, informal* **1** hostile or aggressive behaviour. **2** problems or difficulties. [by shortening and alteration from *aggravation* or AGGRESSION]

aghast /ə'gahst/ *adj* suddenly struck with terror or amazement; shocked: *We watched aghast as the building collapsed.* [Middle English *agast*, past part. of *agasten* to frighten, from A-¹ + *gasten* to frighten, from *gast*, *gost* GHOST¹]

agile /'ajiel/ *adj* **1** quick, easy, and graceful in movement: *with agile steps.* **2** mentally quick and resourceful: *an agile mind.* ➤➤ **agilely** *adv*, **agility** /ə'jiliti/ *noun*. [Middle English via French from Latin *agilis*, from *agere* to drive, act]

agin /ə'gin/ *prep Brit, dialect* against.

aging /'ayjing/ *noun and adj* see AGEING¹, AGEING².

agio /'ajioh/ *noun* (*pl* **agios**) a premium or percentage paid for the exchange of one currency for another. [Italian *agio*, alteration of

Italian dialect *lajjë*, ultimately from Greek *allagē* exchange, from *allos* other]

agism /'ayjiz(ə)m/ *noun* see AGEISM.

agitate /'ajitayt/ *verb trans* **1** to trouble or excite the mind or feelings of (somebody); to disturb (somebody): *She was agitated by his disappearance.* **2** to shake, move, or stir (something): *The drum is agitated by an electric motor.* ➤ *verb intrans* to work to arouse public feeling for or against a cause: *agitating for better schools.* ➤➤ **agitatedly** *adv*, **agitation** /-'taysh(ə)n/ *noun*. [Latin *agitatus*, past part. of *agitare*, frequentative of *agere* to drive]

agitato /aji'tahtoh/ *adj and adv* said of a piece of music: to be performed in a restless and agitated manner. [Italian *agitato*, literally 'agitated', from Latin *agitatus*: see AGITATE]

agitator /'ajitaytə/ *noun* **1** somebody who stirs up public feeling on controversial issues: *political agitators.* **2** a device or apparatus for stirring or shaking.

agitprop /'ajitprop/ *noun* political propaganda, *esp* pro-communist propaganda in the arts. [Russian *Agitpropbyuro* office of agitation and propaganda, from *agitatsiya* agitation + *prop* as in PROPAGANDA]

agit-rock /'ajitrok/ *noun* a form of rock music with polemical, politically and socially committed lyrics on subjects such as social injustice, racism, sexism, and sexuality. [from AGITATE + ROCK³]

agleam /ə'gleem/ *adj* gleaming.

aglet /'aglət/ *noun* **1** a metal tag attached to the end of a lace, cord, or ribbon. **2** = AIGUILLETTE (1). [Middle English *aglet* via early French *aguillette*, *aiguillette* small needle, from late Latin *acicula*, *acucula* ornamental pin, dimin. of Latin *acus* needle, pin]

agley /ə'glay, ə'glee/ *adv chiefly Scot* awry or wrong: *The best-laid schemes o' mice an' men gang aft agley* — Robert Burns. [Scots *agley* squintingly, from A-¹ + *gley* to squint]

aglitter /ə'glitə/ *adj* glittering.

aglow /ə'gloh/ *adj* radiant with warmth or excitement. [A-¹ + GLOW²]

AGM *abbr* annual general meeting, *esp* of a society or company.

agnail /'agnayl/ *noun* **1** a sore or inflammation around a fingernail or toenail. **2** = HANGNAIL. [Old English *angnægl* corn on the foot or toe, from *ang-* (related to *enge* narrow, tight, painful) + *nægl* NAIL¹]

agnate¹ /'agnayt/ *noun* a relative whose kinship is traceable exclusively through the male line of descent; *broadly* any paternal relative: compare COGNATE¹. [Latin *agnatus*, past part. of *agnasci* to be born in addition to, from AD- + *nasci* to be born]

agnate² *adj* **1** related through male descent or on the father's side. **2** allied; akin; related. ➤➤ **agnatic** /-'natik/ *adj*, **agnation** /-'naysh(ə)n/ *noun*.

agnathan /ag'naythən/ *noun* any of a group of primitive aquatic vertebrate animals without jaws, including the lampreys and hagfishes: superclass Agnatha. ➤➤ **agnathan** *adj*. [from the Latin name, from A-² + Greek *gnathos* jaw]

agnosia /ag'nozh(y)ə/ *noun* a disturbance of perception caused *esp* by neurological dysfunction. [scientific Latin *agnosia* from Greek *agnōsia* ignorance, from A-² + *gnōsis* knowledge]

agnostic¹ /ag'nostik/ *noun* **1** somebody who holds the view that any ultimate reality is unknown and prob unknowable. **2** somebody who believes that it is impossible to know whether God or any other supreme being exists or not.

Editorial note
An agnostic holds the view that beliefs should be accepted on the basis of reason and evidence, and that there is insufficient evidence to justify belief in the existence of God. This does not imply that there is no God, but that his existence cannot be known. It is also taken generally to refer to a critical and sceptical view of religious belief — Dr Mel Thompson.

3 somebody who is doubtful or non-committal on a particular question. ➤➤ **agnosticism** /-stisizəm/ *noun*.

Word history
modification of Greek *agnōstos* unknown, unknowable, from A-² + *gnōstos* known, from *gignōskein* to know. The word was created in 1869 as an antonym of *gnostic* by the biologist Thomas Henry Huxley, who felt the need of a label for his own philosophical viewpoint.

agnostic² *adj* of or being an agnostic or relating to the beliefs of agnostics.

Agnus Dei /,agnəs 'dayee/ *noun* a liturgical prayer addressed to Christ as Saviour, often set to music as a movement in a Mass.

[Middle English from late Latin *agnus Dei* lamb of God; from the opening words of the prayer in the Roman Catholic Mass]

ago /ə'goh/ *adv* earlier than now: *ten years ago; How long ago did they leave?* [Middle English *agon, ago*, from *agon* to pass away, from Old English *āgān*, from A-¹ + *gān* to GO¹]

agog /ə'gog/ *adj* full of intense anticipation or excitement; eager: *I was all agog to go* — L P Hartley. [Old French *en gogues* in mirth]

-agogic *comb. form* see -AGOGUE.

a gogo /ə'gohgoh/ *adj informal* (*used after a noun*) in abundance; galore: *movies a gogo.* [from French *à gogo* galore]

-agogue *comb. form* forming words, denoting: a leader or guide: *pedagogue; demagogue.* ⋙ **-agogic** *comb. form.* [via French and Latin from Greek *-agogos* leading, from *agein* to lead]

agonic line /ə'gonik/ *noun* an imaginary line connecting points where there is no magnetic declination. [Greek *agōnos* without angle, from A-² + *gōnia* angle]

agonise /'agəniez/ *verb* see AGONIZE.

agonist /'agənist/ *noun* **1** a muscle that is restricted by the action of an antagonistic muscle with which it is paired: compare ANTAGONIST. **2** a substance capable of combining with a receptor on the surface of a cell and initiating a reaction. [late Latin *agonista* competitor, from Greek *agōnistēs*, from *agōnizesthai* to contend, from *agōn*: see AGONY. Orig in the sense 'protagonistic'; in the above senses prob back-formation from ANTAGONIST]

agonistic /agə'nistik/ *or* **agonistical** *adj* **1** argumentative. **2** said of animal behaviour: aggressive or defensive. **3** of or acting as an agonist. ⋙ **agonistically** *adv.*

agonize *or* **agonise** /'agəniez/ *verb trans* to cause (somebody) to suffer agony. ⋙ *verb intrans* **1** to suffer agony or anguish. **2** to make a great effort. **3** to worry excessively, *esp* in trying to make a decision. [early French *agoniser* to be in agony, via late Latin from Greek *agōnia*: see AGONY]

agonized *or* **agonised** *adj* characterized by, suffering, or expressing agony.

agonizing *or* **agonising** *adj* causing physical or mental agony: *an agonizing reappraisal of his policies.* ⋙ **agonizingly** *adv.*

agony /'agəni/ *noun* (*pl* **agonies**) **1** intense and often prolonged physical pain or mental suffering; anguish. **2** the struggle that precedes death: *his last agony.* [Middle English *agonie* via late Latin from Greek *agōnia* struggle, anguish, from *agōn* gathering, contest for a prize, from *agein* to lead, celebrate]

agony aunt *noun* a journalist who replies to readers' questions about their personal problems in a magazine or newspaper.

agony column *noun* a page or column in a magazine or newspaper in which readers' personal problems are discussed.

agora¹ /'agorə/ *noun* (*pl* **agoras** *or* **agorae** /-ree/) a gathering place for popular political assembly in ancient Greece. [Greek *agora*]

agora² /agə'rah/ *noun* (*pl* **agorot** /-'roht/) a unit of currency in Israel, worth 100th of a shekel. [New Hebrew *ăgōrāh*, from Hebrew, a small coin]

agoraphobia /agrə'fohbi·ə/ *noun* abnormal dread of being in open spaces or public places. ⋙ **agoraphobe** /'ag-/ *noun*, **agoraphobic** *noun and adj.* [scientific Latin *agoraphobia*, from Greek AGORA¹ + PHOBIA]

agorot /agə'roht/ *noun pl* of AGORA².

agouti /ə'goohti/ *noun* (*pl* **agoutis** *or collectively* **agouti**) **1** any of several species of tropical American rodents about the size of a rabbit: genera *Dasyprocta* and *Myoprocta*. **2** fur with alternate dark and light bands on each hair, or an animal with such fur. [French *agouti* from Spanish *agutí* from Guarani]

AGR *abbr* advanced gas-cooled reactor.

agranulocyte /ay'granyooləsiet/ *noun* any of various white blood cells with cytoplasm that does not contain conspicuous granules: compare BASOPHIL, EOSINOPHIL, GRANULOCYTE. ⋙ **agranulocytic** /-'sitik/ *adj.*

agraphia /ay'grafiə/ *noun* total or partial loss of the ability to write, caused by an injury to the brain. [scientific Latin, from A-² + Greek *graphein* to write]

agrarian¹ /ə'greəri·ən/ *adj* **1** to do with farmers, farming, or agricultural life and interests. **2** relating to fields, lands, or their tenure. [Latin *agrarius* from *agr-, ager* field]

agrarian² *noun* a member of a party or movement promoting agricultural interests or land reforms.

agrarianism *noun* a movement to bring about land reforms, e.g. by the redistribution of land.

agree /ə'gree/ *verb trans* **1a** (*usu* + that) to have the same opinion or judgment: *I agree that it would be unwise to interfere.* **b** (*often* + to) to consent to do something: *The present owners have agreed to sell.* **2** *chiefly Brit* to come to terms on (something, e.g. a price), usu after discussion; to accept (something) by mutual consent: *The following articles were agreed* — Winston Churchill. **3** to bring (things, e.g. figures) into harmony. ⋙ *verb intrans* **1** (*often* + to) to give assent; to accede: *I agree to your proposal.* **2a** (*often* + with) to be of the same opinion: *They never seem to agree; I agree with you.* **b** (*often* + with) to suit (somebody) or be on good terms with them; to be compatible: *A man of her own size of understanding would, probably, not agree so well with her* — Mary Wollstonecraft; *Poetry and the stage do not agree well together* — Hazlitt. **c** (*often* + with) to correspond or be consistent: *His statement doesn't agree with the evidence.* **d** (+ with) to suit somebody's health or constitution: *Onions do not agree with me.* **e** (*often* + with) to correspond in grammatical gender, number, case, or person. **3** (*often* + on) to decide together: *We agreed on blue for the kitchen.* [Middle English *agreen* from early French *agreer*, from AD- + *gre* will, pleasure, from Latin *gratus* pleasing, agreeable]

agreeable *adj* **1** to one's liking; pleasing. **2** willing to agree or consent. ⋙ **agreeableness** *noun*, **agreeably** *adv.*

agreed *adj* **1** arranged by mutual consent: *We met at the agreed time.* **2** of the joint opinion: *In this we are agreed.*

agreement *noun* **1a** harmony of opinion or feeling: *We finally reached agreement.* **b** correspondence or consistency: *agreement between the copy and the original.* **c** consent. **2a** an arrangement laying down terms, conditions, etc. **b** a treaty. **c** a legally binding contract. **3** correspondence in grammatical gender, number, case, or person.

agribusiness /'agribiznis/ *noun* all the industries involved in farming. [AGRICULTURE + BUSINESS]

agriculture /'agrikulchə/ *noun* the theory and practice of cultivating and producing crops from the soil and of raising livestock. ⋙ **agricultural** /-'kulchərəl/ *adj*, **agriculturalist** /-'kulchərəlist/ *noun*, **agriculturally** /-'kulchərəli/ *adv*, **agriculturist** /-'kulchərist/ *noun*. [French *agriculture* from Latin *agricultura*, from *agr-, ager* field + *cultura*: see CULTURE¹]

agrimony /'agriməni/ *noun* (*pl* **agrimonies**) a plant of the rose family with spikes of yellow flowers and fruits like burs: genus *Agrimonia*. [Middle English via French and Latin from Greek *argemōnē*]

agro- *comb. form* forming words, with the meanings: **1** fields; soil; agriculture: *agrology.* **2** agricultural and: *agroforestry.* [French *agro-* from Greek *agros* field]

agrobiology /,agrohbie'olǝji/ *noun* the branch of biology that deals with plant nutrition and growth and crop production in relation to soil management.

agrochemical /agroh'kemikl/ *noun* a chemical used in agriculture, e.g. as an insecticide or fertilizer.

agroforestry /agroh'foristri/ *noun* a method of land management that combines pasture and woodland.

agronomy /ə'gronəmi/ *noun* a branch of agriculture dealing with crop production and soil management. ⋙ **agronomic** /agrə'nomik/ *adj*, **agronomically** /agrə'nomikli/ *adv*, **agronomist** *noun*. [prob from French *agronomie*, from AGRO- + -NOMY]

aground /ə'grownd/ *adv and adj* on or onto the shore or the bottom of a body of water: *The ship ran aground.* [Middle English, from A-¹ + GROUND¹]

ague /'aygooh/ *noun* **1** a malarial fever with regularly recurring attacks of chills and sweating: *An untimely ague stay'd me a prisoner in my chamber* — Shakespeare. **2** a fit of shivering. ⋙ **aguish** /'aygooh·ish/ *adj.* [Middle English via French from medieval Latin (*febris*) *acuta* (sharp) fever, from Latin *acutus* sharp]

AH *abbr* used before a date that falls within the Muslim era: *AH 248.* [Latin *Anno Hegirae*, in the year of the HEGIRA (flight of Muhammad from Mecca)]

ah /ah *often prolonged*/ *interj* used to express delight, relief, regret, or comment.

aha /ah'hah/ *interj* used to express surprise, triumph, derision, or amused discovery.

ahead /ə'hed/ *adv and adj* **1a** in a forward direction. **b** in front: *the road ahead.* **2** in, into, or for the future: *plan ahead; the years ahead.*

3 in or towards a better position: *get ahead of the rest.* ✻ **ahead of 1** in front or advance of: *ahead of his time.* **2** better than.

ahem /ə'hem/ *interj* used to attract attention or express mild disapproval. [imitative of clearing the throat]

ahimsa /ə'himsah/ *noun* the Hindu, Buddhist, and Jainist doctrine of refraining from harming any living being. [Sanskrit *ahiṃsā* non-injury]

ahistorical /ayhi'storikl/ *or* **ahistoric** /-storik/ *adj* without regard for history or tradition; concerned only with the present.

-aholic *comb. form* see -HOLIC.

ahoy /ə'hoy/ *interj* used at sea as a greeting or warning: *land ahoy.* [A-¹ + HOY¹]

Ahura Mazda /ah-ˌhooərə 'mazdə/ *noun* the Supreme Being represented as a deity of goodness and light in Zoroastrianism. [Avestan *Ahuramazdā* wise god]

AI *abbr* **1** artificial insemination. **2** artificial intelligence.

ai /'ah·i, ah'ee/ *noun* (*pl* **ais**) a sloth with three claws on each front foot. [Portuguese *ai* or Spanish *aí* from Tupi *ai,* from the sound of its cry]

AID *abbr* artificial insemination by donor.

aid¹ /ayd/ *verb trans* **1** to help or give assistance to (somebody). **2** to bring about the accomplishment of (something); to facilitate (something): *aid restful sleep.* ≫ **aider** *noun.* [Middle English *eyden* via French from Latin *adjuvare,* from AD- + *juvare* to help]

aid² *noun* **1a** help; assistance. **b** money, supplies, or other tangible means of assistance given to those in need, *esp* in another country. **2a** something that helps or supports: *a visual aid; an aid to understanding.* **b** a helper. **3** a tribute paid by a vassal to his lord. ✻ **in aid of 1** in order to help or support (something): *She sold her jewels in aid of charity.* **2** *Brit, informal* for the purpose of (something): *What's this in aid of?*

aide /ayd, ed/ *noun* **1** = AIDE-DE-CAMP. **2** *chiefly NAmer* an assistant: *one of the president's aides.*

aide-de-camp /ayd də 'konh/ *noun* (*pl* **aides-de-camp** /ayd də 'konh/) an officer in the armed forces acting as a personal assistant to a senior officer. [French *aide de camp,* literally 'camp assistant']

aide-mémoire /ayd mem'wah/ *noun* (*pl* **aides-mémoire** /ayd mem'wah/) **1** an aid to the memory, e.g. a note or sketch. **2** a diplomatic memorandum. [French *aide-mémoire,* from *aider* to aid + *mémoire* memory]

Aids *or* **AIDS** /aydz/ *noun* a disease of the immune system, caused by the virus HIV, usu leading to death from infections that the body is no longer able to resist.

Editorial note

Aids is caused by the HIV (Human Immunodeficiency Virus) and is the final or 'full-blown' phase of the HIV disease. Once the body's immune system has been infected with the HIV the virus remains latent in the body for up to ten years or so before the person is diagnosed with Aids. It is characterized by severe immune deficiency and is incurable and fatal at present. Transmission is associated with sexual intercourse and contact with infected blood — Dr John Cormack.

[acronym from *acquired immune deficiency syndrome*]

Aids-related complex *noun* a condition caused by the HIV virus that may produce no symptoms or less severe symptoms than Aids itself, which it sometimes precedes.

aigrette /'aygret, ay'gret/ *noun* **1** a spray of feathers, *esp* of the egret, worn on the head as an ornament. **2** a spray of gems worn on a hat or in the hair. [French *aigrette:* see EGRET]

aiguille /'aygweel/ *noun* a sharp-pointed pinnacle of rock. [French *aiguille* needle, from late Latin *acicula:* see AGLET]

aiguillette /aygwi'let/ *noun* **1** a shoulder cord with metal tags on certain military uniforms. **2** = AGLET (1). [French *aiguillette:* see AGLET]

AIH *abbr* artificial insemination by husband.

aikido /ie'keedoh/ *noun* a martial art with holds and throws similar to those of judo and using non-resistance to cause an opponent's own momentum to work against them. [Japanese *aikidō,* from *ai-* together, mutual + *ki* spirit + *dō* art]

ail /ayl/ *verb trans archaic* to give pain, discomfort, or trouble to (somebody): *What ails you?* ≫ *verb intrans* to be unwell: *She had been ailing for several months.* [Old English *eglan*]

ailanthus /ay'lanthəs/ *noun* (*pl* **ailanthuses**) any of a small Asiatic genus of chiefly tropical trees with unpleasant-smelling greenish flowers, including the tree of heaven: genus *Ailanthus.* [scientific Latin *Ailanthus,* genus name, from Amboinese *ai lanto,* literally 'tree (of) heaven']

aileron /'ayləron/ *noun* a movable surface or flap at the trailing edge of an aircraft wing for giving a rolling motion and providing lateral control. [French *aileron,* dimin. of *aile* wing, from Latin *ala*]

ailing *adj* **1** unwell or chronically ill. **2** in an unsatisfactory condition: *ailing industries.*

ailment /'aylmənt/ *noun* a mild illness or chronic disease.

aim¹ /aym/ *verb intrans* **1a** to direct a course: *Aim for the shore.* **b** to point a weapon at a target. **2** to channel one's efforts; to aspire. **3** to have the intention; to mean: *She aims to marry a duke.* ≫ *verb trans* **1** to direct or point (e.g. a weapon) at a target. **2** to direct (something) at or towards a specified goal: *The show is aimed at children.* [Middle English *aimen* via Old French from Latin *aestimare* to ESTIMATE¹]

aim² *noun* **1** a clear intention or purpose. **2a** the pointing of a weapon at a target: *Take aim.* **b** the ability to hit a target. **c** a weapon's accuracy or effectiveness. ≫≫ **aimless** *adj,* **aimlessly** *adv,* **aimlessness** *noun.*

ain't /aynt/ *contraction non-standard* **1a** am not: *Ain't I a craven? —* Virginia Woolf. **b** are not. **c** is not. **2a** have not. **b** has not. [prob from *an't,* a contraction of *are not* or *am not*]

Usage note

Ain't has never been fully accepted in standard English, though it was commonly used in place of *am not* in the 18th cent. It is still unacceptable in speaking or writing standard English. See also note at AREN'T.

aïoli *or* **aioli** /ie'ohli/ *noun* a garlic-flavoured mayonnaise. [French from Provençal, from *ai* garlic + *oli* oil]

air¹ /eə/ *noun* **1a** the mixture of invisible odourless tasteless gases, mainly nitrogen and oxygen, that surrounds the earth. **b** a light breeze. **c** one of the four elements of the alchemists, the others being earth, fire, and water. **2a** empty unconfined space: *in the open air.* **b** nothingness: *They seem to have vanished into thin air.* **3a** aircraft: *I'll go by air.* **b** aviation: *air safety.* **4** the supposed medium of transmission of radio waves. **5a** the appearance or bearing of a person; demeanour: *an air of dignity.* **b** (*in pl*) an artificial or affected manner; haughtiness: *to put on airs; airs and graces.* **c** the outward appearance of a thing: *an air of luxury.* **d** a surrounding or pervading influence; an atmosphere: *an air of mystery.* **6** a tune or melody. ✻ **in the air** being generally spread round or hinted at: *There are rumours in the air that he will be promoted.* **off (the) air** not or no longer broadcasting on radio or television: *remarks made off air.* **on (the) air** broadcasting on radio or television: *go on the air.* **take the air** to go out of doors for a walk. **up in the air** not yet settled; uncertain. **walk on air** to be filled with elation. [Middle English via Old French and Latin from Greek *aēr;* (sense 6) prob translation of Italian *aria,* from Latin *aer*]

air² *verb trans* **1** to expose (something) to the open air for freshening, drying, etc; to ventilate (something): *air a room.* **2** to expose (something) to warmth so as to remove dampness: *Air the sheets round the fire.* **3** to expose (something, e.g. an opinion) to public view or bring it to public notice: *airing their grievances.* **4** to broadcast (a radio or television programme). ≫ *verb intrans* to become exposed to the open air or to warmth for freshening, drying etc.

air bag *noun* a bag stored inside a motor vehicle and designed to inflate automatically in the event of an impact, cushioning the occupants against injury.

air base *noun* a base of operations for military aircraft.

air bed *noun chiefly Brit* an inflatable mattress.

air bladder *noun* a pouch containing air or other gas, *esp* an organ that controls buoyancy in bony fishes.

airborne *adj* supported or transported by air.

air brake *noun* **1** a brake operated by compressed air. **2** a movable surface projected into the air for slowing an aircraft.

air brick *noun* a building brick or brick-sized metal or plastic box perforated to allow ventilation.

airbrush¹ *noun* an atomizer for spraying paint.

airbrush² *verb trans* **1** to paint or spray (something) with an airbrush. **2** to alter (a photograph) using an airbrush. **3** to alter the record or reputation of (a person) in the public perception: *The former prime minister has been airbrushed out of recent history.*

Airbus *noun trademark* a subsonic jet passenger aeroplane designed for short intercity flights.

air chief marshal *noun* an officer in the Royal Air Force ranking below marshal of the Royal Air Force.

air commodore *noun* an officer in the Royal Air Force ranking below air vice marshal.

air-condition *verb trans* to equip (e.g. a building or vehicle) with air conditioning. ➤ **air-conditioned** *adj*.

air conditioning *noun* an apparatus or system for controlling the temperature, humidity, and cleanness of the air in a building or vehicle. ➤ **air conditioner** *noun*.

air-cool *verb trans* to cool the cylinders of (an internal-combustion engine) directly by air. ➤ **air-cooled** *adj*.

air corridor *noun* an air route over a country along which aircraft are allowed to fly.

air cover *noun* the use of military aircraft to protect ground or naval forces against attack.

aircraft /ˈeəkrahft/ *noun* (*pl* **aircraft**) an aeroplane, helicopter, or other means of transport that can travel through the air and is supported either by its own buoyancy or by the dynamic action of the air against its surfaces.

aircraft carrier *noun* a warship designed so that aircraft can be operated from it.

aircraftman *or* **aircraftwoman** *noun* (*pl* **aircraftmen** *or* **aircraftwomen**) a person of the lowest rank in the Royal Air Force.

aircrew *noun* (*treated as sing. or pl*) the crew of an aircraft, including the pilot and stewards.

air cushion *noun* **1** the layer of air between a hovercraft and the surface over which it moves. **2** an inflatable cushion.

air-cushion vehicle *noun chiefly NAmer* a hovercraft.

airdrop[1] *noun* a delivery of cargo or personnel by parachute from an aircraft.

airdrop[2] *verb trans* (**airdropped, airdropping**) to deliver (cargo or personnel) by parachute.

Airedale /ˈeədayl/ *noun* a large terrier of a breed with a hard wiry coat that is dark on the back and sides and tan elsewhere. [named after *Airedale*, district in Yorkshire, England, where the breed originated]

airer *noun chiefly Brit* a freestanding, usu collapsible, framework for airing or drying clothes, linen, etc.

airfield *noun* an area of land maintained for the landing and take-off of aircraft.

airflow *noun* the motion of air round a moving or stationary object.

airfoil *noun chiefly NAmer* = AEROFOIL.

air force *noun* the branch of a country's armed forces for air warfare.

airframe *noun* the structure of an aircraft or missile, without the engine and related parts.

airfreight[1] /ˈeəfrayt/ *noun* the transport of freight by air, or the charge for this.

airfreight[2] *verb trans* to transport (freight) by air.

airglow *noun* light observed in the sky, *esp* during the night, that originates in the upper atmosphere and is caused by gases reacting to the sun's radiation.

air guitar *noun informal* the playing of an imaginary guitar, *esp* while listening to rock music.

air gun *noun* **1** a gun from which a projectile is propelled by compressed air. **2** any of various hand tools that work by compressed air.

airhead *noun slang* a stupid person.

air hole *noun* a hole to admit or discharge air.

air hostess *noun* a female member of the cabin crew on a passenger aircraft.

airing /ˈeəring/ *noun* **1** exposure to air or warmth for ventilation or drying: *I'll give the bed a good airing*. **2** a walk, ride, or drive in the open air. **3** exposure to discussion or debate: *The proposal will get an airing at the next meeting*.

airing cupboard *noun* a heated cupboard in which household linen, washed laundry, etc is aired and kept dry.

air-kiss *verb trans and intrans* to make the motions of kissing (somebody) without making contact. ➤ **air kiss** *noun*.

air lane *noun* a path customarily followed by aeroplanes.

airless *adj* **1** still or windless. **2** lacking fresh air; stuffy. ➤ **airlessness** *noun*.

air letter *noun* **1** an airmail letter. **2** = AEROGRAM.

airlift[1] *noun* the transport of cargo or passengers by air, usu to or from an otherwise inaccessible area.

airlift[2] *verb trans* to transport (something or somebody) by means of an airlift: *The survivors were airlifted to safety*.

airline *noun* **1** an organization that provides regular public air transport. **2** a pipe or hose supplying air, usu under pressure.

air line *noun chiefly NAmer* = BEELINE.

airliner *noun* a passenger aircraft operated by an airline.

air lock *noun* **1** an airtight chamber, e.g. in a spacecraft or submerged vessel, that allows movement between two areas of different pressures or atmospheres. **2** a stoppage of flow caused by the presence of air in circulating liquid.

airmail[1] *noun* mail transported by aircraft, or this system of transporting mail.

airmail[2] *verb trans* to send (something) by airmail

airman *or* **airwoman** *noun* (*pl* **airmen** *or* **airwomen**) a civilian or military pilot, aircraft crew member, etc.

airman basic *noun* a person of the lowest rank in the US Air Force.

airman first class *noun* a person in the US Air Force ranking below sergeant.

air marshal *noun* **1** an officer in the Royal Air Force ranking below air chief marshal. **2** (*also* **sky marshal**) an armed security guard on a passenger aircraft.

Air Miles *pl noun trademark* points that are awarded to those purchasing certain products, *esp* airline tickets, and that can be used to pay for air travel.

airmiss *noun* a situation in which two aircraft in flight pass dangerously close to each other.

air pistol *noun* a small air gun.

airplane *noun chiefly NAmer* = AEROPLANE.

airplay *noun* the broadcasting of a particular recording, *esp* by a radio station, or a single instance of this.

air pocket *noun* **1** a region of down-flowing or low-density air that causes an aircraft to drop suddenly. **2** a cavity or enclosure containing air, e.g. under water.

airport *noun* a fully-equipped airfield, usu with runways and associated buildings, that is used as a base for the transport of passengers and cargo by air.

air power *noun* the military strength of an air force.

air pump *noun* a pump for removing air from or supplying air to a space or apparatus, often under pressure.

air rage *noun* violence and aggression directed by an aircraft passenger towards other passengers or members of the air crew on the aircraft.

air raid *noun* an attack by armed aircraft on a surface target.

air rifle *noun* an air gun with a rifled bore.

air sac *noun* **1** any of the air-filled spaces in the body of a bird connected with the air passages of the lungs. **2** a thin-walled expanded portion of an insect's trachea.

airscrew *noun* an aircraft propeller.

air-sea rescue *noun* the rescue of people in difficulties at sea by helicopter or other aircraft.

airship *noun* a gas-filled lighter-than-air aircraft that has its own means of propulsion and steering system.

air shot *noun Brit* a golf, cricket, or tennis stroke that misses the ball.

air show *noun* a public display of aircraft and aerobatics.

airsick *adj* suffering from the motion sickness associated with flying. ➤ **airsickness** *noun*.

airside *noun* the area of an airport beyond passport control: compare LANDSIDE (1).

air sign *noun* in astrology, any of the three signs of the Zodiac Gemini, Libra, and Aquarius: compare EARTH SIGN, FIRE SIGN, WATER SIGN.

airspace *noun* the space lying above the earth or a certain area of land or water, *esp* the space lying above a nation and coming under its jurisdiction.

airspeed *noun* the speed of an aircraft relative to the air.

airstrip *noun* a strip of ground where aircraft can take off and land.

air terminal *noun* a building, usu in a city centre, where passengers assemble to be taken to an airport by bus or train.

airtight *adj* **1** impermeable to air. **2** unassailable. >> **airtightness** *noun*.

airtime *noun* the broadcasting of something, e.g. a record or advertisement, on radio or television, or the duration of this.

air-to-air *adj* from one aircraft in flight to or at another: *an air-to-air missile*.

air traffic control *noun* a department that controls the movement of aircraft in flight, or at takeoff or landing, by issuing instructions to pilots regarding their altitude, speed, and course. >> **air traffic controller** *noun*.

air vice-marshal *noun* an officer in the Royal Air Force ranking below air marshal.

airwave *noun* (*usu in pl*) the supposed medium of radio and television transmission.

airway *noun* **1** a designated route along which aircraft fly. **2a** the passage through which air travels to the lungs: *Keep the patient's airway open*. **b** a tube inserted in the throat to let an unconscious person breathe. **3** a passage for air in a mine.

airworthy *adj* said of an aircraft: fit for operation in the air. >> **airworthiness** *noun*.

airy /'eəri/ *adj* (**airier, airiest**) **1a** open to the free circulation of air; well-ventilated. **b** spacious: *an airy room*. **2a** not having solid foundation; illusory: *airy promises*. **b** showing lack of concern; flippant. **3** light and graceful in movement or manner. **4** delicately thin in texture. **5** *literary* high in the air; lofty. >> **airily** *adv*, **airiness** *noun*.

airy-fairy *adj chiefly Brit* whimsically unrealistic: *The report was full of airy-fairy speculation*.

aisle /iel/ *noun* **1** a passage between rows of seats, e.g. in a church or theatre, or between rows of shelving or storage, e.g. in a shop. **2** the side division of a church separated from the nave by columns or piers. * **lead somebody up the aisle** to get married to somebody. >> **aisled** *adj*. [alteration of Middle English *ele, ile*, via French from Latin *ala* wing]

ait /ayt/ *or* **eyot** /ayt, ayət/ *noun Brit* a small island in a river. [Old English *īgeoth*, from *īg* island]

aitch /aych/ *noun* the letter *h*. [French *hache*, from (assumed) vulgar Latin *hacca*]

aitchbone *noun* the hipbone, *esp* of cattle, or the cut of beef containing this. [Middle English *hachbon*, alteration (by incorrect division) of *nachebon*, from Middle English *nache* buttock (via French from Latin *natis*) + *bon* BONE[1]]

ajar /ə'jah/ *adj and adv* said of a door: slightly open. [earlier *on char*, from ON[1] + *char* turn, piece of work, from Old English *cierr*]

AK *abbr* Alaska (US postal abbreviation).

AKA *or* **aka** *abbr* also known as.

Akan /'ahkahn/ *noun* (*pl* **Akans** *or collectively* **Akan**) **1** a member of a people living in Ghana, the Ivory Coast, and Togo. **2** the language of this people, belonging to the Kwa branch of the Niger-Congo family. >> **Akan** *adj*. [the Akan name for the language and people]

akimbo /ə'kimboh/ *adj and adv* said of the position of the arm: with the hand on the hip and the elbow turned outwards: *He stood with one arm akimbo, holding up the glass to the light with the other hand* — Dickens. [Middle English *in kenebowe*, prob from (assumed) Old Norse *i keng boginn* bent in a curve]

akin /ə'kin/ *adj* **1** descended from a common ancestor. **2** (*often* + to) essentially similar, related, or compatible.

akinesia /ayki'neezi-ə/ *noun* total or partial loss of the power of voluntary movement. [Greek *akinēsia*, from A-[2] + *kinein* to move]

Akkadian /ə'kadi-ən/ *noun* **1** a member of a Semitic people inhabiting central Mesopotamia before 2000 BC. **2** the language of this people. >> **Akkadian** *adj*. [*Akkad*, northern region of ancient Babylonia]

AL *abbr* **1** Alabama (US postal abbreviation). **2** Albania (international vehicle registration).

Al *abbr* the chemical symbol for aluminium.

al- *prefix* see AD-.

-al[1] *suffix* forming adjectives from nouns, denoting: character or type: *directional; fictional*. [Middle English via Old French from Latin *-alis*]

-al[2] *suffix* forming nouns from verbs, denoting: an action or process: *rehearsal; withdrawal*. [Middle English *-aille* from Old French from Latin *-alia*, neuter pl of *-alis*]

-al[3] *suffix* forming nouns, denoting: **1** aldehyde: *butanal*. **2** acetal: *butyral*. [French *-al* from *alcool* alcohol, from medieval Latin *alcohol*]

Ala. *abbr* Alabama.

à la /'ah lah (*French* a la)/ *prep* **1** in the manner of (somebody). **2** prepared, flavoured, or served with (something): *spinach à la crème*. [French *à la* from *à la mode* in the style]

alabaster /'aləbahstə, -bastə/ *noun* **1** a fine-textured, usu white and translucent, chalky stone often carved into ornaments: *that whiter skin of hers than snow and smooth as monumental alabaster* — Shakespeare. **2** (*used before a noun*) white or smooth like alabaster. >> **alabastrine** /-'bastrin/ *adj*. [Middle English *alabastre* via French from Latin *alabaster* vase of alabaster, from Greek *alabastros*]

à la carte /ah lah 'kaht/ *adv and adj* according to a menu that prices each item separately: compare TABLE D'HÔTE. [French *à la carte* by the bill of fare]

alack /ə'lak/ *interj archaic* used to express sorrow or regret. [Middle English, prob from AH + LACK[2] in the sense 'fault, loss']

alacrity /ə'lakriti/ *noun formal* promptness or cheerful readiness: *She accepted the offer with alacrity*. [Latin *alacritas* from *alacr-, alacer* lively, eager]

Aladdin's cave /ə'ladinz/ *noun* a hoard of precious things. [*Aladdin*, hero of a tale in *The Arabian Nights*, who gains access to a cave filled with treasure]

à la mode /ah lah 'mohd/ *adj* fashionable or stylish. [French *à la mode* according to the fashion]

alanine /'aləneen, -nien/ *noun* an amino acid found in most proteins. [German *Alanin*, irreg from *Aldehyd*: see ALDEHYDE]

Alar /'aylah/ *noun trademark* a chemical sprayed on fruit or vegetable plants, *esp* apple trees, to improve or increase the crop.

alar /'aylə/ *adj* of or like a wing. [Latin *alaris* from *ala* wing]

alarm[1] /ə'lahm/ *noun* **1** the fear resulting from the sudden sensing of danger. **2** a signal, e.g. a loud noise or flashing light, that warns or alerts, or an automatic device that produces such a signal: *a burglar alarm*. **3** = ALARM CLOCK. [Middle English *alarme, alarom* call to arms, via French from Old Italian *all'arme*, literally 'to the weapon']

alarm[2] *verb trans* **1** to strike (somebody) with fear, apprehension, or anxiety: *Don't be alarmed, it's quite safe!* **2** to warn or alert (somebody). **3** to fit or protect (something) with an automatic alarm. >> **alarming** *adj*, **alarmingly** *adv*.

alarm clock *noun* a clock that can be set to sound an alarm at a required time, usu to rouse somebody from sleep.

alarmist *noun* a person who needlessly alarms other people.

alarum /ə'larəm/ *noun archaic* an alarm or a call to arms: *That ... bell rang out a blood-curdling alarum over my head!* — Mark Twain; *For where a man's intentions are published, it is an alarum, to call up all that are against them* — Bacon. [Middle English *alarom*: see ALARM[1]]

alarums and excursions *pl noun* clamour and confusion. [orig used as a stage direction in Elizabethan drama, indicating martial sounds and the movement of soldiers across the stage]

alas /ə'las/ *interj* used to express unhappiness, pity, or disappointment. [Middle English from Old French, from AH + *las* weary, from Latin *lassus* weary]

alate /'aylayt/ *adj* having wings or wing-like extensions. [Latin from *ala* wing]

alb /alb/ *noun* a full-length white linen vestment, with long tight sleeves and a girdle around the waist, worn by a priest at Mass. [Old English *albe* from Latin *alba*, fem of *albus* white]

albacore /'albəkaw/ *noun* (*pl* **albacores** *or collectively* **albacore**) a large tuna fish with long pectoral fins that is caught for canning:

Thunnus alalunga. [Portuguese *albacor* from Arabic *al-bakūrah* the albacore]

Albanian /al'bayni·ən/ *noun* **1** a native or inhabitant of Albania. **2** the Indo-European language of Albania. ➤➤ **Albanian** *adj.*

albatross /'albatros/ *noun* (*pl* **albatrosses** *or collectively* **albatross**) **1** any of several species of large web-footed seabirds that are related to the petrels and include the largest seabirds: genera *Diomedea* and *Phoebetria*. **2** an encumbrance or handicap. **3** a golf score of three strokes less than par on a hole. [prob alteration of *alcatras* water bird, from Portuguese or Spanish *alcatraz* pelican; (sense 2) from the dead albatross hung round the neck of a sailor in the poem *The Ancient Mariner* by S T Coleridge; (sense 3) suggested by BIRDIE[1](2) and EAGLE[1]]

albedo /al'beedoh/ *noun* (*pl* **albedos**) the fraction of light or other electromagnetic radiation reflected by a surface or body, e.g. the moon or a cloud. [late Latin *albedo* whiteness, from Latin *albus*]

albeit /awl'bee·it/ *conj formal* even though: *He agreed to take part, albeit without enthusiasm.* [Middle English, literally 'all though it be']

albert /'albət/ *noun* a watch chain worn across the front of a waistcoat. [named after Prince *Albert* d.1861, consort of Queen Victoria]

albescent /al'bes(ə)nt/ *adj* becoming or shading into white. [Latin *albescent-, albescens*, present part. of *albescere* to become white, from *albus* white]

Albigenses /albi'jenseez/ *pl noun* members of a Catharistic sect of Christianity in S France between the 11th and 13th cents. ➤➤ **Albigensian** *adj and noun*, **Albigensianism** *noun*. [medieval Latin, pl of *Albigensis*, literally 'inhabitant of Albi', from *Albiga* Albi, commune in S France]

albino /al'beenoh/ *noun* (*pl* **albinos**) an organism with deficient pigmentation, *esp* a human being or other animal with a congenital lack of pigment resulting in a white or translucent skin, white or colourless hair, and eyes with a pink pupil. ➤➤ **albinic** /al'binik/ *adj*, **albinism** /'albiniz(ə)m/ *noun*, **albinotic** /-'notik/ *adj*. [Portuguese *albino*, from Spanish *albo* white, from Latin *albus* white]

Albion /'albi·ən/ *noun literary* Britain or England. [Old English via Latin from Greek *Aloviōn*, of Celtic origin]

albite /'albiet/ *noun* a white to grey feldspar that consists of sodium aluminium silicate and is a common constituent of various rocks, e.g. granite: formula NaAlSi$_3$O$_8$. [Swedish *albit*, from Latin *albus* white]

album /'albəm/ *noun* **1** a book with blank pages used to hold or display a collection, e.g. of stamps or photographs: *Rosamond ... was always that combination of correct sentiments, music, dancing, drawing, elegant note-writing, private album for extracted verse, and perfect blond loveliness* — George Eliot. **2** a recording or collection of recordings issued on one or more compact discs, cassettes, or long-playing records. [Latin *album* a white (blank) tablet, neuter of *albus* white]

albumen /'albyoomin/ *noun* **1** the white of an egg. **2** = ALBUMIN. [Latin *albumen* from *albus* white]

albumin /'albyoomin/ *noun* any of numerous proteins that occur in large quantities in blood plasma, milk, egg white, plant fluids, etc and are coagulated by heat. [ALBUMEN + -IN[1]]

albuminoid /al'byoohminoyd/ *noun* = SCLEROPROTEIN.

albuminous /al'byoohminəs/ *adj* relating to, containing, or like albumen or albumin.

albuminuria /al,byoohmin'nyooəri·ə/ *noun* the presence of albumin in the urine, usu symptomatic of kidney disease. ➤➤ **albuminuric** *adj*.

alburnum /al'buhnəm/ *noun* = SAPWOOD. [Latin *alburnum*, from *albus* white]

alcaic /al'kayik/ *adj* relating to or written in any of several predominantly iambic verse forms, *esp* a four-line stanza consisting of two eleven-syllable lines, one nine-syllable line, and one ten-syllable line. [via late Latin from Greek *Alkaios* Alcaeus, Greek poet of seventh cent. BC who invented the form]

alcaics *pl noun* alcaic verse.

alcalde /al'kaldi/ *noun* the chief administrative and judicial officer of a Spanish or Latin American town. [Spanish *alcalde* from Arabic *al-qāḍī* the judge]

alcazar /al'kazə, ahl'kahzə, al'kahzə, 'alkəzah/ *noun* a Spanish fortress or palace built by the Moors. [Spanish *alcazar*, from Arabic *al-qasr* the castle]

alchemy /'alkəmi/ *noun* (*pl* **alchemies**) **1** a medieval chemical science and philosophical doctrine that sought a means of turning base metals into gold, curing all diseases, and achieving immortality. **2** the transformation of something common into something precious or beautiful: *Full many a glorious morning have I seen ... gilding pale streams with heavenly alchemy* — Shakespeare. ➤➤ **alchemic** /al'kemik/ *adj*, **alchemical** /al'kem-/ *adj*, **alchemist** *noun*. [Middle English *alkamie, alquemie* via Old French or medieval Latin from Arabic *al-kīmiyā'* the alchemy, from late Greek *chēmeia*]

alcheringa /alchə'ring·ga/ *noun* a golden age recorded in the legends of certain Australian Aboriginal peoples as the time when their first ancestors were created. [Aranda *aljerre-nge* in the dreamtime]

alcohol /'alkəhol/ *noun* **1** a colourless volatile inflammable liquid that is the intoxicating agent in fermented and distilled drinks and is also used as a solvent: formula C$_2$H$_5$OH. **2** intoxicating drink containing alcohol. **3** any of various organic compounds, *specif* derived from hydrocarbons, containing the hydroxyl group.

Word history

medieval Latin *alcohol* via Old Spanish from Arabic *al-kuḥul* the powdered antimony. The modern sense of *alcohol* did not emerge until the middle of the 18th cent. As borrowed from Arabic, it orig denoted powdered antimony used as a cosmetic to darken the eyelids. Thence it was taken up by chemists in the 16th cent. to refer to any fine powder. By a further development in the 17th cent., the word was applied in chemistry to any refined liquid obtained by distillation or purification – especially *alcohol of wine*, which in time was shortened to simply *alcohol*.

alcoholic[1] /alkə'holik/ *adj* **1** of, containing, or caused by alcohol. **2** affected with alcoholism. ➤➤ **alcoholically** *adv*.

alcoholic[2] *noun* somebody affected with alcoholism.

alcoholism *noun* excessive and usu compulsive consumption of alcoholic drinks, or the physical and psychological disorders associated with such dependence.

alcopop /'alkohpop/ *noun Brit, informal* a soft drink containing alcohol. [ALCOHOL + POP[2] (2)]

alcove /'alkohv/ *noun* a niche, recess, or arched opening, e.g. in the wall of a room. [French *alcôve* via Spanish from Arabic *al-qubbah* the arch]

aldehyde /'aldihied/ *noun* any of various highly reactive compounds, e.g. acetaldehyde, characterized by the group CHO. ➤➤ **aldehydic** /-'hidik/ *adj*. [German *Aldehyd*, from scientific Latin *al dehyd*, abbr of *alcohol dehydrogenatum* dehydrogenated alcohol]

al dente /al 'denti/ *adj* said of pasta and vegetables: cooked but firm when bitten. [Italian *al dente*, literally 'to the tooth']

alder /'awldə/ *noun* any of a genus of trees or shrubs of the birch family that have toothed leaves, produce wood for turning and bark for tanning, and grow in moist ground: genus *Alnus*. [Old English *alor*]

alderman /'awldəmən/ *noun* (*pl* **aldermen**) **1** in Britain until 1974, a senior member of a county or borough council elected by the other councillors. **2** a person governing a kingdom, district, or shire as viceroy for an Anglo-Saxon king. **3** *NAmer, Aus* an elected member of the governing body of a borough. ➤➤ **aldermanic** /-'manik/ *adj*. [Old English *ealdorman*, from *ealdor* parent (from *eald* old) + *man*]

Aldis lamp /'awldis/ *noun trademark* a hand-held lamp for signalling in Morse code. [named after A C W Aldis d.1953, its British inventor]

aldosterone /al'dostərohn/ *noun* a steroid hormone produced by the adrenal cortex that affects the salt and water balance of the body: formula C$_{21}$H$_{28}$O$_5$. [ALDEHYDE + -O- + STEROL + -ONE]

aldrin /'awldrin/ *noun* a chlorinated insecticide that is very poisonous to human beings: formula C$_{12}$H$_8$Cl$_6$. [named after Kurt *Alder* d.1958, German chemist]

ale /ayl/ *noun* **1** beer. **2** an alcoholic drink made with malt and hops. It is usu more bitter, stronger, and heavier than beer. [Old English *ealu*]

aleatory /'ali·ət(ə)ri, 'ay-/ *or* **aleatoric** /ali·ə'torik, ay-/ *adj* **1** depending on chance. **2** relating to or based on luck, *esp* bad luck. **3** improvisatory or random in character: *aleatory music*. [Latin *aleatorius* of a gambler, from *aleator* gambler, from *alea*, a dice game]

alec *or* **aleck** /'alik/ *noun Aus, informal* a foolish person: compare SMART ALEC.

alee /ə'lee/ *adv and adj* on or towards the leeward side of a boat or ship.

alehouse *noun* dated a pub: *You are to call at all the alehouses and bid those that are drunk get them to bed* — Shakespeare.

alembic /ə'lembik/ *noun* **1** an apparatus formerly used in distillation: *He is as true a man of science as ever distilled his own heart in an alembic* — Nathaniel Hawthorne. **2** a means of refining or transmuting. [Middle English via Old French and medieval Latin from Arabic *al-anbīq* the still, from Greek *ambik-, ambix* cap of a still]

aleph /'ahlef, 'aylef/ *noun* the first letter of the Hebrew alphabet. [Hebrew *āleph*, prob from *eleph* ox]

alert¹ /ə'luht/ *adj* **1** watchful; aware. **2** active; brisk. ➤➤ **alertly** *adv*, **alertness** *noun*. [French *alerte* from Italian *all' erta*, literally 'on the lookout']

alert² *noun* **1** an alarm or other signal that warns of danger, e.g. from hostile aircraft. **2** the danger period during which an alert is in effect. ✻ **on the alert** on the lookout, *esp* for danger or opportunity.

alert³ *verb trans* **1** to call (somebody) to a state of readiness; to warn (somebody). **2** (*often* + to) to cause (somebody) to be aware, e.g. of a need or responsibility.

aleurone /'alyoorohn, ə'lyooərohn/ *or* **aleuron** /-rən/ *noun* minute granules of protein stored in seeds. ➤➤ **aleuronic** /-'ronik/ *adj*. [via German from Greek *aleuron* flour]

Aleut /ə'l(y)ooht, 'al(y)ooht/ *noun* **1** a member of a people of the Aleutian and Shumagin islands and W Alaska. **2** the language of this people. [Russian *aléut*]

A level *noun* **1** an examination in any of various subjects, usu taken at school or college at about the age of 18, or the level of study leading to this. **2** a pass in this examination: *She has four A levels.* [abbr of *Advanced level*]

alevin /'alivin/ *noun* a young fish, *esp* a newly hatched salmon. [French *alevin*, from Old French *alever* to lift up, rear (offspring) from Latin *allevare*, from AD- + *levare* to raise]

alewife /'aylwief/ *noun* (*pl* **alewives**) a N American fish related to the herring that is found in the NW Atlantic: *Alosa pseudoharengus*. [perhaps from French *alose* shad]

alexanders /alig'zahndəz/ *noun* (*pl* **alexanders**) a biennial European plant of the carrot family with flat clusters of greenish yellow flowers and black seeds: *Smyrnium olusatrum*. [Middle English *alexaundre* via Old French from medieval Latin *alexandrum*, prob by folk etymology from Latin *holus atrum* black vegetable]

Alexander technique /alig'zahndə/ *noun* a therapy for the treatment of specific ailments and the improvement of general health and well-being that aims to correct posture and movement, thereby relieving physical, mental, and emotional tension. [named after F M *Alexander* d.1955, Australian actor, who developed it]

Alexandrian /alig'zahndri-ən/ *adj* **1** relating to or characteristic of ancient or modern Alexandria. **2** = HELLENISTIC. [*Alexandria*, city in Egypt, centre of Hellenistic culture]

alexandrine /alig'zahndrin/ *noun* (*also* **Alexandrine**) a twelve-syllable verse line consisting of six iambic feet with a pause after the third. [early French *alexandrin* (adj), from *Alexandre* Alexander; from the use of such lines in a poem about Alexander the Great d.323 BC, king of Macedonia]

alexandrite /alig'zahndriet/ *noun* a green gemstone that appears red in artificial light. [German *Alexandrit*, named after *Alexander I* d.1825, Russian emperor]

alexia /ə'leksi-ə/ *noun* partial or total loss of the ability to read, owing to brain damage: compare APHASIA, APHONIA, DYSLEXIA. [scientific Latin *alexia*, from A-² + Greek *lexis* speech, from *legein* to speak]

alfalfa /al'falfə/ *noun* a deep-rooted plant of the pea family that is widely grown for fodder: *Medicago sativa*. [Spanish *alfalfa*, modification of Arabic dialect *al-faṣfaṣah* the alfalfa]

alfresco *or* **al fresco** /al'freskoh/ *adj and adv* taking place in the open air: *an alfresco lunch*. [Italian *al fresco* in the fresh (air)]

alg- *or* **algo-** *comb. form* forming words, denoting: pain: *algolagnia*. [Latin *alg-*, from Greek *algos*]

alga /'algə/ *noun* (*pl* **algae** /'alji, 'algi/ *or* **algas**) (*usu in pl*) any of a group of chiefly aquatic plants, e.g. seaweeds and pond scums, that lack differentiated stems, roots, and leaves and that often contain a brown or red pigment in addition to chlorophyll. ➤➤ **algal** *adj*, **algoid** *adj*. [Latin *alga* seaweed]

algebra /'aljibrə/ *noun* **1** a branch of mathematics in which letters, symbols, etc representing various entities are combined according to special rules of operation. **2** a system of representing logical arguments in symbols. ➤➤ **algebraist** *noun*.

Word history
medieval Latin *algebra* from Arabic *al-jabr*, literally 'the reduction' (of fractures). The mathematical sense comes from the title of a ninth-cent. Arabic treatise *Yihm al-jabr wa'l-muk ā bala* 'The science of restoring what is missing and equating like with like', by *al-Khuwārizmi*: see ALGORITHM.

Algerian /al'jiəriən/ *noun* a native or inhabitant of Algeria. ➤➤ **Algerian** *adj*.

-algia *comb. form* forming nouns, denoting: pain: *neuralgia*. [Greek *algia*, from *algos*]

algicide /'aljisied/ *noun* a substance that kills algae. [ALGA + -I- + -CIDE]

algin /'aljin/ *noun* alginic acid, an alginate, or a similar substance obtained from seaweed or other marine brown algae. [ALGA+ -IN¹]

alginate /'aljinayt/ *noun* a salt of alginic acid used as a stabilizing, gelling, or thickening agent in the manufacture of ice cream, plastics, etc.

alginic acid /al'jinik/ *noun* an insoluble acid that forms in a thick jelly-like paste when mixed with water and is found in the cell walls of brown algae: formula $(C_6H_8O_6)_n$. [ALGIN + -IC¹]

algo- *comb. form* see ALG-.

Algol *or* **ALGOL** /'algol/ *noun* an early high-level computer language designed primarily for mathematical and scientific use. [acronym from *algorithmic language*]

algolagnia /algoh'lagni-ə/ *noun* sexual pleasure found in inflicting or suffering pain; sadomasochism. ➤➤ **algolagnic** *adj*. [scientific Latin *algolagnia* from ALG- + Greek *lagneia* lust]

algology /al'goləji/ *noun* a branch of biology dealing with algae. ➤➤ **algological** /-'lojik/ *adj*, **algologist** *noun*.

Algonkian /al'gongki-ən/ *noun* see ALGONQUIAN.

Algonkin /al'gongkin/ *noun* see ALGONQUIN.

Algonquian /al'gongkwi-ən/ *or* **Algonkian** /-ki-ən/ *noun* **1** a group of Native American languages spoken *esp* in the eastern parts of Canada and the USA. **2** a member of any of the Native American peoples speaking Algonquian languages. **3** = ALGONQUIN (1), (2). ➤➤ **Algonquian** *adj*.

Word history
ALGONQUIN + -IAN. Words from Algonquian languages that have passed into English include *chipmunk, moccasin, moose, persimmon, powwow, raccoon, skunk, terrapin,* and *toboggan.*

Algonquin /al'gongkwin/ *or* **Algonkin** /-kin/ *noun* **1** a member of a Native American people living in the Ottawa river valley in Canada. **2** the dialect of Ojibwa spoken by the Algonquins. **3** = ALGONQUIAN (1), (2). ➤➤ **Algonquin** *adj*. [French *Algonquin*, alteration of *Algoumequin*, from Micmac *algoomaking* at the place where fish are speared]

algorithm /'algəridhəm/ *noun* a systematic procedure for solving a mathematical problem in a finite number of steps, often using a computer; *broadly* a step-by-step procedure for solving a problem or accomplishing some end. ➤➤ **algorithmic** /-'ridhmik/ *adj*. [alteration of Middle English *algorisme*, via Old French and medieval Latin from Arabic *al-khuwārizmi*, named after *al-Khuwārizmi* fl.825, Arabian mathematician]

alias¹ /'ayli-əs/ *adv* otherwise called or known as: *William Hancock, alias Michael Jones*. [Latin *alias* otherwise, from *alius* other]

alias² *noun* an assumed name.

alibi¹ /'alibie/ *noun* (*pl* **alibis**) **1** the plea of having been elsewhere when a crime was committed, or evidence supporting such a claim. **2** a plausible excuse, usu intended to avert blame or punishment. [Latin *alibi* elsewhere, from *alius* other]

alibi² *verb trans* (**alibis, alibied, alibiing**) to provide (somebody) with an alibi or excuse.

Alice band /'alis/ *noun* a firm headband worn to hold the hair back from the face. [from the illustrations of the character *Alice* in *Through the Looking Glass* by Lewis Carroll]

alicyclic /ali'sieklik, -'siklik/ *adj* combining the properties of aliphatic and cyclic organic chemical compounds. [ALIPHATIC + CYCLIC]

alidade /'alidayd/ *noun* a rule equipped with sights used to determine direction in astronomy or surveying, e.g. as part of an astrolabe. [Middle English *allidatha* via medieval Latin from Arabic *al-'iḍādah* the revolving radius of a circle]

alien[1] /'ayli·ən/ *adj* **1a** relating or belonging to another person, place, or thing; strange. **b** foreign. **2** from another world; extraterrestrial. **3** (+ to) differing in nature or character, *esp* to the extent of being opposed: *They have ideas quite alien to ours.* [Middle English via Old French from Latin *alienus*, from *alius* other]

alien[2] *noun* **1** a foreign-born resident who has not been naturalized; *broadly* a foreign-born citizen. **2** a being from another world; an extraterrestrial. **3** a person, animal, or plant from another family, race, or species. ➤➤ **alienage** *noun*.

alienable *adj* legally capable of being sold or transferred. ➤➤ **alienability** /-'biliti/ *noun*.

alienate /'ayli·ənayt/ *verb trans* **1** to make (somebody) hostile or indifferent, *esp* where attachment formerly existed: *at the risk of alienating his fans.* **2** to cause (something, e.g. affection) to be withdrawn or diverted. **3** to convey or transfer (e.g. property or a right) to another, usu by a specific act: *The grantee of any extensive tract of land generally finds it for his interest to alienate … the greater part of it* — Adam Smith. ➤➤ **alienator** *noun*. [Latin *alienatus*, past part. of *alienare* to estrange, from *alienus*: see ALIEN[1]]

alienation /,ayli·ə'naysh(ə)n/ *noun* **1** withdrawal from or a feeling of apathy towards one's former attachments or society in general.

Editorial note
The concept of alienation in philosophical parlance was popularized by some unfaithful disciples of Hegel: Hess, Feuerbach and, especially, Marx. Alienation is a process whereby products of human work and life gain a quasi-autonomous existence and dominate (or oppress) people like foreign powers; people lose control of their own creations. God is alienated humanity, money is the productive effort alienated from the producers. The word 'alienation' is often used in a vague sense of being injuriously separated from society or one's own milieu — Professor Leszek Kołakowski.

2 a conveyance of property to another.

alienist /'ayli·ənist/ *noun* **1** *NAmer* a specialist in legal aspects of psychiatry. **2** *archaic* somebody who treats mental disorders. [French *aliéniste*, from *aliéné* insane, from Latin *alienatus*, past part. of *alienare*: see ALIENATE]

aliform /'aylifawm/ *adj* wing-shaped or having wing-shaped parts. [Latin *ali-* (from *ala* wing) + -FORM]

alight[1] /ə'liet/ *verb intrans* **1** to come down from something; to dismount or disembark: *passengers alighting at Crewe.* **2** to descend from the air and settle; to land. ➤➤ **alightment** *noun*. [Old English *ālīhtan*, A-[1] + *līhtan* to alight]

alight[2] *adj* **1** *chiefly Brit* on fire; ignited: *The paper caught alight.* **2** animated or alive: *see the place alight with merriment* — Punch. [prob from A-[1] + LIGHT[1]]

align /ə'lien/ *verb trans* **1** to bring (things) into proper relative position or state of adjustment, usu in a straight line. **2** to position (oneself or another) on the side of or against a party or cause: *nations aligned against fascism.* ➤ *verb intrans* **1** to join with others in a common cause. **2** to be or become aligned. ➤➤ **alignment** *noun*. [French *aligner* from Old French, from AD- + *ligne* LINE[2] from Latin *linea*]

alike[1] /ə'liek/ *adj* showing close resemblance without being identical: *alike in their beliefs.* [Old English *onlīc*, from ON[1] + *līc* body]

alike[2] *adv* in the same manner, form, or degree; equally: *a disease that affects children and adults alike.*

aliment /'alimənt/ *noun formal* **1** food or nutriment. **2** sustenance for the body or mind. ➤➤ **alimental** /-'mentl/ *adj*. [Middle English from Latin *alimentum* from *alere* to nourish]

alimentary /ali'ment(ə)ri/ *adj* relating to nourishment or nutrition.

alimentary canal *noun* the tubular passage that extends from the mouth to the anus and functions in the digestion and absorption of food.

alimentation /,alimən'taysh(ə)n/ *noun formal* **1** nourishing or being nourished. **2** sustenance or support. ➤➤ **alimentative** /-'mentətiv/ *adj*.

alimony /'aliməni/ *noun chiefly NAmer* = MAINTENANCE (3). [Latin *alimonia* sustenance, from *alere* to nourish]

A-line *adj* said of a garment: shaped like the lower part of an A, with the bottom wider than the top: *an A-line skirt.*

aliphatic /ali'fatik/ *adj* **1** said of a chemical compound: having an open-chain rather than a cyclic structure: compare AROMATIC[1] (2). **2** of or derived from fat. [Greek *aleiphat-, aleiphar* oil, from *aleiphein* to smear]

aliquot[1] /'alikwot/ *adj* **1** contained an exact number of times in another: *5 is an aliquot part of 15.* **2** constituting a fraction of a whole: *an aliquot part of invested capital.* [medieval Latin *aliquotus* from Latin *aliquot* some, several, from *alius* other + *quot* how many]

aliquot[2] *noun* **1** a small part that is contained an exact number of times in a whole. **2** a small sample, e.g. one taken from a mixture undergoing a chemical reaction to determine what changes have occurred.

alive /ə'liev/ *adj* **1a** having life; not dead: *The fish was still alive.* **b** of all those living: *the proudest mother alive.* **2a** still in existence, force, or operation; active. **b** = LIVE[2] (3B). **3** (+ to) realizing the existence of; aware of: *alive to the danger.* **4** marked by alertness; lively or animated. **5** (*often* + with) showing much activity; swarming: *The sea was alive with large whales* — Herman Melville. ➤➤ **aliveness** *noun*. [Old English *on life*, from ON[1] + *līf* LIFE]

alizarin /ə'lizərin/ *noun* an orange or red dye formerly obtained from madder. [prob from French *alizarine* from *alizari* madder, from Spanish, prob from Arabic *al-'aṣārah* the juice]

alkali /'alkəlie/ *noun* (*pl* **alkalis** *or* **alkalies**) **1** any of various soluble chemical bases, *esp* a hydroxide or carbonate of an alkali metal, that combine with acids to form salts: compare ACID[2], BASE[1] (7). **2** a soluble chemical salt that is present in some soils of dry regions and prevents the growth of crops.

Word history
Middle English via medieval Latin from Arabic *al-qili* the ashes of the plant saltwort. Alkalis were first obtained from the ashes of various plants, including saltwort.

alkali metal *noun* any of the univalent metals lithium, sodium, potassium, rubidium, caesium, and francium.

alkaline /'alkəlien/ *adj* containing or having the properties of an alkali; *specif* having a pH of more than seven. ➤➤ **alkalinity** /-'liniti/ *noun*.

alkaline earth *noun* **1** an oxide of any of the bivalent metals calcium, strontium, barium, magnesium, radium, or beryllium. **2** (*also* **alkaline earth metal**) any of the metals whose oxides are alkaline earths.

alkaloid /'alkəloyd/ *noun* any of numerous nitrogen-containing organic compounds, e.g. morphine, that are usu chemical bases, occur in plants, and are extensively used as drugs. ➤➤ **alkaloidal** /-'loydl/ *adj*.

alkalosis /alkə'lohsis/ *noun* a medical disorder in which the blood, tissues, etc are abnormally alkaline.

alkane /'alkayn/ *noun* any of a series of saturated open-chain hydrocarbons, e.g. methane, ethane, propane, or butane. [ALKYL + -ANE]

alkanet /'alkənet/ *noun* **1a** a plant of the borage family that yields a strong red dye: *Alkanna tinctoria.* **b** the dye obtained from this plant. **2** any of various related plants: genera *Alkanna*, *Pentaglottis*, and *Anchusa*. [Middle English from Old Spanish *alcaneta*, dimin. of *alcana* henna shrub, via medieval Latin from Arabic *al-ḥinnā'* the henna]

alkene /'alkeen/ *noun* any of a series of unsaturated hydrocarbons, e.g. ethylene or propylene, in which the carbon atoms are arranged in a straight line and there is a double bond between two carbon atoms. [ALKYL + -ENE]

alkyd /'alkid/ *or* **alkyd resin** *noun* any of numerous plastics that are produced by heating alcohols with acids and are used to make paints and tough protective coatings. [blend of ALKYL and ACID[2]]

alkyl /'alkil/ *noun* a univalent radical, e.g. methyl, derived from an alkane, e.g. methane, by removal of a hydrogen atom. ➤➤ **alkylic** /al'kilik/ *adj*. [German *Alkyl*, from *Alkohol* alcohol, from medieval Latin *alcohol*: see ALCOHOL]

alkylate /'alkilayt/ *verb trans* to introduce one or more alkyl radicals into (a compound). ➤➤ **alkylation** /-'laysh(ə)n/ *noun*.

alkyne /'alkien/ *noun* any of a series of unsaturated hydrocarbons, e.g. acetylene, in which the carbon atoms are arranged in a straight line and there is a triple bond between two carbon atoms. [ALKYL + -yne, variant of -INE[2]]

all[1] /awl/ *adj* **1a** the whole amount or quantity of: *We sat up all night; all the year round.* **b** as much as possible: *He spoke in all seriousness.* **2** the whole number or sum of: *All dogs love aniseed.* **3** every: *all manner of hardship.* **4** any whatever: *beyond all doubt.* **5a** displaying only: *She was all attention.* **b** having or seeming to have some physical feature conspicuously or excessively: *all thumbs; all ears.* ✳ **all**

there *informal* not mentally subnormal; alert or shrewd. **all very well** a formula used in rejection of advice or sympathy: *It's all very well for you to talk.* **be all one** to be a matter of indifference: *It's all one to me where we go.* **for all** in spite of: *They couldn't open it for all their efforts.* [Old English *eall*]

all² *adv* **1** wholly or altogether: *all alone; I'm all for it.* **2** to a supreme degree: *all-powerful.* **3** for each side: *The score is two all.* ✳ **all but** very nearly; almost: *He … all but burst into hysterical weeping* — James Joyce. **all that** *chiefly in negatives and questions* to a marked or unusual extent; very: *She didn't take his threats all that seriously.* **all the** (+ *compar*) so much: *We'll get there all the sooner.* **all together** all at the same time or in the same place. **all too** emphatically so: *It was all too obvious.*

all³ *pronoun* (*pl* **all**) **1** the whole number, quantity, or amount: *All you need is a bit of patience.* **2** everybody; everything: *He sacrificed all for love.* ✳ **all in all 1** generally; taking everything into account. **2** supremely important: *She was all in all to him.* **all of** fully; no less than: *We lost all of £50.* **all the best** used as an expression of goodwill and usu farewell. **all the way** completely; without reservation: *I'm with you all the way on that.* **for all** to the extent that: *He may be dead for all I know.* **for all one is worth** with all one's might.

all⁴ *noun* one's greatest effort or total resources: *She gave her all for the cause.* ✳ **in all** = ALL TOLD.

alla breve¹ /,alə 'brevi, 'brayvi/ *adj and adv* said of a piece of music: with two or four beats in a bar, a single beat being represented by a minim. [Italian *alla breve*, literally 'according to the breve']

alla breve² *noun* the sign marking a musical piece or passage to be played alla breve, or the time in which it is played.

Allah /'alah, 'alə/ *noun* the name for God used by Muslims or in reference to the Islamic religion. [Arabic *allāh*]

all-American *adj* representative of the ideals of the USA; typically or truly American: *an all-American boy.*

allantois /ə'lantoh·is/ *noun* (*pl* **allantoides** /alən'toh·ideez/) a vascular membrane that surrounds the foetus in reptiles, birds, and mammals and that in some mammals combines with the chorion to form the placenta. ➤➤ **allantoic** /alən'toh·ik/ *adj.* [scientific Latin *allantois* from Greek *allantoeidēs* sausage-shaped, from *allant-, allas* sausage]

allargando /alah'gandoh/ *adj and adv* said of a piece of music: to be performed with gradually decreasing speed and increasing fullness of tone. [Italian *allargando* widening, from *allargare* to widen, from *al-* AD- + *largare* to widen]

all-around *adj chiefly NAmer* = ALL-ROUND.

allay /ə'lay/ *verb trans* (**allays, allayed, allaying**) **1** to reduce the severity of (e.g. pain or grief); to alleviate (something). **2** to reduce or diminish (e.g. fear or suspicion): *The idea of any thing to be done in a moment, was increasing, not lessening, Mr Woodhouse's agitation. The ladies knew better how to allay it* — Jane Austen. [Old English *ālecgan*, from A-¹ + *lecgan* to lay]

All Blacks *pl noun* the New Zealand Rugby Union team. [from the colour of their shirts, shorts, and socks]

all clear *noun* a signal that a danger has passed or that it is safe to proceed: *Wait till you get the all clear.*

allegation /ali'gaysh(ə)n/ *noun* a statement made without proof or that has yet to be proved.

allege /ə'lej/ *verb trans* to assert (something) without proof or before proving it: *The prosecution alleged that she had never seen the man before.* ➤➤ **alleged** /ə'lejd/ *adj*, **allegedly** /ə'lejidli/ *adv*. [Middle English *alleggen* via Old French from Latin *allegare* to dispatch, cite, from AD- + *legare*: see LEGATE]

allegiance /ə'leej(ə)ns/ *noun* **1** dedication to or dutiful support of a person, group, or cause. **2** the obligation of subjects or citizens to their sovereign or government. [Middle English *allegeaunce*, modification of early French *ligeance*, from Old French *lige* LIEGE¹]

allegorical /ali'gorikl/ *or* **allegoric** *adj* constituting or characteristic of allegory. ➤➤ **allegorically** *adv*.

allegorise /'aligəriez/ *verb* see ALLEGORIZE.

allegorist /'aligərist/ *noun* somebody who uses or writes allegory.

allegorize *or* **allegorise** /'aligəriez/ *verb trans or intrans* to compose, express, or interpret (something) as allegory. ➤➤ **allegorization** /-'zaysh(ə)n/ *noun*, **allegorizer** *noun*.

allegory /'alig(ə)ri/ *noun* (*pl* **allegories**) **1a** the expression by means of symbolic figures and actions of truths or generalizations about human existence. **b** a story, poem, painting, etc that con-

tains or consists of allegory. **2** a symbolic representation; an emblem. [Middle English *allegorie* via Latin from Greek *allēgorein* to speak figuratively, from *allos* other + *-agorein* to speak publicly, from *agora* assembly]

allegretto /ali'gretoh/ *adj and adv* said of a piece of music: to be performed faster than andante but not as fast as allegro. ➤➤ **allegretto** *noun*. [Italian *allegretto* from ALLEGRO]

allegro /ə'legroh/ *adj and adv* said of a piece of music: to be performed in a brisk lively manner. ➤➤ **allegro** *noun*. [Italian *allegro* merry, ultimately from Latin *alacr-, alacer* lively]

allele /ə'leel/ *noun* any of two or more genes that occur as alternatives at a given place on a chromosome and are responsible for variations in a hereditary characteristic, e.g. eye colour. ➤➤ **allelic** /ə'leelik/ *adj*. [German *Allel*, short for ALLELOMORPH]

allelomorph /ə'leeləmawf/ *noun* = ALLELE. ➤➤ **allelomorphic** /-'mawfik/ *adj*. [Greek *allēlōn* of each other, from *allos* other + *morphē* form]

alleluia /ali'looh·yə/ *interj and noun* see HALLELUJAH¹, HALLELUJAH². [Middle English via late Latin and Greek from Hebrew *halălūyāh* praise ye Jehovah]

allemande /'aləmand/ *noun* **1** a 17th-cent. and 18th-cent. court or folk dance. **2** music for an allemande, often part of a suite. [French (*danse*) *allemande* German (dance)]

all-embracing *adj* complete or sweeping.

Allen key /'alən/ *noun trademark* a tool with a hexagonal end that is designed to turn a screw with a recess of this shape in the head. [named after the manufacturer, the *Allen Manufacturing Company*, Connecticut]

allergen /'aləjən, -jen/ *noun* a substance that induces allergy. ➤➤ **allergenic** /-'jenik/ *adj*. [ALLERGY + -GEN]

allergic /ə'luhjik/ *adj* **1** (+ to) having an allergy to something: *allergic to strawberries.* **2** of or inducing allergy: *an allergic reaction.* **3** *informal* (+ to) averse or antipathetic to a practice: *allergic to marriage.*

allergy /'aləji/ *noun* (*pl* **allergies**) **1** extreme sensitivity, marked by sneezing, itching, skin rashes, etc, to substances that have no such effect on the average individual.

Editorial note

Allergies are caused by extreme sensitivity (hypersensitivity) of the immune system to innocuous substances, known as 'allergens', which do not usually trigger an immune response in a normal healthy individual. As part of the immune response, the affected tissues release histamine and other chemicals, which results in symptoms such as swelling, itching, constriction of the airways and rashes. A life-threatening allergic reaction is known as anaphylaxis — Dr John Cormack.

2 increased sensitivity to an antigen in response to a first exposure. **3** *informal* a feeling of antipathy or aversion. [German *Allergie*, from Greek *allos* other + *ergon* work]

alleviate /ə'leeviayt/ *verb trans* to relieve (a troublesome situation, state of mind, etc). ➤➤ **alleviation** /-'aysh(ə)n/ *noun*, **alleviative** *adj*, **alleviator** *noun*, **alleviatory** /-ət(ə)ri/ *adj*. [late Latin *alleviatus*, past part. of *alleviare*, from Latin AD- + *levis* light]

alley¹ /'ali/ *noun* (*pl* **alleys**) **1** a narrow back street or passageway between buildings. **2** a garden walk bordered by trees or a hedge. **3** = BOWLING ALLEY. ✳ **up/down one's alley** *chiefly NAmer* suited to one's abilities or tastes. [Middle English from Old French *aler* to go, modification of Latin *ambulare* to walk]

alley² *noun* (*pl* **alleys**) a large or superior playing marble. [by shortening and alteration from ALABASTER]

alleyway *noun* = ALLEY¹ (1).

All Fools' Day *noun* = APRIL FOOLS' DAY.

all found *adv chiefly Brit* with free food and lodging provided in addition to wages: *£200 a week and all found.*

all fours *pl noun* all four legs of a quadruped. ✳ **on all fours** on hands and knees: *crawling around on all fours.*

Allhallows /awl'halohz/ *noun* = ALL SAINTS' DAY. [short for *All Hallows' Day*: see HALLOWEEN]

alliaceous /ali'ayshəs/ *adj* **1** resembling garlic or onion, *esp* in smell or taste. **2** relating or belonging to the genus of plants that includes garlic and onion. [Latin *allium* garlic]

alliance /ə'lie·əns/ *noun* **1** a confederation of nations by formal treaty. **2** a union of families by marriage. **3** an association or bond between groups or individuals who agree to cooperate for mutual benefit: *a closer alliance between government and industry.* **4** a connection or relationship. **5** a botanical category comprising a group of related plant families.

allied /'alied, ə'lied/ *adj* **1** joined in alliance by agreement or treaty. **2** in close association; united. **3a** related by resemblance or common properties: *heraldry and allied subjects.* **b** related genetically. **4** (**Allied**) of the Allies: *an attack by Allied troops.*

Allies /'aliez/ *pl noun* **1** the nations, including Britain, Russia, and France, united against the Central European powers in World War I. **2** the nations, including Britain, the USA, and the Soviet Union, united against the Axis powers in World War II.

alligator /'aligaytə/ *noun* **1** either of two species of large American or Chinese aquatic reptiles that are related to the crocodiles but have broader heads that do not taper towards the snout: genus *Alligator.* **2** leather made from alligator hide. [Spanish *el lagarto* the lizard, from Latin *lacertus, lacerta*]

alligator pear *noun NAmer* = AVOCADO. [by folk etymology from *avocado pear*]

all-important *adj* of very great or greatest importance: *an all-important question.*

all in *adj informal* tired out; exhausted: *You look all in.*

all-in *adj* **1** *chiefly Brit* all-inclusive, *esp* including all costs: *an all-in holiday to Greece.* **2** *Brit* said of wrestling: having almost no holds barred.

all-inclusive *adj* including everything: *a broader and more all-inclusive view.* ⟫⟫ **all-inclusiveness** *noun.*

alliterate /ə'litərayt/ *verb intrans* to use, produce, or contain alliteration. ⟫ *verb trans* to arrange (words) or construct (phrases) so as to cause alliteration. [back-formation from ALLITERATION]

alliteration /ə,litə'raysh(ə)n/ *noun* the repetition of initial consonant sounds in neighbouring words or syllables, e.g. '*threatening throngs of threshers*'. ⟫⟫ **alliterative** /ə'litərətiv/ *adj*, **alliteratively** *adv.* [AD- + Latin *littera* LETTER[1]]

allium /'ali·əm/ *noun* any of a large genus of plants of the lily family including the onion, garlic, chives, leek, and shallot: genus *Allium.* [scientific Latin *Allium*, genus name, from Latin *allium*, garlic]

all-night *adj* **1** lasting throughout the night: *an all-night poker game.* **2** open throughout the night: *an all-night café.*

allo- *comb. form* forming words, with the meanings: **1** other; different; atypical: *allopathy.* **2** being one of a specified group whose members together constitute a structural unit, *esp* of a language: *allophone.* [Greek *all-*, from *allos* other]

allocate /'aləkayt/ *verb trans* **1a** to apportion and distribute (e.g. money or responsibility) in shares. **b** to assign (something limited in supply) to somebody: *We've been allocated one of the new flats.* **2** to earmark or designate (something): *We will allocate a section of the building for research purposes.* ⟫⟫ **allocable** /-kəbl/ *adj*, **allocatable** *adj*, **allocation** /-'kaysh(ə)n/ *noun*, **allocator** *noun.* [medieval Latin *allocatus*, past part. of *allocare*, from AD- + Latin *locare* to place, from *locus* place]

allochthonous or **allocthonous** /ə'lokthənəs/ *adj* said of a plant, animal, or substance: entering a particular ecological region from an outside source: compare AUTOCHTHONOUS. [ALLO- + *-chthonous* (as in AUTOCHTHONOUS)]

allocution /alə'kyoohsh(ə)n/ *noun* a formal speech; *esp* an authoritative or stirring address: *after this vigorous allocution, to one of which sort Lord Steyne treated his 'Hareem' whenever symptoms of insubordination appeared in his household* — Thackeray. [Latin *allocution-, allocutio* from *alloqui* to speak to, from AD- + *loqui* to speak]

allogamy /ə'logəməs/ *noun* reproduction by cross-fertilization: compare AUTOGAMY. ⟫⟫ **allogamous** *adj.*

allograft /'aləgrahft/ *noun* a graft between two genetically unlike members of the same species.

allomorph[1] /'aləmawf/ *noun* any of two or more distinct crystalline forms of the same substance. ⟫⟫ **allomorphic** /-'mawfik/ *adj.* [ALLO- + Greek *morphē* form]

allomorph[2] *noun* any of two or more alternative forms of a morpheme, e.g. the *-es* of *dishes* and the *-s* of *dreams.* ⟫⟫ **allomorphic** *adj.* [ALLO- + MORPHEME]

allopathy /ə'lopəthi/ *noun* conventional medical practice using treatments that produce effects different from those of the disease being treated. ⟫⟫ **allopath** /'aləpath/ *noun*, **allopathic** /alə'pathik/ *adj*, **allopathically** /-'pathikli/ *adv*, **allopathist** /ə'lopəthist/ *noun.* [German *Allopathie*, from ALLO- + -PATHY]

allophone /'aləfohn/ *noun* any of two or more alternative forms of a phoneme, e.g. the aspirated /*p*/ of *pin* and the nonaspirated /*p*/ of *spin*: compare PHONEME. ⟫⟫ **allophonic** /-'fonik/ *adj.*

allopurinol /alə'pyooərinol/ *noun* a drug used to promote excretion of uric acid, e.g. in the treatment of gout. [ALLO- + PURINE + -OL[1]]

all-or-nothing *adj* **1** risking everything: *an all-or-nothing gamble.* **2** accepting no compromises: *an all-or-nothing perfectionist.*

allosaurus /alə'sawrəs/ *noun* a large two-footed flesh-eating dinosaur of the late Jurassic period. [scientific Latin from Greek *allos* other + *sauros* lizard]

allot /ə'lot/ *verb trans* (**allotted, allotting**) **1** to apportion or assign (something); = ALLOCATE (1): *A distinguished post was allotted to 'ancient sirloin', as mine host termed it* — Washington Irving; *Each hour had its allotted task* — Charlotte Brontë. **2** to earmark or designate (something): *Ten minutes have been allotted for your speech.* ⟫⟫ **allotter** *noun.* [Middle English *alotten* from early French *aloter* to share out by drawing lots, from AD- + *lot* lot, of Germanic origin; related to Old English *hlot* LOT[1]]

allotment /ə'lotmənt/ *noun* **1** *Brit* a small plot of land let out to an individual, e.g. by a town council, for cultivation. **2** the act of allotting or a share allotted.

allotrope /'alətrohp/ *noun* any of the two or more different physical forms in which a substance can exist: *Graphite and diamond are allotropes of carbon.* ⟫⟫ **allotropic** /-'tropik/ *adj*, **allotropically** /-'tropikli/ *adv.* [back-formation from ALLOTROPY]

allotropy /ə'lotrəpi/ *noun* the existence of a substance, *esp* an element, in two or more different forms with different physical properties. [ALLO- + *-tropy* from Greek *tropē* turn, turning]

all out *adv* with maximum determination and effort: *She went all out to win.*

all-out *adj* using maximum effort and resources: *an all-out effort to finish on time.*

allover /'awlohvə/ *adj* covering the whole extent or surface: *a sweater with an allover pattern.*

all over *adv* **1** over the whole extent or surface: *decorated all over with a flower pattern.* **2** in every respect: *That's Paul all over.*

allow /ə'low/ *verb trans* **1** to permit (something, or somebody to do something): *Smoking is not allowed.* **2a** to enable or make it possible for (somebody to do something): *The software allows you to copy from one application to another.* **b** to admit the possibility of (something): *The facts allow only one explanation.* **c** to fail to prevent (something, or somebody from doing something): *She had allowed herself to become angry.* **3a** to assign (e.g. time or money) as a share or suitable amount: *Allow an hour for lunch.* **b** to grant (a sum of money) as an allowance to (somebody): *They allowed him £500 a year.* **c** to reckon (an amount) as a deduction or an addition: *Allow a gallon for leakage.* **4** (+ that) to admit (something) as true or valid; to acknowledge (something): *I allowed that I could have been wrong.* ⟫ *verb intrans* **1** (+ of) to admit the possibility of something: *evidence that allows of only one conclusion.* **2** (+ for) to take (special factors or circumstances) into account: *This figure allows for inflation.* [Middle English *allowen* via French from Latin *adlaudare* to extol, from AD- + *laudare* to praise]

allowable *adj* **1** permissible. **2** that may be assigned as an allowance: *expenses allowable against tax.* ⟫⟫ **allowably** *adv.*

allowance[1] *noun* **1a** a share or portion allotted or granted; a ration. **b** a sum granted as reimbursement or for expenses, usu at regular intervals. **c** a reduction from a list price or stated price. **d** an amount deducted or added in reckoning: *an allowance for wastage.* **2** a handicap, e.g. in a race. **3a** permission or sanction. **b** acknowledgment: *allowance of your claim.* **4** (*also in pl*) the taking into account of mitigating circumstances: *We must make allowances for his inexperience.*

allowance[2] *verb trans* **1** *archaic* to put (somebody) on a fixed allowance. **2** to provide (something) in a limited quantity.

allowedly /ə'lowidli/ *adv* as is allowed or acknowledged; admittedly.

alloy[1] /'aloy/ *noun* **1** a solid substance composed of a mixture of metals or of a metal with a non-metal. **2** a metal mixed with a more valuable metal. **3** an addition that impairs or debases something. [early French *aloi* from *aloier* to combine, from Latin *alligare*: see ALLY[1]]

alloy² /əˈloy/ *verb trans* **1** to mix (metals, or a metal with a non-metal) so as to form an alloy. **2** to reduce the purity or value of (something) by addition. **3** to temper or moderate (something): *My happiness was alloyed by a feeling of guilt.*

all-points bulletin *noun NAmer* a police message, e.g. about a suspect wanted for questioning, broadcast to all police officers in an area.

all-powerful *adj* having complete or sole power; omnipotent.

all-purpose *adj* suited for many purposes or uses.

all right¹ *adv* **1** well enough: *She did all right at school.* **2** beyond doubt; certainly: *He has pneumonia all right.* [Middle English *alriht* exactly, from *al* ALL¹ + *riht* RIGHT¹]

all right² *adj* **1** satisfactory or acceptable: *The film is all right for children.* **2** safe or well; in good condition or working order: *I was ill but I'm all right now.* **3** agreeable or pleasing.

all right³ *interj* **1** a formula used for giving assent: *All right, let's go.* **2** an exclamation used in indignant or menacing response: *All right! Just you wait.*

all round *adv* **1** by, for, or to everyone present: *We ordered drinks all round.* **2** in every respect.

all-round *adj* **1** competent in many fields: *an all-round athlete.* **2** having general utility. **3** encompassing all aspects; comprehensive: *an all-round reduction in price.*

all-rounder *noun* somebody who is competent in many fields; *specif* a cricketer who bats and bowls to a relatively high standard.

All Saints' Day *noun* 1 November observed in Christian churches as a festival in honour of all the saints.

all-seater *adj Brit* said of a sports stadium: having no places for standing spectators.

allseed /ˈawlseed/ *noun* any of several plants, e.g. knotgrass, that produce many seeds.

All Souls' Day *noun* 2 November observed in Christian churches as a day of prayer for the souls of believers who have died.

allspice /ˈawlspies/ *noun* **1** a mildly pungent spice prepared from the berry of a W Indian tree belonging to the eucalyptus family. **2** the berry or tree from which allspice is obtained: *Pimenta dioica.* [from its supposed combination of the flavours of cinnamon, cloves, and nutmeg]

all-star *adj* composed wholly or chiefly of stars of the theatre, cinema, etc: *an all-star cast.*

all-terrain vehicle *noun* a motor vehicle with large low-pressure tyres and a low-powered engine, intended for use on rough terrain.

all-ticket *adj* said of a sports match: for which one must buy tickets in advance.

all-time *adj* exceeding all others yet known: *an all-time bestseller.*

all told *adv* altogether; with everything or everybody taken into account.

allude /əˈl(y)oohd/ *verb intrans* (+ to) to make indirect, casual, or implicit reference: *Do you allude to me, Miss Cardew, as an entanglement?* — Wilde. [Latin *alludere*, literally 'to play with', from AD- + *ludere* to play]

all-up *adj* said of an aircraft's weight: including everything necessary for operation.

allure¹ /əˈl(y)ooə/ *verb trans* to entice (somebody) by charm or attraction. ≫ **allurement** *noun*, **alluring** *adj*. [Middle English *aluren* from Old French *aleurer* from Old French, from AD- + *loire* LURE¹]

allure² *noun* power of attraction or fascination; charm.

allusion /əˈl(y)ooh·zh(ə)n/ *noun* **1** an implied or indirect reference, or the use of such references, *esp* in literature. **2** alluding or hinting. ≫ **allusive** *-siv, -ziv/ adj*, **allusively** *adv*, **allusiveness** *noun*. [late Latin *allusion-, allusio* from Latin *alludere*: see ALLUDE]

alluvial¹ /əˈl(y)oohviəl/ *adj* of or forming alluvium: *alluvial soil.*

alluvial² *noun* a deposit of alluvium.

alluvion /əˈl(y)oohvi·ən/ *noun* **1** the wash of water against a shore. **2** = FLOOD¹ (1A). **3** = ALLUVIUM. **4** new land formed by the movement or action of water, e.g. by deposition at the edge of a river, or the formation of such land. [Latin *alluvion-, alluvio* from *alluere* to wash against, from AD- + *lavere* to wash]

alluvium /əˈl(y)oohvi·əm/ *noun* (*pl* **alluviums** *or* **alluvia** /-vi·ə/) clay, silt, or similar material deposited by running water. [late Latin, neuter of *alluvius* alluvial, from *alluere*: see ALLUVION]

ally¹ /ˈalie, əˈlie/ *verb* (**allies, allied, allying**) ≫ *verb trans* **1** (+ with/to) to join or unite (oneself or another person or group): *He allied himself with a wealthy family by marriage.* **2** (+ to) to relate (something) by resemblance or common properties: *Its beak allies it to the finches.* ≫ *verb intrans* (+ with) to form or enter into an alliance. [Middle English *allien* via Old French from Latin *alligare* to bind to, from AD- + *ligare* to bind]

ally² /ˈalie/ *noun* (*pl* **allies**) **1** a state associated with another by treaty or league. **2** a person or group that helps, supports, or cooperates with another.

-ally *suffix* forming adverbs from adjectives that end in *-ic*, with the meaning: in (such) a manner: *terrifically.* [-AL¹ + -LY²]

allyl /ˈalil/ *noun* an organic chemical group, CH_2CHCH_2, that has a valency of 1 and occurs in the compounds that make garlic and mustard pungent. ≫ **allylic** /əˈlilik/ *adj*. [Latin *allium* garlic]

almacantar /almə'kantə/ *noun* see ALMUCANTAR.

alma mater /ˌalmə ˈmahtə, ˈmaytə/ *noun* a school, college, or university that one has attended. [Latin *alma mater* fostering mother]

almanac *or* **almanack** /ˈawlmənak/ *noun* any of various annual publications containing statistical and general information, often in tabular form, *esp* a publication containing astronomical and meteorological data for each day in a particular year. [Middle English *almenak* from medieval Latin *almanach*, from Arabic *al-manākh* the calendar]

almandine /ˈalməndeen, -dien/ *noun* a deep violet to red garnet used as a gemstone. [Middle English *alabandine* from medieval Latin *alabandina* from *Alabanda*, ancient city in Asia Minor]

Almighty /awlˈmieti/ *noun* (**the Almighty**) a title for God.

almighty¹ *adj* **1** (*often* **Almighty**) having absolute power over all: *Almighty God.* **2** having relatively unlimited power: *the almighty dollar.* **3** *informal* great in extent, seriousness, force, etc: *an almighty crash.* [Old English *ælmihtig*, from *eall* ALL¹ + *mihtig* MIGHTY¹]

almighty² *adv informal* to a great degree; very.

almond /ˈahmənd, ˈawl-/ *noun* **1** a small tree of the rose family with pink flowers and edible seeds: *Prunus dulcis.* **2** an edible oval nut obtained from the fruit of this tree, used in cookery and confectionery: *sugared almonds.* **3** (*used before a noun*) containing or flavoured with almonds: *almond essence.* [Middle English *almande* via Old French from late Latin *amandula*, alteration of Latin *amygdala*, from Greek *amygdalē*]

almond-eyed *adj* having narrow slanting eyes.

almoner /ˈahmənə, ˈal-/ *noun* **1** a former name for a social worker attached to a British hospital. **2** somebody who distributed alms in former times. [Middle English *almoiner* from Old French *almosnier* from *almosne* alms, from late Latin *eleemosyna*: see ALMS]

almost /ˈawlmohst/ *adv* very nearly but not exactly or entirely. [Middle English from Old English *ealmǣst*, from *eall* ALL¹ + *mǣst* MOST¹]

alms /ˈahmz/ *pl noun* (*treated as sing. or pl*) money, food, etc given to help the poor, *esp* in former times: *It had been his practice ... to drop his halfpenny duly into the hat of some blind Bartimeus, that sat begging alms by the wayside* — Lamb. ≫ **almsgiver** *noun*, **almsgiving** *noun*. [Old English *ælmesse, ælms* via late Latin *eleemosyna* from Greek *eleēmosynē* pity, alms, from *eleēmōn* merciful, from *eleos* pity]

almshouse *noun Brit* a house founded and financed by charity in which a poor person can live cheaply or free.

almucantar *or* **almacantar** /almə'kantə/ *noun* in astronomy, a line or circle above and parallel to the horizon. [Middle English via medieval Latin or French from Arabic *almukantarāt* lines of celestial latitude]

aloe /ˈaloh/ *noun* **1** any of a large genus of succulent plants of the lily family with tall spikes of flowers: genus *Aloe.* **2** (*usu in pl, but treated as sing.*) the dried juice of the leaves of various aloes used *esp* as a laxative: *bitter aloes.* **3** = CENTURY PLANT. [Middle English via late Latin from Latin *aloe* dried juice of aloe leaves, from Greek *aloē*]

aloe vera /ˈverə, ˈviərə/ *noun* **1** any of a species of aloe with thick fleshy leaves from which an oil is obtained: *Aloe vera.* **2** an extract from the leaves of aloe vera that is used in cosmetic preparations. [modern Latin *aloe vera* true aloe]

aloft /əˈloft/ *adv* **1** at or to a higher place or a great height. **2** at or to the masthead or the upper rigging of a ship: compare ALOW. [Middle English from Old Norse *ā lopt*, from *ā* on, in + *lopt* air]

35

aloha /ə'loh·hə, ə'loh·ə/ *interj* a Hawaiian word used to express greeting or farewell. [Hawaiian from *aloha* love]

alone /ə'lohn/ *adj and adv* **1** considered without reference to any other: *The children alone would eat that much.* **2** separated from others; isolated: *The house stands alone.* **3** exclusive of other factors: *Time alone will show.* **4** free from interference: *Leave my bag alone.* **5** without assistance: *I couldn't have done it alone.* ⟫⟫ **aloneness** *noun*. [Middle English, from *al* ALL[1] + ONE[1]]

along[1] /ə'long/ *prep* **1** over the length of or in a line parallel with (something): *walking along the road.* **2** in the course of (something): *Did you meet anyone along the way?* **3** in accordance with (something): *something along these lines.* [Old English *andlang*, from *and-* against + *lang* LONG[1]]

along[2] *adv* **1** forward; on: *Move along.* **2** as a companion or a necessary or pleasant addition; with one: *Can I bring a friend along?* **3** arriving at a particular place: *I'll be along in five minutes.* **4** at or to a more advanced point or state: *coming along well.* ✳ **all along** all the time: *They knew the truth all along.* **along with 1** in addition to: *chickenpox, along with other childhood ailments.* **2** in company with; simultaneously with: *She arrived along with her solicitor.*

alongshore /ə'long'shaw/ *adv and adj* along the shore or coast: *alongshore currents.*

alongside[1] /ə'long'sied/ *adv* along or at the side of something.

alongside[2] *prep* **1** (*also* + of) side by side with or along the side of (something), usu in a parallel position. **2** (*also* + of) concurrently with (something).

aloof[1] /ə'loohf/ *adv* at a distance; out of involvement.

Word history
obsolete *aloof* to windward, from A-[1] + *loof*, variant of LUFF[1]. This was orig a command to steer a ship to windward and hence away from a lee shore or some obstacle that it might be blown against.

aloof[2] *adj* distant in interest or feeling; reserved or unsympathetic. ⟫⟫ **aloofly** *adv*, **aloofness** *noun*.

alopecia /alə'peeshə/ *noun* abnormal loss of hair in humans or loss of wool, feathers, etc in animals. [Middle English *allopicia* via Latin from Greek *alōpekia*, literally 'fox mange', from *alōpēx* fox]

aloud /ə'lowd/ *adv* **1** with a normal speaking voice; not silently. **2** *archaic* loudly.

alow /ə'loh/ *adv archaic* below, *esp* under the deck of a ship: compare ALOFT. [Middle English, from A-[1] + LOW[3]]

ALP *abbr* Australian Labor Party.

alp /alp/ *noun* **1** a high mountain. **2** in Switzerland, a mountainside pasture. [back-formation from *the Alps*, a mountain system of Europe]

alpaca /al'pakə/ *noun* (*pl* **alpacas** *or collectively* **alpaca**) **1** a type of domesticated mammal, related to the llama, found in Peru: *Lama pacos.* **2** the fine long wool of this mammal, or fabric made from this. [Spanish *alpaca* from Aymara *allpaca*]

alpenglow /'alpəngloh/ *noun* a reddish glow seen near sunset or sunrise on the summits of mountains. [prob partial translation of German *Alpenglühen*, from *Alpen* Alps + *glühen* to glow]

alpenhorn /'alpənhawn/ *noun* a long straight wooden wind instrument used by Swiss herdsmen to call sheep and cattle, *esp* in the past. Also called ALPHORN. [German *Alpenhorn*, from *Alpen* Alps + *Horn* horn]

alpenstock /'alpənstok/ *noun* a long staff with an iron point, used in hill climbing: *He carried in his hand a long alpenstock, the sharp point of which he thrust into everything he approached – the flower beds, the garden-benches, the trains of the ladies' dresses* — Henry James. [German *Alpenstock*, from *Alpen* Alps + *Stock* staff]

alpha[1] /'alfə/ *noun* **1** the first letter of the Greek alphabet (Α, α), equivalent to and transliterated as roman a. **2** a grade given to students showing the highest standard of work. **3** (*used before a noun*) in astronomy, relating to or denoting the chief or brightest star of a constellation: *Alpha Centauri.* [Middle English via Latin from Greek, of Semitic origin; related to Hebrew *āleph*, first letter of the Hebrew alphabet]

alpha[2] *adj informal* alphabetical: *You need to put the words in alpha order.*

alpha and omega /'ohmigə/ *noun* **1a** the beginning and ending. **b** the first and last, used by Christians to denote the eternity of God or as a title for Jesus. **2** the most vital part of something. [from the first and last letters of the Greek alphabet]

alphabet /'alfəbet/ *noun* **1** a set of letters used to write a language, *esp* when arranged in a conventional order.

Editorial note
Our Roman alphabet derives from the one introduced into Greece in the 1st millennium BC, which was adapted from the Phoenician alphabet. Precursors of the earliest Phoenician inscriptions have been found in several Middle Eastern locations from c.1500 BC. But who first created the signs and ordered them, and why, and whether the invention happened more than once, is unknown — Professor David Crystal.

2 a system of signs and signals that can be used in place of letters, e.g. a phonetic alphabet. **3** a set of basic principles about a subject: *learning the electronic alphabet.* [Middle English *alphabete* via late Latin from Greek *alphabētos*, from ALPHA[1] + *bēta* BETA, the first two letters of the Greek alphabet]

alphabetical /alfə'betikl/ *or* **alphabetic** *adj* **1** of or using an alphabet: *alphabetical order.* **2** in the order of the letters of the alphabet: *The list of names is alphabetical.* ⟫⟫ **alphabetically** *adv*.

alphabetize *or* **alphabetise** /'alfəbetiez/ *verb trans* to arrange (a list or sequence) in alphabetical order. ⟫⟫ **alphabetization** /-'zə-ysh(ə)n/ *noun*.

alphabet soup *noun informal* a confused, confusing, or unrelated mixture of things. [so called because of a type of soup that contains pieces of pasta in the shapes of letter of the alphabet]

alpha blocker *noun* any of various drugs that inhibit the type of nervous stimulation that causes constriction of the blood vessels, used *esp* in combating high blood pressure.

alpha decay *noun* the process of radioactive decay that causes the emission of alpha particles.

alpha-foetoprotein /,alfə,feetoh'prohteen/ *noun* a protein that a human foetus produces and is present in the amniotic fluid. If it is detected in abnormally high or low levels, it may indicate the presence of certain congenital disorders, such as spina bifida and Down's syndrome.

alpha-hydroxy acid *noun* an organic acid containing a hydroxyl group adjacent to a carboxylic acid group, a compound used in the manufacture of products used to exfoliate the skin.

alphameric /alfə'merik/ *or* **alphamerical** *adj* alphanumeric. ⟫⟫ **alphamerically** *adv*. [ALPHABET + NUMERICAL]

alphanumeric /,alfənyooh'merik/ *or* **alphanumerical** *adj* **1** consisting of or using both letters and numbers, and sometimes other symbols. **2** said of a letter, number, or symbol: belonging to an alphanumeric system. **3** able to display or use alphanumeric characters. ⟫⟫ **alphanumeric** *noun*, **alphanumerically** *adv*. [ALPHABET + NUMERICAL]

alpha particle *noun* a positively charged nuclear particle, identical with the nucleus of a helium atom, that is ejected at high speed from the nucleus of some radioactive substances when they decay: compare BETA PARTICLE.

alpha ray *noun* a continuous narrow stream of alpha particles.

alpha-receptor *noun* a receptor on the surface of a cell to which neurotransmitters (such as adrenalin) attach themselves, stimulating the sympathetic nervous system.

alpha rhythm *or* **alpha wave** *noun* a variation in a record of the electrical activity of the brain of a frequency of about 10Hz, often associated with states of waking relaxation.

alpha test *noun* a test of a piece of computer software that its manufacturer completes before the more demanding BETA TEST.

alpha-test *verb trans* to subject (computer software) to an alpha test.

alpha wave *noun* see ALPHA RHYTHM.

alphorn /'alphawn/ *noun* = ALPENHORN.

alpine[1] /'alpien/ *noun* any of various plants that grow naturally in mountainous or northern parts of the northern hemisphere.

alpine[2] *adj* **1** (*often* **Alpine**) of or relating to the Alps: *the Alpine scenery.* **2a** of or relating to any high mountains. **b** growing in high mountain areas above the tree line. **3** (**Alpine**) said of competitive ski events: featuring slalom and downhill racing: compare NORDIC[1].

alpinism /'alpiniz(ə)m/ *noun* (*often* **Alpinism**) the climbing of high mountains, *esp* in the Alps. ⟫⟫ **alpinist** *noun*.

already /awl'redi/ *adv* **1** before now or before a particular time: *He had already left*; *There are already four candidates for the post.* **2** previously: *I had seen the film already.* **3** before the expected time: *Surely you're not leaving already?* **4** *chiefly NAmer, informal* used as an intensifier or to express irritation, impatience, etc: *Enough already!* [Middle English *al redy* from *al redy* (adj) wholly ready, from *al* ALL[1] + *redy* READY[1]]

alright /awl'riet/ *adv, adj, and interj* = ALL RIGHT[1].

Usage note
The spelling *alright*, although fairly common, is still considered by many users of English, especially traditionalists, to be an incorrect spelling of *all right*.

Alsatian /al'saysh(ə)n/ *noun* **1** *chiefly Brit* a large dog of a wolflike breed originating in Germany, having a dense brownish or blackish coat and often used as a guard dog or as a guide dog for blind people. Also called GERMAN SHEPHERD. **2** a person from Alsace in eastern France. ➤ **Alsatian** *adj*.

Word history
medieval Latin *Alsatia* Alsace, region of France (formerly of Germany). The German shepherd was first called Alsatian during World War I to avoid the association with Germany; it did not originate in Alsace.

alsike /'alsik, 'alsiek/ *noun* a European perennial clover used as animal feed: *Trifolium hybridum*. [named after *Alsike*, town in Sweden where Linnaeus noted the plant growing]

also /'awlsoh/ *adv* as well; additionally; besides: *You should also take a torch.* [Old English *eallswā*, from *eall* ALL[1] + *swā* SO[1]]

also-ran *noun* **1** an entrant that finishes outside the first three places in a race, *esp* a horse. **2** a person of no distinction or achievement.

alstroemeria /alstrə'miəri·ə/ *noun* a plant of the daffodil family with tuberous roots, cultivated for its brightly coloured trumpet-shaped flowers: genus *Alstroemeria*. [scientific Latin *Alstroemeria*, genus name, named after Baron von *Alstroemer* d.1794, Swedish botanist]

alt. *abbr* **1** alternate. **2** altitude. **3** alto.

Alta. *abbr* Alberta.

Altaic /al'tayik/ *adj* relating to, denoting, or belonging to a language family that includes Turkic, Tungusic, and Mongolian. ➤ **Altaic** *noun*. [the *Altai* mountains in central Asia]

altar /'awltə, 'oltə/ *noun* **1** a table on which the bread and wine used at communion are consecrated in Christian churches. **2** any table-like structure that serves as a centre of worship or ritual, e.g. one on which sacrifices are offered or incense is burned in worship. ✳ **get/lead somebody to the altar** *informal* to succeed in marrying somebody. [Old English *altar* from Latin *altare*]

altar boy *noun* a boy who helps a priest during a service in a Christian church.

altarpiece *noun* a work of art that decorates the space above and behind an altar.

altazimuth /al'taziməth/ *noun* **1** a type of mounting for an astronomical telescope that allows rotation about a vertical axis and a horizontal axis. **2** an instrument with this type of mounting for measuring heights and angles in surveying. [ALTITUDE + AZIMUTH]

alter /'awltə, 'oltə/ *verb* (**altered**, **altering**) ➤ *verb trans* **1** to make (something) different, *esp* in a way that involves only a slight change. **2** *chiefly NAmer, euphem* to castrate or spay (an animal). ➤ *verb intrans* to become different. ➤➤ **alterable** *adj*, **alterably** *adv*. [Middle English *alteren* via French from medieval Latin *alterare*, from Latin *alter* other (of two)]

alteration /awltə'raysh(ə)n, 'ol-/ *noun* **1** a change, *esp* a slight one. **2** the act of changing: *Love is not love which alters when it alteration finds* — Shakespeare.

alterative /'awltərətiv, 'ol-/ *adj* **1** likely to produce alteration. **2** said of a drug: able to make people better. ➤➤ **alterative** *noun*.

altercate /'awltəkayt, 'ol-/ *verb intrans archaic* to quarrel in a heated way.

altercation /awltə'kaysh(ə)n, 'ol-/ *noun* an angry discussion or quarrel. [Middle English *altercacioun* via French from Latin *altercation-, altercatio* from *altercari* to quarrel, dispute, ultimately from *alter* other (of two)]

alter ego /,altə 'eegoh/ *noun* (*pl* **alter egos**) **1** a side of somebody's character that is different from their usual character. **2** a close and trusted friend. [Latin *alter ego*, literally 'another I']

alternate[1] /'awl'tuhnət, 'ol-/ *adj* **1** said of two things: occurring by turns: *It was a day of alternate sunshine and rain.* **2a** arranged one above or alongside the other; forming an alternating series: *alternate layers of brick and stone.* **b** said of plant parts: arranged singly first on one side and then on the other at a different height or point

along the stem, etc: compare OPPOSITE[1] (4). **3** every other; every second: *He works on alternate days.* **4** *chiefly NAmer* = ALTERNATIVE[1] (2). ➤➤ **alternately** *adv*. [Latin *alternatus*, past part. of *alternare* to alternate, from *alternus* every other, from *alter* other (of two)]

Usage note
alternate or alternative? In British English there is a clear distinction between these two words: *alternate* is an adjective and a verb, *alternative* is an adjective and a noun. *Alternate* means 'every other' (*Meetings take place on alternate Wednesdays*) or 'occurring by turns' (*alternate layers of stone and brick*). To *alternate* is 'to do something by turns': *They alternated between urging us to go faster and telling us to slow down.* An *alternative* is 'another different thing that could act as a replacement': *an alternative venue*; *As an alternative to buying a new system, we could try to update the old one.* In American English, however, *alternate* is widely used as an adjective in the sense of *alternative* (*an alternate venue*) and as a noun to mean 'a deputy or substitute'.

alternate[2] /'awltənayt, 'ol-/ *verb trans* (*often* + with) to interchange (somebody or something) with somebody or something else in turn: *Alternate a book of the Old Testament with a book of the New* — Somerset Maugham. ➤ *verb intrans* **1** (*often* + with) said of two things: to occur by turns: *Joy alternated with despair.* **2** (*often* + between) to change repeatedly from one state or action to another: *Her mood alternated between calmness and hysteria.* ➤➤ **alternation** /-'naysh(ə)n/ *noun*.

alternate[3] /'awltuhnət, 'ol-/ *noun chiefly NAmer* somebody who takes the place of or alternates with somebody else; a deputy.

alternate angles *pl noun* in mathematics, two equal angles formed on opposite sides and at opposite ends of a line that intersects two parallel lines, e.g. the angles in the letter Z.

alternating current *noun* an electric current that reverses its direction at regularly recurring intervals. The voltage can be changed by a transformer: compare DIRECT CURRENT.

alternation of generations *noun* the occurrence of two or more forms in the life cycle of a plant or animal, usually involving the regular alternation of a generation produced by sexual reproduction and a generation produced by asexual means.

alternative[1] /awl'tuhnətiv, 'ol-/ *adj* **1** providing a choice, *esp* between two options; able to be used instead of something else: *Is there an alternative route?* **2** constituting an alternative: *We will adopt your alternative suggestion.* **3** of or relating to an activity or procedure that differs from the conventional forms: *alternative technology; alternative theatre.* ➤➤ **alternatively** *adv*.

Usage note
alternative or alternate? See note at ALTERNATE[1].

alternative[2] *noun* **1** an opportunity to choose between two or more possibilities: *I had no alternative but to report him to the police.* **2** one of two or more possibilities between which a choice is to be made.

alternative birth *noun* a method of giving birth that does not rely on conventional hospital procedures.

alternative comedy *noun* a form of comedy that does not rely on old stereotypes about race, sexual politics, relationships within society, etc.

alternative energy *noun* energy produced by methods that do not harm the environment, e.g. by using water or wind power.

alternative medicine *noun* any of a range of medical treatments that are not generally considered to be part of the conventional system of medicine, such as homoeopathy or shiatsu. Also called COMPLEMENTARY MEDICINE.

Editorial note
Also referred to as complementary medicine when used in conjunction with orthodox medicine, alternative medicine encompasses a wide range of treatments and therapies that are not generally considered to be part of the conventional medical system. Alternative medicine, which includes homeopathy, shiatsu, acupuncture and osteopathy, focuses on the relationship between mind and body. 'Energy flow' and 'vital energy', known in some forms as 'Ki' or 'Chi', are central concepts of many alternative practices, which often claim to treat the person as opposed to the illness — Dr John Cormack.

alternative society *noun* (**the alternative society**) a group of people who reject conventional social institutions, practices, and values in favour of a lifestyle based *esp* on communal ownership and self-sufficiency: compare COUNTERCULTURE.

alternative therapy *noun* = ALTERNATIVE MEDICINE.

alternator /'awltənaytə, 'ol-/ *noun* an electric generator for producing alternating current.

althaea (*NAmer* **althea**) /al'thee·ə/ *noun* any of a genus of plants that have tall spikes of flowers, e.g. the hollyhock and marshmallow: genus *Althaea*. [Latin *althaea* marshmallow, from Greek *althaia*]

althorn /'alt·hawn/ *noun* a brass musical instrument of the saxhorn family. [German *Althorn*, from *alt* alto + *Horn* horn]

although /awl'dhoh/ *conj* **1** in spite of the fact or possibility that; though: *I let them do it, although I didn't approve.* **2** but: *She continued reading, although not to the end.* **3** even if or even though: *Prices did fall, although not by much.* [Middle English *although*, from *al* ALL[1] + THOUGH[1]]

altimeter /'altimeetə/ *noun* an instrument used for measuring altitude, *esp* an aneroid barometer that measures height by detecting changes in atmospheric pressure. ⟫⟫ **altimetry** /al'timətri/ *noun*. [Latin *altus* high + -METER[1]]

altitude /'altityoohd/ *noun* **1** the height of an object, e.g. an aircraft, or a place, *esp* above sea level. **2** (*also in pl*) a high place or region. **3** the angular distance of a planet, etc, above the horizon, used with the azimuth to fix the exact position of the planet, etc; elevation. **4** the perpendicular distance from the base of a geometrical figure to the vertex or the side parallel to the base. ⟫⟫ **altitudinal** /-'tyoohdinl/ *adj*. [Middle English from Latin *altitudo* height, depth, from *altus* high, deep]

altitude sickness *noun* a disorder affecting people, *esp* climbers, who breathe air at high altitudes with low oxygen concentrations. The symptoms are nausea, hyperventilation, dizziness, headache, and exhaustion. Also called MOUNTAIN SICKNESS.

Alt key *noun* in computing, a keyboard key that is used in conjunction with another key or keys to give extra functions or special features. [shortening of *Alternative key*]

alto /'altoh/ *noun* (*pl* **altos**) **1a** a low female singing voice, or a singer with this voice. **b** an adult male singing voice above tenor, or a singer with this voice; a countertenor. **2** (*used before a noun*) denoting a musical instrument having a range below that of a soprano. **3** the second highest part in conventional four-part harmony. ⟫⟫ **alto** *adj*. [Italian *alto* high, from Latin *altus*]

alto clef *noun* in music, a C clef that places middle C on the third line of the stave.

altocumulus /altoh'kyoohmyooləs/ *noun* (*pl* **altocumuli** /-lie/) a cloud formation consisting of large whitish globular cloud occurring at medium altitude, higher than cumulus cloud, between about 2000 and 7000m (about 6500 and 23,000ft). [Latin *altus* high + -O- + CUMULUS]

altogether[1] /awltə'gedhə/ *adv* **1** completely; thoroughly; in every way: *That is an altogether different problem.* **2** with everything taken into account: *Altogether it was a good holiday.* [Middle English *altogedere*, from *al* ALL[1] + *togedere* together]

altogether[2] ✳ **in the altogether** *informal* in a naked state.

altostratus /altoh'strahtəs/ *noun* (*pl* **altostrati** /-tie/) a cloud formation consisting of a continuous dark layer occurring at medium altitude, between about 2000 and 7000m (about 6500 and 23,000ft). [Latin *altus* high + -O- + STRATUS]

altricial /al'trish(ə)l/ *adj* **1** said of a bird: hatched in an immature and helpless condition and needing care for some time after birth: compare PRECOCIAL. **2** having altricial young. [Latin *altric-, altrix*, fem of *altor* one who nourishes, from *alere* to nourish]

altruism /'altroohiz(ə)m/ *noun* unselfish regard for or devotion to the welfare of others. ⟫⟫ **altruist** *noun*, **altruistic** /-'istik/ *adj*, **altruistically** /-'istikli/ *adv*. [French *altruisme* from *autrui* other people, ultimately from Latin *alter* other (of two)]

ALU *abbr* in computing, arithmetic logic unit.

alum /'aləm/ *noun* **1** a sulphate of aluminium with potassium, used *esp* as an emetic and astringent: formula $K_2SO_4 \cdot Al(SO_4)_3 \cdot 24H_2O$. **2** any of various double salts with a similar chemical formula and crystal structure to this. [Middle English from early French *alum, alun* from Latin *alumen*]

alumina /ə'l(y)oohminə/ *noun* = ALUMINIUM OXIDE.

aluminate /ə'l(y)oohminayt/ *noun* a chemical compound formed from aluminium oxide and another metal.

aluminise /ə'lyoohminiez/ *verb trans* see ALUMINIZE.

aluminium /alyoo'mini·əm/ (*NAmer* **aluminum** /ə'loohminəm/) *noun* a silver-white metallic chemical element that is light and easily shaped, conducts heat and electricity well, is resistant to rusting, and is used *esp* in kitchen utensils and lightweight alloys: symbol Al, atomic number 13. [scientific Latin from *alumina*: see ALUM]

aluminium oxide *noun* a chemical compound that occurs naturally as corundum and in bauxite, used to produce aluminium, as an abrasive, and as an electrical insulator: formula Al_2O. Also called ALUMINA.

aluminize or **aluminise** /ə'lyoohminiez/ *verb trans* to treat or coat (something) with aluminium.

aluminous /ə'l(y)oohminəs/ *adj* containing alum or aluminium.

aluminum /ə'loohminəm/ *noun NAmer* see ALUMINIUM.

alumna /ə'lumnə/ *noun* (*pl* **alumnae** /-nee/) a former female student of a particular school, college, or university. [Latin *alumna*, fem form of ALUMNUS]

alumnus /ə'lumnəs/ *noun* (*pl* **alumni** /-ni/) a former male student of a particular school, college, or university. [Latin *alumnus* foster son, pupil, from *alere* to nourish]

alveolar[1] /alvi'ohlə, al'vee·ələ/ *adj* **1** of, resembling, or having alveoli or an alveolus. **2** said of a consonant: articulated with the tip of the tongue touching or near the ridge of flesh behind the front teeth.

alveolar[2] *noun* an alveolar consonant, e.g. *d*, *s*, or *t* in English.

alveolate /al'vee·ələt, -layt/ *adj* having regularly arranged deep pits like a honeycomb. ⟫⟫ **alveolation** /-'layshən/ *noun*.

alveolus /alvi'ohləs, al'vee·ələs/ *noun* (*pl* **alveoli** /-lie/) **1** a small cavity or pit, *esp* in a part of the body. **2a** a socket for a tooth. **b** an air cell of the lungs. **c** a socket from which a bristle or hair grows. [Latin *alveolus*, dimin. of *alveus* cavity, hollow, from *alvus* belly]

always /'awlwayz/ *adv* **1a** at all times; continuously: *I have always lived here.* **b** in all cases: *It's always better to be honest.* **2** on every occasion; repeatedly: *We always go to Spain; He's always complaining.* **3** forever; perpetually: *I will always love you.* **4** as a last resort: *You could always ask your parents to help you.* [Middle English *alway, alwayes* from Old English *ealne weg*, literally 'all the way']

always-on *adj* denoting a permanent connection to the Internet that obviates the need to dial up and log on at the beginning of each session.

alyssum /'alisəm/ *noun* any of several species of Eurasian and African plants of the cabbage family that are grown in gardens for their clusters of small white or yellow flowers: genera *Alyssum* and *Lobularia*. [scientific Latin, from Greek *alysson* plant believed to cure rabies, from A-[1] + *lyssa* rabies]

Alzheimer's disease /'alts·hieməz/ *noun* a progressive disease involving the blood vessels of the brain and leading to premature senile dementia. [named after Alois *Alzheimer* d.1915, German neurologist, who identified it]

AM *abbr* **1** Albert Medal. **2** amplitude modulation. **3** Assembly Member, i.e. member of the National Assembly for Wales. **4** associate member. **5** *NAmer* Master of Arts. [(sense 5) from Latin *artium magister*]

Am *abbr* the chemical symbol for americium.

Am. *abbr* **1** America. **2** American. **3** Amos (book of the Bible).

am /əm, m; *strong* am/ *verb* first person sing. present of BE. [Old English *eom*]

a.m. *abbr* ante meridiem, used to indicate the time between midnight and midday.

AMA *abbr* **1** American Medical Association. **2** Australian Medical Association.

amadavat /'amədəvat/ *noun* see AVADAVAT.

amadou /'amədooh/ *noun* = PUNK[3]. [French *amadou*, from Provençal, literally 'lover', from Latin *amator*: see AMATEUR[1]]

amah /'amə, 'ahmə/ *noun* a female servant in the Far East, *esp* a Chinese nursemaid. [Portuguese *ama* wet nurse, from medieval Latin *amma*]

amalgam /ə'malgəm/ *noun* **1** an alloy of mercury with another metal, e.g. silver, that is solid or liquid at room temperature according to the proportion of mercury present, used *esp* in making dental fillings. **2** a mixture of different elements. [Middle English *amalgame*, via French from medieval Latin *amalgama*, prob derivative of Greek *malagma* emollient, from *malassein* to soften]

amalgamate /ə'malgəmayt/ *verb trans* to unite (two or more things) in a mixture; to combine (different things) into a single body. ⟫⟫ **amalgamator** *noun*.

amalgamation /ə,malgə'maysh(ə)n/ *noun* **1** the process of amalgamating or being amalgamated. **2** a consolidation or merger.

amanuensis /ə,manyoo'ensis/ *noun* (*pl* **amanuenses** /-seez/) somebody employed to write from dictation or to copy a manuscript. [Latin *amanuensis*, from (*servus*) *a manu* (slave) with secretarial duties, from AB- + *manus* hand, handwriting + *-ensis* belonging to]

amaranth /'amaranth/ *noun* **1** any of a genus of herbaceous plants, some of which are grown in gardens for their showy purple flowers: genus *Amaranthus*. **2** a dark reddish purple colour. **3** a red dye used to colour medicines and foodstuffs. **4** *chiefly literary* an imaginary flower that never fades. ⮞⮞ **amaranthine** /-'ranthin, -thien/ *adj*. [Latin *amarantus*, a flower, from Greek *amaranton*, neuter of *amarantos* unfading, from A-² + *marainein* to waste away]

amaretti /amə'reti/ *pl noun* small crisp Italian biscuits flavoured with almonds. [from Italian *amaro* bitter]

amaretto /amə'retoh/ *noun* (*pl* **amaretti** /-ti/) an Italian liqueur flavoured with almonds. [Italian *amaretto* from *amaro* bitter]

amaryllis /amə'rilis/ *noun* **1** an African plant of the daffodil family that grows from bulbs and has bright reddish or white lily-like flowers: *Amaryllis belladonna*. **2** any of a genus of tropical S American plants: genus *Hippeastrum*. [scientific Latin, genus name, from the name of a shepherdess in Latin pastoral poetry]

amass /ə'mas/ *verb trans* **1** to collect (something) for oneself; to accumulate: *She managed to amass a great fortune.* **2** to bring (something) together into a mass. ⮞⮞ **amasser** *noun*. [early French *amasser*, from AD- + *masser* to gather into a mass, from Latin *massa*: see MASS²]

amateur¹ /'amatə, -chə/ *noun* **1** somebody who does something as a pastime rather than as a profession, *esp* a sportsman or sportswoman who does not compete for payment. **2** somebody who practises an art or science unskilfully; a dabbler. **3** (+ of) somebody who is fond of something. ⮞⮞ **amateurism** *noun*. [French *amateur* from Latin *amator* lover, from *amare* to love]

amateur² *adj* **1** of or for amateurs rather than professionals. **2** not professional; inexpert: *It was a fairly amateur attempt.*

amateurish *adj* not having or showing professional skill; done badly or carelessly. ⮞⮞ **amateurishly** *adv*, **amateurishness** *noun*.

amative /'amativ/ *adj formal* = AMOROUS. [medieval Latin *amativus* from Latin *amatus*, past part. of *amare* to love]

amatory /'amat(ə)ri/ *adj* of or expressing sexual love or desire: *Moved by amatory curiosity, she turned her eyes critically upon him —* Hardy.

amaurosis /amaw'rohsis/ *noun* (*pl* **amauroses** /-seez/) decay of sight, *esp* due to neurological disease, without obvious change or damage to the eye. ⮞⮞ **amaurotic** /-'rotik/ *adj*. [scientific Latin from Greek *amaurōsis*, literally 'dimming', from *amauroun* to dim, from *amauros* dim]

amaze /ə'mayz/ *verb trans* to fill (somebody) with wonder; to astound. [Old English *āmasian*, from A-¹ + (assumed) *masian* to confuse]

amazement *noun* great astonishment.

amazing *adj* used as a generalized term of approval: *She has the most amazing collection of bottles.* ⮞⮞ **amazingly** *adv*.

Amazon /'amaz(ə)n/ *noun* (*also* **amazon**) a tall strong or athletic woman.

Word history
Middle English via Latin from Greek *Amazōn*, one of a mythological race of female warriors. The Greeks claimed that *Amazōn* came from A-² + *mazos* breast, from the belief that Amazons cut off the right breast in order to wield weapons more easily; the word's true origin is unknown.

Amazonian /amə'zohni-ən/ *adj* **1** (*also* **amazonian**) said of a woman: masculine or aggressive. **2** of the Amazon river or its valley.

ambassador /am'basədə/ *noun* **1** a top-ranking diplomat sent to a foreign country as a resident representative of a government or sovereign, or appointed for a special diplomatic assignment. **2** somebody who represents or promotes a quality, activity, etc: *Yet I have not seen so likely an ambassador of love —* Shakespeare. ⮞⮞ **ambassadorial** /-'dawri-əl/ *adj*, **ambassadorship** *noun*. [Middle English *ambassadour* from early French *ambassadeur*, of Germanic origin]

ambassador-at-large *noun* (*pl* **ambassadors-at-large**) *NAmer* a diplomat or minister who represents a government for a special purpose, but is not assigned to a particular foreign country.

ambassadress /am'basədris/ *noun* **1** a female ambassador. **2** the wife of an ambassador.

amber /'ambə/ *noun* **1** a hard yellow to brown translucent substance that is the fossilized resin of some extinct trees, used chiefly for ornaments and jewellery. **2** a yellowish brown colour. **3** a yellow traffic light that shows between red and green and warns drivers to prepare to stop or go. ⮞⮞ **amber** *adj*. [Middle English *ambre* via French from medieval Latin *ambra*, from Arabic *'anbar* ambergris]

ambergris /'ambəgrees, -gris/ *noun* a waxy substance found floating in tropical waters, which originates in the intestines of the sperm whale and is used in perfumery as a fixative. [Middle English *ambregris* from early French *ambre gris* grey amber (as distinct from *ambre jaune*, literally 'yellow amber', the resin)]

amberjack /'ambəjak/ *noun* any of several species of large fishes found in warm and tropical seas, often hunted for sport: genus *Seriola*. [AMBER + JACK¹]

ambi- *comb. form* forming words, with the meaning: both or two: *ambivalent*; *ambiguous*. [Latin *ambi-*, *amb-* both, around]

ambiance /'ambi-əns (*French* ābiãs)/ *noun* see AMBIENCE.

ambidextrous /ambi'dekstrəs/ *adj* **1** able to use either hand with equal ease. **2** unusually skilful or versatile. ⮞⮞ **ambidexterity** /-'steriti/ *noun*, **ambidextrously** *adv*, **ambidextrousness** *noun*. [late Latin *ambidexter*, from Latin AMBI- + *dexter* on the right, skilful]

ambience /'ambi-əns/ *or* **ambiance** *noun* a surrounding or pervading atmosphere that is characteristic of a place. [French *ambiance* from *ambiant* surrounding, from Latin *ambient-*, *ambiens*: see AMBIENT]

ambient /'ambi-ənt/ *adj* **1** relating to the immediate surroundings: *the ambient temperature*. **2** *formal* surrounding on all sides. [Latin *ambient-*, *ambiens*, present part. of *ambire* to go round, from AMBI- + *ire* to go]

ambient music *noun* music played in the background in supermarkets, restaurants, etc, with the intention of creating a pleasant atmosphere.

ambiguity /ambi'gyooh-iti/ *noun* (*pl* **ambiguities**) **1** the state of being ambiguous or imprecise in meaning. **2** an ambiguous or imprecise word or expression. **3** uncertainty of meaning or significance: *the basic ambiguity of her political stance*.

ambiguous /am'bigyoo-əs/ *adj* **1** capable of more than one interpretation. **2** vague, indistinct, or difficult to classify. ⮞⮞ **ambiguously** *adv*, **ambiguousness** *noun*. [Latin *ambiguus*, from *ambigere* to wander about, from AMBI- + *agere* to drive]

ambisexual /ambi'seks(yoo)əl, -sh(yoo)əl/ *adj* **1** in biology, relating to, denoting, or affecting both sexes. **2** said of a person: having or showing both male and female characteristics; ANDROGYNOUS. ⮞⮞ **ambisexually** *adv*. [from AMBI- + SEXUAL]

ambisonics /'ambisoniks/ *pl noun* (*treated as sing*.) a system of broadcasting high-fidelity sound that uses four loudspeakers to give the effect of sounds coming from spatially distinguishable sources. ⮞⮞ **ambisonic** *adj*. [AMBI- + SONIC]

ambit /'ambit/ *noun* **1** a limiting range or distance: *within an ambit of four metres*. **2** the bounds or limits of a place; the precincts. **3** a sphere of influence; scope. [Middle English from Latin *ambitus* from *ambire*: see AMBIENT]

ambition /am'bish(ə)n/ *noun* a strong drive to do or achieve something, *esp* to attain status, wealth, or power. [Middle English via French from Latin *ambition-*, *ambitio* going round (later, going round canvassing for votes) from *ambire*: see AMBIENT]

ambitious /am'bishəs/ *adj* **1** acting from or showing ambition. **2** motivated by a strong ambition and therefore difficult to achieve: *an ambitious attempt*. ⮞⮞ **ambitiously** *adv*, **ambitiousness** *noun*.

ambivalence /am'bivələns/ *or* **ambivalency** /-si/ *noun* **1** the state of having two opposing and contradictory attitudes or feelings towards an object, person, etc. **2** uncertainty or indecisiveness in making a choice. ⮞⮞ **ambivalent** *adj*, **ambivalently** *adv*. [AMBI- + *valence* as in EQUIVALENCE]

ambivert /'ambivuht/ *noun* a person with both extroverted and introverted characteristics. ⮞⮞ **ambiversion** /-'vuhsh(ə)n/ *noun*. [AMBI- + *-vert* as in INTROVERT¹]

amble¹ /'ambl/ *verb intrans* to move at a leisurely pace. ➤➤ **ambler** *noun*. [Middle English *amblen* via early French *ambler* from Latin *ambulare* to walk]

amble² *noun* **1** a leisurely pace and motion. **2** a leisurely stroll. **3** an easy gait of a horse, in which the legs on each side of the body move together.

amblyopia /ambli'ohpi·ə/ *noun* poor sight without obvious change or damage to the eye, associated *esp* with poisoning or a deficiency of essential nutrients in the diet. ➤➤ **amblyopic** /-pik/ *adj.* [scientific Latin from Greek *amblyōpia*, from *amblys* blunt, dull + *-ōpia* from *ops* eye]

ambo /'amboh/ *noun* (*pl* **ambos** *or* **ambones** /am'bohneez/) a raised platform used as a pulpit in an early Christian church. [medieval Latin *ambon-, ambo* from Greek *ambōn* rim]

amboyna *or* **amboina** /am'boynə/ *noun* **1** an Asian tree of the pea family: *Ptercarpus indicus.* **2** the reddish mottled wood of this tree used in cabinetmaking. [Indonesian *Amboina,* from the island of Ambon]

ambrosia /am'brohzi·ə, zh(y)ə/ *noun* **1** the food of the Greek and Roman gods. **2** something extremely pleasing to eat or smell. **3** = BEEBREAD. ➤➤ **ambrosial** *adj.* [via Latin from Greek *ambrosia* immortality, from *ambrotos* immortal]

ambry /'ambri/ *or* **aumbry** /'awmbri/ *noun* (*pl* **ambries** *or* **aumbries** /-breez/) **1** a recess in a church wall for holding the cup, plate, etc used in communion. **2** *chiefly Brit, archaic* a pantry or cupboard. [Middle English *armarie* via Old French from Latin *armarium* cabinet, cupboard, from *arma* weapons]

ambulance /'ambyooləns/ *noun* a vehicle equipped for transporting injured or sick people to and from hospital. [French *ambulance* field hospital, from *ambulant* itinerant, from Latin *ambulant-, ambulans,* present part. of *ambulare* to walk]

ambulance chaser *noun chiefly NAmer, informal* a lawyer who specializes in cases that seek damages for personal injury. ➤➤ **ambulance chasing** *noun.*

ambulant /'ambyoolənt/ *adj* **1** *formal* said of a patient: not confined to bed; able to walk. **2** moving about. [Latin *ambulant-, ambulans:* see AMBULANCE]

ambulate /'ambyoolayt/ *verb intrans formal or technical* to walk or move around; to wander. ➤➤ **ambulation** /-'laysh(ə)n/ *noun.* [Latin *ambulant-:* see AMBULANCE]

ambulatory¹ /'ambyoolət(ə)ri/ *adj* **1** relating to or adapted for walking. **2** moving or movable from place to place; not fixed. **3a** = AMBULANT (1). **b** of or for a person who is able to walk: *ambulatory treatment.* [Latin *ambulatorius,* from *ambulare* to walk]

ambulatory² *noun* (*pl* **ambulatories**) a sheltered place for walking, *esp* a passage at the east end of a church.

ambuscade¹ /amboo'skayd/ *noun* an ambush: *On the land side stretches a dreary marsh, covered with tall grass and bushes; a fit place for the ambuscade of four thousand Indians* — Charles Kingsley. [early French *embuscade,* modification of Old Italian *imboscata,* from *imboscare* to place in ambush, from IN² + *bosco* forest, perhaps of Germanic origin]

ambuscade² *verb trans archaic* to ambush (somebody). ➤ *verb intrans archaic* to lie in wait.

ambush¹ /'amboosh/ *verb trans* to attack (somebody) from a hidden position. ➤ *verb intrans* to lie in wait; to lurk. [Middle English *embushen* from Old French *embuschier,* from EN-² in (from Latin *in*) + *busche* stick of firewood]

ambush² *noun* **1a** the concealment of a military force or other group in order to carry out a surprise attack from a hidden position. **b** a surprise attack carried out by such a force. **2** a force waiting in ambush, or their position in ambush.

AMDG *abbr* to the greater glory of God. [Latin *ad majorem Dei gloriam*]

ameba /ə'meebə/ *noun NAmer see* AMOEBA.

ameer /ə'miə/ *noun see* EMIR.

ameliorate /ə'meelyərayt/ *verb trans formal* to make (something) better or more tolerable. ➤ *verb intrans formal* to become better or more tolerable. ➤ **amelioration** /-'raysh(ə)n/ *noun,* **ameliorative** /-rətiv/ *adj,* **ameliorator** *noun.* [alteration of MELIORATE]

amen /ah'men, ay'men/ *interj* used at the end of a prayer with the meaning 'so be it', or to express a solemn avowal or approval. [Old English via late Latin and Greek from Hebrew *āmēn* certainly]

amenable /ə'meenəbl/ *adj* **1** easily persuaded to yield or agree; tractable. **2** accountable for one's behaviour; answerable: *citizens amenable to the law.* **3** capable of being judged or tested. ➤➤ **amenability** /-'biliti/ *noun,* **amenableness** *noun,* **amenably** *adv.* [derivative of Old French *amener* to lead up, from AD- + *mener* to lead, from Latin *minare* to drive cattle, from *minari* to threaten]

amend /ə'mend/ *verb trans* **1** to revise or make corrections to (a law, document, etc). **2** to put (something) right. ➤➤ **amendable** *adj,* **amender** *noun.* [Middle English *amenden* via Old French *amender* from Latin *emendare,* from EX-¹ + *menda* fault]

Usage note

amend *or* **emend?** These two words are sometimes confused. To *amend* is a general word meaning to 'correct and improve': *She did her best to amend her behaviour.* It also has a specific meaning in relation to pieces of legislation, to 'alter or add to and improve' (*the Act of 1978 as amended in 1993*). *Emend* has a more limited use. It is used exclusively in relation to texts and means 'to remove errors or irregularities from' (*emended the text to bring it into line with modern spelling conventions*).

amendment *noun* **1** the act of amending something. **2** an alteration to a document, law, etc.

amends /ə'mendz/ ✳ **make amends** to compensate for a loss or injury. [Middle English *amendes* from Old French, pl of *amende* reparation, from *amender:* see AMEND]

amenity /ə'meeniti, ə'men-/ *noun* (*pl* **amenities**) **1** (*usu in pl*) something, e.g. a public facility, that provides or enhances material comfort. **2** (*usu in pl*) something, e.g. a courteous social gesture, conducive to pleasantness and ease of conversation on a social occasion. **3** *formal* pleasantness, *esp* of an environment. [Middle English *amenite* pleasantness, from Latin *amoenitat-, amoenitas* from *amoenus* pleasant]

amenity bed *noun Brit* a hospital bed that provides extra privacy, sometimes available for an additional payment.

amenorrhoea (*NAmer* **amenorrhea**) /əmenə'riə/ *noun* abnormal absence of menstruation. ➤➤ **amenorrhoeic** *adj.* [scientific Latin, from A-² + Greek *mēn* month + -O- + *-rrhoea* discharge from Greek *rhoia* flow]

ament /'aymənt, ə'ment/ *noun* a catkin. ➤➤ **amentaceous** /-'taysi·əs/ *adj.* [Latin *amentum* thong, strap]

amentia /ə'menshə/ *noun dated* severe mental deficiency, *esp* when present from birth. [Latin *amentia* madness, from *ament-, amens* mad, from AB- + *ment-, mens* mind]

Amer. *abbr* **1** America. **2** American.

Amerasian /amə'raysh(ə)n, -zh(ə)n/ *noun* a person of mixed American and Asian parentage, *esp* somebody with an American father and an Asian mother. ➤➤ **Amerasian** *adj.*

amerce /ə'muhs/ *verb trans formal* to punish (somebody), *esp* by a fine. ➤➤ **amercement** *noun,* **amerciable** /-shəbl/ *adj.* [Middle English *amercien,* from Anglo-French *amercier,* from Old French *a merci* at (one's) mercy]

American /ə'merikən/ *noun* **1** a native or inhabitant of N America (or, less often, S or Central America). **2** a native or inhabitant of the USA. **3** the form of English used in the USA. ➤➤ **American** *adj.* [modern Latin *Americanus* from *Americus* Vespucius (Amerigo Vespucci) d.1512, Italian navigator, who explored the east coast of S America and was among the first to identify the new continent]

Americana /əmeri'kahnə/ *pl noun* artefacts or ideas associated with N America, *esp* with the USA.

American aloe *noun* = CENTURY PLANT.

American Dream *noun* (**the American Dream**) the ideals of democracy, freedom, equality, material prosperity, and social welfare to which the USA aspires.

American football *noun* a football game resembling rugby. It is played with an oval ball between teams of eleven players who wear heavy padding and helmets, and involves kicking and running with the ball and forward passing.

American Indian *noun dated* a member of any of the indigenous peoples of N, S, or Central America.

Usage note

American Indian has been largely replaced by *Native American* as the preferred general name for a member of one of the indigenous peoples of, especially, North America. The terms *Indian* and *American Indian* are not considered intrinsically disrespectful, however, and are still quite frequently used by Native Americans themselves. See also note at NATIVE AMERICAN.

Americanise /ə'merikəniez/ *verb see* AMERICANIZE.

Americanism /ə'merikəniz(ə)m/ *noun* **1** a custom, belief, word, etc characteristic of the USA or of its citizens, culture, or language. **2a** adherence or attachment to the USA and its culture. **b** the promotion of the political policies of the USA.

Americanize or **Americanise** /ə'merikəniez/ *verb trans* **1** to make (a country or people) conform to American customs or institutions. **2** to make (something) American in form or character: *Americanize the text for the US market.* ➤ *verb intrans* to become American in character. ➤➤ **Americanization** /-'zaysh(ə)n/ *noun*.

americium /amə'risi·əm/ *noun* a radioactive metallic chemical element produced by bombarding plutonium with neutrons: symbol Am, atomic number 95. [scientific Latin, from *America*, where it was first produced]

Amerindian /amə'rindi·ən/ *noun chiefly NAmer* = NATIVE AMERICAN. ➤➤ **Amerind** /'amərind/ *noun,* **Amerindian** *adj,* **Amerindic** *adj.*

amethyst /ə'məthist/ *noun* **1** a clear purple or violet variety of quartz that is much used as a gemstone. **2** the colour of amethyst. ➤➤ **amethystine** /-'thistin/ *adj.*

Word history
Middle English *amatiste,* via Old French and Latin from Greek *amethystos,* literally 'remedy against drunkenness', from A-² + *methyein* to be drunk, from *methy* wine. It was widely believed that the stone prevented drunkenness.

Amex /'ameks/ *abbr* **1** *trademark* American Express. **2** American Stock Exchange.

Amhara /am'harə/ *noun* (*pl* **Amharas** or *collectively* **Amhara**) a member of an indigenous people inhabiting central Ethiopia. [named after *Amhara,* a region and former kingdom in northwest Ethiopia]

Amharic /am'harik/ *noun* the Semitic language of the people of Ethiopia. ➤➤ **Amharic** *adj.* [named after the *Amhara,* a people of central Ethiopia]

amiable /'aymi·əbl/ *adj* having a friendly and pleasant manner. ➤➤ **amiability** /-'biliti/ *noun,* **amiableness** *noun,* **amiably** *adv.* [Middle English via Old French from late Latin *amicabilis* friendly, from Latin *amicus* friend]

Usage note
amiable or amicable? *Amiable,* meaning 'friendly and pleasant', is used mainly to describe people and their manner: *He seems a very amiable sort of fellow. Amicable,* meaning 'characterized by friendly goodwill', refers chiefly to relationships and dealings between people: *reached an amicable settlement; Their relationship became more amicable once they had agreed the terms of the divorce.*

amianthus /ami'anthəs/ or **amiantus** /-təs/ *noun* a fine silky asbestos. [via Latin from Greek *amiantos,* literally 'unpolluted', from A-² + *miainein* to pollute]

amicable /'amikəbl, ə'mik-/ *adj* characterized by friendly goodwill; peaceable. ➤➤ **amicability** /-'biliti/ *noun,* **amicableness** *noun,* **amicably** *adv.* [Middle English from late Latin *amicabilis,* from Latin *amicus* friend]

Usage note
amicable or amiable? See note at AMIABLE.

AMICE *abbr* Associate Member of the Institution of Civil Engineers.

amice /'amis/ *noun* a vestment made of an oblong piece of white cloth, worn by a priest round the neck and shoulders and partly under the alb. [Middle English *amis,* prob from early French, pl of *amit,* from Latin *amictus* cloak, from *amicire* to wrap round, from AMBI- + *jacere* to throw]

amicus curiae /ə,meekəs 'kyooəri·ee/ *noun* (*pl* **amici curiae** /ə,meekie/) a person who advises a court of law on a particular point concerning a legal action but is not a party to that action. [Latin *amicus curiae,* literally 'friend of the court']

amid /ə'mid/ *prep* **1** *formal* in or to the middle of (something); among. **2** during (something). [Middle English *amidde,* from Old English *onmiddan,* from ON¹ + *midde* MID¹]

amide /'amied, 'amid/ *noun* an organic compound containing the -CONH₂ group. Amides are white crystalline solids: compare IMIDE. ➤➤ **amidic** /ə'midik/ *adj.* [AMMONIA + -IDE]

amidships /ə'midships/ *adv and adj* **1** in or towards the part of a ship midway between the bow and the stern. **2** in or towards the middle of something.

amidst /ə'midst/ *prep literary* = AMID. [Middle English *amiddes,* from *amidde* (see AMID) + *-es, -s* adv suffix]

amigo /ə'meegoh/ *noun* (*pl* **amigos**) *chiefly NAmer, informal* a friend, *esp* in Spanish-speaking communities. [Spanish *amigo* from Latin *amicus* friend]

amine /'ameen/ *noun* any of various usu organic chemical compounds that are bases derived from ammonia by replacement of hydrogen by one or more carbon- and hydrogen-containing groups with a valency of one. ➤➤ **aminic** /ə'minik/ *adj.* [AMMONIA + -INE²]

amino /ə'meenoh/ *adj* of or containing the chemical group NH₂. [AMINE]

amino acid *noun* an organic acid containing the amino group NH₂ and a carboxyl group, *esp* any of the amino acids that are the chief components of proteins and are synthesized by living cells or are obtained as essential components of the diet.

Editorial note
Amino acids possess both an acidic (COO⁻) and a basic (NH₂⁺) group. Each of the 20 naturally occurring amino acids can exist in two optically isomeric forms, only one of which, (-), is found in living organisms. Combined in long chains by linking the NH₂⁺ of one with the terminal CH group of a second (peptide bonds) they constitute proteins — Professor Steven Rose.

amir /ə'miə/ *noun* see EMIR.

Amish /'ahmish, 'amish/ *pl noun* the members of a strict Mennonite sect established in America in the 18th cent. ➤➤ **Amish** *adj.* [prob from German *amisch,* from the name of Jacob *Amman* or *Amen* 17th-cent. Swiss Mennonite bishop]

amiss /ə'mis/ *adv and adj* wrong; not in order: *Something was clearly amiss.* ✳ **not come/go amiss** to be appropriate or welcome. **take it/something amiss** to be offended or upset by something. [Middle English *amis* (adv), from A-¹ + *mis* mistake, wrong]

amitosis /ami'tohsis/ *noun* cell division by simple splitting of the nucleus and division of the cytoplasm without the appearance of chromosomes. ➤➤ **amitotic** /-'totik/ *adj,* **amitotically** /-'totikli/ *adv.* [scientific Latin, from A-² + MITOSIS]

amitriptyline /ami'triptəleen/ *noun* a drug used as a mild tranquillizer to treat depression. [AMINE + TRYPTAMINE + METHYL + -INE²]

amity /'amiti/ *noun* (*pl* **amities**) friendship, *esp* friendly relations between nations: *He was soon led ... to take the child out of her arms with all the unceremoniousness of perfect amity* — Jane Austen. [Middle English *amite* via Old French and medieval Latin from Latin *amicus* friend]

ammeter /'ameetə/ *noun* an instrument for measuring electric current in amperes. [AMPERE + -METER²]

ammo /'amoh/ *noun informal* ammunition. [by shortening]

ammonia /ə'mohni·ə/ *noun* **1** a pungent colourless gas that is a chemical compound of nitrogen and hydrogen, is very soluble in water, forming an alkaline solution, and is used in the manufacture of fertilizers, synthetic fibres, and explosives: formula NH₃. **2** a solution of ammonia in water used *esp* as a cleaning fluid. [modern Latin, from Latin *sal ammoniacus* sal ammoniac, literally 'salt of Ammon' from Greek *ammōniakos* of (Zeus) Ammon, an Egyptian god near whose temple it was prepared]

ammoniac /ə'mohni·ak/ *noun* an aromatic gum resin obtained from an Asian plant of the carrot family and used formerly in medicine as a stimulant and expectorant: *Dorema ammoniacum.* [Middle English via Latin from Greek *ammōniakon,* neuter of *ammōniakos* of Ammon. The resin was first taken from plants found near an Egyptian temple of Zeus Ammon]

ammoniacal /amə'nie·əkl/ or **ammoniac** /ə,mohniak/ *adj* of, containing, or having the properties of ammonia.

ammoniate /ə'mohniayt/ *verb trans* **1** to combine or impregnate (a substance) with ammonia or an ammonium compound. **2** to subject (a substance) to decomposition by ammonification. ➤➤ **ammoniation** /-'aysh(ə)n/ *noun.*

ammonification /ə,mohnifi'kaysh(ə)n/ *noun* **1** the process of ammonifying. **2** decomposition, *esp* of nitrogen-containing organic matter by bacteria, with production of ammonia or ammonium compounds.

ammonify /ə'mohnifei/ *verb trans* (**ammonifies, ammonified, ammonifying**) to treat or impregnate (something) with ammonia or an ammonia compound. ➤➤ **ammonifier** *noun.*

ammonite /'aməniet/ *noun* **1** any of various extinct marine molluscs that were common during the Mesozoic era. **2** a flat spirally-coiled fossil shell of one of these molluscs. ➤➤ **ammonitic** /-'nitik/ *adj.* [scientific Latin *ammonites*, from Latin *cornu Ammonis*, literally 'horn of Ammon', from the fossil's resemblance to the ram's horn associated with Zeus Ammon]

ammonium /ə'mohni-əm/ *noun* an ion, NH_4^+, or a chemical group, NH_4, derived from ammonia by combination with a hydrogen ion or atom. [scientific Latin, from AMMONIA]

ammonium chloride *noun* a white chemical compound that vaporizes readily and is used in dry-cell batteries and as a medicine to clear phlegm from the chest or lungs: formula NH_4Cl.

ammonoid /'amənoyd/ *noun* = AMMONITE.

ammunition /amyoo'nish(ə)n/ *noun* **1a** projectiles that can be fired from a weapon, e.g. bullets or shells, or a collection or supply of these. **b** any object containing explosives, chemicals, etc that can be used as a weapon. **2** arguments and information used to defend or attack a point of view. [obsolete French *amunition*, alteration (by incorrect division) of *la munition* the MUNITION]

amnesia /am'neezyə, -zh(y)ə/ *noun* a partial or total loss of memory, often due to brain injury. ➤➤ **amnesiac** /-ak/ *adj and noun*, **amnesic** /-zik, -zhik/ *adj and noun*, **amnestic** /am'nestik/ *adj.* [scientific Latin from Greek *amnēsia* forgetfulness, prob alteration of *amnēstia*: see AMNESTY[1]]

amnesty[1] /'amnəsti/ *noun* (*pl* **amnesties**) **1** a pardon granted to a large group of individuals, *esp* for political offences. **2a** a suspension of a law for a fixed period during which no official action will be taken against people who admit to having broken the law, provided they satisfy certain conditions: *a drugs amnesty*. **b** the period during which this type of suspension of a law is in force. [Greek *amnēstia* forgetfulness, from *amnēstos* forgotten, from A-[2] + *mnasthai* to remember]

amnesty[2] *verb trans* (**amnesties**, **amnestied**, **amnestying**) to grant (somebody) an amnesty.

amnia /'amni-ə/ *noun* pl of AMNION.

amniocentesis /amniohsen'teesis/ *noun* (*pl* **amniocenteses** /-seez/) the insertion of a hollow needle into the uterus of a pregnant female, *esp* to obtain amniotic fluid from which various abnormalities in the developing foetus can be detected. [scientific Latin, from AMNION + *centesis* puncture, from Greek *kentesis* from *kentein* to prick]

amnion /'amni-ən/ *noun* (*pl* **amnions** or **amnia** /-ə/) a thin membrane forming a closed sac around the embryos of reptiles, birds, and mammals, and containing a watery fluid in which the embryo is immersed. ➤➤ **amniotic** /-'otik/ *adj.* [scientific Latin from Greek *amnion* caul, prob dimin. of *amnos* lamb]

amniotic fluid *noun* the fluid surrounding the foetus in the uterus.

amoeba (*NAmer* **ameba**) /ə'meebə/ *noun* (*pl* **amoebas** or **amoebae** /-bee/, *NAmer* **amebas** or **amebae**) a single-celled organism that has pseudopodia (temporary finger-like extensions of protoplasm; see PSEUDOPOD) with which it feeds and moves, and is widely distributed in water and wet places: genus *Amoeba*. ➤➤ **amoeban** *adj*, **amoebic** *adj.* [scientific Latin *Amoeba*, genus name, from Greek *amoibē* change, from *ameibein* to change]

amoebic dysentery *noun* a short-lived serious intestinal disease of human beings caused by an amoeba and marked by dysentery, griping pain, and erosion of the intestinal wall.

amoeboid (*NAmer* **ameboid**) /ə'meeboyd/ *adj* like an amoeba, *esp* in changing shape or in moving by means of protoplasmic flow.

amok or **amuck** /ə'muk/ *adv* in a frenzied or confused state. ✳ **run amok** **1** to rush about in a wild frenzy. **2** to get completely out of control: *House prices started to run amok*. [Malay *amok* frenzied rush]

among /ə'mung/ or **amongst** /ə'mungst/ *prep* **1** in or through the midst of; surrounded by (a number of things): *wandering among the trees*. **2** in company or association with (a group of people): *living among artists*. **3** by or through the whole group of (things): *discontent among the poor*. **4** in the number or class of (things): *among his many talents*. **5** denoting a division involving three or more people or things: *His estate was divided among his heirs*. [Old English *on gemonge*, from ON[1] + *gemong* crowd]

amontillado /ə,monti'lahdoh/ *noun* (*pl* **amontillados**) a pale fairly dry sherry. [Spanish *amontillado*, from *a* to + *montilla* wine from Montilla, town in Spain]

amoral /ay'morəl, a-/ *adj* **1** lying outside the sphere of moral principles or ethical judgments: compare IMMORAL. **2** said of a person: having no understanding of or concern with morals. ➤➤ **amoralism** *noun*, **amoralist** *noun*, **amorality** /aymə'raliti, amə-/ *noun*, **amorally** *adv*.

Usage note

amoral *or* immoral? An *immoral* person is one who breaks accepted standards of right and wrong. To be *amoral* means that one rejects the whole concept of morality or does not know or cannot know right from wrong. Babies, animals, and robots could be said to be *amoral*.

amoretto /amə'retoh/ *noun* (*pl* **amoretti** /-ti/) a representation of a cupid or cherub, used in art as a conventional symbol of love. [Italian *amoretto*, dimin. of *amore* cupid, love]

amorist /'amərist/ *noun* a person who is in love or who writes about love. ➤➤ **amoristic** /-'ristik/ *adj*.

amoroso[1] /amə'rohzoh/ *noun* (*pl* **amorosos**) a dark sweet sherry. [Spanish *amoroso*, literally 'amorous']

amoroso[2] *adj and adv* said of a piece of music: to be performed in a tender manner. [Italian, from Latin *amorosus*, from *amor* love]

amorous /'amərəs/ *adj* **1** of or relating to love. **2** moved by, inclined to, or indicative of love or desire. ➤➤ **amorously** *adv*, **amorousness** *noun*. [Middle English via Old French from medieval Latin *amorosus* from Latin *amor*: see AMOUR]

amorphous /ə'mawfəs/ *adj* **1a** having no definite form; shapeless. **b** without definite character; unclassifiable. **2** said of rocks, etc: not crystalline. ➤➤ **amorphism** *noun*, **amorphously** *adv*, **amorphousness** *noun*. [Greek *amorphos*, from A-[2] + *morphē* form]

amortize or **amortise** /ə'mawtiez/ *verb trans* **1** to pay off (a mortgage, debt, etc) gradually, usu by periodic instalments or contributions to a sinking fund. **2** to write off the initial cost of (an asset, *esp* in business) over an agreed period. **3** *dated* to transfer (land, etc) in mortmain. ➤➤ **amortizable** *adj*, **amortization** /-'zaysh(ə)n/ *noun*. [Middle English *amortisen* to deaden, alienate in mortmain, modification of early French *amortiss*-, stem of *amortir*, ultimately from AD- + Latin *mort-*, *mors* death]

amosite /'əmosiet/ *noun* a brown asbestos mineral that is an iron-rich AMPHIBOLE (silicate constituent of rocks). [abbr of *Asbestos Mines of South Africa*]

amount[1] /ə'mownt/ *verb intrans* **1** (+ to) to be equal in number or quantity to (something). **2** (+ to) to be equivalent in significance to (something): *acts that amount to treason*. [Middle English *amounten* from Old French *amonter* from *amont* upwards, from AD- + Latin *mont* MOUNTAIN]

amount[2] *noun* **1** a collection of something considered as a unit; a quantity: *She has an enormous amount of energy*. **2** the total of two or more quantities: *The amount for the repairs was higher than I expected*. ✳ **any amount of** plenty of (something). **no amount of** even a great deal of (something): *No amount of persuasion could convince her*.

amour /ə'maw, ə'mooə (*French* amur)/ *noun* a love affair, *esp* an illicit one. [Middle English *amour* love, affection, via Old French and Old Provençal from Latin *amor*, from *amare* to love]

amour propre /'proprə (*French* prɔpr)/ *noun* self-esteem: *Vanity and amour propre played a greater role in her policies than in those of any other ruler of the period* — M S Anderson. [French *amour-propre*, literally 'love of oneself']

AMP *noun* adenosine monophosphate, a chemical compound that is a mononucleotide of adenine and that is reversibly converted in cells to the energy-storing compounds ADP and ATP: formula $C_{10}H_{12}N_5O_3H_2PO_4$.

amp /amp/ *noun* **1** = AMPERE. **2** = AMPLIFIER (1A).

ampelopsis /ampi'lopsis/ *noun* (*pl* **ampelopsis**) either of two species of a genus of deciduous climbing plants with twisting tendrils, native to America and Asia: genus *Ampelopsis*. [scientific Latin *ampelopsis*, from Greek *ampelos* vine + *opsis* appearance]

amperage /'amp(ə)rij/ *noun* the strength of an electric current expressed in amperes.

ampere /'ampeə/ *noun* the basic SI unit of electric current. It is equal to a constant current that, when maintained in two straight parallel conductors one metre apart in a vacuum, produces between the conductors a force equal to 2×10^{-7} newton per metre of length. [named after André M *Ampère* d.1836, French physicist]

ampere-hour *noun* a unit quantity of electricity equal to the quantity carried past any point of a circuit by a steady current of one ampere flowing for one hour.

ampersand /'ampəsand/ *noun* a sign (&) standing for the word *and*. [alteration of *and* (&) *per se and*, 'and (the character &) by itself (is the word) *and*', chanted by children learning the alphabet. The ampersand appeared at the end of the alphabet in children's primers]

amph- *comb. form* see AMPHI-.

amphetamine /am'fetəmeen, -min/ *noun* **1** a synthetic drug that is a powerful stimulant of the central nervous system and that can be strongly addictive if abused. **2** any of various derivatives of amphetamine that have similar properties and uses and have also been used in the treatment of obesity. [ALPHA¹ + *methyl* (from METHYLENE) + obsolete *phene* benzone + ETHYL + AMINE]

amphi- *or* **amph-** *comb form* forming words, with the meanings: **1** on both sides; round: *amphitheatre*. **2** of both kinds; both: *amphibian*. [Latin *amphi-* round, on both sides, from Greek *amphi-*, *amph-*, from *amphi*]

amphibian /am'fibi-ən/ *noun* **1** any of a class of amphibious organisms, *esp* frogs, toads, newts, or other members of a class of cold-blooded vertebrates intermediate in many characteristics between fishes and reptiles and having gilled aquatic larvae and air-breathing adults: class Amphibia. **2** an aeroplane, tank, etc adapted to operate on both land and water. ▶▶ **amphibian** *adj*. [Greek *amphibion* amphibious being, neuter of *amphibios*, literally 'having a double life', from AMPHI- + *bios* life]

amphibious /am'fibi-əs/ *adj* **1** able to live both on land and in water. **2a** relating to or adapted for both land and water: *amphibious vehicles*. **b** involving or trained for coordinated action of land, sea, and air forces organized for invasion: *an amphibious assault*. ▶▶ **amphibiously** *adv*, **amphibiousness** *noun*.

amphibole /'amfibohl/ *noun* any of a group of silicate minerals, e.g. hornblende, that are important constituents of many rocks. [French via late Latin from Greek *amphibolos* ambiguous, from *amphiballein* to throw round, doubt, from AMPHI- + *ballein* to throw]

amphibolite /am'fibəliet/ *noun* a coarse-grained usu metamorphic rock consisting essentially of amphibole. ▶▶ **amphibolitic** /-'litik/ *adj*.

amphibology /amfi'boləji/ *noun* (*pl* **amphibologies**) **1** ambiguity of sentence construction (as in *Are the children safe at home?*). **2** a sentence or phrase of this kind. [Middle English from late Latin *amphibologia*, ultimately from Greek *amphibolos*: see AMBIGUOUS]

amphimictic /amfi'miktik/ *adj* capable of interbreeding freely and of producing fertile offspring. ▶▶ **amphimictically** *adv*. [AMPHI- + Greek *miktos* blended, from *mignynai*]

amphimixis /amfi'miksis/ *noun* (*pl* **amphimixes** /-seez/) the union of reproductive cells in sexual reproduction: compare APOMIXIS. [scientific Latin, from AMPHI- + Greek *mixis* mingling, from *mignynai* to mix]

amphioxus /amfi'oksəs/ *noun* (*pl* **amphioxi** /-sie/ *or* **amphioxuses**) any of several species of lancelets, used as a food fish in parts of Asia: genus *Branchiostoma*. [scientific Latin, from AMPHI- + Greek *oxys* sharp]

amphipod /'amfipod/ *noun* any of various small shrimplike invertebrate animals, e.g. the sandhopper, with a body flattened sideways. ▶▶ **amphipod** *adj*. [Greek AMPHI- + *pod-*, *pous* foot: see FOOT¹]

amphiprostyle /amfi'prohstiel/ *adj* said of a classical building, *esp* a temple: having columns at each end but not at the sides. [via Latin from Greek *amphiprostylos*, from AMPHI- + *prostylos* having pillars in front, from PRO-¹ + *stylos* pillar]

amphisbaena /amfis'beenə/ *noun* **1** (*also* **amphisbaenian**) any of a family of modified wormlike burrowing reptiles that live in warm or tropical countries: family Amphisbaenidae. **2** a mythological serpent with a head at each end, capable of moving in either direction. [via Latin from Greek *amphisbaina*, from AMPHI- + *bainein* to walk, go]

amphitheatre (*NAmer* **amphitheater**) /'amfithiətə/ *noun* **1** an oval or circular building with rising tiers of seats ranged about an arena, of the kind used in ancient Greece and Rome *esp* for contests and public spectacles. **2** a semicircular gallery in a theatre. [via Latin from Greek *amphitheatron*, from AMPHI- + *theatron* theatre]

amphora /'amfərə/ *noun* (*pl* **amphorae** /-ree, -rie/ *or* **amphoras**) a two-handled oval jar or vase with a narrow neck and base, orig used by the ancient Greeks and Romans for holding oil or wine: compare AMPULLA. [Latin *amphora*, modification of Greek *amphoreus*, *amphiphoreus*, from AMPHI- + *phoreus* bearer, from *pherein* to bear]

amphoteric /amfə'terik/ *adj* capable of reacting chemically as both an acid and a base. [Greek *amphoteros* each of two, from *amphō* both]

ampicillin /ampi'silin/ *noun* a type of penicillin used *esp* in treating respiratory infections. [AMINO + PENICILLIN]

ample /'ampl/ *adj* (**ampler, amplest**) **1** enough or more than enough: *They had ample money for the trip*. **2** large or extensive: *a house with an ample garden*. **3** *euphem* buxom; portly: *her ample figure*. ▶▶ **ampleness** *noun*. [French *ample* from Latin *amplus* large, spacious]

amplexus /am'pleksəs/ *noun* the mating embrace of frogs or toads during which eggs are shed into the water and fertilized there. [scientific Latin, from Latin *amplexus* embrace, past part. of *amplecti* to entwine, embrace, from AMBI- + *plectere* to plait]

amplification /,amplifi'kaysh(ə)n/ *noun* **1** an act, example, or product of amplifying. **2a** the particulars used to expand a statement. **b** an expanded statement.

amplifier /'amplifie-ə/ *noun* **1a** an electronic device that makes sounds louder. **b** an electronic device used to increase voltage, current, or power. **2** a person or thing that amplifies something.

amplify /'amplifie/ *verb* (**amplifies, amplified, amplifying**) ▶ *verb trans* **1a** to make (something) larger or greater. **b** to increase the volume of (sound) using an amplifier. **2** to increase the magnitude of (an electronical signal or other input of power). **3** to expand (e.g. a statement) or make it clearer by the use of detail, illustration, etc. ▶ *verb intrans* (*often* + on) to expand on one's remarks or ideas. [Middle English *amplifien* via Old French from Latin *amplificare*, from *amplus* AMPLE]

amplitude /'amplityoohd, -choohd/ *noun* **1** largeness of dimensions or scope; abundance: *Such was his amplitude of learning, and such his copiousness of communication, that it may be doubted whether a day now passes, in which I have not some advantage from his friendship* — Dr Johnson. **2a** the extent of a vibration or oscillation measured from the average position to a maximum. **b** the maximum departure of the value of an alternating current or wave, e.g. a radio wave, from the average value. **3** the position of the horizon between the true east or west point and the foot of a vertical circle passing through any star or object. [Latin *amplitudo*, from *amplus* AMPLE + *-tudo* -TUDE]

amplitude modulation *noun* **1** a modulation of the amplitude of a wave, *esp* a radio carrier wave, by the characteristics of the signal carried. **2** a method of transmitting using this: compare FREQUENCY MODULATION, PHASE MODULATION.

amply /'ampli/ *adv* generously; more than adequately: *amply rewarded*; *amply proportioned*.

ampoule (*NAmer* **ampul** *or* **ampule**) /'ampooh, -pyoohl/ *noun* a small sealed bulbous glass vessel that is used *esp* to hold a sterile solution for hypodermic injection. [Middle English *ampulle* flask, Old English *ampulle* and Old French *ampoule*, both from Latin *ampulla*: see AMPULLA]

ampulla /am'poolə/ *noun* (*pl* **ampullae** /-lee/) **1** an ancient Roman flask of glass or earthenware with two handles, used to hold ointment, perfume, or wine: compare AMPHORA. **2** a bottle for consecrated oil, wine, etc. **3** a bag-like widening of an anatomical duct or canal. ▶▶ **ampullar** *adj*. [Old English *ampulle* from Latin *ampulla*, dimin. of *amphora*: see AMPHORA]

amputate /'ampyootayt/ *verb trans* to remove (all or part of a limb, *esp* a damaged or diseased one) surgically. ▶▶ **amputation** /-'taysh(ə)n/ *noun*, **amputator** *noun*. [Latin *amputatus*, past part. of *amputare*, from AMBI- + *putare* to cut, prune]

amputee /ampyoo'tee/ *noun* somebody who has had all or part of a limb amputated.

amt *abbr* amount.

amu *abbr* atomic mass unit.

amuck /ə'muk/ *adv* see AMOK.

amulet /'amyoolit/ *noun* a natural object such as a stone or piece of jewellery, often inscribed with a magic incantation or symbol, that is believed to protect a person from harm. [Latin *amuletum*]

amuse /ə'myoohz/ *verb trans* **1** to appeal to the sense of humour of (somebody). **2** to entertain or interest (somebody). ⋙ **amused** *adj*, **amusedly** /ə'myoozidli/ *adv*. [early French *amuser*, from AD- + *muser*: see MUSE¹]

amusement *noun* **1** the act or an instance of amusing, or the state of being amused. **2** a means of entertaining or occupying somebody; a pleasurable diversion. **3** a mechanical device or stall for entertainment at a fair, e.g. a roundabout or coconut shy.

amusement arcade *noun chiefly Brit* a covered area with coin-operated games machines for recreation.

amusement park *noun* an enclosed park where various amusements, e.g. roundabouts and sideshows, are permanently set up.

amusing /ə'myoohzing/ *adj* entertaining, *esp* in way that makes one laugh; comical; funny. ⋙ **amusingly** *adv*.

amygdalin /ə'migdəlin/ *noun* a GLUCOSIDE (chemical compound derived from sugar) found *esp* in bitter almonds and used as an expectorant. [scientific Latin *Amygdalus*, genus name, via late Latin from Greek *amygdalos* almond tree]

amyl /'amil/ *noun* **1** the former name for the pentyl group C_5H_{11}, derived from pentane by the removal of a hydrogen atom. **2** *informal* = AMYL NITRITE. [AMYL-]

amyl- *or* **amylo-** *comb. form* forming words, denoting: starch: *amylase*. [late Latin *amyl-* via Latin from Greek *amylon*, neuter of *amylos* not ground at the mill]

amylaceous /ami'layshəs/ *adj* containing or having the characteristics of starch; starchy.

amyl alcohol *noun* any of eight related alcohols used *esp* as solvents and in the manufacture of esters, or a mixture of these.

amylase /'amilayz, -lays/ *noun* any of a number of enzymes that accelerate the breakdown of starch and glycogen, or their products, into simple sugars.

amyl nitrite *noun* a yellowish liquid used as a treatment for angina and sometimes inhaled as a recreational drug.

amylo- *comb. form* see AMYL-.

amyloid¹ /'amiloyd/ *noun* a firm waxy substance consisting of protein and polysaccharides deposited in body organs affected by disease and under other abnormal conditions.

amyloid² *adj* resembling starch.

amyloidosis /,amiloy'dohsis/ *noun* a pathological condition in which amyloid is deposited in organs or tissues.

amylopsin /ami'lopsin/ *noun* an enzyme in pancreatic juice that converts starch into sugar. [AMYL- + -*psin* as in PEPSIN]

amylose /'amilohz, -lohs/ *noun* **1** any of various polysaccharides (complex carbohydrates; see POLYSACCHARIDE) such as starch or cellulose. **2** a component of starch characterized by its straight chains of glucose units and by the tendency of its aqueous solutions to set to a stiff gel. **3** any of various chemical compounds of the general formula $(C_6H_{10}O_5)_n$, obtained by the breakdown of starch.

amylum /'amiləm/ *noun* (*pl* **amylums**) vegetable starch. [via Latin from Greek *amylon*: see AMYL-]

amyotrophic lateral sclerosis /ami-ə'trofik/ *noun* a disorder of the nervous system in which the neurons that control muscle movements degenerate, causing the muscles to weaken and atrophy. Death generally results from the atrophying of the muscles of the organs of respiration. Also called LOU GEHRIG'S DISEASE.

amyotrophy /ami'otrəfi/ *noun* atrophy of muscles. ⋙ **amyotrophic** /ami-ə'trofik/ *adj*. [A-² + MY- + TROPHIC]

Amytal /'amitl/ *noun trademark* a barbiturate occurring as a white crystalline powder, used as a sedative and to induce sleep.

an¹ /(ə)n; *strong* an/ *indefinite article* used in place of *a* (see A¹) before words with an initial vowel sound: *an oak; twice an hour*. [Old English *ān* ONE¹]

Usage note
an or a? See note at A¹.

an² *or* **an'** *conj archaic* if. [Middle English *an*, alteration of AND]

an'¹ *conj informal* = AND.

an'² *conj archaic* see AN².

an- *prefix* see A-², ANA-.

-an¹ *or* **-ean** *or* **-ian** *suffix* forming nouns, denoting: **1** somebody who comes from, belongs to, supports, etc a specified place, thing, or person: *Mancunian; republican*. **2** somebody skilled in or specializing in the subject specified: *phonetician*. [*-an* and *-ian* from Middle English via Old French from Latin *-annus, -ianus; -ean* from such words as *Mediterranean, European*]

-an² *or* **-ean** *or* **-ian** *suffix* forming adjectives, with the meanings: **1** of or belonging to: *American; Christian*. **2** characteristic of; resembling: *Mozartean; Shavian*.

-an³ *suffix* forming nouns, denoting: **1** an unsaturated carbon compound: *furan*. **2** a polymeric anhydride of the carbohydrate specified: *dextran*. [alteration of -ENE, -INE¹, and -ONE]

ana- *or* **an-** *prefix* forming words, with the meanings: **1** up or upwards: *anabasis*. **2** back or backwards: *anapaest*. **3** again: *anabaptism*. [via Latin from Greek *ana-*, up, back, again, from *ana* up]

-ana *or* **-iana** *suffix* forming pl nouns, denoting: collected objects or information relating to or characteristic of the topic, period, place, or individual specified: *Victoriana; Johnsoniana*. [Latin *-ana, -iana*, neuter pl of *-anus, -ianus* -AN¹]

Anabaptism /anə'baptiz(ə)m/ *noun* **1** the Anabaptist movement or its doctrine or practices. **2** (**anabaptism**) the baptism of somebody who was previously baptized. [via Latin from late Greek *anabaptismos* rebaptism, from *anabaptizein* to rebaptize, from ANA- + *baptizein*: see BAPTIZE]

Anabaptist *noun* a member of a Protestant movement that was established in Zurich in 1524. Its chief distinguishing feature was its insistence on baptism or rebaptism of adult believers. ⋙ **Anabaptist** *adj*.

anabas /'anəbas, -bas/ *noun* any of a genus of freshwater fishes of Africa and Asia that can breathe air, live out of water, and move across land, *esp* the climbing perch: genus *Anabas*. [scientific Latin *Anabas*, genus name, from Greek *anabainein* to go up or inland, from ANA- + *bainein* to go]

anabasis /ə'nabəsis/ *noun* (*pl* **anabases** /-seez/) **1** an expedition such as a military advance, *esp* one from the coast inland. **2** a difficult and dangerous military retreat. [Greek *anabasis* inland march, from *anabainein*: see ANABAS; (sense 2) from the retreat of Greek mercenaries in Asia Minor in 401 BC described in the *Anabasis* by Xenophon d.*c*.355 BC, Greek historian who led the retreat]

anabatic /anə'batik/ *adj* said of a wind or air current: moving upwards: compare KATABATIC. [Greek *anabatos*, from *anabainein*: see ANABAS]

anabiosis /,anəbie'ohsis/ *noun* (*pl* **anabioses** /-seez/) a state of suspended animation induced in some organisms, e.g. by desiccation during a drought, and from which they can be revived. ⋙ **anabiotic** /-'otik/ *adj*. [scientific Latin from Greek *anabiōsis* return to life, from *anabioun* to return to life, from ANA- + *bios* life]

anabolic steroid /anə'bolik/ *noun* any of several synthetic steroid hormones that cause a rapid increase in the size and weight of skeletal muscle. They are used legitimately in medicine and illegally to enhance the performance of athletes.

anabolism /ə'nabəliz(ə)m/ *noun* an organism's synthesizing of proteins, fats, and other complex molecules from simpler molecules, with the accompanying storage of energy: compare CATABOLISM. ⋙ **anabolic** /anə'bolik/ *adj*. [ANA- + -*bolism* as in METABOLISM]

anachronism /ə'nakrəniz(ə)m/ *noun* **1** the placing of people, events, objects, or customs in a period to which they do not belong. **2** a person or thing that belongs or seems to belong to an older time. ⋙ **anachronistic** /-'nistik/ *adj*, **anachronistically** /-'nistikli/ *adv*. [prob from early Greek *anachronismos*, ultimately from late Greek *anachronizein* to be late, from ANA- + *chronos* time]

anacoluthon /,anəkə'loohthon/ *noun* (*pl* **anacolutha** /-thə/) **1** grammatical inconsistency in the way in which words are put together to form phrases, sentences, etc, *esp* the shift from one construction to another within a sentence, e.g. in *You really ought — well, do it your own way*. **2** a grammatical construction or sentence, etc of this kind. ⋙ **anacoluthic** /-'thik/ *adj*, **anacoluthically** *adv*. [via late Latin from late Greek *anakolouthon* inconsistency in logic, neuter of Greek *anakolouthos* inconsistent, from AN- + *akolouthos* following, from *ha-, a-* together + *keleuthos* path]

anaconda /anə'kondə/ *noun* any of several species of large semi-aquatic S American snakes of the boa family that crush their prey in their coils: *Eunectes murinus*. [prob modification of Sinhalese *henakandayā* a slender green Sri Lankan snake to which the name was first applied]

anacrusis /anə'kroohsis/ *noun* (*pl* **anacruses** /-seez/) **1** in poetry, one or more unstressed syllables at the beginning of a line. **2** in music, one or more notes preceding the first downbeat of a phrase. [via Latin from Greek *anakrousis* beginning of a song, from *anakrouein* to begin a song: from ANA- + *krouein* to strike]

anadromous /ə'nadrəməs/ *adj* said of a fish: ascending rivers from the sea for breeding: compare CATADROMOUS: *Salmon are anadromous.* [Greek *anadromos* running upwards, from *anadramein* to run upwards, from ANA- + *dramein* to run]

anaemia (*NAmer* **anemia**) /ə'neemi·ə/ *noun* **1** a condition in which the blood is deficient in red blood cells, haemoglobin, or total volume, which results in pallor and a lack of energy. **2** lack of vitality: *She is dying piecemeal of a sort of emotional anaemia* — Ezra Pound. [via Latin from Greek *anaimia* bloodlessness, from A-² + *haima* blood]

anaemic (*NAmer* **anemic**) *adj* **1** suffering from anaemia. **2** with an unhealthily pale complexion.

anaerobe /'anərohb, ə'neərohb/ *noun* an organism, e.g. a bacterium, that lives without or only in the absence of oxygen. [AN- + AEROBE]

anaerobic /anə'rohbik, aneə-/ *adj* **1** living, active, or occurring in the absence of oxygen: *anaerobic bacteria.* **2** of or induced by anaerobes: *The process works by the anaerobic breakdown of organic matter.* ➤➤ **anaerobically** *adv.*

anaesthesia (*NAmer* **anesthesia**) /anəs'theezhə, -zyə/ *noun* **1** loss of sensation of pain induced artificially, e.g. through the injection of drugs or the inhalation of gases. **2** loss of sensation in a part of the body, resulting either from injury or a disorder of the nerves. [via Latin from Greek *anaisthēsia*, from A-² + *aisthēsia* feeling, from *aisthanesthai* to perceive]

anaesthesiology (*NAmer* **anesthesiology**) /,anəs,theezi'oləji/ *noun chiefly NAmer* = ANAESTHETICS. ➤➤ **anaesthesiologist** *noun.*

anaesthetic¹ (*NAmer* **anesthetic**) /anəs'thetik/ *noun* a substance that produces anaesthesia, *esp* a drug or gas administered so that surgery can be carried out painlessly.

anaesthetic² (*NAmer* **anesthetic**) *adj* of or capable of producing anaesthesia. ➤➤ **anaesthetically** *adv.*

anaesthetics *pl noun Brit* (*treated as sing.*) the branch of medical science dealing with anaesthesia and anaesthetic substances.

anaesthetise /ə'neesthətiez/ *verb trans* see ANAESTHETIZE.

anaesthetist (*NAmer* **anesthetist**) /ə'neesthətist/ *noun* a doctor or, in the USA, other qualified person, who is specially trained in administering anaesthetics.

anaesthetize *or* **anaesthetise** (*NAmer* **anesthetize**) /ə'neesthətiez/ *verb trans* to administer an anaesthetic to (somebody). ➤➤ **anaesthetization** /-'zaysh(ə)n/ *noun.*

anaglyph /'anəglif/ *noun* **1** a moving or still picture in which two images in contrasting colours are superimposed to produce a three-dimensional effect when viewed through filters of the same colours. **2** an embossed ornament in low relief. ➤➤ **anaglyphic** /-'glifik/ *adj.* [via late Latin from Greek *anaglyphos* embossed, from *anaglyphein* to emboss, from ANA- + *glyphein* to carve]

Anaglypta /anə'gliptə/ *noun trademark* a heavy usu white wallpaper with an embossed pattern. [Greek *anaglypta* work in low relief, ultimately from ANA- + *glyphein* to carve]

anagram /'anəgram/ *noun* a word or phrase made by rearranging the letters of another, e.g. *ladies* is an anagram of *ideals.* ➤➤ **anagrammatic** /-grə'matik/ *adj,* **anagrammatical** /-grə'matikl/ *adj,* **anagrammatically** /-grə'matikli/ *adv.* [prob from early French *anagramme* via Latin from Greek *anagrammatismos*, from *anagrammatizein* to transpose letters, from ANA- + *gramma* letter]

anagrammatize *or* **anagrammatise** *verb trans* to form (a word) into an anagram. ➤➤ **anagrammatization** *noun.*

anal /'aynl/ *adj* **1** relating to or in the region of the anus. **2** in psychoanalysis, relating to or deriving from the stage of psychosexual development during which the child is particularly concerned with its anal region and faeces, such fixation being linked to personality traits that include fussiness, etc: compare GENITAL, ORAL¹; see ANAL RETENTIVE. ➤➤ **anality** /ay'naliti/ *noun,* **anally** *adv.*

anal. *abbr* **1** analogous. **2** analogy. **3** analysis. **4** analytic.

analects /'analekts/ *or* **analecta** /-'lektə/ *pl noun* selected extracts from miscellaneous writings. [scientific Latin *analecta* from Greek *analekta*, neuter pl of *analektos* gathered together, from *analegein* to collect, from ANA- + *legein* to gather]

analeptic¹ /anə'leptik/ *adj* said *esp* of a medicine: stimulating the central nervous system; restorative. [Greek *analēptikos*, from *analambanein* to take up, restore, from ANA- + *lambanein* to take]

analeptic² *noun* an analeptic medicine.

anal fin *noun* a central unpaired fin of a fish situated behind the anus on the lower side of the body.

analgesia /anəl'jeezh(y)ə, -zyə/ *noun* insensibility to pain without loss of consciousness. [scientific Latin from Greek *analgēsia*, from A-² + *algesia* sense of pain, ultimately from *algos* pain]

analgesic¹ /anəl'jeezik/ *noun* a drug that relieves pain; a painkiller.

analgesic² *adj* relieving pain; painkilling.

analog¹ /'anəlog/ *adj* **1** said of a computer, etc: using data supplied in a stream of numbers represented by directly measurable quantities, e.g. voltages or mechanical rotations: compare DIGITAL. **2** said of a clock or watch, etc: using a pointer or hands rather than having an electronic display of numbers: compare DIGITAL. **3** converting sound waves into a continuous electrical wave form to record sound: compare DIGITAL. [French *analogue* from Greek *analogos*: see ANALOGOUS]

analog² *noun NAmer* see ANALOGUE¹.

analogical /anə'lojikl/ *or* **analogic** *adj* **1** of or based on analogy. **2** expressing or implying an analogy. ➤➤ **analogically** *adv.*

analogise /ə'naləjiez/ *verb* see ANALOGIZE.

analogist /ə'naləjist/ *noun* a person who searches for or reasons from analogies.

analogize *or* **analogise** /ə'naləjiez/ *verb trans* to describe or explain (something) using analogy. ➤ *verb intrans* to use analogy in argumentation, explanation, etc.

analogous /ə'naləgəs/ *adj* **1** (*often* + to/with) similar in some respects: *a kind of numbing affect analogous to the paralysing influence of fear* — Roger Fry. **2** said of plant or animal parts: similar in function but having evolved separately and distinctly. The wings of insects and the wings of birds are analogous structures: compare HOMOLOGOUS. ➤➤ **analogously** *adv,* **analogousness** *noun.* [via Latin from Greek *analogos* proportionate, from ANA- + *logos* reason, ratio]

analogue¹ (*NAmer* **analog**) /'anəlog/ *noun* **1** something that is analogous to something else. **2** an organ or body part similar in function to that of another animal or plant but different in structure and origin: compare HOMOLOGUE. **3** a chemical compound structurally similar to another but differing often by a single chemical element of the same valency and group of the periodic table as the element it replaces: compare HOMOLOGUE. [French *analogue* from Greek *analogos*: see ANALOGOUS]

analogue² *adj* = ANALOG¹.

analogy /ə'naləji/ *noun* (*pl* **analogies**) **1a** an explanation or illustration of something that uses a comparison with something similar. **b** (*often* + between) comparison for the purposes of explanation or illustration. **2a** resemblance in some respects; similarity. **b** something regarded as comparable in this way. **3** correspondence in function between anatomical parts of different structure and origin: compare HOMOLOGY. ➤➤ **analogical** /anə'lojikl/ *adj,* **analogically** /-'lojikl/ *adv.* [prob from Greek *analogia* mathematical proportion, correspondence, from *analogos*: see ANALOGOUS]

anal retentive /ri'tentiv/ *noun* in psychoanalysis, a person who has personality traits, such as meticulousness or over-fussiness, considered to originate in the anal stage of psychosexual development. ➤➤ **anal retention** *noun,* **anal-retentive** *adj,* **anal retentiveness** *noun.*

analysand /ə'nalisand/ *noun* a person who is undergoing psychoanalysis.

analyse (*NAmer* **analyze**) /'anəliez/ *verb trans* **1** to make a close examination of (something) in order to determine its nature, content, or structure; to break (something) down into its components, characteristics, etc. **2a** to determine the chemical components of (a mixture or compound). **b** to determine the factors or elements of (a mathematical formula, equation, etc). **3** = PSYCHOANALYSE. **4** to break (a sentence) down into its grammatical elements. ➤➤ **analysable** *adj,* **analyser** *noun.* [prob from ANALYSIS]

analysis /ə'naləsis/ *noun* (*pl* **analyses** /-seez/) **1a** the examination and identification of the constituents of a complex whole and their relationship to one another. **b** the determination of the chemical components of a mixture or compound or their relative amounts. **c** a statement of such an analysis. **2** the act or process of breaking something up into its constituent elements: compare SYNTHESIS. **3** = PSYCHOANALYSIS. **4** a branch of mathematics concerned with the rigorous treatment of the ideas of limits, functions, calculus, etc. **5** a method in philosophy of resolving complex expressions into simpler or more basic ones. ✳ **in the final/last analysis** when everything else has been duly considered; ultimately. [via Latin from Greek *analysis*, from *analyein* to break up, from ANA- + *lyein* to loosen]

analyst /'anəlist/ *noun* **1** a person who analyses or is skilled in analysis. **2** a psychoanalyst. **3** a systems analyst.

analytical /anə'litikl/ *or* **analytic** *adj* **1** relating to or produced by analysis. **2** skilled in or using analysis, *esp* in reasoning: *a keenly analytical mind*. **3** in logic, self-evidently true or false by virtue of the words used: *'All women are female' is an analytic truth*. **4** said of languages: using word order and grammatical words, not inflection, to indicate grammatical structure and relations. **5** psychoanalytical. ➤➤ **analytically** *adv*, **analyticity** /'tisiti/ *noun*. [via late Latin from Greek *analytikos* from *analyein*: see ANALYSIS]

analytical geometry *noun* the study of geometric properties by means of algebraic operations on coordinates in a coordinate system.

analytical philosophy *noun* a philosophical method which seeks to solve or eliminate philosophical problems by the careful analysis of the words used in formulating them.

analyze /'anəliez/ *verb trans NAmer* see ANALYSE.

anamnesis /anəm'neesis/ *noun* (*pl* **anamneses** /-seez/) **1** in psychology and psychoanalysis, the recalling to mind of past events and experiences, *esp* in the patient's own words. **2** in medicine, a patient's case history. ➤➤ **anamnestic** /-'nestik/ *adj*. [via Latin from Greek *anamnēsis*, from *anamimnēskesthai* to remember, from ANA- + *mimnēskesthai* to call to mind]

anamorphic /anə'mawfik/ *adj* said of a lens or the image produced by it: producing or having a different image magnification in each of two perpendicular directions, thereby either compressing widescreen gauge to fit 35mm film or expanding 35mm film to fill a wide screen. [scientific Latin *anamorphosis* distorted optical image, from late Greek *anamorphoun* to transform, from Greek ANA- + *morphē* form]

anapaest (*NAmer* **anapest**) /'anəpest, -peest/ *noun* a metrical foot consisting of two short syllables followed by one long, or two unstressed syllables followed by one stressed. ➤➤ **anapaestic** /-'pestik, -'peestik/ *adj and noun*. [via Latin from Greek *anapaistos*, literally 'struck back' (i.e. a dactyl reversed), ultimately from ANA- + *paiein* to strike]

anaphase /'anəfayz/ *noun* the stage of MITOSIS and MEIOSIS (cell division) in which the chromosomes move towards the poles of the SPINDLE[1] (stick-shaped cell structure): compare METAPHASE, PROPHASE. ➤➤ **anaphasic** /-'fayzik/ *adj*.

anaphora /ə'nafərə/ *noun* **1** the use of a grammatical substitute, e.g. a pronoun, to refer to a preceding word or phrase, e.g. the word *it* in the sentence *She bought some salmon because it was specially reduced*: compare CATAPHORA. **2** in rhetoric, the repetition of a word or phrase at the beginning of successive clauses, *esp* for effect: compare EPISTROPHE. ➤➤ **anaphoric** /anə'forik/ *adj*, **anaphorically** /-'forikli/ *adv*. [via Latin and late Greek from Greek *anaphora* act of carrying back, reference, from *anapherein* to carry back, refer, from ANA- + *pherein* to carry]

anaphrodisiac[1] /a,nafrə'diziak/ *noun* a drug that tends to lessen sexual desire. [scientific Latin *anaphrodisia* lack of sexual desire, from A-[2] + Greek *aphrodisios*: see APHRODISIAC[1]]

anaphrodisiac[2] *adj* lessening sexual desire.

anaphylactic /,anəfi'laktik/ *adj* of or causing anaphylaxis: *anaphylactic shock*. ➤➤ **anaphylactically** *adv*.

anaphylaxis /,anəfi'laksis/ *noun* (*pl* **anaphylaxes** /-seez/) a sometimes fatal reaction to drugs, insect venom, etc caused by hypersensitivity resulting from earlier contact. [scientific Latin *anaphylaxis*, from ANA- + Greek *phylaxis* guarding]

anaptyxis /anap'tiksis/ *noun* (*pl* **anaptyxes** /-seez/) the development of a vowel between two consonants, e.g. the second *a* in *that-away*. ➤➤ **anaptyctic** *adj*. [via Latin from Greek *anaptyxis* act of unfolding, from *anaptyssein* to unfold, from ANA- + *ptyssein* to fold]

anarchic /a'nahkik/ *or* **anarchical** /-kikl/ *adj* **1** advocating anarchy or likely to bring about anarchy: *anarchic violence*. **2** not adhering to conventions, standards, or expectations: *anarchic experiments in lifestyle* — George Steiner. ➤➤ **anarchically** /-kli/ *adv*.

anarchism /'anəkiz(ə)m/ *noun* **1** a political theory holding that all forms of governmental authority are undesirable and advocating a society based on voluntary cooperation.

Editorial note
Anarchism is split into two distinct branches: one regards individuals as highly egoistic and attempts to release them from the constraints of government to pursue their own concerns; the other deems people to be so socially inclined that mutual cooperation may be attained without state regulation. Either way, it is optimistic about the possibility of life without centralized politics — Professor Michael Freeden.

2 the attacking of the established social order or laws; rebellion.

anarchist /'anəkist/ *noun* somebody who believes in or promotes anarchism, *esp* by attacking the established social order or laws; a revolutionary. ➤➤ **anarchist** *adj*, **anarchistic** /-'kistik/ *adj*, **anarchistically** /-kli/ *adv*.

anarchy /'anəki/ *noun* **1a** absence of government, *esp* a utopian society with complete freedom. **b** a state of lawlessness or political disorder owing to the absence of governmental authority. **2** = ANARCHISM. **3** any state of confusion, disorder or chaos. [via medieval Latin from Greek *anarchia*, from *anarchos* having no ruler, from A-[2] + *archos* ruler]

anastigmat /ə'nastigmat, anə'stigmat/ *noun* a lens that is not ASTIGMATIC (with light rays not converging at a focal point). ➤➤ **anastigmatic** /-'matik/ *adj*. [German *Anastigmat*, back-formation from *anastigmatisch* anastigmatic, from A-[2] + ASTIGMATIC]

anastomose /ə'nastəmohz/ *verb intrans* to interconnect by anastomosis. ➤ *verb trans* to join (parts, e.g. blood vessels) by anastomosis. [prob back-formation from ANASTOMOSIS]

anastomosis /ə,nastə'mohsis/ *noun* (*pl* **anastomoses** /-seez/) **1** the interconnecting of parts or branches of streams, leaf veins, blood vessels, etc. **2** the surgical joining of two hollow organs, e.g. the rejoining of the gut after part has been removed. ➤➤ **anastomotic** /-'motik/ *adj*. [via late Latin from Greek *anastomōsis*, from *anastomoun* to provide with an outlet, from ANA- + *stoma* mouth]

anastrophe /ə'nastrəfi/ *noun* a rhetorical device involving the reversal of the usual order of words, e.g. in *Never have I been so embarrassed* instead of *I have never been so embarrassed*, often used for emphasis. [via medieval Latin from Greek *anastrophē*, literally 'turning back', from *anastrephein* to turn back, from ANA- + *strephein* to turn]

anat. *abbr* **1** anatomical. **2** anatomy.

anathema /ə'nathəmə/ *noun* **1** somebody or something despised or unacceptable: *His opinions are anathema to me*. **2a** a ban or curse solemnly pronounced by ecclesiastical authority and accompanied by excommunication, or the person or thing that is the object of such a ban or curse. **b** a vigorous denunciation; a curse: *Thereupon Dan Cullen sat up on his crazy couch and pronounced anathema upon her and all her breed* — Jack London. [via late Latin from Greek *anathema* thing devoted to evil, curse, from *anatithenai* to dedicate, from ANA- + *tithenai* to put]

anathematize *or* **anathematise** *verb trans* **1** to curse (somebody or something). **2** to proclaim an anathema on (somebody or something).

Anatolian /anə'tohli·ən/ *noun* **1** a native or inhabitant of Anatolia, which forms the greater part of Turkey. **2** a branch of the Indo-European language family consisting of a group of extinct languages of ancient Anatolia, including Hittite. ➤➤ **Anatolian** *adj*.

anatomical /anə'tomikl/ *or* **anatomic** *adj* of anatomy: *an anatomical treatise*. ➤➤ **anatomically** *adv*.

anatomise /ə'natəmiez/ *verb trans* see ANATOMIZE.

anatomist /ə'natəmist/ *noun* **1** somebody who studies or is an expert in anatomy. **2** somebody who analyses something minutely and critically: *an anatomist of modern society*.

anatomize *or* **anatomise** /ə'natəmiez/ *verb trans* **1** to dissect (a corpse). **2** to analyse (something) minutely and critically.

anatomy /ə'natəmi/ *noun* (*pl* **anatomies**) **1a** the branch of biology or medicine that deals with the structure of people, animals, and plants. **b** the process of separating the parts of people, animals, and plants in order to ascertain their position, relations, structure, and function; dissection. **2** structural make-up, *esp* of an organism or part of it. **3** a detailed analysis of any kind: *The anatomy of British society*. **4** *informal* the human body. [Middle English via French and late Latin from Greek *anatomē* dissection, from *anatemnein* to dissect, from ANA- + *temnein* to cut]

anatomy art *noun* **1** a form of sculpture in which preserved human and animal bodies are exhibited in such a way as to show their structure, muscles, and internal organs: compare PLASTINATION. **2** painting that illustrates the structure of human or animal bodies in a creative and artistic way.

anatto /ə'natoh/ *noun* see ANNATTO.

ANC *abbr* African National Congress.

-ance *suffix* forming nouns, denoting: **1** an action or process, or an instance of one: *furtherance*; *performance*. **2** a quality or state, or an instance of one: *brilliance*; *protuberance*. **3** an amount or degree: *conductance*. [Middle English via Old French from Latin *-antia*]

ancestor /'ansestə, -səstə/ *noun* **1** somebody from whom a person is descended, usu more distant than a grandparent. **2** an animal or plant from which a more recent species has evolved. **3** an earlier type or model from which a more recent version has developed. [Middle English *ancestre* via Old French from Latin *antecessor* somebody or something that goes before, from *antecedere* to go before, from ANTE- + *cēdere* to go]

ancestral /an'sestrəl/ *adj* of or inherited from an ancestor: *ancestral estates*. ➤➤ **ancestrally** *adv.*

ancestry /'ansestri, -səstri/ *noun* (*pl* **ancestries**) **1** a line of *esp* noble descent; a lineage. **2** (*treated as sing. or pl*) one's ancestors as a group.

anchor¹ /'angkə/ *noun* **1** a device dropped from a ship or boat to hold it in a particular place, typically a large metal hook that digs into the seabed. **2** something that serves to hold an object firmly in place. **3** somebody or something providing support, stability, and security; a mainstay. **4** an anchorman or anchorwoman. **5** *Brit, informal* (*in pl*) a vehicle's brakes. ✳ **at anchor** said of a ship: held in position by an anchor. **drop anchor** to lower the anchor of a ship to hold it in position. ➤➤ **anchorless** *adj.* [Old English *ancor*, *ancra* via Latin from Greek *ankyra*]

anchor² *verb* (**anchored, anchoring**) ➤ *verb trans* **1** to hold (a boat or ship) in place in the water by means of an anchor. **2** to secure (something) firmly in place. ➤ *verb intrans* **1** to drop anchor. **2** to become fixed; to settle.

anchorage /'angkərij/ *noun* **1** a place where boats and ships are anchored or can anchor. **2** the act or an instance of anchoring a boat or ship, or a charge for this. **3** something that provides a secure hold or attachment. **4** reassurance, security, or stability, or a source of these.

anchoress /'angk(ə)ris/ *noun* a female anchorite.

anchorite /'angkəriet/ *noun* somebody who lives in seclusion, usu for religious reasons; a hermit. ➤➤ **anchoritic** /-'ritik/ *adj.* [Middle English from medieval Latin *anchoreta*, ultimately from Greek *anachōrein* to withdraw]

anchorman *or* **anchorwoman** *noun* (*pl* **anchormen** *or* **anchorwomen**) **1** a man or woman who competes last, e.g. in a relay race. **2** in television and radio broadcasting, a man or woman who links up with outside reporters from a central studio.

anchor person *noun chiefly NAmer* an anchorman or anchorwoman.

anchovy /'anchəvi/ *noun* (*pl* **anchovies** *or collectively* **anchovy**) **1** a common small Mediterranean fish that resembles a herring and is often preserved in oil and salt and used as a garnish: *Engraulis encrasicholus*. **2** any of several species of related fish: genus *Engraulis*. [possibly Spanish *anchova*, ultimately from Greek *aphyē* small fry]

anchusa /ang'kyoosə/ *noun* any of a genus of Eurasian herbaceous plants with hairy leaves and stems and usu bright blue flowers: genus *Anchusa*. [scientific Latin from Greek *ankhousa*]

anchylose /'angkilohz/ *verb intrans* see ANKYLOSE.

anchylosis /angki'lohsis/ *noun* see ANKYLOSIS.

ancien régime /,onsi·an ray'zheem (*French* ɑ̃sjɛ̃ reʒim)/ *noun* (*pl* **anciens régimes** /,onsi·an ray'zheemz (*French* ɑ̃sjɛ̃ reʒim)/) **1** the political and social system of France before the Revolution of 1789. **2** any system or arrangement which has been superseded. [French *ancien régime* old regime]

ancient¹ /'aynsh(ə)nt/ *adj* **1** having existed for many years: *ancient customs*. **2** belonging to a remote period of history, *esp* from the time of the earliest known civilizations to the fall of the western Roman Empire in AD 476. **3** *informal* very old or old-fashioned.

➤➤ **anciently** *adv*, **ancientness** *noun*. [Middle English *ancien* via Old French from Latin *ante* before]

ancient² *noun* (**the ancients**) members of an ancient civilization, *esp* the ancient Greeks and Romans.

ancient history *noun* **1** the history of the ancient civilizations, *esp* those of Greece and Rome. **2** something which has been common knowledge for a long time.

ancient lights *pl noun* (*treated as sing.*) a legally enforceable right to unobstructed daylight from an opening, e.g. a window, in a building.

ancient monument *noun Brit* any structure such as a building or ruin that has been scheduled by the government for preservation because of its historical or architectural value and interest.

ancillary¹ /an'siləri/ *adj* **1** giving support; auxiliary. **2** having a less important position or role; subordinate. [Latin *ancillaris* of a maidservant, ultimately from *anculus* servant]

ancillary² *noun* (*pl* **ancillaries**) *Brit* somebody who assists, *esp* somebody who provides essential support to medical staff but is not medically qualified.

ancon /'angkon/ *noun* (*pl* **ancones** /ang'kohneez/) either of the carved brackets used to support a classical door cornice. [via Latin from Greek *ankōn* elbow]

-ancy *suffix* forming nouns, denoting: a quality or state: *piquancy*; *expectancy*. [Middle English via Old French from Latin *-antia*]

ancylostomiasis /,ansilostə'mie·əsis/ *or* **ankylostomiasis** /,angkilohstə'mie·əsis/ *noun* **1** infestation of the intestine by parasitic bloodsucking hookworms. **2** the condition this causes, which, if untreated, can lead to severe anaemia and malnutrition. [scientific Latin, from *Ancylostoma* the genus name of the hookworm + -IASIS]

AND¹ *abbr* Andorra (international vehicle registration).

AND² *noun* in computing, a logic circuit with two or more inputs and one output, the value of the output being 1 if the values of all inputs are 1, and 0 otherwise.

and /(ə)n, (ə)nd; *strong* and/ *conj* **1** used to join coordinate sentence elements of the same class or function, expressing addition or combination: *She was cold and hungry*; *John and I*. **2** used to express the addition of numbers: *Three and three make six*; *three hundred and seventeen*. **3** used to link clauses to express additional information, consequence, etc: *She's ill and can't travel*; *Water the seeds and they will grow*. **4** used to join repeated words expressing continuation or progression: *They ran and ran*; *It grew larger and larger*. **5** *informal* used instead of *to* after *come*, *go*, *run*, *try*, and *stop*: *Come and look at this*. **6** *archaic* = IF¹. ✳ **and/or** used to indicate that two words or expressions may be taken together or individually. [Old English *and*, *ond*]

-and *suffix* forming nouns, denoting: a person or thing treated in the way specified: *multiplicand*; *analysand*. [Latin *-andus*]

Andalusian /andə'loohsh(ə)n, -syən/ *noun* **1** a native or inhabitant of Andalusia, in southern Spain. **2** the variety of Spanish spoken in Andalusia. ➤➤ **Andalusian** *adj.*

andante /an'dantay/ *adj and adv* said of a piece of music: to be performed moderately slowly. ➤➤ **andante** *noun*. [Italian *andante*, literally 'going', present part. of *andare* to go]

andantino /andan'teenoh/ *adj and adv* said of a piece of music: to be performed slightly faster than andante. ➤➤ **andantino** *noun*. [Italian *andantino*, dimin. of *andante*: see ANDANTE]

Andean /an'dee·ən, 'andi·ən/ *noun* a native or inhabitant of the region of the Andes, a mountain range in S America. ➤➤ **Andean** *adj.*

andiron /'andie·ən/ *noun* either of a pair of metal stands used on a hearth to support burning wood. [Middle English *aundiren* via Old French from assumed Gaulish *anderos* young bull]

Andorran /an'dawrən/ *noun* a native or inhabitant of Andorra, in the S Pyrenees. ➤➤ **Andorran** *adj.*

andr- *or* **andro-** *comb. form* forming words, with the meanings: **1** man: *androgynous*. **2** male: *androecium*. [early French *andr-* via Latin from Greek *andr-*, *anēr* man, male]

androcentric /androh'sentrik/ *adj* focused on or geared towards men. ➤➤ **androcentrism** *noun*.

androecium /an'dreesyəm, -sh(y)əm/ *noun* (*pl* **androecia** /-syə, -sh(y)ə/) all the stamens collectively in the flower of a plant. [scientific Latin *androecium*, from ANDR- + Greek *oikion*, dimin. of *oikos* house]

androgen /'andrəjən/ *noun* any of a number of hormones, such as testosterone, that influence the development of the male reproductive system. >> **androgenic** /-'jenik/ *adj*.

androgyne¹ /'andrəjien/ *noun* = HERMAPHRODITE. [French *androgyne* from Latin *androgynus*: see ANDROGYNOUS]

androgyne² *adj* = ANDROGYNOUS.

androgynous /an'drojinəs/ *adj* **1a** combining features that are typically male with features that are typically female and therefore of uncertain sex. **b** having characteristics of both the male and female forms; hermaphrodite. **2** bearing both male and female flowers in the same cluster. >> **androgyny** /-ni/ *noun*. [via Latin from Greek *androgynos* hermaphrodite, from ANDR- + *gynē* woman]

android /'androyd/ *noun* in science fiction, an automaton that looks and behaves like a human. [late Greek *androeidēs* manlike, from Greek ANDR- + *-oeides* -OID]

andropause /'andrəpawz/ *noun* = MALE MENOPAUSE.

androsterone /an'drostərohn/ *noun* an androgenic steroid hormone that is found in the testes and in the urine of both males and females. formula $C_{19}H_{30}O_2$. [ANDR- + STEROL + -ONE]

-androus *comb. form* forming adjectives, with the meaning: having the number or type of stamens specified: *monandrous*. [scientific Latin *-andrus* from Greek *-andros* having men of a particular kind or number]

ane /ayn/ *adj, noun, and pronoun Scot* one. [Middle English (northern dialect) *an* from Old English *ān*]

-ane *suffix* forming nouns, denoting: a saturated carbon compound, *esp* a hydrocarbon of the alkane series: *methane; alkane*. [alteration of -ENE, -INE², and -ONE]

anecdotage /anik'dohtij/ *noun* **1** anecdotes in general, or the telling of them. **2** *humorous* old age accompanied by a tendency to tell too many stories: *Grandfather's in his anecdotage now*. [(sense 1) ANECDOTE + -AGE; (sense 2) blend of ANECDOTE and DOTAGE]

anecdotal /anik'dohtl/ *adj* **1** existing in the form of an anecdote, *esp* as distinct from corroborated evidence or proof. **2** containing anecdotes or depicting an anecdote: *anecdotal art*. >> **anecdotally** *adv*.

anecdote /'anikdoht/ *noun* a usu short account of an interesting or amusing incident. >> **anecdotalist** /-'dohtəlist/ *noun*, **anecdotic** /-'dotik/ *adj*, **anecdotical** /-'dotikl/ *adj*, **anecdotist** /'anikdohtist/ *noun*. [French *anecdote* from Greek *anekdota* unpublished items, neuter pl of *anekdotos* unpublished, from A-² + *ekdotos* published]

anechoic /ane'kohik/ *adj technical* free from echoes and reverberations.

anem- *or* **anemo-** *comb. form* forming words, denoting: wind: *anemometer*. [prob via French *anémo-* from Greek *anem-, anemo-*, from *anemos*]

anemia /ə'neemi·ə/ *noun NAmer* see ANAEMIA.

anemic *adj NAmer* see ANAEMIC.

anemo- *comb. form* see ANEM-.

anemograph /ə'neməgrahf/ *noun* an anemometer that records its measurements graphically. >> **anemographic** /-'grafik/ *adj*.

anemometer /ani'momitə/ *noun* an instrument for measuring the force or speed of the wind. >> **anemometric** /-moh'metrik/ *adj*, **anemometrical** /-moh'metrikl/ *adj*, **anemometry** *noun*.

anemone /ə'neməni/ *noun* **1** any of various plants of the buttercup family with lobed or divided leaves and brightly coloured flowers: genus *Anemone*. **2** a flower of this plant. **3** = SEA ANEMONE. [via Latin from Greek *anemōnē*, perhaps related by folk etymology to *anemos* wind, but from a word of Semitic origin; related to Hebrew *Na'ǎmān*, epithet of Adonis]

anemophilous /ani'mofiləs/ *adj* said of flowering plants: pollinated by the wind. >> **anemophily** *noun*. [ANEMO- + -PHILOUS]

anencephaly /anin'sefəli, -'kefəli/ *noun* a birth defect in which part or all of the brain is absent. >> **anencephalic** /-'falik/ *adj*. [A-² + Greek *encephalos* brain]

anent /ə'nent/ *prep archaic or Scot* about or concerning (something): *The parlour-maid gave notice, having been terrified ... by an outbreak of sudden temper on the part of the master anent some underdone cutlets* — Saki. [Old English *on efen* alongside, from ON¹ + *efen* EVEN¹]

aneroid /'anəroyd/ *adj* containing no liquid or operated without the use of liquid: *an aneroid manometer*. [French *anéroïde*, from Greek A-² + late Greek *nēron* water + -OID]

aneroid barometer *noun* a barometer in which the action of atmospheric pressure in compressing an evacuated metal capsule is made to move a pointer.

anesthesia /anəs'theezyə, -zh(y)ə/ *noun NAmer* see ANAESTHESIA.

anesthesiology /,anəs,theezi'oləji/ *noun NAmer* see ANAESTHESIOLOGY. >> **anesthesiologist** *noun*.

anesthetic /anəs'thetik/ *noun and adj NAmer* see ANAESTHETIC¹, ANAESTHETIC².

anesthetist /ə'neesthətist/ *noun NAmer* see ANAESTHETIST.

anesthetize /ə'neesthətiez/ *verb NAmer* see ANAESTHETIZE.

anestrus /a'neestrəs/ *noun NAmer* see ANOESTRUS.

aneurysm *or* **aneurism** /'anyooriz(ə)m/ *noun* a permanent blood-filled swelling of a diseased blood vessel. >> **aneurysmal** /anyoo'rizməl/ *adj*. [Greek *aneurysma*, from *aneurynein* to dilate, from ANA- + *eurynein* to stretch]

anew /ə'nyooh/ *adv chiefly literary* **1** one more time; again. **2** in a new form or way. [Old English *of nīwe*, from OF + *nīwe* NEW¹]

angary /'anggəri/ *noun* the right in international law of a nation at war to seize or destroy property of neutrals for military purposes, subject to the payment of compensation. [late Latin *angaria* service to a lord, via Greek from Persian *angaros* courier]

angel /'aynj(ə)l/ *noun* **1a** a spiritual being, usu depicted in human form with wings, believed to serve as a divine intermediary or acting as a heavenly worshipper. **b** a member of the lowest of the nine orders of celestial beings in the traditional hierarchy. **2** a very kind or loving person or a well-behaved child: *Though women are angels, yet wedlock's the devil* — Byron. **3a** an attendant spirit or guardian. **b** a messenger or harbinger: *angel of death*. **4** *informal* a financial backer of a theatrical venture or other enterprise. **5** *informal* an unexplained signal on a radar screen. **6** a former English gold coin portraying St Michael killing a dragon. [Middle English via Old French and late Latin from Greek *angelos* messenger]

angel cake (*NAmer* **angel food cake**) *noun* a pale very light sponge cake.

angel dust *noun informal* the drug phencyclidine.

Angeleno *or* **Angelino** /anjə'leenoh/ *noun* (*pl* **Angelenos** *or* **Angelinos**) a native or inhabitant of Los Angeles. [American Spanish]

angelfish *noun* (*pl* **angelfishes** *or collectively* **angelfish**) **1** any of several species of brightly coloured bony fishes of warm seas with a body that is narrow from side to side and deep from top to bottom: families Chaetodontidae and Pomacanthidae. **2** = SCALARE. **3** = ANGEL SHARK.

angel food cake *noun NAmer* see ANGEL CAKE.

angelic /an'jelik/ *or* **angelical** /-ikl/ *adj* **1** of angels: *the angelic host*. **2** very pretty, kind, or well-behaved. >> **angelically** *adv*.

angelica /an'jelikə/ *noun* **1** candied stalks of a plant related to the carrot and parsley, used as a decoration on cakes and desserts. **2** the plant from whose stalks candied cake decorations are made, having roots and fruit that are used to produce a flavouring oil: *Angelica archangelica*. **3** any of a genus of related plants: genus *Angelica*. [scientific Latin *Angelica*, genus name, short for medieval Latin *herba angelica*, literally 'angelic plant', from its supposed medicinal properties]

Angelino /anjə'leenoh/ *noun* see ANGELENO.

angelology /aynjəl'oləgi/ *noun* the branch of theology concerned with the study of angels.

angel shark *noun* any of several species of sharks that have broad flat heads and bodies and winglike pectoral fins: genus *Squatina*.

angels on horseback *pl noun* (*treated as sing. or pl*) oysters rolled in bacon, grilled, and served, e.g. on cocktail sticks or toast, as an appetizer or a savoury.

Angelus /'anjələs/ *noun* **1** a Roman Catholic devotion said at morning, noon, and evening to commemorate the Incarnation. **2** (*also* **Angelus bell**) a bell rung to mark the time for saying the prayer. [medieval Latin *angelus* from late Latin *angelus* ANGEL, the first word of the opening verse]

anger¹ /'anggə/ *noun* a strong feeling of displeasure aroused by real or imagined offence or injustice and usu accompanied by the desire to retaliate. [Middle English in the senses 'affliction, anger', from Old Norse *angr* grief]

anger² *verb* (**angered, angering**) > *verb intrans* to become angry. > *verb trans* to make (somebody) angry.

Angevin /'anjəvin/ *noun* **1** a native or inhabitant of Anjou in W France. **2** a member of the dynasty of the Plantagenet kings of England. ⫸ **Angevin** *adj.* [French *Angevin* from medieval Latin *andegavinus*, from *Andegavia* Anjou; used in sense 2 because the Plantagenets were descended from Geoffrey of Anjou, and the early Plantagenet kings also held the title Count of Anjou]

angi- *or* **angio-** *comb. form* forming words, denoting: **1** blood or lymph vessels: *angioma*. **2** seed vessels: *angiosperm*. [scientific Latin from Greek *angeion* vessel, blood vessel, dimin. of *angos* vessel]

angina /an'jienə/ *noun* **1** = ANGINA PECTORIS. **2** any condition marked by painful, often suffocating attacks of choking, or an attack of this kind. ⫸ **anginal** *adj*, **anginose** /'anjinohs/ *adj*. [Latin *angina* quinsy, from *angere* to strangle]

angina pectoris /'pektəris/ *noun* a disease marked by brief attacks of intense chest pain, *esp* on exertion, caused by deficient oxygenation of the heart muscles. [scientific Latin *angina pectoris* angina of the chest]

angio- *comb. form* see ANGI-.

angiogram /'anji·əgram/ *noun* an X-ray photograph of blood vessels.

angiography /anji'ogrəfi/ *noun* **1** a technique for imaging blood and lymph vessels using an X-ray examination after a RADIOPAQUE (opaque to radiation) contrast medium has been introduced. **2** an examination of this kind. ⫸ **angiographic** /anjiə'grafik/ *adj*, **angiographically** /anjiə'grafikli/ *adv*.

angioma /anji'ohmə/ *noun* (*pl* **angiomas** *or* **angiomata** /-tə/) a tumour composed chiefly of blood or lymph vessels. ⫸ **angiomatous** *adj*. [scientific Latin *angioma*, from ANGI- + -OMA]

angioplasty /'anjiohplasti/ *noun* (*pl* **angioplasties**) surgical repair of a blood vessel, *esp* the unblocking or widening of a blocked or narrowed artery, e.g. by means of a tiny balloon inflated inside the artery. ⫸ **angioplastic** /-'plastik/ *adj*. [scientific Latin *angioplasty*, from ANGIO- + -*plasty* denoting plastic surgery, ultimately from Greek *plassein* to mould]

angiosperm /'anji·əspuhm/ *noun* any of a large group of plants, including herbaceous plants, shrubs, grasses, and some trees, that produce flowers and reproduce by means of seeds enclosed within a carpel: compare GYMNOSPERM. ⫸ **angiospermous** /-'spuhməs/ *adj*.

Angl. *abbr* Anglican.

Angle /'anggl/ *noun* a member of a Germanic people who, along with the Saxons and Jutes, invaded England during the fifth cent. AD and settled there, mainly in northern and eastern parts of the country. ⫸ **Anglian** /'anggli·ən/ *noun and adj*. [Latin *Angli* (pl), of Germanic origin]

angle[1] *noun* **1a** a geometric figure or space formed by two lines extending from the same point or by two surfaces diverging from the same line. **b** a measure of the inclination of two lines or surfaces that form an angle, expressed in degrees, minutes, and seconds. **2** a corner. **3a** a precise viewpoint from which something is observed, photographed, filmed, or considered; an aspect. **b** a special approach or technique for accomplishing an objective. **4** = ANGLE IRON. ✳ **at an angle** not straight, parallel, vertical, etc; sloping or slanting. ⫸ **angled** *adj*. [Middle English via Old French from Latin *angulus*]

angle[2] *verb trans* **1a** to place, move, or direct (something) in a sloping or slanting position. **b** to bend or shape (something) into an angle. **2** to present (e.g. a news story) from a particular or prejudiced point of view; to slant. ➤ *verb intrans* to turn or proceed at an angle.

angle[3] *verb intrans* **1** to fish with a hook and line. **2** (*usu* + for) to use clever or devious means to attain or try to attain an objective, *esp* by making known indirectly or subtly what one wants: *We angled for an invitation but we didn't get one.* [Middle English *angelen* from Old English *angel* fishhook, from *anga* hook]

angle[4] *noun archaic* a fishhook.

angle bracket *noun* **1** either of a pair of punctuation marks (<>) used to enclose text. Also called BRACKET[1]. **2** a metal bracket with arms set at right angles, used to support shelving, etc.

angle iron *noun* a rolled steel structural member with an L-shaped cross-section.

angle of depression *noun* the angle formed by the line of sight and the horizontal plane for an object below the horizontal.

angle of elevation *noun* the angle formed by the line of sight and the horizontal plane for an object above the horizontal.

angle of incidence *noun* the angle between the direction of a moving body or ray of light where it meets a surface, and a perpendicular at that point.

angle of reflection *noun* the angle between the direction of a moving body or ray of light after reflection from a point on a surface, and a perpendicular at that point.

angle of refraction *noun* the angle between a refracted ray of light and a perpendicular at the point where the ray meets the interface at which refraction occurs.

angle of repose *noun* the steepest angle at which stones or other loose material on a sloping surface will not slide down.

angler *noun* somebody who fishes with a line and hook; a fisherman.

anglerfish *noun* (*pl* **anglerfishes** *or collectively* **anglerfish**) a marine fish with a large flat head and wide mouth with a lure on the head that is used to attract smaller fishes as prey: *Lophius piscatorius* and others.

Anglican[1] /'angglikən/ *adj* belonging or relating to the established episcopal Church of England and Churches of similar faith in communion with it. ⫸ **Anglicanism** *noun*. [medieval Latin *anglicanus* from *anglicus* English, ultimately from Latin *Angli*: see ANGLE]

Anglican[2] *noun* a member of the Anglican Church.

anglicise /'anggliesiez/ *verb trans* see ANGLICIZE.

Anglicism /'angglisiz(ə)m/ *noun* **1** a characteristic feature of English occurring in another language. **2** adherence or attachment to England, English culture, etc. **3** the fact or quality of being English, *esp* typically so. [medieval Latin *anglicus*: see ANGLICAN[1]]

Anglicist /'angglisist/ *noun* a specialist in English language, literature, or culture, usu somebody who is not a native speaker of English.

anglicize *or* **anglicise** /'anggliesiez/ *verb trans* **1** (*often* **Anglicize**) to make (somebody or something) English in tastes or characteristics. **2** to adapt (a foreign word or phrase) to English usage. ⫸ **anglicization** /-sie'zaysh(ə)n, -si'zaysh(ə)n/ *noun*.

angling /'anggling/ *noun* the sport or activity of fishing with hook and line.

Anglo /'anggloh/ *noun* (*pl* **Anglos**) a white person whose first language is English, *esp* one living in the USA. The term is often used as a means of distinguishing such a person from those of Latin, Hispanic, or French origin.

Anglo- *comb. form* forming words, with the meanings: **1** English or British nation, people, or culture: *Anglophobia*. **2** English or British and: *Anglo-American*. [Latin *Anglo*, from late Latin *Angli*: see ANGLE]

Anglo-Catholic *adj* relating to or denoting a High Church movement in Anglicanism fostering Catholic traditions of belief and forms of worship. ⫸ **Anglo-Catholic** *noun*, **Anglo-Catholicism** *noun*.

Anglo-Indian *noun* **1** a British person who lived for a long time in India, *esp* during the time when India was part of the British Empire. **2** a Eurasian of mixed British and Indian birth or descent. ⫸ **Anglo-Indian** *adj*.

Anglo-Irish *pl noun* the formerly dominant group of English Protestant settlers in Ireland. ⫸ **Anglo-Irish** *adj*.

Anglomania /ang·glə'maynyə/ *noun* excessive fondness for English customs, institutions, etc. ⫸ **Anglomaniac** /-'mayni·ak/ *noun*.

Anglo-Norman *adj* **1** relating to or denoting relations between England and Normandy around the time of the Norman invasion. **2** relating to the form of French used in England after the Norman Conquest.

Word history

After the Norman Conquest in 1066, French became the language of the court, government, church, and law in England. Of the numerous French words borrowed into English within the next four centuries, most reflect its status as the language of administration and polite society. French is, for example, the source of many central terms in modern legal vocabulary: *dowry, elope, embezzle, endow, jeopardy, jury, lease, mayhem, nuisance, purloin, trial, verdict, waiver*, and so on. Other borrowings from French in the medieval period include *chronicle, citizen, enhance, exchequer, improve, mariner, noun, packet, perform, pleasant, scourge, several, soil, surgeon, toil, tomb, wager*, and *wreck*. After the political severance of England and

Normandy in 1204, the upper classes gradually acquired English. See also note at FRENCH[2].

Anglophile /'angglәfiel, -fil/ *or* **Anglophil** /-fil/ *noun* (*also* **anglophile**) somebody who is greatly interested in and admires England or Britain, its people, culture, etc. >> **Anglophilia** /-'fili·ә/ *noun*, **Anglophilic** /-'filik/ *adj.* [French *anglophile*, from ANGLO- + -PHILE]

Anglophobe /'angglәfohb/ *noun* (*also* **anglophobe**) somebody who hates or fears England or Britain, its people, culture, etc. >> **Anglophobia** /-'fohbi·ә/ *noun*, **Anglophobic** /-'fohbik/ *adj.* [prob from French *anglophobe*]

Anglophone[1] /'angglәfohn/ *adj* consisting of, belonging to, or relating to an English-speaking population or community, *esp* as contrasted with a French-speaking population or community. compare FRANCOPHONE[1].

Anglophone[2] *noun* a member of an English-speaking population or community, *esp* as contrasted with a member of a French-speaking population or community.

Anglo-Saxon *noun* 1 a member of the Germanic peoples who conquered England in the fifth cent. AD and formed the ruling group until the Norman conquest in 1066. 2 = OLD ENGLISH. 3 loosely, a white person of English or British descent or whose first language is English. 4 *informal* direct or indecent English speech or writing. >> **Anglo-Saxon** *adj.* [Latin *Anglo-Saxones* (pl) alteration of medieval Latin *Angli Saxones*, from Latin *Angli* (see ANGLE) + late Latin *Saxones* (see SAXON)]

Angolan /ang'gohlәn/ *noun* a native or inhabitant of Angola, in SW Africa. >> **Angolan** *adj.*

angora /ang'gawrә/ *noun* 1 the hair of the Angora rabbit or goat. 2a a fabric or yarn made wholly or partly of Angora rabbit or goat hair, used *esp* for knitting: compare MOHAIR. b (*used before a noun*) consisting of or made from this fabric or yarn: *an angora jumper.* 3 (**Angora**) an Angora cat, goat, or rabbit. [*Angora*, former name of Ankara, capital of Turkey]

Angora cat *noun* a cat of a long-haired domestic breed.

Angora goat *noun* a goat of a domestic breed with long silky hair which is the true mohair.

Angora rabbit *noun* a rabbit of a long-haired, usu white, domestic breed.

angostura bark /anggә'stooәrә/ *noun* the aromatic bitter bark of a S American tree of the rue family used as a flavouring and formerly as a tonic and a treatment for fever. [*Angostura*, now called Ciudad Bolívar, town in Venezuela]

Angostura bitters *noun trademark* a bitter aromatic tonic added to alcoholic drinks as a flavouring.

angry /'anggri/ *adj* (**angrier, angriest**) 1a (*often* + about/at/with) feeling or showing anger. b caused by or expressing anger: *angry words.* 2 seeming to show or typify anger: *an angry sky.* 3 painfully inflamed: *an angry rash.* >> **angrily** *adv*, **angriness** *noun*.

angst /angst/ *noun* anxiety and anguish, caused *esp* by considering the state of the world and the human condition. [Danish *Angst* fear; the word was first used in this sense by Søren Kierkegaard d.1855, Danish philosopher]

angstrom /'angstrәm, 'angstrom/ *or* **ångström** /'angstrom/ *noun* a unit of length equal to 10^{-10}m, used *esp* in measuring electromagnetic radiation wavelength. [named after Anders J Ångström d.1874, Swedish physicist]

Anguillan /ang'gwilәn/ *noun* a native or inhabitant of Anguilla, one of the Leeward Islands in the Caribbean. >> **Anguillan** *adj.*

anguilliform /ang'gwilifawm/ *adj* relating to or denoting eels and similar fish. [Latin *anguilla* eel + -iform (see -FORM)]

anguine /'anggwin/ *adj* of or resembling a snake. [Latin *anguinus*, from *anguis* snake]

anguish /'anggwish/ *noun* extreme mental distress or physical pain. [Middle English *angwisshe* via Old French from Latin *angustiae* (pl) straits, distress, from *angustus* narrow]

anguished *adj* suffering or expressing anguish.

angular /'anggyoolә/ *adj* 1a having one or more angles. b forming an angle; sharp-cornered. c placed, attached, etc at an angle. 2 measured by an angle or with reference to the rate at which an angle changes: *angular distance; angular separation.* 3a lean and bony. b stiff in character or manner; awkward. >> **angularity** /-'lariti/ *noun*, **angularly** *adv.* [early French *angulaire* from Latin *angularis*, from *angulus* ANGLE[1]]

angular momentum *noun* a VECTOR[1] (quantity having both magnitude and direction) that is equal to the angular velocity of a rotating body or system multiplied by its MOMENT OF INERTIA (resistance to change of angular velocity) with respect to the rotation axis.

angular velocity *noun* a VECTOR[1] (quantity having both magnitude and direction) that is equal in magnitude to the rate of change of angular position with time and that has direction such that the motion appears clockwise to somebody looking in the direction of the vector.

angulation /anggoo'layshәn/ *noun* 1 the state of having angles or the formation of angles. 2 an angular position or part.

anhedral[1] /an'heedrәl/ *adj* said *esp* of a crystal: having no plane faces. [from A-[2] + -HEDRAL]

anhedral[2] *noun* the angle between a downwardly inclined wing of an aircraft and a horizontal line: compare DIHEDRAL[2].

anhydride /an'hiedried/ *noun* a compound derived from another, *esp* an acid, by removing the elements of water. [ANHYDROUS + -IDE]

anhydrous /an'hiedrәs/ *adj* containing no water, *esp* no WATER OF CRYSTALLIZATION (water chemically combined in a crystal). [Greek *anydros*, from A-[2] + *hydor* water + -OUS]

anil /'anil/ *noun* 1 a shrub of the pea family, found in the W Indies, which is a source of indigo dye: *Indigofera suffruticosa.* 2 the dye itself. [via French and Portuguese from Arabic *an-nīl* the indigo plant, from Sanskrit *nīlī* indigo, from fem of *nīla* dark blue]

aniline /'anilin, -leen/ *noun* a poisonous colourless oily liquid derived from coal tar and used chiefly in the manufacture of dyes and plastics. [German *Anilin* from *anil* indigo: see ANIL]

aniline dye *noun* any synthetic dye made from or chemically related to aniline.

anilingus /ayni'linggәs/ *noun* sexual stimulation of the anus with the tongue or lips. [scientific Latin *anilingus* from ANUS + *-lingus* as in CUNNILINGUS]

anima /'animә/ *noun* 1 an individual's true inner self: compare PERSONA. 2 in Jungian psychology, the inner feminine part of the male personality: compare ANIMUS. [Latin *anima*, literally 'female soul']

animadversion /,animad'vuhsh(ә)n/ *noun formal* 1 a critical and usu censorious remark. 2 hostile criticism. [Latin *animadversion-, animadversio*, from *animadvertere*: see ANIMADVERT]

animadvert /,animad'vuht/ *verb intrans formal* (*usu* + on/upon) to comment, *esp* critically or adversely, on something. [Latin *animadvertere* to pay attention to, censure, from *animum advertere*, literally 'to turn the mind to']

animal[1] /'animәl/ *noun* 1a a living creature, typically differing from a plant in its capacity for spontaneous movement and rapid response to stimulation: *Man is the only animal that blushes. Or needs to* — Mark Twain. b any living creature apart from a human being. c a mammal, or a mammal or reptile, as opposed to a bird, fish, etc. 2a a person considered as a purely physical being. b a coarse, unfeeling, or cruel person. 3 *informal* a person or thing of a particular kind: *a political animal.* [Latin *animal*, from *animalis* animate, from *anima* soul]

animal[2] *adj* 1 of or derived from animals. 2 of the body as opposed to the mind or spirit: *animal lust.* 3 relating to the part of an embryo that contains active cytoplasm.

animalcule /ani'malkyoohl/ *or* **animalculum** /ani'malkyoolәm/ *noun* (pl **animalcules** *or* **animalcula** /-lә/) a minute usu microscopic organism, e.g. an amoeba. >> **animalcular** *adj.* [scientific Latin *animalculum*, dimin. of Latin *animal*: see ANIMAL[1]]

animal husbandry *noun* a branch of agriculture concerned with the breeding and care of domestic animals.

animalise /'animәliez/ *verb trans* see ANIMALIZE.

animalism /'animәliz(ә)m/ *noun* 1a behaviour that demonstrates qualities thought to be typical of animals, *esp* lack of spiritual feeling. b preoccupation with the satisfaction of physical needs and urges; sensuality. 2 a theory that human beings do not have a spiritual nature. >> **animalist** *noun*, **animalistic** /-'listik/ *adj.*

animality /ani'maliti/ *noun* 1a behaviour typical of animals. b behaviour in or characteristics of humans thought to be more typical of animals, e.g. a lack of spiritual feeling or rational thought. 2 the state of being an animal.

animalize *or* **animalise** /'animәliez/ *verb trans* 1 to make (somebody) unfeeling or inhuman; to brutalize (somebody): *The faces of* *men animalized by war.* **2** to cause (somebody) to be ruled by their physical needs and urges, at the expense of their spiritual or emotional side; to sensualize (somebody): *animalized by passion.* ➤➤ **animalization** /-lie'zaysh(ə)n, -li'zaysh(ə)n/ *noun.*

animal kingdom *noun* the one of the three basic groups of natural objects that includes all living and extinct animals: compare MINERAL KINGDOM, PLANT KINGDOM.

animal liberation *noun* **1** the freeing of animals from captivity by people who believe that animals should not be exploited by humans. **2** a movement that advocates the freeing of animals.

animal magnetism *noun* **1** powerful physical charm or sexual attractiveness. **2** *dated* a force that some individuals are said to possess and by which a strong hypnotic influence can be exerted.

animal rights *pl noun* (*treated as sing. or pl*) the rights of animals not to be exploited for human advantage.

animal spirits *pl noun* natural vitality.

animate¹ /'animayt/ *verb trans* **1** to make (something) lively and interesting. **2** to give confidence and support to (somebody); to encourage (somebody). **3** to incite or inspire (somebody) to do something; to move (somebody) to action. **4** to create or film (something) using the techniques of animation. **5** to give life to (something). ➤➤ **animator** *noun.* [Middle English from Latin *animatus,* past part. of *animare* to give life to, from *anima* breath, soul]

animate² /'animət/ *adj* **1** possessing life; alive. **2** relating to animal life. **3** full of energy or life; animated. ➤➤ **animately** *adv,* **animateness** *noun.*

animated /'animaytid/ *adj* **1** full of vigour and spirit; vivacious: *an animated discussion.* **2** full of bustle and activity. **3** made using the techniques of animation: *animated films.* **4** endowed with life or the qualities of life; alive: *Viruses can behave as animated bodies or inert crystals.* ➤➤ **animatedly** *adv,* **animatedness** *noun.*

animated cartoon *noun* a film that creates the illusion of movement by photographing successive positional changes, e.g. of characters in drawings.

animation /ani'maysh(ə)n/ *noun* **1** the state of being lively and full of energy and activity. **2** the technique of filming a sequence of drawings, computer images, or models in different positions so that, in the final film, the characters and other elements in them appear to be moving in a lifelike way: *computer animation.*

animato /ani'mahtoh/ *adj and adv* said of a piece of music: to be performed with liveliness and vigour. [Italian *animato* from Latin *animatus*: see ANIMATE¹]

animatronics /,animə'troniks/ *pl noun* **1** (*treated as sing.*) a branch of theatre and film technology that combines the techniques of traditional puppetry with modern electronics to create animated special effects. **2** the techniques or effects of this. ➤➤ **animatronic** *adj.* [ANIMATION + ELECTRONICS]

anime /'ahneemay/ *noun* a type of animation, orig from Japan, that deals with fantasy relating to the possibilities of modern technology. [Japanese *anime*]

animism /'animiz(ə)m/ *noun* **1** attribution of conscious life, spirits, or souls to nature or natural objects or phenomena. **2** the belief that there is an unseen force that animates the universe. **3** the belief that souls exist independently of bodies. ➤➤ **animist** *noun,* **animistic** /-'mistik/ *adj.* [German *Animismus* from Latin *anima* soul]

animosity /ani'mositi/ *noun* (*pl* **animosities**) a strong feeling of hostility, ill will, or resentment. [Middle English *animosite* via French from Latin *animosus* spirited, from *animus* spirit, mind]

animus /'animəs/ *noun* **1** ill will or hostility; animosity. **2** a pervading attitude or spirit. **3** motivation or sense of purpose. **4** in Jungian psychology, the inner masculine part of the female personality: compare ANIMA. [Latin *animus,* literally 'spirit, mind, courage, anger']

anion /'anie·ən/ *noun* a negatively charged ion that moves towards the anode during electrolysis: compare CATION. ➤➤ **anionic** /-'onik/ *adj,* **anionically** /-'onikli/ *adv.* [Greek *aniōn,* present part. of *anienai* to go up]

anise /'anis/ *noun* a plant of the carrot family with aromatic seeds that have a liquorice-like flavour: *Pimpinella anisum.* [Middle English *anis* via Old French and Latin from Greek *annēson, anison*]

aniseed /'aniseed/ *noun* the seed of anise used as a flavouring in food and drinks. [Middle English *anis* (see ANISE) + SEED¹]

anisette /ani'set (*French* anisεt)/ *noun* a usu colourless liqueur flavoured with aniseed. [French *anisette* from *anis*: see ANISE]

anisotropic /a,niesoh'trohpik, -'tropik/ *adj* said of a crystal: having properties with different values when measured in different directions. ➤➤ **anisotropically** *adv,* **anisotropism** /-'sotrəpiz(ə)m/ *noun,* **anisotropy** /-'sotrəpi/ *noun.* [Greek *aniso* unequal + *tropos* turn + -IC¹]

ankh /angk/ *noun* a cross that has a loop for its upper vertical arm, used in ancient Egypt as an emblem of life. [Egyptian *'nh* life, soul]

ankle /'angkl/ *noun* **1a** the joint between the foot and the leg. **b** the part of the leg between the lower calf and this joint. **2** the joint between the cannon bone and pastern of a horse or related animal. [Old English *anclēow*]

ankle-biter *noun chiefly NAmer, Aus, NZ, informal* a young child.

anklebone *noun* the large protruding bone in the ankle; the TALUS².

anklet /'angklit/ *noun* an ornamental band or chain worn round the ankle.

ankylose *or* **anchylose** /'angkilohz/ *verb intrans* said of a joint or bone: to become stiff or fused owing to ankylosis. [back-formation from *ankylosis*]

ankylosis *or* **anchylosis** /angki'lohsis/ *noun* (*pl* **ankyloses** *or* **anchyloses** /-seez/) **1** the fusing of the bones in a joint resulting in a stiff or immovable joint. **2** union of separate bones or hard parts to form a single bone or part. ➤➤ **ankylotic** /-'lotik/ *adj.* [scientific Latin from Greek *ankylōsis,* from *ankyloun* to make crooked]

ankylostomiasis /,angkilohstə'mie·əsis/ *noun* see ANCYLO-STOMIASIS.

anlage /'anlahgə/ *noun* (*pl* **anlagen** /-gən/ *or* **anlages** /-gəz/) **1** the part of an embryo that will develop into a particular organ. **2** any foundation for future development. [German *Anlage,* literally 'design, construction, foundation']

ann. *abbr* **1** annals. **2** annual. **3** annuity.

anna /'anə/ *noun* a former money unit of India, Pakistan, Bangladesh, and Myanmar, worth one sixteenth of a rupee. [Hindi *ānā*]

annalist /'anəlist/ *noun* a writer of annals; a historian.

annals /'anlz/ *pl noun* **1a** a record of events, activities, etc, arranged in yearly sequence. **b** historical records; chronicles. **2** records of the activities of an organization, e.g. a learned society. ➤➤ **annalistic** /-'listik/ *adj.* [Latin *annales,* pl of *annalis* yearly, from *annus* year]

annates /'anayts/ *pl noun* formerly, a payment to the pope of a newly appointed Roman Catholic bishop's first year of income. [Latin *annata* a year's proceeds, from *annus* year]

annatto *or* **anatto** /ə'natoh/ *noun* (*pl* **annattos** *or* **anattos**) **1** a yellowish red dye made from the pulp that surrounds the seeds of a tropical tree. **2** the tropical American tree from which annatto is obtained: *Bixa orellana.* [of Cariban origin; related to Galibi *annoto* tree producing annatto]

anneal /ə'neel/ *verb trans* **1** to toughen or relieve internal stresses in (steel, glass, etc) by heating and usu gradual cooling. **2** to strengthen (something, e.g. resolve or commitment). ➤➤ **annealer** *noun.* [Old English *onǣlan,* from ON¹ + *ǣlan* to set on fire, burn]

annelid /'anəlid/ *noun* any of a phylum of invertebrate animals, including the earthworms and leeches, that have a long segmented body: phylum Annelida. ➤➤ **annelid** *adj,* **annelidan** /ə'nelidən/ *adj and noun.* [derivative of Latin *anellus,* dimin. of *annulus* ring]

annex¹ /ə'neks/ *verb trans* **1** to add (something) as an extra part; to append. **2** to incorporate (a country or other territory) within the domain of a state. **3** to attach (something) as a consequence or condition. **4** to take or use (something), *esp* without permission: *The true artist is known by the use he makes of what he annexes* — Oscar Wilde. ➤➤ **annexable** *adj,* **annexation** /anek'saysh(ə)n/ *noun,* **annexationist** /-'saysh(ə)nist/ *noun and adj.* [Middle English *annexen* via Old French from Latin *annexus,* past part. of *annectere* to bind to]

annex² *or* **annexe** /'aneks/ *noun* **1** a separate or attached extra structure, *esp* a building providing extra accommodation. **2** something added as an extra part, *esp* an addition to a document.

annihilate /ə'nie·əlayt/ *verb trans* **1** to destroy (something) entirely. **2** *informal* to defeat (somebody) conclusively; to rout or thrash (somebody). ➤ *verb intrans* (*also* + into) said of a subatomic particle and its antiparticle: to undergo annihilation; to be converted to energy by annihilation. ⋙ **annihilator** *noun*. [late Latin *annihilatus*, past part. of *annihilare* to reduce to nothing, from AD- + Latin *nihil* nothing]

annihilation /ə,nie-ə'laysh(ə)n/ *noun* **1** annihilating or being annihilated. **2** *informal* a severe beating or complete defeat. **3** in physics, the process in which a particle and antiparticle, e.g. an electron and a positron, collide and are converted into energy.

anni horribiles /,ani ho'reebileez/ *noun* pl of ANNUS HORRIBILIS.

anni mirabiles /,ani mi'rahbileez/ *noun* pl of ANNUS MIRABILIS.

anniversary /ani'vuhs(ə)ri/ *noun* (*pl* **anniversaries**) **1** the date on which a notable event took place in an earlier year, or the celebration of the event held on that date. **2** (*used before a noun*) of or celebrating an anniversary: *an anniversary present*. [Middle English *anniversarie* via medieval Latin from Latin *anniversarium*, neuter of *anniversarius* returning annually, from *annus* year]

Anno Domini /,anoh 'dominie/ *adv* see AD.

anno Domini *noun* (*also* **anno domini**) *informal* advancing old age: *Anno domini — that's the most fatal complaint of all in the end —* James Hilton.

anno hegirae /hi'jie·əree/ *adv* (*also* **Anno Hegirae**) used to indicate that a year or century comes within the Muslim era: compare HEGIRA. [Latin *anno hegirae* 'in the year of the Hegira']

annotate /'anətayt, 'anohtayt/ *verb trans* to provide (e.g. a literary work) with critical or explanatory notes. ⋙ **annotation** /-'taysh(ə)n/ *noun*, **annotative** *adj*, **annotator** *noun*. [Latin *annotatus*, past part. of *annotare* to mark, from AD- + *nota* mark, note]

announce /ə'nowns/ *verb trans* **1** to make (something) known publicly. **2a** to give notice of the arrival or presence of (somebody, e.g. a guest) or readiness of (something, e.g. dinner). **b** to indicate (something) in advance; to foretell: *The dark clouds and quickening winds announced another storm.* **3** to indicate (something) by action or appearance. ⋙ *verb intrans* NAmer to work as an announcer. ⋙ **announcement** *noun*. [Middle English *announcen* via French from Latin *annuntiare* to report, from AD- + *nuntius* messenger]

announcer /ə'nownsə/ *noun* a person who introduces television or radio programmes, makes commercial announcements, reads news summaries, or gives station identification.

annoy /ə'noy/ *verb trans* **1** to make (somebody) mildly angry; to irritate. **2** to bother (somebody) repeatedly; to pester. ⋙ *verb intrans* to be a source of irritation. ⋙ **annoyance** *noun*, **annoyed** *adj*, **annoying** *adj*, **annoyingly** *adv*. [Middle English *anoien* via Old French from late Latin *inodiare* to make loathsome, from Latin *in odio esse* to be hated, from *odium* hatred]

annual[1] /'anyoo(ə)l/ *adj* **1** covering or lasting for the period of a year: *The country has a low annual rainfall.* **2** occurring or performed once a year; yearly: *an annual reunion.* **3** said of a plant: completing the life cycle in one growing season: compare BIENNIAL[1], PERENNIAL[1]. ⋙ **annually** *adv*. [Middle English via Old French and late Latin from Latin *annuus* yearly and *annalis* yearly, both from *annus* year]

annual[2] *noun* **1** a publication that appears once a year. **2** an annual plant.

annual general meeting *noun* Brit a meeting of all the shareholders of a company or members of a club or society, held once a year, e.g. to elect officebearers, approve accounts, etc.

annualize *or* **annualise** /'anyoo·əliez/ *verb trans* to calculate (a rate of interest, dividends, etc) in such a way as to reflect a full year's rate: *The report gives an annualized rate of growth for the company.*

annual percentage rate *noun* the rate of interest charged on a loan, calculated as the percentage of the amount borrowed that would be charged over a full year.

annual ring *noun* the layer of wood produced by a single year's growth of a tree or other woody plant.

annuitant /ə'nyooit(ə)nt/ *noun* formal somebody who receives or who is entitled to receive an annuity.

annuity /ə'nyooəti/ *noun* (*pl* **annuities**) **1** an amount payable at specified intervals during a specified period, often a person's life. **2** the right to receive or the obligation to pay an annuity, or a contract setting this out. **3** an investment or insurance that will pay an annuity. [Middle English *annuite* via French and medieval Latin from Latin *annuus*: see ANNUAL[1]]

annul /ə'nul/ *verb trans* (**annulled, annulling**) **1** to declare (something, e.g. a marriage) legally invalid. **2** to cancel or abolish (something). ⋙ **annullable** *adj*, **annulment** *noun*. [Middle English

annullen via Old French from late Latin *annullare*, from AD- + Latin *nullus* not any]

annular /'anyoolə/ *adj* in the shape of a ring. ⋙ **annularity** /-'lar-iti/ *noun*, **annularly** *adv*. [French *annulaire* from Latin *annularis*, from *annulus* ring]

annular eclipse *noun* an eclipse of the sun in which a thin outer ring of the sun's disc remains visible.

annulate /'anyoolət/ *or* **annulated** /'anyoolaytid/ *adj* marked with rings or in the shape of a ring. ⋙ **annulation** *noun*.

annulet /'anyoolət/ *noun* a small ring or circle, e.g. a thin ring around an architectural column or a ring-shaped mark on a heraldic shield. [modification of Old French *annelet* small ring, ultimately from Latin *annulus*: see ANNULUS]

annulus /'anyooləs/ *noun* (*pl* **annuli** /-lie/ *or* **annuluses**) *technical* a ring-shaped area, structure, or marking. [Latin *annulus*, dimin. of *anus* ring: see ANUS]

annunciate /ə'nunsiayt/ *verb trans* formal to announce (something). ⋙ **annunciatory** /-si·ət(ə)ri/ *adj*.

annunciation /ə,nunsi'aysh(ə)n/ *noun* **1** (**the Annunciation**). **a** the announcement by the angel Gabriel to the Virgin Mary that she would be the mother of Jesus Christ, related in Luke 1:26–38. **b** a festival of the Christian Church commemorating this, held on Lady Day, 25 March. **2** *archaic or formal* an announcement. [Middle English *annunciacioun* via Old French from Latin *annuntiatus*, past part. of *annuntiare* to announce]

annunciator *noun* a device that shows when an electric circuit has been operated, e.g. a board with bells or lights to show to which room of a large house the servants are being summoned.

annus horribilis /,anəs ho'ribilis/ *noun* (*pl* **anni horribiles** /,ani ho'reebileez/) a year marked by misfortune or disaster. [Latin *annus horribilis*, literally 'terrifying year'; modelled on *annus mirabilis* and used by Queen Elizabeth II to refer to the events of 1992]

annus mirabilis /,anəs mi'rahbilis/ *noun* (*pl* **anni mirabiles** /,ani mi'rahbileez/) a remarkable or wonderful year. [Latin *annus mirabilis*, literally 'remarkable year'; orig applied to 1666, the year of the Great Fire of London]

anoa /ə'noh·ə/ *noun* (*pl* **anoas**) a small water buffalo that resembles a deer, native to Sulawesi (Celebes) in Indonesia: *Anoa depressicornis.* [native name]

anode /'anohd/ *noun* **1** the electrode by which electrons leave a device and enter an external circuit, e.g.: **a** the negative terminal of a battery: compare CATHODE. **b** the positive electrode in an electrolytic cell. **2** the electrode in a thermionic valve or similar electronic device which collects the electrons. ⋙ **anodal** /ə'no-hdl/ *adj*, **anodally** /ə'noh-/ *adv*, **anodic** /ə'nodik/ *adj*, **anodically** /ə'nod-/ *adv*. [Greek *anodos* way up, from ANA- + *hodos* way]

anodize *or* **anodise** /'anədiez/ *verb trans* to subject (something metal) to electrolytic action by making it the anode of a cell in order to coat it with a protective or decorative film. ⋙ **anodization** /-'zaysh(ə)n/ *noun*.

anodyne[1] /'anədien/ *adj* **1** mild or inoffensive to the point of being dull. **2** mentally or emotionally soothing. **3** easing pain. [via Latin from Greek *anōdynos*, from A-[2] + *ōdynē* pain]

anodyne[2] *noun* **1** a painkilling drug. **2** something that soothes or calms. ⋙ **anodynic** /-'dinik/ *adj*.

anoestrus (NAmer **anestrus**) /a'neestrəs/ *noun* a period in which there is no sexual activity between two periods of sexual activity in cyclically breeding mammals, e.g. dogs. [A-[2] + OESTRUS]

anoint /ə'noynt/ *verb trans* **1a** to put oil on the head, feet, etc of (somebody) as part of a religious ceremony. **b** to confer an official, *esp* religious title on (somebody) by anointing them; to consecrate. **2** to smear or rub (something or somebody) with oil or a similar substance. ⋙ **anointer** *noun*, **anointment** *noun*. [Middle English *anointen* via Old French from Latin *inunguere* to smear, from IN-[2] + *unguin-*, *unguen* ointment]

anointing of the sick *noun* the chiefly Roman Catholic and Eastern Orthodox sacrament of anointing and praying over a sick or elderly person, *esp* one who is close to death. Also called EXTREME UNCTION.

anomalistic /ə,nomə'listik/ *or* **anomalistical** *adj* in astronomy, relating to an ANOMALY (angular distance).

anomalistic month *noun* the average time taken by the moon to travel from the point in its orbit nearest the earth round to that point again, equal to about 27½ days.

anomalistic year *noun* the average time taken by the earth to travel from the point in its orbit nearest the sun round to that point again, equal to 365 days, 6 hours, 13 minutes, and 53 seconds.

anomalous /əˈnoməlǝs/ *adj* deviating from what is usual or expected; irregular. ➤➤ **anomalously** *adv*, **anomalousness** *noun*. [via late Latin from Greek *anōmalos* uneven, from A-² + *homalos* even, from *homos* same]

anomaly /əˈnoməli/ *noun* (*pl* **anomalies**) **1** something that deviates from what is usual or expected. **2** deviation from the norm or from expectations. **3** in astronomy, the angular distance of: **a** a planet from its last PERIHELION (closest point to sun). **b** a satellite from its last PERIGEE (closest point to planet). [via Latin from Greek *anōmalia*, from *anōmalos*: see ANOMALOUS]

anomie *or* **anomy** /ˈanomi/ *noun* lack of moral or social standards of conduct and belief in an individual or community, *esp* when these previously existed: *an emphasis on order and stability (as opposed to anarchy or anomie)* — Guardian. ➤➤ **anomic** /əˈnomik/ *adj*. [French *anomie* from Greek *anomia* lawlessness, from *anomos* lawless, from A-² + *nomos* law]

anon /əˈnon/ *adv* *archaic or informal* in a short while; soon. [Old English *on ān* in one]

anon. *abbr* anonymous.

anonym /ˈanənim/ *noun* **1** an anonymous person or publication. **2** a pseudonym. [French *anonyme* from Greek *anōnumous*: see ANONYMOUS]

anonymize *or* **anonymise** /əˈnonimiez/ *verb trans* to withhold the identities of those involved in (something, *esp* medical procedures or tests).

anonymous /əˈnoniməs/ *adj* **1** giving no name, or from somebody whose name is not known: *an anonymous author; anonymous gifts*. **2** having no outstanding distinguishing features; nondescript. ➤➤ **anonymity** /anəˈnimiti/ *noun*, **anonymously** *adv*, **anonymousness** *noun*. [via late Latin from Greek *anōnymos*, from A-² + *ōnyma* name + -OUS]

anopheles /əˈnofileez/ *noun* (*pl* **anopheles**) any of a genus of mosquitoes including all those that transmit malaria to human beings: genus *Anopheles*. ➤➤ **anopheline** /-lien/ *adj* *and noun*. [scientific Latin *Anopheles*, genus name, from Greek *anōphelēs* useless, from A-² + *ōphelein* to help]

anorak /ˈanərak/ *noun* **1** *chiefly Brit* a short weatherproof coat with a hood. **2** *Brit, informal* somebody with laughably unfashionable or boring hobbies. [Greenland Eskimo *ánorâq*]

anorectic /anəˈrektik/ *adj and noun* see ANOREXIC¹, ANOREXIC².

anorexia /anəˈreksi-ə/ *noun* **1** = ANOREXIA NERVOSA. **2** prolonged loss of appetite. [scientific Latin from Greek *anorexia*, from A-² + *orexia* appetite]

anorexia nervosa /nuhˈvohzə/ *noun* a psychological disorder characterized by an aversion to food induced by an obsessive desire to lose weight and sometimes resulting in life-threatening emaciation. [scientific Latin *anorexia nervosa* nervous anorexia]

anorexic¹ /anəˈreksik/ *or* **anorectic** /anəˈrektik/ *adj* **1** suffering from anorexia nervosa. **2** extremely or unhealthily thin.

anorexic² *or* **anorectic** *noun* a person suffering from anorexia nervosa.

anosmia /aˈnozmi-ə/ *noun* partial or total loss of the sense of smell. ➤➤ **anosmic** *adj*. [scientific Latin *anosmia*, from A-² + Greek *osmē* smell]

A N Other *or* **A.N. Other** /ay en ˈudhə/ *noun* *Brit* used, e.g. in a list of competitors, etc, to indicate a person whose name is as yet unknown.

another¹ /əˈnudhə/ *adj* **1** being a different or distinct one: *the same scene viewed from another angle*. **2** some other: *Do it another time*. **3** being one additional: *Have another piece of pie*. **4** patterned after: *another Napoleon*. [Middle English *an other*]

another² *pronoun* **1** an additional one: *Could you eat another?* **2** a different one: *He loved another*.

anoxia /əˈnoksi-ə/ *noun* deficiency of oxygen, e.g. in body tissue, *esp* so severe that it causes permanent damage. ➤➤ **anoxic** *adj*. [scientific Latin *anoxia*, from A-² + OXYGEN]

Anschluss /ˈanshloos (German ˈanʃlʊs)/ *noun* political union; *specif* the annexation by Germany of Austria in 1938. [German *Anschluss* joining, from *anschliessen* to join]

anserine /ˈansərien, -rin/ *adj* of or resembling a goose or geese. [Latin *anserinus*, from *anser* goose]

ANSI /ˈansi/ *abbr* American National Standards Institute.

answer¹ /ˈahnsə/ *noun* **1** a spoken or written reply to a question, remark, etc. **2** a response, reaction, or result: *His only answer was to walk out; I knocked on the door but there was no answer*. **3** the correct solution to a mathematical, etc problem, or any of several solutions offered. **4** an appropriate procedure for dealing with something: *Advice is what we ask for when we already know the answer but wish we didn't* — Erica Jong. **5** a person or thing regarded as competing with or comparable to another that is well known: *The exhibition is the museum world's answer to Disney*. [Old English *andswaru*]

answer² *verb* (**answered, answering**) ➤ *verb trans* **1a** to speak or write in reply to (somebody or something). **b** to provide an answer or solution to (e.g. a question, problem, etc). **c** to reply to (something, e.g. a charge) in justification or explanation. **2** to act in response to (a telephone, signal, etc). **3a** to match or correspond to (something). **b** to be adequate or usable for (a need or purpose). ➤ *verb intrans* **1** to speak, write, or act in reply. **2** to act in response to a sound or other signal. **3a** (+ for) to be responsible or accountable for something. **b** (+ for) to make amends for something. **4** (+ to) to match or correspond to something: *The police have traced nobody answering to the description*. **5** (+ to) to have or accept a name or nickname: *The girl answered to 'Mary'*. **6** (+ to) to respond to a touch, control, etc. **7** to be adequate or usable: *A paper clip will answer for the time being*. [Old English *andswarian*; related to SWEAR]

answerable *adj* **1** (+ to/for) responsible to somebody for something. **2** said of charges, etc: capable of being answered or refuted. ➤➤ **answerability** /-ˈbiliti/ *noun*.

answer back *verb trans and intrans* to reply (to somebody) insolently or rudely.

answering machine *noun* a device that responds to incoming telephone calls with a recorded message and records messages spoken by the callers.

answerphone /ˈahnsəfohn/ *noun* = ANSWERING MACHINE.

ant /ant/ *noun* any of a family of insects related to bees and wasps that live in large social groups with a complex organization and hierarchy in which different castes perform specific duties: family Formicidae. ✳ **have ants in one's pants** *informal* to be fidgety or restless. [Old English *æmette*]

ant. *abbr* antonym.

ant- *prefix* see ANTI-.

-ant¹ *suffix* forming nouns, denoting: **1** somebody or something that performs the action specified: *claimant; deodorant*. **2** a thing that causes the action or process specified: *decongestant*. **3** a thing that is used or acted on in the manner specified: *inhalant*. [Middle English via Old French from Latin *-ant, -ans*]

-ant² *suffix* forming adjectives, with the meanings: **1** performing a specified action or being in the condition specified: *repentant; somnambulant*. **2** causing the action or process specified: *expectorant*.

antacid¹ /anˈtasid/ *noun* a medicine that combats excessive acidity, *esp* in the stomach.

antacid² *adj* correcting excessive activity, e.g. in the stomach.

antagonise /anˈtagəniez/ *verb trans* see ANTAGONIZE.

antagonism /anˈtagəniz(ə)m/ *noun* **1** hostility or antipathy, *esp* when actively expressed. **2** opposition of one substance to the physiological or biochemical action of another.

antagonist /anˈtagənist/ *noun* **1** somebody who opposes or is hostile to another person; an adversary: *He that wrestles with us ... sharpens our skill. Our antagonist is our helper* — Edmund Burke. **2** a drug that opposes or counteracts the action or effects of another. **3** a muscle that contracts with and limits the action of another: compare AGONIST.

antagonistic /an,tagəˈnistik/ *adj* feeling or expressing antagonism; hostile. ➤➤ **antagonistically** *adv*.

antagonize *or* **antagonise** /anˈtagəniez/ *verb trans* **1** to cause (somebody) to become antagonistic. **2** to oppose or counteract (something, *esp* the physiological or biochemical effect of a substance). [Greek *antagōnizesthai*, from ANTI- + *agōnizesthai* to struggle, from *agon*: see AGONY]

Antarctic¹ /anˈtahktik/ *adj* of the S Pole or the surrounding region. [Middle English *antartik* via Latin from Greek *antarktikos*, from ANTI- + *arktikos*: see ARCTIC¹]

Antarctic² *noun* (**the Antarctic**) the area of land, sea, and ice south of the Antarctic Circle.

Antarctic Circle *noun* the parallel of latitude approximately 66½° south of the equator that circumscribes the south polar region.

ant bear *noun* = AARDVARK.

ante¹ /'anti/ *noun* (*pl* **antes**) **1** a poker stake usu put up before the deal. **2** *informal* the importance of something that is under discussion, *esp* something that is at stake: *Her speech was calculated to up the political ante.* **3** *informal* an amount paid or payable: *These improvements would raise the ante.* [ANTE-]

ante² *verb trans* (**antes, anteed** *or* **anted, anteing**) to put up (an ante): compare ANTE UP.

ante- *prefix* forming words, with the meanings: **1a** prior; before: *antecedent*; *antedate*. **b** prior to; earlier than: *antediluvian*. **2** situated before; anterior: *anteroom*. [Middle English from Latin *ante-*, from *ante* before, in front of]

Usage note

ante- *or* anti-? These two prefixes are sometimes confused. *Ante-* means 'before' or 'in front of': *antechamber* ('a room leading into another room'); *antediluvian* ('before Noah's flood'; 'ridiculously outdated'); *antenatal* ('before birth'). The much more common prefix *anti-* means 'in the opposite direction' or 'against' and can be, and is, attached to any number of words: *anticlockwise*; *antidepressant*; *anti-fox-hunting*.

anteater /'anteetə/ *noun* **1** any of several species of Central and S American toothless mammals that feed chiefly on ants and termites, such as the giant anteater, which has a long snout and a long and very bushy tail: family Myrmecophagidae. **2** *informal* = ECHIDNA. **3** *informal* = AARDVARK.

antebellum /anti'beləm/ *adj* existing before a war, *esp* the American Civil War: *an antebellum brick mansion.* [Latin *ante bellum* before the war]

antecedent¹ /anti'seed(ə)nt/ *noun* **1** a preceding thing, event, or circumstance. **2a** (+ of/to) a model or stimulus for later developments: *The bone-shaker was the antecedent of the modern bicycle.* **b** (*in pl*) family origins; ancestry. **c** (*in pl*) a person's social background, history, etc. **3** a word, phrase, or clause functioning as a noun and referred to by a pronoun. **4** in logic, the premise of a conditional proposition, e.g. *if A* in the proposition *if A, then B*: compare CONSEQUENT². **5** the first term of a mathematical ratio. [Middle English via medieval Latin from Latin *antecedent-, antecedens* something that goes before, from *antecēdere* to precede, from ANTE- + *cēdere* to go]

antecedent² *adj* **1** (*often* + to) earlier in time or order. **2** (*often* + to) coming before causally or logically. ⋙ **antecedently** *adv.*

antechamber *noun* = ANTEROOM. [French *antichambre* from Italian *anti-camera*, literally 'preceding chamber']

antedate *verb trans* **1** to precede (something) in time: *His death antedated his brother's.* **2** to attach or assign a date earlier than the true one to (something, e.g. a document or event), *esp* in order to deceive.

antediluvian¹ /antidi'loohvi·ən/ *adj* **1** belonging or relating to the period before the flood described in the Bible. **2** laughably out-of-date; antiquated: *She drives an antediluvian car.* [ANTE- + Latin *diluvium* flood]

antediluvian² *noun* somebody very old or old-fashioned or something antiquated.

antelope /'antilohp/ *noun* (*pl* **antelopes** *or collectively* **antelope**) **1** any of several species of fast-running hoofed mammals native to Africa and Asia, including gazelles, springboks, gnus, and impala: family Bovidae. **2** leather made from antelope hide. [Middle English in the sense of 'fabulous heraldic beast', via French and Latin from late Greek *antholop-, antholops*]

ante meridiem /anti mə'ridi·əm/ *adj* see A.M. [Latin *ante meridiem* before midday]

antenatal¹ /anti'naytl/ *adj* relating to pregnancy, pregnant women, or unborn children: *an antenatal clinic.* ⋙ **antenatally** *adv.*

antenatal² *noun informal* a medical examination, often one of a series, to check the health of a pregnant woman and the development of her baby.

antenna /an'tenə/ *noun* **1** (*pl* **antennae** /-nee/) a movable segmented sense organ on the head of insects, crustaceans, and centipedes and other myriapods. **2** (*pl* **antennas** *or* **antennae**

/-nee/) an aerial, *esp* a large or complex aerial. ⋙ **antennal** *adj*, **antennary** *adj*. [medieval Latin *antenna* from Latin *antemna, antenna* spar supporting a sail]

antepartum /anti'pahtoom/ *adj* relating to or occurring in the period preceding childbirth. [scientific Latin, from Latin *ante partum* before birth]

antepenultimate¹ /antipi'nultimət/ *adj* coming before the next to last; third from last.

antepenultimate² *noun* the person, thing, etc coming before the next to last.

ante-post *adj* said of a bet, etc: placed before the day of a horse race, usu before all the runners are known. [ANTE- + POST¹; from the post on which the numbers of the horses are displayed to run]

anterior /an'tiəri·ə/ *adj* **1** before in time. **2** situated towards the front, *esp* towards the front of the body or near the head: compare POSTERIOR¹. **3** said of a plant part: facing away or furthest away from the stem. ⋙ **anteriorly** *adv*. [Latin *anterior*, compar of *ante* before]

anteroom /'antiroohm/ *noun* an outer room that leads to another usu more important one, often used as a waiting room.

ante up /'anti/ *verb intrans chiefly NAmer, informal* to pay what is due; to pay up: compare ANTE². [ANTE²]

anthelion /ant'heeliən, an'thee-/ *noun* (*pl* **anthelia** /-liə/ *or* **anthelions**) **1** a luminous spot that sometimes appears in the sky opposite the sun: compare PARHELION. **2** a faint halo around a shadow formed on a fog bank or cloud. [Greek *anthēlion*, neuter of *anthēlios* opposite the sun, from ANTI- + *hēlios* sun]

anthelmintic¹ /ant·hel'mintik, anthel-/ *or* **anthelminthic** /'minthik/ *adj* expelling or destroying parasitic worms, e.g. tapeworms. [ANTI- + Greek *helminth-, helmis* worm]

anthelmintic² *or* **anthelminthic** *noun* an anthelmintic substance or drug.

anthem /'anthəm/ *noun* **1** a song of praise or gladness, *esp* a solemn song sung as an expression of national identity. **2** a musical setting of a religious text, sung as part of a church service. **3** any rousing or uplifting song: *rock anthems*. ⋙ **anthemic** /an'themik/ *adj*. [Old English *antefne* via late Latin from Greek *antiphōnos* responsive]

anther /'anthə/ *noun* in flowering plants, the organ at the tip of the stamen that contains and releases pollen. ⋙ **antheral** *adj*. [via Latin from Greek *anthēra*, fem of *anthēros* flowery]

antheridium /anthə'ridi·əm/ *noun* (*pl* **antheridia** /-ə/) the male reproductive organ of ferns, mosses, fungi, and other nonflowering plants. ⋙ **antheridial** *adj*. [scientific Latin *antheridium*, from *anthera*: see ANTHER]

anthesis /an'theesis/ *noun* the period that a plant is in flower, taken from the opening of the flower buds to the time when fertilization is no longer possible. [Greek *anthēsis* flowering]

anthill /'ant·hil/ *noun* **1** a mound of soil, leaves, etc thrown up by ants or termites in digging their nest. **2** a place that is overcrowded and constantly busy: *the human anthill* — H G Wells.

anthocyanin /anthoh'sie·ənin/ *or* **anthocyan** /-'sie·ən/ *noun* any of various blue, violet, or red plant pigments. [Greek *anthos* flower + *kyanos* dark blue + -IN¹]

anthologize *or* **anthologise** /an'tholəjiez/ *verb trans* **1** to compile (an anthology). **2** to publish (something, e.g. a poem) in an anthology. ⋙ **anthologizer** *noun*.

anthology /an'tholəji/ *noun* (*pl* **anthologies**) a collection of selected literary or musical pieces or passages: *An anthology is like all the plums and orange peel picked out of a cake* — Walter A Raleigh. ⋙ **anthologist** *noun*. [Latin *anthologia* collection of epigrams, from Greek *anthologia* flower gathering, from *anthos* flower + *legein* to gather]

anthophilous /an'thofiləs/ *adj* said of insects, birds, etc: visiting flowers. [Greek *anthos* flower + *philos* loving + -OUS]

anthozoan /anthə'zoh·ən/ *noun* any of a class of marine invertebrate animals that includes the corals and sea anemones: class Anthozoa. Also called ACTINOZOAN. ⋙ **anthozoan** *adj*. [Greek *anthos* flower + *zōion* animal]

anthracene /'anthrəseen/ *noun* a colourless crystalline hydrocarbon obtained from coal tar and used in the manufacture of dye and other chemicals: formula $C_{14}H_{10}$. [ANTHRAX + -ENE]

anthraces /'anthrəseez/ *noun* pl of ANTHRAX.

anthracite /'anthrəsiet/ *noun* a hard variety of coal that burns slowly and with a non-luminous flame. >> **anthracitic** /-'sitik/ *adj.* [Greek *anthrakitis*, from *anthrak-, anthrax* coal]

anthrax /'anthraks/ *noun* (*pl* **anthraces** /'anthrəseez/) **1** an often fatal infectious disease of cattle and sheep caused by a spore-forming bacterium and capable of being transmitted to humans. It is characterized by ulcers on the skin, damage to the lungs, or inflammation of the intestines. **2** an ulcer caused by anthrax. [Middle English *antrax* carbuncle, via Latin from Greek *anthrax* coal, carbuncle]

anthrop. *abbr* **1** anthropological. **2** anthropology.

anthrop- *or* **anthropo-** *comb. form* forming words, denoting: human beings: *anthropology.* [via Latin from Greek *anthrōp-, anthrōpo-*, from *anthrōpos* human being]

anthropic /an'thropik/ *or* **anthropical** /-kl/ *adj* of the human race or the period of its existence on earth. [Greek *anthrōpikos*, from *anthrōpos* human being]

anthropic principle *noun* in cosmology, the theory or principle that the fact that human beings exist must place limits on the ways in which the universe could have evolved.

anthropo- *comb. form* see ANTHROP-.

anthropocentric /,anthrəpə'sentrik/ *adj* considering human beings to be the most significant entities of the universe. >> **anthropocentrically** *adv*, **anthropocentricity** /-sen'trisiti/ *noun*, **anthropocentrism** *noun.*

anthropogenesis /,anthrəpə'jenəsis/ *or* **anthropogeny** /anthrə'pojəni/ *noun* the study of the origin and development of human beings. >> **anthropogenetic** /-'netik/ *adj.*

anthropography /anthrə'pogrəfi/ *noun* a branch of anthropology dealing with the geographical distribution of human beings.

anthropoid¹ /'anthrəpoyd/ *adj* **1** resembling human beings in form or behaviour. **2** said of a person: resembling an ape: *anthropoid gangsters.* [Greek *anthrōpoeidēs*, from *anthrōpos* human being]

anthropoid² *noun* any primate of the suborder that includes apes, monkeys, and humans: suborder Anthropoidea.

anthropoid ape *noun* any primate of the group that includes chimpanzees, gorillas, and orang-utans, with long arms, no tail, and a highly developed brain.

anthropology /anthrə'poləji/ *noun* the scientific study of human beings, *esp* in relation to physical characteristics, social relations and culture, and the origin and distribution of races: *Anthropology ... tells us that people are the same the whole world over – except when they are different* — Nancy Banks-Smith. >> **anthropological** /-'lojikl/ *adj*, **anthropologically** /-'lojikli/ *adv*, **anthropologist** *noun.* [modern Latin *anthropologia*, from ANTHROPO- + -LOGY]

anthropometry /anthrə'pomətri/ *noun* the scientific study of the measurement and proportions of the human body. >> **anthropometric** /-pə'metrik, -poh'metrik/ *adj*, **anthropometrical** /-pə'metrikl/ *adj*, **anthropometrically** /-pə'metrikli/ *adv.* [French *anthropométrie*, from ANTHROPO- + *métrie* measuring, ultimately from Greek *metrein* to measure]

anthropomorphic /,anthrəpə'mawfik/ *adj* **1** having a human form or human attributes: *anthropomorphic deities.* **2** ascribing human characteristics to non-human things. >> **anthropomorphically** *adv.* [via late Latin from Greek *anthrōpomorphos*, from ANTHROPO- + *morphē* form]

anthropomorphise /,anthropoh'mawfiez/ *verb trans* see ANTHROPOMORPHIZE.

anthropomorphism /,anthrəpə'mawfiz(ə)m/ *noun* the ascribing of human characteristics, behaviour, form, etc to something that is not human, e.g. a god or an animal. >> **anthropomorphist** *noun.*

anthropomorphize *or* **anthropomorphise** /,anthropoh'mawfiez/ *verb trans* to ascribe human characteristics, behaviour, form, etc to (something non-human).

anthropomorphous /,anthropoh'mawfəs/ *adj* = ANTHROPOMORPHIC. >> **anthropomorphously** *adv.*

anthropophagi /anthrə'pofəgie/ *noun* pl of ANTHROPOPHAGUS.

anthropophagous /anthrə'pofəgəs/ *adj* feeding on human flesh; cannibalistic. >> **anthropophagy** /-ji/ *noun.* [via Latin from Greek *anthrōpophagos*, from ANTHROPO- + *phagein* to eat]

anthropophagus /anthrə'pofəgəs/ *noun* (*pl* **anthropophagi** /-gie/) a cannibal. [Latin from Greek: see ANTHROPOPHAGOUS]

anthroposophy /anthroh'posəfi/ *noun* a system of belief, founded by the Austrian philosopher Rudolf Steiner (d.1925), holding that there is a spiritual world that can be perceived by faculties latent in human beings and that these latent faculties can be developed by systematic training. >> **anthroposophical** /,an-thrəpə'sofikl/ *adj*, **anthroposophist** *noun.* [ANTHROPO- + THEOSOPHY]

anthurium /an'th(y)ooriəm/ *noun* (*pl* **anthuriums**) a tropical American evergreen plant that has flowers with distinctive, usu red, heart-shaped spathes (sheaths enclosing flower clusters; see SPATHE), often used in floral arrangements: genus *Anthurium.* [scientific Latin from Greek *anthos* flower + *oura* a tail, so called because of the projecting tail-like spadix]

anti¹ /'anti/ *noun* (*pl* **antis**) an opponent of a practice or policy. [ANTI-]

anti² *prep and adj* opposed or antagonistic to something or somebody.

anti- *or* **ant-** *prefix* forming words, with the meanings: **1a** opposing or hostile to: *anti-abortion.* **b** preventing: *anti-roll bar.* **c** being a rival: *antipope.* **2** combating or defending against: *antitank.* **3a** opposite in kind to: *anticlimax; anti-hero.* **b** of the same kind but situated opposite or in the opposite direction to: *antipodes; anticlockwise.* **4** being the antimatter counterpart of: *antineutrino.* [Middle English via Old French and Latin from Greek *anti-*]

Usage note
anti- or ante-? See note at ANTE-.

anti-aircraft *adj* designed for or concerned with defence against aircraft: *an anti-aircraft missile.*

antiballistic missile /,antibə'listik/ *noun* a missile for intercepting and destroying ballistic missiles.

antibiosis /,antibie'ohsis/ *noun* antagonistic association between organisms, *esp* micro-organisms, to the detriment of one of them, or between one organism and a metabolic product of another: compare SYMBIOSIS. [scientific Latin *antibiosis*, from ANTI- + *biosis* form of life, ultimately from Greek *bios* life]

antibiotic /,antibie'otik/ *noun* a substance, such as penicillin, able to inhibit the growth of or kill micro-organisms, *esp* bacteria. >> **antibiotic** *adj.* [see ANTIBIOSIS]

antibody /'antibodi/ *noun* (*pl* **antibodies**) a protein, e.g. a blood protein, that is produced by the body in response to a specific ANTIGEN (toxin, virus, etc) and that counteracts its effects by attaching itself to the antigen and neutralizing it or causing its destruction.

antic /'antik/ *adj archaic* grotesque or bizarre: *as I perchance hereafter shall think meet to put an antic disposition on* — Shakespeare. [Italian *antico* ancient, grotesque, from Latin *antiquus* ancient]

anticathode /anti'kathohd/ *noun* the electrode to which the electrons flow in a vacuum tube such as an X-ray tube.

Antichrist /'antikriest/ *noun* (*often* **the Antichrist**) an enemy of Christ, *esp* a great personal opponent of Christ predicted to appear shortly before the end of the world. [Middle English *anticrist* via French and late Latin from Greek *Antichristos*]

anticipate /an'tisipayt/ *verb trans* **1a** to foresee and deal with (something) in advance; to forestall. **b** to act before (another person), *esp* so as to thwart their plans. **2** to discuss or think about (something) in advance or too early. **3** to use or spend (something) before the right or natural time: *We've already anticipated next month's salary.* **4** to look forward to (something) as certain; to expect. >> *verb intrans* to speak or write in knowledge or expectation of something due to happen. >> **anticipant** *noun and adj*, **anticipative** /an'tisipaytiv/ *adj*, **anticipator** *noun*, **anticipatory** /-pət(ə)ri, -paytəri/ *adj.* [Latin *anticipatus*, past part. of *anticipare* to take before, from ANTE- + *capere* to take]

Usage note
At sense (4) you will often find that *expect* is a better word to use, because it is simpler: *we don't expect any trouble* is much more straightforward than *we don't anticipate any trouble,* which has the ring of evasive officialese. It is these associations, rather than any point of grammatical principle, that make *anticipate* so widely disliked in this meaning.

anticipation /an,tisi'paysh(ə)n/ *noun* **1** the state of foreseeing or expecting something: *There is no terror in a bang, only in the anticipation of it* — Alfred Hitchcock. **2** feelings of pleasurable expectation. **3** the foreseeing of something and the action taken to prepare for or forestall it. **4** the use of something in advance or before the right time.

anticlerical /anti'klerikl/ *adj* opposed to the influence of the clergy or church in secular affairs. ⋙ **anticlerical** *noun,* **anticlericalism** *noun,* **anticlericalist** *noun.*

anticlimax /anti'kliemaks/ *noun* **1** an event that is strikingly less important or exciting than expected. **2** the usu sudden and ludicrous descent in writing or speaking from a significant to a trivial idea, or an example of this. ⋙ **anticlimactic** /-'maktik/ *adj,* **anticlimactical** /-'maktikl/ *adj,* **anticlimactically** /-'maktikli/ *adv.*

anticline /'antiklien/ *noun* an arch of stratified rock in which the layers bend downwards in opposite directions from the crest: compare SYNCLINE. ⋙ **anticlinal** /-'kliənl/ *adj.* [ANTI- + Greek *klinein* to lean]

anticlockwise /anti'klokwiez/ *adj and adv* in a direction opposite to that in which the hands of a clock rotate when viewed from the front.

anticoagulant /,antikoh'agyoolənt/ *adj* said of a substance, *esp* a drug: having the effect of inhibiting the clotting of blood. ⋙ **anticoagulant** *noun.*

anticonvulsant /,antikən'vuls(ə)nt/ *adj* said of a drug: having the effect of controlling or preventing convulsions, *esp* epileptic convulsions. ⋙ **anticonvulsant** *noun.*

antics /'antiks/ *pl noun* silly, bizarre, or funny acts or behaviour.

anticyclone /anti'sieklohn/ *noun* a system of winds that rotates about a centre of high atmospheric pressure, usually associated with calm, fine weather. ⋙ **anticyclonic** /-'klonik/ *adj.*

antidazzle /anti'dazl/ *adj* said of a vehicle's rearview mirror: designed to lessen or prevent the dazzling effect of other vehicles' headlights shining onto it from behind.

antidepressant /,antidi'pres(ə)nt/ *adj* said of a drug: used to relieve mental depression. ⋙ **antidepressant** *noun.*

antidiuretic /,antidieyoo'retik/ *adj* tending to reduce the formation of urine. ⋙ **antidiuretic** *noun.*

antidiuretic hormone *noun* = VASOPRESSIN.

antidote /'antidoht/ *noun* **1** a remedy that counteracts the effects of poison. **2** (*usu* + to) something that relieves or counteracts something regarded as unpleasant: *Art is an antidote to the increasing mechanization of our society.* ⋙ **antidotal** /-'dohtl/ *adj.* [Middle English *antidot* via Latin from Greek *antidotos,* from *antididonai* to give as an antidote, from ANTI- + *didonai* to give]

antidromic /anti'dromik/ *adj* said *esp* of a nerve impulse or fibre: proceeding or conducting in a direction opposite to the usual one: compare ORTHODROMIC. [ANTI- + *drom-,* from Greek *dromos* racecourse, running + -IC[1]]

anti-electron /,anti-i'lektron/ *noun* = POSITRON.

anti-emetic /,anti-i'metik/ *adj* said of a drug or treatment: preventing vomiting. ⋙ **anti-emetic** *noun.*

antifreeze /'antifreez/ *noun* a substance added to a liquid, *esp* the water in a car radiator, to lower its freezing point.

antifungal /anti'fung·g(ə)l/ *adj* said e.g. of a drug: effective against fungi; used to treat fungal infections; fungicidal.

antigen /'antijən/ *noun* a chemical, virus, etc that stimulates the production of an antibody when introduced into the body. ⋙ **antigenic** /-'jenik/ *adj,* **antigenically** /-'jenikli/ *adv,* **antigenicity** /-'nisiti/ *noun.*

antigravity /'antigraviti/ *noun* **1** a supposed effect resulting from cancellation or reduction of the force of gravity. **2** (*used before a noun*) reducing or cancelling the effect of gravity, or protecting against it.

Antiguan /an'tigwən/ *noun* a native or inhabitant of the island of Antigua or the state of Antigua and Barbuda in the Caribbean. ⋙ **Antiguan** *adj.*

anti-hero *or* **anti-heroine** *noun* (*pl* **anti-heroes** *or* **anti-heroines**) a man or woman who is a main character in a story, film, play, etc, but who lacks traditional heroic qualities, or whose circumstances do not allow for heroic action. ⋙ **anti-heroic** *adj.*

antihistamine /anti'histəmin, -meen/ *noun* any of various drugs that oppose the actions of histamine and are used *esp* for treating allergies and motion sickness. ⋙ **antihistaminic** /-'minik/ *adj.*

anti-inflammatory *adj* said of a drug: counteracting inflammation. ⋙ **anti-inflammatory** *noun.*

antiknock /anti'nok/ *noun* a substance added to fuel to prevent knocking in an internal-combustion engine.

anti-lock *adj* said of a braking system: designed to prevent the wheels of a vehicle from locking when the brakes are applied suddenly.

antilog /'antilog/ *or* **antilogarithm** /anti'logəridhəm/ *noun* the number corresponding to a given logarithm. ⋙ **antilogarithmic** /-logə'ridhmik/ *adj.*

antimacassar /,antimə'kasə/ *noun* a cover put over the backs or arms of upholstered seats for decoration or protection, orig to protect the backs from soiling by men's hair oil. [ANTI- + MACASSAR OIL]

antimagnetic /,antimag'netik/ *adj* **1** not affected by magnetization or a magnetic field. **2** said of a watch: having a balance unit composed of alloys that will not remain magnetized.

antimalarial /,antimə'leəriəl/ *adj* said of a substance, *esp* a drug: having properties that prevent, halt, or cure malaria. ⋙ **antimalarial** *noun.*

antimatter /'antimatə/ *noun* hypothetical matter composed of antiparticles, e.g. antiprotons instead of protons, positrons instead of electrons, and antineutrons instead of neutrons.

antimetabolite /,antimə'tabəliet/ *noun* a substance, e.g. a sulpha drug, that prevents a living organism from growing normally, often used in the treatment of cancer.

antimissile /anti'misiel/ *adj* directed against or used for intercepting a missile attack: *an antimissile system.* ⋙ **antimissile** *noun.*

antimony /'antiməni; *NAmer* -mohni/ *noun* a silver-white metallic chemical element used *esp* as a constituent of alloys to give added strength and hardness: symbol Sb, atomic number 51. ⋙ **antimonial** /-'mohnyəl, -ni·əl/ *adj,* **antimonious** /-'mohni·əs/ *adj.* [Middle English *antimonie* from medieval Latin *antimōnium,* perhaps modification of Arabic *ithmid,* of Hamitic origin]

antimycotic /,antimie'kotik/ *adj* = ANTIFUNGAL. ⋙ **antimycotic** *noun.*

antineutrino /,antinyooh'treenoh/ *noun* (*pl* **antineutrinos**) the antiparticle corresponding to a neutrino.

antineutron /anti'nyoohtron/ *noun* the antiparticle corresponding to a neutron.

antinode /'antinohd/ *noun* a region of maximum amplitude situated between adjacent nodes in a vibrating body such as the string of a musical instrument. ⋙ **antinodal** /-'nohdl/ *adj.*

antinoise[1] /anti'noyz/ *adj* designed to prevent or put a stop to noise: *antinoise legislation.*

antinoise[2] *noun* sound created in order to reduce the noise level of a piece of machinery, an engine, etc by interference.

antinomian /anti'nohmi·ən/ *noun* a person who denies that moral laws apply to everyone, *esp* an adherent of the view that Christians whose salvation is preordained are freed from all moral restraints. ⋙ **antinomian** *adj,* **antinomianism** *noun.* [medieval Latin *antinomus,* from ANTI- + Greek *nomos* law]

antinomy /an'tinəmi/ *noun* (*pl* **antinomies**) *esp* in philosophy, a contradiction or conflict between two apparently valid principles; a paradox. [German *Antinomie* via Latin from Greek *antinomia,* from ANTI- + *nomos* law]

antinovel /'antinov(ə)l/ *noun* a novel that does not adhere to the traditional or expected conventions of fiction writing, *esp* in having an incoherent plot and lacking the usual narrative structure and character delineations.

antioxidant /anti'oksid(ə)nt/ *noun* a substance that inhibits oxidation reactions, *esp* one added to foods to increase shelf life. ⋙ **antioxidant** *adj.*

antiparticle /'anti'pahtikl/ *noun* an elementary particle identical to another in mass but opposite to it in electric and magnetic properties that, when brought together with its counterpart, produces mutual annihilation.

antipasto /'antipastoh/ *noun* (*pl* **antipastos** *or* **antipasti** /-ti/) a course of savoury food served as a starter before the main course of an Italian meal; an Italian hors d'oeuvre. [Italian *antipasto,* from ANTE- + *pasto* food]

antipathetic /,antipə'thetik, an,tip-/ *or* **antipathetical** *adj* **1** (*usu* + to) opposed in nature or character to something: *I ... should have shunned them as one would fire, lightning, or anything else that is bright* *but antipathetic* — Charlotte Brontë. **2** feeling or causing opposition or hostility. ➤➤ **antipathetically** *adv.*

antipathy /an'tipəthi/ *noun* (*pl* **antipathies**) (*often* + *to*) a deep-seated aversion or dislike; a distaste. [Latin *antipathia* from Greek *antipathēs* of opposite feelings]

antipersonnel /ˌantipuhsə'nel/ *adj* said of a weapon: designed for use against people.

antiperspirant /anti'puhspirənt/ *noun* a substance used to prevent or control perspiration.

antiphon /'antifən, 'antifon/ *noun* a verse, usu from Scripture, said or sung usu before and after a canticle, psalm, or psalm verse as part of a church service. ➤➤ **antiphonal** /an'tifənl/ *adj.* [late Latin *antiphona* from Greek *antiphōnos* responsive]

antiphonary /an'tifən(ə)ri/ *noun* (*pl* **antiphonaries**) a book containing the choral parts of the prescribed form of service in the Roman Catholic Church.

antiphony /an'tifəni/ *noun* (*pl* **antiphonies**) **1** alternation between two groups of singers or musicians, one answering the other. **2** an example of antiphony; a musical response made in antiphony.

antipodal /an'tipədl/ *adj* **1** situated at the opposite side of the earth or moon: *an antipodal meridian; an antipodal continent.* **2** diametrically opposite: *an antipodal point on a sphere.*

antipode /'antipohd/ *noun* (*pl* **antipodes** /an'tipədeez/) *chiefly NAmer* the exact opposite or contrary. [back-formation from ANTIPODES]

antipodes /an'tipədeez/ *pl noun* **1** the region of the earth that is diametrically opposite another. **2** (**the Antipodes**) from the point of view of inhabitants of the northern hemisphere, Australia and New Zealand. ➤➤ **Antipodean** /-'dee-ən/ *adj and noun,* **antipodean** /-'dee-ən/ *adj and noun.* [Middle English *antipodes* people dwelling at opposite points on the globe, via Latin from Greek *antipous* with feet opposite]

antipope /'antipohp/ *noun* a pope who has been elected or a person who claims to be pope in opposition to the pope who has been canonically chosen. [French *antipape* from medieval Latin *antipapa*]

antiproton /anti'prohton/ *noun* the antiparticle corresponding to a proton.

antipruritic /ˌantiproo(ə)'ritik/ *adj* said of a drug or treatment: reducing or preventing itching. ➤➤ **antipruritic** *noun.* [ANTI- + PRURITUS]

antipsychotic /ˌantisie'kotik/ *adj* said of a drug or treatment: preventing psychosis; counteracting the symptoms of a psychosis. ➤➤ **antipsychotic** *noun.*

antipyretic /ˌantipie(ə)'retik/ *adj* said of a drug or treatment: reducing fever. ➤➤ **antipyretic** *noun.* [ANTI- + Latin *pyretic* of fever, ultimately from Greek *pyretos* fever]

antiquarian¹ /anti'kweəri·ən/ *noun* somebody who collects or studies ancient relics or old and rare books and works of art. [Latin *antiquarius* antiquary, from *antiquus*: see ANTIQUE¹]

antiquarian² *adj* **1** of antiquarians or ancient relics. **2** said of books, prints, and other works of art: old and rare. ➤➤ **antiquarianism** *noun.*

antiquark /'antikwahk/ *noun* the antiparticle corresponding to a quark.

antiquary /'antikwəri/ *noun* (*pl* **antiquaries**) = ANTIQUARIAN¹.

antiquated /'antikwaytid/ *adj* **1** outmoded or discredited by reason of age; out-of-date. **2** *informal* very old.

antique¹ /an'teek/ *adj* **1** made in an earlier period and therefore valuable: *antique mirrors.* **2** suggesting the style of an earlier period or imitating the appearance of something old. **3** belonging to or surviving from earlier, *esp* classical, times; ancient: *the ruins of an antique city.* **4** *informal* very old or old-fashioned. [early French *antique,* from Latin *antiquus,* from *ante* before]

antique² *noun* **1a** a piece of furniture, decorative object, or work of art made in an earlier period and sought by collectors and people who prefer old things. **b** (*used before a noun*) dealing in antiques: *an antique shop.* **2** a relic of ancient times. **3** (**the antique**) ancient Greek or Roman style in art.

antique³ *verb trans* (**antiques, antiqued, antiquing**) to finish or refinish (e.g. furniture) in antique style; to give an appearance of age to (a piece of furniture, etc).

antiquity /an'tikwiti/ *noun* (*pl* **antiquities**) **1** ancient times, *esp* the period before the Middle Ages. **2** the quality of being ancient or of ancient lineage: *Antiquity and birth are needless here; 'Tis impudence and money makes a peer* — Defoe. **3** (*in pl*) relics or monuments of ancient times. [Middle English *antiquite* via Old French from Latin *antiquus*: see ANTIQUE¹]

antiracist¹ /anti'raysist/ *adj* **1** opposed to racism. **2** intended to prevent racism.

antiracist² *noun* somebody who is opposed to racism. ➤➤ **antiracism** *noun.*

anti-roll bar *noun* a rubber-mounted bar connecting the suspension system on one side of a motor vehicle to that on the other, intended to reduce rolling while cornering.

antirrhinum /anti'rienəm/ *noun* (*pl* **antirrhinums**) any of a large genus of plants of the foxglove family, e.g. the snapdragon, with brightly-coloured flowers that have petals in the form of two lips: genus *Antirrhinum.* [scientific Latin *antirrhinum,* genus name, from Greek *antirrhinon,* from *anti-* like + *rhin-, rhis* nose]

antiscorbutic /ˌantiskaw'byoohtik/ *adj* said of a substance: counteracting or preventing the development of scurvy. ➤➤ **antiscorbutic** *noun.*

anti-Semitism *noun* hostility towards or discrimination against Jewish people. ➤➤ **anti-Semite** *noun,* **anti-Semitic** *adj.*

antisepsis /anti'sepsis/ *noun* **1** the inhibition of the growth of micro-organisms by antiseptic means. **2** the practice of using antiseptic substances.

antiseptic /anti'septik/ *adj* **1** said of a substance: preventing or inhibiting the growth of disease-causing micro-organisms, *esp* bacteria. **2a** scrupulously clean. **b** extremely neat or orderly, *esp* to the point of being bare or uninteresting. **3** lacking character or passion; impersonal. ➤➤ **antiseptic** *noun,* **antiseptically** *adv.*

antiserum /'antisiərəm/ *noun* (*pl* **antiserums** *or* **antisera** /-rə/) a serum containing antibodies that attack a specific antigen, used in vaccination and in the treatment of disease.

antisocial /anti'sohsh(ə)l/ *adj* **1a** *Brit* said of a person or behaviour: causing annoyance to others, *esp* remorselessly. **b** hostile or harmful to organized society. **2** tending to avoid the company of others; unsociable. ➤➤ **antisocially** *adv.*

Usage note

antisocial, asocial, non-social, unsociable, *or* unsocial? There are slight distinctions in meaning between these five related words that need to be observed. *Antisocial* means 'harmful to society': *antisocial behaviour; It's terribly antisocial to dump rubbish on the side of the road.* *Asocial* is a rarer word and implies total rejection, in this case of society or social contact – a recluse might be described as *asocial. Non-social* is used mainly as a technical term 'not socially oriented' – the life of many animal species could be described as *non-social.* To be *unsociable* usually means 'to be unfriendly and dislike company': *Our new neighbours are totally unsociable and have never even invited us in for a cup of tea.* In British English, *unsocial* is mainly found in the phrase *to work unsocial hours* meaning 'to work at times when most other people are at home'.

antispasmodic /ˌantispaz'modik/ *adj* said of a drug: preventing or relieving spasms or convulsions. ➤➤ **antispasmodic** *noun.*

antistatic /anti'statik/ *adj* said of a substance, fabric, etc: reducing the accumulation or effects of static electricity.

antistrophe /an'tistrəfi/ *noun* **1** in classical Greek drama: **a** the second choral movement in which the chorus dances to the right, in the opposite direction to the STROPHE (the first movement). **b** the section of the ode sung by the chorus during this movement, usu having the same metre as the STROPHE (the section sung during the first movement). **2** in poetry, the second of two contrasting metrical forms. [via late Latin from Greek *antistrophē,* from ANTI- + *strophē*: see STROPHE]

antitank /anti'tangk/ *adj* said of a strategy, weapon, etc: designed for use against armoured vehicles, *esp* tanks.

antithesis /an'tithəsis/ *noun* (*pl* **antitheses** /-seez/) **1a** somebody or something that is a direct opposite: *His ideas are the antithesis of mine.* **b** the quality of being opposite; contrast. **c** a contrast of ideas expressed by a parallel arrangement of words, e.g. in 'action, not words'. **2** in philosophy, the second stage of a reasoned argument: compare THESIS, SYNTHESIS. [via late Latin from Greek *antithesis* opposition, from *antitithenai* to oppose, from ANTI- + *tithenai* to put]

antithetical /anti'thetikl/ *or* **antithetic** *adj* **1** directly opposed or contrary. **2** constituting or marked by antithesis. ➤➤ **antithetically** *adv.*

antitoxin /anti'toksin/ *noun* an antibody capable of neutralizing the specific toxin that stimulated its production in the body, or a serum containing one. ➤➤ **antitoxic** *adj*.

antitrades /anti'traydz/ *pl noun* westerly winds that move counter to the trade winds and become the prevailing westerly winds of middle latitudes.

antitrust /anti'trust/ *adj NAmer* said of laws: protecting trade from monopolies or unfair business practices.

antitussive /anti'tusiv/ *adj* said of a drug or treatment: controlling or preventing coughing. ➤➤ **antitussive** *noun*. [ANTI- + *tussive*, from Latin *tussis* cough]

antitype /'antitiep/ *noun* **1** something or somebody that is represented or foreshadowed by a type or symbol. **2** an opposite type. ➤➤ **antitypical** /-'tipikl/ *adj*.

antivenin /anti'venin/ *or* **antivenom** /anti'venəm/ *noun* an antitoxin to a venom, or a serum containing one. [ANTI- + VENOM + -IN¹]

antiviral /anti'vie-ərəl/ *adj* said of a drug or treatment: directed or effective against viruses.

antivirus /anti'vie-ərəs/ *adj* said of a program: designed to counteract a computer virus. ➤➤ **antivirus** *noun*.

antivivisectionist /,antivivi'sekshənist/ *noun* a person who opposes the use of live animals for scientific research. ➤➤ **antivivisection** *adj*, **antivivisectionism** *noun*, **antivivisectionist** *adj*.

antler /'antlə/ *noun* one of a pair of branched horns of an animal of the deer family, which is shed periodically. ➤➤ **antlered** *adj*. [Middle English *aunteler* via Old French from assumed vulgar Latin *anteoculare*, from neuter of *anteocularis* located before the eye, from ANTE- + Latin *oculus* eye]

ant lion *noun* a large insect that resembles a dragonfly, whose long-jawed larvae dig conical pits in which they lie in wait to catch ants and other insects on which they feed: genus *Myrmeleon*.

antonomasia /,antonə'mayzyə, -zh(y)ə/ *noun* (*pl* **antonomasias**) **1** the substitution of an epithet or title for a proper name, e.g. *his honour* when referring to a judge. **2** the use of a proper name to denote a class of person or thing, e.g. a *Solomon* for a wise ruler. **3** an example of antonomasia. [via Latin from Greek *antonomasia* from *antonomazein* to name instead]

antonym /'antənim/ *noun* a word that means the opposite of another. ➤➤ **antonymous** /an'toniməs/ *adj*, **antonymy** /an'tonimi/ *noun*. [ANTI- + -ONYM]

antrum /'antrəm/ *noun* (*pl* **antra** /'antrə/) **1** a natural cavity or chamber in a body part, *esp* a bone. **2** the part of the stomach that lies just above the PYLORUS (the lowest part of the stomach). ➤➤ **antral** *adj*. [late Latin *antrum* from Greek *antron* cave]

antsy /'antsi/ *adj* (**antsier**, **antsiest**) *chiefly NAmer, informal* **1** fidgety or restless. **2** apprehensive or nervous. [perhaps from the idiom *have ants in one's pants*]

anuria /ə'nyooəriə/ *or* **anuresis** /anyoo'reesis/ *noun* failure or deficiency in the formation and excretion of urine. [scientific Latin, from A-² + URINE]

anus /'aynəs/ *noun* the opening at the end of the alimentary canal through which solid waste matter leaves the body. [Latin *ānus*]

anvil /'anvil/ *noun* **1** a heavy iron block on which metal is shaped by hammering. **2** a small anvil-shaped bone in the middle ear; the INCUS. **3** a towering anvil-shaped cloud. [Old English *anfilte*]

anxiety /ang'zie-iti/ *noun* (*pl* **anxieties**) **1a** uneasiness of mind because of possible impending trouble or danger. **b** a cause of anxiety. **2** a psychiatric disorder, characterized by an abnormal overwhelming sense of apprehension and fear, often with doubt about one's capacity to cope with the threat. **3** (+ to) an ardent or earnest wish: *anxiety to please*. [Latin *anxietas*, from *anxius* anxious: see ANXIOUS]

anxious /'ang(k)shəs/ *adj* **1** uneasy in the mind because of possible or impending trouble or danger. **2** causing anxiety; when anxiety is felt; worrying: *We had a few anxious moments during the storm*. **3** ardently or earnestly wishing to do something. ➤➤ **anxiously** *adv*, **anxiousness** *noun*. [Latin *anxius*, from *angere* to strangle, distress]

any¹ /'eni/ *adj* **1** one or some, no matter which: *Any plan is better than none*. **2** one, some, or all; whatever, e.g.: **a** of whatever number or quantity; even the smallest number or quantity of: *We never get any letters; Have you any money?* **b** no matter how great: *Do it at any cost*. **c** no matter how ordinary or inadequate: *Wear just any old*

thing. **3** (*usu in negatives*) being an appreciable number, part, or amount of: *We didn't stay for any length of time*. ✱ **any time/anytime** *informal* at any time: *Come round any time*. **any day/minute/moment/time etc now** very soon; quite soon. [Old English *ænig*]

any² *pronoun* (*pl* **any**) **1** any person; anybody: *I don't recognize any of them*. **2a** any thing. **b** any part, quantity, or number: *I got hardly any of the cake*. ✱ **not be having any/any of it** *informal* to refuse to tolerate, do, etc something: *He tried to kiss me but I wasn't having any of that!*

Usage note

Any, as a pronoun, may be used with a verb in either the singular or the plural: *I need some glue – is there any left?*; *We sold most of them, and any that were unsold we gave away to friends*. There is sometimes a subtle distinction in the choice of a singular or plural verb. *Is any of these seats free?* would mean, specifically, 'any one', whereas one might ask, equally correctly, *Are any of these seats free?* to mean 'are some of them free?'.

any³ *adv* to any extent or degree: *She's not feeling any better*. ✱ **any more/anymore** any longer; now, as opposed to in the past: *She doesn't live here any more*.

anybody *pronoun* **1** any person: *Has anybody lost their glasses?* **2** *informal* somebody important: *If you have to tell them who you are, you aren't anybody* — Gregory Peck.

anyhow *adv* **1** = ANYWAY. **2** (*also informal* **any old how**) in a haphazard manner: *The clothes were just thrown together anyhow*.

anyone *pronoun* **1** any person. **2** *informal* somebody important: *Everyone who is anyone will be there*.

anyplace *adv NAmer* in, at, or to any place; anywhere.

anyroad *or* **any road** *adv Brit, non-standard* = ANYWAY.

anything¹ *pronoun* **1** any thing whatever: *He'll do anything for a quiet life*. **2** any event, happening, etc: *Who knows? Anything could happen*. ✱ **anything but** not at all; far from: *They were anything but pleased to see us*. **as anything** very: *She's as quick as anything*.

anything² *adv* in any degree; at all: *The water isn't anything like as cold today*.

anyway *adv* **1** in any case; inevitably: *We won't be here anyway*. **2** used when resuming a narrative: *Well, anyway, I rang the bell .... **3** in spite of that; nevertheless: *She told me not to, but I'm going anyway*.

anywhere¹ *adv* **1** in, at, or to any place: *It's too late to go anywhere else now*. **2** to any extent; at all: *Dinner isn't anywhere near ready*. **3** used to indicate limits of variation: *There were anywhere from 40 to 60 of them*. ✱ **get anywhere** to succeed: *I've been trying to do this crossword, but I'm not getting anywhere with it*.

anywhere² *noun* any place.

Anzac /'anzak/ *noun* **1** a soldier from Australia or New Zealand, *esp* in World War I. **2** *informal* any person from Australia or New Zealand. [acronym from *Australian and New Zealand Army Corps*]

A/O *abbr* (*also* **a/o**) account of.

a.o.b. *abbr* (*also* **AOB**) *chiefly Brit* any other business, used at the end of a meeting to refer to points not specified on the agenda.

AOC *abbr* **1** Air Officer Commanding. **2** appellation d'origine contrôlée, a classification of French wine that guarantees that a particular wine comes from a particular region and meets the standards of quality imposed in that region.

ao dai /'ow ,die/ *noun* (*pl* **ao dais**) a traditional Vietnamese garment in the form of a long narrow tunic split up the sides and worn by women over loose trousers.

A-OK *or* **A-okay** /'ayohkay/ *adj and adv informal* in working order or in a perfect state. [orig a term used by US astronauts to indicate 'All systems OK']

AONB *abbr* area of outstanding natural beauty, an area of England or Wales that is officially protected, e.g. against development.

AOR *abbr* adult orientated rock, a style of popular music that combines rock with gentler, more melodic elements, designed to appeal to more mature listeners.

aorist /'ayərist, 'eərist/ *noun* a verb tense, *esp* in Greek, expressing simple occurrence of a past action without reference to its completeness, duration, or repetition. ➤➤ **aoristic** /-'ristik/ *adj*, **aoristically** /-'ristikli/ *adv*. [via late Latin from Greek *aoristos* undefined]

aorta /ay'awtə/ *noun* (*pl* **aortas** *or* **aortae** /-tee/) the main artery in the body, carrying oxygenated blood from the left side of the heart to be distributed by branch arteries throughout the body.

aortal *adj*, **aortic** *adj*. [scientific Latin from Greek *aortē*, from *aeirein* to lift]

à outrance /ah 'oohtronhs (*French* a utrãs)/ *adv* to the bitter end; unsparingly. [French *à outrance*, literally 'to excess']

AP *abbr* Associated Press.

ap-¹ *prefix* see AD-.

ap-² *prefix* see APO-.

apace /ə'pays/ *adv* at a quick pace; swiftly: *Things were developing apace.* [Middle English, prob from French *à pas* on step]

Apache /ə'pachi/ *noun* (*pl* **Apaches** or *collectively* **Apache**) **1** a member of a group of Native American peoples of the SW USA. **2** any of the Na-dene languages of the Apache people. [Spanish, prob from Zuñi *Ápachu* enemy]

apanage /'apənij/ *noun* see APPANAGE.

apart /ə'paht/ *adv* **1a** at a distance from something or somebody else in space or time: *They lived in towns 20 miles apart; Her exams were three days apart.* **b** at a distance in character or quality: *Their ideas are worlds apart.* **2** so as to separate one from another: *You can't tell the twins apart.* **3** excluded from consideration: *Joking apart, what shall we do?* **4** in or into two or more parts: *They had to take the engine apart.* [Middle English, from early French *a part* to the side]

apart from *prep* **1** besides or in addition to (something): *You haven't time, quite apart from the cost.* **2** except for (something): *The script is excellent apart from a few slow scenes.*

apartheid /ə'paht·(h)ayt, -(h)iet/ *noun* **1** a policy of segregation and discrimination against non-whites in the Republic of S Africa, officially abandoned in 1992. **2** any form of racial segregation. [Afrikaans *apartheid* separateness]

aparthotel or **apartotel** /ə'paht(h)ətel/ *noun* a hotel with self-catering apartments as well as normal hotel accommodation. [Spanish *Apartotel*, orig a company name, blend of APARTMENT + HOTEL]

apartment /ə'pahtmənt/ *noun* **1** *chiefly NAmer* a flat. **2** a suite of rooms used for living quarters: *the Royal apartments.* **3** *formal* a single room in a building. ≫ **apartmental** /-'mentl/ *adj*. [French *appartement*, from Italian *appartamento*, ultimately from *a parte* apart]

apartotel /ə'paht(h)ətel/ *noun* see APARTHOTEL.

apathetic /apə'thetik/ *adj* **1** having or showing little or no feeling; spiritless. **2** lacking interest or concern; indifferent. ≫ **apathetically** *adv*.

apathy /'apəthi/ *noun* **1** lack of feeling or emotion; impassiveness. **2** lack of interest or concern; indifference. [Greek *apatheia*, from *apathēs* without feeling, from A¹- + *pathos* feeling]

apatite /'apətiet/ *noun* any of a group of calcium phosphate minerals occurring in phosphate rock, bones, and teeth, *esp* calcium fluorophosphate. [German *Apatit*, from Greek *apatē* deceit, because the mineral takes many forms]

apatosaurus /ə,patə'sawrəs/ *noun* a large herbivorous dinosaur of the Jurassic and Cretaceous periods, with a long neck and tail, its hindlegs being longer than its forelegs, formerly called *brontosaurus*. [scientific Latin *apatosaurus*, from Greek *apatē* deceit + *sauros* lizard]

APB *abbr chiefly NAmer* all points bulletin.

ape¹ /ayp/ *noun* **1** any of several species of large tailless or short-tailed primates belonging to the group which includes gorillas, chimpanzees, orang-utans, and gibbons: families Pongidae and Hylobatidae. **2** *informal* a monkey of any kind. **3a** *archaic* a crass imitator: *Every genius has his apes.* **b** *informal* a large and clumsy or ill-mannered person. **✳ go ape** to run amok; to lose control. ≫ **apelike** *adj*. [Old English *apa*]

ape² *verb trans* to imitate (somebody) closely but often clumsily and ineptly. ≫ **aper** *noun*, **apery** *noun*.

apeman *noun* (*pl* **apemen**) any of various extinct primates believed to be intermediate in character and development between apes and human beings.

aperçu /apuh'sooh (*French* apɛʀsy)/ *noun* (*pl* **aperçus** /-'sooh/) **1** a penetrating or enlightening comment: *interesting observations and aperçus.* **2** a brief survey or résumé; an outline. [French *aperçu*, past part. of *apercevoir* to perceive]

aperient /ə'piəri·ənt/ *noun* a medicine that eases constipation; a laxative. ≫ **aperient** *adj*. [Latin *aperient-, aperiens*, present part. of *aperire* to uncover, open]

aperiodic /,aypiəri'odik/ *adj* **1** happening irregularly: *aperiodic floods.* **2** said of a gauge or instrument: not having periodic vibrations; not oscillatory. ≫ **aperiodically** *adv*, **aperiodicity** /-riə'disiti/ *noun*. [A-² + PERIODIC]

aperitif /əperə'teef, ə'pe-/ *noun* an alcoholic drink taken before a meal to stimulate the appetite. [French *apéritif* from late Latin *aperitivus*, from Latin *aperire* to open]

aperture /'apəchə/ *noun* **1** an open space; a hole or gap. **2a** the opening in a camera or other optical system through which the light passes, or the adjustable size of the opening. **b** the diameter of the objective lens or mirror of a telescope. [Middle English from Latin *apertura*, from *apertus*, past part. of *aperire* to open]

apetalous /a'petələs/ *adj* said of flowers: having no petals. ≫ **apetaly** *noun*. [A-² + PETAL]

APEX /'aypeks/ *abbr* **1** (*also* **Apex**) Advance Purchase Excursion, an airline or rail ticket bought at a cheaper rate a minimum number of days before travelling. **2** Association of Professional, Executive, Clerical, and Computer Staff.

apex *noun* (*pl* **apexes** or **apices** /'aypiseez/) **1** the uppermost point of a triangle, cone, or pyramid. **2** the narrowed or pointed end or tip of something, e.g. a leaf. **3** the highest or culminating point, e.g. of a hierarchy, one's career, etc. [Latin *apex* summit, small rod at top of priest's cap]

aphaeresis or **apheresis** /ə'ferəsis, ə'fiə-/ *noun* (*pl* **aphaereses** or **aphereses** /-seez/) **1** the loss, *esp* by conscious suppression, of one or more sounds or letters at the beginning of a word, e.g. in *bus* for *omnibus*, *cute* for *acute*, *'cos* for *because*: compare APHESIS. **2** a medical technique for removing a component, e.g. plasma, from the blood, and returning the blood to the donor. ≫ **aphaeretic** /afə'retik/ *adj*. [via late Latin from Greek *aphairesis*, literally 'taking off', from *aphairein* to take away]

aphasia /ə'fayzyə, -zh(y)ə/ *noun* full or partial loss of the power to use or understand words, usu resulting from brain damage: compare ALEXIA, APHONIA, DYSLEXIA. ≫ **aphasiac** *adj*, **aphasic** *noun and adj*. [scientific Latin from Greek *aphasia*, from A-² + *phasia* speech]

aphelion /ap'heelyən, ə'feel-/ *noun* (*pl* **aphelia** /-yə/) the point in the path of a planet, comet, etc that is farthest from the sun: compare PERIHELION. [scientific Latin *aphelion*, from AP-² + Greek *hēlios* sun]

apheresis /ə'ferəsis, ə'fiə-/ *noun* see APHAERESIS.

aphesis /'afisis/ *noun* (*pl* **apheses** /-seez/) the gradual and inadvertent loss of an unstressed vowel or syllable from the beginning of a word, as in the case of *squire* (from *esquire*) *bishop* (from *episcopus*), *migraine* (from *hemikrania*), as distinct from the conscious suppression of a vowel or syllable: compare APHAERESIS. ≫ **aphetic** /-'fetik/ *adj*, **aphetically** *adv*. [Greek *aphesis* letting go, from APO- + Greek *hienai* to throw]

aphid /'ayfid/ *noun* any of a family of small insects that suck the juices of plants, e.g. a greenfly: family Aphididae.

aphis /'ayfis/ *noun* (*pl* **aphides** /-deez/) an aphid. [scientific Latin *Aphid-, Aphis*, genus name, from modern Greek *aphis*, perhaps an alteration of *koris* bug]

aphonia /ay'fohniə/ *noun* loss of voice caused by disease or a physical defect rather than by brain damage: compare ALEXIA, APHASIA, DYSLEXIA. [scientific Latin from Greek *aphōnia*, from *aphōnos* voiceless, from A-² + *phonē* sound, voice]

aphorism /'afəriz(ə)m/ *noun* a concise pithy phrase expressing a universal truth; an adage. ≫ **aphorist** *noun*, **aphoristic** /-'ristik/ *adj*, **aphoristically** /-'ristikli/ *adv*. [early French *aphorisme* via late Latin from Greek *aphorizein* to define, from AP-² + *horizein* to separate, divide: see HORIZON]

aphrodisiac¹ /afrə'diziak/ *noun* a food, drink, or drug that stimulates sexual desire. [Greek *aphrodisiakos* sexual, from *aphrodisia* sexual pleasures, neuter pl of *aphrodisios* of Aphrodite, goddess of love]

aphrodisiac² or **aphrodisiacal** /,afrədi'zie·əkl/ *adj* stimulating sexual desire.

aphtha /'afthə/ *noun* (*pl* **aphthae** /-thi/) a type of small ulcer that occurs in groups on the tongue or inside the mouth. [via Latin from Greek *aphtha* thrush]

aphyllous /ə'filəs/ *adj* said of a plant: having no leaves. [Greek *aphyllos*, from A-² + *phyllon* leaf]

apian /'aypi·ən/ *adj* relating to bees. [Latin *apianus*, from *apis* bee]

apiarian /aypi'eəri·ən/ *adj* relating to beekeeping or bees.

apiarist /'aypi·ərist/ *noun* a beekeeper.

apiary /'aypi·əri/ *noun* (*pl* **apiaries**) a place where bees are kept in hives or colonies, *esp* for their honey. [Latin *apiarium* beehive, from *apis* bee]

apical /'aypikl, 'ap-/ *adj* **1** situated at an apex or forming an apex. **2** said of a consonant: produced with the tip of the tongue near or at the front teeth, as with the sound *th*. ⫸ **apically** *adv*. [prob from Latin *apicalis*, from Latin *apic-*, apex]

apices /'aypiseez/ *noun pl of* APEX

apiculture /'aypikulchə/ *noun* the keeping of bees, *esp* on a large scale. ⫸ **apicultural** /-'kulchərəl/ *adj*, **apiculturist** /-'kulchərist/ *noun*. [prob from French *apiculture*, from Latin *apis* bee + French *culture*]

apiece /ə'pees/ *adv* for each one; individually: *selling jars of honey at £1.50 apiece.* [Middle English *a pece*, from A-¹ + *pece* piece]

apish /'aypish/ *adj* **1** resembling an ape. **2** slavishly imitative. **3** extremely silly or affected. ⫸ **apishly** *adv*, **apishness** *noun*.

aplanatic /aplə'natik/ *adj* said *esp* of a lens: free from the kind of image distortion which is caused by the curvature of the lens. [A-² + Greek *planasthai* to wander]

aplasia /ay'playzyə, -zh(y)ə/ *noun* incomplete or faulty development of an organ or part. ⫸ **aplastic** /ay'plastik/ *adj*. [scientific Latin, from A-² + *-plasia* development, ultimately from Greek *plassein* to mould]

aplastic anaemia *noun* a disorder of the bone marrow causing a deficiency of all types of blood cell.

aplenty /ə'plenti/ *adj archaic or literary* enough and to spare; in abundance: *We found fighting aplenty with the members of the various tribes* — Edgar Rice Burroughs.

aplomb /ə'plom/ *noun* complete composure or self-assurance; poise. [French *aplomb* perpendicularity, from early French *a plomb* according to the plummet]

apnoea (*NAmer* **apnea**) /'apni·ə/ *noun* **1** temporary cessation of breathing, *esp* during sleep. **2** = ASPHYXIA. [scientific Latin, from A-² + *-pnoea* breathing, ultimately from Greek *pnein* to breath]

apo- *or* **ap-** *prefix* forming words, with the meanings: **1** away from or off: *aphelion*; *apogee*. **2** detached or separate: *apocarpous*. **3** related to or derived from: *apomorphine*. [Middle English via French or Latin from Greek *apo* from]

Apoc. *abbr* **1** Apocalypse. **2** Apocrypha.

apocalypse /ə'pokəlips/ *noun* **1** a cataclysmic event. **2** (**the Apocalypse**). **a** the ultimate destruction of the world, as depicted in the Book of Revelation in the Bible. **b** the Book of Revelation. **3** something viewed as a prophetic revelation. **4** any of a number of early Jewish and Christian works that describe the future establishment of God's kingdom. [Middle English in the sense 'revelation', via late Latin from Greek *apokalyptein* to uncover, from APO- + *kalyptein* to cover]

apocalyptic /ə,pokə'liptik/ *or* **apocalyptical** *adj* **1** momentous, overwhelming, cataclysmic, or catastrophic. **2** relating to or resembling the biblical Apocalypse. **3** forecasting the ultimate destiny of the world; prophetic. ⫸ **apocalyptically** *adv*.

apocarpous /apə'kahpəs/ *adj* said of flowering plants: having carpels (reproductive parts; see CARPEL) that are separate rather than fused. ⫸ **apocarpy** *noun*.

apochromatic /,apəkrə'matik/ *adj* said *esp* of a lens: free from chromatic and spherical aberration.

apocope /ə'pokəpi/ *noun* the loss of the end of a word, e.g. historically in *sing* from Old English *singan*, and in modern English in shortened forms such as *marge* from *margarine*. [via late Latin from Greek *apocopē* cutting off, from *apokoptein* to cut off]

Apocr. *abbr* Apocrypha.

apocrine /'apəkrin, -kreen/ *adj* relating to or denoting a gland, e.g. a mammary gland or certain sweat glands, that loses cellular tissue in its secretions. [APO- + Greek *krinein* to separate]

apocrypha /ə'pokrifə/ *noun* **1** (**the Apocrypha**) (*treated as sing. or pl*) books included in the SEPTUAGINT (Greek version of Old Testament) and VULGATE (St Jerome's Latin Bible) but excluded from the Jewish and Protestant canons of the Old Testament: compare

PSEUDEPIGRAPHA. **2** writings or statements of dubious authenticity, or a collection of such writings. [medieval Latin *apocrypha*, neuter *pl* of *apocryphus* hidden, ultimately from Greek *apokryptein* to hide away]

apocryphal *adj* **1** said of an account or story: of doubtful authenticity; probably not based on reality or fact. **2** (*often* **Apocryphal**) relating to or resembling the Apocrypha. ⫸ **apocryphally** *adv*.

apodal /'apədl/ *adj* having no feet or parts that look like or are used like feet. [Greek *apod-*, *apous* without feet, from A-² + *pod-*, *pous* foot]

apodictic /apə'diktik/ *or* **apodeictic** /-'diektik/ *adj* said e.g. of logical propositions: expressing, or of the nature of, necessary truth or absolute certainty. ⫸ **apodictically** *adv*. [Latin *apodicticus* demonstrating, giving proof, from Greek *apodeiknynai* to demonstrate, from APO- + *deiknynai* to show]

apodosis /ə'podəsis/ *noun* (*pl* **apodoses** /-seez/) the main clause of a conditional sentence e.g. *tell me* in the sentence *If you know, tell me*: compare PROTASIS. [late Latin *apodosis* from Greek, from *apodidonai* to give back, deliver]

apodous /'apədəs/ *adj* = APODAL.

apogee /'apəjee/ *noun* **1** the point farthest from the earth reached by the moon or a satellite in its orbit: compare PERIGEE. **2** the farthest or highest point; the culmination: *Aegean civilization reached its apogee in Crete.* ⫸ **apogean** /apə'jee·ən/ *adj*. [French *apogée*, ultimately from Greek *apogeios*, *apogaios* far from the earth, from APO- + *gē* earth]

apolitical /aypə'litikl/ *adj* **1** having no interest or involvement in political affairs. **2** having no political significance. ⫸ **apolitically** *adv*. [A-² + POLITICAL]

apologetic /ə,polə'jetik/ *adj* **1** regretfully acknowledging a fault or failure; contrite. **2** offered by way of excuse or apology: *an apologetic smile.* **3** offered in defence or vindication of a doctrine, etc; having the character of an apologia: *an apologetic tract.* ⫸ **apologetically** *adv*. [late Latin *apologeticus* from Greek *apologeisthai* to defend]

apologetics *pl noun* (*treated as sing. or pl*) **1** systematic reasoned argument in defence, e.g. of a doctrine. **2** a branch of theology devoted to the rational defence of Christianity.

apologia /apə'lohjyə/ *noun* **1** a reasoned defence in speech or writing, *esp* of a faith, cause, or institution. **2** a defence of one's conduct, beliefs, etc: *an apologia for his term of office.* [late Latin *apologia*: see APOLOGY]

apologise /ə'poləjiez/ *verb intrans* see APOLOGIZE.

apologist /ə'poləjist/ *noun* a person who speaks or writes in defence of something: *an apologist for fascism; New Labour's apologist.*

apologize *or* **apologise** /ə'poləjiez/ *verb intrans* (*often* + for) to make an apology.

apologue /'apəlog/ *noun* an allegorical narrative, usu with a moral, *esp* an animal fable. [French *apologue* via Latin from Greek *apologos* a story, from APO- + *logos* speech, narrative]

apology /ə'poləji/ *noun* (*pl* **apologies**) **1** an admission of error or discourtesy accompanied by an expression of regret. **2** (+ for) a poor substitute; a specimen: *an apology for a tail.* **3** an excuse or explanation for, or vindication of, something; an apologia: *I offer no apology for my lengthy introduction.* **4** (*in pl*) a formal expression of regret that one is unable to attend a meeting, etc: *send one's apologies.* [via French and late Latin from Greek *apologia* a speech in defence, a vindication, from APO- + *logos* speech]

apolune /'apəloohn/ *noun* the point in the path of a spacecraft, etc orbiting the moon that is farthest from the centre of the moon: compare PERILUNE. [APO- + Latin *luna* moon]

apomixis /apə'miksis/ *noun* (*pl* **apomixes** /-seez/) reproduction involving the production of seed without fertilization: compare AMPHIMIXIS. ⫸ **apomictic** /-'miktik/ *adj*. [scientific Latin, from APO- + Greek *mixis* act of mixing, from *mignynai* to mix]

apomorphine /apə'mawfeen/ *noun* a derivative of morphine used as an emetic, expectorant, hypnotic, and for treating Parkinsonism.

aponeurosis /,apənyoo'rohsis/ *noun* (*pl* **aponeuroses** /-seez/) a sheet of tendinous tissue by which broad sheet-like muscles are attached to the bone. [via scientific Latin from Greek *aponeurōsis*, from APO- + *neuron* sinew]

apophthegm (*NAmer* **apothegm**) /'apəthem/ *noun* a short, pithy, and instructive saying; a maxim. ⫸ **apophthegmatic**

/-theg'matik/ *adj,* **apophthegmatical** /-theg'matikl/ *adj,* **apophthegmatically** /-theg'matikli/ *adv.* [via French from Greek *apophthegmat-, apophthegma,* from *apophthengesthai* to speak out]

apophyllite /ə'pofiliet/ *noun* a mineral occurring as transparent square prisms or whitish masses, chemically a compound of potassium calcium silicate. [APO- + Greek *phyllon* leaf]

apophysis /ə'pofisis/ *noun* (*pl* **apophyses** /-seez/) in anatomy, a projection, *esp* one on a bone to which a muscle attaches. ➤➤ **apophyseal** *adj.* [via scientific Latin from Greek *apophysis* offshoot, from APO- + *phyein* to grow]

apoplectic /apə'plektik/ *adj* **1** relating to or causing apoplexy, or showing symptoms of apoplexy. **2** *informal* bursting with fury; extremely angry. ➤➤ **apoplectically** *adv.*

apoplexy /'apəpleksi/ *noun* (*pl* **apoplexies**) **1** paralysis or loss of consciousness caused by a rupture or blockage in a blood vessel in the brain; a stroke. **2** *informal* speechless, incapacitating rage. [Middle English *apoplexie* via Old French and late Latin from Greek *apoplēxia,* from *apoplēssein* to cripple by a stroke, from APO- + *plēssein* to strike]

aporia /ə'poriə, ə'paw-/ *noun* **1** an unresolvable position, *esp* in philosophy; an impasse. **2** in rhetoric, the expression of doubt, whether in earnest or for effect. [via late Latin from Greek *aporia* difficulty, straits, from A-² + *poros* passage]

aposematic /,apəsi'matik/ *adj* said *esp* of insect coloration: conspicuous and serving to warn off would-be predators, etc. ➤➤ **aposematically** *adv.* [APO- + Greek *sēmat-, sēma* sign]

aposiopesis /,apəzie-ə'peesis/ *noun* (*pl* **aposiopeses** /-seez/) the act of breaking off in mid sentence, sometimes as a rhetorical device, as though prevented by strong feeling from proceeding, as in *Of all the ...!* ➤➤ **aposiopetic** /-'petik/ *adj.* [via late Latin from Greek *aposiōpēsis,* from *aposiōpan* to be quite silent, from APO- + *siōpan* to be silent]

apostasy /ə'postəsi/ *noun* (*pl* **apostasies**) **1** renunciation of a religious faith. **2** abandonment of a previous loyalty; defection. [Middle English *apostasie* via late Latin from Greek *apostasis* revolt, from *aphistasthai* to revolt, from APO- + *histasthai* to stand]

apostate /ə'postayt/ *noun* a person who commits apostasy. ➤➤ **apostate** *adj.*

apostatize or **apostatise** /ə'postətiez/ *verb intrans* to commit apostasy.

a posteriori /,ay postiəri'awri, -rie/ *adj and adv* said of argument or reasoning: proceeding from observed facts to their cause, or from the particular to the general; inductive or inductively: compare A PRIORI: *argue a posteriori.* [Latin 'from what follows', from *a* from + *posterior* later]

apostle /ə'pos(ə)l/ *noun* **1** (*often* **Apostle**) an early Christian teacher sent out to preach the gospel, *esp* one of the group made up of Jesus's original twelve disciples and Paul. **2** any Christian missionary who was the first to preach Christianity in a place or among a people. **3** an advocate, early exponent, or ardent supporter of a system, movement, etc: *Gandhi, a noted apostle of passive resistance as a means of protest; an early apostle of Dadaism.* ➤➤ **apostleship** *noun.* [Middle English from Old French *apostle,* or Old English *apostol,* both from late Latin *apostolus,* from Greek *apostolos* messenger, from *apostellein* to send away]

apostlebird *noun* an Australian bird with grey, black, and brown plumage: *Struthidea cinerea.* [from their supposed habit of moving about in flocks of twelve]

apostle spoon *noun* a teaspoon of a common traditional design, the handle terminating in the figure of a saint or apostle.

apostolate /ə'postələt, -layt/ *noun* **1** the office, mission, or evangelistic work of an apostle. **2** an association of people dedicated to the propagation of a religion or doctrine. [late Latin *apostolatus* from *apostolus:* see APOSTLE]

apostolic /apə'stolik/ *adj* **1** relating to an apostle or the New Testament apostles: *one Catholic and Apostolic Church* — Nicene Creed. **2** relating to the pope as the successor to the apostolic authority vested in St Peter: *the apostolic See.*

apostolic succession *noun* the teaching of the Roman Catholic and Eastern Orthodox Churches that the authority vested in Christian bishops is handed down through successive ordinations from the apostles.

apostrophe¹ /ə'postrəfi/ *noun* a punctuation mark (') used to indicate the omission of letters or figures, the possessive case, or the plural of letters or figures. ➤➤ **apostrophic** /apə'strofik/ *adj.* [early French and late Latin from Greek *apostrophos,* turned away, from *apostrephein* to turn away]

apostrophe² *noun* the rhetorical addressing of a person, usu absent, or a personified thing, as in *O death, where is thy sting? O grave, where is thy victory?* ➤➤ **apostrophic** /apə'strofik/ *adj.* [via Latin from Greek *apostrophē,* literally 'act of turning away', from *apostrephein* to turn away]

apostrophize or **apostrophise** *verb trans* to address (an absent person or a personified thing), *esp* as a rhetorical or poetic device: *Wordsworth's famous line apostrophizing the cuckoo.*

apothecaries' measure or **apothecaries' weight** *noun* the series of units of weight used formerly by pharmacists and based on the ounce of eight drachms and the drachm of three scruples or 60 grains.

apothecary /ə'pothək(ə)ri/ *noun* (*pl* **apothecaries**) *archaic* a pharmacist or pharmacy: *It was Mr Lloyd, an apothecary, sometimes called in by Mrs Reed when the servants were ailing; for herself and the children she hired a physician* — Charlotte Brontë. [Middle English *apothecarie* via Latin from Greek *apothēkē* storehouse, from *apotithenai* to put away]

apothegm /'apəthem/ *noun NAmer* see APOPHTHEGM.

apothem /'apəthem/ *noun* in geometry, the perpendicular extending from the centre of a regular polygon to any of its sides. [APO- + -*them* from Greek *thema* something laid down, THEME¹]

apotheosis /ə,pothi'ohsis/ *noun* (*pl* **apotheoses** /-seez/) **1** elevation to the status of a god; deification. **2** a supreme example of something at its most developed: *It [Treasure Island] is an apotheosis of the boy-story* — Conan Doyle. [via late Latin from Greek *apotheōsis* from *apotheoun* to deify, from APO- + *theos* god]

apotheosize or **apotheosise** /ə'pothee-əsiez, ə'pothi-əsiez/ *verb trans* **1** to deify (somebody). **2** to glorify (something or somebody).

apotropaic /,apətrə'payik/ *adj* said of a ritual, formula, etc: supposedly averting evil or bad luck. [Greek *apotropaios* turning away evil, from APO- + *trepein* to turn, direct]

app. *abbr* **1** appendix. **2** in computing, application. **3** appointed.

appal /ə'pawl/ (*NAmer* **appall**) *verb trans* (**appalled, appalling**) to overcome (somebody) with consternation, horror, or dismay: *The waste appals me; appalled by the squalor.* ➤➤ **appalling** *adj,* **appallingly** *adv.* [Middle English *appallen* via Old French from Latin *pallescere* from *pallēre* to be pale]

Appaloosa /apə'loohsə, -zə/ *noun* a rugged N American saddle horse of a breed with mottled skin and striped hooves. [prob from *Palouse,* a Native American people of Washington and Idaho, USA]

appanage or **apanage** /'apənij/ *noun* **1** formerly, a grant of a province, a lucrative post, or money, made by a monarch or government to a dependent member of a royal family: *bishoprics ... as appanages for the younger sons of great families* — Disraeli. **2** *literary* a usual attribute or prerogative: *as if loveliness were not the special prerogative of woman – her legitimate appanage and heritage* — Charlotte Brontë. [French *apanage* from Old Provençal *apanar* to support, from AP-¹ + *pan* bread, from Latin *panis*]

apparat /'apərat, apə'rat/ *noun* formerly, the administrative set-up of a communist party, *esp* in a communist country. [Russian]

apparatchik /apə'rachik/ *noun* (*pl* **apparatchiks** or **apparatchiki** /-ki/) **1** a member of a communist apparat. **2** a bureaucrat in any organization, *esp* one regarded as bedevilled by bureaucracy. [Russian *apparatchik* from *apparat,* literally 'apparatus']

apparatus /apə'raytəs; *NAmer also* -'ratəs/ *noun* (*pl* **apparatuses** or **apparatus**) **1** equipment designed for a particular use, or a single piece of such equipment: *scientific apparatus; gymnastic apparatus.* **2** the administrative bureaucracy of an organization, *esp* a political party. **3** a group of anatomical organs that have a common physiological function. **4** (*also* **apparatus criticus** or **critical apparatus**) a set of notes accompanying a text, e.g. dealing with disputed readings. [Latin *apparatus,* past part. of *apparare* to prepare, from AP-¹ + *parare* to prepare]

apparel¹ /ə'parəl/ *verb trans* (**apparelled, apparelling,** *NAmer* **appareled, appareling**) *literary* **1** to dress (somebody) or array them in something: *apparelled for the river in a boater and bathing trunks.* **2** to clothe, cover, or adorn (something): *It was still a message of dismissal, apparelled though it was in flowery euphemism.* [Middle English *appareillen* via Old French from Latin *apparēre* to appear]

apparel[2] *noun literary* **1** garments or clothing: *My strange apparel drew no comment.* **2** something that clothes or adorns: *the bright apparel of spring.*

apparent /əˈparənt/ *adj* **1** easily seen or understood; evident: *The reason was all too apparent.* **2** seemingly real but not necessarily so: *The increase is only apparent.* **3** having an absolute right to succeed to a title or estate: *the heir apparent.* ⟩⟩ **apparently** *adv.* [Middle English via Old French from Latin *apparent-, apparens,* present part. of *apparēre:* see APPEAR]

apparent horizon *noun* = HORIZON (1C).

apparent magnitude *noun* the magnitude of a star measured according to its brightness as observed from earth, the brighter stars having a lower value than the fainter ones.

apparent time *noun* the time of day according to the position of the sun, as indicated by a sundial: compare MEAN TIME.

apparition /apəˈrish(ə)n/ *noun* **1a** an unusual or unexpected sight; *esp* the appearance of a ghost. **b** a ghostly figure itself; a phantom. **2** *archaic* the act of becoming visible; appearance: *the apparition of this starre in Bethlehem* — John Gaule. ⟩⟩ **apparitional** *adj.* [Middle English *apparicioun* via late Latin from Latin *apparitus,* past part. of *apparēre:* see APPEAR]

appeal[1] /əˈpeel/ *noun* **1** the power of arousing a sympathetic response; attraction: *The theatre has lost its appeal for him.* **2** an earnest plea, e.g. for mercy; an entreaty. **3** a large-scale coordinated approach to the public for donations to a charity or cause. **4** an application, e.g. to a recognized authority, for corroboration, vindication, or decision. **5** a legal proceeding by which a case is brought to a higher court for review. **6** in cricket, a call by members of the fielding side, *esp* the bowler, for the umpire to declare a batsman out.

appeal[2] *verb intrans (often + to)* **1** to arouse a sympathetic response: *Indian cuisine doesn't appeal to him; the idea appealed.* **2** to make an earnest plea or request: *appeal for help.* **3** to call on another for corroboration, vindication, or decision: *Dorothea appealed to her husband, and he made a silent sign of approval* — George Eliot. **4** to take a case to a higher court for review. **5** to make an appeal in cricket. ⟩ *verb trans* to take (a case) to a higher court. ⟩⟩ **appealable** *adj,* **appealer** *noun.* [Middle English *appelen* to accuse, appeal, via French from Latin *appellare* to address]

appealing *adj* **1** having appeal; attractive: *an appealing grin.* **2** said of a look or expression: marked by earnest entreaty; imploring: *He cast one last appealing look at her – and then he spoke the fatal words* — Wilkie Collins. ⟩⟩ **appealingly** *adv.*

appear /əˈpiə/ *verb intrans* **1a** to be or become visible: *The sun appears on the horizon.* **b** to arrive: *The postman appears promptly at eight each day.* **2** to give the impression of being; to seem: *He appears happy enough.* **3** to come into public view: *She first appeared on a television variety show.* **4** to come formally before an authoritative body: *A man will appear before Chester magistrates today, charged with the assault.* [Middle English *apperen* via Old French from Latin *apparēre,* from AP-[1] + *parēre* to show oneself]

appearance *noun* **1a** a visit or attendance that is seen or noticed by others: *He made a brief appearance at Barbara's party.* **b** participation in a performance, show, programme, etc on screen or on the stage: *the Prime Minister's television appearances.* **2a** an outward aspect; a look: *The animal had a fierce appearance; Her appearance is against her.* **b** an external show; a semblance: *Although hostile, he tried to preserve an appearance of neutrality.* **c** *(in pl)* an outward or superficial look, *esp* one that hides the real situation: *Appearances can be deceptive.* **3** the coming into court of a party in an action, or his or her lawyer: *her expected appearance at Aberdeen Sheriff Court on six charges of theft.* ✳ **keep up appearances** to maintain standards outwardly at least. **put in an appearance** to attend a gathering etc, if briefly. **to all appearances** according to every outward indication: *To all appearances the horse was a no-hoper.*

appease /əˈpeez/ *verb trans* **1** to pacify or calm (somebody). **2** to conciliate (*esp* an aggressor) by making concessions. **3** to assuage or allay (hunger, thirst, etc). ⟩⟩ **appeasable** *adj,* **appeasement** *noun,* **appeaser** *noun.* [Middle English *appesen* from Old French *apaisier,* from AP-[1] + *pais* peace: see PEACE]

appellant[1] /əˈpelənt/ *adj* = APPELLATE.

appellant[2] *noun* a person who appeals against a judicial decision.

appellate /əˈpelət/ *adj* said of a court of law: relating to or recognizing appeals. [Latin *appellatus,* past part. of *appellare* to appeal to, call upon: see APPEAL[2]]

appellation /apəˈlaysh(ə)n/ *noun literary* an identifying name, nickname, or title: *In the navy he [Captain Vere] was popularly known by the appellation Starry Vere* — Herman Melville.

appellation contrôlée /apəˈlasyonh kontrohˈlay (*French* apəlasjɔ̃ kɔ̃trole)/ *noun* a government certification of a French wine guaranteeing that it originates from a specified geographical area and meets that locality's standards of production. [French *appellation contrôlée,* literally 'controlled appellation']

appellative[1] /əˈpelətiv/ *adj* in grammar, denoting a common noun. ⟩⟩ **appellatively** *adv.*

appellative[2] *noun* in grammar, a common noun, *esp* one used as a form of address, e.g. *doctor, waiter, folks.*

appellee /apelˈee/ *noun* the person appealed against in a case taken to a higher court; the defendant in an appeal case.

append /əˈpend/ *verb trans formal* to attach or add (something), *esp* as a supplement, attachment, addition, or appendix to a text: *I deem it proper to append the following brief explanation* — Frederick Douglass; *append one's name to a document.* [French *appendre* from Latin *appendere* to hang on, from AP-[1] + *pendere* to hang]

appendage /əˈpendij/ *noun* **1** a limb or other subordinate or derivative body part: *a useless appendage like the shrivelled wings ... of many insular beetles* — Darwin. **2** something appended to something larger or more important: *A child's nature is too serious a thing to admit of its being regarded as a mere appendage to another being* — Charles Lamb.

appendant /əˈpend(ə)nt/ *adj* **1** associated as an accompaniment or attendant circumstance: *When the Highlanders read the Bible they will naturally wish to ... know the history, collateral or appendant* — Dr Johnson. **2** said of a legal right: attached to the possession of land, etc. **3** attached as an appendage: *an appendant proboscis.* ⟩⟩ **appendant** *noun.*

appendicectomy /əˌpendiˈsektəmi/ *or* **appendectomy** /apənˈdek-/ *noun (pl* **appendicectomies** *or* **appendectomies)** surgical removal of the vermiform appendix. [Latin *appendic-, appendix* (see APPENDIX) + -ECTOMY]

appendices /əˈpendiseez/ *noun* pl of APPENDIX.

appendicitis /əˌpendiˈsietis/ *noun* inflammation of the vermiform appendix. [scientific Latin, from Latin *appendic-,* appendix (see APPENDIX) + -ITIS]

appendix /əˈpendiks/ *noun* **1** *(pl* **appendices** /-seez/) a supplement, e.g. containing explanatory or statistical material, attached at the end of a book or other piece of writing. **2** *(pl* **appendixes)** the vermiform appendix or any similar bodily outgrowth. [Latin *appendic-, appendix* appendage, from *appendere* to hang on, suspend: see APPEND]

apperception /apuhˈsepsh(ə)n/ *noun* **1** an individual's awareness of his or her own mind at work. **2** the realization that an idea or concept newly presented to one belongs to a class or group of ideas already stored in one's mind; the thought 'this is that' or 'this is one of those'. ⟩⟩ **apperceptive** /-ˈseptiv/ *adj.* [French *aperception* from *apercevoir* to perceive]

appertain /apəˈtayn/ *verb intrans (usu + to)* to belong or be connected as a rightful or customary part, possession, or attribute; to pertain: *We were wont to give up all nautical instruments and letters appertaining to any of us* — R H Dana; *In this great stretch of country there is no sign of life nor of anything appertaining to life* — Conan Doyle. [Middle English *apperteinen* via Old French *apartenir* from late Latin *appertinēre,* from Latin AP-[1] + *pertinēre* to belong, PERTAIN]

appestat /ˈapəstat/ *noun* the part of the HYPOTHALAMUS (area of brain regulating bodily needs) that controls the appetite. [APPETITE + -STAT]

appetence /ˈapitəns/ *or* **appetency** /-si/ *noun (pl* **appetences** *or* **appetencies)** **1** *literary* a fixed and strong eagerness or desire; a craving: *Whatsoe'er might please the appetence, here it was poured out in lavish affluence* — Giles Fletcher. **2** a natural attraction or affinity, e.g. between chemicals. ⟩⟩ **appetent** *adj.* [Latin *appetentia,* from *appetent-, appetens,* present part. of *appetere* to crave: see APPETITE]

appetiser /ˈapətiezə/ *noun* see APPETIZER.

appetising *adj* see APPETIZING.

appetite /ˈapətiet/ *noun* **1** a desire to satisfy an internal bodily need; *esp* a desire to eat. **2** a strong desire demanding satisfaction; an inclination: *One loses one's appetite for detective fiction.*

>> **appetitive** *adj.* [Middle English *apetit* via Old French from Latin *appetere* to strive after, from AP-¹ + *petere* to seek]

appetizer *or* **appetiser** /'apətiezə/ *noun* **1** a food or drink that stimulates the appetite, usu served before a meal. **2** a foretaste: *To the Indians death was a very simple thing, for life was just an appetiser* — Ronald Bergan.

appetizing *or* **appetising** *adj* appealing to the appetite, *esp* in appearance or aroma. >> **appetizingly** *adv.*

appl. *abbr* applied.

applaud /ə'plawd/ >> *verb intrans* said of an audience: to express approval by clapping, cheering, etc. >> *verb trans* **1** to express approval of (somebody or something) by clapping the hands. **2** to praise (somebody or something), *esp* publicly: *He was applauded for his presence of mind.* >> **applaudable** *adj*, **applauder** *noun*. [French *applaudir* from Latin *applaudere*, from AP-¹ + *plaudere* to applaud]

applause /ə'plawz/ *noun* **1** approval or admiration expressed by clapping the hands. **2** praise, *esp* when publicly expressed. [medieval Latin *applausus* applause, welcome, earlier clashing noise, noun use of past part. of *applaudere* to clap, applaud: see APPLAUD]

apple /'apl/ *noun* **1a** a round fruit with red or green skin and crisp white flesh. **b** any of a genus of trees of the rose family that bear this fruit: genus *Malus*. **2** a fruit or other plant structure resembling an apple: *crab apples; an oak apple.* ✱ **she's apples** *Aus, informal* everything's fine. **the apple of one's eye** somebody or something greatly cherished [orig the pupil, once believed to be a solid ball, hence something equally precious and delicate]. **upset the apple cart** to ruin a scheme or plan. [Old English *æppel*]

applejack *noun NAmer* brandy distilled from cider.

apple-pie bed *noun Brit* a bed made with the sheet folded back halfway down as a practical joke, so that the occupant cannot lie out straight.

apple-pie order *noun informal* perfect order.

apples and pears *pl noun Brit, informal* stairs. [rhyming slang]

apple sauce *noun* **1** a sauce made of stewed apples, typically served with pork. **2** *NAmer, informal* nonsense.

applet /'aplit/ *noun* in computing, a small application that runs within a larger program, or operates within a web page.

Appleton layer /'aplt(ə)n/ *noun* a layer of the atmosphere containing ionized gases; the F layer. [named after Sir Edward *Appleton* d.1965, English physicist, who discovered it]

appliance /ə'plie·əns/ *noun* **1** an instrument or device designed for a particular use; *esp* a domestic machine, e.g. a food mixer, vacuum cleaner, or cooker. **2** a fire engine. **3** an artificial limb, dental brace, or other device worn to correct a deformity or replace a missing part: *a surgical appliance.* **4** *Brit* the process of applying something; application: *the appliance of science.*

applicable /ə'plikəbl/ *adj* able to be applied rightfully or suitably; appropriate or related. >> **applicability** /ə,plikə'biliti/ *noun.*

applicant /'aplik(ə)nt/ *noun* a person who applies for something, e.g. a job.

application /apli'kaysh(ə)n/ *noun* **1** a request or petition, *esp* a formal request made in writing, e.g. to be considered for a job. **2a** an act of applying. **b** a use to which something is put. **3** capacity for practical use; relevance. **4** close attention; diligence. **5** a computer program that performs a particular function, e.g. word processing. **6** a lotion or other substance applied to the skin. >> **applicative** /ə'plikətiv/ *adj*, **applicatory** /ə'plikət(ə)ri/ *adj*. [Middle English *applicacioun* from Latin *application-, applicatio* a bending towards, attaching, from *applicare*: see APPLY]

applicator /'aplikaytə/ *noun* a device for applying a substance, e.g. medicine or polish.

applied /ə'plied/ *adj* put to practical use; *esp* applying general principles to solve specific problems: *applied sciences; an exhibition of applied art.*

appliqué¹ /ə'pleekay, aplee'kay/ *noun* **1** a cutout decoration fastened, usu by sewing, to a larger piece of material. **2** the decorative work formed in this manner. [French *appliqué*, past part. of *appliquer* to put on, from Latin *applicare*: see APPLY]

appliqué² *verb trans* (**appliqués, appliquéd, appliquéing** /-kay·ing, -'kaying/) to apply (e.g. a decoration or ornament) to a larger surface.

apply /ə'plie/ *verb* (**applies, applied, applying**) >> *verb trans* **1a** to bring (something) to bear or put (something) to use, *esp* for some practical purpose: *We need to apply more pressure to get results; Apply the brakes firmly in an emergency.* **b** to lay or spread (something) on a surface: *Apply varnish to all exposed areas.* **2** (+ to) to devote (oneself or one's efforts) to something with attention or diligence: *They succeed by applying themselves to the job in hand.* >> *verb intrans* **1** (*usu* + to) to have relevance: *This rule applies to new members only; Clause 7 doesn't apply if you're self-employed.* **2** (*usu* + for/to) to make a request, *esp* formally in writing: *Apply in writing to the personnel manager; Will you apply for the job?* >> **applier** /ə'plie·ə/ *noun.* [Middle English *applien* via Old French from Latin *applicare* to fasten to, attach, from AP-¹ + *plicare* to fold]

appoggiatura /ə,pojə'tooərə/ *noun* a GRACE NOTE (musical note added as ornament) preceding an essential melodic note, performed on the beat, normally taking half its time value: compare ACCIACCATURA. [Italian *appoggiatura* support, from *appoggiare* to lean or rest on, ultimately from Latin AP-¹ + *podium* support]

appoint /ə'poynt/ *verb trans* **1** to select (somebody) for an office or position. **2** *formal* to fix or name (something, e.g. a time) officially: *appoint a day for the hearing.* **3** to state in a will that property will be transferred to (somebody), or decide the future ownership of (property) in this way. [Middle English *appointen* from Old French *apointier* to arrange, from *a point* to a point]

appointed *adj* **1** said of a time or place: as previously decided for the event in question: *at the appointed hour.* **2** (*used in combinations*) equipped or furnished as specified: *at their well-appointed premises on Albemarle Street.*

appointee /apoyn'tee, ə-/ *noun* a person who is appointed to a job or post.

appointive /ə'poyntiv/ *adj NAmer* said of a post or office: filled by appointment rather than by election.

appointment *noun* **1** an act of appointing: *the appointment of a new sales manager.* **2** an office or position held by somebody who has been appointed to it rather than voted into it. **3** an arrangement for a meeting or other engagement. **4** (*in pl*) equipment or furnishings: *admiring the cozy apartments and rich but eminently homelike appointments of the place* — Mark Twain. ✱ **by appointment/by appointment to the Queen** selling a commodity or supplying a service to the Queen.

apport /ə'pawt/ *noun* an object supposedly produced by supernatural means at a spiritualist seance. [French *apport* something introduced or added, ultimately from AP-¹ + Latin *portare* to bring, carry]

apportion /ə'pawsh(ə)n/ *verb trans* **1** to divide, distribute, or allot (something) in just proportion or according to a plan: *All around farms were apportioned and allotted in proportion to the standing of each individual* — Conan Doyle. **2** to assign (blame). >> **apportionment** *noun*. [Old French *apportionner*, from AP-¹ + *portionner* to portion]

appose /ə'pohz/ *verb trans technical* to place (one thing) side by side with another; to juxtapose. [from Latin *apponere* to place close to, modelled on COMPOSE, IMPOSE, etc]

apposite /'apəzit/ *adj* highly pertinent or appropriate; apt: *an apposite description.* >> **appositely** *adv*, **appositeness** *noun*. [Latin *appositus*, past part. of *apponere* to place near, from AP-¹ + *ponere* to put]

apposition /apə'zish(ə)n/ *noun* **1** a grammatical construction in which two usu adjacent nouns or noun phrases both refer to the same person or thing and stand in the same syntactic relation to the rest of a sentence, as in 'She lives with *her son, an art historian*', '*My sister Jill* phoned'. **2** *technical* the placing of one thing side by side with another. >> **appositional** *adj*, **appositionally** *adv.*

appraisal /ə'prayz(ə)l/ *noun* an act or instance of appraising, e.g. a valuation of property by an authorized person, or an assessment of a worker's performance.

appraise /ə'prayz/ *verb trans* **1** to evaluate the worth, significance, or status of (somebody or something): *appraising the way in which students approach writing tasks.* **2** to make a valuation of (property, etc) for tax purposes, etc. >> **appraiser** *noun*, **appraising** *adj*, **appraisingly** *adv.* [Middle English *appreisen* from Old French *apprisier*, from AD- + *prisier* to price, prize, from *pris*: see PRICE¹]

Usage note

appraise *or* apprise? These two words are sometimes confused. To *appraise* is a fairly formal word meaning 'to assess' something or 'estimate its value': *appraise the damage caused by the fire.* To *apprise* is an even more formal word meaning 'to inform' and is followed by the preposition *of*: *She had already apprised us of her intentions.*

appreciable /ə'preesh(y)əbl/ *adj* large enough to notice; substantial: *The snail had crawled an appreciable distance.* ➤➤ **appreciably** *adv.*

appreciate /ə'preeshiayt, -siayt/ *verb trans* **1** to recognize the value or importance of (something that one has the benefit of) and be properly grateful: *They don't appreciate their staff; I appreciate your offer.* **2** *informal* (*in negative contexts*) to be pleased at (something): *He doesn't appreciate being kept waiting.* **3** to esteem (something): *appreciate fine wines.* **4** to realize or be aware of (something): *I appreciate that the schedule is tight; I appreciate your difficulty.* **5** *NAmer* to raise the value of (a commodity, currency, etc). ➤ *verb intrans* to increase in value: *The property will have appreciated considerably in six years.* ➤➤ **appreciative** *adj,* **appreciatively** *adv,* **appreciator** *noun,* **appreciatory** *adj.* [late Latin *appretiatus,* past part. of *appretiare,* from Latin AP-[1] + *pretium* PRICE]

appreciation /ə,preeshi'aysh(ə)n, -si'aysh(ə)n/ *noun* **1** sensitive awareness, *esp* recognition of aesthetic values: *appreciation of the fine points; appreciation of good music.* **2** admiration, approval, or gratitude: *show proper appreciation for their generosity.* **3** an increase in value: *an appreciation of 10% over two years.* **4** a judgment or evaluation; *esp* a favourable critical assessment: *The Lancet printed a short appreciation of her life and work.*

apprehend /apri'hend/ *verb trans* **1** *formal or literary* to arrest or seize (a suspected person, etc): *In any other part of the country the drug dealers would have been apprehended in a series of dawn raids* — Independent. **2** to understand or perceive (something): *Society is apprehended as a social system for the organization of production.* **3** *dated* to anticipate (danger, difficulty, etc): *No real danger was at any time apprehended* — Poe. [Middle English *apprehenden* from Latin *apprehendere* to seize]

apprehensible /apri'hensəbl/ *adj* capable of being apprehended. ➤➤ **apprehensibly** *adv.*

apprehension /apri'hensh(ə)n/ *noun* **1** anxiety or fear; nervous anticipation. **2** understanding; comprehension: *that greater clearness of head and quicker apprehension which usually attend temperance in eating and drinking* — Benjamin Franklin. **3** the arrest of a suspected person, etc. [Middle English via late Latin *apprehension-, apprehensio* arrest, seizure, understanding, from Latin *apprehensus,* past part. of *apprehendere,* to seize]

apprehensive /apri'hensiv/ *adj* **1** fearful, anxious, nervous, or uneasy: *Every delay makes one more apprehensive of further delays* — Jane Austen. **2** *archaic* relating to understanding: *our apprehensive faculties* — John Locke. ➤➤ **apprehensively** *adv,* **apprehensiveness** *noun.*

apprentice[1] /ə'prentis/ *noun* **1** a person who is learning an art or trade, either from an employer to whom he or she is bound by contract, or by practical experience under skilled workers. **2** an inexperienced person; a novice. ➤➤ **apprenticeship** *noun.* [Middle English *aprentis* from Old French *apprendre* to learn, from Latin *apprehendere* to seize]

apprentice[2] *verb trans* (*usu in passive*) to take (somebody) on as an apprentice: *She's to be apprenticed to a dressmaker, aren't you, Sally?* — Somerset Maugham; *Arthur, apprenticed as an electrician in Nottingham, was home for the holidays* — D H Lawrence.

apprise *or* **apprize** /ə'priez/ *verb trans formal* (*usu* + *of*) to inform (somebody) of something: *She made certain that all the media were fully apprised of her dissatisfaction.* [French *appris,* past part. of *apprendre* to learn, teach, from Old French *apprendre:* see APPRENTICE[1]]

Usage note
apprise *or* appraise? See note at APPRAISE.

appro /'aproh/ * **on appro** *Brit, informal* on approval.

approach[1] /ə'prohch/ *verb trans* **1a** to draw closer to (something or somebody): *the train now approaching Platform 5.* **b** to come very near to (something) in quality, character, etc: *Something approaching international humour has been achieved by Asterix* — Independent. **2a** to make advances to (somebody), *esp* with an offer of work or a request for support: *She was approached by several film producers; We approached the BBC for a donation.* **b** to begin to consider or deal with (something): *Let's approach the subject with an open mind.* ➤ *verb intrans* to draw nearer. [Middle English *approchen* via Old French from late Latin *appropiare* to draw near, from Latin AP-[1] + *prope* near]

approach[2] *noun* **1** an act or instance of approaching: *She was not aware of his approach.* **2** a means of access: *the northern approaches to the city.* **3** a manner or method of doing something, or the attitude behind this: *They have a highly individual approach to management; I take a different approach.* **4** (*usu in pl*) an advance made to establish personal or business relations: *feminine resistance to his approaches; What he ought to be doing is making approaches to the private sector.* **5** the final part of an aircraft flight before landing. **6** (*used before a noun*) denoting a golf shot from the fairway towards the green. **7** an approximation: *It was an approach to an admission of guilt.*

approachable *adj* not hostile or forbidding in manner and therefore easy to talk to or deal with. ➤➤ **approachability** /.'biliti/ *noun.*

approach road *noun* = SLIP ROAD.

approbation /aprə'baysh(ə)n/ *noun* **1** approval, *esp* if formal or official; sanction: *He did not seek the approbation of the Establishment.* **2** praise; commendation: *where 'outrageous' and 'insane' are terms of approbation.* ➤➤ **approbatory** /ə'prohbət(ə)ri/ *adj* [Middle English via Old French from Latin *approbation-, approbatio,* from *approbare:* see APPROVE]

appropriate[1] /ə'prohpriayt/ *verb trans* **1** to take exclusive possession of (something): *He had appropriated the larger attic as his workroom.* **2** (*often* + *to*) to set (something, *esp* money) apart for a particular purpose or use. **3** to take or make use of (something) without authority or right: *It was not a surprise that Egypt had appropriated the Canal* — Enoch Powell. ➤➤ **appropriable** *adj,* **appropriator** *noun.* [Middle English *appropriaten* from late Latin *appropriatus,* past part. of *appropriare* to make one's own]

appropriate[2] /ə'prohpri-ət/ *adj* **1** suitable: *not an appropriate use of company funds.* **2** apt; fitting: *an appropriate solution; Words appropriate to the occasion.* **3** *archaic* relating or belonging exclusively to a particular person or thing: *a feature ... appropriate and peculiar to the country* — J Fenimore Cooper. ➤➤ **appropriately** *adv,* **appropriateness** *noun.*

appropriate technology *noun* = INTERMEDIATE TECHNOLOGY.

appropriation /ə,prohpri'aysh(ə)n/ *noun* **1** the act or an instance of appropriating: *his free appropriation of whatever might serve his purpose* — Henry James. **2** something appropriated, e.g. money officially set aside for a particular use. ➤➤ **appropriative** /ə'prohpriətiv/ *adj.*

approval /ə'proohvl/ *noun* **1** a favourable opinion or judgment. **2** formal or official permission. * **on approval** said of goods supplied commercially: able to be returned without payment if found unsatisfactory.

approve /ə'proohv/ *verb intrans* (*often* + *of*) to take a favourable view: *He doesn't approve of physical punishment under any circumstances.* ➤ *verb trans* **1** to give formal or official sanction to (something); to ratify: *Parliament approved the proposed measure.* **2** to accept (something) as satisfactory: *The repairs were inspected and approved.* **3** *NAmer* to have or express a favourable opinion of (something). **4** *archaic* to show (e.g. oneself) to be something: *Cornelia ... approved herself so discreet a matron, so affectionate a mother* — Dryden. ➤➤ **approvingly** *adv.* [Middle English *approven* via Old French from Latin *approbare* to judge to be good, from AP-[1] + *probare:* see PROVE]

approved school *noun Brit* a former name for a boarding school for young offenders.

approx. /ə'proks/ *abbr* **1** approximate. **2** approximately.

approximate[1] /ə'proksimət/ *adj* **1** nearly correct or exact. **2** said of a term, etc: loose; inexact. ➤➤ **approximately** *adv.* [late Latin *approximatus,* past part. of *approximare* to come near, from Latin AP-[1] + *proximare:* see PROXIMATE]

approximate[2] /ə'proksimayt/ *verb intrans* **1** (*often* + *to*) to come close, *esp* in quality or character: *The animals are kept as far as possible in conditions approximating to their native habitat.* **2** (*often* + *to*) to average out: *a reading rate approximating to ten books a year.* **3** to make a guess. ➤ *verb trans* **1** to approach or be similar to (something), *esp* in quality or number: *Surgery alters their anatomy so that it approximates that of the preferred sex.* **2** to simulate (something): *Flying conditions can be approximated in the laboratory.* **3** to guess (an amount). ➤➤ **approximative** /ə'proksimətiv/ *adj,* **approximatively** /ə'proksimətivli/ *adv.*

approximation /əˌproksi'maysh(ə)n/ *noun* **1** a roughly calculated amount; an estimate. **2** a loose or inexact account, description, etc. **3** (+ to) something that is approximately similar to a certain thing: *a checked pattern intended as an approximation to a tartan.*

appurtenance /ə'puhtinəns/ *noun* (*also in pl*) an item that belongs to the equipment for something, *esp* a piece of furniture, fitting, household article, etc: *sheets and blankets and knives and forks and pots and pans and more complicated appurtenances of living* — Barbara Vine. ➤➤ **appurtenant** *adj.* [Middle English via Anglo-French from Old French *apartenance*, from *apartenir*: see APPERTAIN]

APR *abbr* annual or annualized percentage rate.

Apr. *abbr* April.

apraxia /ay'praksiə/ *noun* loss or impairment of the ability to execute complex coordinated movements. ➤➤ **apractic** /ay'praktik/ *adj*, **apraxic** *adj.* [scientific Latin from Greek *apraxia*, inaction, from A-² + *prassein* to do]

après-ski /ˌapray 'skee (*French* apre ski)/ *noun* **1** social activity after a day's skiing. **2** (*used before a noun*) relating to this activity: *an après-ski drink.* [French *après* after + *ski* ski, skiing]

apricot /'ayprikot/ *noun* **1a** an oval orange-coloured fruit with soft juicy yellow or orange flesh. **b** the tree of the rose family that bears this fruit, closely related to the peach and plum: *Prunus armeniaca.* **2** an orange-pink colour. [alteration of earlier *abrecock*, from Arabic *al-birqūq* the apricot]

April /'aypril/ *noun* the fourth month of the year. [Middle English via Old French from Latin *Aprilis*]

April fool *noun* the victim of a joke or trick played on April Fools' Day.

April Fools' Day *noun* 1 April, characteristically marked by the playing of practical jokes.

a priori /ˌay prie'awri, -rie/ *adj and adv* **1a** relating to or derived by reasoning from self-evident propositions; deductive: compare A POSTERIORI: *a priori reasoning; argue a priori.* **b** relating to something that can be known by reason alone without recourse to experience. **c** true or false by definition or convention alone, without further investigation: *a priori statements.* **2** said of argument or reasoning: without examination or analysis; presumptive: *something that cannot be assumed a priori.* ➤➤ **apriority** /-'oriti/ *noun.* [Latin *a priori*, from the former]

apron /'aypron/ *noun* **1** a garment tied round the waist and used to protect clothing. **2** something that suggests or resembles an apron in shape, position, or use, e.g.: **a** the part of a theatre stage that projects in front of the curtain. **b** the paved area by an airport terminal or in front of hangars, used for loading and moving aircraft. ✳ **tied to somebody's apron strings** usu said of a man: dominated by a woman, *esp* a mother or wife.

Word history
Middle English, orig *napron*, from early French *naperon*, dimin. of *nape* cloth, modification of Latin *mappa* napkin, towel. The modern form of the word originated in a misunderstanding of *a napron* as *an apron* during the 15th cent. Another word formed in the same way is *adder*.

apropos¹ /apra'poh/ *adv* **1** at the opportune moment: *You could not have arrived more apropos.* **2** by the way; incidentally: *Apropos, I'll be coming too.* [French *à propos*, to the purpose]

apropos² *adj* relevant or opportune: *Read E M Forster's story 'When the machine stopped' – it is rather apropos in today's computer-dependent world.*

apropos³ *prep* (*also* + of) concerning (something); with regard to (something): *apropos our discussions; apropos of your letter.*

apse /aps/ *noun* **1** a projecting and usu rounded and vaulted part of a building, *esp* a church. **2** = APSIS (1). [medieval Latin *apsis*: see APSIS]

apsidal /'apsidl/ *adj* forming or in the form of an apse.

apsis /'apsis/ *noun* (*pl* **apsides** /-deez/) **1** the point in an astronomical orbit at which the distance of the body from the centre of attraction is either greatest or least. **2** = APSE (1). [Latin *apsid-, apsis* from Greek *hapsid-, hapsis*, from *haptein* to fasten]

APT *abbr* Advanced Passenger Train.

apt /apt/ *adj* **1** likely, or having a tendency to do something: *apt to forget.* **2** suited to a purpose; relevant: *an apt choice; an expression that was all too apt.* **3** keenly intelligent and responsive: *an apt pupil.* ➤➤ **aptly** *adv*, **aptness** *noun.* [Middle English, from Latin *aptus*, literally 'fastened', past part. of *apere* to fasten]

Usage note
apt, liable, *and* **likely.** *Apt to, liable to,* and *likely to* are similar in meaning and use and need to be handled with care. *He is apt to exaggerate* means 'he often exaggerates (as we know from our experience of him)'; *he is likely to exaggerate* means 'he can be expected to exaggerate (in this instance)'. *He is liable to exaggerate* can mean either. When referring to a specific time in the future always use *likely*: *It is likely to rain tomorrow.* But *it is apt/liable/likely to rain in November* means in all three forms 'November is often a rainy month'.

apt. *abbr* apartment.

apterous /'aptərəs/ *adj* without wings: *apterous insects.* [Greek *apteros*, from A-² + *pteron* wing]

apteryx /'aptəriks/ *noun* = KIWI (1). [scientific Latin *apteryx*, from A-² + Greek *pteryx* wing]

aptitude /'aptityoohd/ *noun* **1** a natural ability or talent, *esp* for learning. **2** (*usu* + for) general fitness or suitability. ➤➤ **aptitudinal** /-'tyoohdinl/ *adj.*

aqu- *or* **aqua-** *or* **aqui-** *comb. form* forming words, denoting: water: *aquarobics.* [Latin *aqua* water]

aqua¹ /'akwə/ *noun* the colour aquamarine. ➤➤ **aqua** *adj.*

aqua² *noun* in lists of ingredients: water. [Latin *aqua* water]

aqua- *comb. form* see AQU-.

aquaculture /'akwəkulchə/ *noun* the cultivation of aquatic plants or animals for use by humans: compare AQUICULTURE. ➤➤ **aquacultural** /-'kulchərəl/ *adj.* [AQUA- + -*culture* as in *agriculture*]

aquaerobics /akwə'rohbiks/ *pl noun* see AQUAROBICS.

aqua fortis /ˌakwə 'fawtis/ *noun* = NITRIC ACID. [Latin *aqua fortis*, literally 'strong water']

aqualung /'akwəlung/ *noun* an underwater breathing apparatus consisting of cylinders of compressed air or oxygen carried on the back and connected to a face mask. [AQUA- + LUNG]

aquamanile /ˌakwəmə'nieli, -'neeli/ *noun* a medieval ewer, typically shaped like a bird or animal. [via late Latin from Latin *aquaemanalis*, from *aquae* of water + *manale* ewer]

aquamarine /ˌakwəmə'reen/ *noun* **1** a transparent blue to green beryl used as a gemstone: compare BERYL, EMERALD. **2** a pale blue to light greenish blue colour. ➤➤ **aquamarine** *adj.* [Latin *aqua marina* sea water]

aquaplane¹ /'akwəplayn/ *noun* a board for riding on water, towed by a fast motorboat. [AQUA- + PLANE¹]

aquaplane² *verb intrans* **1** to ride on an aquaplane. **2** said of a car: to go out of control by sliding on water lying on the surface of a wet road. ➤➤ **aquaplaner** *noun.*

aqua regia /ˌakwə 'reji·ə, 'ree-/ *noun* a mixture of nitric and hydrochloric acids that dissolves gold or platinum. [Latin *aqua regia*, literally 'royal water']

aquarelle /akwə'rel/ *noun* a painting in thin usu transparent watercolours. ➤➤ **aquarellist** *noun.* [French *aquarelle* from obsolete Italian *acquarella* (now *acquerello*) from *acqua* water, from AQUA-]

aquaria /ə'kweəri·ə/ *noun* pl of AQUARIUM.

aquarist /'akwərist/ *noun* **1** a person who keeps an aquarium. **2** the curator of an aquarium.

aquarium /ə'kweəri·əm/ *noun* (*pl* **aquariums** *or* **aquaria** /-ə/) **1** a glass tank, artificial pond, etc in which living aquatic animals or plants are kept. **2** an establishment where collections of living aquatic organisms are exhibited. [neuter of Latin *aquarius* of water, from AQUA-]

Aquarius /ə'kweəri·əs/ *noun* **1** in astronomy, a constellation (the Water Carrier) depicted as a man pouring water from a jar. **2a** in astrology, the eleventh sign of the zodiac. **b** a person born under this sign. ➤➤ **Aquarian** *adj and noun.* [Latin *aquarius* water carrier, from AQUA-]

aquarobics *or* **aquaerobics** /akwə'rohbiks/ *pl noun* (*treated as sing.*) exercises done to music in a swimming pool. [blend of AQUA- and AEROBICS]

aquatic¹ /ə'kwatik, ə'kwotik/ *adj* **1** growing, living in, or frequenting water. **2** taking place in or on water: *aquatic sports.* ➤➤ **aquatically** *adv.*

aquatic² *noun* **1** an aquatic animal or plant. **2** (*in pl, but treated as sing. or pl*) water sports.

aquatint /'akwətint/ *noun* **1** a method of etching a printing plate that enables tones similar to watercolour washes to be reproduced. **2** a print produced by this method. [Italian *acqua tinta* dyed water]

aquavit /'akwəvit/ *noun* a colourless Scandinavian spirit made with potatoes and flavoured with caraway seeds. [Swedish, Danish, and Norwegian *akvavit* from medieval Latin *aqua vitae*: see AQUA VITAE]

aqua vitae /,akwə 'veetie, 'vie-/ *noun* a strong alcoholic spirit, e.g. brandy or whisky. [Middle English from medieval Latin, literally 'water of life']

aqueduct /'akwədukt/ *noun* **1** a bridge-like structure, usu supported by arches, built to carry a canal across a valley. **2** a channel or passage in the body. **3** any conduit for carrying water. [Latin *aquaeductus*, from *aquae* of water + *ductus* act of leading, from *ducere* to leave]

aqueous /'akwi·əs, 'ay-/ *adj* of or resembling water, or made from, with, or by water. ⟫⟫ **aqueously** *adv.* [late Latin *aqueus* of water, from AQU-]

aqueous humour *noun* a transparent liquid occupying the space between the lens and the cornea of the eye.

aqui- *comb. form* see AQU-.

aquiculture /'akwikulchə/ *noun* = HYDROPONICS: compare AQUA-CULTURE. ⟫⟫ **aquicultural** /-'kulchərəl/ *adj.* [AQUI- + -*culture* as in *agriculture*]

aquifer /'akwifə/ *noun* a water-bearing layer of permeable rock, sand, or gravel. ⟫⟫ **aquiferous** /a'kwifərəs/ *adj.* [scientific Latin *aquifer*, from AQUI- + -*fer* bearing, from *ferre* to carry]

aquilegia /akwi'leej(y)ə/ *noun* = COLUMBINE. [late Latin *aquilegia*; adopted as genus name, prob from Latin *aquilegus* water-gathering, from AQUI- + *legere* to collect]

aquiline /'akwilien/ *adj* **1** relating to or like an eagle. **2** said of the human nose: hooked. ⟫⟫ **aquilinity** /-'liniti/ *noun.* [Latin *aquilinus* of an eagle, from *aquila* eagle]

AR *abbr* **1** annual return. **2** Arkansas (US postal abbreviation). **3** autonomous republic.

Ar *abbr* the chemical symbol for argon.

ar- *prefix* see AD-.

-ar[1] *suffix* forming adjectives from nouns, denoting: **1** nature or composition: *molecular*; *spectacular*. **2** resemblance: *oracular*. [Middle English from Latin -*aris*, alteration of -*alis* -AL[1]]

-ar[2] *suffix* forming nouns, denoting: somebody who engages in a particular activity: *beggar*; *scholar*.

ARA *abbr* Associate of the Royal Academy.

Arab /'arəb/ *noun* **1a** a member of a Semitic people orig of the Arabian peninsula and now widespread throughout the Middle East and N Africa. **b** a member of an Arabic-speaking people. **2** a typically intelligent, graceful, and swift horse of an Arabian stock. ⟫⟫ **Arab** *adj.* [Middle English via Latin and Greek from Arabic *Arab*]

Usage note

Arab, Arabian, or Arabic? *Arab* is the correct adjective to use in political contexts: *Arab nations*; *an Arab leader*. The adjective *Arabian* is mainly used to designate things geographically as belonging to Arabia (the Arabian peninsula, lying between the Red Sea and the Persian Gulf): *in the Arabian desert*. *Arabic* refers principally to the language of the Arab peoples: *to learn Arabic*; *Arabic grammar*; *Arabic poetry*. The numbers in general worldwide use are *Arabic numerals*.

arabesque *noun* **1** a posture in ballet in which the dancer is supported on one leg with one arm extended forwards and the other arm and leg backwards. **2** a decorative design or style that combines natural motifs, e.g. flowers or foliage, to produce an intricate pattern. **3** a musical passage with a highly ornamental melody. [French *arabesque* from Italian *arabesco* in Arabian style, from Latin *Arabus* ARAB]

Arabian[1] /ə'raybi·ən/ *adj* relating to or belonging to Arabia or its people.

Usage note

Arabian, Arabic, or Arab? See note at ARAB.

Arabian[2] *noun* **1** chiefly formerly, a native or inhabitant of Arabia (the Arabian peninsula). **2** an Arab horse.

Arabian camel *noun* = DROMEDARY.

Arabic /'arəbik/ *noun* the Semitic language of the Arab peoples, now spoken in Arabia, Jordan, Lebanon, Syria, Iraq, Egypt, and parts of N Africa. ⟫⟫ **Arabic** *adj.*

Word history

Among the many words of Arabic origin that have passed into English are a significant number reflecting the supremacy of Islamic mathematicians and scientists in the Middle Ages, particularly between the 8th and 12th cents.: *algebra*, *zero*, *cipher*, *alkali*, *alcohol*, *almanac*, *nadir*, and so on. Other Arabic words which have firmly established themselves in English include *alcove*, *assassin*, *candy*, *cotton*, *ghoul*, *giraffe*, *lemon*, *lute*, *magazine*, *mohair*, *monsoon*, *safari*, *saffron*, *sash*, *sofa*, *syrup*, and *tariff*. Recent borrowings, reflecting the resurgence of Islam as a major force in world affairs, include *ayatollah*, *fatwa*, and *intifada*. See also usage note at ARAB.

arabica /ə'rabikə/ *noun* **1** coffee made from a bean that is widely grown in S America. **2** the bean itself. **3** the plant bearing this bean: *Coffea arabica.* [Latin *arabica*, noun use fem of *arabiscus* of Arabia]

Arabic numeral *noun* any of the number symbols 0, 1, 2, 3, 4, 5, 6, 7, 8, 9.

arabinose /'arəbinohz/ *noun* a PENTOSE (sugar containing five carbon atoms) found in pectin and plant gums, used as a culture medium. [ARABICA + -IN[1] + -OSE[2]]

arabis /'arəbis/ *noun* a creeping and trailing plant with pink or white flowers: genus *Arabis.* [via late Latin from Greek *arabis* fem of *Arab-, Araps*, Arab]

Arabist /'arəbist/ *noun* a specialist in the Arabic language or Arab culture.

arable /'arəbl/ *adj* **1** said of land: used or suitable for crop farming. **2** said of crops: suitable for growing on arable land. [Old French *arable* from Latin *arabilis* from *arare* to plough]

arachnid /ə'raknid/ *noun* any of a class of arthropods including the spiders, mites, ticks, and scorpions, with bodies that have two segments, the front segment bearing four pairs of legs: class Arachnida. ⟫⟫ **arachnid** *adj.* [scientific Latin *Arachnida*, name of class, from Greek *arachnē* spider]

arachnoid /ə'raknoyd/ *noun* (*also* **arachnoid membrane**) the thin middle membrane of the three covering the brain and spinal cord, lying between the DURA MATER (outermost membrane) and the PIA MATER (innermost membrane). [scientific Latin *arachnoides* from Greek *arachnoeidēs* like a cobweb, from *arachnē* spider, spider's web + -OID]

arachnophobia /ə,raknə'fohbi·ə/ *noun* irrational fear of spiders. ⟫⟫ **arachnophobe** /ə'raknəfohb/ *noun.* [Greek *arachnē* spider + -PHOBIA]

arak /'arak, 'arək/ *noun* see ARRACK.

Araldite /'arəldiet/ *noun trademark* an epoxy resin used to repair glass, china, plastic, etc. [based on the initials of the manufacturer, *Aero Research Ltd*, Cambridge]

Aramaic /arə'mayik/ *noun* an ancient Semitic language of Syria and Upper Mesopotamia, still spoken by certain minorities, that was used as a lingua franca in SW Asia from the sixth cent. BC, and is important as a major language of Jewish literature. [Latin *Aramaeus* via Greek from Hebrew '*Ărām* Aram, ancient name for Syria]

arame /'arəmi/ *noun* a Pacific seaweed used in Japanese cookery: *Ecklonia bicyclis.* [Japanese *arame*]

Aran /'arən/ *noun* denoting a kind of thick knitwear characterized by cable stitching and lozenge patterns, usu in a thick cream-coloured wool. [*Aran* Islands, off the W coast of Ireland]

Aranda /ə'runtə/ *noun* (*pl* **Arandas** *or* **Aranda**) **1** a member of an aboriginal people of central Australia. **2** the language of this people. ⟫⟫ **Aranda** *adj.* [Aranda name for the people and language]

araneid /ə'rayni·id/ *noun* any of an order of invertebrates constituted by the spiders: order Araneae. [scientific Latin *Araneida* former order name, from *aranea* spider]

arapaima /arə'piemə/ *noun* (*pl* **arapaimas** *or collectively* **arapaima**) a very large edible freshwater fish of tropical S America: *Arapaima gigas.*

araucaria /araw'keəri·ə/ *noun* any of a genus of S American or Australian coniferous trees, *esp* the monkey-puzzle: genus *Araucaria.* [scientific Latin *araucaria*, from *Arauco*, province in Chile]

Arawak /'arəwak/ *noun* (*pl* **Arawaks** *or collectively* **Arawak**) **1** a member of a group of Native American people living chiefly on the coast of Guyana. **2** a family of languages spoken in parts of Central and S America. ⟫⟫ **Arawakan** *adj and noun.* [Carib *aruac*]

arbalest *or* **arbalist** /'ahbəlist/ *noun* a large medieval military steel crossbow. [Old English *arblast* via Old French from late Latin *arcuballista*, from Latin *arcus* bow + *ballista*: see BALLISTA]

arbiter /'ahbitə/ *noun* a person or agency with absolute power of judging and determining. [Middle English from Latin *arbiter* judge, umpire]

arbitrage[1] /'ahbitrij, -trahzh/ *noun* the simultaneous purchase and sale of the same or equivalent security in different markets in order to profit from price discrepancies. [Middle English in the sense 'exercise of individual judgment' via French *arbitrage* from *arbitrer* to give judgment, from Latin *arbitrari*, from *arbiter* judge]

arbitrage[2] *verb intrans* to engage in arbitrage.

arbitrageur /,ahbitrah'zhuh/ *or* **arbitrager** /'ahbitrijə, -trahzhə/ *noun* a dealer on a stock exchange who specializes in arbitrage. [French *arbitrageur* arbitrator, from *arbitrage* judgment, arbitration]

arbitrament /'ahbitrəmənt/ *noun* the judgment given by an arbitrator. [Middle English via Old French from Latin *arbitrari* to give judgment, from *arbiter* ARBITER]

arbitrary /'ahbitrəri/ *adj* **1** said of a decision, judgment, etc: based on whim or random choice rather than reason: *the arbitrary classification of geography as an art rather than a science*. **2** said of a sentence, penalty, etc: that can be imposed at the discretion of a court of law. **3** said of a style of governing or rule: despotic or tyrannical. **4** said of a mathematical constant or other quantity: of unspecified value. ➤➤ **arbitrarily** /'ahbitrərəli, -'trerəli/ *adv*, **arbitrariness** *noun*.

arbitrate /'ahbitrayt/ *verb intrans* to act as an arbitrator. ➤ *verb trans* **1** to act as an arbitrator in (a dispute). **2** to submit (something) for decision to an arbitrator.

arbitration /ahbi'traysh(ə)n/ *noun* the settlement of a disputed issue by an arbitrator.

arbitrator /'ahbitraytə/ *noun* **1** somebody chosen to settle differences between two parties in dispute. **2** = ARBITER.

arbor[1] /'ahbə/ *noun* a spindle or axle of a wheel. [Latin *arbor* tree, shaft]

arbor[2] *noun NAmer* see ARBOUR.

arbor- *or* **arbori-** *comb. form* forming words, denoting: tree: *arboraceous*. [Latin *arbor* tree]

arboraceous /ahbə'rayshəs/ *adj formal* **1** relating to trees or resembling a tree. **2** planted with trees; wooded.

arboreal /ah'bawri·əl/ *adj* of, inhabiting, or relating to trees. ➤➤ **arboreally** *adv*. [Latin *arboreus* of a tree, from *arbor* tree]

arborescent /ahbə'res(ə)nt/ *adj* resembling a tree in properties, growth, structure, or appearance. ➤➤ **arborescence** *noun*, **arborescently** *adv*.

arboretum /ahbə'reetəm/ *noun* (*pl* **arboretums** *or* **arboreta** /-tə/) a place where trees and shrubs are cultivated for study and display. [scientific Latin *arboretum* place grown with trees, from ARBOR-]

arbori- *comb. form* see ARBOR-.

arboriculture /'ahbərikulchə/ *noun* the cultivation of trees and shrubs. ➤➤ **arboriculturist** /-'kulchərist/ *noun*.

arborize *or* **arborise** /'ahbəriez/ *verb intrans* to assume a treelike appearance: *The nerve fibres arborized*. ➤➤ **arborization** /-'zaysh(ə)n/ *noun*.

arbor vitae /,ahbaw 'vietee, -'veetee/ *noun* any of a genus of N American and E Asian ornamental evergreen trees of the cypress family: genus *Thuja*. [Latin *arbor vitae*, literally 'tree of life']

arbour (*NAmer* **arbor**) /'ahbə/ *noun* a garden alcove formed by climbing plants or by branches, or a trelliswork structure on which climbing plants can be grown to form an alcove. ➤➤ **arboured** *adj*. [Middle English *erber* plot of grass, arbour, via Old French from Latin *herba* grass]

arbovirus /'ahbəvie·ərəs/ *noun* any of a group of viruses, including yellow fever and encephalitis, transmitted to vertebrates by mosquitoes, ticks, or other arthropods. [blend of ARTHROPOD + BORNE[2] + VIRUS]

arbutus /ah'byoohtəs/ *noun* any of a genus of shrubs and trees of the heath family, with white or pink flowers: genus *Arbutus*. [Latin *arbutus* the wild strawberry tree]

ARC *abbr* **1** formerly, Agricultural Research Council. **2** Aids-related complex.

arc[1] /ahk/ *noun* **1** something arched or curved. **2** a continuous portion of a curve, e.g. of a circle or an ellipse. **3** the apparent path followed by a planet or other celestial body. **4** a sustained luminous discharge of electricity across a gap in a circuit or between electrodes. **5** = ARC LAMP. **6** in mathematics, used to express the inverse of a trigonometric function as in *arc sine* (written *arcsin* or *sin*[-1]) and *arc cosine* (written *arccos* or *cos*[-1]). [Middle English *ark* via Old French from Latin *arcus* bow, ARCH[1], arc]

arc[2] *verb intrans* (**arced** /ahkt/, **arcing** /'ahking/) **1** to form an arc or follow an arching or curving trajectory. **2** to form an electric arc.

arcade /ah'kayd/ *noun* **1** a long arched gallery or building. **2** a series of arches with their columns or piers. **3** a passageway or covered walk, often with shops on both sides. **4** = AMUSEMENT ARCADE. ➤➤ **arcaded** *adj*. [French *arcade* via Italian from Latin *arcus* bow, ARCH[1]]

arcade game *noun* a computer game of the kind played in an amusement arcade, requiring speedy reactions.

Arcadia /ah'kaydi·ə/ *or* **Arcady** /'ahkədi/ *noun* a usu idealized rural region or scene of simple pleasure and quiet, the typical setting of Greek and Latin pastoral poetry. ➤➤ **Arcadian** *adj*. [via Latin from Greek *Arkadia*, pastoral region of ancient Greece]

arcana /ah'kaynə/ *noun* pl of ARCANUM.

arcane /ah'kayn/ *adj* **1** known or knowable only to a few people to whom secret information has been revealed; esoteric. **2** mysterious. [Latin *arcanus*, shut away, ultimately from *arca* chest]

arcanum /ah'kaynəm/ *noun* (*pl* **arcana** /-nə/) a secret or mystery known only to those who have been initiated. [Latin *arcanum*, neuter of *arcanus*: see ARCANE]

arch[1] /ahch/ *noun* **1** a curved symmetrical structure spanning an opening and supporting a ceiling, roof, wall, bridge, or other part above it. **2** something, e.g. the vaulted bony structure of the foot, resembling an arch in form or function. **3** an archway. [Middle English *arche* via Old French from Latin *arcus*, arch, bow]

arch[2] *verb trans* **1** to form or bend (something) into an arch: *The cat arched its back*. **2** to span (an opening) or provide (a wall or other structure) with an arch. ➤ *verb intrans* to form an arch.

arch[3] *adj* **1a** said of a look, manner, remark, etc: consciously sly or teasing; saucy or playful: *an arch smile*. **b** *archaic* clever; alert: *Oh that arch eye of yours!* — Jane Austen. **2** *archaic* preeminent; exceptional: *the most arch deed of piteous massacre* — Shakespeare. ➤➤ **archly** *adv*, **archness** *noun*. [ARCH-[1] (2), as in *arch-rogue*]

arch. *abbr* **1** archaic. **2** architect. **3** architectural. **4** architecture.

arch-[1] *prefix* forming words, with the meanings: **1** chief or principal: *archbishop*. **2** extreme; most fully embodying the qualities of a specified usu undesirable human type: *arch-rogue*; *arch-enemy*. [Old English *ærce-, arc-* via Latin from Greek *arch-, archi-* from *archein* to begin, rule]

arch-[2] *prefix* see ARCHI-.

-arch *comb. form* forming nouns, denoting: a ruler or leader: *matriarch*; *oligarch*. [Middle English *-arche* via Old French and Latin from Greek *-archēs, -archos* from *archein* to rule]

archae- *or* **archaeo-** (*NAmer* **arche-** *or* **archeo-**) *comb. form* forming words, with the meaning: ancient or primitive: *archaeopteryx*; *archaeology*. [Greek *archaio-* from *archaios* ancient, from *archē* beginning]

Archaean (*NAmer* **Archean**) /ah'kee·ən/ *adj* relating to or dating from the earlier part of the Precambrian aeon, lasting from about 4600 to about 2500 million years ago, before the first living things appeared. Also called AZOIC. ➤➤ **Archaean** *noun*. [Greek *archaios*: see ARCHAE-]

archaeo- *comb. form* see ARCHAE-.

archaeology (*NAmer* **archeology**) /ahki'oləji/ *noun* the scientific study of material remains, *esp* artefacts and dwellings, of past human life and activities.

Editorial note
Literally 'discourse on ancient things', archaeology is the study of the human past through the systematic recovery and analysis of material culture. The discipline aims to recover, describe and classify this material, to describe the form and behaviour of past societies, and to understand the reasons for this behaviour. It has become a truly interdisciplinary subject, drawing on expertise from many other fields — Dr Paul Bahn.

➤➤ **archaeological** /-'lojikl/ *adj*, **archaeologically** /-'lojikəli/ *adv*, **archaeologist** *noun*. [French *archéologie* via late Latin from Greek *archaiologia*, from ARCHAEO- + -LOGY]

archaeopteryx /ahki'optəriks/ *noun* the oldest fossil bird of the late Jurassic period, which combined the wings and feathers of a bird with the teeth and bony tail of a dinosaur. [scientific Latin *archaeopteryx* genus name, from ARCHAEO- + Greek *pteryx* wing]

archaic /ah'kayik/ *adj* 1 antiquated: *archaic methods.* 2 said of vocabulary or expressions: no longer used in ordinary speech or writing. 3 said of art, music, etc: belonging to an early period of development. ➤➤ **archaically** *adv.* [French *archaïque* from Greek *archaïkos*, from *archaios* ancient]

archaise /'ahkay·iez/ *verb* see ARCHAIZE.

archaism /'ahkayiz(ə)m/ *noun* 1 an instance of archaic usage; *esp* an archaic word or expression. 2 the use of archaic diction or style. 3 something outmoded or old-fashioned: *The question is whether these hallowed archaisms are only a surface phenomenon, which a sensible modernization of Parliament would easily sweep away* — Anthony Arblaster. ➤➤ **archaistic** /-'istik/ *adj.* [via Latin from Greek *archaïsmos*, from *archaios* ancient]

archaize *or* **archaise** /'ahkay·iez/ *verb trans* to give (something) an archaic style or character. ➤ *verb intrans* to use, *esp* consciously, archaic language or styles. ➤➤ **archaizer** *noun.*

archangel /'ahk'aynjəl, 'ahk-/ *noun* 1 a chief or principal angel. 2 (*also* **yellow archangel**) a woodland plant of the dead-nettle family, with yellow flowers: *Lamiastrum galeobdolon.* ➤➤ **archangelic** /ahkan'jelik/ *adj.* [Middle English via Old French or late Latin from Greek *archangelos*, from ARCH-[1] + *angelos* angel]

archbishop /ahch'bishəp/ *noun* a bishop at the head of an ecclesiastical province, or one of equivalent honorary rank. ➤➤ **archbishopric** *noun.* [Old English via late Latin from late Greek *archiepiskopos*, from ARCHI- + *episkopos*: see BISHOP]

archdeacon /ahch'deekən/ *noun* a member of the clergy having the duty of assisting a diocesan bishop, *esp* in administrative work. ➤➤ **archdeaconate** /-nət/ *noun,* **archdeaconry** *noun.* [Old English via late Latin from late Greek *archidiakonos*, from Greek ARCHI- + *diakonos* DEACON]

archdiocese /ahch'die·əsis/ *noun* the diocese of an archbishop. ➤➤ **archdiocesan** /-'osisən/ *adj.*

archduchess /ahch'duchis/ *noun* 1 the wife or widow of an archduke. 2 a woman having the rank of archduke in her own right. [French *archiduchesse*, fem of *archiduc* archduke, from early French *archeduc*: see ARCHDUKE]

archduke /ahch'dyoohk/ *noun* a principal duke, *esp* as a former title of the eldest son of the Emperor of Austria. ➤➤ **archducal** *adj,* **archduchy** /ahch'duchi/ *noun,* **archdukedom** *noun.* [early French *archeduc*, from *arche-* ARCH-[1] + *duc*: see DUKE]

arche- *comb. form NAmer* see ARCHAE-.

Archean /ah'kee·ən/ *adj NAmer* see ARCHAEAN.

archegonium /ahki'gohni·əm/ *noun* (*pl* **archegonia** /-ni·ə/) the flask-shaped female sex organ of mosses, ferns, and some conifers. [scientific Latin *archegonium* from Greek *archegonos* originator, from *archein* to begin + *gonos* procreation]

arch-enemy *noun* (*pl* **arch-enemies**) 1 one's most bitter enemy: *She saw her arch-enemy, a neighbor's cat, on top of the high fence* — Nathaniel Hawthorne. 2 (**the arch-enemy**) *archaic* the devil; Satan.

archeo- *comb. form NAmer* see ARCHAE-.

archeology /ahki'oləji/ *noun NAmer* see ARCHAEOLOGY.

archer /'ahchə/ *noun* 1 a person who practises archery. 2 (**the Archer**) the constellation and sign of the zodiac Sagittarius. [Middle English via Old French from late Latin *arcuarius* of a bow, from Latin *arcus* bow, ARCH[1]]

archerfish *noun* (*pl* **archerfishes** *or collectively* **archerfish**) any of several small fishes of SE Asia, Australia, and the Philippines that catch insects by stunning them with drops of water ejected from the mouth: *Toxotes jaculator.*

archery /'ahchəri/ *noun* the art, practice, skill, or sport of shooting arrows from a bow.

archetype /'ahkitiep/ *noun* 1 an original pattern or model; a prototype: *Lancashire's cotton industry provided the archetypes of Blake's 'dark satanic mills'.* 2 a perfect example or model of something: *the Negro in chains, the archetype of exploited humanity* — David Lodge. 3 in Jungian psychology, an inherited idea or mode of thought derived from the collective unconscious. ➤➤ **archetypal** /-'tiepl/ *adj,* **archetypical** /-'tipikl/ *adj.* [via Latin from Greek *archetypon,*

neuter of *archetypos* archetypal, from *archein* to begin, rule + *typos*: see TYPE[1]]

arch-fiend *noun* (**the arch-fiend**) *literary* the devil; Satan.

archi- *or* **arch-** *prefix* forming words, with the meanings: 1 chief or principal: *architrave.* 2 in biology or anthropology, primitive; original; primary. [French *archi-* via Latin from Greek: see ARCH-[1]]

archidiaconal /ˌahkidie'akənl/ *adj* relating to an archdeacon. [late Latin *archidiaconus*: see ARCHDEACON]

archiepiscopal /ahki·i'piskəpl/ *adj* relating to an archbishop. ➤➤ **archiepiscopate** /-pət, -payt/ *noun.* [medieval Latin *archiepiscopalis* from late Latin *archiepiscopus*: see ARCHBISHOP]

archimandrite /ahki'mandriet/ *noun* 1 the superior of a monastery in the Orthodox Church. 2 an honorary title for a monastic priest. [late Latin *archimandrites* via late Greek from Greek ARCHI- + late Greek *mandra* monastery, from Greek, fold, pen]

Archimedes' principle /ahki'meedeez/ *noun* in physics, a law stating that an object floating in a liquid displaces a weight of liquid equal to its own weight. [*Archimedes* d.212 BC, Greek mathematician and inventor]

Archimedes' screw *noun* a device for raising water, consisting of a tube bent spirally round an axis, or of a broad-threaded screw encased by a cylinder.

archipelago /ahki'peləgoh, ahchi-/ *noun* (*pl* **archipelagos** *or* **archipelagoes**) 1 a group of scattered islands. 2 an expanse of sea scattered with islands. ➤➤ **archipelagic** /-pə'lajik/ *adj.* [*Archipelago* Aegean Sea, from Italian *Arcipelago*, literally 'chief sea', from *arci-* ARCHI- + Greek *pelagos* sea]

architect /'ahkitekt/ *noun* 1 a person who designs buildings and superintends their construction. 2 a person who originates or comprehensively plans a system, project, etc: *Lord Beveridge, architect of the Welfare State.* [early French *architecte* via Latin from Greek *architektōn* master builder, from ARCHI- + *tektōn* builder, carpenter]

architectonic /ˌahkitek'tonik/ *adj* 1 relating to architecture or according with its principles: *architectonic requirements; architectonic ornaments.* 2 resembling architecture in structure or organization: *Classification is the architectonic science* — William Whewell. ➤➤ **architectonically** *adv.* [via Latin from Greek *architektonikos*, from *architektōn*: see ARCHITECT]

architectonics *pl noun* (*treated as sing. or pl*) 1 the art or science of architecture. 2 the systematic arrangement of knowledge.

architecture /'ahkitekchə/ *noun* 1 the art, practice, or profession of designing and erecting buildings. 2 a particular method or style of building: *Gothic architecture.* 3 buildings collectively: *the beautiful architecture of Prague.* 4 the design and structure of anything: *the architecture of molecules; software and its architecture.* ➤➤ **architectural** /-'tekchərəl/ *adj,* **architecturally** /-'tekchərəli/ *adv.*

architrave /'ahkitrayv/ *noun* 1 in classical architecture, the lowest part of an ENTABLATURE (upper section supported on columns) resting immediately on the capital of the column. 2a the moulded frame round a rectangular recess or opening, e.g. a door or window. b the exterior moulding round an arch. [early French *architrave* from Old Italian, from ARCHI- + *trave* beam, from Latin *trab-, trabs*]

archive[1] /'ahkiev/ *noun* 1a a collection of historical documents and records. b (*also in pl*) a place in which records or historical documents are preserved. 2 computer data transferred to a disk or tape for long-term storage. ➤➤ **archival** *adj.* [French *archive* via Latin from Greek *archeion* government house (in pl, official documents), from *archē* rule, government]

archive[2] *verb trans* 1 to file or collect (e.g. records or documents) in an archive. 2 to transfer (computer data not needed for immediate access) to a tape or disk for long-term storage.

archivist /'ahkivist/ *noun* an official who organizes and is responsible for archives.

archivolt /'ahkivohlt/ *noun* the lower curve of an arch or a band of moulding ornamenting it.

archlute *noun* a bass lute with a long neck carrying unstopped bass strings.

archon /'ahkon/ *noun* a chief magistrate, one of nine appointed annually, in ancient Athens. [via Latin from Greek *archōn*, present part. of *archein* to rule]

archway /'ahchway/ *noun* an arch with a passage or entrance beneath it, or the passage or entrance itself.

-archy *comb. form* forming nouns, denoting: rule or government: *monarchy*. [Middle English *-archie* via French and Latin from Greek *-archia* from *archein* to rule]

arc lamp *noun* a type of electric lamp that produces light by an arc made when a current passes between two incandescent electrodes surrounded by gas.

Arctic[1] /'ahktik/ *adj* **1** relating to the N Pole or the surrounding region. **2** (**arctic**). **a** extremely cold: *arctic weather; arctic temperatures*. **b** cold in temper or mood. [Middle English *artik* via Latin from Greek *arktikos* from *arktos* bear, Ursa Major, north]

Arctic[2] *noun* **1** (*usu* **the Arctic**) the regions surrounding the N Pole. **2** (**arctic**) *NAmer* a thick warm waterproof overshoe.

Arctic Circle *noun* the parallel of latitude approximately 66½° north of the equator that forms a notional line round the north polar region.

arctic fox *noun* a small fox of arctic regions that is either brownish in summer and white in winter or grey in summer and a light grey-blue in winter: *Alopex lagopus*.

arctic hare *noun* a hare of the N American Arctic whose coat turns white in winter: *Lepus arcticus*.

arctophile /'ahktəfiel/ *noun* a person who likes or collects teddy bears. ➤➤ **arctophilia** /-'fili·ə/ *noun*. [Greek *arktos* bear + -PHILE]

arcuate /'ahkyoo·ət/ *adj* curved like a bow: *an arcuate cloud*. ➤➤ **arcuately** *adv*. [Latin *arcuatus*, past part. of *arcuare* to bend like a bow, from *arcus* bow, ARCH[1]]

arcus senilis /,ahkəs si'neelis/ *noun* (*pl* **arcus seniles** /-leez/) an opaque band that sometimes encircles the cornea of the eye in the elderly. [Latin *arcus senilis*, literally 'senile bow']

arc welding *noun* welding of metal parts by means of an electric arc struck between two electrodes or between one electrode and the metal.

-ard *or* **-art** *suffix* forming nouns, denoting: a person associated with a usu undesirable specified action, state, or quality: *dullard; dotard; laggard; drunkard; braggart*. [Middle English from Old French, of Germanic origin]

ardent /'ahd(ə)nt/ *adj* **1** characterized by strength of feeling; eager or zealous: *ardent passion; an ardent fan*. **2** *archaic or literary* burning; glowing: *I read a sincere nature in your ardent eyes* — Charlotte Brontë. ➤➤ **ardency** *noun*, **ardently** *adv*. [Middle English via Old French from Latin *ardent-, ardens*, present part. of *ardēre* to burn]

ardour (*NAmer* **ardor**) /'ahdə/ *noun* **1** intense feelings, often of passion or love: *His ardour had cooled*. **2** great enthusiasm or zeal: *The weather rather dampened our ardour*. [Middle English via Old French from Latin *ardor* from *ardēre* to burn]

arduous /'ahdyoo·əs/ *adj* **1** hard to accomplish or achieve; difficult or strenuous: *arduous work; an arduous journey*. **2** said of conditions, etc: difficult to endure; harsh. **3** *literary* hard to climb; steep: *The way was rough and arduous*. ➤➤ **arduously** *adv*, **arduousness** *noun*. [Latin *arduus* high, steep, difficult]

are[1] /ə; *strong* ah/ *verb* second person sing. present or pl present of BE. [Old English *earun*]

are[2] /ah/ *noun* a metric unit of area equal to 100m². [French *are* from Latin *area*: see AREA]

area /'eəri·ə/ *noun* **1** the extent of a surface or plane figure measured in square units: *Calculate the area of the triangle*. **2** a piece of ground: *The farm has an area set aside for campers*. **3** a particular space or surface, or one serving a special function: *We plan to have a reception area here; She complains of a pain in the kidney area*. **4** the extent, range, or scope of a concept, operation, or activity; a field: *It lies outside the area of foreign policy*. **5** a sunken court or yard giving access to the basement of a building. ➤➤ **areal** *adj*. [Latin *area* piece of level ground, threshing floor, from *arēre* to be dry]

area code *noun* a set of numbers indicating a particular area of a country, dialled before individual subscriber numbers when making telephone calls from outside that area.

areca /ə'reekə, 'arikə/ *noun* any of a genus of tropical Asian palm trees, *esp* a variety known as betel palm: genus *Areca*. [scientific Latin *Areca*, genus name, via Portuguese from Malayalam *atekka*]

areg /'ahreg/ *noun* pl of ERG[2].

arena /ə'reenə/ *noun* **1** an enclosed area used for public entertainment usu consisting of a level area surrounded by tiered seating. **2** a sphere of interest or activity; a scene: *the political arena*. [Latin *harena, arena* sand, sandy place (from the sand spread on the floor of a Roman arena to soak up the blood)]

arenaceous /ari'nayshəs/ *adj* growing or living in sandy places. [Latin *arenaceus* from *arena*: see ARENA]

aren't /ahnt/ *contraction* **1** are not. **2** used in questions: am not.

Usage note

Aren't I? is the standard less formal alternative for *am I not?: Aren't I clever to have thought of that?; I am on the list, aren't I?* It is incorrect to use *aren't* with *I* except in questions.

areola /ə'ree·ələ/ *noun* (*pl* **areolae** /-lee/) **1** a coloured ring, e.g. round the nipple. **2** a reddened area surrounding a spot, blister, etc. **3** any of the areas between the veins on a leaf or an insect's wing. ➤➤ **areolar** *adj*, **areolate** *adj*. [Latin *areola* small open space, dimin. of *area*: see AREA]

areole /'ariohl, 'eəri-/ *noun* **1** = AREOLA (3). **2** a small hollow in a cactus, from which hairs or spines grow. [French *aréole* from Latin *areola*: see AREOLA]

arête /ə'ret, ə'rayt/ *noun* a narrow sharp-crested mountain ridge. [French *arête*, literally 'fishbone', from Latin *arista* beard of grain]

argali /'ahgali/ *noun* (*pl* **argali**) an Asiatic wild sheep with large horns: *Ovis ammon*. [Mongolian *argali*]

argent /'ahjənt/ *noun* **1** used in heraldry: a silver or white colour. **2** *archaic or literary* the metal or colour silver: *his argent-studded sword* — Cowper. ➤➤ **argent** *adj*. [Middle English via Old French from Latin *argentum* silver]

argentiferous /ahjən'tifərəs/ *adj* producing or containing silver: *argentiferous rock*.

Argentine /'ahjəntien/ *noun and adj* = ARGENTINIAN.

argentine[1] *adj archaic* silver or silvery: *Celestial Dian, goddess argentine, I will obey thee* — Shakespeare.

argentine[2] *noun* a small sea fish with a silvery body: genus *Argentina*.

Argentinian /ahjən'tini·ən/ *noun* a native or inhabitant of Argentina in S America. ➤➤ **Argentinian** *adj*.

argentous /ah'jentəs/ *adj* relating to or containing silver, *esp* in its monovalent form.

argie-bargie /,ahji 'bahji/ *noun* = ARGY-BARGY.

argillaceous /ahji'layshəs/ *adj* relating to or containing clay or clay minerals. [Latin *argillaceus* from *argilla* white clay]

arginine /'ahjinien/ *noun* an amino acid found in most proteins and essential in the nutrition of most vertebrates. [German *Arginin*]

Argive /'ahgiev/ *adj* **1** belonging or relating to Argos in ancient Greece. **2** *literary esp* in Homer, relating to the Greeks; Greek. ➤➤ **Argive** *noun*. [Latin *Argivus* from Greek *Argeios* of Argos, from *Argos*]

argol /'ahgol/ *noun* crude tartar deposited in wine casks during ageing. [Middle English *argoile*, prob from Anglo-French *argoil*, of uncertain origin]

argon /'ahgon/ *noun* a gaseous chemical element of the noble gas group found in the air and volcanic gases and used *esp* as a filler for vacuum tubes and electric light bulbs: symbol Ar, atomic number 18. [Greek *argon*, neuter of *argos* idle, lazy, from A-[2] + *ergon* work; from the gas's relative inertness]

argosy /'ahgəsi/ *noun* (*pl* **argosies**) *literary* a large merchant sailing ship: *Three of your argosies are richly come to harbour* — Shakespeare. [modification of Italian *ragusea* Ragusan vessel, from *Ragusa*, former name of Dubrovnik, city and port in Croatia]

argot /'ahgoh/ *noun* the jargon or slang that is peculiar to a particular group. [orig in the sense 'criminals' cant' from French *argot* cant]

arguable /'ahgyoo·əbl/ *adj* **1** capable of being reasonably asserted or having a case made for it: *It is arguable that she is the best cellist around at present*. **2** open to dispute; debatable: *It is arguable whether such a measure would reduce costs*. ➤➤ **arguably** *adv*.

argue /'ahgyooh/ *verb intrans* **1** to give reasons for or against something; to reason. **2** to contend or disagree in words; to bicker or quarrel. ➤ *verb trans* **1** to give evidence of (something); to indicate. **2** to prove or seek to prove (something) by giving reasons; to maintain. **3** to persuade (somebody) by giving reasons: *They argued him out of going*. **4** to give reasons or arguments in favour of (something): *His letter argues restraint*. ✱ **argue the toss** *chiefly Brit, informal* to dispute a decision that has already been made. [Middle English *arguen* via Old French from Latin *arguere* to make clear]

argufy /'ahgyoofie/ *verb intrans* (**argufies, argufied, argufying**) *informal* to dispute or argue about something trivial.

argument /'ahgyoomənt/ *noun* **1** a quarrel or disagreement. **2a** the act or process of arguing; debate. **b** a coherent series of reasons offered. **3** a reason given as a proof or refutation. **4** an abstract or summary, *esp* of a literary work. **5** in mathematics, any of the variables that determine the value of a function. ✷ **argument from design** the theological argument that God's existence is clear from the evident design of the universe. [Middle English via Old French from Latin *argumentum* from *arguere* to make clear]

argumentation /,ahgyoomen'taysh(ə)n/ *noun* **1** the act or process of forming reasons and drawing conclusions and applying them to a case in discussion. **2** debate or discussion.

argumentative /ahgyoo'mentətiv/ *adj* tending or liking to argue; disputatious ➤➤ **argumentatively** *adv*, **argumentativeness** *noun*.

argus /'ahgəs/ *noun* (*pl* **arguses**) **1** a large Asian pheasant with a long tail and eye-like markings on its wings: *Argusianus argus*. **2** any of various small blue or brown butterflies with eye-like markings: genus *Aricia* and other genera. **3** (**Argus**) *literary* a watchful guardian. [via Latin from Greek *Argos*, a mythological giant with a hundred eyes, the guardian of Io]

argy-bargy /,ahji'bahji/ *noun chiefly Brit, informal* lively discussion or heated dispute, or an instance of this. [reduplication of Scots and English dialect *argy*, alteration of *argue*]

argyle /ah'giel/ *noun* a pattern on knitwear consisting of coloured lozenges on a plain background. [from *Argyll* tartan, that of the Argyll branch of the Campbell clan]

arhat /'ah·hat/ *noun* in Buddhism or Jainism, a person who has achieved a state of enlightenment. [Sanskrit *arhat* deserving]

aria /'ahri·ə/ *noun* (*pl* **arias**) an accompanied melody sung, e.g. in an opera, by one voice. [Italian *aria*, literally 'atmospheric air', modification of Latin *aer*: see AIR[1]]

-arian *suffix* forming nouns, denoting: **1** a believer in something: *Unitarian*. **2** an advocate of something: *vegetarian*. **3** a person who pursues a specified interest or activity: *antiquarian*; *librarian*. **4** somebody who is a specified number of decades old: *octogenarian*. [Latin *-arius* -ARY[1]]

Arianism /'eəri·əniz(ə)m/ *noun* the doctrine, officially declared heretical, that the divinity of the Son is of an inferior nature to that of the Father. ➤➤ **Arian** *adj and noun*. [named after *Arius* d.336, Greek theologian and presbyter of the church]

arid /'arid/ *adj* **1** said of land: excessively dry, *esp* having insufficient rainfall to support agriculture; parched. **2** bleakly unproductive or unrewarding; barren: *arid verse*; *arid scholarship*; *arid argument*. ➤➤ **aridity** /ə'rid-/ *noun*, **aridness** *noun*. [French *aride* from Latin *aridus* dry, parched]

ariel /'eəri·əl/ *noun* an Asian and African gazelle: genus *Gazella*. [Arabic *aryal*, variant of *ayyil* stag]

Aries /'eəriz, 'eəreez/ *noun* **1** in astronomy, a constellation (the Ram) depicted as the ram with the golden fleece sought by Jason. **2a** in astrology, the first sign of the zodiac. **b** a person born under this sign. ➤➤ **Arian** /'eəri·ən/ *adj and noun*, **Arien** *adj and noun*. [Latin *aries* ram]

aright /ə'riet/ *adv* rightly or correctly: *Report me and my cause aright* — Shakespeare; *Agnes had wondered ... if she had heard aright* — Catherine Cookson. [Old English *ariht*, from A-[1] + *riht* RIGHT[1]]

aril /'aril/ *noun* an exterior covering of some seeds, typically hairy or fleshy, like those of yew, that develops after fertilization. ➤➤ **arillate** /-layt/ *adj*. [scientific Latin, probably from late Latin *arillus*, raisin, grape seed]

arioso /ahri'ohsoh, ari-, -zoh/ *noun* (*pl* **ariosos** *or* **ariosi** /-si/) a passage in opera or oratorio intermediate in style between an aria and a recitative, with less formality than the former, and more melody than the latter. [Italian *arioso* like an aria, from *aria*: see ARIA]

arise /ə'riez/ *verb intrans* (*past tense* **arose** /ə'rohz/, *past part.* **arisen** /ə'riz(ə)n/) **1a** (*often* + from) to originate from a source. **b** (*often* + from) to come into being or to somebody's attention. **2** *literary or formal* to get up or rise. [Old English *ārīsan*, from A-[1] + RISE[1]]

aristocracy /ari'stokrəsi/ *noun* (*pl* **aristocracies**) **1** (*treated as sing. or pl*) a usu hereditary nobility ranking socially above the ordinary or common people and below royalty. **2a** a form of government in which power is vested in a small privileged and usu hereditary noble class. **b** a state with such a government. **3** (*treated as sing. or pl*) the whole group of those believed to be superior in some sphere of life or activity; the elite: *the intellectual aristocracy*. [Old French *aristocratie* via late Latin from Greek *aristokratia*, from *aristos* best + *-kratia*: see -CRACY]

aristocrat /'aristəkrat, ə'ris-/ *noun* **1** a member of an aristocracy; *esp* a noble. **2** somebody who has the bearing and viewpoint typical of the aristocracy. **3** a preeminent person or thing: *this aristocrat of freshwater fish*.

aristocratic /,aristə'kratik, ə,ris-/ *adj* belonging to, having the qualities of, or favouring aristocracy. ➤➤ **aristocratically** *adv*. [French *aristocratique* via medieval Latin from Greek *aristokratikos* from *aristokratia*: see ARISTOCRACY]

Aristotelian *or* **Aristotelean** /,aristə'teeli·ən/ *adj* relating to the Greek philosopher Aristotle (d.322 BC), *esp* his doctrines or his principles of logic. ➤➤ **Aristotelian** *noun*, **Aristotelianism** *noun*.

Arita /ə'reetə/ *noun* a Japanese porcelain ware decorated with asymmetric designs. [*Arita*, place of manufacture in Japan]

arithmetic /ə'rithmətik/ *noun* **1** a branch of mathematics that deals with real numbers and calculations made with them. **2** calculation using numbers. **3** a person's skill with numbers: *My arithmetic is improving*. ➤➤ **arithmetic** /arith'metik/ *adj*, **arithmetical** /-'metikl/ *adj*, **arithmetically** /-'metikli/ *adv*, **arithmetician** /-mə'tish(ə)n/ *noun*. [Middle English *arsmetik* via Old French and Latin from Greek *arithmētikē*, ultimately from *arithmos* number]

arithmetic mean *noun* a value found by dividing the sum of a set of terms by the number of terms.

arithmetic progression *noun* a sequence, e.g. 3, 5, 7, 9, in which the difference between any term and its predecessor is constant.

arithmetize *or* **arithmetise** /ə'rithmətiez/ *verb trans* to express (a value, etc) arithmetically.

-arium *suffix* forming nouns, denoting: a thing or place relating to or connected with something: *planetarium*; *aquarium*. [Latin *-arium*, from neuter of *-arius* -ARY[1]]

Ariz. *abbr* Arizona.

Ark. *abbr* Arkansas.

ark /ahk/ *noun* **1** a ship, *esp* the one built by Noah to escape the Flood, or one built as a model of it. **2a** (*often* **Ark/Ark of the Covenant**) the sacred chest containing the Ten Commandments, and representing to the Hebrews the presence of God among them. **b** (*often* **Ark**) a repository for the scrolls of the Torah. ✷ **out of the ark** *informal* deplorably antiquated. [Old English *arc* from a Germanic word borrowed from Latin *arca* chest]

arkose /'ahkohz/ *noun* a coarse-grained sandstone containing a high proportion of feldspar fragments in addition to quartz, derived from the rapid disintegration of granite or gneiss. ➤➤ **arkosic** *adj*. [French *arkose* prob from Greek *archaios* ancient]

arm[1] /ahm/ *noun* **1** either of the human upper limbs that extend from the shoulder, sometimes not including the hand and wrist. **2a** the forelimb of a vertebrate animal. **b** a limb of an invertebrate animal. **3** a support, e.g. on a chair, for the elbow and forearm. **4** the sleeve of a garment. **5** an inlet of water from the sea. **6** a functional division of a group or activity, e.g. a combat branch of an army. ✷ **a baby/babe in arms** a child too young to walk. **arm in arm** with arms linked. **at arm's length** far enough away to avoid unwanted familiarity. **cost an arm and a leg** *informal* to be very expensive. **put the arm on** *NAmer, informal* to try to use force on (somebody). **the long/strong arm of the law** the far-reaching might of the law or the police force. **with open arms** with welcoming enthusiasm. **would give one's right arm for** *informal* want (something) desperately. ➤➤ **armless** *adj*, **armlike** *adj*. [Old English *earm*]

arm[2] *verb trans* **1** to supply or equip (a person, force, or nation) with weapons. **2** to provide (somebody) with something that strengthens, protects, or fortifies. **3** to activate the fuse of (a bomb). ➤ *verb intrans* to prepare oneself for struggle or resistance. [Middle English *armen* via Old French from Latin *armare* from *arma* weapons, tools]

armada /ah'mahdə/ *noun* (*pl* **armadas**) **1** a fleet of warships. **2** the fleet sent against England by Spain in 1588. [Spanish *armada* via medieval Latin from Latin *armata*, past part. of *armare*: see ARM[2]]

armadillo /ahmə'diloh/ *noun* (*pl* **armadillos**) any of several burrowing chiefly nocturnal S American mammals with body and head encased in an armour of small bony plates. [Spanish *armadillo*, dimin. of *armado* armed one, from Latin *armatus*, past part. of *armare*: see ARM[2]]

Armageddon /ahmə'ged(ə)n/ *noun* **1a** a final and conclusive battle between the forces of good and evil, as in the New Testament of the Bible: *I am still as much concerned as ever about the Battle of Armageddon; but I am not as much concerned about the General Election* — G K Chesterton. **b** the place where this will be fought. **2** a vast decisive conflict. [Greek *Armageddōn, Harmagedōn,* scene of the battle foretold in Revelations 16:14–16]

Armalite /'ahməliet/ *noun trademark* a high-velocity lightweight automatic rifle. [named after *Armalite, Inc.,* US manufacturers]

armament /'ahməmənt/ *noun* **1** (*often in pl*) the military strength, *esp* in arms and equipment, of a ship, fort, combat unit, nation, etc. **2** the process of preparing for war. [French *armement* from Latin *armamenta* (pl) utensils, military or naval equipment, from *armare:* see ARM²]

armamentarium /ˌahməmən'teəri-əm/ *noun* (*pl* **armamentaria** /-ə/) the equipment and methods available, *esp* in medical treatment. [Latin *armamentarium* armoury, from *armamenta:* see ARMAMENT]

armature /'ahməchə/ *noun* **1** the central rotating part of an electric motor or generator. **2** a bar of soft iron or steel placed across the poles of a horseshoe magnet to close the magnetic circuit. **3** a framework on which a sculpture or model in clay, wax, etc is assembled. **4a** the protective covering of a plant or animal. **b** an offensive or defensive structure in a plant or animal, e.g. teeth or thorns. **5** *archaic* arms or armour: *the armature of the infantry.* [Latin *armatura* armour, equipment, from *armatus,* past part. of *armare:* see ARM²]

armband /'ahmband/ *noun* **1** a band of material, *esp* cloth, attached over the upper sleeve, usu denoting status, e.g. authority, or condition, e.g. mourning. **2** an inflatable plastic band worn round the upper arm by non-swimmers to keep them afloat.

arm candy *noun informal* a beautiful woman who is seen in a man's company in public.

armchair /'ahmcheə/ *noun* **1** a chair with armrests, usu upholstered. **2** (*used before a noun*) dealing with matters from a theoretical rather than practical angle: *an armchair critic.*

armed forces /ahmd/ *pl noun* the military, naval, and air forces of a nation.

Armenian /ah'meeniən/ *noun* **1** a member of a people living chiefly in Armenia in the Caucasus. **2** the Indo-European language of the Armenians. ➤➤ **Armenian** *adj.*

armful *noun* (*pl* **armfuls**) **1** as much or as many as the arms will hold: *They made off with armfuls of looted goods.* **2** an amount being held in the arms: *She appeared with an armful of washing.*

armhole *noun* an opening for the arm in a garment.

armiger /'ahmijə/ *noun* a person entitled to heraldic arms. [medieval Latin *armiger,* literally 'bearing arms', from *arma* arms + *-ger* bearing]

armillary sphere /'ahmiləri, ah'miləri/ *noun* an old astronomical instrument composed of rings representing the positions of important circles of the celestial sphere. [French *sphère armillaire* via medieval Latin from Latin *armilla* bracelet, iron ring, from *armus* arm, shoulder]

armistice /'ahmistis/ *noun* a suspension of hostilities; a truce. [French *armistice* via modern Latin *armistitium* from Latin *arma* arms + *-stitium* as in *solstitium* SOLSTICE]

Armistice Day *noun* the anniversary of the armistice ending World War I on 11 November 1918.

armlet /'ahmlit/ *noun* **1** a band, e.g. of cloth or metal, worn round the upper arm. **2** a small inlet of the sea.

armoire /ah'mwah/ *noun* a large usu decorative cupboard or wardrobe. [French *armoire* from Old French *armarie,* like AUMBRY from Latin *armarium* closet, from *arma* utensils]

armor /'ahmə/ *noun and verb NAmer* see ARMOUR¹, ARMOUR².

armorial /ah'mawri-əl/ *adj* relating to or bearing heraldic arms. ➤➤ **armorially** *adv.*

armory /'ahməri/ *noun NAmer* see ARMOURY.

armour¹ (*NAmer* **armor**) /'ahmə/ *noun* **1a** a defensive covering for the body; *esp* a covering of metal or chain mail worn by medieval soldiers in combat. **b** a usu metallic protective covering, e.g. for a ship, aircraft, or car. **2** armoured forces and vehicles, e.g. tanks. ➤➤ **armourless** *adj.* [Middle English *armure* via Old French from Latin *armatura:* see ARMATURE]

armour² (*NAmer* **armor**) *verb trans* to equip (somebody) with armour, or fit (something, *esp* a military vehicle) with armour.

armoured (*NAmer* **armored**) /'ahməd/ *adj* **1** said of a vehicle: protected with armour plate. **2** said of an army unit, etc: consisting of or equipped with vehicles protected with armour plate.

armourer (*NAmer* **armorer**) *noun* **1** a person who makes or looks after armour or arms. **2** a person who repairs, assembles, and tests firearms.

armour plate *noun* a defensive covering of hard metal plates for combat vehicles and vessels.

armoury (*NAmer* **armory**) /'ahməri/ *noun* (*pl* **armouries**, *NAmer* **armories**) a collection of or place for storing arms and military equipment, or the equipment itself.

armpit *noun* **1** the hollow beneath the junction of the arm and shoulder. **2** (**the armpit**) *chiefly NAmer, informal* the most unsavoury part of something: *77th Street Station … was the armpit of detective duty* — J Wambaugh.

armrest *noun* a support for the arm, *esp* one on a chair.

arms *noun* **1** weapons, *esp* firearms. **2a** active hostilities. **b** military service or a military profession. **3** the heraldic insignia of a group or body, e.g. a family, corporation, or country. ✳ **a call to arms** a call to get ready to fight. **under arms** equipped or prepared for war. **up in arms** angrily rebellious and protesting strongly: *The entire community are up in arms about the proposed motorway.* [Middle English *armes* (pl) weapons, via Old French from Latin *arma* weapons, tools]

arm-twisting *noun informal* the use of direct personal pressure in order to achieve a desired end.

arm wrestling *noun* a contest in which two opponents sit opposite each other across a table, each with one elbow on its surface, grip each other's hand, and try to force each other's forearm down.

army /'ahmi/ *noun* (*pl* **armies**) **1a** a large organized force for fighting on land. **b** (*often* **Army**) the complete military organization of a nation for land warfare. **2** a large crowd: *An army of tourists arrived in the square.* **3** a body of people organized to advance a cause: *the Salvation Army.* [Middle English *armee* via Old French from medieval Latin *armata,* past part. of *armare:* see ARM²]

army ant *noun* any of a subfamily of blind nomadic ants that travel in huge groups destroying plants and animals in their path: subfamily Dorylinae.

Army List *noun* in the UK, the official list of commissioned officers.

army worm *noun* any of the larvae of several moths, *esp* of the USA and E Africa, that travel in massed columns, destroying crops, *esp* cotton, sugar cane, and maize: family Noctuidae.

arnica /'ahnikə/ *noun* (*pl* **arnicas**) any of a genus of plants of the daisy family with yellow or orange flower heads that yield an oil used in treating sprains and bruises: genus *Arnica.* [scientific Latin *arnica,* of unknown origin]

A-road *noun* a main road of high standard.

aroha /'ahrohə/ *noun NZ* love, affection, or compassion. [Maori *aroha*]

aroid /'eəroyd/ *noun* a plant of the arum family: family Araceae. [ARUM + -OID]

aroma /ə'rohmə/ *noun* (*pl* **aromas**) **1** a distinctive, pervasive, and usu pleasant or savoury smell. **2** a distinctive quality or atmosphere: *The aroma of success hung about her.* [Middle English *aromat* spice, via Old French and Latin from Greek *arōmat-, arōma* herb, spice]

aromatherapy /əˌrohmə'therəpi/ *noun* the use of natural essential oils in a variety of treatments to relieve symptoms, promote healing, and reduce tension. ➤➤ **aromatherapist** *noun.*

aromatic¹ /arə'matik/ *adj* **1** having a pleasant, distinctive, or spicy smell. **2** said of a chemical compound: having a molecular structure containing a ring, *esp* containing a benzene ring or similar chemical group: compare ALIPHATIC. ➤➤ **aromatically** *adv,* **aromaticity** /ˌarəmə'tisiti/ *noun.*

aromatic² *noun* an aromatic substance, plant, drug, or chemical compound.

arose /ə'rohz/ *verb* past tense of ARISE.

around¹ /ə'rownd/ *adv* **1a** in the vicinity: *There was nobody around.* **b** in various directions; to and fro: *walking around; to wave one's arms around.* **c** used with verbs to convey purposelessness: *standing* *around; to mess around.* **d** in existence: *the most intelligent of the artists around today* — R M Coates. **e** *chiefly NAmer* out of bed and active: *up and around by seven.* **f** *chiefly NAmer* approximately: *He's around fifty.* **2** *chiefly NAmer.* **a** in a rough circle surrounding something or somebody: *Gather around and listen.* **b** from person to person: *Pass it around.* **c** so as to face the other way: *She turned around and walked away.* **d** so as to move in a circle: *spinning around.* **✻ have been around** to be sophisticated or worldly-wise. [Middle English, from A-¹ + ROUND⁴]

Usage note _____

around, round, or about? *Round* is in standard use in British English as a preposition (*came round the corner*) or an adverb (*show someone round*), where American English would more commonly have *around.* It is not incorrect in British English either to use *around* in such phrases. Americans also tend to say *around* where most British users would say *about* (*Don't mess around/about with my things; It must have taken around/about five hours*). Again, however, the use of *around* is quite common in British English and perfectly acceptable.

around² *prep* **1** here and there in (a place): *driving around the countryside; papers lying around the room.* **2a** so as to encircle (something): *wearing a medallion around his neck; sitting around the table.* **b** *chiefly NAmer* with a change of direction caused by (a corner, bend, or obstacle): *It's just around the corner.*

arouse /ə'rowz/ *verb trans* **1** to stimulate (a feeling) or evoke (a reaction or response). **2** to awaken (somebody) from sleep. **3** to rouse (somebody) to action. **4** to excite (somebody) sexually. ➤➤ **arousal** *noun.* [A-¹ + ROUSE]

ARP *abbr* air-raid precautions.

arpeggio /ah'pejioh/ *noun* (*pl* **arpeggios**) a chord with notes that are played in succession, not simultaneously. Also called BROKEN CHORD. [Italian *arpeggio* from *arpeggiare* to play on the harp, from *arpa* harp, of Germanic origin]

arquebus /'ahkwibəs/ *or* **harquebus** /'hah-/ *noun* an early type of portable MATCHLOCK (gun with a wick for igniting the gunpowder) usu fired from a support, used in the 15th and 16th cents. [French *harquebuse, arquebuse* from early Low German *hakebusse,* from *haken* hook + *busse* gun]

arr. *abbr* **1** in music, arranged by. **2** arrival. **3** arrives.

arrack *or* **arak** /'arak, 'arək/ *noun* an alcoholic spirit distilled in various Eastern countries from rice, the sap of the coco palm, etc. [Arabic '*araq* sweat, juice, liquor]

arraign /ə'rayn/ *verb trans* **1** to charge (somebody) formally with an offence in a court of law: *arraigned on a charge of treason.* **2** to accuse (somebody) of a fault or wrong: *arraigned in the tabloids for gross ineptitude.* ➤➤ **arraignment** *noun.* [Middle English *arreinen* via Old French, ultimately from Latin *ration-, ratio* REASON¹]

arrange /ə'raynj/ *verb trans* **1** to put (things) in order or into sequence or relationship. **2** to make preparations for (something); to plan. **3** to bring about an agreement concerning (something): *They arranged an exchange of prisoners of war.* **4** to adapt (a musical composition) by scoring it for different voices or instruments. ➤ *verb intrans* to make plans or reach agreement. ➤➤ **arrangeable** *adj,* **arranger** *noun.* [Middle English *arangen* from Old French *arrangier,* from AR- + *rengier:* see RANGE²]

arrangement *noun* **1** a preparation or plan: *travel arrangements.* **2** an informal agreement or settlement, *esp* on personal, social, or political matters. **3** something made by arranging constituents or things together, or the way in which they are arranged: *a floral arrangement.* **4** an adaptation of a musical composition for different voices or instruments.

arrant /'arənt/ *adj* usu intensifying contemptuous terms: complete; utter: *an arrant fool; arrant hypocrisy.* ➤➤ **arrantly** *adv.* [alteration of ERRANT, earlier with the meaning 'outlawed']

arras /'arəs/ *noun* (*pl* **arras**) a wall hanging or screen made of tapestry. [Middle English, from *Arras,* city in France, a medieval centre of tapestry making]

array¹ /ə'ray/ *verb trans* **1** to set or place (things) in order; to marshal. **2** to dress or decorate (somebody), *esp* in splendid or impressive clothes; to adorn. ➤➤ **arrayer** *noun.* [Middle English *arrayen* via Old French, ultimately from AR- + a base of Germanic origin meaning to prepare]

array² *noun* **1** an imposing collection or large number: *an array of goods on display.* **2** an orderly arrangement of things or people, *esp* troops: *drawn up in battle array.* **3** a number of mathematical elements arranged in rows and columns. **4** an arrangement of elements forming a single unit, e.g. a set of data in a computer

memory. **5** *literary or archaic* clothing; apparel: *Thou wolf in sheep's array* — Shakespeare; *I went out in my new array* — Dickens.

arrears /ə'riəz/ *pl noun* **1** an unpaid or overdue debt. **2** an unfinished duty. **✻ in arrears** behind in the payment of a debt or the discharge of an obligation. ➤➤ **arrearage** /-rij/ *noun.* [Middle English *arrere* behind, backwards, via Old French from Latin *ad* to + *retro* backwards]

arrest¹ /ə'rest/ *verb trans* **1** to seize or capture (somebody), *esp* to take or keep (somebody) in custody by authority of law. **2** to catch and fix or hold (something): *The design arrests the attention.* **3a** to bring (something) to a stop. **b** to make (somebody or something) inactive. ➤➤ **arrester** *noun,* **arrestor** *noun.* [Middle English *aresten* via Old French from assumed vulgar Latin *arrestare* to rest stop]

arrest² *noun* **1** the act of taking or keeping somebody in custody by authority of law. **2** a stoppage or cessation, e.g. of the function of an organ: *a cardiac arrest; arrest of growth.* **✻ arrest of judgment** the suspension of court proceedings after the verdict in a criminal trial because of irregularities in the trial. **under arrest** in legal custody.

arrestable offence *noun* a serious offence for which an arrest can be made without a warrant.

arresting *adj* catching the attention; striking. ➤➤ **arrestingly** *adv.*

arrhythmia /ə'ridhmi·ə/ *noun* an abnormal alteration in rhythm of the heartbeat. ➤➤ **arrhythmic** *adj,* **arrhythmical** *adj,* **arrhythmically** *adv.* [scientific Latin from Greek *arrhythmia* lack of rhythm, from A-² + *rhythmos* rhythm]

arrière-pensée /,ariea 'ponsay (*French* arjɛ:r pɔ̃se)/ *noun* a thought, motive, or reservation not revealed to others. [French *arrière-pensée,* from *arrière* behind + *pensée* thought]

arris /'aris/ *noun* (*pl* **arris** *or* **arrises**) the sharp ridge or prominent angle formed by the meeting of two surfaces, *esp* in mouldings. [prob modification of early French *areste,* literally 'fishbone', from late Latin *arista:* see ARÊTE]

arrival /ə'rievl/ *noun* **1** the act or time of arriving. **2** somebody or something that has arrived.

arrive /ə'riev/ *verb intrans* **1** to reach a destination. **2** to come: *The moment has arrived.* **3** to achieve success. **✻ arrive at** to reach (something) by effort or thought: *I have arrived at a decision.* ➤➤ **arriver** *noun.* [Middle English *ariven* to reach the shore, from Old French *arriver,* from AR- + Latin *ripa* shore]

arrivederci /,arive'deachi/ *interj* goodbye. [Italian *arrivederci,* till seeing again]

arriviste /aree'veest/ *noun* a person who puts self-advancement above scruple; a climber or careerist. ➤➤ **arrivisme** /aree'veezm(ə)/ *noun.* [French *arriviste* from *arriver* to arrive]

arrogant /'arəg(ə)nt/ *adj* having a feeling of superiority over others, as revealed in a haughty overbearing manner or in presumptuous claims. ➤➤ **arrogance** *noun,* **arrogantly** *adv.* [Middle English from Latin *arrogant-, arrogans,* present part. of *arrogare:* see ARROGATE]

arrogate /'arəgayt/ *verb trans* to claim or take (something) without justification, on behalf of oneself or another: *She had arrogated to herself the role of moral arbiter; The effect would have been to arrogate constitutional powers to the trade unions.* ➤➤ **arrogation** /-'gaysh(ə)n/ *noun.* [Latin *arrogatus,* past part. of *arrogare* to claim as one's own, from AR- + *rogare* to ask]

Usage note _____

arrogate or abrogate? See note at ABROGATE.

arrondissement /arən'deesmənt (*French* arɔ̃dismã)/ *noun* **1** an administrative district of some large French cities, *esp* Paris. **2** a parliamentary division of a French department. [French *arrondissement* from *arrondir* to make round]

arrow¹ /'aroh/ *noun* **1** a projectile shot from a bow, usu having a slender shaft, a pointed head, and feathers at the end. **2** something shaped like an arrow; *esp* a mark or sign indicating direction. [Old English *arwe*]

arrow² *verb trans* to mark or indicate (something) with an arrow: *The location is arrowed on the map.* ➤ *verb intrans* to move with speed and precision: *The header arrowed its way into the net.*

arrowgrass *noun* a grass-like marsh plant with thin fleshy leaves and a slender spike of inconspicuous flowers: *Triglochin palustris.*

arrowhead *noun* **1** the pointed front part of an arrow. **2** something shaped like an arrowhead. **3** any of several related aquatic plants with leaves shaped like arrowheads.

arrowroot *noun* **1** a tropical American plant with fleshy roots: *Maranta arundinacea*. **2** a nutritive starch obtained from this plant, used *esp* as a thickening agent in cooking. [alteration of Arawak *aru-aru* meal of meals, under the influence of ARROW¹ and ROOT¹, its tubers being used by Native Americans to heal wounds from poisoned arrows]

arrow worm *noun* a small transparent worm-like sea animal found in plankton, with prehensile bristles on its head that grip its prey. Also called CHAETOGNATH.

arroyo /əˈroh-yoh, əˈroyoh/ *noun* (*pl* **arroyos**) *NAmer* **1** a gully or channel carved by running water. **2** a stream in a very dry region. [Spanish *arroyo*]

arse /ahs/ *noun Brit, coarse slang* **1** the buttocks. **2** the anus. [Old English *ærs, ears*]

arse about *verb intrans* (*also* **arse around**) *Brit, coarse slang* to fool around or waste time.

arsehole *noun Brit, coarse slang* **1** the anus. **2** a foolish or stupid person.

arsenal /ˈahsnl/ *noun* **1a** a store of weapons and ammunition. **b** an establishment for the manufacture or storage of arms and military equipment; an armoury. **2** a store or repertory: *Once roused he could draw on a well-stocked arsenal of invective*. [Italian *arsenale*, modification of Arabic *dār sinā'ah* house of manufacture]

arsenic /ˈahsənik/ *noun* **1** a steel-grey metalloid chemical element that forms many poisonous compounds: symbol As, atomic number 33. **2** an extremely poisonous trioxide of arsenic, used *esp* as an insecticide. ▶▶ **arsenic** /ahˈsenik/ *adj*, **arsenical** *adj*, **arsenide** *noun*. [Middle English via Old French and Latin from Greek *arsenikon, arrhenikon* yellow orpiment, from Syriac *zarnīg*, of Iranian origin]

arsenic acid *noun* a poisonous white soluble crystalline solid that is weakly acidic and is used in the production of insecticides: formula H_3AsO_4. ▶▶ **arsenate** *noun*.

arsenopyrite /ˌahsənohˈpie-əriet/ *noun* a metallic mineral that consists of a sulphide of iron and arsenic, and is a principal ore of arsenic.

arses /ˈahseez/ *noun* pl of ARSIS.

arsine /ˈahseen/ *noun* a colourless flammable extremely poisonous gas with a smell like garlic, produced by the reaction of certain arsenic compounds with acids, used in warfare as a poison gas and in electronics to dope transistors: formula AsH_3. [from ARSENIC, on the model of AMINE]

arsis /ˈahsis/ *noun* (*pl* **arses** /ˈahseez/) a stressed syllable in a metrical foot in Greek or Latin verse: compare THESIS (4). [late Latin *arsis* raising of the voice, accented part of metrical foot, from Greek *arsis* act of lifting, from *aeirein, airein* to lift]

arson /ˈahsən/ *noun* the criminal act of setting fire to property in order to cause destruction. ▶▶ **arsonist** *noun*. [via Old French from Latin *ardēre* to burn]

arsphenamine /ahsˈfenəmeen/ *noun* a synthetic arsenic compound formerly used in the treatment of syphilis. [ARSENIC + PHEN- + AMINE]

art¹ /aht/ *noun* **1a** the conscious use of skill and creative imagination, *esp* in the production of aesthetic objects. **b** paintings, sculptures, and other works produced using skill and creative imagination. **c** any of the fine arts or graphic arts. **2a** a skill acquired by experience, study, or observation. **b** an activity which requires a combination of practical knowledge, judgment, and imagination. **3** (**the Arts**) the humanities as contrasted with science. **4** decorative or illustrative elements in books and other printed matter; artwork. **5** (*used before a noun*) devised with artistry or intended for artistic purposes: *an art film; art pottery*. [Middle English via Old French from Latin *art-, ars*]

art² *verb archaic* second person sing. present of BE. [Old English *eart*]

art. *abbr* **1** article. **2** artificial. **3** artillery.

-art *suffix* see -ARD.

art deco /ah(t) ˈdekoh/ *noun* (*also* **Art Deco**) a decorative style of the 1920s and 1930s characterized by bold geometric shapes, bright contrasting colours, and the use of new materials, e.g. plastic. [French *Art Déco*, from *Exposition Internationale des Arts Décoratifs*, an exhibition of decorative arts held in Paris in 1925]

artefact *or* **artifact** /ˈahtifakt/ *noun* **1** a product of human workmanship, e.g. a tool or a pot, often as a subject of archaeological study. **2** a feature or structure that is not normally present, e.g. in a biological specimen, but is introduced during a process of preparation for scientific investigation. ▶▶ **artefactual** /-ˈfaktyooəl, -chooəl/ *adj*. [Latin *arte* by means of skill (from *art-, ars* skill) + *factum* something made, past part. of *facere* to make, do]

artel /ahˈtel/ *noun* a workers' or peasants' cooperative in Russia and other parts of the former USSR. [Russian *artel'* from Italian *artieri*, pl of *artiere* artisan, from *arte* art, from Latin *art-, ars*]

artemisia /ahtəˈmizi-ə/ *noun* any of a genus of strong-smelling herbs or shrubs, e.g. wormwood: genus *Artemisia*. [scientific Latin *artemisia*, genus name, ultimately from Greek]

arterial /ahˈtiəri-əl/ *adj* **1** relating to or located in an artery. **2** denoting the bright red blood contained in an artery. **3** denoting a main road linking large cities and towns. ▶▶ **arterially** *adv*.

arterialize *or* **arterialise** *verb trans* to transform (venous blood) into arterial blood by oxygenation. ▶▶ **arterialization** /-ˈza-ysh(ə)n/ *noun*.

arteriography /ah,tiəriˈografi/ *noun* the X-ray examination of an artery performed after the injection of a substance opaque to radiation.

arteriole /ahˈtiəriohl/ *noun* a small branch of an artery connecting it with capillaries. ▶▶ **arteriolar** /-ˈohlə/ *adj*. [French *artériole*, prob from modern Latin *arteriola*, dimin. of Latin *arteria*: see ARTERY]

arteriosclerosis /ah,tiəriohsklə'rohsis/ *noun* abnormal thickening and hardening of the arterial walls. ▶▶ **arteriosclerotic** /-ˈrotik/ *adj*.

artery /ˈahtəri/ *noun* (*pl* **arteries**) **1** any of the branching elastic-walled blood vessels that carry blood from the heart to the lungs and through the body: compare CAPILLARY¹, VEIN¹. **2** a main channel of transport or communication, *esp* a road, railway line, or river. [Middle English *arterie* via Latin from Greek *artēria* tube, artery]

artesian well /ahˈteezi-ən, -zh(ə)n/ *noun* a well sunk perpendicularly into sloping strata receiving water from a higher level than that of the well, so that the water reaches the surface under its own pressure, with little or no pumping. [French *artésien*, literally 'of Artois', from Old French *Arteis* Artois, region of France, where such wells were sunk in the 18th cent.]

Artex /ˈahteks/ *noun trademark* a type of plaster applied to walls and ceiling to give a textured effect. [blend of ART¹ + TEXTURE¹]

art form *noun* a recognized form or medium of artistic expression.

artful /ˈahtf(ə)l/ *adj* clever in attaining an end, often by deceitful or indirect means; crafty: *the engaging, half-artful, half-artless ways of schoolgirls* — Ralph Waldo Emerson. ▶▶ **artfully** *adv*, **artfulness** *noun*.

art history *noun* the academic study of the development of the fine arts or of all the visual arts. ▶▶ **art historian** *noun*, **art historical** *adj*.

art house *noun* a cinema specializing in films that do not have mass appeal, e.g. artistic or experimental films.

arthr- *or* **arthro-** *comb. form* forming words, denoting: a joint: *arthritis; arthropod*. [via Latin from Greek *arthron* joint]

arthralgia /ahˈthraljə/ *noun* pain in a joint.

arthritic /ahˈthritik/ *adj* relating to or affected with arthritis. ▶▶ **arthritic** *noun*, **arthritically** *adv*.

arthritis /ahˈthrietis/ *noun* an illness causing painful inflammation and stiffness of the joints. [via Latin from Greek *arthritis*, from *arthron* joint + -ITIS]

arthro- *comb. form* see ARTHR-.

arthrodesis /ahˈthrodisis/ *noun* (*pl* **arthrodeses** /-seez/) the surgical immobilization of a joint so that the articulating bones fuse together, used in cases of severe arthritis. [ARTHRO- + Greek *desis* binding, from *dein* to bind]

arthropod /ˈahthrəpod/ *noun* any of a phylum of invertebrate animals, including the insects, arachnids (e.g. scorpions and spiders), and crustaceans (e.g. crabs and lobsters), that have a jointed body and limbs and usu a hard outer skin that is moulted at intervals: phylum Arthropoda. [scientific Latin *Arthropoda* from ARTHRO- + Greek *pod-, pous* foot]

arthroscope /'ahthrəskohp/ *noun* an instrument for examining or operating on the interior of a joint.

Arthurian /ah'th(y)ooəriən/ *adj* relating to the legend of King Arthur and his royal court.

artic /'ahtik/ *noun Brit, informal* an articulated lorry.

artichoke /'ahtichohk/ *noun* **1a** a tall composite plant like a thistle, cultivated for its partly edible flower head. **b** (*also* **globe artichoke**) the flower head of the artichoke, used as a vegetable. **2** = JERUSALEM ARTICHOKE. [Italian dialect *articiocco*, from Arabic *al-khurshūf* the artichoke]

article[1] /'ahtikl/ *noun* **1** a particular or separate object or thing, often viewed as a member of a class of things: *articles of clothing*; *the genuine article*. **2** a piece of non-fictional prose, usu forming an independent part of a magazine, newspaper, etc. **3** a separate clause, item, provision, or point in a text, document, etc. **4** (*in pl*). **a** a written agreement specifying conditions of apprenticeship. **b** a period of work with a firm undertaken by a trainee solicitor, architect, accountant, or surveyor: *He took articles with a Devon firm.* **5** an item of business; a matter. **6** a word or affix, e.g. *a*, *an*, and *the*, used with nouns to specify indefiniteness or definiteness: compare DEFINITE ARTICLE, INDEFINITE ARTICLE. ✳ **article of faith** a strongly held belief. [Middle English via Old French from Latin *articulus* joint, division, dimin. of *artus* joint]

article[2] *verb trans* to bind (somebody) by articles, e.g. of apprenticeship: *articled apprentices*; *He was articled to a firm of solicitors.*

articled clerk *noun Brit* a trainee solicitor.

articular /ah'tikyoolə/ *adj* relating to a joint: *articular cartilage*. [Middle English *articuler* from Latin *articularis* from *articulus*: see ARTICLE[1]]

articulate[1] /ah'tikyoolət/ *adj* **1** expressing oneself readily, clearly, or effectively. **2** said of speech or writing: clearly and intelligibly expressed. **3** having the power of speech. **4** having joints. ➤➤ **articulacy** /-si/ *noun*, **articulately** *adv*, **articulateness** *noun*. [scientific Latin *articulatus* from Latin *articulus*: see ARTICLE[1]]

articulate[2] /ah'tikyoolayt/ *verb trans* **1a** to say (words) clearly and distinctly. **b** to express (an idea) clearly and effectively: *They have not articulated their grievances.* **2** to unite (a body part) with a joint. ➤ *verb intrans* **1** to utter meaningful sounds. **2** said of two bones: to fit together or interconnect to form a joint: *where the clavicle articulates with the sternum.* ➤➤ **articulable** *adj*, **articulative** *adj*, **articulator** *noun*, **articulatory** /-lət(ə)ri/ *adj*. [Latin *articulatus*, past part. of *articulare* from *articulus*: see ARTICLE[1]]

articulated /ah'tikyoolaytid/ *adj* **1** having joints; connected by joints. **2** *chiefly Brit* denoting a commercial vehicle with a tractor and trailer linked by a bar with a pivoting joint: *an articulated lorry.*

articulation /ah,tikyoo'laysh(ə)n/ *noun* **1a** the verbal expression of thoughts and feelings. **b** the act or manner of uttering speech sounds. **2a** a movable joint between plant or animal parts. **b** the state or manner of being jointed or interrelated. **3** the OCCLUSION (meeting together) of the teeth of the upper and lower jaw.

artifact /'ahtifakt/ *noun* see ARTEFACT.

artifice /'ahtifis/ *noun* **1** an artful device, expedient, or stratagem; a trick. **2** clever or artful skill; ingenuity. [early French from Latin *artificium*, from *art-, ars* skill + *facere* to make, do]

artificer /ah'tifisə, 'ah-/ *noun* **1** a skilled or artistic worker or designer. **2** a military or naval mechanic.

artificial /ahti'fish(ə)l/ *adj* **1** made by human skill and labour, often to a natural model; synthetic; fake: *an artificial limb*; *no artificial colouring*. **2** said of somebody's manner: lacking in natural quality; affected or insincere: *bright artificial smiles*. ➤➤ **artificiality** /-shi'aliti/ *noun*, **artificially** *adv*. [Middle English via Old French from Latin *artificialis* from *artificium*: see ARTIFICE]

artificial horizon *noun* a navigational instrument based on a gyroscope, designed to indicate an aircraft's position in relation to the horizontal plane.

artificial insemination *noun* introduction of semen into the uterus or vagina by other than natural means.

artificial intelligence *noun* a branch of computer science concerned with machines or programs that can emulate human behaviour, reasoning, understanding, etc.

artificial respiration *noun* the rhythmic forcing of air into and out of the lungs of somebody whose breathing has stopped.

artillery /ah'tiləri/ *noun* (*pl* **artilleries**) **1** large-calibre mounted firearms, e.g. guns, howitzers, and missile launchers. **2** (*treated as sing. or pl*) a branch of an army armed with artillery. [Middle English *artillerie* military equipment, missile-throwing weapons, from Old French, prob from an alteration of *atirier*: see ATTIRE[2]]

artiodactyl /,ahtioh'daktil/ *noun* any of an order of hoofed mammals, including the pig, camel, and ox, that have an even number of functional toes on each foot: order Artiodactyla. ➤➤ **artiodactyl** *adj*. [Greek *artios* fitting, even-numbered + *daktylos* finger, toe]

artisan /'ahtizan, ahti'zan/ *noun* a skilled manual worker, e.g. a carpenter, plumber, or tailor. [early French *artisan* from Old Italian *artigiano* from *arte art, from Latin art*, ars]

artist /'ahtist/ *noun* **1** a person who practises an imaginative art such as painting or sculpture, *esp* professionally. **2** a skilled performer. **3** somebody whose work requires creativity and imagination, as well as practical skill. **4** *informal* somebody who is proficient in a specified and usu dubious activity; an expert: *a rip-off artist*. **5** *Aus, NAmer, informal* a fellow or character, *esp* of a specified sort. [French *artiste* from Italian *artista*, from *arte* art]

artiste /ah'teest/ *noun* a skilled public performer, *esp* a musical or theatrical entertainer. [French *artiste* artist: see ARTIST]

artistic /ah'tistik/ *adj* **1** concerning or characteristic of art or artists. **2** showing imaginative skill in arrangement or execution. ➤➤ **artistically** *adv*.

artistry /'ahtistri/ *noun* artistic quality or ability.

artless /'ahtlis/ *adj* **1** free from artificiality or affectation; natural: *artless grace*. **2** free from deceit, guile, or artifice; sincerely simple: *artless good nature*. **3** clumsy: *an artless remark*. ➤➤ **artlessly** *adv*, **artlessness** *noun*.

art nouveau /,ah(t) nooh'voh/ *noun* (*often* **Art Nouveau**) a decorative style of late 19th-cent. origin, characterized by flattened curves and plant motifs. [French *art nouveau*, new art]

arts and crafts *pl noun* **1** decorative craftwork and design. **2** (**Arts and Crafts**) a late 19th-cent. movement in building and design aimed at reviving the skilled craftsmanship associated with the medieval guilds.

artsy /'ahtsi/ *adj* (**artsier, artsiest**) *NAmer* = ARTY.

art union *noun Aus, NZ* an officially sanctioned lottery for prizes other than cash. [from the circumstance that the prizes were orig pictures]

artwork *noun* **1** paintings, drawings, and other works of art collectively. **2** the pictures and illustrations in a printed text.

arty /'ahti/ *adj* (**artier, artiest**) showily or pretentiously artistic: *arty lighting and photography.* ➤➤ **artily** *adv*, **artiness** *noun*.

arty-crafty /,ahti 'krahfti/ *adj informal* arty, *esp* affectedly simple or rustic in style. [from the phrase *arts and crafts*]

arty-farty *adj Brit, informal* arty. [alteration of ARTY-CRAFTY]

arugula /ə'roohgyoolə/ *noun NAmer* = ROCKET[3]. [via Italian dialect *arucula* from Italian *rucola*, dimin. of *ruca* ROCKET[3]]

arum /'eərəm/ *noun* any of several species of Old World plants with tiny, densely packed flowers enclosed in a large fleshy SPATHE (leaf-like sheath), e.g. a cuckoopint: family Araceae. [scientific Latin *arum*, genus name, ultimately from Greek *aron* cuckoopint]

arum lily *noun* a lily-like African plant with a large SPATHE (leaf-like sheath): *Zantedeschia aethiopica.*

arvo /'ahvoh/ *noun* (*pl* **arvos**) *Aus, NZ, informal* the afternoon. [alteration of *af* in *afternoon* + -O[1]]

-ary[1] *suffix* forming nouns, with the meanings: **1** belonging to or connected with something: *ovary*. **2** a place or repository for something: *library*; *aviary*. **3** somebody belonging to, connected with, or engaged in something: *functionary*; *missionary*. [Middle English -*arie* via Old French from Latin -*arius, -aria, -arium*, from -*arius*, adj suffix]

-ary[2] *suffix* forming adjectives, with the meaning: relating to or connected with something: *budgetary*; *military*. [Middle English -*arie* via Old French from Latin -*arius*]

Aryan /'eəri·ən/ *noun* **1a** a member of a people speaking an Indo-European language, who appeared as invaders in N India in the second millennium BC. **b** a member of any of the peoples supposedly descended from this people. **c** the language of this people. **2** in Nazi ideology, a white non-Jewish person, *esp* of European origin, held to be racially superior. ➤➤ **Aryan** *adj.* [Sanskrit *ārya* noble]

aryl /'aril/ *noun* a radical, e.g. phenyl, derived from an aromatic hydrocarbon by the removal of one hydrogen atom. [AROMATIC¹ + -YL]

arytenoid /ari'teenoyd/ *adj* **1** denoting either of a pair of small cartilages in the larynx, to which the vocal cords are attached. **2** denoting any of three small muscles in the larynx that narrow the space between the vocal cords. ➤➤ **arytenoid** *noun*. [scientific Latin *arytaenoides* ladle-shaped, from Greek *arytaina* ladle + -OID]

AS *abbr* **1** airspeed. **2** Anglo-Saxon. **3** antisubmarine.

As *abbr* the chemical symbol for arsenic.

as¹ /əz; *strong* az/ *adv* to the same degree or amount; equally; so: *It's like an orange but not as large.* [Old English *eallswā*: see ALSO]

as² *conj* **1** to the same degree that: *I thought as much.* **2** used to introduce a comparison: *as black as night; She lives in the same building as my brother.* **3** used to emphasize an amount: *as many as 250; as long ago as 1930.* **4** used after *so* to introduce a result: *They were so clearly guilty as to leave no doubt.* **5** used after *so* to introduce the idea of purpose: *He hid so as not to get caught.* **6** in the way that: *Do as I say, not as I do.* **7** in accordance with what: *They were late, as usual; She is ill, as you can see.* **8** while or when: *She spilt the milk as she got up.* **9** though: *Naked as I was, I rushed out.* **10** for the reason that: *As it's raining, let's stay at home.* ✳ **as and when** at the time when: *We'll deal with that possibility as and when it crops up.* **as is** *informal* in the present condition without modification: *She bought the clock at an auction as is.* **as it is** in the actual circumstances; really. **as it were** in a manner of speaking; so to speak.

as³ *prep* **1** in the capacity, role, character, state, etc of (a certain class of person or thing): *speaking as your solicitor; They dressed him as a girl; It came as a shock; using books as doorstops.* **2** used with certain verbs of regarding and describing: *It was dismissed as an aberration; They regard her as clever but wayward.*

as⁴ /as/ *noun* (*pl* **asses** /'aseez, 'asiz/) a bronze coin of ancient Rome, or the unit of value represented by it. [Latin *as* a unit]

as- *prefix* see AD-.

ASA *abbr* **1** Advertising Standards Authority. **2** Amateur Swimming Association. **3** American Standards Association.

asafoetida (*NAmer* **asafetida**) /asə'fetidə/ *noun* the fetid gum resin of various oriental plants of the carrot family. It is used in cookery, *esp* in India and the Middle East, to add flavour and aid digestion. [Middle English *asafetida* via medieval Latin, from Persian *azā* mastic + Latin *foetida*, fem of *foetidus*: see FETID]

asana /'ahsənə/ *noun* (*pl* **asanas**) any of the positions used in hatha yoga. [Sanskrit *āsana*]

a.s.a.p. *abbr* as soon as possible.

ASB *abbr* Alternative Service Book.

asbestos /az'bestos, as-/ *noun* any of several minerals composed of thin flexible fibres, *esp* CHRYSOTILE (white asbestos), AMOSITE (brown asbestos), and CROCIDOLITE (blue asbestos), used to make non-combustible, non-conducting, or chemically resistant materials. [Middle English *albestron* mineral supposed to be inextinguishable when set on fire, ultimately from Greek *asbestos* inextinguishable]

asbestosis /azbes'tohsis, as-/ *noun* a disease of the lungs caused by the inhalation of asbestos particles. [scientific Latin *asbestosis*, from ASBESTOS]

ascarid /'askərid/ *or* **ascaris** /-ris/ *noun* any of a family of nematodes, e.g. the common roundworm, parasitic in the human intestine: family Ascaridae. [late Latin *ascarid-*, *ascaris* intestinal worm, from Greek *askarid-*, *askaris*]

ascend /ə'send/ *verb intrans* **1** to move or slope gradually upwards; to rise. **2a** to rise from a lower level or degree: *He ascended through the ranks to become managing director.* **b** to go back in time or in order of genealogical succession. ➤ *verb trans* to go or move up (something, e.g. a slope). ✳ **ascend the throne** to become queen or king. [Middle English *ascenden* from Latin *ascendere*, from AD- + *scandere* to climb]

ascendance *or* **ascendence** /ə'send(ə)ns/ *noun* = ASCENDANCY.

ascendancy *or* **ascendency** /ə'send(ə)nsi/ *noun* (*often* + over) controlling influence; domination.

ascendant¹ *or* **ascendent** /ə'send(ə)nt/ *noun* **1** the degree of the zodiac that rises above the eastern horizon at any moment, e.g. at one's birth. **2** a state or position of dominant power or importance:

The Labour Party was then in the ascendant. [Middle English *ascendent* via medieval Latin from Latin *ascendent-*, *ascendens*, present part. of *ascendere*: see ASCEND]

ascendant² *or* **ascendent** *adj* **1** rising. **2** superior or dominant. ➤➤ **ascendantly** *adv.*

ascendence /ə'send(ə)ns/ *noun* see ASCENDANCE.

ascendency /ə'send(ə)nsi/ *noun* see ASCENDANCY.

ascendent /ə'send(ə)nt/ *noun and adj* see ASCENDANT¹, ASCENDANT².

ascender *noun* the part of a lower-case letter, e.g. 'b', that rises above the main body of the letter, or a letter that has such a part: compare DESCENDER.

ascension /ə'sensh(ə)n/ *noun* **1** the act or process of ascending. **2** (*usu* **Ascension**) in Christianity, Jesus Christ's ascent to heaven after rising from the dead. [Middle English from Latin *ascension-*, *ascensio* from *ascendere*: see ASCEND]

Ascension Day *noun* the Thursday 40 days after Easter observed by Christians in commemoration of Christ's Ascension.

ascent /ə'sent/ *noun* **1a** the act of going, climbing, or travelling up. **b** a way up; an upward slope or path. **2** an advance in social status or reputation; progress: *the ascent of women.* [from *ascend*, by analogy with *descend*: *descent*]

ascertain /asə'tayn/ *verb trans* to find out or learn (something) with certainty. ➤➤ **ascertainable** *adj*, **ascertainment** *noun*. [Middle English *acertainen* to make certain, from early French *acertainer*]

ascesis /ə'seesis/ *noun* severe self-discipline as a regular way of life. [Greek *askēsis* training]

ascetic /ə'setik/ *or* **ascetical** *adj* **1** practising strict self-denial as a spiritual discipline. **2** austere in appearance, manner, or attitude. ➤➤ **ascetic** *noun*, **ascetically** *adv*, **asceticism** /-siz(ə)m/ *noun*. [Greek *askētikos* from *askētēs* a person that exercises, hermit, from *askein* to work, to exercise]

asci /'askie/ *noun* pl of ASCUS.

ascidian /ə'sidi-ən/ *noun* any of several species of invertebrate sea animals including the sea squirt: class Ascidiacea. [scientific Latin *Ascidia*, genus name, from Greek *askidion*, dimin. of *askos* wineskin, bladder]

ASCII /'aski/ *noun* a computer code consisting of 128 seven-bit characters that is used for representing characters as binary numbers storable in a computer memory. [acronym from *American Standard Code for Information Interchange*]

ascites /ə'sieteez/ *noun* (*pl* **ascites**) the accumulation of fluid in the abdomen. ➤➤ **ascitic** /ə'sitik/ *adj*. [Middle English *aschytes* via late Latin from Greek *askitēs* from *askos* wineskin, bladder]

ascomycete /askə'mieseet/ *noun* any of a class of higher fungi, e.g. yeast, in which the spores are formed in an ASCUS (membranous spore sac): class Ascomycetes. ➤➤ **ascomycetous** /-'seetəs/ *adj*. [derivative of Greek *askos* wineskin, bladder + *mykēt-*, *mykēs* fungus]

ascorbate /ə'skawbayt/ *noun* a salt of ascorbic acid.

ascorbic acid /ə'skawbik/ *noun* a compound occurring in citrus fruits and green vegetables that is essential in the diet for the maintenance of healthy connective tissue, a deficiency being the cause of scurvy. Also called VITAMIN C. [A-² + scientific Latin *scorbutus* scurvy]

ascribe /ə'skrieb/ *verb trans* **1** (+ to) to refer or attribute (something) to a supposed cause or source: *The doctor ascribed her symptoms to a lack of fresh air.* **2** to attribute (a quality) to a person or thing: *the healing properties ascribed to this plant.* **3** to attribute (a work of art or literature) to somebody: *The painting known as 'The Bravo' is ascribed variously to Titian and Giorgione.* ➤➤ **ascribable** *adj*. [Middle English *ascriven* via French from Latin *ascribere*, from AD- + *scribere* to write]

ascription /ə'skripsh(ə)n/ *noun* the act of ascribing; attribution. [late Latin *ascription-*, *ascriptio* written addition, from Latin *ascribere*: see ASCRIBE]

ascus /'askəs/ *noun* (*pl* **asci** /'askie/) the membranous oval or tubular spore sac of an ASCOMYCETE (class of fungi). [scientific Latin from Greek *askos* wineskin, bladder]

asdic /'azdik/ *noun* an echo-sounding device for detecting submarines: compare SONAR. [acronym from *Anti-Submarine Detection Investigation Committee*]

-ase *suffix* forming nouns, denoting: an enzyme: *protease*. [French *-ase*]

ASEAN /'asian/ *abbr* Association of South-East Asian Nations.

asepsis /ay'sepsis/ *noun* **1** the condition of being aseptic. **2** a procedure for making or keeping something aseptic.

aseptic /ay'septik/ *adj* **1** preventing infection: *aseptic techniques*. **2** free or freed from disease-causing micro-organisms: *an aseptic operating theatre*. >> **aseptically** *adv*.

asexual /ay'seksyooəl, ay'seksh(ə)l/ *adj* **1** having no sex organs, or apparently without sex. **2** produced without sexual action or differentiation. **3** without expression of or reference to sexual interest. >> **asexuality** *noun*, **asexually** *adv*.

asexual reproduction *noun* reproduction, e.g. by cell division or spore formation, without the union of individuals or gametes.

as far as *conj* to the extent or degree that: *He's OK, as far as I know.*

as for *prep* concerning or in regard to (somebody or something): *As for the others, they'll arrive later.*

as from *prep* not earlier or later than (e.g. a date): *The change takes effect as from July 1st.*

ASH *abbr* Action on Smoking and Health.

ash¹ /ash/ *noun* **1** any of several species of tall pinnate-leaved trees of the olive family: genus *Fraxinus*. **2** the tough elastic wood of this tree. **3** the ligature *æ* used in Old English to represent a low front vowel. [Old English *æsc*; (sense 3) Old English *æsc*, name of the corresponding runic letter]

ash² *noun* **1a** the solid residue left when material is thoroughly burned or oxidized. **b** the fine-grained material ejected from a volcanic crater. **2** (*in pl*) **a** the remains of something destroyed by fire: *a new city built on the ashes of the old*. **b** the remains of a dead body after cremation or disintegration. ✳ **rise from the ashes** to come back into being after apparent destruction. >> **ashless** *adj*. [Old English *asce*]

ashamed /ə'shaymd/ *adj* **1** feeling shame, guilt, or disgrace. **2** restrained by fear of shame: *I was ashamed to ask*. >> **ashamedly** /-midli/ *adv*. [Old English *ascamod*, past part. of *ascamian* to shame, from A-¹ + *scamian* to shame, from *scamu* SHAME¹]

ash blonde *or* **ash blond** *adj* said of hair: of a pale or silvery blonde colour.

ashcan *noun NAmer* a dustbin.

ashen¹ /'ash(ə)n/ *adj* made from the wood of the ash tree.

ashen² *adj* **1** deadly pale; blanched: *His face was ashen with fear*. **2** *literary* resembling ashes in colour.

Ashes /'ashiz/ *pl noun* (**the Ashes**) a trophy played for in a series of cricket Test matches between England and Australia.

Word history
from a jesting reference to the ashes of the dead body of English cricket after an Australian victory in 1882. The newspaper *Sporting Times* published a mock obituary of English cricket stating that 'The body will be cremated and the ashes taken to Australia'. When an English touring team beat Australia in the following winter, some Australian ladies jokingly presented the English captain, Ivo Bligh, with a small terracotta urn containing the ashes of (allegedly) a bail or stump. Ever since, matches between the two countries have been played for this nominal trophy, which remains at Lord's cricket ground and is not physically possessed by the winning side.

ashet /'ashit/ *noun Scot, N English* a large meat plate. [French *assiette* plate]

Ashkenazi /ashkə'nahzi/ *noun* (*pl* **Ashkenazim** /-'nazim/) a Yiddish-speaking Jewish person from central Europe or with central European ancestry: compare SEPHARDI. >> **Ashkenazic** /-'nazik/ *adj*. [Hebrew *Ashkĕnāzī*, from *Ashkenaz*, grandson of Japeth, one of the sons of Noah (Genesis 10:3)]

ash key *noun Brit* the winged fruit of the ash tree, growing in clusters that resemble bunches of keys.

ashlar /'ashlə/ *noun* **1** hewn or squared stone, or masonry consisting of such stone. **2** a thin squared and dressed stone for facing a wall of rubble or brick. [Middle English *asheler* via Old French from Latin *axis* transverse beam, alteration of *assis*]

ashore /ə'shaw/ *adv* on or to the shore.

ashpan *noun* a tray fitted under the grate in a fire to contain falling ashes.

ashram /'ashrəm, 'ashram/ *noun* **1** the religious retreat of a Hindu sage. **2** any religious retreat or sanctuary. [Sanskrit *āśrama*, from *ā* towards + *śrama* religious exercise]

ashtray *noun* a receptacle for tobacco ash and cigar and cigarette ends.

Ash Wednesday *noun* the first day of Lent. [from the Christian custom of sprinkling ashes on penitents' heads]

ashy /'ashi/ *adj* (**ashier, ashiest**) **1** of ashes. **2** = ASHEN² (1).

Asian /'ayzh(ə)n, 'aysh(ə)n/ *adj* relating to or characteristic of the continent of Asia or its people. >> **Asian** *noun*.

Asiatic /ayzi'atik, ayzhi-/ *adj* relating to or belonging to Asia.

A-side *noun* the side of a pop or rock single featuring the song or piece of music that is specifically being marketed.

aside¹ /ə'sied/ *adv and adj* **1** to or towards the side: *He stepped aside to let her pass*. **2** out of the way: *I encouraged him to put his work aside*. **3** in reserve for future use: *They had money set aside for emergencies*. **4** leaving a certain thing out of the argument for the moment: *Taste aside, are you sure it's safe to drink?* [Middle English, from A-¹ + SIDE¹]

aside² *noun* **1** an utterance meant to be inaudible; *esp* an actor's speech supposedly not heard by other characters on stage. **2** a digression.

aside from *prep chiefly NAmer* = APART FROM.

as if *conj* **1** as it would be if: *It was as if he had lost his best friend*. **2** as one would do if: *He shook his head as if to say no*. **3** that: *It's not as if she's poor*. **4** used in emphatic repudiation of a notion: *As if I cared!*

asinine /'asinien/ *adj* lacking intelligence or common sense; stupid. >> **asininely** *adv*, **asininity** /-'niniti/ *noun*. [Latin *asininus* of or like an ass, from *asinus* ASS¹]

-asis *suffix* see -IASIS.

ask /ahsk/ *verb trans* **1a** to call on (somebody) for an answer: *I asked him about his trip*. **b** to put or frame (a question): *We have some questions to ask of you*. **c** to put a question about (something): *I asked his whereabouts*. **2a** to make a request of (somebody): *She asked her teacher for help*. **b** to make a request for (something): *She asked help from her teacher*. **3** (+ to) to behave in such a way as to provoke (an unpleasant response): *They were just asking to be sacked*. **4** (often + for) to set (something) as a price: *She asked £1500 for the car*. **5** to invite (somebody): *Why don't you ask him to dinner?* > *verb intrans* **1** (often + for) to make a request or seek information: *You only have to ask; I asked for guidance*. **2** (+ after) to enquire about somebody's welfare: *He always remembers to ask after my mother*. **3** (+ for) to behave in a way likely to cause something undesirable: *You're asking for trouble; They always ask for it*. ✳ **a big ask** *Aus, NZ, informal* a steep demand; a tall order. **for the asking** with little or no outlay or effort: *The job's yours for the asking*. **I ask you!** an expression of indignation or outrage. >> **asker** *noun*. [Old English *ascian*]

askance /ə'skahns/ ✳ **look askance at** to regard (something or somebody) with disapproval or distrust: *Every householder looked askance at such a woman and child inquiring for accommodation in the gloom* — Hardy. [perhaps from Italian *a scancio* obliquely]

askew /ə'skyooh/ *adv and adj* out of line; awry. [prob from A-¹ + SKEW³]

asking price /'ahsking/ *noun* the price set by the seller.

ask out *verb trans* to invite (somebody) to accompany one somewhere socially, usually as the first step in forming a romantic or sexual relationship.

ask over *or* **ask round** *verb trans* to invite (somebody) to one's house for a social visit.

ASL *abbr* American Sign Language.

aslant /ə'slahnt/ *prep, adv, and adj* in a slanting direction, or over or across (something) in a slanting direction.

asleep /ə'sleep/ *adj* **1** in a state of sleep. **2** said of a limb: lacking sensation; numb. **3** *literary* dead: *and the earth shall restore those that are asleep in her* — Apocrypha.

Aslef /'azlef/ *abbr* Associated Society of Locomotive Engineers and Firemen.

AS level *noun* an examination at an advanced level below that of A level, or a pass in such an examination. [abbr of *Advanced Subsidiary level*]

aslope /ə'slohp/ *adj and adv* in a sloping or slanting position or direction.

ASM *abbr* **1** air-to-surface missile. **2** assistant stage manager.

as much as *prep* (*also* **so much as**) (*used in negative contexts*) even: *They went without as much as a goodbye; not so much as a phonecall in three whole years.*

asocial /ay'sohsh(ə)l/ *adj* **1** avoiding the company of, or interaction with, other people. **2** behaving in a manner inconsiderate of other people.

Usage note
See note at ANTISOCIAL.

as of *prep chiefly NAmer* = AS FROM: *The arrangement is in force as of today.*

asp /asp/ *noun* **1** (*also* **asp viper**) a small viper that has an upturned snout: *Vipera aspis*. **2** a small African cobra: *Naja haje*. [Middle English *aspis* via Latin from Greek]

asparagine /ə'sparəjeen, -jin/ *noun* an amino acid that is an amide of aspartic acid and found in most proteins. [French *asparagine* from Latin *asparagus*: see ASPARAGUS]

asparagus /ə'sparəgəs/ *noun* **1** a tall plant of the lily family widely cultivated for its edible young shoots: *Asparagus officinalis*. **2** the tender spike-shaped shoots of this plant, used as a vegetable. [scientific Latin *asparagus* via Latin from Greek *asparagos*]

asparagus fern *noun* any of several species of plants with decorative feathery foliage, related to asparagus: genus *Asparagus*.

aspartame /ə'spahtaym/ *noun* an artificial sweetener prepared from aspartic acid and phenylalanine.

aspartic acid /ə'spahtik/ *noun* an amino acid found in most proteins. >> **aspartate** *noun*. [irreg from Latin *asparagus*: see ASPARAGUS]

aspect /'aspekt/ *noun* **1a** a particular feature of a situation, plan, or point of view: *There are many aspects to the problem*. **b** appearance to the eye or mind: *The task has a daunting aspect*. **c** *literary or archaic* a person's face or expression: *his grim aspect* — Shakespeare. **2a** a position facing a particular direction: *The house has a southern aspect*. **b** the side of a building facing a particular direction: *the ornamentation on its western aspect*. **c** the position of planets or stars with respect to one another, held by astrologers to influence human affairs. **d** the apparent position of a body in the solar system with respect to the sun. **e** the manner of presentation of an aerofoil, hydrofoil, etc to a gas or liquid through which it is moving. **3** a set of inflected verb forms that indicate the nature of an action in terms of its beginning, duration, completion, or repetition, e.g. in *I swim* and *I am swimming*. >> **aspectual** /a'spekthooəl/ *adj*. [Middle English from Latin *aspectus*, past part. of *aspicere* to look at, from AS- + *specere* to look]

aspect ratio *noun* **1** the ratio of an aerofoil's span to its mean CHORD² (distance between leading and trailing edges). **2** the ratio of the width to the height of a screen or image, e.g. in television or the cinema.

aspen /'aspən/ *noun* any of several species of poplars with leaves that flutter in the lightest wind: genus *Populus*. [Old English *æspe*]

Asperger's syndrome /'aspuhjəz/ *noun* a slight psychiatric disorder related to autism, characterized by difficulty with social interaction and rather narrow preoccupations. [named after Hans Asperger d.1980, Austrian psychiatrist]

aspergilli /aspə'jilie/ *noun* pl of ASPERGILLUS.

aspergillosis /ˌaspəji'losis/ *noun* a condition caused usu by the inhalation of spores from mouldy hay, affecting the lungs and other tissues. Also called FARMER'S LUNG.

aspergillus /aspə'jiləs/ *noun* (*pl* **aspergilli** /-lie/) any of a genus of fungi including many common moulds: genus *Aspergillus*. [scientific Latin *aspergillus*, genus name, from *aspergillum* brush for sprinkling water, from Latin *aspergere* to sprinkle]

asperity /ə'speriti/ *noun* (*pl* **asperities**) **1** roughness of manner or temper; harshness. **2** roughness of surface; unevenness. **3** rigour or hardship. [Middle English *asprete* via Old French from Latin *asper* rough]

asperse /ə'spuhs/ *verb trans archaic or literary* to attack the reputation of (somebody or something); to defame: *Their friend's character hath been falsely and injuriously aspersed* — Henry Fielding. [Latin *aspersus*, past part. of *aspergere* to sprinkle]

aspersion /ə'spuhsh(ə)n/ ✱ **cast aspersions on** to attack the reputation of (somebody or something); to defame: *the aspersions cast upon me through the organs of the Free Church of Scotland* — Frederick Douglass.

asphalt /'asfalt; *NAmer* 'asfawlt/ *noun* **1** a brown to black bituminous substance found in natural beds and also obtained as a residue in petroleum or coal tar refining. **2** an asphaltic composition used for surfacing roads and footpaths. >> **asphaltic** /as'faltik/ *adj*. [Middle English *aspalt* via late Latin from Greek *asphaltos*]

asphodel /'asfədel/ *noun* **1** any of several species of Old World plants of the lily family with long spikes of flowers: genera *Asphodelus* and *Asphodeline*. **2** *literary* an everlasting flower growing in the Elysian fields. [via Latin from Greek *asphodelos*]

asphyxia /ə'sfiksi-ə/ *noun* a lack of oxygen in the body, usu caused by an interruption of breathing, resulting in unconsciousness or death. Also called APNOEA. [scientific Latin from Greek *asphyxia* stopping of the pulse, from A-² + *sphyzein* to throb]

asphyxiate /ə'sfiksi-ayt/ *verb intrans and trans* to suffer or cause (somebody) to suffer a lack of oxygen in the body, e.g. by obstruction of breathing, and become unconscious or die as a result. >> **asphyxiation** /əˌsfiksi-'aysh(ə)n/ *noun*.

aspic /'aspik/ *noun* a clear savoury jelly, e.g. of fish or meat stock, used as a garnish or to make a mould. [French *aspic* asp, because the colours of the jelly were thought to resemble the snake]

aspidistra /aspi'distrə/ *noun* an Asiatic plant of the lily family with large leaves, often grown as a house plant: genus *Aspidistra*. [scientific Latin *aspidistra*, from Greek *aspid-*, *aspis* shield, from the shape of the leaves]

aspirate¹ /'aspirət/ *adj* pronounced with an /h/ sound or a forceful exhalation of breath. [Latin *aspiratus*, past part. of *aspirare*: see ASPIRE]

aspirate² /'aspirayt/ *verb trans* **1** to pronounce (a vowel, consonant, or word) with a forceful exhalation of breath. **2** to draw or remove (e.g. blood) by suction. **3** *technical* to inhale.

aspirate³ /'aspirət/ *noun* **1** an independent /h/ sound, or the character representing this sound. **2** an aspirated consonant, e.g. the *p* of *pit*.

aspirated /'aspiraytid/ *adj* = ASPIRATE¹.

aspiration /aspi'raysh(ə)n/ *noun* **1a** a strong desire to achieve something important; an ambition. **b** the object of this desire. **2** the pronunciation or addition of an aspirate. **3** a drawing of something in, out, up, or through by or as if by suction, e.g. the act of breathing or the withdrawal of fluid from the body.

aspirator /'aspiraytə/ *noun* an apparatus for aspirating fluid, tissue, etc from the body.

aspire /ə'spie-ə/ *verb intrans* (*usu* + to) to seek to attain or accomplish a particular goal: *She aspired to a career in medicine*. >> **aspirant** /'aspirənt/ *noun and adj*, **aspirer** *noun*. [Middle English *aspiren* via French from Latin *aspirare*, literally 'to breathe upon']

aspirin /'asprin/ *noun* (*pl* **aspirin** *or* **aspirins**) **1** the compound acetylsalicylic acid used for relief of pain and fever. **2** a tablet containing this compound. [ACETYL + *spiraeic acid* (former name of salicylic acid), from scientific Latin *Spiraea*, genus of shrubs]

asp viper *noun* see ASP (1).

asquint /ə'skwint/ *adv and adj* from the corner of the eye, in a secretive or conspiratorial way.

as regards /ri'gahdz/ *prep* with respect to or in regard to (somebody or something).

ass¹ /as/ *noun* **1** either of two species of long-eared hardy gregarious mammals related to and smaller than the horse: genus *Equus*. **2** = DONKEY (1). **3** a stupid, obstinate, or perverse person or thing: *The law is an ass*. [Old English *assa*, perhaps via Old Irish *asan* from Latin *asinus*]

ass² *noun chiefly NAmer* = ARSE. [by alteration]

assagai /'asigie/ *noun* see ASSEGAI.

assai /a'sie/ *adv* used with a tempo direction in music: very: *allegro assai*. [Italian *assai* very much]

assail /ə'sayl/ *verb trans* **1** to attack (somebody) violently with blows or words. **2** to prey on (somebody): *He was assailed by doubts*. >> **assailable** *adj*. [Middle English *assailen* via Old French and late Latin *assilire* to leap upon, from AS- + *salire* to leap]

assailant *noun* a person who carries out a physical attack on another.

Assamese *noun* **1** a native or inhabitant of Assam, a state in NE India. **2** an Indic language spoken in Assam, Bhutan, and Bangladesh. >> **Assamese** *adj*.

assassin /ə'sasin/ *noun* **1** a murderer, *esp* of a political or religious leader. **2** (**Assassin**) any of a secret order of Muslims who committed secret murders at the time of the Crusades.

Word history
medieval Latin *assassinus* from Arabic *ḥashshāshīn*, pl of *ḥashshāsh* one who smokes or chews hashish. The original Assassins were members of a heterodox branch, called the Isma'īlites, of the Shiite sect of Islam. Founded at the end of the 11th cent., they were active in Iran and Syria until the 13th cent. The word *assassin* was brought to Europe by crusaders. It was used in Latin texts by English writers as early as the 13th cent., and by the early 17th cent. was used in English in both its original and extended senses.

assassinate /ə'sasinayt/ *verb trans* to kill (somebody, *esp* a political or religious leader) suddenly or secretly. ➤➤ **assassination** /-'naysh(ə)n/ *noun*.

assault[1] /ə'sawlt/ *noun* **1** a violent physical or verbal attack. **2a** in law, an attempt to do or immediate threat of doing unlawful personal violence. **b** rape or other physical attack of a sexual nature. **3** an attempt to attack a fortification by a sudden rush. [Middle English *assaut* via Old French, ultimately from AS- + Latin *salire* to leap]

assault[2] *verb trans* **1** to make an assault on (somebody). **2** to rape or sexually attack (somebody). ➤➤ **assaulter** *noun*, **assaultive** *adj*.

assault and battery *noun* the crime of attacking somebody physically and causing them bodily harm.

assay[1] /ə'say/ *noun* **1** analysis of an ore, drug, etc to determine the presence, absence, or quantity of one or more components. **2** a substance to be analysed in this way. [Middle English from Old French *essai, assai*: see ESSAY[1]]

assay[2] *verb trans* **1a** to analyse (an ore, etc) for one or more valuable components. **b** to determine the purity of (gold, silver, or another precious metal). **2** to judge the worth or quality of (a person or thing). **3** *archaic* to attempt (something) or try (to do something): *I would assay, proud queen, to make thee blush* — Shakespeare. ➤➤ **assayer** *noun*.

assay office *noun* **1** an office at which ores are assayed. **2** *Brit* an institution that awards a hallmark on articles of gold, silver, or platinum.

assegai *or* **assagai** /'asigie/ *noun* (*pl* **assegais** *or* **assagais**) a slender hardwood spear with an iron tip used by tribal societies in southern Africa. [alteration, via French or Portuguese, of Arabic *az-zaghāya* the assegai]

assemblage /ə'semblij/ *noun* **1** a collection of people or things; a gathering or accumulation: *Here was grouped a chaotic assemblage of articles* — Hardy. **2** an artistic work, *esp* of the 1960s, consisting of a three-dimensional collage made from scraps, junk, and odds and ends, e.g. of cloth, wood, and stone.

assemble /ə'sembl/ *verb trans* **1** to bring together (a group of people or a collection of things) in a particular place or for a particular purpose: *He had assembled his voluminous notes* — George Eliot. **2** to fit together the parts of (a kit, model, etc). ➤ *verb intrans* to gather together; to convene. [Middle English *assemblen* from Old French *assembler*, ultimately from AD- + Latin *simul* together]

assembler *noun* **1** a person or device that assembles. **2a** in computing, a program that translates instructions from a low-level symbolic code into MACHINE CODE (information in a form directly usable by the computer). **b** the low-level code itself; ASSEMBLY LANGUAGE.

assembly /ə'sembli/ *noun* (*pl* **assemblies**) **1** a company of people gathered together for a particular purpose; *specif* a regular gathering of staff and pupils of a school for announcements, etc. **2 (Assembly)** a legislative or deliberative body: *the Welsh Assembly*. **3** the process of assembling or of being assembled. **4** a signal for troops to assemble or fall in. **5a** the fitting together of manufactured parts into a complete machine, structure, etc. **b** the collection of parts to be so assembled, or the finished structure. **6** in computing, the translation of assembly language into MACHINE CODE (information in a form directly usable by a computer).

assembly language *noun* a low-level computer language that is a close approximation to MACHINE CODE (information in a form directly usable by a computer) and in which each instruction typically corresponds to a single instruction in machine code.

assembly line *noun* **1** in a factory, an arrangement of machines and equipment by means of which work passes through successive stages and operations until the product is assembled. **2** a process for turning out a finished product in a mechanically efficient but often cursory or impersonal manner.

assent[1] /ə'sent/ *verb intrans* (*usu* + to) to agree to something: *She willingly assented to our proposal.* ➤➤ **assenter** *noun*, **assentor** *noun*. [Middle English *assenten* from Old French *assenter*, ultimately from Latin *assentire*, from AD- + *sentire* to feel]

assent[2] *noun* the act of agreeing; formal agreement or approval.

assert /ə'suht/ *verb trans* **1** to state or declare (something), often forcefully. **2** to give positive demonstration of (a quality or attribute). **3** to insist on (a right or claim). ✳ **assert oneself** to compel recognition of one's individuality, authority, position, or rights. ➤➤ **asserter** *noun*, **assertor** *noun*. [Latin *assertus*, past part. of *asserere*, from AS- + *serere* to join]

assertion /ə'suhsh(ə)n/ *noun* **1** a declaration or positive statement. **2** the act of asserting: *assertion of one's rights*. **3** (*often* **self-assertion**) confidence and firmness in dealing with others; assertiveness

assertive /ə'suhtiv/ *adj* **1** characterized by bold assertion; dogmatic. **2** (*also* **self-assertive**) self-confident and firm in dealing with others and getting one's way. ➤➤ **assertively** *adv*, **assertiveness** *noun*.

assertiveness training *noun* instruction in how to become more assertive and confident without being aggressive

asses /'asiz/ *noun* pl of AS[4], ASS[1], ASS[2].

assess /ə'ses/ *verb trans* **1** to determine the rate or amount of (a tax, claim for damages, etc). **2** to make an official valuation of (property or income) for the purposes of taxation: *Their flat was assessed at over £100,000.* **3** to estimate the quality, nature, or worth of (a person or thing); to evaluate. ➤➤ **assessable** *adj*. [Middle English *assessen*, prob from medieval Latin *assess-*, past part. stem of *assidēre* to sit beside, assist in the office of a judge, from AS- + *sedēre* to sit]

assessment *noun* **1** the act or an instance of assessing. **2** an amount assessed. **3** in Britain, an evaluation made of a student's work, e.g. on a module or assignment.

assessment centre *noun Brit* a centre where juvenile offenders and young people in need of care or protection are sent temporarily while their situation is assessed and longer-term accommodation is found for them.

assessor *noun* **1** a person who makes an assessment. **2** a specialist who is called in to advise a court. **3** an official who assesses property for taxation. **4** a person who investigates and determines the amount of insurance claims.

asset *noun* **1a** (*in pl*) the total property of a person, company, or institution, *esp* that part which can be used to pay debts. **b** a single item of property. **2** an advantage or resource. **3** (*in pl*) the items on a balance sheet showing the book value of property owned. [back-formation from *assets* sufficient property to pay debts and legacies, from Anglo-French *asetz* from Old French *assez* enough, from Latin AS- + *satis* enough]

asset-stripping *noun* the practice of taking over an unsuccessful company and selling its assets separately at a profit.

asseverate /ə'sevərayt/ *verb trans formal* to affirm (something) solemnly: *The man again asseverated that he had let no intruder pass* — G K Chesterton. ➤➤ **asseveration** /-'raysh(ə)n/ *noun*, **asseverative** /-rətiv/ *adj*. [Latin *asseveratus*, past part. of *asseverare*, from AS- + *severus* SEVERE]

asshole /'as·hohl/ *noun NAmer, coarse slang* = ARSEHOLE.

assibilate /ə'sibilayt/ *verb trans* to pronounce (a speech sound) with, or as, a SIBILANT[2] (a sound resembling /s/ or /sh/). ➤ *verb intrans* said of a speech sound: to undergo alteration to a sibilant. ➤➤ **assibilation** /-'laysh(ə)n/ *noun*. [Latin *assibilātus*, past part. of *assībilāre* to hiss at, from AS- + *sībilāre* to hiss]

assiduity /asi'dyoohiti/ *noun* **1** persistent application; diligence: *I found Mr Micawber plying his pen with great assiduity* — Dickens. **2** solicitous or obsequious attention to a person.

assiduous /ə'sidyoo·əs/ *adj* showing careful unremitting attention or persistent application; sedulous: *I was very assiduous in recording his conversation* — James Boswell. ➤➤ **assiduously** *adv*, **assiduousness** *noun*. [Latin *assiduus* from *assidēre*: see ASSESS]

assign[1] /ə'sien/ *verb trans* **1a** to allot (a task, place, accommodation, etc) to somebody. **b** to appoint (somebody) to a particular task, post, duty, etc. **2** to transfer (property) to another person, *esp* in trust or for the benefit of creditors. **3** to specify or fix authoritatively (a date for a future event, etc). **4** to ascribe (something) as a motive or reason. ➤➤ **assignable** *adj*, **assigner** *noun*, **assignor** *noun*. [Middle English *assignen* via Old French from Latin *assignare*, from AS- + *signare* to mark, from *signum* mark, SIGN[1]]

assign² *noun* = ASSIGNEE.

assignation /asig'naysh(ə)n/ *noun* **1** the act or an instance of assigning. **2** a meeting, *esp* a secret one with a lover: *returned from an assignation with his mistress* — W B Yeats. ➤➤ **assignational** *adj.*

assignee /asie'nee/ *noun* **1** a person to whom property or a right is legally transferred. **2** a person appointed to act for another.

assignment *noun* **1a** a position, post, or job to which one is assigned. **b** a specified task or amount of work assigned by somebody in authority, *esp* a teacher or tutor. **2** the legal transfer of property or a document putting this into effect.

assimilate /ə'similayt/ *verb trans* **1a** to take in or absorb (a substance), *esp* as nourishment. **b** to absorb (facts or information) with complete comprehension. **2a** (*usu* + to/with) to make (one thing) similar to another; *specif* to make (a consonant) similar in sound to a following one. **b** (*usu* + to/with) to absorb (e.g. immigrants) into a cultural tradition. ➤ *verb intrans* to become assimilated. ➤➤ **assimilable** *adj*, **assimilative** *adj*, **assimilator** *noun*, **assimilatory** /-lət(ə)ri/ *adj.* [medieval Latin *assimilatus*, past part. of *assimilare* from Latin *assimulare* to make similar, from AS- + *simulare*: see SIMULATE]

assimilation /ə,simə'laysh(ə)n/ *noun* **1a** the act or an instance of assimilating. **b** the process of assimilating or being assimilated. **2** the incorporation or conversion of nutrients into living matter. In animals, this process follows digestion and absorption, and in plants it involves both photosynthesis and absorption of water and minerals from the soil by the roots.

assist¹ /ə'sist/ *verb trans* to help (somebody). ➤ *verb intrans* **1** to help or give support. **2** *formal* (*usu* + at) to be present at a ceremony, etc, *esp* as a helper: *The curate sometimes assisted at weddings and christenings.* ➤➤ **assister** *noun.* [Middle English via French from Latin *assistere*, from AS- + *sistere* to cause to stand]

assist² *noun chiefly NAmer* in baseball and other games, the action of a player who by throwing the ball enables a teammate to put an opponent out or score a goal.

assistance *noun* the act of assisting or the help supplied; aid.

assistant *noun* **1** a person who assists; a helper. **2** (*also* **shop assistant**) a person who serves customers in a shop, etc. **3** (*used before a noun*) denoting a subordinate post in job titles: *an assistant professor.*

assistant referee *noun* an official who assists the referee in various games.

assisted *adj* (*used in combinations*) enhanced or aided in the manner specified: *power-assisted steering.*

assisted place *noun* in Britain, a place at an independent school for a pupil whose fees are supported by a grant from the state.

assisted suicide *noun* a consensual arrangement by which a seriously ill person is helped by a doctor or carer to commit suicide.

assize /ə'siez/ *noun* (*usu in pl*) the periodical sessions of the superior courts formerly held in every English county for trial of civil and criminal cases. [Middle English *assise* via Old French, session, settlement, from *asseoir* to seat, ultimately from Latin *assidēre*: see ASSESS]

assoc. *abbr* association.

associable /ə'sohsh(y)əbl, -si-əbl/ *adj* capable of being associated, joined, or connected in thought. ➤➤ **associability** /-'biliti/ *noun.*

associate¹ /ə'sohsiayt, -shiayt/ *verb trans* **1** (*often* + with) to involve (a person or group) with another, typically more powerful one, e.g. as a business partner or ally. **2** (*often in passive, often* + with) to involve or connect (somebody or something) with a particular thing, quality, feeling, etc: *He began to associate exams with failure; the rituals associated with getting married.* ➤ *verb intrans* **1** (*often* + with) to come together as partners, or mix socially as friends or companions: *She didn't want him associating with drug-takers.* **2** (*often* + with) to combine or join with other parts; to unite: *Cells typically associate with cells of their own class.* ➤➤ **associatory** /-ət(ə)ri/ *adj.* [Middle English *associat* associated, from Latin *associatus*, past part. of *associare* to unite, from AS- + *sociare* to join, from *socius* companion]

associate² /ə'sohsi-ət, -shi-ət/ *adj* **1** sharing a function or office with another: *an associate producer.* **2** having secondary or subordinate status: *associate membership of a society.*

associate³ /ə'sohsi-ət, -shi-ət, -ayt/ *noun* **1** a fellow worker; a partner or colleague. **2** a companion or comrade. **3** something closely connected with or accompanying another thing. **4** a person

admitted to a subordinate degree of membership: *an associate of the Royal Academy.* ➤➤ **associateship** *noun.*

association /ə,sohsi'aysh(ə)n, -shi'aysh(ə)n/ *noun* **1** an organization of people having a common interest; a society or league. **2** a link in memory, thought, or imagination with a thing or person; a connotation: *The room had melancholy associations for her.* **3** associating or being associated; *specif* the formation of mental connections between sensations, ideas, memories, etc: *Words being arbitrary must owe their powers to association* — Dr Johnson. **4** the formation of polymers by loose chemical linkage, e.g. through hydrogen bonds. **5** an ecological community with two or more dominant species uniformly distributed: *a plant association.* ➤➤ **associational** *adj.*

Association Football *noun* football played by teams of eleven players using a round ball which may be kicked and passed to another player but not handled, except by the goalkeepers. [so called because it is played according to rules formulated by the Football Association in the 1860s]

associationism *noun* a theory that explains mental life in terms of the association of ideas.

associative /ə'sohsi-ətiv, -shi-ətiv/ *adj* **1** involving, dependent on, or acquired by association. **2** denoting a mathematical operation that gives the same result regardless of the order of the elements: *Addition is associative since $(a + b) + c = a + (b + c)$.* ➤➤ **associatively** *adv*, **associativity** /-'tiviti/ *noun.*

assonance /'asənəns/ *noun* **1** resemblance of sound in words or syllables. **2** repetition of the vowel sounds in two or more words, e.g. in *stony* and *holy*, or the consonant sounds, e.g. in *stand* and *stoned*, as an alternative to rhyme: compare CONSONANCE. ➤➤ **assonant** *adj and noun.* [French *assonance* from Latin *assonare* to answer with the same sound, from AS- + *sonare* to sound]

as soon as *conj* immediately at or just after the time that: *I'll come as soon as you call.*

assort /ə'sawt/ *verb trans* to distribute (things) into groups of a like kind; to classify. ✷ **assort well/ill with** to fit in well, or not to fit in well, with (a group of things or people). ➤➤ **assortative** *adj*, **assorter** *noun.* [Old French *assortir*, from AD- + *sorte*: see SORT¹]

assorted *adj* **1** consisting of various kinds mixed together. **2** classified into groups. **3** (*used in combinations*) suited to the specified degree by nature, character, or design; matched: *They seemed an ill-assorted pair.*

assortment *noun* a mixed collection of various kinds of things or people.

asst *abbr* assistant.

assuage /ə'swayj/ *verb trans* **1** to ease or lessen the intensity of (suffering, discomfort, etc). **2** to put an end to (thirst, desire, etc) by satisfying; to appease or quench. ➤➤ **assuagement** *noun.* [Middle English *aswagen* via Old French from (assumed) vulgar Latin *assuaviare*, from Latin AS- + *suavis* sweet]

assume /ə'syoohm/ *verb trans* **1** to take (a supposition or hypothesis) as granted or true; to suppose (something) for the sake of argument. **2a** to take (a role etc) upon oneself; to undertake (a task or duty). **b** to invest oneself formally with (an office or its symbols): *They assumed the trappings of power.* **3a** to feign (a certain attitude): *She assumed an air of calm.* **b** to adopt (a new name, identity, etc). **4** to acquire or grow to have (e.g. significance). **5** to seize or usurp (power or authority). ➤➤ **assumable** *adj*, **assumably** *adv.* [Middle English *assumen* from Latin *assumere*, from AS- + *sumere* to take]

Usage note
assume *or* **presume**? *Assume* and *presume* are almost interchangeable in the meaning 'suppose'. *Presume* is rather more formal, tends to suggest that a supposition is made on the basis of a deduction or a reasonable likelihood, and has a slightly unfavourable tinge, possibly picked up from its other meaning ('to take liberties'): *Dr Livingstone, I presume?* (who else could it be?); *From what you said yesterday, I presumed that you'd already made up your mind. Assume* is, however, definitely the word to choose if something is being put forward as a basis for argument: *In drawing up your pension forecast, I assumed that interest rates would remain at about 5%.*

assumed *adj* said of a name: adopted, *esp* for purposes of deception; false.

assumption /ə'sum(p)sh(ə)n/ *noun* **1a** the supposition that something is true. **b** a fact or statement, e.g. a proposition, axiom, or postulate, taken for granted. **2** the act of assuming: *the assumption of a false name.* **3** the act of laying claim to or taking possession of something. **4** (**Assumption**) 15 August, observed by Christians in commemoration of the taking up of the Virgin Mary into heaven.

5 *archaic* arrogance or presumption. [Middle English from late Latin *assumption-*, *assumptio* taking up, from Latin *assumere*: see ASSUME]

assumptive /ə'sum(p)tiv/ *adj* taken for granted; unsupported by evidence.

assurance /ə'shawrəns, ə'shooərəns/ *noun* **1a** the act of assuring; a positive declaration that something is the case. **b** a pledge or guarantee. **2a** the quality or state of being sure or certain; freedom from doubt. **b** confidence of mind or manner; excessive self-confidence: *Thou hast a most agreeable assurance, girl* — John Gay. **3** *chiefly Brit* insurance in which it is certain that the insurer will have to pay out money at some time, *esp* life insurance. **4** something that inspires or tends to inspire confidence

Usage note

assurance *or* insurance? British English uses the term *assurance* to refer to a form of insurance in which money is bound to be paid out at the end of a fixed period of time or on the death of the insured person: *life assurance*. *Insurance* is the general term covering all instances where money will only be paid in particular circumstances: *house contents insurance; travel insurance*.

assure /ə'shaw, ə'shooə/ *verb trans* **1** to inform (somebody) positively that something is the case. **2** to give confidence to (somebody); to reassure. **3** to guarantee the happening or attainment of (something); to ensure: *A word in the right place would assure her promotion*. **4** (*usu in passive*) to make (something) safe; to insure (life, safety, etc). [Middle English *assuren* via early French *assurer* from medieval Latin *assecurare*, from Latin AS- + *securus*: see SECURE[1]]

Usage note

assure, ensure, *or* insure? These three words are sometimes confused. The most common meaning of the verb to *assure* is 'to inform (somebody) positively': *I assured her that she had nothing to worry about*. *Assure* can also mean 'to make certain or safe' – but in this sense it is mainly found in the passive or adjectival form: *Their success is assured; Rest assured that we will do all we can to help you*. The verb generally used in the active form to mean 'to make (something) certain' is *ensure* (often spelt *insure* in American English): *Our first duty is to ensure the safety of the passengers*. *Insure* refers simply to making arrangements to obtain financial compensation in the event of accident or loss: *The painting should be insured for at least a million pounds*.

assured[1] /ə'shawd, ə'shooəd/ *adj* **1** characterized by self-confidence and expertise. **2** characterized by certainty; guaranteed. ➤➤ **assuredly** /-ridli/ *adv*, **assuredness** /-ridnis/ *noun*.

assured[2] *noun* (*pl* **assured**) an insured person.

assurer *or* **assuror** *noun* a person or firm that assures; an insurer.

Assyrian /ə'siri-ən/ *noun* **1** a member of an ancient Semitic kingdom and people of Mesopotamia. **2** the form of Akkadian used by the Assyrians. ➤➤ **Assyrian** *adj*.

Assyriology /ə,siri'oləji/ *noun* the study of the history, language, and antiquities of ancient Assyria and Babylonia. ➤➤ **Assyriological** /-'lojikl/ *adj*, **Assyriologist** *noun*.

AST *abbr* Atlantic Standard Time (time zone).

astable /ay'staybl/ *adj* said of an electrical circuit: having no permanently stable state.

astatic /ə'statik, ay-/ *adj* **1** not stable or steady. **2** in physics, etc, not tending to take a fixed or definite position or direction: *an astatic needle*. ➤➤ **astatically** *adv*, **astaticism** /-siz(ə)m/ *noun*.

astatine /'astəteen, -tin/ *noun* a radioactive chemical element of the halogen group, similar to iodine and formed by radioactive decay or made artificially: symbol At, atomic number 85. [Greek *astatos* unsteady, from A-[2] + *statos* standing, from *histanai* to cause to stand]

aster /'astə/ *noun* any of a genus of composite plants, often with showy heads and leafy stems, that bloom chiefly in the autumn: genus *Aster*. [scientific Latin *Aster*, genus name, via Latin from Greek *aster-*, *astēr* star, aster]

-aster *suffix* forming nouns from nouns, denoting: an inferior, worthless, or false kind of exponent of the art specified: *poetaster*. [Middle English from Latin *-aster*, suffix denoting partial resemblance]

asterisk[1] /'astərisk/ *noun* the sign (*) used as a reference mark, *esp* to denote the omission of letters, to show that something is doubtful, or to link a word to a footnote. [via late Latin from Greek *asteriskos*, dimin. of *aster-*, *astēr* star]

asterisk[2] *verb trans* to mark (a word, passage, etc) with an asterisk.

asterism /'astəriz(ə)m/ *noun* **1a** a pattern of stars within a constellation. **b** a small group of stars. **2** a star shaped figure visible in

some crystals under reflected or transmitted light. **3** three asterisks arranged in the form of a triangle, used in a text to direct attention to a following passage. [Greek *asterismos*, from *asterizein* to arrange in constellations, from *aster-*, *astēr* star]

astern /ə'stuhn/ *adv* **1** behind the stern; to the rear. **2** at or towards the stern of a ship. **3** backwards: *full speed astern*.

asteroid[1] /'astəroyd/ *noun* **1** any of thousands of small planets in the form of rocky bodies mostly between Mars and Jupiter. **2** a starfish: class Asteroidea. ➤➤ **asteroidal** /-'roydl/ *adj*. [Greek *asteroeidēs* starlike, from *aster-*, *astēr* star]

asteroid[2] *adj* **1** starlike. **2** of or like a starfish.

asthenia /əs'theeni-ə/ *noun* lack or loss of strength; debility. ➤➤ **asthenic** /əs'thenik/ *adj*. [scientific Latin from Greek *astheneia*, from *asthenēs* weak, from A-[2] + *sthenos* strength]

asthenosphere /əs'theenəsfiə/ *noun* a zone of the earth beneath the LITHOSPHERE (outer rocky zone of the earth's crust), within which the material is believed to yield readily under stress. [Greek *asthenēs* (see ASTHENIA) + -O- + SPHERE[1]]

asthma /'as(th)mə/ *noun* an allergic condition marked by attacks of laboured breathing with wheezing, coughing, and a sense of constriction in the chest. [Middle English *asma* via medieval Latin from Greek *asthma*]

asthmatic[1] /as(th)'matik/ *adj* associated with or suffering from asthma.

asthmatic[2] *noun* a person who suffers from asthma.

as though *conj* = AS IF.

astigmatic /astig'matik/ *adj* affected with, relating to, or correcting astigmatism. ➤➤ **astigmatically** *adv*.

astigmatism /ə'stigmətiz(ə)m/ *noun* a defect of an optical system, e.g. a lens or the eye, in which rays from a single point fail to meet in a focal point, resulting in patchy blurring of the image. [A-[2] + Greek *stigmat-*, *stigma* mark]

astilbe /ə'stilbi/ *noun* a plant of the saxifrage family grown in gardens for its showy white or purple flowers: genus *Astilbe*. [scientific Latin *Astilbe*, genus name, from A-[2] + Greek *stilbē*, fem of *stilbos* glistening]

astir /ə'stuh/ *adj* **1** in a state of bustle or excitement. **2** out of bed; up. [Scots *asteer*, from A-[1] + *steer*, variant of STIR[1]]

Asti spumante /,asti spoo'manti/ *noun* an Italian sparkling white wine. [Italian *Asti spumante*, literally 'sparkling Asti', from *Asti*, province in Italy where it is made]

as to *prep* **1** used *esp* with questions and speculations: **a** with regard or reference to (something or somebody); about. **b** = AS FOR. **2** by or according to (some means of classification): *They've been graded as to size and colour*.

astonish /ə'stonish/ *verb trans* to affect (somebody) with sudden wonder or surprise. ➤➤ **astonishing** *adj*, **astonishingly** *adv*, **astonishment** *noun*. [prob alteration of earlier *astony*, from Middle English *astonen*, *astonien* via Old French *estoner* from assumed vulgar Latin *extonare* to leave thunderstruck, from Latin EX-[1] + *tonare* to thunder]

astound /ə'stownd/ *verb trans* to affect (somebody) with bewilderment and wonder. ➤➤ **astounding** *adj*, **astoundingly** *adv*. [prob orig *adj*; from Middle English *astoned*, past part. of *astonen*: see ASTONISH]

astr. *abbr* **1** astronomer. **2** astronomy.

astr- *comb. form* see ASTRO-.

astragal /'astrəgl/ *noun* **1** in architecture, a narrow half-round moulding. **2** a wooden bar between window panes. [Latin *astragalus*: see ASTRAGALUS]

astragalus /ə'stragələs, ə-/ *noun* (*pl* **astragali** /-lie/) a bone corresponding to the human anklebone in a bird, mammal, etc. [via Latin from Greek *astragalos* anklebone, moulding]

astrakhan /astrə'kan/ *noun* **1** (*often* **Astrakhan**) karakul sheep wool of Russian origin. **2** a woollen fabric with curled and looped pile. [*Astrakhan*, city in Russia, from which the fleeces were exported]

astral /'astrəl/ *adj* **1** relating to or consisting of stars. **2** relating to or consisting of a spiritual substance held to be the material of which a person's supposed second body is made up, visible to specially gifted people. ➤➤ **astrally** *adv*. [late Latin *astralis* from Latin *astrum* star, from Greek *astron*]

astray /ə'stray/ *adv* **1** off the right path or route. **2** in error; away from a proper or desirable course or development. ✳ **go astray** to become lost. [Middle English from Old French *estraié* wandering, from *estraier*: see STRAY[1]]

astride[1] /ə'stried/ *adv* with the legs wide apart.

astride[2] *prep* **1** on or above (something) and with one leg on each side of it. **2** extending over or across (something); spanning (something).

astringent[1] /ə'strinj(ə)nt/ *adj* **1** said of a lotion or other application: having a contracting and firming effect on the soft tissues of the body. **2** said of wit or remarks: showing little sentiment or sympathy; dry or caustic. **3** sharply refreshing. ➤➤ **astringency** /-si/ *noun*, **astringently** *adv*. [prob via French from Latin *astringent-, astringens*, present part. of *astringere* to bind fast, from AS- + *stringere* to bind tight]

astringent[2] *noun* an astringent liquid.

astro- *or* **astr-** *comb. form* forming words, denoting: stars or the heavens; outer space: *astrophysics*. [Middle English *astro-* via Old French from Latin *astr-, astro-* from Greek, from *astron* star]

astrochemistry /astroh'kemistri/ *noun* the branch of chemistry that deals with heavenly bodies and interstellar space.

astrodome /'astrədohm/ *noun* **1** a transparent dome in the roof of an aircraft, through which astronomical observations can be made. **2** *chiefly NAmer* a sports stadium with a domed roof.

astrol. *abbr* **1** astrologer. **2** astrological. **3** astrology.

astrolabe /'astrəlayb/ *noun* an instrument formerly used to show the positions of the planets and bright stars at any date and time. [Middle English via Old French and medieval Latin from late Greek *astrolabion*, dimin. of Greek *astrolabos*, from *astron* star + *lambanein* to take]

astrology /ə'stroləji/ *noun* the art or practice of determining the supposed influences of the planets and their motions on human affairs and human disposition. ➤➤ **astrologer** *noun*, **astrological** /astrə'lojikl/ *adj*, **astrologically** /-'lojikli/ *adv*. [Middle English *astrologie* via Old French from Latin *astrologia*, from Greek *astron* star + *-logia* -LOGY]

astron. *abbr* **1** astronomer. **2** astronomical. **3** astronomy.

astronaut /'astrənawt/ *noun* a person trained to travel in space. [ASTRO- + *-naut* as in AERONAUT]

astronautics /astrə'nawtiks/ *pl noun* (*treated as sing. or pl*) the science of the construction and operation of vehicles for travel in space. ➤➤ **astronautic** *adj*, **astronautical** *adj*, **astronautically** *adv*.

astronomer /ə'stronəmə/ *noun* a person who is skilled in or practises astronomy.

astronomical /astrə'nomikl/ *or* **astronomic** *adj* **1** of or relating to astronomy. **2** *informal* extremely or excessively large: *They charged us an astronomical sum for the repair*. ➤➤ **astronomically** *adv*.

astronomical clock *noun* **1** a clock that shows astronomical data in addition to normal time. **2** a 24-hour clock based on the SIDEREAL DAY (day equal in duration to one complete rotation of the earth).

astronomical unit *noun* a unit of length used in astronomy, equal to the mean distance of the earth from the sun, or about 149 million km (about 93 million mi).

astronomy /ə'stronəmi/ *noun* the scientific study of the stars, planets, and other bodies of the universe. [Middle English *astronomie* via Old French and Latin from Greek *astronomia*, from *astron* star + *nemein* to order, arrange, distribute]

astrophysics /astroh'fiziks/ *pl noun* (*treated as sing. or pl*) a branch of astronomy dealing with the physical nature of astronomical bodies and phenomena. ➤➤ **astrophysical** *adj*, **astrophysicist** /-sist/ *noun*.

AstroTurf /'astrətuhf/ *noun trademark* an artificial grasslike surface that is used for sports fields. [from the name of the *Astrodome*, indoors arena in Houston, Texas, where it was first used, + TURF[1]]

astute /ə'styooht/ *adj* shrewd and perceptive. ➤➤ **astutely** *adv*, **astuteness** *noun*. [Latin *astutus* from *astus* cunning]

asunder /ə'sundə/ *adv literary* **1** into parts: *The hull broke asunder* — Lew Wallace. **2** apart from each other in position: *The high banks might have been a hundred feet asunder* — J Fenimore Cooper.

as well *adv* **1** in addition; also: *The Victorians expected every building, like every painting, to tell a story, and preferably to point to a moral as well* — Hugh Casson. **2** with an effect that is the same or preferable: *The dead might as well speak to the living as the old to the young* — Willa Cather. ✳ **as well as** in addition to: *They brought a bottle of wine as well as food*.

as yet *adv* up to now, or up to the time mentioned.

asylum /ə'sieləm/ *noun* **1** protection from arrest and extradition given by a nation to political refugees. **2** a place of retreat and security, or the refuge provided by it. **3** *dated* an institution for the care of the destitute or afflicted, *esp* the mentally ill. [Middle English via Latin from Greek *asylon*, neuter of *asylos* inviolable, from A-[2] + *sylon* right of seizure or reprisal]

asymmetric /aysi'metrik/ *or* **asymmetrical** *adj* **1** not symmetrical. **2** said of an atom or group: bonded to several different atoms or groups. ➤➤ **asymmetrically** *adv*, **asymmetry** /ay'simətri/ *noun*. [Greek *asymmetria* lack of proportion, from *asymmetros* ill-proportioned, from A-[2] + *symmetros*: see SYMMETRY]

asymmetric bars *pl noun* a pair of parallel wooden bars, one higher than the other, used in gymnastics.

asymptomatic /ay,simptə'matik/ *adj* said of a patient or a disorder: showing or producing no symptoms of disease. ➤➤ **asymptomatically** *adv*. [A-[2] + SYMPTOM]

asymptote /'asim(p)toht/ *noun* a straight line that is approached more and more closely by a curve but not met by it. ➤➤ **asymptotic** /-'totik/ *adj*, **asymptotically** /-'totikli/ *adv*. [scientific Latin from Greek *asymptōtos* not meeting, from A-[2] + *syn* together + *ptōtos* apt to fall, from *piptein* to fall]

asynchronism /ay'singkrəniz(ə)m/ *noun* see ASYNCHRONY.

asynchronous /ay'singkrənəs/ *adj* not synchronous; proceeding at its own pace; *esp* relating to or denoting a computing operation that does not wait for a communication to end before processing. ➤➤ **asynchronously** *adv*.

asynchrony /ay'singkrəni/ *or* **asynchronism** *noun* an absence or lack of concurrence in time.

asyndeton /ə'sindəton/ *noun* (*pl* **asyndeta** /-tə/ *or* **asyndetons**) the omission of *and*, *or*, or other coordinating conjunction, as a feature of rhetorical or poetic style, as in *I came, I saw, I conquered*. ➤➤ **asyndetic** /asin'detik/ *adj*. [via late Latin from Greek *asyndeton*, neuter of *asyndetos* unconnected, from A-[2] + *syndetos* bound together, from SYN- + *dein* to bind]

asystole /ə'sistəli, ay-/ *noun* the cessation of contractions in the heart muscle, resulting in the absence of a heartbeat; cardiac arrest. ➤➤ **asystolic** /asi'stolik, ay-/ *adj*.

AT *abbr* appropriate technology.

At *abbr* the chemical symbol for astatine.

at[1] /ət/; *strong* at/ *prep* **1** used to indicate presence or occurrence in, on, or near a place: *The train stops at Derby*. **2** used to indicate the direction of an action or motion: *She smiled at me*; *Try to aim at the target*. **3** used to indicate the time when something happens: *They start school at nine*; *at weekends*. **4a** used to indicate position in front of or facing something: *sitting at the table*. **b** used to indicate occupation or employment: *We'll be safe with Dave at the controls*. **c** used in indicating level of competence in any activity: *He's an expert at chess*. **5** used to indicate a situation or condition: *Our daughters are at risk*. **6** used to indicate response or reaction: *I never laugh at his jokes*. **7** used to indicate position on a scale, e.g. of cost, speed, or age: *driving at 90 mph*. **8** used with certain verbs of violence to indicate superficial or incomplete effect: *clawing and tearing at the ferns* — John Steinbeck. ✳ **at a** using no more than a single effort, occasion etc: *He ran up the stairs two at a time*. **at it** busy doing something: *I've been hard at it all day*. **at that 1** used to emphasize some striking aspect; too: *He got a bonus, and a big one at that*. **2** in reaction to something just said or done: *At that she immediately flared up*. **3** just there, without attempting to investigate, etc further: *He let it go at that*. **where it's at** see WHERE[2]. [Old English *æt*]

at[2] /aht/ *noun* (*pl* **at**) a unit of currency in Laos, worth 100th of a kip. [Thai *at*]

at. *abbr* atomic.

at- *prefix* see AD-.

at all *adv* used for emphasis with negatives or in questions: *They don't communicate at all*. ✳ **not at all** used in answer to thanks or to an apology.

ataractic[1] /atə'raktik/ *or* **ataraxic** /-'raksik/ *adj* said of a drug: having a tranquillizing effect. [Greek *ataraktos* calm, unexcited, from A-[2] + *tarassein* to disturb]

ataractic[2] *or* **ataraxic** *noun* a tranquillizing drug.

ataraxia /atə'raksiə/ *or* **ataraxy** /'atəraksi/ *noun* mental calmness or tranquillity; imperturbability. [Greek *ataraxia* serenity, from A-[2] + *tarassein* to disturb]

ataraxic /atə'raksik/ *adj and noun* see ATARACTIC[1], ATARACTIC[2].

ataraxy /'atəraksi/ *noun* see ATARAXIA.

atavism /'atəviz(ə)m/ *noun* **1a** the recurrence in an organism of a form typical of ancestors more remote than the parents. **b** the recurrence of primitive characteristics from the remote past. **2** reversion to an earlier type. **3** an individual or character manifesting atavism; a throwback. ➤➤ **atavistic** /-'vistik/ *adj*, **atavistically** /-'vistikli/ *adv*. [French *atavisme* from Latin *atavus* ancestor]

ataxia /ə'taksi·ə/ *or* **ataxy** /ə'taksi/ *noun* an inability to coordinate voluntary muscular movements that is symptomatic of some nervous disorders. ➤➤ **ataxic** /ə'taksik/ *adj*. [Greek *ataxia* disorder, confusion, from A-[2] + *tassein* to put in order]

ATB *abbr* **1** Advanced Technology Bomber. **2** all-terrain bicycle.

at-bat *noun chiefly NAmer* in baseball, a player's official turn to bat.

ATC *abbr* **1** air traffic control. **2** Air Training Corps.

ate /et, ayt/ *verb* past tense of EAT.

-ate[1] *suffix* forming nouns, denoting: **1** the product of a specified process: *distillate; condensate*. **2** a chemical compound or complex ANION (negatively charged atom or group of atoms) derived from a specified compound or element: *ferrate*. **3** the salt or ester of a specified acid with a name ending in *-ic* and not beginning with *hydro-*: *sulphate*. [Middle English *-at* via Old French from Latin *-atus, -atum*, masc and neuter endings of past part.; (sense 2) scientific Latin *-atum*, from Latin]

-ate[2] *suffix* forming nouns, denoting: **1** the office, function, rank, period of office, etc, of the official or title-bearer specified: *consulate; doctorate*. **2** an individual or group of people holding a specified office or rank or having the function specified: *electorate; magistrate*. [Middle English *-at* via Old French from Latin *-atus*, noun suffix from *-atus*, past part. ending]

-ate[3] *or* **-ated** *suffix* forming adjectives, with the meanings: **1** being in or brought to the state specified: *passionate; inanimate*. **2** characterized by having the thing specified: *craniate; loculated*. **3** resembling or having the shape of the thing specified: *pinnate; foliate*. [Middle English *-at* from Latin *-atus*, past part. ending]

-ate[4] *suffix* forming verbs, with the meanings: **1** to act in a specified way: *pontificate; remonstrate*. **2** to act in the way specified upon (somebody or something): *insulate; assassinate*. **3** to change the state or status of (somebody or something) to that specified: *activate; metricate*. **4** to provide (somebody or something) with the thing specified: *pollinate; populate*. [Middle English *-aten* from Latin *-atus*, past part. ending]

-ated *suffix* see -ATE[3].

atelier /ə'teliay/ *noun* an artist's or designer's studio or workroom. [French *atelier* workshop]

a tempo /ah 'tempoh/ *adj and adv* said of a piece of music: to be performed in the original time. [Italian *a tempo*, literally 'in time']

Athabaskan /'athə'baskən/ *or* **Athapaskan** /-'paskən/ *noun* **1** a language of a family of the Na-Dené group of N America. **2** a member of a people speaking an Athabaskan language. ➤➤ **Athabaskan** *adj*. [Cree *Athap-askaw*, an Athabaskan people, literally 'grass or reeds here and there']

Athanasian Creed /athə'nayzh(ə)n, -sh(ə)n/ *noun* a Christian statement of belief originating in Europe about AD 430 that defines the threefold nature of God in the Trinity and the Incarnation of God as Jesus Christ. [named after St *Athanasius* d.373, Greek theologian, formerly believed to have written it]

Athapaskan /'athə'paskən/ *noun* see ATHABASKAN.

atheism /'aythi·iz(ə)m/ *noun* the belief or doctrine that there is no deity.

Editorial note
Atheism is the denial of the existence of God, although it is made problematic by the fact that some believers may claim that God does not exist in a literal way or in the same sense that other things exist. Atheism includes the claim that 'God' is meaningless, unhelpful or simply mistaken as a way of interpreting the world — Dr Mel Thompson.

➤➤ **atheist** *noun*, **atheistic** /-'istik/ *adj*, **atheistical** /-'istikl/ *adj*, **atheistically** /-'istikli/ *adv*. [early French *athéisme* from Greek *atheos* godless, from A-[2] + *theos* god]

atheling /'athəling/ *noun* an Anglo-Saxon prince or nobleman. [Old English *ætheling*, from *æthelu* nobility]

athematic /aythee'matik/ *adj* **1** denoting music that is not theme-based. **2** in grammar, denoting a verb that contains no THEMATIC (connecting) vowel between the stem and its inflection, e.g. in Latin *est* he is, where *es-* is the stem and *-t* the inflection. [A-[2] + THEMATIC]

athenaeum *or* **atheneum** /athə'nee·əm/ *noun* **1** a literary or scientific association. **2** a library. [Latin *Athenaeum*, a school in ancient Rome for the study of the arts, from Greek *Athēnaion*, a temple of Athene, goddess of wisdom]

Athenian /ə'theeni·ən/ *noun* a native or inhabitant of Athens. ➤➤ **Athenian** *adj*.

atheroma /athə'rohmə/ *noun* a build-up of fatty deposits on the inner lining of the arteries. ➤➤ **atheromatous** /-təs/ *adj*. [scientific Latin *atheromat-, atheroma*, from Latin, a tumour containing matter like gruel, ultimately from Greek *athēra* gruel]

atherosclerosis /,athərohsklə'rohsis/ *noun* arteriosclerosis with the deposition of fatty substances on and fibrosis of the inner lining of the arteries. ➤➤ **atherosclerotic** /-'rotik/ *adj*, **atherosclerotically** /-'rotikli/ *adv*. [scientific Latin, from ATHEROMA + SCLEROSIS]

athlete /'athleet/ *noun* a person who is trained or skilled in exercises, sports, etc that require physical strength, agility, or stamina, *esp* in athletics. [Middle English via Latin *athleta* from Greek *athlētēs*, from *athlein* to contend for a prize, from *athlon* prize, contest]

athlete's foot *noun* a form of RINGWORM (fungal infection) of the feet affecting *esp* the skin between the toes.

athletic /ath'letik/ *adj* **1** relating to athletes or athletics. **2** characteristic of an athlete; vigorous or active. **3** said of a person's build: slim, muscular, and well-proportioned. ➤➤ **athletically** *adv*, **athleticism** /-siz(ə)m/ *noun*.

athletics *pl noun* (*treated as sing. or pl*) **1** *Brit* competitive running, walking, throwing, and jumping sports collectively. **2** *NAmer* exercises, sports, or games in general.

athletic support *noun formal* = JOCKSTRAP.

at home *noun* a reception or party that one gives in one's own house.

-athon *or* **-thon** *comb. form* forming nouns, denoting: a prolonged session of an activity as a feat or contest of endurance, often for charity: *swimathon; telethon*. [from MARATHON]

athwart[1] /ə'thwawt/ *adv* **1** across, *esp* in an oblique direction. **2** across a ship at right-angles to the fore and aft line. **3** in opposition to the right or expected course; awry. [Middle English, from A-[1] + THWART[1]]

athwart[2] *prep* **1** across (something): *The fallen tree lay athwart his path*. **2** against or in opposition to, or so as to thwart (plans or ideas).

-atic *suffix* forming adjectives, with the meaning: having the character or nature of the thing specified: *dramatic*.

-ation *suffix* forming nouns from verbs, denoting: **1** the action or process of doing something: *flirtation; computation*. **2** the result or product of the action or process specified: *alteration; plantation*. **3** the state or condition resulting from the process specified: *elation; agitation*. [Middle English *-acioun* via Old French *-ation* from Latin *-ation-, -atio*, from *-atus* -ATE[1] + *-ion-, -io* -ION]

-ative *suffix* forming adjectives, with the meanings: **1** of, relating to, or connected with the thing or action specified: *authoritative; vocative*. **2** tending to or disposed to do something: *talkative; restorative*. [Middle English via French *-atif* from Latin *-ativus*, from *-atus* past part. ending + *-ivus* -IVE[1]]

atlantes /at'lanteez/ *noun* pl of ATLAS (4).

Atlantic /at'lantik/ *adj* belonging to, relating to, or found near the Atlantic Ocean.

Word history
via Latin from Greek *Atlantikos*, from *Atlantis* Atlantic Ocean, from *Atlant-*, *Atlas* (see ATLAS). Orig applied to the ocean nearest the Atlas Mountains, which were thought to hold up the sky as Atlas held up the earth.

Atlantic Standard Time *or* **Atlantic Time** *noun* the local time in eastern Canada, four hours behind Greenwich Mean Time.

atlas /'atləs/ *noun* **1** a book of maps, charts, or tables: *an atlas of the world; a road atlas*. **2** a book of drawings and diagrams illustrating a particular subject: *an anatomical atlas*. **3** the topmost vertebra of the neck, supporting the skull. **4** (*pl* **atlantes** /at'lanteez/) in architecture, a figure or half figure of a man used as a column to support an ENTABLATURE (upper part of a wall displaying decorative work): compare CARYATID. [from the title used for a book of maps by Gerhardus Mercator d.1594, Flemish cartographer, in reference to *Atlas*, a giant of Greek mythology who supported the heavens on his shoulders]

ATM *abbr* **1** in telecommunications, asynchronous transfer mode. **2** automated teller machine.

atm. *abbr* **1** atmosphere. **2** atmospheric.

atman /'atmən/ *noun* **1** in Hinduism, the innermost essence of each individual. **2** in Hinduism, the supreme universal self; BRAHMAN (1B). [Sanskrit *ātman*, literally 'breath, soul']

atmosphere /'atməsfiə/ *noun* **1** a mass of gas enveloping a celestial body, e.g. a planet; *esp* all the air surrounding the earth. **2** the air or climate of a locality. **3** a surrounding feeling or mood encountered in some environment. **4** a dominant aesthetic or emotional effect or appeal, e.g. of a play, book, film, or musical work. **5** a unit of pressure chosen to be a typical pressure of the air at sea level and equal to 101,325 newtons per square metre (about 14.7lb per square inch). [scientific Latin *atmosphaera*, from Greek *atmos* vapour + *sphaira* SPHERE¹]

atmospheric /atmə'sferik/ *adj* **1** of, occurring in, or like the atmosphere of the earth. **2** having, marked by, or contributing aesthetic or emotional atmosphere: *atmospheric music*. ⪢ **atmospherically** *adv*.

atmospheric pressure *noun* the pressure exerted on the earth's surface by the atmosphere, with a value of 1 atmosphere.

atmospherics /atmə'sferiks/ *pl noun* **1** the audible disturbances produced in a radio receiver by electrical atmospheric phenomena, e.g. lightning. **2** the electrical phenomena causing these.

at. no. *abbr* atomic number.

ATOC /'aytok/ *abbr* Association of Train Operating Companies.

ATOL /'atol/ *abbr* **1** Air Travel Organizers' Licensing. **2** Air Travel Organizer's Licence.

atoll /'atol, ə'tol/ *noun* a coral reef surrounding a lagoon. [*atolu*, native name in the Maldive Islands]

atom /'atəm/ *noun* **1** the smallest particle of an element that can exist either alone or in combination, consisting of electrons, protons, and neutrons. **2** any of the minute indivisible particles of which, according to ancient philosophy, the universe is composed. **3** a tiny particle; a bit: *There's not an atom of truth in it.* [Middle English via Latin from Greek *atomos* indivisible, from A-² + *temnein* to cut]

atom bomb *or* **atomic bomb** *noun* a bomb whose violent explosive power is due to the sudden release of atomic energy derived from the splitting of the nuclei of plutonium, uranium, etc by neutrons in a very rapid chain reaction.

atomic /ə'tomik/ *adj* **1** of or concerned with atoms, atom bombs, or atomic energy. **2** said of a chemical element: existing as separate atoms. ⪢ **atomically** *adv*.

atomic bomb *noun* see ATOM BOMB.

atomic clock *noun* a highly accurate type of clock that is regulated by the natural vibration frequencies of an atomic system, such as a beam of caesium atoms.

atomic energy *noun* energy liberated in an atom bomb, nuclear reactor, etc by changes in the nucleus of an atom.

atomicity /atə'misiti/ *noun* **1** the state of consisting of atoms. **2** the number of atoms in the molecule of a gaseous element. **3** = VALENCY.

atomic mass *noun* the mass of an atom expressed in atomic mass units.

atomic mass unit *noun* a unit of mass used in atomic and nuclear physics, equal to one twelfth of the mass of an atom of carbon-12.

atomic number *noun* the number of protons in the nucleus of an atom, which is characteristic of a chemical element and determines its place in the periodic table.

atomic pile *noun* = REACTOR (1).

atomic structure *noun* the structure of an atom as an electrically neutral entity, having a positively charged nucleus consisting of neutrons and protons, surrounded by negatively charged orbiting electrons, the number of protons and electrons being equal.

atomic theory *noun* **1** the theory that all material substances are composed of atoms of a relatively small number of types and all the atoms of the same type are identical. **2** the theory of atomic structure. **3** = ATOMISM.

atomic weight *noun* a former name for RELATIVE ATOMIC MASS.

atomise /'atəmiez/ *verb* see ATOMIZE.

atomism /'atəmiz(ə)m/ *noun* a doctrine that the universe is composed of simple indivisible minute particles. ⪢ **atomist** *noun*.

atomistic /atə'mistik/ *adj* **1** relating to atoms or atomism. **2** composed of many simple elements; divided into unconnected or antagonistic fragments: *an atomistic society.* ⪢ **atomistically** *adv*.

atomize *or* **atomise** /'atəmiez/ *verb trans and intrans* **1** to reduce (a solid or liquid) or be reduced to minute particles or to a fine spray. **2** to reduce (something) or be reduced to atoms or to small discrete units. ⪢ **atomization** /-'zaysh(ə)n/ *noun*.

atomizer *or* **atomiser** *noun* an instrument for atomizing a perfume, disinfectant, etc.

atomy /'atəmi/ *noun* (*pl* **atomies**) *archaic* a skeleton or emaciated person. [ANATOMY, misunderstood as *an atomy*]

atonal /a'tohnl, ay-/ *adj* said of a musical composition: organized without reference to a musical key and using the notes of the chromatic scale impartially.

Editorial note
To composers in the first decades of the 20th cent., the ever more complex harmonies of late romanticism, especially in the works of Liszt and Wagner, seemed to be leading inevitably towards music in which there was no identifiable sense of key at all. Schoenberg took that final step into the unknown in the finale of his Second String Quartet in 1908. Over the next decade, he and his pupils Berg and Webern produced a series of masterpieces that celebrated the freedom of atonality, before they began to look for a new way of systematizing their language — Andrew Clements.

⪢ **atonalism** *noun*, **atonalist** *noun*, **atonalistic** /-'listik/ *adj*, **atonality** /-'naliti/ *noun*, **atonally** *adv*.

atone /ə'tohn/ *verb intrans* (+ for) to make amends for a crime, sin, or deficiency: *Deeply as I have sinned, I have led a life of martyrdom to atone for it* — Conan Doyle. [Middle English *atonen* to become reconciled, from *at one* in harmony]

atonement *noun* **1** reparation for an offence or injury. **2** (*usu* **Atonement**) the expiation of humankind's original sin through the death of Christ.

atonic /ə'tonik, ay-/ *adj* **1** said of a muscle or other contractile tissue: lacking tone or elasticity. **2** said of a syllable: not accented. ⪢ **atonicity** /ato'nisiti, ay-/ *noun*.

atony /'atəni/ *noun* the lack of tone or elasticity in muscle or other contractile tissue. [via late Latin from Greek *atonia* slackness, from *atonos* without tone, from A-² + *tonos* TONE¹]

atop /ə'top/ *prep literary* at the top of or on top of (something). [A-¹ + TOP¹]

atopy /'atəpi/ *noun* a tendency to asthma, hay fever, dermatitis, and other allergies; hypersensitivity. ⪢ **atopic** /ay'topik/ *adj*. [Greek *atopia* uncommonness, from *atopos* out of the way, uncommon, from A-² + *topos* place]

-ator *suffix* forming nouns, denoting: an agent or doer: *commentator; testator.* [Middle English *-atour* via Old French from Latin *-ator*, from *-atus* -ATE¹ + -OR¹]

-atory¹ *suffix* forming adjectives from verbs, with the meaning: concerned with or tending towards the action or activity specified: *accusatory; explanatory.* [Latin *-atorius*, from *-atus* -ATE¹ + *-orius* -ORY¹]

-atory² *suffix* forming nouns from verbs, denoting: a place concerned with the activity specified: *observatory; reformatory.* [Latin *-atorium*, neuter of *-atorius*: see -ATORY¹]

ATP¹ *noun* adenosine triphosphate, a derivative of adenine that is reversibly converted, *esp* to ADP, with the release of the cellular energy required for many metabolic reactions.

ATP² *abbr* automatic train protection.

atrabilious /atrə'biliəs/ *adj formal* ill-humoured or melancholic. ⪢ **atrabiliousness** *noun*. [Latin *atra bilis* black bile; compare MELANCHOLY¹]

atrazine /'atrəzeen/ *noun* a white crystalline chemical widely used as a weedkiller. [shortening of *amino triazine*]

atresia /ə'treezyə, -zh(y)ə/ *noun* the absence or closure of a natural body passage, such as the anus. [scientific Latin, from A-² + Greek *trēsis* perforation, from *tetrainein* to pierce]

atrium /'atri-əm, 'ay-/ *noun* (*pl* **atria** /-ə/ *or* **atriums**) **1** an inner courtyard open to the sky; *esp* in an ancient Roman house, or with a glazed roof in a modern building. **2** an anatomical cavity or passage; *specif* either of the two upper chambers of the heart that receive blood from the veins and force it into the ventricles (lower chambers; see VENTRICLE). >>> **atrial** *adj.* [Latin *atrium*]

atrocious /ə'trohshəs/ *adj* **1** extremely wicked, brutal, or cruel; barbaric: *atrocious crimes.* **2** *informal* horrifying; appalling: *They are living in atrocious conditions.* **3** *informal* of very poor quality: *atrocious handwriting.* >>> **atrociously** *adv,* **atrociousness** *noun.* [Latin *atroc-, atrox* gloomy, atrocious, from *atr-, ater* black + *-oc-, -ox* looking, appearing]

atrocity /ə'trositi/ *noun* (*pl* **atrocities**) **1** the quality of being atrocious. **2** something shocking or horrifying. **3** (*usu in pl*) a barbarically cruel act. **4** *informal* something ugly; an eyesore.

atrophy[1] /'atrəfi/ *noun* (*pl* **atrophies**) **1** the decrease in size, arrested development, or wasting away of a body part, organ, or tissue. **2** a wasting away or progressive decline of something, *esp* through lack of use; degeneration: *moral atrophy.* >>> **atrophic** /ə'trofik/ *adj.* [late Latin from Greek *atrophia,* from *atrophos* ill fed, from A-[2] + *trephein* to nourish]

atrophy[2] *verb intrans and trans* (**atrophies, atrophied, atrophying**) to undergo or cause (something) to undergo atrophy; to waste away or degenerate.

atropine /'atrəpeen, -pin/ *noun* an alkaloid found in deadly nightshade and used in medicine to inhibit the parasympathetic nervous system, e.g. in order to dilate the pupils, or to inhibit salivation. [German *Atropin,* from scientific Latin *Atropa,* genus name of belladonna, from Greek *Atropos,* one of the three mythical Fates]

att. *abbr* attorney.

attaboy /'atəboy/ *interj NAmer* used to encourage or to express admiration. [alteration of *that's the boy*]

attach /ə'tach/ *verb trans* **1** to fasten (something): *She attached a label to the suitcase.* **2** to ascribe or attribute (something): *We attach too much importance to opinion polls.* **3** to appoint (a person) to serve with an organization for special duties or for a temporary period: *She was attached to NATO.* **4** to involve or include (a proviso, etc) in a deal or agreement: *a loan with no conditions attached.* **5** to bind (somebody) to oneself by ties of affection: *so totally unamiable, so absolutely incapable of attaching a sensible man* — Jane Austen. **6** to bring (oneself) into an association with a person or group: *A Bedouin had attached himself to us* — Henry Tristram. **7** *archaic* to seize (a person or property) by legal authority. >>> *verb intrans* (+ to) to be attributable to somebody or something: *No blame attaches to you.* >>> **attachable** *adj.* [Middle English *attachen* via French *attacher* from Old French *estachier,* from *estache* stake, of Germanic origin]

attaché /ə'tashay/ *noun* a technical expert on a diplomatic staff: *a military attaché.* [French *attaché,* past part. of *attacher:* see ATTACH]

attaché case *noun* a small slim case used for carrying papers.

attached *adj* (+ to) feeling affection or liking for (a person, place, or thing): *The Douglases were very attached to each other* — Conan Doyle.

attachment *noun* **1** the process of attaching one thing to another. **2** a device for attaching to a machine or implement; *esp* one that adds a function: *a sanding attachment for an electric drill.* **3a** (*often* + to) being personally attached to somebody or something; fidelity: *attachment to a cause.* **b** (*often* + to) an affectionate regard for a person, place or thing, *esp* resulting from familiarity: *a deep attachment to the Lake District.* **4** *Brit* a temporary posting to an organization, branch of an organization, or military unit: *working in the BBC on attachment from Radio Zimbabwe.* **5** a computer file or set of data sent with an email message. **6** the physical connection by which one thing is attached to another. **7** *archaic* a seizure of a person or property by legal process.

attack[1] /ə'tak/ *verb trans* **1** to set upon (somebody or something) forcefully in order to damage, injure, or destroy them; to assault. **2** to take the initiative against (the opposing team, etc) in a game or contest. **3** to assail (somebody) with unfriendly or bitter words or hostile criticism. **4** said of a disease, etc: to affect or act on (the body or a part of it) injuriously. **5** to set to work on (a task, etc), *esp* vigorously. >>> *verb intrans* to make an attack: *The away team never attacked with any conviction.* >>> **attacker** *noun.* [early French *attaquer* via (assumed) Old Italian *estaccare* to attach, from *stacca* stake, of Germanic origin]

attack[2] *noun* **1** the act of attacking; an assault. **2** (*often* + on) a belligerent or antagonistic action or verbal assault: *He launched a bitter attack on single-parent families.* **3** the beginning of destructive action, e.g. by a chemical agent. **4** a fit of sickness or disease, often of a recurrent type: *a heart attack.* **5a** an attempt to score or to gain ground in a game. **b** (**the attack**) (*treated as sing. or pl*) the attacking players in a team or the positions occupied by them. **6** a vigorous start made on some undertaking: *I'd better make an attack on the gardening.* **7** the act or manner of beginning or playing a musical passage or composition, *esp* if decisive and clear in tone: *a sharp attack.*

attagirl /'atəguhl/ *interj NAmer* used to encourage or to express admiration. [alteration of *that's the girl*]

attain /ə'tayn/ *verb trans* **1** to achieve (what one has been aiming for); to accomplish (an objective). **2** *formal* to reach (a place). **3** *formal* to reach (a certain age). >>> *verb intrans* (*often* + to) to come or arrive by motion, growth, or effort: *till he hath attained to a state of freedom* — John Locke. >>> **attainability** /-'biliti/ *noun,* **attainable** *adj,* **attainableness** *noun.* [Middle English *atteynen* via Old French *ataindre,* ultimately from Latin *attangere,* from AT- + *tangere* to touch]

attainder /ə'tayndə/ *noun* formerly, a penalty by which a person sentenced to death or outlawry on conviction for treason or felony forfeited property and civil rights. * **act/bill of attainder** a legal provision whereby attainder was imposed without court proceedings. [Middle English *attaynder,* from Old French *ataindre:* see ATTAIN]

attainment *noun* something attained; an accomplishment.

attainment target *noun Brit* a standard level of competence in any subject that schoolchildren are required to have reached at specified stages in the National Curriculum.

attaint /ə'taynt/ *verb trans* **1** formerly, to subject (a person) to the penalty of ATTAINDER (forfeiture of property and civil rights) on sentence of death or outlawry. **2** *archaic* to infect, corrupt, or taint (somebody). [Middle English *attaynten* from Old French *ataint,* past part. of *ataindre:* see ATTAIN]

attar /'atə/ *or* **ottar** /'otə/ *or* **otto** /'otoh/ *noun* a fragrant essential oil or perfume, obtained *esp* from rose petals: *attar of roses.* [Persian *'atir* perfumed, from Arabic *'itr* perfume]

attempt[1] /ə'tempt/ *verb trans* **1** to try (to do something) or make an effort to accomplish (something), *esp* without success: *He attempted to swim across the swollen river; They should never have attempted the crossing in such weather.* **2a** to try to climb (a mountain or mountain face). **b** to try to better or break (a record). >>> **attemptable** *adj.* [Latin *attemptare,* from AT- + *temptare* to touch, try]

attempt[2] *noun* **1** (*often* + at) the act or an instance of attempting something; *esp* an unsuccessful effort: *her attempts at poetry.* **2** (*often* + on) an effort to conquer a mountain or record: *an attempt on the summit.* **3** an attack or assault: *He had survived three attempts on his life.*

attend /ə'tend/ *verb trans* **1** to go to or be present at (an event or performance). **2** to go regularly to (school or another institution) for instruction, treatment etc. **3** said of medical personnel: to look after or tend to (somebody needing treatment). **4** to be in store for, follow, or dog (somebody or their enterprises): *Disaster seemed to attend her every move.* **5** to look after (somebody) in the role of servant, attendant, or companion: *I am most dreadfully attended* — Shakespeare. **6** said of a bridesmaid or best man: to accompany or escort (a bride or bridegroom). >>> *verb intrans* **1** (+ to) to deal with a task, problem, etc. **2** (*often* + to) to listen or watch carefully; to pay attention to what is being said or done. **3** (+ on) to result from something: *the hurt that attends on deception.* >>> **attender** *noun.* [Middle English *attenden* via Old French from Latin *attendere,* literally 'to stretch to', from AT- + *tendere* to stretch]

attendance *noun* **1** the number of people attending an institution, event, exhibition etc: *Attendance at the exhibition reached record levels.* **2** the number of times a person attends an institution, etc, usu out of a possible maximum: *perfect attendance.*

attendance allowance *noun Brit* **1** a state benefit paid to disabled people who require the constant attention of carers at home. **2** money paid to local councillors for the time they spend on council business.

attendance centre *noun* a centre that a young offender is obliged to attend regularly instead of going to prison.

attendant[1] *adj formal* (*often* + on/upon) accompanying or following as a consequence: *the chaos attendant upon earthquakes and other natural disasters; divorce, with its attendant miseries and inconveniences.*

attendant[2] *noun* a person who assists, accompanies, or performs a service for another; *esp* an employee who waits on or looks after customers, etc: *a car-park attendant.*

attendee /aten'dee, ə'tendee/ *noun* a person attending a conference or similar gathering.

attention /ə'tensh(ə)n/ *noun* **1** the activity of attending, *esp* through application of the mind, to an object of sense or thought: *Pay attention!* **2** consideration with a view to action: *She handed him the letters that required his personal attention.* **3a** (*usu in pl*) an act of civility or courtesy, *esp* in courtship. **b** sympathetic consideration of the needs and wants of others. **4** a formal position of readiness assumed by a soldier, etc, standing with feet together and body erect: *standing to attention.* ➤➤ **attentional** *adj.* [Middle English *attencioun* from Latin *attention-, attentio* from *attendere*: see ATTEND]

attention deficit hyperactivity disorder *noun* see ADHD.

attention span *noun* the length of time during which a person is able to concentrate.

attentive /ə'tentiv/ *adj* **1** paying attention: *a class of highly attentive ten-year-olds.* **2** concerned for the welfare of somebody; solicitous. **3** paying attentions to somebody as, or like, a suitor. ➤➤ **attentively** *adv,* **attentiveness** *noun.*

attenuate[1] /ə'tenyooayt/ *verb trans* (*usu in passive*) **1** to cause (a living being or plant) to grow disproportionately long and thin: *the powerful frame attenuated by spare living* — Dickens. **2** to cause (something) to taper or diminish in width. **3** to lessen the force or strength of (something): *If she had had a little more self-control she would have attenuated the emotion to nothing by sheer reasoning* — Hardy. **4** to reduce the amplitude of (an electrical signal or current). **5** to reduce the virulence of (a virus or other pathogen): *killed or attenuated vaccines.* **6** to make (e.g. air or the atmosphere) thin or rarefied in consistency. ➤ *verb intrans* **1** to become long and thin. **2** to grow finer; to diminish or taper. **3** to grow weaker. ➤➤ **attenuation** /-'aysh(ə)n/ *noun.* [Latin *attenuatus,* past part. of *attenuare* to make thin, from AT- + *tenuis* thin]

attenuate[2] *adj* **1** attenuated. **2** tapering gradually: *an attenuate leaf.*

attenuator *noun* a device for attenuating; *esp* one for reducing the amplitude of an electrical signal without introducing distortion.

attest /ə'test/ *verb trans* **1a** to affirm the truth or existence of (something): *Several witnesses attested that he was perfectly sober.* **b** to authenticate (something), *esp* officially: *The testator's intention was attested by the trustees.* **2** to be proof of or bear witness to (something): *Her blushes attest her innocence.* ➤ *verb intrans* (*often* + to) to bear witness to something; to testify to it: *The massive sales of her books attest to her popularity.* ➤➤ **attestable** *adj,* **attester** *noun,* **attestor** *noun.* [French *attester* from Latin *attestari,* from *ad-* + *testis* witness]

attestation /ates'taysh(ə)n/ *noun* **1** the act of attesting. **2** a proof or testimony.

attested /ə'testid/ *adj Brit* said of a dairy herd: certified as free from disease, *esp* tuberculosis.

Attic /'atik/ *noun* a Greek dialect of ancient Attica, which became the literary language of the Greek-speaking world. ➤➤ **Attic** *adj.* [via Latin from Greek *Attikos,* from *Attikē* Attica, state of ancient Greece]

attic *noun* a room or space immediately below the roof of a building. [French *attique* low storey or wall above an entablature, literally 'relating to Attica', from Latin *Atticus*; from the use of this feature in the Attic order of architecture]

Atticism /'atisiz(ə)m/ *noun* **1** a characteristic feature of Attic Greek occurring in another language or dialect. **2** a witty or well-turned phrase.

attire[1] /ə'tie-ə/ *noun formal* dress or clothing.

attire[2] *verb trans formal* (*usu in passive*) to dress (somebody): *She was attired in a startling purple suit.* [Middle English *attiren* from Old French *atirier,* from AT- + *tire* order, rank, of Germanic origin]

attitude /'atityoohd/ *noun* **1** a feeling, emotion, or mental position, *esp* with regard to a situation, topic, person, etc. **2** the arrangement of the parts of a body in sitting, standing, etc; a posture. **3** a manner assumed for a specific purpose: *He adopted a threatening attitude.* **4** *chiefly NAmer, informal* a confrontational or deliberately challenging manner in one's dealings, *esp* with those in authority; studied insolence: *kids with attitude.* **5** the position of an aircraft or spacecraft relative to a particular point of reference such as the horizon. **6** a ballet position in which one leg is raised at the back and bent at the knee. ➤➤ **attitudinal** /-'tyoohdinl/ *adj.* [French *attitude* from Italian *attitudine* aptitude, from late Latin *aptitudin-, aptitudo* fitness, from Latin *aptus* fit]

attitudinize *or* **attitudinise** /ati'tyoohdiniez/ *verb intrans* to assume an affected mental attitude; to pose.

attn *abbr* for the attention of (a specified person).

atto- *comb. form* forming words, denoting: one million million millionth (10^{-18}) part: *attogram.* [Danish or Norwegian *atten* eighteen, from Old Norse *āttjān*]

attorney /ə'tuhni/ *noun* (*pl* **attorneys**) **1** a person who has legal authority to act for another. **2** *NAmer* a lawyer. ➤➤ **attorneyship** *noun.* [Middle English *attourney* from Old French *atorné,* past part. of *atorner* to agree to become tenant to a new owner of the same property, from AT- + *torner:* see TURN[1]]

Attorney General *noun* (*pl* **Attorneys General** *or* **Attorney Generals**) the chief legal officer of a nation or state.

attract /ə'trakt/ *verb trans* **1** to have the power to draw (things) towards itself: *A magnet attracts iron.* **2** to fascinate or arouse the affection or sexual interest of (somebody). **3** to draw the interest of (somebody): *Quite early on the diplomatic life attracted me.* **4** to become the focus of (e.g. notice or attention): *The noise attracted the attention of several passers-by.* **5** to be a reliable proposition for (e.g. funding or investment). **6** in law and insurance, to be liable for (tax, payments, etc): *Estates passing between spouses because of death do not attract capital transfer tax.* ➤ *verb intrans* to possess or exercise the power of attraction: *Opposites attract.* ➤➤ **attractable** *adj,* **attractor** *noun.* [Middle English *attracten,* from Latin *attractus,* past part. of *attrahere* to draw towards, from AT- + *trahere* to draw]

attractant *noun* something that attracts, *esp* a pheromone or other substance that attracts insects or animals. ➤➤ **attractant** *adj.*

attraction /ə'traksh(ə)n/ *noun* **1** (*usu in pl*) a characteristic that arouses interest or admiration; an attractive quality or aspect: *The place has its attractions.* **2** the ability to draw a response in the form of interest or affection: *You underestimate your powers of attraction.* **3** something that draws or is intended to draw crowds of visitors or spectators: *tourist attractions.* **4** a force, e.g. between unlike electrical charges, unlike magnetic poles, or particles of matter, tending to resist separation. **5** personal charm.

attractive *adj* **1** having the power to attract: *attractive forces between molecules; an attractive offer.* **2** good-looking or sexually interesting. **3** arousing interest or pleasure; charming: *an attractive smile.* ➤➤ **attractively** *adv,* **attractiveness** *noun.*

attrib. *abbr* **1** attributive. **2** attributively.

attribute[1] /'atribyooht/ *noun* **1** a characteristic or quality of a person or thing. **2** something associated with or belonging to a person or thing by virtue of which they are what they are; an inherent property or a customary accompaniment: *the attributes of a lady.* [Middle English from Latin *attributus,* past part. of *attribuere,* from AT- + *tribuere* to bestow]

attribute[2] /ə'tribyooht/ *verb trans* **1** (+ to) to credit a certain person, group of people, etc with (something or its invention, creation, or origination): *Popular opinion has always attributed the invention to the Americans; The painting known as 'The Bravo' is now attributed to Titian.* **2** (+ to) to put (a happening, etc) down to a particular circumstance, etc; to regard something as the cause or influence of (something): *To what do you attribute your success?* **3** to ascribe (qualities or feelings) to something or somebody: *The locals attributed amazing healing powers to the spring.* ➤➤ **attributable** *adj,* **attributer** *noun.*

attribution /atri'byoohsh(ə)n/ *noun* the act of attributing; *esp* the ascribing of a work of art to a particular author, artist, or period. ➤➤ **attributional** *adj.*

attributive[1] /ə'tribyootiv/ *adj* **1** relating to or of the nature of an attribute. **2** in grammar, denoting an adjective or modifying noun that directly precedes a noun, as *city* does in *city streets:* compare PREDICATIVE. ➤➤ **attributively** *adv.*

attributive[2] *noun* an attributive word, *esp* an adjective.

attrit /ə'trit/ *verb trans* (**attritted, attritting**) *NAmer, informal* to wear down (an opponent, etc) by sustained harassment. [back-formation from ATTRITION]

attrition /ə'trish(ə)n/ *noun* **1** the wearing away or grinding down of a surface, etc by friction; abrasion. **2** the process of weakening or exhausting an opponent, etc by constant harassment or abuse: *a war of attrition*. **3** sorrow for one's sins arising from fear of punishment: compare CONTRITION. ➤➤ **attritional** *adj.* [Latin *attrition-, attritio*, from *atterere* to rub against, from AT- + *terere* to rub]

attune /ə'tyoohn/ *verb trans* **1** (*often* + to) to cause or allow (people or their bodies) to become used, accustomed, or acclimatized to new circumstances: *to attune the climbers to the altitude*. **2** (*often* + to) to train (the ear) to recognize and respond to certain sounds, etc: *an ear finely attuned to the delicacies of melody* — Poe. **3** to bring (things, people, etc) into harmony with each other. ➤➤ **attunement** *noun.* [AT- + TUNE[1]]

atty. *abbr* attorney.

ATV *abbr* **1** all-terrain vehicle. **2** Associated Television.

at. wt. *abbr* atomic weight.

atypical /ay'tipikl/ *adj* not typical; deviating from a specified type or pattern. ➤➤ **atypicality** /ay,tipi'kaliti/ *noun*, **atypically** *adv.*

AU *abbr* **1** angstrom unit. **2** astronomical unit.

Au *abbr* the chemical symbol for gold. [Latin *aurum*]

aubade /'ohbahd/ *noun* a song, musical work, or poem associated with morning. [French *aubade*, prob from Old Provençal *alba, auba* dawn or dawn song, ultimately from Latin *alba, fem* of *albus* white]

aubergine[1] /'ohbəzheen, -jeen/ *noun* **1a** a plant of the nightshade family widely cultivated for its large purple-skinned oval edible fruit: *Solanum melongena*. **b** a fruit of this plant, used as a vegetable. Also called EGGPLANT. **2** a deep reddish purple colour. [French *aubergine* via Catalan *alberginia* from Arabic *al-bādhinjān* the eggplant, from Persian *badingān*: compare BRINJAL]

aubergine[2] *adj* of a deep reddish purple colour.

aubrietia /aw'breeshə/ *noun* a trailing rock plant of the mustard family, flowering in the spring: *Aubrieta deltoidea*. [scientific Latin, genus name, from Claude *Aubriet* d.1742, French painter of flowers and animals]

auburn[1] /'awbən/ *noun* a reddish brown colour, *esp* of hair. [Middle English *auborne* blond, via Old French from medieval Latin *alburnus* whitish, from Latin *albus* white. The current sense arose by association with *burn*, and because of a 16th-cent. spelling *abroun*, with *brown*]

auburn[2] *adj* said *esp* of hair: dark reddish brown in colour.

AUC *abbr* used to indicate a date reckoned from the traditional foundation of Rome in 753 BC. [Latin *ab urbe condita* from the foundation of the city]

au courant /,oh kooh'ronh (*French* o kurã)/ *adj* **1** fully informed or up to date on developments, etc. **2** fully familiar or conversant with a particular topic, etc. [French *au courant*, literally 'in the current']

auction[1] /'awksh(ə)n/ *noun* **1** a public sale of property in which prospective buyers bid against one another and the sale is made to the buyer offering the highest bid. **2** the act or process of bidding in some card games. [Latin *auction-, auctio*, increase, from *augēre* to increase]

auction[2] *verb trans* (*often* + off) to sell (property) at an auction.

auction bridge *noun* a form of the card game bridge, which differs from contract bridge in that tricks made in excess of the number of tricks the player has contracted to win are scored towards the game.

auctioneer /awkshə'niə/ *noun* a person who sells goods at an auction, conducting the bidding and declaring goods sold. ➤➤ **auctioneering** *noun.*

auction room *noun* **1** (*also in pl*) the premises of an auctioneer. **2** the room in which an auction is conducted.

auctorial /awk'tawri-əl/ *adj* relating to an author or an author's work; authorial: *auctorial intention*. [Latin *auctor* author, originator]

audacious /aw'dayshəs/ *adj* **1a** intrepidly daring; adventurous: *an audacious attempt on the summit*. **b** recklessly bold; rash: *an audacious move that paid off*. **2** insolent or presumptuous. ➤➤ **audaciously** *adv*, **audaciousness** *noun*, **audacity** /aw'dasiti/ *noun.* [French *audacieux*, from *audace* boldness, from Latin *audacia*, from *audac-, audax* bold, from *audēre* to dare]

audible /'awdəbl/ *adj* capable of being heard; loud enough to be heard. ➤➤ **audibility** /-'biliti/ *noun*, **audibly** *adv.* [late Latin *audibilis*, from Latin *audire* to hear]

audience /'awdi-əns/ *noun* **1** (*treated as sing. or pl*) a group of listeners or spectators, e.g. at a theatre or concert performance or a formal lecture. **2** (*treated as sing. or pl*). **a** the people targeted or reached by a television or radio programme or by a particular writer or book. **b** an entertainer's body of fans. **3** a formal hearing or interview: *We were granted an audience with the Pope*. [Middle English via Old French from Latin *audientia*, from *audient-, audiens*, present part. of *audire* to hear]

audile /'awdiel/ *adj* relating to the sense of hearing. [from Latin *audire* to hear, on the pattern of *tactile*]

audio[1] /'awdioh/ *adj* **1** relating to or denoting acoustic, mechanical, or electrical frequencies corresponding to those of audible sound waves, approximately 20 to 20,000Hz. **2** relating to or used in the transmission, reception, or reproduction of sound: compare VIDEO[2]. [from AUDIO-]

audio[2] *noun* the transmission, reception, or reproduction of sound.

audio- *comb. form* forming words, denoting: hearing or sound: *audiotape; audiovisual*. [Latin *audire* to hear]

audiobook /'awdiohbook/ *noun* an audio cassette recording of the text of a book, or an abridged version of it, read aloud.

audio cassette *noun* a cassette of audiotape.

audiology /awdi'oləji/ *noun* the branch of science or medicine concerned with hearing. ➤➤ **audiological** /-'lojikl/ *adj*, **audiologist** *noun.*

audiometer /awdi'omitə/ *noun* an instrument for measuring the sharpness of hearing. ➤➤ **audiometric** /-'metrik/ *adj*, **audiometry** *noun.*

audiophile /'awdiohfiel/ *noun* a person with a keen interest in the reproduction of sounds, *esp* music from high-fidelity broadcasts or recordings.

audiotape *noun* **1** magnetic tape for recording sound. **2** a cassette of this, with or without a recording on it.

audiotypist *noun* a typist trained to type directly from a sound-recording or dictating machine. ➤➤ **audiotyping** *noun.*

audiovisual /,awdioh'viz(h)yooəl/ *adj* said *esp* of teaching methods: using both hearing and sight.

audit[1] /'awdit/ *noun* **1** a formal or official examination and verification of accounts by qualified accountants. **2** a systematic examination of the workings of any organization, business, etc, *esp* with regard to economical use of resources and quality of product or result.

Word history
Middle English from Latin *auditus* act of hearing, past part. of *audire* to hear. The word owes its derivation to the fact that accounts were orig read aloud.

audit[2] *verb trans* (**audited, auditing**) to perform an audit on (accounts, etc). ➤➤ **auditable** *adj.*

audition[1] /aw'dish(ə)n/ *noun* **1** a trial performance to assess the ability of a candidate for a performing role or an applicant for membership of an orchestra, choir, etc. **2** *archaic* the power or sense of hearing. [via Old French or directly from Latin *audition-, auditio*, from *audire* to hear]

audition[2] *verb* (**auditioned, auditioning**) ➤ *verb trans* to test (a performer) for a part, etc by means of an audition. ➤ *verb intrans* (*usu* + for) to give a trial performance before a group of selectors for a play, show, etc.

auditive /'awditiv/ *adj* relating to hearing; auditory.

auditor *noun* **1** a person authorized to perform an audit. **2** a person who hears; a listener: *Both her words and her air seemed intended to excite the amazement of her auditors* — Charlotte Brontë. ➤➤ **auditorial** *adj.* [Latin *auditor* a hearer, from *audire* to hear]

auditorium /awdi'tawri-əm/ *noun* (*pl* **auditoria** /-ə/ *or* **auditoriums**) the part of a theatre, concert hall, etc where an audience sits. [Latin *auditorium* lecture room or court of justice, from *audire* to hear]

auditory /'awdit(ə)ri/ *adj* **1** relating to hearing: *the auditory nerve*. **2** received through the ear: *auditory stimuli*. [late Latin *auditorius* from Latin *audire* to hear]

au fait /oh 'fay/ *adj* (+ with) fully informed about or familiar with (a particular matter or subject): *I expect you're au fait with all this computer jargon.* [French *au fait*, literally 'to the point']

au fond /oh 'fonh/ *adv* basically; fundamentally. [French *au fond*, literally 'at the bottom']

auf Wiedersehen /owf 'veedəzayn (*German* aʊf viːdəzeən)/ *interj* goodbye. [German *auf Wiedersehen*, literally 'till seeing again']

Aug. *abbr* August.

aug. *abbr* in grammar, augmentative.

Augean /aw'jee-ən/ *adj* **1** said of a place: disgustingly dirty. **2** said of a situation: iniquitous or corrupt. [from Greek *Augeias*, whose stable, according to myth, remained uncleaned for 30 years until Hercules cleaned it]

auger /'awgə/ *noun* a tool for boring holes consisting of a shank with a central tapered screw and a pair of cutting lips with projecting spurs: compare GIMLET[1]. [Middle English, alteration (by incorrect division of *a nauger*) of *nauger*, from Old English *nafogār*]

aught /awt/ *pronoun* archaic (*in negative contexts*) anything at all: *for aught I care.* [Old English *āwiht*, from *ā* ever + *wiht* creature, thing]

augite /'awjiet/ *noun* **1** a mineral consisting of a black or dark green pyroxene containing aluminium that is found in igneous rocks. **2** = PYROXENE. ➤➤ **augitic** /aw'jitik/ *adj.* [via Latin from Greek *augitēs*, a type of precious stone, from *augē* brightness]

augment[1] /awg'ment/ *verb trans* **1** to make (something) greater, more numerous, larger, or more intense. **2** to make (a musical interval) a semitone greater than major or perfect: *an augmented fourth.* **3** to add an augment to (a verb). ➤➤ *verb intrans* to become augmented. ➤➤ **augmentable** *adj,* **augmented** *adj,* **augmenter** *noun,* **augmentor** *noun.* [Middle English *augmenten* via Old French from late Latin *augmentare* to increase, from *augmentum* increase, from Latin *augēre* to increase]

augment[2] /'awgment/ *noun* a prefixed or lengthened initial vowel marking past tense, *esp* in Greek and Sanskrit verbs.

augmentation /awgmen'taysh(ə)n/ *noun* **1** the process of augmenting or of being augmented. **2** the amount by which something is augmented.

augmentative[1] /awg'mentətiv/ *adj* **1** tending to augment. **2** said of a word or affix: indicating large size and sometimes awkwardness.

augmentative[2] *noun* **1** an affix or particle, such as *-ón* or *-ote* in Spanish, indicating greatness or largeness and sometimes awkwardness or unattractiveness. **2** a word containing such an affix or particle.

au gratin /oh 'gratin (*French* o gratɛ̃)/ *adj* (*used after a noun*) covered with breadcrumbs or grated cheese and browned under a grill: *cauliflower au gratin.* [French *au gratin*, literally 'with the burned scrapings from the pan']

augur[1] /'awgə/ *noun* a person believed to be able to foretell events by means of omens; a prophet or soothsayer; *specif* an official diviner of ancient Rome. ➤➤ **augural** /'awgərəl, 'awgyərəl/ *adj.* [Latin *augur* prob related to Latin *augēre* to increase]

augur[2] *verb trans* (**augured, auguring**) **1** to foretell (future events), *esp* from omens. **2** to give promise of or presage (some future state or event). ✻ **augur well/ill for** to be an omen of success or failure for (somebody or something).

augury /'awgyoori/ *noun* (*pl* **auguries**) **1** the prediction of the future from omens or portents. **2** an omen or portent.

August /'awgəst/ *noun* the eighth month of the year. [Old English from Latin *Augustus* (*mensis*), the month (formerly *Sextilis* in the Roman calendar) renamed after himself by the first emperor *Augustus* Caesar in 8 BC]

august /aw'gəst/ *adj* marked by majestic dignity or solemn grandeur: *Could so fantastic a pauper get admission to the august presence of a monarch?* — Mark Twain. ➤➤ **augustly** *adv,* **augustness** *noun.* [Latin *augustus*]

Augustan[1] /aw'gust(ə)n/ *adj* **1** relating to or characteristic of Augustus Caesar (d.AD 14), first Roman emperor, his period, or the literature of his reign, e.g. the works of Virgil and Ovid. **2** relating to or characteristic of a neoclassical period in a country's art and literature that is marked by stately refinement and elegance, e.g. the period of the 17th-cent. writers Corneille and Racine in France.

Augustan[2] *noun* an artist or writer of the Augustan period.

Augustinian /awgə'stini-ən/ *noun* a member of a religious order based on the doctrines of St Augustine; *specif* a friar of the Hermits of St Augustine founded in 1256 and devoted to educational, missionary, and parish work. ➤➤ **Augustinian** *adj.* [St *Augustine* d.430, Numidian church father and Bishop of Hippo]

auk /awk/ *noun* any of several species of diving seabirds of the northern hemisphere, with a short neck and black-and-white plumage, e.g. the puffin, guillemot, and razorbill: family Alcidae. [Norwegian or Icelandic *alk, alka* from Old Norse *ālka*]

auld /awld/ *adj Scot* old. [Middle English (northern), variant of Middle English *ald*, from Old English *eald* OLD[1]]

auld lang syne /,awld lang 'sien, 'zien/ *noun* the good old times. [Scots *auld lang syne*, literally 'old long ago']

aumbry /'awmbri/ *noun* see AMBRY.

au naturel /oh natyoo'rel/ *adj and adv* **1** in natural style or condition. **2** uncooked or cooked plainly. **3** naked. [French *au naturel* in the natural state]

aunt /ahnt/ *noun* **1** the sister of one's father or mother, or the wife of one's uncle. **2** used by a child as a term of affection for an adult female friend. [Middle English via Old French *ante* from Latin *amita*]

auntie *or* **aunty** /'ahnti/ *noun* (*pl* **aunties**) **1** *informal* an aunt. **2** (**Auntie**) *Brit, informal* the BBC.

Aunt Sally /'sali/ *noun* (*pl* **Aunt Sallies**) **1** an effigy of a woman at which objects are thrown at a fair. **2** an easy target of criticism or attack.

aunty /'ahnti/ *noun* see AUNTIE.

au pair[1] /oh 'peə/ *noun* a young foreigner, *esp* a young woman, who does domestic work for a family in return for meals and accommodation and the opportunity to learn the language of the family. [French *au pair*, literally 'on even terms']

au pair[2] *or* **au-pair** *verb intrans* to work as an au pair.

aur- *or* **auri-** *comb. form* forming words, denoting: the ear: *aural.* [Latin *auri-* from *auris* ear]

aura /'awrə/ *noun* **1** a distinctive atmosphere surrounding a given source: *Her greatest attraction was the aura of possibility surrounding her* — L M Montgomery. **2** an emanation, invisible except to those with psychic powers, coming from a person or thing. **3** a luminous radiation surrounding a person. **4** a sensation, such as flashing lights or a ringing in the ears, experienced before an attack of a brain disorder, *esp* epilepsy. [Middle English via Latin from Greek *aura* breeze, air]

aural /'awrəl/ *adj* relating to the ear or the sense of hearing. ➤➤ **aurally** *adv.*

Usage note

aural *or* oral? These two words are pronounced the same and are easy to confuse. *Aural* relates to the ears and hearing and is connected with words such as *audible* and *audition*. An *aural* comprehension is one that tests a person's understanding of spoken language. *Oral* relates to the mouth and speaking. Students of foreign languages often have to take an *oral* examination, one that tests their ability to speak the language.

aurar /'owrah/ *noun* pl of EYRIR.

aureate /'awri-ət/ *adj literary* made of gold, or golden in colour: *When all that … dullness of dirty brick trembles in aureate light* — Willa Cather. [from medieval Latin *aureatus* decorated with gold, from *aureus* golden, from *aurum* gold]

aureole /'awriohl/ *or* **aureola** /aw'ree-ələ, ə-/ *noun* **1** a radiant light surrounding the head or body of a representation of a holy figure: compare NIMBUS. **2** the halo surrounding the sun, moon, etc when seen through thin cloud; a corona. [Middle English *aureole* heavenly crown worn by saints, from medieval Latin *aureola* a golden circlet, fem of Latin *aureolus* golden, from *aurum* gold]

au revoir /oh rə'vwah (*French* o ʀəvwaːʀ)/ *interj* goodbye. [French *au revoir*, literally 'till seeing again']

auri- *comb. form* see AUR-.

auric /'awrik/ *adj* of or derived from gold, *esp* trivalent gold. [Latin *aurum* gold]

auricle /'awrikl/ *noun* **1a** = PINNA (2). **b** *no longer in technical use* either ATRIUM (upper chamber) of the heart. **2** an ear-shaped lobe, *esp* one on each atrium of the heart. [Latin *auricula*: see AURICULA]

auricula /aw'rikyoolə/ *noun* an Alpine primula with leaves that are reminiscent of bears' ears: *Primula auricula.* [Latin *auricula*, dimin. of *auris* ear]

auricular /aw'rikyoolə/ *adj* **1** relating to the ear or the sense of hearing. **2** relating to the external ear or to the auricles of the heart. **3** ear-shaped. **4** told privately: *an auricular confession.* [late Latin *auricularis* relating to the external ear, from Latin *auris* ear]

auriculate /aw'rikyoolət/ *adj* having auricles or ear-shaped pouches.

auriferous /aw'rifərəs/ *adj* said of rock: gold-bearing. [Latin *aurifer*, from *aurum* gold + *-fer* bearing, from *ferre* to bear]

Aurignacian /awrig'naysh(ə)n/ *adj* relating to or denoting an Upper Palaeolithic culture characterized by finely made artefacts of stone and bone, cave paintings, and incised drawings. [French *aurignacien* from *Aurignac*, village in France close to a cave site where paintings and artefacts were found in the mid 19th cent.]

aurochs /'awroks/ *noun* (*pl* **aurochs**) an extinct European ox held to be a wild ancestor of domestic cattle: *Bos primigenius.* [German *Aurochs* from Old High German *ūrohso*, from *ūro* aurochs + *ohso* ox]

aurora /aw'rawrə/ *noun* (*pl* **auroras** *or* **aurorae** /-ree/) **1** an atmospheric phenomenon occurring over the northern and southern magnetic poles, consisting of bands or streamers of coloured light passing across the sky. **2** dawn personified. >> **auroral** *adj,* **aurorean** /-ri·ən/ *adj.* [Latin *aurora* dawn]

aurora australis /aw'strahlis, aw'straylis/ *noun* the aurora of the S hemisphere. [Latin *aurora australis,* literally 'southern dawn', from *aurora* dawn + *australis* from *Auster* god of the south wind]

aurora borealis /bawri'ahlis, -'aylis/ *noun* the aurora of the N hemisphere. [Latin *aurora borealis,* literally 'northern dawn', from *aurora* dawn + *borealis* from Greek *Boreas* god of the north wind]

aurorae /aw'rawree/ *noun* pl of AURORA.

aurous /'awrəs/ *adj* of or containing gold, *esp* univalent gold. [Latin *aurum* gold]

AUS *abbr* Australia (international vehicle registration).

Aus. *abbr* **1** Australia. **2** Australian.

auscultation /awskəl'taysh(ə)n/ *noun* the act of listening to the heart, lungs, etc as a medical diagnostic aid. >> **auscultatory** /aw'skultət(ə)ri/ *adj.* [Latin *auscultation-, auscultatio* act of listening, from *auscultare* to listen]

Auslese /'owslayzə/ *noun* a usu sweet white wine produced *esp* in Germany from selected late-gathered ripe grapes. [German *Auslese* selection, choice, choice wine, from *aus* out + *Lese* picking]

auspice /'awspis/ *noun archaic* a favourable prophetic sign. ✳ **under the auspices of** under the patronage or guidance of (a body or person). [Latin *auspicium* from *auspic-, auspex* diviner by birds, from *avis* bird + *specere* to look, look at]

auspicious /aw'spish(ə)s/ *adj* **1** presaging success; propitious: *an auspicious beginning.* **2** prosperous: *the eighty-ninth moon of your Majesty's auspicious reign* — Jonathan Swift. >> **auspiciously** *adv,* **auspiciousness** *noun.*

Aussie[1] /'ozi/ *noun informal* an Australian.

Aussie[2] *adj informal* Australian.

Aust. *abbr* **1** Australia. **2** Australian.

austere /o'stiə, aw-/ *adj* **1** stern and forbidding in appearance and manner: *austere features.* **2** rigidly abstemious; self-denying: *an austere life.* **3** unadorned; simple: *an austere stage set.* **4** succinctly severe in the expression of views: *her austere wit.* >> **austerely** *adv,* **austereness** *noun.* [Middle English via Old French and Latin from Greek *austēros* harsh, severe, rigorous, austere]

austerity /o'steriti, aw-/ *noun* (*pl* **austerities**) **1** enforced or extreme economy. **2** an austere act, manner, or attitude.

Austr-[1] *or* **Austro-** *comb. form* forming nouns and adjectives, with the meaning: south or southern: *Austrasiatic.* [Middle English *austr-,* from Latin *Austr-, Auster* god of the south wind]

Austr-[2] *or* **Austro-** *comb. form* forming nouns and adjectives, with the meaning: Austrian and: *Austro-Hungarian.*

Austral. *abbr* **1** Australasia. **2** Australia. **3** Australian.

austral[1] /'awstrəl/ *adj technical* southern. [Middle English from Latin *australis* southern, from *austr-, auster* the south wind]

austral[2] /'owstrəl/ *noun* (*pl* **australes** /'owstrahles/) the former basic monetary unit of Argentina, divided into 100 centavos. [Spanish *austral,* literally 'southern' from Latin *australis:* see AUSTRAL[1]]

Australasian /ostrə'layzh(y)ən, aw-/ *noun* a native or inhabitant of Australasia, a region comprising Australia, New Zealand, New Guinea, and neighbouring islands in the S Pacific. >> **Australasian** *adj.*

australes /'owstrahles/ *noun* pl of AUSTRAL[2].

Australia Day *noun* the 26th January, observed as a national holiday in Australia in commemoration of the landing of the British at Sydney Cove in 1788 to found a settlement.

Australian[1] *noun* **1** a native or inhabitant of Australia. **2** the speech of the aboriginal inhabitants of Australia. **3** English as spoken and written in Australia.

Word history ____

French *australien* from Latin *australis* in the phrase *Terra Australis* the southern land. Words from the Aboriginal languages of Australia which have become familiar in English mostly refer to indigenous flora and fauna or to Aboriginal practices; they include *boomerang, budgerigar, dingo, kangaroo, koala, kookaburra, wallaby,* and *wombat.* A few words of more general reference have been adopted, such as *barrack* (in the senses 'to jeer' and 'to shout encouragement') and *cooee.*

Australian[2] *adj* **1** characteristic of, relating to, or belonging to Australia. **2** relating to or denoting a biogeographical region that comprises Australia and the islands north of it from the Celebes eastwards, Tasmania, New Zealand, and Polynesia.

Australianism *noun* a characteristic feature of Australian English.

Australian Rules football *noun* a game played between two teams of 18 players on an oval field with four goalposts at each end, using a ball similar to a rugby ball which may be passed from player to player by kicking it or by striking it with the clenched fist.

Australoid[1] /'ostrəloyd/ *adj* relating to or belonging to an ethnic group including the Australian Aboriginals and other peoples of southern Asia and the Pacific islands. [*Australia* + -OID]

Australoid[2] *noun* a member of the Australoid ethnic group.

australopithecine /,ostrəloh'pithəseen/ *noun* an extinct southern African hominid, *esp* of the genus *Australopithecus,* with near-human teeth and a relatively small brain. >> **australopithecine** *adj.* [Latin *australis* (see AUSTRAL[1]) + Greek *pithēkos* ape]

Australorp /'ostrəlawp/ *noun* a black domestic fowl of a breed developed in Australia and valued for its egg production. [blend of *Australia* + *Orpington,* a town in Kent, S England, where the Orpington, ancestor of the Australorp, originated]

Austrian /'ostriən/ *noun* **1** a native or inhabitant of Austria. **2** the dialect of German spoken in Austria. >> **Austrian** *adj.*

Austrian blind *noun* a window blind of soft fabric that gathers into vertical ruches when raised, belonging to an early 19th-cent. style associated with Vienna.

Austro- *comb. form* see AUSTR-[1], AUSTR-[2].

Austroasiatic *or* **Austro-Asiatic** /,ostroh,ayzi'atik, -,ayzhi'atik/ *noun* a family of languages spoken in NE India and SE Asia. >> **Austroasiatic** *adj,* **Austro-Asiatic** *adj.*

Austronesian /ostrə'neezh(ə)n/ *noun* a family of languages including Indonesian, Melanesian, Malagasy, Fijian, and Maori. >> **Austronesian** *adj.* [*Austronesia,* islands of the southern Pacific, from AUSTR-[1] + Greek *nēsos* island]

AUT *abbr Brit* Association of University Teachers.

aut- *or* **auto-** *comb. form* forming words, with the meanings: **1** self; same one; of or by oneself: *autobiography; autodidact.* **2** automatic; self-acting; self-regulating: *autodyne.* [Greek, from *autos* same, -self, self]

autarchy /'awtahki/ *noun* (*pl* **autarchies**) **1** absolute sovereignty; autocracy. **2** see AUTARKY. >> **autarchic** /aw'tahkik/ *adj,* **autarchical** /aw'tahkikl/ *adj.* [Greek *autarchia,* from AUT- + -ARCHY]

autarky /'awtahki/ *or* **autarchy** *noun* (*pl* **autarkies**) **1** self-sufficiency and independence. **2** the policy, or resulting condition, of national economic self-sufficiency. **3** a state that is economically self-sufficient. >> **autarkic** /aw'tahkik/ *adj,* **autarkical** /aw'tahkikl/ *adj.* [German *Autarkie* from Greek *autarkeia* from *autarkēs* self-sufficient, from AUT- + *arkein* to defend, suffice]

autecology /awti'koləji/ *noun* ecology dealing with a single organism or a single species of organism. >> **autecological** /-'lojikl/ *adj.*

auteur /oh'tuh/ *noun* a film director whose personal style and views so distinctively influence the film under production that he or she is thought of as its overall creator.

Editorial note ____

Auteur derives from French criticism of the 1950s and proposes that the collaboration of film-making is beholden to one vision – usually that of the director. This is still in dispute. There are valuable theories that argue how the system, the money, or even the medium itself affects the message. Even among loyal auteurists, it is admitted that the role of auteur can be taken up by producers, writers and, especially, actors and actresses — David Thomson.

[French *auteur* author]

auth. *abbr* authorized.

authentic /aw'thentik/ *adj* **1** worthy of belief as conforming to fact or reality; trustworthy: *an authentic account.* **2** not imaginary, false, or imitation; genuine: *The signature looked authentic enough.* **3** said of a mode in church music: ranging upward from the KEYNOTE[1] (the note on which the mode is based): compare PLAGAL. ⋙ **authentically** *adv*, **authenticity** /-'tisiti/ *noun.* [Middle English *autentik* via Old French from Greek *authentikos* from *authentēs* perpetrator, master]

authenticate /aw'thentikayt/ *verb trans* **1** to prove or declare (a document, signature, etc) genuine. **2** to corroborate (a story, etc) independently. ⋙ **authentication** /-'kaysh(ə)n/ *noun*, **authenticator** *noun.*

author[1] /'awthə/ *noun* **1** the writer of a book, article, etc. **2a** a person whose profession is writing, *esp* a writer of literary works. **b** such a person identified with their works: *She had only to look in her favourite author for an apt quotation.* **3** somebody or something that originates something or gives it existence; a source: *We know who the author of the revolting business is* —Conan Doyle. ⋙ **authorial** /aw'thawri·əl/ *adj.* [Middle English *auctour* via Old North French from Latin *auctor* promoter, originator, author, from *augēre* to increase]

author[2] *verb trans* (**authored, authoring**) to be the writer or originator of (something).

authoress /'awthərəs, -ris/ *noun* a female author.

authoring language *or* **author language** *noun* a computer language system that enables users to create applications, e.g. for computer-aided learning, without any detailed knowledge of programming.

authorise /'awthəriez/ *verb trans* see AUTHORIZE.

authoritarian[1] /aw,thori'teəri·ən/ *adj* **1** said of a regime: enforcing strict obedience to authority, rather than allowing independent decision-making. **2** said of a person in a controlling position: dictatorial, domineering, and tyrannical. ⋙ **authoritarianism** *noun.*

authoritarian[2] *noun* a person in a position of control who brooks no opposition to his or her authority.

authoritative /aw'thoritətiv/ *adj* **1a** having or proceeding from authority; definitive; official: *the authoritative version.* **b** entitled to belief or acceptance; reliable; conclusive: *an authoritative account.* **2** commanding respect and obedience: *in an authoritative tone.* ⋙ **authoritatively** *adv*, **authoritativeness** *noun.*

authority /aw'thoriti/ *noun* (*pl* **authorities**) **1** the power to issue directives accompanied by the right to expect obedience. **2** the position of a person who has such power: *those in authority.* **3** delegated power or authorization: *You had no authority to remove the road blocks.* **4** (**the authorities**) people in command; *specif* a governmental or law-enforcing agency. **5** (*often* **Authority**) a governmental body that administers a public service or enterprise: *the Thames Water Authority.* **6** a citation used in defence or support of one's actions, opinions, or beliefs, or the source from which the citation is drawn. **7** an individual cited or appealed to as an expert: *an authority on D H Lawrence.* **8** effective influence or conviction. **9** the right granted by one person to another to act on his or her behalf. **10** weight, strength, or conviction resulting from practice and expertise: *Voltaire had his enemies but his authority could not be denied.* [Middle English *auctorite* via Old French from Latin *auctoritat-, auctoritas* opinion, decision, power, from *auctor*: see AUTHOR[1]]

authorize *or* **authorise** /'awthəriez/ *verb trans* **1** to invest (somebody) with authority or legal power or empower them to act in a certain way: *He was not authorized to destroy the documents.* **2** to give official permission for (a proceeding, etc); to sanction (an activity, etc): *Who authorized the arrest?* ⋙ **authorization** /-'zaysh(ə)n/ *noun*, **authorizer** *noun.*

Authorized Version *noun* an English version of the Bible prepared under James I, published in 1611, and widely used by Protestants.

author language *noun* see AUTHORING LANGUAGE.

authorship *noun* **1** the profession or activity of writing. **2** the identity of the author of a literary work: *The authorship of the Waverley Novels was for a long time kept secret.*

autism /'awtiz(ə)m/ *noun* a disorder of childhood development marked by inability to form relationships with other people, those affected having only a limited understanding of themselves and others as individuals with independent personalities and thought processes. ⋙ **autistic** /aw'tistik/ *adj and noun.* [scientific Latin *autismus*, from AUT- + -ISM]

auto /'awtoh/ *noun* (*pl* **autos**) *chiefly NAmer* a motor car. [short for AUTOMOBILE]

auto-[1] *comb. form* see AUT-.

auto-[2] *comb. form* forming words, with the meaning: self-propelling; automotive: *autocycle.* [*automobile* (adj) self-propelling]

autoantibody /awtoh'antibodi/ *noun* (*pl* **autoantibodies**) an antibody against one of the constituents of the tissues of the individual that produces it.

autobahn /'awtohbahn/ *noun* a German motorway. [German *Autobahn*, from *Auto* car + *Bahn* track, way]

autobiography /,awtəbie'ogrəfi/ *noun* (*pl* **autobiographies**) an account of one's own life written by oneself. ⋙ **autobiographer** *noun*, **autobiographic** /-'grafik/ *adj*, **autobiographical** /-'grafikl/ *adj.*

autocephalous /awtoh'sefələs/ *adj* said of Eastern national Churches: independent of external, *esp* patriarchal, authority. [late Greek *autokephalos*, from Greek AUTO-[1] + *kephalē* head]

autochthon /aw'tokthən/ *noun* (*pl* **autochthons** *or* **autochthones** /-neez/) **1** an aborigine or native. **2** an autochthonous plant, animal, etc. ⋙ **autochthonism** *noun.* [Greek *autochthōn*, from AUTO-[1] + *chthōn* earth]

autochthonous /aw'tokthənəs/ *adj* indigenous; native: compare ALLOCHTHONOUS. ⋙ **autochthonously** *adv*, **autochthony** *noun.*

autoclave[1] /'awtəklayv/ *noun* an apparatus, e.g. for sterilizing, using superheated steam under pressure. [French *autoclave*, from AUTO-[1] + Latin *clavis* key; so called because it fastens automatically]

autoclave[2] *verb trans* to subject (medical materials, etc) to the action of an autoclave.

autocracy /aw'tokrəsi/ *noun* (*pl* **autocracies**) **1** government by an autocrat. **2** a community or state governed by autocracy.

autocrat /'awtəkrat/ *noun* **1** a person who rules with unlimited power. **2** a dictatorial person. ⋙ **autocratic** /-'kratik/ *adj*, **autocratically** /-'kratikli/ *adv.* [French *autocrate* from Greek *autokratēs* ruling by oneself, absolute, from AUTO-[1] + *kratos* strength, power]

autocross /'awtohkros/ *noun* the sport of racing motor cars on grass tracks against the clock: compare MOTOCROSS, RALLYCROSS. [AUTO + CROSS-COUNTRY[1]]

Autocue /'awtohkyooh/ *noun trademark* a device that enables a television presenter or performer to read a script without averting his or her eyes from the camera.

auto-da-fé /,awtoh dah 'fay/ *noun* (*pl* **autos-da-fé** /,awtoh dah 'fay/) the burning of a heretic; *esp* the ceremonial execution of somebody condemned by the Spanish Inquisition. [Portuguese *auto da fé*, literally 'act of the faith']

autodidact /awtoh'diedakt/ *noun* a person who is self-taught. ⋙ **autodidactic** /-'daktik/ *adj.* [Greek *autodidaktos* self-taught, from AUTO-[1] + *didaktos* taught, from *didaskein* to teach]

auto-erotism /awtoh'erətiz(ə)m/ *or* **auto-eroticism** /,awtohi'rotisiz(ə)m/ *noun* sexual gratification obtained by oneself from one's own body. ⋙ **auto-erotic** /-i'rotik/ *adj*, **auto-erotically** /-i'rotikli/ *adv.*

autofocus /'awtohfohkəs/ *noun* a device in a camera that automatically adjusts the focusing.

autogamy /aw'togəmi/ *noun* self-fertilization: compare ALLOGAMY. ⋙ **autogamous** *adj.* [AUTO-[1] + Greek *gamos* marriage]

autogenic /awtoh'jenik/ *adj* technical produced from the individual's own body; AUTOGENOUS. [Greek *autogenēs*, from AUTO-[1] + *genēs* born, produced]

autogenics *pl noun* (*treated as sing. or pl*) a system of relaxation through conscious control of stress and tension.

autogenic training *noun* = AUTOGENICS.

autogenous /aw'tojənəs/ *adj* originating or derived from sources within the same individual: *an autogenous graft.* ➤➤ **autogenously** *adv.* [Greek *autogenēs*: see AUTOGENIC]

autogenous welding *noun* the welding of metal parts by melting their edges together, as distinct from adding a welding agent.

autogiro *or* **autogyro** /awtə'jie-əroh/ *noun* (*pl* **autogiros** *or* **autogyros**) an aircraft that resembles a helicopter and has a propeller for forward motion and a freely rotating horizontal rotor for lift. [from Spanish *autogiro*, from AUTO-² + *giro* gyration]

autograft /'awtəgrahft, -graft/ *noun* a transplant from one part to another part of the same body.

autograph¹ /'awtəgrahf, -graf/ *noun* **1** a person's handwritten signature, *esp* that of a celebrity. **2** an original manuscript or work of art. ➤➤ **autographic** /-'grafik/ *adj.* [late Latin *autographum*, neuter of Latin *autographus* written with one's own hand, from Greek, from AUTO-¹ + -*graphos* written]

autograph² *verb trans* to write one's signature in (a book, etc) or on (a page, etc).

autogyro /awtə'jie-əroh/ *noun* see AUTOGIRO.

autoharp /'awtohhahp/ *noun* a zither with button-controlled dampers for selected strings.

autohypnosis /,awtohhip'nohsis/ *noun* a self-induced hypnotic state, or the process of producing this. ➤➤ **autohypnotic** /-'notik/ *adj.*

autoimmune /,awtoh-i'myoohn/ *adj* **1** of or caused by autoantibodies. **2** said of a disease: caused by the production of large numbers of autoantibodies. ➤➤ **autoimmunity** *noun*, **autoimmunization** /-,imyoonie'zaysh(ə)n/ *noun.*

autointoxication /,awtoh-in,toksi'kaysh(ə)n/ *noun* the condition of being poisoned by toxic substances produced within one's own body.

autologous /aw'toləgəs/ *adj* derived from the same individual. [AUTO-¹ + -*logous* on the model of *homologous*]

autolysis /aw'toləsis/ *noun* the breakdown of all or part of a cell or tissue by self-produced enzymes. ➤➤ **autolytic** /-'litik/ *adj.* [AUTO-² + Latin *lysis* loosening, from Greek]

automat /'awtohmat/ *noun chiefly NAmer* an automatic vending machine. [German *Automat* via French from Latin *automaton*: see AUTOMATON]

automata /aw'tomətə/ *noun* pl of AUTOMATON.

automate /'awtəmayt/ *verb trans* to convert (a system, etc) to largely automatic operation. ➤➤ **automatable** /-'maytəbl/ *adj.* [back-formation from AUTOMATION]

automated teller machine *noun* = CASH DISPENSER.

automatic¹ /awtə'matik/ *adj* **1a** acting or done spontaneously or unconsciously. **b** resembling an automaton; mechanical. **2** having a self-acting or self-regulating mechanism that requires little or no human intervention: *an automatic car with automatic transmission.* **3** said of a firearm: repeatedly ejecting the empty cartridge shell, introducing a new cartridge, and firing it. **4** happening as a matter of course: *Promotion is no longer automatic after five years' service.* ➤➤ **automatically** *adv,* **automaticity** /-'tisiti/ *noun.* [Greek *automatos* self-acting]

automatic² *noun* an automatic machine or apparatus; *esp* an automatic firearm or a car with automatic transmission.

automatic data processing *noun* the automatic electronic processing of data.

automatic door *noun* a door that opens automatically by electronic means.

automatic exposure *noun* the automatic adjustment of a camera's lens aperture and shutter speed.

automatic gain control *noun* a system of self-adjustment by an amplifier to compensate for variations in the strength of the received signal.

automatic pilot *noun* a device for automatically steering a ship, aircraft, or spacecraft.

automatic transmission *noun* the automatic changing of a motor vehicle's gears, by means of a FLUID DRIVE (device operated by alterations in fluid momentum).

automation /awtə'maysh(ə)n/ *noun* **1** the technique of making an apparatus, process, or system operate automatically. **2** automatic operation of an apparatus, process, or system by mechanical

or electronic devices that take the place of human operators. [irregularly formed from AUTOMATIC¹]

automatise /aw'tomətiez/ *verb* see AUTOMATIZE.

automatism /aw'tomətiz(ə)m/ *noun* **1** an automatic action. **2** the unconscious or subconscious performance of actions. **3** a theory that conceives of the body as a machine, with consciousness being merely an accessory. ➤➤ **automatist** *noun.* [French *automatisme* from *automate*: see AUTOMAT]

automatize *or* **automatise** /aw'tomətiez/ *verb trans* to make (a process, etc) automatic or subject (a system, etc) to automation. ➤➤ **automatization** /,awtoh,matie'zaysh(ə)n/ *noun.*

automaton /aw'tomət(ə)n, -'mayt(ə)n/ *noun* (*pl* **automatons** *or* **automata** /-tə/) **1a** a mechanism having its own power source. **b** a robot. **2** a person who acts in a mechanical fashion. [via Latin from Greek *automaton,* neuter of *automatos* acting on one's own free will]

automobile /'awtəməbeel/ *noun chiefly NAmer* a motor car. ➤➤ **automobilist** /-'mohbəlist, -'beelist/ *noun.* [French *automobile,* from AUTO-¹ + *mobile:* see MOBILE¹]

automobilia /,awtəmoh'biliə/ *pl noun* collectors' items relating to cars and motoring. [AUTO-² + -*bilia* as in MEMORABILIA]

automotive /awtə'mohtiv/ *adj* relating to or concerned with motor vehicles.

autonomic /awtə'nomik/ *adj* **1** acting or occurring involuntarily: *autonomic reflexes.* **2** relating to, affecting, or controlled by the autonomic nervous system. ➤➤ **autonomically** *adv.*

autonomic nervous system *noun* a part of the nervous system of vertebrates that serves and controls the involuntary action of the smooth muscle, cardiac muscle, and glandular tissue.

autonomous /aw'tonəməs/ *adj* self-governing; independent. ➤➤ **autonomously** *adv.* [Greek *autonomos* independent, from AUTO-¹ + *nomos* law]

autonomy /aw'tonəmi/ *noun* (*pl* **autonomies**) **1** self-determined freedom and independence, *esp* moral independence. **2** self-government; *esp* the degree of political independence possessed by a minority group, territorial division, etc. ➤➤ **autonomist** *noun.* [Greek *autonomia* self-government, from AUTO-¹ + *nomos* law]

autopilot /'awtohpielət/ *noun* = AUTOMATIC PILOT.

autopista /'owtohpeestə/ *noun* a Spanish motorway. [Spanish *autopista,* from *auto* automobile + *pista* track]

autopsy /'awtopsi/ *noun* (*pl* **autopsies**) a postmortem examination. [Greek *autopsia* act of seeing with one's own eyes, from AUTO-¹ + -OPSY sight]

autoradiograph /awtoh'raydi-əgrahf, -graf/ *or* **autoradiogram** /-gram/ *noun* an image produced by radiation from a radioactive substance in an object in close contact with a photographic film or plate. ➤➤ **autoradiographic** /-'grafik/ *adj,* **autoradiography** /-'ografi/ *noun.*

autorotate /awtohtoh'tayt/ *verb intrans* said of the rotor of a helicopter or autogiro: to undergo autorotation.

autorotation /,awtohroh'taysh(ə)n/ *noun* the turning of the rotor of a helicopter or autogiro with the resulting lift caused solely by the aerodynamic forces induced by motion of the rotor along its flight path. ➤➤ **autorotational** *adj.*

autoroute /'awtohrooht/ *noun* a French motorway. [French *autoroute,* from *automobile* (see AUTOMOBILE) + *route* road]

autosave /'awtohsayv/ *noun* in computing, a program feature that automatically saves data in an open file at regular intervals.

autos-da-fé /,awtoh dah 'fay/ *noun* pl of AUTO-DA-FÉ.

autosome /'awtəsohm/ *noun* a chromosome other than a sex chromosome. ➤➤ **autosomal** /-'sohml/ *adj,* **autosomally** /-'sohməli/ *adv.* [AUTO-¹ + *sōma* body]

autosport /'awtohspawt/ *noun* motorcycle and motor-vehicle racing and rallying.

autostrada /'owtohstrahdə/ *noun* (*pl* **autostradas** *or* **autostrade** /-day/) an Italian motorway. [Italian *autostrada* from *auto* automobile + *strada* road]

autosuggestion /,awtohsə'jeschən/ *noun* an influencing of one's own attitudes, behaviour, or physical condition by mental processes other than conscious thought.

autotelic /awtoh'telik/ *adj* having a purpose in itself. [Greek *autotelēs,* from AUTO-¹ + *telos* end]

autotomy /aw'totəmi/ *noun* reflex separation of a part, such as a lizard's tail, from the body. >> **autotomic** /-'tomik/ *adj*, **autotomous** *adj*. [AUTO-¹ + Greek *tomē* cutting]

autotoxin /awtə'toksin/ *noun* a poison formed within the organism against which it acts.

autotrophic /awtə'trofik/ *adj* able to live and grow on carbon from carbon dioxide or carbonates and nitrogen from a simple inorganic compound: compare HETEROTROPHIC. >> **autotroph** /'awtətrof/ *noun*, **autotrophically** *adv*. [prob from German *autotroph*, from Greek *autotrophos* supplying one's own food, from AUTO-¹ + *trephein* to nourish]

autumn /'awtəm/ *noun* **1a** *chiefly Brit* the season between summer and winter, in which crops and fruit are gathered and deciduous trees lose their leaves, in the N hemisphere the months of September, October, and November. **b** in astronomy, the period in the N hemisphere extending from the September EQUINOX (time when day and night are of equal length) to the December SOLSTICE (shortest day of the year). **2** a period of maturity or the early stages of decline. >> **autumnal** /aw'tumnəl/ *adj*. [Middle English *autumpne* from Latin *autumnus*]

autumn crocus *noun* a plant of the lily family that blooms in autumn: *Colchicum autumnale*.

aux. *abbr* auxiliary.

auxesis /awk'seesis, awg'zeesis/ *noun* growth; *specif* an increase of cell size without cell division. >> **auxetic** /awk'setik, awg'zetik/ *adj*, **auxetically** /awk'setikli, awg'zet-/ *adv*. [scientific Latin from Greek *auxēsis* increase, growth, from *auxein* to increase]

auxiliary¹ /awg'zilyəri/ *adj* **1** subsidiary: *auxiliary nursing staff*. **2** kept in reserve; supplementary: *an auxiliary power plant*. **3** denoting a verb such as *be, do, have*, or *may*, used with another verb to express tense, voice, or mood. [Latin *auxiliaris* from *auxilium* help]

auxiliary² *noun* (*pl* **auxiliaries**) **1** a person, group, or device serving or used in an auxiliary capacity. **2** a member of a nation's auxiliary troops. **3** an auxiliary verb.

auxiliary troops *pl noun* a foreign force serving a nation that is at war.

auxiliary verb *noun* in grammar, a verb such as *be, do*, or *have*, or a MODAL AUXILIARY VERB (e.g. *will, shall, should, would, may*, or *might*), that helps another verb to form tenses, voices, and moods that cannot be indicated by INFLECTION (verb ending).

auxin /'awksin/ *noun* a plant hormone that promotes growth, or an analogue of one. >> **auxinic** /awk'sinik/ *adj*, **auxinically** /awk'sinikli/ *adv*. [Greek *auxein* to increase]

auxotrophic /awksə'trofik, -'trohfik/ *adj* requiring a specific growth substance beyond the minimum required for normal metabolism and reproduction: *auxotrophic mutants of bacteria*. >> **auxotroph** /'awksətrof, -trohf/ *noun*, **auxotrophically** *adv*. [Greek *auxein* to increase + -o- + -*trophic* from Greek *trophos* nourishing, from *trephein* to nourish]

AV *abbr* **1** ad valorem. **2** audiovisual. **3** Authorized Version (of the Bible).

Av. *abbr* in street names, avenue.

av. *abbr* **1** average. **2** avoirdupois.

avadavat /'avədavat/ *or* **amadavat** /'amə-/ *noun* a green or red Asian bird of the waxbill family: *Amandava formosa* or *Amandava amandava*. [alteration of *Ahmadabad* in India, from where the birds were first exported to Europe]

avail¹ /ə'vayl/ *verb trans* to help or benefit (somebody or their cause). > *verb intrans* to be of use or advantage: *No excuse will avail* — Conan Doyle. * **avail oneself of** to make use of or take advantage of (an opportunity, facility, etc). [Middle English *availen*, prob from *a-* (as in *abaten* to abate) + *vailen* to avail, from Old French *valoir* to be of worth, from Latin *valēre*]

avail² *noun* benefit; use. * **be of little avail/no avail** to be in vain; to prove useless. **to no avail** without success: *I tried arguing, but to no avail*.

available /ə'vayləbl/ *adj* **1** present or ready for immediate use or service. **2** accessible or obtainable. **3** present or free for consultation, etc; not otherwise occupied: *The doctor is not available just now*. **4** present in such chemical or physical form as to be usable, e.g. by a plant: *available nitrogen*. >> **availability** /-'biliti/ *noun*, **availableness** *noun*, **availably** *adv*. [Middle English in the senses 'advantageous', 'beneficial', from *availen* (see AVAIL¹) + -ABLE]

avalanche¹ /'avəlahnch/ *noun* **1a** a large mass of snow or ice falling rapidly down a mountain. **b** = LANDSLIDE (1). **2** a sudden overwhelming rush or accumulation of something: *an avalanche of paperwork*. [French *avalanche*, from French dialect *lavantse, avalantse*]

avalanche² *verb intrans* to descend in an avalanche.

avant-garde¹ /,avong 'gahd/ *noun* (*usu* **the avant-garde**) the group of people who create or apply new ideas and techniques in any field, *esp* the arts. >> **avant-gardism** *noun*, **avant-gardist** *noun*. [French *avant-garde* vanguard]

avant-garde² *adj* said of ideas, works of art, etc: daringly modern or innovative.

avarice /'avəris/ *noun* excessive or insatiable desire for wealth or gain; cupidity. >> **avaricious** /-'rishəs/ *adj*, **avariciously** /-'rishəsli/ *adv*, **avariciousness** /-'rishəsnis/ *noun*. [Middle English via Old French from Latin *avaritia* from *avarus* avaricious, from *avēre* to covet]

avast /ə'vahst/ *interj* a nautical command to stop or cease. [perhaps from Dutch *houd vast* hold fast]

avatar /'avətah/ *noun* **1** an earthly incarnation of a Hindu deity. **2a** an incarnation in human form. **b** an embodiment, e.g. of a concept or philosophy, usu in a person. **3** in computing, a movable icon representing a person in cyberspace or in virtual reality. [Sanskrit *avatāra* descent, from *avatarati* he descends, from *ava-* away + *tarati* he crosses over]

avdp *abbr* avoirdupois.

Ave. *abbr* in street names, avenue.

ave¹ /'ahvay, 'ahvi/ *interj* hail, or farewell. [Middle English from Latin *ave* hail!]

ave² *noun* = HAIL MARY.

Ave Maria /mə'ree-ə/ *noun* = HAIL MARY. [Middle English from medieval Latin *Ave Maria* hail, Mary!]

avenge /ə'venj/ *verb trans* **1** to take vengeance on behalf of (somebody). **2** to exact satisfaction for (a wrong) by punishing the wrongdoer. >> **avenger** *noun*. [Middle English *avengen*, prob from *a-* (as in *abaten* to abate) + *vengen* to avenge, via Old French *vengier* from Latin *vindicare*: see VINDICATE]

avens /'avinz/ *noun* (*pl* **avens**) any of several species of perennial plants of the rose family with white, purple, or yellow flowers: genus *Geum*. [Middle English *avence*, from Old French]

aventurine /ə'ventyoorin, -reen/ *noun* **1** glass containing opaque sparkling particles of foreign material. **2** a translucent quartz spangled with mica or other mineral. [French *aventurine*, from *aventure* chance; because the glass was discovered accidentally]

avenue /'avənyooh/ *noun* **1** a broad street or road, *esp* one bordered by trees. **2** *chiefly Brit* a tree-lined walk or driveway to a large country house. **3** a line of approach: *We explored every avenue in our quest for a solution*. [French *avenue*, fem of *avenu*, past part. of *avenir* to come to, from Latin *advenire* to arrive, reach]

aver /ə'vuh/ *verb trans* (**averred, averring**) **1** *formal* to declare (something) positively: *Some averred that it was a spaniel* — Herman Melville. **2** to allege or assert (something) while pleading in a court of law. >> **averment** *noun*. [Middle English *averren* via Old French *averer* from medieval Latin *adverare* to confirm as authentic, from AD- + Latin *verus* true]

average¹ /'av(ə)rij/ *noun* **1** a single value representative of a set of other values obtained by adding all the values together and dividing by the number of them; ARITHMETIC MEAN: *The average of 7, 10, 3, and 12 is 8*. **2** a level typical of a group, class, or series: *of below-average intelligence*. **3** a ratio expressing the average performance of a sports team or sportsperson as a fraction of the number of opportunities for successful performance. **4** in law: **a** a partial loss or damage sustained by a ship or cargo. **b** a charge arising from this, usu distributed among all those bearing some responsibility for it. [alteration of Old French *avarie* damage to ship or cargo, from Old Italian *avaria*, from Arabic *'awārīyah* damaged merchandise]

average² *adj* **1** equalling an average: *The average age of the participants was 16*. **2a** about midway between extremes: *a man of average build and height*. **b** not out of the ordinary; common; typical: *the average shopper*. >> **averagely** *adv*, **averageness** *noun*.

average³ *verb intrans* (*often* + out) to be or come to an average: *The gain averaged out at 20%*. > *verb trans* **1** to do, get, or have (a certain amount) as an average: *She averages six hours' work a day*. **2** to find the average of (a set of values). **3** (*often* + out) to bring (disparate values) towards the average by redistribution, etc. **4** to have an average or mid-range value of (a certain colour, etc): *a colour averaging a pale purple*.

average-adjuster *noun* a person who acts as assessor for an insurance company in claims relating to loss or damage at sea. ➤➤ **average-adjustment** *noun*.

averse /ə'vuhs/ *adj* (*usu* + to) strongly opposed; disliking: *In principle she was not averse to taking exercise.* ➤➤ **aversely** *adv*, **averseness** *noun*. [Latin *aversus*, past part. of *avertere* to turn away]

Usage note ──────────────

averse or adverse? See note at ADVERSE.

──────────────

aversion /ə'vuhsh(ə)n/ *noun* **1** a feeling of settled dislike for something; antipathy. **2** *chiefly Brit* an object of aversion; a cause of repugnance. [late Latin *aversion-, aversio*, the act of turning away, from Latin *avertere*: see AVERT]

aversion therapy *noun* therapy intended to change antisocial behaviour or a habit by association with unpleasant sensations.

aversive /ə'vuhsiv/ *adj* said of stimuli, etc: tending to cause aversion and hence avoidance.

avert /ə'vuht/ *verb trans* **1** to turn away or aside (the eyes, etc) in avoidance. **2** to see (trouble, etc) coming and ward it off; to avoid or prevent (a problem, etc). ➤➤ **avertable** *adj*, **avertible** *adj*. [Middle English *averten* via Old French from Latin *avertere*, from AB- + *vertere* to turn]

Avesta /ə'vestə/ *noun* the book of the sacred writings of Zoroastrianism. [early Persian *Avastāk*, literally 'original text']

Avestan *noun* the old Iranian sacred language used in the Avesta. ➤➤ **Avestan** *adj*.

avian /'ayvi-ən/ *adj* relating to or derived from birds. [Latin *avis* bird]

aviary /'ayvi-əri/ *noun* (*pl* **aviaries**) a large high enclosure for keeping birds. [Latin *aviarium* from *avis* bird]

aviation /ayvi'aysh(ə)n/ *noun* **1** the operation of aircraft. **2** aircraft manufacture, development, and design. [French *aviation* from Latin *avis* bird]

aviator /'ayviaytə/ *noun dated* the pilot of an aircraft. [French *aviateur*, from *avi-* (from Latin *avis* bird) + *-ateur* (on the pattern of *amateur*)]

aviatrix /'ayviətriks/ *noun* a female aviator.

aviculture /'ayvikulchə/ *noun* the raising and care of birds, *esp* of wild birds in captivity. ➤➤ **aviculturist** *noun*. [Latin *avis* bird + CULTURE[1]]

avid /'avid/ *adj* urgently or greedily eager; keen. ➤➤ **avidity** /ə'viditi/ *noun*, **avidly** *adv*, **avidness** *noun*. [via French *avide* from Latin *avidus*, from *avēre* to covet]

avidin /'avidin, ə'vidin/ *noun* a protein found in white of egg that combines with BIOTIN (B vitamin found in egg yolks) and makes it inactive. [from its avidity for biotin]

avifauna /ayvi'fawnə/ *noun* the birds of a region, period, or environment, or the varieties represented. ➤➤ **avifaunal** *adj*, **avifaunally** *adv*. [scientific Latin from Latin *avis* bird + scientific Latin *fauna*: see FAUNA]

avionics /ayvi'oniks/ *pl noun* **1** (*treated as sing. or pl*) the development and production of electronic equipment for aircraft and space vehicles. **2** (*treated as pl*) the devices and systems so developed. ➤➤ **avionic** *adj*. [blend of AVIATION + ELECTRONICS]

avisandum /avi'zandəm/ *noun* see AVIZANDUM.

avitaminosis /ay,vitəmi'nohsis, a-/ *noun* (*pl* **avitaminoses** /-seez/) disease resulting from a deficiency of one or more vitamins.

avizandum *or* **avisandum** /avi'zandəm/ *noun* in Scots law, private consideration given to a case by the judge, before giving judgment. [medieval Latin *avizandum* something to be considered, from *avizare* to consider]

AVM *abbr* Air Vice Marshal.

avocado /avə'kahdoh/ *noun* (*pl* **avocados** *or* **avocadoes**) **1a** a pulpy green or purple pear-shaped fruit. **b** the tropical American tree of the laurel family that bears this fruit: *Persea americana*. **2** a light green colour. [Spanish *avocado*, alteration of *aguacate*, from Nahuatl *ahuacatl*, short for *ahuacacuahuitl*, literally 'testicle tree', from the shape of the fruit]

avocation /avə'kaysh(ə)n/ *noun* a subordinate occupation pursued in addition to one's vocation, *esp* for enjoyment; a hobby.

➤➤ **avocational** *adj*, **avocationally** *adv*. [Latin *avocation-, avocatio* from *avocare* to call away, from AB- + *vocare* to call]

avocet /'avəset/ *noun* any of several species of black-and-white wading birds with webbed feet and a slender upward-curving bill: genus *Recurvirostra*. [French *avocette* from Italian *avocetta*]

Avogadro's constant /avə'gadrohz/ *or* **Avogadro's number** *noun* the number of molecules that occurs in one mole of substance; 6.023×10^{23}. [named after Count Amedeo *Avogadro* d.1856, Italian chemist and physicist]

Avogadro's law *or* **Avogadro's hypothesis** *noun* the rule that at equal temperature and pressure equal volumes of gases contain the same number of molecules.

Avogadro's number *noun* see AVOGADRO'S CONSTANT.

avoid /ə'voyd/ *verb trans* **1a** to keep away from or shun (somebody or something): *Avoid the M25 at peak times*. **b** to prevent the occurrence of (something): *I changed the subject to avoid an argument*. **c** to refrain from (doing something): *Avoid overwatering*. **2** in law, to make (a plea) legally void. ➤➤ **avoidable** *adj*, **avoidably** *adv*, **avoidance** *noun*, **avoider** *noun*. [Middle English *avoiden* from Old French *esvuidier*, from EX-[1] + *vuidier* to empty]

avoirdupois /,avwahdooh'pwah, ,avədə'poyz/ *or* **avoirdupois weight** *noun* **1** the series of units of weight based on the pound of 16 ounces and the ounce of 16 drams: compare TROY. **2** *informal* bodily heaviness or excess weight. [Middle English *avoir de pois* goods sold by weight, from Old French, literally 'goods of weight']

avouch /ə'vowch/ *verb trans archaic* **1** to declare or affirm (something). **2** to vouch for or corroborate (a statement, etc). **3** to acknowledge (an act) as one's own. ➤➤ **avouchment** *noun*. [Middle English *avouchen* to cite as authority, from Old French *avochier* to summon, from Latin *advocare*: see AVOW]

avow /ə'vow/ *verb trans* **1** to declare (something) with assurance. **2** to acknowledge (one's beliefs or views) openly, bluntly, and without shame. ➤➤ **avowal** *noun*, **avowedly** /-idli/ *adv*, **avower** *noun*. [Middle English *avowen* via Old French *avouer* from Latin *advocare*, from AD- + *vocare* to call]

avulsion /ə'vulsh(ə)n/ *noun* **1** a forcible tearing away of a body part accidentally or surgically. **2** a sudden cutting off of land from a property by flood, currents, etc. [Latin *avulsion-, avulsio*, from *avellere* to tear off, from AB- + *vellere* to pluck, pull]

avuncular /ə'vungkoolə/ *adj* **1** relating to or belonging to an uncle. **2** kindly or genial like an uncle. [Latin *avunculus* maternal uncle]

aw /aw/ *interj chiefly NAmer* used to express mild sympathy, remonstrance, incredulity, or disgust.

AWACS /'aywaks/ *abbr* airborne warning and control system.

await /ə'wayt/ *verb trans* **1** to wait for (somebody or something). **2** said of events: to be in store for (somebody): *A disappointment awaited her*. [Middle English *awaiten*, from early French *awaitier*, from AD- + *waitier*: see WAIT[1]]

awake[1] /ə'wayk/ *verb* (*past tense* **awoke** /ə'wohk/ *or* **awaked**, *past part.* **awoken** /ə'wohkən/) ➤ *verb intrans* **1** to emerge from sleep or a sleeplike state. **2** (*usu* + to) to become conscious or aware of something: *They at last awoke to their danger*. ➤ *verb trans* **1** to arouse (somebody) from sleep or a sleeplike state. **2** to activate or stir up (something lying dormant): *The smell awoke old memories*. [Old English *awacan* from (A-[1] + *wacan* to awake, arise, be born) and Old English *awacian*, from A-[1] + *wacian* to be awake, watch]

awake[2] *adj* **1** not or no longer asleep. **2** (*usu* + to) fully conscious or aware of something: *He wasn't awake to her faults then*.

awaken /ə'waykən/ *verb* (**awakened, awakening**) ➤ *verb trans* to wake (somebody). ➤ *verb intrans* to wake up. ➤➤ **awakener** *noun*. [Old English *awæcnian*, from A-[1] + *wæcnian* to WAKEN]

award[1] /ə'wawd/ *verb trans* **1** to confer or bestow (a scholarship, prize, medal, etc) as being deserved or needed. **2** to give (damages) by judicial decree. ➤➤ **awardable** *adj*, **awarder** *noun*. [Middle English *awarden* to decide, from early French *eswarder*, from EX-[1] + *warder* to guard, of Germanic origin]

award[2] *noun* **1** something that is conferred or bestowed, *esp* on the basis of merit or need. **2** a final decision; *esp* the decision of arbitrators in a case submitted to them.

award wage *noun* in Australia and New Zealand, the statutory minimum rate of pay for a particular type of worker.

aware /ə'weə/ *adj* **1** (*often* + of) having or showing realization; conscious of something: *I was not aware of her presence till she spoke*.

2 having kept oneself informed: *environmentally aware*. ➤➤ **awareness** *noun*. [Old English *gewær*, from *wær* wary]

awash /əˈwosh/ *adj* (*used after a noun*) **1** covered with water; flooded. **2** (+ with) marked by an abundance of (something): *The place was awash with reporters*.

away[1] /əˈway/ *adv* **1** on one's way: *I want to get away early*. **2** from here or there; hence; thence: *Go away and leave me alone!* **3a** in a secure place or manner: *locked away*; *tucked away*. **b** in another direction; aside: *She looked away*. **4** out of existence; to an end: *echoes dying away*; *We lazed the afternoon away*. **5a** on; uninterruptedly: *clocks ticking away*. **b** without hesitation or delay: *Do it right away*. **6** by a long distance or interval; far: *away back in 1910*. **7** from one's possession: *He gave away a fortune*. [Old English *aweg*, *on weg*, from a, ON[1] + *weg* WAY[1]]

away[2] *adj* **1** absent from a place; gone: *My wife is away for the weekend*. **2** (*used after a noun*) distant: *a lake ten miles away*. **3** (*used before a noun*) played on an opponent's grounds: *an away game*.

AWB *abbr* Afrikaner Weerstandsbeweging, a right-wing Afrikaner political group in S Africa.

awe[1] /aw/ *noun* an emotion compounded of dread, veneration, and wonder. [Middle English, from Old Norse *agi* awe, fear]

awe[2] *verb trans* to inspire or fill (somebody) with awe.

awed /awd/ *adj* showing awe: *awed respect*.

aweigh /əˈway/ *adj* said of an anchor: raised just clear of the bottom of a body of water.

awe-inspiring *adj* deserving admiration or wonder; amazing; wonderful.

awesome /ˈaws(ə)m/ *adj* **1** expressing awe: *awesome tributes*. **2** inspiring awe: *an awesome sight*. **3** *informal* excellent; great. ➤➤ **awesomely** *adv*, **awesomeness** *noun*.

awestruck /ˈawstruk/ *or* **awestricken** /ˈawstrikən/ *adj* filled with awe.

awful[1] /ˈawf(ə)l/ *adj* **1** extremely disagreeable or objectionable: *an awful situation*. **2** exceedingly great: *an awful lot to do*. **3** *informal* used as an intensive: *an awful headache*. **4** *archaic* inspiring awe. ➤➤ **awfulness** *noun*.

awful[2] *adv non-standard* very; extremely: *I'm awful thirsty*.

awfully *adv* **1** *informal* used as an intensifier in both favourable and unfavourable contexts: *awfully difficult*; *That's awfully kind of you*. **2** in an awed, or awe-inspiring, manner.

awhile /əˈwiel/ *adv* for a short time: *...and stood awhile in thought* — Lewis Carroll.

awkward /ˈawkwəd/ *adj* **1** lacking dexterity or skill, *esp* in the use of hands; clumsy. **2** lacking ease or grace, e.g. of movement or expression. **3a** lacking social grace and assurance. **b** causing embarrassment: *an awkward moment*. **4** poorly adapted for use or handling. **5** requiring caution: *an awkward diplomatic situation*. **6** deliberately obstructive. ➤➤ **awkwardly** *adv*, **awkwardness** *noun*. [Middle English *awkeward* in the wrong direction, from *awke* turned the wrong way, from Old Norse *öfugr* + -WARD]

awl /awl/ *noun* a pointed instrument for marking surfaces or making small holes, e.g. in leather. [Middle English *al*, from Old Norse *alr*]

awn /awn/ *noun* any of the slender bristles at the end of the flower spikelet in some grasses, e.g. barley. ➤➤ **awned** *adj*. [Old English *agen*, from Old Norse *ögn*]

awning /ˈawning/ *noun* a rooflike cover, often of canvas, used to protect something, e.g. a shop window or a ship's deck from sun or rain. [origin unknown]

awoke /əˈwohk/ *verb* past tense of AWAKE[1].

awoken /əˈwohkən/ *verb* past part. of AWAKE[1].

AWOL /ˈaywol/ *adj* (*often* **awol**) in the armed forces, absent without leave. [acronym from *absent without leave*]

awry /əˈrie/ *adv and adj* **1** in a turned or twisted position or direction; askew. **2** out of the right or hoped-for course; amiss. [Middle English *on wry*, from ON[1] + WRY]

axe[1] (*NAmer* **ax**) /aks/ *noun* **1** a tool that has a head with a cutting edge parallel to the handle and is used for felling trees, chopping wood, etc. **2** (**the axe**) drastic reduction or removal, e.g. of personnel. **3** *informal*. **a** a guitar. **b** in jazz, any musical instrument, *esp* a saxophone. ✳ **get the axe 1** to be sacked; to be made redundant. **2** said of a project: to be cancelled or abandoned. **have an axe to**

grind to have an ulterior, often selfish, purpose to pursue. [Old English *æx*]

axe[2] (*NAmer* **ax**) *verb trans* **1** to remove (personnel from employment or a project from a budget) abruptly. **2a** to hew, shape, or trim (wood or a tree) with an axe. **b** to chop, split, or sever (wood, etc) with an axe.

axel /ˈaksl/ *noun* a jump in ice skating from one skate to the other with one, two, or three and a half turns in the air. [named after *Axel Paulsen* d.1938, Norwegian figure skater]

axeman *noun* (*pl* **axemen**) a person who wields an axe; *specif* a psychopathic criminal.

axes /ˈakseez/ *noun* pl of AXIS.

axial /ˈaksi·əl/ *adj* **1** relating to or functioning as an axis. **2** situated round, in the direction of, or along an axis. ➤➤ **axiality** /-ˈaliti/ *noun*, **axially** *adv*.

axil /ˈaksl/ *noun* the angle between a branch or leaf and the axis from which it arises. [Latin *axilla* armpit]

axilla /akˈsilə/ *noun* (*pl* **axillas** *or* **axillae** /-lee/) *technical* the armpit. [Latin *axilla*]

axillary /akˈsiləri/ *adj* **1** relating to or in the region of the armpit. **2** situated in or growing from an axil.

axiom /ˈaksi·əm/ *noun* **1** a principle, rule, or maxim widely accepted on its intrinsic merit; a generally recognized truth. **2a** a proposition regarded as a self-evident truth. **b** something taken as true for the sake of argument; a postulate. [via Latin from Greek *axiōma* honour, from *axioun* to think worthy, from *axios* worth, worthy]

axiomatic /ˌaksi·əˈmatik/ *adj* of the nature of an axiom; self-evident: *You cannot occupy two places simultaneously. This is axiomatic* — Kipling. ➤➤ **axiomatically** *adv*. [Greek *axiōmatikos*, from *axiōmat-*, *axiōma*: see AXIOM]

axis /ˈaksis/ *noun* (*pl* **axes** /ˈakseez/) **1a** a straight line about which a body or a geometric figure rotates or may be supposed to rotate. **b** a straight line with respect to which a body or figure is symmetrical. **c** any of the reference lines of a coordinate system. **2a** the second vertebra of the neck on which the head and first vertebra pivot. **b** any of various parts that are central or fundamental or that lie on or constitute an axis. **3** any of several imaginary reference lines used in describing a crystal structure. **4** a partnership or alliance, e.g. the one between Germany and Italy in World War II. **5** a plant stem. [Latin *axis* axle]

axis deer *noun* a white-spotted deer of India and other parts of S Asia: genus *Axis*. Also called CHITAL. [Latin *axis* a wild animal of India]

axle /ˈaksl/ *noun* **1** a shaft on or with which a wheel revolves. **2** a rod connecting a pair of wheels of a vehicle. [Middle English *axel-* as in *axeltre*: see AXLETREE]

axletree *noun* a fixed bar or beam with bearings at each end on which wheels, e.g. of a cart, revolve. [Middle English *axeltre* from Old Norse *öxultré*, from *öxull* axle + *tré* tree]

Axminster /ˈaksminstə/ *noun* **1** a carpet weave in which pile tufts are inserted into a backing during its weaving according to a predetermined arrangement of colours and patterns: compare WILTON. **2** a carpet woven in this way. [named after *Axminster*, town in England where such carpets were produced]

axolotl /ˈaksəlotl, -ˈlotl/ *noun* a salamander of mountain lakes of Mexico that matures sexually in the larval stage: genus *Ambystoma*. [Nahuatl *axolotl*, literally 'water doll']

axon /ˈakson/ *noun* a long projecting part of a nerve cell that conducts impulses away from the cell body. ➤➤ **axonal** *adj*, **axonic** /akˈsonik/ *adj*. [scientific Latin from Greek *axōn*]

axonometric projection /ˌaksənohˈmetrik/ *noun* a method of drawing a three-dimensional object in such a way that a rectangular solid appears as inclined and shows three faces. [Greek *axō* axis + -METRIC]

ay[1] /ie/ *interj and noun* see AYE[1], AYE[2].

ay[2] /ay/ *adv* see AYE[3].

ayah /ˈie·ə/ *noun* a native nurse or maid in India. [Hindi *āyā* via Portuguese *aia* from Latin *avia* grandmother]

ayatollah /ˌie·əˈtolə/ *noun* a leader of Iranian Shiite Islam. [Persian *āyatollāh* from Arabic *āyatullāh* manifestation of God]

aye¹ *or* **ay** /ie/ *interj archaic or dialect* **1** yes. **2** used as the correct formal response to a naval order: *Aye, aye, sir.* [perhaps from Middle English *ye, yie*]

aye² *or* **ay** /ie/ *noun* an affirmative vote or voter.

aye³ *or* **ay** /ay/ *adv archaic or Scot* always; ever; continually. [Middle English *aye, ai*, from Old Norse *ei*]

aye-aye /'ie ie/ *noun* a nocturnal lemur of Madagascar. [French *aye-aye*, from Malagasy *aiay*]

Aylesbury /'aylzb(ə)ri/ *noun* (*pl* **Aylesburys**) a bird of a breed of large white domestic ducks. [named after *Aylesbury*, town in England where the breed originated]

Aymara /'iemərah/ *noun* (*pl* **Aymaras** *or collectively* **Aymara**) **1** a member of a Native American people of Bolivia and Peru. **2** the language of this people. [Spanish *Aymará*]

Ayrshire /'eashiə/ *noun* an animal of a breed of hardy dairy cattle that are usu spotted red, brown, or white in colour. [named after *Ayrshire*, former county of Scotland, where the breed originated]

Ayurveda /ahyooə'vaydə, ie-ooə'veedə/ *noun* the traditional Hindu system of medicine based mainly on herbal remedies, homoeopathy, and naturopathy. >>> **Ayurvedic** *adj.* [Sanskrit *āyurveda*, from *āyur* life + *veda* knowledge]

AZ *abbr* **1** Arizona (US postal abbreviation). **2** Azerbaijan (international vehicle registration).

A–Z /,ay tə 'zed/ *noun Brit* an indexed street atlas of a town.

az- *or* **azo-** *prefix* forming words, with the meaning: containing nitrogen, *esp* as the bivalent group -N=N-. [obsolete *azote* nitrogen, from Greek A-² + *zōe* life]

aza- *or* **az-** *prefix* forming words, with the meaning: containing nitrogen in place of carbon and usu the bivalent group NH for the group CH_2 or a single trivalent nitrogen atom for the group CH. [AZ- + -A-]

azalea /ə'zaylyə/ *noun* any of several species of rhododendron with funnel-shaped flowers and deciduous leaves: genus *Rhododendron*. [scientific Latin *Azalea*, genus name, from Greek, from *azaleos* dry]

azeotrope /ə'zee-ətrohp/ *noun* a mixture of liquids with a boiling point that does not change during distillation. >>> **azeotropic** /,ayzi·ə'tropik/ *adj.* [A-² + *zeo-* (from Greek *zein* to boil) + *-trope* from Greek *tropos* turn, way]

Azerbaijani /,azəbie'jahni/ *noun* (*pl* **Azerbaijanis**) **1** a native or inhabitant of Azerbaijan in the Caucasus. **2** the Turkic language spoken in Azerbaijan. >>> **Azerbaijani** *adj.*

Azeri /ə'zeəri/ *noun* **1** a member of a Turkic people living chiefly in N Iran, Armenia, and Azerbaijan. **2** the language of this people. >>> **Azeri** *adj.* [Turkish *azerî* fire, from Persian]

azide /'ayzied, 'azied/ *noun* a compound containing the group -N₃ combined with an element or radical.

azidothymidine /,ayziedoh'thiemideen/ *noun trademark* = AZT.

Azilian /ə'zili-ən/ *adj* relating to or denoting a Mesolithic culture of W Europe of about 10,000–8000 BC. [Mas d'*Azil* in the French Pyrenees, where finds were made]

azimuth /'aziməth/ *noun* **1** an arc of the horizon expressed as the clockwise angle measured between a fixed point, e.g. true north or true south, and the vertical circle passing through the centre of an object. **2** horizontal direction. >>> **azimuthal** /-'moohthl/ *adj,* **azimuthally** /-'moohthli/ *adv.* [Middle English, ultimately from Arabic *as-sumūt* the azimuth, pl of *as-samt* the way]

azimuthal projection *noun* a projection of the earth's surface on a tangential plane.

azine /'azeen, 'azin/ *noun* any of numerous organic chemical compounds having a molecular structure that includes a ring containing six atoms, at least one of which is a nitrogen atom.

azo /'ayzoh, 'azoh/ *adj* relating to or containing the bivalent group -N=N- united at both ends to carbon. [AZ-]

azo- *prefix* see AZ-.

azo dye *noun* any of numerous versatile dyes containing azo groups.

azoic /ay'zohik, a-/ *adj* having no life; *specif* of the geological time that antedates life. [A-² + Greek *zōē* life]

azole /'azohl/ *noun* any of numerous organic chemical compounds having a molecular structure that includes a ring containing five atoms at least one of which is a nitrogen atom.

AZT *abbr trademark* azidothymidine; ZIDOVUDINE.

Aztec /'aztek/ *noun* **1** a member of the Nahuatlan people that founded the Mexican empire conquered by Cortes in 1519. **2** the language of the Aztecs. Also called NAHUATL. >>> **Aztecan** *adj.* [Spanish *Azteca* from Nahuatl, pl of *aztecatl* (the people) from *Aztlan*, their legendary place of origin]

azure¹ /'azyooə, 'azhə, 'ay-/ *adj* of a deep blue colour.

azure² *noun* **1a** sky blue. **b** in heraldry, blue. **2** *archaic* lapis lazuli. [Middle English *asur*, from Old French *azur*, ultimately from Arabic *lāzaward* lapis lazuli, from Persian *lāzhuward*]

azurite *noun* **1** a blue mineral that is a carbonate of copper. **2** a semiprecious stone derived from this. [French *azurite* from *azur*: see AZURE²]

azygous /'azigəs/ *adj* not being one of a pair: *an azygous vein.* [scientific Latin from Greek *azygos* unyoked, from A-² + *zygon* yoke]

B¹ *or* **b** *noun* (*pl* **B's** *or* **Bs** *or* **b's**) **1a** the second letter of the English alphabet. **b** a written character or design denoting this letter. **c** the sound represented by this letter, one of the English consonants. **2** an item designated as B, *esp* the second in a series. **3** a mark or grade rating a student's work as good but short of excellent. **4** in music, the seventh note of the diatonic scale of C major. **5** (*used before a noun*) denoting something that is the less important of two things or a supporting item: *a B-movie*. **6** *euphem* used for any offensive word beginning with the letter *b*.

B² *abbr* **1** bachelor. **2** baryon number. **3** in music, bass. **4** bay. **5** bel. **6** Belgium (international vehicle registration). **7** Bible. **8** in chess, bishop. **9** used on lead pencils: black. **10** used in designating US aircraft, bomber: *B-52*. **11** British. **12** a blood type of the ABO system, containing the B antigen.

B³ *abbr* the chemical symbol for boron.

B⁴ *symbol* magnetic flux density.

b *abbr* **1** in physics, barn. **2** billion. **3** book. **4** born. **5** in cricket, bowled by. **6** breadth. **7** in cricket, bye.

BA *abbr* **1** Bachelor of Arts. **2** British Academy. **3** British Airways. **4** British Association (for the Advancement of Science). **5** Buenos Aires.

Ba¹ *abbr* the chemical symbol for barium.

Ba² *or* **ba** /bah/ *noun* in ancient Egyptian belief, the soul of a person or a god, often depicted in the form of a hawk with a man's head, expressing the soul's mobility after the death of the body: compare KA.

BAA *abbr* British Airports Authority.

baa¹ /bah/ *verb intrans* (**baas, baaed** *or* **baa'd, baaing**) to make the bleat of a sheep, or a sound similar to or in imitation of it. [imitative]

baa² *noun* (*pl* **baas**) the characteristic bleating sound of a sheep, or a similar or imitative sound.

BAAS *abbr* British Association for the Advancement of Science.

baas /bahs/ *noun SAfr* a master or boss. [Afrikaans *baas* from early Dutch *baes*]

baasskap *or* **baaskap** /'bahskap/ *noun SAfr* = WHITE SUPREMACY. [Afrikaans *baasskap* mastership, from *baas* (see BAAS) + *-skap* -ship]

baba /'bahbah, 'bahbə/ *noun* a rich cake leavened with yeast, usu soaked with a rum and sugar syrup. [French from Polish *baba* old woman]

Babbitt /'babit/ *noun chiefly NAmer, derog* a business or professional person who conforms unthinkingly to bourgeois standards and ideals, *esp* of materialism. ➤➤ **Babbittry** /-tri/ *noun*. [named after George French *Babbitt*, character in the novel *Babbitt* by Sinclair Lewis d.1951, US novelist]

babbitt *noun* a babbitt-metal lining for a bearing.

babbitt metal *or* **Babbitt metal** *noun* an alloy, *esp* of tin, copper, antimony, and lead, used for lining bearings. [named after Isaac *Babbitt* d.1862, US inventor]

babble¹ /'babl/ *verb intrans* **1a** to utter meaningless or unintelligible sounds. **b** to talk foolishly; to chatter. **2** said e.g. of a stream: to make a continuous murmuring or bubbling sound. ➤ *verb trans* **1** to utter (something) in an incoherently or meaninglessly repetitious manner. **2** to reveal (something) by talk that is too free. ➤➤ **babblement** *noun*. [Middle English *babelen*, prob of imitative origin]

babble² *noun* **1** meaningless or unintelligible sounds. **2** the murmuring or bubbling sound of a stream, etc.

babbler *noun* **1** somebody who babbles. **2** any of several species of songbirds related to the thrushes and warblers that are found in Asia, Africa, and Australasia and are noted for their loud persistent rapid call: family Timaliidae or subfamily Timaliinae.

babe /bayb/ *noun* **1** *chiefly literary* an infant or baby. **2** a naive inexperienced person. **3a** *informal* a girl or woman, *esp* one regarded as sexually attractive. **b** used as a form of address for a girl or woman. [Middle English, prob imitating infant speech]

babel /'baybl/ *noun* a scene of noise or confusion, *esp* from many voices.

Word history

named after the Tower of *Babel* (Genesis 11:4–9). The tower was intended to reach heaven; this incurred the wrath of God, who punished the builders by making their speech mutually unintelligible.

babirusa *or* **babirussa** *or* **babiroussa** /babə'roohsə/ *noun* a large almost hairless pig of the E Indies, the male of which has large backward-curving tusks: *Babyrousa babyrussa*. [Malay *bābīrūsa*, from *bābī* hog + *rūsa* deer]

Babism /'babiz(ə)m/ *noun* a religious movement that is an offshoot of Shia Islam and was a precursor of Baha'ism, founded in Persia in 1844 by Mirza Ali Muhammad, also known as the Bab. ➤➤ **Babi** *noun*. [Persian from Arabic *bāb* gateway, intermediary; Mirza Ali Muhammad, d. 1850, claimed to be the intermediary of the hidden twelfth imam of Shia Islam]

baboon /bə'boohn/ *noun* any of several species of large African and Asian monkeys that have long doglike muzzles and usu medium-length tails: genera *Papio* and *Mandrillus*. ➤➤ **baboonish** *adj*. [Middle English *babewin* from Old French *babouin*, from *baboue* grimace]

babu /'bahbooh/ *noun* (*pl* **babus**) **1** a form of address for a Hindu man, corresponding to *Mr*. **2** *chiefly derog, dated* an Indian with some education in English; a clerk or office worker. [Hindi *bābū* father]

babul /bah'boohl, 'bahboohl/ *noun* an acacia tree widespread in N Africa and across Asia that yields gum arabic and tannins as well as fodder and timber: *Acacia arabica*. [Persian *babūl*]

babushka /bə'booshkə/ *noun* an elderly Russian woman. [Russian *babushka* grandmother, dimin. of *baba* old woman]

baby[1] /'baybi/ *noun* (*pl* **babies**) **1a** a very young child, *esp* one in the first year or two after birth; an infant. **b** an unborn child: *My baby started kicking before I was four months pregnant.* **c** a very young animal or unborn animal. **2** the youngest of a group. **3** (*used before a noun*) comparatively small of its type: *baby carrots*. **4** a childish or immature person. **5** a person or thing for which one feels special responsibility or pride: *This project is very much her baby.* **6** *informal* an affectionate form of address for a person, *esp* a girl or woman. ✳ **throw the baby out with the bathwater** to get rid of or reject something useful along with other things that are not wanted or not useful: *Parts of her report are good. I don't think we should throw out the baby with the bathwater.* >> **babyhood** *noun*, **babyish** *adj*, **babyishly** *adv*, **babyishness** *noun*. [Middle English, from BABE]

baby[2] *verb trans* (**babies, babied, babying**) to tend or indulge (somebody) with often excessive or inappropriate care.

baby boom *noun* a rapid increase in the birthrate.

baby boomer *noun* somebody born during a baby boom, *esp* a member of the generation born in the UK and USA in the late 1940s and early 1950s.

baby buggy *noun* **1** (**Baby Buggy**) *Brit, trademark* a lightweight foldable pushchair. **2** *NAmer* a pram.

baby carriage *noun chiefly NAmer* a pram.

baby grand *noun* a small grand piano.

Babygro /'baybigroh/ *noun trademark* a one-piece garment for a baby, made of stretchy fabric and typically covering the body, arms, legs, and feet.

Babylon /'babilən, -lon/ *noun derog* any city, place, or group regarded as being given over to corruption, ungodliness, materialism and the pursuit of sensual pleasure such as, as used *esp* by Rastafarians, white Western civilization or, as used by some Protestants, the Roman Catholic Church. [*Babylon*, city of *Babylonia*, ancient country of SW Asia]

Babylonian[1] /babi'lohni·ən/ *adj* belonging or relating to Babylon or ancient Babylonia.

Babylonian[2] *noun* **1** a native or inhabitant of ancient Babylonia or Babylon. **2** the Akkadian language of ancient Babylonia.

babysit *verb intrans* (**babysitting**, *past tense and past part.* **babysat** /-sat/) to care for a child, usu for a short period while the parents are out. >> **babysitter** *noun*. [orig as *babysitter*; *babysit* is a back-formation]

baby-snatcher *noun* **1** somebody who steals a baby from its pram. **2** *humorous* somebody who has a sexual relationship with or marries a much younger person.

baby talk *noun* the imperfect form of speech produced by small children, or an imitation of it used when speaking to small children.

BAC *abbr* British Aircraft Corporation.

baccalaureate /bakə'lawri·ət/ *noun* **1** the academic degree of bachelor. **2** = INTERNATIONAL BACCALAUREATE.

Word history
medieval Latin *baccalaureatus*, from *baccalaureus* bachelor, alteration of *baccalarius* (see BACHELOR). The alteration came about by association with Latin *bacca lauri* laurel berry, because laurels were traditionally awarded to scholars.

baccarat /'bakərah/ *noun* a card game in which three hands are dealt and players may bet on either or both hands against the dealer's, the winning hand having the highest remainder when its face value is divided by ten. [French *baccara*]

bacchanal[1] /'bakənl/ *noun* **1a** a devotee of Bacchus, *esp* one who celebrates the Bacchanalia. **b** a reveller. **2** drunken revelry or carousal; bacchanalia. [Latin *bacchanalis* of *Bacchus*, god of wine, from Greek *Bakchos*]

bacchanal[2] *adj* **1** relating to Bacchus or the Bacchanalia. **2** relating to drunken revelry.

bacchanalia /bakə'nayli·ə/ *pl noun* (*treated as sing. or pl*) **1** (**Bacchanalia**) a Roman festival of Bacchus celebrated with dancing, song, and revelry. **2** a drunken feast; an orgy. >> **bacchanalian** *adj and noun*. [Latin *bacchanalia*, neuter pl of *bacchanalis*: see BACCHANAL[1]]

bacchant /'bakənt/ *noun* (*pl* **bacchants** *or* **bacchantes** /bə'kanteez/) a follower of Bacchus; somebody celebrating the Bacchanalia. [Latin *bacchant-, bacchans*, present part. of *bacchari* to celebrate the festival of Bacchus]

bacchante /bə'kanti/ *noun* a priestess or female follower of Bacchus. [French *bacchante* from Latin *bacchant-, bacchans*: see BACCHANT]

bacchantes /bə'kanteez/ *noun* pl of BACCHANT.

baccy /'baki/ *noun* (*pl* **baccies**) *chiefly Brit, informal* tobacco. [by shortening and alteration]

bach /bach/ *noun* NZ a simple dwelling, *esp* a shack or chalet, e.g. at the seaside or in the country. [prob short for *bachelor*]

bachelor /'bachələ/ *noun* **1a** an unmarried man: *When I said I would die a bachelor, I did not think I should live till I were married* — Shakespeare. **b** a man past the usual age for marrying or one who seems unlikely to marry. **c** (*used before a noun*) suitable for or occupied by a bachelor: *a bachelor flat.* **2** (*often* **Bachelor**) in degree titles: a recipient of what is usu the lowest degree conferred by a college or university: *He's a Bachelor of Arts.* **3** a male animal, e.g. a fur seal, without a mate during breeding time. **4** in medieval times, a young knight who followed the banner of another knight. >> **bachelordom** *noun*, **bachelorhood** *noun*. [Middle English *bacheler* from Old French, prob from medieval Latin *baccalarius* tenant farmer, squire, advanced student, of Celtic origin]

bachelor girl *noun* an unmarried girl or woman who lives independently.

bachelor's buttons *pl noun* (*treated as sing. or pl*) any of various plants with small round double flowers, such as a variety of double-flowered buttercup and certain plants with double daisy-like flowers: *Ranunculus acris, Achillea ptarmica, Kerria japonica*.

Bach flower remedies /bach/ *pl noun trademark* a form of therapy in alternative medicine in which the active ingredient is spring water including tiny amounts of plant extracts. [named after Edward *Bach* d.1936, English physician who devised the system]

bacillary /bə'siləri/ *adj* **1** of or caused by bacilli. **2** = BACILLIFORM. [scientific Latin, from *bacillus*: see BACILLUS]

bacilli /bə'silie/ *noun* pl of BACILLUS.

bacilliform /bə'silifawm/ *adj* **1** rod-shaped. **2** consisting of small rods.

bacillus /bə'siləs/ *noun* (*pl* **bacilli** /-lie/) a usu rod-shaped bacterium, *esp* one that causes disease. [scientific Latin from medieval Latin *bacillus* small staff, rod, dimin. of Latin *baculus* staff, alteration of *baculum*]

back[1] /bak/ *noun* **1a** the rear part of the human body, *esp* from the neck to the end of the spine. **b** the corresponding part of a quadruped or other animal. **c** the spine: *He fell and broke his back.* **d** the main structure of a ship or aircraft. **2a** the side or surface behind the front or face, e.g. the rear part or the farther or reverse side. **b** something at or on the back for support: *The backs of some of the chairs were broken.* **3** a primarily defensive player in some team games, e.g. football, or the position of such a player. **4a** the final section of a book: *There must be an index at the back of the book.* **b** the edge of a book along which the sections or pages are secured or glued. ✳ **at somebody's back 1** following or pursuing somebody closely. **2** supporting somebody. **at the back of one's mind** in one's thoughts but not occupying an important place in them. **back to back** facing in opposite directions with backs touching or close together. **back to front 1** in such a way that the back and the front are reversed in position. **2** in such a way that comprehensive knowledge is gained: *You had to learn the Highway Code back to front.* **behind somebody's back** without a person's knowledge or permission; deceitfully or unfairly. **get/put somebody's back up** to annoy or irritate (somebody). **put one's back into** to make a great effort in carrying out a task. **turn one's back on** to reject or deny (somebody or something): *He turned his back on the past.* **with one's back to/against the wall** in a situation from which one cannot retreat and must either fight or be defeated. >> **backless** *adj*. [Old English *bæc*]

back[2] *adv* **1a** to, towards, or at the rear: *She tied her hair back.* **b** in or into a reclining position: *She told me to lie back.* **2a** away, e.g. from the speaker: *Stand back and give him air.* **b** in or into the past; ago: *It happened three years back.* **c** nearer the beginning: *Go back a couple of pages and read what it says there.* **3a** to, towards, or in a place from which somebody or something came: *He put it back on the shelf.* **b** to or towards a former state: *He was asked to think back* *to his childhood.* **c** in return or reply: *Ring me back.* **4** under restraint: *She was unable to hold back her tears.* **5** in or into a delayed or retarded condition: *That could set the schedule back.* ✳ **back and forth** backwards and forwards repeatedly.

back³ *adj: Come round to the back door.* **1a** at or in the back: *Come round to the back door.* **b** distant from a central or main area; remote: *I stuck to the back roads.* **2** being in arrears: *They owe me £500 in back pay.* **3** not current; published earlier: *Back numbers of the magazine are no longer available.* **4** said of a speech sound: articulated at the back of the mouth.

back⁴ *verb trans* **1a** to support (somebody or something) by giving material or moral assistance. **b** to give financial support to (a scheme or undertaking). **2** to provide a musical backing for (a singer, musician, or song). **3** to cause (a vehicle) to go backwards. **4a** to provide (something, e.g. a chair) with a back. **b** to be at or form the back of (something). **5** to place a bet on (a competitor in a race). **6** to countersign or endorse (a document). ➤ *verb intrans* **1** to move backwards in a vehicle. **2** said of the wind: to shift anticlockwise: compare VEER¹ (2). **3** (+ on/onto) said of a building: to have its back adjacent to or closely facing something specified: *The house backs on to the golf course.* ✳ **back water** to move the oars of a rowing boat in a direction opposite to normal to slow the boat or change its direction. ➤➤ **backer** *noun.*

backache *noun* a pain in the back, *esp* a dull persistent pain.

back away *verb intrans* (*often* + from) to move back, e.g. from a theoretical position; to withdraw.

backbeat *noun* in music, *esp* jazz, rock, or hip hop, an emphatic beat on one of the usu unaccented beats of the bar.

back bench *noun* (*usu in pl*) any of the benches in Parliament on which non-ministerial members sit. ➤➤ **back bench** *adj,* **backbencher** *noun.*

backbite *verb intrans and trans* (*past tense* **backbit,** *past part.* **backbitten**) to say mean or spiteful things about (somebody). ➤➤ **backbiter** *noun.*

backblocks *pl noun Aus, NZ* remote or culturally backward areas: *She's gone to be a nurse somewhere in Queensland's backblocks.* ➤➤ **backblock** *adj.* [from BLOCK¹ in the sense of 'area of land']

backboard *noun* **1** a board worn to support or straighten a person's back. **2** a rounded or rectangular board behind the basket on a basketball court.

back boiler *noun chiefly Brit* a domestic boiler fitted at the back of a coal or gas fire and heated by it.

backbone *noun* **1** = SPINAL COLUMN. **2a** the foundation or most substantial part of something: *these families, who had formed the backbone of the village life in the past, who were the depositaries of village traditions* — Hardy. **b** a chief mountain ridge, range, or system. **3** a firm and resolute character.

backbreaking *adj* physically taxing or exhausting.

backchat *noun chiefly Brit* impudent or argumentative talk made in reply, *esp* by a child or subordinate.

backcloth *noun* **1** *Brit* a painted cloth hung across the rear of a theatre stage. **2** = BACKGROUND (1A), (3A).

backcomb *verb trans* to comb (the hair) against the direction of growth starting with the short underlying hairs in order to produce a bouffant effect.

back country *noun NAmer, Aus, NZ* a sparsely populated rural area.

backdate *verb trans* **1** to apply (a measure or reward) retrospectively. **2** to date (a document) with an earlier date than the actual date.

back door *noun* **1** a door at the rear of a building. **2** an indirect, underhand, or unfair means of access. ➤➤ **backdoor** *adj.*

back down *verb intrans* to concede defeat or give up an argument or claim.

backdrop *noun* = BACKCLOTH.

backed *adj* (*used in combinations*) having a back of the kind specified: *high-backed.*

backfield *noun* in American football, the positions of players who line up behind the line of scrimmage, or the players in these positions.

backfill¹ *verb trans* **1** to fill (a trench or hole) with the soil that was dug out of it. **2** to replace (soil) in a hole or trench, e.g. after an archaeological investigation.

backfill² *noun* soil dug out of a hole or trench and later used to refill it.

backfire¹ *verb intrans* **1** said of a vehicle or its engine: to undergo a premature explosion in a cylinder or in the exhaust system and make a loud bang as a result. **2** to have the reverse of the desired or expected effect, *esp* causing problems that seem to repay unkindness or malicious intent.

backfire² *noun* an instance of a vehicle backfiring.

back-formation *noun* the formation of a word by subtraction of an element from an existing word, or a word formed in this way, e.g. *burgle* from *burglar.*

Word history

Some back-formations are very old: *pea* and *cherry* were both formed in the Middle English period when people removed what they believed to be a plural suffix from the forms *pease* and *cherise,* and *grovel* and *sidle* are long-established verbs created by back-formation from adjectives. In modern English, the great majority of back-formations are verbs formed from nouns.

backgammon /'bakgamən/ *noun* **1** a board game for two players played with dice and counters in which each player tries to move his or her counters along the board and at the same time to block or capture his or her opponent's counters. **2** the most complete form of win in this game. [perhaps from BACK³ + Middle English *gamen, game* GAME¹]

background *noun* **1a** the scenery or ground behind something. **b** the part of a painting or photograph that depicts what lies behind objects in the foreground. **2** an inconspicuous position: *He prefers to remain in the background.* **3a** the conditions that form the setting within which something is experienced. **b** information essential to the understanding of a problem or situation. **c** the total of a person's experience, knowledge, and education. **4** = BACKGROUND NOISE. **5** = BACKGROUND RADIATION. **6** in computing, low-priority tasks and processes performed by a computer without direct involvement of the operator.

background interference *noun* = BACKGROUND NOISE.

background music *noun* **1** music to accompany the action of a film or a radio or television drama, etc. **2** music played in order to create a certain atmosphere, e.g. in a restaurant or airport.

background noise *noun* intrusive sound or signals that interfere with received or recorded electronic signals.

background radiation *noun* a low level of radiation found throughout the natural environment emanating from naturally occurring radioactive isotopes in the soil, etc.

backhand¹ *noun* **1a** a stroke in tennis, squash, etc made with the back of the hand turned in the direction of movement, or the side of the body on which this is made. **b** the side of a court on which such strokes are usu made. **2** handwriting whose strokes slant downward from left to right.

backhand² *adv* with a backhand.

backhand³ *verb trans* to strike (a ball) with a backhand.

backhanded¹ *adj* **1** using or made with a backhand: *a backhanded volley.* **2** said of writing: being backhand. **3** said *esp* of a compliment: ambiguous or ironic; apparently complimentary but with an uncomplimentary edge to it. ➤➤ **backhandedly** *adv.*

backhanded² *adv* with a backhand.

backhander *noun* **1** a backhanded blow or stroke. **2** *Brit* a backhanded compliment or remark. **3** *informal* a bribe.

backing *noun* **1a** support or aid, *esp* financial. **b** endorsement. **2** something forming a back or reverse side. **3** the musical or vocal accompaniment to a song or singer.

backlash *noun* **1** a sudden violent backward movement or reaction. **2** a strong adverse reaction, e.g. to a recent political or social development.

backlift *noun* = BACKSWING.

backlist *noun* a list of a publishing company's publications that are still in print, e.g. because of continuing public demand for them.

backlog *noun* **1** an accumulation of tasks not performed, orders unfulfilled, or materials not processed. **2** a reserve. [BACK³ + LOG¹; orig meaning large log of wood at the back of a fire, which would carry on smouldering after the rest of the wood burned]

backmarker *noun* a competitor at the back of a field in a race.

backmost *adj* farthest back.

back number *noun* **1** an old issue of a periodical or newspaper. **2** *informal* somebody or something regarded as hopelessly outdated.

back of beyond *noun* (**the back of beyond**) a remote inaccessible place: *They lived in an old house in the back of beyond.*

back off *verb intrans* to retreat or shy away from a confrontation.

back out *verb intrans* to withdraw from a commitment or contest.

backpack[1] *noun* **1** = RUCKSACK. **2** a piece of equipment designed to be carried on the back while in use: *Each astronaut carries an oxygen backpack for lunar exploration.*

backpack[2] *verb intrans* to travel or hike carrying food, equipment, or belongings in a backpack. ➤➤ **backpacker** *noun.*

back passage *noun chiefly Brit, euphem* the rectum.

backpedal *verb intrans* (**backpedalled, backpedalling,** *NAmer* **backpedaled, backpedaling**) **1** to pedal the pedals of a bicycle in the opposite direction to normal, e.g. in order to slow down or brake. **2** to back down from or reverse a previous opinion or stand. **3** to move backwards, e.g. in boxing.

back projection *noun* the projecting of a film or slides onto a translucent screen from a projector behind the screen, in order to provide a background for the action of a film or play being enacted in front of the screen, for example to give the illusion of movement.

backroom *adj* **1** relating to a directing group that exercises its authority in an inconspicuous and indirect way. **2** relating to somebody who works behind the scenes, doing work that is often not publicly acknowledged.

back room *noun* a place where work is carried out, decisions are made, etc in secret, supposedly or in fact.

back row *noun* in rugby, the players in the back row of each team's half of a scrum.

backscattering *or* **backscatter** *noun* the scattering of radiation backwards due to reflection from particles of the medium traversed.

backscratch *verb intrans informal* to engage in backscratching.

backscratching *noun informal* doing favours for people in return for favours received, often in a secretive or underhanded way. [from the saying 'You scratch my back and I'll scratch yours']

back seat *noun* an inferior or unobtrusive position: *She won't take a back seat to anyone.*

back-seat driver *noun informal* a car passenger who offers unwanted advice to the driver.

back shift *noun* in shift work, a shift between or overlapping the day shift and the night shift, usu beginning in the afternoon and ending in the evening, or the workers on that shift.

backside *noun informal* the buttocks.

backsight *noun* the sight nearest the eye on a firearm.

back slang *noun* a type of slang created by spelling a word backwards and pronouncing it accordingly, e.g. *yob* for *boy.*

backslapping *noun* excessive cordiality or good fellowship. ➤➤ **backslapper** *noun.*

backslide *verb intrans* (*past tense* **backslid** /'bakslid/, *past part.* **backslid** /'bakslid/ *or* **backslidden** /'bakslid(ə)n/) to lapse morally or in the practice of religion. ➤➤ **backslider** *noun.*

backspace[1] *verb intrans* to press a key on a typewriter or computer keyboard which causes the carriage or cursor to move back one space.

backspace[2] *noun* the key on a typewriter or computer keyboard which when pressed causes the carriage or cursor to move back one space.

backspin *noun* spin of a ball in a direction opposite to that of the ball's forward motion: compare TOPSPIN.

backstabbing *noun* harmful or disloyal behaviour towards somebody to whom one seemed to be a friend. ➤➤ **backstabber** *noun.*

backstage[1] *adv* **1** in or to an area out of view of a theatre audience. **2** in private or secretly.

backstage[2] *adj* **1** of or occurring in the parts of a theatre that cannot be seen by the audience. **2** of the inner working or operation, e.g. of an organization.

backstairs[1] *pl noun* stairs at the back of a building, in some buildings, *esp* formerly, for private use or for the use of servants.

backstairs[2] *or* **backstair** *adj* **1** secret or furtive: *backstairs political deals.* **2** sordid or scandalous: *backstairs gossip.*

backstay *noun* a STAY[3] (rope on a ship) extending aft from a masthead to the stern or side of the ship.

backstitch[1] *noun* a method of hand sewing in which each new stitch is formed by inserting the needle a stitch length behind and bringing it out a stitch length in front of the end of the previous stitch.

backstitch[2] *verb trans and intrans* to sew (something) using backstitch.

backstop *noun* **1** something at the back serving as a stop, e.g. to prevent something from rolling or sliding backwards. **2** a player whose position is behind the batter, *esp* the catcher in baseball.

backstreet[1] *noun* a street, usu small and narrow, that is not a main street or attached to a main street in a town.

backstreet[2] *adj* made, done, or acting illegally or surreptitiously: *backstreet abortions.*

backstroke *noun* a swimming stroke executed on the back using reverse overarm strokes and kicking movements of the feet. ➤➤ **backstroker** *noun.*

backswing *noun* the movement of a bat, arm, etc backwards to a position from which the forward or downward swing is made.

back-to-back *noun* (*pl* **back-to-backs**) a two-storey terraced house built with its back against the back of a parallel terrace.

backtrack *verb intrans* **1** to retrace a path or course. **2** to reverse one's position or stand.

backup *noun* **1** somebody or something that serves as a substitute, auxiliary, or alternative. **2** somebody or something that gives support or is ready to if called upon. **3** in computing, the process of backing up data, or a copy of data made in this way.

back up *verb trans* **1a** to support (somebody) in an argument or proposal. **b** to give support to (an argument, etc). **2** in computing, to make a security copy of (data, a file, etc). **3** to hold (something) back; to cause (something) to accumulate: *The dam was backing up an immense quantity of water.* ➤ *verb intrans* **1** in computing, to make a copy of data, a file, etc, *esp* for security reasons. **2** said of traffic: to form an increasing queue behind a hazard or congestion. **3** in cricket, said of the non-receiving batsman: to move forward down the wicket when the ball is bowled to be ready to make a run.

backveld /'bakfelt/ *noun SAfr* a remote or culturally backward area. [BACK[3] + Afrikaans *veld* field]

backward[1] /'bakwəd/ *adj* **1a** directed or turned backwards. **b** done or executed backwards: *a backward somersault.* **2** affected by a developmental disability. **3** diffident or shy. **4** in cricket, of or occupying a fielding position behind the batsman's wicket. ➤➤ **backwardly** *adv,* **backwardness** *noun.*

backward[2] *adv NAmer* see BACKWARDS.

backwardation /bakwə'daysh(ə)n/ *noun Brit* **1** the difference between the spot price of a commodity and the forward price, *esp* when the forward price is lower. **2** formerly, a premium paid by a seller to a buyer of shares to postpone delivery until a future day of settlement.

backwards (*NAmer* **backward**) *adv* **1** towards the back. **2** with the back foremost. **3** in a reverse direction or towards the beginning: *Why teach them to say the alphabet backwards?* **4** perfectly; thoroughly: *She knows the procedure backwards.* **5** towards the past. **6** towards or into a worse state. ✳ **backwards and forwards** from one place to another and back again repeatedly; to and fro: *My mother has been ill so we have been running backwards and forwards to Glasgow for the past couple of months.* **bend/fall/lean over backwards** to make extreme efforts, *esp* in order to please or conciliate somebody: *They bent over backwards to make us feel welcome.*

backwash *noun* **1a** a backward movement in air, water, etc produced by a propelling force, e.g. the motion of oars. **b** the backward movement of a receding wave. **2** a usu unwelcome consequence or by-product of an event; an aftermath.

backwater *noun* **1** a stagnant pool or inlet kept filled by the opposing current of a river. **2** a place or condition that is isolated or backward, *esp* culturally or intellectually.

backwoods *noun chiefly NAmer* **1** (*usu* **the backwoods**) (*treated as sing. or pl*) heavily forested and uncultivated areas where few people live. **2** a remote or culturally backward area.

backwoodsman /'bakwoodzmən/ *noun* (*pl* **backwoodsmen**) **1** *chiefly NAmer* somebody who lives in the backwoods, or who has the skills and knowledge to survive in the backwoods. **2** an unsociable and uncultured person. **3** *Brit, informal* formerly, a member of the peerage who very rarely attended the House of Lords.

back yard *noun* **1** a yard at the back of one's house. **2** *NAmer* a back garden. **3** any area close to one's home, etc about which one feels some concern or responsibility and over the use of which one feels one should have some control.

bacon /'baykən/ *noun* meat cut from the cured and often smoked side of a pig. **✳ bring home the bacon 1** to achieve success. **2** to provide whatever is necessary for living, etc. **save somebody's bacon** *informal* to save somebody from serious danger or difficulty. [Middle English from Old French, of Germanic origin]

Baconian¹ /bay'kohni·ən/ *adj* **1** relating to the English philosopher and essayist Sir Francis Bacon, d.1626, or his empirical method of research in science. **2** relating to the theory that Sir Francis Bacon was the writer of the plays attributed to William Shakespeare.

Baconian² *noun* **1** a follower of Sir Francis Bacon, his philosophy, or his method of reasoning. **2** a supporter of the theory that Sir Francis Bacon was the writer of the plays attributed to William Shakespeare.

BACS *abbr* Bankers Automated Clearing Services, a company set up by UK banks to process computerized payments such as standing orders and direct debits.

bacteraemia (*NAmer* **bacteremia**) /baktə'reemi·ə/ *noun* the usu transient presence of micro-organisms, *esp* bacteria, in the blood. [scientific Latin *bacteraemia*, alteration of *bacteriaemia*, from BAC- TERI- + *-aemia* from Greek *-aimia*, from *haima* blood]

bacteri- *or* **bacterio-** *comb. form* forming words, denoting: bacteria: *bacteriolysis*. [scientific Latin *bacterium*: see BACTERIUM]

bacteria /bak'tiəri·ə/ *noun* pl of BACTERIUM.

Usage note

Bacteria is a plural noun and takes a plural verb. One single micro-organism is a *bacterium*.

bactericide /bak'tiərisied/ *noun* a substance that kills bacteria. **⟫ bactericidal** /-'siedl/ *adj*, **bactericidally** /-'sied(ə)li/ *adv*.

bacterio- *comb. form* see BACTERI-.

bacteriology /bak,tiəri'oləji/ *noun* **1** a science that deals with bacteria. **2** bacterial life and phenomena: *Let's look at the bacteriology of water supply*. **⟫ bacteriological** /-'lojik(ə)l/ *adj*, **bacteriologically** /-'lojikli/ *adv*, **bacteriologist** *noun*.

bacteriolysis /bak,tiəri'oləsis/ *noun* destruction or dissolution of bacterial cells. **⟫ bacteriolytic** /-'litik/ *adj*. [scientific Latin *bacteriolysis*, from BACTERIO- + -LYSIS]

bacteriophage /bak'tiəri·fayj/ *noun* any of various viruses that attack and destroy bacteria. **⟫ bacteriophagic** /-'fajik/ *adj*, **bacteriophagous** /-'ofəgəs/ *adj*, **bacteriophagy** /-'ofəji/ *noun*. [BAC- TERIO- + Greek *phagein* to eat]

bacteriostasis /bak,tiərioh'staysis/ *noun* inhibition of the growth of bacteria without their destruction. [scientific Latin *bacteriostasis*, from BACTERIO- + STASIS]

bacterium /bak'tiəri·əm/ *noun* (*pl* **bacteria** /-ə/) any of a group of unicellular microscopic organisms that live in soil, water, organic matter, or the bodies of plants and animals. They are important to human beings because of their chemical effects and because many of them cause diseases. **⟫ bacterial** *adj*, **bacterially** *adv*. [scientific Latin *bacterium* from Greek *baktērion* staff]

Bactrian camel /'baktri·ən/ *noun* one of two species of camel, having two humps: *Camelus bactrianus*. [from its habitat in *Bactria*, ancient country of SW Asia]

bad¹ /bad/ *adj* (**worse** /wuhs/, **worst** /wuhst/) **1a** failing to reach an acceptable standard; poor or inadequate. **b** unfavourable. **c** no longer acceptable or usable, because of decay or disrepair: *The apples had all gone bad; The house was in a bad condition*. **2a** morally objectionable. **b** mischievous or disobedient. **3** (*often* + at) unskilful or incompetent: *bad at crosswords*. **4** disagreeable or unpleasant: *bad news*. **5a** (+ for) injurious or harmful: *It is widely acknowledged that smoking is bad for your health*. **b** worse than usual; severe: *a bad cold*. **6** incorrect or faulty: *bad grammar*. **7a** suffering pain or distress; unwell: *If anything, she's worse today*. **b** unhealthy or diseased: *bad teeth*. **8** (*often* + about) regretful or remorseful: *You mustn't feel bad about refusing*. **9** invalid or worthless: *a bad cheque*. **10** said of a debt: not collectible; not going to be paid. **11** (**badder, baddest**) *chiefly NAmer, informal* excellent or admirable. **✳ in a bad way** in

an unfortunate or undesirable state, e.g. ill, in difficulty, etc. **not bad** *informal* quite good. **too bad 1** *informal* regrettable; unfortunate. **2** *informal* said dismissively or philosophically, unfortunate but unable to be changed and therefore to be accepted. **⟫ baddish** *adj*, **badness** *noun*. [Middle English, perhaps from Old English *bæddel* hermaphrodite]

bad² *noun* **1** unfortunate or unhappy circumstances: *You have to take the bad with the good*. **2** an evil, unhappy, or otherwise undesirable state: *They say she's gone to the bad*.

bad³ *adv informal* badly; with ill feeling, sorrow, etc: *Her husband fooling around with other women hit her pretty bad*.

bad blood *noun* **1** dubious or disreputable ancestry, parentage, etc: *She … bade them take good heed of the child, for she came of bad blood* — Dickens. **2** ill feeling or bitterness: *The court heard that there was a background of bad blood between the families* — The Scotsman.

baddie *or* **baddy** /'badi/ *noun* (*pl* **baddies**) *informal* somebody or something bad, frightening, or dangerous, e.g. an opponent of the hero in fiction or the cinema.

bade /bad, bayd/ *verb* past tense of BID¹.

badge¹ /baj/ *noun* **1** a device or token, *esp* of membership in a society or group. **2** a characteristic mark. **3** an emblem awarded for a particular accomplishment. [Middle English *bage, bagge*; earlier history unknown]

badge² *verb trans* to mark or provide (somebody or something) with a badge or emblem.

badger¹ /'bajə/ *noun* **1** either of two species of sturdy burrowing nocturnal mammals widely distributed in the northern hemisphere, typically black or dark grey with white striped facial markings: *Meles meles* and *Taxidea taxus*. **2** the pelt or fur of a badger. [prob from BADGE¹, from the white mark on its forehead]

badger² *verb trans* (**badgered, badgering**) to harass or annoy (somebody) persistently. [from the sport of baiting badgers]

bad hair day *noun informal* a day on which everything goes wrong.

badinage /'badinahzh, -nij/ *noun* playful repartee; banter: *She was waiting for him; waiting with song and story and badinage, sparkling, fanciful, capricious* — Lew Wallace. [French *badinage*, from *badiner* to joke]

badlands *pl noun chiefly NAmer* a barren region marked by extensive rock erosion with fantastic hill formations and deep ravines.

bad lot *noun* a disreputable or dishonest person.

badly *adv* **1** in an unsatisfactory, incorrect, unsuitable, etc way. **2** unkindly; cruelly. **3** unsuccessfully. **4** severely: *She's badly ill*. **5** very much: *I need that money badly*. **✳ badly off** in an unsatisfactory condition, *esp* not having enough money.

badminton /'badmint(ə)n/ *noun* a court game played with light long-handled rackets and a shuttlecock that is volleyed over a net. [named after *Badminton*, estate in SW England, where it was first played]

badmouth *verb trans informal* to criticize or speak badly of (somebody or something): *So why do we keep badmouthing ourselves all the time?* — Punch.

bad news *noun informal* something or somebody likely to cause difficulties and therefore best avoided or got rid of: *She got herself a boyfriend who was really bad news*.

bad-tempered *adj* angry, or easily made angry. **⟫ bad-temperedly** *adv*, **bad-temperedness** *noun*.

BAe *abbr* British Aerospace.

Baedeker /'baydikə/ *noun* any of a series of guidebooks, mainly on European countries and cities, started by Karl *Baedeker*, d. 1859, German publisher.

baffle¹ /'bafl/ *verb trans* **1** to throw (somebody) into puzzled confusion; to perplex (them). **2** to deflect, check, or regulate (fluid, light, sound waves, etc) by means of a baffle. **⟫ bafflement** *noun*, **baffler** *noun*, **baffling** *adj*, **bafflingly** *adv*. [prob alteration of Middle English (Scots) *bawchillen* to denounce, discredit publicly]

baffle² *noun* **1** a device, e.g. a plate, wall, or screen, to deflect, check, or regulate flow, e.g. of a fluid or light. **2** a structure that reduces the exchange of sound waves between the front and back of a loudspeaker.

baffling wind *noun* a light wind that frequently shifts from one point to another.

BAFTA /'baftə/ *abbr* British Academy of Film and Television Arts.

bag¹ /bag/ *noun* **1a** a usu flexible container for holding, storing, or carrying something. **b** a handbag or shoulder bag. **2** something resembling a bag, *esp* a sagging in cloth or a sagging of the skin under the eyes: *Look at the bags under my eyes!* **3a** a quantity of game taken or permitted to be taken. **b** spoils or loot. **4** *chiefly Brit, informal (in pl)* a great deal; lots: *She has bags of money.* **5** *informal, derog* a woman regarded dismissively: *Who cares about that silly old bag?* **6** *informal* something that somebody particularly likes or does: *Crosswords were his bag.* ✳ **bag and baggage 1** with all one's belongings. **2** entirely or wholesale [orig a military term for the personal belongings carried in soldiers' bags plus the regiment's movable equipment; to march out with bag and baggage was to retreat without losing either]. **in the bag** *informal* as good as achieved, or already certain before formally decided or declared. ➤➤ **bagful** (*pl* **bagfuls**) *noun*. [Middle English *bagge* from Old Norse *baggi*]

bag² *verb* (**bagged, bagging**) ➤ *verb intrans* **1** to swell out; to bulge. **2** to hang loosely. ➤ *verb trans* **1** to put (something) into a bag. **2a** to get possession of (something). **b** *informal* to steal (something). **c** *informal* to claim (something) or the right to do (something): *I bag the first shot.* **d** to take (animals) as game. **3** to cause (something) to swell. ➤ **bags I/bags** *Brit, informal* a phrase used, *esp* by children, in claiming something or the right to do something: *Bags I the first shot on the swings.*

bagasse /bə'gas/ *noun* the residue of sugarcane, grapes, etc left after a product, e.g. juice, has been extracted. [French *bagasse* from Spanish *bagazo* pulp]

bagatelle /bagə'tel/ *noun* **1** something unimportant or of little value. **2** a game in which balls must be put into or through cups or arches at one end of an oblong table with pins as obstacles. **3** a short light piece of music. [French *bagatelle* from Italian *bagattella*]

bagel /'baygl/ *noun* a hard glazed ring-shaped bread roll. [Yiddish *beygel*, derivative of Old High German *boug* ring]

baggage /'bagij/ *noun* **1** luggage, *esp* for travel by sea or air. **2** portable equipment, *esp* of a military force. **3** superfluous or useless things, ideas, or practices. **4** the sum of a person's earlier experiences, opinions, or knowledge regarded as a hindrance to or influence on their response to subsequent events and conditions: *You have to jettison your cultural baggage if you're going to succeed as a missionary.* **5** *informal, humorous, or derog* an impudent girl or young woman. [Middle English *bagage* from Old French, from *bague* bundle; (sense 5) prob modification of Old French *bagasse* from Old Provençal *bagassa*]

baggy /'bagi/ *adj* (**baggier, baggiest**) loose, puffed out, or hanging like a bag: *baggy trousers.* ➤➤ **baggily** *adv*, **bagginess** *noun*.

bag lady *noun informal* a homeless woman who lives on the streets, typically carrying all her belongings in shopping bags: *the bag ladies who shuffle their pathetic bundles of possessions into Grand Central Station every night* — The Guardian.

bagman *noun* (*pl* **bagmen**) **1** *chiefly Brit, dated* a sales representative; a travelling salesman. **2** *chiefly NAmer* a person who collects or distributes dishonestly or illegally gained money on behalf of another. **3** *Aus* a tramp; a swagman.

bagnio /'bahnyoh/ *noun* (*pl* **bagnios**) **1** a brothel. **2** formerly, a prison in the Middle or Far East *esp* for slaves. [Italian *bagno* public baths, via Latin from Greek *balaneion*; (sense 2) from the use of Roman baths at Constantinople for imprisonment of Christian prisoners by the Turks]

bagpipe *noun* (*also in pl*) a wind instrument consisting of a mouth tube, chanter, and drone pipes, sounded by the pressure of wind emitted from a leather bag squeezed by the player. ➤➤ **bagpiper** *noun*.

bags /bagz/ *pl noun* = OXFORD BAGS.

baguette /ba'get/ *noun* **1** a long thin French loaf. **2** the shape of a long narrow rectangle, or a gemstone cut into this shape. **3** in architecture, a moulding like the ASTRAGAL (narrow half-round moulding) but smaller. [French *baguette* rod]

bah /bah/ *interj* used to express disdain.

Baha'i¹ /bə'hah-ee/ *noun* (*pl* **Baha'is**) **1** a religious movement originating among Babis in Iran in the 19th cent. and emphasizing the spiritual unity of humankind and all religions. **2** an adherent of this religion. ➤➤ **Baha'ism** *noun*, **Baha'ist** *noun*. [Persian *bahā'ī* of glory, from Arabic *bahā* glory. From Arabic *Bahā'Allāh* the Glory

of God, a name given to Mirza Hussein Ali Nuri (d.1892), founder of the religion]

Baha'i² *adj* relating to Baha'ism.

Bahamian /bə'haymi-ən/ *noun* a native or inhabitant of the Bahamas. ➤➤ **Bahamian** *adj*.

Bahasa Indonesia /bah'hahsə/ *noun* a form of Malay that is the official language of Indonesia. [Indonesian *bahasa indonésia* Indonesian language]

Bahraini *or* **Bahreini** /bah'rayni/ *noun* (*pl* **Bahrainis** *or* **Bahreinis**) a native or inhabitant of Bahrain, a sultanate in the Persian Gulf. ➤➤ **Bahraini** *adj*, **Bahreini** *adj*.

baht /haht/ *noun* (*pl* **bahts** *or* **baht**) the basic monetary unit of Thailand. [Thai *bāt*]

bail¹ /bayl/ *noun* **1** security deposited as a guarantee that somebody temporarily freed from custody will return to stand trial. **2** temporary release on bail. **3** somebody who provides bail. ✳ **go/stand bail** to act as or provide security for somebody who has been freed from custody temporarily. **jump bail** said of somebody who has been released on bail: to fail to appear for trial. [Middle English *bail*, custody, security for appearance, via Old French from Latin *bajulare* to carry a load]

bail² *verb trans* **1** to release (somebody) on bail. **2** (*often* + out) to procure the release of (a person in custody) by giving bail. **3** to deliver (property) in trust to another person for a special purpose and for a limited period. ➤➤ **bailable** *adj*, **bailee** /bay'lee/ *noun*, **bailment** *noun*, **bailor** *noun*. [(senses 1, 2) from BAIL¹; (sense 3) from Anglo-French *baillier* to deliver]

bail³ *noun* **1** in cricket, either of the two crosspieces that lie on the stumps to form the wicket. **2a** *chiefly Brit* a partition for separating animals. **b** *Aus, NZ* a device for holding a cow's head when it is being milked. **3** a bar for holding paper steady on a typewriter or printer. [Middle English *baille* bailey, from Old French]

bail⁴ *or* **bale** *noun* a container used to remove water from a boat. [Middle English *baille* via Old French from medieval Latin *bajula* water vessel]

bail⁵ *or* **bale** *verb trans* (*usu* + out) to clear (water) from a boat by collecting it in a bail, bucket etc and throwing it over the side. ➤ *verb intrans* **1** (*usu* + out) to parachute from an aircraft. **2** *informal* (*usu* + out) to flee a difficult or dangerous situation, often leaving others in trouble or with onerous responsibilities. ➤➤ **bailer** *noun*.

bailey /'bayli/ *noun* (*pl* **baileys**) the outer wall of a castle or any of several walls surrounding the keep, or the area enclosed by it: compare WARD¹. [Middle English *bailli* from Old French *baille, balie* palisade, bailey]

Bailey bridge /'bayli/ *noun* a prefabricated bridge built from interchangeable latticed steel panels. [named after Sir Donald Bailey d.1985, English engineer, who designed it]

bailie /'bayli/ *noun* a Scottish municipal magistrate. [Middle English: see BAILIFF]

bailiff /'baylif/ *noun* **1** *chiefly Brit* an official employed by a sheriff to serve writs, seize property, make arrests, etc. **2** *chiefly Brit* somebody who manages an estate or farm, or who acts as the agent of a landlord. **3** *NAmer* an official in a law court who is responsible for prisoners and keeping order. **4** *Brit* formerly, the chief officer of a sovereign in a district. ➤➤ **bailiffship** *noun*. [Middle English *baillif, bailie*, from Old French *baillif*, from *bail*: see BAIL¹]

bailiwick /'bayliwik/ *noun* **1** the area of jurisdiction of a bailie or bailiff. **2** a person's particular area of responsibility or sphere of knowledge or interest: *But you never do presentations; that's my bailiwick.* [Middle English *baillifwik*, from BAILIFF + *wik* dwelling place, village, from Old English *wīc*]

bail out *or* **bale out** *verb trans* to help (somebody) out of a predicament or free (somebody) from difficulty.

bail up *verb trans Aus, NZ* **1** to secure (a cow's head) in a bail during milking. **2** to make (somebody) a captive, either by force, e.g. in order to rob them, or by engaging them in conversation. ➤ *verb intrans* **1** said of a cow: to be held by a bail while being milked. **2** to surrender; to submit to being robbed.

bain-marie /banh mə'ree/ (*French* bɛ̃ mari)/ *noun* (*pl* **bains-marie** *or* **bain-maries** /banh mə'ree/) a vessel of hot or boiling water into which another vessel, containing food, is placed, in order to cook or heat the food gently: compare DOUBLE SAUCEPAN.

Word history
French *bain marie*, from early French, literally 'bath (of) Mary', from medieval Latin *balneum Mariae*. 'Mary' was an Egyptian alchemist fl. second cent. BC, credited with inventing heating apparatus.

Bairam /bie'rahm, bie'ram, 'bie-/ *noun* either of two annual Muslim festivals, the Lesser Bairam occurring at the end of Ramadan and the Greater Bairam 70 days later at the end of the Muslim year. [Turkish *bayram*]

bairn /bean/ *noun chiefly Scot, N Eng* a child. [Middle English *bern, barn*, from Old English *bearn* and Old Norse *barn*]

bait[1] /bayt/ *noun* **1a** something used in luring an animal, *esp* to a hook or trap. **b** a poisonous material placed where it will be eaten by pests. **2** a lure or temptation of any kind. **3** see BATE[2]. [Old Norse *beit* pasturage and *beita* food; related to Old English *bītan* BITE[1]]

bait[2] *verb trans* **1** to provoke, tease, or exasperate (somebody) with unjust, nagging, or persistent remarks. **2** to harass (e.g. a chained animal) with dogs, usu for sport. **3** to provide (something) with bait: *All the hooks were baited.* ⏵ **baiter** *noun*. [Middle English *baiten* from Old Norse *beita*; related to Old English *bītan* BITE[1]]

baiza /'biezah/ *noun* (*pl* **baiza** *or* **baizas**) a unit of currency in Oman, worth 1000th of a rial. [colloquial Arabic *baiza* from Hindi *paisā* PAISA]

baize /bayz/ *noun* a woollen cloth resembling felt used chiefly as a covering, *esp* for billiard tables and card tables. [early French *baies*, pl of *baie* baize, fem of *bai* bay-coloured, from Latin *badius*]

Bajan /'bayjən/ *noun* a native or inhabitant of Barbados. ⏵⏵ **Bajan** *adj.* [by shortening and alteration from *Barbadian*]

bake[1] /bayk/ *verb trans* **1** to cook (food) by dry heat, *esp* in an oven. **2** to dry or harden (something, *esp* clay articles) by subjecting it to heat. ⏵ *verb intrans* **1** to cook food, e.g. bread and cakes, by baking. **2** to become baked. **3** to become extremely hot: *After a morning's sunbathing, I was beginning to bake.* ⏵ **baker** *noun*. [Old English *bacan*]

bake[2] *noun* **1** a batch of baked food, or a dish containing baked ingredients. **2** *NAmer* a social gathering at which baked food is served.

baked Alaska *noun* a baked dessert consisting of a meringue case filled with sponge cake and ice cream.

baked beans *pl noun* baked haricot beans, *esp* as sold tinned in tomato sauce.

bakehouse *noun* a place for baking food, *esp* bread.

Bakelite /'baykəliet/ *noun trademark* any of various synthetic resins and plastics. [named after L H *Baekeland* d.1944, Belgian-born chemist, who invented it]

baker's dozen /'baykəz/ *noun* thirteen. [prob from a former practice of selling 13 loaves for 12 to prevent accusations of giving short weight]

bakery /'bayk(ə)ri/ *noun* (*pl* **bakeries**) a place for baking or selling baked goods, *esp* bread and cakes.

baking powder *noun* a powder that consists of a bicarbonate and an acid substance, often cream of tartar, used in place of yeast as a raising agent in making scones, cakes, etc.

baking soda *noun* = SODIUM BICARBONATE.

baklava /'bahkləvah, 'bak-/ *noun* a sweet rich dessert of Turkish origin, made of thin layers of pastry containing nuts and honey. [Turkish *baklava*]

baksheesh /bak'sheesh, 'baksheesh/ *noun esp* in the Middle East, money given as a tip or bribe or as alms. [Persian *bakhshīsh*, from *bakhshīdan* to give]

bal. *abbr* in book-keeping, balance.

balaclava /balə'klahvə/ *noun* (*often* **Balaclava** *or* **Balaclava helmet**) a knitted pull-on hood that covers the ears, neck, and throat: *Balaclava helmet in crochet — Queen.*

Word history
named after *Balaclava* (now usu Balaklava), village in the Crimea, Ukraine, where a battle of the Crimean War was fought on 25 October 1854. Soldiers in the Crimea wore balaclavas to protect them from the bitter winter, but the name is not recorded until the 1880s.

balalaika /balə'liekə/ *noun* a musical instrument of Russian origin, having a triangular body and usu three strings, tuned in fourths, which are played by plucking. [Russian *balalaika*]

balance[1] /'baləns/ *noun* **1a** the ability to retain one's physical equilibrium, or the fact of retaining it: *She lost her balance and fell off the*

beam. **b** stability produced by even distribution of weight on each side of a vertical axis. **c** mental and emotional steadiness. **d** an aesthetically pleasing integration of elements. **2a** equilibrium between contrasting, opposing, or interacting elements. **b** equality between the totals of the two sides of an account. **3a** the difference between credits and debits in an account, or a statement of this. **b** something left over; a remainder. **c** an amount in excess, *esp* on the credit side of an account. **4** the weight or force of one side in excess of another: *The balance of the evidence lay on the side of the defendant.* **5a** an instrument for weighing, traditionally a centrally-supported beam that has two scalepans of equal weight suspended from its ends. **b** any device that measures weight and force. **c** (**the Balance**) the constellation and sign of the zodiac Libra. **6a** a counterbalancing weight, force, or influence. **b** = BALANCE WHEEL. **7** the point on the trigger side of a rifle at which the weight of the ends balance each other. * **in the balance** in an uncertain critical position, *esp* with the fate or outcome about to be determined: *The future of democracy was hanging in the balance.* **off balance** unevenly weighted; unstable. **on balance** all things considered. **strike a balance** to adopt a compromise position. ⏵⏵ **balanced** *adj*. [Middle English via Old French from late Latin *bilanc-, bilanx* having two scalepans, from Latin BI-[1] + *lanc-, lanx* plate]

balance[2] *verb intrans* **1** to be or become balanced or established in balance: *She sat balancing on the fence.* **2** (*often* + with) to be an equal counterpoise. **3** to waver or hesitate: *She has a mind that balances and deliberates.* **4** said of accounts, etc: to have the debit and credit totals equal. ⏵ *verb trans* **1** to bring (something) to a state or position of balance. **2a** to equal or equalize (two or more things) in weight, number, or proportion. **b** to counterbalance or offset (something). **3** to compare the relative importance, value, force, or weight of (something); to ponder (something). **4a** to calculate the difference between the debits and credits of (an account). **b** to pay the amount due on (e.g. a credit account). **5** to arrange (something) so that one set of elements exactly equals another: *They were given a number of mathematical equations to balance.* ⏵⏵ **balancer** *noun*.

balance beam *noun* a narrow horizontal wooden beam supported 1.2m (about 4ft) above the floor and used for balancing exercises, or the gymnastic event using this beam.

balance of payments *noun* the difference over a period of time between a country's payments to and receipts from abroad.

balance of power *noun* **1** an equilibrium of power sufficient to prevent one nation from imposing its will upon another. **2** a situation in which one group is in a position to support either of two other groups: *Neither the Tories nor Labour have a majority on the council, and the Lib Dems hold the balance of power.*

balance of trade *noun* the difference in value between a country's imports and exports.

balance sheet *noun* a statement of an organization's financial condition at a given date.

balance wheel *noun* a wheel that regulates or stabilizes the motion of a mechanism, e.g. a watch or clock.

balas ruby /'baləs/ *noun* (*pl* **balas rubies**) a gemstone consisting of a mixture of oxides of aluminium, iron and manganese and having a pale rose-red or orange colour. [Middle English via Old French from Arabic *balakhsh*, named after *Balakhshān*, ancient region of Afghanistan, where it is found]

balata /bə'lahtə/ *noun* **1** the dried juice of certain tropical American trees of the sapodilla family that is used as an alternative to gutta-percha, *esp* in belting and golf balls. **2** the main tree from which balata is obtained: *Manilkara bidentata*. [Spanish *balata*, of Cariban origin]

balboa /bal'boh-ə/ *noun* the basic monetary unit of Panama. [Spanish *balboa*, named after Vasco Núñez de *Balboa* d.1517, Spanish explorer and leader of the first successful Spanish settlement in Panama]

balcony /'balkəni/ *noun* (*pl* **balconies**) **1** a platform built out from the wall of a building and enclosed by a railing or low wall. **2** a gallery inside a building, e.g. a theatre. ⏵⏵ **balconied** *adj*. [Italian *balcone* from Old Italian *balcone* scaffold, of Germanic origin]

bald /bawld/ *adj* **1a** with a scalp on which some or all of the hair has fallen out, or has not yet grown. **b** having little or no tread: *bald tyres.* **c** lacking a natural or normal covering, e.g. of vegetation or nap. **2** blunt and unadorned or undisguised: *Tell me the bald truth.* **3** said of an animal: marked with white, *esp* on the head or face. ⏵⏵ **baldish** *adj*, **baldly** *adv*, **baldness** *noun*. [Middle English *balled*, perhaps of Celtic origin]

baldachin *or* **baldaquin** /'baldəkin/ *noun* **1** a cloth canopy fixed or carried over an important person or a sacred object. **2** an ornamental structure resembling a canopy, *esp* over an altar or shrine in a Christian church. **3** a richly embroidered fabric of silk and gold. [Italian *baldacchino*, from *Baldacco* Baghdad, city in Iraq]

bald eagle *noun* an eagle of N America that has a white head and neck when mature and eats fish and carrion: *Haliaeetus leucocephalus.*

balderdash /'bawldədash/ *noun* nonsense, often used as a general expression of disagreement: *'Such unscientific balderdash,' added the doctor* — Stevenson. [origin unknown]

bald-faced *adj NAmer* = BAREFACED.

baldie /'bawldi/ *noun and adj* see BALDY[1], BALDY[2].

balding /'bawldiŋ/ *adj* becoming bald.

baldric /'bawldrik/ *noun* an often ornamented belt worn over one shoulder and across the body to support a sword, bugle, etc. [Middle English *baudry, baudrik* from Old French *baudre*]

baldy[1] *or* **baldie** /'bawldi/ *noun* (*pl* **baldies**) *informal, derog* somebody who is bald or balding.

baldy[2] *or* **baldie** *adj* (**baldier, baldiest**) *informal, derog* bald or balding.

bale[1] /bayl/ *noun* **1** a large bundle of goods, *esp* a large closely pressed package of merchandise bound and usu wrapped for storage or transportation. **2** the weight of a bale of goods, e.g. 500lb (226.8kg) of cotton. [Middle English from Old French, of Germanic origin]

bale[2] *verb trans* to tie (goods) into bales or bundles. ➤➤ **baler** *noun*.

bale[3] *noun and verb Brit* see BAIL[4], BAIL[5].

bale[4] *noun* **1** great evil. **2** *archaic* sorrow; woe. [Old English *bealu*]

baleen /bə'leen/ *noun* = WHALEBONE. [Middle English *baleine* via Latin from Greek *phallaina* whale]

baleen whale *noun* any of various usu large whales that have whalebone plates instead of teeth which they use to filter KRILL (small shrimplike animals) from large volumes of sea water: suborder Mysticeti.

baleful /'baylf(ə)l/ *adj* **1** deadly or pernicious in influence. **2** gloomily threatening; menacing: *A baleful light sprang up in his gray eyes* — Conan Doyle. ➤➤ **balefully** *adv,* **balefulness** *noun.* [BALE[4]]

bale out *verb trans Brit* see BAIL OUT.

Balinese /bali'neez/ *noun* (*pl* **Balinese**) **1** a native or inhabitant of Bali, island of Indonesia. **2** the Austronesian language of this people. ➤➤ **Balinese** *adj.*

balk[1] (*Brit* **baulk**) /bawlk, bawk/ *verb intrans* **1** (*usu* + at) to stop short and refuse to proceed. **2** (*often* + at) to refuse abruptly: *They balked at the suggestion.* ➤ *verb trans* to check or stop (somebody or something) by an obstacle; to thwart (somebody or something). ➤➤ **balker** *noun.*

balk[2] (*Brit* **baulk**) *noun* **1** a ridge of land left unploughed. **2** a roughly squared beam of timber. **3** the area behind the balk lines on a billiard table. **4** a hindrance or obstacle. **5** in baseball, an illegal movement by the pitcher. [Old English *balca* from Old Norse *bálkr* partition]

Balkan /'bawlkən/ *adj* relating to the Balkan Peninsula in SE Europe, or to the countries occupying it: Albania, Bosnia and Herzegovina, Bulgaria, Croatia, Greece, Macedonia, Romania, part of Turkey, and Yugoslavia: *the Balkan States.* [Turkish *balkan* mountains]

Balkanize *or* **Balkanise** /'bawlkəniez/ *verb trans* to divide (a region) into smaller and often mutually hostile units. ➤➤ **Balkanization** /-'zaysh(ə)n/ *noun.* [named after the *Balkan* Peninsula in SE Europe; from the way in which this territory has been divided into many small states in the 19th and 20th cents]

Balkans /'bawlkənz/ *pl noun* (**the Balkans**) the Balkan Peninsula or the countries occupying it.

balk line *noun* any of four lines parallel to the cushions of a billiard table, *esp* the line at one end behind which the cue balls are placed at the start of many games.

ball[1] /bawl/ *noun* **1a** a solid or hollow spherical or egg-shaped object used in a game or sport. **b** a delivery or play of the ball in cricket, baseball, etc: *It's infuriating when you're bowled by a bad ball.* **c** *chiefly NAmer* any game in which a ball is thrown, kicked, or struck, *esp* baseball. **2a** any round or roundish body or mass: *The wool is gathered into balls.* **b** a spherical or conical projectile, *esp* that

fired by a cannon. **3** the rounded slightly raised fleshy area at the base of a thumb or big toe. **4** *coarse slang.* **a** (*usu in pl*) a testicle. **b** (*in pl*) nonsense, often used to dismiss what somebody else has said. ✳ **on the ball** *informal* marked by being knowledgeable and competent; alert. **start/set/keep the ball rolling** to begin or continue something. **the ball is in your, his, etc court** it is up to you, him, etc to make the next move. [Middle English *bal* from Old Norse *böllr*]

ball[2] *verb trans* **1** to form or gather (something) into a ball. **2** *coarse slang* said of a person: to have sexual intercourse with (somebody). ➤ *verb intrans* to assume the form or shape of a ball.

ball[3] *noun* a large formal gathering for social dancing. ✳ **have a ball** *informal* to enjoy oneself. [French *bal* via Old French and late Latin from Greek *ballizein* to dance]

ballad /'baləd/ *noun* **1** a rhythmic poem of a kind that was orig sung by a strolling minstrel. **2** a slow, romantic or sentimental popular song, *esp* one that tells a story. ➤➤ **balladeer** /balə'diə/ *noun,* **balladic** /bə'ladik/ *adj,* **balladry** *noun.* [Middle English *balade* song sung while dancing, from early French *ballade* via Old Provençal from late Latin *ballare* to dance]

ballade /ba'lahd/ *noun* **1** a fixed verse form of usu three stanzas with recurrent rhymes, a short concluding verse, and an identical refrain for each part. **2** a musical composition, *esp* for piano, intended to suggest a narrative ballad. [Middle English *balade* from early French: see BALLAD]

ball-and-socket joint *noun* a joint in which a rounded part moves within a cuplike socket so as to allow free movement in many directions.

ballast[1] /'baləst/ *noun* **1a** heavy material carried in a ship to improve stability. **b** heavy material that is carried on a balloon or airship to steady it and can be jettisoned to control the rate of descent. **2** gravel or broken stone laid in a bed for railway lines or the lower layer of roads. **3** something that gives stability, *esp* in character or conduct. **4** a device used to stabilize the current in an electrical circuit. [prob from Low German, of Scandinavian origin]

ballast[2] *verb trans* **1** to steady or equip (something) with, or as if with, ballast. **2** to fill in (e.g. a railway bed) with ballast.

ball bearing *noun* a bearing in which hardened steel balls roll with minimal friction in a groove between a shaft and a support, or any of the balls in such a bearing.

ballboy *or* **ballgirl** *noun* a boy or girl who retrieves balls for the players during a tennis match.

ballbreaker *noun coarse slang* **1** a very difficult or demanding task. **2** a woman of strong character perceived as a threat to the dominance of a man or group of men. ➤➤ **ballbreaking** *adj.*

ballcock *noun* an automatic valve, *esp* in a cistern, controlled by the rise and fall of a float at the end of a lever.

ballerina /balə'reenə/ *noun* a female ballet dancer, *esp* the principal female dancer in a company. [Italian *ballerina*, from *ballare* to dance, from late Latin]

ballet /'balay; *NAmer also* ba'lay/ *noun* **1** a form of artistic dancing in which the graceful flowing movements are based on conventional positions and steps. **2** a theatrical art form using ballet dancing, music, and scenery to convey a story, theme, or atmosphere. **3** a group or company of performers of ballet. ➤➤ **balletic** /ba'letik/ *adj,* **balletically** /ba'letik(ə)li/ *adv.* [French *ballet* from Italian *balletto,* dimin. of *ballo* dance, from *ballare*: see BALLERINA]

balletomane /'balitəmayn/ *noun* a devotee of ballet. ➤➤ **balletomania** /-'mayni-ə/ *noun.* [BALLET + -O- + -*mane* from MANIA]

ball game *noun* **1a** a game played with a ball. **b** *NAmer* a baseball game. **2** *informal* a situation or set of circumstances: *That's a whole new ball game.*

ballgirl *noun* see BALLBOY.

ballista /bə'listə/ *noun* (*pl* **ballistae** /-tee/ *or* **ballistas**) an ancient military weapon, often in the form of a crossbow, for hurling large missiles. [Latin *ballista,* from assumed Greek *ballistēs,* from *ballein* to throw]

ballistic /bə'listik/ *adj* **1** of ballistics. **2** said of a measuring instrument: sensitive to sudden brief impulses, e.g. those produced by an electric current. **3** *informal* violently and uncontrollably angry; furious: *She'll go ballistic when you tell her.* ➤➤ **ballistically** *adv.* [Latin *ballista*: see BALLISTA]

ballistic missile *noun* a missile propelled and guided in ascent but falling freely in descent.

ballistics *pl noun* **1** (*treated as sing. or pl*) the science dealing with the motion of projectiles in flight. **2** the individual characteristics of and firing processes in a firearm or cartridge.

ball joint *noun* = BALL-AND-SOCKET JOINT.

ball lightning *noun* a rare form of lightning consisting of luminous balls that may move along solid objects or float in the air.

ballocks /'boləks/ *pl noun* see BOLLOCKS.

balloon[1] /bə'loohn/ *noun* **1a** a baglike fabric, etc container filled with hot air or a gas lighter than air so as to rise and float in the atmosphere. **b** an inflatable usu brightly coloured rubber bag used as a toy. **c** (*used before a noun*) resembling or suggesting a balloon: *a balloon sleeve.* **2** a line enclosing words spoken or thought by a character, *esp* in a cartoon. **3** = BALLOON GLASS. **✻ when the balloon goes up** *informal* when the trouble starts or the action begins. [French *ballon* large football, balloon, from Italian dialect *ballone* large football, augmentative of *balla* ball, of Germanic origin]

balloon[2] *verb intrans* **1** to ascend or travel in a balloon. **2** (*often + out*) to swell or puff out; to expand. **3** to increase rapidly. **4** to travel in a high curving arc. ➤ *verb trans* to cause (something) to inflate or distend. ➤➤ **ballooning** *noun*, **balloonist** *noun*.

balloon angioplasty /'anjiohplasti/ *noun* a medical operation in which a CATHETER (tubular device) with a balloon at the end of it is inserted into a vein or artery, the balloon then being inflated to unblock or widen the blood vessel.

balloon glass *noun chiefly Brit* a short-stemmed drinking glass with a pear-shaped bowl, used *esp* for brandy.

balloon tyre *noun* a large tyre that is inflated to low pressure to provide cushioning over rough surfaces.

ballot[1] /'balət/ *noun* **1** a vote in which votes are recorded and cast in secret. **2** the system of casting votes in secret. **3** a sheet of paper, or orig a small ball, used in a ballot. **4** the right to vote. **5** the number of votes cast. [Italian dialect *ballotta*, dimin. of Italian *balla*: see BALLOON[1]]

ballot[2] *verb* (**balloted, balloting**) ➤ *verb intrans* (*often + for*) to vote by ballot, or decide something in this way. ➤ *verb trans* to ask (somebody) to vote: *All union members will be balloted.* ➤➤ **balloter** *noun*.

ballot box *noun* **1** a sealed box into which ballot papers are put by voters. **2** voting; balloting: *These matters should be decided by the ballot box, not money and influence.*

ballot paper *noun* a paper on which a voter marks his or her vote or votes, e.g. in an election.

ballpark[1] *noun NAmer* a park in which ball games, *esp* baseball, are played. **✻ in the ballpark/in the right ballpark** *informal* roughly accurate.

ballpark[2] *adj informal* approximate: *Can you give me a ballpark figure?*

ballpoint *or* **ballpoint pen** *noun* a pen having as the writing point a small rotating metal ball that inks itself by contact with an inner magazine.

ballroom *noun* a large room for dances.

ballroom dancing *noun* a usu formal type of dancing done *esp* by couples for recreation, exhibition, or competition.

balls-aching *adj coarse slang* boring, tiresome, obnoxious or of a low standard. ➤➤ **balls-achingly** *adv*.

balls up (*NAmer* **ball up**) *verb trans coarse slang* to ruin or make a mess of (something, *esp* a task). ➤ *verb intrans coarse slang* to make a mistake that has this effect.

balls-up (*NAmer* **ball-up**) *noun coarse slang* a muddle; a bungled task or activity.

ballsy /'bawlzi/ *adj* (**ballsier, ballsiest**) *chiefly NAmer, informal* spirited or courageous. ➤➤ **ballsiness** *noun*.

ball up *verb NAmer* see BALLS UP.

ball-up *noun NAmer* see BALLS-UP.

ball valve *noun* a one-way valve consisting of a ball that rests inside a cylindrical seating over a hole and rises and falls by means of a spring, its own weight, or pressure of gases or liquids.

bally /'bali/ *adj and adv Brit, euphem* = BLOODY[1], BLOODY[3]. [alteration of BLOODY[1]]

ballyhoo[1] /bali'hooh/ *noun* (*pl* **ballyhoos**) **1** a noisy demonstration or talk. **2** flamboyant, exaggerated, or sensational advertising or promotion. [origin unknown]

ballyhoo[2] *verb trans* (**ballyhoos, ballyhooed, ballyhooing**) *chiefly NAmer* to give (something) flamboyant, exaggerated, or sensational publicity or propaganda.

ballyrag *verb* see BULLYRAG.

balm /bahm/ *noun* **1a** an aromatic and medicinal resin. **b** any of several species of trees that yield such a resin: genus *Commiphora*. **2** an aromatic preparation, e.g. a healing ointment. **3** something that soothes, relieves, or heals physically or emotionally: *whenever you are out of temper and wish to make yourself unpleasant by way of balm to your soul —* Samuel Butler. **4** any of several species of aromatic plants of the mint family, such as lemon balm: family Labiatae. [Middle English *basme, baume* via Old French and Latin from Greek *balsamon*]

balm of Gilead /'giliad/ *noun* **1a** a fragrant oily resin used *esp* in perfumery. **b** any of several species of small evergreen African and Asian trees from which it is obtained: genus *Commiphora*. **2** either of two poplars: **a** a N American tree with broad heart-shaped leaves: *Populus gileadensis*. **b** = BALSAM POPLAR. **3** a resin obtained from the balsam fir. [named after *Gilead*, region of ancient Palestine known for its balm (Jeremiah 8:22)]

balmoral /bal'morəl/ *noun* **1** a round flat brimless woollen Scottish cap with a pompom and sometimes a plume on one side and ribbons at the back. **2** a type of laced boot. [named after *Balmoral* Castle in NE Scotland]

balmy /'bahmi/ *adj* (**balmier, balmiest**) **1a** having the qualities of balm; soothing. **b** said of weather: pleasantly mild. **2** = BARMY. ➤➤ **balmily** *adv*, **balminess** *noun*. [(sense 2) by alteration]

balneology /balni'oləji/ *noun* the branch of medicine concerned with the therapeutic use of baths and mineral springs. ➤➤ **balneological** /-'lojikl/ *adj*, **balneologist** *noun*. [Latin *balneum* bath + -LOGY]

baloney *or* **boloney** /bə'lohni/ *noun* (*pl* **baloneys** *or* **boloneys**) **1** nonsense, often used as a general expression of disagreement. **2** *NAmer* = BOLOGNA. [perhaps alteration of BOLOGNA]

BALPA /'balpə/ *abbr* British Airline Pilots' Association.

balsa /'bawlsə, 'bolsə/ *noun* **1** (*also* **balsa wood**) the strong very light wood of a tropical American tree. **2** the tree from which balsa is obtained: *Ochroma lagopus*. [Spanish *balsa* raft, because the wood was used to make rafts and small boats]

balsam /'bals(ə)m, 'bols(ə)m/ *noun* **1** an oily and resinous substance released by various plants, or a medicinal preparation containing it. **2a** any of several trees that yield balsam. **b** any of a widely distributed genus of annual plants with watery juice, e.g. touch-me-not: genus *Impatiens*. **3** = BALM (3). ➤➤ **balsamic** /bal'-samik, bol-/ *adj*. [via Latin from Greek *balsamon* BALM]

balsam fir *noun* a coniferous American tree from which Canada balsam is prepared: *Abies balsamea*.

balsamic vinegar /bol'samik/ *noun* a dark Italian vinegar made from the juice of white grapes and matured in wooden casks.

balsam poplar *noun* a N American poplar that is often cultivated as a shade tree and yields balsam: *Populus balsamifera*.

Balti /'bahlti, 'bawlti/ *noun* a Tibeto-Burman language of N Kashmir. [the name in the dialect of Tibetan spoken in Ladakh, a region of NW India, Pakistan, and China]

balti /'balti, 'bawlti/ *noun* (*pl* **baltis**) a style of Indian cooking in which the food is cooked and served in a dish that resembles a small wok. [Urdu *bāltī* pail]

Baltic[1] /'bawltik, 'boltik/ *adj* **1** of the Baltic Sea or the countries that lie on its shores, *esp* Lithuania, Latvia, and Estonia: *the Baltic States*. **2** of a branch of the Indo-European languages including Latvian, Lithuanian, and Old Prussian. [medieval Latin (*mare*) *balticum* Baltic (Sea)]

Baltic[2] *noun* the Baltic languages.

Baltics /'bawltiks/ *pl noun* (**the Baltics**) the Baltic States.

Balto-Slavonic /'bawltoh, 'boltoh/ *noun* according to some, a subfamily of Indo-European languages consisting of the Baltic and the Slavonic branches. Its existence is not accepted by all linguists.

baluster /'baləstə/ *noun* an upright rounded, square, or vase-shaped support, *esp* for the rail of a staircase balustrade. [French *balustre* from Italian *balaustro* via Latin from Greek *balaustion* wild pomegranate flower; from its shape]

balustrade /balə'strayd, 'bal-/ *noun* a row of balusters topped by a rail, *esp* one that runs along the edge of a balcony or bridge. [French *balustrade* from Italian *balaustrata*, from *balaustro*: see BALUSTER]

bambino /bam'beenoh/ *noun* (*pl* **bambinos** *or* **bambini** /-nee/) **1** *informal* any young child. **2** a representation of the infant Christ. [Italian *bambino*, dimin. of *bambo* child]

bamboo /bam'booh/ *noun* (*pl* **bamboos**) **1** any of various chiefly tropical giant grasses including some with strong hollow stems used for building, furniture, or utensils: subfamily Bambusidae. **2** the stem of such a grass. [Malay *bambu*]

bamboo curtain *noun* (*often* **Bamboo Curtain**) a political, military, and ideological barrier between China and the capitalist world, also used to refer to similar barriers between Indochina and the West.

bamboozle /bam'boohzl/ *verb trans* **1** to deceive (somebody) by trickery. **2** to confuse or mystify. ➤➤ **bamboozlement** *noun*, **bamboozler** *noun*. [origin unknown]

ban¹ /ban/ *verb trans* (**banned, banning**) **1** to prohibit (something) or forbid (somebody) to do something, *esp* by legal means or social pressure. [Middle English *bannen* to summon, curse, from Old English *bannan* to summon]

ban² *noun* **1** a legal or social prohibition. **2** *archaic* a denunciation of somebody or something by the church: *a wretch, beneath the ban of Pope and Church* — Scott. **3** a curse: *Thou mixture rank, of midnight weeds collected; with Hecate's ban thrice blasted, thrice infected* — Shakespeare. [Middle English 'summoning of vassals for military service', partly from *bannen* BAN¹ and partly from Old French *ban*, of Germanic origin]

ban³ /bahn/ *noun* (*pl* **bani** /'bahni/) a unit of currency in Romania, worth 100th of a leu. [Romanian *ban* from Serbo-Croat *bān* lord]

banal /bə'nahl, NAmer also 'baynl/ *adj* lacking originality, freshness, or novelty; dull: *And when the remark comes it's always something he has seen and felt for himself – never a bit banal* — Henry James. ➤➤ **banality** /bə'nal-/ *noun*, **banally** *adv*. [French, from early French *banal* 'of compulsory feudal service', later 'possessed in common, commonplace', from *ban*: see BAN²]

BANANA /bə'nahnə/ *noun* a person who objects to a building development even though they will not themselves be inconvenienced by it; a more extreme form of a NIMBY. [acronym from *Build Absolutely Nothing Anywhere Near Anything*]

banana /bə'nahnə/ *noun* **1** an elongated usu tapering fruit with soft pulpy flesh enclosed in a soft usu yellow rind that grows in bunches. **2** any of several species of tropical trees that bear this fruit: genus *Musa*. [Spanish *banana* from Portuguese, ultimately of African origin; related to Wolof *banāna* banana]

banana republic *noun* *derog* a small tropical country that is politically unstable and economically underdeveloped. [from the dependence of some small tropical countries on their fruit-exporting trade]

bananas *adj* *informal* mad: *Call him that and he goes bananas.* [prob from *banana oil* nonsense, insincere or mad talk]

bancassurance /'bangkəshawrəns/ *noun* the selling of life assurance by banks and other financial institutions. [BANK⁴ + ASSURANCE]

band¹ /band/ *noun* **1** a narrow strip serving chiefly as decoration, *esp* a narrow strip of material applied as trimming to an article of dress. **2** a strip distinguishable in some way, e.g. by colour, texture, or composition. **3** an elongated surface or section with parallel or roughly parallel sides. **4** a strip or belt serving to join or hold things together or to transmit motion between e.g. wheels. **5** a ring of elastic used to hold things together. **6a** a more or less well-defined range of wavelengths, frequencies, or energies of light waves, radio waves, sound waves, etc. **b** a range of values. **7** *Brit* a group of pupils assessed as being of broadly similar ability: compare STREAM¹ (5), SET³ (3). **8** in computing, one or more tracks on a compact or floppy disk. **9** (*in pl*) two cloth strips sometimes worn at the front of the neck as part of clerical, legal, or academic dress. [Middle English *bande* strip, from Old French, ultimately of Germanic origin]

band² *verb intrans* **1** (*often* + together) to unite for a common purpose: *They all banded together to fight the enemy.* **2** *Brit* to divide pupils into bands. ➤ *verb trans* **1** to fasten a band to (something) or tie (something) up with a band. **2** to gather (people) together for a purpose; to unite (them). **3** *Brit* to divide (pupils) into bands. ➤➤ **bander** *noun*.

band³ *noun* (*treated as sing. or pl*) **1** a group of people, animals, or things. **2** a group of musicians playing jazz, pop, rock, or marching music. [Middle English from Old French *bande* troop, of Germanic origin]

bandage¹ /'bandij/ *noun* a strip of fabric used to dress and bind up wounds. ➤➤ **bandaging** *noun*. [early French *bandage*, from *bande*: see BAND¹]

bandage² *verb trans* to bind, dress, or cover (a wound or other injury) with a bandage. ➤➤ **bandager** *noun*.

Band-Aid¹ *noun* **1** *trademark* a small adhesive plaster with a gauze pad. **2** (*often* **band-aid**) *often derog* something that provides temporary or superficial relief.

Band-Aid² *adj* (*often* **band-aid**) *often derog* providing temporary or superficial relief; makeshift; ad hoc: *The Opposition derided the Government's band-aid solutions to the financial crisis.* [from BAND-AID¹]

bandanna *or* **bandana** /ban'danə/ *noun* a large colourful patterned handkerchief. [Hindi *bādhnū* tie-dyeing, tie-dyed cloth, from *bādhnā* to tie, from Sanskrit *badhnāti* he ties]

b and b *abbr* (*often* **B and B**) *Brit* bed and breakfast.

bandbox *noun* a usu cylindrical box of cardboard or thin wood used *esp* for holding hats.

bandeau /'bandoh/ *noun* (*pl* **bandeaux** /'bandohz/) a band of material worn round the head to keep the hair in place. [French *bandeau*, dimin. of *bande*: see BAND¹]

banded *adj* marked with bands of colour, etc.

banderilla /bandə'ree(l)yə/ *noun* a decorated barbed dart thrust into the neck or shoulders of the bull in a bullfight. [Spanish *banderilla*, dimin. of *bandera* banner, of Germanic origin]

banderillero /ˌbandəree(l)'yeəroh/ *noun* (*pl* **banderilleros**) a bullfighter whose task is to thrust banderillas into a bull's neck or shoulders in a bullfight. [Spanish *banderillo*, from *banderilla*: see BANDERILLA]

banderole *or* **banderol** /bandə'rohl/ *or* **bannerol** /banə'rohl/ *noun* **1** a long narrow forked flag or streamer. **2** a carved ribbon-like scroll with an inscription. [French *banderole* from Italian *banderuola*, dimin. of *bandiera* banner, of Germanic origin]

bandicoot /'bandikooht/ *noun* **1** (*also* **bandicoot rat**) either of two large rats found in India, Sri Lanka, and SE Asia: *Bandicota indica* and *Nesokia indica*. **2** any of several species of small insect- and plant-eating marsupial mammals of Australia, Tasmania, and New Guinea: family Peramelidae. [Telugu *pandikokku* pig-rat; the bandicoot of India and Sri Lanka is said to grunt like a pig]

bandit /'bandit/ *noun* (*pl* **bandits** *or occasionally* **banditti** /ban'-deeti/) an outlaw, *esp* a member of a band of armed robbers or marauders. ➤➤ **banditry** /-tri/ *noun*. [Italian *bandito*, past part. of *bandire* to banish, of Germanic origin]

bandleader *noun* the conductor of a dance band.

bandmaster *noun* a conductor of a brass band or military band.

bandolier *or* **bandoleer** /bandə'lia/ *noun* a belt worn over the shoulder and across the chest with pockets or loops for cartridges. [early French *bandouliere*, derivative of Old Spanish *bando* band, of Germanic origin]

band saw *noun* a power saw consisting of an endless steel blade running over pulleys.

bandsman *or* **bandswoman** *noun* (*pl* **bandsmen** *or* **bandswomen**) a member of a brass band or military band.

bandstand *noun* a usu roofed stand or platform for a brass band to perform on outdoors: *They ... proceeded to the bandstand ... stood a little while listening to the music of the military performers* — Hardy.

b and w *abbr* black and white.

bandwagon *noun* **1** a wagon for carrying a band in a parade. **2** a party, faction, or cause that attracts adherents by its timeliness, momentum, etc. * **jump/climb on the bandwagon** to attach oneself to a successful cause or enterprise in the hope of personal gain.

bandwidth *noun* a range of frequencies used in radio transmission and telecommunications.

bandy¹ /'bandi/ *verb trans* (**bandies, bandied, bandying**) **1** to exchange (words) in an argumentative, careless, or light-hearted manner. **2** (*often* + about) to use or make reference to (something) in a glib or offhand manner. [prob from early French *bander* to be tight, to hit to and fro, from *bande*: see BAND¹]

bandy² *adj* **1** said of a person's legs: bowed. **2** said of a person: bowlegged. ⟫ **bandy-legged** /-'legid/ *adj.* [prob from obsolete *bandy* hockey stick, of unknown origin]

bandy³ *noun* a game similar to ice hockey played *esp* in the Baltic countries. [perhaps from Old French *bandé*, past part. of *bander*: see BANDY¹]

bane /bayn/ *noun* **1** a cause of death, ruin, or trouble: *Backache was the bane of his life.* **2** (*esp in combination*) poison: *henbane.* ⟫⟫ **baneful** *adj.* [Old English *bana*]

baneberry /'baynb(ə)ri/ *noun* (*pl* **baneberries**) **1** an unpleasant-smelling plant of the buttercup family with small white flowers and black shiny poisonous berries: *Actaea spicata.* Also called HERB CHRISTOPHER. **2** the berry of the baneberry plant.

bang¹ /bang/ *verb trans* **1** to strike (something) sharply; to bump (something): *He fell and banged his knee.* **2** to knock, beat, or strike (something) hard, often with a loud sharp or metallic noise. **3** to cause (something) to make a loud sharp or metallic noise: *Don't bang the door!* **4** *coarse slang* said of a person: to have sexual intercourse with (somebody). ⟩ *verb intrans* **1** to strike, close, etc with a loud sharp noise or thump: *The falling chair banged against the wall.* **2** to produce a sharp often explosive noise or noises. **3** (+ about/around) to move about noisily. **4** *slang* to inject heroin or another drug. ✳ **bang one's head against a brick wall** to waste one's time trying to do something impossible. [prob of Scandinavian origin]

bang² *noun* **1** a resounding blow; a thump. **2** often used as a descriptive interjection: a sudden loud noise. **3** a quick or impressive burst of energy or activity: *The party finished with a bang.* **4** *coarse slang* an act of sexual intercourse. **5** *slang* an injection of heroin or another drug. ✳ **bang goes...** *informal* that is the end of (something, e.g. a plan or hope): *Well, bang goes that scheme for making money.*

bang³ *adv informal* **1** right or directly: *The door hit him bang in the face.* **2** exactly: *They arrived bang on six o'clock.* ✳ **bang on** *Brit, informal* just right; just what is needed; first-rate.

bang⁴ *noun chiefly NAmer* (*usu in pl*) a short squarely-cut fringe of hair. [prob short for BANGTAIL]

bang away *verb intrans informal* (*often* + at) to work with persistent determined effort.

banger *noun Brit* **1** a firework that explodes with a loud bang. **2** *informal* a sausage. **3** *informal* an old usu dilapidated car.

Bangladeshi /banggla'deshi/ *noun* (*pl* **Bangladeshi** *or* **Bangladeshis**) a native or inhabitant of Bangladesh on the Indian subcontinent. ⟫⟫ **Bangladeshi** *adj.*

bangle /'banggl/ *noun* a rigid usu ornamental bracelet or sometimes anklet. [Hindi *baṅglī*]

bang on *verb intrans Brit, informal* (*often* + about) to talk at length and forcefully about something: *He's forever banging on about unmarried mothers.*

bang out *verb trans* **1** to produce (something) quickly: *Could you bang out some new guidelines for us?* **2** to produce (a tune) on a musical instrument such as a piano loudly and with little finesse.

bangra /'banggra, 'bahnggra/ *noun* see BHANGRA.

bangtail /'bangtayl/ *noun* **1** a horse's tail cut very short and across in a straight line. **2** a horse with a tail cut in this way. [prob from BANG¹]

bang up *verb trans chiefly Brit* **1** *informal* to raise (something): *Executive salaries will probably be banged up.* **2** *informal* to imprison (somebody), or lock (a prisoner) in a cell.

bani /'bani/ *noun* pl of BAN³.

banian /'banyan/ *noun* see BANYAN.

banish /'banish/ *verb trans* **1** to require (somebody) by authority to leave a place, *esp* a country. **2** to dispel (something, e.g. an unpleasant thought) from one's mind. ⟫⟫ **banishment** *noun.* [Middle English *banishen* from Old French *baniss-*, stem of *banir*, of Germanic origin]

banister *or* **bannister** /'banista/ *noun* (*also in pl*) a handrail with its upright supports guarding the edge of a staircase. [alteration of BALUSTER]

banjo /'banjoh/ *noun* (*pl* **banjos** *or* **banjoes**) a stringed musical instrument with a round flat body, long neck and usu four or five strings, strummed with the fingers or a plectrum. ⟫⟫ **banjoist** *noun.* [prob of African origin]

bank¹ /bangk/ *noun* **1a** a mound, pile, or ridge, e.g. of earth or snow. **b** a piled-up mass of cloud or fog. **c** an undersea elevation rising *esp* from the continental shelf. **2a** the rising ground bordering a lake or river or forming the embankment along a road or railway. **b** a slope. **3** the lateral inward tilt of a surface along a curve or of a vehicle, *esp* an aircraft, when following a curved path. [Middle English, prob of Scandinavian origin; related to BENCH¹]

bank² *verb intrans* **1** (*often* + up) to rise in or form a bank. **2a** to incline an aircraft laterally when turning. **b** said of an aircraft: to incline laterally. **c** to follow a curve or incline, *esp* in racing. ⟩ *verb trans* **1** to surround (something) with a bank. **2** (*usu* + up) to heap fuel onto (a fire) to ensure slow burning. **3** to build (a road or railway) with the outer edge of a curve higher than the inner.

bank³ *noun* **1** an establishment for keeping, lending, exchanging, or issuing money and for the transmission of funds. **2a** a person conducting a gambling house or game, *esp* the banker in a game of cards. **3** a supply of something held in reserve, e.g.: **a** (**the bank**) the money, chips, etc held by the bank or banker for use in a gambling game. **b** the pool of pieces belonging to a game, e.g. dominoes, from which the players draw. **4** a collection of something kept available for use when needed: *a data bank; a sperm bank.* **5** a container for collecting paper, glass, etc for recycling: *a bottle bank.* [Middle English from early French *banque* or Italian *banca*, literally 'bench', of Germanic origin; related to BENCH¹]

bank⁴ *verb trans* to deposit (money) in a bank. ⟩ *verb intrans* (*often* + with) to deposit money or have an account in a bank: *Where do you bank?* ✳ **bank on** to depend or rely on (somebody or something).

bank⁵ *noun* **1a** a group or series of objects arranged close together in a row or tier. **b** a row of keys on a typewriter or computer keyboard. **2** a bench for the rowers of a galley. [Middle English from Old French *banc* bench, of Germanic origin; related to BENCH¹]

bank⁶ *verb trans* to arrange (objects, etc) in rows or tiers.

bankable *adj* **1** acceptable to or at a bank. **2** regarded as a likely or certain source of profit, *esp* because tending to attract large cinema audiences: *She was no longer a bankable star.* ⟫⟫ **bankability** /-'biliti/ *noun.*

bank bill *noun* a BILL OF EXCHANGE (written order to pay money at a certain date) which is issued by one bank to another or for which payment of the money is guaranteed by a bank.

bankbook *noun* a book held by a depositor, in which a bank enters a record of transactions and interest earned.

bank card *noun* = CHEQUE CARD.

bank draft *noun* an order for payment of money, authorized by a bank and presented to one of its branches or to another bank.

banker¹ *noun* **1** somebody who engages in the business of banking, *esp* a senior bank executive. **2** the player who keeps the bank in various games. **3** *Brit* a certainty; a safe bet. **4** a match-result forecast or an answer to a competition-puzzle clue that a competitor chooses from a number of alternatives and keeps constant through a series of entries, e.g. in a football pool or crossword contest.

banker² *noun Aus, NZ* a river that has overflowed its banks.

banker's card *noun Brit* = CHEQUE CARD.

banker's order *noun* a standing order from a customer to a bank to make a regular payment on his or her behalf.

bank holiday *noun* **1** (*often* **Bank Holiday**) a public holiday in the British Isles on which banks and some businesses are closed. **2** *NAmer* a period when banks are closed, often by government order.

banking¹ *noun* the business of a bank or a banker.

banking² *noun* = BANK¹ (2).

bank manager *noun* somebody who manages a local branch of a bank.

banknote *noun* money in paper form. A banknote is a PROMISSORY NOTE (written promise to pay) issued by a bank, payable to the bearer on demand without interest.

bankroll¹ *noun NAmer* a supply of money; funds.

bankroll² *verb trans* to supply the money required for (something) to function or operate; to finance (somebody or something).

bankrupt¹ /'bangkrupt/ *adj* **1** reduced to a state of financial ruin, *esp* legally declared insolvent. **2a** broken or ruined: *a bankrupt professional career.* **b** (+ of/in) devoid of or totally lacking in (a quality, skill, etc). [early French *banqueroute* from Old Italian *bancarotta*, literally 'broken bank'; the ending changed by association with Latin *rupta* broken]

bankrupt² *noun* **1** an insolvent person whose estate is administered under the bankruptcy laws for the benefit of his or her creditors. **2** somebody who is destitute of a specified quality or thing: *a moral bankrupt.*

bankrupt³ *verb trans* **1** to reduce (a person or organization) to bankruptcy. **2** to impoverish (somebody).

bankruptcy /'bangkrupsi/ *noun* (*pl* **bankruptcies**) **1** being bankrupt. **2** utter failure, or total absence of something desired or required.

bank statement *noun* a printed record of the transactions made on a particular bank account within a particular period.

banner /'banə/ *noun* **1a** a usu square or oblong flag bearing heraldic arms. **b** an ensign displaying a distinctive or symbolic device or legend, *esp* one presented as an award of honour or distinction. **2** a strip of cloth on which a message, slogan, or sign is painted. **3** = BANNER HEADLINE. **4** (*often* + under) a name, slogan, or goal associated with a particular group or ideology. [Middle English *banere* from Old French, of Germanic origin]

banneret *or* **bannerette** /banə'ret/ *noun* a small banner. [Middle English *baneret* from Old French, from *banere*: see BANNER]

banner headline *noun* a headline in large type running across a newspaper page.

bannerol /banə'rohl/ *noun* = BANDEROLE. [early French *bannerol*, variant of *banderole*: see BANDEROLE]

bannister /'banistə/ *noun* see BANISTER.

bannock /'banək/ *noun Scot, N Eng* a round flat loaf of unleavened bread made with oatmeal or barley meal. [Middle English *bannok*, prob from Scottish Gaelic *bannach*]

banns /banz/ *pl noun* the public announcement, *esp* in church, of a proposed marriage. [pl of *bann*, from Middle English *bane, ban* proclamation: see BAN²]

banoffi pie *or* **banoffee pie** /bə'nofi/ *noun* a pie made with bananas, toffee, and cream. [from BANANA and TOFFEE]

banquet¹ /'bangkwit/ *noun* a large and elaborate ceremonial meal for many people often in honour of a person; a feast. [early French *banquet* from Old Italian *banchetto*, dimin. of *banca* bench: see BANK³]

banquet² *verb* (**banqueted, banqueting**) ➤ *verb trans* to provide or entertain (somebody) with a banquet. ➤ *verb intrans* to take part in a banquet. ➤➤ **banqueter** *noun.*

banquette /bang'ket (*French* bɑ̃kɛt)/ *noun* **1** a raised step along the inside of a parapet or trench for soldiers or guns. **2** a built-in upholstered bench along a wall. [French *banquette* from Provençal *banqueta*, dimin. of *banc* bench, of Germanic origin; related to BENCH³]

banshee /'banshee, ban'shee/ *noun* a female spirit in Gaelic folklore whose wailing warns of approaching death in a household. [Scottish Gaelic *ban-sìth* and Irish Gaelic *bean-sídhe*, from Old Irish *ben síde* woman of fairyland]

bantam /'bant(ə)m/ *noun* **1** any of numerous small domestic fowl. **2** a small and tough or aggressive person. [named after *Bantam*, former port in Java. The birds were said to be imported from Bantam, although they are not native there]

bantamweight *noun* **1** a weight in boxing of 51–53.5kg (112–118lb) if professional or 51–54kg (112–119lb) if amateur. **2** a weight in amateur wrestling of usually 52–57kg (115–126lb).

banter¹ /'bantə/ *noun* teasing or badgering; badinage: *He remembered the bitterness of his life at school ... the banter which had made him morbidly afraid of making himself ridiculous —* Somerset Maugham. [origin unknown]

banter² *verb intrans* (**bantered, bantering**) to speak or act playfully or wittily. ➤➤ **banterer** *noun.*

Bantu /'bantooh/ *noun* (*pl* **Bantus** *or collectively* **Bantu**) **1** *derog* a member of a group of indigenous peoples inhabiting central and southern Africa. **2** a group of African languages spoken by these peoples, including Kongo, Swahili, Xhosa, and Zulu. ➤➤ **Bantu** *adj.*

Word history
plural in some African languages of *-ntu*, an element meaning 'person'. Words from Bantu languages that have passed into English include *chimpanzee, mamba, tsetse,* and *zombie,* and possibly *banjo.*

banyan *or* **banian** /'banyan/ *noun* **1** an Indian tree of the fig family with branches that send out shoots which grow down to the soil and root to form secondary trunks: *Ficus benghalensis.* **2** a loose-fitting shirt, jacket, or gown worn *esp* in India. [earlier *banyan* Hindu merchant, from Hindi *baniyā*; from a pagoda erected by merchants under a tree of the species in Iran]

banzai /ban'zie/ *interj* a Japanese cheer or battle cry. [Japanese *banzai* (may you live for) 10,000 years, a greeting to the Japanese emperor, i.e. 'long live the emperor']

baobab /'bayohbab/ *noun* an Old World tropical tree with a thick trunk and an edible acid fruit resembling a gourd: *Adansonia digitata.* Its bark is used in making paper, cloth, and rope. [prob from an African language]

BAOR *abbr* British Army of the Rhine.

bap /bap/ *noun Brit* a soft bread roll with a thin crust and often dusted with flour. [origin unknown]

baptise /bap'tiez, 'baptiez/ *verb trans* see BAPTIZE.

baptism /'baptiz(ə)m/ *noun* **1** the ritual use of water for purification, *esp* in the Christian sacrament of admission to the church. **2** an act, experience, or ordeal by which somebody is purified, sanctified, initiated, or named. ➤➤ **baptismal** /bap'tizmal/ *adj.* [Middle English via Old French and medieval Latin from medieval Greek *baptismos* ceremonial washing, from *baptizein* to BAPTIZE]

baptismal name *noun* = CHRISTIAN NAME (1).

baptism of fire *noun* an initial experience, e.g. a soldier's first battle, that is a severe ordeal. [orig meaning a spiritual baptism by gift of the Holy Spirit, a translation of late Greek *baptisma pyros*; now usu taken to refer to artillery fire]

Baptist /'baptist/ *adj* belonging or relating to the Baptist Church, a Protestant denomination which baptizes full adult believers rather than babies or children.

baptist *noun* **1** somebody who baptizes. **2** (**Baptist**) a member of the Baptist Church.

baptistery *or* **baptistry** /'baptistri/ *noun* (*pl* **baptisteries** *or* **baptistries**) a part of a church or formerly a separate building used for baptism.

baptize *or* **baptise** /bap'tiez, 'baptiez/ *verb trans* **1** to administer baptism to (somebody), *esp* so as to confer membership of the Christian Church. **2** to give a name to (somebody) at baptism, or give (somebody) a name or nickname in general; to christen (them). **3** to initiate or launch (an activity or enterprise). [Middle English *baptizen* via Old French and late Latin from Greek *baptizein* to dip, baptize]

Bar. *abbr* **1** barrister. **2** Baruch (book of the Apocrypha).

bar¹ /bah/ *noun* **1a** a straight piece, e.g. of wood or metal, that is longer than it is wide and has any of various uses, e.g. as a lever, support, barrier, or fastening. **b** a solid piece or block of material that is usu rectangular and longer than it is wide: *a chocolate bar.* **c** = BARRE. **2** something that obstructs or prevents passage, progress, or action, e.g.: **a** an intangible or nonphysical impediment, e.g. to progress or to promotion in a job. **b** the denial or invalidation of a claim in law. **c** a submerged or partly submerged bank, e.g. of sand, along a shore or in a river, often obstructing navigation. **d** in Parliament, a barrier beyond which nonmembers may not pass. **3** in a court of law, the dock or the railing that encloses the dock. **4** (*usu* **the Bar**) **a** *Brit* (*treated as sing. or pl*) the whole body of barristers. **b** *Brit* the profession of barrister. **c** *NAmer* the legal profession. **5** a straight stripe, band, or line much longer than it is wide, e.g.:. **a** any of two or more narrow horizontal stripes on a heraldic shield. **b** = STRIPE¹ (2). **c** a strip of metal attached to a military medal to indicate an additional award of the medal. **6a** a counter at which food or *esp* alcoholic drinks are served. **b** a room or establishment whose main feature is a bar for the serving of alcoholic drinks. **c** a place where goods, *esp* a specified commodity, are sold or served across a counter or a service provided: *There's a heel bar in the high street.* **7** in music, a group of musical notes and rests that add up to a prescribed time value, bounded on each side on the staff by a bar line, or the bar line itself. **8** a small loop or crosspiece of oversewn threads used, *esp* on garments, as a fastening, e.g. for a hook, for joining, or for strengthening something. ✳ **be called to the Bar** *Brit* to become a barrister. **be called within the Bar** *Brit* to be made a Queen's Counsel. **behind bars** in prison. [Middle English *barre* from Old French]

bar² *verb trans* (**barred, barring**) **1a** to fasten (something, e.g. a door) with a bar. **b** to place bars across (something) to prevent movement in, out, or through. **2a** to shut (somebody) in or out by or as if by bars. **b** to set aside the possibility of (something). **3a** to prevent or forbid (something): *No holds barred.* **b** to make a legal objection to (something). **4** to mark (something, e.g. an animal) with stripes.

bar³ *prep* = EXCEPT¹. ✳ **bar none** with no exceptions.

bar⁴ *adv* said of odds in betting: being offered for all the unnamed competitors: *20 to one bar.*

bar⁵ *noun* a unit of pressure equal to 100,000 newtons per square metre (about 14.5lb per square inch). [German *Bar* from Greek *baros* weight]

bar. *abbr* **1** barometer. **2** barometric.

bar- *or* **baro-** *comb. form* forming words, denoting: weight or pressure: *barometer.* [Greek *baros*]

barb¹ /bahb/ *noun* **1a** a sharp projection extending backwards from the point of an arrow, fishhook, etc, and preventing easy extraction. **b** a biting or pointedly critical remark or comment. **2** any of the side branches of the shaft of a feather. **3** a plant hair or bristle ending in a hook. **4** = BARBEL². [Middle English *barbe* barb, beard, via Old French from Latin *barba* beard]

barb² *verb trans* to provide (e.g. an arrow) with a barb.

barb³ *noun* any of a northern African breed of horses that are noted for speed and endurance and are related to Arabs. [French *barbe* from Italian *barbero* of Barbary, from *Barberia* Barbary, former name of the region now comprising Morocco, Algeria, Tunisia, and Libya]

Barbadian /bah'baydi·ən/ *noun* a native or inhabitant of Barbados in the Caribbean. ➤➤ **Barbadian** *adj.*

barbarian¹ /bah'beəri·ən/ *noun* **1** a person belonging to a land, culture, or people regarded as uncivilized or inferior to and more savage than one's own. **2** somebody regarded as lacking refinement, learning, or artistic or literary culture. [Latin *barbarus*: see BARBAROUS]

barbarian² *adj* **1** relating to barbarians or of the nature of a barbarian. **2** lacking refinement, learning, or artistic or literary culture.

barbaric /bah'barik/ *adj* **1** vicious and cruel: *barbaric punishment.* **2** unsophisticated or uncivilized. ➤➤ **barbarically** *adv.*

barbarise /'bahbəriez/ *verb trans* see BARBARIZE.

barbarism /'bahbəriz(ə)m/ *noun* **1** a word, action, or idea that is unacceptable by contemporary standards, or the use of such words, actions, or ideas. **2** primitive or unsophisticated social or intellectual condition. **3** barbarous cruelty.

barbarity /bah'bariti/ *noun* (*pl* **barbarities**) = BARBARISM (2), (3).

barbarize *or* **barbarise** /'bahbəriez/ *verb trans* to make (somebody or something) barbarous. ➤➤ **barbarization** /-'zaysh(ə)n/ *noun.*

barbarous /'bahb(ə)rəs/ *adj* **1** lacking culture or refinement. **2** mercilessly harsh or cruel. **3** with no system of social organization; uncivilized. ➤➤ **barbarously** *adv,* **barbarousness** *noun.* [via Latin from Greek *barbaros* foreign, ignorant]

Barbary ape /'bahbəri/ *noun* a tailless monkey of N Africa and Gibraltar: *Macaca sylvana.* [named after *Barbary*: see BARB³]

barbecue¹ /'bahbikyooh/ *noun* **1** an outdoor, often portable fireplace over which meat and fish are roasted or grilled. **2** a meal or social gathering in the open air at which barbecued food is served. **3** meat roasted or grilled on a barbecue.

Word history
American Spanish *barbacoa,* prob from Taino, an extinct Caribbean language. The word orig meant a wooden frame for drying and storing meat or fish or for sleeping on.

barbecue² *verb trans* (**barbecues, barbecued, barbecuing**) to roast or grill (food) on a barbecue.

barbed /bahbd/ *adj* **1** having barbs. **2** characterized by pointed and biting criticism or sarcasm: *engaging in barbed banter with his opponent* — Daily Telegraph.

barbed wire *noun* twisted wires armed with sharp points set at intervals along it.

barbel¹ /'bahbl/ *noun* a European freshwater fish with four barbels (tactile organs; see BARBEL²) on its upper jaw: *Barbus barbus.* [Middle English via Old French from late Latin *barbellus,* dimin. of Latin *barbus* barbel, from *barba* beard]

barbel² *noun* a slender tactile projecting organ on the lips of certain fishes, e.g. catfish, used in locating food. [early French, dimin. of *barbe*: see BARB¹]

barbell /'bahbel/ *noun* a bar with adjustable weighted discs attached to each end that is used for exercise and in weight-lifting: compare DUMBBELL. [BAR¹ + DUMBBELL]

barber¹ /'bahbə/ *noun* somebody, *esp* a man, who cuts and styles men's hair and shaves or trims beards. [Middle English via Old French from Latin *barba* beard]

barber² *verb trans* (**barbered, barbering**) to cut or trim (a man's hair or beard).

barberry /'bahb(ə)ri, 'bahberi/ *noun* (*pl* **barberries**) any of several species of shrubs having spines, yellow flowers, and oval red berries: genus *Berberis.* [by folk etymology from Middle English *barbere* via French from Arabic *barbārīs*]

barbershop *noun* unaccompanied vocal harmonizing of popular songs, *esp* by a male quartet. [from former custom of men in barbers' shops forming quartets for impromptu singing]

barber's pole *noun* a red and white striped pole traditionally fixed to the front of a barber's shop.

barbette /bah'bet/ *noun* **1** a mound of earth or a protected platform from which guns fire over a parapet. **2** the armour protection of a turret on a warship. [French *barbette,* dimin. of *barbe* headdress]

barbican /'bahbikən/ *noun* a defensive structure, *esp* a tower at a gate or bridge: *Within the barbican a Porter sate, day and night duely keeping watch and ward* — Spenser. [Middle English via Old French from medieval Latin *barbacana*]

barbie /'bahbi/ *noun chiefly Aus, informal* a barbecue. [by shortening and alteration]

bar billiards *noun* a form of billiards sometimes played in public houses, using a small table with holes in the playing area instead of side pockets and obstacles in the form of small upright pegs.

barbital /'bahbital/ *noun NAmer* = BARBITONE. [*barbituric* (see BAR-BITURIC ACID) + *-al* as in VERONAL, an alternative name]

barbitone /'bahbitohn/ *noun Brit* a barbiturate formerly widely used in sleeping pills. [*barbituric* (see BARBITURIC ACID) + -ONE]

barbiturate /bah'bityoorət/ *noun* **1** a salt or ester of barbituric acid. **2** any of several derivatives of barbituric acid, e.g. thiopentone and phenobarbitone, that are used *esp* in the treatment of epilepsy and were formerly widely used in sleeping pills.

barbituric acid /bahbi'tyooərik/ *noun* an organic acid used in the manufacture of barbiturate drugs and plastics: formula $C_4H_4N_2O_3$.

Word history
part translation of German *Barbitursäure,* from the name *Barbara* + URIC + German *Säure* acid. Of the various reasons put forward to explain the name *Barbara,* the most likely is that the substance was discovered on St Barbara's Day.

barbule /'bahbyoohl/ *noun* any of the small outgrowths that fringe the barbs of a feather. [Latin *barbula* little beard]

barcarole *or* **barcarolle** /bahkə'rohl/ *noun* a Venetian boat song with a moderate beat in duple or quadruple compound time suggesting a rowing rhythm, or a piece of music in this style. [French *barcarolle* via Italian from late Latin *barca* BARQUE]

BArch *abbr* Bachelor of Architecture.

bar chart *noun* = BAR GRAPH.

bar code *noun* a code printed on the label of a product for sale, e.g. a food item or book, consisting of parallel lines of varying thickness that indicate price, make, etc and can be read by an electronic scanner to automatically register a price on a cash register or for automatic stock control.

bard¹ /bahd/ *noun* **1** *archaic or literary* somebody, *esp* a Celtic poet-singer, who composed, sang, or recited verses about heroes and their deeds. **2** any poet, *esp* one recognized or honoured at an eisteddfod. **3** (**the Bard**) an epithet for Shakespeare. ➤➤ **bardic** /'bahdik/ *adj.* [Middle English from Scottish Gaelic and early Irish *bard* and Welsh *bardd* poet]

bard² *or* **barde** *noun* a strip of pork fat, bacon, etc for covering lean meat before roasting: compare LARDON. [early French *barde* armour or ornamental covering for a horse, via Old Spanish from Arabic *barda'ah*]

bard³ *or* **barde** *verb trans* to cover (meat to be roasted) with bards to add flavour and seal in moisture.

bardolatry /bah'dolətri/ *noun* extreme or excessive admiration of Shakespeare. ➤➤ **bardolater** *noun.* [the *Bard (of Avon),* epithet of William Shakespeare d.1616, English poet and dramatist + IDOLATRY]

bare[1] /beə/ *adj* **1** lacking a natural, usual, or appropriate covering, *esp* clothing. **2** open to view; exposed. **3a** unfurnished or empty: *The cupboard was bare.* **b** (*usu* + of) devoid or completely lacking in. **4a** having nothing left over or added; mere: *They were given only the bare necessities.* **b** not disguised or embellished in any way: *Let's look at the bare facts.* ✳ **with one's bare hands** without tools or weapons. ➤➤ **bareness** *noun.* [Old English *bær*]

bare[2] *verb trans* to reveal (something, *esp* body parts normally covered up, or thoughts or feelings normally kept private). ✳ **bare one's teeth** to draw back the lips and show the teeth, e.g. in a snarl.

bareback *or* **barebacked** *adv and adj* on the bare back of a horse without a saddle.

bareback sex *or* **barebacking** *noun slang* sexual intercourse without the use of a condom, *esp* when one of the participants is HIV-positive and there is therefore a high risk of the virus being transmitted to their sexual partner.

bare bones *pl noun* the barest essentials, facts, or elements.

barefaced *adj* lacking scruples; shameless. ➤➤ **barefacedly** /beə'faystli, -sidli/ *adv.* **barefacedness** *noun.*

barefoot *or* **barefooted** *adv and adj* without any covering on the feet.

barehanded *adv and adj* **1** without gloves. **2** without tools or weapons: *Not many would take on a crocodile barehanded.*

bareheaded *adv and adj* without a hat or other covering for the head.

bare-knuckle *adj and adv* **1** without wearing boxing gloves: *a bare-knuckle fight.* **2** in an aggressive, unrestrained way.

barely *adv* **1** only just; hardly: *I could barely speak.* **2** in a meagre manner; scantily: *He showed me into a barely furnished room.* **3** not quite; hardly.

barf /bahf/ *verb intrans chiefly NAmer, informal* to vomit. ➤ *verb trans* to vomit (something) up. [prob imitative]

barfly /'bahflie/ *noun* (*pl* **barflies**) *informal* somebody who frequents bars.

bargain[1] /'bahgən/ *noun* **1** an advantageous purchase, or something bought at an advantageous, often reduced price. **2** an agreement between parties concerning the terms of a transaction between them or the course of action each pursues in respect to the other: *A bargain had been struck.* **3** a transaction, situation, or event regarded in the light of its good or bad results: *You have to make the best of a bad bargain.* ✳ **into the bargain** in addition; what is more.

bargain[2] *verb intrans* **1** (*often* + with) to negotiate over the terms of a purchase, agreement, or contract. **2** to come to terms; to agree. ✳ **bargain for** to be prepared for (something). **bargain on** to expect (something). ➤➤ **bargainer** *noun.* [Middle English *bargainen* from Old French *bargaignier*, of Germanic origin]

bargain basement *noun* a section of a shop where merchandise is sold at reduced prices.

barge[1] /bahj/ *noun* **1a** a flat-bottomed boat used chiefly for the transport of goods on inland waterways or between ships and the shore. **b** a long, flat-bottomed, usu brightly decorated boat used on canals and rivers as a pleasure craft or sometimes as a dwelling. **c** a flat-bottomed coastal sailing vessel with leeboards (flat boards attached to a ship's hull; see LEEBOARD) instead of a keel. **2a** a large naval motorboat used by flag officers. **b** an ornate carved vessel used on ceremonial occasions. [Middle English via Old French from late Latin *barca*]

barge[2] *verb intrans* **1** to move in a headlong or clumsy fashion. **2** (+ in/into) to intrude, *esp* noisily or clumsily. [from the slow heavy motion of a barge]

bargeboard *noun* an often ornamented board attached to the sloping edge of a gabled roof. [origin of *barge* unknown]

bargee /bah'jee/ *noun Brit* somebody who works on a barge: *our Deputy Commissioner, who had the manners of a bargee and the tact of a horse* — Kipling.

bargepole *noun* a long thick pole for propelling a barge. ✳ **he/she etc wouldn't touch (something or somebody) with a bargepole** *informal* he, she, etc wouldn't have anything to do with something or somebody under any circumstances.

bar graph *noun* a graph or diagram in which the frequency with which an item occurs is represented by the length of a vertical bar.

baric /'bayrik, 'barik/ *adj* of or containing barium.

barilla /bə'rilə/ *noun* **1** either of two European saltwort plants or a related Algerian plant: genera *Salsola* and *Halogeton*. **2** an impure form of sodium carbonate obtained from barilla ashes and formerly used in making soap and glass. [Spanish *barrilla*]

barista /ba'ristə/ *noun* a person who serves coffee in a coffee bar or coffee shop. [from BAR[1] + -ISTA]

baritone /'baritohn/ *noun* **1** a male singing voice between bass and tenor, or a singer with this voice. **2** (*used before a noun*) denoting a musical instrument having a range below that of tenor: *a baritone horn.* ➤➤ **baritone** *adj.* [French *baryton* or Italian *baritono*, from Greek *barytonos* deep sounding, from *barys* heavy + *tonos* tone]

barium /'beəri-əm/ *noun* a silver-white soft metallic chemical element of the alkaline-earth group; symbol Ba, atomic number 56. [scientific Latin *barium*, from BAR-]

barium meal *noun* a solution of barium sulphate swallowed by a patient to make the stomach or intestines visible in X-ray pictures.

bark[1] /bahk/ *verb intrans* **1** to make the short loud cry characteristic of a dog, or a sound similar to or in imitation of it. **2** to speak in a curt, loud, and usu angry tone; to snap loudly. ➤ *verb trans* to say (something) in a curt, loud, and usu angry tone. ✳ **bark up the wrong tree** to proceed under a misapprehension. ➤➤ **barker** *noun.* [Old English *beorcan*]

bark[2] *noun* **1** the sound made by a barking dog, or a similar or imitative sound. **2** a short sharp peremptory utterance. ✳ **his/her etc bark is worse than his/her etc bite** he/she etc is less fierce than he/she etc seems.

bark[3] *noun* the tough exterior covering of a woody root or stem. ➤➤ **barkless** *adj.* [Middle English from Old Norse *bark-, börkr*]

bark[4] *verb trans* **1** to scrape the skin of (a part of the body, e.g. the knee or shin) by accident. **2** to remove some or all of the bark from (a tree). **3** to tan or dye (something) using substances such as tannin obtained from bark.

bark[5] *noun* **1** *NAmer see* BARQUE: *The only other vessel in port was the Russian government bark, from Asitka, mounting eight guns* — R H Dana. **2** *literary* a boat of any kind. [Middle English via Old French and Old Provençal from late Latin *barca*]

bark beetle *noun* any of several species of beetles that bore under the bark of trees both as larva and adult: family Scolytidae.

barkeeper *or* **barkeep** *noun NAmer* = BARMAN.

barkentine /'bahkənteen/ *noun NAmer see* BARQUENTINE.

barker *noun* a person who stands outside a circus, fair, etc and shouts to encourage people to go in.

barking *or* **barking mad** *adj Brit, informal* completely mad.

barley /'bahli/ *noun* (*pl* **barleys**) a widely cultivated cereal grass whose seed is used to make malt, in foods, e.g. breakfast cereals and soups, and to feed cattle: *Hordeum vulgare.* [Old English *bærlic* (adj), from *bere, bær* barley]

barleycorn *noun* **1a** a grain of barley. **b** barley grain. **2** *archaic* an old measurement of length equal to ⅓ of an inch (about 0.85 cm).

barley sugar *noun* a brittle semi-transparent amber-coloured sweet made of boiled sugar. [because it was formerly made by boiling sugar in a decoction of barley]

barley water *noun* a non-alcoholic drink made by boiling barley in water, often flavoured with fruit.

barley wine *noun* a type of strong sweet ale.

bar line *noun* a vertical line across a musical staff after the last beat of a bar.

barm /bahm/ *noun* yeast formed during the fermenting of beer. [Old English *beorma*]

barman *or* **barmaid** *noun* (*pl* **barmen** *or* **barmaids**) somebody who serves drinks in a bar.

Barmecidal /bahmi'siedl/ *or* **Barmecide** /'bahməsied/ *adj* providing only the illusion of plenty or abundance: *a Barmecidal feast.* [named after *Barmecide*, a wealthy Persian, who, in a tale of *The Arabian Nights*, invited a beggar to a feast of imaginary food]

bar mitzvah *or* **Bar Mitzvah** /bah 'mitsvə/ *noun* **1** the religious ceremony marking a Jewish boy's reaching the age of 13, when adult religious duties and responsibilities are assumed. **2** a Jewish boy who undergoes this ceremony. [Hebrew *bar miṣwāh* son of the (divine) law]

barmy /'bahmi/ *adj* (**barmier, barmiest**) **1** *informal* foolish or slightly mad. **2** frothy with barm.

barn[1] /bahn/ *noun* **1** a usu large farm building for storage, *esp* of feed, harvested grain etc. **2** an unusually large and usu bare building: *They lived in a great barn of a house.* [Old English *bereærn*, from *bere* barley + *ærn* place]

barn[2] *noun* a unit of area equal to 10⁻²⁸ square metres, used *esp* in nuclear physics for measuring the cross-sections of the nuclei of atoms. [from BARN[1]; from its having been considered 'as big as a barn door' for the purposes of nuclear bombardment]

barnacle /'bahnəkl/ *noun* **1** any of numerous species of marine crustaceans that are free-swimming as larvae but fixed to rocks or floating objects as adults: class Cirripedia. **2** often used figuratively to convey tenacious attachment: *From that hour I clove to Queequeg like a barnacle* — Herman Melville. ➤➤ **barnacled** *adj.*

Word history
from the former belief held from at least the 12th cent. to the 17th cent. that barnacle geese hatched from barnacles growing on trees or attached to waterlogged timbers. The mistake probably partly arose from the mystery of the goose's origin (it was not known that they breed in the Arctic). The name of the bird was therefore transferred to the marine animal in the 16th cent.

barnacle goose *noun* a European goose with a white face and black neck that breeds in the Arctic: *Branta leucopsis.* [Middle English *barnakille*, alteration of *bernake*, from medieval Latin *bernaca*]

barn dance *noun* **1** a country dance, *esp* a round dance or a square dance with called instructions. **2** a social gathering for such dances.

barn door *noun* **1** the door of a barn. **2** a movable flap on a light in a theatre or on a film set, used to control the shape of the beam.

barney[1] /'bahni/ *noun* (*pl* **barneys**) *Brit, informal* a quarrel or row. [perhaps from the name *Barney*]

barney[2] *verb intrans* (**barneys, barneyed, barneying**) *Brit, informal* to quarrel or have a row.

barn owl *noun* an owl with a distinctive heart-shaped face that nests *esp* in barns and other buildings and that is found in most parts of the world: *Tyto alba.*

barnstorm *verb intrans chiefly NAmer* **1** to tour rural districts staging usu one-night theatrical performances. **2** to travel from place to place making brief stops, e.g. in the course of a political campaign. **3** to pilot an aeroplane on sightseeing flights or in exhibition stunts, *esp* in rural districts. ➤ *verb trans* to travel across (an area) while barnstorming. ➤ **barnstormer** *noun.* [BARN[1] + STORM[2]; from itinerant actors performing in barns]

barnyard *noun NAmer* = FARMYARD.

baro- *comb. form* see BAR-.

barograph /'barəgrahf/ *noun* a barometer that records its readings, e.g. as a line on a graph. ➤➤ **barographic** /-'grafik/ *adj.*

barometer /bə'romitə/ *noun* **1** an instrument for determining the pressure of the atmosphere and hence for assisting in predicting the weather or measuring the height of an ascent. **2** something that registers fluctuations, e.g. in public opinion. ➤➤ **barometric** /-'metrik/ *adj,* **barometrical** /-'metrikl/ *adj,* **barometrically** /-'metrikli/ *adv,* **barometry** /-tri/ *noun.*

baron /'barən/ *noun* **1a** a member of the lowest rank of the peerage in Britain. **b** a European nobleman of similar rank. **c** formerly, a feudal tenant who received his rights and title directly from the sovereign in return for military or other honourable service. **2** a man of great power or influence in a specified field of activity: *He frequently complained about the power of the press barons.* [Middle English from Old French, of Germanic origin]

baronage /'barənij/ *noun* **1** (*treated as sing. or pl*). **a** barons collectively. **b** the nobility; the peerage. **2** the rank of baron. **3** a list of barons, or of peers.

baroness /'barənes, barə'nes/ *noun* **1** the wife or widow of a baron. **2** a woman having the rank of a baron in her own right.

baronet /'barə'net, 'barənit/ *noun* the holder of a rank of honour below a baron and above a knight.

baronetage /'barənətij/ *noun* **1** (*treated as sing. or pl*) the whole body of baronets. **2** a list of baronets.

baronetcy /'barənətsi/ *noun* (*pl* **baronetcies**) the rank of baronet.

baronial /bə'rohni-əl/ *adj* **1** of or befitting a baron or the baronage. **2** stately and spacious: *a baronial hall.*

baron of beef *noun* a cut of beef consisting of two sirloins joined at the backbone. [origin unknown; perhaps associated with the false understanding of SIRLOIN as *Sir Loin*, supposedly a joint knighted by an English king]

barony /'barəni/ *noun* (*pl* **baronies**) **1** the domain or rank of a baron. **2a** in Ireland, a division of a county. **b** in Scotland, a large estate or manor.

baroque[1] /bə'rok/ *adj* **1** of a style of art, architecture, and music prevalent *esp* in the 17th cent. that is marked by extravagant forms and elaborate and sometimes grotesque ornamentation.

Editorial note
Baroque is the term, originally derogatory, for an architectural style at its peak in 17th- and early 18th-cent. Europe, which developed the Classicism of the Renaissance towards greater extravagance and drama. Its innovations included greater freedom from the conventions of the Orders, much interplay of concave and convex forms, and a preference for the single visual sweep — Simon Bradley.

2 extravagantly intricate or recherché: *the arriviste's tie, complete with baroque coat of arms for the nouveau landowner* — Esquire; *a baroque revenge plot.* ➤➤ **baroquely** *adv.* [French *baroque* irregular from Portuguese *barroco* or Spanish *barrueco* pearl]

baroque[2] *noun* the baroque style in art, architecture, and music.

baroreceptor /'barohriseptə/ *noun* a sense organ, *esp* in the wall of a large artery, that is sensitive to changes in pressure, e.g. of the blood.

barouche /bə'roohsh/ *noun* a four-wheeled horse-drawn carriage with a high driver's seat at the front and a folding top over the rear seats. [German *Barutsche* via Italian from late Latin *birotus* two-wheeled]

barque (*NAmer* **bark**) /bahk/ *noun* **1** a sailing vessel with the rearmost of usu three masts fore-and-aft rigged and the others square-rigged. **2** *literary* a boat. [Middle English *bark* via Old French and Old Provençal from late Latin *barca*]

barquentine (*NAmer* **barkentine**) /'bahkənteen/ *noun* a three-masted sailing vessel with the foremast square-rigged and the other masts fore-and-aft rigged. [BARQUE + -*entine*, alteration of -*antine* as in BRIGANTINE]

barrack[1] /'barək/ *noun* (*usu in pl*) **1** a set or area of buildings providing accommodation for soldiers. **2** a large building characterized by extreme plainness or dreary uniformity with others. [French *baraque* hut, from Catalan *barraca*]

barrack[2] *verb trans* to accommodate (*esp* soldiers) in barracks.

barrack[3] *verb intrans* **1** *chiefly Brit* to jeer or scoff, *esp* at a player or performer. **2** *chiefly Aus, NZ* (*usu* + for) to root or cheer, e.g. for a team. ➤ *verb trans* **1** *chiefly Brit* to shout at (somebody, e.g. a player) derisively. **2** *chiefly Aus, NZ* to support (e.g. a sports team), *esp* by shouting encouragement. ➤➤ **barracker** *noun.* [prob from N Irish dialect *barrack* to brag]

barrack-room lawyer *noun* an opinionated person who persistently and pettily argues over details without having the knowledge or authority to do so.

barrack square *noun* an area for drill practice near a barracks.

barracouta /barə'koohtə/ *noun* (*pl* **barracoutas** or collectively **barracouta**) a large food fish of Pacific seas: *Thyrsites atun.* [modification of American Spanish *barracuda*]

barracuda /barə'kyoohdə/ *noun* (*pl* **barracudas** or collectively **barracuda**) any of several species of predatory fishes of warm seas that include excellent food fishes as well as forms regarded as poisonous: genus *Sphyraena.* [American Spanish *barracuda*]

barrage[1] /'barahzh/ *noun* **1** a wide-ranging bombardment of intensive artillery fire, intended to hinder enemy action. **2** a rapid and overwhelming series of questions or complaints. **3** *Brit* an artificial dam placed in a watercourse or estuary. [French *barrage*, from *barrer* to bar]

barrage[2] *verb trans* to overwhelm (somebody) with questions or complaints.

barrage balloon *noun* a large tethered balloon used to support wires or nets to prevent the approach of low-flying enemy aircraft.

barramundi /barə'moondi/ *noun* (*pl* **barramundis** or **barramunda** /-də/ *noun* (*pl* **barramundis** or **barramundies** or **barramundas** or collectively **barramundi** or **barramunda**) an Australian freshwater fish used for food: *Lates calcarifer.* [native name in Australia]

barrator or **barrater** /'barətə/ *noun* somebody who engages in barratry.

barratry /'barətri/ *noun* (*pl* **barratries**) **1** a fraudulent breach of duty by the master or crew of a ship: *The insurers were obliged to* *answer for the barratry of the master* — Nicolas Magens. **2** persistent litigation. **3** formerly, the buying or selling of church offices. ➤ **barratrous** *adj.* [Middle English *barratrie* from early French *baraterie* deception, from *barater* to deceive, exchange]

barre /bah/ *noun* a horizontal handrail used by ballet dancers while exercising. [French *barre* BAR[1]]

barrel[1] /'barəl/ *noun* **1** an approximately cylindrical container, *esp* for liquids, with bulging sides and flat ends constructed from wooden staves bound together with hoops. **2a** the amount, *esp* of liquid, contained in a barrel. **b** a unit of volume variously reckoned at between 30 and 40 gallons (135 and 180l), depending on the industry. For example, a barrel of oil is 35 gallons (159l), a barrel of beer 36 gallons (164l). **3** the tube of a gun, from which the bullet, etc is fired. **4** the cylindrical part of a pen containing the ink. **5** a cylindrical or tubular part of a machine, e.g. a piece of optical equipment. **6** the trunk of a four-legged animal, e.g. a horse. ✳ **over a barrel** *informal* at a disadvantage or in a position of helplessness: *He had me over a barrel so I had to give in.* ➤ **barrelful** *noun*, **barrelled** *adj.* [Middle English *barel* from early French *baril*]

barrel[2] *verb trans* (**barrelled, barrelling**, *NAmer* **barreled, barreling**) **1** to put or pack (something, *esp* a liquid) in a barrel. **2** *chiefly NAmer, informal* to move at a high speed.

barrel-chested *adj.* having a large rounded chest.

barrelhouse *noun* a style of jazz characterized by a heavy beat and simultaneous improvisation by players. [*barrelhouse* a cheap drinking and dancing establishment]

barrel organ *noun* a musical instrument consisting of a revolving cylinder studded with pegs that open a series of valves to admit air from a bellows to a set of pipes.

barrel roll *noun* a manoeuvre in which an aeroplane moves in a spiral path by turning over sideways while continuing to fly in a straight line.

barrel vault *noun* an arched roof, ceiling, etc having the form of a half cylinder unbroken by joins.

barren /'barən/ *adj* **1** incapable of producing offspring. **2** said e.g. of a tree: habitually failing to fruit. **3** said of land: not productive, *esp* producing inferior or scanty vegetation. **4** (+ of) lacking in or devoid of (a quality, etc). **5** lacking interest, information, or charm. ➤ **barrenly** *adv*, **barrenness** *noun*. [Middle English *bareine* from Old French *baraine*]

barricade[1] /'barikayd, -'kayd/ *noun* **1** an obstruction thrown up across a passage, often a street, to hold back a perceived enemy. **2** any barrier or obstacle. [French *barricade*, from early French *barriquer* to barricade, from *barrique* barrel, because barrels were often used to build barricades]

barricade[2] *verb trans* **1** to block off or defend (a place) with a barricade. **2** to prevent access to (a place) by means of a barricade.

barrier /'bari·ə/ *noun* **1** a fence, bar, or other object that separates, demarcates, or serves as a barricade. **2** something immaterial that impedes or separates: *There was no getting past barriers of reserve.* **3** a factor that tends to restrict the free movement or interacting of individuals or populations. [Middle English *barrere* from Old French *barriere*, from *barre* BAR[1]]

barrier cream *noun* any of various creams for protecting the skin, e.g. from intensive sunlight or chemicals that cause irritation.

barrier reef *noun* a coral reef roughly parallel to a shore and separated from it by a lagoon.

barring /'bahring/ *prep* = EXCEPT[1].

barrio /'bahrioh, 'ba-/ *noun* (*pl* **barrios**) **1** a Spanish-speaking neighbourhood in a city or town in the USA, *esp* in the Southwest. **2** in a Spanish-speaking country, a quarter or district of a city or town. [Spanish *barrio* from Arabic *barrī* of the open country, from *barr* outside, open country]

barrister /'baristə/ *noun* **1** (*also* **barrister-at-law**) *Brit* a lawyer who has the right to plead as an advocate in an English or Welsh superior court: compare SOLICITOR. **2** *Can* a lawyer who pleads in any court. [BAR[1] + *-ister* as in MINISTER[1]]

barroom *noun* = BAR[1] (6B).

barrow[1] /'baroh/ *noun* **1** a cart with a shallow box body, two wheels, and shafts for pushing it, used e.g. by street and market traders. **2** = WHEELBARROW. [Old English *bearwe*; related to Old English *beran* BEAR[2]]

barrow[2] *noun* a large mound of earth or stones over an ancient grave; a tumulus. [Old English *beorg*]

barrow boy *noun* a man or boy who sells goods, e.g. fruit or vegetables, from a barrow.

bar sinister *noun* **1** = BEND SINISTER. **2** the condition of being of illegitimate birth.

Bart *abbr* baronet.

bartender *noun chiefly NAmer* = BARMAN.

barter[1] /'bahtə/ *verb* (**bartered, bartering**) ➤ *verb intrans* **1** to trade by exchanging one commodity for another without the use of money. **2** to bargain or haggle. ➤ *verb trans* **1** to exchange (something) by, or as if by, bartering. **2** (*usu* + away) to part with (something) unwisely or for an unworthy return: *The soul is a terrible reality. It can be bought, and sold, and bartered away* — Oscar Wilde. ➤ **barterer** *noun*. [Middle English *bartren* from early French *barater* to exchange, deceive]

barter[2] *noun* the carrying on of trade by bartering.

bartizan /'bahtiz(ə)n, -'zan/ *noun* a corner turret, parapet, etc projecting from a building: *A bartizan, or projecting gallery before the windows … was crowded with flowers of different kinds* — Scott. [early 19th-cent. modification by Scott of Middle English *bretasinge* from *bretasce*: see BRATTICE]

baryon /'bari·ən/ *noun* any of a group of elementary particles, e.g. a neutron, that are fermions (see FERMION) and have a mass equal to or greater than that of the proton. ➤ **baryonic** /-'onik/ *adj.* [Greek *barys* heavy + -ON[2]]

baryta /bə'rietə/ *noun* **1** barium hydroxide. **2** barium oxide. [scientific Latin: see BARYTES]

barytes /bə'rieteez/ *noun* naturally occurring barium sulphate. [Greek *barytēs* weight, from *barys* heavy]

basal /'bays(ə)l/ *adj* **1** of, situated at, or forming the base. **2** of the foundation, base, or essence of something; fundamental. ➤ **basally** *adv*.

basal metabolic rate *noun* the rate at which heat is given off by an organism at complete rest.

basal metabolism *noun* the rate at which energy is used in a fasting and resting organism using energy solely to maintain vital cellular activity, respiration, and circulation.

basalt /'basawlt, bə'sawlt/ *noun* a dense to fine-grained dark igneous rock consisting essentially of a feldspar and usu pyroxene, low in silica but high in minerals containing iron and magnesium. ➤ **basaltic** /bə'sawltik/ *adj.* [Latin *basaltes*, variant of *basanites* touchstone, via Greek from Egyptian *bhnw*]

bascule /'baskyool, 'baskyoohl/ *noun* **1** a counterbalancing apparatus. **2** (*also* **bascule bridge**) a bridge with sections that are raised and lowered using counterweights on the principle of the seesaw. [French *bascule* seesaw]

base[1] /bays/ *noun* **1a** the bottom of something, *esp* a support or foundation. **b** the lower part of a wall, pier, or column considered as a separate architectural feature. **c** a side or face of a geometrical figure on which it is regarded as standing. **d** that part of an organ by which it is attached to another structure nearer the centre of a living organism. **2** the fundamental part of something; a basis on which other activities or institutions depend: *a financial base.* **3a** a centre from which a start is made in an activity or from which operations proceed: *The police set up a base near the scene of the crime.* **b** a line in a survey which serves as the origin for statistical calculations. **c** the locality or installations on which a military force relies for supplies or from which it starts operations. **d** the number with reference to which a number system is constructed. **e** a number with reference to which logarithms are computed. **f** = ROOT[1] (4). **4a** a main ingredient. **b** a supporting or carrying ingredient. **5a** the starting place or goal in various games. **b** any of the stations at each of the four corners of the inner part of a baseball field to which a batter must run in turn in order to score a run. **6** the middle region of a transistor between the emitter and the collector. **7** any of various typically water-soluble and acrid or salty-tasting chemical compounds that are capable of taking up a hydrogen ion from or donating an unshared pair of electrons to an acid to form a salt: compare ALKALI, ACID[2]. **8** = BASE COMPONENT. [Middle English via Old French and Latin from Greek *basis* step, base, from *bainein* to go]

base[2] *verb trans* **1** to make, form, or serve as a base for (something). **2** (*usu* + on/upon) to use (something) as a base or basis for (something); to found (something). **3** (*usu* + in/at) to have (a place) as an operational base.

base[3] *adj* constituting or serving as a base.

base[4] *adj* **1a** lacking higher values; degrading: *being free from money-craving, with all its base hopes and temptations* — George Eliot. **b** lacking or showing a lack of moral values such as honour, chivalry, or loyalty. **2a** said of a metal: of comparatively low value and having relatively inferior properties, e.g. poor resistance to corrosion: compare NOBLE[1] (7): *gold, silver, and base lead* — Shakespeare. **b** said *esp* of a coin: containing a larger than usual proportion of base metals. **3** morally unworthy: *Men are singularly base* — Henry James; *their base ingratitude to my poor old grandmother* — Frederick Douglass. **4** *archaic* lowly: *his parents base of stock* — Marlowe. ➤➤ **basely** *adv*, **baseness** *noun*. [Middle English *bas* short, low, bass, via Old French from medieval Latin *bassus* short, low]

baseball *noun* **1** a game played, chiefly in North America, with a bat and ball between two teams of nine players each on a large field centring on four bases arranged in a diamond that mark the course a batter must run to score. **2** the ball used in baseball.

baseball cap *noun* a close-fitting round cap of light material with a large peak.

baseboard *noun NAmer* = SKIRTING BOARD.

baseborn *adj* **1** of humble or illegitimate birth. **2** *archaic* dishonourable or ignoble. [BASE[4]]

base component *noun* that part of transformational grammar that consists of rules and a lexicon and that generates the deep structures of a language.

base hit *noun* in baseball, a hit that allows the batter to run to the next base safely.

base hospital *noun* in Australia, a hospital that serves a large rural area.

base-jumping *noun* (*also* **BASE jumping**) parachuting from fixed objects such as buildings, bridges, and mountains. ➤➤ **base-jumper** *noun*. [from *b*uilding, *a*ntenna, *s*pan, and *e*arth, these being the four categories of fixed object from which base-jumpers jump]

baseless *adj* not supported by evidence or fact; unfounded. ➤➤ **baselessly** *adv*, **baselessness** *noun*.

baseline *noun* **1** a line serving as a base, e.g. from which measurements can be made. **2** a basis or starting point for comparisons. **3** the back line at each end of a court in tennis, badminton, etc.

basement /'baysmənt/ *noun* the part of a building that is wholly or partly below ground level.

base metal *noun* a common and relatively cheap metal such as iron or copper, as opposed to e.g. gold and silver.

basenji /bə'senji/ *noun* (*pl* **basenjis**) any of an African breed of small compact curly-tailed dogs that seldom bark. [of Bantu origin; related to Lingala *basenji*, pl of *mosenji* native]

base rate *noun* the rate of interest used by British clearing banks (major banks that issue cheques: see CLEARING BANK) as a basis for calculating charges on loans and interest on deposits.

bases[1] /'baysiz/ *noun* pl of BASE[1].

bases[2] /'bayseez/ *noun* pl of BASIS.

bash[1] /bash/ *verb trans informal* **1** (*often* + in/up) to strike (something or somebody) violently, or to injure (somebody) or damage (something) by striking. **2** (*often* + up) to make a violent physical attack on (somebody). ➤➤ **basher** *noun*. [prob imitative]

bash[2] *noun informal* **1** a forceful blow. **2** *chiefly Brit* (*often* + at) an attempt: *Have a bash at it.* **3** a party.

bashful /'bashf(ə)l/ *adj* **1** socially shy or timid. **2** characterized by, showing, or resulting from extreme sensitiveness or self-consciousness. ➤➤ **bashfully** *adv*, **bashfulness** *noun*. [obsolete *bash* to be abashed, from Middle English *basshen*, short for *abasshen*, *abaishen*: see ABASH]

basho /'bashoh/ *noun* (*pl* **bashos** *or* **basho**) a sumo-wrestling tournament. [Japanese *basho*]

BASIC /'baysik/ *noun* a high-level computer language designed for teaching programming to beginners. [acronym from *Beginner's All-purpose Symbolic Instruction Code*]

basic[1] *adj* **1a** of or forming the base or essence; fundamental. **b** simple; elementary. **2a** constituting or serving as the minimum basis or starting point. **b** simple; without embellishment; of a low but acceptable standard. **3a** of, containing, or having the character of a chemical base. **b** having an alkaline reaction; being an alkali. **4** said of rock: containing relatively little silica. **5** relating to or

made by a steelmaking process in which the furnace is lined with material containing relatively little silica. ➤➤ **basically** *adv*.

basic[2] *noun* (*usu in pl*) something basic; a fundamental.

basically *adv* **1a** essentially; fundamentally: *The plan is basically sound.* **b** in fact: *That's basically all there is to it.* **c** *informal* generally; without being specific: *We were basically thinking of some time in March.* **2** in a simple or unsophisticated way.

Basic English *noun* a simplified version of English with a vocabulary of 850 words designed for teaching and international communication, developed in the 1920s by Charles K Ogden d. 1957, British writer and linguist.

basic industry *noun* any of the industries that are central to the economy of a particular country.

basicity /bay'sisiti/ *noun* (*pl* **basicities**) **1** in chemistry, the fact or condition of being a base. **2a** said of a base: the number of molecules of acid required to neutralize one molecule of the base. **b** said of an acid: the number of hydrogen atoms that are replaceable by a base.

basic slag *noun* a slag formed in the basic process of steelmaking and useful as a fertilizer.

basic wage *noun* the amount that a worker earns before overtime or bonus payments have been added.

basidia /bə'sidi-ə/ *noun* pl of BASIDIUM.

basidiomycete /bə,sidioh'mieseet/ *noun* any of a large class of higher fungi bearing spores on a basidium and including rusts, mushrooms, and puffballs: class Basidiomycetes. ➤➤ **basidiomycetous** /-'seetəs/ *adj*. [BASIDIUM + Greek *mykēt-, mykēs* fungus]

basidiospore /bə'sidiohspaw/ *noun* a SPORE[1] (reproductive body) that is produced by and borne on a basidium and that grows to form a new fungus. [BASIDIUM + -O- + SPORE[1]]

basidium /bə'sidi-əm/ *noun* (*pl* **basidia** /-ə/) a specialized cell on a basidiomycete bearing usu four basidiospores. ➤➤ **basidial** *adj*. [scientific Latin *basidium*, from Latin *basis*: see BASIS]

basil /'baz(ə)l/ *noun* any of several species of aromatic plants of the mint family, *esp* sweet basil, whose leaves are widely used as a herb in cooking: genus *Ocimum*. [Middle English from Old French *basile* via late Latin from Greek *basilikon*, neuter of *basilikos*: see BASILICA]

basilar /'basilə, 'bazilə/ *adj* of or situated at the base. [irreg from BASIS]

basilar membrane *noun* a membrane in the cochlea of the inner ear that vibrates in response to sound waves.

basilica /bə'zilikə, bə'si-/ *noun* **1** an oblong building used in ancient Rome as a place of assembly or as a lawcourt and usu ending in an apse. **2** an early Christian church similar to a Roman basilica. **3** a Roman Catholic church given certain ceremonial privileges. ➤➤ **basilican** *adj*. [via Latin from Greek *basilikē*, fem of *basilikos* royal, from *basileus* king]

basilisk /'basilisk, 'bazilisk/ *noun* **1** a mythical reptile whose breath and glance were fatal: *The stranger turned on him a scowl, into which it seemed as if he would willingly have thrown the power of the fabled basilisk* — Scott. **2** a crested tropical American lizard related to the iguanas: genus *Basiliscus*. [Middle English via Latin from Greek *basiliskos*, dimin. of *basileus* king]

basin /'bays(ə)n/ *noun* **1a** a round open usu metal or ceramic vessel with a greater width than depth and sides that slope or curve inwards to the base, used typically for holding water for washing. **b** a bowl with a greater depth than width used *esp* for holding, mixing, or cooking food: *a pudding basin*. **c** the contents of a basin. **2a** a dock built in a tidal river or harbour. **b** a partly enclosed area of water providing shelter for ships. **3a** a depression in the surface of the land or ocean floor. **b** the region drained by a river and its tributaries. **4** an area of the earth in which the strata dip from the sides towards the centre. ➤➤ **basinal** *adj*, **basined** *adj*, **basinful** *noun*. [Middle English via Old French from late Latin *bacchinon*]

basis /'baysis/ *noun* (*pl* **bases** /'bayseez/) **1** a support or principle on which something is established or constructed: *He has no basis for his beliefs.* **2** a basic principle or way of proceeding: *He receives counselling on a regular basis.* **3** the principal component of something. **4** a foundation or support. [Latin *basis*: see BASE[1]]

bask /bahsk/ *verb intrans* **1** to lie in, or expose oneself to, a pleasant warmth or atmosphere. **2** (*usu* + in) to enjoy somebody's favour or approval. [Middle English *basken* from Old Norse *bathask*, reflexive of *batha* to bathe; related to Old English *bæth* BATH[1]]

basket /'bahskit/ *noun* **1a** a rigid or semirigid receptacle made of interwoven material, traditionally wicker or rattan. **b** any of various lightweight usu wood containers. **c** the contents of a basket. **2** something that resembles a basket, *esp* in shape or use. **3a** a net, open at the bottom and suspended from a metal ring, that constitutes the goal in basketball. **b** a goal scored in basketball. **4** a collection or group: *We looked at a basket of major world currencies.* **5** *Brit, euphem* = BASTARD¹ (2). ⋙ **basketful** *noun*. [Middle English, prob ultimately from Latin *bascauda*, of Celtic origin]

basketball *noun* **1** an indoor court game between two teams of five players each who try to score goals by tossing a large ball through a raised basket. **2** the ball used in basketball.

basket case *noun informal* **1** somebody who has had all four limbs amputated. **2** somebody or something regarded as worn out, incapacitated, or useless: *India was the world's basket case in the 1960s* — The Economist.

basket chair *noun* a wickerwork armchair.

basketry /'bahskitri/ *noun* the art or craft of making baskets or objects woven like baskets, or the woven objects themselves.

basket weave *noun* a textile weave resembling the chequered pattern of a plaited basket.

basketwork *noun* = BASKETRY.

basking shark /'bahsking/ *noun* a large species of shark that often lies near the water surface, feeding on plankton: *Cetorhinus maximus*.

basmati rice /bas'mati, baz-/ *noun* rice of high quality with a delicate flavour, originally grown in northern India and Pakistan. [Hindi *bāsmatī* fragrant]

basophil /'baysəfil/ *or* **basophile** /-fiel/ *noun* a white blood cell with basophilic granules: compare AGRANULOCYTE, EOSINOPHIL, GRANULOCYTE.

basophilic /baysə'filik/ *adj* staining readily with dyes that are chemical bases: *Some blood cells contain basophilic granules.* [BASE¹ + -O- + -PHILIC]

Basque /bask, bahsk/ *noun* **1** a member of a people inhabiting the W Pyrenees. **2** the language of the Basques, not known to be related to any other language. ⋙ **Basque** *adj*. [French *Basque* from Latin *Vasco*]

basque *noun* **1** the lower part of a bodice, that extends a little below the waist. **2** a close-fitting bodice for women: *She appeared in a ... skirt of black paper muslin, a black velvet ... basque* — David Graham Phillips. [French *basque*, ultimately from Old Provençal *basta* seam]

bas-relief /'bas rileef, 'bahs/ *noun* sculptural relief in which the design projects very slightly from the surrounding surface: compare HIGH RELIEF. [French *bas relief*, from *bas* low + *relief* raised work]

bass¹ /bas/ *noun* (*pl* **basses** *or collectively* **bass**) any of numerous edible spiny-finned marine and freshwater fishes: families Centrarchidae, Serranidae. [Middle English *base*, alteration of Old English *bærs*; related to Old English *byrst* bristle]

bass² /bays/ *noun* **1** the lowest adult male singing voice, or a singer with this voice. **2** (*used before a noun*) a musical instrument having the lowest range: *a bass trombone.* **3** a double bass or bass guitar. **4** the lowest singing part in conventional four-part harmony. **5** the lower portion of the audio frequency range considered *esp* in relation to its electronic reproduction. [Middle English *bas*: see BASE⁴]

bass³ /bays/ *adj* **1** of low pitch. **2** deep or grave in tone.

bass⁴ /bas/ *noun* a coarse tough fibre from palm trees. [alteration of BAST]

bass clef /bays/ *noun* in musical notation, a clef placing the F below middle C on the fourth line of the staff.

bass drum /bays/ *noun* a large drum with two heads that gives a low booming sound.

basset /'basit/ *or* **basset hound** *noun* any of a breed of short-legged hunting dogs with long bodies and very long ears. [French from Old French *basset* short, from *bas*: see BASE⁴]

bass guitar /bays/ *noun* a usu electric guitar that has four strings tuned like those of a double bass.

bassi /'basee/ *noun pl* of BASSO.

bassinet /basi'net/ *noun* a baby's basketlike cradle, e.g. of wickerwork or plastic, often with a hood over one end. [prob modification of French *barcelonnette*, dimin. of *berceau* cradle]

bassist /'baysist/ *noun* a musician who plays the double bass or bass guitar.

basso /'basoh/ *noun* (*pl* **bassos** *or* **bassi** /'basee/) a bass voice or singer. [Italian *basso* from medieval Latin *bassus* short, BASE⁴]

bassoon /bə'soohn/ *noun* a large woodwind musical instrument with a DOUBLE REED (two flat pieces of cane that vibrate to make the sound when blown across) and a usual range two octaves lower than the oboe. ⋙ **bassoonist** *noun*. [French *basson* from Italian *bassone*, from *basso*: see BASSO]

basso profundo /prə'foondoh/ *noun* (*pl* **basso profundos** *or* **bassi profundi** /-di/) an exceptionally low bass singing voice, or a singer with this voice. [Italian *basso profundo*, literally 'deep bass']

basso-rilievo /,basoh ri'lyayvoh/ *or* **basso-relievo** /ri'leevoh/ *noun* (*pl* **basso-rilievos** *or* **basso-relievos**) = BAS-RELIEF. [Italian, from *basso* low + *rilievo* raised work]

bass viol /bays/ *noun* = VIOLA DA GAMBA.

bast /bast/ *noun* **1** = PHLOEM. **2** a strong woody fibre obtained chiefly from the phloem of certain plants. [Old English *bæst*]

bastard¹ /'bahstəd, 'bastəd/ *noun* **1** *offensive or archaic* an illegitimate child. **2** *informal*. **a** an offensive or disagreeable person, often used as a general term of abuse. **b** a person of a specified type: *Poor old bastard.* **3** something spurious, irregular, inferior, or of questionable origin. ⋙ **bastardly** *adj*. [Middle English from Old French *bastart*, *bastard*, perhaps from *fils de bast*, literally 'son of the barn' or 'son of the packsaddle']

bastard² *adj* **1** *offensive or archaic* illegitimate. **2** of an inferior or less typical type, stock, or form. **3** lacking genuineness or authority; false.

bastardize *or* **bastardise** *verb trans* **1** *archaic* to declare (somebody) illegitimate. **2** to debase (something). ⋙ **bastardization** /-'zaysh(ə)n/ *noun*.

bastard wing *noun* the projecting part of a bird's wing corresponding to a mammal's thumb and bearing a few short feathers.

bastardy /'bahstədi, 'ba-/ *noun formal or archaic* the quality or state of being a bastard; illegitimacy.

baste¹ /bayst/ *verb trans* to sew (something) temporarily; to tack (it). ⋙ **baster** *noun*, **basting** *noun*. [Middle English *basten* from Old French *bastir*, of Germanic origin; related to Old English *bæst* BAST]

baste² *verb trans* to moisten (e.g. meat) at intervals with melted butter, dripping, etc during cooking, *esp* roasting. ⋙ **baster** *noun*, **basting** *noun*. [origin unknown]

baste³ *verb trans* to beat (somebody) severely or soundly; to thrash (them). ⋙ **basting** *noun*. [prob from Old Norse *beysta*; related to Old English *bēatan* to BEAT¹]

bastinado¹ /basti'naydoh/ *noun* (*pl* **bastinadoes**) a form of punishment or torture by beating the soles of the feet with a stick. [Spanish *bastonada*, from *bastón* stick, from late Latin *bastum*]

bastinado² *verb trans* (**bastinadoes, bastinadoed, bastinadoing**) to punish or torture (somebody) with a bastinado.

bastion /'basti·ən/ *noun* **1** a projecting part of a fortification. **2** a fortified area or position. **3** something or somebody considered as providing defence or protection; a stronghold: *the Académie Française, bastion of French culture.* ⋙ **bastioned** *adj*. [early French *bastion*, from *bastille* fortress, ultimately from Old Provençal *bastir* to build, of Germanic origin]

basuco /bə'soohkoh/ *noun* a cheap impure form of cocaine. [South American Spanish]

bat¹ /bat/ *noun* **1** a usu wooden implement used for hitting the ball in cricket, baseball, table tennis, etc. **2a** a batsman or batswoman. **b** a turn at batting in cricket, baseball, etc. **3** a hand-held implement shaped like a table-tennis bat for guiding aircraft when landing or taxiing. **4** a stout solid stick; a club. **5** a sharp blow. ✱ **off one's own bat** through one's own efforts, *esp* without being prompted. [Old English *batt*, prob of Celtic origin]

bat² *verb* (**batted, batting**) ➤ *verb trans* to strike or hit (something or somebody) with, or as if with, a bat. ➤ *verb intrans* **1** to strike a ball with a bat. **2** to take one's turn at batting, e.g. in cricket or baseball.

bat³ *noun* **1** any of an order of nocturnal flying mammals with forelimbs modified to form wings: order Chiroptera. **2** (**old bat**) *derog* a foolish or disagreeable old woman. [alteration of Middle English *bakke*, prob of Scandinavian origin]

bat[4] *verb trans* (**batted, batting**) to blink (an eye), *esp* in surprise or emotion: *He never batted an eyelid.* [prob alteration of *bate* to beat wings, from Middle English *baten* from Old French *batre* to beat]

batch[1] /'bach/ *noun* **1** a quantity of goods produced or prepared, e.g. baked, at one time. **2** a group of jobs to be run on a computer at one time with the same program. **3** a group of people or things; a lot. [Middle English *bache*; related to Old English *bacan* to BAKE[1]]

batch[2] *verb trans* to gather (things) together as a batch, or process (them) as a batch.

batch file *noun* a computer file that contains a series of commands that are to be processed by a computer consecutively just as if they were keyed in consecutively on the keyboard.

batch processing *noun* a method of processing data in which operations are collected together in batches and run on a computer when time permits.

bate[1] /bayt/ *verb trans archaic* to reduce (something) in bulk, amount, force, etc: *These griefs and losses have so bated me that I shall hardly spare a pound of flesh tomorrow to my bloody creditors* — Shakespeare. **✳ with bated breath 1** with the breath held in anticipation; in agitated suspense: *With parted lips and bated breath the audience hung upon his words* — Mark Twain. **2** in hushed tones: *hang down my head and speak with bated breath* — Frederick Douglass. [Middle English *baten*, short for *abaten*: see ABATE]

bate[2] *or* **bait** *noun informal* a rage or temper. [perhaps back-formation from *baited* harassed, tormented, from BAIT[2]]

bateau /ba'toh/ *noun* (*pl* **bateaux** /ba'toh(z)/) a light flat-bottomed river boat used in N America, *esp* Canada. [Canadian French *bateau*, ultimately from Old English *bāt* boat]

Batesian mimicry /'baytsi·ən/ *noun* the resemblance of a harmless species of animal to another having repellent qualities, e.g. unpalatability, that protect it from predators: compare MÜLLERIAN MIMICRY. [named after Henry Walter *Bates* d. 1892, English naturalist who discovered it]

bath[1] /bahth/ *noun* **1** a vessel for bathing in, *esp* one that is permanently fixed in a bathroom. **2a** a washing or soaking in water, or steam, of all or part of the body. **b** water used for bathing: *I'll just run a bath.* **3a** a specified type of liquid used for a special purpose, e.g. the developing of photographic film, or the vat or tank holding it. **b** a washing or soaking in such a liquid. **4** (*usu in pl*). **a** a building containing a room or series of rooms designed for bathing. **b** = SWIMMING POOL. **c** = SPA. **5** *NAmer* = BATHROOM. [Old English *bæth*]

bath[2] *verb Brit* to give (somebody) a bath. **➤** *verb intrans* to take a bath.

bath- *or* **batho-** *comb. form* forming words, denoting: depth: *bathometer.* [Greek *bathos*, from *bathys* deep]

Bath bun *noun* a sweet yeast-leavened bun containing dried fruit, e.g. raisins and sultanas, and topped with sugar crystals. [named after *Bath*, city in England where it was first made]

bath chair *noun* (*often* **Bath chair**) an old-fashioned usu hooded wheelchair: *being pushed about the grounds by the gardener in a Bath chair* — Conan Doyle. [*Bath*, city in England where many invalids went to bathe in hot springs]

bathe[1] /baydh/ *verb trans* **1** to wash or soak (something) in water or other liquid. **2** to moisten (something). **3** to apply water or a liquid medicament to (a diseased or injured part of the body). **4** to suffuse (something), *esp* with light. **5** *NAmer* to bath (somebody). **➤** *verb intrans* **1** to take a bath. **2** *chiefly Brit* to swim, e.g. in the sea or a river, for pleasure. **3** to become immersed or absorbed. **➤➤** **bather** *noun.* [Old English *bathian*; related to Old English *bæth* BATH[1]]

bathe[2] *noun Brit* an act of bathing, *esp* in the sea.

bathetic /bə'thetik/ *adj* characterized by bathos. **➤➤** **bathetically** *adv.*

bathhouse *noun* a building equipped for people to take baths.

bathing beauty /'baydhing/ *noun* a woman in a swimming costume who is a contestant in a beauty contest.

bathing cap /'baydhing/ *noun* = SWIMMING CAP.

bathing costume /'baydhing/ *noun Brit* = SWIMMING COSTUME.

bathing hut /'baydhing/ *noun* a hut for bathers to undress in.

bathing machine /'baydhing/ *noun* formerly, a bathing hut on wheels that was pulled to the water's edge for the convenience of the bather.

bathing suit /'baydhing/ *noun* = SWIMMING COSTUME.

bath mat *noun* **1** a usu washable mat, often of absorbent material, placed beside a bath. **2** a mat of non-slip material, *esp* rubber, placed in a bath to prevent the bather from slipping.

batho- *comb. form see* BATH-.

batholith /'bathəlith/ *noun* a large dome-shaped mass of igneous rock formed at a great depth below the earth's surface from molten material that forced its way into spaces between existing rocks and later solidified. **➤➤** **batholithic** /-'lithik/ *adj.* [BATHO- + Greek *lithos* stone]

bathometer /bə'thomitə/ *noun* an instrument for measuring depths in water.

bathos /'baythos/ *noun* **1** a sudden descent from something serious or high-minded to something commonplace or trivial. **2** exceptional commonplaceness; triteness. [Greek *bathos*, literally 'depth']

bathrobe *noun* a loose usu absorbent robe, e.g. made of towelling, worn before and after having a bath.

bathroom *noun* **1** a room containing a bath or shower and usu a washbasin and toilet. **2** *orig euphem* a toilet.

bath salts *pl noun* (*treated as sing. or pl*) a usu coloured compound for perfuming or softening bathwater.

bathtub *noun* a bath: **a** *chiefly Brit* one not permanently fixed in a bathroom. **b** *chiefly NAmer* one permanently fixed in a bathroom.

bathy- *comb. form* forming words, with the meanings: **1** deep; depth: *bathymeter.* **2** deep-sea: *bathysphere.* [Greek *bathys* deep]

bathymeter /bə'thimətə/ *noun* an instrument used to measure the depth of oceans, seas, and lakes. **➤➤** **bathymetric** /-'metrik/ *adj,* **bathymetry** *noun.*

bathyscaphe /'bathiskayf, -skaf/ *or* **bathyscaph** /'bathiskaf/ *noun* a navigable submersible ship for deep-sea exploration. [BATHY- + Greek *skaphē* light boat]

bathysphere /'bathisfiə/ *noun* a strongly built diving sphere for deep-sea observation.

batik /'batik, bə'teek/ *noun* an orig Indonesian method of handprinting by coating with wax the parts to be left undyed, or a fabric or design printed using this method. [via Malay from Javanese *batik* painted]

batiste /bə'teest/ *noun* a fine soft sheer fabric of plain weave made of various fibres. [French *batiste*]

batman /'batmən/ *noun* (*pl* **batmen**) a British officer's servant.

Word history
bat pack-saddle, luggage, from Old French. A batman was orig an orderly responsible for the horse that carried the officer's baggage.

bat mitzvah *or* **Bat Mitzvah** /bat 'mitsvə/ *noun* **1** the religious ceremony marking a Jewish girl's reaching the age of 13, when religious responsibilities are assumed. **2** a Jewish girl who undergoes this ceremony. [Hebrew *bath miswāh* daughter of the (divine) law]

baton /'bat(ə)n, 'baton, bə'ton (*French* batɔ̃)/ *noun* **1** a wand with which a conductor directs a band or orchestra. **2** a stick or hollow cylinder passed by each member of a relay team to the succeeding runner. **3** a short stick carried as a symbol of rank, *esp* by a senior military officer. **4** a police officer's truncheon. **5** the long metal rod that is twirled by a drum major or a majorette. [French *bâton* from late Latin *bastum* stick]

baton charge /'bat(ə)n/ *noun* a charge by police or troops wielding batons.

baton round /'bat(ə)n/ *noun* = PLASTIC BULLET.

batrachian[1] /bə'trayki·ən/ *noun* a frog, toad, or other vertebrate amphibian animal. [Greek *batrachos* frog]

batrachian[2] *adj* relating to tailless amphibians such as frogs and toads.

bats /bats/ *adj chiefly Brit, informal* mad; crazy. [prob from the phrase *to have bats in the belfry* to be crazy]

batsman /'batsmən/ *or* **batswoman** /'batswoomən/ *noun* (*pl* **batsmen** *or* **batswomen**) somebody who bats or is batting, *esp* in cricket. **➤➤** **batsmanship** *noun.*

battalion /bə'tali·ən/ *noun* (also in pl, but treated as sing. or pl) **1** a large body of organized troops. **2** a military unit composed of a headquarters and two or more companies. **3** a large group or number of people or things. [Old French *bataillon* via Old Italian from late Latin *battalia*: see BATTLE[1]]

batten¹ /'bat(ə)n/ *noun* **1** a thin narrow strip of squared timber. **2a** a thin strip of wood, plastic, etc, inserted into a sail to keep it flat and taut. **b** a slat used to secure the tarpaulins and hatch covers of a ship. **3** a strip holding a row of floodlights in a theatre. [French *bâton*: see BATON]

batten² *verb trans* (**battened, battening**) (*often* + down) to provide or fasten (*esp* a ship's hatches) with battens.

batten³ *verb intrans* (**battened, battening**) (+ on/upon) to thrive or grow prosperous, *esp* at the expense of somebody or something: *The press of the United States? It is a parasitic growth that battens on the capitalist class* — Jack London. [orig meaning to improve, grow fat, thrive; prob from Old Norse *batna* to improve]

battenberg /'batənbuhg/ *noun* an oblong sponge cake having a cross-section of pink and yellow squares covered in marzipan. [thought to be named after Battenberg, a town in Germany]

batter¹ /'batə/ *verb* (**battered, battering**) ⟩ *verb trans* **1** to beat (somebody or something) persistently or hard so as to bruise, injure, shatter, or demolish them. **2** to wear or damage (something) by hard usage or blows: *a battered old hat.* ⟩ *verb intrans* (+ on/at) to strike heavily and repeatedly; to beat: *She was battering at the door but nobody was in.* [Middle English *bateren*, prob frequentative of *batten* to bat, from *bat*: see BAT¹]

batter² *noun* **1** a mixture that consists essentially of flour, egg, and milk or water, and is thin enough to pour or drop from a spoon: compare DOUGH. **2** batter mixture, e.g. the kind used for coating fish, when cooked. [Middle English *bater*, prob from *bateren*: see BATTER¹]

batter³ *noun* in baseball, etc, the player who is batting.

batter⁴ *verb intrans and trans* (**battered, battering**) to slope or cause (e.g. a wall) to slope upwards and backwards. [origin unknown]

batter⁵ *noun* the slope of the outer face of a structure that slopes upwards and backwards.

battered¹ /'batəd/ *adj* said of food: fried in batter: *battered cod.*

battered² *adj* **1** said of an object: old and damaged or worn. **2** said of a person: injured by repeated violent abuse.

battering ram *noun* a large wooden beam with a head of iron, formerly used for beating down walls.

battery /'bat(ə)ri/ *noun* (*pl* **batteries**) **1** two or more cells connected together to provide an electric current. **2a** (*often* + of) a number of similar articles, items, or devices arranged, connected, or used together; a set or series: *a battery of tests.* **b** *chiefly Brit* a series of cages or compartments for housing, raising, or fattening animals, *esp* poultry: *battery hens.* **c** (*usu* + of) an impressive or imposing group; an array: *a battery of kitchen knives.* **3a** the act of battering somebody. **b** the unlawful application of any degree of force to a person without their consent. **4** (*usu* + of) a grouping of similar artillery guns, e.g. for tactical purposes. **5** (*treated as sing. or pl*) a tactical and administrative army artillery unit equivalent to an infantry company. [early French *batterie* from Old French, from *battre* to beat, from Latin *battuere*: see BATTLE¹]

batting /'bating/ *noun* layers or sheets of raw cotton or wool, used *esp* for lining quilts. [verbal noun from BAT²]

batting average *noun* **1** in cricket, the average score of a batsman's runs per completed innings: compare BOWLING AVERAGE. **2** in baseball, the batter's average score of safe hits per times at bat.

battle¹ /'batl/ *noun* **1** a general hostile encounter between armies, warships, aircraft, etc. **2** a combat between two people. **3** an extended contest, struggle, or controversy: *the battle against cancer.* [Middle English *batel* via Old French from late Latin *battalia* combat, ultimately from Latin *battuere* to beat, of Celtic origin]

battle² *verb intrans* **1** (*often* + against/with) to engage in battle; to fight. **2** (*often* + against/with) to contend with full strength or resources; to struggle: *battling against the elements.* ⟩ *verb trans* **1** to fight against (somebody). **2** to force (e.g. one's way) by battling: *She battled her way to the front of the crowd.* ⟩⟩⟩ **battler** *noun.*

battle-axe *noun* **1** a large axe with a broad head, used formerly in warfare. **2** a quarrelsome domineering woman.

battle cruiser *noun* a large heavily-armed warship faster than a battleship.

battledress *noun* the uniform worn by soldiers in battle.

battlefield *or* **battleground** *noun* a piece of ground where a battle is fought.

battlefield detainee *noun chiefly NAmer* an enemy combatant taken prisoner in time of war but not granted the status or rights of a prisoner of war.

battlement /'batlmənt/ *noun* a parapet with indentations that surmounts a wall and is used for defence or decoration. ⟩⟩⟩ **battlemented** *adj.* [Middle English *batelment* from Old French *bataille* fortifying tower]

battle royal *noun* (*pl* **battles royal** *or* **battle royals**) **1** a fight or contest between more than two opponents, *esp* until only the winner remains on their feet or in the ring. **2** a violent struggle or heated dispute.

battleship *noun* the largest and most heavily armed and armoured type of warship. [short for *line-of-battle ship*]

battue /ba't(y)ooh/ *noun* **1** the beating of woods and bushes to flush game for hunters. **2** a hunt using this method. [French *battue*, from *battre* to beat: see BATTERY]

batty /'bati/ *adj* (**battier, battiest**) *informal* mentally unstable; crazy. ⟩⟩⟩ **battiness** *noun.* [BAT³ + -Y¹. Compare with BATS]

baubee /baw'bee/ *noun* see BAWBEE.

bauble /'bawbl/ *noun* **1** a trinket or trifle: *I value this bauble of a coronet as little as you can, or any philosopher on earth* — Scott. **2** a jester's staff. [Middle English *babel* from Old French]

baud /bawd, bohd/ *noun* (*pl* **baud** *or* **bauds**) any of several units of data transmission speed; *specif* one equal to one bit of data per second. [French *baud*, named after J M E *Baudot* d.1903, French inventor of a code for data transmission]

Bauhaus /'bowhows/ *adj* **1** denoting a German school of design established in 1919 and noted *esp* for a programme that synthesized technology, craftsmanship, and design aesthetics.

Editorial note

The Bauhaus was a hugely influential German school of modernist art and design which existed in Weimar, then Dessau, and finally Berlin until 1933, when it was closed down by the Nazis. Like the English Arts and Crafts movement before it, the Bauhaus aimed to reform the making of everyday objects. But the Bauhaus, rather than rejecting the machine, embraced the functional aesthetic of industrial production — Martin Gayford.

2 characteristic of this school. [German *Bauhaus*, 'architecture house', academy founded in Weimar, Germany]

baulk¹ /'baw(l)k/ *verb Brit* see BALK¹.

baulk² *noun Brit* see BALK².

bauxite /'bawksiet/ *noun* a mineral that is an impure mixture of earthy hydrous aluminium oxides and hydroxides, and is the principal ore of aluminium. ⟩⟩⟩ **bauxitic** /bawk'sitik/ *adj.* [French *bauxite*, named after Les *Baux*, village near Arles, France, near where it was first discovered]

Bavarian /bə'veəri·ən/ *noun* **1** a native or inhabitant of Bavaria, a region in S Germany. **2** the High German dialect of the people of Bavaria. ⟩⟩⟩ **Bavarian** *adj.*

bavarois /bavə'wah/ *or* **bavaroise** /-'wahz/ *noun* a cold dessert made from rich custard set with gelatin in a mould. [French *bavarois* Bavarian]

bawbee *or* **baubee** /baw'bee/ *noun Scot* a halfpenny. [orig a 16th-cent. Scottish coin; prob named after Alexander Orrok fl.1541, laird of *Sillebawby* and master of the mint]

bawd /bawd/ *noun* a woman who keeps a house of prostitution: *As a bawd to a Whore, I grant you, he is to us of great Convenience* — John Gay. [Middle English *bawde*, ultimately from Old French *baud* bold, merry, shameless]

bawdry /'bawdri/ *noun* = BAWDY². [Middle English *bawderie*, from *bawde*: see BAWD]

bawdy¹ /'bawdi/ *adj* (**bawdier, bawdiest**) boisterously or humorously indecent. ⟩⟩⟩ **bawdily** *adv,* **bawdiness** *noun.*

bawdy² *noun* suggestive, coarse, or obscene language. [prob from BAWDY¹]

bawl¹ /bawl/ *verb intrans* **1** to yell or bellow. **2** to cry or wail. ⟩ *verb trans* to yell or bellow (something): *'Shut up!' he bawled.* ⟩⟩⟩ **bawler** *noun.* [Middle English *baulen*, prob of Scandinavian origin]

bawl² *noun* a loud prolonged cry.

bawl out *verb trans chiefly NAmer, informal* to reprimand (somebody) loudly or severely: *The teacher bawled her out for not doing her homework.*

bay[1] /bay/ *noun* **1** an inlet of a sea, lake, etc, usu smaller than a gulf. **2** a land formation resembling this. [Middle English *baye* from Old French *baie* from Spanish *bahia*]

bay[2] *noun* **1** any of several shrubs or trees resembling the laurel. **2** (*in pl*) an honorary garland or crown, *esp* of laurel, given for victory or excellence. [Middle English from Old French *baie* from Latin *baca* berry]

bay[3] *noun* **1** a division of a building or of part of a building, e.g. a recess with a bay window or an area used for a particular purpose. **2** a division of a structure; *esp* a compartment in the fuselage of an aircraft: *the forward instrument bay.* [Middle English from early French *baée* opening, fem past part. of *baer* to gape, yawn, from late Latin *batare*]

bay[4] *adj* said of a horse: reddish brown. [Middle English via Old French *bai* from Latin *badius*]

bay[5] *noun* **1** a horse with a reddish brown body and black mane, tail, and points. **2** a reddish brown colour.

bay[6] *verb intrans* said of dogs and wolves: to bark with prolonged tones. [Middle English *baien, abaien* from Old French *abaiier*, of imitative origin]

bay[7] *noun* **1** the position of an animal or person unable to retreat and forced to face a foe or danger: *The hunter brought his quarry to bay.* **2** the position of somebody or something kept off or repelled with difficulty: *The police kept the rioters at bay.* [Middle English *bay, abay* from Old French *abai*, from *abaiier*: see BAY[6]]

bay leaf *noun* the leaf of the European laurel used dried in cooking.

bayonet[1] /baɪəˈnet, ˈbaɪ-/ *noun* a blade attached to the muzzle of a firearm used in hand-to-hand combat. [French *baïonnette*, named after *Bayonne*, city in France, where they were first made]

bayonet[2] *verb trans* (**bayoneted, bayoneting**) to stab (somebody) with a bayonet.

bayou /ˈbiːuː, ˈbiːoʊ/ *noun* a sluggish marshy tributary of a river or lake, *esp* in the southern USA. [Louisiana French *bayou* from Choctaw *bayuk*]

bay rum *noun* a fragrant cosmetic and medicinal liquid from the oil of the leaves of a W Indian tree of the myrtle family. [BAY[2]]

bay window *noun* a window or series of windows projecting outwards from the wall. [BAY[3]]

bazaar /bəˈzɑː/ *noun* **1** a market, *esp* in the Middle East, consisting of rows of shops or stalls selling miscellaneous goods. **2** a fair for the sale of miscellaneous articles, *esp* for charitable purposes. [Persian *bāzār*]

bazooka /bəˈzuːkə/ *noun* an individual antitank rocket launcher used by infantrymen. [orig a crude musical instrument made of pipes and a funnel; prob of imitative origin]

BB *abbr* **1** Boys' Brigade. **2** used on lead pencils: double black.

BBC *abbr* British Broadcasting Corporation.

BBFC *abbr* British Board of Film Classification.

BBQ *abbr* barbecue.

BBS *abbr* in computing, bulletin board system.

BC *abbr* **1** used after a date: before Christ: *75 BC.* **2** British Columbia.
Usage note
BC *and* AD. See note at AD.

BCD *abbr* binary-coded decimal.

BCE *abbr* before the Common Era, used with cultural neutrality to indicate dates that are BC in Christian reckoning.

BCG vaccine *noun* a vaccine used to protect people against tuberculosis. [abbr of *bacillus Calmette-Guérin*, named after Albert *Calmette* d.1933, and Camille *Guérin* d.1961, French bacteriologists, who developed the vaccine]

BD *abbr* **1** Bachelor of Divinity. **2** Bangladesh (international vehicle registration).

bdellium /ˈdelɪəm/ *noun* a gum resin similar to myrrh, obtained from various trees of the E Indies and Africa. [Middle English via Latin from Greek *bdellion*]

BDS *abbr* **1** Bachelor of Dental Surgery. **2** Barbados (international vehicle registration).

BE *abbr* bill of exchange.

Be *abbr* the chemical symbol for beryllium.

be /bi; *strong* bee/ *verb* (*first person sing. present tense* **am** /əm; *strong* am/, *second person sing. present tense* **are** /ə; *strong* ah/, *third person sing. present tense* **is** /z; *strong* iz/, *pl present tense* **are**, *present subjunctive* **be**, *present part.* **being** /ˈbiːɪŋ/, *first and third person sing. past tense* **was** /wəz; *strong* woz/, *second person sing. past tense and pl past tense* **were** /wə; *strong* wuh/, *past subjunctive* **were**, *past part.* **been** /bin; *strong* been/) ▷ *verb intrans* **1** to exist or be present; to have a particular location: *Your mother is in the garden; Where is the dog?* **2** to be equal or equivalent to something stated as a complement: *Paris is the capital of France; God is love; The first person I saw was your husband.* **3** to occur in time: *The concert was last night.* **4** to have a specified state, function, or value: *The leaves are green; This is for you; The book is £25; Why are you angry?* **5** used with *it* or *there* to introduce general statements: *It is time we went; There are only three minutes left.* **6** used instead of *go* or *come* in the perfect tense: *I have only been to New York once; Has the postman been?* ▷ *verb aux.* **1** used with the present participle to form continuous or progressive tenses: *He is reading; I have been sleeping; We are leaving tomorrow.* **2** used with the past participle of transitive verbs to form the passive voice: *The children were found safe and well; The house is being built on the side of a hill.* **3** used with the past participle of certain intransitive verbs: **a** *archaic* to form perfect tenses: *The wheel is come full circle* — Shakespeare. **b** to form perfect tenses in which the emphasis is on the resulting state rather than the action: *The guests are all gone; The job is not quite finished.* **4** used with *to* and an infinitive to express future action, *esp* to describe destiny, commitment, possibility, or obligation: *He was to become famous; They were to have been married; I am to interview him today; It was nowhere to be found; You are not to smoke.* ✳ **be oneself** to behave normally or naturally. **not be oneself** to feel unwell or not in one's normal frame of mind. **-to-be** in the future, about to be: *She brought along her husband-to-be.* [Old English *bēon*]

be- *prefix* **1** forming verbs from verbs, with the meaning: on; round; all over: *besmear.* **2** forming verbs from verbs, with the meaning: to a great or greater degree; thoroughly: *befuddle.* **3** forming adjectives from adjectives, with the meaning: wearing (a specified article): *bespectacled.* **4** forming verbs from verbs, with the meaning: about; to; at; upon; against; across: *bestride.* **5** forming verbs from adjectives and nouns, with the meaning: to make; to cause to be; to treat as: *belittle.* **6** forming verbs from nouns, with the meaning: to affect, afflict, provide, or cover with, *esp* excessively: *bedevil.* [Old English *bi-, be-*; related to Old English *bī* BY[1]]

beach[1] /beech/ *noun* the shore of a sea or lake, often gently sloping and usu covered by sand or pebbles. [origin unknown]

beach[2] *verb trans* **1** to run or drive (a boat) ashore. **2** to strand (a whale) on a beach.

beachcomber /ˈbeechkohmə/ *noun* a person who searches along a shore for useful or saleable flotsam and jetsam; *esp* somebody who earns a living by doing this.

beachhead /ˈbeechhed/ *noun* an area on a hostile shore occupied to secure further landing of troops and supplies.

beach-la-mar /ˌbeech lə ˈmah/ *noun Brit* = BÊCHE-DE-MER (2). [by folk etymology]

beacon /ˈbeekən/ *noun* **1** a signal fire commonly on a hill, tower, or pole. **2** *Brit* a high conspicuous hill suitable for, or used in the past for, such a fire. **3a** a signal mark used to guide shipping. **b** a radio transmitter emitting signals for the guidance of aircraft. **4** a source of light or inspiration: *He ended by saying that the prospect of a Labour government was a beacon of hope for millions of striving and oppressed people throughout the world* — Independent. [Old English *bēacen* sign]

bead[1] /beed/ *noun* **1** a small ball, e.g. of wood or glass, pierced for threading on a string or wire. **2** (*in pl*). **a** a rosary. **b** a series of prayers and meditations made with a rosary. **3** a small ball-shaped body, *esp* a drop of liquid. **4** a small metal knob on a firearm used as a front sight. **5** a projecting rim, band, or moulding, e.g. on a door.

Word history
Middle English *bede* prayer, prayer bead, from Old English *bed, gebed* prayer; related to Old English *biddan* BID[1]. The development of this word has taken it a long way from its original meaning 'prayer', a sense now surviving only in the compounds *beadsman* and *beadroll*. In the 14th cent. it was transferred to one of the small balls on a string that were used for counting prayers; in the 15th cent. the meaning was broadened to include ornamental beads, and various extended uses, e.g. a drop of liquid, followed.

bead² *verb trans* **1** to adorn or cover (clothing, etc) with beads or beading: *a beaded dress*. **2** to string (things) together like beads. ➤ *verb intrans* to form into a bead.

beading *noun* **1** material adorned with or consisting of beads. **2a** a narrow moulding of rounded, often semicircular, cross section, e.g. on a door. **b** a moulding that resembles a string of beads. **3** a narrow openwork insertion or trimming, e.g. on lingerie.

beadle /'beedl/ *noun* a minor parish official whose duties include ushering and preserving order at church services. [Old English *bydel*]

beady *adj* (**beadier, beadiest**) said of eyes: small, round, and shiny with interest or greed.

beagle /'beegl/ *noun* a hound of a breed with short legs and a smooth coat. [Middle English *begle*; earlier history unknown]

beagling *noun* hunting on foot with beagles. ➤➤ **beagler** *noun*.

beak /beek/ *noun* **1a** the bill of a bird. **b** any of various rigid projecting mouth structures, e.g. of a turtle or dolphin. **c** the long sucking mouth of some insects. **2a** a metal-tipped beam projecting from the bow of an ancient galley for ramming an enemy ship. **b** the pouring spout of a vessel. **3** *informal* the human nose. **4** *chiefly Brit, informal*. **a** a magistrate. **b** a schoolteacher. ➤➤ **beaked** *adj*. [Middle English *bec* via Old French from Latin *beccus*, of Gaulish origin]

beaker /'beekə/ *noun* **1** a large drinking vessel with a wide mouth, *esp* a tall plastic one without a handle. **2** a cylindrical flat-bottomed vessel, usu with a pouring lip, that is used *esp* by chemists and pharmacists. [Middle English *biker* from Old Norse *bikarr*, prob from Old Saxon *bikeri* from a prehistoric West Germanic word borrowed from late Latin *bicarius* beaker, from Greek *bikos* earthen jug]

Beaker Folk *pl noun* a prehistoric people living in Europe in the early Bronze Age whose culture was characterized by finely decorated beakers buried with their dead.

be-all and end-all *noun* (**the be-all and end-all**) the chief factor; the essential element: *Passing exams is not the be-all and end-all of education.*

beam¹ /beem/ *noun* **1a** a long piece of heavy, often squared, timber suitable for use in construction. **b** any of the principal horizontal supporting members of a building or across a ship. **c** the width of a ship at its widest part. **d** the bar of a balance from which scales hang. **e** an oscillating lever joining an engine piston rod to a crank, *esp* in a type of stationary steam engine: *a beam engine*. **2a** a ray or shaft of radiation, *esp* light. **b** a collection of nearly parallel rays, e.g. X-rays, or of particles, moving in nearly parallel paths. **3a** a radio signal transmitted continuously in one direction as an aircraft navigation aid. **b** the course indicated by this. ✱ **broad in the beam** *informal* having wide hips. **off beam/off the beam** wrong; irrelevant: *Your estimate was way off beam*. **on the beam** proceeding or operating correctly. [Old English *bēam* tree, beam]

beam² *verb trans* **1** to emit (light etc) in beams or as a beam. **2** to aim (a broadcast) by directional aerials. ➤ *verb intrans* to smile with joy.

beam-ends *pl noun Brit, informal* buttocks. ✱ **on her beam-ends** said of a ship: about to capsize. **on one's beam-ends** near the end of one's financial resources.

beamer /'beemə/ *noun* in cricket, an intimidatory delivery of the ball that passes or hits the batsman at above waist height before it bounces.

beamy /'beemi/ *adj* said of a ship: broad at its widest part.

bean /been/ *noun* **1a** any of several species of erect or climbing leguminous plants widely cultivated for their usu edible seeds: genus *Phaseolus* and other genera. **b** a seed of any of these plants, often used as a vegetable. **c** a bean pod, used when immature as a vegetable. **d** any of various seeds or fruits that resemble beans or bean pods: *coffee beans*. **e** a plant producing these. **2** *informal*. **a** the smallest possible amount of money: *I gave up my job and haven't a bean*. **b** a valueless item: *It's not worth a bean*. **3** *informal, dated* somebody's head. ✱ **full of beans** full of vigour; very energetic. [Old English *bēan*]

beanbag *noun* **1** a small fabric bag that is filled with beans and used in games or as a toy. **2** a large, loosely stuffed cushion usu containing granules or fragments of plastic foam, used as an informal low chair.

bean curd *noun* a soft cheeselike food that is much used in Eastern cooking and is prepared from soya-bean milk.

beanfeast *noun Brit, informal* a festivity or celebration.

beanie /'beeni/ *noun* a small round hat worn on the back of the head. [BEAN in the sense 'head']

beano /'beenoh/ *noun* (*pl* **beanos**) *Brit, informal* a beanfeast. [by shortening and alteration]

beanpole *noun* **1** a stick used to support a bean plant. **2** *informal* a very tall thin person.

bean sprouts *pl noun* the sprouts of bean seeds, *esp* of the mung bean, used as a vegetable.

bear¹ /beə/ *noun* (*pl* **bears** *or collectively* **bear**) **1** any of a family of large heavy mammals with long shaggy hair and a short tail that feed largely on fruit and insects as well as on flesh: family Ursidae. **2** a surly, uncouth, or shambling person. **3** a person who sells securities or commodities in expectation of a fall in price: compare BULL¹. [Old English *bera*; related to Old English *brūn* BROWN¹; (sense 3) prob from proverbial phrase *selling the bearskin before catching the bear*]

bear² *verb* (*past tense* **bore** /baw/, *past part.* **borne** /bawn/) ➤ *verb trans* **1a** to carry or transport (something): *People came bearing gifts.* **b** to carry or own (something) as equipment: *the right to bear arms.* **c** to entertain (a feeling) mentally: *I bear no malice towards him.* **d** to behave or conduct (oneself): *She bore herself with dignity at all times.* **e** to have or show (something) as a feature: *She bears the scars of a failed marriage.* **f** to give (something) as testimony: *Thou shalt not bear false witness against thy neighbour* — Bible. **g** to have (a name) as an identification. **2a** to give birth to (a baby). **b** to produce (fruit or flowers) as yield. **3a** to support the weight of (something). **b** to tolerate or accept the presence of (something or somebody): *I could hardly bear the pain.* **c** to sustain or incur (something): *The company will bear the cost of the trip.* **d** to allow or admit of (something): *It won't bear repeating.* ➤ *verb intrans* **1** to go or extend in a specified direction: *The road bears to the right.* **2** (*often* + on) to become directed: *The troops brought guns to bear on the target.* **3** (+ on) to apply or have relevance to something: *These are the facts bearing on the situation.* **4** to produce fruit; to yield. **5** (+ with) to show patience or indulgence towards somebody: *Bear with me for a while longer.* ✱ **bear fruit** said of work or efforts: to be productive or have good results. ➤➤ **bearable** *adj*, **bearably** *adv*. [Old English *beran*]

bearbaiting /'beəbayting/ *noun* the practice of setting dogs on a captive bear, which was formerly a popular entertainment.

beard¹ /biəd/ *noun* **1** the hair that grows on the lower part of a man's face, usu excluding the moustache. **2** a hairy or bristly appendage or tuft, e.g. on a goat's chin or an ear of barley. ➤➤ **bearded** *adj*, **beardless** *adj*. [Old English *beard*]

beard² *verb trans* to confront and oppose (somebody) with boldness, resolution, and often effrontery; to defy (somebody): *He was resolved ... at all hazards to retrace his steps and beard the enemy again in his capital* — William Hickling Prescott. [BEARD¹; from the idea of facing an opponent]

bearded tit *noun* a small European bird with a long tail, found in secluded reedy places: *Panurus biarmicus*. Also called REEDLING.

bear down *verb intrans* said of a woman in childbirth: to exert concentrated downward pressure in an effort to expel the baby from the womb. ✱ **bear down on 1** to come towards (somebody) purposefully or threateningly. **2** to weigh heavily on (something).

bearer *noun* **1** a porter. **2** a plant yielding fruit. **3** a pallbearer. **4** a person holding an order for payment, *esp* a bank note or cheque.

bear garden *noun* a scene of great noise or tumult. [from the rowdiness of bearbaiting]

bear hug *noun* a rough tight embrace.

bearing *noun* **1** the manner in which one carries or conducts oneself: *a fine looking man, with a dignified and military bearing* — Edgar Rice Burroughs. **2** (*also in pl*) a machine part in which another part turns or slides. **3** an emblem or figure on a heraldic shield. **4a** the compass direction of a course or of one point with respect to another. **b** a determination of position. **c** (*in pl*) comprehension of one's position, environment, or situation: *He lost his bearings.* **d** (*usu* + on) a relation, connection, significance: *Your opinion has no bearing on the matter.*

bearing rein *noun* = CHECKREIN.

bearish *adj* marked by, tending to cause, or fearful of falling prices, e.g. in a stock market: compare BULLISH. ➤➤ **bearishness** *noun*.

Béarnaise sauce /bayə'nayz/ *noun* a rich sauce made with butter and egg yolks, and flavoured with wine, onion, and tarragon. [French *béarnaise*, fem of *béarnais* of *Béarn*, region and former province of France]

bear out *verb trans* to confirm or substantiate (something): *Research bore out his theory.*

bearskin *noun* an article made of the skin of a bear; *esp* a tall black military hat worn by the Brigade of Guards.

bear up *verb intrans* to summon up courage, resolution, or strength; to endure a difficult situation: *She is bearing up under the strain.*

beast /beest/ *noun* **1a** an animal as distinguished from a plant. **b** a four-legged mammal as distinguished from human beings, lower vertebrates, and invertebrates. **c** an animal under human control. **2** a cruel or contemptible person. [Middle English *beste* via Old French from Latin *bestia*]

beastly *adj* (**beastlier, beastliest**) **1** very unpleasant or disagreeable: *beastly weather.* **2** of beasts; bestial. ➤➤ **beastliness** *noun.*

beast of burden *noun* an animal used to carry heavy material or perform other heavy work, e.g. pulling a plough.

beat[1] /beet/ *verb* (*past tense* **beat**, *past part.* **beaten**) ➤ *verb trans* **1a** to hit (somebody) repeatedly so as to inflict pain. **b** to strike directly against (something) forcefully and repeatedly: *Heavy waves beat the shore.* **c** to flap or thrash at (something) vigorously: *a trapped bird beating the air.* **d** to strike at or range over (something) in order to rouse game, or as if to rouse game. **e** to mix or whip (food). **f** to strike (something) repeatedly in order to produce music or a signal. **2a** to pound (something) into a powder, paste, or pulp. **b** to make (something) by repeated treading or driving over a surface: *A path had been beaten through the woods.* **c** to dislodge (something) by repeated hitting: *We beat the dust from the carpet.* **d** to lodge (something) securely by repeated striking: *He beat a stake into the ground.* **e** to shape (something) by beating; *esp* to flatten (something) thin by blows: *gold beaten into foil.* **f** to sound or express (something), *esp* by drumbeat: *The men beat a tattoo on the drums.* **3** to cause (one's hand or foot) to strike or tap repeatedly: *He beat his foot nervously on the ground.* **4a** to overcome or defeat (somebody). **b** to surpass (somebody). **c** to win by overcoming a restraint imposed by (something): *The oldest entrant beat the odds to win the race.* **5** to indicate (a rhythm) by beating. **6** of a bird's wing: to strike the air. ➤ *verb intrans* **1a** (+ on/at/against) to dash or strike: *The rain was beating on the roof.* **b** to glare or strike with oppressive intensity: *The sun was beating down.* **2a** said of a heart or pulse: to pulsate or throb. **b** to sound on being struck: *The drums were beating.* **3a** to strike the air; to flap: *The bird's wings beat frantically.* **b** to strike cover or range in order to find or rouse game. **4a** to progress with much difficulty. **b** said of a sailing vessel: to make way at sea against the wind by a series of alternate tacks across the wind. ✳ **beat about the bush** to fail to come to the point in conversation by talking indirectly or evasively. **beat a retreat** to withdraw quickly. **beat it** *informal* to hurry away; to leave. **beat somebody to it** to act ahead of somebody, usu so as to forestall them. **it beats me** *informal* I cannot understand: *It beats me why she married him.* **beat somebody down** to make somebody reduce the price of something. ➤➤ **beatable** *adj.* [Old English *bēatan*]

beat[2] *noun* **1a** a metrical or rhythmic stress in poetry or music. **b** the rhythmic effect of this. **c** the tempo indicated to a musical performer. **2a** a pulsation or throb. **b** a sound produced by beating, or as if by beating. **3** each of the pulsations of amplitude produced by the mixing of sine waves, e.g. sound or radio waves, having different frequencies. **4** an area or route regularly patrolled, *esp* by a police officer. **5** a single stroke or blow, *esp* in a series: *three beats on the drum.* **6** = TACK[1] (3B).

beat[3] *adj* **1** of or being beatniks: *beat poets.* **2** *informal* exhausted: *I'm dead beat after driving all day.* [short for *beaten*, past part. of BEAT[1]]

beatbox *noun informal* a drum machine.

beaten[1] *verb* past part. of BEAT[1].

beaten[2] *adj* **1** hammered into a desired shape: *beaten gold.* **2** defeated. ✳ **off the beaten track 1** said of a place: remote or isolated. **2** not well-known; unfamiliar.

beater *noun* **1** any of various hand-held implements for whisking or beating: *a carpet beater; an egg beater.* **2** a person who strikes bushes or other cover to rouse game for hunters.

beatific /bee-ə'tifik/ *adj* **1** of, possessing, or imparting beatitude. **2** having a blissful or benign appearance; saintly or angelic: *a beatific smile.* ➤➤ **beatifically** *adv.* [Latin *beatificus* making happy, from *beatus* happy, blessed, past part. of *beare* to bless]

beatify /bee'atifie/ *verb trans* (**beatifies, beatified, beatifying**) **1** to authorize the veneration of (a dead person) by Roman Catholics by giving the title 'Blessed'. **2** to make (somebody) supremely happy. ➤➤ **beatification** /-fi'kaysh(ə)n/ *noun.* [Old French *beatifier* from late Latin *beatificare*, from Latin *beatus*: see BEATIFIC]

beating *noun* **1** injury or damage inflicted by striking with repeated blows: *a savage beating.* **2** a throbbing: *the beating of your heart.* **3** a defeat: *Our team took a terrible beating in the finals.*

beatitude /bi'atityoohd, -choohd/ *noun* **1a** a state of utmost bliss. **b** used as a title: a primate, *esp* of an Eastern Church. **2** any of a series of sayings of Jesus beginning 'Blessed are' in the Authorized Version of the Bible. [Latin *beatitudo*, from *beatus*: see BEATIFIC]

beatnik /'beetnik/ *noun* in the 1950s and 1960s, a person who rejected the moral attitudes of established society, e.g. by unconventional behaviour and dress.

beat off *verb trans* to drive or force away (a person or animal) with blows. ➤ *verb intrans coarse slang* said of a man: to masturbate.

beat up *verb* to assault and harm (somebody) by repeated punching, kicking, etc.

beau /boh/ *noun* (*pl* **beaux** or **beaus** /bohz/) **1** *chiefly NAmer* a male lover; a boyfriend: *Is that man going to be your beau?* — Gene Stratton Porter. **2** any eligible young male acquaintance: *one never thinks of married men's being beaux – they have something else to do* — Jane Austen. **3** *archaic* sometimes in a nickname: a dandy: *Beau Brummell.* [French *beau* beautiful, from Latin *bellus* pretty]

Beaufort scale /'bohfawt/ *noun* a scale in which the force of the wind is indicated by numbers from 0 (calm) to 12 (hurricane). [named after Sir Francis *Beaufort* d.1857, English admiral, who devised it]

beau ideal /boh eeday'al/ *noun* the perfect type or model: *Her person was of the smallest size that is believed to comport with beauty, and which poets and artists have chosen as the beau ideal of female loveliness* — J Fenimore Cooper. [French *beau idéal* ideal beauty]

Beaujolais /'bohzhəlay/ *noun* a chiefly red table wine made in southern Burgundy in France. [French, named after *Beaujolais*, region of central France]

beaut[1] /byoot/ *noun chiefly Aus, NZ, informal* = BEAUTY (3).

beaut[2] *adj Aus, NZ, informal* fine or marvellous: *a beaut party.*

beauteous /'byoohti-əs/ *adj archaic* beautiful. ➤➤ **beauteousness** *noun.* [Middle English from *beaute*: see BEAUTY]

beautician /byooh'tish(ə)n/ *noun* somebody who gives beauty treatments.

beautiful /'byoohtif(ə)l/ *adj* **1** having qualities of beauty; exciting aesthetic pleasure or delighting the senses. **2** generally pleasing; excellent. ➤➤ **beautifully** *adv.*

beautify /'byoohtifie/ *verb trans* (**beautifies, beautified, beautifying**) to make (somebody or something) beautiful; to embellish. ➤➤ **beautification** /-fi'kaysh(ə)n/ *noun*, **beautifier** *noun.*

beauty /'byoohti/ *noun* (*pl* **beauties**) **1** the qualities in a person or thing that give pleasure to the senses or exalt the mind or spirit; loveliness: *Beauty is truth, truth beauty* — Keats. **2** a beautiful person or thing; *esp* a beautiful woman. **3** a brilliant, extreme, or conspicuous example or instance: *That mistake was a beauty.* **4** a particularly advantageous or excellent quality: *The beauty of my idea is that it costs so little.* [Middle English *beaute* from Old French *biauté*, from *bel, biau* beautiful, from Latin *bellus* pretty]

beauty parlour *noun* = BEAUTY SALON.

beauty queen *noun* a young woman who wins a beauty contest.

beauty salon *noun* an establishment where professional beauty treatments, e.g. hairdressing, treatments for the face, and manicures, are provided, *esp* for women.

beauty sleep *noun* sleep considered as being beneficial to a person's beauty.

beauty spot *noun* **1** a beautiful scenic area. **2** a mark, e.g. a mole or a similar artificial mark, adorning a person's face.

beaux /bohz/ *noun* pl of BEAU.

beaux esprits /ˌbohz e'spree (*French* boz ɛspri)/ *noun* pl of BEL ESPRIT.

beaver[1] /'beevə/ *noun* (*pl* **beavers** *or collectively* **beaver**) **1a** any of several species of large semiaquatic rodents with webbed hind feet and a broad flat tail that build dams and underwater lodges: genus *Castor*. **b** the fur or pelt of the beaver. **2** a hat made of beaver fur or a fabric imitation. **3** a heavy fabric of felted wool napped on both sides. [Old English *beofor*; related to Old English *brūn* BROWN[1]]

beaver[2] *verb intrans* (**beavered, beavering**) (*also* + away) to work energetically: *They are beavering away at the problem.*

beaver[3] *noun* **1** a piece of armour protecting the lower part of the face. **2** a helmet visor. [Middle English *baviere* from Old French]

beaverboard *noun* a fibreboard used for partitions and ceilings. [from *Beaver Board*, a trademark]

bebop /'beebop/ *noun* jazz characterized by unusual chord structures, syncopated rhythm, and harmonic complexity and innovation. Also called BOP[3].

Editorial note
Originally a nonsense word used in scat singing to denote a particular two-beat rhythm, bebop – later more widely recognized in the shorter form 'bop' – became one of the major styles in jazz, developed by young American musicians in the 1940s and characterized by a deeper and more diversified rhythmic and harmonic content than that offered by swing jazz — Richard Cook.

➤➤ **bebopper** *noun*. [imitative of the music's rhythm]

becalm /bi'kahm/ *verb trans* (*usu in passive*) to keep (a sailing vessel) motionless by lack of wind.

became /bi'kaym/ *verb* past tense of BECOME.

because /bi'koz, bi'kaz/ *conj* **1** for the reason that; since: *He rested because he was tired.* **2** and the proof is that: *They must be in, because the light's on.* [Middle English *because that, because*, from *by cause that*]

because of *prep* **1** as a result of (something or somebody): *He was off school because of illness.* **2** for the sake of (something or somebody): *She gave up her job because of the children.*

béchamel /'bayshəmel (*French* beʃamɛl)/ *noun* a white sauce made with ROUX (fat cooked with flour) and milk in which vegetables and herbs have been infused: compare VELOUTÉ. [French *sauce béchamelle*, named after Louis de Béchamel d.1703, French courtier, said to have invented a similar sauce]

bêche-de-mer /,besh də 'meə/ *noun* **1** = TREPANG. **2** (**Bêche-de-Mer**) a pidgin English used *esp* in the W Pacific. Also called BEACH-LA-MAR. [French *bêche-de-mer*, literally 'sea grub']

beck[1] /bek/ *noun* N Eng a brook; *esp* a pebbly mountain stream. [Middle English *bek* from Old Norse *bekkr*]

beck[2] ✳ **at somebody's beck and call** in continual readiness to obey somebody. [Middle English in the senses 'nod', 'bow', 'gesture of command', from *becken, beknen*: see BECKON[1]]

becket /'bekit/ *noun* a bracket, loop of rope, hook, etc for securing tackle or spars on a ship. [origin unknown]

beckon[1] /'bekən/ *verb* (**beckoned, beckoning**) ➤ *verb intrans* **1** to summon or signal, typically with a wave or nod. **2** to appear inviting: *A pint of beer beckoned.* ➤ *verb trans* to beckon to (somebody): *My aunt beckoned me to sit down beside her.* [Middle English *beknen* from Old English *bīecnan*, from *bēacen* sign, later BEACON]

beckon[2] *noun* a summons or signal, typically with a wave or nod.

become /bi'kum/ *verb* (*past tense* **became** /bi'kaym/, *past part.* **become**) ➤ *verb intrans* to come to be: *The sky became darker; The minister became party leader last month.* ➤ *verb trans* to suit or be suitable for (somebody): *That hairstyle becomes her; Such behaviour does not become you.* ✳ **become of** to happen to (somebody): *What became of that girl who lived next door?* [Old English *becuman*, from BE- + *cuman* COME[1]]

becoming *adj* suitable or fitting; *esp* attractively suitable. ➤➤ **becomingly** *adv*.

becquerel /'bek(ə)rəl, bekə'rel/ *noun* the SI unit of radiation activity equal to one unit of disintegration per second. [named after Antoine Henri *Becquerel* d.1908, French physicist]

BEd *abbr* Bachelor of Education.

bed[1] /bed/ *noun* **1a** a piece of furniture or in which one may lie and sleep and that usu includes bedstead, mattress, and bedding. **b** a place of sexual activity. **c** a place for a hospital patient. **d** sleep, or a time for sleeping: *We took a walk before bed.* **2a** a plot of ground, *esp* in a garden, prepared for plants. **b** plants grown in such a plot. **3a** the bottom of a body of water: *the sea bed.* **b** an area of a sea or lake bottom supporting a heavy growth of a specified organism: *an*

oyster bed. **4** a supporting surface or structure; *esp* the foundation that supports a road or railway. **5** = STRATUM. **6** a heap on which something else is laid: *coleslaw on a bed of lettuce.* ✳ **get out of bed on the wrong side** to be in a bad mood at the beginning of the day. **go to bed with** to have sexual intercourse with. **in bed** in the act of sexual intercourse: *His wife found him in bed with another woman.* [Old English *bedd*]

bed[2] *verb* (**bedded, bedding**) ➤ *verb trans* **1a** (*often* + down) to provide (somebody) with a bed or bedding; to settle (somebody) in sleeping quarters: *The children were bedded down for the night.* **b** to have sexual intercourse with (somebody). **2a** to fix (something) firmly in something else; to embed. **b** (*often* + out) to plant or arrange (seedlings, etc) in beds. **3** to lay (something) flat or in a layer. ➤ *verb intrans* **1** (*often* + down) to go to bed: *I need a place to bed down for the night.* **2** (*often* + down) to form a layer.

bed and breakfast *noun* Brit a night's lodging and breakfast the following morning.

bedazzle /bi'daz(ə)l/ *verb trans* to dazzle (somebody) with brilliance; to impress (somebody) greatly. ➤➤ **bedazzlement** *noun*.

bed-blocking *noun* the occupying of hospital beds by patients who do not actually need hospital care because there is no alternative place of care available for them.

bedbug *noun* a wingless bloodsucking bug that sometimes infests beds: *Cimex lectularius.*

bedclothes *pl noun* the covers, e.g. sheets and blankets, used on a bed.

bedder /'bedə/ *noun* **1** a bedding plant. **2** Brit, *informal* a person employed at a Cambridge college to clean rooms.

bedding /'beding/ *noun* **1** = BEDCLOTHES. **2** a bottom layer; a foundation. **3** material used as a bed for livestock. **4** a stratified rock formation.

bedding plant *noun* a plant appropriate or adapted for growing in open-air beds.

bedeck /bi'dek/ *verb trans* to deck out or adorn (a person, place, or thing): *She wears her yellow hair in a high pompadour and is bedecked with rings and chains* — Willa Cather.

bedevil /bi'devl/ *verb trans* (**bedevilled, bedevilling**, NAmer **bedeviled, bedeviling**) **1** to torment (somebody) maliciously; to harass. **2** to change (something) for the worse; to spoil or frustrate. **3** to possess (somebody) with or as if with a devil; to bewitch. ➤➤ **bedevilment** *noun*.

bedfellow *noun* **1** a person who shares a bed. **2** a close associate; an ally: *political bedfellows.*

bedlam /'bedləm/ *noun* a place, scene, or state of uproar and confusion: *It was bedlam at the children's party.* [*Bedlam*, popular name for the Hospital of St Mary of Bethlehem, London, a hospital for the insane, from Middle English *Bedlem* Bethlehem]

bed linen *noun* the sheets and pillowcases used on a bed.

bedmaker *noun* Brit = BEDDER (2).

bedmate *noun* a person who shares one's bed; *esp* a sexual partner.

bed of nails *noun* a difficult or unpleasant situation.

bed of roses *noun* a place or situation of agreeable ease: *It's no bed of roses teaching in a secondary school* — The Daily Mirror.

bedouin *or* **beduin** /'bedwin, 'bedooh·in/ *noun* (*pl* **bedouins** *or* **beduins** *or collectively* **bedouin** *or* **beduin**) (*often* **Bedouin**) a nomadic Arab of the Arabian, Syrian, or N African deserts. [French *bédouin* from Arabic *badāwi, bidwān*, pl of *badawi* desert dweller]

bedpan *noun* a shallow vessel used by a person in bed for urination or defecation.

bedpost *noun* a post of a bedstead, often turned or carved.

bedraggle /bi'dragl/ *verb trans* to wet (somebody or something) thoroughly. [BE- + DRAGGLE]

bedraggled *adj* **1** left wet and limp by rain, or as if by rain. **2** soiled and stained by, or as if by, trailing in mud.

bedridden /'bedrid(ə)n/ *adj* confined to bed, e.g. by illness. [Old English *bedreda* a person confined to bed, from *bedd* BED[1] + *-rida, -reda* RIDER]

bedrock *noun* **1** the solid rock underlying unconsolidated surface materials, e.g. soil. **2** the basis of something: *the bedrock of society.*

bedroll *noun* chiefly NAmer bedding, *esp* that used for sleeping in the open, rolled up for carrying.

bedroom *noun* **1** a room furnished with a bed and intended primarily for sleeping. **2** (*used before a noun*) dealing with, suggestive of, or inviting sexual relations: *a bedroom farce.*

Beds *abbr* Bedfordshire.

bedside *noun* **1** the space at the side of a bed. **2** (*used before a noun*) of or conducted at somebody's bedside: *a bedside vigil.* **3** (*used before a noun*) suitable for a person in bed: *bedside reading.*

bedside manner *noun* the manner with which a doctor deals with patients.

bed-sit *noun Brit, informal* a bed-sitter.

bed-sitter *noun Brit* a single room serving as both bedroom and sitting room.

bed-sitting-room *noun Brit* a bed-sitter.

bedsore *noun* a sore caused by prolonged pressure on part of the body of a bedridden invalid.

bedspread *noun* an ornamental cloth cover for a bed.

bedstead /'bedsted/ *noun* the framework of a bed. [Middle English *bedstede*, from BED[1] + *stede* place]

bedstraw *noun* any of several species of plants of the madder family having angled stems, opposite or whorled leaves, and small flowers: genus *Galium.* [from its use for mattresses]

beduin /'bedwin, 'bedooh·in/ *noun* see BEDOUIN.

bed-wetting /'bedweting/ *noun* involuntary urination in bed during sleep. >> **bed-wetter** *noun.*

bee /bee/ *noun* **1a** any of several species of social four-winged insects often kept in hives for the honey that they produce: genus *Apis.* **b** any of a large group of insects that differ from the related wasps, *esp* in the heavier hairier body and legs, and in sometimes having a pollen basket: superfamily *Apoidea.* **2** *chiefly NAmer* a gathering of people for a specified purpose: *an even more evil fame than attached to the … moonlight husking-bees* — Harold Frederic; *a sewing bee.* ✳ **bee in one's bonnet** an obsession about a specified subject or idea: *He's got a bee in his bonnet about cleanliness.* [Old English *bēo*]

Beeb /beeb/ *noun Brit* the BBC. [by shortening and alteration]

beebread *noun* bitter yellowish brown pollen mixed with honey used by bees as food. Also called AMBROSIA.

beech /beech/ *noun* (*pl* **beeches** *or collectively* **beech**) **1** any of several species of hardwood deciduous trees with smooth grey bark and small edible triangular nuts: genus *Fagus.* **2** the wood of this tree. >> **beechen** *adj.* [Old English *bēce*]

beech mast *noun* the nuts of the beech when lying on the ground.

bee eater *noun* any of several species of brightly coloured insect-eating birds of warm or tropical Europe, Asia, and Australasia, with a slender bill: family Meropidae.

beef[1] /beef/ *noun* (*pl* **beefs**) **1** the flesh of a bullock, cow, or other adult domestic bovine animal. **2a** (*pl* **beeves**, *NAmer* **beefs**) an ox, cow, or bull in a full-grown or nearly full-grown state; *esp* a bullock or cow fattened for food. **b** a dressed carcass of a beef animal. **3** *informal* muscular flesh; brawn. **4** *informal* a complaint. [Middle English from Old French *buef* ox, beef, from Latin *bov-, bos* head of cattle]

beef[2] *verb trans informal* (*usu* + up) to add weight, strength, or power to (something): *Police presence is to be beefed up for the cup final.* > *verb intrans informal* (*often* + about) to complain: *Fans are beefing about the price of the tickets.*

beefburger /'beefbuhgə/ *noun* a hamburger.

beefcake *noun informal* a photographic display of muscular male physiques; compare CHEESECAKE (2).

beefeater *noun* a Yeoman of the Guard. [BEEF[1] + *eater*; orig meaning a well-fed servant]

beefsteak fungus *noun* a bright red edible fungus that grows on dead trees: *Fistulina hepatica.*

beefsteak tomato *noun* = BEEF TOMATO.

beef tea *noun* a hot drink made from beef extract.

beef tomato *noun* a very large variety of tomato.

beef Wellington *noun* a fillet of beef covered with pâté and baked in a casing of pastry.

beefwood *noun* **1** any of several trees of Australia and the W Indies, which yield hard heavy reddish wood: several species, *esp Casuarina equisetifolia.* **2** the wood of any of these trees.

beefy /'beefi/ *adj* (**beefier, beefiest**) **1** tasting of beef. **2** brawny or powerful. >> **beefiness** *noun.*

beehive *noun* **1** a structure for housing a colony of bees. **2** a conically shaped lacquered hairstyle, fashionable for women in the 1960s.

bee-keeper *noun* somebody who keeps bees for their honey. >> **bee-keeping** *noun.*

beeline /'beelien/ ✳ **make a beeline** take a straight direct course: *He made a beeline for the buffet.* [from the belief that nectar-laden bees return to their hives in a direct line]

been /bin; *strong* been/ *verb* past part. of BE.

bee orchid *noun* any of several species of European plants of the orchid family with velvety flowers resembling bees: family Orchidaceae.

beep[1] /beep/ *noun* a sound, e.g. from a horn or electronic device, that serves as a signal or warning. [imitative]

beep[2] *verb intrans* **1** to sound a horn. **2** to make a beep. > *verb trans* to cause (a horn, etc) to sound. >> **beeper** *noun.*

beer /biə/ *noun* **1** an alcoholic drink brewed from fermented malt flavoured with hops. **2** a carbonated non-alcoholic drink, or a fermented, slightly alcoholic drink, flavoured with roots or other plant parts: *ginger beer.* **3** a glass or measure of beer. [Old English *bēor*]

beer and skittles *pl noun* (*treated as sing. or pl*) a situation of agreeable ease: *Being a student is not all beer and skittles.*

beery *adj* (**beerier, beeriest**) **1** affected or caused by beer: *beery voices.* **2** smelling or tasting of beer: *beery breath.*

bee's knees ✳ **the bee's knees** *informal* somebody or something that is outstandingly good: *She thinks her boyfriend is the bee's knees.*

beestings /'beestingz/ *pl noun* (*treated as sing.*) colostrum, *esp* of a cow. [Old English *bȳsting*, from *bēost*]

beeswax /'beezwaks/ *noun* a yellowish plastic substance secreted by bees, which is used by them for constructing honeycombs and by humans as a wood polish.

beeswing /'beezwing/ *noun* a thin crust of tartar that forms on wine when it has been kept for a long time.

beet /beet/ *noun* **1** any of several species of herbaceous plants with a swollen root used as a vegetable, as a source of sugar, or for forage: genus *Beta.* **2** *NAmer* beetroot. [Old English *bēte* from Latin *beta*]

beetle[1] /'beetl/ *noun* **1** any of an order of insects with four wings, of which the front pair are modified into stiff coverings that protect the back pair at rest: order Coleoptera. **2** a game in which the players attempt to be the first to complete a stylized drawing of a beetle in accordance with the throwing of a dice. [Middle English *betylle* from Old English *bitula*, from *bītan* to BITE[1]]

beetle[2] *verb intrans Brit, informal* (*often* + off) to move swiftly: *He beetled off down the road.*

beetle[3] *noun* a heavy wooden tool for hammering or ramming. [Old English *bīetel*; related to Old English *bēatan* to BEAT[1]]

beetling /'beetling/ *adj* prominent and overhanging: *beetling brows.* [Middle English *bitel-browed* with overhanging brows, prob from *betylle, bitel:* see BEETLE[1]]

beetroot /'beetrooht/ *noun* (*pl* **beetroots** *or collectively* **beetroot**) *chiefly Brit* a cultivated beet with a red edible root that is a common salad vegetable: *Beta vulgaris.*

BEF *abbr* British Expeditionary Force.

befall /bi'fawl/ *verb trans and intrans* (*past tense* **befell** /bi'fel/, *past part.* **befallen** /bi'fawlən/) to happen to (somebody or something), *esp* as if by fate: *I hope no disaster has befallen them; whatever befalls.* [Old English *befeallan*, from BE- + *feallan* to FALL[1]]

befit /bi'fit/ *verb trans* (**befitted, befitting**) to be appropriate or suitable for (somebody or something): *He was given a warm welcome, as befits a local hero.* >> **befitting** *adj,* **befittingly** *adv.*

befog /bi'fog/ *verb trans* (**befogged, befogging**) **1** to confuse (something). **2** to make (something) foggy; to obscure (something).

before[1] /bi'faw/ *adv* **1** earlier in time; previously: *They had left a week before; Haven't we met before?* **2** so as to be in advance of others; ahead: *The guide went on before.* [Old English *beforan*, from BE- + *foran* before, from *fore* FORE[1]]

before[2] *prep* **1a** in front of (something or somebody): *standing before the fireplace.* **b** under the jurisdiction or consideration of (somebody or something): *the case before the court.* **2** preceding (an event, date, etc) in time; earlier than (something): *before the war.* **3** in a higher or more important position than (something or somebody): *They put quantity before quality.* **4** under the onslaught of (something): *They retreated before the attack.*

before³ *conj* **1** earlier than the time when. **2** rather than: *I would resign before I would accept a pay cut.*

beforehand /bi'fawhand/ *adv and adj* **1** in anticipation. **2** ahead of time.

befriend /bi'frend/ *verb trans* to become a friend of (somebody) purposely; to show kindness and understanding to (somebody).

befuddle /bi'fudl/ *verb* **1** to muddle or stupefy (somebody) with drink, or as if with drink. **2** to confuse or perplex (somebody). ⟫ **befuddlement** *noun.*

beg /beg/ *verb* (**begged, begging**) ⟫ *verb intrans* **1** to ask for alms or charity. **2** to ask earnestly: *The prisoners begged for mercy; He begged to be allowed out.* **3** said of a dog: to sit up and hold out the forepaws. ⟫ *verb trans* **1** to ask for (something) as charity: *They begged alms.* **2a** to ask earnestly for (something): *She begged a favour.* **b** to ask (somebody) earnestly to do something; to entreat: *He begged her to stay.* ✳ **beg the question** to assume something as established or proved without justification. **go begging** to be available but unwanted. [Middle English *beggen*, prob alteration of Old English *bedecian*]

Usage note ─────────
beg the question. Strictly speaking, a statement that *begs the question* is one that is logically flawed because it is based on an unproven assumption, often taking for granted the very thing that it itself is seeking to establish. If someone argues: *The Loch Ness monster must exist because there have been so many sightings of it,* that statement *begs the question* because it assumes that the sightings were of the monster and not something else – which is the whole point at issue. This is the original meaning of the phrase and the only one allowed by traditionalists. It is, however, probably more frequently used nowadays to mean that a statement raises obvious questions which need to be answered: *Their claim that the scheme will benefit millions begs the question of precisely what benefit those millions will receive.*

began /bi'gan/ *verb* past tense of BEGIN.

beget /bi'get/ *verb trans* (**begetting,** *past tense* **begot** /bi'got/, *archaic* **begat** /bi'gat/, *past part.* **begotten** /bi'gotn/) **1** to produce (offspring) as the father; to sire. **2** to produce or cause (an effect): *Dancing begets warmth, which is the parent of wantonness* — Henry Fielding. ⟫ **begetter** *noun.* [Old English *bigietan*]

beggar¹ /'begə/ *noun* **1** a person who lives by asking for money, food, etc. **2** a very poor person. **3** *informal* a person of a specified kind: *lucky beggar.* [Middle English *beggere, beggare,* from *beggen* to beg + *-ere, -are* -ER²; (sense 3) partly euphemism for BUGGER¹]

beggar² *verb trans* (**beggared, beggaring**) **1** to reduce (somebody) to beggary. **2** to exceed the resources or abilities of (something): *It beggars description.*

beggarly *adj* **1** marked by extreme poverty. **2** contemptibly mean, petty, or paltry: *a beggarly sum.* ⟫ **beggarliness** *noun.*

beggar-my-neighbour *noun* a card game based on luck in which the object is to acquire all the cards held by one's opponents.

beggary /'begəri/ *noun* poverty or penury.

begin /bi'gin/ *verb* (**beginning,** *past tense* **began** /bi'gan/, *past part.* **begun** /bi'gun/) ⟫ *verb intrans* **1a** to do the first part of an action; to start: *If you're all ready, we'll begin.* **b** to undergo initial steps: *Work on the project began in May.* **2a** to come into existence; to arise: *The war began in 1939.* **b** (+ with) to have the specified thing first: *The alphabet begins with A.* ⟫ *verb trans* **1** to set about the activity of (doing something): *The children began laughing.* **2** to call (something) into being; to found: *The dynasty was begun in 1631.* **3** to come first in (something): *A begins the alphabet.* **4** (*usu in negative contexts*) to do or succeed in (something), in the least degree: *I can't begin to describe her beauty.* [Old English *beginnan*]

beginner *noun* somebody who is learning a new activity or doing something for the first time.

beginning *noun* **1** the point at which something begins; the start. **2** the first part. **3** the origin or source. **4** (*usu in pl*) a rudimentary stage or early period: *the beginnings of a cold.*

beg off *verb intrans* to ask to be released from something, e.g. an undertaking.

begone /bi'gon/ *verb intrans* (*usu in imperative*) to go away; to depart. [Middle English from *be gone* (imperative)]

begonia /bi'gohni·ə/ *noun* any of a large genus of tropical plants that have asymmetrical leaves and are widely cultivated as ornamental garden and house plants: genus *Begonia.* [from the Latin genus name, named after Michel *Bégon* d.1710, French governor of Santo Domingo, who introduced the plant to Europe]

begorra /bi'gorə/ *interj Irish* used as a mild oath. [euphemism for *by God*]

begot /bi'got/ *verb* past tense of BEGET.

begotten /bi'gotn/ *verb* past part. of BEGET.

begrime /bi'griem/ *verb trans* to make (somebody or something) dirty; to blacken.

begrudge /bi'gruj/ *verb trans* **1** to give or concede (something) reluctantly: *He begrudged every minute taken from his work.* **2** to envy (somebody) the pleasure or enjoyment of something: *They begrudge him his wealth.* ⟫ **begrudgingly** *adv.*

beguile /bi'giel/ *verb trans* **1** to please or charm (somebody): *the glory of the Jungfrau … the most engaging and beguiling and fascinating spectacle that exists on the earth* — Mark Twain. **2** (*often* + into) to deceive or hoodwink (somebody): *His peculiar specialty is the beguiling of lonely ladies by playing upon their religious feelings* — Conan Doyle. **3** to while (the time) away, *esp* by some agreeable occupation. ⟫ **beguilement** *noun,* **beguiler** *noun,* **beguilingly** *adv.*

beguine /bi'geen/ *noun* a vigorous popular W Indian dance. [American French *béguine* from French *béguin* flirtation]

begum /'baygəm/ *noun* used as a title in some Muslim countries: a woman of high rank. [Urdu *begam*]

begun /bi'gun/ *verb* past part. of BEGIN.

behalf /bi'hahf/ ✳ **on behalf of** in the interest of; as a representative of. [Middle English in the senses 'benefit', 'support', from BY¹ + HALF¹ in the sense 'side']

behave /bi'hayv/ *verb intrans* **1** to conduct oneself in a specified way: *She has been behaving badly.* **2** to conduct oneself properly. ⟫ *verb trans* **1** to conduct (oneself) in a specified way. **2** to conduct (oneself) properly: *Please behave yourself when you go to your grandmother's.* [Middle English *behaven,* from BE- + HAVE¹, hold]

behaviour (*NAmer* **behavior**) /bi'hayvyə/ *noun* **1** the way in which a person conducts himself or herself. **2** anything that an organism does involving action and response to stimulation.

Editorial note ─────────
The simplest behaviour is initiated and controlled by reflexes (input stimuli evoking responses) or by tropisms (movement towards rewarding, or away from noxious, stimuli). Built-in (innate) behaviour can be amazingly elaborate, and appropriate in normal conditions, as for migration or web spinning. Higher animals, especially primates, generalize from past experience to behave with creative intelligence — Professor Richard Gregory.

3 the way in which something, e.g. a machine, functions. ⟫ **behavioural** *adj.* [alteration of Middle English *behavour,* from *behaven:* see BEHAVE]

behaviourism *noun* a theory holding that the proper concern of psychology is the objective study of behaviour and that information derived from introspection is not admissible psychological evidence.

behaviour therapy *noun* therapy intended to change an abnormal behaviour, e.g. a phobia, by conditioning the patient to respond normally.

behead /bi'hed/ *verb trans* to cut off the head of (somebody); to decapitate.

beheld /bi'held/ *verb* past tense and past part. of BEHOLD.

behemoth /bi'heemoth/ *noun* something of oppressive or monstrous size or power. [Middle English via Latin from Hebrew *běhēmōth*]

behest /bi'hest/ *noun* an urgent prompting or insistent request: *He returned home at the behest of his friends.* [Old English *behæs* promise, from *behātan* to promise, from BE- + *hātan* to command, promise]

behind¹ /bi'hiend/ *adv* **1a** in the place that is being or has been departed from: *I've left the keys behind.* **b** in, to, or towards the back: *Look behind.* **2a** in a secondary or inferior position. **b** (*usu* + in/with) in arrears: *He is behind in his payments.* **c** (*usu* + with) late: *I've got behind with my work.* [Old English *behindan,* from BE- + *hindan* from behind]

behind² *prep* **1** at or to the back or rear of (something or somebody): *Look behind you.* **2a** remaining after (somebody who has departed): *He left a great name behind him.* **b** obscured by (something): *There was malice behind the mask of friendship.* **3** less advanced than (somebody or something): *He is behind his class-mates in performance.* **4** used to indicate delay: *behind schedule.* **5** used to indicate deficiency: *Sales are lagging behind last year's figures.* **6a** in the background of (something): *the conditions behind the strike.* **b** in support of (somebody or something): *solidly behind their candidate.*

behind[3] *noun informal* the buttocks.

behindhand *adj* **1a** (*usu* + with) behind schedule: *She is behindhand with her work.* **b** (*usu* + in/with) in arrears: *He was behindhand with the rent.* **2** lagging behind the times; backward.

behind-the-scenes *adj* kept, made, or held in secret: *behind-the-scenes talks.*

behold /bi'hohld/ *verb trans and intrans* (*past tense and past part.* **beheld** /bi'held/) to see or observe (something or somebody). ⟫ **beholder** *noun.* [Old English *behealdan,* from BE- + *healdan* to HOLD[1]]

beholden /bi'hohldn/ *adj* (*usu* + to) under obligation for a favour or gift; indebted: *I want to be beholden to nobody.* [Middle English, past part. of BEHOLD]

behoof /bi'hoof, bi'hoohf/ *noun archaic* advantage or profit. [Old English *behōf*]

behove /bi'hohv/ (*NAmer* **behoove** /bi'hoohv/) *verb trans* to be incumbent on, or necessary, proper, or advantageous for (somebody): *It behoves us to fight.* [Old English *behōfian,* from *behōf* BEHOOF]

beige /bayzh, bayj/ *adj* of a yellowish grey colour. ⟫ **beige** *noun.* [French *beige*]

being /'beeing/ *noun* **1a** the quality or state of having existence: *This law came into being in 1969.* **b** life. **2** the qualities that constitute an existent thing; the essence of somebody or something: *from the depths of his being.* **3** a living thing; *esp* a person. [Middle English, verbal noun from *been, bēon* to BE]

bejewelled (*NAmer* **bejeweled**) *adj* decorated with jewels.

bel /bel/ *noun* ten decibels. [named after Alexander Graham *Bell* d.1922, US inventor of the telephone]

belabour (*NAmer* **belabor**) /bi'laybə/ *verb trans* **1** to work on or at (something) to absurd lengths: *You're belabouring the obvious.* **2a** to beat or thrash (somebody). **b** to assail or attack (somebody).

Belarussian *or* **Belarusian** /belə'rushən/ *noun* see BELORUSSIAN.

belated /bi'laytid/ *adj* delayed beyond the usual time: *belated birthday greetings.* ⟫ **belatedly** *adv,* **belatedness** *noun.* [past part. of archaic *belate* to make late]

belay[1] /bi'lay/ *verb* (**belays, belayed, belaying**) ⟫ *verb trans* **1** to secure or make fast (a rope) by turns round a support. **2** to secure (somebody, e.g. a climber) at the end of a rope. ⟫ *verb intrans* **1** to be belayed. **2** (*usu in imperative*) to stop; to leave off: *Belay there!* [Old English *belecgan,* from BE- + *lecgan* to LAY[1]]

belay[2] *noun* (*pl* **belays**) **1** in mountain climbing, a method or act of belaying a rope or person. **2a** a mountain climber's belayed rope. **b** something to which a belayed rope is attached.

bel canto /bel 'kantoh/ *noun* operatic singing characterized by ease, purity, evenness of tone production, and an agile and precise vocal technique. [Italian *bel canto* beautiful singing]

belch[1] /belch/ *verb intrans* **1** to expel gas suddenly from the stomach through the mouth. **2** (*often* + out) said of smoke, steam, etc: to issue forth spasmodically or forcefully; to gush. ⟫ *verb trans* (*often* + out) to eject or emit (smoke, steam, etc) forcefully. [Old English *bealcian*]

belch[2] *noun* a sudden expulsion of gas from the stomach through the mouth.

beldam *or* **beldame** /'beldəm, 'beldam/ *noun archaic* an old woman; *esp* a hag. [Middle English *beldam* grandmother, from Old French *bel* beautiful + DAM[3]]

beleaguer /bi'leegə/ *verb trans* (**beleaguered, beleaguering**) **1** to beset or harass (somebody): *beleaguered teachers.* **2** to surround (a place) with an army so as to prevent escape; to besiege. [Dutch *belegeren,* from *be-* all around + *leger* camp]

belemnite /'beləmniet/ *noun* a conical pointed fossil shell of any of an order of extinct cephalopod molluscs. [French *bélemnite* from Greek *belemnon* dart]

bel esprit /,bel e'spree (*French* bɛl ɛspri)/ *noun* (*pl* **beaux esprits** /,bohz e'spree (*French* boz ɛspri)/) a person with a fine and gifted mind. [French *bel esprit* fine mind]

belfry /'belfri/ *noun* (*pl* **belfries**) **1** a bell tower, *esp* when associated with a church. **2** a room in which a bell is hung in such a bell tower. [Middle English *belfrey,* alteration by association with *bell,* of *berfrey,* from early French *berfrei*]

Belgian /'belj(ə)n/ *noun* a native or inhabitant of Belgium in NW Europe. ⟫ **Belgian** *adj.*

Belgian hare *noun* a slender dark red rabbit of a domestic breed.

Belial /'beeli·əl/ *noun* often personified in the Bible: worthlessness or wickedness: *children of Belial.* [Greek *Belial* from Hebrew *bĕlīya'al*]

belie /bi'lie/ *verb trans* (**belies, belied, belying**) **1** to give a false impression of (something): *the white frock that ... imparted to her developing figure an amplitude that belied her age* — Hardy. **2** to show (something) to be false: *Harker smiled ... but at the same time his action belied his words, for his hands instinctively sought the hilt of the great Kukri knife* — Bram Stoker. [Old English *belēogan,* from BE- + *lēogan* LIE[4]]

belief /bi'leef/ *noun* **1** something believed; *specif* a tenet or body of tenets held by a group. **2** conviction of the truth of some statement or the reality of some being, thing, or phenomenon, *esp* when based on examination of evidence. **3** trust or confidence in somebody or something.

Editorial note

To believe something is to take it to be true and to use it as a guide to one's actions. Beliefs have generally been thought to be inner states, perhaps present to consciousness, that can be identified through introspection. More recently, the connection between belief and action has been emphasized, especially by economists – beliefs are often just habits of behaviour and expectation which need not be conscious at all — Professor Christopher Hookway.

[Middle English *beleave,* prob alteration of Old English *gelēafa*]

believe /bi'leev/ *verb trans* **1a** to consider (something) to be true or honest: *They believe the reports.* **b** to accept a statement made by (somebody) as the truth: *I don't believe you.* **2** to hold (something) as an opinion; to think: *I believe it will rain soon.* ⟫ *verb intrans* **1a** (*often* + in) to have a firm religious faith: *people who believe in God.* **b** (*often* + in) to accept something trustfully and on faith: *people who believe in the natural goodness of man.* **2** (*often* + in) to have a firm conviction as to the reality or goodness of something: *I don't believe in ghosts; We believe in exercise.* ⟫ **believable** *adj,* **believer** *noun.* [Old English *belēfan,* from BE- + *lyfan, lēfan* to allow, believe]

Belisha beacon /bə'leeshə/ *noun Brit* a flashing light in an amber globe mounted on a black-and-white-striped pole that marks a zebra crossing. [named after Leslie Hore-*Belisha* d.1957, English politician, who was Minister of Transport when they were introduced]

belittle /bi'litl/ *verb trans* to undermine the value of (somebody or something): *He constantly belittles her efforts.* ⟫ **belittlement** *noun,* **belittler** *noun.*

Belizean /be'leeziən/ *noun* a native or inhabitant of Belize in Central America. ⟫ **Belizean** *adj.*

bell[1] /bel/ *noun* **1** a hollow metallic device, either cup-shaped with a flaring mouth or saucer-shaped, that vibrates and makes a ringing sound when struck. **2** the sound of a bell as a signal; e.g. to mark the end of a round in boxing, wrestling, etc. **3** a half-hour subdivision of a watch on a ship, indicated by the strokes of a bell. **4** something with the shape of a bell, e.g. the COROLLA (petals) of any of various flowers or the flared end of a wind instrument. [Old English *belle;* related to Old English *bellan* BELL[3]]

bell[2] *verb trans* **1** to provide (something) with a bell. **2** (+ out) to give (something) the shape or flared mouth of a bell. ⟫ *verb intrans* to take the form of a bell; to flare.

bell[3] *verb intrans* said of a stag or hound: to make a resonant bellowing or baying sound. [Old English *bellan*]

belladonna /belə'donə/ *noun* **1** deadly nightshade. **2** an extract of deadly nightshade containing atropine. [Italian *belladonna* beautiful lady; from its use as a cosmetic to dilute the pupils of the eyes]

belladonna lily *noun* a plant of the daffodil family noted for its fragrant white or pink flowers: *Amaryllis belladonna.*

bell-bottoms *pl noun* trousers with wide flaring bottoms. ⟫ **bell-bottom** *adj.*

bellboy *noun chiefly NAmer* a porter or page in a hotel.

bell buoy *noun* a buoy fitted with a warning bell that is rung by the action of the waves.

bell curve *noun* in mathematics, a graph of a normal distribution.

belle /bel/ *noun* a popular and attractive young woman: *bathing belles; the belle of the ball.* [French *belle*, from fem of *beau*: see BEAU]

belle époque /bel ay'pok (*French* bel epok)/ *noun* the time immediately before World War I, regarded as a time of elegance and prosperity. [French *belle époque* fine period]

belles lettres /,bel 'letrə, 'letə (*French* bɛl lɛtr)/ *pl noun* (*treated as sing. or pl*) literature that has no practical or informative function, *esp* of a light, entertaining, sophisticated nature. >> **belletrist** /bel'letrist/ *noun.* [French *belles lettres* fine letters]

bellflower *noun* = CAMPANULA.

bellhop *noun* NAmer a porter or page in a hotel. [short for *bell-hopper*]

bellicose /'belikohs/ *adj* disposed to or fond of quarrels or wars. >> **bellicosity** /-'kositi/ *noun.* [Middle English from Latin *bellicosus*, from *bellicus* of war, from *bellum* war]

belligerence /bə'lij(ə)rəns/ *or* **belligerency** /-si/ *noun* **1** an aggressive or truculent attitude, atmosphere, or disposition. **2** the state of being at war or in conflict; *specif* the status of a belligerent.

belligerent[1] /bə'lij(ə)rənt/ *adj* **1** engaged in legally recognized war. **2** inclined to or exhibiting aggressiveness, hostility, or combativeness. >> **belligerently** *adv.* [Latin *belligerant-, belligerans,* present part. of *belligerare* to wage war, ultimately from *bellum* war + *gerere* to wage]

belligerent[2] *noun* a country or person engaged in legally recognized war.

bell jar *noun* a bell-shaped glass vessel that is designed to cover objects or to contain gases or a vacuum.

bell metal *noun* bronze with a high tin content, used for bells.

bellow[1] /'beloh/ *verb intrans* **1** to make the loud deep hollow sound characteristic of a bull. **2** to shout in a deep voice. > *verb trans* to bawl (something): *The captain bellows the orders.* [Middle English *belwen* from Old English *bylgian*]

bellow[2] *noun* **1** a bellowing sound. **2** a loud deep shout.

bellows /'belohz/ *pl noun* (*treated as sing.*) **1** a device that by alternate expansion and contraction supplies a current of air, *esp* to a fire. **2** a pleated expandable part in a camera. [Middle English, probably from Old English *belig* bag, skin, BELLY[1]]

bellpull *noun* **1** a cord by which one rings a bell. **2** a handle or knob attached to such a cord.

bell push *noun* a button that is pushed to ring a bell.

bell-ringer *noun* somebody who rings church bells or handbells. >> **bell-ringing** *noun.*

bell tent *noun* a round tent that is supported by a central pole.

bellwether /'belwedhə/ *noun* **1** a male sheep that leads the flock. **2** a leader who is followed blindly. [Middle English from *belle* BELL[1] + *wether*; from the practice of belling the leader of a flock]

belly[1] /'beli/ *noun* (*pl* **bellies**) **1a** the abdomen. **b** the undersurface of an animal's body. **c** a cut of pork consisting of this part of the body. **d** the stomach and associated organs. **2** an internal cavity; the interior: *the belly of the ship.* **3** a surface or object curved or rounded like a human belly: *the belly of a sail.* [Old English *belig* bag, skin, belly]

belly[2] *verb intrans and trans* (**bellies, bellied, bellying**) (*often + out*) to swell or fill, or cause (something) to swell or fill: *The sails bellied out.*

bellyache[1] *noun* colic.

bellyache[2] *verb intrans informal* to complain whiningly or peevishly; to find fault. >> **bellyacher** *noun.*

belly button *noun informal* = NAVEL (I).

belly dance[1] *noun* a solo dance originating in the Middle East, performed by women and emphasizing movements of the belly.

belly dance[2] *verb intrans* to perform a belly dance. >> **belly dancer** *noun.*

belly flop[1] *noun* a dive into water in which the front of the body strikes flat against the surface.

belly flop[2] *verb intrans* to execute a belly flop.

bellyful /'belif(ə)l/ *noun* (*pl* **bellyfuls**) *informal* an excessive amount: *a bellyful of advice.*

belly-land *verb intrans* to land an aircraft on its undersurface without the use of landing gear. >> **belly landing** *noun.*

belly laugh *noun* a deep hearty laugh.

belong /bi'long/ *verb intrans* **1** (+ to) to be somebody's property: *That coat belongs to Jim.* **2** to be in a proper situation, e.g. according to ability or social qualification, or a proper position or place: *I never felt as if I belonged there; These knives belong in the kitchen.* **3** (+ to) to be attached or bound by birth, allegiance, dependency, or membership: *I belong to Glasgow.* **4** (+ to) to be an attribute, part, or function of a person or thing: *nuts and bolts belonging to the engine.* **5** to be properly classified: *Whales belong among the mammals.* [Middle English *belongen*, from BE- + *longen* to be suitable, from *along* (*on*) because (of)]

belonging *noun* **1** (*usu in pl*) possessions: *He packed up his belongings.* **2** close or intimate relationship: *a sense of belonging.*

Belorussian /beloh'rush(ə)n, belə-/ *or* **Belarussian** *or* **Belarusian** *or* **Byelorussian** /bieloh-/ *noun* **1** a native or inhabitant of Belarus (Belorussia) in eastern Europe. **2** the Slavonic language of the Belorussians. >> **Belorussian** *adj.*

beloved[1] /bi'luvid, bi'luvd/ *adj* dearly loved: *his beloved daughter.*

beloved[2] *noun* a dearly loved person: *I'm writing to my beloved.*

below[1] /bi'loh/ *adv* **1** in, on, or to a lower place, floor, or deck. **2** on earth. **3** in a lower rank, number or quantity: *temperatures of 10° and below.* **4** under the surface of the water or earth. [Middle English, from BE- + LOW[1]]

below[2] *prep* **1** in or to a lower place than (something or somebody). **2** inferior to (something or somebody), e.g. in rank. **3** unworthy of (somebody or something). **4** covered by or underneath (something). **5** downstream from (a place). **6** less than (a number or quantity): *below the age of 18.*

Bel Paese /,bel pah'ayzay/ *noun* a mild soft creamy Italian cheese with a thin dark yellow rind. [Italian *bel paese*, literally 'beautiful country']

belt[1] /belt/ *noun* **1** a strip of material worn round the waist or hips for decoration or to hold something, e.g. clothing or a weapon. **2** an endless band of tough flexible material for transmitting motion and power or conveying materials: *a conveyor belt.* **3** an area characterized by some distinctive feature, e.g. of culture, geology, or life forms: *the stockbroker belt.* **4** *informal* a jarring blow; a whack: *a belt on the ear.* ✳ **below the belt** in an unfair way: *Alluding to his past misdeeds in that way was really hitting below the belt.* **belt and braces** using two methods or devices for double security. **tighten one's belt** to reduce expenditure; to take economy measures. **under one's belt** as part of one's experience; having been attained: *She has three hit records under her belt.* >> **belted** *adj.* [Old English *belt*, from a prehistoric Germanic word borrowed from Latin *balteus* belt]

belt[2] *verb trans* **1a** to encircle or fasten (something) with a belt: *a coat belted at the waist.* **b** (*often + on*) to strap (something) on. **2a** to beat (somebody) with or as if with a belt; to thrash. **b** *informal* to strike or hit (somebody): *The man belted him in the mouth.* **3** *informal* (*usu + out*) to sing (a song) in a forceful manner or style. > *verb intrans informal* to move or act in a vigorous or violent manner: *They belted out of the classroom when the bell rang.*

belter *noun informal* **1** an excellent person or thing. **2** a song that is suitable for belting out.

belting /'belting/ *noun* **1** belts collectively. **2** material for belts.

belt up *verb intrans Brit, informal* to stop talking; to be quiet.

beltway /'beltway/ *noun chiefly NAmer* a ring road.

beluga /bi'loohgə/ *noun* **1** a white sturgeon of the Black Sea, the Caspian Sea, and their tributaries: *Huso huso.* **2** a small whale that is white when adult: *Delphinapterus leucas.* [Russian *beluga*, from *belyĭ* white]

belvedere /'belvidiə/ *noun* a structure, e.g. on the roof of a house positioned to command an extensive view: *He chiefly talked of the view from the little belvedere on the roof of the casino* — Henry James. [Italian *belvedere* beautiful view]

BEM *abbr* British Empire Medal.

bemoan /bi'mohn/ *verb trans* to express regret, displeasure, or deep grief over (something); to lament: *She's always bemoaning her fate.*

bemuse /bi'myoohz/ *verb trans* to make (somebody) confused; to bewilder: *I was bemused by all the fuss they were making.* >> **bemusedly** /-zidli/ *adv,* **bemusement** *noun.*

ben[1] /ben/ *noun Scot* used in place names: a mountain or hill. [Scottish Gaelic *beann*]

ben² *noun Scot* the inner room of a house, *esp* a two-roomed cottage. [Old English *binnan* inside]

bench¹ /bench/ *noun* **1** a long backless seat, e.g. of wood or stone, for two or more people. **2** (*often* **the Bench**) a judge's seat in court. **3a** the office of judge or magistrate: *appointed to the bench*. **b** (*treated as sing. or pl*) the judges or magistrates hearing a particular case, or judges or magistrates collectively. **4** a seat for an official, coach, substitute player, etc at the side of a sports field. **5** *Brit* any of the long seats on which members sit in Parliament. **6** a long worktable. [Old English *benc*]

bench² *verb trans* **1** to exhibit (a dog) at a show. **2** *NAmer* to remove (a player) from or keep them out of a game.

bencher *noun Brit* any of the chief or governing members of any of the Inns of Court.

benchmark *noun* **1** a point of reference, e.g. a mark on a permanent object indicating height above sea level, from which measurements may be made, *esp* in surveying. **2** something that serves as a standard by which others may be measured.

bench press *noun* a weightlifting exercise in which a person lies on their back on a bench and lifts a weight with both arms.

bend¹ /bend/ *verb* (*past tense and past part.* **bent** /bent/) ➤ *verb trans* **1** to shape or move (something) into or out of a curve or angle. **2a** to cause (something) to turn from a course; to deflect (something). **b** to turn or direct (something) in a certain direction: *He bent his steps homewards.* **3** (+ to) to direct (oneself or one's attention) strenuously or with interest; to apply (oneself): *They bent themselves to the task.* **4** to interpret or apply (a rule) in a way that suits one's own purpose. **5** to fasten (a sail) to its yard. **6** to subdue (somebody) or make them submissive. ➤ *verb intrans* **1** to move or curve out of a straight line or position. **2** to incline the body, *esp* in submission; to bow. **3** (*often* + to) to yield or compromise: *I refuse to bend to his will.* [Old English *bendan*]

bend² *noun* **1** bending or being bent: *knee bends.* **2** a curved part, *esp* of a road or river. **3** (**the bends**) (*treated as sing. or pl*) = DECOMPRESSION SICKNESS. **4** in heraldry, a band across a shield from top left to bottom right, as viewed from the front. ✻ **round the bend** *informal* mad or crazy.

bend³ *noun* any of various knots for fastening one rope to another or to an object. [Old English *bend* fetter]

bender *noun informal* **1** a drinking spree: *He went on a bender when his wife left him.* **2** a homosexual man. **3** a temporary shelter made from branches that are bent over and covered with plastic or canvas.

bend sinister *noun* in heraldry, a band across a shield from top right to bottom left, as viewed from the front. Also called BAR SINISTER.

bendy *adj* (**bendier, bendiest**) *informal* **1** pliable: *bendy rollers.* **2** having many bends: *a bendy path.*

beneath¹ /bi'neeth/ *prep* **1a** in or to a lower position than (something); below (something): *beneath the stairs.* **b** directly under (something), *esp* so as to be close or touching: *beneath his shirt.* **2** not suitable to (something or somebody); unworthy of (somebody or something): *He thinks it's beneath him to use public transport; She is beneath contempt.* **3** under the control, pressure, or influence of (somebody): *She has six people working beneath her.* [Old English *beneothan*, from BE- + *neothan* below]

beneath² *adv* in or to a lower position; below: *the flat beneath.*

Benedicite /beni'disitay, -tee/ *noun* a hymn of praise to God beginning 'All the works of the Lord, bless ye the Lord'. [Middle English from Late Latin *benedicite* bless ye (first word of the hymn), imperative pl of *benedicere*: see BENEDICTION]

Benedictine /beni'dikteen, -tin/ *noun* **1** a member of a religious order following the rule of St Benedict and devoted *esp* to scholarship. **2** *trademark* a brandy-based liqueur made orig by French Benedictine monks. ➤➤ **Benedictine** *adj.*

benediction /beni'diksh(ə)n/ *noun* **1** the invocation of a blessing; *esp* the short blessing with which public worship is concluded. **2** (*often* **Benediction**) a Roman Catholic or Anglo-Catholic service including the exposition of the HOST⁴ (consecrated bread) and the blessing of the congregation with it. [Middle English *benediccioun* from Latin *benediction-*, *benedictio*, from *benedicere* to bless, speak well of, from *bene* well + *dicere* to say]

Benedictus /beni'diktəs/ *noun* **1** a liturgical text from Matthew 21:9 beginning 'Blessed is he that cometh in the name of the Lord'. **2** a canticle from Luke 1:68 beginning 'Blessed be the Lord God of

Israel'. [late Latin *benedictus* blessed (first word of the text and canticle) past part. of *benedicere*: see BENEDICTION]

benefaction /beni'faksh(ə)n/ *noun* **1** the act of doing good, *esp* by generous donation. **2** a benefit conferred; *esp* a charitable donation. [late Latin *benefaction-*, *benefactio*, from Latin *bene facere* to do good to, from *bene* good, well + *facere* to do]

benefactor /'benifaktə/ *or* **benefactress** /-tris/ *noun* a man or woman who gives aid; *esp* one who makes a gift or bequest to a person, institution, etc.

benefice /'benifis/ *noun* an ecclesiastical office to which an income is attached. ➤➤ **beneficed** *adj.* [Middle English via Old French from late Latin *beneficium* favour, promotion, from *beneficus* beneficent, from *bene* well + *facere* to do]

beneficent /bi'nefis(ə)nt/ *adj* doing or producing good; *esp* performing acts of kindness and charity. ➤➤ **beneficence** *noun*, **beneficently** *adv.* [back-formation from *beneficence* from Latin *beneficentia*, from *beneficus*: see BENEFICE]

beneficial /beni'fish(ə)l/ *adj* **1** (*often* + to) conferring benefits; conducive to personal or social well-being: *beneficial to the health.* **2** receiving or entitling one to receive advantage or profit, *esp* from property: *the beneficial owner of an estate.* ➤➤ **beneficially** *adv.* [Latin *beneficium*: see BENEFICE]

beneficiary¹ /beni'fishəri/ *noun* (*pl* **beneficiaries**) **1** a person who benefits from something. **2** a person who receives the income or proceeds of a trust, will, or insurance policy.

beneficiary² *adj* of a benefice.

benefit¹ /'benifit/ *noun* **1a** something that helps or promotes well-being; an advantage. **b** good or welfare: *I did it for his benefit.* **2** (*also in pl*). **a** financial help in time of need, e.g. sickness, old age, or unemployment. **b** a payment or service provided for by an annuity, pension scheme, or insurance policy. **3** an entertainment, game, or social event to raise funds for a person or cause. ✻ **benefit of the doubt** the assumption of innocence in the absence of proof of guilt: *He said it was an accident and I gave him the benefit of the doubt.* [Middle English from Anglo-French *benfet*, from Latin *bene factum* good deed, from *bene* good, well + *facere* to do]

benefit² *verb* (**benefited** *or* **benefitted, benefiting** *or* **benefitting**) ➤ *verb trans* to be useful or profitable to (somebody). ➤ *verb intrans* (*often* + from) to receive benefit: *You might benefit from taking iron tablets.*

benefit of clergy *noun* **1** the former clerical privilege of being tried in an ecclesiastical court. **2** *humorous* the ministration or sanction of the church: *a couple living together without benefit of clergy.*

Benelux /'beniluks/ *noun* **1** the customs union formed in 1947 between Belgium, the Netherlands, and Luxembourg. **2** these countries collectively. [blend of *Belgium* + *Netherlands* + *Luxembourg*]

benevolent /bi'nevələnt/ *adj* **1** marked by or disposed to doing good; charitable: *a benevolent society.* **2** indicative of or characterized by goodwill: *benevolent smiles.* ➤➤ **benevolence** *noun*, **benevolently** *adv.* [Middle English from Latin *benevolent-*, *benevolens*, from *bene* good, well + *volent-*, *volens*, present part. of *velle* to wish]

BEng *abbr* Bachelor of Engineering.

Bengali /ben'gawli, beng-/ *noun* **1** a native or inhabitant of West Bengal or Bangladesh on the Indian subcontinent. **2** the modern Indic language of the Bengalis. ➤➤ **Bengali** *adj.* [Hindi *Baṅgālī*, from *Baṅgāl* Bengal]

Bengal light /beng'gawl/ *noun* any of various coloured lights or fireworks; *specif* a blue light or flare used, *esp* formerly, for signalling or illumination.

benighted /bi'nietid/ *adj* intellectually, morally, or socially unenlightened: *They diffused the light of Oriental knowledge, through the Western regions of benighted Europe* — Washington Irving. ➤➤ **benightedness** *noun.* [past part. of *benight* to overtake by darkness or night, from BE- + NIGHT]

benign /bi'nien/ *adj* **1** gentle or gracious: *a benign smile.* **2** favourable or mild: *a benign climate.* **3** said of a tumour: not malignant. ➤➤ **benignity** /bi'nigniti/ *noun*, **benignly** *adv.* [Middle English *benigne* via Old French from Latin *benignus*, from *bene* well + *gigni* to be born, passive of *gignere* to beget]

benignant /bi'nignənt/ *adj* = BENIGN. ➤➤ **benignancy** *noun*, **benignantly** *adv.*

bent¹ /bent/ *verb* past tense and past part. of BEND¹.

bent² *adj* **1** changed from an original straight or even condition by bending; curved: *a bent hairpin*. **2** (+ on) determined to have or do something: *He was bent on winning*. **3** *Brit, informal* homosexual. **4** *Brit, informal* corrupt; dishonest.

bent³ *noun* **1** a strong inclination or interest; a bias: *a capitalist bent*. **2** a special ability or talent: *Most Assistant Commissioners develop a bent for some special work after their first hot weather in the country —* Kipling. [irreg from BEND¹]

bent⁴ *noun* **1a** a reedy grass. **b** a stalk of stiff coarse grass. **2** any of several species of grasses including important pasture and lawn grasses: genus *Agrostis*. [Old English *beonot-*]

Benthamism /'benthəmiz(ə)m/ *noun* the utilitarian philosophy of Jeremy Bentham. ⫸ **Benthamite** /-miet/ *noun*. [named after Jeremy *Bentham* d.1832, English philosopher]

benthos /'benthos/ *noun* the organisms that live on or at the bottom of bodies of water. ⫸ **benthic** /'benthik/ *adj*. [scientific Latin from Greek *benthos* depth, deep sea]

bentonite /'bentəniet/ *noun* an absorbent clay used *esp* to give bulk to paper, drugs, etc. [named after Fort *Benton*, Montana, USA, where it is found]

bentwood *noun* wood that is steamed and bent into shape for use in furniture: *a bentwood chair*.

benumb /bi'num/ *verb trans* to make (a person or body part) inactive or numb: *benumbed with fear*. [Middle English *benomen*, *benome*, past part. of *benimen* to deprive, from Old English *beniman*, from BE- + *niman* to take]

Benzedrine /'benzədrin, -dreen/ *noun trademark* a type of amphetamine. [blend of BENZOIC ACID + EPHEDRINE]

benzene /'benzeen/ *noun* an inflammable poisonous liquid hydrocarbon used in the synthesis of organic chemical compounds and as a solvent: formula C_6H_6. ⫸ **benzenoid** /'benzənoyd/ *adj*. [BENZOIC ACID + -ENE]

benzene ring *noun* the structural arrangement of six carbon atoms that exists in the molecules of benzene and in other organic chemical compounds derived from it.

benzine /'benzeen/ *noun* any of various volatile inflammable petroleum distillates used *esp* as solvents or motor fuels. [German *Benzin*, from BENZOIN + -INE²]

benzodiazepine /ˌbenzohdie'ayzipin/ *noun* any of several chemically related synthetic drugs, e.g. diazepam, chlordiazepoxide, and nitrazepam, widely used as tranquillizers, sedatives, and hypnotics. [from BENZOIN + DI-¹ + AZ- + EPOXIDE + -INE²]

benzoic acid /ben'zohik/ *noun* an organic acid used *esp* as a food preservative, in medicine, and in organic synthesis: formula $C_7H_6O_2$. [BENZOIN + ACID²]

benzoin /'benzoh·in, 'benzoyn/ *noun* **1** a hard fragrant yellowish balsamic resin used *esp* in medicines. **2** any of various trees found in SE Asia that yield this resin. [early French *benjoin* via Old Catalan *benjuí* from Arabic *lubān jāwī*, literally 'frankincense of Java']

benzol /'benzol/ *noun* benzene, *esp* when unrefined. [German *Benzol*, from BENZOIN + -OL¹]

bequeath /bi'kweeth, bi'kweedh/ *verb trans* **1** to give or leave (something, *esp* personal property) by will: compare DEVISE¹. **2** to transmit (something); to hand down: *ideas bequeathed to us by the writers of the 19th century*. ⫸ **bequeathal** /bi'kweedhəl/ *noun*. [Middle English *bequethen* from Old English *becwethan*, from BE- + *cwethan* to say]

bequest /bi'kwest/ *noun* **1** the act of bequeathing. **2** a legacy. [Middle English, irreg from *bequethen*: see BEQUEATH]

berate /bi'rayt/ *verb trans* to scold or condemn (somebody) vehemently: *A thousand times I berated myself for being drawn into such a trap —* Edgar Rice Burroughs. [BE- + RATE³]

Berber /'buhbə/ *noun* **1** a member of a Caucasian people of northern Africa. **2** an Afro-Asiatic language spoken by these people. ⫸ **Berber** *adj*. [Arabic *Barbar* from Greek *barbaros* foreign]

berceuse /beə'suhz/ *noun* (*pl* **berceuses** /beə'suhz/) a lullaby or a musical composition in this style. [French *berceuse*, from *bercer* to rock]

bereave /bi'reev/ *verb trans* (*past part*. **bereaved** *or* **bereft**) to rob or deprive (somebody) of something or somebody held dear, *esp* through death: *But I am black, as if bereav'd of light —* Blake. ⫸ **bereavement** *noun*. [Old English *berēafian*, from BE- + *rēafian* to rob]

bereaved *adj* suffering the death of a loved one: *the bereaved relatives*.

bereft *adj* (+ of) deprived or robbed of something; completely without it: *bereft of all hope*. [archaic past part. of BEREAVE]

beret /'beray/ *noun* a cap with a tight headband, a soft flat top, and no peak. [French *béret* from Provençal: see BIRETTA]

berg¹ /buhg/ *noun* an iceberg.

berg² *noun SAfr* often in place-names: a mountain. [Afrikaans *berg* from early Dutch *bergh, berch*]

bergamot /'buhgəmot/ *noun* a pear-shaped orange with a rind that yields an essential oil used in perfumery and as a flavouring. [prob named after *Bergamo*, town in Italy]

bergschrund /'beəgshroont/ *noun* a crevasse at the top of a mountain glacier. [German *Bergschrund*, from *Berg* mountain + *Schrund* crack]

beriberi /'beriberi/ *noun* a deficiency disease marked by degeneration of the nerves, caused by a lack of or inability to assimilate vitamin B_1. [Sinhalese *bæriberi*]

bcrk /buhk/ *noun Brit, slang* see BURK.

berkelium /bə'keeli·əm/ *noun* a radioactive metallic chemical element that is artificially produced: symbol Bk, atomic number 97. [scientific Latin *berkelium*, named after *Berkeley*, city in California, USA, where it was first made]

Berks /bahks/ *abbr* Berkshire.

berm *or* **berme** /buhm/ *noun* **1** a narrow shelf between a ditch and the base of a parapet in a fortification. **2** a narrow path beside a road, canal, etc. [French *berme* from Dutch *berm* strip of ground along a dyke]

Bermuda shorts /bə'myoohdə/ *pl noun* knee-length shorts. [named after *Bermuda*, a group of islands in the W Atlantic]

berry¹ /'beri/ *noun* (*pl* **berries**) **1a** a small, pulpy, and usu edible fruit without a stone, e.g. a strawberry or raspberry. **b** in botany, a simple fruit, e.g. a currant, grape, tomato, or banana, with a pulpy or fleshy PERICARP (structure surrounding the seed or seeds). **2** an egg of a fish or lobster. [Old English *berie*]

berry² *verb intrans* (**berries, berried, berrying**) **1** to gather or seek berries. **2** to bear or produce berries. ⫸ **berried** *adj*.

berserk¹ /bə'zuhk, buh'zuhk/ *noun* an ancient Scandinavian warrior who fought in a wild frenzy. [Old Norse *berserkr*, from *björn* bear + *serkr* shirt, because they wore animal skins rather than armour]

berserk² ✳ **go berserk** to become frenzied, *esp* with anger.

berserker /bə'zuhkə/ *noun* = BERSERK¹.

berth¹ /buhth/ *noun* **1** a place for sleeping, *esp* on a ship or train. **2** an allotted place for a ship at anchor, at a wharf, etc. **3** safe distance for manoeuvring maintained between a ship and another object. **4a** a place or position. **b** *informal* a job or post. ✳ **give a wide berth to** to remain at a safe distance from (somebody or something); to avoid: *I like to give weddings a wide berth*. [prob from BEAR² + -TH²]

berth² *verb trans* **1** to bring (a ship) into a berth; to dock. **2** to allot a berth to (somebody). ⫸ *verb intrans* said of a ship: to come into a berth.

beryl /'beril/ *noun* a mineral that is a silicate of beryllium and aluminium, occurs as green, yellow, pink, or white crystals, and is used as a gemstone: compare AQUAMARINE, EMERALD. [Middle English via Old French and Latin from Greek *bēryllos*, of Indic origin]

beryllium /bə'rili·əm/ *noun* a steel-grey light metallic chemical element: symbol Be, atomic number 4. [scientific Latin from Greek *bēryllion*, dimin. of *bēryllos*: see BERYL]

beseech /bi'seech/ *verb trans* (*past tense and past part*. **beseeched** *or* **besought** /bi'sawt/) **1** to ask (somebody) earnestly to do something; to implore: *Archelaus … humbly besought him to lay aside the thoughts of war, and make peace with Mithridates —* Dryden. **2** to beg for (something) urgently or anxiously: *I should have gone down on my knees to her and besought her forgiveness —* Dickens. ⫸ **beseechingly** *adv*. [Middle English *besechen*, from BE- + *sechen* to SEEK]

beset /bi'set/ *verb trans* (**besetting**, *past tense and past part*. **beset**) **1** to trouble or assail (somebody) constantly: *We were beset by fears*. **2** to surround and attack, or prepare to attack (somebody): *They were beset by the enemy*. ⫸ **besetment** *noun*. [Old English *besettan*, from BE- + *settan* to SET¹]

besetting *adj* constantly causing temptation or difficulty; continuously present: *a besetting sin.*

beside /bi'sied/ *prep* **1a** by the side of (somebody or something): *Walk beside me.* **b** in comparison with (somebody or something): *She is very quiet beside her sister.* **c** unconnected with (something): *beside the point.* **2** *archaic* besides (something). ❋ **beside oneself** in a state of extreme agitation or excitement: *She was beside herself with joy when she found out she was pregnant.* [Old English *be sīdan* at or to the side]

besides¹ *adv* **1** as an additional factor or circumstance: *He has a wife and six children besides.* **2** moreover or furthermore: *I don't like football; besides, I am no good at it.*

besides² *prep* **1** other than (somebody or something): *Who besides John would say that?* **2** as an additional circumstance to (something): *Besides being old, she is losing her sight.*

besiege /bi'seej/ *verb trans* **1** to surround (a place) with armed forces. **2a** to crowd round (somebody); to surround (somebody) closely. **b** to importune (somebody) with questions, requests, etc. ❥❥❥ **besieger** *noun.*

besmear /bi'smiə/ *verb trans literary* to smear or cover (somebody or something).

besmirch /bi'smuhch/ *verb trans* to sully or soil (somebody or their reputation).

besom /'beez(ə)m/ *noun* a broom, *esp* one made of twigs. [Old English *besma*]

besotted /bi'sotid/ *adj* **1** (*usu* + with) infatuated: *He is besotted with his secretary.* **2** drunk or intoxicated. [past part. of *besot* to make dull or foolish, from BE- + *sot* to fool, from Old French *sot* fool]

besought /bi'sawt/ *verb* past tense and past part. of BESEECH.

bespatter /bi'spatə/ *verb trans* (**bespattered, bespattering**) to spatter (something): *Her clothes were bespattered with paint.*

bespeak /bi'speek/ *verb trans* (*past tense* **bespoke** /bi'spohk/, *past part.* **bespoken** /bi'spohkən/) *formal* **1** to indicate or signify (something): *Her performance bespeaks considerable practice.* **2** to hire, engage, order, or claim (something) beforehand: *He … so far recovered … as to ring the bell for the waiter, and bespeak a hot kidney pudding and a plate of shrimps for breakfast* — Dickens. **3** *archaic* to speak to or address (somebody): *And my young mistress thus I did bespeak* — Shakespeare.

bespectacled /bi'spektəkld/ *adj* wearing glasses.

bespoke¹ *adj Brit* **1a** made-to-measure. **b** made or arranged according to particular requirements. **2** dealing in or producing articles that are made to measure: *a bespoke tailor.* [past part. of *bespeak*]

bespoke² /bi'spohk/ *verb* past tense of BESPEAK.

bespoken /bi'spohkən/ *verb* past part. of BESPEAK.

besprinkle /bi'springkl/ *verb trans* (*often* + with) to sprinkle (something) with a liquid.

Bessemer converter /'besimə/ *noun* the furnace used in the Bessemer process.

Bessemer process *noun* a steelmaking process in which air is blasted through molten pig iron in a special type of furnace to oxidize impurities. [named after Sir Henry *Bessemer* d.1898, English engineer and inventor, who developed it]

best¹ /best/ *adj* **1** of the highest quality or most excellent type. **2** most appropriate or advisable: *The best course might be to take them home.* ❋ **the best part of** most of something: *They were stranded for the best part of a week.* [Old English *betst*]

best² *adv* **1** in the best manner; to the best extent or degree: *Friday would suit me best.* **2** as a preference or ideal: *The centre of town is best avoided.* ❋ **as best** in the best way: *She would have to manage as best she could.* **had best** would be well advised to do something: *We had best take the train.*

best³ *noun* (**the best**) what is most excellent or desirable: *He always demands the best of his pupils; That's the best of living in the country.* ❋ **at best** using the most favourable interpretation or in the most favourable circumstances: *The election result was at best uncertain.* **at one's best** in one's best mood, health, state of awareness, etc: *He's never at his best early in the morning.* **do one's best** to do as well as one can; to try one's hardest. **for the best 1** advantageous in the long term: *Your plan to retire is for the best.* **2** having good intentions: *Her mother acted for the best.* **get the best of** to defeat (somebody) or get an advantage over them. **make the best of** to cope

with (an unfavourable situation) so as to get some advantage from it. **the best of three/five/etc.** a greater number of games won in a series, bringing overall victory.

best⁴ *verb trans* to outdo or outwit (somebody).

best before date *noun* a date stamped on food packaging to indicate the date by which it should be used.

best boy *noun* an assistant to a GAFFER (chief lighting electrician) or KEY GRIP (chief equipment handler) in a film or television studio.

best end *noun Brit* a cut of lamb or other meat from the lower end of the neck.

bestial /'besti·əl/ *adj* **1** marked by brutal or inhuman instincts or desires; *specif* sexually depraved. **2** of beasts. ❥❥❥ **bestially** *adv.* [Middle English via Old French from Latin *bestialis*, from *bestia* BEAST]

bestialise *verb* see BESTIALIZE.

bestiality /besti'aliti/ *noun* bestial behaviour; *specif* sexual relations between a human being and an animal.

bestialize *or* **bestialise** /'besti·əliez/ *verb trans* to cause (somebody) to act, live, etc like an animal.

bestiary /'besti·əri/ *noun* (*pl* **bestiaries**) an allegorical or moralizing work of medieval times dealing with real or imaginary animals. [late Latin *bestiarium*, neuter of *bestiarius* of beasts, from Latin *bestia* BEAST]

bestir /bi'stuh/ *verb trans* (**bestirred, bestirring**) to rouse (oneself) to action.

best man *noun* a male friend or relative chosen to attend the bridegroom at his wedding.

bestow /bi'stoh/ *verb trans* (*usu* + on/upon) to present (something) as a gift or honour: *The Queen bestowed a knighthood on him.* ❥❥❥ **bestowal** *noun.* [Middle English *bestowen*, from BE- + *stowe* place, from Old English]

bestrew /bi'strooh/ *verb trans* (*past tense* **bestrewed**, *past part.* **bestrewed** *or* **bestrewn** /bi'stroohn/) **1** to strew (something) somewhere. **2** (+ with) to lie scattered over (a place): *The ground was bestrewn with leaves.*

bestride /bi'stried/ *verb trans* (*past tense* **bestrode** /bi'strohd/, *past part.* **bestridden** /bi'stridn/) **1** to ride, sit, or stand astride (something); to straddle. **2** to tower over (something); to dominate.

bestseller *noun* **1** a book or other product that achieves a high level of sales. **2** the author of such a book. ❥❥❥ **bestselling** *adj.*

bet¹ /bet/ *noun* **1a** the act of risking a sum of money or other stake on the forecast outcome of a future event, e.g. a race or contest, *esp* in competition with another or others. **b** a stake so risked: *a £10 bet.* **c** an outcome or result on which a stake is gambled. **2** an opinion or belief: *My bet is it will pour with rain.* **3** *informal* a plan or course of action: *Your best bet is to call a plumber.* [origin unknown]

bet² *verb* (**betting**, *past tense and past part.* **bet** *or* **betted**) ❥ *verb trans* **1** (*usu* + on) to stake (an amount of money) as a bet. **2** to make a bet with (somebody): *I bet you £10 I can beat you at snooker.* **3** *informal* to be convinced that (a guess or prediction) is true: *I bet they don't turn up.* ❥ *verb intrans* to lay a bet: *betting on the horses.* ❋ **you bet** *informal* you may be sure; certainly: *Do you want to go out for lunch? – You bet!*

beta /'beetə/ *noun* **1a** the second letter of the Greek alphabet (B, β), equivalent to and transliterated as roman b. **b** = B¹ (3). **2** the second brightest star of a constellation. [Greek *bēta*, of Semitic origin; related to Hebrew *bēth*, second letter of the Hebrew alphabet]

beta-blocker *noun* a drug, e.g. propranolol, that inhibits the action of adrenalin and similar compounds and is used *esp* to treat high blood pressure.

beta decay *noun* radioactive decay of an atomic nucleus with the emission of an electron or positron.

betake /bi'tayk/ *verb trans* (*past tense* **betook** /bi'took/, *past part.* **betaken** /bi'taykən/) *literary* (+ to) to take (oneself) off somewhere: *Mrs Gummidge retired with these words, and betook herself to bed* — Dickens.

beta particle *noun* an electron or positron emitted from the nucleus of an atom during beta decay: compare ALPHA PARTICLE.

beta ray *noun* a stream of beta particles.

beta test *noun* a test of a machine or a piece of software, carried out by somebody other than the manufacturer before it is sold to the public: compare ALPHA TEST.

betatron /'beetətron/ *noun* an ACCELERATOR (apparatus used in physics) in which electrons are propelled by the inductive action of a rapidly varying magnetic field. [BETA + -TRON]

betel /'beetl/ *noun* a climbing pepper whose leaves are chewed with betel nut and lime, *esp* by SE Asians, to stimulate the flow of saliva: *Piper betle.* [Portuguese *betel* from Tamil *verrilai*]

betel nut *noun* the astringent seed of the betel palm. [from its being chewed with betel leaves]

betel palm *noun* an Asian palm that has an orange-coloured fruit: genus *Areca catechu.* [BETEL NUT]

bête noire /,bet 'nwah/ *noun* (*pl* **bêtes noires** /,bet 'nwah/) a person or thing strongly detested. [French *bête noire* black beast]

bethel /'beth(ə)l/ *noun* **1** a Nonconformist chapel. **2** a place of worship for seamen. [Hebrew *bēth' ēl* house of God]

bethink /bi'thingk/ *verb trans* (*past tense and past part.* **bethought** /bi'thawt/) *formal or archaic* to remind (oneself) of something; to bring (oneself) to consider something: *That I may be assured, I will bethink me* — Shakespeare.

betide /bi'tied/ *verb trans or intrans formal or literary* to happen, *esp* as if by fate: *We shall remain friends, whatever may betide.* ✳ **woe betide** used as a warning of retribution or punishment: *Woe betide them if they are late!* [Middle English *betiden*, from BE- + *tiden* to happen, from Old English *tīdan*]

bêtise /be'teez/ *noun* (*pl* **bêtises** /be'teez/) **1** stupidity. **2** an act of stupidity: *If it had been pride that interfered with her accepting Lord Warburton such a bêtise was singularly misplaced* — Henry James. [French *bêtise*, from *bête* foolish, from *bête* fool, beast]

betoken /bi'tohkən/ *verb trans* (**betokened, betokening**) **1** to give evidence of (something); to show (something): *Their giggles betokened nervousness.* **2** to presage or portend (something).

betony /'betəni/ *noun* (*pl* **betonies**) **1** a plant of the mint family with purple flowers: *Stachys officinalis.* **2** a related plant, e.g. water betony. [Middle English *betone* via Old French from Latin *vettonica, betonica,* named after the *Vettones,* an ancient Spanish people]

betook /bi'took/ *verb* past tense of BETAKE.

betray /bi'tray/ *verb trans* **1a** to be a traitor to (somebody or something): *He betrayed his people.* **b** to deliver (somebody or something) to an enemy by treachery. **2** to deceive (somebody) or be disloyal to them: *He betrayed his wife by sleeping with her best friend.* **3** to fail or desert (somebody), *esp* in time of need. **4a** to show (one's feelings, etc) inadvertently: *She behaved very well and betrayed no emotion* — Jane Austen. **b** to be an outward sign of (an inner feeling): *His clenched hands betrayed his acute annoyance* — Conan Doyle. **c** to disclose (a secret), deliberately or unintentionally, in violation of confidence. ➤➤ **betrayal** *noun,* **betrayer** *noun.* [Middle English *betrayen,* from BE- + *trayen* to betray, from Old French *traïr* from Latin *tradere:* see TRAITOR]

betroth /bi'trohth, bi'trohdh/ *verb trans* to promise to give (oneself or somebody else) in marriage: *She was betrothed to a teacher.* [Middle English *betrouthen,* from BE- + *trouthe* troth, TRUTH]

betrothal /bi'trohdhəl/ *noun* a mutual promise or contract for a future marriage; engagement.

betrothed *noun* the person to whom one is engaged to be married.

better¹ /'betə/ *adj* **1** of a higher quality or more excellent type. **2** more appropriate or advisable: *It would be better to take them with you.* **3** improved in health; partly or wholly recovered from an illness or injury: *Is she at all better yet?* ✳ **better off** enjoying better circumstances, *esp* financially. **go one better** to improve slightly on what somebody else has achieved. **the better part of** most or nearly all of something: *We waited for the better part of an hour.* [Old English *betera*]

better² *adv* **1** in a way that is more excellent or desirable. **2** to a greater degree; more: *Wait until you are better able to afford it; They like nothing better than a long swim.* **3** more wisely or usefully: *The centre of town is better avoided.* ✳ **had better** would be well advised (to do something): *I thought I had better get in training.*

better³ *noun* **1** (**the better**) what is more excellent or desirable: *It was a change for the better.* **2** dated (*usu in pl*) one's superiors, *esp* in rank or ability. ✳ **for better or worse/or for worse** whether

the outcome is good or bad. **get the better of** to overcome or defeat (somebody).

better⁴ *verb trans* (**bettered, bettering**) **1** to surpass (something) or improve on it: *She bettered the old world record by half a second.* **2** to make (something) more tolerable or acceptable: *The charity has been trying to better the conditions of slum dwellers.* ✳ **better oneself** to improve one's living conditions or social status: *He saw some chance of his children bettering themselves.*

better⁵ *noun* see BETTOR.

better half *noun informal* a spouse or partner.

betterment *noun* **1** improvement; change for the better. **2** in law, the enhanced value of a building or land due to improvements or development in its immediate vicinity.

betting shop /'beting/ *noun Brit* a bookmaker's shop.

bettor *or* **better** /'betə/ *noun* a person who bets.

between¹ /bi'tween/ *prep* **1a** through the common action of (two or more people or things): *Between them, they managed to lay the carpet.* **b** in shares to each of (two or more people or things): *The estate was divided between his four children.* **2a** in or into the time, space, or interval that separates (two or more things): *between the rafters.* **b** in intermediate relation to (two things): *a colour between blue and grey.* **3a** from one to the other of (two places): *travelling between London and Paris.* **b** serving to connect or separate (two things): *The dividing line between fact and fancy.* **4** in point of comparison of (two things or people): *not much to choose between them.* **5** taking together the total effect of (two or more things): *She kept very busy between cooking, writing, and gardening.* ✳ **between you and me** in confidence. [Old English *betwēonum,* from BE- + *-twēonum* (dative pl); related to Old English *twā* TWO]

Usage note

between you and me. Prepositions are followed by the object form of the personal pronoun, not the subject form: *from me to him; for us and against them.* Between is no exception: *We divided it between us* (not *between we*). Having been told repeatedly that it is incorrect to say, for example, *You and me are two of a kind,* people sometimes overcorrect themselves and say *between you and I* when the grammatically correct form is *between you and me.*

between² *adv* in or into an intermediate space or interval: *two adults with a child between.*

betweentimes *adv* at or during intervals.

betweenwhiles *adv* = BETWEENTIMES.

betwixt /bi'twikst/ *adv and prep archaic* between. ✳ **betwixt and between** in a midway position; neither one thing nor the other. [Old English *betwux,* from BE- + *-twux*; related to Old English *twā* TWO]

BeV *abbr* billion electron volts.

bevel¹ /'bevl/ *noun* **1** the angle or slant that one surface or line makes with another when they are not at right angles. **2** an instrument consisting of two rules or arms jointed together and opening to any angle, used for drawing angles or adjusting surfaces to be given a bevel. [Old French *baïf* with open mouth, from *baer* to yawn, from late Latin *batare*]

bevel² *verb* (**bevelled, bevelling,** *NAmer* **beveled, beveling**) ➤ *verb trans* to cut or shape (something) to a bevel. ➤ *verb intrans* to incline or slant.

bevel gear *noun* **1** a pair of toothed wheels that work shafts inclined to each other. **2** a system of gears having such toothed wheels.

beverage /'bev(ə)rij/ *noun* a liquid for drinking; *esp* one that is not water. [Middle English from early French *bevrage,* from *beivre* to drink, from Latin *bibere*]

bevvy /'bevi/ *noun* (*pl* **bevvies**) *Brit, informal* an alcoholic drink: *a couple of bevvies.* [by shortening and alteration from *beverage*]

bevy /'bevi/ *noun* (*pl* **bevies**) a group or collection, *esp* of young women: *a bevy of beauties.* [Middle English *bevey*; earlier history unknown]

bewail /bi'wayl/ *verb trans* to express deep sorrow for (something); to lament.

beware /bi'weə/ *verb trans and intrans* (*usu in imperative*) to be wary of (something): *We were warned to beware of the dog; Beware the Ides of March!* [Middle English *been war,* from *been* to BE + *war* careful, WARY]

bewilder /bi'wildə/ *verb trans* (**bewildered, bewildering**) to perplex or confuse (somebody), *esp* by complexity or variety: *Her* *antagonism bewildered me.* ⟫ **bewilderingly** *adv,* **bewilderment** *noun.* [BE- + archaic *wilder* to lead astray, perplex, prob from WILDERNESS]

bewitch /bi'wich/ *verb trans* **1** to attract (somebody) as if by the power of witchcraft; to enchant: *He was bewitched by her beauty.* **2** to cast a spell over (somebody). ⟫ **bewitchingly** *adv.*

bey /bay/ *noun* **1** a provincial governor in the Ottoman Empire. **2** formerly used as a courtesy title in Turkey and Egypt: Mr: *Ali Bey.* [Turkish *bey* gentleman, chief]

beyond[1] /bi'yond/ *prep* **1** on or to the farther side of (somebody or something); at a greater distance than (somebody or something): *beyond the hedge.* **2a** out of the reach or sphere of (something): *beyond repair.* **b** in a degree or amount surpassing (something): *rich beyond my wildest dreams.* **c** out of the comprehension of (somebody): *How he escaped is beyond me.* **3** = BESIDES[2]. **4** past or later than (a particular time): *beyond six o'clock.* [Old English *begeondan,* from BE- + *geondan* beyond, from *geond* YONDER]

beyond[2] *adv* on or to the farther side; farther: *to the border and beyond.*

beyond[3] *noun* (**the beyond**) something that lies outside the scope of ordinary experience; *specif* the hereafter.

bezant /'bezənt, bə'zant/ *noun* = SOLIDUS (3). [Middle English *besant* via Old French from late Latin *Byzantius* Byzantine, from *Byzantium,* ancient name of Istanbul, city in Turkey]

bezel /'bez(ə)l/ *noun* **1** a sloping edge, *esp* on a cutting tool. **2** the faceted portion, *esp* the upper one, of a gem. **3** a rim or groove that holds a transparent covering of a watch, clock, headlight, etc. [prob French dialect, alteration of French *biseau*]

bezique /bə'zeek/ *noun* **1** a card game for two people that is played with a double pack of 64 cards, including the seven to ace only in each suit. **2** the combination of the queen of spades and the jack of diamonds in this game. [French *bésique*]

BF *abbr* Burkina Faso (international vehicle registration).

bf *abbr Brit, informal* bloody fool.

b/f *abbr* brought forward.

BFI *abbr* British Film Institute.

BFPO *abbr* British Forces Post Office.

BG *abbr* Bulgaria (international vehicle registration).

bhaji *or* **bhajee** /'bahji/ *noun* a spicy Indian vegetable fritter: *onion bhajis.* [Hindi *bhaji* vegetable]

bhang /bang/ *noun* a mild form of cannabis used *esp* in India. [Hindi *bhāṅg*]

bhangra *or* **bangra** /'banggrə, 'bahnggrə/ *noun* a form of traditional Punjabi folk music, sometimes now performed as a form of fusion music influenced by rock and rap. [Punjabi *bhāṅgrā* a traditional Punjab harvest festival dance]

bhp *abbr* brake horsepower.

Bi *abbr* the chemical symbol for bismuth.

bi-[1] *or* **bin-** *prefix* forming words, with the meanings: **1a** two: *bilingual.* **b** appearing or occurring every two: *bimonthly.* **c** into two parts: *bisect.* **2a** twice; doubly; on both sides: *biconvex.* **b** appearing or occurring twice in compare SEMI-: *biweekly.* **3** located between, involving, or affecting two (specified symmetrical parts): *binaural.* **4** DI-[1]: *biphenyl.* **5** acid salt: *bicarbonate.* [Middle English from Latin]

bi-[2] *comb form* see BIO-.

biannual /bie'anyooəl/ *adj* occurring twice a year: compare BIENNIAL[1]. ⟫ **biannually** *adv.*

bias[1] /'bie-əs/ *noun* **1a** an inclination of temperament or outlook; *esp* a personal prejudice. **b** a bent or tendency. **c** in statistics, a tendency of an estimate to deviate in one direction from a true value, e.g. because of non-random sampling. **2** (**the bias**) a line diagonal to the grain of a fabric: *a skirt cut on the bias.* **3a** the tendency of a bowl used in the game of bowls to take a curved path when rolled. **b** the property of shape or weight that causes this. **4** a voltage applied to an electronic device, e.g. the grid of a thermionic valve, to enable it to function normally. [early French *biais* from Old Provençal]

bias[2] *verb trans* (**biased** *or* **biassed**, **biasing** *or* **biassing**) **1** to give a prejudiced outlook to (something or somebody). **2** to influence (somebody) unfairly: *That might bias the jury.*

bias binding *noun* a narrow folded strip of fabric cut on the bias used for hemming, to cover raw edges, or for decoration.

biased /'bie-əst/ *adj* exhibiting or characterized by bias: *biased reporting.*

biathlon /bie'athlən/ *noun* an athletic contest consisting of combined cross-country skiing and rifle shooting. [BI-[1] + Greek *athlon* contest]

Bib. *abbr* **1** Bible. **2** biblical.

bib /bib/ *noun* **1** a covering, e.g. of cloth or plastic, placed over a child's front to protect the clothes. **2** a small rectangular section of a garment, e.g. an apron or dungarees, extending above the waist. [prob from archaic *bib* to drink, from Middle English *bibben,* perhaps from Latin *bibere*]

bib and tucker /'tukə/ ✳ **one's best bib and tucker** *informal* one's best clothes.

bibber /'bibə/ *noun archaic* somebody given to drinking alcohol; a tippler. [archaic *bib* to drink (see BIB) + -ER[2]]

bibcock /'bibkok/ *noun* a tap with a bent-down nozzle. [prob from BIB + COCK[1]]

bibelot /'bib(ə)loh/ *noun* (*pl* **bibelots** /-loh(z)/) a small ornament or decorative object; a trinket or curio: *You'll be tired ... if he shows you all his bibelots and gives you a lecture on each* — Henry James. [French *bibelot*]

bible /'biebl/ *noun* **1a** (**the Bible**) the sacred book of Christians, comprising the Old Testament and the New Testament. **b** any book containing the sacred writings of a religion.

Editorial note
There is no agreement about the exact contents of the Bible. Catholic and Orthodox Bibles contain Old Testament books that were not written in or have not survived in Hebrew; Protestant Bibles usually omit these books. The 'books' were originally written on separate scrolls or sheets of papyrus and were only gathered into one volume hundreds of years after their composition. This process indicates the supreme importance that was attached to these writings — Professor John Rogerson.

2 (**Bible**) a copy or an edition of the Bible. **3** an authoritative book: *the fisherman's bible.*

Word history
Middle English via French and Latin from Greek *biblion* book, from *byblos* papyrus. The word is derived ultimately from *Byblos,* the name of an ancient Phoenician city from which papyrus was exported.

Bible Belt *noun* an area characterized by ardent religious fundamentalism, *esp* such an area in the southern USA.

biblical /'biblikl/ *adj* **1** of or in accordance with the Bible: *a biblical character.* **2** suggestive of the Bible or its times: *biblical times.* ⟫ **biblically** *adv.* [late Latin *biblicus,* ultimately from Greek *biblion:* see BIBLE]

biblio- *comb. form* forming words, denoting: book: *bibliography.* [French *biblio-* via Latin from Greek, from *biblion:* see BIBLE]

bibliography /bibli'ogrəfi/ *noun* (*pl* **bibliographies**) **1** a list of the works referred to in a text or consulted by the author in its production. **2** a list of writings relating to a particular topic, written by a particular author, issued by a particular publisher, etc. **3** the history, identification, or description of writings and publications. ⟫ **bibliographer** *noun,* **bibliographic** /-'grafik/ *adj,* **bibliographical** /-'grafikl/ *adj,* **bibliographically** /-'grafikli/ *adv.* [via Latin from Greek *bibliographia,* the copying of books, from BIBLIO- + *-graphia* -GRAPHY]

bibliomancy /'bibli-əmansi/ *noun* the foretelling of the future by interpreting a passage from a book, *esp* the Bible. [BIBLIO- + -MANCY]

bibliomania /ˌbiblioh'maynyə/ *noun* excessive enthusiasm for books. [BIBLIO- + -MANIA]

bibliophile /'bibli-əfiel/ *noun* a lover or collector of books. ⟫ **bibliophilic** /-'filik/ *adj,* **bibliophilism** /-'ofiliz(ə)m/ *noun,* **bibliophily** /-'ofili/ *noun.* [French *bibliophile,* from BIBLIO- + -PHILE]

bibulous /'bibyooləs/ *adj* prone to over-indulgence in alcoholic drinks. ⟫ **bibulously** *adv,* **bibulousness** *noun.* [Latin *bibulus,* from *bibere* to drink]

bicameral /bie'kam(ə)r(ə)l/ *adj* having two legislative chambers. ⟫ **bicameralism** *noun.* [BI-[1] + Latin *camera* room, CHAMBER]

bicarb /'biekahb/ *noun informal* = SODIUM BICARBONATE.

bicarbonate /bie'kahbənət/ *noun* an acid carbonate; *esp* SODIUM BICARBONATE.

biccy /'biki/ *noun* see BICKY.

bice /bies/ *noun* a dull blue or green pigment. [Middle English *bis* dark grey, from Old French]

bicentenary /biesen'teenəri, -'tenəri/ *noun* (*pl* **bicentenaries**) the celebration of a 200th anniversary.

bicentennial[1] /biesen'teni·əl/ *noun NAmer* a bicentenary.

bicentennial[2] *adj* of a bicentenary.

biceps /'bieseps/ *noun* **1** the large muscle at the front of the upper arm that bends the arm at the elbow when it contracts. **2** any muscle attached in two places at one end. [scientific Latin *bicipit-, biceps* two-headed, from Latin BI-[1] + *capit-, caput* head]

bicker[1] /'bikə/ *verb intrans* (**bickered, bickering**) to engage in petulant or petty argument. ⟫⟫ **bickerer** *noun.* [Middle English *bikeren*; earlier history unknown]

bicker[2] *noun* a petulant or petty argument.

bicky *or* **bikky** *or* **biccy** /'biki/ *noun* (*pl* **bickies** *or* **bikkies** *or* **biccies**) *Brit, informal* a biscuit. [by shortening and alteration]

biconcave /bie'konkayv/ *adj* concave on both sides. Also called CONCAVO-CONCAVE.

biconvex /bie'konveks, -'veks/ *adj* convex on both sides.

biculturalism /bie'kulchərəliz(ə)m/ *noun* the existence of two distinct cultures in one nation: *Canada's biculturalism.* ⟫⟫ **bicultural** *adj.*

bicuspid[1] /bie'kuspid/ *adj* said *esp* of a tooth: having or ending in two points. [scientific Latin *bicuspid-, bicuspis*, from BI-[1] + Latin *cuspid-, cuspis* point]

bicuspid[2] *noun* a tooth with two points.

bicycle[1] /'biesikl/ *noun* a two-wheeled pedal-driven vehicle with handlebars and a saddle. ⟫⟫ **bicycler** *noun*, **bicyclist** *noun.* [BI-[1] + *-cycle* as in TRICYCLE[1]]

bicycle[2] *verb intrans* to ride a bicycle.

bicyclic /bie'siklik, bie'sieklik/ *adj* in chemistry, consisting of or arranged in two cycles or circles.

bid[1] /bid/ *verb* (**bidding**, *past tense* **bid** *or* **bade** /bad/, *past part.* **bid** *or* **bidden** /'bidn/) ⟫ *verb trans* **1a** (*often* + for/against) to offer (a price) for payment or acceptance, e.g. at an auction: *He bid £500 for the vase.* **b** to make a bid of or in (a suit at cards). **2** *archaic* to issue an order to (somebody); to tell (somebody) to do something: *But he ... bids us all prepare against a storm* — Jonathan Swift. **3** *archaic* to give expression to (something): *She bade him a tearful farewell.* ⟫ *verb intrans* to make a bid. ✳ **bid fair** to seem likely; to show promise: *She bids fair to become extremely attractive.* ⟫⟫ **bidder** *noun.* [partly from Old English *biddan*, to request, entreat; partly from Old English *bēodan* to offer, command]

bid[2] *noun* **1a** the act of a person who bids. **b** a statement of what one will give or take for something; *esp* an offer of a price. **c** something offered as a bid: *a bid of £100.* **2** an opportunity to bid. **3a** in cards, the number of tricks to be won, suit to be played in, etc. **b** an announcement of such information. **4** an attempt to win or achieve something: *a bid for power.*

biddable /'bidəbl/ *adj* **1** easily led or controlled; docile. **2** said of a hand or suit of cards: capable of being reasonably bid. ⟫⟫ **biddability** /-'biliti/ *noun.*

bidden /'bidn/ *verb* past part. of BID[1].

bidding *noun* order or command: *He came at my bidding.*

biddy[1] /'bidi/ *noun* (*pl* **biddies**) *informal* a woman: *an eccentric old biddy.* [dimin. of the name *Bridget*]

biddy[2] *noun* (*pl* **biddies**) *chiefly NAmer, informal* a hen or young chicken. [perhaps imitative]

biddy-bid *or* **biddy-biddy** *noun* (*pl* **biddy-bids** *or* **biddy-biddies**) **1** a grassland plant of New Zealand of the rose family: *Acaena anserinifolia.* **2** the burr of this plant. [modification of Maori *piripiri*]

bide /bied/ *verb intrans archaic or dialect* to remain for a while; to stay: *Well, come along home, and don't let's bide out here in the damp* — Hardy. ✳ **bide one's time** to wait until the appropriate time comes to initiate action or to proceed. [Old English *bīdan*]

bidet /'beeday/ *noun* a low bathroom fixture used *esp* for bathing the external genitals and the anus. [French *bidet* small horse, bidet, from *bider* to trot. So called because one sits astride it]

bid up *verb trans* to raise the price of (property in an auction) by a succession of increasing offers.

Biedermeier *or* **Biedermaier** /'beedəmie·ə/ *adj* **1** of or suggesting a conventional and restrained style of furniture and interior decoration popular among the middle classes in Germany in the 19th cent. **2** conventional or philistine in attitude. [named after

Gottlieb *Biedermeier*, fictitious simple German bourgeois, ostensible author of poems by Adolf Kussmaul d.1902, and others]

biennia /bie'eni·ə/ *noun* pl of BIENNIUM.

biennial[1] /bie'eni·əl/ *adj* **1** occurring every two years: compare BIANNUAL. **2** said of a plant: growing vegetatively during the first year and fruiting and dying during the second: compare ANNUAL[1], PERENNIAL[1]. ⟫⟫ **biennially** *adv.*

biennial[2] *noun* **1** an event occurring every two years. **2** a plant growing during the first year and dying during the second.

biennium /bie'eni·əm/ *noun* (*pl* **bienniums** *or* **biennia** /-ə/) a period of two years. [Latin *biennium*, from BI-[1] + *annus* year]

bier /biə/ *noun* **1** a stand on which a corpse or coffin is placed. **2** a coffin together with its stand. [Old English *bǣr*; related to Old English *beran* BEAR[2]]

biff[1] /bif/ *noun informal* a whack or blow. [prob imitative]

biff[2] *verb trans informal* to strike (somebody or something) sharply or roughly.

bifid /'biefid/ *adj* divided into two equal lobes or parts by a central cleft: *a bifid petal.* ⟫⟫ **bifidity** /bie'fiditi/ *noun.* [Latin *bifidus*, from BI-[1] + *-fidus* -FID]

bifocal /bie'fohk(ə)l/ *adj* **1** having two focal lengths. **2** having one part that corrects for near vision and one for distant vision: *a bifocal lens.*

bifocals *pl noun* glasses with bifocal lenses.

bifurcate[1] /'biefuhkayt/ *verb intrans* to divide into two branches or parts. ⟫⟫ **bifurcation** /-'kaysh(ə)n/ *noun.* [late Latin *bifurcatus*, past part. of *bifurcare*, from Latin *bifurcus* two-pronged, from BI-[1] + *furca* FORK[1]]

bifurcate[2] /'biefuhkət, -kayt/ *adj* divided into two branches or parts.

big[1] /big/ *adj* (**bigger, biggest**) **1a** large in size, amount, number, or scale: *a big house.* **b** largest: *the big toe.* **c** large and important in influence, standing, or wealth: *the big four banks.* **2a** elder: *my big sister.* **b** older or grown-up: *When I'm big, I'm going to be a nurse.* **3a** chief, outstanding, or most important: *Housing is the big issue of the campaign; His big moment had finally come.* **b** of great importance, significance, or seriousness: *a big decision; a big problem.* **4** of great force or intensity: *a big storm; a big argument.* **5a** pretentious or boastful: *big talk.* **b** *often ironic* magnanimous or generous: *That's very big of you.* **6** *informal* popular: *Frank Sinatra was very big in Las Vegas.* **7** *literary* advanced in pregnancy: *big with child.* ✳ **too big for one's boots** *informal* excessively self-confident or self-important; conceited. ⟫⟫ **biggish** *adj*, **bigness** *noun.* [Middle English, prob of Scandinavian origin]

big[2] *adv informal* **1a** outstandingly: *She made it big in New York.* **b** on a grand scale: *Think big!* **2** pretentiously or boastfully: *He talks big.*

bigamy /'bigəmi/ *noun* the crime of going through a marriage ceremony with one person while legally married to another. ⟫⟫ **bigamist** *noun*, **bigamous** *adj*, **bigamously** *adv.* [Middle English *bigamie* via late Latin from Latin BI-[1] + Greek *gamos* marriage]

Big Apple *noun* (**the Big Apple**) *chiefly NAmer, informal* New York City. [orig jazz musicians' slang]

big bang *noun* **1** in cosmology, the theoretical explosion of material from which the universe originated. **2a** a sudden reorganization or change. **b** (**Big Bang**) the changes made to many of the regulations governing the British Stock Market in October 1986.

big bang theory *noun* in cosmology, the theory that the universe originated from the explosion of a single mass of material, the components of which are still flying apart: compare STEADY-STATE THEORY.

Big Brother *noun* **1a** a ruthless all-powerful government. **b** an organization perceived as having total control over everybody's lives. **2** the leader of such a government or organization. [named after *Big Brother*, the omnipotent head of state in the novel *1984* by George Orwell d.1950, English writer]

big bud *noun* any of several plant diseases caused by a gall mite and characterized by abnormally swollen buds.

big cat *noun* a large member of the cat family, such as a lion or leopard.

big cheese *noun* = CHEESE[2].

big deal *interj informal* used to show that one is not impressed by something.

big dipper /'dɪpə/ *noun* **1** (*often* **Big Dipper**) *Brit* = ROLLER COASTER. **2** (**the Big Dipper**) *NAmer* = PLOUGH[1] (3).

big end *noun Brit* the end of an engine's connecting rod nearest the crankpin: compare CRANKPIN.

big game *noun* **1** large animals hunted or fished for sport. **2** an important objective, *esp* a risky one.

biggie /'bɪgi/ *noun informal* **1** a very important or well-known person, organization, etc. **2** something that is very complex, difficult, significant, or important.

big gun *noun informal* somebody or something important or powerful: *The stage … is all right if you can be one of the big guns* — Theodore Dreiser.

bighead *noun informal* a conceited person. ➤➤ **bigheaded** *adj,* **bigheadedness** *noun.*

big head *noun informal* an exaggerated opinion of one's importance.

bighearted *adj* generous and kindly. ➤➤ **bigheartedly** *adv,* **bigheartedness** *noun.*

bighorn *noun* (*pl* **bighorns** *or collectively* **bighorn**) a wild sheep of mountainous parts of western N America, the male of which has large curved horns: *Ovis canadensis.*

bight /biet/ *noun* **1a** a bend of a river, coast, mountain chain, etc. **b** a hollow formed by such a bend. **2a** the middle part of a slack rope. **b** a loop in a rope. [Old English *byht*]

bigmouth *noun informal* a loudmouthed or indiscreet person. ➤➤ **bigmouthed** /'bɪgmowdhd, 'bɪgmowtht/ *adj.*

big name *noun* a very famous or important performer or personage. ➤➤ **big-name** *adj.*

big noise *noun informal* an important person.

bigot /'bɪgət/ *noun* somebody who is obstinately or intolerantly devoted to their own religion, opinion, etc: *a religious bigot.* ➤➤ **bigoted** *adj,* **bigotedly** *adv,* **bigotry** /-tri/ *noun.* [early French *bigot* hypocrite, bigot]

big shot *noun informal* an important person.

Big Smoke *noun* (*usu* **the Big Smoke**) *Brit, informal* a large city, *esp* London.

big stick *noun informal* force, or the threat of using force.

big-ticket *adj chiefly NAmer, informal* costing a great deal of money.

big time[1] *noun* (*usu* **the big time**) *informal* success, *esp* in show business: *She's still hoping to make it into the big time.* ➤➤ **big-time** *adj,* **big-timer** *noun.*

big time[2] *adv informal* to a very great extent or degree: *I threw up on the pavement, big time.*

big top *noun* (*usu* **the big top**) the main tent of a circus.

big wheel *noun* **1** (*often* **the big wheel**) a fairground amusement device consisting of a large upright power-driven wheel carrying seats round its rim that remain horizontal while the wheel turns. **2** *chiefly NAmer* = BIG SHOT.

bigwig *noun informal* = BIG SHOT. [from the large wigs worn by important men in the 18th cent.]

BIH *abbr* Bosnia-Herzegovina (international vehicle registration).

Bihari /bi'hahri/ *noun* **1** a native or inhabitant of the state of Bihar in NE India. **2** the Indic language, closely related to Hindi, spoken in the state of Bihar. ➤➤ **Bihari** *adj.* [Hindi *bihārī*]

bijou[1] /'beezhooh/ *noun* (*pl* **bijous** /'beezhoohz/ *or* **bijoux** /'beezhooh/) a small dainty usu ornamental piece of delicate workmanship; a jewel. [French *bijou* from Breton *bizou* ring, from *biz* finger]

bijou[2] *adj* said *esp* of a house: small and attractively elegant.

bijouterie /bi'zhooht(ə)ri/ *noun* a collection of trinkets or ornaments; jewellery. [French *bijouterie,* from *bijou:* see BIJOU[1]]

bijoux /'beezhooh/ *noun* pl of BIJOU[1].

bike[1] /biek/ *noun* **1** a bicycle. **2** a motorcycle. [by shortening and alteration]

bike[2] *verb intrans* to ride a bicycle or motorcycle.

biker *noun* **1** a motorcyclist, *esp* a person who is a member of a gang of motorcyclists. **2** a person who rides a bicycle.

bikini /bi'keeni/ *noun* **1** a woman's brief two-piece garment worn for swimming or sunbathing. **2** (*also in pl*) a pair of woman's very brief underpants.

Word history

French *bikini,* named after the Pacific atoll of *Bikini* where atomic bombs were tested by the USA in 1946. The swimsuit was named by its inventor, Louis Réard d.1984, French engineer, who felt that his creation would cause as big a sensation as the bomb.

bikini line *noun* the limit of the area of skin on a woman's thighs that would be exposed if she were wearing a bikini or similarly brief underwear.

bikini wax *noun* the removal by waxing of a woman's pubic hair, *esp* the visible part outside the bikini line.

bikky /'biki/ *noun* see BICKY.

bilabial[1] /bie'laybi·əl/ *noun* a consonant produced with both lips (e.g. *b, p, m*). [BI-[1] + Latin *labium* lip]

bilabial[2] *adj* said of a consonant: produced with both lips.

bilateral /bie'lat(ə)rəl/ *adj* **1** having two sides. **2** = BIPARTITE (2). ➤➤ **bilateralism** *noun,* **bilaterally** *adv,* **bilateralness** *noun.* [BI-[1] + Latin *later-, latus* side]

bilateral symmetry *noun* a pattern of symmetry (e.g. in animals) in which similar parts are arranged on opposite sides of a central axis so that one and only one plane can divide the individual into essentially identical halves: compare RADIAL SYMMETRY, SYMMETRY.

bilayer /'bielayə/ *noun* a membrane or film with a thickness of two molecules. [BI-[1] + LAYER[1]]

bilberry /'bilb(ə)ri/ *noun* (*pl* **bilberries**) **1** a bluish edible soft fruit. **2** the dwarf bushy European shrub of the heath family that grows on moorland and bears this fruit: *Vaccinium myrtillus.* [*bil-* (prob of Scandinavian origin) + BERRY[1]]

bilbo /'bilboh/ *noun* (*pl* **bilbos**) a sword, *esp* a rapier, with a finely tempered blade. [from *Bilboa,* the former English name for the town of *Bilbao* in northern Spain, where fine sword blades were crafted]

bilboes /'bilbohz/ *pl noun* a long bar of iron with sliding shackles used to confine the feet of prisoners, *esp* on board a ship. [perhaps from *Bilboa,* the former English name for the Spanish town of *Bilbao*]

bilby /'bilbi/ *noun* (*pl* **bilbies**) either of two species of Australian marsupial, similar to a rat, that has large ears, a pointed nose, and a long tail, lives in a burrow and eats other small mammals and lizards: genus *Macrotis.*

Bildungsroman /'bildəngzrohmahn (*German* 'bɪldʊŋsrɔman)/ *noun* a novel that deals with the development of a person's character, *esp* during that person's youth. [German *Bildungsroman,* from *Bildung* development, education + *Roman* novel]

bile /biel/ *noun* **1** a yellow or greenish fluid secreted by the liver into the intestines to aid the digestion of fats. **2** a tendency to become angry; irritability: *But these paroxysms seldom occurred, and in them my big-hearted shipmate vented the bile which more calm-tempered individuals get rid of by continual pettishness* — Herman Melville. [French *bile* from Latin *bilis*]

bile duct *noun* the duct by which bile passes from the liver or gall bladder to the duodenum.

bi-level *adj* having, or organized on, two levels.

bilge[1] /bilj/ *noun* **1a** the lowest part of a ship's hull between the keel and the vertical sides. **b** (*also in pl*) the space inside this part of the hull. **2** = BILGE WATER. **3** *informal* nonsense. [prob modification of Old French *boulge:* see BULGE[1]]

bilge[2] *verb trans* to damage (a ship) in the bilge. ➤ *verb intrans* said of a ship: to suffer damage in the bilge.

bilge keel *noun* a lengthways projection attached to either side of a ship's hull on the bilge to reduce the rolling of the ship and support its weight when grounded.

bilge water *noun* dirty water that collects in the bilge of a ship.

bilharzia /bil'hahzi·ə/ *noun* **1** = SCHISTOSOME. **2** = SCHISTOSOMIASIS. ➤➤ **bilharzial** *adj.* [named after Theodor *Bilharz* d.1862, German zoologist, who discovered the parasite that causes the disease]

bilharziasis /bilhah'zie·əsis/ *noun* (*pl* **bilharziases** /-seez/) = SCHISTOSOMIASIS.

biliary /'biliəri/ *adj* **1** relating to or conveying bile. **2** relating to structures in the body that convey bile. [French *biliare* from Latin *bilis* BILE]

bilingual¹ /bie'linggwəl/ *adj* **1** using or able to use two languages with the fluency of a native speaker. **2** using, relating to, or expressed in two languages: *a bilingual dictionary.* ⟫ **bilingualism** *noun*, **bilingually** *adv.* [Latin *bilinguis*, from BI-¹ + *lingua* tongue]

bilingual² *noun* a bilingual person.

bilious /'bili·əs/ *adj* **1** marked by or suffering from vomiting or a feeling of nausea. **2** *informal* said of colours: extremely distasteful; sickly: *a bilious green.* **3** peevish or ill-natured. **4a** relating to bile. **b** marked by or suffering from excessive secretion of bile. ⟫ **biliously** *adv*, **biliousness** *noun.* [early French *bilieux* from Latin *biliosus*, from *bilis* BILE]

bilirubin /bili'roohbin/ *noun* a reddish yellow pigment occurring in bile, blood, urine, and gallstones. [Latin *bilis* BILE + *ruber* red]

biliverdin /bili'vuhdin/ *noun* a green pigment occurring in bile: formula $C_{33}H_{34}N_4O_6$. [Latin *bilis* bile + obsolete French *verd* green]

bilk /bilk/ *verb trans* **1a** to cheat (somebody), *esp* by swindling them out of money: *defrauded and bilked of all the joys of life* — Jack London. **b** (*usu* + of) to avoid paying (somebody) what is due to them. **2** to block the free development of (something); to frustrate (it): *Fate bilked their hopes.* **3** to slip away from (somebody); to elude (them). ⟫ **bilker** *noun.* [perhaps an alteration of BALK¹]

Bill /bil/ *noun* (*usu* **the Bill**) *Brit, informal* the police. [probably named after *Old Bill*, a grumbling old soldier created during World War I by Bruce Bairnsfather d.1959, British cartoonist. Cartoons often depicted policemen with moustaches similar to Old Bill's]

bill¹ *noun* **1a** the charges made for goods or services. **b** an itemized statement of such charges. **2** a draft of a law presented to a lawmaking body such as Parliament. **3a** a written or printed notice advertising an event of interest to the public (e.g. a theatre show). **b** a programme of entertainment: *Who's top of the bill tonight?* **4** a paper carrying a statement of particulars; see also BILL OF FARE, BILL OF LADING. **5** *chiefly NAmer* = BANKNOTE. **6** a statement of a creditor's claim. ✳ **fill/fit the bill** to serve the required purpose or be suitable. [Middle English via medieval Latin *billa, bulla*: see BULL²]

bill² *verb trans* **1** (*often* + for) to submit a bill of charges to (somebody). **2** (+ as) to announce or proclaim (somebody or something) to be something: *It's being billed as the novel of the decade.* **3a** to advertise (somebody or something), *esp* by posters or placards. **b** to arrange for the presentation of (a person, act, etc) as part of a programme of entertainment.

bill³ *noun* **1a** the hard hooked, pointed, flattened, etc mouthparts of a bird; a bird's beak. **b** the similar mouthparts of an animal such as a turtle or platypus. **2** a narrow piece of land projecting into the sea. [Old English *bile*]

bill⁴ *verb intrans* said of birds, *esp* doves: to stroke each other's bills in courtship. ✳ **bill and coo** said of people, *esp* lovers: to caress and talk lovingly.

bill⁵ *noun* **1** a long staff with a hook-shaped blade, used as a weapon up to the 18th cent. **2** = BILLHOOK. [Old English *bill*]

billabong /'biləbong/ *noun Aus* **1a** a blind channel leading out from a river. **b** a stream bed that is usu dry but is filled seasonally. **2** a backwater forming a stagnant pool. [native name in Australia]

billboard *noun chiefly NAmer* = HOARDING (1). [BILL¹ + BOARD¹]

billet¹ /'bilit/ *noun* **1a** an official order stating that a member of a military force must be provided with board and lodging in a place (e.g. a private home). **b** quarters assigned by a billet or as if by a billet. **2** a position or job: *a lucrative billet.* [Middle English *bylet* short document from early French *billette*, dimin. of *bulle* document, from medieval Latin *bulla*: see BULL²]

billet² *verb trans* (**billeted, billeting**) (*often* + on) to provide (e.g. soldiers) with a billet.

billet³ *noun* **1** a small thick piece of wood (e.g. for firewood). **2** a usu small bar of iron, steel, etc. **3** in architecture, a short cylinder or square projection placed at regular intervals to form a Romanesque moulding or ornament. [Middle English *bylet* from early French *billette*, dimin. of *bille* log, of Celtic origin]

billet-doux /ˌbili 'dooh, ˌbeeyay/ *noun* (*pl* **billets-doux** /-'dooh(z)/) a love letter. [French *billet doux* sweet letter]

billfish *noun* (*pl* **billfishes** *or collectively* **billfish**) a large fish with long spearlike jaws, such as a marlin or swordfish.

billfold *noun NAmer* = WALLET (1). [short for earlier *billfolder*, from BILL¹]

billhead *noun* a printed form used for bills, or the heading of such a form.

billhook *noun* a cutting tool, used *esp* for pruning, that has a blade with a hooked point. [BILL⁵ + HOOK¹]

billiards /'bilyədz/ *pl noun* (*treated as sing.*) **1** any of several games played on an oblong table by hitting small balls against one another or into pockets with a cue. **2** one game of this kind played with three balls, in which scores are made by causing one ball, the cue ball, to hit the other two balls, the object balls, in succession: compare POOL², SNOOKER¹. ⟫ **billiard** *adj.* [early French *billard* billiard cue, billiards, from *bille* log, of Celtic origin]

billiard table *noun* a long rectangular table with a smooth surface covered in green cloth and with pockets at the corners and midway along its long sides, used for playing billiards and similar games.

billing /'biling/ *noun* **1** = ADVERTISING (2): *advance billing.* **2** the relative prominence given to a name (e.g. of an actor) in advertising programmes: *top billing.* [BILL²]

billingsgate /'bilingzgayt/ *noun Brit* swearing or very coarse or obscene language. [named after *Billingsgate*, the main wholesale fish market of London, formerly on the north bank of the Thames near London Bridge, which was notorious for the bad language of its habitués]

billion /'bili·ən/ *noun* **1** a thousand millions or 1,000,000,000 (10^9). **2** *Brit, dated* a million millions or 1,000,000,000,000 (10^{12}). **3** (*also in pl*) an indefinitely large number. ⟫ **billion** *adj*, **billionth** *adj and noun.*

Word history

French *billion* a million millions, from BI-¹ + *-illion* as in MILLION. Large numbers used to be written in groups of six figures; one billion was 1 plus two groups of six noughts (1 000000 000000). In 17th-cent. France it became customary to use groups of three figures; the idea of a million squared was lost and a billion came to be written 1 000 000 000 – a thousand million. This sense was adopted into American English and, to avoid confusion, is now generally used in British English.

billionaire /bilyə'neə/ *noun* somebody whose wealth is estimated at a billion or more units of money (e.g. pounds or dollars). [BILLION + *-aire* as in MILLIONAIRE]

bill of exchange *noun* an unconditional written order from one person to another to pay a specified sum of money to a designated person.

bill of fare *noun* = MENU (1).

bill of health *noun* **1** a certificate given to a ship's captain at the time of leaving port that indicates the state of health of the ship's crew and the condition of the port with regard to infectious diseases. **2** a usu satisfactory report about some condition or situation: *After a thorough investigation into the leaks, the office got a clean bill of health.*

bill of lading *noun* a receipt signed usu by the agent or owner of a ship listing goods that have been or are to be shipped.

Bill of Rights *noun* a summary in law of fundamental rights and privileges guaranteed by the state, such as the English Statute of 1689 or the first ten amendments to the US Constitution, added in 1791.

bill of sale *noun* a formal document for the conveyance or transfer of title to goods and personal property.

billon /'bilən/ *noun* gold or silver heavily alloyed with a less valuable metal. [French *billon*, from *bille*: see BILLIARDS]

billow¹ /'biloh/ *noun* **1** a great wave, *esp* in the open sea. **2** a rolling swirling mass (e.g. of flame or smoke). ⟫ **billowy** *adj.* [prob from Old Norse *bylgja*]

billow² *verb intrans* to rise, roll, bulge, or swell out in or as if in billows. ⟫ *verb trans* to make (something) rise, roll, bulge, or swell out in this way.

billposter *noun* somebody who pastes up advertisements and public notices on hoardings. ⟫ **billposting** *noun.*

billsticker *noun* = BILLPOSTER. ⟫ **billsticking** *noun.*

billy¹ /'bili/ *noun* (*pl* **billies**) a metal or enamelware can with an arched handle and a lid, used for outdoor cooking or carrying food or liquid. [prob from the name *Billy*, nickname for *William*]

billy² *noun* (*pl* **billies**) = BILLY GOAT.

billy³ *noun* (*pl* **billies**) *NAmer* = TRUNCHEON. [prob from *Billy*, nickname for *William*]

billycan *noun chiefly Aus* = BILLY¹.

billy club *noun* = BILLY³.

billy goat *noun informal* a male goat. [from the name *Billy*, nickname for *William*]

billy-o /'bilioh/ ✳ **like billy-o** *informal* very strongly, quickly, or fiercely: *We ran like billy-o but we couldn't catch him.* [origin unknown]

bilobate /bie'lohbayt/ *adj* = BILOBED.

bilobed /'bielohbd/ *adj* divided into two lobes.

biltong /'biltong/ *noun chiefly SAfr* strips of lean meat dried in the sun. [Afrikaans *biltong*, from *bil* buttock + *tong* tongue]

BIM *abbr* British Institute of Management.

bimanal /'bimənl, bie'maynl/ *adj* = BIMANOUS.

bimanous /'bimənəs, bie'maynəs/ *adj* said of humans and the higher primates: having hands or paws that are different in shape and function from the feet. [BI-¹ + Latin *manus* hand]

bimanual /bie'manyooəl/ *adj* done using both hands, or needing to be done with two hands.

bimbo /'bimboh/ *noun* (*pl* **bimbos**) **1** *informal, derog* an attractive but unintelligent person, *esp* a woman. **2** *NAmer, chiefly derog* a fellow. [Italian *bimbo* baby]

bimetallic /biemi'talik/ *adj* **1a** composed of two different metals, *esp* ones that expand by different amounts when heated. **b** denoting a device, such as a thermostat, that has a bimetallic part in it such as a bimetallic strip. **2** relating to bimetallism.

bimetallic strip *noun* a device consisting of strips of two metals, which expand by different amounts for a given change in temperature, welded together so that the whole strip bends when heated. It is used e.g. as an on-off switch in a thermostat.

bimetallism /bie'metəlizəm/ *noun* the use of two metals, e.g. gold and silver, jointly as a monetary standard, with both constituting legal tender at a predetermined ratio. ➤➤ **bimetallist** *noun*, **bimetallistic** /-'listik/ *adj*. [French *bimétallisme*, from BI-¹ + *métal* METAL¹]

bimillenary¹ /biemi'lenəri/ *noun* (*pl* **bimillenaries**) **1** the celebration of a 2000th anniversary. **2** a period of 2000 years.

bimillenary² *adj* **1** relating to a 2000th anniversary. **2** relating to a period of 2000 years.

bimillennial /biemi'leni·əl/ *noun and adj* = BIMILLENARY¹, BIMILLENARY².

bimolecular /biemə'lekyoolə/ *adj* **1** relating to or formed from two molecules. **2** being two molecules thick. ➤➤ **bimolecularly** *adv*.

bimonthly¹ /bie'munthli/ *adv* **1** every two months. **2** twice a month.

bimonthly² *adj* **1** occurring, appearing, etc every two months. **2** occurring, appearing, etc twice a month.

bimonthly³ *noun* (*pl* **bimonthlies**) a bimonthly publication.

bin¹ /bin/ *noun* **1** *Brit* a wastepaper basket, dustbin, or similar container for rubbish. **2** a container used for storage (e.g. of flour, grain, bread, or coal). **3** a partitioned case or stand for storing and ageing bottles of wine. [Old English *binu* manger, basket, prob of Celtic origin]

bin² *verb trans* (**binned, binning**) **1** to dispose of (something) as rubbish. **2** to discard (an idea, etc). **3** to put or store (*esp* bottled wine) in a bin.

bin- *comb. form* see BI-¹. [Middle English from Latin *bini* two by two]

binary¹ /'bienəri/ *adj* **1a** relating to or denoting a system of numbers that has two as its base and uses only the digits 0 and 1: *binary code; a binary number.* **b** involving a choice or condition of two alternatives (e.g. on or off, yes or no): *binary logic.* **2** consisting of or marked by two things or parts. **3** relating or combining two mathematical elements: *a binary operation.* **4** having two musical subjects or two complementary sections: *binary form.* [late Latin *binarius*, from Latin *bini* two by two]

binary² *noun* (*pl* **binaries**) **1** something made of two things or parts. **2** = BINARY STAR. **3** = BINARY WEAPON.

binary fission *noun* asexual reproduction of a cell by division into two parts.

binary star *noun* a system of two stars that revolve round each other.

binary weapon *noun* a weapon for use in chemical warfare, consisting of a shell containing two harmless nontoxic substances which combine when the weapon is fired to produce a toxic gas.

binate /'bienayt/ *adj* said of e.g. leaves: growing in pairs or in two parts. [Latin *bini* twofold]

binaural /bien'awrəl/ *adj* **1** relating to or used with both ears. **2** recorded stereophonically and played as two tracks to the hearer via headphones. ➤➤ **binaurally** *adv*. [Latin BIN- + AURAL]

bind¹ /biend/ *verb* (*past tense and past part.* **bound** /bownd/) ➤ *verb trans* **1a** (*also* + up) to tie (something) together, or make it secure by tying it. **b** to constrain (somebody) by tying them. **2** to put (somebody) under an obligation or legal requirement: *They were bound and thrown into prison.* **3a** to restrain or restrict (somebody, or what somebody does): *He was bound by a sense of fair play.* **b** to put (somebody) under an obligation or legal requirement: *be bound by contract.* **4** (*often* + up) to enclose or cover (something) by wrapping something else around it; *esp* to bandage (a wound, etc). **5** to fasten (something such as a belt) round something. **6** to cause (something) to stick together: *Add an egg to bind the mixture.* **7** to unite (people); to make (somebody) feel attached to somebody else, e.g. through gratitude or affection: *Nothing can break the ties that bind us.* **8** to make (e.g. an agreement or bargain) firm or sure; to settle or seal (something): *A deposit is needed to bind the sale.* **9** to protect, strengthen, or decorate (something) with a band or binding: *The edges of the carpet were bound with yellow tape.* **10** to apply a binding to (a book). **11** to set (somebody) to work as an apprentice; to indenture (somebody). **12** to make (a person or animal) constipated. ➤ *verb intrans* **1** to form a cohesive mass. **2** to become hindered from free operation. **3** to exert a restraining, compelling, or uniting influence on somebody or something: *a promise that binds.* **4** (+ to) to become attached to or combine with something, e.g. by chemical forces: *Enzymes bind to their substrates.* **5** *informal* to complain. [Old English *bindan*]

bind² *noun informal* a nuisance or bore. ✳ **in a bind** *chiefly NAmer, informal* in trouble or difficulty.

binder /'biendə/ *noun* **1** a usu detachable cover (e.g. for holding sheets of paper). **2** a person who binds books. **3** something (e.g. tar or cement) that makes loose substances such as small stones or sand stick together. **4** a harvesting machine that binds straw into bundles.

bindery /'biendəri/ *noun* (*pl* **binderies**) a place where books are bound.

bindi /'bindi/ *noun* (*pl* **bindis**) a decorative mark in the middle of the forehead, worn *esp* by Indian women, *esp* Hindus. [Hindi *bindī*]

bindi-eye /'bindiie/ *noun* a small Australian herbaceous plant with burrlike fruits: *Calotis cuneifolia.* [prob from an Australian Aboriginal language]

binding¹ /'biending/ *noun* **1** a material or device that is used to bind something. **2** a covering that fastens the leaves of a book together. **3** a narrow strip of fabric used to finish raw edges: *bias binding.* [verbal noun from BIND¹]

binding² *adj* (*often* + on) imposing an obligation: *a binding promise.* ➤➤ **bindingly** *adv*.

bind over *verb trans* to impose a specific legal obligation on (somebody): *He was bound over to keep the peace.*

bindweed *noun* any of various twining plants such as convolvulus with widespread root systems and trumpet-shaped flowers that are a nuisance to gardeners.

bine /bien/ *noun* a twining stem or flexible shoot (e.g. of the bindweed or a hop plant). [alteration of BIND² in the sense something that binds]

bin end *noun* one of the last bottles from a particular bin or consignment of wine.

Binet-Simon scale /ˌbeeney see'mohn skayl/ *noun* an intelligence test consisting of graded tasks for children of successive ages. [named after Alfred *Binet* d.1911, and Théodore *Simon* d.1961, the French psychologists who developed the tests]

binge¹ /binj/ *noun informal* a session of unrestrained indulgence in something; *esp* a drinking bout. [English dialect *binge* to drink heavily]

binge² *verb intrans* (**binged, bingeing**) *informal* to indulge in a binge, *esp* of eating or drinking: *I went home and binged on chocolate.*

bingo¹ /'binggoh/ *interj* **1** used to express the suddenness or unexpectedness of an event, or to remark on the successful completion of a task. **2** used as an exclamation to show that one has won a game of bingo. [alteration of *bing* (interj suggesting a sharp ringing sound), of imitative origin]

bingo² *noun* a game of chance played with cards with numbered squares. As numbers are drawn and called out at random, the corresponding squares are covered or marked off, a game being won by covering or marking off all or a predetermined number of squares.

binman *noun* (*pl* **binmen**) *Brit* = DUSTMAN.

binnacle /'bɪnəkl/ *noun* a case, stand, etc containing a ship's compass: *We had no light in the binnacle, but steered by the stars* — R H Dana. [alteration of Middle English *bitakle* via Old Portuguese *bitácola* or Old Spanish *bitácula* from Latin *habitaculum* dwelling place]

binocular /bɪ'nokyoolə/ *adj* relating to, using, or adapted for the use of both eyes: *binocular vision*.

binoculars *pl noun* an optical instrument for viewing things at a distance usu consisting of two small telescopes fixed side by side that can be focused together.

binomial¹ /bɪe'nohmɪ-əl/ *noun* **1** a mathematical expression consisting of two terms connected by a plus sign or minus sign. **2** a Latin name for a species consisting of two parts, the name of its genus followed by another name that designates it specifically. **3** in grammar, a fixed phrase consisting of two nouns joined by *and*, for example *bread and butter*. ➤➤ **binomially** *adv*. [medieval Latin *binomius* having two names, from BI-¹ + Latin *nomin-, nomen* name]

binomial² *adj* consisting of two terms or names: *binomial classification*.

binomial distribution *noun* in statistics, a probability distribution each of whose values corresponds to the probability that a specific combination of two types of possible event will occur in a given proportion of statistical trials.

binomial theorem *noun* a theorem by means of which a binomial may be raised to any power by a formula.

binominal /bie'nominl/ *adj* = BINOMIAL¹ (2).

bint /bint/ *noun Brit, chiefly derog* a girl or woman. [Arabic *bint* girl, daughter]

binturong /'bintyoorong, bin'tooərong/ *noun* an Asiatic civet with a prehensile tail: *Arctictis binturong*. [Malay *binturong*]

bio /'bieoh/ *noun* (*pl* **bios**) *informal* **1** a biography or autobiography. **2** *SAfr* = BIOSCOPE.

bio- *or* **bi-** *comb. form* forming words, denoting: **1** life: *biography*. **2** living organisms or tissue: *biology*. [Greek *bio-*, from *bios* mode of life]

bioactive /bie-oh'aktiv/ *adj* having an effect, *esp* a damaging or destructive one on living things or on something, e.g. blood or sweat, derived from living things.

bioassay¹ /bieoh'asay, -ə'say/ *noun* the determination of the relative strength of a substance, e.g. a drug, by comparing its effect on a test organism with that of a standard preparation. [shortening of *biological assay*]

bioassay² /bieoh'say/ *verb trans* to carry out a bioassay on (e.g. a drug).

bioastronautics /,bie-oh-astrə'nawtiks/ *pl noun* (*treated as sing.*) the study of the effects of space travel on living beings.

bioavailability /,bie-oh-əvaylə'biliti/ *noun* the degree to which a chemical compound, *esp* a drug, administered to a living organism is present and effective in the area of the body where it is intended to have its effect.

biocenosis /,bieohsi'nohsis/ *noun NAmer* see BIOCOENOSIS.

biochemistry /bieoh'kemǝstri/ *noun* chemistry dealing with the chemical compounds and processes that occur in living organisms. ➤➤ **biochemical** *adj*, **biochemically** *adv*, **biochemist** *noun*.

biocide /'bie-əsied/ *noun* a substance, such as DDT, that kills many different living organisms. ➤➤ **biocidal** /-'siedl/ *adj*.

biocoenosis (*NAmer* **biocenosis**) /,bie-ohsi'nohsis/ *noun* (*pl* **biocoenoses** /-'nohseez/) an ecological community made up of a variety of different organisms with its own distinct habitat. ➤➤ **biocoenotic** /-'notik/ *adj*. [scientific Latin, from BIO- + Greek *koinōsis* sharing]

biodegradable /,bieohdi'graydəbl/ *adj* capable of being broken down, *esp* into simpler harmless products, by the action of living organisms, such as bacteria: compare PHOTODEGRAD-

ABLE. ➤➤ **biodegradability** /-'biliti/ *noun*, **biodegradation** /-degrə'daysh(ə)n/ *noun*.

biodiesel /'bieohdeezl/ *noun* a biodegradable fuel produced from organic sources such as rapeseed, soya beans, recycled cooking oil and animal fat, blended with or used as a substitute for petroleum-based diesel oil.

biodiversity /,bie-ohdie'vuhsiti/ *noun* the number and diversity of distinct living species within the world or a particular environment: *The present reduction of biodiversity ... will be the largest setback to life yet* — New Scientist.

bioenergetics /,bieoh,enə'jetiks/ *pl noun* (*treated as sing.*) the biology of energy transformations and exchanges within and between living organisms and their environments. ➤➤ **bioenergetic** *adj*.

bioengineering /,bieoh,enji'niəring/ *noun* the application of engineering principles or equipment to biological or medical science, as, for example, in the production of artificial limbs and industrial biosynthesis.

bioethics /bieoh'ethiks/ *pl noun* (*treated as sing.*) the study of the ethical aspects of various techniques (e.g. genetic engineering and birth control) involving human intervention in biological processes.

biofeedback /bieoh'feedbak/ *noun* the technique of making unconscious or involuntary bodily processes perceptible to the senses in order to allow them to be affected by conscious mental control.

bioflavonoid /bie-oh'flayvənoyd/ *noun* any of a group of chemical compounds occurring in plants, *esp* citrus fruits, rose hips, and blackcurrants, that decrease the fragility of the blood capillaries and reduce their permeability to red blood cells; vitamin P.

biofuel /'bieohfyooh-əl/ *noun* any fuel made from renewable organic resources such as trees, grass, soya beans, rapeseed and seaweed or from waste products such as bark, sawdust, cooking oil, manure and sewage, either used by direct combustion or converted into other forms of fuel such as methane or ethyl alcohol.

biog. *abbr* **1** biographical. **2** biography.

biogas /'bie-ohgas/ *noun* gas, *esp* methane, obtained from processing manure or other biological waste and used as fuel.

biogenesis /bieoh'jenəsis/ *noun* **1** the development of living things from preexisting living things of the same type. **2** = BIOSYNTHESIS. ➤➤ **biogenetic** /-'netik/ *adj*. [scientific Latin, from BIO- + GENESIS]

biogenic /bieoh'jenik/ *adj* produced by living organisms. ➤➤ **biogenicity** /-'nisiti/ *noun*.

biogeographical /,bieohjee-ə'grafikl/ *or* **biogeographic** *adj* **1** relating to biogeography. **2** relating to a geographical region viewed in terms of its plants and animals.

biogeography /,bieohji'ogrəfi/ *noun* a branch of biology that deals with the geographical distribution of animals and plants.

biography /bie'ogrəfi/ *noun* (*pl* **biographies**) **1** a usu written account of a person's life. **2** biographical writing as a literary genre: *Read no history: nothing but biography, for that is life without theory* — Benjamin Disraeli. ➤➤ **biographer** *noun*, **biographic** /-'grafik/ *adj*, **biographical** /-'grafikl/ *adj*, **biographically** /-'grafikli/ *adv*. [late Greek *biographia*, from BIO- + -GRAPHY]

biohazard /'bieohhazəd/ *noun* a danger to health or the environment caused by biological research.

bioindicator /,bieoh'indikaytə/ *noun* see BIOLOGICAL INDICATOR.

bioinformatics /,bieoh-infə'matiks/ *pl noun* (*used as sing. or pl*) the application of data collection and processing methods to the analysis of complex biological phenomena such as genetic codes.

biol. *abbr* **1** biological. **2** biology.

biological /bie-ə'lojikl/ *adj* **1** relating to biology, life, or living organisms: *biological data*. **2** acting on or by means of, or produced by, living organisms: *biological action*. **3** containing a plant or animal product; *specif* being a detergent (e.g. a washing powder) containing an enzyme. ➤➤ **biologically** *adv*.

biological clock *noun* the inherent timing mechanism responsible for various cyclic responses, e.g. changes in hormone levels, of living beings.

biological control *noun* control of pests by interference with their ecological environment, usu by means of natural enemies.

biological indicator *or* **bioindicator** /,bieoh'indikaytə/ *noun* an animal, bird, fish, insect, plant or bacterium whose presence or absence, numbers, and/or condition can be used as an indicator in biological monitoring.

biological monitoring *or* **biomonitoring** /ˌbieohˈmonitəring/ *noun* the monitoring of the condition of some part of the environment, such as levels of atmospheric or water pollution, or, in medicine, the monitoring of the effectiveness of a sterilization procedure, by investigation of the presence or absence, numbers, and/or condition of one or more biological indicators.

biological warfare *noun* warfare involving the use of living organisms, *esp* ones that cause disease, or of chemicals harmful to plants.

biology /bieˈoləji/ *noun* **1** a science that deals with the structure, function, development, distribution, and life processes of living organisms. **2a** the plant and animal life of a region or environment. **b** the physical structure, processes, and functions of a particular organism or group. ≫ **biologist** *noun*. [German *Biologie*, from BIO- + -LOGY]

bioluminescence /ˌbieohloohmiˈnes(ə)ns/ *noun* light from living organisms, or the emission of such light. ≫ **bioluminescent** *adj*.

biomass /ˈbieohmas/ *noun* **1** the amount of living matter present in a region, e.g. in a unit area or volume of habitat. **2** organic materials or waste used as fuel.

biomathematics /ˌbieohmathəˈmatiks/ *pl noun* (*treated as sing. or pl*) the mathematics of biology.

biome /ˈbieohm/ *noun* a major type of ecological community: *the grassland biome*. [BI-² + -OME]

biomedicine /bieˈoh'medəsin/ *noun* a branch of medical science concerned *esp* with the capacity of human beings to survive and function in environments, such as a spacecraft, that cause an abnormal amount of physiological or psychological stress, and also with how such environments can be modified to minimize such stress. ≫ **biomedical** *adj*.

biometrics /bieˈə'metriks/ *pl noun* (*treated as sing. or pl*) = BIOMETRY.

biometry /bieˈomətri/ *noun* the statistical analysis of biological observations and phenomena. ≫ **biometric** /-ˈmetrik/ *adj*, **biometrical** /-ˈmetrikl/ *adj*.

biomonitoring /ˌbieohˈmonitəring/ *noun* SEE BIOLOGICAL MONITORING.

bionic /bieˈonik/ *adj* **1a** involving bionics. **b** having or being an artificial part designed to replace or simulate a living part such as a limb. **2** *not used technically* having exceptional abilities or powers. ≫ **bionically** *adv*.

bionics *pl noun* (*treated as sing. or pl*) **1** a science concerned with the application of biological systems to engineering problems. **2** the use of mechanical parts or artificial substances to replace or simulate damaged, diseased, or missing parts of a living organism. [BI-² + -*onics* as in *electronics*]

bionomics /bieˈoh'nomiks/ *pl noun* (*treated as sing.*) = ECOLOGY. ≫ **bionomic** *adj*, **bionomical** *adj*, **bionomically** *adv*. [*bionomic* (adj) prob from French *bionomique*, from *bionomie* ecology, from BIO- + -NOMY]

biophysics /bieˈoh'fiziks/ *pl noun* (*treated as sing. or pl*) a branch of science concerned with the application of physics to biological problems. ≫ **biophysical** *adj*, **biophysicist** /-sist/ *noun*.

biopic /ˈbieohpik/ *noun* a film based on the life of a well-known person. [shortened from *biographical picture*]

biopsy /ˈbieopsi/ *noun* (*pl* **biopsies**) the removal and examination of tissue, cells, or fluids from the living body. [BI-² + Greek *opsis* appearance]

biorhythm /ˈbieohridhəm/ *noun* (*usu in pl*) a supposed periodic fluctuation in the biological activity of a living thing that is held to affect and determine mood, behaviour, and performance. ≫ **biorhythmic** /-ˈridhmik/ *adj*, **biorhythmically** /-ˈridhmikli/ *adv*.

BIOS /ˈbie-os/ *abbr* Basic Input-Output System, a set of computer instructions controlling input and output functions in the firmware of a computer.

bioscope /ˈbie-əskohp/ *noun chiefly SAfr, informal* = CINEMA.

biosecurity *noun* the protection of people and animals from pests and infectious diseases, and the prevention of the spread of pests and diseases, by isolation, movement restrictions and sanitation.

-biosis *comb. form* (*pl* **-bioses**) forming nouns, denoting: a mode of life: *symbiosis*. ≫ **-biotic** *comb. form*. [scientific Latin from Greek *biōsis*, from *bioun* to live]

biosphere /ˈbie-əsfiə/ *noun* the entirety of those areas of the earth's surface and atmosphere in which life exists.

biosynthesis /bieoh'sinthəsis/ *noun* (*pl* **biosyntheses** /-seez/) the production of a chemical compound by a living organism. ≫ **biosynthetic** /-ˈthetik/ *adj*, **biosynthetically** /-ˈthetikli/ *adv*.

biota /bieˈohtə/ *noun* the flora and fauna of a region. [scientific Latin from Greek *biotē* life]

biotech /ˈbie-ohtek/ *noun informal* = BIOTECHNOLOGY.

biotechnology /ˌbie-ohtekˈnoləji/ *noun* **1** the use of living cells or micro-organisms, such as bacteria, in industry and technology to manufacture drugs and chemicals, create energy, destroy waste matter, etc. **2** *NAmer* the study of the interaction between people and machines they use; = ERGONOMICS. ≫ **biotechnological** /-ˈlojikl/ *adj*, **biotechnologically** /-ˈlojikli/ *adv*, **biotechnologist** *noun*.

bioterrorism /ˌbieoh'terəriz(ə)m/ *noun* terrorism using forms of biological warfare, such as the use of organisms that cause disease. ≫ **bioterrorist** *noun*.

biotic /bieˈotik/ *adj* **1** relating to life or living organisms. **2** caused or produced by living organisms. [Greek *biōtikos*, from *bioun* to live]

-biotic *comb. form* see -BIOSIS.

biotin /ˈbie-ətin/ *noun* a growth-controlling vitamin of the vitamin B complex found *esp* in yeast, liver, and egg yolk. [Greek *biotos* life, sustenance + -IN¹]

biotope /ˈbie-ətohp/ *noun* a small area with its own environmental conditions that is home to a particular ecological community of plant and animal life.

biotype /ˈbie-ətiep/ *noun* a group of organisms whose genetic make-up is identical.

bipartisan /bieˈpahtizn/ *adj* relating to or involving two political parties. ≫ **bipartisanship** *noun*.

bipartite /bieˈpahtiet/ *adj* **1** consisting of two parts. **2** said of a treaty, contract, etc between two parties: **a** having two correspondent parts, one for each party. **b** affecting both parties in the same way. **3** split into two parts or almost into two parts: *a bipartite leaf*. ≫ **bipartitely** *adv*, **bipartition** /-ˈtish(ə)n/ *noun*. [Latin *bipartitus*, past part. of *bipartire* to divide in two, from BI-¹ + *part-*, *pars* PART¹]

biped¹ /ˈbieped/ *noun* a two-footed animal. ≫ **bipedal** /bieˈpeedl/ *adj*. [Latin *biped-*, *bipes*, from BI-¹ + *ped-*, *pes* foot]

biped² *adj* two-footed.

bipinnate /bieˈpinayt/ *adj* said of leaves: made up of branching leaflets that are themselves divided pinnately (in a featherlike arrangement; see PINNATE). ≫ **bipinnately** *adv*.

biplane /ˈbieplayn/ *noun* an aeroplane with two pairs of wings, the one placed above and usu slightly forward of the other.

bipolar /bieˈpohlə/ *adj* **1** having or involving the use of two poles, e.g. north and south geographical or magnetic poles or positive and negative electrical poles. **2** characterized by two opposed statements, views, natures, etc. ≫ **bipolarity** /-ˈlariti/ *noun*.

BIR *abbr* Board of Inland Revenue.

birch¹ /buhch/ *noun* **1a** any of several species of deciduous trees or shrubs typically having a layered outer bark that peels readily: genus *Betula*. **b** the hard pale close-grained wood of this tree. **2a** a birch rod or bundle of twigs for flogging. **b** (**the birch**) punishment by flogging with a birch. ≫ **birchen** *adj*. [Old English *beorc*]

birch² *verb trans* to whip (somebody) with a birch or anything similar.

bird /buhd/ *noun* **1** any of a class of warm-blooded vertebrates whose bodies are more or less completely covered with feathers and whose forelimbs are modified as wings: class Aves. **2a** *chiefly informal* a person, *esp* somebody slightly odd: *He seemed an uppish old bird* — Conan Doyle. **b** *chiefly Brit, informal* a girl. **3** *Brit, informal* a period of imprisonment. ✳ **birds of a feather** people of similar characters, tastes, or interests. **for the birds** *informal* trivial or worthless. **get the bird 1** *chiefly Brit, informal* to be hissed, booed, or jeered at. **2** *chiefly Brit, informal* to be dismissed or fired. **give somebody the bird 1** *chiefly Brit, informal* to hiss, boo, or jeer at (somebody). **2** *chiefly Brit, informal* to dismiss or fire (somebody). **the bird has flown** the person whom one expected to find or capture has escaped. **the birds and the bees** *informal, humorous* the facts of sex and sexual reproduction, *esp* in a form suitable for children. ➤➤ **birdlike** *adj*. [Old English *bridd*; (sense 3) short for rhyming slang *birdlime* time]

birdbath *noun* a usu ornamental basin for birds to bathe in.

birdbrain *noun informal* a silly or stupid person. ➤➤ **birdbrained** *adj*.

birdcage *noun* a cage, usu made of metal wire, for keeping a pet bird in.

birdcall *noun* **1** the characteristic song of a bird. **2** an imitation of, or a device for imitating, the call of a bird.

bird dog *noun NAmer* a gundog trained to hunt or retrieve birds.

bird foot *noun see* BIRD'S FOOT.

birdie[1] /'buhdi/ *noun* **1** used *esp* by or to children: a bird, *esp* a small bird. **2** a golf score of one stroke less than par on a hole.

birdie[2] *verb trans* (**birdies, birdied, birdieing** *or* **birdying** /'buhdiing/) to play (a hole in golf) in one stroke under par.

birdlime *noun* **1** a sticky substance that is smeared on twigs to snare small birds. **2** the droppings of birds.

bird-nesting *noun see* BIRD'S-NESTING.

bird of paradise *noun* any of numerous birds of the New Guinea area, the males of which have brilliantly coloured plumage: family Paradisaeidae.

bird of passage *noun* **1** a migratory bird. **2** a person who leads a wandering or unsettled life.

bird of prey *noun* a hawk, vulture, or other bird that feeds on carrion or on meat taken by hunting.

birdseed *noun* a mixture of hemp, millet, and other seeds used for feeding caged and wild birds.

bird's-eye *noun* (*often in combination*) any of numerous plants with small bright-coloured flowers.

bird's-eye view *noun* **1** a view from above; an aerial view. **2** a brief and general summary; an overview.

bird's-foot *or* **bird-foot** *noun* (*pl* **bird's-foots** *or* **bird-foots**) any of various plants that have some part, such as the flower, that resembles a bird's foot: *Ornithopus perpusillus*.

bird's-foot trefoil *noun* a leguminous plant with claw-shaped pods and usu yellow flowers: *Lotus corniculatus*.

birdshot *noun* very small pellets designed for shooting birds.

bird's-nesting *or* **bird-nesting** *noun* the practice of searching for birds' nests, *esp* in order to steal the eggs.

bird's nest soup *noun* in Chinese cooking, a soup made with gelatinous material formed of dried saliva from the nests of any of several S Asiatic swifts.

birdstrike *noun* a collision between a bird and an aircraft.

bird table *noun* a table, usu on a pole and sometimes with a roof-like cover, on which food is put out for wild birds, *esp* in a garden.

bird-watching *noun* the observation or identification of birds in their natural environment, *esp* as a hobby. ➤➤ **bird-watcher** *noun*.

birefringence /bieri'frinj(ə)ns/ *noun* the refraction of light in two slightly different directions to form two rays. ➤➤ **birefringent** *adj*. [BI-[1] + *refringence*: see REFRINGENT]

bireme /'biereem/ *noun* an ancient galley with two banks of oars. [Latin *biremis*, from BI-[1] + *remus* oar]

biretta /bi'retə/ *noun* a square cap with three ridges on top worn by clergy, *esp* in the Roman Catholic Church. [Italian *berretta* from Old Provençal *berret* cap, from late Latin *birrus* cloak with a hood]

biriani *or* **biryani** /biri'ahni/ *noun* a spicy Indian dish that consists of rice, usu coloured with saffron, mixed with meat, fish, etc. [Hindi *biryāanī* from Persian *biryān* roasted]

birk /buhk/ *noun Brit, slang see* BURK.

birl /buhl/ *verb intrans chiefly Scot* to spin or twirl. ➤ *verb trans NAmer* to spin (a floating log) around in the water with one's feet.

Biro /'bieroh/ *noun* (*pl* **Biros**) *trademark* a kind of ballpoint pen. [named after László *Biró* d.1985, Argentinian inventor, writer, and painter born in Hungary, who with his brother Georg invented and patented the ballpoint pen (first produced commercially in 1945)]

birr /buh/ *noun* the basic monetary unit of Ethiopia, divided into 100 cents. [Amharic *birr*]

birth[1] /buhth/ *noun* **1a** the emergence of a new individual from the body of its parent. **b** the act or process of bringing forth young

from within the body. **2a** the fact of being born: *There is no cure for birth or death save to enjoy the interval* — George Santayana. **b** the fact of being born at a particular time or place: *a Frenchman by birth*. **3** family origin and social status; ancestry or lineage. **4** a beginning or start: *the birth of an idea*. **5** natural or inherited tendency: *an artist by birth*. ✳ **give birth (to) 1** to produce (a baby) as a mother. **2** to cause the development or creation of (something); to give rise to (something). [Middle English from Old Norse *byrth*; related to Old English *beran* BEAR[2]]

birth[2] *verb trans* to give birth to (a baby). ➤ *verb intrans* to give birth.

birth certificate *noun* an official record of somebody's parentage and date and place of birth.

birth control *noun* control of the number of children born, *esp* by preventing or lessening the frequency of conception; *broadly* contraception.

birthday /'buhthday, 'buhthdi/ *noun* **1a** the day of a person's birth. **b** a day of origin. **2** an anniversary of a birth: *A diplomat is a man who always remembers a woman's birthday but never remembers her age* — Robert Frost.

birthday suit *noun humorous* nothing but bare skin; nakedness: *They still like to show a photograph of her at six months in her birthday suit*.

birthing *noun* giving birth, *esp* by methods which aim to assist, but not interfere with, the natural birth process.

birthing pool *noun* a large circular bath in which a woman may sit to give birth.

birthmark *noun* a usu red or brown blemish existing on the skin at birth and remaining either temporarily or permanently.

birth mother *noun* the woman who gives birth to a child, as opposed to, for example, an adoptive mother.

birthplace *noun* the place of somebody's birth or where something originated.

birthrate *noun* the number of live births per unit of population, e.g. 1000 people, in a period of time, e.g. one year.

birthright *noun* something, e.g. a privilege or possession, to which a person is entitled by being born into a particular family, nation, etc.

birthstone *noun* a gemstone associated symbolically with the month of one's birth.

biryani /biri'ahni/ *noun see* BIRIANI.

BIS *abbr* Bank for International Settlements.

biscuit[1] /'biskit/ *noun* **1** *Brit* a small thin dry bakery product that may be either sweet or savoury, is usu crisp in texture and round or rectangular in shape, and is eaten as or with a snack. **2** *NAmer* a soft cake or bread, e.g. a scone, made without yeast. **3** a light yellowish brown colour. **4** earthenware or porcelain after the first firing and before glazing. ✳ **take the biscuit** *Brit, informal* to be the most astonishing or preposterous thing one has heard or seen, *esp* concerning a particular issue: *I've heard some daft ideas in my time, but that one really takes the biscuit*.

Word history
Middle English *bisquite* dry crisp bread, from early French *bescuit*, from *pain bescuit* twice-cooked bread. Biscuits were orig rations carried by soldiers; they were baked and then dried slowly in a very cool oven to make them keep longer.

biscuit[2] *adj* light yellowish brown.

bisect /bie'sekt/ *verb trans* **1** to divide (something) into two parts. **2** to divide (something, *esp* a line or geometrical figure) into two equal parts. ➤ *verb intrans* to cross or intersect. ➤➤ **bisection** /-sh(ə)n/ *noun*.

bisector *noun* a straight line that bisects an angle or a line.

bisexual[1] /bie'seksyooo(ə)l, -sh(ə)l/ *adj* **1a** possessing characteristics of both sexes. **b** sexually attracted to both sexes. **2** of or involving both sexes. ➤➤ **bisexuality** /,bieseksyoo'aliti, -shoo'aliti/ *noun*, **bisexually** *adv*.

bisexual[2] *noun* a bisexual person.

bishop /'bishəp/ *noun* **1** a member of the clergy ranking above a priest, having authority to ordain and confirm, and typically governing a diocese. **2** in chess, either of two pieces of each colour that are allowed to move diagonally across any number of consecutive unoccupied squares. **3** spiced mulled wine. ➤➤ **bishophood** *noun*.

[Old English *bisceop* via Latin from Greek *episkopos*, literally 'overseer', from *epi-* on + *skeptesthai* to look]

bishopric /'bishəprik/ *noun* **1** a diocese. **2** the office of bishop. [Old English *bisceoprīce*, from *bisceop* (see BISHOP) + *rīce* kingdom]

bismuth /'bizməth/ *noun* a reddish white metallic chemical element that is heavy and brittle, is used in alloys and, in the form of its compounds, in certain medical preparations for soothing *esp* stomach disorders: symbol Bi, atomic number 83. ➤➤ **bismuthic** /biz'mudhik, biz'moohdhik/ *adj.* [obsolete German *Bismut* (now *Wismut*), modification of *wismut*, from *wise* meadow + *mut* claim to a mine]

bison /'biesn/ *noun* (*pl* **bison**) **1** either of two species of large shaggy-maned bovine mammals that are now nearly extinct: genus *Bison*. **2** = BUFFALO (1). [Latin *bisont-*, *bison*, of Germanic origin]

bisque¹ /bisk/ *noun* a thick cream soup (e.g. of shellfish or game). [French *bisque* crayfish soup]

bisque² *noun* = BISCUIT¹ (4), *esp* a type of white unglazed ceramic ware. [by shortening and alteration from BISCUIT¹]

bisque³ *noun* in croquet, golf, and tennis, an advantage (e.g. an extra turn or extra point) allowed to an inferior player. [French *bisque*, of unknown origin]

bistable /bie'staybl/ *adj* having two stable states, e.g. off or on.

bister /'beestə, 'beestrə/ *noun* NAmer see BISTRE¹.

bistort /bi'stawt/ *noun* a European plant with twisted roots and a spike of usu pink flowers: *Polygonum bistorta*. [early French *bistorte*, from Latin *bis-* twice + *tortus* past part. of *torquēre* to twist]

bistoury /'bistəri/ *noun* (*pl* **bistouries**) a long surgical knife with a narrow blade. [French *bistouri* dagger]

bistre¹ (*NAmer* **bister**) /'beestə, 'beestrə/ *noun* **1** a pigment used in art, made from wood soot. **2** the dark yellowish brown colour of this pigment. [French *bistre*]

bistre² *adj* dark yellowish brown.

bistro /'beestroh/ *noun* (*pl* **bistros**) a small bar, restaurant, or tavern. [French *bistro*]

bisulphate /bie'sulfayt/ *noun* a salt or ester of sulphuric acid, containing the group HSO_4; an acid sulphate.

bit¹ /bit/ *noun* **1a** a small piece or quantity of anything: *a bit of cake*. **b** a part or section: *Drama is life with the dull bits cut out* — Alfred Hitchcock. **2** *informal.* **a** (**a bit**) a brief period; a while: *Ask her if she'd mind waiting a bit*. **b** (**a bit**) a short distance: *Could everyone shove up a bit, please?* **3** *informal* a very small or insignificant amount or degree: *They're not the slightest bit sorry*. **4** *informal.* **a** (**a bit**) an indefinite but usu quite substantial amount: *That'll cost him a bit*. **b** (**a bit**) an indefinite small fraction: *3 inches and a bit*. **5** *informal* everything appropriate to or associated with a given way of life, sphere of activity, role, etc: *She's rejected the whole love and marriage bit*. **6a** a small coin: *a fivepenny bit*. **b** *NAmer, informal* a monetary unit worth ⅛ of a US dollar: *four bits*. **7** *informal* a young woman, *esp* an attractive one: *She's a right nice bit*. ✱ **a bit** *informal* somewhat; rather: *a bit difficult*. **a bit much** more than one wants to put up with. **a bit of a 1** *informal* to some extent: *He's a bit of a rascal*. **2** *informal* used to play down the seriousness of something: *We're facing a bit of a crisis*. **a bit of all right** *Brit, informal* somebody or something very pleasing, *esp* a sexually attractive person. **bit by bit** by small amounts; little by little. **bit on the side 1** *informal* a casual sexual relationship with somebody other than one's partner. **2** *informal* somebody with whom one has such a relationship. **bits and pieces/bobs** odds and ends, miscellaneous things of little value or substance. **do one's bit** *Brit* to make one's personal contribution to a task or cause. **to bits 1** into pieces: *fell to bits*. **2** to a great extent: *thrilled to bits*. [Middle English, piece bitten off, morsel of food, from Old English *bita*; related to Old English *bītan* to BITE¹]

bit² *noun* **1** a unit of computer information equivalent to the result of a choice between two alternatives (e.g. *on* or *off*). **2** the physical representation of such a unit in a computer or electronic memory. [shortened from *binary digit*]

bit³ *noun* **1** a bar of metal or occasionally rubber attached to the bridle and inserted in the mouth of a horse. **2a** the biting or cutting edge or part of a tool. **b** a replaceable drilling, boring, etc part of a compound tool: *a brace and bit*. **3** something that curbs or restrains. **4** the part of a key that enters the lock and acts on the bolt and tumblers. ✱ **champ/chafe at the bit** to be very impatient to begin to do something. **get/have/take the bit between one's teeth** to begin to do something in a determined manner, or refuse

obstinately to desist from doing something. [Old English *bite* act of biting; related to Old English *bītan* to BITE¹]

bit⁴ *verb trans* (**bitted, bitting**) **1** to put a bit in the mouth of (a horse). **2** to curb or restrain (somebody or something).

bit⁵ *verb* past tense and past part. of BITE¹.

bitch¹ /bich/ *noun* **1** the female of the dog or similar animals. **2a** *slang* a malicious, spiteful, and domineering woman. **b** a woman, girlfriend, or prostitute. **3** *informal* something difficult, trying, or unpleasant. **4** *informal* a complaint or act of complaining. [Old English *bicce*]

bitch² *verb intrans informal* **1** (*often* + about) to make malicious or spiteful comments. **2** (*often* + about) to complain.

bitchy *adj* (**bitchier, bitchiest**) *informal* characterized by malicious or spiteful behaviour. ➤➤ **bitchily** *adv*, **bitchiness** *noun*.

bite¹ /biet/ *verb* (*past tense* **bit** /bit/, *past part.* **bitten** /'bit(ə)n/ *or* **bit**) ➤ *verb trans* **1a** to seize or cut into (somebody or something) with the teeth or jaws. **b** said of an animal or insect: to sting (somebody or something) with a fang or other specialized part of the body. **2** (*often* + off/away) to remove or sever (something) with the teeth. **3** to cut or pierce (somebody or something) with a sharp-edged weapon, or as if with one. **4** to cause sharp pain or stinging discomfort to (somebody). **5** to grip or take a strong hold of (somebody or something). **6** *informal* to annoy or worry (somebody): *What's biting him?* **7** said of acids: to corrode or destroy all or part of (something, *esp* a metal). ➤ *verb intrans* **1** said of an animal or insect: to wound with the teeth, sting with a fang, etc, *esp* by instinct. **2** (+ at) to attempt to bite; to make a biting movement. **3a** to take or maintain a firm hold on something. **b** said of fish: to take a bait. **c** said of a person: to accept an offer, etc. **d** said of an acid: to damage, destroy, or corrode something. **e** said of sanctions, etc: to have an effect. **f** said of a weapon or tool: to cut or pierce. **g** said of food: to have a pungent taste. ✱ **be bitten by/with something** to have great interest in or enthusiasm for (something). **bite off more than one can chew** to undertake to do more than one can successfully manage. **bite one's lip** to show anger or resentment. **bite one's lip/tongue** to stop oneself with an effort from saying something. **bite somebody's head off** to speak to or scold somebody angrily. **bite the bullet** to face up steadfastly to something unwelcome that one has been hesitating over. **bite the dust 1** to fall dead, *esp* in a fight. **2** said of a plan or scheme: to collapse or fail. **bite the hand that feeds one** to harm somebody who has been one's benefactor. **once bitten, twice shy** somebody who has had an unpleasant experience will be more cautious the next time. ➤➤ **biter** *noun*. [Old English *bītan*]

bite² *noun* **1a** the act of biting. **b** a wound made by biting. **2a** an amount of food taken with one bite. **b** a quick meal or snack. **3** a fish that has taken the bait. **4** the grip which establishes physical friction or purchase. **5** a sharp incisive quality or effect. **6** sharpness or pungency of taste. ✱ **put the bite on (somebody) 1** *informal* to borrow or extort money from (somebody). **2 take a bite out of something** to use up a substantial part of it.

bite-size *or* **bite-sized** *adj* **1** small enough to be eaten as one bite. **2** small enough to be easily taken in or understood: *providing the information in bite-size chunks*.

biting /'bieting/ *adj* **1** strong and icy: *a biting wind*. **2** sarcastic: *biting irony*. ➤➤ **bitingly** *adv*.

bitmap¹ *noun* a representation in a computer's memory of an image presented on a computer screen, in which each PIXEL (spot on the screen) is represented by one or more bits (see BIT²) of information.

bitmap² *verb trans* (**bitmapped, bitmapping**) to make a bitmap of (something).

bit of work *noun* (*pl* **bits of work**) *derog* a person: *a nasty bit of work*.

bit part *noun* a small acting part, usu with spoken lines.

bit player *noun* an actor who plays bit parts.

bit rate *noun* the number of bits per second that a digital network is able to carry.

bitstream /'bitstreem/ *noun* a continuous succession of bits (see BIT²) of data.

bitt /bit/ *noun* either of a pair of posts on a ship's deck for securing ropes. [perhaps from Old Norse *biti* beam; related to Old English *bāt* BOAT¹]

bitten /'bit(ə)n/ *verb* past part. of BITE¹.

bitter[1] /'bitə/ *adj* **1** having a sharp taste that is usu more disagreeable than sourness and that is one of the four basic taste sensations: compare SALT[3], SOUR[1], SWEET[1]. **2a** intense or severe: *a bitter struggle.* **b** strongly opposed to one another: *bitter enemies.* **c** harsh and sarcastic; showing or stemming from great dislike or resentment: *bitter contempt; bitter remarks.* **d** very cold: *a bitter winter.* **3a** expressive of severe grief or regret: *bitter tears.* **b** causing great grief, distress, or regret: *But O, how bitter a thing it is to look into happiness through another man's eyes* — Shakespeare. ⟫ **bitterish** *adj,* **bitterly** *adv,* **bitterness** *noun.* [Old English *biter*; related to Old English *bītan* to BITE[1]]

bitter[2] *adv NAmer* bitterly.

bitter[3] *noun* **1** (*in pl, but treated as sing or pl*) a usu alcoholic solution of bitter and often aromatic plant products used *esp* in preparing mixed drinks or as a mild tonic. **2** *Brit* a very dry beer heavily flavoured with hops.

bitter end *noun* (**the bitter end**) the very end, however painful or calamitous. [prob originating from *bitter end* the ship's end of an anchoring cable, from *bitter* a turn of cable round the bitts, from BITT[1]]

bitter lemon *noun* a non-alcoholic fizzy drink flavoured with lemon, with a fairly sharp taste and a light grey-green colour.

bittern /'bitən/ *noun* any of several species of small or medium-sized herons with a characteristic booming cry: genus *Butio.* [Middle English *bitoure,* from early French *butor.* The *n* was added in the 16th cent., probably by association with *heron*]

bittersweet[1] *adj* **1** bitter and sweet at the same time. **2** pleasant but with elements of suffering or regret: *a bittersweet ballad.* ⟫ **bittersweetly** *adv,* **bittersweetness** *noun.*

bittersweet[2] *noun* = WOODY NIGHTSHADE. [from its berries, initially sweet but with a bitter aftertaste]

bitty /'biti/ *adj* (**bittier, bittiest**) scrappy or disjointed. ⟫ **bittily** *adv.*

bitumen /'bityoomin/ *noun* **1** any of various mixtures of hydrocarbons, e.g. tar, that occur naturally or as residues after heating petroleum, coal, etc. **2** (**the bitumen**) *Aus, NZ, informal* a tarred road. ⟫ **bituminoid** /bi'tyoohminoyd/ *adj.* [Middle English *bithumen* mineral pitch, from Latin *bitumin-, bitumen*]

bituminize *or* **bituminise** /bi'tyoohminiez/ *verb trans* **1** to cover or treat (something) with bitumen. **2** to convert (something) into bitumen. ⟫ **bituminization** /-'zaysh(ə)n/ *noun.*

bituminous /bi'tyoohminəs/ *adj* resembling, containing, or impregnated with bitumen.

bituminous coal *noun* a black or dark brown form of coal which has a high calorific value but the burning of which is a major cause of air pollution.

bivalent /bie'vaylənt/ *adj* **1** in chemistry, having a valency of two. **2** said of chromosomes: that become associated in pairs during meiotic cell division. ⟫ **bivalency** /-si/ *noun.*

bivalve[1] /'bievalv/ *adj* said of a mollusc: having a shell composed of two valves.

bivalve[2] *noun* any of a class of aquatic molluscs having a shell composed of two valves: class Bivalvia.

bivouac[1] /'bivooak/ *noun* a usu temporary encampment under little or no shelter. [French *bivouac* from Swiss German *Biwacht* additional night watch]

bivouac[2] *verb intrans* (**bivouacked, bivouacking**) to make a bivouac; to camp.

biweekly[1] /bie'weekli/ *adv* **1** every two weeks. **2** twice a week.

biweekly[2] *adj* issued or occurring every two weeks, or twice a week.

biweekly[3] *noun* (*pl* **biweeklies**) a publication issued every two weeks, or twice a week.

biyearly[1] /bie'yiəli/ *adv* **1** every two years. **2** twice a year.

biyearly[2] *adj* occurring every two years, or twice a year.

biz /biz/ *noun informal* = BUSINESS.

bizarre /bi'zah/ *adj* **1** odd, extravagant, or eccentric. **2** involving sensational contrasts or incongruities. ⟫ **bizarrely** *adv,* **bizarreness** *noun.* [French *bizarre* from Italian *bizzarro*]

Bk *abbr* the chemical symbol for berkelium.

bk *abbr* book.

bkg *abbr* banking.

BL *abbr* **1** in Scotland and Ireland, Bachelor of Law. **2** bill of lading. **3** British Legion. **4** British Library.

blab[1] /blab/ *verb* (**blabbed, blabbing**) ➤ *verb trans* to reveal (a secret). ➤ *verb intrans* to talk indiscreetly or thoughtlessly. ⟫ **blabber** *noun.* [Middle English *blabbe* one who blabs; related to Middle English *blaberen* to BLABBER[1]]

blab[2] *noun* somebody who blabs.

blabber[1] /'blabə/ *verb* (**blabbered, blabbering**) ➤ *verb intrans* to babble. ➤ *verb trans* to say (something) indiscreetly. ⟫ **blabberer** *noun.* [Middle English *blaberen,* prob of imitative origin]

blabber[2] *noun informal* **1** indiscreet or idle chatter. **2** somebody who reveals a secret.

blabbermouth *noun* somebody who talks too much or indiscreetly.

black[1] /blak/ *adj* **1a** of the colour of coal, jet, or tar, the darkest colour from its absorption of all light. **b** having or reflecting little or no light: *black water; a black night.* **c** very dark in colour: *His face was black with rage.* **2** (*often* **Black**). **a** having dark skin pigmentation; *esp* being African, African-American, or Australian Aboriginal in origin: *black Americans.* **b** relating to black people or culture: *black literature.* **3** dirty or soiled: *hands black with dirt.* **4** said of coffee or tea: served without milk or cream. **5a** thoroughly sinister or evil: *a black deed.* **b** indicative of hostility, disapproval, or discredit: *met only with black looks.* **6a** marked by severe depression: *black despair.* **b** gloomy: *The future looks black.* **c** marked by disaster: *black Friday.* **7** showing a profit: compare RED[1] (6): *a black financial statement.* **8** characterized by grim or grotesque humour. **9** bought, sold, or operating illegally and *esp* in contravention of official economic regulations: *the black economy.* **10** *chiefly Brit* subject to boycott by trade-union members. **11** dressed in black: *the Black Prince.* ⟫ **blackish** *adj,* **blackly** *adv,* **blackness** *noun.* [Old English *blæc*]

black[2] *noun* **1a** the colour of coal, jet, or tar, the darkest colour that belongs to objects that neither reflect nor transmit light. **b** total or almost total absence of light: *the black of night.* **2** a black pigment or dye. **3a** something black: *I potted a red, then the black.* **b** black clothing: *He looks good in black.* **4** (*often* **Black**) somebody who belongs wholly or partly to a dark-skinned race, *esp* a person of African, African-American, or Australian Aboriginal origin. **5a** the dark-coloured pieces in a board game (e.g. chess) for two players. **b** the player by whom these are played. ✻ **in the black** financially in credit; solvent; making a profit.

Usage note

black, Negro, *and* coloured. The word *black* (without a capital letter) is currently the most widely accepted non-offensive word for people of African or African-American origin. The terms *Negro* and *coloured,* which both formerly had this function, are no longer felt to be acceptable by black people themselves, although *Coloured* has a specific use in South Africa where it refers to members of a population group of mixed-race origin. Dark-skinned people of Asian origin should not be referred to as *black,* in the context of British society, but as *Asian.*

black[3] *verb trans* **1** to make (something) black. **2** *chiefly Brit* to declare (e.g. a business or industry) subject to boycott by trade-union members.

blackamoor /'blakəmaw, -mooə/ *noun archaic, offensive* = BLACK[1] (2A). [BLACK[1] + MOOR]

black-and-blue *adj* darkly discoloured from blood that has leaked under the skin by bruising.

Black and Tan *noun* a member of the Royal Irish Constabulary formed to resist the armed movement for Irish independence in 1921. [from the colours of their uniform]

black and white *noun* **1** writing or print. **2** a drawing or print done in black and white or in monochrome. **3** black-and-white reproduction of visual images, *esp* by photography or television. **4** an uncompromisingly rigid or simplistic separation into good or bad, right or wrong, etc: *She sees everything in black and white.*

black-and-white *adj* **1** reproducing visual images in black, white, and tones of grey rather than in colours: *black-and-white television.* **2a** sharply divided into two groups or sides. **b** evaluating things as either all good or all bad, etc: *a black-and-white morality.*

black art *noun* = BLACK MAGIC.

blackball *verb trans* **1** to vote against (somebody, *esp* a candidate for membership of a club) in this way. **2** to ostracize (somebody). [from the black ball sometimes used to register an adverse vote in a ballot]

black ban *noun Aus* a blacking or boycott.

black bean *noun* **1a** a black soya bean. **b** a black kidney bean. **2a** an Australian tree of the pea family with thin smooth bark: *Castanospermum australe*. **b** the hard wood of this tree.

black bear *noun* **1** a common medium-sized American bear that lives in forests and has a dark-coloured or black coat: *Ursus americanus*. **2** an Asiatic bear having a black coat with a white V-shaped mark on its chest: *Selenarctos thibetanus*.

black belt *noun* **1a** a rating of expertise in judo, karate, etc. **b** a person who has been rated as an expert in judo, karate, etc. **2** the black belt worn by such a person.

blackberry[1] /'blakb(ə)ri/ *noun* (*pl* **blackberries**) **1** a usu black raspberry-like edible fruit. **2** a prickly shrub of the rose family that bears this fruit: *Rubus fruticosus*.

blackberry[2] *verb intrans* (**blackberries, blackberried, blackberrying**) to pick blackberries: *go blackberrying*.

black bile *noun* in medieval physiology, the one of the four humours that was believed to be secreted by the kidneys or spleen and to cause melancholy.

blackbird *noun* **1** a common Old World thrush, the male of which is black with an orange beak and eye rim: *Turdus merula*. **2** any of several species of American birds, the males of which have black plumage: family Icteridae. **3** *archaic* an African or Polynesian slave.

blackboard *noun* a hard smooth usu dark surface used *esp* in schools and other teaching establishments for writing or drawing on with chalk.

black body *noun* a hypothetical object or surface that completely absorbs all radiant energy falling upon it with no reflection.

black book *noun* a book containing a list of those to be punished, blacklisted, etc. ✳ **in somebody's black books** *informal* in trouble with somebody, or out of favour with them.

black bottom *noun* a popular dance of the 1920s, originating in the USA, involving rotation of the hips.

black box *noun* **1** a usu electronic device, *esp* one that can be plugged in or removed as a unit, and the internal mechanism of which is hidden from or mysterious to the user. **2** = FLIGHT RECORDER.

blackboy *noun* = GRASS TREE.

black bread *noun* coarse dark-coloured bread made from rye flour; pumpernickel.

black bryony *noun* a herbaceous Old World climbing plant that bears red poisonous berries: *Tamus communis*.

blackbuck *noun* a common medium-sized Indian antelope: *Antilope cervicapra*.

black bun *noun Scot* a rich dark fruit cake or bread often encased in pastry and eaten *esp* at New Year.

blackcap *noun* a small Old World warbler, the male of which has a black crown: *Sylvia atricapilla*.

black cap *noun* a black head-covering formerly worn by a judge in Britain when passing the death sentence.

blackcock *noun* the male black grouse.

Black Country *noun* (**the Black Country**) the industrial area in the West Midlands of England.

blackcurrant /'blakkurənt, blak'kurənt/ *noun* **1** a small black edible soft fruit. **2** the widely cultivated European bush that bears this fruit: *Ribes nigrum*.

Black Death *noun* (*usu* **the Black Death**) a form of plague epidemic in Europe and Asia in the 14th cent., or the catastrophic outbreak of this plague in Europe between 1347 and 1350. [from the black patches formed on the skin of its victims]

black diamond *noun* **1** (*in pl*) = COAL. **2** = CARBONADO.

black earth *noun* = CHERNOZEM.

black economy *noun* (*often* **the black economy**) business activity that is carried on unofficially or illegally, *esp* to avoid taxation.

blacken *verb* (**blackened, blackening**) ➤ *verb intrans* to become dark or black: *The sky blackened.* ➤ *verb trans* **1** to make (something) dark or black. **2** to defame or sully (somebody's reputation). ➤➤ **blackener** *noun*.

black eye *noun* a discoloration of the skin round the eye from bruising.

black-eyed bean *noun* = BLACK-EYED PEA.

black-eyed pea *noun* **1** a leguminous plant widely cultivated in warm areas for food and green manure: *Vigna sinensis*. **2** the edible seed of this plant, a beige-coloured bean with a black spot.

black-eyed Susan /'soohzən/ *noun* **1** any of several species of N American plants that have showy flower heads with yellowish orange petals and dark purple or brown centres: genus *Rudbeckia*. **2** an African tropical climbing plant that has flowers with yellow petals and purple centres: *Thunbergia alata*.

blackface *noun* **1** makeup for a non-black actor or performer playing a black role. **b** an actor or performer playing such a role. **2** a sheep with a black face.

blackfish *noun* **1** the female salmon just after spawning. **2** any of numerous dark-coloured fishes, *esp* a tautog.

black flag *noun* a pirate flag, *esp* the JOLLY ROGER.

blackfly *noun* (*pl* **blackflies** *or collectively* **blackfly**) **1** any of several small dark-coloured insects, *esp* a black blood-sucking gnat or a black aphid parasitic on various agricultural and garden plants. **2** an infestation of such insects.

black friar *noun* a Dominican friar. [from the black mantle worn by Dominicans]

black gold *noun* crude oil.

black grouse *noun* a large Eurasian grouse of which the male is black and the female mottled: *Lyrurus tetrix*.

blackguard[1] /'blagəd, 'blagahd/ *noun often humorous* a coarse or unscrupulous person; a scoundrel. ➤➤ **blackguardism** /'blagədiz(ə)m/ *noun*, **blackguardly** /'blagədli/ *adj and adv*. [BLACK[1] + GUARD[1]; orig denoting the kitchen servants of a large household]

blackguard[2] *verb trans* to ridicule (somebody) or address (them) in abusive terms.

blackhead *noun* a small usu dark-coloured oily plug blocking the duct of a sebaceous gland, *esp* on the face.

black hole *noun* **1** a celestial body, prob formed from a collapsed star, with a very high density and an intense gravitational field, from which no radiation can escape. **2** *informal* a place or situation where something (e.g. money) can disappear without leaving a trace or producing any effect.

black ice *noun Brit* transparent slippery ice (e.g. on a road).

blacking *noun* **1** a paste, polish, etc applied to an object to make it black. **2** a boycotting of business, industry, etc by trade-union members.

blackjack[1] *noun* **1** = PONTOON[2]. **2** *NAmer* a cosh. [(sense 1) BLACK[1] + JACK[1] (2); (sense 2) BLACK[1] + JACK[1] (2)]

blackjack[2] *verb trans NAmer* to hit (somebody) with a blackjack.

blacklead /'blakled/ *noun* = GRAPHITE.

blackleg[1] *noun chiefly Brit* a worker acting in opposition to union policies, *esp* by working during a strike.

blackleg[2] *verb intrans* (**blacklegged, blacklegging**) *chiefly Brit* to work during a strike.

black letter *noun* a heavier angular style of type or lettering used *esp* by early European printers.

black light *noun* invisible ultraviolet or infrared light.

blacklist[1] *noun* a list of people or organizations who are disapproved of or are to be punished or boycotted.

blacklist[2] *verb trans* to put (somebody) on a blacklist.

black magic *noun* magic performed with the aim of harming or killing somebody or something, *esp* with the supposed aid of evil spirits.

blackmail[1] *noun* **1a** extortion by threats, *esp* by a threatened exposure of secrets that would lead to loss of reputation, prosecution, etc. **b** money obtained in this way. **2** political, industrial, or moral pressure to do something that is considered undesirable. [BLACK[1] + *mail* tribute, payment, from Old English *māl* agreement, pay]

blackmail[2] *verb trans* (*often* + into) to subject (a person, organization, etc) to blackmail; to force or persuade (them) to do something through blackmail. ➤➤ **blackmailer** *noun*.

Black Maria /,blak mə'rie-ə/ *noun* an enclosed motor vehicle used by police to carry prisoners. [said to be named after *Maria* Lee, the black landlady of a boarding house in Boston, Mass., USA, who helped the police to arrest disorderly clients]

black maria *noun* = HEART (4C).

black mark *noun* a supposed mark indicating somebody's censure or disapproval: *I suppose that'll be a black mark against my name.*

black market *noun* illicit trade in commodities or currencies in violation of official regulations, e.g. rationing.

black marketeer *noun* somebody who trades on a black market.

Black Mass *noun* a travesty of the Christian mass ascribed to worshippers of Satan.

Black Muslim *noun* a member of an exclusively black chiefly US Muslim sect that advocates a strictly separate black community.

black nightshade *noun* see NIGHTSHADE.

blackout *noun* 1 a period of darkness enforced as a precaution against air raids, or caused by a failure of electrical power. 2 a temporary loss or dulling of consciousness, vision, or memory. 3 a holding back or suppression of something: *There was a total news blackout about the invasion.* 4 a usu temporary loss of radio signal, e.g. during the re-entry of a spacecraft.

black out *verb intrans* 1 to be suddenly plunged in darkness. 2 to undergo a temporary loss of consciousness, vision, or memory. 3 to extinguish or screen all lights for protection, *esp* as a precaution against air attack. ⮕ *verb trans* 1 to extinguish or screen (lights) or the lights of (a building, town, etc), *esp* as a precaution against air attack. 2a to suppress (information), *esp* by censorship. b to prevent the broadcasting of (an information programme).

Black Panther *noun* a member of a militant organization of US blacks.

black pepper *noun* a pungent spice prepared from the dried black-husked berries of an E Indian plant used either whole or ground: compare WHITE PEPPER.

Black Power *noun* the mobilization of the political and economic power of US blacks, *esp* to further racial equality.

black pudding *noun chiefly Brit* a very dark sausage made from suet and a large proportion of pigs' blood: compare WHITE PUDDING.

Black Rod *noun* in Britain, the principal usher of the House of Lords. [from his staff of office]

black sheep *noun* a disreputable member of a respectable group, family, etc. [because the fleece of a black sheep was worth less]

Blackshirt *noun* a member of a fascist organization with a black shirt as part of its uniform.

blacksmith *noun* somebody who works iron, *esp* at a forge. ⮕⮕ **blacksmithing** *noun.* [from their working with iron, known as black metal]

black spot *noun Brit* a stretch of road on which accidents occur frequently.

black stump *noun* (*usu* **the black stump**) *Aus, NZ* an imaginary object marking the furthest extent of civilization.

black swan *noun* a swan with black outer feathers and a red beak originally native to Australia: *Cygnus atratus.*

black tea *noun* 1 tea that is dark in colour from complete fermentation of the leaf before drying. 2 tea without milk.

blackthorn *noun* a spiny European shrub of the rose family with hard wood and small white flowers: *Prunus spinosa.*

black tie *noun* 1 a black bow tie worn with a dinner jacket. 2 an ordinary tie of black material, worn as a sign of mourning.

black-tie *adj* said of e.g. a dinner: characterized by or requiring the wearing of semiformal evening dress by men including a dinner jacket and a black bow tie: compare WHITE TIE.

black up *verb intrans* to put on black make-up, *esp* in order to play the role of a black character.

black velvet *noun* a drink that is a mixture of stout and champagne or cider.

blackwater fever /'blakwawtə/ *noun* a severe form of malaria in which the urine becomes dark-coloured.

black widow *noun* a venomous New World spider of which the female is black with an hourglass-shaped red mark on the underside of the abdomen: *Latrodectus mactans.*

bladder /'bladə/ *noun* 1a a membranous sac in animals that serves as the receptacle of a liquid or contains gas, *esp* the urinary bladder. b a hollow balloon-like part in e.g. a frond of seaweed; a VESICLE (1A). 2 a bag filled with a liquid or gas (e.g. the air-filled rubber bag

inside a football). [Old English *blædre*; related to Old English *blāwan* a BLOW¹]

bladder fern *noun* any of several species of ferns that have hooded or bladderlike cases to protect their developing spores: genus *Cystopteris.*

bladderwort /'bladəwuht/ *noun* a plant belonging to the butterwort family, chiefly aquatic plants with bladder-like floats or insect traps: genus *Utricularia.*

bladderwrack /'bladərak/ *noun* a common brown seaweed with air bladders in its fronds, used as a manure and also as a source of iodine: *Fucus vesiculosus.* [BLADDER + WRACK³]

blade /blayd/ *noun* 1 the cutting part of a knife, razor, etc with a sharpened edge or edges. 2a a long narrow leaf, *esp* of a grass, cereal, etc. b the flat expanded part of such a leaf, as distinguished from the stalk. 3 the runner of an ice skate. 4a the broad flattened part of an oar, paddle, bat, etc. b an arm of a screw propeller, electric fan, steam turbine, etc. 5 the broad flat or concave part of a machine, e.g. a bulldozer, that comes into contact with material to be moved. 6 the flat part of the tongue immediately behind the tip. 7 used chiefly in naming cuts of meat: a broad flat body part, *esp* the shoulder blade. 8 *literary.* a a sword. b a swordsman. 9 *archaic or humorous* a dashing lively man. [Old English *blæd*; related to Old English *blōwan* BLOW⁴]

bladed *adj* (*usu used in combinations*) having a blade or blades, *esp* of a specified kind: *broad-bladed leaves.*

blaeberry /'blayb(ə)ri/ *noun* (pl **blaeberries**) *Scot* = BILBERRY. [northern Middle English *blaberie*, from *bla* dark blue (from Old Norse *blār*) + BERRY¹]

blag¹ /blag/ *noun Brit, informal* a mugging or armed robbery. [origin unknown]

blag² *verb trans* (**blagged, blagging**) 1 *Brit, informal.* a to rob (somebody or something), *esp* with violence. b to steal (something): *They blagged a couple of old ladies' handbags.* 2 to bluff: *He had blagged his way into all the big concerts* — The Independent. ⮕⮕ **blagger** *noun.*

blah /blah/ *or* **blah-blah** *noun informal* silly or pretentious chatter or nonsense. [imitative]

blain /blayn/ *noun* an inflamed swelling or sore. [Old English *blegen*; related to Old English *blāwan* BLOW¹]

Blairism /'bleəriz(ə)m/ *noun* the policies associated with Tony Blair, British Labour leader and prime minister from 1997, *esp* regarded as a modified form of traditional socialism. ⮕⮕ **Blairite** *noun.*

blame¹ /blaym/ *verb trans* 1a (*often* + for) to hold (somebody or something) responsible for wrongdoing or an undesirable state of affairs: *I blame him for everything.* b (+ on) to place responsibility for (something reprehensible or unfortunate) on somebody or something: *She blames it on the weather.* 2 to find fault with (somebody); to censure (them). ✳ **be to blame** (*often* + for) to be responsible for wrongdoing or an undesirable state of affairs. **I don't blame you, etc** I think you, etc are/were quite justified. ⮕⮕ **blamable** *adj*, **blamably** *adv*, **blameable** *adj*, **blameably** *adv*, **blamer** *noun.* [Old French *blamer* from late Latin *blasphemare* to blaspheme, from Greek *blasphēmein*]

blame² *noun* 1 (*often* + for) responsibility for wrongdoing or an undesirable state of affairs: *No blame should attach to telling the truth. But it does, it does* — Anita Brookner. 2 disapproval or reproach, or an expression of it. ⮕⮕ **blameful** *adj*, **blamefully** *adv*, **blameless** *adj*, **blamelessly** *adv*, **blamelessness** *noun.*

blameworthy *adj* deserving blame. ⮕⮕ **blameworthiness** *noun.*

blanch /blahnch/ *verb trans* 1a to take the colour out of (something). b to make (a growing plant) pale by excluding light. 2 to scald or parboil (e.g. almonds or food for freezing) in water or steam in order to remove the skin from them, whiten them, or stop enzymatic action. 3 to make (somebody or something) ashen or pale: *Fear blanched her cheeks.* ⮕ *verb intrans* to become white or pale: *He blanched when he heard the news.* ⮕⮕ **blancher** *noun.* [Middle English *blaunchen* from early French *blanchir*, from Old French *blanche* white]

blancmange /blə'monj, blə'monzh/ *noun* a usu sweetened and flavoured dessert made from gelatinous or starchy substances, e.g. cornflour, and milk. [Middle English *blancmanger* from early French *blanc manger* white food]

Blanco /'blangkoh/ *noun trademark* a substance used *esp* in the armed forces to whiten or colour belts and webbing. [French *blanc* white, of Germanic origin]

blanco /'blangkoh/ *verb trans* (**blancoes, blancoed, blancoing**) to whiten or colour (e.g. a belt or webbing) with Blanco.

bland /bland/ *adj* **1a** smooth or soothing: *a bland smile.* **b** showing no emotion or anxiety; unperturbed: *a bland confession of guilt.* **2a** not irritating or stimulating; mild: *a bland diet.* **b** without character or excitement; dull or insipid: *bland stories with little plot or action.* ➤➤ **blandly** *adv,* **blandness** *noun.* [Latin *blandus*]

blandishment /'blandishmənt/ *noun* (*usu in pl*) **1** a coaxing or flattering act or utterance. **2** an enticement or attraction: *I was … proof against the blandishments of the small bottle which she held up … to enforce her persuasions* — Dickens. [*blandish* from Middle English *blandishen* from Old French *blandiss-,* stem of *blandir* to coax or flatter]

blank[1] /blangk/ *adj* **1a** with nothing marked, written, printed, or recorded on it: *blank paper; a blank tape.* **b** not filled in; with spaces to be filled in: *a blank form.* **2a** dazed or nonplussed: *He stared in blank dismay.* **b** expressionless: *a blank stare.* **c** temporarily without thought, memory, or understanding: *My mind went blank.* **3** absolute or unqualified: *a blank refusal.* **4a** lacking interest, variety, or change: *a blank prospect.* **b** having a plain or undecorated surface, or an unbroken surface where an opening is usual: *a blank wall.* ➤➤ **blankly** *adv,* **blankness** *noun.* [Middle English in the sense 'white', from Old French *blanc,* of Germanic origin]

blank[2] *noun* **1a** an empty space, e.g. one to be filled in on a form. **b** a form, etc with blanks to be filled in. **2a** a void, without thought, memory, or understanding: *My mind was a blank during the test.* **b** a vacant or uneventful period: *a long blank in history.* **3** a dash substituted for an omitted word. **4a** a piece of material prepared to be made into something, e.g. a key or coin, by a further operation. **b** = BLANK CARTRIDGE. ✱ **draw a blank 1** to obtain no positive results. **2** to draw a raffle or lottery ticket that does not win.

blank[3] *verb trans NAmer* to keep (an opposing team) from scoring.

blank cartridge *noun* a cartridge loaded with powder but no bullet.

blank cheque *noun* **1** a signed cheque with the amount unspecified. **2** complete freedom of action or control; = CARTE BLANCHE.

blanket[1] /'blangkit/ *noun* **1** a large thick usu rectangular piece of fabric used *esp* as a bed covering, or a similar piece of fabric used as a body covering, e.g. for a horse. **2** a thick covering or layer: *a blanket of snow.* ✱ **born on the wrong side of the blanket** *informal* illegitimate. [Middle English in the sense 'undyed woollen cloth', from Old French *blankete,* from *blanc* white, of Germanic origin]

blanket[2] *verb trans* (**blanketed, blanketing**) **1** to cover (something) with a blanket or with something like a blanket: *New grass blankets the slope.* **2** to obscure, suppress, extinguish, or stifle (something) as if with a blanket. **3** to cover (an area, target group, etc).

blanket[3] *adj* applicable in all instances or to all members of a group or class: *a blanket condemnation of terrorism.*

blanket bath *noun* a wash given to a bedridden person.

blanket bog *noun* a peat bog covering a very wide area, found in cold wet climates and notable for its high acid content.

blanket finish *noun* a finish to a race in which many competitors cross the finishing line very close together.

blanket stitch *noun* a widely spaced loop stitch used *esp* round the edges of thick fabrics, e.g. blankets, instead of hemming in order to prevent fraying.

blankety /'blangkiti/ *adj informal, euphem* a substitute for any adjectival swearword: *That's him and his blankety lawnmower again!*

blank off *verb trans* to block (something): *They blanked off the tunnel.*

blank out *verb trans* **1** to erase (something, e.g. a memory) from one's mind. **2** to make (something) blank.

blank verse *noun* unrhymed verse, *esp* in iambic pentameters.

blanquette /blong'ket/ *noun* a stew of white meat, e.g. veal, in a white sauce. [French *blanquette,* from *blanc:* see BLANKET[1]]

blare[1] /blea/ *verb intrans* to emit loud and harsh sound. ➤ *verb trans* **1** to sound (a horn, etc) loudly and usu harshly. **2** to proclaim (something) loudly or sensationally: *Headlines blared his defeat.* [Middle English *bleren;* related to Old English *blǽtan* to BLEAT[1]]

blare[2] *noun* a loud harsh sound.

blarney[1] /'blahni/ *noun* **1** smooth wheedling talk; flattery. **2** nonsense. [named after the *Blarney Stone,* a stone in Blarney Castle, near Cork, Eire, held to give skill in talking to those who kiss it]

blarney[2] *verb* (**blarneys, blarneyed, blarneying**) ➤ *verb trans* to flatter (somebody) or try to wheedle something from (them). ➤ *verb intrans* to speak flatteringly or coaxingly.

blasé /'blahzay/ *adj* indifferent to pleasure or excitement as a result of real or pretended over-familiarity. [French *blasé,* past part. of *blaser* to exhaust by indulgence]

blaspheme /blas'feem/ *verb trans and intrans* to speak of, address, or use the name of (God or something sacred) with impiety or in profanity. ➤➤ **blasphemer** *noun.* [Middle English *blasfemen* from late Latin *blasphemare:* see BLAME[1]]

blasphemy /'blasfəmi/ *noun* (*pl* **blasphemies**) **1** contempt or lack of reverence for God or something sacred, or an action or speech that shows this. **2** something considered disrespectful to God or sacred things: *All great truths begin as blasphemies* — George Bernard Shaw. ➤➤ **blasphemous** *adj,* **blasphemously** *adv,* **blasphemousness** *noun.*

blast[1] /blahst/ *noun* **1a** an explosion or violent detonation. **b** a violent wave of increased atmospheric pressure produced by such an explosion or detonation. **2** a violent gust of wind. **3** a violent outburst. **4** the sound produced by air blown through a wind instrument or whistle. **5a** a stream of air or gas forced through a hole. **b** the continuous draught forced through a blast furnace. **6a** a sudden pernicious influence or effect: *the blast of a huge epidemic.* **b** a plant disease that causes withering. ✱ **full blast/at full blast** at top speed, full capacity, etc. [Old English *blǽst;* related to Old English *blāwan* BLOW[1]]

blast[2] *verb intrans* **1** to produce loud harsh sounds. **2a** to use an explosive. **b** to shoot. **3** to shrivel or wither. ➤ *verb trans* **1a** to shatter, remove, or open (something) with an explosive or in any similar way: *They blasted a new course for the stream.* **b** to destroy (hopes, etc). **2a** to denounce vigorously: *Judge blasts police methods.* **b** to curse or damn (somebody or something). **3a** to hit (e.g. a ball) vigorously and effectively. **b** to defeat (e.g. an opponent) decisively: *They blasted the home team six-nil.* **4** to injure (something) by the action of wind or in any similar way. **5** to cause (somebody or something) to blast off: *Tomorrow they will blast themselves from the moon's surface.* **6** to apply a forced draught to (something). ➤➤ **blaster** *noun,* **blasting** *noun and adj.*

blast[3] *interj Brit, informal* used to express annoyance.

blast- *or* **blasto-** *comb. form* forming nouns or their derivatives, denoting: bud; embryo; germ: *blastocyst; blastula.* [German *blast-* from Greek *blastos:* see -BLAST]

-blast *comb. form* forming nouns, denoting: **1** formative cell; cell layer: *erythroblast.* **2** formative unit, *esp* of living matter. [scientific Latin from Greek *blastos* bud, shoot]

blasted /'blahstid/ *adj* **1** *informal* infuriating or detestable: *Confound this blasted weather.* **2a** withered. **b** damaged by an explosive, lightning, or the wind, or in a similar way or to a similar extent.

blast furnace *noun* a furnace, *esp* for converting iron ore into iron, in which combustion is forced by a current of air under pressure.

-blastic *comb. form* forming adjectives, with the meaning: having the number or type of buds, cells, or cell layers specified: *megaloblastic.* [-BLAST + -IC[1]]

blasto- *comb. form* see BLAST-.

blastoderm /'blastəduhm/ *noun* a disc-shaped layer of cells formed on top of the yolk in an egg such as a bird's egg and subsequently developing into an embryo.

blast off *verb intrans* said *esp* of rocket-propelled missiles and vehicles: to leave the ground or launch-pad; to take off.

blast-off *noun* the act, action, or time of blasting off.

blastomere /'blastəmiə/ *noun* a cell produced during the cleavage of an egg. ➤➤ **blastomeric** /-'merik/ *adj.* [BLASTO- + -mere from Greek *meros* part]

blastula /'blastyoolə/ *noun* (*pl* **blastulas** *or* **blastulae** /-lee/) the embryo of a metazoan animal at the stage in its development succeeding the MORULA (ball of cells) stage, typically having the form of a hollow fluid-filled cavity bounded by a single layer of cells: compare GASTRULA, MORULA. ➤➤ **blastular** *adj,* **blastula-**

tion /-'laysh(ə)n/ *noun*. [scientific Latin from Greek *blastos* bud, shoot]

blatant /'blayt(ə)nt/ *adj* **1** completely obvious, conspicuous, or obtrusive, *esp* in a crass or offensive manner. **2** noisy, *esp* in a vulgar or offensive manner. ▶▶ **blatancy** /-si/ *noun*, **blatantly** *adv*. [perhaps from Latin *blatire* to chatter. The word is first recorded in the phrase 'blatant beast', referring to a thousand-tongued monster, in Edmund Spenser's poem *The Faerie Queene* (1596)]

Usage note

blatant or **flagrant?** These two words are close together in meaning, both indicating that something is openly outrageous. There is a difference of emphasis, however. *Blatant* emphasizes the obviousness of an offence: *It was such a blatant attempt at emotional blackmail that not even his doting mother could fail to see it. Flagrant*, on the other hand, emphasizes the offence's brazenly shocking or outrageous nature: *If they fail to condemn such a flagrant breach of the regulations, will they ever condemn anything at all?* Both words are spelt with two *a*'s.

blather[1] /'bladhə/ *noun* foolish voluble talk. [Old Norse *blathr* nonsense, from *blathra* to talk nonsense]

blather[2] *verb intrans* (**blathered, blathering**) to talk foolishly or volubly. ▶▶ **blatherer** *noun*.

blatherskite /'bladhəskiet/ *noun* **1** a person who blathers a lot. **2** = BLATHER[1]. [BLATHER[1] + Scots dialect *skate* a contemptible person]

blaze[1] /'blayz/ *noun* **1a** an intensely burning flame or sudden fire. **b** intense direct light, often accompanied by heat: *the blaze of noon*. **2a** a dazzling display: *a blaze of flowers*. **b** brilliance: *the blaze of the jewels*. **3** a sudden outburst: *a blaze of fury*. **4** (*in pl*) a euphemism for HELL: *Tell him to go to blazes; What the blazes are you doing?* ✳ **like blazes** *informal* very hard, fast, etc: *Run like blazes!* [Old English *blæse* torch]

blaze[2] *verb intrans* **1a** to burn intensely: *a blazing fire*. **b** to shine brightly: *The sun blazed overhead*. **2** to be conspicuously brilliant or resplendent. **3** to quickly become very angry: *He suddenly blazed with anger*. **4** (+ away) to shoot rapidly and repeatedly: *They blazed away at the target*. ▶▶ **blazingly** *adv*.

blaze[3] ✳ **blaze abroad** to make (something) public or conspicuous. [Middle English *blasen* from early Dutch *blāsen* to blow]

blaze[4] *noun* **1** a broad white mark on the face of an animal, *esp* a horse. **2** a trail marker, *esp* a mark made on a tree by cutting off a piece of the bark. [German *Blas*]

blaze[5] *verb trans* to mark (e.g. a trail) with blazes. ✳ **blaze a trail** to lead or be a pioneer in some activity.

blazer /'blayzə/ *noun* a jacket, *esp* with patch pockets, that is worn for casual wear or as part of a school uniform. [BLAZE[2] + -ER[2]. So called because of the bright colours of early sporting blazers]

blaze up *verb intrans* **1** to begin to burn fiercely. **2** to quickly become very angry.

blazing /'blayzing/ *adj informal* very intense or very angry: *a blazing row*.

blazon[1] /'blayz(ə)n/ *noun* **1** = COAT OF ARMS. **2** the proper formal description of heraldic arms or charges. [Middle English *blason*, from early French]

blazon[2] *verb trans* (**blazoned, blazoning**) **1** (*often* + forth) to proclaim (something) widely. **2** to describe (heraldic arms or charges) in technical terms, or paint (them). ▶▶ **blazoner** *noun*, **blazoning** *noun*.

blazonry /'blayz(ə)nri/ *noun* **1** dazzling display. **2a** heraldic arms or charges. **b** the art of describing or painting heraldic arms or charges.

bldg *abbr* building.

bleach[1] /bleech/ *verb trans* **1** to remove colour or stains from (e.g. fabric). **2** to make (something) whiter or lighter, *esp* by the physical or chemical removal of colour. ▶▶ **bleachable** *adj*, **bleacher** *noun*. [Old English *blǣcean*; related to Old English *blāc* pale: see BLEAK[1]]

bleach[2] *noun* **1** a strong chemical substance used in bleaching. **2** the degree of whiteness obtained by bleaching.

bleachers /'bleechəz/ *pl noun* (*usu* **the bleachers**) *NAmer* a usu uncovered stand of tiered planks providing inexpensive seating for spectators, e.g. at a sports event. [from its being usu unprotected from the sun]

bleaching powder *noun* a white powder consisting chiefly of calcium hydroxide, calcium chloride, and calcium hypochlorite, used as a bleach, disinfectant, or deodorant.

bleak[1] /bleek/ *adj* **1** exposed, barren, and often windswept. **2** cold or raw: *in the bleak mid-winter* — Christina Rossetti. **3a** lacking in warmth or kindness. **b** not hopeful or encouraging: *a bleak outlook*. **4** severely simple or austere. ▶▶ **bleakish** *adj*, **bleakly** *adv*, **bleakness** *noun*. [Middle English *bleke* pale, from Old English *blāc* pale and Old Norse *bleikr* bleak]

bleak[2] *noun* a small European river fish of the carp family, with silvery-green scales from which a pigment used in making artificial pearls is obtained: *Alburnus lucidus*. [Middle English *bleke*, prob from Old Norse *bleikja*]

blear[1] /bliə/ *verb trans* **1** to make (the eyes) bleary. **2** to blur (something). [Middle English *bleren*, of Germanic origin]

blear[2] *adj* = BLEARY

bleary /'bliəri/ *adj* (**blearier, bleariest**) **1** said of the eyes or vision: dull or dimmed, *esp* from fatigue or sleep. **2** poorly outlined or defined. ▶▶ **blearily** *adv*, **bleariness** *noun*.

bleary-eyed *adj* with blurred vision, from having a weakness of the eyes or from having just wakened.

bleat[1] /bleet/ *verb intrans* **1** to make the cry characteristic of a sheep or goat or any similar sound. **2a** to talk complainingly or with a whine. **b** to blather. ▶ *verb trans* to utter (something) in a bleating manner. ▶▶ **bleater** *noun*, **bleating** *adj and noun*, **bleatingly** *adv*. [Old English *blǣtan*; related to Old English *bellan* BELL[3]]

bleat[2] *noun* **1** the characteristic cry of a sheep or goat or any similar sound. **2** a feeble whining complaint.

bleb /bleb/ *noun* **1** a small blister. **2** an air bubble. [perhaps alteration of BLOB[1]]

bleed[1] /bleed/ *verb* (*past tense and past part.* **bled** /bled/) ▶ *verb intrans* **1a** to emit or lose blood: *If you prick us, do we not bleed?* — Shakespeare. **b** to die or be wounded, *esp* in battle: *Scots wha hae wi' Wallace bled* — Burns. **2** (+ for) to feel anguish, pain, or sympathy: *My heart bleeds for these poor people*. **3a** to lose some constituent (e.g. sap or dye) by exuding it or by diffusion. **b** said of sap, dye, etc: to ooze or flow out. **4** to be printed so as to run off an edge of a page after trimming. ▶ *verb trans* **1** to remove or draw blood from (somebody). **2** to extort money from (somebody). **3** to draw sap from (a tree). **4a** to extract or let out some or all of (a liquid or gas) from a container, etc: *They bled the air from the central-heating system*. **b** to extract or let out some or all of a liquid or gas from (a container system): *bleed the brakes*. **5a** to cause (e.g. a printed illustration) to bleed. **b** to trim (e.g. a page) so that some of the printing bleeds. **6** to drain or drain the vitality or lifeblood from (something): *High taxes are bleeding private enterprise*. [Old English *blēdan*, from *blōd* BLOOD[1]]

bleed[2] *noun* an act or instance of bleeding, *esp* by a haemophiliac.

bleeder *noun Brit, informal* **1** a person or thing regarded as a nuisance, worthless, or objectionable. **2** a haemophiliac.

bleeding *adj and adv informal* = BLOODY[1], BLOODY[3].

bleeding heart *noun* **1** *informal derog* somebody who is considered to show excessive sympathy for e.g. victims of injustice or ill-treatment. **2** any of several species of plants of the fumitory family with usu red or pink heart-shaped flowers: genus *Dicentra*.

bleep[1] /bleep/ *noun* **1** a short high-pitched sound, e.g. from electronic equipment. **2** = BLEEPER. [imitative]

bleep[2] *verb trans* **1** to call (somebody) by means of a bleeper. **2** (*usu* + out) to replace (recorded words) with a bleep or other sound: *All the obscenities were bleeped out*. ▶ *verb intrans* to emit a bleep.

bleeper *noun* a portable radio receiver that emits a bleep as a signal that the wearer is required.

blemish[1] /'blemish/ *noun* **1** a noticeable imperfection; a flaw, stain, or disfiguring mark. **2a** a defect of character. **b** a wrong or blameworthy act: *There are no blemishes on her record*.

blemish[2] *verb trans* to spoil the perfection of (something); to make (it) flawed. [Middle English verb *blemisshen*, from early French *blesmiss-*, stem of *blesmir* to make pale, wound, of Germanic origin]

blench /blench/ *verb intrans* to draw back or flinch from lack of courage. [Old English *blencan* to deceive, influenced in Middle English by *blink*]

blend[1] /blend/ *verb* (*past tense and past part.* **blended** or **blent** /blent/) ▶ *verb trans* **1** to mix or mingle (something), *esp* to combine or associate separate constituents so that they cannot be distinguished. **2** to prepare (e.g. tea or whisky) by thoroughly intermingling different varieties or grades of it. ▶ *verb intrans* **1a** to mix or intermingle thoroughly. **b** to combine into an integrated whole.

c said of colours: to shade into one another. **2a** (*often* + in) to produce a harmonious effect. **b** to fit in well. [Middle English *blenden*, modification of Old Norse *blanda*; related to Old English *blandan* to mix]

blend² *noun* **1** an act or product of blending: *our own blend of tea*. **2** a word produced by combining other words or parts of words, e.g. *smog* from *smoke* and *fog*.

blende /blend/ *noun* = SPHALERITE. [German *Blende*, from *blenden* to blind, deceive; so called because it often resembles galena, but yields no lead]

blender *noun* **1** an electric appliance for grinding or mixing; a liquidizer. **2** any person or thing that blends something.

Blenheim Orange /'blenim/ *noun* an eating apple with a golden-red skin. [named after *Blenheim* Palace in Oxfordshire, England]

blenny /'bleni/ *noun* (*pl* **blennies**) any of numerous usu small and elongated and often scaleless sea fishes with long spiny fins, mostly found in coastal waters: families Blenniidae (scaleless), Clinidae (with scales). [Latin *blennius*, a sea fish, from Greek *blennos*]

blent /blent/ *verb archaic or literary* past tense and past part. of BLEND¹.

blephar- or **blepharo-** *comb. form* forming words, denoting: eyelid: *blepharitis*. [scientific Latin from Greek, from *blepharon* eyelid]

blepharitis /blefə'rietis/ *noun* inflammation of the eyelids. [scientific Latin, from *blephar* + *-itis*]

blepharo- *comb. form* see BLEPHAR-.

blesbok /'blesbok/ or **blesbuck** /'blesbuk/ *noun* (*pl* **blesboks** or **blesbucks** or *collectively* **blesbok** or **blesbuck**) a S African antelope that has a large white spot on the face and lyre-shaped horns and that is closely related to the BONTEBOK: *Damaliscus dorcas phillipsi*. [Afrikaans *blesbok*, from *bles* BLAZE⁴ + *bok* male antelope]

bless /bles/ *verb trans* (*past tense and past part.* **blessed** or **blest** /blest/) **1** to hallow or consecrate (someone or something) by a religious rite, *esp* by making the sign of the cross. **2** to invoke divine care for (someone or something). **3a** to praise or glorify (God): *We bless Your holy name.* **b** (*often* + for) to speak gratefully of (somebody or something); to thank (them): *They blessed him for his kindness.* **4a** (*often* + with) to confer prosperity or happiness on (someone). **b** (+ with) to endow (somebody) with a talent, asset, advantage, etc: *She has been blessed with a beautiful voice.* **5** used in exclamations chiefly to express mild or good-humoured surprise: *Bless my cotton socks, what's happened now?* **6** *archaic* to protect or preserve (somebody or something). ✳ **bless you!/God bless you! 1** words traditionally said to somebody who has just sneezed. **2** an exclamation of surprise, thanks, etc. **Well, I'm blessed!** an exclamation of surprise. [Old English *blēdsian*, from *blōd* BLOOD¹; from the use of blood in consecration in pre-Christian rites]

blessed /'blesid/ *adj* **1a** (*often* **Blessed**) holy; venerated: *the Blessed Sacrament.* **b** (**Blessed**) used as a title for a beatified person: *Blessed Oliver Plunket.* **2a** bringing pleasure or contentment: *The news came as a blessed relief.* **b** used as an intensifier: *No one gave us a blessed penny.* **3** /blest/ enjoying the bliss of heaven. **4** worthy of respect. ⨠ **blessedly** *adv*, **blessedness** *noun*.

blessing *noun* **1a** the invocation of God's favour upon a person: *The congregation stood for the blessing.* **b** the words used in such an invocation. **2** approval: *The chairman has given his blessing to the project.* **3** something conducive to happiness or welfare. **4** grace said at a meal. ✳ **a blessing in disguise** an apparent misfortune that is found in the end to be beneficial.

blest *verb* past tense and past part. of BLESS.

blether¹ /'bledhə/ *verb intrans* (**blethered, blethering**) **1** to talk nonsense or talk volubly; to BLATHER². **2** *chiefly Scot, informal* to have a friendly chat with somebody. ⨠⨠ **bletherer** *noun*. [Scots variant of BLATHER²]

blether² *noun* **1** somebody who talks nonsense; a bletherer. **2** *chiefly Scot, informal* (*in pl*) nonsense. **3** *chiefly Scot, informal* a friendly chat.

blew /blooh/ *verb* past tense of BLOW¹, BLOW⁴.

blewits /'blooh-its/ *noun* (*pl* **blewits**) an edible mushroom that has a lilac-coloured cap and stem when young: *Tricholoma saevum*. [prob irreg from BLUE¹]

blight¹ /bliet/ *noun* **1a** a disease of plants resulting in withering, cessation of growth, and death of parts without rotting. **b** an organism that causes such a disease. **2** something that impairs, frustrates,

or destroys. **3** a condition of disorder or decay: *urban blight.* [origin unknown]

blight² *verb trans* **1** to affect (e.g. a plant) with blight. **2** to impair, frustrate, or destroy (something). ➤ *verb intrans* to suffer from or become affected with blight.

blighter /'blietə/ *noun chiefly Brit, informal* a person or thing regarded as irritating, troublesome, or pitiable. [BLIGHT² + -ER²]

blighty /'blieti/ *noun* (*pl* **blighties**) *informal* **1** used *esp* by British soldiers in World War I: **a** (*usu* **Blighty**) Britain. **b** (*also* **blighty one**) a wound that allows or forces a soldier to be sent home to Britain. **2** leave. [Hindi *bilāyatī, wilāyatī* foreign country, England, from Arabic *wilāyat* province, country]

blimey /'bliemi/ *interj chiefly Brit, informal* used to express surprise. [short for GORBLIMEY]

blimp /blimp/ *noun* **1** a non-rigid airship. **2** (*usu* **Blimp**) a pompous person with out-of-date or extremely conservative views. Also called COLONEL BLIMP. **3** a soundproof cover for a film camera. **4** *NAmer, informal, offensive* a very fat person. ➤ **blimpish** *adj*, **blimpishly** *adv*, **blimpishness** *noun*. [prob based on LIMP³]

blind¹ /bliend/ *adj* **1a** unable to see; sightless. **b** of or for sightless people. **2a** (*often* + to) unable or unwilling to perceive things clearly or judge them rationally: *Love is blind* — Shakespeare; *blind to all arguments.* **b** acting or done without control or judgment: *a blind swipe.* **3a** not based on reason, evidence, or knowledge: *blind faith.* **b** acting without reason or purpose: *blind forces.* **4a** completely insensible: *in a blind stupor.* **b** *informal* drunk. **5** without sight or knowledge of anything that could serve for guidance beforehand. **6** performed solely by the use of instruments within an aircraft: *a blind landing.* **7a** hidden from sight; concealed: *a blind stitch.* **b** unable to be seen round: *a blind corner.* **8** having only one opening or outlet: *a blind alley.* **9** having no opening for light or passage: *a blind wall.* **10** blocked up: *a blind door.* **11** used as an intensifier: *They didn't give us a blind bit of help.* ✳ **(as) blind as a bat** completely, or almost totally, blind. **turn a blind eye** to refuse to react to or take action against somebody's mistakes or wrongdoing. ⨠⨠ **blindly** *adv*, **blindness** *noun*. [Old English *blind*]

blind² *verb trans* **1** to make (somebody) blind. **2** (*often* + to) to rob (somebody) of judgment or discernment. **3** to dazzle (somebody). ➤ *verb intrans Brit, informal* to swear: *cursing and blinding.* ✳ **blind (somebody) with science** to impress or overwhelm (somebody) with a display of usu technical knowledge.

blind³ *noun* **1** (**the blind**) people who are blind: *In the country of the blind the one-eyed man is king* — H G Wells. **2a** a flexible screen for covering a window, e.g. a strip of cloth mounted on a roller. **b** = VENETIAN BLIND. **3** *chiefly Brit* an awning. **4a** anything that hinders sight or keeps out light. **b** a cover or subterfuge. **5** *NAmer* = HIDE². **6** (*also* **blinder**) *Brit, informal* a drinking session.

blind⁴ *adv* **1** to the point of insensibility: *blind drunk.* **2** without seeing outside an aircraft: *They had to fly blind.* **3** used as an intensifier: *He swore blind he wouldn't escape.* ✳ **bake blind** to bake (a pastry case) without a filling, but partly filled with beads, dried peas, etc.

blind alley *noun* **1** = CUL-DE-SAC. **2** a fruitless or mistaken course or direction.

blind date *noun* **1** a date between people who have not previously met. **2** either of the participants in such a meeting.

blinder /'bliendə/ *noun* **1** *Brit, informal* something outstanding, *esp* an outstanding piece of play in cricket or football. **2** *Brit, informal* = BLIND³ (6). **3** *NAmer* = BLINKER³ (3). [BLIND² + -ER²]

blindfold¹ *verb trans* **1** to cover the eyes of (somebody or something) with a piece of material to prevent them from seeing. **2** to hinder (somebody) from perceiving or understanding things clearly. [Middle English *blindfellen, blindfelden* to strike blind, blindfold, from BLIND¹ + *fellen* to FELL²]

blindfold² *noun* something, *esp* a piece of cloth tied around the head that prevents sight or obscures vision or awareness.

blindfold³ *adj and adv* **1** wearing a blindfold. **2** without careful thought.

blind gut *noun* = CAECUM.

blinding¹ /'bliending/ *noun* material, e.g. sand or gravel, used to fill crevices, *esp* in a new road. [from BLIND² in the sense 'to fill gaps in, clog']

blinding² *adj* **1** said of light: so bright as to make seeing difficult or impossible. **2** *informal.* **a** outstanding or extraordinary, *esp* in showing supreme skill; dazzling. **b** extremely obvious; glaring. ⟫ **blindingly** *adv.*

blindman's buff /ˌblIendmanz 'buf/ *noun* a group game in which a blindfolded player tries to catch and identify any of the other players. [*buff* blow, buffet, from Middle English *buffe*, from early French, of imitative origin]

blind side *noun* **1** the side on which one cannot see danger, etc. **2** in rugby, the side nearer to the touchline.

blind spot *noun* **1a** the point in the retina where the optic nerve enters and that is not sensitive to light. **b** a part of a visual field that cannot be seen or inspected: *The car has a bad blind spot.* **2** an area in which one lacks knowledge, understanding, or discrimination. **3** a locality in which radio reception is markedly poorer than in the surrounding area.

blind trust *noun* a trust that manages the financial affairs of a person in public office without that person knowing the details of its financial dealings, so that any possible conflict of interest can be avoided.

blindworm *noun* = SLOWWORM. [because of its small eyes]

bling-bling[1] /ˌblIng-'blIng/ *noun slang* **1** (*also* **bling**) bright or conspicuously extravagant jewellery, *esp* of platinum encrusted with diamonds or false diamonds. **2** a lavish, ostentatious, supposedly status-enhancing lifestyle. [perhaps from the sound of pieces of metallic jewellery hitting lightly against each other]

bling-bling[2] *adj slang* **1** said of jewellery: bright or conspicuously extravagant. **2** said of a person's lifestyle: ostentatiously lavish and extravagant. **3** sexy, stylish, etc.

blini *or* **bliny** /'blIni, 'blee-/ *or* **blinis** *pl noun* in Russian cooking, small pancakes made with yeast and buckwheat flour, usu served with sour cream. [Russian *blini*]

blink[1] /blIngk/ *verb intrans* **1** to close and open the eyes involuntarily. **2** (*often* + at) to look at something with half-shut eyes. **3** to shine intermittently. **4a** (+ at) to condone or ignore a wrongdoing, injustice, etc. **b** (+ at) to look with surprise or dismay at something. ⟫ *verb trans* **1** to cause (one's eyes) to blink. **2** (+ away/back) to remove or stop (something) by blinking: *He blinked back his tears.* **3** to condone or ignore (something). [Middle English *blinken* to open one's eyes, from *blenk*, Scots variant of BLENCH]

blink[2] *noun* **1** a glimmer or sparkle. **2** a usu involuntary shutting and opening of the eye. **3** = ICEBLINK (glare in the sky above ice). ✳ **on the blink** *informal* not working properly: *The light switch is on the blink.*

blinker[1] *noun* **1** a warning or signalling light that flashes on and off. **2** (*in pl*) an obstruction to sight or discernment. **3** *chiefly Brit* either of two flaps, one on each side of a horse's bridle, allowing only frontal vision.

blinker[2] *verb trans* (**blinkered, blinkering**) **1** to put blinkers on (e.g. a horse). **2** to restrict or lessen the understanding, discernment, or awareness of (somebody). ⟫ **blinkered** *adj.*

blinking *adj and adv Brit, euphem* = BLOODY[1], BLOODY[3].

bliny /'blIni, 'blee-/ *pl noun* see BLINI.

blip[1] /blIp/ *noun* **1** a bleep. **2** an image on a radar screen. **3** a brief, and sometimes unwelcome, deviation from the norm; an aberration. [imitative]

blip[2] *verb intrans* (**blipped, blipping**) to deviate briefly from the norm.

bliss /blIs/ *noun* **1** complete happiness: *Bliss was it in that dawn to be alive* — Wordsworth. **2** paradise or heaven. ⟫ **blissful** *adj,* **blissfully** *adv,* **blissfulness** *noun.* [Old English *bliss*; related to Old English *blīthe* BLITHE]

blissed out *adj informal* completely happy.

blister[1] /'blIsta/ *noun* **1** a raised part of the outer skin containing watery liquid. **2** a bubble or raised spot, e.g. in paint, wallpaper, etc, resembling a blister. **3** a disease of plants marked by large swollen patches on the leaves. **4** any of various structures that bulge out: *an aircraft's radar blister.* ⟫ **blistery** *adj.* [Middle English from Old French *blostre* boil or Middle Dutch *bluyster* blister; related to Old English *blǣst* BLAST[1]]

blister[2] *verb* (**blistered, blistering**) ⟫ *verb intrans* to become affected with a blister or blisters. ⟫ *verb trans* **1** to raise a blister or blisters on (e.g. the skin, paint). **2** to attack (somebody) harshly.

blister copper *noun* copper that has a black blistered surface, is almost pure, and occurs as an intermediate product in copper refining.

blistering *adj* **1** extremely intense or severe: *a blistering attack on corruption; blistering heat.* **2** said of speed: extremely fast. ⟫ **blisteringly** *adv.*

blister pack *noun* a pack for small manufactured items, consisting of a transparent covering fastened to a larger usu cardboard backing.

blithe /bliedh/ *adj* **1** light-hearted, merry or cheerful: *Hail to thee, blithe Spirit* — Shelley. **2** casual or heedless: *blithe unconcern.* ⟫ **blithely** *adv,* **blitheness** *noun.* [Old English *blīthe*]

blithering /'blIdhərIng/ *adj informal* **1** stupid: *You blithering idiot!* **2** talking nonsense; babbling. [from *blither,* alteration of BLATHER[1]]

blithesome /'bliedhs(ə)m/ *adj archaic* merry; light-hearted. ⟫ **blithesomely** *adv.*

BLitt *abbr* Bachelor of Letters. [medieval Latin *baccalaureus litterarum*]

blitz[1] /blIts/ *noun* **1** a period of intensive action: *I need to have a blitz on my unpaid bills.* **2a** an intensive aerial bombardment. **b** (**the Blitz**) the bombardment of British cities by the German air force in 1940 and 1941. **3a** = BLITZKRIEG. **b** an intensive attack on or campaign against somebody or something: *a blitz against the unions.* **4** in American football, a concerted charge on the quarterback of the opposing team. [abbr of German *Blitzkrieg*: see BLITZKRIEG]

blitz[2] *verb trans* **1** to deal with (something) in a short, intensive period of action: *I'm going home to blitz the housework.* **2** to attack (somebody or somewhere) in an intensive aerial bombardment.

blitzkrieg /'blItskreeg/ *noun* a violent swift surprise campaign conducted by coordinated air and ground forces. [German *Blitzkrieg,* from *Blitz* lightning + *Krieg* war]

blizzard /'blIzəd/ *noun* **1a** a severe snowstorm. **b** an intensely strong cold wind filled with fine snow. **2** an overwhelming rush or deluge: *We expect the usual blizzard of mail at Christmas.* ⟫ **blizzardy** *adj.* [origin unknown]

bloat[1] /bloht/ *verb trans* **1a** to make (something) swollen with gas or liquid. **b** to enlarge (something) beyond the normal or necessary size. **2** to cure (a herring or mackerel) in smoke. ⟫ *verb intrans* to become swollen with gas or liquid. [*bloat* swollen, perhaps from Old Norse *blautr* soft, soaked]

bloat[2] *noun* a digestive disturbance of domestic animals, *esp* cattle, caused by excessive accumulation of gas in the stomach and resulting in bloating of the abdomen.

bloated *adj* **1a** swollen with liquid or gas. **b** unpleasantly full or distended from eating too much. **2** much larger than is warranted: *a bloated estimate.* **3** puffed up with pride.

bloater /'blohtə/ *noun* a large herring or mackerel lightly salted and briefly smoked.

blob[1] /blob/ *noun* **1a** a small drop of liquid: *a blob of ink.* **b** a small drop or lump of something viscous or thick. **2a** a spot or patch: *a blob of colour.* **b** something ill-defined or amorphous. ⟫ **blobby** *adj.* [Middle English: earlier history unknown]

blob[2] *verb trans* (**blobbed, blobbing**) to apply (a liquid such as paint) in the form of blobs.

bloc /blok/ *noun* a permanent or temporary combination of individuals, parties, or nations for a common purpose. [French *bloc*: see BLOCK[1]]

block[1] /blok/ *noun* **1a** a quantity, number, or section of things dealt with as a unit: *a block of seats.* **b** (*used before a noun*) comprising or relating to a quantity of things dealt with as a unit: *a block booking.* **2a** a large building divided into separate functional units: *a block of flats.* **b** a part of a building or integrated group of buildings devoted to a particular use: *the research block.* **3a** a usu more or less rectangular area, e.g. in a town, enclosed by streets and usu occupied by buildings: *I'm just going for a walk round the block.* **b** *chiefly NAmer* the distance along one side of such an area: *My mother lives just two blocks from here.* **4** a compact usu solid piece of substantial material such as wood or stone, *esp* when specially shaped to serve a particular purpose, e.g. for chopping things on or executions by beheading. **5a** a usu cubical and solid wooden or plastic building toy that is usu provided in sets: *building blocks.* **b** a large rectangular brick. **6** *Brit* a thick pad of paper. **7a** an obstacle or blockage. **b** a wedge or other object for stopping movement, e.g. of a wheel. **8a** interruption of the normal physiological functioning of a body tissue or organ, e.g. transmission of nerve impulses. **b** a psychological factor that prevents normal functioning, reactions, etc. **9** an action or movement intended to obstruct or halt an opponent's manoeuvre in sports, e.g. the action of checking the progress of an opponent in American football by using the body. **10** the metal casting that contains the cylinders of an internal-combustion engine. **11** a wooden or metal case enclosing one or more pulleys. **12** *informal* the head. **13** a heartless, unfeeling, or unemotional person. **14** the standard unit for allocating and transferring data on magnetic disk or tape. **15** a piece of e.g. wood or metal with an engraved or etched design on its surface from which impressions are printed. **16a** a solid toe in a ballet shoe on which a dancer can stand on points. **b** a ballet shoe with such a toe. **17** = STARTING BLOCK. **18** a mould or form on which articles, such as hats, are shaped or displayed. **19** a length of railway track governed by a signal that will allow only one train to pass along it at a time. **20** *Aus, NZ.* **a** an area of land for some purpose. **b** a plot of land in a town with a building on it. ✳ **do one's block** *Aus, informal* to become excited and irrational, e.g. through anger. [Middle English *blok* via early French *bloc* from early Dutch *blok*]

block² *verb trans* **1a** (*often + up*) to make or be a barrier that obstructs (a passage, road, pipe, etc). **b** to hinder the movement or progress of (something) by putting an obstruction in its way. **2** to shut (something) off from view: *The canopy of leaves was blocking the sun.* **3** in various games, to stop or obstruct (an opponent or ball) with one's body. **4** to prevent the normal functioning of (something). **5** to arrange (a timetable or other list) in groups. **6** to prohibit or limit the use of funds or their conversion into foreign exchange. **7** to shape (something such as a hat) by means of a block. **8** to make (two or more lines of writing or type) flush at the left or at both margins. **9** to stamp lettering or a design on (the cover of a book). **10** to secure or mount (something) on a block or provide it with a block. ➤➤ **blocker** *noun*.

blockade¹ /blə'kayd, blo'kayd/ *noun* **1** the surrounding or blocking of a particular enemy area, *esp* a port, to prevent passage of people or supplies. **2** an obstruction.

blockade² *verb trans* **1** to subject (somebody or something) to a blockade. **2** to block or obstruct (something). ➤➤ **blockader** *noun*.

blockage /'blokij/ *noun* **1** an act or instance of blocking, or the state of being blocked: *a blockage in the pipe.* **2** something that causes e.g. a pipe to be blocked: *I used a garden cane to remove the blockage.*

block and tackle *noun* an arrangement of pulley blocks with associated rope or cable for hoisting or hauling.

blockboard *noun* material made of parallel wooden strips glued edge to edge and finished on top and underneath with thin wooden sheets.

blockbuster /'blokbustə/ *noun informal* **1** somebody or something particularly outstanding or effective. **2** a huge high-explosive demolition bomb. ➤➤ **blockbusting** *adj*.

block capitals *pl noun* plain capital letters, printed without serifs or written separately and without embellishment.

block diagram *noun* a diagram, e.g. of a system, process, or computer program, in which labelled shapes, such as rectangles, and interconnecting lines represent the relationship of parts.

blockhead *noun* an extremely dull or stupid person: *No man but a blockhead ever wrote, except for money* — Dr Johnson. ➤➤ **blockheaded** *adj*.

blockhouse /'blok·hows/ *noun* **1** an observation post built to withstand heat, blast, radiation, etc. **2** a building made of heavy timbers with loopholes for firing through, observation, etc, formerly used as a fort. **3** a building built with logs or squared timber.

block in *verb trans* **1** to sketch the outlines of (something) in a design. **2** to keep (somebody or something) in a place by means of a barrier or obstruction.

blockish *adj* **1** stupid or lacking in imagination. **2** dull or lacking in energy.

block letters *pl noun* = BLOCK CAPITALS.

block off *verb trans* to prevent access to or passage through (a place) with a barrier or obstruction.

block out *verb trans* **1** to prevent the passage of (light, sound, etc). **2** to exclude (a memory) from one's consciousness. **3** to sketch the outlines of (something) in a design.

block plane *noun* a small carpenter's plane with the blade mounted at an acute angle, used *esp* for planing across the grain of wood.

block release *noun* a short course of full-time study for which a worker is released by his or her employer: compare DAY RELEASE.

block system *noun* a system whereby a railway line is divided into short sections controlled by signals that do not allow a train into a section until it is completely clear.

block vote *noun* a single vote cast by a representative of a large group, e.g. a trade union delegate at a trades union congress, given a relative value in the total vote that is proportional to the number of people in that group. Also called CARD VOTE.

blog /blog/ *noun* = WEBLOG. ➤➤ **blogger** *noun*, **blogging** *noun*.

bloke /blohk/ *noun chiefly Brit, informal* a man. [perhaps from Shelta]

blokeish *or* **blokish** /'blohkish/ *adj informal* typical or supposedly typical of men, *esp* of men in all-male company; hearty and boisterous, inclined to show off, and interested mainly in sport, drinking, cars, etc.

blond¹ /blond/ *adj* **1a** said of hair: of a flaxen, golden, light auburn, or pale yellowish brown colour. **b** having blond hair and usu a fairly pale skin: *a handsome blond youth.* **2** of a light yellowish brown to dark greyish yellow colour. ➤➤ **blondish** *adj*. [French *blond* from medieval Latin *blondus, blundus* yellow]

Usage note

blond *or* blonde? The two spellings, which are both correct, derive from the masculine (*blond*) and feminine (*blonde*) forms of the word in French. English tends to retain the distinction, at least to the extent of preferring the form *blonde* for women, about whom the word is most often used: *She's gone blonde*; *Gentlemen Prefer Blondes* (novel by Anita Loos). On this basis, it would be logical to write *He is blond* and *She has blonde hair* and to use *blond* in neutral contexts such as *blond-coloured wood*.

blond² *noun* **1** somebody with blond hair and often a light complexion and blue or grey eyes. **2** a light yellowish brown to dark greyish yellow colour.

blonde /blond/ *noun and adj* used *esp* for or in relation to women; = BLOND¹, BLOND². [French *blonde*, fem of *blond*: see BLOND¹]

Usage note

blonde *or* blond? See note at BLOND¹.

blood¹ /blud/ *noun* **1a** the usu red fluid that circulates in the heart, arteries, capillaries, and veins of a vertebrate animal, carrying nourishment and oxygen to, and bringing away waste products from, all parts of the body. **b** a comparable fluid in the body of an invertebrate animal. **2** people or ideas of the specified, *esp* innovative, kind: *We need some fresh blood in the organization.* **3a** lifeblood; life. **b** bloodshed; murder. **4a** human lineage, *esp* the royal lineage: *a prince of the blood.* **b** descent from parents, family background, or ancestors. **5a** temper or passion. **b** in medieval physiology, the one of the four humours (bodily fluids) that was believed to cause optimism or cheerfulness. **6** *archaic* a dashing lively *esp* young man; a rake: *a young blood.* ✳ **after/out for somebody's blood** wanting revenge on somebody. **in one's blood** being an inherent or supposedly inherited part of a person's character or life. **make one's blood boil** to make one very angry: *It makes my blood boil to see such injustice.* **make one's blood run cold** to horrify one. **one's blood is up** one is ready for a fight. [Old English *blōd*]

blood² *verb trans* **1** to stain or wet (somebody or something) with blood, *esp* to mark the face of (an inexperienced fox hunter) with the blood of the fox. **2** to give an initiating experience to (somebody new to a particular field of activity, e.g. battle).

blood-and-thunder *adj informal* violently melodramatic.

blood bank *noun* a place for storage of blood or plasma until required for medical use.

bloodbath *noun* a great slaughter; a massacre.

blood brother *noun* either of two men pledged to mutual loyalty, *esp* by a ceremonial mingling of each other's blood. ➤➤ **blood brotherhood** *noun*.

blood count *noun* the number of blood cells in a definite volume of blood, or the determination of this.

bloodcurdling *adj* arousing horror: *bloodcurdling screams.* ➤➤ **bloodcurdlingly** *adv*.

blood donor *noun* somebody who donates blood, *esp* for blood transfusion.

blood doping *noun* the (illegal) practice of reinjecting an athlete with a quantity of his or her own blood, previously removed and oxygenated, just before an event in an attempt to improve performance.

blooded *adj* (*used in combinations*) **1** having blood (of the stated type): *warm-blooded.* **2** having a (certain type of) character or nature: *cold-blooded.*

blood feud *noun* a murderous feud between clans or families.

blood fluke *noun* = SCHISTOSOME (parasitic flatworm).

blood group *noun* any of the classes into which human beings can be separated on the basis of the presence or absence of specific antigens in their blood. Also called BLOOD TYPE.

blood heat *noun* a temperature approximating to that of the human body, about 37°C or 98.4°F.

blood horse *noun* a thoroughbred.

bloodhound *noun* a large powerful hound of European origin remarkable for its acuteness of smell and poor sight.

bloodless *adj* **1** deficient in or free from blood. **2** not accompanied by the shedding of blood: *a bloodless victory.* **3** lacking in spirit or vitality. **4** lacking in human feeling: *bloodless statistics.* ➤ **bloodlessly** *adv,* **bloodlessness** *noun.*

bloodletting *noun* **1** = BLOODSHED. **2** = PHLEBOTOMY.

bloodline *noun* a group of related individuals, *esp* with distinctive characteristics.

bloodlust *noun* an intense desire to shed blood or kill.

blood money *noun* **1** money obtained at the cost of another's life, *esp* for murder. **2** money paid to the next of kin of a person who has been killed. **3** money given for information about a murder or murderer.

blood orange *noun* a type of eating orange that has red and orange flesh and a reddish skin.

blood plasma *noun* = PLASMA (1B).

blood platelet *noun* any of the minute discs in the blood of vertebrates that assist in blood clotting.

blood poisoning *noun* = SEPTICAEMIA.

blood pressure *noun* pressure that is exerted by the blood on the walls of the blood vessels, *esp* arteries, and that varies with the age and health of the individual.

blood red *adj* of the colour of blood.

blood relation *noun* a person related by birth or descent, as opposed to by marriage.

blood relative *noun* = BLOOD RELATION.

blood serum *noun* **1** the watery portion of the blood excluding the blood cells. **2** blood plasma from which the fibrin has been removed.

bloodshed *noun* **1** the shedding of blood. **2** the taking of life.

bloodshot *adj* said of an eye: having the white part tinged with red.

blood sport *noun derog* a field sport, e.g. fox-hunting or beagling, in which animals are killed.

bloodstain *noun* a discoloration caused by blood.

bloodstained *adj* **1** stained with blood. **2** involved with slaughter; guilty of bloodshed: *We all have bloodstained hands.*

bloodstock *noun* (*treated as sing. or pl*) thoroughbred horses, *esp* when used for racing.

bloodstone *noun* a translucent green quartz gemstone sprinkled with red spots.

bloodstream *noun* the flowing blood in a circulatory system.

bloodsucker *noun* **1** a person who extorts money from another. **2** an animal or insect that sucks blood, *esp* a leech. ➤ **bloodsucking** *adj.*

blood sugar *noun* the glucose, or the amount of glucose, in the blood.

blood test *noun* a test of a person's or animal's blood, e.g. to ascertain the nature of an infection, to detect leukaemia, or to test for illegal substances.

bloodthirsty *adj* **1** eager for or taking pleasure in bloodshed. **2** containing much bloodshed and violence: *a bloodthirsty tale.* ➤ **bloodthirstily** *adv,* **bloodthirstiness** *noun.*

blood type *noun* = BLOOD GROUP.

blood vessel *noun* any of the tubes through which blood circulates in an animal; a vein, artery, or capillary.

bloodworm *noun* **1** any of several genera of reddish segmented worms often used as bait for fish: phylum Annelida. **2** the red aquatic larva of some midges: family Chironomidae.

bloody[1] *adj* (**bloodier, bloodiest**) **1** *informal* used as an intensifier *esp* to express annoyance. **2** smeared with, stained with, or containing blood: *Under the bludgeonings of chance my head is bloody, but unbowed* — W E Henley. **3** accompanied by or involving bloodshed. **4a** murderous or bloodthirsty. **b** merciless or cruel. ➤ **bloodily** *adv,* **bloodiness** *noun.*

Word history

Old English *blōdig,* from *blōd* BLOOD[1]. The use of *bloody* as an intensifier dates back to the 17th cent., but its original connotations are obscure. Since the two earliest uses are both of *bloody drunk,* it has been suggested that this meant 'as drunk as a blood' (sense 6 of blood). Alternatively, it may be that the early combinations *bloody drunk, bloody angry, bloody passionate* all indicate a state in which there may be literally a rush of blood to the face. The oaths *God's blood, sblood, blood* may also have contributed to the sense, but there is no evidence to support the popular belief that it is a corruption of the oath *by our Lady.*

bloody[2] *verb trans* (**bloodies, bloodied, bloodying**) to make (something) bloody.

bloody[3] *adv informal* used as an intensifier: *Not bloody likely!*

Bloody Mary *noun* (*pl* **Bloody Marys**) a cocktail consisting chiefly of vodka and tomato juice. [prob from *Bloody Mary,* nickname of Mary I of England d.1558; from its red colour]

bloody-minded *adj* deliberately obstructive or unhelpful. ➤ **bloody-mindedly** *adv,* **bloody-mindedness** *noun.*

bloom[1] /bloohm/ *noun* **1a** a flower. **b** the state of having flowers: *The roses are in bloom.* **2a** a time of beauty, freshness, and vigour: *the bloom of youth.* **b** a time or state of perfection; prime: *in full bloom.* **3** a rosy or healthy appearance, *esp* on the cheeks. **4** a delicate powdery coating on some fruits and leaves. **5a** cloudiness on a film of varnish or lacquer. **b** a mottled surface that appears on chocolate, often due to incorrect temperatures in manufacture or storage. **6** an excessive growth of algae, e.g. on a pond: *algal bloom.* ➤ **bloomy** *adj.* [Middle English *blome,* from Old Norse *blom;* related to Old English *blōwan* BLOW[4]]

bloom[2] *verb intrans* **1a** to produce or yield flowers. **b** to support abundant plant life: *They are setting out to make the desert bloom.* **2a** to flourish: *blooming with health.* **b** to reach maturity; to blossom: *Their friendship bloomed over the weeks.* **3** said of a body of water: to become densely populated with micro-organisms, *esp* plankton.

bloom[3] *noun* a thick bar of hammered or rolled iron or steel. [Old English *blōma*]

bloomer *noun* **1** *informal* a stupid or embarrassing blunder. **2** *chiefly Brit* a large longish glazed loaf baked at the bottom of the oven and marked with diagonal cuts across the top. **3** a plant or person that blooms, *esp* at a specified time: *She was very much a late bloomer.*

bloomers /ˈbloohməz/ *pl noun* **1** *informal* knickers. **2** a costume worn formerly by women and children, consisting of a short skirt and long loose trousers gathered closely about the ankles. **3a** full loose trousers gathered at the knee, formerly worn by women, *esp* for athletics. **b** an undergarment of similar design. [orig in sense 2: named after Amelia *Bloomer* d.1894, US feminist, who advocated similar dress]

blooming[1] *adj* **1** flourishing. **2** *chiefly Brit, euphem* used as a generalized intensifier, usu expressing annoyance: *You blooming idiot!* [(sense 2) prob euphemism for *bloody*]

blooming[2] *adv chiefly Brit, euphem* used as a generalized intensifier: *It was blooming marvellous!*

blooper /ˈbloohpə/ *noun NAmer, informal* an embarrassing public blunder. [*bloop* a grating or howling sound, of imitative origin]

blossom[1] /ˈblosəm/ *noun* **1** the flower of a plant, *esp* the flower that produces edible fruits. **2a** the mass of flowers on a single plant, *esp* a tree or shrub. **b** the state of having flowers: *in blossom.* **3** a high point or stage of development. ➤ **blossomy** *adj.* [Old English *blōstm;* related to Old English *blōwan* BLOW[4]]

blossom[2] *verb intrans* (**blossomed, blossoming**) **1** to bloom. **2** to come into one's own; to develop in a promising or satisfying way: *a blossoming talent.*

blot[1] /blot/ *noun* **1** a soiling or disfiguring mark; a spot, *esp* a spot of ink or other liquid. **2** a blemish. **3a** a cause for reproach; a fault or bad act. **b** a defect of character. [Middle English, probably of Scandinavian origin]

blot[2] *verb* (**blotted, blotting**) ➤ *verb trans* **1** to spot, stain, or spatter (something) with a discolouring substance. **2** to dry or remove (e.g. ink or spilt liquid) with an absorbing agent such as blotting paper. **3** to spoil (e.g. one's reputation) by committing an error or wrongdoing. ➤ *verb intrans* **1** to make a blot or blots. **2** to become marked with a blot or blots. ✳ **blot one's copybook** to mar one's previously good record or standing.

blotch[1] /bloch/ *noun* **1** an imperfection or blemish. **2** an irregular spot or mark, e.g. of colour or ink. ➤➤ **blotchily** *adv*, **blotchy** *adj*. [prob partly alteration (influenced by BLOT[1]) of *botch* swelling from Old French *boce* BOSS[4], and partly from Old French *bloche* clod of earth]

blotch[2] *verb trans* to make a blotch or blotches with (something). ➤ *verb intrans* to get blotches; to become blotchy: *You have to work very carefully as this paint blotches easily.*

blot out *verb trans* **1** to obscure or eclipse (something); to cover (it) over: *Clouds blotted out the sun.* **2** to shut out from one's consciousness (something unwanted, such as a painful memory). **3** to make one inclined to forgive or ignore (a wrongdoing): *This one good act blots out his many bad ones.* **4** to destroy (something) totally: *One such bomb can blot out a whole city.*

blotter /'blotə/ *noun* a piece of blotting paper.

blotting paper *noun* a spongy unsized paper used to absorb ink.

blotto /'blotoh/ *adj Brit, informal* extremely drunk. [prob from BLOT[2]]

blouse[1] /blowz/ *noun* **1** a usu loose-fitting woman's upper garment that resembles a shirt or smock and is waist-length or longer. **2** a battledress jacket. [French *blouse*]

blouse[2] *verb intrans* to fall in folds. ➤ *verb trans* to make (e.g. part of a piece of clothing) fall in folds.

blouson /'bloohzon/ *noun* a short loose jacket or blouse usu closely fitted at the waist. [French, from *blouse* BLOUSE[1]]

blow[1] /bloh/ *verb* (*past tense* **blew** /blooh/, *past part.* **blown** /blohn/) ➤ *verb intrans* **1** said of air, wind, etc: to move perceptibly or audibly: *The wind of change is blowing through this continent* — Harold Macmillan; *Dust storms had been blowing all night.* **2** to move or be carried by the wind: *Litter was blowing along the street.* **3** to send a current of air through the mouth or nose. **4a** to make a sound by means of air or other gas passing through: *They heard the whistle blow.* **b** said of a wind or brass instrument: to make a sound. **5** said of a whale: to expel air and moisture through its blowhole. **6** said of a tyre: to lose the air inside it through a spontaneous rupture of the casing. **7** said of an electric fuse or a valve: to melt or break when overloaded. **8** *informal* to explode or detonate. **9** *informal* to leave. **10** *chiefly NAmer, informal* to boast. ➤ *verb trans* **1a** to set (air or other gas or vapour) in motion. **b** (*often* + away/in/off) to act on (something) with, or as if with, a current of air or other gas or vapour: *The wind was blowing the curtains; They blew the dust off the shelves.* **2** to force air through (a musical instrument) to produce a sound. **3** to force a strong current of air through (the nose) to clear it of mucus. **4** to produce or shape (e.g. glass or bubbles) by the action of blown or injected air or other gas. **5** to burst or destroy (something) with explosives. **6** *informal* to lose (a chance of success, etc) by failing to use an opportunity. **7** *informal* to spend (money) extravagantly. **8** *informal* to disregard (a difficulty): *We're going on holiday, and blow the expense.* **9** *informal* to reveal (a secret or disguise): *The police operation came to a halt when their cover was blown.* **10** said of an insect: to deposit eggs or larvae on or in (e.g. meat). **11a** to make (a horse) out of breath with exertion. **b** to let (a horse) pause to catch its breath. **12** (*also* + out) to cause (a fuse or valve) to blow. **13** to rupture (something) by excessive pressure: *We've blown a gasket.* **14** *informal* to leave (a place) hurriedly. **15** to remove the liquid contents of (an egg) by blowing through it. ✳ **blow hot and cold** to vary unpredictably in one's support for something; to vacillate. **blow one's lid/stack** *NAmer, informal* to lose one's temper. **blow one's own trumpet** to praise oneself; to boast. **blow one's top** *informal* to lose one's temper. **blow somebody's mind 1** *informal* to amaze (somebody). **2** *informal* to cause (somebody) to hallucinate. **blow the gaff** *Brit, slang* to reveal a secret, *esp* something discreditable. **blow the whistle on somebody/something 1** *informal* to reveal (something secret, *esp* a wrongdoing). **2** *informal* to inform against (somebody). **I'll be blowed/I'm blowed** an expression of surprise or refusal. [Old English *blawan*]

blow[2] *noun* **1** a strong wind or windy storm. **2** an act or instance of blowing or being blown. **3** *informal* a walk or other outing in the fresh air.

blow[3] *noun* **1** a hard hit delivered with a part of the body, *esp* the hand or fist, or with a weapon, tool, or other object. **2** a shock or misfortune. **3** a forcible or sudden act or effort: *We shall strike a blow for freedom.* ✳ **at one blow** in a single action. **come to blows** to start fighting; to end up as a fight. [Middle English (northern) *blaw*; earlier history unknown]

blow[4] *verb trans* (*past tense* **blew** /blooh/, *past part.* **blown** /blohn/) to cause (e.g. flowers or blossom) to open out, usu just before dropping: *These roses are blown.* [Old English *blōwan*]

blow[5] *noun* = BLOOM[1] (1B): *The lilacs are in full blow.*

blow away *verb trans informal* **1** to kill (somebody) with a gun. **2** to defeat or beat (somebody) thoroughly. **3** to impress (somebody).

blowback *noun* **1** a flow of gases through a system in the opposite direction to the one normally taken. **2** the escape to the rear of gases formed while a weapon is being fired. **3** the action of a firearm in which expanding gases of the propellant push back the bolt and so reload the weapon.

blow-by-blow *adj* minutely detailed: *a blow-by-blow account.*

blow-dry[1] *verb trans* (**blow-dries, blow-dried, blow-drying**) to blow warm air over, through, or onto (e.g. the hair) until it is dry. ➤➤ **blow-drier** *noun*.

blow-dry[2] *noun* (*pl* **blow-dries**) an act of drying the hair, usu into a particular style, with a hairdrier: *a cut and blow-dry.*

blower *noun* **1** somebody or something that blows or is blown. **2** a device for producing a current of air or gas. **3** *Brit, informal* the telephone.

blowfish *noun* = GLOBEFISH.

blowfly *noun* (*pl* **blowflies**) any of various two-winged flies that deposit their eggs or maggots *esp* on meat or in wounds, *esp* a bluebottle: family Calliphoridae.

blowgun *noun* = BLOWPIPE (2).

blowhard[1] *noun* a braggart.

blowhard[2] *adj* boastful.

blowhole *noun* **1** a nostril in the top of the head of a whale, porpoise, or dolphin. **2** a hole in the ice to which aquatic mammals, e.g. seals, come to breathe. **3** an opening for letting out air or other gas. **4** a hole in rock or the ground through which air, gas, water etc is forced or released.

blow in *verb intrans* **1** *informal* to arrive casually or unexpectedly. **2** to break inwards because of an explosion. ➤ *verb trans* to make (e.g. a window) break inwards because of an explosion.

blow-in *noun Aus, NZ, informal* somebody who has recently or unexpectedly arrived.

blow-job *noun coarse slang* an act of FELLATIO.

blowlamp *noun* a small portable burner that produces an intense flame and has a pressurized fuel tank.

blown[1] /blohn/ *verb* past part. of BLOW[1], BLOW[4].

blown[2] *adj* **1** swollen. **2** = FLYBLOWN (1). [past part. of BLOW[1]]

blow off *verb intrans informal* **1** to lose one's temper suddenly. **2** to break wind noisily. ➤ *verb trans NAmer* to decline or withdraw from (a commitment).

blowout *noun* **1** *informal* a large meal or other lavish or extravagant entertainment. **2** a bursting of e.g. a tyre or anything else containing air or gas by pressure of the contents on a weak spot. **3** an uncontrolled eruption of an oil or gas well. **4** the melting of a fuse.

blow out *verb intrans* **1** to become extinguished by a breath or gust of air. **2** to break outwards because of an explosion. **3** said of an oil or gas well: to erupt out of control. ➤ *verb trans* **1** to extinguish (e.g. a flame) with the breath or a gust of air. **2** said of a storm: to dissipate (itself) by blowing. **3** to cause (e.g. a window) to break outwards because of an explosion.

blow over *verb intrans* **1** said of a storm: to pass by; to stop. **2** said of a difficulty: to pass by without lasting ill-effects; to be forgotten.

blowpipe *noun* **1** a small tube for blowing air, oxygen, etc into a flame to direct and increase the heat. **2** a tube for propelling a projectile, e.g. a dart, by blowing. **3** a long metal tube used by a glassblower, on which glass is shaped by blowing.

blowsy *or* **blowzy** /'blowzi/ *adj* (**blowsier** *or* **blowzier, blowsiest** *or* **blowziest**) **1** having a coarse ruddy complexion. **2** said *esp* of a woman: slovenly in appearance and usu fat. ⨠ **blowsily** *adv*, **blowsiness** *noun*. [English dialect *blowse, blowze* wench, slattern, of unknown origin]

blowtorch *noun* = BLOWLAMP.

blowup *or* **blow-up** *noun* **1** an explosion. **2** an outburst of temper. **3** a photographic enlargement.

blow up *verb trans* **1** to shatter or destroy (something) by an explosion. **2** to build up or exaggerate (something) to an unreasonable extent. **3** to inflate (something) with air or gas. **4** to make an enlargement of (a photograph). **5** *informal* to reprimand (somebody) angrily. ➤ *verb intrans* **1a** to explode. **b** to be disrupted or destroyed (e.g. by an explosion). **2** *informal* to become violently angry. **3a** to become filled with air or gas. **b** to become expanded to unreasonable proportions. **4a** said of a storm or wind: to start to develop or strengthen. **b** to arise or develop unexpectedly. ✳ **blow up in one's face** said of an action or plan: to fail disastrously with adverse effects for its originator.

blowy *adj* (**blowier, blowiest**) windy: *a blowy March day.*

blowzy /'blowzi/ *adj* see BLOWSY.

BLT *noun informal* a bacon, lettuce, and tomato sandwich.

blub /blub/ *verb* (**blubbed, blubbing**) *informal* = BLUBBER².

blubber¹ /'blubə/ *noun* **1** the fat of large marine mammals, *esp* whales. **2** *informal* body fat. ⨠ **blubbery** *adj*. [Middle English *bluber* bubble, foam, prob of imitative origin]

blubber² *verb* (**blubbered, blubbering**) ➤ *verb intrans informal* to weep noisily. ➤ *verb trans informal* to say (something) while weeping. [Middle English *blubren* to make a bubbling sound, from *bluber*: see BLUBBER¹]

bludge¹ /bluj/ *verb trans Aus, NZ, informal* to scrounge (something). ➤ *verb intrans Aus, NZ, informal* **1** to avoid a task, etc. **2** (+ on) to scrounge something from somebody. ⨠ **bludger** *noun*. [back-formation from slang *bludger* pimp]

bludge² *noun Aus, NZ, informal* **1** an easy task; a doddle. **2** a period of idleness.

bludgeon¹ /'blujən/ *noun* a short club used as a weapon. [perhaps modification of Old French *bougeon*, dimin. of *bouge, bolge* club]

bludgeon² *verb trans* **1** to hit or beat (somebody) with a bludgeon. **2** (*also* + into) to force or persuade (somebody) to do something by aggressive argument.

blue¹ /blooh/ *adj* **1** of the colour of a clear sky, between green and indigo in the spectrum. **2** discoloured through cold, anger, bruising, or fear. **3a** bluish grey: *a blue cat*. **b** having blue or patches of blue as a distinguishing feature: *a blue tit.* **4a** low in spirits. **b** depressing or dismal. **5a** obscene or pornographic: *a blue film.* **b** off-colour or risqué: *blue jokes.* **6** *Brit* supporting the Conservative Party. ✳ **once in a blue moon** very rarely. **until one is blue in the face** unsuccessfully for ever: *You can complain until you're blue in the face but no one will listen.* ⨠ **bluely** *adv*, **blueness** *noun*. [Middle English from Old French *blou*, of Germanic origin]

blue² *noun* **1** the colour of a clear sky, between green and indigo in the spectrum. **2a** a blue pigment or dye. **b** a blue preparation used to whiten clothes in laundering. **3a** a blue object: *He potted the blue but missed the pink.* **b** blue clothing: *dressed in blue.* **4** the sky. **5a** the far distance. **b** the sea. **6** any of numerous small chiefly blue butterflies. **7** (*often* **Blue**) an award given to somebody who has played in a sporting contest between Oxford and Cambridge universities, or somebody who has been given such an award. **8** *Brit* a supporter of the Conservative Party. **9** *Aus, NZ, informal* a quarrel or row. ✳ **out of the blue** without warning; unexpectedly: *She just turned up out of the blue expecting a meal.*

blue³ *verb* (**blues, blued, blueing** *or* **bluing**) ➤ *verb intrans* to turn blue. ➤ *verb trans* **1** to make (something) turn blue. **2** to whiten (laundry) with a blue substance.

blue⁴ *verb trans* (**blues, blued, blueing** *or* **bluing**) *Brit, informal* to spend (money) lavishly and wastefully. [prob from *blew*, past tense of BLOW¹]

blue baby *noun* a baby born with skin of a bluish tint, usu from a congenital heart defect.

bluebeard *noun* a man who marries and kills one wife after another.

Word history

Bluebeard, a folklore character. Bluebeard forbade his wives to look into a certain room, and killed them when they disobeyed. The room held the remains of his earlier wives.

bluebell *noun* **1** any of several species of plants of the lily family bearing blue bell-shaped flowers, *esp* the WILD HYACINTH: genus *Endymion* and other genera. **2** *chiefly Scot* = HAREBELL.

blueberry /'bloohb(ə)ri/ *noun* (*pl* **blueberries**) **1** an edible blue or blackish soft fruit. **2** any of several species of shrubs of the heath family that bear this fruit: genus *Vaccinium.*

bluebird *noun* any of three species of small N American songbird with blue plumage on their head, back, and tail: genus *Sialia.*

blue-black *adj* dark blue.

blue blood *noun* high or noble birth. ⨠ **blue-blooded** *adj*.

blue book *noun* an official parliamentary report or document. [from colour of cover]

bluebottle *noun* **1** a blowfly whose body is iridescent blue and which makes a loud buzzing noise in flight: *Calliphora vomitoria.* **2** = CORNFLOWER **3** *Brit, informal* a police officer. **4** *Aus, NZ, informal* = PORTUGUESE MAN-OF-WAR.

blue cheese *noun* cheese marked with veins of greenish blue mould.

blue chip *noun* a high-quality stock regarded as a very sound investment, usu one issued by a substantial well-established company that enjoys public confidence in its worth and stability. ⨠ **blue-chip** *adj*. [from high-valued gambling chips being blue]

blue-collar *adj* belonging or relating to the class of manual wage-earning employees whose duties often call for the wearing of work clothes or protective clothing: compare WHITE-COLLAR.

Blue Ensign *noun* a blue flag with the union jack in the top inner corner, flown chiefly by auxiliary vessels of the Royal Navy.

blue-eyed boy *noun often derog* a favourite: *Who's teacher's blue-eyed boy, then?*

bluefish *noun* (*pl* **bluefishes** *or collectively* **bluefish**) an active voracious blue-coloured fish that is found in all warm seas and is popular as a game fish: *Pomatomus saltatrix.*

Blue Flag *noun* a plain blue flag awarded to a coastal resort as a sign that its beaches reach the standard of cleanliness and safety prescribed by the European Union.

blue funk *noun* **1** *Brit, informal* a state of great fear or panic. **2** *NAmer, informal* a state of depression.

bluegrass *noun* **1** a type of country music played on unamplified stringed instruments. **2** any of several species of bluish green meadow grass used as fodder and for lawns both in North America and Europe: genus *Poa.* [(sense 1) from *Bluegrass* State, nickname of Kentucky, USA, where such music prob originated]

blue-green alga *noun* = CYANOBACTERIUM.

blue gum *noun* any of several species of Australian eucalyptuses grown for their wood: genus *Eucalyptus.*

blue heeler /'heelə/ *noun* a dog of an Australian breed with a blue-speckled coat mainly used for controlling cattle. [from the fact that the dog snaps at the heels of the animals to drive or control them]

blueish *adj* see BLUISH.

bluejacket *noun informal* a sailor in the navy.

blue jay *noun* a North American bird of the jay family with a blue back and crest: *Cyanocitta cristata.*

blue john *noun* a blue form of fluorite found only in Derbyshire, used *esp* for jewellery and ornaments. [from the name *John*]

blue law *noun NAmer* a law prohibiting certain types of activity on a Sunday, e.g. the sale of alcohol. [from the blue paper on which the puritanical laws of early New England states were printed]

blue mould *noun* any of several genera of fungi that form a bluish mildew on decaying food or other matter: genus *Penicillium* and other genera.

blue murder *noun informal* a scene of noisy commotion. ✳ **cry/scream/yell blue murder** *informal* to make a loud noise of fear, pain, etc.

blue note *noun* a flattened third or seventh note used *esp* in jazz and blues in a chord where a major unflattened interval would be expected.

blue-pencil *verb trans* to edit (a manuscript, film, etc), *esp* by altering or deleting parts considered indecent or otherwise unacceptable; to censor (it).

Blue Peter *noun* a blue signal flag with a white square in the centre, used to indicate that a merchant vessel is ready to sail. [from the name *Peter*]

blue pointer *noun chiefly Aus* = MAKO¹ (a type of shark).

blueprint¹ *noun* **1** a photographic print in white on a bright blue ground, used *esp* for copying maps and plans. **2** a detailed programme of action: *a blueprint for victory*.

blueprint² *verb trans* **1** to make a blueprint of (a plan, etc). **2** to plan out (a programme of action).

blue riband *noun* = BLUE RIBBON.

blue ribbon *noun* a ribbon of blue fabric worn as an honour or award, *esp* by members of the Order of the Garter.

blues *noun* (*pl* **blues**) **1** (**the blues**) (*treated as sing. or pl*) low spirits; melancholy. **2a** (*often* **the blues**) (*usu treated as sing.*) a melancholy style of music which originated among American blacks in the early 20th cent. and is characterized by usu twelve-bar three-line stanzas in which the words of the second line repeat those of the first and by blue notes (flattened thirds or sevenths; see BLUE NOTE) in melody and harmony: *Blues is easy to play, but hard to feel* — Jimi Hendrix. **b** a song or piece of music in this style. **c** (*used before a noun*) written or performing in the style of the blues: *a blues number*; *a blues band*.

Editorial note
Blues is a vocal music, developed by African-Americans in the early 20th cent. that has continuously evolved through many stages of both instrumental and vocal development while remaining essentially and recognizably the same; it also denotes a musical chorus structure of 12 bars, consistently repeated, although open to constant variation through improvisation — Richard Cook.

➤ **bluesy** *adj*.

blue shift *noun* a shift in the wavelengths of the light or other electromagnetic radiations emitted by a celestial body when seen from a distant point, e.g. the earth, from their normal positions in the spectrum towards shorter wavelengths. This is a consequence of the Doppler effect or of the gravity of the body: compare RED SHIFT.

blue-sky *adj* **1** having little or no real value: *blue-sky securities*. **2** having no specific practical application; pure or theoretical: *blue-sky research*.

bluestocking *noun derog* a woman with intellectual or literary interests.

Word history
Bluestocking Society, 18th-cent. literary club in London. Male members wore blue worsted stockings rather than formal black silk ones; women members became known as *bluestocking ladies*.

bluestone *noun* a bluish grey sandstone, used as a building material.

blue tit *noun* a widely distributed European tit that has a bright blue crown and a mostly yellow underside: *Parus caeruleus*.

blue vitriol *noun no longer in technical use* a hydrated copper sulphate.

blue whale *noun* a slate-blue-coloured whale, related to the rorquals, that is the largest living animal and is found *esp* in northern European waters: *Sibbaldus musculus*.

bluey /'blooh·i/ *noun* (*pl* **blueys**) *Aus* a bundle carried by a bushman; swag. [from the blue blanket commonly used to wrap the bundle]

bluff¹ /bluf/ *verb trans* **1** to deceive (somebody) by pretence or an outward appearance of strength, confidence, etc. **2** to deceive (an opponent) in cards by a bold bet on an inferior hand with the result that the opponent withdraws a winning hand. ➤ *verb intrans* to bluff somebody. ➤➤ **bluffer** *noun*. [prob from Dutch *bluffen* to boast]

bluff² *noun* an act or instance of bluffing. ✳ **call somebody's bluff** to challenge (somebody) to prove a claim one believes to be untrue.

bluff³ *adj* **1** good-naturedly frank and outspoken. **2** rising steeply with a broad, flat, or rounded front. ➤➤ **bluffly** *adv*, **bluffness** *noun*. [obsolete Dutch *blaf* flat]

bluff⁴ *noun* a high steep bank; a cliff.

bluish *or* **blueish** /'blooh·ish/ *adj* having a tinge of blue; rather blue. ➤➤ **bluishness** *noun*.

blunder¹ /'blundə/ *verb* (**blundered, blundering**) ➤ *verb intrans* **1** to move unsteadily or confusedly. **2** to make a blunder. ➤ *verb trans* to handle (something) badly; to mismanage (it). ➤➤ **blunderer** *noun*, **blunderingly** *adv*. [Middle English *blundren*, probably of Scandinavian origin]

blunder² *noun* a gross error or mistake resulting from stupidity, ignorance, or carelessness: *Youth is a blunder; manhood a struggle; old age a regret* — Disraeli.

blunderbuss /'blundəbus/ *noun* an obsolete short firearm with a large bore and usu a flaring muzzle. [by folk etymology from obsolete Dutch *donderbus*, from Dutch *donder* thunder + obsolete Dutch *bus* gun]

blunge /blunj/ *verb trans* to mix water and (clay or something similar) to form a paste for pottery. ➤➤ **blunger** *noun*. [blend of BLEND¹ and PLUNGE¹]

blunt¹ /blunt/ *adj* **1a** having an edge or point that is not sharp. **b** without an edge or point. **2a** aggressively outspoken. **b** direct or straightforward. **3** insensitive; dull. ➤➤ **bluntly** *adv*, **bluntness** *noun*. [Middle English, perhaps of Scandinavian origin]

blunt² *verb trans* **1** to make (a knife, etc) less sharp. **2** to make (something) less sharp or severe.

blur¹ /bluh/ *noun* **1** a smear or stain. **2** something vague or indistinct. ➤➤ **blurriness** *noun*, **blurry** *adj*. [perhaps related to Middle English *bleren*: see BLEAR¹]

blur² *verb* (**blurred, blurring**) ➤ *verb trans* **1** to obscure or blemish (something) by smearing. **2** to make (one's memory, perception, etc) indistinct or confused. ➤ *verb intrans* to become vague, indistinct, or confused. ➤➤ **blurringly** *adv*.

blurb /bluhb/ *noun* a short publicity notice, *esp* on a book cover. [coined by Gelett Burgess d.1951, US humorist]

blurt out /bluht/ *verb trans* to utter (something) abruptly and impulsively. [prob imitative]

blush¹ /blush/ *verb intrans* **1** to become red in the face, *esp* from shame, modesty, or embarrassment: *Man is the only animal that blushes. Or needs to* — Mark Twain. **2** to feel shame or embarrassment. ➤➤ **blushingly** *adv*. [Old English *blyscan* to redden, from *blȳsa* flame]

blush² *noun* **1** a reddening of the face, *esp* from shame, confusion, or embarrassment. **2** a red or rosy tint. ✳ **at first blush** when first seen; as a first impression. **spare somebody's blushes** to avoid or refrain from embarrassing (somebody), *esp* by not praising them publicly. ➤➤ **blushful** *adj*.

blusher *noun* a cream or powder for adding colour to the cheeks.

bluster¹ /'blustə/ *verb intrans* (**blustered, blustering**) **1** to talk or act in a noisily self-assertive or boastful manner. **2** to blow in stormy gusts. ➤➤ **blusterer** *noun*, **blusteringly** *adv*. [Middle English *blustren*, prob from early Low German *blüsteren*]

bluster² *noun* **1** loudly boastful or empty threatening talk. **2** a violent blowing; a strong wind. ➤➤ **blusterous** *adj*, **blustery** *adj*.

blvd *abbr* in street names, boulevard.

BM *abbr* **1** Bachelor of Medicine. **2** British Medal. **3** British Museum.

BMA *abbr* British Medical Association.

BMC *abbr* British Medical Council.

BMJ *abbr* British Medical Journal.

B-movie *noun* a film shown, *esp* formerly, as a supporting item in a cinema programme, usu made with a relatively low budget and often with a lower standard of story line and acting than the main film.

BMus *abbr* Bachelor of Music.

BMX *noun* **1** the sport of cross-country or stunt riding on a specially designed bicycle. **2** a bicycle with a strong frame and small wheels designed for use in BMX. [the initials of BICYCLE¹ and MOTOCROSS + X, symbol for *cross*]

Bn *abbr* **1** Baron. **2** Battalion.

bn *abbr* billion.

BO /,bee 'oh/ *noun* a disagreeable smell, *esp* of stale perspiration, given off by a person's body. [short for *body odour*]

bo /boh/ *interj* = BOO¹.

boa /'boh·ə/ *noun* **1** any of several species of large snakes, e.g. the boa constrictor, anaconda, or python, that crushes its prey: family Boidae. **2** a long fluffy scarf of fur, feathers, or delicate fabric. [Latin *boa*, a water snake]

boa constrictor *noun* a tropical American boa that reaches a length of 3m (about 10ft) or more: *Boa constrictor*.

boar /baw/ *noun* **1a** an uncastrated male pig. **b** the male of any of several mammals, e.g. a guinea pig or badger. **2** the Old World wild pig from which most domestic pigs derive; = WILD BOAR: *Sus scrofa*. ⯈ **boarish** *adj*. [Old English *bār*]

board[1] /bawd/ *noun* **1a** a usu long thin narrow piece of sawn timber. **b** (**the boards**) the stage. **2a** a flat usu rectangular piece of material designed or marked for a special purpose, e.g. for playing chess, ludo, backgammon, etc or for use as a blackboard or notice-board. **b** any similar object with a flat surface: *an ironing board; a surfboard*. **3a** (*treated as sing. or pl*) a group of people having managerial, supervisory, or investigatory powers: *board of directors; board of examiners*. **b** an official body: *the gas board*. **4a** any of various wood pulps or composition materials formed into stiff flat rectangular sheets. **b** – CARDBOARD[1]. **5a** daily meals, *esp* when provided in return for payment: *board and lodgings*. **b** *archaic* a table spread with a meal. **b** the side of a ship. **b** the distance that a sailing vessel makes on one tack. ✳ **go by the board** to be neglected; to go out of use [orig of a ship's mast, meaning 'to be broken and swept overboard']. **on board** aboard. **take something on board** *Brit, informal* to apprehend, grasp, accept, or take account of (an idea, etc). ⯈ **boardlike** *adj*. [Old English *bord* piece of sawn lumber, border, ship's side]

board[2] *verb trans* **1** to go aboard (e.g. a ship, train, aircraft, or bus). **2** to come up against or alongside (a ship), usu in order to attack it. **3** (+ over/up) to cover with boards: *We'll need to board up that broken window.* **4** to provide with regular meals and usu lodging for a fixed price. ⯈ *verb intrans* to take one's meals, usu as a paying customer.

boarder *noun* **1** a lodger. **2** a resident pupil at a boarding school. **3** somebody who boards a ship, *esp* in an attack: *Stand by to repel boarders*.

board game *noun* any game that is played by moving pieces on a specially patterned board, e.g. chess, draughts, or snakes and ladders.

boarding card *noun* = BOARDING PASS.

boarding house *noun* a lodging house that supplies meals: *Any two meals at a boarding house are together less than two square meals* — Stephen Leacock.

boarding pass *noun* a document given to a passenger, usu in exchange for a ticket, that enables him or her to board an aircraft or ship.

boarding school *noun* a school at which meals and lodging are provided.

board out *verb trans* to arrange for (somebody or an animal) to receive regular board and usu lodging away from home: *They boarded the cat out while they were on holiday.*

boardroom *noun* a room in which the meetings of a board of directors are held.

boardsailing *noun* = WIND-SURFING.

boardwalk *noun NAmer* a walk often constructed of planking, usu beside the sea.

boart /'boh·ət, bawt/ *noun* see BORT.

boast[1] /bohst/ *noun* **1** an act of boasting. **2** a cause for pride. ⯈ **boastful** *adj*, **boastfully** *adv*, **boastfulness** *noun*. [Middle English *boost*; earlier history unknown]

boast[2] *verb intrans* (*often* + of/about) to praise oneself; to talk with excessive pride about one's abilities, achievements, etc. ⯈ *verb trans* **1** to speak of or assert (something) with excessive pride. **2** to have or display (something that is considered notable or a source of pride): *The library boasts a copy of the First Folio*. ⯈ **boaster** *noun*, **boasting** *noun*, **boastingly** *adv*.

boast[3] *noun* a usu defensive shot in squash made from a rear corner of the court and hitting a side wall before the front wall. [prob from French *bosse* protuberance, place where the ball hits the wall]

boat[1] /boht/ *noun* **1** a small open vessel or craft for travelling across water. **2** a usu small ship: *She left England on the Calais boat*. **3** a boat-shaped utensil or dish: *a gravy boat*. ✳ **in the same boat** in the same situation or predicament. [Old English *bāt*]

boat[2] *verb intrans* to use a boat, *esp* for recreation.

boatbill *noun* a small heron, native to Central and South America, with a broad flattened bill and a black crest: *Cochlearius cochlearius*.

boat deck *noun* the deck of a ship on which its lifeboats are carried.

boatel *or* **botel** /boh'tel/ *noun* a waterside hotel with berths to accommodate people travelling by boat. [blend of BOAT[1] and HOTEL]

boater /'bohtə/ *noun* a stiff straw hat with a shallow flat crown and a brim. [orig worn while boating]

boathook *noun* a pole with a hook at one end, used *esp* for fending off or holding boats alongside.

boathouse /'boht·hows/ *noun* a shed for boats.

boatie /'bohti/ *noun Aus, NZ* a person who enjoys going boating.

boating *noun* the recreative activity of rowing and sailing in boats.

boatload *noun* the quantity of cargo or passengers that a boat is carrying or can carry: *That boatload of people founded Dawson City* — Willa Cather.

boatman *noun* (*pl* **boatmen**) a person who works with, looks after, or hires out boats, *esp* pleasure boats. ⯈ **boatmanship** *noun*, **boatsmanship** *noun*.

boat people *pl noun* refugees, *esp* from Vietnam, who set sail in boats to find a country that is willing to admit them.

boat race *noun* **1** a race between rowing crews. **2** (**the Boat Race**) the annual race between the rowing eights of Oxford and Cambridge Universities, held on the River Thames between Putney and Mortlake in London.

boatswain *or* **bosun** *or* **bo's'n** /'bohs(ə)n/ *noun* a petty officer on a merchant vessel or warrant officer in the navy who supervises all work done on deck and is responsible *esp* for routine maintenance of the ship's structure. [Middle English *bootswein*, from *boot* BOAT[1] + *swein* boy, servant, SWAIN]

boatswain's chair *noun* a support suspended by ropes and pulleys and used for work high on the side of a ship, tall building, etc.

boat train *noun* an express train that takes people to or from a ship.

bob[1] /bob/ *verb* (**bobbed, bobbing**) ⯈ *verb intrans* **1** to move down and up briefly or repeatedly: *His eyes fixed on a cork that bobbed aimlessly on the water* — Kate Chopin. **2** to curtsy briefly. **3** (+ for) to try to seize a suspended or floating apple, etc with the teeth: *bobbing for apples at Halloween*. ⯈ *verb trans* to move (one's head, etc) up and down in a short quick movement. [Middle English *boben* to strike, move with a jerk, prob of imitative origin]

bob[2] *noun* **1** a short quick down-and-up motion. **2** a change of order in bell-ringing.

bob[3] *noun* **1** a short straight hairstyle for women, with the hair cut evenly at about chin level, so that it swings loosely. **2** = FLOAT[1] (1A). **3** a hanging ball or weight on a plumb line or kite's tail. **4** a knot or twist, e.g. of ribbons or hair. **5** *Scot* a nosegay. [Middle English *bobbe* bunch, cluster; earlier history unknown]

bob[4] *verb trans* (**bobbed, bobbing**) **1** to cut (something) shorter; *esp* to crop (a horse's tail). **2** to cut (hair) in a bob.

bob[5] *noun* (*pl* **bob**) *Brit, informal* a shilling. [perhaps from *Bob*, nickname for *Robert*]

bobbejaan /'bobəjahn, -yahn/ *noun SAfr* **1** a baboon. **2** a monkey wrench. [Afrikaans *bobbejaan* from early Dutch *babiaen* baboon]

bobber /'bobə/ *noun* a person who rides a bobsleigh.

bobbin /'bobin/ *noun* **1** a cylinder or spindle on which yarn or thread is wound, for use in sewing, spinning, or lacemaking. **2** a coil of insulated wire or the reel it is wound on. [French *bobine*]

bobbinet /bobi'net/ *noun* a machine-made net of cotton, silk, or nylon, imitating bobbin lace, usu with a six-sided mesh. [blend of BOBBIN and NET[1]]

bobbin lace *noun* = PILLOW LACE.

bobble[1] /'bobl/ *verb intrans* to move jerkily down and up briefly or repeatedly. ⯈ *verb trans NAmer* to fumble (a ball), e.g. in baseball. [frequentative of BOB[1]]

bobble[2] *noun* **1** a small fluffy ball, e.g. of wool, used for ornament or trimming: *curtains with plush bobbles* — H E Bates. **2** a rounded bump or lump on a surface. **3** *NAmer* a fumble in handling the ball, e.g. in baseball. **4** a bobbling movement.

bobble hat *noun* a woollen pull-on hat with a bobble fixed to the crown.

bobby /'bobi/ *noun* (*pl* **bobbies**) *Brit, informal, dated* a police officer. [*Bobby*, nickname for *Robert*, named after Sir *Robert* Peel, d.1850, English statesman, who organized the London police force]

bobby calf *noun* an unweaned calf slaughtered for veal. [prob from *Bob*, nickname for *Robert*]

bobby dazzler /'dazlə/ *noun Brit, dated, informal* something or somebody rather striking or impressive: *She had got a new cotton blouse on. 'Oh, my stars!' he exclaimed. 'What a bobby dazzler!'* — D H Lawrence. [northern English dialect; origin of *bobby* unknown]

bobby pin *noun NAmer, Aus, NZ* = HAIRGRIP. [from BOB³, because used on bobbed hair]

bobby socks *pl noun NAmer* ankle socks of a kind worn by schoolgirls in the 1940s and '50s. [from BOB⁴ in the sense 'to cut short', by association with BOBBY PIN]

bobby-soxer /'bobi soksə/ *noun NAmer, informal, dated* an adolescent girl.

bobcat /'bobkat/ *noun* a common N American lynx with reddish fur and dark spots: *Felis rufus*. [BOB³; from its stubby tail]

bobolink /'bobəlingk/ *noun* a N American songbird that migrates in the autumn, noted for its bubbling call: *Dolichonyx oryzivorus*. [from the sound of its call]

bobotie /bə'boohti/ *noun* a S African baked dish of curried minced meat with a savoury custard topping. [Afrikaans *bobotie*, prob from Malay *burbur* pulp, soup]

bobsled /'bobsled/ *noun NAmer* = BOBSLEIGH. ⟫⟫ **bobsledding** *noun.*

bobsleigh /'bobslay/ *noun* **1** *chiefly Brit* a large sledge for two or four people, with mechanisms for steering and braking, used for racing down an embanked ice-covered slope, as a winter-sports event. **2** either of a pair of short sledges joined by a coupling. ⟫⟫ **bobsleighing** *noun.* [perhaps from BOB³]

bobstay /'bobstay/ *noun* a chain, wire, or rod running from the end of the BOWSPRIT (spar projecting from the bow of a vessel) to the front edge of the bow so as to counteract the upward pull of the FORESTAY (rope running from the foremast to the deck). [prob from BOB²]

bobtail /'bobtayl/ *noun* a horse or dog with a bobbed tail. ⟫⟫ **bobtail** *adj,* **bobtailed** *adj.* [BOB³]

bob up *verb intrans* to emerge, arise, or appear suddenly or unexpectedly.

BOC *abbr* British Oxygen Company.

bocage /bə'kahzh/ *noun* in ceramic work, the representation in relief of plants, leaves, and flowers, e.g. in the modelling of figurines. [French *bocage* copse, via Old French *boscage* from late Latin *boscaticum* thicket, from *boscus* bush]

Boche /bosh/ *noun* (**the Boche**) *informal, dated* Germans, *esp* German soldiers. [French *boche* (slang) rascal, German, prob short for *alboche*, alteration of *allemand* German]

bock /bok/ *noun* a strong dark German beer. [German *Bock* short for *Bockbier*, by shortening and alteration from *Einbecker Bier* beer from *Einbeck*, town in Germany]

BOD *abbr* biochemical oxygen demand.

bod /bod/ *noun informal* **1** a person's body. **2** *chiefly Brit* a person: *an odd bod.* [short for BODY]

bodacious /boh'dayshəs/ *adj NAmer, informal* outstanding or impressive. [blend of BOLD¹ and AUDACIOUS]

bode /bohd/ *verb trans* to presage or foreshadow (*esp* evil or misfortune): *This bodes some strange eruption to our state* — Shakespeare. ✲ **bode ill/well for** to be a bad or good sign for (the future, or some future plan). ⟫⟫ **bodement** *noun.* [Old English *bodian*]

bodega /boh'deega, boh'dayga/ *noun* **1** a storehouse for wine. **2** a shop that sells wine. [Spanish *bodega*, from Latin *apotheca*: see APOTHECARY. Compare BOUTIQUE]

Bode's law /bohdz/ *noun* a simple numerical relation that describes the approximate distances from the sun of the seven inner planets. The formula is $(x + 4) \div 10 =$ distance in astronomical units, where x is 0 for Mercury, 3 for Venus, 6 for earth, 12 for Mars, and so on. [named after Johann *Bode*, d.1826, German astronomer,

who publicized the law. It was discovered by another German astronomer Johann Daniel Titius, d.1796]

bodge /boj/ *verb trans Brit, informal* to make or repair (something) clumsily; to botch (a piece of work). [alteration of BOTCH¹]

bodgie /'boji/ *noun Aus* = TEDDY BOY. [perhaps from Aus *bodger* worthless, from BODGE]

bodhisattva /bodi'sahtvə/ *noun* in Buddhism, a being that has attained perfect enlightenment but compassionately refrains from entering nirvana in order to save others.

Editorial note

Traditionally read as 'one who aspires to enlightenment', a bodhisattva is someone who has set out on a path of many lifetimes in order to become a buddha and liberate all beings from suffering. The bodhisattva doctrine is important in all forms of Buddhism, but receives special emphasis in the Mahayana, where the bodhisattva becomes a figure for both emulation and devotion — Professor Donald Lopez.

[Sanskrit *bodhisattva* a being whose essence is enlightenment, from *bodhi* enlightenment + *sattva* being]

bodhran /'bowrahn, bow'rahn/ *noun* a small Irish drum held in one hand and beaten with a short two-headed stick. [Irish *bodhrán* winnowing drum]

bodice /'bodis/ *noun* **1** the upper part of a woman's dress, from neck to waist, *esp* if close-fitting and constructed as a separate piece from the skirt. **2** *formerly,* a woman's corset-like garment, laced at the front, worn over a blouse or as an undergarment. [alteration of *bodies,* pl of BODY]

bodice-ripper *noun informal, humorous* a romantic novel or film with a high content of excitement, sex, and violence, typically in a historical setting.

bodied *adj* (*used in combinations*) having body, or a body, of the kind specified: *a full-bodied wine; a strong-bodied athlete.*

bodiless /'bodilis/ *adj* **1** lacking a body, or lacking body. **2** incorporeal; insubstantial.

bodily¹ /'bodili/ *adj* **1** relating to or belonging to the body: *bodily needs; bodily functions.* **2** physical or actual, as distinct from spiritual: *in bodily form.*

bodily² *adv* **1** involving the whole body: *He flung himself bodily at his assailant.* **2** in bodily form; in the flesh.

bodkin /'bodkin/ *noun* **1** a blunt thick needle with a large eye used to draw tape or ribbon through a loop or hem. **2** *formerly,* a long ornamental hairpin. **3** a small sharp slender instrument for making holes in cloth. **4** *archaic* a dagger: *when he himself might his quietus make with a bare bodkin* — Shakespeare. [Middle English *boidekyn,* of uncertain origin]

body /'bodi/ *noun* (*pl* **bodies**) **1** the physical structure, made up of bones, flesh and organs, that constitutes a person or animal. **2** a corpse. **3** *informal, dated* a human being; a person. **4** the main part of a human or animal body; the trunk as distinct from the head and limbs. **5a** the part of a garment covering the body or trunk. **b** a woman's garment for the trunk, usu of opaque stretchy material, fastening between the legs. **6** the main, central, or principal part, e.g.:. **a** the nave of a church. **b** the part of a vehicle on or in which the load is placed. **7a** the main or central part of printed or written matter, as distinct from preliminary material or index: *Abbreviations are listed in the body of the dictionary.* **b** the sound box or pipe of a musical instrument. **8** a mass or expanse, *esp* of water. **9** any of the objects in the heavens, that is, the sun, moon, or stars; formerly, any of the seven planets known before the 18th cent.: *the sun and other heavenly bodies.* **10** a material object: *a foreign body.* **11** (*treated as sing. or pl*) a group of people or things, e.g.: **a** a fighting unit: *an armed body of men.* **b** a group of individuals organized for some purpose: *a legislative body.* **12a** compactness or firmness of texture. **b** fullness, e.g. of hair: *a shampoo that gives your hair body.* **c** comparative richness of flavour in wine. ✲ **in a body** in a solid group: *We went in a body to complain to the manager.* **keep body and soul together** to stay alive: *She hardly ate enough to keep body and soul together.* **over my dead body** *informal* not if I can help it: *'I hear he's selling the house' – 'Over my dead body!'* [from Old English *bodig*]

body armour *noun* protective clothing worn on the upper body by the army or the police.

body art *noun* decoration of the body by tattooing and body piercing.

body bag *noun* a bag in which a dead body, e.g. that of a soldier killed in action, is placed for transportation.

body blow *noun* **1** a hard punch on the body. **2** a serious setback.

bodyboard[1] *noun* a type of short surfboard on which the surfer lies prone with the upper part of the body on the board.

bodyboard[2] *verb intrans* to surf on a bodyboard, often using flippers. ≫ **bodyboarder** *noun*, **bodyboarding** *noun*.

body-building *noun* the practice of strengthening the body and developing a conspicuously muscular physique through weight-lifting and diet. ≫ **body-builder** *noun*.

body check *noun* the legal obstruction of an opposing player with the body, e.g. in ice hockey or lacrosse.

body-check *verb trans and intrans* in ice hockey, etc, to obstruct (an opposing player) with the body.

body clock *noun* = BIOLOGICAL CLOCK.

body colour *noun* opaque pigment used in watercolour painting, giving the work a chalky appearance; gouache.

body corporate *noun formal* = CORPORATION (1).

body double *noun* a person whose body substitutes for a film actor, *esp* during stunt scenes.

body forth *verb trans* (**bodies forth, bodied forth, bodying forth**) to give substance to (an idea etc): *as imagination bodies forth the forms of things unknown* — Shakespeare.

bodyguard *noun* an escort whose duty is to protect a person from bodily harm.

body image *noun* a person's concept of their own physical appearance: *a young woman with a poor body image*.

body language *noun* the expressing of feelings, *esp* unconsciously, by looks, movement, and posture.

bodyline bowling /-lien/ *noun* in cricket, intimidatory fast bowling aimed persistently at the batsman's body and directed *esp* towards the leg side.

body louse *noun* a sucking louse that feeds on the body and lives in clothing.

body odour *noun* an unpleasant smell, typically of sweat, given off by a human body.

body piercing *noun* the practice of piercing holes for the insertion of decorative studs, etc in parts of the body other than the ear lobes.

body politic *noun* (**the body politic**) a group of people under a single government.

body-popping *noun* a solo dance form of the 1980s typified by jerky robot-like movements. ≫ **body-popper** *noun*.

body-scanner *noun* a machine that rotates round the body taking cross-sectional X-ray photographs of it that can be used to aid medical diagnosis.

body search *noun* an act, e.g. by airport security staff, of running the hands over a person's body to check for concealed articles such as drugs or weapons.

body-search *verb trans* to carry out a body search on (somebody).

body shop *noun* a workshop where repairs are made to the bodywork of vehicles.

body-snatcher *noun* formerly, a person who dug up corpses illegally for dissection in medical schools, etc.

body stocking *noun* a very light one-piece garment covering the trunk, typically of translucent flesh-coloured nylon jersey, with or without sleeves or legs, worn *esp* by dancers.

body suit *noun* **1** = BODY (5B). **2** a one-piece undergarment for babies, fastening between the legs.

bodysurf /-suhf/ *verb intrans* to surf without a surfboard by planing on the chest and stomach. ≫ **bodysurfer** *noun*.

body swerve *noun* in sport, etc, a swerving action of the whole body to avoid a tackle or collision. ✳ **give something/somebody a body swerve** *Scot* to take steps to avoid (something or somebody).

body-warmer *noun* a padded and usu quilted sleeveless waist-length jerkin.

body wave *noun* in hairdressing, a light permanent wave designed to give the hair body or fullness.

body weight *noun* the weight of one's body.

bodywork *noun* **1** the structure or form of a vehicle body. **2** techniques such as massage, t'ai chi, and yoga that act therapeutically

by releasing tension, balancing energies in the body, and integrating body, mind, and spirit.

body wrap *noun* a kind of beauty therapy for reducing body measurements by wrapping the body in hot bandages.

Boeotian /bi'ohsh(ə)n/ *noun* a dull boorish person. ≫ **Boeotian** *adj*. [named after *Boeotia*, a district of ancient Greece unfairly proverbial for the stupidity of its inhabitants]

Boer /'bawə, 'boh·ə/ *noun* a S African of Dutch descent. ≫ **Boer** *adj*. [Dutch *boer* farmer]

boerbull *or* **boerbul** /'booəbool/ *noun* a breed of mastiff common in S Africa. [Afrikaans *boerboel*, from *boer* country- or Afrikaner-style + Dutch *bulhond* mastiff]

boeremusiek /'boohrəmoosik/ *noun SAfr* the traditional country music of the Afrikaners. [Afrikaans *boeremusiek*, from *boere* country- or Afrikaner-style + *musiek* music]

boerewors /'boohrəvaws/ *noun SAfr* a heavily spiced sausage, usu made from a mixture of beef and pork. [Afrikaans *boerewors*, from *boere* country- or Afrikaner-style + *wors* sausage]

BOF *abbr* in computing, beginning of file.

boffin /'bofin/ *noun chiefly Brit, informal* a scientific expert; *esp* one involved in technological research. [World War II vocabulary, of uncertain origin]

boffo /'bofoh/ *adj NAmer, informal* used mostly in show-business contexts: highly successful: *Batman and Indiana Jones are smash-hit boffo biz movies* — New Statesman & Society. [prob from BOX OFFICE]

Bofors gun /'bohfəz/ *noun* a light automatic anti-aircraft gun. [*Bofors*, munition works in Sweden, where it was first made]

bog /bog/ *noun* **1** wet spongy poorly-drained ground, or an area of this. **2** *Brit, informal* = TOILET (1). ≫ **bogginess** *noun*, **boggy** *adj*. [of Celtic origin; related to Old Irish *bocc* soft; (sense 2) short for *bog-house*]

bogan /'bohgən/ *noun Can* a slow-moving side stream; a backwater. [prob alteration of Algonquian *pokelogan* backwater]

bog asphodel /'asfədel/ *noun* a yellow-flowered bog plant of the lily family: *Narthecium ossifragum*.

bogbean *noun* a bog plant with pink or white hairy flowers and three-lobed leaves: *Menyanthes trifoliata*. Also called BUCKBEAN.

bog cotton *noun* = COTTON GRASS.

bog down *verb trans* (**bogged down, bogging down**) (*usu in passive*) **1** to cause (a vehicle) to sink into mud or a bog, so that it can progress no further. **2** to cause (a person or project) to get stuck and fail to progress.

bogey *or* **bogy** /'bohgi/ *noun* (*pl* **bogeys** *or* **bogies**) **1** a golf score of one stroke over par on a hole. **2** a spectre; a ghost. **3** a source of recurring fear, perplexity, or harassment; = BUGBEAR (1). **4** *Brit, informal* a piece of dried nasal mucus. [prob alteration of BOGLE]

bogeyman *or* **bogyman** /'bohgiman/ *noun* (*pl* **bogeymen** *or* **bogymen**) a monstrous figure invented to threaten children with, so as to frighten them into obedience.

boggle /'bogl/ *verb intrans informal* (+ at) to hesitate to do something because of doubt, fear, or scruples: *Most sensible folk would boggle at paying that price.* ✳ **the mind boggles** used in mock bewilderment or ironic speculation: goodness knows; I haven't a clue: *'What do you suppose they're up to?' 'The mind boggles'.* [perhaps from BOGLE]

bogie *or* **bogy** /'bohgi/ *noun* (*pl* **bogies**) *chiefly Brit* **1** a swivelling framework with one or more pairs of wheels and springs to carry and guide one end of a railway vehicle. **2** a low four-wheeled truck. [origin unknown]

bogle /'bohgl/ *noun* **1** a goblin or spectre. **2** *Scot, N Eng* a scarecrow. [orig Scots and northern dialect, of uncertain derivation]

bog moss *noun* = SPHAGNUM.

bog myrtle *noun* a densely branched shrub that grows in boggy land and has aromatic leaves: *Myrica gale*.

bog oak *noun* an ancient oak preserved in a hardened and blackened state in peat.

bog off *verb intrans* (**bogged off, bogging off**) *Brit, informal* used as an interjection: to go away; = PISS OFF.

bogong /'bohgong/ *or* **bugong** /'boohgong/ *noun* a large brown moth of S Australia, eaten in former times by the Aboriginals: *Agrotis infusa*. [Ngayawong (an Aboriginal language) *bogong*]

bogroll /'bogrohl/ *noun Brit, informal* a roll of toilet paper.

bog-standard *adj informal, derog* of the ordinary or regular standard, without refinements: *bog-standard accommodation.*

bogtrotter /'bogtrotə/ *noun informal, offensive* an Irish person.

bogus /'bohgəs/ *adj* spurious, sham: *a bogus offer.* ➤➤ **bogusly** *adv,* **bogusness** *noun.* [*bogus* a machine for making counterfeit money, of unknown origin]

bogy /'bohgi/ *noun* see BOGEY, BOGIE.

bogyman /'bohgimən/ *noun* see BOGEYMAN.

bohea /boh'hee/ *noun* a black tea. [Chinese (Pekingese) *Wuyi,* named after the hills in China where it was grown]

Bohemian[1] /boh'heemi·ən/ *noun* **1a** a native or inhabitant of Bohemia. **b** the group of Czech dialects spoken in Bohemia. **2** (*often* **bohemian**) a person, typically a writer or artist, living an unconventional life. ➤➤ **Bohemianism** *noun.* [*Bohemia,* region (former kingdom) now forming part of the Czech Republic; (sense 2) from French *bohémien* gypsy, gypsies being thought to come from, or via, Bohemia]

Bohemian[2] *adj* **1** relating to or belonging to the people, dialects, or culture of Bohemia. **2** (*often* **bohemian**) unconventional or dissolute in lifestyle or eccentric, *esp* consciously artistic, in dress: *Painting wasn't a serious profession; it was Bohemian, disreputable, immoral.* — Somerset Maugham.

boho /'boh·hoh/ *adj informal* = BOHEMIAN[2] (2).

bohrium /'bohri·əm/ *noun* a radioactive metallic chemical element artificially produced by atomic collisions at high energy: symbol Bh, atomic number 107. [named after Niels *Bohr,* d.1962, Danish physicist]

Bohr theory /'boh·ə/ *noun* a theory in physics: an electron orbiting an atomic nucleus can exist in only a limited number of energy states. [named after Niels *Bohr,* d.1962, Danish physicist]

boil[1] /boyl/ *verb intrans* **1a** said of a fluid: to reach a temperature, when heated, at which it bubbles and changes into vapour. **b** said of a vessel: to contain a fluid that is boiling: *The kettle's boiling.* **2** said of disturbed water: to bubble or foam violently; to churn. **3** to become furious: *I was boiling with rage.* **4** to undergo the action of a boiling liquid: *The eggs should boil for at least four minutes.* ➤ *verb trans* **1** to subject (food, etc) to the action of a boiling liquid: *I'll boil some eggs.* **2** to heat (a kettle, etc) till its contents boil. [Middle English *boilen* via Old French *boillir* from Latin *bullire* to bubble, from *bulla* bubble]

boil[2] *noun* (**the boil**) the act or state of boiling; = BOILING POINT: *Bring the contents to the boil.*

boil[3] *noun* a localized pus-filled swelling of the skin resulting from infection of a hair follicle. [alteration of Middle English *bile,* from Old English *bȳl*]

boil away *verb intrans* said of a fluid that is being boiled: to turn into vapour; to evaporate. ➤ *verb trans* to boil (a fluid) till it evaporates.

boil down *verb trans* **1** to reduce (a fluid) in bulk by boiling. **2** to condense or summarize (a text). ➤ *verb intrans* (+ to) to amount in essence to a certain thing: *The evidence boils down to you-did-I-didn't* — Harper Lee.

boiled shirt *noun dated* a shirt for wear with formal evening dress, etc, with a starched front.

boiled sweet *noun Brit* a sweet of boiled sugar, usu fruit-flavoured.

boiler *noun* **1** a tank in which water is heated or domestic hot water is stored. **2** the part of a steam generator in which water is converted into steam under pressure. **3** a vessel used for boiling. **4** *Brit, informal* a chicken suitable for boiling rather than roasting.

boilermaker *noun* **1** an industrial metalworker, *esp* a plater or welder. **2** *NAmer* a drink of whisky followed by a glass of beer.

boilerplate /-playt/ *noun* **1** rolled steel plate used *esp* in the construction of boilers. **2** *chiefly NAmer.* **a** journalistic material syndicated to various newspapers, formerly distributed as stereotype plates. **b** speech or writing that merely repeats or rehashes doctrine, etc uncritically. **c** fixed strings of wording for use *esp* in word-processing documents, e.g. clauses in legal contracts: *The rest of the will was boilerplate* — Ed McBain. **3** in rock climbing, a series of overlapping undercut slabs of rock.

boiler room *noun* **1** a room or compartment, e.g. on board ship, that houses a boiler. **2** *chiefly NAmer* (*used before a noun*) of or relating to an organization that tries to sell shares, land, or commodities of dubious value by telephone using high-pressure sales techniques, or the premises used for this purpose: *a boiler-room sales pitch.*

boiler suit *noun chiefly Brit* a one-piece work garment combining shirt and trousers, worn over clothing to protect it; = OVERALL[2].

boiling[1] *adj* **1** *informal* very hot: *The weather was boiling.* **2** suitable for boiling: *a boiling fowl.*

boiling[2] *adv* used as an intensifier: *boiling hot; boiling mad.*

boiling point *noun* **1** the temperature at which a liquid boils. **2** the point at which people lose emotional self-control and become violent or lose their tempers.

boiling-water reactor *noun* a nuclear reactor in which water is used as a coolant and as the force to drive the turbines as it evaporates into steam.

boil over *verb intrans* **1** said of milk or other fluid: to overflow while boiling. **2** to become so angry that one loses one's temper. **3** said of tempers or anger: to get out of control so that violence, etc results.

boil up *verb intrans* **1** said of feelings or a tense situation: to build up towards crisis point so that unrest threatens. **2** said of clouds: to pile up into towering masses on the horizon.

boisterous /'boyst(ə)rəs/ *adj* **1** noisily and cheerfully rough. **2** said of the wind or weather: stormy or wild. ➤➤ **boisterously** *adv,* **boisterousness** *noun.* [variant of Middle English *boisteous, boistuous,* earlier *boistous* rough, of unknown origin]

bok choy /bok 'choy/ *noun NAmer* = PAK CHOI.

Bokmål /'boohkmawl/ *noun* a literary form of Norwegian adapted from written Danish: compare NYNORSK. [Norwegian *Bokmål* book language]

BOL *abbr* Bolivia (international vehicle registration).

bola /'bohlə/ *or* **bolas** /'bohləs/ *noun* (*pl* **bolas** *or* **bolases**) a S American weapon consisting of two or more heavy balls attached to the ends of a cord for hurling at and entangling an animal. [American Spanish *bolas,* orig pl of Spanish *bola* ball]

bold[1] /bohld/ *adj* **1** showing or requiring a fearless adventurous spirit: *a bold child; a bold move.* **2** impudent; presumptuous: *I think he's very bold. It isn't good manners to wink at a strange girl* — L M Montgomery. **3** departing from convention or tradition: *a bold scheme.* **4** standing out prominently; conspicuous: *bold colours.* **5** set, printed, etc in boldface. ✳ **as bold as brass** with brazen self-assurance; without a hint of shame. ➤➤ **boldly** *adv,* **boldness** *noun.* [Old English *bald, beald*]

bold[2] *noun* boldface: *printed in bold.*

boldface *noun* the thickened form of a typeface used to give prominence or emphasis.

bole[1] /bohl/ *noun* the trunk of a tree. [Middle English from Old Norse *bolr*]

bole[2] *noun* a reddish brown clay that can be used as a pigment. [Greek *bōlos* a clod of earth]

bolection /boh'leksh(ə)n/ *noun* a projecting moulding, e.g. framing a panel on a door, etc. [prob alteration of *projection*]

bolero /bə'leəroh/ *noun* (*pl* **boleros**) **1** a type of Spanish dance in moderate triple time, or a piece of music suitable for dancing to it. **2** (*usu* /'boləroh/) a woman's short jacket open at the front. [Spanish *bolero,* perhaps from *bola* ball]

boletus /bə'leetəs/ *noun* (*pl* **boletuses**) any of a genus of fleshy mushrooms and toadstools with a rounded cap that has pores rather than gills on its undersurface, some species of which are edible: genus *Boletus.* [Latin *boletus* a mushroom, from Greek *bōlitēs* a fungus]

bolide /'bohlied, 'bohlid/ *noun* a large bright meteor of a type that tends to explode. [French *bolide* meteor, fireball, via Latin *bolid-, bolis* arrow-shaped meteor, from Greek *bolid-, bolis* missile, javelin, from *ballein* to throw]

bolivar /bo'leevah/ *noun* (*pl* **bolivars** *or* **bolivares** /boli'vahrays/) the basic monetary unit of Venezuela, divided into 100 centimos. [American Spanish *bolívar,* named after Simón *Bolívar* d.1830, Venezuelan soldier and statesman]

Bolivian /bə'livi·ən/ *noun* a native or inhabitant of Bolivia in S America. ➤➤ **Bolivian** *adj.*

boliviano /bə,livi'ahnoh/ *noun* (*pl* **bolivianos**) the basic monetary unit of Bolivia, divided into 100 centavos. [Spanish *boliviano*, literally 'Bolivian']

boll /bohl/ *noun* the seed pod of cotton or similar plants. [Middle English *bolle* bubble, bowl, from Dutch *bolle* rounded object]

bollard /'bolahd, 'boləd/ *noun* **1** *Brit* a short post, e.g. on a kerb or traffic island, to guide vehicles or prevent their access. **2** a post on a wharf round which to fasten mooring lines. **3** a BITT (post on a ship's deck for securing lines to). [perhaps related to or formed irreg from BOLE¹]

bollocking /'boləking/ *noun Brit, coarse slang* a severe reprimand.

bollocks *or* **ballocks** /'boləks/ *pl noun Brit, coarse slang* **1** a man's testicles. **2** (*treated as sing. or pl*) often used as an interjection) utter rubbish; complete nonsense: *a load of bollocks.* [Old English *beallucas* testicles]

bollocks up *verb trans Brit, coarse slang* to make a mess of (an arrangement, operation, etc): *He's managed to bollocks up the timetable again.*

boll weevil /bohl/ *noun* a grey weevil that infests the cotton plant and destroys the bolls: *Anthonomus grandis.*

Bollywood /'boliwood/ *noun informal* the Indian film industry. [blend of *Bombay*, centre of the industry, and HOLLYWOOD]

bolo /'bohloh/ *noun* (*pl* **bolos**) a long heavy single-edged knife of Philippine origin. [Spanish *bolo*]

bologna /bə'lohnyə/ *noun* a large smoked sausage made of beef, veal, and pork. [named after *Bologna*, town in Italy, where it was first made]

bolometer /bə'lomitə, boh-/ *noun* a very sensitive electrical instrument used in the detection and measurement of heat radiation. ➤➤ **bolometric** /bolə'metrik, boh-/ *adj*, **bolometrically** /bolə'met-, boh-/ *adv*. [Greek *bolē* beam of light + -METER²]

boloney /bə'lohni/ *noun* see BALONEY.

Bolshevik /'bolshəvik/ *noun* **1** a member of the more radical wing of the Russian Social Democratic party that seized power in Russia in 1917 and became the Communist party in 1918. **2** *derog* a former term for a Communist, *esp* a Russian Communist. ➤➤ **Bolshevik** *adj*, **Bolshevism** /-viz(ə)m/ *noun*. [Russian *bol'shevik*, from *bol'she* larger; from their forming the majority group of the party]

Bolshevist /'bolshəvist/ *noun* a Bolshevik. ➤➤ **Bolshevist** *adj*.

bolshie¹ *or* **bolshy** /'bolshi/ *noun* (*pl* **bolshies**) *Brit, informal* a Bolshevik.

bolshie² *or* **bolshy** *adj* (**bolshier, bolshiest**) *Brit, informal* obstinate and argumentative; stubbornly uncooperative. ➤➤ **bolshiness** *noun*.

bolster¹ /'bohlstə/ *noun* **1** a long pillow or cushion placed across the head of a bed. **2** a structural part, e.g. in machinery, that eliminates friction or provides support. [Old English *bolster*]

bolster² *verb trans* (**bolstered, bolstering**) (*often* + up) to give support to or reinforce (something): *one of those disheartening instances where truth requires full as much bolstering as error* — Herman Melville; *The thought was sufficient to bolster up his wavering self-esteem.* ➤➤ **bolsterer** *noun*.

bolster³ *noun* a heavy chisel used for cutting bricks or stone slabs. [origin unknown]

bolt¹ /bolt, bohlt/ *noun* **1a** a sliding bar or rod used to fasten a door. **b** the part of a lock that is shot or withdrawn by the key. **2a** a metal rod or pin for fastening objects together. **b** a screw-bolt with a head suitable for turning with a spanner. **3** a rod or bar that closes the breech of a breech-loading firearm. **4** a roll of cloth or wallpaper of a standard length. **5a** a short stout blunt-headed arrow shot from a crossbow. **b** a lightning stroke; a thunderbolt. ✳ **bolt from the blue** a totally unexpected and typically unwelcome happening or development. **have shot one's bolt** *informal* to have used up the resources at one's command to no avail. [Old English *bolt* a crossbow arrow]

bolt² *verb intrans* **1** (*also* + for) to move rapidly; to dash: *She bolted for the exit.* **2a** to dart off or away; to flee. **b** said of a horse: to break from control and make a dash. **3** said of plants: to produce seed prematurely. **4** *NAmer* to break away from or oppose one's political party. ➤ *verb trans* **1** to drive (a fox, rabbit, etc) from its hole; to flush or start (an animal). **2** to secure (a door, etc) with a bolt. **3** to attach or fasten (one part of a machine, etc) to another with bolts. **4** to swallow (food) hastily or without chewing. ➤➤ **bolter** *noun*.

bolt³ *adv* rigidly: *bolt upright.*

bolt⁴ *noun* an escape attempt; a dash or run. ✳ **do a bolt** *informal* to run off, escape, or abscond. **make a bolt for** to dash towards (a door, etc). [BOLT²]

bolt⁵ *or* **boult** *verb trans archaic* to sift (flour, etc). ➤➤ **bolter** *noun*. [Middle English *bulten* from Old French *buleter* to sift, of Germanic origin]

bolt-hole *noun chiefly Brit* a means of rapid escape or place of refuge.

boltrope /'boltrohp, 'bohlt-/ *noun* a strong rope stitched to the edges of a sail to prevent it tearing or fraying.

bolus /'bohləs/ *noun* (*pl* **boluses**) **1** a large pill. **2** a soft mass of food that has been chewed but not swallowed. [late Latin from Greek *bōlos* lump]

bomb¹ /bom/ *noun* **1a** an explosive or incendiary device, typically detonated by impact or a timing mechanism and usu dropped from aircraft, thrown or placed by hand, or fired from a mortar. **b** (**the bomb**) the atom bomb or hydrogen bomb, or nuclear weapons in general. **2** a rounded mass of lava ejected from a volcano. **3** a container for radioactive material, used to treat cancer: *a cobalt bomb*. **4** *Aus, NZ* a dilapidated old car. **5** *informal* a failure or flop: *a terrible bomb of a play* — Paul Newman. ✳ **cost a bomb** *Brit, informal* to be very expensive. **go down a bomb** *Brit, informal* to be received enthusiastically: *Our act goes down a bomb in Britain* — News of the World. **go like a bomb** *informal* to go very fast. **make a bomb** *Brit, informal* to make a lot of money. [French *bombe* from Italian *bomba*, prob via Latin *bombus* from Greek *bombos* deep hollow sound, of imitative origin]

bomb² *verb trans* to drop bombs on (a place) or detonate a bomb in (a building, etc). ➤ *verb intrans informal* said of a show, etc: to be a disastrous failure.

bombard /bom'bahd/ *verb trans* **1** to attack (a place or position) with heavy artillery or with bombs. **2** (*usu* + with) to direct an unremitting flow of questions or facts at (somebody): *We've been bombarded with queries.* **3** to subject (a substance) to the impact of electrons, alpha rays, or other rapidly moving particles. ➤➤ **bombardment** *noun*. [early French *bombarder*, from *bombarde*, kind of cannon, shawm, prob from Latin *bombus*: see BOMB¹]

bombarde /bom'bahd, 'bombahd/ *noun* **1** a SHAWM (medieval wind instrument) of alto pitch. **2** a powerful 16-foot or 32-foot reed STOP² (set of vibrators) on an organ. [French *bombarde* shawm: see BOMBARD]

bombardier /bombə'diə/ *noun* **1** a non-commissioned officer in the British artillery. **2** a US bomber-crew member who aims and releases the bombs.

bombardon /'bombahd(ə)n/ *noun* **1** the bass member of the SHAWM (medieval wind instrument) family. **2** a bass tuba. [Italian *bombardone*, from *bombardo* cannon, prob from Latin *bombus*: see BOMB¹]

bombast /'bombast/ *noun* pretentious inflated speech or writing. ➤➤ **bombastic** /bom'bastik/ *adj*, **bombastically** /bom'bas-/ *adv*. [orig cottonwool padding used in dressmaking, from early French *bombace* raw cotton, from medieval Latin *bombac-, bombax* cotton, ultimately from Greek *bombyk-, bombyx* silkworm, silk garment]

Bombay duck /bom'bay/ *noun* a small fish found off S Asian coasts and eaten dried and salted with curry: *Harpodon nehereus*. Also called BUMMALO. [alteration of *bummalo* (from Marathi *bombil*), by association with *Bombay*, city in India]

Bombay mix *noun* a spicy snack of Indian origin, consisting of a mixture of nuts, lentils, etc.

bombazine /'bombəzeen/ *noun* a silk fabric woven in twill weave and dyed black. [French *bombasin*, via medieval Latin *bombacinum*, *bombycinum* silken texture, neuter of Latin *bombycinus* of silk, from *bombyc-, bombyx* silkworm, silk garment, from Greek]

bomb bay *noun* a bomb-carrying compartment in the underside of a combat aircraft.

bomb disposal *noun* the process of making unexploded bombs safe.

bombe /bomb/ *noun* a frozen dessert made in a round or cone-shaped mould. [French *bombe*: see BOMB¹]

bombed *adj* **1** damaged or destroyed by bombs: *bombed villages*. **2** *informal* heavily under the influence of alcohol or drugs. ✳ **bombed out** having lost home or premises through bombing: *The bombed-out families have been given temporary shelter in a school.*

bomber *noun* **1** an aircraft designed for dropping bombs. **2** somebody who throws or plants bombs.

bomber jacket *noun* a short jacket with elasticated waistband and cuffs, usu with a zipped front. [from the similar jackets worn by some World War II aircrew]

bombora /bom'bawrə/ *noun Aus* a dangerous reef, or the sea breaking over it. [possibly Dharuk (an Aboriginal language) *bumbora*]

bombproof *adj* said *esp* of a purpose-built shelter: strong enough to withstand a bomb blast.

bombshell *noun* **1** an astounding or devastating occurrence or piece of news. **2** *informal* a stunning girl or woman: *a blonde bombshell*. **3** *dated* = BOMB¹ (1A).

bombsight *noun* a sighting device for aiming bombs.

bombsite *noun* an area of ground where buildings have been destroyed by bombing, *esp* from the air.

bomb squad *noun* **1** a branch of the police force that investigates the planting and detonating of bombs by terrorists. **2** a body of police or soldiers specializing in bomb disposal.

bona fide /,bohnə 'fiedi/ *adj* genuine: *Loans will be available to bona fide students only.* [Latin *bona fide* in good faith]

bona fides /,bohnə 'fiediz/ *noun* **1** honest intentions; sincerity: *First gain their trust and establish your bona fides.* **2** *informal* (*treated as pl*) documentary evidence supporting one's claim to be a certain thing; one's credentials. [Latin *bona fides* good faith]

bonanza /bə'nanzə/ *noun* **1** an exceptionally large and rich mass of ore in a mine. **2** widely enjoyed wealth or prosperity resulting from something proving unexpectedly profitable. [Spanish *bonanza*, literally 'calm, fair weather', from medieval Latin *bonacia*, alteration of Latin *malacia* calm at sea, from Greek *malakia* softness, from *malakos* soft]

Bonapartism /'bohnəpahtiz(ə)m/ *noun* support of the French emperors Napoleon I or Napoleon III or their dynasty. ➤➤ **Bonapartist** *noun and adj*. [*Bonaparte, Buonaparte*, family name of the dynasty]

bona vacantia /,bohnə və'kantiə/ *pl noun* in Britain, goods without an owner, which the Crown may have a right to, e.g. articles declared treasure trove, or the estate of a person without heirs who dies intestate. [Latin *bona vacantia*, from *bonum* a piece of property (literally 'something good') + *vacans* ownerless: see VACANT]

bonbon /'bonbon/ *noun* a small item of confectionery; = SWEET² (1). [French *bonbon* (baby talk), reduplication of *bon* good, from Latin *bonus*]

bonbonnière /bonbon'yeə/ *noun* a small decorative container for sweets or confectionery. [French *bonbonnière*, from *bonbon*: see BONBON]

bonce /bons/ *noun Brit, informal* the head. [English dialect *bonce* large marble]

bond¹ /bond/ *noun* **1** something, e.g. a fetter, that binds or restrains. **2** a force of attraction by means of which atoms, ions, or groups of atoms are held together in a molecule or crystal. **3a** an adhesive or cementing material. **b** the adhesion achieved between surfaces cemented together. **4** something that unites or binds: *the bonds of friendship*. **5** a binding agreement, *esp*: **a** a legally enforceable agreement to pay: *You shall not seal to such a bond for me* — Shakespeare. **b** a certificate of intention to pay the holder a specified sum, with or without other interest, on a specified date. **6a** the system of overlapping bricks in a wall. **b** a term used for any of the various patterns for overlapping bricks: *Flemish bond*. **7** = BOND PAPER. **＊ in bond** of dutiable goods: retained in a bonded warehouse pending payment of duty. [Middle English *band, bond* a shackle, fetter, from Old Norse *band*]

bond² *verb trans* **1a** to cause (surfaces) to stick firmly. **b** to hold (atoms) together in a molecule or crystal by chemical bonds. **2** to overlap (bricks, etc) for solidity of construction. **3** to put (goods) in bond until duties and taxes are paid. ➤ *verb intrans* **1** to stick firmly together: *Give the surfaces time to bond.* **2** said of two people, *esp* a mother and newborn child: to form a strong close emotional bond. ➤➤ **bondable** *adj*, **bonder** *noun*.

bondage /'bondij/ *noun* **1** the tenure or service of a villein, serf, or slave. **2a** slavery or serfdom. **b** subjugation to a controlling person or force. **c** a form of sexual gratification involving the physical restraint of one partner: *bondage fantasies*. [Middle English, from *bonde* peasant, serf, from Old English *bōnda* householder, from Old

Norse *bōndi*, a peasant proprietor. The notion of restraint comes from association with BOND¹, in the sense 'fetter']

bonded *adj* **1** denoting items that are imported but held without payment of customs duty: *bonded goods*. **2** composed of two or more layers of fabric held together by an adhesive: *bonded fabrics*. **3** bound by a legal agreement.

bonded warehouse *noun* a warehouse in which imported goods are retained awaiting payment of duty or re-export.

bondholder *noun* a person who holds a government or company bond.

bonding *noun* the forming of a close emotional bond between people, *esp* between a mother and her newborn child.

bondmaid *noun* an unmarried female slave or serf. [from Old English: see BONDAGE]

bondman *or* **bondsman** *noun* (*pl* **bondmen** *or* **bondsmen**) a slave or serf. [Middle English *bonde*: see BONDAGE]

bond paper *noun* writing paper of superior quality.

bondservant *noun* a servant bound to service without wages; a slave. [Old English *bonda*: see BONDAGE]

bondsman /'bondzmən/ *noun* see BONDMAN.

bondstone *noun* a stone long enough to extend through the full thickness of a wall.

bondswoman /'bondzwoomən/ *noun* see BONDWOMAN.

bond-washing *noun Brit* the practice of selling securities just before payment of interest is due, in order to receive a favourable price, which counts as capital gain for tax purposes, rather than the interest, which counts as income.

bondwoman *or* **bondswoman** *noun* (*pl* **bondwomen** *or* **bondswomen**) a female slave or serf. [Old English *bonda*: see BONDAGE]

bone¹ /bohn/ *noun* **1a** the rigid material, made up largely of calcium salts, of which the adult skeleton of most vertebrate animals is chiefly composed. **b** any of the hard structures consisting of this, that together compose the skeleton. **2a** baleen, ivory, or another hard substance resembling bone. **b** any structure composed of this. **3** (*in pl*). **a** a person's mortal remains: *The vault where his bones lie*. **b** one's own body: *Let me rest my weary bones*. **4** a strip of whalebone or steel used to stiffen a corset or dress. **5** (*in pl*) thin bars of bone, ivory, or wood held in pairs between the fingers and used to produce musical rhythms. **6a** (*in pl*) dice. **b** a domino. ＊ **feel in one's bones** to know (something) instinctively or intuitively. **have a bone to pick with** *informal* to have a cause of complaint against (somebody), calling for mutual discussion and settlement. **make no bones about** to have no hesitation in (doing or saying something potentially embarrassing or hurtful). **near/close to the bone** said of a remark: risqué, indecent, or too close to the truth. **on the bone** said of meat: with the bones left in it. **to the bone** reduced to the essentials: *The text has been pared to the bone*. ➤➤ **boneless** *adj*. [Old English *bān*]

bone² *verb trans* to remove the bones from (fish or meat).

bone ash *noun* the white porous residue, chiefly of calcium phosphate, produced from bones heated to a high temperature in air.

bone china *noun* a type of translucent and durable white hard-paste porcelain made from a mixture of bone ash and kaolin.

boned *adj* **1** said of fish or meat: with the bones removed; filleted. **2** stiffened with whalebone or steel: *a boned corset*.

bone-dry *adj* containing no moisture; completely or excessively dry: *We lay in a heather bush … on bone-dry ground* — Robert Louis Stevenson.

bonefish *noun* (*pl* **bonefishes** *or collectively* **bonefish**) any of several species of silvery fishes found in warm shallow waters, remarkable for their numerous bones: genus *Albula*.

bonehead *noun informal* a stupid person. ➤➤ **boneheaded** *adj*.

bone-idle *adj* lazy through and through; incurably lazy.

bone marrow *noun* = MARROW (2A).

bone meal *noun* fertilizer or feed made of crushed or ground bone.

bone of contention *noun* a cause of continuing conflict or disagreement: *Poland was strategically placed between Russia and Germany, and for centuries had been a bone of contention between them* — J Young.

boner /'bohnə/ *noun* **1** *informal* an embarrassing blunder; a howler. **2** *chiefly NAmer, coarse slang* a penile erection. [prob from BONEHEAD]

bonesetter /'bohnsetə/ *noun* formerly, a person, *esp* one who is not a licensed physician, who set broken or dislocated bones.

bone-shaker *noun Brit, informal* an early bicycle with solid tyres.

bone spavin *noun* a bony enlargement on the lower inside of a horse's HOCK[1] (joint corresponding to the human ankle) resulting from osteoarthritis.

bone up *verb intrans informal* (+ on) to try to master necessary information in a short time, *esp* for a special purpose: *I'd better bone up on those theorems before the exam.*

bonfire /'bonfie-ə/ *noun* a large fire built in the open air. [Middle English *bonefire* a fire of bones, from *bon* BONE[1]]

Bonfire Night *noun* = GUY FAWKES NIGHT.

bong[1] /bong/ *verb intrans* to make a deep resonant sound like that of a large bell. [imitative]

bong[2] *noun* a bonging sound.

bong[3] *noun* a water pipe used in smoking narcotic drugs. [Thai *baung* literally 'cylindrical wooden tube']

bongo[1] /'bonggoh/ *noun* (*pl* **bongos** or **bongoes**) either of a pair of small tuned drums played with the hands. [American Spanish *bongó*]

bongo[2] *noun* (*pl* **bongos** or *collectively* **bongo**) a large striped antelope of tropical Africa: *Tragelaphus euryceros*. [from Kikongo (Bantu language)]

bonhomie /'bonəmee, bonə'mee/ *noun* good-natured friendliness. [French *bonhomie*, from *bonhomme* good-natured man, from *bon* good + *homme* man]

bonito /bə'neetoh/ *noun* (*pl* **bonitos**) any of several species of medium-sized tuna with dark stripes: genera *Sarda* and *Katsuwonus*. [Spanish *bonito* pretty, from Latin *bonus* good]

bonk[1] /bongk/ *verb trans informal* **1** to hit (somebody), usu not very hard. **2** *Brit* to have sexual intercourse with (somebody). ⟩ *verb intrans Brit, informal* to have sexual intercourse. ⟩⟩ **bonking** *noun*. [imitative of a hitting noise]

bonk[2] *noun informal* **1** a light blow or hit. **2** *Brit* an act of sexual intercourse.

bonkers /'bongkəz/ *adj Brit, informal* mad or crazy. [origin unknown]

bon mot /ˌbon 'moh (*French* bɔ̃ mo)/ *noun* (*pl* **bons mots** /ˌbon 'moh(z) (*French* bɔ̃ mo)/) a witticism. [French *bon mot*, literally 'good word']

bonne bouche /ˌbon 'boohsh/ *noun* (*pl* **bonnes bouches** /ˌbon 'boohsh/) a tasty morsel of food; a titbit. [French *bonne bouche*, literally 'good mouth']

bonnet /'bonit/ *noun* **1** a cloth or straw hat for a woman or child, tied under the chin. **2** *chiefly Scot* a soft brimless cap. **3** *Brit* the hinged metal covering over the engine of a motor vehicle. **4** formerly, an additional piece of canvas laced to the foot of a jib or foresail to increase sail area. [Middle English *bonet* via Old French from medieval Latin *abonnis* headgear]

bonnet monkey *noun* a MACAQUE (type of monkey) native to India, with tufts of hair on its head giving a bonnet-like effect: *Macaca silenus*.

bonny /'boni/ *adj* (**bonnier, bonniest**) *chiefly Scot, N Eng* **1** attractive or comely. **2** substantial; considerable: *a bonny sum*. ⟩⟩ **bonnily** *adv*, **bonniness** *noun*. [Middle English *bonie* Old French *bon* good, from Latin *bonus*]

bonsai /'bonsie/ *noun* (*pl* **bonsai**) **1** a potted plant dwarfed by special methods of culture. **2** the art of growing dwarfed varieties of trees. [Japanese *bonsai*, from *bon* tray + *sai* planting]

bonspiel /'bonspeel, 'bonspəl/ *noun* a match or tournament between curling clubs. [perhaps from Dutch *bond* league + *spel* game]

bontebok /'bontəbok/ *noun* (*pl* **bonteboks** or *collectively* **bontebok**) a S African antelope that is very closely related to the BLESBOK and is now almost extinct: *Damaliscus pygargus*. [Afrikaans *bontebok*, from *bont* spotted + *bok* male antelope]

bonus /'bohnəs/ *noun* (*pl* **bonuses**) **1** something given in addition to what is usual or strictly due. **2** *chiefly Brit* an extra dividend distributed to shareholders out of profits. **3** money or an equivalent given in addition to an employee's usual remuneration, usu for good performance. **4** an unlooked-for and welcome plus or extra. [Latin *bonus* good]

bonus issue *noun Brit* a distribution of free shares to the shareholders of a company in proportion to the shares they already hold, in place of a dividend.

bon vivant /ˌbonh vee'vonh (*French* bɔ̃ vivã)/ *noun* (*pl* **bon vivants** or **bons vivants** /ˌbonh vee'vonh (*French* bɔ̃ vivã)/) a person with cultivated and refined tastes, *esp* in regard to food and drink. [French *bon vivant* good liver]

bon viveur /ˌbonh vee'vuh (*French* bɔ̃ vivœːr)/ *noun* (*pl* **bon viveurs** or **bons viveurs** /ˌbonh vee'vuhz, vee'vuh (*French* bɔ̃ vivœːr)/) *chiefly Brit* = BON VIVANT.

bon voyage /ˌbon vwah'yahj, -'yahzh (*French* bɔ̃ vwajaʒ)/ *interj* said to somebody embarking on a journey: farewell. [French *bon voyage* good journey]

bonxie /'bongksi/ *noun* = GREAT SKUA. [Shetland dialect *bonxie* from Norwegian *bunksi*]

bony /'bohni/ *adj* (**bonier, boniest**) **1** consisting of or resembling bone. **2a** full of bones. **b** having large or prominent bones. **3** skinny or scrawny. ⟩⟩ **boniness** *noun*.

bony fish *noun* any of a major group of fishes comprising all those with a bony rather than a cartilaginous skeleton and including the salmon, carp, herring, etc; = TELEOST: class Osteichthyes.

bonze /bonz/ *noun* a Chinese or Japanese Buddhist monk. [French *bonze* via Portuguese from Japanese *bonsō*]

bonzer /'bonzə/ *adj Aus, NZ, informal* excellent; especially good. [ultimately connected with French *bon* good]

boo[1] /booh/ *interj* used to express contempt or disapproval or to startle or frighten. [Middle English *bo*; earlier history unknown]

boo[2] *noun* (*pl* **boos**) a shout of disapproval or contempt.

boo[3] *verb* (**boos, booed, booing**) ⟩ *verb intrans* to show scorn or disapproval by shouting 'boo!' ⟩ *verb trans* to shout 'boo!' at (a performer, speaker, etc).

boob[1] /boohb/ *noun Brit, informal* a stupid mistake; a blunder. [short for BOOBY[1]]

boob[2] *verb intrans Brit, informal* to make a stupid mistake.

boob[3] *noun informal* a female breast. [shortening of BOOBY[2]]

booboo /'boohbooh/ *noun* (*pl* **booboos**) *informal* an embarrassing blunder; = BOOB[1]. [reduplicated form of BOOB[1]]

boobook /'boohbook/ *noun* a medium-sized Australian owl with brown plumage; = MOPOKE: *Ninox novaeseelandiae*. [imitative of its call]

boob tube[1] *noun informal* a woman's tube-like garment made of stretchy material for pulling on over the breasts. [from BOOB[3]]

boob tube[2] *noun NAmer, informal* a television set. [from BOOB[1]]

booby[1] /'boohbi/ *noun informal* an awkward foolish person. (*pl* **boobies**) **1** *informal*. **a** an awkward foolish person. **b** the poorest performer in a group. **2** any of several species of small gannets of tropical seas with brightly coloured feet: genus *Sula*. [modification of Spanish *bobo* from Latin *balbus* stammering, prob of imitative origin]

booby[2] *noun* (*pl* **boobies**) *informal* a female breast. [alteration of dialect *bubby*, perhaps imitative of the noise made by a sucking infant]

booby prize *noun* an award for the poorest performance in a contest.

booby trap *noun* **1** a trap for the unwary or unsuspecting. **2** a harmless-looking object concealing an explosive device that is set to explode by remote control or if touched.

booby-trap *verb trans* (**booby-trapped, booby-trapping**) to set a booby trap in or on (something).

boodle /'boohdl/ *noun informal* money, *esp* when stolen or used for bribery. [Dutch *boedel* possessions, lot, from Middle Dutch]

booger /'boohgə/ *noun NAmer, informal* = BOGEY (4). [probably alteration of BUGGER[1]]

boogie[1] /'boohgi/ *noun* **1** = BOOGIE-WOOGIE. **2** *informal* a dance to rock music. [origin unknown]

boogie[2] *verb intrans* (**boogies, boogied, boogieing**) *informal* **1** to dance to rock music. **2** to make love.

boogie board *noun* = BODYBOARD[1].

boogie-woogie /ˌboohgi 'woohgi/ *noun* a style of playing blues on the piano characterized by a steady rhythmic bass and a simple, often improvised, melody. Also called BOOGIE[1]. [reduplication of BOOGIE[1]]

boohai /boo'hie/ ✳ **up the boohai** *NZ* completely lost or astray. [prob from the remote town of *Puhoi* in N Auckland]

boohoo[1] /booh'hooh/ *noun* (*pl* **boohoos**) sometimes used as an interjection: a representation of a sob. [phonetic representation of noisy sobbing]

boohoo[2] *verb intrans* (**boohoos, boohooed, boohooing**) to sob noisily or unrestrainedly.

book[1] /book/ *noun* **1** a set of written, printed, lined, or blank sheets bound together. **2** a long written or printed composition, *esp* a literary one. **3** a major division of a treatise or literary work: *Book 2 of the Aeneid.* **4** (*in pl*) journals, ledgers, etc recording business accounts. **5** (**the Book**) the Bible. **6** (**the book**) a work used as a source or authority for some purpose, e.g. an instruction manual, or the libretto of a play, opera, etc: *That isn't what it says in the book.* **7** *informal* a magazine. **8** a small folder containing a quantity of stamps, tickets, matches, etc, for detaching as required for use. **9** the bets registered by a bookmaker. **10** the number of tricks a card player or side must win before any trick can have scoring value. ✳ **a closed book** a subject about which one is totally ignorant: *The stock market is a closed book to me.* **an open book** something that is only too revelatory: *Her face was an open book.* **a turn-up for the book/books** an unusual occurrence that is worth noting. **bring to book** to punish or reprimand (an offender). **by the book** by following previously laid down instructions and not using personal initiative: *It is safer to go by the book than to risk making a mistake.* **in my book** in my opinion. **in somebody's good/bad books** in favour or disfavour with somebody. **make/open a book** to take bets and pay winnings. **one for the book** an act or occurrence worth noting. **on the books** included in a list of clients, members, or employees. **suit somebody's book** to be convenient for somebody: *It would just have suited her book if that report had been lost.* **take a leaf out of somebody's book** to copy or imitate somebody's behaviour. **throw the book at 1** to charge (a misdoer) with all the offences that can be found. **2** to reprimand (an offender) severely or comprehensively. ➤➤ **bookful** *noun.* [Old English *bōc* beech tree, book, charter, prob from the practice of carving runes on beechwood tablets]

book[2] *verb trans* **1a** to reserve a seat or passage for (somebody): *I've booked you on the 4:30pm train to Edinburgh.* **b** to reserve (seats, tickets, accommodation, etc) in advance: *We'd better book a table for noon; We booked this holiday over two years ago.* **c** to hire the services of (an organization, etc) in advance: *The band is booked for the whole week.* **2a** said of a police officer, etc: to take the name of (a driver, etc) with a view to prosecution: *He was booked for speeding.* **b** to enter the name of (a rugby or football player) in a book for a violation of the rules, usu involving foul play. ➤ *verb intrans* (*also* + *up*) to reserve something in advance: *It's always sensible to book up early.* ➤➤ **booker** *noun.*

bookable *adj* **1** *chiefly Brit* said of theatre seats, tickets, etc: that may be reserved in advance. **2** said of an offence in football or rugby: that makes a player liable to be booked by a referee.

bookbinding /-biending/ *noun* the craft or trade of binding books. ➤➤ **bookbinder** *noun,* **bookbindery** *noun.*

bookcase *noun* a piece of furniture consisting of a set of shelves to hold books.

book club *noun* an association that offers books from a limited range to its members at a discount.

booked up *adj* **1** having no seats, accommodation, etc, available; fully booked: *I'm afraid we're booked up for the whole of June.* **2** having a full schedule with no time free: *Sorry, I'm booked up all next week.*

bookend *noun* a support placed at the end of a row of books.

bookie /'booki/ *noun informal* a bookmaker.

book in *verb intrans* **1** to reserve a room at a hotel. **2** to register one's arrival somewhere, *esp* at a hotel. ➤ *verb intrans* to reserve a room at a hotel for (somebody): *Now don't go and book me in at the Ritz or anything.*

booking *noun* **1** an engagement to perform; a scheduled performance. **2** a reservation: *Bookings are down on last year's.* **3** in football or rugby, an instance of being booked by a referee.

booking clerk *noun* an official who sells tickets, *esp* travel tickets at a railway station: *The booking-clerk said something to the Station-Master* — Kipling.

booking hall *noun* the area of a railway station or other travel terminal where travel tickets are sold.

booking office *noun chiefly Brit* an office where tickets are sold and bookings made, *esp* at a railway station.

bookish *adj* **1** fond of reading and studying. **2** said of language: literary as opposed to colloquial. ➤➤ **bookishly** *adv,* **bookishness** *noun.*

bookkeeper *noun* a person who records the accounts or transactions of a business. ➤➤ **bookkeeping** *noun.*

bookland /'bookland/ *noun Brit* land taken from the common land before the Norman Conquest and granted by 'book' or charter to a private owner. [Old English *bóc* charter, BOOK[1] + LAND[1]]

book learning *noun* knowledge got from books in contrast to practical experience; mere academic theory: *But book-learning is not business; book-learning didn't get me around the world* — Charles Kingsley.

booklet /'booklit/ *noun* **1** a small book with a paper cover and comparatively few pages, usu containing information about a particular subject; a pamphlet. **2** a number of pages of e.g. stamps, tokens, or vouchers, bound together in a stiff cover, to be detached as needed.

book louse *noun* any of several species of small wingless insects whose larvae infest books and destroy them by feeding on the paste that is used in the binding: genus *Liposcelis.*

book lung *noun* a sac-like breathing organ in many arachnids, e.g. spiders and scorpions, containing numerous thin folds of membrane arranged like the leaves of a book.

bookmaker *noun* a person who determines odds and receives and pays off bets. ➤➤ **bookmaking** *noun.*

bookman *noun* (*pl* **bookmen**) *archaic* a literary man; a scholar.

bookmark *noun* **1** a strip of card or leather, or a similar device, used to mark a place in a book. **2** a computing facility whereby the address of a file, web page, etc is recorded for quick future access.

bookmarker *noun* = BOOKMARK (1).

bookmobile /'bookmabeel/ *noun NAmer* a mobile library. [BOOK[1] + AUTOMOBILE]

Book of Common Prayer *noun* until 1980, the official book of procedure for the services of the Anglican Church.

book of hours *noun* a book of prayers to be said at the CANONICAL HOUR (times of day appointed for services), used for private worship by Roman Catholics.

bookplate *noun* a label placed inside the cover of a book, bearing the owner's name.

bookrest *noun Brit* a usu adjustable support for an open book.

bookshelf *noun* (*pl* **bookshelves**) an open shelf for holding books.

bookstall *noun* a stall where books, magazines, and newspapers are sold.

book token *noun Brit* a gift token exchangeable for books.

book value *noun* the value of something as shown by the account books of the business owning it; *esp* the value of a company's buildings, machinery, vehicles, etc that is recognized by the government for accounting and tax purposes, allowing for depreciation: compare MARKET VALUE.

bookworm *noun* **1** *informal* a person unusually fond of reading and study. **2** the BOOK LOUSE or any of various other insect larvae that feed on the binding and paste of books.

Boolean /'boohli·ən/ *adj* relating to or denoting a system in logic that symbolically represents certain relationships between entities, e.g. sets, propositions, or states of computer logic circuits. [named after George *Boole* d.1864, English mathematician, on whose ideas the system is based]

Boolean search *noun* the use of the logical expressions *and, or,* and *not* in search commands relating to a computer database.

boom[1] /boom, boohm/ *noun* **1** a booming sound or cry. **2a** the rapid expansion and development of a town or region. **b** a rapid and widespread expansion of economic activity. **c** a rapid growth or increase in a specified thing: *the baby boom of the late 1950s.* ✳ **boom and bust** over-rapid commercial expansion followed by collapse.

boom[2] /boom, boohm/ *verb intrans* **1** to make a deep hollow sound or cry: *The bitterns boomed and the frogs croaked* — H Rider Haggard. **2** to experience a rapid increase in activity or market success: *Business was booming.* ➤ *verb trans* to cause (something) to resound: *'But somewhat dangerous to navigation,' boomed Richard* — Virginia Woolf. [imitative]

boom³ /boohm/ *noun* **1** a spar at the foot of the mainsail in a fore-and-aft rig that is attached at its fore end to the mast. **2** a long movable arm used to manipulate a microphone. **3** a floating barrier across a river or enclosing an area of water, e.g. to keep logs together, confine an oil spill, etc. **4** a cable or line of spars extended across a river or the mouth of a harbour as a barrier to navigation. [Dutch *boom* tree, beam]

boomer /'boohmə/ *noun* **1** *Aus, informal* a large male kangaroo. **2** a huge wave. [English dialect *boomer* anything large and impressive, prob from BOOM¹]

boomerang¹ /'boohmarang/ *noun* **1** a bent piece of wood shaped so that it returns to its thrower, used by Australian aboriginals as a hunting weapon. **2** an act or utterance that backfires on its originator. [Dharuk Aboriginal language *boomerang*]

boomerang² *verb intrans* said of a plan: to recoil on the utterer or originator, *esp* with unpleasant effects.

boomlet /'boohmlit/ *noun* a small economic boom.

boomslang /'boohmslang/ *noun* a large venomous tree snake of southern Africa: *Dispholidus typus*. [Afrikaans *boomslang*, from *boom* tree + *slang* snake]

boom town *noun* a town that suddenly experiences an increase in size and wealth, resulting typically from the introduction of a new profitable industry.

boon /boohn/ *noun* **1** a timely benefit; a blessing. **2** *archaic* a benefit or favour, *esp* when given in answer to a request: *And ask of Cymbeline what boon thou wilt* — Shakespeare. [Middle English from Old Norse *bōn* petition]

boon companion *noun* a close and congenial friend, with whom one enjoys good times: *The boon companion of the colossal elephant was a common cat!* — Mark Twain. [Middle English *bon* good, via Old French from Latin *bonus*]

boondocks /'boohndoks/ *pl noun NAmer, informal* **1** (**the boondocks**) rough country filled with dense brush. **2** (**the boondocks**) a remote or rural area. **3** (**the boondocks**) *derog* a provincial unsophisticated place. [Tagálog *bundok* mountain]

boondoggle¹ /'boohndogl/ *noun NAmer, informal* a trivial, time-wasting, or dishonest task, typically an activity undertaken for want of something worthwhile to do. [a 1930s term, said to refer orig either to the scouter's plaited leather lanyard or the rancher's leather saddle trimming, as articles crafted by people evidently with time on their hands]

boondoggle² *verb intrans NAmer, informal* to engage in trivial or money-wasting tasks so as to appear busy, *esp* when more serious matters need attention. ⟫⟫ **boondoggler** *noun*, **boondoggling** *noun*.

boong /boohng/ *noun Aus, offensive* an Aboriginal. [from an Aboriginal word meaning 'human being']

boongary /'boohn'geari/ *noun* (*pl* **boongaries**) a tree-dwelling kangaroo native to northern Queensland: *Dendrolagus lumholtzi*. [from an Aboriginal language]

boonies /'boohniz/ *pl noun* (**the boonies**) *NAmer, informal* = BOONDOCKS.

boor /booə, baw/ *noun* a coarse, ill-mannered, or insensitive person. ⟫⟫ **boorish** *adj*, **boorishly** *adv*, **boorishness** *noun*. [Dutch *boer* peasant, farmer]

boost¹ /boohst/ *verb trans* **1** to increase or raise the level of (something). **2** to encourage or give a fillip to (somebody's pride, confidence, or morale). **3a** to increase (a physical quantity, e.g. voltage). **b** to amplify (an electrical signal). **4** to push (somebody) from behind or below to help them. [origin unknown]

boost² *noun* **1** an increase in amount: *Publicity, good or bad, usually results in a boost in sales.* **2** an upward thrust, a fillip. **3** a push from below or behind to assist progress.

booster *noun* **1** (*also* **booster shot**) a supplementary dose of vaccine increasing or renewing the effectiveness of an initial or earlier dose. **2** an auxiliary engine which assists a rocket or spacecraft at take-off by providing a large thrust for a short time. **3** a device that increases voltage or amplifies an electrical signal.

booster seat *noun* a seat placed on top of another seat to raise a small child to a higher level, *esp* in a car.

boot¹ /booht/ *noun* **1a** a piece of footwear that extends above the ankle, sometimes up to the knee, often with a stiff or thick sole and

heel. **b** a stout shoe, *esp* for sports: *football boots*. **2** *informal* a kick: *He got a boot in the ribs.* **3** *Brit* the luggage compartment of a motor car. **4** = BOOTSTRAP¹ (2). **5** formerly, an instrument of torture that crushed the leg and foot. ✴ **boots and all** *Aus, NZ, informal* without reservation; wholeheartedly. **die with one's boots on** to die while still working and active. **get the boot** *informal* to get the sack. **give somebody the boot** *informal* to sack somebody. **put the boot in 1** *chiefly Brit, informal* to kick somebody, *esp* when they are already on the ground. **2** *chiefly Brit, informal* to treat somebody cruelly or unfairly, *esp* when they are already in a vulnerable position. **3** *chiefly Brit, informal* to act with brutal decisiveness. **the boot is on the other foot** the situation is the other way round. **you bet your boots** *informal* you can be quite certain (that something is the case); you bet. ⟫⟫ **booted** *adj*. [Middle English from Old French *bote*]

boot² *verb trans* **1** to kick (somebody): *He booted me in the head.* **2** *informal* (+ out) to eject or discharge (a person) summarily: *She was eventually booted out of office.* **3** = BOOT UP.

boot³ ✴ **to boot** besides; as well: *Her fiancé was a Cambridge graduate, and a lord to boot.* [Old English *bōt* remedy, benefit]

boot⁴ *verb intrans archaic* to be of help, profit, or advantage: *It boots not to look backwards* — Thomas Arnold. ⟫⟫ **verb trans** to be profitable to (a person). [from BOOT³]

bootblack *noun* formerly, a person who cleaned and shone shoes.

bootboy *noun* **1** *informal* a rowdy or violent youth. **2** = BOOTBLACK.

boot camp *noun NAmer* a basic training camp for recruits to the navy and marines.

boot-cut *adj* = BOOTLEG¹ (2).

bootee /'boohtee, booh'tee/ *or* **bootie** /'boohti/ *noun* **1** an infant's boot-shaped sock worn in place of a shoe usu secured by a ribbon. **2** a short boot.

boot fair *noun* = CAR BOOT SALE.

booth /boohth/ *noun* **1** a stall or stand for the sale or exhibition of goods. **2** a small enclosure affording privacy, e.g. for telephoning, vote-casting, etc. [Middle English *bothe*, of Scandinavian origin]

bootie /'boohti/ *noun* see BOOTEE.

bootjack *noun* a device, e.g. of metal or wood, shaped like the letter V and used in pulling off boots.

bootlace *noun Brit* a long stout shoelace.

bootlace fungus *noun* = HONEY FUNGUS.

bootleg¹ *adj* **1** said of alcoholic drink or recordings: smuggled or illegally produced. **2** said of trousers: having legs that flare slightly at the bottom, for wearing over boots. [(sense 1) from former practice of carrying a concealed bottle of liquor in the top of a boot]

bootleg² *verb trans* (**bootlegged, bootlegging**) **1** to manufacture, sell, or transport for sale (alcoholic drink, etc) contrary to law. **2** to record, reproduce, or sell (popular music) without authorization. ⟫⟫ **bootlegger** *noun*.

bootless *adj archaic* useless or unprofitable: *a bootless task.* ⟫⟫ **bootlessly** *adv*, **bootlessness** *noun*. [BOOT³]

bootlick *verb intrans informal* to attempt to gain favour by a cringing or flattering manner. ⟫⟫ **bootlicker** *noun*.

boots *noun* (*pl* **boots**) *Brit, dated* (*treated as sing.*) a servant who polished shoes and carried luggage, *esp* in a hotel. [from *pl* of BOOT¹]

boot sale *noun* = CAR BOOT SALE.

bootstrap¹ *noun* **1** a looped tab at the back of a boot, used for pulling the boot on with. **2** the procedure of starting up a computer in such a way that its operating programs load automatically. ✴ **pull oneself up by one's bootstraps** to improve one's lot through one's own efforts.

bootstrap² *verb trans* (**bootstrapped, bootstrapping**) = BOOT UP.

boot up *verb trans and intrans* to start up (a computer). [from BOOTSTRAP¹]

boot-up *noun* = BOOTSTRAP¹ (2).

booty¹ /'boohti/ *noun* (*pl* **booties**) **1** plunder taken, e.g. in war. **2** a rich gain or prize. [modification of French *butin*, from early Low German *būte* exchange]

booty² *noun* (*pl* **booties**) *NAmer, informal* a person's bottom. [alteration of BODY]

booze[1] /boohz/ *noun informal* **1** intoxicating drink, *esp* spirits. **2** a drinking spree. [Middle English *bousen* from early Dutch or early Flemish *būsen* to drink excessively]

booze[2] *verb intrans informal* to drink intoxicating liquor to excess.

boozer *noun informal* **1** a person who drinks excessively. **2** *Brit* a public house.

booze-up *noun informal* a drunken party or a drinking spree.

boozy *adj* (**boozier, booziest**) *informal* **1** characterized by much intake of alcohol: *a boozy evening at the pub*. **2** given to drinking heavily: *your boozy friends*. ⟩⟩ **boozily** *adv*.

bop[1] /bop/ *noun chiefly Brit, informal* a dance to popular music. [short for BEBOP]

bop[2] *verb intrans* (**bopped, bopping**) *informal* to dance to popular music. ⟩⟩ **bopper** *noun*.

bop[3] *noun* = BEBOP. [short for BEBOP]

bop[4] *verb trans* (**bopped, bopping**) *informal* to punch (somebody) smartly. [imitative]

bop[5] *noun informal* a punch.

bor. *abbr* borough.

bora[1] /'bawrə/ *noun* a violent cold northerly wind of the Adriatic. [Italian dialect, from Latin *boreas* bora: see BOREAL[1]]

bora[2] *noun* an Australian Aboriginal initiation rite marking the passage from boyhood to manhood. [from Kamilaroi (an Aboriginal language) *buuru*]

boracic /bə'rasik/ *adj* **1** = BORIC. **2** *Brit, informal* penniless; = SKINT. [(sense 1) medieval Latin *borac-, borax*: see BORAX; (sense 2) from *boracic lint* rhyming slang for SKINT]

boracic acid /bə'rasik/ *noun* = BORIC ACID.

borage /'borij, 'burij/ *noun* a coarse hairy blue-flowered European herb: *Borago officinalis*. [Middle English *borage* via Old French from medieval Latin *borago*, perhaps from Arabic *'abū ḥurās* father of roughness (because of its hairiness), or *'abū 'āraq* father of sweat (because of its use in inducing sweating)]

borak /'bawrak/ *noun Aus, NZ, informal* banter; teasing; raillery. [Australian pidgin word, from Wathawurung (an Aboriginal language) *burug* no, not]

borane /'bawrayn/ *noun* a chemical compound of the elements boron and hydrogen, or a derivative of such a compound. [BORON + -ANE]

borate /'bawrayt/ *noun* a salt or ester of a boric acid.

borax /'bawraks/ *noun* natural or synthetic hydrated sodium borate used *esp* as a flux, cleansing agent, and water-softener. [Middle English *boras* via French from medieval Latin *borac-, borax*, ultimately from Persian *būrah*]

borazon /'bawrazon/ *noun* a substance that consists of a boron nitride and is as hard as diamond but more resistant to high temperature. [BORON + AZ- + -ON[1]]

borborygmus /bawbə'rigməs/ *noun* (*pl* **borborygmi** /-mie/) a rumbling noise in the stomach. ⟩⟩ **borborygmic** /-mik/ *adj*. [scientific Latin from Greek *borborugmos* intestinal rumbling]

Bordeaux /baw'doh/ *noun* (*pl* **Bordeaux** /baw'doh(z)/) a red or white wine of the Bordeaux region of France.

Bordeaux mixture *noun* a fungicide used *esp* on fruit trees, made by mixing copper sulphate with lime and water. [first used in the vineyards of Bordeaux, SW France]

bordello /baw'deloh/ *noun* (*pl* **bordellos**) *chiefly NAmer* a brothel. [Italian *bordello* from Old French *bordel*, from *borde* hut, of Germanic origin]

border[1] /'bawdə/ *noun* **1** an outer part or edge. **2a** a boundary or frontier. **b** (**the Borders**) the parts of southern Scotland and northern England on either side of the boundary between the two. **c** (**the Border**) the boundary between the Republic of Ireland and Northern Ireland. **3** a narrow bed of planted ground, e.g. beside a path. **4** an ornamental design at the edge of something, e.g. printed matter, fabric, or a rug. [Middle English *bordure* from Old French *bordeure*, of Germanic origin]

border[2] *verb* (**bordered, bordering**) ⟩ *verb trans* **1** to form a border along the edge of (something): *lawns bordered with neat gravel paths*. **2** said of a country or region: to adjoin (another country or region). ⟩ *verb intrans* **1** (+ on) said of a country or region: to adjoin another country or region. **2** (+ on) to be close to a feeling or state: *She began now to have the anxiety which borders on hopelessness* — Jane Austen. ⟩⟩ **bordered** *adj*.

Border collie *noun* a collie of a rough-haired stocky breed commonly used in Britain for herding sheep, usu having a black-and-white coat. [from its origin in the borderlands between England and Scotland]

borderer /'bawdərə/ *noun* a person who lives in a border area between two countries e.g. (**Borderer**) that between Scotland and England.

borderland *noun* **1** the area of country around a border or frontier. **2** the indeterminate territory at the dividing line between two things, belonging definitely to neither one nor the other: *a golden borderland between sleep and waking* — Stevenson.

borderline *adj* **1** verging on one or other place, stake, or concept without being definitely assignable to either. **2** not quite meeting accepted standards, e.g. of morality or good taste: *a borderline joke*.

border line *noun* a line of demarcation.

bordure /'bawdyooə/ *noun* in heraldry, a border round the edge of a shield. [Middle English *bordure* BORDER[1]]

bore[1] /baw/ *verb trans* **1** to make (a hole) in something using a drill. **2** to hollow out (a gun barrel). ⟩ *verb intrans* **1a** to make a hole in something by boring: *They bored through from one cavern into the next*. **b** to drill a mine or well: *Boring for oil will begin next month*. **2** said of a racehorse or athlete: to push another runner out of the way. [Old English *borian*]

bore[2] *noun* **1** a hole made by, or as if by boring. **2a** an interior cylindrical cavity. **b** the barrel of a gun. **3a** the size of a hole. **b** the interior diameter of a tube; calibre. **c** the diameter of an engine cylinder.

bore[3] *noun* a tedious person, situation, or thing. [perhaps from BORE[2]]

bore[4] *verb trans* to weary (somebody) by being dull or monotonous. ⟩⟩ **bored** *adj*.

bore[5] *noun* a tidal flood that moves swiftly in the form of a steep-fronted wave up an estuary, etc. [prob from Old Norse *bāra* wave]

bore[6] *verb* past tense of BEAR[2].

Boreal[1] /'bawri-əl/ *adj* relating to the coniferous forest belt growing in northern and mountainous parts of the northern hemisphere. [Middle English *boriall* from late Latin *borealis*, via Latin *boreas* north wind, north, from Greek *Boreas*, god of the north wind]

Boreal[2] *noun* one of the earliest post-glacial climactic periods in Northern Europe.

boredom /'bawd(ə)m/ *noun* the state of being bored: *No society seems ever to have succumbed to boredom* — J K Galbraith.

borehole *noun* a hole drilled in the earth to obtain water, oil, etc.

borer *noun* a tool used for boring.

boric /'bawrik/ *adj* relating to or containing boron.

boric acid *noun* a white crystalline solid acid used *esp* as a weak antiseptic: formula H_3BO_3.

boride /'bawried/ *noun* a binary compound of boron, usu with a more electropositive element or radical.

boring *adj* causing boredom; tedious; uninteresting. ⟩⟩ **boringly** *adv*.

borlotti bean /baw'loti/ *noun* a speckled pink kidney bean that turns brown when cooked. [plural of Italian *borlotto* kidney bean]

born /bawn/ *adj* **1a** brought into existence by, or as if by, birth: *new-born children; with a courage born of desperation*. **b** (used in combinations) by birth; native: *British-born*. **2** having a specified character, situation, or destiny from birth. **3** (+ of) resulting from (e.g. a feeling or cause): *wisdom born of experience; a born leader*. ✳ **born and bred** by birth and training; through and through: *a countryman born and bred*. **never in all my born days** never in my whole life. **not born yesterday** sufficiently knowing about the ways of the world. [Old English *boren*, past part. of *beran* BEAR[2]]

born-again *adj* having undergone a conversion, *esp* to evangelical Christianity.

borne[1] /bawn/ *verb* past part. of BEAR[2].

borne[2] *adj* (used in combinations) carried by something specified: *airborne; water-borne*.

Bornean /'bawni-ən/ *noun* a native or inhabitant of Borneo in the Malay Archipelago. ⟩⟩ **Bornean** *adj*.

bornite /'bawniet/ *noun* a reddish brown mineral that becomes iridescent from tarnish, consisting of a sulphide of copper and iron and constituting an important source of copper: formula Cu_5FeS_4. [named after Ignaz von *Born* d.1791, Austrian mineralogist]

boron /'bawron/ *noun* a metalloid chemical element found in nature only in combination: symbol B, atomic number 5. ⟫⟫ **boronic** /baw'ronik/ *adj*. [BORAX + *-on* as in *carbon*]

boronia /bə'rohniə/ *noun* a sweet-scented Australian shrub, cultivated for the cut-flower trade: genus *Boronia*. [scientific Latin, named after Francesco *Borone*, d.1794, Italian botanist]

boron nitride *noun* a chemical compound of boron and nitrogen that has a very high melting point and occurs in various forms, e.g. a relatively soft form used in lubricants and in heat-resistant linings for furnaces, etc, and as BORAZON (man-made substance as hard as diamond).

borosilicate glass /bawroh'silikət, -kayt/ *noun* glass containing more boron than usual, used *esp* to make heat-resistant casserole dishes, plates, laboratory flasks, etc. [BORON + SILICATE]

borough /'burə/ *noun* **1** a British urban constituency. **2a** a municipal corporation in certain states of the USA. **b** any of the five political divisions of New York City. [Middle English *burgh*, from Old English *burg* fortified town; Old English *beorg* BARROW[2]]

borrow[1] /'boroh/ *verb trans* **1a** to take or receive (something) with the implied or expressed intention of returning it to its owner or the place where it belongs. **b** to get (a sum of money) from a bank, etc, under an arrangement to pay it back, usu with interest. **2a** to appropriate or adopt (something) for a temporary period: *borrowing prestige from her predecessor*. **b** to take (ideas, etc) from somebody else. **c** to introduce (words from another language) into one's own. **3** in arithmetic, to take (one) from the number of the next highest power of ten when the number being subtracted from is less than the number to be subtracted: *If you subtract 9 from 43, you have to borrow 1 and take 9 from 13*. **4** in executing a stroke in golf, to allow (an amount of deviation from a straight line) to counter the effect of a slope. ⟩ *verb intrans* **1** to borrow something: *Live frugally and you won't have to borrow*. **2** said of a golf ball: to deviate from a straight line because of the slope of the green: *It will borrow from the right*. ✳ **living on borrowed time** continuing to live in spite of being terminally ill. ⟫⟫ **borrower** *noun*. [Old English *borgian*]
Usage note
See note at LEND.

borrow[2] *noun* the tendency of a golf ball to deviate from a straight line because of the slope of the green.

borrow pit *noun* (*also* **borrow hole**) a hole resulting from the excavation of material for use in embanking.

borscht /bawsht/ *or* **borsch** /bawsh/ *noun* a soup of Russian origin, made primarily from beetroots and served hot or cold, often with sour cream. [Russian *borshch*]

Borstal /'bawstl/ *noun Brit* formerly, a penal institution providing training for young offenders. [named after *Borstal*, village in Kent, England, site of first such institution]

bort *or* **boart** /bawt/ *noun* imperfectly crystallized diamond fragments, used as an abrasive. [prob from Dutch *boort*]

borzoi /'bawzoy, baw'zoy/ *noun* a dog of a large long-haired breed developed in Russia, *esp* for pursuing wolves. [Russian *borzoĭ* swift]

boscage *or* **boskage** /'boskij/ *noun* a growth of trees or shrubs. [Middle English *boskage*, ultimately from Old French *bois, bosc* forest]

bosh /bosh/ *noun informal* nonsense. [Turkish *boş* empty, useless]

bosk /bosk/ *noun literary* a small wooded area: *in the bleak tangles of the bosk* — Oscar Wilde. [Middle English *bosk*, variant of *busk* BUSH[1]]

boskage /'boskij/ *noun* see BOSCAGE.

bosky /'boski/ *adj* (**boskier, boskiest**) *literary* full of trees; wooded.

bo's'n /'bohz(ə)n, 'bohs(ə)n/ *noun* see BOATSWAIN.

Bosnian /'bozni-ən/ *noun* **1** a native or inhabitant of Bosnia. **2** a Slavonic language spoken by the Bosnians and written in the Latin alphabet: compare CROATIAN, SERB. ⟫⟫ **Bosnian** *adj*.

bosom /'boozəm/ *noun* **1a** the front of the human chest; *esp* the female breasts. **b** *informal* either of the female breasts. **2** the breast considered as the centre of secret thoughts and emotions: *Hers was not the only dissatisfied bosom* — Jane Austen. **3** the part of a garment covering the breast: *He then drew a pistol from his bosom* — Poe. **4** the deep heart or centre of something: *In the deep bosom of the ocean buried* — Shakespeare. ✳ **in the bosom of one's family** safely surrounded by one's loved ones. [Old English *bōsm*]

bosom companion *noun* = BOSOM FRIEND.

bosomed *adj* (*used in combinations*) having a bosom of the kind specified: *big-bosomed*.

bosom friend *noun* an intimate friend.

bosomy *adj* having large breasts.

boson /'bohson/ *noun* a particle, e.g. a photon, meson, or alpha particle, that obeys relations stated by Bose and Einstein and whose spin is either zero or an integral number. ⟫⟫ **bosonic** /boh'sonik/ *adj*. [from the name of Satyendranath *Bose*, d.1974, Indian physicist + -ON[2]]

BOSS /bos/ *abbr SAfr* Bureau of State Security.

boss[1] /bos/ *noun informal* **1** a person who exercises control or authority; *specif* somebody who directs or supervises workers. **2** a politician who controls a party organization, e.g. in the USA. [Dutch *baas* master]

boss[2] *verb trans informal* **1** to act as director or supervisor of (the staff of an organization, etc). **2** (*usu* + about/around) to give orders to (somebody) in a domineering manner.

boss[3] *adj NAmer, informal* first-rate or excellent.

boss[4] *noun* **1** a stud or knob projecting from the centre of a shield. **2** a carved ornament concealing the intersection of the ribs of a vault or panelled ceiling. **3** the enlarged part of a shaft, on which a wheel is mounted. **4** the middle part of a propeller. **5** a rounded mass of igneous rock protruding through other layers. **6** a protuberant part; a prominence. [Middle English *boce* via Old French from (assumed) vulgar Latin *bottia*]

bossa nova /,bosə 'nohvə/ *noun* a Brazilian dance similar to the samba, or a piece of music for dancing it to. [Portuguese *bossa nova*, literally 'new trend']

boss-eyed *adj Brit, informal* having a squint; cross-eyed. [perhaps connected with dialect *boss* bungle, as in BOSS SHOT]

boss shot *noun dialect or informal* a bad shot or aim; a bungled attempt. [dialect *boss* bungle]

bossy /'bosi/ *adj* (**bossier, bossiest**) *informal* domineering or dictatorial. ⟫⟫ **bossily** *adv*, **bossiness** *noun*.

bossyboots /'bosiboohts/ *noun Brit, informal* a bossy or domineering person.

bosun /'bohz(ə)n, 'bohs(ə)n/ *noun* see BOATSWAIN.

BOT *abbr* Board of Trade.

bot[1] *or* **bott** /bot/ *noun* the larva of the BOTFLY, which develops parasitically in the stomach or intestines of sheep, horses, and cattle. [prob of Low German or Low Dutch origin]

bot[2] *verb* (**botted, botting**) ⟩ *verb trans Aus, informal* to borrow, cadge, or scrounge (something). ⟩ *verb intrans Aus, informal* (*usu* + on) to sponge: *I don't want to bot on my friends all the time*. [prob from BOTFLY in reference to its parasitism]

bot[3] *noun Aus, informal* a scrounger. ✳ **on the bot** on the scrounge.

bot. *abbr* **1** botanical. **2** botany. **3** botanist. **4** bottle.

BOTAC *abbr* British Overseas Trade Advisory Council.

botanic /bə'tanik/ *adj* = BOTANICAL.

botanical /bə'tanikl/ *adj* **1** relating to plants or botany. **2** derived from plants. **3** said of a plant: occurring more or less unchanged from the original wild form. ⟫⟫ **botanically** *adv*. [French *botanique* from Greek *botanikos* of herbs, from *botanē* pasture, herb, from *boskein* to feed]

botanic garden *noun* (*also in pl*) a place in which plant collections are grown for display and scientific study.

botanize *or* **botanise** /'botəniez/ *verb intrans* **1** to collect plants for botanical investigation. **2** to study plants, *esp* on a field trip.

botany /'botəni/ *noun* (*pl* **botanies**) **1** a branch of biology dealing with plant life. **2a** the plant life of a region. **b** the properties and life phenomena exhibited by a plant, plant type, or plant group. ⟫⟫ **botanist** *noun*. [back-formation from *botanic*: see BOTANICAL]

botany wool *noun* a fine grade of merino wool, *esp* from Australian merino sheep. [*Botany* Bay, region of New South Wales in Australia, where it orig came from]

botch[1] /boch/ *verb trans informal* **1** to repair, patch, or assemble (something) in a makeshift or inept way. **2** to foul up or bungle (a task, arrangement, etc) hopelessly. ➤➤ **botcher** *noun*. [Middle English *bocchen* to patch; earlier history unknown]

botch² *noun informal* something botched; a mess: *Somebody's made a botch of the repairs*. ➤➤ **botchy** *adj*.

botel /'boh'tel/ *noun* see BOATEL.

botfly /'botflie/ *noun* (*pl* **botflies**) any of several genera of heavy-bodied two-winged flies with larvae parasitic in the alimentary canals of horses, sheep, cattle, and rarely, human beings: genus *Gasterophilus* and other genera. [BOT¹ + FLY³]

both¹ /bohth/ *adj* being the two; affecting or involving the one as well as the other: *Both his feet were blistered; Both parents were alcoholics*. ✳ **have it both ways** to exploit or profit from each of a pair of contradictory positions, circumstances, etc, or to maintain two contradictory views simultaneously. [Middle English *bothe* from Old Norse *bāthir*]

both² *pronoun* the one as well as the other: *We're both well; I've contacted both of them*.

both³ *conj* used to indicate and stress the inclusion of each of two things specified by coordinated words or word groups: *Both she and my daughter have been invited; She both speaks and writes Swahili*.

bother¹ /'bodhə/ *verb* (**bothered, bothering**) ➤ *verb trans* **1** to disturb, pester, or distract (somebody): *Do stop bothering me while I'm working*. **2** to cause (somebody) to be troubled or perplexed: *His silence bothered her*. **3** to cause (somebody) discomfort or pain: *Her hip bothers her a bit sometimes*. **4** to cause annoyance to (somebody): *Will the radio bother you?* ➤ *verb intrans* **1** (*usu in negative contexts*) to take the trouble to do something: *He didn't bother to answer; Usually she didn't bother putting on make-up at the weekends*. **2** (*usu in negative contexts*) to concern oneself about something: *We don't bother with anniversaries in this family*. **3** to take pains; to take the trouble: *Thanks, but you needn't have bothered*. ✳ **can't be bothered** to be unwilling to take the trouble (to do something): *I can't be bothered learning all these irregular verbs*. [perhaps from Irish Gaelic *bodhraim* I deafen, annoy]

bother² *noun* **1** trouble, *esp* involving violence: *Gangs of ... dropouts ... looking for bother —* George Melly. **2** difficulty or problems: *This time the program loaded without any bother*. **3** unnecessary fuss or effort: *Sorry to cause all this bother*. **4** something that is a nuisance or requires a lot of attention: *I'd love a cup if it's no bother*.

bother³ *interj* (*also* **bother it**) used as a mild expression of annoyance.

botheration /bodhə'raysh(ə)n/ *noun* sometimes used as an interjection: an expression of annoyance or trouble.

bothersome /'bodhəs(ə)m/ *adj* causing bother; annoying.

bothy /'bothi/ *noun* (*pl* **bothies**) *Scot* **1** a small outbuilding on a farm which formerly provided accommodation for farmworkers. **2** a small hut in the mountains which provides shelter for mountaineers and hill-walkers. [Scots *bothy*, prob from Gaelic *bothan* hut, and related to BOOTH]

Botox /'bohtoks/ *noun trademark* a dilute form of the toxin that causes botulism, used as a muscle relaxant in the treatment of a number of disorders such as strabismus and uncontrolled eye blinking, and now also in cosmetic surgery to remove certain types of facial wrinkle. [short for *Botulinum Toxin*]

bo tree /boh/ *noun* the pipal tree: *Ficus religiosa*. [Sinhalese *bō*, from Sanskrit *bodhi*]

botryoidal /botri'oydl/ *adj* having the form of a bunch of grapes: *botryoidal garnets*. [Greek *botryoeidēs*, from *botrys* bunch of grapes]

botrytis /bə'trietəs/ *noun* a rot-causing fungus, *esp* the grey mould *Botrytis cinerea*, which is encouraged to form on grapes used for certain wines; = NOBLE ROT. [scientific Latin, irreg formed from Greek *botrys* bunch of grapes]

Botswanan /bot'swahnən/ *noun* a native or inhabitant of Botswana. ➤➤ **Botswanan** *adj*.

bott /bot/ *noun* see BOT¹.

bottle¹ /'botl/ *noun* **1a** a rigid or semirigid container, *esp* for liquids, usu of glass or plastic, with a comparatively narrow neck or mouth. **b** the contents of a bottle. **c** bottled milk used to feed infants, or its purpose-designed container: *The baby has had her bottle*. **2** *Brit, informal* courage; = NERVE¹ (2): *He didn't have the bottle to go through with it*. ✳ **hit the bottle** *informal* to start drinking alcohol heavily. **on the bottle** *informal* drinking heavily. ➤➤ **bottleful** *noun*. [Middle English *botel* via early French *bouteille* from medieval Latin *butticula*, dimin. of late Latin *buttis* cask]

bottle² *verb trans* **1** to put (liquid, *esp* wine or milk) into a bottle. **2** *Brit* to preserve (fruit, etc) by storage in glass jars. ✳ **bottle it** *Brit, informal* to lose one's nerve; = BOTTLE OUT: *When she was put to the test, she bottled it*.

bottle bank *noun* a large container, sited in a public place, in which people can deposit empty glass bottles for recycling.

bottlebrush *noun* **1** a brush for cleaning bottles; *specif* one with a cylindrical head on a thin stem. **2** any of several species of Australasian shrubs of the eucalyptus family with spikes of brightly coloured, *esp* red, flowers: genera *Callistemon* and *Melaleuca*. Also called CALLISTEMON.

bottled gas *noun* liquefied propane or butane in portable containers, for use as fuel for camping stoves, blowlamps, etc.

bottle-feed *verb trans* (*past tense and past part.* **bottle-fed** /'fed/) to feed (an infant) by means of a bottle.

bottle gas *noun* = BOTTLED GAS.

bottle glass *noun* tough dark green or amber glass used for making bottles.

bottle green *noun* a very dark green.

bottle-green *adj* very dark green.

bottle jack *noun* NZ a large jack used for heavy lifting jobs.

bottleneck *noun* **1** the neck of a bottle. **2a** a narrow stretch of road where the flow of traffic is impeded, so that frequent hold-ups result. **b** a point or situation where free movement or progress is held up. **3** a style of guitar-playing using an object, e.g. a metal bar or the neck of a bottle, pressed against the strings to produce the effect of one note sliding into another.

bottle-nosed dolphin *noun* (*also* **bottlenose dolphin**) a moderately large stout-bodied dolphin with a prominent beak and long curved dorsal fin: *Tursiops truncatus*.

bottle out *verb intrans* *Brit, informal* to lose one's nerve and back out of a plan, challenge, etc.

bottle party *noun* a private party to which guests contribute bottles of drink.

bottler *noun* **1** a person who bottles wine, etc. **2** *Aus, NZ, informal* a term for something or somebody exceptional.

bottle store *noun SAfr* an off-licence.

bottle tree *noun* an Australian tree that has a swollen bottle-shaped trunk: *Adansonia gregorii* and *Brachychiton rupestre*.

bottle up *verb trans* to confine or restrain (one's emotions): *It's no good just bottling up your anger*.

bottom¹ /'botəm/ *noun* **1a** the underside of something. **b** a surface on which something rests. **c** *chiefly Brit* the buttocks or rump. **2** the ground beneath a body of water. **3a** the part of a ship's hull lying below the water. **b** *archaic* a boat or ship, *esp* a merchant ship. **4a** the lowest, deepest, or farthest part or place. **b** the lowest position or last place in order of precedence: *the children at the bottom of the class*. **c** = BOTTOM GEAR. **d** (*also in pl*) the lower part of a two-piece garment: *pyjama bottoms*. **5** (*also in pl*) low-lying grassland along a watercourse. **6** a foundation colour applied to textile fibres before dyeing. **7** *archaic* solidity and firmness of character; staying power, *esp* that of horses: *He has a certain amount of bottom which a lot don't —* The Guardian. ✳ **at bottom** basically, really. **be at the bottom of** to be the real cause of (a situation, problem, etc). **bottoms up!** *informal* used as a toast before starting to drink: cheers! **from the bottom of one's heart** with fervent sincerity. **get to the bottom of** to find out the truth, source, or basis of (a situation, problem, etc). **the bottom falls out of the market, etc** the market, etc collapses suddenly. **touch bottom** to reach a level of morale so low that one can sink no further. [Old English *botm*]

bottom² *verb trans* **1** to provide (a chair, etc) with a bottom. **2** to provide a foundation for (a theory, etc). ➤ *verb intrans* **1** said of a submarine: to reach the sea bed. **2** *Aus, NZ* to excavate (a mine) to the depth of the mineral-bearing strata. ➤➤ **bottomer** *noun*.

bottom³ *adj* **1** belonging to, relating to, or situated at the bottom or lower part of something: *Where's the bottom half of my bikini?* **2** said of fishes: frequenting the bottom of the sea or a river. ➤➤ **bottommost** /-mohst, -məst/ *adj*.

bottom drawer *noun Brit, dated* a young woman's collection of clothes and household articles, kept in anticipation of her marriage, or the drawer in which she stores these things.

bottomed *adj* (*used in combinations*) having a bottom of the kind specified: *copper-bottomed pans*.

bottom gear *noun* the transmission gear of a vehicle giving the lowest speed of travel.

bottomless *adj* **1** extremely deep. **2** boundless or unlimited. ➤ **bottomlessly** *adv*, **bottomlessness** *noun*.

bottom line *noun* **1** (**the bottom line**) the last line of figures in a financial report showing the final profit or loss. **2** (**the bottom line**) *informal* the one important criterion that decides viability: *The bottom line is, will the public buy it?* **3** (**the bottom line**) *informal* the significant point to recognize.

bottom out *verb intrans* said of a situation: to sink to a lowest point and then level out.

bottomry /'botəmri/ *noun dated* a contract by which a ship is pledged as security for a loan to be repaid at the end of a successful voyage. [modification of Dutch *bodemerij*, from *bodem* bottom, ship]

bottom-up *adj* **1** proceeding from the detail to the general principle: compare TOP-DOWN. **2** said of computer-programming: characterized by first developing the simplest operations of a program, followed by integration of the more complex units, the advantage of this order of working being the ability to test as one goes along. **3** said of business decisions: based on the requirements of the ultimate consumer; non-hierarchical.

botty /'boti/ *noun* (*pl* **botties**) *Brit, informal* the bottom or buttocks.

botulin /'botyoolin/ *noun* a toxin that is the direct cause of botulism. [prob from scientific Latin *botulinus*, a spore-forming bacterium, from Latin *botulus* sausage]

botulism /'botyooliz(ə)m/ *noun* acute, often fatal, food poisoning caused by botulin in food, *esp* incompletely sterilized food preserved in an airtight container.

bouclé /'boohklay/ *noun* an uneven yarn of three plies, one of which forms loops at intervals, or fabric made from this. [French *bouclé* curly, past part. of *boucler* to curl, from *boucle* buckle, curl]

boudoir /'boohdwah/ *noun* a woman's dressing room, bedroom, or private sitting room. [French *boudoir*, literally 'sulking place', from *bouder* to pout]

bouffant /'boohfong/ *adj* puffed out: *a bouffant hairstyle*. [French *bouffant* puffed, swelling, present part. of *bouffer* to puff]

bougainvillea or **bougainvillaea** /boohgən'vilyə, -li·ə/ *noun* an ornamental tropical climbing plant with brilliant purple or red floral bracts: genus *Bougainvillea*. [scientific Latin, named after Louis Antoine de *Bougainville*, d.1811, French navigator, who introduced it to Europe]

bough /bow/ *noun* a main branch of a tree. ➤➤ **boughed** *adj*. [Old English *bōg*]

bought /bawt/ *verb* past tense and past part. of BUY[1].

bougie /'boozhi/ *noun* a tapering cylindrical instrument for introduction into a tubular passage of the body. [French *bougie*, literally 'wax candle', named after *Bougie*, seaport in Algeria from which wax was exported]

bouillabaisse /booh·yə'bes (*French* bujabɛs)/ *noun* a highly seasoned fish stew made with at least two kinds of fish. [French *bouillabaisse* from Provençal *bouiabaisso*]

bouillon /'boohyong (*French* bujɔ̃)/ *noun* a thin clear soup made usu from lean beef. [French *bouillon* from Old French *boillon*, from *boillir* to boil]

boulder /'bohldə/ *noun* a large stone or mass of rock greater than 200mm in diameter. ➤➤ **bouldery** *adj*. [short for *boulder stone*, from Middle English *bulder ston*, of Scandinavian origin; related to Swedish dialect *bullersten* large stone in a stream, from *buller* noise + *sten* stone]

boulder clay *noun* a glacial deposit of pebbles, rock, etc in clay.

boule[1] /boohl/ *noun* **1** (*also in pl, but treated as sing.*) an orig French game similar to bowls in which usu metal balls are thrown or rolled in an attempt to place them nearer to a jack than the opponent's balls. **2** a synthetically formed pear-shaped mass of sapphire, spinel, etc with the atomic structure of a single crystal. [French *boule* ball, ultimately from Latin *bulla* bubble]

boule[2] /boohl, byoohl/ *noun* see BUHL.

boule[3] /'boohli/ *noun* **1** the legislative assembly of any of the ancient Greek city states, *esp* that of Athens. **2** the modern Greek parliament. [Greek *boulē* assembly]

boulevard /'boohləvahd, -vah/ *noun* a broad avenue, usu lined by trees. [French *boulevard*, modification of early Dutch *bolwerc*: see BULWARK]

boulle /boohl/ *noun* see BUHL.

boult /bohlt/ *verb trans* see BOLT[5].

bounce[1] /bowns/ *verb trans* **1** to cause (a ball, etc) to rebound. **2** *informal* to return (a cheque) as not good because of lack of funds in the payer's account. ➤ *verb intrans* **1** to rebound after striking the ground or other surface. **2** to move violently, noisily, or with a springing step: *She bounced into the room.* **3** *informal* said of a cheque: to be returned by a bank as not good. ✳ **bounce something off somebody** *informal* to see what somebody's reactions are to an idea, etc. [Middle English *bounsen* to beat, thump, prob of imitative origin]

bounce[2] *noun* **1a** a sudden leap or bound. **b** a rebound. **2** verve, liveliness. **3** the quality of bouncing well; springiness.

bounce back *verb intrans* to recover quickly from a blow or defeat.

bouncer *noun* **1** a person employed in a nightclub or other public place to restrain or remove disorderly people. **2** in cricket, a fast and aggressive short-pitched delivery of the ball that passes or hits the batsman at above chest height after bouncing.

bouncing /'bownsing/ *adj* enjoying good health; robust: *a bouncing baby*.

bouncing bet *noun* (*also* **bouncing Bet**) = SOAPWORT. [*Bet*, nickname for *Elizabeth*]

bouncy /'bownsi/ *adj* (**bouncier, bounciest**) **1** that bounces readily. **2** buoyant; exuberant. ➤➤ **bouncily** *adv*, **bounciness** *noun*.

bouncy castle *noun* (*also* **Bouncy Castle**) *trademark* a large inflatable play structure with a base and sides, typically in the shape of a castle, set up outdoors for children to jump around on, *esp* at fairs, birthday parties, etc.

bound[1] /bownd/ *adj* (*also used in combinations*) going or intending to go somewhere specified: *I was driving along the M5, bound for home; the northbound carriageway*. [Middle English *boun* ready, prepared to go, from Old Norse *būinn*, past part. of *būa* to dwell, prepare]

bound[2] *noun* (*usu in pl, treated as sing. or pl*) **1** a limiting line; a boundary. **2** something that limits or restrains: *beyond the bounds of decency*. ✳ **out of bounds 1** outside the permitted limits: *The town centre was out of bounds for boarding-school pupils*. **2** said of the ball in team sport, etc: outside the area of play. [Middle English via Old French from medieval Latin *bodina*]

bound[3] *verb trans* (*usu in passive*) **1** to set limits to (something): *His views were not bounded by any narrow ideas of expediency* — A Jameson. **2** to form the boundary of (a country, region, etc): *a landlocked country bounded by high mountain ranges*.

bound[4] *adj* **1a** (*usu used in combinations*) confined to a place: *housebound; desk-bound*. **b** certain or sure (to do something): *It's bound to rain soon*. **2** (*also used in combinations*) placed under legal or moral obligation (to do something): *I'm bound to say; We are duty-bound to assist him*. **3** held in chemical or physical combination: *bound water in a molecule*. **4** (*often used in combinations*) said of books: having the kind of binding specified: *a leather-bound volume*. **5** said of a linguistic element: always occurring in combination with another linguistic form, e.g. the negative prefix *un-* as in *unknown* and the agent suffix *-er* as in *speaker*. ✳ **bound up with** closely connected with or dependent on (something): *Logic is bound up with mathematics*. **I'll be bound** I bet; I'll warrant. **I'm bound to say** I must admit. [past part. of BIND[1]]

bound[5] *noun* **1** a leap or jump. **2** a bounce. [early French *bond*, from *bondir* to rebound, earlier to resound, from Latin *bombus*: see BOMB[1]]

bound[6] *verb intrans* **1** to move by leaping. **2** to rebound or bounce.

bound[7] *verb* past tense and past part. of BIND[1].

boundary /'bownd(ə)ri/ *noun* (*pl* **boundaries**) **1** something, *esp* a dividing line, that indicates or fixes a limit or extent. **2** a border or frontier. **3a** the marked limits of a cricket field. **b** a stroke in cricket that sends the ball over the boundary, or the score of four or six made by this. [English dialect *bounder*, from BOUND[2]]

boundary layer *noun* the thin layer of virtually stationary liquid or gas that surrounds a body moving through the medium.

boundary rider *noun Aus, NZ* a person who rides round a sheep or cattle station to maintain the fencing.

boundary umpire *noun* in Australian Rules football, an umpire stationed on the sidelines to signal when the ball is out.

bounden /'bowndən/ ✳ **bounden duty** an obligatory or binding responsibility. [Middle English, archaic past part. of BIND[1]]

bounder /'bowndə/ *noun Brit, dated, informal* a man who behaves badly; a cad. [from BOUND[6]]

boundless /'bowndlis/ *adj* limitless. ➤➤ **boundlessly** *adv*, **boundlessness** *noun*. [from BOUND[2]]

bounteous /'bownti-əs/ *adj* giving or given freely: *Hail, universal Lord, be bounteous still* — Milton; *this bounteous repast* — Charlotte Brontë. ➤➤ **bounteously** *adv*, **bounteousness** *noun*. [Middle English *bountevous* from Old French *bontif* kind, from *bonté*: see BOUNTY]

bountiful /'bowntif(ə)l/ *adj* **1** generous; liberal: *I never met with a young woman to whom Providence has been as bountiful as it has to you, Judith* — J Fenimore Cooper. **2** abundant; plentiful: *a bountiful harvest.* ➤➤ **bountifully** *adv*, **bountifulness** *noun*.

bounty /'bownti/ *noun* (*pl* **bounties**) **1** *literary* generosity. **2** *literary* something given generously; an act of generosity: *the many bounties he studiously concealed, the many acts of humanity he performed in private* — James Boswell. **3a** a financial inducement or reward, *esp* when offered by a government for some act or service. **b** a payment to encourage the killing of vermin or dangerous animals. [Middle English *bounte* goodness, via Old French *bonté* from Latin *bonitat-*, *bonitas*, from *bonus* good]

bounty-hunter *noun* **1** a person who tracks down outlaws or wanted criminals for whose capture a reward is offered. **2** any person who undertakes searches or research for the sake of the reward offered.

bouquet /booh'kay/ *noun* **1** a bunch of flowers fastened together. **2** a distinctive and characteristic fragrance, e.g. of wine. [French *bouquet*, earlier 'thicket', from early French *bosquet*, from Old French *bosc* forest]

bouquet garni /'gahni/ *noun* a small bunch of herbs, e.g. thyme, parsley, and a bay leaf, for use in flavouring stews and soups. [French *bouquet garni*, literally 'garnished bouquet']

bourbon /'buhbən, 'booəbən (*French* burbɔ̃)/ *noun* **1** (**Bourbon**) a member of a royal dynasty who ruled in France, Spain, etc. **2** (*often* **Bourbon**) *chiefly NAmer* an extreme political reactionary. **3** *Brit* a chocolate-flavoured biscuit with a filling of chocolate cream. **4** a whisky distilled from a mash made up of not less than 51% maize plus malt and rye. ➤➤ **bourbonism** *noun*. [*Bourbon*, seigniory in France; (sense 4) *Bourbon* County, Kentucky, USA]

bourdon /'booədn, 'bawdn/ *noun* **1** a 16-foot organ STOP[2] (set of vibrators) that produces low notes. **2** the bass drone on a set of bagpipes. [early French *bourdon* bass pipe, of imitative origin]

bourgeois[1] /'booəzhwah, 'bawzhwah/ *noun* (*pl* **bourgeois** /'booəzhwah, 'bawzhwah/) **1** a middle-class person. **2** a person whose behaviour and views are influenced by middle-class values or interests. **3** (*in pl*) the bourgeoisie. [early French *bourgeois* burgher from Old French *borjois*, from *borc* town, from Latin *burgus* fortified place, of Germanic origin: related to BOROUGH]

bourgeois[2] *adj* **1** middle-class. **2** characterized by a narrow-minded concern for material interests and respectability. **3** capitalist.

bourgeoisie /booəzhwah'zee/ *noun* (*treated as sing. or pl*) the middle class. [French *bourgeoisie*, from *bourgeois*: see BOURGEOIS[1]]

bourn[1] /bawn/ *noun* a small stream. [from Old English *burn*, *bourne*]

bourn[2] *or* **bourne** *noun literary* a boundary or limit: *the undiscovered country from whose bourn no traveller returns* — Shakespeare. [early French *bourne* from Old French *bodne*: see BOUND[2]]

bourrée /'booray/ *noun* a 17th-cent. French dance usu in duple time, or a piece of music suitable for dancing it to. [French *bourrée*, literally 'bundle of twigs', perhaps because performed round a twig fire]

bourse /booəs, baws (*French* burs)/ *noun* **1** a stock exchange of continental Europe. **2** (**the Bourse**) the Paris stock exchange. [French *bourse*, literally 'purse', from medieval Latin *bursa*: see PURSE[1]]

Boursin /booə'sanh/ *noun trademark* a thick cream cheese of French origin that is flavoured with herbs, garlic, or pepper.

boustrophedon /boohstrə'feed(ə)n, bow-/ *adj* denoting a writing system, found e.g. in some ancient Greek inscriptions, with lines running alternately from left to right and from right to left. [Greek *boustrophēdon* literally 'ox-turning-wise', that is, turning like plough-pulling oxen at each end of the furrow, from *bous* ox, cow + *strephein* to turn]

bout /bowt/ *noun* **1** a spell of activity: *a bout of hard work.* **2** a boxing or wrestling match. **3** an outbreak or attack of illness, fever, etc. [English dialect *bout* a trip going and returning in ploughing, from Middle English *bought* bend, prob of Low German origin]

boutique /booh'teek/ *noun* a small fashionable shop selling specialized goods, *esp* clothes, or a small shop within a large department store. [French *boutique* shop, from Latin *apotheca*: see APOTHECARY. Compare BODEGA]

boutonniere /boohto'nyeə/ *noun* = BUTTONHOLE[1]. [French *boutonnière* buttonhole, from *bouton*: see BUTTON]

bouzouki /boo'zoohki/ *noun* (*pl* **bouzoukis**) a long-necked Greek stringed musical instrument that resembles a mandolin. [Modern Greek *mpouzouki*, prob from Turkish *büyük* large]

bovine /'bohvien/ *adj* **1** relating to cattle. **2** like an ox or cow, e.g. in being slow, stolid, or dull. [late Latin *bovinus*, from Latin *bov-*, *bos* ox, cow]

bovine somatotrophin *noun* a hormone that regulates growth in cattle, sometimes given in an artificial form to increase the production of milk.

bovine spongiform encephalopathy *noun* see BSE.

Bovril /'bovril/ *noun trademark* a concentrated beef extract. [Latin *bov-*, *bos* ox + *vril*, an imaginary force in the novel *The Coming Race* by E Bulwer-Lytton d.1873, British novelist]

bovver /'bovə/ *noun Brit, informal* rowdy or violent disturbance; aggro: *bovver boys*. [alteration of BOTHER[2]]

bow[1] /bow/ *verb intrans* **1** (+ to) to submit or yield to something or somebody: *I suppose we must bow to the inevitable.* **2** (*also* + down) to bend the head, body, or knee in respect, submission, or greeting. ➤ *verb trans* **1** to incline (the head, etc), *esp* in respect, submission, or shame. **2** to express (one's assent, etc) by inclining one's head. ✳ **bow and scrape** to act in an obsequious manner. [Old English *būgan*]

bow[2] /bow/ *noun* a bending of the head or body in respect, submission, or greeting. ✳ **make one's bow** to appear in public in a particular role or office for the first time: *when she made her bow as Speaker of the House.* **take a bow** to acknowledge applause or praise.

bow[3] /boh/ *noun* **1** a bend or arch. **2** a weapon for shooting arrows, consisting of a strip of wood, fibreglass, or other flexible material held bent by a strong cord connecting the two ends. **3** a knot that can be pulled undone, tied with two loops and two free ends, used for shoelaces, etc. **4** an implement for playing a violin, etc consisting of a resilient wooden rod with horsehairs stretched from end to end. [Old English *boga*; related to Old English *būgan* BOW[1]]

bow[4] /boh/ *verb trans* **1a** to cause (a person or thing) to bend into a curve: *bowed with age.* **b** (*also* + down) to weigh down or oppress (somebody): *bowed down with care.* **2** to play (a stringed instrument) with a bow. ➤ *verb intrans* **1** to bend or curve. **2** to use a bow to play a violin, etc.

bow[5] /bow/ *noun* **1** (*also in pl*) the forward part of a ship. **2** an oarsman in the front end of a boat; = BOWMAN[2]. ✳ **shot across the bows** a gesture intended as a sharp warning. [Middle English *bowe*, prob from Danish *bov* shoulder, bow, from Old Norse *bōgr*; related to Old English *bōg* BOUGH]

bowdlerize *or* **bowdlerise** /'bowdləriez/ *verb trans* to expurgate (a book, etc) by omitting or modifying parts considered too indecent or offensive for family reading. ➤➤ **bowdlerism** *noun*, **bowdlerization** /-'zayshən/ *noun*, **bowdlerizer** *noun*. [from the name of Thomas *Bowdler*, d.1825, English editor, who produced an expurgated edition of Shakespeare]

bowel /'bowəl/ *noun* **1a** (*in pl*) the intestines. **b** the large intestine or the small intestine. **2** (*in pl*) the innermost parts of something: *in the bowels of the earth.* ➤➤ **bowelless** *adj*. [Middle English from Old French *boel* from Latin *botellus*, dimin. of *botulus* sausage]

bowel movement *noun* **1** the action of discharging faeces from the body; defecation. **2** the stool or faeces discharged from the body.

bower[1] /'bowə/ *noun* **1** an attractive dwelling or retreat. **2** a shelter made e.g. in a garden with tree boughs or vines twisted together.

3 *literary* a boudoir. ⟫ **bowery** /-ri/ *adj*. [Old English *būr* dwelling]

bower² *noun* a ship's principal anchor carried in the bows.

bowerbird *noun* **1** any of several species of songbirds of Australia and New Guinea, the male of which builds a bower-like chamber or passage arched over with twigs and grasses, often adorned with bright-coloured feathers and shells, to attract the female: family Ptilonorhynchidae. **2** *Aus, NZ* a person who hoards odds and ends: *I've always been a bit of a bowerbird.*

bowfin /'bohfin/ *noun* a carnivorous N American freshwater bony fish with a long dorsal fin: *Amia calva.* Also called MUDFISH. [BOW³]

bowhead /'bohhed/ *noun* an Arctic right whale: *Balaena mysticetus.* [BOW³]

bowie knife /'boh·i/ *noun* a stout hunting knife with a sharpened part on the back edge curved concavely to the point. [named after James Bowie d.1836, US soldier, the knife's most famous user]

bowl¹ /bohl/ *noun* **1** any of various round hollow vessels used *esp* for holding liquids or food or for mixing food. **2** the contents of a bowl: *She ate two bowls of porridge.* **3a** the hollow of a spoon or tobacco pipe. **b** the receptacle of a toilet. **4a** a bowl-shaped geographical region or formation. **b** *NAmer* a bowl-shaped structure; *esp* a sports stadium. ⟫ **bowled** *adj*, **bowlful** *noun*. [Old English *bolla*]

bowl² *noun* **1** a ball used in bowls that is weighted or shaped to give it a bias. **2** (*in pl, but treated as sing.*) a game played typically outdoors on a green, in which bowls are rolled at a target jack in an attempt to bring them nearer to it than one's opponent's bowls. [Middle English *boule* via Old French from Latin *bulla* bubble]

bowl³ *verb intrans* **1a** to participate in a game of bowls or bowling. **b** to play or roll a ball in bowls or bowling. **c** to play as a bowler in cricket. **2** (*often* + along) to travel in a vehicle smoothly and rapidly. ⟫ *verb trans* **1a** to roll (a ball) in bowling. **b** to score by bowling: *He bowls 150.* **2a** to deliver (a ball) to a batsman in cricket. **b** said of a bowler: to dismiss (a batsman in cricket) by breaking the wicket.

bowlegged /bohˈleg(i)d/ *adj* having legs that are bowed outwards at the knees; bandy-legged. ⟫ **bowlegs** /'bohˈlegz/ *pl noun.*

bowler¹ *noun* the person who bowls in a team sport; *specif* in cricket, a member of the fielding side who bowls regularly as a specialist.

bowler² *noun* (*also* **bowler hat**) a stiff felt hat with a rounded crown and a narrow brim. [named after *Bowler*, a 19th-cent. family of English hatters]

bowline /'bohlien/ *noun* **1** a rope attached to a square sail that is used to keep the windward edge of the sail taut and at a steady angle to the wind. **2** a knot used to form a non-slipping loop at the end of a rope. [Middle English *bouline*, perhaps from *bowe* BOW⁵ + LINE¹]

bowling *noun* any of several games in which balls are rolled at one or more objects.

bowling alley *noun* a long narrow enclosure or lane with a smooth floor for bowling or playing skittles, or the building or room containing such lanes.

bowling average *noun* the average number of runs scored off the bowling of a cricketer per number of wickets taken, e.g. in a season or his or her career: compare BATTING AVERAGE.

bowling crease *noun* either of the lines drawn perpendicularly across a cricket pitch in line with each wicket: compare POPPING CREASE.

bowling green *noun* a smooth close-cut area of turf for playing bowls.

bowl out *verb trans* to dismiss all the members of (the batting side) in cricket.

bowl over *verb trans* **1** to bump into, or cause something to bump into (a person) so as to knock them down. **2** *informal* to overwhelm (somebody) with surprise: *We were bowled over by the news.*

bowman¹ /'bohmən/ *noun* (*pl* **bowmen**) an archer.

bowman² *noun* (*pl* **bowmen**) a boatman, oarsman, etc in the front of a boat.

Bowman's capsule /'bohmənz/ *noun* the thin membranous capsule surrounding each glomerulus in the kidneys of vertebrates. [named after Sir William *Bowman*, d.1892, English surgeon]

bow out /bow/ *verb intrans* to retire or withdraw.

bow saw /boh/ *noun* a saw having a narrow blade held under tension, *esp* by a light bow-shaped frame.

bowser /'bowzə/ *noun* **1a** a tanker for refuelling aircraft. **b** any tanker delivering fuel. **2** *Aus* a petrol pump. [from *Bowser* trademark for a petrol pump, orig manufactured by S F *Bowser*, Inc., Indiana]

bowshot /'bohshot/ *noun* the distance covered by an arrow shot from a bow.

bowsprit /'bohsprit/ *noun* a spar projecting forward from the bow of a ship. [Middle English *bouspret*, prob from Middle Low German *bōchsprēt*, from *bōch* bow + *sprēt* pole]

Bow-Street runner /'boh street/ *noun* a member of a police force in London in the early 19th cent.: *He was … giving such a show of excitement as would have convinced an Old Bailey judge or a Bow Street runner* — Stevenson. [named after *Bow Street* in London, site of the chief metropolitan police court]

bowstring /'bohstring/ *noun* the string that joins the ends of a bow for shooting arrows.

bow tie /boh/ *noun* a short tie fastened in a bow, *esp* a small black one for use with formal evening dress.

bow window /boh/ *noun* a curved bay window.

bow-wow¹ /bow'wow/ *interj* used to represent the bark of a dog.

bow-wow² /'bowwow/ *noun* used *esp* by or to children: a dog.

bowyangs /'bohyangz/ *pl noun* *Aus, NZ, informal* strings tied below the knee round each leg of a pair of trousers. [English dialect *bowy-yanks* leather leggings, of unknown origin]

bowyer /'bohyə/ *noun* a person who makes or sells bows for archery.

box¹ *noun* **1a** a rigid container, typically rectangular, having sides, a bottom, and usu a lid. **b** the contents of a box: *I ate a whole box of chocolates.* **2** (**the box**) *chiefly Brit, informal* television. **3** a small compartment, e.g. for a group of spectators in a theatre, for transporting a horse, or for housing a public telephone, etc. **4** = PENALTY BOX (2). **5** a square or oblong division or storage compartment. **6** = POST OFFICE BOX. **7** a boxlike protective case, e.g. for a bearing in machinery. **8** a shield to protect the genitals, worn *esp* by batsmen and wicket-keepers in cricket. **9** a square or rectangle containing, or to be filled in with, information, e.g. on a proforma, or on a computer screen. **10** a grid marked out on the road, e.g. at a junction, for guiding traffic. **11** = PENALTY AREA. **12** (**the box**) in baseball, the area occupied by the batter. **13** (*also* **Christmas box**) a small gift of money to a tradesman, postman, etc, at Christmas. ✳ **out of one's box** *Brit, informal* high on drugs or intoxicated with alcohol. ⟫ **boxful** *noun*, **box-like** *adj*. [Old English via late Latin *buxis* from Greek *pyxis*, from *pyxos* BOX⁵]

box² *verb trans* **1** to provide (something) with a box. **2** (*often* + up) to enclose (something) in a box. **3** (+ in). **a** to build a box round (pipes, etc). **b** to enclose or confine (somebody); to hem (them) in. ✳ **box the compass 1** to name the 32 points of the compass in their order. **2** to make a complete reversal.

box³ *verb intrans* to engage in boxing. ⟫ *verb trans* **1** to slap (somebody's ears) with the hand. **2** to engage in boxing with (somebody). ✳ **box clever** *Brit, informal* to outdo an opponent by cunning. [Middle English; earlier history unknown]

box⁴ *noun* a punch or slap, *esp* on the ear.

box⁵ *noun* an evergreen shrub or small tree used *esp* for hedges: *Buxus sempervivens* and *Casearia praecox.* [Old English via Latin *buxus* from Greek *pyxos*]

Box and Cox *adv and adj* *Brit* alternating; turn and turn about. [characters who share a room but never meet, in a play by J M Morton d.1891, English dramatist]

box camera *noun* an unsophisticated box-shaped camera with a simple lens and shutter.

boxcar *noun* *NAmer* an enclosed goods wagon on a train; = VAN¹ (2).

box elder *noun* a N American maple cultivated for the shade it provides: *Acer negundo.*

Boxer *noun* a member of a Chinese secret society which was opposed to foreign influence in China and whose rebellion was suppressed in 1900. [approximate translation of Chinese (Pekingese) *yi he quan*, literally 'righteous harmonious fist']

boxer¹ /'boksə/ *noun* a person who engages in the sport of boxing.

boxer[2] *noun* a dog of a breed originating in Germany, having a compact medium-sized body, short hair, and a flat pug-like face. [German *Boxer* from BOXER[1]]

boxer shorts *pl noun* men's loose-fitting underpants.

box girder *noun* a hollow rectangular girder.

boxing *noun* the art of attack and defence with the fists, practised as a sport. [BOX[3]]

Boxing Day *noun* 26 December, observed as a public holiday in Britain, on which service workers, e.g. postmen, were traditionally given Christmas boxes.

boxing glove *noun* a heavily padded leather mitten worn in boxing.

box junction *noun* a road junction at which a pattern of cross-hatched yellow lines on the road warns the road-user not to enter until their exit is clear.

box kite *noun* a tailless kite consisting of two or more open-ended connected boxes.

box number *noun* the number of a box or pigeon hole at a newspaper or post office where arrangements are made for replies to advertisements or other mail to be sent.

box office *noun* **1** an office, e.g. in a theatre, where tickets of admission are sold. **2** something that enhances ticket sales: *The publicity is all good box office.*

box pleat *noun* a pleat made by forming two folded edges, one facing right and the other left.

boxroom *noun Brit* a small storage room in a house.

box spanner *noun Brit* a spanner that is shaped to enclose a nut, bolt head, etc.

box spring *noun* **1** a spiral spring, one of a number attached to a foundation and enclosed in a cloth-covered frame, for use in mattresses or chair bases. **2** a set of spiral springs.

boxty /'boksti/ *noun* (*also* **boxty bread**) an Irish type of bread with raw potatoes as a chief ingredient. [Irish *bacstaí*]

boxwood *noun* the very close-grained heavy tough hard wood of the box tree.

boxy *adj* (**boxier, boxiest**) **1** resembling a box; box-like. **2** said of clothing, *esp* a jacket: square-cut; chunky. **3** said of a room: cramped or poky. **4** said of recorded sound: restricted in tone, so that the higher and lower frequencies are not accurately reproduced. ➤➤ **boxiness** *noun.*

boy[1] /boy/ *noun* **1a** a male child from birth to puberty. **b** a son. **c** an immature male; a youth. **d** a boyfriend. **2** (**the boys**) *informal* a man's male friends, work colleagues, team mates, etc: *a drink with the boys.* **3** *dated, offensive* a male black servant. ➤➤ **boyhood** *noun,* **boyish** *adj,* **boyishly** *adv,* **boyishness** *noun.* [Middle English, of Germanic origin]

boy[2] *interj* (*also* **oh boy**) *chiefly NAmer* an exclamation of surprise, delight, excitement, etc.

boyar /'bohyah/ *noun* a member of the pre-imperial Russian aristocracy. [Russian *boyárin* grandee]

boy-band *noun* a pop group consisting of several young men who sing and dance but generally do not play musical instruments.

boycott[1] /'boykot/ *verb trans* to engage in a concerted refusal to have dealings with (a person, shop, organization, etc) or buy (certain goods), usu to express disapproval or to force acceptance of certain conditions. ➤➤ **boycotter** *noun.* [named after C C Boycott, d.1897, English land agent in Ireland who was ostracized for refusing to reduce rents]

boycott[2] *noun* an act of boycotting.

boyfriend *noun* a frequent or regular male companion; a male lover.

Boyle's law /boylz/ *noun* a law in chemistry: the volume of a fixed mass of gas is inversely proportional to the pressure at a constant temperature. [named after Robert *Boyle*, Irish physicist and chemist, d.1691, who first stated it]

boyo /'boyoh/ *noun* (*pl* **boyos**) *Irish and Welsh, informal* a boy or lad. [BOY[1]]

boy racer *noun* a young man who likes to drive fast cars and is inclined to drive aggressively.

Boys' Brigade *noun* a Christian organization for boys founded in 1883 for the encouragement of discipline, manly virtues, and self-respect.

Boy Scout *noun dated* a Scout.

boysenberry /'boyzənb(ə)ri/ *noun* (*pl* **boysenberries**) **1** a large raspberry-like fruit. **2** the spring shrub developed by crossing several varieties of blackberry and raspberry that bears this fruit: *Rubus loganobaccus.* [named after Rudolph *Boysen,* d.1950, US horticulturalist who developed it + BERRY[1]]

bozo /'bohzoh/ *noun* (*pl* **bozos**) *NAmer, informal* a thick-witted fellow; a dolt. [origin unknown]

BP *abbr* **1** used after dates, *esp* in geology and archaeology: before the present. **2** blood pressure. **3** boiling point. **4** British Petroleum. **5** British Pharmacopoeia.

Bp *abbr* Bishop.

BPhil *abbr* Bachelor of Philosophy.

bpi *abbr* **1** in computing, bits per inch. **2** in computing, bytes per inch.

B-picture *noun* = B-MOVIE.

bps *abbr* bits per second.

b.pt. *abbr* boiling point.

Bq *abbr* becquerel.

BR *abbr* **1** Brazil (international vehicle registration). **2** formerly, British Rail.

Br *abbr* the chemical symbol for bromine.

Br. *abbr* **1** British. **2** brother.

bra /brah/ *noun* a woman's closely fitting undergarment with cups for supporting the breasts. ➤➤ **braless** *adj.* [short for BRASSIERE]

braai[1] /brie/ *noun SAfr* **1** a portable grill for roasting meat, etc; = BARBECUE[1]. **2** a barbecue party. **3** an area, e.g. a patio, designed for a braai. [short for BRAAIVLEIS]

braai[2] *verb trans* (**braais, braaied, braaiing** *or* **braaing**) *SAfr* to barbecue (meat, etc).

braaivleis /'brieflays/ *noun SAfr* a grill for barbecuing, or a barbecue party. [Afrikaans *braaivleis* grilled meat, from *braai* to grill + *vleis* meat]

brace[1] /brays/ *noun* **1** an appliance for supporting a weak leg or other body part. **2** a dental fitting worn to correct irregular teeth. **3** a diagonal piece of structural material that serves to strengthen. **4** a rope attached to a yard on a ship that swings the yard horizontally to trim the sail. **5** something, e.g. a clasp, that connects or fastens. **6a** a mark ({ or }) used to connect words or items to be considered together. **b** this mark connecting two or more musical staves the parts of which are to be performed simultaneously. **7** (*pl* **brace**) two of a kind; a pair: *several brace of quail.* **8** (*also* **brace and bit**) a crank-shaped instrument for using with and turning a drilling bit. [Middle English *brace* pair, clasp, via Old French *brace,* literally 'two arms', from Latin *bracchium* arm, from Greek *brachiōn* shorter, used to mean 'the upper arm', which is shorter than the forearm]

brace[2] *verb trans* **1a** to prepare (oneself, or a part of one's body) for receiving an impact: *She braced herself by holding the truck-side* — John Steinbeck. **b** to prepare or steel (oneself): *Brace yourself for a shock.* **2** to turn (a sail yard) by means of a brace. **3** to fit or support (a limb, the front teeth, etc) with a brace: *He had polio as a child and his legs were heavily braced.*

bracelet /'brayslit/ *noun* **1** an ornamental band or chain worn round the wrist. **2** *informal* (*in pl*) handcuffs. [Middle English from Old French *bracelet,* dimin. of *bras* arm, from Latin *bracchium*: see BRACE[1]]

bracer[1] /'braysə/ *noun* an arm- or wrist-protector, *esp* for use by an archer. [Middle English from early French *braciere* from Old French *braz* arm, from Latin *bracchium*: see BRACE[1]. Compare BRASSIERE]

bracer[2] *noun informal* a drink, e.g. of an alcoholic beverage, taken as a stimulant.

braces *pl noun Brit* a pair of elasticated straps attached to the waistband of trousers and worn over the shoulders, for holding the trousers up. [from BRACE[1]]

brace up *verb intrans* to take courage, or bear one's troubles cheerfully. ➤ *verb trans* to give (somebody) courage or moral strength.

brachi- *or* **brachio-** *comb. form* forming words, denoting: an arm: *brachiate*; *brachiopod.* [Latin *bracchium, brachium*: see BRACE[1]]

brachia /'brayki-ə, 'braki-ə/ *noun* pl of BRACHIUM.

brachial /'brayki-əl, 'braki-əl/ *adj* **1** relating to or located in an arm: *a brachial artery.* **2** resembling an arm; arm-like: *brachial appendages.*

brachiate[1] /'braykiayt, 'brakiayt/ *verb intrans* said of a monkey or ape: to progress by swinging from one hold to another by the arms. ➤ **brachiation** /-'aysh(ə)n/ *noun*, **brachiator** *noun*.

brachiate[2] /'brayki·ət, 'braki·ət/ *adj* **1** having arms. **2** branched, *esp* having paired branches on alternate sides, diverging almost at right angles from the stem.

brachio- *comb. form* see BRACHI-.

brachiopod /'brayki·əpod, 'braki-/ *noun* any of a phylum of marine invertebrate animals with shells composed of two halves hinged together: phylum Brachiopoda. [Latin *bracchium* (see BRACE[1]) + Greek *pod-, pous* foot]

brachiosaurus /,braki·ə'sawrəs, ,bray-/ *noun* a huge plant-eating dinosaur up to 30m (about 100ft) in length. [from the Latin genus name, from BRACHIO- arm (from its long forelegs) + Greek *sauros* lizard]

brachistochrone /brə'kistəkrohn/ *noun* the curve down which a body being acted on by gravity will travel in the shortest possible time from one point to another. [from Greek *brachistos* (superlative of *brachys* short) + *chronos* time]

brachium /'brayki·əm, 'braki·əm/ *noun* (*pl* **brachia** /'brayki·ə, 'braki·ə/) **1** the upper part of the arm or forelimb from the shoulder to the elbow. **2** a part of an invertebrate animal, e.g. a starfish, that corresponds to an arm. ➤ **brachial** *adj*. [Latin *bracchium, brachium*: see BRACE[1]]

brachy- *comb. form* forming words, with the meaning: short: *brachydactylous*. [Greek *brachy-*, from *brachys* short]

brachycephalic /,brakisi'falik/ *adj* having a short or broad head: compare DOLICHOCEPHALIC. ➤ **brachycephaly** /-'sefəli/ *noun*. [scientific Latin *brachycephalus*, from Greek *brachy-* + *kephalē* head]

brachylogy /bra'kiləji/ *noun* **1** conciseness or over-conciseness of expression. **2** a condensed expression from which a word or words essential to the construction or sense have been omitted, as in *Thank you!* or *Morning!* [Greek *brachylogia*, from BRACHY- + *-logia* speech]

bracing /'braysing/ *adj* refreshing or invigorating: *a bracing breeze*. ➤ **bracingly** *adv*, **bracingness** *noun*.

bracken /'brakən/ *noun* **1** a common large coarse fern *esp* of moorland areas, which is poisonous to grazing animals: *Pteridium aquilinum*. **2** a dense growth of this: *We pushed our way through shoulder-length bracken*. [Middle English *braken*, prob of Scandinavian origin]

bracket[1] /'brakit/ *noun* **1a** (*usu in pl*) either of a pair of marks () used in writing or printing to enclose matter; = PARENTHESIS (1B). **b** either of a pair of marks [] used in writing and printing to enclose matter or in mathematics and logic to show that a complex expression should be treated as a single unit. **c** either of a pair of marks <> used to enclose matter; = ANGLE BRACKET (1). **d** either of a pair of marks { } for connecting words, etc; = BRACE[1] (6A). **2** any of a graded series of social groups: *the £20,000 income bracket*. **3** in building or construction, an overhanging projecting fixture or strut that is designed to support a vertical load or strengthen an angle. **4** a pair of shots fired usu in front of and beyond a target to aid in range-finding, or the distance between these. [from early French *braguette* codpiece (from its similarity to the architectural bracket), dimin. of *brague* breeches, via Old Provençal and Latin from Gaulish *brāca*, of Germanic origin]

bracket[2] *verb trans* (**bracketed, bracketing**) **1** to place (written or printed matter) within brackets. **2** (+ together) to put (two or more people or things) in the same category or associate them mentally. **3** to attach or support (a beam, overhanging part, etc) with brackets. **4a** to get a range by firing in front of and behind (a target). **b** to establish a margin on either side of (an estimation, etc).

bracket fungus *noun* a BASIDIOMYCETE (type of fungus) that forms shelf-like spore-bearing bodies, e.g. on tree trunks: order Aphyllophorales.

brackish /'brakish/ *adj* said of water: slightly salty. ➤ **brackishness** *noun*. [Dutch *brac* salty + -ISH]

bract /brakt/ *noun* **1** a small leaf near a flower or floral axis. **2** a leaf borne on a floral axis. ➤ **bracteal** /'brakti·əl/ *adj*, **bracteate** /'brakti·ət, -ayt/ *adj*, **bracted** *adj*. [Latin *bractea* thin metal plate]

bracteole /'braktiohl/ *noun* a small or secondary bract, *esp* on a floral axis. ➤ **bracteolate** /brak'teeələt, -layt, 'brakti·əlayt/ *adj*. [scientific Latin *bracteola*, dimin. of Latin *bractea* thin metal plate]

brad /brad/ *noun* a thin wedged-shaped nail having a slight projection at the top of one side instead of a head. [Middle English from Old Norse *broddr* spike; related to Old English *byrst* BRISTLE[1]]

bradawl /'bradawl/ *noun* an awl; *esp* one used by a woodworker.

bradycardia /bradi'kahdi·ə/ *noun* relatively slow heart action, whether physiological or pathological: compare TACHYCARDIA. [scientific Latin from Greek *bradys* slow + *kardia* heart]

bradykinin /bradi'kienin/ *noun* a polypeptide that is formed in injured tissue, causes contraction of smooth muscle, dilates blood vessels, and probably plays a part in inflammatory processes. [Greek *bradys* slow + KININ]

brae /bray/ *noun Scot* **1** a hillside, steep river bank, or steep hill on a road. **2** (*in pl*) *esp* in placenames, an upland area: *in such a part of the Highlands as the Braes of Balquhidder* — Robert Louis Stevenson. [Middle English *bra* from Old Norse *brā* eyelash; related to Old English *bregdan* BRAID[1]]

Braeburn /'braybuhn/ *noun* a New Zealand eating apple with a green and red skin and crisp juicy flesh. [named after *Braeburn* Orchards, where it was first grown on a commercial scale]

brag[1] /brag/ *verb intrans* (**bragged, bragging**) to talk boastfully. ➤ *verb trans* to assert (something) boastfully: *... who had bragged that they knew every landmark of the way* — Jack London. ➤ **bragger** *noun*.

brag[2] *noun* **1** a card game resembling poker. **2** a boastful statement. [*brag* boast (from the boast or challenge made by one player to another), from Middle English *brag* boastful, of unknown origin]

braggadocio /bragə'dochioh, -'dokioh/ *noun* empty boasting. [modification of *Braggadocchio*, the name of an archetypal braggart in the poem *The Faerie Queene* by Edmund Spenser, d.1599, English poet, formed prob from BRAGGART[1] + Italian *-occio* 'big, great']

braggart[1] /'bragət/ *noun* a loud arrogant boaster: *O, I could play the woman with mine eyes and braggart with my tongue!* — Shakespeare. [French *bragard*, from *braguer* to boast, brag]

braggart[2] *adj* boastful.

Brahma /'brahmə/ *noun* **1** = BRAHMAN (1B). **2** the creator deity of the Hindu sacred triad: compare SIVA, VISHNU. [Sanskrit *brahman*]

Brahman /'brahmən/ *noun* (*pl* **Brahmans**) **1a** (*also* **Brahmin**) a Hindu of the highest caste traditionally assigned to the priesthood: compare KSHATRIYA, SUDRA, VAISYA. **b** the impersonal ground of all being in Hinduism. Also called BRAHMA, BRAHMIN. **2a** *NAmer* see BRAHMIN (3). **b** a large vigorous heat-resistant and tick-resistant animal developed in the USA by interbreeding Indian cattle. ➤ **Brahmanic** /brah'manik/ *adj*, **Brahmanical** /brah'man-/ *adj*. [Sanskrit *brahman* prayer, praise, worship]

Brahmanism *noun* orthodox Hinduism adhering to the pantheism of the Vedas and to the ancient sacrifices and family ceremonies.

Brahmin /'brahmin/ *noun* **1** = BRAHMAN (1A). **2** = BRAHMAN (1B). **3** any of the ZEBU breed of cattle or a US cross-breed developed from this. *NAmer* Also called BRAHMAN. **4** *NAmer* an intellectually and socially cultivated but aloof person. ➤ **Brahminical** /brah'minikl/ *adj*, **Brahminism** *noun*.

braid[1] /brayd/ *verb trans* **1** *chiefly NAmer* to plait (the hair). **2** (*usu in passive*) to ornament (clothing, etc) with ribbon or braid. ➤ **braider** *noun*. [Old English *bregdan* to interweave, literally 'to move suddenly']

braid[2] *noun* **1** a narrow strip of fabric, *esp* plaited cord or ribbon, used for trimming. **2a** *chiefly NAmer* a length of plaited hair; = PLAIT[1] (1). **b** a very narrow plait of hair with coloured threads interlaced and decorative beads at the end.

brail[1] /brayl/ *noun* a rope fastened to the edge or end of a sail and used for hauling the sail up or in. [Middle English *brayle* from Old French *braiel* strap]

brail[2] *verb trans* to take in (a sail) by the brails.

braille /brayl/ *noun* (*also* **Braille**) a system of writing or printing for the blind that uses characters made up of raised dots. [named after Louis *Braille*, d.1852, French teacher of the blind, who devised it]

brain[1] /brayn/ *noun* **1a** the portion of the vertebrate central nervous system that constitutes the organ of thought and neural coordination, is made up of neurons and supporting and nutritive structures, is enclosed within the skull, and is continuous with the spinal cord. **b** a nervous centre in invertebrates comparable in position and function to the vertebrate brain. **c** (*usu in pl*) this part of an animal's brain used as food.

Editorial note
The human brain is the most complicated structure known with its 100 billion nerve cells, each with around 2000 connections. Having evolved from simple ganglia, the brain handles information from the senses, controls movements, creates intelligent solutions to problems, and so on, in specialized regions. How it generates consciousness remains mysterious — Professor Richard Gregory.

2 an intellect or mind: *She has a good brain.* **3a** (*in pl*) intellectual endowment; intelligence: *They need somebody with plenty of brains.* **b** *informal* a very intelligent or intellectual person. **c** a person thought of in terms of their intellect: *She's one of the best scientific brains in the country.* **d** (**the brain/the brains**) the chief planner of an organization or enterprise; the mastermind: *He was usually the brains behind those schemes.* **4** an automatic device, e.g. a computer, that performs one or more of the functions of the human brain for control or computation. **✳ have something on the brain** to have a snatch of music, song, or verse constantly recurring in one's head. **rack/wrack one's brains** to make a great mental effort; to think hard. [Old English *brægen*]

brain² *verb trans* **1** to kill (somebody) by smashing their skull. **2** *informal* to hit (somebody) hard on the head.

brainbox /'braynboks/ *noun Brit, informal* **1** the skull or cranium. **2** a very intelligent person.

brainchild *noun* something that is the product of a specified person's creative imagination: *The automation of the catalogue had been the librarian's brainchild.*

brain coral *noun* any of several genera of coral that have surface convolutions resembling those of the brain: genus *Diploria* and other genera.

brain-dead *adj* **1** having suffered brain death. **2** *informal* totally lacking in intelligence: *brain-dead politicians.*

brain death *noun* the death of a human being determined by the assessment that their brain has irreversibly ceased to function.

brain drain *noun* (**the brain drain**) *informal* loss of highly qualified workers and professionals through emigration.

brainiac /'brayniak/ *noun NAmer, informal* a very intelligent or intellectual person.

brainless *adj* stupid; foolish. **≫ brainlessly** *adv*, **brainlessness** *noun.*

brainpan *noun chiefly NAmer, informal* the skull.

brainpower *noun* intellectual ability; intelligence.

brain stem *noun* the part of the brain comprising the medulla oblongata, the midbrain, and the pons.

brainstorm *noun* **1** *informal* a transitory disturbance in the brain, resulting in uncharacteristic behaviour or a lapse in concentration; a mental aberration. **2** an instance of brainstorming. **3** *chiefly NAmer, informal* an inspiration; a brainwave.

brainstorming *noun* **1** a problem-solving technique that involves the spontaneous contribution of ideas from all members of a group. **2** (*used before a noun*) of or relating to brainstorming: *a brainstorming session.*

brains trust *noun chiefly Brit* a group of expert advisers assembled to answer questions of immediate or current interest in public or on radio or television: compare BRAIN TRUST.

brainteaser *noun* a logical or mathematical puzzle.

brain trust *noun NAmer* a group of expert advisers to a government, department, or politician: compare BRAINS TRUST.

braintwister *noun* = BRAINTEASER.

brainwash *verb trans* to attempt systematically to instil beliefs into (somebody), often in place of beliefs already held. **≫ brainwasher** *noun*, **brainwashing** *noun*. [from brainwashing, translation of Chinese (Pekingese) *xi nao*]

brain wave *noun* **1** a rhythmic fluctuation of voltage between parts of the brain. **2** *informal* a sudden bright idea.

brainy *adj* (**brainier, brainiest**) *informal* intelligent; clever. **≫ braininess** *noun.*

braise /brayz/ *verb trans* to cook (meat, etc) slowly by first sautéeing it in hot fat and then simmering it gently in very little liquid in a closed container. [French *braiser*, from *braise* live coals, from Old French *brese*]

brak /brak/ *noun SAfr* a mongrel dog; a cur. [Afrikaans *brak*, from Dutch *brak* setter]

brake¹ /brayk/ *noun* **1** (*also in pl*) a device for slowing down or stopping a vehicle, usu by friction against the wheels. **2** something that slows down or stops movement or activity. **✳ put the brake on** to take steps to slow the progress of something thought to be developing too precipitately. **≫ brakeless** *adj.* [Middle English, bridle, curb; earlier history unknown]

brake² *verb intrans* **1** to operate, manage, or apply a brake, *esp* on a vehicle. **2** said of a vehicle: to become slowed by a brake. **≫** *verb trans* to slow or stop (a vehicle) using a brake.

brake³ *noun literary* **1** a thicket: *This green plot shall be our stage, this hawthorn brake our tiring-house* — Shakespeare. **2** an area of overgrown rough or marshy land. **≫ braky** /'brayki/ *adj.* [Old English *bracu*]

brake⁴ *noun* **1** an open horse-drawn four-wheeled carriage. **2** = SHOOTING BRAKE. [variant of BRAKE² in the sense 'carriage frame used for breaking in horses']

brake⁵ /brayk/ *noun* = BRACKEN. [Middle English *brake*, prob introduced as a sing. of *braken* (see BRACKEN), misapprehended as a pl]

brake⁶ *noun* **1** a toothed instrument used for crushing flax and hemp. **2** (*also* **brake harrow**) a machine formerly used for breaking up large clumps of earth. [Middle English, perhaps related to BREAK²]

brake⁷ *verb trans* to crush (flax and hemp) with a brake.

brake⁸ *verb* archaic past tense of BREAK¹.

brake disc *noun* in a disc brake, the disc attached to the wheel, on which the brake pad presses.

brake drum *noun* in a drum brake, the short broad cylinder attached to the wheel, against which the brake shoe presses.

brake-fade *noun* a decrease in the efficiency of a braking system due to the brakes overheating, sometimes resulting in a total loss of stopping capacity.

brake fluid *noun* the oily fluid used to transmit pressure in a hydraulic brake system or clutch system.

brake horsepower *noun* the useful power of an engine as calculated from the resistance to a brake or dynamometer applied to the shaft or flywheel.

brake light *noun* either of a pair of red lights at the rear of a vehicle that light up when the brakes are applied.

brake lining *noun* an asbestos strip riveted to a brake shoe to increase its friction.

brakeman *noun* (*pl* **brakemen**) **1** *chiefly NAmer* a railway worker responsible for the brakes and for general maintenance of rolling stock, who may also act as assistant guard. *Brit* Also called BRAKESMAN. **2** the person sitting at the rear of a bobsleigh who operates the brakes.

brake pad *noun* in a disc brake, the block that presses on the disc.

brake shoe *noun* in a drum brake, a long curved block that presses on the drum.

brakesman /'brayksmən/ *noun* (*pl* **brakesmen**) *Brit* = BRAKEMAN (1).

brake van *noun Brit* on a railway train, the coach or wagon from which the brakes can be applied; = GUARD'S VAN.

bramble /'brambl/ *noun* **1** a prickly rambling shrub of the rose family, *esp* a blackberry. **2** *chiefly Scot* the fruit of this shrub; = BLACKBERRY¹. **≫ brambly** *adj.* [Middle English *brembel* from Old English *brēmel*; related to Old English *brōm* BROOM]

brambling /'brambling/ *noun* a brightly coloured Old World finch: *Fringilla montifringilla.* [prob from BRAMBLE + -LING]

Bramley /'bramli/ *noun* a large green variety of cooking apple. [named after Matthew *Bramley*, fl 1850, English butcher and reputed first grower of the fruit]

bran /bran/ *noun* the broken husk of cereal grain separated from the flour or meal by sifting. [Middle English from Old French]

branch¹ /brahnch/ *noun* **1** a secondary woody shoot arising from the trunk of a tree, or from a bough, or from the main axis of a shrub. **2a** *chiefly NAmer* the tributary of a river. **b** a side road or way. **c** a slender projection, e.g. the tine of an antler. **3** a distinct part of a complex whole, e.g.: **a** a division of a family descending from a particular ancestor. **b** a distinct section of a particular subject of study: *Pathology is a branch of medicine.* **c** a division or separate part of an organization. **≫ branched** *adj*, **branchless** *adj*, **branchlet**

/'brahnchlit/ *noun*, **branchy** *adj*. [Middle English via Old French from late Latin *branca* paw]

branch[2] *verb intrans* **1** to put forth branches. **2** to spring out, e.g. from a main stem.

branchia /'brangki·ə/ *noun* (*pl* **branchiae** /'brangkiee/) the gill of a fish or other aquatic animal. ➤ **branchial** *adj*, **branchiate** /'brangki·ət, -ayt/ *adj*. [via Latin from Greek *branchion* gill]

branchiopod /'brangki·əpod/ *noun* any of a class of aquatic crustaceans, e.g. a brine shrimp, typically having a long body, a carapace, and many pairs of leaflike appendages: class Branchiopoda. ➤ **branchiopodan** /ˌbrangki'opədən, ˌbrangki·ə'pohdən/ *adj*, **branchiopodous** /ˌbrangki'opədəs, ˌbrangki·ə'pohdəs/ *adj*. [Greek *branchia* gills + *pod-*, *pous* foot]

branch out *verb intrans* to extend one's activities or try new experiences.

brand[1] /brand/ *noun* **1a** a class of goods identified by name as the product of a single firm or manufacturer. **b** a characteristic or distinctive kind: *his own lively brand of humour*. **2a** a mark made by burning with a hot iron, or with a stamp or stencil, to identify manufacture or quality or to designate ownership, e.g. of cattle. **b** formerly, a mark put on criminals with a hot iron. **c** a mark conveying disgrace: *the brand of poverty*. **3a** a tool used to produce a brand; = BRANDING IRON. **b** a charred or smouldering piece of wood. **c** a flaming torch. **d** *literary* a sword: *So this great brand the King took, and by this will beat his foemen down* — Tennyson. [Old English *brand* torch, sword; related to Old English *bærnan* BURN[1]]

brand[2] *verb trans* **1** to mark (goods, cattle, slaves, or criminals) with a brand: *And now I must become her branded slave* — Dryden. **2** to stigmatize (somebody, or their conduct): *There are certain actions which the consent of all nations and individuals has branded with the unchangeable name of meanness* — Thomas Paine. **3** to impress (something) indelibly: *a day that is forever branded on my memory* — Oscar Wilde. ➤ **brander** *noun*.

branded /'brandid/ *adj* labelled with the manufacturer's brand.

branding iron *noun* an iron implement that is heated and used to brand cattle, etc.

brandish /'brandish/ *verb trans* to shake or wave (a weapon, etc) menacingly or ostentatiously. [Middle English *braundisshen* from Old French *brandiss-*, stem of *brandir*, from *brand* sword, of Germanic origin]

brandleader /'brandleedə/ *noun* the best-known best-selling brand of a type of product.

brandling /'brandling/ *noun* a red earthworm with brighter-coloured rings, found in manure and used as angling bait: *Eisenia fetida*. [from BRAND[1] + -LING]

brand name *noun* the name or trademark that a manufacturer gives to a product or range of products; = TRADE NAME.

brand-new *adj* conspicuously new and unused. [literally 'fresh from the fire', as if newly forged or minted; from BRAND[1]]

brandy /'brandi/ *noun* (*pl* **brandies**) **1** a spirit made by distilling wine or fermented fruit juice. **2** a glass or measure of brandy. [short for *brandywine*, from Dutch *brandewijn*, from early Dutch *brant* burned, distilled + *wijn* wine]

brandy butter *noun Brit* a hard sauce served *esp* with Christmas pudding, made by beating butter with sugar and brandy.

brandy snap *noun* a very thin cylindrical ginger biscuit sometimes flavoured with brandy, usu served filled with cream.

brant /brant/ *noun* (*pl* **brants** *or collectively* **brant**) *chiefly NAmer* = BRENT GOOSE.

bran tub *noun Brit* a tub filled with bran, with small wrapped presents concealed within it; = LUCKY DIP.

brash[1] /brash/ *adj* **1** aggressively or insensitively self-assertive; impudent. **2** tastelessly showy: *brash new houses*. **3** impetuous or rash. ➤ **brashly** *adv*, **brashness** *noun*. [origin unknown]

brash[2] *noun* **1** a mass of fragments, e.g. of ice. **2** in farming, stony soil, excellent for growing corn. ➤ **brashy** *adj*. [obsolete *brash* to breach a wall, prob from early French *breche* breach]

brass /brahs/ *noun* **1** an alloy of copper and zinc. **2a** the brass instruments of an orchestra or band. **b** *Brit* a brass memorial tablet, *esp* set into the wall or floor of a church. **c** bright metal fittings, e.g. nails and doorknobs, or utensils: *He polishes the brass every day*. **d** a round flat brass ornament for attaching to a horse's harness. **3** *informal* brazen self-assurance; cheek. **4** (*also* **the top brass**) *informal*

the senior office-bearers; the people in authority. **5** *Brit, informal* money. ➤ **brass** *adj*. [Old English *bræs*]

brassard /'brasahd/ *noun* **1** a distinguishing armband worn on the sleeve of a uniform, etc. **2** formerly, a piece of armour for protecting the arm. [French *brassard* via early French *brassal* from Old Italian *bracciale*, from *braccio* arm, from Latin *bracchium*: see BRACE[1]]

brass band *noun* a band consisting, or chiefly consisting, of brass and percussion instruments.

brassed off *adj Brit, informal* miserably bored, dissatisfied, or fed up.

brasserie /'bras(ə)ri/ *noun* a small informal French-style restaurant. [French *brasserie*, orig 'brewery', from early French *brasser* to brew, ultimately from Gallo-Latin *brace*, a kind of wheat]

brass farthing *noun* a trivial amount. * **not have two brass farthings to rub together** to have no money; to be quite destitute.

brass hat *noun Brit, informal* a high-ranking military officer.

brassica /'brasikə/ *noun* any of a large genus of plants of the mustard family that includes many important vegetables and crop plants, e.g. cabbage, turnip, mustard, and rape: genus *Brassica*. [from the Latin genus name, from *brassica* cabbage]

brassie *or* **brassy** /'brasi, 'brahsi/ *noun* (*pl* **brassies**) an old name for a No. 2 wood golf club, which has a wooden head with a metal sole plate and is used *esp* for long shots from the fairway. [so called because the sole plate was orig brass]

brassiere /'brazi·ə/ *noun formal* the full form of BRA. [via obsolete French *brassiere*, from Old French *braciere* arm-protector, formed from *braz* arm, from Latin *bracchium*: see BRACE[1]. Compare BRACER[1]]

brass instrument *noun* any of a group of wind instruments with a long, usu curved, cylindrical or conical metal tube, a mouth-piece against which the player's lips vibrate, and usu valves or a slide for producing all the notes within the instrument's range.

brass neck *noun informal* calm audacity; nerve: *Would you have the brass neck to go to the bank and ask for a loan of £97 million?* — Daily Mirror.

brass rubbing *noun* **1** the activity of taking an impression from an engraved brass plaque by rubbing a sheet of paper laid over it with heelball or chalk. **2** an impression taken in this way.

brass tacks *pl noun informal* details of immediate practical importance. * **get down to brass tacks** to tackle the real or practical issues.

brassy[1] *adj* (**brassier**, **brassiest**) **1** shamelessly bold; brazen. **2** resembling brass, *esp* in colour. ➤ **brassily** *adv*, **brassiness** *noun*.

brassy[2] /'brasi, 'brahsi/ *noun* see BRASSIE.

brat /brat/ *noun informal* a child, *esp* an ill-disciplined one. ➤ **brattish** *adj*, **brattishness** *noun*, **bratty** *adj*. [perhaps from English dialect *brat* ragamuffin]

bratpack *noun informal* **1** a group of precociously successful and fashionable young performers, writers, etc. **2** a group of self-important and ill-mannered young people. ➤ **bratpacker** *noun*.

brattice /'bratis/ *noun* a wooden or cloth partition, *esp* a temporary one, for directing air in a mine. ➤ **bratticed** *adj*. [Middle English *bretais*, *bretasce* parapet via Old French *bretesche* from medieval Latin *breteschia*, from Old English *brittise* British]

bratwurst /'brahtvooəst/ *noun* a German sausage, usu of pork, for frying. [German *Bratwurst*, from Old High German *brāt* meat without waste + *Wurst* sausage]

bravado /brə'vahdoh/ *noun* swaggering conduct intended to impress or deceive people. [early French *bravade* and Spanish *bravada*, both from Italian *bravata*, from *bravare* to challenge, show off, from *bravo*: see BRAVE[1]]

brave[1] /brayv/ *adj* **1** courageous; fearless. **2** excellent; splendid: *at least thirty thousand men, and it was a brave sight for the eye to look on* — William Hickling Prescott. ➤ **bravely** *adv*. [French *brave* from Italian and Spanish *bravo* courageous, wild, from Latin *barbarus*: see BARBAROUS]

brave[2] *verb trans* to face or endure (unpleasant or dangerous conditions) with courage: *I don't feel like braving that blizzard tonight*. * **brave it out** to make an effort to get through a difficult, embarrassing, or painful experience with an appearance of confidence or unconcern.

brave[3] *noun dated* a Native N American warrior.

brave new world *noun* the prospect of a new and better society in the future: *This brave new world of social engineering produces the opposite of community contact* — B Campbell. [with allusion to Shakespeare, *The Tempest* v.i.182–3: 'How beauteous mankind is! O brave new world That has such people in 't!', also used as the title of a novel by Aldous Huxley (1932)]

bravery /'brayv(ə)ri/ *noun* courage or valour.

bravo[1] /brah'voh/ *interj* used *esp* by audience members to applaud a performer: well done! [Italian *bravo*: see BRAVE[1]]

bravo[2] *noun* (*pl* **bravos**) a shout of 'Bravo!'

bravo[3] /'brahvoh/ *noun* (*pl* **bravos** *or* **bravoes**) a villain or desperado; *esp* a hired assassin.

bravura /brə'v(y)oоərə/ *noun* **1** a flamboyant brilliant style, *esp* in the performance of a musical piece requiring technical expertise. **2** a musical passage requiring exceptional agility and technical skill in execution. **3** a display of flamboyant recklessness. [Italian *bravura* expertise, from *bravare*: see BRAVADO]

braw /braw/ *adj Scot* fine or beautiful. [Scot variant of BRAVE[1]]

brawl[1] /brawl/ *verb intrans* **1** to quarrel or fight noisily. **2** said of water: to make a loud confused bubbling sound. ⋙ **brawler** *noun*. [Middle English *brawlen*, perhaps imitative]

brawl[2] *noun* **1** a noisy quarrel or fight. **2** a brawling noise.

brawn /brawn/ *noun* **1a** strong muscles. **b** muscular strength. **2** *Brit* pork trimmings, *esp* the meat from a pig's head, boiled, chopped, and pressed into a mould. [Middle English from Old French *braon* muscle, of Germanic origin]

brawny /'brawni/ *adj* (**brawnier, brawniest**) muscular; strong. ⋙ **brawnily** *adv*, **brawniness** *noun*.

bray[1] /bray/ *verb intrans* **1** to utter the loud harsh cry characteristic of a donkey: *a braying laugh*. **2** said of a trumpet, etc: to produce a loud and brilliant noise. ➤ *verb trans* to utter or play (something) loudly or harshly. [Middle English *brayen* from Old French *braire* to cry, prob of Celtic origin]

bray[2] *noun* the characteristic cry of a donkey.

bray[3] *verb trans archaic* to crush or grind (something) finely, *esp* in a mortar: *a delicate paste of brayed wheat* — Lew Wallace. [Middle English *brayen* from early French *broiier*, of Germanic origin]

braze /brayz/ *verb trans* to solder (metals) with an alloy, e.g. of brass and silver, that melts on contact with the heated metals being joined. ⋙ **brazer** *noun*. [prob from French *braser* to solder, from Old French *brese* live coals]

brazen[1] /'brayz(ə)n/ *adj* **1** shamelessly or contemptuously bold. **2** *chiefly literary* resembling or made of brass: *brazen cauldrons* — Thomas Bulfinch. **3** sounding harsh and loud like struck brass. ⋙ **brazenly** *adv*, **brazenness** *noun*. [Old English *bræsen*, from *bræs* BRASS]

brazen[2] ✲ **brazen it out** to face danger, trouble, or criticism with defiance or impudence.

brazen-faced *adj* shamelessly bold; = BRAZEN[1] (1).

brazier[1] /'brayzi-ə, 'brayzhə/ *noun* a receptacle or stand for holding burning coals. [French *brasier* fire of hot coals, from Old French *brese* hot coals]

brazier[2] /'brayzyə, 'brayzhə/ *noun* a person who works in brass. ⋙ **braziery** *noun*. [Middle English *brasier*, from *bras* BRASS]

brazil /brə'zil/ *noun* **1** (**brazil nut**) a roughly triangular oily edible nut. **2** the tall S American tree that bears this nut: *Bertholletia excelsa*. **3** = BRAZILWOOD. **4** a dye obtained from brazilwood. [named after *Brazil*, country in S America]

Brazilian /brə'zilyən/ *noun* a native or inhabitant of Brazil in S America. ⋙ **Brazilian** *adj*.

brazilwood *noun* the heavy red wood of a tropical leguminous tree: genus *Caesalpinia*. [Spanish *brasil*, from *brasa* live coals; from its colour]

breach[1] /breech/ *noun* **1** infringement or violation, e.g. of a law, obligation, or standard: *breach of contract*. **2** a gap, e.g. in a wall, made by battering. **3** a break in customarily friendly relations: *I attempted familiarities ... which she repulsed with proper resentment ... This made a breach between us* — Benjamin Franklin. **4** a leap, *esp* of a whale out of water: *the sublime breach* — Herman Melville. ✲ **step into the breach** to replace somebody who has been prevented from doing a certain job, *esp* at short notice. [Old English *bryce*; related to BREAK[2]]

breach[2] *verb trans* **1** to make a breach in (a barrier). **2** to break or violate (an agreement, etc).

breach of promise *noun* violation of a promise, *esp* to marry somebody.

breach of the peace *noun* an instance of disorderly conduct causing a public disturbance, treated as a criminal offence.

bread[1] /bred/ *noun* **1** a food consisting essentially of flour or meal which is baked and usu leavened, *esp* with yeast. **2** food or sustenance: *our daily bread*. **3** *informal*. **a** livelihood: *He earned his daily bread as a labourer.* **b** money. ✲ **cast one's bread upon the waters** to do good without expectation of thanks or reward. **know which side one's bread is buttered** to know where one's best interest lies. **take the bread out of somebody's mouth** to take away somebody's livelihood. [Old English *brēad*]

bread[2] *verb trans* (*usu in passive*) to cover (a piece of fish or meat) with breadcrumbs; = BREADCRUMB[2]: *a breaded pork chop*.

bread and butter *noun* one's means of sustenance or livelihood: *Writing is my bread and butter.*

bread-and-butter *adj* **1a** basic; fundamental: *wages, housing, and other bread-and-butter issues.* **b** said of work, etc: that can be depended on to earn money; routine or reliable: *the bread-and-butter repertoire of an orchestra.* **2** said of a letter: expressing thanks for hospitality.

bread and circuses *noun* political measures or policies aimed at pleasing large numbers of people. [translating Latin *panem et circenses* (Juvenal, *Satires* x.81), the two things that most interested the people of Imperial Rome]

breadbasket *noun informal* the stomach.

breadboard *noun* **1** a board on which to cut bread or knead dough. **2** a board on which electric or electronic components may be arranged and interconnected experimentally.

breadcrumb[1] *noun* a small fragment of bread.

breadcrumb[2] *verb trans* (*usu in passive*) to cover (a piece of fish or meat) with breadcrumbs.

breadfruit *noun* **1** a large starchy fruit that has white flesh with a breadlike texture. **2** the tree that bears this fruit: *Artocarpus altilis*.

breadline *noun NAmer* a queue of people waiting to receive food given in charity. ✲ **on the breadline** *Brit* earning no more than the minimum for survival.

bread sauce *noun* a spicy sauce made with breadcrumbs, milk, cream and onion, traditionally served with turkey.

breadstick /-stik/ *noun* a stick of crisp bread.

breadth /bretth, bredth/ *noun* **1** the distance from side to side of something; = WIDTH (1A). **2a** wide range or scope; catholicity: *breadth of learning*. **b** liberality of views or taste: *breadth of vision*. **3** *dated* a piece of cloth of full width: *a breadth of tweed*. [Old English *brēdu* + -TH[2], modelled on LENGTH]

breadthways *or* **breadthwise** *adv and adj* in the direction of the breadth: *a course of bricks laid breadthways*.

breadwinner *noun* the member of a family whose earnings are their chief means of support. ⋙ **breadwinning** *noun*.

break[1] /brayk/ *verb* (*past tense* **broke** /brohk/, *past part.* **broken** /'brohkən/) ➤ *verb trans* **1a** to damage (something) by causing it to separate into pieces with suddenness or violence. **b** to damage (a machine, etc) and stop it working. **c** to fracture (a limb, etc). **d** to rupture (a surface). **e** to split (something) or divide it into smaller units, parts, or processes. **f** in battle, to cause (drawn-up lines) to scatter. **2a** to fail to observe (a rule or law), *esp* deliberately. **b** to fail to keep or abide by (a promise, agreement, or contract); = BREACH[2]. **3a** to defeat (an opponent or enemy) decisively. **b** (*also* + to) to train (an animal, *esp* a horse) to adjust to the service or convenience of human beings. **c** to crush the spirit of (a person). **d** to exhaust (somebody) in health, strength, or capacity. **e** to ruin (somebody) financially. **f** to reduce (somebody) in rank, or cashier them. **4** to reduce the force or impact of (a fall). **5a** to take measures to make (a strike) fail, e.g. by using alternative labour. **b** to resolve (a deadlock). **c** to end (a fast) by eating. **d** to interrupt (a journey) by stopping for a rest or a meal. **6a** to interrupt (somebody's train of thought), so that continuity is lost. **b** to interrupt (a silence) with a sound. **7** to open (an electric circuit) so that operation is suspended. **8** to destroy the unity or completeness of (a collection): *We're auctioning the spoons as a unit, so as not to break the set.* **9** to interrupt the uniformity of (something): *A chimney breaks the line of the roof.* **10a** to exceed or surpass (a record). **b** said of a golfer: to score less than (a specified total). **c** to run a race in less than (a specified time). **11** said of the player receiving service in tennis: to get the better of (one's opponent's serve) by winning the game. **12** to demonstrate the falsity of (an alibi or excuse). **13** to solve or discover the principles of (a code or cipher system). **14** to cause (somebody) to discontinue a habit: *how to break yourself of the smoking habit*. **15** to make (news, etc) known to people. ➤ *verb intrans* **1a** to come apart or split into pieces; to burst or shatter. **b** said of a machine, etc: to stop working as a result of damage or wear. **c** to fold, bend, lift, or come apart at a seam, groove, or joint. **d** said of a wave: to curl over and disintegrate in surf or foam, against a rock or on a beach. **2a** said of the day: to dawn. **b** said of a storm: to develop suddenly, with thunder, lightning, and rain. **c** said of weather: to change. *esp* suddenly after a settled period. **d** said of a line of troops: to give way in disorderly retreat. **e** said of a person's health or spirit: to fail under pressure. **3a** (*often* + from) to escape with sudden forceful effort: *He broke from his captors*. **b** (*often* + from) to work loose and become detached: *The boat broke from its moorings*. **c** said of the fluid or 'waters' surrounding an unborn baby: to be released from the AMNION (membrane enclosing the baby) as it ruptures during labour. **d** (*often* + off) to make the opening shot of a game of snooker, billiards, or pool. **e** said of a ball bowled in cricket: to change direction on bouncing. **f** said of boxers: to separate after a clinch. **4a** said of news: to become known or made public. **b** said of a fish, *esp* a trout or salmon: to emerge through the surface of the water. **c** to make a sudden dash for cover. **5a** said of the voice or the sound of a wind instrument: to alter sharply in tone, pitch, or intensity; to shift abruptly from one register to another. **b** said of a boy's voice: to deepen at puberty. **6** said of a horse: to fail to keep moving in the desired manner, e.g. by reverting to trotting when cantering. **7** to interrupt one's work or activity for a brief period. **8** said of cream: to separate during churning into liquid and fat. **9** *chiefly NAmer* to happen or develop: *For the team to succeed, everything has to break right*. ✳ **break a leg!** *informal* said to somebody about to perform: best of luck! [from the superstition that to wish somebody good luck invites misfortune]. **break camp** to take tents down and leave. **break cover** said of a person or animal on the run: to emerge from concealment. **break even** to recoup one's initial outlay or investment but no more. **break into 1a** to start (an activity) with vigour: *The horse broke into a gallop*. **b** said of a person or a person's face: to relax into (a smile, etc). **2a** to contrive to enter (a certain area of activity). **b** to interrupt (a conversation, etc). **break jail** to escape from prison. **break loose** to escape. **break new/fresh ground** to try something new; to make an innovation. **break one's duck** said of a batsman in cricket: to score for the first time. **break one's word** to fail to keep one's promise. **break open** to open (something) forcibly. **break rank** said of troops drawn up in line: to move out of formation. **break somebody's serve/break somebody's service/break service** in tennis, to win a game against the server. **break somebody's heart** to cause somebody deep hurt or sorrow. **break step** said of marching troops: to stop marching in step. **break the back of something** to complete the most arduous part of a task. **break the bank** *often humorous* to cause financial ruin. **break the ice** to do or say something that overcomes the initial reserve of a group. **break wind** to release intestinal gas from the anus. **break with something** to do something different from (a custom or tradition). **break with somebody** to end a relationship with (a partner or friend) after a quarrel, etc. [Old English *brecan*]

break² *noun* **1a** an act or action of breaking. **b** the opening shot in a game of snooker, billiards, or pool. **2a** a condition produced by, or as if by, breaking; a gap: *a break in the clouds*. **b** a discontinuation of previously good relations; = BREACH¹ (3). **c** a gap in an otherwise continuous electric circuit. **3** the action or act of breaking in, out, or forth: *a jail break*. **4** a dash or rush: *They made a break for it*. **5** the act of separating after a clinch in boxing. **6** a discontinuity in space or time, e.g.: **a** an abrupt or noteworthy departure from tradition in manners, morals, artistic production, etc. **b** an abrupt or noteworthy change or interruption in a continuous process or trend: *It makes a break*. **c** a respite from work or duty. **d** *Brit* a daily pause for play and refreshment at school: *We played rounders during break*. **e** a planned interruption in a radio or television programme: *a break for the commercials*. **f** a brief holiday: *taking a weekend break in Paris*. **7a** the change in direction of forward travel of a cricket ball on bouncing, usu resulting from spin imparted by the bowler. **b** the deviation of a pitched baseball from a straight line. **c** a slow ball bowled in cricket that moves in a specified direction on bouncing: *an off break*. **8** failure of a horse to continue in a required manner. **9a** (*also* **break of service**) the action

or an instance of breaking an opponent's service at tennis. **b** a sequence of successful shots or strokes, or a score thus made: *a break of 86 in snooker*. **10** a marked change in the quality of the sound of a voice or musical instrument. **11** a place, situation, or time at which a break occurs, e.g.: **a** the point where one musical register changes to another. **b** a short intermediate passage between phrases in jazz. **c** the place at which a word is divided, *esp* at the end of a line of print or writing. **12** *informal*. **a** a stroke of good luck. **b** an opportunity or chance: *I'm still waiting for my big break*. **13** an act of moving ahead of the main body of riders in a bicycle road race, or the group of riders who have moved ahead in this manner: *the eight-man break* — Cycling. ✳ **a bad break** a piece, or a run, of bad luck. **break of day** dawn. **give me/us a break!** *informal* expressing impatient irritation: spare me!

breakable¹ *adj* capable of being broken; fragile.

breakable² *noun* a breakable or fragile object.

breakage /'braykij/ *noun* **1** (*usu in pl*) something broken. **2** allowance for things broken, e.g. in transit.

breakaway¹ *noun* **1** somebody or something that breaks away. **2** a breaking away, e.g. from a group or tradition; a withdrawing.

breakaway² *adj* **1** favouring independence from an affiliation; withdrawing: *A breakaway faction formed a new party*. **2** *chiefly NAmer* made to break or bend easily: *breakaway road signs for highway safety*.

break away *verb intrans* **1** to escape from restraint or captivity: *She managed to break away from him and run*. **2** to detach oneself from, and move ahead of, the main group, e.g. in a race. **3** (*often* + from) to make a deliberate effort to escape from the restrictions of a tradition, or the influence of a person or group: *I'm afraid I couldn't break away from the habit of fulsome adulation and suddenly change my style* — Saki.

break-dance *verb intrans* to perform break dancing. ➤➤ **break dancer** *noun*.

break dancing *noun* an athletic form of street dance developed in the 1980s by African Americans, in which performers spin on head and shoulders.

breakdown *noun* **1** a failure to function. **2** a physical, mental, or nervous collapse. **3** failure to progress or have effect: *a breakdown in negotiations*. **4** the process of decomposing. **5** a division into categories; a classification. **6** a whole analysed into parts; *specif* an account in which the transactions are recorded under various categories.

break down *verb trans* **1a** to cause (a structure or barrier) to fall or collapse by breaking or shattering it. **b** to remove (a hindrance to progress, etc). **2a** to divide (something) into parts or categories for purposes of analysis. **b** to separate (a chemical compound, etc) into simpler substances. **c** to take (something) apart, *esp* for storage or shipment and for later reassembly. ➤ *verb intrans* **1a** said of a vehicle or other machine: to become inoperative through breakage or wear. **b** to deteriorate or fail: *Relations broke down*. **2a** to allow of analysis or subdivision: *The outline breaks down into three parts*. **b** to undergo decomposition. **c** to lose one's composure completely.

breakdown lorry *noun* a lorry fitted with equipment suitable for repairing or towing disabled or immobilized motor vehicles.

breakdown truck *noun* = BREAKDOWN LORRY.

breaker¹ *noun* **1** a wave breaking into foam. **2** *informal* a user of Citizens' Band radio; *specif* somebody who interrupts a conversation in order to transmit a message. **3** a break dancer.

breaker² *noun* a small water cask. [by folk etymology from Spanish *barrica*]

break-even *noun* **1** the point at which profit equals loss: *break-even fares*. **2** (*used before a noun*) of or relating to break-even.

breakfast¹ /'brekfəst/ *noun* the first meal of the day, *esp* when taken in the morning, or the food prepared for or eaten at this meal. [Middle English *brekfast*, from BREAK¹ + FAST⁴]

breakfast² *verb intrans* to have breakfast. ➤➤ **breakfaster** *noun*.

breakfront *noun* **1** a sideboard or other piece of furniture whose front is broken by a curve or angle. **2** (*used before a noun*) of or relating to a breakfront: *a breakfront chest of drawers*.

break in *verb intrans* **1** to enter a house or building by force. **2** (*often* + on) to intrude or interrupt. ➤ *verb trans* **1a** to train (a horse) to carry a rider or pull a load. **b** to accustom (somebody) to a certain activity. **2** to wear (new boots or shoes) to make them soften and become comfortable.

break-in *noun* an act of forcing an entry into a building, usu with the intention of committing burglary.

breaking point *noun* the point at which a person gives way under stress.

breakneck *adj* denoting a dangerously fast pace: *driving at break-neck speed.*

break off *verb intrans* **1** to become detached; to separate. **2** to stop abruptly while speaking, working, etc. ➤ *verb trans* **1** to detach (something) from the main part. **2** to discontinue (a connection or relationship).

breakout[1] *noun* an escape using force, e.g. from imprisonment or a siege.

breakout[2] *adj NAmer, informal* wildly successful: *a breakout movie.*

break out *verb intrans* **1** (+ of) to escape from confinement. **2** said of something violent or unpleasant, such as a disease: to develop or emerge with suddenness and force. **3** (+ in) to become affected with a skin eruption. ➤ *verb trans* to unfurl (a flag) at the mast.

break point *noun* **1** in tennis, the stage in a game at which the player receiving service needs only one more point to win the game. **2** a point, e.g. in a computer program, at which an interruption can be made.

breakthrough *noun* **1** a sudden advance, *esp* in knowledge or technique: *a medical breakthrough.* **2** an act or point of breaking through an obstruction. **3** an attack that penetrates enemy lines.

breakthrough bleeding *noun* irregular bleeding from the uterus occurring between menstrual periods.

breakup *noun* **1** a dissolution or disruption: *the breakup of a marriage.* **2** a division into smaller units. **3** *chiefly Can* the spring thaw.

break up *verb trans* **1** to break (something) into pieces or into its component parts. **2a** to disrupt the continuity of (something). **b** to bring (a relationship) to an end. **3** *informal.* **a** to cause (somebody) great distress: *His wife's death broke him up.* **b** *chiefly NAmer* to cause (somebody) to laugh uncontrollably. ➤ *verb intrans* **1a** said of a relationship: to come to an end. **b** (+ with) to separate from another person. **c** said of a meeting, etc: to disperse on completion of business. **d** *Brit* said of a school: to leave for the holidays. **2** to lose morale or composure. **3** *informal* to laugh uncontrollably.

breakwater *noun* an offshore structure, e.g. a wall used to protect a harbour or beach from the force of waves.

bream[1] /breem/ *noun* (*pl* **breams** or collectively **bream**) **1** a silvery European freshwater fish related to the carp, with a deep narrow body: *Abramis brama.* **2** any of various similar or related fishes, including several freshwater sunfishes. **3** the sea bream. [Middle English *breme* from early French, of Germanic origin]

bream[2] *verb trans archaic* = GRAVE[4]. [prob from Dutch *brem* furze]

breast[1] /brest/ *noun* **1** either of two protuberant milk-producing glandular organs situated on the front of the chest in the human female and some other mammals. **2a** the front part of the body between the neck and the abdomen; the chest. **b** the corresponding part of an animal's body, or a cut of meat taken from this part. **3** *formal* the place where emotions and thoughts reside; the bosom. [Old English *brēost*]

breast[2] *verb trans* **1** to contend with (something) resolutely; to confront (it): *It was time to breast the rush-hour traffic.* **2a** to meet or lean against (something) with the breast or front: *The swimmer breasted the waves.* **b** to thrust the chest against (something): *The sprinter breasted the tape.* **3** *chiefly Brit* to reach the top of (a hill or mountain).

breast-beating *noun* an ostentatious and noisy display of emotion.

breastbone *noun* = STERNUM.

breast-feed *verb trans* (*past tense and past part.* **breast-fed**) to feed (a baby) with milk from the breast rather than with formula milk from a bottle.

breast implant *noun* a sac filled with fluid, e.g. silicone, implanted in the chest in a surgical operation to reconstruct or enhance a breast.

breastpin *noun* a brooch or pin worn on the breast, *esp* to fasten a garment.

breastplate *noun* **1** a metal plate worn as defensive armour for the chest. **2** = PLASTRON (2).

breast pump *noun* a suction device used to get milk from a woman's breasts if she wants to store it or donate it to another baby.

breaststroke *noun* a swimming stroke executed on the front by thrusting the arms forwards while kicking outwards and backwards with the legs, then sweeping the arms backwards.

breastsummer /'bres(t)səmə/ *noun* see BRESSUMER. [BREAST[1]+ SUMMER[4]]

breastwork /'brestwuhk/ *noun* a temporary fortification, usu consisting of a wall of earth built to about chest height.

breath /breth/ *noun* **1a** the faculty of breathing. **b** an act of breathing. **c** opportunity or time to breathe; respite. **2** a slight movement of air. **3** air inhaled and exhaled in breathing. **4a** a slight fragrance or smell. **b** a slight indication; a suggestion: *There was not the faintest breath of scandal.* **5** *literary* something that injects new life or energy: *You felt the heady breath of a new age.* ✳ **catch one's breath 1** to rest long enough to restore normal breathing. **2** to stop breathing briefly, usu under the influence of strong emotion. **out of breath** breathing very rapidly, e.g. from strenuous exercise. **under one's breath** in a whisper. [Middle English *breth* from Old English *brǣth*; related to Old English *beorma* BARM]

breathable /'breedhəbl/ *adj* **1** suitable for breathing: *breathable air.* **2** allowing air to pass through; porous: *a breathable synthetic fabric.* ➤➤ **breathability** /-'biliti/ *noun.*

breathalyse or **breathalyze** /'brethəliez/ *verb trans* to test (a driver) for the level of alcohol in exhaled breath, using a breathalyser. [back-formation from BREATHALYSER]

breathalyser or **breathalyzer** /'brethəliezə/ *noun* a device used to test the alcohol content in the blood of a motorist, usu consisting of a plastic bag into which the subject blows through crystals which turn green if the alcohol level is too high. [BREATH + ANALYSE + -ER[2]]

breathe /breedh/ *verb intrans* **1** to draw air into and expel it from the lungs. **2** to be alive: *Such a move would not be countenanced while she still breathed.* **3** to pause and rest before continuing. **4** said of wine: to be exposed to the beneficial effects of air after being kept in a bottle. **5** said of wind: to blow softly. ➤ *verb trans* **1a** (*often* + out) to send (something) out by exhaling: *She breathed garlic over him.* **b** to instil (something) as if by breathing: *Her speech was to breathe new life into the movement.* **2a** to utter or express (something): *Don't breathe a word of it to anyone.* **b** to make (something) manifest; to display (it): *The novel breathes despair.* **3** to allow (e.g. a horse) to rest after exertion. **4** to inhale (something). ✳ **breathe easily/freely** to enjoy relief, e.g. from pressure or danger. **breathe down somebody's neck** to keep somebody under constant or too close surveillance. [Middle English *brethen* from Old English *brǣth* BREATH]

breather /'breedhə/ *noun* **1** *informal* a break in activity for rest or relief. **2** a small vent in an otherwise airtight enclosure, e.g. an engine's crankcase.

breathing /'breedhing/ *noun* either of the marks ' or ' used in writing ancient Greek to indicate ASPIRATION (the audible release of air) or its absence in the pronunciation of an initial vowel or the letter rho.

breathing space *noun* a pause in a period of activity, *esp* for rest and recuperation.

breathless /'brethlis/ *adj* **1** not breathing, *esp* holding one's breath due to excitement or suspense. **2a** gasping for breath, e.g. after strenuous exercise. **b** gripping or intense: *breathless tension.* **3** without any breeze; stuffy: *It was a breathless summer's afternoon.* ➤➤ **breathlessly** *adv,* **breathlessness** *noun.*

breathtaking /'brethtayking/ *adj* hugely impressive, exciting, or thrilling: *a breathtaking turn of speed.* ➤➤ **breathtakingly** *adv.*

breath test *noun Brit* a test made with a breathalyser.

breathy /'brethi/ *adj* (**breathier, breathiest**) characterized or accompanied by the audible passage of breath. ➤➤ **breathily** *adv,* **breathiness** *noun.*

breccia /'breki-ə, 'brechi-ə/ *noun* a rock consisting of angular fragments embedded in sand, clay, etc. [Italian *breccia* gravel, of Germanic origin]

Brechtian /'brekhti-ən/ *adj* relating to or suggestive of the writings of the German dramatist Bertolt Brecht, *esp* using dramatic techniques aimed at getting the audience to distance itself from the action and therefore adopt a more critical approach to it. [Bertolt *Brecht* d.1956, German dramatist]

bred /bred/ *verb* past tense and past part. of BREED[1].

breech /breech/ *noun* **1** the part of a firearm at the rear of the barrel. **2** the buttocks. [Old English *brēc*, pl of *brōc* leg covering; related to Old English *brecan* to BREAK[1]]

breech birth *noun* a birth in which the feet or the buttocks of the baby appear first. Also called BREECH DELIVERY.

breechblock *noun* in breech-loading firearms, the block that closes the rear of the barrel against the force of the charge.

breech delivery *noun* = BREECH BIRTH.

breeches /'brichiz, 'breechiz/ *pl noun* **1** knee-length trousers, usu closely fastened at the lower edges. **2** jodhpurs that are baggy at the thigh and close fitting and fastened with buttons from the knee to the ankle. **3** *humorous* trousers. [Middle English, pl of BREECH]

breeches buoy *noun* a life-saving apparatus in the form of a pair of canvas breeches hung from a lifebuoy running on a rope leading from a ship in distress to a rescue ship or to the shore.

breeching /'breeching/ *noun* the part of a harness that passes round the haunches of a draught animal.

breechloader *noun* a firearm that is loaded at the breech. ➤➤ **breech-loading** *adj*.

breed[1] /breed/ *verb* (*past tense and past part.* **bred** /bred/) ➤ *verb trans* **1a** to produce (offspring) by hatching or gestation. **b** to bring (somebody) up: *She was born and bred in Somerset.* **2** to produce or engender (something): *Despair often breeds violence.* **3** to propagate (plants or animals) sexually and usu under controlled conditions. **4** to inculcate (something) by training: *We aim to breed good behaviour.* **5** to produce (fissile material for use in nuclear reactors or warheads) in a nuclear chain reaction in a breeder reactor. ➤ *verb intrans* **1** to produce offspring by sexual union. **2** to propagate animals or plants. [Old English *brēdan*; related to Old English *brōd* BROOD[1]]

breed[2] *noun* **1** a group of animals or plants, often specially selected, visibly similar in most characteristics. **2** race or lineage. **3** a class or kind: *We're seeing a new breed of radical.*

breeder /'breedə/ *noun* **1** an animal or plant kept for propagation. **2** a person engaged in the breeding of a specified animal or plant. **3** = BREEDER REACTOR.

breeder reactor *noun* a nuclear reactor in which more radioactive fuel is produced than is consumed.

breeding *noun* **1** the sexual propagation of plants or animals, *esp* the development of new or improved varieties. **2** behaviour, *esp* when it shows good manners. **3** ancestry.

breeding ground *noun* a place or set of circumstances favourable to the propagation of certain ideas, movements, etc.

breeks /breeks/ *pl noun chiefly Scot* trousers. [Middle English (northern) *breke* from Old English *brēc*: see BREECH]

breeze[1] /breez/ *noun* **1** a light gentle wind; *specif* a wind of between 4 and 31mph. **2** *chiefly NAmer, informal* something easily done; a cinch. **3** *chiefly Brit, dated, informal* a slight disturbance or quarrel. ➤➤ **breezeless** *adj*. [early French *brise* NE wind, perhaps alteration of *bise* cold north wind]

breeze[2] *verb intrans* **1** (+ in/into/along) to come in or into, or move along, swiftly and casually or nonchalantly: *She breezed in as if nothing had happened.* **2** *informal* to make progress quickly and easily: *He'll breeze through these books.*

breeze[3] *noun* ashy residue from the making of coke or charcoal. [prob modification of French *braise*: see BRAISE]

breeze-block *noun* a rectangular building block made of breeze mixed with sand and cement.

breezeway *noun NAmer* a covered passage, e.g. between a house and garage.

breezy *adj* (**breezier, breeziest**) **1** quite windy; fresh. **2** brisk or lively. **3** carefree or careless; insouciant. ➤➤ **breezily** *adv*, **breeziness** *noun*.

bremsstrahlung /'bremshtrahləng, 'bremstrahləng/ *noun* the electromagnetic radiation produced by the sudden slowing down of a charged particle in an intense electric field. [German *Bremsstrahlung*, from *bremsen* to brake + *Strahlung* radiation]

Bren gun /bren/ *noun* a gas-operated magazine-fed light machine gun. [blend of *Brno*, city in Czechoslovakia where it was first made + *Enfield*, town in England where it was subsequently produced]

brent goose /brent/ *noun* a small dark goose that breeds in the Arctic and migrates southwards: *Branta bernicla.* [origin unknown]

bressumer /'bresəmə/ *or* **breastsummer** /'bres(t)səmə/ *noun* a large supporting beam set across an opening, e.g. a fireplace. [alteration of BREASTSUMMER]

brethren /'bredhrin/ *noun* used in formal address and to refer to members of a religious order or a society: pl of BROTHER.

Breton /'bret(ə)n/ *noun* **1** a native or inhabitant of Brittany. **2** the Celtic language of the Bretons. ➤➤ **Breton** *adj*. [French *breton* via late Latin from Latin *Briton-, Brito*: see BRITON]

breve /breev/ *noun* **1** a musical note with the time value of two semibreves or four minims. **2** a curved mark (•) placed over a vowel in some languages to show a short or unstressed vowel or syllable. [Latin *breve*, neuter of *brevis* BRIEF[1]]

brevet[1] /'brevit/ *noun* a commission giving a military officer higher nominal rank than that for which he or she receives pay. [Middle English in the sense 'an official message', from Old French *brevet*, dimin. of *bref, brief* letter: see BRIEF[2]]

brevet[2] *verb trans* (**breveted** *or* **brevetted, breveting** *or* **brevetting**) to confer a usu specified rank on (somebody) by brevet.

breviary /'brevi·əri, 'bree-, 'brevyəri/ *noun* (*pl* **breviaries**) **1** (*often* **Breviary**) a book containing the prayers, hymns, psalms, and readings for the canonical hours. **2** = DIVINE OFFICE. [Latin *breviarium*, from *brevis* BRIEF[1]]

brevity /'breviti/ *noun* **1** the quality of being brief, *esp* shortness of duration. **2** expression in few words; conciseness: *Since brevity is the soul of wit … I will be brief* — Shakespeare. [Latin *brevitas*, from *brevis* BRIEF[1]]

brew[1] /brooh/ *verb trans* **1** to prepare (e.g. beer or ale) by steeping, boiling, and fermentation or by infusion and fermentation. **2** to prepare (e.g. tea) by infusion in hot water. **3** (*often* + up) to contrive or plot (something): *They were brewing up a plan.* ➤ *verb intrans* **1** to brew beer or ale. **2** *chiefly Brit* to undergo infusion: *He left the tea to brew.* **3** (*often* + up) to be in the process of formation: *A storm is brewing in the east.* ➤➤ **brewer** *noun*. [Old English *brēowan*]

brew[2] *noun* **1a** a brewed beverage. **b** a product of brewing. **2** a combination or mixture.

brewer's droop /'brooh·əz/ *noun Brit, informal* a man's inability to achieve erection after drinking too much alcohol.

brewer's yeast *noun* a yeast used in brewing and as a source of vitamins of the B complex.

brewery /'brooh·əri/ *noun* (*pl* **breweries**) a place in which beer or ale is brewed commercially on a large scale.

brew up *verb intrans Brit, informal* to make tea.

briar[1] /'brie·ə/ *noun* see BRIER[1].

briar[2] *noun* **1** see BRIER[2]. **2** a tobacco pipe made from the root of a brier.

bribe[1] /brieb/ *verb trans* to induce or influence (somebody) by bribery. ➤ *verb intrans* to practise bribery. ➤➤ **bribable** *adj*, **briber** *noun*.

bribe[2] *noun* **1** something, *esp* money, given or promised to influence somebody's judgment or conduct. **2** anything that serves to induce or persuade. [Middle English in the sense 'something stolen', from Old French *bribe* bread given to a beggar]

bribery /'brieb(ə)ri/ *noun* the act or practice of giving or taking a bribe.

bric-a-brac /'brik ə brak/ *noun* miscellaneous small articles, usu of ornamental or sentimental value; curios. [French *bric-à-brac*, from obsolete *à bric à brac* at random]

brick[1] /brik/ *noun* **1** a rectangular block of baked clay and sand used for building or paving purposes, ranging in colour from a deep bluish black through a rich red brown to a pale yellowish fawn. **2** a rectangular compressed mass, e.g. of ice cream. **3** *Brit, informal, dated* a reliable, resolute, or undaunted person; a stalwart: *Angela, you're a real brick.* [Middle English *bryke* via Old French *brique* from early Dutch *bricke*; related to Old English *brecan* BREAK[1]]

brick[2] *verb trans* (+ up) to close, face, or pave (something) with bricks: *The disused entrance had been bricked up.*

brickbat *noun* **1** a piece of something hard used as a missile. **2** a critical remark.

brickie /'briki/ *noun Brit, informal* a bricklayer.

bricklayer *noun* a person who is employed to lay bricks. ➤➤ **bricklaying** *noun*.

brick red *adj* of a reddish brown colour. ➤➤ **brick red** *noun*.

brickwork /'brikwuhk/ *noun* the parts of a structure that are made from bricks and mortar.

brickworks /'brikwuhks/ *noun* (*pl* **brickworks**) a place where bricks are produced.

brickyard *noun* = BRICKWORKS.

bricolage /brikə'lahzh/ *noun* something made using a mixture of materials, or the effect created by this. [French *bricolage* from *bricole* trifle]

bridal /'briedl/ *adj* of or for a bride or wedding; nuptial.

bride /bried/ *noun* a woman at the time of her wedding. [Old English *brȳd*]

bridegroom *noun* a man at the time of his wedding. [Old English *brȳdguma*, from *bryd* BRIDE + *guma* man; the spelling altered by association with GROOM[1]]

bride price *noun* money, property, or other gifts that a bridegroom's family gives to a bride at the time of their marriage, *esp* in tribal societies.

bridesmaid /'briedzmayd/ *noun* an unmarried woman or girl who attends a bride.

bridge[1] /brij/ *noun* **1a** a structure spanning a gap or obstacle, e.g. a river, and supporting a roadway, railway, canal, or path. **b** a time, place, or means of connection or transition: *Humour helped to build a bridge across the age gap.* **2a** the upper bony part of the nose. **b** the part of a pair of glasses that rests on this. **c** an arch serving to raise the strings of a musical instrument. **d** a raised platform on a ship from which the captain and officers control it. **e** in billiards and snooker, a cue rest with a wide span. **3** a partial denture permanently attached to adjacent natural teeth, filling a gap. [Old English *brycg*]

bridge[2] *verb trans* **1** to make a bridge over or across (something, e.g. a river). **2** to bring together people or things that are separated by (something). >> **bridgeable** *adj*.

bridge[3] *noun* a card game related to whist for usu four players in two partnerships in which players bid for the right to name a trump suit and try to win tricks, and in which the hand of the declarer's partner is exposed and played by the declarer. [alteration of earlier *biritch*, of unknown origin]

bridgehead *noun* **1a** a fortification protecting the end of a bridge nearest an enemy. **b** the area round the end of a bridge. **2** an advanced position, usu beyond a bridge, seized or targeted in hostile territory as a foothold for further advance.

bridge loan *noun NAmer* = BRIDGING LOAN.

bridge roll *noun* a small finger-shaped soft roll. [BRIDGE[1] or BRIDGE[3]]

bridgework /'brijwuhk/ *noun* a dental bridge.

bridging loan *noun* a short-term loan made to somebody awaiting finalization of a long-term loan or mortgage.

bridle[1] /'briedl/ *noun* **1** a framework of leather straps buckled together round the head of a horse or other draught or riding animal, including the bit and reins, used to direct and control it. **2** a length of secured cable, *esp* on a boat, to which a second cable can be attached, e.g. for mooring. **3** something that curbs or restrains: *They set a bridle on his power.* [Old English *brīdel*; related to Old English *bregdan* BRAID[1]]

bridle[2] *verb trans* **1** to put a bridle on (an animal). **2** to restrain or control (something): *You must learn to bridle your tongue.* >> *verb intrans* to show hostility or resentment in response to a perceived affront to pride or dignity, *esp* by drawing back the head and chin.

bridle path *noun* a track or right of way suitable for horse riding.

bridleway *noun* = BRIDLE PATH.

Brie /bree/ *noun* a large round cream-coloured soft cheese that becomes runny as it ripens. [named after *Brie*, district in France where it was orig made]

brief[1] /breef/ *adj* **1** short in duration or extent. **2** expressed in few words; concise. >> **briefly** *adv*, **briefness** *noun*. [Middle English *bref*, *breve* via Old French from Latin *brevis*]

brief[2] *noun* **1a** a set of instructions outlining what is required, and usu setting limits to one's powers, e.g. in negotiating. **b** a statement of a client's case drawn up for the instruction of legal counsel. **c** a case given to a barrister. **d** *Brit, informal* a barrister or solicitor assigned to somebody. **e** a synopsis or summary. **2** a papal directive, less binding than a BULL[2]. ✱ **hold a brief for** *Brit* to be retained as counsel for (somebody). **in brief** in a few words; briefly.

[Middle English *bref* from Old French *bref* summary, ultimately from Latin *brevis* BRIEF[1]]

brief[3] *verb trans* **1** to provide (somebody) with final instructions or necessary information: *It was my job to brief journalists about the situation.* **2** *Brit* to retain (a barrister) as legal counsel.

briefcase *noun* a flat rectangular case for carrying papers or books.

briefing *noun* a meeting to give out final instructions or necessary information, or the instructions or information given out.

briefs /breefs/ *pl noun* short underpants for men or women.

brier[1] *or* **briar** /'brie·ə/ *noun* any plant with woody and thorny or prickly stems, *esp* a wild plant of the rose family. >> **briery** *adj*. [Old English *brēr*]

brier[2] *or* **briar** *noun* a HEATH (plant) of S Europe with a root used for making pipes: *Erica arborea.* [French *bruyère* heath, from late Latin *brucus* heather, of Celtic origin]

Brig. *abbr* **1** brigade. **2** brigadier.

brig[1] /brig/ *noun* a two-masted square-rigged sailing ship. [short for BRIGANTINE]

brig[2] *noun* a prison in the US Navy. [orig a detention cell on a warship; prob from BRIG[1]]

brig[3] *noun Scot* a bridge.

brigade[1] /bri'gayd/ *noun* **1** a large section of an army usu composed of a headquarters, several fighting units, e.g. infantry battalions or armoured regiments, and supporting units. **2** an organized or uniformed group of people, e.g. firefighters. [French *brigade* from Italian *brigata*, from *brigare*: see BRIGAND]

brigade[2] *verb trans* to form or unite (people) into a brigade.

brigadier /brigə'diə/ *noun* an officer in the British Army and the Royal Marines ranking below a major general. [French *brigadier*, from *brigade*: see BRIGADE[1]]

brigadier general *noun* an officer in the US army, air force, and marines ranking below a major general.

brigalow /'brigəloh/ *noun Aus* any of several species of acacia forming thick scrub: genus *Acacia.* [Aboriginal name in Australia]

brigand /'brigənd/ *noun* somebody who lives by plunder, usu as a member of a gang of marauding thieves; a bandit. >> **brigandage** *noun*, **brigandry** *noun*. [Middle English *brigaunt* via Old French *brigand* from Old Italian *brigante*, from *brigare* to fight, of Celtic origin]

brigantine /'brigənteen/ *noun* a two-masted square-rigged sailing ship differing from a brig in not carrying a square mainsail. [Old French *brigantin* from Old Italian *brigantino*, from *brigante*: see BRIGAND]

Brig.-Gen. *abbr* brigadier general.

bright /briet/ *adj* **1a** radiating or reflecting light; shining. **b** radiant with happiness, animation, or good fortune: *bright faces.* **2** said of a colour: of high saturation or brilliance. **3a** quick to learn or understand; intelligent. **b** lively and charming: *Be bright and jovial among your guests*— Shakespeare. **c** successful, or promising success or good fortune: *She has a bright future ahead of her.* ✱ **bright and early** very early in the morning. **bright spark** an intelligent person. >> **bright** *adv*, **brightly** *adv*, **brightness** *noun*. [Old English *beorht*]

brighten /'brietn/ *verb intrans and trans* (**brightened, brightening**) (*often* + up) to become, or make (something or somebody), bright or brighter. >> **brightener** *noun*. [Old English *beorhtnian*, from *beorht* BRIGHT]

bright lights *pl noun* (**the bright lights**) an urban area offering a variety of entertainments, or the false gaiety and allure of such an area.

Bright's disease /'briets/ *noun* a kidney disease marked by albumin in the urine. [named after Richard *Bright* d.1858, English physician who first described it]

brightwork /'brietwuhk/ *noun* polished or plated metalwork, *esp* the exposed and often decorative metal parts of ships and motor vehicles.

brill[1] /bril/ *noun* (*pl* **brill**) a European flatfish related to the turbot: *Scophthalmus rhombus.* [perhaps from Cornish *brythel* mackerel]

brill[2] *adj Brit, informal* excellent. [short for BRILLIANT[1]]

brilliant[1] /'brilyənt, 'brili·ənt/ *adj* **1** very bright, *esp* sparkling or glittering with light. **2a** having great intellectual ability: *a brilliant scholar.* **b** strikingly impressive or distinctive: *a brilliant example.* **3** *Brit, informal* of high quality; good: *The food was brilliant.*

>>> **brilliance** *noun,* **brilliancy** *noun,* **brilliantly** *adv.* [French *brillant,* present part. of *briller* to shine, via Italian from Latin *beryllus:* see BERYL]

brilliant[2] *noun* a gem, *esp* a diamond, cut with numerous facets for maximum brilliance.

brilliant cut *noun* a cut for gems, consisting of two pyramids with numerous facets joined at the base.

brilliantine /'brilyənteen/ *noun dated* a scented oil for making men's hair glossy and smooth.

brim[1] /brim/ *noun* **1** the edge or rim of something, *esp* a container. **2** the projecting rim of a hat. >>> **brimless** *adj.* [Middle English *brimme,* of Germanic origin]

~~brim² verb intrans (brimmed, brimming) to be full to the brim~~

brimful /brim'fool/ *adj* full to the brim, *esp* about to overflow.

brimmed *adj* (*used in combinations*) having a brim of the kind specified: *wide-brimmed.*

brim over *verb intrans* to be so full as to overflow.

brimstone /'brimstohn/ *noun* **1** *archaic* = SULPHUR[1] (1). **2** a yellow butterfly common in Britain and N Europe: *Gonepteryx rhamni.* [Middle English *brinston,* prob from *birnan* (see BURN[1]) + *ston* STONE[1]]

brindled /'brind(ə)ld/ *or* **brindle** /'brind(ə)l/ *adj* said of an animal: having dark streaks or flecks on a grey or tawny background. [alteration of archaic *brinded* from Middle English *brende, brended;* prob related to Old English *brand* BRAND[1]]

brine[1] /brien/ *noun* **1** a solution of water and common salt. **2** sea water. **3** the sea itself. [Old English *brȳne*]

brine[2] *verb trans* to pickle (something, e.g. meat) with brine.

bring /bring/ *verb trans* (*past tense and past part.* **brought** /brawt/) **1** to carry or convey (something or somebody) to a place or person: *Will you bring me some tea?* **2** to cause (something) to reach or result in a particular condition: *Bring the water to the boil.* **3** to force or compel (oneself) to do something: *I cannot bring myself to speak to him.* **4** to cause (something) to occur; to lead to (a result): *Winter will bring snow and ice.* **5** to initiate (an action, *esp* in law). **6** to prefer (a charge). **7** to offer or present (something): *Did they have an argument to bring?* **8** to sell for (a price). *** bring to bear 1** to apply (something); to put (something) to use: *He wanted her to bring her vast knowledge to bear on the problem.* **2** to exert (pressure). >>> **bringer** *noun.* [Old English *bringan*]

bring about *verb trans* to cause (something) to take place; to effect (something).

bring and buy sale *noun Brit* a sale of goods donated by members of the community, usu held to raise money for charity.

bring around *verb trans NAmer* see BRING ROUND

bring down *verb trans* **1** to cause (something) to fall or come down. **2** to reduce (something, e.g. a price). **3** (*usu in passive*) to cause (somebody) to be in a depressed state. **4** to cause (a government) to lose power. **5** to kill (an animal) by shooting it.

bring forth *verb trans formal* **1** to bear (produce): *The tree brought forth fruit.* **2** to give birth to (offspring). **3** to offer or present (something).

bring forward *verb trans* **1** to schedule (something) for an earlier time. **2** in bookkeeping, to carry (a total) forward, e.g. to the top of the next page.

bring in *verb trans* **1** to produce or earn (income). **2** to introduce (a measure or procedure). **3** to pronounce (a verdict) in court.

bring off *verb trans* **1** to achieve or conclude (something) successfully. **2** *coarse slang* to give (somebody) an orgasm.

bring on *verb trans* **1** to cause (a feeling or symptom) to occur. **2** to help (somebody or something) to develop or make better progress.

bring out *verb trans* **1** to make (something) more clearly visible or noticeable. **2** to publish (something) or make it public. **3** (+ in) to cause (somebody) to be afflicted with a rash or other visible symptoms of illness. **4** to encourage (somebody) to be less reticent. **5** to utter (something). **6** *chiefly Brit* to instruct or cause (workers) to strike. **7** *Brit* to introduce (a young woman) formally to society.

bring round (*NAmer* **bring around**) *verb trans* **1** to persuade (somebody) to adopt a particular opinion or course of action. **2** to revive (somebody) who has been unconscious.

bring to *verb trans* **1** = BRING ROUND (2). **2** to cause (a boat) to lie to or come to a standstill.

bring up *verb trans* **1** to educate or rear (a child) to adulthood. **2** to mention (something). **3** to vomit (something).

brinjal /'brinjəl/ *noun Indian, SAfr* = AUBERGINE[1]. [Portuguese *bringella, beringela* via Arabic *bādhinjan* from Persian *bādingān.* Compare with AUBERGINE[1]]

brink /bringk/ *noun* **1** an edge, *esp* the edge at the top of a steep place. **2** the point at which something is about to happen; the verge: *We are on the brink of war.* [Middle English, prob of Scandinavian origin]

brinkmanship /'bringkmənship/ *noun* the art of going to the very brink of conflict, danger, etc before drawing back, as a tactic to intimidate an enemy into conceding or backing down.

briny[1] /'brieni/ *noun* (**the briny**) *Brit, informal* sea water, or the sea itself.

briny[2] *adj* (**brinier, briniest**) of brine; salty. >>> **brininess** *noun.*

brio /'breeoh/ *noun* enthusiasm and liveliness; verve. [Italian *brio*]

brioche /bree'osh/ *noun* a light, slightly sweet bread roll made with a rich yeast dough. [French *brioche* from early French *brier* to knead, of Germanic origin]

briquette *or* **briquet** /bri'ket/ *noun* a compacted block, e.g. a block of coal-dust used as fuel for a barbecue. [French *briquette,* dimin. of *brique:* see BRICK[1]]

brisk /brisk/ *adj* **1** energetic and fast: *a brisk pace.* **2** fresh and invigorating: *brisk weather.* **3** keenly alert; lively. **4** sharp in tone or manner: *I found her a little too brisk for my liking.* >>> **briskly** *adv,* **briskness** *noun.* [prob modification of French *brusque:* see BRUSQUE]

brisket /'briskit/ *noun* a joint of beef cut from the breast. [Middle English *brusket;* related to Old English *brēost* BREAST[1]]

brisling /'brizling, 'brisling/ *noun* (*pl* **brislings** *or collectively* **brisling**) a small herring that resembles a sardine and is processed in the same way: *Clupea sprattus.* [Norwegian *brisling* from Low German *bretling,* from *bret* broad; related to Old English *brād* BROAD[1]]

bristle[1] /'brisl/ *noun* **1** a short stiff coarse hair or filament. **2** a material consisting of natural rather than synthetic filaments, used to make artists' brushes. [Middle English *bristil,* from *brust* bristle, from Old English *byrst*]

bristle[2] *verb intrans* **1a** to rise and stand stiffly erect: *Notice how its quills bristle in all directions.* **b** said of an animal: to raise the bristles, e.g. in anger. **2** to take on an aggressive attitude or appearance, e.g. in response to an insult or criticism. **3** (+ with) to be filled or thickly covered with something suggestive of bristles: *The rooftops bristled with chimneys.* >>> *verb trans* **1** to provide (something, e.g. a brush) with bristles. **2** to make (something) bristly; to ruffle (it).

bristletail *noun* any of several species of wingless insects, e.g. the silverfish, with two or three slender bristles at the rear end of the body: orders Thysanura and Diplura.

bristly /'brisli/ *adj* (**bristlier, bristliest**) **1a** consisting of or resembling bristles. **b** thickly covered with bristles. **2** tending to bristle easily; belligerent.

Bristol board /'bristl/ *noun* fine cardboard with a smooth surface used by artists. [named after *Bristol,* city and port in S W England]

Bristol fashion *adj Brit, informal, dated* in good order; spick-and-span.

bristols *pl noun Brit, slang, dated* a woman's breasts. [rhyming slang *Bristol (City)* titty]

Brit /brit/ *noun informal* a British person.

Brit. *abbr* **1** Britain. **2** British.

Britannia /bri'tanyə/ *noun* Great Britain or the British Empire personified in the form of a seated female figure wearing a helmet and carrying a trident. [poetic name for Great Britain, from Latin]

Britannia metal *noun* a silver-white alloy of tin, antimony, and copper.

Britannia silver *noun* silver of at least 95.84% purity.

Britannic /bri'tanik/ *adj dated* British: *Her Britannic Majesty.*

britches /'brichiz/ *pl noun* breeches.

Briticism /'britisiz(ə)m/ *or* **Britishism** /'britishiz(ə)m/ *noun* a characteristic feature of British English. [BRITISH[1] + *-icism* as in GALLICISM]

British[1] /'british/ *noun* (**the British**) (*treated as pl*) the people of Britain. [Old English *Brettisc,* of Celtic origin]

British[2] *adj* of Britain, its people, or the variety of the English language that they speak. ➤ **Britishness** *noun*.

Britisher *noun chiefly NAmer, informal* a British person.

Britishism *noun* see BRITICISM.

British Summer Time *noun* time one hour ahead of Greenwich Mean Time that is used in Britain during the summer and is the same as Central European Time: compare DAYLIGHT SAVING TIME.

British thermal unit *noun* the quantity of heat required to raise the temperature of 1lb of water by 1°F under standard conditions.

Briton /'brit(ə)n/ *noun* **1** a native or inhabitant of Britain. **2** a member of any of the peoples inhabiting Britain before the Anglo-Saxon invasions. [Middle English *Breton* via French from Latin *Briton-, Brito*, of Celtic origin]

Britpop /'britpop/ *noun* pop music typical of a style produced by some British groups in the mid 1990s.

brittle[1] /'britl/ *adj* **1** easily broken or cracked. **2** liable not to survive setbacks or upsets; fragile: *A brittle glory shineth in that face; as brittle as the glory is the face* — Shakespeare. **3** light and thin in tone; sharp: *a brittle sound.* **4** lacking warmth or depth of feeling: *brittle gaiety.* ➤ **brittlely** /'britl-li/ *adv,* **brittleness** *noun,* **brittly** *adv.* [Middle English *britil,* of Germanic origin]

brittle[2] *noun* a sweet made with caramelized sugar and nuts: *peanut brittle.*

brittle bone disease *noun* = OSTEOPOROSIS.

brittle star *noun* any of a subclass or class of starfish that have slender flexible arms: class Ophiuroidea.

BRN *abbr* Brunei (international vehicle registration).

bro. *abbr* brother.

broach[1] /brohch/ *verb trans* **1** to open up (a subject) for discussion. **2a** to pierce (a container, *esp* a cask or bottle) prior to using the contents; to tap (it). **b** to open up or break into (e.g. a store or stock of something) and start to use it. [Middle English *broche* from Old French, ultimately from Latin *broccus* projecting]

broach[2] *noun* **1a** a metal-cutting hand tool for smoothing the inside of holes. **b** a tool for tapping casks. **2** a spit for roasting meat.

broach[3] *verb intrans* (+ to) said of a boat: to change direction dangerously, *esp* so as to lie broadside to the waves. ➤ *verb trans* to cause (a boat) to broach. [perhaps from BROACH[1]]

B-road *noun* a road of a lower standard than an A-road.

broad[1] /brawd/ *adj* **1a** large in size or extent from side to side or between limits: *broad shoulders.* **b** of a specified size in width: *They made the path ten feet broad.* **2** widely applicable or applied; general: *in broad terms.* **3** relating to main points or features rather than to details: *broad outlines.* **4** easily understood or noticed; obvious: *a broad hint.* **5** extending far and wide; vast: *the broad plains.* **6** dialectal, *esp* in pronunciation: *She spoke broad Somerset.* **7** said of a vowel: open. **8** marked by lack of restraint or delicacy; coarse: *Some of the jokes he cracked were rather broad.* ✳ **broad daylight** full daylight. [Old English *brād*]

broad[2] *noun* **1** the broad part: *The broad of his back took the full impact.* **2** *NAmer, informal* a woman. **3** (*usu* **the Broads**) a large area of fresh water formed by the broadening of a river, *esp* such stretches of water found in E England: *the Norfolk Broads.*

broad[3] *adv dated* in a broad manner; fully: *They were broad awake.*

broad arrow *noun* **1** an arrow with a flat barbed head. **2** *Brit* a mark like a broad arrow that identifies government property, including clothing formerly worn by convicts.

broadband /'brawdband/ *noun* any of several telecommunications systems that allow the user a permanent connection to the Internet and are capable of transmitting digital data at significantly higher speeds than traditional dial-up modem connections. ➤ **broadband** *adj.*

broad bean *noun* **1** a Eurasian leguminous plant widely cultivated for its large flat edible seeds: *Vicia faba.* **2** a seed of this plant, used as a vegetable.

broad-brush *adj* dealing with main elements rather than details; general: *a broad-brush strategy for electoral reform.*

broadcast[1] *verb* (past tense **broadcast,** past part. **broadcast** or **broadcasted**) ➤ *verb trans* **1** to transmit (a television or radio programme), or make (something) known by featuring it in such a programme. **2** to make (something) widely known. **3** to scatter or sow (seed) over a broad area. ➤ *verb intrans* **1** to transmit a

broadcast. **2** to speak or perform on a broadcast programme. ➤ **broadcaster** *noun.*

broadcast[2] *noun* a single radio or television programme.

broadcast[3] *adj* said *esp* of seed: cast or scattered in all directions.

broadcast[4] *adv* to or over a broad area.

Broad Church *adj* relating to a liberal form of Anglicanism that flourished in the late 19th cent.

broadcloth *noun* a twilled napped woollen or worsted fabric with a smooth lustrous finish and dense texture.

broaden *verb trans and intrans* (**broadened, broadening**) to become broad or broader, or make (something) broad or broader.

broad gauge *noun* a size of railway track that is wider than the standard.

broad-leaved /'brawdleevd/ *or* **broadleaf** *adj* having broad leaves, *esp* not coniferous.

broadloom *noun* a carpet woven on a wide loom.

broadly *adv* in general terms; overall: *The problem is broadly one of organization.*

broad-minded *adj* **1** tolerant of varied views, unconventional behaviour, etc; liberal. **2** not easily shocked or offended, *esp* in relation to aspects of sex. ➤ **broad-mindedly** *adv,* **broad-mindedness** *noun.*

broadsheet *noun* **1** a large-format newspaper, technically one with a page depth the full size of a rotary press plate: compare TABLOID. **2** a large sheet of paper printed on one side only, or something, e.g. an advertisement, printed on a broadsheet.

broadside[1] *noun* **1a** the simultaneous firing of all the guns on one side of a ship, or the bank of guns itself. **b** a forceful verbal or written attack. **2** the side of a ship above the waterline. **3** = BROADSHEET (2).

broadside[2] *adv* with the broadside or broader side towards a given object or point; sideways.

broadsword /'brawdsawd/ *noun* a sword with a broad blade for cutting rather than thrusting.

broadtail *noun* a very young karakul lamb with fur that resembles moiré silk, or the fur from such a lamb.

Brobdingnagian /brobding'nagi-ən/ *adj* of colossal size; towering. [*Brobdingnag,* imaginary country inhabited by giants in *Gulliver's Travels* by Jonathan Swift d.1745, Irish satirist]

brocade /brə'kayd/ *noun* a rich usu silk fabric woven with raised patterns often in gold or silver thread. ➤ **brocaded** *adj.* [Spanish *brocado* via Catalan from Italian *broccato,* ultimately from Latin *broccus* projecting]

broccoli /'brokəli/ *noun* **1** a plant of the cabbage family widely cultivated for its clusters of edible green or purplish flower heads that are cooked and eaten before the buds have opened: *Brassica oleracea italica.* **2** a flower head of this plant, used as a vegetable. [Italian *broccoli,* pl of *broccolo* flowering top of a cabbage, dimin. of *brocco* small nail, sprout, from Latin *broccus* projecting]

broch /brok, brokh/ *noun* an ancient fortified circular tower found in the N and W of Scotland and adjacent islands. [Scottish *broch, bruch* borough, from Middle English (Scottish) *brugh,* alteration of Middle English *burgh:* see BOROUGH]

brochette /bro'shet, broh'shet/ *noun* a skewer of roasted or grilled food. [French *brochette* from Old French *broche* pointed tool: see BROACH[2]]

brochure /'brohshə, broh'shooə/ *noun* a small pamphlet, typically printed on glossy paper, containing advertising or promotional material. [French *brochure,* from *brocher* to sew, from Old French *brochier* from *broche:* see BROACH[2]]

brock /brok/ *noun Brit* used as a name: a badger. [Old English *broc,* of Celtic origin]

Brocken spectre /'brokən/ *noun* a phenomenon in which a person's shadow is cast by the sun onto a bank of mist, seen *esp* on the top of a hill or mountain. [a mountain in the Harz Mountains, Germany]

brocket /'brokit/ *noun* any of several species of small S American deer with unbranched horns: genus *Mazama.* [Middle English *broket,* prob modification of early French *brocard, brockart* fallow deer one year old]

broderie anglaise /,brohdəri 'ongglez, ong'glez/ *noun* **1** openwork embroidery, usu in white thread, on white fine cloth. **2** cloth embroidered with broderie anglaise. [French *broderie anglaise* English embroidery]

brogue¹ /brohg/ *noun* a stout shoe characterized by decorative perforations on the uppers. [Irish Gaelic *bróg* and Scottish Gaelic *bròg*, ultimately from Old Norse *brōk* leg covering; related to Old English *brōc* leg covering]

brogue² *noun* a dialect or regional pronunciation, *esp* an Irish accent. [perhaps from Irish Gaelic *barróg* wrestling hold, bond (as in *barróg teangan* lisp, literally 'hold of the tongue')]

broil /broyl/ *verb trans NAmer* to grill (food). ➤ *verb intrans* to become extremely hot. [Middle English *broilen* from Old French *bruler* to burn, from Latin *ustulare* to singe]

broiler /'broylə/ *noun* **1** a bird suitable for grilling, *esp* a young chicken. **2** *NAmer* a grill.

broke¹ /brohk/ *verb* past tense of BREAK¹.

broke² *adj informal* with no money at all; penniless. [Middle English, alteration of BROKEN²]

broken¹ /'brohkən/ *verb* past part. of BREAK¹.

broken² *adj* **1** violently separated into parts; shattered. **2** having undergone or been subjected to fracture: *a broken leg*. **3** not in working order; defective. **4** cut off or disconnected: *a broken transmission*. **5** not fulfilled; violated: *a broken promise*. **6** discontinuous; having gaps, *esp* at regular intervals: *a broken line*. **7** adversely affected or disrupted by marital separation or divorce. **8a** subdued completely; crushed: *a broken spirit*. **b** made weak or infirm. **9** said of a land surface: irregular, interrupted, or full of obstacles. **10** lacking fluency: *broken English*. ➤➤ **brokenly** *adv*, **brokenness** *noun*. [Old English *brocen*, past part. of *brecan* to break]

broken chord *noun* = ARPEGGIO.

broken-down *adj* **1** in a state of disrepair; dilapidated. **2** spiritually or physically ill or exhausted.

brokenhearted *adj* overcome by sorrow or grief.

broken home *noun* a family that has been adversely affected or disrupted by marital separation or divorce.

broken wind /wind/ *noun* a chronic respiratory disease of horses marked by a persistent cough and heaving of the flanks. ➤➤ **broken-winded** *adj*.

broker /'brohkə/ *noun* **1** an agent who negotiates contracts of purchase and sale, *esp* in the financial and insurance sectors. **2** somebody who acts as an intermediary, e.g. in a business deal or political negotiation. [Middle English in the sense 'negotiator', from Anglo-French *brocour*]

brokerage /'brohk(ə)rij/ *noun* **1** the business of a broker. **2** the fee or commission for transacting business as a broker.

brolga /'brolgə/ *noun* a large grey Australian bird that is a species of crane: *Grus rubicunda*. [native name in Australia]

brolly /'broli/ *noun* (*pl* **brollies**) *Brit, informal* an umbrella. [by shortening and alteration]

brom- *comb. form* see BROMO-.

bromeliad /broh'meeliad/ *noun* any of a family of chiefly tropical American plants including the pineapple and various ornamental plants with fleshy spiky leaves: family Bromeliaceae. [scientific Latin *Bromelia*, genus of tropical American plants, named after Olaf *Bromelius* d.1705, Swedish botanist]

bromide /'brohmied/ *noun* **1** a chemical compound of bromine with another element or radical, *esp* any of various bromides, for example potassium bromide, formerly used as sedatives. **2** in publishing, a page proof photographed and reproduced on paper coated with silver bromide emulsion, giving a high-quality image. **3** a commonplace or hackneyed statement or notion, *esp* one calculated to avoid giving a critical response: *Not for him the inane bromides of lesser managers —* The Economist.

bromide paper *noun* photographic paper coated with silver bromide emulsion.

bromine /'brohmeen/ *noun* a non-metallic chemical element of the halogen group, usu occurring as a deep red corrosive toxic liquid with a pungent, often irritating vapour: symbol Br, atomic number 35. [French *brome* + -INE² (from Greek *brōmos* bad smell)]

bromo- *or* **brom-** *comb. form* forming words, denoting: bromine. [prob from French *brome*: see BROMINE]

bronch- *comb. form* see BRONCHO-.

bronchi /'brongki, 'brongkie/ *noun* pl of BRONCHUS.

bronchial /'brongki-əl/ *adj* relating to or in the region of the bronchi or the smaller tubes branching off them in the lungs. ➤➤ **bronchially** *adv*.

bronchiectasis /brongki'ektəsis/ *noun* abnormal dilation of the bronchial tubes, often as a result of infection. [scientific Latin *bronchiectasis*, from BRONCHO- + Greek *ectasis* dilatation]

bronchiole /'brongkiohl/ *noun* a minute thin-walled branch of a bronchus. ➤➤ **bronchiolar** /-'ohlə/ *adj*. [scientific Latin *bronchiolum*, dimin. of *bronchia*: see BRONCHO-]

bronchitis /brong'kietis/ *noun* acute or chronic inflammation of the bronchial tubes accompanied by a cough and catarrh. ➤➤ **bronchitic** /brong'kitik/ *adj and noun*.

broncho- *or* **bronch-** *comb. form* forming words, with the meaning: bronchial tube or bronchial: *bronchitis*; *bronchodilator*. [late Latin *bronch-* from Greek *bronchus* BRONCHUS]

bronchodilator /ˌbrongkohdie'laytə/ *noun* any drug that relieves the symptoms of asthma and bronchitis by relaxing the bronchial muscles and so dilating the bronchial tubes.

bronchopneumonia /ˌbrongkohnyoo'mohni-ə/ *noun* pneumonia affecting many widely scattered but small areas of lung tissue.

bronchoscope /'brongkəskohp/ *noun* a tubular, usu flexible, illuminated instrument used for inspecting or passing instruments into the bronchi.

bronchus /'brongkəs/ *noun* (*pl* **bronchi** /'brongki, 'brongkie/) either of the two main branches of the windpipe that lead into the lungs. [via Latin from Greek *bronchos*]

bronco /'brongkoh/ *noun* (*pl* **broncos**) a wild or partially broken horse of western N America, *esp* a mustang. [Mexican Spanish *bronco* from Spanish *bronco* rough, wild]

brontosaurus /brontə'sawrəs/ *or* **brontosaur** /'brontəsaw/ *noun* dated an apatosaurus. [former genus name, from Greek *brontē* thunder + *sauros* lizard]

Bronx cheer /brongks/ *noun* a rude sound made by sticking the tongue out and blowing noisily; a raspberry. [*the Bronx*, a borough in New York City]

bronze¹ /bronz/ *noun* **1** any of various copper-base alloys, *esp* one containing a high proportion of tin. **2** a sculpture or artefact made of bronze. **3** a yellowish brown colour. **4** a bronze medal: *He won a bronze in the 100 metres*. ➤➤ **bronzy** *adj*. [French *bronze* from Italian *bronzo*, perhaps from Persian *birinj, pirinj* copper]

bronze² *adj* **1** made of bronze. **2** of a yellowish brown colour.

bronze³ *verb trans* **1** to give the appearance of bronze to (something). **2** to make (somebody) brown or suntanned.

Bronze Age *noun* (**the Bronze Age**) the period of human history characterized by the use of bronze or copper tools and weapons, coming between the Stone Age and the Iron Age.

Editorial note
The Bronze Age is the period of antiquity in the Old World in which bronze became the primary material for tools and weapons. Bronze is a combination of copper and (usually) tin, metals which do not normally occur in proximity to each other, and the resulting rise in trade led to considerable differentiation of status, power, and wealth. In Europe the period conventionally spans the period from 2000 to about 700 BC, while in the Far East it is of similar or later date — Dr Paul Bahn.

bronzed *adj* with pale skin made attractively dark by exposure to the sun; tanned.

bronze medal *noun* a medal of bronze awarded to somebody who comes third in a competition, *esp* in athletics or other sports. ➤➤ **bronze medallist** *noun*.

brooch /brohch/ *noun* an ornament worn on clothing and fastened by means of a pin. [Middle English *broche* pointed tool, brooch: see BROACH²]

brood¹ /broohd/ *noun* **1a** young birds, insects, etc hatched or cared for at one time. **b** *humorous or derog* the children in one family. **2** a group of similar or related people or things. [Old English *brōd*; related to Old English *beorma* BARM]

brood² *verb intrans* **1** said of a bird: to sit on eggs in order to hatch them. **2a** (+ on/over/about) to dwell gloomily on, or worry over or about something. **b** to be in a state of depression. **3** to hover or seem to hover menacingly: *the brooding hills*. ➤➤ **broodingly** *adv*.

brood³ *adj* said of an animal: kept for breeding: *a brood mare*.

brooder *noun* a heated house or other structure used for raising young birds.

broody *adj* (**broodier, broodiest**) **1** said of a hen or other female fowl: being in a state of readiness to brood eggs. **2** *informal* said of a woman: feeling a strong desire or urge to be a mother. **3** tending to be occupied with thoughts, *esp* dwelling on depressing thoughts; introspective. ➤➤ **broodily** *adv*, **broodiness** *noun*.

brook[1] /brook/ *noun* a usu small freshwater stream. ➤➤ **brooklet** *noun*. [Old English *brōc*]

brook[2] *verb trans formal* (*in negative contexts*) to tolerate (something); to stand for (it): *She would brook no interference with her plans*. [Old English *brūcan* to use, enjoy]

brooklime *noun* either of two plants with blue flowers that are varieties of speedwell, found in wet areas of Europe, Asia, and N America: *Veronica americana* or *Veronica beccabunga*. [BROOK[1] + Old English *hleomoce* brooklime]

broom /broohm, broom/ *noun* **1** a long-handled brush for sweeping, orig one consisting of a bundle of broom twigs, now usu composed of bristles or nylon fibres. **2** any of several species of shrubs of the pea family with long slender branches, small leaves, and usu showy yellow flowers: genus *Cytisus*, *Genista*, and other genera. [Old English *brōm*]

broomrape /'broohmrayp/ *noun* a plant that grows as a parasite on the roots of other plants: genus *Orobanche*. [part translation of late Latin *rapum genistae* broom tuber, from the parasitic growth of one species on the roots of broom]

broomstick /'broohmstik/ *noun* the long thin handle of a broom, or the whole broom when ridden by a witch in children's stories.

bros. *or* **Bros.** *abbr* brothers.

brose /brohz/ *noun chiefly Scot* a porridge made with boiling milk, water, or other liquid and oatmeal. [perhaps alteration of Scottish *bruis* broth, from Old French *broez*, ultimately of Germanic origin]

broth /broth/ *noun* **1a** the stock in which meat, fish, cereal grains, or vegetables have been cooked. **b** a thin soup made from stock. **2** a liquid medium for culturing *esp* bacteria. [Old English *broth*]

brothel /'broth(ə)l/ *noun* a premises in which the services of prostitutes can be bought. [Middle English in the senses 'worthless person', 'prostitute', ultimately from Old English *brēothan* to waste away]

brothel creepers *pl noun informal* men's shoes, usu of suede, with a thick crepe sole, popular in the 1950s: compare CREEPER. [because the wearer can walk silently]

brother /'brudhə/ *noun* **1** a male having the same parents as another person. **2** *NAmer, informal* a black man. **3** (*pl* **brothers** *or* **brethren** /'bredhrin/) a male who shares a common tie or interest, e.g. a fellow member of a trade union or fellow member of an all-male club or society. **4** (*pl* **brothers** *or* **brethren**) a member of a men's religious order who is not in holy orders: *a lay brother*. **5** (*pl* **brothers** *or* **brethren**) used as a title in some evangelical denominations: *a fellow male member of the Christian Church*. [Old English *brōthor*]

brotherhood *noun* **1** the quality or state of being brothers. **2a** an association, e.g. a religious body, founded for a particular purpose. **b** fellowship between all human beings, or the idea of it: *universal brotherhood*. [Middle English *brotherhede, brotherhod*, alteration of *brotherrede*, from Old English *brōthorrǣden*, from *brōthor* BROTHER + *rǣden* condition]

brother-in-law *noun* (*pl* **brothers-in-law**) **1** the brother of one's husband or wife. **2** the husband of one's sister.

brotherly *adj* **1** relating or appropriate to brothers, *esp* in feeling or showing platonic affection. **2** based on feelings of brotherhood with others; compassionate: *brotherly love*. ➤➤ **brotherliness** *noun*.

brougham /'brooh(ə)m/ *noun* **1** a light closed four-wheeled horse-drawn carriage in which the driver sits high up at the front: *A brougham and pair of grays, under the glare of a gas-lamp, stood before the doctor's door* — Conan Doyle. **2** a large car with an open compartment for the driver. [named after Henry Peter *Brougham* d.1868, Scottish jurist, who designed it]

brought /brawt/ *verb* past tense and past part. of BRING.

brouhaha /'broohhahhah/ *noun* a scene of noisy confusion or protest; an uproar. [French *brouhaha*, prob imitative]

brow /brow/ *noun* **1a** the forehead. **b** an eyebrow. **2** the face, or the expression on it: *a troubled brow*. **3** the top or edge of a hill, cliff, etc. [Old English *brū*]

browbeat /'browbeet/ *verb trans* (*past tense* **browbeat**, *past part.* **browbeaten**) to intimidate, coerce, or bully (somebody) by a persistently threatening or dominating manner: *They were browbeaten into accepting a cut in salary*.

browed *adj* (*used in combinations*) having a brow or brows of the kind specified: *beetle-browed*.

brown[1] /brown/ *adj* **1** of the colour of wood or soil, between red and yellow in hue. **2** of dark or tanned complexion. **3** said of foodstuffs: partially or wholly unrefined, or made with such ingredients. **4** said of bread: made with wholemeal or wheatmeal flour, or a mixture of either of these and a proportion of white flour. ➤➤ **brownness** *noun*. [Old English *brūn*]

brown[2] *noun* the colour of wood or soil, between red and yellow in hue. ➤➤ **brownish** *adj*, **browny** *adj*.

brown[3] *verb trans and intrans* to make (e.g. meat) brown by cooking, or to become brown.

brown ale *noun Brit* a sweet, dark, heavily malted beer, usu sold in bottles.

brown algae *pl noun* any of a large class of algae that are predominantly brown in colour, most of which are seaweeds: class Phaeophyceae.

brown bagging *noun NAmer, informal* **1** taking a packed lunch to work. **2** taking one's own alcoholic drink to a restaurant or other establishment that is not licensed to sell alcohol.

brown bear *noun* a large and fierce bear that is predominantly brown in colour, found in the forests of Europe, Asia, and N America: *Ursus arctos*.

brown coal *noun* = LIGNITE.

brown dwarf *noun* a cool faint star with a mass less than about one tenth of that of the sun.

browned-off *adj informal* annoyed or disheartened; = FED UP.

brown fat *noun* a heat-producing tissue that is present in significant amounts in hibernating mammals, human infants, and adults acclimatized to cold.

brownfield *adj* relating to or located in urban areas where buildings previously existed and have since been demolished: *brownfield developments*.

brown goods *pl noun* electrical consumer goods, e.g. television sets, hi-fi systems, and home computers, that are chiefly used for recreation: compare WHITE GOODS.

Brownian motion /'browni·ən/ *noun* a random movement of microscopic particles suspended in liquids or gases resulting from the impact of molecules of the liquid or gas surrounding the particles. [named after Robert *Brown* d.1858, Scottish botanist who first described the motion]

brownie /'browni/ *noun* **1** (**Brownie**) a member of the most junior section of the Guide movement for girls aged from seven to ten. **2** a small square or rectangle of rich chocolate cake containing nuts. **3** a good-natured goblin believed to perform household chores at night. [BROWN[1]]

Brownie Guide *noun Brit* = BROWNIE (1).

brownie point *noun informal* a mark of merit gained in the eyes of somebody else for having done something helpful or kind.

browning *noun Brit* a substance, e.g. caramelized sugar, used to give a brown colour to soups and gravies.

brown-nose[1] *verb trans NAmer, informal* to behave in a servile and flattering manner towards (somebody). ➤ *verb intrans NAmer, informal* to be obsequious; to crawl.

brown-nose[2] *noun NAmer, informal* a servile and flattering person; a crawler.

brown-noser *noun* = BROWN-NOSE[2].

brown owl *noun* **1** (**Brown Owl**) *informal* the leader of a pack of Brownies. **2** a tawny owl.

brown rat *noun* the common domestic rat: *Rattus norvegicus*.

brown rice *noun* rice that has been hulled but not polished, so that it retains the germ and bran.

brown sauce *noun* **1** a sauce usu made from a roux (a mixture of flour and fat heated together) combined with meat stock: compare WHITE SAUCE. **2** *Brit* a commercially prepared condiment with a dark brown colour and a strong taste of vinegar.

Brownshirt *noun* **1** a Nazi stormtrooper. **2** a member of any fascist party, or a Nazi sympathizer. [translation of German *Braunhemd*; from the uniform worn by Nazi stormtroopers]

brownstone /'brownstohn/ *noun NAmer* a building, usu an apartment block, made of a reddish brown sandstone, or this kind of sandstone itself.

brown study *noun dated* an absent-minded or daydreaming state; a reverie.

brown sugar *noun* **1** unrefined or partially refined sugar. **2** refined sugar having crystals that are covered with a film of brown syrup.

brown trout *noun* a speckled trout which is the common native species in Europe, widely fished and used for food: *Salmo trutta*.

browse[1] /browz/ *verb intrans* **1** to read or search idly through a book or mass of things, e.g. in a shop, in the hope of finding something interesting. **2** said of animals: to nibble at leaves, grass, or other vegetation. ➤ *verb trans* **1** in computing, to look at (the contents of a file, disk, directory, or website). **2** to nibble at (vegetation). [French *broster* from Old Saxon *brustian* to sprout]

browse[2] *noun* **1** tender shoots, twigs, and leaves of trees and shrubs that provide food for animals, e.g. deer. **2** a period of time spent browsing: *I had a good browse in the library.* [prob modification of early French *brouts*, pl of *brout* sprout, from Old French *brost*, of Germanic origin]

browser *noun* **1** a customer in a shop who is merely browsing, not intending to buy. **2** an animal that browses. **3** a computer program used for finding and viewing information on the World Wide Web. Also called WEB BROWSER.

BRS *abbr* British Road Services.

brucellosis /broohsə'lohsis, -siz/ *noun* a serious long-lasting infectious disease affecting cattle, often causing miscarriage in pregnant cattle, and humans, causing fever, pain, and swelling of the joints. [scientific Latin *Brucella*, a genus of bacteria, named after Sir David *Bruce* d.1931, Scottish bacteriologist, who identified the bacterium that causes it]

brucite /'broohsiet/ *noun* a mineral consisting essentially of magnesium hydroxide: formula $Mg(OH)_2$. [named after Archibald *Bruce* d.1818, US mineralogist]

bruin /'brooh·in/ *noun* used as a name: a bear. [Dutch *bruin*, name of the bear in the medieval poem *Reynard the Fox*]

bruise[1] /broohz/ *noun* **1a** an injury involving rupture of small blood vessels and discoloration without a break in the skin. **b** an injury to plant tissue involving underlying damage and discoloration without a break in the skin. **2** an injury to the feelings.

bruise[2] *verb trans* **1** to inflict a bruise on (somebody, or a part of somebody's body). **2** to crush (e.g. leaves or berries) by pounding. **3** to wound (somebody) emotionally or psychologically. ➤ *verb intrans* to be damaged by a bruise: *Tomatoes bruise easily.* [Middle English *brusen* from Old French *bruisier* to break and Old English *brȳsan* to harm by hitting]

bruiser *noun informal* a large burly person, *esp* a man, orig a boxer.

bruit[1] /brooht/ *verb trans literary* (*often* + abroad) to spread (a report or rumour); to noise (something) abroad: *These acts of justice and benevolence were bruited abroad* — Scott; *This dark tale, whispered at first, was now bruited far and wide* — Nathaniel Hawthorne.

bruit[2] /brooh·ee/ *noun* **1** an abnormal sound, e.g. a heart murmur, that can be detected in a medical examination. **2** *archaic*. **a** a loud noise, or a loud protest or outcry: *according to the French proverb ... Much bruit little fruit* — Bacon. **b** a report or rumour: *The bruit is Hector's slain, and by Achilles* — Shakespeare. [Middle English from Old French *bruit* noise]

brumby /'brumbi/ *noun* (*pl* **brumbies**) *Aus* a wild or unbroken horse. [prob native name in Queensland, Australia]

brume /broohm/ *noun literary* mist or fog. ➤➤ **brumous** /'broohməs/ *adj.* [French *brume* fog, winter, from Latin *bruma* winter solstice, winter, from *brevis* BRIEF[1]]

Brummagem /'bruməjim/ *adj* cheap, inferior, or showy. [*Brummagem*, alteration of *Birmingham* city in England, formerly famed for cheap manufactured goods]

Brummy[1] *or* **Brummie** /'brumi/ *noun* (*pl* **Brummies**) *Brit, informal* **1** a native or inhabitant of Birmingham. **2** the dialect or accent of Birmingham. [by shortening and alteration from BRUMMAGEM]

Brummy[2] *or* **Brummie** *adj Brit, informal* belonging or relating to Birmingham.

brunch /brunch/ *noun* a meal, usu taken in the middle of the morning, that combines a late breakfast and an early lunch. [blend of BREAKFAST[1] + LUNCH[1]]

brunette[1] (*NAmer* **brunet**) /brooh'net/ *noun* a girl or woman with dark brown hair. [French *brunet* (masc) and *brunette* (fem) via Old French *brun* brown, from late Latin *brunus*, of Germanic origin; related to BROWN[1]]

brunette[2] *adj* said of hair: dark brown.

brunt /brunt/ *noun* the principal force, e.g. of an attack or a blow: *The town bore the brunt of the tornado.* [Middle English in the senses 'blow', 'attack'; earlier history unknown]

bruschetta /broo'sketə/ *noun* thick slices of bread flavoured with garlic and olive oil and toasted. [Italian *bruschetta*]

brush[1] /brush/ *noun* **1** an implement composed of filaments of hair, bristle, nylon, or wire set into a firm piece of material and used for grooming hair, painting, sweeping, or scrubbing. **2** an act of brushing: *Give your hair a brush.* **3** a quick light touch or momentary contact in passing: *I felt the brush of her coat.* **4** a conductor, e.g. a piece of carbon or braided copper wire, that makes electrical contact between a stationary and a moving part. **5** the bushy tail of a fox. [Middle English *brusshe* from Old French *broce*]

brush[2] *verb trans* **1a** to apply a brush to (something, e.g. hair). **b** to apply (something, e.g. paint) with a brush. **2** (+ away/off) to remove (something) with sweeping strokes: *She brushed the dirt off her coat.* **3** to pass lightly over or across (something) or touch gently against (it) in passing.

brush[3] *verb intrans* (+ by/past) to move lightly, heedlessly, or rudely. [Middle English *bruschen* to rush, from Old French *brosser* to dash through underbrush]

brush[4] *noun* **1** scrub vegetation, or land covered with it. **2** *chiefly NAmer, Aus* = BRUSHWOOD. [Middle English *brusch* from Old French *broce*]

brush[5] *noun* a brief antagonistic encounter or skirmish: *I had a brush with authority.* [Middle English *brusche* rush, hostile collision, from *bruschen*: see BRUSH[3]]

brush aside *verb trans* = BRUSH OFF (2).

brush discharge *noun* an undirected electrical discharge that takes place when a low potential difference prevents a spark or arc from being formed.

brushed *adj* said of a fabric: with the nap raised to give a softer texture: *brushed cotton.*

brush off *verb trans* **1** to reject (somebody) in an offhand way; to dismiss (them). **2** to dismiss (something, e.g. a criticism) swiftly and with nonchalant ease.

brush-off *noun informal* a quietly curt or disdainful dismissal; a rebuff.

brush turkey *noun* a flightless bird that is native to Australia and New Guinea and is known for its habit of building mounds of earth: *Alectura lathami.*

brushup *noun Brit* a smartening of one's appearance: *He went off for a quick wash and brushup.*

brush up *verb trans* (*often* + on) to renew one's skill in (something) or refresh one's memory of (it): *She'll have to brush up on her French.* ➤ *verb intrans* to tidy one's clothes, hair, etc.

brushwood *noun* **1** twigs or small branches, *esp* when cut or broken. **2** a thicket of shrubs and small trees.

brushwork /'brushwuhk/ *noun* the technique of applying paint with a brush, or a particular artist's use of the brush in painting or as visible in a painting.

brusque /broosk, broohsk/ *adj* blunt or abrupt in manner or speech, often to the point of rudeness. ➤➤ **brusquely** *adv*, **brusqueness** *noun.* [French *brusque* via Italian *brusco* from late Latin *bruscus* butcher's-broom]

Brussels carpet /'bruslz/ *noun* a carpet with a looped woollen pile fixed onto a strong linen base. [named after *Brussels*, city in Belgium]

Brussels lace *noun* any of various fine laces, *esp* with appliqué floral designs.

Brussels sprout *or* **Brussel sprout** *noun* **1** a plant of the cabbage family widely cultivated for its small edible buds: *Brassica oleracea gemmifera.* **2** a bud of this plant, used as a vegetable.

brut /brooht (*French* bryt)/ *adj* said of champagne: very dry. [French *brut*, literally 'rough']

brutal /'brooohtl/ *adj* **1** cruel and cold-blooded: *a brutal attack.* **2** harsh or severe: *brutal weather.* **3** unpleasantly accurate and incisive: *brutal truth.* >> **brutality** /brooh'taliti/ *noun,* **brutally** *adv.*

brutalise *verb* see BRUTALIZE.

brutalism /'broohtǝliz(ǝ)m/ *noun* a style of modern architecture characterized by massiveness and lack of ornamentation. >> **brutalist** *adj and noun.*

brutalize *or* **brutalise** *verb trans* **1** to make (somebody) brutal, unfeeling, or inhuman: *They are a people brutalized by poverty and disease.* **2** to treat (somebody) brutally. >> **brutalization** /-'zaysh(ǝ)n/ *noun.*

brute[1] /brooht/ *noun* **1** a brutal person. **2** an animal, *esp* when its animal qualities are contrasted to human qualities. >> **brutish** *adj,* **brutishly** *adv,* **brutishness** *noun.* [Middle English via Old French from Latin *brutus* stupid, heavy]

brute[2] *adj* **1** purely physical: *brute strength.* **2a** cruel or savage. **b** not working by reason; mindless: *brute instinct.*

bruxism /'bruksiz(ǝ)m/ *noun* the habit of unconsciously gritting or grinding the teeth, *esp* in situations of stress or during sleep. [Greek *brychein* to gnash the teeth + -ISM]

bryology /brie'olǝji/ *noun* a branch of botany that deals with mosses and liverworts. >> **bryological** /-'lojikl/ *adj,* **bryologist** *noun.* [Greek *bryon* moss + -LOGY]

bryony /'brie-ǝni/ *noun* (*pl* **bryonies**) any of a genus of climbing plants of the cucumber family with large leaves and red or black fruit: genus *Bryonia.* [via Latin from Greek *bryōnia*]

bryophyte /'brie-ǝfiet/ *noun* any of a division of nonflowering plants comprising the mosses and liverworts. >> **bryophytic** /-'fitik/ *adj.* [Greek *bryon* moss + *phyton* plant]

bryozoan /brie-ǝ'zoh-ǝn/ *noun* any of a phylum of aquatic invertebrate animals that reproduce by budding and usu form colonies that live permanently attached to rocks, seaweed, etc: phylum Bryozoa. [from the Latin phylum name, from Greek *bryon* moss + -ZOA]

Brythonic /bri'thonik/ *noun* the group of the Celtic languages comprising Welsh, Cornish, and Breton: compare GOIDELIC. >> **Brythonic** *adj.* [Welsh *Brython* Britons]

BS *abbr* **1** *NAmer* Bachelor of Science. **2** Bachelor of Surgery. **3** Bahamas (international vehicle registration). **4** British Standard.

BSC *abbr* **1** British Steel Corporation. **2** British Sugar Corporation.

BSc *abbr* Bachelor of Science.

BSE *abbr* bovine spongiform encephalopathy, a fatal disease of cattle affecting their central nervous system, causing them to become agitated and stagger violently.

BSI *abbr* **1** British Standards Institution. **2** Building Societies Institute.

B-side *noun* the side of a vinyl record that features a song or piece of music regarded as less important than the song or music on the A-side.

BSL *abbr* British Sign Language.

BST *abbr* **1** bovine somatotrophin. **2** British Summer Time.

BT *abbr* British Telecommunications.

Bt *abbr* Baronet.

BTh *abbr* Bachelor of Theology.

Btu *or* **BTU** *abbr* British thermal unit.

B2B *abbr* business-to-business.

B2C *abbr* business-to-customer.

bub /bub/ *noun NAmer, informal* used to address a boy or man. [prob by shortening and alteration from BROTHER]

bubble[1] /'bubl/ *noun* **1a** a usu small body of gas within a liquid or solid. **b** a thin, spherical, usu transparent, film of liquid inflated with air or vapour. **c** a transparent dome. **2** something that resembles a bubble in shape, *esp* the circle enclosing the words or thoughts of characters in comics. **3** something that lacks firmness or reality, *esp* an unreliable or speculative scheme. **4** a sound like that of bubbling. [Middle English, prob imitative of the noise of bubbling]

bubble[2] *verb intrans* **1** to form or produce bubbles. **2** to make a sound like the bubbles rising in liquid: *A brook bubbled over rocks.* **3** to be highly excited or overflowing with a feeling: *She was bubbling over with happiness.*

bubble and squeak *noun Brit* a dish consisting of usu leftover potato, cabbage, and sometimes meat, fried together. [from the noise of frying]

bubble bath *noun* a perfumed, usu liquid or granular preparation that produces foam when added to water.

bubble car *noun chiefly Brit* a small usu three-wheeled car with a domed, often transparent roof, popular in the 1960s.

bubble chamber *noun* a chamber in which the path of an ionizing particle is made visible by a track of bubbles, usu in liquid hydrogen.

bubble gum *noun* chewing gum that can be blown into large bubbles.

bubble memory *noun* in computing, a kind of memory formerly used to permit a large amount of information to be stored as tiny areas of magnetization in a semiconductor.

bubble pack *noun* = BLISTER PACK.

bubble wrap *noun* wrapping material in the form of sheets of plastic with air pockets at regular intervals.

bubbly[1] *adj* (**bubblier, bubbliest**) **1** full of bubbles. **2** overflowing with good spirits or liveliness; vivacious: *a bubbly personality.*

bubbly[2] *noun informal* champagne, or any sparkling wine.

bubo /'byoohboh/ *noun* (*pl* **buboes**) an inflamed swelling of a lymph gland, *esp* in the groin or armpit. >> **bubonic** /byooh'bonik/ *adj.* [late Latin *bubon-, bubo,* from Greek *boubōn* groin, gland, bubo]

bubonic plague *noun* a highly infectious and fatal form of plague characterized by the formation of buboes: compare PLAGUE[1].

buccal /'bukl/ *adj technical* relating to or in the region of the cheeks or the cavity of the mouth. [Latin *bucca* cheek]

buccaneer[1] /bukǝ'niǝ/ *noun* **1** a pirate, *esp* one preying on Spanish ships and settlements in the W Indies in the 17th cent. **2** an unscrupulous adventurer, *esp* in politics or business. [orig referring to French hunters in the Caribbean; French *boucanier,* from *boucaner* to smoke meat on a grid over a fire, ultimately from Tupi]

buccaneer[2] *verb intrans* to act unscrupulously or boldly like a buccaneer.

buccinator /'buksinaytǝ/ *noun* either of the flat thin muscles of the cheeks that are used for chewing. [Latin *buccina* trumpet]

buck[1] /buk/ *noun* **1a** a male animal, *esp* a male deer, antelope, rabbit, or rat. **b** *SAfr* an antelope. **2** *archaic* a man, *esp* a young and virile, spirited, or impudent man. [Old English *bucca* stag, he-goat]

buck[2] *verb intrans* **1** said of a horse or mule: to spring into the air with the back curved and come down with the forelegs stiff and the head lowered. **2** to refuse to agree or cooperate; to balk. **3** *chiefly NAmer* to move or react jerkily. >> *verb trans* **1** to throw (e.g. a rider) by bucking. **2** to fight against or refuse to comply with (something); to oppose (it): *They always wanted to buck the system.*

buck[3] *noun NAmer, Aus, NZ, informal* a dollar. [perhaps short for *buckskin,* regarded as a unit of exchange in early N American commerce]

buck[4] *noun* **1** an object formerly used in poker to mark the next player to deal. **2** anything that serves as a reminder. ✳ **pass the buck** *informal* to shift a responsibility to somebody else. **the buck stops here** *informal* the responsibility cannot be shifted to somebody else. [short for earlier *buckhorn knife,* used as a buck in poker]

buckbean *noun* = BOGBEAN.

buckboard *noun NAmer* a four-wheeled horse-drawn vehicle with the seat mounted on a sprung platform fixed between the front and back wheels. [obsolete *buck* body of a wagon + BOARD[1]]

bucket[1] /'bukit/ *noun* **1** a large open container, usu round, with tapering sides, a flat bottom, and a semicircular handle on top, used *esp* for holding or carrying liquids. **2** the amount contained in a bucket; a bucketful. **3a** the scoop of an excavating machine. **b** any of the scooped-out blades on the rim of a waterwheel. **c** any of the vanes of a turbine rotor. **4** *informal* (*in pl*) large quantities. [Middle English via Anglo-French *buket* from Old English *būc* pitcher, belly]

bucket[2] *verb intrans* (**bucketed, bucketing**) to move about jerkily or recklessly.

bucket down *verb intrans Brit* said of rain: to fall heavily.

bucketful /'bukitf(ǝ)l/ *noun* (*pl* **bucketfuls**) as much as a bucket will hold.

bucket seat *noun* in a sports car, aeroplane, etc, an individual seat with a rounded back and sides that extend slightly forward to give extra sideways support when cornering or banking.

bucket shop *noun informal* **1** *Brit* a small-scale business, *esp* a travel agent selling low-priced air tickets, that operates on the edge of the law and may default on its commitments to its customers. **2** a dishonest stockbroking firm that speculates and gambles on stocks and commodities using the funds of its clients. [orig a shady establishment where small quantities of liquor were dispensed in buckets]

buckeye *noun* any of several species of N American trees and shrubs with large red or white flowers and sticky buds: genus *Aesculus*.

buckhorn *noun* horn from a buck used *esp* for knife-handles.

buckjumper *noun Aus, NZ* an often untamed horse given to bucking.

buckle[1] /'bukl/ *noun* a fastening consisting of a rigid rim, usu with a hinged pin, used to join together two loose ends, *esp* of a belt or strap, or for decoration. [Middle English *bocle* via Old French from Latin *buccula* cheek strap of a helmet, dimin. of *bucca* cheek]

buckle[2] *verb trans* **1** to fasten (something, e.g. a belt) with a buckle. **2** to cause (something, e.g. metal) to bend, give way, or crumple. ➤ *verb intrans* **1** to bend or warp: *The pavement buckled in the heat.* **2** to give up a struggle or abandon resistance; to yield: *He buckled under the pressure and said that she could go.*

buckle[3] *noun* a bulge or similar distorted formation caused by buckling.

buckle down *verb intrans* to apply oneself vigorously: *It's about time she buckled down to her work.*

buckler *noun* a small round shield held by a handle at arm's length: *He took possession of the city in the name ... of the Catholic sovereigns, and would maintain and defend the same with sword and buckler* — William Hickling Prescott. [Middle English *bocler* from Old French *bocler* shield with a boss]

buckle to *verb intrans* to brace oneself or gather up one's strength to put effort into work: *We must buckle to and get on with the job.*

Buckley's /'bukliz/ *noun Aus, NZ, informal* a remote chance. [perhaps from William *Buckley* d.1856, escaped convict who lived among Aboriginals]

buckminsterfullerene /ˌbukminstə'fooləreen/ *noun* a form of carbon in which the 60 carbon atoms form pentagonal and hexagonal rings arranged in a spherical shape. [named after Richard *Buckminster Fuller* d.1983, US architect who invented the geodesic dome structure of buildings, which the molecule resembles]

bucko /'bukoh/ *noun* (*pl* **buckoes** or **buckos**) *chiefly Irish, informal* (*often as a form of address*) a young fellow; a lad: *How the hell are ye, me young bucko?* — Iain Banks. [BUCK[1](2) + -O[1]]

buckram /'bukrəm/ *noun* a fabric stiffened for use as an interlining in garments, a stiffening in hats, and in bookbinding. [Middle English *bukeram* via Old French from Old Provençal *bocaran*, named after *Bokhara*, city in central Asia]

Bucks /buks/ *abbr* Buckinghamshire.

buck's fizz /ˌbuks 'fiz/ *noun Brit* a drink of champagne mixed with orange juice. [named after *Buck's* Club in Mayfair, London, where it was concocted]

buckshee /buk'shee, 'bukshee/ *adj chiefly Brit, informal* without charge; free. [Hindi *bakhśiś* gratuity, gift, from Persian *bakhshīsh*: see BAKSHEESH]

buckshot *noun* a coarse lead shot used *esp* for shooting large animals.

buckskin *noun* **1** a soft pliable usu suede-finished leather. **2** thick heavy cotton or woollen fabric with a smooth finish.

buckthorn *noun* any of several species of often thorny trees or shrubs with berries that were formerly used as a laxative: genus *Rhamnus*.

bucktooth *noun* a large projecting front tooth. ➤➤ **bucktoothed** *adj*.

buck up *verb intrans* **1** to become encouraged or more cheerful. **2** to hurry up. ➤ *verb trans* **1** to raise the morale or spirits of (somebody): *The news bucked her up no end.* **2** to improve or smarten (something). [BUCK[2]]

buckwheat *noun* **1** an Asian plant of the dock family that has pinkish white flowers and triangular edible seeds used to make flour: genus *Fagopyrum*. **2** the seed of this plant, used as a cereal grain and for flour. [Dutch *boekweit* from early Dutch *boecweit* literally 'beech wheat', from *boec-* beech + *weit* wheat. So called because its grains resemble beech mast]

buckyball /'bukibawl/ *noun informal* in chemistry, a spherical molecule of carbon, *esp* buckminsterfullerene.

buckytube /'bukityoohb/ *noun informal* in chemistry, a cylinder of carbon atoms.

bucolic /byooh'kolik/ *adj* **1** relating to shepherds; pastoral. **2** relating to or typical of the countryside, rural life, or its lack of sophistication: *the bucolic confusion between the functions of knives and forks* — Harold Frederic. ➤➤ **bucolically** *adv*. [via Latin from Greek *boukolikos*, from *boukolos* cowherd, from *bous* head of cattle]

bud[1] /bud/ *noun* **1** a small protuberance on the stem of a plant that develops into a flower, leaf, or shoot. **2a** an incompletely opened flower. **b** an outgrowth of an organism that becomes a new individual. **3** anything that is not yet mature or fully developed. [Middle English *budde*; earlier history unknown]

bud[2] *verb* (**budded, budding**) ➤ *verb intrans* **1** said of a plant: to produce buds. **2** to begin to grow or develop. **3** to reproduce asexually by forming buds that develop into new individuals. ➤ *verb trans* to graft a bud into (a plant of another kind), usu in order to propagate a desired variety.

Buddha /'boodə/ *noun* **1** somebody who has attained the perfect enlightenment sought in Buddhism. **2** a statue, painting, or other representation of Gautama Buddha. [Sanskrit *buddha* enlightened]

Buddhism /'boodiz(ə)m/ *noun* a religion or philosophy that developed in India in the fifth and sixth cents BC out of the teaching of Gautama Buddha, maintaining that one can be liberated from the suffering inherent in life by ridding oneself of desire and self-delusion.

Editorial note
A term of relatively recent coinage used to describe the various Asian traditions that derive inspiration and authority from the stories about and teachings of an itinerant Indian teacher of the 5th cent. BCE known as the Buddha ('Awakened One'). Although the Buddha wrote nothing and scholars debate what he did and did not teach, myriad doctrines have been ascribed to him over the centuries — Professor Donald Lopez.

➤➤ **Buddhist** *noun and adj*.

budding /'buding/ *adj* in an early and usu promising stage of development: *There is a budding morrow in midnight* — Keats.

buddleia /'budli·ə/ *noun* any of a genus of shrubs or trees with showy clusters of usu yellow or violet flowers, many of which are attractive to butterflies: genus *Buddleia*. [from the Latin genus name; named after Adam *Buddle* d.1715, English botanist]

buddy[1] /'budi/ *noun* (*pl* **buddies**) *informal* **1** *chiefly NAmer* a friend, colleague, or partner. **2** *chiefly NAmer* used as a familiar form of address to a man. **3** a volunteer who acts as a companion and helper to a person with Aids. [prob childish alteration of BROTHER]

buddy[2] *verb intrans* (**buddies, buddied, buddying**) to act as a friend.

buddy movie *noun* a film that centres on the relationship between two friends.

budge /buj/ *verb intrans* (*usu in negative contexts*) **1** to move: *The donkey would not budge.* **2** to change an opinion or abandon a standpoint: *In spite of the opinion polls the minister is refusing to budge on this issue.* ➤ *verb trans* (*usu in negative contexts*) **1** to make (somebody or something) move. **2** to make (somebody) change an opinion or abandon a standpoint. [French *bouger*, ultimately from Latin *bullire*: see BOIL[1]]

budge over *verb intrans* = BUDGE UP.

budgerigar /'buj(ə)rigah/ *noun* a small Australian bird that belongs to the same family as the parrots and is often kept in captivity, typically light green with yellow and black markings: *Melopsittacus undulatus*. [native name in Australia]

budget[1] /'bujit/ *noun* **1** a statement of a financial position for a definite period of time, e.g. for the following year, based on estimates of expenditures and proposals for financing them. **2** (**the Budget**) a statement of the British government's financial position presented annually to the British parliament by the Chancellor of the Exchequer, including proposals for financing planned expenditure. **3** a plan of how money will be spent or allocated: *a weekly budget*. **4** the amount of money available for, required for, or assigned to a particular purpose. **5** (*used before a noun*) designed or suitable for people with a limited income or a limited amount of money to spend: *budget holidays; budget prices.* **6** *archaic* a bundle, package, or letter, *esp* as bringing news: *The Thursday produced a second budget of news from Penelope* — Wilkie Collins. ✳ **on a budget** having, using, or requiring only a small amount of money. **open one's budget** *archaic* to speak one's mind. ➤➤ **budgetary** /-t(ə)ri/ *adj.*

Word history
Middle English *bowgette* pouch, wallet, via Old French from Latin *bulga* leather bag, of Gaulish origin. In the 18th cent. the Chancellor of the Exchequer was said to 'open the budget' (wallet) when presenting his statement, and the word came to mean the statement itself, and later any financial plan or provision.

budget² *verb* (**budgeted, budgeting**) ➤ *verb trans* to plan or provide for the use of (e.g. money, time, or personnel) in detail. ➤ *verb intrans* **1** to arrange or plan a budget. **2** (+ for) to allocate money for some purpose: *We haven't budgeted for a holiday this year.*

budget account *noun* **1** *Brit* an account with a large shop that allows a customer to buy goods on credit up to an agreed limit and pay for them in monthly instalments. **2** *Brit* a bank account for the payment of household bills, being credited with regular or equal monthly payments from the customer's current account.

budge up *verb intrans informal* to move along, *esp* so that somebody else can sit down.

budgie /'buji/ *noun informal* a budgerigar. [by shortening and alteration]

buff¹ /buf/ *noun* **1** a pale yellowish brown colour. **2** a strong supple oil-tanned leather produced chiefly from cattle hides. **3** a device, e.g. a stick or pad, with a soft absorbent surface used for polishing something. **4** *informal* somebody who has a keen interest in and wide knowledge of a specified subject; an enthusiast: *a film buff.* ✳ **in the buff** *informal* naked. [French *buffle* wild ox, from Old Italian *bufalo*: see BUFFALO; (sense 4) earlier 'someone who is enthusiastic about going to see fires', from the buff overcoats worn by volunteer firemen in New York City around 1820]

buff² *adj* of a pale yellowish brown colour.

buff³ *verb trans* **1** to polish or shine (something). **2** to give a velvety surface like that of buff to (leather).

buffalo /'bufəloh/ *noun* (*pl* **buffaloes** *or collectively* **buffalo**) **1** a large shaggy N American wild ox with short horns, heavy forequarters, and a large muscular hump: *Bison bison.* Also called BISON. **2** a large African ox with a short mane and large horns that curve outwards and backwards: *Synceros caffer.* **3** a water buffalo. [Italian *bufalo* and Spanish *búfalo* via Latin from Greek *boubalos* African gazelle, from *bous* head of cattle]

buffalo grass *noun* **1** a low-growing grass that is native to the plains of N America: *Stenotaphrum americanum.* **2** a grass that is widely grown in Australia and New Zealand: *Stenotaphrum secundatum.*

buffer¹ /'bufə/ *noun* **1** any of various devices for reducing the effect of an impact, *esp* a spring-loaded metal disc on a railway vehicle or at the end of a railway track. **2** a device that serves to protect something, or to cushion against shock. **3** a person who shields another, *esp* from annoying routine matters. **4** a chemical substance capable in solution of neutralizing both acids and bases and thereby maintaining original acidity or basicity, or a solution containing this substance. **5** a temporary storage area in a computer, *esp* one that accepts information at one rate and delivers it at another. [obsolete *buff* to react like a soft body when struck, of imitative origin]

buffer² *verb trans* (**buffered, buffering**) **1** to lessen the shock of (something); to cushion (it). **2** to add a buffer to (e.g. a solution), or to buffer a solution of (a substance).

buffer³ *noun Brit, informal* a silly or ineffectual man. [origin unknown]

buffer solution *noun* = BUFFER¹ (4).

buffer state *noun* a small neutral state lying between two larger potentially rival powers.

buffer stock *noun* a stock of a basic commodity, e.g. tin, that is built up when supply is plentiful and prices are relatively low, and distributed when the supply is less plentiful, thus offsetting fluctuations in the availability of the commodity and stabilizing its price.

buffet¹ /'boofay/ *noun* **1** a meal set out on tables or a sideboard for diners to help themselves. **2** a counter for refreshments. **3** *chiefly Brit* a self-service restaurant or snack bar. **4** *Brit* a buffet car. **5** /'boo-fay, 'bufit/ a sideboard or cupboard often used for the display of tableware. [French *buffet*]

buffet² /'bufit/ *verb trans* (**buffeted, buffeting**) **1** to strike (something) repeatedly; to batter (it): *The waves buffeted the shore.* **2** to treat (somebody) roughly or unpleasantly: *He had been buffeted by life.* **3** to strike (somebody) sharply, *esp* with the hand; to cuff (them). [Middle English from Old French *buffet* (noun), dimin. of *buffe* a blow, of imitative origin]

buffet³ /'bufit/ *noun* **1** = BUFFETING. **2** *dated* a blow, *esp* with the hand: *I began instead to rain kicks and buffets on the door* — Stevenson.

buffet car /'boofay/ *noun Brit* a railway carriage with a counter at which snacks and drinks can be bought.

buffeting /'bufiting/ *noun* the shaking or vibrating of an aircraft or part of an aircraft caused by irregular air currents.

buffi /'boofi/ *noun pl* of BUFFO.

bufflehead /'buflhed/ *noun* a small N American diving duck, the male of which has a black and white head: *Bucephala albeola.* [archaic *buffle* buffalo + HEAD¹]

buffo /'boofoh/ *noun* (*pl* **buffi** /'boofi/ *or* **buffos**) a male singer of comic roles in opera, or the comic role itself. [Italian *buffo*, from *buffone*: see BUFFOON]

buffoon /bə'foohn/ *noun* **1** a person who behaves ludicrously in order to amuse others; a clown. **2** a noisy, clumsy, or incompetent fool. ➤➤ **buffoonery** *noun.* [French *bouffon* from Old Italian *buffone*, ultimately from Latin *bufo* toad]

bug¹ /bug/ *noun* **1** *technical* any of an order of insects with mouthparts that enable them to pierce and suck: order Hemiptera. **2** any creeping or crawling insect commonly considered unpleasant or a pest, e.g. a bedbug. **3** *informal* any micro-organism, *esp* a disease-producing bacterium, or a disease caused by it. **4** an unexpected defect or imperfection. **5** a fault in a computer program: *We'll need to iron the bugs out.* **6** *informal* a temporary enthusiasm; a craze. **7** a concealed listening device. [Middle English *bugge* spectre, goblin, of Scandinavian origin]

bug² *verb trans* (**bugged, bugging**) **1** *informal* to bother or annoy (somebody): *The noise was beginning to bug me.* **2a** to plant a concealed listening device in (a place). **b** to eavesdrop on (somebody) by means of a concealed listening device.

bugaboo /'bugəbooh/ *noun* (*pl* **bugaboos**) *chiefly NAmer* a source of often imaginary fear or anxiety; a bogey. [prob of Celtic origin and related to Welsh *bwcibo* the Devil, Cornish *buccaboo*]

bugbear *noun* **1** a source of persistent dread, concern, or difficulty: *Inflation was the national bugbear.* **2** in folklore, a hobgoblin, traditionally one in the form of a bear. [prob from BUG¹ + BEAR¹]

bug-eyed *adj* with eyes that protrude.

bugger¹ /'bugə/ *noun coarse slang* **1a** a disagreeable or contemptible person, *esp* a man or boy. **b** a person of a specified kind: *You poor bugger.* **2** *chiefly Brit* a cause of annoyance or difficulty: *It's a bugger of a thing to move.* **3** a man who has anal intercourse.

Word history
Old French *bougre* heretic, sodomite, from late Latin *Bulgarus* Bulgarian. Bulgarians belonging to the Orthodox Church were regarded as heretics by the Catholic Church; heretics were traditionally suspected of forbidden sexual practices.

bugger² *verb* (**buggered, buggering**) ➤ *verb trans coarse slang* **1** (*often* + up) to damage or ruin (something), usu because of incompetence. **2** to exhaust (somebody). **3** *Brit* (+ around/about) to cause (somebody) problems, *esp* by being deliberately evasive or misleading: *Don't bugger me about.* **4** used interjectionally to express contempt or annoyance: *Bugger Tom! We'll go without him.* **5** to have anal intercourse with (somebody). ➤ *verb intrans Brit, coarse slang* (+ around/about) to fool around, *esp* by dithering or being indecisive.

bugger all *noun Brit, coarse slang* nothing: *There's bugger all else to do.*

bugger off *verb intrans Brit, coarse slang* to go away.

buggery *noun* anal intercourse.

Buggin's turn *or* **Buggins's turn** /'buginz/ *noun Brit, informal* the system or principle of awarding an appointment or promotion to the person next in line according to seniority, length of service, etc, regardless of merit. [the name *Buggins*]

buggy¹ /'bugi/ *noun* (*pl* **buggies**) **1** a lightweight foldable pushchair. **2** a motor vehicle of basic design, *esp* one for use on beaches or a lunar exploration vehicle. **3** a light one-horse carriage: *Go get your horse and buggy and we'll go tonight!* — Emily Dickinson. [origin unknown]

buggy[2] *adj* (**buggier, buggiest**) infested with bugs.

bugle[1] /'byoohgl/ *noun* a valveless brass musical instrument that resembles a small trumpet, used *esp* for military calls. [Middle English, orig in the senses 'buffalo', 'instrument made of buffalo horn', 'bugle', via Old French from Latin *buculus*, dimin. of *bos* head of cattle, from Greek *bous*]

bugle[2] *verb intrans* to sound a bugle. ➤➤ **bugler** *noun*.

bugle[3] *noun* a European annual plant of the mint family that has spikes of usu blue but occasionally white or pink flowers: *Ajuga reptans*. [Middle English via Old French from late Latin *bugula*]

bugloss /'byoohglos/ *noun* any of several species of coarse hairy plants of the borage family that grow mainly in dry and sandy areas: genera *Lycopsis* and *Echium*. [Old French *buglosse* via Latin from Greek *bouglõssos*, from *bous* head of cattle + *glõssa* tongue]

bugong /'boohgong/ *noun* see BOGONG.

buhl *or* **boulle** *or* **boule** /boohl/ *noun* inlaid decoration of tortoise shell or ornamental metalwork, e.g. brass, used in cabinetwork. [German translation of the name of André Charles *Boulle* d.1732, French cabinet-maker]

build[1] /bild/ *verb* (*past tense and past part.* **built** /bilt/) ➤ *verb trans* **1** to construct (something) by putting together materials gradually into a composite whole. **2** to cause (something) to be constructed, *esp* to give instructions or provide finance for its construction. **3** (+ on) to develop (a concept, scheme, or relationship) according to specified principles: *Good teamwork is built on openness.* **4** to increase, enlarge, or develop (an organization or undertaking) gradually: *The family has built the business over several generations.* ➤ *verb intrans* **1** to carry out building work, *esp* to build houses or other premises. **2** to increase gradually in size or intensity: *In the following bars the music builds to a climax.* [Old English *byldan*]

build[2] *noun* the physical proportions of a person or animal, *esp* a person's figure of a usu specified type: *an athletic build.*

builder *noun* somebody who works in the construction industry, *esp* somebody who works as a contractor or somebody who supervises building operations.

build in *verb trans* to construct or develop (something) as an integral part.

building *noun* **1** a permanent structure, e.g. a school or house, usu having walls and a roof. **2** the art, business, or act of assembling materials into a structure.

building society *noun* any of various organizations providing their members with financial services similar to those of a bank, *esp* traditionally investment accounts and loans in the form of mortgages.

buildup *noun* **1** something that develops or increases gradually: *We need to deal with the buildup of traffic.* **2** praise or publicity, *esp* given in advance: *Sales were slow in spite of the buildup the product received.*

build up *verb trans* **1** to develop (something) gradually by increments: *If you start investing now you can build up a useful sum by the age of fifty.* **2** to praise (somebody or something) or publicize (them) favourably. **3** to improve the health or strength of (somebody), *esp* after an illness. ➤ *verb intrans* to accumulate or develop: *The traffic was steadily building up.*

built /bilt/ *adj* proportioned or formed in a specified way: *a slightly built girl.*

built-in *adj* **1** forming an integral part of a structure: *built-in cupboards.* **2** existing naturally or as a basic or essential feature; intrinsic: *built-in safeguards.*

built-up *adj* **1** made of several sections or layers fastened together. **2** said of an area: in which many houses and other buildings are situated.

bulb /bulb/ *noun* **1a** a short stem base of a plant, e.g. the lily, onion, or hyacinth, with one or more buds enclosed in overlapping membranous or fleshy leaves, that is formed underground as a resting stage in the plant's development: compare CORM, TUBER. **b** a tuber, corm, or other fleshy structure resembling a bulb in appearance. **c** a plant having or developing from a bulb. **2a** a light bulb. **b** a part shaped like a bulb, e.g. the mercury reservoir of a thermometer. **3** a rounded or swollen anatomical structure. [via Latin from Greek *bolbos* bulbous plant]

bulbil /'bulbil/ *noun* in botany, a small or secondary bulb, *esp* a bud that grows in the angle between the stem and the leaf or in place of flowers on some plants and is capable of producing a new plant. [French *bulbille*, dimin. of *bulbe* bulb, from Latin *bulbus*: see BULB]

bulbous /'bulbəs/ *adj* **1** resembling a bulb, *esp* in roundness: *a bulbous nose.* **2** growing from or bearing bulbs.

bulbul /'boolbool/ *noun* any of several species of songbirds of Asia and Africa that live in groups: family Pycnonotidac. [Persian *bulbul* from Arabic]

Bulgar /'bulgah/ *noun* a member of a group of peoples inhabiting Bulgaria in the seventh cent.

bulgar /'bulgə/ *noun* see BULGUR.

Bulgarian /bul'geəri-ən, bool-/ *noun* **1** a native or inhabitant of Bulgaria in SE Europe. **2** the Slavonic language of this people. ➤➤ **Bulgarian** *adj*.

bulge[1] /bulj/ *noun* **1** a swelling or convex curve on a surface, usu caused by pressure from within or below. **2** *informal* a sudden and usu temporary expansion, e.g. in population. ➤➤ **bulging** *adj*, **bulgy** *adj*. [Old French *boulge, bouge* leather bag, curved part, from Latin *bulga*: see BUDGET[1]]

bulge[2] *verb intrans* to swell or curve outwards.

bulgur *or* **bulgar** /'bulgə/ *noun* wheat grain that has been parboiled, dried, and broken into pieces, popular in Middle Eastern cookery; cracked wheat. Also called BURGHUL. [Turkish *bulgur* bruised grain]

bulimia /byooh'limi-ə/ *noun* an emotional disorder in which the sufferer follows periods of compulsive overeating with periods of fasting or self-induced vomiting, often accompanied by depression. ➤➤ **bulimic** *adj and noun*. [scientific Latin from Greek *boulimia* great hunger, from *bous* head of cattle + *limos* hunger]

bulimia nervosa /nuh'vohsə/ *noun* = BULIMIA.

bulk[1] /bulk/ *noun* **1** thickness, volume, size, or extent, *esp* when great. **2a** a large, heavy, or substantial mass. **b** a structure, *esp* when viewed as a mass of material: *The only things visible were the shrouded bulks of snow-covered cars.* **3** (+ of) the main or greater part. **4** dietary fibre; roughage. ✳ **in bulk** in large amounts or quantities, *esp* in amounts or quantities much larger than as usu packaged or purchased. [Middle English in the senses 'heap', 'bulk', from Old Norse *bulki* cargo]

bulk[2] *verb trans* **1** (*often* + out) to cause (something) to swell or to be thicker or fuller; to pad (it): *I had to bulk the text out to 20,000 words.* **2** to gather (things) into a mass or a single unit. ➤ *verb intrans* to appear as a factor; to loom: *It is a consideration that bulks large in everyone's thinking.*

bulk[3] *adj* said of materials: bought or sold in large quantities, usu unpackaged: *bulk cement.*

bulkhead *noun* a partition or wall separating compartments, e.g. in an aircraft or ship, *esp* one built to resist pressure or to contain water, fire, or gas in the event of damage to one part. [*bulk* from Old Norse *bálkr* partition + HEAD[1]]

bulk modulus *noun* in physics, the ratio of stress, e.g. hydrostatic stress, to volumetric strain in a body.

bulky *adj* (**bulkier, bulkiest**) **1** having too much bulk, *esp* unwieldy or cumbersome. **2** *euphem* overweight. ➤➤ **bulkily** *adv*, **bulkiness** *noun*.

bull[1] /bool/ *noun* **1a** an adult male bovine animal. **b** an adult male elephant, whale, or other large animal. **2** somebody who resembles a bull in aggressiveness, strength, or brawny build. **3** somebody who buys securities or commodities in expectation of a price rise or who acts to effect such a rise: compare BEAR[1]. **4** (**the Bull**) the constellation and sign of the zodiac Taurus. **5** *Brit* a bull's-eye. ✳ **like a bull in a china shop** clumsy or tactless. **take the bull by the horns** to face up to a problem. [Old English *bula*; (sense 3) prob developed as a companion to *bear*]

bull[2] *noun* **1** a papal edict on a subject of major importance. **2** an edict or decree of any kind. [Middle English *bulle* from medieval Latin *bulla* seal, sealed document, from Latin *bulla*, bubble, amulet]

bull[3] *noun informal* nonsense, *esp* empty, boastful, or insincere talk. [short for BULLSHIT[1]]

bullace /'boolis/ *noun* a European plum tree that bears small oval fruit in clusters, the cultivated variety of which is the damson: *Prunus domestica insititia.* [Middle English *bolace* via Old French from medieval Latin *bolluca* sloe]

bull ant *noun* = BULLDOG ANT.

bull bar *noun* a protective metal grille fitted to the front of a vehicle.

bulldog *noun* **1** a sturdy breed of dog with widely separated forelegs, a short neck, and a wide head with a projecting lower jaw. **2** a courageous, stubborn, or tenacious person. **3** *informal* a proctor's attendant at Oxford or Cambridge University.

bulldog ant *noun* a large Australian ant with a painful sting. Also called BULL ANT.

bulldog bat *noun* a fish-eating bat of Central and S America: *Noctilio leporinus*.

bulldog clip *noun* *Brit, trademark* a large clip made from two flat metal bars and a spring, used to clamp sheets of paper together.

bulldoze *verb trans* **1** to move, clear, demolish, or level (something) with a bulldozer. **2** to force (*esp* one's way) insensitively or ruthlessly. **3** *informal* (*often* + into) to bully or intimidate somebody. [perhaps from BULL¹ + alteration of DOSE¹]

bulldozer *noun* an earth-moving vehicle fitted with caterpillar tracks, with a broad blunt horizontal blade at one end, mounted on a pivoting arm.

bullet /'boolit/ *noun* **1** a small round or elongated projectile designed to be fired from a pistol, rifle, or other firearm, often also taken to include its cartridge. **2** something resembling a bullet in shape, speed, or intensity of impact. **3** in printing, a large dot used to introduce each of several lines or passages of text, e.g. points in a list. [French *boulette* small ball and *boulet* missile, dimin. of *boule* ball, ultimately from Latin *bulla* bubble]

bulletheaded *adj* **1** having a rounded solid-looking head. **2** bullheaded.

bulletin /'boolǝtin/ *noun* **1** a brief public notice, *esp* a brief news item intended for immediate publication. **2** a short programme of news items on radio or television. **3** a journal published at regular intervals, *esp* the journal of an institution or association. [French *bulletin* from Italian *bullettino*, dimin. of *bulla* papal edict, from medieval Latin: see BULL²]

bulletin board *noun* **1** *NAmer* a noticeboard. **2** a computer-based exchange system that is not part of the Internet but that authorized users access by direct telephone communication, participating in discussion groups, placing advertisements, exchanging software, etc.

bulletproof *adj* **1** designed to withstand the impact of gunfire and not to allow bullets to pass through. **2** unchallengeable; unassailable; not open to question or criticism.

bullet train *noun* *informal* a Japanese high-speed train.

bullfight *noun* a spectacle in an arena in which bulls are ceremonially excited, fought with, and in Hispanic tradition killed, for public entertainment. ➤➤ **bullfighter** *noun*, **bullfighting** *noun*.

bullfinch *noun* a European finch, the male of which has a rosy red breast and throat, a blue-grey back, and a black cap, chin, tail, and wings: *Pyrrhula pyrrhula*.

bullfrog *noun* a large frog with a deep croak, native to N America: *Rana catesbiana*.

bullhead *noun* any of various small river fishes with a large spiny head, *esp* a species known as MILLER'S-THUMB: family Cottidae.

bullheaded *adj* stupidly stubborn; headstrong. ➤➤ **bullheadedly** *adv*, **bullheadedness** *noun*.

bullhorn *noun* *chiefly NAmer* a megaphone.

bullion /'boolyǝn/ *noun* gold or silver in bars that has not been minted. [Middle English from Anglo-French *bullion* mint, ultimately from Latin *bullire*: see BOIL¹]

bullish /'boolish/ *adj* **1** suggestive of a bull, e.g. in brawniness. **2** marked by, tending to cause, or hopeful of rising prices, e.g. in a stock market: compare BEARISH. **3** energetically optimistic or enterprising: *An immensely confident batsman, Gooch is at his most bullish against the West Indians* — Daily Telegraph. ➤➤ **bullishly** *adv*, **bullishness** *noun*.

bull neck *noun* a thick short powerful neck. ➤➤ **bullnecked** *adj*.

bullock /'boolǝk/ *noun* a young castrated bull. [Old English *bulluc*, dimin. of *bula* BULL¹]

bullring *noun* an arena for bullfights.

bull-roarer *noun* a wooden slat tied to the end of a thong and whirled to make a roaring sound, used *esp* by Australian aboriginals in religious rites.

bull's-eye *noun* **1a** the centre of a target, or a shot that hits it. **b** something that precisely attains a desired end. **2** a very hard round usu peppermint sweet. **3** *dated* a small thick disc of glass inserted, e.g. in a ship's deck, to let in light. **4** a simple lens of short focal distance, or a lantern fitted with one.

bullshit¹ *noun coarse slang* nonsense, *esp* empty, boasting, or insincere talk. [BULL¹ + SHIT¹]

bullshit² *verb* (**bullshitting**, *past tense and past part.* **bullshit** or **bullshitted**) ➤ *verb intrans coarse slang* to talk loudly or confidently about something of which one has no knowledge. ➤ *verb trans coarse slang* to try to deceive or impress (somebody) by bullshitting. ➤➤ **bullshitter** *noun*.

bull terrier *noun* a short-haired breed of terrier, originated in England by crossing the bulldog with a breed of terrier.

bully¹ /'booli/ *noun* (*pl* **bullies**) **1** a browbeating person, *esp* somebody who is habitually cruel to other weaker people. **2** *archaic* a hired ruffian: *a knot of pedlars, pickpockets, highwaymen, and bullies* — Jonathan Swift. [orig meaning 'sweetheart', 'fine fellow' prob modification of Dutch *boel* lover, from early High German *buole*]

bully² *verb trans* (**bullies, bullied, bullying**) to intimidate or coerce (somebody) with persistently aggressive or violent behaviour, or by using threats of violence.

bully³ *noun* (*pl* **bullies**) in hockey, a procedure for starting play in a match, in which two opposing players face each other and alternately strike the ground and the opponent's stick three times before attempting to gain possession of the ball. [origin unknown]

bully⁴ *adj and interj* used, sometimes ironically, as a general expression of approval: excellent: *Bully for them!*

bully⁵ *verb* (**bullies, bullied, bullying**) ➤ *verb trans* to put (a hockey ball) in play with a bully. ➤ *verb intrans* (+ off) to start or restart a hockey match with a bully.

bully⁶ *noun* = BULLY BEEF.

bully beef *noun informal* beef that has been preserved with salt and tinned. [prob modification of French *bœuf bouilli* boiled beef]

bullyboy *noun* an aggressive or violent man, *esp* a hired thug.

bully-off *noun* (*pl* **bully-offs**) = BULLY³.

bullyrag /'boolirag/ or **ballyrag** /'balirag/ *verb trans* (**bullyragged** or **ballyragged, bullyragging** or **ballyragging**) *NAmer, informal* to torment or bully (somebody), *esp* by mocking or playing cruel practical jokes. [origin unknown]

bulrush /'boolrush/ *noun* **1** any of several species of annual or perennial grasslike plants that grow in wet areas and are varieties of sedge: genus *Scirpus*. **2** either of two plants that have a tall stem topped with a thick furry spike of densely packed flowers and are varieties of reedmace: *Typha latifolia* and *Typha angustifolia*. **3** used in the Bible: the papyrus plant. [Middle English *bulrysche*, prob from BULL¹ as something large or coarse + *rysche* RUSH³]

bulwark /'boolwǝk/ *noun* **1a** a solid wall-like structure built, e.g. around a fort, for defence; a rampart. **b** a breakwater or seawall. **2a** a strong support or protection: *Education is regarded as a bulwark of democracy*. **b** anything that acts as a defence: *A pay rise of 30% would certainly be a bulwark against inflation*. **3** (*usu in pl*) the side of a ship above the upper deck. [Middle English *bulwerke* via early Dutch *bolwerc* from early High German, from *bole* plank + *werc* work]

bum¹ /bum/ *noun Brit, informal* the buttocks. [Middle English *bom*; earlier history unknown]

bum² *adj informal* **1** *chiefly NAmer* inferior or worthless: *bum advice*. **2** injured or damaged: *a bum knee*.

bum³ *noun NAmer, informal* **1** an idler or loafer. **2** a homeless person who lives on the streets. **3** an incompetent person. **4** somebody who devotes his or her time to a specified recreational activity: *a ski bum; a beach bum*. [prob short for BUMMER²]

bum⁴ *verb* (**bummed, bumming**) ➤ *verb intrans chiefly NAmer, informal* (+ around) to spend time idly and often travelling casually: *She bummed around for three years before she got a job*. ➤ *verb trans informal* to obtain (something) by begging; to cadge (it): *Can I bum a fag off you?* [prob back-formation from BUMMER²]

bum⁵ *verb trans* (**bummed, bumming**) *Brit, coarse slang* to have anal intercourse with (somebody).

bum bag *noun Brit, informal* a small bag for personal belongings, attached to a belt worn around the waist.

bumbailiff *noun Brit, derog* formerly, a bailiff employed to seize property or collect debts. [BUM¹; from the close pursuit of debtors]

bumble[1] /'bumbl/ *verb intrans* **1** to speak in a faltering or rambling manner. **2** (*often* + along) to move, act, or proceed in a clumsy, unsteady, or incompetent manner. ➤➤ **bumbler** *noun*, **bumblingly** *adv*. [prob alteration of BUNGLE[1]]

bumble[2] *verb intrans* said of an insect: to drone. [Middle English *bomblen* to boom, of imitative origin]

bumblebee *noun* any of many species of large hairy bees with a deep loud hum: genus *Bombus*.

bumboat *noun* a boat that brings commodities for sale to larger ships. [prob from Low German *bumboot*, from *bum* tree + *boot* boat]

bumf or **bumph** /bumf/ *noun chiefly Brit, informal* documents, brochures, forms, and other paperwork regarded as superfluous, long-winded, or unwanted: *When the registration forms came through she apparently mistook them for election bumf and threw them away* — Daily Telegraph. [orig meaning 'toilet paper'; short for *bumfodder*, from BUM[1] + FODDER[1]]

bumfluff *noun Brit, informal derog* the fine hairs that form the beard on the chin of an adolescent. ➤➤ **bumfluffed** *adj*.

bummalo /'buməloh/ *noun* (*pl* **bummalo**) = BOMBAY DUCK. [prob modification of Marathi *bombil*]

bummer[1] /'bumə/ *noun informal* an unpleasant experience, *esp* a piece of bad luck or a bad reaction to a hallucinogenic drug. [prob from BUM[1]]

bummer[2] *noun NAmer* = BUM[3] (1). [prob modification of German *Bummler* loafer, from *bummeln* to dangle, loaf]

bump[1] /bump/ *verb trans* **1** to strike or knock (something) with force. **2** to injure or damage (something) by striking it on something hard, usu accidentally. **3** to collide with (something or somebody). **4** to dislodge (something) with a jolt. **5** *informal* to exclude (an airline passenger) from a flight because of overbooking. ➤ *verb intrans* **1** to move in a series of bumps, e.g. in a vehicle along an uneven road. **2** (*often* + against/into) to knock against something with a forceful jolt. ✴ **bump into** to meet (somebody) unexpectedly or by chance. [imitative]

bump[2] *noun* **1** a sudden forceful blow or jolt. **2a** a swelling of tissue caused by an injury to a part that has been struck by accident. **b** a natural protuberance of the skull. **3** a dancer's thrusting of the hips forwards in an erotic manner: compare GRIND[2]. **4** (**the bumps**) the act of holding somebody by the arms and legs and swinging him or her into the air and back to the ground: *They gave her the bumps on her birthday*.

bumper[1] *noun* **1** a metal, rubber, or more commonly, plastic fitting, at either end of a motor vehicle for absorbing shock or minimizing damage in collision. **2** in cricket, a bouncer.

bumper[2] *adj* unusually large or fine: *a bumper crop*.

bumper[3] *noun* **1** *archaic* a brimming cup or glass. **2** something unusually large. [prob from BUMP[1] in an obsolete sense 'to bulge']

bumper car *noun* a car used in dodgems.

bumph /bumf/ *noun* see BUMF.

bumpkin /'bum(p)kin/ *noun* an awkward and unsophisticated person, *esp* from the country. [perhaps from Flemish *bommekijn* small cask, from early Dutch *bomme* cask]

bump off *verb trans informal* to murder (somebody).

bump start[1] *verb trans chiefly Brit* to push-start (a motor vehicle).

bump start[2] *noun* a push-start.

bumptious /'bum(p)shəs/ *adj* self-assertive in a presumptuous and often noisy manner; overbearing. ➤➤ **bumptiously** *adv*, **bumptiousness** *noun*. [BUMP[1] + -tious as in FRACTIOUS]

bump up *verb trans* **1** *informal* to raise or increase (something, e.g. a price). **2** *informal* to promote (somebody) to a higher grade or rank.

bumpy *adj* (**bumpier, bumpiest**) **1** having or covered with bumps; uneven: *a bumpy road*. **2** marked by jolts: *a bumpy ride*. ➤➤ **bumpily** *adv*, **bumpiness** *noun*.

bum rap *noun chiefly NAmer, informal* an unfair accusation or prison sentence.

bum's rush *noun NAmer, informal* forcible ejection from a place or dismissal from a position: *They gave him the bum's rush*.

bun /bun/ *noun* **1** a small round bread roll or cake that may contain added ingredients, e.g. currants or spice. **2** a usu tight knot of hair worn on the back of the head. **3** *NAmer, informal* (*in pl*) buttocks. ✴ **have a bun in the oven** *informal* to be pregnant. [Middle English *bunne*; earlier history unknown]

bunch[1] /bunch/ *noun* **1** a compact group formed by a number of things of the same kind, *esp* when growing or loosely held together; a cluster. **2** *informal* a group of people. **3** (*in pl*) a style in which the hair is divided into two lengths and tied on each side of the head. ➤➤ **bunchy** *adj*. [Middle English *bunche*; earlier history unknown]

bunch[2] *verb trans and intrans* (*often* + up) to form (people or things) into a group or cluster.

bunco /'bungkoh/ *noun* (*pl* **buncos**) *NAmer, informal* a swindle, often a confidence trick. [prob from Spanish *banca* bench, bank (in gambling)]

buncombe /'bungkəm/ *noun* see BUNKUM.

bundle[1] /'bundl/ *noun* **1a** a collection of things held loosely together. **b** a number of things wrapped for carrying; a package. **2** a small band of mostly parallel nerve or other fibres. **3** a great deal; a mass: *Man is an embodied paradox, a bundle of contradictions* — C C Colton. **4** *informal* a sizable sum of money. ✴ **go a bundle on** *Brit, informal* (*usu in negative contexts*) to like or enjoy. [Middle English *bundel* from early Dutch]

bundle[2] *verb trans* **1** to make (things) into a bundle or package. **2** *informal* to hustle or hurry (somebody) unceremoniously: *He bundled the children off to school.* **3** (+ into) to hastily deposit or stuff (something) into a suitcase, box, drawer, etc. ➤ *verb intrans* to sleep with a boyfriend or girlfriend without undressing, a former custom.

bundle up *verb trans and intrans* to dress (somebody) warmly.

bundu /'boondooh/ *noun SAfr* an area of uncultivated land covered by scrub; the bush. [Bantu *bundu*]

bun-fight *noun Brit, informal* a social gathering at which food is served, *esp* a tea party.

bung[1] /bung/ *noun* something used to plug an opening, *esp* the stopper in the bunghole of a cask. [Middle English via early Dutch from Latin *puncta*, fem past part. of *pungere* to prick]

bung[2] *verb trans* **1** (*often* + up) to plug, block, or close (something) with, or as if with, a bung. **2** *chiefly Brit, informal* to throw, toss, or put (something): *Bung me that pen.*

bung[3] *noun Brit, informal* a bribe.

bung[4] *adj Aus, NZ, informal* **1** broken or useless. **2** dead. ✴ **go bung 1** to die. **2** to fail. [from an Aboriginal language]

bungalow /'bunggəloh/ *noun* a single-storeyed house. [Hindi *banglā* (house) in the Bengal style]

bungee jumping /'bunji/ *noun* the activity or sport of diving from a high place, e.g. a bridge or a crane, with the feet attached to an elasticated rope designed to pull the jumper up just before he or she would hit the ground. ➤➤ **bungee jump** *noun*. [origin of *bungee* unknown]

bunghole *noun* a hole for emptying or filling a cask.

bungle[1] /'bunggl/ *verb trans* to perform or handle (something) clumsily; to botch (it). ➤➤ **bungler** *noun*, **bungling** *adj*. [perhaps of Scandinavian origin]

bungle[2] *noun* something done clumsily; a botch.

bunion /'bunyən/ *noun* an inflamed swelling at the side of the foot on the first joint of the big toe. [prob from obsolete *bunny* swelling, from Middle English *bony*, prob from early French *bugne* bump on the head]

bunk[1] /bungk/ *noun* **1** a built-in bed, e.g. on a ship, that is often one of a tier of berths. **2** a bunk bed. **3** *informal* any sleeping place, *esp* one that is temporary or makeshift. [prob short for BUNKER[1]]

bunk[2] *verb intrans* (*often* + down) to sleep or bed down, *esp* in a makeshift bed.

bunk[3] *noun informal, dated* empty or foolish talk; nonsense: *History is bunk* — Henry Ford. [short for BUNKUM]

bunk[4] ✴ **do a bunk** *chiefly Brit, informal* to make a hurried departure, *esp* in order to escape. [origin unknown]

bunk bed *noun* either of two single beds constructed so as to sit one above the other.

bunker[1] /'bungkə/ *noun* **1** a bin or compartment for storage, *esp* one for storing coal or other fuel. **2** a protective embankment or dugout, *esp* a fortified chamber built of reinforced concrete and set mostly below ground. **3** a golf course hazard that is an area of sand-covered bare ground with one or more embankments. [Scottish *bonker* chest, box]

bunker[2] *verb trans* (**bunkered, bunkering**) **1** to place or store (*esp* fuel) in a bunker. **2** in golf, to hit (a ball) into a bunker.

bunkhouse *noun NAmer* a rough simple building providing sleeping quarters, e.g. for workers on a ranch.

bunk off *verb intrans chiefly Brit, informal* to leave, *esp* to play truant from school.

bunkum *or* **buncombe** /'bungkəm/ *noun informal, dated* insincere or foolish talk; nonsense.

Word history
named after *Buncombe* County, North Carolina, USA. The county's congressional representative in 1820 made a seemingly irrelevant speech in order to impress his constituents.

bunny /'buni/ *noun* (*pl* **bunnies**) **1** *informal* used by or to children: a rabbit. **2** *Aus, informal* a victim or dupe. [English dialect *bun* rabbit]

bunny girl *noun* a nightclub hostess who wears a costume that includes a stylized rabbit's tail and ears.

Bunsen burner /'buns(ə)n/ *noun* a gas burner in which air is mixed with the gas to produce an intensely hot blue flame. [named after Robert *Bunsen* d.1899, German chemist who designed it]

bunt[1] /bunt/ *noun* **1a** the middle part of a square sail. **b** the bunched part of a furled sail. **2** the baggy part of a fishing net. [perhaps from Low German *bunt* bundle, from early Low German]

bunt[2] *noun* a disease of wheat caused by either of two parasitic fungi. [origin unknown]

bunt[3] *verb trans* to strike or push (*esp* a ball) with little force. ➤➤ **bunter** *noun*. [alteration of BUTT[1]]

bunting[1] /'bunting/ *noun* any of various birds that have short strong beaks and are related to the finches: genus *Emberiza* and others. [Middle English; earlier history unknown]

bunting[2] *noun* **1** flags, pennants, streamers, and other decorations collectively. **2** a lightweight, loosely woven fabric orig used for flags and other decorations. [perhaps from English dialect *bunt* to sift]

buntline /'buntlin, 'buntlien/ *noun* any of the ropes attached to a square sail for hauling it up to the yard for furling.

bunya /'bunyə/ *or* **bunya bunya** /'bunyə bunyə/ *noun* a tall tree with edible cones that is native to Australia: *Araucaria bidwillii*. [native name in Australia]

bunyip /'bunyip/ *noun Aus* a mythical monster that is supposed to inhabit swamps in remote parts of Australia. [native name in Australia]

buoy[1] /boy/ *noun* **1** a distinctively shaped and marked float moored to the bottom of a body of water, as a navigational aid to mark a channel or hazard, or for mooring a ship. **2** = LIFEBUOY. [Middle English *boye* from assumed French *boie*, of Germanic origin]

buoy[2] *verb trans* **1a** (+ up) to keep (something) afloat. **b** (+ up) to support or sustain (something or somebody). **2** (+ up) to raise the spirits of (somebody): *He is buoyed up by hope*. **3** to mark (something) by a buoy. [(senses 1 and 2) prob from Spanish *boyar* to float, from *boya* buoy, from assumed early French *boie* BUOY[1]; (sense 3) from BUOY[1]]

buoyancy /'boyənsi/ *noun* **1a** the tendency of a body to float or to rise when submerged in a fluid. **b** the power of a fluid to exert an upward force on a body placed in it. **2** the ability to recover quickly from discouragement or disappointment; resilience. **3** the capacity, e.g. of prices or business activity, to maintain or return rapidly to a satisfactorily high level.

buoyant /'boyənt/ *adj* **1** capable of floating. **2** cheerful or resilient. **3** said of prices or business activity: maintaining a satisfactorily high level. ➤➤ **buoyantly** *adv*.

BUPA /'b(y)oohpə/ *abbr* British United Provident Association, a private health insurance company.

BUR *abbr* Burma (international vehicle registration for Myanmar).

bur /buh/ *noun* see BURR[1] (I).

burb /buhb/ *noun NAmer, informal* a suburb. [short for SUBURB]

burble[1] /'buhbl/ *verb intrans* **1** to make a bubbling sound; to gurgle. **2** to speak rapidly or ramblingly; to prattle. **3** said of airflow: to become turbulent. ➤➤ **burbler** *noun*. [Middle English *burblen*, prob of imitative origin]

burble[2] *noun* **1** a burbling sound. **2** a burst of rapid speech or a bout of rambling speech. **3** a turbulent airflow.

burbot /'buhbət/ *noun* (*pl* **burbots** *or collectively* **burbot**) a freshwater fish of the cod family that has barbels on its mouth and is found in cold rivers and lakes of Europe, Asia, and N America: *Lota*

lota. [Middle English *borbot* from Old French *borbot*, from *bourbe* mud]

burden[1] /'buhd(ə)n/ *noun* **1** something that is carried; a load. **2** something, e.g. a responsibility or debt, regarded as oppressive or wearisome; an encumbrance. **3** capacity for carrying cargo: *a ship of a hundred tons' burden*. [Old English *byrthen*; related to Old English *beran* BEAR[2]]

burden[2] *verb trans* (**burdened, burdening**) to give (somebody) a burden of some kind to bear: *I'll not burden you with a lengthy account*.

burden[3] *noun* **1** the chorus or refrain of a song or poem. **2** a central topic; a theme. [alteration of *bourdon* drone bass, e.g. in a bagpipe, from early French *bourdon* bass pipe, of imitative origin]

burden of proof *noun* the duty of proving an assertion.

burdensome /'buhd(ə)ns(ə)m/ *adj* imposing or constituting a burden; oppressive.

burdock /'buhdək/ *noun* any of several species of sturdy plants of the daisy family that have prickly purple spherical flower heads similar to those of the thistles: genus *Arctium*. [BURR[1] + DOCK[1]]

bureau /'byooəroh/ *noun* (*pl* **bureaus** *or* **bureaux** /'byooərohz/) **1a** a specialized administrative unit, *esp* a government department in the USA or continental Europe. **b** an office or agency where information or contacts are provided, *esp* one offering a public service. **2a** *Brit* a writing desk, *esp* one with drawers and a sloping top. **b** *NAmer* a chest of drawers, *esp* a low one for use in a bedroom. [French *bureau* desk, cloth covering for desks, from late Latin *burra* shaggy cloth]

bureaucracy /byooə'rokrəsi/ *noun* (*pl* **bureaucracies**) **1** government characterized by specialization of functions, adherence to fixed rules, and a hierarchy of authority. **2** government officials collectively. **3** any administrative system that is marked by excessive officialism. **4** any complex and inflexible set of procedures, or the infuriatingly inflexible and apparently obstructive attitudes of those who enforce them. ➤➤ **bureaucratic** /,byooərə'kratik/ *adj*, **bureaucratically** /,byooərə'kratikli/ *adv*. [French *bureaucratie*, from *bureau* (see BUREAU) + *-cratie* -CRACY]

bureaucrat /'byooərəkrat/ *noun* **1** a member of a bureaucracy, *esp* a government official. **2** any official or representative who rigidly adheres to inflexible rules or procedures.

bureaucratize *or* **bureaucratise** /byooə'rokrətiez/ *verb trans* to make (something) bureaucratic. ➤➤ **bureaucratization** /-rətie'zaysh(ə)n/ *noun*.

bureau de change /də 'shonzh/ *noun* (*pl* **bureaux de change** /'byooəroh də 'shonzh/) an office or part of a bank where money can be changed into other currencies. [French *bureau de change* office of exchange]

bureaux /'byooərohz/ *noun* pl of BUREAU.

bureaux de change *noun* pl of BUREAU DE CHANGE.

burette (*NAmer* **buret**) /byoo'ret/ *noun* a graduated glass tube with a small hole at the bottom that is opened and closed by a tap, used for dispensing measured, usu small, quantities of liquid. [French *burette* from Old French *buie* pitcher, of Germanic origin]

burg /buhg/ *noun* **1** an ancient or medieval fortress or walled town. **2** *NAmer, informal* a city or town. [Old English: see BOROUGH]

burgage /'buhgij/ *noun* formerly, a tenure by which land in an English or Scottish town was held for a yearly rent or in return for services provided to a king or lord. [Middle English in the sense 'property held by burgage tenure', via Old French from Latin *burgus* fortified place, of Germanic origin; related to BOROUGH]

burgee /'buhjee/ *noun* a swallow-tailed or triangular flag flown, *esp* by racing yachts, for identification. [perhaps from French dialect *bourgeais* shipowner, from Old French *borjos*: see BOURGEOIS[1]]

burgeon /'buhj(ə)n/ *verb intrans* (**burgeoned, burgeoning**) **1** to send forth new growth, e.g. buds or branches. **2** to grow and expand rapidly. [Middle English *burjonen*, from *burjon* bud, via Old French from late Latin *burra* shaggy cloth]

burger /'buhgə/ *noun* = HAMBURGER.

burgess /'buhjis/ *noun* **1** *archaic* a citizen of a British borough. **2** formerly, a Member of Parliament for a borough, city, or university. [Middle English *burgeis* from Old French *borjois*: see BOURGEOIS[1]]

burgh /'burə/ *noun* **1** *archaic* a borough. **2** a town in Scotland that has a charter that orig gave it legal rights and privileges and that until 1975 had distinct local government functions. [Middle English: see BOROUGH]

burgher /'buhgə/ *noun* **1** *archaic* an inhabitant of an *esp* medieval borough or a town. **2** *SAfr* formerly, a citizen of one of the Boer republics.

burghul /'buhgool/ *noun* = BULGUR. [Persian *burghul*]

burglar /'buhglə/ *noun* somebody who commits burglary. [Anglo-French *burgler* via medieval Latin from Latin *burgus* fortified place]

burglarize *or* **burglarise** *verb trans NAmer* to burgle (a building or person).

burglary *noun* (*pl* **burglaries**) **1** the offence of unlawfully entering a building with criminal intent, *esp* to steal. **2** an instance of burglary.

burgle /'buhgl/ *verb trans* to commit an act of burglary in (a building) or against (a person). [back-formation from BURGLAR]

burgomaster /'buhgəmahstə/ *noun* the mayor of a town in certain European countries. [Dutch *burgemeester*, from *burg* town + *meester* master]

Burgundy /'buhgəndi/ *noun* (*pl* **Burgundies**) a red or white table wine from the Burgundy region of France.

burgundy *adj* of a deep purplish red colour. ➤➤ **burgundy** *noun*.

burial /'beri·əl/ *noun* the act, process, or ceremony of burying a dead body. [Old English *byrgels*]

burial ground *noun* a cemetery.

burin /'byooərin/ *noun* **1** an engraver's steel cutting tool. **2** a prehistoric flint tool with a bevelled point. [French *burin*]

burk *or* **berk** *or* **birk** /buhk/ *noun Brit, slang* a stupid person; a fool. [short for rhyming slang *Berkshire* or *Berkeley Hunt* cunt]

burl[1] /buhl/ *noun* **1** a knot or lump in thread or cloth. **2** *NAmer* a hard rounded outgrowth on a tree or veneer made from this. [Middle English *burle* via (assumed) early French from late Latin *burra* shaggy cloth]

burl[2] *verb trans* to finish (cloth), *esp* by repairing loose threads and knots. ➤➤ **burler** *noun*.

burl[3] *noun Aus* a try: *I'll give it a burl.* [prob alteration of *whirl* as in *give it a whirl*]

burlap /'buhlap/ *noun* a coarse heavy plain-woven fabric, usu of jute or hemp, used for sacking and in furniture and linoleum manufacture. [alteration of earlier *borelapp*, of unknown origin]

burlesque[1] /buh'lesk/ *noun* **1** a literary or dramatic work that uses exaggeration or imitation to ridicule. **2** mockery, usu by imitation or caricature, or an instance of this. **3** *NAmer* a stage show usu consisting of short turns, comic sketches, and striptease acts. [*burlesque* (adj) comic, droll, via French and Italian from Spanish *burla* joke]

burlesque[2] *adj* of the nature of a burlesque, *esp* designed to ridicule or parody.

burlesque[3] *verb trans* (**burlesques, burlesqued, burlesquing**) to imitate (somebody or something) in a humorous or derisive manner; to mock (them).

burly /'buhli/ *adj* (**burlier, burliest**) strongly and heavily built. ➤➤ **burliness** *noun*. [Middle English in the senses 'comely', 'noble', 'well-built', of Germanic origin]

Burmese /buh'meez/ *noun* (*pl* **Burmese**) **1** a native or inhabitant of Myanmar. **2** the Tibeto-Burman language spoken by the people of Myanmar. ➤➤ **Burmese** *adj*. [*Burma*, former name of Myanmar, country in SE Asia]

Burmese cat *noun* a cat of a breed resembling the Siamese cat but of solid and darker colour, typically dark brown or grey, and usu with orange or yellow eyes.

burn[1] /buhn/ *verb* (*past tense and past part.* **burned** *or* **burnt** /buhnt/) ➤ *verb intrans* **1a** said of a fire: to consume fuel and give off heat, light, and gases. **b** said of a fuel or other material: to undergo combustion: *The wood burns well.* **c** said of a building etc: to be consumed or destroyed by fire. **2** to give off light: *A lamp was burning in the window.* **3** to become charred, scorched, or destroyed by fire or the action of heat: *I think the food must be burning.* **4** said of the skin: to become reddened and sore from exposure to heat. **5a** to be longing: *They were burning to tell the story.* **b** (+ with) to experience an emotion or desire strongly: *She was burning with fury.* **6** *informal* to drive very fast. ➤ *verb trans* **1a** to cause (something) to undergo combustion by fire. **b** to use (something) as fuel. **2a** to injure or damage (something) by exposure to fire, heat, radiation, corrosive chemicals, or electricity. **b** to char or scorch (something) by exposure to fire or heat. **c** to put (somebody) to death by burning. **3** to produce (something) by burning: *He managed to burn a*

hole in the sleeve. ✳ **burn one's bridges/boats** to commit oneself to a course of action that cannot be reversed. **burn one's fingers** see FINGER[1]. **burn the candle at both ends** to be active at night as well as by day. **burn the midnight oil** to work or study far into the night. [Middle English *birnan* from Old English *byrnan* (verb intrans), *bærnan* (verb trans)]

burn[2] *noun* **1a** an injury or damage resulting from burning. **b** a burned area: *I noticed a burn on the table top.* **c** a burning sensation: *I can still feel the burn of the iodine on the cut.* **2** a firing of a spacecraft rocket engine in flight. **3** *Brit, informal* tobacco or a cigarette.

burn[3] *noun chiefly Scot* a small stream. [Old English *burn*, *bourne* BOURN[1]]

burner *noun* the part of a fuel-burning device, e.g. a stove or furnace, where the flame is produced.

burnet /'buhnit/ *noun* **1** any of several species of plants of the rose family with red or purplish flowers arranged in spikes: genus *Sanguisorba*. **2** = BURNET MOTH. [Middle English from Old French *burnete*, from *brun*: see BRUNETTE[1]]

burnet moth *noun* any of several species of day-flying moths with bright metallic green or blue front wings and red hind wings: family Zygaenidae. [Middle English *burnet*: see BURNET]

burning *adj* **1a** on fire. **b** ardent or intense: *burning enthusiasm*. **2a** producing heat or the sensation of heat: *a burning fever*. **b** resembling that produced by a burn: *a burning sensation on the tongue*. **3** of fundamental importance; urgent: *It is one of the burning issues of our time*. ➤➤ **burningly** *adv*.

burning bush *noun* **1** any of several plants with red fruit or foliage, *esp* the summer cypress, with leaves that turn red in autumn. **2** = GAS PLANT.

burning glass *noun* a lens used to produce fire from the rays of the sun.

burnish[1] /'buhnish/ *verb trans* to make (something, *esp* metal) shiny or lustrous, *esp* by rubbing; to polish (it). ➤➤ **burnished** *adj*, **burnisher** *noun*. [Middle English *burnischen* from early French *bruniss-*, stem of *brunir* to make brown, from *brun*: see BRUNETTE[1]]

burnish[2] *noun* a shine or lustre.

burnous (*NAmer* **burnoose**) /buh'noohs/ *noun* a hooded cloak traditionally worn by Arabs and Moors. [French *burnous* via Arabic from Greek *birros*]

burnout *noun* **1** a condition of extreme exhaustion and disillusionment caused by overwork and stress. **2** the moment at which a jet or rocket engine uses up its fuel and ceases to operate.

burn out *verb trans* **1** to cause (something) to fail as a result of too much heat, friction, or electric current. **2** to cause (something) to be no longer active: *The disease had burned itself out.* **3** to exhaust (somebody) from overwork or stress: *He had burned himself out by the age of thirty.* ➤ *verb intrans* **1** said of a fuse or other electrical device: to cease to conduct electricity when the filament has melted. **2** said of a jet or rocket engine: to cease to operate having used up all its fuel. **3** to become exhausted from overwork or stress.

burnt /buhnt/ *verb chiefly Brit* past tense and past part. of BURN[1].

burnt offering *noun* **1** a sacrifice offered to a deity and usu burned on or at an altar. **2** *humorous* a burned or overcooked meal or piece of food.

burnt sienna[1] *adj* of a reddish brown or deep reddish orange colour.

burnt sienna[2] *noun* **1** SIENNA (natural brownish yellow earthy substance) heated to give it a reddish or orange hue and used as a pigment: compare RAW SIENNA[2]. **2** the reddish brown or deep reddish orange colour of this.

burnt umber[1] *adj* of a dark reddish brown colour.

burnt umber[2] *noun* **1** UMBER (a natural dark brown earthy substance) heated to give it a reddish hue and used as a pigment: compare RAW UMBER[2]. **2** the dark reddish brown colour of this.

burn up *verb trans informal* to obsess (somebody): *Jealousy was burning him up.*

burn-up *noun informal* the act or an instance of driving at high speed.

burp[1] /buhp/ *noun informal* a belch. [imitative]

burp[2] *verb intrans informal* to belch. ➤ *verb trans* to relieve the indigestion of (a baby) by patting or rubbing its back until excess gas is released through the mouth.

burr[1] /buh/ *noun* **1** (*also* **bur**) a rough or prickly covering of a fruit or seed. **2** something that sticks or clings. **3** a thin rough edge left after cutting or shaping metal, plastic, etc. **4** a hard rounded outgrowth on a tree trunk or branch. **5a** the rolled pronunciation of /r/ made at the back of the throat, as in a West Country or Northumberland accent. **b** the rolled /r/ made at the front of the mouth in some Scottish accents. **c** generally, a dialectal pronunciation: '*A Yorkshire burr,*' *he affirmed,* '*was ... much better than a Cockney's lisp.*' — Charlotte Brontë. **6** a small drill, e.g. one used by a dentist or surgeon. **7** a rough whirring sound. [Middle English *burre*, of Germanic origin; related to Old English *byrst* BRISTLE[1]]

burr[2] *verb intrans* to make a whirring sound. ➤ *verb trans* to pronounce (an 'r') with a burr.

burrito /bə'reetoh/ *noun* (*pl* **burritos**) a tortilla rolled round a savoury filling and baked. [American Spanish *burrito*, literally 'little donkey', dimin. of Spanish *burro*: see BURRO]

burro /'booroh/ *noun* (*pl* **burros**) *chiefly NAmer* a small donkey used as a pack animal. [Spanish *burro*, ultimately from late Latin *burricus* small horse]

burrow[1] /'buroh/ *noun* a hole or excavation in the ground made by a rabbit, fox, etc for shelter and habitation. [Middle English *borow*, variant of BOROUGH]

burrow[2] *verb trans* **1** to construct or excavate (e.g. a hole or passage) by tunnelling. **2** to make a motion suggestive of burrowing with (something); to nestle (it): *She burrowed her tiny hand into mine.* ➤ *verb intrans* **1** to conceal oneself in, or as if in, a burrow. **2a** to make a burrow. **b** to progress by digging or tunnelling. **3** to make a motion suggestive of burrowing; to snuggle: *The piglets burrowed against their mother's back for warmth.* **4** to make a search as if by digging: *She burrowed into her pocket for some change.* ➤➤ **burrower** *noun.*

bursa /'buhsə/ *noun* (*pl* **bursas** *or* **bursae** /'buhsee/) a small sac or pouch in the body, *esp* a fluid-filled sac between a tendon and a bone. ➤➤ **bursal** *adj.* [scientific Latin from medieval Latin *bursa* bag, PURSE[1]]

bursar /'buhsə/ *noun* **1** *chiefly Brit* an officer, e.g. of a monastery or college, in charge of funds. **2** *Scot* the holder of a bursary. [medieval Latin *bursarius*, from *bursa*: see BURSA]

bursary /'buhs(ə)ri/ *noun* (*pl* **bursaries**) **1** a bursar's office. **2** a grant of money awarded to a student; a scholarship. [medieval Latin *bursaria*, from *bursa*: see BURSA]

bursitis /buh'sietis/ *noun* inflammation of a BURSA (fluid-filled sac) of the knee, shoulder, elbow, or other joint. [scientific Latin *bursitis*, from BURSA]

burst[1] /buhst/ *verb* (*past tense and past part.* **burst**) ➤ *verb intrans* **1** to break suddenly and violently apart or into pieces. **2a** to give vent suddenly to a repressed emotion: *He burst into tears.* **b** to begin suddenly and forcefully: *The next moment he had burst into song.* **3** to emerge or appear suddenly: *She burst out of the house.* **4** (+ with) to be filled to breaking point or to the point of overflowing: *The cupboard was bursting with packets of every kind.* ➤ *verb trans* **1** to cause (something) to break suddenly and violently: *She burst a blood vessel; He burst the balloon by sitting on it.* **2** to produce (something) by bursting: *The weight had burst a hole in the bag.* [Old English *berstan*]

burst[2] *noun* **1** a sudden usu temporary outbreak or eruption: *There were several bursts of applause.* **2** a sudden, usu brief, intense effort or exertion; a spurt: *She produced a burst of speed.* **3** a temporary marked increase or display: *It was an uncharacteristic burst of generosity.* **4** a volley of shots from a usu automatic firearm.

burst out *verb intrans* **1** to begin suddenly: *He burst out laughing.* **2** to exclaim suddenly.

burthen /'buhdhən/ *noun archaic* a burden: *The vapours weep their burthen to the ground* — Tennyson.

burton /'buht(ə)n/ ✳ **go for a burton** *Brit, informal* to be broken, destroyed, or ruined: *Once again, our plans went for a burton.*

Word history
prob from *Burton* ale, a type of strong ale brewed in Burton-upon-Trent in Staffordshire. The original sense 'go for a drink', prob led to 'be ruined by indulgence in drink'.

bury /'beri/ *verb trans* (**buries, buried, burying**) **1a** to place (a corpse) in the earth or a tomb with the appropriate funeral rites. **b** to lose (somebody) by death: *She has buried three husbands.* **2** to hide or dispose of (something) by depositing it in the earth. **3** to cover (something) from view; to conceal (it): *The report was buried under miscellaneous papers.* **4** to put (something) completely out of mind: *They would have to bury their differences.* **5** (+ in) to submerge or engross (somebody, *esp* oneself): *She buried herself in her books.* ✳ **bury the hatchet** to settle a disagreement and become reconciled [from the custom among Native Americans of burying all weapons during peace negotiations]. [Old English *byrgan*]

bus[1] /bus/ *noun* (*pl* **buses**, *NAmer* **busses**) **1** a large motor-driven passenger vehicle operating usu according to a timetable along a fixed route. **2** *informal* a car or aircraft, *esp* an old and unreliable one. **3** a conductor or an assembly of conductors connected to several similar circuits in an electrical or electronic system, e.g. one that carries data from one part of a computer to another or from the central processing unit to a printer or other peripheral. [short for OMNIBUS]

bus[2] *verb* (**bused** *or* **bussed, busing** *or* **bussing**) ➤ *verb intrans* to travel by bus. ➤ *verb trans* **1** to transport (people) by bus. **2** *NAmer* to transport (children) by bus to a school in another district where the pupils are of a different race, in order to create integrated classes.

bus. *abbr* business.

busbar /'busbah/ *noun* a solid rod or rail designed as a conductor for high currents. [BUS[1] + BAR[1]]

busboy /'busboy/ *noun NAmer* a waiter. [OMNIBUS in an earlier sense 'assistant in a restaurant' (prob suggesting 'somebody who does all tasks')]

busby /'buzbi/ *noun* (*pl* **busbies**) **1** a military full-dress fur hat that has a small bag hanging one side, worn *esp* by hussars. **2** *informal* the bearskin worn by the Brigade of Guards. [prob from the name *Busby*]

bush[1] /boosh/ *noun* **1a** a shrub, *esp* one with a woody stem and branches that grow thickly from it at a low level. **b** a dense thicket of shrubs. **2** (*usu* **the bush**) a large uncleared or sparsely settled area, e.g. in Africa or Australia, that is usu covered with scrub or forest. **3** *coarse slang* the pubic hair. **4** a bushy tuft or mass: *a bush of black hair.* **b** a bushy tail of a fox, squirrel, or other animal; a brush. **5** a bunch of ivy formerly hung up as the sign of a wineseller or a tavern. [Middle English, of Germanic origin]

bush[2] *verb intrans* to grow thickly or spread like a bush.

bush[3] *or* **bushing** *noun* a usu removable cylindrical lining for an opening through which a shaft passes, e.g. in a car's suspension system, used to limit the size of the opening, resist abrasion, or serve as a guide. [Dutch *bus* bushing, box, via early Dutch *busse* box, from late Latin *buxis*]

bush[4] *verb trans* to provide (a bearing, shaft, etc) with a bush.

bush baby *noun* any of several species of small active nocturnal tree-dwelling African primates with large eyes and ears, and a long tail and hind limbs: genus *Galago*.

bushbuck *noun* (*pl* **bushbucks** *or collectively* **bushbuck**) a small striped antelope of tropical African forests, the male of which has spirally twisted horns: *Tragelaphus scriptus.* [translation of Afrikaans *bosbok*]

bushed *adj informal* **1** thoroughly tired out; exhausted. **2** perplexed or confused. **3** *chiefly Aus* lost, *esp* in the bush.

bushel /'booshl/ *noun* **1** a British unit of volume used for grain and other dry goods and for liquids, equal to 8 imperial gallons (about 36.4l). **2** a US unit of volume used for dry goods, equal to 64 US pints (about 30.3l). **3** a container with a capacity equal to a bushel. ✳ **hide one's light under a bushel** see HIDE[1]. [Middle English *busshel* from Old French *boissel*, of Celtic origin]

bushfire *noun* a rapidly spreading and uncontrolled fire in the Australian bush.

Bushido /boohshi'doh/ *noun* the Japanese code of chivalry that originated with the Samurai warriors, valuing honour above life, and stressing loyalty to the feudal lord or emperor. [Japanese *bushidō*, from *bushi* warrior + *dō* doctrine]

bushing /'booshing/ *noun* see BUSH[3].

Bushism /'booshiz(ə)m/ *noun* a verbal slip or illogicality uttered by George W. Bush, the 43rd president of the United States.

bush jacket *noun* a cotton jacket with patch pockets and a belt, resembling a shirt. [from its orig use in rough country]

bush lawyer *noun Aus, NZ, informal* somebody who offers legal advice without having any qualifications.

bush-league *adj NAmer, informal* of low value or merit; inferior. [*bush league* minor baseball league]

bushman *noun* (*pl* **bushmen**) **1** (**Bushman**) a member of a race of nomadic hunting people of southern Africa. **2** *dated* the San languages spoken by these peoples. **3** *chiefly Aus* somebody who lives in the bush. [(sense 1) modification of obsolete Afrikaans *boschjesman*, from *boschje* (dimin. of *bosch* forest) + *man* man]

bushmaster *noun* a large tropical American pit viper that is the largest New World venomous snake: *Lachesis muta.*

bushmeat *noun* in parts of Africa, chimpanzee meat.

bushpig *noun* a wild pig of southern Africa that has long reddish brown body hair, white face markings, and a white crest on the back: *Potamochoerus porcus.* [translation of Dutch *bosvark*]

bushranger *noun* **1** *NAmer* somebody who lives in a sparsely populated uncultivated or forested area away from civilization; a woodsman. **2** *Aus* an outlaw living in the bush.

bush telegraph *noun* the rapid unofficial communication of news, rumours, etc by word of mouth.

bushveld /'booshvelt, -felt/ *noun* (**the bushveld**) an area of scrub or wild country in S Africa.

bushwhack *verb intrans* **1** *NAmer, Aus, NZ* to clear a path through thick woods, *esp* by chopping down bushes and low branches. **2** *NAmer, Aus, NZ* to live or hide out in the woods. **3** *NAmer* to fight as a guerrilla or bandit in the bush or attack from the bush. ➤ *verb trans* to ambush (somebody). ➤➤ **bushwhacker** *noun,* **bushwhacking** *noun.* [earliest as *bushwhacker*; *bushwhack* is a back-formation]

bushy[1] *adj* (**bushier, bushiest**) **1** growing thickly or densely: *bushy eyebrows.* **2** full of or overgrown with bushes. ➤➤ **bushily** *adv,* **bushiness** *noun.*

bushy[2] *noun* (*pl* **bushies**) *Aus, NZ, informal* somebody who lives in the bush.

business /'biznis/ *noun* **1a** a usu commercial activity engaged in as a means of livelihood: *They're in the fruit-importing business.* **b** one's regular employment, profession, or trade. **c** a commercial or industrial enterprise: *She sold her business and retired.* **d** commercial and industrial enterprises as a whole, or the sector of the economy they represent: *This news is bad for business.* **e** economic transactions or dealings; custom: *He is ready to take his business elsewhere unless service improves.* **2a** somebody's role or function: *She certainly knows her business.* **b** an immediate task or objective; a mission. **c** a particular field of endeavour: *They're the best in the business.* **3** an affair of some kind; a matter: *It was a strange business.* **4a** personal concern: *It was none of your business.* **b** proper motive; justification: *You have no business asking me that.* **5** movements or actions performed by an actor as a way of communicating something about the character or simply to create something for the audience to watch. **6** serious activity: *We immediately got down to business.* **7** (**the business**) *informal* excellent, or precisely what is needed: *This potato salad is the business!* ✳ **like nobody's business** extraordinarily well or rapidly. **mean business** to speak or act with serious intent; to be in earnest. [Middle English *bisinesse*, from *bisy* BUSY[1] + *-nesse* -NESS]

business card *noun* a visiting card for business purposes, giving the owner's name, position, company, and address.

business class *noun* a class of air travel accommodation that is intermediate between first class and tourist class.

business end *noun informal* the end of a tool, machine, etc that performs the work or at which the intended action occurs.

businesslike *adj* **1** efficient and systematic, often to the point of being cool or abrupt. **2** serious and purposeful.

businessman *or* **businesswoman** *noun* (*pl* **businessmen** *or* **businesswomen**) **1** somebody professionally engaged in commercial transactions, *esp* in an executive capacity. **2** somebody with financial flair: *I'm not much of a businessman.*

business park *noun* a landscaped area, usu on the edge of a town, designed for offices or light industry.

business process re-engineering *noun* the analysis and restructuring of a company's methods and organization.

business studies *pl noun* (*treated as sing.*) economics and management studied as part of a school or college course.

busk /busk/ *verb intrans* to sing or play an instrument in the street in order to earn money from passers-by. ➤➤ **busker** *noun.* [perhaps obsolete *busk* to seek after, prob from obsolete French *busquer* to steal, ultimately of Germanic origin]

buskin /'buskin/ *noun* **1** formerly, a laced boot reaching halfway up the calf or to the knee, e.g. the high thick-soled boot worn by

actors in ancient Athenian tragedy. **2** the high thick-soled boot (the *cothurnus*) worn by actors in ancient Athenian tragedy, often contrasted with the 'sock' (*soccus*) worn by actors in comedy: *to hear thy buskin tread and shake the stage* — Ben Jonson. **3** tragic drama, *esp* tragedy resembling that of ancient Greek drama. [perhaps modification of Spanish *borcegui*]

bus lane *noun Brit* a traffic lane for buses only.

busman *noun* (*pl* **busmen**) a bus driver.

busman's holiday *noun* a holiday spent doing the kind of thing one normally does at work.

buss[1] /bus/ *verb trans archaic* to kiss (somebody or something). [prob imitative]

buss[2] *noun archaic* a kiss.

bus shelter *noun* a covered structure giving protection against bad weather to people waiting at a bus stop.

bus stop *noun* a place, usu marked by a standardized sign, where people may board and alight from buses.

bus-stop surgery *noun* rejuvenating cosmetic surgery involving rapidly performed operations such as injections of Botox or gel-fillers or removal of dead skin.

bust[1] /bust/ *noun* **1a** a woman's breasts. **b** used in clothing sizes: the circumference of a woman's torso at breast height. **2** a sculpture of the upper part of the human figure including the head, neck, and usu shoulders. [French *buste* via Italian from Latin *bustum* tomb, statue on a tomb]

bust[2] *verb* (*past tense and past part.* **busted** *or* **bust**) ➤ *verb trans informal* **1** to break or smash (something) or make it inoperative: *I bust my watch this morning.* **2** *chiefly NAmer.* **a** to arrest (somebody). **b** to raid (a place): *Police busted the flat below looking for heroin.* **3** *NAmer* to demote (somebody), *esp* to a lower military rank. ➤ *verb intrans informal* **1a** to burst: *We were laughing fit to bust.* **b** to stop working or become inoperative through breakage or wear; to break down. **2** to lose a game or turn by exceeding a limit, e.g. the count of 21 in pontoon. [alteration of BURST[1]]

bust[3] *adj informal* **1** broken. **2** bankrupt: *The company has gone bust.*

bust[4] *noun informal* **1** a police raid or arrest. **2** *NAmer* a blow. **3** a failure or bankruptcy: *boom and bust.*

bustard /'bustəd/ *noun* any of several species of large long-legged and long-necked Eurasian, African, and Australian game birds that build nests on the ground, have a slow stately walk, and are capable of powerful swift flight when alarmed: family Otididae. [Middle English via Old French and Old Italian from Latin *avis tarda* slow bird]

buster /'bustə/ *noun* **1** *chiefly NAmer, informal* used as an often disrespectful form of address to a man or boy: *Thanks a million, buster.* **2** (*used in combinations*) somebody or something that attacks or destroys a specified thing: *ghostbusters.*

bustier /'boostiay/ *noun* an article of women's clothing similar to a bodice, worn as a top. [French *bustier*, from *buste*: see BUST[1]]

bustle[1] /'busl/ *verb intrans* **1** to move briskly and often with an ostentatious show of activity or purpose. **2** to be full of people and activity: *It was a town bustling at all times of the day and night.* ➤➤ **bustling** *adj.* [prob alteration of obsolete *buskle* to prepare, frequentative of BUSK]

bustle[2] *noun* noisy and energetic activity: *They longed to escape the hustle and bustle of the big city.*

bustle[3] *noun* a pad or framework worn formerly to expand and support fullness at the back of a woman's skirt. [origin unknown]

bust up *verb trans informal* to bring (something) to an end, *esp* abruptly. ➤ *verb intrans informal* to come to an *esp* abrupt end.

bust-up *noun informal* **1** a breaking up or breaking apart: *It followed the bust-up of their marriage.* **2** a quarrel or brawl.

busty *adj* (**bustier, bustiest**) *informal* said of a woman: having large breasts.

busy[1] /'bizi/ *adj* (**busier, busiest**) **1** engaged in an activity and giving it full attention; occupied. **2** full of activity; bustling: *a busy seaport.* **3** foolishly or intrusively active; meddlesome. **4** full or too full of detail: *a busy design.* **5** *chiefly NAmer* said of a telephone line: in use. ➤➤ **busily** *adv,* **busyness** *noun.* [Old English *bisig*]

busy[2] *verb trans* (**busies, busied, busying**) to make (*esp* oneself) busy; to occupy (*esp* oneself): *He busied himself with the ironing.*

busybody *noun* (*pl* **busybodies**) a meddlesome or inquisitive person.

busy lizzie /'lizi/ *noun* a common house plant that bears usu pink, scarlet, or crimson flowers almost continuously: *Impatiens balsamina*. [BUSY[1] + *Lizzie*, nickname for *Elizabeth*]

but[1] /bət; *strong* but/ *conj* **1** used to join coordinate sentence elements of the same class or function expressing contrast: on the other hand: *I meant to tell you but you weren't here.* **2** and nevertheless; yet: *They were poor but proud.* **3** used to introduce an expression of protest or enthusiasm: *But that's ridiculous!* **4** used to signal that a new topic is being embarked on: *But to continue* .... **5a** *formal* were it not; save: *He would have collapsed but for your help.* **b** *formal (in negative contexts)* without the necessary accompaniment that: *They never meet but there's a skirmish of wit between them* — Shakespeare. **c** *dialect* otherwise than; that ... not: *That was how I was brought up, and I don't know but what it was just as good a way as all these new-fangled notions for training children* — L M Montgomery. [Old English *būtan* (prep and conj) outside, without, except, except that, from Old English *be* BY[1] and *ūtan* outside]

but[2] *prep* **1** with the exception of (something or somebody); barring (them): *We're all here but Mary.* **2** other than (something): *This letter is nothing but an insult.* **3** not counting (something): *They live in the next house but two.*

but[3] *adv* **1** only or merely: *He is but a child.* **2** to the contrary: *Who knows but that he may succeed.* **3** used for emphasis: *Get there but fast.* **4** *NE Eng, Aus* however or though: *It's pouring with rain, warm but.*

but[4] *noun* a doubt or objection: *There are no buts about it.*

but[5] *noun Scot* the kitchen or living quarters of a two-room cottage. [Scots *but* outer, from BUT[1]]

butadiene /byoohtə'die-een/ *noun* an inflammable gaseous hydrocarbon used in making synthetic rubbers: formula C_4H_6. [BUTANE + DI-[1] + -ENE]

butane /'byoohtayn/ *noun* an inflammable gas that is a member of the alkane series of organic chemical compounds, is obtained usu from petroleum or natural gas and used *esp* as a fuel, e.g. in cigarette lighters: formula C_4H_{10}. [BUTYRIC + -ANE]

butanoic acid /byoohtə'noh·ik/ *noun* = BUTYRIC ACID.

butch[1] /booch/ *adj informal* said of a woman or homosexual man: aggressively masculine in appearance or behaviour. [*Butch*, a nickname for boys, prob short for BUTCHER[1]]

butch[2] *noun informal* a butch person, *esp* a lesbian who adopts the masculine role in a relationship.

butcher[1] /'boochə/ *noun* **1a** somebody who slaughters animals bred for meat or cuts up and prepares them for sale. **b** somebody who sells or deals in meat. **2** somebody who kills people ruthlessly or brutally. ✳ **have/take a butcher's** *Brit, slang* to have a look [rhyming slang *butcher's hook* 'look']. [Middle English *bocher* from Old French *bouchier*, from *bouc* he-goat, prob of Celtic origin]

butcher[2] *verb trans* (**butchered, butchering**) **1** to slaughter and prepare (an animal) for sale. **2** to kill (people) ruthlessly or indiscriminately. **3** to spoil or ruin (something), *esp* by clumsy or unthinking treatment. ➤➤ **butcherer** *noun*.

butcher-bird *noun* **1** any of various birds of the shrike family that often impale their prey on thorns: family Laniidae. **2** any of several species of Australian songbirds: genus *Cracticus*.

butcher's-broom *noun* a European plant of the lily family with stiff-pointed leaflike twigs formerly used for brooms: *Ruscus aculeatus*.

butchery *noun* (*pl* **butcheries**) **1** the preparation of meat for sale. **2** cruel and ruthless slaughter of human beings. **3** the action of spoiling or ruining something, *esp* by clumsy or unthinking treatment. **4** *chiefly Brit, dated* a slaughterhouse.

butler /'butlə/ *noun* the chief male servant of a large household, who is in charge of the other servants, directs the serving of meals, and is a personal attendant to the householder: *Motkin, the butler, who ... had grown prematurely grey in Lady Susan's service, added to his other excellent qualities an intelligent interest in matters connected with the Turf* — Saki. [Middle English *buteler* from Old French *bouteillier* bottle bearer, from *bouteille*: see BOTTLE[1]]

butt[1] /but/ *verb trans* to strike or shove (something) with the head or horns. [Middle English *butten* from Old French *boter*, of Germanic origin]

butt[2] *noun* a blow or thrust, usu with the head or horns.

butt[3] *noun* **1** the thicker or handle end of a tool or weapon. **2** an unused remainder, *esp* the unsmoked remnant of a cigar or cigarette. **3** the end of a plant or tree nearest the roots. **4** *NAmer,*

informal the buttocks. [Middle English, of Germanic origin; prob related to Old English *buttuc* BUTTOCK]

butt[4] *noun* **1** an object of abuse or ridicule; a victim. **2a** a mound or bank of earth for catching bullets, arrows, etc shot at a target. **b** a target used in archery or rifle practice. **c** (*in pl*) a shooting range for archery or rifle practice. **d** a low mound, wall, etc from behind which hunters shoot at game birds. [Middle English; partly from early French *but* target, end, of Germanic origin, partly via early French *bute* backstop]

butt[5] *verb trans* **1** to place (things) end to end or side to side without overlapping. **2** to join (pieces, e.g. of wood) by means of a butt joint. ➤ *verb intrans* (+ against/on to) to abut. [partly from BUTT[4], partly from BUTT[3]]

butt[6] *noun* a large barrel, *esp* for water, wine, or beer. [Middle English via Old French and Old Provençal from late Latin *buttis*]

butte /byooht/ *noun NAmer or technical* an isolated hill with steep sides, usually with a smaller summit area than a mesa. [French *butte* knoll, from early French *bute* mound of earth serving as a backstop: see BUTT[4]]

butter[1] /'butə/ *noun* **1** a pale yellow solid substance that is used as food, e.g. for spreading on bread and in baking, in the form of an emulsion of fat globules, air, and water made by churning milk or cream. **2a** any of various vegetable oils that remain solid or semisolid at ordinary temperatures: *cocoa butter.* **b** any of various food spreads made with butter or having the consistency of butter: *peanut butter.* ✳ **look as if butter wouldn't melt (in one's mouth)** to have an innocent or meek appearance that may well be deceptive. [Old English *butere* from a prehistoric West Germanic word which came via Latin *butyrum* from Greek *boutyron*, from *bous* cow + *tyros* cheese]

butter[2] *verb trans* (**buttered, buttering**) to spread (e.g. bread) or coat (e.g. a cake tin) with butter.

butterball *noun informal* an overweight person.

butter bean *noun* a large dried lima bean.

butterbur /'butəbuh/ *noun* a large Eurasian plant of the daisy family with very large leaves and reddish purple flowers, found *esp* in damp places: *Petasites hybridus.*

buttercup *noun* any of various species of plants with usu bright yellow flowers that commonly grow in fields and as weeds: genus *Ranunculus.*

butterfat *noun* the natural fat of milk and chief constituent of butter.

butterfingered *adj informal* apt to let things fall or slip through the fingers; careless.

butterfingers *noun* (*pl* **butterfingers**) *informal* somebody who tends to drop things.

butterfish *noun* (*pl* **butterfishes** or *collectively* **butterfish**) any of various species of small long fishes with spiny fins and a slippery coating of mucus, found *esp* in warm seas: family Stromateidae.

butterfly *noun* (*pl* **butterflies**) **1** any of an order of slender-bodied insects that fly by day and have large, broad, often brightly coloured wings and long thin antennae: order Lepidoptera. **2** a frivolous person, *esp* one chiefly occupied with the pursuit of pleasure. **3** a swimming stroke executed on the front by moving both arms together forwards out of the water and then sweeping them back through the water while kicking the legs up and down together. **4** *informal* (*in pl*) queasiness caused *esp* by nervous tension. [Old English *buterflēoge*, from *butere* butter + *flēoge* fly; perhaps from former belief that butterflies steal milk and butter]

butterfly effect *noun* the progressive production of a vast and far-reaching effect by a small and apparently insignificant cause. [from the theory that the flapping of a butterfly's wings can initiate a chain of events producing a hurricane]

butterfly fish *noun* **1** a European blenny: *Blennius ocellaris.* **2** any of a family of deep-bodied fish of tropical waters: family Chaetodontidae.

butterfly nut *noun* = WING NUT.

butterfly valve *noun* a valve that controls the flow of gas or liquid along a pipe, consisting of a disc turning round an axis on the diameter of the disc.

buttermilk *noun* **1** the liquid left after butter has been churned from milk or cream, used for making scones and some kinds of bread. **2** fermented, slightly sour milk made by the addition of suitable bacteria to milk.

butter muslin *noun Brit* thin muslin with a fine mesh, of a kind orig used to wrap butter.

butternut *noun* **1** an American tree of the walnut family: *Juglans cinerea*. **2** the edible oily nut of this tree.

butternut squash *noun* a pear-shaped winter squash with a pale rind.

butterscotch *noun* **1** a brittle toffee made from brown sugar, syrup, butter, and water. **2** a flavouring resembling butterscotch.

butter up *verb trans informal* to charm (somebody) with lavish flattery; to cajole (them).

butterwort *noun* any of several species of insect-eating plants that grow in damp places and have fleshy, usu light green, leaves that produce a sticky secretion: genus *Pinguicula*.

buttery[1] /ˈbʌt(ə)ri/ *noun* (*pl* **butteries**) *Brit* a room, e.g. in a college, in which food and drink are served or sold: *then, to take a peep in … at the butteries, and sculleries, redolent of antique hospitality* — Charles Lamb. [Middle English *boterie*, ultimately from Old French *botte* cask, BUTT[6]]

buttery[2] *adj* similar to or containing butter. >>> **butteriness** *noun*.

buttie /ˈbʌti/ *noun* see BUTTY[1].

butt in *verb intrans* **1** to meddle or intrude. **2** to interrupt.

butt joint *noun* a joint made by placing the ends or sides of the parts together without overlap and often with reinforcement.

buttock /ˈbʌtək/ *noun* the back of a hip that forms one of the two fleshy parts on which a person sits, or the corresponding part of a cow or other mammal. [Old English *buttuc*]

buttock-clenching *adj* **1** terrifying. **2** extremely embarrassing or tedious. >>> **buttock-clenchingly** *adv*.

button[1] /ˈbʌt(ə)n/ *noun* **1** a small knob or disc secured to an article, e.g. of clothing, and used as a fastener by passing it through a buttonhole or loop. **2** *chiefly NAmer* a usu circular badge bearing a design or slogan. **3** a knob on an item of electrical or electronic equipment that is pressed to activate a function. **4** a guard on the tip of a fencing foil. **5** something of little value: *Her advice is not worth a button*. ✱ **on the button** *informal* with absolute precision; exactly. >>> **buttonless** *adj*. [Middle English *boton* from Old French *bouton*, of Germanic origin]

button[2] *verb* (**buttoned, buttoning**) > *verb trans* (often + up) to close or fasten (something) with buttons: *Button up your overcoat*. > *verb intrans* to have buttons for fastening: *This dress buttons at the back*.

button-down *adj* **1** said of a collar: having the ends fastened to the garment with buttons. **2** *NAmer* boringly conventional or conservative, *esp* in dress or attitudes.

buttonhole[1] *noun* **1** a slit or loop in the edge of a piece of material, through which a button is passed. **2** *chiefly Brit* a flower worn in a buttonhole or pinned to the lapel.

buttonhole[2] *verb trans* **1** to provide (a garment) with buttonholes. **2** to sew (something) with buttonhole stitch.

buttonhole[3] *verb trans informal* to detain (somebody) in conversation. [alteration of *buttonhold* to detain somebody by holding the buttons on his or her clothes]

buttonhole stitch *noun* a delicate sewing stitch with loops very close together, used to make a firm or neat edge, e.g. on a buttonhole.

buttonhook *noun* a hook for pulling small buttons through buttonholes: *A hundred times in my boyhood days had I picked locks with a buttonhook* — Edgar Rice Burroughs.

button mushroom *noun* an immature whole mushroom.

button quail *noun* any of several species of small ground-living birds of Africa, Europe, and Asia, resembling quails and related to the cranes and bustards: family Turnicidae.

buttons *noun* (*pl* **buttons**) *Brit, informal* used as a name: a page boy. [from rows of buttons on his jacket]

button-through *adj Brit* said of a garment: fastened from the top to the bottom with buttons: *a button-through skirt*.

buttress[1] /ˈbʌtrɪs/ *noun* **1** a supporting structure built against a wall or building to provide reinforcement. **2** a projecting part of mountain, *esp* on a rock cliff. **3** something that supports or strengthens: *a buttress of the cause of peace*. [Middle English *butres* from Old French *boterez*, from *boter* to thrust, of Germanic origin]

buttress[2] *verb trans* **1** to support (a wall) with a buttress. **2** to give support or strength to (something, e.g. an argument). >>> **buttressed** *adj*.

butt weld *noun* a butt joint made by welding. >>> **butt welding** *noun*.

butt-weld *verb trans* to join (metal parts) by means of a butt weld.

butty[1] *or* **buttie** /ˈbʌti/ *noun* (*pl* **butties**) *Brit, informal* a sandwich. [BUTTER[1] + -Y[4]]

butty[2] *noun* (*pl* **butties**) **1** *chiefly Brit, informal* a fellow worker; a friend or mate. **2** *Brit* a middleman between a mine-owner and the miners. [origin unknown]

butut /ˈbuːtuːt/ *noun* a unit of currency in The Gambia, worth 100th of a dalasi. [native name in The Gambia]

butyl /ˈbjuːtɪl, ˈbjuːtiːl/ *noun* any of various chemical groups derived from butane: formula C_4H_9. [BUTYRIC + -YL]

butyl rubber *noun* a kind of synthetic rubber used to make the inner tubes for tyres and liners for ponds.

butyric /bjuːˈtɪrɪk/ *adj dated* relating to or producing butyric acid: *butyric fermentation*. [French *butyrique* from Latin *butyrum*. see BUTTER[1]]

butyric acid *noun dated* an unpleasant-smelling fatty acid found *esp* in rancid butter: formula $CH_3(CH_2)_2COOH$.

buxom /ˈbʌks(ə)m/ *adj* said of a woman: with an attractively rounded figure and large breasts. >>> **buxomness** *noun*.

Word history ════════════════

Middle English *buxsum* compliant, gracious, ultimately from Old English *būgan* to bend. The Middle English sense evolved into 'blithe, lively' and then into 'plump' (from the traditional association of plumpness and cheerfulness). Originally applied to both sexes, now usu to women.

buy[1] /bie/ *verb* (*past tense and past part.* **bought** /bawt/) > *verb trans* **1** to become the owner of (something) by paying or agreeing to pay money for it. **2** to obtain (something), often by some sacrifice: *We have bought ourselves a little more time*. **3** to secure the cooperation of (somebody) by bribery. **4** to be the purchasing equivalent of (an amount): *The pound buys less today than it used to*. **5** *informal* to believe or accept (something said or proposed): *I don't buy that*. > *verb intrans* to work as a buyer for a shop or other business. [Old English *bycgan*]

buy[2] *noun informal* a purchase, *esp* considered in terms of its value for money.

buyback *noun* **1** a system in which something is repurchased by the seller at a later date, often under the terms of a contract. **2** a system in which a supplier of industrial machinery or facilities is repaid in the output of the plant.

buyer *noun* somebody who selects and buys stock to be sold in a shop or other business.

buyer's market *noun* a market in which supply exceeds demand, buyers have a wide range of choice, and prices tend to be low: compare SELLER'S MARKET.

buy in *verb trans* **1** to buy (a stock of goods) for a purpose. **2** to buy (stocks, shares, etc that a seller has not handed over at the agreed time), charging the extra cost to the defaulting or delaying seller. **3** to withdraw (an item) from an auction because it has failed to reach the reserve price.

buy-in *noun* the purchase of a majority holding in a company by a group of outside executives who take over its management.

buy off *verb trans* to secure the cooperation of (somebody) by bribery.

buyout *noun* the purchase of all the shares in a business, or a controlling proportion of them, *esp* by its managers.

buy out *verb trans* **1** to buy the shares or controlling interest of (a company). **2** to buy the share of (somebody) to get control of a company. **3** to free (somebody, *esp* oneself) from military service by payment.

buy up *verb trans* **1** to secure a controlling interest in (e.g. a company), *esp* by acquiring shares. **2** to buy all or a great deal of (a commodity).

buzz[1] /bʌz/ *verb intrans* **1** to make a continuous low humming sound like that of a bee. **2** to be filled with the murmur of voices, or with gossip or rumours: *Oil-industry publications buzz with talk of further cutbacks* — The Times. **3** to make a signal with a buzzer. **4** to move in a hurried, energetic, or busy manner. > *verb trans* **1** to summon (somebody) or signal (somebody or something) with a buzzer. **2** *informal* to telephone (somebody). **3** *informal* to fly over or close to (somebody or something) in order to threaten or warn (them): *The airliner was buzzed by fighters during its approach.* [Middle English *bussen*, of imitative origin]

buzz² *noun* **1** a continuous low humming sound. **2** a confused murmur or flurry of activity. **3** rumour or gossip. **4** a signal conveyed by a buzzer or bell. **5** *informal* a telephone call. **6** *informal* a pleasant stimulation; a kick.

buzzard /'buzəd/ *noun* **1** *chiefly Brit* any of several species of large European hawks with broad rounded wings and a soaring flight: genus *Buteo*. **2** *chiefly NAmer* any of various large birds of prey, e.g. the turkey buzzard. **3** *informal* a contemptible, greedy, or grasping person. [Middle English *busard* via Old French from Latin *buteon-, buteo*]

buzzer *noun* an electrical signalling device that makes a buzzing sound.

buzz off *verb intrans informal* to go away quickly.

buzz saw *noun NAmer* a circular saw.

buzzword *noun informal* **1** a usu technical word or phrase that has become fashionable and is frequently bandied about. **2** any catchword or slogan.

BV *abbr* Blessed Virgin.

BVI *abbr* British Virgin Islands (international vehicle registration).

BVM *abbr* Blessed Virgin Mary.

b/w *abbr* black and white.

bwana /'bwahnə/ *noun* often used in former times by an E African person to a European settler: master or boss. [Swahili *bwana* from Arabic *abūna* our father]

BY *abbr* Byelorussia (international vehicle registration for Belarus).

by¹ /bie/ *prep* **1a** in proximity to (somebody or something); near (them): *standing by the window.* **b** on the person or in the possession of (somebody): *I always keep a spare set by me.* **2a** through, or through the medium of (something); via (it): *Enter by the door; delivered by hand.* **b** up to and then beyond (somebody or something); past (them): *The bullet went right by him.* **3a** in the circumstances of (something); during (it): *She studies by night.* **b** not later than (a time): *I was in bed by two.* **4** through the instrumentality or use of (something): *I travel by bus.* **5a** through the action or creation of (somebody): *a trio by Mozart.* **b** sired by (somebody). **c** with the participation of (the other parent): *his daughter by his first wife.* **6** with the witness or sanction of (somebody or something): *I swear by Heaven.* **7a** in conformity with (something): *You must act by the rules; She opened it by mistake.* **b** in terms of (something): *They pay by the hour; Did you call her by name?* **c** from the evidence of (something): *Never judge by appearances alone.* **d** with the action of (something): *I began by scolding her; She alarmed him by driving too fast.* **8** with respect to (something): *He is French by birth.* **9** to the amount or extent of (something): *better by far.* **10** in successive units or increments of (something): *by inches; day by day.* **11** used in division as the inverse of 'into': *Divide 70 by 35.* **12** used in multiplication: *Multiply ten by four.* **13** used in measurements: *a room 4m by 5m.* ✳ **by oneself 1** unaccompanied: *standing by himself.* **2** unaided: *She did her shoes up all by herself.* [Old English (prep) *be, bī*]

by² *adv* **1** past: *We saw him go by.* **2a** at or to another's home: *I said I'd stop by for a chat.* **b** close at hand; near: *They live close by.* **3** aside or away, *esp* in or into reserve: *Keep a few bottles by.*

by- *or* **bye-** *prefix* forming words, with the meanings: **1** off the main route; side. **2** incidental or secondary: *by-election.*

by and by *adv* soon.

by and large *adv* when all things are considered; on the whole.

by-blow *noun* **1** *Brit, dated* an illegitimate child: *Yes, Billy Budd was a foundling, a presumable by-blow, and, evidently, no ignoble one* — Herman Melville. **2** an indirect blow.

bye¹ /bie/ *noun* **1** the passage to the next round of a tournament allowed to a competitor who has no opponent or whose opponent has withdrawn. **2** in cricket, a run scored off a ball that passes the batsman without striking the bat or body: compare LEG BYE, EXTRA² (4). **3** in golf, one or more unplayed holes, played after the match is over. **4** something of secondary importance. ✳ **by the bye** by the way. [alteration of BY²]

bye² *interj informal* used as an expression of farewell. [short for GOODBYE¹]

bye- *prefix* see BY-.

bye-bye *interj informal* used as an expression of farewell. [childish reduplication of GOODBYE¹]

bye-byes *noun* used by or to children: bed or sleep: *Go to bye-byes.*

byelaw /'bielaw/ *noun* see BYLAW.

by-election *noun Brit* a special election held between regular elections to fill a vacancy that has arisen unexpectedly, e.g. from the death or resignation of a Member of Parliament.

bye-line *noun informal* = BY-LINE (2).

Byelorussian /byeloh'rush(ə)n, beloh-/ *noun* see BELORUSSIAN.

bygone¹ /'biegon/ *adj* belonging to an earlier time, and often now outmoded.

bygone² *noun* a domestic or industrial implement of an early and now disused type. ✳ **let bygones be bygones** to forgive and forget past quarrels.

bylaw *or* **byelaw** /'bielaw/ *noun* **1** a law or regulation made by a local authority and having effect only within an area controlled by the authority. **2** a rule concerning the affairs of a club, company, etc. [Middle English *bilawe*, ultimately from Old Norse *bȳr* town + *lög* law]

by-line *noun* **1** the author's name printed with a newspaper or magazine article. **2** a goal line. **3** a touchline. **4** a secondary line.

BYOB *abbr* bring your own bottle.

bypass¹ *noun* **1** a road built so that through traffic can avoid a town centre. **2** a channel carrying a fluid round a part and back to the main stream. **3** a passage created surgically between two blood vessels to divert blood from one part to another.

bypass² *verb trans* **1** to avoid (something, e.g. a town centre) by means of a bypass. **2** to neglect or ignore (something or somebody), usu intentionally; to circumvent (them).

bypath *noun* a little-used road.

byplay *noun* action engaged in on the side while the main action proceeds, e.g. during a film or play.

by-product *noun* **1** something produced, e.g. in manufacturing, in addition to a principal product. **2** a secondary and sometimes unexpected result.

byre /'bie·ə/ *noun Brit* a cow shed. [Old English *bȳre*]

byroad *noun* a secondary road.

Byronic /bie'ronik/ *adj* displaying a self-conscious romanticism. ➤➤ **Byronically** *adv.* [from the characteristics of the life and writings of George Gordon, Lord *Byron* d.1824, English poet]

byssi /'bisie/ *noun* pl of BYSSUS.

byssinosis /bisi'nohsis/ *noun* a chronic lung disorder associated with the prolonged inhalation of cotton dust. [scientific Latin *byssinosis*, ultimately from Greek *byssos*: see BYSSUS]

byssus /'bisəs/ *noun (pl* **byssuses** *or* **byssi** /'bisie/*)* **1** a fine cloth of ancient times that was probably linen. **2** a tuft of filaments by which mussels and some other bivalve molluscs attach themselves to a surface. [via Latin from Greek *byssos* flax, of Semitic origin]

bystander /'biestandə/ *noun* somebody present but not involved in a situation or event.

byte /biet/ *noun* in computing, a string of eight adjacent bits (binary digits) that is capable of representing numbers from 0 to 255, processed by a computer as a unit. [perhaps alteration of BITE²]

byway *noun* **1** a little-used road. **2** a secondary or little-known aspect: *The author takes us down the byways of medieval literature.*

byword *noun* **1** a proverb. **2** somebody or something taken as representing some usu bad quality: *a byword for cruelty.*

by-your-leave *noun* a request for permission: *He grabbed my hand without so much as a by-your-leave.*

Byzantine¹ /bi'zantien, bie-, -teen/ *adj* **1** relating to or belonging to the ancient city of Byzantium or its empire. **2** of or in a style of architecture developed in the Byzantine Empire in the fourth to sixth cents, featuring a central dome built over a square space and extensive use of mosaics. **3** complex to the point of being confusing or obscure; labyrinthine. **4** characterized by trickery and deception; underhand. [late Latin *Byzantinus*, from *Byzantium*, ancient name of Istanbul, city in Turkey]

Byzantine² *noun* a native or inhabitant of Byzantium.

BZ *abbr* Belize (international vehicle registration).

C¹ *or* **c** *noun* (*pl* **C's** *or* **Cs** *or* **c's**) **1a** the third letter of the English alphabet. **b** a written character or design denoting this letter. **c** the sound represented by this letter, one of the English consonants. **2** an item designated as C, *esp* the third in a series. **3** a mark or grade rating a student's work as fair or mediocre in quality. **4** in music, the first note of the diatonic scale of C major. **5** the Roman numeral for 100. **6** *informal* cocaine. **7** a computer programming language.

C² *abbr* **1** Cape (on maps). **2** capacitance. **3** Catholic. **4** Celsius. **5** centigrade. **6** century. **7** in Britain, Conservative. **8** corps. **9** coulomb. **10** Cuba (international vehicle registration).

C³ *abbr* the chemical symbol for carbon.

© *symbol* copyright.

c *abbr* **1** carat. **2** in cricket, caught by. **3** cent. **4** centi-. **5** century. **6** chapter. **7** circa. **8** cold. **9** colt. **10** cubic. **11** in physics, the speed of light in a vacuum.

c/- *abbr Aus* care of.

CA *abbr* **1** California (US postal abbreviation). **2** chartered accountant. **3** Consumers' Association.

Ca *abbr* the chemical symbol for calcium.

ca *abbr* circa.

CAA *abbr Brit* Civil Aviation Authority.

Caaba /'kahbə/ *noun* see KAABA.

CAB *abbr* formerly, Citizens' Advice Bureau.

cab /kab/ *noun* **1** a taxi. **2** the part of a locomotive, truck, crane, etc that houses the driver and operating controls. **3** in former times, a cabriolet or similar horse-drawn carriage used for hire. [short for CABRIOLET]

cabal /kə'bal/ *noun* a clandestine or unofficial faction, *esp* in political intrigue.

Word history
French *cabale* via medieval Latin *cabbala* from late Hebrew *qabbālāh* received (lore). The word orig meant 'secret', soon extended to 'secret meeting' and 'clandestine group'. The latter was particularly applied to a committee of the privy council. By coincidence, from 1670 to 1674, the initials of five principal members of this committee spelt the word *cabal*: Clifford, Arlington, Buckingham, Ashley, Lauderdale. Contemporary pamphleteers seized on this coincidence to attack the five men, and thereby gave wider currency to the word.

cabala *or* **cabbala** *or* **kabala** *or* **kabbala** *or* **kabbalah** /kə'bahlə, 'kabələ/ *noun* **1** (*often* **Cabala**) a system of esoteric Jewish belief based on the extraction of hidden meanings and predictions from the Old Testament and other texts. **2** any occult or secret subject or doctrine. **>> cabalism** /'kabəliz(ə)m/ *noun*, **cabalist** /'kabəlist/ *noun*, **cabalistic** /kabə'listik/ *adj*. [medieval Latin *cabbala*: see CABAL]

caballero /kabə'lyeəroh, -'yeəroh/ *noun* (*pl* **caballeros**) a Spanish gentleman or knight. [Spanish *caballero* from late Latin *caballarius*: see CAVALIER¹]

cabana /kə'bahnə/ *noun NAmer* a hut near a beach or swimming pool for bathers to change in. [Spanish *cabaña* from late Latin *capanna, cavanna* CABIN¹]

cabaret /'kabəray/ *noun* **1** a stage show or series of acts provided at a nightclub, restaurant, etc. **2** such entertainment in general. **3** a nightclub or other venue providing such entertainment. [French *cabaret* tavern, prob ultimately from late Latin *camera*: see CHAMBER]

cabbage /'kabij/ *noun* **1a** a cultivated plant that has a short stem and a dense round head of usu green leaves eaten as a vegetable: *Brassica oleracea capitata*. **b** the leaves of this plant, used as a vegetable. **2a** *derog* somebody who has lost control of their mental and usu physical faculties as the result of illness, brain damage, or accident. **b** *informal* an inactive and apathetic person. [Middle English *caboche* from early French *caboce* head]

cabbage palm *noun* a palm tree with cabbage-like buds that are eaten as a vegetable: *Roystonea oleraceae*.

cabbage rose *noun* a rose with a large compact flower.

cabbage tree *noun* a palmlike tree grown *esp* for ornament in New Zealand: *Cordyline australis*.

cabbage white *noun* any of several species of largely white butterflies whose caterpillars feed on cabbage plants: family Pieridae.

cabbala /kə'bahlə, 'kabələ/ *noun* see CABALA.

cabby *or* **cabbie** /'kabi/ *noun* (*pl* **cabbies**) *informal* a taxi driver.

caber /'kaybə/ *noun* a roughly trimmed tree trunk that is thrown in the Scottish sport of tossing the caber. [Scottish Gaelic *cabar*]

Cabernet Franc /,kabənay 'fronh/ *noun* **1** a variety of grape related to Cabernet Sauvignon and often blended with it in the production of typically dry red wine. **2** a wine produced from this grape. [French *Cabernet Franc*]

Cabernet Sauvignon /,kabənay sohvi'nyonh/ *noun* **1** a variety of grape widely used in the production of dry red wine. **2** a wine produced from this grape. [French *Cabernet Sauvignon*]

cabin¹ /'kabin/ *noun* **1a** a private room or compartment on a ship or boat for passengers or crew. **b** a compartment in an aircraft for cargo, crew, or passengers. **2** a small usu single-storeyed dwelling of simple construction, *esp* one made of wood. **3** *chiefly Brit* a cab in a truck, crane, etc. [Middle English *cabane* via Old French and Old Provençal from medieval Latin *capanna* hut]

cabin² *verb trans* (**cabined, cabining**) *chiefly literary* to confine (somebody) in a small space.

cabin boy *noun* a boy employed as a servant on board a ship.

cabin class *noun* a class of accommodation on a passenger ship superior to tourist class and inferior to first class.

cabin cruiser *noun* a large private motorboat with living accommodation.

cabinet /'kabinit/ *noun* **1a** a case or cupboard usu with doors, shelves, and compartments for storing or displaying articles. **b** an upright case housing a radio, television, etc. **2** (*often* **Cabinet**) (*treated as sing. or pl*) a body of advisers to a head of state, e.g.: **a** in Britain, a body consisting of the prime minister and senior ministers who together formulate government policy. **b** in the USA, the heads of the executive departments of government collectively. [French *cabinet* small room, dimin. of early French *cabine* gambling house]

cabinetmaker *noun* a craftsman who makes fine furniture in wood. ➤➤ **cabinetmaking** *noun*.

cabinetwork *noun* high quality woodwork produced by a cabinetmaker.

cabin fever *noun chiefly NAmer, informal* depression or irritability resulting from a long period spent in cramped quarters or otherwise confined, e.g. indoors during the winter.

cable¹ /'kaybl/ *noun* **1a** a strong thick rope, *esp* one over 8cm (3in.) in thickness. **b** a wire rope or metal chain of great strength, *esp* one connected to a ship's anchor. **2** an assembly of electrical wires insulated from each other and surrounded by a sheath. **3** = CABLEGRAM. **4** = CABLE TELEVISION. **5** a nautical unit of length equal to 608ft (about 185m) in Britain and 720ft (about 219m) in the USA. **6** = CABLE STITCH. [Middle English via French and medieval Latin from Latin *capere* to take]

cable² *verb trans* **1** to fasten or provide (something) with a cable or cables. **2a** to send (a message) in the form of a cablegram. **b** to communicate with or inform (somebody) by cablegram. ➤ *verb intrans* to communicate by means of a cablegram.

cable car *noun* **1** any of a series of cabins suspended from an overhead cable along which they are pulled, *esp* to transport passengers up and down a mountainside. **2** a carriage that is pulled along a cable railway.

cablegram /'kayblgram/ *noun* a telegram sent by an underwater cable.

cable-laid *adj* said of a rope: composed of three ropes twisted together, each containing three strands.

cable length *noun* = CABLE¹ (5).

cable railway *noun* a railway along which the carriages are pulled by an endless cable operated by a stationary motor.

cable stitch *noun* a knitting stitch that produces a twisted rope-like pattern.

cable television *noun* a television broadcasting system in which subscribers receive programmes via a cable, rather than by aerial, typically supplied by a company providing a range of communications and information services.

cableway *noun* an overhead system along which goods carriers or cable cars can be pulled.

cabochon /'kabəshon/ *noun* a highly polished gem cut in a dome-shaped form without facets. [French *cabochon*, augmentative of early French *caboce* head]

caboodle /kə'boohdl/ ✳ **the whole caboodle** *informal* the whole lot: *There is an argument ... for slashing costs by abolishing the whole caboodle: ballot papers, polling booths, town hall declarations and all.* — Daily Telegraph. [prob from *ca*- (intensive prefix, prob of imitative origin) + obsolete *boodle* lot, large amount]

caboose /kə'boohs/ *noun* **1** a ship's GALLEY (kitchen), *esp* when housed in a cabin on the deck. **2** *NAmer* a wagon attached to a goods train, usu at the rear, mainly for the crew to eat and sleep in. [prob via Dutch *kabuis* from early Low German *kabūse*]

cabotage /'kabətahzh/ *noun* **1** coastal shipping, navigation, trade, or transport. **2** a country's limiting of traffic within its territory, *esp* air traffic within its airspace, to its own domestic carriers. [French *cabotage* from *caboter* to sail along the coast]

cabriole /'kabriohl/ *noun* **1** (*also* **cabriole leg**) a curved furniture leg, often ending in an ornamental foot, characteristic of the early 18th cent. **2** a ballet leap in which one leg is extended to the side, front, or back in mid-air and the other struck against it. [French *cabriole*: see CABRIOLET]

cabriolet /ˌkabriohˈlay/ *noun* **1** a light two-wheeled carriage with a hood, pulled by a single horse. **2** a car with a folding or removable roof; a convertible. [French *cabriolet*, dimin. of *cabriole* caper, from early French *capriole*: see CAPRIOLE¹]

cac- or **caco-** *comb. form* forming words, with the meaning: bad; unpleasant: *cacography*. [scientific Latin *cac*-, *caco*-, ultimately from Greek *kakos* bad]

cacao /kə'kah·oh, kə'kayoh/ *noun* (*pl* **cacaos**) **1a** any of the fatty seeds of a S American tree that are used in making cocoa, chocolate, and cocoa butter; a cocoa bean. **b** these seeds considered collectively. **2** the S American tree that bears fleshy pods containing these seeds: *Theobroma cacao*. [Spanish *cacao* from Nahuatl *cacahuatl* cacao beans]

cachalot /'kashəlot/ *noun* = SPERM WHALE. [French *cachalot*]

cache¹ /kash/ *noun* **1** a hiding place, *esp* for provisions or weapons. **2** something hidden or stored in a cache. **3** = CACHE MEMORY. [French *cache* from *cacher* to press, hide, ultimately from Latin *cogere*: see COGENT]

cache² *verb trans* to place, hide, or store (something) in a cache.

cache memory *noun* a small computer memory that keeps frequently used data within the central processing unit so that it can be accessed at a higher speed than from main memory. Also called CACHE¹.

cachepot /'kashpoh, 'kashpot/ *noun* an ornamental container for a houseplant in a flowerpot. [French *cache-pot*, from *cacher* to hide + *pot* pot]

cache-sexe /'kashseks/ *noun* a small garment worn to cover only the genitals. [French *cache-sexe*, from *cacher* to hide + *sexe* genitals]

cachet /'kashay, kə'shay/ *noun* **1** prestige, or a characteristic feature or quality that confers prestige: *The smells of cellars are a rare treat to dogs, especially ancient Brooklyn cellars which have a cachet all their own* — Christopher Morley. **2** a seal on a document, *esp* one used as a mark of official approval. **3** something other than the postmark that is stamped by hand on a postal item. **4** a capsule of rice paper or flour paste containing an unpleasant-tasting medicine. [early French *cachet* from *cacher*: see CACHE¹]

cachexia /kə'keksi·ə/ *or* **cachexy** /kə'keksi, ka-/ *noun* general physical wasting and malnutrition, usu associated with chronic disease. ➤➤ **cachectic** /kə'kektik/ *adj*. [via late Latin from Greek *kachexia* bad condition]

cachinnate /'kakinayt/ *verb intrans formal* to laugh loudly or immoderately. ➤➤ **cachinnation** /-'naysh(ə)n/ *noun*. [Latin *cachinnatus*, past part. of *cachinnare*, of imitative origin]

cachou /'kashooh, kə'shooh/ *noun* (*pl* **cachous**) **1** = CATECHU. **2** a pill or lozenge used to sweeten the breath. [French *cachou* via Portuguese from Malayalam *kāccu*]

cachucha /kə'choohchə/ *noun* a lively Andalusian solo dance in triple time performed with castanets. [Spanish *cachucha* small boat, cachucha]

cacique /kə'seek/ *noun* **1** a Native American chief in an area in which Spanish culture is predominant. **2** a local political leader in Spain and Latin America. [Spanish *cacique*, of Arawakan origin]

cack-handed /kak 'handid/ *adj Brit, informal* **1** awkward or clumsy. **2** *derog* left-handed. ➤➤ **cack-handedly** *adv*, **cack-handedness** *noun*. [from dialect *cack* excrement]

cackle¹ /'kakl/ *verb intrans* **1** to make the sharp squawking noise or cry characteristic of a hen, *esp* after laying. **2** to laugh in a way suggestive of a hen's cackle. **3** to talk noisily about trivialities; to chatter. ➤ *verb trans* to say (something) in a voice suggestive of a hen's cackle. [Middle English *cakelen*, of imitative origin]

cackle² *noun* **1** a cackling noise made by a hen. **2** a cackling laugh. **3** *informal* noisy chat about nothing in particular. ✳ **cut the cackle** *informal* to stop talking.

caco- *comb. form* see CAC-.

cacodemon /kakə'deemən/ *noun* an evil spirit; a demon. [Greek *kakodaimōn*, from *kakos* bad + *daimōn* spirit]

cacodyl /'kakədil/ *noun* **1** a chemical group containing arsenic, with compounds that usu have a vile smell and are often poisonous: formula $As(CH_3)_2$. **2** a colourless liquid with the odour of garlic, consisting of two cacodyl groups joined together: formula $As_2(CH_3)_4$. ➤➤ **cacodylic** /-'dilik/ *adj*. [from Greek *kakōdēs* ill-smelling]

cacoëthes /kakoh'eetheez/ *noun formal* an insatiable desire or uncontrollable urge. [via Latin from Greek *kakoëthes* wickedness]

cacography /kə'kogrəfi, ka-/ *noun formal* **1** bad handwriting. **2** incorrect spelling. ➤➤ **cacographic** /-'grafik/ *adj.*

cacomistle /'kakəmisl/ *noun* a carnivorous tree-dwelling mammal found in the S parts of N America that is related to and resembles the raccoon: *Bassariscus astutus*. [Mexican Spanish *cacomistle* from Nahuatl *tlacomiztli*, from *tlaco* half + *miztli* mountain lion]

cacophony /kə'kofəni/ *noun* (*pl* **cacophonies**) a harsh or discordant combination or confusion of sounds: *so deafening a cacophony of howls, groans, and thumps* — Charles Kingsley. ➤➤ **cacophonous** *adj.* [French *cacophonie* via Latin from Greek *kakophōnia*, from *kakos* bad + *phōnē* sound]

cactus /'kaktəs/ *noun* (*pl* **cacti** /'kaktie/ *or* **cactuses**) any of a family of plants that have fleshy stems and scales or spines instead of leaves, often bear brightly coloured flowers, and are found *esp* in deserts and other dry areas: family Cactaceae. [Latin genus name *Cactus* from Greek *kaktos*, a kind of thistle]

cacuminal /kə'kyoohminl/ *adj* said of a speech sound: made with the tip of the tongue curled back against the roof of the mouth; retroflex. [Latin *cacumin-, cacumen* top, point]

CAD /kad/ *abbr* computer-aided design.

cad /kad/ *noun* dated an unscrupulous or dishonourable man: *I tell you, sir, a man who would insult his sister before a stranger is an oaf and a cad* — Christopher Morley. ➤➤ **caddish** *adj.* [English dialect *cad* unskilled assistant, short for CADDIE[1]]

cadastral /kə'dastrəl/ *adj* showing the ownership, boundaries, and value of land and buildings, *esp* for the purposes of taxation: *a cadastral register.* [French *cadastral* from *cadastre* register of property used in assessing taxes, ultimately from late Greek *katastichon* notebook]

cadaver /kə'davə, kə'dahvə, kə'dayvə/ *noun* a corpse, *esp* one intended for dissection. ➤➤ **cadaveric** /kə'davərik/ *adj.* [Latin *cadaver* from *cadere* to fall]

cadaverous /kə'dav(ə)rəs/ *adj* **1** resembling a corpse, *esp* in being unhealthily pale or thin. **2** gaunt or haggard.

CADCAM /'kadkam/ *abbr* computer-aided design and manufacture.

caddie[1] *or* **caddy** /'kadi/ *noun* (*pl* **caddies**) somebody who carries a golfer's clubs and may also give other assistance or advice. [French *cadet*: see CADET]

caddie[2] *or* **caddy** *verb intrans* (**caddies, caddied, caddying**) to act or work as a golfer's caddie.

caddis fly /'kadis/ *noun* any of an order of insects with four membranous wings, long thin antennae with many joints, and aquatic larvae: order Trichoptera.

caddis worm *noun* the aquatic larva of a caddis fly, which protects itself with a case made from silk covered with bits of debris, e.g. grains of sand. [prob alteration of obsolete *codworm*, from *cod* bag (from Old English *codd*) + WORM[1]; from the case in which it lives]

caddy[1] /'kadi/ *noun* (*pl* **caddies**) a small container, *esp* a box or tin used for holding tea. [Malay *kati* a unit of weight]

caddy[2] *noun see* CADDIE[1].

caddy[3] *verb intrans see* CADDIE[2].

-cade *comb. form* forming nouns from nouns, denoting: a procession: *motorcade*. [from CAVALCADE]

cadence /'kayd(ə)ns/ *or* **cadency** /-si/ *noun* (*pl* **cadences** *or* **cadencies**) **1a** the rhythmic flow and intonations of speech. **b** a fall in the pitch of the voice, e.g. at the end of a sentence. **c** the rhythm of poetry or prose. **2** in music, a sequence of chords moving to a harmonic close or point of rest and giving the sense of harmonic completion. **3a** the beat, time, or measure of a rhythmical motion or activity, e.g. rowing or marching. **b** the rhythmic recurrence of a sound. ➤➤ **cadenced** *adj,* **cadential** /kay'densh(ə)l/ *adj.* [Middle English via Old Italian from Latin *cadere* to fall]

cadent /'kayd(ə)nt/ *adj* having a rhythmic fall in pitch or tone. [Latin *cadent-, cadens,* present part. of *cadere* to fall]

cadenza /kə'denzə/ *noun* **1** a technically showy, sometimes improvised, solo passage in a concerto. **2** a flourish or other showy embellishment by a solo singer or instrumentalist, usu just before a cadence, that was popular *esp* in 18th-cent. music.

Editorial note

A cadenza is an extended passage at the final cadence of a concerto movement for a soloist to show off his or her improvising skills; the orchestra stops on an unresolved chord and the performer sets off alone on an often prolonged virtuoso display ending in a trill to summon the orchestra for the final resolution. Cadenzas first featured in 18th-cent. Neapolitan opera arias and string works of Corelli and Vivaldi, whence classical composers adopted the idea. For the 'Emperor' concerto Beethoven wrote the cadenzas as part of the whole and inspired 19th-cent. composers and performers to make the cadenza an opportunity to pre-compose elaborate fantasies based on thematic material from the work — Amanda Holden.

[Italian *cadenza* cadence, cadenza, from Latin *cadere* to fall]

cadet /kə'det/ *noun* **1** somebody training to be an officer in the armed forces or the police force. **2** a young person receiving basic military training, *esp* at school. **3a** a younger brother or son. **b** a younger branch of a family, or a member of that branch. ➤➤ **cadetship** *noun.*

Word history

French *cadet* younger son, from French dialect *capdet*, literally 'little chief', ultimately from Latin *caput* head. It was a common practice before the Revolution for younger sons of the French nobility to join the army without a commission and try to advance themselves by ability and experience. This led to the idea of a trainee or unskilled assistant, and hence to CADDIE[1] and CAD.

cadge /kaj/ *verb informal* to ask for and get (something) by imposing on somebody's hospitality or good nature: *cadge a lift into town; He cadged a fiver from his brother.* ➤➤ **cadger** *noun.* [backformation from Scots *cadger* carrier, huckster, from Middle English *caggen* to tie]

cadi /'kahdi, 'kaydi/ *noun see* QADI.

cadmium /'kadmi-əm/ *noun* a bluish white soft metallic chemical element used *esp* in protective platings and batteries, and in alloys for making tramway wires and electric fuses: symbol Cd, atomic number 48.

Word history

scientific Latin *cadmium*, from Latin *cadmia*: see CALAMINE. Cadmium is so named because it is found with calamine in zinc ore.

cadmium yellow *noun* a vivid yellow colour, or a pigment of this colour containing cadmium sulphide.

cadre /'kahdə/ *noun* **1** a permanent group of trained people forming the nucleus of a military force or other organization, capable of rapid expansion if required. **2a** a group of activists working for the Communist Party or a similar cause. **b** any group of activists. **3** a member of a cadre. [French *cadre* via Italian from Latin *quadrum* square]

caduceus /kə'dyoohsi-əs/ *noun* (*pl* **caducei** /-si-ie/) **1** the symbolic staff of an ancient Greek or Roman herald, with two entwined snakes and two wings at the top, carried by the messenger god Hermes or Mercury. **2** a representation of this staff used as the insignia of the medical profession. ➤➤ **caducean** /-si-ən, -shən/ *adj.* [Latin *caduceus*, ultimately from Greek *karyx, kēryx* herald]

caducity /kə'dyoohsiti/ *noun formal* **1** the quality of being transitory or perishable. **2** senility. [French *caducité* from *caduc* transitory, from Latin *caducus*: see CADUCOUS]

caducous /kə'dyoohkəs/ *adj* said *esp* of a petal or other plant part: falling off easily, often at an early stage. [Latin *caducus* tending to fall, transitory, from *cadere* to fall]

caeca /'seekə/ *noun* pl of CAECUM.

caecilian /see'sili-ən/ *noun* any of numerous species of mainly tropical burrowing amphibian animals that resemble worms: order Gymnophiona. ➤➤ **caecilian** *adj.* [Latin *caecilia* lizard, slowworm, from *caecus* blind]

caecum (*NAmer* **cecum**) /'seekəm/ *noun* (*pl* **caeca**, *NAmer* **ceca** /'seekə/) **1** the pouch in which the large intestine begins and into which the ileum of the small intestine opens from one side. **2** any body part or other structure that ends in a sac or pouch. ➤➤ **caecal** *adj.* [scientific Latin *caecum*, from Latin *intestinum caecum* blind intestine]

caen- *or* **caeno-** *comb. form see* CEN-.

Caerphilly /keə'fili, kah-, kə-/ *noun* a mild white moist cheese. [named after *Caerphilly*, urban district in Wales, where it was orig made]

Caesar /'seezə/ *noun* **1** used as a title for a Roman emperor, *esp* those from Augustus to Hadrian. **2** (*often* **caesar**) any emperor, dictator, or powerful ruler. [family name of Gaius Julius *Caesar* d.44 BC, Roman statesman]

Caesarean[1] *or* **Caesarian** /si'zeəri-ən/ *adj* of or relating to any of the Caesars.

Caesarean[2] (*NAmer* **Cesarean**) *noun* a surgical operation carried out to deliver a baby, involving an incision of the abdominal and uterine walls. [from the belief that Julius Caesar was born in this way]

Caesarean section (*NAmer* **Cesarean section**) *noun* = CAESAREAN[2].

Caesarian /si'zeəri·ən/ *adj* see CAESAREAN[1].

caesious (*NAmer* **cesious**) /'seezi·əs/ *adj* bluish or greyish green. [Latin *caesius* bluish grey]

caesium (*NAmer* **cesium**) /'seezi·əm/ *noun* a silver-white soft metallic chemical element of the alkali metal group that is used in photoelectric cells and atomic clocks: symbol Cs, atomic number 55. [scientific Latin *caesium* from Latin *caesius* bluish grey]

caesium clock *noun* an atomic clock using the vibration of caesium atoms as its standard of time.

caesura /si'zyooərə, si'zhooərə/ *noun* (*pl* **caesuras** *or* **caesurae** /-ree/) **1** a break or pause in a line of verse, usu at or near the middle. **2** in classical Greek or Latin verse, a break within a metrical FOOT[1] (unit comprising fixed combination of syllables) caused by the ending of a word. >> **caesural** *adj.* [late Latin *caesura*, ultimately from Latin *caedere* to cut]

café /'kafay/ *noun* **1** *chiefly Brit* a small restaurant serving light meals and usu non-alcoholic drinks. **2** *NAmer* a bar or nightclub. [French *café* coffee, café, from Turkish *kahve*: see COFFEE]

café au lait /,kafay oh 'lay (*French* kafɛ o lɛ)/ *noun* **1** coffee with milk. **2** the light brown colour of coffee with milk. [French *café au lait*]

café noir /,kafay 'nwah (*French* kafe nwar)/ *noun* coffee without milk; black coffee. [French *café noir*]

cafeteria /kafə'tiəri·ə/ *noun* a restaurant in which the customers serve themselves or are served at a counter and take the food to tables to eat. [American Spanish *cafetería* retail coffee store, from Spanish *café* coffee]

cafetière /kaf'tyeə/ *noun* a coffee pot with a plunger inside that is used to push the grounds to the bottom of the pot before the coffee is poured. [French *cafetière*]

caff /kaf/ *noun Brit, informal* a café, *esp* one serving cheap plain food in simple surroundings. [by shortening and alteration]

caffeine /'kafeen/ *noun* a chemical compound that occurs naturally in tea and coffee and acts as a stimulant and DIURETIC[2] (substance that increases the production of urine). [German *kaffein* from *kaffee* coffee, via French *café* from Turkish *kahve*: see COFFEE]

caffè latte /,kafay 'latay/ *noun* a drink made by adding a little espresso coffee to frothy steamed milk. [Italian *caffè latte* milk coffee]

caftan /'kaftan/ *noun* see KAFTAN.

cage[1] /kayj/ *noun* **1** a box or enclosure of open construction, usu with bars or netting, for confining or carrying animals. **2** something resembling a cage in form or purpose, *esp* the moving enclosed platform of a lift. **3** a framework serving as a support: *the steel cage of a skyscraper.* **4** a barred cell or fenced area for confining prisoners. [Middle English via Old French from Latin *cavea* cavity, cage, from *cavus* hollow]

cage[2] *verb trans* **1** to put or keep (e.g. an animal) in a cage. **2** to confine (somebody) as if in a cage.

cage bird *noun* a bird that is kept in a cage, or a bird of a kind that people keep in cages.

cagey *or* **cagy** /'kayji/ *adj* (**cagier, cagiest**) *informal* **1** hesitant about committing oneself, communicating one's intentions, etc. **2** wary of being trapped or deceived. >> **cageyness** *noun*, **cagily** *adv*, **caginess** *noun.* [origin unknown]

cagoule *or* **kagoul** /kə'goohl/ *noun* a lightweight waterproof jacket with a hood, *esp* one that is pulled over the head rather than fastened with a zip. [French *cagoule* hood, cowl, from late Latin *cuculla* monk's cowl]

cagy /'kayji/ *adj* see CAGEY.

cahoots /kə'hoohts/ * **in cahoots** *informal* (*often* + with) working together secretly, *esp* with some dishonest or evil intention: *This particular supermarket assistant, in cahoots with a customer, wrapped the goods and deliberately understated the price.* [perhaps from French *cahute* cabin, hut]

CAI *abbr* **1** computer-aided instruction. **2** computer-assisted instruction.

caiman /'kaymən/ *noun* see CAYMAN.

cain- *comb. form* see CEN-.

-caine *comb. form* forming nouns, denoting: a synthetic anaesthetic resembling cocaine: *lignocaine.* [German *-kain*, from *Kokain* cocaine]

caino- *comb. form* see CEN-.

Cainozoic /kaynə'zoh·ik/ *adj and noun* see CENOZOIC.

caïque /kie'eek/ *noun* **1** any of various small sailing vessels used in the E Mediterranean. **2** a light rowing boat used on the Bosphorus. [Turkish *kayik*]

Cairene /'kie(ə)reen/ *noun* a native or inhabitant of Cairo, capital city of Egypt. >> **Cairene** *adj.*

cairn /keən/ *noun* **1** a pile of stones built as a memorial or landmark, e.g. at the top of a mountain. **2** = CAIRN TERRIER. [Middle English *carne* from Scottish Gaelic *càrn*]

cairngorm /'keəngawm/ *noun* a yellow or smoky-brown quartz used as a gemstone. [named after *Cairngorm*, mountain in Scotland, where it is found]

cairn terrier *noun* a terrier of a breed originating in Scotland, having a small compact body and coarse hair. Also called CAIRN. [from its use in hunting among cairns]

caisson /'kays(ə)n, kə'soohn/ *noun* **1** a chest or wagon for carrying ammunition, *esp* for use by large guns and cannons. **2a** a watertight chamber, usu with a supply of compressed air, used to house people doing construction work under water. **b** a float for raising a sunken vessel. **c** a watertight structure used to keep water in or out of a dock, harbour, etc. [French *caisson*, augmentative of *caisse* box, via Old Provençal from Latin *capsa*: see CASE[2]]

caisson disease *noun* = DECOMPRESSION SICKNESS.

caitiff /'kaytif/ *noun archaic or literary* a base, cowardly, or despicable person. [Middle English *caitif* prisoner, wretched person, via French from Latin *captivus* CAPTIVE[1]]

cajole /kə'johl/ *verb trans* to persuade (somebody) with flattery or deception, *esp* in the face of reluctance to do something; to coax (them): *Why must they [women] be cajoled into virtue by artful flattery and sexual compliments?* — Mary Wollstonecraft. >> **cajolement** *noun*, **cajoler** *noun*, **cajolery** /-ləri/ *noun.* [French *cajoler* to chatter like a jay in a cage, cajole, ultimately from Latin *cavea*: see CAGE[1]]

Cajun[1] /'kayjən/ *noun* **1** a descendant of the French Canadians who settled in Louisiana in the 18th cent. **2** (*also* **cajun**) the syncopated folk music of the Cajuns, often with French vocals and steel guitar, fiddle, and accordion accompaniment. [alteration of ACADIAN]

Cajun[2] *adj* of or relating to the Cajuns or their culture, *esp* their music or their style of cookery.

cake[1] /kayk/ *noun* **1** any of various sweet foods made from a basic mixture of flour and sugar, usu with fat, eggs, and a raising agent, and typically baked in a round, square, or oblong mould. **2** (*usu in combination*) a flattened usu round mass of fried or baked savoury food: *a fishcake.* **3** (*usu in combination*) a breadlike food made from an unleavened dough and usu baked or fried in small flat shapes: *an oatcake.* **4** a block or crust of something solid, *esp* compacted or congealed matter: *a cake of ice.* * **go/sell like hot cakes** to sell extremely quickly; to be very popular. [Middle English from Old Norse *kaka*]

cake[2] *verb trans* to cover (something) with a layer of something solid or semi-solid; to encrust (it): *shoes caked with mud.* >> *verb intrans* to form or harden into a mass.

cakewalk *noun* **1** a dance characterized by stylish walking steps and figures and typically involving high strutting movements, or the marching music to which such a dance is traditionally performed. **2** *informal* an easy task. >> **cakewalker** *noun.* [from the former practice of giving a cake as a prize to the most accomplished dancer]

CAL /kal/ *abbr* **1** computer-aided learning. **2** computer-assisted learning.

Cal. *abbr* **1** California. **2** large calorie.

cal. *abbr* **1** calibre. **2** small calorie.

Calabar bean /'kaləbah/ *noun* the dark brown poisonous seed of a tropical African climbing plant of the pea family, used as a source of the drug physostigmine. [named after *Calabar*, city and port in Nigeria, from which it was exported]

calabash /'kaləbash/ *noun* **1a** the large hard-skinned flask-shaped fruit of a tropical American tree. **b** the tropical American tree that bears this fruit: *Crescentia cujete*. **2** something made from the hollowed-out and dried skin of the calabash fruit, e.g. a water container or a tobacco pipe. [French *calebasse* gourd, from Spanish *calabaza*, prob from Arabic *qar'ah yābisah* dry gourd]

calaboose /'kaləboohs, -'boohs/ *noun* NAmer, informal a jail, *esp* a local jail. [Spanish *calabozo* dungeon]

calabrese /kalə'brayzi, -'breezi/ *noun* a type of sprouting broccoli. [Italian *calabrese* Calabrian, from *Calabria*, region of Italy]

calamander /kalə'mandə/ *noun* the hard hazel-brown black-striped wood of an E Indian tree of the ebony family, used for furniture. [prob from Dutch *kalamanderhout* calamander wood]

calamari /kalə'mahri/ *pl noun* squid, *esp* served as food. [via Italian from Latin *calamarius* of a pen, from *calamus* reed; from the shape of the squid's inner shell]

calamine /'kaləmien/ *noun* a pink powder of zinc oxide or carbonate with a small amount of ferric oxide, used in soothing or cooling lotions. [French *calamine* zinc ore, via medieval Latin from Latin *cadmia* Theban (earth), ultimately named after *Cadmus*, legendary founder of Thebes, ancient city of Greece, near to which the ore was first found]

calamint /'kaləmint/ *noun* a plant of the mint family with aromatic purple or pink flowers: genus *Calamintha*. [Middle English *calament* via Old French and medieval Latin from Greek *kalaminthē*]

calamity /kə'lamiti/ *noun* (*pl* **calamities**) **1** an extremely grave event; a disaster: *Calamities are of two kinds: misfortune to ourselves, and good fortune to others* — Ambrose Bierce. **2** a state of deep distress caused by misfortune or loss. >> **calamitous** *adj*, **calamitously** *adv*, **calamitousness** *noun*. [French *calamité* from Latin *calamitat-, calamitas*]

calamus /'kaləməs/ *noun* (*pl* **calami** /-mie/) **1a** = SWEET FLAG. **b** the aromatic root of the sweet flag, or a preparation made from this. **2** the central shaft of a feather; a quill. [Latin *calamus* reed, reed pen, from Greek *kalamos*]

calando /kə'landoh/ *adj and adv* said of a piece of music: to be performed with gradually increasing speed and volume. [Italian *calando* dropping, from *calare* to lower, drop]

calandria /kə'landri·ə/ *noun* a closed vessel through which a set of pipes pass, used as a HEAT EXCHANGER (device transferring heat), e.g. in a nuclear reactor. [Spanish *calandria*, literally 'lark']

calash /kə'lash/ *or* **calèche** /-'lesh/ *noun* **1** a light horse-drawn carriage with a folding top and small wheels. **2** a hood on a framework worn by women over high elaborate wigs in the 18th cent. [French *calèche* from German *Kalesche* from Czech *kolesa* wheels, carriage]

calc- *or* **calci-** *comb. form* forming words, denoting: lime, calcium, or calcium compounds: *calcify*; *calcifuge*. [Latin *calc-, calx*: see CHALK[1]]

calcaneus /kal'kayni·əs/ *or* **calcaneum** /-ni·əm/ *noun* (*pl* **calcanei** /-ni·ie/ *or* **calcanea** /-ni·ə/) the bone that forms the heel. [late Latin *calcaneus*, alteration of Latin *calcaneum*, from *calc-, calx* heel]

calcareous /kal'keəri·əs/ *adj* **1** resembling, containing, or consisting of calcium compounds, *esp* calcium carbonate. **2** growing on limestone or in soil with a high lime or chalk content. >> **calcareously** *adv*, **calcareousness** *noun*. [Latin *calcarius* of lime, from *calc-, calx*: see CHALK[1]]

calceolaria /,kalsi·ə'leəri·ə/ *noun* a tropical American plant of the foxglove family with brightly coloured pouch-shaped flowers: genus *Calceolaria*. [from the Latin genus name, from *calceolus* small shoe, dimin. of *calceus* shoe, from *calc-, calx* heel]

calces /'kalseez/ *noun* pl of CALX.

calci- *comb. form* see CALC-.

calcicole /'kalsikohl/ *noun* a plant that usually grows on soils containing lime or other calcium compounds: compare CALCIFUGE. >> **calcicolous** /kal'sikələs/ *adj*. [French *calcicole* calcicolous, from CALCI- + Latin *colere* to inhabit]

calciferol /kal'sifərol/ *noun* a synthetic vitamin D used to treat rickets and as a rat poison; vitamin D$_2$. [blend of CALCIFEROUS and ERGOSTEROL]

calciferous /kal'sif(ə)rəs/ *adj* producing or containing calcium carbonate.

calcifuge /'kalsifyoohj/ *noun* a plant that does not normally grow on soils containing lime or other calcium compounds: compare CALCICOLE. >> **calcifugous** /kal'sifəgəs/ *adj*. [French *calcifuge* calcifugous, from CALCI- + Latin *fugere* to flee]

calcify /'kalsifie/ *verb* (**calcifies, calcified, calcifying**) >> *verb trans* **1** to harden (something, e.g. body tissue) by the deposition of calcium carbonate or other calcium compounds. **2** to convert (something) into a solid compound of calcium. >> *verb intrans* to become calcified. >> **calcific** /kal'sifik/ *adj*, **calcification** /-fi'kaysh(ə)n/ *noun*.

calcine /'kalsin, 'kalsien/ *verb trans* to heat (*esp* a metal ore or other inorganic material) to a high temperature, usu in order to cause it to lose water, combine with oxygen, or turn to powder. >> *verb intrans* to be calcined. >> **calcination** /kalsi'naysh(ə)n/ *noun*. [Middle English *calcenen* via French from Latin *calc-, calx*: see CHALK[1]]

calcite /'kalsiet/ *noun* calcium carbonate in the form of limestone, chalk, marble, etc. >> **calcitic** /kal'sitik/ *adj*.

calcitonin /kalsi'tohnin/ *noun* a hormone produced by the thyroid gland that acts to reduce the amount of calcium present in the blood by lowering the rate at which it leaves the bones. [CALCI- + TONIC[2] + -IN[1]]

calcium /'kalsi·əm/ *noun* a silver-white metallic chemical element of the alkaline-earth group found in nature only in combination: symbol Ca, atomic number 20. [scientific Latin *calcium*, from Latin *calc-, calx*: see CHALK[1]]

calcium carbide *noun* a usu dark grey solid chemical compound that produces acetylene when mixed with water and is used *esp* in acetylene lamps: formula CaC_2.

calcium carbonate *noun* a chemical compound that occurs naturally in bones and shells and as chalk, marble, limestone, etc, and is used industrially in cement, fertilizers, and animal feed: formula $CaCO_3$.

calcium chloride *noun* a white chemical compound used in its ANHYDROUS (water-free) state as a drying agent and in a hydrated (chemically combined with water; see HYDRATE[2]) state for melting ice on roads: formula $CaCl_2$.

calcium hydroxide *noun* a white chemical compound used to make plaster and cement; slaked lime: formula $Ca(OH)_2$.

calcium oxide *noun* a white chemical compound used in the manufacture of steel and glass; quicklime: formula CaO.

calcium phosphate *noun* any of various chemical compounds that occur naturally in certain rocks, teeth, and bones and are used in fertilizers and animal feeds.

calculable /'kalkyooləbl/ *adj* able to be calculated or estimated. >> **calculability** /-'bilati/ *noun*, **calculably** *adv*.

calculate /'kalkyoolayt/ *verb trans* **1** to determine (something) by mathematical processes. **2** to reckon (something) by exercise of practical judgment; to estimate (it). >> *verb intrans* **1** to make a calculation. **2** (+ on) to count or rely on (doing something): *They had calculated on selling the house first*. >> **calculative** /-lətiv/ *adj*. [Latin *calculatus*, past part. of *calculare*, from *calculus* pebble (used in reckoning)]

calculated *adj* **1a** worked out by mathematical calculation. **b** undertaken after reckoning or estimating the probability of success: *a calculated risk*. **2a** (*often* + to) shrewdly planned or contrived to accomplish a purpose: *a look calculated to enrage his opponent*. **b** intentional; deliberate: *a calculated insult*. >> **calculatedly** *adv*.

calculating *adj* **1** used for making calculations: *a calculating machine*. **2** marked by shrewd consideration of one's own interests; scheming: *In the present play [King Lear], that which aggravates the sympathy of the reader ... is the cold, calculating, obdurate selfishness of his daughters* — Hazlitt. >> **calculatingly** *adv*.

calculation /kalkyoo'laysh(ə)n/ *noun* **1** the process or result of calculating something. **2** an act of calculating something. **3** studied care in planning, *esp* to promote one's own interests.

calculator *noun* **1** a machine for performing mathematical operations, *esp* a small hand-held electronic device. **2** a set or book of tables used in calculating.

calculi /'kalkyoolie/ *noun* pl of CALCULUS.

calculous /'kalkyooləs/ *adj* in medicine, caused or characterized by a stony calculus or several calculi.

calculus /'kalkyooləs/ *noun* **1** (*pl* **calculi**). **a** a hard stony mass, e.g. of cholesterol, that forms abnormally in the kidney, gall bladder, or other hollow organ or tube, may cause a painful blockage, and often requires removal by a surgical operation. **b** tartar that accumulates on the teeth. **2** (*pl* **calculuses**). **a** a branch of mathematics, comprising differential and integral calculus, that deals with rates of change of functions and the ideas of limits and has applications to the calculation of arcs, areas, volumes, etc. **b** any system of calculation that uses a special symbolic notation. [Latin *calculus* pebble, stone in the bladder or kidney, stone used in reckoning]

caldera /kal'deərə/ *noun* a wide volcanic crater formed by violent eruption followed by subsidence of the central part of the volcano. [Spanish *caldera* cauldron, from late Latin *caldaria*]

caldron /'kawldrən/ *noun* see CAULDRON.

calèche /kə'lesh/ *noun* see CALASH.

Caledonian[1] /kalə'dohni·ən/ *adj* relating to Scotland, *esp* to the Scottish Highlands or ancient Scotland. [*Caledonia* Latin name of part of N Britain, later applied to Scotland]

Caledonian[2] *noun literary or humorous* a native or inhabitant of Scotland.

calefacient[1] /kali'fayshənt/ *adj* having a warming effect. [Latin *calefacient-*, *calefaciens*, present part. of *calefacere*: see CHAFE[1]]

calefacient[2] *noun* any medicinal preparation that has a warming effect, e.g. a mustard plaster.

calendar[1] /'kaləndə/ *noun* **1** a system for fixing the beginning, length, and divisions of the year and arranging days and longer divisions of time, e.g. weeks and months, in a definite order. **2** a table or set of tables displaying the days of one year. **3** a chronological list of events or activities: *a major event in the sporting calendar*. [Middle English *calender* via Anglo-French or medieval Latin from Latin *kalendarium* moneylender's account book, from *kalendae* CALENDS, the day of the month on which accounts were traditionally settled]

calendar[2] *verb trans* (**calendared, calendaring**) to enter (something) in a calendar.

calendar month *noun* = MONTH (1A).

calendar year *noun* = YEAR (2A).

calender[1] /'kaləndə/ *noun* a machine for pressing cloth, rubber, paper, etc between rollers or plates, e.g. to produce a smooth or glossy surface. [French *calandre*, modification of Greek *kylindros*: see CYLINDER]

calender[2] *verb trans* (**calendered, calendering**) to press (e.g. cloth, rubber, or paper) in a calender.

calends *or* **kalends** /'kalindz/ *pl noun* (*treated as sing. or pl*) the first day of each month in the ancient Roman calendar: compare IDES, NONES. [Middle English *kalendes* from Latin *kalendae*, *calendae*]

calendula /kə'lendyoolə/ *noun* **1** any of a genus of plants of the daisy family with orange or yellow flowers, e.g. the pot marigold: genus *Calendula*. **2** the essential oil obtained from a calendula.

Word history ──────────
from the Latin genus name, via medieval Latin from Latin *calendae* CALENDS. Probably so called because the marigold flowers for most of the year, and can usually be seen each calends.

calf[1] /kahf/ *noun* (*pl* **calves** /kahvz/ *or* **calfs**) **1a** the young of the domestic cow or any other bovine mammal, e.g. the bison. **b** the young of some other large animals, e.g. the elephant or whale. **2** = CALFSKIN. **3** a mass of floating ice detached from an iceberg, a glacier that runs into the sea, etc. ✳ **in calf** said of a cow: pregnant. ➤➤ **calflike** *adj*. [Old English *cealf*]

calf[2] *noun* (*pl* **calves**) the fleshy back part of the leg below the knee. [Middle English from Old Norse *kālfi*]

calf love *noun* = PUPPY LOVE.

calfskin *noun* a high-quality leather made from the skin of a calf.

caliber /'kalibə/ *noun NAmer* see CALIBRE.

calibrate /'kalibrayt/ *verb trans* **1** to determine the correct reading of (an arbitrary or inaccurate scale or instrument) by comparison with a standard. **2** to determine, adjust, or mark the graduations of (e.g. a thermometer). **3** to measure the diameter of (e.g. a gun barrel). ➤➤ **calibration** /-braysh(ə)n/ *noun*, **calibrator** *noun*.

calibre (*NAmer* **caliber**) /'kalibə/ *noun* **1** the internal diameter of a hollow cylinder, *esp* a gun barrel. **2** the external diameter of a round or cylindrical object, *esp* a bullet, shell, or other projectile. **3a** degree of mental capacity or moral quality. **b** degree of excellence or importance. [French *calibre* via Old Italian from Arabic *qālib* mould, shoemaker's last]

calices /'kaliseez, 'kay-/ *noun* pl of CALIX.

caliche /kə'leechi/ *noun* a sodium-rich gravel or crumbly rock found in Chile and Peru and used as a source of nitrogen compounds, e.g. fertilizers. [American Spanish *caliche* via Spanish from Latin *calc-*, *calx*: see CHALK[1]]

calico /'kalikoh/ *noun* (*pl* **calicoes** *or* **calicos**) **1** white or unbleached cotton cloth of medium weight, orig imported from India. **2** *NAmer* any brightly printed cotton fabric. [named after *Calicut*, city in India, where it originated]

calico bush *noun* = MOUNTAIN LAUREL.

calico printing *noun* a process of making coloured designs on cotton fabrics, e.g. calico.

Calif. *abbr* California.

calif /'kaylif, 'kalif/ *noun* see CALIPH.

califate /'kaylifayt, 'kal-/ *noun* see CALIPHATE.

Californian /kali'fawni·ən/ *noun* a native or inhabitant of the US state of California. ➤➤➤ **Californian** *adj*.

California poppy /kali'fawni·ə/ *noun* a N American plant of the poppy family with bright yellow or orange flowers: *Eschscholtzia californica*.

californium /kali'fawni·əm/ *noun* a radioactive metallic chemical element that is artificially produced by bombarding curium 244 and americium 243 with neutrons: symbol Cf, atomic number 98. [scientific Latin *californium*, named after *California*, state of USA, where it was first made]

calipash /'kalipash/ *noun* a fatty gelatinous edible substance of a dull greenish colour found next to the upper shell of a turtle. [perhaps native name in West Indies]

calipee /'kalipee/ *noun* a fatty gelatinous edible substance of a light yellow colour found next to the lower shell of a turtle. [perhaps native name in West Indies]

caliper[1] /'kalipə/ *noun NAmer* see CALLIPER[1].

caliper[2] *verb trans NAmer* see CALLIPER[2].

caliph *or* **calif** /'kalif, 'kaylif/ *noun* in former times, a secular and spiritual head of Islam claiming descent from Muhammad. ➤➤ **caliphal** *adj*. [Middle English *caliphe* via French from Arabic *khalīfah* successor]

caliphate *or* **califate** /'kalifayt, -fət, 'kay-/ *noun* the position of caliph or the area ruled by a caliph.

calisthenics /kalis'theniks/ *pl noun NAmer* see CALLISTHENICS.

calix /'kaliks, 'kayliks/ *noun* (*pl* **calices** /'kaliseez, 'kay-/) a cup, *esp* one used in church; a chalice. [Latin *calic-*, *calix*]

calk /kawk/ *verb trans* see CAULK.

call[1] /kawl/ *verb intrans* **1a** to speak loudly or distinctly. **b** to cry out to attract attention or make somebody come. **c** said of a bird or animal: to utter its characteristic note or cry. **2a** (*often* + in/by/round) to make a brief visit: *I'll call by later*. **b** (+ at) said e.g. of a train: to stop at (a specified place along a route). **3** (*often* + up) to telephone. **4** to make a demand in card games, e.g. to see a player's hand. **5** to predict the result of tossing a coin. ➤ *verb trans* **1a** (*often* + out) to utter or announce (something) in a loud distinct voice. **b** (*often* + out) to read (something, e.g. a list of names) aloud. **2a** to command or request (somebody) to come or be present, especially in an official context such as a witness in a lawcourt. **b** to invite or command people to come together at (e.g. a meeting); to convoke (a meeting). **c** to rouse (somebody) from sleep. **d** to attract (e.g. game) by imitating a characteristic cry. **3** to give the order for (something) or bring it into action: *The unions have called a strike*. **4a** to apply a particular name or description to (somebody or something): *We call her Kitty; I call that generous*. **b** to consider (something) from an estimate or for convenience: *Let's call it a round £100*. **5** (*often* + up) to communicate or attempt to communicate with (somebody) by telephone or radio. **6a** to rule on the status of (e.g. a tennis serve): *The serve was called out*. **b** said of a cricket umpire: to judge the delivery of (a bowler) to be illegal. **7** to call out the instructions for (a dance). **8a** to make a demand in bridge for (a card or suit). **b** to require (a player) to show their hand in poker by making an equal bet. **9** to predict or guess the outcome of (something): *The election is too close to call*. ✳ **call for 1** to visit or stop at a place in order to take (something or somebody) away; to collect. **2** to require (something) as necessary or appropriate: *The task called for all her strength*. **3** to demand or order (something): *legislation calling for the establishment of new schools*. **call in/into question** to cast doubt on (something): *evidence that called into question the validity of his statement*. **call on/upon** to require or oblige (somebody) to do something: *You may be called on to attend*. **call the shots/the tune** to be in charge or in control, e.g. determining policy or procedure. **call to account 1** to hold (somebody) responsible. **2** to reprimand (somebody). **3** to demand an explanation from (somebody). **call to mind** to remember (something). **call to order** to order (a meeting) to observe the customary rules. ➤➤ **callable** *adj.* [Middle English *callen*, prob from Old Norse *kalla*]

call² *noun* **1a** an act of calling with the voice. **b** the cry of a bird or animal, or an imitation of this. **2a** a request or command to come or assemble. **b** a summons or signal on a drum, bugle, or pipe. **3a** a demand or request. **b** need or justification: *There was no call for such rudeness.* **4a** a strong inner prompting to a course of action, e.g. a divine vocation; a calling. **b** the attraction or appeal of a particular activity or place: *the call of the wild.* **c** admission to the bar as a barrister. **5** a short usu formal visit. **6** an act of telephoning somebody. **7** a usu vocal ruling made by an official of a sports contest. **8** the act of calling in a card game. ✳ **on call 1** ready to be used or summoned when needed. **2** said of a loan: to be repaid on demand. **within call** within hearing or reach of a call or summons.

calla /'kalə/ *noun* **1** a poisonous European plant of the arum family with heart-shaped leaves that grows in wet places: *Calla palustris.* **2** an African plant of the arum family with brightly coloured or brilliant white flowers: genus *Zantedeschia.* [from the Latin genus name, modification of Greek *kallaia* cock's wattles]

calla lily *noun* = CALLA.

Callanetics /kalə'netiks/ *pl noun trademark* (*treated as sing. or pl*) a system of exercises involving small precise movements designed to trim and strengthen the body by developing deep muscles. [from the name of its inventor *Callan* Pinckney b.1939, US fitness teacher + *-etics* as in ATHLETICS]

call box *noun Brit* a public telephone box.

callboy *noun* a person who tells actors when it is time to go on stage.

call centre *noun* an office or department handling telephone calls received *esp* from customers of a company or other organization.

call down *verb trans* to invoke (somebody or something) or cause them to appear.

caller *noun* **1** somebody who makes a telephone call or pays a visit. **2** *Aus* somebody who gives a running commentary at a race meeting.

call girl *noun* a prostitute who accepts appointments by telephone: compare STREETWALKER.

calligraphy /kə'ligrəfi/ *noun* the art of producing beautiful or elegant handwriting, or the handwriting itself. ➤➤ **calligrapher** *noun,* **calligraphic** /kali'grafik/ *adj,* **calligraphist** *noun.* [French *calligraphie* from Greek *kalligraphia,* from *kallos* beauty + *-graphia* -GRAPHY]

call in *verb trans* **1** to summon (somebody) to consult them or seek their help. **2a** to demand repayment of (a loan). **b** to withdraw (currency) from circulation.

calling /'kawling/ *noun* **1** a strong inner impulse towards a particular course of action, *esp* when accompanied by conviction of divine influence. **2** any profession or occupation, *esp* one demanding dedication.

calling card *noun* **1** a small printed card bearing a person's name and other details, presented by way of personal introduction; a visiting card. **2** *informal* anything that serves as evidence that somebody or something has been somewhere: *Some dog has left its calling card on my front step.*

calliope /kə'lie-əpi/ *noun NAmer* a keyboard musical instrument resembling an organ and consisting of a series of whistles sounded by steam or compressed air. [named after *Calliope,* the Muse of epic poetry in Greek mythology]

calliper¹ (*NAmer* **caliper**) /'kalipə/ *noun* **1** (*usu in pl*) a measuring instrument with two hinged arms that can be adjusted to determine thickness, diameter, or distance between surfaces: *a pair of callipers.* **2** a support for the human leg extending from the knee or thigh to the foot. [alteration of CALIBRE]

calliper² (*NAmer* **caliper**) *verb trans* (**callipered, callipering,** *NAmer* **calipered, calipering**) to measure (something) with callipers.

callipygian /kali'piji-ən/ *adj literary* having well-shaped attractive buttocks. [Greek *kallipygos,* from *kalli-* beautiful + *pygē* buttocks]

callistemon /kali'steemən, kə'listəmən/ *noun* = BOTTLEBRUSH (2). [from the Latin genus name, from Greek *kallos* beauty + *stēmōn* thread, stamen]

callisthenics (*NAmer* **calisthenics**) /kalis'theniks/ *pl noun* (*treated as sing. or pl*) the art or practice of performing systematic rhythmic bodily exercises, usu without apparatus, or the exercises themselves. ➤➤ **callisthenic** *adj.* [Greek *kallos* beauty + *sthenos* strength]

call loan *noun* money lent that is liable to be repaid whenever the lender wishes.

call money *noun* = CALL LOAN.

call off *verb trans* **1** to cancel (a plan or arrangement). **2** to give a command to (an animal) to leave somebody alone.

call of nature *noun euphem* the urge to urinate or defecate.

call option *noun* an option to buy a specified amount of a share issue, security, commodity, etc at a fixed agreed price at or within an agreed time: compare PUT OPTION.

callose /'kalohs/ *noun* a carbohydrate that is a component of plant cell walls. [Latin *callosus:* see CALLOUS]

callosity /kə'lositi/ *noun* (*pl* **callosities**) *technical* an area of marked or abnormal hardness and thickness on skin, bark, etc.

callous /'kaləs/ *adj* **1** feeling no sympathy for others; cruelly unsympathetic. **2** said *esp* of skin or bark: hardened and thickened. ➤➤ **callously** *adv,* **callousness** *noun.* [French *calleux* from Latin *callosus,* from *callum, callus* callous skin]

call out *verb trans* **1** to summon (people) to action. **2** to instruct (workers) to strike.

call-out *noun* an occasion on which somebody is summoned, e.g. to give medical treatment or to carry out emergency repairs.

callow /'kaloh/ *adj* **1** lacking adult attitudes; immature: *a callow youth.* **2** said of a bird: not yet fully fledged. ➤➤ **callowness** *noun.* [Old English *calu* bald]

call sign *noun* the combination of letters and numbers assigned to a radio operator or station for identification.

call up *verb trans* **1** to summon (somebody), *esp* for military service or some other duty. **2** to bring (something) to mind.

call-up *noun* an order to report for military service.

callus /'kaləs/ *noun* (*pl* **calluses**) **1** a hard thickened area on skin or bark. **2** a mass of connective tissue that forms round a break in a bone and changes into bone as the break heals. **3** soft tissue that forms over a wounded or cut plant surface. **4** a tumour of plant tissue. [Latin *callus* callous skin]

calm¹ /kahm; *NAmer* kah(l)m/ *adj* **1** free from anger, nervousness, excitement, etc. **2** marked by the absence of wind or rough water; still: *a calm sea.* ➤➤ **calmly** *adv,* **calmness** *noun.* [Middle English *calme* via French, Old Italian, and late Latin from Greek *kauma* heat of the day, from *kaiein* to burn]

calm² *noun* **1** an emotional state free from anger, nervousness, excitement, etc. **2** the absence of wind or rough water; stillness.

calm³ *verb trans* (*often* + down) to make (somebody or something) calm. ➤ *verb intrans* (*often* + down) to become calm.

calmative /'kahmətiv; *NAmer* 'kah(l)mətiv/ *adj* said of a drug: having a calming effect; sedative. ➤➤ **calmative** *noun.* [CALM³ + *-ative* as in SEDATIVE¹]

calomel /'kaləmel, -məl/ *noun* a white tasteless powder consisting largely of mercurous chloride, used medicinally, e.g. as a purgative. [scientific Latin *calomelas,* from Greek *kalos* beautiful + *melas* black; probably so called because it was orig obtained from a black compound of mercury]

Calor gas /'kalə/ *noun trademark* butane gas in liquid form that is contained in portable cylinders and used as a fuel, e.g. for domestic heating. [Latin *calor* heat]

caloric¹ /kə'lorik/ *noun* a hypothetical weightless fluid formerly held to be responsible for the phenomena of heat and combustion. [French *calorique,* from Latin *calor:* see CALORIE]

caloric² *adj* of heat or calories. ➤➤ **calorically** *adv.*

calorie *or* **calory** /'kaləri/ *noun* (*pl* **calories**) **1a** the quantity of heat required to raise the temperature of 1g of water by 1°C under standard conditions, equal to 4.1868 joules. Also called SMALL CALORIE. **b** the amount of heat required to raise the temperature of 1kg of water by 1°C under standard conditions. Also called KILOCALORIE, LARGE CALORIE. **2a** a unit equivalent to the kilocalorie expressing the energy-producing value of food when used in the body. **b** an amount of food that has an energy-producing value of one kilo-calorie. [French *calorie* from Latin *calor* heat, from *calēre* to be warm]

calorific /kalə'rifik/ *adj* **1** of heat production. **2** relating to the energy-producing content of food, fuel, etc. [French *calorifique* from Latin *calorificus*, from *calor*: see CALORIE]

calorific value *noun* the quantity of heat or energy, usu expressed in joules per kilogram, produced by burning a specified amount of fuel or food.

calorimeter /kalə'rimitə/ *noun* any of several devices for measuring heat taken up or given out, e.g. during a chemical reaction. ⏩ **calorimetric** /-'metrik/ *adj*, **calorimetry** /-tri/ *noun*. [Latin *calor* (see CALORIE) + -METER[2]]

calory /'kaləri/ *noun* see CALORIE.

calque /kalk/ *noun* = LOAN TRANSLATION. [French *calque* copy, from *calquer* to trace, via Italian from Latin *calcare* to trample]

caltrop *or* **caltrap** /'kaltrəp/ *noun* **1** = WATER CHESTNUT (2). **2** a device with four metal points arranged so that one always projects upwards, used to hinder enemy horses, vehicles, etc. [Old English *calcatrippe* a plant that catches the feet, from medieval Latin *calcatrippa* from *calc-*, *calx* heel]

calumet /'kalyoomet/ *noun* a long highly ornamented pipe smoked by Native Americans, *esp* on ceremonial occasions in token of peace. [American French *calumet* via French and Latin from Greek *kalamos* reed]

calumniate /kə'lumniayt/ *verb trans formal* to maliciously make false statements about (somebody); to slander (them). ⏩ **calumniation** /-'aysh(ə)n/ *noun*, **calumniator** *noun*.

calumny /'kaləmni/ *noun* (*pl* **calumnies**) **1** a false charge or misrepresentation maliciously calculated to damage another person's reputation. **2** the making of such a false charge or misrepresentation. ⏩ **calumnious** /kə'lumni-əs/ *adj*. [early French *calomnie* from Latin *calumnia*, from *calvi* to deceive]

Calvados /'kalvədos/ *noun* apple brandy made in the Calvados department of Normandy.

calvary /'kalvəri/ *noun* (*pl* **calvaries**) **1** a sculpture of the crucifixion of Christ. **2** an experience of intense mental suffering. [named after *Calvary*, the hill near Jerusalem where Christ was crucified]

calve /kahv/ *verb trans and intrans* **1** said of a cow, whale, etc: to give birth to (a calf). **2** said of an iceberg, glacier, etc: to release (a floating mass of ice). [Old English *cealfian*, from *cealf* CALF[1]]

calves[1] /'kahvz/ *noun* pl of CALF[1].

calves[2] *noun* pl of CALF[2].

Calvin cycle *noun* in photosynthesis, a series of reactions in which carbon dioxide is converted to glucose. [named after Melvin *Calvin* d.1997, US biochemist]

Calvinism /'kalviniz(ə)m/ *noun* the Christian doctrines of John Calvin and his followers, marked by emphasis on the sovereignty of God and *esp* by the doctrine of predestination. ⏩ **Calvinist** *noun and adj*, **Calvinistic** /-'nistik/ *adj*, **Calvinistical** /-'nistikl/ *adj*. [named after John *Calvin* d.1564, French theologian]

calx /kalks/ *noun* (*pl* **calxes** *or* **calces** /'kalseez/) the crumbly residue left when a metal or mineral has been subjected to intense heat. [Middle English *cals*, from Latin *calx*: see CHALK[1]]

calyces /'kaliseez, 'kay-/ *noun* pl of CALYX.

calypso /kə'lipsoh/ *noun* (*pl* **calypsos**) **1** a style of West Indian music in which improvised lyrics, usu satirizing current events, are sung to music with a syncopated rhythm. **2** a song in this style. ⏩ **calypsonian** /-'sohni-ən, kalip-/ *noun and adj*. [perhaps named after *Calypso*, island nymph in Homer's *Odyssey*]

calyx /'kaliks, 'kayliks/ *noun* (*pl* **calyxes** *or* **calyces** /'kaliseez, 'kay-/) **1** the outer usu green or leafy part of a flower, consisting of a ring of sepals that protect the developing bud. **2** any cup-shaped body part, *esp* any of several cavities in the kidney through which urine passes before it reaches the bladder. [via Latin from Greek *kalyx*]

calzone /kalt'sohnay/ *noun* (*pl* **calzoni** /-ni/ *or* **calzones**) an Italian dish consisting of a pizza base folded over a generous filling. [Italian *calzone*, literally 'trouser leg', because of its shape]

CAM /kam/ *abbr* **1** Cameroon (international vehicle registration). **2** computer-aided manufacture.

cam /kam/ *noun* a mechanical device, e.g. a wheel or shaft with a projecting part, that transforms circular motion into intermittent

or back-and-forth motion. [perhaps via French *came* from German *Kamm*, literally 'comb']

camaraderie /kamə'rahdəri, -'radəri/ *noun* a spirit of good humour and trust among friends. [French *camaraderie* from *camarade*: see COMRADE]

camarilla /kamə'rilə/ *noun* a group of unofficial often secret and scheming advisers. [Spanish *camarilla*, literally 'small room']

camber[1] *noun* **1** a slight arching or upward sloping from the sides to the middle of a road, deck, beam, etc. **2** the degree to which an aircraft wing or other aerofoil curves up from its front edge and down again to its back edge. **3** a positioning of the wheels of a motor vehicle so that they are closer together at the bottom than at the top.

camber[2] /'kambə/ *verb* (**cambered, cambering**) ⏩ *verb intrans* to curve upwards in the middle. ⏩ *verb trans* to cause (e.g. a road or deck) to curve in this way. [French *cambrer* from Latin *camurus* curved]

Camberwell Beauty /'cambəwel/ *noun* a dark brown butterfly with a broad yellow border on the wings: *Nymphalis antiopa*. [named after *Camberwell*, district of London, where the first specimens were collected]

cambium /'kambi-əm/ *noun* (*pl* **cambiums** *or* **cambia** /'kambi-ə/) a thin layer of cells between the XYLEM (water-conducting tissue) and PHLOEM (food-conducting tissue) of many plants that divides to form more xylem and phloem as the plant grows. ⏩ **cambial** *adj*. [scientific Latin *cambium*, ultimately from Latin *cambiare* to exchange, of Celtic origin]

Cambodian /kam'bohdi-ən/ *noun* **1** a native or inhabitant of Cambodia in SE Asia. **2** the official language of Cambodia; Khmer. ⏩ **Cambodian** *adj*.

Cambrian /'kambri-ən/ *adj* **1** Welsh. **2** relating to or dating from a geological period, the earliest period of the Palaeozoic era, lasting from about 570 to about 510 million years ago, and marked by the presence of every type of invertebrate animal. ⏩ **Cambrian** *noun*. [medieval Latin *Cambria* Wales, from Welsh *Cymry* Welshmen]

cambric /'kambrik/ *noun* a fine white linen or cotton fabric. [obsolete Flemish *Kameryk* Cambrai, city in France where it was first made]

Cambs *abbr* Cambridgeshire.

camcorder /'kamkawdə/ *noun* a video camera with a built-in video recorder. [blend of CAMERA + RECORDER]

came[1] /kaym/ *verb* past tense of COME[1].

came[2] *noun* a slender grooved lead rod used to hold together panes of glass, *esp* in a lattice or stained-glass window. [origin unknown]

camel /'kaməl/ *noun* **1** either of two large RUMINANT[1] (cud-chewing) mammals with humped backs and long necks used for riding and for carrying goods in desert regions, *esp* in Africa and Asia: **a** the one-humped Arabian camel; the dromedary: *Camelus dromedarius*. **b** the two-humped Bactrian camel: *Camelus bactrianus*. **2** a float attached to a ship to increase its buoyancy. **3** a light yellowish brown colour. [Old English via French and Latin from Greek *kamēlos*, of Semitic origin]

cameleer /kamə'liə/ *noun* somebody who rides or controls a camel.

camel hair *noun* **1** soft silky cloth made from the hair of a camel, sometimes mixed with wool, usu light tan in colour. **2** the hair of a camel or a substitute for it, e.g. hair from squirrels' tails, used *esp* in paintbrushes.

camellia /kə'meelyə/ *noun* any of a genus of shrubs with glossy evergreen leaves and showy roselike flowers: genus *Camellia*. [from the Latin genus name, from *Camellus*, Latin name of Georg Josef Kamel d.1706, Moravian Jesuit missionary, who first described the plant]

camelopard /kə'meləpahd/ *noun archaic* a giraffe. [late Latin *camelopardus* from Greek *kamēlopardalis*, from *kamēlos* camel + *pardalis* leopard]

Camembert /'kaməmbeə (*French* kamãbɛːr)/ *noun* a round soft cheese with a thin greyish white rind. [named after *Camembert*, town in Normandy, France, near to which it was orig made]

cameo /'kamioh/ *noun* (*pl* **cameos**) **1a** a small piece of stone, e.g. onyx, carved in such a way that the background is a different colour from the raised design. **b** a small medallion, e.g. on a ring or brooch, with a profiled head in relief. **2** a short literary or dramatic piece that reveals or highlights character, plot, or scene.

3 a small role, *esp* in a film or television drama, played by a well-known actor and often confined to a single scene. [Italian *cameo*]

camera /'kamrə/ *noun* **1** a device for recording still or moving images in the form of a lightproof box with an aperture and a lens, using light-sensitive film or electronic array to produce a still photograph, cinema film, or video signal. **2** (*often* **Camera**) the treasury department of the papal CURIA (court and government of the Catholic Church). ✳ **in camera** in private, often in a judge's private rooms, with members of the public excluded. **on camera** within the range of a camera, e.g. during the making of a film or television broadcast, and therefore visible or recorded. [late Latin *camera* room, from Latin: see CHAMBER]

cameraman *noun* (*pl* **cameramen**) somebody who operates a camera in television or films.

camera obscura /əb'skyooərə/ *noun* a darkened box or room with an aperture through which light from outside enters through an optical system to form an image of the exterior view on a flat surface, e.g. a screen, inside. [Latin *camera obscura* dark chamber]

camerlengo /kamə'lenqgoh/ *noun* (*pl* **camerlengos**) a cardinal who heads the papal treasury. [Italian *camarlingo*, of Germanic origin]

Cameroonian /kamə'roohni-ən/ *noun* a native or inhabitant of Cameroon in W Africa. ➤➤ **Cameroonian** *adj.*

camiknickers /'kaminikəz/ *pl noun Brit* a women's one-piece undergarment that combines a camisole and knickers. ➤➤ **camiknicker** *adj.*

camisole /'kamisohl/ *noun* a short bodice worn as an undergarment by women. [French *camisole*, prob via Old Provençal from late Latin *camisia* shirt]

camomile *or* **chamomile** /'kaməmiel/ *noun* any of several species of strong-scented plants of the daisy family with leaves and flowers that are used medicinally, *esp* in herbal remedies: genus *Anthemis*. [Middle English *camemille* via Latin from Greek *chamaimēlon*, from *chamai* on the ground + *mēlon* apple]

camouflage[1] /'kaməflahzh, -flahj/ *noun* **1** the disguising of military or other equipment or installations with nets, paint, foliage, etc, or the disguise applied. **2** animal markings, colouring, etc that match the natural surroundings and conceal the animal from predators. **3a** concealment by means of disguise. **b** something, e.g. a disguise or way of behaving, designed to deceive or conceal. [French *camouflage* from *camoufler* to disguise, from Italian *camuffare*]

camouflage[2] *verb trans* to conceal or disguise (something or somebody) by camouflage. ➤➤ **camouflageable** *adj.*

camp[1] /kamp/ *noun* **1a** an area of ground on which tents or other temporary shelters are erected, or the area together with the shelters and inhabitants regarded as a unit: *set up camp in the foothills*. **b** a place where troops are housed or trained. **c** a place with temporary accommodation and other facilities, e.g. for holiday-makers, prisoners, etc: *a holiday camp; a concentration camp*. **d** (*used before a noun*) suitable for use in a camp or while travelling, e.g. by being lightweight or collapsible. **2** (*treated as sing. or pl*) a group of people who share a particular view, e.g. members of a political party or supporters of a particular doctrine: *split into two camps*. **3a** *SAfr* a field for grazing animals. **b** *Aus* a place where sheep, cattle, etc congregate. **4** an ancient or prehistoric fortified site. [early French *camp*, prob via Old Provençal from Latin *campus* plain, field]

camp[2] *verb intrans* **1** to pitch or occupy a camp. **2** to live temporarily in a tent or other outdoor accommodation, e.g. on holiday. **3** to settle down as if to a siege: *Reporters have been camping outside the house for weeks*. ➤➤ **camping** *noun*.

camp[3] *adj informal* **1** exaggeratedly effeminate. **2** deliberately and outrageously affected or inappropriate, *esp* to the point of tastelessness, in order to amuse. **3** said of a man: homosexual. ➤➤ **campily** *adv*, **campness** *noun*, **campy** *adj.* [origin unknown]

camp[4] *verb intrans informal* to adopt a camp style or behave in a camp manner. ✳ **camp it up** *informal* to act or behave in an exaggeratedly theatrical or effeminate manner that is intended to be amusing.

camp[5] *noun* a camp style of acting or way of behaving: *a marvellous piece of high camp*.

campaign[1] /kam'payn/ *noun* **1** a series of coordinated events or operations designed to bring about a particular result, *esp* a social or political objective, e.g. a candidate's election. **2a** a connected series of military operations forming a distinct phase of a war. **b** active military life: *be on campaign*.

Word history
French *campagne* open country, ultimately from Latin *campus* plain, field. In military use the word orig applied to time spent camping and exercising in open country.

campaign[2] *verb intrans* to go on, engage in, or conduct a campaign. ➤➤ **campaigner** *noun*.

campanile /kampə'neeli/ *noun* (*pl* **campaniles** *or* **campanili** /-lee/) a bell tower, *esp* one that is freestanding. [Italian *campanile*, from *campana* bell, from late Latin]

campanology /kampə'noləji/ *noun* the art of bell ringing. ➤➤ **campanological** /-nə'lojikl/ *adj*, **campanologist** *noun*. [modern Latin *campanologia*, from late Latin *campana* bell + *-logia* -LOGY]

campanula /kəm'panyoolə/ *noun* any of a genus of plants of the harebell family with bell-shaped blue, white, or purple flowers: genus *Campanula*. Also called BELLFLOWER. [from the Latin genus name, dimin. of late Latin *campana* bell]

campanulate /kəm'panyoolət, -layt/ *adj* said *esp* of flowers or other plant parts: bell-shaped. [scientific Latin *campanula* bell-shaped part, dimin. of late Latin *campana* bell]

camp bed *noun* a small collapsible bed, usu of fabric stretched over a lightweight frame.

camper /'kampə/ *noun* **1** a person who stays temporarily in a tent, caravan, etc, or at a holiday camp. **2** a motor vehicle equipped for use as temporary accommodation, e.g. while holidaying.

camp follower *noun* **1** a civilian, *esp* a prostitute, who follows a military unit in order to provide services to military personnel. **2** somebody who is temporarily attached to a group, *esp* for opportunistic reasons.

camphor /'kamfə/ *noun* a gummy fragrant chemical compound obtained from the wood and bark of the camphor tree and used as a liniment and insect repellent: formula $C_{10}H_{16}O$. ➤➤ **camphoric** /kam'forik/ *adj.* [Middle English *caumfre* via French, Arabic, and Malay from Sanskrit *kapūra*]

camphorate /'kamfərayt/ *verb trans* to impregnate or treat (something) with camphor.

camphor tree *noun* a large evergreen tree of the laurel family grown in most warm countries as a source of camphor: *Cinnamomum camphora*.

camping site *noun* = CAMPSITE.

campion /'kampi-ən/ *noun* any of numerous species of plants of the carnation family with delicate red, pink, or white flowers: genera *Silene* and *Lychnis*.

Word history
prob from obsolete *campion* champion. The campion is said to have been used by the Greeks and Romans in victors' garlands.

campo /'kampoh/ *noun* (*pl* **campos**) a type of grassland plain in S America. [via American Spanish from Spanish *campo* field from Latin *campus*]

campsite *noun* an area of land set aside for tents, caravans, etc and often having toilets, washrooms, and other facilities for holidaymakers.

campus /'kampəs/ *noun* (*pl* **campuses**) **1** the grounds and buildings of a university, *esp* one that is geographically self-contained. **2** *NAmer* the grounds of a school, college, etc. [Latin *campus* field, plain]

campylobacter /,kampiloh'baktə/ *noun* a rod-shaped bacterium that causes food poisoning and gastroenteritis: genus *Campylobacter*. [scientific Latin *campylobacter*, from Greek *kampylos* bent + Latin *bacterium*: see BACTERIUM]

CAMRA /'kamrə/ *abbr* Campaign for Real Ale.

camshaft /'kamshahft/ *noun* a shaft to which a cam is attached.

Can. *abbr* **1** Canada. **2** Canadian.

can[1] /kan, kən/ *verb aux* (*third person sing. present tense* **can,** *past tense* **could** /kood, kəd/) **1** to be able to; to know how to: *She can speak seven languages; I can't make the door open*. **2** to have permission to; may: *You can go if you want*. **3** to have a certain tendency or likelihood: *It can be cold at night*. **4** used in the negative to express surprise or disbelief: *They cannot be serious*. [Old English *cunnan* to know, later 'to know how to'] can or may? Can is nowadays used far more frequently than may when routinely asking or giving permission (Can I go now, please? You can go if you want), despite the argument by traditionalists that this loses a useful distinction between can 'be able to' and may 'be allowed to'. May is however more usual in polite requests (Jane, may I introduce you to Mrs Potter?), and when may is needed to avoid ambiguity (They seem doubtful about what they may and may not do).

can² /kan/ noun **1a** a usu cylindrical metal container, esp for liquids: an oil can. **b** a usu cylindrical metal container in which food or drink is sealed for sale or long-term storage; a tin: a can of beans. **2** Brit, informal (in pl) headphones. **3** NAmer, informal a toilet. **4** chiefly NAmer, informal jail. ✳ **in the can** said of a film, videotape, etc: completed and ready for release. ⮞⮞ **canful** adj. [Old English canne]

can³ /kan/ verb trans (**canned, canning**) **1** to pack or preserve (esp food or drink) in a can. **2** chiefly NAmer, informal to put a stop or end to (something): Can that racket. — Nathaniel Bust. ⮞⮞ **canner** noun.

Canaanite /'kaynəniet/ noun a member of a Semitic people who inhabited ancient Palestine and Phoenicia from about 3000 BC. ⮞⮞ **Canaanite** adj. [Greek Kananitēs from Kanaan Canaan, ancient region in Palestine]

Canada balsam /'kanədə/ noun a sticky yellowish or greenish resin from the balsam fir that is used as an adhesive, esp in mounting subjects on microscope slides. [named after Canada, country in N America]

Canada day noun July 1, observed as a public holiday in Canada in commemoration of the proclamation of dominion status in 1867.

Canada goose noun a wild goose that is grey and brown with a black head and neck and a white patch under the throat, introduced into Europe from N America: Branta canadensis.

Canadian /kə'naydi·ən/ noun a native or inhabitant of Canada. ⮞⮞ **Canadian** adj, **Canadianism** noun.

Canadian football noun a field game resembling American football that is played with teams of twelve players each.

Canadian pondweed noun an aquatic plant that thrives in slow-moving water, introduced into Europe from N America and used in garden ponds to increase the oxygen content of the water: Elodea canadensis.

Canadien /kənadi'en (French kanadjē/ or **Canadienne** /(French kanadjɛn)/ noun a male or female French Canadian.

canaille /kə'nayəl, kə'nie (French kanaj/ noun derog (treated as sing. or pl) the common people; the rabble. [French canaille via Italian from Latin canis dog]

canal /kə'nal/ noun **1** an artificial waterway for commercial vessels and pleasure boats. **2** any channel or watercourse used for drainage, for irrigation, or to convey water for power. **3** a tubular passage in an animal or plant; a duct: the alimentary canal. [Middle English from Latin canalis pipe, channel, from canna reed]

canal boat noun a boat for use on a canal, esp a barge.

canalize or **canalise** /'kanəliez/ verb trans **1** to provide (an area) with a canal or canals. **2** to convert (a river) into a canal. **3** to direct (something, e.g. a flow of liquid or gas) into a preferred channel or outlet. ⮞⮞ **canalization** /-'zaysh(ə)n/ noun.

canapé /'kanəpay, -pi/ noun an appetizer consisting of a small piece of bread, biscuit, pastry, etc with a savoury topping. [French canapé sofa (the base being seen as a 'couch' on which to 'seat' toppings), from medieval Latin canopeum, canapeum: see CANOPY¹]

canard /kə'nahd, 'kanahd/ noun **1** a false or unfounded report or story; a hoax. **2a** a small wing-shaped device mounted near an aircraft's nose to provide extra stability or control. **b** an aircraft with such a device fitted. [French canard duck; (sense 1) from early French vendre des canards à moitié to cheat, literally 'to half-sell ducks']

canary /kə'neəri/ noun (pl **canaries**) **1** a small usu yellow finch native to the Canary Islands, widely kept as a cage bird: Serinus canaria. **2** a sweet white wine of the Canary Islands. [French canarie from Old Spanish canario, from Islas Canarias Canary Islands]

canary yellow adj of a vivid yellow colour. ⮞⮞ **canary yellow** noun.

canasta /kə'nastə/ noun **1** a card game resembling rummy usu for four players using two full packs plus jokers, in which players or partnerships win points for sets of three or more cards of the same rank and score bonuses for seven-card sets. **2** a combination of seven cards of the same rank in canasta. [Spanish canasta basket]

cancan /'kankan/ noun an energetic stage dance performed by women, often in a row, who kick their legs high while holding up the front of their skirt. [French cancan]

cancel¹ /'kansl/ verb (**cancelled, cancelling,** NAmer **canceled, canceling**) ⮞ verb trans **1** to decide that (something arranged) will not take place, usu without intending to reschedule it. **2a** to make (something) void; to annul or revoke (it): cancel a magazine subscription. **b** (often + out) to match (something) in force or effect; to counterbalance or offset (it): His irritability cancelled out his natural kindness — Osbert Sitwell. **c** formal to put an end to (something); to destroy (it). **3** to mark (something written or printed) for deletion. **4a** in mathematics, to remove (a common divisor) from a numerator and denominator. **b** to remove (equivalents) on opposite sides of an equation or account. **5** to deface (e.g. a postage stamp), usu with a set of lines, so as to prevent reuse. ⮞ verb intrans (+ out) to neutralize each other's strength or effect; to be counterbalanced. ⮞⮞ **canceller** noun. [Middle English cancellen via Old French and late Latin from Latin cancellare to make like a lattice, ultimately from carcer prison]

cancel² noun **1** a cancellation. **2** a loose page in a book containing missing or revised text or instructions for correction or deletion of existing text. **3** NAmer = NATURAL² (3A).

cancellation (NAmer **cancelation**) /kansə'layshən/ noun **1** something cancelled, esp a cancelled booking for a theatre seat, hotel room, place on a flight, etc that may become available for others to book. **2** a mark made to cancel something, e.g. a postage stamp. **3** the cancelling of something.

cancellous /'kansələs, kan'seləs/ adj said of bone: having a porous structure. [scientific Latin cancelli intersecting bony plates and bars in cancellous bone, from Latin cancelli lattice, from carcer prison]

cancer /'kansə/ noun **1a** a malignant tumour that develops when cells multiply in an unlimited way. **b** the medical condition that is characterized by the presence of such a tumour or tumours.

Editorial note
A cancer is a malignant tumour that develops when cells multiply in an abnormal and uncontrolled manner. Cancerous cells can invade and destroy nearby tissues and spread (or 'metastasise') to other areas of the body – by direct spread or via the blood and/or lymphatic systems — Dr John Cormack.

2 a spreading evil in a person, society, etc: the cancer of hidden resentment — Irish Digest. **3** (**Cancer**) in astronomy, a constellation (the Crab) depicted as a crab crushed beneath Hercules' foot. **4** (**Cancer**). **a** in astrology, the fourth sign of the zodiac. **b** a person born under this sign. ⮞⮞ **Cancerian** /kan'siəri·ən, kan'seə-/ adj and noun, **cancerous** adj. [Middle English from Latin cancer crab, cancer]

cancroid¹ /'kangkroyd/ adj **1** resembling a crab. **2** resembling a cancer in appearance or rapid growth. [Latin cancr-, cancer crab, cancer]

cancroid² noun any of various forms of slow-growing skin cancer.

candela /kan'daylə, kan'deelə/ noun the basic SI unit of luminous intensity. Also called CANDLE¹. [Latin candela: see CANDLE¹]

candelabrum /kandl'ahbrəm/ or **candelabra** /-'ahbrə/ noun (pl **candelabra** or **candelabrums** or **candelabras**) a branched candlestick or lamp with several lights. [Latin candelabrum from candela: see CANDLE¹]

candescent /kan'des(ə)nt/ adj formal glowing or dazzling with heat. ⮞⮞ **candescence** noun. [Latin candescent-, candescens, present part. of candescere to cause to shine, from candēre to shine]

candid /'kandid/ adj **1** indicating or suggesting complete sincerity; frank or open. **2** tending to criticize severely; blunt or outspoken. **3** said of photographs, etc: featuring subjects acting naturally and unposed, and often taken without their knowledge. ⮞⮞ **candidly** adv, **candidness** noun. [French candide from Latin candidus bright, white, from candēre to shine, glow]

candida /'kandidə/ noun any of a genus of parasitic fungi that resemble yeasts, including the fungus that causes THRUSH²: genus Candida. [from the Latin genus name, from candidus white]

candidate /'kandidayt, -dət/ noun **1** somebody who is competing with others for something, e.g. a job, a political position, or an award. **2** somebody who is taking an examination. **3** somebody or something regarded as suitable for something, or likely to suffer something. ⮞⮞ **candidacy** /-dəsi/ noun, **candidature** noun. [Latin *candidatus* clothed in white, from *candidus* white; from the white toga worn by candidates for office in ancient Rome]

candid camera *noun* **1** a usu small camera equipped with a fast lens that is used for taking informal photographs of unposed subjects, often without their knowledge. **2** the style of still photography or documentary filming that captures subjects in this way.

candidiasis /kandi'die-əsis/ *noun* THRUSH² or a similar disease caused by infection with a CANDIDA fungus. [scientific Latin *candidiasis*, from CANDIDA]

candied /'kandid/ *adj* sweetened or preserved with a thick coating of sugar.

candle¹ /'kandl/ *noun* **1** a usu long slender cylindrical mass of tallow or wax enclosing a wick that is burned to give light. **2** something resembling a candle in shape or use: *a sulphur candle for fumigation.* **3** = CANDELA. ✳ **not hold a candle to** to be much inferior to (something else). **not worth the candle** *chiefly Brit* not worth the effort, or not justified by the result. [Old English *candel* from Latin *candela*, from *candēre* to shine]

candle² *verb trans* to examine (eggs) for staleness, blood clots, or fertility by holding them between the eye and a light. ⟫⟫ **candler** *noun.*

candleberry /'kandlb(ə)ri/ *noun* (*pl* **candleberries**) = WAX MYRTLE.

candleholder *noun* = CANDLESTICK.

candlelight *noun* **1** the light given off by a candle. **2** *archaic* the time for lighting up; twilight. ⟫⟫ **candlelit** *adj.*

Candlemas /'kandlməs/ *noun* a Christian feast commemorating the presentation of Christ in the temple and the purification of the Virgin Mary, observed on 2 February. [Old English *candelmæsse*, from *candel* (see CANDLE¹) + *mæsse* feast: see MASS¹; from the candles blessed and carried in celebration of the feast]

candlenut /'kandlnut/ *noun* **1** a tropical tree of the spurge family that is a source of oil used in paints and varnishes: *Aleurites moluccana.* **2** any of the seeds of this tree, formerly burned as candles.

candlepower *noun* luminous intensity expressed in candelas.

candlestick *noun* a holder with a socket for a candle.

candlewick *noun* **1** a fabric made with thick soft cotton yarn cut in a raised tufted pattern, used *esp* for bedspreads. **2** the yarn used to make this fabric.

candlewood *noun* slivers of resinous wood burned for light.

can-do *adj informal* marked by determination to press on and get things done, regardless of difficulties: *A can-do attitude is beginning to replace the inertia bred of vested interests* — The Economist.

candour (*NAmer* **candor**) /'kandə/ *noun* **1** sincerity or honesty of expression; frankness or openness. **2** directness in stating something or in criticizing somebody; bluntness. [French *candeur* from Latin *candor* whiteness]

C and W *abbr* country and western.

candy¹ /'kandi/ *noun* (*pl* **candies**) **1** crystallized sugar formed by boiling down sugar syrup. **2** *chiefly NAmer.* **a** sweets, chocolate, and other confectionery. **b** a sweet. [Middle English *sugre candy* via Old French from Old Italian *zucchero candi*, from *zucchero* sugar + Arabic *qandī* candied, from *qand* cane sugar]

candy² *verb trans* (**candies, candied, candying**) to encrust or glaze (e.g. fruit or fruit peel) with sugar by cooking it in a heavy syrup.

candy floss *noun Brit* **1** a light fluffy mass of spun sugar, usu wound round a stick as a sweet. **2** something attractive but insubstantial.

candy-striped *adj* said *esp* of fabric: with a regular pattern of usu narrow stripes of colour, often pink, on a white background.

candytuft *noun* any of several species of plants of the mustard family cultivated for their white, pink, or purple flowers: genus *Iberis.* [*Candy*, former name of Crete, Greek island + TUFT¹]

cane¹ /kayn/ *noun* **1a** a hollow or pithy usu flexible jointed stem of some reeds and grasses, e.g. bamboo. **b** any of various tall woody grasses or reeds, *esp* sugarcane. **c** a long woody flowering or fruiting stem, *esp* of a raspberry. **2a** a walking stick, *esp* one made from a cane. **b** a cane or rod used to give beatings, or the punishment so inflicted. **c** a length of split rattan used in basketry, wickerwork, etc. [Middle English via Old French and Old Provençal from Latin *canna*, from Greek *kanna*, of Semitic origin]

cane² *verb trans* **1a** to beat (somebody) with a cane. **b** *informal* to punish or reprimand (somebody) severely. **c** *informal* to defeat (somebody) convincingly; to trounce (them). **2** to weave or furnish (something) with cane: *cane the seat of a chair.*

canebrake /'kaynbrayk/ *noun NAmer* a thicket of canes.

cane sugar *noun* sugar obtained from sugarcane.

canine¹ /'kaynien/ *adj* **1** of, resembling, or being a dog or a member of the family of carnivorous mammals that includes dogs, wolves, jackals, and foxes. **2** of or being any of the four conical pointed teeth lying between the incisor and the first premolar on each side of both jaws. [Latin *caninus* from *canis* dog]

canine² *noun* **1** a canine tooth. **2** a canine animal.

caning *noun* **1** a beating with a cane or rod. **2** *informal* a severe reprimand or punishment. **3** *informal* a convincing defeat; a trouncing.

canister /'kanistə/ *noun* **1** a small usu metal box or tin for holding a dry product, e.g. tea or shot. **2** in former times, a metal cylinder containing shot or shrapnel, designed to explode on impact when fired from a cannon, or the contents of such a cylinder. [via Latin from Greek *kanastron* basket, from *kanna* reed]

canker¹ /'kangkə/ *noun* **1** an ulcer or spreading sore, *esp* one affecting the mouth. **2a** an area of dead tissue or an open wound in a plant: *as killing as the canker to the rose* — Milton. **b** any of various inflammatory diseases of animals, e.g. an ear disease of dogs, cats, and rabbits, or a disease of horses that softens the underside of the hooves. **3** a source of spreading corruption or evil. ⟫⟫ **cankerous** /-rəs/ *adj.* [Middle English via French from Latin *cancer* crab, cancer]

canker² *verb* (**cankered, cankering**) ⟫ *verb trans* **1** to corrupt or undermine (somebody or something): *God help that country, cankered deep by doubt* — Archibald MacLeish. **2** to infect (somebody or something) with canker. ⟫ *verb intrans* **1** to become infected with canker. **2** to be corrupted or undermined.

cankerworm *noun* any of the larvae of various N American moths that are harmful to trees, *esp* by feeding on buds and leaves.

canna /'kanə/ *noun* any of a genus of tropical plants grown for their bright red or yellow flowers and decorative leaves: genus *Canna.* [from the Latin genus name from Greek *kanna* reed]

cannabin /'kanəbin/ *noun* = CANNABIS RESIN. [Latin *cannabis*: see CANNABIS]

cannabis /'kanəbis/ *noun* **1** the dried leaves and flowering tops of female hemp plants, which yield cannabis resin and are sometimes smoked or eaten for their intoxicating effect. **2** = HEMP (1C). [via Latin from Greek *kannabis* hemp]

cannabis café *noun* a café in which the selling and smoking of cannabis is permitted or tolerated.

cannabis resin *noun* a dark resin obtained from female hemp plants that contains the physiologically active ingredients of cannabis. Also called CANNABIN.

canned /kand/ *adj* **1** recorded for mechanical or electronic reproduction, *esp* prerecorded for addition to a soundtrack or a videotape: *canned laughter; canned music.* **2** sold or preserved in a can; tinned. **3** *informal* drunk.

cannel coal /'kanl/ *noun* a bituminous coal that burns brightly. [prob from English dialect *cannel* candle, from Old English *candel*: see CANDLE¹]

cannelloni /kanə'lohni/ *pl noun* (*treated as sing. or pl*) large tubular rolls of pasta served with a filling, e.g. of meat, vegetables, or cheese. [Italian *cannelloni*, literally 'large tubes', ultimately from *canna* cane, reed, from Latin: see CANE¹]

cannery /'kanəri/ *noun* (*pl* **canneries**) a factory for canning foods.

cannibal /'kanibl/ *noun* **1** a human being who eats human flesh. **2** an animal that eats its own kind. ⟫⟫ **cannibalism** *noun,* **cannibalistic** /-'listik/ *adj.* [Spanish *Canibales*, the name of a West Indian tribe said to be cannibals, from Arawakan *Caniba, Carib,* of Cariban origin]

cannibalize or **cannibalise** /'kanibəliez/ *verb trans* to dismantle (e.g. a machine) in order to provide spare parts for others. ⟫⟫ **cannibalization** /-'zaysh(ə)n/ *noun.*

cannon¹ /'kanən/ *noun* (*pl* **cannons** or **cannon**) **1a** a large gun mounted on a carriage, used formerly in warfare. **b** an automatic shell-firing gun mounted *esp* in an aircraft. **2** a heavy tube or drum that rotates freely on its supporting shaft. **3** *Brit* a shot in billiards in which the cue ball strikes two object balls in succession, or a shot in snooker or pool in which the ball struck by the cue ball strikes a second ball close to it. [French *canon* via Italian from Latin *canna*: see CANE[1]; (sense 3) alteration of CAROM[1]]

Usage note
cannon or canon? These two words are easily confused. The noun *cannon* means 'a large gun' or 'a shot in billiards or snooker'. *Cannon* is also a verb: *The shot cannoned off the far post*. *Canon* is only used as a noun and means 'a clergyman', 'a musical composition', 'a body of principles or rules', or 'an authoritative list of books'.

cannon[2] *verb intrans* (**cannoned, cannoning**) **1a** (+ into) to collide with (somebody or something). **b** (+ off) to collide with and be deflected off (something). **2** *Brit* to make a cannon in billiards, snooker, or pool.

cannonade[1] /kanəˈnayd/ *noun* a burst or period of continuous heavy artillery fire.

cannonade[2] *verb trans* to attack (e.g. troops) with a cannonade.

cannonball[1] *noun* a round solid missile made for firing from the type of cannon used in former times.

cannonball[2] *verb intrans* to move or progress at a very fast pace.

cannon bone *noun* the leg bone between the hock joint and the fetlock of a horse or other hoofed mammal. [French *canon*: see CANNON[1]]

cannoneer /kanəˈniə/ *noun* in former times, a soldier who fired a cannon.

cannon fodder *noun* soldiers regarded merely as material to be expended in battle.

cannot /ˈkanot, ˈkanət, kəˈnot/ *contraction* can not. ✳ **cannot but/cannot help but** to be bound to; must: *I could not but smile at the answer*.

cannula /ˈkanyoolə/ *noun* (*pl* **cannulas** *or* **cannulae** /-lee/) a small tube for inserting into a body cavity or duct, e.g. for draining off fluid or for introducing medicine. [scientific Latin *cannula*, dimin. of Latin *canna*: see CANE[1]]

cannulate /ˈkanyoolayt/ *verb trans* to insert a cannula into (a body cavity or duct). ➤ **cannulation** /-ˈlaysh(ə)n/ *noun*.

canny /ˈkani/ *adj* (**cannier, canniest**) **1** cautious and shrewd; astute. **2** *Scot, NE Eng* careful, *esp* where money is concerned; thrifty. **3** *NE Eng* pleasant or attractive. ➤ **cannily** *adv*, **canniness** *noun*. [CAN[1] in an obsolete sense 'to know' + -Y[1]]

canoe[1] /kəˈnooh/ *noun* a long light narrow boat with pointed ends and curved sides usu propelled with a paddle. [French *canoe* via Spanish and Arawakan from Carib *canaoua*]

canoe[2] *verb intrans* (**canoes, canoed, canoeing**) to travel in or paddle a canoe. ➤ **canoeist** *noun*.

can of worms *noun informal* a potentially awkward or complicated matter, situation, etc.

canon[1] /ˈkanən/ *noun* **1** a regulation or dogma decreed by a church council. **2a** an accepted principle, rule, or criterion. **b** a body of principles, rules, or standards. **3a** an authoritative list of books accepted as Holy Scripture. **b** the authentic works of a writer. **4** the series of prayers forming the set part of the Roman Catholic Mass and including the consecration of the bread and wine. **5** a musical composition for two or more vocal or instrumental parts in which the melody is repeated by the voices or instruments entering in succession and overlapping. [Old English via Latin from Greek *kanōn* rule]

Usage note
canon or cannon? See note at CANNON[1].

canon[2] *noun* **1** a clergyman belonging to the chapter of a cathedral or collegiate church. **2** = CANON REGULAR. [Middle English *canoun* via Anglo-French from late Latin *canonicus* a person living under a rule, from Greek *kanonikos*, from *kanōn* rule]

Usage note
canon or cannon? See note at CANNON[1].

cañon /ˈkanyən/ *noun* see CANYON.

canonic /kəˈnonik/ *adj* = CANONICAL.

canonical /kəˈnonikl/ *adj* **1** of a canon, *esp* an ecclesiastical or musical one. **2a** conforming to a general rule; orthodox. **b** conforming to CANON LAW. **3** accepted as forming part of the canon of Holy Scripture or of a writer's works. **4** of a cathedral chapter. ➤ **canonically** *adv*, **canonicity** /kanəˈnisiti/ *noun*.

canonical hour *noun* **1** in the Roman Catholic Church, any of the daily religious services that make up the Divine Office: compare MATINS, LAUDS, PRIME[1], TERCE, SEXT, NONE[3], VESPERS, COMPLINE.

2 in the Church of England, any time of the day at which the marriage ceremony may lawfully be performed.

canonicals *pl noun* the vestments prescribed by canon for an officiating clergyman.

canonise /ˈkanəniez/ *verb trans* see CANONIZE.

canonist /ˈkanənist/ *noun* a specialist in canon law.

canonize *or* **canonise** /ˈkanəniez/ *verb trans* **1** to recognize (somebody) officially as a saint. **2** to give official sanction or approval to (something), *esp* by ecclesiastical authority. ➤ **canonization** /-ˈzaysh(ə)n/ *noun*. [Middle English *canonizen* from late Latin *canon* catalogue of saints, ultimately from Greek *kanōn* rule]

canon law *noun* the codified law governing a church.

canon regular *noun* (*pl* **canons regular**) a member of any of several Roman Catholic institutes of priests belonging to a religious order and living in a community.

canonry /ˈkanənri/ *noun* (*pl* **canonries**) **1** the office of a canon. **2** the endowment that financially supports a canon. **3** the building in which a canon resides.

canoodle /kəˈnoohdl/ *verb intrans informal* to kiss and cuddle amorously with somebody; to pet. [perhaps from English dialect *canoodle* donkey, fool, silly lover]

Canopic jar /kəˈnohpik/ *noun* a jar in which the ancient Egyptians preserved the viscera of an embalmed body.

Word history
named after *Canopus*, city of ancient Egypt. The Egyptian god Osiris was worshipped there in the form of a jar with a human head, and the name *Canopic* was wrongly given to the funerary jars, one of which represents Imset, the human-headed son of the god Horus.

canopy[1] /ˈkanəpi/ *noun* (*pl* **canopies**) **1a** a cloth covering suspended over a bed. **b** a cover, often of cloth, fixed or carried above a person of high rank or a sacred object. **c** an awning or marquee. **d** anything that seems like a cover: *the canopy of the heavens*. **2** an ornamental rooflike structure. **3a** the transparent enclosure over an aircraft cockpit. **b** the lifting or supporting surface of a parachute. **4** the uppermost layer of a forest, composed of spreading leafy branches. [Middle English *canope* from medieval Latin *canopeum*, ultimately from Greek *kōnōpion* couch with mosquito net, from *kōnōps* mosquito]

canopy[2] *verb trans* (**canopies, canopied, canopying**) to cover (something) with or as if with a canopy: *a canopied bed*.

canst /kənst; *strong* kanst/ *verb archaic* second person sing. present tense of CAN[1].

Cant. *abbr* Canticles (book of the Bible).

cant[1] /kant/ *noun* **1** the insincere or hypocritical expression of platitudes or sentiments, *esp* those suggesting piety. **2** the jargon of a specific group of people; *specif* the slang used by thieves, beggars, etc. **3** set or stock phrases: *I won't be called names ... as wife, spouse, my dear, joy, jewel, love, sweetheart, and the rest of that nauseous cant, in which men and their wives are so fulsomely familiar* — Congreve.

cant[2] *verb intrans dated* to speak in cant or jargon. [prob from early French *canter* to tell, literally 'to sing', from Latin *cantare*: see CHANT[1]]

cant[3] *noun* **1a** an oblique or slanting surface. **b** an inclination from a given line; a slope. **2a** a sudden thrust that produces some displacement. **b** the displacement so caused. [Middle English, prob from early Dutch *cant* edge, corner, via French from Latin *canthus*, *cantus* iron tyre, perhaps of Celtic origin]

cant[4] *verb trans* **1** to set (something) at an angle; to tilt (it). **2** to give an oblique edge to (something); to bevel (it). **3** to overturn (something); to tip (it) over. ➤ *verb intrans* **1** to slope. **2** to pitch to one side; to lean.

can't /kahnt/ *contraction* can not.

Cantab. /ˈkantab/ *abbr* used with academic awards: of Cambridge: *MA Cantab*. [Latin *Cantabrigiensis*, from *Cantabrigia* Cambridge]

cantabile /kanˈtahbili, -lay/ *adj and adv* said of a piece of music: to be performed in a singing manner. ➤ **cantabile** *noun*. [Italian *cantabile* from late Latin *cantabilis* worthy to be sung, from Latin *cantare*: see CHANT[1]]

Cantabrigian /kantəˈbriji-ən/ *noun* **1** a student or graduate of Cambridge University. **2** a native or inhabitant of Cambridge. ➤ **Cantabrigian** *adj*. [Latin *Cantabrigia* Cambridge]

Cantal /kon'tahl (*French* kătal)/ *noun* a hard strong-flavoured French cheese similar to Cheddar. [named after *Cantal,* department in S France where it is made]

cantaloupe *or* **cantaloup** /'kantəloohp/ *noun* a MUSKMELON (type of cultivated melon) with a hard ridged rind and orange flesh. [named after *Cantalupo,* former papal villa near Rome, Italy, the first place in Europe where it was grown]

cantankerous /kan'tangkərəs/ *adj* ill-natured or quarrelsome. ➤➤ **cantankerously** *adv,* **cantankerousness** *noun.* [perhaps irreg from obsolete *contack* contention]

cantata /kan'tahtə/ *noun* a choral composition, often a musical setting of a religious text, comprising choruses, solos, recitatives, and interludes. [via Italian from Latin *cantata* sung mass, ecclesiastical chant, fem past part. of *cantare*: see CHANT[1]]

cant dog *noun* = CANT HOOK.

canteen /kan'teen/ *noun* **1** a dining hall, *esp* in a school or factory. **2** a shop providing supplies in a camp. **3** *Brit* a partitioned box for holding cutlery. **4** a small flask used by a soldier, traveller, etc to carry liquid, *esp* drinking water. [French *cantine* bottle case, sutler's shop, from Italian *cantina* wine cellar, from *canto* corner, from Latin *canthus* iron tyre, perhaps of Celtic origin]

canter[1] /'kantə/ *noun* **1** a three-beat gait of a horse or similar animal that is smoother and slower than a gallop. **2** a ride at this speed. ✳ **at a canter** easily; with little or no effort. [short for obsolete *canterbury,* named after the city of *Canterbury,* England; from the supposed gait of pilgrims to the shrine of St Thomas à Becket at Canterbury]

canter[2] *verb* (**cantered, cantering**) ➤ *verb intrans* to progress or ride at a canter. ➤ *verb trans* to cause (a horse) to canter.

Canterbury bell /'kantəb(ə)ri/ *noun* a tall European plant cultivated for its large showy bell-shaped flowers: *Campanula medium.* [said to be from bells on the harness of pilgrims' horses going to *Canterbury,* city in England]

cantharides /kan'tharideez/ *pl noun* (*treated as sing. or pl*) = SPANISH FLY (2). [Middle English *cantharide* (sing.) via Latin from Greek *kantharid-, kantharis*]

canthi /'kanthie/ *noun* pl of CANTHUS.

cant hook *noun* a stout wooden lever with a metal-clad end, used *esp* in handling logs. [CANT[3]]

canthus /'kanthəs/ *noun* (*pl* **canthi** /'kanthie/) either of the angles formed where the upper and lower eyelids meet. [via Latin from Greek *kanthos*]

canticle /'kantikl/ *noun* a song; *specif* any of several songs, e.g. the Magnificat, taken from the Bible and used in services of worship. [Middle English from Latin *canticulum,* dimin. of *canticum* song, from *canere* to sing]

cantilena /kanti'laynə/ *noun* **1** a simple fluid style in vocal music. **2** the part carrying the main tune in choral music. [via Italian from Latin *cantilena* song, from *cantus*]

cantilever /'kantileevə/ *noun* **1** a projecting beam or member supported at only one end. **2** a bracket-shaped member supporting a balcony or a cornice. **3** either of the beams or trusses that form a span of a cantilever bridge. [perhaps from CANT[3] + -I- + LEVER[1]]

cantilever bridge *noun* a bridge formed from beams or trusses that are supported at one end, project towards each other, and are joined directly or by a suspended connecting member.

cantillate /'kantilayt/ *verb trans* to recite (passages of religious text) on musical notes, *esp* in a Jewish service of worship. ➤➤ **cantillation** /-'laysh(ə)n/ *noun.* [Latin *cantillatus,* past part. of *cantillare* to sing low, from *cantare* to sing]

cantina /kan'teenə/ *noun* a small bar or wine shop, *esp* in a Spanish-speaking area. [Spanish *cantina* canteen, from Italian *cantina* wine cellar: see CANTEEN]

canting /'kanting/ *adj* in heraldry, expressing a name by means of a visual pun: *canting arms.*

cantle /'kantl/ *noun* the upward-curving rear part of a saddle. [Middle English from early French *cantel,* dimin. of *cant* edge, corner: see CANT[3]]

canto /'kantoh/ *noun* (*pl* **cantos**) a major division of a long poem. [Italian *canto* from Latin *cantus* song, past part. of *canere* to sing]

canton[1] /'kanton/ *noun* **1** a small territorial division of a country, e.g.: **a** any of the states of the Swiss confederation. **b** a division of a French arrondissement. **2** /'kant(ə)n/ a square in the top left corner of a heraldic shield. ➤➤ **cantonal** /'kant(ə)nl, kan'tonl/ *adj.* [Old French *canton* corner, ultimately from Latin *canthus* iron tyre; (sense 1) via Italian *canto* corner; (sense 2) via Old Provençal *cant* edge, corner]

canton[2] /kan'ton/ *verb trans* (**cantoned, cantoning**) **1** to divide (e.g. a country) into cantons. **2** /kən'toohn/ to allot quarters to (e.g. a body of troops).

Cantonese /kantə'neez/ *noun* (*pl* **Cantonese**) **1** a native or inhabitant of Canton, city in China. **2** the dialect of Chinese spoken in and around Canton. ➤➤ **Cantonese** *adj.*

cantonment /kən'toohnmənt/ *noun* **1** the billeting of troops. **2** a group of structures providing temporary or permanent accommodation for troops; a military camp or situation. [French *cantonnement* from *cantonner* to billet troops, from Old French *canton:* see CANTON[1]]

cantor /'kantaw/ *noun* **1** a singer who leads the choir or congregation in Christian church services. **2** a synagogue official who sings or chants liturgical music and leads the congregation in prayer. [Latin *cantor* singer, from *canere* to sing]

cantorial /kan'tawri-əl/ *adj* **1** of a cantor or precentor. **2** of the north side of the choir, e.g. in a cathedral, where the cantor or precentor sits: compare DECANAL.

cantoris /kan'tawris/ *noun* the part of a church choir sitting on the north side and taking the second or lower part in music for two groups: compare DECANI. [Latin *cantoris* of the cantor: see CANTOR]

Cantuar. *abbr* used chiefly in the signature of the Archbishop of Canterbury: of Canterbury. [Latin *Cantuariensis*]

cantus firmus /ˌkantəs 'fuhməs/ *noun* (*pl* **cantus firmi** /'fuhmie/) **1** the plainchant or simple Gregorian melody, orig sung in unison and with a prescribed form and use. **2** a melodic theme or subject, *esp* one for contrapuntal treatment. [medieval Latin *cantus firmus,* literally 'fixed song']

Canuck /kə'nuk/ *noun chiefly NAmer, informal* **1** a Canadian, *esp* a French Canadian. **2** *derog* the language of the French Canadians. [prob alteration of CANADIAN]

canvas /'kanvəs/ *noun* (*pl* **canvases** *or* **canvasses**) **1a** a strong closely woven cloth, usu of linen, hemp, or cotton, used for clothing, sails, tents etc. **b** sails or tents considered collectively. **2a** a cloth surface suitable for painting on in oils. **b** a painting on such a surface. **3** a coarse cloth woven to form an open mesh for embroidery or tapestry. **4** in rowing, either end of a racing boat, orig covered with canvas: *They won by a canvas.* **5** the floor of a boxing or wrestling ring. ✳ **under canvas 1** in a tent; camping. **2** with sails set; under sail. [Middle English *cenevas* via French from Latin *cannabis:* see CANNABIS]

Usage note

canvas *or* canvass? The material that tents are traditionally made of is *canvas.* Before an election, political parties *canvass* the voters to try to obtain their support.

canvasback *noun* a N American wild duck closely related to the European pochard: *Aythya valisineria.* [from its colour]

canvass[1] /'kanvəs/ *verb trans* **1** to visit (e.g. voters) in order to solicit political support or to ascertain opinions. **2** to discuss or debate (something). **3a** to examine (something) in detail. **b** *NAmer* to examine (votes) officially for authenticity. ➤ *verb intrans* to solicit orders, votes, opinions, etc. ➤➤ **canvasser** *noun.*

Word history

obsolete *canvas* to toss in a canvas sheet, from CANVAS. Tossing in a sheet was a rough affair, often done as a punishment; the sense evolved via 'to handle roughly', 'to castigate or criticize', 'to debate vigorously', 'to actively seek support'. See also usage note at CANVAS.

canvass[2] *noun* **1** the act of canvassing. **2** a survey to ascertain the probable vote before an election. **3** *chiefly NAmer* a scrutiny, *esp* of votes.

canyon *or* **cañon** /'kanyən/ *noun* a deep valley or gorge. [American Spanish *cañón,* prob alteration of early Spanish *callón,* augmentative of *calle* street, from Latin *callis* footpath]

canyoning *noun* the sport of jumping into a mountain stream in protective clothing and being carried along by the water through rapids and down falls.

canzonetta /kanzə'netə/ *noun* (*pl* **canzonettas** *or* **canzonette** /-'netay/) a light and graceful song, *esp* one in the Italian style of the 16th to 18th cents. [Italian *canzonetta,* dimin. of *canzone* song, from Latin *cantion-, cantio,* ultimately from *canere* to sing]

caoutchouc /'kowchoohk/ *noun* = RUBBER¹ (1A). [French *caoutchouc* via early Spanish *cauchuc* from Quechua *kauchuk*]

CAP *abbr* Common Agricultural Policy.

cap¹ /kap/ *noun* **1a** a soft close-fitting head covering without a brim and often with a peak. **b** a head covering that denotes the rank or occupation of the wearer, e.g. a nurse. **c** *chiefly Brit* a head covering awarded to a member of a sports team, *esp* a player selected for a national team, or somebody to whom such a cap has been awarded. **d** an academic mortarboard: *students dressed in cap and gown.* **2a** a natural cover or top. **b** the PILEUS (upper dome-shaped part) of a mushroom or toadstool. **3** something that serves as a cover or protection, *esp* for the end or top of an object. **4** an upper financial limit: *a cap on the level of community charge any council may make* — Daily Telegraph. **5** the uppermost part; the top. **6** a small container holding an explosive charge, e.g. for a toy pistol or for priming the charge in a firearm. **7** *Brit* = DUTCH CAP. **8** an artificial substitute or protective covering for the external part of a tooth. ✲ **cap in hand** in a deferential manner: *He went cap in hand to various companies asking for sponsorship.* **set one's cap at** *dated* said of a woman: to try to attract (a particular man), *esp* with a view to marriage. ⪢ **capful** (*pl* **capfuls**) *noun.* [Old English *cæppe* from late Latin *cappa* head covering, cloak]

cap² *verb trans* (**capped, capping**) **1** to provide or protect (something) with a cap: *have a tooth capped.* **2** to form a cap over (something); to crown (it): *The mountains were capped with mist* — John Buchan. **3a** *chiefly Brit* to select (a player) for a sports team: *capped for England.* **b** *chiefly Scot, NZ* to award an academic degree to (somebody). **4a** to follow (something) with a more impressive or significant example; to outdo (it): *I can cap that story with a better one.* **b** to put the finishing touch to (something). **5** to impose an upper financial limit on (e.g. a tax or charge). ✲ **to cap it all** as the last and usu most infuriating, outrageous, etc of a series of events: *To cap it all, they expected us to pay the bill!*

cap. *abbr* **1** capacity. **2** capital. **3** capitalize. **4** capital letter.

capability /kaypə'biliti/ *noun* (*pl* **capabilities**) **1** being capable. **2** a feature or faculty capable of development; potential.

capable /'kaypəbl/ *adj* **1** able or competent: *her capable fingers.* **2** (+ of) having the required attributes or inclination to perform (a specified deed or action): *He is capable of murder.* **3** (+ of) susceptible of (something): *a remark capable of being misunderstood.* ⪢ **capableness** *noun,* **capably** *adv.* [orig in the sense 'able to take in or understand'; early French *capable* from late Latin *capabilis,* from Latin *capere* to take]

capacious /kə'payshəs/ *adj* able to hold a great deal; roomy. ⪢ **capaciously** *adv,* **capaciousness** *noun.* [Latin *capac-, capax,* from *capere* to take]

capacitance /kə'pasit(ə)ns/ *noun* **1** the ability of a conductor or system of conductors and insulators to store electric charge. **2** the measure of this ability, equal to the ratio of the charge induced to the potential difference. ⪢ **capacitive** /-tiv/ *adj.* [CAPACITY + -ANCE]

capacitor /kə'pasitə/ *noun* a component in an electrical circuit that provides capacitance and usu consists of an insulator sandwiched between two oppositely charged conductors.

capacity /kə'pasiti/ *noun* (*pl* **capacities**) **1a** the ability to receive, accommodate, or deal with something. **b** a measured ability to contain; volume: *a tank with a capacity of 40 litres.* **c** the maximum amount that can be contained or produced: *working at capacity.* **d** (*used before a noun*) being such a maximum amount: *a capacity crowd.* **2a** ability or talent. **b** power or potential: *a capacity for violence.* **3** a position or role assigned or assumed: *in her capacity as judge.* **4** legal competence or authority. **5a** the quantity of electricity that a battery, motor, etc can deliver under particular conditions. **b** *dated* = CAPACITANCE (2). [Middle English *capacite* via French from Latin *capacitat-, capacitas,* from *capac-, capax:* see CAPACIOUS]

cap and bells *noun* the traditional dress of a court jester, including a cap with bells attached.

caparison¹ /kə'paris(ə)n/ *noun* **1** an ornamental covering for a horse, *esp* for a warhorse in former times. **2** rich clothing; adornment. [French *caraçon* from Old Spanish *caparazón*]

caparison² *verb trans* (**caparisoned, caparisoning**) to put a caparison on (something or somebody).

cape¹ /kayp/ *noun* a sleeveless outer garment, or part of a garment, that fits closely at the neck, hangs loosely from the shoulders, and

is usu shorter than a cloak. ⪢ **caped** *adj.* [prob via Spanish *capa* cloak, from late Latin *cappa* head covering, cloak]

cape² *noun* a point or area of land jutting out into a sea as a headland or promontory. [Middle English *cap* via French and Old Provençal from Latin *caput* head]

Cape Coloured *noun* a person of mixed black and white ancestry in S Africa. ⪢ **Cape Coloured** *adj.* [named after Cape Province, former province of S Africa]

Cape doctor *noun* a strong SE wind of S Africa. [from the belief that it blows away disease and germs]

Cape Dutch *noun archaic* = AFRIKAANS.

Cape gooseberry *noun* **1** an edible yellow fruit. **2** the tropical plant of the potato family that bears this fruit and yellow flowers: *Physalis peruviana.*

capelin /'kap(ə)lin/ *or* **caplin** /'kaplin/ *noun* a small food fish of northern seas related to the smelts: *Mallotus villosus.* [Canadian French *capelan* via French from Old Provençal *capelan* chaplain, codfish, from medieval Latin *cappellanus:* see CHAPLAIN]

caper¹ /'kaypə/ *verb intrans* (**capered, capering**) to leap about in a playful or carefree way; to prance. [prob by shortening and alteration from CAPRIOLE¹ (noun)]

caper² *noun* **1** a playful or carefree leap. **2** a high-spirited escapade; a prank. **3** *informal* a frivolous, disreputable, dangerous, or illegal activity or enterprise.

caper³ *noun* **1** (*usu in pl*) any of the greenish flower buds or young berries of a Mediterranean shrub, which are pickled and used as a seasoning, garnish, etc. **2** the low prickly shrub that bears these buds and berries: *Capparis spinosa.* [back-formation from *capers* (taken as a pl), from Middle English *caperis* via Latin from Greek *kapparis*]

capercaillie /kapə'kayli/ *or* **capercailzie** /-'kaylzi/ *noun* the largest grouse of Europe, Asia, and Africa, found *esp* in N European forests: *Tetrao urogallus.* [Scottish Gaelic *capull coille,* literally 'horse of the woods']

Capetian /kə'peesh(ə)n/ *noun* a member of the dynasty that ruled France from 987 to 1328. ⪢ **Capetian** *adj.* [French *capétien,* from Hugh *Capet* d.996, French king who founded the dynasty]

Cape Verdean /'vuhdi-ən/ *noun* a native or inhabitant of Cape Verde, archipelago and republic in the Atlantic Ocean off the coast of NW Africa. ⪢ **Cape Verdean** *adj.*

capias /'kaypi-as, 'kap-/ *noun* (*pl* **capiases**) in law, a writ ordering that the named person be arrested. [Latin *capias,* literally 'you are to take']

capillarity /kapi'lariti/ *noun* the phenomenon in which the surface of a liquid in contact with a solid, e.g. in a fine-bore tube, is raised or lowered depending on the relative attraction of the molecules of the liquid for each other and for those of the solid. Also called CAPILLARY ACTION. [CAPILLARY² + -ITY]

capillary¹ *noun* (*pl* **capillaries**) a capillary tube or passage, *esp* any of the smallest blood vessels connecting arterioles (small arteries; see ARTERIOLE) with venules (small veins; see VENULE) and forming networks throughout the body: compare ARTERY, VEIN¹.

capillary² /kə'piləri/ *adj* **1a** resembling a hair, *esp* in slender elongated form. **b** said of a tube, passage, etc: having a very fine bore. **2** of capillaries or capillarity. [French *capillaire* from Latin *capillaris,* from *capillus* hair]

capillary action *noun* = CAPILLARITY.

capital¹ /'kapitl/ *noun* **1a** a city serving as a seat of government: *the capital of France.* **b** a place that is preeminent in some specified field of activity: *the antiques capital of the world.* **2a** wealth or goods used to produce further wealth or goods. **b** a sum of money saved, lent, borrowed, or invested. **c** a stock of accumulated possessions, or their value, *esp* at a particular time and in contrast to income received during a particular period. **d** the excess of the assets of a business over its liabilities. **e** (*treated as sing. or pl*) people holding capital; the capitalist class. **3** a capital letter. ✲ **make capital out of** to turn (a situation) to one's advantage. [French *capital* from Italian *capitale* chief, principal, from Latin *capitalis* (see CAPITAL²); (senses 2 and 3) from CAPITAL²]

capital² *adj* **1** punishable by death: *a capital crime.* **2** said of a letter: of the series used to begin sentences or proper names, e.g. *A, B, C* rather than *a, b, c.* **3** of the greatest significance or influence: *the capital importance of criticism in the work of creation itself* — T S Eliot.

4 *dated* excellent: *a capital book.* ⨠ **capitally** *adv.* [Middle English from Latin *capitalis*, from *capit-, caput* head]

capital³ *noun* the uppermost part of an architectural column. [Middle English *capitale* via French from late Latin *capitellum* small head, top of column, dimin. of Latin *capit-, caput* head]

capital assets *pl noun* = FIXED ASSETS.

capital gain *noun* (*usu in pl, but treated as sing.*) the profit from the sale of an asset, e.g. a house.

capital gains tax *noun* tax levied on capital gains.

capital goods *pl noun* goods used in producing other commodities rather than for sale to consumers.

capital-intensive *adj* involving a proportionately large investment in buildings, machinery, etc in the process of production: compare LABOUR-INTENSIVE.

capitalise /'kapitl·iez/ *verb* see CAPITALIZE.

capitalism *noun* an economic system characterized by the profit motive and by private ownership and control of the means of production, distribution, and exchange.

capitalist¹ *noun* **1** a person with capital, *esp* invested in business; *broadly* a very wealthy person. **2** a person who favours capitalism.

capitalist² *or* **capitalistic** /-'listik/ *adj* **1** owning capital: *the capitalist class.* **2** of, practising, or advocating capitalism: *capitalist nations.* ⨠ **capitalistically** /-'listikli/ *adv.*

capitalize *or* **capitalise** *verb trans* **1** to write or print (e.g. a word) in capitals or with an initial capital. **2** to convert (something) into capital: *They capitalized the company's reserve fund.* **3** to convert (a periodic payment) into an equivalent lump sum: *capitalized annuities.* **4** to supply capital for (somebody or something). **5** to calculate the present value of (an income extended over a period of time). ⨠ *verb intrans* (+ on) to gain by turning (something) to advantage: *The party capitalized on the country's growing social unrest.* ⨠ **capitalization** /-'zaysh(ə)n/ *noun.*

capital levy *noun* a levy on personal or industrial capital in addition to income tax and other taxes; a general property tax.

capital punishment *noun* the legal killing of criminals as punishment for their crimes; the death penalty.

capital ship *noun* a warship, e.g. a battleship, of the first rank in size and importance.

capital transfer tax *noun* in Britain, between 1975 and 1986, a tax levied on the estate of a dead person: compare DEATH DUTY, INHERITANCE TAX.

capitate /'capitayt/ *noun* (*also* **capitate bone**) the largest of the bones of the CARPUS (wrist), which articulates with the central bone of the METACARPUS (bones between wrist and fingers) at the base of the hand. [Latin *capitatus* headed, from *capit-, caput* head]

capitation /kapi'taysh(ə)n/ *noun* a payment or charge based on a fixed amount per person. [late Latin *capitation-, capitatio* poll tax, from Latin *capit-, caput* head]

capitol /'kapitl/ *noun* **1** (**Capitol**) the building in which the US Congress meets in Washington DC. **2** a building in which a US state legislative body meets. [Latin *Capitolium*, temple of Jupiter on the Capitoline hill in Rome]

capitula /kə'pityoolə/ *noun* pl of CAPITULUM.

capitular /kə'pityoolə/ *adj* of a cathedral chapter. [medieval Latin *capitularis*, from *capitulum* chapter, dimin. of Latin *capit-, caput* head]

capitulate /kə'pityoolayt/ *verb intrans* **1** to surrender, often after negotiation of terms. **2** to cease resisting; to acquiesce. [medieval Latin *capitulatus*, past part. of *capitulare* to distinguish by heads or chapters, from late Latin *capitulum*: see CAPITULAR]

capitulation /kə,pityoo'laysh(ə)n/ *noun* **1** the act of capitulating. **2** an agreement setting out terms of surrender. **3** a set of terms or articles constituting an agreement between governments, *esp* in former times.

capitulum /kə'pityoolǝm/ *noun* (*pl* **capitula** /-lə/) **1** a rounded or flattened cluster of stalkless flowers, often simulating one larger flower. **2** a rounded enlarged part on the end of an anatomical structure, e.g. a bone. [via scientific Latin from Latin *capitulum*: see CAPITULAR]

caplet /'kaplit/ *noun trademark* a medicinal tablet, usu oval in shape, with a hard smooth soluble outer coating. [blend of CAPSULE + TABLET]

caplin /'kaplin/ *noun* see CAPELIN.

capo /'kapoh/ *noun* (*pl* **capos**) a movable bar attached to the fingerboard of a guitar or similar musical instrument to raise the pitch of all the strings uniformly. [short for *capotasto*, from Italian *capotasto*, literally 'head of fingerboard']

capoeira /kapooh'ayrǝ/ *noun* a Brazilian martial art and dance form which originated among slaves of African descent. ⨠ **capoeirista** /kapoo·i'reestǝ/ *noun.* [Portuguese, possibly from an African language]

capon /'kaypǝn/ *noun* a castrated male chicken fattened for eating: *and then the justice, in fair round belly with good capon lined* — Shakespeare. [Old English *capūn*, prob via French from Latin *capon-, capo*; related to Greek *koptein* to cut]

caponize *or* **caponise** /'kaypǝniez/ *verb trans* to castrate (a male chicken) and fatten it for eating.

capote /kǝ'poht/ *noun* a long hooded cloak or overcoat. [French *capote* from *cape* cloak, from late Latin *cappa*]

cappuccino /kapoo'cheenoh/ *noun* (*pl* **cappuccinos**) frothy coffee made with espresso and steamed milk. [Italian *cappuccino* Capuchin; from the likeness of its colour to that of a Capuchin's habit]

capriccio /kǝ'prichioh/ *noun* (*pl* **capriccios**) an instrumental piece in free form, usu lively in tempo. [Italian *capriccio*: see CAPRICE]

capriccioso /kǝprichi'ohzoh/ *adj and adv* said of a piece of music: to be performed in a free and lively manner. [Italian *capriccioso* from *capriccio*: see CAPRICE]

caprice /kǝ'prees/ *noun* **1a** a sudden and seemingly unmotivated change of mind. **b** a disposition to change one's mind impulsively. **2** a sudden and unpredictable change or series of changes: *the caprices of the weather.* **3** = CAPRICCIO. [French *caprice* from Italian *capriccio*, literally 'head with hair standing on end', later 'a sudden start', from *capo* head (from Latin *caput*) + *riccio* hedgehog, from Latin *ericius*]

capricious /kǝ'prishǝs/ *adj* governed or characterized by caprice; apt to change suddenly or unpredictably. ⨠ **capriciously** *adv,* **capriciousness** *noun.*

Capricorn /'kaprikawn/ *noun* **1** (*also* **Capricornus**) in astronomy, a constellation (the Goat) depicted as a creature resembling a goat with the tail of a fish. **2a** in astrology, the tenth sign of the zodiac. **b** a person born under this sign. ⨠ **Capricornian** /-'kawni·ǝn/ *adj and noun.* [Middle English *Capricorne* from Latin *Capricornus*, from *caper* goat + *cornu* horn]

caprine /'kaprien/ *adj* of or resembling a goat. [Latin *caprinus*, from *capr-, caper* goat]

capriole¹ /'kapriohl/ *noun* a vertical leap made by a trained horse with a backward kick of the hind legs at the height of the leap. [early French *capriole* from Old Italian *capriola*, from *capriolo* roebuck, from Latin *capreolus* goat, roebuck, from *capr-, caper* he-goat]

capriole² *verb intrans* said of a horse: to perform a capriole.

caps. *abbr* **1** capital letters. **2** capsule.

Capsian /'kapsi·ǝn/ *adj* of a Palaeolithic culture of N Africa and S Europe. [French *capsien*, from Latin *Capsa* Gafsa, oasis in Tunisia where traces of this culture were found]

capsicum /'kapsikǝm/ *noun* **1** any of a genus of tropical plants and shrubs of the nightshade family bearing fruit with many seeds and fleshy walls, e.g. the hot pepper and sweet pepper: genus *Capsicum.* **2** a fruit of this plant, which comes in a variety of colours and is used as a vegetable, for flavouring, etc; a pepper. [from the Latin genus name, perhaps from Latin *capsa* case, chest, from *capere* to take]

capsid¹ /'kapsid/ *noun* any of a large family of bugs that are mostly plant-feeding and cause damage to crops: family Miridae. Also called MIRID. [derivative of Greek *kapsis* gulping, from *kaptein* to gulp down]

capsid² *noun* the outer protein shell of a virus particle. [Latin *capsa* (see CAPSICUM) + -ID²]

capsize /kap'siez/ *verb trans* to cause (a boat) to overturn. ⨠ *verb intrans* said of a boat: to overturn. [origin unknown]

capstan /'kapstǝn/ *noun* **1** a mechanical device consisting of an upright drum round which a rope, cable, etc is wound, used for moving or raising heavy weights. **2** a rotating shaft that drives tape at a constant speed in a tape recorder. [Middle English via Old Provençal from Latin *capistrum* halter, from *capere* to seize]

capstan lathe *noun* a lathe with a rotatable holder for mounting a number of tools to be used in succession.

capstone /'kapstohn/ *noun* = COPINGSTONE.

capsulated /'kapsyoolaytid/ *adj* enclosed in a capsule.

capsule /'kapsyoohl, 'kapsyool/ *noun* **1** a gelatin shell enclosing a drug for swallowing. **2a** a detachable pressurized compartment, *esp* in a spacecraft or aircraft, containing crew and controls. **b** a spacecraft. **3** a membrane or sac enclosing a body part. **4a** a dry fruit composed of two or more carpels (female reproductive organs; see CARPEL) that burst open spontaneously when mature to release their seeds. **b** the spore-producing sac of a moss. **5** a metal, wax, or plastic covering that encloses the top of a bottle, *esp* of wine, and protects the cork. **6** (*used before a noun*) brief or compact: *capsule criticism*. >> **capsular** /'kapsyoolə/ *adj*, **capsulate** *adj*. [French *capsule* from Latin *capsula*, dimin. of *capsa*: see CASE²]

capsulize or **capsulise** /'kapsyooliez/ *verb trans* to formulate or state (information) in a brief or compact way.

Capt. *abbr* captain.

captain¹ /'kaptin/ *noun* **1a** a person in command of a ship or boat. **b** a pilot of a civil aircraft. **2a** in the Royal Navy and US Navy, an officer ranking below a commodore and above a commander. **b** in the army, marines, and some air forces, an officer ranking below a major and above a lieutenant. **3** a leader of a team, *esp* a sports team. **4** a dominant figure: *captains of industry*. **5** *NAmer* a fire or police officer. >> **captaincy** /-si/ *noun*, **captainship** *noun*. [Middle English *capitane* via Old French from late Latin *capitaneus* chief, from Latin *capit-, caput* head]

captain² *verb trans* to be captain of (something).

caption¹ /'kapsh(ə)n/ *noun* **1** a comment or description accompanying a pictorial illustration. **2** a heading or title, *esp* of an article or a legal document. **3** a subtitle or other piece of textual information on a film or television screen.

Word history
Middle English *capcioun* from Latin *caption-, captio* act of taking, from *capere* to take. Caption orig meant 'arrest' or 'an arrest warrant', later the statement of when, where, and by whose authority the warrant was issued, hence a heading or title.

caption² *verb trans* (**captioned, captioning**) to supply a caption or captions for (something).

captious /'kapshəs/ *adj* having or showing an ill-natured inclination to find fault and raise objections. >> **captiously** *adv*, **captiousness** *noun*. [Middle English *capcious* via Old French from Latin *captiosus*, from *caption-, captio* act of taking, deception, from *capere* to take]

captivate /'kaptivayt/ *verb trans* to fascinate or charm (somebody) irresistibly: *He was captivated by her beauty.* >> **captivating** *adj*, **captivatingly** *adv*, **captivation** /-'vaysh(ə)n/ *noun*.

captive¹ /'kaptiv/ *adj* **1a** taken and held prisoner, *esp* by an enemy in war. **b** kept within bounds; confined. **c** held under control. **2** in a situation that makes departure or inattention difficult: *a captive audience*. >> **captivity** /kap'tiviti/ *noun*. [Middle English from Latin *captivus*, from *captus*, past part. of *capere* to take]

captive² *noun* somebody who is taken and held prisoner.

captor /'kaptə/ *noun* somebody who takes and holds another captive. [late Latin *captor*, from Latin *captus*: see CAPTIVE¹]

capture¹ /'kapchə/ *noun* **1** the act of gaining control or possession. **2** somebody or something that has been captured. **3** in physics, the acquisition by an atom, molecule, ion, or nucleus of an additional elementary particle, often with associated emission of radiation. **4** the collection and storing of data by computer. [French *capture* from Latin *captura*, from *captus*: see CAPTIVE¹]

capture² *verb trans* **1** to take (a person, animal, or place) captive. **2** to represent or preserve (something) in words, pictures, etc: *how well the scene was captured on film*. **3** to remove (e.g. a chess piece) from the playing board according to the rules of a game. **4** in physics, to bring about the capture of (an elementary particle). **5** to store (data) in a computer.

capuchin /kə'pyoohchin, -shin/ *noun* **1** (**Capuchin**) a member of a strict branch of the Franciscan order of missionary friars. **2** a hooded cloak worn by women in former times. **3** any of several species of S American monkeys with hair on their crown shaped like a monk's cowl: genus *Cebus*. **4** a domestic fancy pigeon of a breed with head and neck feathers resembling a monk's cowl. [early French *capuchin* from Old Italian *cappuccino*, from *cappuccio* hood, from *cappa* cowl, cloak, from late Latin]

capybara /kapi'bahrə/ *noun* (*pl* **capybaras**) a mainly aquatic S American rodent with no tail that resembles a large guinea pig: *Hydrocherus hydrochaeris*. [Portuguese *capibara*, from Tupi]

car /kah/ *noun* **1** a usu four-wheeled motor vehicle designed for transporting a small number of people and typically propelled by an internal-combustion engine. **2** a railway carriage, *esp* one used for a specific purpose: *the buffet car; a sleeping car*. **3** the passenger compartment of an airship or balloon. **4** *chiefly literary* a chariot or war or of triumph: *like captives bound to a triumphant car* — Shakespeare. >> **carful** (*pl* **carfuls**) *noun*. [Middle English *carre* from Anglo-French, ultimately from Latin *carrus*, of Celtic origin]

carabineer or **carabinier** /,karəbi'niə/ *noun* a soldier armed with a carbine. [French *carabinier*, from *carabine* carbine, from early French *carabin* carabineer]

carabiner /karə'beenə/ *noun* see KARABINER.

carabinier /karəbi'niə/ *noun* see CARABINEER.

carabiniere /,karəbi'nyeəri/ *noun* (*pl* **carabinieri** /-ri/) a member of the Italian national police force. [Italian *carabiniere* from French *carabinier*: see CARABINEER]

caracal /'karəkal/ *noun* a medium-sized wild cat of Africa and Asia that has long legs and sharply pointed ears with black tufts: *Felis caracal*. [French *caracal* via Spanish from Turkish *karakulak*, literally 'black-ear', from *kara* black + *kulak* ear]

caracara /kahrə'kahrə/ *noun* (*pl* **caracaras**) any of several species of large mostly S American birds of prey that have long legs and bare faces and feed on carrion: family Falconidae. [via Spanish or Portuguese from Tupi *caracará*, of imitative origin]

caracole¹ /'karəkohl/ *noun* in dressage, a half turn to the right or left executed by a horse and rider. [via French from Spanish *caracol* snail, spiral stair, caracole]

caracole² *verb intrans* to perform a caracole.

caracul /'karəkl/ *noun* see KARAKUL.

carafe /kə'rahf, kə'raf/ *noun* a glass container, typically with a flaring lip and open top, used to hold water or wine, *esp* at table. [French *carafe* via Italian from Arabic *gharrāfah*]

carambola /karəm'bohlə/ *noun* **1** a greenish yellow fruit with a sweet-sour taste and a distinctive lobed appearance that gives it a star-shaped cross-section. Also called STARFRUIT. **2** the E Indian tree of the wood-sorrel family that bears this fruit: *Averrhoa carambola*. [Portuguese *carambola* from Marathi *karambal*]

caramel /'karəməl, 'karəmel/ *noun* **1** a dark brown substance obtained by heating sugar and used as a colouring and flavouring agent. **2** a chewy soft toffee. [French *caramel* via Spanish from Portuguese *caramelo* icicle, caramel, from late Latin *calamellus* small reed]

caramelize or **caramelise** /'karəməliez/ *verb trans* to change (sugar or the sugar content of a food) into caramel. > *verb intrans* to change to caramel. >> **caramelization** /-'zaysh(ə)n/ *noun*.

carapace /'karəpays/ *noun* a hard case, e.g. of chitin, covering the back or part of the back of a turtle, crab, etc. [French *carapace* from Spanish *carapacho*]

carat /'karət/ *noun* **1** a unit of weight used for precious stones equal to 200mg. **2** (*NAmer chiefly* **karat**) a unit of fineness for gold equal to one twenty-fourth part of pure gold in an alloy. [French *carat*, prob via medieval Latin from Arabic *qīrāt* bean pod, a small weight, from Greek *keration* carob bean, a small weight, dimin. of *kerat-, keras* horn; referring to the long seed pod of the carob]

caravan¹ /'karəvan/ *noun* **1** *Brit* an enclosed or covered vehicle designed to be towed by a car or horse and to serve as a dwelling when parked. **2a** (*treated as sing. or pl*) a company of travellers, often with pack animals, on a journey through desert or hostile regions. **b** a group of vehicles travelling together. [Italian *caravana* from Persian *kārwān*]

caravan² *verb intrans* (**caravanned, caravanning**, *NAmer* **caravaned, caravaning**) to have a holiday in a caravan. >> **caravanner** *noun*, **caravanning** *noun*.

caravanserai /karə'vansərie/ (*NAmer* **caravansary** /-səri/) *noun* (*pl* **caravanserais** or **caravansaries**) a large inn in Eastern countries that is built round a courtyard and used as a resting place for travellers and their animals. [Persian *kārwānsarāī*, from *kārwān* CARAVAN¹ + *sarāī* palace, inn]

caravel /'karəvel/ or **carvel** /'kahvl/ *noun* a small Spanish and Portuguese ship of the 15th and 16th cents with broad bows, a high narrow POOP[1] (superstructure at stern), and triangular sails. [French *caravelle* from Old Portuguese *caravela*]

caraway /'karəway/ *noun* **1** an aromatic plant of the carrot family with white flowers and pungent seeds used for flavouring food: *Carum carvi*. **2** the seeds of this plant used in cookery. [Middle English via medieval Latin from Arabic *karawyā*, prob from Greek *karon* cumin]

carb /kahb/ *noun informal* = CARBURETTOR.

carb- *or* **carbo-** *comb. form* forming words, denoting: carbon: *carbide*; *carbohydrate*. [French *carbone*: see CARBON]

carbamate /'kahbəmayt/ *noun* a salt or ester of carbamic acid.

carbamic acid /kah'bamik/ *noun* an acid occurring in the form of salts and esters in the blood and urine of mammals. formula NH_2COOH. [CARB- + AMIDE + -IC[1]]

carbaryl /'kahbəril/ *noun* a synthetic insecticide used to kill head lice, fleas, and plant pests. [CARBAMATE + -YL]

carbide /'kahbied/ *noun* a chemical compound of carbon usu with a metallic element.

carbine /'kahbien/ *noun* **1** a short light automatic or semi-automatic rifle. **2** a short light rifle or musket orig carried by cavalry. [French *carabine* from early French *carabin* carabineer]

carbo- *comb. form* see CARB-.

carbohydrate /kahbə'hiedrayt, kahboh-/ *noun* any of various compounds of carbon, hydrogen, and oxygen, e.g. sugars, starches, and celluloses, often formed by plants and constituting a major class of energy-providing animal foods.

carbolic acid /kah'bolik/ *noun* = PHENOL (1). [CARB- + -IC[1] + Latin *oleum* oil]

car bomb *noun* an explosive device concealed in a motor vehicle, *esp* one intended for use against people or property in the vicinity of the vehicle.

carbon /'kahb(ə)n/ *noun* **1** a non-metallic chemical element occurring naturally as diamond, graphite, etc or forming a constituent of coal, petroleum, limestone and other carbonates, and organic compounds: symbol C, atomic number 6. **2a** = CARBON PAPER (2). **b** = CARBON COPY (1). **3** a piece of carbon used as a component of a battery. [French *carbone* from Latin *carbon-*, *carbo* ember, charcoal]

carbon 14 *noun* a radioactive carbon isotope of mass number 14, used in CARBON DATING.

carbonaceous /kahbə'nayshəs/ *adj* relating to, resembling, or containing carbon.

carbonade /'kahbənayd/ *noun* see CARBONNADE.

carbonado /kahbə'naydoh/ *noun* (*pl* **carbonados**) an opaque dark-coloured diamond used as an abrasive. [Portuguese *carbonado*, literally 'carbonated', from *carbone* carbon, from French: see CARBON]

carbonara /kahbə'nahrə/ *noun* a pasta dish served with a sauce containing ham, cheese, cream, and eggs. [Italian *carbonara*, from *alla carbonara* on the charcoal grill]

carbonate[1] /'kahbənət, -nayt/ *noun* a salt or ester of carbonic acid.

carbonate[2] /'kahbənayt/ *verb trans* **1** to convert (something) into a carbonate. **2** to impregnate (a drink) with carbon dioxide; to aerate (it). >>> **carbonation** /-'naysh(ə)n/ *noun*.

carbon black *noun* any of various black substances consisting of very small particles of carbon that are obtained usu as soot and are used *esp* as pigments.

carbon copy *noun* **1** a copy made with carbon paper. **2** a duplicate or exact replica: *He is a carbon copy of his father.*

carbon cycle *noun* the cycle of carbon in living things in which carbon dioxide from the air is processed by plants during photosynthesis to form organic nutrients and is ultimately restored to the inorganic state by respiration and rotting.

carbon dating *noun* the determination of the age of ancient organic material, e.g. wood or fossil bones, by recording the deterioration of carbon 14 in the material.

carbon dioxide *noun* a heavy colourless gas that does not support combustion, is formed *esp* by the burning and decomposition of organic substances, and is absorbed from the air by plants in photosynthesis: formula CO_2.

carbon disulphide *noun* a colourless flammable poisonous liquid, used *esp* as a solvent for rubber: formula CS_2.

carbon fibre *noun* a strong lightweight material made from filaments of pure carbon.

carbonic /kah'bonik/ *adj* of, containing, or derived from carbon or carbon dioxide.

carbonic acid /kah'bonik/ *noun* a weak acid that is a solution of carbon dioxide in water: formula H_2CO_3.

carboniferous /kahbə'nif(ə)rəs/ *adj* **1** producing or containing carbon or coal. **2** (**Carboniferous**) relating to or dating from a geological period, the fifth period of the Palaeozoic era, lasting from about 363 million to about 290 million years ago, and marked by the formation of coal deposits. >>> **Carboniferous** *noun*.

carbonize *or* **carbonise** *verb trans* to convert (something) into carbon or a carbon-containing residue. > *verb intrans* to become carbonized. >>> **carbonization** /-'zaysh(ə)n/ *noun*.

carbon monoxide *noun* a very toxic gas with no colour or odour, formed as a product of the incomplete combustion of carbon: formula CO.

carbonnade *or* **carbonade** /kahbə'nayd/ *noun* a rich beef stew made with beer. [orig in the sense 'meat or fish cooked on hot coals'; French *carbonnade*, from Latin *carbon-*, *carbo* ember, charcoal]

carbon paper *noun* **1** thin paper coated on one side with dark pigment that is placed between two sheets of paper to make a copy, the pigment being transferred by the pressure of writing or typing on the upper sheet. **2** a sheet of this paper.

carbon sink *noun* a forest or any other area of land or sea rich in the plant life that absorbs large amounts of the carbon dioxide produced by the burning of fossil fuels.

carbon tax *noun* a tax on fossil fuels, e.g. petrol, with the aim of reducing their use in order to protect the environment.

carbon tetrachloride /tetrə'klawried/ *noun* a colourless non-flammable poisonous liquid used as an industrial solvent and a starting material for making other organic compounds: formula CCl_4.

carbonyl /'kahbənil/ *noun* a chemical group occurring in aldehydes, ketones and carboxylic acids: formula CO, valency 2.

car boot sale *noun Brit* a sale of miscellaneous secondhand articles usu from the boots of the sellers' cars parked on a designated site.

Carborundum /kahbə'rundəm/ *noun trademark* any of various abrasive materials. [blend of CARBON + CORUNDUM]

carboxyl /kah'boksil/ *noun* a chemical group that is typical of acidic organic chemical compounds: formula COOH. [CARB- + OXYGEN + -YL]

carboxylate /kah'boksilayt/ *noun* a salt or ester of a carboxylic acid.

carboxylic acid /kahbok'silik/ *noun* an organic acid, e.g. acetic acid, containing one or more carboxyl groups.

carboy /'kahboy/ *noun* a large usu spherical container for corrosive liquids, often in a protective frame. [Persian *qarāba* from Arabic *qarrābah* demijohn]

carbuncle /'kahbungkl/ *noun* **1** a painful boil-like inflammation of the skin and deeper tissues with several openings for the discharge of pus: *What is proposed [as an extension to the National Gallery] is like a monstrous carbuncle on the face of a much-loved and elegant friend* — Charles, Prince of Wales. **2** a red gemstone, usu a garnet, cut in a domed shape without facets. >>> **carbuncular** /kah'bungkyoolə/ *adj*. [Middle English via Old French from Latin *carbunculus* small coal, carbuncle, dimin. of *carbon-*, *carbo* charcoal, ember]

carburation /kahbyoo'raysh(ə)n/ *noun* the process of mixing air with fuel in a carburettor to produce an explosive mixture for an internal-combustion engine.

carburet /'kahbyooret/ *verb trans* (**carburetted, carburetting,** *NAmer* **carbureted, carbureting**) to combine or enrich (e.g. a gas) with carbon or carbon compounds. [obsolete *carburet* carbide]

carburettor *or* **carburetter** (*NAmer* **carburetor**) /kahbyoo'retə, kahbə'retə/ *noun* an apparatus for supplying an internal-combustion engine with a fixed quantity of vaporized fuel mixed with air in an explosive mixture.

carcajou /'kahkəjooh, -zhooh/ *noun NAmer* = WOLVERINE. [Canadian French *carcajou*, of Native American origin]

carcass or **carcase** /'kahkəs/ noun 1 a dead body, esp the body of an animal slaughtered for meat. 2 the decaying or worthless remains of a structure: *the half-submerged carcass of a wrecked vessel.* 3 a framework, esp the framework of a tyre as distinct from the tread. 4 *humorous or derog* a living human body: *Shift your carcass!* [French *carcasse* from Old French *carcois*]

carcinogen /kah'sinəjən/ noun something, e.g. a chemical compound, that causes cancer. >> **carcinogenesis** /-'jenəsis/ noun, **carcinogenic** /-'jenik/ adj, **carcinogenicity** /,kahsinəjə'nisiti/ noun. [Greek *karkinos* crab, cancer + -GEN]

carcinoma /kahsi'nohmə/ noun (pl **carcinomas** or **carcinomata** /-mətə/) a cancerous tumour originating in the EPITHELIUM (tissue covering an external surface or lining a body cavity). >> **carcinomatous** /-mətəs/ adj. [via Latin from Greek *karkinōma* cancer, from *karkinos* crab, cancer]

car coat noun a short coat orig designed for car drivers.

card[1] /kahd/ noun 1a thin cardboard or stiff paper. b a piece of card, usu small and rectangular in shape, used for any of various purposes: *an identity card; an index card.* 2a a postcard. b a greetings card. c a visiting card. 3a a playing card. b (*in pl, but treated as sing. or pl*) a game played with cards. 4 a rectangular piece of plastic issued by a bank or other organization, usu having machine-readable information about the holder and used to obtain credit, withdraw cash, etc. 5 a programme, esp one for a sporting event. 6 a valuable asset, advantage, or right for use in negotiations: *They hold all the cards.* 7 Brit, informal (*in pl*) the official documents relating to an employee's income tax, national insurance, etc, held by their employer. 8 *informal* an amusing or eccentric person. * **a card up one's sleeve** a secret plan or asset kept in reserve until needed. **get/ask for one's cards** Brit, informal to be dismissed/resign from employment. **on the cards** quite possible; likely to occur. **put/lay one's cards on the table** to divulge or declare one's intentions, position, resources, etc. [Middle English *carde* from Old French *carte*, prob from Old Italian *carta* leaf of paper, from Latin *charta* leaf of papyrus, from Greek *chartēs*]

card[2] noun an implement or machine for carding fibres or raising a nap on cloth. [Middle English *carde* via Old French from late Latin *cardus* thistle, from Latin *carduus*]

card[3] verb trans to cleanse and disentangle (fibres) with a toothed implement or machine preparatory to spinning. >> **carder** noun.

cardamom /'kahdəməm/ noun 1 an aromatic fruit containing seeds used as a spice or condiment. 2 the E Indian plant of the ginger family that bears this fruit: *Elettaria cardamomum.* [via Latin from Greek *kardamōmon*, blend of *kardamon* peppergrass and *amōmon*, an Indian spice plant]

cardboard[1] noun a thick stiff material made from the same ingredients as paper and used for boxes, packaging, etc.

cardboard[2] adj 1 made of cardboard. 2 unreal or insubstantial: *The story has too many cardboard characters.*

cardboard city noun a place where many homeless people sleep in makeshift shelters, e.g. cardboard boxes.

card-carrying adj 1 being a fully paid-up member, esp of a political party or trade union. 2 dedicated or committed to a cause. [from the assumption that such a person carries a membership card]

cardi- or **cardio-** comb. form forming words, with the meanings: 1 heart; cardiac: *cardiogram; cardiology.* 2 cardiac and: *cardiovascular.* [Greek *kardi-, kardio-*, from *kardia* heart]

cardiac[1] /'kahdiak/ adj 1 relating to or in the region of the heart. 2 relating to or in the region of the part of the stomach into which the oesophagus opens. [via scientific Latin from Greek *kardiakos*, from *kardia* heart]

cardiac[2] noun somebody suffering from heart disease.

cardie or **cardy** /'kahdi/ noun (pl **cardies**) informal a cardigan. [by shortening and alteration]

cardigan /'kahdigən/ noun a knitted garment with sleeves for the upper body that opens down the front and is usu fastened with buttons.

Word history

named after James Thomas Brudenell, seventh Earl of *Cardigan* d.1868, English soldier. Cardigan's troops wore jackets resembling this garment while serving in the Crimea.

cardinal[1] /'kahdinl/ noun 1 a member of a body of high officials of the Roman Catholic Church whose powers include the election of a new pope. 2 a deep scarlet colour. 3 any of several species of finches of the USA, the male of which has bright red plumage: subfamily Cardinalinae. >> **cardinalate** /-dinələt, -dinəlayt/ noun, **cardinalship** noun. [Middle English via Old French from Latin *cardinalis* of a hinge, from *cardin-, cardo* hinge; (senses 2, 3) from the colour of a cardinal's robes]

cardinal[2] adj of primary importance; fundamental. >> **cardinally** adv.

cardinal flower noun a N American lobelia with bright scarlet flowers: *Lobelia cardinalis.*

cardinal number noun a number, e.g. one, two, three, that is used in simple counting and that indicates how many items there are in a set: compare ORDINAL NUMBER.

cardinal point noun any of the four principal compass points: north, south, east, and west.

cardinal red noun = CARDINAL[1] (2).

cardinal virtue noun any of the four traditionally defined natural virtues, i.e. prudence, justice, temperance, and fortitude; *broadly* any important moral quality.

cardinal vowel system noun a set of standard reference points for describing or classifying the vowel sounds of any language according to the shape of the mouth and the position of the tongue.

card index noun Brit a filing or cataloguing system in which each item is entered on a separate card.

card-index verb trans to make a card index of (something).

cardio- comb. form see CARDI-.

cardiogram /'kahdiəgram/ noun the curve or tracing made by a cardiograph.

cardiograph /'kahdi-əgrahf, -graf/ noun an instrument that registers movements of the heart in the form of a graph. >> **cardiographer** /-'ogrəfə/ noun, **cardiographic** /-'grafik/ adj, **cardiography** /-'ogrəfi/ noun.

cardioid /'kahdioyd/ noun a heart-shaped curve traced by a point on the circumference of a circle as it rolls completely round a fixed circle of equal radius.

cardiology /kahdi'oləji/ noun the branch of medical science concerned with the heart, its diseases, and their treatment. >> **cardiological** /-'lojikl/ adj, **cardiologist** noun.

cardiopulmonary /kahdioh'pulmən(ə)ri, -'poolmən(ə)ri/ adj relating to or in the region of the heart and lungs.

cardiovascular /,kahdioh'vaskyoolə/ adj relating to or in the region of the heart and blood vessels.

cardoon /kah'doohn/ noun a large plant of the daisy family that is related to the globe artichoke and cultivated for its edible root and leafstalks: *Cynara cardunculus.* [French *cardon* from late Latin *cardon-, cardo* thistle, from Latin *carduus* thistle, artichoke]

cardsharp noun a person who habitually cheats at cards.

cardsharper noun = CARDSHARP.

card vote noun = BLOCK VOTE.

cardy /'kahdi/ noun see CARDIE.

care[1] /keə/ noun 1a anxiety: *a face lined with care.* b a cause for anxiety: *without a care in the world.* 2 close attention; effort: *She took care over the drawing.* 3a charge; supervision: *under the doctor's care.* b Brit legal responsibility for or guardianship of children by a local authority: *taken into care.* c a sense of loving protectiveness or solicitude: *a father's care.* d attention to or provision for the welfare, maintenance, etc of somebody or something: *the care of the elderly.* 4 somebody or something that is an object of attention, anxiety, or solicitude: *The flower garden was her special care.* * **care of** at the address of. **take care** to be careful or watchful; to exercise caution or prudence. **take care of 1** to attend to (something): *We'll take care of the catering.* **2** to deal with (somebody): *If there are any troublemakers, I'll take care of them.* **3** to look after (somebody): *As she became older, she was no longer able to take care of herself.* [Old English *caru*]

care[2] verb intrans 1a to feel trouble or anxiety: *She doesn't care if she hurts people's feelings.* b (*often* + about) to feel interest or concern: *He doesn't care about politics.* 2 to give care: *They care for the sick.* 3 (+ for) to have a liking or taste for (something or somebody): *I don't care for brandy.* > verb trans 1 to be concerned about (something or somebody): *Nobody cares what I do.* 2 to wish (to do something): *if you care to go.*

careen /kə'reen/ *verb trans* **1** to cause (e.g. a boat) to lean over to one side. **2** to clean, caulk, or repair (a boat) in this position. ➤ *verb intrans* **1** said *esp* of a boat: to lean over to one side; to heel over. **2** *chiefly NAmer* = CAREER². [French *carène* keel, via Old Italian from Latin *carina*, literally 'nutshell']

career¹ /kə'riə/ *noun* **1a** the course of somebody's working life or a specified part of it: *Churchill's career as a politician.* **b** a field of employment in which one expects to spend a significant part of one's working life, *esp* a field requiring special qualifications or training and having opportunities for advancement. **c** (*used before a noun*) of or engaged in an occupation that offers a long-term series of opportunities for advancement, usu within some specified organization or business: *a career diplomat.* **2a** a course or path through history. **b** a headlong course or path. * **in full career** at full speed; in headlong progress: *The Earl of Chester's horse … came in full career at him* — Keats. [French *carrière* via Old Provençal *carriera* street, from medieval Latin *carraria* road for vehicles, from Latin *carrus* CAR]

career² *verb intrans* to move swiftly in an uncontrolled fashion: *The car careered off the road.*

careerist *noun* somebody who is intent on advancing their career, often at the expense of personal integrity. ➤➤ **careerism** *noun*.

career woman *noun* a woman who puts advancement in her career or profession before marriage or motherhood: *Birth rates soared and career women sank in prestige to the level of drop-outs.*

carefree *adj* free from anxiety or responsibility: *carefree holidays.* ➤➤ **carefreeness** *noun*.

careful /'keəf(ə)l/ *adj* **1** exercising or taking care: *a careful driver.* **2a** marked by attentive concern. **b** cautious; prudent: *Be careful of the horses.* ➤➤ **carefully** *adv*, **carefulness** *noun*.

caregiver *noun chiefly NAmer* a person who looks after a child or somebody who is ill, elderly, or disabled, *esp* in the home.

care label *noun* a label attached to a garment, bearing instructions for washing, ironing, etc.

careless *adj* **1** not taking care: *a careless workman.* **2a** negligent or slovenly: *writing that is careless and full of errors.* **b** unstudied; spontaneous: *careless grace.* **3a** free from care; untroubled: *careless days.* **b** indifferent; unconcerned: *careless of the consequences.* ➤➤ **carelessly** *adv*, **carelessness** *noun*.

carer *noun Brit* a person who looks after somebody who is ill, elderly, or disabled, *esp* in the home.

caress¹ /kə'res/ *noun* **1** a gentle or loving touch or stroke. **2** a kiss. [French *caresse* from Italian *carezza*, from *caro* dear, from Latin *carus*]

caress² *verb trans* **1** to touch or stroke (somebody or something) lightly and lovingly. **2** to touch or affect (something or somebody) gently or soothingly: *music that caresses the ear.* ➤➤ **caressingly** *adv*.

caret /'karət/ *noun* a mark (^) or (⁁) used on written or printed matter to indicate an insertion to be made. [Latin *caret* it is lacking, from *carēre* to lack, be without]

caretaker *noun* **1** a person who takes care of the house or land of an owner, *esp* during their absence. **2** a person who looks after a usu large public building, e.g. a school, attending to maintenance, cleaning, security, etc. **3** somebody or something temporarily installed in office: *a caretaker government.*

careworn *adj* showing the effects of grief or anxiety: *a careworn face.*

cargo /'kahgoh/ *noun* (*pl* **cargoes** or **cargos**) the goods conveyed in a ship, aircraft, or vehicle; freight. [Spanish *cargo* load, charge, from *cargar* to load, from late Latin *carricare*: see CHARGE¹]

cargo cult *noun* a movement of the SW Pacific characterized by a belief in the imminent arrival of divine benefactors in ships and aircraft bringing an abundance of goods.

Carib /'karib/ *noun* (*pl* **Caribs** or **Carib**) **1** a member of a Native American people of northern S America and the Lesser Antilles. **2** the language of the Caribs. [modern Latin *Caribes* (pl), via Spanish from Arawakan *Carib*]

Caribbean /kari'bee-ən/ *adj* **1** of the Caribbean Sea and its islands, *esp* the W Indies. **2** of the Caribs or their language. [modern Latin *Caribbaeus* from *Caribes*: see CARIB]

caribou /'kariboo/ *noun* (*pl* **caribous** or collectively **caribou**) any of several species of large N American deer that have broad

branching antlers and are related to the reindeer: genus *Rangifer*. [Canadian French *caribou*, of Algonquian origin]

caricature¹ /'karikətyooə/ *noun* **1a** exaggeration of personal features or characteristics, often to a ludicrous or grotesque degree. **b** a representation, *esp* in literature or art, that makes use of such exaggeration for comic or satirical effect. **2** an imitation or distortion so gross or inferior as to seem like a caricature: *I've got to take under my wing, tra-la, a most unattractive old thing, tra-la, with a caricature of a face* — W S Gilbert. ➤➤ **caricatural** *adj*, **caricaturist** *noun*. [Italian *caricatura* from *caricare* to load, exaggerate, from late Latin *carricare*: see CHARGE¹]

caricature² *verb trans* to make a caricature of (somebody or something); to represent (them) in caricature.

CARICOM /'karikom/ *abbr* Caribbean Community and Common Market.

caries /'keəreez/ *noun* (*pl* **caries**) progressive decay of a tooth or bone, caused by micro-organisms. [Latin *caries* decay]

carillon /kə'rilyən/ *noun* **1** a set of tuned bells sounded by hammers controlled from a keyboard. **2** a tune played on such a set of bells. [French *carillon*, alteration of Old French *quarregnon* peal of four bells, from late Latin *quaternion-*, *quaternio* set of four]

carina /kə'reenə, kə'rienə/ *noun* (*pl* **carinas** or **carinae** /-nee/) a keel-shaped part, e.g. on a bird's breastbone. [Latin *carina* keel]

carinate /'karinayt/ *adj* having a carina, keel, or ridge: *a carinate sepal.*

carinated /'karinaytid/ *adj* = CARINATE.

caring /'keəring/ *adj* **1** showing concern for others: *a caring partner.* **2** involved with the welfare of others: *the caring professions.*

carioca /kari'ohkə/ *noun* **1** (**Carioca**) a native or inhabitant of Rio de Janeiro. **2** a dance resembling the samba, or the music for this dance. [Portuguese *carioca*, from Tupi]

cariogenic /,keərioh'jenik/ *adj* causing caries, *esp* tooth decay.

cariole /'kariohl/ *noun* see CARRIOLE.

carious /'keəri-əs/ *adj* said of a tooth or bone: affected with caries; decayed. [Latin *cariosus*, from *caries* decay]

carjacking *noun* the act or an instance of hijacking a car. ➤➤ **carjacker** *noun*.

cark /kahk/ *verb intrans archaic* to be anxious. ➤ *verb trans archaic* to cause (somebody) to be anxious: *Clym had passed from the dullness of sorrow to the fluctuation of carking incertitude* — Hardy. ➤➤ **carking** *adj*. [Middle English *carken* to load, burden, via early French *carquier* from late Latin *carricare*: see CHARGE¹]

carl or **carle** /kahl/ *noun archaic* a man of the common people. [Old English from Old Norse *karl* man, carl; related to Old English *ceorl* CHURL]

carline /'kahlin/ *noun* **1** (*also* **carling**) a fore-and-aft timber supporting a ship's deck or framing a deck opening. **2** *chiefly Scot* an old woman or witch. [Middle English *kerling* from Old Norse, from *karl* man, CARL]

carload *noun* a load that fills a car, *esp* a number of people so transported.

Carlovingian¹ /kahloh'vinji-ən/ *adj* = CAROLINGIAN¹. [French *carlovingien*, prob from medieval Latin *Carlus* Charles + French *-ovingien* as in *mérovingien* Merovingian]

Carlovingian² *noun* = CAROLINGIAN².

Carmelite /'kahməliet/ *noun* a member of a Roman Catholic order of mendicant friars founded in the 12th cent. or a corresponding order of nuns founded in the 15th cent. ➤➤ **Carmelite** *adj*. [Middle English from medieval Latin *carmelita*, named after Mount *Carmel*, Palestine, where the order was founded]

carminative¹ /kah'minətiv/ *adj* causing expulsion of gas from the digestive tract to relieve flatulence.

Word history ────────────
French *carminatif* from Latin *carminatus*, past part. of *carminare* to card, from *carmin-*, *carmen* card, from *carrere* to card. The connection with carding comes from the idea of 'combing out' the bad humours that produce the gas.

carminative² *noun* a carminative drug.

carmine /'kahmin/ *noun* **1** a rich crimson or scarlet pigment. **2** a vivid red colour. [French *carmin* from medieval Latin *carminium*, from Arabic *qirmiz* kermes + Latin *minium* red lead]

carnage /'kahnij/ *noun* great slaughter, e.g. in battle. [French *carnage* flesh of slain animals or men, from medieval Latin *carnaticum* tribute consisting of animals or meat, from Latin *carn-, caro* flesh]

carnal /'kahnl/ *adj* **1** of or given to physical, *esp* sexual, pleasures and appetites. **2** temporal; worldly. ➤➤ **carnality** /kah'naliti/ *noun*, **carnally** *adv.* [Middle English via French from late Latin *carnalis*, from Latin *carn-, caro* flesh]

carnal knowledge *noun* used *esp* as a legal term: sexual intercourse: *He had carnal knowledge of his brother's wife.*

carnassial /kah'nasi·əl/ *adj* of or being the large long cutting teeth of a carnivore. [French *carnassier* carnivorous, from Latin *carn-, caro* flesh]

carnation /kah'naysh(ə)n/ *noun* **1a** any of numerous cultivated varieties of the clove pink with fragrant typically red, pink, or white flowers: *Dianthus caryophyllus.* **b** a flower of this plant. **2** a light red or pink colour. [French *carnation* from Old Italian *carnagione*, from *carne* flesh, from Latin *carn-, caro*]

carnauba /kah'nowbə/ *noun* **1** a Brazilian palm with an edible root and fan-shaped leaves that yield a wax used in polishes: *Copernicia cerifera.* **2** a hard brittle wax obtained from the leaves of this tree. [Portuguese *carnauba*, from Tupi]

carnelian /kah'neeli·ən/ *noun* see CORNELIAN.

carnet /'kahnay (*French* karnɛ)/ *noun* **1** a customs document permitting free movement of a vehicle across a frontier or temporary duty-free importation, e.g. of goods en route to another country. **2** a book of tickets, usu at a discount, e.g. for use on public transport. [French *carnet* notebook, via early French *quernet* from Latin *quaterni* set of four]

carnival /'kahnivl/ *noun* **1** a period or instance of public merrymaking or feasting, *esp* one just before Lent in some Roman Catholic countries. **2a** an exhibition or organized programme of entertainment; a festival. **b** a travelling circus or funfair. [Italian *carnevale*, alteration of *carnelevare*, literally 'removal of meat', ultimately from Latin *carn-, caro* flesh + *levare* to raise, remove]

carnivore /'kahnivaw/ *noun* **1** any of an order of flesh-eating mammals: order Carnivora. **2** any animal or plant that feeds on flesh or animal tissue. [Latin *carnivorus*: see CARNIVOROUS]

carnivorous /kah'niv(ə)rəs/ *adj* **1** said of an animal: feeding on flesh; *specif* belonging to the order Carnivora. **2** said of a plant: feeding on nutrients obtained from animal tissue, *esp* insects. ➤➤ **carnivorously** *adv*, **carnivorousness** *noun*. [Latin *carnivorus*, from *carn-, caro* flesh + *-vorus* -VOROUS]

carnosaur /'kahnəsaw/ *noun* any of a group of large flesh-eating dinosaurs that walked on two legs, including tyrannosaurus and allosaurus. [Latin *carn-, caro* flesh + *sauros* lizard]

carob /'karəb/ *noun* **1** a Mediterranean evergreen tree of the pea family with red flowers: *Ceratonia siliqua.* **2** the edible dark-coloured pod of this tree, used for animal fodder and as the source of a chocolate substitute. [Old French *carobe* via medieval Latin *carrubium* from Arabic *kharrūbah*]

carol¹ /'karəl/ *noun* a popular seasonal song or ballad, usu a religious one, *esp* a Christmas song or hymn. [Middle English *carole* via Old French from late Latin *choraula* choral song, ultimately from Greek *choraulēs* choral accompanist, from *choros* CHORUS¹ + *aulein* to play a reed instrument]

carol² *verb* (**carolled, carolling**, *NAmer* **caroled, caroling**) ➤ *verb trans* to sing (something), *esp* joyfully. ➤ *verb intrans* **1** to sing, *esp* joyfully. **2** to sing carols, *esp* at Christmas.

Caroline /'karəlien/ *or* **Carolean** /-'lee·ən/ *adj* used *esp* with reference to the reigns of Charles I (1625–49) and Charles II (1660–85) of England: of or relating to Charles. [medieval Latin *Carolus* Charles]

Carolingian¹ /karə'linji·ən/ *adj* of a medieval Frankish dynasty, named after Charles Martel, that ruled in France (751–987), Germany (752–911), and Italy (744–961). [French *carolingien* from medieval Latin *karolingi* French people, ultimately from Old High German *Karl* Charles]

Carolingian² *noun* a member of the Carolingian dynasty.

carol-singing *noun* the singing of Christmas carols, *esp* in a group outdoors or going from house to house to raise money. ➤➤ **carol-singer** *noun*.

carom¹ /'karəm/ *noun NAmer* = CANNON¹ (3). [by shortening and alteration from obsolete *carambole*, from Spanish *carambola*]

carom² *verb intrans* (**caromed, caroming**) *NAmer* = CANNON² (2).

carotene /'karəteen/ *noun* any of several orange or red plant pigments, found *esp* in carrots, that are converted to vitamin A in the body. [late Latin *carota* carrot]

carotenoid /kə'rotənoyd/ *noun* a carotene or similar pigment occurring in plants and some animal tissues.

carotid¹ /kə'rotid/ *adj* of or being either of the pair of arteries that supply the head with blood. [French *carotide* from Greek *karōtides* carotid arteries, from *karoun* to stupefy; from the belief that pressure on these arteries causes stupor]

carotid² *noun* the carotid artery or arteries.

carousal /kə'rowzl/ *noun* = CAROUSE².

carouse¹ /kə'rowz/ *verb intrans* **1** to take part in a drinking spree or drunken revel: *If that death were so near, he would not banquet and carouse and swill amongst the students, as even now he doth —* Marlowe. **2** to drink alcoholic beverages heavily or freely. [early French *carrousse*, from *carous* completely, all out, in *boire carous* to empty the cup, from German *gar aus trinken* to drink all out]

carouse² *noun* a drunken revel.

carousel *or* **carrousel** /karə'sel, -'zel/ *noun* **1** *chiefly NAmer* a merry-go-round. **2** a rotating stand or delivery system, e.g. for slides in a projector or for baggage at an airport. [French *carrousel* tournament for horsemen, from Italian *carosello*]

carp¹ /kahp/ *noun* (*pl* **carps** *or collectively* **carp**) **1** a large soft-finned freshwater fish often farmed for food: *Cyprinus carpio.* **2** any of various similar or related fishes. [Middle English *carpe* via Old French from late Latin *carpa*, prob of Germanic origin]

carp² *verb intrans informal* (+ at) to find fault or complain querulously and often unnecessarily. ➤➤ **carper** *noun*. [Middle English *carpen*, of Scandinavian origin]

carp- *or* **carpo-** *comb. form* forming words, denoting: fruit or seed: *carpology.* [via French and Latin from Greek *karp-, karpo-*, from *karpos* fruit]

-carp *comb. form* forming nouns, denoting: **1** part of a fruit: *mesocarp.* **2** fruit: *schizocarp.* [via Latin from Greek *-karpion*, from *karpos* fruit]

carpaccio /kah'pachioh/ *noun* an Italian delicacy comprising thin slices of raw meat or fish served with a dressing. [Italian *carpaccio*, named after Vittore *Carpaccio* d.1525, Italian painter, noted for his use of red pigments resembling raw meat]

carpal¹ /'kahpl/ *adj* of or forming part of the wrist. [scientific Latin *carpalis*, from *carpus*: see CARPUS]

carpal² *noun* a carpal bone.

carpal tunnel syndrome *noun* a condition caused by pressure on the nerve passing through the wrist and resulting in pain and tingling in the hand and fingers.

car park *noun chiefly Brit* an area or building set aside for parking cars.

carpel /'kahpl/ *noun* the female reproductive organ of a flowering plant, which usu forms the innermost part of a flower and consists of an ovary attached to a STIGMA (pollen-receiving structure) by a thin tubular STYLE¹. ➤➤ **carpellary** /-ləri/ *adj.* [scientific Latin *carpellum*, from Greek *karpos* fruit]

carpenter¹ /'kahpintə/ *noun* a woodworker, *esp* one who builds or repairs large-scale structural woodwork: compare JOINER. [Middle English via French from Latin *carpentarius* carriage-maker, from *carpentum* carriage, of Celtic origin]

carpenter² *verb* (**carpentered, carpentering**) ➤ *verb intrans* to follow the trade of a carpenter. ➤ *verb trans* **1** to make (something) by or as if by carpentry. **2** to put (something) together, often in a rough-and-ready manner.

carpentry /'kahpintri/ *noun* **1** the art or trade of a carpenter; *specif* the art of shaping and assembling structural woodwork. **2** woodwork produced by a carpenter.

carpet¹ /'kahpit/ *noun* **1** a heavy woven or felted material used as a floor covering, or a floor covering made of this material. **2** a covering that resembles a carpet: *a carpet of leaves.* *** on the carpet** before an authority for censure or reprimand. [Middle English via Old French from Old Italian *carpita*, ultimately from Latin *carpere* to pluck]

carpet² *verb trans* (**carpeted, carpeting**) **1** to cover (something) with or as if with a carpet: *Bluebells carpeted the ground.* **2** *informal* to reprimand (somebody).

carpetbag *noun* a travelling bag made of carpet-like fabric, common in the 19th cent.

carpetbagger *noun* **1** in the USA in former times, a Northerner who went to the South after the American Civil War in search of personal gain. **2** a non-resident who meddles in the politics of a locality, *esp* somebody seeking election to public office. **3** an opportunist. [from their carrying all their belongings in carpetbags]

carpet beetle *noun* any of several species of small beetles whose larvae feed on fabrics and woollen goods: genus *Anthrenus*.

carpet bomb *verb trans* to drop bombs on (an area) so as to cause extensive uniform damage.

carpeting *noun* carpets, or material for carpets.

carpet shark *noun* any of several species of sharks with mottled skin found in shallow waters of the Pacific Ocean: family Orectolobidae.

carpet slipper *noun* a slipper for indoor wear. [from the uppers being orig made of carpet-like fabric]

carpet sweeper *noun* a manual device with a revolving brush used to clean household carpets.

car phone *noun* a cellular phone for use in a motor vehicle.

carpi /'kahpie/ *noun* pl of CARPUS.

carpo- *comb. form* see CARP-.

carpology /kah'poləji/ *noun* a branch of botany dealing with the study of fruit and seeds.

carport *noun* an open-sided shelter for cars, attached to a house.

-carpous *comb. form* forming adjectives, with the meaning: having (such) fruit or (so many) fruits: *polycarpous*. [scientific Latin *-carpus* from Greek *-karpos*, from *karpos* fruit]

carpus /'kahpəs/ *noun* (*pl* **carpi** /'kahpie/) the wrist, or the bones that form the wrist. [scientific Latin *carpus*, from Greek *karpos* wrist]

carrack /'karak/ *noun* a large square-rigged trading vessel of the 14th to 17th cents that was sometimes equipped for warfare. [Middle English *carrake* via Old French and Old Spanish from Arabic *qarāqīr*, pl of *qurqūr* merchant ship]

carrageen or **carragheen** /'karəgeen/ *noun* a dark purple branching edible seaweed found on the coasts of N Europe and N America: *Chondrus crispus*. [named after *Carragheen*, town near Waterford, Eire]

carrageenan /karə'geenən/ *noun* a carbohydrate extracted *esp* from carrageen and used e.g. as an emulsifying agent in foods.

carragheen /'karəgeen/ *noun* see CARRAGEEN.

carrel /'karəl/ *noun* a partitioned area or cubicle used for individual study, *esp* in a library. [alteration of Middle English *carole* in the old senses 'round dance', 'ring': see CAROL[1]]

carriage /'karij/ *noun* **1** *Brit* a railway passenger vehicle; a coach. **2** a wheeled vehicle, *esp* a horse-drawn passenger vehicle. **3** a movable part of a machine that supports some other part: *a typewriter carriage*. **4a** the act of carrying or conveying something, *esp* items of merchandise. **b** the price or cost of this: *carriage paid*. **5** the manner of bearing the body; posture. [Middle English *cariage* from early French, from *carier*: see CARRY[1]]

carriage clock *noun* a small clock enclosed in a glass-sided metal frame, usu with a handle at the top.

carriage return *noun* a mechanism or key used to start a new line on a typewriter or computer.

carriage trade *noun* trade from rich people.

carriageway *noun Brit* the part of a road used by vehicular traffic, often consisting of several lanes; see LANE (2).

carrick bend /'karik/ *noun* a knot used to join the ends of two large ropes. [prob from obsolete *carrick*, from Middle English *carrake*: see CARRACK]

carrier /'kari-ə/ *noun* **1** a bearer or messenger. **2** an individual or organization that undertakes to transport goods, messages, people, etc for payment. **3a** a container for carrying something. **b** *Brit* = CARRIER BAG. **c** a device or mechanism that carries something. **4** a bearer and transmitter of a causative agent of disease, *esp* a person or animal that is immune to the disease. **5a** a usu inactive accessory substance: *a carrier for a drug*. **b** a substance, e.g. a catalyst, by means of which some element or group is transferred from one chemical compound to another. **6** a radio or electrical wave of relatively high frequency that can be modulated to carry a signal representing sound, vision, or other information, *esp* in order to transmit that signal. Also called CARRIER WAVE. **7** in physics, a mobile electron or HOLE[1] (vacancy resulting from the absence of an electron) capable of carrying an electric charge in a semiconductor. **8** = AIRCRAFT CARRIER.

carrier bag *noun Brit* a usu disposable bag of plastic or thick paper used for carrying goods, *esp* shopping.

carrier pigeon *noun* a homing pigeon used to carry messages.

carrier wave *noun* = CARRIER (6).

carriole or **cariole** /'kariohl/ *noun* **1** *chiefly Can* a light sleigh drawn by dogs or horses. **2** in former times, a small open horse-drawn carriage with two wheels. **3** a covered cart. [French *cariole* from Old Provençal *carriola* two-wheeled carriage, ultimately from Latin *carrus* vehicle]

carrion /'kari-ən/ *noun* **1** (*also used before a noun*) dead and putrefying flesh: *You'll ask me why I rather choose to have a weight of carrion flesh than to receive three thousand ducats* — Shakespeare. **2** something corrupt or rotten. [Middle English *caroine* from Anglo-French, ultimately from Latin *carn-*, *caro* flesh]

carrion crow *noun* the common European black crow: *Corvus corone*.

carrot /'karət/ *noun* **1a** a plant with feathery leaves widely cultivated for its long orange tapering or conical edible root: *Daucus carota*. **b** the root of this plant, used as a vegetable. **2** a promised and often illusory reward or advantage: *He offered them the carrot of promotion*. [early French *carotte* via late Latin from Greek *karōton*]

carroty *adj* said of hair: bright orange-red in colour.

carrousel /karə'sel, -'zel/ *noun* see CAROUSEL.

carry[1] /'kari/ *verb* (**carries, carried, carrying**) ➤ *verb trans* **1** to move or transport (something) from one place to another. **2** to support (something): *A thick beam carries the weight of the upper storeys.* **3** to wear or have (something) on one's person: *I never carry much money.* **4** to be pregnant with (an unborn child). **5** to have (something) as a mark or attribute: *She will carry the scars of this incident for a very long time.* **6** to bear or transmit (a disease). **7** to lead or influence (people), *esp* by appealing to their emotions. **8** in arithmetic, to transfer (a digit corresponding to a multiple of ten) to the next higher power of ten. **9** to have (something) as a consequence: *The crime carried a heavy penalty.* **10** to hold (oneself) in a specified manner: *He carries himself well.* **11** to sing (a tune) with reasonable correctness of pitch. **12** to keep (goods) in stock for sale. **13** to maintain (something) through financial support or personal effort: *She carried the project from beginning to end.* **14** to make up for the poor performance of (a member of a team) by performing well oneself. **15** to extend and apply (something): *You can carry a principle too far.* **16** to broadcast or publish (a feature or story): *Later editions carried the full budget speech.* **17a** to win acceptance of (a proposal). **b** *NAmer* to win a majority of votes in (a state or district etc). **18** said of a ship: to have (a sail or sails) hoisted. ➤ *verb intrans* **1** to act as a bearer. **2** to be transported, conveyed, or transmitted to a distance: *Their voices carry well.* ✱ **carry all before one** to win with wide support or approval. **carry a torch for somebody** to remain in love with somebody, *esp* without reciprocation. **carry the can** *informal* to bear the responsibility or blame [said to be from the 'can' or keg of beer which one soldier carried for himself and his comrades]. **carry the day** to win or prevail. [Middle English *carien* from early French *carier* to transport in a vehicle, from *car* vehicle, from Latin *carrus*, of Celtic origin]

carry[2] *noun* (*pl* **carries**) **1** the act or a method of carrying. **2a** the range of a gun or projectile. **b** the distance travelled by a struck ball, *esp* in golf. **3** = PORTAGE[1] (2).

carryall /'kariawl/ *noun NAmer* = HOLDALL.

carry away *verb trans* (*usu in passive*) to cause (somebody) to become over-emotional or lose self-control.

carrycot *noun chiefly Brit* a small lightweight boxlike bed with two handles, in which a baby can be carried.

carry forward *verb trans* in accounting: **a** to transfer (a total) to the next column, page, or book relating to the same account. **b** to apply (a loss or an unused credit) to the taxable income of a subsequent period.

carrying-on *noun* (*pl* **carryings-on**) *informal* rowdy, excited, or improper behaviour, or an instance of this.

carry off *verb trans* **1** said of a disease: to cause the death of (somebody). **2** to perform (something) easily or successfully. **3** to gain possession or control of (something); to win or capture (it): *They carried off the prize.*

carry on *verb trans* to conduct or manage (a business or undertaking). ➤ *verb intrans* **1** to continue one's course or activity, *esp* in spite of obstacles or discouragement. **2** *informal* to behave in a rowdy, excited, or improper manner. **3** *Brit, informal* (*usu* + with) to flirt or have a love affair with somebody.

carry-on *noun Brit, informal* a fuss or to-do.

carryout /'kariowt/ *noun* **1** *chiefly Scot* alcoholic drink bought to be consumed off the premises. **2** *chiefly NAmer & Scot* = TAKEAWAY².

carry out *verb trans* **1** to put (a plan or idea) into execution. **2** to bring (something) to a successful conclusion; to complete or accomplish (something).

carry over *verb trans* **1** = CARRY FORWARD. **2** to postpone (something). **3** to hold over (goods) for use, sale, etc in the future. ➤ *verb intrans* to persist from one stage or sphere of activity to another: *The aggressiveness he shows on screen sometimes carries over into his private life.*

carry-over *noun* **1** the act or process of carrying over. **2** something carried over.

carry through *verb trans* = CARRY OUT. ➤ *verb intrans* to survive or persist.

carse /kahs/ *noun Scot* low fertile land beside a river. [Middle English *cars, kerss,* perhaps of Old Norse origin]

carsick /'kahsik/ *adj* suffering from motion sickness caused by travelling in a motor vehicle. ➤➤ **carsickness** *noun.*

cart¹ /kaht/ *noun* **1** a heavy two-wheeled or four-wheeled vehicle used for transporting loads. **2** a lightweight two-wheeled vehicle drawn by a horse, pony, or dog. **3** a small wheeled vehicle. **4** *NAmer* a supermarket trolley. ✳ **in the cart** in a difficult situation. **put the cart before the horse** to do things in the reverse of the normal order. [Middle English, prob from Old Norse *kartr*; related to Old English *cradol* CRADLE¹]

cart² *verb trans* **1** to carry or convey (something or somebody) in or as if in a cart. **2** *informal* (+ off) to take or drag (somebody) away without ceremony or by force: *They carted him off to jail.* **3** *informal* to carry (*esp* something heavy) by hand: *I had to cart my suitcase up three flights of stairs.* ➤➤ **carter** *noun.*

cartage /'kahtij/ *noun* the act of conveying goods by cart or the charge for this.

carte blanche /ˌkaht 'blonhsh (*French* kart blãʃ), ˌkaht 'blonhsh/ *noun* full discretionary power: *He was given carte blanche to furnish the house.* [French *carte blanche* blank document]

cartel /kah'tel/ *noun* an association of independent commercial enterprises designed to limit competition, e.g. by regulating prices. [French *cartel* letter of defiance, from Old Italian *cartello* placard, from *carta*: see CARD¹]

Cartesian¹ /kah'teezhən, -zyən/ *adj* of or used in the philosophy of René Descartes. ➤➤ **Cartesianism** *noun.* [Latin *cartesianus,* from Renatus *Cartesius,* the Latin name of René Descartes d.1650, French philosopher]

Cartesian² *noun* a follower of René Descartes.

Cartesian coordinate *noun* (*usu in pl*) any of a set of numbers fixing the position of a point by its distance from each of two or three lines or planes at right angles to one another.

Carthaginian /ˌkahthə'jini-ən/ *noun* a native or inhabitant of the ancient city of Carthage in N Africa on the Bay of Tunis. ➤➤ **Carthaginian** *adj.*

carthorse *noun* a large strong horse bred or used for pulling heavy loads.

Carthusian /kah'thyoohzyən/ *noun* a member of an austere contemplative order of monks or nuns founded by St Bruno in 1084. ➤➤ **Carthusian** *adj.* [medieval Latin *Cartusiensis,* from *Carthusia,* Latin name of *Chartreuse,* mother house of the order, near Grenoble, town in France]

cartilage /'kahtilij/ *noun* a translucent firm elastic tissue that makes up most of the skeleton of very young vertebrates and becomes mostly converted into bone in adult higher vertebrates, e.g. mammals, remaining in structures such as the external ear and the larynx. ➤➤ **cartilaginous** /-'lajinəs/ *adj.* [Latin *cartilagin-, cartilago*]

cartilaginous fish *noun* any of a major group of fishes comprising all those with a cartilaginous rather than a bony skeleton, and including the sharks, dogfishes, and rays: class Chondrichthyes.

cartload *noun* the quantity that a cart can hold.

cartogram /'kahtəgram/ *noun* a map showing statistical information presented in diagrammatic form. [French *cartogramme,* from *carte* (see CARD¹) + -O- + *-gramme* -GRAM]

cartography /kah'tografi/ *noun* the art, science, or technology of drawing or compiling maps and charts. ➤➤ **cartographer** *noun,* **cartographic** /-'grafik/ *adj,* **cartographical** /-'grafikl/ *adj.* [French *cartographie,* from *carte* (see CARD¹) + -O- + *-graphie* -GRAPHY]

cartomancy /'kahtəmansi/ *noun* the telling of fortunes by the use of playing cards. [French *cartomancie,* from *carte* (see CARD¹) + -O- + *mancie* -MANCY]

carton /'kaht(ə)n/ *noun* a box or container made of cardboard, plastic, etc. [French *carton* from Italian *cartone*: see CARTOON¹]

cartoon¹ /kah'toohn/ *noun* **1** a satirical drawing commenting on public and usu political matters. **2** = STRIP CARTOON. **3** = ANIMATED CARTOON. **4** a preparatory design, drawing, or painting, e.g. for a fresco. [Italian *cartone* pasteboard, cartoon, augmentative of *carta*: see CARD¹]

cartoon² *verb trans* to draw a cartoon of (something or somebody). ➤ *verb intrans* to draw cartoons. ➤➤ **cartoonist** *noun.*

cartouche /kah'toohsh/ *noun* **1** a scroll-shaped ornamental tablet, drawing, or architectural feature. **2** an ornate frame. **3** an oval or oblong outline, e.g. on ancient Egyptian monuments, enclosing a ruler's name. [French *cartouche* cartridge with paper case, from Italian *cartoccio,* from *carta*: see CARD¹]

cartridge /'kahtrij/ *noun* **1a** a tube of metal, paper, etc containing the charge and often the bullet or shot for a firearm. **b** a case containing an explosive charge for blasting. **2** a container of usu consumable material for insertion into a larger apparatus, e.g.: **a** a case containing a reel of magnetic tape, photographic film, etc, designed for easy insertion. **b** a replaceable container of ink or a similar substance for insertion into a pen, printer, etc. **3** the part of the arm of a record player holding the stylus and the mechanism that converts movements of the stylus into electrical signals. [alteration of *cartage,* modification of French *cartouche*: see CARTOUCHE]

cartridge belt *noun* a belt with a series of loops for holding cartridges for firearms.

cartridge paper *noun* thick paper with a rough surface, e.g. for drawing.

cartwheel *noun* **1** a sideways handspring with arms and legs extended. **2** a wheel of a cart.

cartwright /'kahtriet/ *noun* somebody who makes and repairs carts.

caruncle /'karəngkl/ *noun* **1** a naked fleshy outgrowth, e.g. the comb or wattle of a domestic fowl. **2** an outgrowth near the MICROPYLE (opening through which pollen enters) of a seed. ➤➤ **caruncular** /kə'rungkyoolə/ *adj.* [obsolete French *caruncule* from Latin *caruncula* little piece of flesh, dimin. of *caro* flesh]

carve /kahv/ *verb trans* **1a** to cut (e.g. wood or stone) so as to shape it. **b** to produce (a statue, design, etc) by cutting: *He carved his initials in the soft sandstone.* **2** (*often* + out) to make or acquire (a career, reputation, etc) through one's own efforts: *She carved out a place for herself in the firm.* **3** to cut (food, *esp* meat) into pieces or slices. ➤ *verb intrans* **1** to cut up and serve meat. **2** to work as a sculptor or engraver. [Old English *ceorfan*]

carvel /'kahvl/ *noun* see CARAVEL. [Middle English *carvile* via early French *caravelle, carvelle* from Portuguese *caravela*]

carvel-built *adj* said of a boat: built with the planks meeting flush at the seams: compare CLINKER-BUILT. [prob from Dutch *karveel* caravel, from early French *carvelle*: see CARVEL]

carven /'kahvən/ *adj archaic or literary* wrought or ornamented by carving; carved: *A casement high and triple-arched there was, all garlanded with carven imag'ries* — Keats.

carver *noun* **1a** a long sharp knife used for carving meat. **b** (*in pl*) a knife and fork used for carving and serving meat. **2** *Brit* a chair with armrests forming part of a set of dining-room chairs.

carvery /'kahvəri/ *noun* (*pl* **carveries**) *chiefly Brit* a buffet-style restaurant where the customers' choice of roast meat is carved in their presence.

carve up *verb trans* **1** to divide (something) into parts or shares: *They carved up the inheritance between them.* **2** *Brit, informal* to overtake (a vehicle or its driver) in an aggressive manner.

carve-up *noun informal* **1** a competitive event in which the result has been illegally decided beforehand. **2** a division into parts, *esp* the sharing out of loot.

carving noun **1** the act, art, or craft of somebody who carves. **2** a carved object or design.

car wash noun **1** an automatic machine for washing cars, usu consisting of large revolving brushes through which water and soap are sprayed. **2** an area or establishment containing such a machine or machines.

caryatid /kari'atid/ noun (pl **caryatids** or **caryatides** /-deez/) an architectural column in the form of a draped female figure used to support an entablature: compare ATLAS. [via Latin from Greek *karyatides* priestesses of Artemis at Caryae, caryatids, from *Karyai* Caryae, town in Greece]

caryopsis /kari'opsis/ noun (pl **caryopses** /-seez/) a dry fruit, e.g. of grasses, in which the fruit and seed are fused together in a single grain. [scientific Latin *caryopsis*, from Greek *karyon* nut + -OPSIS appearance]

Casanova /kasə'nohvə/ noun a promiscuous and unscrupulous male lover: *One doesn't need much literary skill to be the Casanova of Tulse Hill* — Wendy Cope. [named after Giacomo Girolamo *Casanova* d.1798, Italian adventurer who wrote memoirs describing his sexual and other exploits]

casbah /'kazbah/ noun see KASBAH.

cascade[1] /kas'kayd/ noun **1** a steep small fall of water, *esp* one of a series of such falls. **2** a series or succession of stages, processes, etc in which each item derives from, is triggered by, or acts on the product of the one before. **3** an arrangement of fabric, e.g. lace, that falls in a wavy or zigzag line. **4** something falling or rushing forth in profusion: *a cascade of coins*. [French *cascade* from Italian *cascata*, from *cascare* to fall, from Latin *casus*, past part. of *cadere* to fall]

cascade[2] verb intrans to fall or pour in or as if in a cascade.

cascara /kas'kahrə/ noun **1** a buckthorn tree or shrub of the Pacific coast of the USA: *Rhamnus purshiana*. Also called CASCARA BUCK-THORN. **2** the dried bark of this tree or shrub, used as a mild laxative. Also called CASCARA SAGRADA. [Spanish *cáscara* bark, from *cascar* to crack, break, from Latin *quassare* to shake, break; (sense 2) American Spanish *cascara sagrada* sacred bark]

cascara buckthorn noun = CASCARA (1).

cascara sagrada noun = CASCARA (2).

case[1] /kays/ noun **1a** a set of circumstances or conditions; a situation. **b** a situation or object requiring investigation or action: *the case of the missing money box*. **2** a form of a noun, pronoun, or adjective indicating its grammatical relation to other words. **3a** a suit or action that reaches a court of law. **b** the evidence supporting a conclusion. **c** an argument, *esp* one that is convincing: *He made a good case for changing the rule*. **4a** an instance that directs attention to a situation or exhibits it in action; an example: *a case of mistaken identity*. **b** an instance of disease or injury, or a patient suffering from a specific condition: *three cases of food poisoning*. **c** a person or family receiving the attention or services of a social worker. **5** *informal* a peculiar person; a character. ✳ **case in point** a relevant example. **in any case** without regard to or in spite of other considerations: *War is inevitable in any case*. **in case 1** for use in or as a precaution against the event that: *Take a towel in case you want to swim*. **2** as a precaution: *You'd better lock the door, just in case*. **in case of 1** in the event of: *In case of fire, press the alarm button*. **2** as a precaution against: *They posted sentries in case of attack*. [Middle English *cas* via Old French from Latin *casus* fall, chance, past part. of *cadere* to fall]

case[2] noun **1** a box or receptacle for holding something, e.g.: **a** *chiefly Brit* a suitcase. **b** a glass-panelled box for the display of specimens, e.g. in a museum. **2** a box together with its contents: *a case of wine*. **3a** an outer covering: *a pastry case*. **b** a stiff book cover that is made apart from the book and glued onto it. **4** a shallow divided tray for holding printing type. [Middle English *cas* via early French *casse*, from Latin *capsa* chest, case, from *capere* to take]

case[3] verb trans **1** to enclose (something) in a case; to encase (it). **2** *informal* to inspect or study (e.g. a house), *esp* with intent to rob it.

casebook noun a book containing records of illustrative cases for reference, e.g. in law or medicine.

casebound /'kaysbownd/ adj said of a book: being a hardback.

cased /kayst/ adj = CASEBOUND.

case-harden verb trans (**case-hardened, case-hardening**) **1** to harden the surface of (iron or steel). **2** to make (somebody) callous. ▶▶ **case-hardened** adj.

case history noun a record of history, environment, and relevant details, e.g. of individual behaviour or condition, *esp* for use in analysis, illustration, or diagnosis.

casein /'kaysin, 'kayseen/ noun a protein in milk that is precipitated by lactic acid or rennet, is the chief constituent of cheese, and is used in making paints or plastics. [prob via French *caséine* from Latin *caseus* cheese]

case law noun law established by previous judicial decisions.

case load noun the number of cases handled in a particular period, e.g. by a court or clinic.

casemate noun a fortified position or chamber, or an armoured enclosure on a warship, from which guns are fired. [early French *casemate* from Old Italian *casamatta*]

casement noun a window that opens on hinges at the side. [Middle English in the sense 'hollow moulding', prob from early French *encassement* frame, from *encasser* to enshrine, frame, from EN-[1] + *casse*: see CASE[2]]

caseous /'kaysi-əs/ adj of or like cheese. [Latin *caseus* cheese]

case-sensitive adj in computing, sensitive to the difference between upper-case and lower-case letters.

case shot noun an artillery projectile consisting of a number of balls or metal fragments enclosed in a case.

case study noun an analysis of a person, institution, or community based on details concerning development, environment, etc.

casework noun social work involving direct consideration of the problems of individual people or families. ▶▶ **caseworker** noun.

cash[1] /kash/ noun **1** money in the form of notes and coins, *esp* when immediately available; ready money. **2** money or its equivalent paid promptly at the time of purchase. **3** (*used before a noun*) of or involving cash: *a cash transaction*. ▶▶ **cashless** adj. [early French *casse* money box, from Old Italian *cassa*, from Latin *capsa*: see CASE[2]]

cash[2] verb trans to pay or obtain cash for (a cheque, money order, etc).

cash[3] noun (pl **cash**) a Chinese or Indian coin of low monetary value. [Portuguese *caixa* from Tamil *kācu*, a small copper coin, from Sanskrit *karsa*, a weight of gold or silver]

cash-and-carry[1] adj said of goods sold wholesale: paid for immediately and taken away by the purchaser.

cash-and-carry[2] noun a shop selling goods on a cash-and-carry basis, *esp* one selling goods in bulk to the retail trade.

cashback noun **1** an arrangement by which customers can obtain cash from a shop when paying for their purchases by debit card, or the cash so obtained. **2** a discount or cash refund offered as an incentive to purchase: *mortgages with cashback*.

cashbook noun a book in which a record is kept of all money received and paid out.

cash card noun a card that is issued by a bank or building society and allows the holder to operate a cash dispenser.

cash cow noun *informal* a business or product from which liquid assets can be easily and consistently derived.

cash crop noun a crop, e.g. cotton or sugar beet, produced for sale rather than for use by the grower.

cash desk noun a desk, e.g. in a shop, where payment for purchases is made.

cash dispenser noun an electronic machine, usu on the exterior of a bank, supermarket, etc, from which cash can be withdrawn by inserting a cash card or credit card and keying in a personal identification number.

cashew /'kashooh, kə'shooh, ka'shooh/ noun **1** the edible kidney-shaped nut of a tropical American tree. **2** the tree, belonging to the sumach family, that bears this nut: *Anacardium occidentale*. [Portuguese *acajú, cajú*, from Tupi *acajú*]

cash flow noun **1** the flow of money into and out of a business; the pattern of income and expenditure. **2** a record, assessment, or forecast of this.

cashier[1] /ka'shiə/ noun a person employed to handle cash or deal with payment and receipts in a shop, bank, etc. [Dutch *kassier* from early French *cassier*, from *casse* money box: see CASE[2]]

cashier[2] verb trans to dismiss (somebody), usu with dishonour, *esp* from service in the armed forces. [Dutch *casseren* from French *casser* to discharge, annul]

cash in *verb trans* to convert (something) into cash: *He cashed in all his bonds.* ➤ *verb intrans* (*usu* + on) to exploit (a financial or other advantage): *cashing in on the success of recent peace initiatives.*

cashmere /kash'miə, 'kashmiə/ *noun* **1** fine wool from the undercoat of the Kashmir goat. **2** yarn or fabric made from this. [from *Cashmere*, variant of *Kashmir*, region of the Indian subcontinent]

cash on delivery *noun* payment for merchandise at the time of delivery.

cashpoint *noun Brit* = CASH DISPENSER.

cash register *noun* a machine with a drawer for cash that is used in shops etc to record and display the amount of a sale and the money received.

cash up *verb intrans Brit* to add up the day's takings at the close of business.

casing /'kaysing/ *noun* **1** an outer cover or shell, *esp* for protection, or material for encasing. **2** an enclosing frame, *esp* round a door or window opening.

casino /kə'seenoh/ *noun* (*pl* **casinos**) a building or room used for gambling. [Italian *casino*, from *casa* house, from Latin *casa* cabin]

cask /kahsk/ *noun* **1** a barrel-shaped container, usu for holding liquids. **2** a cask and its contents, or the quantity contained in a cask. [French *casque* helmet, from Spanish *casco* potsherd, skull, helmet, from *cascar*: see CASCARA]

casket /'kahskit/ *noun* **1** a small chest or box, usu ornamental, e.g. for jewels. **2** *chiefly NAmer* a coffin. [Middle English, modification of Old French *cassette*, dimin. of *casse*: see CASE[2]]

casque /kask/ *noun* **1** a helmet. **2** in zoology, a structure resembling a helmet, e.g. on the bill of a hornbill. [French *casque*: see CASK]

Cassandra /kə'sandrə/ *noun* a person who predicts misfortune or disaster.

Word history
named after *Cassandra*, daughter of King Priam of Troy in Greek legend. Cassandra was given the gift of prophecy by Apollo, but he later decreed that she should never be believed.

cassava /kə'sahvə/ *noun* **1** any of several species of tropical plants of the spurge family: genus *Manihot*. **2** the fleshy edible rootstock of this plant, which yields a nutritious starch. [Spanish *cazabe* cassava bread, from Taino *caçábi*]

casserole[1] /'kasərohl/ *noun* **1** a heatproof covered dish in which food may be cooked, usu slowly in an oven, and served. **2** the savoury food cooked and served in a casserole. [French *casserole* saucepan, from early French *casse* ladle, dripping pan, ultimately from Greek *kyathos* ladle]

casserole[2] *verb trans* to cook (food) slowly in a casserole.

cassette /kə'set/ *noun* **1** a small case containing magnetic tape that can be inserted in a recording or playback device. **2** a lightproof container holding film that can be inserted into a camera. [French *cassette* casket, dimin. of early French *casse*: see CASE[2]]

cassia /'kasi-ə/ *noun* **1** = SENNA (I). **2** a coarse cinnamon bark obtained from a tropical Asian tree. [Old English via Latin from Greek *kassia*, of Semitic origin]

cassis /ka'sees/ *noun* a sweet purple liqueur made from blackcurrants. [French *cassis* blackcurrant, from Latin *cassia*]

cassiterite /kə'sitəriet/ *noun* a brown or black mineral that is a naturally occurring form of tin dioxide and is the chief source of tin: formula SnO_2. [French *cassitérite* from Greek *kassiteros* tin]

cassock /'kasək/ *noun* an ankle-length garment worn *esp* by the Roman Catholic and Anglican clergy. [early French *casaque* from Persian *kazhāghand* padded jacket, from *kazh* raw silk + *āghand* stuffed]

cassoulet /'kasəlay/ *noun* a stew of haricot beans and mixed meats. [French *cassoulet*, dimin. of *cassolo* bowl, ultimately from Greek *kyathos* ladle]

cassowary /'kasəweəri/ *noun* (*pl* **cassowaries**) any of various species of large flightless birds found *esp* in New Guinea and Australia and closely related to the emu: genus *Casuarius*. [Malay *kěsuari*]

cast[1] /kahst/ *verb* (*past tense and past part.* **cast**) ➤ *verb trans* **1** to cause (something) to move by forcibly throwing it. **2** to direct (something): *Cast your mind back to last year.* **3** to send forth or emit (something): *The fire casts a warm glow.* **4** to place (somebody or something) as if by throwing: *He was cast into prison.* **5a** to cause (something) to fall on or affect something or somebody: *The*

results *cast doubt on our theory.* **b** to cause (a spell) to have an effect. **6** to deposit (a vote) formally. **7** to throw (something) off or away; to discard (it). **8** to shed or moult (skin, hair, feathers, etc). **9a** to assign the parts for (a film, play, etc). **b** to select (an actor) for a particular role. **10** to arrange (facts, figures, etc) into a suitable form or order. **11a** to shape (metal, plastic, etc) by pouring it into a mould when molten and letting it harden. **b** to form (an object) in this way. **12** to calculate (a horoscope) by means of astrology. ➤ *verb intrans* **1** to throw out a line and bait with a fishing rod. **2** (+ about/around) to look or search. **3** to veer. [Middle English *casten* from Old Norse *kasta*]

cast[2] *noun* **1** the act or an instance of casting something, e.g. a fishing line. **2** the distance to which something can be thrown. **3** (*treated as sing. or pl*) the set of performers in a dramatic production. **4a** a turning or cue in a particular direction. **b** a slight squint in the eye. **5a** a reproduction, e.g. of a statue, formed by casting. **b** an impression taken from an object with a molten or plastic substance. **c** = PLASTER[1] (3). **d** a mould used in casting. **6** a modification of a colour by a trace of some added colour: *grey with a greenish cast.* **7** a shape or appearance: *the delicate cast of her features.* **8** something shed, ejected, or discarded, e.g. the excrement of an earthworm or a pellet regurgitated by a bird. **9** a wide sweep made by a sheepdog or hunting hound.

castanet /kastə'net/ *noun* (*usu in pl*) either of a pair of small wooden or plastic shells clicked together in the hand, *esp* by flamenco dancers. [Spanish *castañeta*, dimin. of *castaña* chestnut, from Latin *castanea*]

castaway[1] /'kahstəway/ *noun* a person who is cast adrift or ashore as a result of a shipwreck or as a punishment.

castaway[2] *adj* **1** cast adrift or ashore. **2** rejected or discarded.

cast away *verb trans* (*usu in passive*) to shipwreck or maroon (somebody or something).

cast down *verb trans* (*usu in passive*) to depress (somebody).

caste /kahst/ *noun* **1** any of the hereditary social groups in Hinduism that restrict the occupations of their members and their association with members of other castes.

Editorial note
From the Portuguese 'casta', social class, caste is a term used specifically to refer to the social structure of Hindu India. The fourfold division of society into priests, warriors, merchants, and servants, sanctioned in ancient scriptures and said to structure all social relations, has been both defended and opposed over the course of Indian history and to the present day — Professor Donald Lopez.

2a a social class. **b** the prestige conferred by social class. **3** the system of social division by castes. **4** a specialized form of a social insect, e.g. a soldier or worker ant, adapted to carry out a particular function in the colony. ✴ **lose caste** *informal* to fall in status or prestige. [Portuguese *casta* race, lineage, fem of *casto* pure, chaste, from Latin *castus*]

castellan /'kastilən/ *noun* a governor or warden of a castle or fort. [Middle English *castelleyn* via French from Latin *castellanus* occupant of a castle, from *castellum*: see CASTLE[1]]

castellated /'kastilaytid/ *adj* **1** having battlements like a castle. **2** said of a nut or similar part: having indentations, grooves, or slots resembling battlements. ➤➤ **castellation** /-'laysh(ə)n/ *noun*. [medieval Latin *castellatus*, past part. of *castellare* to fortify, from Latin *castellum*: see CASTLE[1]]

caster *noun* **1** see CASTOR[2]. **2** somebody or something that casts. [CAST[1] + -ER[2]]

caster sugar *or* **castor sugar** *noun* finely granulated white sugar.

castigate /'kastigayt/ *verb trans formal* to punish or reprimand (somebody) severely. ➤➤ **castigation** /-'gaysh(ə)n/ *noun*, **castigator** *noun*. [Latin *castigatus*, past part. of *castigare*: see CHASTEN]

Castile soap /ka'steel/ *noun* a fine hard mild soap made from olive oil and sodium hydroxide. [named after *Castile*, region of Spain where it was first made]

Castilian /ka'stilyən/ *noun* **1** a native or inhabitant of Castile, region and former kingdom of Spain. **2** the Spanish dialect of Castile, or the official and literary language of Spain based on it. ➤➤ **Castilian** *adj*.

casting /'kahsting/ *noun* **1** something cast in a mould. **2** something cast out or off. **3** the assignment of parts in a dramatic production to actors.

casting couch *noun informal* the practice of assigning parts in a dramatic production to those who have sexual relations with the director, or the couch on which such encounters allegedly take place.

casting vote *noun* a deciding vote cast by a presiding officer in the event of a tie.

cast iron *noun* a hard brittle alloy of iron, carbon, and silicon, cast in a mould.

cast-iron *adj* **1** made of cast iron. **2a** capable of withstanding great strain; strong or unyielding: *a cast-iron stomach.* **b** impossible to disprove or falsify: *a cast-iron alibi.*

castle[1] /'kahsl/ *noun* **1** a large fortified building or set of buildings. **2** a stronghold. **3** = ROOK[3]. [Old English *castel* via French from Latin *castellum* fortress, castle, dimin. of *castrum* fortified place]

castle[2] *verb intrans and trans* in chess, to move (a king) two squares towards a rook and then place the rook on the square passed over by the king.

castle in Spain *noun* = CASTLE IN THE AIR.

castle in the air *noun* (*usu in pl*) an impractical scheme; a daydream.

castoff *noun* **1** (*also in pl*) a cast-off article, e.g. a piece of clothing. **2** an estimate of the space that will be required for a piece of text when printed.

cast off *verb trans* **1** to unfasten or untie (a boat or line). **2** to remove (a stitch or stitches) from a knitting needle to form an edge that will not unravel. **3** to get rid of or discard (something): *She cast off all restraint.* **4** to estimate or calculate the amount of space that (text) will take up when printed. ➤ *verb intrans* **1** to unfasten or untie a boat or a line. **2** to finish a knitted article by casting off all the stitches.

cast-off *adj* given up or discarded, *esp* because outgrown or no longer wanted: *cast-off clothes; a cast-off lover.*

cast on *verb trans or intrans* to place (a stitch or stitches) on a knitting needle, *esp* for beginning a knitted article.

castor[1] /'kahstə/ *noun* a strong-smelling substance obtained from glands near the anus of the beaver, used *esp* in making perfume. [Middle English in the sense 'beaver', via Latin from Greek *kastōr*, named after *Castor*, hero or demigod of Greek mythology]

castor[2] *or* **caster** *noun* **1** a small wheel set in a swivel mounting on the base of a piece of furniture, machinery, etc. **2** a container with a perforated top for sprinkling powdered or granulated foods, *esp* sugar. [CAST[1] + -OR[1], -ER[2]]

castor oil *noun* a pale viscous oil obtained from the seeds of the castor-oil plant, used *esp* as a laxative. [prob from its former use as a substitute for castor in medicine]

castor-oil plant *noun* a tropical plant of the spurge family widely grown for its oil-rich beans: *Ricinus communis.*

castor sugar *noun* see CASTER SUGAR.

cast out *verb trans* to drive out or expel (somebody or something).

castrate[1] /ka'strayt/ *verb trans* **1a** to remove the testes of (a male animal); to geld (it). **b** to remove the ovaries of (a female animal); to spay (it). **2** to deprive (somebody or something) of vitality or effect; to emasculate (them). ➤ **castration** *noun.* [Latin *castratus*, past part. of *castrare*]

castrate[2] /'kastrayt/ *noun* an animal or man that has been castrated: *I am a woman, not a castrate* — Germaine Greer.

castrato /ka'strahtoh/ *noun* (*pl* **castrati** /-tee/) a male singer castrated pre-puberty to preserve the high range of his voice. [Italian *castrato*, past part. of *castrare* to castrate, from Latin]

casual[1] /'kazh(y)ooəl, 'kazyoo-/ *adj* **1** subject to, resulting from, or occurring by chance: *a casual meeting.* **2a** occurring without regularity; occasional: *casual work.* **b** employed for irregular periods: *a casual labourer.* **3a** feeling or showing little concern; nonchalant or offhand: *a casual attitude.* **b** informal, *esp* designed for informal wear: *casual clothes.* ➤ **casually** *adv,* **casualness** *noun.* [Middle English via Old French from late Latin *casualis*, from Latin *casus*: see CASE[1]]

casual[2] *noun* **1** a casual or migratory worker. **2** (*in pl*) casual clothes or shoes. **3** *Brit* a member of a youth culture characterized by expensive casual dress and usu by aggressive behaviour.

casualty /'kazh(y)ooəlti, 'kazyoo-/ *noun* (*pl* **casualties**) **1** a member of a military force killed or wounded in action. **2** a person or thing injured, lost, or destroyed: *Small firms will be the first casualties of these policies.* **3** the accident and emergency department of a

hospital. [Middle English *casuelte* chance, mischance, loss, from medieval Latin *casualitas*, from late Latin *casualis*: see CASUAL[1]]

casuarina /kasyooə'rienə/ *noun* an Australian and SE Asian tree that has thin drooping jointed twigs and yields a heavy hard wood: genus *Casuarina.* [from the Latin genus name, from Malay (*pohon*) *kĕsuari,* literally 'cassowary tree'; from the resemblance of its twigs to cassowary feathers]

casuist /'kazh(y)ooist, 'kazyooist/ *noun* a person skilled in or given to casuistry. ➤ **casuistic** /-'istik/ *adj,* **casuistical** /-'istikl/ *adj.* [French *casuiste* from Spanish *casuista,* from Latin *casus*: see CASE[1]]

casuistry /'kazhyooistri, 'kazyoo-/ *noun* **1** a method or doctrine dealing with cases of conscience and the resolution of conflicting moral obligations. **2** the false application of general principles to particular instances, *esp* with regard to morals or law: *Under every creed ... self-deception and dishonest casuistry get in* — John Stuart Mill.

casus belli /,kahsoos 'belee/ *noun* (*pl* **casus belli** /'belie/) an event or action that brings about a war. [Latin *casus belli* occasion of war]

CAT /kat/ *abbr* **1** computer-aided testing. **2** computerized axial tomography.

cat[1] /kat/ *noun* **1a** a small furry flesh-eating mammal kept as a pet or for catching rats and mice: *Felis catus.* **b** any of a family of carnivores that includes the domestic cat, lion, tiger, leopard, jaguar, cougar, lynx, and cheetah: family Felidae. **2** *informal* a malicious woman. **3** = CAT-O'-NINE-TAILS. **4** *informal.* **a** a player or devotee of jazz. **b** a person, *esp* a man. ✳ **let the cat out of the bag** to divulge a secret, *esp* inadvertently. **like a cat on a hot tin roof/on hot bricks** very agitated or uneasy. **put/set the cat among the pigeons** to do or say something that causes trouble. ➤ **catlike** *adj.* [Old English *catt* from a Germanic word prob borrowed from Latin *cattus, catta* cat]

cat[2] *verb trans* **1** to raise (an anchor) to the cathead. **2** to flog (somebody) with a cat-o'-nine-tails.

cat[3] *noun informal* = CATAMARAN (1).

cat[4] *noun informal* = CATALYTIC CONVERTER.

cata- *or* **cat-** *or* **cath-** *prefix* forming words, with the meanings: **1** down: *catheter.* **2** wrong: *catachresis.* **3** completely: *cathexis.* **4** against: *catatonia.* [Greek *kata-, kat-, kath-,* from *kata* down, in accordance with, by]

catabolism *or* **katabolism** /kə'tabəliz(ə)m/ *noun* destructive metabolism involving the release of energy and resulting in the breakdown of complex materials, e.g. glucose: compare ANABOLISM. ➤ **catabolic** /katə'bolik/ *adj.* [Greek *katabolē* throwing down, from *kataballein* to throw down, from *kata-* CATA- + *ballein* to throw]

catachresis /katə'kreesis/ *noun* (*pl* **catachreses** /-seez/) use of the wrong word for the context. ➤ **catachrestic** /-'krestik/ *adj,* **catachrestical** /-'krestikl/ *adj.* [via Latin from Greek *katachrēsis* misuse, from *katachrēsthai* to use up, misuse, from *kata-* CATA- + *chrēsthai* to use]

cataclysm /'katəkliz(ə)m/ *noun* **1** a violent geological change of the earth's surface. **2** a momentous event marked by violent upheaval and destruction. **3** a flood or deluge. ➤ **cataclysmal** /-'klizməl/ *adj,* **cataclysmic** /-'klizmik/ *adj,* **cataclysmically** /-'klizmikli/ *adv.* [French *cataclysme* via Latin from Greek *kataklysmos,* from *kataklyzein* to flood, from *kata-* CATA- + *klyzein* to wash]

catacomb /'katəkoohm/ *noun* (*also in pl*) **1** a galleried subterranean cemetery with recesses for tombs. **2** an underground passageway or group of passageways; a labyrinth. [early French *catacombe,* prob via Old Italian *catacomba* from late Latin *catacumbae* (pl), the name of a subterranean cemetery near Rome]

catadioptric /,katədie'optrik/ *adj* involving both reflection and refraction.

catadromous /kə'tadrəməs/ *adj* said of a fish: living in fresh water and going to the sea to spawn: compare ANADROMOUS. [scientific Latin *catadromus,* from CATA- + -*dromus* running]

catafalque /'katəfalk/ *noun* an ornamental structure supporting or bearing a coffin, e.g. while the body lies in state. [Italian *catafalco,* ultimately from CATA- + Latin *fala* siege tower]

Catalan /'katəlan/ *noun* **1** a native or inhabitant of Catalonia, region of NW Spain. **2** the Romance language of Catalonia, Valencia, and the Balearic islands. ➤ **Catalan** *adj.* [Spanish *Catalán*]

catalectic /katə'lektik/ *adj* lacking a syllable at the end of a line of verse. [late Latin from Greek *katalēktikos*, from *katalēgein* to leave off, from *kata-* CATA- + *lēgein* to stop]

catalepsy /'katəlepsi/ *noun* a trancelike state associated with schizophrenia in which the body remains rigid and immobile for prolonged periods. ➤➤ **cataleptic** /-'leptik/ *adj and noun*. [Middle English *catalempsi*, ultimately from Greek *katalēpsis* act of seizing, from *katalambanein* to seize, from *kata-* CATA- + *lambanein* to take]

catalogue¹ (*NAmer* **catalog**) /'katəlog/ *noun* **1** a complete list of items arranged systematically with descriptive details, or a brochure or book containing such a list: *'We are men, my liege.' 'Ay, in the catalogue ye go for men'* — Shakespeare. **2** a list or series: *a catalogue of disasters*. [Middle English *cateloge* via Old French and late Latin from Greek *katalogos*, from *katalegein* to list, enumerate, from *kata-* CATA- + *legein* to gather, speak]

catalogue² (*NAmer* **catalog**) *verb trans* (**catalogues, catalogued, cataloguing,** *NAmer* **catalogs, cataloged, cataloging**) **1** to enter (an item) in a catalogue. **2** to make a catalogue of (a collection of things).

catalpa /kə'talpə/ *noun* an American and Asian tree of the jacaranda family with heart-shaped leaves and pale showy flowers: genus *Catalpa*. [Creek *kutuhlpa*, literally 'head with wings']

catalyse (*NAmer* **catalyze**) /'katəliez/ *verb trans* to bring about the catalysis of (a chemical reaction).

catalysis /kə'taləsis/ *noun* (*pl* **catalyses** /-seez/) a change, *esp* an increase, in the rate of a chemical reaction induced by a catalyst. [Greek *katalysis* dissolution, from *katalyein* to dissolve, from *kata-* CATA- + *lyein* to dissolve, release]

catalyst /'katəlist/ *noun* **1** a substance that changes, *esp* increases, the rate of a chemical reaction but itself remains chemically unchanged. **2** somebody or something whose action inspires further and usu more important events. [from CATALYSIS, by analogy to *analysis*: *analyst*]

catalytic /katə'litik/ *adj* causing or involving catalysis.

catalytic converter *noun* a device in a motor vehicle that uses catalysts to reduce the poisonous and polluting substances in exhaust fumes.

catalyze /'katəliez/ *verb trans NAmer* see CATALYSE.

catamaran /'katəmərən/ *noun* **1** a boat with twin hulls side by side. **2** a raft made of logs or pieces of wood lashed together. [Tamil *kaṭṭumaram*, from *kaṭṭu* to tie + *maram* tree]

catamite /'katəmiet/ *noun archaic* a boy kept for homosexual intercourse.

Word history
Catamitus, Latin name of Ganymede (via Etruscan from Greek *Ganymēdēs*). Ganymede was a beautiful young Trojan prince who was carried off by Zeus and made cupbearer to the gods.

catamount /'katəmownt/ *noun* a lynx, puma, or similar wild cat. [Middle English *cat-a-mountain* from *cat of the mountain*]

catamountain /katə'mowntin/ *noun* = CATAMOUNT.

cataphora /kə'tafərə/ *noun* the use of a grammatical form, e.g. a pronoun, to refer to a following word or group of words: compare ANAPHORA. ➤➤ **cataphoric** /katə'forik/ *adj*. [Greek *kataphora* carrying down, conveyance, from *kataphorein* to carry down, from *kata-* CATA- + *pherein* to carry]

cataplexy /'katəpleksi/ *noun* sudden temporary paralysis following a strong emotional stimulus, e.g. shock. [German *Kataplexie* from Greek *kataplēxis*, from *kataplēssein* to strike down, terrify, from *kata-* CATA- + *plēssein* to strike]

catapult¹ /'katəpult/ *noun* **1** *chiefly Brit* a Y-shaped stick with a piece of elastic material fixed between the two prongs, used for shooting small objects, e.g. stones. **2** in former times, a military device used for hurling missiles. **3** a device for launching an aircraft at flying speed, e.g. from an aircraft carrier. [French *catapulte* via Latin from Greek *katapaltēs*, from *kata-* CATA- + *pallein* to hurl, brandish]

catapult² *verb trans* **1** to throw or launch (a missile) by means of a catapult. **2** to cause (somebody or something) to move suddenly or abruptly: *She was catapulted from rags to riches overnight.* ➤ *verb intrans* to move suddenly or abruptly.

cataract /'katərakt/ *noun* **1a** a waterfall, *esp* a large one descending steeply or in steps. **b** steep rapids in a river. **c** a downpour or deluge. **2** a clouding of the lens of the eye or its enclosing membrane, obstructing the passage of light. [via Latin from Greek *kataraktēs*

waterfall, portcullis, from *katarassein* to dash down, from *kata-* CATA- + *arassein* to strike, dash; (sense 2) from the idea of a barrier coming down in front of the eye]

catarrh /kə'tah/ *noun* inflammation of a mucous membrane, *esp* in the human nose and throat, or the resulting excessive discharge of mucus. ➤➤ **catarrhal** /-rəl/ *adj*. [French *catarrhe* via late Latin from Greek *katarrhous*, from *katarrhein* to flow down, from *kata-* CATA- + *rhein* to flow]

catarrhine /'katərien/ *adj* of or being any of a division of primates that includes the Old World monkeys, apes, and humans and is characterized by having nostrils close together and directed downwards: compare PLATYRRHINE. [Greek *katarrhin* having a hooked nose, from *kata-* CATA- + *rhin-, rhis* nose]

catastrophe /kə'tastrəfi/ *noun* **1** a momentous, tragic, and unexpected event of extreme severity. **2** = CATACLYSM (1). **3** the final events of a play, *esp* a tragedy; the denouement. ➤➤ **catastrophic** /katə'strofik/ *adj*, **catastrophically** /katə'strofikli/ *adv*. [Greek *katastrophē*, from *katastrephein* to overturn, from *kata-* CATA- + *strephein* to turn]

catastrophism /kə'tastrəfiz(ə)m/ *noun* the theory that geological changes, e.g. in the earth's crust, have occurred in response to sudden violent stimuli rather than by gradual processes. ➤➤ **catastrophist** *noun and adj*.

catatonia /katə'tohni-ə/ *noun* **1** a form of schizophrenia, marked by catalepsy. **2** = CATALEPSY. ➤➤ **catatonic** /-'tonik/ *adj and noun*. [scientific Latin *catatonia* from German *Katatonie*, from *kata-* CATA- + Latin *tonus* tone, tension]

catboat *noun* a sailing boat with a mast positioned close to the bows and a single sail. [perhaps from *cat*, a former type of cargo ship]

cat burglar *noun* a burglar who enters buildings by skilful or daring feats of climbing.

catcall¹ *noun* a loud or raucous cry expressing disapproval.

catcall² *verb intrans* to utter a catcall.

catch¹ /kach/ *verb* (*past tense and past part.* **caught** /kawt/) ➤ *verb trans* **1a** to capture or seize (a person or an animal), *esp* after pursuit. **b** to take or entangle (a person or an animal) in or as if in a snare: *caught in a web of deceit.* **c** to discover (somebody) unexpectedly; to surprise (them): *We caught them kissing.* **d** to cause (something) to become entangled, fastened, or stuck: *I caught my sleeve on a nail.* **2a** to intercept and keep hold of (a moving object), *esp* in the hands. **b** to dismiss (a batsman in cricket) by catching the ball after it has been hit and before it has touched the ground. **c** to seize (something): *Catch hold of the railing.* **d** to take in and retain (something): *a barrel to catch the rainwater.* **3a** to contract or become infected with (a disease). **b** to hit or strike (something): *I caught my elbow on the counter.* **c** to be struck or affected by (something): *She caught the spirit of the occasion.* **4** to attract or arrest (somebody's attention). **5** to take or get (something) momentarily or quickly: *He caught a glimpse of his friend.* **6** to be in time for (something): *I want to catch the last post.* **7** to grasp (something) with the senses or the mind: *I didn't catch your name.* **8** to capture a likeness of (somebody or something). ➤ *verb intrans* **1** to become caught: *My sleeve caught on a nail.* **2** said of a fire: to start to burn. ✱ **catch it** *informal* to incur blame or punishment. **catch sight of** to see (something or somebody) suddenly or momentarily. ➤➤ **catchable** *adj*. [Middle English *cacchen* from early French *cachier* to hunt, ultimately from Latin *captare* to chase, from *capere* to take]

catch² *noun* **1a** something caught, *esp* the total quantity caught at one time: *a large catch of fish.* **b** the act or an instance of catching. **2** a game in which a ball is thrown and caught. **3** something that retains or fastens something: *The safety catch of her brooch was broken.* **4** a concealed difficulty; a snag: *There must be a catch in it somewhere.* **5** *informal* an eligible marriage partner: *He's a good catch.* **6** an often humorous or bawdy round for three or more voices. **7** a break in the voice, *esp* one caused by emotion.

catch-22 *noun* a predicament from which a victim is unable to extricate himself or herself because the means of escape depends on mutually exclusive prior conditions.

Word history
named after *Catch-22*, novel by Joseph Heller d.1999, US writer. In the novel a bomber pilot feigns insanity so as to be excused from flying, but his wish to avoid combat is taken as proof of his sanity; this is referred to as Catch-22.

catchall /'kachawl/ *noun* **1** something intended to include or cover miscellaneous cases, items, circumstances, etc. **2** (*used before a noun*) including miscellaneous cases, items, etc: *a catchall category*.

catch-as-catch-can *noun* a style of wrestling in which all mutually agreed holds are allowed.

catch crop *noun* a crop planted between the rows of the main crop or grown between the harvesting of one crop and the planting of another: compare COVER CROP.

catcher /'kachə/ *noun* a baseball player who stands behind the batter to catch balls that the batter fails to hit.

catchfly *noun* any of various genera of plants of the pink family with sticky stems on which small insects are caught: genera *Silene*, *Lychnis*, and other genera.

catching *adj* **1** infectious; contagious: *Chickenpox is catching*; *Her enthusiasm was catching*. **2** alluring or attractive.

catchment *noun* the action of collecting something, *esp* water, or the amount collected.

catchment area *noun* **1** the area from which a river, lake, reservoir, etc gets its water. **2** a geographical area from which people are drawn to attend a particular school, hospital, etc.

catch on *verb intrans* **1** to become popular. **2** *informal* (*often* + to) to understand or become aware.

catch out *verb trans* to expose or detect (somebody) in wrongdoing or error.

catchpenny *adj derog* designed to sell quickly and cheaply by superficial appeal, showiness, sensationalism, etc: *You have manufacturers contriving tens of thousands of catchpenny devices, storekeepers displaying them, and newspapers and magazines filled up with advertisements of them —* Upton Sinclair.

catchphrase *noun* a phrase that enjoys often short-lived popularity; *specif* one associated with a particular person or group.

catchup *noun NAmer* see KETCHUP.

catch up *verb intrans and trans* **1** to succeed in reaching or drawing level with (somebody ahead). **2** (*also* + on/with) to complete (work or commitments) that remain or are overdue: *I must catch up on the accounts.* ❋ **be/get caught up in** to become involved or engrossed in (an activity). **catch up with 1** to exchange (information) with somebody one has not seen for a while. **2** said of bad consequences or effects: to affect (somebody) eventually.

catchweight *adj* of or being a wrestling contest in which normal weight restrictions do not apply.

catchword *noun* **1** a word or expression associated with some school of thought or political movement; a slogan. **2** a word printed under the last line of a page that duplicates the first word of the following page.

catchy *adj* (**catchier, catchiest**) **1** tending to attract interest or attention: *a catchy title*. **2** easy to remember and reproduce: *a catchy tune*.

cat door *noun* = CAT FLAP.

cate /kayt/ *noun archaic* (*usu in pl*) a dainty or choice item of food; a delicacy. [Middle English *cate*, *acate* article of purchased food, from early French *acat* a purchase, from *acater* to buy, ultimately from Latin *acceptare*: see ACCEPT]

catechetical /kati'ketikl/ *adj* **1** relating to the oral instruction of people preparing to become members of a Christian Church. **2** relating to a system of teaching, *esp* religious instruction, by question and answer. [Greek *katēkhētikos* from *katēkhētēs* catechist, from *katēkhein*: see CATECHIZE]

catechise /'katikiez/ *verb trans* see CATECHIZE.

catechism /'katəkiz(ə)m/ *noun* **1** instruction by question and answer. **2** a manual for systematic teaching; *specif* a summary of religious doctrine in the form of questions and answers. **3** a set of formal questions put as a test. ❯❯ **catechismal** /-'kizməl/ *adj.*

catechize *or* **catechise** /'katəkiez/ *verb trans* **1** to teach (somebody) systematically, *esp* by using question and answer; *specif* to give (them) religious instruction in such a manner. **2** to question (somebody) systematically or searchingly: *You may catechise me about the battle of Flodden, or ask particulars about Bruce and Wallace —* Scott. ❯❯ **catechist** *noun,* **catechizer** *noun.* [late Latin *catechizare* from Greek *katēchein* to teach, literally 'to din into', from *kata-* CATA- + *ēchein* to resound, from *ēchē* sound]

catecholamine /katə'kohləmeen/ *noun* any of various amines (chemical compounds; see AMINE), e.g. adrenalin and dopamine, that function as hormones, neurotransmitters, or both.

catechu /'katəchooh/ *noun* any of several dry or resinous astringent substances obtained from tropical Asiatic plants and used in tanning, dyeing, etc. Also called CACHOU. [prob from Malay *kachu*, of Dravidian origin]

catechumen /katə'kyoohmen/ *noun* a person receiving instruction in Christian doctrine and discipline before admission to membership of a church. [Middle English *cathecumyn* via French and late Latin from Greek *katēchoumenos*, present part. passive of *katēchein*: see CATECHIZE]

categoric /katə'gorik/ *adj* = CATEGORICAL.

categorical /katə'gorikl/ *adj* absolute; unqualified: *a categorical denial.* ❯❯ **categorically** *adv.* [via late Latin from Greek *katēgorikos*, from *katēgoria* affirmation: see CATEGORY]

categorical imperative *noun* a moral obligation that is unconditionally and universally binding.

categorize *or* **categorise** /'katəgəriez/ *verb trans* to put (somebody or something) into a category; to classify (them). ❯❯ **categorization** /-'zaysh(ə)n/ *noun.*

category /'katəg(ə)ri/ *noun* (*pl* **categories**) **1** a division within a system of classification. **2a** a general or fundamental form or class of terms, things, or ideas, e.g. in philosophy. **b** any of the underlying concepts to which an object of experience must conform. ❯❯ **categorial** /-'gawri-əl/ *adj.* [via late Latin from Greek *katēgoria* predication, category, from *katēgorein* to accuse, affirm, predicate, from *kata-* CATA- + *agora* public assembly]

catena /kə'teenə/ *noun* (*pl* **catenae** /-nee/ *or* **catenas**) a connected series of related things, *esp* of comments on the Bible by early Christian theologians. [Latin *catena* chain]

catenary[1] /kə'teenəri/ *noun* (*pl* **catenaries**) the curve formed by a perfectly flexible cord of uniform density and cross section hanging freely from two fixed points. [Latin *catenaria*, fem of *catenarius* of a chain, from *catena* chain]

catenary[2] *adj* of or being a catenary.

catenate /'katənayt/ *verb trans formal* to connect (things) in a series; to link (them). ❯❯ **catenation** /-'naysh(ə)n/ *noun.* [Latin *catenatus*, past part. of *catenare*, from *catena* chain]

cater /'kaytə/ *verb intrans* (**catered, catering**) **1** (*often* + for) to provide and serve a supply of prepared food: *I had to cater for ten people at Christmas.* **2** (+ for/to) to supply what is required or desired by (somebody or something): *The concert hall caters for disabled people*; *They catered to her whims all day long.* ❯❯ **caterer** *noun,* **catering** *noun.* [obsolete *cater* buyer of provisions, from Middle English *catour*, *acatour*, from early French *acater*: see CATE]

catercorner /'kaytəkawnə/ *adv and adj NAmer* in a diagonally opposite position: *The house stood catercorner across the square.* [obsolete *cater* a four on cards or dice (from Latin *quattuor* four) + CORNER[1]]

cater-cornered /'kaytəkawnəd/ *adv and adj* = CATERCORNER.

Caterpillar /'katəpilə/ *noun trademark* **1** a tractor or other vehicle designed to travel over rough or soft ground and propelled by two endless metal belts. **2** either of the endless metal belts used to propel such a vehicle.

caterpillar *noun* a wormlike larva; *specif* the larva of a butterfly or moth. [Middle English *catyrpel* from early French *catepelose*, literally 'hairy cat']

caterwaul[1] /'katəwawl/ *verb intrans* to make a loud wailing cry. [Middle English *caterwawen*, of imitative origin]

caterwaul[2] *noun* a loud wailing cry.

catfish *noun* (*pl* **catfishes** *or collectively* **catfish**) any of numerous species of large-headed fishes with barbels (tactile organs; see BARBEL[2]) round the mouth: order Siluriformes.

cat flap *noun* a small hinged flap in the lower part of a door through which a cat may pass.

catgut *noun* a tough cord usu made from sheep intestines and used *esp* for the strings of musical instruments and sports rackets.

Cath. *abbr* **1** Cathedral. **2** Catholic.

cath- *prefix* see CATA-.

Cathar /'kathah/ *noun* (*pl* **Cathars** *or* **Cathari** /-ree/) a member of any of several ascetic Christian sects flourishing in the late Middle Ages, *esp* in Provence, and teaching that the material world is evil.

➤➤ **Catharism** *noun*, **Catharist** *noun and adj.* [late Latin *cathari* (pl), via late Greek from Greek *katharoi*, from *katharos* pure]

catharsis /kə'thahsis/ *noun* (*pl* **catharses** /-seez/) **1** purification or purgation of the emotions through drama. **2** the process of bringing repressed ideas and feelings to consciousness and expressing them, *esp* during psychoanalysis. **3** purgation of the bowels. ➤➤ **cathartic** *adj*, **cathartically** *adv.* [via Latin from Greek *katharsis*, from *kathairein* to cleanse, purge, from *katharos* pure]

Cathay /ka'thay/ *noun literary or archaic* China. [medieval Latin *Cataya, Kitai*, of Turkic origin]

cathead /'kat·hed/ *noun* a projecting part near the bow of a ship to which the anchor is hoisted and secured.

cathedral /kə'theedrəl/ *noun* a church that is the official seat of a diocesan bishop. [late Latin *cathedralis*, prob short for (assumed) *ecclesia cathedralis* church containing a bishop's throne, from Latin *cathedra*: see CHAIR[1]]

Catherine wheel /'kath(ə)rin/ *noun* a firework in the form of a flat coil that spins as it burns. [named after St *Catherine* of Alexandria d.c.307, Christian martyr tortured on a spiked wheel]

catheter /'kathətə/ *noun* a flexible tubular device for insertion into a hollow body part, e.g. the bladder, usu to draw off or inject fluids or to keep a passage open. [via late Latin from Greek *kathetēr*, from *kathienai* to send down, from *kata-* CATA- + *hienai* to send]

catheterize or **catheterise** /'kathitəriez/ *verb trans* to introduce a catheter into (a hollow body part). ➤➤ **catheterization** /-'zaysh(ə)n/ *noun.*

cathexis /kə'theksis/ *noun* (*pl* **cathexes** /-seez/) in psychology, investment of mental or emotional energy in a person, object, or idea. ➤➤ **cathectic** *adj.* [scientific Latin *cathexis* (intended as translation of German *Besetzung*), from Greek *kathexis* holding, from *katechein* to hold fast, occupy, from *kata-* CATA- + *echein* to have, hold]

cathode /'kathohd/ *noun* **1** the electrode by which electrons leave an external circuit and enter a device, e.g.: **a** the positive terminal of a battery: compare ANODE. **b** the negative electrode in an electrolytic cell. **2** the electrode in a thermionic valve or similar electronic device that emits the electrons. ➤➤ **cathodal** /kə'thohdl/ *adj*, **cathodic** /kə'thodik/ *adj.* [Greek *kathodos* way down, from *kata-* CATA- + *hodos* way]

cathode ray *noun* a beam of high-speed electrons projected from the heated cathode of a vacuum tube.

cathode-ray tube *noun* a vacuum tube in which a beam of electrons is projected onto a fluorescent screen to provide a spot of light that produces a visual display, e.g. a television picture.

Catholic /'kath(ə)lik/ *noun* a member of the Roman Catholic Church.

catholic *adj* **1a** comprehensive; universal. **b** broad in sympathies, tastes, or interests. **2** (**Catholic**). **a** of or forming the ancient undivided Christian Church or a Church claiming historical continuity from it, *esp* the Roman Catholic Church. **b** of or forming the entire body of worshippers that constitutes the Christian Church.

Editorial note ─────
Originally denoting in the New Testament an inclusive church containing Greeks as well as Jews, the term 'catholic' was used in an exclusive sense in the third and fourth cents to define a church whose agreed beliefs and doctrines excluded anyone who held contrary opinions. These two senses continue today in the notions of the church as catholic (i.e. universal and inclusive) and Catholic (i.e. having a specific and exclusive historical identity) — Professor John Rogerson.

➤➤ **Catholicism** /kə'tholəsiz(ə)m/ *noun.* [Old French *catholique* via late Latin from Greek *katholikos* universal, general, from *katholou* in general, from *kata* by + *holos* whole]

Catholicise /kə'tholəsiez/ *verb see* CATHOLICIZE.

catholicity /kathə'lisiti/ *noun* **1** liberality of sentiments or views. **2** universality; comprehensiveness.

Catholicize or **Catholicise** /kə'tholəsiez/ *verb trans* to convert (a person or group) to Catholicism. ➤ *verb intrans* to become converted to Catholicism.

cation /'katie·ən/ *noun* a positively charged ion that moves towards the cathode during electrolysis: compare ANION. ➤➤ **cationic** /-'onik/ *adj.* [Greek *kation*, neuter present part. of *katienai* to go down, from *kata-* CATA- + *ienai* to go]

catkin /'katkin/ *noun* a densely crowded spike of flowers without petals hanging from a tree, e.g. a willow or hazel. [early Dutch *katteken* kitten; from its resemblance to a cat's tail]

cat litter *noun* absorbent material placed in a receptacle or location where a domestic cat urinates and defecates.

catmint *noun* any of several species of blue-flowered plants of the mint family with small pale purple-spotted flowers and a strong scent that is attractive to cats: *Nepeta cataria* and other species.

catnap[1] *noun* a brief period of sleep, *esp* during the day.

catnap[2] *verb intrans* (**catnapped, catnapping**) to have a catnap.

catnip *noun* = CATMINT. [CAT[1] + obsolete *nep* catnip, via Old English *nepte* from Latin *nepeta*]

cat-o'-nine-tails *noun* (*pl* **cat-o'-nine-tails**) a flogging whip made of nine knotted cords fastened to a handle. [from the resemblance of its scars to the scratches of a cat]

catoptric /ka'toptrik/ *adj* of a mirror or reflected light, or produced by reflection. [Greek *katoptrikos* from *katoptron* mirror, from *katopsesthai* to be going to observe, from *kata-* CATA- + *opsesthai* to be going to see]

cat's cradle *noun* a game in which different patterns are formed in a loop of string held between the hands by moving the fingers or by transferring the string to the hands of another.

Catseye /'katsie/ *noun trademark* each of a series of small reflecting studs set in the road to mark the middle or edge of the carriageway by reflecting light from the beams of vehicle headlights.

cat's-eye *noun* (*pl* **cat's-eyes**) any of various gems, e.g. a chrysoberyl or a chalcedony, that reflect a narrow band of light from within.

cat's-paw *noun* (*pl* **cat's-paws**) **1** somebody used by another as a tool or dupe. **2** a light breeze that ruffles the surface of water in irregular patches. [(sense 1) from the fable of a monkey that used a cat's paw to draw chestnuts from a fire]

cat's pyjamas *pl noun* = CAT'S WHISKERS.

cat's-tail *noun* = REEDMACE.

CAT standard *noun* a set of voluntary minimum standards set down by the Government to designate ISAs and mortgages that are subject to fair and clearly stated charges, terms, and conditions and that are accessible to customers with limited funds. [from *Charges, Access and Terms*]

catsuit *noun* a tightly fitting one-piece garment combining top and trousers.

catsup /'katsəp/ *noun NAmer* = KETCHUP.

cat's whisker *noun* a fine wire used as a metallic electrode in a crystal radio receiver.

cat's whiskers *pl noun* (**the cat's whiskers**) *informal* an excellent person or thing: *He thinks he's the cat's whiskers.*

cattery /'katəri/ *noun* (*pl* **catteries**) a place for the breeding or care of cats.

cattle /'katl/ *pl noun* bovine animals, e.g. cows or oxen, *esp* those reared for domestic use and kept on a farm, ranch, etc. [Middle English from early French *catel* personal property, via medieval Latin from Latin *capitalis*: see CAPITAL[2]]

cattle cake *noun* cattle food in a concentrated compressed form.

cattle grid *noun Brit* a shallow ditch in a road covered by parallel bars spaced far enough apart to prevent livestock but not wheeled vehicles from crossing.

cattleman *noun* (*pl* **cattlemen**) somebody who tends or raises cattle.

cattlestop *noun NZ* = CATTLE GRID.

catty /'kati/ *adj* (**cattier, cattiest**) **1** spiteful; malicious. **2** of or resembling a cat. ➤➤ **cattily** *adv*, **cattiness** *noun.*

CATV *abbr* community antenna television.

catwalk *noun* **1** a narrow stage extending into the audience at a fashion show: *The catwalk is theatre. It's about provocation and outrage* — Vivienne Westwood. **2** a narrow walkway, e.g. round a piece of machinery.

Caucasian /kaw'kayzhən/ *adj* **1** of the white race of humankind as classified according to physical features. **2** of the Caucasus or its inhabitants. ➤➤ **Caucasian** *noun*, **Caucasoid** /'kawkəsoyd/ *noun.* [*Caucasus, Caucasia*, region of SW Russia]

Caucasoid /'kawkəsoyd/ *adj* = CAUCASIAN (1).

caucus[1] /'kawkəs/ *noun* (*pl* **caucuses**) **1** a closed political meeting to decide on policy, select candidates, etc. **2** a group of people forming a faction within a larger body or organization, *esp* a political party. [prob of Algonquian origin]

caucus[2] *verb intrans* (**caucused, caucusing**) to hold or form a caucus.

caudal /'kawdl/ *adj* **1** of, being, or resembling a tail. **2** relating to or in the region of the hind part of the body. ⟫⟫ **caudally** *adv*. [scientific Latin *caudalis*, from Latin *cauda* tail]

caudal fin *noun* the tail fin of a fish or similar aquatic animal.

caudate /'kawdayt/ *adj* having a tail or a tail-like appendage.

caudated /'kawdaytid/ *adj* = CAUDATE.

caudillo /kaw'deelyoh, kow-/ *noun* (*pl* **caudillos**) in Spanish-speaking countries, a military dictator. [Spanish *caudillo* from late Latin *capitellum* small head, from Latin *capit-, caput* head]

caught /kawt/ *verb* past tense of CATCH[1].

caul /kawl/ *noun* **1** the inner foetal membrane of higher vertebrate animals, e.g. humans, *esp* when covering the head at birth. **2** the large fatty fold of membrane covering the intestines. [Middle English *calle* from Old French *cale*]

cauldron *or* **caldron** /'kawldrən/ *noun* **1** a large open metal pot used for cooking over an open fire. **2** something that resembles a boiling cauldron: *a cauldron of intense emotions*. [Middle English from early French *caudron* from Latin *caldaria* warm bath, cooking pot, ultimately from *calēre* to be warm]

cauliflower /'koliflowə/ *noun* **1** a plant of the cabbage family cultivated for its compact head of usu white undeveloped edible flowers: *Brassica oleracea botrytis*. **2** the flower head of this plant, used as a vegetable. [Italian *cavolfiore*, literally 'cabbage flower', ultimately from Latin *caulis* stem, cabbage + *flor-, flos* FLOWER[1]]

cauliflower ear *noun* an ear thickened and deformed through injury, e.g. from repeated blows in boxing.

caulk *or* **calk** /kawk/ *verb trans* **1** to stop up and make watertight (the seams of a boat, cracks in wood, etc) by filling or sealing them with a waterproof material. **2** to make (a boat or ship) watertight in this way. ⟫⟫ **caulker** *noun*. [Middle English *caulken* via early French *cauquer* to trample, from Latin *calcare*, from *calc-, calx* heel]

causal /'kawzl/ *adj* **1** of or being a cause: *the causal agent of a disease*. **2** expressing or indicating a cause or causation: *a causal clause*. ⟫⟫ **causally** *adv*.

causality /kaw'zaliti/ *noun* (*pl* **causalities**) **1** a causal quality or agency. **2** the relationship between a cause and its effect. **3** the principle that everything has a cause.

causation /kaw'zaysh(ə)n/ *noun* **1** the act or process of causing. **2** the act or agency by which an effect is produced. **3** the relationship between cause and effect.

causative[1] /'kawzətiv/ *adj* **1** effective or operating as a cause or agent. **2** in grammar, expressing causation: *a causative verb*. ⟫⟫ **causatively** *adv*.

causative[2] *noun* a class of verbs expressing causation, or a member of this class.

cause[1] /kawz/ *noun* **1a** somebody or something that brings about an effect or result. **b** a reason for an action or condition; a motive: *a cause for complaint*. **2a** a ground for legal action. **b** a suit or action that reaches a court of law. **3** a principle or movement worth defending or supporting: *a worthy cause*. ⟫⟫ **causeless** *adj*. [Middle English via Old French from Latin *causa*]

cause[2] *verb trans* to serve as the cause of (something); to bring (it) about: *Your carelessness nearly caused an accident*. ⟫⟫ **causer** *noun*.

'cause /kəz; *strong* koz/ *conj informal* because.

cause célèbre /,kohz say'leb(rə) (*French* ko:z selɛbr)/ *noun* (*pl* **causes célèbres** /,kohz say'leb(rə)/) a legal case or controversial issue that excites widespread interest. [French *cause célèbre* celebrated case]

causerie /'kohz(ə)ri/ *noun* **1** an informal conversation; a chat. **2** a short informal written composition, *esp* on a literary subject. [French *causerie*, from *causer* to chat, from Latin *causari* to plead, discuss, from *causa* CAUSE[1]]

causeway /'kawzway/ *noun* a raised road or path, *esp* across wet ground or water. [Middle English *cauciwey*, from *cauci* raised path + *wey* WAY[1]]

caustic[1] /'kostik, 'kawstik/ *adj* **1** capable of destroying or eating away by chemical action; corrosive. **2** bitterly sarcastic or cutting: *The Badger's caustic, not to say brutal, remarks, may be imagined* — Kenneth Grahame. **3a** in physics, of or being a curve formed by rays coming from a point and reflected or refracted by a curved surface. **b** of or being a surface with the shape of such a curve.

⟫⟫ **caustically** *adv*, **causticity** /ko'stisiti, kaw-/ *noun*. [via Latin from Greek *kaustikos*, from *kaiein* to burn]

caustic[2] *noun* **1** a caustic substance. **2** in physics, a caustic curve or surface.

caustic potash *noun* = POTASSIUM HYDROXIDE.

caustic soda *noun* = SODIUM HYDROXIDE.

cauterize *or* **cauterise** /'kawtəriez/ *verb trans* to sear or burn (a wound or body tissue) with a cautery, *esp* in order to stop bleeding or destroy infection. ⟫⟫ **cauterization** /-'zaysh(ə)n/ *noun*.

cautery /'kawtəri/ *noun* (*pl* **cauteries**) **1** the act of cauterizing a wound or body tissue. **2** an instrument, e.g. a hot iron, or a caustic chemical used in cauterization. [via Latin from Greek *kautērion* branding iron, from *kaiein* to burn]

caution[1] /'kawsh(ə)n/ *noun* **1** prudent forethought intended to minimize risk; care: *Proceed with caution*. **2** a warning or admonishment; *specif* an official warning given to somebody who has committed a minor offence. **3** *informal* somebody or something that causes astonishment or amusement: *She's a proper caution*. [Latin *caution-, cautio* precaution, from *cavēre* to be on guard]

caution[2] *verb trans* **1** to warn or advise caution to (somebody). **2** to warn (somebody under arrest) that their words will be recorded and may be used in evidence. **3** to admonish or reprove (somebody); *specif* to give (them) an official warning: *He was cautioned for disorderly conduct*. ⟫ *verb intrans* (*often* + against) to urge, advise, or warn: *They cautioned against the use of excessive force*.

cautionary /'kawshən(ə)ri/ *adj* serving or intended to serve as a warning: *a cautionary tale*.

cautious /'kawshəs/ *adj* careful; prudent: *a cautious approach*. ⟫⟫ **cautiously** *adv*, **cautiousness** *noun*.

cava /'kahvə/ *noun* a sparkling white wine produced in Spain by the champagne method. [Spanish *cava*]

cavalcade /'kavlkayd, kavəl'kayd/ *noun* **1** a procession, *esp* one of people on horseback or in carriages or other vehicles. **2** a dramatic sequence or procession; a series: *a cavalcade of events*. [French *cavalcade* ride on horseback, from Old Italian *cavalcata*, from *cavalcare* to go on horseback, ultimately from Latin *caballus* horse]

cavalier[1] /kavə'liə/ *noun* **1** a gallant gentleman of former times, *esp* one in attendance on a lady. **2** *archaic* a man trained in arms and horsemanship; *specif* a mounted soldier. **3** (**Cavalier**) a supporter of Charles I of England, *esp* during the Civil War. [early French *cavalier* via Old Italian and Old Provençal from late Latin *caballarius* horseman, from Latin *caballus* horse]

cavalier[2] *adj* **1** offhand or dismissive with regard to important matters, other people's feelings, etc: *Individual writings of would-be psychohistorians have consistently been characterized by a cavalier attitude towards fact* — David E Stannard. **2** debonair. **3** (**Cavalier**) of the party of Charles I of England. ⟫⟫ **cavalierly** *adv*.

cavalry /'kavəlri/ *noun* (*pl* **cavalries**) (*treated as sing. or pl*) **1** a branch of an army consisting of mounted troops. **2** a branch of a modern army consisting of armoured vehicles. ⟫⟫ **cavalryman** *noun*. [Italian *cavalleria* cavalry, chivalry, from *cavaliere* horseman, from late Latin *caballarius*: see CAVALIER[1]]

cavalry twill *noun* a strong fabric woven in a double twill and used orig for riding breeches.

cavatina /kavə'teenə/ *noun* (*pl* **cavatine** /-nee, -nay/ *or* **cavatinas**) **1** a short simple operatic solo. **2** an instrumental composition in a similar style, usu with a slow tempo. [Italian *cavatina*, from *cavata* production of sound from an instrument, from *cavare* to dig out, from Latin *cavus* hollow]

cave[1] /kayv/ *noun* **1a** a natural chamber, usu underground or in the side of a hill or cliff, with an opening on the surface. **b** (*used before a noun*) living or found in a cave or caves: *cave dweller; cave painting*. **2** *Brit* a formal withdrawal from a political party, or a group of people who do this. [Middle English via Old French from Latin *cava*, from *cavus* hollow; (sense 2) from *cave of Adullam*, where David was joined by malcontents (I Samuel 22:1, 2)]

cave[2] *verb trans* to form a cave in or under (something); to hollow (it) out. ⟫ *verb intrans* to explore underground systems of caves or potholes. ⟫⟫ **caver** *noun*.

cave[3] /'kayvee/ *interj Brit* used as a warning call among schoolchildren, *esp* at public school. ✱ **keep cave** *Brit* to act as a lookout at school. [Latin *cave* beware, from *cavēre* to beware, be on guard]

caveat /'kaviat/ *noun* **1** *formal* a cautionary statement or warning. **2** an official notice to a court to suspend a proceeding until the opposition has been heard. [Latin *caveat* let him beware, from *cavēre* to beware]

caveat emptor /'emptaw/ *noun* the principle in commerce stating that buyers who purchase goods without a guarantee take the risk of quality upon themselves. [Latin *caveat emptor* let the buyer beware]

cave in *verb intrans* **1** to fall in or collapse: *The roof of the tunnel caved in.* **2** *informal* to cease to resist; to submit: *He caved in under pressure from his colleagues.* ➤ *verb trans* to cause (something) to fall in or collapse.

cave-in *noun* **1** a collapse or falling in: *a cave-in at the old mine.* **2** an instance of submission or ceasing to resist: *another cave-in from the government.*

caveman *noun* (*pl* **cavemen**) **1** somebody who lives in a cave, *esp* a cave dweller of the Stone Age. **2** a man who acts in a rough primitive manner, *esp* towards women.

Cavendish /'kavəndish/ *noun* tobacco that is softened by moisture, usu sweetened, and pressed into flat cakes. [prob from the name *Cavendish*]

cavern /'kavən/ *noun* a large usu underground chamber or cave. [Middle English *caverne* via Old French from Latin *caverna*, from *cavus* hollow]

cavernous /'kavənəs/ *adj* **1** having caverns or cavities: *cavernous rocks.* **2** constituting or resembling a cavern: *a cavernous hall.* ➤➤ **cavernously** *adv.*

caviar *or* **caviare** /'kaviah/ *noun* the salted roe of large fish, e.g. sturgeon, eaten as a delicacy. ✳ **caviar to the general** something considered too delicate, refined, or lofty for mass appreciation. [obsolete Italian *caviaro* from Turkish *havyar*]

cavil[1] /'kav(i)l/ *verb intrans* (**cavilled, cavilling**, *NAmer* **caviled, caviling**) (*often* + at) to raise trivial and frivolous objections. ➤➤ **caviller** *noun.* [Latin *cavillari* to jest, cavil, from *cavilla* raillery]

cavil[2] *noun* a trivial or frivolous objection.

caving *noun* the exploration of caves as a sport or pastime.

cavitation /kavi'taysh(ə)n/ *noun* **1** the formation of cavities in something. **2** the formation of partial vacuums in a liquid by the swift movement of a solid body, e.g. a propeller, or by high-frequency sound waves.

cavity /'kaviti/ *noun* (*pl* **cavities**) an empty or hollowed-out space within a mass; *specif* a decaying hollow in a tooth. [French *cavité* from late Latin *cavitas*, from Latin *cavus* hollow]

cavity wall *noun* a wall built in two thicknesses with an insulating air space between them.

cavity wall insulation *noun* a substance inserted into the space between the thicknesses of a cavity wall in order to reduce heat loss from a building.

cavort /kə'vawt/ *verb intrans* **1** to prance or leap about: *He's the Morris dancer, isn't he? I've seen him cavorting about on summer nights outside the Olive and Dove* — Ruth Rendell. **2** to behave in an extravagant manner. [perhaps alteration of CURVET[1]]

cavy /'kayvi/ *noun* (*pl* **cavies**) any of several species of short-tailed S American rodents including the guinea pig: family Caviidae. [Latin genus name *Cavia*, from obsolete Portuguese *çavía* from Tupi *sawiya* rat]

caw[1] /kaw/ *verb intrans* to utter the harsh raucous cry of the crow or a similar sound. [imitative]

caw[2] *noun* the harsh raucous cry of the crow, or a similar sound.

cay /kay, kee/ *noun* a low island or reef of sand or coral. [Spanish *cayo*, from Lucayo (a language formerly spoken in the Bahamas)]

cayenne /kay'en/ *noun* = CAYENNE PEPPER.

cayenne pepper /kay'en/ *noun* **1** a pungent red condiment consisting of the ground dried pods and seeds of hot peppers: compare CHILLI, PAPRIKA. **2** a hot pepper, *esp* a cultivated variety with long twisted red pods. [alteration (by association with *Cayenne*, town in French Guiana) of *cayan*, from Tupi *kyinha*]

cayman *or* **caiman** /'kaymən/ *noun* (*pl* **caymans** *or collectively* **cayman**) any of several species of Central and S American reptiles of the crocodile family closely related to the alligators: genus *Caiman*. [Spanish *caimán*, prob from Carib *caymán*]

Cayuga /kee'oohgə, kay-, kie-/ *noun* (*pl* **Cayugas** *or collectively* **Cayuga**) **1** a member of a Native American people of New York State. **2** their Iroquoian language. [prob from an Iroquoian place name]

Cayuse /'kieyoohs, kie'yoohs/ *noun* (*pl* **Cayuses** *or collectively* **Cayuse**) **1** a member of a Native American people of Oregon and Washington. **2** (**cayuse**) *NAmer* an American Indian-bred pony. [the name of the people in Chinook Jargon]

CB *abbr* **1** in radio, citizens' band. **2** *Brit* Companion of the (Order of the) Bath.

CBC *abbr* Canadian Broadcasting Corporation.

CBE *abbr* Brit Commander of the (Order of the) British Empire.

CBI *abbr* Confederation of British Industry.

CBS *abbr* Columbia Broadcasting System.

CC *abbr* **1** Chamber of Commerce. **2** City Council. **3** County Council. **4** Cricket Club.

cc *abbr* **1** carbon copy. **2** chapters. **3** cubic centimetre.

CCD *abbr* charge-coupled device.

C clef *noun* in music, a symbol indicating middle C by its position on one of the lines of the stave.

CCTV *abbr* closed-circuit television.

CD *abbr* **1** civil defence. **2** compact disc. **3** diplomatic corps. [(sense 3) French *corps diplomatique*]

Cd *abbr* the chemical symbol for cadmium.

cd *abbr* candela.

CD-I *abbr* compact disc interactive.

CDN *abbr* Canada (international vehicle registration).

CD player *noun* a piece of audio equipment for playing compact discs.

Cdr *abbr* Commander.

Cdre *abbr* Commodore.

CD-ROM /seedee'rom/ *noun* a compact disc on which very large amounts of data can be stored for use by a computer. [short for *compact disc read-only memory*]

CDT *abbr* **1** Central daylight time (time zone). **2** craft, design, and technology.

CDV *abbr* CD video.

CD video *noun* a system for the recording and reproduction of high-quality sound synchronized with video images on a compact disc.

CE *abbr* **1** Church of England. **2** civil engineer. **3** Common Era. **4** Council of Europe.

Ce *abbr* the chemical symbol for cerium.

ceanothus /see-ə'nohthəs/ *noun* a shrub or small tree of the buckthorn family that is grown for its showy clusters of blue or white flowers: genus *Ceanothus*. [scientific Latin, genus name, from Greek *keanōthos* a thistle]

cease[1] /sees/ *verb trans* to bring (something) to an end; to terminate (it): *The company has ceased trading.* ➤ *verb intrans* **1** to come to an end: *When will the fighting cease?* **2** to stop an activity or action to an end; to stop or discontinue: *The baby cried for hours without ceasing.* [Middle English *cesen* via Old French from Latin *cessare* to delay, from *cedere* to yield]

cease[2] *noun* stopping; cessation: *without cease.*

cease-fire *noun* **1** a military order to stop firing. **2** a suspension of active hostilities.

ceaseless *adj* continuing endlessly; constant. ➤➤ **ceaselessly** *adv.*

ceca /'seekə/ *noun NAmer* pl of CECUM.

cecum /'seekəm/ *noun NAmer* see CAECUM.

cedar /'seedə/ *noun* **1** any of several species of usu tall evergreen coniferous trees of the pine family: genera *Cedrus* and *Thuja*. **2** the fragrant durable wood of a cedar tree. [Middle English *cedre* via Old French and Latin from Greek *kedros*]

cedar of Lebanon /'lebənən/ *noun* a tall evergreen tree with short leaves in small bundles and upright cones that is native to Asia Minor: *Cedrus libani*. [named after *Lebanon*, country in Asia Minor]

cede /seed/ *verb trans* to yield or surrender (e.g. territory), usu by treaty. ➤➤ **ceder** *noun.* [French *céder* or Latin *cedere* to go, withdraw, yield]

cedi /'saydi/ *noun* (*pl* **cedi** /'saydi/) the basic monetary unit of Ghana, divided into 100 pesewas. [Akan *sedie* cowrie]

cedilla /sə'dilə/ *noun* a mark (ç) placed under a letter in some languages to show an alteration of its usual pronunciation, e.g. under *c* in French to change its sound from the /k/ of *café* to the /s/ of *façade*. [Spanish *cedilla*, the obsolete letter ç (actually a medieval form of the letter z), dimin. of *ceda, zeda* the letter z, via late Latin from Greek *zēta*]

Ceefax /'seefaks/ *noun trademark* a service provided by the BBC transmitting information, e.g. the weather or sports results, that can be viewed in the form of printed text on a television set adapted for this facility. [from the initial syllables of *seeing* and FACSIMILE[1]]

CEGB *abbr* Central Electricity Generating Board.

ceiba /'saybə/ *noun* a large tropical tree of the baobab family that bears large pods filled with seeds covered with a silky floss that yields the fibre kapok: *Ceiba pentandra*. [Spanish, prob of Arawakan origin]

ceilidh /'kayli/ *noun* **1** a party, e.g. after a wedding, with traditional country dancing and music, *esp* in Scotland or Ireland. **2** an informal gathering of friends and neighbours for singing, storytelling, and music, *esp* in Scotland and Ireland in former times. [Irish Gaelic *céilí* and Scottish Gaelic *céilidh* visit, visiting, from Old Irish *céle, céile* companion]

ceiling /'seeling/ *noun* **1** the overhead inside surface of a room. **2** an upper prescribed limit: *a ceiling on price increases*. **3** a prescribed or actual maximum height at which an aircraft can fly. **4** the height above the ground of the base of the lowest layer of clouds. [Middle English *celing* from *celen* to furnish with a ceiling, prob via French from Latin *caelare* to carve, from *caelum* chisel, from *caedere* to cut]

cel *or* **cell** /sel/ *noun* a transparent plastic sheet on which drawings for animated cartoons are made or which is used as an overlay in artwork. [short for *Celluloid*]

celadon /'seləd(o)n/ *noun* **1** a greyish green colour. **2** a greyish green ceramic glaze or pottery with such a glaze, *esp* a type of Chinese porcelain. ➤➤ **celadon** *adj*. [named after *Céladon*, languid lover in the romance *L'Astrée* by Honoré d'Urfé d.1625, French writer]

celandine /'seləndien/ *noun* **1** a common yellow-flowered European perennial plant of the buttercup family: *Ranunculus ficaria*. Also called LESSER CELANDINE: *There's a flower that shall be mine, 'tis the little celandine* — Wordsworth. **2** a yellow-flowered biennial plant of the poppy family: *Chelidonium majus*. Also called GREATER CELANDINE.

Word history
Middle English *celidoine* via Old French and Latin from Greek *chelidonios*, from *chelidōn* swallow. The flowering season of the plant was believed to coincide with the arrival and departure of migrating swallows.

-cele *comb. form* forming nouns, denoting: hernia: *hydrocele*. [French *-cele* via Latin from Greek *kēlē* tumour]

celeb /sə'leb/ *noun informal* = CELEBRITY (1).

celebrant /'selibrənt/ *noun* the priest officiating at the Eucharist.

celebrate /'selibrayt/ *verb trans* **1a** to mark (a special occasion) with festivities or suspension of routine activities: *celebrate an anniversary*. **b** to mark (a holy day or feast day) ceremonially. **2** to perform (a sacrament or solemn ceremony) publicly and with appropriate rites: *celebrate the Eucharist*. **3** to hold (something) up for public acclaim; to extol (it): *His poetry celebrates the glory of nature*. ➤ *verb intrans* **1** to observe a special occasion with festivities. **2** to officiate at a religious ceremony. ➤➤ **celebration** /-'braysh(ə)n/ *noun*, **celebrator** *noun*, **celebratory** /-brət(ə)ri/ *adj*. [Latin *celebratus*, past part. of *celebrare* to frequent, celebrate, from *celebr-, celeber* much frequented, famous]

celebrated *adj* widely known or acclaimed; famous.

celebrity /sə'lebriti/ *noun* (*pl* **celebrities**) **1** a well-known and widely acclaimed person: *To become a celebrity is to become a brand name* — Philip Roth. **2** the state of being famous.

celeriac /sə'leriak/ *noun* a type of celery grown for its thickened edible root. [irreg from CELERY]

celerity /sə'leriti/ *noun formal* rapidity of motion or action. [Middle English *celerite* via French from Latin *celeritat-, celeritas*, from *celer* swift]

celery /'seləri/ *noun* a European plant of the carrot family with leafstalks that are eaten raw or cooked as a vegetable: *Apium graveolens*. [prob from Italian dialect *seleri*, pl of *selero*, ultimately from Greek *selinon* parsley]

celery salt *noun* salt and ground celery seed, used as seasoning.

celesta /sə'lestə/ *or* **celeste** /sə'lest/ *noun* a keyboard musical instrument with hammers that strike steel plates producing a tinkling bell-like sound. [French *célesta*, alteration of *céleste* heavenly, from Latin *caelestis*: see CELESTIAL]

celestial /sə'lesti-əl/ *adj* **1** of or suggesting heaven or divinity; divine. **2** of or in the sky: *a celestial body*. ➤➤ **celestially** *adv*. [Middle English via Old French from Latin *caelestis*, from *caelum* sky]

celestial equator *noun* the great circle on the celestial sphere midway between the two points round which the daily rotation of the stars appears to take place.

celestial mechanics *noun* a branch of astronomy that deals with the application of the laws of dynamics and gravitation to the motions of bodies in orbit, e.g. moons, planets, and binary stars.

celestial navigation *noun* navigation using the position of the stars.

celestial pole *noun* either of the two points on the celestial sphere round which the daily rotation of the stars appears to take place.

celestial sphere *noun* an imaginary sphere of infinite radius against which the celestial bodies appear to be projected.

celiac /'seeliak/ *adj NAmer* see COELIAC.

celibate[1] /'selibət/ *adj* **1** abstaining from sexual intercourse, *esp* because of a religious vow. **2** unmarried. ➤➤ **celibacy** /-bəsi/ *noun*. [Latin *caelibatus* from *caelib-, caelebs* unmarried]

celibate[2] *noun* a celibate person: *It's about time we accepted total celibates are no more deranged, inefficient, unhappy or unhealthy than any other section of the population* — Germaine Greer.

cell[1] /sel/ *noun* **1a** a small room in a prison for one or more inmates. **b** a barely furnished room for one person, e.g. in a convent or monastery. **c** a one-roomed dwelling occupied by a solitary person, e.g. a hermit or recluse. **2** the smallest structural unit of living matter, consisting of a nucleus surrounded by CYTOPLASM (jelly-like material) and bounded by a membrane, capable of functioning either alone or with others in all fundamental life processes: *blood cell*.

Editorial note
That all living organisms are composed of cells has been known since the work of microscopists in the mid 19th cent. The simplest independently living organisms such as bacteria are single-celled, whilst in multicellular organisms different tissues contain cells specialized for distinct functions, like nerve or muscle. The ten trillion cells of the human body include some 250 different cell types — Professor Steven Rose.

3 a small compartment, or a bounded space, e.g. a compartment of a honeycomb or a receptacle for seeds in a plant. **4** the primary unit of a political, *esp* subversive, organization: *terrorist cell*. **5** a small religious house dependent on a monastery or convent. **6a** a vessel containing electrodes and an electrolyte either for generating electricity by chemical action or for use in electrolysis. **b** a single unit in a device for producing electricity as a result of exposure to radiant energy. **7** a basic subdivision of a computer memory that is addressable and can hold one unit, e.g. a word, of a computer's basic operating data. **8** any of the individual geographical regions of a cellular radio system. [Old English via Old French from Latin *cella* small room]

cell[2] *noun* see CEL.

cella /'selə/ *noun* the principal chamber of an ancient temple containing the shrine to the divinity; *broadly* the main body of any classical building: compare NAOS. [Latin *cella* small room, cella]

cellar[1] /'selə/ *noun* **1** an underground room, *esp* one used for storage. **2** a stock of wine. [Middle English *celer* via Anglo-French from Latin *cellarium* storeroom, from *cella* small room]

cellar[2] *verb trans* (**cellared, cellaring**) to store or place (e.g. wine) in a cellar.

cellarage /'selərij/ *noun* **1** cellar space, *esp* for storage. **2** the charge made for storage in a cellar.

cellarer *noun* an official in charge of provisions in a monastery.

cellaret *or* **cellarette** /selə'ret/ *noun* a case or sideboard for holding bottles of alcoholic drink, *esp* wine.

cell block *noun* a block of cells in a prison.

cell division *noun* the process by which two daughter cells are formed from a parent cell: compare MEIOSIS (1), MITOSIS. Also called CLEAVAGE.

celled *adj* (*used in combinations*) having cells of the kind or number specified: *single-celled organisms*.

Cellnet *noun trademark* a cellular radio network for users of mobile phones.

cello /'cheloh/ *noun* (*pl* **cellos**) a stringed musical instrument of the violin family that is intermediate in range between the viola and the double bass and is held between the player's knees, supported on the ground by an adjustable metal spike. >>> **cellist** *noun*. [short for VIOLONCELLO]

Cellophane /'seləfayn/ *noun trademark* thin transparent sheets of cellulose, used *esp* for wrapping goods. [from CELLULOSE + *diaphane*, a fine, semi-transparent silk fabric, from Latin *diaphanus*: see DIAPHANOUS]

cellphone *noun* a mobile phone for use in a cellular radio system. [short for *cellular telephone*]

cellular /'selyoolə/ *adj* **1** relating to or consisting of cells. **2** containing cavities; porous. **3** having a very open weave: *a cellular blanket*. **4** relating to or used in a cellular radio system: *a cellular telephone*. >>> **cellularity** /-'lariti/ *noun*. [scientific Latin *cellularis*, from *cellula* living cell, from Latin, dimin. of *cella* small room]

cellular radio *noun* a communications system for mobile phones in which an area is divided into cells, each with its own transmitter, and the receiver automatically switches from one to another as the user crosses the borders between them.

cellule /'selyoohl/ *noun* a small cell. [Latin *cellula*: see CELLULAR]

cellulite /'selyooliet/ *noun* a type of body fat, possibly caused by water retention, that produces a dimpled effect on the skin, e.g. of the thigh: *I'm extremely lucky in that I have no cellulite* — Joan Collins. [French *cellulite*, from *cellule* small cell, from Latin *cellula*: see CELLULAR]

cellulitis /selyoo'lietis/ *noun* inflammation of body tissue, *esp* below the surface of the skin.

celluloid /'selyoolooyd/ *noun* **1** (**Celluloid**) *trademark* a tough inflammable thermoplastic that is composed mainly of cellulose nitrate and camphor and was formerly used to coat film. **2a** film for the cinema: *her first appearance on celluloid*. **b** (*used before a noun*) relating or belonging to the cinema: *celluloid heroes*. [CELLULOSE + -OID]

cellulose /'selyoolohs, -lohz/ *noun* **1** a carbohydrate made up of glucose units that constitutes the chief part of plant cell walls and is the raw material of many manufactured goods, e.g. paper, rayon, and cellophane. **2** paint or lacquer of which the main constituent is cellulose nitrate or acetate. [French *cellulose*, from *cellule* living cell, from scientific Latin *cellula*: see CELLULAR]

cellulose acetate *noun* a chemical compound formed by the action of acetic acid on cellulose and used for making textile fibres, packaging sheets, photographic films, and varnishes. Also called ACETATE.

cellulose nitrate *noun* a chemical compound formed by the action of nitric acid on cellulose and used for making explosives, plastics, rayon, and varnishes.

cell wall *noun* the firm outer layer, formed usu from cellulose, that encloses and supports most plant cells.

celom /'seeləm/ *noun NAmer* see COELOM.

Celsius /'selsi·əs/ *adj* of or being a scale of temperature on which water freezes at 0° and boils at 100° under standard conditions: *24 degrees Celsius; the Celsius scale*. [named after Anders *Celsius* d.1744, Swedish astronomer, who devised a similar scale]

Usage note

Celsius or **centigrade**? *Celsius* has been internationally adopted as the name of the temperature scale and is always used, for example, in giving weather forecasts. *Centigrade* is no longer in technical use.

Celt *or* **Kelt** /kelt/ *noun* **1** a member of a division of the early Indo-European peoples extending at various times from the British Isles and Spain to Asia Minor. **2** a native or inhabitant of Highland Scotland, Ireland, Wales, Cornwall, the Isle of Man, or Brittany, *esp* one speaking a Celtic language. [French *Celte* from Latin *Celtae* (pl), from Greek *keltoi*]

celt /selt/ *noun* a prehistoric stone or metal implement shaped like a chisel or axe head. [late Latin *celtis* chisel]

Celtic[1] *or* **Keltic** /'keltik/ *adj* of the Celts or their languages.

Usage note

The standard pronunciation of *Celtic* (and *Celt*) in England and Wales is with an initial *k*- sound. The variant pronunciation with an initial *s*- sound is much less common and mainly used in the name of the Glasgow football team *Celtic*.

Celtic[2] *or* **Keltic** *noun* a branch of Indo-European languages comprising Welsh, Cornish, Breton, Irish and Scottish Gaelic, and Manx. >>> **Celticism** *noun*.

Celtic cross *noun* a Latin cross with a ring around the intersection of the crossbar and upright.

Celtic fringe *noun* Cornwall, Wales, Ireland, and Highland Scotland, or the people of these areas, considered as a cultural and political grouping.

cembalo /'chembəloh/ *noun* (*pl* **cembali** /-lee/ *or* **cembalos**) = HARPSICHORD. [Italian *cembalo*, short for *clavicembalo*, from medieval Latin *clavis* key + *cymbalum*: see CYMBAL]

cement[1] /si'ment/ *noun* **1a** a powder containing lime and clay that is used as the binding agent in mortar and concrete. **b** concrete or mortar. **2** a substance used for sticking objects together. **3** something serving to unite firmly: *the cement that holds the community together*. **4** = CEMENTUM. **5** an adhesive preparation used for filling teeth, attaching dental crowns, etc. [Middle English *sement* via Old French from Latin *caementum* stone chips used in making mortar, from *caedere* to cut]

cement[2] *verb trans* **1** to join (things) together firmly by the application of cement or a similar substance. **2** to cover or fill (something) with concrete or mortar. **3** to make (e.g. a relationship) firm and strong: *cement a friendship*.

cementation /seemen'taysh(ə)n, sem-/ *noun* the process of heating a solid surrounded by a powder so that the solid is changed by chemical combination with the powder, *esp* the heating of iron surrounded by charcoal to make steel.

cement mixer *noun* a machine with a revolving drum in which cement, aggregate, and water are mixed to make concrete.

cementum /si'mentəm/ *noun* the thin bony layer enclosing the base of a tooth. [scientific Latin *cementum*, from Latin *caementum*: see CEMENT[1]]

cemetery /'semət(ə)ri/ *noun* (*pl* **cemeteries**) a burial ground, *esp* one not in a churchyard. [Middle English *cimitery* via French and late Latin from Greek *koimētērion* sleeping chamber, burial place, from *koiman* to put to sleep]

cen- *or* **ceno-** *or* **cain-** *or* **caino-** *or* **caen-** *or* **caeno-** *comb. form* forming words, with the meaning: new or recent: *Cenozoic*. [Greek *kain-, kaino-*, from *kainos*]

-cene *comb. form* forming adjectives and nouns, denoting: a recent geological period: *Eocene*. [Greek *kainos* new]

CEng /,see 'eng/ *abbr* Chartered Engineer.

ceno- *comb. form* see CEN-.

cenobite /'seenəbiet/ *noun NAmer* see COENOBITE.

cenotaph /'senətahf/ *noun* **1** a tomb or monument erected in honour of a dead person or group of people whose remains are elsewhere. **2** (**the Cenotaph**) a monument in Whitehall, London, erected in memory of the dead of World Wars I and II. [French *cénotaphe* via Latin from Greek *kenotaphion*, from *kenos* empty + *taphos* tomb]

Cenozoic /seenə'zoh·ik/ *or* **Cainozoic** /kaynə-/ *adj* relating to or dating from a geological era (extending from the end of the Mesozoic era until the present time, and including the Tertiary and Quaternary periods) lasting from about 65 million years ago to the present, and marked *esp* by a rapid evolution of mammals, birds, and flowering plants. >>> **Cenozoic** *noun*.

cense /sens/ *verb trans* to perfume (something), *esp* with a censer. [Middle English *censen*, prob short for *encensen* to incense, via French from late Latin *incensare*, from *incensum* incense]

censer *noun* a covered incense burner swung on chains during certain religious rituals.

censor[1] /'sensə/ *noun* **1** an official who examines publications, films, letters, etc and has the power to suppress objectionable, e.g. obscene or libellous, matter. **2** either of two magistrates of early Rome who acted as census takers, inspectors of morals, etc. **3** a supposed mental agency that represses certain unacceptable ideas and desires before they reach consciousness. >>> **censorial** /sen'sawri·əl/ *adj*. [Latin *censor*, from *censēre* to assess, tax]

censor[2] *verb trans* (**censored, censoring**) to examine and remove objectionable matter from (e.g. a publication, film, letter).

censorious /sen'sawri·əs/ *adj* severely critical; given to censure: *The censorious said she slept in a hammock and understood Yeats's poems, but her family denied both stories* — Saki. ⟫⟫ **censoriously** *adv*, **censoriousness** *noun*. [Latin *censorius* of a censor, from *censor*: see CENSOR[1]]

censorship *noun* **1a** the practices, powers, or duties of a censor, *esp* repressive censorial control. **b** the act of censoring something.

Editorial note ───────────

Originally, censorship was the power wielded in ancient Rome by the Censor, official guardian of public morals. Now, it denotes suppression or eradication of words, images, or messages deemed harmful to others, e.g. by corrupting minds (obscenity) or outraging feelings (indecency). Political censorship represses ideas disquietening to rulers: Stalin censored history by eliminating (in person or in photo) those who made it. Only communications with oneself defy censorship: thought is free — Geoffrey Robertson.

2 the office, power, or term of a Roman censor. **3** the repression in the mind of unacceptable ideas and desires.

censure[1] /'senshə/ *noun* **1** a judgment involving condemnation. **2** the act of blaming or condemning sternly. **3** an official reprimand. [Latin *censura*, from *censēre*: see CENSOR[1]]

censure[2] *verb trans* to find fault with and criticize (somebody) as blameworthy. ⟫⟫ **censurable** *adj*.

census /'sensəs/ *noun* (*pl* **censuses**) **1** a periodic counting of the population and gathering of related statistics, e.g. age, sex, or social class, carried out by a government. **2** an official count or tally: *a traffic census*. [Latin *census*, from *censēre*: see CENSOR[1]]

cent /sent/ *noun* a unit of currency worth 100th of the basic monetary unit of certain countries, e.g. the dollar (in EU countries up to the introduction of the euro in 2002). [French *cent* hundred, from Latin *centum*]

cent. *abbr* century.

centas /'sentas, 'tsantas/ *noun* (*pl* **centas** or **centai** /-tie/) a unit of currency in Lithuania, worth 100th of a litas. [Lithuanian *centas*]

centaur /'sentaw/ *noun* any of a race of mythological creatures with the head, arms, and upper body of a man, and the lower body and back legs of a horse. [Middle English via Latin from Greek *Kentauros*, name of a tribe of skilled horsemen in Thessalonia]

centaury /'sentawri/ *noun* (*pl* **centauries**) any of a genus of low-growing plants of the gentian family, formerly used in medicine: genus *Centaurium*.

Word history ───────────

Middle English *centaure* via French and Latin from Greek *kentaureion*, from *Kentauros*: see CENTAUR. According to legend, this plant was discovered by the centaur Chiron.

centavo /sen'tahvoh/ *noun* (*pl* **centavos**) a unit of currency worth 100th of the basic monetary unit of certain Spanish- or Portuguese-speaking countries (in Portugal up to the introduction of the euro in 2002). [Spanish *centavo* hundredth, from Latin *centum* hundred]

centenarian[1] /sentə'neəri·ən/ *noun* somebody who is 100 years old or older.

centenarian[2] *adj* at least 100 years old.

centenary[1] /sen'teenəri, sen'tenəri/ *noun* (*pl* **centenaries**) a 100th anniversary, or a celebration marking this. [late Latin *centenarium*, from Latin *centenarius* of a hundred, from *centum* hundred]

centenary[2] *adj* **1** relating to a 100th anniversary or a period of 100 years. **2** occurring every 100 years.

centennial[1] /sen'teni·əl/ *adj* **1** marking a 100th anniversary: *centennial celebrations*. **2** occurring every 100 years. **3** relating to or lasting for a period of 100 years. ⟫⟫ **centennially** *adv*. [Latin *centum* + *-ennial* as in BIENNIAL[1]]

centennial[2] *noun* = CENTENARY[1].

center /'sentə/ *noun and verb NAmer* see CENTRE[1], CENTRE[2].

centesimal /sen'tesiməl/ *adj* marked by or relating to division into hundredths. ⟫⟫ **centesimally** *adv*. [Latin *centesimus* hundredth, from *centum* hundred]

centésimo /sen'tesimoh/ *noun* (*pl* **centesimos**) a unit of currency worth 100th of the basic monetary unit of Panama and Uruguay. [Spanish *centésimo* from Latin *centesimus*: see CENTESIMAL]

centi- *comb. form* forming words, with the meanings: **1** hundred: *centipede*. **2** one hundredth part: *centimetre*. [French *centi-* hundredth, from Latin *centum* hundred]

centigrade /'sentigrayd/ *adj* of or being a scale of 100 degrees, *esp* the Celsius scale of temperature. [French *centigrade*, from Latin *centum* hundred + *gradus* step]

Usage note ───────────
centigrade or Celsius? See note at CELSIUS.

centigram /'sentigram/ *noun* a metric unit of mass equal to 100th of a gram.

centilitre (*NAmer* **centiliter**) /'sentileetə/ *noun* a metric unit of capacity equal to 100th of a litre (about 0.35fl oz).

centime /'sonteem/ *noun* a unit of currency worth 100th of the basic monetary unit of France and certain French-speaking countries (in EU countries up to the introduction of the euro in 2002). [French *centime* from *cent* hundred, from Latin *centum*]

centimetre (*NAmer* **centimeter**) /'sentimeetə/ *noun* a metric unit of length equal to 100th of a metre (about 0.4in.).

centimetre-gram-second *adj* of or being a system of units based on the centimetre, the gram, and the second.

centimo /'sentimoh/ *noun* (*pl* **centimos**) a unit of currency worth 100th of the basic monetary unit of Spain and certain Spanish-speaking countries (in Spain up to the introduction of the euro in 2002). [Spanish *céntimo* from French *centime*: see CENTIME]

centipede /'sentipeed/ *noun* any of a class of long invertebrate animals with a flattened body divided into many segments, each bearing one pair of legs: class Chilopoda. [Latin *centipeda*, from *centi-* + *ped-*, *pes* foot]

cento /'sentoh/ *noun* (*pl* **centones** /sen'tohneez/ or **centos**) a literary work made up of quotations from other works. [Latin *cento* patchwork garment]

centr- or **centri-** or **centro-** *comb. form* forming words, with the meaning: centre: *centrifugal*; *centroid*. [Greek *kentr-*, *kentro-*, from *kentron*: see CENTRE[1]]

centra /'sentrə/ *noun pl* of CENTRUM.

central /'sentrəl/ *adj* **1a** at, in, or near the centre: *an office in central London*. **b** easily accessible; convenient: *Our house is very central for the shops*. **2** containing or constituting a centre: *the central point*. **3** of primary importance; principal: *the central character of the novel*. **4** having overall power or control: *decided by the central committee*. ⟫⟫ **centrality** /sen'traliti/ *noun*, **centrally** *adv*. [Latin *centralis* from *centrum*: see CENTRE[1]]

Central America *noun* the isthmus between North America and South America and the countries it contains, e.g. Guatemala, Nicaragua, and Costa Rica. ⟫⟫ **Central American** *adj*.

central bank *noun* the main banking institution of a country, usu dealing with government or interbank transactions rather than those of private individuals.

Central European Time *noun* the standard time, one hour ahead of Greenwich Mean Time, that is used by most countries of continental Europe.

central heating *noun* a system of heating in which heat is produced at a central source, e.g. a boiler, and carried by pipes to radiators or air vents throughout a building.

centralise *verb* see CENTRALIZE.

centralism *noun* the practice or principle of concentrating power and control in a central authority. ⟫⟫ **centralist** *noun and adj*, **centralistic** /-'listik/ *adj*.

centralize or **centralise** *verb trans* to bring (something) to a centre; to consolidate (it); *specif* to bring (power, authority, administration, etc) under central control. ⟫ *verb intrans* to come to or gather round a centre; *specif* to come under central control. ⟫⟫ **centralization** /-'zaysh(ə)n/ *noun*.

central locking *noun* a system by which all or some of the doors of a motor vehicle can be locked or unlocked simultaneously by turning the key in a single lock.

central nervous system *noun* the part of the nervous system that in vertebrates consists of the brain and spinal cord and that coordinates the activity of the entire nervous system.

central processing unit *noun* the part of a computer system that carries out all the arithmetical and logical operations.

central reservation *noun* a strip in the middle of a road, *esp* a motorway or dual carriageway, that is usu covered with grass or tarmac.

Central Standard Time *noun* the standard time, six hours behind Greenwich Mean Time, used in the central states and provinces of North America.

Central Time *noun* = CENTRAL STANDARD TIME.

centre[1] (*NAmer* **center**) /'sentə/ *noun* **1a** the point lying at the same distance from both ends of a line, all sides of a polygon, or all points on the circumference of a circle. **b** the middle part of something: *at the centre of the stage; chocolates with soft centres.* **c** the point or axis about which a system is arranged, or about which it pivots or rotates: *Things fall apart; the centre cannot hold* — W B Yeats. **2a** a place, *esp* a building or collection of buildings, in which a particular activity is concentrated: *a shopping centre; a health centre.* **b** the part of a town or city where most of the shops, banks, offices, etc are situated: *the town centre.* **c** somebody or something on whom or which interest is concentrated: *the centre of the controversy.* **d** a source from which something originates: *a centre of academic excellence.* **3** (*often* **Centre**) a group, party, etc holding moderate political views. **4a** in some sports, e.g. football or hockey, a player occupying a middle position in the forward line of a team. **b** an instance of passing the ball from the side to the middle of a pitch or field, e.g. in football. **5** a group of nerve cells having a common function: *respiratory centre.* **6** a rod with a conical end that supports a workpiece in a lathe or grinding machine and about which the workpiece revolves. **7** = CENTRING. **8** (*used before a noun*) at or relating to a centre: *the centre hole; a centre kick.* [Middle English via French from Latin *centrum*, from Greek *kentron* sharp point, point of a pair of compasses, centre of a circle, from *kentein* to prick]

Usage note

Centre is the correct British English spelling for both the noun and the verb; *center* is the equivalent spelling in American English. As a verb, *centre* ought logically to be followed by the prepositions *at, in, on,* or *upon: The debate centres on the issue of funding.* Despite its illogicality with respect to physical midpoints that cannot go around anything, the phrase *centre around* or *round* is well established and has been used by many respected writers such as Conrad and Kipling. Some traditionalists may prefer, however, to use another verb such as *revolve* in its place: *The whole debate revolves around the issue of funding.*

centre[2] (*NAmer* **center**) *verb intrans* **1** (+ on/round/around) to have (something) as a centre; to focus on (it): *The conversation centred on the royal wedding.* **2** to come to or towards a centre or central area. **3** in sports, to centre a ball, puck, etc. ➤ *verb trans* **1** to place or fix (something) in or at a centre or central area: *Centre the picture on the wall.* **2** to gather (things) to a centre; to concentrate (them): *She centred her hopes on her son.* **3** in sports, to pass (e.g. a ball or puck) from either side towards the middle of the playing area.

centre back *noun* a player or position in football in the middle of the defence.

centre bit *noun* a drilling tool with a central point for guidance and two side cutters, used for boring holes in wood.

centreboard *noun* a retractable keel used *esp* in small sailing boats.

centred *adj* **1** (*used in combinations*) having a centre of the specified kind: *a dark-centred flower.* **2** at or in the centre: *a centred dot.* **3** *chiefly NAmer* said of a person: emotionally stable.

centrefold *noun* **1** an illustration covering the two facing pages in the centre of a newspaper or magazine. **2** the two facing pages in the centre of a newspaper or magazine.

centre forward *noun* a player or position in hockey, football, etc in the middle of the forward line.

centre half *noun* a player or position in hockey, football, etc in the middle of the halfback line.

centre of curvature *noun* the centre of the circle that has the same curvature as a curve at a given point.

centre of gravity *noun* the point from which the whole weight of a body may be considered to act.

centre of mass *noun* the point at which the entire mass of a body or system of bodies may be considered as concentrated.

centrepiece *noun* **1** an ornament, e.g. a flower arrangement, placed in the centre of a table. **2** the most important or outstanding item: *the centrepiece of the plan.*

centre spread *noun* = CENTREFOLD.

centre stage *noun* **1** the centre of a theatre stage. **2** a position of prominence; the focus of attention: *take centre stage.*

centre three-quarter *noun* either of the two players or positions in rugby in the middle of the three-quarter-back line.

centri- *comb. form* see CENTR-.

centric /'sentrik/ *adj* **1** central. **2** of a nerve centre. ➤➤ **centricity** /sen'trisiti/ *noun.* [Greek *kentrikos* of the centre, from *kentron*: see CENTRE[1]]

-centric *comb. form* forming adjectives, with the meanings: **1** having a specified kind of centre or number of centres: *polycentric.* **2** having the specified thing as a centre: *heliocentric.* **3** having the specified thing as one's central point of view or interest: *Eurocentric.* [medieval Latin *-centricus*, from Latin *centrum*: see CENTRE[1]]

centrical *adj* = CENTRIC.

centrifugal /sentri'fyoohg(ə)l, sen'trif-/ *adj* **1** proceeding or acting in a direction away from a centre or axis: compare CENTRIPETAL (1). **2** using or acting by centrifugal force: *a centrifugal pump.* **3** tending away from centralization; separatist: *centrifugal tendencies in modern society.* ➤➤ **centrifugally** *adv.* [scientific Latin *centrifugus*, from CENTRI- + Latin *fugere* to flee]

centrifugal force *noun* the force that appears to act on an object moving along a circular path and that acts outwardly from the centre of rotation.

centrifuge[1] /'sentrifyoohj, -fyoohzh/ *noun* a rotating machine that uses centrifugal force to separate substances of different densities, remove moisture, or simulate gravitational effects. [French *centrifuge* centrifugal, from scientific Latin *centrifugus*: see CENTRIFUGAL]

centrifuge[2] *verb trans* to subject (something) to centrifugal action, *esp* in a centrifuge. ➤➤ **centrifugation** /-'gaysh(ə)n/ *noun.*

centring /'sent(ə)ring/ *noun* a temporary wooden framework on which an arch is supported during construction.

centriole /'sentriohl/ *noun* either of a pair of organelles (specialized cell parts; see ORGANELLE), each consisting of nine microtubules arranged cylindrically, that are found in many animal cells and function in the formation of the apparatus that separates pairs of corresponding chromosomes during cell division. [German *Zentriol*, from *Zentrum* centre, from Latin *centrum*: see CENTRE[1]]

centripetal /sentri'peetl, sen'tripitl/ *adj* **1** proceeding or acting in a direction towards a centre or axis: compare CENTRIFUGAL (1). **2** tending towards centralization; unifying. ➤➤ **centripetally** *adv.* [scientific Latin *centripetus*, from CENTRI- + Latin *petere* to go to, seek]

centripetal force *noun* the force that is necessary to keep an object moving in a circular path and that is directed inwards towards the centre of rotation.

centrist /'sentrist/ *noun* (*often* **Centrist**) a member of a moderate political party; *broadly* somebody holding moderate political views. ➤➤ **centrism** *noun.*

centro- *comb. form* see CENTR-.

centroid /'sentroyd/ *noun* = CENTRE OF MASS.

centromere /'sentrəmiə/ *noun* the point on a chromosome by which it appears to attach to the spindle during cell division. [CENTRO- + -*mere* part, segment, from Greek *meros*]

centrosome /'sentrəsohm/ *noun* the region of clear cytoplasm in a cell that contains the centriole and is adjacent to the nucleus. [German *Zentrosom*, from CENTRO- + -SOME[1]]

centrum /'sentrəm/ *noun* (*pl* **centrums** or **centra** /'sentrə/) **1** a centre. **2** the body of a VERTEBRA (bone of the spine). [Latin: see CENTRE[1]]

centuple[1] /'sentyoopl, sen'tyoohpl/ *adj* one hundred times as great or as many. [French *centuple* from Latin *centuplus, centuplex,* from *centum* hundred + -*plex* -fold]

centuple[2] *noun* an amount 100 times as great as another.

centuple[3] *verb intrans* to become 100 times as great or as many. ➤ *verb trans* to make (something) 100 times as great or as many.

centurion /sen'tyooəri·ən/ *noun* **1** an officer commanding an ancient Roman century. **2** somebody who scores a century in cricket. [Middle English via French from Latin *centurion-, centurio,* from *centuria*: see CENTURY]

century /'sench(ə)ri/ *noun* (*pl* **centuries**) **1** a period of 100 years, *esp* any of the 100-year periods reckoned forwards or backwards from the conventional date of the birth of Christ. **2** a group, sequence, or series of 100 like things; *specif* 100 runs made by a cricketer in one innings. **3** a subdivision of the ancient Roman legion orig consisting of 100 men. **4** a division of the ancient Roman people for voting purposes. [Latin *centuria,* from *centum* hundred]

century plant *noun* a Mexican agave with long lance-shaped leaves that matures and flowers once after many years of growth and then dies: *Agave americana*. Also called AMERICAN ALOE.

CEO *abbr* Chief Executive Officer.

cep /sep/ *noun* an edible fungus with a shiny brown cap and white sponge-like underside that is considered a delicacy, *esp* in France and Germany: *Boletus edulis*. [French *cèpe* from French dialect *cep* tree trunk, mushroom, from Latin *cippus* stake, post]

cephal- *or* **cephalo-** *comb. form* forming words, with the meanings: **1** head: *cephalometry*. **2** head and: *cephalothorax*. [via Latin from Greek *kephal-*, *kephalo-*, from *kephalē* head]

cephalic /si'falik/ *adj* **1** relating to the head. **2** situated on, in, or near the head. ➤➤ **cephalically** *adv.* [French *cephalique* via Latin from Greek *kephalikos*, from *kephalē* head]

-cephalic *comb. form* forming adjectives, with the meaning: having a specified kind of head or number of heads: *brachycephalic*.

cephalic index *noun* the ratio of the maximum breadth of the head to its maximum length multiplied by 100: compare CRANIAL INDEX.

cephalization *or* **cephalisation** /sefəlie'zaysh(ə)n/ *noun* an evolutionary tendency to specialization of the body with concentration of sense organs and nerve centres in an anterior head.

cephalo- *comb. form* see CEPHAL-.

cephalochordate /,sefəloh'kawdayt/ *noun* any of a subphylum of small slender fish-like marine animals including the lancelets that have a NOTOCHORD (supporting skeleton-like rod) but no vertebral column: subphylum Cephalochordata. [derivative of CEPHAL- + Latin *chorda* cord]

cephalometry /sefə'lomətri/ *noun* the science of measuring the head. ➤➤ **cephalometric** *adj.*

cephalopod /'sef(ə)ləpod/ *noun* any of a class of molluscs including the squids, cuttlefishes, and octopuses, that have muscular tentacles around the head, usu furnished with suckers, and highly developed eyes: class Cephalopoda. ➤➤ **cephalopod** *adj,* **cephalopodan** /sefə'lopədən, -'pohdən/ *adj and noun.* [CEPHALO- + Greek *pod-, pous* foot]

cephalosporin /,sef(ə)lə'spawrin/ *noun* any of several antibiotics derived from the fungus *Cephalosporium*, resembling penicillin. [scientific Latin *Cephalosporium*, genus of fungi from which they are derived + -IN¹]

cephalothorax /,sef(ə)lə'thawraks/ *noun* (*pl* **cephalothoraxes** *or* **cephalothoraces** /-rəseez/) the united head and thorax of a spider, scorpion, crab, or related animal.

-cephalous *comb. form* = -CEPHALIC.

Cepheid /'seefiid, 'sef-/ *noun* any of a class of pulsating stars with regularly varying light intensities.

Word history
Latin *Cepheus*, a northern constellation, named after *Cepheus*, mythical king of Ethiopia and father of Andromeda, from Greek *Kēpheus*. One of the stars in this constellation is a typical cepheid.

Cepheid variable *noun* = CEPHEID.

ceramic¹ /sə'ramik/ *adj* **1** relating to a product, e.g. porcelain or brick, made from clay or similar material by firing at high temperatures. **2** relating to the manufacture of ceramic articles. [Greek *keramikos* from *keramos* potter's clay, pottery]

ceramic² *noun* **1** (*in pl, but treated as sing.*) the art or process of making ceramic articles. **2** a product of ceramic manufacture. **3** a substance used to make ceramic articles. ➤➤ **ceramicist** /-sist/ *noun.*

ceramic hob *noun* a flat cooking surface made of ceramic material with heating elements underneath.

cerastes /si'rasteez/ *noun* a venomous viper of the Near East that has a horny projection over each eye: *Cerastes cornutus*. [Middle English via Latin from Greek *kerastēs* horned, from *keras* horn]

ceratopsian /serə'topsi-ən/ *noun* any of a group of horned plant-eating dinosaurs, including triceratops, that walked on four legs and had a protective bony frill around the neck. [via Latin from Greek *keras, kerat-* horn + *ōps* face]

cercaria /suh'keəri-ə/ *noun* (*pl* **cercariae** /-ri-ee/) a larva of a parasitic flatworm, e.g. a liver fluke, that is usu tadpole-shaped and develops in an intermediate host, e.g. a snail. [scientific Latin *cercaria* from Greek *kerkos* tail]

cercus /'suhkəs, 'kuh-/ *noun* (*pl* **cerci** /-see, -sie, 'kuhkee/) either of a pair of simple or segmented structures at the hind end of various insects, e.g. a cockroach, and other arthropods. [scientific Latin from Greek *kerkos* tail]

cere /siə/ *noun* a waxy swelling at the base of a bird's upper beak. [Middle English *sere* via French from Latin *cera* wax, prob from Greek *kēros*]

cereal /'siəri-əl/ *noun* **1a** a grass or other plant, e.g. wheat or rice, yielding grain suitable for food. **b** the edible grain of such a plant. **2** a food made from grain and usu eaten with milk at breakfast. **3** (*used before a noun*) relating to edible grain, the plants that produce it, or food made from it: *cereal crops*. [French *céréale* from Latin *cerealis* of grain, from *Ceres*, the Roman goddess of agriculture]

Usage note
cereal or **serial**? These two words, which are pronounced the same, are sometimes confused. *Cereal* refers to grain and food (*breakfast cereal; cereal crops*). The word derives from the name of the Roman goddess of corn and agriculture *Ceres*, which is why it is spelt with two *e*'s. *Serial* derives from the word *series* and refers to things that happen in a series: *a serial killer; a TV serial*.

cerebellum /serə'beləm/ *noun* (*pl* **cerebellums** *or* **cerebella** /-lə/) a large part of the back of the brain that projects outwards and is concerned with coordinating muscles and maintaining balance: *When in that House MPs divide, if they've a brain and cerebellum too, they've got to leave that brain outside, and vote just as their leaders tell 'em to* — W S Gilbert. ➤➤ **cerebellar** *adj.* [Latin *cerebellum*, dimin. of CEREBRUM]

cerebr- *or* **cerebro-** *comb. form* forming words, with the meanings: **1** brain; cerebrum: *cerebrate*. **2** of the brain or cerebrum and: *cerebrospinal*.

cerebra /'seribrə/ *noun* pl of CEREBRUM.

cerebral /'serəbrəl/ *adj* **1a** of the brain. **b** of the cerebrum. **2a** appealing to the intellect: *cerebral drama*. **b** primarily intellectual in nature: *a cerebral society*. **3** said of a speech sound: RETROFLEX (2). ➤➤ **cerebrally** *adv.* [French *cérébral* from Latin *cerebrum* brain]

cerebral haemorrhage *noun* bleeding from an artery of the brain, which may cause a stroke.

cerebral hemisphere *noun* either of the two convoluted halves of the cerebrum of the brain.

cerebral palsy *noun* a disability resulting from damage to the brain before or during birth and characterized by speech disturbance and lack of muscular coordination: compare SPASTIC PARALYSIS.

cerebrate /'serəbrayt/ *verb intrans formal* to use the mind; to think. ➤➤ **cerebration** /-'braysh(ə)n/ *noun.* [CEREBRUM]

cerebro- *comb. form* see CEREBR-.

cerebrospinal /,serəbroh'spienl/ *adj* of the brain and spinal cord.

cerebrospinal fluid *noun* a watery liquid of the brain that fills the spaces between the membranes that surround the spinal cord and the brain.

cerebrovascular /,serəbroh'vaskyoolə/ *adj* of the brain and the blood vessels supplying it.

cerebrum /'seribrəm/ *noun* (*pl* **cerebrums** *or* **cerebra** /-brə/) **1** the expanded front portion of the brain that in higher mammals consists of the two cerebral hemispheres and is considered to be the seat of conscious mental processes. **2** the brain in its entirety. [Latin *cerebrum* brain]

cerecloth /'siəkloth/ *noun* waxed cloth formerly used for wrapping a dead body. [alteration of earlier *cered cloth* waxed cloth, from *cere*: see CEREMENT]

cerement /'siəmənt/ *noun archaic* (*usu in pl*) a shroud for the dead: *Thy canoniz'd bones, hearsed in death, have burst their cerements* — Shakespeare. [*cere* to wax, wrap in a cerecloth (via French from Latin *cerare*, from *cera*: see CERE) + -MENT]

ceremonial¹ /serə'mohni-əl/ *adj* marked by or used in ceremony: *ceremonial sword.* ➤➤ **ceremonialism** *noun,* **ceremonialist** *noun,* **ceremonially** *adv.*

Usage note
ceremonial or **ceremonious**? These two adjectives, both derived from *ceremony*, are sometimes confused. *Ceremonial* describes the nature of an occasion or thing, the fact that it is a ceremony or is used in ceremonies: *a ceremonial wreath-laying; ceremonial robes*. *Ceremonious* describes the elaborate and formal manner in which something is done: *a ceremonious bow*. People may be described as *ceremonious*, but not usually as *ceremonial*.

ceremonial[2] *noun* **1a** an act or action involving ceremony. **b** a prescribed system of formalities or rituals. **2** the order of service in the Roman Catholic Church, or a book containing this.

ceremonious /serə'mohni-əs/ *adj* **1** devoted to form and ceremony; punctilious: *with ceremonious politeness.* **2** = CEREMONIAL[1]. ➤➤ **ceremoniously** *adv*, **ceremoniousness** *noun*.

Usage note
ceremonious or ceremonial? See note at CEREMONIAL[1].

ceremony /'serəməni/ *noun* (*pl* **ceremonies**) **1** a formal act or series of acts prescribed by ritual, protocol, or convention: *the marriage ceremony.* **2a** established procedures of civility or politeness. **b** exaggeratedly polite, correct, or formal behaviour: *with great ceremony.* ✳ **stand on ceremony** to act in a formally correct manner: *There's no need to stand on ceremony.* [Middle English *ceremonie* via French from Latin *caerimonia*]

Cerenkov radiation *or* **Cherenkov radiation** /chi'r(y)engkof/ *noun* light produced by charged particles, e.g. electrons, passing through a transparent medium at a speed greater than that of light in the same medium. [named after P A *Cherenkov* d.1990, Russian physicist, who discovered its cause]

cereology /siəri'oləji/ *noun* the study of crop circles. ➤➤ **cereologist** *noun*. [from Latin *Ceres* the Roman goddess of agriculture + -LOGY]

ceresin /'serisin/ *noun* a hard mineral wax used as a substitute for beeswax, *esp* in paints and polishes. [derivative of Latin *cera* wax]

cerise /sə'rees, sə'reez/ *adj* of a light purplish red colour. ➤➤ **cerise** *noun*. [French *cerise* cherry via late Latin *ceresia* from Greek *kerasos* cherry tree]

cerium /'siəri-əm/ *noun* a grey soft metallic chemical element, the most abundant of the rare-earth group, that is used to make lighter flints: symbol Ce, atomic number 58. [scientific Latin, named after *Ceres*, asteroid discovered around the same time as the element, which in turn was named after the Roman goddess of agriculture]

cermet /'suhmit/ *noun* an alloy of a heat-resistant ceramic material and a metal, used *esp* for turbine blades. [blend of CERAMIC[1] + METAL[1]]

CERN /suhn/ *abbr* European Organization for Nuclear Research. [French *Conseil Européen pour la Recherche Nucléaire*]

cerography /siə'rogrəfi/ *noun* the art or technique of engraving on wax, *esp* to make a printing plate. [Greek *kērographia*, from *kēros* wax + -GRAPHY]

ceroplastic /siəroh'plastik/ *adj* **1** relating to modelling in wax. **2** modelled in wax. [Greek *kēroplastikos*, from *kēros* wax + *plastikos*: see PLASTIC[2]]

cert /suht/ *noun Brit, informal* a certainty, *esp* a horse that is sure to win a race: *a dead cert for the 4.30.*

cert. *abbr* **1** certificate. **2** certified. **3** certify.

certain[1] /'suhtn/ *adj* **1** assured in mind; convinced: *I'm certain she saw me.* **2a** established beyond doubt or question; indisputable: *It is certain that the problem exists.* **b** unerring; dependable: *Her judgment was certain.* **3a** inevitable: *the certain advance of age and decay.* **b** incapable of failing; destined: *She is certain to do well.* **4a** of a known but unspecified character, quantity, or degree: *The house has a certain charm.* **b** named but not known: *a certain Mr Brown.* **c** moderate: *to a certain extent.* **5** fixed; settled: *The time of the meeting is not yet certain.* ✳ **for certain** without doubt; assuredly. [Middle English via Old French from Latin *certus*, past part. of *cernere* to sift, discern, decide]

certain[2] *pronoun* some; unspecified ones: *Certain of the questions were irrelevant.*

certainly /'suht(ə)nli/ *adv* **1** undoubtedly: *It certainly makes a difference.* **2** yes; of course: *Certainly not!* **3** in a confident manner.

certainty *noun* (*pl* **certainties**) **1a** something indisputable or inevitable. **b** somebody or something that cannot fail. **2** the quality or state of being certain. ✳ **for a certainty** without doubt.

CertEd /,suht 'ed/ *abbr Brit* Certificate in Education.

certifiable /suhti'fie-əbl/ *adj* **1** able to be certified. **2** *informal* insane.

certificate[1] /sə'tifikət/ *noun* a document containing an official statement; *esp* one declaring the status or qualifications of the holder: *a birth certificate.* [Middle English *certificat* via French from late Latin *certificatum*, neuter past part. of *certificare*: see CERTIFY]

certificate[2] /sə'tifikayt/ *verb trans* to authorize or provide (somebody or something) with a certificate. ➤➤ **certification** /,suhtifi-'kaysh(ə)n/ *noun*, **certificatory** /-kət(ə)ri, ,suhtifi'kayt(ə)ri/ *adj*.

Certificate of Secondary Education *noun* a British examination in any of many subjects intended for the majority of children and taken typically at about the age of 16, which was replaced in 1988 by the General Certificate of Secondary Education.

certified cheque *noun* a cheque that bears a guarantee of payment by the bank on which it is drawn.

certify /'suhtifie/ *verb trans* (**certifies, certified, certifying**) **1a** to confirm (something), *esp* officially in writing. **b** to declare (something) officially as being true or as meeting a standard. **c** to declare officially the insanity of (somebody). **2** to award a certificate or licence to (somebody): *a certified teacher.* [Middle English *certifien* via French from late Latin *certificare*, from Latin *certus* certain]

certiorari /,suhtiaw'reərie/ *noun* a writ of a superior court calling for the records of proceedings in an inferior court. [Middle English from Latin *certiorari* to be informed; from the use of this word in the writ]

certitude /'suhtityoohd/ *noun* the state of being or feeling certain: *Certitude is not the test of certainty. We have been cocksure of many things that were not so* — Oliver Wendell Holmes. [Middle English from late Latin *certitudo*, from Latin *certus* certain]

cerulean /si'roohli-ən/ *adj literary* deep sky blue in colour. ➤➤ **cerulean** *noun*. [Latin *caeruleus* dark blue]

cerumen /si'roohmən/ *noun* = EARWAX. ➤➤ **ceruminous** /-nəs/ *adj*. [scientific Latin from Latin *cera* wax, prob from Greek *kēros*]

ceruse /'siəroohs, si'roohs/ *noun* white lead as a pigment. [Middle English via early French *céruse* from Latin *cerussa*]

cervelat /'suhvəlat, -lah/ *noun* a smoked sausage made from pork and beef. [obsolete French *cervelat* from Italian *cervellata*]

cervic- *or* **cervico-** *comb. form* forming words, with the meanings: **1** neck; cervix: *cervicitis.* **2** cervical and: *cervicothoracic.* [Latin *cervic-, cervix* neck]

cervical /'suhvikl, sə'viekl/ *adj* **1** of a cervix, *esp* the cervix of the uterus: *cervical cancer.* **2** of the neck: *cervical vertebrae.*

cervical smear *noun* a test for the early detection of cancer in which cells from the cervix of the uterus are examined under a microscope, or a specimen spread on a microscope slide for this purpose.

cervices /'suhviseez/ *noun* pl of CERVIX.

cervicitis /suhvi'sietəs/ *noun* inflammation of the neck of the womb. [scientific Latin]

cervico- *comb. form* see CERVIC-.

cervine /'suhvien/ *adj* of or resembling deer. [Latin *cervinus* of a deer, from *cervus* stag, deer]

cervix /'suhviks/ *noun* (*pl* **cervices** /-seez/ *or* **cervixes**) **1** a constricted portion of an organ or body part, *esp* the narrow outer end of the uterus. **2** the neck. [Latin *cervic-, cervix* neck]

Cesarean /si'zeəri-ən/ *noun NAmer* see CAESAREAN[2].

cesious /'seezi-əs/ *adj NAmer* see CAESIOUS.

cesium /'seezi-əm/ *noun NAmer* see CAESIUM.

cess[1] /ses/ *noun* a tax or levy, *esp* in Scotland or Ireland. [prob short for obsolete noun *assess* assessment]

cess[2] *noun chiefly Irish* luck: *Bad cess to you!* [prob short for SUCCESS]

cessation /si'saysh(ə)n/ *noun* a temporary or final stop; an ending. [Middle English *cessacioun* via French from Latin *cessation-, cessatio* delay, idleness, from *cessare*: see CEASE[1]]

cesser /'sesə/ *noun* an ending or cessation in law, e.g. of interest or liability. [early French *cesser* to cease from Latin *cessare*: see CEASE[1]]

cession /'sesh(ə)n/ *noun* **1** the act or an instance of yielding rights or property, *esp* territory. **2** territory yielded by cession. [Middle English via French from Latin *cession-, cessio*, from *cedere* to withdraw, CEDE]

cessionary *noun* somebody to whom property, rights, etc are transferred.

cesspit /'sespit/ *noun* **1** a pit for the disposal of refuse, *esp* sewage. **2** a corrupt or squalid place. [CESSPOOL + PIT[1]]

cesspool /'sespoohl/ *noun* **1** an underground basin for liquid waste, e.g. household sewage. **2** a corrupt or squalid place. [by folk etymology from Middle English *suspiral* vent, cesspool, from early

French *souspirail* ventilator, from *souspirer* to sigh, from Latin *suspirare* to draw a long breath, from SUB- up + *spirare* to breathe]

cestode /'sestohd/ *noun* any of a subclass of parasitic flatworms including the tapeworms, usu living in the intestines: subclass Cestoda. ➤➤ **cestode** *adj*. [Greek *kestos* girdle]

CET *abbr* Central European Time (time zone).

cetacean /si'taysh(ə)n/ *noun* any of an order of aquatic, mostly marine, mammals, including the whales, dolphins, and porpoises, that have a fish-like nearly hairless body and paddle-shaped forelimbs: order Cetacea. ➤➤ **cetacean** *adj*, **cetaceous** /-shəs/ *adj*. [Latin *cetus* (see CETANE)]

cetane /'seetayn/ *noun* a colourless oily hydrocarbon found in petroleum: formula $C_{16}H_{34}$. ➤➤ **cetyl** /'seetl/ *adj*.

Word history ⎯⎯⎯⎯⎯⎯⎯⎯⎯⎯⎯⎯⎯⎯
Latin *cetus* whale (from Greek *kētos*) + -ANE. So called because similar compounds were orig obtained from spermaceti.

cetane number *noun* a number that is used to measure the ignition properties of a diesel fuel: compare OCTANE NUMBER.

cetane rating *noun* = CETANE NUMBER.

ceteris paribus /,ketəris 'paribəs, ,set-/ *adv formal* all other things being equal. [Latin]

ceviche /se'veechay/ *noun* a S American dish of marinaded raw fish or seafood, served as a starter. [from Latin American Spanish]

CF *abbr* **1** cystic fibrosis. **2** Chaplain to the Forces.

Cf *abbr* the chemical symbol for californium.

cf. *abbr* compare. [Latin *confer*, imperative of *conferre* to compare]

c/f *abbr* carried forward.

CFC *abbr* chlorofluorocarbon.

CFE *abbr* College of Further Education.

cg *abbr* centigram.

CGS *abbr Brit* Chief of General Staff.

cgs *abbr* centimetre-gram-second (system): *cgs units*.

CH *abbr* **1** central heating. **2** Companion of Honour. **3** *Confédération Helvétique* (international vehicle registration for Switzerland).

ch *abbr* **1** chain (unit of length). **2** chapter. **3** in chess, check. **4** child. **5** children. **6** church.

cha /chah/ *noun* see CHAR⁵.

chaat /chaht/ *noun* an Indian dish of boiled vegetables and spices. [Hindi]

chabazite /'kabəziet/ *noun* a complex mineral consisting of sodium calcium aluminium silicate and used in water softeners: formula $(Ca,Na_2)(Al_2Si_4O_{12}) \cdot 6H_2O$. [German *Chabasit* from French *chabasie*, derivative of Greek *chalaza* hailstone]

Chablis /'shabli/ *noun* (*pl* **Chablis** /'shabli/) a dry white table wine produced in northern Burgundy. [named after *Chablis*, town in France where it is produced]

cha-cha¹ /'chah chah/ *or* **cha-cha-cha** /'chah chah chah/ *noun* (*pl* **cha-chas** *or* **cha-cha-chas**) **1** a fast rhythmic ballroom dance of Latin American origin. **2** music written for this dance or with its rhythm. [American Spanish *cha-cha-cha*]

cha-cha² *or* **cha-cha-cha** *verb intrans* (**cha-chas** *or* **cha-cha-chas**, **cha-chaed** *or* **cha-cha-chaed**, **cha-chaing** *or* **cha-cha-chaing**) to dance the cha-cha.

chacma /'chakmə/ *noun* a large grey-coated southern African baboon: *Papio* or *Chaeropithecus comatus*. [Hottentot]

chaconne /shə'kon/ *noun* **1** a musical composition typically consisting of variations on a repeated succession of chords. **2** an old Spanish dance tune resembling the passacaglia. [French *chaconne* from Spanish *chacona*]

chad *noun* small pieces of paper or card punched out from paper tape, data cards, etc, or a single piece of this. [of unknown origin]

chador *or* **chadar** *or* **chuddar** /'chudə/ *noun* a large cloth serving as a veil and head covering worn by women in India and Iran, *esp* a black one worn by some Muslim women as a sign of religious orthodoxy. [Hindi *caddar* from Persian *chaddar*]

chaetognath /'keetəgnath/ *noun* any of a phylum of small free-swimming marine worms with movable curved bristles on either side of the mouth: phylum Chaetognatha. ➤➤ **chaetognath** *adj*, **chaetognathan** /kee'tognəthən/ *adj and noun*. [Greek *chaitē* long flowing hair + *gnathos* jaw]

chafe¹ /chayf/ *verb trans* **1a** to make (something) sore by rubbing. **b** to rub (something) so as to wear it away. **2** to warm (part of the body) by rubbing. **3** to irritate or vex (somebody). ➤ *verb intrans* **1** to feel irritation or discontent; fret: *chafing at the limitations of the software*. **2** to become sore or damaged as a result of rubbing. [Middle English *chaufen* to warm, via French from Latin *calefacere*, from *calēre* to be warm + *facere* to make]

chafe² *noun* injury or wear caused by friction.

chafer *noun* any of numerous species of large beetles, e.g. the cockchafer, whose larvae do great damage to plant roots: family Scarabaeidae. [Old English *ceafor*]

chaff¹ /chaf/ *noun* **1** the husks and other debris separated from the seed in threshing grain. **2** chopped straw, hay, etc used for animal feed. **3** strips of foil or other material ejected into the air to reflect enemy radar waves and so prevent detection. **4** worthless matter. ➤➤ **chaffy** *adj*. [Old English *ceaf*]

chaff² *noun* light jesting talk; banter. [prob from CHAFE¹]

chaff³ *verb trans* to tease (somebody) good-naturedly. ➤ *verb intrans* to jest or banter.

chaffer¹ /'chafə/ *verb intrans* (**chaffered, chaffering**) to bargain or haggle. [Old English *ceapfaru*, from *ceap* trade + *faru* journey]

chaffer² *noun* bargaining or haggling.

chaffinch /'chafinch/ *noun* a European finch with a reddish breast, a bluish head, and white wing bars: *Fringilla coelebs*. [Old English *ceaffinc*, from *ceaf* CHAFF¹ + *finc* FINCH]

chafing dish /'chayfing/ *noun* a dish for cooking or keeping food warm, *esp* over a spirit burner at the table: *He found Ottenberg in the act of touching a match to a chafing-dish, at a table laid for two in his sitting-room* — Willa Cather. [Middle English *chafing*, present part. of *chaufen, chafen*: see CHAFE¹]

Chagas' disease /'shahgəs(iz)/ *noun* an often fatal tropical American disease caused by a TRYPANOSOME (parasitic micro-organism) and characterized by high fever and swelling, e.g. of the lymph nodes. [named after Carlos *Chagas* d.1934, Brazilian physician who first described it]

chagrin¹ /'shagrin, shə'grin/ *noun* mental distress caused by humiliation, disappointment, or failure. [French *chagrin* sadness]

chagrin² *verb trans* (**chagrined, chagrining**) (*usu in passive*) to cause (somebody) mental distress; to disappoint or annoy (them): *I was chagrined to learn that my proposal had been rejected*.

chain¹ /chayn/ *noun* **1a** a series of usu metal links or rings connected to one another and used for various purposes, e.g. support, restraint, or decoration. **b** a piece of jewellery or badge of office consisting of such a series of links. **c** a unit of length equal to 66ft (about 20.12m). **d** a measuring instrument of 100 links used in surveying. **2** (*usu in pl*) something that confines, restrains, or secures: *the chains of ignorance*. **3a** a series of linked or connected things: *a chain of events*; *a mountain chain*. **b** a group of associated establishments, e.g. shops or hotels, under the same ownership. **c** a number of atoms or chemical groups united like links in a chain. [Middle English *cheyne* via Old French from Latin *catena*]

chain² *verb trans* (*often* + up/down) to fasten, restrict, or confine (somebody or something) with, or as if with, a chain.

chainé /she'nay/ *noun* a series of short regular usu fast turns by which a ballet dancer moves across the stage. [French, from past part. of *chaîner* to chain]

chain gang *noun* (*treated as sing. or pl*) a gang of convicts chained together, usu while doing hard labour outside prison.

chain letter *noun* a letter requesting that the recipient send copies of it, sometimes together with money or goods, to a specified number of other people who should then repeat the process.

chain mail *noun* flexible armour made of interlinked metal rings.

chain reaction *noun* **1** a series of related events, each one initiating the next. **2** a self-sustaining chemical or nuclear reaction yielding energy or products that cause further reactions of the same kind.

chain saw *noun* a portable power saw that has teeth linked together to form a continuous revolving chain.

chain-smoke *verb intrans* to smoke continually, usu lighting one cigarette from the butt of the previous one. ➤ *verb trans* to smoke (cigarettes etc) in this way. ➤➤ **chain-smoker** *noun*.

chain stitch *noun* an ornamental embroidery or crochet stitch that resembles the links of a chain.

chain store *noun* any of several shops under the same ownership and selling the same lines of goods.

chainwheel *noun* a toothed wheel, e.g. on a bicycle, that transmits power by means of a chain.

chair[1] /chea/ *noun* **1** a seat for one person, usu with four legs and a back and sometimes with arms. **2a** an office or position of authority or dignity; *specif* a professorship: *a university chair*. **b** a chairman or chairwoman. **3** = SEDAN CHAIR. **4** (**the chair**) *NAmer* = ELECTRIC CHAIR. **5** a deep-grooved metal block fastened to a railway sleeper to hold a rail in place. [Middle English via Old French *chaiere* and Latin *cathedra* from Greek *kathedra*, from *kata*- CATA- + *hedra* seat]

chair[2] *verb trans* **1** to preside as chairman or chairwoman of (a meeting, committee, etc). **2** *chiefly Brit* to carry (somebody) shoulder-high in acclaim: *the time you won your town the race we chaired you through the market place* — A E Housman. **3** to install (somebody) in office.

chair lift *noun* a ski lift with seats for passengers.

chairman *or* **chairwoman** *noun* (*pl* **chairmen** *or* **chairwomen**) **1** somebody who presides over or heads a meeting, committee, organization, or board of directors. **2** a radio or television presenter, *esp* one who coordinates unscripted or diverse material. ➤➤ **chairmanship** *noun*.

chairperson *noun* (*pl* **chairpersons**) a chairman or chairwoman.

chaise /shayz, shez/ *noun* **1** a light horse-drawn carriage, usu with two wheels and a folding top. **2** = POST CHAISE. **3** = CHAISE LONGUE. [French *chaise* chair, chaise, alteration of Old French *chaiere*: see CHAIR[1]]

chaise longue /ˌshayz ˈlongg/ *noun* (*pl* **chaise longues** *or* **chaises longues** /ˈlongg(z)/) a low sofa with a partial backrest and only one armrest, on which one may recline. [French *chaise longue* long chair]

chakra /ˈshakrə, ˈshukrə/ *noun* in yoga, a centre of spiritual power in the human body. [Sanskrit *cakra* wheel, circle]

chalaza /kəˈlahzə, kəˈlayzə/ *noun* (*pl* **chalazae** /-zie/ *or* **chalazas**) either of a pair of spiral bands in the white of a bird's egg that extend from the yolk and are attached to opposite ends of the shell membrane. ➤➤ **chalazal** *adj*. [scientific Latin from Greek *khalaza* hailstone]

chalcedony /kalˈsedəni/ *noun* (*pl* **chalcedonies**) a translucent quartz, often pale blue or grey in colour, that is used as a gemstone. ➤➤ **chalcedonic** /-ˈdonik/ *adj*. [Middle English *calcedonie* via late Latin from Greek *Chalkēdōn* Chalcedon, former city in Turkey]

chalcolithic /kalkəˈlithik/ *adj* relating to a prehistoric period in which both stone and bronze implements were used. [Greek *chalkos* copper + -LITH]

chalcopyrite /kalkəˈpieriet/ *noun* a yellow mineral consisting of copper-iron sulphide that is a common ore of copper: formula $CuFeS_2$. [scientific Latin *chalcopyrites*, from Greek *chalkos* copper + Latin *pyrites*]

Chaldean /kalˈdee-ən/ *noun* **1** a member of an ancient Semitic people who once ruled in Babylonia. **2** the Semitic language of the Chaldeans. **3** an astrologer. ➤➤ **Chaldean** *adj*. [Latin *Chaldaeus* Chaldean, astrologer, from Greek *Chaldaios*, from *Chaldaia* Chaldea, region of ancient Babylonia]

Chaldee /ˈkaldee, kalˈdee/ *noun* **1** the Aramaic vernacular that was the original language of some parts of the Old Testament. **2** a Chaldean, or the language of the Chaldeans. [Middle English *Caldey*, prob via early French *chaldée* from Latin *Chaldaeus*: see CHALDEAN]

chalet /ˈshalay/ *noun* **1a** a small house with a steeply sloping roof and widely overhanging eaves, *esp* a type of wooden house common in rural Switzerland. **b** a small house or hut used *esp* for temporary accommodation, e.g. at a holiday camp. **2** a hut used by herdsmen in the Alps. [French *chalet*, ultimately from Latin *casa* hut]

chalice /ˈchalis/ *noun* **1** *literary* a drinking cup; a goblet: *This even-handed justice commends the ingredients of our poisoned chalice to our own lips* — Shakespeare. **2** a gold or silver cup used to hold the wine at Communion in some Christian churches. [Middle English via Anglo-French from Latin *calic-, calix*]

chalk[1] /chawk/ *noun* **1** a soft white, grey, or buff limestone composed chiefly of the shells of small marine organisms. **2** a short stick of chalk or chalky material, often coloured, used *esp* for writing and drawing. ❋ **as alike/different as chalk and cheese**

very different from each other. [Old English *cealc* via West Germanic from Latin *calc-, calx* lime, from Greek *chalix* pebble]

chalk[2] *verb trans* **1** to rub, mark, or whiten (something) with chalk: *chalk the end of a snooker cue*. **2** to write or draw (something) with chalk: *I chalked my name on the wall*.

chalkboard /ˈchawkbawd/ *noun NAmer* = BLACKBOARD.

chalkface /ˈchawkfays/ *noun* the classroom, considered as the workplace of teachers: *how the council's ... programme is actually working out at the chalkface* — Daily Telegraph. [modelled on COAL-FACE]

chalk out *verb trans* to delineate (something) roughly; to sketch (it) out: *chalk out a plan of action*.

chalk pit *noun* a quarry from which chalk is obtained.

chalk up *verb trans* **1** to ascribe or credit (something); *specif* to charge (something) to an account: *You can chalk it up to expenses*. **2** to attain or achieve (something): *We chalked up a record score that season*. **3** to set (something) down or add (it) up with, or as if with, chalk: *chalk up the total*.

chalky *adj* (**chalkier, chalkiest**) **1** containing or consisting of chalk: *chalky soil*. **2** resembling chalk in colour or texture, *esp* as white as chalk.

challah /ˈhahlə, khah-/ *noun* a white leavened bread in a plaited loaf, traditionally eaten on the Jewish sabbath. [Hebrew *hallah*]

challenge[1] /ˈchalinj/ *verb trans* **1a** to defy (somebody) boldly; to dare (them): *I challenge you to do better*. **b** to invite or call (somebody) to fight or compete. **2** to dispute (something), *esp* as being unjust, invalid, or outmoded: *new data that challenges old assumptions*. **3** to question formally the legality or legal qualifications of (e.g. a juror). **4** to order (somebody) to halt and provide proof of identity. **5** to test the skill of (somebody) in a stimulating way. **6** to administer infective material to (an organism) in order to ascertain whether experimental immunization has been effective. ➤➤ **challengeable** *adj*, **challenger** *noun*. [Middle English *chalengen* to accuse, via Old French from Latin *calumniari* to accuse falsely, from *calumnia*: see CALUMNY]

challenge[2] *noun* **1** an invitation or summons to fight or compete; *specif* a call to a duel. **2a** a calling to account or into question; a protest or demand for justification. **b** a command given by a sentry, watchman, etc to halt and prove identity. **c** a formal objection to a juror or jury. **3** the quality of being demanding or stimulating, or something with such a quality: *The job presented a real challenge*. **4** a test of immunity by re-exposure to infective material.

challenged *adj euphem* (*usu used in combinations*) lacking or deficient in the specified physical or mental attribute: *visually challenged*.

Usage note
The word *challenged* was put forward in the 1980s as a solution to the problem of how to describe, sensitively and positively, the various disabilities from which some people suffer – thus, *physically challenged* (disabled) and *visually challenged* (blind or with deficient eyesight). The word quickly came to be seen as a clear example of euphemism and political correctness and to be ridiculed in such combinations as *cerebrally challenged* (stupid) and *vertically challenged* (short). The question of how physical disabilities can be referred to in a way that is not demeaning to the sufferer is an ongoing one, but *challenged* is no longer recommended for serious use.

challenging *adj* stimulating interest, thought, action, or effort; demanding. ➤➤ **challengingly** *adv*.

challis /ˈshali, ˈshalis/ *noun* a lightweight soft clothing fabric made of cotton, wool, or synthetic yarn. [prob from the name *Challis*]

chalone /ˈkalohn/ *noun* an internal secretion that depresses activity and inhibits the growth and differentiation of the cells in a tissue: compare HORMONE. [Greek *chalōn*, present part. of *chalan* to slacken]

chalumeau /ˈshalumoh/ *noun* (*pl* **chalumeaux** /ˈshalumoh/) **1** an early reed musical instrument from which the clarinet developed in the 18th cent. **2** the lowest register of the clarinet. [via French from Latin *calamellus* little reed]

chalybeate /kəˈlibi-ət/ *adj* said of water: impregnated with iron-containing chemical compounds: *chalybeate springs*. [scientific Latin *chalybeatus* from Latin *chalybs* steel, from Greek *chalyb-, chalyps*, from *Chalybes*, the name of an ancient people in Asia Minor famous for their iron-working skills]

chamber /ˈchaymbə/ *noun* **1** a natural or artificial enclosed space or cavity. **2** (*usu in pl*) a room where a judge hears private cases. **3** a legislative or judicial body, *esp* either of two houses of a legislature, or a hall used by such a body: *Chamber of Deputies*. **4a** (*in pl*) a set of rooms used by a group of barristers. **b** a reception room in an official or state building. **5** the part of a gun that holds the charge or cartridge. **6** *archaic* a room, *esp* a bedroom. **7** = CHAMBER POT. **8** (*used before a noun*) relating to or involving a small group of musical instruments or a small orchestra: *a chamber concert*. [Middle English via Old French *chambre* from Latin *camera* arched roof, from Greek *kamara* vault]

chamberlain /ˈchaymbəlin/ *noun* **1** a chief officer of a royal or noble household. **2** a treasurer, e.g. of a corporation.

Word history
Middle English from Old French *chamberlayn*, from a Germanic word borrowed: see CHAMBER. The word orig referred to a servant of the bed-chamber.

chambermaid *noun* a woman who cleans bedrooms and makes beds, *esp* in a hotel.

chamber music *noun* music written for a small group of instruments.

Chamber of Commerce *noun* an association of business people to promote commercial and industrial interests in the community.

chamber of horrors *noun* a hall in which objects of macabre interest, e.g. instruments of torture, are exhibited; *broadly* any horrifying or frightening place, situation, etc.

chamber orchestra *noun* a small orchestra, usu with one player for each part.

chamber pot *noun* a bowl-shaped receptacle for urine and faeces, used chiefly in the bedroom.

chambray /ˈshambray/ *noun* a lightweight clothing fabric with coloured warp and white weft yarns. [irreg from *Cambrai*, the name of the city in N France where it was orig made]

chambré /ˈshombray (*French* ʃɑ̃bre), ˈshombray/ *adj* said of wine: at or brought to room temperature. [French *chambré*, past part. of *chambrer* to put in a room, from *chambre*: see CHAMBER]

chameleon /kəˈmeeli·ən/ *noun* **1** any of numerous species of African and Eurasian lizards with a long tongue, a grasping tail, eyeballs that move independently, and the ability to change the colour of the skin: genus *Chamaeleo* and other genera. **2** somebody or something changeable; *specif* a fickle person. ⋙ **chameleonic** /-ˈonik/ *adj*. [Middle English *camelion* via French and Latin from Greek *chamaileōn*, from *chamai* on the ground + *leōn* lion]

chamfer[1] /ˈchamfə/ *noun* an edge that has been cut back from a right angle to form a narrow flat surface with two oblique angles. [back-formation from *chamfering*, from early French *chanfreint*, past part. of *chanfraindre* to bevel, from *chant* edge (from Latin *canthus* iron tyre) + *fraindre* to break, from Latin *frangere*]

chamfer[2] *verb trans* (**chamfered, chamfering**) to cut a chamfer on (something).

chammy *or* **shammy** /ˈshami/ *noun* = CHAMOIS (2). [by shortening and alteration]

chamois /ˈshamwah/ *noun* (*pl* **chamois** /ˈshamwah(z)/) **1** a small goatlike antelope of Europe and the Caucasus: *Rupicapra rupicapra*. **2** a soft pliant leather prepared from the skin of the chamois or sheep, used *esp* as a cloth for polishing. [early French *chamois* from late Latin *camox*]

chamois leather /ˈshami, ˈshamwah/ *noun* = CHAMOIS (2).

chamomile /ˈkaməmiel/ *noun* see CAMOMILE.

champ[1] /champ/ *verb trans* **1** to munch (food) noisily. **2** to gnaw or bite (something). ⋙ *verb intrans* **1** to make biting or gnashing movements. **2** to eat noisily. ✳ **champ at the bit** to show impatience or eagerness: *The children were champing at the bit to get on board*. [perhaps imitative]

champ[2] *noun informal* a champion, *esp* in a sport or game.

champagne /shamˈpayn/ *noun* **1** a white sparkling wine made in the former province of Champagne in France. **2** a pale golden cream colour.

champagne socialist *noun derog* somebody who holds socialist opinions but enjoys an affluent lifestyle.

champaign /shamˈpayn/ *noun literary* an expanse of level open country; a plain. [Middle English *champaine* via French *champagne*, from late Latin *campania*, from Latin *campus* plain, field]

champers /ˈshampəz/ *noun Brit, informal* champagne.

champerty /ˈchampəti/ *noun* (*pl* **champerties**) an illegal action whereby an outsider aids somebody involved in a law suit, e.g. by paying for their defence, in the hope of receiving a share of the property, money, etc at stake. ⋙ **champertous** /-təs/ *adj*. [Middle English *champartie* from early French *champart* field rent, from *champ* field (from Latin *campus*) + *part* portion]

champion[1] /ˈchampi·ən/ *noun* **1** somebody or something that shows marked superiority; *specif* the winner of a competitive event. **2** a militant supporter of, or fighter for, a cause or person: *an outspoken champion of civil rights*. **3** in former times, somebody who did battle on behalf of another, *esp* in a tournament: *God will raise me up a champion* — Sir Walter Scott. [Middle English via Old French from medieval Latin *campion-, campio*, of West Germanic origin]

champion[2] *verb trans* (**championed, championing**) to protect or fight for (something or somebody) as a champion.

champion[3] *adj chiefly N Eng, informal* superb; splendid.

championship *noun* **1a** a contest held to determine a champion: *tennis championship*. **b** the position or title of champion. **2** the act of championing, defence: *his championship of freedom of speech*.

champlevé[1] /ˈshomləvay (*French* ʃɑ̃ləve)/ *noun* a style of enamel decoration in which the enamel colours are fired in shallow depressions pressed or cut into a metal surface: compare CLOISONNÉ. [French *champlevé* raised field, from *champ* field (from Latin *campus*) + *levé*, past part. of *lever* to raise, from Latin *levare*]

champlevé[2] *adj* relating to or decorated with champlevé.

chance[1] /chahns/ *noun* **1a** the incalculable assumed element in existence that renders events unpredictable: *leave it to chance*. **b** an event without discernible human intention or observable cause: *This is a strange chance that throws you and me together* — Dickens.

Editorial note
The chance of a coin landing heads is a property of the coin which explains how often it lands heads when tossed. Determinists would claim that nothing ever really happens by chance: talk of chances always reflects our ignorance of many of the causes that act on the coin — Professor Christopher Hookway.

2 a situation favouring some purpose; an opportunity. **3a** the possibility of a specified or favourable outcome in an uncertain situation: *We have almost no chance of winning*. **b** (*in pl*) the more likely indications: *Chances are he's already heard the news*. **4** a risk: *I took a chance on it*. **5** an opportunity of scoring a goal in football or dismissing a batsman in cricket. ✳ **by chance** accidentally; without planning or intention: *We met by chance*. [Middle English via Old French from Latin *cadent-, cadens*, present part. of *cadere* to fall]

chance[2] *adj* accidental or casual; happening by chance: *a chance remark*.

chance[3] *verb intrans* **1** to take place or come about by chance; to happen: *It chanced that the street was empty*. **2** (+ on/upon) to find or happen upon (something) by chance: *chance on an idea*. ⋙ *verb trans* to accept the hazard of (something); to risk (it). ✳ **chance one's arm** *informal* to risk something with little chance of success.

chancel /ˈchahnsl/ *noun* the part of a church containing the altar and seats for the clergy and choir. [Middle English via French from Latin *cancelli* lattice; from the latticework enclosing it]

chancellery *or* **chancellory** /ˈchahnsələri/ *noun* (*pl* **chancelleries** *or* **chancellories**) **1** the position, department, or official residence of a chancellor. **2** *NAmer* the office or staff of an embassy or consulate.

chancellor /ˈchahns(ə)lə/ *noun* **1** the titular head of a British university. **2** the chief minister of state in some European countries. **3a** = CHANCELLOR OF THE EXCHEQUER. **b** = LORD CHANCELLOR. **c** in former times, the secretary of a nobleman, prince, or king. **4a** a usu lay legal officer of an Anglican diocese. **b** a Roman Catholic priest heading a diocesan chancery. ⋙ **chancellorship** *noun*.

Word history
Middle English *chanceler* via Old French *chancelier* from late Latin *cancellarius* doorkeeper, secretary, from *cancellus* lattice. The term orig denoted a court official at the latticework partition between the judge and the people.

Chancellor of the Duchy of Lancaster *noun* a British government minister who has no direct responsibility for a government department but is usu a member of the cabinet.

Chancellor of the Exchequer *noun* a member of the British cabinet in charge of public finances.

chancellory *noun* see CHANCELLERY.

chance-medley *noun* (*pl* **chance-medleys**) a fight that begins spontaneously, without premeditation, and in which one of the participants is killed. [Anglo-French *chance medlee*, literally 'mixed chance']

chancer *noun Brit, informal* an unprincipled person; an opportunist.

chancery /'chahnsəri/ *noun* (*pl* **chanceries**) **1a** (**Chancery**) a division of the High Court having jurisdiction over causes in equity. **b** a US court of equity. **2** a record office for public archives or those of ecclesiastical, legal, or diplomatic proceedings. **3a** a chancellor's court or office. **b** the office in which the business of a Roman Catholic diocese is transacted and recorded. **c** = CHANCELLERY (2). ✲ **in chancery 1** said of a lawsuit: being heard in a court of chancery. **2** said of a wrestler: with the head locked under the arm of one's opponent. **3** in a hopeless predicament. [Middle English *chancerie*, alteration of *chancellerie* chancellery, from Old French *chancelier*: see CHANCELLOR]

Chancery Division *noun* = CHANCERY (IA).

chancre /'shangkə/ *noun* an initial sore or ulcer of some diseases, e.g. syphilis. ⟫⟫ **chancrous** /'shangkrəs/ *adj*. [French *chancre* from Latin *cancer* crab, CANCER]

chancroid /'shangkroyd/ *noun* a bacterial venereal disease causing ulceration in the genital area, or an ulcer so caused. ⟫⟫ **chancroidal** /shang'kroydl/ *adj*.

chancy /'chahnsi/ *adj* (**chancier, chanciest**) uncertain in outcome or prospect; risky. ⟫⟫ **chancily** *adj*, **chanciness** *noun*.

chandelier /shandə'liə/ *noun* a branched ornamental lighting fixture suspended from a ceiling. [French *chandelier* candlestick, modification of Latin *candelabrum*, from *candela*: see CANDLE[1]]

chandler /'chahndlə/ *noun* a retail dealer in supplies and equipment of a specified kind: *a ship's chandler; a corn chandler*. [Middle English *chandeler* maker or seller of candles, via Old French from Latin *candela*: see CANDLE[1]]

chandlery *noun* (*pl* **chandleries**) the business, shop, or merchandise of a chandler.

change[1] /chaynj/ *verb trans* **1a** to make (something or somebody) different. **b** to give a different status or aspect to (something): *They seem to have changed their thinking on the matter.* **2** (*often* + into) to convert or transform (something). **3** (*often* + for) to replace (one thing) with another: *She has changed her name; We've changed our old van for a hatchback.* **4** (*often* + over/round) to exchange or reverse (things). **5a** to exchange (something) for a comparable item. **b** to exchange (a sum of money) for an equivalent sum in another currency. **6** to select (a new gear) in a motor vehicle. **7** to undergo a loss or modification of (some quality): *The foliage was changing colour.* **8** to put fresh clothes or covering on (somebody or something). ⟩ *verb intrans* **1** to become different. **2** (*often* + to) to undergo transformation, transition, or conversion: *Most industries have changed to the metric system.* **3** to go from one vehicle of a public transport system to another: *We have to change at Paris.* **4** to put on different clothes. **5** (*usu* + with) to engage in giving something and receiving something in return. **6** said of the moon: to pass from one phase to another. **7** said of the male voice: to shift to a lower register; = BREAK[1] (‼LINK‼) ✲ **change hands** to become the property of a different owner. **change the subject** to begin talking about something different during a conversation. ⟫⟫ **changer** *noun*. [Middle English *changen* via Old French from Latin *cambiare* to exchange, of Celtic origin]

change[2] *noun* **1a** an alteration: *a change in the weather.* **b** a substitution: *a change of players.* **c** variety or novelty: *for a change.* **2** an alternative set, *esp* of clothes. **3a** money returned when a payment exceeds the amount due: *She gave me the wrong change.* **b** money of lower denominations or different currency received in exchange for an equivalent sum: *Have you got change for a ten-pound note?* **c** coins of low denominations: *a pocketful of change.* **4** an order in which a set of bells is struck in change ringing. **5** the passage of the moon from one phase to another; *specif* the coming of the new moon. **6** (**the change**) the menopause. ✲ **get no change out of** *informal* to fail to get information from, exploit, or outwit (somebody). ⟫⟫ **changeful** *adj*, **changeless** *adj*, **changelessness** *noun*.

changeable *adj* **1** able or apt to vary. **2** capable of being altered or exchanged. **3** fickle: *young men especially, they are amazingly changeable and inconstant* — Jane Austen. ⟫⟫ **changeability** /-'biliti/ *noun*, **changeableness** *noun*, **changeably** *adv*.

change down *verb intrans* to select a lower gear in a motor vehicle.

changeling /'chaynjling/ *noun* a child secretly exchanged for another in infancy; *specif* one believed to have been left in place of a human child by fairies.

change of heart *noun* a complete reversal in attitude.

change of life *noun* (**the change of life**) the menopause.

change-over *noun* a conversion to a different system or function.

change ringing *noun* the art or practice of ringing a set of tuned bells, *esp* church bells, in continually varying order.

change up *verb intrans* to select a higher gear in a motor vehicle.

changing room *noun* a room in which one changes one's clothes, e.g. before or after sporting activity.

channel[1] /'chanl/ *noun* **1a** the bed where a stream of water runs. **b** the deeper navigable part of a river, harbour, or strait. **c** a narrow region of sea between two land masses. **d** (**the Channel**) the English Channel separating Britain and France. **2** (*also in pl*) a course or direction of thought, action, or communication: *use official channels.* **3a** a path along which information passes or can be stored, e.g. on a recording tape. **b** a band of frequencies of sufficient width for a transmission, e.g. from a radio or television station. **c** a television station: *switch over to another channel.* **4** a usu tubular passage, *esp* for liquids. **5** a long gutter, groove, or furrow. [Middle English *chanel* via Old French from Latin *canalis*: see CANAL]

channel[2] *verb trans* (**channelled, channelling**, *NAmer* **channeled, channeling**) **1** to direct (something) towards a particular purpose: *He should channel his energy into more constructive activities.* **2** to convey (something) through a channel. **3** to form or wear a channel in (something). **4** to act as a medium through whom (the spirits of the dead) can communicate with living people.

channel-hop *verb intrans* (**channel-hopped, channel-hopping**) *informal* to repeatedly change television channels using a remote control device.

channelize *or* **channelise** /'chanəliz/ *verb trans* = CHANNEL[2] (2). ⟫⟫ **channelization** /-'zaysh(ə)n/ *noun*.

channel-surf *verb intrans NAmer* = CHANNEL-HOP.

chanson /'shonsonh (*French* ʃɑ̃sɔ̃)/ *noun* (*pl* **chansons** /'shonsonhz (*French* ʃɑ̃sɔ̃)/) a French song, *esp* a cabaret song. [French *chanson*, from Latin *cantion-, cantio*, from *canere* to sing]

chanson de geste /də 'zhest (*French* də ʒɛst)/ *noun* (*pl* **chansons de geste** /də 'zhest (*French* də ʒɛst)/) any of several Old French epic poems of the 11th to the 14th cents that recount feats of heroism. [French *chanson de geste* song of heroic deeds]

chant[1] /chahnt/ *verb trans* to utter (e.g. a slogan) in a rhythmic monotonous tone: *The crowd chanted his name.* ⟩ *verb intrans* **1** to sing a chant. **2** to recite in a rhythmic monotonous tone. [Middle English *chaunten* via French from Latin *cantare*, from *canere* to sing]

chant[2] *noun* **1a** a repetitive melody used for liturgical singing in which as many syllables are assigned to each note as required. **b** a psalm or canticle sung in this way. **2** a rhythmic monotonous utterance, recitation, or song.

chanter /'chahntə/ *noun* the REED PIPE (pipe producing sound by the vibration of a reed) of a bagpipe with finger holes on which the melody is played.

chanterelle /shantə'rel, shon-/ *noun* an edible mushroom that has a rich yellow colour, funnel-shaped cap, and a pleasant smell: *Cantharellus cibarius.* [French *chanterelle* from Latin *cantharella*, dimin. of *cantharus* drinking-vessel]

chanteuse /shon'tuhz/ *noun* (*pl* **chanteuses** /shon'tuhz/) a female nightclub or cabaret singer. [French *chanteuse*, fem of *chanteur* singer, from *chanter* to sing, from Latin *canere*]

chanticleer /'chantikliə/ *noun literary* a name for the domestic cock: *My lungs began to crow like chanticleer ... and I did laugh sans intermission* — Shakespeare. [Middle English *Chantecleer* from Old French *Chantecler*, the name of the cock in the poem *Roman de Renart*]

Chantilly /shon'tili, shan-/ *noun* **1** a delicate lace with a floral or scrolled design on a hexagonal mesh background. **2** sweetened whipped cream. [named after *Chantilly*, town in France]

chantry /'chahntri/ *noun* (*pl* **chantries**) a chapel or altar founded under an endowment for the chanting of masses for the founder's soul. [Middle English from Old French *chanterie* singing, from *chanter*: see CHANTEUSE]

chanty /'chanti/ *noun* = SHANTY[2].

Chanukah /'hahnookah/ *noun* see HANUKKAH.

chaology /kay'oləji/ *noun* the scientific study of chaos theory. ➤➤ **chaologist** *noun*.

chaos /'kayos/ *noun* **1a** a state of utter confusion. **b** a confused mass. **2** (*often* **Chaos**) the confused unorganized state of original matter before the creation of distinct forms: compare COSMOS (1). ➤➤ **chaotic** /kay'otik/ *adj*, **chaotically** /kay'otikli/ *adv*. [via Latin from Greek *chaos* abyss]

chaos theory *noun* a scientific theory relating to the irregular and unpredictable behaviour of complex systems that nevertheless have an underlying order.

chap[1] /chap/ *noun informal* a man; a fellow. [short for *chapman* merchant, pedlar, from Old English *cēapman*, from *cēap* trade + MAN[1]]

chap[2] *verb* (**chapped, chapping**) ➤ *verb trans* to cause (something, *esp* the skin) to open in slits or cracks, usu by exposure to wind, cold, or dryness: *chapped lips.* ➤ *verb intrans* to open in slits or cracks. [Middle English *chappen*, of Germanic origin]

chap[3] *noun* a crack in the skin caused by exposure to wind, cold, or dryness.

chap[4] *noun* (*usu in pl*) **1** a jaw or its fleshy covering. **2** the lower front part of the face. [prob from CHAP[2]]

chap. *abbr* **1** chaplain. **2** chapter.

chaparajos /chapə'rah·khohs/ *or* **chaparejos** /-'ray·khohs/ *pl noun* = CHAPS. [Mexican Spanish *chaparreras*, from Spanish *chaparro*: see CHAPARRAL]

chaparral /shapə'ral/ *noun* in the USA, a dense area of shrubs or dwarf trees, *esp* evergreen oaks. [Spanish *chaparral*, from *chaparro* dwarf evergreen oak, from Basque *txapar*]

chapati *or* **chapatti** /chə'pati, chə'pahti/ *noun* (*pl* **chapatis** *or* **chapattis**) in Indian cookery, a thin unleavened usu round bread. [Hindi *capati* from Sanskrit *carpaṭi* thin cake, from *carpaṭa* flat]

chapbook /'chapbook/ *noun* a small book formerly sold by pedlars, containing ballads, tales, etc. [CHAPMAN + BOOK[1]]

chape /chayp/ *noun* **1** the metal mounting or trimming of a scabbard or sheath and *esp* of its point. **2** the part of a buckle by which it is fixed to a strap, belt, etc. [Middle English *chape* scabbard, via French from late Latin *cappa* head covering, cloak]

chapel[1] /'chapl/ *noun* **1a** a place of worship serving a residence or institution. **b** a room or bay in a church for prayer or minor religious services. **2a** a place of worship used by a Nonconformist Christian group. **b** the doctrines or practices of such a group. **3** a choir of singers belonging to a chapel. **4** a chapel service or assembly. **5** (*treated as sing. or pl*) the members of a trade union, *esp* in a printing or publishing house.

Word history
Middle English via Old French from medieval Latin *cappella*, dimin. of late Latin *cappa* cloak. The first chapel was built to house the cloak of St Martin of Tours.

chapel[2] *adj chiefly Brit* belonging to a Nonconformist church.

chapel of ease *noun* a dependent church built to accommodate parishioners living in remote areas.

chapel of rest *noun* an undertaker's mortuary.

chaperon[1] *or* **chaperone** /'shapərohn/ *noun* somebody delegated to supervise others and ensure propriety, *esp* a married or older woman who accompanies a younger woman on social occasions.

Word history
French *chaperon* hood, via French from late Latin *cappa* head covering, cloak. The underlying idea is of giving protection.

chaperon[2] *or* **chaperone** *verb trans* (**chaperoned, chaperoning**) to act as chaperon to (somebody); to escort (them). ➤➤ **chaperonage** /-nij/ *noun*.

chapfallen /'chapfawlən/ *adj* depressed or dejected: *He … sallied forth … with an air quite desolate and chapfallen. – Oh these women! these women!* — Washington Irving. [CHAP[4] + FALLEN[1]]

chaplain /'chaplin/ *noun* **1** a clergyman in charge of a chapel. **2** a clergyman officially attached to a branch of the armed forces, an institution, a family, etc. [Middle English *chapelain* via Old French from medieval Latin *cappellanus* custodian of the cloak of St Martin of Tours, from *cappella*: see CHAPEL[1]]

chaplaincy /'chaplinsi/ *noun* (*pl* **chaplaincies**) **1** the position or office of a chaplain. **2** the building where a chaplain works.

chaplet /'chaplit/ *noun* **1** a wreath to be worn on the head. **2** a string of prayer beads; one third of the rosary. **3** a beaded

moulding. ➤➤ **chapleted** *adj*. [Middle English *chapelet* from Old French, dimin. of *chapel* hat, garland, from medieval Latin *cappellus* head covering, from late Latin *cappa*]

chapman /'chapmən/ *noun* (*pl* **chapmen**) *archaic* an itinerant pedlar; a trader. [Middle English from Old English *cēapman*, from *cēap* trade + MAN[1]]

chappie /'chapi/ *noun informal* a man; a fellow.

chaps *pl noun* leather leggings worn over the trousers, *esp* by N American ranch hands. [short for CHAPARAJOS]

chaptalize *or* **chaptalise** /'shaptl·iez/ *verb trans* to add sugar to (the juice of wine grapes). ➤➤ **chaptalization** *noun*. [French *chaptaliser*, from Jean-Antoine *Chaptal* d.1832, French chemist]

chapter /'chaptə/ *noun* **1a** a major division of a book. **b** something resembling a chapter in being a significant specified unit or sequence of events: *a chapter of accidents; the final chapter of his career.* **2a** the canons of a cathedral or collegiate church, or the members of a religious house. **b** a regular meeting of a religious chapter. **3** a local branch of a society or fraternity. [Middle English *chapitre* division of a book, meeting of canons, via Old French from Latin *capitulum*, dimin. of *capit-, caput* head]

chapter and verse *noun* a full specification of the source of a piece of information. [from custom of citing passages in the Bible by chapter and verse number]

chapter house *noun* the building or rooms where a chapter meets.

char[1] /chah/ *verb* (**charred, charring**) ➤ *verb trans* **1** to burn (something) slightly; to scorch (it). **2** to convert (something) to charcoal or carbon, usu by heat; to burn (it). ➤ *verb intrans* to become charred. [back-formation from CHARCOAL]

char[2] *or* **charr** *noun* (*pl* **chars** *or* **charrs** *or collectively* **char** *or* **charr**) any of several species of freshwater and sea fishes related to the trout and salmon: genus *Salvelinus*. [origin unknown]

char[3] *verb intrans* (**charred, charring**) to work as a cleaning woman, *esp* in a private house. [back-formation from CHARWOMAN]

char[4] *noun Brit, informal* = CHARWOMAN.

char[5] *or* **cha** *noun Brit, informal* = TEA (1C). [Hindi *cā*, from Chinese (Pekingese) *cha*]

charabanc /'sharəbang/ *noun Brit, dated* a motor coach used for sightseeing. [French *char à bancs* wagon with benches]

characin /'karəsin/ *noun* any of several species of a family of usu small brightly coloured tropical fishes: family Characidae. ➤➤ **characin** *adj*. [derivative of Greek *charak-, charax* pointed stake, a fish]

character /'karəktə/ *noun* **1a** the mental or moral qualities that make up and distinguish a particular person, or any of these qualities considered individually. **b** the sum of the distinctive qualities of something; its main or essential nature: *the unique character of the town.* **c** a feature used to categorize things, e.g. organisms, or a group or kind so distinguished. **d** an inherited characteristic. **2a** any of the people portrayed in a novel, film, play, etc. **b** *informal* a person, *esp* one marked by notable or conspicuous traits: *His aunt is quite a character.* **3** good reputation: *a character reference.* **4** moral strength; integrity: *a man of character.* **5** a written testimonial of a person's qualities. **6a** a symbol, e.g. a letter, numeral, or punctuation mark, used in writing or printing. **b** a symbol that represents information, *esp* in a code that can be understood by computer. **c** a distinctive mark, usu in the form of a stylized graphic device. **d** a style of writing or printing. ✳ **in/out of character** in/not in accord with a person's usual qualities, traits, or behaviour. ➤➤ **characterful** *adj*, **characterless** *adj*. [Middle English *caracter* via French from Latin *character* mark, distinctive quality, from Greek *charaktēr*, from *charassein* to scratch, engrave]

character actor *noun* an actor capable of playing unusual or eccentric personalities often markedly different in age.

character assassination *noun* an attempt to destroy somebody's reputation by malicious defamation.

characterise *verb trans* see CHARACTERIZE.

characteristic[1] /,karəktə'ristik/ *adj* serving to reveal individual character and distinguish one person or thing from another; typical: *a characteristic odour.* ➤➤ **characteristically** *adv*.

characteristic[2] *noun* **1** a distinguishing trait, quality, or property. **2** the integral part of a common logarithm.

characterize *or* **characterise** *verb trans* **1** to describe the character or quality of (somebody or something): *She characterized him as soft-spoken yet ambitious.* **2** to be a characteristic of (something); to distinguish (it): *The cheese is characterized by its delicate flavour.* ⯮ **characterization** /-'zaysh(ə)n/ *noun.*

character recognition *noun* the recognition of printed or written characters by a computer.

character sketch *noun* a brief description of a person's character.

character witness *noun* a person who gives evidence concerning the reputation, conduct, and moral nature of somebody involved in a legal action.

charade /shə'rahd/ *noun* **1** (*in pl, but treated as sing. or pl*) a game in which one team acts out a word or phrase syllable by syllable while the other tries to guess what is being represented. **2** a ridiculous pretence. [French *charade* from Provençal *charrado* conversation]

charbroil /'chahbroyl/ *verb trans NAmer* = BARBECUE². [CHARCOAL + BROIL]

charcoal /'chahkohl/ *noun* **1** a black porous carbon prepared by partly burning wood, bone, or other vegetable or animal substances. **2a** fine charcoal used in pencil form for drawing. **b** a drawing done with charcoal. **3** (*also* **charcoal grey**) a very dark grey colour. [Middle English *charcole*; earlier history unknown]

charcuterie /shah'koohtəri (*French* ʃarkytri)/ *noun* **1** cooked cold meats. **2** a shop selling cooked cold meats. [French *charcuterie* from early French *chaircuiterie* from *chaircuitier* seller of pork, from *chair cuite* cooked meat]

chard /chahd/ *noun* a beet with large dark green leaves and succulent stalks that are often cooked as a vegetable: *Beta vulgaris cicla.* Also called SEA KALE (2). [French *carde* via Old Provençal from Latin *carduus* thistle, artichoke]

Chardonnay /'shahdənay/ *noun* **1** a variety of grape used in Burgundy, Australia, California, and elsewhere in the production of dry white wines. **2** a wine produced from this grape. [French *Chardonnay*]

Charentais /sharon'tay (*French* ʃarᾶtɛ)/ *noun* a small round melon with a yellowish green rind and faintly scented orange flesh. [French *charentais* of *Charente*, department of France]

charge¹ /chahj/ *verb trans* **1a** to set or ask (a price or fee). **b** to ask payment of (a person). **c** (*often* + *to*) to record (an item) as an expense, debt, obligation, or liability. **d** to impose a financial obligation on (something). **2a** (*often* + *with*) to accuse (somebody) formally of having committed an offence. **b** to assert (something) as an accusation: *The report charges that they altered the data.* **3a** (*often* + *with*) to entrust (somebody) with a task or responsibility. **b** to command or exhort (somebody) with right or authority: *I charge you not to leave.* **4** to rush violently at (somebody or something); to attack them. **5a** to load or fill (something) to capacity: *charge the blast furnace with ore.* **b** (*often* + *up*) to restore the active materials in (a battery) by the application of a current. **c** to give an electric charge to (a battery or similar device). **d** to place a usu powder charge in (a firearm). **e** to fill (somebody or something) with passionate emotion, feeling, etc: *a highly charged issue.* **6** to place a heraldic charge on (a shield, banner, etc). ⯮ *verb intrans* **1** to rush forwards, *esp* in attack. **2** to set a price: *They don't charge for parking.* **3** said of a battery: to receive and store electricity. ⯮ **chargeable** *adj.* [Middle English *chargen* via Old French from late Latin *carricare*, from Latin *carrus*: see CAR]

charge² *noun* **1** the price demanded or paid for something. **2** an accusation, indictment, or statement of complaint. **3a** an instruction or command. **b** instructions given by a judge to a jury. **4a** an obligation or requirement: *To maintain this readiness … is … a first charge upon our military effort* — Sir Winston Churchill. **b** supervision or custody: *I left them in her charge.* **c** somebody or something committed to the care of another. **5** a violent rush forwards, *esp* in attack. **6a** the quantity that something is intended or fitted to receive and hold, *esp* the quantity of explosive for a gun or cannon. **b** power or force: *the emotional charge of the drama.* **c** a basic property of matter that occurs in discrete natural units and is considered as negative or positive. **d** a definite quantity of electricity, *esp* the quantity held by a battery. **7** a design or image depicted on a heraldic shield: compare DEVICE (2A). ✱ **in charge** in control or command. **in charge of** responsible for (an activity or function). **take charge** (*often* + *of*) to assume care or control.

charge account *noun* = CREDIT ACCOUNT.

charge-cap *verb trans* (**charge-capped, charge-capping**) *Brit* to restrict the level of local taxation that can be levied by (a local authority). ⯮ **charge-capping** *noun.*

charge card *noun* a card, usu provided by a shop, authorizing the purchase of goods or services that are charged to the holder's account with the shop.

charge-coupled device *noun* a data recording device consisting of an array of light-sensitive semiconductor cells on a silicon chip that is used chiefly in imaging systems, e.g. in television cameras.

chargé d'affaires /,shahzhay da'feə/ *noun* (*pl* **chargés d'affaires** /,shahzhay da'feə(z)/) **1** a diplomat who substitutes for an ambassador or minister in their absence. **2** a diplomatic representative inferior in rank to an ambassador. [French *chargé d'affaires*, literally 'one charged with affairs']

chargehand *noun Brit* a worker in charge of a group of other workers or a particular piece of work.

charge nurse *noun* a nurse in charge of a hospital ward, *esp* a male nurse: compare SISTER (4).

charger¹ *noun* **1** a horse for battle or parade. **2** a device used to charge a battery.

charger² *noun* a large flat meat dish used in former times. [Middle English *chargeour* from Anglo-French *chargir* to load, from late Latin *carricare*: see CHARGE¹]

charge sheet *noun* a police record of charges made and people to be tried in a magistrate's court.

chargrill *verb trans* to grill (food) quickly over charcoal. [CHARCOAL + GRILL²]

chariot /'chari·ət/ *noun* **1** a two-wheeled horse-drawn vehicle of ancient times used in warfare and racing. **2** a light four-wheeled carriage used in former times, *esp* on state occasions. **3** *literary* a stately vehicle. [Middle English via Old French *char* from Latin *carrus*: see CAR]

charioteer /,chari·ə'tiə/ *noun* the driver of a chariot.

charisma /kə'rizmə/ *noun* (*pl* **charismata** /-mətə/) **1** the special magnetic appeal, charm, or power of an individual, e.g. a political leader, that inspires popular loyalty and enthusiasm. **2** an extraordinary power divinely given to a Christian. [Greek *charisma* favour, gift, from *charizesthai* to favour, from *charis* grace]

charismatic /kariz'matik/ *adj* **1** having charisma. **2** relating to the charismatic movement. **3** said of a power or gift: divinely given to a Christian. ⯮ **charismatically** *noun.*

charismatic movement *noun* a group within a Christian church whose members display charismatic powers, e.g. speaking in tongues.

charitable /'charitəbl/ *adj* **1a** liberal in giving to the poor; generous. **b** of or giving charity: *charitable institutions.* **2** merciful or kind in judging others; lenient. ⯮ **charitableness** *noun,* **charitably** *adv.*

charity /'chariti/ *noun* (*pl* **charities**) **1a** kindly generosity and helpfulness, *esp* aid given to those in need. **b** an institution engaged in helping those in need. **c** (*used before a noun*) relating to or in aid of charity: *charity concert; charity shop.* **2** benevolent goodwill towards or love of humanity: *All mankind's concern is charity* — Pope. **3** lenient judgment of others. **4a** a gift for public benevolent purposes. **b** an institution, e.g. a hospital, funded by such a gift. [Middle English *charite* via Old French from late Latin *caritat-, caritas* Christian love, ultimately from Latin *carus* dear]

charivari /shahri'vahri/ *noun* **1** a noisy and discordant serenade, made by banging saucepans, kettles, etc, to a newly married couple. **2** a noisy and raucous medley of sounds; a din. [French *charivari* via late Latin from Greek *karēbaria* headache, from *kara, karē* head + *barys* heavy]

charka *or* **charkha** /'chahkə/ *noun* a domestic spinning wheel used in India chiefly for spinning cotton. [Hindi *carkha*]

charlady /'chahlaydi/ *noun* (*pl* **charladies**) *Brit* = CHARWOMAN.

charlatan /'shahlət(ə)n/ *noun* somebody who pretends, usu ostentatiously, to have special knowledge or ability; a quack: *The word charlatan once thrown on the air could not be let drop* — George Eliot. ⯮ **charlatanism** *noun,* **charlatanry** /-ri/ *noun.* [Italian *ciarlatano,* alteration of *cerretano,* literally 'inhabitant of *Cerreto',* village in Italy]

Charles's Wain /ˌchahlziz 'wayn/ *noun* = URSA MAJOR. [Old English *Charles Wægn* the wagon of Charles, named after Charlemagne d.814, Frankish king]

charleston[1] /'chahlstən/ *noun* a lively ballroom dance, popular in the 1920s, in which the knees are turned inwards and heels are swung sharply outwards on each step. [named after *Charleston*, city in South Carolina, USA]

charleston[2] *verb intrans* (**charlestoned**, **charlestoning**) to dance the charleston.

charley horse /'chahli/ *noun* NAmer, *informal* muscle strain or bruising resulting from strenuous exercise. [*Charley*, nickname for *Charles*]

charlie /'chahli/ *noun* **1** an absurd or stupid person; a fool: *I felt a proper charlie.* **2** *informal* cocaine. [*Charlie*, nickname for *Charles*]

charlock /'chahlok/ *noun* a wild mustard with yellow flowers that is a weed of cultivated ground: *Sinapis arvensis*. [Old English *cerlic*]

charlotte /'shahlət/ *noun* a hot baked dessert consisting of fruit layered or covered with breadcrumbs or sponge cake. [French *charlotte*, prob from the name *Charlotte*]

charlotte russe /roohs/ *noun* a cold dessert consisting of a mixture of whipped cream, custard, and sometimes fruit, surrounded by sponge fingers and set in a mould. [French *charlotte russe* Russian charlotte]

charm[1] /chahm/ *noun* **1a** the quality of fascinating, alluring, or delighting others. **b** (*also in pl*) a particularly pleasing or attractive quality or feature. **2** something, e.g. an act or phrase, believed to have magic power; an incantation. **3** something worn to ward off evil or to ensure good fortune. **4** a small ornament worn on a bracelet or chain: *charm bracelet*. **5** a property of some elementary particles, e.g. quarks, proposed to account for their unexpectedly long lifetimes compared with otherwise identical particles. ✱ **like a charm** perfectly: *It worked like a charm*. ⟫⟫ **charmless** *adj*. [Middle English *charme* via Old French from Latin *carmen* song, from *canere* to sing]

charm[2] *verb trans* **1a** to fascinate or delight (somebody) by compelling attraction: *I was charmed by his suave manner.* **b** to gain (something) or influence (somebody) by the use of personal charm: *She charmed me into accepting her offer.* **2a** to affect (somebody or something) by magic or as if by supernatural powers; to bewitch (them). **b** to control (an animal) by the use of rituals, e.g. the playing of music, held to have magical powers: *charm a snake*. ⟫ *verb intrans* **1** to have the effect of a charm. **2** to be fascinating or delightful. ⟫⟫ **charmer** *noun*.

charmed[1] /chahmd/ *adj* **1** free of any difficulty or misfortune as if protected by supernatural powers: *a charmed life*. **2** in physics, relating to a particle having charm.

charmed[2] *interj dated* used to express pleasure at meeting somebody for the first time.

charming[1] *adj* extremely pleasing or delightful; entrancing: *It is absurd to divide people into good and bad. People are either charming or tedious* — Oscar Wilde. ⟫⟫ **charmingly** *adv*.

charming[2] *interj* used to express disapproval or displeasure, *esp* in response to rudeness.

charm offensive *noun* a campaign to achieve a particular goal, *esp* in politics, by the strategic use of charm.

charnel house /'chahn(ə)l/ *noun* a building or chamber in which dead bodies or bones are deposited. [Middle English *charnel* via French from late Latin *carnale*, neuter of *carnalis* of the flesh, from Latin *carn-*, *caro* flesh]

Charolais /'sharəlay/ *noun* (*pl* **Charolais**) an animal of a French breed of large white cattle used primarily for beef and crossbreeding. [named after *Charolais*, district in France where the breed originated]

charpoy /'chahpoy/ *noun* a lightweight Indian bedstead. [Hindi *cārpāī*]

charr /chah/ *noun* see CHAR[2].

chart[1] /chaht/ *noun* **1a** a map used for navigation by sea or air. **b** an outline map showing the geographical distribution of something, e.g. climatic variations. **2a** a sheet giving information in the form of a table or graph. **b** (**the charts**) a list of best-selling popular records produced weekly. **c** a schematic, usu large, diagram. **d** a sheet of paper ruled and graduated for use in a recording instrument, e.g. an electrocardiograph. [early French *charte* from Latin *charta* piece of papyrus, document, from Greek *chartēs*]

chart[2] *verb trans* **1** to make a chart of (something). **2** to lay out a plan for (something). **3** to display, mark, or record (something) on a chart. **4** to outline (the course or progress of something): *The book charts the progress of her career.* ⟫ *verb intrans* said of a record: to appear in the charts.

charter[1] /'chahtə/ *noun* **1** a formal written instrument or contract. **2a** a document that creates and defines the rights of a city, educational or professional institution, or company. **b** = CONSTITUTION (2). **3** a special privilege, immunity, or exemption. **4a** a total or partial lease of a ship, aeroplane, etc for a particular use or group of people. **b** (*used before a noun*) relating to such a lease: *charter flights*. [Middle English *chartre* via Old French from Latin *chartula*, dimin. of *charta*: see CHART[1]]

charter[2] *verb trans* (**chartered**, **chartering**) **1** to grant a charter to (something or somebody). **2** to hire or lease (something) for usu exclusive and temporary use: *charter a boat*. ⟫⟫ **charterer** *noun*.

chartered *noun* having passed the examinations or satisfied other requirements for membership of a professional institution: *chartered accountant*; *chartered engineer*.

charter member *noun* an original member of a society or corporation.

charterparty *noun* (*pl* **charterparties**) a contract for the hire of all or part of a ship for the conveyance of cargo or passengers. [French *charte partie* from medieval Latin *charta partita*, literally 'divided charter']

Chartism *noun* the principles and practices of a body of 19th–cent. English political reformers. ⟫⟫ **Chartist** *noun*. [medieval Latin *charta* charter from Latin: see CHART[1]]

chartreuse /shah'truhz/ *noun* **1** an aromatic liqueur, usu green or yellow in colour. **2** a brilliant yellowish green colour. [French *chartreuse*, named after *La Grande Chartreuse*, Carthusian monastery near Grenoble where the liqueur was first produced]

charwoman /'chahwoomən/ *noun* (*pl* **charwomen**) a cleaning woman; *esp* one employed in a private house. [*chare* (see CHORE) + WOMAN]

chary /'cheəri/ *adj* (**charier**, **chariest**) **1** cautious, *esp* wary of taking risks: *chary of giving such information to strangers.* **2** slow to grant or accept: *a man very chary of compliments.* ⟫⟫ **charily** *adv*, **chariness** *noun*. [Old English *cearig* sorrowful, from *caru* sorrow]

chase[1] /chays/ *verb trans* **1** to follow (somebody or something) rapidly or persistently; to pursue (them). **2** to cause (somebody or something) to depart or flee; to drive (them): *chase the dog out of the kitchen.* **3** *chiefly Brit* (+ up) to investigate (a matter) or contact (a person, company, etc) in order to obtain information or hasten results: *chase up an invoice.* **4** *informal* to attempt to establish a romantic or sexual relationship with (somebody) in a persistent or unsubtle manner. ⟫ *verb intrans* **1** (+ after) to chase an animal, person, or thing. **2** to rush or hasten: *We chased all over town looking for a place to stay.* [Middle English *chasen* from French, ultimately from Latin *captare*: see CATCH[1]]

chase[2] *noun* **1a** the act or an instance of chasing; pursuit. **b** (**the chase**) the hunting of wild animals. **2** something pursued; a quarry. **3** a tract of unenclosed land set aside for the breeding of animals for hunting and fishing. **4** = STEEPLECHASE. ✱ **give chase** to go in pursuit.

chase[3] *verb trans* **1** to ornament (something) with raised or incised work, e.g. by engraving or inlaying. **2** to make (a mark, design, etc) by this process: *chase a monogram.* [Middle English *chassen*, modification of early French *enchasser* to set (a jewel): see ENCHASE]

chase[4] *noun* **1** a groove cut in a surface for a pipe, wire, etc. **2** the part of a cannon enclosing the barrel between the trunnions (points on which the gun is swivelled; see TRUNNION) and the mouth of the muzzle. [French *chas* eye of a needle, from late Latin *capsus* enclosed space, ultimately from Latin *capsa*: see CASE[2]]

chase[5] *noun* a rectangular steel or iron frame into which printing type or blocks are locked for printing or platemaking. [prob from French *châsse* frame, from Latin *capsa*: see CASE[2]]

chaser *noun* **1** an alcoholic drink taken immediately after another that is milder or stronger, e.g. beer after spirits. **2** a horse used in steeplechasing.

chasm /'kaz(ə)m/ *noun* **1** a deep cleft in the earth. **2** an apparently unbridgeable gap: *a political chasm between the two countries.* ⟫⟫ **chasmic** *adj*. [via Latin from Greek *chasma*]

chassé[1] /'shasay/ *noun* a sliding dance step. [French *chassé*, past part. of *chasser* to chase]

chassé² *verb intrans* (**chassés, chasséd, chasséing**) to make a sliding dance step.

chasseur /sha'suh (*French* ʃasœr)/ *adj* (*used after a noun*) cooked in a sauce made with wine and mushrooms: *chicken chasseur*. [French *chasseur* from early French *chasser*]

chassis /'ʃasi/ *noun* (*pl* **chassis** /'ʃasiz/) **1** a supporting framework for the body of a vehicle, e.g. a car. **2** the frame on which the electrical parts of a radio, television, etc are mounted. [French *châssis*, ultimately from Latin *capsa*: see CASE²]

chaste /chayst/ *adj* **1** abstinent from sexual intercourse, or from unlawful or immoral sexual intercourse. **2** pure in thought and behaviour; modest. **3** severely simple in design or execution; austere: *written in a chaste style*. ⪢ **chastely** *adv*, **chasteness** *noun*. [Middle English via Old French from Latin *castus* pure]

chasten /'chays(ə)n/ *verb trans* (**chastened, chastening**) **1** to correct (somebody) by punishment or suffering; to discipline (them). **2** to subdue or restrain (somebody): *chastened by their defeat*. ⪢ **chastener** *noun*. [alteration of obsolete *chaste* from Middle English *chastien* via Old French from Latin *castigare*, from *castus* pure + *-igare* from *agere* to drive]

chastise /chas'tiez/ *verb trans* **1** to inflict punishment on (somebody), *esp* by beating. **2** to subject (somebody) to severe reproof or criticism. ⪢ **chastisement** *noun*, **chastiser** *noun*. [Middle English *chastisen* via Old French from Latin *castigare*: see CHASTEN]

chastity /'chastiti/ *noun* **1** the state of being chaste; purity. **2a** abstinence from sexual intercourse, *esp* extramarital sexual intercourse: *A false morality is even established, which makes all the virtue of women consist in chastity, submission, and the forgiveness of injuries* — Mary Wollstonecraft. **b** virginity.

chastity belt *noun* a device consisting of a belt with an attachment passing between the legs, used in former times to prevent a woman from having sexual intercourse.

chasuble /'chazyoobl/ *noun* a sleeveless outer vestment worn by the officiating priest at mass. [French *chasuble* from late Latin *casubla* hooded garment]

chat¹ /chat/ *verb intrans* (**chatted, chatting**) to talk in an informal or familiar manner. [Middle English *chatten*, short for *chatteren*: see CHATTER¹]

chat² *noun* **1a** light familiar talk. **b** a friendly conversation. **2** a stonechat, whinchat, or related bird with a harsh chattering call. [(sense 2) prob imitative]

château /'shatoh/ *noun* (*pl* **châteaus** *or* **châteaux** /'shatohz/) **1** a feudal castle or large country house in France. **2** a French vineyard estate. [French *château* via Old French *chastel* from Latin *castellum*: see CASTLE¹]

chateaubriand /,shatohbree'onh (*French* ʃatobrijã)/ *noun* a large thick fillet steak. [named after François René de *Chateaubriand* d.1848, French writer and statesman, whose chef is said to have first served it]

châteaux /'shatohz/ *noun* pl of CHÂTEAU.

chatelaine /'shatəlayn/ *noun* **1** the mistress of a castle or large house. **2** a clasp with a short chain formerly used to attach small articles, e.g. keys, to a woman's belt. [French *châtelaine*, fem of *châtelain*, from Latin *castellanus* occupant of a castle]

chatline *noun* a telephone service that people call to join in a general conversation with other users of the service.

chatoyant /shə'toyənt/ *adj* said of a gem: having a changeable lustre or colour and reflecting an undulating narrow band of white light. ⪢ **chatoyance** *noun*, **chatoyancy** /-si/ *noun*. [French *chatoyant*, present part. of *chatoyer*, literally 'to shine like a cat's eyes']

chat room *noun* a facility on the Internet where people with similar interests can exchange messages, views, etc.

chat show *noun* a television or radio programme in which people, *esp* celebrities, are interviewed informally or engage in discussion.

chattel /'chatl/ *noun* an item of personal property: *goods and chattels*. [Middle English *chatel* property, via Old French from medieval Latin *capitale*, from Latin *capitalis*: see CAPITAL²]

chatter¹ /'chatə/ *verb intrans* (**chattered, chattering**) **1** to talk idly, incessantly, or fast. **2** said of birds and other animals: to produce rapid successive inarticulate sounds suggestive of language: *Squirrels chattered angrily*. **3a** said of teeth: to click together repeatedly or uncontrollably, e.g. from cold. **b** said of a drill or

other tool: to vibrate rapidly while cutting. ⪢ **chatterer** *noun*. [Middle English *chatteren*, of imitative origin]

chatter² *noun* **1** the sound or action of chattering. **2** idle talk; prattle.

chatterbox *noun informal* somebody who talks incessantly.

chattering classes *pl noun informal, derog* the educated section of society considered as always talking about political and cultural issues.

chatty *adj* (**chattier, chattiest**) *informal* **1** fond of chatting; talkative. **2** having the style and content of light familiar conversation: *a chatty letter*. ⪢ **chattily** *adv*, **chattiness** *noun*.

chat up *verb trans Brit, informal* to engage (somebody) in friendly conversation flirtatiously or for an ulterior motive.

chaudfroid /'shoh'fwah (*French* ʃofrwa)/ *noun* a dish of cold meat, fish, etc cooked with a creamy sauce containing aspic that sets to a jelly. [French *chaudfroid*, literally 'hot-cold', from *chaud* hot (from Latin *calidus*) + *froid* cold (from Latin *frigidus*)]

chauffeur¹ /'shohfə, shoh'fuh/ *or* **chauffeuse** /shoh'fuhz/ *noun* a person employed to drive a private car or similar motor vehicle.

Word history ────────────
French *chauffeur*, literally 'stoker', from *chauffer* to heat, from Latin *calefacere*: see CHAFE¹. In French, *chauffeur* orig meant the driver of an early steam-powered car.

chauffeur² *verb intrans* to work as a chauffeur. ⪢ *verb trans* to transport (somebody) as the driver or as a chauffeur: *I chauffeured them to the airport.*

chaulmoogra /chawl'moohgrə/ *noun* an E Indian tree that yields an acrid oil formerly used in treating leprosy and skin diseases: *Hydnocarpus kurzii*. [Bengali *cāulmugrā*]

chauvinism /'shohvəniz(ə)m/ *noun* **1** excessive or blind patriotism. **2** undue partiality to or belief in the superiority of one's own group, cause, etc: *male chauvinism*. ⪢ **chauvinist** *noun and adj*, **chauvinistic** /-'nistik/ *adj*, **chauvinistically** /-'nistikli/ *adv*. [French *chauvinisme*, named after Nicolas *Chauvin* fl.1815, French soldier of excessive patriotism and devotion to Napoleon]

chayote /chay'ohtee/ *noun* **1** a tropical American climbing plant of the marrow family, with pale green pear-shaped edible fruit and an edible tuberous root: *Sechium edule*. **2** a fruit of this plant, used as a vegetable. [Spanish from Nahuatl *chayotli*]

ChB *abbr* Bachelor of Surgery. [medieval Latin *Chirurgiae Baccalaureus*]

cheap¹ /cheep/ *adj* **1a** relatively low in price, *esp* lower than the market price or the real value: *a cheap ticket*. **b** charging a low price: *a cheap supermarket*. **2a** of inferior quality or worth: *cheap furniture*. **b** contemptible because of lack of any fine or redeeming qualities: *cheap election gimmickry*. **3a** gained with little effort: *a cheap victory*. **b** gained by contemptible means: *cheap laughs*. **4** said of money: obtainable at a low rate of interest. **5** *NAmer* miserly or stingy. ✳ **cheap and cheerful** inexpensive but acceptable or serviceable. **cheap and nasty** inexpensive and of poor quality. ⪢ **cheapish** *adj*, **cheaply** *adv*, **cheapness** *noun*. [Middle English *chep* bargain, from Old English *cēap* trade]

cheap² *adv* at or for a low price; cheaply.

cheap³ ✳ **on the cheap** at minimum expense; cheaply: *clothes produced on the cheap.*

cheapen *verb* (**cheapened, cheapening**) ⪢ *verb trans* **1a** to make (something) cheap or cheaper in price or value. **b** to make (somebody) lower in esteem: *Don't cheapen yourself*. **2** to make (something) tawdry, vulgar, or inferior. ⪢ *verb intrans* to become lower in price, value, quality, or esteem.

cheap-jack¹ *noun* somebody, *esp* a pedlar, who sells cheap wares. [CHEAP¹ + the name *Jack*]

cheap-jack² *adj* **1** inferior, cheap, or worthless: *cheap-jack film companies*. **2** characterized by unscrupulous opportunism: *cheap-jack speculators*.

cheapo /'cheepoh/ *adj informal* inexpensive and often of inferior quality: *cheapo video tapes*.

cheapskate *noun informal* (*often before a noun*) a miserly or stingy person. [CHEAP¹ + *skate* fellow, miser, of unknown origin]

cheat¹ /cheet/ *verb trans* **1** to deprive (somebody) of something valuable, *esp* by deceit or fraud. **2** to deceive, trick, or swindle (somebody). **3** to avoid, defeat the purpose of, or blunt the effects of (something): *cheat winter of its dreariness* — Washington Irving. ⪢ *verb intrans* **1a** to violate rules dishonestly, e.g. at a game or in an examination. **b** to practise fraud or deception. **2** (+ on) to be sexually unfaithful to (somebody): *She had been cheating on her husband.* ➤➤ **cheater** *noun.* [Middle English *chet* escheat, short for *eschete*: see ESCHEAT¹]

cheat² *noun* **1** somebody who cheats; a pretender or deceiver. **2** a fraudulent deception; a trick or fraud.

Chechen /'chechən/ *noun* **1** a native or inhabitant of Chechnya in the Caucasus. **2** the Caucasian language of the Chechens. ➤➤ **Chechen** *adj.* [obsolete Russian *chechen*]

check¹ /chek/ *noun* **1a** an inspection, test, or verification. **b** a standard or criterion for testing and evaluation. **2** a sudden pause or stoppage in the forward progress of something. **3** somebody or something that arrests or restrains, a restraint. **4** (*often used as an interj*) in chess, exposure of a king to an attack from which it must be protected or moved to safety: *in check.* **5a** a pattern of squares, usu of alternating colours, or a square in such a pattern. **b** a fabric woven or printed with such a design. **6** a crack or break, *esp* in a piece of timber. **7** *NAmer* see CHEQUE. **8a** *chiefly NAmer* a ticket or token showing ownership or indicating payment made: *a luggage check.* **b** *NAmer* a counter in various games. **c** *NAmer* a bill, *esp* for food and drink in a restaurant. **9** *NAmer* = TICK¹ (1). ✳ **in check** under restraint or control: *hold the enemy in check.*

Word history
Middle English *chek* from Old French *eschec*, via Arabic from Persian *shāh* king. The word was first used in chess as a warning that the king was under threat; this led to the sense 'stoppage', 'restraint' (as no piece could move except to protect the king), leading in turn to the idea of an inspection or verification as something causing delay; (sense 6) Middle English *chek*, short for *cheker* chequer (via Old French *eschequier* to play chess, from *eschec*) comes from the squared pattern of a chessboard.

check² *verb trans* **1a** to inspect (something) for satisfactory condition, accuracy, safety, or performance. **b** to verify (something) to ensure that it is the case: *Check that you have enough money.* **c** to compare (something) with a source, original, or authority. **2a** to slow (something) or bring it to a stop. **b** to block the progress of (somebody). **3a** to restrain or diminish the action or force of (something). **b** to ease off and then secure again (e.g. a rope). **4** *chiefly dialect* to rebuke or reprimand (somebody). **5** in chess, to put (an opponent's king) in check. **6** *chiefly NAmer* (*often* + in) to note or mark (e.g. an item on a list) with a tick. **7** *chiefly NAmer* (*often* + in) to leave or accept (something) for safekeeping in a cloakroom or left-luggage office. ➤ *verb intrans* **1a** to investigate and make sure: *check on the passengers' safety.* **b** *chiefly NAmer* to correspond point for point; to tally: *The description checks with the photograph.* **2a** to halt through caution, uncertainty, or fear. **b** said of a dog: to stop in a chase, *esp* when scent is lost. ✳ **check into** to check in at (a hotel etc). **check up on 1** to examine (something) for accuracy or truth, *esp* in order to corroborate information. **2** to make thorough inquiries about (somebody or something). ➤➤ **checkable** *adj.*

checked *adj* marked with a pattern of squares, *esp* of alternating colours: *a checked shirt.*

checker¹ *noun* **1** somebody or something that checks, verifies, or inspects things, e.g. for faults or errors. **2** *NAmer* a cashier in a supermarket.

checker² *noun* **1** *informal* see CHEQUER¹. **2** *NAmer* a piece used in the game of draughts. [sense (2) back-formation from CHECKERS]

checker³ *verb trans NAmer* see CHEQUER².

checkerboard *noun NAmer* = CHESSBOARD.

checkered /'chekəd/ *adj NAmer* see CHEQUERED.

checkers *pl noun NAmer* = DRAUGHTS. [pl of *checker* chessboard, via Middle English *cheker*: see CHECK¹]

check in *verb intrans* to report one's presence or arrival, *esp* to arrive and register at a hotel or airport. ➤ *verb trans* **1** to deposit (luggage) for transport, *esp* by air. **2** to register the arrival of (somebody or something).

check-in *noun* the act of checking in, e.g. at a hotel or airport, or the place where this is done.

checklist *noun* a list of things, people, etc, *esp* a complete list of checks to be made or tasks to be done.

checkmate¹ *noun* **1a** (*often used as an interj*) the act of putting a chess opponent's king in check from which escape is impossible and thereby winning the game. **b** the situation of a king in this position. **2** complete defeat. [Middle English *chekmate*, interj used to announce checkmate, via Old French and Arabic from Persian *shāh māt*, literally 'the king is left helpless'; compare CHECK¹]

checkmate² *verb trans* **1** to put (a chess opponent's king) in checkmate. **2** to thwart or counter (somebody or something) completely.

checkout *noun* **1** a cash desk equipped with a cash register in a self-service shop. **2** the act of checking out of a hotel etc.

check out *verb intrans* **1** to complete the formalities before leaving a hotel etc. **2** *chiefly NAmer* to correspond or tally. ➤ *verb trans* **1** to cause the removal of (something) to be recorded. **2** *chiefly NAmer* to confirm or verify (something).

checkpoint *noun* a location where inspection, e.g. of people or vehicles crossing a border, may take place.

checkrein *noun* a short rein attached from the bit to the saddle to prevent a horse from lowering its head.

checkroom *noun NAmer* a room in which luggage, parcels, or coats may be left for safekeeping.

checksum *noun* in computing, a digit derived from the sum of the digits appearing in a piece of data, used as a check to detect errors in the data.

checkup *noun* an examination, *esp* a general medical or dental examination.

Cheddar /'chedə/ *noun* a hard smooth-textured cheese with a flavour that ranges from mild to strong as the cheese matures. [named after *Cheddar*, village in Somerset, England where it was orig made]

cheder /'khaydə, 'khedə/ *noun* see HEDER.

cheek¹ /cheek/ *noun* **1** the fleshy side of the face below the eye and above and to the side of the mouth. **2** insolent boldness; impudence. **3** *informal* a buttock. **4** either of two paired facing parts, e.g. the jaws of a vice. ✳ **cheek by jowl** very close together. **turn the other cheek** to respond to injury or unkindness with patience; to forgo retaliation [from Christ's instruction 'whosoever shall smite thee on thy right cheek, turn to him the other also' (Matthew 5:39)]. [Old English *cēace*]

cheek² *verb trans informal* to speak rudely or impudently to (somebody).

cheekbone *noun* the bone forming the prominence below the eye.

cheeky *adj* (**cheekier, cheekiest**) impudent or insolent. ➤➤ **cheekily** *adv,* **cheekiness** *noun.*

cheep¹ /cheep/ *noun* a faint shrill sound characteristic of a young bird. [imitative]

cheep² *verb intrans* to utter a cheep or a series of cheeps.

cheer¹ /chiə/ *noun* **1** a shout of applause or encouragement. **2** happiness; gaiety. **3** state of mind or heart; spirit: *Be of good cheer* — Bible. [Middle English *chere* face, mood, via Old French and Latin from Greek *kara* head]

cheer² *verb trans* **1a** (*usu* + up) to make (somebody) happy or happier. **b** (*usu* + up) to instil (somebody) with hope or courage; to comfort (them). **2** (+ on) to urge on or encourage (somebody), *esp* by shouts: *We cheered the team on.* **3** to applaud (somebody) with shouts. ➤ *verb intrans* **1** (*usu* + up) to become happy or less sad. **2** to utter a shout of applause or triumph. ➤➤ **cheerer** *noun.*

cheerful /'chiəf(ə)l/ *adj* **1a** full of good spirits; happy. **b** ungrudging: *cheerful obedience.* **2** conducive to good spirits; likely to dispel gloom: *a cheerful sunny room.* ➤➤ **cheerfully** *adv,* **cheerfulness** *noun.*

cheerio /chiəri'oh/ *interj chiefly Brit* used as an informal farewell or, *esp* in former times, as a drinking toast. [CHEERY + -O²]

cheerleader *noun* somebody who leads organized cheering, *esp* a member of a team of young women who do this at N American sports events.

cheerless *adj* gloomy or miserable: *a cheerless November afternoon.* ➤➤ **cheerlessly** *adv,* **cheerlessness** *noun.*

cheers *interj* used as a drinking toast and sometimes as an informal farewell or expression of thanks.

cheery *adj* (**cheerier, cheeriest**) marked by or causing good spirits; cheerful. ➤➤ **cheerily** *adv,* **cheeriness** *noun.*

cheese¹ /cheez/ *noun* **1a** a food consisting of coagulated, compressed, and usu ripened milk curds. **b** a cake of cheese, often cylindrical in shape. **2** a fruit preserve with the consistency of cream cheese: *lemon cheese.* **3a** something resembling cheese in consistency. **b** something round and flat like a cheese. [Old English *cēse* from a prehistoric West Germanic word borrowed from Latin *caseus* cheese]

cheese² *noun informal* an important person; a boss. [prob from Hindi *chīz* thing, from Persian]

cheeseboard *noun* **1** a board on which cheese is served. **2** a selection of cheeses served as a course of a meal.

cheeseburger *noun* a burger with a slice of cheese on top, usu in a soft bread roll.

cheesecake *noun* **1** a baked or refrigerated dessert consisting of a soft filling, usu containing cheese, on a biscuit or pastry base. **2** *informal* a photographic display of shapely and scantily clothed women: compare BEEFCAKE.

cheesecloth *noun* a lightweight loosely woven cotton fabric. [from its use in cheesemaking]

cheesed off *adj chiefly Brit, informal* annoyed or bored; fed up. [prob from *cheese* to stop, run away, of unknown origin]

cheesehead *adj* said of a screw or bolt: having a squat cylindrical head.

cheeseparing¹ /'cheezpeəring/ *noun* miserly or petty economizing; stinginess.

cheeseparing² *adj* miserly or stingy.

cheese plant *noun* = SWISS CHEESE PLANT.

cheese straw *noun* a stick of pastry flavoured with cheese, eaten as a snack.

cheesy *adj* (**cheesier, cheesiest**) **1** resembling cheese in smell, taste, appearance, or consistency. **2** *informal* said of a smile: very broad and often insincere: *a cheesy grin.* **3** *informal* of poor quality and lacking in good taste.

cheetah /'cheetə/ *noun* a long-legged spotted African and formerly Asiatic cat that resembles a small leopard and is the fastest land animal: *Acinonyx jubatus.* [Hindi *cītā* from Sanskrit *citrakāya* tiger, from *citra* bright + *kāya* body]

chef /shef/ *noun* a skilled cook; *esp* the chief cook in a restaurant or hotel. [French *chef*, short for *chef de cuisine* head of the kitchen]

chef d'oeuvre /shay 'duhvrə (*French* ʃɛ dœːvr)/ *noun* (*pl* **chefs d'oeuvre** /shay 'duhvrə (*French* ʃɛ dœːvr)/) a masterpiece, *esp* in art or literature. [French *chef-d'oeuvre* leading work]

Chekhovian /che'kohvi·ən/ *adj* characteristic of the style or works of Anton Chekhov. [Anton *Chekhov* d.1904, Russian writer]

chela¹ /'keelə/ *noun* (*pl* **chelae** /'keelee/) a pincerlike claw of a crustacean, e.g. a crab, or an arachnid, e.g. a scorpion. [scientific Latin from Greek *chēlē* claw]

chela² /'chaylə/ *noun* (*pl* **chelas**) in Hinduism, a disciple or pupil of a religious teacher. [Hindi *celā* servant]

chelae /'keelee/ *noun* pl of CHELA¹.

chelate¹ /'keelayt/ *adj* **1** resembling or having chelae. **2** of or having a molecular structure in which a metal ION (electrically charged atom or group of atoms) is held by two or more coordinate bonds.

chelate² *verb intrans* to form a chelate. ⟫⟫ **chelation** /ki'laysh(ə)n/ *noun.*

chelate³ *noun* a chelate chemical compound.

chelicera /ki'lisərə/ *noun* (*pl* **chelicerae** /-rie/) either of the front pair of appendages on the heads of spiders and other arachnids, often modified as fangs or pincers. ⟫⟫ **cheliceral** *adj,* **chelicerate** /-rət/ *adj and noun.* [scientific Latin from French *chélicère,* from Greek *chēlē* claw + *keras* horn]

chelonian /ki'lohni·ən/ *noun* any of an order of reptiles including the tortoises and turtles, characterized by a bony shell: order Chelonia. ⟫⟫ **chelonian** *adj.* [Greek *chelōnē* tortoise]

Chelsea bun /'chelsi/ *noun* a sweet bun made with yeast and dried fruit, e.g. currants, raisins, etc, and shaped in a flat coil. [named after *Chelsea,* district of London]

Chelsea pensioner *noun* a veteran or disabled soldier living at the Chelsea Royal Hospital.

chem. *abbr* **1** chemical. **2** chemist. **3** chemistry.

chem- *or* **chemi-** *or* **chemo-** *comb. form* forming words, with the meanings: **1** chemical; chemistry: *chemotherapy; chemotaxis.* **2** chemically: *chemisorb.* [scientific Latin from late Greek *chēmeia* alchemy, prob from *chyma* fluid, from *chein* to pour]

chemical¹ /'kemikl/ *adj* **1** of, used in, or produced by chemistry: *chemical reaction.* **2** using, involving, or made from chemicals: *chemical weapon.* ⟫⟫ **chemically** /'kemikli/ *adv.*

chemical² *noun* a substance obtained by a chemical process or used to produce a chemical effect.

chemical bond *noun* = BOND¹ (2).

chemical engineering *noun* engineering dealing with the industrial application of chemistry. ⟫⟫ **chemical engineer** *noun.*

chemical formula *noun* = FORMULA (2B).

chemical toilet *noun* a toilet in which faeces and urine are treated with chemicals, *esp* one used on a boat or in a caravan.

chemical warfare *noun* warfare using poisonous or harmful chemicals.

chemico- *comb. form* forming words, with the meaning: chemical; chemistry: *chemicophysical.*

chemiluminescence /,kemiloohmi'nes(ə)ns/ *noun* light produced by chemical reaction. ⟫⟫ **chemiluminescent** *adj.*

chemin de fer /sha,manh də 'feə/ *noun* a card game resembling baccarat in which only two hands are dealt and any number of players may bet against the dealer. [French *chemin de fer* railway; from the speed at which the game is played]

chemise /shə'meez/ *noun* **1** a woman's loose-fitting undergarment. **2** a loose straight-hanging dress without a waist. [Middle English via Old French from late Latin *camisia* shirt]

chemist /'kemist/ *noun* **1** somebody who is trained in chemistry. **2** *Brit* a pharmacist. **3** *Brit* a retail shop where medicines and other articles, e.g. cosmetics and films, are sold. [scientific Latin *chimista,* short for medieval Latin *alchimista* alchemist]

chemistry /'kemistri/ *noun* (*pl* **chemistries**) **1** a science that deals with the composition, structure, and properties of substances and of the transformations they undergo.

Editorial note
Chemistry is divided into several branches. Physical chemistry deals with the principles of chemistry and its basis in physics. Organic chemistry deals with the structures and reactions of compounds of carbon; inorganic chemistry with the properties of all the other elements. Biochemistry deals with the compounds and reactions that participate in the processes of life. These divisions are becoming increasingly blurred — Professor Peter Atkins.

2a the composition and chemical properties of a substance. **b** chemical processes and phenomena, e.g. of an organism: *blood chemistry.* **3** the complex nature of a relationship, feeling, phenomenon, etc, *esp* seen as inexplicable or instinctive: *We don't really know what sexual chemistry is. We can't explain it.*

chemo- *comb. form* see CHEM-.

chemoautotrophic /keemohawtə'trohfik, kemoh-/ *adj* said *esp* of a bacterium: AUTOTROPHIC (capable of making sugars, proteins, etc from carbon dioxide and other simple chemical compounds) and deriving energy from the reaction between a chemical and oxygen: compare PHOTOAUTOTROPHIC. ⟫⟫ **chemoautotrophically** *adv,* **chemoautotrophy** *noun.*

chemoreceptor /'keemohriseptə/ *noun* a sense organ, e.g. a taste bud, that responds to chemical stimuli.

chemosynthesis /keemoh'sinthəsis/ *noun* the formation of organic chemical compounds, e.g. in living cells, using energy derived from chemical reactions rather than from light: compare PHOTOSYNTHESIS.

chemotherapy /keemoh'therapi/ *noun* the use of chemical agents in the treatment or control of disease, *esp* cancer. ⟫⟫ **chemotherapist** *noun.*

chemurgy /'kemuhji/ *noun* the industrial use of organic raw materials, or the branch of chemistry concerned with this. ⟫⟫ **chemurgic** /ki'muhjik/ *adj.*

chenille /shə'neel/ *noun* **1** a soft velvety yarn of silk, cotton, wool, or synthetic fibre with a long pile. **2** a fabric made from this yarn. [French *chenille,* literally 'caterpillar', from Latin *canicula,* dimin. of *canis* dog; from its hairy appearance]

cheongsam /'chongsam/ *noun* a dress with a slit skirt and a mandarin collar worn *esp* by Chinese women. [Chinese (Cantonese) *cheung saam* long gown]

cheque (*NAmer* **check**) /chek/ *noun chiefly Brit* a written order for a bank to pay money as instructed or the printed form on which it is written. [alteration of CHECK¹]

chequebook *noun* a book containing unwritten cheques.

chequebook journalism *noun* sensationalist journalism consisting of exclusive reports acquired by paying large amounts of money, e.g. to friends and relations of people in the public eye.

cheque card *noun* a card guaranteeing that the holder's cheques up to a specified amount will be honoured by the issuing bank.

chequer[1] (*NAmer* **checker**) /'chekə/ *noun* (*also in pl*) = CHECK[1] (5A). [Middle English *cheker* from Old French *eschequier*: see CHECK[1]]

chequer[2] (*NAmer* **checker**) *verb trans* (**chequered, chequering**, *NAmer* **checkered, checkering**) to variegate (something) with different colours or shades, *esp* to mark it with squares of alternating colours: *chequered flag*.

chequered (*NAmer* **checkered**) *adj* characterized by variations in fortune: *a chequered career*.

Cherenkov radiation /chi'r(y)engkof/ *noun* see CERENKOV RADIATION.

cherish /'cherish/ *verb trans* **1a** to hold (somebody or something) dear; to feel or show affection for (them). **b** to keep or cultivate (something) with care and affection; to nurture (it). **2** to keep (something) in the mind with hope or affection: *I still cherish that memory*. ➤➤ **cherishable** *adj*. [Middle English *cherisshen* via French from Old French *chier* dear, from Latin *carus*]

chernozem /'chuhnəzem/ *noun* a dark-coloured humus-rich soil found in temperate to cool climates, *esp* in the Russian steppes. [Russian *chernozem* black earth]

Cherokee /'cherəkee/ *noun* (*pl* **Cherokees** *or collectively* **Cherokee**) **1** a member of a Native N American people orig of Tennessee and N Carolina. **2** the Iroquoian language of this people. ➤➤ **Cherokee** *adj*. [prob from Creek *tciloki* people of a different speech]

cheroot /shə'rooht/ *noun* a cigar cut square at both ends. [Tamil *curuṭṭu* roll]

cherry /'cheri/ *noun* (*pl* **cherries**) **1a** a smooth yellow to deep red or blackish fruit with sweet flesh and a hard stone. **b** any of numerous species of trees and shrubs of the rose family that bear this fruit and are often cultivated for their ornamental flowers: genus *Prunus*. **c** the wood of the cherry tree or shrub. **2** a bright red colour. **3** *informal* virginity. ➤➤ **cherry** *adj*. [Middle English *chery* from early French *cherise* (taken as a plural) via Latin from Greek *kerasos* cherry tree]

cherry brandy *noun* a sweet liqueur in which cherries have been steeped.

cherry-pick *verb intrans informal* to select the most desirable things or people and ignore other items or members of the group. ➤ *verb trans informal* to select (something or somebody) in this way.

cherry picker *noun informal* a hydraulic crane that supports a platform, used for raising and lowering people working at high levels.

cherry plum *noun* an Asiatic plum tree used extensively in Europe as a stock onto which buds from domestic varieties are grafted: *Prunus cerasifera*.

cherry tomato *noun* a very small tomato with a strong sweet flavour.

chersonese /'kuhsəneez, -nees/ *noun chiefly literary* a peninsula. [via Latin from Greek *chersonēsos*, from *chersos* dry land + *nēsos* island]

chert /chuht/ *noun* a rock resembling flint and consisting essentially of quartz. ➤➤ **cherty** *adj*. [origin unknown]

cherub /'cherəb/ *noun* **1** (*pl* **cherubim** /-bim/) a biblical attendant of God or of a holy place, often represented as a being with large wings, a human head, and an animal body. **2** (*pl* **cherubs**). **a** a beautiful usu winged and chubby child in painting and sculpture. **b** an innocent-looking usu chubby and pretty person, *esp* a child. ➤➤ **cherubic** /chi'roohbik/ *adj*, **cherubically** /chi'rooh-/ *adv*. [via Latin from Greek *cherub*, from Hebrew *kĕrūbh*]

chervil /'chuhvil/ *noun* an aromatic plant of the carrot family with leaves that are used as a herb or a salad vegetable: *Anthriscus cerefolium*. [Old English *cerfille*]

Ches. *abbr* Cheshire.

Cheshire cheese /'cheshə/ *noun* a white or pinkish orange cheese with a crumbly texture. [named after *Cheshire*, county in England where it was orig made]

chess /ches/ *noun* a board game for two players who have 16 pieces each and try to get the opposing king into a position called CHECKMATE[1] (a direct attack from which the king cannot escape). [Middle English *ches* from Old French *esches*, accusative pl of *eschec*: see CHECK[1]]

chessboard *noun* a board used in chess, draughts, etc that is divided into 64 equal squares of two alternating colours.

chessman *noun* (*pl* **chessmen**) any of the pieces (one king, one queen, two rooks, two bishops, two knights, and eight pawns) used by each player in the game of chess.

chest[1] /chest/ *noun* **1a** a box with a lid used *esp* for the safekeeping of belongings. **b** a small cupboard used *esp* for storing medicines or first-aid supplies. **c** a case in which a commodity, e.g. tea, is shipped. **2a** the part of the body enclosed by the ribs and breastbone. **b** the front of the body from the neck to the waist. ✳ **get something off one's chest** to relieve the burden of a problem, worry etc by talking about it. ➤➤ **chestful** *noun*. [Old English *cest*]

chest[2] *verb trans* to strike (a football) with the chest: *He chested the ball down to his feet*.

chesterfield /'chestəfeeld/ *noun* **1** a heavily padded usu leather sofa with arms and back of the same height. **2** a man's semifitted overcoat with a velvet collar. [prob named after a 19th-cent. Earl of *Chesterfield*]

chestnut /'ches(t)nut/ *noun* **1a** a tree or shrub of the beech family: *Castanea sativa*. **b** the edible nut of the chestnut tree. **c** the hard wood of the chestnut tree. **2** a reddish brown colour. **3** = HORSE CHESTNUT. **4** a chestnut-coloured horse. **5** *informal* an often repeated joke or story; *broadly* anything repeated excessively. **6** the small hard patch on the inner side of a horse's leg. ➤➤ **chestnut** *adj*. [Middle English *chasteine, chesten* chestnut tree, via French and Latin from Greek *kastanea*]

chest of drawers *noun* a piece of furniture containing a set of drawers.

chesty *adj* (**chestier, chestiest**) **1** inclined to, symptomatic of, or suffering from disease of the chest: *a chesty cough*. **2** *informal* having prominent breasts. ➤➤ **chestiness** *noun*.

chetrum /'cheetrəm, 'chet-/ *noun* (*pl* **chetrums** *or* **chetrum**) a unit of currency in Bhutan, worth 100th of a ngultrum. [native name in Bhutan]

cheval glass /shə'val/ *noun* a full-length mirror in a frame by which it may be tilted. [French *cheval* horse, support]

chevalier /shevə'liə/ *noun* **1** a member of any of various orders of merit, e.g. the French Legion of Honour. **2** a chivalrous man. **3** *archaic* a knight. [French *chevalier* knight, horseman, from late Latin *caballarius*: see CAVALIER[1]]

Cheviot /'cheevi-ət, 'che-/ *noun* **1** a sheep of a hardy hornless breed. **2** (**cheviot**) a fabric made from the wool of Cheviot sheep. [named after the *Cheviot* Hills on the border between England and Scotland, where the sheep were bred]

chèvre /'shevrə/ *noun* a soft goat's-milk cheese. [French *chèvre*, goat, she-goat, from Latin *capra* she-goat, fem of *capr-, caper* he-goat]

chevron /'shevrən/ *noun* **1** a figure, pattern, or object having the shape of a V or an inverted V, e.g.: **a** a sleeve badge that consists of one or more chevron-shaped stripes and indicates the wearer's rank. **b** a V-shaped heraldic design with the point uppermost. **2** (*in pl*) a row of horizontal black and white V-shaped stripes indicating that a road bends sharply. [Middle English from early French *chevron* rafter, chevron, from (assumed) vulgar Latin *caprion-, caprio* rafter]

chevrotain /'shevrətayn, -tin/ *noun* any of several species of very small hornless RUMINANT[1] (related to cattle and deer) mammals of tropical Asia and W Africa: family Tragulidae. Also called MOUSE DEER. [French *chevrotain*, dimin. of early French *chevrot* kid, fawn, dimin. of *chèvre* goat: see CHÈVRE]

chew[1] /chooh/ *verb trans* (*also* + up) to crush, grind, or gnaw (food, etc) with, or as if with, the teeth. ➤ *verb intrans* (*also* + on) to crush, grind, or gnaw food, etc. ✳ **chew the fat/rag** *informal* to make friendly conversation; to chat or gossip. ➤➤ **chewable** *adj*, **chewer** *noun*, **chewiness** *noun*, **chewy** *adj*. [Old English *cēowan*]

chew[2] *noun* **1** the act of chewing. **2** something for chewing, e.g. a chewy sweet or something made for a pet dog to chew.

chewing gum *noun* a flavoured sweetened substance, e.g. chicle, for chewing.

chewing tobacco *noun* tobacco prepared for chewing, e.g. by the addition of flavourings, rather than smoking.

chew over *verb trans informal* to meditate on (something); to think about (it) carefully.

Cheyenne /shie'an/ *noun* (*pl* **Cheyennes** /shie'an/ *or collectively* **Cheyenne**) 1 a Native American people of the western plains of the USA, or a member of this people. 2 the Algonquian language of this people. [Canadian French *Cheyenne* from Dakota *Shaiyena*, from *shaia* to speak strangely]

chez /shay/ *prep* at or to the home of: *chez Louis*. [French *chez*, ultimately from Latin *casa* cottage]

chi¹ /kie/ *noun* the 22nd letter of the Greek alphabet (X, χ), equivalent to and transliterated as roman ch. [Greek *chei*]

chi² *or* **ch'i** *or* **qi** /chee/ *noun* in traditional Chinese medicine, philosophy, and martial arts, the life-force or energy that flows within an individual's body. [Chinese (Pekingese) *ch'i*, also written *qi*, air, energy]

chiack¹ /'chieak/ *verb trans chiefly Aus, informal* to make derisive or teasing remarks about (somebody or something). [alteration of *chi-hike*, *chi-ike* a shout of greeting or derision]

chiack² *noun chiefly Aus, informal* derisive remarks.

Chianti /ki'anti/ *noun* a dry red Italian table wine. [Italian, named after *Chianti*, district of Tuscany, Italy, where it is made]

chiaroscuro /ki,ahrə'skooəroh/ *noun* (*pl* **chiaroscuros**) 1 pictorial representation in terms of light and shade. 2 the arrangement or treatment of light and shade in a painting. [Italian *chiaroscuro*, from *chiaro* clear, light + *oscuro* obscure, dark]

chiasma /ki'azmə/ *noun* (*pl* **chiasmas** *or* **chiasmata** /-tə/) an anatomical cross-shaped configuration, e.g. one between paired chromatids (part of chromosome; see CHROMATID) considered to be the point where genetic material is exchanged. [scientific Latin from Greek *chiasma* crosspiece, cross-shaped mark, from *chiazein* to mark with a chi, from CHI¹, written χ]

chiasmus /kie'azməs/ *noun* (*pl* **chiasmi** /-mie/) inversion of the relationship between the elements of parallel phrases, e.g. as in Goldsmith's *to stop too fearful, and too faint to go*, or an example of this. ▶▶ **chiastic** *adj*. [Latin *chiasmus* from Greek *chiasmos*, from *chiazein*: see CHIASMA]

chibouk *or* **chibouque** /chi'boohk/ *noun* a long-stemmed Turkish tobacco pipe. [French *chibouque* from Turkish *çibuk*]

chic¹ /sheek, shik/ *adj* (**chicer, chicest**) having or showing elegance and sophistication, *esp* of dress or manner. ▶▶ **chicly** *adv*, **chicness** *noun*. [French *chic*]

chic² *noun* elegance and sophistication.

Chicana /chi'kahnə/ *noun* (*pl* **Chicanas**) *NAmer* an American woman or girl of Mexican origin or descent. [modification of Spanish *mejicana*, fem of *mejicano* Mexican: see CHICANO]

chicane¹ /shi'kayn/ *noun* 1 a series of tight turns in opposite directions in an otherwise straight stretch of a road-racing course. 2 a hand of cards containing no trumps. [French *chicane* deception, obstacle, from early French *chicaner* to quibble, obstruct justice]

chicane² *verb trans* to deceive (somebody) by the use of chicanery. ▶ *verb intrans* to use chicanery.

chicanery /shi'kayn(ə)ri/ *noun* (*pl* **chicaneries**) 1 deception by the use of fallacious or irrelevant arguments. 2 a piece of sharp practice or legal trickery: *Nothing is so mistaken as the supposition that a person is to extricate himself from a difficulty by intrigue, by chicanery, by dissimulation ... This increases the difficulties tenfold* — Thomas Jefferson.

Chicano /chi'kahnoh/ *noun* (*pl* **Chicanos**) *NAmer* an American man or boy of Mexican origin or descent. [modification of Spanish *mejicano* Mexican]

chichi¹ /'sheeshee/ *adj* 1 showy, frilly, or elaborate. 2 unnecessarily elaborate or affected. [French *chichi*]

chichi² *noun* 1 showy ornamentation. 2 unnecessarily elaborate style.

chick /chik/ *noun* 1a a young bird. b a newly hatched chicken. 2 *informal, dated* a young woman: *Johnny's going out with a real cool chick*. [short for CHICKEN¹]

chickadee /'chikədee/ *noun* any of numerous species of crestless N American songbirds of the tit family: *esp* family Paridae. [imitative]

chicken¹ /'chikn/ *noun* 1a the common domestic fowl, *esp* when young. b the flesh of a chicken used as food. 2 *informal*. a an informal contest in which the participants put themselves in danger to see who is brave. b a coward. 3 *informal* a young and inexperienced person. ✳ **he/she is no chicken/spring chicken** he/she is no longer young. [Old English *cicen* young chicken; related to Old English *cocc* COCK¹]

chicken² *adj informal* scared to do something: *Don't be chicken. There's not really a ghost in there.*

chicken feed *noun informal* a small and insignificant amount, *esp* of money.

chicken-hearted *adj* timid; cowardly.

chicken-livered *adj* = CHICKEN-HEARTED.

chicken out *verb intrans* (**chickened, chickening**) *informal* (*often* + of) to lose one's nerve: *He chickened out of asking her*.

chickenpox *noun* an infectious virus disease, *esp* of children, that is marked by mild fever and a rash of small blisters.

chicken wire *noun* a light galvanized wire netting with a hexagonal mesh. [from its use for making enclosures for chickens]

chick-lit *noun* a genre of literature dealing with the lives of young city-based women and their social or romantic problems and aspirations.

chick-pea /'chik pee/ *noun* 1 an Asiatic leguminous plant: *Cicer arietinum*. 2 the hard edible seed of this plant. [by folk etymology from Middle English *chiche*, via French from Latin *cicer*]

chickweed /'chikweed/ *noun* any of numerous species of small-leaved plants of the pink family that occur commonly as weeds: family Caryophyllaceae.

chicle /'chikl/ *noun* a gum from the latex of the sapodilla, used as the chief ingredient of chewing gum. [Spanish *chicle* from Nahuatl *chictli*]

chicory /'chik(ə)ri/ *noun* (*pl* **chicories**) 1 a blue-flowered European perennial composite plant of the daisy family, widely cultivated for its edible thick roots and as a salad plant: *Cichorium intybus*. 2 the ground roasted root of this plant, used as a coffee additive. [Middle English *cicoree* via French and Latin from Greek *kichoreia*]

chide /chied/ *verb trans* (*past tense* **chided** *or* **chid** /chid/, *past part.* **chided** *or* **chidden** /'chid(ə)n/) to rebuke (somebody) angrily; to scold (them). ▶▶ **chider** *noun*, **chidingly** *adv*. [Old English *cidan* to quarrel, chide, from *cid* strife]

chief¹ /cheef/ *noun* 1 the head of a body of people or an organization; a leader: *the chief of police*. 2 the upper third of a heraldic FIELD¹ (surface on which coat of arms is displayed), or a broad horizontal band across the top of a shield. ▶▶ **chiefdom** *noun*. [Middle English from Old French, head, chief, from Latin *caput* head]

chief² *adj* 1 of the highest rank or office; head: *the chief librarian*. 2 of greatest importance or influence; main: *The chief reason for holidaying abroad is the weather*.

chief constable *noun* the principal officer of a British police force.

Chief Executive *noun* 1 the most senior executive of a business organization, etc. 2a the chief officer of an executive body, e.g. the governor of a state. b *NAmer* the president of the United States.

Chief Executive Officer *noun* = CHIEF EXECUTIVE (1).

chief inspector *noun* a British police officer ranking between an inspector and a superintendent.

chief justice *noun* the presiding judge of a supreme court of justice, e.g. the US Supreme Court.

chiefly *adv* 1 most importantly; principally or especially. 2 for the most part; mostly or mainly.

chief of staff *noun* 1 the senior officer of an armed forces staff that serves a commander. 2 the senior officer of a branch of the armed forces.

chief petty officer *noun* a non-commissioned officer in the Royal Navy and US Navy ranking above a petty officer.

chief superintendent *noun* an officer in the British police ranking next above superintendent.

chieftain /'cheeftən/ *noun* a chief, *esp* of a band, tribe, or clan. ▶▶ **chieftainship** *noun*. [Middle English *chieftaine* from early French *chevetain* from late Latin *capitaneus*: see CAPTAIN¹]

chieftaincy /'cheeftǝnsi/ *noun* (*pl* **chieftaincies**) **1** the rank, dignity, office, or rule of a chieftain. **2** a region or a people ruled by a chief.

chief technician *noun* a non-commissioned officer in the Royal Air Force ranking below a flight sergeant.

chiffchaff /'chifchaf/ *noun* a small greenish European warbler: *Phylloscopus collybita*. [imitative]

chiffon /'shifon, shi'fon/ *noun* a sheer fabric of silk, etc. [French *chiffon* from *chiffe* old rag, alteration of early French *chipe* from Middle English *chip* CHIP¹]

chiffonier /shifǝ'niǝ/ *noun* a high narrow chest of drawers. [French *chiffonnier*, from *chiffon*: see CHIFFON]

chigger /'chigǝ/ *noun* = CHIGOE. [by alteration]

chignon /'sheenyon/ *noun* a smooth knot of hair worn *esp* at the nape of the neck. [French *chignon* from early French *chaignon* chain, collar, nape]

chigoe /'chigoh/ *noun* **1** a tropical flea, the female of which burrows under the skin: *Tunga penetrans*. **2** *NAmer* = HARVEST MITE. [of Cariban origin]

Chihuahua /chi'wahwǝ/ *noun* any of a breed of very small dog of Mexican origin with a round head and large ears. [Mexican Spanish, named after *Chihuahua*, state and city in Mexico]

chilblain /'chilblayn/ *noun* an inflammatory sore, *esp* on the feet or hands, caused by exposure to cold. ⟫⟫ **chilblained** *adj*. [CHILL³ + BLAIN]

child /cheeld/ *noun* (*pl* **children** /'childrǝn/) **1** a young person, *esp* between infancy and youth. **2** an unborn or recently born person. **3a** a son or daughter: *She left the estate to her children*. **b** *archaic or literary* (+ of) a descendant: *the Children of David*. **4** a childlike or childish person. **5** (+ of) a person who is strongly influenced by another or by a place or state of affairs: *As a writer, she was very much a child of the depression*. **6** (+ of) a product or result: *... dreams; which are the children of an idle brain* — Shakespeare. ✻ **with child** said of a woman: PREGNANT. ⟫⟫ **childless** *adj*, **childlessness** *noun*. [Old English *cild*]

child abuse *noun* the sexual or violent mistreatment of children by those who have responsibility for their welfare.

childbearing *noun* the act or process of giving birth to children.

childbed *noun archaic* = CHILDBIRTH.

child benefit *noun* a state allowance paid weekly or monthly to a parent for each child in the family.

childbirth *noun* the action or process of giving birth to a child or children.

childcare *noun* the care and supervision of children.

Childe /cheeld/ *noun archaic* a young man of noble birth. [variant of CHILD]

childhood *noun* the state or period of being a child.

childish *adj* **1** of or befitting a child or childhood. **2** marked by or suggestive of immaturity: *a childish tantrum*. ⟫⟫ **childishly** *adv*, **childishness** *noun*.

childlike *adj* marked by the innocence and trust associated with children: *a childlike devotion*.

childminder *noun chiefly Brit* a person who looks after other people's children, *esp* in their own home, when the parents are at work. ⟫⟫ **childminding** *noun*.

childproof *adj* not liable to damage or misuse by children; *specif* designed to be impossible for children to open: *a childproof lock*.

children /'childrǝn/ *noun* pl of CHILD.

Children of Israel *pl noun* (**the Children of Israel**) the Jewish people.

child's play *noun* an extremely simple task or act.

Chilean /'chili·ǝn/ *noun* a native or inhabitant of Chile in S America. ⟫⟫ **Chilean** *adj*.

Chile pine /'chili/ *noun* = MONKEY-PUZZLE. [named after *Chile*, country in S America, where it originated]

Chile saltpetre *noun* naturally occurring sodium nitrate.

chili /'chili/ *noun NAmer* see CHILLI.

chiliad /'kiliad/ *noun* **1** a group of 1000. **2** a period of 1000 years. [late Latin *chiliad-*, *chilias* from Greek, from *chilioi* thousand]

chiliasm /'kiliaz(ǝ)m/ *noun* = millenarianism (see MILLENARIAN). ⟫⟫ **chiliast** /-ast/ *noun*, **chiliastic** /-'astik/ *adj*. [Latin *chiliasmus*

from late Latin *chiliastes* those who believe in chiliasm, from *chilias*: see CHILIAD]

chill¹ /chil/ *verb trans* **1a** to make (somebody or something) cold or chilly. **b** to make (food or drink) cool, *esp* without freezing. **2** to affect (somebody) as if with cold; to dispirit (them): *His lack of conscience chilled me*. **3** to harden the surface of (metal) by sudden cooling. ⟫ *verb intrans* **1** to become cold. **2** *informal* = CHILL OUT. ⟫⟫ **chillingly** *adv*. [Middle English *chillen*, from *chile* cold, frost, from Old English *cele*; related to Old English *ceald* COLD¹]

chill² *noun* **1a** a disagreeable sensation of coldness. **b** a feverish cold, causing shivering, etc. **2** a moderate but disagreeable degree of cold. **3** coldness of manner: *He felt the chill of his opponent's stare*.

chill³ *adj* = CHILLY (1), (2).

chiller *noun* **1** something that chills something or somebody: *a wine chiller*. **2** a terrifying film or story, usu with a supernatural element; a SPINE-CHILLER.

chilli (*NAmer* **chili**) /'chili/ *noun* (*pl* **chillies**, *NAmer* **chilies**) **1** the pod of a hot pepper used either whole or ground as a pungent condiment: compare CAYENNE PEPPER, PAPRIKA. **2** = CHILLI POWDER. **3** = CHILLI CON CARNE. [Spanish *chile* from Nahuatl *chilli*]

chilli con carne /kon 'kahni/ *noun* a spiced Mexican stew of minced beef and beans, strongly seasoned with chillies or chilli powder. [Spanish *chile con carne* chilli with meat]

chilli powder *noun* a reddish powder made from ground chillies mixed with other spices, used as a flavouring.

chill out *verb intrans informal* to relax.

chilly *adj* (**chillier, chilliest**) **1** noticeably cold, *esp* unpleasantly so. **2** lacking warmth of feeling; distant or unfriendly: *The atmosphere in the office was distinctly chilly*. **3** tending to arouse fear or apprehension: *I didn't want to dwell on the chilly details of the murder*. ⟫⟫ **chilliness** *noun*.

Chiltern Hundreds /'chiltǝn/ *pl noun* a nominal office for which an MP applies in order to resign their seat.

Word history

named after the *Chiltern Hundreds*, district of Buckinghamshire, England. An MP is not normally allowed to resign before the next General Election, but must do so if he or she accepts an office of profit under the Crown. Stewardship of the Chiltern Hundreds, while purely nominal, is technically such an office. Once an MP has been appointed to the stewardship and vacated the Parliamentary seat, he or she then resigns the stewardship so that it is available for the next MP who wishes to leave Parliament.

chimaera /ki'miǝrǝ, kie-/ *noun* (*pl* **chimaeras** *or* collectively **chimaera**) any of a family of marine cartilaginous fishes with a tapering tail: family Chimaeridae. **2** (*pl* **chimaeras**) see CHIMERA. [(sense 1) scientific Latin genus name *Chimaera*, from Latin: see CHIMERA]

chimb /chiem, chim/ *noun* see CHIME³.

chime¹ /chiem/ *noun* **1a** a bell or musically tuned set of bells. **b** a set of objects, e.g. hanging metal bars or tubes, that sound like bells when struck. **c** apparatus for chiming a bell or set of bells. **2** the sound of a bell, e.g. on a clock. **3** (*usu in pl*). **a** the sound of a set of bells. **b** a musical sound like that of bells. [Middle English in the sense of 'cymbal', via Old French from Latin *cymbalum*]

chime² *verb intrans* **1** to make the sounds of a chime. **2** (*usu* + together/with) to be or act in accord: *The music and the mood chimed well together*. ⟫ *verb trans* **1** to cause (a bell) to chime. **2** to signal or indicate (the time) by chiming: *The clock chimed midnight*. ⟫⟫ **chimer** *noun*.

chime³ /chiem, chim/ *or* **chimb** *noun* the projecting rim of a barrel. [Middle English *chimbe*, of Germanic origin]

chime in *verb intrans* **1** (*often* + with) to break into a conversation or discussion, *esp* in order to express an opinion: *At this point David chimed in with his version of the story*. **2** (*often* + with) to combine harmoniously with a person or policy.

chimenea *noun* a round, somewhat pear-shaped, open-fronted, wood-burning clay stove or fireplace with a chimney, orig from Mexico. [Spanish *chimenea* chimney, fireplace, hearth]

chimera *or* **chimaera** /ki'miǝrǝ, kie-/ *noun* (*pl* **chimeras** *or* **chimaeras**) **1a** (**Chimera, Chimaera**) in Greek mythology, a fire-breathing female monster that had a lion's head, a goat's body, and a serpent's tail. **b** an imaginary monster made up of incongruous parts. **2a** an illusion or fabrication of the mind, *esp* an unrealizable dream: *There is no chimera vainer than the hope that one human heart shall find sympathy in another* — Edward Bulwer-Lytton. **b** a terror that exists only in the mind. **3** an individual, organ, or part consisting of tissues of diverse genetic constitution, occurring *esp* in plants and most frequently at a graft union. ➤➤ **chimeric** /ki'merik, kie-/ *adj,* **chimerical** /ki'merikl, kie-/ *adj,* **chimerically** /ki'merikli, kie-/ *adv.* [Latin *chimaera* from Greek *chimaira* she-goat, chimera]

chimney /'chimni/ *noun* (*pl* **chimneys**) **1** a vertical structure incorporated into a building and enclosing a flue or flues for carrying off smoke; *esp* the part of such a structure extending above a roof. **2** a structure through which smoke and gases, e.g. from a furnace or steam engine, are discharged. **3** a tube, usu of glass, placed round a flame, e.g. of an oil lamp, to serve as a shield. **4** a narrow cleft, vent, etc, e.g. in rock. [Middle English from early French *cheminée*, via Latin from Greek *kaminos* furnace, fireplace]

chimney breast *noun* the wall that encloses a chimney and projects into a room.

chimneypiece *noun Brit* = MANTELPIECE.

chimney pot *noun* a pipe, usu made of earthenware, at the top of a chimney.

chimney stack *noun* **1** a chimney made of masonry, brickwork, etc, rising above a roof and usu containing several flues. **2** a tall chimney, typically of circular section, serving a factory, power station, etc.

chimney sweep *noun* somebody whose occupation is cleaning soot from chimney flues.

chimp /chimp/ *noun informal* = CHIMPANZEE.

chimpanzee /chimpan'zee/ *noun* an anthropoid ape of equatorial Africa with predominantly black coloration: *Pan troglodytes* and *Pan paniscus.* [Kongo *chimpenzi*]

Chin. *abbr* Chinese.

chin[1] /chin/ *noun* the lower portion of the face lying below the lower lip and including the prominence of the lower jaw. ✻ **keep one's chin up** to remain cheerful in trying circumstances. **take it on the chin** to accept (a difficult situation) bravely or stoically. [Old English *cinn*]

chin[2] *verb trans* (**chinned, chinning**) **1** to bring (something) to or hold (something) with the chin: *He chinned his violin and began to play.* **2** e.g. in gymnastics, to raise one's chin to the level of (e.g. a bar) by pulling oneself up with one's arms.

china /'chienə/ *noun* **1a** porcelain. **b** vitreous porcelain ware, e.g. dishes and vases, for domestic use. **2** *chiefly Brit* = BONE CHINA. **3a** = CHINAWARE. **b** crockery: *Set the table with the good china.* [Persian *chini* Chinese porcelain]

china clay *noun* = KAOLIN.

chinagraph /'chienəgrahf/ *noun* a pencil that will write on china or glass.

chinagraph pencil *noun* = CHINAGRAPH.

chinaman *noun* (*pl* **chinamen**) **1** (**Chinaman**) *dated* a native of China. **2** in cricket, a ball bowled by a slow left-hander that breaks from the off to the leg side on bouncing as viewed by a right-handed batsman. [(sense 2) perhaps from bowling of this type by Ellis Achong d.1986, Chinese-born West Indian cricketer]

china stone *noun* **1** a form of partially decomposed kaolinized granite with unaltered feldspar, that is pulverized and used in the manufacture of certain types of porcelain. **2** a type of smooth-textured, fine-grained limestone.

China tea *noun* a kind of tea that is made from a tea plant grown in China and is smoke-cured.

Chinatown *noun* the Chinese quarter of a city.

chinaware /'chienəweə/ *noun* tableware made of china.

chincherinchee /chinchə'rinchee, -rin'chee, chingkə-/ *noun* a plant of the lily family of S African origin with long fleshy leaves and tall stems carrying many white, cream, or yellow flowers: *Ornithogalum thyrsoides.* [imitative of the sound of the flower-stalks rubbing together in the wind]

chinchilla /chin'chilə/ *noun* **1a** either of two species of S American rodents the size of a large squirrel: genus *Chinchilla.* **b** its soft pearly-grey fur. **2a** a breed of domestic rabbit with long white or greyish fur. **b** a breed of cat with similar fur. **c** the fur of the chinchilla rabbit. [Spanish *chinchilla*]

chin-chin /,chin 'chin/ *interj Brit* used as an informal greeting, farewell, or toast. [Chinese (Pekingese) *qing, qingqing* phrase of salutation]

Chindit /'chindit/ *noun* a member of an Allied force fighting behind Japanese lines in Burma (now Myanmar) during WWII. [Burmese *chinthé*, a fabulous lionlike animal]

chine[1] *noun* **1a** the backbone, *esp* of an animal. **b** a cut of meat including the whole or part of the backbone: *a prodigious chine of roasted bear's meat* — J Fenimore Cooper. **2** a mountain ridge. **3** the intersection of the bottom and sides of a boat. [Middle English from early French *eschine*, of Germanic origin]

chine[2] *verb trans* to separate the backbone from the ribs of (a joint of meat), or to cut through the backbone of (a carcass).

chine[3] /chien/ *noun Brit* a steep-sided ravine, *esp* in Dorset or the Isle of Wight. [Old English *cine, cinu* crack, chasm]

Chinese /chie'neez/ *noun* (*pl* **Chinese**) **1** a native or inhabitant of China. **2** a group of related Sino-Tibetan languages of the people of China, *esp* Mandarin. ➤➤ **Chinese** *adj.*

Word history
China, country in Asia. Words from Chinese that are well established in English include *kowtow, tea, tycoon, typhoon,* and *yen.* More recent borrowings, often reflecting western interest in Chinese cookery, medicine, and philosophy, include *chop suey, ginseng, wok, yang,* and *yin.*

Chinese cabbage *noun* either of two Asian varieties of cabbage widely used in oriental cookery: *Brassica pekinensis* and *Brassica chinensis.*

Chinese chequers (*NAmer* **Chinese checkers**) *pl noun* (*treated as sing.*) a board game for two to six players in which each player tries to be the first to transfer a set of pegs or marbles from a home point to the opposite point of a star-shaped board by single moves or jumps.

Chinese gooseberry *noun* = KIWI FRUIT.

Chinese lantern *noun* **1** a collapsible lantern of thin coloured paper. **2** a widely cultivated plant related to the nightshade and petunia, which has thin-walled bulbous calyxes (outer part of flower; see CALYX) that are a brilliant orange-red when mature: *Physalis alkekengi.*

Chinese leaf *noun* (*usu in pl*) an Asiatic type of cabbage widely used in oriental cookery: *Brassica chinensis.*

Chinese puzzle *noun* an intricate or ingenious puzzle.

Chinese wall *noun* **1** an apparently insurmountable barrier, *esp* a serious obstacle to understanding. **2** a code of practice prohibiting the exchange of sensitive information among different departments of a financial institution in order to avoid conflicts of interest and insider dealing. [probably with reference to the *Great Wall of China,* a defensive wall built in the third cent. BC between China and Mongolia]

Chinese white *noun* a white zinc oxide pigment.

Chink /chingk/ *noun offensive or derog* a Chinese person. [alteration of *Chinese*]

chink[1] /chingk/ *noun* **1** a small slit or fissure: *They could see in through a chink in the curtain.* **2** a means of evasion or escape; a loophole: *He found a chink in the law.* [prob alteration of CHINE[3]]

chink[2] *noun* a short sharp metallic sound. [imitative]

chink[3] *verb intrans* to make a sharp light metallic or ringing sound. ➤ *verb trans* to cause (something) to make such a sound.

Chinkie or **Chinky** /'chingki/ *noun* (*pl* **Chinkies**) *Brit, informal* **1** *offensive or derog* a Chinese person. **2** *dated.* **a** a Chinese meal, *esp* a takeaway meal. **b** a restaurant or takeaway where one can buy a Chinese meal.

chinless *adj Brit, informal, derog* lacking firmness of purpose; ineffectual.

chinless wonder *noun Brit, informal, derog* a person, *esp* a male of the upper classes, who is weak and foolish.

chinned /chind/ *adj* (*used in combinations*) having a chin of the kind specified: *double-chinned.*

Chino- *comb. form* forming words, with the meaning: Chinese; = SINO-: *Chino-Japanese.*

chino /'cheenoh/ *noun* (*pl* **chinos**) **1** a cotton twill fabric, usu khaki-coloured. **2** (*in pl*) trousers made of chino. [American Spanish *chino*]

chinoiserie /shee'nwahzəri/ *noun* **1** a style in art and interior design that copies Chinese features or motifs. **2** an object or a decoration in this style. [French *chinoiserie*, from *chinois* Chinese, from *Chine* China]

Chinook /chi'noohk, chi'nook/ *noun* (*pl* **Chinooks** *or collectively* **Chinook**) **1** a member of a Native American people of Oregon. **2** the language of this people. ⟫ **Chinook** *adj*. [Salish *Tsinúk*]

chinook *noun* **1** a warm moist southwesterly wind of the NW coast of the USA. **2** a warm dry westerly wind of the E slopes of the Rocky Mountains. [named after the CHINOOK]

Chinook Jargon *noun* a mixture of Chinook and other Native American languages, French, and English, formerly used as a lingua franca in the NW USA and in W Canada and Alaska.

chintz /chints/ *noun* a printed plain-weave fabric, usu of glazed cotton. [earlier *chints*, pl of *chint*, from Hindi *chīt*]

chintzy *adj* (**chintzier, chintziest**) **1** made or decorated with, or as if with, chintz. **2** gaudy; cheap. ⟫ **chintziness** *noun*.

chinwag *noun informal* a conversation or chat: *I had a good chinwag with my sister*.

chip¹ /chip/ *noun* **1a** a small thin flat piece, e.g. of wood or stone, cut, struck, or flaked off. **b** a small thin slice or piece of chocolate, etc. **2** a flaw left after a chip is removed: *There's a chip in this cup*. **3a** *chiefly Brit* a strip of potato fried in deep fat. **b** *NAmer, Aus* = CRISP². **4** a counter used as a token for money in gambling games. **5** an integrated circuit or the small piece of semiconductor, *esp* silicon, on which it is constructed. **6a** = CHIP SHOT. **b** in football, rugby, etc, a kick in which the ball is lifted into the air and travels over a short distance. **7** a thin strip of wood or similar material used for weaving baskets, hats, etc. ✳ **a chip off the old block** a person who resembles either of their parents. **a chip on one's shoulder** a challenging, belligerent, or embittered attitude. **have had one's chips** *informal* to be beaten, doomed, dead, etc. **when the chips are down** when the crucial or critical point has been reached: *When the chips are down, you have only yourself to depend on*. [Middle English, of Germanic origin]

chip² *verb* (**chipped, chipping**) ⟩ *verb trans* **1a** to cut or hew (something) with an edged tool. **b** (*often* + off/away) to cut or break (a small piece) from something. **c** to cut or break a fragment from (something). **2** to kick or hit (a ball, pass, etc) in a short high arc. **3** *Brit* to cut (potatoes) into chips. ⟩ *verb intrans* **1** to break off in small pieces. **2** to play a chip shot.

chipboard *noun* a board made from compressed wood chips and glue, used e.g. for flooring.

chip in *verb intrans informal* **1** to contribute: *Everyone chipped in for the gift*. **2** *Brit* to interrupt or add a comment to a conversation between other people. ⟩ *verb trans Brit, informal* to contribute (something): *She chipped in £5 for the gift*.

chipmunk /'chipmungk/ *noun* any of numerous species of small striped American squirrels: genera *Tamias* and *Eutamius*. [alteration of earlier *chitmunk*, of Algonquian origin]

chipolata /chipə'lahtə/ *noun* a small sausage. [French *chipolata* from Italian *cipollata*, fem of *cipollato* with onions, from *cipolla* onion, ultimately from Latin *cepa*]

Chippendale /'chipəndayl/ *adj* of an 18th-cent. English furniture style characterized by graceful outline and fine ornamentation. [named after Thomas *Chippendale* d.1779, English cabinetmaker and designer]

chipper /'chipə/ *adj informal* cheerful; bright: *She, Rosie, was game for anything, but poor Carlo hadn't been feeling exactly chipper* — John Mortimer. [prob from northern English dialect *kipper* lively]

chipping /'chiping/ *noun* (*usu in pl*) a fragment of stone used in surfacing roads.

chippy¹ /'chipi/ *noun* (*pl* **chippies**) *Brit, informal* **1** a shop selling fish and chips. **2** a carpenter.

chippy² *adj* (**chippier, chippiest**) touchy; sensitive.

chip shot *noun* a short shot in golf that lofts the ball to the green and allows it to roll.

chir- *or* **chiro-** *comb. form* forming words, denoting: hand: *chiropractic*. [via Latin from Greek *cheir-, cheiro-*, from *cheir* hand]

chiral /'kierəl/ *adj* said of a crystal or molecule: not able to be superimposed on its mirror image. ⟫ **chirality** /kie'raliti/ *noun*. [CHIR- + -AL¹, literally 'handed', i.e. asymmetric]

Chi-Rho /,kie 'roh/ *noun* (*pl* **Chi-Rhos**) a Christian monogram and symbol formed from the first two letters, χ and ρ, of the Greek word for *Christ*. [CHI¹ + RHO]

chiro- *comb. form* see CHIR-.

chirography /kie'rogrəfi/ *noun* handwriting; penmanship. ⟫ **chirographer** *noun*, **chirographic** /-'grafik/ *adj*, **chirographical** /-'grafikl/ *adj*.

chiromancy /'kierəmansi/ *noun* = PALMISTRY. ⟫ **chiromancer** *noun*. [prob from early French *chiromancie* from medieval Latin *chiromantia*, from Greek *cheir-* CHIRO- + *-manteia* -MANCY]

chiropody /ki'ropədi/ *noun* the care and treatment of the human foot in health and disease. ⟫ **chiropodist** *noun*. [CHIRO- + -POD, from its original concern with both hands and feet]

chiropractic /kierə'praktik/ *noun* a system of healing disease that employs manipulation and adjustment of body structures, e.g. the spinal column. ⟫ **chiropractor** /'kie-/ *noun*. [CHIRO- + Greek *praktikos*. see PRACTICAL]

chiropteran¹ /kie'roptərən/ *noun* = BAT³ (1). [CHIRO- + -PTERAN]

chiropteran² *adj* relating to bats.

chirp¹ /chuhp/ *verb intrans* **1** said of a small bird or insect: to make a short shrill sound. **2** to make a sound or speak in a tone resembling the short shrill sound of a small bird or insect. ⟩ *verb trans* to say (something) in a lively chirping manner. [imitative]

chirp² *noun* the short shrill sound of a small bird or insect, or a sound resembling this.

chirpy *adj* (**chirpier, chirpiest**) *informal* lively; cheerful. ⟫ **chirpily** *adv*, **chirpiness** *noun*.

chirr¹ /chuh/ *verb intrans* said of a grasshopper, etc: to make a characteristic trilled sound. [imitative]

chirr² *noun* the trilled sound of a grasshopper, etc.

chirrup¹ /'chirəp/ *verb intrans* (**chirruped, chirruping**) said *esp* of a bird: to chirp. ⟫ **chirrupy** *adj*. [imitative]

chirrup² *noun* a chirp.

chisel¹ /'chizl/ *noun* a metal tool with a cutting edge at the end of a blade, used in dressing, shaping, or working wood, stone, or metal. [Middle English from early French, prob alteration of *chisoir* goldsmith's chisel, from (assumed) vulgar Latin *caesorium* cutting instrument, from Latin *caesus*, past part. of *caedere* to cut]

chisel² *verb* (**chiselled, chiselling**, *NAmer* **chiseled, chiseling**) ⟩ *verb trans* **1** to cut or work (something) with, or as if with, a chisel. **2** *informal*. **a** to trick or cheat (somebody): *He's chiselled me out of my prize*. **b** to obtain (something) by cheating: *He chiselled £100 out of them*. ⟩ *verb intrans informal* to trick or cheat. ⟫ **chiseller** *noun*.

chiselled (*NAmer* **chiseled**) *adj* sharply defined; clear-cut: *chiselled features*.

chi-square test /kie/ *or* **chi-squared test** *noun* a statistical test that indicates the agreement between a set of observed values and a set of values derived from a theoretical model.

chit¹ /chit/ *noun* an immature, often disrespectful, young woman, *esp* one of slight build: *I'm not going to be ordered about by a mere chit of a girl*. [Middle English *chitte* kitten, cub; earlier history unknown]

chit² *noun* a small slip of paper with writing on it, *esp* an order for goods or a note of money owed. [Hindi *ciṭṭhī*]

chital /'cheetl/ *noun* = AXIS DEER. [Hindi *cītal* from Sanskrit *citrala* variegated, from *citra* spotted, bright]

chitchat¹ /'chitchat/ *noun informal* small talk; gossip. [reduplication of CHAT¹]

chitchat² *verb intrans* (**chitchatted, chitchatting**) *informal* to make small talk; to gossip.

chitin /'kietin/ *noun* a horny POLYSACCHARIDE (type of carbohydrate) that forms part of the hard outer covering of *esp* insects and crustaceans. ⟫ **chitinous** *adj*. [French *chitine* from Greek *chitōn* chiton, tunic]

chiton /'kiet(o)n/ *noun* any of a class of marine molluscs with a shell of many plates: class Polyplacophora. [Latin genus name of one genus of the class, from Greek *chitōn* tunic, of Semitic origin]

chitterling /'chitəling/ *noun* (*usu in pl*) a section of the smaller intestines of pigs, *esp* when prepared as food. [Middle English *chiterling*]

chitty /'chiti/ *noun* (*pl* **chitties**) *Brit, informal* = CHIT².

chivalrous /'shiv(ə)lrəs/ *adj* **1a** honourable; generous. **b** graciously courteous and considerate, *esp* to women. **2** having the characteristics of a knight, e.g. valour or gallantry. **3** of or characteristic of knight-errantry. ⟫ **chivalrously** *adv*, **chivalrousness** *noun*.

[Middle English from early French *chevalereus*, from *chevalier*: see CHEVALIER]

chivalry /'shiv(ə)lri/ *noun* **1** the system, spirit, or customs of medieval knighthood. **2a** the qualities, e.g. courage, integrity, and consideration, of an ideal knight; chivalrous conduct. **b** courteous behaviour, *esp* towards women: *I admit it is more fun to punt than be punted, and that a desire to have all the fun is nine-tenths of the law of chivalry* — Dorothy L Sayers. **3** *archaic* (*treated as sing. or pl*). **a** knights. **b** mounted men-at-arms. ➤➤ **chivalric** /shi'valrik, 'shiv-/ *adj*. [Middle English *chivalrie* from Old French *chevalerie*, from *chevalier*: see CHEVALIER]

chive /chiev/ *noun* (*usu in pl*) a perennial plant related to the onion whose long thin leaves are used to flavour and garnish food: *Allium schoenoprasum*. [Middle English via French from Latin *cepa* onion]

chivvy *or* **chivy** /'chivi/ *verb trans* (**chivvies** *or* **chivies, chivvied** *or* **chivied, chivvying** *or* **chivying**) *informal* **1** to tease or annoy (somebody) with persistent petty attacks; to harass (them). **2** (*often* + up/along) to rouse (somebody) to activity. [prob from English dialect *Chevy Chase* chase, confusion, the title of a ballad celebrating a battle in the Cheviot Hills in 1388]

chlamydia /klə'midi·ə/ *noun* (*pl* **chlamydia** *or* **chlamydiae** /-ee/) any of a genus of micro-organisms that are intracellular parasites causing infections of the eye and the urinogenital system: genus *Chlamydia*. [Latin genus name, from Latin *chlamyd-, chlamys* mantle]

chlamydomonas /ˌklamidə'mohnəs/ *noun* a single-celled green alga that has two flagella (whip-like extensions; see FLAGELLUM) and is common in soil and fresh water: genus *Chlamydomonas*. [Latin genus name, from Latin *chlamyd-, chlamys* mantle + *monas* monad]

chlor- *or* **chloro-** *comb. form* forming words, with the meanings: **1** green: *chlorophyll; chlorosis*. **2** chlorine: *chloride; chlorpromazine*. [scientific Latin from Greek, from *chlōros* greenish yellow]

chloral /'klawrəl/ *noun* = CHLORAL HYDRATE.

chloral hydrate *noun* a synthetic drug used as a sedative and hypnotic.

chloramphenicol /klawram'fenikol/ *noun* an antibiotic that is effective against a wide range of micro-organisms and is used *esp* to treat typhoid fever. [CHLOR- + *amid-* + PHEN- + NITR- + GLYCOL]

chlorate /'klawrayt/ *noun* a salt containing the radical ClO₃.

chlordane /'klawdayn/ *noun* a chlorinated insecticide. [CHLOR- + *indane*, an oily cyclic hydrocarbon]

chlorella /klə'relə/ *noun* (*pl* **chlorellas** *or* **chlorellae** /-ee/) a single-celled green alga: genus *Chlorella*. [Latin genus name, from Greek *chlōros* greenish yellow]

chloride /'klawried/ *noun* a compound of chlorine with another element or radical, *esp* a salt or ester of hydrochloric acid. [German *Chlorid*, from CHLOR- + *-id* -IDE]

chlorinate /'klawrinayt/ *verb trans* to treat (something) or cause (something) to combine with chlorine or a compound of chlorine. ➤➤ **chlorination** /-'naysh(ə)n/ *noun*, **chlorinator** *noun*.

chlorine /'klawreen/ *noun* a gaseous chemical element of the halogen group that is isolated as a pungent dense greenish yellow gas: symbol Cl, atomic number 17. [CHLOR- + -INE²]

chlorite /'klawriet/ *noun* a salt containing the radical ClO₂. [prob from French, from CHLOR-]

chloro- *comb. form* see CHLOR-.

chlorofluorocarbon /ˌklawroh,flooəroh'kahbən/ *noun* any of various compound methane-based gases containing chlorine and fluorine that are used as refrigerants and as propellant gases in aerosol cans. Chlorofluorocarbons are greenhouse gases and have been held responsible for damage to the earth's ozone layer.

chloroform¹ /'klorəfawm/ *noun* a colourless volatile liquid used *esp* as a solvent and formerly as a general anaesthetic. [French *chloroforme*, from CHLORO- + *formyle* formyl, the chemical group HCO, from its having been regarded as a trichloride of this radical]

chloroform² *verb trans* to treat (somebody) with chloroform or administer chloroform to (them), *esp* so as to produce unconsciousness or death.

Chloromycetin /ˌklorohmie'seetin/ *noun trademark* = CHLORAMPHENICOL. [CHLORO- + Greek *myket-, mykes* fungus + -IN¹]

chlorophyll (*NAmer also* **chlorophyl**) /'klorəfil/ *noun* **1** the green photosynthetic colouring matter of plants. **2** a waxy green

substance containing chlorophyll, extracted from green plants and used as a colouring agent or deodorant. ➤➤ **chlorophyllous** /-'filəs/ *adj*. [French *chlorophylle*, from CHLORO- + Greek *phyllon* leaf]

chloroplast /'klawrohplast/ *noun* a chlorophyll-containing ORGANELLE (part of cell) that is the site of photosynthesis and starch formation in plant cells.

chloroquine /'klawrohkween/ *noun* an antimalarial drug. [CHLORO- + QUINOLINE]

chlorosis /klaw'rohsis/ *noun* **1** an iron-deficiency anaemia of young girls characterized by a greenish colour of the skin. **2** a diseased condition in green plants marked by yellowing or blanching. ➤➤ **chlorotic** /klaw'rotik/ *adj*.

chlorous /'klawrəs/ *adj* of or obtained from trivalent chlorine.

chlorpromazine /klaw'prohməzeen/ *noun* a derivative of phenothiazine used widely as a tranquillizer, *esp* to suppress disturbed behaviour, e.g. in the treatment of schizophrenia. [CHLOR- + PROPYL + METHYL + PHENOTHIAZINE]

ChM *abbr* Master of Surgery. [medieval Latin *Chirurgiae Magister*]

chocaholic /chokə'holik/ *noun* see CHOCOHOLIC.

choc-ice /'chok ies/ *noun Brit* a bar of ice cream covered in chocolate. [short for *chocolate ice*]

chock¹ /chok/ *noun* a wedge or block placed under a door, barrel, wheel, etc to prevent movement. [origin unknown]

chock² *verb trans* **1** to stop (something) or make (something) secure with, or as if with, chocks; to provide (something) with chocks or something similar. **2** to raise or support (a boat, etc) on blocks.

chock-a-block *adj and adv* tightly packed; in a very crowded condition. [CHOCK¹ + A-¹ on + BLOCK¹, orig the position of a tackle when both blocks are together]

chocker /'chokə/ *adj Brit, informal* **1** absolutely full; chock-a-block. **2** *dated* annoyed; fed up.

chock-full *adv* as full as possible. [CHOCK¹]

chocoholic *or* **chocaholic** /chokə'holik/ *noun* somebody who is addicted to or extremely fond of chocolate. [blend of CHOCOLATE¹ and ALCOHOLIC¹]

chocolate¹ /'choklət/ *noun* **1** a paste, powder, or solid block of food prepared from ground roasted cacao seeds, usu sweetened or flavoured: compare COCOA. **2** a sweet made or coated with chocolate. **3** a beverage made by mixing chocolate with hot water or milk. **4** dark brown. ➤➤ **chocolatey** *adj*, **chocolaty** *adj*. [Spanish *chocolate* from Nahuatl *xocoatl*]

chocolate² *adj* dark brown.

chocolate-box *adj* superficially pretty or sentimental: *a chocolate-box painting of a farmhouse.* [from the pictures commonly seen on boxes of chocolates]

Choctaw /'choktaw/ *noun* (*pl* **Choctaws** *or collectively* **Choctaw**) **1a** a member of a Native American people of Mississippi, Alabama, and Louisiana. **b** the language of this people. **2** (**choctaw**) a half turn in ice-skating from either edge of one foot to the opposite edge of the other foot: compare MOHAWK. [Choctaw *Chahta*]

choice¹ /choys/ *noun* **1** the act of choosing; selection.

Editorial note ⸺⸺⸺
To choose is to select one option in preference to others, and to do so for a reason. Rational choice, in this sense, is commonly held to be the product of two things: how much one wants something and one's estimation of the chances of getting it. Social choice is a matter of how the rational choice for a group is determined by the individual rational choices of its members. Choosing is not picking. Choice requires reasons — Professor Jonathan Dancy.

2 the power of choosing; option: *Marriages would in general be as happy, and often more so, if they were all made by the Lord Chancellor … without the parties having any choice in the matter* — Dr Johnson. **3a** somebody or something chosen: *The first candidate would be my choice.* **b** the best part; the elite. **4** a sufficient number and variety to choose among: *I was looking for new shoes, but there wasn't much choice.* [Middle English *chois* from Old French, from *choisir* to choose, of Germanic origin]

choice² *adj* **1** of high quality: *choice meat.* **2** selected with care; well chosen. **3** said of language, etc: vulgar; rude; obscene. ➤➤ **choicely** *adv*, **choiceness** *noun*.

choir /kwie·ə/ *noun* **1** (*treated as sing. or pl*). **a** an organized group of singers. **b** a group of instruments of the same type playing together. **2** the part of a church occupied by the singers or the clergy; *specif* the part of the chancel between the sanctuary and the nave. [Middle English *quer* via Old French *cuer* from Latin *chorus*: see CHORUS[1]]

choirboy *or* **choirgirl** *noun* a boy or girl singer in a choir, *esp* in church.

choir organ *noun* a keyboard and related stops of an organ having mostly soft stops.

choir school *noun* a school primarily intended for the boys of a cathedral choir.

choke[1] /chohk/ *verb trans* **1** to stop the normal breathing of (a person or an animal) by compressing or obstructing the windpipe, or by poisoning available air. **2a** (*often* + back/down) to stop or suppress (something, e.g. tears) or the expression of (something, e.g. emotion). **b** to silence (something): *The government issued a ban designed to choke discussion.* **c** to fill (also + up) to make (somebody) speechless with emotion. **3a** to restrain the growth or activity of (a plant, etc): *The flowers were choked by the weeds.* **b** to obstruct (something) by filling it up or clogging it: *Leaves choked the drain.* **c** to fill (something completely; to jam (it). **4** to enrich the fuel mixture of (a petrol engine) by partially shutting off the air intake of the carburettor. ➤ *verb intrans* **1** to become unable to breathe e.g. because of an obstruction in the windpipe. **2a** to become obstructed or checked. **b** (*also* + up) to become speechless or incapacitated, *esp* from strong emotion. **3** to lose one's composure and fail to perform effectively in a critical situation: *After beating the other contestants, he choked when he had to answer the final question.* [Old English *acēocian*]

choke[2] *noun* **1** the act or sound of choking. **2** a valve in the carburettor of a petrol engine for controlling the amount of air in a fuel-air mixture. **3** = INDUCTOR.

choke[3] *noun* the inedible fibrous central part of a globe artichoke. [back-formation from ARTICHOKE, prob by confusion with CHOKE[2]]

chokeberry /'chohkb(ə)ri/ *noun* (*pl* **chokeberries**) **1** a shrub of the rose family that has brilliant autumn foliage: genus *Aronia*. **2** the small astringent berry of this shrub.

choke chain *noun* a chain collar that may be tightened as a noose and is used in training and controlling dogs.

choked *adj informal* **1** *Brit* angry or resentful. **2** emotionally moved; touched: *in a choked voice.*

chokedamp *noun* a nonexplosive gas containing carbon dioxide that occurs in mines and is incapable of supporting animal life or a flame.

choker *noun* **1** a short necklace or decorative band that fits closely round the throat. **2** a high stiff collar, *esp* a clerical collar.

chokey *or* **choky** *noun* (*pl* **chokeys** *or* **chokies**) *Brit, slang* = PRISON. [Hindi *caukī* shed, lock-up]

choko /'chohkoh/ *noun* (*pl* **chokos**) *Aus, NZ* the succulent green or white pear-shaped fruit of a tropical American vine that tastes like cucumber and is used as a vegetable. [American Spanish *chocho* from Nahuatl *chayotli*]

choky /'chohki/ *noun* see CHOKEY.

chol- *or* **chole-** *or* **cholo-** *comb. form* forming words, denoting: bile; gall: *cholesterol.* [Greek *chol-, cholē-, cholo-,* from *cholē, cholos*]

cholangiography /kə,lanji'ogrəfi/ *noun* X-ray photography of the bile ducts. ➤➤ **cholangiogram** /kə'lanji·əgram/ *noun.* [CHOL- + ANGIO- + -GRAPHY]

chole- *comb. form* see CHOL-.

cholecalciferol /,kohlikal'sifərol/ *noun* the main naturally occurring vitamin D, found in most fish liver oils, formed in the skin of human beings on exposure to sunlight, and essential for the deposition of calcium in bones; vitamin D₃.

choler /'kolə/ *noun* **1** *formal* anger; irascibility: *He had the choler of the obese, easily roused and as easily calmed* — Somerset Maugham. **2** *archaic* = YELLOW BILE. [Middle English *coler* via French from Latin *cholera* bilious disease, from Greek *cholē* bile]

cholera /'kolərə/ *noun* an often fatal infectious epidemic disease caused by a bacterium and marked by severe gastrointestinal disorders, or any of several similar diseases of human beings and domestic animals. ➤➤ **choleraic** /-'rayik/ *adj.* [Middle English *colera* bile, from Latin *cholera*: see CHOLER]

choleric /'kolərik/ *adj formal* angry; irate.

cholesteric /kə'lesterik/ *adj* of or being the form of a liquid crystal characterized by the arrangement of the molecules in layers with the long axes of the molecules parallel to the plane of the layers: compare NEMATIC, SMECTIC.

cholesterol /kə'lestərol/ *noun* a steroid that is present in animal and plant cells and is a possible factor in hardening of the arteries. [French *cholésterine,* from CHOLE- + Greek *stereos* solid]

choli /'chohli/ *noun* (*pl* **cholis**) a short-sleeved close-fitting bodice worn under a sari. [Hindi *colī* from Sanskrit *cola, coḍa*]

choline /'kohleen/ *noun* a naturally occurring substance that is a vitamin of the vitamin B complex essential to liver function. [Greek *cholē* bile + -INE[2]]

cholo- *comb. form* see CHOL-.

chomp[1] /chomp/ *verb trans and intrans* to chew (something) noisily. [by alteration from CHAMP[1]]

chomp[2] *noun* a bite or chew.

Chomskyan[1] *or* **Chomskian** /'chomski·ən/ *adj* characteristic of the work or theories of Noam Chomsky (b.1928), US linguist who argues that the structure of language depends on the structure of the human mind and that linguistics is an integral part of psychology and philosophy.

Chomskyan[2] *or* **Chomskian** *noun* a supporter of Noam Chomsky and his linguistic theories.

chondrite /'kondriet/ *noun* a type of stony meteorite containing chondrules. ➤➤ **chondritic** /kon'dritik/ *adj.* [Greek *chondros* grain + -ITE[1]]

chondrule /'kondroohl/ *noun* a rounded stony granule often found embedded in meteorites and sometimes in marine sediments. [Greek *chondros* grain]

chook /chook/ *noun Aus, NZ* a chicken or fowl. [imitative]

choose /choohz/ *verb* (*past tense* **chose** /chohz/, *past part.* **chosen** /'chohz(ə)n/) ➤ *verb trans* **1a** to select (somebody or something) freely and after consideration. **b** to decide on (somebody), *esp* to elect (them): *They chose her as leader.* **2a** to decide (to do something): *She chose to go by train.* **b** to wish (to do something): *Supposing I don't choose to stay?* ➤ *verb intrans* **1** (*also* + between) to make a selection; to decide: *We had to choose between chicken and fish.* **2** to wish to do something: *I'll go if I choose.* ➤➤ **chooser** *noun.* [Old English *cēosan*]

choosy *or* **choosey** /'choohzi/ *adj* (**choosier, choosiest**) fastidiously selective; particular. ➤➤ **choosily** *adv,* **choosiness** *noun.*

chop[1] /chop/ *verb* (**chopped, chopping**) ➤ *verb trans* **1a** (*usu* + off/down) to cut into (something) or sever (it), usu by a blow or repeated blows of a sharp instrument: *They chopped down the tree.* **b** (*often* + up) to cut (something) into pieces: *First chop an onion.* **2** to dispense with (something) or to limit the extent, force, or amount of (it): *We were forced to severely chop the budget for this project.* **3a** to strike (a ball) so as to impart backspin. **b** to strike (an opponent, etc) with a short, sharp blow, *esp* with the side of the hand. **4** to subject (a beam of light) to the action of a CHOPPER (6). ➤ *verb intrans* to make a quick stroke or repeated strokes with, or as if with, a sharp instrument. [Middle English *chappen, choppen,* of Germanic origin]

chop[2] *noun* **1** a forceful, usu slanting, blow or stroke with, or as if with, an axe or cleaver or with the side of the hand. **2** a small cut of meat often including part of a rib. **3** an uneven motion of the sea, *esp* when wind and tide are opposed. ✱ **get the chop** *informal* to be dismissed or brought to an abrupt end: *I think this project is going to get the chop.* **give somebody/something the chop** *informal* to dismiss (somebody); to bring (something) to an abrupt end.

chop[3] *verb intrans* (**chopped, chopping**) said *esp* of the wind: to change direction. ✱ **chop and change** *Brit* to keep changing one's mind, plans, etc. **chop logic** to argue with minute oversubtle distinctions. [Old English *cēapian* to barter]

chop[4] *noun Brit, archaic* a seal or official stamp such as was formerly used in China or India, or a licence validated by such a seal. ✱ **not much chop** *Aus, NZ, informal* not very good. [Hindi *chāp* stamp]

chop-chop *adv and interj informal* without delay; quickly. [Pidgin English, reduplication of *chop* fast, from Chinese (Cantonese) *gap* urgent]

chophouse /'chophows/ *noun* a restaurant specializing in meat dishes, *esp* chops or steaks.

chopper *noun* **1a** somebody or something that chops. **b** *Brit* a short-handled axe or cleaver. **2** *informal* a helicopter. **3** *informal* (in *pl*) teeth. **4** *informal* a customized motorcycle, *esp* one with high handlebars. **5** *coarse slang* a penis. **6** a device that interrupts an electric current or a beam of radiation, e.g. light, at short regular intervals.

choppy *adj* (**choppier, choppiest**) said of the sea or other expanse of water: rough with small waves. ➤➤ **choppiness** *noun*. [CHOP³]

chops *pl noun* jaws, or the fleshy covering of the jaws: *The hungry dog licked his chops.* ✳ **lick one's chops** *informal* to show that one is looking forward to something with great pleasure. [alteration of CHAP⁴]

chopstick *noun* either of two slender sticks held between thumb and fingers, used chiefly in oriental countries to lift food to the mouth. [Pidgin English, from *chop* fast (of Chinese origin: see CHOP-CHOP) + STICK¹]

chop suey /'sooh·i/ *noun* (*pl* **chop sueys**) a Chinese-style dish of shredded meat or chicken with bean sprouts and other vegetables, usu served with rice and soy sauce. [Chinese (Cantonese) *jaahp seui* odds and ends, from *jaahp* various + *seui* bits]

choral¹ /'kawrəl/ *adj* accompanied with or designed for singing, *esp* by a choir. ➤➤ **chorally** *adv*. [French *choral* from medieval Latin *choralis*, from Latin *chorus*: see CHORUS¹]

choral² /kə'rahl/ *noun* = CHORALE.

chorale /kə'rahl/ *noun* **1** a traditional hymn or psalm, usu German, for singing in church, or the music composed for one. **2** *chiefly NAmer* (*treated as sing. or pl*) a chorus or choir. [German *Choral*, short for *Choralgesang* choral song]

chord¹ /kawd/ *noun* a combination of notes sounded together. [alteration of Middle English *cord*, short for ACCORD²]

chord² *noun* **1** = CORD¹ (2). **2** a straight line joining two points on the circumference of a circle. **3** an individual emotion or disposition: *That touched the right chord.* **4** the straight line joining the leading and trailing edges of an aerofoil. **5** in building either of the two outside members of a TRUSS¹ (wooden or metal framework used as a structural support). [alteration of CORD¹]

chord³ *verb trans* to add notes to (a melody) to form chords.

chordal *adj* **1** of or suggesting a chord. **2** relating to music characterized more by harmony than by counterpoint.

chordate¹ /'kawdayt/ *noun* any of a large phylum of animals, including the vertebrates, that have at some stage of development a NOTOCHORD (supporting skeleton-like rod), a central nervous system along the back, and gill clefts: phylum Chordata. [derivative of Latin *chorda*: see CORD¹]

chordate² *adj* relating to the chordates.

chore /chaw/ *noun* **1** a routine task or job, *esp* a household one. **2** a difficult, disagreeable, or boring, task. [alteration of *chare*, from Middle English *char* turn, piece of work, from Old English *cierr*]

chorea /ko'ree·ə/ *noun* a nervous disorder marked by spasmodic movements of limbs and facial muscles and by lack of coordination. [scientific Latin from Latin *chorea* dance, from Greek *choreia*, from *choros* CHORUS¹]

choreograph /'koriəgrahf, -graf/ *verb trans* to compose or arrange the steps and dances for (a ballet or piece of music). ➤➤ **choreographer** /-'ogrəfə/ *noun*.

choreography /kori'ogrəfi/ *noun* **1** the composition and arrangement of a ballet or other dance for the stage. **2** stage dancing as distinguished from social or ballroom dancing. **3** the art of representing dance steps and sequences in symbols. ➤➤ **choreographic** /-'grafik/ *adj*, **choreographically** /-'grafikli/ *adv*. [French *chorégraphie*, from Greek *choreia* dance (from *choros* CHORUS¹) + French *-graphie* -GRAPHY]

choric /'korik/ *adj* of or being in the style of a chorus, *esp* a Greek chorus.

chorion /'kawri·ən/ *noun* the outer embryonic membrane of higher vertebrates. ➤➤ **chorionic** /-'onik/ *adj*. [scientific Latin from Greek *chorion*]

chorister /'koristə/ *noun* a singer in a choir; *specif* a choirboy or choirgirl. [Middle English *querister* via Anglo-French *cueristre* from medieval Latin *chorista*, from Latin *chorus*: see CHORUS¹]

chorizo /chə'reezoh/ *noun* (*pl* **chorizos**) a dried pork sausage that is highly seasoned with paprika, pimientos, garlic, and spices. [Spanish *chorizo*]

choroid¹ /'kawroyd/ *noun* a membrane of the eye containing large pigment cells that lies between the RETINA (inner membrane) and the SCLERA (outer coating). [scientific Latin *choroides* from Greek *chorioeidēs* resembling the chorion, from *chorion* CHORION]

choroid² *adj* relating to the choroid.

choroid coat *noun* = CHOROID¹.

choropleth /'korohpleth, 'korəpleth/ *noun* a map presenting the subject under study in terms of average value per unit area within specific boundaries, e.g. density of population per square kilometre shown within local, regional, or national administrative areas, often using a range of colours or shading to show orders of density. [Greek *chōros* place + *plēthos* quantity]

chortle¹ /'chawtl/ *verb intrans* to laugh or chuckle, *esp* in satisfaction or exultation: *'O frabjous day! Callooh! Callay!' he chortled in his joy* — Lewis Carroll; *'Ah well,' he chortled. 'In Tonga we hear things a little late.'* — Simon Winchester. ➤➤ **chortler** *noun*. [blend of CHUCKLE¹ and SNORT¹, portmanteau word invented by Lewis Carroll]

chortle² *noun* a laugh or chuckle.

chorus¹ /'kawrəs/ *noun* **1a** (*treated as sing. or pl*) an organized company of singers who sing in concert; *specif* a body of singers who sing the choral parts of a work, e.g. in opera. **b** a group of dancers and singers supporting the featured players in a musical or revue: *a chorus girl.* **2a** a part of a song or hymn recurring at intervals. **b** a composition sung by a chorus. **3** something performed, sung, or uttered simultaneously by a number of people or animals. **4a** a character, e.g. in Elizabethan drama, who comments on the action, or the part spoken by this character. **b** a group of singers and dancers, e.g. in Greek drama, who comment on the action, or the part sung by them. ✳ **in chorus** in unison. [Latin *chorus* from Greek *choros* ring dance, chorus]

chorus² *verb trans and intrans* (**choruses, chorused, chorusing**) to sing or utter (something) in chorus.

chorus girl *noun* a young woman who sings or dances in the chorus of a musical, cabaret, etc.

chose /chohz/ *verb* past tense of CHOOSE.

chosen¹ /'chohz(ə)n/ *verb* past part. of CHOOSE.

chosen² *adj* selected or marked for favour or special privilege: *This is a privilege granted only to a chosen few.*

chosen³ *pl noun* (**the chosen**) people who are the object of divine favour.

chough /chuf/ *noun* any of several species of birds of the crow family found in Europe and Asia that have red legs and glossy black plumage: genus *Pyrrhocorax*. [Middle English, probably imitative of its call]

choux pastry /shooh/ *noun* a light pastry made with an egg-enriched dough, used for profiteroles, eclairs, etc. [French *choux*, pl of *chou*, literally 'cabbage', denoting a round cake of choux pastry filled with cream, from Latin *caulis* stalk]

chow¹ /chow/ *noun informal* food. [perhaps from Chinese (Pekingese) *jiao* meat dumpling]

chow² *or* **chow chow** *noun* a dog of a breed having a blue-black tongue, a heavy coat, and a broad head. [from a Chinese dialect word related to Cantonese *kau* dog]

chow-chow *noun* a Chinese preserve of ginger, fruits, and peel in heavy syrup. [Pidgin English *chow-chow* mixture]

chowder /'chowdə/ *noun* a thick soup or stew made with clams or other seafood. [French *chaudière* kettle, contents of a kettle, from Latin *caldaria*: see CAULDRON]

chow mein /'mayn/ *noun* a Chinese-style dish of fried noodles usu mixed with shredded meat or poultry and vegetables. [Chinese (Pekingese) *chao mian*, from *chao* to fry + *mian* dough]

CHP *abbr* combined heat and power.

Chr. *abbr* **1** Christ. **2** Christian. **3** relating to the Bible: Chronicles.

chrestomathy /kre'stomuthi/ *noun* (*pl* **chrestomathies**) an anthology of passages of texts, compiled as an aid to learning a language. [Latin *chrestomathia* from Greek *chrēstomatheia*, from *chrēstos* useful + *manthanein* to learn]

chrism /'kriz(ə)m/ *noun* consecrated oil used in Greek and Roman Catholic churches, *esp* in baptism, confirmation, and ordination. [Old English *crisma* via late Latin from Greek *chrisma* chrism, ointment, from *chriein* to anoint]

chrisom /'kriz(ə)m/ *noun* a white cloth or robe put on a child at baptism as a symbol of innocence and formerly also used as a shroud for infants. [Middle English *crisom*, short for *crisom cloth*, from *crisom* CHRISM + CLOTH]

Christ[1] /kriest/ *noun* = MESSIAH (1). ➤➤ **Christlike** *adj*. [Old English *Crist* via Latin from Greek *Christos* anointed, from *chriein* to anoint]

Christ[2] *interj informal* an exclamation of surprise, horror, etc.

Christadelphian[1] /kristə'delfiən/ *noun* a member of a Christian sect that claims to follow the practices of the earliest disciples, interprets the Bible literally, and holds that only the righteous will finally have eternal life, whilst the wicked are to be completely obliterated and the ignorant and unconverted not raised from the dead. [*Christ* + Greek *adelphos* brother]

Christadelphian[2] *adj* relating to the Christadelphians.

christen /'kris(ə)n/ *verb trans* (**christened, christening**) **1a** = BAPTIZE (1), (2). **b** to name (somebody) at baptism. **2** to name or dedicate (a ship, bell, etc) by a ceremony suggestive of baptism. **3** to name (something or somebody): *He christened his car 'Thunderball'*. **4** *informal* to use (something) for the first time. [Old English *cristnian* from *cristen* Christian, via Latin from Greek *christianos*, from *christos*: see CHRIST[1]]

Christendom /'kris(ə)ndəm/ *noun* the community of people or nations professing Christianity. [Old English *cristendōm*, from *cristen* (see CHRISTEN) + -DOM]

christening *noun* **1** the ceremony of baptizing and naming a child. **2** any ceremony or event in which something is christened.

Christian[1] /'krischən/ *noun* **1a** an adherent of Christianity. **b** a member of a Christian denomination, *esp* by baptism. **2** *informal* a good or kind person regardless of religion. [via Latin from Greek *christianos*, from *Christos*: see CHRIST[1]]

Christian[2] *adj* **1** of or consistent with Christianity or Christians. **2** *informal* commendably decent or generous: *She has a very Christian concern for others*. ➤➤ **Christianly** *adv*.

Christian era *noun* (**the Christian era**) the period dating from the birth of Christ.

Christianise /'kristi-əniez/ *verb trans* see CHRISTIANIZE.

Christianity /kristi'aniti/ *noun* **1** the religion based on the life and teachings of Jesus Christ and the Bible.

Editorial note
Christianity is a religion claiming that the life, death, and resurrection of Jesus of Nazareth are the most complete revelation of the nature of God, and that the actions of Jesus were the actions of God and are a means by which individuals can know themselves to be accepted as God's children and become members of the Church — Professor John Rogerson.

2 conformity to the Christian religion, or a branch of it: *I do not ask whether this is Christianity or morality, I ask whether it is decency* — Thomas Paine.

Christianize *or* **Christianise** /'kristi-əniez/ *verb trans* to make (somebody or something) Christian. ➤➤ **Christianization** /-'zaysh(ə)n/ *noun*, **Christianizer** *noun*.

Christian name *noun* **1** a name given at christening or confirmation. **2** a forename.

Christian Science *noun* a religion founded by Mary Baker Eddy d.1910, that includes a practice of spiritual healing. ➤➤ **Christian Scientist** *noun*.

christie *or* **christy** /'kristi/ *noun* (*pl* **christies**) a skiing turn used for stopping or for changing direction during descent, and executed, usu at high speed, by shifting the body weight forwards and swinging round with skis parallel. [by shortening and alteration from *christiania*, from *Christiania*, former name of Oslo in Norway]

Christingle /'kristinggl/ *noun* an orange stuck with a lighted candle and pieces of fruit that is held by children at a Protestant religious service during the Advent or Christmas period as a symbol of the world, Christ as the light of the world, and the fruits of the earth. [prob modification of German *Christkindl* Christ child]

Christmas /'krismas/ *noun* **1** a festival of the Christian Church commemorating the birth of Christ and usu observed as a public holiday, celebrated on 25 December. **2** the festival season from Christmas Eve till the Epiphany on 6 January. ➤➤ **Christmassy** *adj*. [Old English *Cristes mæsse* Christ's mass]

Christmas box *noun Brit* a small gift, usu of money, given at Christmas to people such as postmen or refuse collectors for their services throughout the year.

Christmas cactus *noun* a branching S American cactus with flat stems, short joints, and showy red flowers, commonly grown as a winter-flowering house plant: *Schlumbergera truncata*.

Christmas Eve *noun* the day before Christmas day; *specif* the evening of that day.

Christmas pudding *noun* a rich steamed pudding containing dried fruit, candied peel, spices, brandy, etc, traditionally eaten at Christmas.

Christmas rose *noun* a European plant of the buttercup family that flowers in winter and has white or purplish flowers: *Helleborus niger*.

Christmastide /'krismastied/ *noun* = CHRISTMAS (2).

Christmastime /'krismastiem/ *noun* the Christmas season.

Christmas tree *noun* an evergreen or artificial tree decorated with lights, tinsel, etc at Christmas.

Christo- *comb. form* forming words, denoting: Christ: *Christology*.

Christology /kri'stoləji/ *noun* (*pl* **Christologies**) **1** the branch of theology concerned with the person, character, and role of Christ. **2** any particular theological description of the person, character, and role of Christ. ➤➤ **Christological** /kristə'lojikl/ *adj*.

christy /'kristi/ *noun* (*pl* **christies**) see CHRISTIE.

chrom- *or* **chromo-** *comb. form* forming words, with the meanings: **1** chromium: *chromate*. **2** colour; coloured: *chromolithograph*. [French *chrom-* from Greek *chrōma* colour]

chroma /'krohmə/ *noun* a quality of colour combining hue and saturation. [Greek *chrōma* colour]

chromakey /'krohməkee/ *noun* a digital technique by which a block of a particular colour in a video image can be replaced by another colour or image.

chromat- *or* **chromato-** *comb. form* forming words, with the meaning: colour: *chromaticity*. [Greek *chrōmat-*, *chrōma*]

chromate /'krohmayt/ *noun* a salt or ester of chromic acid. [French *chromate* from Greek *chrōma* colour]

chromatic /kroh'matik/ *adj* **1** relating to colour sensation or intensity of colour. **2a** of or giving all the notes of the chromatic scale. **b** characterized by frequent use of intervals or notes outside the diatonic scale. ➤➤ **chromatically** *adv*, **chromaticism** /-siz(ə)m/ *noun*. [Greek *chrōmatikos* from *chrōmat-*, *chrōma* skin, colour, modified tone]

chromatic aberration *noun* distortion in an optical image caused by the differences in refraction of the different colours of the spectrum and characterized by coloured outlines round an image.

chromaticity /krohmə'tisiti/ *noun* a quality of a colour in terms of its purity and dominant or complementary wavelength.

chromatic scale *noun* a musical scale consisting entirely of semitones.

chromatid /'krohmətid/ *noun* either of the paired strands of a chromosome.

chromatin /'krohmətin/ *noun* a complex of DNA with proteins that forms the chromosomes in the cell nucleus and is readily stained.

chromato- *comb. form* see CHROMAT-.

chromatography /krohmə'togrəfi/ *noun* the separation of chemicals from a mixture by passing the mixture as a solution or vapour over or it through a substance, e.g. paper, which adsorbs the chemicals to differing extents. ➤➤ **chromatograph** /-'matəgrahf/ *noun*, **chromatographic** /-matə'grafik/ *adj*.

chrome[1] /krohm/ *noun* **1** chromium, or a pigment formed from it. **2** a plating of chromium, or something with such a plating. [French *chrome* from Greek *chrōma* colour; because of the bright colours of some chromium compounds]

chrome[2] *verb trans* **1** to treat (something) with a compound of chromium, e.g. in dyeing. **2** to plate (something) with chromium.

-chrome *comb. form* forming nouns and adjectives, with the meanings: **1** coloured; coloured thing: *polychrome*. **2** colouring matter: *urochrome*. [medieval Latin *-chromat-*, *-chroma* coloured thing, from Greek *chrōmat-*, *chrōma* colour]

chrome yellow *noun* a yellow pigment consisting essentially of lead chromate.

chromic /'krohmik/ *adj* of or derived from trivalent chromium.

chrominance /'krohminəns/ *noun* the colour information in a colour television signal. [CHROM- + LUMINANCE]

chromite /'krohmiet/ *noun* a mineral that consists of a magnetic oxide of iron and chromium. [German *Chromit*, from CHROM-]

chromium /'krohmi·əm/ *noun* a blue-white metallic chemical element found naturally only in combination and used *esp* in alloys and in electroplating: symbol Cr, atomic number 24. [scientific Latin *chromium* from French *chrome*: see CHROME¹]

chromo /'krohmoh/ *noun* (*pl* **chromos**) = CHROMOLITHOGRAPH.

chromo- *comb. form* see CHROM-.

chromolithograph /krohmoh'lithəgrahf/ *noun* a picture printed in colours from a series of stones prepared by the lithographic process. ➤➤ **chromolithographer** /-li'thografə/ *noun*, **chromolithographic** /-'grafik/ *adj*, **chromolithography** /-'thografi/ *noun*.

chromosome /'krohməsohm/ *noun* any of the gene-carrying bodies that contain DNA and protein and are found in the cell nucleus. ➤➤ **chromosomal** /-'sohml/ *adj*. [CHROMO- + -SOME³]

chromosphere /'krohməsfiə/ *noun* the lower layer of the sun's atmosphere that is immediately above the PHOTOSPHERE (luminous surface), or a similar part of the atmosphere of any star. ➤➤ **chromospheric** /-'sferik/ *adj*.

chromous /'krohməs/ *adj* of or derived from bivalent chromium.

Chron. *abbr* Chronicles (books of the Bible).

chron- *or* **chrono-** *comb. form* forming words, denoting: time: *chronology*. [Greek *chron-* from *chronos*]

chronic /'kronik/ *adj* **1a** said *esp* of an illness: marked by long duration or frequent recurrence: compare ACUTE¹. **b** suffering from a chronic disease: *a chronic alcoholic*. **2a** always present or encountered, *esp* constantly troubling: *chronic financial difficulties*. **b** habitual; persistent: *a chronic grumbler*. **3** *Brit, informal* bad; terrible: *His singing is absolutely chronic*. ➤➤ **chronically** *adv*, **chronicity** /kro'nisiti/ *noun*. [French *chronique* from Greek *chronikos* of time, from *chronos* time]

chronic fatigue syndrome *noun* a condition characterized by extreme and long-lasting tiredness that is not alleviated by bed rest and is made worse by any physical or mental exertion, often accompanied by muscle and joint pains, weakness, slight fever, sore throat, and depression. The cause is unknown and it can last for years.

chronicle¹ /'kronikl/ *noun* **1** a continuous and detailed historical account of events arranged chronologically without analysis or interpretation. **2** a narrative. [Middle English from Anglo-French *cronicle*, alteration of Old French *chronique*, via Latin from Greek *chronika*, neuter pl of *chronikos*: see CHRONIC]

chronicle² *verb trans* to record (events) in or as if in a chronicle. ➤➤ **chronicler** *noun*.

Chronicles *pl noun* (*treated as sing. or pl*) either of two historical books of canonical Jewish and Christian Scripture.

chrono- *comb. form* see CHRON-.

chronograph /'krohnəgrahf/ *noun* an instrument for accurately measuring and recording time intervals. ➤➤ **chronographic** /-'grafik/ *adj*.

chronologic /kronə'lojik/ *adj* = CHRONOLOGICAL.

chronological /kronə'lojikl/ *adj* of or arranged in or according to the order of time: *chronological tables of British history*. ➤➤ **chronologically** *adv*.

chronology /krə'noləji/ *noun* (*pl* **chronologies**) **1** a method for setting past events in order of occurrence, or the scientific study or use of such a method. **2** an arrangement in order of occurrence; *specif* such an arrangement presented in tabular or list form. ➤➤ **chronologist** *noun*. [Latin *chronologia*, from CHRONO- + -LOGY]

chronometer /krə'nomitə/ *noun* an instrument for measuring time, *esp* one designed to keep time with great accuracy.

chronometry /krə'nometri/ *noun* the science of accurate time measurement. ➤➤ **chronometric** /kronə'metrik/ *adj*, **chronometrical** /kronə'metrikl/ *adj*, **chronometrically** /kronə'metrikli/ *adv*.

chrys- *or* **chryso-** *comb. form* forming words, with the meaning: gold; yellow: *chrysolite*. [Greek *chrys-* from *chrysos* gold, of Semitic origin]

chrysalid /'krisəlid/ *noun* = CHRYSALIS.

chrysalis /'krisəlis/ *noun* (*pl* **chrysalises** *or* **chrysalides** /kri'salideez/) **1** a pupa, *esp* of a butterfly or moth, or the case enclosing it.

2 a sheltered state or stage of being or growth: *ready to emerge from the chrysalis of adolescence*. [Latin *chrysallid-, chrysallis* gold-coloured pupa of a butterfly, from Greek *chrysos* gold, of Semitic origin]

chrysanthemum /kri'zanthiməm/ *noun* any of various species of plants with brightly coloured often double flower heads: genera *Chrysanthemum* and *Dendranthema*. [Latin genus name, from Greek *chrysanthemon*, from CHRYS- + *anthemon* flower]

chryselephantine /kriseli'fantin/ *adj* said *esp* of classical Greek sculpture: made of, overlaid with, or decorated with gold and ivory. [Greek *chryselephantinos*, from CHRYS- + *elephantinos* made of ivory, from *elephant-, elephas* ivory, elephant]

chryso- *comb. form* see CHRYS-.

chrysoberyl /'krisəberil/ *noun* a yellow or pale green mineral consisting of beryllium aluminium oxide, used as a gem. [via Latin from Greek *chrysobēryllos*, from CHRYS- + *bēryllos* BERYL]

chrysolite /'krisəliet/ *noun* = OLIVINE. [Middle English *crisolite* via Old French and Latin from Greek *chrysolithos* from CHRYSO- + *-lithos* -LITE]

chrysoprase /'krisəprayz/ *noun* an apple-green variety of chalcedony that is used as a gemstone. [Middle English *crisopace* via French from Latin *chrysoprasus* from Greek *chrysoprasos*, from CHRYSO- + *prason* leek]

chrysotile /'krisətiel/ *noun* a type of fibrous silky asbestos. [German *Chrysotil*, from CHRYSO- + *-til* fibre, from Greek *tillein* to pluck]

chthonian /'thohni-ən/ *adj* = CHTHONIC.

chthonic /'thonik/ *adj* of the underworld; infernal: *chthonic deities*. [Greek *chthon-, chthōn* earth]

chub /chub/ *noun* (*pl* **chubs** *or collectively* **chub**) **1** a European freshwater fish of the carp family: *Leuciscus cephalus*. **2** any of several species of similar marine or freshwater fish: family Cyprinidae. [Middle English *chubbe*; previous history unknown]

Chubb /chub/ *noun trademark* a type of lock with a device for jamming the bolt if an attempt is made to pick it. [named after Charles *Chubb* d.1846, English locksmith]

chubby /'chubi/ *adj* (**chubbier, chubbiest**) plump: *a chubby boy*. ➤➤ **chubbiness** *noun*. [CHUB (because of its short thick body) + -Y¹]

chuck¹ /chuk/ *verb trans* **1** to pat or tap (somebody): *He chucked her under the chin*. **2** *informal*. **a** (*often* + away) to toss or throw (something). **b** (*often* + out/away) to discard (something). **3** *informal* (+ *in/up*) to leave (something or somebody); to GIVE UP: *He chucked his job after a couple of weeks*. * **chuck it down** *informal* to rain heavily. [perhaps from early French *chuquer, choquer* to knock]

chuck² *noun* **1** a pat or nudge under the chin. **2** *informal* a throw. * **get the chuck** *Brit, informal* to be dismissed or rejected, *esp* from a relationship. **give somebody the chuck** *Brit, informal* to dismiss or reject somebody, *esp* from a relationship.

chuck³ *noun* **1** a cut of beef that includes most of the neck and the area about the shoulder blade. **2** a device for holding a workpiece, e.g. for turning on a lathe, or a tool, e.g. in a drill. [English dialect *chuck* lump, log, prob variant of CHOCK¹]

chuck⁴ *noun dialect* a term of endearment: *Be innocent of the knowledge, dearest chuck, till thou applaud the deed* — Shakespeare. [Middle English *chuk*, from *chukken* to make a clucking noise, of imitative origin]

chuckle¹ /'chukl/ *verb intrans* to laugh inwardly or quietly. [prob frequentative of *chuck* to make a clucking noise, of imitative origin]

chuckle² *noun* an inward or quiet laugh.

chucklehead *noun informal* a stupid person. ➤➤ **chuckleheaded** /-'hedid/ *adj*. [obsolete *chuckle* lumpish (prob from CHUCK³) + HEAD¹]

chuck out *verb trans informal* to eject (somebody) from a place or an office; to dismiss (them). ➤➤ **chucker-out** *noun*.

chuck steak *noun* = CHUCK³ (1).

chuck wagon *noun NAmer* a wagon carrying a stove and provisions for cooking, e.g. on a ranch. [English dialect *chuck* food]

chuddar /'chudə/ *noun* see CHADOR.

chuff¹ /chuf/ *verb intrans* to produce or move with a sound made by, or as if by, a steam engine releasing steam regularly. [imitative]

chuff² *noun* the sound of a steam engine releasing steam regularly.

chuffed *adj Brit, informal* pleased. [English dialect *chuff* fat, proud, happy]

chug[1] /chug/ *verb intrans* (**chugged, chugging**) to move or go with a repetitive dull explosive sound made by, or as if by, a labouring engine. [imitative]

chug[2] *noun* a dull repetitive explosive sound made by e.g. an engine labouring.

chukar /chu'kah/ *or* **chukor** /chu'kaw/ *noun* (*pl* **chukar** *or* **chukors** *or collectively* **chukar** *or* **chukor**) a largely grey-and-black Indian partridge: *Alectoris chukar*. [Hindi *cakor*]

chukka /'chukə/ *noun* **1** see CHUKKER. **2** (*also* **chukka boot**) an ankle-length leather boot worn for playing polo.

chukker *or* **chukka** /'chukə/ *noun* any of the periods of play in a polo game. [Hindi *cakkar* circular course, from Sanskrit *cakra* wheel, circle]

chukor /chu'kaw/ *noun* see CHUKAR.

chum[1] /chum/ *noun informal, dated* a close friend; a mate. [perhaps by shortening and alteration from *chamber fellow* roommate]

chum[2] *verb intrans* (**chummed, chumming**) *Scot, informal* to accompany (somebody) as a friend. ✻ **chum up** *dated* (*often* + with) to form a friendship, *esp* a close one.

chummy *adj* (**chummier, chummiest**) *informal* friendly; intimate. ➤➤ **chummily** *adv,* **chumminess** *noun.*

chump /chump/ *noun* **1** a cut of meat taken from between the loin and hindleg, *esp* of a lamb, mutton, or pork carcass. **2** *informal* a fool; a stupid person: *Chumps always make the best husbands. When you marry, Sally, grab a chump* — P G Wodehouse. ✻ **off one's chump** *Brit, slang* crazy; mad. [perhaps blend of CHUNK and LUMP[1]]

chunder /'chundə/ *verb intrans* (**chundered, chundering**) *chiefly Aus, informal* to vomit. [origin unknown]

chunk /chungk/ *noun* **1** a lump, *esp* one of a firm or hard material, e.g. wood. **2** *informal* a fairly large quantity: *He put a sizable chunk of money on the race.* [perhaps alteration of English dialect *chuck:* see CHUCK[3]]

chunky *adj* (**chunkier, chunkiest**) **1** broad and heavy; stocky. **2** filled with chunks: *chunky marmalade.* **3** said of materials, clothes, etc: thick and heavy. ➤➤ **chunkiness** *noun.*

Chunnel /'chunl/ *noun* (**the Chunnel**) *informal* the railway tunnel under the English Channel linking England and France. [blend of CHANNEL[1] and TUNNEL[1]]

chunter /'chuntə/ *verb intrans* (**chuntered, chuntering**) *Brit, informal* (*often* + on) to talk or mutter incessantly and usu irrelevantly. [prob imitative]

church[1] /chuhch/ *noun* **1a** a building for public worship, *esp* Christian worship. **b** a place of worship used by an established denomination, *esp* the Church of England, as opposed to a Nonconformist body: compare CHAPEL[1] (2A). **2** (**the Church**) institutionalized Christian religion, *esp* the established Christian religion of a country. **3a** (**the Church**) a body or organization of religious believers, e.g. the whole body of Christians. **b** = DENOMINATION (1). **c** = CONGREGATION (2). **4** an occasion for public worship: *He goes to church every Sunday.* **5** (**the church**) the clerical profession: *She considered the church as a possible career.* ➤➤ **churchly** *adj,* **churchman** *noun,* **churchwoman** *noun.* [Old English *circe* from a prehistoric West Germanic word derived from Greek *kyriakos* of the lord, from *kyrios* lord, master, from *kyros* power]

church[2] *verb trans* to put (a woman) through the ceremony of churching.

Church Army *noun* an Anglican organization for social work and evangelism founded on the model of the Salvation Army.

Church Commissioner *noun* a member of a body of trustees responsible for overseeing and administering the finances, investments, and properties of the Church of England.

churchgoer /'chuhchgoh·ə/ *noun* somebody who attends church regularly. ➤➤ **churchgoing** *adj and noun.*

churching /'chuhching/ *noun* a ceremony in which a woman is received and blessed in church after childbirth.

Church of England *noun* the established episcopal church of England: *The Church of England should no longer be satisfied to represent only the Conservative Party at prayer* — Agnes Maude Royden.

Church of Scotland *noun* the main Presbyterian denomination in Scotland, belonging to the Calvinist tradition, in which each congregation is governed by an elected body of ordained lay elders.

church school *noun* a primary school controlled in part by a church.

churchwarden *noun* **1** either of two lay parish officials in Anglican churches with responsibility *esp* for parish property and alms. **2** *Brit* a long-stemmed clay tobacco pipe.

churchy *adj* (**churchier, churchiest**) marked by strict conformity or zealous adherence to the forms or beliefs of a church. ➤➤ **churchiness** *noun.*

churchyard *noun* an enclosed piece of ground surrounding a church; *esp* one used as a burial ground.

churinga /chə'ring·gə/ *noun* (*pl* **churinga** *or* **churingas**) among Australian aborigines, a sacred stone amulet or similar object. [native name in Australia]

churl /chuhl/ *noun* **1a** a rude ill-bred person. **b** *archaic* a mean morose person. **2** *archaic* a rustic or country person. [Old English *ceorl* man, churl]

churlish /'chuhlish/ *adj* **1** rudely uncooperative; surly. **2** lacking refinement or sensitivity. ➤➤ **churlishly** *adv,* **churlishness** *noun.*

churn[1] /chuhn/ *noun* **1** a vessel used in making butter in which milk or cream is agitated to separate the oily globules from the watery medium. **2** *Brit* a large metal container for transporting milk. [Old English *cyrin,* related to Old English *corn* CORN[1]; from the granular appearance of cream as it is churned]

churn[2] *verb trans* **1** to agitate (milk or cream) in a churn in order to make butter. **2** to stir or agitate (liquid) violently. ➤ *verb intrans* **1** to produce or be in violent motion. **2** to work a churn.

churn out *verb trans chiefly informal* to produce (something) prolifically and mechanically, usu without great concern for quality: *She has been churning out short stories for years.*

churn rate *noun* the rate at which a business loses customers or loses and has to replace staff.

churr[1] /chuh/ *verb intrans* to make a vibrant or whirring noise characteristic of certain insects and birds, e.g. the partridge. [imitative]

churr[2] *noun* the vibrant or whirring noise of certain insects and birds.

chute /shoot/ *noun* **1** an inclined plane, channel, or passage down which things may pass: *a rubbish chute.* **2** a slide into a swimming pool. **3** a waterfall, rapid, etc. **4** *informal* a parachute. **5** *Scot* = SLIDE[2] (1A). [French *chute* from Old French *cheoir* to fall, from Latin *cadere*]

chutney /'chutni/ *noun* (*pl* **chutneys**) a thick condiment or relish of Indian origin that contains fruits, sugar, vinegar, and spices: compare PICKLE[1] (1B). [Hindi *caṭnī*]

chutzpah /'khootspə, 'hootspə/ *noun informal* brazen audacity. [Yiddish *chutzpah* from late Hebrew *ḥuspāh*]

chyle /kiel/ *noun* LYMPH (liquid containing white blood cells) that is milky from emulsified fats and is produced during intestinal absorption of fats. ➤➤ **chylous** /'kieləs/ *adj.* [late Latin *chylus* from Greek *chylos* juice, chyle, from *chein* to pour]

chyme /kiem/ *noun* the semifluid mass of partly digested food expelled by the stomach into the duodenum. ➤➤ **chymous** /'kieməs/ *adj.* [scientific Latin *chymus* via late Latin from Greek *chymos* juice]

CI *abbr* **1** Channel Islands. **2** Côte d'Ivoire (international vehicle registration).

Ci *abbr* curie.

CIA *abbr NAmer* Central Intelligence Agency.

ciabatta /chə'bahtə/ *noun* (*pl* **ciabattas** *or* **ciabatte** /-tay/) **1** a type of flattish white Italian bread made with olive oil. **2** a loaf of this bread. [Italian dialect *ciabatta* slipper; from its shape]

ciao /chow/ *interj* used to express greeting or farewell. [Italian dialect *ciao,* alteration of *schiavo* (I am your) slave, from medieval Latin *sclavus:* see SLAVE[1]]

ciborium /si'bawri·əm/ *noun* (*pl* **ciboria** /-ri·ə/) **1** a goblet-shaped vessel for holding the consecrated bread used at Communion. **2** a free-standing vaulted canopy supported by four columns over a high altar. [medieval Latin *ciborium* via Latin from Greek *kibōrion* cup]

cicada /si'kahdə/ *noun* (*pl* **cicadas** *or* **cicadae** /-dee/) any of a family of insects that have large transparent wings and the males of which produce a shrill singing noise: family Cicadidae. [Latin *cicada*]

cicatrice /'sikətris/ *noun* = CICATRIX.

cicatrices /sikə'trieseez/ *noun* pl of CICATRIX.

cicatrise /'sikətriez/ *verb trans and intrans* see CICATRIZE.

cicatrix /'sikətriks/ *noun* (*pl* **cicatrices** /-'trieseez/) **1** a scar resulting after a flesh wound has healed. **2a** a mark left on a stem after the fall of a leaf or bract. **b** = HILUM (I). ⋙ **cicatricial** /-'trish(ə)l/ *adj.* [Latin *cicatric-, cicatrix*]

cicatrize *or* **cicatrise** /'sikətriez/ *verb trans* = SCAR². ⋙ *verb intrans* to heal by forming a scar. ⋙ **cicatrization** /-'zaysh(ə)n/ *noun.*

cicely /'sisəli/ *noun* = SWEET CICELY.

cicerone /sisə'rohni, chichə-/ *noun* (*pl* **cicerones** *or* **ciceroni** /-nee/) **1** a person who acts as a guide to antiquities. **2** a guide or mentor.

Word history
Italian *cicerone*, named after *Cicero* d.43 BC, Roman orator and statesman. The word is probably a humorous allusion to Cicero's learning and eloquence.

cichlid /'siklid/ *noun* any of a family of mostly tropical freshwater fishes with spiny fins: family Cichlidae. [Greek *kichlē* thrush, also a kind of wrasse]

CID *abbr* Brit Criminal Investigation Department.

-cide *comb. form* forming nouns, denoting: **1** killer: *insecticide*. **2** killing: *suicide*. ⋙ **-cidal** *comb. form*. [French (sense 1) from Latin *-cida*, (sense 2) from Latin *-cidium*, both from *caedere* to cut, kill]

cider /'siedə/ *noun* **1** fermented, often sparkling, apple juice. **2** *NAmer* an unfermented apple-juice drink. [Middle English *sidre* via Old French and late Latin from Greek *sikera* strong drink, from Hebrew *shēkhār*]

c.i.f. *abbr* cost, insurance, and freight.

cig /sig/ *noun informal* a cigarette.

cigar /si'gah/ *noun* a roll of tobacco leaf for smoking. ✳ **close but no cigar** *chiefly NAmer, informal* a comment made in response to an answer that is not quite correct, an attempt that is not quite successful, etc. [Spanish *cigarro*]

cigarette (*NAmer also* **cigaret**) /sigə'ret/ *noun* a narrow cylinder of cut tobacco enclosed in paper for smoking, or a similar roll of a herbal or narcotic substance. [French *cigarette*, dimin. of *cigare* cigar, from Spanish *cigarro* CIGAR]

cigarette card *noun* a small oblong card with a picture on one side and information on the other, formerly given away in a packet of cigarettes.

cigarillo /sigə'riloh, -'reelyoh/ *noun* (*pl* **cigarillos**) a very small cigar. [Spanish *cigarrillo*, dimin. of *cigarro* CIGAR]

ciggie *or* **ciggy** /'sigi/ *noun* (*pl* **ciggies**) *informal* a cigarette. [by shortening and alteration]

cilia /'sili·ə/ *noun* pl of CILIUM.

ciliary /'sili·əri/ *adj* **1** relating to cilia. **2** of the ciliary body.

ciliary body *noun* the ringlike muscular body supporting the lens of the eye.

cilium /'sili·əm/ *noun* (*pl* **cilia** /'sili·ə/) **1** a minute hairlike part, *esp* one capable of a lashing movement that produces locomotion in a single-celled organism. **2** an eyelash. ⋙ **ciliate** /siliət, -ayt/ *adj,* **ciliated** /-aytid/ *adj,* **ciliation** /-'aysh(ə)n/ *noun.* [Latin *cilium* eyelid]

C in C *abbr* Commander in Chief.

cinch¹ /sinch/ *noun informal* **1a** something certain to happen: *It's a cinch that Mike will win the high jump.* **b** a task performed with ease: *Finding the way here was a cinch.* **2** *NAmer* = GIRTH¹ (2). [Spanish *cincha* from Latin *cingula* girdle, girth, from *cingere* to gird]

cinch² *verb trans chiefly NAmer* **1a** *informal* (*often + up*) to fasten or tighten a girth round (a horse). **b** (*often + in*) to tighten (a garment) as if with a girth: *She was wearing a dress cinched at the waist.* **2** *informal* to make certain of (something); to assure (it).

cinchona /sing'kohnə/ *noun* **1** any of a genus of S American trees and shrubs of the madder family: genus *Cinchona*. **2** the dried bark of any of these trees, which contains quinine. [Latin genus name, named after the Countess of *Chinchón* d.1641, vicereine of Peru, who introduced the drug into Spain]

cinchonine /'singkəneen/ *noun* an alkaloid found *esp* in cinchona bark and used like quinine.

cincture /'singkchə/ *noun* a girdle or belt, *esp* a cloth cord or sash worn round an ecclesiastical vestment or the habit of a religious order. [Latin *cinctura* girdle, from *cinctus*, past part. of *cingere* to gird]

cinder /'sində/ *noun* **1** slag, e.g. from a blast furnace or volcano, or a fragment of this. **2** (*usu in pl*) a fragment of ash. **3** a piece of partly burned material, e.g. coal, that will burn further but will not flame. ⋙ **cindery** *adj.* [Old English *sinder*]

Cinderella /sində'relə/ *noun* **1** somebody or something that suffers undeserved neglect. **2** somebody or something that is suddenly raised from obscurity to honour or importance.

Word history
named after *Cinderella*, heroine of a fairy-tale. Neglected and used as a servant by her family, Cinderella is helped by her fairy godmother to meet and eventually marry Prince Charming.

cine- *comb. form* forming words, with the meanings: **1** moving pictures: *cinecamera*. **2** relating to the cinema: *cineaste*. [CINEMA or CINEMATOGRAPHY]

cineaste *or* **cineast** /'siniast/ *noun* a devotee of the cinema. [French *cinéaste*, from *cinéma* CINEMA + *-aste* as in *enthousiaste* enthusiast]

cinecamera /'sinikamərə/ *or* **ciné camera** *noun* a simple hand-held camera for making amateur films.

cinefilm /'sinifilm/ *or* **ciné film** *noun* film for making moving pictures on cinecameras.

cinema /'sinimə/ *noun* **1** *chiefly Brit* a theatre where films are shown. **2a** (**the cinema**) films considered as an art form, entertainment, or industry. **b** (**the cinema**) the art or technique of making films, or the effects appropriate to film. [French *cinéma*, short for *cinématographe*: see CINEMATOGRAPH]

cinematic /sini'matik/ *adj* **1** made and presented as a film: *cinematic fantasies*. **2** of or suitable for the making of films. ⋙ **cinematically** *adv.*

cinematograph /sini'matəgrahf/ *noun chiefly Brit* a film camera or projector. [French *cinématographe*, from Greek *kinēmat-, kinēma* movement (from *kinein* to move) + -O- + -GRAPH]

cinematography /ˌsinimə'togrəfi/ *noun* the art or science of cinema photography. ⋙ **cinematographer** *noun,* **cinematographic** /-matə'grafik/ *adj,* **cinematographically** /-matə'grafikli/ *adv.*

cinema vérité /'veritay/ *noun* the art or technique of film-making so as to convey documentary-style realism. [French *cinéma-vérité*, literally 'truth cinema']

cineraria /sinə'reəri·ə/ *noun* any of several composite pot plants with heart-shaped leaves and clusters of bright flower heads: genus *Pericallis* (formerly *Cineraria*). [scientific Latin *cineraria*, from Latin *cinerarius* of ashes, from *ciner-, cinis* ashes; from the pale grey down on the leaves]

cinerarium /sinə'reəri·əm/ *noun* (*pl* **cineraria** /-ri·ə/) a place where the ashes of the cremated dead are kept. ⋙ **cinerary** /'sinərəri/ *adj.* [Latin *cinerarium*, from *ciner-, cinis* ashes]

Cingalese /singgə'leez/ *noun and adj* (*pl* **Cingalese**) = SINHALESE.

cinnabar /'sinəbah/ *noun* **1** naturally occurring red mercuric sulphide. **2** a European moth with greyish black fore wings marked with red and clear reddish pink hind wings: *Tyria jacobaeae*. [Middle English *cynabare* via French and Latin from Greek *kinnabari*, of Semitic origin]

cinnabar moth *noun* = CINNABAR (2).

cinnamon /'sinəmən/ *noun* **1a** any of a genus of trees of the laurel family with an aromatic bark used as a spice: genus *Cinnamomum*. **b** this spice. **2** a light yellowish brown. [Middle English *cynamone* via Latin from Greek *kinnamōmon, kinnamon*, of Semitic origin]

cinque /singk/ *noun* in certain games, e.g. dice, five. [Middle English from Old French *cinc* from Latin *quinque*]

cinquecento /chingkwi'chentoh/ *noun* (*often* **Cinquecento**) the 16th cent., *esp* in Italian art.

Word history
Italian, literally 'five hundred', from *cinque* five (from Latin *quinque*) + *cento* hundred (from Latin *centum*). Italian *cinquecento* in this case is short for *milcinquecento* fifteen hundred, referring to the years 1500–99.

cinquefoil /'singkfoyl/ *noun* **1** a plant of the rose family with five-lobed leaves: genus *Potentilla*. **2** in architecture, a design enclosed by five joined arcs arranged in a circle. [Middle English *sink foil* via French from Latin *quinquefolium*, from *quinque* five + *folium* leaf]

Cinque Ports /singk/ *pl noun* orig five and now seven towns on the SE coast of England with ancient privileges because of their importance in naval defence. [Middle English from Old French *cinq ports* five ports, from Latin *quinque portus*]

cion /'sie·ən/ *noun NAmer* see SCION (I).

cipher¹ or **cypher** /'siefə/ noun **1a** a method of transforming a text in order to conceal its meaning. **b** a message in code. **c** a key to such a code. **2** a combination of symbolic letters, esp a monogram. **3a** archaic = ZERO¹ (1). **b** somebody who or something that has no worth or influence; a nonentity: 'There I shall see mine own figure.' 'Which I take to be either a fool or a cipher' — Shakespeare. **4** any of the Arabic numerals. [Middle English from early French cifre via medieval Latin from Arabic ṣifr empty, cipher, zero]

cipher² or **cypher** verb trans (**ciphered** or **cyphered**, **ciphering** or **cyphering**) **1** to encode (something). **2** to compute (something) arithmetically. **3** NAmer, archaic to figure (something) out: Leave me alone to cipher out a way — Mark Twain. ➤ verb intrans chiefly NAmer, archaic to make arithmetical or other calculations; to figure.

circa /'suhkə/ prep used esp with dates: at, in, or of approximately: She was born circa 1600. [Latin circa, from circum round, from circus: see CIRCLE¹]

circadian /suh'kaydi·ən/ adj being, having, characterized by, or occurring in approximately day-long periods or cycles, e.g. of biological activity or function: circadian rhythms; circadian leaf movements. [Latin circa about + dies day + -AN²]

circinate /'suhsinayt/ adj technical rolled or coiled with the top as a centre: circinate fern fronds. [Latin circinatus, past part. of circinare to make round, from circinus pair of compasses, from circus: see CIRCLE¹]

circle¹ /'suhkl/ noun **1a** a closed flat curve every point of which is equidistant from the centre. **b** something in the form of a circle: The children quickly formed a circle. **2** a balcony or tier of seats in a theatre. **3** a cycle or round. **4** (treated as sing. or pl) a group of people sharing a common interest, activity, or leader: the gossip of court circles. **5** an instance of circular reasoning. **6** a circle formed on the surface of a sphere, e.g. the earth, by the intersection of a plane: a circle of latitude. **✳ come/turn full circle** to return to the position or condition in which the thing in question started; to go back to the beginning. **go/run round in circles** to be frantically active without making any progress. [Middle English cercle via Old French from Latin circulus, dimin. of circus ring, circus, from or related to Greek krikos, kirkos ring]

circle² verb trans **1** to move or revolve round (somebody or something). **2** to enclose (something) in or as if in a circle. ➤ verb intrans to move in or as if in a circle. ➤➤ **circler** noun.

circlet /'suhklit/ noun something in the form of a little circle, esp a circular ornament.

Circlip /'suhklip/ noun trademark a clip that encircles a tubular fitting and is held in place by its natural tension. [blend of CIRCLE¹ or CIRCULAR¹ + CLIP²]

circs /suhks/ pl noun chiefly Brit, informal circumstances. [by shortening]

circuit¹ /'suhkit/ noun **1** a closed loop encompassing an area, or the area enclosed. **2a** a course round a periphery. **b** a racetrack. **c** the act of going round such a course or a racetrack. **3a** a regular tour, e.g. by a judge, round an assigned area or territory. **b** the route travelled. **c** a group of church congregations with one pastor, e.g. in the Methodist Church. **4a** a complete path of an electric current. **b** an array of electrical components connected so as to allow the passage of current. **c** a two-way communication path between points, e.g. in a computer. **5a** an association or league of similar groups. **b** a chain of theatres at which productions are presented successively. **c** a regular series of sports competitions in which the same competitors take part, or the players themselves. [Middle English via French from Latin circuitus, past part. of circumire, circuire to go round, from CIRCUM- + ire to go]

circuit² verb (**circuited**, **circuiting**) ➤ verb trans **1** to make a circuit round (something). **2** to provide (something) with an electrical circuit. ➤ verb intrans to make a circuit.

circuit breaker noun a switch that automatically interrupts an electric circuit under an infrequent abnormal condition.

circuitous /suh'kyooh·itəs/ adj indirect in route or method; roundabout. ➤➤ **circuitously** adv, **circuitousness** noun, **circuity** noun.

circuitry /'suhkitri/ noun (pl **circuitries**) electrical circuits, or a system of circuits.

circular¹ /'suhkyoolə/ adj **1** of circles; having the form of a circle. **2a** moving in or describing a circle or spiral. **b** circuitous. **3** marked by the fallacy of assuming something which is to be demonstrated: circular arguments. **4** marked by or moving in a cycle. **5** said of a letter or advertising material: intended for circulation to a number

of people, e.g. by mail. ➤➤ **circularity** /-'lariti/ noun, **circularly** adv. [Middle English circuler via French from late Latin circularis, from Latin circulus: see CIRCLE¹]

circular² noun a paper, e.g. a leaflet or advertisement, intended for wide distribution.

circularize or **circularise** verb trans **1** to send circulars to (people). **2** to publicize (something), esp by means of circulars. **3** to make (something) circular. ➤➤ **circularization** /-'zaysh(ə)n/ noun.

circular saw noun a power-driven saw that has its teeth set on the edge of a revolving metal disc.

circulate /'suhkyoolayt/ verb intrans **1** to move in a circle, circuit, or orbit, esp to follow a course that returns to the starting point: Blood circulates through the body. **2a** to flow without obstruction. **b** to become well known or widespread: Rumours circulated through the town. **c** to go from group to group at a social gathering. **d** said of a newspaper, etc: to come into the hands of readers; specif to be sold or distributed. ➤ verb trans to cause (something) to circulate. ➤➤ **circulative** /-lətiv/ adj, **circulator** /-laytə/ noun, **circulatory** /-lət(ə)ri/ adj. [Latin circulatus, past part. of circulare, from circulus: see CIRCLE¹]

circulating library noun a small library which moves from one place to another, e.g. between hospitals.

circulation noun **1** a flow. **2** orderly movement through a circuit, esp the movement of blood through the vessels of the body induced by the pumping action of the heart. **3a** passage or transmission from person to person or place to place, esp the interchange of currency: Does anyone know how many coins are in circulation? **b** the extent of dissemination, esp the average number of copies of a publication sold over a given period. **✳ out of circulation** not participating in social life.

circulatory system /'suhkyoolət(ə)ri, suhkyoo'layt(ə)ri/ noun the system of blood and lymphatic vessels and the heart concerned with the circulation of the blood and lymph.

circum- prefix forming words, with the meaning: round; about: circumnavigate. [Old French from Latin, from circum, from circus: see CIRCLE¹]

circumambient /suhkəm'ambiənt/ adj formal or literary on all sides; encompassing. ➤➤ **circumambience** noun, **circumambiently** adv. [late Latin circumambient-, circumambiens, present part. of circumambire to surround in a circle, from Latin CIRCUM- + ambire to go round]

circumambulate /suhkəm'ambyoolayt/ verb trans formal to walk round (a place), esp in a ritual fashion. ➤➤ **circumambulation** /-'laysh(ə)n/ noun. [late Latin circumambulatus, past part. of circumambulare, from CIRCUM- + ambulare to walk]

circumcise /'suhkəmsiez/ verb trans to cut off all or part of the foreskin of (a male) or the clitoris of (a female). [Middle English circumcisen from Latin circumcisus, past part. of circumcidere, from CIRCUM- + caedere to cut]

circumcision /suhkəm'sizh(ə)n/ noun **1** the act of circumcising somebody, e.g.: **a** a Jewish rite of circumcising performed on male infants as a sign of inclusion in the Jewish religious community. **b** (often **female circumcision**) the rite of circumcising a female. **2** (**Circumcision**) 1 January, observed as a festival in some Christian churches in commemoration of the circumcision of Jesus.

circumference /suh'kumfərəns/ noun **1** the perimeter of a circle. **2** the external boundary or surface of a figure or object. ➤➤ **circumferential** /-'rensh(ə)l/ adj, **circumferentially** /-'renshəli/ adv. [Middle English via French from Latin circumferentia, from circumferre to carry round, from CIRCUM- + ferre to carry]

circumflex¹ /'suhkəmfleks/ noun a mark, usu (^) but also (ˆ) or (˜), placed over a vowel in some languages to show length, contraction, or a particular quality of a vowel. [Latin circumflexus, past part. of circumflectere to bend round, mark with a circumflex, from CIRCUM- + flectere to bend]

circumflex² adj **1** said of a vowel: marked with or having the sound indicated by a circumflex. **2** in anatomy, curved.

circumfuse /suhkəm'fyoohz/ verb trans formal or technical **1** to surround or envelop (something). **2** to pour (a liquid) round something. ➤➤ **circumfusion** /-'fyoohzh(ə)n/ noun. [Latin circumfusus, past part. of circumfundere to pour round, from CIRCUM- + fundere to pour]

circumlocution /suhkəmlə'kyoohsh(ə)n/ noun **1** the use of an unnecessarily large number of words to express an idea. **2** evasive language or an evasive expression: His circumlocutions are roundly called lies — Somerset Maugham. ⟫ **circumlocutory** /-'lokyoot(ə)ri/ adj. [Latin circumlocution-, circumlocutio, from CIRCUM- + locutio speech, from loqui to speak]

circumlunar /suhkəm'loohnə/ adj revolving round or surrounding the moon.

circumnavigate /suhkəm'navigayt/ verb trans to go round (the earth), esp to travel completely round it, esp by sea or air. ⟫ **circumnavigation** /-'gaysh(ə)n/ noun, **circumnavigator** noun. [Latin circumnavigatus, past part. of circumnavigare to sail round, from CIRCUM- + navigare: see NAVIGATE]

circumpolar /suhkəm'pohlə/ adj 1 surrounding or found near a pole of the earth. 2 said of a celestial body: continually visible above the horizon at a particular latitude.

circumscribe /'suhkəmskrieb/ verb trans 1 to surround (something) by a physical or imaginary line. 2 to restrict the range or activity of (something) definitely and clearly. 3 to draw round (a geometrical figure) so as to touch it at as many points as possible. [Latin circumscribere, from CIRCUM- + scribere to write, draw]

circumscription /suhkəm'skripsh(ə)n/ noun circumscribing or being circumscribed, esp a restriction, or the act of imposing one. [Latin circumscription-, circumscriptio, from circumscribere: see CIRCUMSCRIBE]

circumsolar /suhkəm'sohlə/ adj revolving about or found in the vicinity of the sun.

circumspect /'suhkəmspekt/ adj careful to consider all circumstances and possible consequences; prudent. ⟫ **circumspection** /-'speksh(ə)n/ noun, **circumspectly** adv. [Middle English via French from Latin circumspectus, past part. of circumspicere to look around, be cautious, from CIRCUM- + specere to look]

circumstance /'suhkəmstans/ noun **1a** (usu in pl, but treated as sing. or pl) a state of affairs; the situation one finds oneself in: He claimed he was a victim of circumstances and had had no option but to steal. **b** (in pl) one's situation with regard to material or financial welfare: He was living in easy circumstances. **c** a condition or event that accompanies, causes, or determines another, or the totality of such conditions or events: There was a period of rapid change in economic circumstance. **2a** a fact or detail pertinent to an event, story, etc; an incident viewed as part of a narrative or course of events. **b** something that happens by chance: It was just an unfortunate circumstance that she was there too. **c** an occurrence: Open rebellion was a rare circumstance. **3** ceremonial formalities: He loved the pomp and circumstance of the coronation. ✳ **in/under no circumstances** on no account; never. **in/under the circumstances** because of the conditions; considering the situation. [Middle English via French from Latin circumstantia, from circumstare to stand around, from CIRCUM- + stare to stand]

circumstanced adj formal placed in specified circumstances, esp in regard to property or income: She was obviously well circumstanced.

circumstantial /suhkəm'stansh(ə)l, -'stahnsh(ə)l/ adj **1a** belonging to, consisting in, or dependent on circumstances. **b** said of evidence: tending to prove a fact indirectly by proving other events or circumstances which afford a basis for a reasonable inference of the occurrence of the fact at issue: The presence of a suspect's fingerprints is circumstantial evidence. **c** said of a law case: based on or using circumstantial evidence. **2** pertinent but not essential; incidental. **3** abounding in factual details. ⟫ **circumstantiality** /-shi'aliti/ noun, **circumstantially** adv.

circumstantiate /suhkəm'stanshiayt/ verb trans to supply (something) with circumstantial evidence or support.

circumvallate /suhkəm'valayt/ verb trans to surround (something) by, or as if by, a rampart. ⟫ **circumvallation** /-'laysh(ə)n/ noun. [Latin circumvallatus, past part. of circumvallare to surround with a wall, from CIRCUM- + vallare to fortify with a wall, from vallum rampart]

circumvent /suhkəm'vent/ verb trans **1** to find a way round (a problem), esp by ingenuity. **2** to evade (e.g. an enemy), esp by means of a stratagem. **3** archaic to outwit (somebody). **4** archaic to encircle (an enemy) so as to capture them. ⟫ **circumvention** /-'vensh(ə)n/ noun. [Latin circumventus, past part. of circumvenire to skirt around, from CIRCUM- + venire to come]

circus /'suhkəs/ noun (pl **circuses**) **1a** an entertainment in which a variety of performers, e.g. acrobats and clowns, and performing animals are involved in a series of unrelated acts, or the covered arena housing it. **b** an activity suggestive of a circus, e.g. in being

a busy scene of noisy or frivolous action. **2** (**Circus**) Brit usu in proper names: a large open road junction in a town partly surrounded by a circle of buildings: Piccadilly Circus. **3a** a large circular or oval stadium used esp for sports contests or spectacles. **b** a public spectacle. [Latin circus: see CIRCLE¹]

ciré /'siray (French sire)/ noun a highly glazed finish, usu achieved by waxing and heating, or a fabric with such a finish. [French ciré, past part. of cirer to wax, from cire wax, from Latin cera, prob from Greek kēros]

cire perdue /,siə peə'dooh (French sir pɛrdy)/ noun a process used in metal casting in which a clay impression of an object, e.g. a statue, is formed from a wax model which is then melted away leaving a mould into which molten metal can be poured. [French (moulage à) cire perdue lost wax (casting)]

cirque /suhk/ noun **1** a deep steep-walled glacially excavated hollow on a mountain flank. **2** archaic = CIRCUS (3A). [French cirque from Latin circus: see CIRCLE¹]

cirr- or **cirri-** or **cirro-** comb. form forming words, with the meaning: cirrus: cirriped; cirrostratus. [scientific Latin, from cirrus]

cirrhosis /si'rohsis/ noun (pl **cirrhoses** /-seez/) hardening, esp of the liver, caused by excessive formation of connective tissue. ⟫ **cirrhotic** /si'rotik/ adj and noun. [scientific Latin cirrhosis from Greek kirrhos orange-coloured; because the liver often becomes orange-coloured]

cirri /'sirie/ noun pl of CIRRUS.

cirri- comb. form see CIRR-.

cirriped /'siriped/ or **cirripede** /-peed/ noun any of a class of marine crustaceans including the barnacles, that are permanently attached to a rock, etc as an adult: class Cirripedia. [CIRRI- + Latin ped-, pes foot]

cirro- comb. form see CIRR-.

cirrocumulus /siroh'kyoohmyoolas/ noun (pl **cirrocumuli** /-lie/) a cloud formation consisting of small white rounded masses occurring at high altitude, usu in regular groupings forming a mackerel sky, between about 5000 and 10,000m (about 16,600 and 35,000ft).

cirrostratus /siroh'strahtəs/ noun (pl **cirrostrati** /-tie/) a cloud formation consisting of a uniform layer of high stratus clouds that are darker than cirrus, occurring at high altitude, between about 5000 and 10,000m (about 16,600 and 35,000ft).

cirrus /'sirəs/ noun (pl **cirri** /'sirie/) **1** a wispy white cloud formation, usu consisting of minute ice crystals, occurring at high altitudes, between about 5000 and 10,000m (about 16,600 and 35,000ft). **2** technical. **a** = TENDRIL **b** a slender, usu flexible, animal appendage. [scientific Latin from Latin cirrus curl]

CIS abbr Commonwealth of Independent States, a successor to the USSR.

cis- prefix forming words, with the meaning: on this side of: cisalpine. [Latin, from cis]

cisalpine /sis'alpien/ adj south of the Alps, i.e. on 'this' side of the Alps as looked at from Rome.

cisco /'siskoh/ noun (pl **ciscoes** or **ciscos**) any of several species of herring-like North American freshwater food fishes of the salmon family: genus Coregonus. [back-formation from Canadian French ciscoette from Ojibwa bemidewiskawed the one with oily skin]

cislunar /sis'loohnə/ adj between the earth and the moon: cislunar space.

cisplatin /sis'platin/ noun a platinum compound used in the treatment of certain forms of cancer. [CIS- + PLATINUM]

cissing /'sising/ noun the occurrence of unwanted holes and cracks in paintwork. [origin unknown]

cissy¹ or **sissy** /'sisi/ noun (pl **cissies** or **sissies**) Brit, informal **1** an effeminate boy or man. **2** a cowardly person. [sis (short for SISTER) + -Y²]

cissy² or **sissy** adj (**cissier, cissiest**) Brit, informal **1** effeminate. **2** cowardly.

cist¹ /sist/ or **kist** /kist/ noun a Neolithic or Bronze Age stone burial chamber. [Welsh cist chest, from Latin cista]

cist² noun in ancient Greece and Rome, a box for holding sacred utensils. [Latin cista from Greek kistē]

Cistercian¹ /si'stuhsh(ə)n/ noun a member of an austere Benedictine order founded by St Robert of Molesme in 1098 at Cîteaux in France. [medieval Latin Cistercium Cîteaux]

Cistercian[2] *adj* of the Cistercians.

cistern /'sist(ə)n/ *noun* **1** a water reservoir for a toilet. **2** a tank at the top of a house or building. **3** *chiefly NAmer* a tank, usu underground, for storing rainwater. [Middle English via French from Latin *cisterna*, from *cista* box, chest]

cistus /'sistəs/ *noun* a shrub of the rockrose family with large red or white flowers: genus *Cistus*. [Latin genus name, from Greek *kistos* rockrose]

citadel /'sitədl, -del/ *noun* **1** a fortress, *esp* one that commands a city. **2** a stronghold. **3** a Salvation Army church. [early French *citadelle* from Old Italian *cittadella*, dimin. of *cittade* city, from medieval Latin *civitat-, civitas*: see CITY]

citation /sie'taysh(ə)n/ *noun* **1a** an act of citing or quoting. **b** a quotation. **2** a mention, *esp* of something praiseworthy; *specif* specific reference in a military dispatch to meritorious conduct. **3** *chiefly NAmer* an official summons to appear before a court of law, or the document containing it. **4** in law, the act of quoting legal authority, or a case cited as authority or precedent. ➤➤ **citational** *adj*.

cite /siet/ *verb trans* **1** to quote (something) by way of example, authority, precedent, or proof: *The devil can cite Scripture for his purpose* — Shakespeare. **2** to refer to or name (somebody), *esp* to mention (them) formally in commendation or praise. **3** to call upon (somebody) to appear before a court of law. ➤➤ **citable** *adj*. [early French *citer* to cite, summon, from Latin *citare* to put in motion, rouse, summon, from *citus*, past part. of *ciēre* to stir, move]

CITES /'sieteez/ *abbr* Convention on International Trade in Endangered Species.

cithara /'sithərə/ *noun* an ancient Greek stringed musical instrument of the lyre family with a wooden sounding board. [via Latin from Greek *kithara*]

citified *or* **cityfied** /'sitified/ *adj often derog* having adopted city ways: *Even the trees seem citified and self-conscious* — Helen Keller. ➤➤ **citification** /-fi'kaysh(ə)n/ *noun*.

citizen /'sitiz(ə)n/ *noun* **1** a member of a state, *esp* a native or naturalized one. **2** an inhabitant of a city or town. ➤➤ **citizenship** *noun*. [Middle English *citizein* from Anglo-French *citezein*, alteration of Old French *citeien*, from *cité*: see CITY]

citizenry /'sitiz(ə)nri/ *noun* (*pl* **citizenries**) *formal* (*treated as sing. or pl*) the whole body of citizens.

Citizens' Advice Bureau *noun* in Britain, an office at which members of the public can get information about their civil rights, the law, etc, or the organization that runs such offices.

citizen's arrest *noun* a legally permitted arrest by a member of the public.

Citizens' Band *noun* a system of radio communication by which private individuals, *esp* drivers, can transmit messages to one another.

Citizen's Charter *noun* a document produced by the British government in 1991 that sets out the standards of service expected from various public bodies and private companies and guarantees redress where such standards are not met, or any similar document.

citrate /'sitrayt, 'sietrayt/ *noun* a salt or ester of citric acid.

citric acid /'sitrik/ *noun* an acid occurring in lemons, limes, etc, formed as an intermediate in cell metabolism, and used as a flavouring: formula $C_6H_8O_7$.

citric acid cycle *noun* = KREBS CYCLE.

citrine[1] /'sitrin/ *adj* resembling a lemon, *esp* in colour. [Middle English via French from medieval Latin *citrinus*, from Latin *citrus* citron tree]

citrine[2] *noun* semiprecious yellow quartz.

citron /'sitrən/ *noun* **1a** a fruit like the lemon but larger and with a thicker rind. **b** the tree that bears this fruit: *Citrus medica*. **2** the preserved rind of the citron, used *esp* in cakes and puddings. [Middle English via French from Old Provençal, modification of Latin *citrus* citron tree]

citronella /sitrə'nelə/ *noun* **1** a fragrant S Asian grass that yields an oil used in perfumery and as an insect repellent: *Cymbopogon nardus*. **2** the oil obtained from the grass. [scientific Latin *citronella* from French *citronnelle* lemon balm, from *citron*: see CITRON]

citrous /'sitrəs/ *adj* relating to citrus trees or their fruit.

citrus[1] /'sitrəs/ *noun* (*pl* **citruses**) any of a genus of thorny trees and shrubs of the rue family grown in warm regions for their edible thick-rinded juicy fruit, e.g. the orange or lemon: genus *Citrus*. [Latin genus name, from Latin *citrus* citron tree]

citrus[2] *adj* of the citrus or the fruit of a citrus.

cittern /'sitən/ *noun* a plucked stringed musical instrument with an oval belly and back and wire strings, popular *esp* in Renaissance England. [blend of CITHARA and GITTERN]

city /'siti/ *noun* (*pl* **cities**) **1a** a large town. **b** *Brit* a town that has a cathedral or has had city status conferred on it by charter. **c** *NAmer* a chartered municipality, usu a large one. **2** (**the City**) *Brit*. **a** the financial and commercial area of London. **b** (*treated as sing. or pl*) influential financial interests of the British economy. [Middle English *citie* large or small town, from Old French *cité* capital city, from medieval Latin *civitat-, civitas*, from Latin, citizenship, state, city of Rome, from *civis* citizen]

City Chambers *pl noun* the building occupied by the administration of a Scottish city.

city desk *noun* **1** *Brit* the department dealing with the financial section of a journal or newspaper. **2** *NAmer* the section of a newspaper office in charge of local news.

city editor *noun* the editor in charge of the city desk.

city father *noun* an important official or prominent citizen of a city.

cityfied /'sitified/ *adj* see CITIFIED.

city hall *noun* *NAmer* **1** the chief administrative building of a city. **2** (*often* **City Hall**) the administration of a city.

cityscape /'sitiskayp/ *noun* a view of a city, or its pictorial representation.

city slicker *noun* *NAmer, informal* = SLICKER (2B).

city-state *noun* an autonomous state consisting of a city and surrounding territory, e.g. in ancient Greece or medieval Italy.

city technology college *noun* a British secondary school providing a science-based education in an inner-city area.

civet /'sivit/ *noun* **1** a thick yellowish musky-smelling substance extracted from a pouch near the sexual organs of the civet cat and used in perfumery: *Give me an ounce of civet, good apothecary, to sweeten my imagination* — Shakespeare. **2** = CIVET CAT. [early French *civette* via Old Italian *zibetto* from Arabic *zabād* civet perfume]

civet cat *noun* any of several species of flesh-eating mammals of Africa, Asia, and S Europe having a long body and short legs, from which civet is obtained: family Viverridae.

civic /'sivik/ *adj* of a citizen, a city, or citizenship. ➤➤ **civically** *adv*. [Latin *civicus*, from *civis* citizen]

civic centre *noun* *Brit* an area where a planned group of the chief public buildings of a town are situated, or the buildings themselves.

civics *pl noun* (*treated as sing. or pl*) a social science dealing with the rights and duties of citizens.

civies /'siviz/ *pl noun* see CIVVIES.

civil /'sivl/ *adj* **1** adequately courteous and polite; not rude: *We will never be friends but we can at least be civil to each other*. **2** of citizens: *civil liberties*. **3** of or involving the general public as distinguished from special, e.g. military or religious, affairs. **4** relating to private rights as distinct from criminal proceedings: *a civil case*. **5** said of time: based on the movements of the sun and legally recognized for use in ordinary affairs. ➤➤ **civilly** *adv*. [Middle English via French from Latin *civilis*, from *civis* citizen]

civil defence *noun* **1** (*often* **Civil Defence**) protective measures organized by and for civilians against hostile attack, *esp* from the air, or natural disaster. **2** (**the Civil Defence**) the organization concerned with this.

civil disobedience *noun* refusal to obey governmental demands, e.g. payment of tax, as a means of protest or of obtaining concessions or something demanded.

civil engineer *noun* an engineer who deals with the design and construction of large-scale public works, e.g. roads or bridges. ➤➤ **civil engineering** *noun*.

civilian[1] /si'vilyən/ *noun* somebody who is not in the army, navy, air force, or other uniformed public body.

civilian[2] *adj* relating to people who are not in the armed forces: *civilian casualties*.

civilianize or **civilianise** /si'vilyəniez/ *verb trans* to convert (something or somebody) from military to civilian status or control. ⪢ **civilianization** /-'zaysh(ə)n/ *noun*.

civility /si'viliti/ *noun* (*pl* **civilities**) **1** courtesy; politeness. **2** (*usu in pl*) a polite act or expression.

civilization or **civilisation** /,sivilie'zaysh(ə)n/ *noun* **1a** a relatively high level of cultural and technological development. **b** the culture characteristic of a particular time or place. **2** the process of becoming civilized. **3** *often humorous* life in a place that offers the comforts of the modern world; *specif* life in a city: *After a week in the wilderness, it was good to get back to civilization.*

civilize or **civilise** /'siv(ə)liez/ *verb trans* **1** to cause (a society) to develop out of a primitive state; *specif* to bring (it) to a technically advanced and rationally ordered stage of cultural development. **2** to educate or refine (somebody). ⪢ **civilizable** *adj*, **civilizer** *noun*.

civilized or **civilised** *adj* **1** of or being peoples or nations in a state of civilization. **2** polite, decent, refined, or enlightened: *There must be a more civilized way of resolving our differences.*

civil law *noun* **1** the body of private law developed from Roman law as distinct from common law. **2** (*often* **Civil Law**) = ROMAN LAW.

civil liberty *noun* **1** a right or freedom of the individual citizen in relation to the state, e.g. freedom of speech. **2** such rights or freedoms considered collectively. ⪢ **civil libertarian** *noun*.

civil list *noun* (**the civil list**) an annual allowance by Parliament for the household expenses of the monarch and royal family.

civil marriage *noun* a marriage involving a civil contract but no religious rite.

civil rights *pl noun* civil liberties, *esp* those of status equality between races or groups: *We can never get civil rights in America until our human rights are first restored* — Malcolm X.

Editorial note
Civil rights are the basic freedoms and opportunities an individual can receive from society balanced with the needs of society as a whole (unlike human rights, which are vested in an individual as his or her intrinsic right). By mutual agreement they are enshrined in law. Those who disobey the law cannot exercise them. Successive struggles for civil rights in the 20th cent. have borne great leaders such as Gandhi and Martin Luther King — Helena Kennedy.

civil servant *noun* a member of a civil service.

civil service *noun* (*treated as sing. or pl*) the administrative service of a government or international agency, exclusive of the armed forces and the judiciary.

civil war *noun* war, or a war, between opposing groups of citizens of the same country.

civvies or **civies** /'siviz/ *pl noun informal* civilian as distinguished from military clothes. [by shortening and alteration]

civvy street /'sivi/ *noun* (*often* **Civvy Street**) *Brit, informal* civilian life, as opposed to life in the services: *He is back on civvy street after five years in the army.*

CJ *abbr* Chief Justice.

CJD *abbr* Creutzfeldt-Jakob disease.

CL *abbr* Ceylon (international vehicle registration for Sri Lanka).

Cl *abbr* the chemical symbol for chlorine.

cl *abbr* centilitre.

clack[1] /klak/ *verb intrans* **1** to make an abrupt striking sound or sounds. **2** *informal* to chatter. ⪢ *verb trans* to cause (something) to make a clatter. ⪢ **clacker** *noun*. [Middle English *clacken*, of imitative origin]

clack[2] *noun* **1** a sound of clacking. **2** *informal* rapid continuous talk; chatter.

clad[1] /klad/ *verb* past tense and past part. of CLOTHE.

clad[2] *verb* past tense and past part. of CLAD[4].

clad[3] *adj* covered or clothed: *ivy-clad buildings*; *He was clad in tweeds*. [from CLAD[1]]

clad[4] *verb trans* (**cladded** or **clad, cladding**) to cover (a surface) with cladding. [from CLAD[1]]

cladding *noun* a thin covering or overlay, e.g. of stone on a building or metal on a metal core.

clade /klayd/ *noun technical* a group of organisms, e.g. all animals with backbones, that includes all the descendants of a single common ancestor. ⪢ **cladism** /'kladiz(ə)m/ *noun*, **cladistic** /klə'distik/ *adj*. [Greek *klados* branch]

cladistics /klə'distiks/ *pl noun* (*treated as sing. or pl*) a theory that describes the relationship between types of organism on the assumption that their sharing of a unique characteristic, e.g. the hair of mammals, possessed by no other organism indicates their descent from a single common ancestor. [CLADE + *-istics* as in STATISTICS]

cladode /'kladohd/ *noun technical* a branch that closely resembles a leaf and often bears leaves or flowers. [scientific Latin *cladodium* from Greek *klados* branch]

claim[1] /klaym/ *verb trans* **1a** to ask for (something), *esp* as a right: *She claimed Income Support*. **b** to require or demand (something). **c** to take or account for (something, *esp* a life): *Bubonic plague claimed thousands of lives*. **2** to take (something) as the rightful owner. **3** to assert (something) in the face of possible contradiction; to maintain (it): *He claimed that he'd been cheated*. ⪢ *verb intrans* **1** to make a claim; to claim something: *Amazingly, some Lottery winners fail to claim*. **2** (+ for) to make a claim under the terms of e.g. an insurance policy. ⪢ **claimable** *adj*, **claimer** *noun*. [Middle English *claimen* via Old French from Latin *clamare* to cry out, shout]

claim[2] *noun* **1** a demand for something due, or believed to be due: *an insurance claim*. **2a** (+ to/on) a right or title to something: *The whole family had claims on her attention*. **b** an assertion open to challenge: *Some of her claims are just ridiculous*. **3** something claimed, *esp* a tract of land staked out.

claimant /'klaymənt/ *noun* (*also* + to) somebody who asserts a right or entitlement, e.g. to a title or a benefit: *There were three claimants to the throne*; *social security claimants*.

clairvoyance /kleə'voyəns/ *noun* **1** the power or faculty of discerning objects not apparent to the physical senses. **2** the ability to perceive matters beyond the range of ordinary perception. ⪢ **clairvoyant** *adj and noun*. [French *clairvoyance*, from *clairvoyant* clear-sighted, from *clair* clear (from Latin *clarus*) + *voyant*, present part. of *voir* to see, from Latin *vidēre*]

clam /klam/ *noun* any of numerous species of marine molluscs living in sand or mud, many of which are eaten as food: class Bivalvia. [Old English *clamm* bond, fetter; from the clamping action of the shells]

clamant /'klaymənt/ *adj* **1** *formal* demanding attention; urgent. **2** clamorous. **3** demanding attention. ⪢ **clamantly** *adv*. [Latin *clamant-, clamans*, present part. of *clamare* to cry out]

clambake *noun NAmer* **1** an outdoor party, *esp* a seashore outing where food is cooked on heated rocks covered by seaweed. **2** a gathering characterized by noisy sociability, *esp* a political rally. [CLAM + BAKE[1]]

clamber /'klambə/ *verb intrans* (**clambered, clambering**) to climb awkwardly or with difficulty. ⪢ **clamberer** *noun*. [Middle English *clambren*, prob from *clamb*, old past tense of CLIMB[1]]

clammy /'klami/ *adj* (**clammier, clammiest**) **1** damp, clinging, and usu rather cold: *clammy hands*. **2** said of the weather: humid. **3** said of a person, their personality, etc: making one feel uncomfortable or uneasy. ⪢ **clammily** *adv*, **clamminess** *noun*. [Middle English, prob from *clammen* to smear, stick, from Old English *clæman*; related to Old English *clæg* CLAY]

clamour[1] (*NAmer* **clamor**) /'klamə/ *noun* **1** noisy shouting. **2** a loud continuous noise. **3** (*often* + against/for) insistent public expression, e.g. of support or protest: *The Government ignored the clamour for representation*. ⪢ **clamorous** /-rəs/ *adj*, **clamorously** /-rəsli/ *adv*, **clamorousness** /-rəsnis/ *noun*. [Middle English *clamor* via French from Latin *clamor*, from *clamare* to cry out]

clamour[2] (*NAmer* **clamor**) *verb* (**clamoured, clamouring**, *NAmer* **clamored, clamoring**) ⪢ *verb intrans* **1** to make a din. **2** (*usu* + against/for) to become loudly insistent: *The public clamoured for his impeachment*. ⪢ *verb trans* to utter or proclaim (something) insistently and noisily.

clamp[1] /klamp/ *noun* **1** a device that holds or compresses two or more parts firmly together. **2** = WHEEL CLAMP. [Middle English, prob from (assumed) early Dutch *klampe*]

clamp[2] *verb trans* **1** to fasten (something) with, or as if with, a clamp: *The surgeon clamped the artery to stop the bleeding*. **2** to hold (something) tightly. **3** to wheel-clamp (a vehicle). ⪢ **clamper** *noun*.

clamp[3] *noun Brit* a heap of potatoes, turnips, etc covered over with straw or earth. [prob from Dutch *klamp* heap]

clamp down *verb intrans* (*often* + *on*) to impose restrictions on something or somebody, or to make restrictions more stringent: *The police are clamping down on drink-driving.* ⟩⟩ **clamp-down** *noun.*

clam up *verb intrans* (**clammed up, clamming up**) *informal* to become silent: *When I asked about her boyfriend, she suddenly clammed up.*

clan /klan/ *noun* **1a** the whole body of people belonging to a particular family or group of families of Scottish descent and sharing a common surname or one of a number of surnames. **b** a group of people related by family: *the Kennedy clan.* **2** a close-knit group united by a common interest or common characteristics: *I was never in the biker clan.* ⟩⟩ **clansman** *noun,* **clanswoman** *noun.* [Middle English from Scottish Gaelic *clann* offspring, clan, from Old Irish *cland* plant, offspring, from Latin *planta* plant]

clandestine /klan'destin, 'klandestin/ *adj* held in or conducted with secrecy; surreptitious: *a clandestine meeting.* ⟩⟩ **clandestinely** *adv.* [early French *clandestin* from Latin *clandestinus,* irreg from *clam* secretly]

clang[1] /klang/ *verb intrans* to make a loud metallic ringing sound, or do something with such a sound: *The gate clanged shut.* ⟩ *verb trans* to cause (something) to clang: *He clanged the bell.* [Latin *clangere* to resound]

clang[2] *noun* a loud ringing metallic sound.

clanger *noun Brit, informal* a blunder.

clangour[1] (*NAmer* **clangor**) /'klang-ə/ *noun* **1** a resounding clang or series of clangs: *the clangour of hammers.* **2** uproar. ⟩⟩ **clangorous** *adj,* **clangorously** *adv.* [Latin *clangor,* from *clangere* to resound]

clangour[2] (*NAmer* **clangor**) *verb intrans* (**clangoured, clangouring,** *NAmer* **clangored, clangoring**) to make a clangour.

clank[1] /klangk/ *verb intrans* to make a sharp brief metallic sound or a series of such sounds. ⟩ *verb trans* to cause (something) to clank. ⟩⟩ **clankingly** *adv.* [prob imitative]

clank[2] *noun* a sharp brief metallic sound.

clannish /'klanish/ *adj* tending to associate only with a select group of similar background, status, or interests. ⟩⟩ **clannishly** *adv,* **clannishness** *noun.*

clap[1] /klap/ *verb* (**clapped, clapping**) ⟩ *verb trans* **1a** to strike (the hands) together repeatedly, usu in applause. **b** to applaud (a person or an act). **2a** to strike (two flat hard surfaces) together so as to produce a loud sharp percussive noise. **b** said of a bird: to flap (the wings) noisily. **3** to strike (somebody) with the flat of the hand in a friendly way: *He clapped his friend on the back.* **4a** to place, put, or set (something or somebody) in a certain place or condition, *esp* energetically: *They clapped him in irons; He clapped a hand to his head in dismay.* **b** to impose (e.g. a restriction). ⟩ *verb intrans* **1** to applaud. **2** to produce a sharp percussive noise. ✳ **clap eyes on** see EYE[1]. **clap hold of** *informal* to seize (somebody or something) suddenly and energetically. [Old English *clæppan*]

clap[2] *noun* **1** the sound of clapping hands, *esp* applause. **2** a loud sharp percussive noise, *esp* of thunder. **3** a friendly slap: *He gave her a clap on the shoulder.*

clap[3] *noun* (*often* **the clap**) *slang* = SEXUALLY TRANSMITTED DISEASE, *esp* gonorrhoea. [early French *clapoir* bubo]

clapboard[1] /'klabəd, 'klapbawd/ *noun NAmer* = WEATHERBOARD (1). [partial translation of Dutch *klaphout* stave wood]

clapboard[2] *verb trans NAmer* to cover (a structure) with weatherboards.

clapped out *adj chiefly Brit, informal* said *esp* of machinery: old and worn-out; liable to break down irreparably.

clapper *noun* the tongue of a bell. ✳ **go/run like the clappers** *Brit, informal* to move as fast as possible.

clapperboard *noun* a hinged board containing identifying details of the scene to be filmed that is held before the camera and banged together to mark the beginning and end of each take.

claptrap *noun informal* pretentious nonsense; rubbish: *The more rigorously materialistic Darwinists dismissed Teilhard's philosophy as pretentious claptrap* — Phillip E Johnson. [CLAP[2] + TRAP[1]; from its attempt to win applause]

claque /klak/ *noun* (*treated as sing. or pl*) **1** a group hired to applaud at a performance. **2** a group of self-interested obsequious flatterers. [French *claque,* from *claquer* to clap, of imitative origin]

clarence /'klarəns/ *noun* a closed four-wheeled horse-drawn carriage for four passengers. [named after the Duke of *Clarence,* later William IV of England d.1837]

claret[1] /'klarit/ *noun* **1** a dry red Bordeaux wine. **2** a dark purplish red colour. [Middle English from early French *vin claret* clear wine, from *claret* clear, from Latin *clarus* CLEAR[1]]

claret[2] *adj* of a dark purplish red colour.

clarify /'klarifie/ *verb* (**clarifies, clarified, clarifying**) ⟩ *verb trans* **1** to make (something) understandable. **2** to make (a situation) free from confusion. **3a** to make (a liquid, etc) clear or pure, usu by freeing it from suspended matter. **b** to melt (butter) to make it clear. ⟩ *verb intrans* to become clear. ⟩⟩ **clarification** /-fi'kaysh(ə)n/ *noun,* **clarificatory** /-fi'kaytəri/ *adj,* **clarifier** *noun.* [Middle English *clarifien* via French from late Latin *clarificare,* from Latin *clarus* CLEAR[1]]

clarinet /klari'net/ *noun* a woodwind musical instrument with a single REED (flat piece of cane that vibrates to make the sound when blown across), a cylindrical tube flared at the end, and holes stopped by keys. ⟩⟩ **clarinettist** *noun.* [French *clarinette,* prob derivative of medieval Latin *clarion-, clario:* see CLARION[1]]

clarion[1] /'klari-ən/ *noun* a medieval trumpet, or the sound of one. [Middle English via French from medieval Latin *clarion-, clario,* from Latin *clarus* CLEAR[1]]

clarion[2] *adj* loud and clear: *Friends! This is a clarion call to action!*

clarity /'klariti/ *noun* (*pl* **clarities**) the quality or state of being clear. [Middle English *clarite,* from Latin *claritat-, claritas,* from *clarus* CLEAR[1]]

clarkia /'klahki-ə/ *noun* a showy annual garden plant, orig from N America, of the evening-primrose family with white, purple, pink, red, or orange flowers: genus *Clarkia.* [Latin genus name, named after William *Clark* d.1838, US explorer, who discovered it]

clarsach /'klahsəkh, -shəkh, -s(h)akh/ *noun* the ancient small harp of Ireland and Scotland. [Scottish Gaelic *clàrsach* and Irish Gaelic *cláirseach*]

clary /'kleari/ *noun* (*pl* **claries**) any of several species of plants of the mint family, closely related to sage: genus *Salvia.* [Middle English *clarie* via early French *sclaree* from medieval Latin *sclareia*]

clash[1] /klash/ *noun* **1** a noisy, usu metallic, sound of collision. **2a** a hostile encounter: *The police had to deal with a clash between rival fans.* **b** a sharp conflict: *a clash of opinions.* [imitative]

clash[2] *verb intrans* **1** to make a clash: *Cymbals clashed.* **2a** (*often* + *with*) to come into conflict: *He has clashed with every member of the department at some point.* **b** (*often* + *with*) to form a displeasing combination; not to match: *These colours clash; Her lipstick clashes with her hair.* **c** said of opinions, etc: to be incompatible or irreconcilable. ⟩ *verb trans* to cause (something) to clash. ⟩⟩ **clasher** *noun.*

clasp[1] /klahsp/ *noun* **1** a device for holding objects or parts of something together: *the clasp of a necklace.* **2** a holding or enveloping with, or as if with, the hands or arms. **3** a device, e.g. a bar, attached to a military medal ribbon to indicate the action or campaign at which the bearer was present. [Middle English *claspe;* earlier history unknown]

clasp[2] *verb trans* **1** to fasten (something) with, or as if with, a clasp. **2** to enclose and hold (somebody or something) with the arms; to embrace (them). **3** to seize (something) with, or as if with, the hand; to grasp (it). ⟩⟩ **clasper** *noun.*

claspers *pl noun* a male copulatory structure of some insects and fishes.

clasp knife *noun* a large single-bladed folding knife having a catch to hold the blade open.

class[1] /klahs/ *noun* **1a** (*treated as sing. or pl*) a group sharing the same economic or social status in a society consisting of several groups with differing statuses: *the working class.* **b** social rank. **c** the system of differentiating society by classes: *Class! Yes, it's still here. Terrific staying power, and against the historical odds* — Martin Amis. **d** *informal* high quality; elegance: *That picture gives the room a touch of class.* **2a** (*treated as sing. or pl*) a body of students meeting regularly with a teacher to study the same subject. **b** a meeting of students with a teacher to study a subject. **c** *NAmer* the students who graduate in a particular year: *the class of '94.* **3a** a category in biological classification ranking above the order and below the phylum or division. **b** a grammatical category: *Parts of speech are word classes.* **c** a collection of elements; = SET[3] (5). **4a** a division or rating based on grade or quality: *first class.* **b** *Brit* a level of university honours degree awarded to a student according to merit. [French *classe* from Latin *classis* group called to arms, class of citizens]

class² *verb trans* **1** (*usu* + *as*) to classify (something or somebody): *A tomato is classed as a fruit.* **2** to assign (people or things) to particular classes; to grade (them).

class action *noun NAmer* a lawsuit taken to court by one or more plaintiffs on behalf of both themselves and any others who have a shared interest in the alleged wrong.

class-conscious *adj* **1** actively aware of one's common status with others in a particular class. **2** taking part in class war. ➤➤ **class-consciousness** *noun*.

classic¹ /'klasik/ *adj* **1a** of recognized value or merit; serving as a standard of excellence: *classic recordings*. **b** both traditional and enduring: *a classic heritage*. **c** characterized by simple tailored and elegant lines that remain in fashion year after year: *a classic suit*. **2a** authoritative, definitive. **b** being an example that shows clearly the characteristics of some group of things or occurrences; archetypal: *a classic case of first-night nerves*. **3** = CLASSICAL (1). [French *classique* from Latin *classicus* of the highest class of Roman citizens, of the first rank, from *classis*: see CLASS¹]

Usage note

classic *or* classical? These two adjectives are not usually interchangeable in modern English. If something is described as *classic*, it usually either sets a standard of excellence (*a classic recording*) or perfectly illustrates a particular phenomenon (*a classic case of mistaken identity*). *Classical* generally refers to the world of ancient Greece and Rome (*classical antiquity*), to serious music (*classical composers such as Beethoven and Mozart*) and to long-standing or formerly authoritative forms when contrasted with modern ones (*classical mechanics as opposed to quantum mechanics*). The distinction was considerably less clear-cut, however, in former times.

classic² *noun* **1a** a work of lasting excellence, or the author of one. **b** an authoritative or definitive work. **2** (*in pl*). **a** (**the classics**) literary works of ancient Greece or Rome. **b** (*often* **Classics**) Greek and Latin literature, history, and philosophy considered as an academic subject. **3** a classic example; an archetype. **4a** an important long-established sporting event. **b** in Britain, any of five flat races for horses, the Derby, the Oaks, the St Leger, the One Thousand Guineas, and the Two Thousand Guineas.

classical *adj* **1a** of the ancient Greek and Roman world, or its literature, art, architecture, or ideals. **b** copying or showing the influence of ancient Greek and Roman forms or principles.

Editorial note

Classical is a term used for the architecture of ancient Greece and Rome, revived at the Renaissance and subsequently imitated around the Western world. It uses a range of conventional forms, the roots of which are the Orders, or types of column each with its fixed proportions and ornaments (especially Doric, Ionic and Corinthian). Classical buildings tend also to be symmetrical, both externally and on plan — Simon Bradley.

2a of or being music of the late 18th and early 19th cents characterized by an emphasis on simplicity, objectivity, and proportion, or of a composer of such music. **b** of or being music in the European tradition that includes such forms as chamber music, opera, and symphony as distinguished from folk, popular music, or jazz. **3a** both authoritative and traditional. **b** of a system or method that constitutes an early, or an accepted although not necessarily modern, approach to a subject; standard: *classical Mendelian genetics*. **c** said of physics: not involving relativity, wave mechanics, or quantum theory. **4** concerned with instruction in the classics: *a classical education*. **5** = CLASSIC¹ (2). [Latin *classicus*: see CLASSIC¹]

Usage note

classical *or* classic? See note at CLASSIC¹.

classicalism /klasikl·iz(ə)m/ *noun* = CLASSICISM.

classicalist /klasikl·ist/ *noun* = CLASSICIST.

classicality /klasi'kaliti/ *noun* the quality or state of being classic or classical.

classically *adv* **1** in a classic or classical manner: *classically beautiful*. **2** in classical music: *She sings folk music, but she's classically trained*.

classic car *noun Brit* an old motor car; *specif* one manufactured between 1925 and 1942.

classicise /'klasisiez/ *verb trans* see CLASSICIZE.

classicism /'klasisiz(ə)m/ *noun* **1** adherence to traditional standards, e.g. of simplicity, restraint, and proportion, that are considered to have universal and lasting worth. **2a** the principles or style embodied in classical literature, art, or architecture. **b** a classical idiom or expression.

classicist /'klasisist/ *noun* **1** an advocate or student of classicism. **2** a scholar or student of Classics.

classicize *or* **classicise** /'klasisiez/ *verb trans* to make (something) classic or classical in style.

classification /,klasifi'kaysh(ə)n/ *noun* **1** classifying or being classified. **2a** systematic arrangement in groups according to established criteria; *specif* taxonomy. **b** a class or category. ➤➤ **classificatory** *adj*.

classified /'klasified/ *adj* **1** divided into classes or placed in a class. **2** said of information, a document, etc: withheld from general circulation for reasons of national or military security. **3** said of a road: given a classification as a motorway, an A-road, or a B-road, according to its relative size and importance, as opposed to a minor unclassified road.

classified ad *noun* (*usu in pl*) an advertisement in a newspaper or periodical, usu in small type and grouped according to subject.

classify /'klasifie/ *verb trans* (**classifies, classified, classifying**) **1a** to arrange (people or things) in classes. **b** (*often* + *as*) to assign (somebody or something) to a category. **2** to designate (a document, information, etc) as secret and not to be made available to the general public. ➤➤ **classifiable** *adj*, **classifier** *noun*.

classless *adj* **1** free from class distinction: *a classless society*. **2** belonging to no particular social class: *a classless accent*. ➤➤ **classlessness** *noun*.

classmate *noun* a member of the same class in a school or college.

classroom *noun* a room where classes are held, *esp* in a school.

class struggle *noun* (*often* **the class struggle**) the conflict between social classes; *specif* in Marxist theory, the struggle for economic and political power between the workers and the capitalists and ruling class in a capitalist society.

class war *noun* = CLASS STRUGGLE.

classy *adj* (**classier, classiest**) *informal* elegant; stylish. ➤➤ **classiness** *noun*.

clastic /'klastik/ *adj* said of a rock: made up of fragments of pre-existing rocks. [Greek *klastos* broken, from *klan* to break]

clathrate /'klathrayt/ *noun* in chemistry, a compound formed by the inclusion of molecules of one kind in the crystal lattice of another. [Latin *clathratus* from *clathri* (pl) lattice, from Greek *klēithron* bar, from *kleiein* to close]

clatter¹ /'klatə/ *verb* (**clattered, clattering**) ➤ *verb intrans* **1** to make a loud rattling or banging noise: *The dishes clattered on the shelf*. **2** to move or go with a loud rattling or banging noise: *She clattered down the stairs*. **3** to prattle or chatter. ➤ *verb trans* to cause (dishes, etc) to clatter. ➤➤ **clatterer** *noun*, **clatteringly** *adv*. [Middle English *clatren*, of imitative origin]

clatter² *noun* **1** a loud rattling or banging noise, e.g. of hard bodies striking together: *the clatter of pots and pans*. **2** a commotion: *the midday clatter of the business district*.

claudication /klawdi'kaysh(ə)n/ *noun technical* lameness or limping. [Latin *claudication-, claudicatio*, from *claudicare* to limp, from *claudus* lame]

clause /klawz/ *noun* **1** a string of words containing a subject and predicate and functioning either as a sentence or as a member of a complex or compound sentence. **2** a distinct article or condition in a formal document. ➤➤ **clausal** *adj*. [Middle English via Old French from medieval Latin *clausa* close of a rhetorical period, from Latin, fem past part. of *claudere* to close]

claustral /'klawstrəl/ *adj* = CLOISTRAL. [Middle English from medieval Latin *claustralis*, from *claustrum*: see CLOISTER¹]

claustrophobia /klostrə'fohbi·ə, klaw-/ *noun* abnormal dread of being in closed or confined spaces. ➤➤ **claustrophobe** /'klos-, 'klaws-/ *noun*. [scientific Latin *claustrophobia*, from Latin *claustrum* (see CLOISTER¹) + -PHOBIA]

claustrophobic¹ /klostrə'fohbik, klaw-/ *adj* **1** suffering from claustrophobia. **2** said of a place or situation: making one feel uncomfortable, as if suffering from claustrophobia: *I hate lifts. They're so claustrophobic.*

claustrophobic² *noun* somebody who suffers from claustrophobia.

clavate /'klayvayt, 'klayvət/ *adj* said of e.g. a leaf: club-shaped. ➤➤ **clavately** *adv*. [scientific Latin *clavatus*, from Latin *clava* club, from *clavus* nail, knot in wood]

clave¹ /'klayv/ *verb archaic* past tense of CLEAVE².

clave² /klayv, klahv/ *noun* either of a pair of small wooden sticks struck together rhythmically, e.g. in accompanying a rumba. [American Spanish *clave* from Spanish, keystone, clef, from Latin *clavis* key]

clavichord /'klavikawd/ *noun* an early keyboard musical instrument, usu rectangular in shape with strings that are struck by small brass blades, producing soft silvery notes. [medieval Latin *clavichordium*, from Latin *clavis* key + *chorda*: see CORD¹]

clavicle /'klavikl/ *noun* a shoulder bone typically linking the shoulder blade and breastbone in humans and other vertebrates; the collarbone. ➤➤ **clavicular** /klə'vikyoolə/ *adj*. [French *clavicule* from Latin *clavicula*, dimin. of *clavis* key]

clavier /'klavi-ə/ *noun* 1 a keyboard instrument. 2 the keyboard of a keyboard instrument. [German *Klavier* from French *clavier*, ultimately from Latin *clavis* key]

claviform /'klavifawm/ *adj* said of e.g. a leaf: club-shaped. [Latin *clava*: see CLAVATE]

claw¹ /klaw/ *noun* 1 a sharp slender curved nail on an animal's toe, or a part resembling or a limb having one. 2 any of the pincer-like organs on the end of some limbs of a lobster, scorpion, or similar arthropod. 3 something, e.g. the forked end of a claw hammer, resembling a claw. ➤➤ **clawed** *adj*, **clawless** *adj*. [Old English *clawu* hoof, claw]

claw² *verb trans* to rake, seize, dig, remove, or make (something) with, or as if with, claws. ➤ *verb intrans* (*often* + at) to scrape, scratch, dig, or pull something with, or as if with, claws.

claw back *verb trans* 1 to get or take (something) back with difficulty or harshness. 2 to take (money) back, *esp* by taxation. ➤➤ **claw-back** *noun*.

claw hammer *noun* a hammer with one end of the head forked for pulling out nails.

clay /klay/ *noun* 1a an earthy material that is soft when moist but hard when fired, is composed mainly of fine particles of aluminium silicates, and is used for making brick, tile, and pottery, or soil composed chiefly of this. b thick and clinging earth or mud. 2a a substance that resembles clay and is used for modelling. b the human body as distinguished from the spirit. ➤➤ **clayey** /'klayi/ *adj*, **clayish** *adj*. [Old English *clæg*]

claymore /'klaymaw/ *noun* 1 a large two-edged broadsword formerly used by Scottish Highlanders. 2 a type of single-edged broadsword. [Scottish Gaelic *claidheamh mór* great sword]

clay pigeon *noun* a saucer-shaped object usu made of baked clay and thrown into the air by a TRAP¹ (device for hurling clay pigeons) as a target for shooting at with a shotgun for sport.

clean¹ /kleen/ *adj* 1a free or relatively free from dirt: *We changed into clean clothes*. b habitually keeping oneself clean: *Cats are clean animals*. 2a free from contamination, pollution, infection, or disease. b relatively free from, or producing little or no, radioactive fallout. 3a free from illegal, immoral, or disreputable activities: *He's got a clean record*. b said of a driving licence: free from endorsements or penalty points. c *NAmer, informal* carrying no concealed weapons, illegal drugs, etc. d *informal* innocent. 4 free from the use of obscenity: *I just don't know any clean jokes!* 5 observing the rules; fair: *a clean fight*. 6 thorough; complete: *a clean break with the past*. 7a pure; unadulterated. b free, or relatively free, from errors or blemishes. c said of a sheet of paper, etc: unused; without anything on it. d legible and with few corrections or alterations: *clean copy*. 8a characterized by clarity, precision, or deftness: *architecture with clean, almost austere, lines; a clean throw*. b not jagged; smooth: *a clean edge*. c said of a ship or aircraft: well streamlined. d said of a taste or smell: fresh; invigorating. 9 ritually or spiritually pure. ✳ **clean sheet/slate** a situation in which no record is kept of past errors, previous decisions, etc. **a clean sweep 1** the removal of everything and everyone that is not wanted. 2 the winning of all prizes, etc. **make a clean breast of it** to make a full confession. ➤➤ **cleanly** *adv*, **cleanness** *noun*. [Old English *clæne*]

clean² *adv* 1 all the way; completely: *The bullet went clean through his arm*. 2a so as to leave something clean: *New brooms sweep clean*. b in a fair manner; according to the rules: *Fight clean*.

clean³ *verb trans* 1 to make (something or somebody) clean. 2a (*often* + out) to strip or empty (something). b (*often* + out) to deprive (somebody) of money or possessions: *They cleaned him out completely*. ➤ *verb intrans* to undergo cleaning; to be cleanable. ➤➤ **cleanable** *adj*.

clean⁴ *noun* an act of cleaning away dirt: *Give your room a good clean*.

clean-cut *adj* 1 sharply defined; clear. 2 said of a person: clean and neat in appearance. 3 cut so that the surface or edge is smooth and even.

cleaner *noun* 1 somebody whose occupation is cleaning rooms or clothes. 2 a substance, implement, or machine for cleaning: *a bathroom cleaner*. ✳ **take somebody to the cleaners** *informal* to rob (somebody) or defraud (them). 2 *informal* to criticize (somebody).

cleaning *noun* making something clean; *specif* cleaning and tidying a house or room.

cleanliness /'klenlinis/ *noun* fastidiousness in keeping things or one's person clean. ➤➤ **cleanly** *adj*.

cleanse /klenz/ *verb trans* 1 to clean (something or somebody) thoroughly, e.g. with a lotion or cleanser. 2 to make (somebody or something) ritually pure. 3 *archaic* to cure (somebody). [Old English *clǣnsian* to purify, from *clǣne* CLEAN¹]

cleanser *noun* a preparation, e.g. a scouring powder or skin cream, used for cleaning.

clean-shaven *adj* with the hair of the beard and moustache shaved off.

cleansing /'klenzing/ *noun* 1 the street-cleaning and collection of household and business refuse carried out by or on behalf of a local authority. 2 a process of improvement or purification, *esp* by the removal of somebody or something considered undesirable: *ethnic cleansing; They saw the clamp-down on drugs as a form of social cleansing*.

clean up *verb intrans* 1 to make somebody or something clean. 2 *informal* to make a large *esp* sweeping gain, e.g. in business or gambling. ➤ *verb trans* 1 to remove (a mess) by cleaning. 2 to make (somebody or something) clean. ➤➤ **clean-up** *noun*.

clear¹ /kliə/ *adj* 1a bright; luminous: *clear blue*. b free from cloud, mist, haze, or dust: *a clear day*. c untroubled; serene: *a clear gaze*. 2a clean or pure; free from blemishes: *a clear skin*. b easily seen through; transparent: *a clear liquid*. 3a easily heard; not muffled. b pure; not rough or hoarse: *She has a beautifully clear singing voice*. 4a easily visible; plain. b free from obscurity or ambiguity; easily understood: *Do I make myself clear?* 5a capable of sharp discernment; keen: *This problem needs a clear mind*. b free from doubt; sure: *We are not clear what to do*. 6 free from guilt: *a clear conscience*. 7a net: *a clear profit*. b unqualified; absolute: *a clear victory*. c full: *six clear days*. 8a said of a road, etc: free from obstruction or entanglement. b (+ of) away from; not at or touching: *You're clear of the wall at this side*. c (+ of) rid of something; no longer troubled by it: *We'll be OK once we're clear of these teething troubles*. 9 in showjumping, without faults: *a clear round*. ✳ **as clear as mud** *informal* not at all clear. ➤➤ **clearly** *adv*, **clearness** *noun*. [Middle English *clere* via Old French from Latin *clarus* clear]

clear² *adv* 1 clearly: *They cried loud and clear*. 2 *chiefly NAmer* all the way: *You can see clear to the mountains today*.

clear³ *verb trans* 1a (*often* + out) to free (something) from unwanted material: *I must clear out the cupboard*. b to evacuate (an area, a building). 2a (*often* + off/up/away) to remove or dispose of (something) that is no longer wanted: *We cleared the plates from the table; They cleared away the rubbish*. b to form (something) by removing material: *They cleared a path through the snow*. 3 in football, to kick (the ball) away from the goal as a defensive measure. 4a (+ of) to free (somebody) from accusation or blame: *He was cleared of murder*. b to certify (somebody) as trustworthy: *They have all been cleared for top security work*. 5a to rid (the throat) of phlegm. b to erase accumulated totals or stored data from (a calculator or computer memory). 6a to free (somebody) from financial obligation. b (*often* + off) to settle or discharge (a debt, etc). c to deal with (work) until it is finished or settled. d to earn (a certain sum of money) without deduction. e to put (a cheque) through a clearing house. 7a to authorize (something) or cause it to be authorized. b to authorize (somebody or something) to do something. 8 to go over (an obstacle) without touching it. 9 to make (something) transparent or translucent. 10 to satisfy the requirements of (customs) at an airport etc. ➤ *verb intrans* 1a (*often* + up) said of the weather: to become free from rain, mist, etc. b (*often* + away) to go away; to vanish: *The symptoms cleared gradually; After the mist cleared away we had a lovely view*. 2 said of a cheque: to pass through a clearing house and so be accepted. ✳ **clear the air** to remove tension or hostility by open discussion. **clear the decks** to prepare for action. ➤➤ **clearable** *adj*, **clearer** *noun*.

clear⁴ *noun* 1 a clear space or part; a clearing. 2 a high long arcing shot in badminton. 3 the position or colour of a signal when indicating that traffic may pass. ✳ **in the clear 1** free from guilt or suspicion. **2** out of trouble. **3** having funds; solvent.

clearance *noun* **1** authorization: *The pilot is waiting to get clearance to land.* **2** (*also* **clearance sale**) a sale to clear out stock. **3a** the removal of buildings, people, etc from the space they previously occupied: *the Highland Clearances*; *slum clearance*. **b** a clearing of the ball in football. **4** the distance by which one object clears another, or the clear space between them. **5** the passing of cheques and other claims among banks through a clearing house.

clearcole /'kliəkohl/ *noun* a priming of size mixed with ground chalk or white lead, formerly used *esp* in house painting. [partial translation of French *claire colle*, from *claire* clear + *colle* glue]

clear-cut *adj* **1** sharply outlined; distinct. **2** free from ambiguity or uncertainty: *a clear-cut case of sabotage.*

clearheaded *adj* **1** not confused; sensible; rational. **2** having no illusions about a state of affairs; realistic.

clearing *noun* an area of land cleared of wood and brush.

clearing bank *noun* a bank that is a member of a clearing house.

clearing house /'kliəringhows/ *noun* **1** an establishment maintained by banks for settling mutual claims and accounts. **2** an agency for collecting, classifying, and distributing something, *esp* information.

clear off *verb intrans informal* to go away.

clear out *verb trans* to use or empty all of (something). ➤ *verb intrans informal* to go away; to leave a place. ➤➤ **clearout** *noun.*

clear-sighted *adj* CLEARHEADED (2), *esp* having perceptive insight.

clearstory *noun* see CLERESTORY.

clear up *verb trans* **1a** to remove (a mess, etc). **b** to tidy (a room, etc) by removing unwanted things. **2** to provide a solution or explanation for (a problem or mystery). ➤ *verb intrans* said of an illness, etc: to be cured or alleviated.

clearway *noun Brit* a road on which vehicles may stop only in an emergency.

cleat /kleet/ *noun* **1a** a projecting piece, e.g. on the bottom of a shoe, that provides a grip. **b** (*in pl*) shoes equipped with cleats. **2a** a wedge-shaped piece fastened to something and serving as a support or check. **b** a wooden or metal fitting, usu with two projecting horns, round which a rope may be made fast. [Middle English *clete* wedge, of Germanic origin]

cleavage /'kleevij/ *noun* **1** the space between a woman's breasts, *esp* when exposed by a low-cut garment: *One or two of Miss Loren's films have been more notable for the depth of cleavage displayed than any profoundness of plot* — Guardian. **2** a division. **3** = CELL DIVISION. **4** the property of a crystal or rock, e.g. slate, of splitting along definite planes. **5** the splitting of a molecule into simpler molecules.

cleave[1] /kleev/ *verb* (*past tense* **clove** /klohv/ *or* **cleft** /kleft/ *or* **cleaved**, *past part.* **cloven** /'klohv(ə)n/ *or* **cleft** *or* **cleaved**) ➤ *verb trans* **1** to divide or pass through (something or somewhere) by, or as if by, a cutting blow; to split (something). **2** to create (a path) through something as if by cleaving. ➤ *verb intrans* **1** to split, *esp* along the grain. **2** to divide. **3** to move as if cleaving a path through something. ➤➤ **cleavable** *adj.* [Old English *clēofan*]

cleave[2] *verb intrans* (*past tense* **cleaved** *or archaic* **clave** /klayv/) (+ to) to stick firmly and closely or loyally and steadfastly to somebody or something. [Old English *clifian*; related to Old English *clǣg* CLAY]

cleaver *noun* a butcher's implement for cutting animal carcasses into joints or pieces.

cleavers *pl noun* (*treated as sing. or pl*) an annual plant of the madder family that bears small white flowers and whose stem, leaves, and fruit are covered with stiff prickles that make it stick to surfaces: *Galium aparine*. Also called GOOSEGRASS. [Middle English *clivre*, alteration of Old English *clife* burdock, cleavers; related to Old English CLEAVE[1]]

clef /klef/ *noun* a sign placed on a musical stave to indicate the pitch represented by the notes following it. [French *clef* key, from Latin *clavis*]

cleft[1] /kleft/ *noun* **1** a space or opening made by splitting; a fissure. **2** a V-shaped indented formation; a hollow between ridges or protuberances. [Middle English *clift* from Old English *geclyft*; related to Old English *clēofan* CLEAVE[1]]

cleft[2] *verb* past tense and past part. of CLEAVE[1].

cleft lip *noun* = HARELIP.

cleft palate *noun* a congenital fissure of the roof of the mouth.

cleft stick *noun chiefly Brit* a dilemma.

cleg /kleg/ *noun Brit* = HORSEFLY. [Middle English, from Old Norse *kleggi*]

clematis /klə'maytəs, 'klemətis/ *noun* a climbing plant of the buttercup family with white, pink, or purple flowers: genus *Clematis*. [Latin genus name, from Greek *klēmatis* brushwood, clematis, from *klēmat-*, *klēma* twig, from *klan* to break]

clemency /'klemənsi/ *noun* **1** an inclination to moderate the severity of punishment due; mercifulness or leniency. **2** general pleasantness and mildness of weather.

clement /'klemənt/ *adj* **1** said of the weather: pleasantly mild. **2** acting mercifully or inclined to be merciful; lenient: *a clement judge.* [Middle English from Latin *clement-*, *clemens*]

clementine /'klemənteen, -tien/ *noun* a small citrus fruit that is a cross between an orange and a tangerine and has slightly acid flesh. [French *clémentine*, from the male forename *Clément*]

clench /klench/ *verb trans* **1** to close or hold together (the fists, teeth, etc) tightly. **2** to grip or clutch (something) firmly. ➤ *verb intrans* **1** said of a set of muscles: to contract suddenly. **2** said of the fist or jaw: to become firmly closed or set as the muscles tauten. [Old English *-clencan*; related to Old English *clingan* CLING[1]]

clepsydra /'klepsidrə/ *noun* (*pl* **clepsydras** *or* **clepsydrae** /-dree/) a water clock. [via Latin from Greek *klepsydra*, from *kleptein* to steal + *hydōr* water]

clerestory *or* **clearstory** /'kliəstawri/ *noun* (*pl* **clerestories, clearstories**) **1** the part of an outside wall of a room or building, *esp* a church, that rises above an adjoining roof: *clerestory windows*. **2** *chiefly NAmer* a raised ventilating section of a railway carriage roof. [Middle English, from *clere* clear + *story* storey]

clergy /'kluhji/ *noun* (*treated as sing. or pl*) the group of people ordained to act as priests or ministers in an organized religion, *esp* a Christian Church. [Middle English *clergie* via Old French from Latin *clericus*: see CLERK[1]]

clergyman *or* **clergywoman** *noun* (*pl* **clergymen** *or* **clergywomen**) an ordained priest or minister.

cleric /'klerik/ *noun* a member of the Christian clergy, or an equivalent minister or leader from another religion. [late Latin *clericus*: see CLERK[1]]

clerical *adj* **1** denoting or involving office work of a fairly routine kind, such as typing and filing. **2** relating to or characteristic of the clergy, a clergyman, or a cleric. ➤➤ **clerically** *adv.*

clerical collar *noun* a narrow stiff upright white collar fastening at the back and worn by clergymen and clergywomen.

clerical error *noun* a mistake in a document made when it was being written or copied out.

clericalism *noun* a policy promoting ecclesiastical influence in secular matters. ➤➤ **clericalist** *noun.*

clericals *pl noun* clothes worn by the clergy.

clerihew /'klerihooh/ *noun* a witty pseudo-biographical four-line verse. [named after Edmund *Clerihew* Bentley d.1956, English writer, who invented the form]

clerk[1] /klahk; *NAmer* kluhk/ *noun* **1a** somebody whose occupation is keeping records or accounts or doing general office work: *a filing clerk*. **b** *NAmer* a shop assistant. **2** = CLERIC. **3** *archaic* a scholar. ➤➤ **clerkly** *adj,* **clerkship** *noun.* [Old English *cleric*, *clerc* via Latin *clericus* of the clergy, from late Greek *klērikos*, from Greek *klēros* lot, inheritance; because in the Middle Ages the clergy kept the local records]

clerk[2] *verb intrans* to act or work as a clerk.

clerk of the course *noun* (*pl* **clerks of the course**) an official who has direct charge of the running of a horse-racing or motor-racing meeting.

clerk of the works *noun* (*pl* **clerks of the works**) the person in charge of building works in a particular place.

clever /'klevə/ *adj* (**cleverer, cleverest**) **1a** mentally quick and resourceful; intelligent. **b** characterized by intelligence, wit, or ingenuity. **2** witty or ingenious but lacking depth or soundness. **3** skilful or adroit with the hands or body. ➤➤ **cleverly** *adv,* **cleverness** *noun.* [Middle English *cliver*, prob of Scandinavian origin]

clever-clever *adj derog* over-ingenious, or trying too hard to be or appear clever.

clever clogs *noun* = CLEVER DICK.

clever dick *noun Brit, informal* a person who is ostentatiously or annoyingly clever.

clevis /'klevis/ *noun* a usu U-shaped metal shackle with the ends drilled to receive a pin or bolt used for attaching or suspending parts. [earlier *clevi*, prob of Scandinavian origin]

clew[1] /klooh/ *noun* **1** either of the lower corners of a square sail, or the lower aft corner of a triangular sail. **2** a ball of thread or yarn. **3** *archaic* = CLUE[1] (I). [Old English *cliewen*: see CLUE[1]]

clew[2] *verb trans* to haul (a sail) up or down by ropes through the clews.

clianthus /klie'anthəs/ *noun* a leguminous plant of Australia and New Zealand that has clusters of slender scarlet flowers: genus *Clianthus*. [Latin genus name, prob from Greek *klei-*, *kleos* glory + *anthos* flower]

cliché /'kleeshay/ *noun* **1** a hackneyed phrase or expression, or the idea expressed by it: *forever poised between a cliché and an indiscretion* — Harold Macmillan. **2** a hackneyed theme or situation. **3** *Brit* in printing, a stereotype or electrotype plate. ⟫⟫ **clichéd** *adj,* **cliché'd** *adj.* [French *cliché* stereotype, past part. of *clicher* to stereotype]

click[1] /klik/ *noun* **1** a light sharp sound, of the kind made when one metal or plastic part makes contact with or locks into another. **2** a sharp speech sound in some languages made by the sudden inrush of air when the tongue is released after being pressed against the palate or the back of the teeth. **3** in computing, an action of pressing and releasing a button on a mouse. [prob imitative]

click[2] *verb trans* **1** to make (something) produce a click. **2a** to press and release (a button on a mouse). **b** (*often + on*) in computing, to select (a function) by pressing and releasing a button on a mouse: *On the toolbar, click the printer icon.* ⟫ *verb intrans* **1** to operate with or make a click. **2** *informal.* **a** (*often + with*) to strike up an immediately warm friendship with somebody. **b** (*usu + with*) to become successful or popular: *The film really clicked with London audiences.* **3** *Brit* to cause sudden insight or recognition: *The name clicked.* **4** (*usu + on*) in computing, to press a button on a mouse or select an option in this way: *Click on any part of the map.* ⟫⟫ **clicker** *noun.*

click beetle *noun* any of a family of beetles able to right themselves with a click when turned over: family Elateridae.

client /'klie·ənt/ *noun* **1a** somebody who engages or receives the advice or services of a professional person or organization. **b** a customer. **2a** in computing, a computer or workstation to which data is provided by a server. **b** in computing, a program used to contact another computer or a network and request data from it. **3** a person, state, etc under the protection of another: *client states.* **4** a plebeian in ancient Rome who was granted protection by a patron. ⟫⟫ **clientage** /-tij/ *noun,* **cliental** /klie'entl, 'klie·əntl/ *adj.* [Middle English via French from Latin *client-*, *cliens*, client, dependent, ultimately from *cluere* to obey]

client-centred therapy *noun* a method of therapy designed to encourage people to learn to take responsibility for their own actions and to solve their own problems.

clientele /kleeon'tel/ *noun* (*treated as sing. or pl*) a body of clients: *a shop with an exclusive clientele.* [French *clientèle*, from Latin *clientela*, from *client-*, *cliens*: see CLIENT]

clientelism /klee·on'telizm/ *noun usu derog* a situation in which patronage is used extensively and often misused.

clientism /'klie·əntizm/ *noun* = CLIENTELISM.

cliff /klif/ *noun* a very steep high face of rock, earth, etc, *esp* on the coast. ⟫⟫ **cliffy** *adj.* [Old English *clif*]

cliffhanger *noun* **1** a story, or an episode in a story, that ends in extreme suspense; any suspenseful situation. ⟫⟫ **cliff-hanging** *adj.* [from early film serials in which each episode ended with at least one character hanging from a cliff or in some other precarious situation; the audience had to see the next episode to learn their fate]

climacteric[1] /klie'maktərik, kliemək'terik/ *adj* **1** of crucial importance, or having vital consequences or implications. **2** relating to a climacteric. [via Latin from Greek *klimaktērikos*, from *klimaktēr* critical point, literally 'rung of a ladder', from *klimak-*, *klimax*: see CLIMAX[1]]

climacteric[2] *noun* **1** a major turning point or critical stage; *specif* one supposed to occur at intervals of seven years. **2** the menopause, or a corresponding period in men during which sexual activity is reduced.

climactic /klie'maktik/ *adj* causing or forming a climax. ⟫⟫ **climactically** *adv.*

Usage note
climactic *or* climatic? These two words are easily confused, but can be just as easily distinguished if the nouns they come from are borne in mind. *Climactic* comes from *climax*: *the climactic moment of the play. Climatic* comes from *climate*: *the climatic conditions in northern Borneo.*

climate /'kliemət/ *noun* **1a** the average course or condition of the weather in a particular area over a period of years as shown by temperature, wind, rain, etc. **b** a region of the earth having a particular type of weather conditions. **2** the prevailing state of affairs or feelings of a group or period; a milieu: *a climate of fear.* ⟫⟫ **climatic** /klie'matik/ *adj,* **climatical** /klie'matikl/ *adj,* **climatically** /klie'matikli/ *adv.* [Middle English *climat* via French and Latin from Greek *klimat-*, *klima* inclination, latitude, climate, from *klinein* to lean]

Usage note
climatic *or* climactic? See note at CLIMACTIC.

climate control *noun* = AIR CONDITIONING.

climatology /kliemə'toləji/ *noun* the branch of meteorology dealing with climates. ⟫⟫ **climatological** /-'lojikl/ *adj,* **climatologically** /-'lojikli/ *adv,* **climatologist** *noun.*

climax[1] /'kliemaks/ *noun* **1a** the highest point or point of maximum intensity; a culmination. **b** the point of highest dramatic tension or a major turning point in some action (e.g. of a play). **2** = ORGASM. **3** a technique in or passage of rhetoric in which a series of phrases or sentences are arranged in increasing order of forcefulness. **4** a relatively stable final stage reached by a plant community in its ecological development. [via Latin from Greek *klimax* ladder, from *klinein* to lean]

climax[2] *verb intrans and trans* to come to or bring (something) to a climax.

climb[1] /kliem/ *verb intrans* **1a** to go up, down, etc on a more or less vertical surface using the hands to grasp or give support. **b** said of a plant: to ascend while growing, e.g. by twining. **2a** to go gradually upwards; to rise: *The aircraft climbed to 10,000ft before levelling off.* **b** to slope upwards: *The road climbs steadily.* **3** to increase in amount or value: *Inflation climbed to 27%.* **4** to get into or out of clothing, a confined space, etc, usu with some awkwardness or effort. **5** to go up mountains for sport. ⟫ *verb trans* **1** to go upwards on, to the top of, or over (something): *climb a hill.* **2** to draw or pull oneself up, over, or to the top of (something), by using the hands and feet: *climb a tree.* **3** said of a plant: to grow up or over (something). ✳ **be climbing the walls** *informal* to be extremely frustrated, impatient, anxious, etc. ⟫⟫ **climbable** *adj.* [Old English *climban*]

climb[2] *noun* **1** an act of climbing; an ascent by climbing. **2a** a route taken by climbers. **b** a steep slope or ascent. **3** an increase, *esp* a sudden one, in amount or value.

climb down *verb intrans* to withdraw from a position in an argument; to back down. ⟫⟫ **climbdown** *noun.*

climber *noun* **1** a person who climbs hills or mountains. **2** a climbing plant. **3** *chiefly Brit* = SOCIAL CLIMBER.

climbing frame *noun Brit* a framework for children to climb on.

climbing iron *noun* = CRAMPON.

climbing perch *noun* a small Indian fish resembling a perch that travels overland by means of its spiny projecting fins, and has modified gills for breathing air: *Anabas testudineus.*

climbing wall *noun* a wall fitted with artificial hand- and footholds to provide practice in rock climbing.

clime /kliem/ *noun chiefly literary* (*usu in pl*) = CLIMATE (IB): *Match me such marvel save in Eastern clime, a rose-red city – 'half as old as Time'!* — J W Burgon. [late Latin *clima*, zone, from Greek *klima*: see CLIMATE]

clinch[1] /klinch/ *verb trans* **1** to make (e.g. an arrangement) final; to settle (something): *That clinched the argument; We set up a meeting to clinch the deal.* **2** to turn over or flatten the protruding pointed end of (e.g. a driven nail). **3** to fasten (something) by clinching a nail, etc. ⟫ *verb intrans* **1** in boxing or wrestling, to hold an opponent at close quarters. **2** *informal* to embrace or hug somebody. [prob alteration of CLENCH]

clinch² *noun* **1** in boxing or wrestling, the act or an instance of clinching. **2** *informal* an embrace. **3** a fastening by means of a clinched nail, rivet, or bolt.

clincher *noun informal* a decisive fact, argument, act, or remark: *'Why cannot I communicate with the young lady's friends?' ... 'Because they live one hundred miles from here.' ... 'That's a clincher,' said Mr Weller, aside.* — Dickens.

cline /klien/ *noun* a graded series of differences in shape or physiology shown by a group of related organisms, usu along a line of environmental or geographical transition; *broadly* a continuum. ➤➤ **clinal** *adj.* [Greek *klinein* to lean]

-cline *comb. form* forming nouns, denoting: a slope: *monocline.* [Greek *klinein* to lean]

cling¹ /kling/ *verb intrans* (*past tense and past part.* **clung** /klung/) **1a** (+ to/onto) to hold on tightly or tenaciously. **b** (+ to/onto) to stick as if glued firmly. **2a** to have a strong emotional attachment or dependence. **b** (+ to) to refuse to give up; to remain stubbornly attached to or convinced of something: *They clung to the hope that their son would be found alive.* **3** said *esp* of a smell: to linger. ➤➤ **clingy** *adj.* [Old English *clingan*]

cling² *noun* = CLINGSTONE.

clingfilm *noun* a thin transparent plastic film used to wrap foodstuffs and keep them fresh.

clingstone *noun* a fruit, e.g. a peach, whose flesh sticks strongly to the stone.

clinic /ˈklinik/ *noun* **1a** a place where treatment or advice is given in a specified area of medicine: *an antenatal clinic.* **b** a hospital, or part of a hospital, where medical treatment is given to outpatients. **2** a bedside class for medical students in which patients are examined and discussed. **3a** a meeting held by an expert or person in authority, to which people bring problems for discussion and resolution: *an MP's weekly clinic for her constituents.* **b** a session in which skills or knowledge, usu in a specified field, are taught by an expert, *esp* remedially: *a golf clinic.* [French *clinique* from Greek *klinikē* medical practice at the sickbed, from *klinē* bed]

clinical *adj* **1** involving, based on, or noticeable from direct observation of the patient: *clinical psychology.* **2** analytic or detached. **3** said of a room, surroundings, etc: severely plain and functional, lacking any ornament or colour. ➤➤ **clinically** *adv.*

clinical psychology *noun* the branch of psychology concerned with the diagnosis and treatment of mental illness.

clinical thermometer *noun* a thermometer for measuring body temperature.

clinician /kliˈnish(ə)n/ *noun* somebody qualified in clinical medicine, psychiatry, etc as distinguished from somebody specializing in laboratory or research techniques.

clink¹ /klingk/ *verb intrans and trans* to make or cause (something) to make a slight sharp short metallic sound. [Middle English *clinken,* of imitative origin]

clink² *noun* a sharp short ringing sound.

clink³ *noun slang* prison. [*Clink,* the name of a former prison in *Clink* Street, Southwark, London]

clinker /ˈklingkə/ *noun* **1** stony matter fused by fire; slag. **2** a vitrified brick. **3** *informal* something unsatisfactory or of poor quality. [alteration of *klincard* a hard yellowish Dutch brick, from obsolete Dutch *klinkaard*]

clinker-built *adj* said of a boat or ship: having the lower edge of each external plank or plate overlapping the upper edge of the one below it: compare CARVEL-BUILT. [*clinker* noun, variant of CLINCH²]

clinometer /kliˈnomitə, ˈklie-/ *noun* any of various instruments for measuring angles of slope. ➤➤ **clinometric** /klinəˈmetrik, klie-/ *adj,* **clinometry** *noun.*

clint /klint/ *noun* a limestone block in a horizontal limestone surface broken up by clefts: compare GRIKE. [Middle English, perhaps from early German *klint* cliff, crag]

clip¹ /klip/ *verb* (**clipped, clipping**) ➤ *verb trans* to clasp or fasten (something) with a clip. ➤ *verb intrans* (*often* + on) to be attached by means of a clip. [Old English *clyppan*]

clip² *noun* **1** any of various devices that grip, clasp, or hold objects together or in position. **2** a piece of jewellery held in position by a spring clip. **3a** a device to hold cartridges that is inserted into a magazine from which ammunition is fed into the chamber of an automatic firearm. **b** such a magazine.

clip³ *verb trans* (**clipped, clipping**) **1a** to cut (hair or wool) with or as if with shears. **b** to clip the hair or wool of (an animal). **2a** to cut off the end or outer part of (something). **b** to remove (something) by or as if by cutting it out. **3** to abbreviate (letters or words) in speech or writing. **4** *informal* to hit (somebody or something) with a sharp or glancing blow: *She clipped him round the ear.* **5** *NAmer, informal* to cheat or swindle (somebody). ✳ **clip the wings of** to restrict the freedom or power of (somebody). [Middle English *clippen,* from Old Norse *klippa*]

clip⁴ *noun* **1a** the product of a single shearing, e.g. of sheep. **b** an act of clipping, or the manner in which something is clipped. **2** a section of filmed material, *esp* an excerpt from a feature film. **3** *informal* a sharp blow. **4** *informal* a rapid pace or speed.

clip art *noun* in computing, ready-drawn pictures, symbols, etc provided in software programs for users to insert into their own documents.

clipboard *noun* **1** a small writing board with a spring clip for holding papers. **2** a temporary storage area in word-processing and other computer programs in which data removed or copied from a file is held until it is reinserted elsewhere.

clip-clop /klip ˈklop/ *verb intrans* (**clip-clopped, clip-clopping**) *informal* to make the rhythmic repeated sound characteristically produced by horses' hooves. ➤➤ **clip-clop** *noun.* [imitative]

clip joint *noun informal* a place of public entertainment, e.g. a nightclub, that defrauds, overcharges, etc. [CLIP³ in the sense 'to overcharge, swindle' + JOINT¹]

clip-on *adj* incorporating a clip for easy fastening to something else: *clip-on earrings.*

clip-ons *pl noun* **1** sunglasses that clip onto spectacles. **2** earrings that clip onto ears.

clipped /klipt/ *adj* said of a person's way of speaking: tersely quick and distinct.

clipper /ˈklipə/ *noun* **1** (*usu in pl*) an implement for cutting or trimming hair or nails. **2** a fast sailing ship, *esp* with long slender lines, a sharply raked bow, and a large sail area.

clippie /ˈklipi/ *noun Brit, informal, dated* a female bus conductor. [CLIP³ in the sense 'to punch a hole', i.e. in a bus ticket]

clipping *noun chiefly NAmer* a piece that has been cut or trimmed from something, e.g. from a newspaper or from a fingernail.

clique /kleek/ *noun* (*treated as sing. or pl*) a highly exclusive and often aloof group of people held together by common interests, views, etc: *'I hear you have such pleasant society in America.' 'There are cliques in America as elsewhere, Lady Hunstanton'* — Oscar Wilde. ➤➤ **cliquey** *adj,* **cliquish** *adj.* [French *clique* from Old French *cliquer* to make a noise, clap]

CLit /ˌsee ˈlit/ *abbr* Companion of Literature.

clitoridectomy /ˌklitəriˈdektəmi/ *noun* (*pl* **clitoridectomies**) surgical removal of the clitoris; female circumcision.

clitoris /ˈklitəris/ *noun* a mainly internal erectile organ at the front or top part of the vulva that is a centre of sexual sensation in females. ➤➤ **clitoral** *adj.* [scientific Latin, from Greek *kleitoris*]

Cllr *abbr Brit* councillor.

Clo. *abbr* in street names, close.

cloaca /klohˈaykə/ *noun* (*pl* **cloacae** /-kee, -see/) **1** a conduit for sewage. **2** the body cavity into which the intestinal, urinary, and reproductive canals discharge, *esp* in birds, reptiles, amphibians, and many fishes. ➤➤ **cloacal** *adj.* [Latin *cloaca*]

cloak¹ /klohk/ *noun* **1** a sleeveless outer garment that usu fastens at the neck, hangs loosely from the shoulders, and is longer than a cape. **2** something that conceals; a pretence or disguise. [Middle English *cloke* via French from medieval Latin *clocca* bell; from its shape]

cloak² *verb trans* to cover or hide (somebody or something) with, or as if with, a cloak.

cloak-and-dagger *adj* dealing in or suggestive of melodramatic intrigue and secrecy.

cloakroom *noun* **1** a room in which outdoor clothing or bags may be left during one's stay. **2** *chiefly Brit, euphem* a room with a toilet.

clobber¹ /ˈklobə/ *noun Brit, informal* gear, paraphernalia; *esp* clothes worn for a usu specified purpose or function. [prob alteration of CLOTHES]

clobber[2] *verb trans* (**clobbered, clobbering**) *informal* **1** to hit (somebody or something) with force. **2** to defeat (somebody) overwhelmingly. [origin unknown]

cloche /klosh/ *noun* **1** a translucent cover used for protecting outdoor plants. **2** a woman's usu soft close-fitting hat with a deeply rounded crown and narrow brim. [French *cloche* bell, from medieval Latin *clocca*]

clock[1] /klok/ *noun* **1** a device with a dial and hands or a digital display for indicating or measuring time. **2** *informal* a recording or metering device with a dial and indicator attached to a mechanism, *esp* a speedometer or milometer. **3** *Brit, informal* a person's face. **4** *Brit* the fluffy head of a dandelion when it has gone to seed. ✳ **against the clock** within a strictly limited space of time. **round the clock** continuously all day and night. **turn back the clock** to revert to an earlier or past state or condition. [Middle English *clok* via Middle Dutch and early French from medieval Latin *clocca* bell]

clock[2] *verb trans* **1** *esp* in sports, to time (somebody or something) with a stopwatch or electric timing device. **2a** to register (a time, distance, or speed) on a mechanical recording device. **b** *Brit, informal* (*often* + up) to attain (a time, speed, etc) or achieve (a victory, success, etc). **3** *informal* to hit (somebody): *He clocked him on the jaw.* **4** *Brit, informal* to see or observe (somebody or something). **5** *Brit, informal* to turn back the milometer of (a vehicle) illegally to make it appear to have done a lower mileage.

clock[3] *noun* an ornamental pattern on the outside ankle or side of a stocking or sock. [prob from CLOCK[1] in its original sense 'bell'; from its original bell-like shape]

clock golf *noun* a lawn game in which players putt a golf ball into a hole from twelve points in a circle round it.

clock in *verb intrans* to record the time of one's arrival at or start of work by means of a time clock.

clockmaker *noun* somebody who makes and mends clocks and watches.

clock off *verb intrans* = CLOCK OUT.

clock on *verb intrans* = CLOCK IN.

clock out *verb intrans* to record the time of one's departure from or stopping of work by means of a time clock.

clock radio *noun* a radio that has a built-in alarm clock.

clock speed *noun* in computing, the speed at which a processor is able to perform its operations, usu measured in megahertz.

clocktower /'kloktowə/ *noun* a usu square tower often forming part of a building (e.g. a church or town hall) and having a clock face on each side at or near the top.

clock-watcher *noun* a worker who keeps close watch on the passage of time in order not to work a single moment longer than he or she has to. ➤ **clock-watching** *noun*.

clockwise *adv* in the direction in which the hands of a clock rotate as viewed from the front. ➤➤ **clockwise** *adj*.

clockwork *noun* machinery that operates in a manner similar to that of a mechanical clock; *specif* machinery powered by a coiled spring: *a clockwork toy.* ✳ **like clockwork** smoothly and with no hitches.

clod /klod/ *noun* **1** a lump or mass, *esp* of earth or clay. **2** a clumsy or stupid person. **3** a gristly cut of beef taken from the neck. ➤➤ **cloddish** *adj*, **cloddishly** *adv*, **cloddishness** *noun*, **cloddy** *adj*. [Middle English, alteration of CLOT[1]]

clodhopper /'klodhopə/ *noun informal* **1** a large heavy shoe. **2** an awkward or clumsy person. ➤➤ **clodhopping** *adj*.

clog[1] /klog/ *noun* **1** a shoe, sandal, or overshoe with a thick typically wooden sole. **2a** a weight attached, *esp* to an animal, to hinder movement. **b** an impediment or encumbrance. [Middle English *clogge* short thick piece of wood; earlier history unknown]

clog[2] *verb* (**clogged, clogging**) ➤ *verb trans* **1** (*often* + up) to block or obstruct (something), *esp* with thick, sticky, or matted material. **2** to halt or retard the progress, operation, or growth of (somebody or something). ➤ *verb intrans* to become blocked up. ➤➤ **cloggy** *adj*.

cloisonné /'klwazonay, klwah'zonay/ *noun* a style of enamel decoration in which the enamel is fired in raised sections separated by fine wire or thin metal strips: compare CHAMPLEVÉ[1]. [French *cloisonné*, past part. of *cloisonner* to partition]

cloister[1] /'kloystə/ *noun* **1** a covered passage on the side of an open court, usu having one side walled and the other an open arcade or

colonnade. **2a** a monastery or convent. **b** the monastic life. [Middle English *cloistre* via Old French and medieval Latin from Latin *claustrum* bar, bolt, from *claudere* to close]

cloister[2] *verb trans* (**cloistered, cloistering**) to seclude (somebody or oneself) from the world in or as if in a monastic establishment: *Her work was top secret and she had to cloister herself in the laboratory.*

cloistered *adj* **1a** kept apart or sheltered from everyday life. **b** suggestive of the seclusion of a monastic establishment: *cloistered calm.* **2** surrounded with a cloister: *cloistered gardens.*

cloistral /'kloystrəl/ *adj* suggestive of or relating to a cloister.

clomp /klomp/ *verb intrans* to tread clumsily; to clump. [imitative]

clone[1] /klohn/ *noun* **1a** an individual that is asexually produced and is identical to its parent. **b** *technical* all such progeny of a single parent. **2** *informal* an exact or very close copy or replica of somebody or something else. **3** a counterfeit credit or debit card onto which the details from the magnetic strip of another card have been copied. ➤➤ **clonal** *adj*. [Greek *klōn* twig, slip]

clone[2] *verb trans* **1** to cause (a cell or organism) to grow as a clone. **2** to make a clone or a very close copy of (something or somebody). **3** *informal* to give (e.g. a mobile phone) the same electronic identifying code as another machine to avoid being charged for using it. **4** to make a counterfeit credit or debit card by copying onto it the details from the magnetic strip of another card.

clonk[1] /klongk/ *verb intrans* to make a dull heavy thumping sound as if from the impact of a hard object on a hard but hollow surface. ➤ *verb trans informal* to hit (somebody or something). [imitative]

clonk[2] *noun* a dull heavy thumping sound.

clonus /'klohnəs/ *noun* a rapid succession of alternating contractions and partial relaxations of a muscle that occurs in some nervous diseases. ➤➤ **clonic** *adj*, **clonicity** /kloh'nisiti/ *noun*. [Greek *klonos* turmoil]

clop /klop/ *verb intrans* (**clopping, clopped**) to make the sound of a hoof or shoe on a hard surface. ➤➤ **clop** *noun*.

close[1] /klohs/ *adj* **1** near in space or time: *Our house is close to the station.* **2** said of relatives: near in relationship. **3** intimate or affectionate: *The two boys were close friends.* **4a** said of a connection: strong: *We have close links with a town in Italy.* **b** said of a resemblance: almost exact, showing only small variations. **5** having little space in between; dense: *The fabric has a close weave.* **6** said of a game or contest: having only a small gap or score between participants; evenly contested. **7** very careful and concentrated: *He kept a close watch on the children; Pay close attention to the teacher.* **8** said of the weather, or a room or building: hot and stuffy; airless. **9a** secretive or reticent: *She had always kept very close about her time in Australia.* **b** not generous, *esp* with money; mean. **10** confined or restricted. **11** said of a vowel: articulated with some part of the tongue close to the palate. ✳ **close to home** see HOME[1]. ➤➤ **closely** *adv*, **closeness** *noun*. [Middle English *clos* via French from Latin *clausus*, past part. of *claudere* to shut or close]

close[2] /klohs/ *adv* (**closer, closest**) in or into a close position or manner; near: *They held each other close.* ✳ **close on** almost: *There were close on 100 people at the party.* **come close to doing something** to almost do something: *The recession had come close to ruining them.*

close[3] /klohs/ *noun* **1** *Brit* a road closed at one end. **2** *Brit* the precinct of a cathedral. **3** *Scot* an entry from the street to the common stairway of a building.

close[4] /klohz/ *verb trans* **1** to move (a door, window, lid, etc) to cover a corresponding opening. **2** to prevent access to (a road or entrance). **3** to cover or shut (something that is open, e.g. a book or suitcase) by bringing together the edges or parts of it. **4** to bring (an activity or operation) to an end: *He decided to close his account.* **5** (*often* + down) to suspend or stop the operations of (a business, shop, etc). **6a** to finish discussing or negotiating (an issue or topic). **b** to settle or agree (a business deal). ➤ *verb intrans* **1** said of a door, window, lid, etc: to move so as to cover a corresponding opening. **2** to come to an end; to conclude: *The meeting closed just before midnight.* **3a** to stop trading for the day: *The shops close early on Tuesdays.* **b** (*often* + down) to cease operation permanently. **4** (*often* + with) to come closer to somebody, *esp* in order to fight. **5** (+ on) to catch up with somebody ahead, *esp* in pursuit. ✳ **close one's doors 1** to refuse admission. **2** to go out of business. **close ranks** to unite to meet a challenge. ➤➤ **closable** *adj*. [Middle English *closen* via Old French from Latin *claudere* to shut]

close⁵ /klohz/ *noun* the end or conclusion of something: *The decade drew to a close.*

close call /klohs/ *noun* a narrow escape.

close-cropped /klohs/ *adj* clipped short: *close-cropped hair.*

closed /klohzd/ *adj* **1a** not open: *The bookshop is closed on Sundays; Is the gate closed?* **b** not allowing entry; blocked. **2a** said of a system or society: forming a self-contained unit; self-sufficient. **b** limited or restricted. **3** said of a curve: fully enclosing an area; returning to its starting point without retracing its path. **4** said of a mathematical set: characterized by elements that when subjected to an operation produce only elements of the same set. **5** said of a syllable: ending in a consonant. ✳ **behind closed doors** in secret.

closed book *noun* something that one does not or cannot understand: *Physics is a closed book to me.*

closed chain *noun* = RING¹ (8).

closed circuit *noun* a connected array of electrical components that form a complete circuit and allow the passage of current.

closed-circuit television *noun* a television system or installation, used *esp* for surveillance in which the signals are transmitted by wire from one or more cameras to a limited number of receivers, usu in one location.

closed-end *adj* **1** not allowed to exceed a predetermined number or extent. **2** *NAmer* said of an investment company: having a fixed capitalization and number of shares.

close down /klohz/ *verb intrans Brit* to stop broadcasting for the day. ➤ *verb trans* in football, to prevent (an opponent) from playing freely, by close marking.

close-down *noun* the act or result of closing down; *esp* the end of a period of broadcasting.

closed season /klohzd/ *noun chiefly NAmer* = CLOSE SEASON.

closed shop /klohzd/ *noun* an establishment which employs only union members: compare OPEN SHOP.

close-fisted /klohs/ *adj* not generous with money; mean.

close harmony /klohs/ *noun* harmony using chords in which the notes are close together.

close-hauled /klohs/ *adj and adv* said of a ship: with the sails set for sailing as near directly into the wind as possible.

close in /klohz/ *verb intrans* **1** (*often* + on) to approach and surround a place from various directions: *At dawn police closed in on the scene.* **2** to grow progressively darker in the evenings towards the winter solstice.

close-knit /klohs/ *adj* bound together by strong ties of familiarity and affection.

close out /klohz/ *verb intrans* **1** *chiefly NAmer* to dispose of goods or a business, *esp* at a reduced price. **2** to put an account in order for disposal or transfer.

close quarters /klohs/ *pl noun* (*usu* + at) immediate contact or short range: *Most of the fighting took place at close quarters.*

close season /klohs/ *noun Brit* **1** a period during which it is illegal to kill or catch certain game or fish. **2** a period of the year when there is no play in a particular sport.

close shave /klohs/ *noun informal* a narrow escape.

closet¹ /'klozit/ *noun* **1** a small or private room. **2** *archaic* = WATER CLOSET. **3** *chiefly NAmer* a cupboard. **4** (*used before a noun*) being privately but not overtly as specified; secret: *a closet romantic.* ✳ **come out of the closet** to declare oneself to be a homosexual. [Middle English from early French, dimin. of *clos* enclosure]

closet² *verb trans* (**closeted, closeting**) to shut (somebody or oneself) away in a private place: *She was closeted with her three advisers in the library; He closeted himself in the study.*

close up /klohz/ *verb intrans* **1** to come closer together: *The troops were ordered to close up.* **2** said of a wound: to heal completely.

close-up /klohs/ *noun* **1** a photograph or film shot taken at close range. **2** a view or examination of something from a small distance away.

closing time /'klohzing/ *noun Brit* a time set by law at which public houses must close and stop selling alcoholic drinks.

clostridium /klo'stridi·əm/ *noun* (*pl* **clostridia** /-di·ə/) any of various spore-forming soil or intestinal bacteria that cause gas gangrene, tetanus, and other diseases. ➤➤ **clostridial** *adj*. [Latin genus name, from Greek *klōstēr* spindle, from *klōthein* to spin; from their being shaped like a rod or spindle]

closure¹ /'klohzhə/ *noun* **1** the act of closing or the state of being closed. **2** in cricket, the ending of a side's innings by declaration. **3** the closing of debate in a legislative body, *esp* by calling for a vote: compare GUILLOTINE¹. **4** a device that closes or seals a container. [Middle English via Old French *closure* from Latin *clausura*, from *claudere* to close]

closure² *verb trans* to close (a debate) by closure.

clot¹ /klot/ *noun* **1a** a roundish viscous lump formed by coagulation of liquid, e.g. cream. **b** a coagulated mass produced by clotting of blood. **2** *Brit, informal* a stupid person. [Old English *clott*]

clot² *verb* (**clotted, clotting**) ➤ *verb intrans* **1** to become a clot; to form clots. **2** said of blood: to undergo a sequence of complex chemical and physical reactions that results in conversion into a coagulated mass. ➤ *verb trans* to cause (a liquid) to clot.

cloth /kloth/ *noun* (*pl* **cloths** /kloths/) **1** a pliable material made usu by weaving, felting, or knitting natural or synthetic fibres. **2** a piece of cloth used for a particular purpose, e.g. a tablecloth, dishcloth, or duster. **3** (**the cloth**) the clergy: *a man of the cloth.* [Old English *clāth*]

cloth-cap *adj Brit, informal* working-class. [from the cloth caps commonly worn, *esp* formerly, by working-class men]

clothe /klohdh/ *verb trans* (*past tense and past part.* **clothed** *or* **clad** /klad/) **1a** to cover (somebody) with or as if with clothing; to dress. **b** to provide (somebody) with clothes. **2** to express or enhance (something) by suitably significant language. [Old English *clāthian* from *clāth* CLOTH, garment]

cloth-eared *adj Brit, informal* irritatingly deficient in hearing.

clothes /klohdhz/ *pl noun* **1** articles made of cloth or other material worn to cover the body, for warmth, protection, or decoration: *The naked every day he clad when he put on his clothes* — Goldsmith. **2** = BEDCLOTHES. [Old English *clāthas*, pl of *clāth* CLOTH, garment]

clotheshorse *noun* **1** a frame on which to hang clothes, *esp* for drying or airing indoors. **2** *chiefly NAmer, derog* a conspicuously dressy person.

clothesline *noun* a line, e.g. of cord or nylon, on which clothes may be hung to dry, *esp* outdoors.

clothes moth *noun* any of several species of small yellowish or buff-coloured moths whose larvae eat wool, fur, hair, or feathers: family Tineidae; *esp* the common clothes moth: *Tineola bisselliella.*

clothes peg *noun* a wooden or plastic clip or forked device used for holding clothes or washing on a line.

clothespin *noun NAmer* = CLOTHES PEG.

clothier /'klohdhiə/ *noun* somebody who makes or sells cloth or clothing. [Middle English, alteration of *clother*, from CLOTH]

clothing /'klohdhing/ *noun* = CLOTHES.

cloth of gold *noun* a sumptuous fabric of gold thread interwoven with silk or wool.

clotted cream /klotid/ *noun* a thick cream made chiefly in Cornwall and Devon by slowly heating whole milk and then skimming the cooled cream from the top: *attempting to … have a weighty and concerned look in matters of marmalade, honey, and clotted cream* — Hardy.

clotting factor *noun* any of a number of substances, including Factor 8, which is needed in the blood to allow clotting.

cloture¹ /'klohchə/ *noun NAmer* = CLOSURE¹ (3). [French *clôture* from Old French *closure*: see CLOSURE¹]

cloture² *verb trans NAmer* = CLOSURE².

cloud¹ /klowd/ *noun* **1a** a visible mass of particles of water or ice at a usu great height in the air. **b** a light puffy or billowy mass, e.g. of smoke or dust, in the air. **2** a mass of opaque matter in interstellar space. **3** a great crowd or multitude; a swarm, *esp* of insects: *clouds of mosquitoes.* **4** something that obscures or blemishes or causes a feeling of gloom. ✳ **on cloud nine** *informal* feeling extremely elated or happy. **under a cloud** under suspicion or in a bad mood. **with one's head in the clouds** out of touch with reality. ➤➤ **cloudless** *adj*, **cloudlessly** *adv*, **cloudlet** /'klowdlit/ *noun*. [Old English *clūd*]

cloud² *verb intrans* **1** (+ over/up) to grow cloudy. **2a** said of facial features: to become troubled, apprehensive, etc. **b** to become blurred, dubious, or ominous. ➤ *verb trans* **1a** to envelop or obscure (something) with or as if with a cloud. **b** to make (something) opaque or murky by condensation, smoke, etc. **2** to make (something) unclear or confused. **3** to taint or sully (something): *a clouded reputation.* **4** to cast gloom over (something).

cloud base *noun* the altitude of the lowest level of a mass of cloud.

cloudberry /'klowdb(ə)ri/ *noun* **1** a creeping plant closely related to the raspberry: *Rubus chamaemorus.* **2** the pale amber edible fruit of this plant. [CLOUD[1] + BERRY[1]; perhaps from its shape]

cloudburst *noun* a sudden very heavy fall of rain.

cloud chamber *noun* a vessel containing saturated water vapour whose sudden expansion reveals the passage of an ionizing particle, e.g. an alpha particle, by a trail of visible droplets.

cloud cover *noun* the clouds obscuring the sky, or the extent of sky that is obscured by clouds.

cloud-cuckoo-land *noun* a utopian world that exists only in the mind of someone who is resolutely idealistic and impractical. [translation of Greek *Nephelokokkygia,* imaginary realm in the play *The Birds* by Aristophanes, fifth-cent. BC Greek dramatist]

cloud forest *noun* a type of rainforest found in mountainous regions of the Caribbean, central and south America, and southeast Asia, generally at a height of between 1500 and 3500 metres (4900 and 11500 feet) above sea level, in which the forest or its tree canopy is for much of the time shrouded by cloud.

cloudy *adj* (**cloudier, cloudiest**) **1a** said of the sky: overcast with clouds. **b** said of the weather: characterized by overcast skies and little sunshine. **2** not clear or transparent: *cloudy beer; a cloudy mirror.* **3** anxious or gloomy. ⟫⟫ **cloudily** *adv,* **cloudiness** *noun.*

clough /kluf/ *noun Eng dialect* a ravine or steep valley. [Old English *clōh*]

clout[1] /klowt/ *noun* **1** *informal* a blow or hit with the hand, a cricket bat, etc. **2** *informal* influence; *esp* effective political power. **3** *chiefly N Eng, Scot dialect* a piece of cloth, *esp* one used for household tasks (e.g. polishing or cleaning): *dishclout.* [Old English *clūt*]

clout[2] *verb trans informal* to hit (somebody or something) forcefully.

clout nail *noun* a nail with a large flat head. [CLOUT[1] in the sense 'iron plate used to keep wood from wearing']

clove[1] /klohv/ *noun* any of the small bulbs, e.g. in garlic, that make up a larger bulb. [Old English *clufu*]

clove[2] *noun* **1** the dried unopened flower bud of a tropical tree, shaped like a small brown spike, used as a spice and for making oil. **2** the tree from which these buds are taken: *Eugenia aromatica.* [alteration of Middle English *clowe,* from Old French *clou de girofle,* literally 'nail of clove', from Latin *clavus* nail]

clove[3] *verb* past tense of CLEAVE[1].

clove hitch *noun* a knot used to secure a rope temporarily to a spar or another rope. [Middle English *cloven, clove* divided, past part. of *clevien* to cleave]

cloven /'klohv(ə)n/ *verb* past part. of CLEAVE[1].

cloven foot *noun* a foot, e.g. of a sheep, that is divided into two parts. ⟫⟫ **cloven-footed** *adj.*

cloven hoof *noun* **1** = CLOVEN FOOT. **2** the sign of Satan or the devil: *At the core, they [aunts] are all alike. Sooner or later, out pops the cloven hoof* — P G Wodehouse. ⟫⟫ **cloven-hoofed** *adj.*

clove oil *noun* an aromatic oil obtained from clove buds and used medicinally, *esp* in dentistry, to relieve pain.

clover /'klohvə/ *noun* any of numerous species of leguminous fodder plants with leaves that have three leaflets and flowers in dense heads: genus *Trifolium.* ✳ **in clover** in prosperity or in pleasant circumstances. [Old English *clāfre*]

cloverleaf *noun* a road junction resembling the shape of a four-leaved clover and connecting two major roads at different levels.

clown[1] /klown/ *noun* **1** an entertainer who wears a grotesquely comic costume and makeup and performs simple knockabout comedy routines; *specif* a traditionally dressed comedy performer in a circus. **2** somebody who habitually acts in a ridiculously comical way or plays the fool; a joker. **3** *archaic* an unsophisticated person, *esp* a rustic. ⟫⟫ **clownery** *noun,* **clownish** *adj.* [perhaps from early French *coulon* settler, from Latin *colonus* colonist, farmer, from *colonia* colony]

clown[2] *verb intrans* (*usu* + about/around) to act as or like a clown.

clownfish *noun* (*pl* **clownfishes** *or collectively* **clownfish**) a small brightly coloured tropical fish that generally lives in close contact with sea anemones.

cloy /kloy/ *verb trans and intrans* to make (somebody) weary or satiated with an excess, usu of something orig pleasing. ⟫⟫ **cloyingly** *adv.* [Middle English *acloien* to lame, via French from medieval Latin *inclavare* to drive a nail into, from Latin *in* + *clavus* nail]

cloze test /klohz/ *noun* an educational test in which the reader has to replace words that have been deleted from a text. [by shortening and alteration from CLOSURE[1]]

club[1] /klub/ *noun* **1** an association of people with a common interest or who jointly engage in a particular activity, usu one that holds periodic meetings: *a judo club.* **2a** an association of people that has premises available for members to stay, eat, or socialize. **b** the meeting place or premises of a club. **3** a group of people who agree to make regular payments or purchases in order to secure some advantage: *a book club.* **4** = NIGHTCLUB. **5a** a heavy stick thicker at one end than the other and used as a hand weapon. **b** in golf and other games, a stick or bat used to hit a ball. **6a** a playing card marked with one or more black figures in the shape of a clover leaf. **b** (*in pl, but treated as sing. or pl*) the suit comprising cards identified by this figure. ✳ **in the club** *informal* said of a woman: pregnant.

Word history

Middle English *clubbe* from Old Norse *klubba;* (sense 6) translation of Spanish *basto* or Italian *basto,* from the figure of a stick on Spanish and Italian cards. The relationship between the meanings 'heavy stick' and 'association of people' is not altogether clear. The latter meaning arose in the mid-17th cent., perhaps from the verb *club* in the senses 'to gather into a club-like mass' or 'to collect together'.

club[2] *verb* (**clubbed, clubbing**) ⟩ *verb trans* to beat or strike (a person or an animal) with or as if with a club. ⟩ *verb intrans* **1** (+ together) to combine to share a common expense or object. **2** *informal* to go to nightclubs: *They were out clubbing until dawn.*

clubbable *adj* sociable.

clubber *noun* somebody who frequents nightclubs.

clubby *adj* (**clubbier, clubbiest**) **1** liking company; sociable. **2** forming or characteristic of an exclusive group: *Underwriting is probably the clubbiest of all City activities* — Financial Weekly.

club car *noun NAmer* a lounge car on a train.

club class *noun Brit* a class of air travel used *esp* by business travellers that is less luxurious than first class but provides better facilities than economy class.

club foot *noun* a misshapen foot twisted out of position from birth. ⟫⟫ **clubfooted** *adj.*

clubhouse *noun* **1** a building occupied by a club or used for club activities. **2** a building that has changing rooms and social facilities for a sports club.

clubland *noun Brit* the area or world of clubs, *esp*: **a** the area around St James's in London. **b** an area containing a large number of working men's clubs.

clubman *or* **clubwoman** *noun* (*pl* **clubmen** *or* **clubwomen**) a member of a club, *esp* of an exclusive social club.

club moss *noun* any of a class of primitive vascular plants: order Lycopsida. [translation of scientific Latin *muscus clavatus;* from the club-shaped spore-producing vessels in some species]

clubroot *noun* a disease of cabbages and related plants characterized by swellings or distortions of the root.

club sandwich *noun* a sandwich of three slices of bread with two layers of filling.

club soda *noun NAmer* soda water.

clubwoman *noun* see CLUBMAN.

cluck[1] /kluk/ *verb intrans* **1** to make the characteristic guttural sound of a hen. **2** *informal* (+ over) to express fussy interest or concern. ⟩ *verb trans* to express (something) by clucking: *She couldn't help clucking her disapproval.* [imitative]

cluck[2] *noun* a clucking sound.

clucky *adj* (**cluckier, cluckiest**) **1** said of a hen: sitting on or ready to sit on eggs. **2** *Aus, informal* said of a woman: obsessed with children; broody.

clue[1] /klooh/ *noun* **1** something that helps to solve a problem or mystery or to indicate the perpetrator of or motive for a crime. **2** a cryptic phrase, anagram, etc that has to be solved as part of a crossword puzzle. ✳ **not have a clue 1** to know nothing; to have no idea: *I haven't a clue where he's gone.* **2** to be incompetent.

Middle English variant of CLEW[1], from Old English *cliewen* rounded mass, ball of thread. The forms *clew* and *clue* were used more or less interchangeably until at least the 18th cent. Sense 1 comes from the story of Theseus in Greek mythology, who took a ball of thread into the labyrinth, paying it out on the way in and winding it up again to find his way out.

clue[2] *verb trans* (**clues, clued, clueing** *or* **cluing**) *informal* (*usu* + in/up) to inform (somebody) of something: *Clue me in on how it happened.*

clued-up *adj* well informed.

clueless *adj Brit, informal* hopelessly ignorant or lacking in ability, knowledge, or common sense.

clump[1] /klump/ *noun* **1** a compact group of things of the same kind, *esp* trees or bushes; a cluster. **2** a compact mass. **3** a heavy tramping sound. ➤➤ **clumpy** *adj.* [prob from Low German *klump*]

clump[2] *verb intrans* **1** to tread clumsily and noisily. **2** to form clumps. ➤ *verb trans* to arrange (something) in clumps or cause (something) to form clumps.

clumsy /'klumzi/ *adj* (**clumsier, clumsiest**) **1a** awkward and ungraceful in movement or action. **b** lacking tact or subtlety: *a clumsy joke.* **2** awkwardly or poorly made; unwieldy. ➤➤ **clumsily** *adv,* **clumsiness** *noun.* [prob from obsolete *clumse* benumbed with cold, of Scandinavian origin]

clunch /klunch/ *noun Brit* a soft type of limestone. [perhaps from dialect adjective *clunch* lumpy]

clung /klung/ *verb* past tense and past part. of CLING[1].

Cluniac /'kloohniak/ *adj* relating to or inspired by the monastery of Cluny and the reformed Benedictine order founded there in 910. [from *Cluny*, town in Burgundy, eastern France]

clunk[1] /klungk/ *noun* the sound made when one heavy or metallic object strikes another. [imitative]

clunk[2] *verb intrans* to make the sound of a clunk.

clunky *adj* (**clunkier, clunkiest**) **1** *informal* that is solid or heavy and tends to make a clunking sound. **2** *NAmer* ponderous and awkward; clodhopping.

cluster[1] /'klustə/ *noun* **1** a compact group formed by a number of similar things or people; a bunch. **2** a group of faint stars or galaxies that appear close together and have common properties, e.g. distance and motion. **3** two or more consonants or vowels grouped together in a word. **4** in statistics, a naturally occurring and statistically significant subgroup within a population. ➤➤ **clustery** *adj.* [Old English *clyster*]

cluster[2] *verb intrans and trans* (**clustered, clustering**) to form or cause (people or things) to form a cluster.

cluster bomb *noun* a bomb that explodes to release many smaller usu incendiary or fragmentation missiles.

clutch[1] /kluch/ *verb trans* to grasp or hold (something) with or as if with the hand or claws, *esp* tightly or suddenly. ➤ *verb intrans* **1** (*often* + at) to seek to grasp and hold. **2** to operate the clutch on a motor vehicle. [Old English *clyccan*]

clutch[2] *noun* **1a** the claws or a hand in the act of grasping or seizing firmly. **b** (*in pl*) control or possession: *At last she was in his clutches.* **2** a device for gripping an object, e.g. attached to the end of a chain or tackle. **3a** a coupling used to connect and disconnect a driving and a driven part of a mechanism. **b** a lever or pedal operating such a clutch, *esp* in a motor vehicle. **4** *NAmer* a critical or decisive moment, *esp* in a game; cf CRUNCH[2] (2).

clutch[3] *noun* **1** a nest of eggs or a brood of chicks. **2** a group of people or things. [alteration of English dialect *cletch* hatching, brood]

clutch bag *noun* a small handbag with no handle.

clutter[1] /'klutə/ *verb trans* (**cluttered, cluttering**) (*often* + up) to fill or cover (a surface or room) with scattered or disordered things. [Middle English *clotteren* to clot, from CLOT[2]]

clutter[2] *noun* **1a** a crowded or confused mass or collection. **b** scattered or disordered material: *This wicker screen is ideal for dividing your lounge or concealing unwanted clutter — Best.* **2** interfering echoes visible on a radar screen caused by reflection from objects other than the target.

Clydesdale /'kliedzdayl/ *noun* a horse of a heavy breed used for pulling loads, having long shaggy growths of hair on its legs. [named after *Clydesdale*, region of Scotland, where it originated]

clypeus /'klipi·əs/ *noun* (*pl* **clypei** /'klipiie/) a plate on the front of an insect's head. ➤➤ **clypeal** /'klipi·əl/ *adj,* **clypeate** /'klipi·ət/ *adj.* [Latin *clypeus* round shield]

Cm *abbr* the chemical symbol for curium.

cm *abbr* centimetre.

Cmdr *abbr* Commander.

Cmdre *abbr* Commodore.

CMEA *abbr* Council for Mutual Economic Assistance.

CMG *abbr Brit* Companion of the Order of St Michael and St George.

CMOS /'seemos/ *noun* a technology evolved to create low-voltage integrated circuits, or a chip carrying such an integrated circuit. [acronym of *complementary metal oxide semiconductor*]

CMV *abbr* cytomegalovirus.

CNAA *abbr* Council for National Academic Awards.

CND *abbr* Campaign for Nuclear Disarmament.

CNN *abbr* Cable News Network.

CNS *abbr* central nervous system.

CO *abbr* **1** Colombia (international vehicle registration). **2** Colorado (US postal abbreviation). **3** commanding officer. **4** Commonwealth Office. **5** conscientious objector.

Co *abbr* the chemical symbol for cobalt.

co. *or* **Co.** *abbr* **1** company. **2** county.

c/o *abbr* **1** care of. **2** in bookkeeping, carried over.

co- *prefix* forming words, with the meanings: **1** with; together; joint: *coexist; coheir; co-education.* **2** in or to the same degree: *coextensive.* **3a** associate; fellow: *co-author; co-star.* **b** deputy; assistant: *copilot.* [Middle English from Latin, from COM-]

coach[1] /kohch/ *noun* **1** *chiefly Brit.* **a** a bus used for long-distance or charter work, usu having a single deck. **b** a railway carriage. **2** a large, usu closed, four-wheeled horsedrawn carriage. **3a** somebody who instructs or trains a performer, sportsperson, team, etc. **b** a private tutor. [Middle English *coche* via French from German *kutsche,* prob from Hungarian *kocsi (szekér)* wagon from *Kocs,* village in Hungary]

coach[2] *verb trans* **1** to act as coach to (a person or team). **2** to train (somebody) intensively in a particular skill by instruction, demonstration, and practice. ➤ *verb intrans* **1** to travel in a coach. **2** to instruct, direct, or prompt as a coach. ➤➤ **coacher** *noun.*

coach bolt *noun Brit* a large bolt with a round head above a square upper shank, used for fixing pieces of timber together.

coach-built *adj* said of a vehicle body: built to individual requirements by craftsmen. ➤➤ **coachbuilder** *noun.*

coachman *noun* (*pl* **coachmen**) a man who drives a horsedrawn coach or carriage.

coachwork *noun* the bodywork of a road or rail vehicle.

coadjutor /koh'ajətə/ *noun* a bishop assisting a diocesan bishop and often having the right of succession. ➤➤ **coadjutor** *adj.* [Middle English *coadjutour* via French from Latin *coadjutor,* from CO- + *adjutor* aid, from *adjuvare* to help]

coagula /koh'agyoolə/ *noun* pl of COAGULUM.

coagulant /koh'agyoolənt/ *noun* something that produces coagulation.

coagulate[1] /koh'agyoolayt/ *verb intrans and trans* to become or cause (a fluid) to become viscous or thickened into a coherent mass; to curdle or clot. ➤➤ **coagulable** *adj,* **coagulation** /-'laysh(ə)n/ *noun,* **coagulative** /-lətiv/ *adj,* **coagulator** *noun.* [Latin *coagulatus,* past part. of *coagulare* to curdle]

coagulate[2] /koh'agyoolət/ *noun* a substance produced by coagulation.

coagulum /koh'agyooləm/ *noun* (*pl* **coagula** /-lə/ *or* **coagulums**) a coagulated mass. [Latin *coagulum* coagulant]

coal /kohl/ *noun* **1a** a black or blackish solid combustible mineral, mined from the ground, consisting chiefly of carbonized vegetable matter and widely used as a natural fuel. **b** a small piece or broken up quantity of this. **2** a piece of glowing, burning, or burned carbonized material. ✲ **coals to Newcastle** something taken or sent to a place that already has plenty of it. ➤➤ **coaly** *adj.* [Old English *col*]

coal black *adj* absolutely black; very black.

coaler *noun* a ship or train used to transport or supply coal.

coalesce /koh·ə'les/ *verb intrans* to unite into a whole; to fuse. ⟫⟫ **coalescence** *noun*, **coalescent** *adj*. [Latin *coalescere*, from CO- + *alescere* to grow]

coalface *noun* the exposed seam ready to be worked in a coalmine. ✳ **at the coalface** engaged in practical or hard physical work; *esp* as opposed to theoretical or managerial work.

coalfield *noun* a region in which deposits of coal occur.

coalfish *noun* (*pl* **coalfishes** *or collectively* **coalfish**) any of several blackish or dark-backed fishes, *esp* coley.

coal gas *noun* gas made from burning coal; *esp* gas made by carbonizing bituminous coal and used for heating and lighting.

coalhole *noun* **1** a hole or chute for receiving coal, **2** *Brit* a compartment for storing coal.

coalition /koh·ə'lish(ə)n/ *noun* **1** (*treated as sing. or pl*) a temporary alliance, e.g. of political parties, for joint action such as forming a government. **2a** an act of coalescing; a union. **b** a body formed by the union of orig distinct elements. ⟫⟫ **coalitionist** *noun*. [early French *coalition* from Latin *coalitus*, past part. of *coalescere*: see COALESCE]

coal measures *pl noun* beds of coal with the associated rocks.

coalmine *noun* a mine from which coal is extracted. ⟫⟫ **coalminer** *noun*, **coalmining** *noun*.

coal scuttle *noun* a container like a bucket, used for carrying or storing coal indoors.

coal tar *noun* tar obtained by the distilling of bituminous coal and used *esp* in making dyes and drugs.

coal tit *noun* a small European tit with a black crown and a white patch on the neck: *Parus ater*.

coaming /'kohming/ *noun* a raised frame, e.g. round a hatchway in the deck of a ship, to keep out water. [perhaps irreg from COMB[1]]

coarctate /koh'ahktayt/ *adj technical* **1** constricted or compressed, *esp* having the abdomen separated from the THORAX (central body region) by a narrow constriction. **2** said of an insect larva or pupa: enclosed in the skin from the larval stage. ⟫⟫ **coarctation** /-'taysh(ə)n/ *noun*. [Latin *coarctatus*, past part. of *coarctare* to press together]

coarse /kaws/ *adj* **1a** rough in texture or tone: *coarse cloth; a coarse cry*. **b** adjusted or designed for heavy, fast, or less delicate work: *a coarse saw with large teeth*. **2** composed of relatively large particles: *coarse sand*. **3a** crude or unrefined in taste, manners, or language; common. **b** said of language: vulgar or obscene. **4** of ordinary or inferior quality or value. ⟫⟫ **coarsely** *adv*, **coarseness** *noun*. [Middle English *cors*, prob from COURSE[1] in the sense 'the common run of things']

coarse fish *noun chiefly Brit* any freshwater fish not belonging to the salmon family. ⟫⟫ **coarse fishing** *noun*.

coarse-grained *adj* **1** having a rough or large grain and usu a rough texture. **2** unrefined, common, or boorish in manner; uncouth.

coarsen *verb* (**coarsened, coarsening**) ⟩ *verb trans* to make (somebody or something) coarse. ⟩ *verb intrans* to become coarse.

coast[1] /kohst/ *noun* **1a** the edge of a landmass or country where it reaches the sea. **b** the land near a shore; the seashore. **2** *NAmer*. **a** a slope suitable for tobogganing down. **b** a ride down a slope on a toboggan. ✳ **the coast is clear** there is no danger, or the danger is past. ⟫⟫ **coastal** *adj*. [Middle English *cost* via French from Latin *costa* rib, side]

coast[2] *verb intrans* **1a** to slide, glide, etc downhill by the force of gravity. **b** to move along without, or as if without, further application of propulsive power. **c** to proceed easily without making any special effort or becoming greatly involved. **2** to sail along the shore. ⟩ *verb trans* to sail along the shore of (a country or land mass).

coaster *noun* **1** a small vessel trading from port to port along a coast. **2** a small mat used, *esp* under a drinks glass, to protect a surface. **3** *NAmer*. **a** a roller coaster. **b** a toboggan.

coastguard *noun* **1** a force responsible for maintaining lookout posts round the coast of a country, mounting rescues at sea, preventing smuggling, etc. **2** a member of such a force.

coastline *noun* a coast, *esp* considered with respect to its shape or characteristics.

coast-to-coast *adj* extending or operating across the whole of a country or landmass, from one side to the other.

coat[1] /koht/ *noun* **1a** a full-length outer garment, *esp* one worn outdoors in cold weather, that has sleeves and usu opens the full length of the centre front. **b** a jacket. **2** the external covering of hair, fur, etc on an animal. **3** a protective layer; a coating, e.g. of paint. ⟫⟫ **coated** *adj*. [Middle English *cote* from Old French, of Germanic origin]

coat[2] *verb trans* to cover or spread (something) with a protective or enclosing layer. ⟫⟫ **coater** *noun*.

coat hanger *noun* a shaped piece of wood, rigid wire, or plastic with a hook, for hanging clothes.

coati /koh'ahti/ *noun* (*pl* **coatis**) any of several species of tropical American mammals related to the raccoon but with a longer body and tail and a long flexible snout: genera *Nasua* and *Nasuella*. [Portuguese *coatí* from Tupi]

coatimundi /koh,ahti'moondi/ *noun* (*pl* **coatimundis**) = COATI. [Tupi *coatimundi*]

coating *noun* a layer of one substance covering another.

coat of arms *noun* (*pl* **coats of arms**) a set of distinctive heraldic shapes or representations, usu depicted on a shield, belonging to a particular family, institution, etc. [translation of French *cotte d'armes*]

coat of mail *noun* a garment of overlapping metal scales or chain mail formerly worn as armour.

coat tails *pl noun* two long tapering flaps at the back of a man's tailcoat. ✳ **on somebody's coat tails** with the help, usu undeserved, of somebody else: *He was elected on the President's coat tails*.

co-author[1] /'koh·awthə/ *noun* a joint or associate author.

co-author[2] *verb trans* (**co-authored, co-authoring**) to be a joint author of (a book, article, etc).

coax /kohks/ *verb trans* **1** to influence or gently urge (somebody) by caresses or flattery; to wheedle. **2** to extract or gain (something) by means of gentle urging or flattery: *I coaxed an answer out of her*. **3** to manipulate (something) with great perseverance and skill towards a desired condition: *He spent hours coaxing his hair into a quiff*. ⟫⟫ **coaxer** *noun*, **coaxingly** *adv*. [earlier *cokes*, from *cokes* noun simpleton]

coaxial /koh'aksi·əl/ *adj* **1** mounted on a common axis. **2** using or connected to a coaxial cable. ⟫⟫ **coaxially** *adv*.

coaxial cable *noun* a conductor for high-frequency electrical signals, e.g. telephone or television signals, consisting of a tube of electrically conducting material containing and insulated from a central conducting wire.

cob[1] /kob/ *noun* **1** a male swan. **2a** = CORNCOB. **b** = COBNUT. **3** a horse of a short-legged stocky breed used mainly for riding. **4** *Brit* a small rounded usu crusty loaf. ⟫⟫ **cobby** *adj*. [Middle English *cobbe* leader, of Germanic origin]

cob[2] *noun* **1** a building material used chiefly in SW England and consisting of natural clay or chalk mixed with straw or hair as a binder. **2** a house built of cob. [perhaps from COB[1] in the sense 'rounded mass, lump']

cobalt /'kohbawlt/ *noun* a silver-white magnetic metallic chemical element used in many alloys: symbol Co, atomic number 27. ⟫⟫ **cobaltic** /koh'bawltik/ *adj*, **cobaltous** /koh'bawltəs/ *adj*. [German *Kobalt*, alteration of *kobold* goblin; from its occurrence in silver ore, believed to be due to goblins]

cobalt blue *noun* a greenish blue pigment consisting essentially of cobalt oxide and alumina.

cobalt bomb *noun* a device containing a radioactive isotope of cobalt, cobalt 60, used in radiotherapy.

cobber /'kobə/ *noun Aus, informal* a man's male friend; a mate. [prob from Yiddish *chaber* comrade, from Hebrew]

cobble[1] /'kobl/ *verb trans* **1** to repair or make (*esp* shoes). **2** (+ together) to make or assemble (something) roughly or hastily. [Middle English *coblen*, perhaps back-formation from *cobelere* COBBLER]

cobble[2] *noun* a naturally rounded stone of a size suitable for paving a street. [Middle English, from COB[1] in the sense 'round object']

cobble[3] *verb trans* to pave (a road) with cobbles.

cobbler *noun* **1** a mender or maker of leather goods, *esp* shoes. **2** *Brit, slang* (*in pl*) often used interjectionally: nonsense, rubbish. **3** an iced drink consisting of sherry or wine mixed with lemon juice and sugar. **4a** *NAmer* a deep-dish fruit pie with a thick crust. **b** *Brit* a dish of stewed meat with a topping of scones. [Middle English *cobelere*; (sense 2) rhyming slang *cobbler's (awls)* balls]

cobblestone *noun* = COBBLE². ➤➤ **cobblestoned** *adj.*

cobelligerent *or* **co-belligerent** /ˈkohbəˈlijərənt/ *noun* a country fighting with another power against a common enemy. ➤➤ **cobelligerence** *noun*, **cobelligerency** *noun*, **cobelligerent** *adj.*

coble /ˈkohbl, ˈkobl/ *noun* a flat-bottomed fishing boat with a LUG-SAIL (four-sided fore-and-aft sail). [Middle English, prob of Celtic origin]

cobnut /ˈkobnut/ *noun* **1** a European hazel tree: *Corylus avellana grandis*. **2** the nut of this tree. [COB¹ in the sense 'lump, round object']

Cobol *or* **COBOL** /ˈkohbol/ *noun* a high-level computer language designed for business applications. [acronym from *common business oriented language*]

cobra /ˈkohbrə, ˈkobrə/ *noun* any of several species of venomous Asiatic and African snakes that have grooved fangs and can expand the skin of the neck into a hood: genus *Naja*. [Portuguese *cobra de capello* hooded snake, from Latin *colubra* snake]

cobweb /ˈkobweb/ *noun* **1** a spider's web, *esp* one indicating long disuse or neglect. **2** a single thread spun by a spider. ➤➤ **cobwebbed** *adj*, **cobwebby** *adj*. [Middle English *coppeweb*, from obsolete *coppe* spider + WEB¹]

coca /ˈkohkə/ *noun* **1** a S American shrub with yellow flowers whose leaves contain cocaine and other alkaloids: *Erythroxylum coca*. **2** the dried leaves of this shrub, chewed as a stimulant. [Spanish *coca* from Quechua *kúka*]

Coca-Cola /ˌkohkə ˈkohlə/ *noun* trademark a brand of cola.

cocaine /koh'kayn, kə'kayn/ *noun* an alkaloid that is obtained from coca leaves, has been used as a local anaesthetic, and is a common drug of abuse that can result in psychological dependence.

cocci /ˈkok(s)ie/ *noun* pl of COCCUS.

coccidia /kok'sidiə/ *noun* pl of COCCIDIUM.

coccidiosis /ˌkokˌsidi'ohsis/ *noun* (*pl* **coccidioses** /-seez/) a disease of birds and mammals, e.g. poultry and sheep, caused by coccidia in the intestines. [scientific Latin *coccidiosis* from Greek *kokkos* a berry]

coccidium /kok'sidi-əm/ *noun* (*pl* **coccidia** /-di-ə/) any of an order of protozoans that are usu parasitic in the lining of the digestive tract of vertebrates: order Coccidia. [scientific Latin *coccidium*, dimin. of *coccus* from Greek *kokkos* a berry]

coccus /ˈkokəs/ *noun* (*pl* **cocci** /ˈkok(s)ie/) a spherical bacterium. ➤➤ **coccal** *adj*, **coccoid** *adj*. [scientific Latin from Greek *kokkos* a berry]

coccyx /ˈkoksiks/ *noun* (*pl* **coccyges** /ˈkoksijeez/ *or* **coccyxes**) the small triangular bone at the end of the spinal column below the sacrum in human beings and the tailless apes. ➤➤ **coccygeal** /kok'siji-əl/ *adj*. [scientific Latin from Greek *kokkyx* cuckoo, coccyx; from its resemblance to a cuckoo's beak]

cochineal /kochi'neel/ *noun* a red dyestuff consisting of the dried bodies of female cochineal insects, used *esp* as a colouring agent for food. [French *cochenille* or Spanish *cochinilla* woodlouse, cochineal]

cochineal insect *noun* a small bright red insect that feeds on cacti: *Dactylopius coccus*.

cochlea /ˈkokli-ə/ *noun* (*pl* **cochleas** *or* **cochleae** /-li-ee/) a coiled part of the inner ear of higher vertebrates that is filled with liquid through which sound waves are transmitted to the auditory nerve. ➤➤ **cochlear** *adj*. [scientific Latin from Greek *kochlias*, from *kochlos* land snail]

cock¹ /kok/ *noun* **1a** the male, *esp* the adult male, of various birds; *specif* the domestic fowl. **b** a male crab, lobster, or salmon. **2** a device, e.g. a tap or valve, for regulating the flow of a liquid. **3** the hammer of a firearm, or its position when cocked ready for firing: *at full cock*. **4** *Brit* used as a term of informal address to a man: pal. **5** *coarse slang* the penis. **6** *Brit, informal* nonsense, rubbish. **7** an upward tilt: *a cock of the head*. [Old English *cocc*, of imitative origin]

cock² *verb trans* **1a** to set (something) erect: *The dog cocked its ears*. **b** to turn, tip, or tilt (something), usu to one side: *He cocked his head inquiringly*. **2a** to draw back and set the hammer of (a firearm) for firing. **b** to draw or bend (the hand, arm, or wrist) back in preparation for throwing or hitting. **3** to turn up (e.g. the brim of a hat). ✴ **cock a snook** to react with disdain or defiance: *It was his way of*

cocking a snook at authority. [*cock* to swagger, stick up, from Middle English *cocken* to quarrel, fight, from *cok* COCK¹]

cock³ *noun* a small pile (e.g. of hay). [Middle English *cok*, of Scandinavian origin]

cockabully /ˈkokəbooli/ *noun* (*pl* **cockabullies**) a small blunt-nosed freshwater fish found in New Zealand: genus *Gobiomorphus*. [Maori *kokopu*]

cockade /ko'kayd/ *noun* an ornament, e.g. a rosette or knot of ribbon, worn on the hat as a badge. ➤➤ **cockaded** *adj*. [modification of French *cocarde*, fem of *cocard* vain]

cock-a-doodle-doo /ˌkok ə ˌdoohdl 'dooh/ *interj* used to represent the crowing of a cockerel. [imitative]

cock-a-hoop /ˌkok ə 'hoohp/ *adj informal* triumphantly boastful; exulting. ➤➤ **cock-a-hoop** *adv*. [from the phrase *to set cock a hoop* to be festive, of unknown origin]

cock-a-leekie /ˌkok ə 'leeki/ *noun* a chicken and leek soup. [alteration of *cockie* (dimin. of COCK¹) + *leekie*, dimin. of LEEK]

cockalorum /ˌkokə'lawrəm/ *noun* a self-important little man. [prob modification of obsolete Flemish *kockeloeren* to crow, of imitative origin]

cockamamie /ˌkokə'maymi/ *adj NAmer* ridiculous or nonsensical. [prob alteration of DECALCOMANIA]

cock-and-bull story *noun* an incredible and apparently fabricated story.

cockatiel /ˌkokə'teel/ *noun* a small grey Australian parrot with a crested yellow head: *Nymphicus hollandicus*. [Dutch *kaketielje* from Malay *kakatua*]

cockatoo /ˌkokə'tooh/ *noun* (*pl* **cockatoos**) **1** any of numerous species of large noisy chiefly Australasian parrots with crests and brightly coloured plumage: family Cacatuidae, *esp* genus *Kakatoe*. **2** *Aus, NZ, informal* a small farmer. **3** *Aus, informal* a lookout. [Dutch *kaketoe* from Malay *kakatua*, from *kakak* elder sibling + *tua* old; (sense 3) from the belief that a flock of cockatoos post a sentry while feeding]

cockatrice /ˈkokətris, -tries/ *noun* **1** a mythical creature, half snake and half cock, hatched from a cock's egg and able to kill with a look: *O my accursed womb ... A cockatrice hast thou hatched to the world, whose unavoided eye is murderous* — Shakespeare. **2** = BASILISK (1). [Middle English *cocatrice* via French from medieval Latin *cocatric-, cocatrix* mongoose]

cockboat /ˈkokboht/ *noun* a small boat; *esp* one used as a tender to a larger boat. [obsolete *cock* small boat, from Middle English *cok* via Old French from medieval Latin]

cockchafer /ˈkokchayfə/ *noun* a large European beetle destructive to vegetation: *Melolontha melolontha*. [COCK¹ + CHAFER]

cockcrow *noun literary* dawn.

cocked hat *noun* a hat with a brim turned up at three places to give a three-cornered shape. ✴ **knock into a cocked hat** *informal* to defeat or surpass (somebody or something) completely.

cockerel /ˈkok(ə)rəl/ *noun* a young male domestic fowl. [Middle English *cokerelle*, from Old French dialect *kokerel*, dimin. of Old French *coc* cock]

cocker spaniel *noun* a small spaniel with long ears and silky coat.

Word history
from *cocking* woodcock hunting. The cocker was used to find and flush woodcock for shooting.

cock-eyed /ˈkokˈied/ *adj informal* **1a** askew or awry. **b** somewhat foolish or mad: *a cock-eyed scheme*. **2** having a squint.

cockfighting *noun* the setting of specially bred cocks, usu fitted with metal spurs, to fight each other for public entertainment. ➤➤ **cockfight** *noun*.

cockle¹ /ˈkokl/ *noun* = CORN COCKLE. [Old English *coccel*]

cockle² *noun* **1** a common edible bivalve mollusc: genus *Cardium*. **2** the ribbed shell of this mollusc. ✴ **warm the cockles of one's heart** to give one a feeling of pleasure mixed with slightly sentimental tenderness. [Middle English *cokille* from early French *coquille*, via Latin from Greek *konchylion*, from *konchē* CONCH]

cockle³ *noun* a pucker or wrinkle. [early French *coquille*: see COCKLE²]

cockle⁴ *verb intrans and trans* to wrinkle or pucker, or cause (e.g. fabric) to wrinkle to pucker.

cockleshell *noun* **1** the shell of a cockle, scallop, or similar mollusc. **2** a light flimsy boat.

cockney /'kokni/ *noun* (*pl* **cockneys**) **1** a native of London, *esp* of the East End of London; traditionally somebody born within the sound of the bells of St Mary-le-Bow. **2** the dialect of London, *esp* the East End of London: *If it were not for talking cockney, we might call him a 'regular swell'* — Poe. ⟫⟫ **cockney** *adj*, **cockneyism** *noun*. [Middle English *cokeney* pampered child, (effeminate) townsman, literally 'cock's egg', from *cok* COCK[1] + *ey* egg, from Old English *ǣg*; from the belief that small misshapen eggs were laid by cocks]

cock of the walk *noun* somebody who dominates or is self-assertive, *esp* overbearingly.

cockpit *noun* **1a** a space in the fuselage of an aeroplane for the pilot and crew. **b** the driver's compartment in a racing or sports car. **2a** the rear part of the lowest deck of a sailing warship used as officers' quarters and for treating the wounded. **b** a recess below deck level from which a small vessel, e.g. a yacht, is steered. **3a** a pit or enclosure for cockfights. **b** a place noted for bloody, violent, or prolonged conflict.

cockroach /'kokrohch/ *noun* any of numerous species of insects resembling beetles that have flattened bodies and long antennae and include some domestic pests: suborder Blattodea, *esp Periplaneta americana* and *Blatta orientalis*. [by folk etymology from Spanish *cucaracha*, from *cuca* caterpillar]

cockscomb /'kokskohm, 'kokskoom/ *noun* **1** see COXCOMB. **2** a pot plant of the amaranth family grown for its red, yellow, or purple flowers: *Celosia cristata*.

cockshy /'kokshie/ *noun* (*pl* **cockshies**) *Brit* **1** a target that things may be thrown at in a game. **2** a throw at this target.

Word history ⸻
COCK[1] + SHY[4]. Orig the target was a clay pot containing a cock; the contestant who succeeded in breaking the pot won the bird.

cocksure *adj informal* = COCKY[1]. ⟫⟫ **cocksurely** *adv*, **cocksureness** *noun*. [prob from COCK[1] + SURE[1]]

cocktail /'koktayl/ *noun* **1a** a drink of mixed spirits or of spirits mixed with flavourings. **b** something resembling or suggesting such a drink; *esp* a mixture of diverse elements: *a deadly cocktail of chemicals*. **2** a dish served as a starter or dessert usu consisting of seafood or chopped fruit with a sauce or dressing **3** (*used before a noun*) suitable for social occasions involving cocktails: *a cocktail dress*.

Word history ⸻
prob from COCK[1] + TAIL[1]. The word orig meant a horse with a tail that stuck up like a cock's, caused by cutting the tail muscles. As this was usually done to carriage horses and hunters, the word was then applied to a racehorse that had one of these in its pedigree, i.e. that was not pure bred; hence a mixture.

cock up *verb trans chiefly Brit, coarse slang* to spoil (something) or render it a failure by bungling or incompetence. ⟫⟫ **cock-up** *noun*.

cocky[1] /'koki/ *adj* (**cockier, cockiest**) *informal* marked by arrogant overconfidence or presumptuousness. ⟫⟫ **cockily** *adv*, **cockiness** *noun*. [COCK[1] + -Y[1]]

cocky[2] *noun* (*pl* **cockies**) *Aus, NZ* somebody who owns a small farm. [by shortening and alteration from COCKATOO]

coco /'kohkoh/ *noun* (*pl* **cocos**) **1** = COCONUT. **2** = COCONUT PALM. [Spanish *coco* from Portuguese *côco*, literally 'bogeyman'; because the base of the coconut looks like a face]

cocoa /'kohkoh/ *noun* **1a** powdered ground roasted cacao seeds from which some fat has been removed: compare CHOCOLATE[1]. **b** a hot drink made by mixing cocoa with milk: *Cocoa is a cad and a coward, cocoa is a vulgar beast* — G K Chesterton. **2** the cacao tree of S America, which has fleshy yellow pods containing many seeds: *Theobroma cacao*. [modification of Spanish *cacao*: see CACAO]

cocoa bean *noun* the seed of the cacao tree.

cocoa butter *noun* a pale vegetable fat with a low melting point obtained from cacao seeds.

coconut /'kohkənut/ *noun* the large oval fruit of the coconut palm whose outer fibrous husk yields coir and whose nut contains thick edible white flesh and a thick sweet milk.

coconut ice *noun* a sweet with the consistency of fudge that is made with sugar and desiccated coconut and is usu coloured pink or white.

coconut matting *noun* a coarse matting made from the outer fibrous husk of the coconut and used *esp* for doormats.

coconut milk *noun* **1** the sweet juice contained in the coconut. **2** a liquid obtained from the flesh of the coconut by pressing or boiling, used in Asian cookery.

coconut oil *noun* an almost colourless oil extracted from coconuts and used *esp* in making soaps and cosmetics.

coconut palm *noun* a tall American tropical palm tree that produces coconuts: *Cocos nucifera*.

coconut shy *noun* a stall at a funfair where people throw balls at coconuts on stands.

cocoon[1] /kə'koohn/ *noun* **1a** a silk envelope which an insect larva forms about itself and in which it passes the pupa stage. **b** an animal's protective covering similar to this. **2** a protective covering like a cocoon, e.g. for an aeroplane in storage. **3** a sheltered or insulated state of existence. [French *cocon* from Provençal *coucoun*, from *coco* shell]

cocoon[2] *verb trans* to wrap or envelop (somebody or something), *esp* tightly, in or as if in a cocoon.

cocotte /ko'kot, kə'kot/ *noun* **1** a small ovenproof dish in which an individual portion of a dish is cooked and served. **2** *dated* a female prostitute. [French *cocotte*, orig baby-talk for a hen]

cocuswood /'kohkəswood/ *noun* **1** a West Indian hardwood tree: *Brya ebenus*. **2** the dark-coloured hard wood of this tree, which turns black as it ages and is used to make musical instruments and in inlays.

COD *abbr* **1** cash on delivery. **2** *NAmer* collect on delivery.

cod[1] /kod/ *noun* (*pl* **cods** or collectively **cod**) **1a** a large grey soft-finned fish with barbels (tactile organs; see BARBEL[2]) that is found in the colder parts of the N Atlantic and is a major food fish: *Gadus morhua*. **b** any of several species of fish of the cod family, *esp* a Pacific fish closely related to the Atlantic cod: family Gadidae. **2** any of various spiny-finned fishes resembling the true cods. **3** the flesh of the cod used as food. [Middle English; earlier history unknown]

cod[2] *noun Brit, informal, dated* nonsense. [short for CODSWALLOP]

cod[3] *verb trans* (**codded, codding**) *Brit, informal* to trick or kid (somebody). [origin unknown]

cod[4] *noun* a trick or hoax.

coda /'kohdə/ *noun* **1** a concluding section to a piece of music that is formally distinct from its main structure. **2** something that serves to round off or conclude something, *esp* a literary or dramatic work, and that has an interest of its own. [Italian *coda* tail, from Latin *cauda*]

coddle /'kodl/ *verb trans* **1** to cook (*esp* eggs) slowly in a liquid just below the boiling point. **2** to treat (a person or animal) with extreme care; to pamper. ⟫⟫ **coddler** *noun*. [perhaps from *caudle*, a warm drink given to invalids, from Latin *caldum* hot drink]

code[1] /kohd/ *noun* **1** a system of letters, numbers, words, or symbols used to represent and replace those conveying the meaning of a text, e.g. to keep it secret or to communicate it briefly. **2** a system of numbers, symbols, etc that conveys information or instructions to a computer. **3** a particular set of letters, numbers, etc identifying or representing a particular object. **4** = AREA CODE. **5** = GENETIC CODE. **6a** a systematic body of laws, *esp* one established by statutes. **b** a set of rules or principles governing the behaviour of a particular group or individual. ⟫⟫ **coded** *adj*. [Middle English via French from Latin *caudex, codex* trunk of a tree, tablet of wood covered with wax for writing on, book]

code[2] *verb trans* **1** to put (words) into the form or symbols of a code. **2** to specify (an amino acid, protein, etc) in terms of the genetic code. ⟫ *verb intrans* to be or contain the genetic code for an amino acid, protein, etc. ⟫⟫ **codable** *adj*, **coder** *noun*.

codeine /'kohdeen/ *noun* a derivative of morphine with a less powerful effect that is given orally to relieve pain and coughing. [French *codéine* from Greek *kōdeia* poppyhead, from *kōos* cavity]

code name *noun* a name that for secrecy or convenience is used in place of an ordinary name.

code of conduct *noun* (*pl* **codes of conduct**) the rules, written or unwritten, that govern the way the people in a particular group, occupation, or situation are expected to behave.

code of practice *noun* (*pl* **codes of practice**) the set of rules, written or unwritten, that govern the way the people in a particular profession are expected to go about their work.

co-dependency /kohdi'pendənsi/ *noun* a state of mutual dependency, *esp* a situation where a carer comes to rely psychologically on the person he or she is caring for.

co-determination /ˌkohdiˌtuhmi'naysh(ə)n/ *noun* the participation of the workforce with management in the determination of business policy.

codex /'kohdeks/ *noun* (*pl* **codices** /'kohdiseez/) a manuscript book, *esp* of biblical or classical texts. [Latin *codex*]

codfish *noun* (*pl* **codfishes** or *collectively* **codfish**) = COD¹.

codger /'kojə/ *noun informal* an old and mildly eccentric man. [prob alteration of *cadger*: see CADGE]

codices /'kohdiseez/ *noun* pl of CODEX.

codicil /'kohdisil/ *noun* **1** a modifying clause added to a will. **2** an appendix or supplement. ➤ **codicillary** /-'siləri/ *adj.* [early French *codicille* from Latin *codicillus*, dimin. of *codic-, codex* book]

codicology /kohdi'kolaji/ *noun* the study of manuscripts. ➤ **codicological** /-kə'lojikl/ *adj.* [from French *codicologie*, from Latin *codic-*, stem of *codex* codex + -OLOGY]

codify /'kohdifie/ *verb trans* (**codifies, codified, codifying**) to collect and arrange (e.g. laws or rules) in a systematic form. ➤ **codification** /-fi'kaysh(ə)n/ *noun*, **codifier** *noun*.

codlin /'kodlin/ *noun* see CODLING².

codling¹ /'kodling/ *noun* a young cod. [Middle English, from COD¹ + -LING]

codling² or **codlin** *noun* any of several elongated greenish cooking apples. [alteration of Middle English *querdlyng*, from Anglo-French *quer de lion* lion heart; from its tapering shape and because it is very hard when raw]

codling moth or **codlin moth** *noun* a small moth whose larva lives in apples, pears, etc: *Cydia pomonella*.

cod-liver oil *noun* an oil obtained from the liver of the cod and closely related fishes and used as a source of vitamins A and D.

codon /'kohdon/ *noun* in genetics, a group of three adjacent nucleotides (structural units; see NUCLEOTIDE) in RNA or DNA that codes for a particular amino acid or starts or stops protein synthesis. [CODE¹ + -ON²]

codpiece *noun* a flap or bag concealing an opening in the front of men's breeches, *esp* in the 15th and 16th cent: *Why, what a ruthless thing is this … for the rebellion of a codpiece to take away the life of a man!* — Shakespeare. [Middle English *codpese*, from *cod* bag, scrotum (from Old English *codd*) + *pese* PIECE¹]

codswallop /'kodzwoləp/ *noun chiefly Brit, informal* nonsense.

Word history
origin uncertain. Sometimes said to be named after Hiram Codd, 19th-cent. inventor of a bottle for fizzy drinks, *Codd's Wallop* becoming a derogatory term for gassy beer; there is no evidence to support this.

co-ed /koh'ed/ *noun* **1** a co-educational school. **2** *NAmer* a female student in a co-educational institution. ➤ **co-ed** *adj.* [short for *co-educational*]

co-education /ˌkoh-edyoo'kaysh(ə)n, ˌkoh-ejoo-/ *noun* the education of students of both sexes at the same institution. ➤ **co-educational** *adj*, **co-educationally** *adv.*

coefficient /koh-i'fish(ə)nt/ *noun* **1** a constant, usu a number, placed before the variable factor or factors in an algebraic expression and multiplying them: *In the expression $5xy$ the coefficient of xy is 5.* **2** a number that serves as a measure of some property or characteristic, e.g. of a device or process: *the coefficient of expansion of a metal.* [scientific Latin *coefficient-, coefficiens*, from Latin CO- + *efficient-, efficiens*: see EFFICIENT]

coelacanth /'seeləkanth/ *noun* a fish with fleshy pectoral fins, known only from fossils until a living specimen was caught in S African waters in 1938: genus *Coelacanthus*. [Greek *koilos* hollow + *akantha* thorn, spine; because of the hollow spines in its fins]

coelenterate /see'lentərayt, -rət/ *noun* any of a phylum of invertebrate animals including the corals, sea anemones, and jellyfishes: phylum Coelenterata. ➤ **coelenterate** *adj.* [Latin phylum name, from Greek *koilos* hollow + *enteron* intestine]

coeliac (*NAmer* **celiac**) /'seeliak/ *adj* relating to or in the region of the abdominal cavity. [via Latin from Greek *koiliakos*, from *koilia* cavity, from *koilos* hollow]

coeliac disease *noun* defective digestion of fats in the intestines, *esp* in young children.

coelom (*NAmer* **celom**) /'seeləm/ *noun* (*pl* **coeloms** or **coelomata** /see'lohmətə/, *NAmer* **celoms** or **celomata**) the space between the body wall and the digestive tract in animals more advanced than the lower worms. ➤ **coelomic** /see'lohmik/ *adj.* [German *Koelom* from Greek *koilōma* cavity, from *koilos* hollow]

coelomate /'seeləmayt/ *noun* an animal with a coelom. ➤ **coelomate** *adj.*

coelurosaur /si'lyooərəsaw/ *noun* a small flesh-eating dinosaur that walked on two legs and is believed to be an ancestor of the birds. [Greek *koilos* hollow + *oura* tail + *sauros* lizard]

coen- or **coeno-** *comb. form* forming words, with the meaning: common; general: *coenobite*. [scientific Latin, from Greek *koin-, koino-*, from *koinos*]

coenobite (*NAmer* **cenobite**) /'seenəbiet/ *noun* a member of a monastic community. ➤ **coenobitic** /-'bitik/ *adj*, **coenobitical** /-'bitikl/ *adj.* [late Latin *coenobita* from *coenobium* monastery, from late Greek *koinobion*, derivative of Greek *koin-* COEN- + *bios* life]

coenzyme /koh'enziem/ *noun* a nonprotein compound that combines with a protein to form an active enzyme and whose activity cannot be destroyed by heat.

coequal /koh'eekwəl/ *adj* equal with one another. ➤ **coequal** *noun*, **coequality** /koh-i'kwoliti/ *noun*, **coequally** *adv.*

coerce /koh'uhs/ *verb trans* **1** (*often* + into) to compel (somebody) to do something by force or threats. **2a** to restrain or dominate (somebody) by authority or force. **b** to bring about (something) by force or threat. ➤ **coercible** *adj*, **coercive** *adj.* [Latin *coercēre*, from CO- + *arcēre* to shut up or hold off]

coercion /koh'uhsh(ə)n/ *noun* **1** the use of force or threats to make somebody do something or to bring something about. **2** government using force.

coercive force *noun* in physics, the opposing magnetic intensity that must be applied to a magnetized material to demagnetize it.

coercivity /koh-uh'siviti/ *noun* the property of a material determined by the value of the coercive force when the material has been fully magnetized.

coeval /koh'eevl/ *adj* of the same or equal age, antiquity, or duration. ➤ **coeval** *noun*, **coevality** /-'valiti/ *noun*, **coevally** *adj.* [Latin *coaevus*, from CO- + *aevum* age, lifetime]

coexist /koh-ig'zist/ *verb intrans* **1** to exist together or at the same time. **2** to live in peace with each other. ➤ **coexistence** *noun*, **coexistent** *adj.*

coextensive /koh-ik'stensiv/ *adj* having the same scope or boundaries in space or time. ➤ **coextensively** *adv.*

C of C *abbr* Chamber of Commerce.

C of E *abbr* **1** Church of England. **2** Council of Europe.

coffee /'kofi/ *noun* **1a** a hot drink made from the ground roasted seeds of a coffee tree. **b** these seeds, *esp* after roasting and grinding. **2** = COFFEE TREE. **3** a cup of coffee. **4** a light brown colour. ➤ **coffee** *adj.* [Italian *caffè* via Turkish *kahve* from Arabic *qahwa*]

coffee bar *noun* an establishment where coffee and light refreshments are served; a cafe or snack bar.

coffee house *noun* an establishment that sells coffee and refreshments and, historically, often served as an informal club.

coffee mill *noun* a small machine used for grinding roasted coffee beans.

coffee morning *noun Brit* a morning social gathering at which coffee is served; *esp* one at which funds are raised for a charity.

coffee pot *noun* a pot for brewing or serving coffee.

coffee shop *noun* a small restaurant where light snacks are served.

coffee table *noun* a low table usu placed in a living room.

coffee-table book *noun* a book that is large in format and lavishly produced, e.g. with extensive use of full-colour illustrations, as if for display on a coffee table.

coffee tree *noun* any of several species of large African evergreen shrubs or small trees of the madder family that are widely cultivated in warm regions for their seeds: genus *Coffea*.

coffer¹ /'kofə/ *noun* **1** a chest or box; *esp* a strongbox. **2** (*usu in pl*) a treasury or exchequer; *broadly* a store of wealth: *The national coffers have been emptied to pay for this war.* **3a** = CAISSON (2). **b** = COFFERDAM. **4** a recessed decorative panel in a vault, ceiling, etc.

[Middle English *coffre* via Old French from Latin *cophinus* basket, from Greek *kophinos*]

coffer² *verb trans* (**coffered, coffering**) to decorate (a vault, ceiling, etc) with recessed decorative panels.

cofferdam *noun* a watertight enclosure from which water is pumped to allow construction or repair, e.g. of a pier or ship's hull.

coffin¹ /'kofin/ *noun* **1** a box or chest for the burial of a corpse. **2** the horny body forming the hoof of a horse's foot. [Middle English, basket, receptacle, via French from Latin *cophinus*: see COFFER¹]

coffin² *verb trans* (**coffined, coffining**) to enclose or place (somebody or something) in or as if in a coffin.

coffin bone *noun* the bone enclosed within the hoof of a horse.

coffin nail *noun informal* a cigarette.

coffle /'kofl/ *noun* a train of slaves or animals fastened together. [Arabic *qāfila* caravan]

C of S *abbr* Church of Scotland.

cog¹ /kog/ *noun* **1** a tooth on the rim of a wheel or gear. **2** a subordinate person or part. ➤➤ **cogged** *adj* [Middle English *cogge*, of Scandinavian origin]

cog² *noun* = TENON¹. [prob alteration of *cock* (tenon), perhaps from Old French *coque* notch]

cogent /'kohj(ə)nt/ *adj* said of an argument or evidence: appealing forcibly to the mind or reason; convincing. ➤➤ **cogency** *noun*, **cogently** *adv*. [Latin *cogent-, cogens*, present part. of *cogere* to drive together, from CO- + *agere* to drive]

cogitate /'kojitayt/ *verb intrans and trans formal* to ponder, usu intently and objectively, about (something); to meditate. ➤➤ **cogitation** /-'taysh(ə)n/ *noun*, **cogitative** *adj*, **cogitator** *noun*. [Latin *cogitatus*, past part. of *cogitare* to think or think about, from CO- + *agitare* to turn over (in the mind)]

cogito /'kogitoh, 'koj-/ *noun* in philosophy, the principle that one's existence can be conclusively established by the fact that one thinks. [Latin *cogito, ergo sum* I think, therefore I am (theorem stated by René Descartes d.1650, French philosopher)]

cognac /'konyak/ *noun* a French brandy; *specif* one from the departments of Charente and Charente-Maritime distilled from white wine. [French *cognac*, named after *Cognac*, town in France, where it is produced]

cognate¹ /'kognayt/ *adj* **1** related by blood, *esp* on the mother's side: compare AGNATE¹. **2a** related by derivation or borrowing or by descent from the same ancestral language: *The German word Vater is cognate with father.* **b** denoting a noun that is related in form and meaning to the verb of which it is the object (e.g. to die a death). **3** of the same or similar nature. ➤➤ **cognately** *adv*, **cognateness** *noun*, **cognation** /kog'naysh(ə)n/ *noun*. [Latin *cognatus*, from CO- + *gnatus, natus*, past part. of *nasci* to be born]

cognate² *noun* a thing, e.g. a word, that is cognate with another.

cognisable /'kognizəbl, kog'niez-/ *adj* see COGNIZABLE.

cognisance /'kogniz(ə)ns/ *noun* see COGNIZANCE.

cognisant /'kogniz(ə)nt/ *adj* see COGNIZANT.

cognition /kog'nish(ə)n/ *noun* **1** the mental act or process of acquiring knowledge that involves the processing of sensory information and includes perception, awareness, and judgment. **2** an insight, intuition, or perception that is a product of this process.

Editorial note

Since the 1950s, the cognitive sciences have urged that we understand cognition on the model of a computer. Perception, inference, language use, and memory all depend upon extensive unconscious computation and upon cognitive structures and dispositions which are innate, perhaps to be explained by natural selection — Professor Christopher Hookway.

➤➤ **cognitional** *adj*. [Middle English from Latin *cognition-, cognitio*, from *cognoscere* to become acquainted with, know]

cognitive /'kognitiv/ *adj* **1** relating to cognition. **2** based on or reducible to empirical knowledge. ➤➤ **cognitively** *adv*, **cognitivity** /-'tiviti/ *noun*.

cognitive dissonance *noun* psychological conflict resulting from incompatible beliefs and attitudes held simultaneously.

cognitive science *noun* the scientific study of the mental and other processes involved in obtaining and using knowledge.

cognitive therapy *noun* a method of treating psychological disorders that encourages patients to face up to and resolve their own distorted ways of thinking about themselves and the world.

cognizable *or* **cognisable** /'kognizəbl, kog'niez-/ *adj formal or technical* **1** perceptible. **2** capable of being heard and determined by a court of law. ➤➤ **cognizably** *adv*.

cognizance *or* **cognisance** /'kogniz(ə)ns/ *noun formal or technical* **1** jurisdiction or control. **2** the ability to perceive or understand. **3** notice or heed: *The tribunal takes cognizance of the exceptional circumstances in this case.* **4** in heraldry, a distinctive badge or mark. [Middle English *conisaunce* via French from Latin *cognoscere* to know]

cognizant *or* **cognisant** /'kogniz(ə)nt/ *adj formal or technical* having special or certain knowledge, often from first-hand sources. [back-formation from COGNIZANCE]

cognomen /kog'nohmen/ *noun (pl* **cognomens** *or* **cognomina** /-minə/) **1** a surname, *esp* the family (and usu third) name of a citizen of ancient Rome. **2** *formal or humorous* a name, *esp* a descriptive nickname. ➤➤ **cognominal** /kog'nominl/ *adj*. [Latin *cognomen*, from CO- + *nomen* name]

cognoscente /konyoh'shenti/ *noun (pl* **cognoscenti** /-ti/) a person having or claiming expert knowledge; a connoisseur. [Italian *cognoscente* wise, from Latin *cognoscent-, cognoscens*, present part. of *cognoscere* to know]

cogwheel *noun* a wheel with cogs or teeth.

cohabit /koh'habit/ *verb intrans* (**cohabited, cohabiting**) to live or exist together, *esp* as unmarried sexual partners. ➤➤ **cohabitant** *noun*, **cohabitation** /-'taysh(ə)n/ *noun*, **cohabitee** /-'tee/ *noun*, **cohabiter** *noun*. [late Latin *cohabitare*, from Latin CO- + *habitare* to inhabit]

coheir /koh'eə/ *noun* somebody who inherits something jointly with somebody else.

cohere /koh'hiə/ *verb intrans* **1** to hold together firmly as parts of the same whole; *broadly* to stick together. **2** to be logically or aesthetically consistent. [Latin *cohaerēre*, from CO- + *haerēre* to stick]

coherent /koh'hiərənt/ *adj* **1** able to speak clearly and make oneself understood. **2a** logically consistent: *a coherent argument.* **b** showing a unity of thought or purpose. **3** having the quality of cohering. **4** said *esp* of electromagnetic waves: having a definite relationship to each other: *coherent light.* ➤➤ **coherence** *noun*, **coherency** *noun*, **coherently** *adv*. [Latin *cohaerent-, cohaerens*, present part. of *cohaerēre*: see COHERE]

cohesion /koh'heezh(ə)n/ *noun* **1a** the fact or state of being coherent, *esp* acting or working together effectively as a unit. **b** the act of cohering. **2** in physics, molecular attraction by which the particles of a body are united throughout its mass. **3** union between similar plant parts or organs. ➤➤ **cohesive** *adj*, **cohesively** *adv*, **cohesiveness** *noun*. [Latin *cohaesus*, past part. of *cohaerēre*: see COHERE]

coho *or* **cohoe** /'koh·hoh/ *noun (pl* **cohos** *or* **cohoes** *or collectively* **coho** *or* **cohoe**) a N Pacific salmon having deep red flesh: *Oncorhynchus kisutch*. [origin unknown]

cohort /'kohhawt/ *noun* **1a** a group of soldiers; *esp* a division of a Roman legion. **b** a band or group. **2** a group of individuals having age, class membership, or other statistical factors in common in a study of the population. **3** *chiefly NAmer* a companion or accomplice. [Old French *cohorte* from Latin *cohort-, cohors* court, retinue]

Usage note

The use in sense (3) arises from a misunderstanding of the plural form *cohorts* as meaning a group of which each member is a *cohort*, whereas a *cohort* is a group and *cohorts* are several groups. This misunderstanding is reinforced by confusion of the first syllable *co-* with words such as *co-author* and *co-star*, as if the spelling might be *co-hort*, a fellow *hort* (whatever that is). This meaning is creeping into British English: *his chief cohort was an Englishman*. There are much better alternatives: for example *supporter, collaborator, henchman*, and *associate*, as well as the two words given in the definition above.

cohune /koh'hoon/ *noun* a palm tree native to Central America that has feathery leaves and produces a nut containing a valuable oil similar to coconut oil.

COI *abbr* Central Office of Information.

coif¹ /koyf/ *noun* **1** a close-fitting cap worn by nuns under a veil. **2** a protective usu metal skullcap formerly worn under a hood of mail. [Middle English *coife* via French *coife* from late Latin *cofea*]

coif² /koyf, kwahf/ *verb trans* (**coiffed, coiffing,** *NAmer* **coifed, coifing**) **1** to arrange (hair) by brushing, combing, or curling. **2** to cover or dress (hair) with or as if with a coif.

coiffeur /kwah'fuh (*French* kwafø:r)/ *noun* a hairdresser. [French *coiffeur*, from *coiffer* to arrange the hair, earlier 'to cover with a coif', from *coife*: see COIF[1]]

coiffeuse /kwah'fuhz (*French* kwafø:z)/ *noun* a female hairdresser. [French *coiffeuse*, fem of COIFFEUR]

coiffure /kwah'f(y)ooə (*French* kwafy:r)/ *noun* a hairstyle. >>> **coiffured** *adj.* [French *coiffure*, from *coiffer*: see COIFFEUR]

coign of vantage /koin/ *noun formal* an advantageous position. [*coign*, earlier spelling of COIN[1] in the sense 'corner']

coil[1] /koyl/ *verb trans* to wind (something long) into rings or spirals. >>> *verb intrans* **1** to move in a circular, spiral, or winding course. **2** to form a coil. [early French *coillir, cuillir* to gather, from Latin *colligere*: see COLLECT[1]]

coil[2] *noun* **1a** a length of rope, cable, etc gathered into a series of loops. **b** a series of loops; a spiral. **2** a single loop of a coil. **3a** a number of turns of wire, *esp* in spiral form, used for electromagnetic effect or for providing electrical resistance. **b** an electrical coil that supplies a high voltage to the spark plugs of an internal-combustion engine. **4** an intrauterine contraceptive device in the form of a metal or plastic coil. **5** a series of connected pipes in rows, layers, or windings, e.g. in a condenser.

coil[3] *noun archaic* turmoil or trouble: *I am not worth this coil that's made for me* — Shakespeare. [origin unknown]

coin[1] /koyn/ *noun* **1** a usu thin round piece of metal issued as money. **2** metal money. ✳ **pay somebody back in their own coin** *informal* to treat somebody as they have treated others. [Middle English via French *coin* wedge, corner, die, from Latin *cuneus* wedge]

coin[2] *verb trans* **1a** to make (a coin), *esp* by stamping; to mint. **b** to convert (metal) into coins. **2** to create or invent (a word or phrase). **3** to make or earn (money) rapidly and in large quantity. ✳ **to coin a phrase** said, usu ironically, when one uses an idiom or cliché: *I think he was being economical with the truth, to coin a phrase.*

coinage /'koynij/ *noun* **1a** coins collectively. **b** the coins in use as money in a particular country. **2a** the act of coining or inventing something. **b** something, e.g. a word, that is made up or invented.

coin-box *noun* **1** a telephone whose operation is paid for by inserting coins. **2** a box on such a telephone that receives the coins.

coincide /koh·in'sied/ *verb intrans* **1** (*often* + with) to occur at the same time or in the same place. **2** (*often* + with) to correspond in nature, character, function, or position. **3** (*often* + with) to be in accord or agreement; to concur. [medieval Latin *coincidere*, from Latin CO- + *incidere* to fall on, from IN-[2] + *cadere* to fall]

coincidence /koh'insid(ə)ns/ *noun* **1** the chance occurrence at the same time or place of two or more events that appear to be related or similar: *It's just a coincidence; The thing is beyond coincidence* — Conan Doyle. **2** the act or condition of coinciding; a correspondence. >>> **coincidental** /-'dentl/ *adj*, **coincidentally** /-'dentəli/ *adv*.

coincident /koh'insid(ə)nt/ *adj* **1** occupying the same space or time; coinciding: *coincident points.* **2** of similar nature; harmonious. >>> **coincidently** *adv*.

coiner *noun chiefly Brit* somebody who makes counterfeit coins.

coin-op /'koin op/ *noun* a self-service laundry where the machines are operated by coins.

Cointreau /'kwontroh/ *noun trademark* a colourless liqueur flavoured with oranges. [named after the *Cointreau* family, French liqueur manufacturers]

coir /'koyə/ *noun* a stiff coarse fibre from the husk of a coconut. [Malayalam *kāyar* rope]

coition /koh'ish(ə)n/ *noun* = COITUS. >>> **coitional** *adj*. [Latin *coition-, coitio* a coming together, from *cuire*: see COITUS]

coitus /'koytəs, 'koh·itəs/ *noun technical* sexual intercourse involving insertion of the penis into the vagina and culminating in ejaculation. >>> **coital** *adj*, **coitally** *adv*. [Latin *coitus*, past part. of *coire* to come together, from CO- + *ire* to go]

coitus interruptus /intə'ruptəs/ *noun* coitus in which the penis is withdrawn before orgasm in order to prevent ejaculation of sperm into the vagina. [scientific Latin *coitus interruptus*, interrupted coitus]

Coke /kohk/ *noun trademark* short for Coca-Cola.

coke[1] /kohk/ *noun* a solid porous fuel that remains after gases have been driven from coal by heating. [Middle English; earlier history unknown]

coke[2] *verb trans* to convert (coal) into coke.

coke[3] *noun slang* cocaine. [by shortening and alteration]

Col. *abbr* **1** Colonel. **2** Colorado. **3** Colossians (book of the Bible).

col /kol/ *noun* **1** a depression or pass in a mountain ridge or range. **2** in meteorology, a region of low pressure between two anticyclones. [French *col* from Latin *collum* neck]

col. *abbr* **1** colour; coloured. **2** column.

col- *prefix* see COM-.

cola *or* **kola** /'kohlə/ *noun* **1** a carbonated soft drink flavoured with extract from coca leaves, kola nut, sugar, caramel, and acid and aromatic substances. **2** any of a genus of small W African trees that have seeds containing caffeine: genus *Cola*. [(sense 1) from COCA-COLA; (sense 2) from W African *kolo* nut]

colander /'koləndə, 'kul-/ *or* **cullender** /'kuləndə/ *noun* a perforated bowl-shaped utensil for washing or draining food. [Middle English *colyndore*, prob modification of Old Provençal *colador* from Latin *colatus*, past part. of *colare* to sieve]

cola nut *noun* see KOLA NUT.

co-latitude /koh'latityoohd/ *noun* the difference between a degree of latitude and 90°.

colcannon /kol'kanən/ *noun* an Irish dish of potatoes and cabbage boiled and mashed together usu with cream or buttermilk. [Irish Gaelic *cál ceannan* white-headed cabbage]

colchicine /'kolchiseen, 'kolkiseen/ *noun* an alkaloid extracted from the corms or seeds of the meadow saffron and used to inhibit division of the cell nucleus in mitosis and in the treatment of gout. [Latin *Colchicum*, genus name of the meadow saffron]

colchicum /'kolchikəm, 'kolkikəm/ *noun* (*pl* **colchicums**) **1** any of a genus of African and Eurasian plants of the lily family with flowers that resemble crocuses: genus *Colchicum*. **2** the colchicine-containing dried corm or dried ripe seeds of the meadow saffron. [Latin genus name, from Greek *kolchikon* product of *Colchis*, an ancient region in Asia, home of the sorceress Medea; the plant was believed to be poisonous]

cold[1] /kohld/ *adj* **1** having a low temperature, often below the normal temperature or below that compatible with human comfort: *But this place is too cold for hell* — Shakespeare. **2a** said of food: previously cooked but served at a low temperature: *cold meat.* **b** not served at the correct high temperature: *This soup is cold.* **3** refrigerated: *cold drinks.* **4a** characterized by lack of feeling or sociability; unemotional; unresponsive. **b** unfriendly or hostile: *a cold stare.* **5** producing a sensation of cold; chilling, depressing, or cheerless: *cold blank walls.* **6** said of a colour: producing an impression of being cool; *specif* in the range blue to green. **7a** dead. **b** unconscious: *knocked out cold.* **8a** retaining only faint scents, traces, or clues: *a cold trail.* **b** far from a goal, object, or solution sought. **9** presented or regarded in a straightforward way; impersonal: *the cold facts.* **10** unprepared. **11** said of a process: performed on an unheated material: *cold conditioning of steel prior to rolling.* ✳ **give somebody the cold shoulder** to be unfriendly towards somebody. **in cold blood** with premeditation; deliberately. **in the cold light of day** when a situation is considered soberly and objectively. **leave somebody cold** to fail to excite, impress, or move somebody. >>> **coldish** *adj*, **coldly** *adv*, **coldness** *noun*. [Old English *ceald, cald*]

cold[2] *noun* **1a** a condition of low temperature. **b** cold weather. **2** bodily sensation produced by relative lack of heat; chill. **3** an infection characterized by a sore throat, runny nose, sneezing, etc; COMMON COLD. ✳ **catch a cold** *informal* to be in trouble, *esp* in financial difficulties as a result of speculating unwisely. **out in the cold** ignored or neglected.

cold[3] *adv* **1** with utter finality; absolutely: *She was turned down cold.* **2** without any preparation: *He had to do it cold.*

cold-blooded *adj* **1a** done or acting without consideration or compunction; ruthless: *cold-blooded murder.* **b** concerned only with the facts; emotionless. **2** having a body temperature not internally regulated but approximating to that of the environment: compare WARM-BLOODED. >>> **cold-bloodedly** *adv*, **cold-bloodedness** *noun*.

cold call *noun* an unsolicited visit or telephone call made by a salesperson to a prospective customer.

cold-call *verb intrans and trans* **1** to make a cold call to (somebody). **2** to sell (goods or services) by a cold call.

cold cathode *noun* a cathode that emits electrons at an ambient temperature.

cold chisel *noun* a chisel made of steel suitable for chipping or cutting cold metal.

cold comfort *noun* something intended to console or compensate somebody but inadequate for the purpose.

cold cream *noun* a thick oily often perfumed cream for cleansing and soothing the skin of the neck, face, etc.

cold cuts *pl noun* sliced assorted cold cooked meats.

cold feet *pl noun* *informal* fear or doubt strong enough to prevent a planned course of action.

cold frame *noun* a usu glass-covered frame without artificial heat used to protect plants and seedlings.

cold front *noun* an advancing edge of a cold air mass.

cold fusion *noun* the supposed production of energy by nuclear fusion at ordinary temperatures, without the application of great heat and pressure.

cold-hearted *adj* marked by lack of sympathy, interest, or sensitivity. >>> **cold-heartedly** *adv*, **cold-heartedness** *noun*.

cold-rolled *adj* said of metal: rolled into sheets while cold and so having a smooth hard surface.

cold sore *noun* a blister or group of blisters appearing round or inside the mouth, caused by a viral infection: compare HERPES SIMPLEX.

cold start *noun* **1** an act of starting something, *esp* an engine or a machine, without preparation. **2** in computing, the reloading of a program.

cold-start *verb trans* **1** to start (something) without preparation. **2** in computing, to reload (a program).

cold storage *noun* **1** storage, e.g. of food, in a cold place for preservation. **2** a condition of being held or continued without being acted on; abeyance.

cold store *noun* a building for cold storage.

cold sweat *noun* concurrent perspiration and chill, usu associated with fear, pain, or shock.

cold turkey *noun* **1** *informal*. **a** the abrupt complete cessation of the use of an addictive narcotic drug by an addict. **b** the shivering, nausea, feelings of fear, etc resulting from this. **2** *NAmer* blunt language or procedure.

cold war *noun* **1a** a conflict carried on by methods other than military action. **b** (**the Cold War**) the period of intense rivalry and hostility between the Western and Soviet blocs between 1945 and 1989. **2** a hostile but nonviolent relationship.

cold wave *noun* **1** a period of unusually cold weather. **2** a permanent wave applied to the hair using chemicals.

cole /kohl/ *noun* cabbage, broccoli, kohlrabi, or a related edible plant of the cabbage family. [Old English *cāl* from Latin *caulis* stem, cabbage]

colectomy /kə'lektəmi/ *noun* (*pl* **colectomies**) a surgical operation to remove all or part of the colon.

coleopteran /koli'optərən/ *noun* any of an order of beetles typically with shell-like forewings: order Coleoptera. >>> **coleopteran** *adj*. [scientific Latin *coleoptera*, from Greek *koleon* sheath + *pteron* wing]

coleoptile /koli'optiel/ *noun* the first leaf produced by a germinating seed of grasses and some related plants, which forms a protective sheath round the bud that develops into the shoot. [scientific Latin *coleoptilum*, from Greek *koleon* sheath + *ptilon* down]

coleorhiza /kolia'riezə/ *noun* (*pl* **coleorhizae** /-zi/) the protective sheath that in some plants (e.g. grasses) covers the part of the seedling that develops into the first root. [scientific Latin, from Greek *koleon* sheath + -RHIZA]

coleslaw /'kohlslaw/ *noun* a salad of raw sliced or chopped white cabbage, carrots, etc. [Dutch *koolsla*, from *kool* cabbage + *sla* salad]

coleus /'kohli-əs/ *noun* (*pl* **coleuses**) any of a genus of plants of the mint family including many grown for their brightly coloured and variegated foliage: genus *Solenostemon* (formerly *Coleus*). [Latin *coleus*, former genus name, from Greek *koleos*, *koleon* sheath; because the stamens are joined together, resembling a sheath]

coley /'kohli/ *noun* (*pl* **coleys** or collectively **coley**) *Brit* a N Atlantic food fish closely related to the cod. [prob by shortening and alteration from COALFISH]

colic /'kolik/ *noun* a paroxysm of abdominal pain localized in the intestines or other hollow organ and caused by spasm, obstruction, or twisting. >>> **colicky** *adj*. [Middle English via French and Latin from Greek *kōlikos* colicky, from *kōlon*, alteration of *kolon* colon]

coliseum or **colosseum** /kolə'see-əm/ *noun* a large building, e.g. a stadium or theatre, used for public entertainments.

Word history
medieval Latin from Latin *Colosseum* the amphitheatre in Rome, from *colossus*: see COLOSSUS. The Coliseum stood near a large statue of Nero.

colitis /kə'lietəs, koh-/ *noun* inflammation of the colon. [scientific Latin *colitis*, from COLON[1] + -ITIS]

coll. *abbr* college.

collaborate /kə'labərayt/ *verb intrans* **1** (*often* + with) to work together or to work with somebody else on a common project or with a common aim. **2** (*often* + with) to cooperate with an enemy of one's country. >>> **collaboration** /-'raysh(ə)n/ *noun*, **collaborative** /-rətiv/ *adj*, **collaboratively** /-rətivli/ *adv*, **collaborator** *noun*. [late Latin *collaboratus*, past part. of *collaborare* to labour together, from CO- + Latin *laborare* to work]

collaborationism *noun* collaboration with an enemy. >>> **collaborationist** *adj and noun*.

collage /'kolahzh/ *noun* **1** a composition made of pieces of paper, wood, cloth, etc fixed to a surface. **2** an assembly of diverse fragments: *a collage of ideas*. >>> **collagist** *noun*. [French *collage* gluing, from *coller* to glue, from *colle* glue, ultimately from Greek *kolla*]

collagen /'koləjən/ *noun* an insoluble protein that occurs as fibres in connective tissue, e.g. tendons, and in bones, and yields gelatin and glue on prolonged heating with water. [Greek *kolla* glue + -GEN]

collapsar /kə'lapsah/ *noun* an old star that has collapsed; *esp* a BLACK HOLE.

collapse[1] /kə'laps/ *verb intrans* **1** to fall down or break completely; to disintegrate. **2** to fall inward and become flat abruptly and completely, e.g. through compression: *a collapsed lung*. **3** to fail suddenly and completely. **4** to suffer a breakdown in energy, stamina, or self-control through exhaustion or disease; *esp* to fall helpless or unconscious. **5** to fold down into a more compact shape: *a telescope that collapses*. > *verb trans* to cause (something) to collapse. >>> **collapsible** *adj*. [Latin *collapsus*, past part. of *collabi*, from COL- + *labi* to fall, slide]

collapse[2] *noun* **1** an instance of falling down, falling in, or disintegration. **2** total failure or breakdown. **3** a sudden, incapacitating loss of energy, strength, or self-control. **4** an airless state of a lung or part of a lung.

collar[1] /'kolə/ *noun* **1** a band of fabric that serves to finish or decorate the neckline of a garment; *esp* one that is turned over. **2** a band fitted around the neck of an animal. **3** a protective or supportive device worn round the neck. **4** something resembling a collar, e.g. a ring or round flange to restrain motion or hold something in place. **5** any of various animal markings similar to a collar in appearance or form. **6** a cut of bacon from the neck of a pig. >>> **collared** *adj*, **collarless** *adj*. [Middle English *coler* via Old French from Latin *collare*, from *collum* neck]

collar[2] *verb trans* (**collared, collaring**) *informal* **1a** to seize (somebody) by or as if by the collar or neck; to apprehend. **b** to get control of (something): *With our machine ... we can collar nearly the whole of this market* — Roald Dahl. **2** to stop and detain (somebody) in conversation; to buttonhole.

collar beam *noun* a horizontal beam in a roof that connects two opposite rafters at a place higher than their base: compare TIE-BEAM.

collarbone *noun* = CLAVICLE.

collard /'koləd/ *noun* *NAmer*, *Brit dialect* the leaves of a variety of cabbage, used as a vegetable. [variant of *colewort* kale]

collard greens *pl noun* = COLLARD.

collared dove *noun* a dove with grey-brown plumage and a narrow band of black around its neck: *Streptopelia decaocto*.

collate /kə'layt/ *verb trans* **1** to collect and compare (information, statements, etc) carefully in order to verify them and often to integrate them or arrange them in order. **2** to assemble (pages) in proper order: *This machine can collate the printed sheets*. **3** to appoint (a priest) to a Church of England benefice of which the bishop is the patron. >>> **collator** *noun*. [back-formation from COLLATION]

collateral[1] /kə'lat(ə)rəl/ *adj* **1** accompanying as secondary or subordinate. **2** belonging to the same ancestral stock but not in a direct line of descent: compare LINEAL. **3** parallel or corresponding in position, time, or significance. ➤➤ **collaterality** /-'raliti/ *noun,* **collaterally** *adv.* [Middle English, prob via French from medieval Latin *collateralis,* from COL- + Latin *lateralis* lateral]

collateral[2] *noun* **1** property pledged by a borrower to protect the interests of the lender. **2** a collateral relative.

collateral damage *noun* unintended destruction or casualties in non-military areas caused by a military operation.

collation /kə'laysh(ə)n/ *noun* **1** the act, process, or result of collating. **2** a light meal; *specif* one allowed on fast days in place of lunch or supper. [Middle English via Old French from Latin *collation-, collatio* bringing together, from *conferre*: see CONFER]

colleague /'koleeg/ *noun* a fellow worker, *esp* in a profession. [French *collegue* from Latin *collega,* from COL- + *legare* to appoint, depute]

collect[1] /kə'lekt/ *verb trans* **1a** to bring (things) together in one place; *specif* to assemble a collection of (things) as a hobby. **b** to gather or exact (e.g. payments or contributions) from a number of sources: *collect taxes.* **2** to fetch (something or somebody) from a place: *It's your turn to collect the children from school.* **3** to accumulate or gather (something) passively: *Books collect dust.* **4** to gain or regain control of (something or oneself): *He tried to collect his thoughts.* **5** to claim as due and receive possession or payment of (something): *She is entitled to collect social security.* **6** *chiefly Brit* to gain or obtain (something). ➤ *verb intrans* **1** to come together in a band, group, or mass; to gather. **2** (*often* + on) to receive payment: *By collecting on his insurance he was able to replace the camera.* [Latin *collectus,* past part. of *colligere* to collect, from COL- + *legere* to gather]

collect[2] /'kolikt/ *noun* **1** a short prayer comprising an invocation, petition, and conclusion. **2** a prayer preceding the Epistle read at Communion. [Middle English *collecte* via Old French from medieval Latin *collecta,* short for *oratio ad collectam* prayer upon assembly]

collect[3] /kə'lekt/ *adj and adv NAmer* to be paid for by the receiver: *a collect telephone call; Send the package collect.*

collectable[1] *or* **collectible** /kə'lektəbl/ *adj* **1** able to be collected. **2** worth making a collection of or putting into a collection; of interest to a collector.

collectable[2] *or* **collectible** *noun* an object that is worth collecting.

collected /kə'lektid/ *adj* **1** exhibiting calmness and composure. **2** assembled from a number of sources: *the collected works of Jane Austen.* ➤➤ **collectedly** *adv,* **collectedness** *noun.*

collectible /kə'lektəbl/ *adj and noun* see COLLECTABLE[1], COLLECTABLE[2].

collection /kə'leksh(ə)n/ *noun* **1** the act or process of collecting. **2** something collected, *esp* an accumulation of objects gathered for study, comparison, or exhibition. **3** a range of similar products, e.g. new garments, presented to the public: *Christian Dior's spring collection.*

collective[1] /kə'lektiv/ *adj* **1** denoting a number of individuals considered as one group: *Flock is a collective word.* **2** = MULTIPLE[1] (5). **3** of, made, or held in common by a group of individuals: *collective responsibility; collective control.* **4** collectivized: *a collective farm.* ➤➤ **collectively** *adv,* **collectiveness** *noun,* **collectivity** /kolek'tiviti/ *noun.*

collective[2] *noun* **1** (*treated as sing. or pl*) a collective body; a group. **2** a cooperative organization; *specif* a collective farm.

collective bargaining *noun* negotiation between an employer and union representatives usu on wages, hours, and working conditions.

collective farm *noun* a large farm that is worked jointly by a group of people, but is usually owned and supervised by the state.

collective noun *noun* in grammar, a noun that denotes a number of individuals considered as one group.

Usage note

The following list gives some of the special terms used to describe groups of animals, birds, and people. Some of them are in general use but others come from antiquarians' lists and have no real basis in usage: apes: shrewdness; asses: herd; bees: hive, swarm, drift, or bike; birds: flock or flight; boar: sounder; boys: blush; buffalo: herd or gang; cattle: herd or drove; chickens: brood; cranes: herd; curlew: herd; deer: herd or mob; dogs: pack or kennel; doves: flight; ducks (on water): raft, bunch, or padding; ducks (in flight): team; elephants: herd; elk: herd; finches: charm; fish: shoal; flies: cloud; geese: gaggle or (in the air) skein, team, or wedge; giraffes: herd; goats:

flock or herd; grouse: pack or covey; hawks: cast; horses: team or (breeding) stud; hounds: pack, kennel, or cry; insects: flight or swarm; kangaroos: mob or troop; kittens: kindle; ladies: bevy; lions: pride; monkeys: troop; partridges: covey; penguins: rookery; pheasants: head; pigeons: kit (flying together); pigs: herd; plovers: stand or wing; porpoises: herd, pod, or school; pups: litter; quail: bevy or drift; racehorses: string; roes: bevy; rooks: parliament; seals: herd, rockery, or pod (small herd); sheep: flock or herd; snipe: wisp; swallows: flight; swans: game or herd or (in the air) wedge; swine: herd; waterfowl: bunch or knob; whales: school, herd, gam, or pod (small school); widgeon: company or trip; wildfowl: bunch, trip, plump, or knob (less than 30); wolves: pack; women: gaggle; wrens: herd.

collective ownership *noun* the ownership of something, e.g. land, by a group of people who have collective control.

collective unconscious *noun* that part of a person's unconscious which is inherited and shared with all other people.

collectivise /kə'lektiviez/ *verb* see COLLECTIVIZE.

collectivism /kə'lektiviz(ə)m/ *noun* a political or economic theory advocating collective control, *esp* over production and distribution. ➤➤ **collectivist** *adj and noun,* **collectivistic** /-'vistik/ *adj.*

collectivize *or* **collectivise** /kə'lektiviez/ *verb trans* to organize (something) under collective control. ➤➤ **collectivization** /-'zaysh(ə)n/ *noun.*

collector /kə'lektə/ *noun* **1** somebody who collects things of a certain type: *a stamp collector.* **2** an official who collects funds, *esp* money: *a debt collector.* **3a** a conductor that maintains contact between moving and stationary parts of an electric circuit. **b** a region in a transistor that collects charge carriers. ➤➤ **collectorship** *noun.*

collector's item *noun* an object that is of special interest and value to collectors.

colleen /ko'leen/ *noun Irish* a girl or young woman. [Irish Gaelic *cailín*]

college /'kolij/ *noun* **1** a building used for an educational or religious purpose. **2a** a self-governing constituent body of a university offering instruction and often living quarters. **b** an institution offering vocational or technical instruction: *business college; art college.* **3** an organized body of people engaged in a common pursuit. **4a** *chiefly Brit* a public school or private secondary school. **b** a state school for older pupils: *a sixth-form college.* [Middle English via French from Latin *collegium* society, from *collega*: see COLLEAGUE]

college of education *noun* a college for the training of teachers.

collegial /kə'leeji·əl/ *adj* **1** = COLLEGIATE (1), (2). **2** characterized by equal sharing of authority, *esp* by Roman Catholic bishops. ➤➤ **collegiality** /-'aliti/ *noun,* **collegially** *adv.*

collegian /kə'leejən/ *noun* a member of a college.

collegiate /kə'leeji·ət/ *adj* **1** relating to a collegiate church. **2** relating to or comprising a college. **3** = COLLEGIAL (2). ➤➤ **collegiately** *adv.* [medieval Latin *collegiatus* from Latin *collegium* society, from *collega*: see COLLEAGUE]

collegiate church *noun* **1** a church other than a cathedral that has a chapter of canons. **2** *NAmer, Scot* a church or corporate group of churches with two or more ministers of equal rank.

col legno /kol 'legnoh/ *adv* said of a passage of music for stringed instruments: to be played by tapping the strings with the back of the bow. [Italian *col legno,* literally 'with the wood']

collenchyma /kə'lengkimə/ *noun* a plant tissue found in growing stems, leaf midribs, etc that consists of living cells with irregularly thickened walls: compare PARENCHYMA, SCLERENCHYMA. ➤➤ **collenchymatous** /kolən'kiemətəs, -'kimətəs/ *adj.* [scientific Latin, from Greek *kolla* glue + *enkhuma* infusion]

Colles' fracture /'kolis/ *noun* a fracture of the radius just above the wrist in which the hand is displaced backwards. [named after Abraham *Colles* d.1843, Irish surgeon]

collet /'kolit/ *noun* a metal band, collar, ferrule, or flange; *esp* a circle or flange in which a gem is set. [early French *collet,* dimin. of *col* collar, from Latin *collum* neck]

collide /kə'lied/ *verb intrans* **1** to come together forcibly. **2** to come into conflict. [Latin *collidere,* from COL- + *laedere* to injure by striking]

collider *noun* a ring-shaped particle beam accelerator in which electrons and positrons circulate in opposite directions and collide with each other, thereby producing other elementary particles used in research into the nature of matter.

collie /'koli/ *noun* a large dog of a breed orig used to herd sheep, having a pointed nose and long hair. [prob from English dialect *colly* black, from *col* COAL]

collier /'koli·ə/ *noun* 1 a coal miner. 2 a ship for transporting coal. [Middle English *colier* charcoal-burner, from *col* coal]

colliery /'koli·əri, 'kolyəri/ *noun* (*pl* **collieries**) a coal mine and its associated buildings.

colligative /kə'ligətiv/ *adj* depending on the number rather than the nature of particles, e.g. molecules: *Pressure is a colligative property*. [Latin *colligatus*, past part. of *colligare* to bind together, from COL- + *ligare* to tie]

collimate /'kolimayt/ *verb trans* 1 to make (e.g. rays of light) parallel. 2 to adjust the line of sight of (a telescope, theodolite, etc). ⮞⮞ **collimation** /-'maysh(ə)n/ *noun*. [Latin *collimatus*, past part. of *collimare*, variant of *collineare* to make straight, from COL- + *linea* line]

collimator *noun* 1 a device for producing a beam of parallel rays or radiation. 2 a small telescope fixed to a larger one to adjust its line of sight.

collinear /koh'lini·ə/ *adj* said of points: lying on or passing through the same straight line. ⮞⮞ **collinearity** /-'ariti/ *noun*.

collision /kə'lizh(ə)n/ *noun* 1 an act or instance of colliding; a clash. 2 in physics, an encounter between particles, e.g. atoms or molecules, resulting in the exchange or transformation of energy. ⮞⮞ **collisional** *adj*. [Middle English from Latin *collision-, collisio*, from *collidere* to collide]

collision course *noun* a course or approach that would result in collision or conflict if continued unaltered.

collocate[1] /'koləkayt/ *verb trans formal* to set or arrange (things) in a particular place or position, *esp* side by side. ⮞ *verb intrans* (*often* + with) said of a linguistic element: to form part of a collocation. [Latin *collocatus*, past part. of *collocare*, from COL- + *locare* to place, from *locus* place]

collocate[2] *noun* a word that is typically, or very frequently, used in conjunction with another word.

collocation /kolə'kaysh(ə)n/ *noun* the act or result of placing or arranging together; *specif* a combination of two or more words that is well established by usage. ⮞⮞ **collocational** *adj*.

collocutor /'koləkyoohtə, kə'lokyootə/ *noun* somebody taking part in a conversation. [late Latin *collocutor* from *colloqui*: see COLLOQUY]

collodion /kə'lohdi·ən/ *noun* a viscous solution of PYROXYLIN (mixture of cellulose nitrates), used as a coating for wounds or for photographic films. [modification of scientific Latin *collodium* from Greek *kollōdēs* glutinous, from *kolla* glue]

collogue /ko'lohg/ *verb intrans* to conspire or speak furtively.

colloid /'koloyd/ *noun* 1a a substance composed of particles that are too small to be seen with a light microscope but too large to form a true solution: compare CRYSTALLOID[1]. b a system consisting of a colloid together with the gaseous, liquid, or solid medium in which it is dispersed. 2 a gelatinous substance found in tissues, *esp* in disease. ⮞⮞ **colloidal** /ko'loydl/ *adj*, **colloidally** /ko'loydəli/ *adv*.

collop /'koləp/ *noun* a small slice, *esp* of meat; an escalope. [Middle English, prob of Scandinavian origin]

colloq. *abbr* 1 colloquial. 2 colloquially.

colloquia /kə'lohkwi·ə/ *noun* pl of COLLOQUIUM.

colloquial /kə'lohkwi·əl/ *adj* used in, characteristic of, or using the style of familiar and informal conversation; conversational. ⮞⮞ **colloquially** *adv*. [Latin *colloquium*: see COLLOQUY]

colloquialism *noun* 1 a colloquial expression. 2 colloquial style.

colloquium /kə'lohkwi·əm/ *noun* (*pl* **colloquiums** *or* **colloquia** /-kwi·ə/) a conference or seminar. [Latin *colloquium*: see COLLOQUY]

colloquy /'koləkwi/ *noun* (*pl* **colloquies**) 1 a formal conversation or dialogue. 2 a religious conference. [Latin *colloquium*, from *colloqui* to converse, from COL- + *loqui* to speak]

collotype /'kolətiep/ *noun* 1 a process for printing illustrations directly from a hardened film of gelatin. 2 a print made by collotype.

collude /kə'loohd/ *verb intrans* (*often* + with) to cooperate with, or give support or approval to, somebody in secret; to conspire or plot. ⮞⮞ **colluder** *noun*. [Latin *colludere*, from COL- + *ludere* to play, from *ludus* game]

collusion /kə'loohzh(ə)n/ *noun* secret agreement or cooperation for an illegal or deceitful purpose. ⮞⮞ **collusive** /-siv/ *adj*, **collusively** /-sivli/ *adv*. [Middle English via French from Latin *collusion-, collusio*, from *colludere*: see COLLUDE]

collyrium /kə'liri·əm/ *noun* (*pl* **collyriums** *or* **collyria** /-ri·ə/) an eye lotion. [via Latin from Greek *kollyrion* pessary, eye salve, dimin. of *kollyra* roll of bread]

collywobbles /'koliwoblz/ *pl noun informal* 1 (*usu* the collywobbles) pain or discomfort in the stomach. 2 (*usu* the collywobbles) a nervous or anxious feeling; butterflies. [prob alteration of COLIC + WOBBLE[2]]

Colo. *abbr* Colorado.

colobus monkey /'koləbəs/ *noun* any of several species of long-tailed African monkeys that live in trees, eat leaves, have long silky fur, and have no thumb, or only a vestigial thumb, on their paws: genera *Colobus* and *Procolobus*. [Latin genus name, from Greek *kolobos* docked, mutilated; from its rudimentary thumb]

cologne /kə'lohn/ *noun* scented toilet water. [named after *Cologne*, city in Germany, where it was first made]

Colombian *noun* a native or inhabitant of Colombia in S America. ⮞⮞ **Colombian** *adj*.

colon[1] /'kohlon/ *noun* the part of the large intestine that extends from the caecum to the rectum. ⮞⮞ **colonic** /kə'lonik/ *adj*. [via Latin from Greek *kolon* colon]

colon[2] *noun* 1 a punctuation mark (:) used chiefly to introduce a quotation or list of items, or to direct attention to matter that follows. 2 the sign (:) used in various technical contexts, *esp* to show a ratio, e.g. 4:1 = 'four to one'. [via Latin from Greek *kōlon* limb, part of a strophe]

colón /koh'lohn, koh'lon/ *noun* (*pl* **colones** /-nays/) the basic monetary unit of Costa Rica and El Salvador. [Spanish *colón*, named after Cristóbal *Colón* (Christopher Columbus) d.1506, Italian navigator]

colonel /'kuhnl/ *noun* an officer in the army or US air force ranking below brigadier or brigadier general, often in overall command of a regiment in the British army. ⮞⮞ **colonelcy** /-si/ *noun*. [alteration of *coronel* from early French, modification of Old Italian *colonnello* column of soldiers, colonel, dimin. of *colonna* column, from Latin *columna*: see COLUMN]

Colonel Blimp /blimp/ *noun* a pompous person with out-of-date or extreme conservative views; a reactionary. ⮞⮞ **Colonel Blimpism** *noun*. [named after *Colonel Blimp*, cartoon character created by David Low d.1963, Brit cartoonist]

colones /koh'lonays, koh'lohnays/ *noun* pl of COLÓN.

colonial[1] /kə'lohni·əl/ *adj* 1 relating to or characteristic of a colony. 2 (*often* **Colonial**) made or prevailing in America before 1776: *colonial architecture*. 3 possessing or composed of colonies: *Britain's colonial empire*. ⮞⮞ **colonially** *adv*.

colonial[2] *noun* a member or inhabitant of a colony.

colonialism *noun* 1 control by a state over a dependent area or people. 2 a policy based on this. ⮞⮞ **colonialist** *noun and adj*.

colonic irrigation *noun* the injection of fluid into the colon via the anus as a cleansing or therapeutic operation.

colonise /'koləniez/ *verb* see COLONIZE.

colonist /'kolənist/ *noun* 1 a member or inhabitant of a colony. 2 somebody who colonizes or settles in a new country.

colonize *or* **colonise** /'koləniez/ *verb trans* 1 to establish a colony in (a place) or extend colonial control over (an indigenous people): *Those people who were once colonized by the [English] language are now rapidly remaking it, domesticating it, becoming more and more relaxed about the way they use it* — Salman Rushdie. 2 said of plants and animals: to begin to live and breed in (a new area or environment). 3 *often humorous* to take over and occupy (a room, building, or area). ⮞⮞ **colonization** /-'zaysh(ə)n/ *noun*, **colonizer** *noun*.

colonnade /kolə'nayd/ *noun* a row of columns placed at regular intervals, usu supporting an entablature and often a roof. ⮞⮞ **colonnaded** *adj*. [French *colonnade* from Italian *colonnato*, from *colonna* column, from Latin *columna*: see COLUMN]

colonoscope /kə'lonəskohp/ *noun* a long medical instrument with which the colon can be examined and operated upon. ⮞⮞ **colonoscopy** /-'noskəpi/ *noun*.

colony /'koləni/ *noun* (*pl* **colonies**) 1a a body of settlers living in a new territory, often already occupied by an indigenous people, that is subject to control by the settlers' parent state. **b** the territory settled or controlled in this way. **2a** a group of individuals with common interests or origins living close together: *an artists' colony.* **b** the area occupied by such a group. **3** a group of people segregated from the general public: *a leper colony; a penal colony.* **4** a distinguishable localized population within a species: *a colony of termites.* **5a** a mass of micro-organisms, usu growing in or on a solid medium. **b** all the units of a compound animal, e.g. a coral. **6a** (**the colonies**) all Britain's former territorial possessions overseas collectively. **b** (**the colonies**) the thirteen established areas of British settlement in North America that became the original United States after independence. [Middle English via French from Latin *colonia* settlement, farm, from *colere* to cultivate]

colophon /'koləfon/ *noun* **1** a statement at the end of a book or manuscript, giving facts about its production. **2** an identifying symbol used by a printer or publisher. [via Latin from Greek *kolophōn* summit, finishing touch]

colophony /ko'lofəni/ *noun* = ROSIN¹. [Middle English *colophonie* from Latin *colophonia resina* resin from *Colophon*, an Ionian city]

color /'kulə/ *verb and noun NAmer* see COLOUR¹ and COLOUR².

colorable /'kul(ə)rəbl/ *adj NAmer* see COLOURABLE.

Colorado beetle /kolə'rahdoh/ *noun* a black-and-yellow striped beetle that feeds on the leaves of the potato plant: *Leptinotarsa decemlineata.* [named after *Colorado*, state of USA]

coloration (*Brit also* **colouration**) /kulə'raysh(ə)n/ *noun* **1** colouring or complexion: *the dark coloration of his skin.* **2** use or choice of colours, e.g. by an artist. **3** an arrangement or range of colours: *the brilliant coloration of a butterfly's wing.*

coloratura /,kolərə'tyooərə/ *noun* **1** elaborate embellishment in vocal music. **2** a singer who uses such embellishment. [Italian *coloratura* literally 'colouring' ultimately from Latin *colorare* to colour, from *color* COLOUR¹]

colored /'kul(ə)rd/ *adj and noun NAmer* see COLOURED¹, COLOURED².

colorful /'kul(ə)rf(ə)l/ *adj NAmer* see COLOURFUL.

colorific /kulə'rifik/ *adj* producing or capable of giving colour.

colorimeter /kulə'rimitə/ *noun* an instrument used for chemical analysis by comparison of a liquid's colour with standard colours. ➤➤ **colorimetric** /-'metrik/ *adj*, **colorimetry** *noun.*

coloring /'kul(ə)ring/ *adj NAmer* see COLOURING.

colorist /'kul(ə)rist/ *noun NAmer* see COLOURIST.

coloristic /kul(ə)'ristik/ *adj NAmer* see COLOURISTIC.

colorless /'kul(ə)rləs/ *adj NAmer* see COLOURLESS.

colossal /kə'los(ə)l/ *adj* **1** of very great size or degree: *a colossal building; a colossal blunder.* **2** said of a statue: twice life size or larger: compare HEROIC (4). **3** said of columns of a particular architectural order: extending over more than one storey of a building. ➤➤ **colossally** *adv.* [French *colossal* from *colosse*, from Latin *colossus*: see COLOSSUS]

colosseum /kolə'see·əm/ *noun* see COLISEUM.

colossus /kə'losəs/ *noun* (*pl* **colossuses** *or* **colossi** /-sie/) **1** a statue of gigantic size, often in particular reference to the Colossus of Rhodes of antiquity, erroneously believed to bestride the harbour: *Why man, he doth bestride the narrow world like a Colossus, and we petty men walk under his huge legs* — Shakespeare. **2** somebody or something remarkably preeminent. [via Latin from Greek *kolossos*]

colostomy /kə'lostəmi/ *noun* (*pl* **colostomies**) the surgical formation of an artificial anus in the wall of the abdomen after a shortening of the colon, or the artificial anus so formed. [COLON¹ + -*stomy* from STOMA]

colostrum /kə'lostrəm/ *noun* the milk that is secreted for a few days after giving birth and is characterized by high protein and antibody content. ➤➤ **colostral** *adj.* [Latin *colostrum* beastings]

colotomy /kə'lotəmi/ *noun* (*pl* **colotomies**) an incision into the colon.

colour¹ (*NAmer* **color**) /'kulə/ *noun* **1a** a visual sensation, e.g. of redness, blueness, etc, caused by the wavelength of perceived light. **b** the property of objects and light sources that enables them to be described as green, yellow, brown, etc. **2a** a hue, e.g. red or blue, or such hues in general, *esp* as opposed to black, white, and grey. **b** a substance, or a pigment used in painting, that gives colour when applied to an object. **3** the use or combination of colours, e.g. by painters. **4a** the skin pigmentation characteristic of a particular race. **b** skin pigmentation other than white. **5** the tint characteristic of good health. **6** (*usu in pl*). **a** an identifying badge or flag, e.g. of a ship or regiment. **b** coloured clothing distinguishing somebody as a member of a usu specified group, e.g. a sports team, or as a representative of a usu specified person or thing. **7** any of the five principal heraldic tinctures, i.e. azure, vert, sable, gules, and purpure. **8** vitality or interest: *The play had a good deal of colour to it.* **9** tonal quality in music. **10** an outward often deceptive show; an appearance, e.g. of authenticity: *His wounds gave colour to his story.* **11** *Brit* (*usu in pl*) the award made to a regular member of a team: *I got my cricket colours.* **12** in physics, each of three properties of quarks (hypothetical particles; see QUARK¹) called blue, green, and red. ✳ **nail one's colours to the mast** to make one's beliefs or intentions completely plain, *esp* in a defiant manner [from the idea of a commander nailing up his colours so that they could not be lowered in surrender]. **sail under false colours** to assume a false identity or character in order to deceive. **show** (**oneself in**) **one's true colours** to reveal one's true nature or character. **with flying colours** see FLYING¹. [Middle English *colour* via Old French from Latin *color*]

colour² (*NAmer* **color**) *verb trans* **1a** to give colour to (something). **b** to change the colour of (something). **2a** to misrepresent or distort (something). **b** to influence or affect (something): *He didn't let it colour his judgment.* ➤ *verb intrans* to take on or impart colour; *specif* to blush. ➤➤ **colourant** *noun.*

colourable (*NAmer* **colorable**) *adj* **1** seemingly valid or genuine; plausible. **2** able to be coloured. ➤➤ **colourably** *adv.*

colouration /kulə'raysh(ə)n/ *noun Brit* see COLORATION.

colour bar *noun* a social or legal barrier that prevents non-white people from participating with white people in various activities or restricts their opportunities.

colour-blind *adj* unable or partially unable to distinguish one or more colours. ➤➤ **colour blindness** *noun.*

colour code *noun* a system of colours, used as a way of identifying something, e.g. wires or papers.

colour-code *verb trans* to mark or colour (something) according to a colour code.

coloured¹ (*NAmer* **colored**) *adj* **1** having colour. **2** marked by exaggeration or bias. **3** *offensive.* **a** of a race other than white; *esp* BLACK¹ (2). **b** (*often* **Coloured**) said *esp* of S Africans: of mixed race.

coloured² (*NAmer* **colored**) *noun* (*often* **Coloured**) *offensive* a person of mixed descent.

Usage note
Negro, black, *and* coloured. See note at BLACK².

colourfast *adj* having colour that will not fade or run. ➤➤ **colourfastness** *noun.*

colour filter *noun* = FILTER¹ (3B).

colourful (*NAmer* **colorful**) /'kuləf(ə)l/ *adj* **1** having striking colours. **2** full of variety or interest. **3** said of language: coarse or vulgar. ➤➤ **colourfully** *adv,* **colourfulness** *noun.*

colouring (*NAmer* **coloring**) *noun* **1a** the application or combination of colours. **b** the effect produced by combining or applying colours. **2** something that produces colour. **3** the natural colour of somebody's hair, skin, and eyes, *esp* their complexion: *her dark colouring.* **4** an influence or bias. **5** a timbre or quality.

colourist (*NAmer* **colorist**) *noun* somebody, *esp* a painter, who colours or deals with colour.

colouristic (*NAmer* **coloristic**) *adj* **1** involving or relating to the use of colour or special colour effects. **2** in music, relating to or involving the use of tone colour for expressive purposes.

colourless (*NAmer* **colorless**) *adj* **1** lacking colour. **2** dull or uninteresting. ➤➤ **colourlessly** *adv,* **colourlessness** *noun.*

colour scheme *noun* a systematic combination of colours: *the colour scheme of a room.*

colour sergeant *noun* **1** the senior sergeant in a British infantry company. **2** a non-commissioned officer of the highest rank in the Royal Marines. [because the sergeant is responsible for the regimental colours on ceremonial occasions]

colour supplement *noun Brit* an illustrated colour magazine published as a supplement to a newspaper.

colourwash *noun* a coloured distemper.

colourway *noun* = COLOUR SCHEME.

colporteur /'kolpawtə/ *noun* a seller of religious books. [French *colporteur*, alteration of early French *comporteur*, from *comporter* to bear, peddle, from Latin *comportare*, from COM- + *portare* to carry]

colposcope /'kolpəskohp/ *noun* an instrument for examining the cervix and vagina. >> **colposcopy** /kol'poskəpi/ *noun*. [Greek *kolpos* womb + -SCOPE]

colt /kohlt/ *noun* **1** a young male horse that is sexually immature or that has not attained a particular age. **2** a novice; *esp* a player in a junior team. [Old English; related to Old English *cild* CHILD]

colter /'kohltə/ *noun* NAmer see COULTER.

coltish *adj* **1** frisky or playful. **2** of or resembling a colt. >> **coltishly** *adv*, **coltishness** *noun*.

coltsfoot *noun* (*pl* **coltsfoots**) a composite plant with yellow flower heads that appear early in spring before the leaves: *Tussilago farfara*. [from the shape of the leaves]

colubrid /kə'loohbrid, -'lyoohbrid/ *noun* any of a large family of nonvenomous snakes found in many parts of the world, including the grass snake and the whip snake: family Colubridae. >> **colubrid** *adj*. [from Latin *coluber, colubra* snake + -ID¹]

colubrine /'koləbrin, -brien/ *adj* relating to or resembling a snake. [Latin *colubrinus* from *coluber, colubra* snake]

columbarium /koləm'beəri·əm/ *noun* (*pl* **columbaria** /-ri·ə/) a structure, e.g. in a crematorium, lined with recesses for urns containing ashes of those who have been cremated. [Latin *columbarium* dovecote, from *columba* dove]

columbine /'koləmbien/ *noun* any of several species of plants of the buttercup family with showy spurred flowers: genus *Aquilegia*. Also called AQUILEGIA. [Middle English via medieval Latin *columbina herba* dovelike plant, from Latin *columba* dove; because the flower is supposed to resemble a group of doves]

columella /kolyoo'melə/ *noun* (*pl* **columellae** /-li/) **1a** the bony or partly cartilaginous rod connecting the eardrum with the inner ear in birds and in many reptiles and amphibians. **b** the bony central axis of the COCHLEA (spirally coiled hearing organ) of the ear. **2** the central column or axis of a spiral shell (e.g. of a snail). **3** the axis of the spore-bearing capsule in mosses and some liverworts. >> **columellar** *adj*, **columellate** *adj*. [scientific Latin *columella*, from Latin, dimin of *columna* column]

column /'koləm/ *noun* **1** a pillar that usu consists of a round shaft, a capital, and a base. **2a** something resembling a column in form, position, or function: *a column of water*. **b** a rod or shaft used to control the operations of a machine or vehicle: *the steering column*. **3** a long narrow formation of soldiers, vehicles, etc in rows. **4a** a vertical arrangement of items or a vertical section of printing on a page: *a column of figures*. **b** a special and usu regular feature in a newspaper or periodical. >> **columned** *adj*. [Middle English *columne* via French from Latin *columna*, from *columen* top]

columnar /kə'ləmnə, kə'lumnə/ *adj* **1** relating to or characterized by columns. **2** denoting, relating to, or composed of tall narrow cylindrical epithelial cells.

column inch *noun* a unit of measure for printed matter one column wide and one inch deep.

columnist /'koləmnist/ *noun* somebody who writes a newspaper or magazine column.

colure /kə'lyooə, 'kohlyooə/ *noun* the great circle on the celestial sphere passing through the poles and either the equinoxes or solstices. [via late Latin from Greek *kolouroi*, pl of *kolouros* stumptailed, from *kolos* docked + *oura* tail; from the lower part being cut off from sight by the horizon]

colza /'kolzə/ *noun* **1** rape or another COLE (plant of the cabbage family) whose seed is used as a source of oil. **2** = RAPESEED. [French *colza* from Dutch *koolzaad*, from early Dutch *coolsaet*, from *coole* cabbage + *saet* seed]

COM *abbr* computer output on microfilm.

com- *or* **col-** *or* **con-** *or* **cor-** *prefix* forming words, with the meaning: with, together or jointly: *commingle; collinear; concentrate; correlation*. [Middle English via Old French from Latin, with, together, thoroughly: see CO-]

coma¹ /'kohmə/ *noun* (*pl* **comas**) a state of deep unconsciousness caused by disease, injury, etc. [scientific Latin from Greek *kōma* deep sleep]

coma² *noun* (*pl* **comae** /'kohmee/) **1** the head of a comet, usu containing a nucleus. **2** an optical aberration in which the image of a point source becomes a comet-shaped blur. **3** a tuft of hairs

attached to a seed. >> **comatic** /koh'matik/ *adj*. [via Latin from Greek *komē* hair]

Comanche /kə'manchi/ *noun* (*pl* **Comanches** *or collectively* **Comanche**) **1** a member of a Native American people who live over an area ranging from Wyoming and Nebraska into New Mexico and NW Texas. **2** the language of this people. [Spanish *Comanche* from Ute, a Native American language of Utah and New Mexico)]

comatose /'kohmətohs, -tohz/ *adj* **1** in a state of coma. **2** characterized by lethargy and sluggishness; torpid: *a comatose economy*. [French *comateux*, from Greek *kōmat-, kōma* deep sleep]

comb¹ /kohm/ *noun* **1a** a toothed instrument used *esp* for arranging, untangling, or holding the hair. **b** a structure resembling a comb, *esp* any of several toothed devices used in separating or ordering textile fibres. **2** = CURRYCOMB. **3** a fleshy crest on the head of a domestic fowl or a related bird. **4** a honeycomb. >> **combed** *adj*. [Old English *camb*]

comb² *verb trans* **1** to draw a comb through (the hair) for the purpose of arranging or untangling it. **2** to prepare (e.g. wool or cotton) for use in manufacturing by cleaning and arranging its fibres with a comb. **3** to search or examine (something) systematically. >> *verb intrans* said of a wave: to roll over or break into foam.

combat¹ /'kombat/ *noun* **1** a fight or contest between individuals or groups. **2a** active fighting in a war: *He died in combat*. **b** (*used before a noun*) of or for combat: *combat troops*. [early French *combattre*, ultimately from COM- + Latin *battuere* to beat, of Celtic origin]

combat² /'kombat, kəm'bat/ *verb* (**combated** *or* **combatted**, **combating** *or* **combatting**) >> *verb intrans* to engage in combat; to fight. >> *verb trans* **1** to struggle against (something); *esp* to strive to reduce or eliminate (something): *strategies to combat inflation*. **2** to fight with (an individual or group); to battle.

combatant¹ /'kombətənt/ *noun* a person, nation, etc that is engaged in or prepared for combat.

combatant² *adj* actively participating in combat.

combat fatigue *noun* = SHELL SHOCK.

combative /'kombətiv/ *adj* marked by eagerness to fight or contend. >> **combatively** *adv*, **combativeness** *noun*.

combat trousers *pl noun* loose-fitting trousers, usu made of strong cotton, with patch pockets on the back and on the legs.

combe /koohm/ *noun* Brit see COOMB.

comber /'kohmə/ *noun* **1** a long heavy wave; a roller. **2** somebody or something that combs.

combination /kombi'naysh(ə)n/ *noun* **1** an act or the process of combining. **2a** a result or product of combining. **b** a group of people working as a team. **3** in mathematics, any of the different sets of a specified number of individuals that can be chosen from a group and are considered without regard to order within the set: compare PERMUTATION. **4** the sequence of letters or numbers that will open a combination lock. **5** (*in pl*) a one-piece undergarment for the upper and lower parts of the body and legs. >> **combinational** *adj*.

combination lock *noun* a lock with a mechanism operated by the selection of a specific combination of letters or numbers.

combinative /'kombinətiv, -naytiv/ *adj* **1** tending or able to combine. **2** resulting from combination.

combinatorial /,kombinə'tawri·əl/ *adj* of or relating to the ordering and arrangement of discrete mathematical elements within finite sets: *combinatorial mathematics*.

combine¹ /kəm'bien/ *verb trans* **1a** to bring (people or things) together; to unite, mix, or merge. **b** to cause (substances) to unite into a chemical compound. **2** to possess (certain qualities) in combination. >> *verb intrans* **1** to act together. **2a** to become one by joining or merging. **b** said of substances: to unite to form a chemical compound. >> **combinable** *adj*. [Middle English *combinen* via French *combiner* from late Latin *combinare*, from COM- + Latin *bini* two by two]

combine² /'kombien/ *noun* **1** a combination of people or organizations, *esp* in industry or commerce, to further their interests. **2** = COMBINE HARVESTER.

combine harvester *noun* a harvesting machine that cuts, threshes, and cleans grain while moving over a field.

combing wool /'kohming/ *noun* wool with long fibres suitable for combing, used *esp* in the manufacture of worsteds.

combining form *noun* in grammar, a linguistic form, e.g. *Franco-*, that cannot stand alone but forms compounds with other forms.

comb jelly *noun* = CTENOPHORE.

combo /'komboh/ *noun* (*pl* **combos**) *informal* **1** a small jazz or dance band. **2** *chiefly NAmer* any combination. [COMBINATION + -O¹]

combust /kəm'bust/ *verb trans and intrans* to burn (something) or be burned. [Latin *combustus*, past part. of *comburere* to burn up, from COM- + *urere* to burn]

combustible¹ /kəm'bustəbl/ *adj* **1** capable of being set on fire. **2** easily excited. ➤➤ **combustibility** /-'biliti/ *noun*.

combustible² *noun* a substance that is capable of being set on fire.

combustion /kəm'buschən/ *noun* **1** an act of burning. **2** a chemical reaction, *esp* an oxidation, in which light and heat are produced; the process of burning: *The cook hung over her crucibles in a frame of body and mind threatening spontaneous combustion —* Charlotte Brontë. ➤➤ **combustive** /-tiv/ *adj*.

combustion chamber *noun* a chamber, e.g. in a boiler furnace or an internal-combustion engine, in which combustion occurs.

Comdr *abbr* Commander.

Comdt *abbr* Commandant.

come¹ /kum/ *verb* (*past tense* **came** /kaym/, *past part.* **come**) ➤ *verb intrans* **1a** to move towards somebody or something nearer, *esp* towards the speaker; to approach. **b** to accompany somebody in an activity: *Can we come sailing?* **2a** to reach a specified position in a progression: *Now we come to the section on health.* **b** to arrive, appear, or occur: *The time has come.* **c** used in the subjunctive mood before an expression of future time: *a year ago come March.* **3a** (*often + to*) to approach or fulfil a specified condition: *You'll come to no harm; He came to his senses.* **b** to happen to or affect somebody or something: *No harm will come to you.* **4a** used to express arrival at a specified condition: *I came to regard him as a friend.* **b** used to express a chance occurrence: *How did you come to be invited?* **5a** to extend or reach: *Her dress came to her ankles.* **b** to amount: *That comes to £20 exactly.* **6a** to fall within the specified limits, scope, or jurisdiction: *This comes within the terms of the treaty.* **b** (+ from) to issue or originate: *A sob came from her throat; Comedy comes from conflict, from hatred —* Warren Mitchell. **7a** to be available or turn out, usu as specified: *This model comes in several sizes; The holiday didn't come cheap.* **b** to occur or belong in a specified place or relation: *The address comes above the date; Monday comes after Sunday.* **8a** to reach a specified state: *The string came loose; It all came right in the end.* **b** to take form: *The story won't come.* **9** *informal* to have a sexual orgasm. ➤ *verb trans* **1** to move nearer by traversing (a specified distance): *He has come several miles.* **2** *informal* to take on the aspect of (somebody); to play the role of: *Don't come the old soldier with me.* ✳ **as it comes** without stipulated additions: *I'll take my whisky as it comes.* **come across** to meet with or find (somebody or something) by chance. **come again?** *informal* used as a request for a remark to be repeated. **come by** to get possession of (something); to acquire: *Good jobs are hard to come by.* **come clean** *informal* to tell the whole story; to confess. **come into** to acquire (something) as a possession or inheritance: *He came into a fortune.* **come it** *chiefly Brit, informal* to act with bold disrespect: *Don't come it with me.* **come of 1** to be descended from (e.g. a family or line). **2** to result from (something). **come off it** *informal* an expression of disbelief at what somebody has said. **come over** to affect (somebody) suddenly and strangely: *What's come over you?* **come somebody's way** to fall to somebody's lot. **come through** to survive an illness, etc. **come to 1** to recover consciousness. **2** to be a question of (something): *I'm hopeless when it comes to arithmetic.* **3** to total (an amount): *The bill came to over £50.* **come to oneself** to recover consciousness or self-control. **come to pass** *formal or literary* to happen. **come upon** to meet with or find (somebody or something) by chance. **have it coming to one** *informal* to deserve what one is going to get. **not know whether one is coming or going** to be in a state of frantic disorder and bewilderment. **to come** in the future; coming: *in years to come.* [Old English *cuman*]

come² *interj* used to express encouragement or to urge reconsideration: *Come, come, it's not as bad as that.*

come³ *noun informal* semen.

come about *verb intrans* **1** to occur; to take place. **2** said of a ship: to turn onto a new tack.

come across *verb intrans* **1** to produce a specified impression: *His ideas didn't come across very well.* **2** *informal* (+ with) to provide something demanded or expected, *esp* money or sexual favours.

come along *verb intrans* **1** to appear unexpectedly or by chance. **2** (*usu in imperative*) to hurry. **3** to progress or develop.

comeback *noun* **1** a return to a former state or condition. **2a** a means of redress. **b** a retrospective criticism of a decision. **3** *informal* a sharp or witty reply; a retort.

come back *verb intrans* **1** said of past events: to be gradually recalled. **2** to regain a former condition or position. **3** *NAmer* to reply or retort.

Comecon /'komikon/ *noun* an economic organization (1949–91) formed by the countries of the Soviet bloc to coordinate their economies and promote mutual aid. [acronym from *Council for Mutual Economic Assistance*]

comedian /kə'meedi-ən/ *noun* **1** a person, *esp* a professional entertainer, who aims to be amusing. **2** an actor who plays comic roles. [French *comédien* from Old French *comedie*: see COMEDY; *comedienne* from French *comédienne*, fem of *comédien*]

comedic /kə'meedik/ *adj* of comedy: *comedic talent*.

comedienne /kəmeedi'en/ *noun* **1** a woman, *esp* a professional entertainer, who aims to be amusing. **2** an actress who plays comic roles.

comedo /'komidoh/ *noun* (*pl* **comedones** /-'dohneez/) = BLACK-HEAD.

> **Word history**
> scientific Latin from Latin *comedo* glutton, from *comedere* to eat up, from COM- + *edere* to eat. The word was orig applied to a kind of parasitic worm; the current sense comes from the wormlike material that can be squeezed from a blackhead.

comedown *noun informal* **1** a striking descent in rank or dignity. **2** a disappointment.

come down *verb intrans* **1** said of prices, values, etc: to decrease. **2** said of e.g. an aircraft: to land or crash. **3** to formulate and express an opinion or decision one way or the other: *They came down in favour of the proposal.* **4** to be passed down from an earlier generation. **5** to return to normal after taking a narcotic drug. **6** *Brit* to return from a university. ✳ **come down to** to amount to or be reduced to (something). **come down on** to criticize or punish (somebody). **come down with** to become affected by (an ailment).

comedy /'komədi/ *noun* (*pl* **comedies**) **1a** a play, film, etc of light and amusing character, typically with a happy ending. **b** the genre of dramatic literature dealing with comic or serious subjects in a light or satirical manner, or a work in this genre: compare TRAGEDY. **c** entertainment intended to make people laugh. **2** a ludicrous or farcical event or series of events. **3** the comic aspect of something. [Middle English via Old French and Latin from Greek *kōmōidia*, from *kōmos* revel + *aeidein* to sing]

comedy of manners *noun* a comedy that portrays satirically the manners and fashions of a particular class or set of people.

come-hither *adj informal* sexually inviting: *that come-hither look in his eyes.*

come in *verb intrans* **1a** to be useful, or to function as specified: *This will come in handy.* **b** to assume a role or function: *That's where you come in.* **2a** said of news, etc: to be circulated or become known. **b** said of income: to be received. **c** said of a radio signal: to be received as specified: *He was coming in loud and clear.* **3** said of a competitor: to finish in a specified position: *His horse came in last.* ✳ **come in for** to become subject to (something unwelcome, e.g. criticism).

comely /'kumli/ *adj* (**comelier, comeliest**) of pleasing appearance; not plain. ➤➤ **comeliness** *noun*. [Middle English *comly*, alteration of Old English *cȳmlic* glorious, from *cȳme* lovely, fine]

come off *verb intrans* **1** *informal* said of a plan, etc: to succeed. **2** to finish or emerge from something in a specified condition: *You came off best.* **3** to become detached. **4** *Brit, informal* to have an orgasm.

come on *verb intrans* **1** to begin or become established: *as winter came on.* **2** used to express encouragement or conviction: *Come on, you can do it.* **3** (*usu in imperative*) to hurry. **4** to make an entrance, *esp* on a stage. ✳ **come on to** *informal* to make a sexual proposal to (somebody).

come-on *noun* **1** *informal* an instance of sexually provocative enticement. **2** an attraction or enticement, e.g. in sales promotion, to induce an action.

come out *verb intrans* **1** to be published or become known. **2a** (+ in favour of/against) to support or oppose (a person, proposal, etc) publicly. **b** to present oneself openly as homosexual. **3** to end up as specified: *It will all come out right.* **4** said of a photograph: to appear satisfactory or as specified. **5** *Brit* to go on strike. **6** *Brit, dated* to make one's first appearance in society as a debutante. **✳ come out in** said of skin: to show or be covered with (*esp* spots). **come out with** to utter or say (something), usu unexpectedly.

come over *verb intrans* **1** to make a casual visit. **2** to change from one side or opinion to an opposing one. **3** *Brit informal* to be affected by a feeling: *She came over all peculiar.* **4** to produce a specified impression.

comer /'kumə/ *noun* **1** (*used in combinations*) somebody who comes or arrives: *a newcomer to the town.* **2** *NAmer, informal* somebody making rapid progress or showing promise.

come round *verb intrans* **1** to recover consciousness. **2** to be persuaded to adopt a particular opinion or course of action. **3** said of a recurring date or time: to be approaching again.

comestible /kə'mestəbl/ *noun formal* (*usu in pl*) food. [early French *comestible* edible, via medieval Latin from Latin *comestus*, past part. of *comedere* to eat up, from COM- + *edere* to eat]

comet /'komit/ *noun* a celestial body that typically follows a highly elliptical orbit round the sun and consists of an icy nucleus surrounded by a cloud of gas and dust, some of which trails away from the sun to form long tails. ➤➤ **cometary** *adj.* [Old English *cometa* via Latin from Greek *kometes*, literally 'long-haired', from *kome* hair]

come through *verb intrans* **1** to survive danger or difficulty. **2** said of a radio signal, etc: to be received clearly. **3** said of a person: to fulfil hopes or expectations.

come up *verb intrans* **1** said of a circumstance, *esp* an unwelcome one: to arise or occur unexpectedly. **2** to rise in rank or status. **3** to be improved as specified, *esp* after cleaning: *The table came up like new.* **✳ come up against** to encounter (a difficulty). **come up roses** to happen in the most desirable or enjoyable way: *Everything's coming up roses* — Stephen Sondheim. **come up with** to produce (something needed), *esp* to resolve a lack or difficulty.

comeuppance /kum'up(ə)ns/ *noun informal* a deserved rebuke or punishment: *He'll get his comeuppance in the end.*

comfit /'kumfit/ *noun archaic* a sweet consisting of a nut, seed, piece of fruit, etc coated and preserved with sugar. [Middle English *confit* from early French *confit*, past part. of *confire* to prepare, from Latin *conficere*: see CONFECT]

comfort[1] /'kumfət/ *noun* **1** consolation or encouragement in time of trouble or worry, or somebody or something that provides this. **2** contented well-being; physical ease: *a life of comfort.* ➤➤ **comfortless** *adj.*

comfort[2] *verb trans* **1** to cheer (somebody) up. **2** to ease the grief, trouble, or anxiety of (somebody); to console or reassure (somebody). ➤➤ **comforting** *adj,* **comfortingly** *adv.* [Middle English *comforten* via Old French from late Latin *confortare* to strengthen greatly, from COM- + Latin *fortis* strong]

comfortable *adj* **1a** providing or enjoying physical comfort: *a comfortable armchair.* **b** providing or enjoying contentment and security: *a comfortable income.* **2a** causing no worry or doubt: *comfortable assumptions that require no thought.* **b** free from stress or tension: *a comfortable routine.* **3** easy: *a comfortable win.* ➤➤ **comfortably** *adv.*

comforter *noun* **1** somebody who gives consolation or reassurance. **2** *Brit* a baby's dummy. **3** *dated* a knitted scarf. **4** *NAmer* a quilt or eiderdown.

comfort station *noun NAmer, euphem* a public toilet.

comfrey /'kumfri/ *noun* (*pl* **comfreys**) any of several species of tall plants of the borage family, with coarse hairy leaves that are much used in herbal medicine: genus *Symphytum.* [Middle English *cumfirie* via Old French from Latin *conferva* a water plant, from *confervere* to boil together, heal, from CON- + *fervere* to boil]

comfy /'kumfi/ *adj* (**comfier, comfiest**) *informal* comfortable. [by shortening and alteration]

comic[1] /'komik/ *adj* **1** of or marked by comedy. **2** causing laughter or amusement; funny. [via Latin from Greek *komikos*, from *komos* revel]

comic[2] *noun* **1** a comedian. **2** a magazine consisting mainly of strip cartoon stories. **3** *NAmer* (*in pl*) comic strips.

comical *adj* causing laughter, *esp* because of a startlingly or unexpectedly humorous impact: *He thought her hat was comical.* ➤➤ **comically** *adv.*

comic opera *noun* opera with humorous episodes and usu some spoken dialogue and a sentimental plot.

comic strip *noun* a strip cartoon.

coming[1] /'kuming/ *noun* the act or an instance of arriving: *comings and goings.*

coming[2] *adj* **1** immediately due in sequence or development; next: *the coming year.* **2** gaining in importance; up-and-coming: *It's the coming thing.*

Comintern /'komintuhn/ *noun* an international Socialist organization operating from 1919 to 1943. [Russian *Komintern*, from *Kommunisticheskii Internatsional* Communist International]

comity /'komiti/ *noun* (*pl* **comities**) **1** a loose widespread community. **2** = COMITY OF NATIONS. **3** *formal* harmony or fellowship. [Latin *comitat-, comitas* courtesy, from *comis* courteous]

comity of nations *noun* the courtesy and friendship of nations, marked *esp* by recognition of each other's laws.

comma /'komə/ *noun* **1** a punctuation mark (,) used principally as a mark of separation within a sentence or list. **2** a butterfly with a silvery comma-shaped mark on the underside of the hind wing: *Polygonia c-album.* [late Latin *comma*, via Latin from Greek *komma* segment, clause, from *koptein* to cut]

command[1] /kə'mahnd/ *verb trans* **1** to direct (somebody) authoritatively; to order. **2a** to be able to ask for and receive (something): *He commands a high fee; She commands a great deal of respect.* **b** to overlook or dominate (something) from or as if from a strategic position. **c** to have military command of (troops) as senior officer. ➤ *verb intrans* to be commander; to be supreme. [Middle English *comanden* via Old French *comander* from Latin *commendare*: see COMMEND]

command[2] *noun* **1a** an authoritative order. **b** (*used before a noun*) done on command or request: *a command performance.* **2a** an electrical signal that actuates a device, e.g. a control mechanism in a spacecraft, or the activation of a device by means of such a signal. **b** a computer instruction that actuates the performance of a function. **3a** the ability or power to control; mastery. **b** the authority or right to command: *the officer in command.* **c** facility in use: *a good command of French.* **4** (*treated as sing. or pl*) the unit, personnel, etc under a commander.

commandant /komən'dant/ *noun* a commanding officer.

command economy *noun* see PLANNED ECONOMY.

commandeer /komən'diə/ *verb trans* **1** to seize (something) for military purposes. **2** to take arbitrary or forcible possession of (something). [Afrikaans *kommandeer* via French *commander* to command, from Latin *commendare*: see COMMEND]

commander *noun* **1** a commanding officer. **2** the presiding officer of a society or organization. **3** an officer in the Royal Navy or the US Navy ranking below a captain. ➤➤ **commandership** *noun.*

commander-in-chief *noun* (*pl* **commanders-in-chief**) an officer who is in supreme command of an armed force.

commanding *adj* **1** having command; being in charge: *a commanding officer.* **2** deserving or expecting respect and obedience: *a commanding voice.* **3** dominating or having priority: *a commanding view; a commanding lead.* ➤➤ **commandingly** *adv.*

command language *noun* in computing, a simplified language that enables the operator to enter sets of commands.

commandment *noun* something commanded; *specif* any of the biblical Ten Commandments.

command module *noun* a part of a spacecraft designed to carry the crew, the main communication equipment, and the equipment for re-entry.

commando /kə'mahndoh/ *noun* (*pl* **commandos**) **1** a soldier trained to carry out surprise raids. **2** a unit of such soldiers. [Afrikaans *kommando* via Dutch from Spanish *comando*, from *comandar* to command, from French *commander*: see COMMANDEER]

command paper *noun Brit* a government report laid before Parliament at the command of the Crown.

command performance *noun* a performance of a play, film, etc for a member of the royal family.

command post *noun* the headquarters of a military unit in the field.

commedia dell'arte /kə,maydi·ə del 'ahti/ *noun* Italian comedy of the 16th–18th cents, improvised from standardized situations and stock characters. [Italian *commedia dell'arte* comedy of art]

comme il faut /,kom eel 'foh/ *adj* conforming to accepted standards; proper: *Our house is very far from the center [of Venice] but the little canal is very comme il faut* — Henry James. [French *comme il faut* as it should be]

commemorate /kə'memərayt/ *verb trans* **1** to mark or formally remember (an event or a person) by some ceremony or observation. **2** said of a plaque, monument, etc: to serve as a memorial of (somebody or something). ➤ **commemoration** /-'raysh(ə)n/ *noun*, **commemorative** /-rətiv/ *adj*. [Latin *commemoratus*, past part. of *commemorare*, from COM- + *memorare* to remind of, from *memor* mindful]

commence /kə'mens/ *verb trans and intrans* to start or begin (something). [Middle English *comencen* from Old French, ultimately from COM- + Latin *initiare* to begin: see INITIATE[1]]

commencement /kə'mensmənt/ *noun* **1** a beginning. **2** *NAmer* a day on which degrees or diplomas are conferred by a school or college.

commend /kə'mend/ *verb trans* **1** to praise or express approval of (somebody or something): *She did commend my yellow stockings of late* — Shakespeare. **2** to recommend (something or somebody) as worthy of confidence or notice. **3** (+ to) to entrust (something) to somebody for care or preservation. **4** (+ to) to pass on the good wishes of (somebody): *Please commend me to your father.* ➤ **commendable** *adj*, **commendably** *adv*. [Middle English *commenden* from Latin *commendare*, from COM- + *mandare* to entrust]

commendation /koman'daysh(ə)n/ *noun* something, e.g. a formal citation, that commends somebody or something. ➤ **commendatory** /kə'mendət(ə)ri/ *adj*.

commensal[1] /kə'mens(ə)l/ *adj* living in a state of commensalism. [Middle English from medieval Latin *commensalis*, from Latin COM- + late Latin *mensalis* of the table, from Latin *mensa* table]

commensal[2] *noun* an organism living in a state of commensalism.

commensalism *noun* the association of two species whereby one species obtains benefits, e.g. food or protection, from the association without the other species being harmed.

commensurable /kə'mensh(ə)rəbl/ *adj* (*often* + with/to) having a common measure; *esp* divisible by a common unit an integral number of times. ➤ **commensurability** /-'biliti/ *noun*, **commensurably** *adv*.

commensurate /kə'menshərət/ *adj* **1** (*usu* + with) equal or approximately equal in measure or extent; coextensive. **2** (*often* + to/with) corresponding in size, extent, amount, or degree; proportionate: *He was given a job commensurate with his abilities.* ➤ **commensurately** *adv*, **commensuration** /-'raysh(ə)n/ *noun*. [late Latin *commensuratus*, from COM- + *mensuratus*, past part. of *mensurare* to measure, from Latin *mensura*: see MEASURE[1]]

comment[1] /'koment/ *noun* **1a** an observation or remark expressing an opinion or attitude. **b** a judgment expressed indirectly: *This film is a comment on current moral standards.* **2** a note explaining or criticizing the meaning of a piece of writing. **3** discussion, *esp* of a topical issue. [Middle English via late Latin from Latin *commentum* invention, neuter past part. of *comminisci* to invent, from COM- + -*minisci* (related to *ment*-, *mens* mind)]

comment[2] *verb intrans* **1** (*often* + on/upon) to make a comment. **2** (*often* + on/upon) to explain or interpret something by comment.

commentary /'komənt(ə)ri/ *noun* (*pl* **commentaries**) **1** a systematic series of explanations or interpretations, e.g. of a piece of writing. **2** a series of spoken remarks and comments used as a broadcast description of some event: *a running commentary on the match.*

commentate /'koməntayt/ *verb intrans* (*often* + on) to act as a commentator; *esp* to give a broadcast commentary. [back-formation from COMMENTATOR]

commentator *noun* a person who provides a commentary; *specif* somebody who reports and discusses news or sports events on radio or television.

commerce /'komuhs/ *noun* **1** the exchange or buying and selling of commodities, *esp* on a large scale. **2** *archaic* = SEXUAL INTERCOURSE. **3** *dated* the exchange of ideas, etc; social interaction. [early French *commerce* from Latin *commercium*, from COM- + *merc*-, *merx* merchandise]

commercial[1] /kə'muhsh(ə)l/ *adj* **1** of or characteristic of commerce. **2** engaged in work to be sold. **3a** having or being a good financial prospect: *They found oil in commercial quantities.* **b** said of a chemical: supplied in bulk and average or inferior in quality. **c** producing work to a standard determined only by market criteria. **4a** viewed with regard to profit: *a commercial success.* **b** designed for a large market. **5** supported by advertisers: *commercial TV.* ➤ **commercially** *adv*.

commercial[2] *noun* an advertisement broadcast on radio or television.

commercial art *noun* graphic art put to commercial use, *esp* in advertising. ➤ **commercial artist** *noun*.

commercial break *noun* a break in a television or radio programme, or between programmes, for advertisements.

commercialise *verb* see COMMERCIALIZE.

commercialism *noun* **1** commercial spirit, institutions, or methods. **2** excessive emphasis on profit.

commercialize *or* **commercialise** *verb trans* **1** to make (something) commercial. **2** to exploit (somebody or something) for profit. ➤ **commercialization** /-'zaysh(ə)n/ *noun*.

commercial paper *noun* short-term negotiable instruments, e.g. cheques and bills of exchange, usu sold by one company to another for immediate cash needs.

commercial traveller *noun Brit, dated* a travelling sales representative.

commercial vehicle *noun* a vehicle designed for carrying goods or fare-paying passengers.

commie /'komi/ *noun informal, derog* a communist. [by shortening and alteration]

commination /komi'naysh(ə)n/ *noun* a warning of vengeance; a denunciation. ➤ **comminatory** /'komtnət(ə)ri/ *adj*. [Middle English via French from Latin *commination*-, *comminatio*, from *comminari* to threaten severely, from COM- + *minari* to threaten]

commingle /ko'ming·gl/ *verb trans and intrans literary* to combine or mix (something).

comminute /'kominyooht/ *verb trans* to reduce (something) to minute particles; to pulverize. ➤ **comminution** /-'nyoohsh(ə)n/ *noun*. [Latin *comminutus*, past part. of *comminuere*, from COM- + *minuere* to lessen]

commis /'komi/ *noun* (*pl* **commis** /'komi/) (*used before a noun*) a junior or assistant in a hotel, catering establishment, etc: *a commis chef*. [French *commis*, past part. of *commettre* to commit, entrust, from Latin *committere*: see COMMIT]

commiserate /kə'mizərayt/ *verb intrans* (+ with) to feel or express sympathy; to condole: *I commiserated with them over their hard luck.* ➤ **commiseration** /-'raysh(ə)n/ *noun*, **commiserative** /-rətiv/ *adj*. [Latin *commiseratus*, past part. of *commiserari*, from COM- + *miserari* to pity, from *miser* wretched]

commissar /komi'sahr/ *noun* **1** a Communist party official assigned to a military unit to teach party principles and ideals. **2** the head of a government department in the Soviet Union until 1946. [Russian *komissar* from German *Kommissar*, from medieval Latin *commissarius*, from Latin *committere*: see COMMIT]

commissariat /komi'seəri·ət, -at/ *noun* **1** the department of an army that organizes food supplies. **2** a government department in the Soviet Union until 1946. [modern Latin *commissariatus*, from medieval Latin *commissarius* person in charge, from Latin *committere*: see COMMIT; (sense 2) Russian *komissariat* via German *Kommissariat*, from modern Latin *commissariatus*]

commissary /'komis(ə)ri/ *noun* (*pl* **commissaries**) **1** an officer in charge of military supplies. **2** a bishop's deputy. **3** *NAmer* a restaurant, *esp* on a military base or in a film studio. **4** *NAmer* a store selling equipment and food supplies. [Middle English *commissarie* from medieval Latin *commissarius*, from Latin *committere*: see COMMIT]

commission[1] /kəˈmish(ə)n/ *noun* **1** an authorization or command to perform a prescribed act or task, e.g. to produce a work of art. **2a** (*treated as sing. or pl*) a group of people directed to perform some duty. **b** (*often* **Commission**) (*treated as sing. or pl*) a government agency: *the Commission for Racial Equality*. **3** a fee, *esp* a percentage, paid to an agent or employee for transacting a piece of business or performing a service. **4a** a formal warrant granting various powers. **b** military rank above a certain level, or a certificate conferring such rank. **5** an act of committing something: *the commission of a crime*. **6** authority to act as agent for another, or something to be done by an agent. **✳ in commission** said of a ship, machine, etc: in use or ready for use. **on commission** with commission serving as partial or full pay for work done. **out of commission** said of a ship, machine, etc: out of use or working order. [Middle English via French from Latin *commission-*, *commissio* act of bringing together, from *committere*: see COMMIT]

commission[2] *verb trans* **1a** to order, appoint, or assign (somebody) to perform a task or function: *His grandson was commissioned to write his biography*. **b** to order (a task) to be done: *She has commissioned a portrait*. **2** to confer a formal commission on (a member of the armed forces). **3** to make (a ship) ready for active service. **4** to put (equipment or machinery) into working order.

commissionaire /kə,mishəˈneə/ *noun chiefly Brit* a uniformed attendant at a cinema, theatre, office, etc. [French *commissionnaire*, from *commission*: see COMMISSION[1]]

commissioner /kəˈmish(ə)nə/ *noun* **1** a member or the head of a commission. **2** the government representative in a district, province, etc.

commissioner for oaths *noun Brit* a solicitor authorized to administer oaths or affirmations or to take affidavits.

commissure /ˈkomisyooə/ *noun* **1** the place where two parts are joined. **2** a connecting band of nerve tissue in the brain or spinal cord. ➤➤ **commissural** /-ˈsyooərəl/ *adj*. [Middle English via French from Latin *commissura* a joining, from *committere*: see COMMIT]

commit /kəˈmit/ *verb trans* (**committed, committing**) **1** to carry out (a crime, sin, etc). **2a** to obligate or bind (oneself or somebody else) to a course of action or a set of beliefs: *a committed Christian*. **b** to assign (somebody or something) to some particular course or use: *All available troops were committed to the attack*. **3a** (*usu +* to) to entrust (something or somebody) to somebody's care. **b** to place (somebody) in a prison or psychiatric hospital. **c** to transfer or consign (something) to a place or a process: *He refused to commit anything to paper*. **d** to refer (e.g. a legislative bill) to a committee. ➤➤ **committable** *adj*, **committer** *noun*. [Middle English *committen* from Latin *committere* to connect, entrust, from COM- + *mittere* to send]

commitment *noun* **1a** an agreement or pledge to do something in the future. **b** something pledged; an engagement or obligation. **c** loyalty to a system of thought or action. **2** an act of committing to a charge or trust.

committal /kəˈmitl/ *noun* **1** the sending of somebody to prison or a psychiatric hospital, or for trial. **2** the burial of a body.

committee /kəˈmiti/ *noun* **1** (*treated as sing. or pl*) a body of people delegated to organize or administrate a society, event, etc. **2** (*treated as sing. or pl*) a body of people delegated to report on or investigate some matter. **3** formerly, somebody entrusted with the charge of a mentally ill or mentally handicapped person. [Middle English in the sense 'a person to whom a charge is committed', from *committen*: see COMMIT]

Committee of the Whole House *noun* in Britain, the whole membership of the House of Commons operating as a committee under informal rules.

committee stage *noun* the stage in British parliamentary procedure between the second reading and the third reading, when a bill is discussed in detail in committee.

commode /kəˈmohd/ *noun* **1** a boxlike structure or chair with a removable seat covering a chamber pot. **2** a low chest of drawers. **3** a washstand. [French *commode* suitable, convenient, from Latin *commodus*, from COM- + *modus* measure]

commodious /kəˈmohdi-əs/ *adj formal* comfortably or conveniently spacious; roomy: *The two gentlemen ... sent for a hackney coach, and in this commodious vehicle they rolled comfortably downtown* — Henry James. ➤➤ **commodiously** *adv*, **commodiousness** *noun*. [Middle English, in the sense 'useful', via French from medieval Latin *commodiosus*, from Latin *commodum* convenience, neuter of *commodus*: see COMMODE]

commodity /kəˈmoditi/ *noun* (*pl* **commodities**) **1a** something that can be bought and sold. **b** an article of trade or commerce, *esp* when delivered for shipment. **2** something useful or valuable. [Middle English *commoditee* via French from Latin *commoditat-*, *commoditas*, from *commodus*: see COMMODE]

commodore /ˈkomədaw/ *noun* **1** the senior captain of a merchant shipping line. **2** the chief officer of a yacht club. [prob modification of Dutch *komandeur* commander, from French *commandeur*, ultimately from Latin *commendere*: see COMMEND]

common[1] /ˈkomən/ *adj* **1a** occurring or appearing frequently; familiar: *a common sight*. **b** of the familiar kind: *common salt*. **2a** widespread or general: *common knowledge*. **b** characterized by a lack of privilege or special status: *the common people*. **c** simply satisfying accustomed criteria and no more; elementary: *common decency*. **3** lacking refinement. **4** belonging to or shared by two or more individuals or by all members of a group: *a common acquaintance*. **5** of the community at large; public: *for the common good*. **6** in grammar, belonging to a gender that includes masculine and feminine. **7** in mathematics, belonging to more than one quantity: *a common multiple*. **8** said of a syllable: able to be short or long. **✳ common or garden** ordinary or everyday. **make common cause with** to unite with (somebody) in a shared objective. ➤➤ **commonly** *adv*, **commonness** *noun*. [Middle English *commun* via Old French from Latin *communis*]

Usage note

common, mutual, *or* **reciprocal?** See note at MUTUAL.

common[2] *noun* **1a** a more or less treeless expanse of undeveloped land available to all for recreation. **b** undivided land used *esp* for pasture. **2** *Brit, informal* common sense. **3** a religious service suitable for any of various festivals. **4** (*also* **right of common**) in law, a right which somebody has on another person's land. **5✳ in common 1** said of interests, attitudes, or experience: shared together: *We had a lot in common*. **2** used jointly. **in common with** like: *In common with many other women of her generation, she didn't go out to work*.

commonable /ˈkomənəbl/ *adj Brit* **1** said of land, *esp* formerly: jointly owned and used. **2** said of an animal, *esp* formerly: allowed to be put on a common.

commonage /ˈkomənij/ *noun* **1** community land. **2** the right to use such land, e.g. to pasture animals. **3** the common people.

commonality /koməˈnaliti/ *noun* (*pl* **commonalities**) **1** possession of common features or attributes or of some degree of standardization; commonness. **2** a common feature or attribute. **3** (**the commonality**) = COMMONALTY. [Middle English *communalitie*, alteration of *communalte*: see COMMONALTY]

commonalty /ˈkomənəlti/ *noun* (**the commonalty**) the common people, or the political estate formed by them. [Middle English *communalte* from Old French *comunalté*, from *comunal*: see COMMUNAL]

common carrier *noun* an individual or company undertaking to transport people or goods for payment.

common chord *noun* = TRIAD (1B).

common cold *noun* inflammation of the mucous membranes of the nose, throat, mouth, etc caused by a virus and lasting for a short time.

common denominator *noun* **1** in mathematics, a number into which the denominators of several fractions can be divided with no remainder. **2** a common trait or theme.

Common Entrance *noun Brit* an examination taken by children, usu at the age of 13, for admission to a public school.

commoner *noun* **1** a member of the common people; somebody not of noble rank. **2** *Brit* a student, e.g. at Oxford, who is not supported by the college endowments. **3** somebody who has a right on another person's land.

Common Era *noun* the Christian era.

common fraction *noun* a fraction in which both the numerator and denominator are expressed as numbers and are separated by a horizontal or slanted line: compare DECIMAL[2]. Also called SIMPLE FRACTION.

common ground *noun* an area of agreement, *esp* between people with different opinions, attitudes, beliefs, etc.

common law *noun* **1** the body of uncodified English law that forms the basis of the English legal system: compare EQUITY (2),

STATUTE LAW. **2** (*used before a noun*) recognized in law without solemnization of marriage: *his common law wife*.

common logarithm *noun* a logarithm whose base is ten.

common market *noun* **1** an economic unit formed to remove trade barriers among its members. **2** (**the Common Market**) an informal name for the European Economic Community (now the European Union).

common noun *noun* a noun that designates any one of a class of beings or things, e.g. *teacher, city*: compare PROPER NOUN.

commonplace[1] *adj* routinely found; ordinary or unremarkable: *Depend upon it, there is nothing so unnatural as the commonplace —* Conan Doyle. ⪢ **commonplaceness** *noun*. [translation of Latin *locus communis* widely applicable argument, translation of Greek *koinos topos*]

commonplace[2] *noun* **1** an obvious or trite observation. **2** something taken for granted. **3** an item in a commonplace book.

commonplace book *noun* a notebook into which somebody copies memorable writings or sayings.

common room *noun chiefly Brit* a room or set of rooms in a school or college for the recreational use of the staff or students.

commons /'komənz/ *pl noun* **1** (**the Commons**) the House of Commons. **2** the common people, *esp* thought of as a political group. **3** *archaic* food or provisions shared jointly by all members of an institution; rations: *short commons*.

common salt *noun* salt; sodium chloride.

commonsense *adj* showing sound and prudent judgment.

common sense *noun* sound and prudent judgment. ⪢ **commonsensical** *adj*.

common time *noun* the musical metre marked by four crotchets per bar.

commonweal /'komənweel/ *noun archaic* **1** the general welfare. **2** a commonwealth.

commonwealth *noun* **1** an independent state; a republic. **2** (**the Commonwealth**) a loose association of autonomous states under a common allegiance; *specif* an association consisting of Britain and states that were formerly British colonies. **3** (**the Commonwealth**) the British state from 1649 to 1660. **4** a formal title of certain states of the USA. **5** the federal union of Australian states. **6** (**the commonwealth**) *archaic* a political unit founded on law and united by agreement of the people for the common good.

Editorial note ───────
A commonwealth is defined by Locke (1632–1704) in his second treatise, On Government, as 'an independent Community'. Today, however, the term means a collection of communities, or rather a community of free and independent states, as opposed to an empire, a form of government in which dependent peoples are ruled by a superior — Professor Vernon Bogdanor.

[Middle English *commen wealthe*, from *commen, commun* (see COMMON[1]) + *wealthe, welthe* welfare: see WEALTH]

Commonwealth of Nations *noun* = COMMONWEALTH (2).

commotion /kə'mohsh(ə)n/ *noun* **1** a disturbance or tumult. **2** noisy confusion and bustle. **3** a state of civil unrest or insurrection. [Middle English via French from Latin *commotion-, commotio*, from *commovēre* to agitate, from COM- + *movēre* to MOVE[1]]

communal /'komyoonl/ *adj* **1** shared or used in common by members of a group or community: *communal changing rooms*. **2** of a community: *communal riots*. **3** of a commune or communes. ⪢ **communality** /-'naliti/ *noun*, **communally** *adv*. [French *communal* from late Latin *communalis*, from Latin *communis* COMMON[1]]

communalise /'komyoonəliez/ *verb* see COMMUNALIZE.

communalism *noun* social organization on a communal basis. ⪢ **communalist** *noun*, **communalistic** *adj*.

communalize *or* **communalise** /'komyoonəliez/ *verb trans* to make (something) the property of a community. ⪢ **communalization** /-lie'zaysh(ə)n/ *noun*.

communard /'komyoonahd/ *noun* **1** (**Communard**) a person who participated in the Commune of Paris in 1871. **2** a person who lives in a commune. [French *communard*, from *commune*: see COMMUNE[1]]

commune[1] /'komyoohn/ *noun* **1** an often rural community of unrelated individuals or families organized on a communal basis. **2** the smallest administrative district of a number of European

countries. [French *commune*, ultimately from Latin *communis* COMMON[1]]

commune[2] /kə'myoohn/ *verb intrans* **1** (*usu* + with) to communicate intimately: *communing with nature*. **2** *NAmer* to receive Communion. [Middle English *communen* to converse, administer Communion, via French and late Latin from Latin *communicare*: see COMMUNICATE]

communicable /kə'myoohnikəbl/ *adj* said *esp* of a disease: able to be communicated or transmitted to others. ⪢ **communicability** /-'biliti/ *noun*, **communicably** *adv*.

communicant /kə'myoohnikənt/ *noun* **1** a church member who receives or is entitled to receive Communion. **2** *archaic* an informant.

communicate /kə'myoohnikayt/ *verb trans* **1** to convey knowledge of or information about (something); to make known. **2** to cause (something) to pass from one person to another. ⪢ *verb intrans* **1** to transmit information, thought, or feeling so that it is satisfactorily received or understood. **2** said of rooms: to give access to each other; to connect. **3** to receive Communion. ⪢ **communicator** *noun*, **communicatory** /-kat(ə)ri/ *adj*. [Latin *communicatus*, past part. of *communicare* to impart, participate, from *communis* COMMON[1]]

communication /kə,myoohni'kaysh(ə)n/ *noun* **1** the exchange of information, or the use of a common system of symbols, signs, behaviour, etc for this. **2** a verbal or written message. **3** (*in pl*). **a** a system, e.g. of telephones, for communicating. **b** a system of routes for moving troops, supplies, etc. **4** (*in pl, but treated as sing. or pl*) techniques for the effective transmission of information, ideas, etc. ⪢ **communicational** *adj*.

communication cord *noun Brit* a device, e.g. a chain or handle, in a railway carriage that may be pulled in an emergency to sound an alarm.

communication satellite *or* **communications satellite** *noun* an artificial satellite used to relay telephone, radio, and television signals.

communicative /kə'myoohnikətiv/ *adj* **1** tending to communicate; talkative. **2** of communication. ⪢ **communicatively** *adv*.

communion /kə'myoohnyən/ *noun* **1** (*often* **Communion**) the religious service celebrating the Eucharist in Protestant churches, the act of receiving the Eucharist, or the consecrated elements of the Eucharist. **2** intimate fellowship or rapport: *communion with nature*. **3** a body of Christians having a common faith and discipline. [Middle English from Latin *communion-, communio* mutual participation, from *communis* COMMON[1]]

communiqué /kə'myoohnikay/ *noun* an official announcement; a bulletin. [French *communiqué*, from past part. of *communiquer* to communicate, from Latin *communicare* to impart, participate]

communise /'komyooniez/ *verb* see COMMUNIZE.

communism /'komyooniz(ə)m/ *noun* **1a** a theory advocating elimination of private property. **b** a system in which goods are held in common and are available to all as needed. **2** (**Communism**). **a** a doctrine based on revolutionary Marxian socialism and Marxism-Leninism that was the official ideology of the former Soviet Union. **b** a totalitarian system of government in which a single party controls state-owned means of production. [French *communisme*, from *commun* common, from Latin *communus*]

communist /'komyoonist/ *noun* **1** (*often* **Communist**) an adherent or advocate of communism. **2** a left-wing revolutionary. ⪢ **communist** *adj*, **communistic** /-'nistik/ *adj*.

communitarian[1] /kə,myoohni'teəri-ən/ *adj* of or based on social organization in small communes.

communitarian[2] *noun* a supporter of social organization in small collectivist communities. ⪢ **communitarianism** *noun*.

community /kə'myoohniti/ *noun* (*pl* **communities**) **1** (*treated as sing. or pl*). **a** a group of people living in a particular area. **b** all the interacting populations of various living organisms in a particular area. **c** a group of individuals with some common characteristic, e.g. profession, religion, or status. **d** a body of people or nations having a common history or common interests: *the international community*. **2** society in general. **3a** joint ownership or participation. **b** common character; likeness: *They were bound by community of interests*. **c** social ties; fellowship. [Middle English *comunete* via French *comuneté*, from Latin *communitat-, communitas*, from *communis* COMMON[1]]

community care *noun* the provision of care, e.g. nursing, to enable people to stay in their own community rather than in a hospital or institution.

community centre *noun* a building or group of buildings for the educational and recreational activities of a community.

community charge *noun Brit* a tax formerly levied on individuals, in place of domestic rates, to pay for local government expenditure.

community chest *noun* a general fund accumulated from subscriptions to pay for social welfare requirements in a community.

community home *noun Brit* a centre for housing young offenders and other young people requiring similar care.

community policing *noun* policing by officers who are familiar with the community in which they serve. ➤➤ **community policeman** *noun*, **community policewoman** *noun*.

community service *noun* unpaid work undertaken for the benefit of the community, *esp* by a convicted person as an alternative to a prison term.

communize *or* **communise** /'komyooniez/ *verb trans* **1** to make (something) communal or public. **2** to make (a person or a country) communist. ➤➤ **communization** /-'zaysh(ə)n/ *noun*.

commutate /'komyootayt/ *verb trans* to reverse the direction of (an electric current); *esp* to convert (alternating current) to direct current. [back-formation from COMMUTATION]

commutation /komyoo'taysh(ə)n/ *noun* **1** an act or the process of commuting; *esp* the substitution by executive authority of a legal penalty less severe than that imposed judicially. **2** the process of converting an alternating current to a direct current. **3** a replacement; *specif* a substitution of one form of payment or charge for another. [Middle English via French from Latin *commutation-, commutatio*, from *commutare*: see COMMUTE]

commutative /kə'myoohtətiv/ *adj* **1** denoting the combination of elements in a mathematical operation that produces a result that is independent of the order in which the elements are taken: *Addition of the positive integers is commutative.* **2** of or showing commutation.

commutator /'komyootaytə/ *noun* a device for reversing the direction of an electric current; *esp* a device on a motor or generator that converts alternating current to direct current.

commute /kə'myooht/ *verb intrans* **1** to travel back and forth regularly, *esp* between home and work. **2** said of two mathematical operators: to give a commutative result. ➤ *verb trans* **1** (*usu* + to) to exchange (a penalty) for another less severe: *He had his death sentence commuted to life imprisonment.* **2** (*often* + into/for) to convert (e.g. a payment) into another form. ➤ **commutable** *adj*, **commuter** *noun*. [Latin *commutare* to change, exchange, from COM- + *mutare* to change]

comp[1] /komp/ *noun informal* **1** *Brit* a competition. **2** *Brit* a comprehensive school. **3** a compositor. **4** *NAmer* a complimentary ticket. **5** compensation. **6** a musical accompaniment.

comp[2] *verb trans* to play (music) as an accompaniment.

comp. *abbr* **1** comparative. **2** compare. **3** compiled. **4** composer. **5** composition. **6** comprehensive.

compact[1] /kəm'pakt/ *adj* **1** having parts or units closely packed or joined. **2** succinct or terse: *a compact statement.* **3** occupying a small volume because of efficient use of space: *a compact camera.* **4** *archaic* (+ of) composed. ➤➤ **compactly** *adv*, **compactness** *noun*. [Middle English, in the sense 'firmly put together', from Latin *compactus*, past part. of *compingere* to put together, from COM- + *pangere* to fasten]

compact[2] /kəm'pakt/ *verb trans* **1** to press (something or its component parts) together; to compress or consolidate. **2** (*usu* + of) to make (something) up by connecting or combining elements; to compose. ➤➤ **compaction** /-sh(ə)n/ *noun*, **compactor** *noun*.

compact[3] /'kompakt/ *noun* a small slim case for face powder.

compact[4] /'kompakt/ *noun* an agreement or contract. [Latin *compactum*, neuter of *compactus*, past part. of *compacisci* to make an agreement, from COM- + *pacisci* to contract]

compact disc /'kompakt/ *noun* a small plastic aluminium-coated disc on which sound or information is stored in digital form in microscopic pits that can be read by a laser beam.

compadre /kom'pahdray/ *noun chiefly NAmer, informal* a companion. [Spanish *compadre*, literally 'godfather']

companion[1] /kəm'panyən/ *noun* **1** a person who accompanies or spends time with another. **2** something belonging to a pair or set of matching things. **3** a person employed to live with and provide company and service for somebody. **4** a member of the lowest rank of certain orders of knighthood. **5** a guide or handbook on a subject. ➤➤ **companionship** *noun*. [Middle English *compainoun* via Old French from late Latin *companion-, companio*, from Latin COM- + *panis* bread, food]

companion[2] *noun* **1** a companionway, or a covering at the top of one. **2** a raised frame allowing light to reach the windows of a lower deck. [by folk etymology from Dutch *kampanje* poop deck]

companionable *adj* marked by, conducive to, or suggestive of companionship; sociable: *a companionable silence.* ➤➤ **companionableness** *noun*, **companionably** *adv*.

companionate marriage /kəm'panyənət/ *noun* a proposed form of marriage in which the partners would be treated as equals. Birth control would be used, divorce permitted for childless couples by mutual consent, and no financial or economic claim could be made by one party on the other.

companionway *noun* a ship's stairway from one deck to another.

company[1] /'kump(ə)ni/ *noun* (*pl* **companies**) **1** (*treated as sing. or pl*) an association of people for carrying on a commercial or industrial enterprise. **2a** friendly association with another; fellowship: *I enjoy her company.* **b** companions or associates: *I'm not happy with the company he keeps.* **c** (*treated as sing. or pl*) visitors or guests: *We're having company for dinner.* **3** (*treated as sing. or pl*). **a** a group of people or things: *a company of horsemen.* **b** a unit of soldiers composed usu of two or more platoons. **c** an organization of musical or dramatic performers. **d** the officers and crew of a ship. **e** *Brit* a unit of Guides. ✳ **keep company with** to associate or spend time with (somebody) on a regular basis. **keep somebody company** to accompany or spend time with somebody so that they will not be lonely, bored, etc. [Middle English *companie* from Old French *compagnie*, from *compain* companion, from late Latin *companio*: see COMPANION[1]]

company[2] *verb trans* (**companies, companied, companying**) *literary* to accompany or keep company with (somebody).

company car *noun* a car provided by a company for the use of an employee.

company officer *noun* an army officer of the rank of second lieutenant, lieutenant, or captain.

company secretary *noun* a senior officer of a company with chief responsibility for its financial and legal aspects.

company sergeant major *noun* the senior noncommissioned officer of a company.

compar. *abbr* comparative.

comparable /'komp(ə)rəbl/ *adj* **1** (*often* + with/to) capable of or suitable for comparison. **2** approximately equivalent; similar: *fabrics of comparable quality.* ➤➤ **comparability** /-'biliti/ *noun*, **comparably** *adv*.

comparative[1] /kəm'parətiv/ *adj* **1** considered as if in comparison to something else as a standard; relative: *a comparative stranger.* **2** involving comparison between different branches of a subject: *comparative anatomy.* **3** in grammar, of or constituting the degree of comparison expressing increase in quality, quantity, or relation: compare SUPERLATIVE[1] (2): *The comparative form of 'hot' is 'hotter'.* ➤➤ **comparatively** *adv*.

comparative[2] *noun* the comparative degree or form in a language.

comparator /kəm'parətə/ *noun* in engineering, a device for comparing something with a similar thing or with a standard measure.

compare[1] /kəm'peə/ *verb trans* **1** (*usu* + to) to represent (something or somebody) as similar to another thing or person; to liken: *Shall I compare thee to a summer's day?* — Shakespeare. **2** (*often* + to/with) to examine the character or qualities of (something or somebody) in order to discover resemblances or differences: *We compared the two paintings*; *I compared her signature with the one on the letter.* **3** in grammar, to inflect or modify (an adjective or adverb) according to the degrees of comparison. ➤ *verb intrans* (+ with) to be similar, or different in a specified way: *This year's sales figures compare favourably with last year's.* ✳ **compare notes** to exchange information or opinions. [Middle English *comparen* via French from Latin *comparare* to couple, compare, from *compar* like, from COM- + *par* equal]

Usage note

compare to and compare with. Both prepositions, to and with, can be used following compare. Neither is more correct than the other, but a slight distinction can be made in meaning. To has traditionally been preferred when the similarity between two things is the point of the comparison and compare means 'liken': I hesitate to compare my own works to those of someone like Dickens. With, on the other hand, suggests that the differences between two things are as important as, if not more important than, the similarities: We compared the facilities available to most city-dwellers with those available to people living in the country; to compare like with like.

compare² noun comparison: beauty beyond compare.

comparison /kəm'paris(ə)n/ noun **1a** the representing of one thing or person as similar to or like another. **b** an examination of two or more items to establish similarities and dissimilarities. **2** identity or similarity of features: There are several points of comparison between the two authors. **3** in grammar, the modification of an adjective or adverb to denote different levels of quality, quantity, or relation. [Middle English from Latin comparation-, comparatio, from comparare: see COMPARE¹]

compartment¹ /kəm'pahtmənt/ noun **1** any of the parts into which an enclosed space is divided. **2** a separate division or section. ⟩⟩ **compartmental** /kompaht'mentl/ adj, **compartmentally** adv. [French compartiment via Italian from late Latin compartiri to share out, from Latin COM- + partiri to share, from part-, pars PART¹]

compartment² verb trans **1** to put (things) into compartments. **2** to divide (something) into compartments.

compartmentalize or **compartmentalise** /kompaht'ment(ə)liez/ verb trans to separate (things) into isolated compartments or categories: compartmentalized knowledge. ⟩⟩ **compartmentalization** /-'zaysh(ə)n/ noun.

compass¹ /'kumpəs/ noun **1a** an instrument that indicates directions, typically by having a needle that points to magnetic north. **b** (usu in pl) an instrument for drawing circles or transferring measurements that consists of two legs joined at one end by a pivot. **2a** a boundary or circumference: within the compass of the city walls. **b** range or scope: the compass of a voice.

compass² verb trans archaic **1** to devise or contrive (something), often with craft or skill; to plot. **2a** to encompass (something). **b** to travel entirely round (a place): compass the earth. [Middle English compassen via Old French from (assumed) vulgar Latin compassare to pace off, from COM- + Latin passus pace]

compass card noun a circular rotating card in a compass showing the 32 points of the compass.

compassion /kəm'pash(ə)n/ noun sympathetic awareness of others' distress together with a desire to alleviate it. [Middle English via French from late Latin compassion-, compassio, from compati to sympathize, from COM- + Latin pati to bear, suffer]

compassionate /kəm'pash(ə)nət/ adj **1** having or showing compassion; sympathetic. **2** granted because of unusual distressing circumstances affecting an individual: compassionate leave. ⟩⟩ **compassionately** adv.

compassion fatigue noun growing public reluctance to help people in need as prolonged exposure to their plight breeds indifference.

compass rose noun a graduated, often decorated, circle printed on a chart, usu showing both magnetic and true directions.

compass saw noun a saw with a narrow blade for cutting curves.

compatible /kəm'patəbl/ adj **1** (often + with) capable of existing or living together in harmony. **2** said of equipment: able to be used in combination without modification. **3** consistent. ⟩⟩ **compatibility** /-'biliti/ noun, **compatibly** adv. [early French compatible from medieval Latin compatibilis sympathetic, from compati: see COMPASSION]

compatriot /kəm'patri·ət/ noun a person from the same country: But I have always found that a true Scot resents your admiration of his compatriot [Burns], even more than he would your contempt of him — Charles Lamb. [French compatriote from late Latin compatriota, from COM- + patriota: see PATRIOT]

compeer /'kompiə/ noun formal an equal or peer. [modification of Latin compar, from compar (adj) like: see COMPARE¹]

compel /kəm'pel/ verb trans (**compelled, compelling**) **1** to drive or force (somebody) irresistibly to do something: Poverty compelled him to work. **2** to cause (something) to occur by overwhelming pressure: Exhaustion of ammunition compelled their surrender. [Middle English compellen via French from Latin compellere, from COM- + pellere to drive]

compellable /kom'peləbl/ adj said of a witness: able to be forced to give evidence or appear as a witness.

compelling adj having an irresistible power of attraction. ⟩⟩ **compellingly** adv.

compendia /kəm'pendi·ə/ noun pl of COMPENDIUM.

compendious /kəm'pendi·əs/ adj formal comprehensive but relatively brief. ⟩⟩ **compendiously** adv, **compendiousness** noun.

compendium /kəm'pendi·əm/ noun (pl **compendiums** or **compendia** /-di·ə/) **1** a brief summary of a larger work or of a field of knowledge; an abstract. **2** a collection of indoor games and puzzles. [Latin compendium saving, shortcut, from compendere to weigh together, from COM- + pendere to weigh]

compensate /'kompənsayt/ verb trans **1** (often + for) to make amends to (somebody), esp by appropriate payment: She compensated her neighbour for damage to his property. **2** to have an equal and opposite effect to (something); to counterbalance. ⟩ verb intrans (+ for) to supply an equivalent: He compensated for his bad memory by taking plenty of notes. ⟩⟩ **compensative** /-sətiv/ adj, **compensator** noun, **compensatory** /-'sayt(ə)ri, kəm'pensət(ə)ri/ adj. [Latin compensatus, past part. of compensare, from compensus, past part. of compendere: see COMPENDIUM]

compensation /kompen'saysh(ə)n/ noun **1** a recompense; specif payment for damage or loss. **2a** increased functioning or development of one organ to compensate for a defect in another. **b** the alleviation of feelings of inferiority, frustration, failure, etc in one field by increased endeavour in another. ⟩⟩ **compensational** adj.

comper /'kompə/ noun Brit, informal somebody who enters many competitions, esp as a hobby.

compere¹ /'kompeə/ noun Brit the presenter of a radio or television programme, esp a light entertainment programme, or a variety show. [French compère, literally 'godfather', from medieval Latin compater, from COM- + Latin pater father]

compere² verb trans and intrans Brit to present or introduce (a show).

compete /kəm'peet/ verb intrans (often + with) to strive against others for an objective; to be in a state of rivalry: The boy is competing with his sister for his mother's attention. [late Latin competere to seek together, from Latin competere to come together, agree, be suitable, from COM- + petere to go to, seek]

competence /'kompit(ə)ns/ or **competency** /-si/ noun (pl **competences** or **competencies**) **1** the quality or state of being competent. **2** in linguistics, the innate human capacity to acquire, use, and understand language: compare PERFORMANCE. **3** formal a sufficiency of income for the necessities and conveniences of life.

competent /'kompit(ə)nt/ adj **1a** having requisite or adequate ability: a competent electrician. **b** showing clear signs of production by a competent person, e.g. a worker or writer: a competent novel. **2** legally qualified to deal with a particular matter. ⟩⟩ **competently** adv. [Middle English, in the sense 'suitable', via French from Latin competent-, competens, present part. of competere: see COMPETE]

competition /kompə'tish(ə)n/ noun **1** the act or process of competing; rivalry. **2** an organized test of comparative skill, performance, etc. **3** the competing of two or more parties to do business with another.

Editorial note

In economic analysis, competition comes in several forms, each sometimes defined by the degree of power companies have to change market prices by changing their output. More pure competition implies each company is a smaller part of its market, and has less power to determine its own prices. This is held to promote short-run benefits (such as lower consumer prices) and more significant long-run advantages (such as enhancing incentives for innovation); although some forms of so-called 'imperfect competition' can promote wasteful and spurious product distinctions — Evan Davis.

4 (treated as sing. or pl) the others competing with one: keeping ahead of the competition. **5** competing demand by two or more organisms or kinds of organisms for some environmental resource in short supply. [late Latin competition-, competitio, from Latin competitus, past part. of competere: see COMPETE]

competitive /kəm'petitiv/ adj **1** relating to, characterized by, or based on competition. **2** said of wages and prices: at least as good as those offered by rivals. **3** inclined or desiring to compete. ⟩⟩ **competitively** adv, **competitiveness** noun.

competitor /kəmˈpetitə/ *noun* somebody or something that competes; a contestant or rival.

compilation /kompiˈlaysh(ə)n/ *noun* 1 the act or process of compiling. 2 something compiled from a number of different sources.

compile /kəmˈpiel/ *verb trans* 1 to collect (material) into one work. 2 to compose (a book, record, etc) out of materials from other sources. 3 in computing, to translate (e.g. a program) using a compiler. [Middle English *compilen* via French from Latin *compilare* to plunder]

compiler *noun* 1 a computer program that translates instructions written in a high-level symbolic language into machine code. 2 a person who compiles a book, etc.

comping /ˈkomping/ *noun Brit, informal* the practice or hobby of entering competitions.

complacency /kəmˈplays(ə)nsi/ *or* **complacence** *noun* self-satisfaction accompanied by unawareness of actual dangers or deficiencies: *Nothing is to me more distasteful than that entire complacency and satisfaction which beam in the countenances of a new-married couple* — Charles Lamb.

complacent /kəmˈplays(ə)nt/ *adj* self-satisfied: *a complacent smile.* ➤➤ **complacently** *adv.* [Latin *complacent-, complacens,* present part. of *complacēre* to please greatly, from COM- + *placēre* to PLEASE[1]]

complain /kəmˈplayn/ *verb intrans* 1 to express feelings of discontent. 2 to announce that one has a pain or symptom: *He complained of toothache.* ➤➤ **complainer** *noun,* **complainingly** *adv.* [Middle English *compleynen* via Old French *complaindre* from (assumed) vulgar Latin *complangere,* from COM- + Latin *plangere* to lament]

complainant *noun* in law, the party in a legal action or proceeding who makes a complaint; a plaintiff.

complaint /kəmˈplaynt/ *noun* 1 an expression of discontent. 2a something that is the cause or subject of protest or outcry. b a minor illness or disease. 3 a formal allegation by the plaintiff in a civil action. [Middle English *compleynte* from Old French *complainte,* from *complaindre:* see COMPLAIN]

complaisant /kəmˈplays(ə)nt/ *adj* having or marked by an inclination to please or comply: *Miss Crawford, complaisant as a sister, was careless as a woman and a friend* — Jane Austen. ➤➤ **complaisance** *noun.* [French *complaisant,* present part. of *complaire* to gratify, acquiesce, from Latin *complacēre:* see COMPLACENT]

compleat /komˈpleet/ *adj archaic* complete, *esp* having a complete range of relevant qualities: *the compleat conductor.*

complement[1] /ˈkomplimənt/ *noun* 1a something that completes a whole, or adds extra features to enhance it. b the quantity required to make something complete; a counterpart. 2 either of two mutually completing parts; a counterpart. 2 in grammar, an added word or phrase by which a predicate is made complete, e.g. *president* in the sentence *They elected him president.* 3 the protein in blood serum that in combination with antibodies causes the destruction of antigens, e.g. bacteria. 4 in geometry, an angle or arc that when added to a given angle or arc equals 90°. ➤➤ **complemental** /-ˈmentl/ *adj.* [Middle English from Latin *complementum,* from *complēre:* see COMPLETE[1]]

Usage note —————
complement *or* **supplement**? Both these words convey the idea of adding something. If one thing *complements* another, however, it goes well with it and enhances it when they are put together: *A hat should complement the rest of one's outfit, not draw attention to itself.* If one thing *supplements* another, it adds to it and reinforces it: *She supplements her income by giving private music lessons.* A good wine may be a *complement* to a meal, but a person might need a dietary *supplement* if some essential element is lacking from the food they normally eat. Note that neither of these words is spelt with an *i.* See also note at COMPLIMENT[1].

complement[2] /ˈkompliment/ *verb trans* to be complementary to (something): *He found her a flower that would complement her dress.*

complementary /kompliˈment(ə)ri/ *adj* 1 serving to complete or enhance something. 2 mutually supplying each other's lack. 3 using or relating to complementary medicine. ➤➤ **complementarily** *adv,* **complementariness** *noun,* **complementarity** /-ˈtariti/ *noun.*
Usage note —————
complementary *or* **complimentary**? See note at COMPLIMENTARY.

complementary angle *noun* either of two angles that have the sum of 90°.

complementary colour *noun* either of a pair of contrasting colours that produce a neutral colour when combined.

complementary DNA *noun* a strand of DNA paired precisely with a strand of RNA so that the sequence of bases on one strand determines that on the other.

complementary medicine *noun* = ALTERNATIVE MEDICINE.

complementation /ˌkomplimənˈtaysh(ə)n/ *noun* 1 in mathematics, the determination of the complement of a given set. 2 the production of a normal organism from the mating of two mutant organisms.

complete[1] /kəmˈpleet/ *adj* 1 having all necessary parts, elements, or steps: *a complete set.* 2 whole or concluded: *two complete revolutions about the sun.* 3a fully carried out; thorough: *a complete renovation.* b total or absolute: *complete silence.* 4 thoroughly competent; highly proficient: *the complete interviewer* ➤➤ **completely** *adv,* **completeness** *noun.* [Middle English *complet* via French from Latin *completus,* past part. of *complēre* to fill up, complete, from COM- + *plēre* to fill]

complete[2] *verb trans* 1 to bring (something) to an end; to finish doing (something): *I have completed my painting.* 2a to make (something) whole or perfect. b to mark the end of (something): *A rousing chorus completes the show.* c to execute or fulfil (something): *They completed the contract.* d to enter information on (a form). ➤ *verb intrans* to carry out all the legal requirements for transfer of a property. ➤➤ **completion** /kəmˈpleesh(ə)n/ *noun.*

completist /kəmˈpleetist/ *noun* somebody who has an obsession with collecting everything belonging to a particular set, e.g. all the recordings made by an artist.

complex[1] /ˈkompleks/ *adj* 1 composed of two or more parts. 2 hard to separate, analyse, or solve; intricate: *a complex problem.* 3 in mathematics, of or being a complex number. ➤➤ **complexity** /komˈpleksiti/ *noun,* **complexly** *adv.* [Latin *complexus,* past part. of *complecti* to embrace, comprise (a multitude of objects), from COM- + *plectere* to braid]

complex[2] *noun* 1 a whole made up of interrelated parts: *a shopping complex.* 2a a group of repressed related desires and memories that usu adversely affects personality and behaviour: *a persecution complex.* b *informal* an exaggerated reaction to or anxiety about something: *She has a complex about flying.* 3 in chemistry, a substance or compound in which the constituents are more intimately associated than in a simple mixture.

complex fraction *noun* a fraction that has fractions for the numerator, the denominator, or both.

complexion *noun* 1 the appearance of the skin, *esp* of the face. 2 the overall aspect or character of something: *That puts a different complexion on things.* ➤➤ **complexional** *adj,* **complexioned** *adj.* [Middle English via French from medieval Latin *complexion-, complexio* physical constitution, from Latin *complecti:* see COMPLEX[1]]

complex number *noun* a number containing both real and imaginary parts.

complex sentence *noun* a sentence that consists of a main clause and one or more subordinate clauses.

compliance /kəmˈplie-əns/ *noun* 1 the act or process of complying with the wishes of others. 2 a disposition to yield to others. 3 in physics, the ability of an object to yield elastically when a force is applied, or a measure of this. ➤➤ **compliant** *adj,* **compliantly** *adv.*

complicate /ˈkomplikayt/ *verb trans* 1 to make (something) complex or difficult: *Then, to complicate matters, his ex-wife turned up at the wedding.* 2 to combine (things), *esp* in an involved or inextricable manner. [Latin *complicatus,* past part. of *complicare* to fold together, from COM- + *plicare* to fold]

complicated *adj* 1 difficult to analyse, understand, or explain. 2 consisting of parts intricately combined. ➤➤ **complicatedly** *adv.*

complication /kompliˈkaysh(ə)n/ *noun* 1a intricacy or complexity. b the act or an instance of making something difficult, involved, or intricate. c a complex or intricate feature or element. d a factor or issue that occurs unexpectedly and changes existing plans, methods, or attitudes. 2 a secondary disease or condition developing in the course of a primary disease or condition: *Eclampsia is a serious complication of pregnancy.*

complicit /kəmˈplisit/ *adj* participating in a wrongful act.

complicity /kəmˈplisiti/ *noun* association or participation in a wrongful act. [French *complicité,* from *complice* accomplice, from late Latin *complic-, complex* partner, from Latin *complicare:* see COMPLICATE]

compliment[1] /'komplimənt/ *noun* **1** an expression of esteem, affection, or admiration; *esp* a flattering remark: *That is one great difference between us. Compliments always take you by surprise, and me never* — Jane Austen. **2** (*in pl*) best wishes; regards: *with the compliments of the management*. ✴ **return the compliment** to respond in kind. [French *compliment* via Italian from Spanish *cumplimiento*, from *cumplir* to be courteous]

Usage note

compliment *or* complement? These two words are easily confused. An expression of admiration is a *compliment*: *My compliments to the chef; The remark was intended as a compliment*. A *complement* is an accompaniment to something that sets off its good qualities (*Wine is the perfect complement to a good meal*), the full number of something (*The baby had the usual complement of arms and legs*), or a word or expression that completes a predicate. The verbs *compliment* and *complement* work in the same way: *May I compliment you on your cooking?*; *Their characters may be different, but they complement each other well*. See also note at COMPLEMENT[1].

compliment[2] /'kompliment/ *verb trans* **1** (*often* + on) to pay a compliment to (somebody): *She complimented him on his singing*. **2** *archaic* (*often* + with) to present (somebody) with a token of esteem: *He complimented her with a bouquet of flowers*.

complimentary /kompli'ment(ə)ri/ *adj* **1** expressing or containing a compliment: *a complimentary remark*. **2** given free as a courtesy or favour: *complimentary tickets*. ➤➤ **complimentarily** *adv*.

Usage note

complimentary *or* complementary? There is the same difference in meaning between *complimentary* and *complementary* as between their respective nouns. A *complimentary* remark is flattering and expresses admiration. A *complimentary* ticket or *complimentary* copy of a book is given free. *Complementary*, on the other hand, refers to the relationship between things or people that go well together: *complementary colours*.

compliment slip *or* **compliments slip** *noun Brit* a slip of paper bearing a company's name and address, sent with goods in place of a covering letter.

compline /'komplin/ *noun* the last of the canonical hours, said before retiring at night. [Middle English *complie*, *compline* from Old French *complie*, modification of late Latin *completa*, fem past part. of *complēre*: see COMPLETE[1]]

comply /kəm'plie/ *verb intrans* (**complies, complied, complying**) **1** (*usu* + with) to conform or adapt one's actions to somebody else's wishes or to a rule: *She refused to comply with his demands*. **2** (*usu* + with) to meet a certain standard: *The toy doesn't comply with European safety legislation*. [Italian *complire* via Spanish from Latin *complēre*: see COMPLETE[1]]

compo[1] /'kompoh/ *noun* (*pl* **compos**) a material made of a mixture of others; a composite. [short for COMPOSITION]

compo[2] *noun* (*pl* **compos**) *Brit* a supply of food for several days, made up of various items and carried by a soldier, etc when fresh food is unavailable. [short for COMPOSITE[1]]

component[1] /kəm'pohnənt/ *noun* **1** a constituent part, *esp* of a machine. **2** in mathematics, any of the vector terms added to form a vector sum or resultant. ➤➤ **componential** /kompə'nensh(ə)l/ *adj*. [Latin *component-, componens*, present part. of *componere*: see COMPOUND[3]]

component[2] *adj* said of parts: serving or helping to constitute a whole; constituent.

compo rations *pl noun* = COMPO[2].

comport /kəm'pawt/ *verb trans formal* to behave (oneself) in a manner that conforms with what is right, proper, or expected. ➤ *verb intrans archaic* (+ with) to be fitting; to accord: *acts that comport with ideals*. [early French *comporter* to bear, conduct, from Latin *comportare* to bring together, from COM- + *portare* to carry]

comportment /kom'pawtmənt/ *noun informal* bearing or demeanour.

compose /kəm'pohz/ *verb trans* **1a** to create (something) by mental or artistic labour: *He composed a sonnet*. **b** to formulate and write (a piece of music). **2a** to form (something) by putting it together. **b** (*usu in passive*) to form the substance of (something); to make (something) up. **c** to arrange (type) for printing; to set. **3** to free (oneself) from agitation; to calm or settle (oneself). **4** *archaic* to settle (a point of disagreement). [early French *composer* from Latin *componere*: see COMPOUND[3]]

composed *adj* free from agitation; calm and collected. ➤➤ **composedly** /-zidli/ *adv*.

composer *noun* a person who writes music.

composite[1] /'kompəzit/ *adj* **1** made up of distinct parts or constituents. **2** combining the typical or essential characteristics of individuals making up a group: *a composite portrait of mystics known to the painter*. **3** (**Composite**) of a Roman order of architecture that combines Ionic with Corinthian. **4** /'kompəziet/ of or belonging to a very large family of plants, including the dandelion, daisy, and sunflower, typically having florets arranged in dense heads that resemble single flowers. **5** in mathematics, having two or more factors; not prime. ➤➤ **compositely** *adv*, **compositeness** *noun*. [Latin *compositus*, past part. of *componere*: see COMPOUND[3]]

composite[2] /'kompəziet/ *noun* **1** a composite material, *esp* a building material. **2** /'kompəziet/ a plant of the composite family. **3** /'kompəziet/a motion or proposal created from several related motions for the purpose of discussion, e.g. at a national conference.

composite[3] /'kompəziet/ *verb trans* to merge (several things) to form a composite whole; *esp* to combine (visual images) to produce a single picture.

composition /kompə'zish(ə)n/ *noun* **1a** a piece of writing; *esp* a school essay: *Read your own compositions, and when you meet with a passage which you think is particularly fine, strike it out* — Dr Johnson. **b** a written piece of music. **2** a product of mixing or combining various elements or ingredients. **3** the factors or parts that make up something, or the way in which the factors or parts make up the whole. **4a** the act or process of composing; *specif* arrangement into proper proportion or relation and artistic form. **b** an arrangement of type for printing, or the production of this. **5** an agreement by which a creditor accepts partial payment. ➤➤ **compositional** *adj*, **compositionally** *adv*. [Middle English *composicioun* via French from Latin *composition-, compositio*, from *componere*: see COMPOUND[3]]

compositor /kəm'pozitə/ *noun* somebody who sets type.

compos mentis /,kompəs 'mentis/ *adj* of sound mind, memory, and understanding. [Latin, literally 'having mastery of one's mind']

compost[1] /'kompost/ *noun* a mixture of decayed organic matter used as a fertilizer. [early French *composte* via medieval Latin from Latin *compositum*, neuter past part. of *componere*: see COMPOUND[3]]

compost[2] *verb trans* **1** to convert (plant debris, etc) to compost. **2** to add compost to (something).

composter /kəm'postə/ *noun* a barrel or similar container in which organic matter is collected for composting.

composure /kəm'pohzhə/ *noun* calmness of mind, bearing, or appearance.

compote /'kompot/ *noun* fruit cooked in syrup and usu served cold. [French *compote* via Old French from Latin *composta*, fem past part. of *componere*: see COMPOUND[3]]

compound[1] /'kompownd/ *noun* **1** something formed by a union of elements or parts. **2** in chemistry, a distinct substance formed by combination of chemical elements in fixed proportion. **3** a word consisting of components that are words, e.g. *houseboat* or *whitewash*. [Middle English *compouned*, past part. of *compounen*: see COMPOUND[3]]

compound[2] /'kompownd/ *adj* **1** composed of or resulting from a union of usu similar separate elements, ingredients, or parts. **2** said of a sentence: having two or more main clauses.

compound[3] /kəm'pownd/ *verb trans* **1** to put together (parts) so as to form a whole; to combine. **2** to form (something, e.g. a medicine) by combining parts. **3a** to calculate (interest) on both the principal and accumulated interest. **b** to augment or add to (something). **b** to augment or add to (something bad): *He compounded the error by covering it up*. **4** in law, to agree not to prosecute (an offence) in return for payment, etc. ➤➤ **compoundable** *adj*, **compounder** *noun*. [Middle English *compounen* via French from Latin *componere* to put together, from COM- + *ponere* to put]

compound[4] /'kompownd/ *noun* a fenced or walled-in area containing a group of buildings. [by folk etymology from Malay *kampong* group of buildings, village]

compound eye *noun* an eye of insects and other arthropods that consists of a number of separate visual units.

compound fracture *noun* a bone fracture produced in such a way as to form an open wound.

compound interest *noun* interest calculated on the principal plus accumulated interest.

compound leaf *noun* a divided leaf that has two or more leaflets on a common stalk.

compound lens *noun* a combination of two or more simple lenses.

compound time *noun* in music, a tempo with two or more groups of simple time units in each bar: compare SIMPLE TIME.

comprehend /kompri'hend/ *verb trans* **1** to grasp the nature, significance, or meaning of (something); to understand (something). **2** *formal* to include (something): *The park comprehends all of the land beyond the river.* [Middle English *comprehenden* from Latin *comprehendere*, from COM- + *prehendere* to grasp, understand, comprise]

comprehensible /kompri'hensəbl/ *adj* capable of being comprehended; intelligible. ➤➤ **comprehensibility** /-'biliti/ *noun*, **comprehensibly** *adv*.

comprehension /kompri'hensh(ə)n/ *noun* **1a** grasping with the intellect; understanding. **b** the capacity for understanding fully. **2** *Brit* a school exercise testing understanding of a passage. [French *comprehension* from Latin *comprehension-*, *comprehensio*, from *comprehendere*: see COMPREHEND]

comprehensive[1] /kompri'hensiv/ *adj* **1** covering completely or broadly; inclusive: *comprehensive insurance.* **2** wide-ranging: *comprehensive knowledge.* **3** *Brit* relating to, applying, or denoting the principle of educating in one secondary school children of all abilities from a given area: *comprehensive education; a comprehensive school.* ➤➤ **comprehensively** *adv*, **comprehensiveness** *noun*.

comprehensive[2] *noun Brit* a comprehensive school.

compress[1] /kəm'pres/ *verb trans* **1** to press or squeeze (something) together. **2** to reduce (something, e.g. a computer file) in size or volume as if by squeezing. ➤ *verb intrans* to be compressed. ➤➤ **compressibility** /-'biliti/ *noun*, **compressible** *adj*. [Middle English *compressen* via late Latin from Latin *compressus*, past part. of *comprimere* to compress, from COM- + *premere* to PRESS[1]]

compress[2] /'kompres/ *noun* a pad pressed on a body part, e.g. to ease the pain and swelling of a bruise. [early French *compresse*, from *compresser* to compress, from late Latin *compressare*,frequentative of *comprimere*: see COMPRESS[1]]

compressed /kəm'prest/ *adj* **1** pressed together. **2** reduced in size or volume, e.g. by pressure. **3** flattened as though subjected to compressing.

compressed air *noun* air under pressure greater than that of the atmosphere.

compression /kəm'presh(ə)n/ *noun* **1** the action of compressing or being compressed. **2** the process of compressing the fuel mixture in a cylinder of an internal-combustion engine, or the quality of this process.

compressor /kəm'presə/ *noun* **1** something that compresses. **2** a machine for compressing gases. **3** a muscle that compresses a part. **4** an electrical device that reduces the variation in range of a transmitted signal.

comprise /kəm'priez/ *verb trans* **1** to be made up of (something): *The family comprised two adults and three children.* **2** to make up or constitute (something). [Middle English *comprisen* from early French *compris*, past part. of *comprendre*, from Latin *comprehendere*: see COMPREHEND]

Usage note

Comprise is a difficult word to use, because it is close in meaning to, but should be treated differently from, such verbs as *consist (of)*, *compose*, and *make up*. There are two rules to remember. First, a whole *comprises* (consists of or is composed of) its parts; the parts *make up* or *constitute* the whole, but do not *comprise* it: *The collection comprises over 500 items; The meal comprised no less than fifteen courses.* Second, *comprise* should not be followed by *of*, even when it is used in the passive.

compromise[1] /'komprəmiez/ *noun* **1a** a settlement reached by mutual concession. **b** the settling of differences through arbitration or mutual concession. **c** something blending qualities of two different things: *a compromise solution.* **2** a shameful concession, e.g. a lowering of standards for expediency: *a compromise of principles.* [Middle English, in the sense 'mutual promise to abide by an arbiter's decision', via French from Latin *compromissum*, neuter past part. of *compromittere* to promise mutually, from COM- + *promittere*: see PROMISE[1]]

compromise[2] *verb intrans* to come to agreement by mutual concession. ➤ *verb trans* **1** to expose (somebody or something) to discredit or danger. **2** to go against (one's principles, etc) for

expediency. **3** *archaic* to settle (a disagreement) by mutual concessions. ➤➤ **compromiser** *noun*.

compromising /'komprəmiezing/ *adj* likely to lead to discredit or scandal: *They were caught in a compromising situation.*

comptroller /kən'trohlə/ *noun* a public finance officer. [Middle English, alteration of *conterroller* controller]

compulsion /kəm'pulsh(ə)n/ *noun* **1a** compelling or being compelled. **b** a force or agency that compels. **2** a strong impulse to perform an irrational act: *a compulsion to steal.* [Middle English via French from late Latin *compulsion-*, *compulsio*, from Latin *compellere*: see COMPEL]

compulsive /kəm'pulsiv/ *adj* of, caused by, or suffering from a psychological compulsion or obsession: *a compulsive liar.* ➤➤ **compulsively** *adv*, **compulsiveness** *noun*.

compulsory /kəm'pulsəri/ *adj* **1** mandatory or enforced: *compulsory arbitration.* **2** involving compulsion or obligation; coercive: *compulsory legislation.* ➤➤ **compulsorily** *adv*.

compulsory purchase *noun Brit* the purchase of private land or property for public use or development whether the owner wishes to sell it or not.

compunction /kəm'pungksh(ə)n/ *noun* **1** anxiety arising from awareness of guilt; remorse. **2** a twinge of misgiving; a scruple. ➤➤ **compunctious** /-shəs/ *adj*, **compunctiously** *adv*. [Middle English *compunccioun* via French from late Latin *compunction-*, *compunctio*, from Latin *compungere* to prick hard, sting, from COM- + *pungere* to prick]

compurgation /kompuh'gaysh(ə)n/ *noun* in law, a method of trial abolished in 1833 by which a person could be acquitted if witnesses swore to his or her innocence and veracity. [late Latin *compurgation-*, *compurgatio*, from Latin *compurgare* to clear completely, from COM- + *purgare*: see PURGE[1]]

compurgator /'kompuhgaytə/ *noun* in law, formerly, a person testifying to the innocence or veracity of another.

computation /kompyoo'taysh(ə)n/ *noun* **1a** the act or process of calculating, or a system of calculating. **b** the result of calculating; an amount calculated. **2** the use or operation of a computer. ➤➤ **computational** *adj*, **computationally** *adv*.

compute /kəm'pyooht/ *verb trans* to determine or calculate (a quantity or number), *esp* by mathematical means or using a computer. ➤ *verb intrans* **1** to make calculations; to reckon. **2** to use a computer. **3** *informal* (*in negative contexts*) to make sense. ➤➤ **computability** /-'biliti/ *noun*, **computable** *adj*. [Latin *computare*, from COM- + *putare* to settle an account]

computer *noun* a programmable electronic device that can store, retrieve, and process data.

computer-aided design *noun* industrial design using computer graphics to construct models.

computerate /kəm'pyooht(ə)rət/ *adj informal* computer-literate.

computer dating *noun* the use of computers by introduction agencies to match the personal details of their clients.

computer game *noun* a game played on a computer by keying in instructions or by using keys, a mouse, or a joystick to move a point or figure on a screen.

computerize *or* **computerise** *verb trans* **1** to equip (an office, company, etc) with computers. **2** to carry out, control, or conduct (something) by means of a computer. ➤➤ **computerization** /-'zaysh(ə)n/ *noun*.

computer language *noun* an artificial language used to program a computer.

computer-literate *adj* able to use a computer competently. ➤➤ **computer literacy** *noun*.

computer science *noun* the study of the construction, operation, and use of computers.

comrade /'komrid, 'komrayd/ *noun* **1a** an intimate friend or associate; a companion. **b** a fellow soldier: *comrades in arms.* **2** a fellow communist. ➤➤ **comradely** *adj*, **comradeship** *noun*. [early French *comarade* group sleeping in one room, roommate, companion, from Old Spanish *cámara* room, from late Latin *camera, camara* room, from Latin: see CHAMBER; (sense 2) from its use as a form of address by communists]

Comsat /'komsat/ *noun trademark* an artificial satellite used for relaying radio waves, e.g. for intercontinental communication. [short for *communications satellite*]

Con *abbr* **1** Conservative. **2** Constable.

con¹ /kon/ *noun informal* a confidence trick.

con² *verb trans* (**conned, conning**) *informal* to swindle or trick (somebody): *She was conned out of her savings.*

con³ *noun informal* a convict.

con⁴ *noun* the opposing or negative position, or somebody holding it: compare PRO¹. [Middle English from Latin *contra* against, opposite]

con⁵ *adv* on the negative side; in opposition: compare PRO²: *So much has been written pro and con.*

con⁶ (*NAmer* **conn**) *verb trans* (**conned, conning**) to conduct or direct the steering of (a ship). [alteration of Middle English *condien* to conduct, via French from Latin *conducere*: see CONDUCE]

con⁷ (*NAmer* **conn**) *noun* the control exercised by a person steering a ship.

con⁸ *verb trans* (**conned, conning**) *archaic* **1** to study or examine (something) closely. **2** to learn (something) by heart. [Middle English *connen* to know, learn, study, alteration of *cunnen* to know]

con⁹ *prep* used in music: with: *con brio.* [Italian *con*]

con- *prefix* see COM-.

con amore /kon a'mawray/ *adv* said of a piece of music: to be performed in a tender manner. [Italian *con amore* with love]

conation /kə'naysh(ə)n/ *noun* an instinct, drive, wish, craving, etc to act purposefully. ⨠ **conative** /'konətiv, 'koh-/ *adj.* [Latin *conation-, conatio* act of attempting, from *conari* to attempt]

con brio /kon 'breeoh/ *adv* said of a piece of music: to be performed in a vigorous or brisk manner. [Italian *con brio* with vigour]

concatenate /kon'katənayt/ *verb trans formal or technical* to link (things) together in a series or chain. ⨠ **concatenation** /-'naysh(ə)n/ *noun.* [late Latin *concatenatus*, past part. of *concatenare* to link together, from Latin CON- + *catenare* to chain, from *catena* chain]

concave /'konkayv, kon'kayv/ *adj* hollowed or rounded inwards like the inside of a bowl: compare CONVEX. ⨠ **concavely** *adv.* [early French *concave* from Latin *concavus*, from CON- + *cavus* hollow]

concavity /kon'kaviti/ *noun* (*pl* **concavities**) **1** the quality or state of being concave. **2** a concave line or surface or the space included in it.

concavo-concave /kon,kayvoh kon'kayv/ *adj* having both sides concave; biconcave.

concavo-convex /kon,kayvoh kon'veks/ *adj* **1** concave on one side and convex on the other. **2** said of a lens: having the concave side more curved than the convex.

conceal /kən'seel/ *verb trans* **1** to place (something) out of sight. **2** (*often* + from) to prevent disclosure or recognition of (something): *Hear me, ye women who adorn yourselves alluringly and conceal your thoughts from your men* — George Bernard Shaw. ⨠ **concealment** *noun.* [Middle English *concelen* via French from Latin *concelare*, from CON- + *celare* to hide]

concealer *noun* somebody or something that conceals; *specif* a flesh-coloured cosmetic product used to conceal facial blemishes.

concede /kən'seed/ *verb trans* **1a** to accept (something) as true, valid, or accurate. **b** to acknowledge (something) grudgingly or hesitantly. **2** to grant or yield (a right or privilege). **3** to allow (e.g. a goal or point) involuntarily: *United conceded two more goals.* ⨠ *verb intrans* to make concession; to yield. ⨠ **conceder** *noun.* [French *concéder* from Latin *concedere*, from CON- + *cedere* to yield, CEDE]

conceit /kən'seet/ *noun* **1** excessively high opinion of oneself: *Conceit spoils the finest genius* — Louisa M Alcott. **2** *literary.* **a** a fanciful idea. **b** an elaborate, unusual, and cleverly expressed figure of speech. [Middle English, in the sense 'thought, opinion' from *conceiven*: see CONCEIVE]

conceited *adj* having an excessively high opinion of oneself. ⨠ **conceitedly** *adv,* **conceitedness** *noun.*

conceivable /kən'seevəbl/ *adj* capable of being conceived in the mind; imaginable: *I have searched in every conceivable place.* ⨠ **conceivability** /-'biliti/ *noun,* **conceivably** *adv.*

conceive /kən'seev/ *verb trans* **1** to become pregnant with (a baby). **2a** to cause (something) to originate in one's mind: *He conceived a prejudice against her.* **b** to form a conception of (something); to visualize or imagine. ⨠ *verb intrans* **1** to become pregnant. **2** (+ of) to form a conception in the mind: *Most parents couldn't conceive of*

giving their children away. ⨠ **conceiver** *noun.* [Middle English *conceiven* via Old French from Latin *concipere* to take in, conceive, from CON- + *capere* to take]

concelebrate /kən'seləbrayt, kon-/ *verb trans* to celebrate or officiate at (Mass or the Eucharist) jointly with another priest. ⨠ **concelebrant** *noun,* **concelebration** /-'braysh(ə)n/ *noun.* [Latin *concelebratus,* past part. of *concelebrare* to celebrate in great numbers, from CON- + *celebrare* to celebrate]

concenter /kən'sentə/ *verb trans and intrans NAmer* see CONCENTRE.

concentrate¹ /'kons(ə)ntrayt/ *verb trans* **1a** to focus or direct (one's mind or attention) on or towards a common centre or objective: *Depend upon it, Sir, when a man knows he is to be hanged in a fortnight, it concentrates his mind wonderfully* — Dr Johnson. **b** to gather (something) into one body, mass, or force: *Power was concentrated in a few able hands.* **2a** to make (a solution) less dilute. **b** to express or exhibit (something) in condensed form: *The author concentrates his message in the last paragraph.* ⨠ *verb intrans* **1** (*often* + on) to concentrate one's powers, efforts, or attention: *Try to concentrate on your work.* **2** to gather or collect. **3** to go towards or meet at a common centre. ⨠ **concentrative** /-traytiv/ *adj,* **concentrator** *noun.* [French *concentrer* from CON- + Latin *centrum*: see CENTRE¹]

concentrate² *noun* something in concentrated form, *esp* food.

concentration /konsən'traysh(ə)n/ *noun* **1** direction of attention to a single object, activity, etc. **2** a concentrated mass or thing. **3** the relative amount of a substance in a mixture or a solution.

concentration camp *noun* a camp where political prisoners, refugees, etc are confined; *esp* any of the Nazi camps for the internment or mass execution of prisoners during World War II.

concentre (*NAmer* **concenter**) /kən'sentə/ *verb trans and intrans* to collect (something) at or come to a common centre. [early French *concentrer*]

concentric /kən'sentrik/ *adj* said of shapes: having a common centre: *concentric circles.* ⨠ **concentrically** *adv,* **concentricity** /konsen'trisiti/ *noun.* [medieval Latin *concentricus,* from CON- + Latin *centrum*: see CENTRE¹]

concept /'konsept/ *noun* **1** something conceived in the mind; a thought or notion. **2** a generic idea abstracted from particular instances. **3** (*used before a noun*) developed to test or implement new ideas: *a concept car.* ⨠ **conceptual** /kən'septyooəl/ *adj,* **conceptually** *adv.* [Latin *conceptum,* neuter past part. of *concipere*: see CONCEIVE]

conception /kən'sepsh(ə)n/ *noun* **1** conceiving or being conceived; the beginning of pregnancy. **2** a general idea; a concept: *He has no conception of what it is like to be short of money.* **3** the originating of something in the mind: *the conception of a plan.* ⨠ **conceptional** *adj,* **conceptive** /-tiv/ *adj.* [Middle English *concepcioun* via Old French from Latin *conception-, conceptio,* from *concipere*: see CONCEIVE]

conceptual art *noun* an artistic genre in which the concept that the artist wishes to convey is considered more important than the form or composition of the work of art by which it is conveyed, and in which a mere statement of the concept itself may sometimes serve as the artwork. ⨠ **conceptual artist** *noun.*

conceptualise /kən'septyooəliez/ *verb* see CONCEPTUALIZE.

conceptualism /kən'septyooəliz(ə)m/ *noun* in philosophy, a theory asserting that classes and universals exist only as mental concepts. ⨠ **conceptualist** *noun.*

conceptualize *or* **conceptualise** *verb trans* to form a concept of (something). ⨠ **conceptualization** /-'zaysh(ə)n/ *noun.*

conceptus /kən'septəs/ *noun* (*pl* **conceptuses**) *technical* an embryo or foetus. [Latin *conceptus* one conceived, past part. of *concipere*: see CONCEIVE]

concern¹ /kən'suhn/ *verb trans* **1** to be about or relate to (something or somebody): *The novel concerns three soldiers.* **2** to involve or have an influence on (somebody): *The problem concerns us all.* **3** to be a cause of trouble or distress to (somebody): *His ill health concerns me.* **4** to engage or occupy (oneself): *He concerns himself with trivia.* ✳ **as far as somebody or something is concerned** with regard to somebody or something. **to whom it may concern** used at the beginning of a letter that is not addressed to anybody in particular. [Middle English *concernen* via French from medieval Latin *concernere,* from CON- + Latin *cernere* to sift]

concern[2] *noun* **1** something that relates to or involves one: *It's not my concern.* **2** anxiety, or a cause of anxiety. **3** a matter for consideration. **4** a marked interest or regard. **5** a business or manufacturing organization or establishment: *a going concern.* **6** *informal, dated* a contrivance or thing.

concerned *adj* **1** anxious. **2** (*used after a noun*) involved: *The police arrested the men concerned.*

concerning *prep* relating to (something); with reference to (something): *I'd like some information concerning French classes.*

concernment /kən'suhnmənt/ *noun archaic* something in which one is concerned.

concert[1] /'konsət/ *noun* **1** a public performance of music or dancing; *esp* a musical performance made up of several individual compositions. **2** agreement. **✳ in concert 1** working together. **2** said of a musician: performing live. [French *concert* from Italian *concerto* harmony, agreement, from *concertare* to negotiate, ultimately from CON- + Latin *certare* to strive, from *certus*: see CERTAIN[1]]

concert[2] /kən'suht/ *verb trans* to establish (a plan) by agreement between those involved.

concertante /konchə'tantay, -tanti/ *adj* said of a piece of music, *esp* a symphony: having parts for solo instruments. [Italian *concertante*, present part. of *concertare* to be in harmony]

concerted /kən'suhtid/ *adj* **1a** planned or done together; combined: *a concerted effort.* **b** performed in unison. **2** said of music: arranged in parts for several voices or instruments.

concert grand *noun* a grand piano of the largest size, used for concerts.

concerti /kən'shuhtee, kən'chuhtee/ *noun* pl of CONCERTO.

concerti grossi /'grosi/ *noun* pl of CONCERTO GROSSO.

concertina[1] /konsə'teenə/ *noun* a small hexagonal musical instrument of the accordion family.

concertina[2] *verb intrans* (**concertinas, concertinaed** *or* **concertina'd** /-nəd/, **concertinaing**) to collapse or fold up like the bellows of a concertina.

concertino /konchə'teenoh/ *noun* (*pl* **concertinos**) **1** a short concerto. **2** the solo instruments in a CONCERTO GROSSO (piece for solo instruments and full orchestra). [Italian *concertino*, dimin. of *concerto*: see CONCERT[1]]

concertmaster *noun chiefly NAmer* the principal first violinist and usu assistant conductor of an orchestra. [German *Konzertmeister*, from *Konzert* concert + *Meister* master]

concerto /kən'shuhtoh, kən'chuhtoh/ *noun* (*pl* **concertos** *or* **concerti** /-tee/) a piece for one or more soloists and orchestra, usu with three contrasting movements.

Editorial note
Concerto is now used to designate a work in which one solo instrument, sometimes more, is contrasted with a larger instrumental group (conventionally a full symphony orchestra); the term was first used in the 17th cent. to describe music written for voices and instruments. But it was the concerto grosso, as perfected by Corelli at the turn of the 18th cent., that began the evolution of the form, which reached its high point in the vehicles for virtuoso display of the romantic era — Andrew Clements.

[Italian *concerto*: see CONCERT[1]]

concerto grosso /'grosoh/ *noun* (*pl* **concerti grossi** /'grosi/) a piece for a small group of solo instruments and full orchestra. [Italian *concerto grosso* big concerto]

concert party *noun* a concert by a number of people performing variety acts.

concert pitch *noun* **1** in music, a tuning standard of usu 440 Hertz for A above middle C. **2** a high state of fitness, tension, or readiness.

concession /kən'sesh(ə)n/ *noun* **1** the act or an instance of conceding. **2** a reduced price or fare for people in certain categories, e.g. children, pensioners, or the unemployed. **3** a grant of land, property, or a right made, *esp* by a government, in return for services or for a particular use. **4a** a small shop or business that is allowed to operate on the premises of a larger business. **b** the right to operate such a concession. **5** a reduction of demands or standards made *esp* to accommodate shortcomings. **➤➤ concessionary** *adj.* [French *concession* from Latin *concession-, concessio*, from *concedere*: see CONCEDE]

concessionaire /kən,seshə'neə/ *noun* the owner, operator, or beneficiary of a concession. [French *concessionnaire*, from *concession*: see CONCESSION]

concessive /kən'sesiv/ *adj* **1** making or being a concession. **2** in grammar, said of a word or clause: showing the concession of a point.

conch /kongk, konch/ *noun* (*pl* **conchs** *or* **conches** /'konchiz/) **1a** any of numerous species of large marine gastropod molluscs: family Strombidae. **b** the spiral shell of such a mollusc. **2** in architecture, an apse, or the plain semidome of an apse. [Latin *concha* mussel, mussel shell, from Greek *konchē*; (sense 2) Italian *conca* semidome, apse, via late Latin from Latin *concha*]

concha /'kongkə/ *noun* (*pl* **conchae** /'kongkee/) something shell-shaped; *esp* the largest and deepest concavity of the external ear. [Latin *concha* shell, from Greek *konchē*]

conchie /'konchi/ *noun* see CONCHY.

conchoidal /kong'koydl/ *adj* said *esp* of a crystal fracture: shaped like the smooth curved inner surface of a mussel or oyster shell. [Greek *konchoeidēs* like a mussel, from *konchē* mussel, shell]

conchology /kong'koləji/ *noun* the study of shells. **➤➤ conchologist** *noun.*

conchy *or* **conchie** /'konchi/ *noun* (*pl* **conchies**) *chiefly Brit, informal, derog* a conscientious objector to war. [by shortening and alteration]

concierge /konsi'eəzh/ *noun* somebody who is employed as a doorkeeper, caretaker, etc, *esp* in France. [French *concierge*, modification of Latin *conservus* fellow slave, from CON- + *servus* slave]

conciliar /kən'sili-ə/ *adj* of or issued by a council. [Latin *concilium*: see COUNCIL]

conciliate /kən'siliayt/ *verb trans* **1** to appease or pacify (somebody). **2** *formal* to reconcile (people). **➤➤ conciliation** /-'aysh(ə)n/ *noun,* **conciliative** /-ətiv/ *adj,* **conciliator** *noun,* **conciliatory** /-ət(ə)ri/ *adj.* [Latin *conciliatus*, past part. of *conciliare* to assemble, unite, win over, from *concilium*: see COUNCIL]

concinnity /kən'siniti/ *noun formal* neatness and elegance, *esp* of literary style. [Latin *concinnitas*, from *concinnus* skilfully put together]

concise /kən'sies/ *adj* brief and clear, without unnecessary details. **➤➤ concisely** *adv,* **conciseness** *noun.* [Latin *concisus*, past part. of *concidere* to cut up, from CON- + *caedere* to cut, strike]

concision /kən'sizh(ə)n/ *noun* conciseness. [Middle English from Latin *concision-, concisio*, from *concidere*: see CONCISE]

conclave /'kongklayv, 'konklayv/ *noun* **1** a private meeting or secret assembly. **2** the assembly of Roman Catholic cardinals secluded continuously while electing a pope. [Middle English via French from Latin *conclave* room that can be locked up, from CON- + *clavis* key]

conclude /kən'kloohd/ *verb trans* **1** to bring (something) to an end, *esp* in a particular way or with a particular action: *Let us conclude the meeting with a prayer.* **2a** to arrive at (an opinion), *esp* by logical inference or reasoning: *I concluded that her argument was sound.* **b** to come to an agreement on (something, e.g. a deal or treaty). **➤ verb intrans** to end. [Middle English *concluden* from Latin *concludere* to shut up, end, infer, from CON- + *claudere* to shut]

conclusion /kən'kloohzh(ə)n/ *noun* **1** the act or an instance of concluding. **2** a final summing up, e.g. of an essay. **3a** a reasoned judgment; an inference. **b** in logic, the inferred proposition of a syllogism. **4** a result or outcome: *It was a foregone conclusion.* **✳ jump to conclusions** to reach a decision too quickly, without considering all the circumstances. [Middle English via French from Latin *conclusion-, conclusio*, from *concludere*: see CONCLUDE]

conclusive /kən'kloohsiv/ *adj* putting an end to debate or question, *esp* by reason of irrefutability. **➤➤ conclusively** *adv,* **conclusiveness** *noun.*

concoct /kən'kokt/ *verb trans* **1** to prepare (e.g. a meal) by combining diverse ingredients. **2** to devise or invent (e.g. a story). **➤➤ concocter** *noun,* **concoction** /kən'koksh(ə)n/ *noun.* [Latin *concoctus*, past part. of *concoquere* to cook together, from CON- + *coquere* to cook]

concomitance /kən'komitəns/ *noun* **1** the state of being concomitant. **2** in Christianity, the doctrine that the bread and wine of the Eucharist contain the body and blood of Christ.

concomitant[1] /kon'komit(ə)nt, kən-/ *adj formal* accompanying, *esp* in a subordinate or incidental way. **➤➤ concomitantly** *adv.* [Latin *concomitant-, concomitans*, present part. of *concomitari* to accompany, from CON- + *comitari* to accompany, from *comit-, comes* companion]

concomitant[2] *noun* something that accompanies or is connected with something else.

concord /'kongkawd, 'konkawd/ *noun* **1** *formal* a state of agreement; harmony: *living in concord.* **2** a treaty or covenant. **3** grammatical agreement. **4** in music, a harmonious combination of simultaneously heard notes. [Middle English via Old French from Latin *concordia*, from *concord-*, *concors* agreeing, from CON- + *cord-*, *cor* heart]

concordance /kən'kawd(ə)ns/ *noun* **1** an alphabetical index of the principal words in a book or an author's works, with their immediate contexts. **2** *formal* agreement. [Middle English via French from medieval Latin *concordantia*, from Latin *concordant-*, *concordans*, present part. of *concordare* to agree, from *concord-*, *concors*: see CONCORD]

concordant /kən'kawd(ə)nt/ *adj* **1** in agreement. **2** harmonious. >> **concordantly** *adv.* [Middle English via French from Latin *concordant-*, *concordans*, present part. of *concordare* to agree, from *concord-*, *concors*: see CONCORD]

concordat /kon'kawdat, kən-/ *noun* a compact or covenant; *specif* one between a pope and a sovereign or government. [French *concordat* from medieval Latin *concordatum*, neuter past part. of Latin *concordare*: see CONCORD]

concourse /'kongkaws, 'konkaws/ *noun* **1a** an open space where roads or paths meet. **b** an open space or main hall, e.g. in a station. **2** *formal* a coming, gathering, or happening together: *a large concourse of people.* [Middle English via early French *concours* from Latin *concursus*, past part. of *concurrere*: see CONCUR]

concrescence /kən'kres(ə)ns/ *noun* in biology, the growing together of parts or organs, e.g. of an embryo. >> **concrescent** *adj.* [Latin *concrescentia*, from *concrescent-*, *concrescens*, present part. of *concrescere*: see CONCRETE[1]]

concrete[1] /'kongkreet, 'konkreet/ *adj* **1a** real or tangible: *Halstead presented no concrete evidence of any Marxist motivation among the Museum's scientists — Phillip E Johnson.* **b** specific or particular: *concrete proposals.* **c** characterized by or belonging to immediate experience of actual things or events. **2** said of a noun: naming a thing rather than a quality, state, or action. >> **concretely** *adv*, **concreteness** *noun.* [Middle English, in the sense 'coalesced', from Latin *concretus*, past part. of *concrescere* to grow together, from CON- + *crescere* to grow]

concrete[2] *noun* a hard strong building material made by mixing a cementing material and a mineral aggregate, e.g. sand and gravel, with sufficient water to cause the cement to set and bind the entire mass.

concrete[3] *verb trans* **1** to cover (something) with or set (something) in concrete. **2** /kən'kreet/ *archaic* to form (something) into a solid mass. >> *verb intrans* /kən'kreet/ to become solid.

concrete mixer *noun* = CEMENT MIXER.

concrete music *noun* = MUSIQUE CONCRÈTE.

concrete poetry *noun* poetry which uses typographical arrangement for its effect.

concretion /kən'kreesh(ə)n/ *noun* **1** a hard, usu inorganic, mass formed abnormally in a living body. **2** a mass of deposited mineral matter in rock. >> **concretionary** *adj.*

concretize or **concretise** /'kongkritiez, 'konkritiez/ *verb trans* to make (e.g. an idea) concrete, specific, or definite. >> **concretization** /-tie'zaysh(ə)n/ *noun.*

concubinage /kon'kyoobinij/ *noun* being or having a concubine.

concubine /'kongkyoobien, 'konkyoobien/ *noun* in a polygamous society, a woman who lives with a man in addition to his lawful wife or wives. [Middle English via Old French from Latin *concubina*, from CON- + *cubare* to lie]

concupiscence /kən'kyoohpis(ə)ns/ *noun* *formal* strong desire; *esp* lust. >> **concupiscent** *adj.* [Middle English via French from late Latin *concupiscentia*, from Latin *concupiscent-*, *concupiscens*, present part. of *concupiscere* to desire ardently, from CON- + *cupere* to desire]

concur /kən'kuh/ *verb intrans* (**concurred, concurring**) **1** (*often* + with) to express agreement: *She concurred with my opinion.* **2** said of events: to happen together; to coincide. [Middle English *concurren* from Latin *concurrere*, from CON- + *currere* to run]

concurrence /kən'kurəns/ *noun* **1** occurrence at the same time. **2a** agreement or union in action; cooperation. **b** agreement in opinion. **c** consent.

concurrent /kən'kurənt/ *adj* **1** operating or occurring at the same time. **2** in mathematics, said of lines: convergent; *specif* meeting at a common point. >> **concurrently** *adv.* [Middle English via French from Latin *concurrent-*, *concurrens*, present part. of *concurrere*: see CONCUR]

concuss /kən'kus/ *verb trans* to affect (somebody) with concussion. [Latin *concussus*, past part. of *concutere*: see CONCUSSION]

concussion /kən'kush(ə)n/ *noun* **1** a jarring injury to the brain, often resulting in unconsciousness, caused by a hard blow. **2** a hard blow or collision. >> **concussive** /kən'kusiv/ *adj.* [early French *concussion* from Latin *concussion-*, *concussio*, from *concutere* to shake violently, from CON- + *quatere* to shake]

condemn /kən'dem/ *verb trans* **1** to declare (a person or an action) to be utterly reprehensible, wrong, or evil, usu after considering evidence. **2a** to prescribe punishment for (somebody); *specif* to sentence (somebody) to death. **b** (*usu* + to) to cause (somebody) to suffer something unpleasant; to doom: *He was condemned to a life of solitude.* **3** to declare (something) unfit for use. >> **condemnable** /kən'demnəbl/ *adj*, **condemnation** /kondem'naysh(ə)n/ *noun*, **condemnatory** /kən'demnət(ə)ri/ *adj.* [Middle English *condemnen* via Old French from Latin *condemnare*, from CON- + *damnare*: see DAMN[1]]

condemned cell *noun* *Brit* formerly, a prison cell for people condemned to death.

condensate /kən'densayt/ *noun* a liquid product of condensation.

condensation /kondən'saysh(ə)n/ *noun* **1** droplets of water formed, e.g. on a window, when water vapour in the air cools and becomes liquid. **2** the act or process of changing from a vapour or a gas to a liquid. **3** in chemistry, a reaction that involves union between molecules to form a new chemical compound that is more complex. **4** something that has been condensed, e.g. an abridgment of a literary work.

condensation trail *noun* = VAPOUR TRAIL.

condense /kən'dens/ *verb trans* to make (something) denser or more compact; to compress. >> *verb intrans* to undergo condensation. >> **condensable** *adj.* [Middle English *condensen* via French from Latin *condensare*, from CON- + *densare* to make dense, from *densus* DENSE]

condensed milk *noun* milk thickened by evaporation and sweetened.

condenser *noun* **1a** an apparatus for condensing gas or vapour. **b** a lens or mirror used to concentrate light on an object. **2** a capacitor.

condescend /kondi'send/ *verb intrans* **1** to adopt a patronizing attitude of superiority. **2a** to descend to less formal or dignified action or speech: *She actually condescended to join us in the pub.* **b** to waive the privileges of rank: *The general condescended to eat with his subordinates.* >> **condescending** *adj*, **condescension** *noun.* [Middle English *condescenden* via French from late Latin *condescendere*, from CON- + Latin *descendere*: see DESCEND]

condign /kən'dien/ *adj* *literary* well-deserved; merited: *'Speak thou this in my praise, master?' 'In thy condign praise.'* — Shakespeare. >> **condignly** *adv.* [Middle English *condigne* via French from Latin *condignus* very worthy, from CON- + *dignus* worthy]

condiment /'kondimənt/ *noun* a flavouring for food, such as salt, pepper, or mustard. [Middle English via French from Latin *condimentum*, from *condire* to pickle, from *condere* to build, store up, from CON- + *-dere* to put]

condition[1] /kən'dish(ə)n/ *noun* **1** the state of something, e.g. with regard to appearance or fitness for use: *There had been complaints about the condition of the road.* **2a** a usu defective state of health: *a heart condition.* **b** a state of physical fitness: *out of condition.* **c** (*in pl*) attendant circumstances: *under present conditions.* **d** *archaic* social status; rank. **3** something essential to the occurrence of something else; a prerequisite: *One of the necessary conditions for producing a pure chemical acid is clean apparatus.* ✳ **on condition that** providing that. [Middle English *condicion* via French from Latin *condicion-*, *condicio* terms of agreement, condition, from *condicere* to agree, from CON- + *dicere* to say, determine]

condition[2] *verb trans* **1a** to adapt or modify the behaviour of (a person or animal) so that they act or respond in a particular way. **b** to cause (a response) to be triggered by one stimulus because of previous association with another. **2** to put (something) into a proper or desired state for work or use. **3** to give a certain condition to (something). **4** to use conditioner on (the hair). **5** to make (something) subject to or dependent on a condition.

conditional¹ *adj* **1** subject to, implying, or dependent on a condition: *Her university place was conditional on getting the required grades.* **2** in grammar, expressing a condition, often with the word 'if'. ➤➤ **conditionality** /-'naliti/ *noun,* **conditionally** *adv.*

conditional² *noun* in grammar, a conditional clause or mood.

conditional discharge *noun* a penalty involving compliance with some condition, rather than actual punishment, imposed by a court for a minor or technical offence.

conditioned *adj* **1** subject to, implying, or dependent on a condition; CONDITIONAL¹. **2** brought or put into a specified state, *esp* a high level of fitness. **3** said cap of a reflex determined or established by conditioning.

conditioner *noun* a substance applied to the hair, fabric, etc, to improve the condition.

condo /'kondoh/ *noun* (*pl* **condos**) *NAmer, informal* a condominium.

condole /kən'dohl/ *verb intrans* (+ with) to express sympathetic sorrow: *He condoled with us over the loss of our aunt.* [late Latin *condolēre,* from CON- + Latin *dolēre* to feel pain]

condolence /kən'dohləns/ *noun* **1** sympathy with somebody in sorrow. **2** (*also in pl*) an expression of sympathy.

condom /'kondəm, 'kondom/ *noun* a rubber sheath worn over the penis or in the vagina during sexual intercourse to prevent conception or sexually transmitted disease.

Word history
origin uncertain. This word is first recorded in the early 18th cent. (although the device certainly existed earlier), in the forms *condum, condon, cundum.* It has long been popularly supposed to have owed its name to a Dr or Colonel Condom, its alleged inventor, but he almost certainly did not exist. Various other origins have been proposed (e.g. from the town of *Condom* in France, from Latin *quondam* 'formerly, on occasion', or from medieval Latin *condoma* 'house, dome'), but none is generally accepted.

condominium /kondə'mini-əm/ *noun* (*pl* **condominiums**) **1** joint sovereignty by two or more nations, or a territory under joint sovereignty. **2** *NAmer.* **a** an individually owned unit in a multi-unit structure, e.g. a block of flats. **b** a block of individually owned flats. [from CON- + Latin *dominium:* see DOMAIN]

condone /kən'dohn/ *verb trans* to pardon or overlook (an offence) voluntarily; to accept (something) tacitly: *I don't condone corruption in politics.* ➤➤ **condonation** /kondə'naysh(ə)n/ *noun,* **condoner** *noun.* [Latin *condonare* to forgive, from CON- + *donare* to give]

condor /'kondaw/ *noun* a very large vulture of the high Andes with a bare head and neck: *Vultur gryphus.* [Spanish *cóndor* from Quechua *kúntur*]

condottiere /kondo'tyeəri/ *noun* (*pl* **condottieri** /-ri/) **1** a leader of a troop of mercenaries, in Italy or elsewhere in Europe, between the 14th and 16th cents. **2** a member of a condottiere's troop: *And now it shall be seen whether Spanish and Italian condottieri can hold their own on British ground against the men of Devon* — Charles Kingsley. [Italian *condottiere,* from *condotta* act of hiring, troop of mercenaries, from Latin *conducti* hired mercenaries, from *conducere:* see CONDUCE]

conduce /kən'dyoohs/ *verb intrans formal* (+ to) to lead or contribute to a particular and usu desirable result. [Middle English *conducen* to conduct, from Latin *conducere* to conduct, bring together, hire, from CON- + *ducere* to lead]

conducive /kən'dyoohsiv/ *adj* (+ to) likely to bring about a certain desirable result: *The disruptive mood of many of today's classrooms is hardly conducive to profitable study.*

conduct¹ /'kondukt/ *noun* **1** a mode or standard of personal behaviour, *esp* as based on moral principles. **2** the act, manner, or process of carrying on, organizing or directing an operation, etc; management: *the conduct of war.* [medieval Latin *conductus* escort, guide, past part. of *conducere:* see CONDUCE]

conduct² /kən'dukt/ *verb trans* **1** to guide or escort (somebody) somewhere: *He got a job conducting tourists through the museum.* **2a** to carry on or direct (an operation) from a position of command or control: *He conducted a siege.* **b** to carry out (an exercise or operation): *We're going to conduct an experiment.* **3a** to convey (water or other fluid material) in a channel, pipe, etc. **b** to act as a medium for transmitting (heat or light). **4** to behave (oneself) in a specified manner: *He conducted himself appallingly.* **5** to direct the performance or execution of (a musical work or group of musicians).

➤ *verb intrans* **1** to act as leader or director, *esp* of an orchestra. **2** to have the property of transmitting heat, sound, electricity, etc. ➤➤➤ **conductibility** /-'biliti/ *noun,* **conductible** *adj,* **conductive** /-tiv/ *adj.*

conductance /kən'dukt(ə)ns/ *noun* the ability of a material to conduct electricity.

conducti /kən'duktie/ *noun* pl of CONDUCTUS.

conduction /kən'duksh(ə)n/ *noun* **1** the transfer of heat from an area of higher temperature to one of lower temperature in a conducting medium. **2** the transmission of sound or electricity through a medium. **3** the transmission of an electrical impulse through nerve tissue. **4** the conducting or conveying, e.g. of water, through a channel, etc. **5** = CONDUCTIVITY.

conductive education /kən'duktiv/ *noun* an educational system for children with severely impaired motor coordination, in which they are encouraged repeatedly to attempt a simple action until they can perform it.

conductivity /konduk'tiviti/ *noun* (*pl* **conductivities**) the ability of a material to conduct or transmit heat or electricity, or the degree of this. Also called CONDUCTION.

conductor /kən'duktə/ *noun* **1** a person who directs the performance of an orchestra or other group of musicians. **2** a substance or body capable of transmitting electricity, heat, sound, etc. **3a** *esp* formerly, a collector of fares on a bus or tram. **b** *chiefly NAmer* a railway officer in charge of a train; = GUARD¹ (7). ➤➤ **conductorial** /konduk'tawri-əl/ *adj,* **conductorship** *noun.*

conductor rail *noun* a rail for conducting current to an electric locomotive or train.

conductress /kən'duktris/ *noun esp* formerly, a female collector of fares on a bus or tram.

conductus /kən'duktəs/ *noun* (*pl* **conducti** /-tie/) a choral work of the 12th or 13th cent., with a metrical Latin text of moral, religious, or political content set either to specially composed music, or to a secular tune, rather than based on plainsong. [Latin *conductus,* past part. of *conducere:* see CONDUCE]

conduit /'kondit, 'kondwit, 'kondyoo-it/ *noun* **1** a channel through which something, e.g. a fluid, is conveyed. **2** a pipe, tube, or tile for protecting electric wires or cables. **3** an agency of communication or transmission: *a conduit for information.* [French *conduit* pipe, channel, from medieval Latin *conductus* water pipe, past part. of Latin *conducere:* see CONDUCE]

condyle /'kondil/ *noun* a rounded prominence at the end of a bone, forming part of the joint with another bone. ➤➤ **condylar** *adj,* **condyloid** /-loyd/ *adj.* [French *condyle* via Latin from Greek *kondylos* knuckle]

condyloma /kondi'lohmə/ *noun* (*pl* **condylomas** or **condylomata** /-mətə/) a warty growth on the skin or mucous membrane, usu near the anus and genitals, resulting from syphilis or a viral infection. ➤➤ **condylomatous** /-'lomətəs, -'lohmətəs/ *adj.* [scientific Latin, from Greek *kondylōma,* from *kondylos* knuckle, knob, lump]

cone¹ /kohn/ *noun* **1a** the tapering fruit of a coniferous tree, made up of a mass of overlapping woody scales arranged on an axis and bearing seeds between them. **b** any of several similar flower or fruit clusters. **2** in solid geometry: **a** a solid generated by rotating a right-angled triangle about a side other than its hypotenuse. **b** a solid figure tapering evenly to a point from a circular base. **3** a plastic cone-shaped portable marker set up on a road surface to re-route traffic. **4** a crisp cone-shaped wafer for holding a portion of ice cream. **5** the apex of a volcano. **6** any of the relatively short light-receptors in the retina of vertebrates that are sensitive to bright light and function in colour vision: compare ROD (5). **7** a conical gastropod mollusc related to snails, whelks, and limpets: genus *Conus.* [French *cône* via Latin from Greek *kōnos* pine cone, geometrical cone]

cone² *verb trans* **1** to bevel (something) like the slanting surface of a cone. **2** *Brit* (+ off) to close (part of a road, *esp* a lane or carriageway of a motorway) with a line of traffic cones.

coney /'kohni/ *noun* = CONY (1), (2).

confab¹ /'konfab/ *noun informal* a chat or discussion. [short for *confabulation*]

confab² *verb intrans* (**confabbed, confabbing**) *informal* to have a chat or discussion.

confabulate /kən'fabyoolayt/ *verb intrans formal* **1** to chat. **2** to hold a discussion. ➤➤ **confabulation** /-'laysh(ə)n/ *noun,*

confabulatory /-lət(ə)ri/ *adj.* [Latin *confabulatus*, past part. of *confabulari*, from COM- + *fabulari* to talk, from *fabula* story]

confect /kən'fekt/ *verb trans* to put together or prepare (an elaborate dish, artistic work, etc) from assorted ingredients or materials: *She was at work confecting another best-seller.* [Latin *confectus*, past part. of *conficere* to prepare, put together, from CON- + *facere* to make]

confection /kən'feksh(ə)n/ *noun* **1** an elaborately prepared item of sweet food, e.g. a cake or dessert. **2** an elaborately contrived article of dress, e.g. a woman's hat. **3** the process of assembling, composing, or confecting something. [Latin *confection-, confectio* preparation, from *conficere*: see CONFECT]

confectioner *noun* a manufacturer of or dealer in confectionery.

confectioner's custard *noun* a thick sweet custard used as a filling in pastries, etc.

confectioner's sugar *noun NAmer* = ICING SUGAR.

confectionery *noun* (*pl* **confectioneries**) **1** sweets, chocolate, cakes, and biscuits. **2** the confectioner's art or business. **3** a confectioner's shop.

confederacy /kən'fed(ə)rəsi/ *noun* (*pl* **confederacies**) **1** a league or compact for mutual support or common action; an alliance of independent states. **2** an unlawful association; a conspiracy. **3a** a league or alliance for common action. **b** (**the Confederacy**) the eleven southern states that withdrew from the USA in 1860 and 1861. >> **confederal** *adj.*

confederate[1] /kən'fed(ə)rət/ *adj* **1** united in a league; allied. **2** (**Confederate**) belonging or relating to the Confederacy. [late Latin *confoederatus*, past part. of *confoederare* to unite by a league, from CON- + Latin *foeder-, foedus* compact]

confederate[2] *noun* **1** an ally or accomplice: *He will fall upon us with his confederates and slay us all* — Edgar Rice Burroughs. **2** (**Confederate**) an adherent of the Confederacy.

confederate[3] /kən'fedərayt/ *verb trans* to unite (states, bodies, etc) in a confederacy. > *verb intrans* to band together to form a confederacy.

confederation /kən,fedə'raysh(ə)n/ *noun* **1** a league or alliance. **2** a union of self-governing states under the minimal control of a central authority. **3** the act of forming such a union or league.

confer /kən'fuh/ *verb* (**conferred, conferring**) > *verb trans* (*often* + on) to bestow (an honour, award, or title) on somebody: *An honorary doctorate had been conferred on him by Edinburgh University.* > *verb intrans* (*often* + with) to come together to compare views or take counsel; to consult: *You may confer with your team.* >> **conferrable** *adj,* **conferral** *noun,* **conferrer** *noun.* [Latin *conferre* to bring together, from CON- + *ferre* to carry]

conferee or **conferree** /konfuh'ree/ *noun* **1** a person on whom an award, etc is conferred. **2** a person who is conferred with on some matter. **3** any of the participants or delegates attending a conference.

conference /'konf(ə)rəns/ *noun* **1a** a usu formal interchange of views; a consultation. **b** a discussion held between people linked by telephone or computer. **2** a meeting of people, e.g. members of a certain profession, for the discussion of matters of common concern, typically lasting several days and including the presentation of papers. **3** a representative assembly or administrative organization of a denomination, organization, association, etc. * **in conference** taking part in a meeting. >> **conferential** /konfə'rensh(ə)l/ *adj.*

conference call *noun* a telephone discussion between three or more people whose telephones lines have been temporarily linked for the purpose.

Conference pear *noun* a sweet firm-fleshed variety of pear. [apparently named after the 1885 National Pear Conference; the pear was first exhibited in that year]

conferencing *noun* group discussion between people linked by telephone, by telephone and video equipment, or by computer.

conferree /konfuh'ree/ *noun* see CONFEREE.

confess /kən'fes/ *verb trans* **1a** to make known or admit (wrongdoing, etc on one's part). **b** to acknowledge (a fact), *esp* reluctantly: *I must confess that I am still in the dark* — Conan Doyle. **2a** to acknowledge (sin) to God or a priest. **b** said of a priest: to receive the confession of (a penitent). > *verb intrans* **1a** to acknowledge one's sins or the state of one's conscience to God or a priest. **b** said of a priest: to hear a confession. **2** to admit something: *Come,*

confess, and be an honest girl for once — Henry Fielding. >> **confessable** *adj.* [French *confesser* from Latin *confessus*, past part. of *confitēri* to confess, from CON- + *fatēri* to confess]

confessant *noun* in the Roman Catholic Church, a person who attends confession and confesses to a priest.

confessedly /kən'fesidli/ *adv* by confession; admittedly.

confession /kən'fesh(ə)n/ *noun* **1a** an acknowledgement of a fault, etc: *Valentin de Bellegarde was, by his own confession, at all times a great chatterer* — Henry James. **b** (*in pl*) revelations of a private nature about one's life: *Confessions of an English Opium Eater* — de Quincey. **2** a formal or written acknowledgment of guilt by a person accused of an offence. **3** in the Roman Catholic Church, a disclosure of one's sins in confidence to a priest, or the procedure of attending a church for this purpose. **4** a formal statement of religious beliefs: *a confession of faith.* **5** (*also* **Confession**) an organized religious body having a common creed. * **hear confession** said of a priest: to listen in private to somebody's confession of sin and give them absolution. >> **confessional** *adj,* **confessionalism** *noun,* **confessionalist** *noun,* **confessionally** *adv,* **confessionary** *adj.*

confessional *noun* **1** the enclosed cubicle in a church where a priest hears confessions, divided by a screen from the person making confession. **2** the practice of confessing to a priest.

confessor *noun* **1** in the Roman Catholic Church: **a** a priest who hears confessions and gives absolution. **b** a priest who acts as one's regular spiritual adviser: *His wife was accustomed, in all grave matters, to seek the counsel and ministry of her confessor Fray Simon* — Washington Irving. **c** a person who witnesses heroically to the Christian faith but does not suffer actual martyrdom. **2** a person who makes a confession.

confetti /kən'feti/ *noun* (*treated as sing.*) small bits of coloured paper for throwing at celebrations, *esp* weddings. [Italian *confetti*, pl of *confetto* a sweet, from Latin *confectum* something prepared, neuter past part. of *conficere*: see CONFECT; from the Italian practice of throwing sweets, real or imitation, at carnivals]

confidant *or* **confidante** /'konfidant, -'dant/ *noun* a male or female friend to whom one entrusts one's secrets; an intimate. [French *confident* (fem *confidente*) a confidant, via Italian from Latin *confident-, confidens*, past part. of *confidere*: see CONFIDE]

Usage note

confidant(e) or **confident?** A *confidant* is a person to whom one entrusts one's secrets. It is spelt *confidante* when the person in question is a woman or girl. *Confident* is the adjective meaning 'assured, certain': *We know we're facing tough opposition, but we're confident we can win.*

confide /kən'fied/ *verb intrans* (+ in) to impart one's secrets and other private matters to somebody: *I had nobody to confide in.* > *verb trans* **1** to tell (something) confidentially: *She once confided to me that she disliked both her children.* **2** *dated* to entrust (something) to somebody's care: *The power confided in me will be used to hold, occupy, and possess the property and places belonging to the government* — Abraham Lincoln. >> **confider** *noun.* [Latin *confidere* to entrust utterly, from CON- + *fidere* to trust]

confidence /'konfid(ə)ns/ *noun* **1** a consciousness of one's powers being sufficient, or a feeling of reliance on one's circumstances; self-assurance. **2** faith or trust in something or somebody: *As a mark of our confidence in you, we are promoting you to manager.* **3** certainty or strong expectation: *They had every confidence of success.* **4** reliance on the discretion of one's hearers: *She told me her story in strictest confidence.* **5** something said or written in confidence; a secret. * **in somebody's confidence** on intimate enough terms with somebody for them to tell one their private concerns. **take somebody into one's confidence** to tell somebody something in private. [Latin *confidentia* from *confidere*: see CONFIDE]

confidence game *noun NAmer* = CONFIDENCE TRICK.

confidence interval *noun* a set of values within which there is a specified probability, e.g. 95%, of including the true value of a statistical mean, average, variance, etc.

confidence man *noun dated* the full form of CONMAN.

confidence trick *noun* a swindle performed *esp* by somebody pretending to be something they are not. >> **confidence trickster** *noun.*

confident /'konfid(ə)nt/ *adj* **1** characterized by assurance; self-reliant. **2** (*also* + of) full of conviction; certain: *confident of success.* >> **confidently** *adv.* [Latin *confident-, confidens*, present part. of *confidere*: see CONFIDE]

Usage note
confident or confidant(e)? See note at CONFIDANT.

confidential /konfi'densh(ə)l/ *adj* 1 said of information: intended to be kept secret. 2 characterized by intimacy or willingness to confide. 3 said of a secretary or assistant: entrusted with private or confidential information. ➤➤ **confidentiality** /-shi'aliti/ *noun*, **confidentially** *adv*, **confidentialness** *noun*.

confiding *adj* tending to confide; trustful: *I'm a very confiding soul by nature* — Jean Webster. ➤➤ **confidingly** *adv*, **confidingness** *noun*.

configuration /kən,figyoo'raysh(ə)n, kən,figə-/ *noun* 1a an arrangement of parts, *esp* as relative one to another. b the figure, contour, pattern, workings, etc, produced by such an arrangement. 2 the process of configuring a computer program or system, or the resulting set-up. 3 the relative positions in space of the atoms in a chemical compound. 4 a set of separate psychological features functioning as a unit; = GESTALT. ➤➤ **configurational** *adj*, **configurationally** *adv*, **configurative** /kən'figyoorətiv, kən'figə-/ *adj*.

configure /kən'figə/ *verb trans* 1 to give (a thing or things) a certain shape, pattern or configuration. 2 to set up (a computer system along with its peripherals, or a computer program) to operate according to a certain pattern or sequence. ➤➤ **configurable** *adj*. [from Latin *configurare* to shape according to a pattern, from CON- + *figura* shape, figure]

confine /kən'fien/ *verb trans* 1 (*often* + to) to restrict or keep (somebody or something) within certain limits: *I had to confine myself to a brief summary; Please confine your questions to matters that are directly relevant*. 2 to shut (somebody) up: *He had been confined to barracks for insubordination*. 3 (+ to) said of an illness, etc: to keep (somebody) in bed, a wheelchair, etc: *He was confined to bed with gout*. 4 *dated* to keep (a woman) indoors or in bed immediately before, during, and just after childbirth. ➤➤ **confiner** *noun*. [French *confiner* to confine, from Latin *confinis*: see CONFINES]

confinement /kən'fienmənt/ *noun* 1 the act of confining or the state of being confined. 2 *dated* the period immediately before, during, and just after, childbirth.

confines /'konfienz/ *pl noun* limits or boundaries: *An achievement of this nature ... was not ... to a bold spirit, beyond the confines of the possible* — Edgar Allan Poe; *We had to keep within the confines of the school grounds*. [French *confins* (pl), ultimately from Latin *confinis* bordering, from CON- + *finis* end, limit]

confirm /kən'fuhm/ *verb trans* 1 to establish or give official notice of the correctness of (a report, suspicion, fear, etc). 2 (+ in) to vindicate or strengthen (somebody) in a belief, etc: *We were soon confirmed in our suspicions of foul play*. 3 to be evidence of or prove (something). 4 to commit oneself definitely to (a booking, arrangement, etc). 5 to administer the rite of confirmation to (a candidate). ➤➤ **confirmability** /-'biliti/ *noun*, **confirmable** *adj*, **confirmative** /-tiv/ *adj*, **confirmatory** /-mət(ə)ri/ *adj*. [French *confirmer* to confirm, from Latin *confirmare* to strengthen, confirm, from CON- + *firmare* to make firm, from *firmus* FIRM[1]]

confirmand /'konfəmand/ *noun* a person who is a candidate for the religious ceremony of confirmation. [Latin *confirmandus*, verbal noun from *confirmare*: see CONFIRM]

confirmation /konfə'maysh(ə)n/ *noun* 1 confirming proof; corroboration. 2 the confirming of a booking, arrangement, etc. 3 a religious ceremony admitting a person to full membership of a Christian church. ➤➤ **confirmational** *adj*.

confirmed *adj* 1 being so fixed in habit or attitude as to be unlikely to change: *a confirmed bachelor*. 2 having been admitted to full membership of a Christian church through the religious ceremony of confirmation. ➤➤ **confirmedly** /-midli/ *adv*, **confirmedness** /-m(i)dnis/ *noun*.

confiscable /kən'fiskəbl, kon-/ *adj* liable to confiscation.

confiscate /'konfiskayt/ *verb trans* 1 to seize (somebody's property) by authority. 2 to appropriate (somebody's land) and add it to the public treasury as a penalty. ➤➤ **confiscation** /-'skaysh(ə)n/ *noun*, **confiscator** *noun*, **confiscatory** /kən'fiskət(ə)ri/ *adj*. [Latin *confiscatus*, past part. of *confiscare*, from CON- + *fiscus* treasury]

confit /'konfi/ *noun* a dish of meat, typically duck or goose, cooked slowly in its own fat. [French *confit*, past part. of *confire* to prepare, preserve, from Latin *conficere*: see CONFECT]

confiteor /kon'fitiaw/ *noun* a liturgical form of confession of sins used *esp* in the Roman Catholic Church. [Latin *confiteor* I confess, from *confitēri*: see CONFESS]

conflab[1] /'konflab/ *noun informal* = CONFAB[1]. [humorous alteration]

conflab[2] *verb intrans* (**conflabbed, conflabbing**) *informal* = CONFAB[2].

conflagration /konflə'graysh(ə)n/ *noun* a fire, *esp* a large and disastrous one. [Latin *conflagration-, conflagratio*, from *conflagrare* to burn, from CON- + *flagrare* to burn]

conflate /kən'flayt/ *verb trans* to combine or fuse (two or more things, ideas, texts, stories, etc) into one: *Two of the characters in the original novel have been conflated in the film*. ➤➤ **conflation** /-sh(ə)n/ *noun*. [Latin *conflatus*, past part. of *conflare* to blow together, fuse, from CON- + *flare* to blow]

conflict[1] /'konflikt/ *noun* 1 a sharp disagreement or clash: *my conflict with and victory over Mrs Reed* — Charlotte Brontë. 2 mental struggle resulting from incompatible impulses: *There is no conflict of opposite feelings in his breast* — Hazlitt. 3 a hostile encounter, e.g. a fight, battle, or war. [Latin *conflictus* act of striking together, contest, from *confligere* to strike together, from CON- + *fligere* to strike]

conflict[2] /kən'flikt/ *verb intrans* to be incompatible or in opposition to each other; to clash. ➤➤ **conflicted** *adj*, **confliction** *noun*.

conflicting /kən'flikting/ *adj* being in conflict or opposition; incompatible: *conflicting reports*. ➤➤ **conflictingly** *adv*.

confluence /'konfloo-əns/ *noun* 1 a coming or flowing together; a meeting or gathering at one point. 2 the union of two or more streams, or the place where this occurs. ➤➤ **confluent** *adj*. [Latin *confluent-, confluens*, present part. of *confluere* to flow together, from CON- + *fluere* to flow]

conflux /'konfluks/ *noun* = CONFLUENCE. [medieval Latin *confluxus*, past part. of Latin *confluere*: see CONFLUENCE]

confocal /kon'fohkl/ *adj* having a common focus or common foci. ➤➤ **confocally** *adv*.

conform /kən'fawm/ *verb intrans* 1 to be obedient or compliant; *esp* to adapt oneself to prevailing standards or customs: *She refuses to conform*. 2 (+ to/with) to accord with a certain standard or pattern: *All our equipment conforms to official safety standards*. ➤➤ **conformer** *noun*. [French *conformer* from Latin *conformare*, from CON- + *formare* to form, from *forma* FORM[1]]

conformable *adj* 1 (+ to) consistent with, or corresponding to (a certain mood, type, standard, etc). 2 said of geological strata: following in unbroken sequence and stratified at the same angle. ➤➤ **conformability** /-'biliti/ *noun*, **conformably** *adv*.

conformal *adj* said of a transformation: leaving the size of the angle between corresponding curves unchanged; *esp* denoting a map that represents small areas in their true shape. ➤➤ **conformally** *adv*. [late Latin *conformalis* having the same shape, from CON- + Latin *forma* shape, FORM[1]]

conformance *noun* = CONFORMITY.

conformation /konfə'maysh(ə)n/ *noun* 1 the way in which something is formed; shape, structure. 2 the arrangement of the parts of something, or the points within something, *esp* with relation to each other; = CONFIGURATION (1). 3 any three-dimensional arrangement that atoms in a molecule may adopt, *esp* by rotation about individual bonds (groups of atoms held together). ➤➤ **conformational** *adj*.

conformist *noun* 1 a person who conforms to the orthodox view or accepted social practice. 2 formerly, a person who conformed to the practices of an established Church, *esp* the Church of England. ➤➤ **conformist** *adj*.

conformity /kən'fawmiti/ *noun* 1 (+ with) correspondence or accordance with a certain model or standard: *Alterations are needed to bring everything into conformity with required standards*. 2 (+ to) behaviour that is in compliance with a convention or specified requirements: *Conformity to the party line was not her strong point*. 3 similarity in form. 4 formerly, compliance with the practices of an established Church, *esp* the Church of England.

confound[1] /kən'fownd/ *verb trans* 1 to surprise or disconcert (somebody). 2 to prove (an argument, prediction, etc) wrong. 3 to defeat or overthrow (somebody or their plans). 4 (*usu in passive, often* + with) to confuse (things) or confuse (one thing) with another: *confusion worse confounded* — Milton. [Latin *confundere* to pour together, muddle, disorder, from CON- + *fundere* to pour]

confound[2] *interj dated* a mild interjection of annoyance: *Confound it! Where's my pen?*

confounded *adj dated* used to express annoyance: damned: *I don't understand your confounded scientific nomenclature* — Henry James. ➤➤ **confoundedly** *adv.*

confraternity /konfrə'tuhniti/ *noun* (*pl* **confraternities**) a brotherhood devoted to a religious or charitable cause. [medieval Latin *confraternitat-, confraternitas* brotherhood, from CON- + *frater* brother]

confrère /'konfreə/ *noun* a colleague or a fellow member of one's profession, association, etc: *Several times she turned her head toward one or other of her confrères and smiled her appreciation* — Jack London. [French *confrère* from medieval Latin *confrater* colleague, fellow, brother, from CON- + *frater* brother; re-adopted into English after becoming obsolete in the 17th cent.]

confront /kən'frunt/ *verb trans* **1** said of a problem, etc: to lie before (somebody): *the difficulties that confront us.* **2** to have (something) before one to face or tackle: *just some of the problems that we confront every day.* **3** to face up to (a problem or an opponent) and prepare to tackle them: *They confronted each other across the table.* **4** to present (somebody) with irrefutable and unwelcome facts, etc. [French *confronter* to border on, confront, from Latin *confrontare* to bound, from CON- + *front-, frons* forehead]

confrontation /konfrən'taysh(ə)n/ *noun* **1** a face-to-face meeting or debate. **2** the clashing of forces or ideas; a conflict: *sit-ins, confrontations and riot* — Power & Authority in British Universities. ➤➤ **confrontational** *adj,* **confrontationism** *noun,* **confrontationist** *noun.*

Confucian /kən'fyoohsh(ə)n/ *noun* a follower of Confucius. ➤➤ **Confucian** *adj.* [named after *Confucius* d.479 BC, Chinese philosopher]

Confucianism /kən'fyoohsh(ə)niz(ə)m/ *noun* a system of social and moral teachings founded by the Chinese philosopher Confucius, emphasizing harmonious behaviour, human sympathy, and filial piety. ➤➤ **Confucianist** *noun and adj.*

confuse /kən'fyoohz/ *verb trans* **1** to bewilder or perplex (somebody). **2** *archaic* to embarrass or abash (somebody). **3** to muddle or befuddle (a person or their mind, etc): *He had not drunk enough wine to confuse his wits.* **4** to make (something) more incomprehensible: *Don't try to explain; you'll just confuse the issue.* **5** (*often* + with) to muddle (two or more usu similar things) or mistake (one thing) for another: *I often confuse the twins; People confuse 'mitigate' with 'militate'.* [back-formation from CONFUSED]

confused *adj* **1** unable to sort out one's thoughts or emotions; bewildered. **2** muddled in one's mind, usu because of old age. **3** *archaic* embarrassed: *Instead of answering, Harriet turned away confused* — Jane Austen. **4** disorganized or muddled: *a confused and disjointed account.* **5** composed of a bewildering mixture of elements: *a confused din.* ➤➤ **confusedly** /-zidli/ *adv.* [French *confus* from Latin *confusus,* past part. of *confundere*: see CONFOUND[1]]

confusing *adj* tending to cause mental confusion or bewilderment. ➤➤ **confusingly** *adv.*

confusion /kən'fyoohzh(ə)n/ *noun* **1** uncertainty or perplexity: *There is a certain amount of confusion over the new labelling system.* **2** a muddled or bewildered mental state: *The old man is showing signs of confusion and disorientation.* **3** a state of disorder or muddle: *The lights failed and in the confusion I mislaid my briefcase.* **4** a jumble: *She stared blankly at the confusion of papers on the desk.* **5** the muddling of two things, or the mistaking of one thing for another. **6** embarrassment: *He turned away to hide his confusion.*

confute /kən'fyooht/ *verb trans* **1** to defeat (somebody) thoroughly in argument: *Very fond we were of argument and very desirous of confuting one another* — Benjamin Franklin. **2** to refute (an argument) conclusively. ➤➤ **confutation** /konfyooh'taysh(ə)n/ *noun.* [Latin *confutare,* from CON- + *-futare* to beat]

conga /'konggə/ *noun* **1** a dance involving three steps followed by a kick, performed by a group, usu in single file. **2** a tall narrow bass drum beaten with the hands. [American Spanish *conga* from Spanish, fem of *congo* of the *Congo,* region in Africa]

congé /'konzhay/ *noun* **1** formal permission to depart. **2a** a farewell or leave-taking: *make one's congé.* **b** a farewell salutation or bow. **3** *humorous* an unceremonious dismissal: *give somebody their congé.* [French *congé* from Latin *commeatus* going back and forth, leave to go, past part. of *commeare* to go back and forth]

congeal /kən'jeel/ *verb intrans* **1** to pass from a fluid to a solid state in the process of cooking or freezing; to coagulate. **2** to become rigid, inflexible, or immobile. ➤ *verb trans* to cause (something) to

congeal. ➤➤ **congealable** *adj,* **congealment** *noun,* **congelation** *noun.* [French *congeler* from Latin *congelare,* from CON- + *gelare* to freeze]

congener /kən'jeenə/ *noun* **1** a member of the same taxonomic genus as another plant or animal. **2** somebody or something resembling another in nature or action. **3** a secondary product, e.g. an aldehyde or ester, retained in an alcoholic beverage, an important factor in determining its flavour and in causing hangovers. ➤➤ **congeneric** /konjə'nerik/ *adj,* **congenerous** /kən'jenərəs/ *adj.* [Latin *congener* of the same kind, from CON- + *gener-, genus* kind]

congenial /kən'jeeni·əl/ *adj* **1** pleasant; *esp* agreeably suited to one's nature, tastes, or outlook. **2** (*often* + with) suited to or fitting in well with something: *For every one who feels inclined; some post we undertake to find; congenial with his frame of mind* — W S Gilbert. ➤➤ **congeniality** /-'aliti/ *noun,* **congenially** *adv.* [CON- + Latin *genialis* pleasant, from *genius* task, inclination]

congenital /kən'jenitl/ *adj* **1** said of a disease or abnormality: existing at or dating from birth. **2** *informal* having an ingrained tendency to be a certain thing: *He's a congenital liar.* ➤➤ **congenitally** *adv.* [Latin *congenitus,* from CON- + *genitus,* past part. of *gignere* to beget]

conger /'konggə/ *noun* any of several species of large edible sea eels: genus *Conger* and other genera. [Middle English *congre* via Old French from Latin *congr-, conger,* from Greek *gongros*]

conger eel *noun* = CONGER.

congeries /'konjəreez; kən'jiəreez/ *noun* (*pl* **congeries**) an accumulation or aggregation: *The upper part of Durnover was mainly composed of a curious congeries of barns and farmsteads* — Hardy. [Latin *congeries* heap, pile, from *congerere* to bring together, accumulate, from CON- + *gerere* to bear]

congested *adj* **1** overcrowded, e.g. with people or traffic. **2** said of the lungs or respiratory system: filled with mucus, so as to make breathing difficult. **3** said of other parts of the body: over-full of blood. ➤➤ **congestion** *noun,* **congestive** *adj.*

congestion charging *noun* the imposition of a charge on motorists who drive into a city or the centre of a city. ➤➤ **congestion charge** *noun.*

congius /'konji·əs/ *noun* (*pl* **congii** /'konji·ie/) **1** a liquid pharmaceutical measure equal to one imperial gallon. **2** an ancient Roman liquid measure roughly equal to 0.7 of an imperial gallon. [Latin *congius,* alteration of Greek *konchion,* dimin. of *konchē* cockle, mussel]

conglobate /'kong·glohbayt, kong'globayt/ *verb trans* to form (something) into a round compact mass. ➤➤ **conglobate** *adj,* **conglobation** /-'baysh(ə)n/ *noun.* [Latin *conglobatus,* past part. of *conglobare* to press into a ball or mass, from CON- + *globus* GLOBE[1]]

conglobulate /kon'globyoolayt/ *verb intrans* to join together into a crowd or mass: *Swallows … conglobulate together, by flying round and round* — Dr Johnson. [Latin *globulus* (see GLOBULE), on the model of CONGLOBATE]

conglomerate[1] /kən'glomərayt/ *verb intrans* to gather into a mass; to accumulate: *Numbers of dull people conglomerated round her* — Virginia Woolf. ➤➤ **conglomeration** /-'raysh(ə)n/ *noun,* **conglomerative** /-rətiv/ *adj.*

conglomerate[2] /kən'glomərət/ *noun* **1** a composite mixture; *specif* a type of rock composed of variously-sized rounded fragments in a cement-like bed. **2** a widely diversified business company formed through successive acquisitions of other firms. ➤➤ **conglomerate** *adj,* **conglomeratic** /-'ratik/ *adj.*

Congolese /'kong·gəleez, -'leez/ *noun* (*pl* **Congolese**) **1** a native or inhabitant of the Congo, or the Democratic Republic of Congo, formerly Zaïre. **2** any of the Bantu languages spoken in the Congo area. ➤➤ **Congolese** *adj.*

congrats /kən'grats/ *pl noun and interj informal* congratulations.

congratulate /kən'gratyoolayt/ *verb trans* (+ on) to express one's pleasure to (somebody) at their success or good fortune: *He congratulated her on her promotion.* ➤➤ **congratulation** /-'laysh(ə)n/ *noun,* **congratulator** *noun,* **congratulatory** /-lət(ə)ri/ *adj.* [Latin *congratulatus,* past part. of *congratulari* to wish joy, from CON- + *gratulari* to show joy, from *gratus* pleasing]

congratulations /kən,gratyoo'laysh(ə)nz/ *pl noun and interj* (*also* + on) an expression of pleasure at somebody's success or good fortune: *Congratulations on winning!*

congregant /'konggrigənt/ *noun* a member of a congregation.

congregate /'konggrigayt/ *verb intrans* to gather together: *People began to congregate in the square.* ⟩ *verb trans* (*usu in passive*) to assemble (people or things) together. [Latin *congregatus*, past part. of *congregare*, from CON- + *greg-, grex* flock]

congregation /konggri'gaysh(ə)n/ *noun* 1 an assembly of people, *esp* gathered in a church, etc, for religious worship. 2 a religious community; *esp* an organized body of believers in a particular locality. ⟩⟩ **congregational** *adj.*

Congregationalism /kong-gri'gaysh(ə)nlizm/ *noun* a Protestant denomination in which each church is governed by the assembly of the local congregation. ⟩⟩ **Congregationalist** *noun and adj.*

congress /'konggres, 'konggris/ *noun* 1 a formal meeting or programme of meetings between delegates for discussion and usu action on some question. 2a the supreme legislative body of a nation. b (**Congress**) the supreme legislative body of the USA. 3 an association, usu made up of delegates from constituent organizations. 4 *formal* the act or action of coming together and meeting. ⟩⟩ **congressional** /kən'gresh(ə)nl/ *adj,* **congressionally** *adv.* [Latin *congressus,* past part. of *congredi* to come together, from CON- + *gradi* to go]

congressman *or* **congresswoman** *noun* (*pl* **congressmen** *or* **congresswomen**) a member of a congress.

congruent /'konggrooənt/ *adj* 1 = CONGRUOUS. 2 geometrically identical; equal in size and shape: *congruent triangles.* ⟩⟩ **congruence** *noun,* **congruency** /-si/ *noun,* **congruently** *adv.* [Latin *congruent-, congruens,* present part of *congruere*]

congruous /'konggrooəs/ *adj* 1 (+ with) in agreement, harmony, or accordance with something: *carrying a certain air of distinction congruous with good family* — T S Eliot. 2 *formal* conforming to the circumstances or requirements of a situation; appropriate: *a congruous room to work in* — George Bernard Shaw. ⟩⟩ **congruity** /kən'grooh-iti/ *noun,* **congruously** *adv,* **congruousness** *noun.* [Latin *congruus* harmonious, concordant, from *congruere* to run together, coincide, agree, from CON- + *ruere* to fall, rush]

coni /'kohnie/ *noun* pl of CONUS.

conic[1] /'konik/ *adj* 1 relating to cones. 2 having the shape of a cone; = CONICAL. [Latin *conicus* from Greek *kōnikos,* from *kōnos* CONE[1]]

conic[2] *noun* = CONIC SECTION.

conical /'konikl/ *adj* 1 having the shape of a cone. 2 relating to cones. ⟩⟩ **conically** *adv.*

conical projection *noun* = CONIC PROJECTION.

conic projection *noun* a map projection of the earth's surface appearing as it would if projected onto the inside surface of a cone surrounding the globe, the cone being then unrolled and laid flat. This projection is useful for sections of the globe only, since the distortion over a small area is almost negligible.

conics *pl noun* (*treated as sing. or pl*) the geometry of the cone and its sections, that is, the circle, ELLIPSE, PARABOLA, and HYPERBOLA (open curves).

conic section *noun* any of the closed or open curves produced by the intersection of a plane with a cone, that is, the circle, ELLIPSE, PARABOLA, or HYPERBOLA.

conidia /koh'nidi-ə/ *noun* pl of CONIDIUM.

conidiophore /koh'nidi-əfaw/ *noun* a specialized HYPHA (filament of a fungus) that bears conidia (spores; see CONIDIUM). ⟩⟩ **conidiophorous** /-'of(ə)rəs/ *adj.* [scientific Latin *conidium* (from Greek *konis* dust) + -PHORE]

conidium /koh'nidi-əm/ *noun* (*pl* **conidia** /-di-ə/) an asexual spore, e.g. of a fungus or bacterium. ⟩⟩ **conidial** *adj.* [scientific Latin *conidium* from Greek *konis* dust]

conifer /'konifə, 'koh-/ *noun* any of an order of trees and shrubs, e.g. the pine, cypress, and yew, that bear ovules naked on the surface of scales, e.g. in cones, rather than enclosed in an ovary: order Coniferales. ⟩⟩ **coniferous** /kə'nif(ə)rəs/ *adj.* [Latin *conifer* cone-bearing, from *conus* cone (from Greek *kōnos*) + -FER]

coniform /'kohnifawm/ *adj* having the shape of a cone; = CONICAL.

coniine /'kohni-een, -in, 'kohneen/ *noun* an alkaloid that is the principal poison in hemlock. [German *Koniin* via late Latin *conium* from Greek *kōneion* hemlock]

conj. *abbr* 1 conjugation. 2 conjunction.

conjectural /kən'jekch(ə)rəl/ *adj* 1 of the nature of, involving, or based on conjecture. 2 existing only in conjecture: *notional and conjectural essences* — Charles Lamb. ⟩⟩ **conjecturally** *adv.*

conjecture[1] /kən'jekchə/ *noun* 1 the drawing of conclusions from incomplete evidence. 2 a conclusion reached by surmise or guesswork. 3 in textual criticism, a suggested reading. [Latin *conjectura,* from *conjectus,* past part. of *conicere* to throw or put together, from CON- + *jacere* to throw]

conjecture[2] *verb trans* 1 to guess (something): *I conjectured that he would head for Dover.* 2 to suggest (a certain reading) in a disputed text. ⟩ *verb intrans* to form conjectures. ⟩⟩ **conjecturer** *noun.*

conjoin /kən'joyn/ *verb trans formal* to join (people or things) together. ⟩ *verb intrans formal* to unite or combine: *Now let Richmond and Elizabeth, the true succeeders of each royal house ... conjoin together!* — Shakespeare. [French *conjoindre* from Latin *conjungere* to join together, unite in marriage, from CON- + *jungere* to JOIN[1]]

conjoint /kən'joynt/ *adj* involving two or more in combination; joint, united. ⟩⟩ **conjointly** *adv.*

conjugal /'konjoogl/ *adj* relating to the married state or married people and their relationship. ⟩⟩ **conjugality** /-'galiti/ *noun,* **conjugally** *adv.* [Latin *conjugalis,* from *conjug-, conjux* husband, wife, from *conjungere*: see CONJOIN]

conjugal rights *pl noun* the rights implied by and involved in the marriage relationship, *esp* the right of sexual intercourse between husband and wife.

conjugant /'konjoogənt/ *noun* either of a pair of conjugating gametes (reproductive cells; see GAMETE) or organisms.

conjugate[1] /'konjoogayt/ *verb trans* 1 to give in prescribed order the various inflectional forms of (a verb). 2 to join or combine (two substances), *esp* reversibly. ⟩ *verb intrans* 1 to become joined together. 2 said of reproductive cells: to pair and fuse in genetic conjugation. 3 said of a verb: to inflect. [Latin *conjugatus,* past part. of *conjugare* to unite, from CON- + *jugare* to join, from *jugum* yoke]

conjugate[2] /'konjoogət/ *adj* 1 joined together, *esp* in pairs; coupled. 2 acting or operating as if joined. 3 having features in common but opposite or inverse in some particular, e.g. having an opposite sign or lying on the opposite side of an axis: *conjugate roots; conjugate focuses.* 4 (*often* + to) denoting an acid or base related by the difference of a proton. 5 said of words: derived from the same root and therefore usu alike in meaning. ⟩⟩ **conjugacy** /-si/ *noun,* **conjugately** *adv,* **conjugateness** *noun.*

conjugate[3] /'konjoogət/ *noun* 1 something conjugate; a product of conjugating. 2 an element of a mathematical group that is equal to a given element of the group multiplied on the right by another element and on the left by the inverse of the latter element.

conjugated /'konjoogaytid/ *adj* formed by the combination of two compounds or combined with another compound: *a conjugated protein.*

conjugation /konjoo'gaysh(ə)n/ *noun* 1a inflection of a verb for number, person, tense, voice, and mood. b the inflectional forms of a verb, *esp* in a tabular arrangement. c a class of verbs having the same type of inflectional forms. 2 the fusion of gametes (reproductive cells; see GAMETE), *esp* of similar size, with union of their nuclei that in algae, fungi, etc replaces the typical fertilization of higher forms. 3 the one-way transfer of DNA between bacteria in cellular contact. 4 the pairing of corresponding chromosomes during the early stage of MEIOSIS (cell division). 5 the combination, *esp* if reversible, of two substances. ⟩⟩ **conjugational** *adj,* **conjugationally** *adv,* **conjugative** /-gaytiv/ *adj.*

conjunct[1] /kən'jungkt/ *adj* joint or united. [Latin *conjunctus,* past part. of *conjungere*: see CONJOIN]

conjunct[2] /'konjungkt/ *noun* 1 each of two or more combined or associated things. 2 in logic, any of the components of a CONJUNCTION (syllogism). 3 in grammar, an adverb such as *therefore* or *however,* that connects sentences, etc.

conjunction /kən'jungksh(ə)n/ *noun* 1 in grammar, a word such as *and, or, but, if,* or *when,* that joins together sentences, clauses, phrases, or words. 2 the process of joining, or state of being joined. 3 in astrology: a the apparent meeting or passing of two or more planets, stars, or other celestial bodies in the same part of the sky. b a configuration in which two celestial bodies have their least apparent separation. 4 in logic, a SYLLOGISM (compound statement of the type *All As are Bs; Cs are As; therefore Cs are Bs*) that is true if and only if each of its components is true. 5 occurrence together in time or space; concurrence: *Could you possibly wish for a more favorable conjunction of circumstances?* — Thomas Paine. ✱ **in conjunction with** combined with (something). ➤➤ **conjunctional** *adj*, **conjunctionally** *adv*.

conjunctiva /kənˈjungktivə, konjungkˈtievə/ *noun* the mucous membrane that lines the inner surface of the eyelids and is continued over part of the eyeball. ➤➤ **conjunctival** /kənˈjungktivl, konjungkˈtievl/ *adj*. [scientific Latin from Latin *conjunctivus* serving to connect, from *conjungere*: see CONJOIN]

conjunctive[1] /kənˈjungktiv/ *adj* **1** connective. **2** in grammar, behaving as a conjunction: *conjunctive phrases like 'in case' and 'as soon as'*. **3** in logic, denoting a compound preposition. ➤➤ **conjunctively** *adv*.

conjunctive[2] *noun* in grammar, a conjunction.

conjunctivitis /kənˌjungktiˈvietis/ *noun* inflammation of the CONJUNCTIVA (membrane lining the eyelid and covering the eyeball), *esp* a contagious type with overproduction of mucus, causing eyelashes to adhere. Also called PINKEYE.

conjuncture /kənˈjungkchə/ *noun* a combination of circumstances or events usu producing a crisis; = JUNCTURE.

conjure /ˈkonjə, ˈkunjə/ *verb trans* **1** (+ up) to produce (something) from one's imagination or by using one's creative powers. **2** (+ up) said of a word, sensation, etc: to evoke (ideas, images, etc). **3** *archaic* to summon (spirits, demons, etc) by means of a magic ritual. **4** *ˌˌˌ ˌˌˌˌˌˌˌˌˌˌˌ ˌˌˌˌˌˌˌˌˌ (ˌˌˌˌˌˌˌˌ)* ˌˌ ˌˌ ˌˌˌˌˌˌˌˌˌˌˌˌˌ ˌˌ ˌˌˌˌˌˌ *thee to pardon Rome* — Shakespeare. ➤ *verb intrans* **1** to perform conjuring tricks. **2** *archaic* to use magical powers: *I'll learn to conjure, and raise devils* — Shakespeare. ✱ **a name to conjure with** a name that commands awed respect. ➤➤ **conjuration** /-ˈraysh(ə)n/ *noun*, **conjuring** *noun*. [French *conjurer* from Latin *conjurare* to swear together, from CON- + *jurare* to swear]

conjurer or **conjuror** /ˈkonjoorə, ˈkun-/ *noun* a person who performs tricks by sleight of hand or illusion.

conjuring trick *noun* a trick using sleight of hand that deceives the eye or apparently defies nature.

conjuror *noun* see CONJURER.

conk[1] /kongk/ *noun informal* **1** *Brit* the nose. **2** the head. [prob alteration of CONCH]

conk[2] *verb trans informal* to hit (somebody) on the head.

conker /ˈkongkə/ *noun* **1** the large hard shiny brown nut of the horse chestnut, *esp* as used in playing conkers. **2** *Brit* (*in pl, but treated as sing.*) a game in which each player in turn swings a conker on a string to try to break one held on its string by their opponent. [dialect *conker* a snail shell, from the original use of a snail shell on a string in the game, perhaps from CONCH]

conk out *verb intrans dated, informal* **1** said of a motor vehicle or its driver or a machine, or body part: to break down. **2** said of a person: to collapse, faint, die, or fall asleep. [prob imitative of a failing engine]

conman /ˈkonman/ *noun* (*pl* **conmen**) *informal* a person who uses confidence tricks to cheat others; a swindler.

con moto /kon ˈmohtoh/ *adv* said of a piece of music: to be performed with spirit and liveliness. [Italian *con moto* with movement]

Conn. *abbr* Connecticut.

conn[1] /kon/ *verb trans NAmer* see CON[6].

conn[2] *noun* see CON[7].

connate /ˈkonayt/ *adj* **1** said of plant or animal parts: congenitally or firmly united. **2** said of water: entrapped in sediments at the time of their deposition. **3** said of characteristics: innate; inborn. ➤➤ **connately** *adv*. [Latin *connatus*, past part. of *connasci* to be born together, from CON- + *nasci* to be born]

connatural /kəˈnachərəl/ *adj* **1** (*often* + to) said of abilities or tendencies: natural to (a person or thing) because inborn or inherent. **2** of the same nature: *Linked to her connatural tree, co-twisting her limbs with its own … his Dryad lay* — Charles Lamb. ➤➤ **connaturally** *adv*. [medieval Latin *connaturalis*, from CON- + Latin *naturalis*: see NATURAL[1]]

connect /kəˈnekt/ *verb trans* **1** to link (two things) together: *Assemble the two halves before connecting them*. **2** to link (an electrical apparatus) with a power supply: *connect the laptop to the mains*. **3** (*often* + with) to associate (two things) mentally: *I failed to connect the face with the name*. **4** to constitute a link between (two things): *What connects them?* **5** to link (two callers) by telephone: *Just trying to connect you*. ➤ *verb intrans* **1** (*often* + with) to be joined: *The*

bathroom connects with the bedroom. **2** (*often* + with) said of a train, bus, etc: to be timed to reach its destination in time for passengers to transfer to another train, bus, or other form of transport. **3** *informal* (*also* + with) said of a hit or shot: to find its target; to hit home: *My fist connected with his jaw*. [Latin *connectere*, from CON- + *nectere* to bind]

connected *adj* **1** joined or linked together. **2** associated: *The re-emergence of tuberculosis is connected with people sleeping rough*. **3** having a social, professional, or commercial relationship: *She's connected with television*. ➤➤ **connectedly** *adv*, **connectedness** *noun*.

connecting rod *noun* a rod that transmits power from a part of a machine in reciprocating motion, e.g. a piston, to another that is rotating, e.g. a crankshaft.

connection (*Brit* **connexion**) /kəˈneksh(ə)n/ *noun* **1** something that connects; a link: *a loose connection in the wiring*. **2** a relationship or association: *I no longer have any connection with the Nationalist Party*. **3** a train, bus, plane, etc, that one is scheduled to transfer to: *I missed my connection*. **4** (*also in pl*) somebody connected to one by friendship, kinship, professional interests, etc: *She has connections in high places*. **5** *chiefly NAmer, informal* a supplier or source of narcotics. **6** formerly, a fellowship of Methodist churches. ✱ **in connection with** with relation to (something). **in this/that connection** in reference to this or that.

connective /kəˈnektiv/ *adj* tending or serving to connect. ➤➤ ˌˌˌˌˌˌˌˌˌˌˌˌˌˌ ˌˌˌ ˌˌˌˌˌˌˌˌˌˌˌ /ˌˌˌ ˌˌˌˌˌˌˌ/ ˌˌˌˌ

connective tissue *noun* any of various tissues, e.g. bone or cartilage, that pervade, support, and bind together other tissues and organs.

connexion /kəˈneksh(ə)n/ *noun Brit* see CONNECTION.

conning tower /ˈkoning/ *noun* a raised observation tower, usu incorporating an entrance on the deck of a submarine. [*conning* verbal noun from CON[6]]

conniption /kəˈnipsh(ə)n/ *noun NAmer, informal* a fit of rage, hysteria, or alarm. [prob invented]

conniption fit *noun NAmer, informal* = CONNIPTION.

connivance /kəˈniev(ə)ns/ *noun* knowledge of and active or passive consent to wrongdoing: *Drug-dealing went on with the connivance of certain police officers*.

connive /kəˈniev/ *verb intrans* **1** (*often* + in/at) to pretend ignorance of or fail to take action against something one ought to oppose: *Parents connived at their daughters' dishonesty*. **2** (*often* + with) to cooperate secretly or have a secret understanding; to conspire: *conniving with certain unscrupulous elements to get the bill accepted*. ➤➤ **conniver** *noun*. [French *conniver* from Latin *conivēre*, *connivēre* to close the eyes, connive, from CON- + *-nivēre* (related to *nictare* to wink)]

conniving *adj* scheming, calculating, or coldly manipulative.

connoisseur /konəˈsuh/ *noun* an expert judge in matters of taste or appreciation, e.g. of art or food: *a connoisseur of fine wines*. ➤➤ **connoisseurship** *noun*. [obsolete French *connoisseur* (now *connaisseur*), from Old French *connoistre* to know, from Latin *cognoscere* to become acquainted with]

connotation /konəˈtaysh(ə)n/ *noun* **1a** (*also in pl*) something suggested by a word as distinct from its direct meaning or DENOTATION: *For me, henceforth, the word 'coffee-house' will have anything but an agreeable connotation* — Jack London; *Use a term free of clerical connotations* — William James. **b** the process by which this kind of association is made. **2** in philosophy, the essential characteristic or characteristics implied by a concept or term; = INTENSION (2): *The connotation of the word 'fir' is the set of characteristics, e.g. needle-shaped leaves and fir cones, that distinguish a fir from other trees*. ➤➤ **connotational** *adj*.

connote /kəˈnoht/ *verb trans* **1** said of a word, etc: to convey (a range of ideas or feelings) in addition to its exact explicit meaning: *the barbaric savagery that the term 'ethnic cleansing' connotes*. **2** said of a fact or circumstance: to imply or indicate as a logically essential attribute of something: *the personal shame connoted by redundancy*. ➤➤ **connotative** /ˈkonətaytiv/ *adj*. [medieval Latin *connotare*, from CON- + *notare*: see NOTE[2]]

connubial /kəˈnyoohbi·əl/ *adj* concerning marriage or the relationship between husband and wife; = CONJUGAL. ➤➤ **connubiality** /-ˈaliti/ *noun*, **connubially** *adv*. [from Latin *conubialis*, formed from *conubium*, *connubium* marriage, from CON- + *nubere* to marry]

conodont /'kohnədont/ *noun* **1** a tiny tooth-like fossil found in marine sedimentary rocks, associated with animals that lived between the CAMBRIAN and TRIASSIC periods (from 540 to 208 million years ago). **2** the small worm-like invertebrate animal at the entrance to whose gut these tooth-like structures were probably sited. [Greek *kōnos* CONE[1] + -ODONT]

conoid[1] /'kohnoyd/ *adj* having the shape, or approximate shape, of a cone. ⟫⟫ **conoidally** *adv*.

conoid[2] *noun* a conoid object.

conoidal /koh'noydl/ *adj* = CONOID[1].

conquer /'kongkə/ *verb* (**conquered, conquering**) ⟫ *verb trans* **1** to gain control over, acquire by force of arms, or subjugate (a country, etc or its people). **2** to overcome by force of arms, or vanquish (an army or general). **3** to master (a personal problem or weakness): *He conquered his fear of flying*. **4** to climb and reach the summit of (a mountain). ⟫ *verb intrans* to be victorious. ⟫⟫ **conqueror** *noun*. [Old French *conquerre*, ultimately from Latin *conquirere* to gain, win, from CON- + *quaerere* to seek]

conquest /'kon(q)kwest/ *noun* **1a** the act or process of conquering. **b** (**the Conquest**) the invasion and subjugation of England by William of Normandy in 1066. **2** (*also in pl*). **a** something conquered; *esp* territory appropriated in war. **b** a person who has been won over, *esp* by love or sexual attraction. [Old French *conquest, conqueste*, ultimately from Latin *conquisitus*, past part. of *conquirere*: see CONQUER]

conquistador /kon'k(w)istədaw/ *noun* (*pl* **conquistadores** /-'dwarays, -reez/ *or* **conquistadors**) a conqueror; *specif* any of the Spanish conquerors of America. [Spanish *conquistador* from *conquistar* to conquer, from Latin *conquistus* won, gained, from *conquirere*: see CONQUER]

con rod *noun Brit, informal* = CONNECTING ROD.

consanguineous /konsang'gwini-əs/ *adj* of the same blood or origin; *specif* descended from the same ancestor. ⟫⟫ **consanguineously** *adv*, **consanguinity** /-'gwiniti/ *noun*. [Latin *consanguineus*, from CON- + *sanguin-, sanguis* blood]

conscience /'konsh(ə)ns/ *noun* **1** the consciousness of the moral quality of one's own conduct or intentions, together with a feeling of obligation to refrain from doing wrong. **2** conformity to the dictates of conscience; conscientiousness: *Conscience argues against it*. ✳ **in all conscience** by any standard of fairness. **on one's conscience** said of a misdeed or omission: causing one to feel guilty. ⟫⟫ **conscienceless** *adj*. [Latin *conscientia* from *conscient-, consciens*, present part. of *conscire* to be conscious, be conscious of guilt, from CON- with (oneself) + *scire* to know]

conscience clause *noun* a clause in a law exempting those who object on moral or religious grounds.

conscience money *noun* money paid, usu anonymously, to relieve the conscience.

conscience-stricken *adj* feeling guilty or ashamed about something that one has done or failed to do.

conscientious /konshi'enshəs/ *adj* **1** governed by or conforming to the dictates of conscience; scrupulous. **2** meticulous or careful, *esp* in one's work; hard-working. ⟫⟫ **conscientiously** *adv*, **conscientiousness** *noun*. [French *conscientieux* from medieval Latin *conscientiosus*, from Latin *conscientia*: see CONSCIENCE]

conscientious objector *noun* a person who refuses to serve in the armed forces or bear arms, *esp* on moral or religious grounds. ⟫⟫ **conscientious objection** *noun*.

conscious[1] /'konshəs/ *adj* **1** aware of one's surroundings and responding to them normally; awake. **2** (+ of) aware of something: *She was conscious of a chilliness in his tone*. **3** (+ of) recognizing a feeling in oneself: *He was conscious of a certain sense of disappointment*. **4** (+ of) appreciative of something: *conscious of the honour being done to me*. **5** (+ of) painfully aware of, or sensitive about something: *He behaved as if continually conscious of his lack of height*. **6** self-conscious; put-on: *a rather conscious display of bonhomie*. **7** deliberate: *Try to make a conscious effort to look at people when addressing them*. **8** (*used in combinations*) showing concern for the thing specified: *bargain-conscious shoppers*. **9** *archaic* shy: *Mr Elton only looked very conscious and smiling* — Jane Austen. **10** in psychology, denoting the part of the mind the workings of which one is aware. ⟫⟫ **consciously** *adv*. [from Latin *conscius*, from *conscire*: see CONSCIENCE]

conscious[2] *noun* in Freudian psychology, the part of the mind's workings that one is aware of.

consciousness *noun* **1** the state of being awake and aware of one's surroundings, and of responding to them normally. **2** that level of mental response and activity of which one is aware, as distinct from unconscious processes: *The sound of the telephone suddenly intruded itself into his consciousness*.

Editorial note

In psychology and neuroscience consciousness means subjective experience. Once excluded from scientific study, consciousness is now considered one of its greatest challenges. We know that physical changes in the brain are related to changes in consciousness, but the 'hard problem' of consciousness is to understand how private subjective experience can arise from objective events such as the firing of brain cells — Dr Susan Blackmore.

3 the state of knowing about or being conscious of something: *her consciousness of her own attractiveness*. **4** (*often as comb. form*) concern about a specific matter or area of activity: *political consciousness; class-consciousness*.

consciousness-raising *noun* **1** the process of increasing people's understanding of and concern about a topic, *esp* a social or political question. **2** (*used before a noun*) concerned with consciousness-raising: *consciousness-raising groups*.

conscript[1] /'konskript/ *noun* a person who has been conscripted. [Latin *conscriptus*, past part. of *conscribere* to enrol, from CON- + *scribere* to write]

conscript[2] /kən'skript/ *verb trans* to enlist (somebody) compulsorily, *esp* for military service. ⟫⟫ **conscription** /-sh(ə)n/ *noun*.

consecrate /'konsikrayt/ *verb trans* **1** to make or declare (a church, etc) sacred by a solemn ceremony. **2** to prepare (bread and wine used at communion) to be received as Christ's body and blood. **3** (*usu* + to) to devote (one's life) to a purpose with deep solemnity or dedication. **4** to ordain (somebody) to a religious office, *esp* that of bishop. **5** to make (something) inviolable or venerable: *customs consecrated by time*. ⟫⟫ **consecration** /-'kraysh(ə)n/ *noun*, **consecrator** *noun*, **consecratory** /-'kraytəri/ *adj*. [Latin *consecratus*, past part. of *consecrare*, from CON- + *sacrare* to consecrate, from *sacer* sacred]

Consecration /konsi'kraysh(ə)n/ *noun* in the Roman Catholic Church, the moment during Mass when the bread and wine are believed to change into the body and blood of Christ.

consecutive /kən'sekyootiv/ *adj* **1** following one after the other in order without gaps: *on three consecutive days*. **2** in grammar, denoting a clause expressing result. ⟫⟫ **consecutively** *adv*, **consecutiveness** *noun*. [French *consécutive* from medieval Latin *consecutivus*, from Latin *consecutus*, past part. of *consequi* to follow closely, from CON- + *sequi* to follow]

consensual /kən'sensyoo-əl/ *adj* **1** relating to consent or consensus. **2** said of a contract, etc: concluded by mutual consent, not formerly validated in writing. ⟫⟫ **consensually** *adv*. [Latin *consensus*: see CONSENSUS]

consensus /kən'sensəs/ *noun* **1** general agreement; unanimity. **2** the judgment arrived at by most of those concerned. **3** (*used before a noun*) arrived at by consensus: *a consensus decision*. [Latin *consensus* agreement, past part. of *consentire*: see CONSENT[1]]

Usage note

The only *c* in *consensus* is at the beginning of the word – it is spelt with three *s's*.

consensus sequence *noun* a sequence of DNA found with a similar function and only minor structural variations in organisms of widely different type.

consent[1] /kən'sent/ *verb intrans* (*often* + to) to give assent or approval to something; to agree to it: *They consented to the proposals*. ⟫ *verb trans* to agree (to do something): *She consented to be nominated*. ⟫⟫ **consenter** *noun*, **consentingly** *adv*. [Latin *consentire*, from CON- + *sentire* to feel]

consent[2] *noun* compliance in or approval of what is done or proposed by another; acquiescence: *Get her consent in writing*. ✳ **by common consent** with the agreement of everybody. **informed consent** agreement to a procedure, typically a surgical one, in the full knowledge of the risks.

consentient /kən'sensh(ə)nt/ *adj archaic* consenting; in agreement: *the consentient testimony of several eye witnesses*.

consenting adult *noun* an adult who consents to a sexual act.

consequence /'konsikwəns/ *noun* **1** a result or effect. **2** importance or relevance: *The exact time is of no consequence as long as we know the date*. **3** *dated* social importance: *people of consequence*. **4** (*in pl, but treated as sing.*) a game in which a story is made up by consecutive players, each of whom is ignorant of what the previous player contributed, and which concludes with a contribution beginning 'and the consequence was ... '. ✳ **in consequence** as a result; consequently. **take/bear the consequences** to accept responsibility for the possibly undesirable results of one's decision. [Latin *consequentia* consequence, result, from *consequent-, consequens*, present part. of *consequi*: see CONSECUTIVE]

consequent[1] /'konsikwənt/ *adj* **1** *formal* (+ to) following as a result or effect: *the complications consequent on lying*. **2** observing logical sequence; rational. [Latin *consequent-, consequens*, present part. of *consequi*: see CONSECUTIVE]

consequent[2] *noun* **1** in philosophy, a logical deduction. **2** in logic, the conclusion of a conditional proposition, e.g. *then B* in *if A, then B*: compare ANTECEDENT[1].

consequential /konsi'kwensh(ə)l/ *adj* **1** occurring as a secondary result; indirect: *consequential loss*. **2** having significant consequences; important: *consequential matters*. **3** self-important; pompous: *It was amusing to note how the consequential Jones was already beginning to give himself airs* — Conan Doyle. ⯈⯈ **consequentiality** /-shi'aliti/ *noun*, **consequentially** *adv*, **consequentialness** *noun*.

consequentialism *noun* in ethics, the teaching that the morality of an action is to be assessed solely in the light of how desirable or undesirable its consequences are.

consequently *adv* as a result; in view of the foregoing.

conservancy /kən'suhv(ə)nsi/ *noun* (*pl* **conservancies**) **1a** conservation. **b** an organization designated to conserve and protect the environment. **c** an area protected by such a body. **2** *Brit* a board regulating a river or port. [alteration of obsolete *conservacy* conservation from medieval Latin *conservatia*, from Latin *conservatus*, past part. of *conservare*: see CONSERVE[1]]

conservation /konsə'vaysh(ə)n/ *noun* **1** careful preservation and protection, *esp* of a natural resource, the quality of the environment, or a plant or animal species, to prevent exploitation, destruction, or neglect. **2** the preservation of historic or archaeological artefacts or sites. **3** in physics, the conserving of a quantity: *conservation of momentum*. ⯈⯈ **conservational** *adj*, **conservationist** *noun*. [Latin *conservation-, conservatio*, from *conservare*: see CONSERVE[1]]

conservation of energy *noun* a principle in physics: the total amount of energy in an isolated system remains constant and is independent of any changes occurring within the system.

conservation of mass *noun* a principle in physics: the total mass of any isolated system remains constant regardless of any reactions occurring between the parts of the system.

conservation of momentum *noun* a principle in physics: the total linear or angular momentum of any isolated system remains constant, provided no external force is applied.

conservatism /kən'suhvətiz(ə)m/ *noun* **1** the disposition to preserve what is established, or a political philosophy based on this. **2** (**Conservatism**) the principles and policies of a Conservative party. **3** the tendency to prefer an existing situation to change.

Editorial note ⎯⎯⎯⎯⎯⎯⎯⎯⎯⎯⎯⎯⎯⎯⎯
Most people exhibit some attachment to what they know and like – conservatism with a small 'c'. Political Conservatism (with a big 'C') can be an extension of this sort of pragmatic scepticism about change: but not always. Instead it may take the form of radical Conservatism (e.g. that of Margaret Thatcher), sponsoring drastic and doctrinaire reforms, albeit of a right-wing nature — Professor Peter Clarke.

conservative[1] /kən'suhvətiv/ *adj* **1a** relating to or denoting a philosophy of conservatism; traditional. **b** (**Conservative**) advocating conservatism; *specif* relating to or constituting a British political party associated with support of established institutions and opposed to radical change. **2a** moderate; cautious: *a conservative estimate*. **b** characterized by or relating to traditional norms of taste, elegance, style, or manners: *a conservative suit*. ⯈⯈ **conservatively** *adv*, **conservativeness** *noun*.

conservative[2] *noun* **1** (**Conservative**) a supporter of a Conservative party: *I often think it's comical ... how Nature always does contrive ... that every boy and every gal that's born into this world alive is either a little Liberal or else a little Conservative* — W S Gilbert. **2** a person who keeps to traditional methods or views.

Conservative Judaism *noun* Judaism as practised *esp* among some US Jews, with adherence to the TORAH and TALMUD (Jewish scriptures) but with allowance for some departures in keeping with circumstances.

conservatoire /kən'suhvətwah/ *noun* a school specializing in any one of the fine arts: *a conservatoire of music*. [French *conservatoire* from Italian *conservatorio* home for foundlings, music school, from Latin *conservatus*, past part. of *conservare*: see CONSERVE[1]]

conservator /kən'suhvətə, 'konsəvaytə/ *noun* **1** a museum official responsible for the care, restoration, etc of exhibits. **2** an official charged with the protection of something affecting public welfare and interests, e.g. as a member of a conservancy. ⯈⯈ **conservatorial** /kən,suhvə'tawri-əl/ *adj*.

conservatorium /kən,suhvə'tawri-əm/ *noun* (*pl* **conservatoriums** *or* **conservatoria**) *Aus* a college for the study of music or any of the other arts; = CONSERVATOIRE. [German *Conservatorium* from late Latin, from Latin *conservare*: see CONSERVE[1]]

conservatory /kən'suhvət(ə)ri/ *noun* (*pl* **conservatories**) **1** a greenhouse, usu forming a room of a house, for growing or displaying ornamental plants. **2** *chiefly NAmer* a specialist academy in one of the arts; = CONSERVATOIRE.

conserve[1] /kən'suhv/ *verb trans* **1a** to keep (something, such as wildlife) in a state of safety or wholeness. **b** to avoid wasteful or destructive use of (a resource). **2** to preserve (fruit, etc), *esp* with sugar. **3** to maintain (mass, energy, momentum, etc) at a constant level during a process of chemical or physical change. ⯈⯈ **conserver** *noun*. [Latin *conservare*, from CON- + *servare* to keep, guard, observe]

conserve[2] /kən'suhv, 'konsuhv/ *noun* a preserve of fruit boiled with sugar that is used like jam.

consider /kən'sidə/ *verb* (**considered, considering**) ⯈ *verb trans* **1** to think about (something) carefully. **2** to deem or judge (something or someone to be something): *She was considered a reliable historian; I considered that it was a good time to invest*. **3** to have sympathetic regard for (somebody, their wishes, etc). **4** to look at (something) appraisingly. **5** to bear (something) in mind. ⯈ *verb intrans* to reflect or deliberate: *Take time to consider*. ✳ **all things considered** on the whole: *The party was quite a success, all things considered*. [Latin *considerare* to consider, contemplate, perhaps from *sider-, sidus* star, therefore literally 'to observe the stars']

considerable *adj* **1** worth consideration; significant: *a considerable contribution to literature*. **2** large in extent or degree: *a considerable number*. ⯈⯈ **considerably** *adv*.

considerate /kən'sid(ə)rət/ *adj* showing concern for the rights, needs, and feelings of others. ⯈⯈ **considerately** *adv*, **considerateness** *noun*.

consideration /kən,sidə'raysh(ə)n/ *noun* **1** continuous and careful thought: *after mature consideration*. **2** a factor taken into account in making a decision, etc. **3** the bearing of something in mind: *consideration of the possible risks*. **4** concern for others; considerateness. **5** a payment for a service: *for a small consideration*. **6a** an element of benefit or loss that distinguishes a legally binding contract from a mere promise. **b** something of value given in return for a promise. **7** *dated* respect or esteem: *... became people of consideration* — V S Pritchett. ✳ **in consideration of** in return for (a service, etc). **take something into consideration** to take something into account; *specif* said of a judge: to consider (additional offences admitted by a defendant). **under consideration** being considered.

considered *adj* matured by extended thought: *his considered opinion*.

considering[1] *prep* taking (something) into account: *He did well considering his limitations*.

considering[2] *conj* in view of the fact that (something is the case): *Considering he was new at the job, he did quite well*.

considering[3] *adv informal* all things considered: *You did pretty well, considering*.

consign /kən'sien/ *verb trans* **1** to entrust (something) to somebody's care. **2** to send or address (something) to an agent to be cared for or sold. **3** to commit (something) to a place where it will be got rid of: *Thousands of photographs were consigned to the flames*. ⯈⯈ **consignable** *adj*, **consignor** *noun*. [Latin *consignare* to put one's seal on, from CON- + *signum* mark, seal, SIGN[1]]

consignee /konsie'nee/ *noun* a person to whom something is consigned.

consignment *noun* a batch of goods for delivery: *a consignment of furniture*.

consist /kən'sist/ *verb intrans* **1** (+ in) to lie or reside in something: *Liberty consists in the absence of obstructions* — A E Housman. **2** (+ of) to be made up or composed of one or several things: *Breakfast* consisted of cereal, milk, and fruit. [Latin consistere to exist, stand firm, from CON- + sistere to stand]

consistency /kən'sist(ə)nsi/ or **consistence** noun **1** the degree of thickness, viscosity, or firmness of a substance: Boil the juice to the consistency of a thick syrup. **2** the quality of being mutually consistent, or of not being contradictory: a lack of consistency between the eye-witness accounts. **3** the quality of not varying over a period of time: the consistency of her stroke play on court.

consistent adj **1** (often + with) in agreement; not contradictory: Contemporary witnesses are remarkably consistent on this point. **2** not varying over a period of time: maintaining a consistent standard. **3** hanging together logically; not self-contradictory: His characters are believable and consistent. **4** (+ with) fitting in with (certain conjectural circumstances): injuries consistent with a knife attack. ⨠ **consistently** adv. [Latin consistent-, consistens, present part. of consistere: see CONSIST]

consistory /kən'sist(ə)ri/ noun (pl **consistories**) a church tribunal or governing body; esp one made up of the pope and cardinals. ⨠ **consistorial** /konsi'stawri·əl/ adj. [medieval Latin consistorium church tribunal, from Latin consistere: see CONSIST]

consistory court noun a diocesan court in the Church of England.

consociation /kən,sohsi'aysh(ə)n, -shi'aysh(ə)n/ noun an ecological community with a single dominant organism. ⨠ **consociational** adj. [Latin consociation-, consociatio alliance, from consociare to associate, from CON- + socius companion]

consolation /konsə'laysh(ə)n/ noun **1** comfort given to or received by somebody who has suffered loss or disappointment. **2** something that affords comfort: The grandchildren are a great consolation.

consolation prize noun a prize given to somebody who just fails to gain a major prize in a contest.

console[1] /kən'sohl/ verb trans to comfort or serve to comfort (somebody) in their grief or disappointment: I was consoled by the thought that she had not suffered. ⨠ **consolable** adj, **consolatory** /kən'solət(ə)ri/ adj, **consolingly** adv. [Latin consolari to console, from CON- + solari to soothe]

console[2] /'konsohl/ noun **1** a control panel, or switchboard, or a cabinet or other unit in which a control panel is mounted. **2** an electronic device dedicated to playing computerized video games using a television set as display. **3** the desk containing the keyboards, stops, etc of an organ. **4** a cabinet, e.g. for a radio or television set, designed to rest directly on the floor. **5** a carved bracket projecting from a wall to support a shelf or cornice. [French console architectural bracket, corbel, support, possibly shortened from consolateur comforter (perhaps a reference to the similarly shaped misericords for resting on in choir stalls), from Latin consolator consoler, from consolari: see CONSOLE[1]]

console table /'konsohl/ noun a table fixed to a wall and supported by brackets.

consolidate /kən'solidayt/ verb trans **1** to strengthen (something) or make it more solid and stable: A lining of brickwork was added to consolidate the structure. **2** to cause (something) to solidify or form a compact mass. **3** to strengthen (a leading position) or make (it) more secure: He consolidated his lead during the succeeding laps. **4** to combine (several elements) into a unit: consolidated securities. ⨠ verb intrans **1** to coagulate or solidify. **2** to combine or amalgamate. ⨠ **consolidation** /-'daysh(ə)n/ noun, **consolidator** noun. [Latin consolidatus, past part. of consolidare to make solid, from CON- + solidus SOLID[1]]

Consols /'konsolz/ pl noun esp formerly, interest-bearing government securities without a maturity date: I have heard of an old dowager countess whose money was all in Consols — Samuel Butler. [shortening of consolidated annuities]

consommé /kən'somay/ noun a thin clear soup made from meat broth. [French consommé, past part. of consommer to complete, boil down, from Latin consummare to complete, from CON- + summa: see SUM[1]]

consonance /'kons(ə)nəns/ noun **1a** in verse, etc, correspondence or recurrence of sounds, esp consonant sounds, as in shall surely follow: compare ASSONANCE. **b** a harmonious combination of musical notes: compare DISSONANCE. **2** formal harmony or agreement: These things suggested a want of easy consonance with the deeper rhythms of life — Henry James. [Latin consonantia, from consonant-, consonans, present part. of consonare: see CONSONANT[1]]

consonant[1] /'kons(ə)nənt/ noun **1** any of a class of speech sounds, e.g. /p/, /g/, /n/, /l/, /s/, /r/, characterized by constriction or closure at one or more points in the breath channel. **2** a letter or symbol representing any of these sounds. ⨠ **consonantal** /-'nantl/ adj. [Latin consonant-, consonans, present part. of consonare to sound together, from CON- + sonare to sound, from sonus sound]

consonant[2] adj **1** said of musical notes: producing a harmonious sound or chord: compare DISSONANT. **2** said of words: having similar sounds. **3** formal (+ with) in agreement or harmony with (something): It was not constant with his image to attend such a function. ⨠ **consonantly** adv.

con sordino /kon saw'deenoh/ adv said of a piece of music: to be performed with the use of a MUTE[2] (device to muffle sound). [Italian con sordino]

consort[1] /'konsawt/ noun **1** a husband or wife, esp that of a reigning monarch. **2** a companion or associate. **3** a ship acting as escort. [Latin consort-, consors a partner, literally 'one who shares a common lot', from CON- + sort-, sors lot, share]

consort[2] noun **1** a group of musicians performing together, esp playing early music. **2** a set of musical instruments, esp of the same family, played together. ✳ **in consort** together; in conjunction or harmony. [CONSORT[3]]

consort[3] /kən'sawt/ verb intrans formal **1** (+ with) to keep company with certain people: consorting with criminals. **2** (+ with) to accord or harmonize with something: The illustrations consort admirably with the text — Times Literary Supplement.

consortium /kən'sawti·əm/ noun (pl **consortia** /-ti·ə/ or **consortiums**) a temporary combination of businesses providing or bidding for services for a project. [Latin consortium, fellowship, from consort-, consors: see CONSORT[1]]

conspectus /kən'spektəs/ noun a survey or summary; esp a brief one providing an overall view. [Latin conspectus, past part. of conspicere: see CONSPICUOUS]

conspicuous /kən'spikyooəs/ adj **1** obvious to the eye or mind. **2** attracting attention; striking. ✳ **conspicuous by one's absence** only too obviously missing or absent from a gathering one should be attending. ⨠ **conspicuity** /konspi'kyooh·iti/ noun, **conspicuously** adv, **conspicuousness** noun. [Latin conspicuus, from conspicere to observe, get sight of, from CON- + specere to look]

conspicuous consumption noun lavish or wasteful spending thought to enhance social prestige.

conspiracy /kən'spirəsi/ noun (pl **conspiracies**) **1** the activity of conspiring together: conspiracy to murder. **2** the offence of conspiring to do something criminal or illegal. **3a** an agreement reached by a group of conspirators; a plot. **b** (treated as sing. or pl) a group of conspirators. [Old French conspiration, from Latin conspirare: see CONSPIRE]

conspiracy of silence noun an agreement to keep silent, esp in order to promote or protect selfish interests.

conspiracy theory noun a theory that an otherwise unexplained event was caused by the secret concerted action of powerful individuals or groups, rather than by a combination of circumstances.

conspirator /kən'spirətə/ noun a person who conspires; a plotter.

conspiratorial /kən,spirə'tawri·əl/ adj **1** of a conspiracy or conspirator. **2** said of somebody's manner, etc: suggestive of conspiracy: in a conspiratorial whisper. ⨠ **conspiratorially** adv.

conspire /kən'spie·ə/ verb intrans **1** to plot secretly with others, esp to do something wrong or illegal: They conspired to defraud the business. **2** to act together as if deliberately, with undesirable results: Circumstances conspired to defeat his efforts. [Latin conspirare to agree, conspire, literally 'to breathe together', from CON- + spirare to breathe]

con spirito /kon 'spiritoh/ adv said of a piece of music: to be performed in a lively or spirited style. [Italian con spirito with spirit]

Const. abbr Constable.

const. abbr constant.

constable /'konstəbl, 'kun-/ noun **1** Brit a police officer; specif one ranking below sergeant. **2** a high officer of a medieval royal or noble household. **3** the warden or governor of a royal castle or a fortified town. [Middle English conestable, ultimately from late Latin comes stabuli, literally 'officer of the stable']

constabulary[1] /kən'stabyooləri/ noun (pl **constabularies**) (treated as sing. or pl) **1** the police force of a district or country. **2** an armed police force organized on military lines: *the Royal Ulster Constabulary.*

constabulary[2] *adj* relating to a constable or constabulary: *When constabulary duty's to be done, a policeman's lot is not a happy one* — W S Gilbert.

constancy /ˈkɒnstənsi/ *noun* **1** fidelity or loyalty. **2** the quality of being unchanging: *constancy of purpose.*

constant[1] /ˈkɒnst(ə)nt/ *adj* **1** characterized by steadfast resolution or faithfulness; exhibiting constancy of mind or attachment: *constant friend.* **2** invariable or uniform: *at a constant temperature.* **3** continually occurring or recurring; regular: *constant interruptions.* ➤➤ **constantly** *adv.* [Latin *constant-, constans*, present part. of *constare* to stand firm, be consistent, from CON- + *stare* to stand]

constant[2] *noun* **1** something with an invariable or unchanging value, e.g.: **a** a number that has a fixed value in a given situation or universally or that is characteristic of some substance or instrument. **b** a number that is assumed not to change value in a given mathematical discussion. **2** a term in logic with a fixed designation.

constantan /ˈkɒnstəntən/ *noun* an alloy of copper and nickel used for electrical resistors and in thermocouples. [coined from CONSTANT[1], from the constancy of its resistance under change of temperature]

constative /kənˈstaytiv, ˈkɒnstətiv/ *adj* denoting an utterance that constitutes a statement and can be true or false, such as *I sneezed* as distinct from a PERFORMATIVE utterance, such as *I promise.* [from Latin *constat-, constare* establish + -IVE[1]]

constellation /kɒnstəˈlaysh(ə)n/ *noun* **1** any of 88 arbitrary configurations of stars supposed to fill the outlines of usu mythical figures. **2** a cluster, group, or pattern of things, e.g. medical symptoms, factors, or ideas. **3** a dazzling circle of people: *the Alexandrians, a constellation of genius* — Ralph Waldo Emerson. ➤➤ **constellatory** /kənˈstelət(ə)ri/ *adj.* [late Latin *constellation-, constellatio*, from *constellatus* studded with stars, from CON- + Latin *stella* star]

consternate /ˈkɒnstənayt/ *verb trans* (*usu in passive*) to fill (somebody) with anxiety or consternation. [Latin *consternatus*, past part. of *consternare*: see CONSTERNATION]

consternation /kɒnstəˈnaysh(ə)n/ *noun* amazed dismay that throws one into confusion. [Latin *consternation-, consternatio*, from *consternare* to bewilder, alarm, from CON- + *sternare* to prostrate]

constipate /ˈkɒnstipayt/ *verb trans* (*usu in passive*) to cause constipation in (somebody): *Some pain-killers make you constipated.* [Latin *constipatus*, past part. of *constipare* to crowd together, from CON- + *stipare* to press together]

constipation /kɒnstiˈpaysh(ə)n/ *noun* abnormally delayed or infrequent passage of faeces, *esp* when these are hard and compacted.

constituency /kənˈstityoo-ənsi/ *noun* (*pl* **constituencies**) an electoral district or the body of voters resident in it.

constituent[1] /kənˈstityoo-ənt/ *noun* **1** an essential part; a component: *the constituents of rain water.* **2** a member of an MP's constituency: *appreciative letters from his constituents.* [French *constituant*, present part. of *constituer* to constitute, establish, from Latin *constituere*: see CONSTITUTE]

constituent[2] *adj* **1** serving to form, compose, or make up a unit or whole; component: *constituent elements.* **2** having the power to frame or amend a constitution: *a constituent assembly.* ➤➤ **constituently** *adv.* [Latin *constituent-, constituens*, present part. of *constituere*: see CONSTITUTE]

constitute /ˈkɒnstityooht/ *verb trans* **1** said of a group of people or things: to compose (something) together: *Seven members constitute a quorum.* **2** to be or amount to (something): *Does singing in the street at night constitute a breach of the peace?* **3** to appoint (somebody) to an office, function, or dignity: *formally constituted office-bearers.* **4** to establish or set up (an organization, etc). **5** to give legal form to (an assembly, court, etc). [Latin *constitutus*, past part. of *constituere* to set up, constitute, from CON- + *statuere* to set up]

constitution /kɒnstiˈtyoohsh(ə)n/ *noun* **1** the fundamental principles and laws of a nation, state, or social group that guarantee certain rights to the people in it, determine the powers and duties of the government, and state how the government is appointed and what its structure will be.

Editorial note
A constitution is a collection of fundamental rules, generally codified in a single legal document, although three democracies – Britain, New Zealand and Israel – have unwritten or uncodified constitutions. States are also regulated by unwritten rules generally known as conventions. Most modern constitutions contain, in addition to rules regulating government, a Bill of Rights to protect the citizen — Professor Vernon Bogdanor.

2 a written document embodying the rules of a political or social organization. **3** an established law or custom; an ordinance. **4** the act of establishing, making, or setting up. **5** the make-up of something in terms of the elements of which it consists; composition. **6** the physical and mental make-up of a person: *She's lucky to have a strong constitution.* ➤➤ **constitutionless** *adj.*

constitutional[1] *adj* **1** in accordance with or authorized by the constitution of a state or society: *a constitutional government.* **2** regulated by or ruling according to a constitution: *a constitutional monarchy.* **3** relating to the constitution of a state: *constitutional studies.* **4** relating to the fundamental make-up of something; essential. **5** relating to the constitution of body or mind.

constitutional[2] *noun dated* a walk taken for the sake of one's health.

constitutionalism *noun* **1** adherence to constitutional principles. **2** constitutional government. ➤➤ **constitutionalist** *noun.*

constitutional law *noun* law dealing with the powers, organization, and responsibilities of government.

constitutionally *adv* **1** with relation to the constitution of a country, association, union, etc: *She was not constitutionally eligible for office.* **2** with relation to structure, composition, or physical constitution: *The material does not alter constitutionally when heated.* **3a** with relation to one's bodily constitution: *Constitutionally, he had never been robust.* **b** *humorous* as a result of one's moral or mental shortcomings: *She's constitutionally incapable of being punctual for anything.*

constitutive /kənˈstityootiv/ *adj* **1** having the power to enact or establish something. **2** forming a constituent part of something. ➤➤ **constitutively** *adv.*

constrain /kənˈstrayn/ *verb trans* **1** said *esp* of circumstances: to force (somebody) to do something: *Such is now the necessity which constrains them to alter their former systems of government* — Thomas Jefferson. **2** to inhibit (something): *For whatever may be said of Spanish pride, it rarely chills or constrains the intercourse of social or domestic life* — Washington Irving. [French *constraindre* from Latin *constringere* to constrict, constrain, from CON- + *stringere* to draw tight]

constrained *adj* said of conversation, smiles, etc: forced or unnatural, e.g. as a result of embarrassment: *The 'How d'ye do's' were quiet and constrained on each side* — Jane Austen. ➤➤ **constrainedly** /-nidli/ *adv.*

constraint /kənˈstraynt/ *noun* **1** the state of being forced into a course of action: *Bitter constraint and sad occasion dear compels me to disturb your season due* — Milton. **2** a constraining force; a check: *the constraints of poverty.* **3** inhibition that represses one's natural freedom of behaviour; embarrassment: *Lydgate found it more and more agreeable to be with her, and there was no constraint now* — George Eliot.

constrict /kənˈstrikt/ *verb trans* **1a** to make (a passage or opening) narrow: *Deposits build up, constricting the arteries.* **b** to compress or squeeze (a nerve, etc). **2** to limit or inhibit (something): *leading a somewhat constricted existence.* ➤➤ **constriction** *noun,* **constrictive** /-tiv/ *adj.* [Latin *constrictus*, past part. of *constringere*: see CONSTRAIN]

constrictor *noun* **1** a muscle that contracts a cavity or orifice or compresses an organ. **2** a snake, e.g. a boa or python, that kills prey by compressing it in its coils.

construct[1] /kənˈstrukt/ *verb trans* **1** to make, form, build, or erect (something). **2** to form (a sentence, etc) according to grammatical rules. **3** to build up (a theory or hypothesis) from pieces of evidence. **4** to draw (a geometrical figure) with suitable instruments and under given conditions. ➤➤ **constructible** *adj,* **constructor** *noun.* [Latin *constructus*, past part. of *construere* to build, from CON- + *struere* to build]

construct[2] /ˈkɒnstrukt/ *noun* **1** something constructed or formulated. **2** a product of thought; an idea or concept: *a construct of the imagination.* **3** in linguistics, a group of words constituting a phrase.

construction /kən'struksh(ə)n/ *noun* **1** the activity of building, or the process of being built. **2** a building or other structure. **3** a geometrical figure constructed to help solve a mathematical problem. **4** the formation of a clause or sentence according to grammatical rules. ✳ **put a certain construction on** to interpret (somebody's behaviour or words) in a certain way: *Now don't go putting a wrong construction on what I said.* ⟫⟫ **constructional** *adj*, **constructionally** *adv*.

constructive /kən'struktiv/ *adj* **1** relating to or involved in construction. **2** said of criticism, etc: offering ideas for improvement; positive rather than negative and destructive. **3** inferred rather than explicit: *constructive dismissal.* ⟫⟫ **constructively** *adv*, **constructiveness** *noun*.

constructivism *noun* a non-figurative art movement originating in Russia about 1914 and concerned with the aesthetic effects of the juxtaposition of geometric forms and various kinds of surface quality, e.g. colour, tone, or texture, and the use of modern industrial materials, e.g. glass and plastic. ⟫⟫ **constructivist** *adj and noun*.

construe /kən'strooh/ *verb* (**construes, construed, construing**) ⟫ *verb trans* **1** to interpret (words, actions, evidence, etc) in a certain way: *She had evidently construed my remarks as criticism.* **2a** to analyse the syntax of or parse (a sentence or sentence part). **b** to translate (a passage, e.g. of Latin or Greek) by parsing it step by step. ⟫ *verb intrans* to analyse grammatically a sentence or passage for translation. ⟫⟫ **construable** *adj*, **construal** *noun*. [from Latin *construere* to construct or (later) construe: see CONSTRUCT¹]

consubstantial /konsəb'stansh(ə)l/ *adj* in Christian theology, said *esp* of the three persons of the Trinity: of the same substance. ⟫⟫ **consubstantiality** /-shi'aliti/ *noun*. [late Latin *consubstantialis*, from CON- + *substantia*: see SUBSTANCE]

consubstantiation /,konsəbstansi'aysh(ə)n, -shi'aysh(ə)n/ *noun* in Christian theology, the Lutheran doctrine of the actual presence and combination of the body and blood of Christ with the bread and wine used at Communion: compare REAL PRESENCE.

consuetude /'konswityoohd/ *noun esp Scot* a custom or established usage, *esp* one that has legal force: *Long consuetude and custome ... haue established their authoritie* — John Knox. [Old French *consuetude* from Latin *consuetudo*: see CUSTOM¹]

consul /'kons(ə)l/ *noun* **1** an official appointed by a government to reside in a foreign country and there look after the interests of citizens of the appointing country. **2a** either of two elected chief magistrates of the Roman republic. **b** any of three chief magistrates of France from 1799 to 1804. ⟫⟫ **consular** /'konsyoolə/ *adj*, **consulship** *noun*. [Latin *consul*, based on *consulere* to consult]

consulate /'konsyoolət/ *noun* **1** the premises where a consul works. **2** government by consuls. **3** the period of office of a consul. **4** (**Consulate**) the government of the first French republic by consuls.

consul general *noun* (*pl* **consuls general**) a senior diplomatic consul stationed in an important place or having jurisdiction in several places or over several consuls.

consult /kən'sult/ *verb trans* **1** to ask the advice or opinion of (a doctor or other professional). **2** to look up (a reference book, etc). ⟫ *verb intrans* **1** to deliberate together; to confer. **2** to serve as a consultant; to give consultations: *Dr Mann consults daily between two and five.* ⟫⟫ **consultee** /konsul'tee/ *noun*, **consulter** *noun*, **consultor** *noun*. [Latin *consultare*, from *consulere* to deliberate, consult]

consultancy /kən'sult(ə)nsi/ *noun* (*pl* **consultancies**) **1** an agency that provides consulting services. **2** the post of a consultant.

consultant *noun* **1** an expert who gives professional advice or services. **2** the most senior grade of British hospital doctor, usu having direct clinical responsibility for hospital patients. **3** a person who consults somebody or something. ⟫⟫ **consultantship** *noun*.

consultation /kons(ə)l'taysh(ə)n/ *noun* **1** a meeting for discussion or debate. **2** a session or appointment with a doctor or other expert. **3a** the act of consulting or process of being consulted. **b** the activity of conferring.

consultative /kən'sultətiv/ *adj* relating to or intended for consultation; advisory: *a consultative committee.*

consulting *adj* **1** providing professional or expert advice: *a consulting architect.* **2** of a consultation or consultant: *The doctor's consulting hours are from two to five.*

consumables /kən'syoohməblz/ *pl noun* food or provisions.

consume /kən'syoohm/ *verb trans* **1** to ingest (food or drink). **2** to be a customer for (goods or services). **3** to use or use up (a fuel or other resource). **4** said *esp* of fire: to destroy (something) completely. **5** (*usu in passive*) said of an emotion, *esp* an unworthy one: to obsess the heart or mind of (somebody): *She was consumed with jealousy.* ⟫⟫ **consumable** *adj*. [Latin *consumere* to devour, destroy, from CON- + *sumere* to take up, take, from SUB- up + *emere* to take]

consumedly /kən'syoohmidli/ *adv archaic* (*used as an informal intensifier*) acutely or excessively: *He laughed consumedly over the joke* — Samuel Butler.

consumer *noun* **1** a customer for goods or services. **2** an organism requiring complex organic compounds for food, which it obtains by preying on other organisms or by eating particles of organic matter. ⟫⟫ **consumership** *noun*.

consumer durable *noun* (*also in pl*) a relatively expensive household item that is expected to last and have plenty of use, such as a car or washing machine.

consumer goods *pl noun* goods such as food, clothes, books, that satisfy immediate personal requirements and are not used in further manufacturing processes

consumerism *noun* **1** the promotion and protection of the consumer's interests. **2** the theory that an increasing consumption of goods is economically desirable. ⟫⟫ **consumerist** *noun and adj*.

consumer terrorism *noun* the deliberate contamination of food products on sale to the public, as a means of blackmailing the producers or sellers of the products. ⟫⟫ **consumer terrorist** *noun*.

consuming *adj* said of enthusiasms, etc: totally absorbing: *a consuming passion for all things mechanical.* ⟫⟫ **consumingly** *adv*.

consummate¹ /kən'sumət, 'konsyoomət, 'konsəmət/ *adj* **1** said of the practiser of an art: extremely skilled and accomplished: *a consummate liar.* **2** of the highest degree: *consummate skill.* ⟫⟫ **consummately** *adv*. [Latin *consummatus*, past part. of *consummare* to sum up, finish, from CON- + *summa*: see SUM¹]

consummate² /'konsyoomayt, 'konsəmayt/ *verb trans* **1** to make (a marriage) complete by sexual intercourse. **2** to finish (e.g. a business deal). ⟫⟫ **consummative** /-tiv/ *adj*, **consummator** *noun*.

consummation /konsyoo'maysh(ə)n, konsə-/ *noun* **1** the consummating of a marriage. **2** the ultimate end; a goal.

consumption /kən'sum(p)sh(ə)n/ *noun* **1** the act of consuming or process of being consumed: *fit for human consumption.* **2** an amount consumed: *increased fuel consumption.* **3** the buying of goods and services to satisfy immediate needs. **4** *dated* a wasting disease, *esp* tuberculosis of the lungs. [Latin *consumption-, consumptio*, from *consumere*: see CONSUME]

consumptive¹ /kən'sum(p)tiv/ *adj dated* related to or affected with consumption, *esp* of the lungs. ⟫⟫ **consumptively** *adv*.

consumptive² *noun* someone suffering from consumption.

cont. *abbr* **1** contents. **2** continued.

contact¹ /'kontakt/ *noun* **1** the action or condition of physically touching: *My head made contact with the ceiling.* **2** meeting or communication: *people you come into contact with in your everyday life.* **3** communication in the form of a significant signal observed or received from a person or object: *radar contact with Mars.* **4** a useful business acquaintance or relationship: *our contact in Berlin.* **5** any of the people who have been in association with an infected person. **6a** the junction of two electrical conductors. **b** a part of an electrical device for such a junction. **7** (*used before a noun*) caused by or involving touch: *contact dermatitis.* **8** (*in pl*) contact lenses. ⟫⟫ **contactual** /-tyooəl/ *adj*. [Latin *contactus* contact, touching, past part. of *contingere* to touch, have contact with, pollute, from CON- + *tangere* to touch]

contact² *verb trans* to communicate with (somebody). ⟫⟫ **contactable** *adj*.

contact inhibition *noun* the cessation of movement and growth of one cell when in contact with another, observed *esp* in tissue cultures.

contact lens *noun* a thin lens designed to fit over the cornea of the eye, *esp* for the correction of a visual defect.

contact print *noun* a photographic print made with a negative in contact with a photographic paper, plate, or film.

contact sheet *noun* a sheet of contact prints.

contact sport *noun* any sport that of its nature brings participants into direct physical contact, such as wrestling, karate, or boxing, or, in a lesser way, football, rugby, or basketball.

contagion /kən'tayj(ə)n/ *noun* **1a** the transmission of a disease from one person to another by contact. **b** a contagious disease. **c** an infection. **2** a corrupting influence or contact. [Latin *contagion-, contagio* infection, from *contingere*: see CONTACT[1]]

contagious /kən'tayjəs/ *adj* **1** said of a disease: communicable by contact; catching. **2** said of a person: suffering from a contagion and likely to communicate it; infectious. **3** said of somebody's mood or attitude: tending to communicate itself to others; infectious: *Her enthusiasm was contagious.* ➤➤ **contagiously** *adv*, **contagiousness** *noun*.

Usage note

contagious or infectious? A *contagious* disease is spread by direct physical contact with an affected person or by touching something previously touched by an affected person: athlete's foot is a contagious disease. An *infectious* disease is transmitted by airborne micro-organisms: chickenpox and influenza are highly *infectious* diseases.

contagious abortion *noun* brucellosis or another disease of domestic animals that causes spontaneous abortion.

contain /kən'tayn/ *verb trans* **1** to have or hold (something) within itself: *The tin contained some stale biscuits.* **2** to comprise or include (something): *The revised bill contains several new clauses.* **3** to keep (something) within limits or hold (it) back or down: *The flood waters could not be contained.* **4** to check or halt (something): *They tried to contain the spread of the infection.* **5** to restrain or control (oneself or one's excitement): *She could contain herself no longer.* **6** said of a number: to be divisible by (a factor), usu without a remainder. ➤➤ **containable** *adj*. [Latin *continēre* to hold together, hold in, contain, from CON- + *tenēre* to hold]

container *noun* **1** an object, such as a box or tin, that contains things. **2** a metal packing case for the transport of goods, standardized for mechanical handling, usu forming a single load for a lorry or railway wagon.

containerize or **containerise** *verb trans* **1** to transport (goods) in containers. **2** to convert (a port or goods-transporting system) to the use of containers.

container ship *noun* a ship for carrying cargo in containers.

containment *noun* the action of keeping something under control, *esp* of preventing the expansion of a hostile power or ideology.

contaminant /kən'taminənt/ *noun* a contaminating substance.

contaminate /kən'taminayt/ *verb trans* **1** to render (something) impure or unfit for use through contact with or the admixture of a polluting or poisonous substance. **2** to make (something) radioactive through exposure to a radioactive substance. **3** to destroy the purity and innocence of (somebody or something) through unwholesome or undesirable influences. ➤➤ **contamination** /-'naysh(ə)n/ *noun*, **contaminative** /-nativ/ *adj*, **contaminator** *noun*. [Latin *contaminatus*, past part. of *contaminare*, from *contamen* contact, defilement, from CON- + a word related to *tangere* to touch]

contango /kən'tanggoh/ *noun Brit* **1** in a commodity market or stock exchange, a situation where a commodity's cash price or the price of a security is lower than its forward price. **2** a premium paid by a buyer to a seller of shares or commodities to postpone delivery until a future day of settlement. [prob a coinage based on Latin verbs in which the first person pres sing. ends in *-o*, perhaps meant to express the idea 'I make contingent']

contd *abbr* continued.

conte /konht, kawnt (*French* kɔ̃t)/ *noun* a tale or short story, *esp* of adventure. [French *conte* tale, ultimately from Latin *computare*: see COMPUTE]

conté /'kontay/ or **Conté** *noun* a hard non-greasy crayon used by artists, typically black, brown, or red, made of graphite and clay. [named after Nicolas J. *Conté* d.1805, French chemist, who developed it]

contemn /kən'tem/ *verb trans archaic* to despise (something) or treat (it) with contempt: *worldlings … who are apt to contemn holy things* — Bacon. ➤➤ **contemner** *noun*, **contemnor** /kən'temnə/ *noun*. [Latin *contemnere*, from CON- + *temnere* to despise]

contemplate /'kontəmplayt/ *verb trans* **1** to consider or meditate on (something). **2** to look at (something) attentively. **3** (*usu in negative contexts*) to envisage (something) with equanimity: *I could not contemplate life without him.* **4** to consider (something) as a course of action: *She contemplated suicide.* ➤ *verb intrans* to ponder or meditate. ➤➤ **contemplator** *noun*. [Latin *contemplatus*, past part. of *contemplari* to survey, observe, from CON- + *templum* space marked out for observation of auguries]

contemplation /kontəm'playsh(ə)n/ *noun* **1** the activity of looking at, considering, or studying something attentively. **2** meditation on spiritual things as a private devotion; *specif* in Christian devotions, seeking to feel God's presence through prayer.

contemplative[1] /kən'templətiv, 'kontəmplaytiv/ *adj* **1** relating to or involving contemplation. **2** denoting a religious order devoted to prayer and penance. ➤➤ **contemplatively** *adv*, **contemplativeness** *noun*.

contemplative[2] *noun* a person who practises contemplation.

contemporaneous /kən,tempə'rayni-əs, ˌkon-/ *adj* belonging to, existing during, or happening during the same period of time. ➤➤ **contemporaneity** /-'neeiti, -'nayiti/ *noun*, **contemporaneously** *adv*, **contemporaneousness** *noun*. [Latin *contemporaneus*, from CON- + *tempor-, tempus* time]

contemporary[1] /kən'temp(ə)rəri/ *adj* **1** happening, existing, living, or coming into being during the same period of time. **2** reflecting today's design or fashion trends; modern: *contemporary furniture.* ➤➤ **contemporarily** *adv*. [medieval Latin *contemporarius*, from CON- + Latin *tempor-, tempus* time]

contemporary[2] *noun* (*pl* **contemporaries**) a person who is contemporary with the person in question, *esp* somebody of the same age: *a contemporary of Wordsworth's.*

contemporize or **contemporise** /kən'tempəriez/ *verb trans* **1** to place (things) in or regard (them) as belonging to the same period. **2** to update or modernize (something) or make (it) contemporary. ➤ *verb intrans* to be contemporary.

contempt /kən'tempt/ *noun* **1** the feeling one has towards someone or something that one despises or has no respect for. **2** (**contempt of court**) the offence of obstructing the administration of justice in court; *esp* wilful disobedience to or open disrespect for a court. ✳ **beneath contempt** utterly despicable. **hold somebody/something in contempt** to despise somebody or something. **hold somebody in contempt** to judge somebody to be in contempt of court. [Latin *contemptus*, past part. of *contemnere*: see CONTEMN]

contemptible *adj* deserving contempt. ➤➤ **contemptibility** /-'biliti/ *noun*, **contemptibleness** *noun*, **contemptibly** *adv*.

contemptuous /kən'temptyooəs/ *adj* manifesting, feeling, or expressing contempt. ➤➤ **contemptuously** *adv*, **contemptuousness** *noun*.

contend /kən'tend/ *verb intrans* **1** to strive or vie in contest or rivalry: *the line-up of those contending for a medal this year.* **2** (+ with) to try to overcome difficulties: *He had a lot of problems to contend with.* **3** to strive in debate; to argue. ➤ *verb trans* to maintain or assert (something): *She contended that it was their error, not hers.* ➤➤ **contender** *noun*. [Latin *contendere* to strive, from CON- + *tendere* to stretch]

content[1] /kən'tent/ *adj* (*also* + with) happy or satisfied: *She was content with her progress.* ✳ **not content with** in spite of having achieved something: *Not content with having secured the lion's share, she set about stealing everybody else's.* ➤➤ **contentment** *noun*. [Latin *contentus*, past part. of *continēre*: see CONTAIN]

content[2] *verb trans* to satisfy (somebody) or appease their desires: *It takes very little to content him.* ✳ **content oneself with** to accept (something that is less than one really wants): *He had to content himself with a single helping seeing no more was on offer.*

content[3] *noun* a state of happy satisfaction; *esp* freedom from care or discomfort. ✳ **to one's heart's content** as much as one wants: *You can wander round the countryside to your heart's content.*

content[4] /'kontent/ *noun* **1** (*in pl*) the things that are contained in something: *The contents of the drawer were strewn over the floor.* **2** (*also* **table of contents**) (*in pl*) the topics and material advertised as treated in a written work. **3** the matter dealt with in a literary work, lecture, speech, etc, as distinct from its form or style of presentation: compare FORM[1] (9B). **4** the amount or proportion of a specified material contained in something: *the lead content of paint.* ➤➤ **contentless** *adj*. [medieval Latin *contentum* (*pl* **contenta**) thing(s) contained, past part. of *continēre*: see CONTAIN]

contented /kən'tentid/ *adj* **1** satisfied with one's situation, status, possessions, etc; happy. **2** reflecting such satisfaction: *a contented expression.* ➤➤ **contentedly** *adv*, **contentedness** *noun*.

contention /kən'tensh(ə)n/ *noun* **1** rivalry or competition. **2** disagreement or argument. **3** a point advanced or maintained in a debate or argument. ✳ **in contention** contending for a prize, etc. [Latin *contention-, contentio*, from *contendere*: see CONTEND]

contentious /kən'tenshəs/ *adj* 1 exhibiting a tendency to quarrels and disputes. 2 likely to cause contention: *a contentious issue*. 3 denoting a legal case involving a dispute between parties: *contentious suits*. ➤➤ **contentiously** *adv*, **contentiousness** *noun*.

conterminous /kon'tuhminəs/ *adj* see COTERMINOUS. ➤➤ **conterminously** *adv*. [Latin *conterminus*, from CON- + *terminus* boundary]

contessa /kon'tesə/ *noun* an Italian countess. [Italian *contessa* from late Latin *comitissa*, fem of *comes* COUNT³]

contest¹ /'kontest/ *noun* 1 a struggle for superiority or victory. 2 a competition or competitive event. [early French *contester* from Latin *contestari litem* to bring an action at law, from *contestari* to call to witness, from CON- + *testis* witness]

contest² /kən'test/ *verb trans* 1 to stand as a candidate in (an election) or for (an elected post). 2 to dispute (a will, claim, decision, etc), sometimes through the law. ➤ *verb intrans* (+ with/against) to strive or vie. ➤➤ **contestable** *adj*, **contester** *noun*.

contestant /kən'test(ə)nt/ *noun* 1 one of the participants in a contest. 2 a person who contests an award or decision.

contestation /konte'staysh(ə)n/ *noun formal* arguing or disputing; controversy.

context /'kontekst/ *noun* 1 the parts surrounding a written or spoken word or passage that can throw light on its meaning. 2 the interrelated conditions in which something exists or occurs. ➤➤ **contextual** /kən'tekstyooəl/ *adj*, **contextually** *adv*. [Latin *contextus* connection of words, coherence, past part. of *contexere* to weave together, from CON- + *texere* to weave]

contextualise /kən'tekstyooəliez/ *verb* see CONTEXTUALIZE.

contextualism /kən'tekstyooəliz(ə)m/ *noun* in philosophy, insistence on establishing the context of enquiry as a prerequisite to solving problems or analysing the meaning of terms. ➤➤ **contextualist** *noun*.

contextualize *or* **contextualise** /kən'tekstyooəliez/ *verb trans* to put (something) into its appropriate context: *Contextualizing the earliest occurrences of slang terms will sometimes lead you to their origin*. ➤➤ **contextualization** /-'zaysh(ə)n/ *noun*.

contiguity /konti'gyooh·iti/ *noun* 1 the condition of being contiguous. 2 in psychology, the closeness of two events, leading to their association in the mind.

contiguous /kən'tigyooəs/ *adj* 1 in actual contact: *contiguous molecules*. 2 touching along a boundary or at a point; adjacent: *contiguous counties*. 3 next or near in time or sequence. ➤➤ **contiguously** *adv*, **contiguousness** *noun*. [Latin *contiguus*, from *contingere*: see CONTACT¹]

continence /'kontinəns/ *noun* 1 self-restraint from yielding to impulse or desire. 2 the ability to control one's bladder and bowels; the condition of being continent.

continent¹ /'kontinənt/ *noun* 1 any of the great divisions of land on the globe, that is, Europe, Asia, Africa, N and S America, Australia, Antarctica. 2 (**the Continent**) the continent of Europe, as distinguished from the British Isles. [Latin *continent-*, *continens*, present part. of *continēre*: see CONTAIN]

continent² *adj* 1 exercising self-restraint. 2 able to control the passing of urine and faeces. ➤➤ **continently** *adv*. [Latin *continent-*, *continens*, present part. of *continēre*: see CONTAIN]

continental¹ /konti'nentl/ *adj* relating to or characteristic of a continent, *esp* Europe. ➤➤ **continentally** *adv*.

continental² *noun* an inhabitant of a continent, *esp* Europe.

continental breakfast *noun* a light breakfast, typically of bread rolls with preserves and coffee.

continental climate *noun* the climate typical of the interior of a continent, with hot summers, cold winters, and comparatively little rainfall.

continental day *noun Brit* a school day that starts in the early morning and ends in the early afternoon, and does not include a long midday break.

continental drift *noun* 1 the drifting apart of the continents across the earth's surface from a single solid land mass over geological time. 2 the theory that such drifting is taking place.

continental quilt *noun Brit* = DUVET.

continental shelf *noun* the gently sloping part of the ocean floor that borders a continent and ends in a steeper slope to the ocean depths.

Continental System *noun* (**the Continental System**) the attempt to blockade Britain begun by Napoleon Bonaparte in 1806.

contingency /kən'tinj(ə)nsi/ *noun* (*pl* **contingencies**) 1 an event, especially an undesirable one, that may occur but cannot be definitely predicted; an eventuality. 2 the absence of certainty in the occurrence of events. 3 in philosophy, the absence of necessity, or the circumstance that something is so without having to be. 4 (*used before a noun*) intended for use if an event should occur: *contingency plans*.

contingency table *noun* a table that shows the correlation between two variables.

contingent¹ /kən'tinj(ə)nt/ *adj* 1 happening by or subject to chance or unforeseen causes. 2 happening as a secondary rather than direct consequence. 3 not logically necessary. 4 (+ on/upon) dependent on or conditioned by (something): *Half of that income I have secured to you ... for life contingent on your undertaking the guardianship* — H Rider Haggard. ➤➤ **contingently** *adv*. [Latin *contingent-*, *contingens*, present part. of *contingere*: see CONTACT¹]

contingent² *noun* a quota or share, *esp* of people supplied from or representative of an area, group, or military force: *the arrival of the Irish contingent*.

continua /kən'tinyoo·ə/ *noun* pl of CONTINUUM.

continual /kən'tinyooəl/ *adj* 1 continuing indefinitely without interruption: *living in continual fear*. 2 recurring in steady rapid succession: *continual interruptions*. ➤➤ **continually** *adv*. [French *continuel* from Latin *continuus* continuous, from *continēre*: see CONTAIN]

> **Usage note**
>
> **continual** *or* **continuous**? The classic illustration of the difference between these two closely related adjectives compares a dripping tap (*continual* – occurring constantly, again and again and again with breaks in between) with a flowing tap (*continuous* – continuing in an unbroken stream). It follows from this that *continual* is generally the word to use with a plural noun (*continual interruptions*; *continual requests for this record*), whereas either word may accompany a singular noun: *a continual* (constantly renewed) *or continuous* (unceasing) *bombardment by the enemy*.

continuance /kən'tinyooəns/ *noun* 1 the act or process of continuing: *the continuance of hostilities*. 2 the time during which an arrangement, etc lasts or is in force: *during the continuance of the contract*. 3 *NAmer* adjournment of court proceedings.

continuant /kən'tinyooənt/ *noun* a consonant (e.g. /l/ or /f/) that may be prolonged, as distinct from a STOP² (consonant that closes the vocal passage, e.g. /p/). ➤➤ **continuant** *adj*.

continuation /kən,tinyoo'aysh(ə)n/ *noun* 1 the process of continuing or of being continued. 2 resumption after an interruption. 3 something that continues, increases, or adds to something: *Leith is a district community, not just a continuation of Edinburgh*.

continuative¹ /kən'tinyooətiv/ *adj* 1 denoting a word or phrase, such as *well* or *so*, that has the function of moving discourse along. 2 denoting a relative clause that adds the next point in a narrative, as in *then I met Jane, who offered to drive me home*.

continuative² *noun* a continuative word or phrase.

continue /kən'tinyooh/ *verb intrans* 1 to maintain a condition, course, or action without interruption. 2 to remain in existence; to endure. 3 to remain in a place or condition; to stay. 4 to resume an activity after interruption. ➤ *verb trans* 1a to maintain (a condition, course, or action) without interruption; to carry on (doing something). b to prolong (an activity) or resume (it) after interruption. 2 to cause (something) to continue. 3 to say (something) further: *'And we love this house,' she continued*. 4 *NAmer* to postpone or adjourn (a legal proceeding). ➤➤ **continuer** *noun*. [Latin *continuare* to make continuous, from *continuus* continuous, from *continēre*: see CONTAIN]

continuing education *noun* an educational programme for adults supplementary to the formal education system, typically consisting of short or part-time courses intended to update skills and increase knowledge.

continuity /konti'nyooh·iti/ *noun* (*pl* **continuities**) 1a uninterrupted connection, succession, or union. b persistence without essential change. c uninterrupted duration in time: *Viewers enjoy the feeling of continuity that soaps provide*. 2 something that has, displays, or provides continuity, e.g.: a a script or scenario in the performing arts; *esp* one giving the details of the sequence of individual shots. **b** speech or music used to link parts of an entertainment, *esp* a radio or television programme. **3** the property characteristic of a continuous mathematical function.

continuity girl *or* **continuity man** *noun* a person who is responsible for ensuring consistency between individual shots after a break in filming.

continuo /kən'tinyoooh/ *noun* a bass part for a keyboard instrument with or without a bass string instrument written as a succession of bass notes with figures that indicate the required chords, used as an accompaniment in baroque music. [Italian *continuo* continuous, from Latin *continuus*, from *continēre*: see CONTAIN]

continuous /kən'tinyooəs/ *adj* **1** uninterrupted; unbroken: *a continuous line.* **2** said of a mathematical function: having an arbitrarily small numerical difference between the value at any one point and the value at any other point sufficiently near the first point. **3** in grammar, denoting tenses formed with the present participle; = PROGRESSIVE¹ (5). ➤➤ **continuously** *adv,* **continuousness** *noun.* [Latin *continuus*, from *continēre*: see CONTAIN]
Usage note
continuous *or* continual? See note at CONTINUAL.

continuous assessment *noun* appraisal of the value of a student's work throughout a course as a means of awarding their final mark or degree.

continuous creation *noun* creation seen as a continuous process, as proposed by the STEADY-STATE THEORY, rather than a sudden single event.

continuous stationery *noun* a continuous strip of paper folded concertina-wise and perforated for division into sheets, used e.g. in dot-matrix printers.

continuum /kən'tinyoo-əm/ *noun* (*pl* **continua** /-ə/) **1** a continuous homogeneous extent or succession, such that adjacent parts are not distinguishable one from the other: *the space-time continuum.* **2** a sequence of minute gradations between extremes: *All such traits are marked by a continuum from one extreme to another —* David E Stannard. [Latin *continuum*, neuter of *continuus* continuous, from *continēre*: see CONTAIN]

contort /kən'tawt/ *verb trans* **1** to twist (something) out of shape: *I saw a grim smile contort Mr Rochester's lips —* Charlotte Brontë. **2** to write or put (something) in a wordy, awkward, and unnatural way: *his strange contorted sentences.* ➤➤ *verb intrans* said *esp* of a face or features: to twist in fury, agony, etc. ➤➤ **contortion** /-sh(ə)n/ *noun,* **contortive** /-tiv/ *adj.* [Latin *contortus,* past part. of *contorquēre,* from CON- + *torquēre* to twist]

contortionist /kən'tawsh(ə)nist/ *noun* **1** an acrobat who specializes in unnatural, *esp* convoluted, body postures. **2** somebody who gets themselves out of difficulties by means of complicated but doubtful arguments. ➤➤ **contortionistic** /-'nistik/ *adj.*

contour¹ /'kontooə/ *noun* **1** an outline, *esp* of a curving or irregular figure, or a line representing this. **2** a line, e.g. on a map, connecting points of equal elevation or height. [French *contour* from Italian *contorno,* from *contornare* to round off, sketch in outline, from CON- + Latin *tornare* to turn on a lathe, from *tornus* lathe]

contour² *verb trans* **1a** to shape the contour or outline of (something). **b** to shape (something) so as to fit contours. **2** to construct (a road, etc) in conformity to a contour. **3** said of a road, etc: to follow the contours of (a natural feature). **4** to enter the contours on (a map, etc).

contour feather *noun* any of the medium-sized feathers that form the general covering of a bird and determine the external contour.

contour line *noun* = CONTOUR¹ (2).

contour ploughing *noun* ploughing that follows the contours of the land, so as to reduce soil erosion.

contr. *abbr* contralto.

contra /'kontrə/ *noun* a member of a US-backed military organization in revolt against the left-wing SANDINISTA government of Nicaragua during the 1980s. [American Spanish *contra,* shortening of *contrarevolucionario* counterrevolutionary]

contra- *prefix* forming words, with the meanings: **1** against: *contraception.* **2** contrary; contrasting: *contradistinction.* **3** pitched below normal: *contrabass.* [Latin *contra, contra-* against, opposite]

contraband /'kontrəband/ *noun* **1** goods or merchandise whose import, export, or possession is forbidden. **2** smuggled goods.

➤➤ **contraband** *adj.* [Italian *contrab(b)ando* from medieval Latin *contrabannum,* from CONTRA- + *bannus, bannum* decree, of Germanic origin]

contrabass /'kontrəbays/ *noun* = DOUBLE BASS.

contrabassoon /ˌkontrəbə'soohn/ *noun* a woodwind musical instrument with a DOUBLE REED (two flat pieces of cane that vibrate to make the sound when blown across) having a range an octave lower than that of the bassoon.

contraception /ˌkontrə'sepsh(ə)n/ *noun* prevention of conception or impregnation, *esp* by artificial means. [CONTRA- + CONCEPTION]

contraceptive¹ /ˌkontrə'septiv/ *adj* denoting a method, device, or drug used to prevent conception.

contraceptive² *noun* a contraceptive method, device, or drug.

contract¹ /'kontrakt/ *noun* **1a** a legally binding agreement between two or more people or parties. **b** a document stating the terms of such an agreement. **2** an undertaking to win a specified number of tricks in bridge. **3** *informal* an arrangement for the murder of somebody by a hired killer. [Latin *contractus,* past part. of *contrahere* to draw together, make a contract, from CON- + *trahere* to draw]

contract² /kən'trakt/ *verb trans* **1a** to establish or undertake (something) by contract: *The firm was contracted to build the road in 18 months.* **b** to transfer or convey (something) by contract: *The copyright was contracted to the publisher.* **2** to catch (a disease): *From the inclemency of the weather and the fatigue of the journey he soon contracted a slow illness —* Edward Gibbon. **3** to incur (a debt). **4** to knit or wrinkle (one's brows) when frowning. **5** to reduce (something) to a smaller size by or as if by squeezing or forcing it together. **6** to shorten (a word) by omitting one or more sounds or letters. ➤ *verb intrans* to draw together or tighten, so as to shorten or become reduced in size: *Metal contracts on cooling.*

contractable /kən'traktəbl/ *adj* said of a disease or habit: that can be caught or passed on. ➤➤ **contractability** /-'biliti/ *noun.*

contract bridge /'kontrakt/ *noun* a form of the card game bridge, which differs from AUCTION BRIDGE in that overtricks do not count towards game bonuses.

contractible /kən'traktəbl/ *adj* **1** said of tissues, etc: that can contract; CONTRACTILE. **2** said of a word or name: that can be shortened. ➤➤ **contractibility** /-'biliti/ *noun.*

contractile /kən'traktiel/ *adj* having the ability to contract or cause contraction: *a contractile protein.* ➤➤ **contractility** /kontrak'tiliti/ *noun.*

contractile vacuole *noun* a spherical sac in a single-celled organism that contracts to discharge fluid from the body.

contract in /'kontrakt, kən'trakt/ *verb intrans Brit* to agree to be included in a particular scheme.

contraction /kən'traksh(ə)n/ *noun* **1** the contracting of a muscle or muscle fibre. **2** a shortening of a word, syllable, or word group, or the resultant short form: *contractions such as 'can't' and 'won't'.* ➤➤ **contractional** *adj,* **contractive** /-tiv/ *adj.*

contract killing /'kontrakt/ *noun* **1** a murder carried out by a hired killer. **2** the practice of hiring killers to commit murders.

contractor /kən'traktə/ *noun* a person who contracts to perform work, *esp* building work, or to provide supplies, usu on a large scale.

contractorize *or* **contractorise** /kən'traktəriez/ *verb trans and intrans Brit* to farm out (the work of providing a service, *esp* a public one) to a contractor. ➤➤ **contractorization** /-'zaysh(ə)n/ *noun.*

contract out /'kontrakt, kən'trakt/ *verb intrans* to opt not to be included in a particular scheme.

contractual /kən'traktyooəl/ *adj* relating to or constituting a contract. ➤➤ **contractually** *adv.*

contracture /kən'trakchə/ *noun* a permanent shortening of a muscle or tendon or of other tissue, e.g. scar tissue, producing deformity. ➤➤ **contractural** *adj.*

contradance *or* **contredanse** /'kontrədahns/ *noun* a country dance with couples in two lines facing each other. [variant of CONTREDANSE]

contradict /kontrə'dikt/ *verb trans* **1** to state the contrary of (a statement or speaker). **2** to deny the truthfulness of (a statement or speaker). ➤➤ **contradictable** *adj,* **contradictor** *noun.* [Latin *contradictus,* past part. of *contradicere,* from CONTRA- + *dicere* to say, speak]

contradiction /kontrə'diksh(ə)n/ *noun* **1** the act of contradicting. **2** an expression or proposition containing contradictory parts; logical inconsistency. **3** opposition of factors inherent in a system or situation. ✳ **contradiction in terms** a group of words or a concept that associates incompatible elements: *A 'high contralto' sounds like a contradiction in terms.*

contradictory /kontrə'dikt(ə)ri/ *adj* **1** constituting a contradiction; incompatible or inconsistent. **2** said of a person: inclined to contradict. **3** said of a pair of propositions: logically such that one and only one must be true: compare CONTRARY[1]. ➤➤ **contradictorily** *adv*, **contradictoriness** *noun*.

contradistinction /,kontrədi'stingksh(ə)n/ *noun* a distinction made between things by contrasting their different qualities. ✳ **in contradistinction to** in contrast to (something else). ➤➤ **contradistinctive** /-tiv/ *adj*, **contradistinctively** /-tivli/ *adv*.

contradistinguish /,kontrədi'stinggwish/ *verb trans* to distinguish (two things) by contrasting their qualities.

contrafactive /kontrə'faktiv/ *adj* in linguistics, said of a verb such as *wish* or *pretend*: taking as its object a clause that conveys something that is not true. compare FACTIVE, NON-FACTIVE.

contrafactual /kontrə'faktyooəl/ *adj* = COUNTERFACTUAL.

contraflow /'kontrəfloh/ *noun* a temporary two-way traffic-flow system introduced on one carriageway of a motorway, etc while the other is closed off, e.g. for repair.

contrail /'kontrayl/ *noun chiefly NAmer* = VAPOUR TRAIL. [short for CONDENSATION TRAIL]

contraindicate /kontrə'indikayt/ *verb trans* to render (a treatment or procedure) inadvisable: *a drug that is contraindicated in pregnancy.* ➤➤ **contraindication** /-'kaysh(ə)n/ *noun*, **contraindicative** /-'dikətiv/ *adj*.

contralateral /kontrə'lat(ə)rəl/ *adj* situated on, appearing on, or affecting the opposite side of the body: compare IPSILATERAL.

contralto /kən'traltoh/ *noun* (*pl* **contraltos**) the lowest female singing voice, or a singer with this voice. [Italian *contralto* from CONTRA- + ALTO]

contra mundum /,kontrə 'moondoom/ *adv* said of an individual stand somebody has taken: defying the rest of the world; in a minority of one: *Griffin contra mundum - with a vengeance!* — H G Wells. [Latin *contra mundum* against the world]

contraposition /,kontrəpə'zish(ə)n/ *noun* in logic, the conversion of a proposition so that its terms are negated and their order reversed, e.g. *All A is B* would be converted into *All not-B is not-A.*

contrapposto /kontrə'postoh/ *noun* (*pl* **contrapposti** /-tee/) in painting or sculpture of the human form, a twisting of the body on its own axis, so that the position of head and shoulders contrasts with that of the hips and legs. [Italian *contrapposto*, past part. of *contrapporre* to oppose, contrast, from Latin *contraponere* to place against, oppose to, from CONTRA- + *ponere* to put]

contraption /kən'trapsh(ə)n/ *noun* a newfangled or complicated device; a gadget. [perhaps a fanciful coinage based on CONTRIVE]

contrapuntal /kontrə'puntl/ *adj* relating to musical counterpoint. ➤➤ **contrapuntally** *adv*. [Italian *contrap(p)unto* counterpoint, from medieval Latin *contrapunctum*, neuter of *contrapunctus*: see COUNTERPOINT[1]]

contrarian /kən'treəri·ən/ *noun* a person who opposes a current trend; *esp* an investor who deliberately acts against the tendency of the stock market. ➤➤ **contrarian** *adj*, **contrarianism** *noun*.

contrariety /kontrə'rieti/ *noun* opposition, disagreement, or inconsistency between two things. [late Latin *contrarietat-, contrarietas*, from *contrarius*: see CONTRARY[1]]

contrariwise /kən'treəriwiez, 'kontrə-/ *adv* **1** conversely; vice versa. **2** on the contrary. **3** in contrast; on the other hand.

contrary[1] /'kontrəri/ *adj* **1** completely different or opposed in nature. **2** /kən'treəri, 'kontrəri/ obstinately self-willed; inclined to oppose the wishes of others. **3** said of the wind or weather: unfavourable. **4** /kən'treəri/ opposite in position or direction: *They are gone a contrary way* — Shakespeare. **5** said of a pair of propositions: logically such that one, or neither, but not both, must be true: compare CONTRADICTORY. ➤➤ **contrarily** *adv*, **contrariness** *noun*. [Latin *contrarius* from *contra* opposite]

contrary[2] *noun* (*pl* **contraries**) **1** a fact or condition incompatible with another. **2** either of a pair of opposites. **3** either of two contrary propositions, e.g. *true* and *false*, that cannot both simultaneously be said to be true of the same subject. ✳ **on/quite the**

contrary just the opposite; no. **to the contrary 1** to the opposite effect: *If I hear nothing to the contrary, I'll accept that explanation.* **2** notwithstanding.

contrary to /'kontrəri/ *prep* in opposition to (something): *Contrary to expectation, he passed.*

contrast[1] /'kontrahst/ *noun* **1a** juxtaposition of dissimilar elements, e.g. colour, tone, or emotion, in a work of art. **b** degree of difference between the lightest and darkest parts of a painting, photograph, television picture, etc. **2** comparison of similar objects to set off their dissimilar qualities. **3** a person or thing against which another may be contrasted: *He's such a contrast to his father.* ➤➤ **contrastive** /kən'trahstiv/ *adj*, **contrastively** /kən'trahstivli/ *adv*.

contrast[2] /kən'trahst/ *verb intrans* (+ with) to exhibit contrast: *Today's falls contrast with last month's bullishness.* ➤ *verb trans* **1** to put (two things or people) in contrast. **2** to compare (two things) in respect to differences. ➤➤ **contrastable** *adj*, **contrasting** *adj*, **contrastingly** *adv*. [French *contraster*, ultimately from Latin CONTRA- + *stare* to stand]

contrast medium /'kontrahst/ *noun* a substance, such as barium sulphate, that is opaque to X-rays and can be introduced into a part of the body that is undergoing radiography in order to improve contrast and therefore visibility.

contrasty /kən'trahsti, 'kon-/ *adj informal* said of a film, photograph, or television picture: showing strong contrast between highlights and shadows.

contrasuggestible /,kontrəsə'jestibl/ *adj* tending to respond to a suggestion by doing or thinking the opposite. ➤➤ **contrasuggestibility** /-'biliti/ *noun*, **contrasuggestion** *noun*.

contravene /kontrə'veen/ *verb trans* to act, or be, contrary to (a law, agreement, principle, etc). ➤➤ **contravener** *noun*. [late Latin *contravenire*, from CONTRA- + Latin *venire* to come]

contravention /kontrə'vensh(ə)n/ *noun* a violation or infringement. ✳ **in contravention of** in such a manner as to infringe (a law or principle). [late Latin *contraventus*, past part. of *contravenire*: see CONTRAVENE]

contredanse /'kontrədahns (French kɔ̃trədɑ̃s)/ *noun* (*pl* **contredanses** /-siz (French -dɑ̃s)/) **1** an 18th-cent. French country dance related to the quadrille. **2** a piece of music for a contredanse. **3** see CONTRADANCE. [French *contredanse*, by folk etymology (influenced by *contre-* COUNTER-) from COUNTRY DANCE]

contre-jour /'kontrəzhooə (French kɔ̃trəʒuːr)/ *adj* of or relating to the technique of photographing into the light, so that the light source is behind the subject: *contre-jour shots.* [French *contre-jour*, from *contre* COUNTER- + *jour* day, daylight]

contretemps /'konhtrətonh, 'kon- (French kɔ̃trətɑ̃)/, 'konhtrətonh, 'kon-/ *noun* (*pl* **contretemps** /-tonhz (French kɔ̃trətɑ̃)/) a minor setback, disagreement, or confrontation. [French *contretemps*, from *contre-* COUNTER- + *temps* time]

contribute /kən'tribyooht, 'kon-/ *verb trans* **1** to give (money, etc) in common with others for a common cause. **2** to supply (an article, etc) for a publication. ➤ *verb intrans* **1** (+ to) to help bring about an end or result: *factors contributing to the collapse of Communism.* **2** to supply articles to a publication. ➤➤ **contributive** /kən'tribyootiv/ *adj*, **contributively** /kən'tribyootivli/ *adv*, **contributor** /kən'tribyootə/ *noun*. [Latin *contributus*, past part. of *contribuere* to bring together, from CON- + *tribuere* to grant]

Usage note

Contribute is usually pronounced with the stress on the second syllable *-trib-*. Pronunciation with the stress on the first syllable *con-* is disliked by many people.

contribution /kontri'byoohsh(ə)n/ *noun* **1** the act of contributing. **2** something contributed.

contributory[1] /kən'tribyoot(ə)ri/ *adj* **1** having helped to cause something: *contributory factors.* **2** denoting a pension scheme or insurance plan that is contributed to by both employers and employees. **3** contributing to a common fund or enterprise: *contributory bodies.*

contributory[2] *noun* (*pl* **contributories**) a person liable in British law to contribute towards meeting the debts of a bankrupt company.

contributory negligence *noun* in law, insufficient care and attention on the part of an injured person, judged to have been a factor in the circumstances of their injury.

con trick *noun informal* = CONFIDENCE TRICK.

contrite /kən'triet/ *adj* **1** grieving and penitent for one's sin or shortcomings. **2** showing contrition: *a contrite expression.* ▶▶ **contritely** *adv*, **contriteness** *noun*. [medieval Latin *contritus* literally 'ground down, bruised', past part. of *conterere* to grind, bruise, from CON- + *terere* to rub]

contrition /kən'trish(ə)n/ *noun* sorrow for one's sins, arising *esp* from the love of God rather than fear of punishment: compare ATTRITION.

contrivance /kən'triev(ə)ns/ *noun* **1** the process of contriving something. **2** something contrived, e.g. a mechanical device or a clever ploy: *the first European fire-arm, a clumsy contrivance* — Herman Melville. **3** rather too obvious artificiality in achieving an effect.

contrive /kən'triev/ *verb trans* **1a** to devise or plan (something). **b** to create (something) in an inventive or resourceful manner: *They contrived a stretcher from a couple of branches.* **2a** to bring about or manage (something): *Perhaps he could contrive another encounter with her.* **b** to manage (to do something stupid): *He contrived to lock himself out.* ▶▶ **contrivability** /-'biliti/ *noun*, **contrivable** *adj*, **contriver** *noun*. [earlier *controve* from late Latin *contropare* to compare, from CONTRA- + Latin *tropus* turn, manner, from Greek *tropos*]

contrived *adj* said of artistic or literary effects, language, etc: unnatural or forced.

control¹ /kən'trohl/ *verb trans* (**controlled, controlling**) **1** to supervise and direct (something). **2** to operate (a machine). **3** to restrain (oneself or one's emotions). **4** to regulate (the finances of an organization, etc). ▶▶ **controllability** /-'biliti/ *noun*, **controllable** *adj*. [from French *controleur* from *contrerolle* copy of an account, audit, from *contre-* COUNTER- + *rolle* roll, account]

control² *noun* **1** power or authority to control: *He lost control of the car.* **2** the activity or situation of controlling. **3** direction, review, regulation, and coordination of business activities. **4** mastery in the use of a tool, instrument, technique, or artistic medium. **5** restraint or reserve. **6** a checking device. **7a** = CONTROL EXPERIMENT. **b** in a control experiment, a subject not given the treatment under trial, for purposes of comparison. **8** (*in pl*) the devices and mechanisms used to regulate or guide the operation of a machine, apparatus, or system. **9** (*treated as sing. or pl*) an organization that directs a space flight: *mission control.* **10** a personality or spirit believed to be responsible for the utterances or performances of a spiritualistic medium at a séance. ✳ **in control** in control or command. **out of control** dangerously unrestrained. **under control** being properly supervised and regulated.

control character *noun* in computing, a keyboard character that is not printed, but initiates an operation or controls a device.

control experiment *noun* an experiment or trial in which parallel testing is carried out on a CONTROL² (a subject not given the treatment under trial).

control key *noun* a key on a computer keyboard that another key causes to emit a command sequence when pressed simultaneously with it.

controlled *adj* **1** said of a person's expression or behaviour: deliberately calm: *His tone was quiet and controlled* — Edith Wharton. **2** said of an experiment or trial: in which testing is simultaneously carried out on a CONTROL² (a subject not given the treatment under trial), or in which possible extraneous factors are controlled for, or taken into account. **3** said of a drug: that has legal restrictions on its use and possession. **4** said of an aircraft's flight: directed from the ground or from another aircraft.

controlled experiment *noun* = CONTROL EXPERIMENT.

controller *noun* **1** a person who controls or directs something: *the controller of Radio 3.* **2** the chief financial officer of an organization or business enterprise. ▶▶ **controllership** *noun*.

controlling interest *noun* sufficient share ownership in a company to have control over policy.

control panel *noun* a panel on which are mounted devices, e.g. dials and switches, used in the remote control and monitoring of electrified or mechanical apparatus.

control rod *noun* one of a set of rods, usu containing a neutron-absorber, e.g. boron, that can be moved up or down along their axis into the core of a nuclear reactor to control the rate of the reaction.

control surface *noun* a movable aerofoil or fin of an aircraft or ship that allows the position of the vehicle relative to the ground or water to be changed.

control tower *noun* a tall airport building from which movements of aircraft on the ground and in the air are controlled.

control unit *noun* **1** formerly, a section of a prison providing a special punitive regime of total isolation for especially violent prisoners. **2** a section of the central processing unit in a computer that controls the movement of information between the memory, the arithmetic and logic unit, and other registers in order to execute a program.

controversial /kontrə'vuhsh(ə)l/ *adj* tending to cause controversy. ▶▶ **controversialism** *noun*, **controversialist** *noun*, **controversially** *adv*.

controversy /'kontrəvuhsi, kən'trovəsi/ *noun* (*pl* **controversies**) **1** debate or disagreement, *esp* in public or in the media. **2** a dispute over a specific issue. [Latin *controversia* from *controversus* disputed, literally 'turned against', from CONTRA- + *versus*, past part. of *vertere* to turn]

Usage note
The traditional pronunciation of *controversy* places the stress on the first syllable *con-*. This is the only standard pronunciation in American English. In British English the stress is frequently placed on the second syllable *-trov-*. All modern British dictionaries accept this pronunciation, but many traditionalists dislike it.

controvert /'kontrəvuht, -'vuht/ *verb trans formal* to deny or dispute the truth of (something). ▶▶ **controverter** *noun*, **controvertible** /-'vuhtəbl/ *adj*. [back-formation from CONTROVERSY]

contumacious /kontyoo'mayshəs/ *adj formal* stubbornly disobedient; rebellious: *to reduce the contumacious monks to obedience* — History and Antiquities of Rochester. ▶▶ **contumaciously** *adv*, **contumacy** /'kontyooməsi/ *noun*. [Latin *contumacia* from *contumac-, contumax* insubordinate, from CON- + *tumēre* to swell, be proud]

contumely /kon'tyoohmili, 'kontyoomli/ *noun formal* abusive and contemptuous language or treatment: *the proud man's contumely* — Shakespeare. ▶▶ **contumelious** /-'meeli-əs/ *adj*, **contumeliously** /-'meeli-əsli/ *adv*. [Latin *contumelia* abuse, insult, invective; perhaps related to Latin *contumacia*: see CONTUMACIOUS]

contuse /kən'tyoohz/ *verb trans* to injure (part of the body) without breaking the skin; to bruise (it). [Latin *contusus*, past part. of *contundere* to crush, bruise, from CON- + *tundere* to beat]

contusion /kən'tyoohzh(ə)n/ *noun* a bruise.

conundrum /kə'nundrəm/ *noun* (*pl* **conundrums**) **1** a riddle; *esp* one whose answer is or involves a pun. **2** an intricate and difficult problem. [perhaps a fanciful coinage; orig applied to a crank or pedant, later a whim]

conurbation /konuh'baysh(ə)n/ *noun* a vast urban area, formed when the suburbs of a large city coalesce with nearby towns. [CON- + Latin *urb-, urbs* city]

conus /'kohnəs/ *noun* (*pl* **coni** /'kohnie/) **1** the cone-shaped upper front part of the right ventricle of the heart. **2** the cone-shaped lower end of the spinal cord. [Latin *conus* from Greek *kōnos* CONE¹]

conus arteriosus /ah,tiəri'ohsəs/ *noun* = CONUS (1).

conus medullaris /,medə'lahris/ *noun* = CONUS (2).

convalesce /konvə'les/ *verb intrans* to recover gradually after sickness or weakness. ▶▶ **convalescence** *noun*, **convalescent** *adj* and *noun*. [Latin *convalescere*, from CON- + *valescere* to grow strong, from *valēre* to be strong or well]

convect /kən'vekt/ *verb intrans* to transfer heat by convection. ▶ *verb trans* to circulate (warm air) by convection. [back-formation from CONVECTION]

convection /kən'veksh(ə)n/ *noun* the transfer of heat by the circulatory motion that occurs in a gas or liquid at a non-uniform temperature owing to the variation of density with temperature. ▶▶ **convectional** *adj*, **convective** /-tiv/ *adj*. [late Latin *convection-, convectio*, from Latin *convehere* to bring together, from CON- + *vehere* to carry]

convector /kən'vektə/ *noun* a heating unit from which heated air circulates by convection.

convene /kən'veen/ *verb intrans* to assemble for a meeting, etc. ▶ *verb trans* **1** to cause (a committee, etc) to assemble. **2** *archaic* to summon (a person) before a tribunal. [Middle English *convenen* via

French from Latin *convenire* to come together, be suitable, from CON- + *venire* to come]

convener *noun* see CONVENOR.

convenience /kən'veenyəns/ *noun* **1** ease of use or access; handiness: *the convenience of email*. **2** one's personal comfort or advantage: *Our passengers' convenience comes first*. **3** an appliance, device, or service conducive to comfort: *every modern convenience*. **4** Brit = PUBLIC CONVENIENCE. ✻ **at one's convenience** when it suits one to do something. **at one's earliest convenience** as soon as it suits one to do something.

convenience food *noun* commercially prepared food, e.g. frozen ready-cooked meals, requiring little or no further preparation before eating.

convenience store *noun* chiefly NAmer a small shop that stocks general groceries and household goods, and stays open late and at weekends.

convenient /kən'veenyənt/ *adj* **1** suited to personal comfort or to easy use: *a convenient mode of transport*. **2** suited to a particular situation: *a convenient place to start*. **3** near at hand; easily accessible: *We found a convenient restaurant*. ➤➤ **conveniently** *adv*. [Latin *convenient-*, *conveniens*, present part. of *convenire*: see CONVENE]

convenor *or* **convener** *noun* **1** chiefly Brit. **a** a member of a group, *esp* a committee, responsible for calling meetings. **b** a chairperson. **2** an elected union official responsible for coordinating the work of shop stewards in an establishment.

convent /'konv(ə)nt/ *noun* **1** a local community or house of a religious order or congregation; *esp* an establishment of nuns. **2** a school attached to a convent, at which the majority of teachers are nuns. [medieval Latin *conventus* convent, earlier 'an assembly', past part. of *convenire*: see CONVENE]

conventicle /kən'ventikl/ *noun* **1** formerly, an (irregular or unlawful) assembly or meeting, *esp* of dissenters (people not conforming to the Church of England; see DISSENTER), for religious worship. **2** the small chapel or meetinghouse used for this purpose. ➤➤ **conventicler** *noun*. [Latin *conventiculum*, dimin. of *conventus* assembly, past part. of *convenire*: see CONVENE]

convention /kən'vensh(ə)n/ *noun* **1** accepted social custom or practice, or a specific form or use. **2** a generally agreed principle or practice. **3** an agreement between states that regulates matters affecting all of them. **4** a compact between opposing military commanders, *esp* one concerning prisoner exchange or armistice. **5** an assembly of people met for a common purpose; a conference. **6** a meeting of the delegates of a US political party for the purpose of formulating policies and selecting candidates for office. **7** an established artistic technique or practice: *the conventions of the stream-of-consciousness novel*. **8** an agreed system of bidding or playing that conveys information between partners in bridge or other card games. [Latin *convention-*, *conventio*, from *convenire*: see CONVENE]

conventional *adj* **1a** conforming to or sanctioned by convention: *Galbraith challenged the conventional wisdom that everything would be all right if only the Gross National Product were big enough* — Peter Lewis. **b** lacking originality or individuality. **2** said of warfare: not using atom bombs or hydrogen bombs. ➤➤ **conventionalism** *noun*, **conventionalist** *noun*, **conventionality** /-'naliti/ *noun*, **conventionally** *adv*.

conventionalize *or* **conventionalise** /kən'vensh(ə)nliez/ *verb trans* to make (something or somebody) conventional. ➤➤ **conventionalization** /-'zaysh(ə)n/ *noun*.

conventioneer /kən,venshə'niə/ *noun* chiefly NAmer a person attending a convention.

convent school *noun* = CONVENT (2).

conventual[1] /kən'ventyoo(ə)l/ *adj* relating to, belonging to, or befitting a convent or monastic life. ➤➤ **conventually** *adv*. [medieval Latin *conventualis*, from *conventus* convent, past part. of *convenire*: see CONVENE]

conventual[2] *noun* a member of a convent.

converge /kən'vuhj/ *verb intrans* **1** said of lines: to move together towards a common point and finally meet. **2** (+ on/upon) to come together in a common interest or focus: *Groups of protesters converged on the embassy*. **3** said of a mathematical sequence: to ultimately approach a finite limit. [medieval Latin *convergere*, from CON- + *vergere* to bend, incline]

convergence *or* **convergency** /-si/ *noun* **1** a converging, *esp* towards union or uniformity; *esp* coordinated movement of the eyes resulting in reception of an image on corresponding retinal

areas. **2** independent development in unrelated organisms of similar characters, often associated with similar environments or behaviour.

convergent *adj* **1** tending to move towards one point or to approach each other. **2** said of unrelated organisms: exhibiting convergence. **3** mathematically converging to a limit: *a convergent series or sequence*. **4** denoting STRABISMUS (squinting), in which the eyes are turned towards each other.

conversable /kən'vuhsəbl/ *adj* **1** literary pleasant and easy to converse with: *Mrs Bardell let lodgings to many conversable single gentlemen* — Dickens. **2** archaic relating to or suitable for conversation or social interaction: *The evening was quiet and conversable* — Jane Austen.

conversant /kən'vuhs(ə)nt/ *adj* (+ with) fully acquainted or familiar with facts, principles, etc: *conversant with the details of the contract*. ➤➤ **conversantly** *adv*. [Latin *conversant-*, *conversans*, present part. of *conversari*: see CONVERSE[1]]

conversation /konvə'saysh(ə)n/ *noun* **1a** informal verbal exchange of feelings, opinions, or ideas. **b** an instance of this. **2** an exchange similar to conversation; *esp* interaction with a computer, *esp* through a keyboard. ➤➤ **conversational** *adj*, **conversationally** *adv*. [Latin *conversation-*, *conversatio*, from *conversari*: see CONVERSE[1]]

conversationalist *noun* a person who enjoys or excels in conversation.

conversation piece *noun* **1** a group picture or portrait, e.g. of members of a family, in which the subjects are posed in a rural or domestic setting. **2** an object whose unusualness arouses interest and prompts conversation: *The jail was Maycomb's only conversation piece; its detractors said it looked like a Victorian privy* — Harper Lee.

conversazione /,konvəsatsi'ohni/ *noun* (*pl* **conversaziones** /-neez/ *or* **conversazioni** /-nee/) a meeting for informal discussion of intellectual or cultural matters. [Italian *conversazione* conversation, from Latin *conversation-*, *conversatio*, from *conversari*: see CONVERSE[1]]

converse[1] /kən'vuhs/ *verb intrans* **1** to exchange thoughts and opinions in speech; to talk. **2** to carry on an exchange similar to a conversation; *esp* to interact with a computer. ➤➤ **converser** *noun*. [Latin *conversari* to keep company with, from *convertere* to turn round, from CON- + *vertere* to turn]

converse[2] /'konvuhs/ *noun* literary conversation.

converse[3] /'konvuhs/ *adj* reversed in order, relation, or action; opposite. ➤➤ **conversely** *adv*. [Latin *conversus*, past part. of *convertere*: see CONVERSE[1]]

converse[4] /'konvuhs/ *noun* **1** a situation, event, fact, etc that is the opposite of something else. **2** a theorem or statement obtained by interchanging the premise and conclusion of a given theorem or statement, e.g. the converse of 'if male then mortal' is 'if mortal then male'.

conversion /kən'vuhsh(ə)n/ *noun* **1** the converting of something or its converted state. **2** something converted from one use to another. **3a** the alteration of a building to a different purpose. **b** a building so altered. **4** a definite and decisive adoption of a religious faith, or an experience that prompts this or is associated with it. **5** the unlawful exercising of rights to personal property belonging to another. **6** in rugby or American football, an opportunity to score extra points awarded after a try or touchdown, or the score that results from this. **7** an opportunity to kick a goal awarded to the scoring team after a try in rugby, or the score that results from a successful kick. **8** bodily symptoms, e.g. paralysis, appearing as a result of mental conflict without a physical cause. ➤➤ **conversional** *adj*. [Middle English via French from Latin *conversion-*, *conversio*, a turning around, from *convertere*: see CONVERSE[1]]

conversion hysteria *noun* = CONVERSION (8).

convert[1] /kən'vuht/ *verb trans* **1** to change (something) from one form or function to another, e.g. to make structural alterations to (a building or part of a building). **2** to alter the physical or chemical nature or properties of (something), *esp* in manufacturing. **3** to exchange (e.g. a security or bond) for something of equivalent value. **4a** to win (somebody) over from one persuasion or party to another. **b** to cause (somebody) to experience a religious conversion. **5a** in rugby, to complete (a try) by successfully kicking a conversion. **b** in American football, to complete (a touchdown) by successfully kicking a conversion. ➤ *verb intrans* **1** to undergo conversion. **2** to be able to be converted. **3** in American football, to make a conversion. **4** in logic, to interchange the SUBJECT[1] (3B) and PREDICATE[1] (2) to obtain a new proposition. [Middle English *converten* via Old French *convertir* from Latin *convertere*: see CONVERSE[1]]

convert[2] /ˈkonvuht/ *noun* a person who has been converted, *esp* one who has undergone a religious conversion.

converter *or* **convertor** /kənˈvuhtə/ *noun* **1** somebody or something that converts. **2** the furnace used in the Bessemer process of steel-making, or a device employing mechanical rotation to change electrical energy from one form to another. **3** an electronic device for converting signals from one frequency to another. **4** a device that accepts data in one form and converts it to another, e.g. an analogue-to-digital converter.

converter reactor *noun* a nuclear reactor that converts one kind of fuel into another, usu fertile material into fissile material.

convertible[1] /kənˈvuhtəbl/ *adj* **1** capable of being converted. **2** said of a car: having a top that may be lowered or removed. **3** said of currency: capable of being exchanged for a specified equivalent, e.g. another currency. **4** said of a bond, stock, etc: capable of being exchanged for other assets, e.g. shares. ⫸ **convertibility** /-vuhtəˈbiliti/ *noun*, **convertibly** *adv*.

convertible[2] *noun* **1** a convertible car. **2** a convertible bond, stock, or currency.

convertible marka /ˈmahkə/ *noun* the basic monetary unit of Bosnia-Herzegovina, divided into 100 fennigs.

convertor /konˈvuhtə/ *noun* see CONVERTER.

convex /konˈveks/ *adj* curved or rounded outwards like the outside of a bowl: compare CONCAVE. ⫸ **convexly** *adv*. [early French *convexe* from Latin *convexus* vaulted, concave, convex]

convexity /kənˈveksiti/ *noun* (*pl* **convexities**) **1** the quality or state of being convex. **2** a convex line, surface, or part.

convexo-concave /kən,veksoh konˈkayv/ *adj* **1** concave on one side and convex on the other. **2** said of a lens: having the convex side curved more than the concave.

convexo-convex *adj* having both sides convex; biconvex.

convey /kənˈvay/ *verb trans* **1** to take or carry (something or somebody) from one place to another. **2** to impart or communicate (e.g. a feeling or idea). **3** in law, to transfer (property or the rights to property) to another person. ⫸ **conveyable** *adj*. [Middle English *conveyen* via French from Latin *conviare* to escort, from CON- + *via* way]

conveyance *noun* **1** the conveying of something. **2** a means of transport; a vehicle. **3** a document by which rights to property are transferred, or the transfer itself.

conveyancing *noun* the act or business of transferring rights to property. ⫸ **conveyancer** *noun*.

conveyor *or* **conveyer** *noun* **1** somebody who conveys something. **2** a conveyor belt.

conveyor belt *noun* a mechanical apparatus for carrying articles, in the form of an endless moving belt or set of linked plates.

convict[1] /kənˈvikt/ *verb trans* to find or prove (somebody) to be guilty of a crime. [Middle English *convicten* from Latin *convictus*, past part. of *convincere* to refute, convict, from CON- + *vincere* to conquer]

convict[2] /ˈkonvikt/ *noun* a person who has been found guilty and is serving a prison sentence.

conviction /kənˈviksh(ə)n/ *noun* **1a** a strongly held persuasion or belief. **b** the state of being convinced. **2** the convicting of somebody, or the state of being convicted, *esp* in judicial proceedings.

convince /kənˈvins/ *verb trans* **1** to cause (somebody) to believe or accept something. **2** to persuade (somebody) to a course of action. ⫸ **convincer** *noun*, **convincible** *adj*. [Latin *convincere*: see CONVICT[1]]

convincing *adj* **1** removing doubt or disbelief; plausible. **2** said of a victory, etc: secured easily and by a large margin. ⫸ **convincingly** *adv*.

convivial /kənˈvivi·əl/ *adj* **1** sociable or friendly: *convivial company*. **2** occupied with or fond of eating, drinking, and good company. ⫸ **conviviality** /-ˈaliti/ *noun*, **convivially** *adv*. [late Latin *convivialis* from Latin *convivium* banquet, from CON- + *vivere* to live]

convocation /konvəˈkaysh(ə)n, konvoh-/ *noun* **1** either of the two provincial assemblies of bishops and representative clergy of the Church of England (Canterbury and York). **2a** *Brit* a legislative assembly of a university. **b** *NAmer* a ceremonial assembly of graduates of a college or university. **3** the act of calling people together. ⫸ **convocational** *adj*. [Middle English via French from Latin *convocation-*, *convocatio* a calling together, from *convocare*: see CONVOKE]

convoke /kənˈvohk/ *verb trans formal* to call (a formal meeting). [early French *convoquer* from Latin *convocare*, from CON- + *vocare* to call]

convoluted *adj* **1** complex and difficult to understand or unravel; involved: *a convoluted argument*. **2** *technical* having twists or coils. ⫸ **convolutedly** *adv*. [Latin *convolutus*, past part. of *convolvere*: see CONVOLVE]

convolution /konvəˈloohsh(ə)n/ *noun* **1** a twist or coil. **2** any of the irregular ridges on the surface of the brain, *esp* of the CEREBRUM (anterior portion of the brain) of higher mammals. **3** something intricate or complicated. ⫸ **convolutional** *adj*.

convolve /kənˈvolv/ *verb trans* to roll or twist (something) together. [Latin *convolvere*, from CON- + *volvere* to roll]

convolvulus /kənˈvolvyooləs/ *noun* (*pl* **convolvuluses**) any of a genus of trailing or twining plants of the bindweed family, many of which have trumpet-shaped flowers and broadly triangular leaves: genus *Convolvulus*. [Latin *convolvulus*, from *convolvere*: see CONVOLVE]

convoy[1] /ˈkonvoy/ *noun* (*treated as sing. or pl*) a group of ships, military vehicles, etc moving together, *esp* with a protective escort. ✱ **in convoy** travelling together.

convoy[2] *verb trans* to accompany or escort (something or somebody in transit) for protection. [Middle English *convoyen* via French from Latin *conviare*: see CONVEY]

convulsant[1] /kənˈvuls(ə)nt/ *adj* said of a drug: causing convulsions.

convulsant[2] *noun* a convulsant drug.

convulse /kənˈvuls/ *verb trans* **1** to cause (a person) to be shaken violently by spasms, e.g. of rage, laughter, etc. **2** to cause upheaval in (a community, etc): *He threatened to raise a scandal that would convulse the nation* — Conan Doyle. ⫸ *verb intrans* to be convulsed. ⫸ **convulsive** *adj*, **convulsively** *adv*. [Latin *convulsus*, past part. of *convellere* to pluck up, convulse, from CON- + *vellere* to pull]

convulsion /kənˈvulsh(ə)n/ *noun* **1** an abnormal violent and involuntary contraction or series of contractions of the muscles. **2** a violent disturbance. **3** (*in pl*) an uncontrolled fit of laughter.

cony *or* **coney** /ˈkohni/ *noun* (*pl* **conies** *or* **coneys**) **1** a rabbit. **2** rabbit fur. **3** a hyrax. [Middle English *conies* (pl), via early French *conis* from Latin *cuniculus* rabbit]

coo[1] /kooh/ *verb intrans* (**coos, cooed, cooing**) **1** to make the low soft cry characteristic of a dove or pigeon, or a sound similar to it. **2** to talk lovingly or appreciatively. [imitative]

coo[2] *noun* the low soft cry of a dove or pigeon.

coo[3] *interj Brit, informal* used to express surprise, awe, etc. [origin unknown]

cooee[1] /ˈkooh-ee/ *interj informal* used to make one's presence known or to attract somebody's attention at a distance. ✱ **within cooee** *Aus, NZ* in earshot. [imitative of an Aboriginal signal]

cooee[2] *verb intrans* (**cooees, cooeed, cooeeing**) to call 'cooee'.

cook[1] /kook/ *verb intrans* **1** to prepare food for eating, *esp* by subjecting it to heat. **2** said of food: to undergo the process of being cooked. **3** *informal* to falsify (e.g. financial accounts) in order to deceive: *She was accused of cooking the books*. **4** *informal* to occur or happen: *What's cooking?* **5** *NAmer, informal* to be working or performing well, or progressing successfully: *Now we're really cooking!* ⫸ *verb trans* **1** to prepare (food) for eating by a heating process. **2** to subject (something) to the action of heat or fire. ✱ **cook somebody's goose** *informal* to ruin somebody's plans irretrievably. ⫸ **cookable** *adj*, **cooking** *noun*.

cook[2] *noun* a person who prepares food for eating, *esp* as a job. [Old English *cōc*, ultimately from Latin *coquus*]

cookbook *noun* = COOKERY BOOK.

cook-chill *noun Brit* a method of preparing food in which dishes are pre-cooked and quickly chilled for reheating later. ⫸ **cook-chill** *adj*.

cooker *noun Brit* **1** an apparatus, appliance, etc for cooking, typically consisting of an oven, hot plates or rings, and a grill fixed in position. **2** *informal* a variety of fruit, *esp* an apple, not usu eaten raw.

cookery /'kook(ə)ri/ *noun* (*pl* **cookeries**) **1** the art or practice of cooking. **2** *NAmer* a kitchen.

cookery book *noun* a book of recipes and instructions for preparing and cooking food.

cookhouse /'kookhows/ *noun* a kitchen set up outdoors, e.g. at a campsite, or on board ship.

cookie /'kooki/ *noun* **1a** *NAmer* a sweet flat or slightly leavened biscuit. **b** *Scot* a plain bun. **2** *informal* a person of a specified type: *a tough cookie*. **3** in computing, a string of data relating to a particular website, downloaded to a user's hard disk and accessed whenever he or she visits that site. ✳ **the way the cookie crumbles** *chiefly NAmer, informal* what inevitably happens. [Dutch *koekje*, dimin. of *koek* cake]

cooking apple *noun* an apple suitable for cooking.

cook-off *noun chiefly NAmer* a cookery contest, typically involving the preparation of a speciality, e.g. barbecued ribs.

cookout *noun NAmer* an outing at which food is cooked and served in the open.

cook shop *noun* a shop that sells kitchenware.

Cook's tour /kooks/ *noun informal* a quick tour in which attractions are viewed briefly and cursorily. [named after Thomas *Cook* and Son, English travel agency, which first organized guided tours]

cook up *verb trans informal* to concoct or improvise (something).

cool¹ /koohl/ *adj* **1** moderately cold; lacking in warmth. **2** bringing or suggesting relief from heat: *a cool dress*. **3** lacking friendliness or enthusiasm. **4** dispassionately calm and self-controlled. **5** said of a colour: producing an impression of being cool: *a bathroom decorated in cool blues and lilacs*. **6** *informal* used as an intensive: *We made a cool million on the deal*. **7** *informal* fashionable or attractive: *We admired his cool sunglasses*. **8** *informal* very good: *I've had a cool idea*. **9** said of jazz: of or being an understated, restrained, and melodic style that became popular in the 1940s. ➤➤ **coolish** *adj*, **coolly** *adv*, **coolness** *noun*. [Old English *cōl*]

cool² *verb intrans* **1** to lose heat or warmth. **2** to lose enthusiasm or passion. ➤ *verb trans* **1** (*often* + off/down) to make (something or somebody) cool or cooler. **2** to moderate the excitement, force, or activity of (something, e.g. somebody's temper). ✳ **cool it** *informal* to become calm or quiet; to relax: *Just cool it, will you, so I can think*. **cool one's heels** to wait or be kept waiting for a long time, *esp* from disdain or discourtesy.

cool³ *noun* **1** a cool atmosphere or place. **2** *informal* poise or composure: *Don't lose your cool*. **3** *informal* the quality of being impressively fashionable or attractive. ✳ **keep/lose one's cool** *informal* to stay, or fail to stay, calm and composed.

cool⁴ *adv informal* in a casual and nonchalant manner: *Play it cool*.

coolabah *or* **coolibah** /'koohləbah/ *noun* a eucalyptus or gum tree that typically grows in cool conditions near rivers and streams: *Eucalyptus microtheca*. [native name in Australia]

coolant /'koohlənt/ *noun* a liquid or gas used in cooling, *esp* in an engine.

cool bag *noun* an insulated bag used for keeping food or drink cool.

cool box *noun* an insulated box with a handle, used for keeping food or drink cool.

cool down *verb intrans* to allow a violent emotion, e.g. rage, to pass.

cooldrink *noun SAfr* a soft drink. [translation of Afrikaans *koeldrank*]

cooler *noun* **1a** a container for cooling liquids. **b** *NAmer* a refrigerator. **c** *NAmer* a cool bag or cool box. **2** (**the cooler**) *informal* prison or a prison cell. **3** a drink consisting of wine, fruit juice, and soda water.

coolheaded *adj* not easily made angry, flustered, or excited.

coolibah /'koohləbah/ *noun* see COOLABAH.

coolie /'koohli/ *noun* **1** *dated* an unskilled labourer or porter, usu in or from the Far East, hired for low or subsistence wages. **2** *offensive* somebody from India. [Hindi *kulī*]

coolie hat *noun* a shallow conical hat, usu of straw.

cooling-off period *noun* an interval to allow passions to cool, to permit negotiation between parties, or to allow a recently signed contract to be cancelled.

cooling tower *noun* a tall wide concrete tower in which steam from an industrial process, e.g. the generation of electricity, is allowed to condense.

coomb *or* **coombe** *or* **combe** /koohm/ *noun Brit* a valley or basin, *esp* on a hillside or running up from the coast. [Old English *cumb*, of Celtic origin]

coon /koohn/ *noun* **1** *NAmer* a raccoon. **2** *informal, offensive* a black person. [short for RACCOON]

cooncan /'koohnkan/ *noun* a card game for two players with a pack of 40 cards, similar to rummy. [modification of Mexican Spanish *con quien* with whom?]

coonskin *noun* the skin or pelt of a raccoon.

coop¹ /koohp/ *noun* **1** a cage or small enclosure or building, *esp* for housing poultry. **2** a confined space. **3** a wicker basket used for catching fish. [Middle English *cupe*, ultimately from Latin *cupa* cask]

coop² *verb trans* (*usu* + up) to confine (a person or animal) in a restricted space.

co-op /'koh op/ *noun informal* a cooperative enterprise.

cooper¹ /'koohpə/ *noun* a person who makes or repairs barrels, casks, etc. ➤➤ **cooperage** /-rij/ *noun*. [Middle English *couper*, *cowper* via early Dutch *cūper* from Latin *cupa* cask]

cooper² *verb trans* (**coopered, coopering**) to make or repair (barrels, casks, etc).

cooperate *or* **co-operate** /koh'opərayt/ *verb intrans* **1** to act or work with another person or other people for a common purpose. **2** to do or agree to what is asked. ➤➤ **cooperator** *noun*. [late Latin *cooperatus*, past part. of *cooperari* to work together, from CO- + *operare*: see OPERATE]

cooperation *or* **co-operation** /koh·opə'raysh(ə)n/ *noun* **1** the action of cooperating. **2** willingness to do or agree to what is asked. **3** the organization of people into cooperatives, or the functioning of cooperatives.

cooperative¹ *or* **co-operative** /koh'op(ə)rətiv/ *adj* **1** showing cooperation or a willingness to work with others. **2** of, or organized as, a cooperative. ➤➤ **cooperatively** *adv*, **cooperativeness** *noun*.

cooperative² *or* **co-operative** *noun* an enterprise, e.g. a shop, or organization, e.g. a society, owned by and operated for the benefit of those using its services: *a housing cooperative*.

co-opt /koh 'opt/ *verb trans* **1** said of a committee or other body: to choose or elect (somebody) as a member. **2** to take (e.g. a faction or movement) into a larger group; to assimilate (it). **3** to take (something) and use it as one's own; to appropriate (it). ➤➤ **co-optation** /-'taysh(ə)n/ *noun*, **co-option** /-sh(ə)n/ *noun*, **co-optive** /-tiv/ *adj*. [Latin *cooptare*, from CO- + *optare* to choose]

coordinate¹ *or* **co-ordinate** /koh'awd(ə)nayt/ *verb trans* **1** to combine (diverse elements) into a common action, movement or condition; to harmonize (them). **2** in chemistry, to combine to form a coordinate bond to (e.g. an atom). ➤ *verb intrans* to combine or act together harmoniously. ➤➤ **coordinative** /-tiv/ *adj*, **coordinator** *noun*. [late Latin *coordinatus*, past part. of *coordinare* to arrange together, from CO- + *ordinare* to arrange]

coordinate² *or* **co-ordinate** *noun* **1** in mathematics, any of a set of numbers used in specifying the location of a point on a line, on a surface, or in space. **2** (*in pl*) outer garments, usu separates, in harmonizing colours, materials, and pattern.

coordinate³ *or* **co-ordinate** /koh'awd(ə)nət/ *adj* **1** equal in rank, quality, or significance. **2** of equal rank in a sentence: *coordinate clauses*. **3** relating to or marked by coordination. **4** involving coordinates: *coordinate geometry*.

coordinate bond *or* **co-ordinate bond** *noun* in chemistry, a COVALENT BOND (bond formed by shared pairs of electrons) for which the electrons are supplied by only one of the two atoms it joins.

coordinate clause *or* **co-ordinate clause** *noun* a clause that begins with a coordinating conjunction and ranks equally with the other clause or clauses in a sentence.

coordinated *or* **co-ordinated** /koh'awd(ə)naytid/ *adj* able to move one's body efficiently and usu gracefully in sports, gymnastics, etc.

coordinate geometry *or* **co-ordinate geometry** *noun* = ANALYTICAL GEOMETRY.

coordinating conjunction or **co-ordinating conjunction** /koh'awd(ə)nayting/ *noun* a conjunction such as *and* or *but* that joins together clauses or other grammatical elements of equal rank: compare SUBORDINATING CONJUNCTION.

coordination or **co-ordination** /kohawdi'naysh(ə)n/ *noun* **1** the act or action of coordinating. **2** the state of being coordinate or coordinated.

coot /kooht/ *noun* (*pl* **coot**) **1** any of several species of water birds with dark plumage and a white bill: genus *Fulica*. **2** *informal* a foolish or eccentric person. [Middle English *coote*, of Germanic origin]

cootie /'koohti/ *noun NAmer, NZ, informal* a body louse. [perhaps modification of Malay *kutu*]

co-own /koh 'ohn/ *verb trans* to own (something) with somebody else. ➤➤ **co-owner** *noun.*

cop[1] /kop/ *noun* **1** *informal* a police officer. **2** an arrest. ✳ **not much cop** *Brit, informal* fairly bad; worthless: *The film wasn't much cop.* [prob from obsolete *cap* arrest, via French from Latin *capere*]

cop[2] *verb trans* (**copped, copping**) *informal* **1** to get hold of or capture (somebody); *specif* to arrest (them). **2** to suffer (something): *He copped a beating.* **3** *NAmer* to get (illegal drugs). ✳ **cop a plea** *NAmer, informal* to plea bargain. **cop hold of** *Brit, informal* to hold onto (something). **cop it 1** *Brit, informal* to be in serious trouble. **2** *Brit, informal* to be killed. [perhaps from Dutch *kapen* to steal, from Frisian *kāpia* to take away]

cop[3] *noun* **1** a conical or cylindrical mass of thread, yarn, or twisted strands of wool or cotton wound on a spindle. **2** *Brit, dialect* a top or crest, e.g. of a hill. [Old English *copp* top]

copacetic /kohpə'setik, -'seetik/ *adj NAmer, informal* very satisfactory. [origin unknown]

copaiba /koh'pieba, koh'paybə/ *noun* **1** an oleoresin used *esp* in varnishes. **2** a S American tree that yields the oleoresin: genus *Copaifera*. [Spanish *copaíba* from Portuguese, of Tupian origin]

copal /'kohp(ə)l/ *noun* a resin from various tropical trees used in varnishes. [Spanish *copal* from Nahuatl *copalli* resin]

coparcener /koh'pahs(ə)nə/ *noun* in law, a person who inherits jointly or equally with others; a joint heir. [Middle English, from CO- + *parcener* partner, from early French *parçonier*, ultimately from Latin *partition-, partitio*: see PARTITION[1]]

copartner or **co-partner** /koh'pahtnə/ *noun* an equal partner in a business or other enterprise. ➤➤ **copartnership** *noun.*

COPD *abbr* chronic obstructive pulmonary disease.

cope[1] /kohp/ *verb intrans* to deal with something effectively: *He couldn't cope with such a noisy class; Her heart couldn't cope with the extra strain placed on it.* [Middle English *copen* to fight, from early French *couper* to cut, strike, from *coup* cut, blow, ultimately from Greek *kolaphos* punch, blow]

cope[2] *noun* a long ecclesiastical vestment resembling a cape, worn on special occasions. [Middle English, ultimately from late Latin *cappa* head covering]

cope[3] *verb trans* to supply (e.g. a wall) with a coping.

copeck /'kohpek/ *noun* see KOPECK.

copepod /'kohpəpod/ *noun* any of a large subclass of usu minute freshwater and marine crustaceans: subclass Copepoda. [Greek *kōpē* oar + *pod-, pous* foot]

coper /'kohpə/ *noun Brit* a horse dealer; *esp* a dishonest one. [English dialect *cope* to trade, from Middle English *copen* to buy, from early Dutch]

Copernican /kə'puhnikən/ *adj* of Copernicus or the Copernican system. ➤➤ **Copernican** *noun,* **Copernicanism** *noun.* [Nicolaus *Copernicus* d.1543, Polish astronomer]

Copernican system *noun* the theory put forward by Nicolaus Copernicus that the earth rotates daily on its axis and the planets revolve in orbits round the sun: compare PTOLEMAIC SYSTEM.

copestone /'kohpstohn/ *noun* = COPINGSTONE.

copier /'kopi-ə/ *noun* a machine for making copies, *esp* a photocopier.

co-pilot /'koh pielət/ *noun* a qualified aircraft pilot who assists or relieves the pilot but is not in command.

coping /'kohping/ *noun* the final, usu sloping, course of brick, stone, etc on the top of a wall. [COPE[3], ultimately from late Latin *cappa* head covering]

coping saw *noun* a narrow-bladed saw used in cutting curved outlines in thin wood. [*coping*, present part. of obsolete *cope* to cut, notch]

copingstone *noun* a stone forming part of a coping.

copious /'kohpi-əs/ *adj* **1** yielding something in abundance; plentiful: *a copious harvest.* **2** present in large quantities, or taking place on a large scale: *copious eating and still more copious drinking* — Aldous Huxley. **3** profuse in words or expression: *a copious talker.* ➤➤ **copiously** *adv,* **copiousness** *noun.* [Middle English from Latin *copiosus*, from *copia* abundance]

copita /koh'peetə/ *noun* a tulip-shaped glass used *esp* for sherry. [Spanish *copita*, dimin. of *copa* cup]

coplanar /koh'playnə/ *adj* in geometry, lying or acting in the same plane. ➤➤ **coplanarity** /-'nariti/ *noun.*

cop off *verb intrans informal* to have a casual sexual encounter with somebody.

copolymer /koh'polimə/ *noun* a POLYMER (large molecule composed of many repeating subunits) in which two or more chemically different subunits are present. ➤➤ **copolymeric** /-'merik/ *adj.*

copolymerize or **copolymerise** *verb trans* to form a copolymer by combining (molecules of two or more chemical compounds). ➤➤ **copolymerization** /-'zaysh(ə)n/ *noun.*

cop out *verb intrans informal* to avoid an unwanted responsibility or fail to fulfil a commitment.

cop-out *noun informal* the act or an instance of copping out.

copper[1] /'kopə/ *noun* **1** a common reddish metallic chemical element that is ductile and malleable and one of the best conductors of heat and electricity, and is used for electrical wiring and as a constituent of certain alloys: symbol Cu, atomic number 29. **2** the colour of copper. **3** *Brit* a coin or token made of copper or bronze and usu of low value. **4** any of various small butterflies with usu copper-coloured wings. **5** *Brit* a large metal vessel used, *esp* formerly, for boiling laundry. ➤➤ **coppery** *adj.* [Old English *coper* from late Latin *cuprum*, from Latin *cyprium aes* Cyprus metal, because Cyprus was a major source]

copper[2] *adj* of the reddish colour of copper.

copper[3] *verb trans* (**coppered, coppering**) to coat or sheathe (something) with copper.

copper[4] *noun Brit, informal* a police officer. [COP[1] + -ER[2]]

copperas /'kopərəs/ *noun* a green hydrated ferrous sulphate used in making inks and pigments: formula $FeSO_4 . 7H_2O$. [alteration of Middle English *coperose* via Old French from late Latin *cuprum* (see COPPER[1]) + Latin *rosa* ROSE[1]]

copper beech *noun* a variety of beech tree with copper-coloured leaves.

copper-bottomed *adj Brit* completely safe; reliable: *a copper-bottomed currency; a copper-bottomed promise.* [from the former practice of coating the bottoms of timber-frame ships with copper to prevent rotting]

copperhead *noun* **1** a venomous N American snake with a coppery-brown head: *Agkistrodon contortrix.* **2** a venomous Australian snake with a coppery band around its head: *Austrelaps superbus.*

copperplate *noun* **1** a style of fine handwriting that is marked by lines of sharply contrasting thickness. **2** an engraved or etched copper printing plate, or a print made from such a plate.

copper pyrites *noun* = CHALCOPYRITE.

coppersmith *noun* a person who produces articles of copper.

copper sulphate (*NAmer* **copper sulfate**) *noun* a chemical compound that usu occurs chemically associated with water in the form of blue crystals but also occurs as a white powder when free from water. It is used in fungicides, electroplating solutions, textile dyeing, and as a timber preservative: symbol $CuSO_4$.

coppice[1] /'kopis/ *noun* a thicket, grove, etc of small trees in which the trees are regularly cut back to promote growth and supply wood for poles and firewood. [early French *copeiz*, from *couper* to cut]

coppice[2] *verb trans* to cut back (trees) to produce a dense growth of small trees.

copr- *comb. form* see COPRO-.

copra /'koprə/ *noun* dried coconut kernels yielding coconut oil. [Portuguese *copra* from Malayalam *koppara*]

copro- or **copr-** comb. form forming words, with the meaning: dung or faeces: coprolite. [via Latin from Greek kopr-, kopro- from kopros dung]

coproduce or **co-produce** /kohprə'dyoohs/ verb trans to produce (e.g. a film or television programme) in cooperation with each other or with another producer. ⟫⟫ **coproducer** noun, **coproduction** noun.

coprolalia /koprə'layli·ə/ noun a psychiatric condition characterized by the involuntary and frequent use of obscene language. [COPRO- + Greek lalia speech]

coprolite /'koprəliet/ noun fossil excrement.

coprophagia /koprə'fayji·ə/ noun see COPROPHAGY.

coprophagous /ko'profəgəs/ adj feeding on dung: a coprophagous beetle. [Greek koprophagos, from kopros dung + -phagos -eating, from phagein to eat]

coprophagy /ko'profəji/ or **coprophagia** /koprə'fayji·ə/ noun the eating of dung.

coprophilia /koprə'fili·ə/ noun a marked, esp sexual, interest in excrement and defecation.

copse /kops/ noun a coppice. [by alteration]

cop shop noun Brit, informal a police station.

Copt /kopt/ noun 1 a member of a people descended from the ancient Egyptians. 2 a member of the Coptic Church. [Arabic qubt Copts, via Coptic gyptios from Greek aigyptios Egyptian]

Copt. abbr Coptic.

Coptic[1] /'koptik/ noun the Afro-Asiatic language of the Copts, which is no longer spoken but survives in the liturgy of the Coptic Church.

Coptic[2] adj of or relating to the Copts, the Coptic language, or the Coptic Church.

Coptic Church noun the ancient branch of the Christian Church that developed in Egypt and survives today.

copula /'kopyoolə/ noun a verb, e.g. a form of be or seem, that links a subject and a complement, as in the sentence She became rich. ⟫⟫ **copular** adj. [Latin copula bond, from CO- + apere to fasten]

copulate /'kopyoolayt/ verb intrans to engage in sexual intercourse. ⟫⟫ **copulation** /-'laysh(ə)n/ noun, **copulatory** /-lət(ə)ri/ adj. [Latin copulatus, past part. of copulare to join, from copula: see COPULA]

copulative[1] /'kopyoolətiv/ adj 1a in grammar, joining together coordinate words or word groups and expressing the sum of their meanings: a copulative conjunction. b in grammar, functioning as a copula. 2 relating to copulation. ⟫⟫ **copulatively** adv.

copulative[2] noun a copulative word.

copy[1] /'kopi/ noun (pl **copies**) 1 an imitation, transcript, or reproduction of an original work. 2 a single specimen of a printed book, CD, etc. 3 material ready to be printed or photoengraved. 4 written material as distinct from illustrations or other graphic material. 5 newsworthy material: Reporters found anything she did to be good copy. 6 archaic a model to be copied, esp a specimen of fine handwriting. [Middle English copie via French and medieval Latin from Latin copia abundance]

copy[2] verb (**copies, copied, copying**) ⟫ verb trans 1 to make a copy of (something). 2 to model oneself on (somebody). 3 to make a copy of (somebody else's work); to imitate (it). ⟫ verb intrans 1 to make a copy. 2 to undergo copying: The document did not copy well.

copybook noun 1 a book formerly used in teaching handwriting, containing models for imitation. 2 (used before a noun) completely correct and conforming to established standards: The church, a copybook model of renaissance perfection, imposes most beautifully, if rather donnishly upon the pastoral scene — Guardian.

copycat noun informal 1 somebody, esp a child, who slavishly imitates the behaviour or practices of another. 2 (used before a noun) imitating something else: copycat murders.

copy-edit verb trans (**copy-edited, copy-editing**) to prepare (manuscript copy) for printing, esp by correcting errors and making the style consistent throughout. ⟫⟫ **copy editor** noun.

copyhold noun a former type of land tenure in England established by a transcript of the manorial records, or a piece of land held in this way.

copyholder noun 1 formerly, a holder of land in copyhold. 2 a device for holding copy, esp for a typesetter in a printing house.

copyist noun 1 a person who makes written copies of documents. 2 a person who imitates the work of others, e.g. somebody who copies works of art.

copyreader noun 1 an editor in a publishing house who reads and corrects manuscript copy; a copy editor. 2 somebody who edits and adds headlines to newspaper or magazine copy; a subeditor.

copyright[1] noun the exclusive legal right to reproduce, publish, and sell a literary, musical, or artistic work for a fixed number of years.

copyright[2] verb trans to secure a copyright on (a literary, musical, or artistic work).

copyright library noun a library that receives a copy of every book published in Britain.

copytaster noun Brit a journalist who selects potential copy.

copy typist noun a typist who types up written notes or drafts, rather than typing from dictation.

copywriter noun a writer of advertising or publicity copy. ⟫⟫ **copywriting** noun.

coq au vin /kok oh 'van/ noun a dish of chicken cooked in red wine with bacon and shallots. [French coq au vin cock in wine]

coquet or **coquette** /ko'ket, kə'ket/ verb intrans (**coquetted, coquetting**) 1 to play the coquette; to flirt. 2 to deal with something playfully rather than seriously; to trifle.

coquette /ko'ket, kə'ket/ noun 1 a woman who tries to gain the attention and admiration of men without sincere affection; a flirt: I like a woman who lays herself out a little more to please us … something of the coquette. A man likes a sort of challenge — George Eliot. 2 a hummingbird of Central and S America with a prominent crest: genus Lophornis. ⟫⟫ **coquetry** /'kokətri/ noun, **coquettish** adj, **coquettishly** adv, **coquettishness** noun. [French coquette, fem of coquet wanton, dimin. of coq cock]

coquina /ko'keenə/ noun a soft whitish limestone formed of broken shells and corals. [Spanish coquina, prob irreg dimin. of concha shell]

Cor. abbr 1 Corinthians (books of the Bible). 2 NAmer coroner.

cor /kaw/ interj Brit, informal used to express surprise, incredulity, or admiration. [euphemism for God]

cor- prefix see COM-.

coracle /'korəkl/ noun a small round boat of a traditional Welsh or Irish design made by covering a wicker frame with waterproof material. [Welsh corwgl]

coracoid /'korəkoyd/ noun the coracoid process. [via Latin from Greek korakoeidēs like a raven, from korak-, korax raven]

coracoid process noun a bone of many vertebrate animals that extends from the SCAPULA (shoulder blade or its equivalent) to or towards the STERNUM (breastbone or its equivalent). In mammals it is reduced to a small peg projecting from the scapula.

coral /'korəl/ noun 1a a hard substance, usu containing calcium, produced by certain marine invertebrate animals related to the sea anemones. b a rich red precious type of coral secreted by a gorgonian coral: Corallium nobile. 2 a marine invertebrate animal of a group that secrete an external chalky or horny skeleton and usu occur united into branching, encrusting, or more or less solid colonies. They have a hollow cylindrical body with a ring of tentacles round the mouth: orders Scleractinia, Madreporaria, Gorgonacea, and Alcyonacea. 3 a bright reddish mass of edible ovaries, e.g. of a lobster or scallop. 4 a deep orange-pink colour. ⟫⟫ **coral** adj, **coralloid** /-loyd/ adj. [Middle English via French from Latin corallium from Greek korallion]

coralline[1] /'korəlien/ adj of or like coral or a coralline. [French corallin via late Latin from Latin corallium: see CORAL]

coralline[2] noun 1 any of a family of hardened calcium-containing red seaweeds: family Corallinaceae. 2 any of various aquatic invertebrate animals, esp a bryozoan or hydroid, that live in colonies and resemble coral.

coralroot noun 1 any of several species of leafless orchids with branching stems that give them a superficial resemblance to coral: genus Corallorhiza. 2 a related orchid of N America with colourful flowers: genus Hexalectris.

coral snake noun 1 any of several species of venomous snakes with grooved fangs and brilliant bands of black, yellow, or white, found in tropical regions of N and S America: genus Micrurus. 2 any of various similar but harmless snakes found in Africa and Asia.

cor anglais /ˌkawr 'ongglay, kawr ong'glay (French kɔr ɑ̃glɛ), ˌkawr 'ongglay, kawr ong'glay/ noun (pl **cors anglais**) a woodwind musical instrument with a double reed similar to, and with a range a fifth lower than, the oboe. [French cor anglais English horn]

corbel[1] /'kawbl/ noun a stone or brick projection from a wall which supports a weight, esp one stepped upwards and outwards. [Middle English from early French corbel, literally 'little raven', from Latin corvus raven; perhaps because a corbel was thought to resemble a raven's beak]

corbel[2] verb trans (**corbelled, corbelling**, NAmer **corbeled, corbeling**) to supply (a wall) with a corbel, or lay (stone or brick) in the form of a corbel.

corbie /'kawbi/ noun chiefly Scot a carrion crow or a raven. [Middle English via early French corbin from Latin corvus raven]

corbie gable noun a gable with stepped sides.

corbie step noun any of the series of steps on the sloping sides of a corbie gable.

cord[1] /kawd/ noun 1 a length of long thin flexible material consisting of several strands, e.g. of thread or yarn, woven or twisted together, or such material in general. 2 an anatomical structure, e.g. a nerve, resembling a cord. 3 an electric flex. 4a corduroy. b (in pl) trousers made of corduroy. 5 a unit of cut wood usu equal to 3.63m³ (128ft³), or a stack containing this amount of wood. [Middle English via early French corde and Latin chorda from Greek chordē]

cord[2] verb trans to provide or bind (something) with a cord, or connect (things) with a cord.

cordage /'kawdij/ noun ropes, esp in a ship's rigging.

cordate /'kawdayt/ adj heart-shaped. [Latin cordatus, from cord-, cor heart]

corded adj 1 striped or ribbed with or as if with cord; twilled. 2 bound or fastened with cords. 3 said of a muscle: ridged.

cord grass noun a robust grass that grows in salt marshes: genus Spartina.

cordial[1] /'kawdi-əl/ adj 1 warmly and genially affable. 2 sincerely or deeply felt: a cordial and active dislike for both his parents — Samuel Butler. ⟫ **cordiality** /-'aliti/ noun, **cordially** adv. [Middle English from medieval Latin cordialis, from Latin cor heart]

cordial[2] noun 1 Brit a non-alcoholic sweetened fruit drink. 2 NAmer a liqueur. 3 a stimulating medicine.

cordierite /'kawdiəriet/ noun a blue mineral with a glassy lustre that consists of a silicate of aluminium, iron, and magnesium, and exhibits strong DICHROISM (property of appearing as two different colours when viewed from different directions): formula (MgFe)₂Al₄Si₅O₁₈. [French cordierite, named after Pierre Cordier d.1861, French geologist]

cordillera /ˌkawdi'lyeərə/ noun a system of mountain ranges, esp in western N America, consisting of a number of more or less parallel chains of mountain peaks. [Spanish cordillera from Latin chorda: see CORD[1]]

cordite /'kawdiet/ noun a smokeless explosive made from nitroglycerine, guncotton, and petroleum jelly. [CORD[1] + -ITE[1]]

cordless adj said of an electrical device: operating without direct connection to the mains supply or power source.

cordoba /'kawdəbə/ noun the basic monetary unit of Nicaragua, divided into 100 centavos. [Spanish córdoba, named after Francisco Fernández de Córdoba d.1526, Spanish explorer and governor of Nicaragua]

cordon[1] /'kawd(ə)n/ noun 1 (treated as sing. or pl) a line of troops, police, etc enclosing an area and preventing access to it. 2 a plant, esp a fruit tree, trained to a single stem by pruning off all side shoots. 3 a ribbon worn as a badge of honour or as a decoration. 4 = STRING COURSE. [French cordon ornamental cord, ribbon, dimin. of corde: see CORD[1]]

cordon[2] verb trans (**cordoned, cordoning**) (+ off) to form a protective or restrictive cordon round (an area).

cordon bleu[1] /ˌkawdonh 'bluh (French kɔrdɔ̃ blø), ˌkawdonh 'bluh/ adj said of cookery: of the highest standard. [French cordon bleu blue ribbon; the insignia of the highest order of chivalry in the reign of the Bourbon kings of France]

cordon bleu[2] noun (pl **cordons bleus**) 1 the highest distinction in cookery. 2 a person with a high degree of skill or distinction in cookery, esp in classical French cuisine.

cordon sanitaire /ˌkawdonh sani'teə (French sanitɛːr)/ noun (pl **cordons sanitaires**) 1 a barrier round an infected region, policed to prevent the spread of infection. 2 a buffer zone. [French cordon sanitaire sanitary cordon]

cordovan /'kawdəv(ə)n/ noun a soft fine-grained leather, often of horsehide, orig made in Cordoba. [Old Spanish cordován, from Córdova (now Córdoba), city in Spain where it was first produced]

corduroy /'kawd(ə)roy/ noun a durable usu cotton pile fabric with lengthways ribs. [perhaps from CORD[1] + obsolete duroy, a coarse woollen fabric, of unknown origin]

corduroy road noun a road built of logs laid side by side.

cordwainer /'kawdwaynə/ noun Brit, archaic a shoemaker. [Middle English cordwain cordovan, via French from Old Spanish cordován: see CORDOVAN]

cordwood noun wood piled or sold in cords.

CORE abbr NAmer Congress of Racial Equality.

core[1] /kaw/ noun 1 the usu inedible central part of some fruits, e.g. a pineapple; esp the papery parts encasing the seeds in fruit such as apples and pears. 2a the essential, basic, or central part, e.g. of an individual, class, or entity. b the inmost or most intimate part: He was honest to the core. 3 the central part of a planet, esp the earth, which has physical properties, e.g. heat conductivity and density, that are different from those of the surrounding parts. 4 a cylindrical portion removed from a mass for inspection; specif such a portion of rock obtained by boring. 5 the part of a nuclear reactor that contains the rods of fuel, e.g. uranium, and in which the energy-producing reaction occurs. 6 a piece of ferromagnetic material, e.g. soft iron, that serves to concentrate and intensify the magnetic field resulting from passing an electric current through a surrounding coil. 7 the part of a mould used for casting metal objects that shapes a depression, cavity, or hole in the object. 8 a small rounded lump of stone, e.g. flint, from which flakes have been struck for making primitive weapons or tools. [Middle English; earlier history unknown]

core[2] verb trans to remove a core from (a fruit). ⟫⟫ **corer** noun.

coreferential /koh-refə'rensh(ə)l/ adj said of two words: referring to the same person or thing.

coreligionist or **co-religionist** /koh-ri'lijənist/ noun a person of the same religion.

coreopsis /kori'opsis, koh-/ noun a plant of the daisy family, widely grown for its showy yellow or yellow and red flowers: genus Coreopsis. [Latin genus name, from Greek koris bedbug (because of the seed shape) + -OPSIS]

corepressor /kohri'presə/ noun a substance that activates a particular genetic REPRESSOR (substance that inhibits the synthesis of a protein), e.g. by combining with it.

co-respondent or **corespondent** /ˌkoh ri'spond(ə)nt/ noun a person alleged to have committed adultery with the respondent in a divorce case.

core subject noun a school subject that is compulsory, esp for pupils at each key stage of the National Curriculum in British schools.

core time noun Brit the period of each day which is a compulsory working period for employees on flexitime.

corf /kawf/ noun (pl **corves** /kawvz/) Brit a basket formerly used in a mine to convey ore or coal. [Middle English via early Dutch corf or medieval Latin korf from Latin corbis basket]

corgi /'kawgi/ noun (pl **corgis**) a short-legged dog of a breed with a fox-like head, orig developed in Wales. Also called WELSH CORGI. [Welsh corgi, from cor dwarf + ci dog]

coria /'kawriə/ noun pl of CORIUM.

coriander /kori'andə, 'ko-/ noun 1 an aromatic plant of the carrot family, native to Europe and Asia and cultivated for its leaves and seeds that are used as a flavouring in cooking: Coriandrum sativum. 2 the leaves or seeds of this plant, or the spice prepared from the seeds. [Middle English coriandre via French and Latin from Greek koriandron]

Corinthian[1] /kə'rinthiən/ noun 1 a native or inhabitant of Corinth in Greece. 2 an amateur sportsman or yachtsman.

Corinthian[2] adj 1 relating to the modern city or the ancient city-state of Corinth. 2 denoting the lightest and most ornate of the three Greek orders of architecture characterized by its bell-shaped CAPITAL[3] (upper part of a column) enveloped with large spiny leaves modelled on the acanthus plant: compare DORIC[1], IONIC[1].

Coriolis force /kori'ohlis/ *noun* a force arising as a result of the earth's rotation that deflects moving objects, e.g. projectiles or air currents, to the right in the northern hemisphere and to the left in the southern hemisphere. [named after Gaspard *Coriolis* d.1843, French civil engineer]

corium /'kawriəm/ *noun* (*pl* **coria** /'kawri·ə/) = DERMIS. [Latin *corium* leather]

cork[1] /kawk/ *noun* **1** the elastic tough outer tissue of the cork oak used *esp* for stoppers and insulation. **2** a cork stopper for a bottle. **3** an angling float made from cork. [Middle English, in the senses 'cork', 'bark', ultimately from Latin *cortic-, cortex* bark]

cork[2] *verb trans* to fit or close (something, *esp* a bottle) with a cork.

corkage /'kawkij/ *noun* a charge made in a restaurant for serving wine that has been bought elsewhere by a customer.

corked *adj* said of wine: having an unpleasant smell and taste as a result of being kept in a bottle sealed with a leaky cork.

corker *noun informal, dated* an astonishing person or thing.

corking /'kawking/ *adj informal, dated* extremely good; excellent.

cork oak *noun* a S European and N African oak with bark that yields cork: *Quercus suber*.

corkscrew[1] *noun* **1** an implement for removing corks from bottles, typically consisting of a pointed spiral piece of metal attached to a handle. **2** (*used before a noun*) spiral: *corkscrew curls*.

corkscrew[2] *verb intrans* to move or twist in a spiral.

corkwood *noun* a small tree with light or corky wood, e.g. a deciduous tree of the southeastern USA: *Leitneria floridana*.

corky /'kawki/ *adj* (**corkier, corkiest**) **1** resembling cork, e.g. in consistency. **2** corked.

corm /kawm/ *noun* a rounded thick underground plant stem base with buds and scaly leaves that stores food and produces new shoots each year: compare BULB, TUBER. [Latin *cormus* from Greek *kormos* tree trunk, from *keirein* to cut]

cormorant /'kawmərənt/ *noun* any of several species of common dark-coloured European seabirds with a long neck, hooked bill, webbed feet, and white throat and cheeks: genus *Phalacrocorax*. [Middle English *cormeraunt* from early French *cormareng*, from *corp* raven + *marenc* of the sea]

corn[1] /kawn/ *noun* **1** *chiefly Brit* the important cereal crop of a particular region, usu wheat, barley, or oats in Britain, or the seeds of any such crop. **2** *NAmer, Aus, NZ* maize. **3** a small hard seed. **4** *informal* something corny. [Old English]

corn[2] *verb trans* to preserve or season (food) with salt or brine: *corned beef*.

corn[3] *noun* a local hardening and thickening of skin, e.g. on the top of a toe. [Middle English *corne* via French from Latin *cornu* horn, point]

cornball *adj NAmer, informal* corny.

corn borer *noun* a moth of eastern N America with a larva that is a major pest of maize, potatoes, and dahlias: *Ostrinia nubilalis*.

corn bread *noun* bread made from maize flour.

corn bunting *noun* a European bird with streaky grey-brown plumage, found in marshy fields and scrub: *Miliaria calandra*.

corncob *noun* the core on which the edible kernels of sweet corn are arranged.

corn cockle *noun* a poisonous annual purple-flowered plant, formerly found as a weed of cornfields: *Agrostemma githago*.

corncrake *noun* a common Eurasian bird of the rail family with a short bill, tan-coloured speckled plumage, and a reddish tail: *Crex crex*.

corn dog *noun NAmer* a hot dog fried in batter and served on a stick.

corn dolly *noun Brit* an article of woven straw, orig having ritual significance but now used for decoration.

cornea /'kawni·ə, kaw'nee·ə/ *noun* the hard transparent membrane of the eyeball that covers the iris and pupil. ➤➤ **corneal** *adj*. [Latin *cornea*, fem of *corneus* horny, from *cornu* horn]

corned beef /kawnd/ *noun* chopped and pressed beef that has been preserved in brine.

cornel /'kawnl/ *noun* any of several species of shrubs, *esp* the dogwood: genus *Cornus*. [Latin *cornus* cornelian cherry]

cornelian /kaw'neeli·ən/ *or* **carnelian** *noun* a hard reddish form of the mineral chalcedony, used in jewellery. [Middle English *corneline* from early French *corneline*, perhaps from *cornelle* cornel, from Latin *cornus* cornelian cherry]

cornelian cherry *noun* **1** an edible oval-shaped scarlet fruit. **2** the deciduous shrub or small tree of the dogwood family that bears this fruit: *Cornus mas*. [CORNEL + -IAN]

corneous /'kawni·əs/ *adj formal* like horn in texture. [Latin *corneus*, from *cornu* horn]

corner[1] /'kawnə/ *noun* **1a** the point where converging lines, edges, or sides meet; an angle. **b** the place of intersection of two streets or roads. **2a** the area of a playing field or court near the intersection of the sideline and the goal line or baseline. **b** any of the four angles of a boxing or wrestling ring, *esp* one in which a fighter rests between rounds. **3a** a private, secret, or remote place: *a quiet corner of a small Welsh town*. **b** a difficult or embarrassing situation; a position from which escape or retreat is difficult or impossible: *He talked himself into a tight corner*. **4** (*treated as sing. or pl*) a contestant's group of supporters or adherents. **5a** = CORNER KICK. **b** = CORNER HIT. **6** in economics, control or ownership of enough of the available supply of a commodity to allow manipulation of the price. **7** a triangular cut of gammon or ham from the top of the hind leg. **8** (*used before a noun*) on or suitable for a corner: *a corner cupboard*. ✳ **in somebody's corner** on somebody's side. **round/around the corner** imminent. [Middle English from early French *cornere*, ultimately from Latin *cornu* horn, corner]

corner[2] *verb* (**cornered, cornering**) ➤ *verb trans* **1a** to drive (a person or animal) into a corner. **b** to detain (somebody); *esp* to force (them) into conversation. **2** to gain control of (an economic market) by acquiring a substantial supply of a commodity: *They were able to corner the wheat market*. ➤ *verb intrans* to turn corners: *This car corners well*.

cornerback *noun* in American football, a defensive back who plays outside the linebacker and is chiefly responsible for covering the wide receiver of the opposing team.

cornered *adj* (*used in combinations*) having a specified number of corners: *a three-cornered hat*.

corner hit *noun* in hockey or shinty, a free hit awarded to the attacking side when a member of the defending side has sent the ball over his or her own goal line.

corner kick *noun* in football, a free kick that is taken from the corner of the field and is awarded to the attacking team when a member of the defending team has sent the ball behind his or her own goal line.

corner shop *noun Brit* a small shop selling food, household supplies, and sometimes newspapers and magazines.

cornerstone *noun* **1** a block of stone forming a part of a corner or angle in a wall, *esp* one forming the base of a corner and often laid ceremonially to mark the beginning of construction. **2** the most basic element of something; a foundation: *This Declaration of Right ... is the cornerstone of our constitution* — Edmund Burke.

cornerwise *adv* diagonally.

cornet[1] /'kawnit/ *noun* **1** a brass musical instrument with finger-operated valves to vary the pitch. It resembles a trumpet but has a shorter tube and less brilliant tone. **2** *Brit* an ice cream cone. ➤➤ **cornetist, cornettist** /'kawnitist, kaw'netist/ *noun*. [Middle English via French from Latin *cornu* horn]

cornet[2] *noun* formerly, the fifth commissioned officer of a British cavalry troop who carried the standard.

Word history
early French *cornette* type of headdress, standard, standard-bearer, ultimately from Latin *cornu* horn, point. The word orig meant a woman's headdress such as that worn by the Sisters of Charity, which had large stiff wings or horns. It later came to mean a flap or strip of lace hanging down from a woman's headdress, hence the standard of a cavalry troop (orig a long tapering pennon), and the standard-bearer.

cornett /kaw'net/ *noun* a Renaissance woodwind musical instrument with a cup-shaped mouthpiece like a trumpet and a tapered tube with finger holes like a recorder. [Middle English *cornette, cornet*]

corn exchange *noun* a building in which corn was formerly traded.

cornflakes *pl noun* toasted flakes of maize eaten as a breakfast cereal.

cornflour *noun Brit* a finely ground flour made from maize, rice, etc and used as a thickening agent in cooking.

cornflower *noun* any of several species of European plants with narrow leaves and delicate blue, purple, or white flowers that resemble daisies: *Centaurea cyanus* and other species.

cornice /'kawnis/ *noun* **1a** an ornamental projecting piece that forms the top edge of a building, pillar, etc, *esp* the top projecting part of the entablature of a classical building. **b** an ornamental plaster moulding between the wall and ceiling of a room. **2** a decorative band of metal or wood used to conceal curtain fixtures. **3** an overhanging mass of snow or ice on a mountain. ➤➤ **corniced** *adj.* [early French *cornice* from Italian *cornice*]

corniche /kaw'neesh/ *noun* a road built along a coast, *esp* along the face of a cliff. [French *cornice, corniche* cornice]

Cornish[1] /'kawnish/ *noun* the Celtic language of Cornwall. [Middle English, from the first element of *Cornwall* + -ISH]

Cornish[2] *adj* of or from Cornwall or the Cornish language. ➤➤ **Cornishman** *noun,* **Cornishwoman** *noun.*

Cornish pasty *noun Brit* a pasty consisting of a circular piece of pastry folded over a savoury filling of meat, potato, and vegetables.

Corn Laws *pl noun* a series of laws in force in Britain before 1846 restricting the importing of foreign grain.

corn marigold *noun* a European plant of the daisy family that has golden-yellow flowers and is a weed of cornfields: *Chrysanthemum segetum.*

cornmeal *noun* meal made from maize.

corn oil *noun* oil obtained from maize, used in cooking.

corn pone /pohn/ *noun NAmer* a bread made with maize and baked or fried. [CORN[1] + obsolete *pone* bread, of Algonquian origin]

cornrows /'kawnrohz/ *pl noun* a hairstyle formed by tightly plaiting the hair in parallel rows.

corn salad *noun* = LAMB'S LETTUCE.

corn silk *noun* the silky tuft at the top of an ear of maize.

corn snake *noun* a long harmless snake found in N American cornfields: *Elaphe guttata.*

cornstarch *noun NAmer* = CORNFLOUR.

cornu /'kawnyooh/ *noun* (*pl* **cornua** /'kawnyooh·ə/) a horn-shaped anatomical structure. ➤➤ **cornual** *adj.* [Latin *cornu* horn]

cornucopia /kawnyoo'kohpi·ə/ *noun* **1** a goat's horn overflowing with flowers, fruit, and corn, used to symbolize plenty. **2** an inexhaustible store; an abundance: *The States always had that image of the cornucopia of goodies and pleasurable things, with no whiff of European austerity and rationing —* Daily Telegraph. **3** a container shaped like a horn or cone. ➤➤ **cornucopian** *adj.* [late Latin *cornucopia* from Latin *cornu copiae* horn of plenty]

corny /'kawni/ *adj* (**cornier, corniest**) *informal* **1** tiresomely simple and sentimental; trite. **2** unoriginal and overused; hackneyed. ➤➤ **cornily** *adv,* **corniness** *noun.* [CORN[1], orig in the sense 'appealing to country folk']

corolla /kə'rolə/ *noun* in botany, the petals of a flower collectively, constituting the inner floral envelope. [Latin *corolla,* dimin. of *corona:* see CROWN[1]]

corollary /kə'roləri/ *noun* (*pl* **corollaries**) **1** in logic, a direct conclusion from a proved proposition. **2** something that naturally follows or accompanies something else. ➤➤ **corollary** *adj.* [Middle English *corolarie* via late Latin from Latin *corollarium* money paid for a garland, gratuity, from *corolla:* see COROLLA]

corona[1] /kə'rohnə/ *noun* (*pl* **coronas** *or* **coronae** /-nee/) **1a** a usu coloured circle of usu diffracted light seen round and close to a luminous celestial body, e.g. the sun or moon. **b** the tenuous outermost part of the atmosphere of the sun and other stars appearing as a halo round the moon's black disc during a total eclipse of the sun. **2** the upper portion of a bodily part, e.g. a tooth or the skull. **3** in botany, a circular appendage on the inner side of the corolla in the daffodil, jonquil, and similar flowers. **4** a circular chandelier, *esp* in a church. **5** the concave moulding on the upper part of the cornice on a classical building. [Latin *corona:* see CROWN[1]]

corona[2] *noun* a long straight-sided cigar of uniform thickness. [*La Corona,* orig a trademark, from Spanish *corona* crown]

coronach /'korənəkh, -nək/ *noun* a Scottish or Irish funeral song. [Scottish Gaelic *corranach* and Irish Gaelic *coránach,* from early Irish *comh-* together + *rànach* outcry, weeping]

coronae /kə'rohnee/ *noun* pl of CORONA[1].

coronagraph /kə'rohnəgrahf/ *noun* see CORONOGRAPH.

coronal /'korənl/ *adj* **1** of a corona or crown. **2** lying in the direction of the coronal suture. **3** relating to or in the region of the coronal plane.

coronal plane *noun* in anatomy, the frontal plane that passes through the long axis of the body and divides it into front and back parts.

coronal suture *noun* in anatomy, the join between the parietal and frontal bones extending across the top of the skull.

coronary[1] /'korən(ə)ri/ *adj* relating to or in the region of the arteries and veins that supply and encircle the heart. [CORONA[1] + -ARY[2]]

coronary[2] *noun* (*pl* **coronaries**) = CORONARY THROMBOSIS.

coronary artery *noun* either of two arteries, one on the right and one on the left of the heart, that arise from the AORTA (large artery carrying blood away from the heart) and supply blood to the tissues of the heart itself.

coronary thrombosis *noun* the blocking of a coronary artery of the heart by a blood clot, usu causing death of heart muscle tissue.

coronation /korə'naysh(ə)n/ *noun* the act or ceremony of crowning a sovereign or his or her consort. [Middle English *coronacion* from early French *coronation,* from *coroner:* see CROWN[2]]

coronation chicken *noun* a dish of cold cooked chicken in a spicy mayonnaise sauce. [created in 1953 in honour of the coronation of Elizabeth II]

coroner /'korənə/ *noun* a public officer whose principal duty is to enquire into the cause of any death which there is reason to suppose might not be due to natural causes. [Middle English, in the sense 'an officer of the crown', via Anglo-French from Latin *corona:* see CROWN[1]]

coronet /'korənit/ *noun* **1** a small crown. **2** an ornamental wreath or band for the head. **3** the lower part of a horse's foot between the fetlock and the hoof, where the horn ends in skin. **4** a knob of bone at the base of a deer's antler. [early French *coronete,* dimin. of *corone:* see CROWN[1]]

coronograph *or* **coronagraph** /kə'rohnəgrahf/ *noun* a telescope for observing the sun's coronas.

Corp. *abbr* **1** Corporal. **2** *NAmer* Corporation.

corpora /'kawpərə/ *noun* pl of CORPUS.

corpora allata /ə'laytə/ *noun* pl of CORPUS ALLATUM.

corpora callosa /kə'lohsə/ *noun* pl of CORPUS CALLOSUM.

corpora cavernosa /kavə'nohsə/ *noun* pl of CORPUS CAVERNOSUM.

corporal[1] /'kawp(ə)rəl/ *noun* **1** a non-commissioned officer in the British and US armies, Royal Air Force, Royal Marines, and US Marines, ranking below a sergeant. **2** a petty officer in the Royal Navy. [early French *corporal,* lowest non-commissioned officer, alteration of *caporal,* ultimately from Latin *caput* head]

corporal[2] *adj* of or affecting the body: *corporal punishment.* ➤➤ **corporality** /-'raliti/ *noun,* **corporally** *adv.* [Middle English via French from Latin *corporalis,* from *corpor-, corpus* body]

corporal[3] *noun* a linen cloth on which the bread and wine are placed during a Communion service. [Middle English via French and medieval Latin from Latin *corporalis,* from *corpus* body; from the doctrine that the bread of the Eucharist becomes or represents the body of Christ]

corporal punishment *noun* physical punishment, e.g. caning.

corpora lutea /'loohti·ə/ *noun* pl of CORPUS LUTEUM.

corpora spongiosa /spunji'ohsə/ *noun* pl of CORPUS SPONGIOSUM.

corporate /'kawp(ə)rət/ *adj* **1** relating to companies or the people, *esp* the executives, who work in them. **2** in law, forming a company; incorporated. **3** of or belonging to a unified body of individuals. ➤➤ **corporately** *adv.* [Latin *corporatus,* past part. of *corporare* to make into a body, from *corpor-, corpus* body]

corporate hospitality *noun* entertainment offered by a business to valuable clients and associates, e.g. at a prestigious cultural or sporting event.

corporate identity *noun* the way that a business or other organization presents itself, e.g. in its choice of logo, vehicle livery, and letterheads.

corporate raider *noun* a person who pursues a strategy of making or threatening to make takeover bids for companies.

corporate state *noun* a state in which government is by elected representatives from businesses and other organizations, rather than from geographical areas.

corporation /ˌkawpəˈraysh(ə)n/ *noun* **1** a body made up of more than one person which is formed and authorized by law to act as a single person with its own legal identity, rights, and duties. **2** (*treated as sing. or pl*) the municipal authorities of a British town or city. **3** *dated* a paunch.

corporation tax *noun* tax levied on the profits of companies.

corporatise /ˈkawp(ə)rətiez/ *verb* see CORPORATIZE.

corporatism *noun* the organization of a society into corporations serving as organs of political representation, e.g. in Fascist Italy. **➤➤ corporatist** *adj and noun*.

corporative /ˈkawp(ə)rətiv/ *adj* **1** of corporatism: *a corporative state*. **2** of a corporation.

corporatize or **corporatise** /ˈkawp(ə)rətiez/ *verb trans* to turn (an organization, *esp* a government department) into a corporation. **➤➤ corporatization** /-tiezaysh(ə)n/ *noun*.

corporeal /kawˈpawri·əl/ *adj* **1** having, consisting of, or relating to a physical material body; not spiritual. **2** not immaterial or intangible; substantial. **➤➤ corporeality** /-ˈaliti/ *noun*, **corporeally** *adv*. [Latin *corporeus* of the body, from *corpor-, corpus* body]

corposant /ˈkawpəz(ə)nt/ *noun archaic* an instance of St Elmo's fire. [Portuguese *corpo-santo* holy body]

corps /kaw/ *noun* (*pl* **corps** /kawz/) **1** (*treated as sing. or pl*) an army unit usu consisting of two or more divisions organized for a particular purpose. **2** a body of people engaged in a specific activity: *the diplomatic corps*. [French *corps* from Latin *corpus* body]

corps de ballet /ˌkaw də ˈbalay, NAmer baˈlay/ *noun* (*pl* **corps de ballet** /ˌkaw/) (*treated as sing. or pl*) the members of a ballet company. [French *corps de ballet*]

corpse[1] /kawps/ *noun* a dead body, *esp* a dead human body. [Middle English *corps* via French from Latin *corpus* body]

corpse[2] *verb intrans informal* to stifle laughter with difficulty, e.g. on a solemn occasion or while acting in a play.

corpulent /ˈkawpyoolənt/ *adj* excessively fat; obese. **➤➤ corpulence** *noun*, **corpulency** *noun*. [early French *corpulence* (noun) from Latin *corpulentia*, ultimately from Latin *corpus* body]

cor pulmonale /ˌkaw poolmoˈnahli, -ˈnayli/ *noun* disease of the heart characterized by an increase in size and volume of the right-hand VENTRICLE (lower chamber of the heart), resulting from disease of the lungs or their blood vessels. [Latin *cor pulmonale*, literally 'pulmonary heart']

corpus /ˈkawpəs/ *noun* (*pl* **corpora** /ˈkawpərə/ *or* **corpuses**) **1a** a collection or body of writings or works, e.g. of one author or artist, *esp* of a particular kind or on a particular subject. **b** a body of spoken or written language for linguistic study. **2** in anatomy, the main body or corporeal substance of a thing, *esp* the main part of a bodily structure or organ: *the corpus of the uterus*. [Middle English from Latin *corpus* body]

corpus allatum /əˈlaytəm/ *noun* (*pl* **corpora allata** /-tə/) either of a pair of organs that lie behind the brain of many insects and secrete *esp* juvenile hormones. [Latin *corpus allatum*, literally 'applied body']

corpus callosum /kəˈlohs(ə)m/ *noun* (*pl* **corpora callosa** /-sə/) a wide band of nerve fibres joining the cerebral hemispheres in the brains of humans and other higher mammals. [Latin *corpus callosum*, literally 'callous body']

corpus cavernosum /ˈkawpəs kavəˈnohsəm/ *noun* (*pl* **corpora cavernosa** /kawpərə kavəˈnohsə/) in anatomy, a section of erectile tissue in the penis or the clitoris: compare CORPUS SPONGIOSUM. [Latin *corpus* body + cavernosum, neuter of *cavernosus* containing hollows]

Corpus Christi /ˈkristi/ *noun* a Christian feast in honour of the Eucharist, observed on the Thursday after Trinity Sunday. [Middle English from medieval Latin *corpus Christi*, literally 'body of Christ']

corpuscle /ˈkawpəsl, ˈkawpusl, kawˈpusl/ *noun* **1** a living cell, *esp* a blood cell. **2** any of various very small multicellular parts of an organism. **3** a minute particle. **➤➤ corpuscular** /kawˈpuskyoolə/ *adj*. [Latin *corpusculum*, dimin. of *corpus* body]

corpus delicti /diˈlikti/ *noun* in law, the body of facts showing that a breach of the law has taken place, *esp* the body of the victim in a case of murder. [Latin *corpus delicti* body of the crime]

corpus luteum /ˈloohti·əm/ *noun* (*pl* **corpora lutea** /-ti·ə/) a reddish yellow mass of hormone-secreting tissue that forms in the ovary of a mammal after ovulation and quickly returns to its original state if the ovum is not fertilized. [Latin *corpus luteum* yellowish body]

corpus spongiosum /ˈkawpəs spunjiˈohsəm/ *noun* (*pl* **corpora spongiosa** /kawpərə spunjiˈohsə/) in anatomy, part of the tissue making up the erectile tissue in the penis: compare CORPUS CAVERNOSUM. [Latin *corpus spongiosum* porous body]

corral[1] /kəˈrahl, kəˈral/ *noun NAmer* **1** a pen or enclosure for confining livestock. **2** formerly, a ring of covered wagons around a camp to provide protection against potential attack. [Spanish *corral*, ultimately from Latin *currus* cart]

corral[2] *verb trans* (**corralled, corralling**) **1** *chiefly NAmer* to enclose (livestock) in a corral. **2** *NAmer* to arrange (wagons) so as to form a corral. **3** to collect (people) together.

correct[1] /kəˈrekt/ *adj* **1** true or right: *Is that the correct time?* **2** conforming to an approved or conventional standard: *the correct way of addressing a bishop*. **3** conforming to a specified ideology: *politically correct*. **➤➤ correctly** *adv*, **correctness** *noun*. [Middle English from Latin *correctus*, past part. of *corrigere* to make straight, from COR- + *regere* to guide]

correct[2] *verb trans* **1a** to make or set (something) right; to amend (it). **b** to alter or adjust (something) so as to remove an error, imperfection, or failing. **2** to point out the faults in (a piece of writing). **3** *archaic* to punish (e.g. a child) with a view to reforming or improving them: *Could you bear to be corrected for your faults?* — Charles Lamb. **➤➤ correctable** *adj*, **corrector** *noun*.

correction /kəˈreksh(ə)n/ *noun* **1** an amendment made to remove an error. **2** something, *esp* something written, substituted in place of what is wrong. **3** a quantity added or subtracted in order to improve accuracy, e.g. in adjusting an instrument. **4** *NAmer or dated* punishment. **5** the act or an instance of correcting something.

correctional *adj NAmer* relating to prisons or other places or methods of punishment: *a correctional facility*.

correction fluid *noun* a white or coloured liquid used to cover an error in writing or typing.

corrective /kəˈrektiv/ *adj* intended to correct: *corrective lenses; corrective punishment*. **➤➤ correctively** *adv*.

correlate[1] /ˈkorilayt/ *verb intrans* to have a reciprocal or mutual relationship. **➤** *verb trans* **1** to establish a mutual or reciprocal relation between (things). **2** in mathematics, to relate (variables) so that each member of one set or series has a corresponding member of another set or series assigned to it. **3** to bring (things) together for the purposes of comparison: *correlating the research findings of several groups*. [back-formation from CORRELATION]

correlate[2] /ˈkorilayt, -lət/ *noun* in philosophy, either of two things related in such a way that one directly implies the other, e.g. husband and wife.

correlation /koriˈlaysh(ə)n/ *noun* **1** a mutual or reciprocal relationship between things. **2** in statistics, an association between two variables such that a change in one implies a proportionate change in the other. **3** the act or an instance of correlating two things. **➤➤ correlational** *adj*. [medieval Latin *correlation-, correlatio*, from COR- + *relation-, relatio*: see RELATION]

correlation coefficient *noun* in statistics, a number or function that indicates the degree of correlation between two sets of data or between two variables.

correlative[1] /kəˈrelativ, ko-/ *adj* **1** naturally related; corresponding. **2** said of words or parts of words: grammatically related and regularly used together, e.g. *neither* and *nor*. **➤➤ correlatively** *adv*, **correlativity** /-ˈtiviti/ *noun*.

correlative[2] *noun* a correlative word.

correspond /koriˈspond/ *verb intrans* **1a** (*usu* + to/with) to conform or be compatible; to match. **b** (*usu* + to/with) to be equivalent or similar. **2** (*usu* + with) to communicate by exchanging letters. [early French *correspondre* from medieval Latin *correspondēre* to respond together, from COR- + *respondēre*: see RESPOND[1]]

correspondence *noun* **1** letters, or communication by letter: *Nor can [I] form the remotest conjecture of the position of New South Wales, or Van Diemen's Land. Yet I do hold a correspondence with a very dear* *friend in the first-named of these two Terrae Incognitae* — Charles Lamb. **2a** the agreement of things with one another. **b** a particular similarity. **c** in mathematics, an association of one or more members of one set with each member of another set.

correspondence course *noun* a course of study in which students send and receive material by post.

correspondence principle *noun* in physics, the principle that states that there must be agreement in the predictions of quantum and classical mechanics in the limit of very large quantum numbers (number describing an elementary particle; see QUANTUM NUMBER).

correspondent[1] *noun* **1** a person who contributes news or comment to a publication or radio or television network: *a war correspondent.* **2** a person who communicates with another by letter.

correspondent[2] *adj* **1** similar. **2** conforming to something or agreeing with it.

corresponding *adj* **1a** agreeing in some respect, e.g. kind, degree, position, or function. **b** related or accompanying. **2** participating at a distance and by post: *a corresponding member of the society.* ⋙ **correspondingly** *adv.*

corrida /ko'reedhə, -də/ *noun* a bullfight. [Spanish *corrida de toros* running of bulls]

corridor /'koridaw, -də/ *noun* **1** a passage, e.g. in a hotel or railway carriage, onto which compartments or rooms open. **2** a narrow strip of land through foreign-held territory. **3** a restricted path for air traffic. **4** a strip of land that by geographical characteristics is distinct from its surroundings. ✴ **the corridors of power** the highest levels of administration in government, business, etc. [French *corridor* from early Italian *corridore*, ultimately from Latin *currere* to run]

corrie /'kori/ *noun Scot* a steep-sided glacially excavated hollow in the side of a mountain; a cwm or cirque. [Scottish Gaelic *coire* kettle]

corrigendum /kori'jendəm/ *noun* (*pl* **corrigenda** /-də/) an error in a printed work. [Latin *corrigendum*, from *corrigere*: see CORRECT[1]]

corrigible /'korijəbl/ *adj* capable of being corrected. ⋙ **corrigibility** /-ə'biliti/ *noun.* [Middle English via French from medieval Latin *corrigibilis*, from Latin *corrigere*: see CORRECT[1]]

corroborant /kə'robərənt/ *adj archaic* said of a medicine: having an invigorating effect. [Latin *corroborant-*, *corroborans*, present part. of *corroborare*: see CORROBORATE]

corroborate /kə'robərayt/ *verb trans* to support (e.g. a claim or an opinion) with evidence or authority. ⋙ **corroboration** /-'raysh(ə)n/ *noun,* **corroborative** /-tiv/ *adj,* **corroborator** *noun,* **corroboratory** /-ət(ə)ri/ *adj.* [Latin *corroboratus,* past part. of *corroborare* to give added strength, from COR- + *robor-, robur* strength]

corroboree /kə'robəree, -'ree/ *noun* **1** an Australian Aboriginal ceremony with songs and symbolic dances to celebrate important events. **2** *Aus.* **a** a noisy party. **b** a commotion or uproar. [native name in New South Wales, Australia]

corrode /kə'rohd/ *verb trans* **1** to eat or wear (*esp* metal) away gradually by chemical action. **2** to weaken or destroy (something) gradually, as if by chemical action. ⋙ *verb intrans* to undergo corroding. ⋙ **corrodible** *adj.* [Middle English *corroden* from Latin *corrodere* to gnaw to pieces, from COR- + *rodere* to gnaw]

corrosion /kə'rohzh(ə)n/ *noun* **1** the action or process of corroding. **2** a corroded part or area.

corrosive[1] /kə'rohsiv, -ziv/ *adj* **1** causing corrosion: *corrosive acids; corrosive action.* **2** harmful or destructive, *esp* insidiously so: *This priest … took it absurdly amiss that I should point out to him the corrosive effect which modern science must have on his beliefs* — Conan Doyle. ⋙ **corrosively** *adv,* **corrosiveness** *noun.*

corrosive[2] *noun* a substance, *esp* an acid, that causes corrosion.

corrugate /'korəgayt/ *verb trans and intrans* to fold (something) or become folded into alternating ridges and grooves: *The remnants of last week's blizzard had frozen into corrugated patches of ice in the car park* — David Lodge. ⋙ **corrugated** *adj,* **corrugation** /-'gaysh(ə)n/ *noun.* [Latin *corrugatus,* past part. of *corrugare,* from COR- + *rugare* to wrinkle]

corrugated iron /'korəgaytid/ *noun* sheet iron or sheet steel shaped into straight parallel regular and equally curved alternate ridges and grooves.

corrupt[1] /kə'rupt/ *adj* **1a** open to or characterized by bribery or other improper conduct. **b** morally degenerate and perverted;

depraved. **2a** said of computer data: damaged in a way that may make the program, file, etc unusable. **b** said of a text: containing errors. **3** *archaic* tainted. ⋙ **corruptly** *adv.* [Middle English from Latin *corrumpere* to spoil, from COR- + *rumpere* to break]

corrupt[2] *verb trans* **1** to make (somebody or something) corrupt. **2a** to alter (a manuscript, text, etc) from the original or correct form or version. **b** to damage (computer data). **3** *archaic* to taint (something) or make (it) putrid. ⋙ **corrupter** *noun,* **corruptibility** /-'biliti/ *noun,* **corruptible** *adj,* **corruptibly** *adv,* **corruptive** /-tiv/ *adj.*

corruption /kə'rupsh(ə)n/ *noun* **1a** inducement by bribery to do wrong. **b** bribery or dishonesty of any kind. **2** impairment of integrity, virtue, or moral principle. **3** decay or decomposition. **4** an alteration, e.g. to a manuscript.

corsage /kaw'sahzh/ *noun* **1** an arrangement of flowers worn by a woman, pinned to a dress or a lapel. **2** the bodice of an evening dress. [French *corsage* bust, bodice, ultimately from Latin *corpus* body]

corsair /'kawseə/ *noun* a pirate, *esp* a privateer of the Barbary coast. [early French *corsaire* pirate, from medieval Latin *cursus* a raid, plunder, from Latin: see COURSE[1]]

corse /kaws/ *noun archaic* a corpse. [Middle English *cors* from Old French *cors* body]

corselet /'kaws(ə)lit/ *noun* **1** see CORSLET. **2** see CORSELETTE.

corselette /kawsə'let/ *or* **corselet** /'kawslit/ *noun* a one-piece undergarment combining girdle and bra. [orig a trademark; from French *corselet*: see CORSLET]

corset /'kawsit/ *noun* **1** a stiffened or elasticated supporting undergarment for women, extending from beneath the bust to below the hips, designed to give shape to the figure. **2** a similar garment worn by men and women to give support in cases of injury, *esp* to the back. **3** a close-fitting outer garment covering the torso, worn in the Middle Ages. ⋙ **corseted** *adj.* [Middle English from early French *corset,* dimin. of *cors* body, from Latin *corpus*]

corsetière /,kawseti'eə/ *noun* a woman who makes, fits, or sells corsets. [French *corsetière,* from *corset*: see CORSET]

corsetry /'kawsitri/ *noun* undergarments, *esp* women's undergarments, that give support or shape.

Corsican /'kawsikən/ *noun* **1** a native or inhabitant of Corsica, an island off the W coast of Italy. **2** the language of Corsica. ⋙ **Corsican** *adj.*

corslet *or* **corselet** /'kawslit/ *noun* a piece of armour that covers the torso but usu not the arms or legs. [early French *corselet,* dimin. of *cors* body, bodice, from Latin *corpus* body]

cortège *or* **cortege** /kaw'tezh/ *noun* **1** a procession, *esp* a funeral procession. **2** a train of attendants; a retinue. [French *cortège* from Italian *corteggio,* ultimately from Latin *cohort-, cohors* court, retinue]

cortex /'kawteks/ *noun* (*pl* **cortices** /'kawtiseez/) **1** in anatomy, the outer part of an organ of the body, *esp* the outer layer of grey matter of the brain. **2** in botany, the layer of tissue between the inner vascular tissue and the outer epidermal tissue of a green plant. [Latin *cortic-, cortex* bark]

cortical /'kawtikl/ *adj* **1** of or consisting of a cortex. **2** involving or resulting from the action or condition of the cerebral cortex.

corticate /'kawtikət, -kayt/ *adj* in botany, having a cortex.

cortices /'kawtiseez/ *noun* pl of CORTEX.

cortico- *comb. form* forming words, with the meaning: cortex: *corticosteroid.*

corticosteroid /,kawtikoh'stiəroyd/ *noun* **1** any of several steroids, e.g. cortisone, produced by the cortex of the adrenal gland. **2** a synthetic drug with actions similar to those of natural corticosteroids.

corticosterone /,kawtikoh'sterohn/ *noun* a steroid hormone produced by the outer part of the adrenal gland, which regulates the synthesis and breakdown of proteins and carbohydrates: formula $C_{21}H_{30}O_4$.

corticotrophin /,kawtikoh'trohfin/ *or* **corticotropin** /-'trohpin/ *noun* = ADRENOCORTICOTROPHIC HORMONE.

cortisol /'kawtisol, -zol/ *noun* = HYDROCORTISONE.

cortisone /'kawtisohn, -zohn/ *noun* a steroid hormone that is produced by the cortex of the adrenal gland and is often used, in synthetic form, as a treatment for various conditions, e.g. skin disorders. [alteration of CORTICOSTERONE]

corundum /kə'rundəm/ *noun* a very hard natural or synthetic mineral that consists of aluminium oxide, exists in various colours, and is used as an abrasive and a gemstone. [Tamil *kuruntam* from Sanskrit *kuruvinda* ruby]

coruscate /'korəskayt/ *verb intrans literary* to give off flashes of light; to sparkle; to scintillate: *a coruscating radiance of glance —* Charlotte Brontë; *coruscating wit.* ➤➤ **coruscation** /-'skaysh(ə)n/ *noun.* [Latin *coruscatus*, past part. of *coruscare* to flash]

corvée /'kawvay/ *noun* **1** unpaid labour that under a feudal system was due to a lord from a tenant. **2** labour exacted in lieu of taxes by public authorities, e.g. for road construction. [Middle English *corvee*, ultimately from Latin *corrogare* to collect, requisition, from COR- + *rogare* to beg]

corves /kawvz/ *noun* pl of CORF.

corvette /kaw'vet/ *noun* **1** a small highly manoeuvrable armed escort ship. **2** a small sailing warship with a single tier of guns. [French *corvette* from Dutch *korf* basket, small ship, from Latin *corbis* basket]

corvine /'kawvien/ *adj* **1** of or related to crows. **2** resembling a crow. [Latin *corvinus*, from *corvus* raven]

corybantic /kori'bantik/ *adj* wildly ecstatic. [Latin *Corybantes*, the attendants or priests of the goddess Cybele in classical mythology, noted for orgiastic processions and rites, from Greek *Korybant-, Korybas*]

corymb /'korim(b)/ *noun* in botany, any kind of flower that grows in the form of a flat-topped cluster; *specif* one in which the flower stalks are attached at different levels on the main axis. ➤➤ **corymbose** /-bohs/ *adj.* [French *corymbe* from Latin *corymbus* cluster of fruit or flowers, from Greek *korymbos* cluster]

coryphée /kori'fay/ *noun* a leading dancer in the corps de ballet of a ballet company. [French *coryphée* via Latin *coryphaeus* from Greek *koryphaios* leader, from *koryphē* summit]

coryza /kə'riezə/ *noun* a short-lasting infectious inflammation of the upper respiratory tract, *esp* the common cold. [via late Latin from Greek *koryza* nasal mucus]

cos¹ /kəz; *strong* koz/ *conj informal* because. [by shortening and alteration]

cos² /koz/ *noun* (*also* **cos lettuce**) a crisp long-leaved variety of lettuce. [*Cos*, Greek island where it was first grown]

cos³ /koz/ *abbr* cosine.

Cosa Nostra /kohzə 'nostrə/ *noun* the N American branch of the Mafia organization. [Italian *cosa nostra*, literally 'our thing']

cosec /'kohsek/ *abbr* cosecant.

cosecant /koh'seek(ə)nt, koh'sek(ə)nt/ *noun* in mathematics, the trigonometric function that is the reciprocal of the sine. [Latin *cosecant-, cosecans*, from CO- + *secant-, secans*: see SECANT]

cosech /'kohsech/ *abbr* hyperbolic cosecant.

coseismal /koh'siezmǝl/ *adj* said of points: simultaneously affected by the same phase of seismic shock during an earthquake.

coset /'kohset/ *noun* in mathematics, a subset of a mathematical group that consists of all the products obtained by multiplying, either on the right or on the left, a fixed element of the group by each of the elements of a given subgroup.

cosh¹ /kosh/ *noun Brit* a short heavy rod often enclosed in a softer material and used as a hand weapon. [perhaps from Romany *kosh* stick]

cosh² *verb trans Brit* to strike (somebody) with a cosh.

cosh³ *abbr* hyperbolic cosine. [shortening of COSINE + *h* for HYPERBOLIC²]

cosignatory *or* **co-signatory** /koh'signət(ə)ri/ *noun* (pl **cosignatories**) a joint signer of a document or treaty.

cosine /'kohsien/ *noun* in mathematics, the trigonometric function that for an acute angle in a right-angled triangle is the ratio between the side adjacent to the angle and the hypotenuse: compare SINE, TANGENT¹. [Latin *cosinus*, from CO- + *sinus* curve, sine]

cosmetic¹ /koz'metik/ *noun* a preparation designed to be applied to the skin or hair to improve its appearance or texture.

cosmetic² *adj* **1** of or intended to improve beauty, e.g. of the hair or complexion. **2** intended to improve the outward appearance only, often in order to conceal underlying or fundamental shortcomings. ➤➤ **cosmetically** *adv.* [Greek *kosmētikos* skilled in adornment, from *kosmein* to arrange, adorn, from *kosmos* COSMOS]

cosmetician /kozmi'tish(ə)n/ *noun NAmer* a person who is professionally trained in the use of cosmetics.

cosmetology /kozmi'tolǝji/ *noun* the cosmetic treatment of the skin, hair, and nails. ➤➤ **cosmetologist** *noun.* [French *cosmétologie*]

cosmic /'kozmik/ *adj* **1** of the universe in contrast to the earth alone. **2** relating to the region of space that lies outside the earth's atmosphere. ➤➤ **cosmical** *adj.* great in extent, intensity, or comprehensiveness. ➤➤ **cosmically** *adv.* [Greek *kosmikos*, from *kosmos* COSMOS]

cosmical /'kozmikl/

cosmic dust *noun* very fine particles of solid matter in any part of the universe.

cosmic ray *noun* (*usu in pl*) a stream of high energy radiation reaching the earth from outer space.

cosmic string *noun* a string of matter of infinite thinness but immense mass and length, postulated by some physicists to explain the formation of galaxies at the beginning of time.

cosmo- *comb. form* forming words, denoting: the world or the universe: *cosmology.* [Greek *kosmos* order, universe]

cosmogony /koz'mogəni/ *noun* (pl **cosmogonies**) the study of the creation or origin of the universe, or of a particular part of it. ➤➤ **cosmogonic** /-'gonik/ *adj*, **cosmogonical** /-'gonikl/ *adj*, **cosmogonist** *noun.* [via Latin from Greek *kosmogonia*, from *kosmos* COSMOS + *gonos* offspring]

cosmography /koz'mogrǝfi/ *noun* (pl **cosmographies**) **1** the branch of science dealing with the constitution of the universe, *esp* of the solar system. **2** a general description of the world or the universe. ➤➤ **cosmographer** *noun*, **cosmographic** /-'grafik/ *adj*, **cosmographical** /-'grafikl/ *adj.* [Middle English *cosmographie* via late Latin from Greek *kosmographia*, from *kosmos* COSMOS + *-graphia* -GRAPHY]

cosmological /kozmǝ'lojikl/ *adj* of or relating to cosmology.

cosmological constant *noun* in astronomy, a constant used in theoretical models of the universe, orig used by Einstein in equations of general relativity.

cosmological principle *noun* in astronomy, the theory that the universe appears the same no matter where the observer stands.

cosmology /koz'molǝji/ *noun* (pl **cosmologies**) **1** the branch of astronomy dealing with the origin, structure, and space-time relationships of the universe. **2** a theoretical account of the nature of the universe. ➤➤ **cosmologist** *noun.* [Latin *cosmologia* from Greek *kosmos* COSMOS + Latin *-logia* -LOGY]

cosmonaut /'kozmǝnawt/ *noun* a Russian astronaut. [partial translation of Russian *kosmonavt*, from Greek *kosmos* COSMOS + Russian *-navt* as in *aeronavt* aeronaut]

cosmopolitan¹ /kozmǝ'polit(ə)n/ *adj* **1** composed of people, constituents, or elements from many parts of the world. **2** marked by a sophistication that comes from wide and often international experience: *It is surely nothing less than martyrdom to a man of cosmopolitan sympathies to absorb in silent resignation the news of a county town —* Wilkie Collins. **3** having worldwide rather than provincial scope or bearing. **4** said of a plant or animal: found in most parts of the world and under varied ecological conditions. ➤➤ **cosmopolitanism** *noun.* [Latin *cosmopolites*: see COSMOPOLITE]

cosmopolitan² *noun* a cosmopolitan person, plant, or animal.

cosmopolite /koz'mopǝliet/ *noun* a cosmopolitan person. [Latin *cosmopolites* from Greek *kosmopolitēs*, from *kosmos* COSMOS + *politēs* citizen]

cosmos /'kozmos/ *noun* **1** the universe, *esp* when regarded as an orderly system: compare CHAOS (2). **2** any of a genus of tropical American plants of the daisy family grown for their yellow or red flower heads: genus *Cosmos*. [Greek *kosmos* order, universe, ornamentation; (sense 2) from Greek *kosmos* in the sense 'ornamentation']

Cossack /'kosak/ *noun* **1** a member of a people of S Russia and the Ukraine famous for their horseriding skill. **2** a member of a unit of Cossack cavalrymen who fought under the Russian tsars. [Russian *kazak* and Ukrainian *kozak* from Turkish *kazak* free person]

cosset /'kosit/ *verb trans* (**cosseted, cosseting**) to treat (a person or animal) with great or excessive indulgence and protection; to pamper (them). [obsolete *cosset* pet lamb, perhaps from Old English *cotsæta* cottager]

cossie or **cozzie** /'kozi/ noun informal a swimming costume. [by shortening and alteration]

cost¹ /kost/ noun **1** the price paid or charged for something. **2** the expenditure, e.g. of effort or sacrifice, made to achieve an objective. **3** the loss or penalty incurred in gaining something. **4** (in pl) expenses incurred in litigation, esp those ordered by the court to be paid to the successful party. ✳ **at all costs** regardless of the price or difficulties. **at any cost** regardless of the price or difficulties. **at cost** at the price paid by the retailer. **to one's cost** to one's disadvantage or loss.

cost² verb trans (past tense and past part. **cost**) **1** to have a price of (a specified amount). **2** informal to have a high price for (somebody). **3** to cause (somebody) to pay, suffer, or lose something: Frequent absences cost him his job; Your suggestion would cost us too much time. **4** (past tense and past part. **costed**) to estimate or set the cost of (something). [Middle English costen via early French coster from Latin constare to stand firm, to cost, from CON- + stare to stand]

costa /'kostə/ noun (pl **costae** /'kostee/) **1** in botany and zoology, a rib or riblike part. **2** the front vein of an insect wing or other part that resembles a rib. ⏩ **costal** adj, **costate** /'kostayt/ adj. [Latin costa rib, side]

cost accounting noun the systematic recording and analysis of the costs of material, labour, and overheads of a particular business. ⏩ **cost accountant** noun.

costae /'kosti/ noun pl of COSTA.

co-star¹ /'koh stah/ noun a star who has equal billing with another leading performer in a film or play.

co-star² verb (**co-starred, co-starring**) ⏵ verb intrans to appear as a co-star in a film or play. ⏵ verb trans to feature (an actor) as a co-star.

Costa Rican /kostə 'reekən/ noun a native or inhabitant of Costa Rica in Central America. ⏩ **Costa Rican** adj.

cost-benefit adj involving an assessment of the cost of an enterprise weighed against its potential benefits.

cost-effective adj economically worthwhile. ⏩ **cost-effectively** adv, **cost-effectiveness** noun.

costermonger /'kostəmunggə/ noun Brit, dated a person who sells articles, esp fruit or vegetables, from a street barrow or stall. [alteration of obsolete costardmonger, from costard a kind of large apple + -MONGER]

costive /'kostiv/ adj affected with constipation. ⏩ **costiveness** noun. [Middle English from early French costivé, past part. of costiver to constipate, from Latin constipare: see CONSTIPATE]

costly adj (**costlier, costliest**) **1** expensive or valuable. **2** made at great expense or with considerable sacrifice. ⏩ **costliness** noun.

costmary /'kostmeəri/ noun (pl **costmaries**) a plant of the daisy family that resembles tansy and is used as a herb and was formerly used in place of hops for flavouring beer: Balsamita major. [Middle English costmarie, from coste costmary (ultimately from Greek kostos a fragrant root) + Marie the Virgin Mary, because it was formerly used medicinally]

cost of living noun the cost of purchasing those goods and services that are regarded as necessary for maintaining an acceptable standard of living.

cost-of-living index noun = RETAIL PRICE INDEX.

cost-plus adj said of pricing: calculated on the basis of a fixed fee or a percentage added to actual cost.

cost price noun the price paid by a retailer for an article of merchandise to be resold.

cost-push noun an increase or upward trend in production costs, sometimes considered to result in increased consumer prices irrespective of the level of demand.

costume¹ /'kostyoohm, 'kostyoom/ noun **1** a set of garments belonging to a specific time, place, or character, worn in order to assume a particular role, e.g. in a play or as fancy dress. **2** a swimming costume. **3** Brit, dated a matching jacket and skirt. [French costume via Italian from Latin consuetudin-, consuetudo: see CUSTOM¹]

costume² verb trans **1** to provide (somebody) with a costume. **2** to design costumes for (a play, film, or other performance).

costume drama noun a film or television drama set in a particular historical period.

costume jewellery noun inexpensive jewellery, orig of a kind typically worn attached to clothing rather than on the body.

costumier /ko'styoohmi·ə/ (NAmer **costumer** /'kostyoohmə/) noun a person who deals in or makes costumes, e.g. for theatrical productions. [French costumier, from costume: see COSTUME¹]

cosy¹ (NAmer **cozy**) /'kohzi/ adj (**cosier, cosiest**, NAmer **cozier, coziest**) **1** enjoying or affording warmth and comfort; snug. **2** marked by the intimacy of the family or a close group. **3a** informal, derog suggesting close association or connivance: a cosy agreement. **b** complacent: cosy morality. ⏩ **cosily** adv, **cosiness** noun. [prob of Scandinavian origin]

cosy² (NAmer **cozy**) noun (pl **cosies**, NAmer **cozies**) a cover, esp for a teapot, designed to keep the contents hot.

cosy up (NAmer **cozy up**) verb intrans (**cosies, cosied, cosying**, NAmer **cozies, cozied, cozying**) informal (usu + to) to attempt to gain friendship or intimacy, esp in an ingratiating and self-serving way: The government has been cosying up to opposition leaders.

cot¹ /kot/ noun **1** Brit a small bed for a baby or young child, with high enclosing sides consisting of vertical bars. **2** a small or narrow bed for occasional use. **3** NAmer a camp bed. **4** a hammock on a ship. [Hindi khāṭ bedstead, from Sanskrit khatvā, of Dravidian origin]

cot² noun **1** archaic a small house or cottage. **2** a shelter for sheep, birds, etc; a cote. [Old English]

cot³ abbr cotangent.

cotangent /koh'tanj(ə)nt, 'koh-/ noun in mathematics, the trigonometric function that is the reciprocal of the tangent. [Latin cotangent-, cotangens, from CO- + tangent-, tangens: see TANGENT¹]

cot death noun Brit the death of a baby or very young child during sleep, from no apparent disease.

cote /koht/ noun a shed or coop for small domestic animals, esp pigeons. [Old English cote cottage]

coterie /'kohtəri/ noun a small and usu exclusive group of people with a unifying common interest or purpose: And he did not join the intellectual coterie in the afternoon, as he usually did — Kate Chopin. [French côterie, orig 'a group of tenants', ultimately from medieval Latin cotarius tenant of a cottage, of Germanic origin]

coterminous /koh'tuhminəs/ or **conterminous** adj **1** having the same boundaries: coterminous states. **2** having the same scope or lasting the same time: coterminous interests. ⏩ **coterminously** adv. [alteration of obsolete conterminous, from Latin conterminous, from CON- + terminus boundary]

coth /koth/ noun hyperbolic cotangent.

cotidal /koh'tiedl/ adj indicating equality in the tides or a coincidence in the time of high or low tide.

cotillion /kə'tilyən/ noun **1** an elaborate 18th-cent. French dance with frequent changing of partners. **2** NAmer a quadrille. **3** NAmer a formal ball. [French cotillon, literally 'petticoat', from early French cote coat, of Germanic origin]

cotinga /kə'tinggə/ noun any of numerous species of brightly coloured birds with hooked beaks, found in the tropical regions of Central and S America: genus Cotinga. [Latin genus name, from Tupi cutinga]

cotoneaster /kə,tohni'astə/ noun a flowering shrub of the rose family, with small white flowers followed by red or black berries: genus Cotoneaster. [Latin genus name, from cotoneum (see QUINCE) + -ASTER]

Cotswold /'kotswohld, 'kotswəld/ noun an animal of a breed of large sheep with long wool, originating in England. [named after the Cotswold Hills, England, where the breed originated]

cotta /'kotə/ noun a waist-length surplice worn by members of a choir and some Roman Catholic priests and servers. [medieval Latin cotta, of Germanic origin]

cottage¹ /'kotij/ noun **1** a small simple house, esp in the country. **2** informal a public lavatory considered as a venue for homosexual activity. ⏩ **cottagey** adj. [Middle English cotage from Anglo-French cotage or Anglo-Latin cotagium, both of Germanic origin, related to COT²]

cottage² verb intrans informal said of men: to engage in homosexual activity in a public toilet. ⏩ **cottaging** noun.

cottage cheese noun a soft white mild-tasting cheese made from the curds of skimmed milk.

cottage garden *noun* a garden of a type supposedly common round country cottages in the 19th and early 20th cents, devoted mainly to vegetables, herbs, and informal borders of flowers.

cottage hospital *noun Brit* a small hospital without resident doctors.

cottage industry *noun* an industry with a work force consisting of family units working at home with their own equipment.

cottage loaf *noun* a loaf of bread with a distinctive shape formed by placing a small round mass of dough on top of a larger one.

cottage pie *noun Brit* a shepherd's pie *esp* made with minced beef: compare SHEPHERD'S PIE.

cottager *noun* somebody who lives in a cottage.

cottar *or* **cotter** /'kotə/ *noun* in Scotland and Ireland formerly, a person occupying a cottage, sometimes with a small holding of land, usu in return for services. [Middle English, from COT² + -AR²]

cotter pin *noun* **1** a pin for fastening parts of a machine or other mechanism together. **2** a split pin that passes through the holes in two or more parts and is spread open at its ends to secure the fastening. [origin unknown]

cotton /'kot(ə)n/ *noun* **1a** a soft usu white fibrous substance composed of the hairs surrounding the seeds of the cotton plant. **b** a freely branching tropical and subtropical plant that produces these seeds: genus *Gossypium*. **2a** fabric made of cotton. **b** yarn spun from cotton. **c** *NAmer* cotton wool. ➤➤ **cottony** *adj*. [Middle English *coton* via French from Arabic *qutn*]

cotton bud *noun Brit* a short plastic stick with a small wad of cotton wool on each end, used for cleaning ears, etc and for removing make-up.

cotton cake *noun* = COTTONSEED CAKE.

cotton candy *noun NAmer* candy floss.

cotton gin *noun* a machine for separating the seeds, seed cases, and waste material from cotton.

cotton grass *noun* a sedge with tufted spikes: genus *Eriophorum*. Also called BOG COTTON.

cotton on *verb intrans informal* (often + to) to become aware of something, usu after initially not realizing it.

cotton-picking *adj NAmer, informal* used to express irritation or anger. [prob because cotton picking is a hard menial task]

cottonseed cake *noun* a compressed mass of cotton seeds used for feeding cattle.

cotton swab *noun NAmer* a cotton bud.

cottontail *noun* a rather small N American rabbit that is sandy brown in colour with a white fluffy tail: genus *Sylvilagus*.

cottonwood *noun* a poplar tree of N America that has a tuft of cottony hairs on the seed and is often cultivated for its rapid growth and luxuriant foliage: *Populus deltoides*.

cotton wool *noun* **1** *Brit* fluffy balls or pads, orig made from raw cotton and now made from bleached cotton, often with a proportion of synthetic fibre, used for cleaning wounds, removing make-up, etc. **2** *NAmer* raw cotton.

cotyledon /koti'leed(ə)n/ *noun* in botany, the first leaf or either of the first pair of leaves developed by the embryo of a seed plant. ➤➤ **cotyledonal** *adj*, **cotyledonary** *adj*, **cotyledonous** /-nəs/ *adj*. [via Latin from Greek *kotylēdōn* cup-shaped hollow, from *kotylē* cup]

coucal /'kookəl/ *noun* any of numerous species of ground-dwelling birds found in Africa, S Asia, and Australia: genera *Centropus* and *Coua*. [French *coucal*, perhaps a blend of *coucou* cuckoo and *alouette* lark]

couch¹ /kowch/ *noun* **1** a long upholstered piece of furniture for sitting or lying on, either with a back and armrests or with a low back and raised head-end. **2** a long upholstered seat with a headrest for patients to lie on during medical examination or psychoanalysis.

couch² *verb trans* **1** to phrase (something) in a specified manner: *The letter was couched in hostile terms.* **2** formerly, to treat (a cataract) by displacing the lens of the eye. **3** to lower (a weapon) to an attacking position. **4** to embroider (a design) by attaching a thread to a fabric using small regularly spaced stitches. ➤ *verb intrans* **1** said of an animal: to lie down to sleep. **2** *literary* to lie in ambush. [Middle English via Old French *coucher* to lie down, from Latin *collocare*: see COLLOCATE¹]

couch³ /'kowch, 'koohch/ *noun* = COUCH GRASS.

couchant /'kowch(ə)nt/ *adj* (*used after a noun*) in heraldry, said of an animal: lying down with the head up: *a lion couchant*. [Middle English from early French *couchant*, present part. of *coucher* to lie down, from Latin *collocare*: see COLLOCATE¹]

couchette /kooh'shet/ *noun* **1** a railway carriage that has seats which convert into bunks. **2** a bunk in a railway carriage. [French *couchette*, dimin. of *couche*: see COUCH²]

couch grass /kowch, koohch/ *noun* any of several species of grasses that spread rapidly by long creeping underground stems and are difficult to eradicate: genus *Elymus*. [alteration of *quitch* grass: see QUITCH]

couch potato *noun informal* an inactive person, *esp* somebody who spends a lot of time watching television.

coudé /'koohday, kooh'day/ *adj* said of a telescope: constructed so that light is reflected to a focus at a fixed place where the holder for a photographic plate, spectrograph, etc may be mounted. [French *coudé* bent like an elbow, from *coude* elbow, from Latin *cubitum*]

cougar /'koohgə/ *noun* (*pl* **cougars** *or collectively* **cougar**) *NAmer* a puma. [French *couguar* from Latin *cuguacuarana*, from Tupi *suasuarana*, literally 'deer-like' from *suasu* deer + *rana* resembling]

cough¹ /kof/ *verb intrans* **1** to expel air from the lungs suddenly with an explosive noise. **2** to make a noise like that of coughing. **3** *Brit, informal* to reveal information: *We questioned him, but he didn't cough.* ➤ *verb trans* to utter (something) with a cough or by coughing. [Middle English *coughen*, of imitative origin]

cough² *noun* **1** a condition marked by repeated or frequent coughing. **2** an act or sound of coughing. ➤➤ **cougher** *noun*.

cough drop *noun* a cough sweet.

cough mixture *noun Brit* any of various medicated liquids used to relieve coughing.

cough sweet *noun* a medicated sweet sucked to relieve coughing and soothe a sore throat.

cough up *verb trans* **1** to expel (e.g. mucus) by coughing. **2** *informal* to produce or hand over (e.g. money or information) unwillingly. ➤ *verb intrans informal* to produce or hand something over.

could /kəd, *strong* kood/ *verb aux* the past tense of CAN¹, used: **1** to express possibility in the past: *He realized he could go.* **2** to express a condition: *He said he would go if he could.* **3** to express a possibility: *You could be right.* **4** as a polite form in the present: *Could you do this for me?* **5** to express expectation or obligation: *You could at least apologize.* [Middle English *coude* from Old English *cuthe*, past tense of *cunnan* CAN¹]

couldn't /'koodnt/ *contraction* could not.

coulee /'koohli/ *noun NAmer* a deep ravine. [Canadian French *coulée* from French *coulée*, flowing, flow of lava, ultimately from Latin *colum* sieve]

coulibiac *or* **koulibiac** /koohli'byak/ *noun* a Russian dish of meat or fish, e.g. salmon, baked in pastry. [Russian *kulebyaka*]

coulis /kooh'lee/ *noun* (*pl* **coulis**) a thin sauce made from puréed fruit or vegetables. [French *coulis* from *couler* to flow, ultimately from Latin *colum* sieve]

couloir /'koohlwah/ *noun* a gorge in a mountainside. [French *couloir* gully, literally 'strainer', ultimately from Latin *colum* sieve]

coulomb /'koohlom, 'koohlohm/ *noun* the SI unit of electric charge, equal to the charge transported in one second by a current of one ampere. [named after Charles A de *Coulomb* d.1806, French physicist]

Coulomb's law *noun* in physics, a law stating that the mutual force, e.g. attraction or repulsion, exerted by one electrostatic point charge on another is proportional to the product of the charges and is inversely proportional to the square of their separation.

coulter (*NAmer* **colter**) /'kohltə/ *noun* a blade or sharp disc attached to the beam of a plough that makes a vertical cut in the ground in front of the ploughshare. [Middle English *colter* via French from Latin *culter* ploughshare]

coumarin /'koohmərin/ *noun* a chemical compound with the smell of vanilla, obtained from plants or made synthetically and used *esp* in perfumery: formula $C_9H_6O_2$. [French *coumarine*, from *coumarou* tonka bean tree, via Spanish or Portuguese from Tupi *cumarú* tonka bean]

coumarone /'koohmərohn/ *noun* a chemical compound obtained from coal tar and used to make resins for varnishes, printing inks, etc: formula C_8H_6O. [COUMARIN + -ONE]

Coun. *abbr* councillor.

council /'kownsl/ *noun* **1a** (*treated as sing. or pl*) an elected or appointed body with administrative, legislative, or advisory powers. **b** (*treated as sing. or pl*) a locally-elected body having power over a district, county, parish, etc. **2** *Brit* (*used before a noun*) provided and often subsidized by a local authority: *council housing*. [Middle English *counceil* via early French *concile* from Latin *concilium*, from CON- + *calare* to call]

Usage note

council *or* counsel? These two words, which are pronounced the same, are sometimes confused. A *council* is an administrative, advisory, or executive body of people: *She stood for election to the local council*; *council workers*. A member of a *council* is a *councillor*. *Counsel* is a formal word for advice (*He always gave wise counsel*), and also means a lawyer or group of lawyers (*the counsel for the prosecution*). *Counsel* is also used as a verb meaning to give help with psychological, social, or personal problems, and a person who gives such help is a *counsellor*: *Friends of the murdered teenager are receiving help from counsellors.*

councillor (*NAmer* **councilor**) /'kowns(ə)lə/ *noun* a member of a council. >>> **councillorship** *noun*.

councilman /'kownslmən/ *or* **councilwoman** *noun* (*pl* **councilmen** *or* **councilwomen**) *chiefly NAmer* a man or woman who is a member of a town or city council.

Council of Ministers *noun* (*treated as sing. or pl*) the group of senior government ministers who form the Prime Minister's advisory body; the cabinet.

councilor /'kownslə, -silə/ *noun NAmer* see COUNCILLOR.

council tax *noun* a tax based on the value of property, paid by householders in Britain as a way of funding the provision of services by their local authority.

counsel [1] /'kownsl/ *noun* **1a** advice, *esp* when given following consultation. **b** *archaic* deliberation or consultation itself: *Here thou, great Anna! whom three realms obey, dost sometimes counsel take – and sometimes tea —* Pope. **2a** (*pl* **counsel**) a barrister engaged in the trial of a case in court. **b** (*pl* **counsel**) a lawyer appointed to advise a client. ✳ **keep one's own counsel** to keep one's thoughts or intentions to oneself. [Middle English *conseil* via Old French from Latin *consilium*, from *consulere*: see CONSULT]

Usage note

counsel *or* council? See note at COUNCIL.

counsel [2] *verb trans* (**counselled, counselling,** *NAmer* **counseled, counseling**) **1** to advise (somebody). **2** to give (somebody) help with psychological, social, or personal problems. >>> **counselling** *noun*.

counsellor (*NAmer* **counselor**) /'kownsl·ə/ *noun* **1** a person who gives professional advice or guidance: *a marriage guidance counsellor*. **2** a senior diplomatic officer. **3** *NAmer* a person who has supervisory duties at a summer camp for children. **4** *NAmer, Irish* a lawyer; *specif* a barrister.

counsel of perfection *noun* a piece of excellent but impracticable advice.

counselor /'kownsl·ə/ *noun NAmer* see COUNSELLOR.

count [1] /kownt/ *verb trans* **1** to find the total number of (something). **2** to include (somebody or something) in a tallying and reckoning: *There are about 100 copies if you count the damaged ones.* **3** to think of (somebody or something) as having a particular quality or fulfil a particular role: *Count yourself lucky.* **4** to include or exclude (somebody) as if by counting: *You can count me in.* > *verb intrans* **1** to name the numbers in order by units or groups. **2** to have value or significance: *These are the people who really count.* **3** to be thought of as having a particular quality or fulfilling a particular role: *Does dancing count as a sport?* ✳ **count on 1** to look forward to (something) as certain. **2** to rely on (somebody). **count one's blessings** to remind oneself of the good things in one's life. >>> **countable** *adj*. [Middle English *counten* via early French *compter* from Latin *computare*: see COMPUTE]

count [2] *noun* **1a** the act or process of counting. **b** a total obtained by counting. **2a** in law, an allegation in an indictment: *She was found guilty on all counts.* **b** a specific point under consideration; an issue: *They disagreed on several counts.* **3** in boxing, the calling out of the seconds from one to ten when a boxer has been knocked down. **4** any of various measures of the fineness of a textile yarn.

✳ **out for the count** in boxing, having been knocked down and staying down for a count of ten.

count [3] *noun* a European nobleman corresponding in rank to a British earl. [early French *comte* via late Latin *comit-, comes* from Latin *comes* companion, member of the imperial court]

countdown *noun* **1** a continuous counting backwards to zero of the time remaining before an event, *esp* the launching of a rocket. **2** the remaining time before an important event: *the countdown to lift-off*.

count down *verb intrans* to count backwards to zero, *esp* to show the time remaining before the launch of a rocket.

countenance [1] /'kownt(ə)nəns/ *noun* **1** a person's face, *esp* as an indication of mood, emotion, or character: *A merry heart maketh a cheerful countenance —* Bible. **2** *formal* moral support or approval. **3** composure: *She kept her countenance.* [Middle English *contenance* via Old French and medieval Latin from Latin *continentia* restraint, ultimately from *continēre*: see CONTAIN]

countenance [2] *verb trans* to consider or allow (something): *Perhaps the most audacious thing about this exhibition is that the British Museum should have countenanced it at all —* Economist.

counter [1] *noun* **1** a level surface, e.g. a table, over which transactions are conducted or food is served or on which goods are displayed. **2** *NAmer* a kitchen work top. **3** a small disc of metal, plastic, etc used in counting or in games. **4** something of value in bargaining; an asset. **5** a person or machine that counts, *esp* a device that detects ionizing particles: *a Geiger counter.* ✳ **over the counter 1** without a prescription. **2** through a broker's office rather than through a stock exchange. **under the counter** by surreptitious means, often in an illicit and private manner. [Middle English *countour* via early French *comptour* from medieval Latin *computatorium* computing place, from Latin *computare*: see COMPUTE]

counter [2] *verb* (**countered, countering**) > *verb trans* to act in opposition to (something or somebody); to oppose (them). > *verb intrans* **1** to meet attacks or arguments with defensive or retaliatory steps. **2** in boxing or fencing, to attack while warding off a blow.

counter [3] *adv* (+ *to*) in an opposite, contrary, or wrong direction: *values that run counter to those of established society.* [Middle English via early French *contre* from Latin *contra* against, opposite]

counter [4] *noun* **1** something that counters something else. **2** an overhanging stern of a ship or boat. **3a** in boxing or fencing, the making of an attack while warding one off. **b** a blow given in this way. **4** in printing, an area within a piece of type, e.g. for the letter O, which is hollow and does not print.

counter [5] *adj* opposite, or showing opposition.

counter- *prefix* forming words, with the meanings: **1a** opposing or retaliatory: *counteroffensive.* **b** in the opposite direction: *countermarch.* **2** complementary or corresponding: *counterpart.* **3** duplicate or substitute: *counterfoil.* [Middle English *contre-* from early French *contre*: see COUNTER [3]]

counteract *verb trans* to lessen or neutralize the usu ill effects of (something) by an opposing action. >>> **counteraction** *noun*, **counteractive** /-tiv/ *adj*.

counterattack [1] *or* **counter-attack** /'kowntərətak/ *noun* an attack made in reply to an enemy's attack.

counterattack [2] *or* **counter-attack** *verb intrans* to make a counterattack.

counterattraction *or* **counter-attraction** *noun* an attraction that competes with another.

counterbalance [1] *noun* **1** a weight that balances another. **2** a force or influence that offsets or checks an opposing force.

counterbalance [2] *verb trans* to oppose or balance (something) with an equal weight or force.

counterblast *noun* often as the title of a militant writing: an energetic and often vociferous reaction or response: *Besides, we must get through another chapter of 'A Counterblast to Agnosticism' before we turn in —* Hardy; *The Female Nude by Lynda Nead (£35) promises to be a counterblast to Kenneth Clarke's classic —* The Art Newspaper.

counterchange [1] *verb trans literary* to design or decorate (something) with contrasting colours; to chequer (it).

counterchange [2] *noun* a reversal or transposition.

countercharge *noun* a charge made to counter another charge or to oppose an accuser.

counterclaim[1] *noun* **1** an opposing claim. **2** in law, an opposing claim made by a defendant against somebody who is claiming against him or her.

counterclaim[2] *verb intrans* in law, to make a counterclaim.

counterclockwise *adj and adv NAmer* anticlockwise.

counterculture *noun* a way of life with values that run counter to established social norms: compare ALTERNATIVE SOCIETY.

counterespionage *or* **counter-espionage** *noun* activities directed towards detecting and thwarting enemy espionage.

counterexample *noun* an example that disproves a theorem, proposition, etc.

counterfactual /kowntə'faktyooəl/ *adj* in philosophy, denoting a statement expressing something that is not the case.

counterfeit[1] /'kowntəfit, -feet/ *adj* **1** made in imitation of something else with intent to deceive or defraud. **2** *archaic* insincere or feigned: *counterfeit sympathy*. [Middle English *countrefet* from early French *contrefait*, past part. of *contrefaire* to imitate, from CONTRA- + Latin *facere* to make]

counterfeit[2] *noun* a forgery.

counterfeit[3] *verb trans* to imitate or copy (something) closely, *esp* with intent to deceive or defraud. ⟫ **counterfeiter** *noun*.

counterfoil *noun chiefly Brit* the part of a cheque, ticket, etc that is kept as a record or receipt.

counterinsurgency *or* **counter-insurgency** *noun* organized military activity designed to suppress rebellion.

counterintelligence *or* **counter-intelligence** *noun* organized activity designed to block an enemy's sources of information; counterespionage.

counterintuitive *or* **counter-intuitive** *adj* going against common sense or what one might expect. ⟫ **counterintuitively** *adv*.

counterirritant *noun* something applied to the skin locally to produce surface inflammation with the object of reducing inflammation in tissue underneath.

countermand[1] /kowntə'mahnd/ *verb trans* **1** to revoke (a command) by a contrary order. **2** to order back (e.g. troops) by a superseding contrary order. [Middle English *countermaunden* from early French *contremander*, from *contre-* COUNTER- + *mander* to command]

countermand[2] *noun* a contrary order revoking an earlier one.

countermarch[1] *noun* a movement in marching by which a unit of troops reverses direction while keeping the same order.

countermarch[2] *verb intrans* to reverse direction in marching.

countermeasure *noun* a measure designed to counter another action or state of affairs.

countermove *noun* a move designed to counter another move.

counteroffensive *noun* a military offensive undertaken from a previously defensive position.

counterpane *noun dated* a bedspread.

Word history
alteration of Middle English *countrepointe*, modification of early French *coute pointe*, literally 'embroidered quilt'. The spelling changed by association with PANE in an old sense 'piece of cloth'.

counterpart *noun* **1** a person or thing with the same function or characteristics as another; an equivalent. **2** in law, a duplicate of a legal document.

counterpoint[1] *noun* **1a** the combination of two or more independent melodies into a single harmonic texture. **b** one or more independent melodies added above or below a given melody. **2a** the use of contrast or interplay of elements in a work of art. **b** a complementing or contrasting idea. [early French *contrepoint* from medieval Latin *contrapunctum* or *cantus contrapunctus* song pricked or marked against (the original melody), from CONTRA- + *punctus* point, musical note, from Latin *pungere* to prick; the notes of the second melody being marked against or underneath the notes of the original]

counterpoint[2] *verb trans* **1** to compose or arrange (a musical work) in counterpoint. **2** to set off or emphasize (something) by contrast or juxtaposition.

counterpoise[1] *noun* **1** a force, influence, etc that acts as a counterbalance. **2** *archaic* a state of balance; equilibrium. **3** a counterbalance. [Middle English *countrepeis* from early French *contrepeis, contrepois*, from *contre-* COUNTER- + *peis, pois* weight]

counterpoise[2] *verb trans* to balance (something); to act as a contrast to (it).

counterproductive *adj* having effects that are the opposite to those intended.

Counter-Reformation *noun* the reform movement in the Roman Catholic Church in the 16th and 17th cents, in response to the Protestant REFORMATION (16th-cent. religious movement rejecting papal authority and advocating reform).

counterrevolution *or* **counter-revolution** *noun* a revolution directed towards overthrowing the system established by a previous revolution. ⟫ **counterrevolutionary** *adj and noun*.

counterscarp *noun* the outer wall or slope of a ditch in a fortification. [early French *countrescarpe*, from *contre-* COUNTER- + *escarpe* scarp]

countershading /'kowntəshayding/ *noun* a pattern of coloration on an animal in which the upper surface normally exposed to light is darker in colour than those parts normally in shadow, giving the body a uniform appearance.

countershaft *noun* a machine shaft that is driven by a main shaft and transmits motion to a working part.

countersign[1] *verb trans* to add one's signature to (a document) as a witness of another signature. ⟫ **countersignature** *noun*.

countersign[2] *noun archaic* a password or secret signal in response to one spoken by a military guard.

countersink *verb trans* (*past tense and past part.* **countersunk** /-sungk/) **1** to enlarge (a hole), *esp* by bevelling, so that the head of a bolt, screw, etc will fit below or level with the surface. **2** to set the head of (e.g. a screw) below or level with the surface.

countertenor *noun* a male singing voice higher than tenor, or a singer with this voice. [Middle English *countretenour* from early French *contreteneur*, from *contre* COUNTER- + *teneur* tenor]

countertrade /'kowntətrayd/ *noun* a form of international trading in which goods are exchanged for other goods or services rather than for money.

countervail /kowntə'vayl/ *verb trans* to counterbalance the effect of (something); to offset (it). [Middle English *countrevailen* from early French *contrevaloir*, from *contre-* COUNTER- + *valoir* to be worth]

countervailing duty /kowntə'vayling/ *noun* an import tax on goods, e.g. those that are produced cheaply or subsidized in their country of origin, imposed to protect domestic producers.

counterweight *noun* a counterbalance.

countess /'kowntis, 'kowntes/ *noun* **1** the wife or widow of an earl or count. **2** a woman who has the rank of earl or count in her own right.

countinghouse /'kowntinghows/ *noun* formerly, a building, room, or office used for keeping account books and transacting business.

countless *adj* too numerous to be counted; innumerable.

count noun *noun* in grammar, a noun, e.g. *bean* or *sheet*, that forms a plural and can be used with a number or the indefinite article: compare MASS NOUN.

count palatine *noun* (*pl* **counts palatine**) **1** an earl or other lord of a county palatine in England or Ireland. **2** a count of the Holy Roman Empire with imperial powers in his own domain.

countrified *or* **countryfied** /'kuntrified/ *adj* rural in style or manner, *esp* lacking the sophistication of the city. [COUNTRY + *-fied* as in *glorified*]

country /'kuntri/ *noun* (*pl* **countries**) **1** a political state or nation or its territory. **2** rural as opposed to urban areas; countryside. **3** an indefinite usu extended expanse of land; a region: *inhospitable hill country*. ✱ **go to the country** *Brit* to dissolve Parliament and have a general election. [Middle English *contree* via early French *contrée* from medieval Latin *contrata terra* land lying opposite, from Latin *contra* against, on the opposite side]

country and western *noun* country music.

country club *noun* a sporting or social club set in a rural area.

country cousin *noun* somebody who is unaccustomed to or confused by the bustle and sophistication of city life.

country dance *noun* any of various folk dances typically arranged in square or circular figures or in two long rows with dancers facing their partners.

countryfied /'kuntrified/ *adj* see COUNTRIFIED.

country house *noun* a house, mansion, or estate in the country.

countryman *or* **countrywoman** *noun* (*pl* **countrymen** *or* **countrywomen**) **1** a man or woman who lives in the country or has country ways. **2** a man or woman who comes from the same country as oneself; a compatriot.

country music *noun* music derived from or imitating the folk style of the southern or western USA, typically featuring acoustic guitars, simple melodies, and narrative, often sentimental lyrics.

country seat *noun* a mansion or estate in the country that is the hereditary property of one family.

countryside *noun* a rural area.

country-wide /'kuntriwied/ *adj and adv* nationwide.

county /'kownti/ *noun* (*pl* **counties**) **1** a territorial division of Britain and Ireland constituting the chief unit for administrative, judicial, and political purposes. **2** the largest local government unit in various countries, e.g. the USA. **3** *Brit* (*used before a noun*) characteristic of or belonging to the English landed gentry: *a county accent.* [Middle English *counte* via French and medieval Latin from late Latin *comitatus* office of a count, from *comes*: see COUNT³]

county borough *noun* a borough of England, Wales, and Northern Ireland which until 1974 had the local government powers of a county.

county council *noun* an elected government body responsible for the administration of a county. ➤➤ **county councillor** *noun.*

county court *noun* a local civil court in England which is presided over by a judge and deals with relatively minor claims.

county palatine *noun* (*pl* **counties palatine**) a county in England or Ireland over which an earl or other lord formerly had royal powers.

county seat *noun NAmer* = COUNTY TOWN.

county town *noun chiefly Brit* a town that is the seat of the government of a county.

coup¹ /kooh/ *noun* (*pl* **coups** /koohz/) **1** = COUP D'ÉTAT. **2** a brilliant, sudden, and usu highly successful stroke or act. [French *coup*: see COPE¹]

coup² /kowp/ *verb chiefly Scot* to overturn or upset (something). [Middle English *coupen* to strike, from French *couper*: see COPE¹]

coup de foudre /ˌkooh də 'foohdrə (*French* fudr)/ *noun* (*pl* **coups de foudre**) an unexpected overwhelming happening. [French *coup de foudre*, literally 'stroke of lightning']

coup de grâce /ˌkooh də 'grahs, 'gras (*French* ku də gras)/ *noun* (*pl* **coups de grâce**) **1** a fatal blow or shot administered to end the suffering of a mortally wounded person or animal. **2** a decisive finishing stroke. [French *coup de grâce* stroke of mercy]

coup de main /ˌkooh də 'manh (*French* də mɛ̃)/ *noun* (*pl* **coups de main**) a sudden forceful attack. [French *coup de main* stroke of the hand]

coup d'état /ˌkooh day'tah (*French* deta)/ *noun* (*pl* **coups d'état**) the violent overthrow of an existing government by a small group of rebels. [French *coup d'état*, literally 'stroke of state']

coup de théâtre /ˌkooh də tay'ahtr(ə)/ *noun* (*pl* **coups de théâtre**) **1** a sudden sensational turn of events, *esp* in a play. **2** a spectacular piece of staging or stagecraft. [French *coup de théâtre* stroke of theatre]

coup d'oeil /ˌkooh 'duh·i (*French* dœ:j)/ *noun* (*pl* **coups d'oeil**) a glance: *We ... endeavour now to present to the reader a coup d'oeil of the whole suite of apartments* — Edward Bulwer-Lytton. [French *coup d'oeil* stroke of the eye]

coupe /kooh/ *noun* **1** a small shallow dish with a stem. **2** a cold dessert of fruit and ice cream served in a coupe. [French *coupe* cup, from late Latin *cuppa*]

coupé /'koohpay/ *noun* **1** a two-door car that has a fixed roof and a sloping rear. **2** a four-wheeled horse-drawn carriage for two passengers with an outside seat for the driver. [French *coupé*, from past part. of *couper*: see COPE¹]

couple¹ /'kupl/ *noun* **1** two things considered together; a pair. **2** (*treated as sing. or pl*) two people paired together; *esp* two people who are married or living together. **3** *informal* an indefinite small number; a few. **4** in mechanics, two equal and opposite forces that act along parallel lines and cause rotation. ➤➤ **coupledom** *noun.* [Middle English, in the sense 'pair, bond' via early French *cople* from Latin *copula* bond]

couple² *verb trans* **1** to unite or link (one thing) with another: *He coupled his praise with a request.* **2** to fasten (e.g. railway carriages) together; to connect (them). ➤ *verb intrans* **1** to copulate. **2** to come together to form a unit; to join.

coupler *noun* **1** something that couples two things. **2** a device on a keyboard instrument by which keyboards or keys are connected to play together.

couplet /'kuplit/ *noun* a unit of two successive, usu rhyming, lines of verse. [early French *coplet*, dimin. of *cople*: see COUPLE¹]

coupling *noun* a device that serves to connect the ends of adjacent parts or objects, e.g. electrical circuits or railway carriages.

coupon /'koohpon/ *noun* **1** a ticket or voucher that entitles the holder to something, e.g. a free gift, discount, etc. **2** a voucher that entitles the holder to a share in rationed food, clothing, etc. **3** a part of a printed advertisement to be cut off for use as an order or enquiry form. **4** a printed entry form for a competition, *esp* the football pools. **5a** a part of a bond, stating how much and when interest is due, that is detached and presented for the payment of this interest. **b** the rate of interest paid upon a fixed-interest stock or bond. [French *coupon*, literally 'piece cut off', from *couper*: see COPE¹]

courage /'kurij/ *noun* mental or moral strength to confront and withstand danger, fear, or difficulty; bravery. ✳ **have the courage of one's convictions** to be brave enough to do what one thinks is right, irrespective of the obstacles in one's way. **take courage** to summon up the necessary courage to do something difficult or dangerous. [Middle English *corage* via French from Latin *cor* heart]

courageous /kə'rayjəs/ *adj* having or showing courage; brave. ➤➤ **courageously** *adv,* **courageousness** *noun.*

courante /kooh'rahn(h)t (*French* kurɑ̃:t)/ *noun* a dance of Italian origin consisting of quick running steps. [early French *courante* from *courir* to run, from Latin *currere*]

courgette /kooə'zhet/ *noun Brit* a variety of small vegetable marrow used as a vegetable. Also called ZUCCHINI. [French dialect *courgette*, dimin. of *courge* gourd, from Latin *cucurbita*]

courier¹ /'koori·ə/ *noun* **1** a person whose job is collecting and delivering parcels, papers, etc. **2** a person employed by a holiday company to assist tourists abroad and liaise between them and the company in matters of difficulty. [early French *courrier* from early Italian *corriere*, ultimately from Latin *currere* to run]

courier² *verb trans* to send (e.g. a parcel) by courier.

course¹ /kaws/ *noun* **1** the path over which something moves: *the course of a river.* **2** the direction of travel, *esp* of an aircraft, usu measured as a clockwise angle from north. **3** a movement or progression in space or time: *We were surprised by the course of events.* **4a** the usual procedure or normal action of something: *The law must take its course.* **b** a chosen manner of conducting oneself; a plan of action: *Our wisest course is to retreat.* **5** a series of lessons or lectures relating to a subject. **6** a part of a meal served at one time. **7** a particular medical treatment administered over a designated period. **8** an area of land marked out for a particular sport, e.g. a racecourse or golf course. **9** a row or layer, *esp* a continuous horizontal layer of brick or masonry throughout a wall. **10** the lowest sail on the masts of a square-rigged vessel. [Middle English via French from Latin *cursus*, past part. of *currere* to run]

course² *verb intrans* said of a liquid: to run or flow: *He could feel the blood coursing through his veins.* ➤ *verb trans* to hunt or pursue (e.g. hares) with dogs that follow by sight rather than smell.

coursebook *noun Brit* a textbook for students that covers a particular syllabus.

courser¹ *noun* any of several species of African and Asian birds noted for their swift running: genus *Cursorius.*

courser² *noun literary* a swift powerful horse; a charger. [Middle English from early French *coursier*, from *course* course, run, ultimately from Latin *currere* to run]

coursework *noun* work done by a student on a course, *esp* for a course marked by continuous assessment.

court¹ /kawt/ *noun* **1a** an official assembly of people authorized to hear judicial cases. **b** a place in which a such a court is held. **2** a rectangular space walled or marked off for playing lawn tennis, squash, basketball, etc. **3** a space enclosed wholly or partly by buildings or circumscribed by a single building. **4a** (*treated as sing. or pl*) the family and retinue or total body of courtiers of a sovereign. **b** the residence or establishment of a sovereign. **5** (*treated as sing. or pl*) the body of members of an assembly or board with legislative or administrative powers. ✳ **out of court** without having a court hearing. [Middle English via French *cort* from Latin *cohort-, cohors* enclosure, throng, cohort]

court² *verb trans* **1a** *dated* to seek the affections of (somebody); to woo (them). **b** said of an animal: to perform actions to attract (a mate). **2** to seek to win the favour or support of (somebody). **3** to act so as to invite or provoke (a specified outcome): *She courts disaster.* ➤ *verb intrans dated* said of a man and woman: to be involved in a romantic relationship.

court bouillon /ˌkaw boohˈyonh/ *noun* a stock made with vegetables, herbs, and often wine, used with fish. [French *court-bouillon*, from *court* short + *bouillon* bouillon]

court card *noun Brit* a king, queen, or jack in a pack of cards. [alteration of *coat card*, from the coats worn by the figures depicted]

court circular *noun Brit* a daily report of the engagements and other activities of the members of the royal family, published in newspapers.

court cupboard *noun* a 16th- or 17th-cent. sideboard or cabinet with an open base and a closed top section with one or more doors.

Courtelle /kawˈtel/ *noun trademark* an acrylic fibre.

courteous /ˈkuhti·əs/ *adj* showing respect and consideration for others; polite. ➤ **courteously** *adv*, **courteousness** *noun*. [Middle English *corteis* from early French *corteis*, from *cort* COURT¹]

courtesan /ˈkawtizan, -ˈzan/ *noun* a prostitute, *esp* one with a wealthy or upper-class clientele. [early French *courtisane* via early Italian *cortigiana* woman courtier, ultimately from Latin *cohort-, cohors* enclosure, throng, cohort]

courtesy /ˈkuhtəsi/ *noun* (*pl* **courtesies**) **1** courteous behaviour. **2** a courteous act or expression: *Fair sir, you spit on me on Wednesday last, you spurned me such a day; another time you called me dog; and for these courtesies I'll lend you thus much moneys* — Shakespeare. **3** (*used before a noun*) done or provided by way of courtesy: *a courtesy call.* **4** *archaic* a curtsy. ✳ **by courtesy of/courtesy of** through the kindness, generosity, or permission granted by (a person or organization). [Middle English *corteisie* from early French *corteis* courteous, from *cort* COURT¹]

courtesy light *noun* a small light inside a motor vehicle that comes on automatically when a door is opened.

courtesy title *noun* a title given to somebody, e.g. the son or daughter of a peer, which is without legal validity but commonly accepted.

courthouse /ˈkawt·hows/ *noun* **1** a building in which a court of law is held. **2** the administrative building of a US county.

courtier /ˈkawti·ə/ *noun* an attendant or companion to a king or queen. [Middle English from Old French *cortoyer* to be present at court, from *cort* COURT¹]

courtly *adj* (**courtlier**, **courtliest**) elegant and refined. ➤ **courtliness** *noun*.

courtly love *noun* a medieval conventionalized code prescribing the conduct and emotions of ladies and their lovers.

court-martial¹ *noun* (*pl* **courts-martial** *or* **court-martials**) **1** a court of commissioned officers that tries members of the armed forces. **2** a trial by such a court.

court-martial² *verb trans* (**court-martialled**, **court-martialling**, *NAmer* **court-martialed**, **court-martialing**) to try (somebody) by court-martial.

Court of Appeal *noun* a court hearing appeals from the decisions of lower courts.

court of first instance *noun* a law court in which proceedings are started.

court of inquiry *noun* a board of people appointed to ascertain the causes of an accident, disaster, etc.

court of law *noun* = COURT¹ (1A).

court of record *noun* a court whose recorded proceedings are valid as evidence of fact.

Court of Session *noun* the highest civil court in Scotland.

Court of St James's *noun* the court of the British sovereign. [*St James's* Palace, London, former seat of the British court]

court order *noun* an order issuing from a court of law that requires a person to do or abstain from doing a specified act.

court plaster *noun* an adhesive plaster, *esp* of silk coated with isinglass and glycerin, formerly used to cover wounds. [from its use for beauty spots by ladies at royal courts]

court roll *noun Brit* a register of land holdings of a manor.

courtroom *noun* a room in which the sessions of a court of law are held.

courtship /ˈkawtship/ *noun* **1** a period of courting. **2** the courting rituals of animals. **3** the process of courting favour.

court shoe *noun Brit* a plain high-heeled woman's shoe with no fastenings. [from its use as part of dress at court]

court tennis *noun NAmer* = REAL TENNIS.

courtyard *noun* an open court or enclosure adjacent to a building.

couscous /ˈkoohskoohs/ *noun* a N African dish of crushed or coarsely ground wheat steamed and served with meat or vegetables. [French *couscous* from Arabic *kuskus*, from *kuskasa* to pound, pulverize]

cousin /ˈkuzn/ *noun* **1** a child of one's uncle or aunt. **2** a kinsman or relative: *our American cousins.* **3** formerly used as a title by a sovereign in addressing a nobleman. ➤➤ **cousinhood** *noun*, **cousinly** *adj*, **cousinship** *noun*. [Middle English *cosin* via French from Latin *consobrinus*, from CON- + *sobrinus* cousin on the mother's side, from *soror* sister]

cousin-german *noun* (*pl* **cousins-german**) *dated* a first cousin. [Middle English *cosin germain* via French from Old French *cosin germain*, from *cosin* cousin + *germain* from Latin *germanus* having the same parents]

couth /koohth/ *adj* sophisticated or polished: *couth and kempt in creaseless suits* — Punch. [back-formation from UNCOUTH]

couture /koohˈtyooə/ *noun* the business of designing and making fashionable custom-made women's clothing. [French *couture* from early French *couture* sewing, ultimately from Latin *consuere* to sew together, from CON- + *suere* to sew]

couturier /koohˈtyooəri·ə, -riay/ *or* **couturière** /koohˌtyooəriˈeə/ *noun* a man or woman who makes and sells couture clothes. [French *couturier* dressmaker, from early French *cousturier* tailor's assistant, from *cousture*: see COUTURE]

couvade /koohˈvahd/ *noun* a custom among some peoples by which a father takes to his bed at the birth of his child as if bearing it himself. [French *couvade* from *couver* to sit on, brood, from Latin *cubare* to lie down]

couverture /ˈkoohvəchə, koohvˈeəˈtooə/ *noun* chocolate containing a high percentage of cocoa butter, used by chefs for coating, icing, or decorating confectionery. [French *couverture* covering, from *couvert*, past part. of *couvrir* to cover, from Old French *covrir*]

covalent /kohˈvaylənt/ *adj* said of chemical bonds: created by shared electrons or pairs of electrons between combining atoms. ➤➤ **covalence** *noun*, **covalency** *noun*, **covalently** *adv*.

covalent bond *noun* a non-ionic chemical bond formed by shared pairs of electrons between combining atoms.

covariance /kohˈveəri·əns/ *noun* **1** in mathematics, the ARITHMETIC MEAN (average value) of the products of the differences of corresponding values of two random variables from their respective means. **2** in statistics, the expected value of the product of the deviations of two random variables from their respective means.

covariant /kohˈveəri·ənt/ *adj* in mathematics, said of a variable: changing in proportion to another variable: *covariant distribution.*

cove¹ /kohv/ *noun* **1** a small sheltered inlet or bay. **2** a concave architectural moulding, *esp* at the point where a wall meets a ceiling or floor. [Old English *cofa*]

cove² *verb trans* to fit (a wall or ceiling) with a cove.

cove³ *noun Brit, informal, dated* a man: *Is this cove trying to be funny, or what?* — Conan Doyle. [prob from Romany *kova* thing, person]

coven /ˈkuvn/ *noun* (*treated as sing. or pl*) a group or gathering of witches. [Middle English *covin* band, via French and medieval Latin from *convenire* to convene]

covenant¹ /ˈkuv(ə)nənt/ *noun* **1** a solemn agreement; a contract. **2** a contract that binds a person to make regular payments of money to a charitable organization. **3** in the Bible, an agreement between God and the Israelites. ➤➤ **convenantal** /kuvəˈnantl/ *adj*. [Middle English via French from Latin *convenire*: see CONVENE]

covenant² *verb intrans* to enter into a covenant. ➤ *verb trans* to agree to or promise (something) by entering into a covenant.

covenanter *or* **covenantor** *noun* **1** somebody who makes a covenant. **2** (**Covenanter**) an adherent of the Scottish National Covenant of 1638 that established and set out a defence of Presbyterianism.

Coventry /'kov(ə)ntri, 'kuv-/ ✳ **send to Coventry** to exclude or ostracize (somebody).

Word history
from *Coventry*, city in England. The phrase is sometimes said to come from the unpopularity of soldiers billeted in the city, or because Royalist prisoners in the English Civil War were sent to Coventry, which was staunchly Parliamentarian.

cover[1] /'kuvə/ *verb* (**covered, covering**) ➤ *verb trans* **1a** to place or set a cover or covering over (something). **b** to lie or spread over (something); to envelop. **c** to extend thickly or conspicuously over the surface of (something): *Her face was covered in spots.* **d** to travel (a specified distance). **2** to hide (something) from sight or knowledge; to conceal. **3a** to include, consider, or take (a matter) into account; to treat (a subject). **b** to report news about (something). **c** to have (something) as one's territory or field of activity. **4a** to insure against (a specified risk or contingency). **b** to provide protection against or compensation for (loss, risk, etc). **c** to make sufficient provision for (a demand or charge) by means of a reserve or deposit. **5a** to protect (somebody) by being in a position to fire at an attacker. **b** to hold (somebody) within range of an aimed firearm. **6a** in sport, to mark (a member of an opposing team) in order to obstruct a play. **b** in baseball, to have (a base) protected. **c** in chess, to protect (a piece on a chess board) from attack by an opponent. **7a** said of a male animal: to copulate with (a female animal). **b** said of a bird: to sit on and incubate (eggs). **8** to record a cover version of (a song). **9** in bridge, to play a higher-ranking card on (a previously played card). ➤ *verb intrans* **1** (+ for) to act as a substitute or replacement for somebody during an absence. **2** (+ for) to provide an alibi for somebody who is absent or doing something wrong. ✳ **cover one's back** *informal* to take precautions against blame for something. **cover one's tracks** to conceal evidence of one's past actions. ➤➤ **coverable** *adj.* [Middle English *coveren* via early French *covrir* from Latin *cooperire*, from CO- + *operire* to close, cover]

cover[2] *noun* **1** something wrapped or spread over to conceal or give protection, *esp*: **a** something flat placed over a container to close it; a lid or top. **b** an overlay or outer layer, e.g. for protection. **c** (*usu in pl*) a blanket, eiderdown, etc used on a bed. **d** a protective covering, e.g. a binding or jacket, for a book. **2a** natural shelter, e.g. undergrowth, for an animal, or the materials that provide this. **b** a position or situation affording shelter from attack. **c** the protection offered by a force, e.g. of aircraft, supporting a military operation. **3** a condition or circumstance that helps to conceal or obscure: *under cover of darkness.* **4** a pretext or disguise: *The project was a cover for intelligence operations.* **5** *Brit* protection under an insurance policy. **6** a single place setting in a restaurant. **7** = COVER VERSION. **8a** in cricket, the fielding position of cover-point, extra cover, or any position in between them. **b** (**the covers**) the fielding positions on the off side of a cricket pitch that lie between point and mid-off.

coverage /'kuv(ə)rij/ *noun* **1** an area or amount covered. **2** inclusion within the scope of discussion or reporting: *news coverage.* **3** the number or percentage of people reached by a communications medium.

cover-all *adj* taking everything into account; comprehensive.

cover charge *noun* a charge, e.g. for service, made by a restaurant or nightclub in addition to the charge for food and drink.

cover crop *noun* a crop, e.g. clover, planted in otherwise bare fields, *esp* between the planting of main crops, to enrich the soil and prevent erosion: compare CATCH CROP.

cover girl *noun* an attractive young woman whose picture appears on a magazine cover.

cover glass *noun* a piece of very thin glass used to cover material on a glass microscope slide.

covering *noun* something that covers or conceals.

covering letter *noun* a letter containing an explanation of or additional information about an accompanying item.

coverlet /'kuvəlit/ *noun* a bedspread. [Middle English, alteration of *coverlite* from Anglo-French *coverelyth*, from early French *covrir*: see COVER[1] + *lit* bed]

cover letter *noun* NAmer a covering letter.

cover note *noun* Brit a provisional insurance document providing cover between acceptance of a risk and issue of a full policy.

cover-point *noun* in cricket, a fielding position further from the batsman than point and situated between mid-off and point.

coverslip *noun* = COVER GLASS.

covert[1] /'kuvət, ko'vuht/ *adj* not openly shown or acknowledged; secret. ➤➤ **covertly** *adv,* **covertness** *noun.* [Middle English from early French *covert,* past part. of *covrir:* see COVER[1]]

covert[2] *noun* **1** a thicket providing cover for game. **2** a feather covering the bases of the wing or tail feathers of a bird.

coverture /'kuvətyə/ *noun literary* shelter or concealment of any kind.

cover-up *noun* a device or course of action that conceals an error or a crime.

cover version *noun* a new version of a pop song previously recorded by another artist.

covet /'kuvit/ *verb trans* (**coveted, coveting**) to long to have (something that belongs to somebody else): *For what satisfaction hath a man, that he shall 'lie down with kings and emperors in death', who in his lifetime never greatly coveted the society of such bed-fellows?* — Charles Lamb. ➤➤ **covetable** *adj.* [Middle English *coveiten* via early French *coveitier* from Latin *cupere* to desire]

covetous /'kuvitəs/ *adj* showing an inordinate desire to have something, *esp* somebody else's wealth or possessions. ➤➤ **covetously** *adv,* **covetousness** *noun.*

covey /'kuvi/ *noun* (*pl* **coveys**) a small flock of birds, *esp* grouse or partridge. [Middle English from early French *couver* to sit on, brood over, from Latin *cubare* to lie]

coving /'kohving/ *noun* = COVE[1] (2).

cow[1] /kow/ *noun* **1a** the mature female animal of cattle, *esp* domestic cattle. **b** a cow that has had more than one calf. **2** a mature female of various other animals, e.g. the whale, seal, or moose. **3** *informal* a woman, *esp* one who is unpleasant in some way. **4** *Aus, NZ, informal* a cause of annoyance or difficulty. ✳ **till the cows come home** for ever. [Old English *cū*]

cow[2] *verb trans* to intimidate (somebody) with threats or a show of strength. [prob from Old Norse *kúga* to oppress]

coward /'kowəd/ *noun* somebody who lacks courage or resolve. ➤➤ **cowardliness** *noun,* **cowardly** *adj.* [Middle English via early French *coart* from Latin *cauda* tail, perhaps in reference to an animal with its tail between its legs]

cowardice /'kowədis/ *noun* lack of courage or resolve. [Middle English *cowardise* from early French *coardise* from *coart:* see COWARD]

cowbane /'kowbayn/ *noun* any of several species of tall perennial Eurasian plants growing on marshy ground, some varieties of which are poisonous: genus *Cicuta.*

cowbell *noun* a bell hung round the neck of a cow to make a sound by which it can be located.

cowberry /'kowberi/ *noun* (*pl* **cowberries**) **1** a low-growing shrub of the heather family that grows on open ground and is closely related to the bilberry: *Vaccinium vitis-idaea.* **2** the red edible fruit of this plant.

cowbird *noun* any of several species of N American songbirds that often feed near grazing cattle and lay their eggs in other birds' nests: genus *Molothrus.*

cowboy *noun* **1** a man who tends or drives cattle, *esp* a cattle ranch hand in N America. **2** *informal* a person who employs irregular or unscrupulous methods, *esp* a tradesman who is incompetent or dishonest.

cowboy boot *noun* a boot with a high arch and heel and usu fancy stitching.

cowboy hat *noun* a wide-brimmed hat with a large soft crown.

cowcatcher *noun chiefly NAmer* an apparatus on the front of a locomotive or tram for removing obstacles from the track.

cow-cocky *noun* (*pl* **cow-cockies**) *Aus, NZ, informal* a small dairy farmer. [COW[1] + COCKY[2]]

cower /'kowə/ *verb intrans* (**cowered, cowering**) to crouch down or shrink away, e.g. in fear, from something menacing. [Middle English *couren,* of Scandinavian origin]

cowfish *noun* (*pl* **cowfish**) **1** any of several species of small brightly coloured fishes with projections resembling horns over the eyes: *Lactoria diaphana* and other species. **2** a tropical herbivorous aquatic animal, *esp* the manatee or dugong: order Sirenia.

cowgirl *noun* a woman who tends or drives cattle, *esp* a cattle ranch hand in N America.

cowherd *noun* a person who tends cows.

cowhide *noun* **1** leather made from the hide of a cow. **2** *NAmer* a coarse leather whip.

cowl /kowl/ *noun* **1** a hood or long hooded cloak, *esp* of a monk. **2a** a chimney covering designed to improve ventilation. **b** a cowling. ⟫ **cowled** *adj*. [Middle English *cowle* from Old English *cugele*, ultimately from Latin *cucullus* hood]

cowlick *noun* a tuft of hair that sticks up, *esp* over the forehead. [from its appearance of having been licked by a cow]

cowling *noun* a removable metal covering over an engine, *esp* in an aircraft.

cowl neck *noun* a draped neckline on a garment, which falls in loose folds at the front. ⟫ **cowl-necked** *adj*.

cowman *noun* (*pl* **cowmen**) a cowherd or cowboy.

co-worker /'kohwuhkə/ *noun* a fellow worker.

cow parsley *noun* a coarse tall plant of the carrot family of Europe, Asia, and Africa with clusters of tiny white flowers and leaves that resemble those of parsley: *Anthriscus sylvestris*.

cowpat *noun* a small heap of cow dung.

cowpea *noun* = BLACK-EYED PEA.

Cowper's gland /'koohpəz, 'kow-/ *noun* either of two small glands in males that discharge into the URETHRA (canal carrying urine from the bladder) a liquid that makes up a small proportion of the seminal fluid. [named after William *Cowper* d.1709, English surgeon]

cowpoke *noun* *NAmer, informal* a cowboy.

cowpox *noun* a mild viral disease of cows causing vesicles on the udders, that when communicated to humans gives protection against smallpox, matter from cowpox vesicles having been used in the earliest vaccine developed by Edward Jenner in 1796.

cowpuncher *noun* *NAmer, informal* a cowboy.

cowrie or **cowry** /'kowri/ *noun* (*pl* **cowries**) **1** any of numerous species of marine gastropod molluscs with glossy and often brightly coloured shells: genus *Cypraea*. **2** the shell of a cowrie, formerly used as money in parts of Africa and Asia. [Hindi *kaur*]

co-write *verb trans* to collaborate with another in the writing of (something): *the body of songs that were co-written by Lennon and McCartney*. ⟫ **co-writer** *noun*.

cowry /'kowri/ *noun* see COWRIE.

cowshed *noun* a farm building for housing cattle or for milking cows.

cowslip /'kowslip/ *noun* a common European plant of the primrose family with fragrant yellow or purplish flowers: *Primula veris*. [Old English *cūslyppe* cow dung, from *cū* cow + *slypa, slyppe* paste]

cow wheat *noun* any of several species of plants with yellow flowers found in Europe, Asia, and N America, that are partly parasitic on the roots of other plants: *Melampyrum pratense* and other species.

Cox /koks/ *noun* a variety of green eating apple with a red tinge. [named after R *Cox*, English fruitgrower]

cox[1] /koks/ *noun* a coxswain. ⟫ **coxless** *adj*.

cox[2] *verb intrans* to be a cox. ⟫ *verb trans* to be cox of (a boat).

coxa /'koksə/ *noun* (*pl* **coxae** /'koksee/) **1** the hipbone or hip joint. **2** the basal segment of a limb of an insect, spider, etc. ⟫ **coxal** *adj*. [Latin *coxa* hip]

coxalgia /kok'saljə/ *noun* **1** a painful disease of the hip joint. **2** pain in the hip joint. ⟫ **coxalgic** *adj*. [COXA + -ALGIA]

coxcomb /'kokskohm/ *noun archaic* **1** a conceited foolish person; a fop: *If he is only a chattering coxcomb, he will not occupy much of my time or thoughts* — Jane Austen. **2** a jester's cap, decorated with a red crest: *Thou must needs wear my coxcomb* — Shakespeare. **3** *humorous* the head; the pate: *That slate descended on the bald coxcomb of Sir Vindex Brindlecombe* — Charles Kingsley. ⟫ **coxcombry** *noun*. [Middle English *cokkes comb* cock's comb]

Coxsackie virus *noun* a virus of the gastro-intestinal tract that can affect the nervous system, causing respiratory and muscular disease. [named after *Coxsackie* in New York State, where it was first recognized]

Cox's orange pippin /'koksiz/ *noun* = COX.

coxswain[1] /'koksn, 'kokswayn/ *noun* **1** the steersman of a racing rowing boat who usu directs the crew. **2** a sailor who commands and usu steers a ship's boat. ⟫ **coxswainship** *noun*. [Middle English *cokswayne*, from *cok* (see COCKBOAT) + SWAIN]

coxswain[2] *verb intrans* to command or steer as coxswain. ⟫ *verb trans* to command or steer (a boat) as coxswain.

coy /koy/ *adj* (**coyer, coyest**) **1a** affectedly shy. **b** provocatively playful or coquettish. **2** (*often* + about) showing reluctance to reveal details, *esp* over a sensitive issue: *He was coy about revealing his salary*. ⟫ **coyly** *adv*, **coyness** *noun*. [Middle English, quiet, shy, via French from Latin *quietus*: see QUIET[1]]

coy. *abbr* used in the armed forces: company.

coyote /koy'ohti, kie-/ *noun* (*pl* **coyotes** or collectively **coyote**) a predatory wild dog of N America, of wolflike appearance: *Canis latrans*. [Mexican Spanish *coyote* from Nahuatl *coyotl*]

coypu /'koypooh/ *noun* (*pl* **coypus** or collectively **coypu**) a S American semi-aquatic beaver-like rodent with webbed feet, farmed for its fur (NUTRIA) and now commonly found in E Anglia: *Myocastor coypus*. [American Spanish *coipú* from Araucan *coypu*]

coz /kuz/ *noun* *NAmer or archaic* used *esp* as a form of address: a cousin or other relation: *'Farewell gentle cousin.' 'Coz, farewell.'* — Shakespeare. [by shortening and alteration]

cozen /'kuz(ə)n/ *verb trans* (**cozened, cozening**) *archaic or literary* to deceive, trick, or beguile (somebody): *I think't no sin to cozen him that would unjustly win* — Shakespeare; *He's supposed to have cozened me out of four hundred dollars* — Christopher Morley. ⟫ **cozenage** /-nij/ *noun*, **cozener** *noun*. [prob from obsolete Italian *cozzonare* from Italian *cozzone* horse trader, from Latin *cocion-, cocio* trader]

cozy[1] /'kohzi/ *adj* (**cozier, coziest**) *NAmer* see COSY[1].

cozy[2] *noun* (*pl* **cozies**) *NAmer* see COSY[2].

cozy up *verb NAmer* see COSY UP.

cozzie *noun* *Aus, informal* see COSSIE.

CP *abbr* **1** Communist Party. **2** *Aus* Country Party.

cp *abbr* **1** candlepower. **2** compare.

CPAG *abbr* Child Poverty Action Group.

cpd *abbr* compound.

CPI *abbr* in the US, consumer price index.

Cpl *abbr* Corporal.

CPO *abbr* Chief Petty Officer.

CPR *abbr* **1** Canadian Pacific Railway. **2** cardiopulmonary resuscitation.

CPRE *abbr* Council for the Protection of Rural England.

CPS *abbr* in England and Wales, Crown Prosecution Service.

cps *abbr* **1** in computing, characters per second. **2** cycles per second.

CPSA *abbr* *Brit* Civil and Public Services Association.

CPU *abbr* central processing unit.

CPVC *abbr* chlorinated polyvinyl chloride.

CPVE *abbr* *Brit* Certificate of Pre-Vocational Education.

CR *abbr* Costa Rica (international vehicle registration).

Cr[1] *abbr* councillor.

Cr[2] *abbr* the chemical symbol for chromium.

cr. *abbr* **1** credit. **2** creditor.

crab[1] /krab/ *noun* **1a** any of numerous chiefly marine crustaceans usu with the front pair of limbs modified as grasping pincers and a short broad flattened carapace: order Decapoda. **b** the flesh of this cooked and eaten as food. **2** (*in pl*) infestation with crab lice. **3** (**the Crab**) the constellation and sign of the zodiac Cancer. **4** a lifting device, e.g. attached to a crane, with a pincer-like action. ✳ **catch a crab** to make a faulty stroke in rowing. ⟫ **crablike** *adj*. [Old English *crabba*]

crab[2] *verb intrans* (**crabbed, crabbing**) **1** to move sideways or obliquely like a crab. **2** to go fishing for crabs. ⟫ **crabber** *noun*.

crab[3] *noun* a crab apple. [Middle English *crabbe*, perhaps related to Swedish *skrabbe* crab apple]

crab[4] *noun* *informal* a bad-tempered person.

crab[5] *verb* (**crabbed, crabbing**) ⟫ *verb intrans informal* to carp or grouse: *She's always crabbing about the weather*. ⟫ *verb trans NAmer, informal* to interfere with, ruin, or spoil (something): *trying to crab my act as usual*. [orig of hawks, to claw each other, from CRAB[1]]

crab apple *noun* **1** a small wild sour apple. **2** a tree that bears these apples: *Malus sylvestris*. [see CRAB³]

crabbed /'krabid/ *adj* **1** morose or peevish; = CRABBY: *I'm a crusty, lonesome, crabbed old chap* — L M Montgomery. **2** said of writing: difficult to read or understand. ➤➤ **crabbedly** *adv*, **crabbedness** *noun*. [Middle English, partly from *crabbe* CRAB¹, partly from *crabbe* CRAB³]

crabby /'krabi/ *adj* (**crabbier, crabbiest**) *informal* cross; ill-tempered. [CRAB⁴]

crabgrass *noun* a grass with freely rooting creeping stems that grows as a weed in lawns: *Digitaria sanguinalis*.

crab louse *noun* (*also in pl*) a sucking louse that infests human body hair, e.g. in the pubic area: *Phthirus pubis*.

crab spider *noun* any of numerous species of spiders with long front legs that have a crablike sideways motion: family Thomisidae.

crab stick *noun* a stick of compressed fish meat flavoured with crab.

crabwise *adv* **1** sideways. **2** in a sidling or cautiously indirect manner.

crack¹ /krak/ *verb intrans* **1** to make a sudden sharp explosive noise: *The whip cracks.* **2a** to break or split apart. **b** to develop fissures. **3** said of the voice: to change pitch suddenly: *His voice cracked with emotion.* **4** to collapse emotionally under stress. **5** said of hydrocarbons: to break up into simpler chemical compounds when heated, usu with a catalyst. ➤ *verb trans* **1a** to break (something) so that fissures appear on the surface: *The snowball cracked the windowpane.* **b** to break (something) with a crack: *another gadget for cracking nuts.* **2** to tell (a joke). **3a** to puzzle out and expose, solve, or reveal the mystery of (a code, etc). **b** to break into (a safe). **c** to break through (a barrier, etc) so as to gain acceptance or recognition. **4** to cause (something) to make a sudden sharp noise: *crack one's knuckles.* **5a** to subject (heavy hydrocarbons) to cracking, *esp* to produce petrol. **b** to produce (petrol) by cracking. **6** *informal* to open (a can or bottle) for drinking. [Old English *cracian*]

crack² *noun* **1** a sudden sharp loud noise: *the crack of rifle fire.* **2a** a line or narrow opening that marks a break; a fissure: *a crack in the ice.* **b** a narrow opening; a chink: *Leave the door open a crack.* **3** a break or unsteadiness in the voice. **4** a sharp resounding blow: *He got a crack on the head from the corner of the mantelpiece.* **5** *informal* a witty remark; a quip. **6** *informal* (+ at) an attempt or try at something: *have a crack at the championship.* **7** (**the crack**) *dialect, informal* conversation, *esp* amusing conversation. **8** (*also* **crack cocaine**) *slang* a purified, potent, and highly addictive variety of cocaine, in the form of white pellets that are smoked by users. ✳ **at the crack of dawn** very early in the morning. **the crack of doom** the thunderclap heralding the Day of Judgment: *Once fairly out on a round, it would take the crack of doom to stop a true golfer* — Conan Doyle; *It seemed that the list would stretch out to the crack of doom* — Mark Twain.

crack³ *adj informal* of superior quality or ability: *a crack shot.*

crackbrained *adj informal* idiotic; crazy: *a crackbrained scheme.*

crackdown *noun informal* an act or instance of cracking down.

crack down *verb intrans informal* (+ on) to take regulatory or disciplinary action against (something or somebody): *The police are cracking down on drink-driving.*

cracked *adj* **1** marked by unsteadiness or sudden changes of pitch: *a cracked voice.* **2** *informal* mentally disordered; crazy: *You must be cracked!*

cracked wheat *noun* whole wheat that has been cut or crushed into small pieces and boiled and dried for use e.g. with savoury dishes; = BULGUR.

cracker *noun* **1a** a brightly coloured paper and cardboard tube that makes a cracking noise when pulled sharply apart and usu contains a toy, paper hat, or other party item, used *esp* at Christmas. **b** a folded paper cylinder containing an explosive that is discharged to make a noise. **2** (*in pl*) a nutcracker. **3** a thin savoury biscuit. **4** *Brit, informal* something or somebody exceptional; *esp* an outstandingly attractive person. **5** the apparatus in which cracking, *esp* of petroleum, is carried out.

cracker-barrel *adj NAmer* said *esp* of somebody's ideology or philosophy: homespun; unsophisticated. [from the notion of discussions taking place around the biscuit barrel in country stores]

crackerjack¹ /'krakəjak/ *noun chiefly NAmer, informal* somebody or something of marked excellence.

crackerjack² *adj chiefly NAmer, informal* of marked excellence.

crackers *adj chiefly Brit, informal* mad; crazy: *His family are all completely crackers.* [prob alteration of CRACKED]

crackhead *noun informal* a person addicted to the drug CRACK² (form of cocaine).

cracking *adv informal, dated* used as an approving intensive: *a cracking good story.*

crackjaw *adj archaic* said of a word: difficult to pronounce: *a Polish nobleman, a Count somebody; I never can remember their crack-jaw names* — Disraeli.

crackle¹ /'krakl/ *verb* ➤ *verb intrans* to make a series of small cracking noises: *Soon a good fire was crackling in the hearth.* ➤ *verb trans* **1** to cause (something) to make a crackling sound: *He crackled the fresh notes between his fingers.* **2** to craze (pottery or porcelain). [frequentative of CRACK¹]

crackle² *noun* **1** the noise of repeated small cracks or reports. **2** a network of fine cracks on an otherwise smooth surface. **3** pottery or porcelain decorated with a network of fine cracks. ➤➤ **crackly** *adj*.

crackleware *noun* = CRACKLE² (3).

crackling *noun* the crisp skin of roast meat, *esp* pork.

cracknel /'kraknl/ *noun* a hard brittle biscuit. [Middle English *krakenelle*, prob modification of early French *craquelin* from early Dutch *crākeline*, from *crāken* to crack]

crack on *verb intrans informal* (*often* + with) to make speedy progress with a task, etc: *We'll be able to crack on with the work once these few details are sorted out.*

crackpot¹ *noun informal* (*often before another noun*) somebody with eccentric ideas: *a crackpot scheme.* [CRACK¹ + POT¹, in the sense 'head']

crackpot² *adj informal* eccentric or cranky: *his crackpot ideas.*

cracksman *noun* (*pl* **cracksmen**) *informal* a burglar.

crack up *verb intrans informal* **1** to undergo a physical or mental collapse: *Most people crack up under the strain of the job.* **2** to laugh uncontrollably. ✳ **not all it's cracked up to be** *informal* not as good as one has been led to expect: *The restaurant isn't all it's cracked up to be.*

crack-up *noun informal* a collapse or breakdown.

crack willow *noun* a Eurasian willow of damp habitats with branches that break off readily, often rooting themselves to produce new growth: *Salix fragilis.*

-cracy *comb. form* forming nouns, denoting: **1** rule; government: *democracy.* **2** a powerful or dominant social or political class: *aristocracy.* **3** a state having a specified government or ruling class: *meritocracy.* [early French *-cratie* via late Latin *-cratia* from Greek *-kratia*, from *kratos* strength, power]

cradle¹ /'kraydl/ *noun* **1a** a baby's bed or cot, usu on rockers. **b** a framework of wood or metal used as a support, scaffold, etc. **2** a place of origin: *An English gentleman who had lived some years in this region [of Switzerland] said it was the cradle of compulsory education* — Mark Twain. ✳ **from the cradle** from earliest infancy: *The children were trained from the cradle to deadly hatred against the Mexicans* — William Hickling Prescott. **from the cradle to the grave** throughout one's life: *Trace a man's career from his cradle to his grave and mark how Fortune has treated him* — Samuel Butler. [Old English *cradol*]

cradle² *verb trans* **1** to place or keep (somebody) in or as if in a cradle. **2** to shelter or hold (somebody or something) protectively.

cradle cap *noun* a scaly skin condition of the scalp, affecting small babies.

cradle-snatcher *noun informal* a person who is romantically or sexually involved with a much younger person.

cradlesong *noun* a lullaby.

craft¹ /krahft/ *noun* **1a** an activity or trade requiring manual dexterity or artistic skill. **b** a trade or profession. **2** (*often in combination*) skill in planning, making, or executing something; dexterity: *stagecraft.* **3** (*treated as sing. or pl*) the members of a trade or trade association. **4** (*pl* **craft** *or* **crafts**). **a** a boat. **b** an aircraft. **c** a spacecraft. **5** skill in deceiving to gain an end.

Word history
from Old English *cræft* strength, skill. The basic meaning of *craft*, common to most Germanic languages, is 'strength'. In English it also acquired, as

early as the ninth cent., the sense 'skill, cleverness'. In reference to manual dexterity, this sense has retained a positive force; but in reference to mental agility, which may be viewed with suspicion or envy, it gradually became derogatory and by the 13th cent. often signified guile or fraud. The derivative adjective *crafty* developed in the same way; today it is used only in a negative sense.

craft² *verb trans* to form or construct (something) using or as if using skill and dexterity: *a beautifully crafted novel.*

craftsman *or* **craftswoman** *noun* (*pl* **craftsmen** *or* **craftswomen**) **1** a man or woman who practises a skilled trade or handicraft. **2** a person who displays a high degree of manual dexterity or artistic skill. ➤➤ **craftsmanship** *noun.*

crafty *adj* (**craftier, craftiest**) **1** showing subtlety and guile. **2** *archaic* highly trained; skilful: *The king ... brocht right crafty masonis to big [= build] this abbay [of Holyrood]* — John Bellenden. ➤➤ **craftily** *adv,* **craftiness** *noun.*

crag /krag/ *noun* a steep rugged rock or cliff. [Middle English, of Celtic origin: compare Gaelic *creag* rock, cliff]

craggy /'kragi/ *adj* (**craggier, craggiest**) rough; rugged: *his hard, deep-lined, craggy features* — Conan Doyle. ➤➤ **cragginess** *noun.*

cragsman *noun* (*pl* **cragsmen**) a skilled or experienced rock-climber.

crake /krayk/ *noun* any of numerous species of short-billed rails, e.g. the corncrake: genus *Porzana* and other genera. [Middle English, prob from Old Norse *krāka* crow or *krākr* raven; related to Old English *crāwan* CROW²]

cram /kram/ *verb* (**crammed, cramming**) ➤ *verb trans* **1** to pack or jam (a container) tight: *She crammed her suitcase with clothes.* **2** (+ in/into) to thrust (something) forcefully into something: *He crammed the notes into his wallet.* **3** *informal* to prepare (a student) hastily for an examination: *cram foreigners for English-proficiency exams.* **4** *informal* to eat (something) voraciously; to bolt (one's food). ➤ *verb intrans* **1** to study hastily and intensively for an examination. **2** *informal* to eat greedily or until uncomfortably full. [Old English *crammian*]

crambo /'kramboh/ *noun* a game in which a player gives a word or line of verse to be matched in rhyme by other players. [alteration of *crambe* cabbage, from Latin *crambe repetita* cabbage served up again, used by Juvenal for any unwanted repetition]

cram-full *adj* as full as can be: *It's a wonderful reference work – cram-full of facts.*

crammer /'kramə/ *noun Brit, informal* a school or teacher that prepares students intensively for an examination.

cramp¹ /kramp/ *noun* **1** a painful involuntary spasmodic contraction of a muscle. **2** (*in pl*) severe abdominal pain, e.g. in menstruation. [Middle English *crampe* from Old French, of Germanic origin]

cramp² *noun* **1** a usu metal device bent at the ends and used to hold timbers or blocks of stone together. **2** a clamp. [Low German or obsolete Dutch *krampe* hook; related to Old English *cradol* CRADLE¹]

cramp³ *verb trans* **1** to affect (somebody) with cramp: *Suppose she grew so tired and cramped that she could hold on no longer!* — L M Montgomery. **2** to confine or restrain (somebody or something): *Their researches were severely cramped by niggardly funding.* **3** to fasten or hold (something) with a clamp. ✳ **cramp somebody's style** to be an inhibiting influence on them.

cramp ball *pl noun* a hard round shiny black fungus found on dying wood, *esp* ash, formerly carried as a charm against cramp: *Daldinia concentrica.*

cramped /krampt/ *adj* **1** said of conditions or accommodation: too small or crowded for comfort. **2** said of handwriting: small and hard to read.

cramp-iron *noun* = CRAMP² (I).

crampon /'krampon/ *noun* **1** a metal frame with downward- and forward-pointing spikes that is fixed to the sole of a boot for climbing slopes of ice or hard snow. **2** (*usu in pl, but treated as sing.*) a hooked mechanical device for lifting heavy objects. [early French *crampon*, of Germanic origin]

cran /kran/ *noun* formerly, a unit of measurement for fresh herrings, equal to 37.5gall. [Gaelic *crann* herring measure]

cranberry /'kranb(ə)ri/ *noun* (*pl* **cranberries**) **1** any of several species of plants of the heath family: genus *Vaccinium*. **2** the red acid berry of such plants, used in making sauces and jellies. [partial translation of Low German *kraanbere*, from *kraan* crane + *bere* berry]

crane¹ /krayn/ *noun* **1** a machine for moving heavy weights by means of a projecting swinging arm or a hoisting apparatus supported on an overhead track. **2** any of several species of tall wading birds, typically with white or grey plumage: family Gruidae. [Old English *cran*]

crane² *verb trans* **1** to stretch (one's neck), *esp* in order to see better. **2** to raise or lift (something) by or as if by a crane: *There was no car ramp and vehicles had to be craned aboard.* ➤ *verb intrans* to stretch one's neck, *esp* in order to see better.

crane fly *noun* any of numerous species of long-legged slender flies that resemble large mosquitoes but do not bite: family Tipulidae.

cranesbill *noun* any of several species of plants with lobed leaves and pink or purple five-petalled flowers; *esp Geranium pratense*: genus *Geranium*. [from the long beaked fruit of some species, thought to resemble a crane's bill: compare GERANIUM, PELARGONIUM]

crani- *or* **cranio-** *comb. form* forming words, with the meaning: cranium: *craniate.* [medieval Latin *cranium*: see CRANIUM]

crania /'krayni·ə/ *noun* pl of CRANIUM.

cranial index /'krayni·əl/ *noun* the ratio of the maximum breadth of the skull to its maximum height multiplied by 100: compare CEPHALIC INDEX.

cranial nerve *noun* any of the twelve pairs of nerves that leave the lower surface of the brain to connect with the body, *esp* the head and face.

craniate¹ /'krayni·ət, -ayt/ *adj* having a skull.

craniate² *noun* a person or animal having a skull; a vertebrate.

cranio- *comb. form* see CRANI-.

craniology /krayni'olǝji/ *noun* a science dealing with variations in size, shape, and proportions of the skull among the different races of human beings. ➤➤ **craniological** /-'lojikl/ *adj,* **craniologist** *noun.*

craniometry /krayni'omǝtri/ *noun* a science dealing with the measurement of the skull. ➤➤ **craniometric** /-'metrik/ *adj.*

craniotomy /krayni'otǝmi/ *noun* (*pl* **craniotomies**) **1** a surgical incision into the skull. **2** surgical perforation of the skull of a dead foetus in order to facilitate its extraction.

cranium /'krayni·əm/ *noun* (*pl* **craniums** *or* **crania** /'krayni·ə/) the skull; *specif* the part that encloses the brain. ➤➤ **cranial** *adj.* [medieval Latin *cranium* from Greek *kranion*]

crank¹ /krangk/ *noun* **1** a part of an axle or shaft bent at right angles by which reciprocating motion is changed into circular motion or vice versa. **2** an eccentric person, or one who is excessively enthusiastic or fastidious about something: *The man with a new idea is a crank until the idea succeeds* — Mark Twain. [Old English *cranc-*; related to Old English *cradol* CRADLE¹]

crank² *verb trans* **1** (*often* + up) to start (an engine) using a crank. **2** (+ up) to increase (something, e.g. the volume of a sound) in intensity. **3** to bend (a shaft, etc) into the shape of a crank. ➤ *verb intrans* **1** to turn a crank, e.g. to start an engine. **2** *informal* to inject a narcotic drug.

crank³ *adj archaic* said of a boat: easily capsized: *The stowage was clumsily done, and the vessel consequently crank* — Poe. [short for *crank-sided* easily tipped]

crankcase *noun* the housing of a crankshaft.

crankpin *noun* the pin which forms the handle of a crank or to which the connecting rod is attached: compare BIG END.

crankshaft *noun* a shaft driven by or driving a crank.

cranky *adj* (**crankier, crankiest**) **1** *informal* strange; odd; eccentric. **2** *NAmer* bad-tempered. **3** said of machinery: working erratically; unpredictable. ➤➤ **crankily** *adv,* **crankiness** *noun.* [CRANK¹ and CRANK³]

crannog /'kranəg/ *noun* an artificial, often fortified, island dwelling constructed in a lake or marsh in prehistoric and early medieval Ireland and Scotland. [Gaelic *crannag* and Irish *crannóg*]

cranny /'krani/ *noun* (*pl* **crannies**) a small crack or slit; a chink. ➤➤ **crannied** *adj.* [Middle English *crany* from early French *cren, cran* notch]

crap¹ /krap/ *noun coarse slang* **1** sometimes used as an interjection: nonsense; rubbish: *Their new album is a load of crap.* **2a** excrement.

b the act or an instance of defecating. [Middle English *crappe* chaff, residue from rendered fat, from early Dutch *krappe* piece torn off, from *krappen* to break off]

crap² *verb intrans* (**crapped, crapping**) *coarse slang* to defecate.

crape /krayp/ *noun* **1** any crinkly material; = CREPE (1). **2** *esp* formerly: **a** black silk or artificial silk, from which mourning clothes were made. **b** a band of this fabric worn, *esp* on a hat, as a sign of mourning. [modification of French *crêpe*: see CREPE]

crap out *verb intrans* **1** *coarse slang* (often + of) to withdraw from a commitment or a planned course of action through loss of courage: *He crapped out of doing a bungee jump.* **2** *NAmer, Aus, NZ, coarse slang* to fail or wear out; to give up. **3** *NAmer, slang* to make a losing throw in the game of craps.

crapper *noun coarse slang* a toilet.

crappy /'krapi/ *adj* (**crappier, crappiest**) *coarse slang* of very poor quality. [CRAP¹]

craps /kraps/ *pl noun* (*treated as sing. or pl*) a gambling game played with two dice where players try to throw a seven or eleven. [Louisiana French *craps* via French *crabs, craps*, from English *crabs* lowest throw (two ones) at dice, either pl of CRAB¹ or from *crab's eyes*]

crapulent /'krapyoolənt/ *adj literary* crapulous. ➤➤ **crapulence** *noun*. [late Latin *crapulentus* from Latin *crapula* drunkenness, from Greek *kraipalē*]

crapulous /'krapyooləs/ *adj literary* **1** suffering the effects of excessive drinking of alcohol. **2** characterized by excessive indulgence, *esp* in alcohol: *leading a crapulous life; crapulous habits.* [late Latin *crapulosus* from Latin *crapula*: see CRAPULENT]

craquelure /'krakəlyooə/ *noun* fine cracks on the surface of old paintings caused by decay of pigment and varnish. [French *craquelure* from *craqueler* to crack, crackle, of imitative origin]

crases /'krayseez/ *noun* pl of CRASIS.

crash¹ /krash/ *verb trans* **1a** to break or smash (something) violently and noisily. **b** to damage (an aircraft) in landing. **c** to damage (a vehicle) by collision. **2a** to cause (something) to make a crashing sound: *He crashed the cymbals together.* **b** to force (one's way) somewhere noisily. **3** *informal* to enter (a party, etc) without invitation or payment. **4** to cause (a computer system or program) to fail. ➤ *verb intrans* **1a** to break or split into pieces with or as if with violence and noise. **b** to crash an aircraft or vehicle. **c** to be involved in a crash. **2** to make a crashing noise. **3** to move noisily. **4** *informal* (also + out) to spend the night, *esp* in a makeshift place; to go to sleep: *Can I crash on your floor tonight?* **5** said of a computer system or program: to become completely inoperative, *esp* suddenly. [Middle English *crasschen*, of imitative origin]

crash² *noun* **1a** a loud noise: *a crash of thunder.* **b** the noise of things smashing: *There was a loud crash in the kitchen.* **2** the act or an instance of crashing; a violent collision: *a plane crash.* **3** a sudden decline or failure, e.g. of a business: *the Wall Street crash.*

crash³ *adj* designed to achieve an intended result in the shortest possible time: *a crash diet; a crash course in computer studies.*

crash⁴ *noun dated* (often before a noun) a coarse fabric made orig of linen, used for draperies, clothing, etc: *strong white crash bags* — Pall Mall Gazette. [prob from Russian *krashenina* coloured linen]

crash barrier *noun Brit* a barrier to prevent vehicles accidentally colliding or leaving the road.

crash dive *noun* a steep descent in an aircraft.

crash-dive *verb intrans* said *esp* of an aircraft or submarine: to descend or dive steeply and quickly. ➤ *verb trans* to cause (an aircraft or submarine) to dive steeply and quickly.

crash helmet *noun* a helmet that is worn, e.g. by motorcyclists, to protect the head in the event of an accident.

crashing ✳ **a crashing bore** *informal* the ultimate in insupportable bores: *the sort of man who, amusing initially, can rapidly become a crashing bore; The whole thing is a crashing bore.*

crash-land *verb intrans* said of an aircraft or pilot: to land under emergency conditions, usu with some damage to the craft. ➤ *verb trans* to land (an aircraft) in this way. ➤➤ **crash landing** *noun*.

crash pad *noun informal* a place where free temporary sleeping accommodation is available.

crash team *noun* a medical team equipped to deal at a moment's notice with cardiac arrest.

crash-test *verb trans* to crash (a new vehicle) deliberately in controlled conditions so as to assess its strength under impact.

crashworthiness *noun* the capacity of a vehicle to protect its occupants in a collision.

crasis /'kraysis/ *noun* (*pl* **crases** /-seez/) in phonetics, the contraction of two vowels or diphthongs into one long vowel or diphthong. [Greek *krasis* mixing, combination, from *kerannynai* to mix]

crass /kras/ *adj* **1** insensitive; coarse: *crass behaviour.* **2** deplorably great; complete: *crass stupidity.* ➤➤ **crassitude** /'krasityoohd/ *noun*, **crassly** *adv*, **crassness** *noun*. [Latin *crassus* thick, gross]

-crat *comb. form* forming nouns, denoting: **1** an advocate or partisan of a specified form of government: *democrat.* **2** a member of a specified ruling class: *plutocrat; technocrat.* ➤➤ **-cratic** *comb. form*. [French *-crate*, back-formation from *-cratie*: see -CRACY]

crate¹ /krayt/ *noun* **1** a framework or box, usu wooden, for holding goods, e.g. fruit, bottles, etc, *esp* during transit. **2** the contents of a crate. **3** *informal* an old dilapidated car, aeroplane, etc. ➤➤ **crateful** (*pl* **cratefuls**) *noun*. [Latin *cratis* wickerwork]

crate² *verb trans* to pack (something) in a crate: *The wine is then crated and loaded into trucks for distribution.*

crater¹ /'kraytə/ *noun* **1a** a bowl-shaped depression forming the mouth of a volcano. **b** a bowl-shaped depression formed by the impact of a meteorite. **2** a hole in the ground made by an explosion. **3** a jar or vase with a wide mouth used in classical antiquity for mixing wine and water. [Latin *crater* mixing bowl, crater, from Greek *kratēr*, from *kerannynai* to mix]

crater² *verb trans* (**cratered, cratering**) to form craters in (something).

-cratic *comb. form* see -CRAT.

craton /'krayton/ *noun* a stable, relatively immobile area of the earth's crust that forms the central mass of a continent or the central basin of an ocean. ➤➤ **cratonic** *adj*. [German *kraton*, modification of Greek *kratos* strength]

cravat /krə'vat/ *noun* a decorative band or scarf worn round the neck by men. [French *cravate*, from *Cravate* Croatian; from the scarf worn by Croatian mercenaries in France]

crave /krayv/ *verb trans* **1** to have a strong or urgent desire for (something): *The sufferer craves water but cannot drink.* **2** *formal* to ask for or beg (something) earnestly: *I crave the court's indulgence.* **3** *formal* to require (attention): *Another matter craves my immediate attention.* ➤ *verb intrans* (+ after/for) to have a strong desire for; to yearn for: *I crave for mental exaltation* — Conan Doyle. ➤➤ **craver** *noun*. [Old English *crafian*]

craven¹ /'krayv(ə)n/ *adj* completely lacking in courage; cowardly. ➤➤ **cravenly** *adv*, **cravenness** *noun*. [Middle English *cravant*, perhaps from Old French *cravante*, present part. of *cravanter* to burst, break, from Latin *crepare*]

craven² *noun* a cowardly person: *Ain't I a craven?* — Virginia Woolf.

craving *noun* (*usu* + for) a great desire or longing: *a craving for tobacco.*

craw /kraw/ *noun* **1** the crop of a bird or insect. **2** the stomach, *esp* of an animal. ✳ **stick in one's craw** to be difficult to swallow, do, accept, or utter: *What sticks in the craw is saying 'Sir' to people you despise.* [Middle English *crawe* from (assumed) Old English *crawa*]

crawfish *noun* (*pl* **crawfish**) *chiefly NAmer* a crayfish.

crawl¹ /krawl/ *verb intrans* **1** to move slowly on hands and knees or by dragging the body using the arms. **2** to move or progress slowly or laboriously. **3** said of a plant: to creep. **4** (often + with) to be alive or swarming with or as if with creeping things: *The path was crawling with ants.* **5** *informal* (often + to) to behave in a servile manner: *He'll just go crawling to the boss as usual.* [Middle English *crawlen* from Old Norse *krafla*; related to Old English *crabba* CRAB¹]

crawl² *noun* **1a** the act or an instance of crawling. **b** slow or laborious motion: *traffic moving at a crawl.* **2** the fastest swimming stroke, executed lying on the front and consisting of alternating overarm strokes combined with kicks with alternate legs.

crawler *noun* **1** *Brit, informal* a servile person. **2** a vehicle, e.g. a crane, that travels on caterpillar tracks. **3** a heavy slow-moving vehicle. **4** a computer program that scans the World Wide Web so as to compile an index of data.

crawler lane *noun* a lane on an uphill stretch of a major road for the use of heavy slow-moving vehicles.

crawly *adj* (**crawlier, crawliest**) creepy: *a sort of crawly sensation, as of a … ghost flitting about the place* — Thackeray.

crayfish /'krayfish/ *noun* (*pl* **crayfish** or **crayfishes**) **1** any of numerous species of freshwater crustaceans resembling the lobster but usu much smaller: genera *Astacus* and *Cambarus* and other genera. **2** any of several other crustaceans, *esp* the SPINY LOBSTER. [by folk etymology from Middle English *crevis* crayfish, from early French *crevice*, of Germanic origin]

crayon[1] /'krayən, 'krayon/ *noun* a stick of coloured chalk or wax used for writing or drawing. [French *crayon* crayon, pencil, dimin. of *craie* chalk, from Latin *creta*]

crayon[2] *verb trans* (**crayoned, crayoning**) to draw or colour (something) with a crayon.

craze[1] /krayz/ *verb trans* **1** (*usu as past part.*) to madden (somebody) or send (them) crazy: *crazed by pain and fear.* **2** to produce minute cracks on the surface or glaze of (pottery). ➤ *verb intrans* to develop a mesh of fine cracks. [Middle English *crasen* to crush, craze, of Scandinavian origin]

craze[2] *noun* (*often* + for) an exaggerated and often short-lived enthusiasm; a fad: *the 17th-cent. craze for exotic tulips.*

crazy[1] *adj* (**crazier, craziest**) *informal* **1** mad; insane. **2a** impractical: *a crazy idea.* **b** unusual; eccentric. **3** (+ about) extremely enthusiastic about or very fond of (somebody or something): *She's crazy about John Travolta.* **4** spectacularly precarious: *The door was hanging at a crazy angle.* ➤ **crazily** *adv*, **craziness** *noun*.

crazy[2] *noun* (*pl* **crazies**) *chiefly NAmer, informal* an insane person.

crazy paving *noun* a paved surface made up of irregularly shaped paving stones.

CRC *abbr* camera-ready copy.

creak[1] /kreek/ *verb intrans* to make a prolonged grating or squeaking noise: *creaking floorboards.* [Middle English *creken* to croak, of imitative origin]

creak[2] *noun* a prolonged rasping, grating, or squeaking noise, e.g. of an unoiled hinge. ➤➤ **creakily** *adv*, **creaky** *adj*.

cream[1] /kreem/ *noun* **1a** the yellowish part of milk containing butterfat, which forms a surface layer when milk is allowed to stand. **b** this separated as a distinct commodity: *strawberries and cream.* **2a** a food, e.g. a sauce or a cake filling, prepared with or resembling cream in consistency, richness, etc. **b** a biscuit, chocolate, etc filled with whipped cream or a soft preparation resembling it: *Have a coffee cream.* **c** something with the consistency of thick cream; *esp* an emulsified medicinal or cosmetic preparation: *hand cream.* **3** (**the cream**) (+ of) the choicest part: *The cream of the Scottish nobility fell at the Battle of Flodden.* **4** a pale yellowish white colour. ➤➤ **creamily** *adv*, **creaminess** *noun*, **creamy** *adj.* [Middle English *creime, creme*, via French from late Latin *cramum*, of Celtic origin]

cream[2] *verb intrans* **1** said of milk, ale, etc: to form cream or a surface layer like the cream on milk. **2** to break into a creamy froth: *the creaming breakers* — Conan Doyle. ➤ *verb trans* **1** to skim (milk). **2** to cause (milk) to form a surface layer of cream. **3a** to prepare (food) with a cream sauce: *creamed chicken.* **b** to mash (vegetables) with added milk or cream: *creamed potatoes.* **4** to work or blend (butter and sugar) to the consistency of cream. **5** to add cream to (coffee). **6** to rub a cosmetic cream into (the skin). **7** *NAmer, informal* to defeat (somebody) completely.

cream[3] *adj* of a pale yellowish white colour: *a cream carpet.*

cream cheese *noun* a mild white soft unripened cheese made from whole milk enriched with cream.

cream cracker *noun Brit* a crisp thin savoury biscuit.

creamer *noun* **1** a device for separating cream from milk. **2** a powdered cream substitute for use in coffee. **3** *NAmer* a small vessel, e.g. a jug, for serving cream.

creamery *noun* (*pl* **creameries**) an establishment where butter and cheese are made or where milk and milk products are prepared or sold: compare DAIRY (2).

cream off *verb trans* to select and remove (the choicest part or items) from the main body: *The American firms cream off the brightest students.*

cream of tartar *noun* potassium hydrogen tartrate occurring as a white powder and used *esp* in baking powder. [see TARTAR]

cream puff *noun* **1** a cake consisting of choux pastry filled with cream. **2** *chiefly NAmer, informal* an ineffectual person.

cream sherry *noun* a full-bodied sweet sherry.

cream soda *noun* a soft drink containing carbon dioxide to make it fizzy, flavoured with vanilla, and sweetened with sugar.

cream tea *noun Brit* afternoon tea at which scones are served with whipped or clotted cream and jam.

creance /'kreeəns/ *noun* in falconry, a length of fine cord attached to the hawk's leash to prevent its escape during training. [French *créance* faith]

crease[1] /krees/ *noun* **1a** a mark made in fabric, paper, etc by crumpling or crushing. **b** a ridge made, e.g. in a trouser leg, by folding and pressing. **c** a facial wrinkle. **2a** an area surrounding the goal in lacrosse, ice hockey, etc into which an attacking player may not precede the ball or puck. **b** the BOWLING CREASE, POPPING CREASE, or RETURN CREASE of a cricket pitch. [prob from Middle English *creste*: see CREST[1]]

crease[2] *verb trans* **1** to crush or crumple (cloth or paper) or fold and press it. **2** *chiefly Brit, informal.* **a** (*often* + up) to double (a person) up with laughter, or cause (them) much amusement. **b** to tire (a person) out. ➤ *verb intrans* to become creased: *The fabric creases badly.*

create /kri'ayt/ *verb trans* **1** to bring (something) into existence: *And God created great whales, and every living thing that moveth* — Bible. **2a** to produce or cause (something): *create a disturbance; His accomplice created a diversion.* **b** to invest (somebody) with a new form, office, or rank: *He was created a peer of the realm.* **3** to make, design, or invent (something): *the cartoonist who created Snoopy.* ➤ *verb intrans Brit, informal* to make a loud fuss about something: *A woman at the next table started to create; Next door's baby was creating.* [Middle English *createn* from Latin *creatus*, past part. of *creare* to create]

creatine /'kree-əteen/ *noun* a compound present in the body that is produced during the metabolism of protein and has a part in supplying energy for muscle contraction. [Greek *kreat-, kreas* flesh + -INE[2]]

creatinine /kree'atineen/ *noun* a product of the metabolism of CREATINE that is excreted in the urine, the rate of excretion being an indicator of kidney function and muscle mass.

creation /kri'aysh(ə)n/ *noun* **1a** something created: *We are God's creations.* **b** an original work of art. **c** *often derog* a product of some art or craft, e.g. dressmaking or cookery, *esp* if somewhat striking: *a hideous creation in mauve and magenta tulle.* **d** the world: *Novels … are the stupidest things in creation* — Jane Austen. **e** creatures singly or collectively: *The appetite for joy which pervades all creation* — Hardy. **2** (**the Creation**) the act of bringing the world into ordered existence.

creationist *noun* an adherent of a theory that all forms of life were created simultaneously by God and did not evolve from earlier forms. ➤➤ **creationism** *noun*, **creationist** *adj*.

creation science *noun* the interpretation of scientific knowledge so that it accords with the doctrine of creationism (see CREATIONIST).

creative /kri'aytiv/ *adj* **1** showing the ability or power to create; given to creating: *creative people.* **2** having the quality of something imaginatively created: *creative writing.* **3** containing misleading inventions designed to falsify or conceal the facts: *creative accounting.* ➤➤ **creatively** *adv*, **creativeness** *noun*, **creativity** /kree-ə'tiviti/ *noun*.

creator *noun* **1** a person who creates, usu by bringing something new or original into being: *the creator of Tintin.* **2** (**the Creator**) God.

creature /'kreechə/ *noun* **1a** a lower animal: *the creatures of the woods.* **b** an animate being, *esp* a non-human one: *the least of God's creatures.* **2** a human being; a person: *She's a pathetic creature.* **3** a person who is the servile dependant or tool of another: *Sir Francis Windebank … was a creature of [Archbishop] Laud's* — David Hume. **4** a thing that is the product or offspring of something; a figment: *mere creatures of fantasy.* **5** something created: *I felt what the duties of a creator towards his creature were* — Mary Shelley. ➤➤ **creatural** *adj*, **creaturely** *adj*. [Middle English via Old French from late Latin *creatura*, from Latin *creatus*: see CREATE]

creature comforts *pl noun* material things that give bodily comfort.

crèche /kresh/ *noun* **1** *Brit* a centre where young children are looked after while their parents are at work, shopping, etc. **2** *NAmer* a representation of the Nativity scene: compare CRIB[1] (5). [French *crèche* from Old French *creche* manger, crib, of Germanic origin]

cred /kred/ *noun Brit, informal* street credibility.

credal *or* **creedal** /'kreedl/ *adj* of or relating to a creed.

credence /'kreed(ə)ns/ *noun* **1** acceptance of something as true or real: *I don't give credence to gossip.* **2** = CREDENCE TABLE. ✳ **lend credence to** said of circumstantial details, etc: to bear out (a report, rumour, etc) or give (it) credibility. [Middle English via French from medieval Latin *credentia*, from Latin *credent-, credens*, present part. of *credere* to believe, trust]

credence shelf *noun* = CREDENCE TABLE (2).

credence table *noun* **1** a side table or sideboard. **2** in a church, a shelf on which the bread and wine of the Eucharist are placed before consecration. [French *credence* from Old Italian *credenza* belief, confidence, from medieval Latin *credentia*; prob from CREDENCE in its obsolete sense of a precautionary tasting, presumably at a side table, of food about to be served to a great personage, to guard against poisoning: see CREDENCE]

credential /kri'densh(ə)l/ *noun* (*usu in pl, but treated as sing.*) something, *esp* a letter, that gives proof of identity, status, or authority.

credenza /kri'denzə/ *noun* = CREDENCE TABLE. [Italian *credenza*: see CREDENCE TABLE]

credibility /kredi'biliti/ *noun* **1** the quality of being believable. **2** trust or belief in somebody based on their track record: *The government has lost credibility over this and other recent incidents.* **3** = STREET CREDIBILITY.

credibility gap /kredi'biliti/ *noun* a discrepancy between what is claimed and what is perceived to be true, or a lack of credibility arising from this.

credible /'kredəbl/ *adj* offering reasonable grounds for belief. ➤➤ **credibly** *adv*. [Middle English from Latin *credibilis*, from *credere* to believe]

credit[1] /'kredit/ *noun* **1** a source of honour or repute: *She is a credit to her parents.* **2** acknowledgment; approval: *Give credit where credit is due.* **3** influence derived from enjoying the confidence of others; standing: *John Gilpin was a citizen of credit and renown* — Cowper. **4** credence: *rumours that deserve no credit.* **5a** the balance in a person's favour in an account. **b** an amount or sum placed at a person's disposal by a bank and usu to be repaid with interest. **c** time given for payment for goods or services provided but not immediately paid for: *long-term credit.* **d** an entry on the right-hand side of an account constituting an addition to a revenue, net worth, or liability account. **6a** a line, note, or name that acknowledges the source of an item. **b** (*usu in pl*) an acknowledgment of a contributor by name that appears at the beginning or end of a film or television programme. **7a** recognition that a student has fulfilled a course requirement. **b** *Brit* the passing of an examination at a level well above the minimum though not with distinction. ✳ **do somebody credit/do credit to somebody** said of a quality, etc that somebody evinces: to show somebody in a worthy light: *Your solicitude does you credit.* **give somebody credit for** to allow that they must have (usu some quite normal quality): *Give me credit for some common sense.* **have to one's credit** to number (something) among one's achievements: *She has several publications to her credit.* **in credit** said of a bank account: having money in it. **on credit** with the cost charged to one's account and paid later: *He bought his new tape recorder on credit.* **on the credit side** as a positive aspect: *On the credit side, the acting, costumes, and set are excellent.* **take credit for** to claim responsibility for (something satisfactory): *Managers typically take credit for success and blame failure on their subordinates.* **to somebody's credit** as a creditable effort in difficult circumstances: *To her credit, she never once blamed her husband.* [French *crédit* via Old Italian from Latin *creditum* something entrusted to another, loan, neuter past part. of *credere* to believe, trust]

credit[2] *verb trans* (**credited, crediting**) **1** to believe (something): *I couldn't credit it when her ex-husband turned up at her wedding.* **2a** to enter (an amount) on the credit side of an account. **b** to place an amount to the credit of (an account): compare DEBIT[2]. **3a** (+ with) to ascribe some favourable characteristic to (somebody): *Credit me with some intelligence.* **b** (+ to) to attribute (e.g. an invention, a saying, etc) to some person: *a bon mot wrongly credited to David Garrick.* [partly from CREDIT[1]; partly from Latin *creditus*, past part. of *credere* to believe, trust]

creditable *adj* said of a performance or effort: deserving acknowledgment even if not successful; very respectable: *She went out with*

a creditable 6–4, 4–6, 3–6 against the reigning champion. ➤➤ **creditability** /-'biliti/ *noun*, **creditably** *adv*.

credit account *noun* an account, e.g. that of a customer with a shop, that allows the deferment of payments for the purchase of goods.

credit card *noun* a card provided by a bank, etc, allowing the holder to obtain goods and services on credit.

credit note *noun* a note given by a shop to a customer who has returned goods on account of their unsuitability, which can be exchanged for other goods of the same value.

creditor *noun* a person to whom a debt is owed.

credit rating *noun* the proved ability of a person or company to honour their financial commitments.

credit title *noun* an acknowledgment of a contributor's role, shown at the beginning or end of a film, programme, etc; = CREDIT[1] (6B).

credit transfer *noun* a transfer of money directly from one bank account to another.

credit union *noun* a cooperative association of people who save money in a common fund, make loans to members at a low rate of interest, and share interest payments.

creditworthy *adj* qualifying for commercial credit. ➤➤ **creditworthiness** *noun*.

credo /'kreedoh, 'kraydoh/ *noun* (*pl* **credos**) **1** a creed. **2** (**Credo**) a musical setting of the creed in a sung mass. [Middle English from Latin *credo* I believe: see CREED]

credulity /kri'dyoohliti/ *noun* undue willingness to believe; gullibility: *A little credulity helps one on through life very smoothly* — Elizabeth Gaskell.

credulous /'kredyooləs/ *adj* ready to believe, *esp* on slight evidence. ➤➤ **credulously** *adv*, **credulousness** *noun*. [Latin *credulus*, from *credere* to believe]

Cree /kree/ *noun* (*pl* **Crees** *or collectively* **Cree**) **1** a member of a Native American people of Manitoba and Saskatchewan. **2** the Algonquian language of this people. ➤➤ **Cree** *adj*. [short for earlier *Christens* from Canadian French *Christino*, prob modification of Ojibwa *Kenistenoag*]

creed /kreed/ *noun* **1** a set of religious beliefs: *regardless of nationality, colour, or creed.* **2** a tenet or set of tenets: *It is only in the lonely emergencies of life that our creed is tested* — William James. **3a** a conventionalized statement of religious belief. **b** (**the Creed**) the Apostles' Creed or the Nicene Creed, said or sung as part of Christian worship. [Old English *crēda* from Latin *credo* I believe (first word of the Apostles' and Nicene Creeds), from *credere* to believe, trust, entrust]

creedal *adj* see CREDAL.

Creek /kreek/ *noun* **1** a member of a confederacy of Native American peoples of Alabama, Georgia, and Florida. **2** the Muskogean language spoken by many in this confederacy. [CREEK, because of the large number of creeks and waterways in their territory]

creek /kreek/ *noun* **1** *chiefly Brit* a small narrow inlet of a lake, sea, etc. **2** *chiefly NAmer, Aus* a brook. ✳ **up the creek 1** *informal* in trouble. **2** *informal* wrong; mistaken. [Middle English *crike, creke*, from Old Norse *-kriki* bend]

creel /kreel/ *noun* a wickerwork container, e.g. for newly caught fish. [Middle English *creille, crele*, prob via French from Latin *craticula*, dimin. of *cratis* wickerwork]

creep[1] /kreep/ *verb intrans* (*past tense and past part.* **crept** /krept/) **1** to move along with the body prone and close to the ground; to crawl: *all creeping things* — Bible. **2** to go very slowly: *The hours crept by.* **3** to move cautiously or quietly so as to escape notice: *She had crept into the room and was standing beside him.* **4** (+ into) to become increasingly evident as an element in somebody's manner, etc: *A note of irritation crept into her voice.* **5** *informal* to behave in a servile manner. **6** said of a plant: to spread or grow over a surface by clinging with tendrils, roots, etc or rooting at intervals. **7** said of a material: to change shape permanently due to prolonged stress or exposure to high temperatures. [Old English *crēopan*]

creep[2] *noun* **1** a creeping movement. **2** *Brit, informal* an ingratiatingly servile person. **3** *informal* a contemptuous term for a person one dislikes, *esp* a man. **4** the slow change of dimensions of an object due to prolonged exposure to high temperature or stress. ✳ **give one the creeps** *informal* to repel one; to make one's flesh creep: *That picture gives me the creeps.*

creeper *noun* **1** a creeping plant. **2** a bird that creeps about on trees or bushes, *esp* the TREECREEPER. **3** a creeping insect or reptile. **4** a type of grapnel used for dragging the sea bed. **5** a shoe with a thick crepe sole that allows the wearer to pad about silently: compare BROTHEL CREEPERS.

creeping Jenny or **creeping jennie** *noun* a trailing plant of the primrose family with yellow flowers, that grows in damp places throughout Europe: *Lysimachia nummularia.* Also called MONEYWORT.

creeping Jesus *noun informal* a cringing, sanctimonious person.

creepy /'kreepi/ *adj* (**creepier, creepiest**) **1** producing a sensation of shivery apprehension: *a creepy story.* **2** *informal* slightly sinister or unpleasant: *a creepy personality.*

creepy-crawly /ˌkreepi 'krawli/ *noun* (*pl* **creepy-crawlies**) *Brit, informal* a small creeping or scuttling creature, e.g. a spider.

creese /krees/ *noun* = KRIS: *These [arrows] ... resembled in some respects the writhing creese of the Malay* — Poe.

cremaster /kri'mastə/ *noun* a usu hooked projection at the hind end of the pupa of butterflies and moths, that serves to suspend the pupa. [scientific Latin from Greek *kremastēr* suspender, from *kremannynai* to hang]

cremate /kri'mayt/ *verb trans* to reduce (a dead body) to ashes by burning. ⟫ **cremation** /kri'maysh(ə)n/ *noun,* **crematory** /'krem-/ *adj.* [Latin *crematus,* past part. of *cremare* to burn up, cremate]

crematorium /kremə'tawri·əm/ *noun* (*pl* **crematoriums** or **crematoria** /-ri·ə/) a place where dead bodies are cremated.

crème (*French* krɛm)/ *noun* (*pl* **crèmes** /krem(z) (*French* krɛm))/) a food, e.g. a sauce or cake filling, prepared with or resembling cream. [French *crème* from late Latin *cramum:* see CREAM[1]]

crème brûlée /ˌkrem brooh'lay/ *noun* a thick custard made with eggs and cream and topped with caramelized sugar. [French *crème brûlée* burned cream]

crème caramel /ˌkrem karə'mel/ *noun* an egg custard made in an oven dish lined with caramel.

crème de la crème /ˌkrem də lah 'krem/ *noun* (**the crème de la crème**) the finest of the finest; the most exclusive set: *All my pupils are the crème de la crème* — Muriel Spark. [French *crème de la crème* cream of the cream]

crème de menthe /ˌkrem də 'month (*French* də mã:t)/ *noun* a sweet green or white mint-flavoured liqueur. [French *crème de menth,* literally 'cream of mint']

crème fraîche /ˌkrem 'fresh/ *noun* a type of slightly fermented thick cream. [French *crème fraîche* fresh cream]

crenate /'kreenayt/ *adj* said of a leaf: having a scalloped edge. ⟫ **crenation** /kri'naysh(ə)n/ *noun.* [scientific Latin *crenatus* from medieval Latin *crena* notch]

crenated /kri'naytid/ *adj* = CRENATE.

crenel /'krenl/ *noun* a crenellation. [early French *crenel* from Old French, dimin. of *cren* notch, from *crener* to notch]

crenellated /'krenəlaytid/ *adj* having battlements.

crenellation /krenə'laysh(ə)n/ *noun* an indentation in a battlement.

crenelle /krə'nel/ *noun* = CRENEL.

crenulate /'krenyoolət, -layt/ *adj* having an irregularly wavy or serrated outline: *a crenulate shoreline; a crenulate leaf.* ⟫ **crenulation** *noun.* [scientific Latin *crenulatus* from *crenula,* dimin. of medieval Latin *crena* notch]

crenulated /'krenyoolaytid/ *adj* = CRENULATE.

creodont /'kree·ədont/ *noun* any of an order of fossil carnivorous mammals of the Tertiary period, the ancestors of modern carnivores: order Creodonta. [scientific Latin *Creodonta,* order name, from Greek *kreas* flesh + *odont-, odous* tooth]

Creole /'kreeohl/ *noun* **1** a person of European descent in the W Indies or Spanish America. **2** a white descendant of early French or Spanish settlers of the Gulf States of the USA. **3** a person of mixed French or Spanish and black descent. ⟫ **Creole** *adj.* [French *créole* via Spanish *criollo* from Portuguese *crioulo* white person born in the colonies, from *criar* to breed, from Latin *creare* to produce, CREATE]

creole *noun* a language based on two or more languages, *esp* one developed through the interaction of a local language, e.g. an African tongue spoken in the W Indies, with a European one: compare PIDGIN. ⟫ **creole** *adj.*

creolized or **creolised** /'kree·əliezd/ *adj* denoting a variety of a language, *esp* a European one, that has developed the status of a creole: *the creolized varieties of English spoken in the Caribbean.*

creosol /'kree·əsol/ *noun* an aromatic oily liquid chemical compound that is one of the active constituents of creosote. [CREOSOTE[1] + -OL[1]]

creosote[1] /'kree·əsoht/ *noun* **1** a brownish oily liquid obtained from coal tar and used *esp* as a wood preservative. **2** a clear or yellowish oily liquid obtained from wood tar and used as an antiseptic. ⟫ **creosotic** /-'sotik/ *adj.* [German *Kreosot,* from Greek *kreas* flesh + *sōtēr* preserver, ultimately from *sōs* safe; from its antiseptic properties]

creosote[2] *verb trans* to treat (something) with creosote.

creosote bush *noun* a shrub that forms dense scrub in Mexico and surrounding arid areas, with leaves that smell like creosote and yield an antiseptic: *Larrea tridentata.*

creosote plant *noun* = CREOSOTE BUSH.

crepe or **crêpe** /krayp, krep/ *noun* **1** (*also* **crape**) a light crinkled fabric woven from any of various fibres. **2** a small very thin pancake. **3** = CREPE RUBBER. ⟫ **crepey** *adj,* **crepy** *adj.* [French *crêpe,* from early French *crespe* curled, from Latin *crispus*]

crepe de Chine /ˌkrayp də 'sheen/ *noun* a soft fine crepe, orig of silk. [French *crêpe de Chine* crepe from China]

crepe paper *noun* thin paper with a crinkled or puckered texture.

creperie or **crêperie** /'kraypəri (*French* krɛpri)/ *noun* (*pl* **creperies**) a restaurant that specializes in crepes. [French *crêperie*]

crepe rubber *noun* crude or synthetic rubber in the form of crinkled sheets, used *esp* for shoe soles.

crêpe suzette /ˌkrayp sooh'zet, krep/ *noun* (*pl* **crêpes suzette** /ˌkrayp, ˌkrep/) a thin folded or rolled pancake in a hot orange-butter sauce that is sprinkled with a liqueur, e.g. cognac, and set alight for serving. [French *crêpe suzette,* from *crêpe* pancake + *Suzette,* dimin. of *Suzanne;* said to be named after *Suzanne* Reichenberg d.1924, French actress]

crépinette /kraypi'net (*French* krɛpinet)/ *noun* a flat sausage containing minced meat and stuffing, encased in pork caul. [French *crépinette* dimin. of *crépine* caul]

crepitate /'krepitayt/ *verb intrans* to crackle. [Latin *crepitatus,* past part. of *crepitare* to crackle, from *crepare* to rattle, crack]

crepitation /krepi'taysh(ə)n/ *noun* **1** a crackling sound heard from the lungs that is characteristic of pneumonia. **2** a grating sound produced by the parts of a broken bone moving against each other at the site of fracture.

crepitus /'krepitəs/ *noun* = CREPITATION. [Latin *crepitus* a creaking noise, noun from past part. of *crepare* to rattle, crack]

crept /krept/ *verb* past tense and past part. of CREEP[1].

crepuscular /kri'puskyoolə/ *adj* **1** *formal* relating to or resembling twilight; dim; dusky: *a crepuscular horizon on a plain at dawn* — Joseph Conrad. **2** active in the twilight: *crepuscular insects.* [Latin *crepusculum* twilight, from *creper* dusky]

Cres. *abbr* Crescent.

cresc. *abbr* in music, crescendo.

crescendo[1] /krə'shendoh/ *noun* (*pl* **crescendos** or **crescendi** /-dee/) **1** a gradual increase; *esp* a gradual increase in volume in a musical passage. **2** a crescendo musical passage. [Italian *crescendo* growing, from Latin *crescendum,* verbal noun from *crescere* to grow]

Usage note

Strictly speaking a *crescendo* is a process rather than a point reached, and so *climax* and *peak* are sometimes better words to use, especially in figurative uses after words like *reach* or *rise* to: e.g. *the excitement reached a peak* rather than *the excitement reached a crescendo.*

crescendo[2] *adj and adv* said of a piece of music: to be performed with an increase in volume.

crescendo[3] *verb intrans* (**crescendoes, crescendoed, crescendoing**) to increase in force or volume.

crescent[1] /'kres(ə)nt, 'krez(ə)nt/ *noun* **1** the figure of the moon at any stage between new moon and first quarter or last quarter and the succeeding new moon. **2** something shaped like a crescent and consisting of a concave and a convex curve. **3** *Brit* a curved street. **4** (**the Crescent**) *esp* formerly: **a** a crescent as the symbol of Islam: *Neighbouring states of opposite creeds, were occasionally linked together in alliances ... so that the Cross and Crescent were to be seen side by side, fighting against some common enemy* — Washington Irving. **b**

Islam itself. [Middle English *cressant* from Old French *creissant*, present part. of *creistre* to grow, increase, from Latin *crescere*]

crescent² *adj* **1** said of the moon: in its first or last quarter. **2** *archaic or literary* growing; increasing; waxing: *My powers are crescent* — Shakespeare.

cresol /'kreesol/ *noun* a phenol used *esp* as a disinfectant. [CREOSOTE¹ + -OL¹]

cress /kres/ *noun* any of numerous species of plants of the mustard family that have mildly pungent leaves and are used in salads and as a garnish: genus *Barbarea* and other genera. [Old English *cærse, cressa*]

cresset /'kresit/ *noun* formerly, an iron basket mounted on a pole or wall, holding material, e.g. pitch or wood, that is burned for illumination or as a beacon. [Middle English from Old French *craisset*, from *craisse* grease]

crest¹ /krest/ *noun* **1a** a showy tuft or projection on the head of an animal, *esp* a bird. **b** a plume, emblem, etc worn on a knight's helmet. **c** a symbol of a family, office, etc, that appears as a figure above the shield in a heraldic ACHIEVEMENT (coat of arms). **d** *not used technically* in heraldry: a coat of arms. **e** the upper muscular ridge of a horse's neck from which the mane grows. **2** the ridge or top, *esp* of a wave, roof, or mountain. **3** the climax; culmination: *at the crest of her fame.* ✻ **on the crest of a wave** enjoying great success. ➤➤ **crestless** *adj.* [Middle English *creste* via French, from Latin *crista* crest, cock's comb]

crest² *verb trans* to reach the crest of (a hill, ridge, wave, etc): *They were cresting a corner of London which is almost as precipitous as Edinburgh* — G K Chesterton. ➤ *verb intrans* said of a wave: to rise to a crest.

crested *adj* **1** said *esp* of a bird: having a crest: *the crested grebe.* **2** topped or crowned with something suggestive of a crest: *Each [island] was crested with a knot of lofty palms* — Charles Kingsley. **3** marked or decorated with the crest of a family, etc: *crested crockery.*

crestfallen *adj* disheartened or dejected.

cretaceous /kri'tayshəs/ *adj* **1** resembling or containing chalk. **2** (**Cretaceous**) relating to or dating from a geological period, the last period of the Mesozoic era, lasting from about 146 million to about 65 million years ago, and marked by the dominance of dinosaurs. ➤➤ **Cretaceous** *noun.* [Latin *cretaceus* from *creta* chalk]

Cretan /'kreetn/ *noun* a native or inhabitant of the island of Crete in the eastern Mediterranean. ➤➤ **Cretan** *adj.*

cretic /'kreetik/ *noun* in prosody, a metrical foot containing one short syllable between two long ones, giving the rhythm *dah-di-dah.* [via Latin from Greek *Krētikos* of Crete]

cretin /'kretin/ *noun* **1** somebody afflicted with cretinism. **2** *offensive* an imbecile; an idiot. ➤➤ **cretinous** /-nəs/ *adj.*

Word history
French *crétin* from French dialect *cretin* Christian, human being, from Latin *christianus*: see CHRISTIAN¹. French dialect *cretin* was applied to sufferers from cretinism, apparently as a reminder that they were human beings with Christian souls.

cretinism *noun* congenital physical stunting and mental retardation caused by severe deficiency of the thyroid hormone in infancy.

cretonne /'kreton, kre'ton/ *noun* a strong unglazed cotton or linen cloth used *esp* for curtains and upholstery. [French *cretonne*, named after *Creton*, town in Normandy, France]

Creutzfeldt-Jakob disease /kroytsfelt 'yakob/ *noun* (*often* **CJD**) a progressive disease of middle age, characterized by dementia, muscular wasting, spasticity, and involuntary movements, believed to be caused by a PRION (infectious protein particle). ✻ **new variant Creutzfeldt-Jakob disease** (*often* **new variant CJD**) a form of the disease characterized by early onset, thought to be the human variety of BSE. [named after H G *Creutzfeldt* d.1964 and A M *Jakob* d.1931, German neurologists]

crevasse /krə'vas/ *noun* a deep fissure in a glacier. [French *crevasse* from Old French *crevace*: see CREVICE]

Usage note
crevasse or crevice? A *crevasse* is a large crack, for example in a mountain, glacier, or ice field. An unlucky mountaineer might fall down a *crevasse*. A *crevice* is a small or tiny crack, where dirt lodges or where one might lose a small coin.

crevice /'krevis/ *noun* a narrow opening resulting from a split or crack. [Middle English from Old French *crevace*, from *crever* to break, from Latin *crepare* to crack]

Usage note
crevice or crevasse? See note at CREVASSE.

crew¹ /krooh/ *noun* (*treated as sing. or pl*) **1a** the personnel of a ship or boat, excluding the captain and officers. **b** members of a crew: *the captain and 50 crew.* **c** the people who man an aircraft in flight. **2** a company of people working on one job or under one supervisor. **3** *informal, derog* a number of people temporarily associated: *that crew of deadbeats.* ➤➤ **crewman** *noun.* [Middle English *crue* military reinforcement, from early French *creue* increase, from *creistre* to grow, from Latin *crescere*]

crew² *verb chiefly Brit* past tense of CROW².

crew³ *verb trans* to serve as a member of a crew on (a ship, aircraft, etc). ➤ *verb intrans* to serve as a member of a crew, *esp* to act as the subordinate partner on a yacht.

crew cut *noun* a very short bristly haircut, *esp* for a man. ➤➤ **crew-cut** *adj.*

crewel /'krooh-əl/ *noun* loosely twisted worsted yarn used in embroidery and tapestry. [Middle English *crule*; earlier history unknown]

crewelwork *noun* embroidery design worked with crewel.

crew neck *noun* a round flat neckline on a knitted pullover. ➤➤ **crew-necked** *adj.* [from the pullovers worn by crews of rowing boats]

crib¹ /krib/ *noun* **1** *chiefly NAmer* a child's cot with barred or slatted sides. **2** *archaic* a baby's cradle. **3** a cattle stall. **4** a manger or rack for animal fodder. **5** *Brit* a model of the Nativity scene, with the infant Christ lying in a manger: compare CRÈCHE (2). **6** a literal translation of a text, *esp* one used surreptitiously by students. **7** a work that has been plagiarized: *a flagrant crib.* **8a** *archaic* a room or small place to live: *a mean little airless lodging … a mere crib for two.* **b** *NAmer* an apartment. **c** *NZ* a weekend cottage. **9a** the card game CRIBBAGE. **b** the discard pile in cribbage. **10** *Aus, NZ, informal* a snack. **11** heavy timber framework used in constructing foundations, etc. [Old English *cribb* crib, stall]

crib² *verb* (**cribbed, cribbing**) ➤ *verb trans* **1** to copy (somebody else's work) without permission or acknowledgment. **2** *archaic* to steal (something): *Child … cribbed the necklace, hid it, played with it, cut the string, and swallowed a bead* — Dickens. **3** *archaic* to confine or restrain (a person, etc): *But now I am cabined, cribbed, confined, bound in* — Shakespeare. ➤ *verb intrans* **1** to copy from a crib or from a classmate, etc. **2** *Brit, dated* to grumble: *She's out half the time and doesn't answer the telephone, and when I start cribbing she just laughs* — L P Hartley. ➤➤ **cribber** *noun.*

cribbage /'kribij/ *noun* a card game for two to four players who each try to form various counting combinations of cards. [prob from CRIB¹]

crib-biting *noun* a habit that some horses have of gnawing at the woodwork in their stable, slobbering, salivating, and sucking in air.

crib death *noun NAmer* = COT DEATH.

cribriform /'kribrifawm/ *adj* denoting an anatomical structure that is pierced with small holes, e.g. for the passage of nerves: *a cribriform plate.* [Latin *cribrum* sieve + -FORM]

cribwork *noun* the timber framework used in constructing foundations, etc; = CRIB¹ (11).

crick¹ /krik/ *noun* a painful spasmodic condition of the muscles of the neck, back, etc. [Middle English *cryk*; earlier history unknown]

crick² *verb trans* to cause a crick in (the neck, etc).

cricket¹ /'krikit/ *noun* a game played with a bat and ball on a large field with two wickets near its centre by two sides of eleven players each who try to score runs by hitting the ball and running between the wickets. ✻ **not cricket** *Brit, informal* against the dictates of fair play; not honourable. ➤➤ **cricketer** *noun.* [French *criquet* stake used as goal in a bowling game]

cricket² *noun* any of numerous species of leaping insects noted for the chirping sounds produced by the male: family Gryllidae. [Middle English *criket* from early French *criquet*, of imitative origin]

cricoid /'kriekoyd/ *adj* denoting the ring-shaped cartilage of the larynx. [via scientific Latin from Greek *krikoeidēs* ring-shaped, from *krikos* ring + -OID]

cri de coeur /kree də 'kuh/ *noun* (*pl* **cris de coeur** /kree/) a passionate plea or protest. [French *cri de coeur* cry from the heart]

cried /kried/ *verb* past tense and past part. of CRY¹.

crier /'krie·ə/ *noun* an officer who makes announcements in a court.

crikey /'krieki/ *interj chiefly Brit, dated* used to express surprise. [euphemism for CHRIST²]

crime /kriem/ *noun* **1** violation of law, or an instance of this, punishable by the state: *Petty laws breed great crimes* — Ouida. **2** a grave offence, *esp* against morality. **3** criminal activity: *victims of crime.* **4** *informal* something deplorable, foolish, or disgraceful: *It's a crime to waste good food.* [Middle English from Latin *crimen* accusation, fault, crime]

crime passionnel /,kreem pasyo'nel/ *noun* (*pl* **crimes passionnels** /,kreem pasyo'nel/) a crime, usu murder, prompted by sexual jealousy. [French *crime passionnel* crime of passion]

crime writer *noun* a writer of detective fiction or thrillers.

crimin- *or* **crimino-** *comb. form* forming words, denoting: crime or criminals. [Latin *crimin-, crimen* accusation, offence]

criminal¹ /'kriminl/ *adj* **1** involving or constituting a crime: *criminal negligence.* **2** relating to crime or its punishment: *criminal law.* **3** guilty of crime: *the criminal classes; the criminal mind.* **4** *informal* disgraceful; deplorable: *a criminal waste of money.* ➤➤ **criminality** /-'naliti/ *noun,* **criminally** *adv.* [Middle English via French from late Latin *criminalis,* from Latin *crimin-, crimen* CRIME]

criminal² *noun* a person who has committed or been convicted of a crime.

criminal conversation *noun* a former legal term for adultery, *esp* as constituting grounds for the husband's recovery of damages from the wife's adulterous partner.

criminalize *or* **criminalise** *verb trans* **1** to make (an activity) illegal; to outlaw (it). **2** to outlaw the activities of (a person) and so turn them into a criminal.

criminal law *noun* the law relating to crimes and their punishments.

crimino- *comb. form* see CRIMIN-.

criminogenic /kriminoh'jenik/ *adj* likely to lead to criminal behaviour: *the question of whether television violence is or is not criminogenic; Corporate crime can be linked to criminogenic factors associated with upward mobility.*

criminology /krimi'noləji/ *noun* the study of crime, criminals, and penal treatment. ➤➤ **criminological** /-'lojikl/ *adj,* **criminologist** *noun.*

crimp¹ /krimp/ *verb trans* **1** to make (the hair) wavy or curly. **2** to roll or curl the edge of (a steel panel, etc). **3** to pinch or press (material) together in order to seal or join it. **4** *NAmer, informal* to hinder or hamper (a person or operation): *research crimped by a lack of funding.* ➤➤ **crimper** *noun.* [Dutch or Low German *krimpen* to shrivel]

crimp² *noun* **1** a rolled, folded, or compressed edge. **2** a tight curl or wave in the hair.

Crimplene /'krimpleen/ *noun trademark* a textured continuous-filament polyester yarn. [prob from CRIMP² + *-lene* as in TERYLENE]

crimson¹ /'krimz(ə)n/ *adj* of a deep purplish red colour. ➤➤ **crimson** *noun.* [Middle English *crimisin* via Old Spanish *cremesín* from Arabic *qirmizī,* from *qirmiz* KERMES]

crimson² *verb* (**crimsoned, crimsoning**) ➤ *verb intrans literary* **1** to become crimson: *The sky crimsoned towards the west.* **2** to blush: *She crimsoned when he kissed her.* ➤ *verb trans* to make (something) crimson.

cringe¹ /krinj/ *verb intrans* **1** to shrink or cower in fear. **2** to adopt a cowering posture expressive of humility. **3** (*often* + to) to behave with fawning self-abasement: *It is not my nature, sir, to cringe to any man* — Conan Doyle; *The elder advanced with a cringing smile* — Somerset Maugham. **4** to feel acute embarrassment: *The patronizing tone her father used to her friends made her cringe.* [Middle English *crengen* of Germanic origin]

cringe² *noun* the act or an instance of cringing.

cringeworthy *adj informal* embarrassingly awful: *cringeworthy lyrics.*

cringle /'kring·gl/ *noun* an eyelet or loop worked into the edge of a sail for attaching a rope. [Low German *kringel,* dimin. of *kring* ring; related to Old English *cradol* CRADLE¹]

crinkle¹ /'kringkl/ *verb intrans* **1** to wrinkle. **2** to rustle. ➤ *verb trans* to cause (something) to crinkle. [Middle English *crynkelen,* of Germanic origin]

crinkle² *noun* a wrinkle. ➤➤ **crinkly** *adj.*

crinoid /'krienoyd/ *noun* any of a large class of echinoderms having a cup-shaped body with five or more feathery arms: class Crinoidea. ➤➤ **crinoid** *adj,* **crinoidal** /-'noidl/ *adj.* [Latin class name, from Greek *krinon* lily + -OID]

crinoline /'krinəlin/ *noun* a full skirt as worn by women in the 19th cent., or a padded or hooped petticoat supporting it. [French *crinoline* from Italian *crinolino,* from *crino* horsehair (from Latin *crinis* hair) + *lino* flax, linen, from Latin *linum*]

criollo /kri'oh(l)yoh/ *noun* (*pl* **criollos**) **1** a person born and usu raised in S America; *esp* one of Spanish descent. **2** a domestic animal of a breed or strain developed in Latin America; *esp* a breed of strong hardy horses developed in Argentina. ➤➤ **criollo** *adj.* [Spanish *criollo:* see CREOLE]

cripes /krieps/ *interj informal, dated* an expression of surprise or dismay. [euphemism for CHRIST²]

cripple¹ /'kripl/ *noun* **1** *offensive* a lame or partly disabled person. **2** a person who is impaired in a non-physical way: *an emotional cripple.* [Old English *crypel;* related to Old English *crēopan* CREEP¹]

cripple² *verb trans* **1** to make (somebody) a cripple; to lame (them). **2** to impair (a person) mentally, emotionally, etc: *emotionally crippled by the traumatic experience.* **3** to hamper or severely limit (a person, operation, etc): *a crippling interest rate.*

crisis /'kriesis/ *noun* (*pl* **crises** /'krieseez/) **1** a time of acute difficulty or danger, *esp* on a national or international scale: *The Cuban missile crisis of 1962.* **2a** the turning point for better or worse in an acute disease, e.g. pneumonia. **b** a sudden attack of pain, distress, etc. [via Latin from Greek *krisis* decision, from *krinein* to decide]

crisp¹ /krisp/ *adj* **1a** easily crumbled; brittle. **b** desirably firm and fresh: *a crisp apple; crisp lettuce leaves.* **c** newly made or prepared: *a crisp pound note.* **d** said of curly hair: strong and wiry. **2** sharp, clean-cut, and clear: *a crisp illustration.* **3** decisive; sharp: *a crisp manner.* **4** said of the weather: briskly cold; fresh; *esp* frosty. ➤➤ **crisply** *adv,* **crispness** *noun.* [Old English *crisp* curled, from Latin *crispus*]

crisp² *noun Brit* a thin slice of flavoured or salted fried potato, usu eaten cold: *a packet of crisps.*

crisp³ *verb trans* **1** to make or keep (food) crisp: *Crisp the bread in the oven.* **2** *archaic* to curl or crimp (hair). ➤ *verb intrans* to become crisp: *Allow the breadcrumbs time to crisp under the grill.*

crispate /'krispeit, -pit/ *adj* said e.g. of leaves: having a wavy or undulating edge.

crispbread *noun* a plain dry unsweetened biscuit made from crushed grain, e.g. rye.

crisper *noun* a compartment at the bottom of a refrigerator for keeping vegetables, *esp* salad vegetables, fresh.

Crispin /'krispin/ *noun* a sweet eating apple of Japanese origin with a greenish yellow skin.

crispy *adj* (**crispier, crispiest**) **1** firm and fresh. **2** made crisp by deep frying: *crispy noodles.* ➤➤ **crispiness** *noun.*

crisscross¹ /'kriskros/ *noun* a crisscrossed pattern. [obsolete *christcross* Christ's cross, from the cross symbol traditionally printed before the alphabet on children's hornbooks]

crisscross² *adj* marked or characterized by a crisscrossing pattern or network.

crisscross³ *verb trans* **1** to pass back and forth through or over (a place). **2** to mark (something) with intersecting lines. ➤ *verb intrans* to go or pass back and forth.

crista /'kristə/ *noun* (*pl* **cristae** /'kristee/) **1** in biology, a ridge or crest. **2** any of the inwardly projecting folds of the inner membrane of a MITOCHONDRION (part of plant and animal cells involved in energy production). [Latin *crista* CREST¹]

cristobalite /kri'stohbəliet/ *noun* a white silica that is stable at high temperatures and is found in volcanic rocks. [German *Cristobalit* from Cerro San Cristóbal, site in Mexico]

crit. *abbr* **1** critical. **2** criticism.

criterion /krie'tiəri·ən/ *noun* (*pl* **criteria** /-ri·ə/ *or* **criterions**) a standard on which a judgment or decision may be based: *The group chosen for testing had to meet certain criteria; It would be interesting to know on what criteria some were selected and some rejected.* ➤➤ **criterial** *adj.* [Greek *kritērion* from *kritēs* judge, from *krinein* to judge, decide]

Usage note
criterion *and* criteria. Criteria is the plural form of *criterion.* A phrase such as *this criteria* is incorrect. If a thing is judged by such and such *criteria,* then

more than one standard of judgment is being applied to it: *Value for money is surely not the only relevant criterion in this case; the criteria by which schools will be judged to have succeeded or failed are set out in the report.*

critic /'kritik/ *noun* **1** a person who evaluates works of art, literature, or music, *esp* as a profession: *The critic must educate the public; the artist must educate the critic* — Oscar Wilde. **2** a person who tends to judge harshly or to be over-critical of minor faults: *I am my own harshest critic.* [via Latin from Greek *kritikos* able to discern or judge, from *krinein* to judge]

critical *adj* **1a** inclined to criticize severely and unfavourably. **b** consisting of or involving criticism: *critical writings.* **c** exercising or involving careful judgment or judicious evaluation: *Would you cast a critical eye over this article, please?* **2a** relating to or denoting a measurement, point, etc at which some quality, property, or phenomenon undergoes a marked change: *critical temperature.* **b** crucial; decisive: *a critical test.* **c** being in or approaching a state of crisis. **3** said of a nuclear reactor: sustaining an energy-producing chain reaction. ➤➤ **criticality** /-'kaliti/ *noun,* **critically** *adv.*

critical angle *noun* **1** the smallest angle of incident light reflected onto a surface at which total reflection takes place. **2** the angle of attack at which the flow about an aerofoil changes abruptly, with corresponding abrupt changes in the lift and drag.

critical mass *noun* the minimum mass of fissile material that can sustain a nuclear chain reaction.

critical path *noun* a sequence of activities that forms part of a complex activity, the timing of which determines the expected completion time of the complex activity.

critical point *noun* **1** in chemistry, the stage at which the liquid and gas phases of a substance have the same density and are indistinguishable. **2** *NAmer* in mathematics, = STATIONARY POINT.

critical state *noun* in chemistry, the state of a substance when it is at the CRITICAL POINT.

critical temperature *noun* the temperature of a gas above which it cannot be liquefied by pressure alone.

criticise /'kritisiez/ *verb* see CRITICIZE.

criticism /'kritisiz(ə)m/ *noun* **1a** the act of criticizing, usu unfavourably. **b** a critical observation or remark. **c** a detailed or reasoned assessment; a critique. **2** the art or act of analysing and evaluating *esp* the fine arts, literature, or literary documents.

criticize *or* **criticise** /'kritisiez/ *verb trans* **1** to find fault with (somebody or something). **2** to consider the merits and demerits of (something, *esp* a literary or artistic work) and judge or evaluate it accordingly. ➤ *verb intrans* to criticize something or somebody.

critique /kri'teek/ *noun* a critical estimate or discussion, e.g. an article or essay. [French *critique* critic, criticism, from Greek *kritikē*, from *krinein* to judge]

critter /'kritə/ *noun dialect* a creature. [by alteration]

croak¹ /krohk/ *verb intrans* **1a** to give the characteristic cry of a frog or crow. **b** to speak in a hoarse throaty voice. **c** *archaic* to make gloomy predictions; to be pessimistic: *'I doubt our being able to do so much.' ... 'You croaking fellow! ... We shall be able to do ten times more'* — Jane Austen. **2** *informal* to die. ➤ *verb trans* **1** to utter (something) in a hoarse raucous voice. **2** to announce or forbode (something gloomy or momentous): *the raven ... that croaks the fatal entrance of Duncan* — Shakespeare. **3** *informal* to kill (somebody). ➤➤ **croaker** *noun.* [Middle English *croken*, of imitative origin]

croak² *noun* a deep hoarse cry characteristic of a frog or crow, or a sound resembling this. ➤➤ **croaky** *adj.*

Croat /'kroh-ət/ *noun* = CROATIAN.

Croatian /kroh'aysh(ə)n/ *noun* **1** a native or inhabitant of Croatia in SE Europe. **2** the form of Serbo-Croatian spoken by the Croatians and written in the Roman alphabet: compare BOSNIAN, SERB. ➤➤ **Croatian** *adj.*

croc /krok/ *noun informal* a crocodile.

crochet¹ /'krohshay/ *noun* crocheted work. [early French *crochet* hook, crochet, dimin. of *croche* hook, of Scandinavian origin]

crochet² *verb* (**crocheted** /'krohshayd/, **crocheting** /-shaying/) ➤ *verb trans* to make (a garment or design) by drawing a single continuous yarn or thread into a pattern of interlocked loops using a hooked needle. ➤ *verb intrans* to do crochet work. ➤➤ **crocheter** /'krohshayə/ *noun.*

croci /'krohkie, 'krohsie/ *noun* pl of CROCUS.

crocidolite /kroh'sidəliet/ *noun* a blue or green asbestos mineral that is a fibrous silicate of sodium and iron. [German *Krokydolith*, from Greek *krokyd-, krokys* nap on cloth + German *-lith* -LITE]

crock¹ /krok/ *noun Brit, informal* **1** an elderly infirm person. **2** an old, often broken-down, vehicle. [Middle English *crok* old disabled animal, prob of Scandinavian origin]

crock² *noun* **1** a thick earthenware pot or jar. **2** a piece of broken earthenware used *esp* to cover the bottom of a flowerpot. **3** an item of crockery. **4** *chiefly NAmer, informal* a lie, fabrication, or piece of nonsense. [Old English *crocc*]

crock³ *verb trans informal* **1** (*also* + up) to injure, weaken, or disable (somebody or something): *I've crocked my back.* **2** *NAmer* to make (somebody) drunk: *The man was crocked.* ➤ *verb intrans informal* (*also* + up) to break down; to collapse.

crockery /'krokəri/ *noun* earthenware or china tableware, *esp* for everyday domestic use.

crocket /'krokit/ *noun* an architectural ornament in the form of curved and bent foliage placed at regular intervals on the edge of a gable, spire, or canopy. [Middle English *croket* from early French *croquet,* dimin. of *croc* hook, of Scandinavian origin]

crocodile /'krokədiel/ *noun* **1a** any of several species of tropical or subtropical large voracious semi-aquatic reptiles with a thick skin and long body: genus *Crocodylus* and other genera. **b** a CROCODILIAN of any kind. **2** (*often before a noun*) the skin of a crocodile, leather prepared from this, or an imitation of it: *Crocodile handbags.* **3** *Brit* a line of people, e.g. schoolchildren, walking in pairs. [Middle English *cocodrille* via Old French and medieval Latin from Latin *crocodilus,* from Greek *krokodilos* lizard, crocodile, from *krokē* pebble + *drilos* worm]

crocodile clip *noun* a peg-like metal clip with long notched edges, used for joining wires or making other electrical connections.

crocodile tears *pl noun* false or affected tears; hypocritical sorrow. [from ancient belief that crocodiles shed tears over their prey]

crocodilian /krokə'dili-ən/ *noun* any of an order of reptiles including the crocodiles, alligators, caymans, gavial, and related extinct animals: order Crocodylia. ➤➤ **crocodilian** *adj.*

crocus /'krohkəs/ *noun* (*pl* **crocuses** *or* **croci** /'krohkie, 'krohsie/) an early-flowering plant of the iris family bearing a single brightly-coloured flower: genus *Crocus.* [Latin genus name from Greek *krokos* saffron, of Semitic origin]

Croesus /'kreesəs/ *noun* a fabulously wealthy person. [from Croesus, king of Lydia in the mid-sixth cent. BC, famed for his wealth]

croft /kroft/ *noun* **1** *Brit* a small enclosed field usu adjoining a house. **2** a small farm, *esp* in Scotland, worked by a tenant. ➤➤ **crofter** *noun.* [Old English; related to Old English *crēopan* CREEP¹]

crofting *noun Brit* the system of working the land as crofts.

Crohn's disease /krohnz/ *noun* a chronic inflammatory disease of the bowel, causing scarring and thickening of the bowel wall, fistulae, and abscesses, with resultant malabsorption of nutrients. [named after B B *Crohn* d.1983, US physician, who was one of the first to describe it]

croissant /'krwahsong (*French* krwasɔ̃)/ *noun* a flaky rich crescent-shaped roll of bread or yeast-leavened pastry. [French *croissant* crescent, from Old French *creissant*: see CRESCENT¹]

Croix de Guerre /krwa də 'geə/ *noun* the highest French military decoration. [French *Croix de Guerre* cross of war]

Cro-Magnon /,kroh 'manyon, 'magnən/ *noun* (*used before a noun*) denoting a tall erect race of human beings who appeared about 35,000 years ago, and flourished from the Upper Palaeolithic to Neolithic period, known from skeletal remains found chiefly in S France and classified as the same species as recent human beings.

Editorial note
Cro-Magnon is a rock shelter in the Dordogne, southwest France, which gave its name to the modern form of human (Homo sapiens) after several late Palaeolithic burials were discovered there in 1868. The skeletons indicated tall, muscular people with a long skull, high forehead, and broad face, with prominent chin — Dr Paul Bahn.

[named after *Cro-Magnon,* a cave near Les Eyzies, France, where remains were found]

crombec /'krombek/ *noun* any of several species of small African warblers with colourful plumage and a very short tail: genus *Sylvietta*. [via French from Dutch *krom* crooked + *bek* beak]

cromlech /'kromlek/ *noun* **1** *no longer used technically* in Wales, a megalithic burial chamber consisting of a flat stone laid on upright ones; = DOLMEN. **2** in Brittany, a circle of standing stones. [Welsh *cromlech*, from *crom* curved + *llech* slab]

crone /'krohn/ *noun* a withered old woman. [Middle English from early French *carogne* carrion, ultimately from Latin *carn-*, *caro* flesh]

croning /'krohning/ *noun esp* in the US or Australia, a feminist celebration honouring older women. [punning blend of CROWN[1] and CRONE]

crank /krangk/ *adj Aus, NZ, informal, dated* **1** unsound or unfit. **2** dishonest; fraudulent. [perhaps from CRANK[3], or via German or Yiddish *krank* ill, from early High German *kranc* weak]

crony /'krohni/ *noun* (*pl* **cronies**) *informal, often derog* a close friend, *esp* of long standing; a chum: *a crony of former president Marcos*; *They're old cronies*. [alteration of obsolete *chrony*, prob from Greek *chronios* long-lasting, from *chronos* time]

cronyism *noun* favouritism shown to friends, *esp* in making political appointments.

crook[1] /krook/ *noun* **1** an implement or part of something having a bent or hooked shape. **2a** a shepherd's staff. **b** a bishop's crozier. **3** a bend or curve: *She carried the parcel in the crook of her arm*. **4** *informal* a person given to criminal practices; a thief or swindler. ⟩⟩ **crookery** *noun*. [Middle English *crok* from Old Norse *krōkr* hook]

crook[2] *verb trans* to bend (something): *crook one's finger*. ⟩ *verb intrans* to curve or wind.

crook[3] *adj Aus, NZ, informal* **1** ill; sick. **2** not in correct working order. **3** bad; unpleasant. ✱ **go crook** *Aus, NZ, informal* (*usu* + *at/on*) to lose one's temper. [shortening of CROOKED, perhaps influenced by CRANK[3]]

crookback *noun archaic* a person with a hump; a hunchback: *this scolding crookback … misshapen Dick* — Shakespeare.

crooked /'krookid/ *adj* **1** having a crook or curve; bent. **2** *informal* not morally straightforward; dishonest. **3** *Aus, NZ, informal* bad-tempered; angry. ⟩⟩ **crookedly** *adv*, **crookedness** *noun*.

croon[1] /kroohn/ *verb intrans* to sing, *usu* sentimental popular songs, in a low or soft voice. ⟩ *verb trans* to sing (a song) in a crooning manner. ⟩⟩ **crooner** *noun*. [Middle English *croynen* to bellow, from early Dutch *cronen*; related to Old English *cran* CRANE[1]]

croon[2] *noun* **1** an instance of singing in a low or soft voice. **2** a crooning voice or tone.

crop[1] /krop/ *noun* **1** a plant product that can be grown and harvested extensively, or the total production of it: *a large apple crop*. **2** a group or quantity appearing at any one time: *a new crop of students*; *Any change in procedure will produce a fresh crop of mistakes and misunderstandings*. **3** a riding whip, *esp* with a short stock and a loop on the end, or its stock or handle. **4** a short haircut. **5** a pouched enlargement of the gullet of many birds in which food is stored and prepared for digestion. **6** the whole tanned hide of an animal. [Old English *cropp*]

crop[2] *verb* (**cropped, cropping**) ⟩ *verb trans* **1a** to cut (hair) short: *the new cropped style*. **b** said of an animal: to graze on (grass, etc). **c** to cut and harvest (mature plant produce). **d** to trim (a photograph). **2a** to grow (something) as a crop: *We plan to crop more wheat next year*. **b** to plant (land) so as to bear a crop. ⟩ *verb intrans* **1** to yield or bear a crop. **2** said of an animal: to graze on grass, etc.

crop circle *noun* a ring or other pattern of flattened corn appearing within a field of standing corn, *esp* in S England, and attributed to meteorological, paranormal, or extraterrestrial forces, or to hoaxers.

crop-dusting *noun* the spraying of crops from the air with fertilizer, insecticide, or fungicide in powdered form.

crop-eared *adj* **1** said *esp* of a dog or horse: having the tops of the ears cut off, e.g. for identification. **2** used contemptuously of the 17th-cent. Roundheads, in reference to their severely cropped hair.

cropper[1] /'kropə/ *noun* a plant that yields a crop of a usu specified quality or amount.

cropper[2] ✱ **come a cropper 1** *informal* to have a fall: *I tripped over the wire and came a cropper*. **2** *informal* to suffer a severe reversal: *A lot of those speculators came a cropper*. [prob from English dialect *crop neck*, from CROP[1]]

crop rotation *noun* the practice of growing different crops in succession on the same land, chiefly to preserve the productive capacity of the soil.

crop top *noun* a woman's close-fitting vest-like garment *esp* of cotton jersey, cut short beneath the bust to leave the midriff bare.

crop up *verb intrans informal* to happen or appear unexpectedly or casually: *Another problem has cropped up*.

croque-monsieur /krok mə'syuh/ *noun* a cheese and ham sandwich grilled or fried. [French *croque-monsieur*, literally 'munch-man']

croquet[1] /'krohkay/ *noun* **1** a game in which wooden balls are driven by mallets through a series of hoops set out on a lawn, the winner being the first player to hit the central post. **2** the driving away of an opponent's croquet ball by striking one's own ball placed against it. [French dialect *croquet* hockey stick, from early French, dimin. of *croc* hook, of Scandinavian origin]

croquet[2] *verb trans* (**croqueted** /'krohkayd/, **croqueting** /-kay-ing/) to drive away (an opponent's croquet ball) by striking one's own ball placed against it.

croquette /kroh'ket/ *noun* a small piece of minced meat, vegetable, etc coated with breadcrumbs and fried in deep fat. [French *croquette* from *croquer* to crunch, of imitative origin]

crore /kraw/ *noun* a unit of currency in India worth 10 million rupees or 100 lakhs. [Hindi *karōr*]

crosier or **crozier** /'krohzi-ə/ *noun* a staff resembling a shepherd's crook, carried by bishops as a symbol of office. [Middle English *croser* crosier-bearer, from early French *crossier*, from *crosse* crosier, of Germanic origin]

cross[1] /kros/ *noun* **1a** a figure formed by two intersecting lines + or x. **b** the figure (x) used to mark something incorrect in a school exercise, etc (compare TICK[1]), or to represent a kiss in a letter, etc. **2a** an upright stake with a transverse beam used, *esp* by the ancient Romans, for execution. **b** (**the Cross**) in Christianity, the cross on which Christ was crucified, or the Crucifixion itself. **c** the Cross as a symbol of Christianity, or any representation of it. **d** a monument in the form of a cross. **3a** the crossing of dissimilar individuals, or the resulting hybrid. **b** (+ between) somebody or something that combines characteristics of two different types or individuals. **4** a hook delivered over the opponent's lead in boxing. **5** the act of crossing the ball in football. ✱ **at cross purposes** misunderstanding each other or having different objectives. **have one's cross to bear** to have personal troubles to bear like everybody else [from the practice of making someone condemned to crucifixion carry his cross to the place of execution]. **make the sign of the cross 1** said *esp* of a Roman Catholic: as an act of reverence, to indicate the shape of the Cross, gesturing towards one's forehead, centre body, and each shoulder in turn. **2** said of a priest, etc: to indicate the shape of the Cross with one's hand in blessing a congregation, etc. **on the cross** on the bias; diagonally. [Old English via Old Norse or Old Irish from Latin *cruc-*, *crux*]

cross[2] *verb trans* **1a** to lie or be situated across (something): *The path crosses two fields*. **b** said of one line, road, etc: to intersect (another). **2** to go across (e.g. a road, river, room, boundary): *Only two crossed the finishing line*. **3a** (+ off/out/through) to cancel (an item) by drawing a line across it. **b** to draw two parallel lines across (a cheque) so as to allow only direct payment into a bank account, not encashment. **c** to finish off (a letter *t* or *f*) with the horizontal bar. **4a** in sitting, to position (one's legs) so that one thigh is resting on the other. **b** to fold (one's arms) or place them crosswise. **5** to make the sign of the cross in front of (oneself). **6** to oppose or frustrate (somebody). **7** to hybridize (an animal or plant) by causing it to interbreed with one of a different kind. **8** to kick or pass (the ball) across the field in football. ⟩ *verb intrans* **1** said of two lines, etc: to lie or be across each other. **2** said of letters, messages, etc: to pass simultaneously in opposite directions before the sender of each has received the other. **3** said of plant or animal species: to interbreed or hybridize. **4** in football, to cross the ball. ✱ **cross my heart** used to guarantee the truth of what one is saying. **cross somebody's palm with silver** *often humorous* to pay somebody to tell one's fortune or perform some other service. **cross swords** (*often* + with) to come into conflict. **cross the floor** *Brit* to join the opposing party, or change parties, in Parliament. **get one's lines or wires crossed** *informal* to misunderstand something. ⟩⟩ **crosser** *noun*.

cross[3] *adj* **1** (*often* + with) angry; annoyed. **2** irritable; grumpy. ⟩⟩ **crossly** *adv*, **crossness** *noun*.

cross- *comb. form* forming words, denoting: **1** movement from one side to the other: *cross-channel services.* **2** transverse position: *crossbeams.* **3** interrelation or interaction: *cross-dating; cross-fertilization.* **4** the form of a cross: *crossroads; crossbones.*

crossbar *noun* a transverse bar, e.g. between goalposts.

crossbeam *noun* a beam lying transversely between beams positioned lengthways, e.g. in a roof.

cross bench *noun* any of the benches in the House of Lords for members who belong to neither government nor opposition parties. ⟫ **crossbencher** *noun.* [because the benches are at right angles to the government and opposition benches]

crossbill *noun* any of several species of finches whose bills have strongly curved crossed tips, adapted for extracting seeds from fir cones: genus *Loxia.*

crossbones *pl noun* two leg or arm bones placed or depicted crosswise: compare SKULL AND CROSSBONES.

crossbow *noun* a short bow mounted crosswise near the end of a wooden support and used, *esp* formerly, to fire bolts and stones. ⟫ **crossbowman** *noun.*

crossbred *adj* hybrid; *esp* produced by interbreeding two pure but different breeds, strains, or varieties: compare STRAIGHTBRED. ⟫ **crossbred** *noun.*

crossbreed¹ *verb* (*past tense and past part.* **crossbred**) ⟩ *verb trans* to hybridize or cross (two varieties or breeds of the same species). ⟩ *verb intrans* to undergo crossbreeding.

crossbreed² *noun* a hybrid.

cross-check¹ *verb* to check (information) for validity or accuracy by reference to more than one source.

cross-check² *noun* a check by reference to more than one source.

cross-country¹ *adj and adv* **1** proceeding over countryside rather than by roads: *cross-country rambling; cycle cross-country.* **2** said of a race: held over the countryside instead of over a track.

cross-country² *noun* (*pl* **cross-countries**) **1** cross-country running, horse-riding, etc. **2** a cross-country race.

cross-cultural *adj* **1** embracing different cultures: *meetings that make for better cross-cultural understanding.* **2** drawing a comparison between different cultures.

crosscurrent *noun* **1** a current in a river or the sea that flows across the main current. **2** a conflicting tendency: *political crosscurrents.*

crosscut¹ *verb trans* to cut across the grain of (wood).

crosscut² *noun* something that cuts across or through; *specif* a mine passage driven through a body of ore or from a shaft to a body of ore.

crosscut saw *noun* a saw designed to cut across the grain of wood: compare RIPSAW.

cross-dating *noun* the dating of archaeological finds from one site by relating them to material from a comparable site.

cross-dresser *noun* a transvestite. ⟫ **cross-dressing** *noun.*

crosse /kros/ *noun* a long-handled stick with a shallow triangular net of leather thongs at the end, used in lacrosse. [French *crosse* crosier, of Germanic origin]

crossed *adj* said of a telephone line: connected in error to two or more telephones.

cross-examine *verb trans* to question closely (a witness in a law court) in order to check answers or elicit new information. ⟫ **cross-examination** *noun,* **cross-examiner** *noun.*

cross-eye *noun* **1** a squint in which the eye turns towards the nose. **2** (*in pl*) eyes that squint inwards. ⟫ **cross-eyed** *adj.*

cross-fertilization *or* **cross-fertilisation** *noun* **1a** fertilization by the joining of ova with pollen or sperm from a different individual: compare SELF-FERTILIZATION. **b** cross-pollination. **2** interaction, *esp* of a broadening or productive nature.

crossfire *noun* **1** firing from two or more points in crossing directions. **2** rapid or heated interchange: *He was caught in the crossfire between his feuding parents.*

cross-grained *adj* **1** said of timber: having the grain or fibres running diagonally, transversely, or irregularly. **2** said of a person: difficult to deal with; intractable.

cross hair *noun* a fine wire or thread, usu one of two, seen through the eyepiece of an optical instrument and used as a reference.

crosshatch *verb trans* to shade (something) with a series of intersecting parallel lines. ⟫ **cross-hatching** *noun.*

crosshead *noun* **1** a sliding metal block between a piston rod and a connecting rod, *esp* in a steam engine. **2** a centred headline, *esp* between paragraphs in a newspaper column.

cross-index *verb trans* to provide (e.g. an item in a text) with a cross-reference. ⟫ **cross-index** *noun.*

cross infection *noun* **1** *esp* in a hospital, the transfer of an infection to patients suffering from different ones. **2** the transfer of infections between different species of plants or animals.

crossing *noun* **1** a journey across something, e.g. a strip of sea, a mountain range, etc: *a sea-crossing; Hannibal's crossing of the Alps.* **2a** part of a road marked by studs, stripes, etc, where pedestrians may cross; = PEDESTRIAN CROSSING. **b** a place where a railway crosses a road; = LEVEL CROSSING. **c** a place where roads, etc cross each other: *Turn right at the next crossing.*

crossing-over *noun* the interchange of genes between HOMOLOGOUS (pairing) chromosomes during meiotic cell division.

cross-legged /kros'legid, kros'legd/ *adv and adj* said of a person seated *esp* on the floor: with ankles crossed and knees bent outwards.

cross-link *noun* an atom, group, etc connecting parallel chains in a polymer or other complex chemical molecule. ⟫ **cross-linkage** *noun.*

cross-match *verb trans* to determine the compatibility of (a donor's and a recipient's blood) before transfusion. ⟫ **cross-matching** *noun.*

crossopterygian /krosoptə'rijiən/ *noun* any of a subclass (Crossopterygia) of fishes with fleshy lobe-shaped fins that are the probable ancestors of the amphibians, the COELACANTH being the only extant representative. [derivative of Greek *krossoi* tassels, fringe + *pteryg-, pteryx* wing, fin]

crossover¹ *noun* **1a** a crossing on a street or over a river. **b** a short track joining two adjacent railway lines. **2** an instance or product of genetic CROSSING-OVER. **3** the act or an instance of changing the style of popular music, *esp* to broaden its appeal, or of combining styles.

crossover² *adj* **1** representing a crossover in popular music: *a crossover album.* **2** having or combining two or more styles, functions, purposes, etc: *not quite a health food shop and not quite a supermarket; it's a crossover store.*

crosspatch *noun informal* a bad-tempered person. [CROSS³ + obsolete *patch* fool, of unknown origin]

crosspiece *noun* a transverse beam, joist, or bar.

crossply *adj* said of a tyre: having the cords arranged crosswise to strengthen the tread: compare RADIAL¹ (2). ⟫ **crossply** *noun.*

cross-pollination *noun* the transfer of pollen from one flower to the stigma of another: compare SELF-POLLINATION.

cross product *noun* in mathematics, = VECTOR PRODUCT.

cross-question *verb trans* **1** to cross-examine (a witness). **2** to question (somebody) intensively.

cross-refer *verb* (**cross-referred, cross-referring**) ⟩ *verb trans* **1** to direct (a reader) from one page or entry, e.g. in a book, to another. **2** to refer from (a secondary entry) to a main entry. ⟩ *verb intrans* to make a cross-reference.

cross-reference¹ *noun* an indication at one place, e.g. in a book or filing system, of the existence of relevant information at another place.

cross-reference² *verb trans* to provide (an item in a text, etc) with a cross-reference. ⟫ *verb intrans* to cross-refer.

crossroad *noun* (*usu in pl, but treated as sing. or pl*) **1** the place where two or more roads intersect. **2** a crucial point or stage, *esp* where a decision must be made: *She is at a crossroads in her career.*

crossruff /'krosruf/ *noun* a series of plays in a card game, *esp* whist or bridge, in which partners (or in bridge the declarer playing both his or her own hand and his or her partner's) alternately trump different suits and lead to the other partner's hand for that purpose: *We set up a crossruff in hearts and diamonds.*

cross-section *noun* **1** a surface made by cutting across something, *esp* at right angles to its length, or a drawing of one. **2** a representative sample: *a cross-section of society.* **3** the probability of an encounter between particles, resulting in a specified effect: *the ionization cross-section.* ⟫ **cross-sectional** *adj.*

cross-sell *verb trans* (*past tense and past part.* **cross-sold**) to sell (an additional product or service) to a client or customer who has already purchased some product or service: compare UPSELL.

cross-selling *noun* the marketing ploy of offering a range of additional products and services to existing customers.

cross-stitch[1] *noun* a stitch in the shape of an X formed by crossing one stitch over another, or needlework using such a stitch.

cross-stitch[2] *verb trans* to sew (something) using cross-stitches.

cross-subsidization *noun* the funding of one particular group or activity by money generated by a related group or activity. >>> **cross-subsidy** *noun*

cross-talk *noun* **1** unwanted signals in a communications channel or storage location that come from another channel or storage location. **2** rapid witty exchanges; repartee.

crosstie *noun NAmer* a railway sleeper.

cross training *noun* training of a sportsperson in other, usu related, sports in order to improve performance in their chosen sport.

crosstrees *pl noun* a pair of horizontal crosspieces on a mast to which supporting ropes are attached.

crosswalk *noun NAmer, Aus* a specially paved or marked path for pedestrians crossing a street or road: compare ZEBRA CROSSING.

crossways *adv* crosswise; diagonally.

crosswind /'kroswind/ *noun* a wind blowing in a direction not parallel to the course of a vehicle, aircraft, etc.

crosswise *adv* so as to cross something; across: *logs laid crosswise.*

crossword *noun* a puzzle in which words are entered in a pattern of numbered squares in answer to correspondingly numbered clues in such a way that the words reading horizontally have letters in common with those reading vertically where they meet or interact.

crossword puzzle *noun* = CROSSWORD.

crostini /kro'steenee/ *pl noun* small pieces of toast or fried bread with a savoury topping, served as canapés. [Italian *crostini*, pl of *crostino* little crust, ultimately from Latin *crusta* CRUST[1]]

crotal /'krotl/ *noun* see CROTTLE.

crotch /kroch/ *noun* **1** the angle between the inner thighs where they meet the human body. **2** a fork in a tree. >>> **crotched** *adj.* [prob alteration of CRUTCH]

crotchet /'krochit/ *noun Brit* a musical note with the time value of half a minim or two quavers. *NAmer* Also called QUARTER NOTE. [Middle English *crochet* hook, from early French: see CROCHET[1]]

crotchety /'krochiti/ *adj informal* bad-tempered or irritable. >>> **crotchetiness** *noun.* [CROTCHET in the sense 'idiosyncrasy']

croton /'kroht(ə)n/ *noun* **1** a tropical plant whose seeds yield an oil formerly used as a strong purgative: *Croton tiglium.* **2** any of a genus of plants of the spurge family: genus *Croton.* **3** a small tropical evergreen shrub with colourful leaves: *Codiaeum variegatum.* [Latin genus name, from Greek *krotōn* castor-oil plant]

crottle *or* **crotal** /'krotl/ *noun* any of several lichens found in Scotland, used to dye wool in tweed-making: *esp Parmelia saxatilis.* [Gaelic *crotal*]

crouch[1] /krowch/ *verb intrans* to lower the body by bending one's knees and bending the upper body forward. [Middle English *crouchen*, perhaps from early French *crochir* to become hook-shaped, from *croche*: see CROCHET[1]]

crouch[2] *noun* a crouching position.

croup[1] /kroohp/ *noun* inflammation of the larynx and trachea in children and babies, typically causing laboured, rasping breathing and a hoarse cough. >>> **croupous** /'kroohpəs/ *adj,* **croupy** *adj.* [English dialect *croup* to cry hoarsely, cough, prob of imitative origin]

croup[2] *noun* the rump or hindquarters, *esp* of a horse. [Middle English from Old French *croupe*, of Germanic origin]

croupier /'kroohpiay, 'kroohpi-ə/ *noun* an employee of a gambling casino who collects and pays out bets at the gaming tables.

Word history

French *croupier* pillion rider, literally 'rider on the croup of a horse', from *croupe*: see CROUP[2]. The word orig meant someone who stood behind a gambler and gave advice.

croustade /krooh'stahd/ *noun* a crisp shell of bread, pastry, potatoes, etc that is fried or baked and filled with food. [French *croustade* from Provençal *croustado*, from *crousto* crust]

croute /krooht/ *noun* **1** a round slice of crisply fried, baked, or toasted bread on which savouries may be served. **2** a pastry cover; a crust. [French *croûte* crust]

crouton /'kroohton/ *noun* a small cube of crisp toasted or fried bread served with soup or used as a garnish. [French *croûton*, dimin. of *croûte* crust, from Latin *crusta*]

Crow /kroh/ *noun* (*pl* **Crow** *or* **Crows**) **1** a member of a Native American people of the region between the Platte and Yellowstone rivers. **2** the Siouan language of this people. [Siouan *apsáloke* crow people]

crow[1] /kroh/ *noun* **1** any of several species of large birds with glossy plumage, a heavy beak, rounded wings, and a raucous cry, *esp* the CARRION CROW (*Corvus corone*) or HOODED CROW (*Corvus corone cornix*): genus *Corvus.* **2** *informal* an ugly old woman. ✳ **as the crow flies** in a direct line, usu as distinct from the overland route. **eat crow** *NAmer, informal* to be forced to accept humiliation or defeat; to eat humble pie. [Old English *crāwe*; related to Old English *crāwan* CROW[2]]

crow[2] *verb intrans* (*past tense* **crowed** *or* **crew**, *past part.* **crowed**) **1** said of a cock: to make its shrill long-drawn-out cry. **2** said *esp* of an infant: to utter sounds of happiness or pleasure. **3a** (+ over) to triumph over somebody in their defeat: *Her father's comfort ... will consist of his crowing over her and saying 'I always told you so!'* — Henry James. **b** (*often* + over/about) to brag about one's success: *crowing about her promotion.* [Old English *crāwan*; related to Old English *crāwe* CROW[1]]

crow[3] *noun* **1** the characteristic cry of the cock. **2** a triumphant cry.

crowbar *noun* an iron or steel bar for use as a lever that is wedge-shaped at the working end. [CROW[1] + BAR[1]; prob from the forked end, like a crow's foot, it sometimes has]

crowberry /'krohb(ə)ri/ *noun* (*pl* **crowberries**) **1** a low shrubby evergreen plant, *esp* of arctic or mountainous regions: *Empetrum nigrum.* **2** the tasteless black berry of this plant.

crowd[1] /krowd/ *noun* **1a** (*treated as sing. or pl*) a large number of people gathered together without order; a throng. **b** a mass of spectators: *playing before a 20,000-strong crowd.* **2** (**the crowd**) people in general: *the desire to stand out from the crowd and be different.* **3** a large number of things close together and in disorder; a huddle: *a crowd of telegraph poles.* **4** a specified social group: *the in crowd; He got in with a bad crowd.*

crowd[2] *verb intrans* **1** (*often* + round) to press close: *People crowded round to listen.* **2** to collect in numbers; to throng: *Spectators crowded onto the pitch; She couldn't sleep for the thoughts crowding into her head.* >>> *verb trans* **1a** to fill (a place) by pressing or thronging together: *The centre was crowded with Christmas shoppers.* **b** to force or thrust (objects) into a small space: *the tendency to crowd too much furniture into a room.* **2** (+ off/out of) said of a throng: to push (others) out of the way: *The army of fans crowded us off the pavement.* **3** to press close to (somebody) or jostle them: *Don't crowd him – he needs air.* **4** *informal* to put pressure on (somebody): *I can't think straight if you crowd me.* [Old English *crūdan*]

crowded /'krowdid/ *adj* **1** filled with numerous people or things: *the crowded shopping centre; hunting for something on his crowded desktop.* **2** full of events: *her crowded engagement diary; a life crowded with incident.* >>> **crowdedness** *noun.*

crowdie /'krowdi/ *noun* a fine-grained cottage cheese. [Scots, of unknown origin]

crowd in on *verb trans* to overwhelm (somebody): *She tried to shut out the fears that kept crowding in on her.*

crowd out *verb trans* **1** to exclude (somebody or something) by depriving them of space or attention: *allow one's business commitments to crowd out family duties.* **2** said of a crowd: to fill (a place, etc) to capacity: *The event proved unexpectedly popular and the venue was crowded out with enthusiasts.*

crowdpuller *noun chiefly Brit, informal* somebody or something that attracts a large audience or mass of spectators. >>> **crowdpulling** *adj.*

crowfoot *noun* any of several species of typically aquatic plants of the buttercup family, with lobed leaves shaped like a crow's foot: *esp Ranunculus aquatilis:* genus *Ranunculus.*

crown[1] /krown/ *noun* **1** a gold and jewel-encrusted headdress worn as a symbol of sovereignty. **2** (**the Crown**). **a** the government under a constitutional monarchy. **b** the sovereign as head of state, or sovereignty. **3** a reward of victory or mark of honour; *esp* the title representing the championship in a sport: *winners of this year's* *coveted crown.* **4** a wreath, band, or circular ornament for the head, *esp* worn as a symbol of victory. **5a** the topmost part of the skull or head. **b** the summit of a slope, mountain, etc. **c** the part of a hat or cap that covers the crown of the head. **d** the part of a tooth visible outside the gum, or an artificial substitute or covering for it. **e** the upper portion of a cut gem. **f** the middle of the road where there is a camber on either side. **g** the slight convex curve of a bowling green. **h** the upper part of the foliage of a tree or shrub. **i** the part of a flowering plant at which stem and root merge. **6** the high point or culmination: *the crown of human endeavour.* **7** a British coin worth 25 pence (formerly five shillings), now minted only for a commemorative purpose. **8** any of various foreign monetary units, e.g.: **a** the Czech or Slovak koruna. **b** the Swedish krona. **c** the Danish or Norwegian krone. **9** any of various paper or book sizes, e.g.: **a** (*in full* **metric crown**) the size 384×504mm. **b** (*in full* **crown octavo**) the size 186×123mm. **c** (*in full* **crown quarto**) the size 246×189mm. ⟩⟩ **crowned** *adj.* [Middle English *coroune, crowne,* via Old French *corone* from Latin *corona* wreath, crown, from Greek *korōnē*]

crown² *verb trans* **1** to place a crown on the head of (somebody), *esp* as a symbol of investiture: *In 1650, Christina had herself crowned 'king' rather than 'queen'.* **2** to recognize (somebody), usu officially, as the leader in a particular field, *esp* a sport: *crowned champion three years running.* **3** *literary* to surmount (something): *the battlemented structure that crowned the hill.* **4** to put a draughtsman on top of (another draughtsman) to make a king. **5** to bring (something) to a successful conclusion: *Success finally crowned her efforts.* **6** to put an artificial crown on (a tooth). **7** *informal* to hit (somebody) on the head: *A slate fell off the roof and crowned a passer-by.* ⟩ *verb intrans* said of a baby's head: to appear in the vaginal opening fully, before emerging. ✳ **to crown it all** as the final and worst of a series of misfortunes. [Middle English *corounen,* via Old French *coroner* from Latin *coronare,* from *corona*]

Crown Colony *noun* a colony of the Commonwealth over which the British government retains some control.

Crown Court *noun* a local criminal court in England and Wales having jurisdiction over serious offences.

Crown Derby *noun* a type of porcelain manufactured in Derby from the mid 18th to mid 19th cent., typically stamped with a D surmounted by a crown.

crowned head *noun* a king or queen: *the crowned heads of Europe.*

crown gall *noun* a plant disease that is destructive *esp* to fruit trees and roses and is caused by a bacterium, *Agrobacterium tumefaciens,* which forms tumorous enlargements just below the ground on the trunk or stem.

crown glass *noun* a glass of relatively low refractive index and dispersion, used *esp* in lenses.

crown green *noun Brit* a bowling green which slopes downwards slightly from its centre to its outer edge.

crown imperial *noun* a tall garden plant of the lily family, with usu orange bell-shaped flowers in a cluster of leaves at the top of the stem: *Fritillaria imperialis.*

crowning *noun* in obstetrics, the stage of labour when the baby's head passes through the vaginal opening.

crown jewels *pl noun* the jewels, e.g. crown and sceptre, belonging to a sovereign's regalia.

Crown Office *noun* in England and Wales, an office of the Supreme Court with the responsibility for deciding which cases are to be tried in the High Court.

crown of thorns *noun* a starfish of the Pacific region that is covered with long spines and feeds on the coral of coral reefs: *Acanthaster planci.*

crown prince *noun* a male heir apparent to a crown or throne.

crown princess *noun* **1** the wife of a crown prince. **2** a female heir apparent or heir presumptive to a crown or throne.

Crown Prosecution Service *noun* In England and Wales, a body set up in 1986 under the Director of Public Prosecutions to take over all prosecutions initiated by the police.

crown saw *noun* a saw with teeth at the edge of a hollow cylinder that is used to cut circular holes.

crown wheel *noun* a gearwheel of the kind used in motor-vehicle gears, whose teeth are at right angles to its face.

crow's-foot *noun* (*pl* **crow's-feet**) (*usu in pl*) any of the wrinkles round the outer corners of the eyes.

crow's nest *noun* a partly enclosed high lookout platform, e.g. on a ship's mast.

crow step *noun* (*usu in pl*) one of a series of steps forming the edge of a gable; = CORBIE STEP. ⟩⟩ **crow-stepped** *adj.*

croze /krohz/ *noun* **1** a groove made round the trimmed stave-ends of a barrel to receive the edge of the lid. **2** the cooper's tool used for making this groove. [perhaps French *creux, creuse* hollow]

crozier /'krohzi·ə/ *noun* see CROSIER.

CRT *abbr* cathode-ray tube.

cru /krooh (*French* kry)/ *noun* (*pl* **crus** /krooh (*French* kry)/) in France, a vineyard, or group of vineyards, used in the classification of certain fine French wines, e.g. Bordeaux. [French *crû* past part. of *croître* to grow]

cruces /'kroohseez/ *noun* pl of CRUX.

crucial /'kroohshəl/ *adj* **1** important or essential to the resolving of a crisis; decisive: *Talks are at a crucial stage.* **2** (*often* + to) of the greatest importance or significance: *Your contribution is crucial to the operation.* **3** *informal* wonderful or excellent. ⟩⟩ **crucially** *adv.*

Word history
French *crucial* from Latin *cruc-, crux* cross. Although *crucial* entered English in the early 18th cent. in the literal meaning 'cross-shaped', its modern senses did not appear until the 19th cent. They derived from Francis Bacon's Latin phrase *instantia crucis* 'instance of the cross' (i.e. a signpost at a fork in a road, where a decision has to be made), referring to an instance that settles the claims of two rival arguments.

crucian /'kroohsh(ə)n/ *noun* a small carp of a colour ranging from olive green to reddish brown, farmed in eastern Europe: *Carassius carassius.* [modification of Low German *karuse* via early High German from Lithuanian *karusis*]

crucian carp *noun* = CRUCIAN.

cruciate /'kroohshiayt/ *adj* **1** in anatomy, cross-shaped: *cruciate ligaments.* **2** said of a plant: having leaves or petals arranged in the form of a cross; cruciform. ⟩⟩ **cruciately** *adv.* [scientific Latin *cruciatus* from Latin *cruc-, crux* cross]

crucible /'kroohsibl/ *noun* **1** a vessel for melting or calcining (reducing, e.g. to powder; see CALCINE) a substance at a very high temperature. **2** a severe test: *During the next half-century and more, my race [black people] must continue passing through the severe American crucible* — Booker T Washington. **3** a situation in which interacting influences produce something new: *the encounter between the Arts and Crafts movement and pre-Raphaelitism that was the crucible of Art Nouveau.* [Middle English *corusible* from medieval Latin *crucibulum,* ultimately from Latin *cruc-, crux* CROSS¹]

crucifer /'kroohsifə/ *noun* **1** any of several species of plants of the mustard family, including the cabbage, stock, cress, etc: family Cruciferae. **2** a person who carries a cross, *esp* at the head of an ecclesiastical procession. ⟩⟩ **cruciferous** /krooh'sif(ə)rəs/ *adj.* [Latin *cruc-, crux* CROSS¹ + -FER]

crucifix /'kroohsifiks/ *noun* a representation of Christ on the cross. [Middle English from late Latin *crucifixus* the crucified Christ, past part. of *crucifigere* to crucify, from Latin *cruc-, crux* CROSS¹ + *figere* to fasten]

crucifixion /kroohsi'fiksh(ə)n/ *noun* **1** the act of crucifying. **2** (**Crucifixion**) the crucifying of Christ.

cruciform /'kroohsifawm/ *adj* forming or arranged in a cross. ⟩⟩ **cruciformly** *adv.* [Latin *cruc-, crux* CROSS¹ + -FORM]

crucify /'kroohsifie/ *verb trans* (**crucifies, crucified, crucifying**) **1** to execute (somebody) by nailing or binding their hands and feet to a cross and leaving them to die. **2** to cause (a person) anguish or agony: *The pain was crucifying.* **3** *informal* to defeat (a person or team) decisively. **4** to condemn, ridicule, or criticize (somebody) unmercifully: *The critics would crucify us.* [Middle English *crucifien* via Old French from late Latin *crucifigere:* see CRUCIFIX]

cruck /kruk/ *noun Brit* formerly, either of a pair of curved timbers forming a main roof support and extending to the ground: *cruck-framed roofs.* [Middle English *crokke,* prob variant of *crok:* see CROOK¹]

crud /krud/ *noun informal* **1** a deposit or incrustation of filth, grease, etc. **2** a contemptuous term for a person one dislikes. **3** rubbish; nonsense: *a lot of pretentious mould-be-academic crud.* ⟩⟩ **cruddy** *adj.* [Middle English *curd, crudd* CURD]

crude¹ /kroohd/ *adj* **1** existing in a natural state and unaltered by processing: *crude oil.* **2** said of language, behaviour, etc: vulgar; gross: *Their table manners were crude to say the least.* **3** rough or inexpert in plan or execution: *That's the proposal in crude outline.* **4** in statistics, tabulated without being broken down into classes: *a crude death rate.* ⟫ **crudely** *adv*, **crudeness** *noun*. [Middle English from Latin *crudus* raw, rough]

crude² *noun* a substance, *esp* petroleum, in its natural unprocessed state: *20,000 tonnes of crude.*

crudités /'kroohditay/ *pl noun* a dish of small pieces of raw carrot, onion, celery, etc cut into thin slices and served as an hors d'oeuvre, usu with a dip. [French *crudité* crudity, rawness, from Latin *cruditas*, from *crudus* raw, rough]

crudity /'kroohditi/ *noun* (*pl* **crudities**) **1** the quality of being crude; crudeness. **2** a crude remark.

cruel /'krooh·əl/ *adj* (**crueller**, **cruellest**, *NAmer* **crueler**, **cruelest**) **1** (*often* + to) liking to inflict pain or suffering; pitiless: *dog-owners who are cruel to their pets.* **2** causing suffering; painful: *cruel remarks; for I do see the cruel pangs of death right in thine eye* — Shakespeare. ⟫ **cruelly** *adv*, **cruelness** *noun*. [Middle English via Old French from Latin *crudelis*, from *crudus* raw, rough]

cruelty /'krooh·əlti/ *noun* (*pl* **cruelties**) **1** the quality of being cruel; a sadistic or callous turn of mind. **2** cruel behaviour, or an instance of it: *divorce on the grounds of mental cruelty.* [Middle English *cruelte* via Old French from Latin *crudelitas*, from *crudelis*: see CRUEL]

cruelty-free *adj* denoting cosmetics or related products that have been developed by methods not involving tests on animals.

cruet /'krooh·it/ *noun* **1** *Brit* a small container, e.g. a pot, shaker, or small bottle, for holding a condiment, esp salt, pepper, or mustard, at table. **2** *Brit* a set of cruets on a stand. **3** a vessel to hold wine or water for the Eucharist: *a pair of pewter Communion cruets.* [Middle English from Anglo-French, dimin. of Old French *crue*, of Germanic origin; related to Old English *crocc* CROCK²]

cruet stand *noun* = CRUET (2).

cruise¹ /'kroohz/ *verb intrans* **1** to travel by sea for pleasure. **2** to go about or patrol the streets without any definite destination: *a cruising taxi.* **3a** said of an aircraft: to fly at the most efficient operating speed. **b** said of a vehicle: to travel at an economical speed that can be maintained for a long distance. **4** to make progress easily: *They cruised to victory.* **5** *informal* to search, e.g. in public places, for a partner, *esp* a homosexual one. ⟫ *verb trans informal* to search (the streets) for a sexual partner, *esp* a homosexual one. [Dutch *kruisen* to cross, cruise, via early Dutch *crūce* cross, from Latin *cruc-*, *crux*]

cruise² *noun* the act or an instance of cruising; *esp* a sea voyage for pleasure.

cruise control *noun* a control in a motor vehicle that can be operated to select and maintain a constant speed without the use of the accelerator pedal.

cruise missile *noun* a long-distance low-flying missile that is guided by an inbuilt computerized navigation system and typically carries a nuclear warhead.

cruiser *noun* **1** a yacht or motor boat with passenger accommodation; = CABIN CRUISER. **2** a large fast lightly armoured warship. **3** *NAmer* a police patrol car.

cruiserweight *noun chiefly Brit* a professional boxer who weighs between 12st 7lb (about 79.4kg) and 13st 8lb (almost 86.2kg).

cruller /'krullə/ *noun NAmer* a small deep-fried cake made of twisted or curled dough. [Dutch *kruller* from *krullen* to curl]

crumb¹ /krum/ *noun* **1** a small fragment of bread, cake, biscuit, or cheese. **2** a small amount: *a crumb of comfort.* **3** the soft inner part of a loaf of bread, as distinct from the outer crust. **4** loose crumbly soil. **5** *NAmer, informal* a contemptuous term for somebody one despises. [Middle English *crumme*, from Old English *cruma*]

crumb² *verb trans* **1** to cover or thicken (food) with crumbs. **2** to break up (food or some other substance) into crumbs: *Add the crumbed biscuits to the melted mixture.*

crumble¹ /'krumbl/ *verb* (**crumbling**) ⟫ *verb trans* to break (something) into small pieces: *crumbling his bread between his fingers.* ⟫ *verb intrans* (*often* + away) to disintegrate: *crumbling masonry; Support for him began to crumble away.* [alteration of Middle English *kremelen*, frequentative of Old English *gecrymian* to crumble, from *cruma* CRUMB¹]

crumble² *noun* **1** a crumbly mixture of fat, flour, and sugar. **2** a dessert of stewed fruit with this topping: *apple crumble.*

crumbly¹ *adj* inclined to crumble: *crumbly bread; crumbly cheese.*

crumbly² *noun* (*pl* **crumblies**) *informal, humorous* an old person: *Very nice of you to invite an old crumbly like me.*

crumbs *interj chiefly Brit, informal* used to express surprise or consternation. [euphemism for CHRIST¹]

crumby /'krumi/ *adj* see CRUMMY.

crumhorn /'krumhawn/ *noun* see KRUMMHORN.

crummy *or* **crumby** /'krumi/ *adj* (**crummier**, **crummiest**) *informal* **1** disagreeable; inferior; squalid: *a crummy existence; crummy accommodation.* **2** ill: *feel crummy.* ⟫ **crummily** *adv*, **crumminess** *noun*. [Middle English *crumme*: see CRUMB¹]

crump¹ /krump/ *verb intrans* **1** to crunch. **2** *informal* to explode heavily. [imitative]

crump² *noun* **1** a crunching sound. **2** *informal* a shell or bomb.

crumpet /'krumpit/ *noun* **1** a small round cake made from an unsweetened leavened batter that is cooked on a griddle and usu toasted before serving. **2** *Brit, informal, offensive* women collectively as sexual objects: *a piece of crumpet.* [perhaps from Middle English *crompid cake* wafer, literally 'curled-up cake', from *crumped*, past part. of *crumpen* to curl up, from Old English *crump*, *crumb* crooked]

crumple¹ /'krumpl/ *verb trans* to crush (something) out of shape: *crumpled bedclothes; a mass of twisted crumpled metal.* ⟫ *verb intrans* **1** to become crumpled: *Satin crumples so easily.* **2** to collapse: *Opposition to the scheme suddenly crumpled.* **3** said of the face or features: to lose form or distort: *Her face crumpled at the news.* [frequentative of Middle English *crumpen*: see CRUMPET]

crumple² *noun* a wrinkle or crease made by crumpling.

crumple zone *noun* a part of a motor vehicle, *esp* the boot or the bonnet, which is designed to buckle on impact, thus protecting the passenger area by absorbing much of the force of that impact.

crunch¹ /krunch/ *verb trans* **1** to chew or bite (something) with a noisy crushing sound: *crunch popcorn.* **2** to cause (something) to make a crushing sound: *crunching the gravel underfoot.* **3** to make (one's way) with a crushing sound: *crunch one's way through the snow.* ⟫ *verb intrans* **1** to crunch something. **2** to make a crushing sound: *The car crunched across the gravel.* [alteration of *craunch*, prob of imitative origin]

crunch² *noun* **1** an act or sound of crunching. **2** (**the crunch**) *informal* the critical or decisive situation or moment: *When it came to the crunch he sided against me.*

cruncher *noun* **1** a crucially important or difficult issue. **2** *informal* a finishing blow; a coup de grâce. **3** a computer, program, or operator that can perform complex tasks at speed: compare NUMBER-CRUNCHER.

crunchy *adj* (**crunchier**, **crunchiest**) crisp; brittle. ⟫ **crunchiness** *noun*.

crupper /'krupə/ *noun* a leather loop passing under a horse's tail and buckled to the saddle to prevent the saddle from slipping forwards. [Middle English *cruper* from Old French *crupiere*, from *croupe*: see CROUP²]

crural /'krooərəl/ *adj* relating to the leg or thigh. [Latin *cruralis* from *crur-*, *crus* leg]

crusade¹ /krooh'sayd/ *noun* **1** (*usu* **the Crusades**) (*also in pl*) any of the medieval Christian military expeditions to win the Holy Land from the Muslims. **2** a reforming enterprise undertaken with zeal and enthusiasm: *a moral crusade.* [blend of early French *croisade* and Spanish *cruzada*, both from Latin *cruc-*, *crux* CROSS¹]

crusade² *verb intrans* to engage in a crusade: *crusading for better prison conditions.* ⟫ **crusader** *noun*.

cruse /kroohz/ *noun archaic* a small earthenware jar or pot for holding oil, water, etc. [Old English *crūse* pitcher]

crush¹ /krush/ *verb trans* **1** to alter or destroy the structure of (something) by pressure or compression: *He got his fingers crushed in the machinery.* **2** to reduce (something) to particles by pounding or grinding: *Crush a pound of digestive biscuits; crushed ice.* **3** to subdue or overwhelm (somebody or something): *crush a revolt; a crushing remark.* **4** (*often* + into/against) to crowd or push (people, animals, etc) into a confined space: *Goodness knows how many of us were crushed into that tiny lobby.* ⟫ *verb intrans* to become crushed: *Eggshells crush easily.* ⟫ **crushable** *adj*, **crusher** *noun*, **crushing** *adj*, **crushingly** *adv*. [Middle English *crusshen* from early French *cruisir*, of Germanic origin]

crush² *noun* **1** a crowding together, *esp* of many people. **2** a soft drink made from the juice of pressed fruit: *orange crush.* ✳ **have a crush on somebody** *informal* to be infatuated with somebody, *esp* somebody unsuitable or unattainable.

crush bar *noun* a bar in a theatre or opera house where drinks can be bought in the interval.

crush barrier *noun Brit* a barrier erected to control crowds.

crushed velvet *noun* velvet whose nap leans in a variety of directions, giving the fabric the appearance of having been squashed.

crust[1] /krust/ *noun* **1a** the hardened exterior of bread. **b** a piece of this or of bread grown dry or hard. **2** the pastry cover of a pie. **3a** a hard or brittle surface layer, e.g. of soil or snow. **b** the outer rocky layer of the earth. **c** a hard deposit on the skin; *esp* a scab. **d** a deposit built up on the inside of a wine bottle during long ageing. **4** a superficial hardness of behaviour: *He broke through her crust of reserve.* ⋙ **crustal** *adj.* [Middle English, from Latin *crusta* rind, shell, crust]

crust[2] *verb trans* to form a crust on, or encrust (something): *rocks crusted with barnacles.* ➤ *verb intrans* to form a crust: *Blood and matter crusted around the wound.*

crustacean /kru'staysh(ə)n/ *noun* any of a large subphylum of mostly aquatic arthropods, including the lobsters, crabs, and woodlice, with a carapace, a pair of appendages on each segment, and two pairs of antennae: subphylum Crustacea. ⋙ **crustacean** *adj,* **crustaceous** /-shəs/ *adj.* [Latin group name, neuter pl of *crustaceus,* from *crusta* rind, shell, CRUST[1]]

crusted *adj* covered with or having formed a crust.

crustie /'krusti/ *noun* see CRUSTY[2].

crustose /'krustohs/ *adj* denoting a lichen or alga that develops or resembles a crust.

crusty[1] *adj* (**crustier, crustiest**) **1** having a hard well-baked crust. **2** surly; uncivil; truculent. ⋙ **crustily** *adv,* **crustiness** *noun.*

crusty[2] *or* **crustie** *noun* (*pl* **crusties**) *informal* a young person of unkempt appearance who follows an alternative lifestyle, often involving squatting: *free washing facilities for all crusties* — New Musical Express.

crutch /kruch/ *noun* **1a** a staff of wood or metal typically fitting under the armpit to support a disabled person in walking. **b** any prop or support: *a device commonly resorted to as a crutch for a lame argument.* **2** the crotch of an animal or human: *I clapt my hand under his crutch and … pitched him head-foremost into the river* — Benjamin Franklin. **3** the part of a garment that covers the human crotch. [Old English *crycc*]

crux /kruks/ *noun* (*pl* **cruxes** *or* **cruces** /'kroohseez/) **1** an essential or decisive point: *the crux of the matter.* **2** a puzzling or difficult problem: *textual cruxes.* [Latin *cruc-, crux* CROSS[1]]

cruzeiro /krooh'zeəroh/ *noun* (*pl* **cruzeiros**) the former basic monetary unit of Brazil, divided into 100 centavos. [Portuguese *cruzeiro* large cross (because the coin was marked with a cross), from Latin *cruc-, crux* CROSS[1]]

cry[1] /krie/ *verb* (**cries, cried, crying**) ➤ *verb intrans* **1** to weep or sob. **2** *archaic or literary* to call loudly; to shout, e.g. in fear or pain: *when Agamemnon cried aloud* — T S Eliot. **3** said of a bird or animal: to utter a characteristic sound or call. **4** *informal* (+ out for) to require or suggest strongly a certain treatment, remedy, etc: *entries that cry out for a diagram or illustration.* ➤ *verb trans* **1** *literary* to utter (something) loudly. **2** said of a hawker: to proclaim (one's wares) publicly. ✳ **cry for the moon** to want the unattainable. **cry over spilt milk** to express vain regrets for what cannot be recovered or undone. **cry stinking fish** to belittle one's own product. **for crying out loud** *informal* used to express exasperation and annoyance. [Middle English *crien* via Old French from Latin *quiritare* to cry out for help (from a citizen), to scream, from *Quirit-, Quiris* Roman citizen]

cry[2] *noun* (*pl* **cries**) **1** a spell of weeping: *Have a good cry.* **2** an inarticulate utterance of distress, rage, pain, etc. **3** a loud shout. **4** a watchword or slogan: *The universal cry of France and of Europe in 1814 was … 'Assez de Bonaparte'* — Ralph Waldo Emerson. **5** a general public demand or complaint. **6** the characteristic sound or call of an animal or bird. ✳ **cry from the heart** a heartfelt appeal; = CRI DE COEUR. **in full cry** in pursuit.

cry- *or* **cryo-** *comb. form* forming words, denoting: cold; low temperature; freezing: *cryogenics.* [German *kryo-* from Greek, from *kryos* frost]

crybaby *noun* (*pl* **crybabies**) *informal* a person who cries or complains too easily or frequently.

cry down *verb trans* to disparage or depreciate (somebody or something).

crying ✳ **a crying shame** a shocking thing; a matter for great self-reproach: *It would be a crying shame to miss the opportunity.*

cryo- *comb. form* see CRY-.

cryobiology /,krieohbie'oləji/ *noun* the study of the effects of extremely low temperature on biological systems. ⋙ **cryobiological** /-'lojikl/ *adj,* **cryobiologist** *noun.*

cry off *verb trans* to call off (an agreement, etc). ➤ *verb intrans chiefly Brit* to withdraw; to back out.

cryogen /'krie-əjən/ *noun* a substance used in producing low temperatures; a refrigerant.

cryogenics *pl noun* (*treated as sing. or pl*) the physics of the production and effects of very low temperatures. ⋙ **cryogenic** *adj.*

cryolite /'krie-əliet/ *noun* a mineral consisting of sodium-aluminium fluoride, found in Greenland and used in making soda and aluminium.

cryonics /krie'oniks/ *pl noun* (*treated as sing. or pl*) the freezing procedure by which a patient is preserved after his or her legal death in the hope of restoration to life and health at some future time when medical science will have advanced sufficiently to bring this about. ⋙ **cryonic** *adj.* [shortening of CRYOGENICS]

cryoprecipitate /,krieohpri'sipitayt/ *noun* a precipitate obtained from a frozen solution thawing under controlled conditions, as Factor VIII, used in the treatment of haemophilia, is obtained from frozen blood.

cryoprotectant /,krie-ohprə'tekt(ə)nt/ *noun* a chemical, e.g. glycerol, or a mixture of chemicals, that is able to penetrate living cells and prevent their damage, e.g. from the formation of ice crystals, when they are subjected to low temperatures and cryopreservation.

cryostat /'krie-əstat/ *noun* an apparatus for maintaining a constant low temperature.

cryosurgery /,krieoh'suhj(ə)ri/ *noun* surgery in which extreme chilling is used to destroy or cut tissue.

crypt /kript/ *noun* a chamber, e.g. a vault, wholly or partly underground; *esp* a vault under the main floor of a church. [via Latin from Greek *kryptē,* fem of *kryptos* hidden, from *kryptein* to hide]

crypt- *or* **crypto-** *comb. form* forming words, with the meanings: **1** hidden; obscure: *cryptogenic.* **2** secret; unavowed: *cryptofascist.* [scientific Latin from Greek *kryptos:* see CRYPT]

cryptanalysis /kriptə'naləsis/ *noun* the deciphering of cryptograms or cryptographic systems. ⋙ **cryptanalyst** /-'tanəlist/ *noun,* **cryptanalytical** /-'litikl/ *adj.* [blend of CRYPTOGRAM + ANALYSIS]

cryptic /'kriptik/ *adj* **1** secret; occult. **2** intended to be obscure or mysterious. **3** serving to conceal: *cryptic coloration in animals.* ⋙ **cryptically** *adv.* [via late Latin from Greek *kryptikos,* from *kryptos:* see CRYPT]

crypto- *comb. form* see CRYPT-.

cryptococcosis /,kriptəko'kohsis/ *noun* an infectious disease that is caused by a fungus, *Cryptococcus neoformans,* and is characterized by the production of lumps or abscesses in the lungs, the tissues under the skin, joints, and *esp* the brain and MENINGES (membranes enclosing the brain and spinal cord). [*Cryptococcus,* genus name + -OSIS]

cryptocrystalline /,kriptoh'kristəlien/ *adj* having minute crystals distinguishable only under the microscope.

cryptogam /'kriptəgam/ *noun dated* a plant, e.g. a fern, moss, or fungus, reproducing by means of spores and not producing flowers or seed. ⋙ **cryptogamous** /krip'togəməs/ *adj.* [Greek *kryptos* + *-gamia* -GAMY]

cryptogamic /kriptə'gamik/ *adj* **1** relating to cryptogams. **2** in ecology, denoting a surface crust or desert soil consisting of mosses, lichens, and cyanobacteria (blue-green algae; see CYANOBACTERIUM), significant in the prevention of erosion.

cryptogenic /kriptə'jenik/ *adj* of obscure or unknown origin: *a cryptogenic disease.*

cryptogram /'kriptəgram/ *noun* a communication, etc in cipher or code. [French *cryptogramme,* from CRYPT- + -gramme -GRAM]

cryptography /krip'togrəfi/ *noun* **1** secret writing; cryptic symbolization. **2** the preparation of cryptograms, ciphers, or codes. ⋙ **cryptographer** *noun,* **cryptographic** /-'grafik/ *adj.* [Latin *cryptographia,* from CRYPTO- + -graphia -GRAPHY]

cryptology /krip'toləji/ *noun* **1** the scientific study of codes. **2** the art of devising a code. ⋙ **cryptologic** /-'lojik/ *adj,* **cryptological** /-'lojikl/ *adj,* **cryptologist** *noun.*

cryptomeria /kriptə'miəriə/ *noun* an evergreen tree of the cypress family with curved needle-like leaves and small cones that is a valuable timber tree of China and Japan: *Cryptomeria japonica.* [scientific Latin from CRYPTO- + Greek *meros* part; from the seeds of its cones being hidden within bracts]

cryptonym /'kriptənim/ *noun* a code name. ⋙ **cryptonymous** /-'toniməs/ *adj,* **cryptonymy** /-'tonimi/ *noun.*

cryptorchid /krip'tawkid/ *noun* a person affected with CRYPT-ORCHIDISM. [CRYPT- + Greek *orchid-, orchis* testicle]

cryptorchidism /krip'tawkidiz(ə)m/ *noun* a condition in which one or both of a boy's testes fail to descend normally.

cryptozoology /,kriptohzooh'oləji, -zooh'oləji/ *noun* the study of animals, e.g. the yeti, which are generally believed to be extinct or mythical. ⋙ **cryptozoologist** *noun.*

crystal¹ /'kristl/ *noun* **1a** a piece of a solid material with a naturally regular geometrical structure and plane faces that are symmetrically arranged: *graphite crystals.* **b** any solid chemical substance that has a regularly repeating internal arrangement of atoms or molecules. **c** an electronic component containing crystalline material used as a frequency-determining element. **d** a clear transparent mineral, *esp* colourless quartz. **e** = CRYSTAL BALL. **2a** a clear colourless glass of superior quality. **b** collectively, articles made of such glass: *the family crystal.* **c** the transparent cover over a watch or clock dial. [Middle English *cristal* via Old French and Latin from Greek *krystallos* ice, crystal]

crystal² *adj* **1** relating to or using a crystal: *a crystal microphone.* **2** composed of crystal glass: *a crystal chandelier.* **3a** composed of clear quartz: *a crystal ball.* **b** resembling clear quartz; clear; lucid: *crystal waters.*

crystal ball *noun* **1** a usu crystal sphere traditionally used by fortune-tellers. **2** a means or method of predicting future events.

crystal class *noun* any of 32 categories of crystals classified according to the disposition of atoms in the CRYSTAL LATTICE.

crystal-clear *adj* perfectly clear: *crystal-clear lakes; a crystal-clear tone; The instructions were crystal-clear.*

crystal-gazing *noun* **1** the art or practice of concentrating on a crystal ball to aid divination. **2** the attempt to predict future events or make difficult judgments, *esp* without adequate data. ⋙ **crystal-gazer** *noun.*

crystal glass *noun* = CRYSTAL¹ (2A).

crystalize *or* **crystalise** *verb see* CRYSTALLIZE.

crystall- *or* **crystallo-** *comb. form* forming words, denoting: crystal: *crystalliferous.* [Greek *krystallos*]

crystal lattice *noun* the symmetrical three-dimensional disposition of atoms within a crystal.

crystalline /'kristəlien/ *adj* **1** composed of crystal or crystals. **2** having the form or structure of a crystal. **3** like crystal in transparency or clarity: *the crystalline depths.* ⋙ **crystallinity** /-'liniti/ *noun.* [Middle English *cristallin* via French and Latin from Greek *krystallinos,* from *krystallos* CRYSTAL¹]

crystalline lens *noun* the lens of the eye in vertebrates.

crystallise *verb see* CRYSTALLIZE.

crystallite /'kristəliet/ *noun* a minute unspecific mineral form, *esp* in glassy volcanic rocks, that marks the first step in crystallization. ⋙ **crystallitic** /-'litik/ *adj.* [German *Kristallit* from Greek *krystallos* CRYSTAL¹]

crystallize *or* **crystallise** *or* **crystalize** *or* **crystalise** *verb trans* **1** to cause (a substance) to form crystals or assume crystalline form. **2** to cause (a thought or idea) to take a definite form: *I need time to crystallize my ideas.* **3** to coat or impregnate (fruit, etc) with sugar: *crystallized pears.* **4** to convert (a financial liability) from a FLOATING CHARGE to a FIXED CHARGE. ⋗ *verb intrans* to become crystallized. ⋙ **crystallizable** *adj,* **crystallization** /-'zaysh(ə)n/ *noun,* **crystallized** *adj.*

crystallo- *comb. form see* CRYSTALL-.

crystallography /kristə'logrəfi/ *noun* the science dealing with the forms and structures of crystals. ⋙ **crystallographer** *noun,* **crystallographic** /-'grafik/ *adj,* **crystallographically** /-'grafikli/ *adv.*

crystalloid¹ /'kristəloyd/ *noun* **1** a substance that forms a true solution and is capable of being crystallized: compare COLLOID. **2** a crystal-like accumulation of protein in a plant cell.

crystalloid² *adj* denoting or resembling a crystal.

crystal meth *noun* = METHAMPHETAMINE.

crystal set *noun* a simple early form of radio receiver that has no amplifier or source of power and uses a crystal detector to convert radio signals into a form that produces sound when passed through an earphone.

crystal system *noun* any of the six or, in some classifications, seven categories into which a crystal is placed according to the arrangement of its atoms.

cry up *verb trans* to praise (somebody or something) highly; to extol (them).

CS *abbr* **1** chartered surveyor. **2** Civil Service. **3** Court of Session.

Cs *abbr* the chemical symbol for caesium.

c/s *abbr* cycles per second.

CSA *abbr* Child Support Agency.

csardas /'chahdash/ *noun see* CZARDAS.

CSC *abbr* Civil Service Commission.

CSE *abbr Brit* Certificate of Secondary Education, a former public examination, a first-grade pass in which was equivalent to a GCE O level.

CS gas *noun* a gas that causes irritation and watering of the eyes when dispersed in the air as a means of controlling riots. [from the surname initials of Ben *Corson* b.1896, and Roger *Stoughton* d.1957, US chemists, who developed it]

CSIRO *abbr Aus* Commonwealth Scientific and Industrial Research Organization.

CSM *abbr* Company Sergeant Major.

CST *abbr NAmer, Can* Central Standard Time.

CT *abbr* **1** computerized *or* computed tomography. **2** Connecticut (US postal abbreviation).

ct *abbr* **1** carat. **2** cent. **3** (*often* **Ct**) court.

CTC *abbr* City Technology College.

ctenidium /ti'nidiəm/ *noun* (*pl* **ctenidia** /-'nidiə/) any of a mollusc's comb-like respiratory gills. [via scientific Latin from Greek *ktenidion,* dimin. of *kten-, kteis* comb]

ctenoid /'teenoyd/ *adj* said of the scales of fish: having a toothed margin: compare GANOID, PLACOID: *a ctenoid fish.* [Greek *ktenoeidēs,* from *kten-, kteis* comb]

ctenophore /'teenəfaw/ *noun* any of a phylum of sea animals superficially resembling jellyfishes but swimming by means of eight bands of fused cilia (hairlike structures; see CILIUM): phylum Ctenophora. ⋙ **ctenophoran** /tee'nofərən/ *adj and noun.* [scientific Latin *Ctenophora,* phylum name, from Greek *kten-, kteis* comb + -PHORE]

CTS *abbr* carpal tunnel syndrome.

CTT *abbr* capital transfer tax.

CU *abbr* **1** Christian Union. **2** in computing, control unit.

Cu *abbr* the chemical symbol for copper. [late Latin *cuprum* copper]

cu. *abbr* cubic.

cuadrilla /kwah'dree(l)yə/ *noun* (*treated as sing. or pl*) the team helping the matador in a bullfight. [Spanish *cuadrilla,* dimin. of *cuadra* square, from Latin *quadra*]

cub¹ /kub/ *noun* **1** the young of a flesh-eating mammal, e.g. a fox, bear, or lion. **2** (**Cub**) = CUB SCOUT. **3** *dated* a young man: *A loose-jointed, long-legged, tow-headed, jeans-clad countrified cub of about sixteen lounged in one day* — Mark Twain. [origin unknown]

cub² *verb intrans* (**cubbed, cubbing**) to give birth to cubs.

cubage /'kyoohbij/ *noun* cubic capacity or contents; = CUBATURE.

Cuban /'kyoohb(ə)n/ *noun* a native or inhabitant of Cuba in the West Indies. ⋙ **Cuban** *adj.*

Cuban heel *noun* a broad medium-high heel on a shoe or boot.

cubature /'kyoohbəchə/ *noun* **1** the determination of the volume of a solid. **2** cubic contents or capacity.

cubbing /'kubing/ *noun* the hunting of young foxes.

cubby /'kubi/ *noun* (*pl* **cubbies**) *chiefly NAmer* a snug space or room, e.g. one used as a children's play area; = CUBBYHOLE. [obsolete *cub* cattle-pen, from Dutch *kub* thatched roof]

cubbyhole *noun* a small room or enclosed space: *the cubbyhole under the stairs.* [obsolete *cub* cattle pen, related to Dutch *kub* thatched roof]

cube[1] /kyoohb/ *noun* **1a** a polyhedron with six equal square faces. **b** a block of anything so shaped: *a bouillon cube.* **2** the product got by multiplying a number by its square, represented by a superscript number 3: *The cube of 4 is 64.* [Middle English via French from Latin *cubus* from Greek *kybos* cube, vertebra]

cube[2] *verb trans* **1** to raise (a number) to the third power by multiplying it by its square. **2** to cut (food) into small cubes; = DICE[2] (1A). ⋙ **cuber** *noun.*

cubeb /'kyoohbeb/ *noun* **1** any of several species of tropical shrubs of the pepper family: *Piper cubeba* and other species. **2** the dried unripe berry of this shrub, used as a stimulant and diuretic, and formerly to treat infections of the urinary tract. [Old French *cubebe* via medieval Latin from Arabic *kubābah*]

cube root *noun* the number that, when cubed, produces the number in question: *The cube root of 27 is 3.*

cubic /'kyoohbik/ *adj* **1** cube-shaped. **2** denoting a crystal system characterized by three equal axes at right angles. **3a** three-dimensional. **b** used before a unit of length: denoting a volume equal to that of a cube whose edges are of the specified unit: *a cubic metre*; *6 cubic centimetres.* **4** relating to or involving the cube of a quantity: *a cubic equation.*

cubical *adj* cubic; *esp* shaped like a cube. ⋙ **cubically** *adv.*

cubicle /'kyoohbikl/ *noun* **1** a small partitioned space or compartment: *changing cubicles.* **2** a sleeping compartment partitioned off from a large room. [Latin *cubiculum* bedroom, from *cubare* to lie, recline]

cubiform /'kyoohbifawm/ *adj* cube-shaped. [Latin *cubus* CUBE[1] + -FORM]

cubism /'kyoohbiz(ə)m/ *noun* a 20th-cent. art movement that abandoned perspective represented from a single viewpoint by displaying several aspects of the same object simultaneously through the device of interlocking planes.

Editorial note ──────────

Cubism was the decisive movement in early 20th-cent. art. Picasso and Braque, the two key cubists – 'like climbers roped together' – abandoned the perspective box of post-Renaissance painting. In its place, they substituted forms and space constructed out of angular planes and facets, flattened against the picture plane. From this novel method of building a picture much modernist art developed — Martin Gayford.

⋙ **cubist** *adj,* **cubist** *noun,* **cubistic** /kyooh'bistik/ *adj.* [French *cubisme*, from *cube* (see CUBE[1]) + *-isme* -ISM]

cubit /'kyoohbit/ *noun* any of various ancient units of length based on the length of the forearm from the elbow to the tip of the middle finger: *The length of the Ark shall be three hundred cubits* — Bible. [Middle English from Latin *cubitum* elbow, cubit]

cubital /'kyoohbitəl/ *adj* relating to the forearm or elbow. [Middle English from Latin *cubitalis* from *cubitum* elbow, forearm]

cuboid[1] /'kyoohboyd/ *adj* cube-shaped. ⋙ **cuboidal** /kyooh'boydl/ *adj.*

cuboid[2] *noun* **1** a three-dimensional geometric shape having six rectangular faces at right angles to each other. **2** an approximately cube-shaped bone that is the outermost of the bones of the ankle.

cuboid bone *noun* = CUBOID[2] (2).

cub reporter *noun informal, dated* a junior newspaper reporter.

Cub Scout *noun* a member of the most junior section of the Scout Association.

cucking stool /'kuking/ *noun* a seat to which offenders were formerly tied to be pelted, jeered at, or plunged into water. [Middle English *cucking stol*, literally 'defecating chair'; because a commode was often used for the purpose]

cuckold[1] /'kukohld/ *noun* a man whose wife is adulterous, traditionally a figure of fun. [Middle English *cokewold*, prob from Old French *cucuault*, from *cucu* CUCKOO[1]; from the idea of invading somebody else's nest]

cuckold[2] *verb trans* said of a man: to make a cuckold of (a married man) by having an adulterous relationship with his wife. ⋙ **cuckoldry** /-ri/ *noun.*

cuckoo[1] /'kookooh/ *noun* (*pl* **cuckoos**) **1a** a greyish brown European bird that lays its eggs in the nests of small songbirds, which hatch them and rear the offspring: *Cuculus canorus.* **b** any of a large family of related birds: family Cuculidae. **2** the characteristic

two-note call of the male cuckoo. [Middle English *cuccu* from Old French *cucu*, imitative of the bird's call]

cuckoo[2] *adj informal* insane; crazy.

cuckoo clock *noun* a clock containing a mechanical cuckoo on a spring, that shoots out on the hour and delivers the appropriate number of cuckoo calls.

cuckooflower *noun* a European and American plant of the mustard family with lilac flowers, which grows in wet places: *Cardamine pratensis.* [from its flowering when the cuckoo is first heard calling]

cuckoopint *noun* a European arum that has a pale green leaflike bract surrounding tiny purple flowers, and bears a cluster of red berries: *Arum maculatum.* [Middle English *cuccupintel*, from *cuccu* (see CUCKOO[1]) + *pintel* PINTLE]

cuckoo spit *noun* a frothy secretion exuded on plants by the larva of a froghopper.

cucumber /'kyoohkumbə/ *noun* **1** a climbing plant cultivated as a garden vegetable for its long green edible fruit: *Cucumis sativus.* **2** a fruit of this plant, used as a vegetable, *esp* in salads: *A cucumber should be well sliced, and dressed with pepper and vinegar, and then thrown out, as good for nothing* — Dr Johnson. ✴ **as cool as a cucumber** perfectly calm and composed. [Middle English from early French *cocombre*, from Latin *cucumer-, cucumis*]

cucurbit /kyooh'kuhbit/ *noun chiefly NAmer* a plant of the cucumber family: family Cucurbitaceae. ⋙ **cucurbitaceous** *adj.* [Middle English *cucurbite* via French from Latin *cucurbita* gourd]

cud /kud/ *noun* food brought up into the mouth by a ruminating animal from its first stomach to be chewed again. ✴ **chew the cud 1** said of a ruminant animal: to re-chew partly digested food. **2** to turn things over in the mind; to ruminate: *Which sentiment being a pretty hard morsel … we shall leave the reader to chew the cud upon it to the end of the chapter* — Henry Fielding. [Old English *cwudu*]

cuddie /'kudi/ *noun* see CUDDY.

cuddle[1] /'kudl/ *verb trans* to hold (somebody) close for warmth or comfort or in affection. ⋗ *verb intrans* (*often* + up to) to lie close; to nestle or snuggle: *The child cuddled up to her mother.* [origin unknown]

cuddle[2] *noun* an act of cuddling: *Here, give us a cuddle.*

cuddlesome /'kudls(ə)m/ *adj* cuddly.

cuddly /'kudl·i/ *adj* (**cuddlier, cuddliest**) **1** attractively soft and plump. **2** enjoying a cuddle: *He was never a cuddly child.*

cuddy /'kudi/ *or* **cuddie** *noun* (*pl* **cuddies**) *Brit, dialect* **1** a donkey. **2** a stupid person. [perhaps from *Cuddy*, nickname for *Cuthbert*]

cudgel[1] /'kuj(ə)l/ *noun* a short heavy club. ✴ **take up the cudgels** to engage vigorously in a defence: *always ready to take up the cudgels on behalf of some oppressed minority.* [Old English *cycgel*]

cudgel[2] *verb trans* (**cudgelled, cudgelling,** *NAmer* **cudgeled, cudgeling**) to beat (somebody) with or as if with a cudgel. ✴ **cudgel one's brains** to force oneself to a supreme effort of cogitation or recollection.

cudweed /'kudweed/ *noun* a plant of the daisy family with silky or woolly foliage: genera *Gnaphalium* and *Filago.*

cue[1] /kyooh/ *noun* **1a** a signal to a performer to begin a specific speech or action. **b** something serving a comparable purpose; a hint. **2** in psychology, a feature of something that determines the way in which it is perceived. **3** a facility in video or audio equipment for feeding a recording through at high speed and picking it up at a preselected point. ✴ **on cue** at exactly the right time: *Jack arrived right on cue, just as we were about to serve dinner.* [prob from *qu,* abbr of Latin *quando* when, used as a direction in actors' copies of plays]

cue[2] *verb trans* (**cuing, cueing**) **1** to give a cue to (somebody); to prompt (them): *Could you cue me in?* **2** to serve as a prompt or reminder to (somebody): *He had all his points on a postcard, to cue him in case he had a blank.* **3** to set audio or video equipment to play (a preselected section of a recording).

cue[3] *noun* a long tapering rod for striking the ball in billiards, snooker, etc. ⋙ **cueist** *noun.* [variant of QUEUE[1]]

cue[4] *verb* (**cuing, cueing**) ⋗ *verb trans* to strike (a ball) with a cue. ⋗ *verb intrans* to use a cue.

cue ball *noun* the ball in billiards, snooker, etc that is struck by a cue.

cue card *noun* a card held up alongside a television camera for a newscaster, etc to read from while appearing to be looking into the camera.

cuesta /'kwestə/ *noun* (*pl* **cuestas**) a hill or ridge with a steep face on one side and a gentle slope on the other. [Spanish *cuesta* from Latin *costa* side, rib]

cuff[1] /kuf/ *noun* **1** a fold or band at the end of a sleeve which encircles the wrist. **2** *chiefly NAmer* a turned-up hem of a trouser leg. **3** *informal* (*usu in pl*) a handcuff. * **off the cuff** in reference either to speaking in public or to pronouncing on some matter: without preparation; impromptu, as though from notes hastily made on one's shirt cuff. ≫ **cuffed** *adj*. [Middle English in the sense 'glove, mitten'; previous history unknown]

cuff[2] *verb trans* to strike (somebody), *esp* with or as if with the palm of the hand. [perhaps from CUFF[1], in the obsolete sense 'glove']

cuff[3] *noun* a blow with the hand, *esp* when open; a slap.

cuff link *noun* an ornamental device consisting of two linked parts used to fasten a shirt cuff.

Cufic /'koohfik, 'kyoohfik/ *noun* see KUFIC.

cui bono /kwee 'bonoh/ *phrase* a principle that probable responsibility for an act or event lies with somebody having something to gain. [Latin *cui bono* to whose advantage?]

cuirass /kwi'ras/ *noun* **1** formerly, a piece of armour consisting of a joined backplate and breastplate. **2** an artificial ventilator that encloses the trunk and forces air into and out of the lungs. [Middle English *curas* via French from late Latin *coreaceus* leathern, from Latin *corium* skin, leather, of which a cuirass was orig made]

cuirassier /kwirə'siə/ *noun* formerly, a cavalry soldier wearing a cuirass.

cuisine /kwi'zeen/ *noun* **1** a manner of preparing or cooking food, *esp* as typical of a certain country or region. **2** the food so prepared and cooked: *We enjoy Malay cuisine.* [French *cuisine* kitchen, from late Latin *coquina*: see KITCHEN]

cuisse /kwis/ *noun* formerly, a piece of armour for the front of the thigh. [Middle English *cusseis* (pl) from early French *cuissaux*, pl of *cuissel*, from *cuisse* thigh, from Latin *coxa* hip]

culch /kulch/ *noun* see CULTCH.

Culdee /'kul'dee/ *noun* a member of any of a number of small religious communities living a reclusive life without monastic vows, loosely attached to the ancient Celtic Church and continuing in Scotland till the 14th cent., when they were absorbed into regular religious orders. [Middle English via medieval Latin from early Irish *céle dé* companion of God]

cul-de-sac /'kul di sak/ *noun* (*pl* **culs-de-sac** /'kul/ *or* **cul-de-sacs** /saks/) **1** a street, usu residential, closed at one end. **2** a dead end; an impasse. [French *cul-de-sac*, orig in anatomy, literally 'bottom of a bag']

-cule *suffix* forming nouns, denoting: a small example of the thing specified: *animalcule; fascicule*. [via French *-cule* from Latin *-culus*, dimin. suffix]

culex /'kyoohleks/ *noun* (*pl* **culices** /'-liseez/) any of a large widely distributed genus of mosquitoes that includes the common house mosquito (*Culex pipiens*) of Europe and N America: genus *Culex*. ≫ **culicine** *adj and noun*. [via scientific Latin from Latin *culex* gnat]

culinary /'kulin(ə)ri/ *adj* relating to the kitchen or cookery. [Latin *culinarius* from *culina*: see KILN]

cull[1] /kul/ *verb trans* **1** to control the size of a population of (animals) by killing a limited number. **2** to identify and remove the rejects from (a flock, herd, etc) for slaughter. **3** to select (a body of people or things) from a source or a range of sources: *a linguistic analysis of material culled from various radio interviews.* ≫ **culler** *noun*. [Middle English *cullen* via French from Latin *colligere*: see COLLECT[1]]

cull[2] *noun* **1** an operation to cull animals. **2** a livestock animal selected for culling.

cullender /'kuləndə/ *noun* see COLANDER.

cullet /'kullit/ *noun* broken or waste glass added to new material in glass manufacture, to increase the rate of melting and as a means of recycling glass. [alteration of obsolete *collet*, literally 'neck', glass-making term for glass left on the blowing iron when the finished article is removed]

culm[1] /kulm/ *noun* coal dust or slack. [Middle English, perhaps from Old English *col* COAL]

culm[2] *noun* the hollow jointed stem of a grass or similar plant. [Latin *culmus* stalk]

culminant /'kulminənt/ *adj* said of a celestial body: on the meridian.

culminate /'kulminayt/ *verb intrans* **1** said of a celestial body: to be at the meridian; to be directly overhead. **2** (*often + in*) to reach the highest or a climactic or decisive point: *He had had no love affair since that which culminated in his marriage* — Theodore Dreiser. ≫ **culmination** /-'naysh(ə)n/ *noun*. [medieval Latin *culminatus*, past part. of *culminare* to exalt, crown, from *culmin-*, *culmen* top]

culottes /kyoo'lots/ *pl noun* women's knee-length shorts, cut very full so as to resemble a skirt. [French *culotte* breeches, dimin. of *cul* backside, from Latin *culus*]

culpable /'kulpəbl/ *adj* meriting condemnation or blame: *culpable negligence.* ≫ **culpability** /-'biliti/ *noun*, **culpably** *adv*. [Middle English *coupable* via French from Latin *culpabilis*, from *culpare* to blame, from *culpa* guilt]

culpable homicide *noun* in Scotland and certain other jurisdictions, an act that causes a person's death but does not amount to murder; manslaughter.

culprit /'kulprit/ *noun* a person who is guilty of a crime or a fault.

Word history

Anglo-French *cul* (abbr of *culpable* CULPABLE) + *prest*, *prit* ready (from Latin *praestus*), prob from the legal phrase *Cupable; prest d'averer* (you are) guilty; (we are) ready to prove it. In English courts after the Norman Conquest, a prisoner's plea of not guilty was answered by the clerk of the crown, who said *culpable* (guilty) and that he was *prest* (ready) to proceed with the prosecution. The formula *cul. prest* or *cul. prit* was then entered on the official record of proceedings. Later, these words were mistakenly taken as a single word referring to the prisoner (the earliest record of this use is not before the late 17th cent.).

cult /kult/ *noun* **1a** a system of religious beliefs and ritual, or the body of adherents of one: *the cult of the Virgin Mary.* **b** a religion regarded as unorthodox or spurious, or the body of adherents of one: *A cult is a religion with no political power* — Tom Wolfe. **2** (*often before a noun*) great devotion, often regarded as a fad, to a person, idea, or thing, or a group showing such devotion: *Burns rapidly became a cult figure; the cult of youth.* ≫ **cultic** *adj*, **cultish** *adj*, **cultism** *noun*, **cultist** *noun*. [French *culte* from Latin *cultus* care, adoration, past part. of *colere* to cultivate]

cultch *or* **culch** /kulch/ *noun* the material composing an oyster bed, consisting of grit, stones, and broken shells. [origin unknown]

cultigen /'kultij(ə)n/ *noun* a plant species that is known only in cultivation, with no known wild forebear. [*cultivated* + -GEN]

cultivar /'kultivah/ *noun* a plant variety that has been developed in cultivation by selective breeding from natural species. [short for *cultivated variety*]

cultivate /'kultivayt/ *verb trans* **1** to prepare or use (land, soil, etc) for the growing of crops. **2** to grow (a plant or crop), *esp* on a large scale. **3** to grow (bacteria, tissue, viruses, etc) in a culture; = CULTURE[2]. **4** to improve or refine (*esp* one's mind) through study, edifying pursuits, etc: *cultivating the mind.* **5** to affect (a manner, etc) with assiduous practice: *cultivate an air of nonchalance.* **6** to encourage or foster the friendship of (a person, *esp* who can be useful to one). ≫ **cultivatable** *adj*, **cultivation** /-'vaysh(ə)n/ *noun*. [medieval Latin *cultivatus*, past part. of *cultivare*, from Latin *cultus*: see CULT]

cultivated *adj* refined; educated: *cultivated manners; her cultivated friends.*

cultivator *noun* an implement to break up the soil while crops are growing.

cultural /'kulchərəl/ *adj* **1** relating to education and the arts. **2** relating to a society's culture and traditions. ≫ **culturally** *adv*.

cultural anthropology *noun* a branch of anthropology that deals with the study of culture rather than the evolution, physical characteristics, etc of human beings: compare PHYSICAL ANTHROPOLOGY. Also called ETHNOLOGY. ≫ **cultural anthropologist** *noun*.

cultural attaché *noun* a member of an ambassadorial staff responsible for promoting cultural relations between the country of residence and the country he or she represents.

culture¹ /'kulchə/ *noun* **1** the development of the mind, *esp* by education. **2a** enlightenment and excellence of taste acquired by intellectual and aesthetic training. **b** intellectual and artistic enlightenment as distinguished from vocational and technical skills. **3a** the customary beliefs, social forms, etc of a racial, religious, or social group: *a dismissive attitude towards cultures different from one's own.* **b** the socially transmitted pattern of human behaviour that includes thought, speech, action, institutions, and artefacts.

Editorial note
'When I hear the word "culture" I reach for my revolver.' Hanns Johst's phrase, often attributed to Goering, refers to the fine and performing arts. Yet culture, which entails all of the ways in which people perceive, make intelligible and organize their being, can also embrace sport, science, and religion — Dr Maria Tippett.

4 the cultivation of living cells, tissue, viruses, etc in prepared nutrient media, or a product of this. **5** cultivation; tillage. **6** the attitude and behaviour of a particular social group or of society as a whole: *drug culture; blame culture.* [Middle English via French from Latin *cultura*, from *cultus*: see CULT]

culture² *verb trans* **1** to grow (bacteria, viruses, etc) in a culture. **2** to start a culture from (a specimen, etc): *culture a specimen of urine.*

-culture *comb. form* forming nouns, denoting: the cultivation or tending of the thing specified: *viticulture; apiculture; arboriculture.*

cultured *adj* cultivated: *As she became more irate her voice lost its cultured tones.*

cultured pearl *noun* a natural pearl grown under controlled conditions and usu induced by inserting a foreign body into the mantle of the oyster.

culture shock *noun* psychological and social disorientation caused by confrontation with a new or alien culture.

culture vulture *noun humorous* a person who has an avid, sometimes uncritical, interest in culture.

cultus /'kultəs/ *noun* (*pl* **cultus**) a cult, or the ritual associated with it: *the cultus of the Blessed Virgin* — Edward Pusey; *A cultus, or ceremonial worship ... constituted the sum-total of religion in the idea of a Pagan* — De Quincey. [Latin *cultus*: see CULT]

culverin /'kulvərin/ *noun* **1** a long cannon of relatively light construction used in the 16th and 17th cent. **2** an early musket. [Middle English from early French *couleuvrine*, from *couleuvre* snake, from Latin *colubra*]

culvert /'kulvət/ *noun* a small tunnel that allows water to pass under a road, railway, etc. [origin unknown]

cum /kum/ *prep* with; combined with; along with: *a lounge-cum-dining room.* [Latin *cum*; related to Latin COM-]

cumber /'kumbə/ *verb trans* (**cumbered, cumbering**) *dated* **1** to clutter up (a place or surface): *my own writing table ... cumbered with little bottles* — Dickens. **2** to burden or hamper (somebody): *The little woman ... bustled about like a true Martha, cumbered with many cares* — Louisa M Alcott. [Middle English *cumbren*, prob from ENCUMBER]

Cumberland sauce *noun* a spicy sauce made from redcurrant jelly, containing shreds of orange rind, served with game, turkey, etc. [named after *Cumberland*, a former county in NW England]

Cumberland sausage /'kumbələnd/ *noun Brit* a large coarse type of sausage.

cumbersome /'kumbəs(ə)m/ *adj* unwieldy because of heaviness and bulk. ➤ **cumbersomely** *adv*, **cumbersomeness** *noun.*

cumbrous /'kumbrəs/ *adj literary* cumbersome; unwieldy: *large bucks ... armed with their cumbrous antlers* — Darwin. ➤ **cumbrously** *adv*, **cumbrousness** *noun.*

cum grano salis /koom 'grahnoh 'sahlis/ *adv* with a pinch of salt; with due scepticism. [Latin *cum grano salis* with a grain of salt]

cumin or **cummin** /'kumin/ *noun* **1** a plant of the carrot family cultivated for its aromatic seeds: *Cuminum cyminum.* **2** these seeds used as a flavouring. [Old English *cymen*]

cummerbund /'kuməbund/ *noun* a broad waist sash worn *esp* with men's formal evening wear. [Hindi *kamarband* from Persian, from *kamar* waist + *band*]

cummin /'kumin/ *noun* see CUMIN.

cumquat /'kumkwot/ *noun* see KUMQUAT.

cumulate¹ /'kyoohmyoolayt/ *verb trans* to accumulate (things). ➤ **cumulation** /-'laysh(ə)n/ *noun.* [Latin *cumulatus*, past part. of *cumulare*, from *cumulus* mass]

cumulate² /'kyoohmyoolət/ *adj* accumulated.

cumulative /'kyoohmyoolətiv/ *adj* increasing by successive additions: *The treatment has a cumulative effect.* ➤ **cumulatively** *adv*, **cumulativeness** *noun.*

cumulative index *noun* **1** an index formed by the constant addition of items. **2** an index that amalgamates a series of indexes, e.g. those of a set of periodicals.

cumulative voting *noun* an electoral voting system whereby voters have as many votes as there are candidates.

cumuli /'kyoohmyoolie, -lee/ *noun* pl of CUMULUS.

cumulonimbus /,kyoohmyooloh'nimbəs/ *noun* (*pl* **cumulonimbi** /-bie/) a cumulus cloud formation often in the shape of an anvil, occurring at low altitude, between about 300 and 1500m (about 1000 and 5000ft), but extending to great heights and characteristic of thunderstorm conditions.

cumulus /'kyoohmyooləs/ *noun* (*pl* **cumuli** /-lie, lee/) a massive cloud formation consisting of a flat base and rounded outlines often piled up like a mountain, occurring at low altitude, between about 350 and 2000m (about 1200 and 6000ft). [Latin *cumulus* mass]

cuneate /'kyoohni-ət, -ayt/ *adj* having a narrow triangular shape with the smallest angle towards the base: *a cuneate leaf.* ➤ **cuneatus** *adv.* [Latin *cuneatus* from *cuneus* wedge]

cuneiform¹ /'kyoohnifawm/ *adj* **1** wedge-shaped. **2** composed of or written in the wedge-shaped characters used in ancient Assyrian, Babylonian, and Persian inscriptions: *cuneiform alphabet.* [prob from French *cunéiforme*, from Latin *cuneus* + French *-iforme* -IFORM]

cuneiform² *noun* cuneiform writing.

cunjevoi /'kunjivoy/ *noun* **1** a sea squirt of Australian waters, used as fishing bait: *Pyura praeputialis.* **2** an Australian plant grown for its edible corms: *Alocasia macrorrhiza.* [from a N Australian Aboriginal language]

cunjie or **cunjy** /'kunji/ *noun* = CUNJEVOI (1).

cunnilinctus /kuni'lingktəs/ *noun* = CUNNILINGUS. [scientific Latin *cunnilinctus*, from Latin *cunnus* vulva + *linctus* act of licking, from *lingere* to lick]

cunnilingus /kuni'linggəs/ *noun* oral stimulation of the vulva or clitoris. [Latin *cunnilingus* a person who licks the vulva, from *cunnus* vulva + *lingere* to lick]

cunning¹ /'kuning/ *adj* **1** devious; crafty. **2** dexterous; ingenious: *cunning workmanship.* **3** *NAmer* prettily appealing; cute. ➤ **cunningly** *adv*, **cunningness** *noun.*

Word history
Middle English, present part. of *cunnan* to know how to, from Old English: see CAN¹. The original meaning of *cunning*, from the 14th cent., was 'learned'. From this derived the sense 'skilful, clever' which in modern use rarely appears except in reference to craftsmanship. Because 'clever' is often seen as 'too clever' or 'deceitful', by the late 16th cent. the word acquired the derogatory sense which prevails today.

cunning² *noun* **1** craftiness; slyness: *with the cunning of a fox; The greatest cunning is to have none at all* — Carl Sandburg. **2** skill; dexterity; ingenuity: *high-ribbed vault with perfect cunning framed* — Wordsworth.

cunt /kunt/ *noun taboo* **1** the female genitals. **2** an abusive term for a person one dislikes. [Middle English *cunte*, of Germanic origin]

cup¹ /kup/ *noun* **1** a small open drinking vessel that is bowl-shaped and has a handle on one side. **2** in ecclesiastical use, the chalice holding the Communion wine, or the consecrated wine itself. **3** an ornamental metal cup offered as a prize, or a competition or championship with a cup as a prize. **4a** something resembling a cup, e.g. a plant or body part. **b** either of two parts of a bra or swimsuit that are shaped to fit over the breasts. **c** in golf, the hole on a putting green, or its metal lining. **5** any of various alcoholic cold drinks made from mixed ingredients: compare PUNCH⁵: *cider cup.* **6a** the capacity of a cup. **b** *chiefly NAmer* a cupful, usu as a specific measurement: *a cup of flour.* **7** (*in pl*) the name of one of the four suits in a pack of tarot cards. ✲ **in one's cups** *informal* drunk: *He probably said it in his cups.* **one's cup of tea** *informal* what is thoroughly congenial to one: *Committee meetings were not her cup of tea.* ➤ **cuplike** *adj.* [Old English *cuppe* from late Latin *cuppa*]

cup² *verb trans* (**cupped, cupping**) **1a** to curve (one's hands) into the shape of a cup: *He cupped his hands round the mug of tea.* **b** to curve one's hands round (something): *with one's chin cupped in one's* *hands; She cupped his face in her hands.* **2** formerly, to treat or draw blood from (somebody) by CUPPING.

cup-and-ring mark *noun* a CUP MARK surrounded by one or more concentric rings.

cupboard /'kubəd/ *noun* a recess with a door, usu shelved, or a freestanding piece of furniture with doors, for storage of utensils, food, clothes, etc. [Middle English *cupbord*, a table or sideboard on which crockery was displayed, from *cuppe* CUP¹ + *bord* BOARD¹, table]

cupboard love *noun* insincere love professed in order to get something.

cup cake *noun* a small round cake that is baked in a cup-shaped paper or foil container and is covered with a thick layer of icing.

cupel¹ /'kyoohpl, kyoo'pel/ *noun* a small shallow porous cup used to separate gold and silver from lead. ➤➤ **cupellation** /-'laysh(ə)n/ *noun.* [French *coupelle*, dimin. of *coupe* cup, from late Latin *cuppa*]

cupel² *verb trans* (**cupelled, cupelling,** *NAmer* **cupeled, cupeling**) to refine (precious metals) in a cupel. ➤➤ **cupeller** *noun.*

cup final *noun* the final match that decides the winner of a competition for a cup.

cupful /'kupf(ə)l/ *noun* (*pl* **cupfuls**) **1** as much as a cup will hold. **2** *chiefly NAmer* a unit of measure equal to 8fl oz (0.227l).

cupidity /kyooh'piditi/ *noun* inordinate desire for wealth or possessions; avarice; greed. [Middle English *cupidite* via French from Latin *cupiditat-, cupiditas,* from Latin *cupere* to desire]

Cupid's bow *noun* the double curve made by the edge of a person's top lip, reminiscent of the bow traditionally depicted as carried by the Roman god of love Cupid.

cup mark *noun* (*usu in pl*) a small circular depression gouged in a rock or standing stone in prehistoric times, of uncertain purpose.

cupola /'kyoohpələ/ *noun* (*pl* **cupolas**) **1** a small domed structure built on top of a roof. **2** a domed gun turret on a tank, warship, etc. **3** a vertical cylindrical furnace for melting pig iron, orig domed. [Italian *cupola* from Latin *cupula,* dimin. of *cupa* tub]

cuppa /'kupə/ *noun* (*pl* **cuppas**) *chiefly Brit, informal* a cup of tea: *Fancy a cuppa?* [short for *cuppa tea,* representing the pronunciation of *cup of tea*]

cupping /'kuping/ *noun* formerly, the application to the skin of a previously heated glass vessel, in which a partial vacuum develops, in order to draw blood to the surface, e.g. for bleeding.

cupr- *or* **cupri-** *or* **cupro-** *comb. form* forming words, denoting: **1** copper: *cupriferous.* **2** copper and: *cupro-nickel.* [late Latin *cuprum:* see COPPER¹]

cuprammonium rayon /kyoohprə'mohni-əm/ *noun* a rayon made from cellulose dissolved in a copper solution containing ammonia.

cupreous /'kyoohpri-əs/ *adj archaic or literary* resembling copper; coppery: *bright cupreous fishes* — Henry David Thoreau. [late Latin *cupreus,* from *cuprum:* see COPPER¹]

cupri- *comb. form* see CUPR-.

cupric /'kyoohprik/ *adj* relating to or containing bivalent copper.

cupriferous /kyooh'prifərəs/ *adj* said of an ore, etc: containing copper.

cuprite /'kyoohpriet/ *noun* red copper oxide occurring as a mineral. [German *Kuprit* from late Latin *cuprum:* see COPPER¹]

cupro- *comb. form* see CUPR-.

cupro-nickel /'kyoohproh/ *noun* an alloy, usu of seven parts of copper and three parts of nickel, used *esp* in British silver coins.

cuprous /'kyoohprəs/ *adj* relating to or containing univalent copper.

cuptie *noun* a match in a knockout competition for a cup.

cupule /'kyoohpyoohl/ *noun* a cup-shaped anatomical or plant structure. [from late Latin *cupula,* dimin. of Latin *cupa* tub]

cur /kuh/ *noun* **1** a mongrel or inferior dog. **2** *informal* a surly or cowardly fellow. [Middle English, prob short for *cur-dog,* perhaps related to Old Norse *kurra* to growl]

curaçao *or* **curaçoa** /kyoʊərə'soh/ *noun* a liqueur flavoured with the peel of bitter oranges. [Dutch *curaçao,* named after *Curaçao,* island in the Netherlands Antilles, where the oranges are grown]

curacy /'kyooərəsi/ *noun* (*pl* **curacies**) the office or term of office of a curate.

curare *or* **curari** /kyoo'rahri/ *noun* **1** any of various highly toxic extracts from plants (of the genus *Curarea* and other genera), used by S American Indians as arrow poison. **2** the alkaloid TUBOCURARINE, extracted from the woody climbing plant *Chondodendron tomentosum* and used medicinally as a muscle relaxant. [Portuguese and Spanish *curare* from Carib *kurari*]

curassow /'kyooərəsoh/ *noun* any of several species of large tree-dwelling game birds of S and Central America related to the domestic fowl: genus *Crax.* [alteration of *Curaçao*]

curate¹ /'kyooərət/ *noun* **1** a clergyman serving as assistant, e.g. to a rector, in a parish. **2** *archaic* a clergyman in charge of a parish. **3** *Irish, informal* a barman. [Middle English from medieval Latin *curatus* clergyman, one having the care of souls, from Latin *cura* care]

curate² /kyoo'rayt/ *verb trans* to manage (a museum, exhibition, etc) as a curator. [back-formation from CURATOR]

curate's egg *noun Brit* something with both good and bad parts.
Word history ———————————————————————
from a cartoon depicting a curate who, given a stale egg by his bishop, declared that parts of it were excellent.

curative¹ /'kyooərətiv/ *adj* relating to or used in the cure of diseases. ➤➤ **curatively** *adv.*

curative² *noun* a medicine or agent used to cure something.

curator /kyoo'raytə/ *noun* a person in charge of a museum, art gallery, etc, or a collection within one. ➤➤ **curatorial** /kyooərə'tawri-əl/ *adj,* **curatorship** *noun.* [Latin *curator,* from *curare* to care, from *cura* care]

curb¹ /kuhb/ *noun* **1** a check or restraint. **2a** a chain or strap used to restrain a horse, attached to the sides of the bit and passing below the lower jaw. **b** a bit used *esp* with a curb chain or strap, usu in a double bridle. **3** a sprain in a ligament just below a horse's hock. **4** *chiefly NAmer* = KERB. [early French *courbe* curve, curved piece of wood or iron, from Latin *curvus* curved]

curb² *verb trans* **1** to check or control (somebody or something). **2** to put a curb on (a horse).

curbstone *noun NAmer* = KERBSTONE.

curcuma /'kuhkyoomə/ *noun* any of a genus of tropical plants of the ginger family with short fleshy roots, including the plant from which turmeric is obtained: genus *Curcuma.* [scientific Latin from Arabic *kurkum* saffron]

curd /kuhd/ *noun* **1** (*also in pl*) the thick casein-rich part of coagulated milk used as a food or made into cheese. **2** a fatty substance occurring as small deposits in poached salmon. **3** a rich thick fruit preserve made with eggs, sugar, and butter: *lemon curd.* **4** the edible head of a cauliflower or a similar related plant. ➤➤ **curdy** *adj.* [Middle English; earlier history unknown]

curd cheese *noun* a smooth sharp-tasting soft cheese made from the curds of skimmed milk.

curdle /'kuhdl/ *verb trans* **1** to cause (milk) to separate into solid curds and liquid: *Any acid curdles milk.* **2** to cause (any liquid or soft mixture) to break up in this manner. ➤ *verb intrans* to separate into curds or lumps and liquid: *Add the egg, alternately with the flour, to prevent the mixture from curdling.* * **make one's blood curdle** to fill one with dread. [frequentative of obsolete *curd* to thicken or congeal, from CURD]

cure¹ /kyooə/ *noun* **1a** a drug, treatment, etc that gives relief or recovery from a disease. **b** relief or recovery from a disease. **2** something that corrects a harmful or troublesome situation; a remedy. **3** a process or method of curing meat, fish, etc or of hardening rubber, concrete, etc. **4a** a spiritual or pastoral charge. **b** a parish. ➤➤ **cureless** *adj.*
Word history ———————————————————————
Middle English from Old French, ultimately from Latin *cura* care. The original sense was 'care, concern', *esp* the spiritual care of souls; later 'care of the sick', hence 'remedy'.

cure² *verb trans* **1** to restore (somebody) to health, soundness, or normality: *The new treatment cured many of tuberculosis.* **2** to bring about recovery from (an illness or other disorder): *He claimed that an alternative remedy had cured his cancer.* **3** to rectify (a harmful or troublesome situation): *Nothing will cure rampant inflation overnight.* **4** to free (somebody) from something objectionable or harmful: *He desperately wants to be cured of his drug habit.* **5a** to preserve (meat, fish, etc) by salting, drying, smoking, etc. **b** to harden (rubber, plastic, concrete, etc) by some chemical process such as vulcanization. **c** to prepare (skins or hides) for use by tanning, etc. ➤ *verb* *intrans* **1** to effect a cure: *Thirty-month-old Samuel Johnson was taken to Queen Anne suffering from scrofula, but unfortunately her touch failed to cure.* **2** to undergo a curing or hardening process. ➤➤ **curability** /-'biliti/ *noun*, **curable** *adj*, **curableness** *noun*, **curer** *noun*.

curé /'kyooəray/ *noun* (*pl* **curés** /'kyooərayz/) a parish priest in France or another French-speaking country. [Old French *curé* from medieval Latin *curatus*: see CURATE¹]

cure-all *noun* a remedy for all ills; a panacea.

curet /kyoo'ret/ *noun* see CURETTE¹.

curettage /kyoo'retij, kyooəri'tahzh/ *noun* a surgical scraping or cleaning, e.g. of the womb, by means of a curette.

curette¹ *or* **curet** /kyoo'ret/ *noun* a scoop, loop, or ring used in curettage. [French *curette* from *curer* to clean or cure, from Latin *curare* to care for, from *cura* care]

curette² *verb trans* to perform curettage on (a patient).

curfew /'kuhfyooh/ *noun* **1** a regulation imposed on all or particular people, *esp* during times of civil disturbance, requiring their withdrawal from the streets by a stated time. **2** a signal, e.g. the sounding of a bell, announcing the beginning of a time of curfew. **3a** the hour at which a curfew becomes effective. **b** the period during which a curfew is in effect. [Middle English from early French *covrefeu*, a signal given to bank the hearth fire, from *covrir* (see COVER¹) + *feu* fire, from Latin *focus* hearth]

curia /'kyooəri·ə/ *noun* (*pl* **curiae** /'kyooəri·ee/) **1** (*often* **Curia**) the administration and governmental apparatus of the Roman Catholic Church. **2** any of the ten divisions of an ancient Roman tribe. ➤➤ **curial** *adj*. [Latin *curia*, from CO- + *vir* man]

curie /'kyooəri/ *noun* (*pl* **curies**) a unit of radioactivity equal to 3.7 × 10¹⁰ disintegrations per second. [named after Pierre *Curie* d.1906, French physicist, and his Polish-born wife Marie d.1934, physicist and chemist, who studied radioactivity]

curio /'kyooərioh/ *noun* (*pl* **curios**) something considered novel, rare, or bizarre: *He bought up a lot of [em]balmed human heads (great curios, you know)* — Herman Melville. [short for CURIOSITY]

curiosa /kyooəri'ohsə/ *pl noun* **1** curiosities. **2** *euphem* erotic or pornographic books, etc. [Latin *curiosa*, neuter pl of *curiosus*: see CURIOUS]

curiosity /kyooəri'ositi/ *noun* (*pl* **curiosities**) **1** desire to know: *Curiosity is one of the most permanent and certain characteristics of a vigorous intellect* — Dr Johnson. **2** inquisitiveness or nosiness. **3a** a strange, interesting, or rare object, custom, etc: *collect curiosities.* **b** an abstruse fact: *the curiosities of anatomical science* — Charles Lamb.

curious /'kyooəri·əs/ *adj* **1** eager to investigate and learn. **2** inquisitive or nosy. **3** strange, novel, or odd. **4** *euphem* said of books: erotic or pornographic. ➤➤ **curiously** *adv*, **curiousness** *noun*. [Middle English via French from Latin *curiosus* careful, inquisitive, from *cura* care]

curium /'kyooəri·əm/ *noun* a radioactive metallic chemical element produced by bombarding plutonium with high speed particles: symbol Cm, atomic number 96. [scientific Latin, named after Pierre and Marie *Curie*: see CURIE]

curl¹ /kuhl/ *verb trans* **1** to form (hair) into waves or coils. **2** to form (something) into a curved, twisted, or spiral shape. **3** in weight-training, to lift (a weight) using only the hands, wrists, and forearms. ➤ *verb intrans* **1a** said of hair: to grow in coils or spirals. **b** to form curls or twists. **2** to move or progress in curves or spirals: *The smoke curled up into the sky.* **3** to play the game of curling. ✱ **curl one's lip** to lift the corner of one's mouth in a sneer; to sneer. **make one's hair curl** to horrify one: *stories that would make your hair curl.* [Middle English *curlen*, from *crul* curly, from early Dutch *krul*]

curl² *noun* **1** a curled lock of hair. **2** something with a spiral or winding form; a coil. **3** a curling movement: *a curl of the lip.* **4** a weightlifting manoeuvre using only the hands, wrists, and forearms. **5** in mathematics, a function of the vector expressing the rotation of the vector field.

curler *noun* **1** a small cylinder on which hair is wound for curling; a roller. **2** a person who plays the game of curling.

curlew /'kuhlyooh/ *noun* (*pl* **curlews** *or collectively* **curlew**) any of various brownish migratory wading birds with long legs and a long slender down-curved bill: *Numenius arquata* and others. [Middle English from early French *corlieu*, of imitative origin]

curlicue *or* **curlycue** /'kuhlikyooh/ *noun* a decorative curve or flourish, e.g. in handwriting. [CURLY + CUE³, in the sense 'braid of hair']

curling *noun* a game in which two teams of four players each slide heavy round flat-bottomed stones over ice towards a target circle marked on the ice. [verbal noun from CURL¹]

curling iron *noun* = CURLING TONGS.

curling irons *pl noun* = CURLING TONGS: *She got out her curling irons and lighted the gas and went to work repairing the ravages* — O Henry.

curling tongs *pl noun* a rod-shaped instrument with a hinged clamp, operated like scissors, that is heated so that locks of hair can be wound round it to be curled.

curly *adj* (**curlier, curliest**) tending to curl; having curls. ➤➤ **curliness** *noun*.

curlycue /'kuhlikyooh/ *noun* see CURLICUE.

curly endive *noun* a variety of endive with curled leaves: *Cichorium endivia.*

curmudgeon /kə'mujən/ *noun* a crusty ill-tempered or miserly person, *esp* an old man: *a tight-fisted old curmudgeon.* ➤➤ **curmudgeonly** *adj*. [origin unknown]

currach *or* **curragh** /'kurə, 'kurəkh/ *noun* a coracle. [Scottish Gaelic *curach* and Irish Gaelic *currach* small boat]

curragh /'kurə, 'kurəkh/ *noun* in Ireland and the Isle of Man, a marshy area. [Irish Gaelic *corrach*, Manx *curragh* bog, marsh, fen]

currant /'kurənt/ *noun* **1** a small seedless type of dried grape used in cookery. **2** a shrub of the gooseberry family bearing a redcurrant, blackcurrant, or similar acid edible fruit, or the fruit it bears. [Middle English *raison of Coraunte* raisin of *Corinth*, region and city of Greece]

Usage note

currant *or* current? See note at CURRENT¹.

currawong /'kurəwong/ *noun* any of three species of an Australian songbird similar to a crow, with black, grey, and white plumage: genus *Strepera*. [Aboriginal]

currency /'kurənsi/ *noun* a system of money that is in circulation as a medium of exchange. (*pl* **currencies**) **1a** a system of money, usu in the form of coins and bank notes, that is in circulation as a medium of exchange: *The baht is the main unit of currency in Thailand; the stronger world currencies; Halfpennies are no longer legal currency.* **b** a figurative medium of exchange: *the threats and sulks that were the currency of negotiation in our household.* **2** general use, acceptance, or prevalence, or the state of being in general use, etc: *I have doubts about the currency of some of these expressions.* ✱ **in currency 1** in vogue: *theories about grammar-learning that were in currency in the 1950s.* **2** said of coins or notes: in circulation: *The large ten-penny pieces are no longer in currency.*

current¹ /'kurənt/ *adj* **1a** elapsing now: *during the current week.* **b** occurring in or belonging to the present time: *the current president; my current job; current events.* **2** valid as a medium of exchange: *current coins.* **3** generally accepted, used, or practised at the moment: *Only two senses of the word are still current; current treatments.* ➤➤ **currently** *adv*, **currentness** *noun*. [Middle English *curraunt* from Old French *curant*, present part. of *courre* to run, from Latin *currere*]

Usage note

current *or* currant? *Current* with an *e* has a wide range of meanings: *current affairs; the current month; also electric current; strong currents make swimming dangerous* (see CURRENT²). *Currant* with an *a* is a fresh or dried berry: *redcurrants; currants and raisins.*

current² *noun* **1a** the part of a body of gas or liquid that moves continuously in a certain direction. **b** the swiftest part of a stream. **c** a movement of lake, sea, or ocean water. **2a** a flow of electricity resulting from the movement in a certain direction of electrically charged particles. **b** a quantity, usu measured in amperes, representing the rate of such flow. **3** a tendency to follow a certain or specified course: *an increasing current of radicalism.*

current account *noun Brit* a bank account against which cheques may be drawn and on which interest is usu not payable: compare DEPOSIT ACCOUNT.

current assets *pl noun* cash itself, or assets that will convert to cash in the current year: compare FIXED ASSETS.

curricle /'kurikl/ *noun* a light, open carriage drawn by two horses harnessed side by side: *She found herself with Henry in the curricle, as happy a being as ever existed* — Jane Austen. [Latin *curriculum* racing chariot]

curricula /kə'rikyoolə/ *noun* pl of CURRICULUM.

curricula vitae /'veetie/ *noun* pl of CURRICULUM VITAE.

curriculum /kə'rikyooləm/ *noun* (*pl* **curricula** /-lə/ *or* **curriculums**) the courses offered by an educational institution or followed by an individual or group. ➤➤ **curricular** *adj*. [Latin *curriculum* running, course, from *currere* to run]

curriculum vitae /'veetie/ *noun* (*pl* **curricula vitae**) a summary of somebody's career and qualifications, *esp* as relevant to a job application. [Latin *curriculum vitae* course of (one's) life]

currish /'kuhrish/ *adj* **1** bad-tempered; snappish. **2** ignoble. ➤➤ **currishly** *adv*. [literally 'like a CUR']

curry¹ /'kuri/ *verb trans* (**curries, curried, currying**) **1** to dress the coat of (a horse) with a currycomb. **2** to dress (tanned leather). ★ **curry favour** to seek to gain favour by flattery or attention; to ingratiate oneself. ➤➤ **currier** *noun*. [Middle English *currayen* from Old French *correer* to prepare, curry, from (assumed) vulgar Latin *conredare*, from CON- + prehistoric Germanic word]

curry² *noun* (*pl* **curries**) a food or dish seasoned with a mixture of spices or curry powder. [Tamil-Malayalam *karī* sauce]

curry³ *verb trans* (**curries, curried, currying**) to flavour or cook (food) with curry powder or sauce.

currycomb *noun* a metal comb with rows of teeth or serrated ridges, used *esp* to clean grooming brushes or to curry horses.

curry powder *noun* a condiment consisting of several pungent ground spices, e.g. cayenne pepper, fenugreek, and turmeric.

curse¹ /kuhs/ *noun* **1a** an appeal to a deity that invokes harm or injury on another; an imprecation. **b** a swearword or other offensive expression used in anger: *The ringing of the telephone occasioned another string of curses.* **2** an influence for evil or misfortune that comes in or as if in response to imprecation or as retribution: *There seemed to be a curse on the family.* **3** a cause of misfortune: *Extreme conscientiousness can be more of a curse than an advantage.* **4** (**the curse**) *informal, dated* menstruation. [Old English *curs*]

curse² *verb trans* **1** to call upon divine or supernatural power to cause harm or injury to (somebody or something); to doom or damn (somebody or something). **2** to use profanely insolent language against (somebody). **3** (*often* + with) to bring evil upon (somebody); to afflict (them) with something: *I'm cursed with poor eyesight.* ➤ *verb intrans* to utter curses; to swear.

cursed /'kuhsid, kuhst/ *or* **curst** /kuhst/ *adj* **1** *informal, dated* under or deserving a curse: *those cursed hounds.* **2** (*often* **curst**) *archaic* vicious, cantankerous, or contrary: *God sends a curst cow short horns* — Shakespeare. ➤➤ **cursedly** /'kuhsidli/ *adv*, **cursedness** /'kuhsidnis/ *noun.*

cursive¹ /'kuhsiv/ *adj* said of handwriting: executed in flowing strokes with the characters joined in each word. ➤➤ **cursively** *adv*, **cursiveness** *noun*. [French *cursif* from medieval Latin *cursivus* running, from Latin *currere* to run]

cursive² *noun* cursive writing.

cursor /'kuhsə/ *noun* **1** a movable pointer, usu pulsing on and off, on a visual display unit, radar screen, etc for indicating the specific position that will be immediately affected by input. **2** a transparent slide with a reference hairline for precisely locating marks on a scientific instrument, e.g. a slide rule. [Middle English, in the sense 'runner', from Latin, from *currere* to run]

cursorial /kuh'sawri-əl/ *adj* said of an animal, etc or a part of one: adapted to running: *cursorial birds.*

cursory /'kuhsəri/ *adj* rapid and often superficial; hasty: *a cursory glance.* ➤➤ **cursorily** /'kuhs(ə)rəli/ *adv*, **cursoriness** *noun*. [late Latin *cursorius* of running, from Latin *currere* to run]

curst /kuhst/ *adj archaic* see CURSED.

curt /kuht/ *adj* characterized by rude or peremptory shortness; brusque: *a curt manner; curt comments.* ➤➤ **curtly** *adv*, **curtness** *noun*. [Latin *curtus* shortened]

curtail /kuh'tayl/ *verb trans* to cut (something) short; to limit (it): *Art is allowed ... indecent license ... but the privileges of literature in this respect have been sharply curtailed* — Mark Twain. ➤➤ **curtailer** *noun*, **curtailment** *noun*. [alteration of obsolete *curtal* to dock an animal's tail, ultimately from Latin *curtus* shortened, short]

curtain¹ /'kuht(ə)n/ *noun* **1** a hanging fabric screen that can usu be drawn back or up, *esp* one used at a window. **2a** (**the curtain**) the movable screen separating the stage from the auditorium of a theatre. **b** the ascent or opening, e.g. at the beginning of a play, of a stage curtain or its descent or closing. **3** *informal* (*in pl*) the end; *esp* death: *This means curtains for the research programme; It's curtains*

for yours truly. **4** a device or agency that conceals or acts as a barrier: compare IRON CURTAIN. **5a** a castle wall between two neighbouring bastions. **b** an exterior wall that carries no load. [Middle English *curtine* via Old French from late Latin *cortina* from Latin *cohort-, cohors* enclosure, court]

curtain² *verb trans* **1** to furnish (a window or opening) with curtains: *a curtained recess.* **2** to veil (something) or shut it off with, or as if with, a curtain: *keep one's private life curtained from the public gaze.*

curtain call *noun* an appearance by a performer after the final curtain of a play, opera, etc in response to the applause of the audience.

curtain lecture *noun humorous, archaic* a litany of complaints delivered by a wife to her husband in the privacy of the curtained bed.

curtain-raiser *noun* **1** a short play presented before the main full-length drama. **2** a short preliminary to a main event.

curtain wall *noun* = CURTAIN¹ (5).

curtal-axe /'kuhtl/ *noun* see CURTLE-AXE.

curtana /kuh'tahnə, kuh'taynə/ *noun* a sword without a point, carried at the coronation of English monarchs as a symbol of mercy. [Middle English via Anglo-French from Old French *curtain*, name of the broken sword of the legendary hero Roland, from *cort* short, from Latin *curtus*]

curtilage /'kuhtəlij/ *noun* a piece of ground within the fence surrounding a house. [Middle English from Old French *cortillage*, from *cortil* courtyard, from *cort*: see COURT¹]

curtle-axe *or* **curtal-axe** /'kuhtl/ *noun archaic* a broad slashing sword: *a gallant curtle-axe upon my thigh* — Shakespeare. [alteration of CUTLASS]

curtsy¹ *or* **curtsey** /'kuhtsi/ *noun* (*pl* **curtsies**) a woman's brief sinking movement, the equivalent of a man's bow, performed by putting one leg behind the other and flexing the knees, at the same time dropping the head, formerly as a general gesture of respect, now chiefly used in greeting royalty; a bob. [alteration of COURTESY]

curtsy² *or* **curtsey** *verb intrans* (**curtsies, curtsied, curtsying**) to make a curtsy.

curule /'kyooəroohl/ *adj* in ancient Rome, denoting the authority of an aedile, consul, or praetor, who were entitled to use the *sella curulis*, a folding stool. [Latin *curulis* from *currus* chariot, in reference to the carriage conveying the senior magistrate to the seat of office, from *currere* to run]

curvaceous /kuh'vayshəs/ *adj* said of a woman: having a pleasingly well-developed figure with attractive curves.

curvature /'kuhvəchə/ *noun* **1a** the circumstance of being curved. **b** the degree to which something is curved: *The curvature can be measured.* **2a** an abnormal curving, e.g. of the spine. **b** (*also* **greater curvature, lesser curvature**) the left and right curved sides of the stomach. [Latin *curvatura*, from *curvare*: see CURVE¹]

curve¹ /kuhv/ *verb intrans* to have or make a turn, change, or deviation from a straight line without sharp breaks or angularity. ➤ *verb trans* to cause (something) to curve. [Latin *curvare* from *curvus* curved]

curve² *noun* **1** a curving line or surface. **2** something curved, e.g. a curving line of the human body. **3** a representation on a graph of a varying quantity, e.g. speed, force, or weight. **4** (*also* **curve ball**) in baseball, a delivery by the pitcher that causes the ball to swerve away from a straight line. ➤➤ **curvy** *adj*.

curvet¹ /'kuh'vet/ *noun* **1** a prancing leap of a horse in which all legs are in the air at once, the forelegs being raised first. **2** a graceful leap. [Italian *corvetta*, dimin. of *corva*, earlier *curva* a curve, from Latin *curvus* bent]

curvet² *verb intrans* (**curvetted, curvetting**, *NAmer also* **curveted, curveting**) **1** said of horse: to make a curvet. **2** to prance, caper, or leap about gracefully.

curvilinear /kuhvi'lini-ə/ *adj* consisting of or bounded by curved lines. ➤➤ **curvilinearity** /-'ariti/ *noun*, **curvilinearly** *adv*. [Latin *curvus* curved + *linea*: see LINE¹]

cuscus /'kuskəs/ *noun* (*pl* **cuscuses**) any of several tree-dwelling New Guinea phalangers (small marsupials with prehensile tails; see PHALANGER): *esp Spilocuscus maculatus.* [via French and Dutch from a native name in New Guinea]

cusec /'kyoohsek/ *noun* a unit of flow used *esp* for water, equal to one cubic foot per second. [shortened from *cubic foot per second*]

cushat /'kushət/ *noun chiefly Scot* a woodpigeon. [Old English *cūscote*]

Cushing's disease /'kooshingz/ *noun* = CUSHING'S SYNDROME when caused by a tumour of the pituitary gland.

Cushing's syndrome *noun* obesity, *esp* of the face, and muscular weakness, caused by an excess of corticosteroid hormone, often resulting from prolonged therapeutic administration. [named after Harvey *Cushing* d.1939, US surgeon]

cushion¹ /'koosh(ə)n/ *noun* **1** a soft pillow or padded bag, *esp* one used for sitting, reclining, or kneeling on. **2** a pad of springy rubber along the inside of the rim of a billiard table off which balls bounce. **3** something serving to mitigate the effects of disturbances or disorders: *a cushion against fluctuation in demand.* ≫ **cushiony** *adj.* [Middle English *cusshin* from early French *coissin*, ultimately from Latin *coxa* hip]

cushion² *verb trans* **1** to furnish (something) with a cushion. **2a** to mitigate the effects of (something unpleasant). **b** to protect (somebody or something) against force or shock.

Cushitic /koo'shitik/ *noun* a branch of the Afro-Asiatic language family comprising various languages of E Africa, *esp* Ethiopia and Somalia. ≫ **Cushitic** *adj.* [named after *Cush* (Kush), ancient country of NE Africa]

cushy /'kooshi/ *adj* (**cushier, cushiest**) *informal* entailing little hardship or effort; easy: *a cushy job.* ≫ **cushiness** *noun.* [Hindi *khush* pleasant, from Persian *khūsh*]

cusp /kusp/ *noun* **1** either horn of a crescent moon. **2a** a pointed projection formed by or arising from the intersection of two arcs in Gothic tracery: compare FOIL¹ (4A). **b** in mathematics, a point at which a curve is sharply reversed. **3** a point on the grinding surface of a tooth. **4** a fold or flap of a valve, in the heart or a blood vessel. **5** the initial point of an astrological house. ✳ **on the cusp** in transition between one state and another. ≫ **cuspate** /'kuspit, 'kuspayt/ *adj.* [Latin *cuspis* point]

cuspid /'kuspid/ *noun* a tooth with a single point; a canine tooth. ≫ **cuspidate** /-dayt/ *adj.* [Latin *cuspid-, cuspis* point, apex]

cuspidor /'kuspidaw/ *noun* a spittoon. [Portuguese *cuspidouro* place for spitting, from *cuspir* to spit, from Latin *conspuere*, from COM- + *spuere* to spit]

cuss¹ /kus/ *noun informal* **1** a curse. **2** a fellow: *a harmless old cuss.* [alteration of CURSE¹]

cuss² *verb trans informal* to curse (somebody or something). ≫ *verb intrans informal* to curse.

cussed /'kusid/ *adj informal* obstinate; cantankerous. ≫ **cussedly** *adv,* **cussedness** *noun.*

custard /'kustəd/ *noun* **1** a semisolid, sweetened, and often baked mixture made with milk and eggs. **2** a sweet sauce made with milk and eggs or a commercial preparation of coloured cornflour. [Middle English *custarde, crustade,* a kind of pie, prob from Old French *crouste* crust, from Latin *crusta*]

custard apple *noun* **1** a large tropical fruit with sweet yellow pulp. **2** any of several species of chiefly tropical American trees or shrubs bearing this fruit: genus *Annona.*

custard pie *noun* **1** an open pastry case containing egg custard. **2** this type of pie or an artificial substitute used in slapstick comedy for throwing at somebody or applying forcefully to their face.

custodial /ku'stohdi-əl/ *adj* **1** said of a sentence imposed by a judge: involving detention, usu in prison. **2** relating to guardianship or custody.

custodian /ku'stohdi-ən/ *noun* a person who guards and protects or maintains; *esp* the curator of a public building. ≫ **custodianship** *noun.*

custody /'kustədi/ *noun* **1a** the state of being cared for or guarded; guardianship: *archives in the custody of the County Record Office.* **b** imprisonment; detention: *remain in custody; deaths in police custody.* **2** the act or right of caring for a minor, *esp* when granted by a court of law; guardianship: *regain custody of one's child.* [Middle English *custodie* from Latin *custodia* guarding, from *custod-, custos* guardian]

custom¹ /'kustəm/ *noun* **1a** an established socially accepted practice: *It is a custom more honoured in the breach than the observance.* **b** long-established practice having the force of law. **c** the usual practice of an individual: *sleeping within my orchard, my custom always of the afternoon* — Shakespeare. **d** the usages that regulate social life.

2 (*in pl*). **a** duties or tolls imposed on imports or exports. **b** (*treated as sing. or pl*) the agency, establishment, or procedure for collecting such customs. **3** *chiefly Brit* business patronage: *threaten to withdraw one's custom.* [Middle English *custume* via Old French from Latin *consuetudin-, consuetudo,* from *consuescere* to accustom, from CON- + *suescere* to become accustomed]

custom² *adj NAmer* made to personal order or specifications: *custom clothes.*

customary *adj* established by or according to custom; usual. ≫ **customarily** *adv,* **customariness** *noun.*

custom-built *adj* built to individual specifications.

customer /'kustəmə/ *noun* **1** a person who purchases a commodity or service. **2** an individual, usu having some specified distinctive trait: *a tough customer.* [Middle English *custumer,* from *custume:* see CUSTOM¹]

customhouse *noun* see CUSTOMSHOUSE.

customize *or* **customise** *verb trans* **1** to build, fit, or alter (something) according to individual specifications. **2** to program (computer keys) to perform some dedicated task.

custom-made *adj* made to individual specifications: *a custom-made suit.*

customshouse *or* **customhouse** *noun* a building where customs are collected and where vessels are cleared for entry.

customs union *noun* an agreement between two or more states to allow free trade between themselves but to impose a common external tariff on imports from non-member states.

cut¹ /kut/ *verb* (**cutting,** *past tense and past part.* **cut**) ≫ *verb trans* **1a** to penetrate or make an opening in (something or somebody) with a sharp instrument or object. **b** to injure (oneself or a part of the body) in this way. **c** to trim or pare (something). **2a** to hurt the feelings of (somebody). **b** to ignore (an acquaintance) deliberately or spitefully. **3a** to shorten or edit (a piece of writing, stage performance, etc) by making omissions. **b** to reduce (expenditure, costs, etc). **c** *chiefly NAmer* to dilute (a drink) or adulterate (a drug). **4a** to mow or reap (grass, hay, etc). **b** to fell or hew (timber). **5a** to divide (e.g. food) into parts with an edged instrument. **b** to slice or separate (a piece) from a whole with a knife, etc. **c** to divide (something) into segments. **6** said of a line, etc: to intersect (another line, etc). **7** to break or interrupt (a flow, supply, etc): *They cut our supply lines.* **8a** to divide (a pack of cards) into two portions. **b** to draw (a card) from the pack. **9a** to strike (a ball) so as to impart backspin; = CHOP¹ (3A). **b** in cricket, to play a horizontal stroke to the off at (a ball) or at the bowling of (a bowler). **10** to stop (a motor) by opening a switch. **11** to stop or interrupt the filming of (a scene). **12** to make, shape, or fashion (an article) with or as if with an edged tool, scissors, etc: *a place where diamonds are cut; a well-cut suit.* **13** to record sounds on (a recording medium). **14** *informal.* **a** to stop or cease (something): *Cut the nonsense.* **b** to absent oneself from (a class). ≫ *verb intrans* **1a** said of an instrument or object: to have the capacity to penetrate or make an opening. **b** to be able to be separated, divided, or marked with a sharp instrument: *Cheese cuts easily.* **c** to perform the operation of dividing, severing, incising, or intersecting. **2** to make a stroke with a whip, sword, etc. **3** in cricket, to play a cut. **4** to cause constriction or chafing: *The garters cut into our thighs.* **5** to have a telling effect, influence, or significance: *an analysis that cuts deep.* **6a** to divide a pack of cards, *esp* in order to decide who deals. **b** to draw a card from the pack. **7a** to move swiftly: *The yacht cut through the water.* **b** to move in a direct course: *The fox cut across the field.* **c** to change sharply in direction; to swerve: *Another car cut in front of us.* **d** to change from one sound or image to another in film, radio, or television: *cut to the garden scene.* **8** to stop filming or recording. ✳ **cut a caper** to skip or frolic in a playful manner. **cut a dash** to look smart or handsome. **cut a fine/poor figure** to look impressive or pathetic. **cut and run** *informal* to make a speedy and undignified escape [referring to sailors cutting the anchor cable and allowing the ship to run before the wind]. **cut a tooth** said of a baby: to produce a new tooth. **cut both ways 1** said of a statement, etc: to be equally valid for and against an argument. **2** said of a procedure: to have disadvantages as well as advantages. **cut corners** to do something cheaply or quickly by making risky economies. **cut from the same cloth** having similar qualities or character. **cut in line** *NAmer* to jump a queue. **cut it fine** see FINE¹. **cut no ice** *informal* to fail to impress; to have no importance or influence. **cut one's teeth** to get early practice or initiation in an activity. **cut somebody dead** to ignore somebody deliberately. **cut something short 1** to abbreviate something. **2** to interrupt (a speaker or speech). **cut the mustard** *informal* to come up to standard. **cut to the chase** *NAmer, informal* to get to the point. [Middle English *cutten*, probably of Germanic origin]

cut² *noun* **1** something cut or cut off. **2a** a length of cloth varying from 44–109m (40–100yd) in length. **b** the yield of products cut, *esp* during one harvest. **c** a piece from a meat carcass or a fish, or a slice cut from it. **d** *informal* a share: *He took his cut of the profits.* **3a** an opening made with an edged instrument. **b** a gash or wound. **c** a surface or outline left by cutting. **4a** a stroke or blow with the edge of something sharp. **b** a gesture or expression that hurts somebody's feelings: *the unkindest cut of all.* **c** a reduction or paring: *a cut in pay.* **d** a cutting of playing cards, or the result of this. **5a** a sharp downward blow or stroke. **b** backspin. **c** in cricket, an attacking stroke played with the bat held horizontally, sending the ball on the off side. **6** an abrupt transition from one sound or image to another in film, radio, or television. **7a** the style in which something is cut or shaped: *with eyes severe and beard of formal cut* — Shakespeare; *clothes of a good cut.* **b** a pattern or type. **c** a haircut: *have a cut and blow-dry.* ✴ **a cut above 1** superior to or of higher quality or rank than (somebody or something else). **2** superior; of higher quality or rank. **cut and thrust** a competitive and stimulating environment.

cut-and-dried *adj* said of a situation: completely decided; not open to further discussion.

cut-and-paste *noun* a word-processing technique in which a portion of text can be deleted and reinserted in a different position.

cutaneous /kyooh'tayni-əs/ *adj* relating to or affecting the skin. [scientific Latin *cutaneus* from Latin *cutis* skin]

cutaway *adj* having parts cut away or absent: *a cutaway coat.*

cutback *noun* a reduction or decrease.

cut back *verb trans* **1** to shorten or prune (a plant). **2** to reduce (costs or expenditure). ➤ *verb intrans* to economize.

cut down *verb trans* **1** to make (something, esp something growing) fall by cutting through it. **2** to kill or incapacitate (somebody). ➤ *verb intrans* (*often* + on) to reduce or restrict an activity, expenditure, etc. ✴ **cut down to size** to expose somebody's excessive self-importance.

cute /kyooht/ *adj* **1** *informal* attractive or pretty, *esp* in a dainty or delicate way. **2** sexually attractive. **3** shrewd; knowing: *And then, these exchanges, they don't answer when you have cute jockeys to deal with* — George Eliot. ➤➤ **cutely** *adv*, **cuteness** *noun*. [short for ACUTE¹]

cutes /'kyoohteez/ *noun* pl of CUTIS.

cutesy /'kyoohtsi/ *adj* (**cutesier, cutesiest**) odiously sweet or cute.

cutesy-pie *adj* = CUTESY.

cut glass *noun* glass ornamented with patterns cut into its surface by an abrasive wheel and then polished.

cuticle /'kyoohtikl/ *noun* **1** dead or horny skin; *esp* the skin surrounding the base and sides of a fingernail or toenail. **2** the thick or horny epidermis of an animal. **3** a thin fatty film on the external surface of many higher plants. **4** the outer layer of a hair. ➤➤ **cuticular** /kyooh'tikyoolə/ *adj*. [Latin *cuticula*, dimin. of *cutis* skin]

cutie /'kyoohti/ *noun* (*pl* **cuties**) *informal* an attractive person.

cutin /'kyoohtin/ *noun* a water-repellent substance containing waxes and fats, that becomes impregnated into plant cell walls and forms a continuous layer on the external surface of plants. [CUTIS + -IN¹]

cut in *verb intrans* **1** to interrupt abruptly. **2** to pull in too closely after overtaking another vehicle. **3** said of a motor or device: to start operating, *esp* after an automatic connection. ➤ *verb trans informal* to include (somebody) in a deal or payment.

cut-in *noun* an edited-in shot in a film sequence.

cutis /'kyoohtis/ *noun* (*pl* **cutes** /'kyoohteez/ *or* **cutises**) the true skin; = DERMIS. [Latin *cutis* skin]

cutlass /'kutləs/ *noun* a short curved sword, *esp* as used formerly by sailors. [early French *coutelas*, augmentative of *coutel* knife, from Latin *cultellus*, dimin. of *culter* knife, ploughshare]

cutler /'kutlə/ *noun* a person who deals in, makes, or repairs cutlery. [Middle English from early French *coutelier*, from Latin *cultellus*: see CUTLASS]

cutlery /'kutləri/ *noun* **1** edged or cutting tools; *esp* implements, e.g. knives, forks, and spoons, for cutting and eating food. **2** the business of a cutler.

cutlet /'kutlit/ *noun* **1** a small slice of meat from the neck of lamb, mutton, or veal, or a burger or croquette of minced food in this shape. **2** a cross-sectional slice from between the head and centre of a large fish: compare STEAK (3). [French *côtelette* from Old French *costelette*, dimin. of *coste* rib, side, from Latin *costa*]

cutline *noun* **1** a horizontal line marked about 1.8m (6ft) from the floor on the front wall of a squash court, above which the ball must be hit when serving. **2** *NAmer* a caption under a photograph, cartoon, illustration, etc.

cutoff *noun* **1** the process of cutting something, e.g. a supply, off, or a device for doing this. **2** (*often before a noun*) a stopping-point for some treatment, etc, or the point, date, or period for this: *Where's the cutoff point?* **3** (*in pl*) shorts made from a pair of jeans by cutting the legs off at the thigh.

cut off *verb trans* **1** to remove (something) by cutting. **2** to stop the passage of (something): *Supplies were cut off.* **3** to separate or restrict (somebody or something): *A line of trees cut off the view; He cut himself off from his family.* **4** to cause the untimely death of (somebody). **5** to disinherit (an heir). **6** to stop the operation of (a motor). **7** to disconnect (somebody) during a telephone call. **8** to deprive (somebody) of a supply of something, *esp* gas or electricity.

cutout *noun* **1** something cut out: *a cardboard cutout of the President.* **2** a device that cuts out; *esp* one that is operated automatically by an excessive electric current.

cut out¹ *verb trans* **1** to form or shape (something) by cutting, erosion, etc. **2** to eliminate (somebody or something) from a process or activity: *cut out the middleman.* **3** to stop doing (something). **4a** to remove or exclude (somebody or something). **b** to make (an engine, etc) inoperative. ➤ *verb intrans* **1** said of an engine: to cease operating. **2** *NAmer* to swerve out from a lane of traffic. **3** *NAmer* to leave. ✴ **cut it out** *informal* stop it.

cut out² *adj* (*usu in negative contexts*) naturally fitted or suited: *He is not cut out to be an actor; I'm not cut out for teaching.*

cut-price *adj* selling or sold at a discount.

cutpurse *noun archaic* a purse-stealer; a pickpocket: *cutpurse quick of hand* — Shakespeare. [with reference to the theft of purses by cutting the strings attaching them to the belt]

cutter *noun* **1a** a person whose work is cutting or involves cutting, e.g. of cloth or film. **b** an instrument, machine, machine part, or tool that cuts. **2a** a ship's boat for carrying stores or passengers. **b** formerly, a fore-and-aft rigged sailing boat with a single mast and two foresails.

cutthroat¹ *noun dated* a murderous thug.

cutthroat² *adj* **1** murderous; cruel. **2** ruthless; unprincipled: *cutthroat competition.*

cutthroat razor *noun Brit* a razor with a rigid steel cutting blade hinged to a case that forms a handle when the razor is open for use.

cutting¹ *noun* **1** something cut off or out: *clear the cuttings off the floor.* **2** a part of a plant stem, leaf, root, etc capable of developing into a new plant. **3** an excavation or cut, *esp* through high ground, for a canal, road, etc. **4** *Brit* an item cut out of a publication. *NAmer* Also called CLIPPING: *press cuttings.* **5** a gramophone record; a disc. **6** a harvesting.

cutting² *adj* **1** designed for cutting; sharp; edged: *a cutting tool.* **2** said of a remark: likely to wound the feelings of another; sarcastic. **3** said of wind: strong and piercingly cold. ➤➤ **cuttingly** *adv*.

cutting and shutting *noun informal* the illegal practice of welding together two halves of different cars.

cutting edge *noun* the most advanced point, where important action is taken: *at the cutting edge of new technology.*

cuttlebone /'kutlbohn/ *noun* the internal shell of the cuttlefish used in the form of a powder for polishing or as a mineral supplement to the diet of cage birds. [Middle English *cotul* cuttlefish (from Old English *cudele*) + BONE¹]

cuttlefish /'kutlfish/ *noun* (*pl* **cuttlefishes** *or collectively* **cuttlefish**) any of several genera of ten-armed marine CEPHALOPOD molluscs differing from the related squids in having a hard internal shell: genus *Sepia* and other genera. [Middle English *cotul* (see CUTTLEBONE) + FISH¹]

cut up¹ *verb trans* **1** to cut (something) into parts or pieces. **2** to criticize (somebody) severely or hostilely. **3** said of a driver: to swerve in front of (another driver). ➤ *verb intrans NAmer, informal* to behave in a comic or unruly manner. ✳ **cut up rough** to behave aggressively or vindictively.

cut up² *adj informal* deeply distressed; grieved.

cutwater *noun* the foremost part of a ship's bow.

cutwork *noun* a type of embroidery or lace with parts cut out, the edges being decoratively oversewn.

cutworm *noun* any of several species of chiefly nocturnal caterpillars that feed on plant stems near ground level: family Noctuidae.

cuvée /'kyoohvay (*French* kyve)/ *noun* a blend or batch of wine, *esp* champagne. [French *cuvée* vatful, from *cuve*: see CUVETTE]

cuvette /kyooh'vet/ *noun* a small transparent laboratory vessel, *specif* for holding samples in a SPECTROPHOTOMETER (instrument for measuring light absorption). [French *cuvette*, dimin. of *cuve* tub, from Latin *cupa*]

CV *abbr* curriculum vitae.

CVO *abbr Brit* Commander of the Royal Victorian Order.

CVS *abbr* chorionic villus sampling, a test for foetal abnormality.

Cwlth *abbr* Commonwealth.

cwm /koohm/ *noun* a basin-shaped hollow in a mountain, *esp* in Wales; = CIRQUE (1). [Welsh *cwm* valley]

cwo *abbr* cash with order.

CWS *abbr* Cooperative Wholesale Society.

cwt *abbr* hundredweight.

CY *abbr* Cyprus (international vehicle registration).

-cy *suffix* forming nouns from nouns and adjectives, denoting: **1** action or practice of: *mendicancy*; *piracy*. **2** rank or office of: *baronetcy*; *papacy*. **3** body or class of: *magistracy*. **4** quality or state of: *accuracy*; *bankruptcy*. [Middle English *-cie*, via Old French *-cie*, *-tie* from Latin *-cia*, *-tia* and Greek *-ti(e)ia*, *t(e)ia*]

cyan /'siean, 'sie-ən/ *noun* a greenish blue colour. [Greek *kyanos* dark blue]

cyan- *or* **cyano-** *comb. form* forming words, with the meanings: **1** dark blue; blue: *cyanosis*. **2** cyanide: *cyanogen*. **3** containing a cyanide group: *cyanobenzene*. [German *cyan-*, from Greek *kyan-*, *kyano-*, from *kyanos* dark blue]

cyanamide /sie'anəmied/ *noun* **1** calcium cyanamide. **2** a caustic organic acid whose calcium salt is calcium cyanamide. [blend of CYANOGEN + AMIDE]

cyanic /sie'anik/ *adj* **1** relating to or containing CYANOGEN. **2** of a blue or bluish colour.

cyanic acid /sie'anik/ *noun* a strongly acidic, colourless, poisonous, and volatile liquid, HOCN.

cyanide /'sie-ənied/ *noun* an extremely poisonous salt of HYDROCYANIC ACID or a NITRILE (organic compound), containing the univalent chemical radical -CN. [CYANOGEN + -IDE]

cyano- *comb. form see* CYAN-.

cyanoacrylate /,sie-ənoh'akrilayt/ *noun* any of several liquid acrylate monomers (unit of a polymer; see MONOMER) that are used as very rapidly setting strong adhesives in industry and medicine.

cyanobacterium /,sie-ənohbak'tiəri-&schwam/ *noun* (*pl* **cyanobacteria** /-riə/) any of a division of blue-pigmented microorganisms capable of PHOTOSYNTHESIS (using light to synthesize organic compounds, as plants do) and formerly regarded as algae; = BLUE-GREEN ALGA.

cyanocobalamin /,sie-ənohkoh'baləmin/ *noun* a water-soluble vitamin B containing cobalt, that occurs *esp* in liver, is essential for normal blood formation and nerve function, and whose lack or malabsorption results in pernicious anaemia; vitamin B_{12}. [CYANO- + COBALT + VITAMIN]

cyanogen /sie'anəjən/ *noun* a colourless inflammable extremely poisonous gas. [French *cyanogène*, from CYANO- + *gène* -GEN]

cyanosis /sie-ə'nohsis/ *noun* bluish or purplish discoloration of the skin due to deficient oxygenation of the blood. ➤ **cyanotic** /-'notik/ *adj*. [scientific Latin from Greek *kyanōsis* dark blue colour, from *kyanos* dark blue]

cyber- *comb. form* forming words, denoting: information technology, *esp* the Internet: *cybercafé*. [back-formation from CYBERNETICS]

cybercafé /'siebəkafay, -fi/ *noun* a café that offers the public access to information technology, *esp* the Internet, for a fee.

cyberchondriac /siebə'kondriak/ *noun* somebody who having consulted a medical self-diagnosis site on the Internet goes to a doctor complaining of an ailment or ailments they have convinced themselves they are suffering from. [from CYBER- + HYPOCHONDRIAC]

cyber-crime *noun* computer-based crime such as computer hacking, financial fraud and the dissemination of illegal pornography through the Internet.

cyberflirtation /'siebəfluhtaysh(ə)n/ *noun* flirtation via the Internet.

cybernated /'siebənaytid/ *adj* involving CYBERNATION: *a cybernated bakery*.

cybernation /siebə'naysh(ə)n/ *noun* the automatic control of a process or operation, e.g. in manufacturing, by means of computers. [CYBERNETICS + -ATION]

cybernetics /siebə'netiks/ *pl noun* (*treated as sing. or pl*) the comparative study of the automatic control systems formed by the nervous system and brain and by mechanical-electrical communication systems. ➤ **cybernetic** *adj*. [Greek *kybernētēs* pilot, governor (from *kybernan* to steer, govern) + -ICS]

cyberphobia /siebə'fohbi-ə/ *noun* fear or distrust of computers and information technology, *esp* the Internet. ➤ **cyberphobe** /'sie-/ *noun*, **cyberphobic** /'fohbik/ *adj*.

cyberpunk /'siebəpungk/ *noun* **1** a genre of science fiction which envisages a bleak and violent future society in which the world is controlled by a computer network. **2** a creator or devotee of cyberpunk.

cybersex /'siebəseks/ *noun* sexual activity on the Internet involving the use of pornographic websites, sexual titillation in chat rooms, etc.

cyberspace /'siebəspays/ *noun* the notional environment in which on-line communication takes place.

cybersquatter /'siebəskwotə/ *noun* somebody who registers an Internet domain name that is likely to be wanted by another person, a business organization, or other body in the hope of selling it to them at a profit.

cyberstalking /'siebə,stawking/ *noun* obsessive or threatening communication with a person by email. ➤ **cyberstalker** *noun*.

cyberterrorism /'siebəterəriz(ə)m/ *noun* politically motivated disruptive or destructive attacks on computer systems and databases via the Internet.

cyborg /'siebawg/ *noun* an unemotional fictional character that is part human and part machine. [short for *cybernetic organism*]

cycad /'siekad/ *noun* any of a genus of tropical gymnospermous (producing seeds not encased in an ovary; see GYMNOSPERM) trees resembling palms: genus *Cycas*. [Latin genus name, ultimately from Greek *koix* Egyptian palm]

cycl- *or* **cyclo-** *comb. form* forming words, with the meanings: **1** circle: *cyclometer*. **2** having a cyclic molecular structure: *cyclohexane*. [Greek *kykl-*, *kyklo-*, from *kyklos* circle]

Cycladic /si'kladik/ *adj* denoting the Bronze-Age culture and artefacts of the Cyclades, islands of the S Aegean Sea, in the period 3000–1050 BC.

cyclamate /'sikləmayt, 'sie-/ *noun* a synthetic compound used, *esp* formerly, as an artificial sweetener. [*cyclohexyl* (from CYCLOHEXANE + -YL) + *sulphamate* (from SULPHUR¹ + AMIDE + -ATE¹)]

cyclamen /'sikləmən/ *noun* (*pl* **cyclamen** *or* **cyclamens**) any of a genus of plants of the primrose family with drooping pink, red, or white flowers: genus *Cyclamen*. [Latin genus name, from Greek *kyklaminos*]

cycle¹ /'siekl/ *noun* **1a** a series of related events happening in a regularly repeated order, or the time needed to complete it: *the cycle of reproduction*. **b** one complete performance of a periodic process, e.g. a vibration or electrical oscillation. **2** a group of poems, plays, novels, operas, or songs on a central theme: *the Ring Cycle*. **3** a bicycle, motorcycle, tricycle, etc. [French *cycle* via late Latin *cyclus* from Greek *kyklos* circle, wheel, cycle]

cycle² *verb intrans* **1** to ride a cycle; to bicycle. **2a** to pass through a cycle. **b** to recur in cycles. ➤ **cycling** *noun*.

cyclic /'siklik, 'sieklik/ *adj* **1** of or belonging to a cycle. **2** said of a compound, e.g. benzene: containing a ring of atoms. **3** of a figure whose vertices lie on the circumference of a circle.

cyclical /'siklikl, 'sieklikl/ *adj* = CYCLIC.

cycling shorts *pl noun* **1** tight-fitting Lycra shorts reaching to mid-thigh or just above the knee and having a padded seat, worn for cycling. **2** a similar garment without padding, for casual wear.

cyclise /'siekliez/ *verb* see CYCLIZE.

cyclist /'sieklist/ *noun* a person who rides a bicycle.

cyclize *or* **cyclise** /'siekliez/ *verb trans* to make (a chemical compound) form one or more rings in the molecular structure. ≫ **cyclization** /-'zaysh(ə)n/ *noun*.

cyclo- *comb. form* see CYCL-.

cycloalkane /siekloh'alkayn/ *noun* any of a group of saturated chemical compounds of the general formula C_nH_{2n} that contain only carbon and hydrogen atoms arranged in rings.

cyclo-cross /'siekloh kros/ *noun* the sport of racing bicycles on cross-country courses that usu require contestants to carry their bicycles at some stage.

cyclohexane /siekloh'heksayn/ *noun* a cyclic hydrocarbon found in petroleum and used *esp* as a solvent and in organic synthesis.

cycloid¹ /'siekloyd/ *noun* a curve resembling a series of arches traced by a point on the circumference of a circle that is rolling along a straight line. ≫ **cycloidal** /sie'kloydl/ *adj*. [French *cycloïde*, from Greek *kykloeidēs* circular, from *kyklos* circle]

cycloid² *adj* circular; *esp* arranged or progressing in circles.

cyclometer /sie'klomitə/ *noun* a device designed to record the revolutions of a wheel and often the distance traversed by a wheeled vehicle, *esp* a bicycle.

cyclone /'sieklohn/ *noun* **1** a storm or system of winds that rotates about a centre of low atmospheric pressure, advances at high speeds, and often brings abundant rain. **2** a tornado. **3** a region of low atmospheric pressure; = LOW² (2). ≫ **cyclonic** /sie'klonik/ *adj*, **cyclonically** /sie'klonikli/ *adv*. [Greek *kyklōma* wheel, coil, from *kykloun* to go round, from *kyklos* circle]

cyclopaedia /sieklə'peedi·ə/ *noun* see CYCLOPEDIA.

cyclopean /sieklə'pee·ən, sie'klohpiən/ *adj* **1** relating to or resembling a Cyclops. **2** huge; massive: *the cyclopean wall of granite cliff which forms the western side of Lundy* — Charles Kingsley. **3** denoting a style of masonry typical in Greece during the Mycenaean period, using massive blocks of undressed stone.

cyclopedia *or* **cyclopaedia** /sieklə'peedi·ə/ *noun archaic* an encyclopedia. ≫ **cyclopedic** /-dik/ *adj*. [shortening]

Cyclops /'sieklops/ *noun* (*pl* **Cyclopses** *or* **Cyclopes** /-peez/) **1** in Greek mythology, a member of a race of savage giants with a single eye in the centre of the forehead. **2** (**cyclops**) any of several species of a tiny predatory CRUSTACEAN with a cylindrical body and a single eye: genus *Cyclops* and other genera. [Greek *Kyklops* round-eyed]

cyclorama /sieklə'rahmə/ *noun* (*pl* **cycloramas**) **1** a scene painted on the interior wall of a cylindrical room, appearing in natural perspective to a central observer. **2** in the theatre, a cloth or wall curved in an arc at the back of the stage, often painted to represent the sky. [CYCLO- + Greek *horama* spectacle, modelled on PANORAMA]

cyclosis /sie'klohsis/ *noun* the slow, usu circular, movement of CYTOPLASM within a living cell. [scientific Latin from Greek *kyklōsis* encirclement, from *kykloun*: see CYCLONE]

cyclosporin /siekloh'spawrin/ *noun* a drug produced by certain fungi, which suppresses the immune response and is used to prevent rejection after transplant surgery. [scientific Latin *Cyclosporinae*, class of brown algae from which it is obtained]

cyclostome /'siekləstohm/ *noun* any of a class of primitive fishlike vertebrates, including the hagfishes and lampreys, that have a round sucking mouth: class Cyclostomata. [CYCLO- + Greek *stoma* mouth]

cyclostyle¹ /'siekləstiel/ *noun* a machine for making multiple copies that uses a stencil cut by a pen whose tip is a small ROWEL¹ (toothed wheel). [orig a trademark; from CYCLO- + STYLE¹]

cyclostyle² *verb trans* to make multiple copies of (something) by using a cyclostyle.

cyclothymia /siekloh'thiemi·ə/ *noun dated* a condition marked by abnormal swings between elated and depressed moods. ≫ **cyclothymic** /-mik/ *adj*. [scientific Latin *cyclothymia* from German *Zyklothymie*, from *zykl*- CYCLO- + *-thymie* -thymia]

cyclotron /'sieklətron/ *noun* a particle accelerator in which protons, ions, etc are propelled by an alternating electric field in a constant magnetic field. [CYCLO- + -TRON; from the circular movement of the particles]

cyder /'siedə/ *noun Brit, archaic* = CIDER.

cygnet /'signit/ *noun* a young swan. [Middle English *sygnett* from early French *cygne* swan, via Latin from Greek *kyknos*]

cylinder /'silində/ *noun* **1a** a surface traced by a straight line moving parallel to a fixed straight line and passing through all the points of a circle in other closed curves. **b** the space bounded by a cylinder and two parallel planes that cross it. **c** a hollow or solid object with the shape of a cylinder and a circular or oval cross-section. **2a** the piston chamber in a steam or internal-combustion engine. **b** any of various rotating parts, e.g. in printing presses. **c** a metal container for gas under pressure. [early French *cylindre* via Latin from Greek *kylindros* roller, from *kylindein* to roll]

cylinder block *noun* the metal moulding that contains the cylinders of an internal-combustion engine; = BLOCK¹ (10).

cylinder head *noun* the top cover of the CYLINDER BLOCK of an internal-combustion engine, providing a gas-tight seal.

cylinder seal *noun* a barrel-shaped stone seal incised with cuneiform characters, of a kind used in ancient Mesopotamia.

cylindric /si'lindrik/ *adj* see CYLINDRICAL.

cylindrical /si'lindrikl/ *adj* of, or in the form of, a cylinder. ≫ **cylindrically** *adv*.

cymbal /'simbl/ *noun* a percussion instrument consisting of a concave brass plate that produces a clashing tone when struck with a drumstick or against another cymbal. ≫ **cymbalist** *noun*. [Middle English, from Old English *cymbal* and early French *cymbale*, both via Latin from Greek *kymbalon*, from *kymbē* bowl]

cymbidium /sim'bidi·əm/ *noun* a tropical *esp* Asian and Australasian orchid with showy boat-shaped flowers: genus *Cymbidium*. [Latin genus name, from Latin *cymba* boat, from Greek *kymbē* bowl, boat]

cyme /siem/ *noun* an inflorescence in which all floral axes end in a single flower and the main axis bears the central and first-opening flower with subsequent flowers developing from side shoots: compare RACEME. ≫ **cymose** /'siemohs, 'siemohz/ *adj*, **cymosely** /'sie-/ *adv*. [Latin *cyma* cabbage sprout, from Greek *kyma* swell, wave, cabbage sprout, from *kyein* to be pregnant]

Cymric /'kimrik/ *adj dated* denoting the Welsh language or Welsh culture. [Welsh *Cymry* Brythonic Celts, Welshmen, pl of *Cymro* Welshman]

cynic /'sinik/ *noun* **1a** a person who doubts the existence of human sincerity or of any motive other than self-interest: *'What is a cynic?' 'A man who knows the price of everything and the value of nothing'* — Oscar Wilde. **b** a person who is habitually pessimistic or sardonic. **2** (**Cynic**) an adherent of an ancient Greek school of philosophers who held that virtue is the highest good and that its essence lies in mastery over one's desires and wants.

Editorial note
The Cynics of ancient Greece, among whom Diogenes is most famous, taught that the only way to attain peace of mind is to reject the ordinary amenities of life and to live simply and austerely. It is probably because they disdained all conventions and attempted to live naturally, like animals, that they were called 'cynic', literally 'doglike' — Dr Anthony Grayling.

≫ **cynicism** /-siz(ə)m/ *noun*. [early French *cynique* via Latin from Greek *kynikos*, literally 'like a dog' from *kyn-*, *kyōn* dog, which became a nickname for a Cynic]

cynical *adj* **1** sceptical about the existence of altruism; believing that people are motivated by self-interest. **2** manifesting this kind of motivation: *the cynical exploitation of cheap labour; the kind of inferior work you'd expect from a cynical clock-watcher*.

cynosure /'sinəzyooə, 'sie-/ *noun* a centre of attraction, interest, or attention: *where perhaps some beauty lies, the cynosure of neighbouring eyes* — Milton.

Word history
French *cynosure* Ursa Minor, guide, via Latin from Greek *kynosoura*, from *kynos oura* dog's tail. Ursa Minor contains the pole star, used as a guide by navigators and therefore the centre of their attention.

Cynthia /'sinthi·ə/ *noun literary* the moon personified. [Latin *Cynthia*, goddess of the moon, fem of *Cynthius* of *Cynthus*, mountain on Delos, Greek island, where she was born]

cypher¹ /'siefə/ *noun* see CIPHER¹.

cypher² *verb trans* see CIPHER².

cypress /'sieprəs/ *noun* **1** any of several species of evergreen gymnospermous trees with aromatic overlapping leaves resembling scales: *Cupressus sempervirens* and other species. **2** the wood of any of these trees. [Middle English via Old French and Latin from Greek *kyparissos*]

cyprinid /'siprinid/ *noun* any of a family of bony fishes that includes the carp, dace, and tench: family Cyprinidae. [scientific Latin *Cyprinidae* from Greek *kyprinos* carp]

Cypriot /'sipri·ət/ *or* **Cypriote** /-oht/ *noun* **1** a native or inhabitant of Cyprus in the eastern Mediterranean. **2** the form of Greek spoken on Cyprus. ➤➤ **Cypriot** *adj.* [French *cypriote*, ultimately from Greek *Kypriōtēs*, from *Kypros* Cyprus]

Cypriot Greek *noun* = CYPRIOT (2).

cypripedium /sipri'peedi·əm/ *noun* any of a genus of orchids with large showy drooping flowers including the lady's slipper: genus *Cypripedium*. [Latin genus name, from late Latin *Cypris*, a name for Venus, goddess of love and beauty + Greek *pedilon* sandal]

cypsela /'sipsələ/ *noun* (*pl* **cypselae** /-lee/) a one-seeded fruit, e.g. that of the daisy, formed by fusion of two carpels (female reproductive organs; see CARPEL) and surrounded by a tubular CALYX (circle of leaflike structures supporting a flower). [via scientific Latin, from Greek *kypselē* vessel, box]

Cyrenaic /sie·ərinayik/ *adj* relating to a hedonistic (regarding pleasure as the greatest good; see HEDONISM) school of philosophy founded by Aristippus of Cyrene in about 400 BC. [*Cyrene*, ancient Greek city in N Africa]

Cyrillic /si'rilik/ *adj* denoting an alphabet used for writing various Slavic languages, e.g. Old Church Slavonic, Russian, and Bulgarian. ➤➤ **Cyrillic** *noun*. [named after St *Cyril* d.869, apostle of the Slavs, reputed inventor of the Cyrillic alphabet]

cyst /sist/ *noun* **1** a closed sac, e.g. of watery liquid or gas, with a distinct membrane, *esp* one developing abnormally in a plant or animal. **2a** a micro-organism in a resting or spore stage, or a capsule formed about it. **b** a resistant cover about a parasite when inside the host. ➤➤ **cystoid** /'sistoyd/ *adj and noun*. [scientific Latin *cystis* from Greek *kystis* bladder, pouch]

cyst- *or* **cysto-** *comb. form* forming words, denoting: **1** bladder: *cystitis*; *cystoscope*. **2** sac: *cystocarp*. [French *cyst-* from Greek *kyst-*, *kysto-*, from *kystis*]

-cyst *comb. form* forming nouns, denoting: a bladder or sac: *blastocyst*. [scientific Latin *-cystis* from Greek *kystis*]

cystectomy /si'tektəmi/ *noun* (*pl* **cystectomies**) surgical removal of: **a** the urinary bladder. **b** the gall bladder. **c** a diseased cyst.

cysteine /'sisti·een, 'sistayn/ *noun* a sulphur-containing amino acid found in many proteins and readily convertible to CYSTINE. [CYSTINE + *-ein* -IN¹]

cystic /'sistik/ *adj* **1** of, composed of, or containing a cyst or cysts. **2** of the urinary or gall bladder.

cystic fibrosis *noun* a common, often fatal, hereditary disease appearing in early childhood and marked *esp* by faulty digestion and difficulty in breathing.

cystine /'sisteen, 'sistin/ *noun* an oxidized dimeric form of cysteine. [CYST- + -INE² from its discovery in bladder stones]

cystitis /si'stietəs/ *noun* inflammation of the urinary bladder, causing frequency of urination, accompanied by a burning sensation. [scientific Latin *cystitis*]

cysto- *comb. form* see CYST-.

cystocarp /'sistəkahp/ *noun* the fruiting structure, containing spores borne on filaments, produced in red algae after fertilization.

cystoscope /'sistəskohp/ *noun* an instrument that is passed through the URETHRA (tube that discharges urine from the bladder) for the visual examination of the bladder and the introduction of instruments into the bladder under visual control. ➤➤ **cystoscopic** *adj*, **cystoscopy** *noun*.

cyt- *or* **cyto-** *comb. form* forming words, denoting: **1** cell: *cytology*. **2** cytoplasm: *cytokinesis*. [German *zyt-*, *zyto-*, from Greek *kytos* hollow vessel]

-cyte *comb. form* forming nouns, denoting: a cell: *leucocyte*. [scientific Latin *-cyta* from Greek *kytos* hollow vessel]

cytidine /'sietədeen/ *noun* a NUCLEOSIDE containing CYTOSINE. [CYTOSINE + -IDE + -INE²]

cyto- *comb. form* see CYT-.

cytoarchitectonics /sitoh·ahkitek'toniks/ *pl noun* (*treated as sing.*) = CYTOARCHITECTURE.

cytoarchitecture /sietoh'ahkitektchə/ *noun* **1** the structure of cells. **2** the arrangement of cells in tissue.

cytochrome /'sietəkrohm/ *noun* any of several enzymes that function in intracellular energy generation as transporters of electrons, *esp* to oxygen, by undergoing successive oxidation and reduction.

cytogenetics /sitohji'netiks/ *pl noun* (*treated as sing. or pl*) a branch of genetics that investigates the structure of chromosomes in relation to heredity and variation.

cytokinesis /sietohki'neesis/ *noun* the cleavage of the cytoplasm of a cell into daughter cells following division of the nucleus. [scientific Latin *cytokinesis*, from CYT- + Greek *kinēsis* motion]

cytokinin /sietoh'kienin/ *noun* any of various plant-growth hormones that promote cell division and are concerned with a variety of developmental processes, e.g. initiation of shoot formation and seed germination. [CYT- + KININ]

cytology /sie'toləji/ *noun* the biology of the structure, function, multiplication, pathology, etc of cells. ➤➤ **cytological** /-'lojikl/ *adj*, **cytologically** /-'lojikli/ *adv*, **cytologist** *noun*.

cytolysis /sie'tolisis/ *noun* the dissolution or disintegration of cells, usu associated with disease. ➤➤ **cytolytic** /-'litik/ *adj*.

cytomegalic /sietohmi'galik/ *adj* characterized by or producing enlarged cells. [scientific Latin *cytomegalia* condition of having enlarged cells (from CYT- + MEGAL- + -IA¹) + -IC¹]

cytomegalovirus /sietohmegaloh'vie·ərəs/ *adj* any of a large group of highly species-specific DNA-containing viruses that are widely distributed in human beings and that affect *esp* the salivary glands and kidney, causing enlargement of the infected cells.

cytoplasm /'sietohplaz(ə)m/ *noun* the substance of a plant or animal cell outside the organelles, e.g. the nucleus and mitochondria. ➤➤ **cytoplasmic** /-'plazmik/ *adj*, **cytoplasmically** /-'plazmikli/ *adv*.

cytosine /'sietəseen/ *noun* a pyrimidine base that is one of the four bases whose order in a DNA or RNA chain codes genetic information: compare ADENINE, GUANINE, THYMINE, URACIL. [CYT- + -OSE² + -INE²]

cytosol /'sietohsol/ *noun* the portion of the cytoplasm excluding the organelles (parts with a special function; see ORGANELLE).

cytotoxin /sietoh'toksin/ *noun* a substance with a toxic effect on cells. ➤➤ **cytotoxic** /-'sik/ *adj*, **cytotoxicity** /-'sisiti/ *noun*.

CZ *abbr* Czech Republic (international vehicle registration).

czar /zah/ *noun* see TSAR.

czardas *or* **csardas** /'chahdash/ *noun* (*pl* **czardas** *or* **csardas** /chahdash/) a Hungarian dance in which the dancers start slowly and finish rapidly. [Hungarian *csárdás*]

czarevich /'zahrəvich/ *noun* see TSAREVICH.

czarina /zah'reenə/ *noun* see TSARINA.

Czech /chek/ *noun* **1** a native or inhabitant of the Czech Republic; *specif* a Slav of the former W Czechoslovakia. **2** the Slavonic language of the Czechs. ➤➤ **Czech** *adj*.

Word history

Czech *Čech*. Czech words that have passed into English include *howitzer*, *pistol*, *polka*, and *robot*.

Czechoslovak /chekə'slohvak/ *or* **Czechoslovakian** /-vakiən/ *noun* a native or inhabitant of the former country of Czechoslovakia, separated since 1993 into the two independent countries of the Czech Republic and Slovakia. ➤➤ **Czechoslovakian** *noun*.

D¹ *or* **d** *noun* (*pl* **D's** *or* **Ds** *or* **d's**) **1a** the fourth letter of the English alphabet. **b** a written character or design denoting this letter. **c** the sound represented by this letter, one of the English consonants. **2** an item designated as D, *esp* the fourth in a series. **3** a mark of grade rating a student's work as below average. **4** in music, the second note of the diatonic scale of C major. **5** the Roman numeral for 500.

D² *abbr* **1** *NAmer* Democrat. **2** *NAmer* Democratic. **3** depth (of an object). **4** Deutschland (international vehicle registration for Germany). **5** dimensional (used after a number). **6** dimensions (used after a number). **7** drawn (used in tables of match results).

D³ *abbr* the chemical symbol for deuterium.

d *abbr* **1** daughter. **2** day(s). **3** deci-. **4** departs (used in timetables). **5** diameter. **6** died. **7** *Brit* pence (before decimalization). **8** *Brit* penny (before decimalization).

d' *contraction* do: *D'you know what the time is?*

'd *contraction* **1** had. **2** would.

DA *abbr* **1** *NAmer* district attorney. **2** *informal* duck's arse (hairstyle).

D/A *abbr* in electronics, digital to analogue.

da¹ /dah/ *noun Brit, dialect* an affectionate name for one's father. [imitating baby talk]

da² *abbr* deca-.

dab¹ /dab/ *verb* (**dabbed, dabbing**) ➤ *verb trans* **1** to touch (a surface) lightly and repeatedly, *esp* with a cloth, brush, etc. **2** to apply (a liquid or powder) with light strokes: *She dabbed powder on her cheeks.* ➤ *verb intrans* to pat something gently: *dabbing ineffectually at the cut with a tissue.*

dab² *noun* **1** a small amount of something soft or moist: *a dab of paint.* **2** a gentle touch or stroke, e.g. with a sponge; a pat. **3** *Brit, informal* (*in pl*) fingerprints. [Middle English *dabbe*, prob of imitative origin]

dab³ *noun* any of several species of common brown flatfish found *esp* in the North Atlantic: genus *Limanda*. [Anglo-French *dabbe*]

dabber /'dabə/ *noun* in printing, a pad used to ink type or engraving plates.

dabble /'dabl/ *verb trans* to dip (the fingers or toes) in water and move them about. ➤ *verb intrans* **1** said of a water bird: to reach with the beak to the bottom of shallow water to obtain food. **2** (*often* + in) to work or concern oneself casually or superficially: *She dabbles in art.* ➤➤ **dabbler** *noun*. [perhaps frequentative of DAB¹]

dabchick *noun* any of several small grebes, *esp* the little grebe. [prob irreg from obsolete *dop* to dive + CHICK]

dab hand *noun Brit, informal* a person who is skilful at something; an expert. [*dab* perhaps alteration of ADEPT¹]

DAC *abbr* in electronics, digital to analogue converter.

da capo /dah 'kahpoh/ *adj and adv* used as a direction in music: repeat or repeated from the beginning: compare DAL SEGNO. [Italian *da capo* from the head]

dace /days/ *noun* (*pl* **dace**) a small slender freshwater European fish: *Leuciscus leuciscus*. [Middle English from early French *dars*: see DART¹; from the way it darts around in the water]

dacha *or* **datcha** /'dahchə/ *noun* (*pl* **dachas** *or* **datchas**) a Russian country cottage, *esp* one used as a second or holiday home. [Russian *dacha* gift, grant of land; because it was often the gift of a ruler]

dachshund /'daksənd/ *noun* a dog of a breed originating in Germany, having a long body, short legs, and long drooping ears. [German *Dachshund* from *Dachs* badger + *Hund* dog; because the dogs were orig bred to hunt badgers]

dacite /'daysiet/ *noun* a fine-grained volcanic rock containing quartz. ➤➤ **dacitic** *adj.* [*Dacia*, a Roman province + -ITE¹]

dacoit /də'koyt/ *noun* in India and Myanmar (formerly Burma), a member of an armed gang of robbers. [Hindi *ḍakait*]

Dacron /'dakron/ *noun NAmer, trademark* a synthetic polyester textile fibre.

dactyl /'daktil/ *noun* a metrical foot consisting of one long and two short, or one stressed and two unstressed, syllables, e.g. in *tenderly*. [Middle English *dactile* via Latin from Greek *daktylos* finger; from the first of the three syllables being the longest, like the joints of the finger]

dactylic¹ /dak'tilik/ *adj* of or containing dactyls.

dactylic² *noun* (*also in pl*) verse containing dactyls.

dad /dad/ *noun informal* an affectionate name for one's father. [prob imitating baby talk]

Dada /'dahdah/ *noun* an early 20th-cent. movement in art and literature based on deliberate irrationality and negation of traditional artistic values. Dada was one of the main influences on surrealism.

Editorial note ━━━━━━
Dada was not a style. It was, as André Breton (1896–1966) said, a state of mind. Born during World War I in Zurich, it took the utter bankruptcy of conventional society, art, literature and thought as its starting point. Instead, it inculcated anti-art and unreason through ironic and anarchic gestures (which paradoxically often proved a fertile inspiration for later art) — Martin Gayford.

➤➤ **Dadaism** *noun,* **Dadaist** *noun and adj,* **Dadaistic** /-'istik/ *adj.* [French *dada* hobbyhorse, title of a review; said to have been chosen because it sounded meaningless or childish]

daddy /'dadi/ *noun* (*pl* **daddies**) *informal* an affectionate name for one's father. [DAD + -Y⁴]

daddy longlegs /'longlegz/ *noun* (*pl* **daddy longlegs**) **1** *Brit* = CRANE FLY. **2** *NAmer* = HARVESTMAN.

dado /'daydoh/ *noun* (*pl* **dados** or **dadoes**) **1** the lower part of an interior wall when decorated or faced differently from the upper part. **2** in architecture, the part of a pedestal or plinth between the base and the cornice. **3** *NAmer* a rectangular groove made across the grain of a piece of wood, so that another piece can be fitted to form a joint. [Italian *dado* die, plinth]

dado rail *noun* a decorative moulding attached to an interior wall, usu at the height of the windowsills.

daemon /'deemən/ or **daimon** /'diemohn/ *noun* **1** a supernatural being of Greek mythology; a demigod. **2** an attendant power or spirit; a genius: *The fairest fortune that can befall a man is to be guided by his daemon to that which is truly his own* — Ralph Waldo Emerson. **3** *archaic* = DEMON (1). ➤➤ **daemonic** /dee'monik/ *adj*. [late Latin *daemon*: see DEMON]

daff /daf/ *noun informal* a daffodil.

daffodil /'dafədil/ *noun* any of several species of bulb-producing plants with flowers that have a large typically yellow corona elongated into a trumpet shape: genus *Narcissus*. [prob from Dutch *de affodil* the asphodel, via early French *afrodille* via Latin from Greek *asphodelos*]

daffodil yellow *adj* of a bright yellow colour. ➤➤ **daffodil yellow** *noun*.

daffy /'dafi/ *adj* (**daffier, daffiest**) *informal* crazy or foolish. ➤➤ **daffiness** *noun*. [obsolete *daff* fool, coward]

daft /dahft/ *adj chiefly Brit, informal* **1** silly or foolish. **2** (+ about) fanatically enthusiastic or infatuated. [Old English *gedæfte* mild, gentle]

dag[1] /dag/ *noun Aus, NZ* a piece of matted or manure-coated wool on a sheep's hindquarters. * **rattle one's dags** *informal* to hurry up. [Middle English *dagge* a part hanging down; earlier history unknown]

dag[2] *verb trans* (**dagged, dagging**) *Aus, NZ* to remove dags from (a sheep).

dag[3] *noun Aus, NZ, informal* an eccentric or socially awkward person. [prob from English slang *dagen* artful criminal, from *dagen*, *degen* sword, from German *Degen*]

Dagestanian /dagi'stahniən, -'staniən/ *noun* **1** a native or inhabitant of Dagestan in SW Russia. **2** the NE Caucasian language of the people of Dagestan. ➤➤ **Dagestanian** *adj*.

dagga /'dahkhə/ *noun chiefly SAfr* cannabis. [Afrikaans *dagga* from Khoikhoi *dachab*]

dagger /'dagə/ *noun* **1** a short sharp pointed weapon used for stabbing: *I will speak daggers to her but use none* — Shakespeare. **2** in printing, a sign (†) used as a reference mark or to indicate a death date; an obelus. * **at daggers drawn** in bitter conflict. **look daggers at** to look angrily at (somebody). [Middle English, prob from obsolete *dag* to stab, pierce]

daggy /'dagi/ *adj* (**daggier, daggiest**) *Aus, NZ, informal* **1** slovenly. **2** dowdy or unfashionably dressed. [DAG[3]]

dago /'daygoh/ *noun* (*pl* **dagos** or **dagoes**) *informal, offensive* a person of Italian, Spanish, or Portuguese birth or descent. [alteration of *diego*, from the Spanish first name *Diego*]

daguerreotype or **daguerrotype** /də'geratiep/ *noun* an early photograph produced on a silver or a silver-covered copper plate. [French *daguerréotype*, named after L J M *Daguerre* d.1851, French painter and physicist who invented it]

dah /dah/ *noun* = DASH[2] (2). [imitative]

dahlia /'dayli·ə, 'daylyə/ *noun* any of a genus of Mexican composite plants with showy flower heads and roots that form tubers, including many ornamental garden plants: genus *Dahlia*. [named after Anders *Dahl* d.1789, Swedish botanist who discovered the genus]

daikon /'diek(ə)n, 'diekon/ *noun* = MOOLI. [Japanese *daikon*]

Dáil /doyl, diel/ or **Dáil Éireann** /'eərən/ *noun* the lower house of parliament in the Republic of Ireland: compare SEANAD ÉIREANN. [Irish Gaelic *dáil* assembly]

daily[1] /'dayli/ *adj* **1** of or occurring every day or every weekday. **2** said of a newspaper: issued every weekday. [Old English *dæglīc*]

daily[2] *adv* every day.

daily[3] *noun* (*pl* **dailies**) **1** *informal* a newspaper published daily from Monday to Saturday. **2** *Brit, dated* a cleaning woman who works on a daily basis.

daimio /'diemyoh/ *noun* see DAIMYO.

daimon /'diemohn/ *noun* see DAEMON.

daimyo or **daimio** /'diemyoh/ *noun* a Japanese feudal baron. [Japanese *daimyo*, from *dai* great + *myō* name]

dainty[1] /'daynti/ *adj* (**daintier, daintiest**) **1** delicately beautiful. **2** graceful or elegant. **3** fastidious, *esp* about food. ➤➤ **daintily** *adv*, **daintiness** *noun*.

dainty[2] *noun* (*pl* **dainties**) something pleasant to eat; a delicacy. [Middle English *deinte* via Old French from Latin *dignitat-*, *dignitas*: see DIGNITY]

daiquiri /'dakiri/ *noun* (*pl* **daiquiris**) a cocktail made of rum, lime juice, and sugar. [named after *Daiquirí*, town in Cuba where rum was produced]

dairy /'deəri/ *noun* (*pl* **dairies**) **1** a room, building, etc where milk is processed and butter or cheese is made. **2** an establishment for the sale or distribution of milk and milk products: compare CREAMERY. **3** (*used before a noun*) relating to or containing milk, butter, or cheese: *dairy produce*. ➤➤ **dairying** *noun*. [Middle English *deyerie*, from *deye* dairymaid, female servant, from Old English *dæge* kneader of bread]

dairymaid *noun archaic* a woman employed in a dairy.

dairyman *noun* (*pl* **dairymen**) a man who runs a dairy farm or who works in a dairy.

dais /'day·is/ *noun* a raised platform in a hall or large room, e.g. for a speaker using a lectern. [Middle English *deis* via Old French from Latin *discus* dish, quoit, DISC]

daisy /'dayzi/ *noun* (*pl* **daisies**) **1** a common short European plant with a yellow disc and white or pink ray flowers: *Bellis perennis*. **2** used in the names of various other similar plants, e.g. the Michaelmas daisy or oxeye daisy. * **pushing up (the) daisies** *informal* dead and in one's grave. [Old English *dægesēage*, from *dæg* DAY + *ēage* EYE[1]; because the flower opens in daylight]

daisy chain *noun* **1** a string of linked daisies threaded through their stalks. **2** a series of linked events, people, or things. **3** in computing, a way of linking hardware in a linear series using cables.

daisy-chain *verb trans* in computing, to connect (hardware) in a linear series using cables.

daisy-cutter *noun* in cricket and baseball, a ball that is bowled or hit along the ground or that keeps low on pitching.

daisy wheel *noun* a device in a typewriter or printer that carries the letter type to be printed. It is shaped like a wheel with a different character at the end of each spoke.

Dak. *abbr* Dakota.

Dakota /də'kohtə/ *noun* (*pl* **Dakotas** or *collectively* **Dakota**) **1** a member of a Native American people of the N Mississippi valley. **2** the Siouan language of this people. ➤➤ **Dakotan** *adj*. [the Dakotan name of the people, literally 'allies']

daks /daks/ *pl noun Aus, informal* trousers. [from proprietary name Daks]

dal[1] /dahl/ *noun* see DHAL.

dal[2] *abbr* decalitre(s).

Dalai Lama /,dalie 'lahmə/ *noun* the spiritual head of Tibetan Buddhism and, until 1959, the ruler of Tibet. [Mongolian *dalai lama* ocean lama, so called because he is said to be an ocean of compassion]

dalasi /dah'lahsi/ *noun* (*pl* **dalasis** or **dalasi**) the basic monetary unit of the Gambia, divided into 100 butut. [local name in the Gambia]

dale /dayl/ *noun* a vale or valley. [Old English *dæl*]

Dalek /'dahlek/ *noun* a fictional creature with a tinny monotonous voice, protected by a distinctive metallic shell containing its life-support system. [name of creatures in television science-fiction series 'Dr Who', said to have been taken from an encyclopedia volume covering the alphabetic sequence *dal-* to *-lek*]

dalesman /'daylzmən/ or **daleswoman** *noun* (*pl* **dalesmen** or **daleswomen**) a person living in the Yorkshire Dales in N England.

Daliesque /dahli'esk/ *adj* in the surrealist, dream-like style of Salvador Dali. [Salvador *Dali* d.1989, Spanish artist]

Dalit /'dahlit/ *noun* in India, a member of the lowest caste in the traditional caste system: compare SCHEDULED CASTE, UNTOUCHABLE[2]. [Hindi *Dalit* from Sanskrit *dalita* oppressed]

dally /'dali/ *verb intrans* (**dallies, dallied, dallying**) **1** to waste time; to dawdle. **2a** (+ with) to act playfully or flirtatiously with somebody. **b** (+ with) to take a passing interest in something.

dalliance *noun.* [Middle English *dalyen* from Anglo-French *dalier* to chat]

Dalmatian /dal'maysh(ə)n/ *noun* **1** a large dog of a breed having a white short-haired coat with black or brown spots. **2** a native or inhabitant of Dalmatia. ⟫ **Dalmatian** *adj.* [(sense 1) from the supposed origin of the breed in *Dalmatia*, region of Croatia]

dalmatic /dal'matik/ *noun* a long outer garment with slit sides and wide sleeves, of a kind worn by deacons or prelates, and by a king or queen at a coronation. [late Latin *dalmatica*, fem of *dalmaticus* Dalmatian, from *Dalmatia*; because they were orig made of Dalmatian wool]

dal segno /dal 'senyoh/ *adj and adv* used as a direction in music: return to the sign that marks the beginning of a section to be repeated: compare DA CAPO. [Italian *dal segno* from the sign]

dalton /'dawlt(ə)n/ *noun* = ATOMIC MASS UNIT. [named after John *Dalton* d.1844, English chemist and physicist who laid the foundations of modern atomic theory]

daltonism /'dawltəniz(ə)m/ *noun* = PROTANOPIA. [named after John *Dalton* (see DALTON), who suffered from and studied colour blindness]

dam[1] /dam/ *noun* **1** a barrier built across a watercourse to hold back and raise the level of the water, *esp* to form a reservoir. **2** a barrier built by a beaver in a stream for the construction of a lodge. **3** *chiefly NAmer* in dentistry, a rubber sheet used as a barrier for saliva in the mouth. [Middle English, of Germanic origin]

dam[2] *verb trans* (**dammed, damming**) **1** to build a dam across (a river or lake). **2** to block or stop (e.g. a flow of water).

dam[3] *noun* a female parent of a domestic animal. [Middle English *dam, dame*: see DAME]

dam[4] *abbr* decametre(s).

damage[1] /'damij/ *noun* **1** loss or harm resulting from injury to person, property, or reputation. **2** (*in pl*) compensation in money imposed by law for loss or injury. ✳ **what's the damage?** *informal* what does it cost? [Middle English via Old French from Latin *damnum* damage, loss, fine]

damage[2] *verb trans* to cause damage to (something). ⟫ *verb intrans* to become damaged. ⟫ **damaging** *adj*, **damagingly** *adv*.

Damascene[1] /'daməseen/ *noun* a native or inhabitant of Damascus, capital of Syria.

Damascene[2] *adj* **1** of or relating to Damascus. **2** of or like the conversion of St Paul, which occurred on the road to Damascus. **3** of or relating to Damascus steel. **4** relating to the art of damascening metal. [Latin *Damascenus* (adj) of *Damascus*, city in Syria formerly famous for steelworking and silk]

damascene[1] *verb trans* to ornament (e.g. iron or steel) with wavy patterns like those of watered silk or with inlaid work of precious metals. [from DAMASCENE[2]]

damascene[2] *noun* the characteristic markings of damascened steel.

Damascus steel /də'maskəs/ *noun* damascened steel used *esp* for sword blades.

damask[1] /'daməsk/ *noun* **1a** a reversible lustrous fabric, e.g. of linen, cotton, or silk, having a plain background woven with patterns. **b** a tablecloth made from such a fabric. **2** = DAMASCUS STEEL. **3** the colour of a damask rose, a greyish pink. [Middle English *damaske* via medieval Latin from Latin *Damascus*: see DAMASCENE[2]]

damask[2] *adj* of the colour of a damask rose, a greyish pink.

damask rose *noun* a large fragrant greyish pink rose cultivated *esp* as a source of attar of roses: *Rosa damascena*.

dame /daym/ *noun* **1** (**Dame**) in the UK, a title given to a woman who has been awarded an order of knighthood, e.g. the Order of the British Empire. **2** *archaic* an elderly woman. **3** *Brit* a comic ill-tempered old woman in a pantomime, usu played by a male actor. **4** *NAmer, informal* a woman. [Middle English *dam, dame* lady, dam, via Old French from Latin *domina*, fem of *dominus* master]

dame school *noun* formerly, a school in which reading and writing were taught by a woman in her home.

dame's violet *noun* a Eurasian plant of the mustard family widely cultivated for its spikes of fragrant white or purple flowers: *Hesperis matronalis*.

damfool[1] /dam'foohl/ *adj informal, dated* extremely foolish or stupid. [alteration of DAMN[3] + FOOL[1]]

damfool[2] *noun informal, dated* a foolish or stupid person.

damn[1] /dam/ *verb trans* **1** to condemn (somebody) to a punishment or fate, *esp*, in some beliefs, to eternal punishment. **2** to condemn (somebody or something) as a failure by public criticism: *a play damned by the critics.* **3** to bring ruin on (somebody). **4** to curse (somebody or something). ⟫ *verb intrans* to curse or swear. ✳ **damn with faint praise** to praise (somebody or something) in a feeble or ambiguous way that seems like criticism. **I'll be damned** *informal* used to express astonishment. **I'll be damned if** *informal* used to express firm refusal: *I'll be damned if I'll go.* [Middle English *dampnen* via Old French from Latin *damnare*, from *damnum* DAMAGE[1], loss, fine]

damn[2] *noun* (*usu in negative contexts*) the slightest bit: *I couldn't give a damn.*

damn[3] *adj informal* used as an intensive: *It's a damn nuisance.* ✳ **damn all** *Brit, informal* nothing at all. **damn well** *informal* beyond doubt or question; certainly: *better damn well marry that boy* — Spare Rib.

damn[4] *interj informal* used to express annoyance.

damnable /'damnəbl/ *adj* **1** very bad; detestable: *damnable weather.* **2** deserving damnation. ⟫ **damnably** *adv*.

damnation[1] /dam'naysh(ə)n/ *noun* condemnation to hell: *We're't not for gold and women, there would be no damnation* — Cyril Tourneur.

damnation[2] *interj* used to express annoyance.

damnatory /'damnət(ə)ri/ *adj* expressing or causing condemnation.

damned /damd/ *adj* (**damnedest**) *informal* used as an intensive: *I can't get my damned shoe on.*

damnedest ✳ **do one's damnedest** *informal* to try one's best to do something.

damnify /'damnifie/ *verb trans* (**damnifies, damnified, damnifying**) in law, to cause loss or injury to (somebody). ⟫ **damnification** /-fi'kayshən/ *noun*. [Old French *damnifier*, ultimately from Latin *damnificus* injurious, from *damnum* DAMAGE[1]]

damning /'daming/ *adj* attesting to or suggesting guilt or error: *The witness presented some damning evidence.* ⟫ **damningly** *adv*.

damosel or **damozel** /'daməzel/ *noun archaic* a damsel. [Old French *dameisele*: see DAMSEL]

damp[1] /damp/ *adj* slightly or moderately wet. ⟫ **dampish** *adj*, **damply** *adv*, **dampness** *noun*.

damp[2] *noun* **1** moisture or humidity. **2** *archaic* (*in pl*) moist air. **3** *archaic* discouragement. [early Dutch or German *damp* vapour]

damp[3] *verb trans* **1** to dampen (something). **2** (*often* + down) to restrain or control (an activity, condition, etc). **3** (*often* + down) to reduce the air supply to (a fire) so that it becomes less intense. **4** in physics, to decrease the amplitude of (an oscillation or wave) progressively. **5** in music, to decrease the vibration of (the strings of an instrument).

damp course *noun* a horizontal damp-resistant layer near the ground in a masonry wall.

dampen *verb trans* (**dampened, dampening**) **1** to make (something) damp. **2** to reduce the strength or intensity of (feelings): *Nothing could dampen his spirits.* **3** to decrease the vibration or oscillation of (sound waves). ⟫ **dampener** *noun*.

damper *noun* **1** in music, a small felted block which prevents or stops the vibration of a piano string. **2** a device, e.g. a shock absorber, designed to bring a mechanism to rest with minimum oscillation. **3** a valve or plate in the flue of a furnace for regulating the draught. **4** *chiefly Aus, NZ* a loaf or scone of unleavened bread made with flour and water and baked in the ashes of a fire. ✳ **put a damper on** to have a dulling or restraining influence on (somebody or something).

damping /'damping/ *noun* **1** in physics, a decrease of amplitude of oscillation, e.g. caused by friction or resistance. **2** a method for decreasing amplitude of oscillation.

damping-off *noun* a diseased condition of seedlings or cuttings caused by fungi.

damp-proof[1] *adj* impervious to damp.

damp-proof[2] *verb trans* to make (a wall or building) impervious to damp by means of a damp course.

damp-proof course *noun* = DAMP COURSE.

damp squib *noun Brit* something that ends feebly, *esp* after a promising start.

damsel /'damzəl/ *noun archaic or literary* a young unmarried woman. [Middle English *dameisel* from Old French *dameisele*, ultimately from Latin *domina*: see DAME]

damselfish *noun* (*pl* **damselfishes** *or collectively* **damselfish**) any of several small brightly coloured marine fishes of tropical and warm seas: *Chromis chromis* and other species.

damselfly *noun* (*pl* **damselflies**) a slender insect related to the dragonfly, having projecting stalked wings that are folded above the body when the insect is at rest: suborder Zygoptera.

damson /'damzən/ *noun* **1** a small purple fruit similar to a plum. **2** the small tree that bears this fruit: *Prunus domestica*. [Middle English, from Latin *prunum damascenum* plum of *Damascus*, city in Syria]

damson cheese *noun* a preserve made with sieved damsons and sugar, which is potted and aged before eating.

Dan. *abbr* Daniel (book of the Bible).

dan /dan/ *noun* a level of expertise in judo or karate, or a person who has achieved a specified level. There are ten levels. [Japanese *dan*]

dance[1] /dahns/ *verb intrans* **1** to move the body in a rhythmic way, *esp* in a set sequence of steps and in time to music: *Fine dancing, I believe, like virtue, must be its own reward* — Jane Austen. **2** to move quickly and lightly. ➤ *verb trans* to perform (a dance or a role in a ballet). ✳ **dance attendance on** to attend to the needs of (somebody); to try to please (somebody). **dance to somebody's tune** to do what somebody wants. ➤➤ **danceable** *adj*, **dancer** *noun*, **dancing** *noun*. [Middle English *dauncen* from Old French *dancier*]

dance[2] *noun* **1** a series of steps and bodily movements, usu in time to music. **2** a social gathering at which dancing takes place. **3** a piece of music for dancing to. **4** = DANCE MUSIC. ✳ **lead somebody a merry dance** to cause somebody a lot of trouble.

dance band *noun* a band that plays music for people to dance to.

dance floor *noun* a separate part of the floor in a disco, nightclub, etc where people can dance.

dance hall *noun* a public hall with facilities for dancing.

dance music *noun* rhythmic electronic music played in clubs.

dance of death *noun* **1** a medieval artistic theme in which a figure personifying death leads people to the grave. **2** a dance symbolizing this.

D and C *abbr* dilatation and curettage, a gynaecological procedure in which the womb is gently stretched open to allow its temporary lining to be scraped clean.

dandelion /'dandilie·ən/ *noun* any of several species of plants of the daisy family with yellow flowers and downy seed heads, occurring virtually worldwide as a weed: *Taraxacum officinale* and other species. [early French *dent de lion* lion's tooth, because of the indentations on the leaves]

dandelion clock *noun* the downy pale seed head of a dandelion.

dander[1] /'dandə/ ✳ **get/have one's dander up** *informal* to lose one's temper. [perhaps from *dander*, *dunder* ferment]

dander[2] *noun* minute scales from hair, feathers, or skin. [alteration of DANDRUFF]

dandify /'dandifie/ *verb trans* (**dandifies**, **dandified**, **dandifying**) to make (somebody) ostentatiously fashionable.

dandle /'dandl/ *verb trans* to move (a baby or small child) up and down in one's arms or on one's knee in affectionate play. [origin unknown]

dandruff /'dandruf/ *noun* dead skin that comes off the scalp in small white or greyish scales. ➤➤ **dandruffy** *adj*. [from *dand-* (origin unknown) + *-ruff*, of Scandinavian origin]

dandy[1] /'dandi/ *noun* (*pl* **dandies**) **1** a man who is obsessively concerned with looking fashionable. **2** *informal, dated* something excellent in its class. ➤➤ **dandyish** *adj*, **dandyism** *noun*. [perhaps from *Dandy*, nickname for *Andrew*]

dandy[2] *adj* (**dandier**, **dandiest**) *chiefly NAmer, informal* very good; first-rate.

dandy brush *noun* a coarse brush used in grooming horses.

Dane /dayn/ *noun* a native or inhabitant of Denmark. [Old English *Dene* or Old Norse *Danr*]

Danegeld /'dayngeld/ *noun* **1** in Anglo-Saxon England, a tax levied to finance resistance to the Danish invaders. **2** a similar tax levied by the Norman kings of England in the 11th and 12th cents.

[Middle English, from DANE + *geld* tribute, payment, from Old Norse *gjald*]

Danelaw *noun* **1** the part of England held by the Danes before the Norman Conquest in 1066. **2** the law in force in this area.

dang[1] /dang/ *verb trans chiefly NAmer, informal, euphem* = DAMN[1] (4).

dang[2] *adj chiefly NAmer, informal, euphem* = DAMN[3].

dang[3] *interj chiefly NAmer, informal, euphem* = DAMN[4].

danger /'daynjə/ *noun* **1** exposure to the possibility of injury, pain, or loss: *Boldness is ever blind; for it seeth not danger* — Bacon. **2** a case or cause of danger: *I was well aware of the dangers of mining.* **3** the possibility of something unwelcome: *Is there any danger of her dying?*

Word history
Middle English *daunger* from Old French *dangier*, ultimately from Latin *dominium* ownership, power, from *dominus* lord. The original sense was 'power', *esp* the power to harm or injure, later 'injury, damage', hence the risk of these.

danger list *noun Brit* a list of hospital patients who are critically ill.

danger money *noun* extra payment for dangerous work.

dangerous /'daynj(ə)rəs/ *adj* **1** able or likely to do harm or inflict injury. **2** involving danger; risky or perilous. ➤➤ **dangerously** *adv*, **dangerousness** *noun*.

dangle /'danggl/ *verb intrans* to hang or swing loosely. ➤ *verb trans* **1** to cause (something) to swing or dangle. **2** to offer (something) enticingly. ➤➤ **dangler** *noun*, **dangly** *adj*. [prob of Scandinavian origin]

dangling participle /'danggling/ *noun* in grammar, a verbal phrase that is not grammatically related to the noun to which it logically refers, e.g. *Driving home last night, a rabbit made me swerve*.

Danish[1] /'daynish/ *adj* from or relating to Denmark. [Old English *Denisc* from *Dene* DANE]

Danish[2] *noun* the Scandinavian language spoken in Denmark.

Danish blue *noun* a soft white Danish cheese with blue veins and a strong flavour.

Danish pastry *noun* a small cake made from a rich yeast dough with a sweet filling.

dank /dangk/ *adj* unpleasantly moist or wet. ➤➤ **dankly** *adv*, **dankness** *noun*. [Middle English *danke*, prob of Scandinavian origin]

danse macabre /,dahns mə'kahbrə (*French* dã:s maka:br)/ *noun* = DANCE OF DEATH. [French *danse macabre* macabre dance]

danseur /dahn'suh (*French* dãsœ:r)/ *noun* a male ballet dancer. [French *danseur*, from *danser* to dance]

danseuse /dahn'suhz (*French* dãsø:z)/ *noun* a female ballet dancer. [French *danseuse*, fem of DANSEUR]

Dantean /'dantiən, dan'tiən/ *adj* of or in the style of the Italian poet Dante Alighieri (1265–1321), *esp* reminiscent of his description of a journey through hell and the punishments suffered there. ➤➤ **Dantean** *noun*, **Dantesque** *adj*.

Danubian /də'nyooh·biən/ *adj* of or relating to the Danube, a river in central and SE Europe.

dap[1] /dap/ *verb intrans* (**dapped**, **dapping**) to fish by allowing the bait to touch the surface of the water lightly. [perhaps alteration of DAB[1]]

dap[2] *noun* **1** in fishing, a fly that allows the bait to touch the surface of the water. **2** *dialect* a plimsoll.

daphne /'dafni/ *noun* a small ornamental shrub with evergreen leaves and fragrant bell-shaped pinkish flowers: genus *Daphne*. [via Latin from Greek *daphnē* laurel, named after *Daphne*, a nymph in Greek mythology who was changed into a laurel to escape from Apollo's advances]

daphnia /'dafni·ə/ *noun* (*pl* **daphnia**) a minute freshwater crustacean used as food for aquarium fish: genus *Daphnia*. [Latin genus name, from *Daphne*: see DAPHNE]

dapper /'dapə/ *adj* said of a man: neat and spruce in dress and demeanour. ➤➤ **dapperly** *adv*, **dapperness** *noun*. [Middle English *dapyr* from early Dutch *dapper* quick, strong]

dapple[1] /'dapl/ *verb trans* to mark (a surface) with rounded patches of varying shade. [Middle English *dappel-grey* (adj) grey variegated with spots of different colour, perhaps of Scandinavian origin]

dapple[2] *noun* **1** a spot or patch of a colour different from its background. **2** a dappled horse or other animal.

dapple-grey *noun* a horse with a grey coat marked with spots of a darker colour. **>> dapple-grey** *adj*.

dapsone /'dapsohn/ *noun* a synthetic antibacterial drug used to treat leprosy: formula $(H_2NC_6H_4)_2SO_2$. [shortened from *diamin-odiphenyl-sulphone*]

darbies /'dahbiz/ *plural noun Brit, informal, archaic* handcuffs. [short for obsolete *Father Darby's (Derby's) bands* rigid bond binding a debtor, perhaps from the name of a money-lender]

Darby and Joan /,dahbi ən 'john/ *noun chiefly Brit* a happily married elderly couple. [prob from *Darby and Joan*, couple in an 18th-cent. song]

Darby and Joan club *noun Brit* a club for elderly people.

dare[1] /deə/ *verb* (*third person sing. present tense before an expressed or implied infinitive without 'to'* **dare**) **>** *verb intrans* to have sufficient courage or boldness to do something: *No one dared say a word; He says he dare not try.* **>** *verb trans* to challenge (somebody) to do something: *I dared him to jump.* *** don't you dare** used to tell somebody in an angry way not to do something. **how dare you?** used to express anger: *How dare you open my letters?* **I dare say/daresay** it is likely or probable that: *I dare say we could come to an agreement about the money.* **>> darer** *noun*. [Old English *durran*]

dare[2] *noun* a challenge to do something bold or rash.

daredevil *noun* somebody who is recklessly bold. **>> daredevilry** /-ri/ *noun*.

daren't /deənt/ *contraction* dare not.

darg /dahg/ *noun Aus, NZ or dialect* a fixed amount of work; a task. [Old English *dægweorc*, from *dæg* DAY + *weorc* WORK[1]]

daring[1] /'deəring/ *adj* adventurously bold in action or thought. **>> daringly** *adv*.

daring[2] *noun* adventurous boldness.

dariole /'dariohl/ *noun* a small cup-shaped mould in which a single portion of a sweet or savoury dish is cooked and served. [French *dariole* pastry filled with cream]

Darjeeling /dah'jeeling/ *noun* a high-quality tea grown in the mountainous districts of N India. [named after *Darjeeling*, town in India famous for its tea plantations]

dark[1] /dahk/ *adj* **1** with little or no light. **2a** wholly or partially black. **b** said of a colour: not light or pale. **3a** said of the hair or complexion: not fair. **b** said of a person: having brown or black hair. **4** secret or mysterious: *He kept his plans dark.* **5a** sinister or evil: *dark deeds.* **b** angry: *dark looks.* **c** dismal or sad: *Those were dark times for us.* **6** remote or uncivilized: *darkest Peru.* **7** *archaic* lacking knowledge; ignorant. **>> darkish** *adj*, **darkly** *adv*, **darkness** *noun*. [Old English *deorc*]

dark[2] *noun* **1a** the absence of light; darkness: *She was scared of the dark.* **b** night or nightfall: *owls that come out after dark.* **2** a dark or deep colour. *** in the dark** in a state of ignorance.

Dark Ages *pl noun* **1** (*also* **dark ages**) the period of European history from the fall of the Roman Empire in the West (AD 476) to about 1000, typically perceived as a time devoid of culture, learning, or civilized attitudes: *Her intellect reached forward into the twentieth century; her social prejudices and family affections reached back into the dark ages* — George Bernard Shaw. **2** (*also* **dark ages**) any period or existence seen as similarly primitive or deprived: *For in those dark ages, even all-perfect America read rubbish* — Louisa M Alcott.

dark chocolate *noun* chocolate that is dark in colour and slightly bitter; plain chocolate.

dark current *noun* the residual current in a device, e.g. a photocell or video camera tube, when there is no light falling on it.

darken *verb* (**darkened, darkening**) **>** *verb trans* **1** to make (something) dark or darker. **2** said of something unwelcome: to spoil or blight (something): *lives darkened by poverty.* **3** to make (somebody) unhappy or angry. **>** *verb intrans* **1** to become dark or darker. **2** to become unhappy or angry. **3** said of the eyes or face: to show a strong emotion, *esp* anger. *** not darken somebody's door** to keep away from somebody. **>> darkener** *noun*.

darkey /'dahki/ *noun* (*pl* **darkeys**) see DARKY.

dark horse *noun* **1** somebody or something that is little known but is likely to succeed, *esp* a competitor in a race or contest. **2** a secretive person.

darkie /'dahki/ *noun* see DARKY.

dark lantern *noun* a lantern that can be closed to conceal the light.

darkling /'dahkling/ *adj literary* of or in the dark: *And we are here as on a darkling plain* — Matthew Arnold.

dark matter *noun* invisible and unidentified matter that is believed by astronomers to account for up to 90% of the universe's mass.

dark reaction *noun* in biochemistry, the phase of PHOTO-SYNTHESIS (use of sunlight by green plants to obtain nutrients) that does not require the presence of light. It involves the formation of sugars and other carbohydrates from carbon dioxide using stored energy. Compare LIGHT REACTION.

darkroom *noun* a room with specially subdued light for handling and processing light-sensitive photographic materials.

darksome /'dahksəm/ *adj literary* dark.

darky *or* **darkie** *or* **darkey** /'dahki/ *noun* (*pl* **darkies** *or* **darkeys**) *offensive* a black person.

darling[1] /'dahling/ *noun* **1** used as a familiar or affectionate form of address. **2** a dearly loved person. **3** a favourite: *He is the critics' darling.* [Old English *dēorling*, from *dēore* DEAR[1]]

darling[2] *adj* **1** dearly loved; favourite. **2** charming: *a darling little house.*

darn[1] /dahn/ *verb trans* **1** to mend (knitted material) with interlacing stitches woven across a hole or worn part. **2** to embroider (material) using a long running stitch. **>> darning** *noun*. [prob from French dialect *darner*, ultimately of Celtic origin]

darn[2] *noun* a darned area of a garment: *He was wearing a sweater full of darns.*

darn[3] *verb trans informal, euphem* = DAMN[1] (4).

darn[4] *adj informal, euphem* = DAMN[3].

darned /dahnd/ *adj informal, euphem* = DAMNED.

darnel /'dahnl/ *noun* any of several species of grasses that are common weeds in fields of grain: genus *Lolium*. [Middle English; earlier history unknown]

darner /'dahnə/ *noun* **1** a darning needle. **2** *NAmer* any of several species of large dragonflies: family Aeshnidae. [(sense 2) prob because of its shape]

darning needle *noun* **1** a long needle with a large eye for use in darning. **2** *NAmer* = DARNER (2).

dart[1] /daht/ *noun* **1** a small projectile with a pointed shaft and flights of feather or plastic, used as a weapon or in the game of darts. **2** a stitched tapering fold put in a garment to shape it to the figure. **3** a quick movement or dash. [Middle English from early French *dars*, of Germanic origin]

dart[2] *verb intrans* to move suddenly or rapidly: *He darted across the road.* **>** *verb trans* to throw or thrust (something) with a sudden movement.

dartboard *noun* a circular target used in the game of darts, marked into sections that have different scores.

darter /'dahtə/ *noun* **1** a fish-eating bird that has a long slender neck and flies with darting movements: genus *Anhinga*. **2** either of two genera of small, brightly coloured freshwater fishes of N America: genera *Etheostoma* and *Percina*. **3** any of several species of dragonflies with a wide body that catch prey by darting out from a perch: family Libellulidae and related families.

Dartmoor pony /'dahtmaw/ *noun* an animal of an old breed of small shaggy English ponies. [named after *Dartmoor*, region of SW England where the breed originated]

darts /dahts/ *pl noun* (*usu treated as sing.*) an indoor game in which darts are thrown at a dartboard to score points.

Darwinism /'dahwiniz(ə)m/ *noun* a theory of evolution developed by Charles Darwin. It asserts that widely divergent groups of plants and animals have arisen from common ancestors as a result of natural selection of offspring which develop slight variations that make them better adapted to their environment.

Editorial note
A term used for evolution itself (which Darwin did most to establish) and for Darwin's theory of its mechanism – natural selection. Darwin himself recognized other causes of evolution, but only natural selection accounts for the apparent 'design' of organisms. Neo-Darwinism unites Darwinism with Mendelism: particulate genes have a frequency in the gene pool,

which is biased over the generations by non-random selection — Professor Richard Dawkins.

>> **Darwinian** /dah'wini·ən/ *noun and adj*, **Darwinist** *noun and adj*. [Charles *Darwin* d.1882, English naturalist]

dash[1] /dash/ *verb intrans* **1** to move with speed or haste. **2** to smash against something. > *verb trans* **1a** to hurl or fling (something) with great force. **b** to strike or knock (something) violently. **2** to destroy or ruin (a hope or plan). [Middle English *dasshen*, prob of imitative origin]

dash[2] *noun* **1** a punctuation mark (—) used to indicate a break in the structure of a sentence, or to stand for missing words or letters. **2** in Morse code, a signal, e.g. a flash or audible tone, of relatively long duration: compare DOT[1] (5). **3** in music, a vertical line written above or below a note, showing that it is to be played staccato. **4a** a speedy or hasty movement or journey. **b** *chiefly NAmer* a sprint. **5** a small amount of a substance: *a dash of salt*. **6** liveliness of style and action; panache. **7** = DASHBOARD.

dash[3] *interj Brit, informal, dated* used to express annoyance.

dashboard *noun* a panel containing dials and controls in a car or other vehicle.

Word history
DASH[1], in an obsolete sense 'to splash, splatter', + BOARD[1]. A dashboard was orig a board or panel that protected the driver of a carriage from being splattered with mud.

dashed /dasht/ *adj Brit, informal, dated* used for emphasis: *a dashed pity*.

dashiki /də'sheeki/ *noun* (*pl* **dashikis**) a loose brightly coloured shirt without buttons, traditionally worn by men in W Africa. [alteration of Yoruba *danshiki*]

dashing *adj* **1** marked by vigorous action; spirited. **2** smart and stylish in dress and manners. >> **dashingly** *adv*.

dash off *verb trans* to complete or execute (e.g. writing or drawing) hastily.

dashpot *noun* a device for cushioning or damping a movement, e.g. of a mechanical part, to avoid shock.

dassie /'dahsi/ *noun* any of several species of hyraxes of Africa and SW Asia, *esp* the rock hyrax: family Procaviidae. [Afrikaans *dassie* from Dutch *das* badger]

dastard /'dastəd/ *noun archaic* a coward, *esp* one who commits malicious acts. [Middle English, perhaps from Old Norse *dœstr* exhausted]

dastardly *adj dated* despicably malicious or cowardly: *One could do a dastardly thing if one chose, but it was contemptible to regret it afterwards* — Somerset Maugham. >> **dastardliness** *noun*.

dasyure /'dasiyooə/ *noun* any of a genus of tree-dwelling flesh-eating marsupial mammals of Australia and Tasmania resembling large weasels: genus *Dasyurus*. Also called QUOLL. [Greek *dasys* thick with hair + *oura* tail]

DAT /dat/ *abbr* digital audiotape.

dat. *abbr* dative.

data /'daytə/ *pl noun* (*treated as sing. or pl*) **1** factual information, e.g. measurements or statistics, used as a basis for reasoning, discussion, or calculation. **2** in computing, the numbers, characters, etc on which a computer operates. [pl of DATUM]

Usage note
Data is, strictly speaking, a plural noun with a comparatively rare singular form *datum*. With the advent of computers and data processing, *data* has come increasingly to be seen and used as a singular mass noun like *information* or *news*: *The data is currently being processed*. Traditionalists insist however that this should be: *The data are currently being processed*.

databank *noun* a collection of computer data organized for rapid search and retrieval, e.g. by computer.

database *noun* a set of data held in structured form by a computer.

database management system *noun* a software system that organizes the structure of data in a database and controls access to, input to, and output of that data.

datable *or* **dateable** /'daytəbl/ *adj* able to be given a particular date.

data capture *noun* in computing, the act of collecting data and converting it into a form that a computer can use.

data compression *noun* in computing, the reorganization or restructuring of data so that it takes up less storage space.

dataglove *noun* a glove fitted with sensors that transmits the hand movements of the person wearing it to a virtual-reality system.

data mining *noun* in marketing, counterespionage, etc: the computer analysis of large databases for the purpose of extracting from them useful but previously undiscovered information.

data processing *noun* the entering, storing, maintaining, and arranging of data, *esp* by a computer. >> **data processor** *noun*.

data protection *noun Brit* legal protection of the privacy and security of information stored in computers.

datcha /'dahchə/ *noun* see DACHA.

date[1] /dayt/ *noun* **1** a particular day of the month or year, identified by a number or phrase. **2a** the time at which a particular event has occurred or will occur. **b** the period of time to which something belongs. **c** (*in pl*) the two dates marking the beginning and end of something, *esp* the dates of somebody's birth and death. **3** *informal*. **a** an appointment, *esp* a romantic or social engagement. **b** a person with whom one has arranged such an appointment. **4** a show or concert, *esp* one that is part of a series being performed in different venues. **※ to date** until the present moment. [Middle English via French from Latin *data*, as in *data Romae* (letter) given at Rome, fem past part. of *dare* to give]

date[2] *verb trans* **1** to determine the date of (something). **2** to mark (a document, letter, etc) with a date. **3** to make (somebody) appear old-fashioned: *His record collection dates him*. **4** *informal* to go on a date with (somebody). > *verb intrans* **1** (*usu* + from) to have been in existence for a specified time: *coins dating from Anglo-Saxon times*. **2** to become old-fashioned: *clothes that won't date*. **3** *informal* said of two people: to go out together.

date[3] *noun* **1** a small brown oval fruit with a long thin stone and a sweet taste, eaten fresh or dried. **2** the tall tropical palm that bears this fruit: *Phoenix dactylifera*. [Middle English via Old French and Latin from Greek *daktylos* finger; because the leaves resemble the fingers of a hand]

dateable /'daytəbl/ *adj* see DATABLE.

dated *adj* out of date or old-fashioned.

dateless *adj* **1** having no date. **2** timeless.

Date Line *noun* = INTERNATIONAL DATE LINE.

dateline *noun* a line in a written document or publication giving the date and place of composition or issue.

date rape *noun* a rape committed on a victim who is on a date with the assailant.

date stamp *noun* **1** a device for stamping a date. **2** the impression or mark made by this.

dating agency *noun* an agency that arranges introductions for people seeking a companion or partner.

dative[1] /'daytiv/ *adj* in Greek, Latin, German, etc: denoting a grammatical case expressing an indirect object. [Middle English *datif* from Latin *dativus* relating to giving, from *datus*, past part. of *dare* to give]

dative[2] *noun* the dative case or a word in this case.

datum /'daytəm/ *noun* (*pl* **data**) **1** a piece of information, e.g. a number, fixed point, or assumed value, used as a basis for measuring or calculating. **2** something given or admitted, *esp* as a basis for reasoning or drawing conclusions. [Latin *datum* something given, neuter past part. of *dare* to give]

datum line *or* **datum level** *noun* a horizontal line or plane used as a reference point for taking measurements, e.g. in engineering or surveying.

datura /də'tyooərə/ *noun* any of a genus of widely distributed, strong-scented, and often poisonous plants that includes the thorn apple: genus *Datura*. [Latin genus name, from Hindi *dhatūrā* jimsonweed]

daub[1] /dawb/ *verb trans* **1** to cover or coat (a surface) crudely with a soft thick substance. **2** to apply (a substance) crudely to a surface. >> **dauber** *noun*. [Middle English *dauben* via Old French from Latin *dealbare* to whiten, from DE- + *albus* white]

daub[2] *noun* **1** in building, *esp* formerly, a mixture of plaster or clay and straw, used with WATTLE[1] (sticks, twigs, etc) to form a wall. **2** something daubed on; a smear. **3** a crude painting.

daube /dohb/ *noun* a stew of meat, *esp* beef, braised in wine. [French *daube* via Italian from Catalan *a la adoba* stewed]

daughter /'dawtə/ *noun* **1a** a girl or woman having the relation of child to parent. **b** a female descendant. **2** a woman having a specified origin or affiliation: *a daughter of the Church.* **3** in physics, an isotope formed as the immediate product of the radioactive decay of an element. **4** (*used before a noun*) in biology, of the first generation of offspring, molecules, etc produced by reproduction, division, or replication: *a daughter cell.* ⟫⟫ **daughterhood** *noun*, **daughterly** *adj.* [Old English *dohtor*]

daughter-in-law *noun* (*pl* **daughters-in-law**) the wife of one's son.

daunt /dawnt/ *verb trans* to discourage or dishearten (somebody). ⟫⟫ **daunting** *adj*, **dauntingly** *adv.* [Middle English *daunten* via Old French from Latin *domitare* to tame, from *domare* to tame]

dauntless *adj* courageous and fearless. ⟫⟫ **dauntlessly** *adv*, **dauntlessness** *noun*.

dauphin /'dohfanh (*French* dofɛ̃)/ *noun* (*often* **Dauphin**) used, formerly, as a title: the eldest son of a king of France.

Word history
French *dauphin* from Old French *dalfin* (see DOLPHIN) title of lords of the Dauphiné, whose coat of arms featured three dolphins. The title passed to the monarch's son after the province was sold to the French crown in 1343.

dauphine /'dohfeen (*French* dofin)/ *noun* (*often* **Dauphine**) the wife of a dauphin. [French *dauphine*, feminine of DAUPHIN]

dauphinois /dohfi'nwa/ *or* **dauphinoise** /-'nwaz/ *adj* said of potatoes: thinly sliced and baked in layers with milk and cream. [French *dauphinois* of Dauphiné]

daven /'dahv(ə)n/ *verb intrans* (**davened, davening**) in Judaism, to recite the prayers of the liturgies, or to lead the prayers. [Yiddish *davnen* to pray]

davenport /'davənpawt/ *noun* **1** *Brit* a writing desk with a sloping top and drawers. **2** *NAmer* a large upholstered sofa, *esp* one that converts into a bed. [prob from the name *Davenport*]

davit /'davit/ *noun* a projecting arm, similar to a crane, used on a vessel for lowering equipment, e.g. a lifeboat. [prob from the name *David*]

Davy Jones's locker /,dayvi 'johnziz/ *noun informal* the bottom of the sea, regarded as the resting place for those who have drowned. [named after *Davy Jones*, legendary spirit of the sea]

Davy lamp *noun* an early safety lamp used in mines. It was an oil-burning lamp with a wire mesh around the flame to minimize the risk of explosions. [named after Sir Humphry *Davy* d.1829, English chemist and inventor]

dawdle /'dawdl/ *verb intrans* **1** to move slowly or lackadaisically. **2** to spend time idly. ⟫⟫ **dawdler** *noun.* [origin unknown]

dawn[1] /dawn/ *noun* **1** the first appearance of light in the morning. **2** a first appearance; a beginning: *the dawn of the space age.*

dawn[2] *verb intrans* **1** to begin to grow light as the sun rises. **2** to begin to appear or develop. **3** (*usu* + on) to begin to be perceived or understood by somebody: *The truth finally dawned on him.* [Middle English *dawnen*, back-formation from *dawning* daybreak, from Old English *dagian* to dawn]

dawn chorus *noun* the singing of large numbers of birds at dawn.

dawn raid *noun* **1** a raid taking place very early in the day, *esp* by police. **2** *Brit* an attempt by a business company to buy a significant proportion of another company's shares at one time, typically at the start of a day's trading and in order to mount a takeover.

day /day/ *noun* **1a** a period of 24 hours beginning at midnight, corresponding to one rotation of the earth on its axis. **b** the period of daylight between sunrise and sunset. **c** the time established by usage or law for work, school, etc: *an eight-hour day.* **2** the time taken by a planet to turn once on its axis; a solar day. **3** a day set aside for a particular activity: *a business day.* **4a** (*also in pl*) a particular time or period in the past: *in my grandmother's day.* **b** an era: *the dawn of a new day in Anglo-French relations.* ✳ **all in a day's work** part of what one normally does. **any day 1** *informal* at any time. **2** *informal* used to emphasize a preference: *in any circumstances: I'd rather have meat than fish any day.* **at the end of the day** *informal* when one considers everything. **call it a day** to stop work or activity for the time being. **day and night** at all times. **day in, day out** continuously or repeatedly over a long period. **make a day of it** to spend a whole day celebrating or enjoying oneself. **one day/one of these days** at some future time. **that will be the day** *informal* used to express doubt about a possibility. **these days** in the present times. [Old English *daeg*]

Dayak /'dieak/ *noun* see DYAK.

daybed *noun* **1** a narrow bed or couch for rest or sleep during the day. **2** *NAmer* a couch or sofa that can be converted into a bed.

daybook *noun* **1** *NAmer* a diary or journal. **2** in accounting, a book used for recording the transactions of the day.

dayboy *noun Brit* a boy who attends a boarding school during the day but lives at home.

daybreak *noun* dawn.

day care *noun* supervision and facilities for those unable to look after themselves during the day, e.g. preschool children or the elderly.

day-care centre *noun* = DAY CENTRE.

day centre *noun* a place providing supervision and facilities for elderly or handicapped people during the day.

daydream[1] *noun* **1** a pleasant fantasy or reverie indulged in while one is awake. **2** an unrealistic scheme or plan.

daydream[2] *verb intrans* to have a daydream. ⟫⟫ **daydreamer** *noun.*

daygirl *noun Brit* a girl who attends a boarding school during the day but lives at home.

Day-Glo /'dayglow/ *noun trademark* a type of fluorescent paint which glows in natural daylight.

day labourer *noun* an unskilled labourer who is paid by the day.

daylight *noun* **1** the light of the sun during the day; sunshine. **2** dawn. **3** *informal* (*in pl*) consciousness or wits: used to intensify an expression of fear, violence, etc: *You scared the living daylights out of me.* ✳ **see daylight** to understand something that has been obscure.

daylight robbery *noun Brit, informal* exorbitant pricing or charging.

daylight saving time *noun chiefly NAmer* time set usu one hour ahead of standard time and used *esp* during the summer: compare BRITISH SUMMER TIME.

daylight time *noun* = DAYLIGHT SAVING TIME.

day lily *noun* a Eurasian plant of the lily family cultivated for its large red, orange, or yellow flowers lasting for one day: genus *Hemerocallis.*

Day of Atonement *noun* = YOM KIPPUR.

Day of Judgment *noun* = JUDGMENT DAY.

day of reckoning *noun* a time when the results of mistakes or misdeeds are felt, or when offences are punished.

day release *noun* a system in Britain whereby employees are allowed days off work to attend educational courses: compare BLOCK RELEASE.

day return *noun Brit* a bus or train ticket sold at a reduced fare for a return journey completed on the same day.

day room *noun* a living room in a hospital or other institution, for use during the day.

daysack *noun Brit* a small bag carried on the back, e.g. by hikers.

day school *noun* **1** a private school for students living at home. **2** a school that holds classes during the day rather than the evening.

day surgery *noun* surgery that can be carried out without an overnight stay in hospital.

daytime *noun* the time when it is light, between sunrise and sunset.

day-to-day *adj* **1** happening every day; regular or routine: *day-to-day problems.* **2** providing for a day at a time with little thought for the future: *an aimless day-to-day existence.*

day trip *noun* a journey or outing that is completed in one day, *esp* one made for pleasure. ⟫⟫ **day tripper** *noun.*

daze[1] /dayz/ *verb trans* to stupefy or stun (somebody), *esp* by a blow or shock. ⟫⟫ **dazedly** /'dayzidli/ *adv.* [Middle English *dasen* from Old Norse *dasathr* exhausted]

daze[2] *noun* a state of confusion or shock.

dazzle[1] /'dazl/ *verb trans* **1** to blind (a person or animal) temporarily by sudden bright light. **2** to greatly impress or overwhelm (somebody). ⟫⟫ **dazzler** *noun.* [frequentative of DAZE[1]]

dazzle[2] *noun* sudden blinding brightness.

dazzling /'dazling/ *adj* **1** shining very brightly. **2** amazing or impressive. ➤➤ **dazzlingly** *adv.*

dB *abbr* decibel(s).

Db *abbr* the chemical symbol for dubnium.

DBE *abbr* Dame Commander of the Order of the British Empire.

DBMS *abbr* database management system.

DBS *abbr* **1** direct broadcasting by satellite. **2** direct-broadcasting satellite.

dbx *noun trademark* in electronics, a system used to increase the dynamic range of reproduced sound and reduce noise. [DB + x standing for *expander*]

DC *abbr* **1** in music, da capo. **2** direct current. **3** District of Columbia (US postal abbreviation). **4** District Commissioner.

DCB *abbr Brit* Dame Commander of the Order of the Bath.

DCC *abbr* digital compact cassette.

DCh *abbr* Doctor of Surgery. [medieval Latin *Chirurgiae Doctor*]

DCL *abbr* Doctor of Civil Law.

DCM *abbr Brit* Distinguished Conduct Medal.

DCMG *abbr Brit* Dame Commander of the Order of St Michael and St George.

DCVO *abbr Brit* Dame Commander of the Royal Victorian Order.

DD *abbr* **1** direct debit. **2** Doctor of Divinity.

D-day *noun* **1** 6 June 1944, the day on which the Allies began the invasion of France in World War II. **2** a day set for beginning something important. [*D* abbr for *day*]

DDE *abbr* dynamic data exchange, a method formerly used to exchange information between computer files.

DDR *abbr* Deutsche Demokratische Republik, the former East Germany.

DDS *abbr* Doctor of Dental Surgery.

DDT *noun* a synthetic chlorinated water-insoluble insecticide that tends to accumulate in food chains and is poisonous to many vertebrates. [short for *dichloro-diphenyl-trichloro-ethane*]

DE *abbr* Delaware (US postal abbreviation).

de- *prefix* forming verbs and their derivatives, denoting: **1** the opposite of a specified action: *depopulate; decompose; deindustrialization.* **2** removal of something: *delouse; decapitate.* **3** a reduction in something: *devalue.* **4** alighting from a vehicle: *deplane.* [Middle English from Old French *de-, des-,* partly from Latin *de-* from, down, away and partly from Latin *dis-* apart]

deaccession /dee-ək'sesh(ə)n/ *verb trans* to sell or otherwise dispose of (an article belonging to a museum, library, or art gallery).

deacon /'deek(ə)n/ *noun* **1** in Catholic, Anglican, and Orthodox Churches, an ordained minister ranking below a priest. **2** in various Protestant Churches, a lay minister with administrative and sometimes spiritual duties. **3** formerly, a minister appointed to dispense charity. ➤➤ **deaconship** *noun.* [Old English *dēacon* via late Latin *diaconus* from Greek *diakonos* servant]

deaconess /deekə'nes/ *noun* in some Churches, a woman with the duties of a deacon.

deactivate /dee'aktivayt/ *verb trans* to make (e.g. a bomb or a virus) inactive or ineffective. ➤➤ **deactivation** /-'vaysh(ə)n/ *noun,* **deactivator** *noun.*

dead¹ /ded/ *adj* **1a** no longer alive. **b** having no life: *a dead planet.* **2a** said of a body part: lacking feeling; numb. **b** unfeeling or unresponsive. **3a** said of equipment: no longer working. **b** said of a bottle or glass: empty or finished with. **c** said of a ball: temporarily out of play. **4** no longer used, active, or relevant: *dead languages; dead coals.* **5** *informal* lacking in activity or interest; dull: *The campus is dead at weekends.* **6a** said of a colour: not bright. **b** said of a sound: dull. **7** *informal* complete or absolute: *a dead giveaway.* ✱ **dead as a doornail** utterly dead. **dead as a dodo** no longer living or existing; quite dead. **dead from the neck up** *informal* stupid. **dead in the water** said of a ship: not able to move or function. **dead meat** *informal* doomed, *esp* facing death. **dead on one's feet** *informal* very tired. **dead to the world** *informal* asleep or otherwise unaware of one's surroundings. ➤➤ **deadness** *noun.* [Old English *dēad*]

dead² *noun* **1** (**the dead**) (*treated as pl*) people or animals who are dead. **2** the time when something is at its most intense: *the dead of winter.*

dead³ *adv* **1** absolutely, completely, or exactly: *dead ahead.* **2** *Brit, informal* very: *dead lucky.*

dead-ball line *noun* **1** in rugby, a line at each end of the pitch, not more than 23m (about 25yd) behind the goal line, beyond which the ball is out of play. **2** in football, a goal line.

deadbeat¹ *noun informal* **1** an idle person; a loafer. **2** *NAmer* somebody who consistently fails to pay debts.

deadbeat² *adj* said of a mechanism: without recoil.

dead beat *adj informal* very tired; exhausted.

deadbolt *noun* a bolt that is operated directly by a key or knob rather than having a spring mechanism.

dead centre *noun* either of the two positions at the ends of a stroke in a crank and connecting rod when the crank is directly in line with the rod.

dead duck *noun informal* somebody or something that is unlikely to succeed.

deaden *verb trans* (**deadened, deadening**) **1** to reduce the resonance of (a sound); to muffle. **2a** to reduce the sensation of (feeling, pain, etc). **b** to deprive (e.g. a part of the body) of sensation: *fingers deadened by frostbite.* **3a** to deprive (something) of liveliness or excitement. **b** to cause (somebody) to become insensitive. ➤➤ **deadener** *noun.*

dead end *noun* **1** an end of a street or passage without an exit. **2** a situation or course of action in which no progress can be made.

deadening *noun* material used to soundproof walls or floors.

deadeye *noun* **1** in sailing, a circular or semicircular wooden block through which a rope may be secured, used to tighten stays or shrouds. **2** *chiefly NAmer, informal* a marksman.

deadfall *noun NAmer* a type of trap in which the prey is killed or disabled by a heavy object, e.g. a log, falling on it.

dead hand *noun* an oppressive influence: *the dead hand of bureaucracy.*

deadhead¹ *verb trans* **1** *chiefly Brit* to remove dead flower heads from (a plant). **2** *NAmer, informal* to drive (a vehicle) without carrying any passengers or other load. ➤ *verb intrans NAmer, informal* to drive a vehicle that is empty.

deadhead² *noun* **1** *informal* a dull or stupid person. **2** *chiefly NAmer, informal* a person who has not paid for a ticket, e.g. for a journey or performance. **3** *chiefly Brit* a dead flower head.

dead heat *noun* a race or contest that ends with more than one competitor finishing level or achieving the highest score.

dead leg *noun informal* a sensation of numbness in the leg caused by a blow.

dead-leg *verb trans* (**dead-legged, dead-legging**) *informal* to give (somebody) a dead leg.

dead letter *noun* **1** a law, custom, or treaty that has fallen out of use without being formally repealed or abolished. **2** a letter that cannot be delivered or returned because it lacks adequate directions.

deadlight *noun* **1** a metal cover or shutter fitted inside a porthole or window on a ship to keep out light and water. **2** *NAmer* a skylight that does not open.

deadline *noun* **1** a date or time before which something must be completed. **2** a boundary beyond which it is not possible or permitted to pass.

Word history
The word was coined in the Confederate prisoner of war camp, Andersonville, during the American Civil War (1861–5), when a line was marked out a little distance from the perimeter wire fence and the instruction was given that any prisoner crossing the line should be shot on sight.

dead load *noun* in engineering, a static load or force on a structure resulting from the weight of its component parts: compare LIVE LOAD.

deadlock¹ *noun* **1** a situation in which no progress can be made or agreement reached; a standstill. **2** *Brit* a lock that can be opened and shut only by a key.

deadlock² *verb trans* **1** to bring (traffic, negotiations, etc) to a standstill. **2** *Brit* to secure (a door, window, etc) with a deadlock.

dead loss *noun* a person or thing that is useless or unproductive.

deadly¹ *adj* (**deadlier, deadliest**) **1** likely to cause or capable of producing death: *a deadly disease.* **2** aiming to kill or destroy; implacable: *a deadly enemy.* **3** unerring: *deadly accuracy.* **4** *informal* lacking animation or sparkle; dull or tedious: *a deadly conversation.* **5** intense or extreme: *in deadly earnest.* ⟫⟫ **deadliness** *noun.*

deadly² *adv* **1** suggesting death: *His face was deadly pale.* **2** extremely: *I am deadly serious.*

deadly nightshade /'niet·shayd/ *noun* a European poisonous nightshade that has dull purple flowers and black berries: *Atropa belladonna.*

deadly sin *noun* in Christian belief, any of the seven sins of pride, covetousness, lust, anger, gluttony, envy, and sloth, regarded as leading to damnation.

dead man's fingers *pl noun* a fleshy soft coral of European coastal waters, thought to resemble the fingers of a corpse: *Alcyonium digitatum.*

dead man's handle *or* **dead man's pedal** *noun* a handle or pedal that requires constant pressure to allow operation, e.g. of a train or tram. If pressure is released, the brakes are automatically applied.

dead march *noun* a piece of solemn funeral music intended to accompany or suggest a funeral procession: *'Tis worse than whistlin' the 'Dead March' in barricks* — Kipling.

dead men's fingers *noun* = DEAD MAN'S FINGERS.

deadnettle *noun* any of several species of European and Asian plants of the mint family, resembling a stinging nettle but without stinging hairs: genus *Lamium.*

deadpan¹ *adj and adv* without feeling or expression. [DEAD¹ + PAN¹ in the sense 'face']

deadpan² *verb intrans* (**deadpanned, deadpanning**) to say something, *esp* something amusing, without expression or emotion.

dead reckoning *noun* the calculation of the position of a ship or aircraft from the record of the courses followed, the distance travelled, etc, without the use of external navigational aids such as observation of the sun or stars.

dead ringer *noun* a person or thing that strongly resembles another.

dead shot *noun* a person who is skilled at shooting.

dead time *noun* in physics, the period after a particle has been recorded in a device when no further particle can be detected.

deadweight *noun* **1** the unrelieved weight of an inert person or object. **2** a ship's total weight including cargo, fuel, stores, crew, and passengers. **3** = DEAD LOAD.

deadwood *noun* **1** wood that is dead on a tree. **2** people or things that have become useless or unproductive.

deaf¹ /def/ *adj* **1** lacking or deficient in the sense of hearing. **2** (+ to) unwilling to hear or listen to somebody or something; not to be persuaded: *She was deaf to reason.* ✻ **fall on deaf ears** to be ignored or unheeded. **turn a deaf ear** to refuse to listen. ⟫⟫ **deafness** *noun.* [Old English *dēaf*; related to Old English *dumb* DUMB]

deaf² *pl noun* (**the deaf**) people who are deaf.

deaf aid *noun Brit* a hearing aid.

deaf-blind *adj* severely deficient in both hearing and vision.

deafen *verb trans* (**deafened, deafening**) to overpower (somebody) with noise.

deafening *adj* extremely loud. ⟫⟫ **deafeningly** *adv.*

deaf-mute *noun offensive* somebody who is unable to hear or speak.

deal¹ /deel/ *verb* (*past tense and past part.* **dealt** /delt/) ➤ *verb trans* **1a** to distribute (cards) to players in a game. **b** (+ in) to include (somebody) in a game or hand. **2** (+ out) to distribute or apportion (something). **3** to administer or inflict (e.g. a blow). ➤ *verb intrans* **1** (*often* + in) to sell or trade in something commercially. **2** *informal* to buy and sell drugs illegally. **3** to distribute cards to players in a game. ✻ **deal with 1a** to take action with regard to (somebody or something): *I'll deal with my letters tomorrow.* **b** to cope with (somebody or something). **c** to have business relations with (somebody). **2** to be concerned with (a theme or subject). ⟫⟫ **dealing** *noun.* [Old English *dǣlan*]

deal² *noun* **1** an advantageous bargain or transaction. **2** a particular kind of treatment: *a raw deal.* **3** the process of distributing cards to players in a game. ✻ **a good/great deal 1** a lot: *a great deal of money.* **2** considerably: *It was raining a good deal harder now.* **it's a deal** *informal* used to confirm or assent to an agreement.

deal³ *noun* fir or pine timber, or a sawn piece of this. [early Dutch or early Low German *dele* plank]

dealer *noun* **1a** a person who deals in goods or services: *an antique dealer.* **b** a person who deals in shares, securities, etc, as a PRINCIPAL² (person for whom somebody acts as an agent). **c** somebody who deals in illegal drugs; a pusher. **2** the player who deals the cards in a game or round of play. ⟫⟫ **dealership** *noun.*

dealings /'deelingz/ *pl noun* business or personal relationships or activities.

dealt /delt/ *verb* past tense and past part. of DEAL¹.

dean¹ /deen/ *noun* **1a** the head of the chapter of a collegiate or cathedral church. **b** = RURAL DEAN. **2a** the head of a university division, faculty, or school. **b** a college or secondary school administrator in charge of guidance and discipline. [Middle English *deen* via French from late Latin *decanus*, literally 'chief of ten', from Latin *decem* ten]

dean² *or* **dene** *noun Brit* usu in place names: a narrow wooded valley with a stream running through it. [Old English *denu*]

deanery /'deenəri/ *noun* (*pl* **deaneries**) the office, jurisdiction, or official residence of a clerical dean.

dear¹ /diə/ *adj* **1a** much loved; precious or cherished: *a dear friend.* **b** used as a polite form of address in letters: *Dear Sir.* **c** sweet; appealing. **2** expensive. ✻ **for dear life** desperately; as if to escape death: *I clung on for dear life.* ⟫⟫ **dearness** *noun.* [Old English *dēore*]

dear² *noun* **1a** a loved one; a sweetheart. **b** used as a familiar or affectionate form of address. **2** a lovable person: *For I should be a perfect dear on fifty thousand pounds a year* — A P Herbert.

dear³ *adv* at a high cost; dearly: *Neglecting his family cost him dear.*

dear⁴ *interj* used to express annoyance or dismay: *Oh dear.* [prob short for *dear God* or *dear Lord*]

dearest¹ /'diərist/ *adj* **1a** most loved: *her dearest friend.* **b** most cherished: *his dearest wish.* **2** most expensive.

dearest² *noun* used as an affectionate form of address.

dearie /'diəri/ *noun* see DEARY.

Dear John *or* **Dear John letter** *noun informal* a letter written by a woman to a man to break off a relationship or engagement.

dearly *adv* **1** very much: *I would dearly like to help you.* **2** at a great cost.

dearth /duhth/ *noun* an inadequate supply; a scarcity. [Middle English *derthe*, from *dere* DEAR¹, costly]

deary *or* **dearie** /'diəri/ *noun* (*pl* **dearies**) *chiefly Brit* used as a familiar or condescending form of address. ✻ **deary me!** used to express surprise or consternation.

death /deth/ *noun* **1a** a permanent cessation of all vital functions; the end of life. **b** an instance of somebody or something dying. **c** the cause or occasion of loss of life: *Drinking was the death of him.* **2** the state of being dead. **3** (**Death**) death personified, usu represented as a skeleton with a scythe. **4** extinction or disappearance: *language death.* ✻ **at death's door** seriously ill. **be in at the death** to be a witness to the death of (somebody or something). **be the death of** *often humorous* to cause the death of (somebody). **like death warmed up** *informal* looking very pale and ill. **to death** beyond all acceptable limits; excessively: *I was bored to death.* ⟫⟫ **deathlike** *adj.* [Old English *dēath*]

death adder *noun* any of several species of poisonous Australian snakes with a thick body and a very thin tail: *Acanthophis antarcticus* and other species.

deathbed *noun* the bed in which a person is dying or has died: *But I should not think the better of a man who should tell me on his deathbed, he was sure of salvation* — Dr Johnson.

deathblow *noun* a destructive or killing stroke or event.

death camp *noun* a prison camp in which large numbers of people, e.g. prisoners of war or political prisoners, are put to death or die.

death cap *noun* a poisonous toadstool with a pale green cap and milky white gills, found in most parts of the British Isles, *esp* in beech and oak woodland: *Amanita phalloides.*

death cell *noun* = CONDEMNED CELL.

death certificate *noun* an official document issued by a doctor, stating the time and cause of a person's death.

death duty *noun* in Britain until 1975, a tax levied on the estate of a dead person: compare CAPITAL TRANSFER TAX, INHERITANCE TAX.

death futures *pl noun NAmer, informal* life insurance policies of people who are terminally ill, bought from them by others as a financial investment.

death knell *noun* **1** the ringing of a bell to mark a person's death. **2** an indication of the end or failure of something.

deathless *adj* immortal; lasting for ever: *only the deep sense of some deathless shame* — John Webster. ➤➤ **deathlessness** *noun.*

deathly *adj* (**deathlier, deathliest**) **1** suggestive of death: *a deathly pallor.* **2** *archaic or literary* fatal: *a deathly blow.*

death mask *noun* a cast taken from the face of a dead person.

death penalty *noun* punishment by death.

death rate *noun* the number of deaths per 1000 people in a population per year.

death rattle *noun* a gurgling sound produced by air passing through mucus in the lungs and throat of a dying person.

death row *noun* a part of a prison containing the cells of those condemned to death: *Unlike other prisoners, death-row inmates are not 'doing time'* — Mumia Abu-Jamal.

death's-head *noun* a human skull symbolizing death.

death's-head hawkmoth *noun* = DEATH'S-HEAD MOTH.

death's-head moth *noun* a large European hawkmoth with skull-shaped markings on its back: *Acherontia atropos.*

death squad *noun* a group of people who track down and kill the opponents of a person or organization.

death tax *noun NAmer* = INHERITANCE TAX.

death toll *noun* the number of people or animals dying as a result of something.

death trap *noun* a potentially lethal structure or place.

death warrant *noun* a warrant for the execution of a death sentence.

deathwatch *noun* a vigil kept with the dead or dying.

deathwatch beetle *noun* a small beetle common in old buildings, where it bores into woodwork making an ominous ticking sound: *Xestobium rufovillosum.*

death wish *noun* a usu unconscious desire for one's own death.

deb /deb/ *noun informal* a debutante.

debacle /di'bahkəl/ *noun* a complete failure; a fiasco. [French *débâcle* from *débâcler* to unbar, from early French DE- + *bacler* to bar, ultimately from Latin *baculum* staff]

debag /dee'bag/ *verb trans* (**debagged, debagging**) *Brit, informal* to remove the trousers of (somebody) as a joke or punishment.

debar /di'bah/ *verb trans* (**debarred, debarring**) (+ from) to bar or preclude (somebody) from having or doing something. ➤➤ **debarment** *noun.* [Middle English *debarren* from early French *desbarrer* to unbar, from DE- + *barrer* to bar]

debark¹ /dee'bahk/ *verb intrans* to disembark. ➤➤ **debarkation** /-bah'kayshən/ *noun.* [early French *debarquer*, from DE- + *barque* bark]

debark² *verb trans* to remove the bark from (a tree).

debase /di'bays/ *verb trans* **1** to lower (something) in status or quality. **2a** to reduce the intrinsic value of (a coin) by increasing the content of low-value metal. **b** to reduce the exchange value of (a monetary unit). ➤➤ **debasement** *noun,* **debaser** *noun.* [DE- + BASE⁴]

debatable /di'baytəbl/ *adj* open to debate; questionable. ➤➤ **debatably** *adv.*

debate¹ /di'bayt/ *noun* **1** a formal discussion of a motion by a legislative body. **2** an argument or controversy.

debate² *verb intrans* **1** to discuss a question by considering opposed arguments. **2** to participate in a debate. ➤ *verb trans* **1** to argue about (a matter). **2** to consider (a matter) from different viewpoints. ➤➤ **debater** *noun.* [Middle English *debaten* from Old French *debatre,* from DE- + *batre* to beat, from Latin *battuere*]

debauch¹ /di'bawch/ *verb trans* to corrupt or pervert (a person or institution): *the veracity of language, which cannot be debauched* — Ralph Waldo Emerson. ➤➤ **debauched** *adj,* **debaucher** *noun.* [French *débaucher* from Old French *desbauchier* to scatter, roughhew (timber), from DE- + *bauch* beam, of Germanic origin]

debauch² *noun* a bout of indulgence in sensual pleasures.

debauchee /dibaw'chee/ *noun* somebody given to debauchery. [French *débauché,* past part. of *débaucher:* see DEBAUCH¹]

debauchery /di'bawchəri/ *noun* excessive indulgence in sensual pleasures.

debeak /dee'beek/ *verb trans* to remove part of the beak of (a chicken or other bird) to prevent injury to other birds.

debenture /di'benchə/ *noun* **1** *Brit* a loan secured on the assets of a company in respect of which the company must pay a fixed interest before any dividends are paid to its own shareholders. **2** (*also* **debenture bond**) *NAmer* an unsecured bond that is backed only by the credit standing of the issuer. [Latin *debentur* they are due, from *debēre* to owe]

debilitate /di'biliteyt/ *verb trans* to impair the strength of (somebody); to enfeeble: *a debilitating illness.* ➤➤ **debilitation** /-'taysh(ə)n/ *noun,* **debilitative** *adj.* [Latin *debilitatus,* past part. of *debilitare* to weaken, from *debilis* weak]

debility /di'biliti/ *noun* weakness or infirmity. [early French *debilité* from Latin *debilitat-, debilitas,* from *debilis* weak]

debit¹ /'debit/ *noun* **1a** an entry in an account recording money owed. **b** the sum of such entries. **2** a charge against a bank account. [Latin *debitum:* see DEBT]

debit² *verb trans* (**debited, debiting**) **1** to record (an amount) as a debit. **2** said of a bank: to take (a sum of money) from an account as payment: compare CREDIT².

debit card *noun* a card issued by a bank authorizing the purchase of goods or services which are charged electronically to the holder's account.

debonair /debə'neə/ *adj* **1** suave or urbane. **2** light-hearted or nonchalant. ➤➤ **debonairly** *adv.* [Middle English *debonere* from Old French *debonaire,* from *de bonne aire* of good family or nature]

debouch /di'bowch/ *verb intrans* to emerge or issue from a narrow space into a wider area. [French *déboucher,* from DE- + *bouche* mouth, from Latin *bucca* cheek]

debouchment *noun* a mouth or outlet, *esp* of a river.

debridement /di'breedmənt/ *noun* in medicine, the surgical removal, *esp* from a wound, of dead, lacerated, or contaminated tissue or foreign bodies. [French *débridement* from *débrider* to remove unhealthy tissue, literally 'to unbridle', from DE- + *bride* bridle]

debrief /dee'breef/ *verb trans* to interrogate (a soldier, diplomat, etc) about a mission or task after its completion. ➤➤ **debriefer** *noun,* **debriefing** *noun.*

debris /'debri/ *noun* **1** the remains of something broken down or destroyed. **2a** an accumulation of fragments of rock. **b** accumulated rubbish or waste. [French *débris* from Old French, from *debrisier* to break to pieces, from DE- + *brisier* to break, of Celtic origin]

debt /det/ *noun* **1** money owed or due. **2** the state of owing something, *esp* money: *They are heavily in debt.* ✳ **in somebody's debt** owing somebody gratitude; indebted to somebody.

Word history
Middle English *dette, debte* from Old French *dette* something owed, from Latin *debitum,* past part. of *debēre* to owe. The *b* was introduced in the 14th or 15th cent. to conform with Latin *debitum,* but has never been pronounced: compare DOUBT¹.

debt collector *noun* a person employed by a creditor to collect debts.

debt of honour *noun* a debt that cannot be legally enforced but is regarded as morally binding, *esp* a gambling debt.

debtor *noun* somebody who owes a debt.

debug /dee'bug/ *verb trans* (**debugged, debugging**) **1** to eliminate errors or malfunctions in (computer software or equipment). **2** to remove a concealed microphone or wiretapping device from (a room or building). **3** *NAmer* to remove insects from (e.g. a building), *esp* with pesticide. ➤➤ **debugger** *noun.*

debunk /dee'bungk/ *verb trans* **1** to expose the falseness of (a statement or idea): *Deadly pseudo-solutions, such as the blocking of research, will lose the battle of ideas if enough people debunk them* — K Eric Drexler. **2** to expose the inflated reputation of (somebody). ➤➤ **debunker** *noun.* [DE- + BUNK³]

debus /dee'bus/ *verb* (**debussed, debussing**) ➤ *verb trans Brit, informal* to unload (e.g. military stores) from a vehicle. ➤ *verb intrans Brit, informal* to alight from a motor vehicle.

debut[1] /'dayb(y)ooh/ *noun* **1** a first public appearance. **2** *dated* a formal entrance into society. **3** (*used before a noun*) denoting a first recording, publication, etc: *debut novel*. [French *début* from *débuter* to begin, from DE- + *but* starting point, goal]

debut[2] *verb intrans* (**debuted, debuting**) to make a debut.

debutant /'debyootont/ *noun* somebody making a debut. [French *débutant*, present part. of *débuter*: see DEBUT[1]]

debutante /'debyootont/ *noun* a woman making a debut; *esp* an aristocratic young woman making her formal entrance into society. [French *débutante*, fem of *débutant*: see DEBUTANT]

Dec. *abbr* December.

dec. *abbr* **1** deceased. **2** decimal. **3** decimetre. **4** in cricket, declared. **5** declension. **6** declination. **7** decrease. **8** in music, decrescendo.

deca- *or* **dec-** *or* **deka-** *or* **dek-** *comb. form* forming words, with the meaning: **1** ten: *decahedron; decathlon*. **2** containing ten atoms, groups, or chemical equivalents in the molecular structure. [via Latin from Greek *deka-, dek-*, from *deka* ten]

decade /'dekayd, di'kayd/ *noun* **1** a period of ten years. **2a** a group, set, or sequence of ten. **b** in physics, a ratio of 10:1, *esp* the interval between frequencies of this ratio. ⏵ **decadal** *adj*. [Middle English via French and late Latin from Greek *dekad-, dekas*, from *deka* ten]

decadence /'dekəd(ə)ns/ *noun* **1** a period or process of moral or cultural decay or decline. **2** self-indulgence, *esp* the unrestrained gratification of desires or appetites. [early French via medieval Latin *decadentia* from late Latin *decadent-, decadens*, present part. of *decadere* to fall, sink, from DE- + *cadere* to fall]

decadent /'dekəd(ə)nt/ *adj* **1** marked by decay or decline, *esp* in moral or cultural standards. **2** self-indulgent in an uninhibited or immoral way. ⏵ **decadently** *adv*. [back-formation from DECADENCE]

decaf /'deekaf/ *noun informal* decaffeinated coffee.

decaffeinate /dee'kafinayt/ *verb trans* to remove most of the caffeine from (coffee or tea). ⏵ **decaffeination** /-'nayshən/ *noun*.

decagon /'dekəgon/ *noun* a polygon with ten angles and ten sides. ⏵ **decagonal** /di'kagənl/ *adj*. [Greek *dekagōnon*, from DECA- + -GON]

decahedron /dekə'heedrən/ *noun* (*pl* **decahedra** *or* **decahedrons**) a polyhedron with ten faces. ⏵ **decahedral** *adj*. [DECA- + -HEDRON]

decal /'deekal, 'dekəl/ *noun chiefly NAmer* a design or picture on prepared paper for transfer to another surface; a transfer. [short for DECALCOMANIA]

decalcify /dee'kalsifie/ *verb trans* (**decalcifies, decalcified, decalcifying**) to remove calcium or calcium compounds from (bones, teeth, soil, etc). ⏵ **decalcification** /-fi'kaysh(ə)n/ *noun*, **decalcifier** *noun*.

decalcomania /di,kalkə'mayni-ə/ *noun* **1** the process of transferring a design from specially prepared paper to another surface such as glass. **2** a design transferred in this way. [French *décalcomanie*, from *décalquer* to copy by tracing + *manie* mania; from the mid 19th-cent. craze for the process]

decalitre (*NAmer* **decaliter** *or* **dekaliter**) /'dekəleetə/ *noun* a metric unit of capacity equal to ten litres (about 2.2gall).

Decalogue /'dekəlog/ *noun* the Ten Commandments. [Middle English *decaloge* via late Latin from Greek *dekalogos*, from DEKA- + *logos* word]

decametre (*NAmer* **decameter** *or* **dekameter**) /'dekəmeetə/ *noun* a metric unit of length equal to 10m (about 10.94yd). ⏵ **decametric** /-'metrik/ *adj*. [French *décamètre*, from DECA- + *mètre* METRE[1]]

decamp /di'kamp/ *verb intrans* **1** to depart secretly or suddenly; to abscond: *But plunder was there none. Lucy had decamped with all her moveable wealth — Charles Kingsley.* **2** *archaic* to break up a camp. ⏵ **decampment** *noun*. [French *décamper* from early French *descamper*, from DE- + *camper* to camp]

decanal /di'kaynl/ *adj* **1** of a dean or deanery. **2** of the south side of the choir, e.g. in a cathedral, where the dean sits: compare CANTORIAL. [medieval Latin *decanus*: see DEAN[1]]

decane /'dekayn/ *noun* any of several liquids that belong to the alkane series of organic chemical compounds and that have the same molecular formula but a different structural arrangement of atoms: formula $C_{10}H_{22}$. [DECA- + -ANE]

decani /di'kaynie/ *noun* the part of a church choir sitting on the south side and taking the first or higher part in music for two groups: compare CANTORIS. [medieval Latin *decani* of the dean, from late Latin *decanus*: see DECANAL]

decant /di'kant/ *verb trans* to pour (liquid) gradually from one vessel into another, *esp* without disturbing the sediment. [medieval Latin *decanthare*, from DE- + *cantus* edge, rim]

decanter *noun* an ornamental glass bottle into which an alcoholic drink, *esp* wine, is decanted.

decapitate /di'kapitayt/ *verb trans* to cut off the head of (a person). ⏵ **decapitation** /-'taysh(ə)n/ *noun*, **decapitator** *noun*. [late Latin *decapitatus*, past part. of *decapitare*, from DE- + *capit-, caput* head]

decapod /'dekəpod/ *noun* any of an order of crustaceans including the shrimps, lobsters, and crabs, having stalked eyes, five pairs of appendages, and the head and thorax fused and covered by a carapace: order Decapoda. ⏵ **decapod** *adj*. [Latin *Decapoda*, order name, from DECA- + Greek *pous, pod-* foot]

decarbonize *or* **decarbonise** /dee'kahbəniez/ *verb trans* to remove carbon from (a surface, machinery, etc). ⏵ **decarbonization** /-'zayshən/ *noun*, **decarbonizer** *noun*.

decarboxylase /deekah'boksilayz, -lays/ *noun* in biochemistry, any of a group of enzymes that speed up the rate of removal of a carboxylic acid group from a compound, *esp* an amino acid.

decarboxylate /,deekah'boksilayt/ *verb trans* in chemistry, to remove a carboxylic acid group from (an organic compound). ⏵ **decarboxylation** /-'layshən/ *noun*.

decastyle /'dekəstiel/ *adj* in architecture, said of a temple or portico: having ten columns.

decasyllabic /,dekəsi'labik/ *adj* consisting of ten syllables.

decathlete /di'kathleet/ *noun* an athlete who competes in the decathlon.

decathlon /di'kathlon/ *noun* an athletic contest in which each competitor takes part in ten events: the 100m, 400m and 1500m races, the 110m high hurdles, and the javelin, discus, shot put, pole vault, high jump, and long jump. [French *décathlon*, from DECA- + Greek *athlon* contest]

decay[1] /di'kay/ *verb intrans* **1a** to rot or decompose because of the action of bacteria or fungi. **b** to decrease gradually in soundness, strength, or vigour; to deteriorate. **2** in physics, to undergo radioactive decay. ⏵ *verb trans* to destroy (a substance) by decomposition. [Middle English *decayen* via French from Latin *decidere*: see DECIDE]

decay[2] *noun* **1** the state or process of decaying. **2** the product of decay; rot or decomposition.

decease[1] /di'sees/ *noun formal* death. [Middle English *deces* via French from Latin *decessus* departure, death, from *decedere* to depart, die, from DE- + *cedere* to go]

decease[2] *verb intrans archaic* to die.

deceased[1] *noun* (*pl* **deceased**) (**the deceased**) *formal* a person who has recently died.

deceased[2] *adj formal* recently dead.

decedent /di'seed(ə)nt/ *noun NAmer* in law, a deceased person. [Latin *decedent-, decedens*, present part. of *decedere*: see DECEASE[1]]

deceit /di'seet/ *noun* **1a** the act or practice of deceiving; deception. **b** an attempt to deceive; a trick. **2** the quality of being deceitful. [Middle English *deceite* via Old French from Latin *decepta*, fem past part. of *decipere*: see DECEIVE]

deceitful /di'seetf(ə)l/ *adj* having a tendency or disposition to deceive; dishonest. ⏵ **deceitfully** *adv*, **deceitfulness** *noun*.

Usage note

deceitful *or* deceptive? *Deceitful* implies an intention to deceive. Generally speaking, only people and their words and actions can be described as *deceitful*. *Deceptive* is applied to things that are able to mislead the unwary: *Appearances can be deceptive.*

deceive /di'seev/ *verb trans* to cause (somebody) to accept as true or valid what is false or invalid; to delude: *O let not Time deceive you, you cannot conquer Time — W H Auden.* ⏵ *verb intrans* to practise deceit. ⏵ **deceivable** *adj*, **deceiver** *noun*. [Middle English *deceiven* via Old French *deceivre* from Latin *decipere*, from DE- + *capere* to take]

decelerate /dee'selərayt/ *verb trans and intrans* to move or cause (something) to move at decreasing speed. ⏵ **deceleration** /-'raysh(ə)n/ *noun*, **decelerator** *noun*. [DE- + ACCELERATE]

December /di'sembə/ *noun* the twelfth month of the year. [Middle English *Decembre* via Old French from Latin *December* tenth month, from *decem* ten; because it was the tenth month of the Roman year: see SEPTEMBER]

decency /'deesənsi/ *noun* (*pl* **decencies**) **1** behaviour or attitudes that conform to normal standards of propriety or morality. **2a** (*usu in pl*) a standard of propriety. **b** (*in pl*) the things considered necessary for an adequate standard of living.

decennial /di'seni·əl/ *adj* **1** lasting for ten years. **2** occurring every ten years. ⟩⟩ **decennial** *noun*, **decennially** *adv*. [Latin *decennis*, from *decem* ten + *annus* year]

decent /'dees(ə)nt/ *adj* **1a** conforming to normal standards of propriety or morality: *All decent people live beyond their income* — Saki. **b** free from obscenity. **2a** adequate or satisfactory: *decent housing*. **b** *chiefly Brit, informal* obliging; considerate: *It was decent of him to own up.* **3** *informal* clothed or sufficiently covered to be seen without impropriety. ⟩⟩ **decently** *adv*. [French *décent* from Latin *decent-*, *decens*, present part. of *decēre* to be fitting]

decentralisation *noun* see DECENTRALIZATION.

decentralise *verb* see DECENTRALIZE.

decentralization or **decentralisation** /dee,sentrəlie'zaysh(ə)n/ *noun* **1** the distribution of functions and powers from a central authority to regional authorities, departments, etc. **2** the redistribution of population and industry from urban centres to outlying areas.

decentralize or **decentralise** /dee'sentrəliez/ *verb trans* to bring about the decentralization of (e.g. an authority or government). ⟩⟩ **decentralist** *noun and adj.*

deception /di'sepsh(ə)n/ *noun* **1a** the act or an instance of deceiving. **b** the fact or condition of being deceived. **2** something that deceives; a trick. [Middle English *decepcioun* via French from late Latin *deception-*, *deceptio*, from Latin *decipere*: see DECEIVE]

deceptive /di'septiv/ *adj* tending or having the power to deceive; misleading. ⟩⟩ **deceptively** *adv*, **deceptiveness** *noun*.

Usage note ──────────
deceptive or *deceitful?* See note at DECEITFUL. In phrases like *a deceptively spacious house*, which are characteristic of marketing and advertising jargon, *deceptively* is used in a seemingly odd way. In this phrase, the house is spacious only in the sense that appearances suggest otherwise; *deceptively* here is equivalent to *surprisingly* rather than *misleadingly* (which *deceptively* means in a phrase such as *her voice was deceptively calm*: it was indeed calm in a way that the house is not spacious). Logically we might expect the wording to be *a deceptively cramped house*; but for obvious reasons this is not usually found.

decerebrate /dee'serəbrayt/ *verb trans* to remove or inactivate the brain of (an animal in a laboratory). ⟩⟩ **decerebrate** /-brət/ *adj,* **decerebration** /-'braysh(ə)n/ *noun.*

deci- *comb. form* forming words, denoting: one tenth part of (the unit specified): *decilitre.* [French *déci-* from Latin *decimus* tenth, from *decem* ten]

decibel /'desibel/ *noun* **1** a unit for expressing the intensity of sounds. **2** a unit for expressing the ratio of two amounts of electric or acoustic signal power equal to ten times the common logarithm of this ratio. [DECI- + BEL]

decide /di'sied/ *verb intrans* **1** to make a definite choice or come to a firm conclusion in a situation where more than one option or possibility is open: *He decided on the blue shirt.* **2** to make a judgment: *She decided in favour of the defendant.* ⟩ *verb trans* **1** (*often* + *to/that*) to make a choice or come to a conclusion about (something): *I decided to go by bus; They decided that they couldn't afford a holiday.* **2** to influence (somebody) to make a choice or resolution: *In the end, her screaming decided me and I left the room.* **3** to settle the outcome of (something): *Her goal decided the match.* ⟩⟩ **decidable** *adj.* [Middle English *deciden* via French from Latin *decidere* to cut or fall off, from DE- + *caedere* to cut]

decided *adj* **1** unquestionable: *We had a decided advantage.* **2** free from doubt or hesitation: *My mother is a woman of decided opinions.* ⟩⟩ **decidedly** *adv*, **decidedness** *noun.*

decider *noun* **1** a game, point, or goal that decides the winner of a competition or match. **2** an additional contest held to determine the winner of a series of contests when the final score is even.

deciduous /di'sidyooəs/ *adj* **1a** said of a tree: having leaves that are shed seasonally: compare EVERGREEN[1] (1). **b** said of leaves, teeth, etc: shed at a particular stage in development. **2** *formal*

ephemeral or transitory. ⟩⟩ **deciduousness** *noun*. [Latin *deciduus*, from *decidere* to fall off, from DE- + *cadere* to fall]

decigram /'desigram/ *noun* one tenth of a gram (0.0035oz). [French *décigramme*, from DECI- + *gramme*: see GRAM[1]]

decile /'desiel/ *noun* in statistics, any of ten groups containing equal numbers of items and each representing a particular frequency distribution within a statistical population. [Latin *decem* ten + -ILE]

decilitre (*NAmer* **deciliter**) /'desileetə/ *noun* one tenth of a litre (about 0.18pt).

decillion /di'silyən/ *noun* **1** *Brit* the number one followed by 60 zeros (10^{60}). **2** *NAmer* the number one followed by 33 zeros (10^{33}). [Latin *decem* ten + English *-illion* (as in MILLION)]

decimal[1] /'desiməl/ *adj* **1a** based on the number ten. **b** subdivided into units which are tenths, hundredths, etc of another unit. **c** expressed in a decimal fraction. **2** numbered or proceeding by tens. **3** using a decimal system (e.g. of coinage). ⟩⟩ **decimally** *adv.* [Latin *decima* tithe, from *decimus* tenth, from *decem* ten]

decimal[2] *noun* a fraction that is expressed as a series of integral numbers representing powers of one tenth, shown by writing a dot followed by one digit for the number of tenths, one digit for the number of hundredths, and so on (e.g. 0.25 = 25/100): compare COMMON FRACTION.

decimal currency *noun* (*pl* **currencies**) a currency in which the basic monetary unit is divided into ten or a hundred smaller units.

decimal fraction *noun* = DECIMAL[2].

decimalize or **decimalise** *verb trans* **1** to express (a number) as a decimal. **2** to convert (a system) to a decimal system. ⟩⟩ **decimalization** /-'zaysh(ə)n/ *noun.*

decimal place *noun* the position of a digit to the right of a decimal point.

decimal point *noun* the dot placed to the left of a decimal fraction, often between it and a whole number.

decimal system *noun* a system of numbering or classification based on the number ten, so that its most important structural values are ten, the various multiples of ten, a tenth.

decimate /'desimayt/ *verb trans* **1a** to kill a large number of people from among (a group or population): *Typhus fever decimated the school periodically* — Charlotte Brontë. **b** to destroy a large part of (something). **2** to kill every tenth man of (e.g. a regiment of mutinous soldiers). ⟩⟩ **decimation** /-'maysh(ə)n/ *noun*, **decimator** *noun.* [Latin *decimatus*, past part. of *decimare*, from *decimus* tenth, from *decem* ten]

Usage note ──────────
Historically, the word *decimate* refers to the practice in the Roman army of killing every tenth man in a mutinous unit in order to ensure loyalty of the surviving 90%. Although the Latin word for 'tenth' is embedded in *decimate* (compare *decimal, decimetre* etc), the word is now accepted by all but the most historically minded as meaning 'kill or destroy a large number or part of something': *The famine decimated the population; The industry has been decimated.* It goes against the grain of the word, however, to link it with a specific quantity (*decimate by 50%*), to apply it to an individual or indivisible thing, or to use it as a substitute for *annihilate* or *exterminate.*

decimetre (*NAmer* **decimeter**) /'desimeetə/ *noun* one tenth of a metre (about 3.9in.).

decipher /di'siefə/ *verb trans* (**deciphered**, **deciphering**) **1** to convert (something coded) into intelligible form; to decode (it). **2** to make out the meaning of (something) despite its obscurity. ⟩⟩ **decipherable** *adj*, **decipherment** *noun.*

decision /di'sizh(ə)n/ *noun* **1a** a choice in favour of a particular object or course of action reached after considering various alternatives. **b** the act or process of deciding. **2** promptness and firmness in deciding: *He is a man of courage and decision.* [early French *decision* from Latin *decision-*, *decisio*, from *decidere*: see DECIDE]

decision tree *noun* a graphical representation of the choices open to a decision-maker, with each possible decision and its consequences presented as a branch off a central stem so that the whole diagram looks like a tree.

decisive /di'siesiv/ *adj* **1** of crucial importance in determining the outcome of something: *the decisive battle.* **2** clearly and unambiguously settling an issue; conclusive: *a decisive victory.* **3** marked by or indicative of the ability to make clear or firm decisions. ⟩⟩ **decisively** *adv*, **decisiveness** *noun.*

deck[1] /dek/ *noun* **1a** a platform in a ship dividing the hull horizontally into different compartments. **b** the upper platform, open to the air, roughly level with the top of a ship's hull. **2** something resembling the deck of a ship, e.g. the floor of a bus. **3** *chiefly NAmer* a flat roof or platform at the side of a building, where people can sit or walk. **4a** a platform forming the upper operating surface of a record player with the turntable on it. **b** = TAPE DECK. **5** *NAmer* a pack of playing cards. **6** (**the deck**) *informal* the ground or floor. ✳ **clear the decks** to remove all objects or obstacles from an area or surface, *esp* in order to prepare for another activity. [Middle English from early Dutch *dec* roof, covering, cloak, from *decken* to cover]

deck² *verb trans* **1** (*often* + out) to decorate or adorn (something or somebody): *Rich women decked out in furs.* **2** *informal* to hit (somebody) hard; to floor (them). **3** to add a deck to (a vessel). [Dutch *dekken* to cover]

deck chair *noun* an adjustable folding chair made of canvas stretched over a wooden frame.

-decker *comb. form* forming nouns or adjectives, denoting: objects with the number of levels, floors, or layers specified: *a double-decker bus; a triple-decker cheeseburger.*

deckhand *noun* a seaman who performs manual duties.

deckle /'dekl/ *noun* a part of a paper-making machine that determines the width of the web. [German *Deckel* cover, from *decken* to cover]

deckle edge *noun* a rough untrimmed edge of paper. ⟩⟩ **deckle-edged** *adj.*

declaim /di'klaym/ *verb intrans* **1** to speak loudly and with dramatic or rhetorical expression. **2** to speak pompously or bombastically. ⟩ *verb trans* to deliver (a speech) or speak (words) in a loud and rhetorical or bombastic way. ⟩⟩ **declaimer** *noun.* [Middle English *declamen* from Latin *declamare*, from DE- + *clamare* to cry out]

declamation /deklə'maysh(ə)n/ *noun* **1** the art or act of declaiming. **2a** a speech given as a rhetorical exercise. **b** a speech showing strong feeling.

declamatory /di'klamət(ə)ri/ *adj* in the style of a declamation; impassioned, rhetorical, or bombastic. [Latin *declamatorius*, from *declamare*: see DECLAIM]

declarant /di'kleərənt/ *noun* somebody who makes a legal declaration.

declaration /deklə'raysh(ə)n/ *noun* **1a** an emphatic announcement or statement. **b** a document containing a formal statement of terms, rights, etc. **2** *Brit* the formal announcement of the number of votes cast for each candidate in an election. **3** the act or an instance of declaring. **4a** a plaintiff's formal statement of a claim. **b** an unsworn witness statement. **5** in cricket, an announcement of a decision to end the innings before all the batsmen are out. **6a** the announcement of trumps in a card game. **b** in some card games, the announcement by a player that he or she holds a particular combination of cards.

declarative /di'klarətiv/ *adj* **1** constituting a statement rather than a command or a question: *a declarative sentence.* **2** making a declaration. ⟩⟩ **declaratively** *adv.*

declaratory /di'klarət(ə)ri/ *adj* serving to declare, set forth, or explain.

declare /di'kleə/ *verb trans* **1** to make (something) known formally or explicitly. **2** to make (something) evident; to show (it). **3** to state (something) emphatically; to affirm (it): *They declared their innocence.* **4** to make a full statement of (one's taxable or dutiable income or property): *I have nothing to declare except my genius —* Oscar Wilde. **5a** to announce (e.g. a trump suit) in a card game. **b** to announce that one has (a combination of playing cards) in canasta, rummy, etc. ⟩ *verb intrans* **1** to make a declaration. **2** (*often* + for) to make a public statement of one's support. **3** said of a cricket captain or team: to announce a decision to end the team's innings before all the batsmen are out. ✳ **declare war** to commence hostilities; *specif* to make a formal declaration of intention to go to war. ⟩⟩ **declarable** *adj*, **declarer** *noun.* [Middle English *declaren* via French from Latin *declarare*, from DE- + *clarare* to make clear, from *clarus* clear]

déclassé /day'klasay/ *adj* brought down to a lower social class or status. [French *déclassé*, past part. of *déclasser* to declass]

declassify /dee'klasifie/ *verb trans* (**declassifies, declassified, declassifying**) to declare (e.g. documents, information) no longer secret. ⟩⟩ **declassification** /-fi'kaysh(ə)n/ *noun.*

declension /di'klensh(ə)n/ *noun* **1** a schematic arrangement of noun, adjective, or pronoun inflections. **2** a class of nouns or adjectives having the same type of inflectional forms. **3** a deterioration or decline. ⟩⟩ **declensional** *adj.* [early French *declinaison* from *decliner*: see DECLINE¹]

declination /dekli'naysh(ə)n/ *noun* **1** the angular distance, e.g. of a star, N or S from the celestial equator. **2** the angle between a compass needle and the geographical meridian, equal to the difference between magnetic and true north. **3** a formal refusal. ⟩⟩ **declinational** *adj.* [Middle English *declinacioun* via French from Latin *declination-, declinatio* turning aside, altitude of the pole, from Latin *declinare*: see DECLINE¹]

decline¹ /di'klien/ *verb intrans* **1a** to become gradually less strong, effective, or good; to weaken or deteriorate. **b** to become smaller or fewer in number; to diminish. **2** to refuse. **3a** to slope downwards; to descend. **b** to bend down; to droop. **4a** said of a celestial body: to sink towards setting. **b** to draw towards a close; to wane. ⟩ *verb trans* **1a** to refuse (e.g. an offer) courteously: *I declined her invitation.* **b** *formal* to refuse to undertake, engage in, or comply with (something): *to decline battle.* **2** in grammar, to list the inflectional forms of (a noun, pronoun, or adjective) in the prescribed order. ⟩⟩ **declinable** *adj*, **decliner** *noun.* [Middle English *declinen* via early French *decliner* from Latin *declinare* to turn aside, inflect, from DE- + *clinare* to incline]

decline² *noun* **1a** a gradual reduction or change for the worse. **b** a gradual physical or mental decay. **2** the period during which something is approaching its end. **3** a downward slope. **4** *archaic* a wasting disease, *esp* tuberculosis of the lungs.

declivity /di'kliviti/ *noun* (*pl* **declivities**) *formal* a descending slope. ⟩⟩ **declivitous** /-təs/ *adj.* [Latin *declivitat-, declivitas*, from *declivis* sloping down, from DE- + *clivus* slope, hill]

declutch /dee'kluch/ *verb intrans* to disengage the clutch of a motor vehicle or other machine.

declutter /dee'klutə/ *verb trans* (**decluttered, decluttering**) to remove unnecessary clutter from (a room, a desk, one's life, etc).

decoct /di'kokt/ *verb trans* to extract the essence of (something) by boiling. [Latin *decoctus*, past part. of *decoquere*, from DE- + *coquere* to cook]

decoction /di'koksh(ə)n/ *noun* **1** the extraction of the essence of a substance by boiling. **2** the concentrated liquor extracted.

decode /dee'kohd/ *verb trans* **1** to convert (a coded message) into intelligible language. **2** to convert (e.g. computer characters or electrical signals) from one coded form to another. ⟩⟩ **decoder** *noun.*

decoke /dee'kohk/ *verb trans Brit* to remove carbon deposits from (e.g. an internal-combustion engine).

décolletage /daykol'tahzh (*French* dekɔlta:ʒ)/ *noun* the low-cut neckline of a dress. [French *décolletage* from *décolleter*: see DÉCOLLETÉ¹]

décolleté¹ /daykol'tay, day'koltay (*French* dekɔlte)/ *adj* **1** said of a woman: wearing a strapless or low-necked dress. **2** said of a dress: low-necked. [French *décolleté*, past part. of *décolleter* to give a low neckline to, from DE- + *collet* collar, from Latin *collum* neck]

décolleté² *noun* = DÉCOLLETAGE.

decolonize or **decolonise** /dee'koləniez/ *verb trans* to free (a country) from colonial status; to grant (it) independence. ⟩⟩ **decolonization** /-'zaysh(ə)n/ *noun.*

decolorize or **decolorise** /dee'kuləriez/ (*Brit chiefly* **decolourize** or **decolourise**) *verb trans* to remove colour from (something). ⟩⟩ **decolorization** /-'zaysh(ə)n/ *noun.*

decommission /deekə'mish(ə)n/ *verb trans* **1** to remove (a ship, weapon, etc) from service. **2** to shut down and abandon (a nuclear reactor).

decompose /deekəm'pohz/ *verb intrans* to undergo chemical breakdown; to decay or rot. ⟩ *verb trans* **1** to separate (something) into its constituent parts, elements, atoms, etc. **2** to cause (something) to rot. ⟩⟩ **decomposition** /,deekompə'zish(ə)n/ *noun.* [French *décomposer*, from DE- + *composer* to compose]

decomposer *noun* any of various organisms (e.g. many bacteria and fungi) that break down organic matter, *esp* dead tissue, into inorganic products.

decompress /deekəm'pres/ *verb trans* **1** to release (something) from pressure or compression. **2** to expand (computer data) to its normal size after it has been compressed. ➤➤ **decompression** /-'presh(ə)n/ *noun*.

decompression chamber *noun* a chamber in which air pressure can be gradually reduced until it reaches the level of atmospheric pressure, used *esp* by deep-sea divers returning to the surface.

decompression sickness *noun* a sometimes fatal condition suffered *esp* by deep-sea divers, characterized by intense pains, *esp* in the joints, paralysis, and difficulty in breathing, caused by the expansion of nitrogen bubbles in the blood and tissue after a rapid transfer from a pressurized to a non-pressurized environment.

decongest /deekən'jest/ *verb trans* to relieve the congestion in (something).

decongestant /deekən'jest(ə)nt/ *noun* something, e.g. a drug, that relieves congestion. ➤➤ **decongestant** *adj*.

deconsecrate /dee'konsikrayt/ *verb trans* to declare (a building or area) to be no longer sacred and return it to secular use. ➤➤ **deconsecration** /-'kraysh(ə)n/ *noun*.

deconstruct /deekən'strukt/ *verb trans* **1** to analyse (e.g. a film or text) by deconstruction. **2** to take (something) to pieces; to dismantle (it). ➤➤ **deconstructive** /-tiv/ *adj*.

deconstruction /deekən'struksh(ə)n/ *noun* a critical technique, e.g. in literary or film criticism, which claims that there is no single innate meaning and thus no single correct interpretation of a text, but that the task of the critic or reader is to dismantle the implied unity of a work of art to reveal the variety of interpretations that are possible.

Editorial note
Loosely applied to any rejection of the usual conventions of construction (in the case of avant-garde films, or even fashion garments that show their seams), deconstruction in a more specific sense is attributable to the philosopher Jacques Derrida (b.1930), who shows how, when two terms are opposed, each owes its meaning to its difference from the other. This trace of difference, and so of the other in the selfsame, deconstructs the apparent antithesis between them — Professor Catherine Belsey.

➤➤ **deconstructionism** *noun*, **deconstructionist** *noun and adj*.

decontaminate /deekən'taminayt/ *verb trans* to rid (some-thing) of contamination, e.g. radioactivity. ➤➤ **decontamination** /-'naysh(ə)n/ *noun*.

decontextualize *or* **decontextualise** /deekon'tekstyoooəliez/ *verb trans* to remove (something) from its context and consider it in isolation. ➤➤ **decontextualization** /-lie'zaysh(ə)n/ *noun*.

decontrol[1] /deekən'trohl/ *verb trans* (**decontrolled, decontrolling**) to end control of (e.g. commodity prices).

decontrol[2] *noun* the act of decontrolling something.

decor *or* **décor** /'dekaw/ *noun* **1** the style and layout of interior decoration and furnishings. **2** a stage setting. [French *décor* from *décorer* to decorate, from Latin *decorare*: see DECORATE]

decorate /'dekərayt/ *verb trans* **1a** to give (something) a more attractive appearance by adding colour or ornamental shapes or objects to it. **b** to apply new coverings of paint, wallpaper, etc to the interior or exterior surfaces of (a room or a building). **2** to award a medal or other mark of honour to (somebody). [Latin *decoratus*, past part. of *decorare*, from *decor-, decus* ornament, honour]

Decorated /'dekəraytid/ *adj* denoting or relating to a style of Gothic architecture prevalent in Britain from the late 13th to the mid 14th cent., characterized by ogee arches and elaborate ornamentation.

decoration /dekə'raysh(ə)n/ *noun* **1** the act or process of decorating. **2** an ornament: *Christmas decorations*. **3** a badge of honour, e.g. a medal.

decorative /'dek(ə)rətiv/ *adj* serving to decorate; *esp* purely ornamental rather than functional. ➤➤ **decoratively** *adv*, **decorativeness** *noun*.

decorator *noun* somebody whose job is painting and wallpapering rooms or buildings.

decorous /'dekərəs/ *adj* marked by propriety and good taste; decent or restrained. ➤➤ **decorously** *adv*, **decorousness** *noun*. [Latin *decorus*, from *decor* beauty, grace]

decorticate /dee'kawtikayt/ *verb trans* **1** to peel the husk, bark or other outer covering from (something). **2** to remove (part of) the cortex from (e.g. the brain). ➤➤ **decortication** /-'kaysh(ə)n/ *noun*. [Latin *decorticatus*, past part. of *decorticare* to remove the bark from, from DE- + *cortic-, cortex* bark]

decorum /di'kawrəm/ *noun* behaviour that is in accordance with the dictates of propriety and good taste: *I would hardly walk from this room to the next to look at the raw efforts of those who have not been bred to the trade [of acting]: a set of gentlemen and ladies who have all the disadvantages of education and decorum to struggle through* — Jane Austen. [Latin *decorum*, neuter of *decorus*: see DECOROUS]

decoupage /daykooh'pahzh (*French* dekupa:ʒ)/ *noun* the art of applying decorative cutouts, e.g. of paper, to a surface and then coating them with varnish, lacquer, etc. [French *découpage*, literally 'act of cutting out', from *découper* to cut out, from DE- + *couper* to cut]

decouple /dee'kupl/ *verb trans chiefly Brit* to isolate (*esp* oscillating electrical systems) from one another so that they behave independently.

decoy[1] /'deekoy, di'koy/ *noun* **1** something used to lure or lead another person or animal into a trap. **2** somebody or something used to distract or divert the attention, e.g. of an enemy. **3** a pond into which wildfowl are lured for capture. [prob from Dutch *de kooi*, literally 'the cage']

decoy[2] *verb trans* to lure or entice (somebody) by or as if by a decoy.

decrease[1] /di'krees/ *verb intrans* to become progressively less, e.g. in size, amount, number, or intensity. ➤ *verb trans* to cause (something) to decrease. ➤➤ **decreasingly** *adv*. [Middle English *decreessen* from Latin *decrescere*, from DE- + *crescere* to grow]

decrease[2] /'deekrees, di'krees/ *noun* **1** the process of decreasing. **2** the amount by which something decreases.

decree[1] /di'kree/ *noun* **1** an order, *esp* one having legal force. **2** a judicial decision, *esp* in an equity, probate, or divorce court. [Middle English via French from Latin *decretum*, neuter past part. of *decernere* to decide, from DE- + *cernere* to sift or decide]

decree[2] *verb trans* (**decrees, decreed, decreeing**) to command or impose (something) by decree: *The emperor decreed an amnesty.*

decree absolute *noun* a decree making a divorce final.

decree nisi /'niesie/ *noun* a provisional decree of divorce that is made absolute after a fixed period unless cause to the contrary is shown. [Latin *nisi* unless]

decrement /'dekrimənt/ *noun* **1** a gradual decrease in quality or quantity. **2** the quantity lost by diminution or waste. **3** in mathematics, a negative increment. **4** in physics, a measure of the amount by which an oscillator damps the oscillation of the alternating current that it produces, expressed as a ratio of successive amplitudes. [Latin *decrementum*, from *decrescere*: see DECREASE[1]]

decrepit /di'krepit/ *adj* **1** wasted and weakened, *esp* by the infirmities of old age. **2a** worn-out. **b** fallen into ruin or disrepair. ➤➤ **decrepitude** /-tyoohd/ *noun*. [Middle English via French from Latin *decrepitus*, from DE- + *crepitus*, past part. of *crepare* to crack or creak]

decrepitate /di'krepitayt/ *verb trans* to roast or calcine (e.g. a salt) so as to cause crackling or until crackling stops. ➤ *verb intrans* to become decrepitated. ➤➤ **decrepitation** /-'taysh(ə)n/ *noun*. [Latin DE- + *crepitare* to crackle, from *crepitus*: see DECREPIT]

decrescendo /deekrə'shendoh/ *adj and adv* in music, = DIMINUENDO. ➤➤ **decrescendo** *noun*. [Italian *decrescendo* decreasing, from Latin *decrescendum*, verbal noun from *decrescere*: see DECREASE[1]]

decrescent /di'kres(ə)nt/ *adj* said of the moon: decreasing or waning. [alteration of *decressant*, ultimately from Latin *decrescent-, decrescens*, present part. of *decrescere*: see DECREASE[1]]

decretal /di'kreetl/ *noun* an authoritative papal decision on a point of canon law. [Middle English *decretale* via French and late Latin from Latin *decretum*: see DECREE[1]]

decriminalize *or* **decriminalise** /dee'kriminəliez/ *verb trans* to stop treating (something) as a criminal offence; to legalize (it): *Attempts have been made to decriminalize prostitution.* ➤➤ **decriminalization** /-'zaysh(ə)n/ *noun*.

decry /di'krie/ *verb trans* (**decries, decried, decrying**) **1** to express strong disapproval of (something). **2** to depreciate (e.g. a coin) officially or publicly. ➤➤ **decrier** *noun*. [French *décrier* from Old French *descrier*, from DE- + *crier* to cry]

decrypt /dee'kript, di'kript/ *verb trans* to decode (a cryptogram), *esp* without prior knowledge of the key. ➤➤ **decryption** *noun*. [DE- + CRYPTOGRAM, *cryptograph*]

decumbent /di'kumb(ə)nt/ *adj* said of a plant: lying on the ground except for a raised apex or extremity. [Latin *decumbent-*, *decumbens*, present part. of *decumbere* to lie down, from DE- + *-cumbere* to lie down]

decussate /di'kusayt, -sət/ *adj* **1** shaped like an X. **2** said of leaves: arranged in pairs each at right angles to the next pair above or below. [Latin *decussatus*, past part. of *decussare* to intersect, from *decussis* the Roman numeral X, intersection]

decussation /deekə'saysh(ə)n/ *noun* a crossed tract of nerve fibres passing between parts of the body on opposite sides of the brain or spinal cord.

dedicate /'dedikayt/ *verb trans* **1** (+ to) to make a solemn long-term commitment of (oneself or one's time) to achieving a particular goal or pursuing a particular way of life. **2a** to set (something) apart for a specific use or purpose. **b** to set (something, e.g. a building) apart for a sacred purpose, *esp* to devote (it) to the worship of God or the commemoration of a particular individual (e.g. a saint). **3** to inscribe or address (a book, song, etc) to somebody or something as a mark of esteem or affection: *He dedicated the new book to a friend.* ⟫⟫ **dedicatee** /-kə'tee/ *noun*, **dedicator** *noun*. [Middle English from Latin *dedicatus*, past part. of *dedicare* to affirm, dedicate, from DE- + *dicare* to proclaim]

dedicated *adj* **1** devoted to a cause, ideal, or purpose; zealous: *a dedicated scholar*. **2** given over to a particular purpose: *a dedicated process control computer.* ⟫⟫ **dedicatedly** *adv*.

dedication /dedi'kaysh(ə)n/ *noun* **1** a devoting or setting aside for a particular purpose, *esp* a religious one. **2** a phrase or sentence used to dedicate a book, song, etc to somebody. **3** commitment to achieving a particular purpose, ideal, etc; self-sacrificing devotion.

dedicative /'dedikətiv/ *adj* = DEDICATORY.

dedicatory /'dedikət(ə)ri/ *adj* serving to dedicate something or acting as a dedication.

deduce /di'dyoohs/ *verb trans* **1** to establish (a fact, the truth, etc) by reasoning and making use of the information available; *specif* to infer (a conclusion) from a general principle: compare INDUCE. **2** *archaic* to trace the course or derivation of (something). ⟫⟫ **deducible** *adj*. [Latin *deducere* to lead out or away, from DE- + *ducere* to lead]

deduct /di'dukt/ *verb trans* (*often* + from) to subtract (an amount) from a total. [Latin *deductus*, past part. of *deducere*: see DEDUCE]

deductible¹ *adj* that can be deducted: *Your petrol expenses are deductible for tax purposes.* ⟫⟫ **deductibility** /-'biliti/ *noun*.

deductible² *noun NAmer* an insurance excess.

deduction /di'duksh(ə)n/ *noun* **1a** the act or an instance of taking away or subtracting. **b** an amount that is or may be subtracted. **2a** the use of reasoning and the available information to discover the truth or reach a conclusion about something; *specif* the process of drawing a particular conclusion from a general premise. **b** a conclusion reached by this process.

deductive /di'duktiv/ *adj* based on or using deduction. ⟫⟫ **deductively** *adv*.

deed¹ /deed/ *noun* **1** something that is done; an action: *evil deeds*. **2** an illustrious act or action; a feat or exploit. **3** the act of doing something: *Never mistake the word for the deed.* **4** in law, a signed and sealed written document containing a transfer, bargain, or contract. [Old English *dæd*]

deed² *verb trans NAmer* to convey or transfer (e.g. property) by deed.

deed of covenant *noun Brit* an agreement to pay a certain amount of money regularly, *esp* one that benefits a charity by allowing it to reclaim the tax paid on the sum.

deed poll *noun* (*pl* **deeds poll**) a deed made and executed by one party only, often used to change a person's name. [DEED¹ + *poll* having the edges cut straight rather than indented, from POLL¹]

deejay /'deejay/ *noun informal* a disc jockey.

deem /deem/ *verb trans formal* to judge or consider (something) to be something: *I would deem it an honour.* [Middle English *demen* from Old English *dōm* judgment]

de-emphasize *or* **de-emphasise** /dee'emfəsiez/ *verb trans* to reduce emphasis on or commitment to (something): *He had proposed that the firm de-emphasized currently troubled departments —* Newsweek.

deemster /'deemstə/ *noun* a High Court judge in the Isle of Man. [Middle English *demestre* judge, from *demen*: see DEEM]

de-energize *or* **de-energise** /dee'enəjiez/ *verb trans* to disconnect (an electrical circuit) from a power source.

deep¹ /deep/ *adj* **1** extending far downwards or back from a surface or area: *a deep well; a deep cupboard*. **2** extending well inwards from an outer surface: *a deep cut*. **3** having a specified extension in an implied direction: *a shelf 20 centimetres deep; cars parked three deep*. **4** coming from very low in the chest: *He gave a deep sigh*. **5a** said of a colour: high in saturation and low in lightness; dark and full. **b** having a low musical pitch or pitch range. **6a** intellectually demanding or difficult to understand: *The poem is too deep for me*. **b** capable of serious and significant thought: *a deep thinker*. **7a** (+ in) experiencing or involved in something to a great extent or with great intensity: *deep in debt*. **b** (+ in) absorbed or engrossed: *deep in thought*. **8** intense or extreme: *deep sleep*. **9** *informal* cunning or devious. **10** remote in time or space. **11a** in sport, near or towards the outer limits of the playing area, or far from an attacking movement. **b** in cricket, of or occupying a fielding position far from the batsman. ✱ **go off the deep end 1** to become very excited or angry. **2** *chiefly NAmer* to enter recklessly on a course of action. **in deep water** in difficulty or distress; unable to manage. ⟫⟫ **deeply** *adv*, **deepness** *noun*. [Old English *dyppan* DIP¹]

deep² *adv* **1** to a great depth: *They had to dig deep*. **2** far in: *a house deep in the woods*. **3** far on; late: *They danced deep into the night*. **4** in a deep position in sport: *The wingers were playing deep*. **5** far back in space or time: *The tradition had its roots deep in the Dark Ages*.

deep³ *noun* **1a** (**the deep**) the sea. **b** any of the very deep portions of a body of water, *esp* the sea. **2** a vast or immeasurable extent; an abyss: *the black deep of space*. **3** the middle or most intense part: *the deep of winter*. **4** in cricket, the part of the playing area near the boundary and far from the batsman.

deep-discount *adj* **1** said of financial securities: issued at a discount to the redemption value and having a low rate of interest, thus giving capital gain rather than income. **2** *NAmer* enormously reduced in price.

deep-dish *adj* cooked in a deep dish and thus more substantial than usual.

deepen *verb* (**deepened, deepening**) ⟫ *verb trans* to make (something) deeper or more profound. ⟫ *verb intrans* to become deeper or more profound.

deep freeze *noun* **1** a freezer. **2** the condition of being held in temporary suspension.

deep-freeze *verb trans* (*past tense* **deep-froze**, *past part.* **deep-frozen**) to freeze or store (e.g. food) in a freezer.

deep-fry *verb trans* (**deep-fries, deep-fried, deep-frying**) to fry (food) by complete immersion in hot fat or oil. ⟫⟫ **deep-fryer** *noun*.

deep-laid *adj* carefully and cunningly contrived: *deep-laid plots*.

deep-pan *adj* said of a pizza: cooked in a pan with raised sides and with a thicker crust than usual.

deep-rooted *adj* firmly established; held or felt with great intensity or conviction: *You have a deep-rooted loyalty to your family*.

deep-sea *noun* (*used before a noun*) relating to or occurring in the deeper parts of the sea: *deep-sea fishing*.

deep-seated *adj* firmly established and difficult to change or remove: *a deep-seated tradition*.

deep-set *adj* said *esp* of eyes: set firmly or deeply.

Deep South *noun* the southernmost part of the eastern USA, including Alabama, Georgia, Louisiana, and Mississippi.

deep space *noun* space well beyond the limits of the earth's atmosphere, including space outside the solar system.

deep structure *noun* in grammar, a formal representation of the underlying meaning of a sentence.

deep vein thrombosis *noun* the development of a blood clot in a deep-lying vein in the calf or thigh, caused *esp* by injury or inactivity, and sometimes giving rise to a pulmonary embolism.

deer /diə/ *noun* (*pl* **deers** *or collectively* **deer**) any of numerous species of ruminant mammals of which most of the males and some of the females bear antlers: family Cervidae. [Old English *dēor* beast]

deerhound *noun* a tall dog of a breed with a rough coat resembling the greyhound.

deer-lick *noun* a block or area of salt that deer can lick.

deerskin *noun* **1** leather from a deer's hide. **2** (*used before a noun*) made from this.

deerstalker /'diəstawkə/ *noun* **1** a close-fitting hat with peaks at the front and the back and ear-flaps. **2** somebody who stalks deer. [because they were often worn by people stalking deer]

de-escalate /dee'eskəlayt/ *verb trans* to reduce the intensity or gravity, extent, or scope of (something): *Officers tried to de-escalate the situation.* ➤ *verb intrans* to decrease in intensity, extent, or scope. ➤➤ **de-escalation** /-'laysh(ə)n/ *noun.*

def /def/ *adj slang* excellent. [prob short for DEFINITIVE¹]

def. *abbr* **1** defective. **2** defence. **3** defendant. **4** used *esp* for deferred shares: deferred. **5** definite. **6** definition.

deface /di'fays/ *verb trans* to spoil the external appearance of (something). ➤➤ **defaceable** *adj,* **defacement** *noun,* **defacer** *noun.* [Middle English *defacen* from Old French *desfacier,* from DE- + *face:* see FACE¹]

de facto¹ /day 'faktoh/ *adv* in reality; actually. [Latin *de facto,* literally 'of fact']

de facto² *adj* existing in fact; effective: compare DE JURE: *a de facto state of war.*

defalcate /'deefalkayt/ *verb intrans formal* to embezzle. ➤➤ **defalcation** /-'kaysh(ə)n/ *noun,* **defalcator** *noun.* [late Latin *defalcatus,* past part. of *defalcare* to deduct, literally 'to cut down', from Latin DE- + *falc-, falx* sickle]

defame /di'faym/ *verb trans* to injure the reputation of (somebody) by libel or slander. ➤➤ **defamation** /defə'maysh(ə)n/ *noun,* **defamatory** /di'famət(ə)ri/ *adj,* **defamer** *noun.* [Middle English via French from Latin *diffamare,* from DIS- + *fama* FAME]

defat /dee'fat/ *verb trans* (**defatted, defatting**) to remove fat from (food).

default¹ /di'fawlt/ *noun* **1** failure to do something required by duty or law, e.g.: **a** failure to pay debts. **b** failure to appear at the required time in a legal proceeding. **2** failure to be present; absence. **3a** in computing, an option that has been pre-selected and that remains in effect until it is overridden or cancelled. **b** (*used before a noun*) pre-selected and remaining in effect until overridden or cancelled. ✳ **by default** in the absence of an alternative: *She won by default since her opponent refused to compete.* **in default** guilty of non-payment of a debt or of failing to appear in court. **in default of** in the absence of. [Middle English *defaute, defaulte,* from Latin *defallere* to be lacking, from DE- + *fallere* to deceive]

default² *verb intrans* **1** (*often* + on) to fail to meet an obligation, *esp* a financial one. **2** to fail to appear in court. ➤ *verb trans* to declare (somebody) to be in default.

defaulter /di'fawltə/ *noun* **1** somebody who defaults. **2** *Brit* a member of the armed forces who commits a military offence.

defeasible /di'feezəbl/ *adj* capable of being annulled. ➤➤ **defeasibility** /-'biliti/ *noun.*

defeat¹ /di'feet/ *verb trans* **1** to win a victory over (somebody or something): *We managed to defeat the opposing team.* **2** to frustrate (e.g. a hope). **3** in law, to nullify (something). [Middle English *deffeten* from Old French *deffaire, desfaire,* ultimately from Latin *disfacere* to undo, from DIS- + *facere* to do]

defeat² *noun* **1a** failure to win, or to achieve an aim: *We are not interested in the possibilities of defeat; they do not exist* — Queen Victoria. **b** a contest, battle, etc in which one is the loser. **2** (*usu* + of) the act or an instance of defeating somebody or something.

defeatism *noun* a pessimistic view of the chances of overcoming difficulties or achieving success; acceptance of or resignation to defeat. ➤➤ **defeatist** *noun and adj.*

defecate /'defəkayt/ *verb intrans* to discharge faeces from the bowels. ➤➤ **defecation** /-'kaysh(ə)n/ *noun,* **defecator** *noun,* **defecatory** *adj.* [Latin *defaecatus,* past part. of *defaecare,* from DE- + *faec-, faex* dregs]

defect¹ /'deefekt/ *noun* **1** an imperfection that impairs the worth or usefulness of something; a fault or shortcoming: *a hearing defect.* **2** a deficiency. [Middle English *defaicte* via French from Latin *defectus* lack, past part. of *deficere* to desert or fail, from DE- + *facere* to make, do]

defect² /di'fekt/ *verb intrans* to desert a cause or party, often in favour of another. ➤➤ **defection** *noun,* **defector** *noun.*

defective¹ /di'fektiv/ *adj* **1** having a defect and unable to fulfil its function properly; faulty: *a defective pane of glass; defective eyesight.* **2** *offensive* said of a person: subnormal, *esp* in intelligence. **3** in grammar, lacking one or more of the usual inflections. ➤➤ **defectively** *adv,* **defectiveness** *noun.*

Usage note

defective *or* **deficient?** These two words are close together in meaning and can sometimes be used to describe the same thing, but there is a significant difference between them. *Defective* is applied to functioning things that fail to function properly: a *defective* component is faulty and does not work: *defective brakes. Deficient* primarily means 'lacking' or 'inadequate': *a diet deficient in the vitamins necessary for healthy growth.*

defective² *noun offensive* somebody who is subnormal physically or mentally.

defence (*NAmer* **defense**) /di'fens/ *noun* **1a** the act or an instance of defending. **b** a means or method of defending. **2a** an argument in support or justification. **b** a defendant's denial, answer, or strategy. **3** (*in pl*) a defensive structure. **4** (*treated as sing. or pl*). **a** a defending party or group, e.g. in a court of law. **b** defensive players, acts, or moves in a game or sport. **5** the military resources of a country: *the defence budget.* ➤➤ **defenceless** *adj,* **defencelessly** *adv,* **defencelessness** *noun.* [Middle English via Old French from Latin *defensa,* fem past part. of *defendere:* see DEFEND]

defence mechanism *noun* **1** a reaction used by a living organism to defend itself against bacteria and viruses. **2** a usu unconscious mental process, e.g. projection or repression, that prevents the entry of unacceptable or painful thoughts into consciousness.

defend /di'fend/ *verb trans* **1a** (*often* + from/against) to protect (somebody or something) from attack. **b** to attempt to retain (something that one holds, e.g. a military position, sporting title, or parliamentary seat) in the face of efforts by others to gain it. **2** to maintain (something) by argument in the face of opposition or criticism. **3** to attempt to prevent an opponent from scoring (e.g. a goal). **4** to act as legal representative in court for (somebody). ➤ *verb intrans* **1** to take action against attack or challenge. **2** to play or be in defence. ➤➤ **defendable** *adj.* [Middle English *defenden* via Old French from Latin *defendere,* from DE- + *-fendere* to strike]

defendant *noun* a person, company, etc against whom a criminal charge or civil claim is made: compare PLAINTIFF.

defender *noun* somebody who plays in a defensive position in a sport.

defenestration /dee,feni'straysh(ə)n/ *noun chiefly humorous* the act of throwing somebody out of a window. [DE- + Latin *fenestra* window]

defense /di'fens/ *noun NAmer* see DEFENCE.

defensible *adj* capable of being defended, e.g. by argument or in a war. ➤➤ **defensibility** /-'biliti/ *noun,* **defensibly** *adv.* [Middle English from late Latin *defensibilis,* from *defendere:* see DEFENCE]

defensive /di'fensiv/ *adj* **1a** serving to defend. **b** devoted to resisting or preventing aggression, attack, criticism, or attempts by an opponent to score. **2** anticipating criticism, sensitive to it, and eager to defend one's own actions or views. ✳ **on the defensive** having to defend oneself against attack or criticism. ➤➤ **defensively** *adv,* **defensiveness** *noun.*

defer¹ /di'fuh/ *verb trans* (**deferred, deferring**) **1** to postpone (an action, decision, etc). **2** *NAmer* to postpone the military drafting of (somebody). ➤➤ **deferment** *noun,* **deferrable** *adj,* **deferral** *noun.* [Middle English *deferren, differren* via French from Latin *differre:* see DIFFER]

defer² *verb intrans* (**deferred, deferring**) (*usu* + to) to acknowledge somebody else's superiority, usu out of respect, *esp* to allow somebody else's opinion to prevail. [Middle English *deferren, differren* via French from Latin *deferre* to bring or bring down, from DE- + *ferre* to carry]

deference /'def(ə)rəns/ *noun* **1** the respect and esteem due to a superior or an elder. **2** compliance with the wishes or opinion of another. ✳ **in deference to** because of respect for.

deferent¹ /'def(ə)rənt/ *adj* serving to carry down or out: *a deferent duct.* [Latin *deferent-, deferens,* present part. of *deferre* to carry down]

deferent² *adj* = DEFERENTIAL. [back-formation from DEFERENCE]

deferential /defə'rensh(ə)l/ *adj* **1** showing or expressing deference; respectful. **2** showing or expressing excessive deference; obsequious. ➤➤ **deferentially** *adv.* [Latin *deferent-, deferens,* present part. of *deferre:* see DEFER²]

deferred /di'fuhd/ *adj* said of a payment: withheld for or until a stated time.

defiance /di'fie-əns/ *noun* bold resistance or disobedience. ✳ **in defiance of** despite; contrary to. ➤➤ **defiant** *adj,* **defiantly** *adv.*

defibrillation /dee,fibri'laysh(ə)n/ *noun* the restoration of the normal regular beating and rhythm of the heart.

defibrillator /dee'fibrilaytə/ *noun* an apparatus used to apply an electric current to the heart to restore its normal rhythm.

deficiency /di'fish(ə)nsi/ *noun* (*pl* **deficiencies**) **1** being deficient; inadequacy. **2** a lack or shortage.

deficiency disease *noun* a disease, e.g. scurvy, caused by a lack of essential vitamins, minerals, etc in the diet.

deficient /di'fish(ə)nt/ *adj* **1** (*usu* + in) lacking in some necessary quality or element: *I had been deficient in judgment*. **2** not up to a normal standard or complement; inadequate. ➤➤ **deficiently** *adv.* [Latin *deficient- deficiens*, present part. of *deficere*: see DEFECT[1]]

Usage note
deficient or defective? See note at DEFECTIVE[1].

deficit /'defisit/ *noun* **1** a deficiency in amount or quality. **2a** in economics, an excess of expenditure over revenue. **b** an excess of liabilities over assets. [French *déficit* from Latin *deficit* it is wanting, from *deficere*: see DEFECT[1]]

deficit financing *noun* spending that is financed by borrowing.

defilade[1] /defi'layd/ *verb trans* to arrange (fortifications) so as to protect the lines from enemy fire. [prob from DE- + *-filade* as in ENFILADE[1]]

defilade[2] *noun* the act or process of defilading.

defile[1] /di'fiel/ *verb trans* **1** to make (something) unclean or impure. **2** *archaic* to deprive (a woman) of her virginity. ➤➤ **defilement** *noun*, **defiler** *noun*. [Middle English *defilen*, alteration of *defoulen* to trample or defile, from Old French *defouler* to trample, from DE- + *fouler* to trample, literally 'to full']

defile[2] *verb intrans* to march off in a file. [French *défiler*, from DE- + *filer* to move in a column]

defile[3] *noun* a narrow passage or gorge. [French *défilé*, past part. of *défiler*: see DEFILE[2]]

define /di'fien/ *verb trans* **1a** to be or describe the essential quality or qualities of (somebody or something); to identify (them). **b** to set forth the meaning of (e.g. a word): *To define true madness, what is't but to be nothing else but mad?* — Shakespeare. **2a** to fix or mark the limits of (something); to demarcate (it). **b** to make (something) clear or precise in outline: *The issues aren't too well defined.* ➤➤ **definable** *adj*, **definer** *noun*. [Middle English *definen* via French from Latin *definire*, from DE- + *finire* to limit, end, from *finis* boundary, end]

definite /'definət/ *adj* **1a** free of all ambiguity, uncertainty, or obscurity. **b** clearly apparent; unquestionable: *I had a definite advantage.* **2** having distinct or certain limits. ➤➤ **definitely** *adv*, **definiteness** *noun*. [Latin *definitus*, past part. of *definire*: see DEFINE]

Usage note
definite or definitive? These two words are sometimes confused. Both *definite* and *definitive* suggest that something is unlikely to be changed: a *definite* answer is clear, firm, and unambiguous; a *definite* date is one that has been decided on and fixed by the people involved. *Definitive* has connotations of being authoritative and conclusive: the *definitive* answer to a problem is one that solves it once and for all. If someone writes a *definitive* biography or plays the *definitive* Hamlet, that person's book or performance becomes the standard by which all later ones are judged.

definite article *noun* in grammar, a word (*the* in English) that designates an identified or immediately identifiable person or thing: compare INDEFINITE ARTICLE.

definite integral *noun* in mathematics, a number that is the difference between the values of an integral at two given limits: compare INDEFINITE INTEGRAL.

definition /defi'nish(ə)n/ *noun* **1a** a statement of what a word or phrase means. **b** a word or phrase expressing the essential nature of a person or thing. **2** the act or an instance of defining. **3** the action or power of making definite and clear. **4a** distinctness of outline or detail, e.g. in a photograph. **b** clarity, *esp* of musical sound in reproduction. ➤➤ **definitional** *adj.*

definitive[1] /di'finətiv/ *adj* **1a** serving to provide a final solution: *a definitive victory.* **b** serving to define or specify something precisely: *definitive laws.* **2** authoritative and apparently exhaustive: *a definitive biography.* **3** fully differentiated or developed: *the definitive form of an organ of the body.* **4** said of a postage stamp: issued as one of the normal stamps of the country or territory of use. ➤➤ **definitively** *adv.*

Usage note
definitive or definite? See note at DEFINITE.

definitive[2] *noun* a definitive postage stamp.

deflagrate /'defləgrayt/ *verb intrans* to burn rapidly with sparks and intense heat. ➤ *verb trans* to cause (a substance) to burn in this way. ➤➤ **deflagration** /-'graysh(ə)n/ *noun.* [Latin *deflagratus*, past part. of *deflagrare* to burn down, from DE- + *flagrare* to burn]

deflate /di'flayt, dee'flayt/ *verb trans* **1** to release air or gas from (e.g. a balloon or a tyre). **2a** to reduce (something) in size or importance. **b** to reduce (somebody) in self-confidence or self-importance, *esp* suddenly. **3** to reduce (a price level) or cause (the economy or the availability of credit) to contract. ➤ *verb intrans* to lose firmness through or as if through the escape of contained gas. ➤➤ **deflator** *noun.* [DE- + *-flate* as in INFLATE]

deflation /di'flaysh(ə)n, dee-/ *noun* **1** the act or an instance of deflating; the state of being deflated. **2a** a contraction in the volume of available money and credit, and a resulting decline in economic activity, *esp* as a result of government policy. **b** a decline in the general level of prices. **3** in geology, the erosion of soil by the wind. ➤➤ **deflationary** *adj*, **deflationist** *noun and adj.*

deflect /di'flekt/ *verb trans* to turn (somebody or something) from a straight course or fixed direction. ➤ *verb intrans* to turn aside; to deviate. ➤➤ **deflective** /-tiv/ *adj*, **deflector** *noun.* [Latin *deflectere* to bend down, turn aside, from DE- + *flectere* to bend]

deflection or **deflexion** /di'fleksh(ə)n/ *noun* **1a** the act of deflecting; the condition of being deflected. **b** the amount or degree by which something is deflected. **2** the movement, usu as a departure from the zero reading, of an indicator or pointer on the scale of an instrument, *esp* an electrical one.

deflocculate /di'flokyoolayt/ *verb trans and intrans* to disperse (something) or become dispersed into fine particles: *The soil deflocculated.*

defloration /deeflaw'raysh(ə)n/ *noun* deflowering or being deflowered. [Middle English *defloracioun* from Latin *deflorare*: see DEFLOWER]

deflower /dee'flowə/ *verb trans* (**deflowered, deflowering**) *dated or literary* **1** to deprive (a woman) of her virginity; to ravish (her). **2** to spoil (something) or take away its beauty: *They found a great deal of entertainment at the hotel, an enormous wooden structure, for the erection of which it seemed to them that the virgin forests of the West must have been terribly deflowered* — Henry James. [Middle English *deflouren* via French from Latin *deflorare*, from DE- + *flor-, flos* flower]

defocus /dee'fohkəs/ *verb trans* (**defocused** or **defocussed, defocusing** or **defocussing**) to put (e.g. an image or lens) out of focus. ➤ *verb intrans* to go out of focus.

defoliant /dee'fohli-ənt/ *noun* a chemical applied to plants to cause the leaves to drop off prematurely.

defoliate /dee'fohliayt/ *verb trans* to deprive (a tree or an area) of leaves, *esp* prematurely or as a tactic in warfare. ➤➤ **defoliate** *adj*, **defoliation** /-'aysh(ə)n/ *noun*, **defoliator** *noun.* [late Latin *defoliatus*, past part. of *defoliare* to strip of leaves, from DE- + *folium* leaf]

deforest /di'forist/ *verb trans* to clear (an area) of forests. ➤➤ **deforestation** /-'staysh(ə)n/ *noun.*

deform /di'fawm/ *verb trans* **1** to spoil the form or appearance of (something). **2** to make (something) ugly or monstrous. **3** to alter the shape of (something) by stress. ➤ *verb intrans* to become misshapen or changed in shape. ➤➤ **deformable** *adj*, **deformation** /defə'maysh(ə)n/ *noun*, **deformational** /defə'maysh(ə)nl/ *adj.* [Middle English *deformen* via French from Latin *deformare*, from DE- + *formare* to form, from *forma* FORM[1]]

deformed /di'fawmd/ *adj* distorted or unshapely in form.

deformity *noun* (*pl* **deformities**) **1a** the state of being deformed; ugliness. **b** a deformed person or thing. **2** a physical blemish or distortion; a disfigurement. **3** a moral or aesthetic flaw or defect. [Middle English *deformite* via French from Latin *deformitat-, deformitas*, from *deformis* deformed, from DE- + *forma* FORM[1]]

DEFRA *abbr* Brit Department for Environment, Food and Rural Affairs.

defraud /di'frawd/ *verb trans* (*often* + of) to cheat (somebody) of something. ➤➤ **defrauder** *noun.* [Middle English *defrauden* via French from Latin *defraudare*, from DE- + *fraudare* to cheat, from *fraud-, fraus* FRAUD]

defray /di'fray/ *verb trans* to provide for the payment of (an expense). ⟫ **defrayable** *adj,* **defrayal** *noun,* **defrayment** *noun.* [early French *deffrayer,* from DE- + *frayer* to expend from Old French *frai* expenditure, literally 'damage by breaking', from Latin *fractum,* neuter past part. of *frangere* to break]

defrock /dee'frok/ *verb trans* to unfrock (e.g. a priest).

defrost /dee'frost/ *verb trans* **1** to thaw out (food) from a frozen state. **2** to free (a refrigerator or freezer) from ice. **3** *NAmer* to demist (a windscreen). ⟩ *verb intrans* to thaw out, *esp* from a deep-frozen state.

defroster *noun* a device for removing or preventing frost, e.g. in a refrigerator.

deft /deft/ *adj* marked by facility and skill; nimble. ⟫ **deftly** *noun,* **deftness** *noun.* [Middle English *defte,* variant of DAFT]

defunct /di'fungkt/ *adj* **1** no longer existing or in use. **2** dead; extinct: *snipping off the heads of defunct roses, and thinking of nothing in particular* — Saki. [Latin *defunctus,* from past part. of *defungi* to finish or die, from DE- + *fungi* to perform]

defuse /dee'fyoohz/ *verb trans* **1** to remove the fuse from (a mine, bomb, etc). **2** to make (something) less harmful, potent, or tense: *The ministers held talks to try to defuse the crisis.*

defy /di'fie/ *verb trans* (**defies, defied, defying**) **1** to resist (somebody) by refusing to do what they want; to show no fear of nor respect for (them): *They would be unwise to defy public opinion.* **2** to challenge (somebody) to do something considered impossible; to dare (them). **3** to resist attempts at (something): *The paintings defy classification.* **4** *archaic* to challenge (somebody) to fight. ⟫ **defier** *noun.* [Middle English *defyen* to renounce faith in or challenge, via Old French from Latin DIS- + *fidere* to trust]

deg. *abbr* degree.

dégagé /dayga'zhay/ *adj* **1** free and easy in manner; nonchalant; unconcerned. **2** politically uncommitted. [French *dégagé,* from past part. of *dégager* to redeem a pledge, free, from Old French *des-gagier,* from *des-* DE- + *gage* pledge]

degas /dee'gas/ *verb trans* (**degassed, degassing**) to remove gas from (something).

degauss /dee'gows/ *verb trans* to demagnetize (something); *esp* to demagnetize (a steel ship) as a protection against magnetic mines. ⟫ **degausser** *noun.*

degenerate[1] /di'jen(ə)rət/ *adj* **1** having sunk to a condition below that which is normal to a type; *esp* having sunk to a lower and usu peculiarly corrupt state. **2** said of a plant or animal: having lost an ancestral structure, function, etc; e.g. loss of gut and eyes in tapeworm. ⟫ **degeneracy** /-si/ *noun,* **degenerately** *adv.* [Middle English *degenerat* from Latin *degeneratus,* past part. of *degenerare,* from DE- + *gener-, genus* race, kind]

degenerate[2] *noun* somebody who or something which is degenerate.

degenerate[3] /di'jenərayt/ *verb intrans* **1** to pass from a higher to a lower type or condition; to deteriorate: *The road degenerated into a bumpy track.* **2** to decline from a former thriving or healthy condition. **3** said of organisms: to evolve into a less complex form. ⟫ **degenerative** /-rətiv/ *adj.*

degeneration /di,jenə'raysh(ə)n/ *noun* **1a** the process or an instance of degenerating. **b** the state of being degenerate. **2a** in medicine, the damage caused to cells or tissues in the body by disease or ageing. **b** in biology, the loss of function or structure in an organism, as an evolutionary process.

deglaze /dee'glayz/ *verb trans* to add wine, cream, stock, etc to (a pan in which food has been braised or cooked) in order to dilute the juices remaining and make a sauce.

deglutition /deeglooh'tish(ə)n/ *noun technical* the act or process of swallowing. [French *déglutition* from Latin *deglutitus,* past part. of *deglutire* to swallow down, from DE- + *glutire, gluttire* to swallow]

degradation /degrə'daysh(ə)n/ *noun* **1a** the process of degrading or being degraded. **b** an action or condition that is considered humiliating. **2** a state of physical or moral debasement or squalor. **3** a gradual loss of quality or deterioration in performance. **4** the wearing down of rocks by erosion. **5** the breaking down of a chemical substance into simpler substances, molecules, or atoms.

degrade /di'grayd/ *verb trans* **1** to cause (somebody) to lose the respect of others or self-respect; to demean (them). **2** to reduce the quality of (something); *specif* to impair (it) with respect to some physical property. **3** *archaic* to lower (somebody) in grade, rank, or status; to demote (them). **4** in chemistry, to decompose (a compound). **5** in geology, to wear (rocks) down by erosion. ⟩ *verb intrans* **1** to become qualitatively worse; to degenerate. **2** to decompose or disintegrate. ⟫ **degradable** *adj,* **degrader** *noun.* [Middle English *degraden* via French and late Latin from Latin *degradere,* from DE- + *gradus* step, GRADE[1]]

degrading *adj* humiliating; debasing: *degrading punishments.* ⟫ **degradingly** *adv.*

degree /di'gree/ *noun* **1a** the extent or measure of an action, condition, or relation: *The whole case rests on the degree of force that victims are entitled to use in defending themselves.* **b** an amount or measure: *a high degree of probability.* **2a** a division or interval of a scale of measurement; *specif* any of various units for measuring temperature. **b** a 360th part of the circumference of a circle. **3** a step or stage in a process, course, or order of classification. **4** an academic title conferred on students in recognition of proficiency or honorarily. **5** the rank or status of a person: *people of high degree.* **6** a legal measure of guilt or negligence: *She was found guilty of murder in the first degree.* **7** in medicine, a measure of damage caused to tissue by burning. **8** in mathematics: **a** the rank of algebraic expression that for a monomial term is the sum of the exponents of the variable factors and for a polynomial is the sum of the exponents of the variable factors of the highest degree. **b** the greatest power of the derivative of highest order in a differential equation. **9** in music, the position of a note on a scale. ✻ **by degrees** gradually. **to a degree 1** to some extent; somewhat. **2** to a remarkable extent: *the man is eccentric to a degree.* [Middle English via French from Latin *degradus,* from DE- + *gradus* step, GRADE[1]]

degree of freedom *noun* **1** in physics, any of a limited characteristic number of ways in which a body or system may move. **2** in statistics, the number of independent values or quantities that must be specified to define a statistical situation completely.

degrees of frost *pl noun Brit* degrees of temperature below zero.

de haut en bas /də ,oh on(h) 'bah (*French* də o ã ba)/ *adj and adv* with a superior or condescending manner. [French *de haut en bas* from top to bottom]

dehisce /di'his/ *verb intrans* said of seedpods, etc: to split open; to discharge the contents by splitting. ⟫ **dehiscence** *noun,* **dehiscent** *adj.* [Latin *dehiscere* to split open, from DE- + *hiscere* to gape]

dehorn /dee'hawn/ *verb trans* to remove, or prevent the growth of, the horns of (e.g. cattle).

dehumanize or **dehumanise** /dee'hyoohməniez/ *verb trans* to deprive (somebody) of human qualities or personality. ⟫ **dehumanization** /-'zaysh(ə)n/ *noun.*

dehumidify /deehyooh'midifie/ *verb trans* (**dehumidifies, dehumidified, dehumidifying**) to remove moisture from (e.g. air). ⟫ **dehumidification** /-fi'kaysh(ə)n/ *noun,* **dehumidifier** *noun.*

dehydrate /deehie'drayt/ *verb trans* **1** to remove water from (a chemical compound, foodstuff, etc). **2** to make (something) dry and uninteresting in style or character. ⟩ *verb intrans* to lose water or body fluids. ⟫ **dehydration** /-'draysh(ə)n/ *noun,* **dehydrator** *noun.*

dehydrogenate /dee'hiedrəjənayt, deehie'drojənayt/ *verb trans* to remove hydrogen from (a chemical compound). ⟫ **dehydrogenation** /-'naysh(ə)n/ *noun.*

dehydrogenize or **dehydrogenise** /dee'hiedrəjəniez, deehie'drojəniez/ *verb trans* = DEHYDROGENATE.

de-ice /dee'ies/ *verb trans* to keep (something) free from ice or rid (it) of ice.

de-icer *noun* **1** a substance used to remove ice or frost from a windscreen, e.g. an aerosol spray. **2** a device used on aircraft to remove ice from, or prevent the formation of ice on, their outer surfaces.

deictic /'diektik/ *adj* in grammar, dependent on context and a reference to something already mentioned for its full meaning: *This, that, and those have a deictic function.* [Greek *deiktikos* from *deiknynai* to show]

dei ex machina /,dayee eks 'makinə/ *noun* pl of DEUS EX MACHINA.

deify /'deeifie, 'day-/ *verb trans* (**deifies, deified, deifying**) **1a** to make a god of (somebody or something). **b** to take (somebody or something) as an object of worship. **2** to glorify (something) as of supreme worth. ⟫ **deification** /-fi'kaysh(ə)n/ *noun.* [Middle English *deifyen* via French and late Latin from Latin *deificare,* from *deus* god]

deign /dayn/ *verb intrans* to see fit to act in a less dignified, haughty, or indifferent way than usual; to condescend: *She barely deigned to acknowledge their greeting.* ➤ *verb trans archaic* to condescend to give or offer (something). [Middle English *deignen* via Old French from Latin *dignare, dignari* to consider worthy, from *dignus* worthy]

de-industrialization *or* **de-industrialisation** /,dee-industri·əlie'zaysh(ə)n/ *noun* the loss of industrial capability or strength.

deinonychus /die'nonikəs/ *noun* a large flesh-eating dinosaur of the Cretaceous period that walked on two legs. [via Latin from Greek *deinos* terrible + *onyx, onykh-* claw]

deionize *or* **deionise** /dee'ie·əniez/ *verb trans* to remove ions from (*esp* water). ➤ **deionization** /-zaysh(ə)n/ *noun*, **deionizer** *noun*

deism /'deeiz(ə)m, 'day-/ *noun* a movement or system of thought advocating natural religion based on human reason rather than revelation; *specif* a chiefly 18th-cent. doctrine asserting that although God created the universe He does not intervene in its functioning. ➤ **deist** *noun*, **deistic** /-'istik/ *adj*, **deistical** /-'istikl/ *adj*, **deistically** /-'istikli/ *adv*. [French *déisme* from Latin *deus* god]

deity /'deeiti, 'day-/ *noun* (*pl* **deities**) **1** a god or goddess: *the deities of ancient Greece.* **2a** the rank or essential nature of a god. **b** (**the Deity**) the Supreme Being; God. **3** somebody exalted or revered as supremely good or powerful. [Middle English *deitee* via French from late Latin *deitat-, deitas,* from Latin *deus* god]

déjà vu /,dayzhah 'vooh (*French* deʒa vy)/ *noun* **1** the illusion of remembering scenes and events when they are experienced for the first time. **2** something excessively or unpleasantly familiar. [French *déjà vu* already seen]

deject /di'jekt/ *verb trans* to make (somebody) feel sad or depressed. [from Middle English *dejecten* to throw down, from Latin *dejectus,* past part. of *deicere* throw down, from DE- + *jacere* to throw]

dejected /di'jektid/ *adj* cast down in spirits; depressed. ➤ **dejectedly** *adv*.

dejection /di'jeksh(ə)n/ *noun* lowness of spirits; depression or melancholy.

de jure /di 'jooəri/ *adv and adj* by right, *esp* full legal right: compare DE FACTO[2]: *Recognition was extended de jure to the new government.* [Latin *de jure,* literally 'of law']

deka- *or* **dek-** *comb. form* see DECA-.

dekaliter *noun NAmer* see DECALITRE.

dekameter *noun NAmer* see DECAMETRE.

deke[1] /deek/ *verb trans* in ice hockey, to draw (an opposing player) out of position by feinting to make a move or play a shot. [by shortening from DECOY[2]]

deke[2] *noun* in ice hockey, a pretend move or shot to draw an opposing player out of position.

dekko /'dekoh/ *noun Brit, informal* a look or glance. [Hindi *dekho* look!, imperative pl of *dekhnā* to see, from Sanskrit *dṛś*]

Del. *abbr* Delaware.

del. *abbr* delegate.

delay[1] /di'lay/ *noun* **1a** the act or an instance of delaying. **b** the act or an instance of being delayed. **2** the time during which something is delayed.

delay[2] *verb trans* **1** to leave the doing of (something) to a later time; to postpone (something). **2** to stop, detain, or hinder (somebody or something) for a time. ➤ *verb intrans* to fail to act or move immediately. ➤ **delayer** *noun*. [Middle English *delayen* from Old French *delaier,* from DE- + *laier* to leave, ultimately from Latin *laxare* to slacken]

delayed action *noun* (*used before a noun*) said of e.g. a bomb or camera: that does not operate until an often preset period of time has elapsed.

delayed drop *noun* a parachute drop in which the parachute is not opened until a predetermined time has elapsed.

delayering /dee'layəring/ *noun* the simplification of the hierarchical structure within an organization by removing some of the intermediate levels of responsibility.

dele[1] /'deeli/ *verb trans* (**deles, deled, deleing**) in printing, to delete (e.g. a character) from typeset matter. [Latin *dele,* imperative sing. of *delēre*: see DELETE]

dele[2] *noun* any of several proofreading marks used to indicate a deletion from a text.

delectable /di'lektəbl/ *adj* **1** highly pleasing; delightful. **2** said of food: delicious. ➤ **delectability** /-'biliti/ *noun*, **delectableness** *noun*, **delectably** *adv*. [Middle English via French from Latin *delectabilis,* from *delectare*: see DELIGHT[1]]

delectation /delek'taysh(ə)n, dee-/ *noun formal* delight or enjoyment. [Middle English *delectacioun* via French from Latin *delectation-, delectatio,* from *delectare*: see DELIGHT[1]]

delegacy /'deligəsi/ *noun* (*pl* **delegacies**) **1a** the act of delegating. **b** an appointment as delegate. **2** (*treated as sing. or pl*) a body of delegates; a board.

delegate[1] /'deligət/ *noun* **1** a person delegated to act for somebody else, e.g. a representative of a state or organization at a conference. **2** a representative of a territory of the USA in the House of Representatives. [Middle English *delegat* via late Latin from Latin *delegatus,* past part. of *delegare* to send on a mission, from DE- + *legare* to send]

delegate[2] /'deligayt/ *verb trans* **1** to entrust (e.g. a duty or responsibility) to another. **2** to appoint (somebody) as one's representative. ➤ *verb intrans* to assign responsibility or authority to other people.

delegation /deli'gaysh(ə)n/ *noun* **1** (*treated as sing. or pl*) a group of people chosen to represent others. **2** the act of delegating or being delegated.

delegitimize *or* **delegitimise** /deeli'jitimiez/ *verb trans* to take away the legal status, civil rights, or legitimacy of a person, group, etc. ➤ **delegitimization** /-mie'zaysh(ə)n/ *noun*.

delete /di'leet/ *verb trans* to eliminate (something) *esp* by crossing out, cutting out, or erasing. ➤ **deletion** *noun*. [Latin *deletus,* past part. of *delēre* to wipe out, destroy, from DE- + *-lēre* (related to Latin *linere* to smear)]

deleterious /deli'tiəri·əs/ *adj formal* harmful or detrimental: *a bill to forbid the manufacture, exportation, importation, purchase, sale, borrowing, lending, stealing, drinking, smelling, or possession ... of each and every deleterious beverage known to the human race, except water* — Mark Twain. ➤ **deleteriously** *adv*, **deleteriousness** *noun*. [Greek *dēlētērios,* from *dēleisthai* to hurt]

delft /delft/ *noun* tin-glazed Dutch earthenware with blue and white or polychrome decoration. [named after *Delft,* town in the Netherlands where it originated]

delftware /'delftweə/ *noun* = DELFT.

deli /'deli/ *noun* (*pl* **delis**) *informal* = DELICATESSEN (1).

deliberate[1] /di'lib(ə)rət/ *adj* **1** characterized by awareness of the nature of the action involved and of its consequences; wilful. **2** characterized by or resulting from careful and thorough consideration. **3** slow or unhurried: *He walked with a deliberate step.* ➤ **deliberately** *adv*, **deliberateness** *noun*. [Latin *deliberatus,* past part. of *deliberare* to weigh in the mind, ponder, from DE- + *libra* scale, pound]

deliberate[2] /di'libərayt/ *verb trans* to think about (something) carefully and thoroughly and often discuss it formally before reaching a decision. ➤ *verb intrans* to ponder issues and decisions carefully. ➤ **deliberator** *noun*.

deliberation /di,libə'raysh(ə)n/ *noun* **1a** careful and serious thought. **b** a discussion and consideration of pros and cons. **2** slow and careful movement or action. ➤ **deliberative** /di'lib(ə)rətiv/ *adj*, **deliberatively** /di'lib-/ *adv*, **deliberativeness** /di'lib-/ *noun*.

delicacy /'delikəsi/ *noun* (*pl* **delicacies**) **1** something pleasing to eat that is considered rare or luxurious. **2a** the quality or state of being dainty: *lace of great delicacy.* **b** frailty or fragility. **3a** refined sensibility in feeling or conduct; tact. **b** avoidance of anything offensive or disturbing; squeamishness. **4** precise and refined perception or discrimination.

delicate /'delikət/ *adj* **1a** very finely made: *a gown of delicate silk.* **b** easily torn; fragile: *a delicate butterfly wing.* **2a** pleasing to the senses in a mild or subtle way: *a delicate shade of blue.* **b** marked by daintiness or charm of colour, line, or proportion. **3a** marked by extreme precision. **b** having or showing extreme sensitivity: *a delicate instrument.* **4** calling for or involving meticulously careful treatment: *the delicate balance of power.* **5** marked by or requiring tact; sensitive: *The book touches on a delicate subject.* **6** weak or sickly: *She was a delicate child.* **7** fastidious or squeamish: *a lady of delicate tastes.* ➤ **delicately** *adv*, **delicateness** *noun*. [Middle English *delicat* from Latin *delicatus* charming, self-indulgent, effeminate]

delicatessen /,delikə'tes(ə)n/ *noun* **1** a shop where delicacies and foreign foods, e.g. cooked meats, are sold. **2** foods of this type.

[obsolete German *delicatessen* delicacies, via French from Old Italian *delicatezza*, from *delicato* delicate, from Latin *delicatus*]

delicious /di'lishəs/ *adj* **1** highly pleasing to one of the bodily senses, *esp* that of taste. **2** affording great pleasure; delightful. ➤➤ **deliciously** *adv*, **deliciousness** *noun*. [Middle English via Old French and late Latin from Latin *deliciae* delight, from *delicere*: see DELIGHT[1]]

delight[1] /di'liet/ *verb intrans* (often + in) to take great pleasure in doing something: *He delighted in teasing her.* ➤ *verb trans* to give enjoyment or satisfaction to (somebody): *The pianist delighted the audience with his performance.*

Word history
Middle English *deliten* via Old French from Latin *delectare*, from *delectus*, past part. of *delicere* to allure, from DE- + *lacere* to allure. The -*gh*- was added in the 16th cent. by association with LIGHT[1].

delight[2] *noun* **1** great pleasure or satisfaction; joy. **2** something that gives great pleasure: *The room was a delight to behold.*

delighted *adj* highly pleased. ➤➤ **delightedly** *adv*.

delightful /di'lietf(ə)l/ *adj* highly pleasing; charming. ➤➤ **delightfully** *adv*, **delightfulness** *noun*.

Delilah /di'lielə/ *noun* a treacherous and seductive woman. [named after *Delilah* in the Old Testament (Judges 16: 4–20), a woman whom Samson loved, who discovered the secret of his strength and betrayed him to the Philistines]

delimit /di'limit/ *verb trans* (**delimited, delimiting**) to fix the limits of (something). [French *délimiter* from Latin *delimitare*, from DE- + *limitare* to limit, from *limit-, limes* boundary, LIMIT[1]]

delimitate /di'limitayt/ *verb trans* to delimit (something). ➤➤ **delimitation** /-'taysh(ə)n/ *noun*, **delimitative** /-tiv/ *adj*.

delineate /di'liniayt/ *verb trans* **1** to show (something) by drawing lines in the shape of it; to portray (it). **2** to describe (something) in usu sharp or vivid detail. ➤➤ **delineation** /-'aysh(ə)n/ *noun*, **delineative** /-tiv/ *adj*, **delineator** *noun*. [Latin *delineatus*, past part. of *delineare*, from DE- + *linea*: see LINE[1]]

delinquency /di'lingkwənsi/ *noun* (*pl* **delinquencies**) **1** antisocial or illegal conduct. **2** an offence or crime. **3** failure to fulfil one's obligations.

delinquent[1] /di'lingkwənt/ *noun* somebody who has behaved in an antisocial or criminal way, *esp* a young person.

delinquent[2] *adj* **1** guilty of wrongdoing or of neglect of duty. **2** marked by delinquency: *delinquent behaviour.* ➤➤ **delinquently** *adv*. [Latin *delinquent-, delinquens*, present part. of *delinquere* to fail, offend, from DE- + *linquere* to leave]

deliquesce /deli'kwes/ *verb intrans* **1** to melt away. **2** said of a compound: to dissolve gradually in water attracted and absorbed from the air. ➤➤ **deliquescence** *noun*, **deliquescent** *adj*. [Latin *deliquescere*, from DE- + *liquescere* to make fluid, from *liquēre* to be fluid]

delirious /di'liri-əs/ *adj* **1a** confused and disturbed as a result of delirium. **b** characteristic of delirium. **2** wildly joyful; ecstatic. ➤➤ **deliriously** *adv*, **deliriousness** *noun*.

delirium /di'liri-əm/ *noun* **1** confusion, frenzy, disordered speech, hallucinations, etc, occurring as a mental disturbance. **2** frenzied excitement or emotion. [Latin *delirium*, from *delirare* to deviate, be crazy, from DE- + *lira* furrow]

delirium tremens /'tremenz/ *noun* a violent delirium with tremors induced by chronic alcoholism. [Latin *delirium tremens* trembling delirium]

delist /dee'list/ *verb trans* to remove (somebody or something) from a list, *esp* to remove (a security) from a stock exchange's official list.

deliver /di'livə/ *verb* (**delivered, delivering**) ➤ *verb trans* **1a** (often + to) to bring or take (something or somebody) to a specified place or to the person or people expecting to receive them: *We deliver the milk to your doorstep.* **b** (often + up) to hand over (something or somebody) formally; to surrender (them). **2** to aim or guide (e.g. a blow) to an intended target or destination. **3a** to utter (something): *She delivered her speech effectively.* **b** to announce (something, e.g. a verdict) formally. **4** to set (somebody) free; to save (them). **5a** to assist in the birth of (a baby). **b** to assist (somebody) in giving birth. **6** (often **be delivered of**) to give birth to (a baby). ➤ *verb intrans* **1** to take goods purchased or ordered to customers' homes: *Sorry, we don't deliver on Saturdays.* **2** *informal* to produce the promised, desired, or expected results: *He made many promises, but will he deliver?* ✴ **deliver oneself of** *formal* to say or utter. **deliver the**

goods *informal* to deliver what has been promised. ➤➤ **deliverable** *adj*, **deliverer** *noun*. [Middle English *deliveren* via Old French from Latin *deliberare*, from DE- + *liberare*: see LIBERATE]

deliverance *noun* **1** liberation or rescue. **2** *formal* an opinion or verdict expressed publicly.

delivery /di'liv(ə)ri/ *noun* (*pl* **deliveries**) **1a** the act or an instance of delivering something. **b** something delivered at one time or in one unit: *milk deliveries.* **2** the act of giving birth. **3a** the uttering of a speech. **b** the manner or style in which a speech is spoken. **4** an instance of throwing or bowling, *esp* of a ball in cricket. **5** liberation or rescue. **6** a physical or legal transfer. ✴ **take delivery of** to receive, and often sign for, something or somebody delivered. [Middle English *deliverie*, from *deliveren*: see DELIVER]

dell /del/ *noun* a small secluded hollow or valley, *esp* in a forest. [Old English *dæl* valley]

delouse /dee'lows/ *verb trans* to remove lice from (a person or an animal).

Delphian /'delfi-ən/ *adj* = DELPHIC.

Delphic /'delfik/ *adj* **1** (*also* **delphic**) said of an utterance: ambiguous, obscure, or enigmatic: *The right hon. and learned Member for Pentlands made a speech of an accomplished delphic nature in which he said that, if change were to be allowed, independence would be the least advantageous change* — Hansard. **2** relating to ancient Delphi or its oracle. ➤➤ **delphically** *adv*.

Word history
from *Delphi*, town in ancient Greece. The oracle at Delphi spoke through a priestess in a state of trance; her answers were often cryptic and ambiguous but were regarded as having great authority.

delphinium /del'fini-əm/ *noun* (*pl* **delphiniums**) any of a genus of plants of the buttercup family with deeply cut leaves and blue or purple flowers in showy spikes: genus *Delphinium*. [Latin genus name, from Greek *delphinion* larkspur, dimin. of *delphin-, delphis* DOLPHIN; because the spur on the back of the larkspur flower was thought to resemble a dolphin's back]

delta /'deltə/ *noun* **1** a triangular alluvial deposit at the mouth of a river. **2** the fourth letter of the Greek alphabet (Δ, δ), equivalent to and transliterated as roman d. **3** in mathematics, an increment of a variable. ➤➤ **deltaic** /del'tayik/ *adj*. [Middle English *deltha* from Greek *delta*, of Semitic origin; related to Hebrew *dāleth*, fourth letter of the Hebrew alphabet; (sense 1) from the triangular shape of the Greek character]

delta connection *noun* a type of connection, used in a three-phase electrical system, that is triangular in form with input and output capability at its three junctions.

delta particle *noun* a type of HYPERON with a very short life span.

delta ray *noun* an electron that acquires sufficient energy to eject from an atom as a result of the interaction of a charged particle with matter.

delta rhythm *noun* the electrical activity of the brain during deep sleep.

delta stock *noun* active securities of the fourth grade among those on the London stock exchange, whose prices are not required to be continuously displayed.

delta wave *noun* = DELTA RHYTHM.

delta wing *noun* an approximately triangular aircraft wing with a nearly straight rearmost edge.

deltiology /delti'oləji/ *noun* the hobby of collecting and studying postcards. ➤➤ **deltiologist** *noun*. [Greek *deltion* small writing tablet + -LOGY]

deltoid /'deltoyd/ *noun* a large triangular muscle covering the shoulder joint and acting to raise the arm to the side. [via Latin from Greek *deltoeidēs* shaped like a delta, from DELTA]

delude /di'loohd/ *verb trans* to mislead the mind or judgment of (somebody); to deceive or trick (them). ➤➤ **deluder** *noun*. [Middle English *deluden* from Latin *deludere*, from DE- + *ludere* to play]

deluge[1] /'delyoohj/ *noun* **1** a great flood. **2** (**the Deluge**) the Flood recorded in the Old Testament (Genesis 6:8). **3** a drenching fall of rain. **4** an overwhelming amount or number: *This person was a deluge of words and a drizzle of thought* — Peter de Vries. [Middle English via French from Latin *diluvium*, from *diluere* to wash away, from DIS- + *lavere* to wash]

deluge[2] *verb trans* **1** to overwhelm or swamp (somebody). **2** to flood (something).

delusion /di'loohzh(ə)n/ *noun* **1a** a false belief or impression: *Darwinism is the story of humanity's liberation from the delusion that its destiny is controlled by a power higher than itself* — Phillip E Johnson. **b** a mental state characterized by false beliefs about the self or others that persists despite the contrary evidence of fact and occurs in psychotic states. **2** the act of deluding or the state of being deluded. ➤➤ **delusional** *adj*. [Middle English from Latin *delusion-, delusio*, from *deludere*: see DELUDE]

delusive /di'loohsiv, -ziv/ *adj* giving a false impression; misleading or deceptive. ➤➤ **delusively** *adv*, **delusiveness** *noun*.

delusory /di'loohz(ə)ri, -s(ə)ri/ *adj* = DELUSIVE.

delustre (*NAmer* **deluster**) /dee'lustə/ *verb trans* (**delustring**, *NAmer* **delustering**) to reduce the sheen of (e.g. yarn or fabric).

de luxe /di 'luks/ *adj* notably luxurious or elegant; of a superior quality. [French *de luxe* of luxury]

delve /delv/ *verb intrans* **1** to make a careful or detailed search for information: *I began to wish I hadn't delved into my past*. **2** to reach inside something and search about in it; to rummage: *She delved into the box*. **3** *archaic* to dig. ➤ *verb trans archaic or literary* to dig or excavate (something). [Old English *delfan*]

Dem. *abbr NAmer* **1** Democrat. **2** Democratic.

demagnetize *or* **demagnetise** /dee'magnitiez/ *verb trans* to cause (something) not to have magnetic properties or a magnetic field. ➤➤ **demagnetization** /-'zaysh(ə)n/ *noun*, **demagnetizer** *noun*.

demagogue /'deməgog/ (*NAmer* **demagog**) *noun* **1** an agitator who makes use of popular prejudices in order to gain power. **2** a leader of the common people in ancient times. ➤➤ **demagogic** /-'gogik, -'gojik/ *adj*, **demagoguery** /-gəri/ *noun*, **demagogy** /-gi, -ji/ *noun*. [Greek *dēmagōgos*, from *dēmos* people + *agōgos* leading, from *agein* to lead]

demand[1] /di'mahnd/ *noun* **1a** an act of demanding or asking, *esp* in an authoritative or peremptory way; a claim: *a 10% wage demand*. **b** (*in pl*) claims or requirements: *Studying makes great demands on my time*. **2** desire or need: *There is a great demand for teachers*. **3** in economics, the quantity of a commodity or service wanted at a specified price and time: compare SUPPLY[2]. * **in demand** sought after; popular. **on demand** whenever the demand is made: *You must show your tickets on demand*.

demand[2] *verb trans* **1** to ask or call for (something) with authority; to claim (it) as due or just: *They demanded payment of the debt*. **2** to call for (something) urgently, peremptorily, or insistently. **3** to ask authoritatively or earnestly to be informed of (something): *The man demanded the reason for her visit*. **4** to require (something): *The task demands your full attention*. ➤➤ **demander** *noun*. [Middle English *demaunden* via French from Latin *demandere*, from DE- + *mandare*: see MANDATE[1]]

demand feeding *noun* the practice of feeding babies whenever they cry for milk, rather than at set times.

demanding *adj* **1** needing much effort or skill; exacting. **2** said of a person: difficult to please, *esp* requiring hard work or high standards from other people. ➤➤ **demandingly** *adv*.

demand-led *adj* in economics, determined or driven by customer demand.

demarcate /'deemahkayt/ *verb trans* **1** to mark the limits of (something). **2** to set (things) apart; to separate (them). [back-formation from DEMARCATION]

demarcation *or* **demarkation** /deemah'kaysh(ə)n/ *noun* **1** the marking of limits or boundaries. **2** *Brit* the separation of areas of work to be carried out by members of particular trade unions: *a demarcation dispute*.

Word history ━━━━━━━━
Spanish *demarcación* and Portuguese *demarcação*, from *demarcar* to delimit, from DE- + *marcar* to mark, ultimately of Germanic origin. The word was orig used in the phrase *line of demarcation* (translating Spanish *línea de demarcación* and Portuguese *linka de demarcação*), a line fixed by the pope in 1493 which separated Spanish and Portuguese territories in the New World.

démarche /'daymahsh/ *noun* a course of action; a manoeuvre, *esp* a diplomatic one. [French *démarche* gait, from Old French *demarchier* to take steps, from DE- + *marchier* to march, of Germanic origin]

demarkation /deemah'kaysh(ə)n/ *noun* see DEMARCATION.

dematerialize *or* **dematerialise** /deemə'tiəri-əliez/ *verb intrans* to lose material form or qualities; to vanish. ➤ *verb intrans* to cause (something) to vanish.

deme /deem/ *noun* **1** a local community in ancient Attica or modern Greece. **2** in biology, a local population of closely related organisms. [Greek *dēmos* people]

demean[1] /di'meen/ *verb trans* to degrade or debase (somebody or something): *Don't demean yourself by taking that job*. [DE- + MEAN[1]]

demean[2] *verb trans archaic* to behave or conduct (oneself). [Middle English *demenen* from Old French *demener* to conduct or guide, from DE- + *mener* to lead]

demeanour (*NAmer* **demeanor**) /di'meenə/ *noun* behaviour towards others; outward manner: *I turned to Aunt Agatha, whose demeanour was ... like that of one who, picking daisies on the railway, has just caught the down express in the small of the back* — P G Wodehouse. [earlier *demeanure*, from DEMEAN[2] + -URE]

demented /di'mented/ *adj* insane; crazy. ➤➤ **dementedly** *adv*, **dementedness** *noun*. [archaic *dement* to drive mad, from late Latin *dementare*, from Latin *dement-, demens*: see DEMENTIA]

dementia /di'menshə/ *noun* a state of chronic impairment of a person's mental functions caused by damage to or deterioration of the brain and characterized by memory failure and personality changes while control of physical functions remains largely unaffected: *senile dementia*. [Latin *dementia*, from *dement-, demens* mad, from DE- + *ment-, mens* mind]

dementia praecox /'preekoks/ *noun* = SCHIZOPHRENIA. [Latin *dementia praecox* premature dementia]

demerara sugar /demə'reərə/ *noun* brown crystallized unrefined cane sugar from the W Indies. [named after *Demerara*, region of Guyana where it is produced]

demerge /'deemuhj/ *verb trans* to split up (a conglomerate formed by a previous merger) into separate companies.

demerger /dee'muhjə/ *noun* an act of demerging a company.

demerit /dee'merit, 'dee-/ *noun* **1** a quality that deserves blame or lacks merit; a fault or defect. **2** *NAmer* a bad mark given to an offender. ➤➤ **demeritorious** /-'tawri-əs/ *adj*. [Middle English from early French *demerite*, from DE- + *merite*: see MERIT[1]]

demersal /di'muhsl/ *adj* said of fish: living near the bottom of the sea: compare PELAGIC. [Latin *demersus*, past part. of *demergere* to sink, from DE- + *mergere* to dip, sink or plunge]

demesne /di'mayn, di'meen/ *noun* **1** land surrounding e.g. a manor, which is actually occupied by the owner and not held by tenants. **2** legal possession of land as one's own. **3** landed property; an estate. **4** a region or realm. [Middle English from Old French *demaine*, ultimately from Latin *dominus* master]

demi- *prefix* **1** forming words, with the meaning: half: *demisemiquaver*. **2** forming nouns, denoting: a person or thing partly belonging to the type or class specified: *demigod*. [Middle English via French from Latin *dimidius*, prob back-formation from *dimidiare* to halve, from DIS- + *medius* mid]

demi-glace /'demiglahs/ *noun* a brown sauce reduced in volume by boiling until sufficiently thick to coat and give a glazed appearance to food. [French *demi-glace*, literally 'half-glaze']

demigod /'demigod/ *or* **demigoddess** /-dis/ *noun* **1a** a mythological superhuman being with less power than a god. **b** an offspring of a union between a mortal and a god. **2** a person so outstanding that they seem to approach the divine.

demijohn /'demijon/ *noun* a large narrow-necked bottle made of glass or stoneware. [by folk etymology from French *dame-jeanne* Lady Jane]

demilitarize *or* **demilitarise** /dee'militəriez/ *verb trans* to strip (an area) of military forces, weapons, etc. ➤➤ **demilitarization** /-'zaysh(ə)n/ *noun*.

demimondaine /,demimon'dayn/ *noun* a woman thought to be outside respectable society, usu a courtesan or kept woman. [French *demi-mondaine*, fem of *demi-mondain*, from *demi-monde*: see DEMIMONDE]

demimonde /demi'mond/ *noun* (*treated as sing. or pl*) **1** a class of women, *esp* in the 19th cent., who were on the fringes of respectable society, generally consisting of courtesans and kept women. **2** a group engaged in activity of doubtful legality or propriety. [French *demi-monde*, literally 'half-world', from DEMI- + *monde* world, from Latin *mundus*]

demineralize or **demineralise** /dee'min(ə)rəliez/ *verb trans* to remove the mineral matter from (e.g. water). **»** **demineralization** /-'zaysh(ə)n/ *noun*.

demi-pension /demi'ponhsyonh/ *noun* in French-speaking countries, hotel accommodation providing bed, breakfast and a main meal per day; = HALF-BOARD. [French *demi-pension* half-board]

demise¹ /di'miez/ *noun* **1a** *technical or euphem* death. **b** the end of something, e.g. an industry or enterprise. **2a** the conveyance of an estate by a will or lease. **b** the transfer of sovereignty by succession or inheritance. [early French *demise* fem past part. of *demettre* to dismiss, from Latin *demittere* to send down or away, from DE- + *mittere* to send]

demise² *verb trans* **1** to convey (e.g. an estate) by will or lease. **2** to transmit (a sovereign's title) by succession or inheritance. **»** *verb intrans* to pass by descent or bequest: *The property demised to the king.*

demi-sec /demi'sek/ *adj* said of wine: medium dry. [French *demi-sec*, from DEMI- + *sec* dry]

demisemiquaver /,demisemi'kwayvə/ *noun* a musical note with the time value of half a semiquaver or a quarter of a quaver.

demist /dee'mist/ *verb trans Brit* to remove mist from (e.g. a car windscreen). **»** **demister** *noun*.

demit /di'mit/ *verb trans* (**demitted, demitting**) *formal* to resign from (a post). **»** **demission** *noun*. [early French *demettre* from Latin *demittere*: see DEMISE¹]

demitasse /'demitas/ *noun* a small cup of, or for, black coffee. [French *demi-tasse*, from DEMI- + *tasse* cup]

demiurge /'demiuhj/ *noun* **1** a deity who, according to the philosophy of Plato, is the creator of the material universe. **2** a Gnostic deity who is the creator of the material world but is inferior to the supreme being. **»** **demiurgic** /-'uhjik/ *adj*, **demiurgical** /-'uhjikl/ *adj*. [via late Latin from Greek *dēmiourgos*, literally 'one who works for the people', from *dēmios* of the people + -*ourgos* worker]

demi-vegetarian *noun* a person who avoids red meat but occasionally eats white meat and fish.

demo /'demoh/ *noun* (*pl* **demos**) **1** *informal*. **a** = DEMONSTRATION (2), (3). **b** (*used before a noun*) used for the purposes of demonstration. **2** (**Demo**) *NAmer* = DEMOCRAT (2). **3** a version of a computer game or piece of recorded music used for demonstration purposes.

demob¹ /dee'mob/ *verb trans* (**demobbed, demobbing**) *chiefly Brit, informal* to demobilize (troops).

demob² *noun chiefly Brit, informal* demobilization.

demobilize or **demobilise** /dee'mohbiliez/ *verb trans* to disband (troops) or to release (somebody) at the end of a period of military service. **»** **demobilization** /-'zaysh(ə)n/ *noun*.

democracy /di'mokrəsi/ *noun* (*pl* **democracies**) **1a** a form of government in which the supreme power is exercised by the people, directly or indirectly through a system of representation usu involving free elections. **b** a state governed in this way.

Editorial note
Democracy is government conducted by representatives freely and periodically elected by adult citizens. Neither voters nor candidates may be disqualified by reference to status, race, or political party: votes (usually by secret ballot) must be cast without intimidation and counted under objective scrutiny. A right to democracy may slowly be emerging in international law: Churchill's opinion, that democracy is the worst form of government except for all the others, is widely shared — Geoffrey Robertson.

2 the absence of class distinctions or privileges in a society. **3** control of a group by its own members or the will of a majority of them. [via French and Latin from Greek *dēmokratia*, from *dēmos* people + -*kratia* -CRACY]

democrat /'deməkrat/ *noun* **1a** an adherent of democracy. **b** somebody who practises social equality. **2** (**Democrat**) a member of the Democratic party of the USA.

democratic /demə'kratik/ *adj* **1** relating to or favouring democracy or social equality. **2** (*often* **Democratic**) denoting or relating to a political party of the USA associated with policies of social reform and internationalism. **»** **democratically** *adv*.

democratize or **democratise** /di'mokrətiez/ *verb trans* to make (a state or organization) democratic. **»** **democratization** /-'zaysh(ə)n/ *noun*, **democratizer** *noun*.

démodé /daymoh'day/ *adj* no longer fashionable; out-of-date. [French *démodé*, from dé- DE- + *mode* fashion]

demodulate /dee'modyoolayt/ *verb trans* to extract the information, e.g. a video signal, from (a modulated carrier wave). **»** **demodulation** /-'laysh(ə)n/ *noun*, **demodulator** *noun*.

demographics /demə'grafiks/ *pl noun* statistical trends revealed by demography: *demographics which indicate that young workers will be in short supply in the next decade* — The Guardian.

demographic timebomb *noun* a marked increase or decrease in the present birthrate that is expected to cause very serious social problems in the future.

demography /di'mogrəfi/ *noun* the statistical study of human populations, *esp* with reference to size and density, distribution, and vital statistics. **»** **demographer** *noun*, **demographic** /demə'grafik/ *adj*, **demographically** /-'grafikli/ *adv*. [French *démographie* from Greek *dēmos* people + French -*graphie* -GRAPHY]

demoiselle /demwah'zel/ *noun* **1** a small crane with predominantly blue-grey plumage, characteristic tufts of white behind each eye, and elongated black breast feathers: *Anthropoides virgo*. **2** = DAMSELFLY. **3** = DAMSELFISH. **4** *archaic or literary* a young lady. [French *demoiselle* from Old French *dameisele*: see DAMSEL]

demolish /di'molish/ *verb trans* **1** to destroy, smash, or tear down (something). **2** to defeat or refute (an argument). **3** *informal* to eat up or devour (food): *It only took the kids five minutes to demolish the whole bowl of spaghetti.* **»** **demolisher** *noun*. [early French *demoliss-*, stem of *demolir* from Latin *demoliri*, from DE- + *moliri* to construct, from *moles* mass]

demolition /demə'lish(ə)n/ *noun* the act or an instance of demolishing. **»** **demolitionist** *noun*.

demon /'deemən/ *noun* **1a** an evil supernatural being; a devil. **b** an evil, cruel, or undesirable person. **2a** somebody who has unusual drive, enthusiasm, or effectiveness: *a demon for work.* **b** (*used before a noun*) very forceful, effective, or enthusiastic. **3** *Aus, NZ* a police officer, *esp* in plain clothes. **4** = DAEMON (1), (2). [Middle English from Latin *daemon* evil spirit, from Greek *daimōn* deity]

demonetize or **demonetise** /dee'munitiez/ *verb trans* to stop using (a metal) as a money standard. **»** **demonetization** /-'zaysh(ə)n/ *noun*. [French *démonétiser*, from dé- DE- + Latin *moneta* coin]

demoniac¹ /di'mohniak/ *adj* **1** = DEMONIC. **2** possessed or influenced by a demon. **»** **demoniacally** /-'nie·əkli/ *adv*. [Middle English *demoniak* via late Latin from Greek *daimoniakos*, from *daimon-, daimōn* deity]

demoniac² *noun* somebody regarded as possessed by a demon.

demoniacal /deemə'nie·əkl/ *adj* = DEMONIAC¹.

demonic /di'monik/ or **demonical** *adj* **1** relating to or resembling a demon or evil spirit. **2** intense, frantic, or frenzied. **»** **demonically** *adv*.

demonise /'deeməniez/ *verb* see DEMONIZE.

demonism /'deeməniz(ə)m/ *noun* **1** belief in demons. **2** the worship of demons.

demonize or **demonise** /'deeməniez/ *verb trans* to make (somebody or something) seem evil or wicked. **»** **demonization** /-'zaysh(ə)n/ *noun*.

demonolatry /deemə'nolətri/ *noun* the worship of demons.

demonology /deemə'noləji/ *noun* the study of or belief in demons. **»** **demonologist** *noun*.

demonstrable /di'monstrəbl/ *adj* capable of being demonstrated. **»** **demonstrability** /-'biliti/ *noun*, **demonstrably** /di'monstrəbli, 'demən-/ *adv*.

demonstrate /'demənstrayt/ *verb trans* **1** to show (something) clearly. **2a** to prove or make (something) clear by reasoning or evidence. **b** to illustrate and explain (something), *esp* with many examples. **3** to show or prove the application, value, or efficiency of (e.g. a car) to a prospective buyer. **»** *verb intrans* **1** to make or give a demonstration. **2** to take part in a demonstration: *Hundreds of people demonstrated against the abortion bill.* [Latin *demonstratus*, past part. of *demonstrare*, from DE- + *monstrare* to show]

demonstration /demən'straysh(ə)n/ *noun* **1** an outward expression or display. **2** a mass meeting, procession, etc to display group feelings, e.g. about grievances or political issues. **3a** a showing and explanation of an action or process, *esp* to inform or instruct other people: *a cookery demonstration.* **b** a showing and explanation of the merits of a product to a prospective buyer. **4** (*used before a noun*) used for purposes of demonstration, *esp* to prospective buyers: *demonstration model.* **5a** conclusive evidence; proof. **b** a proof in which the conclusion is the immediate sequence of reasoning from premises. **6** a show of armed force. ➤➤ **demonstrational** *adj*.

demonstrative¹ /di'monstrətiv/ *adj* **1a** inclined to display feelings openly. **b** expressing a feeling or intention clearly. **2** (+ of) demonstrating something to be real or true. **3** pointing out the particular person or thing referred to and distinguishing him, her, or it from others of the same class: *'That' is a demonstrative pronoun.* ➤➤ **demonstratively** *adv*, **demonstrativeness** *noun*.

demonstrative² *noun* in grammar, a demonstrative word or morpheme.

demonstrator /'demənstraytə/ *noun* **1** somebody who participates in a demonstration: *The demonstrators were given a police escort.* **2** somebody who demonstrates equipment, products, etc. **3** somebody who teaches something by demonstration.

demoralize or **demoralise** /di'morəliez/ *verb trans* to weaken the morale or self-respect of (somebody); to discourage or dispirit (them). ➤➤ **demoralization** /-'zaysh(ə)n/ *noun*, **demoralizing** *adj*, **demoralizingly** *adv*.

demote /di'moht/ *verb trans* to reduce (somebody) to a lower grade or rank. ➤➤ **demotion** *noun*. [DE- + -*mote* as in PROMOTE]

demotic¹ /di'motik/ *adj* **1** said of language: typical of the common people; popular. **2** denoting or written in a simplified form of ancient Egyptian writing. **3** denoting or written in the language spoken in modern Greece. [Greek *dēmotikos*, from *dēmotēs* commoner, from *dēmos* people]

demotic² *noun* **1** ancient Egyptian demotic script. **2** demotic Greek.

demotivate /dee'mohtivayt/ *verb trans* to make (somebody) less motivated to do something. ➤➤ **demotivation** /-'vaysh(ə)n/ *noun*.

demount /dee'mownt/ *verb trans* **1** to remove (e.g. a gun) from a mounting. **2** to disassemble or dismantle (something). ➤➤ **demountable** *adj*.

demulcent¹ /di'muls(ə)nt/ *adj* said of a medicine: relieving inflammation or irritation; soothing. [Latin *demulcent-, demulcens*, present part. of *demulcēre* to soothe, from DE- + *mulcēre* to soothe]

demulcent² *noun* a substance used to reduce irritation and pain, e.g. in the mucous membranes of the mouth.

demur¹ /di'muh/ *verb intrans* (**demurred, demurring**) **1** to show hesitation or to raise doubts or objections about accepting something. **2** in law, to put in a demurrer. ➤➤ **demurrable** *adj*, **demurral** *noun*. [Middle English *demeoren* to linger, via Old French from Latin *demorari*, from DE- + *morari* to linger, from *mora* delay]

demur² *noun* hesitation or objection: *Many teenagers simply follow fashion without demur.*

demure /di'myooə/ *adj* (**demurer, demurest**) **1** reserved or modest: *A girl not out has always the same sort of dress: a close bonnet, for instance; looks very demure, and never says a word —* Jane Austen. **2** affectedly modest, shy, or serious; coy. ➤➤ **demurely** *adv*, **demureness** *noun*. [Middle English, perhaps from early French *demorer, demourer* to linger, from Latin *demorari*: see DEMUR¹]

demurrage /di'muhrij/ *noun* **1** the detention of a ship or vehicle, e.g. for loading or unloading, beyond the time agreed upon between the owner and the charterer. **2** a charge paid to the owner by the charterer for this.

demurrer *noun* an objection, *esp* a legal one that assumes the truth of the matter alleged by the opponent, but asserts that it is insufficient in law to sustain the opponent's claim, and that therefore the action should not be allowed to proceed. [early French *demorer*: see DEMURE]

demutualize or **demutualise** /dee'myoohtyooəliez/ *verb intrans* said of a building society or insurance company: to change from being run on mutual principles to being a public limited company. ➤ *verb trans* to change (e.g. a building society) in this way. ➤➤ **demutualization** /-'zaysh(ə)n/ *noun*.

demy /di'mie/ *noun* **1** a size of paper usu 572 × 444mm (22½ × 17½in). **2** (*also* demy octavo) a book size 216 × 135mm (8¹/₂ × 5¼in). [Middle English *demi* half: see DEMI-]

demystify /dee'mistifie/ *verb trans* (**demystifies, demystified, demystifying**) to eliminate the mystery from (something); to clarify (it). ➤➤ **demystification** /-fi'kaysh(ə)n/ *noun*.

demythologize or **demythologise** /deemi'tholəjiez/ *verb trans* to eliminate the mythical elements or associations of (a belief, tradition, etc).

den /den/ *noun* **1** the lair of a wild, usu predatory, animal. **2** a centre of secret, *esp* unlawful, activity: *an opium den.* **3** a comfortable usu secluded room. [Old English *denn*]

denar /'deenə/ *noun* the basic monetary unit of Macedonia. [see DINAR]

denarii /di'neəriie/ *noun* pl of DENARIUS.

denarius /di'neəri-əs/ *noun* (pl **denarii**) a small silver coin of ancient Rome. [Middle English from Latin *denarius*: see DENIER¹]

denary /'deenəri/ *adj* of a system of numbers having ten as its base; decimal. [Latin *denarius*: see DENIER¹]

denationalize or **denationalise** /dee'nash(ə)nəliez/ *verb trans* **1** to remove (something) from ownership or control by the state. **2** to divest (a person or a country) of national status, character, or rights. ➤➤ **denationalization** /-'zaysh(ə)n/ *noun*.

denaturalize or **denaturalise** /dee'nachərəliez/ *verb trans* **1** to make (something) unnatural. **2** to deprive (somebody) of the rights and duties of a citizen. ➤➤ **denaturalization** /-'zaysh(ə)n/ *noun*.

denature /dee'naychə/ *verb trans* **1** to take away the natural qualities of (something or somebody). **2a** to modify (e.g. a protein) by heat, acid, etc so that some of the original structure of the molecule is lost and its properties are changed. **b** to make (alcohol) unfit for drinking (e.g. by adding an obnoxious substance). ➤➤ **denaturant** /dee'naychərənt, dee'na-/ *noun*, **denaturation** /,deenaychə'raysh(ə)n, ,deenachə'raysh(ə)n/ *noun*.

dendr- or **dendro-** *comb. form* forming words, denoting: a tree or trees: *dendrochronology*. [Greek, from *dendron* tree]

dendrite /'dendriet/ *noun* **1a** a mineral marked with a branching crystal form. **b** these marks. **2** a branching form of a crystal. **3** any of the branching extensions from a nerve cell that conduct impulses towards the cell body. ➤➤ **dendritic** /den'dritik/ *adj*, **dendritically** /den'dritikli/ *adv*.

dendro- *comb. form* see DENDR-.

dendrochronology /,dendrohkrə'noləji/ *noun* the dating of events and variations in climate by comparative study of the annual growth rings in wood.

dendrology /den'droləji/ *noun* the study of trees. ➤➤ **dendrological** /-'lojikl/ *adj*, **dendrologist** *noun*.

Dene /'deni/ *noun* **1** a member of a group of indigenous peoples of NW Canada and Alaska. **2** any of the Athabaskan languages of these peoples. [French *Déné* from Athabaskan *dene* people, tribe]

dene¹ /deen/ *noun* see DEAN².

dene² *noun* Brit a bare sandy area or sand dune by the sea. [Middle English *den, denne*; prob related to Old English *dūn* down]

denervate /'deenuhvayt/ *verb trans* to deprive (a body part) of a nerve supply, e.g. by cutting a nerve. ➤➤ **denervation** /-'vaysh(ə)n/ *noun*.

dengue /'denggi/ *noun* an infectious short-lasting viral disease transmitted by mosquitoes and characterized by a headache and pain in the joints. [Spanish *dengue* from Kiswahili *dinga*]

deni /'deeni/ *noun* (pl **deni**) a unit of currency in Macedonia, worth 100th of a denar.

deniable /di'nie-əbl/ *adj* capable of being denied.

denial /di'nie-əl/ *noun* **1** a refusal to satisfy a request or desire. **2a** a refusal to admit the truth or reality, e.g. of a statement or charge. **b** an assertion that an allegation is false. **3** a refusal to acknowledge somebody or something; a disavowal: *Peter's denial of Christ.* **4** self-denial. **5** in psychology, an unconscious refusal to acknowledge feelings or thoughts that may be painful.

denier¹ /'deeni-ə, 'deni-ə/ *noun* a unit of fineness for silk, rayon, or nylon yarn equal to the fineness of a yarn weighing 1g for each 9000m.

Word history

Middle English *denere* via French from Latin *denarius*, coin worth ten asses, from *denarius* containing ten, from *deni* ten each, from *decem* ten. A denier was orig a small coin used in France and W Europe between the 8th cent. and 19th cent.

denier² /di'nie-ə/ *noun* somebody who denies.

denigrate /'denigrayt/ *verb trans* to make negative or critical statements, usu unjustly, about (somebody or something); to belittle (them). ➤➤ **denigration** /-'graysh(ə)n/ *noun*, **denigrator** *noun*, **denigratory** *adj*. [Latin *denigratus*, past part. of *denigrare*, from DE- + *nigrare* to blacken, from *nigr-, niger* black]

denim /'denəm/ *noun* **1** a firm durable twilled usu blue cotton fabric used for jeans and work clothes. **2** *informal* (*in pl*) denim clothes; *esp* blue jeans. [French *serge de Nîmes* serge of Nîmes, a town in France]

denitrify /dee'nietrifie/ *verb trans* (**denitrifies, denitrified, denitrifying**) to remove nitrates or nitrites from (e.g. soil). ➤➤ **denitrification** /-fi'kaysh(ə)n/ *noun*.

denizen /'deniz(ə)n/ *noun* **1** *literary or humorous* an inhabitant or resident. **2** somebody who is allowed to live in a foreign country. **3** a naturalized plant or animal. [Middle English *denysen* via French from Latin *deintus*, from DE- + *intus* within]

denominate /di'nominayt/ *verb trans formal* to give a name to (somebody or something). [Latin *denominatus*, past part. of *denominare*, from DE- + *nominare* to name, from *nomin-, nomen* name]

denomination /dinomi'naysh(ə)n/ *noun* **1** a religious organization or sect. **2** a grade or degree in a series of values or sizes, e.g. of money. **3** a name or designation; *esp* a general name for a category.

denominational *adj* belonging or relating to a particular religious denomination: *a denominational school.*

denominationalism *noun* the narrowly exclusive emphasizing of denominational differences. ➤➤ **denominationalist** *noun.*

denominative /di'nominətiv/ *adj* giving or constituting a name.

denominator *noun* the part of a vulgar fraction that is below the line and that indicates how many parts the numerator is divided into; a divisor.

denotation /deenoh'taysh(ə)n/ *noun* **1** an act or process of denoting. **2** a meaning; *esp* a direct specific meaning as distinct from a suggested or implied meaning. **3** a denoting term; a name. **4** a sign or indication.

denote /di'noht/ *verb trans* **1** to signify or indicate (something): *Their swollen bellies denote starvation.* **2** to be a sign or mark for (something); to symbolize (it): *Red denotes danger.* **3** to have the meaning of or mean (something). ➤➤ **denotative** /-tiv/ *adj.* [early French *denoter* from Latin *denotare*, from DE- + *notare* to note, from *nota* a mark]

denouement /day'noohmonh/ *noun* **1** the final part of a literary work in which all the complications of the plot are resolved. **2** the outcome of a complex sequence of events: *half afraid that I might be too late to assist at the denouement of the little mystery* — Conan Doyle. [French *dénouement* untying, ultimately from DE- + Latin *nodare* to tie, from *nodus* knot]

denounce /di'nowns/ *verb trans* **1** to condemn (somebody), *esp* publicly, as deserving censure or punishment. **2** to inform against or accuse (somebody): *They denounced him to the authorities.* **3** to announce formally the termination of (e.g. a treaty). ➤➤ **denouncement** *noun,* **denouncer** *noun.* [Middle English *denouncen* via Old French from Latin *denuntiare*, from DE- + *nuntiare* to report]

de novo /di 'nohvoh/ *adv* over again; anew. [Latin *de novo* from new]

dense /dens/ *adj* **1** marked by high density, compactness, or crowding together of parts: *dense undergrowth; a dense fog.* **2** *informal* dull; stupid. **3** demanding concentration if it is to be followed or understood: *dense prose.* ➤➤ **densely** *adv,* **denseness** *noun.* [Middle English from Latin *densus*]

densitometer /densi'tomitə/ *noun* an instrument for determining optical or photographic density.

density /'densiti/ *noun* (*pl* **densities**) **1** the quantity or state of being dense. **2a** the mass of a substance or distribution of a quantity per unit of volume or space. **b** the average number of individuals or units per unit of space: *a population density.* **3** the degree of opaqueness of something translucent. **4** *informal* stupidity; dullness.

dent[1] /dent/ *noun* **1** a depression or hollow made by a blow or by pressure. **2** an adverse effect: *The extra petrol made a dent in the weekly budget.* [Middle English alteration of DINT[1]]

dent[2] *verb trans* to make a dent in or on (something).

dent- or **denti-** or **dento-** *comb. form* forming words, denoting: a tooth or the teeth: *dentifrice.* [Middle English *denti-* from Latin, from *dent-, dens* tooth]

dental /'dentl/ *adj* **1** relating to the teeth or to dentistry. **2** said of a consonant: articulated with the tip or blade of the tongue against or near the upper front teeth, e.g. the sound 'th' in English. [Latin *dentalis*, from *dent-, dens* tooth]

dental floss *noun* a waxed thread used to clean between the teeth.

dental hygienist *noun* a person who is trained in the care and cleaning of teeth, who acts as an assistant to a dentist.

dentalium /den'tayli·əm/ *noun* (*pl* **dentalia** /-li·ə/) any of a genus of shellfish including the tooth shell: genus *Dentalium*. [Latin genus name, from Latin *dentalis*: see DENTAL]

dental surgeon *noun* = DENTIST.

dentate /'dentayt/ *adj* having teeth or pointed conical projections: *a dentate leaf.* ➤➤ **dentately** *adv.* [Latin *dentatus*, from *dent-, dens* tooth]

denti- *comb. form* see DENT-.

denticle /'dentikl/ *noun* a small tooth or other conical pointed projection. [Middle English from Latin *denticulus*, dimin. of *dent-, dens* tooth]

denticulate /den'tikyoolət/ *adj* **1** covered with small pointed projections: *a denticulate shell.* **2** cut into dentils: *a denticulate cornice.*

denticulated /den'tikyoolaytid/ *adj* = DENTICULATE.

dentifrice /'dentifris/ *noun* a powder, paste, or liquid for cleaning the teeth. [early French *dentifrice* from Latin *dentifricium*, from *dent-, dens* tooth + *fricare* to rub]

dentil /'dentil/ *noun* any of a series of small projecting rectangular blocks, *esp* under a cornice on a building. [obsolete French *dentille*, dimin. of *dent* tooth, from Latin *dent-, dens*]

dentine (*NAmer* **dentin**) /'denteen/ *noun* a calcium-containing material, similar to but harder and denser than bone, of which the principal mass of a tooth is composed. ➤➤ **dentinal** *adj.*

dentist /'dentist/ *noun* somebody who treats diseases, malformations, and injuries to the teeth, mouth, etc and who makes and inserts false teeth. ➤➤ **dentistry** /-tri/ *noun.* [French *dentiste*, from *dent*: see DENTIL]

dentition /den'tish(ə)n/ *noun* **1** the number, kind, and arrangement of a human being's or animal's teeth. **2** the emergence of teeth from the gums. [Latin *dentition-, dentitio*, from *dentire* to cut teeth, from *dent-, dens* tooth]

dento- *comb. form* see DENT-.

denture /'denchə/ *noun* **1** an artificial replacement for one or more teeth. **2** (*in pl*) a set of false teeth. [French *denture* from *dent*: see DENTIL]

denuclearize or **denuclearise** /dee'nyoohkliəriez/ *verb trans* to remove nuclear arms from (a country). ➤➤ **denuclearization** /-'zaysh(ə)n/ *noun.*

denude /di'nyoohd/ *verb trans* **1a** to strip (something) of all covering. **b** to lay (an area) bare by erosion. **2** to remove an important possession or something (from somebody or something): *He had been denuded of his dignity.* ➤➤ **denudation** /deenyooh'daysh(ə)n/ *noun.* [Latin *denudare*, from DE- + *nudus* bare]

denumerable /di'nyoohm(ə)rəbl/ *adj* said of a mathematical set: having elements that can be numbered successively; countable. ➤➤ **denumerability** /-'biliti/ *noun,* **denumerably** *adv.*

denunciate /di'nunsiayt/ *verb trans* = DENOUNCE. ➤➤ **denunciator** *noun,* **denunciatory** /-ət(ə)ri/ *adj.* [Latin *denuntiatus*, past part. of *denuntiare*: see DENOUNCE]

denunciation /di,nunsi'aysh(ə)n/ *noun* the act or an instance of denouncing; public condemnation.

deny /di'nie/ *verb trans* (**denies, denied, denying**) **1** to declare (something) to be untrue or invalid; to refuse to accept (it). **2a** to refuse to give or permit something to (somebody, oneself). **b** to refuse to grant (e.g. a request, access). **3** to disown or repudiate (somebody or something). ✳ **deny oneself** to refrain ascetically from self-indulgence or pleasure. [Middle English *denyen* via Old French from Latin *denegare*, from DE- + *negare* to deny]

Usage note

deny, refute, reject, or repudiate? See note at REFUTE.

deoch an doris or **doch an dorris** /,dokh hən 'dowris/ *noun Scot, Irish* a parting drink. [Scottish Gaelic and Irish Gaelic *deoch an doruis* a drink at the door]

deodar /'deeohdah, 'dee·ədah/ *noun* an East Indian cedar with drooping branches: *Cedrus deodara.* [Hindi *deodār* from Sanskrit *devadāru* timber of the gods, from *deva* god + *dāru* wood]

deodorant /dee'ohdərənt/ *noun* a preparation that destroys or masks unpleasant smells.

deodorize *or* **deodorise** /dee'ohdəriez/ *verb trans* to remove or mask the unpleasant smell of (something). ➤➤ **deodorization** /-'zaysh(ə)n/ *noun*, **deodorizer** *noun*.

deontic /dee'ontik/ *adj* in philosophy, relating to duty or obligation. [Greek *deont-*, *deon* that which is obligatory, neuter present part. of *dein* to lack, be needful]

deontology /deeon'toləji/ *noun* in philosophy, a theory or examination of the nature of moral obligation. ➤➤ **deontological** /-'lojikl/ *adj*, **deontologist** *noun*.

Deo volente /,dayoh vo'lenti/ *adv* God being willing. [Latin *deo volente*]

deoxygenate /dee'oksijinayt/ *verb trans* to remove oxygen from (something). ➤➤ **deoxygenation** /-'naysh(ə)n/ *noun*.

deoxyribonuclease /di,oksirieboh'nyoohkliayz/ *noun* an enzyme that breaks DNA down into smaller molecules. [DE- + OXY-² + RIBOSE + NUCLEASE]

deoxyribonucleic acid /,deeoksi,riebohnyooh'klayik, -'kleeik/ *noun* see DNA. [DEOXYRIBOSE + NUCLEIC ACID]

deoxyribose /,deeoksi'riebohz/ *noun* a sugar that is part of the repeating structure forming the long chains of a DNA molecule. [DE- + OXY-² + RIBOSE]

dep. *abbr* **1** department. **2** departs. **3** departure. **4** deposed. **5** deposit. **6** depot. **7** deputy.

depart /di'paht/ *verb intrans* **1** (*usu* + from) to go away; to leave. **2** (*usu* + for) to set out: *We'll be departing for Bristol in five minutes.* **3** (*usu* + from) to turn aside; to deviate. **4** to die. ➤ *verb trans chiefly NAmer* to leave (a place). ✳ **depart this life** to die. [Middle English *departen* to divide, go away, from Old French *departir*, from DE- + *partir* to divide, ultimately from Latin *part-*, *pars* PART¹]

departed¹ *adj euphem* having died, *esp* recently.

departed² *noun euphem* **1** (**the departed**) (*treated as sing.*) a person who has recently died. **2** (**the departed**) (*treated as pl.*) people who have recently died.

department *noun* **1a** a major division of a government. **b** a division of an institution or business that provides a specified service or deals with a specified subject: *the sales department*; *the geography department.* **2** a major administrative subdivision, e.g. in France. **3** a section of a department store. **4** *informal.* **a** a distinct sphere, e.g. of activity or thought; an area of responsibility; a speciality: *That's not my department.* **b** a particular aspect, *esp* of somebody's physical or mental makeup: *rather deficient in the brains department.* ➤➤ **departmental** /deepaht'mentl/ *adj*, **departmentally** /deepaht'mentəli/ *adv*. [French *département*, from Old French *departir*: see DEPART]

departmentalize *or* **departmentalise** /deepaht'mentəliez/ *verb trans* to divide (something) into departments. ➤➤ **departmentalization** /-'zaysh(ə)n/ *noun*.

department store *noun* a large shop selling a wide variety of goods, arranged in several sections each devoted to a particular type of merchandise.

departure /di'pahchə/ *noun* **1a** the act or an instance of going away. **b** (*also used before a noun*) the setting off of an aircraft from an airport, a train from a station, etc: *the departure gate.* **2** (*usu* + from) deviation or divergence from a straight or prescribed course, a customary way of behaving, etc, or an instance of this. **3** the distance due east or west travelled by a ship in its course. ✳ **a new departure** a course of action, line of business, etc different from any previously pursued.

depend /di'pend/ *verb intrans* **1** (*usu* + on/upon) to be determined by or based on some condition or action: *It all depends on what you mean by 'correct'.* **2** (*usu* + on/upon) to place reliance or trust in (a claim, statement, etc): *That certain kings reigned, and certain battles were fought, we can depend upon as true; but all the colouring, all the philosophy of history is conjecture* — Dr Johnson. **3** (+ on/upon) to rely on (somebody) for assistance, financial support, etc: *I have to depend on my neighbours a good deal.* **4** *archaic or literary* to hang down. [Middle English *dependen* via early French *dependre* from Latin *dependēre*, from DE- + *pendēre* to hang]

dependable *adj* reliable or trustworthy. ➤➤ **dependability** /-'biliti/ *noun*, **dependableness** *noun*, **dependably** *adv*.

dependance *noun NAmer* see DEPENDENCE.

dependant (*NAmer* **dependent**) *noun* a person who relies on another person, *esp* for financial support.

Usage note
dependant *or* **dependent?** In British English *dependent* is an adjective (*dependent on her mother for support; too dependent on overseas imports*) and *dependant* is a noun meaning 'a dependent person' (*not earning enough to be able to provide adequately for her dependants*). In American English the form *dependent* is generally used both as an adjective and noun.

dependence (*NAmer* **dependance**) *noun* **1** the fact of being wholly determined by or based on something else. **2** the fact of needing somebody or something else in order to be able to live or function satisfactorily. **3** reliance or trust. **4** a psychological or physiological need for a drug; addiction or habituation.

dependency /di'pend(ə)nsi/ *noun* (*pl* **dependencies**) **1** a territorial unit under the jurisdiction of a nation but not formally annexed to it. **2** something that is dependent on something else. **3** dependence.

dependent¹ *adj* **1** (*often* + on/upon) relying on somebody or something else for support or help. **2** (*often* + on/upon) determined or conditioned by somebody else; contingent. **3** subject to the jurisdiction of e.g. another state; subordinate. **4** having a need for something, e.g. a drug. **5** in mathematics, said of a variable: having a value that is determined by that of one or more independent variables in a function. **6** in grammar, = SUBORDINATE¹. ➤➤ **dependently** *adv*. [Middle English *dependant*, from early French present part. of *dependre*: see DEPEND]

Usage note
dependent *or* **dependant?** See note at DEPENDANT.

dependent² *noun NAmer* see DEPENDANT.

depersonalize *or* **depersonalise** /dee'puhsənəliez/ *verb trans* **1** to deprive (somebody or something) of the sense of personal identity. **2** to make (something) impersonal. ➤➤ **depersonalization** /-'zaysh(ə)n/ *noun*.

depict /di'pikt/ *verb trans* **1** to represent (something) by a picture. **2** to describe (something). ➤➤ **depicter** *noun*, **depiction** *noun*, **depictive** /-tiv/ *adj*, **depictor** *noun*. [Latin *depictus*, past part. of *depingere*, from DE- + *pingere* to paint]

depilate /'depilayt/ *verb trans* to remove hair from (a part of the body). ➤➤ **depilation** /-'laysh(ə)n/ *noun*. [Latin *depilatus*, past part. of *depilare*, from DE- + *pilus* hair]

depilatory /di'pilət(ə)ri/ *noun* (*pl* **depilatories**) an agent, e.g. a cream wax, for removing hair, wool, or bristles. ➤➤ **depilatory** *adj*.

deplane /dee'playn/ *verb intrans chiefly NAmer* to get off an aircraft.

deplete /di'pleet/ *verb trans* **1** to lessen (something) markedly in quantity, content, power, or value. **2** to empty (something) wholly or partially. ➤➤ **depletion** *noun*. [Latin *depletus*, past part. of *deplēre*, from DE- + *plēre* to fill]

depleted uranium *noun* uranium from which most of the U-235 isotope has been removed, usually through being used as nuclear fuel.

depletion layer *noun* a layer in a semiconductor with few charge carriers, conveying an electrical charge between areas of different conductivity.

deplorable /di'plawrəbl/ *adj* **1** extremely bad. **2** lamentable: *a deplorable accident.* ➤➤ **deplorably** *adv*.

deplore /di'plaw/ *verb trans* to regret or disapprove of (something) strongly. ➤➤ **deploringly** *adv*. [French *déplorer* from Latin *deplorare*, from DE- + *plorare* to wail]

deploy /di'ploy/ *verb trans* **1** to spread out (e.g. troops or ships); *esp* in battle formation. **2** to put (something) to use; to bring (it) into action: *By deploying all his considerable powers of persuasion, he managed to get his way.* ➤ *verb intrans* said of troops: to move into position ready for action. ➤➤ **deployment** *noun*. [French *déployer* from Latin *displicare* to scatter, unfold, from DIS- + *plicare* to fold]

deplume /dee'ploohm/ *verb trans* to pluck the feathers of (a bird). [Middle English *deplumen* via French from Latin *deplumare*, from DE- + *pluma* feather]

depolarize *or* **depolarise** /dee'pohləriez/ *verb trans* in physics, to remove or reduce the polarization of (e.g. a dry battery or a cell membrane). ➤➤ **depolarization** /-'zaysh(ə)n/ *noun*.

depoliticize *or* **depoliticise** /deepə'litisiez/ *verb trans* to make (something) nonpolitical: *We want to depoliticize foreign aid.* ➤➤ **depoliticization** /-'zaysh(ə)n/ *noun*.

deponent[1] /di'pohnənt/ *adj* said of a verb: occurring with passive or middle voice forms but with active voice meaning. [Latin *deponent-, deponens*, present part. of *deponere* to put down, from DE- + *ponere* to put]

deponent[2] *noun* 1 in grammar, a deponent verb. 2 in law, somebody who gives evidence, under oath.

depopulate /dee'popyoolayt/ *verb trans* to reduce greatly the population of (an area). ➤ *verb intrans* to decrease in population. ➤➤ **depopulation** /-'laysh(ə)n/ *noun*. [Latin *depopulatus*, past part. of *depopulari*, from DE- + *populari* to ravage, from *populus* people]

deport /di'pawt/ *verb trans* 1 to expel (e.g. an alien) legally from a country; to exile (somebody). 2 *formal* to behave or conduct (oneself) in a specified manner. ➤➤ **deportable** *adj*, **deportation** /deepaw'taysh(ə)n/ *noun*. [Latin *deportare* to carry away, from DE- + *portare* to carry]

deportee /deepaw'tee/ *noun* a person who has been deported or is under sentence of deportation.

deportment *noun Brit* the manner in which one stands, sits, or walks; posture.

depose /di'pohz/ *verb trans* 1 to remove (somebody) from a position of authority, e.g. a throne. 2 to testify (something) under oath or by affidavit. ➤ *verb intrans* to bear witness. [Middle English *deposen* via French from Latin *deponere*: see DEPONENT[1]]

deposit[1] /di'pozit/ *verb trans* (**deposited, depositing**) 1a to place (something) *esp* for safekeeping or as a pledge. b to put (money) in a bank. 2a to lay down (something); to place (it). b to let fall (e.g. sediment). [Latin *depositus*, past part. of *deponere*: see DEPONENT[1]]

deposit[2] *noun* 1a money given as a pledge or down payment. b money or valuables deposited in a bank. 2 a depository. 3 something laid down; *esp* matter deposited by a natural process. ✴ **on deposit** 1 paid into a deposit account. 2 paid as an instalment.

deposit account *noun chiefly Brit* an account, e.g. in a bank, on which interest is usu payable and from which withdrawals can be made usu only by prior arrangement: compare CURRENT ACCOUNT.

depositary /di'pozit(ə)ri/ *noun* (*pl* **depositaries**) a person to whom something is entrusted.

deposition /depə'zish(ə)n, dee-/ *noun* 1 the removal of somebody from a position of authority. 2 a usu written and sworn statement presented as evidence. 3 an act or process of depositing. 4 (**the Deposition**) the taking down of Christ's body from the Cross.

depositor *noun* somebody who places money on deposit in a bank or building society.

depository /di'pozit(ə)ri/ *noun* (*pl* **depositories**) 1 a place where something is deposited, *esp* for safekeeping; a storehouse. 2 a trustee; a depositary.

depot /'depoh/ *noun* 1a *Brit* a place where buses or trains are kept when not in use or taken for maintenance. b *NAmer* a railway or bus station. 2 a place for storing goods; a storehouse. 3a a place for the storage of military supplies. b a place for the reception and training of military recruits; a regimental headquarters. [French *dépôt* from medieval Latin *depositum*, neuter past part. of *deponere*: see DEPONENT[1]]

deprave /di'prayv/ *verb trans* to corrupt (somebody) morally; to pervert (them). ➤➤ **depravation** /deprə'vaysh(ə)n/ *noun*, **depraved** *adj*. [Middle English *depraven* via French from Latin *depravare* to pervert, from DE- + *pravus* crooked, bad]

depravity /di'praviti/ *noun* (*pl* **depravities**) 1 moral corruption: *His was not gay, wanton, unfeeling depravity; he [Guy Fawkes] did not murder in sport* — Charles Lamb. 2 an instance of this.

deprecate /'deprikayt/ *verb trans* 1 to express disapproval of (something or somebody), *esp* mildly or regretfully. 2 to disparage or depreciate (something). ➤➤ **deprecatingly** *adv*, **deprecation** /-'kaysh(ə)n/ *noun*, **deprecator** *noun*. [Latin *deprecatus*, past part. of *deprecari* to avert by prayer, from DE- + *precari* to pray]

Usage note

deprecate *or* **depreciate**? The difference in meaning of these two words is being eroded. To *deprecate* is a rather formal verb meaning to 'feel or express disapproval of (something)': *She deprecated their lack of courtesy toward the old lady*. To *depreciate* means both to 'fall in value' or 'lower the value of (something)' (*The currency is depreciating*) and, more formally, to 'belittle (somebody or something)': *My efforts were depreciated and I was made to feel useless*. The distinction between expressing disapproval and belittling or disparaging is sometimes so fine that the words *deprecate* and *depreciate* are increasingly being used interchangeably.

deprecatory /'deprikayt(ə)ri/ *adj* 1 apologetic: *'Oh,' said Rosamond, with a slight deprecatory laugh, 'I was only going to say we sometimes have dancing, and I wanted to know whether you would feel insulted if you were asked to come.'* — George Eliot. 2 disapproving. ➤➤ **deprecatorily** *adv*.

depreciate /di'preeshiayt, -siayt/ *verb trans* 1 to lower the price or estimated value of (something). 2 to belittle or disparage (somebody or something). ➤ *verb intrans* to lessen in value; to fall. ➤➤ **depreciative** /-shətiv/ *adj*, **depreciatory** /-shi-ət(ə)ri, -si-ət(ə)ri/ *adj*. [late Latin *depretiatus*, past part. of *depretiare*, from Latin DE- + *pretium* price]

Usage note

depreciate *or* **deprecate**? See note at DEPRECATE.

depreciation /di,preeshi'aysh(ə)n, -si'aysh(ə)n/ *noun* 1 a reduction or loss in the value of something, e.g. because of wear and tear or market conditions. 2 in accounting, an allowance made for a loss in value. 3 in economics, a reduction in the value of a currency. 4 an instance of something depreciating or being depreciated.

depredate /'depridayt/ *verb trans and intrans formal* to plunder or ravage (a place). ➤➤ **depredator** *noun*, **depredatory** *adj*. [late Latin *depraedatus*, past part. of *depraedari*, from Latin DE- + *praedari* to plunder, from *praeda* booty, PREY[1]]

depredation /depri'daysh(ə)n/ *noun* (*usu in pl*) an act of plundering, pillage, or robbery. [via French from Latin *depraedation-, depraedatio*, from *depraedari*: see DEPREDATE]

depress /di'pres/ *verb trans* 1 to sadden or dispirit (somebody). 2 to lessen the activity or strength of (something). 3 to decrease the market value or marketability of (something). 4 to push or press (something) down: *This lever depresses the key*. [Middle English *depressen* via French from Latin *depressus*, past part. of *deprimere* to press down, from DE- + *premere* to press]

depressant *noun* something, e.g. a drug, that depresses function or activity: *Alcohol acts as a depressant of the brain*. ➤➤ **depressant** *adj*.

depressed *adj* 1 low in spirits; sad, *esp* suffering from depression. 2 suffering from economic depression: *a depressed area*. 3 lowered or sunken, *esp* in the centre. 4 said *esp* of a plant: flattened as if by external pressure.

depressing *adj* causing emotional depression: *a depressing story*. ➤➤ **depressingly** *adv*.

depression /di'presh(ə)n/ *noun* 1 a mental disorder marked by inactivity, difficulty in thinking and concentration, and *esp* by sadness or dejection. 2 an unhappy state or mood; dejection. 3 a lowering of activity, vitality, amount, force, etc. 4a a period of low general economic activity marked by rising levels of unemployment. b (**the Depression**) the period of economic stagnation, mass unemployment, and hardship worldwide in the early 1930s. 5 a depressed place or part; a hollow. 6 an atmospheric low. 7 a pressing down; a lowering. 8 in astronomy, the angular distance of a celestial body below the horizon.

depressive[1] /di'presiv/ *adj* 1 tending to depress. 2 characterized by or liable to psychological depression. ➤➤ **depressively** *adv*.

depressive[2] *noun* somebody who suffers from periods of psychological depression.

depressor *noun* 1 a muscle that draws down a part of the body: compare LEVATOR. 2 a device for pressing a part down or aside, e.g. a surgical instrument. [late Latin *depressor*, from Latin *deprimere*: see DEPRESS]

depressurize *or* **depressurise** /dee'preshəriez/ *verb trans* to cause the pressure of a gas to drop within (a container or vehicle). ➤➤ **depressurization** /-'zaysh(ə)n/ *noun*.

deprivation /depri'vaysh(ə)n/ *noun* 1a the state of being without or of being denied something, *esp* something vital to one's wellbeing; loss. b lack of basic necessities such as food or shelter; hardship. 2 the act or an instance of depriving somebody of something.

deprive /di'priev/ *verb trans* 1 (*usu +* of) to prevent (somebody) from making use of or benefiting from something: *He threatened to deprive them of their rights*. 2 (*usu +* of) to take something away from (somebody). 3 to remove (e.g. a clergyman) from office. [Middle English *depriven* from late Latin *deprivare*, from Latin DE- + *privare*: see PRIVATE[1]]

deprived *adj* lacking the necessities of life or a good environment: *culturally deprived children; a deprived area*.

deprogramme (*NAmer* **deprogram**) /dee'prohgram/ *verb trans* to free (somebody) from the effects of intensive short-term conditioning, e.g. that received by a convert to a religious group.

dept *abbr* department.

depth /depth/ *noun* **1** the quality of being deep; deepness. **2a** the perpendicular measurement downwards from a surface. **b** the distance from front to back. **3** a part that is far from the outside or surface: *the depths of the woods*. **4** a profound or intense state, e.g. of thought or feeling: *the depths of despair*. **5** the worst, most intensive, or severest part: *the depths of winter*. **6** the degree of intensity: *depth of a colour*. **7** the quality of being profound (e.g. in insight) or full (e.g. of knowledge). **8** (*in pl*) a deep place in a body of water: *found in the depths of the ocean*. *** in depth** with great thoroughness: *I haven't studied it in depth*. **out of one's depth 1** in water that is deeper than one's height. **2** beyond one's ability to understand. [Middle English from DEEP¹ + -TH²]

depth bomb *noun* = DEPTH CHARGE.

depth charge *noun* an explosive projectile for use underwater, *esp* against submarines.

depth of field *noun* the range of distances within which something viewed through a camera or microscope will be in focus.

depth psychology *noun* the investigation of the unconscious; psychoanalysis.

depurate /'depyoorayt/ *verb trans* to purify (e.g. the body). **≫** *verb intrans* to become free of impurities. **≫** **depuration** /-'raysh(ə)n/ *noun*. [late Latin *depuratus*, past part. of *depurare*, from Latin DE- + *purare* to purify, from *purus* clean, PURE]

deputation /depyoo'taysh(ə)n/ *noun* (*treated as sing. or pl*) a small group of people chosen to represent the members of a larger, usu unofficial group, *esp* in negotiations with authority.

depute¹ /di'pyooht/ *verb trans* **1** to appoint (somebody) to act as a deputy. **2** to delegate (something). [Middle English *deputen* to appoint, via French from Latin *deputare* to consider (as), from DE- + *putare* to consider]

depute² /'depyooht/ *noun Scot* a deputy. [Middle English from early French *député, depute*: see DEPUTY]

deputize *or* **deputise** /'depyootiez/ *verb intrans* (*usu* + for) to act as a deputy.

deputy /'depyooti/ *noun* (*pl* **deputies**) **1** a person, e.g. a second-in-command, appointed as a substitute with power to act for another. **2** a member of the lower house of some legislative assemblies. [Middle English from early French *député*, past part. of *deputer*, from Latin *deputare*: see DEPUTE¹]

deracinate /dee'rasinayt/ *verb trans formal or literary* to uproot (something). **≫** **deracination** /-'naysh(ə)n/ *noun*. [French *déraciner*, from *dé-* DE- + *racine* root, ultimately from Latin *radic-, radix*]

derail /di'rayl/ *verb trans* to cause (e.g. a train) to leave the rails. **≫** *verb intrans* to be derailed. **≫** **derailment** *noun*. [French *dérailler*, from *dé-* DE- + *rail*, from RAIL¹]

derailleur /di'raylə/ *noun* **1** a mechanism for changing gear on a bicycle, by moving the chain from one set of exposed gears to another. **2** a bicycle with such a mechanism. [French *dérailleur*, from *dérailler*: see DERAIL]

derange /di'raynj/ *verb trans* **1** to disturb the operation or functions of (something); to disarrange (it). **2** to make (somebody) insane. **≫** **derangement** *noun*. [French *déranger* from Old French *desrengier* to put out of line, from DE- + *reng* place, rank]

deranged *adj* mad or insane.

derby /'dahbi/ *noun* (*pl* **derbies**) **1** (**the Derby**) a flat race for three-year-old horses held annually at Epsom in England. **2** a usu informal race or contest for a specified category of contestant: *a donkey derby*. **3** a sporting match against a major local rival. **4** *chiefly NAmer* a bowler hat. [named after Edward Stanley, twelfth Earl of *Derby* d.1834, who founded the horse race in 1780; (sense 4) said to be because bowler hats were worn at the Epsom Derby]

derecognize *or* **derecognise** /dee'rekəgniez/ *verb trans* to withdraw official recognition from (a trade union). **≫** **derecognition** /-'nish(ə)n/ *noun*.

deregulate /dee'regyoolayt/ *verb trans* **1** to remove (something) from legal jurisdiction by law. **2** to remove from government control or management: *Bus services were deregulated in the 1980s*.
Editorial note ────
In economics to deregulate can refer to many different types of measure, in particular the removal of price controls; the removal of government

subsidies to preferred producers; or the removal of barriers to entry of new competitors into a sector. The term sometimes loosely refers to the removal of any impediment to competition, even if privately created — Evan Davis.

≫ **deregulation** /-'laysh(ə)n/ *noun*.

derelict¹ /'derəlikt/ *adj* **1** left to decay; abandoned or ruined. **2** *chiefly NAmer* lacking a sense of duty; negligent. [Latin *derelictus*, past part. of *derelinquere* to abandon, from DE- + *relinquere*: see RELINQUISH]

derelict² *noun* **1** a down-and-out: *Each time a derelict asks for a dime, he feels a coward if he pays the money* — Norman Mailer. **2** something voluntarily abandoned, e.g. a ship.

dereliction /derə'liksh(ə)n/ *noun* **1a** conscious neglect: *dereliction of duty*. **b** a fault or shortcoming. **2** abandonment or being abandoned, *esp* when this is intentional. **3** a recession of water leaving permanently dry land.

derestrict /deeri'strikt/ *verb trans* to cancel or remove a restriction, *esp* a speed limit, from (something). **≫** **derestriction** *noun*.

deride /di'ried/ *verb trans* to mock or scorn (something). **≫** **derider** *noun*, **deridingly** *adv*. [Latin *deridēre*, from DE- + *ridēre* to laugh]

de rigueur /də ri'guh (*French* də rigœːr)/ *adj* required by fashion, etiquette, or custom: *an evening shirt even frillier than those currently de rigueur at Oxford* — Len Deighton. [French *de rigueur* compulsory, literally 'of strictness']

derision /di'rizh(ə)n/ *noun* scorn or ridicule. [Middle English via French from Latin *derision-, derisio*, from *deridēre*: see DERIDE]

derisive /di'riesiv, -ziv/ *adj* showing derision; mocking or scornful. **≫** **derisively** *adv*, **derisiveness** *noun*.
Usage note ────
derisive *or* derisory? See note at DERISORY.

derisory /di'riez(ə)ri/ *adj* **1** ridiculously small and inadequate: *a derisory pay offer*. **2** derisive: *derisory laughter*.
Usage note ────
derisory *or* derisive? These two words are sometimes confused. Both derive from the word *derision*. The main meaning of *derisory* in modern English is 'ridiculously small and inadequate' (and therefore deserving derision): *a derisory pay offer*. The only meaning of *derisive* is 'mocking' (expressing derision): *derisive jeers*.

derivation /deri'vaysh(ə)n/ *noun* **1a** the fact of being obtained or originating from a particular source. **b** the act or an instance of deriving. **2a** the history or formation of a word from another word or root. **b** an act of tracing or stating the derivation of a word. **3a** a source or origin. **b** descent: *a family of Scottish derivation*. **4** something that is derived; a derivative. **≫** **derivational** *adj*.

derivative¹ /di'rivətiv/ *adj* **1** made up of derived elements; not original. **2** formed by derivation. **≫** **derivatively** *adv*.

derivative² *noun* **1** something derived, e.g. a word formed by derivation. **2** in mathematics, the limit of the ratio of the change in a function to the corresponding change in its independent variable as the latter change approaches zero. **3** in chemistry, a chemical related structurally to and derivable from another. **4** a financial product, such as a futures contract, linked to a commodity, currency, etc and dependent on the value of that for its own value.

derive /di'riev/ *verb trans* **1a** to obtain or receive (something), *esp* from a specified source. **b** to obtain (a chemical) from a parent substance. **2** to infer or deduce (something). **3a** to trace the process by which one thing is obtained or develops from another. **b** to form (something) by derivation. **≫** *verb intrans* (+ from) to come as a derivative. **≫** **derivable** *adj*. [Middle English *deriven* to draw off liquid, via French from Latin *derivare*, from DE- + *rivus* stream]

derived unit *noun* a unit of measurement, e.g. a newton, pascal, or watt, defined in terms of the basic units of a system (e.g. the SI system).

derm /duhm/ *noun* = DERMIS. [Latin *derma* from Greek (see DERM-) and Latin *dermis*: see DERMIS]

derm- *or* **derma-** *or* **dermat-** *or* **dermo-** *or* **dermato-** *comb. form* forming words, denoting: the skin. [via Latin from Greek *derm-, dermo-*, from *dermat-, derma* skin, from *derein* to skin]

-derm *comb. form* forming nouns, denoting: skin; layer: *ectoderm; pachyderm*. [prob via French *-derme* from Greek *derma*: see DERM-]

derma /'duhmə/ *noun* = DERMIS. [via Latin from Greek *derma*: see DERM-]

-derma *comb. form* forming nouns, denoting: the skin or a skin ailment: *scleroderma*. [via Latin from Greek *dermat-, derma*: see DERM-]

dermabrasion /duhmə'brayzh(ə)n/ *noun* cosmetic exfoliation of the skin by means of a rapidly spinning abrasive wheel or wire brush.

dermat- *or* **dermato-** *comb. form* see DERM-. [Greek, from *dermat-, derma*: see DERM-]

dermatitis /duhmə'tietis/ *noun* a disease or inflammation of the skin.

dermatology /duhmə'toləji/ *noun* the branch of medicine dealing with the skin and skin diseases. >>> **dermatological** /-'lojikəl/ *adj*, **dermatologist** *noun*.

dermis /'duhmis/ *noun* **1** the skin. **2** the sensitive vascular inner layer of the skin. >>> **dermal** *adj*, **dermic** /'duhmik/ *adj*. [scientific Latin *dermis*, back-formation from EPIDERMIS]

dermo- *comb. form* see DERM-.

dernier cri /,deəniay 'kree (*French* dɛrnje kri)/ *noun* the latest fashion. [French *dernier cri* last cry]

derogate /'derəgayt/ *verb intrans formal* **1** (+ from) to take away a desirable aspect or feature; to detract. **2** (+ from) to deviate or go astray from (e.g. a principle or standard). >>> *verb trans formal* **1** to express a negative opinion of (something or somebody); to disparage (them). **2** to reduce the applicability of (a law or regulation). >>> **derogative** /di'rogətiv/ *adj*. [Latin *derogatus*, past part. of *derogare* to annul (a law), detract, from DE- + *rogare* to ask, propose (a law)]

derogation /derə'gaysh(ə)n/ *noun* **1** exemption from a regulation; *specif* exemption granted by the European Community to a member state. **2** disparagement; debasement.

derogatory /di'rogət(ə)ri/ *adj* expressing a low opinion; insulting or disparaging. >>> **derogatorily** *adv*.

derrick /'derik/ *noun* **1** a hoisting apparatus employing a tackle rigged at the end of a beam. **2** a framework over an oil well or similar hole, for supporting drilling tackle. [orig meaning 'a hangman, the gallows': from *Derrick*, surname of 17th-cent. English hangman]

derrière /'deri·eə/ *noun euphem or humorous* the buttocks. [French *derrière* hinder, behind, from Latin *de retro*, from DE- + *retro* back]

derring-do /,dering 'dooh/ *noun archaic or literary* daring action: *deeds of derring-do*.

Word history
alteration of Middle English *dorring don* daring to do, from *dorring* (noun from *dorren* to dare) + *don* to do. The phrase appeared as *derrynge do* in a 15th-cent. manuscript; the poet Edmund Spenser took this to mean 'manhood, chivalry', and used it in *The Shepheardes' Calendar* (1579) and later in the *Faerie Queen*. Sir Walter Scott revived it in *Ivanhoe* (1820), using it to mean 'desperate courage'.

derringer /'derinjə/ *noun* a short-barrelled pistol of large calibre. [named after Henry *Deringer* d.1868, US gunsmith, who invented it]

derris /'deris/ *noun* **1** a tropical climbing plant of the pea family, that is a source of poisons and insecticides: genus *Derris*. **2** a preparation of derris roots and stems used as an insecticide. [Latin genus name, from Greek *derein* to skin]

derv /duhv/ *noun* fuel oil for diesel engines. [acronym from *diesel-engined road vehicle*]

dervish /'duhvish/ *noun* a member of a Muslim religious order noted for devotional exercises, e.g. bodily movements leading to a trance. [Turkish *derviş* beggar, from Persian *darvēsh* poor; from the vow of poverty made by dervishes]

desalinate /dee'salinayt/ *or* **desalinize** *or* **desalinise** *verb trans* to remove salt from (*esp* sea water). >>> **desalination** /-'naysh(ə)n/ *noun*. [DE- + SALINE[1] + -ATE[4]]

desalt /dee'sawlt/ *verb trans* to desalinate (sea water).

descale /dee'skayl/ *verb trans* to remove scale deposits from (pipes, kettles, etc).

descant[1] /'deskant/ *noun* a counterpoint superimposed on a simple melody and usu sung by some or all of the sopranos. [Middle English *dyscant* via Old French from late Latin *discantus*, from Latin DIS- + *cantus* song]

descant[2] /des'kant, dis'kant/ *verb intrans* **1** to sing or play a descant. **2** (+ on/upon) to talk or write at considerable length: *He descanted to his heart's content on his favourite topic* — George Bernard Shaw.

descant recorder *noun chiefly Brit* the member of the recorder family with a range of two octaves above the C above middle C.

descend /di'send/ *verb intrans* **1a** to pass from a higher to a lower level. **b** to incline, lead, or extend downwards: *The road descends to the river*. **2** (+ from) to derive or come from; to have as an ancestor: *We are descended from apes*. **3** to pass by inheritance: *The house descended to her when her aunt died*. **4a** (+ on/upon) to make a sudden attack or be suddenly inflicted on somebody: *The plague descended on their people*. **b** *chiefly humorous* (+ on/upon) to make a sudden disconcerting visit or appearance: *The starving hordes descended upon the kitchen*. **5a** to proceed from higher to lower in a sequence or gradation. **b** to pass from the general to the particular. **6** (+ to) to sink in status or dignity; to stoop: *I couldn't descend to such abusive language*. >>> *verb trans* to pass, move, or extend down, or down along (something): *She descended the steps*. [Middle English *descenden* via Old French *descendre* from Latin *descendere*, from DE- + *scandere* to climb]

descendant (*NAmer* **descendent**) *noun* somebody or something descended or deriving from somebody or something else. [via French from Latin *descendent-, descendens*, present part. of *descendere*: see DESCEND]

descender *noun* **1** the part of a lower-case letter, e.g. 'p', that descends below the main body of the letter. **2** a letter that has such a part: compare ASCENDER.

descent /di'sent/ *noun* **1** the act or process of descending. **2a** a downward inclination; a slope. **b** a descending way, e.g. a staircase. **3** a downward step, e.g. in status or value. **4a** (*often* + from) derivation from an ancestor; birth or lineage: *of French descent*. **b** (*often* + from) a transmission from a usu earlier source; a derivation. **5** (*often* + on) a sudden hostile raid or attack. **6** the transmission of an estate by inheritance. [Middle English from early French *descente*, from *descendre*: see DESCEND]

describe /di'skrieb/ *verb trans* **1** to give an account of (something) in words. **2** to trace the outline of (something): *The footsteps described a perfect circle on the ground*. >>> **describable** *adj*, **describer** *noun*. [Latin *describere*, from DE- + *scribere* to write]

description /di'skripsh(ə)n/ *noun* **1** an account intended to convey a mental image of something experienced. **2** a kind or sort: *people of every description*. [Middle English *descripcioun* via French from Latin *description-, descriptio*, from *describere*: see DESCRIBE]

descriptive /di'skriptiv/ *adj* **1** serving to describe, *esp* vividly: *a descriptive account*. **2** characterized by description: *the descriptive basis of science*. **3a** in grammar, said of a modifier: expressing the quality, kind, or condition of what is denoted by the modified term; not limiting or demonstrative. **b** in grammar, said of a clause or phrase: non-restrictive. **4** in linguistics, serving to describe the structure of a language at a particular time without making value judgments and usu excluding historical and comparative data. >>> **descriptively** *adv*, **descriptiveness** *noun*.

descry /di'skrie/ *verb trans* (**descries, descried, descrying**) *formal* to notice or see (something), *esp* at a distance. [Middle English *descrien* from Old French *descrier*: see DECRY]

desecrate /'desikrayt/ *verb trans* **1** to violate the sanctity of (something sacred); to profane (it). **2** to treat (a sacred place) irreverently or contemptuously. >>> **desecration** /-'kraysh(ə)n/ *noun*, **desecrator** *noun*. [DE- + *-secrate* as in CONSECRATE]

desegregate /dee'segrigayt/ *verb trans* to eliminate racial segregation in (e.g. a school). >>> **desegregation** /-'gaysh(ə)n/ *noun*.

deselect /deesi'lekt/ *verb trans* **1** to drop (somebody) from a team or group. **2** said of a constituency political party in Britain: to refuse to readopt (somebody) as a parliamentary candidate. >>> **deselection** *noun*.

desensitize *or* **desensitise** /dee'sensatiez/ *verb trans* **1a** to make (somebody) less sensitive or responsive to feelings or situations, e.g. to the suffering of others. **b** to make (somebody previously sensitive) insensitive or nonreactive to a sensitizing agent. **2** to make (a photographic material) less sensitive or completely insensitive to radiation. >>> **desensitization** /-'zaysh(ə)n/ *noun*, **desensitizer** *noun*.

desert[1] /'dezət/ *noun* **1a** a barren region incapable of supporting much life. **b** an uninhabited place; a place of solitude; a wilderness: *'Sometimes I have been in the humour of wishing to retire to a desert.' 'Sir, you have desert enough in Scotland.'* — Dr Johnson. **2** an area or place that is deprived of or devoid of something important: *a cultural desert*. [Middle English via Old French and late Latin from

Latin *desertum*, neuter past part. of *deserere* to desert, from DE- + *serere* to join together]

Usage note

desert or **dessert**? *Dessert* is a noun meaning 'the sweet course in a meal'. The stress in *dessert* is on the second syllable. A barren wilderness is a *desert* (a noun, with stress on the first syllable). The verb to *desert* (stress on the second syllable) means to 'abandon (somebody or something)' or to 'absent oneself from military duty without leave' (see DESERT³ (2B)). To *get one's just deserts* (plural noun, with stress on the second syllable) is to 'be treated as one deserves' (see DESERT²).

desert² /di'zuht/ *noun* **1** (*usu in pl*) deserved reward or punishment: *She got her just deserts.* **2** the quality or fact of deserving reward or punishment. [Middle English *deserte* from Old French, fem past part. of *deservir*: see DESERVE]

desert³ /di'zuht/ *verb trans* **1** to leave (somebody or something), usu without intending to return. **2a** to abandon or forsake (somebody) *esp* in time of need. **b** to abandon (military service) without leave: *He was shot for deserting his post.* ➤ *verb intrans* to quit one's post, military service, etc without leave or justification. ➤➤ **deserter** *noun.* [French *déserter* from late Latin *desertare*, from *desertus*, past part. of *deserere*: see DESERT¹]

desert boot /'dezət/ *noun* an ankle-high laced suede boot with a rubber sole.

desertification /di,zuhtifi'kaysh(ə)n/ *noun* the reduction of fertile land to barren land or desert, *esp* as a result of overuse and poor irrigation.

desertion /di'zuhsh(ə)n/ *noun* the abandonment of a post or relationship and the moral and legal obligations attached to it: *She sued for divorce on grounds of desertion.*

desert island *noun* a remote tropical island; *esp* one that is uninhabited.

desert rat /'dezət/ *noun* **1** a jerboa found in the deserts of N Africa: *Jaculus orientalis.* **2** *Brit* a soldier of the British 7th Armoured Division who served in the N African desert campaign during World War II.

desert varnish *noun* a hard, dark-coloured surface coating of oxides that forms on exposed rock surfaces in deserts.

deserve /di'zuhv/ *verb trans* to be worthy of or suitable for (some recompense or treatment): *At 50, everyone has the face he deserves —* George Orwell. ➤➤ **deservedly** /-vidli/ *adv,* **deservedness** /-vidnis/ *noun.* [Middle English *deserven* via Old French *deservir* to serve zealously, from DE- + *servire*: see SERVE¹]

deserving *adj* meriting something, *esp* financial aid. ➤➤ **deservingly** *adv,* **deservingness** *noun.*

desex /dee'seks/ *verb trans* **1** to castrate or spay (an animal). **2** to desexualize (somebody).

desexualize or **desexualise** /dee'seksyoo(ə)liez, -shəliez/ *verb trans* to deprive (somebody) of sexuality, sexual power, or the qualities appropriate to one or other sex. ➤➤ **desexualization** /-'zaysh(ə)n/ *noun.*

déshabillé /dayza'beeay/ or **deshabille** /-'beel, disə'beel/ *noun* the state of being only partially or carelessly dressed. [French *déshabillé,* past part. of *déshabiller* to undress, from *dés* DIS- + *habiller* to dress]

desiccate /'desikayt/ *verb trans* **1** to dry (something) up. **2** to preserve (a food) by drying; to dehydrate. ➤➤ **desiccant** *noun,* **desiccation** /-'kaysh(ə)n/ *noun,* **desiccative** /-tiv/ *adj,* **desiccator** *noun.* [Latin *desiccatus,* past part. of *desiccare* to dry up, from DE- + *siccare* to dry, from *siccus* dry]

desiderata /di,zidə'rahtə/ *noun* pl of DESIDERATUM.

desiderate /di'zidərayt/ *verb trans formal* to harbour or express a wish to have or attain (something). ➤➤ **desideration** /-'raysh(ə)n/ *noun,* **desiderative** /-ərətiv/ *adj.* [from Latin *desideratus,* past part. of *desiderare* to desire]

desideratum /di,zidə'rahtəm/ *noun* (*pl* **desiderata** /-tə/) *formal* something desired as necessary. [Latin *desideratum,* neuter past part. of *desiderare*: see DESIRE¹]

design¹ /di'zien/ *verb trans* **1a** to conceive and plan (something) out in the mind. **b** to devise (something) for a specific function or end: *It was designed as a school textbook.* **2a** to draw the plans for (e.g. a building). **b** to create or execute (something) according to a plan. ➤ *verb intrans* **1** to conceive or execute a plan. **2** to draw, lay out, or prepare a design. [early French *designer* from Latin *designare,* from DE- + *signare* to mark, mark out, from *signum* SIGN¹]

design² *noun* **1** a drawing, plan, or pattern showing the details of how something is to be constructed. **2** the act of producing such a plan. **3** a decorative pattern. **4** the arrangement of the elements of a work of art or artefact. **5a** a particular purpose held in view. **b** deliberate purposeful planning: *more by accident than by design.* **6** a mental plan or scheme. **7** (*in pl,* + on) dishonest, hostile, or acquisitive intent.

designate¹ /'dezignayt/ *verb trans* **1** to nominate (somebody) for a specified purpose, office, or duty. **2** to call (somebody or something) by a distinctive name or title. **3** to indicate or point (something) out. ➤➤ **designator** *noun.*

designate² /'dezignət, -nayt/ *adj* chosen for an office but not yet installed: *ambassador designate.* [Latin *designatus,* past part. of *designare*: see DESIGN¹]

designation /dezig'naysh(ə)n/ *noun* **1** a distinguishing name or title. **2** the act of indicating or identifying.

designedly /di'zienidli/ *adv* on purpose.

designer *noun* **1** somebody who designs; *esp* somebody who creates the design of a manufactured object (e.g. a garment). **2** (*used before a noun*). **a** made by a well-known fashion designer: *designer jeans.* **b** worn or used by people who want to seem fashionable: *designer stubble.* **3** (*used before a noun*) altered by genetic engineering: *a designer virus that attacks caterpillars.*

designer baby *noun informal* a baby conceived for a special purpose by in-vitro fertilization.

designer drug *noun* a synthetic drug that has effects similar to those of an illegal narcotic but can be made legally.

designing *adj* crafty or scheming.

desirable /di'zie-ərəbl/ *adj* **1** worth seeking or doing as advantageous, beneficial, or wise: *Legislation is desirable.* **2** causing desire; attractive, *esp* sexually. ➤➤ **desirability** /-'biliti/ *noun,* **desirableness** *noun,* **desirably** *adv.*

desire¹ /di'zie-ə/ *verb trans* **1** to long or hope for (something). **2** to express a wish for (something); to request (it). **3** to wish to have sexual relations with (somebody). **4** *archaic or formal* to express a wish to (somebody); to ask (them): *She desires you to wait outside.* [Middle English *desiren* via Old French from Latin *desiderare,* from DE- + *sider-, sidus* star]

desire² *noun* **1** a longing or craving; *esp* a sexual longing. **2** a formal request or petition. **3** something desired: *It was my heart's desire.*

desirous /di'zie-ərəs/ *adj formal* (*usu* + of/to) eagerly wanting; desiring: *He was desirous of fame.*

desist /di'zist/ *verb intrans formal* (*often* + from) to cease to proceed or act: *They were asked to desist from playing loud music late at night.* [early French *desister* from Latin *desistere,* from DE- + *sistere* to stand, stop]

desk /desk/ *noun* **1a** a table with a sloping or horizontal surface and often drawers and compartments, designed *esp* for writing and reading. **b** a table, counter, or booth at which cashiers, clerks, etc work. **c** a music stand, *esp* as shared by two players in an orchestra, or the position shared by two such players. **d** a church lectern. **2** a division of an organization specializing in a usu specified type or phase of activity, *esp* a section of the editorial staff of a newspaper or news programme: *And now, over to our sports desk for the football results.* [Middle English *deske* via medieval Latin from Latin *discus* dish, disc]

deskbound *adj* working or involving work in an office rather than travelling.

desk editor *noun* an editor in a publishing company whose responsibility it is to copy-edit and proofread manuscripts for publication, texts received from printers, etc.

de-skill /dee'skil/ *verb trans* **1** to remove or diminish the element of skill in (a job) by the introduction of automation. **2** to deprive (a worker) of a chance to use their skill, through changes in manufacturing patterns or processes.

desk job *noun* a clerical or administrative job, requiring that one spend one's time working at a desk.

desktop¹ *noun* **1** the working surface of a desk. **2** a desktop computer. **3** the visible screen produced on a VDU by computer software, on which icons, the cursor, etc are displayed.

desktop² *adj* **1** of a compact size suitable for use on a desk or table. **2** of or using a compact computer system that can fit on a desk, usu comprising a keyboard, VDU, microcomputer, and printer, as opposed e.g. to a laptop or hand-held portable computer.

desktop publishing *noun* the production of printed material by a desktop system essentially comprising a personal computer, software, and a laser printer.

desman /'desmən/ *noun* (*pl* **desmans**) either of two aquatic insect-eating mammals resembling moles with long tails and long snouts, found in Russia and the Pyrenees: *Desmana moschata* and *Galemys pyrenaicus*. [short for Swedish *desmansråtta*, from *desman* musk + *råtta* rat]

desolate[1] /'desələt/ *adj* **1** deserted; uninhabited. **2** barren; lifeless: *a desolate landscape.* **3** devastated; laid waste. **4** forsaken, forlorn, hopeless; extremely unhappy. **5** sad; giving no comfort or hope: *desolate memories.* ➤➤ **desolately** *adv,* **desolateness** *noun.* [Middle English *desolat* from Latin *desolatus,* past part. of *desolare* to abandon, from DE- + *solus* alone]

desolate[2] /'desəlayt/ *verb trans* **1** to deprive (a place) of inhabitants. **2** to lay waste to (a place). **3** to make (somebody) feel forlorn, forsaken, or extremely unhappy. ➤➤ **desolated** *adj,* **desolatingly** *adv,* **desolator** *noun.*

desolation /desə'laysh(ə)n/ *noun* **1** devastation; ruin. **2** misery; wretchedness: *He knew the hopelessness of the search for work and the desolation which is harder to bear than hunger* — Somerset Maugham. **3** a barren wasteland. **4** the act or an instance of desolating.

desorb /dee'sawb/ *verb trans* to free (a substance) from an absorbed or adsorbed state. ➤➤ **desorption** /dee'sawpsh(ə)n/ *noun.* [DE- + -*sorb* as in ABSORB and ADSORB]

despair[1] /di'speə/ *verb intrans* (*often* + of) to lose all hope or confidence: *We began to despair of winning.* ➤➤ **despairing** *adj,* **despairingly** *adv.* [Middle English *despeiren* via French from Latin *desperare,* from DE- + *sperare* to hope]

despair[2] *noun* **1** utter loss of hope. **2** (**the despair of**) a cause of hopelessness or great exasperation: *That child is the despair of his parents.*

despatch[1] /di'spach/ *verb see* DISPATCH[1].

despatch[2] *noun see* DISPATCH[2].

desperado /despə'rahdoh/ *noun* (*pl* **desperadoes** *or* **desperados**) *dated* a bold, reckless, or violent person, *esp* a criminal. [alteration, by association with Spanish words ending in -*ado,* of obsolete *desperate* desperado, from DESPERATE]

desperate /'desp(ə)rət/ *adj* **1** in despair because beyond or almost beyond hope. **2a** reckless because of despair. **b** undertaken as a last resort: *A situation like this calls for desperate remedies.* **3** (*often* + for) suffering extreme need or anxiety: *We were desperate for money.* **4** fraught with extreme danger or impending disaster: *a desperate situation.* **5** violent or dangerous: *desperate criminals.* **6** *informal* said of the weather, etc: very bad; severe. ➤➤ **desperateness** *noun.* [Latin *desperatus,* past part. of *desperare,* from DE- + *sperare* to hope]

desperately *adv* **1** in a desperate manner; in despair or desperation. **2** *informal* extremely: *I was desperately unhappy at school.*

desperation /despə'raysh(ə)n/ *noun* **1** loss of hope and surrender to despair: *The mass of men lead lives of quiet desperation* — Henry David Thoreau. **2** extreme recklessness caused by hopelessness.

despicable /di'spikəbl/ *adj* morally contemptible: *The dress of a clergyman should be in order, and nothing is more despicable than conceited attempts at avoiding the appearance of the clerical order* — James Boswell. ➤➤ **despicableness** *noun,* **despicably** *adv.* [late Latin *despicabilis* from Latin *despicari:* see DESPISE]

despise /di'spiez/ *verb trans* **1** to regard (somebody) with contempt or distaste. **2** to regard (something) as negligible or worthless, or as contemptible or distasteful. ➤➤ **despiser** *noun.* [Middle English *despisen* via French from Latin *despicere,* from DE- + *specere* to look]

despite[1] /di'spiet/ *prep* notwithstanding; in spite of: *She ran despite her injury.* ✳ **despite oneself** in spite of one's intentions, wishes, character, etc. [short for *in despite of:* see DESPITE[2]]

despite[2] *noun formal* **1** harm or injury; disservice or disadvantage: *I know of no government which stands to its obligations, even in its own despite, more solidly* — Winston Churchill. **2** active opposition: *I hate fox-hunting. My entire life has been lived in its despite.* **3** *archaic* the feeling or attitude of despising; contempt. **4** *archaic* malice or spite. ✳ **in despite of** *archaic* in spite of. [Middle English *despite* contempt, defiance, via Old French from Latin *despectus,* from *despectus,* past part. of *despicere:* see DESPISE]

despoil /di'spoyl/ *verb trans* to plunder or pillage (a place). ➤➤ **despoiler** *noun,* **despoilment** *noun.* [Middle English *despoylen* via French from Latin *despoliare,* from DE- + *spoliare* to strip, rob]

despoliation /di,spohli'aysh(ə)n/ *noun* the act or an instance of plundering or being plundered. [Late Latin *despoliation-, despoliatio,* from *despoliare:* see DESPOIL]

despond[1] /di'spond/ *verb intrans archaic or literary* to become despondent. [Latin *despondēre* to give up, become discouraged, from DE- + *spondēre* to promise solemnly]

despond[2] *noun archaic* despondency.

despondent *adj* feeling extreme discouragement or dejection. ➤➤ **despondency** /-si/ *noun,* **despondently** *adv.* [Latin *despondent-, despondens,* present part. of *despondēre:* see DESPOND[1]]

despot /'despot/ *noun* **1** a ruler with absolute power. **2** a person exercising power abusively or tyrannically. ➤➤ **despotic** /di'spotik/ *adj,* **despotically** /di'spotikli/ *adv.* [French *despote* from Greek *despotēs* master, absolute ruler]

despotism /'despətiz(ə)m/ *noun* **1** rule by a despot; absolutism: *If despotism failed for want of a capable benevolent despot, what chance has democracy, which requires a whole population of capable voters* — George Bernard Shaw. **2** despotic exercise of power.

desquamate /'deskwəmayt/ *verb intrans technical* said *esp* of the outer layer of skin: to peel off in scales. ➤➤ **desquamation** /-'maysh(ə)n/ *noun.* [Latin *desquamatus,* past part. of *desquamare,* from DE- + *squama* scale]

des. res. /,dez 'rez/ *noun Brit, informal* a house with desirable characteristics. [short for *desirable residence*]

des res *abbr* desirable residence.

dessert /di'zuht/ *noun* a sweet course or dish served at the end of a meal.

Word history
French *dessert,* from *desservir* to clear the table, from DE- + *servir* to serve, from Latin *servire:* see SERVE[1]. Dessert was orig dishes of fruit and nuts put out after the table was cleared at the end of the meal. See also usage note at DESERT[1].

dessertspoon *noun* **1** a spoon intermediate in size between a teaspoon and a tablespoon and used for eating dessert. **2** a dessertspoonful. ➤➤ **dessertspoonful** *noun.*

dessert wine *noun* a sweet wine often served with dessert.

destabilize *or* **destabilise** /dee'staybəliez/ *verb trans* to make (a government or the economy of a country, etc) unstable. ➤➤ **destabilization** /-'zaysh(ə)n/ *noun.*

destination /desti'naysh(ə)n/ *noun* a place which is set for the end of a journey or to which something is sent.

destine /'destin/ *verb trans* (*usu in passive*) **1** (+ for) to designate or dedicate (something or somebody) in advance; to set (them or it) apart for a specified purpose or goal: *She believed she was destined for great things.* **2** (*usu* + for) to direct (something) to a place: *At the harbour there was freight destined for various English ports.* [Middle English *destinen* via French from Latin *destinare* to make firm, establish]

destiny /'destini/ *noun* (*pl* **destinies**) **1** the power or agency held to determine the course of events; fate. **2** something to which a person or thing is destined; their fate or fortune. **3** a predetermined course of events. [Middle English *destinee* from French, fem past part. of *destiner:* see DESTINE]

destitute /'destityooht/ *adj* **1** lacking the basic necessities of life; extremely poor. **2** (+ of) lacking something necessary or desirable: *Hers was a heart destitute of feeling.* ➤➤ **destitution** /-'tyoohsh(ə)n/ *noun.* [Middle English from Latin *destitutus,* past part. of *destituere* to abandon, deprive, from DE- + *statuere* to set up]

destrier /'destri-ə/ *noun archaic* a war-horse or charger. [Middle English via French from Latin *dextra,* fem of *dexter* right; because when it was not being ridden on by the knight, the destrier was led by the squire on the right of his own horse]

destroy /di'stroy/ *verb trans* **1** to demolish or ruin (something): *The nation that destroys its soil destroys itself* — Franklin D Roosevelt. **2a** to put an end to (somebody); to kill (them). **b** to kill (an animal) humanely. **3** to make (something) ineffective; to neutralize (it). **4** *informal* to beat (somebody) thoroughly: *The lads went out there and totally destroyed the United defence.* [Middle English *destroyen* via French from Latin *destruere,* from DE- + *struere* to build]

destroyer *noun* **1** somebody or something that destroys. **2** a fast multi-purpose warship smaller than a cruiser.

destruct[1] /di'strukt/ *verb trans* to destroy (something or somebody, *esp* a missile or rocket of one's own, e.g. on grounds of safety).

>> **destructibility** /-'biliti/ *noun,* **destructible** *adj.* [back-formation from DESTRUCTION]

destruct² *noun* **1** the deliberate destruction of a device, e.g. one's own missile or rocket. **2** (*used before a noun*) used for destroying a device: *Something's gone wrong! Press the destruct button.*

destruction /di'struksh(ə)n/ *noun* **1** the act or an instance of destroying or being destroyed. **2** a cause of ruin or downfall. [Middle English *destruccioun* via French from Latin *destruction-, destructio,* from *destruere* to destroy]

destructive /di'struktiv/ *adj* **1a** causing destruction. **b** designed or tending to destroy. **2** said of criticism, etc: pointing out faults and failings without offering ideas for improvement; not constructive. >> **destructively** *adv,* **destructiveness** *noun*

destructive distillation *noun* decomposition of a substance, e.g. wood, coal, or oil, by heating in a closed container and collecting the volatile products.

destructor *noun* **1** an incinerator for refuse. **2** a device for destroying a missile or rocket.

desuetude /'deswityoohd, di'syooh-ityoohd/ *noun formal* discontinuance from use; disuse: *The rules of life which he had drawn about himself fell into desuetude* — James Joyce. [French *désuétude* from Latin *desuetudo,* from *desuetus,* past part. of *desuescere* to become unaccustomed, from DE- + *suescere* to become accustomed]

desulphurize *or* **desulphurise** (*NAmer* **desulfurize**) /dee-'sulfəriez/ *verb trans* to remove sulphur or sulphur compounds from (e.g. petroleum products). >> **desulphurization** /-'zaysh(ə)n/ *noun,* **desulphurizer** *noun.*

desultory /'desəlt(ə)ri, 'dez-/ *adj* **1** passing aimlessly from one subject or activity to another. **2** random; haphazard; happening on and off: *There has been desultory guerrilla warfare in the region for years.* >> **desultorily** *adv,* **desultoriness** *noun.* [Latin *desultorius* superficial, literally 'leaping off', from *desilire* to leap down, from DE- + *salire* to leap]

Det. *abbr* Detective.

detach /di'tach/ *verb trans* **1** to separate (something), *esp* from a larger mass and usu without causing damage. **2** to separate (something) from a parent organization or larger group for a special purpose: *A ship was detached from the fleet and sent to intercept the destroyer.* **3** (*often* + from) to keep (oneself) emotionally detached from something. >> **detachability** /-'biliti/ *noun,* **detachable** *adj,* **detachably** *adv.* [French *détacher* from Old French *destachier,* from DE- + *-tachier* as in *atachier* to ATTACH]

detached *adj* **1** said of a house: standing by itself; not sharing any wall with another building. **2** said of a person: free from prejudice or emotional involvement; aloof. **3** said of the retina of the eye: having become separated from the CHOROID¹ (tissue behind the retina), so causing loss of vision in the affected part. >> **detachedly** *adv,* **detachedness** *noun.*

detachment *noun* **1a** freedom from bias or emotional involvement. **b** indifference to worldly concerns. **2** (*treated as sing. or pl*) a body of troops, ships, etc separated from the main body for a special mission. **3** the act or an instance of detaching; separation.

detail¹ /'deetayl/ *noun* **1a** a part considered separately from the whole. **b** (*usu in pl*) an individual relevant part or fact: *Can you let me have the details by tonight, please?* **c** a small and subordinate part; *specif* part of a work of art considered or reproduced in isolation. **2** extended treatment of or attention to particular items: *attention to detail.* **3a** (*treated as sing. or pl*) a small military detachment selected for a particular task. **b** the task to be performed by a military detail. ✳ **in detail** item by item; thoroughly. [French *détail,* from Old French, literally 'slice, piece', from *détaillier* to cut up, from DE- + *taillier* to cut]

detail² *verb trans* **1** to report (something) in detail. **2** to assign (somebody) to a particular task or place.

detailed *adj* marked by abundant detail or thorough treatment: *He gave a detailed account of the battle.*

detain /di'tayn/ *verb trans* **1** to delay (somebody); to hold (them) back. **2** to hold or retain (somebody) in custody, or as if in custody: *She was detained in hospital overnight.* >> **detainable** *adj,* **detainment** *noun.* [Middle English *deteynen* via Old French *detenir* from Latin *detinēre,* from DE- + *tenēre* to hold]

detainee /deetay'nee/ *noun* a person held in custody, *esp* for political reasons.

detainer *noun* **1** the withholding from the rightful owner of something which has lawfully come into the possession of the holder. **2** detention in custody, or a writ authorizing it. [Anglo-French *detener,* from Old French *detenir:* see DETAIN]

detect /di'tekt/ *verb trans* **1** to discover the existence or discern the presence of (something or somebody). **2** to discover (a crime or criminal). >> **detectability** /-'biliti/ *noun,* **detectable** *adj,* **detection** *noun.* [Middle English *detecten* from Latin *detectus,* past part. of *detegere* to uncover, detect, from DE- + *tegere* to cover]

detective¹ /di'tektiv/ *noun* **1** a police officer or other person engaged in investigating crimes, detecting lawbreakers, etc. **2** somebody involved in or good at getting information that is not readily accessible.

detective² *adj* **1** of detectives or their work: *a detective novel. After a bit of detective work, I discovered I was related to the Archbishop of Canterbury.* **2** used in detecting something.

detector *noun* **1** a device used to detect the presence of radiation, particles, or physical substances or objects. **2** a part of an electrical circuit used in extracting the audio or visual information from a radio wave; a demodulator

detent /di'tent/ *noun* a device that locks or unlocks one mechanical part in relation to another, *esp* in a clock. [French *détente* from early French *destente,* from DE- + *tendre* to stretch, from Latin *tendere*]

détente *or* **detente** /day'tonht/ *noun* a relaxation of strained relations, e.g. between ideologically opposed nations. [French *détente:* see DETENT]

detention /di'tensh(ə)n/ *noun* **1** the act or an instance of detaining or being detained, *esp* in custody. **2** *chiefly Brit* the act or an instance of keeping in a pupil after school hours as a punishment. [via French from late Latin *detention-, detentio,* from Latin *detinēre:* see DETAIN]

detention centre *noun* an institution for the detention of young offenders for short periods.

deter /di'tuh/ *verb trans* (**deterred, deterring**) **1** (*often* + from) to discourage or prevent (somebody) from acting. **2** to prevent (something) happening; to discourage people from doing (something). [Latin *deterrēre,* from DE- + *terrēre* to frighten]

detergent¹ /di'tuhj(ə)nt/ *noun* a cleansing agent; *specif* any of various synthetic water-soluble compounds that are chemically different from soaps but have similar cleansing properties. [French *détergent* from Latin *detergent-, detergens,* present part. of *detergēre* to wipe off, cleanse, from DE- + *tergēre* to wipe]

detergent² *adj* cleaning or cleansing: *a substance with strong detergent properties.*

deteriorate /di'tiəri-ərayt/ *verb intrans* to grow worse. >> *verb trans* to make (something) worse. >> **deterioration** /-'raysh(ə)n/ *noun,* **deteriorative** /-rətiv/ *adj.* [late Latin *deterioratus,* past part. of *deteriorare,* from Latin *deterior* worse]

determinable /di'tuhminəbl/ *adj* **1** capable of being determined, definitely ascertained, or decided upon. **2** in law, liable to be terminated; terminable.

determinant /di'tuhminənt/ *noun* **1** something that determines, fixes, or conditions. **2** something that is inherited and produces a genetic effect, *esp* a gene. **3** in mathematics: **a** an array of symbols or numbers written in the form of a square matrix bordered on either side by a vertical line. **b** a value assigned to a determinant obtained by manipulating its elements according to a certain rule.

determinate /di'tuhminət/ *adj* **1** fixed; established. **2** conclusively determined; definitive. **3** said of a flowering plant: cymose (see CYME). >> **determinacy** /-si/ *noun,* **determinately** *adv,* **determinateness** *noun.* [Middle English from Latin *determinatus,* past part. of *determinare:* see DETERMINE]

determination /di,tuhmi'naysh(ə)n/ *noun* **1a** firm intention. **b** the ability to make and act on firm decisions; resoluteness. **2** the act or an instance of determining something. **3** a judicial decision settling a dispute. **4** in law, the terminating of a contract, right, etc.

determinative¹ /di'tuhminətiv/ *adj* serving to determine. >> **determinatively** *adv.*

determinative² *noun* **1** something serving to determine. **2** = DETERMINER (2).

determine /di'tuhmin/ *verb trans* **1a** to fix (something) conclusively or authoritatively. **b** to settle or decide (something): *You have to determine the rights and wrongs of the case.* **2a** to fix (something) beforehand. **b** to regulate (something): *Demand determines the price.* **c** in mathematics, to specify the value, position, or form of (a quantity, a point, a figure, etc). **3a** to ascertain the intent, nature, or scope of (something). **b** *archaic* to set an end to (an estate, etc). **4** in law, to put or set an end to (something); to terminate (a contract, etc). ➤ *verb intrans* **1** to come to a decision: *He determined to ask her out.* **2** *archaic* in law, to come to an end or become void. [Middle English *determinen* via French from Latin *determinare*, from DE- + *terminare* to limit, from *terminus* limit, end]

determined *adj* **1** decided; resolved: *I was determined to learn to drive.* **2** firm; resolute: *a very determined woman.* ➤➤ **determinedly** *adv*, **determinedness** *noun*.

determiner *noun* **1** something or somebody that determines. **2** a word that limits the meaning of a noun and comes before a descriptive adjective modifying the same noun, e.g. *his* in 'his new car'.

determinism *noun* **1** a doctrine that all phenomena are determined by preceding occurrences, *esp* the doctrine that all human acts, choices, etc are causally determined and that free will is illusory. **2** a belief in predestination. ➤➤ **determinist** *noun and adj*, **deterministic** /-'nistik/ *adj*, **deterministically** /-'nistikli/ *adv*.

deterrent[1] /di'terənt/ *noun* something that deters; *specif* a weapon, *esp* a nuclear weapon, that is held in readiness by one nation or alliance in order to deter another from attacking. [Latin *deterrent-, deterrens*, present part. of *deterrēre*: see DETER]

deterrent[2] *adj* serving to deter. ➤➤ **deterrence** *noun*, **deterrently** *adv*.

detest /di'test/ *verb trans* to feel intense dislike for (something or somebody); to loathe (it or them). ➤➤ **detester** *noun*. [Middle English *detesten* from Latin *detestari*, literally 'to curse while calling a deity to witness', from DE- + *testari* to call to witness]

detestable /di'testabl/ *adj* arousing or deserving intense dislike; hateful. ➤➤ **detestably** *adv*.

detestation /deetes'taysh(ə)n/ *noun* extreme dislike; abhorrence.

dethrone /dee'throhn/ *verb trans* **1** to depose (a monarch). **2** to depose or remove (somebody) from a position of power or authority. ➤➤ **dethronement** *noun*.

detinue /'detinyooh/ *noun* the unlawful detention of a piece of personal property. [Middle English *detenewe* from early French *detenue* detention, past part. of *detenir*: see DETAIN]

detonate /'detənayt/ *verb trans* to cause (a bomb, etc) to explode with sudden violence. ➤ *verb intrans* said of a bomb, etc: to explode. ➤➤ **detonation** *noun*, **detonative** /-tiv/ *adj*. [Latin *detonatus*, past part. of *detonare* to thunder down, from DE- + *tonare* to thunder]

detonator *noun* **1** a device used for detonating a high explosive. **2** *Brit* a device, clipped onto a railway line, that detonates as a train passes to warn of *esp* fog or emergency.

detour[1] /'deetooə/ *noun* a deviation from a course or procedure; *specif* a way that is an alternative to a shorter or planned route. [French *détour* from Old French *destor*, from *destorner* to divert, from DE- + *torner* to turn, from Latin *tornare*]

detour[2] *verb intrans* to make a detour. ➤ *verb trans* to send (somebody or something) by a roundabout route.

detox[1] /'deetoks/ *noun informal* detoxification, or a detoxification centre: *He's been in detox three times.*

detox[2] *verb trans* = DETOXIFY. ➤ *verb intrans* to be detoxified.

detoxicate /dee'toksikayt/ *verb trans* = DETOXIFY. ➤➤ **detoxicant** *noun*, **detoxication** /-'kaysh(ə)n/ *noun*. [DE- + Latin *toxicum* poison]

detoxification centre /dee,toksifi'kaysh(ə)n/ *noun* a place, e.g. a clinic, where patients are treated for alcoholism or drug addiction.

detoxify /dee'toksifie/ *verb trans* (**detoxifies, detoxified, detoxifying**) **1** to remove a poison or toxin from (something or somebody). **2** to treat (somebody) for dependency on alcohol or drugs. ➤➤ **detoxification** /di,toksifi'kaysh(ə)n/ *noun*.

DETR *abbr Brit* formerly, Department of the Environment, Transport, and the Regions.

detract /di'trakt/ *verb intrans* (+ from) to take away something desirable from something; to make something less valuable, desirable, interesting, etc. [Middle English *detracten* from Latin *detractus*, past part. of *detrahere* to withdraw, disparage, from DE- + *trahere* to draw]

detraction /di'traksh(ə)n/ *noun* belittling; disparagement. ➤➤ **detractive** /-tiv/ *adj*.

detractor *noun* a person who denigrates somebody or their ideas or beliefs: *Her detractors were more vociferous than her supporters.*

detrain /dee'trayn/ *verb intrans* to alight from a railway train. ➤ *verb trans* to remove (somebody or something) from a train. ➤➤ **detrainment** *noun*.

detriment /'detrimənt/ *noun* injury or damage, or a cause of this. [Middle English via French from Latin *detrimentum*, from *deterere* to wear away, impair, from DE- + *terere* to rub]

detrimental /detri'mentl/ *adj* harmful, damaging. ➤➤ **detrimentally** *adv*.

detrition /di'trish(ə)n/ *noun* the act or an instance of wearing away, *esp* by rubbing. [Latin *detrition-, detritio*, from *deterere*: see DETRIMENT]

detritus /di'trietəs/ *noun* **1** loose material, e.g. rock fragments or organic particles, produced by disintegration. **2** debris or waste material: *The floods carry along the waste and detritus of a large population.* ➤➤ **detrital** *adj*. [French *détritus* from Latin *detritus*, past part. of *deterere*: see DETRIMENT]

de trop /də 'troh (*French* də tro)/ *adj* not wanted or needed; superfluous. [French *de trop* excessive]

detumescence /deetyooh'mes(ə)ns/ *noun* subsidence or diminution of swelling. ➤➤ **detumescent** *adj*.

deuce /dyoohs/ *noun* **1** a playing card or the face of a dice representing the number two. **2** a tie in a game, e.g. tennis, after which a side must score two consecutive clear points to win. **3** *informal* (*formerly used as an interjection or intensive*). **a** (**the deuce**) the devil; the dickens. **b** something very bad or remarkable of its kind: *a deuce of a mess.* [early French *deus* two, from Latin *duo*; (sense 3) prob from Low German *duus* deuce, the worst throw with a pair of dice]

deuced[1] /'dyoohsid, dyoohst/ *adj informal* damned or confounded. ➤➤ **deucedly** /'dyoohsidli/ *adv*.

deuced[2] /dyoohst/ *adv* deucedly: *It's deuced good of you to help.*

deus ex machina /,dayəs eks 'makinə/ *noun* (*pl* **dei ex machina** /'dayee/) somebody or something, e.g. in fiction or drama, that appears or is introduced suddenly and unexpectedly and provides a contrived solution to an apparently insoluble difficulty.

Word history
In Greek theatre actors representing gods were suspended above the stage on a kind of crane, by which they could be lowered to intervene in the action and bring about the denouement:

The beast is evidently as much of a pawn as Jonah; its providential appearance just as the sailors are tossing Jonah overboard smacks far too heavily of a deus ex machina — Julian Barnes.

Word history
Latin *deus ex machina* a god from a machine, translation of Greek *theos ek mēchanēs*. In Greek theatre actors representing gods were suspended above the stage on a kind of crane, by which they could be lowered to intervene in the action and bring about the denouement.

Deut. *abbr* Deuteronomy.

deuter-[1] *or* **deutero-** *comb. form* forming words, with the meaning: second or secondary: *deuterium.* [Greek *deuteros* second]

deuter-[2] *or* **deutero-** *comb. form* forming words, with the meaning: deuterium; containing deuterium: *deuterate.*

deuteranopia /,dyoohtərə'nohpi·ə/ *noun* a form of colour blindness resulting in the inability to distinguish between greens, reds, and yellows. It is caused by insensitivity to green light: compare PROTANOPIA, TRITANOPIA. [DEUTER-[1] + AN- + -OPIA]

deuterate /'dyoohtərayt/ *verb trans* to introduce deuterium into (a compound). ➤➤ **deuteration** /-'raysh(ə)n/ *noun*.

deuteride /'dyoohtəried/ *noun* any of various compounds containing deuterium in place of hydrogen.

deuterium /dyooh'tiəri·əm/ *noun* the hydrogen isotope that is twice the mass of ordinary hydrogen: symbol D: compare HYDROGEN, PROTIUM, TRITIUM. [scientific Latin *deuterium*, from DEUTER-[1]; because it is the second of the series of possible hydrogen isotopes]

deutero- *comb. form* see DEUTER-[1], DEUTER-[2].

Deutschmark /'doychmahk/ *or* **Deutsche Mark** /'doychə mahk (*German* 'dɔɪtʃə mark)/ *noun* the basic monetary unit of Germany, divided into 100 pfennig. [German *Deutschmark* German mark]

deutzia /'dyoohtsi·ə, 'doytsi·ə/ *noun* an ornamental shrub of the saxifrage family with white or pink flowers: genus *Deutzia*. [Latin genus name, named after Jean *Deutz* d.1784?, Dutch patron of botanical research]

devaluate /dee'valyoohayt/ *verb* = DEVALUE.

devaluation /dee,valyoo'aysh(ə)n/ *noun* **1** a reduction in the exchange value of a currency. **2** a lessening, *esp* of status or stature.

devalue /dee'valyooh/ *verb trans* **1** to reduce the exchange value of (money). **2** to lessen the value or reputation of (something or somebody). ⪢ *verb intrans* to institute devaluation.

Devanagari /dayvə'nahg(ə)ri/ *noun* the alphabet used for writing Sanskrit and various modern languages of India. [Sanskrit *devanāgarī*, from *deva* divine + *nāgarī* script of the city]

devastate /'devəstayt/ *verb trans* **1** to reduce (a place) to ruin; to lay (it) waste. **2** to have a shattering effect on (somebody or something); to overwhelm (them), e.g. with grief or horror: *He was utterly devastated by the news of his mother's death.* ⪢ **devastation** /-'staysh(ə)n/ *noun*, **devastator** *noun*. [Latin *devastatus*, past part. of *devastare*, from DE- + *vastare* to lay waste]

devastating /'devəstayting/ *adj* **1** causing great destruction. **2** overwhelming with e.g. grief or horror: *devastating news.* **3** *informal* extremely attractive or impressive: *You look absolutely devastating, my darling.* ⪢ **devastatingly** *adv*.

develop /di'veləp/ *verb* (**developed, developing**) ⪢ *verb intrans* **1a** to go through a process of natural growth, differentiation, or evolution by successive changes. **b** to evolve; to grow. **2** to become gradually visible or apparent. **3** in chess, to move one's pieces to positions providing more opportunity for effective use. ⪢ *verb trans* **1a** to unfold (an idea) gradually or in detail; to expound (it). **b** to show signs of (an illness). **c** to subject (exposed photographic material) to chemicals, in order to produce a visible image, or to make (it) visible by such a method. **d** to elaborate (a musical theme) by the working out of rhythmic and harmonic changes. **2** to bring out the possibilities of (something). **3a** to promote the growth of (something): *She developed her muscles.* **b** to make (resources, etc) more available or usable. **c** to build on or change the use of (a tract of land). **d** to move (a chess piece) to a position providing more opportunity for effective use. **4** to cause (something) to grow, mature, or increase. **5** to acquire (something) gradually: *He developed a taste for good wine.* ⪢ **developable** *adj*. [French *développer* from Old French *desvoloper* to unwrap, from DE- + *voloper* to wrap]

developed *adj* said of a country: having achieved a high economic level of industrialization and a high standard of living.

developer *noun* **1** a chemical used to develop exposed photographic materials. **2** a person who develops real estate, *esp* somebody who improves and subdivides land and builds and sells houses on it.

developing *adj* said of a country: underdeveloped.

development *noun* **1a** the act or an instance of developing or being developed. **b** the result of this, e.g. an innovation or new product. **2** something which changes a situation: *There's been a new development and the strike has been called off.* **3** an area of new building: *There's going to be a major housing development here.* **4** in music, the treatment of previously heard themes and phrases, *esp* the central section of a musical movement written in sonata form. ⪢ **developmental** /-'mentl/ *adj*, **developmentally** /-'mentəli/ *adv*.

developmental disorder *noun* a psychological disorder that develops during infancy and childhood and is characterized by a delay in the development in one or more mental functions that develop during that period.

development area *noun Brit* an area of high unemployment where government encouragement is given to new industries.

deviant[1] /'deevi·ənt/ *adj* **1** deviating, *esp* from a norm. **2** characterized by deviation. ⪢ **deviance** *noun*, **deviancy** /-si/ *noun*.

deviant[2] *noun* a person whose behaviour differs markedly from the norm, *esp* with regard to their sexual or social behaviour.

deviate[1] /'deeviayt/ *verb intrans* to stray, *esp* from a topic, principle, or accepted norm, or from a straight course. ⪢ **deviator** *noun*, **deviatory** /-ət(ə)ri/ *adj*. [late Latin *deviatus*, past part. of *deviare*, from Latin DE- + *via* way]

deviate[2] /'deevi·ət/ *noun dated* = DEVIANT[2].

deviation /deevi'aysh(ə)n/ *noun* **1** departure from accepted norms of behaviour, *esp* sexual or social behaviour. **2** departure from an established party line. **3** the difference between a value in a frequency distribution and a fixed number. **4** deflection of a compass needle caused by local magnetic influences. ⪢ **deviationism** *noun*, **deviationist** *noun and adj*.

device /di'vies/ *noun* **1a** a piece of equipment or a mechanism designed for a special purpose or function. **b** a scheme to trick or deceive. **c** something, e.g. a figure of speech or a dramatic convention, designed to achieve a particular artistic effect. **d** something elaborate or intricate in design. **2a** an emblematic design with a motto used as a heraldic bearing: compare CHARGE[2] (7). **b** a motto. ⁕ **leave somebody to their own devices** to leave somebody alone to do as they please. [Middle English *devis, devise* division, intention, from Old French from *deviser* to divide, regulate, tell, from Latin *dividere*: see DIVIDE[1]]

devil[1] /'devl/ *noun* **1** (*usu* **the Devil**) the supreme spirit of evil in Jewish and Christian belief. **2** a malignant spirit; a demon. **3** an extremely cruel or wicked person; a fiend. **4** a high-spirited, reckless, or energetic person. **5** *informal* a person of the specified type: *You're a lucky devil.* **6a** (**the devil**) *informal* something provoking, difficult, or trying: *This type of bottle is the very devil to open.* **b** used as an interjection or intensive: *What the devil is that?* **7a** *dated, informal* a junior legal counsel working without payment to gain experience. **b** = PRINTER'S DEVIL. **8** any of various machines or devices, e.g. a paper shredder. ⁕ **between the devil and the deep blue sea** faced with two equally unwelcome alternatives. **give the devil his due** to give desired credit to an opponent or an unpleasant person. **go to the devil 1** to fail completely; to be ruined. **2** to become depraved. **3** said in anger, rejection, etc: to go away: *Tell him to go to the devil!* **like the devil** *informal* with great speed, intensity, etc. **play the devil with** to cause damage or disruption to (something): *This cold wind plays the devil with my sinuses.* **speak/talk of the devil** said when somebody appears who has just been mentioned [from the proverb *talk of the devil and he's sure to appear*]. **the devil to pay** a lot of trouble: *There'll be the devil to pay if she catches us.* [Old English *dēofol* via late Latin *diabolus* from Greek *diabolos*, literally 'slanderer']

devil[2] *verb* (**devilled, devilling**, *NAmer* **deviled, deviling**) ⪢ *verb trans* **1** to season (food) highly, *esp* with peppery condiments: *devilled kidneys.* **2** *NAmer, informal* to tease or annoy (somebody). ⪢ *verb intrans* to serve or function as a legal devil.

devilfish *noun* (*pl* **devilfishes** *or collectively* **devilfish**) **1** *Brit* = ANGLERFISH. **2** *chiefly NAmer* = MANTA RAY. **3** a large octopus, squid, or similar creature.

devilish[1] *adj* of or characteristic of a devil; wicked: *devilish tricks.* ⪢ **devilishly** *adv*, **devilishness** *noun*.

devilish[2] *adv dated, informal* very or extremely: *He's devilish handsome.*

devil-may-care *adj* heedless of authority or convention.

devilment *noun* wild mischief.

devil ray *noun NAmer* = MANTA RAY.

devilry /'devlri/ *noun* (*pl* **devilries**) **1** mischief, or an act of mischief. **2** action performed with the help of the devil; witchcraft.

devil's advocate *noun* **1** a person who champions the less accepted or approved cause, *esp* for the sake of argument. **2** formerly, the Roman Catholic official who presented the possible objections to a deceased person's claims to canonization or to the title 'Blessed'. [translation of Latin *advocatus diaboli*]

devil's coach horse *noun* a large predatory ROVE BEETLE: *Staphylinus olens.*

devil's food cake *noun chiefly NAmer* a type of rich dark chocolate cake.

deviltry /'devltri/ *noun* (*pl* **deviltries**) *archaic* devilry.

devious /'deevi·əs/ *adj* **1** said of a person: not straightforward or wholly sincere. **2** tortuously underhand: *by devious means.* **3** roundabout or circuitous: *We went by a rather devious route.* ⪢ **deviously** *adv*, **deviousness** *noun*. [Latin *devius*, from DE- + *via* way]

devise[1] /di'viez/ *verb trans* **1a** to formulate (a plan) in the mind; to invent (it). **b** to plan or plot (something). **2** to give or leave (real property) by will: compare BEQUEATH. ⪢ **devisable** *adj*, **deviser** *noun*. [Middle English *devisen* via French from Latin *divisus*, past part. of *dividere*: see DIVIDE[1]]

devise[2] *noun* **1** a devising act or clause. **2** property devised by will.

devisee /divie'zee/ *noun* somebody to whom a devise of property is made.

devisor *noun* somebody who devises property in a will.

devitalize *or* **devitalise** /dee'vietəliez/ *verb trans* to deprive (somebody) of life, vigour, or effectiveness. >> **devitalization** *noun*.

devoice /dee'voys/ *verb trans* to pronounce (a sometimes or formerly voiced sound) without vibration of the vocal cords.

devoid /di'voyd/ *adj* (+ of) not having or using; lacking: *I am dotingly fond of music … and my friends tell me I am not entirely devoid of taste* — Jane Austen. [Middle English from Old French *desvoidier* to empty out, from DE- + *vuidier*: see VOID³]

devoir /'devwah, dəv'wah/ *noun* **1** *archaic* duty; responsibility. **2** *archaic or literary* (*in pl*) respects; compliments: *We must of course call on them to pay our devoirs*. [Middle English, alteration of *dever* from Old French *deveir*, from *devoir, deveir* to owe, be obliged, from Latin *debēre*]

devolution /deevə'loohsh(ə)n/ *noun* **1** the surrender of functions and powers to regional or local authorities by a central government.

Editorial note
Devolution is literally a handing down from a superior to an inferior. In politics, it may be defined as consisting of three elements: the transfer to a subordinate body; on a geographical basis; of functions exercised by the legislature or by ministers. Devolution offers a way of transferring power without undermining the basis of the unitary state — Professor Vernon Bogdanor.

2 delegation or conferral to a subordinate. **3** the passage of rights, property, etc to a successor. >> **devolutionary** *adj*, **devolutionist** *noun*. [Latin *devolution-, devolutio*, from *devolvere*: see DEVOLVE]

devolve /di'volv/ *verb trans* **1** (*usu* + on/upon/to) to transfer (property or a responsibility or duty) from one person to another; to hand (it) down. **2** (*usu* + on/upon/to) to surrender (power) by devolution. > *verb intrans* **1** (*usu* + on/upon/to) to pass by transmission or succession. **2** (*usu* + on/upon/to) to fall or be passed, usu as an obligation or responsibility. [Middle English *devolven* from Latin *devolvere* to roll down, from DE- + *volvere* to roll]

Devonian /de'vohni·ən/ *adj* **1** of Devon. **2** relating to or dating from a geological period, the fourth period of the Palaeozoic era, lasting from about 409 million to about 363 million years ago, and marked by the first appearance of insects and amphibians. >> **Devonian** *noun*. [*Devon*, county in England; (sense 2) from the large formation of rocks of this period centred in Devon]

devoré /də'vawray/ *noun* a velvet fabric having a pattern etched with acid. [French *dévoré* devoured, past part. of *dévorer*: see DEVOUR]

devote /di'voht/ *verb trans* **1** (+ to) to set (something) apart for a special purpose; to dedicate (it) to something. **2** (+ to) to give (oneself) over wholly to something or somebody. [Latin *devotus*, past part. of *devovēre*, from DE- + *vovēre* to vow]

devoted *adj* **1** (*also* + to) very loving: *a devoted mother*. **2** (*also* + to) loyally attached: *a devoted friend*. **3** (*usu* + to) giving a lot of time, effort, etc to something; dedicated: *He was devoted to his garden*. >> **devotedly** *adv*.

devotee /devə'tee/ *noun* **1** a keen follower or supporter; an enthusiast: *a devotee of opera*. **2** a deeply religious person.

devotion /di'vohsh(ə)n/ *noun* **1a** (*also* + to) great love, affection, or dedication. **b** (*usu* + to) the act or an instance of devoting or being devoted. **2a** religious zeal; piety. **b** (*usu in pl*) a special act of prayer or supplication. >> **devotional** *adj*.

devour /di'vowə/ *verb trans* **1** to eat (food) up greedily or ravenously. **2** *literary* to swallow (something) up; to consume (it): *The house was devoured by the fire*. **3** (*usu in passive*) said *esp* of a feeling: to preoccupy or absorb (somebody): *preyed upon by a devouring curiosity to be informed of all I had seen and heard* — Dickens. **4** to take (something) in eagerly through the mind or senses: *She absolutely devours books*. >> **devourer** *noun*. [Middle English *devouren* from early French *devorer* from Latin *devorare*, from DE- + *vorare* to devour]

devout /di'vowt/ *adj* **1** devoted to religion; pious. **2** sincere; genuine: *a devout hope*. >> **devoutly** *adv*, **devoutness** *noun*. [Middle English *devot* via French from late Latin *devotus*, from Latin, past part. of *devovēre*: see DEVOTE]

DEW *abbr* distant early warning.

dew¹ /dyooh/ *noun* **1** moisture that condenses on the surfaces of cool bodies, *esp* at night. **2** any minute droplets of moisture, e.g. tears or sweat. [Old English *dēaw*]

dew² *verb trans literary* to cover (something) with dew or other beads of moisture.

dewan /di'wahn/ *noun* an Indian official, *esp* the prime minister or finance minister of an Indian state. [Hindi *dīwān* from Persian, account book]

Dewar flask /'dyooh·ə/ *noun* a glass or metal vacuum flask that is used *esp* in laboratories for storing liquefied gases. [named after Sir James *Dewar* d.1923, Scots chemist and physicist, who invented it]

dewberry /'dyoohb(ə)ri/ *noun* (*pl* **dewberries**) **1** any of several species of shrubs resembling the blackberry: genus *Rubus*. **2** the berry of the dewberry.

dewclaw *noun* a vestigial digit not reaching to the ground on the foot of a mammal, or a claw or hoof at the end of this. >> **dewclawed** *adj*.

dewdrop *noun* a drop of dew.

Dewey decimal classification /'dyooh·i/ *noun* a book classification whereby main classes are shown by a three-digit number and subdivisions by numbers after a decimal point. [named after Melvil *Dewey* d.1931, US librarian, who devised the system]

dewfall *noun literary* the time when dew forms.

dewlap *noun* a hanging fold of skin under the neck of an animal, e.g. a cow.

dew point *noun* the temperature of the air at which dew begins to be deposited.

dew pond *noun* a shallow, usu artificial, pond thought to be filled by the condensation of dew.

dewy *adj* (**dewier, dewiest**) moist with dew, or as if with dew. >> **dewily** *adv*, **dewiness** *noun*.

dewy-eyed *adj* naively credulous or trusting.

Dexedrine /'deksədreen, -drin/ *noun trademark* a preparation of the stimulatory drug dextroamphetamine sulphate. [prob from DEXTR-, modelled on BENZEDRINE]

dexter /'dekstə/ *adj* of or on the right-hand side of a heraldic shield from the bearer's point of view: compare SINISTER (3). [Latin *dexter* of or on the right]

dexterity /dek'steriti/ *noun* **1** skill and ease in using the hands. **2** physical or mental nimbleness or agility: *O most wicked speed, to post with such dexterity to incestuous sheets!* — Shakespeare. [via French from Latin *dexteritat-, dexteritas*, from *dexter* right]

dexterous /'dekst(ə)rəs/ *or* **dextrous** /'dekstrəs/ *adj* **1** skilful with the hands. **2** mentally adroit. >> **dexterously** *adv*. [Latin *dexter* dextral, skilful; because for most people the right hand is more skilful]

dextr- *or* **dextro-** *comb. form* forming words, with the meaning: on or towards the right; right: *dextral*. [late Latin, from Latin *dexter* right]

dextral /'dekstrəl/ *adj* **1** of or inclined to the right. **2a** right-handed. **b** said of the shell of a gastropod mollusc: having whorls that turn in an anticlockwise direction from the top to the bottom: compare SINISTRAL. >> **dextrality** /dek'straliti/ *noun*, **dextrally** *adv*.

dextran /'dekstrən/ *noun* **1** any of numerous polysaccharides (chemicals whose molecules consist of chains of sugar molecules: see POLYSACCHARIDE) that yield only glucose on hydrolysis. **2** a compound obtained from dextran and used as a plasma substitute. [DEXTR- + -AN³]

dextrin /'dekstrin/ *noun* any of various soluble gummy polysaccharides (chemicals whose molecules consist of chains of sugar molecules: see POLYSACCHARIDE) used as adhesives and as sizes for paper and textiles. [French *dextrine*, from DEXTR- + -INE²]

dextro- *comb. form* see DEXTR-.

dextrorotary /dekstroh'roht(ə)ri/ *adj* = DEXTROROTATORY.

dextrorotatory /dekstroh'rohtət(ə)ri, -'taytəri/ *adj* turning clockwise or towards the right, *esp* rotating the plane of polarization of light towards the right: compare LAEVOROTATORY. >> **dextrorotation** /-'taysh(ə)n/ *noun*.

dextrorse /'dekstraws/ *adj* said of a plant: twining spirally upwards round an axis from left to right: compare SINISTRORSE. >> **dextrorsely** *adv*. [Latin *dextrorsus* towards the right, from DEXTR- + *versus*, past part. of *vertere* to turn]

dextrose /'dekstrohz, 'dekstrohs/ *noun* dextrorotatory glucose.

dextrous /'dekstrəs/ *adj* see DEXTEROUS.

DF *abbr* **1** Defender of the Faith. **2** direction finder. [(sense 1) medieval Latin *defensor fidei*]

DFC *abbr Brit* Distinguished Flying Cross.

DfEE *abbr* formerly, Department for Education and Employment.

DfES *abbr Brit* Department for Education and Skills.

DFM *abbr Brit* Distinguished Flying Medal.

DG *abbr* **1** by the grace of God. **2** director-general. **3** Thanks be to God. [(sense 1) late Latin *Dei gratia*; (sense 3) late Latin *Deo gratias*]

dg *abbr* decigram.

DH *abbr* Department of Health.

dhal *or* **dal** /dahl/ *noun* **1** a plant of the pea family that is cultivated in India and the tropics. *Cajanus cajan*. **2** a purée made up from the seeds of this plant. [Hindi *dāl*]

dhansak /'dunsahk/ *noun* an Indian dish *esp* of chicken or lamb, cooked in a thick sauce with lentils and spices. [Gujarati *dhansak*]

dharma /'dahmə/ *noun* in Hinduism and Buddhism, the fundamental concept of law, both natural and moral, based on the principle of everything in the universe acting according to its essential nature or proper station. [Sanskrit *dharma* decree, custom, from *dhārayati* he holds]

Dharuk /'durook/ *noun* an Aboriginal language, now extinct, of New South Wales.

dhobi /'dohbi/ *noun* (*pl* **dhobis**) an Indian washerman or washerwoman. [Hindi *dhobī*]

dhoti /'dohti/ *noun* (*pl* **dhotis**) a loincloth worn by Hindu men. [Hindi *dhotī*]

dhow /dow/ *noun* an Arab lateen-rigged (with triangular sail set at an angle: see LATEEN) boat, usu having a long overhanging bow and a high poop. [Arabic *dāwa*]

DHSS *abbr Brit* formerly, Department of Health and Social Security.

dhurrie *or* **durrie** /'duri/ *noun* an Indian woven rug, typically of thick coarse cotton yarn. [Hindi *darī*]

DI *abbr* **1** Detective Inspector. **2** donor insemination.

di-[1] *comb. form* forming words, with the meanings: **1** twice; twofold; double: *dichromatic*. **2** containing two atoms, groups, or chemical equivalents in the molecular structure: *dichloride*. [Middle English via French and Latin from Greek]

di-[2] *prefix* see DIA-.

dia. *abbr* diameter.

dia- *or* **di-** *prefix* forming words, with the meanings: **1** through: *diapositive*; *dielectric*. **2** across: *diameter*. [Middle English via Old French and Latin from Greek *dia* through, apart]

diabetes /die-ə'beetis, -teez/ *noun* any of various abnormal conditions characterized by the secretion and excretion of excessive amounts of urine, *esp* DIABETES MELLITUS. [via Latin from Greek *diabētēs*, from *diabainein* to go through, from DIA- + *bainein* to go; so called because of the thirst and excessive urination associated with diabetes]

diabetes insipidus /in'sipidəs/ *noun* a disorder of the pituitary gland characterized by intense thirst and by the excretion of large amounts of urine. [Latin *diabetes insipidus* insipid diabetes]

diabetes mellitus /'melitəs/ *noun* a disorder of the process by which the body uses sugars and other carbohydrates in which not enough insulin is produced or there is increased resistance to its action and which is characterized typically by abnormally great amounts of sugar in the blood and urine. [Latin *diabetes mellitus* honey-sweet diabetes]

diabetic[1] /die-ə'betik/ *adj* **1** of diabetes or diabetics: *diabetic chocolate*. **2** affected with diabetes.

diabetic[2] *noun* a person affected with diabetes.

diablerie /dee'ahbləri/ *noun* diabolical power; sorcery; = BLACK MAGIC: *The very diablerie of the woman, while it horrified and repelled, attracted in an even greater degree* — H Rider Haggard. [French *diablerie* via Old French from late Latin *diabolus*: see DEVIL[1]]

diabolic /die-ə'bolik/ *adj* **1** of or characteristic of the devil; fiendish. **2** dreadful; = DIABOLICAL (2). >> **diabolically** *adv*, **diabolicness** *noun*. [Middle English *deabolik* via French from late Latin *diabolicus*, from *diabolus*: see DEVIL[1]]

diabolical *adj* **1** of the devil. **2** *chiefly Brit*, *informal* dreadful; appalling: *It's diabolical the way he treats his wife*. >> **diabolically** *adv*, **diabolicalness** *noun*.

diabolism /die'abəliz(ə)m/ *noun* dealings with, possession by, or worship of the devil. >> **diabolist** *noun*.

diabolo /di'abəloh, dee-/ *noun* (*pl* **diabolos**) **1** a game in which a two-headed top is balanced and spun on a string stretched between two sticks. **2** the two-headed top used in the game of diabolo. >> **diabolist** *noun*. [Italian *diabolo* devil]

diachronic /die-ə'kronik/ *adj* of or dealing with the historical development of phenomena, *esp* language: compare SYNCHRONIC. >> **diachronically** *adv*.

diaconal /die'akənəl/ *adj* of a deacon or deaconess. [late Latin *diaconalis*, from *diaconus*: see DEACON]

diaconate /die'akənit, -nayt/ *noun* **1** the office of a deacon or deaconess, or their period of office. **2** the body of deacons or deaconesses.

diacritic[1] /die-ə'kritik/ *noun* a mark near or through an orthographic or phonetic character or combination of characters indicating a changed phonetic value.

diacritic[2] *adj* = DIACRITICAL.

diacritical *adj* **1** said of a mark or sign: serving as a diacritic. **2** serving to distinguish; distinctive. [Greek *diakritikos* separative, from *diakrinein* to distinguish, from DIA- + *krinein* to separate]

diadelphous /die-ə'delfəs/ *adj* said of stamens: united so as to form two sets. [DI-[1] + Greek *adelphos* brother]

diadem /'die-ədem/ *noun* **1** a crown; *specif* a headband worn as a badge of royalty. **2** regal power or dignity. [Middle English *diademe* via French and Latin from Greek *diadēma*, from *diadein* to bind round, from DIA- + *dein* to bind]

diaeresis (*NAmer* **dieresis** /die'erisis/) *noun* (*pl* **diaereses** /-seez/, *NAmer* **diereses**) **1** a mark (¨) placed over a vowel to indicate pronunciation as a separate syllable, e.g. in *naïve*, or for any other purpose. **2** the break in a verse caused by the coincidence of the end of a foot with the end of a word. >> **diaeretic** /-'retik/ *adj*. [via late Latin from Greek *diairesis*, from *diairein* to divide, from DIA- + *hairein* to take]

diag. *abbr* diagram.

diagnose /'die-əgnohz/ *verb trans* to recognize (a disease, etc) by signs and symptoms. *verb intrans* to make a diagnosis. >> **diagnosable** /-'nohzəbl/ *adj*. [back-formation from *diagnosis*]

diagnosis /die-əg'nohsis/ *noun* (*pl* **diagnoses** /-seez/) **1** the art or act of identifying a disease from its signs and symptoms, or a statement resulting from this. **2** the investigation of the cause or nature of a problem or phenomenon, or a statement resulting from this. [via Latin from Greek *diagnōsis*, from *diagignōskein* to distinguish, from DIA- + *gignōskein* to know]

diagnostic[1] /die-əg'nostik/ *adj* of or involving diagnosis. >> **diagnostically** *adv*.

diagnostic[2] *noun* (*also in pl, but treated as sing. or pl*) the art or practice of diagnosis. >> **diagnostician** /-'stish(ə)n/ *noun*.

diagonal[1] /die'ag(ə)nl/ *adj* **1** said of a line: running in an oblique direction from a reference line, e.g. the vertical. **2** joining two non-adjacent angles of a polygon or polyhedron. >> **diagonally** *adv*. [Latin *diagonalis* from Greek *diagōnios* from angle to angle, from DIA- + *gōnia* angle]

diagonal[2] *noun* **1** a diagonal straight line or plane. **2** a diagonal direction. **3** a diagonal row. **4** = SOLIDUS (1).

diagram[1] /'die-əgram/ *noun* **1** a line drawing made for mathematical or scientific purposes. **2** a drawing or design that shows the arrangement and relations, e.g. of parts. >> **diagrammatic** /-grə'matik/ *adj*, **diagrammatically** *adv*. [Greek *diagramma*, from *diagraphein* to mark out by lines, from DIA- + *graphein* to write]

diagram[2] *verb trans* (**diagrammed, diagramming**, *NAmer* **diagramed, diagraming**) to represent (something) in the form of a diagram.

dial[1] /die-əl/ *noun* **1** the graduated face of a timepiece. **2a** a face on which some measurement is registered, usu by means of numbers and a pointer. **b** a sometimes disc-shaped control or indicator on an electrical or mechanical device: *a telephone dial*. **3** a sundial. **4** *Brit*, *informal* a person's face. [Middle English, ultimately from Latin *dies* day]

dial[2] *verb* (**dialled, dialling**, *NAmer* **dialed, dialing**) *verb trans* **1** to operate a dial so as to select (a telephone number, etc). **2** to indicate, control, etc (something) by means of a dial. *verb intrans* **1** to make a call on a dial telephone. **2** to manipulate a dial. >> **dialler** *noun*.

dial. *abbr* dialect.

dialect /'die-əlekt/ *noun* **1a** a regional, social, or subordinate variety of a language, usu differing distinctively in grammar and vocabulary from the standard language. **b** such varieties collectively. **2** a variant of a computer programming language. ⧉ **dialectal** /-'lektl/ *adj*. [early French *dialecte* via Latin from Greek *dialektos* conversation, dialect, from *dialegesthai*: see DIALOGUE]

dialectic[1] /die-ə'lektik/ *noun* **1** (*usu in pl, but treated as sing. or pl*) a systematic reasoning, exposition, or argument that juxtaposes opposed or contradictory ideas and seeks to resolve their conflict. **2** the dialectical tension or opposition between two interacting forces or elements. **3** (*usu in pl, but treated as sing. or pl*) development through the stages of thesis, antithesis, and synthesis in accordance with Hegel's logic or systems derived from it. [Middle English *dialetik* intellectual investigation by means of dialogue, via French and Latin from Greek *dialektikē*, from *dialektos* conversation, from *dialegesthai*: see DIALOGUE]

dialectic[2] *adj* = DIALECTICAL.

dialectical *adj* of or in accordance with dialectic. ⧉ **dialectically** *adv*.

dialectical materialism *noun* the Marxist theory that the material basis of a reality constantly changes in a dialectical process that is independent of thought.

dialectician /,die-əlek'tish(ə)n/ *noun* somebody who is skilled in or practises dialectic.

dialectology /,die-əlek'toləji/ *noun* the study of dialect. ⧉ **dialectological** /-'lojikl/ *adj*, **dialectologist** *noun*.

dialling code *noun* the part of a telephone number that refers to an exchange rather than an individual subscriber.

dialling tone *noun* a sound heard over a telephone indicating that a number may be dialled.

dialog *noun NAmer* see DIALOGUE.

dialog box *noun NAmer* see DIALOGUE BOX.

dialogic /die-ə'lojik/ *adj* of or characterized by dialogue: *dialogic writing*.

dialogical /die-ə'lojikl/ *adj* = DIALOGIC.

dialogue (*NAmer* **dialog**) /'die-əlog/ *noun* **1a** a conversation between two or more people or between a person and a computer. **b** an exchange of ideas and opinions. **2** the conversational element of literary or dramatic composition. **3** discussion or negotiation between two nations, factions, groups, etc with conflicting interests: *One can only approve the governmental policy of dialogue between East and West*. **4** a literary work in conversational form. [early French *dialogue* via Latin from Greek *dialogos*, from *dialegesthai* to converse, from DIA- + *legein* to speak]

dialogue box (*NAmer* **dialog box**) *noun* a small window on a computer screen that prompts a response from the user.

dial tone *noun NAmer* = DIALLING TONE.

dial up *verb intrans* to connect to the Internet by means of a modem. ⧉ **dial-up** *adj and noun*.

dialysate (*NAmer* **dialyzate**) /die'alizayt/ *noun* the material that passes through the membrane in dialysis, or the liquid into which this material passes. [DIALYSIS or DIALYSE + -ATE[1]]

dialyse (*NAmer* **dialyze**) /'die-əliez/ *verb trans* to subject (a person, blood, etc) to dialysis. ⧉ *verb intrans* to undergo dialysis. ⧉ **dialysable** *adj*, **dialysation** /-'zaysh(ə)n/ *noun*, **dialyser** *noun*.

dialysis /die'alisis/ *noun* (*pl* **dialyses** /-seez/) the separation of substances in solution by means of their unequal diffusion through semipermeable membranes, *esp* the purification of blood by such means. ⧉ **dialytic** /-'litik/ *adj*. [via Latin from Greek *dialysis* separation, from *dialyein* to dissolve, from DIA- + *lyein* to loosen]

dialyze *verb trans NAmer* see DIALYSE.

diam. *abbr* diameter.

diamagnet /'die-əmagnit/ *noun* a diamagnetic substance. [back-formation from DIAMAGNETIC]

diamagnetic /,die-əmag'netik/ *adj* of or being a substance that in a magnetic field is slightly attracted towards points of lower field intensity. ⧉ **diamagnetism** /-'magnitiz(ə)m/ *noun*.

diamanté /die-ə'manti, dee-ə'montay/ *noun* **1** sparkling particles, *esp* powdered crystal, or cloth or other material decorated with these. **2** (*used before a noun*) decorated with diamanté: *a diamanté*

necklace. [French *diamanté*, past part. of *diamanter* to set with diamonds, from *diamant*: see DIAMOND[1]]

diamantiferous /,die-əmən'tifərəs/ *adj* yielding diamonds.

diameter /die'amitə/ *noun* **1** a line passing through the centre of a geometrical figure or body. **2** the length of a straight line through the centre of an object, e.g. a circle. **3** the thickness or width of something round, e.g. a pole or hole. ⧉ **diametral** *adj*. [Middle English *diametre* via French and Latin from Greek *diametros*, from DIA- + *metron* measure]

diametric /die-ə'metrik/ *adj* **1** completely opposed or opposite. **2** of or constituting a diameter. ⧉ **diametrically** *adv*.

diametrical /die-ə'metrikl/ *adj* = DIAMETRIC.

diamond[1] /'diemənd/ *noun* **1** a very hard crystalline carbon, or a piece of it, which is highly valued as a precious stone and used industrially as an abrasive and in rock drills: *I never hated a man enough to give him diamonds back* — Zsa Zsa Gabor. **2** a square or rhombus orientated so that the diagonals are horizontal and vertical. **3a** a playing card marked with one or more red diamond-shaped figures. **b** (*in pl, but treated as sing. or pl*) the suit comprising cards identified by this figure. **4** the entire playing field or the area enclosed by the bases in baseball. ⧉ **diamondiferous** /-'dif(ə)rəs/ *adj*. [Middle English *diamaunde* via early French *diamant* from late Latin *diamant-, diamas*, alteration of Latin *adamant-, adamas*, hardest metal, diamond, ultimately from Greek]

diamond[2] *adj* of a 60th or, less often, 75th anniversary: *They're celebrating their diamond wedding*.

diamondback *noun* **1** either of two species of large and deadly rattlesnakes of the southern USA with diamond-shaped markings on their back: genus *Crotalus*. **2** a terrapin with diamond-shaped markings on its shell, found on the western and Gulf coasts of the USA: genus *Malaclemys*. [from the diamond-shaped markings]

diamorphine /die-ə'mawfeen/ *noun* heroin. [contraction of *diacetylmorphine*, scientific name of heroin, from DI-[1] + ACETYL + MORPHINE]

dianthus /die'anthəs/ *noun* (*pl* **dianthuses** or **dianthi** /-thie/) = PINK[3]. [Latin *dianthus*, genus name, from Greek *dios* heavenly + *anthos* flower]

diapason /die-ə'pays(ə)n, -z(ə)n/ *noun* **1a** a principal organ stop extending through the range of the instrument. **b** a full deep burst of harmonious sound. **2** the entire range of musical tones. **3** range, scope. [Middle English via Latin from Greek (*hē*) *dia pasōn* (*chordōn symphōnia*) the concord through all the notes]

diapause /'die-əpawz/ *noun* a period of arrested development between periods of activity, e.g. in an insect. [Greek *diapausis* pause, from *diapauein* to pause, from DIA- + *pauein* to stop]

diaper[1] /'die-əpə/ *noun* **1** *chiefly NAmer* a nappy. **2** a soft, usu white, linen or cotton fabric used for tablecloths or towels. **3** an ornamental pattern consisting of one or more small repeated units of design, e.g. geometric figures. [Middle English *diapre* via French and Latin from Greek *diaspros* completely white, from DIA- + *aspros* white]

diaper[2] *verb trans* (**diapered, diapering**) **1** to put a diaper on (a baby). **2** to ornament (something) with diaper designs.

diaphanous /die'afənəs/ *adj* said of fabrics: so fine as to be almost transparent. ⧉ **diaphanously** *adv*. [via Latin from Greek *diaphanēs*, from *diaphainein* to show through, from DIA- + *phainein* to show]

diaphoresis /,die-əfə'reesis/ *noun* sweating, *esp* profuse sweating brought about by artificial means. [via late Latin from Greek *diaphorēsis*, from *diaphorein* to perspire, from DIA- + *pherein* to carry]

diaphoretic /,die-əfə'retik/ *adj* said of a drug: causing sweating. [via late Latin from Greek *diaphorētikos*, from *diaphorein*: see DIAPHORESIS]

diaphragm /'die-əfram/ *noun* **1** the partition separating the chest and abdominal cavities in mammals. **2** a dividing membrane or thin partition, *esp* in a tube. **3** a partition in a plant or the body or shell of an invertebrate animal. **4** = DUTCH CAP. **5** a device that limits the amount of light entering an optical system. **6** a thin flexible disc that is free to vibrate, e.g. in an earphone. ⧉ **diaphragmatic** /-frag'matik/ *adj*. [Middle English *diafragma* via late Latin from Greek *diaphragma*, from *diaphrassein* to barricade, from DIA- + *phrassein* to enclose]

diaphysis /die'afisis/ *noun* (*pl* **diaphyses** /-iseez/) the shaft of a long bone, e.g. the tibia: compare EPIPHYSIS. [via Latin from Greek *diaphysis* spinous process of the tibia, from *diaphyesthai* to grow between]

diapositive /die-ə'pozətiv/ *noun* a transparent photographic positive; *specif* a SLIDE².

diapsid¹ /'die'apsid/ *adj* relating to reptiles, e.g. crocodiles, lizards, snakes, and dinosaurs, having two pairs of openings in the bones of the skull that cover the temples. [from *Diapsida*, Latin name of subclass, from DI-¹ + Greek *hapsid-, hapsis* arch]

diapsid² *noun* a diapsid animal.

diarchy /'dieahki/ *noun* (*pl* **-ies,** *pl* **diarchies**) see DYARCHY.

diarist /'die-ərist/ *noun* somebody who keeps a diary.

diarrhoea (*NAmer* **diarrhea**) /die-ə'riə/ *noun* abnormally frequent intestinal evacuations with more or less fluid faeces. ▶ **diarrhoeal** *adj,* **diarrhoeic** /-'reeik/ *adj.* [Middle English *diaria* via late Latin from Greek *diarrhoia*, from *diarrhein* to flow through, from DIA- + *rhein* to flow]

diary /'die-əri/ *noun* (*pl* **diaries**) **1** a daily record of personal experiences or observations, or a book containing such a record: *I never travel without my diary. One should always have something sensational to read in the train* — Oscar Wilde. **2** *chiefly Brit* a book with dates marked in which memoranda can be noted. [Latin *diarium,* from *dies* day]

Diaspora /die'aspərə/ *noun* **1a** (**the Diaspora**) (*treated as sing. or pl*) the Jews living outside Palestine or modern Israel. **b** the settling, or area of settlement, of Jews outside Palestine after the Babylonian exile. **2** (*also* **diaspora**) a dispersion or migration, e.g. of people orig coming from the same country or having a common culture: *The American diaspora.* [Greek *diaspora* dispersion, from *diaspeirein* to scatter, from DIA- + *speirein* to sow]

diastalsis /die-ə'stalsis/ *noun* (*pl* **diastalses** /-seez/) a downward wave of contraction that occurs in the intestine during the digestion of food. ▶ **diastaltic** /-'staltik/ *adj.* [DIA- + *-stalsis* as in PERISTALSIS]

diastase /'die-əstayz/ *noun* amylase, *esp* a mixture of amylases from malt. ▶ **diastasic** /-'stayzik/ *adj.* [French *diastase* from Greek *diastasis* separation, interval, from DIA- + *stasis* placing]

diastole /die'astəli/ *noun* a rhythmically recurrent expansion; *esp* the dilation of the cavities of the heart during which they fill with blood: compare SYSTOLE. ▶ **diastolic** /-'stolik/ *adj.* [Greek *diastolē* dilatation, from *diastellein* to expand, from DIA- + *stellein* to send]

diastrophism /die'astrəfiz(ə)m/ *noun* the process of deformation of the earth's crust that produces continents, ocean basins, mountains, etc. ▶ **diastrophic** /-'strofik/ *adj,* **diastrophically** /-'strofikli/ *adv.* [Greek *diastrophē* twisting, from *diastrephein* to distort, from DIA- + *strephein* to twist]

diathermanous /die-ə'thuhmənəs/ *adj* transmitting infrared radiation. ▶ **diathermancy** /-'thuhmənsi/ *noun.*

diathermic /die-ə'thuhmik/ *adj* **1** transmitting heat. **2** relating to diathermy.

diathermy /'die-əthuhmi/ *noun* the generation of heat in tissue by electric currents for medical or surgical purposes. [Latin *diathermia,* from Greek DIA- + *thermē* heat]

diathesis /die'athəsis/ *noun* (*pl* **diatheses** /-seez/) a constitutional predisposition towards an abnormality or disease. [via Latin from Greek *diathesis* arrangement, from *diatithenai* to arrange, from DIA- + *tithenai* to set]

diatom /'die-ətəm/ *noun* a minute single-celled alga with a hard shell-like skeleton composed of silica: class Bacillariophyceae. ▶ **diatomaceous** /-'mayshəs/ *adj.* [Greek *diatomos* cut in half, from *diatemnein* to cut through, from DIA- + *temnein* to cut]

diatomic /die-ə'tomik/ *adj* consisting of two atoms.

diatomite /die'atəmiet/ *noun* a light crumbly material derived from diatom remains and used as a filter and for thermal insulation: compare KIESELGUHR.

diatonic /die-ə'tonik/ *adj* relating to a major or minor musical scale of eight notes to the octave without chromatic deviation. [via late Latin from Greek *diatonikos,* from *diatonos* stretching, from DIA- + *teinein* to stretch]

diatribe /'die-ətrieb/ *noun* a lengthy piece of bitter and abusive criticism. [via Latin from Greek *diatribē* pastime, discourse, from *diatribein* to spend (time), wear away, from DIA- + *tribein* to rub]

diazepam /die'azəpam/ *noun* a synthetic tranquillizer that is also used as a sedative and muscle relaxant, *esp* before surgical operations. Also called VALIUM. [DI-¹ + AZ- + EPOXIDE + AMIDE]

diazo /die'azoh/ *adj* **1** of or containing a radical composed of two nitrogen atoms united to a single carbon atom. **2** of or containing a DIAZONIUM ion.

diazonium /die-ə'zohni-əm/ *noun* an ion that is composed of two nitrogen atoms united to one carbon atom and usu exists in salts that are used in the manufacture of azo dyes. [DIAZO + AMMONIUM]

dibasic /die'baysik/ *adj* **1** said of an acid: having two replaceable hydrogen atoms. **2** said of a base or a basic salt: having two HYDROXYL groups. ▶ **dibasicity** /-'sisiti/ *noun.*

dibber /'dibə/ *noun* a dibble. [by alteration]

dibble¹ /'dibl/ *noun* a small pointed hand implement used to make holes in the ground for plants, seeds, or bulbs. [Middle English *debylle*; earlier history unknown]

dibble² *verb trans* **1** to plant (seeds, etc) with a dibble. **2** to make holes in (soil) with, or as if with, a dibble.

dibs /dibz/ *pl noun* **1** *informal* money, *esp* in small amounts. **2** *chiefly NAmer, informal* (+ on) the right to have first choice: *If there's only one chocolate cookie, I've got dibs on it.* [prob short for *dibstones* jacks, from obsolete *dib* to dab]

dice¹ /dies/ *noun* (*pl* **dice**) **1a** a small cube that is marked on each face with from one to six spots used to determine arbitrary values in various games. **b** a gambling game played with dice. **2** (*usu in pl*) small cubical pieces of food. **✻ no dice** *informal* of no avail; no use. [Middle English *dyce,* plural of *dee* DIE²]

Usage note

dice *and* **die**. Strictly and historically speaking, *dice* is the plural of *die.* The use of *dice* to mean a single small cube is, however, long established and perfectly acceptable. *Dice* therefore is both the singular and plural form: *to throw the dice* could refer to one or more cubes.

dice² *verb trans* **1a** to cut (food) into small cubes. **b** to ornament (something) with square markings. **2** to gamble (money) using dice: *He diced his money away.* ▶ *verb intrans* to play games with dice. **✻ dice with death** to take a big risk. ▶ **dicer** *noun.* [Middle English *dycen,* from *dyce:* see DICE¹]

dicey *adj* (**dicier, diciest**) *informal* risky; unpredictable.

dich- *or* **dicho-** *comb. form* forming words, with the meaning: in two; apart: *dichotomy.* [late Latin from Greek, from *dicha*]

dichloride /die'klawried/ *noun* a compound containing two atoms of chlorine combined with an element or radical.

dichlorodiphenyltrichloroethane /die,klawrohdie,feeniel-trie,klawroh'eethayn/ *noun* = DDT.

dicho- *comb. form* see DICH-.

dichotomy /die'kotəmi/ *noun* (*pl* **dichotomies**) **1** a division into two mutually exclusive or contradictory groups or things, or a contrast between them. **2** in botany, a repeated branching into two parts. ▶ **dichotomous** *adj,* **dichotomously** *adv.* [Greek *dichotomia* from *dichotomos,* from DICHO- + -TOMY]

dichroism /'diekrohiz(ə)m/ *noun* **1** the property of certain crystals differing in colour when viewed in the direction of two different axes. **2** the property of a surface of reflecting light of one colour and transmitting light of other colours. ▶ **dichroic** /die'krohik/ *adj.* [Greek *dichroos* two-coloured, from DI-¹ + *chrōs* colour]

dichromate /die'krohmayt/ *noun* an orange-to-red chromium salt containing two atoms of chromium in the molecule.

dichromatic /diekroh'matik/ *adj* **1** having or using two colours. **2** said of e.g. a bird species: having two colour varieties or colour phases independent of age or sex: *Female cuckoos are dichromatic.* ▶ **dichromatism** /die'krohmətiz(ə)m/ *noun.*

dichromic /die'krohmik/ *adj* = DICHROMATIC.

dick /dik/ *noun* **1** *coarse slang* the penis. **2** *coarse slang* a contemptible person. **3** *chiefly NAmer, dated, informal* a detective. [*Dick,* nickname for *Richard;* (sense 3) prob by shortening and alteration]

dickens /'dikinz/ *noun* (**the dickens**) *informal* (used as an interjection or intensive) devil; deuce: *What the dickens is going on?* [euphemism]

Dickensian /di'kenzi-ən/ *adj* **1** of Charles Dickens d.1870, English novelist who wrote about contemporary social problems, or his novels. **2** of or suggestive of aspects of Victorian England, *esp* urban squalor or conviviality.

dicker[1] /'dikə/ *verb intrans* (**dickered, dickering**) **1** to bargain or haggle. **2** to hesitate or dither. ➤➤ **dickerer** *noun*. [origin unknown]

dicker[2] *noun* **1** the act or an instance of bargaining or haggling. **2** something got by bargaining or haggling.

dickey *or* **dicky** /'diki/ *noun* (*pl* **dickeys** *or* **dickies**) **1a** a false front of a shirt. **b** = DICKEY BOW. **2** *chiefly Brit, dated*. **a** the driver's seat in a carriage. **b** a folding seat at the back of a carriage or motor car. [*Dicky*, nickname for *Richard*]

dickeybird *noun* **1** used by or to children: a small bird. **2** *informal* so much as a single word: *I never said a dickeybird*. [*Dicky*, nickname for *Richard*; (sense 2) rhyming slang *dickeybird* word]

dickey bow *or* **dicky bow** *noun Brit, informal* a bow tie. [see DICKEY]

dickhead *noun coarse slang* a stupid or incompetent person.

dicky[1] *adj* (**dickier, dickiest**) *Brit, informal* in a weak or unsound condition: *He's got to be careful. He's got a dicky heart*. [origin unknown]

dicky[2] *noun* (*pl* **dickies**) see DICKEY.

dicky bow *noun* see DICKEY BOW.

diclinous /'die'klienəs/ *adj* said of a plant: having the stamens and ovaries in separate flowers: compare MONOCLINOUS. [scientific Latin *diclinus*, literally 'having two beds', from DI-[1] + Greek *klinē* bed]

dicot /'diekot/ *noun* = DICOTYLEDON.

dicotyledon /ˌdiekoti'leedn/ *noun* any of a class of flowering plants that have two cotyledons (leaves produced by a germinating seed: see COTYLEDON): class Dicotyledoneae: compare MONOCOTYLEDON. ➤➤ **dicotyledonous** /-nəs/ *adj*.

dicrotic /die'krotik/ *adj* said of the pulse: having a double beat, e.g. in certain feverish states. [Greek *dikrotos* having a double beat]

dict. *abbr* **1** dictation. **2** dictator. **3** dictionary.

dicta /'diktə/ *noun* pl of DICTUM.

Dictaphone /'diktəfohn/ *noun trademark* a dictating machine. [DICTATE[1] + -PHONE]

dictate[1] /dik'tayt/ *verb intrans* **1** to give dictation. **2** to speak or act with authority; to prescribe. ➤ *verb trans* **1** to speak or read (a letter, etc) for a person to transcribe or for a machine to record. **2** to impose, pronounce, or specify (something) with authority. [Latin *dictatus*, past part. of *dictare* to assert, dictate, compose, from *dictus*, past part. of *dicere* to say]

dictate[2] /'diktayt/ *noun* **1** an authoritative rule, prescription, or command. **2** (*usu in pl*) a ruling principle: *We must all act according to the dictates of our consciences*.

dictating machine /dik'tayting/ *noun* a machine designed for the recording of dictated matter.

dictation /dik'taysh(ə)n/ *noun* **1a** the act or manner of uttering words to be transcribed. **b** material that is dictated or transcribed. **2** the action of laying down authoritative rules or directions; = PRESCRIPTION (2).

dictator /dik'taytə/ *noun* **1** an absolute ruler, *esp* one who has seized power unconstitutionally and uses it oppressively. **2** a domineering person. **3** a person granted absolute emergency power, *esp* in ancient Rome. [Latin *dictator*, from *dictatus*: see DICTATE[1]]

dictatorial /ˌdiktə'tawri·əl/ *adj* **1** of a dictator: *I am not invested with dictatorial powers. If I were, I should be quite ready to dictate* — Winston Churchill. **2** arrogantly domineering. ➤➤ **dictatorially** *adv*.

dictatorship *noun* **1** the office of dictator. **2** total or absolute control; leadership, rule. **3** a state or form of government where absolute power is concentrated in one person or a small clique.

diction /'diksh(ə)n/ *noun* **1** choice of words, *esp* with regard to correctness or clearness. **2** pronunciation and enunciation of words in speaking or singing. [Latin *diction-, dictio* speaking, style, word, from *dicere* to say]

dictionary /'dikshən(ə)ri/ *noun* (*pl* **dictionaries**) **1a** a reference book containing words and usu phrases, usu alphabetically arranged, together with information about them, *esp* their forms, pronunciations, and meanings. **b** a reference book giving for words or phrases of one language equivalents in another language. **2** a reference book that lists alphabetically terms or names, e.g. related to a specific subject or sphere of activity, along with information

about them: *a biographical dictionary*; *a dictionary of philosophy*. [Latin *dictionarium*, from *diction-, dictio*: see DICTION]

dictum /'diktəm/ *noun* (*pl* **dicta** /'diktə/ *or* **dictums**) **1** an authoritative statement on some topic; a pronouncement: *the dictum of a well-known headmaster ... that all parents were fools, but more especially mothers* — Samuel Butler. **2** = OBITER DICTUM (I). [Latin *dictum*, from neuter of *dictus*: see DICTATE[1]]

did /did/ *verb* past tense of DO[1].

didactic /di'daktik, die-/ *adj* **1** intended to teach something, *esp* a moral lesson. **2** having a tendency to teach in an authoritarian manner. ➤➤ **didactically** *adv*, **didacticism** /-siz(ə)m/ *noun*. [Greek *didaktikos*, from *didaskein* to teach]

didactics *pl noun* (*treated as sing. or pl*) the art or science of teaching or instruction.

diddicoy /'didikoy/ *noun* see DIDICOI.

diddle /'didl/ *verb trans informal* to cheat or swindle (somebody). ➤➤ **diddler** *noun*. [prob named after Jeremy *Diddler*, character in the play *Raising the Wind* by James Kenney d.1849, English dramatist]

diddly-squat /'didli'skwot/ *or* **doodly-squat** *noun NAmer, informal* nothing: *He knows diddly-squat about baseball*. [prob from NAmer slang *doodle* excrement + SQUAT[1] in the sense 'to defecate']

diddums /'didəmz/ *interj Brit, informal* used to express commiseration to, or as if to, a child. [baby-talk alteration of *did you/he/she*]

diddy *adj* (**diddier, diddiest**) *Brit, informal* charmingly small. [prob baby-talk for *little*]

didgeridoo /ˌdijəri'dooh/ *noun* (*pl* **didgeridoos**) an Australian wind instrument consisting of a long wooden tube. [imitative]

didicoi *or* **didicoy** *or* **diddicoy** /'didikoy/ *noun* (*pl* **didicois** *or* **didicoys** *or* **diddicoys**) *dialect* an itinerant tinker, traveller, etc who is not a true Romany. [Romany]

didn't /'didnt/ *contraction* did not.

didst /didst/ *verb archaic* second person sing. past tense of DO[1].

didymium /di'dimi·əm, die-/ *noun no longer in technical use* a mixture of rare-earth elements made up chiefly of neodymium and praseodymium. [Latin *didymium* from Greek *didymos* double, twin, testicle, from *dyo* two]

die[1] /die/ *verb* (**dies, died, dying**) ➤ *verb intrans* **1** to stop living; to undergo the ending of physical life. **2a** to pass out of existence, to cease: *His anger died at these words*. **b** to be forgotten: *His name will never die*. **3** (*also* + for) to long keenly or desperately: *I was dying to go to the loo*. **4** (*also* + on) to stop: *The engine died on me just when I was overtaking*. **5** (+ of) to be almost overwhelmed with (e.g. boredom). ➤ *verb trans* to suffer (a particular death). ✴ **die hard** said of habits or attitudes: to take a long time to change or disappear. **I'd die first** I'd rather die (than do the thing in question). **never say die** *informal* never give up. **to die for** *informal* excellent or desirable: *They serve chocolate cheesecake to die for*. [Middle English *dien*, from or related to Old Norse *deyja* to die]

die[2] *noun* **1** (*pl* **dice** /dies/) a dice. **2** (*pl* **dies**) any of various tools or devices for giving a desired shape, form, or finish to a material or for impressing an object or material. **3** (*pl* **dies**) a dado or plinth. ✴ **the die is cast** the irrevocable decision or step has been taken. [Middle English *dee* via French from Latin *datum* something given, neuter past part. of *dare* to give]

Usage note
die *and* **dice**. See note at DICE[1].

die away *verb intrans* to become weaker or fainter and then disappear: *The sound of cheering eventually died away*.

dieback /'diebak/ *noun* a condition in woody plants in which young shoots, branches, etc are killed as a result of frost damage, pollution such as acid rain, or fungal infection.

die back *verb intrans* said of a plant, shoots, etc: to die as far as the roots of the plant, e.g. at the end of the growing season.

die-cast *verb trans* (*past tense and past part.* **die-cast**) to make (an object) by forcing molten plastic, metal, etc into a die.

diecious /'die'eeshəs/ *adj NAmer* see DIOECIOUS.

die down *verb intrans* **1** to diminish or subside. **2** said of a plant, shoots, etc: = DIE BACK.

die-hard *noun* **1** a person who strongly resists change. **2** (*used before a noun*) strongly resisting change: *a die-hard conservative*.

dieldrin /'deeldrin/ *noun* an insecticide that contains chlorine. [from the name of Otto *Diels* d.1954, German chemist + ALDRIN]

dielectric¹ /die·ə'lektrik/ *adj* able to transmit an electrical effect by electrostatic induction but not by conduction. ➤➤ **dielectrically** *adv.* [DIA- + ELECTRIC²]

dielectric² *noun* a dielectric substance; an insulator.

diene /'die·een/ *noun* a chemical compound containing two carbon-carbon double bonds.

die off *verb intrans* to die one by one, sometimes until none exist.

die out *verb intrans* **1** to become extinct. **2** to disappear; to cease to exist, be done, etc: *Widows always used to wear black, but the practice has died out now.*

dieresis /die'erisis/ *noun NAmer* see DIAERESIS.

diesel /'deezl/ *noun* **1** a diesel engine, or a vehicle driven by one. **2** a heavy mineral oil used as fuel in diesel engines. [named after Rudolf *Diesel* d.1913, German mechanical engineer, who designed the engine]

diesel-electric¹ *adj* of or using the combination of a diesel engine driving an electric generator: *a diesel-electric locomotive.*

diesel-electric² *noun* a diesel-electric locomotive.

diesel engine *noun* an internal-combustion engine in which fuel is ignited by air compressed to a sufficiently high temperature.

diesel oil *noun* = DIESEL (2).

Dies Irae /,deeayz 'iəray/ *noun* a medieval Latin hymn sung in requiem masses. [Latin *Dies Irae* day of wrath; the first words of the hymn]

diesis /'die·isis/ *noun* (*pl* **dieses** /-seez/) in printing, = DOUBLE DAGGER. [via Latin from Greek *diesis* a quarter tone in music; the symbol was orig used in musical notation]

diestock *noun* a piece of equipment to hold dies used for cutting threads.

diet¹ /'die·ət/ *noun* **1** the food and drink habitually taken by a group, animal, or individual. **2** the kind and amount of food prescribed for a person for a special purpose, e.g. losing weight. **3** (*used before a noun*) said of food or drinks: low in calories or fat content: *diet cola.* [Middle English *diete* via French and Latin from Greek *diaita* manner of living, from DIA- + -*aita*, from *aisa* share]]

diet² *verb intrans* (**dieted, dieting**) to eat and drink sparingly or according to prescribed rules, *esp* in order to lose weight. ➤➤ **dieter** *noun.*

diet³ *noun* **1** any of various national or provincial legislatures. **2** in Scotland, a meeting or session of a lawcourt or other official body. [Latin *dieta* day's journey, day for an assembly, from *dies* day]

dietary¹ /'die·ət(ə)ri/ *adj* of a diet.

dietary² *noun* (*pl* **dietaries**) the kinds and amounts of food available to or eaten by an individual, group, or population.

dietary fibre *noun* the fibrous content of food that helps digestion and is present in large amounts in roughage.

dietetic /die·ə'tetik/ *adj* **1** of diet. **2** adapted for use in special diets. ➤➤ **dietetically** *adv.*

dietetics *pl noun* (*treated as sing. or pl*) the application of the principles of nutrition to feeding.

dietitian *or* **dietician** /die·ə'tish(ə)n/ *noun* a specialist in dietetics.

differ /'difə/ *verb intrans* (**differed, differing**) **1** (+ from) to be unlike; to be distinct from: *In what way does his story differ from mine?* **2** said of people: to disagree: *We differ on religious matters.* [Middle English *differen* via early French *differer* to postpone, be different, from Latin *differre*, from DIS- + *ferre* to carry]

difference /'difrəns/ *noun* **1a** (*often* + between) unlikeness between two or more people or things: *The only difference between a saint and a sinner is that every saint has a past and every sinner has a future* — Oscar Wilde. **b** (*often* + between) the degree or amount by which things differ. **2** a disagreement or dispute; dissension: *They were unable to settle their differences.* **3** the degree or amount by which things differ in quantity or measure; *specif* a remainder. **4** a significant change in or effect on a situation.

different /'difrənt/ *adj* **1** partly or totally unlike; dissimilar. **2** *informal* unusual; special. **3a** distinct. **b** other. ✷ **make a difference 1** to have an effect: *Do you think it would make a difference if I apologized?* **2** to treat (people, etc) differently: *I don't make any difference between boys and girls.* **with a difference** with some new and special feature. ➤➤ **differently** *adv,* **differentness** *noun.* [early

French *different* from Latin *different-, differens,* present part. of *differre:* see DIFFER]

Usage note
different from/to/than. The combination preferred by traditionalists is *different from,* which keeps *different* in line with *differ* (*How does this version differ* (or *How is this version different*) *from the previous one?*). *Different to* has, however, been used for a very long time in British English, and most modern authorities on British English accept it as an alternative, at least in anything but very formal writing. *Different than* is in widespread use in American English and is cautiously accepted in British English when followed by a clause: *It's altogether different than I expected* (strictly: *different from what I expected*). *Different than* is not usually acceptable in either British or American English when followed by a noun.

differentia /difə'renshi·ə/ *noun* (*pl* **differentiae** /-shi·ee/) the mark or feature that distinguishes one member of a general class from another, *esp* a trait distinguishing one species from other species of the same genus. [Latin *differentia* difference, from *different-, differens:* see DIFFERENT]

differential¹ /difə'renshəl/ *adj* **1a** of or constituting a difference. **b** based on or resulting from a differential: *differential freight charges.* **2** in physics, of quantitative differences, or producing effects by reason of quantitative differences. **3** in mathematics, relating to a differential or differentiation. ➤➤ **differentially** *adv.*

differential² *noun* **1** the amount of a difference between comparable individuals or classes; *specif* the amount by which the remuneration of distinct types of worker differs. **2** in mathematics, the product of the derivative of a function of one variable with the increment of the independent variable: *For a function f(x) the differential is f'(x)dx.* **3** = DIFFERENTIAL GEAR.

differential calculus *noun* a branch of mathematics dealing chiefly with the rate of change of functions with respect to their variables.

differential equation *noun* an equation containing differentials or derivatives of functions.

differential gear *noun* an arrangement of gears in a vehicle that allows one of the wheels imparting motion to turn, e.g. in going round a corner, faster than the other.

differentiate /difə'renshiayt/ *verb trans* **1** to mark or show a difference in (things). **2** to cause differentiation of (something) in the course of development. **3** to obtain the mathematical derivative of (a function, etc). ➤ *verb intrans* **1** (+ between) to recognize or make a difference between (people, etc). **2** to become distinct or different in character. **3** to undergo differentiation. ➤➤ **differentiability** /-shi·ə'biliti/ *noun,* **differentiable** /-shi·əbl/ *adj,* **differentiator** *noun.*

differentiation /,difə,renshi'aysh(ə)n/ *noun* **1** the act or an instance of differentiating. **2** development into more complex, numerous, or varied forms. **3a** modification of body parts for performance of particular functions. **b** all the processes whereby apparently similar cells, tissues, and structures attain their adult forms and functions.

difficult /'difik(ə)lt/ *adj* **1** hard to do, make, carry out, or understand: *a difficult climb; a difficult text.* **2** hard to deal with, manage, or please: *a difficult child.* ➤➤ **difficultly** *adv.* [back-formation from DIFFICULTY]

difficulty *noun* (*pl* **difficulties**) **1** the state of being difficult. **2** an obstacle or impediment. **3** (*usu in pl*) a cause of trouble or embarrassment, *esp* of a financial nature. **4** a disagreement: *We've had some little difficulties, but it's all sorted out now.* [Middle English *difficulte* from Latin *difficultas,* from *difficilis* difficult, from DIS- + *facilis* easy]

diffident /'difid(ə)nt/ *adj* lacking in self-confidence; reserved; unassertive. ➤➤ **diffidence** *noun,* **diffidently** *adv.* [Latin *diffident-, diffidens,* present part. of *diffidere* to distrust, from DIS- + *fidere* to trust]

diffract /di'frakt/ *verb trans* to cause (a beam of light) to become a set of light and dark or coloured bands in passing by the edge of an opaque body, through narrow slits, etc. ➤➤ **diffraction** *noun,* **diffractive** /-tiv/ *adj,* **diffractively** /-tivli/ *adv,* **diffractiveness** /-tivnəs/ *noun.* [Latin *diffraction-, diffractio,* from *diffringere* to break apart, from DIS- + *frangere* to break]

diffraction grating *noun* = GRATING¹ (2).

diffuse¹ /di'fyoohs/ *adj* **1** not concentrated or localized; scattered. **2** lacking conciseness; verbose. ➤➤ **diffusely** *adv,* **diffuseness** *noun.* [Latin *diffusus,* past part. of *diffundere* to spread out, from DIS- + *fundere* to pour]

diffuse² /di'fyoohz/ *verb trans* **1** to spread (something) out freely in all directions. **2** to break up and distribute (incident light) by reflection. ➤ *verb intrans* **1** to spread out or become transmitted. **2** to undergo diffusion. ➤➤ **diffuser** *noun,* **diffusibility** /-'biliti/ *noun,* **diffusible** *adj,* **diffusive** /-siv/ *adj,* **diffusively** /-sivli/ *adv,* **diffusiveness** /-sivnəs/ *noun.* [Middle English from early French *diffus* from Latin *diffusus:* see DIFFUSE¹]

diffusion /di'fyoohzh(ə)n/ *noun* **1** the act or an instance of diffusing or being diffused. **2** the state of being long-winded. **3a** the process whereby particles of liquids, gases, or solids intermingle as the result of their spontaneous movement. **b** reflection of light by a rough reflecting surface. **4** the spread of a cultural characteristic, e.g. an artefact or custom, from one area or culture to another, e.g. by migration or trade.

diffusionism *noun* the theory in anthropology that similarities between different cultures are the result of diffusion. ➤➤ **diffusionist** *noun and adj.*

dig¹ /dig/ *verb* (**digging,** *past tense and past part.* **dug** /dug/) ➤ *verb intrans* **1a** to turn up, loosen, or remove earth. **b** (+ for) to look for something by digging: *The children were in the garden digging for treasure.* **2** *slang, dated* to understand. ➤ *verb trans* **1** to break up, turn, or loosen (earth) with an implement. **2** to bring (something) to the surface by, or as if by, digging; to unearth (it). **3** to hollow out (a hole or tunnel) by removing earth; to excavate (it). **4** to poke or prod (somebody): *She kept on digging him in the ribs.* **5** *slang, dated.* **a** to understand or appreciate (something): *I don't dig rap music.* **b** to pay attention to (something or somebody); to look at or notice (it or them): *Dig that hat over there.* [Middle English *diggen,* perhaps from Old English *dīc* DITCH¹]

dig² *noun* **1a** a thrust or poke. **b** *informal* a cutting or snide remark. **2** an archaeological excavation site. **3** *chiefly Brit, informal* (in pl) lodgings. [(sense 3) short for DIGGINGS]

digastric /die'gastrik/ *adj* said of a muscle: having two enlarged parts separated by a tendon. [Latin *digastricus,* from DI-¹ + *gastricus* gastric]

digest¹ /di'jest, die'jest/ *verb trans* **1** to convert (food) into a form the body can use. **2** to soften or decompose or extract soluble ingredients from (a substance) by heat and moisture or chemicals. **3** to assimilate (something) mentally: *Some books are to be tasted, others to be swallowed, and some few to be chewed and digested —* Bacon. **4** to distribute or arrange (something) systematically. **5** to compress (material or information) into a short summary. ➤ *verb intrans* to become digested. ➤➤ **digester** *noun,* **digestibility** /-'biliti/ *noun,* **digestible** *adj.* [Middle English *digesten* from Latin *digestus:* see DIGEST²]

digest² /'diejest/ *noun* **1** a literary abridgment. **2** a systematic compilation of laws. [Middle English *Digest,* compilation of Roman laws ordered by Justinian, from Latin *Digesta* collection of writings arranged under headings, from *digestus,* past part. of *digerere* to arrange, distribute, digest, from DIS- + *gerere* to carry]

digestion /di'jeschən, die-/ *noun* the process or power of digesting something, *esp* food. ➤➤ **digestional** *adj.*

digestive¹ /di'jestiv, die-/ *noun* **1** something that aids digestion. **2** *Brit* = DIGESTIVE BISCUIT.

digestive² *adj* of, causing, or promoting digestion. ➤➤ **digestively** *adv.*

digestive biscuit *noun Brit* a slightly sweet biscuit made from wholemeal flour.

digger /'digə/ *noun* **1a** somebody or something that digs. **b** a tool or machine for digging. **2** (**Digger**) *informal* a private soldier from Australia or New Zealand, *esp* in World War I.

diggings /'digingz/ *pl noun* **1** a place of excavating, *esp* for ore, metals, or precious stones. **2** material dug out. **3** *Brit, informal, dated* lodgings.

dight /diet/ *verb trans archaic* to dress or adorn (somebody or something). [Old English *dihtan* to arrange, compose, ultimately from Latin *dictare* to dictate, compose]

dig in *verb intrans* **1** said of a soldier: to dig defensive positions. **2** *informal* to hold stubbornly to a position. **3** *informal* to begin eating. ➤ *verb trans* to incorporate (a substance) in the soil by digging. ✳ **dig one's heels in** *informal* to refuse to move or change one's mind; to be stubborn.

digit /'dijit/ *noun* **1a** any of the Arabic numerals from one to nine, usu also including 0. **b** any of the elements that combine to form numbers in a system other than the decimal system. **2** a finger or toe. [Middle English from Latin *digitus* finger, toe; (sense 1) from counting on the fingers]

digital *adj* **1a** relating to calculation or data storage using discrete values rather than continuously variable ones. **b** relating to data presented, stored, or manipulated in the form of numerical digits. **c** said of a computer: operating with numbers expressed as discrete pulses representing digits, usu in the form of binary notation: compare ANALOG¹. **d** said of a clock or watch, etc: presenting information in the form of numerical digits rather than by a pointer moving round a dial: compare ANALOG¹. **e** said of a way of recording sound: involving the conversion of sounds into digital form so that background noise and distortion are reduced: compare ANALOG¹. **2a** of the fingers and toes. **b** done with a finger or the fingers: *a digital examination of the rectum.* ➤➤ **digitally** *adv.*

digital audiotape *noun* magnetic tape that records and stores sound in digital form.

digital camera *noun* a camera which produces digital images that can be stored on a computer, displayed on a screen, and printed.

digital compact cassette *noun* a magnetic tape cassette on which sound can be recorded in digital form.

digital divide *noun* the gap in educational potential, earning potential, etc that exists between those who have access to computing facilities and the Internet and those who do not.

digitalin /diji'taylin/ *noun* a compound obtained from digitalis and used in the treatment of heart disease.

digitalis /diji'talis/ *noun* the dried leaf of the common foxglove, containing several compounds which are important as drugs used *esp* as powerful heart stimulants. [Latin *digitalis* of a finger, from *digitus* finger, toe; from its finger-shaped corolla]

digitalize or **digitalise** *verb trans* to digitize (data, etc).

digital recording *noun* a recording process in which sound or images are converted into numbers and stored for reproduction.

digital television *noun* television in which the picture information is transmitted in digital form and decoded at the receiver.

digital versatile disc *noun* = DIGITAL VIDEO DISC.

digital video disc *noun* a type of high-capacity optical compact disc that can store a much larger quantity of video, audio, or other information than a conventional compact disc.

digitate /'dijitayt/ *adj* **1** said of a leaf: having divisions arranged like the fingers of a hand. **2** said of an animal: having fingers or toes. ➤➤ **digitately** *adv,* **digitation** /-'taysh(ə)n/ *noun.*

digitigrade¹ /'dijitigrayd/ *adj* said of a mammal: walking on the toes with the back of the foot more or less raised: compare PLANTIGRADE¹. [French *digitigrade,* from Latin *digitus* finger, toe + *-gradus* walking]

digitigrade² *noun* a digitigrade animal.

digitize or **digitise** *verb trans* to put (data, etc) into digital notation. ➤➤ **digitization** /-'zaysh(ə)n/ *noun,* **digitizer** *noun.*

digitoxin /diji'toksin/ *noun* a compound that is the most active constituent of DIGITALIS. [DIGITALIS + TOXIN]

dignified /'dignified/ *adj* showing or having dignity. ➤➤ **dignifiedly** *adv,* **dignifiedness** *noun.*

dignify /'dignifie/ *verb trans* (**dignifies, dignified, dignifying**) to confer dignity or distinction on (something or somebody), sometimes something or somebody unworthy. [early French *dignifier* from late Latin *dignificare,* from Latin *dignus* worthy]

dignitary /'dignit(ə)ri/ *noun* (*pl* **dignitaries**) a person of high rank or holding a position of dignity or honour.

dignity /'digniti/ *noun* **1** being worthy, honoured, or esteemed: *No race can prosper till it learns there is as much dignity in tilling a field as in writing a poem —* Booker T Washington. **2** high rank, office, or position. **3** a high opinion of oneself; self-esteem. **4** stillness of manner; gravity. ✳ **beneath one's dignity** not worthy of being done by somebody as important as one considers oneself to be. **stand on one's dignity** to demand to be treated with respect. [Middle English *dignete* via French from Latin *dignitat-, dignitas,* from *dignus* worthy]

dig out *verb trans* **1** to remove (something) by digging. **2** to search for and find (something): *Can you dig out last month's sales figures, please?*

digoxin /di'joksin/ *noun* a poisonous compound obtained from some foxgloves and used similarly to DIGITALIS. [blend of DIGITALIS + TOXIN]

digraph /'diegrahf/ *noun* **1** a group of two successive letters, with the phonetic value of a single sound, e.g. *sh* or *th*. **2** = LIGATURE (4). ➤➤ **digraphic** /die'grafik/ *adj*.

digress /die'gres/ *verb intrans* to turn aside, *esp* from the main subject in writing or speaking. ➤➤ **digresser** *noun*, **digressive** /-siv/ *adj*, **digressively** /-sivli/ *adv*, **digressiveness** /-sivnəs/ *noun*. [Latin *digressus*, past part. of *digredi* to step aside, from DIS- + *gradi* to step]

digression /die'gresh(ə)n/ *noun* the act or an instance of digressing.

dig up *verb trans* **1a** to find or produce (something) by digging. **b** to remove (something) by digging. **2** to discover (something) by searching: *See if you can dig up any info about him.*

dihedral¹ /die'heedrəl/ *adj* having or contained by two flat surfaces.

dihedral² *noun* **1** the angle between two intersecting planes or faces of a solid. **2** the angle between an upwardly inclined wing of an aircraft and a horizontal line: compare ANHEDRAL².

dihybrid /die'hiebrid/ *noun* an organism, cell, etc having two different versions of each of two genes; or a cross producing such individuals.

dik-dik /'dikdik/ *noun* any of several species of small E African antelopes: genus *Madoqua*. [native name in East Africa]

dike¹ /diek/ *noun* see DYKE¹.

dike² *verb trans* see DYKE².

dike³ *noun informal, derog* see DYKE³.

diktat /'diktat/ *noun* a harsh settlement or ruling imposed by a victor or authority. [German *Diktat* something dictated, from Latin *dictatum*, neuter past part. of *dictare*: see DICTATE¹]

dilapidate /di'lapidayt/ *verb intrans* to become dilapidated. ➤ *verb trans* to cause (something) to become dilapidated. [Latin *dilapidatus*, past part. of *dilapidare* to squander, destroy, from DIS- + *lapidare* to throw stones, from *lapidus* stone]

dilapidated /di'lapidaytid/ *adj* decayed or fallen into partial ruin, *esp* through neglect or misuse. ➤➤ **dilapidation** /-'daysh(ə)n/ *noun*.

dilatation /dielə'taysh(ə)n, dilə-/ *noun* **1a** the condition of being stretched beyond normal dimensions: *dilatation of the stomach*. **b** = DILATION (2). **2** a dilated part or formation.

dilatation and curettage *noun* = D AND C.

dilate /di'layt, die'layt/ *verb trans* to distend (something). ➤ *verb intrans* **1** to become wide. **2** (+ on/upon) to comment at length on (something). ➤➤ **dilatability** /-'biliti/ *noun*, **dilatable** *adj*, **dilative** /-tiv/ *adj*, **dilator** *noun*. [Middle English *dilaten* via French from Latin *dilatare* to spread wide, from DIS- + *latus* wide]

dilation /di'laysh(ə)n, die-/ *noun* **1a** the act or an instance of dilating or being dilated. **b** the state of being dilated. **2** the stretching or enlarging of an organ or other part of the body.

dilatory /'dilət(ə)ri/ *adj* **1** tending or intended to cause delay. **2** slow, tardy. ➤➤ **dilatorily** *adv*, **dilatoriness** *noun*. [late Latin *dilatorius* from Latin *dilatus*, past part. of *differre*: see DIFFER]

dildo /'dildoh/ *noun* (pl **dildos** or **dildoes**) an object serving as an artificial penis for inserting into the vagina for sexual stimulation. [perhaps modification of Italian *diletto* delight, from Latin *delectare*: see DELIGHT¹]

dilemma /di'lemə, die-/ *noun* **1a** a situation involving choice between two equally unsatisfactory alternatives. **b** *informal* a problem seemingly incapable of a satisfactory solution: *The tormenting dilemma of the Middle East is this: either we have one people too many or one state too few* — Afief Safieh. **2** an argument in which an opponent's position is refuted by being shown to lead to two or more unacceptable alternatives. ➤➤ **dilemmatic** /dilə'matik/ *adj*. [via late Latin from late Greek *dilēmmat-, dilēmma*, prob back-formation from Greek *dilēmmatos* involving two assumptions, from DI-¹ + *lēmmat-, lēmma* assumption]

Usage note ————

Strictly, a *dilemma* refers to a situation in which one is faced by two, and only two, equally unpleasant alternatives – as in the slightly old-fashioned phrase *to be on the horns of a dilemma*. A situation where there are more than two unpleasant alternatives is, strictly speaking, a *quandary*, though many dictionaries define a *dilemma* as involving 'two or more' unpleasant

alternatives. *Dilemma* ought not to be used if there is an open choice as to how to deal with a problem or if the alternatives faced are not unpleasant.

dilettante¹ /dili'tanti/ *noun* (pl **dilettantes** or **dilettanti** /-tee/) a person with a superficial interest in an art or a branch of knowledge. ➤➤ **dilettantish** *adj*, **dilettantism** *noun*. [Italian *dilettante*, present part. of *dilettare* to delight, from Latin *delectare*: see DELIGHT¹]

dilettante² *adj* of or denoting a dilettante.

dilettanti /dili'tantee/ *noun* pl of DILETTANTE¹.

diligence¹ /'dilij(ə)ns/ *noun* steady application and effort. [early French *diligence* from Latin *diligentia*, from *diligent-, diligens*: see DILIGENT]

diligence² *noun* a stagecoach, *esp* one formerly used in France. [French, from *carosse de diligence* literally 'coach of haste']

diligent /'dilij(ə)nt/ *adj* showing steady application and effort. ➤➤ **diligently** *adv*. [Middle English via French from Latin *diligent-, diligens*, present part. of *diligere* to esteem, love, from DIS- + *legere* to select]

dill¹ /dil/ *noun* a European plant with aromatic foliage and seeds, both of which are used in flavouring foods, e.g. pickles: *Anethum graveolens*. [Old English *dile*]

dill² *noun Aus, NZ, informal* a foolish or crazy person. [back-formation from DILLY²]

dill pickle *noun* a small pickled cucumber seasoned with dill.

dilly¹ /'dili/ *noun* (pl **dillies**) *NAmer, informal* a remarkable or outstanding person or thing. [obsolete *dilly* delightful, alteration of DELIGHTFUL]

dilly² *adj* (**dillier, dilliest**) *Aus, NZ, informal, dated* foolish, crazy. [English dialect *dilly* eccentric]

dilly bag *noun* an Australian mesh bag of native grass or fibres. [*dilli*, native name in Australia]

dillydally /dili'dali/ *verb intrans* (**dillydallies, dillydallied, dillydallying**) *informal* to waste time by loitering; to dawdle. [reduplication of DALLY]

diluent¹ /'dilyoo-ənt/ *noun* an agent for diluting. [Latin *diluent-, diluens*, present part. of *diluere*: see DELUGE¹]

diluent² *adj* making thinner or less concentrated; diluting.

dilute¹ /die'l(y)ooht, di-/ *verb trans* **1** to make (a liquid) thinner or more liquid by adding another liquid. **2** to diminish the strength, force, brilliance, etc of (something). ➤➤ **diluter** *noun*, **dilution** /-sh(ə)n/ *noun*, **dilutive** /-tiv/ *adj*. [Latin *dilutus*, past part. of *diluere*: see DELUGE¹]

dilute² *adj* weak; diluted.

diluvial /di'loohvi-əl/ *adj* of or brought about by a flood. [late Latin *diluvialis* from Latin *diluvium*: see DELUGE¹]

diluvian /di'loohvi-ən/ *adj* = DILUVIAL.

dim¹ /dim/ *adj* (**dimmer, dimmest**) **1** giving out a weak or insufficient light. **2** seen indistinctly: *A dim shape loomed out of the fog.* **3** not seeing clearly: *The old man's eyes were dim.* **4** *informal* lacking intelligence; stupid. **5** not remembered clearly: *I have only a dim memory of what happened.* ✳ **take a dim view of** to have an unfavourable or pessimistic attitude to (something). ➤➤ **dimly** *adv*, **dimness** *noun*. [Old English]

dim² *verb* (**dimmed, dimming**) ➤ *verb trans* **1** to make (something) dim. **2** *NAmer* to dip (a vehicle's headlights). ➤ *verb intrans* to become dim.

dim. *abbr* **1** dimension. **2** diminuendo. **3** diminutive.

dime /diem/ *noun* a coin worth a tenth of a US dollar. ✳ **a dime a dozen** *NAmer, informal* very cheap. [Middle English, in the sense 'tenth part, tithe', via French from Latin *decima*, fem of *decimus* tenth, from *decem* ten]

dime novel *noun NAmer* a melodramatic paperback novel. ➤➤ **dime novelist** *noun*.

dimension¹ /di'mensh(ə)n, die-/ *noun* **1a** (in pl) size in one or all directions. **b** (usu in pl) the range over which something extends; the scope. **2** an aspect: *The oral dimension of the novel is very important* — Karl Miller. **3a** extension in one direction; *specif* any of three or four coordinates determining a position in space or in space and time. **b** any of a group of parameters necessary and sufficient to determine uniquely each element of a system of mathematical entities: *The surface of a sphere has two dimensions.* **c** (usu in pl) any of the fundamental quantities, *specif* mass, length, and time, which combine to make a derived unit: *Velocity has the dimensions of length divided by time.* ➤➤ **dimensional** *adj,* **dimensionless** *adj.* [Middle English via French from Latin *dimension-, dimensio,* from *dimetiri* to measure out, from DIS- + *metiri* to measure]

dimension² *verb trans* (**dimensioned, dimensioning**) to indicate the dimensions on (a drawing).

dimer /'diemə/ *noun* a compound formed by the union of two radicals or two molecules of a simpler compound. ➤➤ **dimeric** /die'merik/ *adj.* [DI-¹ + -MER]

dimerize *or* **dimerise** /'diemǝriez/ *verb trans* to combine with (a similar molecule) to form a dimer. ➤➤ **dimerization** /-'zaysh(ǝ)n/ *noun.*

dimerous /'dimǝrǝs/ *adj* said of an insect or plant part: consisting of two parts. ➤➤ **dimerism** *noun.* [Latin *dimerus,* from DI-¹ + -*merus* having that many parts, from Greek *meros* part]

dimeter /'dimitǝ/ *noun* a line of verse consisting of two metrical feet. [late Latin from Greek *dimetros,* adj, being a dimeter, from DI-¹ + *metron* measure]

dimethylformamide /die,methil'fawmǝmied, die,meethiel-/ *noun* a colourless liquid used as a solvent and catalyst.

dimethylsulphoxide (*NAmer* **dimethylsulfoxide**) /die,me-thilsul'foksied, die,meethiel-/ *noun* a compound obtained as a by-product in wood-pulp manufacture and used *esp* as a solvent, e.g. for drugs applied to the skin.

diminish /di'minish/ *verb trans* **1** to cause (something) to be or appear less. **2** to reduce (a person or thing) in standing or perceived worth: *Any man's death diminishes me* — John Donne. **3** in architecture, to make (something) taper. **4** in music, to decrease (an interval) by a semitone. ➤ *verb intrans* **1** to become gradually less; to dwindle. **2** to taper. ➤➤ **diminishable** *adj.* [Middle English *deminishen* via French from late Latin *diminuere,* alteration of Latin *deminuere,* from DE- + *minuere* to lessen]

diminished *adj* said of a musical interval: made a semitone less than perfect or minor: *a diminished fifth.*

diminished responsibility *noun* limitation of a person's criminal responsibility due to mental abnormality or instability.

diminishing returns *pl noun* a rate of yield that beyond a certain point fails to increase in proportion to additional investments of labour or capital.

diminuendo /di,minyoo'endoh/ *adj and adv* said of a piece of music: to be performed with a decrease in volume. ➤➤ **diminuendo** *noun.* [Italian *diminuendo* diminishing, from late Latin *diminuendum,* verbal noun from *diminuere:* see DIMINISH]

diminution /dimi'nyoohsh(ǝ)n/ *noun* a diminishing or decrease. [Middle English *diminucioun* via French from Latin *deminution-, deminutio,* from *deminuere:* see DIMINISH]

diminutive¹ *adj* **1** exceptionally small; tiny. **2** said of certain affixes, e.g. *-ling,* and words formed with them, e.g. *duckling:* indicating small size and sometimes lovableness or triviality. ➤➤ **diminutively** *adv,* **diminutiveness** *noun.*

diminutive² /di'minyootiv/ *noun* a diminutive word, affix, or name. [Middle English *diminutif* from late Latin *diminutivum,* from Latin *deminuere:* see DIMINISH]

dimissory /di'misǝri/ *adj* **1** *technical* giving permission to be ordained in another bishop's diocese: *a dimissory letter.* **2** *formal* granting leave to depart. [Latin *dimissorius* submitting a matter to a higher court, from *dimittere* to dismiss]

dimity /'dimiti/ *noun* (*pl* **dimities**) a corded cotton fabric woven with checks or stripes. [alteration of Middle English *demyt,* prob from early Greek *dimitos* of double thread, from Greek DI-¹ + *mitos* warp thread]

dimmer /'dimǝ/ *noun* **1** a device for regulating the brightness of electric lighting. **2** *NAmer* a dipped headlight on a vehicle.

dimmer switch *noun* = DIMMER (1).

dimorphism /die'mawfiz(ǝ)m/ *noun* the occurrence, combination, or existence of two distinct forms, e.g.: **a** the existence of two different forms of a species, distinguished by size, colour, etc. **b** the existence of an organ, e.g. the leaves of a plant, in two different forms. **c** crystallization of a chemical compound in two different forms. ➤➤ **dimorphic** /-fik/ *adj,* **dimorphous** /-fǝs/ *adj.*

dimple¹ /'dimpl/ *noun* **1** a slight natural indentation in the cheek or another part of the human body. **2** a depression or indentation on a surface. ➤➤ **dimply** *adj.* [Middle English *dympull,* of Germanic origin]

dimple² *verb trans* to mark (something) with dimples: *a baby's dimpled knuckles.* ➤ *verb intrans* to form dimples, e.g. by smiling.

dim sum /,dim 'sum/ *noun* Chinese food consisting of small pieces of meat or vegetable wrapped in pastry and fried or steamed. [Chinese (Cantonese) *dim sam* small centre]

dimwit /'dimwit/ *noun informal* a stupid or mentally slow person. ➤➤ **dim-witted** /dim'witid/ *adj,* **dim-wittedly** /dim'wit-/ *adv,* **dim-wittedness** /dim'wit-/ *noun.*

DIN /din/ *abbr* German Industrial Standards. [German *Deutsche Industrie-Norm*]

din¹ /din/ *noun* a loud continued discordant noise. [Old English *dyne*]

din² *verb intrans* (**dinned, dinning**) to make a din: *The music dinned in their ears.* ✳ **din something into** to instil something into (somebody) by perpetual repetition.

dinar /'deenah/ *noun* the basic monetary unit of certain N African and Middle Eastern countries, of Bosnia-Herzegovina, and Yugoslavia. [Arabic *dīnār* via Greek from Latin *denarius:* see DENIER¹]

dine /dien/ *verb intrans* to eat dinner: *One cannot think well, love well, sleep well, if one has not dined well* — Virginia Woolf. ➤ *verb trans* to entertain (somebody) to dinner: *They wined and dined us splendidly.* ✳ **dine off/on/upon** to eat (something) as one's meal, *esp* dinner. **dine out on** to be socially in demand as a result of (an amusing or interesting story one has to tell): *You'll be able to dine out on the story of your shipwreck for years.* [Middle English *dinen* from Old French *disner, diner* from Latin DIS- + late Latin *jejunare* to fast, from Latin *jejunus* fasting]

diner *noun* **1** somebody who is dining. **2a** *NAmer* a small restaurant, often beside the road. **b** *chiefly NAmer* a dining car.

dinette /die'net/ *noun* a small room or part of a room set aside for eating meals in.

ding¹ /ding/ *verb trans* **1** to cause (e.g. a bell) to make a ringing sound. **2** (+ into) to din (something) into somebody. ➤ *verb intrans* to make a ringing sound. [prob imitative]

ding² *noun* a ringing sound.

dingbat /'dingbat/ *noun* an eccentric or stupid person. [origin unknown]

dingbats /'dingbats/ *pl noun* (**the dingbats**) *Aus, NZ, informal* (*treated as sing. or pl*) an attack of nervous anxiety. [origin unknown]

dingdong¹ /'dingdong/ *noun* **1** the ringing sound produced by repeated strokes, *esp* on a bell. **2** *Brit, informal* a rapid heated exchange of words or blows. [imitative]

dingdong² *adj* **1** of or resembling the sound of a bell. **2** *Brit, informal* with the advantage, e.g. in an argument, fight, or race, passing continually back and forth from one participant, side, etc to the other.

dinges /'dingǝs/ *noun chiefly SAfr, informal* = DINGUS.

dinghy /'ding·gi/ *noun* (*pl* **dinghies**) **1** a small boat often carried on a ship and used *esp* as a lifeboat or to transport passengers to and from shore. **2** a small open sailing boat. **3** a rubber life raft. [Bengali *dingi* and Hindi *ḍiṅgī*]

dingle /'ding·gl/ *noun* a small narrow wooded valley. [Middle English, in the sense 'abyss'; earlier history unknown]

dingo /'ding·goh/ *noun* (*pl* **dingoes** *or* **dingos**) a wild dog of Australia: *Canis dingo.* [native name in Australia]

dingus /'dingǝs, 'ding·gǝs/ *noun informal* something whose name is unknown or forgotten or that one does not wish to use. [Afrikaans and Dutch *dinges,* prob from German *Dings,* from genitive of *Ding* thing]

dingy /'dinji/ *adj* (**dingier, dingiest**) **1** dirty; discoloured. **2** shabby; squalid. ➤➤ **dingily** *adv,* **dinginess** *noun.* [origin unknown]

dining car *noun* a railway carriage where meals are served.

dining room *noun* a room set aside for eating meals in.

dinkie /'dingki/ *noun* see DINKY².

dinkum /'dingkǝm/ *adj Aus, NZ, informal* real or genuine. [prob from English dialect *dinkum* work]

dinkum oil *noun Aus, NZ, informal* the truth.

dinky¹ /'dingki/ *adj* (**dinkier, dinkiest**) *informal* **1** *chiefly Brit* neat and dainty. **2** *chiefly NAmer* small; insignificant. [Scots *dink* neat + -Y¹]

dinky² *or* **dinkie** *noun* (*pl* **dinkies**) *informal* a partner in a couple with two careers and no children. [from the initial letters of *double income, no kids* + -Y¹]

dinky-di /dingki'die/ *adj Aus, NZ, informal* = DINKUM. [by alteration]

dinner /'dinə/ *noun* **1** the principal meal of the day taken either in the evening or at midday. **2** a formal evening meal or banquet. [Middle English *diner* from Old French: see DINE]

dinner-dance *noun* an entertainment at which a formal evening meal is followed by dancing.

dinner jacket *noun* a jacket, usu black, for men's semiformal evening wear.

dinner lady *noun Brit, informal* a woman who serves meals and supervises children during mealtimes at school.

dinner service *noun* a set of dishes used for serving and eating a meal.

dinosaur /'dinəsawr/ *noun* **1** any of a group of extinct, typically very large reptiles of the Mesozoic era, most of which lived on the land: orders Saurischia and Ornithischia. **2** a person, organization, or institution that is outdated and unwilling or unable to adapt to change: *Britain's industrial dinosaurs*. ⟫⟫ **dinosaurian** /-'sawri·ən/ *adj and noun*. [Greek *deinos* terrible + *sauros* lizard]

dint¹ /dint/ *noun archaic* a blow or stroke. ✳ **by dint of** by means or application of. [Old English *dynt* stroke, blow]

dint² *verb trans* **1** to make a dent in (something). **2** to impress (something) or drive (it) in with force.

diocesan /die'osisən/ *noun* a bishop having jurisdiction over a diocese.

diocese /'die·əsis/ *noun* the area under the jurisdiction of a bishop. ⟫⟫ **diocesan** *adj*. [Middle English *diocise* via French and Latin from Greek *dioikēsis* administration, administrative division, from *dioikein* to keep house, govern, from DIA- + *oikein* to dwell, manage, from *oikos* house]

diode /'dieohd/ *noun* **1** a semiconductor device having only two terminals. **2** a thermionic valve having only an anode and a cathode.

dioecious (*NAmer* **diecious**) /die'eeshəs/ *adj* having male and female reproductive organs in different individuals: compare MONOECIOUS. [Greek DI-¹ + *oikos* house]

Dionysiac /die·ə'niziak/ *adj* = DIONYSIAN. [Latin *dionysiacus* from Greek *dionysiakos*, from *Dionysos* Dionysus]

Dionysian /die·ə'nizi·ən/ *adj* **1** of or relating to Dionysus, the Greek god of wine. **2** frenzied; orgiastic.

Diophantine equation /die·ə'fantien/ *noun* in mathematics, an indeterminate POLYNOMIAL² (having two or more variables) equation with integral coefficients for which it is required to find all integral solutions. $x^2 + y^2 = z^2$ is one Diophantine equation. [named after *Diophantus* fl about 275, Greek mathematician]

dioptre (*NAmer* **diopter**) /die'optə/ *noun* a unit of measurement of the refractive power of lenses equal to the reciprocal of the focal length in metres. [*diopter* orig denoting an optical instrument, via French and Latin from Greek *dioptra* from DIA- + *opsesthai* to be going to see]

dioptric /die'optrik/ *adj* **1** causing or serving to cause the convergence or divergence of a beam of light; refractive. **2** produced by means of refraction. [Greek *dioptrikos* of a diopter (instrument), from *dioptra*: see DIOPTRE]

dioptrics *pl noun* (*treated as sing. or pl*) the branch of optics concerned with the refraction of light.

diorama /'die·ərahmə/ *noun* **1** a scenic representation in which an artificially lit translucent painting is viewed through an opening. **2a** a three-dimensional representation in which miniature modelled figures, buildings, etc are displayed against a painted background. **b** a life-size museum exhibit of an animal or bird in realistic natural surroundings against a painted background. **3** a small-scale set used in films and television. ⟫⟫ **dioramic** /-'ramik/ *adj*. [French *diorama*, from DIA- + *-orama* as in PANORAMA]

diorite /'die·əriet/ *noun* a medium- to coarse-grained intrusive igneous rock rich in plagioclase. ⟫⟫ **dioritic** /-'ritik/ *adj*. [French *diorite* from Greek *diorizein* to distinguish, from DIA- + *horizein* to define]

dioxide /die'oksied/ *noun* an oxide containing two atoms of oxygen: *carbon dioxide*.

dioxin /die'oksin/ *noun* any of a group of poisonous chemical compounds that are chlorinated hydrocarbons produced as by-products during the manufacture of certain herbicides or during burning at high temperatures.

DIP *abbr* **1** document image processing. **2** Dual Inline Package.

Dip. *abbr* Diploma.

dip¹ /dip/ *verb* (**dipped, dipping**) ⟫ *verb trans* **1a** to plunge or immerse (something or somebody) in a liquid. **b** to immerse (a sheep, etc) in an antiseptic or parasite-killing solution, or (wood, grain, etc) in a preservative. **c** to moisten, cool, dye, or coat (something) by immersion. **d** to make (a candle) by immersing a wick repeatedly in hot wax. **2** to lift up (water, grain etc) by scooping or ladling. **3** to lower (something) and then raise it again: *They dipped the flag in salute*. **4** to lower (the beam of a vehicle's headlights) so as to reduce glare. **5** (+ in/into) to reach (a hand, etc) into a container, *esp* so as to take something out. **6** to baptize (somebody) by total immersion. ⟫ *verb intrans* **1a** to plunge into a liquid and quickly emerge. **b** to immerse something in a processing liquid or finishing material. **2a** to drop or decrease suddenly, often only temporarily and by a small amount. **b** said of an aircraft: to drop suddenly before climbing. **3** (+ in/into) to reach inside or below something, *esp* so as to take out part of the contents: *He dipped into the packet of biscuits*. **4a** to slope down. **b** to incline downward from the plane of the horizon. **5** said of a flag: to be lowered and raised. ✳ **dip into 1** to make inroads into (something) for funds or supplies: *She dipped into the family's savings*. **2** to read (something) superficially or in a random manner: *He dipped into a book while he was waiting*. [Old English *dyppan*]

dip² *noun* **1** the act or an instance of dipping or being dipped. **2** a brief bathe for sport or exercise. **3a** a sauce or soft mixture into which food is dipped before being eaten: *salsa dip*. **b** a liquid preparation into which an object or animal may be dipped, e.g. for cleaning or disinfecting: *sheep dip*. **4** a brief drop followed by a rise. **5a** a hollow or depression. **b** a short downward slope, e.g. in a road, followed by a rise. **6** = MAGNETIC DIP. **7** the angle that a stratum or similar geological feature makes with a horizontal plane.

DipAD *abbr Brit* Diploma in Art and Design.

DipEd /,dip 'ed/ *abbr Brit* Diploma in Education.

dipeptide /die'peptied/ *noun* a peptide having two molecules of amino acid in its molecular structure.

DipHE *abbr Brit* Diploma of Higher Education.

diphtheria /dip'thiəri·ə, dif-/ *noun* an acute infectious disease caused by a bacterium and marked by fever and the formation of a false membrane, *esp* in the throat, causing difficulty in breathing. ⟫⟫ **diphtherial** *adj*, **diphtheritic** /diptha'ritik, dif-/ *adj*, **diphtheroid** /'dipthəroyd, 'dif-/ *adj*. [scientific Latin *diphtheria* via French from Greek *diphthera* leather; from the toughness of the false membrane]

Usage note

The common pronunciation in which the first syllable is pronounced as though it were *dip-* is recognized as correct by all modern dictionaries. The traditional pronunciation, with the first syllable pronounced as *diff-* is equally correct but becoming less common. Note that the correct spelling is *-phth-*.

diphthong /'difthong, 'dip-/ *noun* **1** a gliding monosyllabic vowel sound, e.g. /oy/ in *toy*, that starts at the articulatory position for one vowel and moves to the position of another. **2a** a group of two letters representing a single sound; = DIGRAPH (1). **b** either of the ligatures æ or œ. ⟫⟫ **diphthongal** /dif'thong·gl/ *adj*. [Middle English *diptonge* via French and late Latin from Greek *diphthongos*, from DI-¹ + *phthongos* voice, sound]

diphthongize *or* **diphthongise** /'difthong·giez, 'dip-/ *verb intrans* said of a vowel: to become a diphthong. ⟫ *verb trans* to pronounce (a vowel) as a diphthong. ⟫⟫ **diphthongization** /-ie'zaysh(ə)n/ *noun*.

dipl- *or* **diplo-** *comb. form* forming words, with the meaning: double; twofold: *diplopia*. [Greek, from *diploos* double]

diplococcus /diploh'kokəs/ *noun* (*pl* **diplococci** /-'koksie/) any of a genus of bacteria that usu occur in pairs and that includes some serious pathogens: genus *Diplococcus*. [Latin *diplococcus*, genus name, from DIPL- + COCCUS]

diplodocus /di'plodəkəs/ *noun* a large plant-eating dinosaur with a long neck and long tail. [Latin *diplodocus*, genus name, from DIPL- + Greek *dokos* beam, bar]

diploid[1] /'diployd/ *adj* said of a cell or organism: having double the basic number of chromosomes arranged in homologous pairs: compare HAPLOID[1], POLYPLOID[1].

diploid[2] *noun* a diploid cell, individual, or generation.

diploma /di'plohmə/ *noun* **1** a certificate of a qualification, usu in a more specialized subject or at a lower level than a degree. **2** formerly, an official or State document. [Latin *diploma* passport, diploma, from Greek *diplōma* folded paper, passport, from *diploun* to double, from *diploos* double]

diplomacy /di'plohməsi/ *noun* **1** the art and practice of conducting international relations. **2** skill and tact in handling affairs or dealing with people: *His diplomacy was as wrongheaded as a buffalo's* — Hardy.

diplomat /'dipləmat/ *noun* **1** a person, e.g. an ambassador, employed in diplomacy. **2** a person skilled in dealing with people tactfully and adroitly. [French *diplomate*, back-formation from *diplomatique*: see DIPLOMATIC]

diplomate /'dipləmayt/ *noun* a person who holds a diploma. [DIPLOMA + -ATE[2]]

diplomatic /diplə'matik/ *adj* **1** of diplomats or international relations: *the diplomatic service*. **2** employing tact and conciliation: *She maintained a diplomatic silence.* **3** exactly reproducing the original: *a diplomatic edition of a manuscript.* >> **diplomatically** *adv*. [(senses 1 and 2) French *diplomatique* connected with documents regulating international relations, from Latin *diplomaticus*; (sense 3) Latin *diplomaticus* from *diplomat-, diploma*: see DIPLOMA]

diplomatic bag *noun chiefly Brit* a bag or container in which official mail is sent, exempt from customs inspection, to or from an embassy.

diplomatic corps *noun* the whole body of diplomats representing foreign governments in a country.

diplomatic immunity *noun* the exemption from local laws and taxes accorded to diplomatic staff abroad.

diplomatic service *noun* a government department that sends diplomats to represent their country in foreign countries.

diplomatist /di'plohmətist/ *noun* a person skilled or employed in diplomacy; a diplomat.

diplopia /di'plohpi·ə/ *noun* = DOUBLE VISION.

diplopod /'dipləpod/ *noun* any of a class of arthropods, including the millipedes, with two pairs of feet on each body segment: class Diplopoda.

diplotene /'diplohteen/ *noun* a stage of meiotic cell division during which the paired chromosomes begin to separate. [DIPL- + -*tene*, from Latin *taenia* ribbon, band]

dipole /'diepohl/ *noun* **1a** a pair of equal and opposite electric charges, or magnetic poles of opposite sign, separated by a small distance. **b** a molecule having such charges. **2** a radio aerial consisting of two horizontal rods in line, with their ends slightly separated. >> **dipolar** /die'pohlə/ *adj*.

dipole moment *noun* **1** the product of one of the equal but opposite charges on two atoms in a molecule and the distance separating them. **2** the product of two equal and opposite magnetic poles or electric charges that are separated by a short distance.

dipper /'dipə/ *noun* **1** somebody or something that dips. **2** any of several species of small birds somewhat resembling blackbirds that are notable for swimming underwater in rivers and streams to feed: genus *Cinclus*. **3** something, e.g. a long-handled cup, used for dipping.

dippy /'dipi/ *adj* (**dippier, dippiest**) *informal* crazy; eccentric. [perhaps alteration of *dipso*, short for *dipsomaniac*: see DIPSOMANIA]

dipso /'dipsoh/ *noun* (*pl* **dipsos**) *informal, offensive* an alcoholic or dipsomaniac.

dipsomania /dipsoh'mayni·ə/ *noun* acute and relatively short-lived bouts of craving for alcohol. >> **dipsomaniac** /-ak/ *noun*. [scientific Latin *dipsomania*, from Greek *dipsa* thirst + *mania*: see MANIA]

dipstick /'dipstik/ *noun* **1** a graduated rod for measuring the depth of a liquid, e.g. the oil in a car's engine. **2** *informal* a stupid or contemptible person.

dipswitch /'dipswich/ *noun chiefly Brit* a switch that dips headlight beams.

dipteran /'diptərən/ *noun* any of an order of insects that has a single pair of wings: order Diptera. >> **dipteran** *adj*. [scientific Latin from Greek *dipteros*: see DIPTEROUS]

dipterous /'diptərəs/ *adj* **1** having two wings or winglike appendages. **2** of the two-winged flies. [scientific Latin from Greek *dipteros*, from DI-[1] + *pteron* wing]

diptych /'diptik/ *noun* **1** a two-leaved hinged writing tablet. **2** a painting or carving done on two hinged panels and used *esp* as an altarpiece. [late Latin *diptycha* (pl) from Greek, neuter pl of *diptychos* folded in two, from DI-[1] + *ptychē* fold]

dir. *abbr* director.

dire /die·ə/ *adj* **1** warning of disaster; ominous: *a dire forecast.* **2** desperately urgent: *After the floods, the country was in dire need of international aid.* **3** *informal* dreadful; awful: *That new sitcom is absolutely dire.* >> **direly** *adv*, **direness** *noun*. [Latin *dirus*]

direct[1] /di'rekt, die'rekt/ *verb trans* **1a** to control and regulate the activities or course of (something). **b** to control the organization and performance of (a film, play, or broadcast); to supervise (it): *He directed the latest science fiction film.* **c** to order or instruct (somebody) with authority: *Police directed the crowd to move back.* **d** to train and usu lead performances of (people, *esp* musicians): *He directed the orchestra in a new work.* **e** *chiefly NAmer* to conduct (musicians). **2** to show or point out the way for (somebody). **3** to cause (something) to turn, move, point, or follow a straight course: *She directed her eyes heavenward.* **4a** to mark (a letter or parcel) with a name and address. **b** to address or aim (a remark). >> *verb intrans* to act as director. [Middle English *directen* from Latin *directus*, past part. of *dirigere*, from DIS- + *regere* to put straight]

direct[2] *adj* **1a** going from one point to another in time or space without deviation or interruption; straight. **b** going by the shortest way: *We'll take the direct route.* **2a** stemming immediately from a source, cause, or reason: *The rioting was a direct result of the government's imposition of new taxes.* **b** passing in a straight line of descent from parent to offspring: *Thackeray is a direct ancestor of my wife.* **c** arguing from a premise to a conclusion: *a direct proof.* **3** frank; straightforward: *I always admired her direct manner.* **4a** operating without an intervening agency. **b** effected by the action of the people or the electorate and not by representatives. **5** consisting of or reproducing the exact words of a speaker or writer: *direct speech.* **6** diametric; exact: *That was a direct contradiction of all he'd said before.* **7** said of a celestial body: moving in the general planetary direction from west to east; not retrograde. >> **directness** *noun*. [Middle English from Latin *directus*: see DIRECT[1]]

direct[3] *adv* **1** from point to point without deviation; by the shortest way: *You should write to him direct.* **2** without an intervening agency or stage: *They want to sell oil direct to the government.*

direct access *noun* a fast method of finding data in a storage medium, *esp* on magnetic disk or in random-access memory, where the access time is independent of the location of the data: compare SEQUENTIAL ACCESS.

direct action *noun* action that seeks to achieve an end by the most immediately effective means, e.g. a boycott or strike.

direct current *noun* an electric current flowing in one direction only, *esp* such a current that is substantially constant in value: compare ALTERNATING CURRENT.

direct debit *noun* an order to a bank to accept charges for amounts not specified in advance on an account from another named account at specified times: compare STANDING ORDER.

direct grant *noun* **1** in Britain, formerly, a grant of money given direct by the government to certain British schools, which were obliged to admit a number of non-fee-paying pupils. **2** (*used before a noun*) in Britain, formerly, receiving such a grant: *a direct-grant school.*

direction /di'reksh(ə)n, die-/ *noun* **1a** the line or course along which somebody or something moves or is aimed: *They drove off in the direction of London.* **b** the point towards which somebody or something faces: *Which direction does this house face?* **2a** a tendency or trend. **b** a guiding or motivating purpose: *After that, I had a new sense of direction.* **c** a course of action. **3a** the act or an instance of directing or being directed. **b** guidance or supervision of action. **c** the act, art, or technique of directing an orchestra, film, or theatrical production. **4** (*in pl*) explicit instructions on how to do something or get to a place: *Read the directions on the packet; I asked for directions to King's Cross.* **5** a word, phrase, or sign indicating the appropriate tempo, mood, or intensity of a passage or movement in music. >> **directionless** *adj*.

directional *adj* **1** of or indicating direction in space. **2a** suitable for detecting the direction from which radio signals come, or for sending out signals in one direction only: *a directional aerial.* **b** relating to a device that operates more efficiently in one direction than in others. **c** concentrated in a particular direction. **3** relating to direction or guidance, *esp* of thought or effort. ⋙ **directionality** /-'naliti/ *noun.*

direction finder *noun* an aerial used to determine the direction of incoming radio waves.

directive¹ /di'rektiv, die-/ *noun* an authoritative instruction issued by a high-level body or official.

directive² *adj* **1** serving to direct, guide, or influence. **2** serving to provide a direction.

direct labour *noun* labour that is employed directly rather than via a contractor.

directly¹ *adv* **1** in a direct manner. **2a** without delay; immediately. **b** *dated* soon or shortly.

directly² *conj chiefly Brit, informal* immediately after; as soon as.

direct mail *noun* unsolicited advertising material posted by a company to potential customers.

direct marketing *noun* the selling of goods by a company directly to its customers through mail order, telephone sales, newspaper advertising, etc rather than through retailers.

direct method *noun* a method of foreign-language teaching, placing the emphasis on oral work and minimal use of the student's own language.

direct object *noun* a grammatical object representing the primary goal or the result of the action of a verb, e.g. *me* in 'He hit me' and *a house* in 'We built a house'.

directoire /direk'twah/ *adj Brit* formerly, said of furniture and women's clothes: in the style of the period of the French Directory: *directoire knickers.* [French *Directoire* Directory, from Latin *directorium*: see DIRECTORY]

director *noun* **1** the head of an organized group or administrative unit. **2** a member of a governing board entrusted with the overall direction of a company. **3** somebody who has responsibility for supervising the artistic and technical aspects of a film or play: compare PRODUCER. ⋙ **directorial** /-'tawri·əl/ *adj,* **directorship** *noun.*

directorate /di'rektərət, die-/ *noun* **1** (*treated as sing. or pl*) a board of directors, e.g. of a company. **2** the office of director.

director-general *noun* (*pl* **directors-general** *or* **director-generals**) the senior director of a large organization.

Director of Public Prosecutions *noun* **1** in England and Wales, a government legal official with responsibility for instituting, undertaking, or advising on prosecutions in important criminal cases. **2** in Australia, a government legal official with responsibility for undertaking prosecutions on behalf of the Crown.

director's chair *noun* a lightweight folding armchair, usu with a canvas back and seat. [from its use by film directors on set]

directors-general *noun* pl of DIRECTOR-GENERAL.

Directory /di'rekt(ə)ri, die-/ *noun* (**the Directory**) the French Revolutionary government which ruled France from 1795 to 1799, consisting of a bicameral legislature and an executive comprising five 'directors'. [French *Directoire* Directory]

directory /di'rekt(ə)ri, die-/ *noun* (*pl* **directories**) **1** an alphabetical or classified list, e.g. of names, addresses, telephone numbers, etc. **2** on a computer, a list of the files contained in a disk. **3** formerly, a book or collection of directions or rules, *esp* concerning forms of worship. [Latin *directorium*, neuter of *directorius* directorial, from *dirigere*: see DIRECT¹]

directory assistance *noun NAmer* = DIRECTORY ENQUIRIES.

directory enquiries *pl noun* (*treated as sing. or pl*) a telephone service providing enquirers with the telephone numbers of people and organizations except those who are ex-directory.

direct proportion *noun* a proportion of two variables whose ratio is constant: compare INVERSE PROPORTION: *Isabel's silence about Mr Osmond … was in direct proportion to the frequency with which he occupied her thoughts* — Henry James.

directress /di'rektris, die-/ *or* **directrice** /di'rektrees/ *noun* a female director. [*directress* from DIRECTOR + -ESS; *directrice* from French]

directrix /di'rektriks, die-/ *noun* (*pl* **directrixes** *or* **directrices** /-triseez/) in geometry, a fixed curve by relation to which a conic section is described. [Latin *directrix*, fem of Latin *director*, from *dirigere*: see DIRECT¹]

direct selling *noun* = DIRECT MARKETING.

direct speech *noun* in grammar, the exact words uttered by a person or to somebody as opposed to their words in the form in which they are reported or referred to, e.g. *I told you so* as opposed to *I said I'd told him so*: compare INDIRECT SPEECH.

direct tax *noun* a tax on income or resources exacted directly from the person, organization, etc on whom it is levied: compare INDIRECT TAX.

dirge /duhj/ *noun* **1** a song or hymn of grief or lamentation, *esp* intended to accompany funeral or memorial rites. **2** a slow mournful song or piece of music. ⋙ **dirgeful** *adj.* [Middle English *dirige*, the Office of the Dead (from the first word of a late Latin antiphon used in the Office), imperative of Latin *dirigere*: see DIRECT¹]

dirham /'diərəm, 'diəhəm/ *noun* **1** the basic monetary unit of Morocco and the United Arab Emirates. **2a** a unit of currency in Libya, worth 1000th of a dinar. **b** a unit of currency in Qatar, worth 100th of a riyal. [Arabic *dirham* from Latin *drachma*: see DRACHMA]

dirigible¹ /'dirijəbl/ *adj* capable of being steered. [Latin *dirigere*: see DIRECT¹]

dirigible² *noun* an airship. [short for *dirigible balloon*]

dirigisme /deeree'zheez(ə)m (*French* diriʒizm)/ *noun chiefly derog* state control of the economy and social institutions. ⋙ **dirigiste** /-'zheest (French -ʒist)/ *adj.* [French *dirigisme*, from *diriger* to direct, from Latin *dirigere*: see DIRECT¹]

dirk /duhk/ *noun* a long straight-bladed dagger, formerly used *esp* by Scottish Highlanders. [Scots *durk*]

dirndl /'duhndl/ *noun* **1** (*also* **dirndl skirt**) a full skirt with a tight waistband. **2** a traditional Alpine style of woman's dress with a tight bodice and a dirndl skirt. [short for German *Dirndlkleid*, from German dialect *Dirndl* girl + German *Kleid* dress]

dirt /duht/ *noun* **1a** a filthy or soiling substance, e.g. mud or grime. **b** *informal* excrement: *dog dirt.* **c** somebody or something worthless or contemptible. **2** earth; soil. **3** *informal.* **a** obscene or pornographic speech or writing. **b** scandalous or malicious gossip: *Do you have any dirt on the new manager?* ⁕ **do somebody dirt** *informal* to deliberately do something that will harm the reputation, position, etc of (somebody). **treat like dirt** *informal* to treat (somebody) very badly, as if they are of no value or significance. [Middle English *drit*, from Old Norse]

dirt cheap *adj and adv informal* at a very low price.

dirt track *noun* a track of earth, cinders, etc used for motorcycle races or flat races.

dirty¹ *adj* (**dirtier, dirtiest**) **1a** not clean or pure; marked or contaminated with dirt. **b** causing somebody or something to become soiled or covered with dirt: *I do all the dirty jobs around the house.* **2a** base; sordid: *War is a dirty business.* **b** unsportsmanlike; unfair: *Some of the teams are noted for their dirty play.* **c** low; despicable: *That was a dirty trick to play on her!* **3a** indecent; obscene: *She won't tolerate dirty language in her pub.* **b** involving illicit sexual activity: *a dirty weekend.* **4** said of the weather: rough or stormy. **5** said of a colour: not clear and bright; dull: *drab dirty-pink walls.* **6** conveying resentment or disgust: *She gave him a dirty look.* **7** producing considerable nuclear fallout: *dirty bombs.* ⁕ **do the dirty on** to play a mean, underhanded, or treacherous trick on (somebody). ⋙ **dirtily** *adv,* **dirtiness** *noun.*

dirty² *verb* (**dirties, dirtied, dirtying**) ➤ *verb trans* to make (something) dirty. ➤ *verb intrans* to become dirty.

dirty³ *adv* **1** *informal* very: *There's a dirty great dog in the garden.* **2a** in an unfair, unsportsmanlike, or underhanded manner: *His motto is 'If you're losing, fight dirty'.* **b** using obscene or indecent language: *He thinks it's smart to talk dirty.*

dirty bomb *noun* a bomb made by surrounding a conventional explosive with radioactive material.

dirty old man *noun informal* **1** an elderly man who shows an interest in sex that is considered lewd or immoral or distasteful in a person of his age. **2** a man who shows an indecent and lascivious interest in younger members of the opposite sex.

dirty word *noun* **1** an obscene word or swearword. **2** *informal* something somebody has a strong dislike of: *Effort is a dirty word in his book.*

dirty work *noun informal* behaviour or an act that is unfair, treacherous, or criminal: *They sent her to do their dirty work for them.*

dis *or* **diss** /dis/ *verb trans* (**dissed, dissing**) *informal, chiefly NAmer* to insult (somebody); to speak to (them) in a disrespectful manner. [prob shortened from DISRESPECT²]

dis- *prefix* forming words, with the meanings: **1a** to do the opposite of (a specified action): *disestablish; disappear.* **b** to deprive of, remove (something specified) from: *disarm; dismember.* **c** to exclude or expel from: *disbar.* **2** opposite or absence of: *disarray; disbelief.* **3** not: *disagreeable; dishonest.* **4** completely: *disannul; disgruntled.* **5** = DYS-: *disfunction.* [Middle English *dis-, des-* via Old French *des-, dis-* from Latin DIS-, literally 'apart'; (sense 5) by folk etymology]

disability /disə'biliti/ *noun* (*pl* **disabilities**) **1a** the condition of being disabled; *specif* inability to do something because of physical or mental impairment. **b** something that disables; a handicap. **2** a legal disqualification.

disable /dis'aybl/ *verb trans* **1a** to make (somebody or something) incapable or ineffective. **b** to deprive (somebody or something) of physical soundness; to cripple (them or it). **2** to deprive (somebody) of a legal right, qualification, or capacity. ➤➤ **disablement** *noun*.

disabled¹ *adj* **1** having physical disabilities. **2** having been made incapable of operating.

disabled² *pl noun* (**the disabled**) people who are disabled.

disabuse /disə'byoohz/ *verb trans* (*usu* + of) to free (somebody) from a mistaken impression or judgment. [French *désabuser*, from *dés-* DIS- + *abuser*: see ABUSE¹]

disaccharide /die'sakəried/ *noun* any of a class of sugars, e.g. sucrose, which, on hydrolysis, yield two MONOSACCHARIDE (simple sugar) molecules.

disadvantage¹ /disəd'vahntij/ *noun* **1a** an unfavourable, inferior, or prejudicial situation: *With some of their best players unavailable, United were at a serious disadvantage.* **b** somebody or something which causes one to be in an unfavourable condition or position; a handicap: *Her poor health is a great disadvantage to her.* **2** loss or damage, *esp* to reputation or finances. [Middle English *disavauntage* from Old French, from DIS- + *avantage*: see ADVANTAGE]

disadvantage² *verb trans* to place (somebody) at a disadvantage.

disadvantaged *adj* underprivileged, *esp* socially.

disadvantageous /,disadvahn'tayjəs/ *adj* **1** causing a disadvantage. **2** prejudicial; unfavourable: *His actions were viewed by many in a disadvantageous light.* **3** derogatory; disparaging. ➤➤ **disadvantageously** *adv*, **disadvantageousness** *noun*.

disaffect /disə'fekt/ *verb trans* to alienate the affection or loyalty (of somebody). ➤➤ **disaffection** *noun*.

disaffected *adj* discontented and resentful, *esp* towards authority. ➤➤ **disaffectedly** *adv*.

disaffiliate /disə'filiayt/ *verb trans* to end an affiliation or connection with (a group or organization). ➤ *verb intrans* to separate from an affiliation or connection. ➤➤ **disaffiliation** /-'aysh(ə)n/ *noun*.

disaffirm /disə'fuhm/ *verb trans* to annul or repudiate (a legal settlement, etc). ➤➤ **disaffirmation** /,disafə'maysh(ə)n/ *noun*.

disafforest /disə'forist/ *verb trans chiefly Brit* to deforest (an area). ➤➤ **disafforestation** /-'staysh(ə)n/ *noun*.

disaggregate /dis'agrigayt/ *verb trans* to separate (something) into its component parts. ➤ *verb intrans* to break up into component parts. ➤➤ **disaggregation** /-'gaysh(ə)n/ *noun*.

disagree /disə'gree/ *verb intrans* **1** (*often* + with) to differ in opinion. **2** (*often* + with) to be unlike or at variance with (something). **3** (+ with) to have a bad effect on (somebody): *Fried foods disagree with me.* [Middle English *disagreen* from early French *desagreer*, from DIS- + *agreer*: see AGREE]

disagreeable *adj* **1** unpleasant; objectionable. **2** peevish; ill-tempered. ➤➤ **disagreeableness** *noun*, **disagreeably** *adv*.

disagreement *noun* **1** (*often* + with) a difference of opinion; an argument. **2** (*often* + between) a lack of correspondence; a disparity.

disallow /disə'low/ *verb trans* **1** to refuse to allow (something); to prohibit (it). **2** to refuse to admit or recognize the truth or validity of (something). ➤➤ **disallowance** *noun*.

disambiguate /disam'bigyooayt/ *verb trans* to remove possible ambiguity from (a phrase, sentence, etc). ➤➤ **disambiguation** /-'aysh(ə)n/ *noun*.

disappear /disə'piə/ *verb intrans* **1** to pass from view suddenly or gradually. **2** to cease to be or to be known. **3** *informal* to leave or depart, *esp* secretly. ➤ *verb trans* to cause (somebody) to disappear from their home or from society by imprisoning or killing them secretly. ➤➤ **disappearance** *noun*.

disapplication /dis,apli'kaysh(ə)n/ *noun* in British education, exemption from the requirements of the National Curriculum.

disappoint /disə'poynt/ *verb trans* to fail to meet the expectation or hope of (somebody), or to sadden (them) by so doing. ➤➤ **disappointing** *adj*, **disappointingly** *adv*. [early French *desapointier*, from DIS- + *apointier*: see APPOINT]

disappointed *adj* defeated in expectation or hope; thwarted: *She did not know whether to pity him for disappointed love of her, or to be angry with him for having got over it* — Hardy. ➤➤ **disappointedly** *adv*.

disappointment *noun* **1** the act or an instance of disappointing or being disappointed. **2** somebody or something that disappoints.

disapprobation /dis,aprə'baysh(ə)n/ *noun formal* disapproval.

disapproval /disə'proohv(ə)l/ *noun* unfavourable opinion; censure.

disapprove /disə'proohv/ *verb intrans* (*often* + of) to have or express an unfavourable opinion of (something or somebody). ➤ *verb trans* to refuse approval to (something); to reject (it). ➤➤ **disapprover** *noun*, **disapproving** *adj*, **disapprovingly** *adv*.

disarm /dis'ahm/ *verb trans* **1a** to deprive (somebody) of a weapon or weapons. **b** to deprive (a country or force) of a means of attack or defence. **c** to make (a bomb, etc) harmless, *esp* by removing a fuse or warhead. **2** to dispel the hostility or suspicion of (somebody). ➤ *verb intrans* **1** to lay aside arms. **2** to reduce or abolish weapons and armed forces. ➤➤ **disarmer** *noun*. [Middle English *desarmen* from Old French *desarmer*, from DIS- + *armer*: see ARM²]

disarmament /dis'ahməmənt/ *noun* the relinquishment or reduction of weapons and armed forces.

disarming *adj* allaying criticism or hostility: *a disarming smile.* ➤➤ **disarmingly** *adv*.

disarrange /disə'raynj/ *verb trans* to disturb the arrangement or order of (something). ➤➤ **disarrangement** *noun*.

disarray¹ /disə'ray/ *noun* a lack of order or sequence; disorder.

disarray² *verb trans* to throw or place (something) into disorder. [Middle English *disarayen* from Old French *desareer*, from DIS- + *areer* to array]

disarticulate /disah'tikyoolayt/ *verb trans* to cause (bones) to become disjointed. ➤ *verb intrans* said of bones: to become disjointed. ➤➤ **disarticulation** /-'laysh(ə)n/ *noun*.

disassemble /disə'sembl/ *verb trans* to take (a machine, etc) apart. ➤➤ **disassembly** *noun*.

disassembler *noun* somebody or something that disassembles something; *specif* a computer program that translates something written in machine code into assembly language.

disassociate /disə'sohsiayt, -shiayt/ *verb trans* = DISSOCIATE. ➤➤ **disassociation** /-'aysh(ə)n/ *noun*.

disaster /di'zahstə/ *noun* **1a** a sudden event bringing great damage, loss, or destruction. **b** an unfortunate occurrence; a calamity: *if you can meet with Triumph and Disaster and treat those two impostors just the same* — Kipling. **2** *informal* a failure: *He was a complete disaster as a teacher.* ➤➤ **disastrous** /-strəs/ *adj*, **disastrously** *adv*. [early French *desastre* from Old Italian *disastro*, literally 'unfavourable aspect of a star', from DIS- (from Latin) + *astro* star, from Latin *astrum*]

disaster area *noun* **1** an area officially declared to be the scene of a disaster and therefore qualified to receive emergency loans and supplies. **2** *informal* somebody or something that is disorderly, confused, or inadequate.

disavow /disə'vow/ *verb trans formal* to deny knowledge of or responsibility for (something); to repudiate (it). ➤➤ **disavowal** *noun*. [Middle English *desavowen* from Old French *desavouer*, from DIS- + *avouer*: see AVOW]

disband /dis'band/ *verb intrans* said of a group: to break up and separate; to disperse. ➤ *verb trans* to break up (a group). ➤➤ **disbandment** *noun*. [early French *desbander*, from DIS- + *bande* BAND³]

disbar /dis'bah/ *verb trans* (**disbarred, disbarring**) to deprive (a barrister) of the right to practise; to expel (them) from the bar. ➤➤ **disbarment** *noun*.

disbelief /disbi'leef/ *noun* mental rejection of something as untrue.

disbelieve /disbi'leev/ *verb trans* **1** to reject or withhold belief in (something). **2** to believe that (somebody) is not speaking the truth. ➤ *verb intrans* (*usu* + in) to reject or withhold belief: *He was … the sort of atheist who does not so much disbelieve in God as personally dislike him* — George Orwell. ➤➤ **disbeliever** *noun*, **disbelieving** *adj*.

disbud /dis'bud/ *verb trans* (**disbudded, disbudding**) to remove superfluous buds from (a plant), *esp* in order to improve the quality of bloom.

disburden /dis'buhd(ə)n/ *verb trans* (**disburdened, disburdening**) **1** to unburden (oneself or one's mind): *Mercedes … disburdened herself of copious opinions on that matter* — Jack London. **2** to unload (something). ➤➤ **disburdenment** *noun*.

disburse /dis'buhs/ *verb trans* to pay out (money), *esp* from a fund. ➤➤ **disbursement** *noun*, **disburser** *noun*. [early French *desbourser* from Old French *desborser*, from DIS- + *borser* to get money, from *borse* purse, from medieval Latin *bursa*]

disc (*NAmer* **disk**) /disk/ *noun* **1a** a thin flat circular object. **b** an apparently flat figure or surface, e.g. of a planet: *the solar disc.* **2** a disk for a computer. **3** *dated* a gramophone record. **4** any of various round flat anatomical structures, *esp* any of the cartilaginous discs between the spinal vertebrae: *She was suffering from a slipped disc and could barely move.* **5** any of the sharp-edged concave circular cutting blades of a harrow. **6** the central part of the flower head of a plant such as the daisy, which is made up of many closely packed small tubular flowers. [Latin *discus* from Greek *diskos* disc, platter, DISCUS]

Usage note

disc or **disk**? *Disc* is the correct spelling of the word in British English, except in the context of computers where the usual American English spelling *disk* is generally preferred: *a slipped disc* but *a disk drive*.

disc. *abbr* **1** discount. **2** discovered. **3** discoverer.

discalced /dis'kalst/ *adj* said of a friar or nun: barefoot or wearing only sandals. [part translation of Latin *discalceatus*, from DIS- + *calceatus*, past part. of *calceare* to put on shoes, from *calceus* shoe, from *calc-, calx* heel]

discard[1] /dis'kahd/ *verb trans* **1** to get rid of (something or somebody) as useless or superfluous. **2a** to throw out (a playing card) from one's hand. **b** to play (any card from a suit different from the one led except a trump) when unable to follow suit. ➤ *verb intrans* to discard a playing card. [DIS- + CARD[1]]

discard[2] /'diskahd/ *noun* **1** somebody or something discarded, *esp* a discarded card. **2** the act of discarding in a card game.

disc brake *noun* a brake that operates by the friction of pads pressing against the sides of a rotating disc.

disc camera *noun* a camera using film contained on a disc that rotates in the camera after each exposure.

discern /di'suhn/ *verb trans* **1** to detect (something or somebody) with one of the senses, *esp* vision. **2** to perceive (something) or recognize (it) mentally. ➤➤ **discerner** *noun*, **discernible** *adj*, **discernibly** *adv*. [Middle English *discernen* via French from Latin *discernere* to separate, distinguish between, from DIS- + *cernere* to sift]

discerning *adj* showing insight and understanding; discriminating. ➤➤ **discerningly** *adv*.

discernment *noun* skill in discerning; keen insight.

disc floret *noun* = DISC FLOWER.

disc flower *noun* any of the small tubular flowers that make up the central part of the flower head of a plant such as the daisy: compare RAY FLOWER.

discharge[1] /dis'chahj/ *verb trans* **1a** to dismiss (somebody) from employment or service. **b** to release (somebody) from custody or care. **2a** to fulfil (a debt or obligation) by performing an appropriate action. **b** to release (somebody) from an obligation. **3a** to send or pour out (a liquid or gas); to emit (it). **b** to shoot (a firearm). **4** to annul (an order of court) legally. **5a** to unload (a charge, load, or burden). **b** to unload (a boat, etc). **6** to remove an electric charge from (something) or reduce the electric charge of (it). ➤ *verb intrans* **1** to throw off or deliver a load, charge, or burden. **2a** said

of a gun: to be fired. **b** to pour out fluid contents. **3** to lose or reduce an electric charge. ➤➤ **dischargeable** *adj*, **discharger** *noun*. [Middle English *dischargen* via French from late Latin *discarricare*, from Latin DIS- + *carricare*: see CHARGE[1]]

discharge[2] /'dischahj, dis'chahj/ *noun* **1** release or dismissal, *esp* from an office or employment, or a document stating this. **2a** the act or an instance of relieving somebody of an obligation, accusation, or penalty. **b** a certificate of release or payment. **3a** legal release from confinement. **b** an acquittal. **4** the act or an instance of discharging or unloading. **5** the act or an instance of firing a missile or missiles: *an artillery discharge.* **6a** the act or an instance of flowing or pouring out. **b** something that is discharged or emitted: *a purulent discharge.* **7a** a brief flow of an electric charge through a gas, usu with associated light emission. **b** the conversion of the chemical energy of a battery into electrical energy.

discharge tube *noun* a tube which contains gas or vapour, usu at very low pressure, in which a discharge of electricity, usu producing light, occurs when a high voltage is applied to electrodes in the tube.

disc harrow *noun* a harrow with sharp-edged discs set at an angle for cutting or loosening soil.

disciple /di'siepl/ *noun* **1** a person who learns from, and is much in the company of, a teacher or instructor; a pupil or follower: *I found it [the group] to consist of a veteran angler and two rustic disciples* — Washington Irving. **2** any of the followers of Christ during his life on earth; *esp* any of Christ's twelve appointed followers. ➤➤ **discipleship** *noun*. [Old English via French from Latin *discipulus* pupil, from *discere* to learn]

disciplinarian /disipli'neəri·ən/ *noun* a person who enforces or advocates strict discipline or order.

disciplinary /'disiplinəri/ *adj* **1** of or involving discipline; corrective: *disciplinary action.* **2** of a particular field of study.

discipline[1] /'disiplin/ *noun* **1a** order obtained by enforcing obedience, e.g. in a school or army. **b** self-control. **2** training of the mind and character designed to produce obedience and self-control. **3** punishment or chastisement. **4** a system of rules governing conduct. **5** a field of study. ➤➤ **disciplinal** *adj*. [Middle English via French from Latin *disciplina* teaching, learning, from *discipulus*: see DISCIPLE]

discipline[2] *verb trans* **1** to punish or penalize (a person or animal) for the sake of discipline. **2** to train (a person or animal) by instruction and exercise, *esp* in obedience and self-control. **3** to bring (a group, e.g. troops) under control. ➤➤ **disciplinable** *adj*, **discipliner** *noun*.

discipular /di'sipyoolə/ *adj formal* of a disciple.

disc jockey *noun* a person who plays and introduces recorded music on a radio programme or at a nightclub or party.

disclaim /dis'klaym/ *verb trans* **1** to deny or disavow (something). **2** to renounce a legal claim to (property). ➤ *verb intrans* to make a disclaimer. [Anglo-French *disclaimer*, from DIS- + *claimer* to claim, from Old French *clamer*, from Latin *clamare*: see CLAIM[1]]

disclaimer *noun* **1** a denial or repudiation. **2a** a denial of legal responsibility. **b** a renunciation of a legal claim. [Anglo-French *disclaimer*, from the verb: see DISCLAIM]

disclose /dis'klohz/ *verb trans* **1** to make (information) known; to reveal (it) to public knowledge. **2** to expose (something) to view. ➤➤ **discloser** *noun*. [Middle English *disclosen* via French from Latin *disclaudere* to open, from DIS- + *claudere* to close]

disclosing agent *noun* a substance that indicates the presence of something, e.g. plaque on teeth.

disclosing tablet *noun* a tablet containing a disclosing agent.

disclosure /dis'klohzhə/ *noun* **1** something disclosed; a revelation. **2** the act or an instance of disclosing or exposing.

disco /'diskoh/ *noun* (*pl* **discos**) *informal* **1** a discotheque. **2** a collection of popular records together with the equipment for playing them. **3** a type of soul-based dance music. [short for DISCOTHEQUE]

discobolus or **discobolos** /di'skobələs/ *noun* (*pl* **discoboli** /-lie/ or **discoboloi** /-loy/) **1** a discus thrower, *esp* in classical Greece. **2** a classical statue of a discus thrower. [via Latin from Greek *diskobolos*, from *diskos* DISCUS + *ballein* to throw]

discography /di'skografi/ *noun* (*pl* **discographies**) **1** a descriptive list of recordings, *esp* by a particular artist or band. **2** the study of recorded music. ➤➤ **discographer** *noun*, **discographic** /-'grafik/

adj, **discographical** /-'grafikl/ adj. [DISC + -O- + -GRAPHY, on the pattern of *biography*]

discoid /'diskoyd/ adj resembling a disc or discus; disc-shaped. [via late Latin from Greek *diskoeidēs*, from *diskos* DISC]

discolour (*NAmer* **discolor**) /dis'kulǝ/ verb trans to cause (something) to change colour for the worse; to stain (it). ➤ verb intrans to become discoloured. ➤➤ **discolouration** /-'raysh(ǝ)n/ noun. [Middle English *discolouren* via French and late Latin from Latin *discolor* of another colour, from DIS- + *color* COLOUR¹]

discombobulate /diskǝm'bobyoolayt/ verb trans *NAmer, informal* to upset or confuse (somebody). [prob alteration of DISCOMPOSE]

discomfit /dis'kumfit/ verb trans (**discomfited, discomfiting**) **1** to cause perplexity and embarrassment to (somebody); to disconcert (them): *He imagined himself to be ... accomplished ... because he could spell his own name; and was marvellously discomfited that I didn't think the same* — Emily Brontë. **2** to frustrate the plans of (somebody); to thwart (them). ➤➤ **discomfiture** /-fichǝ/ noun. [Middle English *discomfiten* from Old French *desconfit*, past part. of *desconfire*, from DIS- + *confire*: see COMFIT]

Usage note
discomfit or **discomfort**? *Discomfit* originally meant to 'defeat' and from that came to mean to 'thwart': *His attempts at persuasion were of no avail and he retired discomfited.* Because it is usually pronounced the same, or virtually the same, as the commoner and weaker verb *discomfort*, it is now often treated as having the same meaning to 'make (somebody) feel uneasy'.

discomfort¹ noun mental or physical unease, or something causing this.

discomfort² /dis'kumfǝt/ verb trans to make (somebody) uncomfortable or uneasy. [Middle English *discomforten* from Old French *desconforter*, from DIS- + *conforter* to COMFORT²]

Usage note
discomfort or **discomfit**? See note at DISCOMFIT.

discommode /diskǝ'mohd/ verb trans to inconvenience or incommode (somebody). [early French *discommoder* from DIS- + *commode*: see COMMODE]

discompose /diskǝm'pohz/ verb trans *formal* to disturb the composure of (somebody). ➤➤ **discomposure** /-'pohzhǝ/ noun.

disconcert /diskǝn'suht/ verb trans to disturb the composure of (somebody); to fluster (them). ➤➤ **disconcerted, disconcerting** adj, **disconcertingly** adv, **disconcertion** /-'suhsh(ǝ)n/ noun. [obsolete French *disconcerter*, from DIS- + *concerter* to bring together, from Latin *concertare*: see CONCERT¹]

disconfirm /diskǝn'fuhm/ verb trans to indicate that (a theory, etc) is not correct. ➤➤ **disconfirmation** /,diskonfǝ'maysh(ǝ)n/ noun.

disconnect /diskǝ'nekt/ verb trans **1** to break the connection of (something), e.g. to a power supply: *Disconnect the lawnmower before cleaning the blades.* **2a** to cut off the supply of (a public service, e.g. electricity or the telephone). **b** to cut off the supply of e.g. electricity or the telephone to (a person, etc). **3** to cut (somebody) off during a telephone call. ➤ verb intrans to become disconnected or be able to be disconnected. ➤➤ **disconnection** /-'neksh(ǝ)n/ noun.

disconnected adj **1** disjointed or incoherent: *Her essay was just a stream of disconnected thoughts.* **2** not connected; having been disconnected. ➤➤ **disconnectedly** adv, **disconnectedness** noun.

disconsolate /dis'konsǝlǝt/ adj dejected; downcast. ➤➤ **disconsolately** adv, **disconsolateness** noun, **disconsolation** /-'laysh(ǝ)n/ noun. [Middle English from Latin *disconsolatus*, from DIS- + *consolatus*, past part. of *consolari*: see CONSOLE¹]

discontent¹ /diskǝn'tent/ noun **1** lack of contentment; dissatisfaction. **2** somebody who is discontented; a malcontent.

discontent² verb trans to make (somebody) discontented.

discontent³ adj = DISCONTENTED.

discontented adj restlessly unhappy; dissatisfied. ➤➤ **discontentedly** adv, **discontentedness** noun, **discontentment** noun.

discontinue /diskǝn'tinyooh/ verb (**discontinues, discontinued, discontinuing**) ➤ verb trans **1** to cease or stop (something). **2** to cease production of (something): *This line has been discontinued.* ➤ verb intrans to come to an end. ➤➤ **discontinuance** noun, **discontinuation** /-'aysh(ǝ)n/ noun. [Middle English *discontinuen* via French from Latin *discontinuare*, from DIS- + *continuare*: see CONTINUE]

discontinuous /diskǝn'tinyooǝs/ adj lacking sequence, coherence, or continuity. ➤➤ **discontinuity** /,diskonti'nyooh·iti/ noun, **discontinuously** adv.

discord¹ /'diskawd/ noun **1** lack of agreement or harmony; conflict. **2a** a combination of musical sounds that strikes the ear very harshly; dissonance. **b** a harsh unpleasant combination of sounds. [Middle English *discorde* from Latin *discord-, discors* discordant, from DIS- + *cord-, cor* heart]

discord² /'diskawd, dis'kawd/ verb intrans to disagree or clash. [Middle English *discorden* via French from Latin *discordare*, from *discord-, discors* discordant, from DIS- + *cord-, cor* heart]

discordant /dis'kawd(ǝ)nt/ adj **1** relating to a discord; dissonant: *discordant tones.* **2** disagreeing; at variance. ➤➤ **discordance** noun, **discordancy** /-si/ noun, **discordantly** adv.

discotheque /'diskǝtek/ noun a nightclub for dancing to recorded music. [French *discothèque*, from *disque* disc, record + -O- + -*thèque* as in *bibliothèque* library]

discount¹ /'diskownt/ noun **1** a reduction made from the gross amount or value of something, e.g.: **a** a reduction in the price of goods, accorded *esp* to special or trade customers. **b** a reduction in the amount due on a bill of exchange, debt, etc when paid promptly or before the specified date. **2** (*used before a noun*) selling goods or services at a discount, or relating to such goods and services. ✳ **at a discount** below the usual price.

discount² /'diskownt/ verb trans **1a** to make a deduction from (a price), usu for cash or prompt payment. **b** to sell (an item) or offer (it) for sale at a discount. **c** to buy or sell (a bill of exchange) before maturity at below the stated price. **2** /dis'kownt/. **a** to leave (something) out of account as unimportant, unreliable, or irrelevant; to disregard (it). **b** to underestimate the importance of (something); to minimize (it). **3** to take (a future event) into account in present arrangements or calculations in order to lessen its effect. ➤➤ **discountable** /dis'kowntǝbl/ adj. [modification of French *décompter* via French and medieval Latin from Latin DIS- + *computare*: see COUNT¹]

discounted cash flow noun a method of assessing the present value of an anticipated future sum.

discountenance /dis'kownt(ǝ)nǝns/ verb trans **1** to abash or disconcert (somebody). **2** *formal* to discourage (something or somebody) by showing disapproval.

discount house noun **1** *chiefly Brit* an organization whose business is discounting bills of exchange before their due date. **2** *chiefly NAmer* a shop where goods are sold at a discount from the recommended price.

discount market noun the part of the money market, including banks and, formerly, discount houses, involved in discounting bills of exchange and other financial securities.

discount rate noun **1** the interest on an annual basis deducted in advance on a loan, e.g. a bank loan. **2** the charge levied by a central bank for advances and rediscounts.

discount store noun *NAmer* = DISCOUNT HOUSE (2).

discourage /dis'kurij/ verb trans **1** to deprive (somebody) of confidence; to dishearten (them). **2a** to hinder or deter (somebody) from doing something: *They tried to discourage their son from buying a motorbike.* **b** to attempt to prevent (something), *esp* by showing disapproval of it or taking some action to counter it. ➤➤ **discouragement** noun, **discouraging** adj, **discouragingly** adv. [Old French *descoragier*, from DIS- + *corage*: see COURAGE]

discourse¹ /'diskaws/ noun **1** talk, conversation, or continuous text, *esp*, in linguistics, with regard to logical flow and progression through choice of expression, etc. **2** a formal speech or piece of writing. **3** *archaic* the power of reasoning. [Middle English *discours* from late Latin *discursus* conversation, literally 'running to and fro', past part. of Latin *discurrere* to run about, from DIS- + *currere* to run]

discourse² /dis'kaws/ verb intrans *literary* **1** (*often* + on/upon) to express one's ideas in speech or writing: *For two hours he discoursed upon celts, arrowheads, and shards* — Conan Doyle. **2** (*also* + on/upon) to talk or converse. ➤➤ **discourser** noun.

discourse marker /'diskaws/ noun in linguistics, a word used in conversation or discourse to signal the kind of communication one is making, e.g. *certainly* for concessions, *besides, I mean,* for additions and reinforcements, *therefore* for conclusions, and *but* for counter arguments.

discourteous /dis'kuhti·əs/ *adj* rude or impolite; lacking in manners or consideration for others. ➤➤ **discourteously** *adv*, **discourteousness** *noun*.

discourtesy /dis'kuhtəsi/ *noun* (*pl* **discourtesies**) rudeness, incivility, or an instance of either.

discover /di'skuvə/ *verb trans* (**discovered, discovering**) 1 to find (something) by searching or by chance. 2 to be the first to see, find, or know about (something): *Sir Alexander Fleming discovered penicillin.* 3 to realize or find out (a fact). 4 *archaic* to disclose (something): *I grew more and more astonished as she discovered her plan to me.* ➤➤ **discoverable** *adj*, **discoverer** *noun*. [Middle English *discoveren* via Old French *descovrir* from late Latin *discooperire* to disclose, from DIS- + *cooperire*: see COVER¹]

discovered check *noun* in chess, the putting of one's opponent's king in check from a piece other than the one used for the move.

discovery /di'skuv(ə)ri/ *noun* (*pl* **discoveries**) 1 the act or process of discovering or revealing something; the process of being discovered or revealed. 2a somebody or something discovered. b a divulgence or revelation. 3 in law, an obligatory disclosure of documents or facts by a party to a legal action. 4 (**Discovery**) a variety of eating apple with a red and green skin and crisp moderately sweet flesh.

discredit¹ /dis'kredit/ *verb trans* (**discredited, discrediting**) 1 to reject (a story or statement) as untrue. 2 to cast doubt on the accuracy, authority, or reputation of (a person or their ideas, work, etc).

discredit² *noun* 1a loss of credit or reputation: *I knew stories to the discredit of England* — W B Yeats. b a person or thing that brings disgrace. 2 loss of belief or confidence; doubt: *Contradictions cast discredit on his testimony.*

discreditable *adj* bringing discredit or disgrace; shameful. ➤➤ **discreditably** *adv*.

discreet /di'skreet/ *adj* 1 judicious in speech or conduct; *esp* capable of maintaining a prudent silence. 2 subtle; trying not to attract attention. 3 unpretentious or modest; showing quiet good taste: *The house was furnished with discreet elegance.* ➤➤ **discreetly** *adv*, **discreetness** *noun*. [early French *discret* from Latin *discretus* separate, past part. of *discernere* (see DISCERN); the sense influenced by late Latin *discretion-, discretio* discernment]

Usage note

discreet *or* discrete? Though they are pronounced the same and look very similar, these two words have distinct and different meanings. When used of people, *discreet* means 'careful, reliable, and not likely to gossip' (*Can we rely on her to be discreet?*): when used about actions, it means 'unlikely to attract attention' (*We have made a few discreet inquiries*). Discrete is a more technical word meaning 'separate' or 'individually distinct': *The process can be broken down into a number of discrete stages.*

discrepancy /di'skrep(ə)nsi/ *noun* (*pl* **discrepancies**) 1 the state of being at variance, or of not agreeing. 2 an instance of inconsistency between two accounts, etc.

discrepant /di'skrep(ə)nt/ *adj* said of two reports, etc: not agreeing; having discrepancies; at variance. ➤➤ **discrepantly** *adv*. [Latin *discrepant-, discrepans*, present part. of *discrepare* to sound discordantly, from DIS- + *crepare* to rattle, creak]

discrete /di'skreet/ *adj* 1 individually distinct: *They form two discrete categories.* 2 consisting of distinct or unconnected elements; discontinuous. ➤➤ **discretely** *adv*, **discreteness** *noun*. [Middle English from Latin *discretus*: see DISCREET]

Usage note

discrete *or* discreet? See note at DISCREET.

discretion /di'skresh(ə)n/ *noun* 1 the quality of being discreet, e.g. in employing self-control, and in safeguarding the dignity and privacy of others. 2 the ability to make responsible decisions: *She has reached the age of discretion.* 3 the freedom to act as one sees fit in any particular situation: *I leave the matter to your discretion.*

discretionary *adj* 1 left to or exercised at one's own discretion: *discretionary powers.* 2 subject to the discretion of another: *a discretionary grant.*

discretionary income *noun* what remains of one's income after obligatory charges and basic living expenses have been deducted: compare DISPOSABLE INCOME.

discretionary trust *noun* a trust in which the number of shares allocated to each beneficiary is determined not by the SETTLOR (creator of the trust) in the trust, but at the discretion of the trustees.

discriminant /di'skriminənt/ *noun* 1 a distinguishing characteristic. 2 a mathematical expression providing a criterion for the behaviour of another more complicated expression, relation, or set of relations.

discriminate¹ /di'skriminayt/ *verb intrans* 1a (+ between) to make a distinction between (two things): *He can't discriminate between fact and fancy.* b to show good judgment or discernment. 2 (+ against) to treat (somebody) differently and *esp* unfavourably on the grounds of race, sex, religion, etc: *Women feel discriminated against.* [Latin *discriminatus*, past part. of *discriminare* to divide, from *discrimin-, discrimen* distinction, difference, from *discernere*: see DISCERN]

discriminate² /di'skriminət/ *adj* showing discrimination.

discriminating *adj* 1 discerning or judicious in matters of taste, etc. 2 observant of fine differences and distinctions: *a discriminating eye.* 3 said of a duty or tariff: imposed at differential rates rather than at a flat rate. ➤➤ **discriminatingly** *adv*.

discrimination /di,skrimi'naysh(ə)n/ *noun* 1 prejudicial treatment, e.g. on the grounds of race or sex. 2 the recognition or appreciation of the difference between one thing and another. 3 discernment and good judgment, *esp* in matters of taste. ➤➤ **discriminational** *adj*.

discriminative /di'skriminətiv/ *adj* = DISCRIMINATORY.

discriminator *noun* somebody or something that discriminates; *specif* an electronic circuit that can be adjusted to accept or reject signals above a specific value.

discriminatory /di'skriminət(ə)ri/ *adj* showing discrimination, *esp* of an unfavourable kind: *a discriminatory law.* ➤➤ **discriminatorily** *adv*.

discursive /di'skuhsiv, -ziv/ *adj* 1 said of a person's writing or lecturing style, etc: passing unmethodically from one topic to another; digressive. 2 relating to discourse of various kinds. 3 in philosophy, proceeding by logical argument or reason. ➤➤ **discursively** *adv*, **discursiveness** *noun*. [late Latin *discursivus* from Latin *discursus*: see DISCOURSE¹]

discus /'diskəs/ *noun* 1 a solid disc, between 180mm and 219mm (about 7–9in) in diameter, that is thicker in the centre than at the edge, thrown as an event in ancient Greek games and in modern athletic contests. 2 the athletic event of throwing the discus. [Latin *discus* quoit, disc, dish, from Greek *diskos*, from *dikein* to throw]

discuss /di'skus/ *verb trans* 1 to consider or examine (a topic) in speech or writing. 2 to talk about (an issue, problem, etc) so as to make decisions: *Let's discuss holiday dates.* ➤➤ **discussable** *adj*, **discusser** *noun*, **discussible** *adj*. [Middle English *discussen* from Latin *discussus*, past part. of *discutere* to shatter, later 'to analyse in detail', from DIS- apart + *quatere* to shake]

discussion /di'skush(ə)n/ *noun* 1 consideration of a question in open debate or conversation. 2 a conversation or debate about something.

disdain¹ /dis'dayn/ *noun* the feeling one has for something one despises; contempt or scorn. [Middle English *desdeynen* via French from Latin *dedignari* to scorn, from DE- + *dignari* to deem worthy, from *dignus* worthy]

disdain² *verb trans* 1 to regard (a person or thing) with disdain. 2 to refuse (to do something) because of disdain: *She disdained to answer him.*

disdainful /dis'daynf(ə)l/ *adj* feeling or showing disdain; superior: *a disdainful smile.* ➤➤ **disdainfully** *adv*, **disdainfulness** *noun*.

disease /di'zeez/ *noun* 1 a condition of a living animal or plant body, or of a specific part of one, that impairs the performance of a vital function; a sickness or malady.

Editorial note

Diseases are the result of something going wrong with the normal everyday functions of the body. They may result from a multitude of causes – such as in-built (or genetic) errors, auto-immune disorders (where the body's own defence mechanisms turn inwards on itself), or damage from without by, for example, viruses, bacteria, toxins or chemicals; they can result in impairment of both mental and physical function and may in some cases be preventable — Dr John Cormack.

2 a harmful or corrupt development, situation, condition, etc: *the disease of self-doubt.* ➤➤ **diseased** *adj*. [Middle English *disese* uneasiness, sickness, from early French *desaise*, from DIS- + *aise*: see EASE¹]

diseconomy /disi'konəmi/ *noun* (*pl* **diseconomies**) 1 a lack of economy. 2 an increase in costs, or a factor responsible for this.

disembark /disim'bahk/ *verb intrans* to alight from a ship, plane, etc. ➤ *verb trans* to put (passengers, etc) on land from a ship, plane, etc. ➤➤ **disembarkation** /dis,embah'kaysh(ə)n/ *noun.* [early French *desembarquer*, from DIS- + *embarquer*: see EMBARK]

disembarrass /disim'barəs/ *verb trans formal* (*usu* + of) to free (somebody) from something troublesome or superfluous: *He disembarrassed himself of the autograph-hunters by jumping into a cab.* ➤➤ **disembarrassment** *noun.*

disembodied /disim'bodid/ *adj* 1 denoting a soul existing apart from the body it inhabited: *We were in some mysterious way invisible, and as free to come and go as disembodied spirits* — Lewis Carroll. 2 coming from an invisible source: *a disembodied voice.*

disembowel /disim'bowəl/ *verb trans* (**disembowelled, disembowelling**, *NAmer* **disemboweled, disemboweling**) to remove the bowels or entrails of or eviscerate (a person or animal). ➤➤ **disembowelment** *noun.*

disempower /disim'powə/ *verb trans* (**disempowered, disempowering**) to deprive (a person or group) of initiative or confidence. ➤➤ **disempowerment** *noun.*

disenchant /disin'chahnt/ *verb trans* to rid (somebody) of an illusion; to disillusion (them): *The Darwin who wrote The Descent of Man was disenchanted with natural selection* — Phillip E Johnson. ➤➤ **disenchanted** *adj,* **disenchanter** *noun,* **disenchanting** *adj,* **disenchantingly** *adv,* **disenchantment** *noun.* [early French *desenchanter*, from DIS- + *enchanter*: see ENCHANT]

disencumber /disin'kumbə/ *verb trans* (**disencumbered, disencumbering**) to free (somebody, *esp* oneself) from an encumbrance. [early French *desencombrer*, from DIS- + *encombrer*: see ENCUMBER]

disendow /disin'dow/ *verb trans* to strip (a church, etc) of an endowment. ➤➤ **disendowment** *noun.*

disenfranchise /disin'franchiez/ *verb trans* 1 to deprive (a person) of any citizen's rights, *esp* that of voting. 2 to deprive (a place) of the right to send representatives to an elected body. ➤➤ **disenfranchisement** /-chizmənt/ *noun.*

disengage /disin'gayj/ *verb trans* 1 to release or detach (somebody, *esp* oneself, or a part of one) from something that holds, engages, or entangles: *He disengaged himself from her embrace.* 2 to remove (troops) from combat areas. ➤ *verb intrans* 1 said of troops or combatants: to withdraw, or retire from engagement. 2 in fencing, to move one's sword to the other side of an opponent's sword in order to attack. ➤➤ **disengagement** *noun.* [French *désengager*, from *dés*-DIS- + *engager*: see ENGAGE]

disentail /disin'tayl/ *verb trans* in law, to free (an estate) from entail. ➤➤ **disentailment** *noun.*

disentangle /disin'tanggl/ *verb* 1 to free (somebody or something) from entanglements: *if I can disentangle myself from a prior commitment.* 2 to unravel (tangled wool, string, etc). ➤➤ **disentanglement** *noun.*

disenthral (*NAmer* **disenthrall**) /disin'thrawl/ *verb trans* (**disenthralled, disenthralling**) *literary* to set (a person or thing) free. ➤➤ **disenthralment** *noun.*

disentitle /disin'tietl/ *verb trans* to deprive (somebody) of a right or entitlement: *Certain factors may disentitle you to benefit.* ➤➤ **disentitlement** *noun.*

disequilibrium /dis,eekwi'libri·əm, dis,ek-/ *noun* loss or lack of equilibrium.

disestablish /disi'stablish/ *verb trans* to deprive (*esp* a national Church) of established status. ➤➤ **disestablishment** *noun.*

disesteem[1] /disi'steem/ *noun dated* disfavour; lack of esteem.

disesteem[2] *verb trans dated* to regard (a person or thing) with disfavour, or think little of (them): *I would not therefore be thought to disesteem … the study of nature* — John Locke.

diseur /dee'zuh/ *noun* (*pl* **diseurs** /dee'zuh/) a male reciter or entertainer, *esp* a professional one. [French *diseur*, from *dire* to say, from Latin *dicere*]

diseuse /dee'zuhz/ *noun* (*pl* **diseuses** /dee'zuhz/) a female reciter or entertainer, *esp* a professional one. [French *diseuse* from *dire* to say, from Latin *dicere*]

disfavour[1] (*NAmer* **disfavor**) /dis'fayvə/ *noun* 1 disapproval or dislike. 2 the state of being disapproved of: *He fell into disfavour.* [prob from early French *desfaveur*, from DIS- + Old French *favor*: see FAVOUR[1]]

disfavour[2] (*NAmer* **disfavor**) *verb trans* to regard or treat (a person or thing) with disfavour.

disfigure /dis'figə/ *verb trans* to mar or spoil the appearance or quality of (somebody or something). ➤➤ **disfigurement** *noun.* [early French *desfigurer*, from DIS- + *figure* form, face, figure, from Latin *figura*]

disforest /dis'forist/ *verb trans* = DEFOREST.

disfranchise /dis'franchiez/ *verb trans* = DISENFRANCHISE.

disfunction /dis'fungksh(ə)n/ *noun* = DYSFUNCTION.

disgorge /dis'gawj/ *verb trans* 1 to vomit (food) from the stomach. 2 to discharge (a load or contents): *The bus disgorged its load at the camp.* 3 to give up (dishonestly acquired funds) on request or under pressure. ➤ *verb intrans* to discharge contents. ➤➤ **disgorgement** *noun.* [early French *desgorger*, from DIS- + *gorge* throat]

disgorger *noun* a device for extracting a hook from a fish's gullet.

disgrace[1] /dis'grays/ *verb trans* 1 to bring reproach or shame to (somebody) through unacceptable conduct. 2 to cause (somebody) to lose favour or standing, *esp* as a consequence of dishonourable behaviour: *the disgraced minister.*

disgrace[2] *noun* 1 loss of favour, honour, or respect; shame. 2 somebody or something shameful: *His manners are a disgrace; You're a disgrace to the school.* ✲ **in disgrace** out of somebody's favour, e.g. because of unacceptable conduct. [via French from Old Italian *disgrazia*, from DIS- + *grazia* grace, from Latin *gratia* favour: see GRACE[1]]

disgraceful /dis'graysf(ə)l/ *adj* shameful or shocking. ➤➤ **disgracefully** *adv,* **disgracefulness** *noun.*

disgruntled /dis'gruntld/ *adj* aggrieved and dissatisfied. ➤➤ **disgruntlement** *noun.* [from DIS- (used intensively) + *gruntle* to grumble, from Middle English *gruntlen*, frequentative of GRUNT[1]]

disguise[1] /dis'giez/ *verb trans* 1 to change the appearance or nature of (a person or thing) in order to conceal their identity. 2 to hide the true state or character of (something): *The facts cannot be disguised any longer.* ➤➤ **disguisedly** /-zidli/ *adv,* **disguisement** *noun.* [Middle English *disgisen* to change one's dress, from Old French *desguisier*, from DIS- + *guise* fashion, of Germanic origin]

disguise[2] *noun* 1 a costume or other means of disguising oneself or concealing one's identity. 2 the state of being disguised: *The Duke returns to Vienna in disguise.*

disgust[1] /dis'gust/ *noun* 1 the loathing or revulsion one feels for something that sickens one, or that one cannot bear. 2 the indignation one feels at a moral outrage. ✲ **in disgust** because of disgust, boredom, or frustration: *I gave up in disgust after the third unsuccessful attempt.* [early modern French *desgoust*, from DIS- + *goust* taste, from Latin *gustus*]

disgust[2] *verb trans* to arouse repugnance, aversion, or indignation in (somebody). ➤➤ **disgusted** *adj,* **disgustedly** *adv,* **disgusting** *adj,* **disgustingly** *adv.*

dish[1] /dish/ *noun* 1a a shallow open often circular vessel used *esp* for holding or serving food. b any vessel from which food is eaten or served. c the amount a dish will hold; a dishful: *He ate two dishes of pasta.* d (**the dishes**) the utensils and tableware used in preparing, serving, and eating a meal: *I have to wash the dishes.* 2 a type of food prepared in a particular way: *a fish dish.* 3 something resembling a dish in shape, e.g.: a a directional aerial, *esp* for receiving radio or television transmissions or microwaves, having a concave *usu* parabolic reflector. b a hollow or depression, e.g. a concavity in a spoked wheel. 4 *informal* an attractive person. ➤➤ **dishful** (*pl* **dishfuls**) *noun,* **dishlike** *adj.* [Old English *disc* plate, ultimately from Latin *discus*: see DISCUS]

dish[2] *verb trans* 1 to make (a surface) concave like a dish. 2 *chiefly Brit, informal* to ruin or spoil (a person or their hopes). ➤ *verb intrans NAmer* to gossip. ✲ **dish the dirt** *informal* to spread gossip.

dishabille /disə'beel/ *noun* = DÉSHABILLÉ.

dish aerial *noun* = DISH[1] (3A).

disharmony /dis'hahməni/ *noun* lack of harmony; discord. ➤➤ **disharmonious** /-'mohni·əs/ *adj.*

dishcloth *noun* 1 a cloth for washing dishes. 2 a cloth for drying dishes; = TEA TOWEL.

dishcloth gourd *noun NAmer* = LOOFAH.

dishdasha /dishdashə/ *or* **dishdash** /'dishdash/ *noun* a long-sleeved full-length robe worn by men from the Arabian peninsula. [from Arabic *dišdāša*]

dishearten /dis'haht(ə)n/ *verb trans* (**disheartened, disheartening**) to discourage (somebody) or cause (them) to lose enthusiasm or morale. ➤➤ **disheartening** *adj*, **dishearteningly** *adv*, **disheartenment** *noun*.

dished *adj* **1** slightly concave. **2** said of a pair of vehicle wheels: fixed so as to be nearer together at the bottom than the top.

dishevel /di'shevl/ *verb trans* (**dishevelled, dishevelling**, *NAmer* **disheveled, disheveling**) to make (hair or clothes) untidy or disordered. [back-formation from DISHEVELLED]

dishevelled (*NAmer* **disheveled**) *adj* said *esp* of a person's hair or appearance: unkempt or untidy. [Middle English *discheveled* with the hair uncovered, from early French *descheveler*, past part. of *descheveler*, from DIS- + *chevel* hair, from Latin *capillus*]

dishonest /dis'onist/ *adj* not honest, truthful, or sincere; deceitful. ➤➤ **dishonestly** *adv*. [early French *deshoneste*, from DIS- + *honeste* HONEST]

dishonesty *noun* lack of honesty or integrity; deceitfulness.

dishonor /dis'onə/ *noun and verb NAmer* see DISHONOUR[1], DISHONOUR[2].

dishonorable *adj NAmer* see DISHONOURABLE.

dishonour[1] (*NAmer* **dishonor**) /dis'onə/ *noun* **1** loss of honour or reputation. **2** a state of shame or disgrace. **3** an insult or affront. [Old French *deshonor*, from DIS- + *honor* HONOUR[1]]

dishonour[2] (*NAmer* **dishonor**) *verb trans* **1** to treat (a person, or a thing deserving respect) in a degrading or disrespectful manner. **2** to bring shame on (somebody). **3** said of a bank, etc: to refuse to accept or pay (a cheque, etc).

dishonourable (*NAmer* **dishonorable**) *adj* base or shameful; discreditable. ➤➤ **dishonourably** *adv*.

dish out *verb trans* **1** to serve out (food) from a dish, pan, etc. **2** *informal* to give or distribute (advice, criticism, etc) freely. ✳ **dish it out** *informal* to criticize people or inflict punishments indiscriminately.

dish towel *noun Scot, NAmer* = TEA TOWEL.

dish up *verb trans* **1** to serve (food) onto dishes from a pan, etc. **2** to produce or present (facts or information). ➤ *verb intrans* to serve food onto dishes ready to be eaten: *I'm dishing up now*.

dishwasher *noun* **1** an electrical machine that washes dishes; a washing-up machine. **2** a person employed to wash dishes.

dishwater *noun* water in which dishes have been washed.

dishy *adj* (**dishier, dishiest**) *chiefly Brit, informal* said of a person, *esp* a man: attractive. [DISH[1] (4)]

disillusion[1] /disi'loohzh(ə)n, -'lyoohzh(ə)n/ *noun* the state of being disillusioned or disabused; loss of a cherished ideal or belief.

disillusion[2] *verb trans* to reveal the unpleasant truth about somebody or something admired to (somebody); to disenchant (them). ➤➤ **disillusionment** *noun*.

disillusioned *adj* bitter or depressed as a result of having been disillusioned.

disincentive /disin'sentiv/ *noun* something that discourages action or effort; a deterrent.

disinclination /,disingkli'naysh(ə)n/ *noun* unwillingness to do something.

disinclined /disin'kliend/ *adj* unwilling to do something.

disinfect /disin'fekt/ *verb trans* to cleanse (a place, etc) of infection, *esp* by destroying harmful micro-organisms. ➤➤ **disinfection** *noun*. [early French *desinfecter*, from DIS- + *infecter* to infect, from Latin *infectus*: see INFECT]

disinfectant[1] /disin'fekt(ə)nt/ *noun* a chemical that destroys harmful micro-organisms.

disinfectant[2] *adj* destroying harmful micro-organisms.

disinfest /disin'fest/ *verb trans* to rid (a place, etc) of insects, rodents, or other pests. ➤➤ **disinfestation** /dis,infe'staysh(ə)n/ *noun*.

disinflation /disin'flaysh(ə)n/ *noun* a reduction of the rate of inflation. ➤➤ **disinflationary** *adj*.

disinformation /,disinfə'maysh(ə)n/ *noun* deliberately false or misleading information, e.g. supplied to an enemy. [based on Russian *desinformatsiya*]

disingenuous /disin'jenyoo·əs/ *adj* insincere, especially in pretending ignorance of something one knows about; falsely naïve. ➤➤ **disingenuously** *adv*, **disingenuousness** *noun*.

disinherit /disin'herit/ *verb trans* (**disinherited, disinheriting**) **1** to deprive (an heir) of the right to inherit, *esp* by altering one's will.

2 *formal* to deprive (any person or group) of a rightful heritage: *My constituency is the desperate, the disinherited, the disrespected, and the despised* — Jesse Jackson. ➤➤ **disinheritance** *noun*.

disinhibit /disin'hibit/ *verb trans* (**disinhibited, disinhibiting**) to remove inhibiting restraints from (somebody). ➤➤ **disinhibition** /-'bish(ə)n/ *noun*.

disintegrate /dis'intigrayt/ *verb intrans* **1** to break into fragments or constituent elements. **2** to lose unity or cohesion: *His family was slowly disintegrating*. **3** said *esp* of a nucleus or other subatomic particle: to undergo a change in composition, *esp* by emitting radioactive particles or dividing into smaller units. ➤ *verb trans* to cause (something) to disintegrate. ➤➤ **disintegrative** /-tiv/ *adj*, **disintegrator** *noun*.

disintegration /dis,inti'graysh(ə)n/ *noun* **1** the act or an instance of disintegrating. **2** the process by which a nucleus or other subatomic particle emits radioactive particles or divides into smaller units.

disinter /disin'tuh/ *verb trans* (**disinterred, disinterring**) **1** to remove (somebody's corpse) from a grave or tomb. **2** to bring to light or unearth (something hidden or forgotten): *Finding that ... there were objections to an invented name, I disinterred the old one* — Hardy. ➤➤ **disinterment** *noun*.

disinterest /dis'intrest, -trast/ *noun* **1** lack of self-interest; disinterestedness; impartiality. **2** *non-standard* lack of interest; apathy.

disinterested *adj* **1** free from selfish motive or interest; impartial. **2** *non-standard* uninterested. ➤➤ **disinterestedly** *adv*, **disinterestedness** *noun*.

Usage note

disinterested *or* **uninterested**? *Disinterested* is now so often used to mean 'unconcerned' or 'bored' (in other words *uninterested*), that it can easily be misinterpreted when used in its primary meaning in modern English of 'impartial' or 'not motivated by selfishness'. A *disinterested* observer is somebody who is not on anybody's side; an *uninterested* observer simply does not care about what is going on. Careful users of English should try to preserve this distinction.

disintermediation /,disintəmeedi'aysh(ə)n/ *noun* the practice in corporate finance of borrowing money directly from lenders, e.g. by issuing bonds, instead of using an intermediary, e.g. a bank.

disinvent /disin'vent/ *verb intrans* (*usu in negative contexts*) to undo the invention of (something): *You can't disinvent the nuclear bomb*.

disinvest /disin'vest/ *verb intrans* to reduce or terminate investment.

disinvestment /disin'vestmənt/ *noun* reduction or termination of investment, *esp* by realizing assets or not replacing capital equipment.

disjecta membra /dis,yektə 'membrə/ *pl noun* scattered fragments, *esp* of a literary work. [Latin *disjecta membra* scattered limbs (from *disicere* to throw about + *membrum* limb), alteration of Horace (*Satires* 1.4): *disjecti membra poetae* the limbs of a dismembered poet, that is, random quotations]

disjoin /dis'joyn/ *verb literary* (*usu in passive*) to detach: *He that outlives a wife whom he has long loved sees himself disjoined from the only mind that has the same hopes, and fears, and interest* — Dr Johnson. [early French *desjoindre* from Latin *disjungere* to separate, from DIS- + *jungere* to join]

disjoint[1] /dis'joynt/ *verb trans* **1** to disturb the orderly structure or arrangement of (something). **2** *dated* to take (a meat carcass) apart at the joints. ➤ *verb intrans* *dated* to come apart at the joints.

disjoint[2] *adj* **1** *archaic* dislocated: *Fortinbras ... thinking by our late dear brother's death our state to be disjoint and out of frame* — Shakespeare. **2** said of mathematical sets: having no elements in common.

disjointed *adj* lacking orderly sequence; incoherent: *a disjointed narrative*. ➤➤ **disjointedly** *adv*, **disjointedness** *noun*.

disjunct /'disjungkt/ *noun* = SENTENCE ADVERB. [Latin *disjunctus*, past part. of *disjungere*: see DISJOIN]

disjunction /dis'jungksh(ə)n/ *noun* **1** a lack of coordination; a mismatch. **2** a cleavage or separation. **3** in logic: **a** a compound sentence consisting of two sentences linked by *or*, whether an INCLUSIVE DISJUNCTION or an EXCLUSIVE DISJUNCTION. **b** the relation between two such sentences. **c** the operator or element denoting *or*.

disjunctive[1] /dis'jungktiv/ *adj* **1** lacking coordination or cohesiveness. **2a** said of a proposition: constituting a logical disjunction. **b** said of a conjunction, e.g. *or* or *but*: expressing an alternative or opposition between the meanings of the words connected by it. ➤➤ **disjunctively** *adv.*

disjunctive² *noun* **1** in grammar, a disjunctive conjunction. **2** in logic, a disjunctive proposition.

disjuncture /dis'jungkchə/ *noun* a separation, split, discontinuity, or dichotomy.

disk /disk/ *noun* **1a** (*Brit also* **disc**) a round flat plate coated with a magnetic substance on which data for a computer is stored. **b** a computer storage device consisting of a stack of disks rotating at high speed, each disk having its own head to read and write data. **2** *chiefly NAmer* = DISC.
Usage note
disk *or* disc? See note at DISC.

disk drive *noun* a device that enables a computer to transfer data to and retrieve it from magnetic disks.

diskette /dis'ket/ *noun* = FLOPPY DISK.

disk-operating system *noun* the part of a computer's operating system that reads and writes data to and from disk drives. Also called DOS.

disk pack *noun* = DISK (1B).

dislike¹ /dis'liek/ *noun* **1** a feeling of aversion or disapproval. **2** something one has an aversion for: *likes and dislikes.* **✳ take a dislike to** to develop an aversion for (a person or thing).

dislike² *verb trans* to regard (somebody or something) with dislike. ➤➤ **dislikable** *adj,* **dislikeable** *adj.*

dislocate /'disləkayt/ *verb trans* **1** to displace (a bone) from its normal articulation. **2** to disrupt the normal order or organization of (a timetable, etc). **3** to put (machinery) out of order. [late Latin *dislocatus,* past part. of *dislocare,* from DIS- + *locare* to position, from *locus* place]

dislocation /dislə'kaysh(ə)n/ *noun* **1** displacement of one or more bones at a joint. **2** a discontinuity in the lattice structure of a crystal. **3** disruption of an established order or course: *The flu epidemic had caused much dislocation in the school timetable.*

dislodge /dis'loj/ *verb trans* to force (something or somebody) out of a fixed or entrenched position. ➤➤ **dislodgement** *noun.* [Old French *deslogier,* from DIS- + *loger* to lodge, from *loge* LODGE¹]

disloyal /dis'loyəl/ *adj* not loyal to obligations or ties; unfaithful. ➤➤ **disloyally** *adv,* **disloyalty** *noun.* [Old French *desloial,* from DIS- + *loial:* see LOYAL]

dismal /'dizm(ə)l/ *adj* **1** causing or expressing gloom or sadness: *'Now if you're ready, Oysters dear, we can begin to feed.' 'But not on us!' the Oysters cried, turning a little blue. 'After such kindness, that would be a dismal thing to do!'* — Lewis Carroll. **2** *informal* incompetent: *a dismal effort.* **✳ the dismal science** *humorous* political economy, so nicknamed by Carlyle. ➤➤ **dismally** *adv,* **dismalness** *noun.* [Middle English from Anglo-French *dismal* days marked as unlucky in medieval calendars, from late Latin *dies mali* evil days]

dismantle /dis'mantl/ *verb trans* **1** to take (something) to pieces. **2** to break up (an organization, etc due for termination). **3** to strip (a fortified place) of equipment, etc or (a ship) of sails and rigging. ➤➤ **dismantlement** *noun.* [early French *desmanteler* to destroy a fortification, from DIS- + *manteler* to fortify, from Latin *mantellum* cloak, mantle]

dismast /dis'mahst/ *verb trans* to remove or break off the mast of (a ship).

dismay¹ /dis'may/ *verb trans* to fill (somebody) with consternation or sadness. ➤➤ **dismayingly** *adv.* [Old French *esmaier* to trouble, from Latin EX-¹ + Germanic stem *-mag* to be able, with change of prefix to DIS-]

dismay² *noun* consternation or sadness.

dismember /dis'membə/ *verb trans* (**dismembered, dismembering**) **1** to cut or tear off the limbs of (a person or animal). **2** to divide up (a territory, etc) into parts. ➤➤ **dismembered** *adj,* **dismemberment** *noun.* [Old French *desmembrer,* from DIS- + *membre,* from Latin *membrum* limb]

dismiss /dis'mis/ *verb trans* **1** to order or allow (somebody) to leave; to send (somebody) away. **2** to discharge (somebody) from employment or service. **3** to put (a suggestion, etc) out of one's mind or reject it as unworthy of serious consideration. **4** said of a judge: to refuse a further hearing to (a court case). **5** in cricket, to bowl out (a batsman or side). ➤➤ **dismissal** *noun,* **dismissible** *adj.* [late Latin *dismissus,* modification of Latin *dimissus,* past part. of *dimittere,* from DIS- apart + *mittere* to send]

dismissive /dis'misiv/ *adj* **1** said of somebody's attitude to something: disparaging or disdainful. **2** serving to dismiss a topic, etc. ➤➤ **dismissively** *adv,* **dismissiveness** *noun: a dismissive wave of the hand.*

dismount /dis'mownt/ *verb intrans* to alight from a horse, bicycle, etc. ➤ *verb trans* **1** to make (a computer disk or disk drive) unavailable for use. **2** to throw down or unseat (a rider) from horseback. **3** to remove (a cannon, etc) from a mounting or support.

Disneyfy /'diznifie/ *verb trans* (**Disneyfies, Disneyfied, Disneyfying**) *derog* to give (a historical building or site, etc) a popularizing and simplistic theme-park treatment that merely serves to trivialize it. ➤➤ **Disneyfication** /-fi'kaysh(ə)n/ *noun.* [from the *Disneyland* theme park in California, inspired by the cartoon films of Walt *Disney* d.1966, US animator and producer]

disobedient /disə'beedi·ənt/ *adj* refusing or failing to obey. ➤➤ **disobedience** *noun,* **disobediently** *adv.* [Old French *desobedient,* from DIS- + *obedient:* see OBEDIENT]

disobey /disə'bay/ *verb trans* to fail to obey (somebody, an order, etc). ➤ *verb intrans* to be disobedient. [early French *desobeir,* from DIS- + *obeir:* see OBEY]

disoblige /disə'bliej/ *verb trans* **1** to act counter to the wishes of (somebody). **2** *informal* to inconvenience (somebody). [French *désobliger,* orig in the sense 'to set free from an obligation', from DIS- + Latin *obligare:* see OBLIGE]

disomic /die'sohmik/ *adj* in genetics, having one or more of the set of chromosomes duplicated but not the entire set. ➤➤ **disomy** *noun.* [coined from DI-¹ + CHROMOSOME]

disorder¹ /dis'awdə/ *verb trans* (**disordered, disordering**) (*usu in passive*) to disrupt, disarrange, or upset (something): *disordered lives; disordered clothing.*

disorder² *noun* **1** lack of order; untidiness; confusion. **2** breach of the peace or public order: *civil disorder.* **3** an abnormal physical or mental condition; an ailment: *a skin disorder.*

disorderly *adj* **1** untidy or disarranged. **2** unruly, violent, or disruptive of public order: *drunk and disorderly.* ➤➤ **disorderliness** *noun.*

disorderly house *noun* in law, a brothel.

disorganise /dis'awgəniez/ *verb trans* see DISORGANIZE.

disorganised *adj* see DISORGANIZED.

disorganize *or* **disorganise** /dis'awgəniez/ *verb trans* to disrupt (an arrangement, system, etc). ➤➤ **disorganization** /-'zaysh(ə)n/ *noun.* [French *désorganiser,* from *dés-* DIS- + *organiser* to organize]

disorganized *or* **disorganised** *adj* **1** lacking coherence or system. **2** said of a person: unmethodical.

disorient /dis'awrient, -ənt/ *verb trans chiefly NAmer* = DISORIENTATE. [French *désorienter* from *dés-* DIS- + *orienter* to orient, from *orient* east]
Usage note
disorient *or* disorientate? See note at DISORIENTATE.

disorientate /dis'awri·əntayt/ *verb trans* **1** (*usu in passive*) to deprive (somebody) of the normal sense of position, relationship, or identity. **2** to confuse (somebody). ➤➤ **disorientation** /-'taysh(ə)n/ *noun.*
Usage note
disorientate *or* disorient? Both forms of the word are correct. *Disorient* is more often used in American English, *disorientate* in British English.

disown /dis'ohn/ *verb trans* **1** to refuse to acknowledge (a relative, *esp* one's own child) as one's own. **2** to repudiate any connection with (principles or beliefs that other people might associate one with).

disparage /di'sparij/ *verb trans* to speak slightingly of or belittle (somebody or something). ➤➤ **disparagement** *noun,* **disparaging** *adj,* **disparagingly** *adv.* [Middle English *disparagen* to degrade by an unequal marriage, from Old French *desparagier* to marry below one's class, from DIS- + *parage* extraction, lineage, from Latin *par* equal]

disparate¹ /'dispərət/ *adj* quite separate and distinct: *They were discovered to be two quite disparate genera.* ➤➤ **disparately** *adv,* **disparateness** *noun.* [Latin *disparatus,* past part. of *disparare* to separate, from DIS- + *parare* to prepare]

disparate² *noun* (*in pl*) things or people that are completely separate or distinct.

disparity /di'spariti/ *noun* (*pl* **disparities**) difference or inequality, or an instance of this: *the disparity between their ages.* [early French *desparité* from late Latin *disparitat-*, *disparitas*, from DIS- + *paritat-*, *paritas*: see PARITY¹]

dispassionate /dis'pash(ə)nət/ *adj* not influenced by strong feeling; impartial: *a dispassionate observer.* ➤➤ **dispassionately** *adv*, **dispassionateness** *noun*.

dispatch¹ *or* **despatch** /di'spach/ *verb trans* **1a** to send (a letter, etc) somewhere. **b** to send (personnel) to carry out a particular, usu official, task: *Mounted police were dispatched to quell the riot.* **2a** to carry out or complete (a task) rapidly or efficiently: *Having dispatched the morning's business, he went to the golf course.* **b** *informal* to consume or make short work of (food or drink). **3** *euphem* to kill (somebody), *esp* with quick efficiency. ➤ *verb intrans archaic* **1** to hasten somewhere: *And now despatch we toward the court* — Shakespeare. **2** to make haste: *The hour steals on; I pray you sir, dispatch* — Shakespeare. ➤➤ **dispatcher** *noun*. [Spanish *despachar* or Italian *dispacciare* to hasten, from Old French *despeechier* to set free, ultimately from DIS- + Latin *pedica* a fetter]

Usage note

dispatch *or* **despatch**? Both spellings are equally acceptable; *dispatch* is the more common of the two.

dispatch² *or* **despatch** *noun* **1** a message; *esp* an important official diplomatic or military message. **2** a news item sent in by a correspondent to a newspaper. **3** promptness and efficiency: *She conducts her business with despatch.* **4** the act of dispatching, e.g.: **a** the sending of a communication or personnel: *the dispatch of troops to the frontier.* **b** *euphem* the killing of a person or animal.

dispatch box *noun* **1** a case or container for carrying dispatches or documents, *esp* concerning affairs of state. **2** (**the Dispatch Box**) either of a pair of boxes in front of the Speaker's or Lord Chancellor's seat in the British Parliament, from which ministers or shadow ministers speak.

dispatch case *noun* a case for carrying state or official papers; = DISPATCH BOX (1).

dispatch rider *noun* a motorcyclist or, formerly, horseman, carrying urgent dispatches.

dispel /di'spel/ *verb trans* (**dispelled, dispelling**) to drive away or disperse (fears, doubts, depression, etc). [Latin *dispellere*, from DIS- + *pellere* to drive, beat]

dispensable /di'spensəbl/ *adj* that can be dispensed with; inessential: *dispensable items.* ➤➤ **dispensability** /-'biliti/ *noun*.

dispensary /di'spens(ə)ri/ *noun* (*pl* **dispensaries**) **1** a part of a hospital or chemist's shop where drugs, medical supplies, etc are dispensed. **2** a clinic where medical, dental, or veterinary aid is provided.

dispensation /dispen'saysh(ə)n/ *noun* **1** *esp* in religion and theology: **a** a general administration or ordering of things, *esp* a divine ordering of human affairs. **b** a particular arrangement or provision made by God, providence, or nature; a bestowal of favour by God. **c** a particular religious system, *esp* considered as controlling human affairs during a specified period: *the patriarchal dispensation.* **2a** an exemption from a law, vow, etc; *specif* permission to disregard or break a rule of Roman Catholic Church law: *Their marriage was annulled by special dispensation.* **b** a formal authorization. **3a** the act or an instance of dispensing. **b** something that is dispensed or distributed. ➤➤ **dispensational** *adj.*

dispensationalism *noun* in Christian theology, the interpretation of history as a series of divine dispensations (bestowals of favour; see DISPENSATION) or periods progressively revealing God and his plan of salvation. ➤➤ **dispensationalist** *noun.*

dispensatory /di'spensət(ə)ri/ *noun* (*pl* **dispensatories**) a technical book listing the composition, preparation, and use of various drugs: compare PHARMACOPOEIA.

dispense /di'spens/ *verb trans* **1** to deal out or distribute (something) in portions. **2** to prepare and give out (drugs, medicine, etc on prescription). **3** to administer (law or justice). **4a** (+ with) to get rid of or discard (something): *We could almost dispense with the fax machine now that we have email.* **b** (+ with) to do without (something): *Shall we dispense with the formalities?* **5** (*usu* + from) to give a dispensation to (somebody) or exempt (them) from a duty, etc. [Middle English *dispensen* from late Latin *dispensare* to grant dispensation, earlier 'to distribute', from *dispendere* to weigh out, from DIS- + *pendere* to weigh]

dispenser *noun* **1** a container or machine that dispenses items, e.g. of food, or fixed quantities, e.g. of drink. **2** a person who dispenses medicines.

dispensing chemist *noun* a chemist qualified and licensed to prepare, dispense, and advise on, medicines.

dispensing optician *noun* an optician qualified and licensed to prescribe and dispense spectacles and contact lenses in addition to making them.

dispersant /di'spuhs(ə)nt/ *noun* a dispersing agent; *esp* a liquid or gas used to disperse and stabilize fine particles of a substance in a particular medium.

disperse¹ /di'spuhs/ *verb trans* **1** to spread or distribute (something) widely: *Air currents disperse the pollen.* **2** to break up (a crowd, etc). **3** to cause (fog, etc) to evaporate or vanish. **4** to break up (something) into fine particles: *The violence of the waves dispersed the oil without damage to bird life.* **5** in physics, to separate (light) into its constituent wavelengths. **6** (*usu in passive*) in chemistry, to spread particles of (a substance) evenly throughout a colloid or suspension. ➤ *verb intrans* **1** to break up in random fashion: *The protesters dispersed as armed police approached.* **2** to become dispersed; to dissipate or vanish: *The fog dispersed towards morning.* ➤➤ **disperser** *noun*, **dispersible** *adj*, **dispersive** /-siv/ *adj.* [Middle English *dysparsen* via French from Latin *dispersus*, past part. of *dispergere* to scatter, from DIS- + *spargere* to scatter]

disperse² *adj* in chemistry, denoting the state of a substance held in particle form within a colloid or suspension.

dispersion /di'spuhsh(ə)n/ *noun* **1** the act or an instance of dispersing. **2** in chemistry, the even spread of a substance in particle form throughout a colloid or suspension; the substance so dispersed. **3** in statistics, the extent to which the values of a frequency distribution vary. **4a** in physics, the separation of light into colours by refraction or diffraction with formation of a spectrum. **b** the separation of radiation or a stream of particles into components of different wavelength, mass, etc. **5** (**the Dispersion**) the scattering of Jews outside Israel; = DIASPORA.

dispirit /di'spirit/ *verb trans* (**dispirited, dispiriting**) to dishearten or discourage (somebody). ➤➤ **dispirited** *adj*, **dispiritedly** *adv*, **dispiritedness** *noun*, **dispiriting** *adj*, **dispiritingly** *adv.*

displace /dis'plays/ *verb trans* **1a** to take the place of (something) or replace it: *English has now largely displaced Irish as the lingua franca.* **b** to take the place of (an atom) in a chemical reaction. **c** to cause displacement of (a quantity of water). **2a** to remove (something) from or force (it) out of its usual or proper place: *The pain was traced to a displaced vertebra.* **b** to remove (somebody) from office. ➤➤ **displaceable** *adj*. [Old French *desplacer*, from DIS- + *place*: see PLACE¹]

displaced person *noun* a person who has been forced to leave their country because of war, revolution, etc; a refugee.

displacement *noun* **1** the action of displacing or process of being displaced. **2** the volume or weight of a fluid, e.g. water, displaced by a body, e.g. a ship, of equal weight floating in it, used as a measure of the ship's size. **3** the difference between the initial position of a body and any later position. **4** the volume displaced by a piston in a pump or engine, or the total volume so displaced by all the pistons in an internal-combustion engine. **5** the transfer of emotions from the object that orig evoked them to a substitute, e.g. in dreams.

displacement activity *noun* in psychology, the substitution of another form of behaviour for what is normal or expected, typically when there is a conflict of impulses.

displacement pump *noun* a pump in which the displacement of fluid is effected by a plunger, steam, or compressed air in combination with non-return valves.

displacement ton *noun* a unit approximately equal to one long ton of seawater, used in reckoning the displacement of ships, and equal to 35ft³ (0.991m³).

display¹ /di'splay/ *verb trans* **1** to set out (a collection of things) for public viewing. **2** to expose (something) to view, e.g. by spreading it out. **3** said of a computer, etc: to show (information) on screen. **4** to demonstrate (a quality): *He displayed tact and tolerance.* **5** to make a deliberate play of (something one prides oneself on) to impress others: *He liked to display his erudition.* **6** said of a bird, reptile, or fish: to go through a ritual of showy behaviour in order to attract a mate. ➤➤ **displayer** *noun*. [Middle English *displayen* via

Anglo-French from Latin *displicare* to scatter, unfold, from DIS- + *plicare* to fold]

display[2] *noun* **1** a public presentation in the form of a performance or exhibition: *a fireworks display*. **2** the displaying of something, e.g. the demonstration of a quality or of a type of behaviour: *a display of bad temper*. **3** ostentation; showing off: *Those long words she uses are mere display*. **4** type, page design, or printing designed to catch the eye, e.g. in headlines and title pages. **5** an eye-catching arrangement by which something, e.g. a range of goods for sale, is exhibited: *a window display*. **6** an electronic device for presenting pictures or data on screen, the process of presenting them, or the pictures and data so presented. **7a** a distinctive pattern of behaviour exhibited by an animal, e.g. in defending its territory, and designed to evoke a particular response in other animals, *esp* members of the same species. **b** a pattern of courting behaviour exhibited *esp* by male birds in the breeding season to attract the attention of a female. ✳ **put on display** to set out (something) for public viewing: *The archaeological finds will be put on display next week.*

display cabinet *noun* = DISPLAY CASE.

display case *noun* a glazed case for the display of museum exhibits, etc, or jewellery for sale.

displayed *adj* in heraldry, denoting a bird of prey with wings outspread.

display type *noun* in printing, a flamboyant or eye-catching font used for posters, headings, or advertisements.

displease /dis'pleez/ *verb trans* to annoy or upset (somebody). ➤ *verb intrans* to cause annoyance or displeasure. ➤ **displeased** *adj*, **displeasing** *adj*, **displeasingly** *adv*. [Middle English *displesen* from early French *desplaisir*, ultimately from DIS- + Latin *placēre* to PLEASE[1]]

displeasure /dis'plezhə/ *noun* disapproval or annoyance.

disport /di'spawt/ *verb trans archaic* to divert or amuse (oneself) actively: *a crowd of boys who were running, jumping, playing at ball and leap-frog and otherwise disporting themselves* — Mark Twain. ➤ *verb intrans archaic* to frolic or gambol: *dolphins disporting in the waves*. [Middle English *disporten* from early French *desporter* carry off, from DIS- + *porter* to carry]

disposable[1] /di'spohzəbl/ *adj* **1** designed to be used once and then thrown away. **2** said of financial resources: available for use. ➤ **disposability** /-'biliti/ *noun*.

disposable[2] *noun* (*usu in pl*) a disposable article.

disposable goods *pl noun* consumer goods bought for immediate short-term use, such as newspapers, clothing, food, and drink.

disposable income *noun* what is left of one's income after taxes and social-security charges have been paid: compare DISCRETIONARY INCOME.

disposal /di'spohzl/ *noun* **1** the action or process of getting rid of something: *waste disposal*. **2** *NAmer* = WASTE-DISPOSAL UNIT. **3** the sale of assets, shares, or property. **4** positioning or organization; = DISPOSITION (3). ✳ **at one's disposal** available for one's use. **be at somebody's disposal** to be ready to attend to somebody's needs or requests.

dispose /di'spohz/ *verb trans* **1** to put (things or personnel) in position. **2** to give (somebody) a tendency towards something: *Faulty diet disposes one to sickness*. ➤ *verb intrans* **1** (+ of) to transfer (a possession) to somebody else or sell it on: *I've disposed of my old computer*. **2** to get rid of (rubbish or waste): *Please dispose of glass bottles with care*. **3** *euphem* to kill or murder (somebody). **4** to deal conclusively with (a theory, etc) or demolish (it): *The new evidence effectively disposes of my hypothesis*. **5** to control the course of events: *Man proposes, God disposes*. [Middle English *disposen* via early French *disposer* from Latin *disponere* to arrange, from DIS- + *ponere* to place]

disposed *adj* **1** (*usu in negative contexts*) inclined or willing (to do something): *I'm not disposed to wait indefinitely while you make up your mind*. **2** inclined a certain way in one's attitude to somebody or something: *She seemed kindly disposed to us*.

disposition /dispə'zish(ə)n/ *noun* **1** a person's temperamental make-up: *an outgoing disposition*. **2** a tendency or inclination: *a disposition to behave childishly*. **3** the action of arranging people or things in a certain way, or the result of this: *the disposition of troops over the sloping ground*. **4** the transfer of property to the possession of another person, *esp* by will or deed. **5** *archaic* the determination of events, *esp* by divine ordination. ➤ **dispositional** *adj*. [Latin *disposition-, dispositio*, from *disponere*: see DISPOSE]

dispositive /dis'pozitiv/ *adj* **1** tending towards the settlement of an issue. **2** said of a will: effecting the disposition of property.

dispossess /dispə'zes/ *verb trans* **1** to deprive (somebody) of possession or occupancy. **2** in football, etc, to deprive (an opponent) of the ball. ➤ **dispossession** /-'zesh(ə)n/ *noun*, **dispossessor** *noun*. [Old French *despossesser*, from DIS- + *possesser*: see POSSESS]

dispossessed[1] *adj* deprived of homes, possessions, and security: *hordes of dispossessed Kosovar Albanians*.

dispossessed[2] *pl noun* (**the dispossessed**) dispossessed people considered as a group.

dispraise[1] /dis'prayz/ *verb trans archaic* to comment on (somebody or something) disapprovingly: *I will not dispraise your sister Cassandra's wit* — Shakespeare. ➤ **dispraisingly** *adv*. [Middle English *dispraisen* from Old French *despreisier*, ultimately from Latin *depretiare*: see DEPRECIATE]

dispraise[2] *noun archaic* disapproval or criticism; disparagement: *There is not a syllable of either praise or dispraise* — Samuel Butler.

disproof /dis'proohf/ *noun* **1** the act or an instance of disproving. **2** evidence that disproves: *The law of gravity, for example … makes exact predictions that leave it wide open to disproof* — K Eric Drexler.

disproportion /disprə'pawsh(ə)n/ *noun* lack of proportion, symmetry, or proper relation, or an instance of this. ➤ **disproportional** *adj*.

disproportionate /disprə'pawsh(ə)nət/ *adj* out of proportion: *The fare was lavish, and quite disproportionate to the small number of guests*. ➤ **disproportionately** *adv*.

disprove /dis'proohv/ *verb trans* to prove (a statement, etc) to be false, or refute (it) by argument. ➤ **disprovable** *adj*. [Middle English *disproven* from early French *desprover*, from DIS- + *prover*: see PROVE]

disputable /di'spyoohtəbl/ *adj* **1** open to doubt or debate; questionable. **2** *archaic* inclined to dispute; = DISPUTATIOUS: *He is too disputable for my company* — Shakespeare. ➤ **disputableness** *noun*, **disputably** *adv*.

disputant /di'spyooht(ə)nt, 'dispyoot(ə)nt/ *noun* one of the people engaged in a dispute or a disputation.

disputation /dispyooh'taysh(ə)n/ *noun* **1** debate or argument, or an instance of this. **2** *esp* formerly, the oral defence of an academic thesis by formal logic.

disputatious /dispyoo'tayshəs/ *adj* inclined to dispute; argumentative. ➤ **disputatiously** *adv*, **disputatiousness** *noun*.

dispute[1] /di'spyooht/ *verb intrans* (*often* + about) to argue, *esp* angrily and persistently. ➤ *verb trans* **1** to make (something) the subject of disputation: *They disputed the issue vehemently for some hours*. **2** to call (a statement, etc) into question: *I dispute those statistics*. **3** to struggle over or contest (a reigning or leading position): *She is disputing the championship with Graf*. **4** to struggle against or resist (an advance or landing by an enemy). ➤ **disputative** /-tətiv/ *adj*, **disputer** *noun*. [Middle English *disputen* via Old French from Latin *disputare* to discuss, contend, from DIS- + *putare* to think]

dispute[2] /di'spyooht, 'dispyooht/ *noun* **1** controversy or debate. **2** a quarrel or disagreement. **3** a disagreement with management over pay, etc: *an industrial dispute*. ✳ **beyond dispute** true, or proved, without a shadow of doubt. **in dispute 1** quarrelling: *The parties are still in dispute*. **2** disputed: *His victory is now in dispute*.

disqualification /dis,kwolifi'kaysh(ə)n/ *noun* **1** the act or an instance of disqualifying. **2** something that disqualifies: *Some see homosexuality as a disqualification for a career in the services*.

disqualify /dis'kwolifie/ *verb trans* (**disqualifies, disqualified, disqualifying**) **1** to make or declare (somebody) unfit or unsuitable to do something: *She was disqualified from driving for a year*. **2** to declare (somebody) ineligible, e.g. for a prize, because of violation of the rules: *She was disqualified after a positive drugs test*.

disquiet[1] /dis'kwie-ət/ *noun* anxiety or worry.

disquiet[2] *verb trans* (**disquieted, disquieting**) to make (somebody) uneasy or worried. ➤ **disquieted** *adj*, **disquieting** *adj*.

disquietude /dis'kwie-ətyoohd/ *noun formal* disquiet or anxiety.

disquisition /diskwi'zish(ə)n/ *noun* a long or elaborate discussion or essay on a subject. ➤ **disquisitional** *adj*. [Latin *disquisition-, disquisitio*, from *disquirere* to enquire diligently, from DIS- + *quaerere* to seek]

disrate /dis'rayt/ *verb trans* to reduce (e.g. a sailor) in rank.

disregard[1] /disri'gahd/ *verb trans* **1** to pay no attention to (something). **2** to treat (somebody or something) as not worthy of regard or notice.

disregard[2] *noun* lack of attention or regard; neglect: *He showed complete disregard for his own and others' safety.* >>> **disregardful** *adj.*

disrelish[1] /dis'relish/ *verb trans archaic* to find (something) unpalatable or distasteful: *Mrs Hudson ... found herself disrelishing the singular situation of seeming to side against her own flesh and blood —* Henry James.

disrelish[2] *noun archaic* a feeling of distaste.

disremember /disri'membə/ *verb trans* (**disremembered, disremembering**) *chiefly NAmer* to forget (something).

disrepair /disri'peə/ *noun* the state of being in need of repair: *The house had fallen into disrepair.*

disreputable /dis'repyootəbl/ *adj* **1** having a bad reputation; not respectable. **2** said of clothing, etc: dirty or untidy in appearance. >>> **disreputability** /-'biliti/ *noun,* **disreputableness** *noun,* **disreputably** *adv.*

disrepute /disri'pyooht/ *noun* lack of good reputation or respectability: *Sexist advertising brought the product into disrepute.*

disrespect[1] /disri'spekt/ *noun* lack of respect or politeness. >>> **disrespectful** *adj,* **disrespectfully** *adv,* **disrespectfulness** *noun.*

disrespect[2] *verb trans chiefly NAmer* to show disrespect for or insult (somebody).

disrobe /dis'rohb/ *verb intrans* **1** *formal* to take off ceremonial clothing. **2** *esp humorous* to undress. >>> *verb trans* to remove clothing from (somebody): *Officious menials hastily disrobed him of his tattered cloak —* Scott. [early French *desrober,* from DIS- + *robe* garment, of Germanic origin]

disrupt /dis'rupt/ *verb trans* **1** to throw (something) into disorder: *Protesters disrupted the meeting.* **2** to interrupt the continuity of (a schedule, etc). >>> **disrupter** *noun,* **disruption** /-sh(ə)n/ *noun,* **disruptive** /-tiv/ *adj,* **disruptively** /-tivli/ *adv,* **disruptiveness** /-tivnəs/ *noun.* [Latin *disruptus,* past part. of *disrumpere,* from DIS- + *rumpere* to break]

diss /dis/ *verb trans* see DIS.

dissatisfaction /di,satis'faksh(ə)n/ *noun* lack of satisfaction; discontent.

dissatisfy /di'satisfie, dis'sa-/ *verb trans* to disappoint or fail to satisfy (somebody). >>> **dissatisfied** *adj.*

dissave /di'sayv/ *verb intrans NAmer* to spend more than one earns in a particular period, and so fall back on savings. >>> **dissaving** *noun.*

dissect /di'sekt, die'sekt/ *verb trans* **1** to cut (an animal or plant) into pieces, *esp* for scientific examination. **2** to analyse and interpret (a literary work, etc) in detail. >>> **dissection** /-sh(ə)n/ *noun,* **dissector** *noun.* [Latin *dissectus,* past part. of *dissecare* to cut apart, from DIS- + *secare* to cut]

dissected *adj* **1** said of a leaf: cut deeply into several fine lobes. **2** said of a plateau: sliced by gorges.

dissemble /di'sembl/ *verb intrans* to conceal facts, intentions, or feelings under some pretence. >>> *verb trans* **1** to hide (something) under a false appearance. **2** to put on the appearance of (something); to feign (it). >>> **dissemblance** *noun,* **dissembler** *noun.* [alteration of obsolete *dissimule,* via French from Latin *dissimulare:* see DISSIMULATE]

disseminate /di'seminayt/ *verb trans* to spread (ideas, information, etc) about freely or widely. >>> **dissemination** /-'naysh(ə)n/ *noun,* **disseminator** *noun.* [Latin *disseminatus,* past part. of *disseminare,* from DIS- + *seminare* to sow, from *semin-, semen* seed]

disseminated sclerosis *noun* = MULTIPLE SCLEROSIS.

disseminule /di'seminyoohl/ *noun* a part or organ, e.g. a seed or spore, that is produced by a plant and serves to propagate it. [DISSEMINATE + -ULE]

dissension /di'sensh(ə)n/ *noun* disagreement in opinion that makes for discord. [via French from Latin *dissension-, dissensio,* from *dissentire:* see DISSENT[1]]

dissensus /di'sensəs/ *noun* widespread dissent or disagreement. [DIS- + CONSENSUS, or directly from Latin *dissensus* disagreement, discord, past part. of *dissentire:* see DISSENT[1]]

dissent[1] /di'sent/ *verb intrans* **1** to differ in opinion. **2** to reject the doctrines of an established Church. **3** to withhold assent. >>> **dissenter** *noun.* [Middle English *dissenten* from Latin *dissentire* to disagree, from DIS- + *sentire* to feel]

dissent[2] *noun* difference of opinion; *esp* religious or political nonconformity.

Dissenter *noun* formerly, a person who refuses to conform to the established, usu Anglican, Church; = NONCONFORMIST (2).

dissentient[1] /di'senshi-ənt/ *adj* disagreeing or dissenting, *esp* from a majority view. [Latin *dissentient-, dissentiens,* present part. of *dissentire:* see DISSENT[1]]

dissentient[2] *noun* a person who dissents, *esp* from a majority view.

dissertation /disə'taysh(ə)n/ *noun* a long detailed written treatment of a subject; *specif* one submitted for a degree, diploma, etc. >>> **dissertational** *adj.* [Latin *dissertation-, dissertatio,* from *dissertare* to discourse, frequentative of *disserere,* from DIS- + *serere* to join, arrange]

disservice /di'suhvis/ *noun* an action or deed which works to somebody's disadvantage.

dissever /di'sevə/ *verb* (**dissevered, dissevering**) *formal* **1** (+ from) to sever or separate (one thing) from another. **2** to divide or fragment (something). >>> **disseverance** *noun,* **disseverment** *noun.* [Middle English *disseveren* via Old French *dessevrer* from late Latin *disseparare,* from Latin DIS- + *separare:* see SEPARATE[1]]

dissident[1] /'disid(ə)nt/ *noun* a person who disagrees strongly or rebelliously with the policies of the government or with established opinion. >>> **dissidence** *noun.* [Latin *dissident-, dissidens,* present part. of *dissidere* to sit apart, disagree, from DIS- + *sedere* to sit]

dissident[2] *adj* disagreeing, *esp* strongly or rebelliously, with an opinion or group.

dissimilar /di'similə, dis'si-/ *adj* (*often* + to/from) not similar; unlike: *a dance step not dissimilar to a polka.* >>> **dissimilarity** /-'lariti/ *noun,* **dissimilarly** *adv.*

dissimilate /di'similayt/ *verb trans* (*usu in passive*) in linguistics, to alter (a consonant sound) so that it diverges from a similar one in proximity to it: *'Glamour' is a doublet of 'grammar', with 'r' dissimilated to 'l'.* >>> *verb intrans* said of consonant sounds: to become dissimilar in this way. >>> **dissimilation** /-'laysh(ə)n/ *noun,* **dissimilatory** /-ət(ə)ri/ *adj.* [DIS- + Latin *similis* same, modelled on ASSIMILATE]

dissimilitude /disi'milityoohd/ *noun formal* lack of resemblance; dissimilarity. [Latin *dissimilitudo,* from *dissimilis* unlike, from DIS- + *similis* like]

dissimulate /di'simyoolayt, dis'si-/ *verb* **1** to conceal one's real feelings or motives, or disguise them; = DISSEMBLE. **2** to disguise the true nature of (something). >>> **dissimulation** /-'laysh(ə)n/ *noun,* **dissimulator** *noun.* [Latin *dissimulatus,* past part. of *dissimulare,* from DIS- + *simulare* to simulate, from *similis* like, same]

dissipate /'disipayt/ *verb trans* **1** to dispel (something) or cause (it) to disappear or scatter: *The walk soon dissipated his resentment.* **2** to spend or use up (money, energy, etc) aimlessly or foolishly. **3** to cause (energy) to be lost on its conversion to heat. >>> *verb intrans* to separate and scatter, or fade away and vanish. >>> **dissipater** *noun,* **dissipative** /-tiv/ *adj,* **dissipator** *noun.* [Latin *dissipatus,* past part. of *dissipare* disperse, from DIS- + *supare* to throw]

dissipated *adj* given to dissipation; dissolute. >>> **dissipatedly** *adv,* **dissipatedness** *noun.*

dissipation /disi'paysh(ə)n/ *noun* **1** the process of dissipating or of being dissipated. **2** dissolute living; debauchery; *esp* excessive indulgence in alcohol. **3** wasteful expenditure.

dissociate /di'sohsiayt, -shiayt/ *verb trans* **1a** to declare (oneself) aloof from association or union with somebody or something else: *I dissociate myself from my colleague's remarks.* **b** to separate (two ideas) in the mind: *It's difficult to dissociate him from his television persona.* **2** to subject (a compound) to chemical dissociation. >>> *verb intrans* said of a chemical compound: to undergo dissociation. >>> **dissociative** /-i-ətiv/ *adj.* [Latin *dissociatus,* past part. of *dissociare,* from DIS- + *sociare* to join, from *socius* companion]

dissociation /disohsi'aysh(ə)n, -shi'aysh(ə)n/ *noun* **1** the process of dissociating or of being dissociated; disassociation. **2** the process by which a chemical combination breaks up into simpler constituents, *esp* as a result of the action of heat or a solvent. **3** in psychiatry, the separation of a more or less autonomous group of ideas or activities from the mainstream of consciousness, *esp* in cases of mental disorder.

dissoluble /di'solyoobl, dis'sol-/ *adj* capable of being dissolved, disconnected, or undone. ➤➤ **dissolubility** /-'biliti/ *noun*. [Latin *dissolubilis*, from *dissolvere*: see DISSOLVE¹]

dissolute /'disəlooht, -lyooht/ *adj* morally unrestrained; debauched. ➤➤ **dissolutely** *adv*, **dissoluteness** *noun*. [Latin *dissolutus*, from past part. of *dissolvere*: see DISSOLVE¹]

dissolution /disə'loohsh(ə)n, -'lyoohsh(ə)n/ *noun* 1 the act or an instance of dissolving. 2 the termination of an association or union, *esp* a marriage. 3 the breaking up or dispersal of a group, assembly, etc: *the Dissolution of the monasteries*. 4 dissolute behaviour or lifestyle. 5 disintegration or decay.

dissolve¹ /di'zolv/ *verb trans* 1a to terminate (a partnership, *esp* a marriage) officially. b to dismiss (an assembly, etc) or cause (it) to break up or cease operating: *Parliament was dissolved before the election*. 2a to cause (a substance) to pass into solution. b to melt or liquefy (a substance). 3 to fade out (one film or television scene) whilst fading in another. ➤ *verb intrans* 1a to pass into solution. b to become fluid or melt. 2 to fade away; to disperse: *The vision dissolved before his eyes*. 3 (*usu* + into) to be emotionally overcome: *She dissolved into tears*. ➤➤ **dissolvable** *adj*, **dissolver** *noun*. [Middle English *dissolven* from Latin *dissolvere*, from DIS- + *solvere*: see SOLVE]

dissolve² *noun* an effect used in films and television in which one scene is dissolved into the next.

dissolvent /di'zolv(ə)nt/ *noun* a substance that is capable of dissolving another substance; a solvent.

dissonance /'disənəns/ *noun* 1 in music, an unresolved note or chord, *esp* an interval not included in a major or minor triad or its inversions; the sound made by this. 2 a combination of discordant sounds: compare CONSONANCE. 3 lack of harmony or agreement; a clash.

dissonant /'disənənt/ *adj* 1 said of a musical combination: discordant or harmonious: compare CONSONANT². 2 clashing or incongruous in combination or juxtaposition. ➤➤ **dissonantly** *adv*. [via French from Latin *dissonant-*, *dissonans*, present part. of *dissonare* to be discordant, from DIS- + *sonare* to sound]

dissuade /di'swayd/ *verb trans* (+ from) to deter or discourage (somebody) from a course of action by persuasion. ➤➤ **dissuasion** /-'swayzh(ə)n/ *noun*, **dissuasive** /-siv, -ziv/ *adj*, **dissuasively** /-sivli, -zivli/ *adv*, **dissuasiveness** /-sivnəs, -zivnəs/ *noun*. [French *dissuader* from Latin *dissuadēre* to advise against, from DIS- + *suadēre* to urge]

dissyllable /di'siləbl, die-/ *noun* see DISYLLABLE.

dissymmetry /dis'simətri/ *noun* 1 lack of symmetry. 2 mirror-image symmetry, as between an object and its mirror image, or between the left and right hands. ➤➤ **dissymmetric** /-'metrik/ *adj*.

dist. *abbr* 1 distance. 2 distilled. 3 district.

distaff /'distahf/ *noun* 1 in spinning, a staff for holding the flax, wool, etc that is to be spun. 2 woman's work or domain: *I must change arms at home and give the distaff into my husband's hands* — Shakespeare. 3 the female side of a family; = DISTAFF SIDE: *The crown of France never falls to the distaff* — Edward Phillips. [Old English *distæf*, from *dis-* (related to Middle Low German *dise* bunch of flax) + *stæf* STAFF¹]

distaff side *noun* the female side of a family: *They inherit Plantagenet blood by direct descent, and Tudor on the distaff side* — Conan Doyle.

distal /'distl/ *adj* said *esp* of an anatomical part: far from the centre or point of attachment or origin; terminal: compare PROXIMAL. ➤➤ **distally** *adv*. [DISTANT + -AL²]

distance¹ /'dist(ə)ns/ *noun* 1 the space between two points or places, or the length of this: *the distance from Oxford to Manchester*. 2 a far-off point: *Look at the picture from a distance*. 3 (**the distance**) the part of a scene furthest away from the viewer: *I could see a light in the distance*. 4 wide separation or remoteness: *I never found the distance a problem*. 5 (*often* **distance in time**) an interval or time gap. 6 aloofness, coolness, or reserve in a relationship between people. 7 *Brit*. a in horse-racing, a gap of more than 20 lengths between two finishers. b in horse-racing, a point 240 yards short of the winning post. 8 *NAmer* in horse-racing, the distance from the winning post that any other horse must have reached before the winner finishes, in order to qualify for the next heat. ✳ **go the distance** to keep going until the end of a contest, etc. **keep one's**

distance 1 to maintain a coolness or reserve; to avoid getting involved. 2 to preserve a physical gap between oneself and another person, etc. **keep somebody at a distance** to treat somebody with reserve. **the middle distance** the area between foreground and distance. **within striking distance of** very close to (a point that represents one's destination or goal). **within walking/shouting distance** not too far away to walk or shout: *I like to be within walking distance of the shops*. [via French from Latin *distantia*, from *distant-*: see DISTANT]

distance² *verb trans* 1 to separate (one person from another) or make them less close. 2 to keep (oneself) aloof from, or become less involved with, a situation, etc: *You have to distance yourself from even the most tragic cases*. 3 *NAmer* in horse-racing, to beat (a horse) by a distance. 4 to outstrip (a competitor); = OUTDISTANCE.

distance learning *noun* the activity of studying at home, e.g. for a degree, from broadcast, audio, or video material, with correspondence, email, or the telephone as the tutorial medium, sometimes with the support of occasional local tutorials.

distance runner *noun* a runner who takes part in long-distance or middle-distance races.

distant /'dist(ə)nt/ *adj* 1 a certain distance away: *a few miles distant*. 2 remote in space or time: *the distant hills*. 3 said of travels, etc: to faraway places. 4 not closely related: *a distant cousin*. 5 reserved or aloof in personal relationships; cold: *polite but distant*. 6 said of somebody's eyes or expression: abstracted from the immediate present. ➤➤ **distantly** *adv*, **distantness** *noun*. [via French from Latin *distant-*, *distans*, present part. of *distare* to stand apart, be distant, from DIS- + *stare* to stand]

distantiate /di'stanshi·ayt/ *verb trans* to set or keep (a person or thing) at a distance. ➤➤ **distantiation** /-'aysh(ə)n/ *noun*. [Latin *distantia* distance, from *distant-*: see DISTANT]

distant signal *noun* a preliminary railway signal that indicates how the next home signal is set.

distaste /dis'tayst/ *noun* 1 (*often* + for) a dislike of or aversion to something. 2 disapproval: *He regarded his fellow passengers with distaste*.

distasteful /dis'taystf(ə)l/ *adj* causing distaste; offensive. ➤➤ **distastefully** *adv*, **distastefulness** *noun*.

distemper¹ /di'stempə/ *noun* 1 a viral disease of certain animals, *esp* a highly infectious disease of dogs, with fever and coughing and sometimes disturbance of the nervous systems. 2 *archaic* an illness: *My distemper was a pleurisy* — Benjamin Franklin. 3 a social or political evil. [archaic *distemper* to upset, derange, from late Latin *distemperare* to temper or mix badly, from Latin DIS- + *temperare* to temper, mingle]

distemper² *noun* 1 a method of painting in which pigments are mixed with white or yolk of egg or size, *esp* for mural decoration. 2a the paint used in the distemper process. b any of numerous water-based paints for general, *esp* household, use.

distemper³ *verb trans* (**distempered, distempering**) to paint (something) in or with distemper. [Middle English *distemperen* to mix with liquid, soak, via Old French from Latin DIS- + *temperare*, to temper, mingle]

distend /di'stend/ *verb trans* to cause (a part of the body, e.g. the belly) to swell from internal pressure. ➤ *verb intrans* to swell. ➤➤ **distended** *adj*, **distensibility** /-sə'biliti/ *noun*, **distensible** /-səbl/ *adj*, **distension** /-sh(ə)n/ *noun*. [Middle English *distenden* from Latin *distendere*, from DIS- + *tendere* to stretch]

distich /'distik/ *noun* in prosody, a two-line unit of verse; a couplet. ➤➤ **distichal** *adj*. [via Latin from Greek *distichon*, neuter of *distichos* having two rows, from DI-¹ + *stichos* row, verse]

distichous /'distikəs/ *adj* said of leaves: arranged in two opposite vertical rows. ➤➤ **distichously** *adv*. [via late Latin from Greek *distichos*: see DISTICH]

distil (*NAmer* **distill**) /di'stil/ *verb* (**distilled, distilling**) ➤ *verb trans* 1 to produce (a liquid) in purified form by heating it till it evaporates as steam, and cooling it till it again becomes liquid. 2 to make (whisky or other spirits) by this method. 3 to extract the essence of (a plant, etc) by heating it with a solvent. 4 to produce (an oil, etc) by this means. 5 (+ out/off) to obtain, or separate (a volatile ingredient) by heating. 6 to derive (ideas, a written work, etc) from a body of previously amassed material. 7 to extract the essential matter from (previously amassed material): *It's time you distilled all those random jottings into a book*. ➤ *verb intrans* 1 to undergo distillation. 2 to condense or drop from a still after distillation. **3** to exude in drops or in a fine mist. **4** to appear slowly or in small quantities at a time. ➤➤ **distillatory** /-ət(ə)ri/ *adj.* [Middle English *distillen* via French from late Latin *distillare*, alteration of *destillare* from DE- + *stillare* to drip, from *stilla* drop]

distillate /'distilət, -layt/ *noun* **1** a product of distillation. **2** a concentrated form.

distillation /disti'laysh(ə)n/ *noun* a process that consists of condensing the gas or vapour obtained from heated liquids or solids and that is used *esp* for purification, fractionation, or the formation of new substances.

distiller *noun* a person or company that makes alcohol, *esp* spirits, by distilling.

distillery /di'stiləri/ *noun* (*pl* **distilleries**) the works where whisky or another spirit is distilled.

distinct /di'stingkt/ *adj* **1** (*often* + from) different or separate: *'Courage' has a meaning distinct from 'bravery'.* **2** readily perceptible to the senses or mind; clear: *The image remained distinct in her memory.* **3** definite: *a distinct possibility of rain.* ✳ **as distinct from** as opposed to or in contrast to. ➤➤ **distinctness** *noun.* [Middle English via French from Latin *distinctus*, past part. of *distinguere*: see DISTINGUISH]

Usage note
distinct or **distinctive**? These two words are sometimes confused. *Distinct* means 'separate and different', 'clear', or 'clearly noticeable': *a distinct air of unease; The word has two distinct meanings.* Something that is *distinctive* has its own special or unmistakable character: *a distinctive flavour.*

distinction /di'stingksh(ə)n/ *noun* **1** a discrimination made between things that are similar but not the same: *the distinction between 'ceremonial' and 'ceremonious'.* **2** a division resulting from discrimination: *class distinctions.* **3** outstanding merit or special talent: *a writer of distinction.* **4** the highest level of excellence in passing an exam: *a distinction in physics.* ✳ **draw/make a distinction between** to regard (two things) as different. **have the distinction of** to be unique in (being or doing something): *He had the distinction of being the first male graduate of a women's college.* **without distinction** indiscriminately: *The plague attacked rich and poor without distinction.*

distinctive /di'stingktiv/ *adj* clearly marking somebody or something as different from others; characteristic: *a very distinctive voice.* ➤➤ **distinctively** *adv,* **distinctiveness** *noun.*

Usage note
distinctive or **distinct**? See note at DISTINCT.

distinctly *adv* **1** clearly: *Another shot rang out distinctly.* **2** definitely: *I distinctly heard her say 'Tuesday'.* **3** very or remarkably: *a distinctly unhelpful attitude.*

distingué or **distinguée** /di'stanggay (*French* distēge)/ *adj* distinguished in appearance or manner. [French *distingué,* past part. of *distinguer:* see DISTINGUISH]

distinguish /di'sting·gwish/ *verb trans* **1** to perceive (something) as being separate or different. **2** (*often* + from) to recognize a difference between (one thing) and another: *You are old enough to distinguish right from wrong.* **3** to separate (things or people) into kinds, classes, or categories: *The kids are great at distinguishing makes of cars.* **4** to define (something) or list its characteristics: *Can you distinguish it further?* **5** said of a feature, etc: to serve to identify (a person or thing): *Pale ring-shaped markings distinguish the seal species Phoca hispida.* **6** to do something to make (oneself) notable, *esp* achieve something worthy: *He distinguished himself by winning the sack race.* ➤ *verb intrans* (+ between) to recognize the difference between (two or more things): *You are old enough to distinguish between right and wrong.* ➤➤ **distinguishability** /-'biliti/ *noun,* **distinguishable** *adj,* **distinguishably** *adv.* [French *distinguer* from Latin *distinguere,* literally 'to separate by pricking', from DIS- + *stinguere* to quench, earlier 'to prick']

distinguished *adj* **1** characterized by eminence, distinction, or excellence: *a distinguished scholar.* **2** dignified in manner, bearing, or appearance.

distort /di'stawt/ *verb trans* **1** to alter the true meaning of or misrepresent (words, a statement, etc). **2** to cause (something) to take on an unnatural or abnormal shape. **3** to reproduce or broadcast (radio sound, a television picture, etc) poorly or inaccurately owing to a change in the wave form of the original signal. ➤➤ **distorted** *adj,* **distortedly** *adv,* **distortedness** *noun.* [Latin *distortus,* past part. of *distorquēre,* from DIS- + *torquēre* to twist]

distortion /di'stawsh(ə)n/ *noun* **1** the act or an instance of distorting. **2** the quality or state of being distorted; a product of distortion, e.g.: **a** a lack of proportion in an optical image resulting from defects in the optical system. **b** faulty reproduction of radio sound, a television picture, etc, caused by a change in the wave form of the original signal. ➤➤ **distortional** *adj.*

distract /di'strakt/ *verb trans* **1** to draw (somebody or their attention) away from the task in hand, etc. **2** to divert (somebody): *Think of something to distract the baby.* **3** *archaic* to drive (somebody) mad. ➤➤ **distractibility** /-tə'biliti/ *noun,* **distractible** *adj,* **distracting** *adj,* **distractingly** *adv,* **distractive** /-tiv/ *adj.* [Middle English *distracten* from Latin *distractus,* past part. of *distrahere* to draw apart, from DIS- + *trahere* to draw]

distracted *adj* **1** not able to concentrate on the matter in hand, etc. **2** agitated. ➤➤ **distractedly** *adv,* **distractedness** *noun.*

distraction /di'straksh(ə)n/ *noun* **1** something that distracts one's attention: *I worked at night because there were too many distractions during the day.* **2** an amusement or activity: *There are plenty of distractions to keep the family amused.* ✳ **drive somebody to distraction** said of a constant irritation, etc: to reduce somebody to a state of nervous agitation.

distractor *noun* **1** something that distracts one's attention from the important issue, etc. **2** an inappropriate option in a multiple-choice question.

distrain /di'strayn/ *verb* **1** to seize the property of (a debtor) in compensation for money owed. **2** to seize (property) in compensation for money owed. ➤➤ **distrainable** *adj,* **distrainee** /-'nee/ *noun,* **distrainer** *noun,* **distrainment** *noun.* [Middle English *distreynen* via Old French from late Latin *distringere* to draw apart, detain, from DIS- + *stringere* to bind tight]

distraint /di'straynt/ *noun* the act of distraining. [DISTRAIN + -t as in CONSTRAINT]

distrait /di'stray (*French* distrɛ)/ *adj* absentminded. [French *distrait,* past part. of *distraire* to distract, from Latin *distrahere:* see DISTRACT]

distraught /di'strawt/ *adj* mentally agitated; frantic. ➤➤ **distraughtly** *adv.* [Middle English, alteration of obsolete *distract,* from Latin *distractus,* past part. of *distrahere:* see DISTRACT]

distress[1] /di'stres/ *noun* **1** mental or physical anguish. **2** hardship or suffering caused *esp* by lack of money or the necessities of life. **3** a state of danger or desperate need: *a ship in distress.* **4** a medical condition in which there is strain on the vital functions, *esp* difficulty in breathing. **5** seizure of property by a creditor as satisfaction for a debt; = DISTRAINT. ➤➤ **distressful** *adj.* [Middle English *destresse* from Old French, ultimately from Latin *districtus,* past part. of *distringere:* see DISTRAIN]

distress[2] *verb trans* **1** to cause distress to (somebody). **2** to simulate marks of usage, wear and tear, etc on (new furniture, etc) to give an appearance of antiquity. ➤➤ **distressing** *adj,* **distressingly** *adv.*

distressed *adj* **1** suffering distress. **2** impoverished: *distressed gentlefolk.*

distress signal *noun* a signal from a ship or aircraft that is in danger and needing assistance.

distributary /di'stribyoot(ə)ri/ *noun* (*pl* **distributaries**) a river branch flowing from and never returning to the main stream, as in a delta.

distribute /di'stribyooht, 'dis-/ *verb trans* **1** to divide or apportion (something) among a number of recipients. **2** (*usu in passive*) to disperse or scatter (something) over an area: *The species is distributed throughout Britain.* **3** to supply (goods) to the shops or outlets that are to sell them to consumers. **4** in logic, to use (a term) so as to refer to every member of the class named: *The proposition 'all men are mortal' distributes 'man' but not 'mortal'.* **5** to divide or separate (things) into classes or categories. **6** in printing, to return (type) to the right compartments for each character. ➤➤ **distributable** *adj.* [Middle English *distributen* from Latin *distributus,* past part. of *distribuere,* from DIS- + *tribuere* to allot]

Usage note
Distribute is traditionally pronounced with the stress on the second syllable *-trib-.* Modern dictionaries also recognize the pronunciation with the stress on the first syllable *dis-.*

distributed logic *noun* a computer system in which processing is shared between many processors linked by a network or bus.

distributed system *noun* a network of linked computers.

distribution /distri'byoohsh(ə)n/ *noun* **1** the act or an instance of distributing. **2a** the position, arrangement, or frequency of occurrence, e.g. of the members of a group, over an area or throughout a space or unit of time. **b** the natural geographical range of an organism. **3** in statistics, the set of possible values of a variable presented in terms of frequency. **4** the means by which something, e.g. electric power, is distributed. **5** the transport and delivery of goods to the shops or outlets that are to sell them to the consumers. ➤➤ **distributional** *adj*.

distributive[1] /di'stribyootiv/ *adj* **1** relating to or concerned with distribution. **2** in grammar, denoting a pronoun or determiner such as *each, either, every*, or *none*, that refers singly and without exception to all the members of a group. **3** in mathematics, denoting a law that relates the operations of addition and multiplication, such that $x(y + z) = xy + xz$. ➤➤ **distributively** *adv*, **distributiveness** *noun*, **distributivity** /-'tiviti/ *noun*.

distributive[2] *noun* a distributive word such as *each, either, every*, or *none*.

distributor /di'stribyootə/ *noun* **1** somebody or something that distributes. **2** a person employed to manage the distribution of goods. **3** an apparatus for directing current to the sparking plugs of an internal-combustion engine.

district[1] /'distrikt/ *noun* **1** a territorial division made *esp* for administrative purposes; *specif* in Britain, a division of a region or county that elects its own councillors. **2** an area or region with a specified character or feature: *a residential district*. [via French from medieval Latin *districtus* jurisdiction, district, past part. of *distringere*: see DIS-TRAIN]

district[2] *verb trans* to divide (an area) into districts.

district attorney *noun* the prosecuting officer of a judicial district in the USA.

district auditor *noun* in Britain, a civil servant who audits the accounts of local authorities.

district court *noun* in the USA, a federal court in which a case is heard in the first instance.

district high school *noun* in New Zealand, a school in a country area that provides both primary and secondary education.

district nurse *noun* in Britain, a qualified nurse, employed by a local authority, who visits and treats patients in their own homes.

distrust[1] /dis'trust/ *noun* suspicion or lack of trust. ➤➤ **distrustful** *adj*, **distrustfully** *adv*, **distrustfulness** *noun*.

distrust[2] *verb trans* to regard (somebody or something) as untrustworthy or unreliable. ➤➤ **distruster** *noun*.

disturb /di'stuhb/ *verb trans* **1** to break in upon (somebody) or interrupt them. **2** to alter the position or arrangement of (something). **3** to destroy the peace of mind or composure of (somebody). **4** to put (somebody) to inconvenience. **5** to disrupt the calm tenor of (something): *The arrival of their grandchildren disturbed their quiet Sunday afternoon*. ➤➤ **disturber** *noun*, **disturbing** *adj*, **disturbingly** *adv*. [Middle English *disturben, destourben* via Old French from Latin *disturbare*, from DIS- + *turbare* to throw into disorder]

disturbance *noun* **1** the act or an instance of disturbing. **2** an interruption. **3** in law, a riot or outbreak of public disorder. **4** a small earthquake. ✱ **disturbance of the peace** the offence of behaving in a riotous or unruly manner in a public place.

disturbed *adj* suffering from emotional or mental instability.

disubstituted /die'substityoohtid/ *adj* said of a molecule: having two substituted atoms or groups.

disulfiram /diesul'fiərəm/ *noun* a compound used in the treatment of alcoholism, which acts by causing severe nausea when alcohol is drunk. [*disulfide* (NAmer for DISULPHIDE) + THIOUREA + AMYL]

disulphide /die'sulfied/ *noun* a compound containing two atoms of sulphur combined with an element or radical.

disunion /dis'yoohnyən/ *noun* **1** the termination of union; separation. **2** disunity.

disunite /disyoo'niet/ *verb trans* to divide or separate (people or things). ➤➤ **disunited** *adj*.

disunity /dis'yoohniti/ *noun* lack of unity; dissension.

disuse /dis'yoohs/ *noun* the state of no longer being used: *a word that has fallen into disuse*.

disused /dis'yoohzd/ *adj* no longer used; abandoned.

disutility /disyooh'tiliti/ *noun esp* in economics, a drawback or disadvantage associated with a particular activity or procedure.

disyllable *or* **dissyllable** /di'siləbl, die-/ *noun* a word, metrical foot, etc consisting of two syllables. ➤➤ **dissyllabic** /disi-/ *adj*, **disyllabic** /disi'labik, die-/ *adj*. [French *disyllabe* via Latin from Greek *disyllabos* having two syllables, from DI-[1] + *syllabē*: see SYLLABLE]

dit /dit/ *noun* used to articulate the Morse Code DOT[1] (5). [imitative]

ditch[1] /dich/ *noun* a long narrow excavation dug in the earth for defence, drainage, irrigation, etc. [Old English *dic* dyke, ditch]

ditch[2] *verb trans* **1** to dig ditches throughout (an area) for drainage, etc. **2** to make a forced landing of (an aircraft) on water. **3** *informal* to get rid of or abandon (a plan, project, etc). **4** *NAmer, informal* to play truant from (school). ➤ *verb intrans* **1** to dig ditches or repair them. **2** said of a pilot: to come down in the sea. ➤➤ **ditcher** *noun*, **ditching** *noun*.

ditchwater *noun* stagnant water as found in ditches. ✱ **dull as ditchwater** said *esp* of people: irredeemably boring.

diterpene /die'tuhpeen/ *noun* any of a group of unsaturated hydrocarbons, mainly vegetable products, with the formula $C_{20}H_{32}$. ➤➤ **diterpenoid** /-'noyd/ *adj*.

ditheism /'dietheeiz(ə)m/ *noun* belief in two supreme gods, *esp* as opposing forces of good and evil. ➤➤ **ditheist** *noun*, **ditheistic** /-'istik/ *adj*, **ditheistical** /-'istikl/ *adj*.

dither[1] /'didhə/ *verb intrans* (**dithered, dithering**) to act nervously or indecisively; to vacillate. ➤➤ **ditherer** *noun*. [Middle English *didderen*, prob related to DODDER[1]]

dither[2] *noun* a state of indecision or nervous excitement: *all of a dither*. ➤➤ **dithery** *adj*.

dithi- *or* **dithio-** *comb. form* forming words, with the meaning: containing two atoms of sulphur, usu in place of two oxygen atoms, in the molecular structure. [DI-[1] + THI-]

dithyramb /'dithəram(b)/ *noun* **1** a rapturous Greek hymn in honour of Bacchus. **2** a short poem or other piece of writing in a rapturous or exalted style. ➤➤ **dithyrambic** /-'rambik/ *adj*, **dithyrambically** /-'rambikli/ *adv*. [Greek *dithyrambos*]

ditransitive /die'tranzitiv, die'transitiv/ *adj* denoting a verb that can take two objects, typically a direct and an indirect one, such as *give, tell, buy*. ➤➤ **ditransitivity** /-'tiviti/ *noun*.

ditsy /'ditsi/ *adj* (**ditsier, ditsiest**) see DITZY.

dittany /'ditəni/ *noun* **1** a pink-flowered plant that is native to Crete: *Origanum dictamnus*. **2** = GAS PLANT. [Middle English *ditoyne* via French and Latin from Greek *diktamnon*]

ditto[1] /'ditoh/ *noun* **1** used to avoid repeating a word: a thing mentioned previously or above; the same. **2** a mark (,, or ") used as a sign indicating repetition usu of a word directly above in a previous line. [Italian dialect, past part. of Italian *dire* to say, from Latin *dicere*]

ditto[2] *adv* as before or aforesaid; in the same manner.

ditto[3] *verb trans* (**dittos, dittoed, dittoing**) to copy or repeat (something).

dittography /di'tografi/ *noun* the unintentional repetition of letters or words in copying or printing. ➤➤ **dittographic** /-'grafik/ *adj*. [Greek *dittographia*, from *dittos* two-fold + *-graphia* -GRAPHY]

ditto mark *noun* = DITTO[1] (2).

ditty /'diti/ *noun* (*pl* **ditties**) a short simple song. [Middle English *ditee* from Old French *ditié* poem, past part. of *ditier* to compose, from Latin *dictare*: see DICTATE[1]]

ditty bag *noun* a bag used *esp* by sailors to hold small articles of gear, e.g. thread, needles, and tape. [origin uncertain]

ditty box *noun* a box used for the same purpose as a ditty bag.

ditz /dits/ *noun NAmer, informal* a ditzy person; a scatterbrain. [back-formation from DITZY]

ditzy *or* **ditsy** *adj* (**ditzier, ditziest**) *chiefly NAmer, informal* silly or scatterbrained. [perhaps alteration of DIZZY[1]]

diuresis /dieyoo'reesis/ *noun* an increased excretion of urine. [DI-[1] + Greek *ourēsis* urination, from *ouron* urine]

diuretic[1] /dieyoo'retik/ *adj* said of a drug: acting to increase the flow of urine. ➤➤ **diuretically** *adv*. [Middle English via French and Latin from Greek *diourētikos*, from *diourein* to urinate, from DIA- + *ouron* urine]

diuretic[2] *noun* a diuretic medicine.

diurnal /die'uhnl/ *adj* **1** having a daily cycle: *diurnal tides*. **2** occurring during the day or daily: *diurnal tasks*. **3** said of flowers: opening during the day and closing at night. **4** said of animals: active during the day. ➤ **diurnally** *adv*. [Middle English from late Latin *diurnalis*, from *diurnus* daily, from *dies* day]

div /div/ *noun* = DIVVY³. [Romany *div*]

div. *abbr* division.

diva /'deevə/ *noun* (*pl* **divas** *or* **dive** /'deevee/) **1a** a principal female opera singer; = PRIMA DONNA (1). **b** any distinguished female singer. **2** a haughty or temperamental woman. [Italian, literally 'goddess', from Latin *diva*, fem of *divus* divine, god]

divagate /'dievəgayt/ *verb intrans literary* to wander from one place or subject to another; to stray. ➤ **divagation** /-'gaysh(ə)n/ *noun*. [late Latin *divagatus*, past part. of *divagari* to wander about, from DIS- + *vagari* to wander]

divalent /die'vaylənt/ *adj* in chemistry, having a valency of two; bivalent.

Divali /di'vahli/ *noun* see DIWALI.

divan /di'van/ *noun* **1a** a long low couch, usu without arms or back, placed against a wall. **b** a bed of a similar style without a head or foot board. **2a** the privy council of the Ottoman Empire. **b** a council chamber in some Muslim countries, *esp* Turkey; the council itself. **3** an anthology of poems in Persian or Arabic, usu by a single author.

Word history
Turkish *dīvan* from Persian *dīwān* account book, court, bench. Persian *dīwān* orig meant a brochure or booklet, hence a collection of poems or of the records of an assembly, the assembly itself, a bench built along the wall of a courtroom or council chamber, a couch.

divaricate¹ /die'varikayt/ *verb intrans* to branch off; to diverge. ➤ **divarication** /-'kaysh(ə)n/ *noun*. [Latin *divaricatus*, past part. of *divaricare*, from DIS- + *varicare* to straddle]

divaricate² /die'varikət/ *adj* branching off; diverging.

dive¹ /div/ *verb intrans* (*past tense and past part.* **dived** *or NAmer* **dove** /dohv/, **diving**) **1a** to plunge into water headfirst, with arms extended forward. **b** to do this as a competitive sport, with a variety of prescribed moves: *She dives for the British team*. **2** to swim underwater using breathing equipment. **3** said of a submarine: to submerge. **4** said of a bird or an aircraft: to descend steeply through the air. **5** said of prices or profits: to plummet. **6** (+ into) to plunge one's hand into (a container, etc): *She dived into her shopping bag and brought out a crumpled receipt*. **7** (+ into) to plunge into (some activity): *He dived eagerly into his work*. **8** (+ for) to dash for (cover or shelter). **9** to lunge: *He dived at her and she sidestepped*. [Old English *dyfan* to dip, and *dūfan* to dive]

Usage note
dived and **dove**. *Dove* is an alternative past tense form of to *dive* in American English. It is not used in British English.

dive² *noun* **1** a headlong plunge into water, e.g. one performed with prescribed moves in competitive diving. **2** the submerging of a submarine. **3** a steep descent by an aircraft. **4** a sharp decline: *a steep dive in profits*. **5** *informal* a disreputable bar or meeting place. **6** a ploy in football in which a player falls over deliberately and ostentatiously after being tackled in order to give the effect of having been fouled. ✳ **make a dive for** to reach out for or rush towards (something): *He made a dive for the exit*. **take a dive** said of a boxer: to pretend to be knocked out.

dive³ /'deevee/ *noun pl* of DIVA.

dive-bomb *verb trans* to bomb (a place) from an aeroplane while making a steep dive towards the target. ➤ **dive-bomber** *noun*.

dive in *verb intrans informal* to involve oneself in some activity with alacrity, *esp* eating.

diver /'dievə/ *noun* **1** a person who dives as a competitive sport. **2** a person who works or explores underwater for long periods, either carrying a supply of air in cylinders or having it sent from the surface. **3a** any of several species of large fish-eating diving birds of the northern part of the northern hemisphere that have the legs placed far back under the body and as a result have a clumsy floundering gait on land: genus *Gavia*. **b** any of various diving birds.

diverge /die'vuhj, di-/ *verb intrans* **1** to move in different directions from a common point: *Their paths diverged*. **2** (*often* + from) to differ in character, form, or opinion: *This is the point at which Aristotle diverges from Plato* — James Martineau. **3** (*often* + from) to turn aside from a course or norm. **4** to be mathematically DIVERGENT. [late Latin *divergere* to turn away, from Latin DIS- + *vergere* to incline]

divergence *noun* **1a** the act or an instance of diverging. **b** the amount by which something diverges; = DIFFERENCE (3). **2** the acquisition of dissimilar characteristics by related organisms living in different environments.

divergency /die'vuhjənsi/ *noun* = DIVERGENCE.

divergent *adj* **1** diverging or differing from each other. **2a** said of a mathematical series: having a sum that continues to increase or decrease as the number of terms increases without limit. **b** said of a sequence: increasing or decreasing without limit. **3** causing divergence of rays: *a divergent lens*. ➤ **divergently** *adv*. [Latin *divergent-, divergens*, present part. of *divergere*: see DIVERGE]

divergent thinking *noun* thinking that is consciously directed away from conventional routes and assumptions, so as to generate a variety of conclusions or solutions.

divers /'dievəz/ *adj archaic* various: *Time travels in divers paces with divers persons* — Shakespeare. [Middle English *divers* via Old French from Latin *diversus*, past part. of *divertere*: see DIVERT]

diverse /die'vuhs, di'vuhs/ *adj* **1** different or unlike: *diverse interests*. **2** varied or assorted: *pursuits as diverse as rock-climbing and palaeography*. ➤ **diversely** *adv*, **diverseness** *noun*. [Middle English *diverse*, variant of DIVERS]

diversify /die'vuhsifie, di-/ *verb trans* (**diversifies, diversified, diversifying**) **1** to make (things) diverse or vary them. **2** to divide (investment of funds, etc) among different securities to reduce risk. ➤ *verb intrans* said *esp* of a company: to engage in varied business operations or lines of production in order to reduce risk. ➤ **diversification** /-fi'kaysh(ə)n/ *noun*, **diversifier** *noun*.

diversion /di'vuhsh(ə)n, die-/ *noun* **1** a turning aside from a course or activity. **2** a detour designated for traffic when the usual route is closed. **3** an amusement or pastime. **4** something that draws the attention away from the main scene of activity or operations: *The accomplice created a diversion in the street*. ➤ **diversionary** *adj*.

diversity /di'vuhsiti, die-/ *noun* (*pl* **diversities**) **1** the condition of being different or having differences: *the English countryside in all its diversity*. **2** a variety or assortment: *a diversity of topics*.

divert /die'vuht, di-/ *verb trans* **1a** to redirect (something) from one course or use to another. **b** to distract (somebody): *something diverted his attention*. **2** to entertain or amuse (somebody): *She's trying to divert the kids*. [Middle English *diverten* via French from Latin *divertere* to turn in opposite directions, from DIS- + *vertere* to turn]

diverticula /dievuh'tikyoolə/ *noun* pl of DIVERTICULUM.

diverticular disease /dievuh'tikyoolə/ *noun* DIVERTICULOSIS, with related muscle spasms and abdominal pain.

diverticulitis /,dievuh,tikyoo'lietis/ *noun* inflammation of a DIVERTICULUM, *esp* in the large bowel, causing pain and difficulty with bowel movements.

diverticulosis /,dievuh,tikyoo'lohsis/ *noun* a condition of the bowel, *esp* the large bowel, characterized by the presence of many diverticula.

diverticulum /dievə'tikyooləm/ *noun* (*pl* **diverticula** /-lə/) a pocket or closed branch opening off a main passage, *esp* an abnormal pouch opening off the intestine. ➤ **diverticular** *adj*. [Latin *diverticulum* bypath, prob alteration of *deverticulum* from *devertere* to turn aside, from DE- + *vertere* to turn]

divertimento /di,vuhti'mentoh/ *noun* (*pl* **divertimenti** /-tee/ *or* **divertimentos**) an instrumental chamber work in several movements and usu light in character. [Italian *divertimento* diversion, from *divertire* to divert, amuse, via French from Latin *divertere*: see DIVERT]

diverting *adj* amusing; entertaining: *And love! What diverting scenes would it produce!* — Mary Wollstonecraft. ➤ **divertingly** *adv*.

divertissement /di'vuhtismənt (*French* divɛrtismã)/ *noun* (*pl* **divertissements** /-mənts (*French* -mã)/) **1a** a ballet or ballet suite serving as an interlude. **b** a virtuoso solo dance within a ballet. **2** = DIVERTIMENTO. **3** a diversion or entertainment. [French *divertissement* diversion, from *divertir* to divert, from Latin *divertere*: see DIVERT]

Dives /'dieveez/ *noun literary* the archetypal rich man. [Latin *dives* rich, used in the Vulgate translation of the New Testament (Luke

16) as the name of the rich man at whose gate the beggar Lazarus sat]

divest /die'vest/ *verb trans* **1** (+ of) to deprive or dispossess (somebody) of property, authority, title, etc. **2a** (+ of) to rid or free (oneself) of something oppressive: *Now we will divest us both of rule, interest of territory, cares of state* — Shakespeare. **b** *humorous* (+ of) to relieve (oneself) of clothing: *divesting herself of her out-of-door attire* — Dickens. **3** to strip (something) of an attribute, etc: *Christmas had long since been divested of its magic.* **4** to take away (property or vested rights) from somebody. **5** to sell off (subsidiary companies) or dispose of (investments). [alteration of *devest* via early French *desvestir* from late Latin *disvestire*, from DIS- + *vestire* to clothe]

divestiture /die'vesticha/ *or* **divesture** /die'vescha/ *noun* **1** the compulsory transfer of title or disposal of interests on government order. **2** the selling off of subsidiary companies, or withdrawal from investment; = DISINVESTMENT.

divestment *noun* **1** the act of divesting. **2** = DIVESTITURE.

divesture /die'vescha/ *noun* = DIVESTITURE.

divi /'divi/ *noun* see DIVVY[1].

divide[1] /di'vied/ *verb trans* **1** to split (people, things, etc) into two or more parts or groups. **2** to split (a territory) into areas. **3** to separate (something) into categories. **4** to share (something) between recipients. **5** to be what separates (one thing and another): *The Alps divide Switzerland from Italy and France.* **6** to be the issue that provokes disagreement in (a body) or between (parties): *The question of gay clergy is dividing the Church.* **7** to distribute (one's time) between one thing and another. **8** in mathematics, to operate on (a number) to find out how many times it contains a smaller number: *Divide 20 by 5.* ➤ *verb intrans* **1** to separate in parts, branches, groups, etc: *the point where the river divides.* **2** said of a legislative body: to separate into groups for voting. **3** in mathematics, said of a number: to allow of division without a remainder: *20 does not divide by 3.* ➤➤ **dividable** *adj.* [Middle English *dividen* from Latin *dividere* to split, from DIS- + *-videre* to separate]

divide[2] *noun* **1** a line of division; a split: *the great divide between the haves and the have-nots.* **2** *chiefly NAmer* a dividing ridge between drainage areas; a watershed.

divided highway *noun NAmer* = DUAL CARRIAGEWAY.

divided skirt *noun* wide-legged knee-length shorts for women, skirt-like in appearance; = CULOTTES.

dividend /'dividend, -dand/ *noun* **1a** a sum of money to be divided and distributed, *esp* the part of a company's profits payable to shareholders. **b** an individual shareholder's portion of this. **2** (*usu in pl*) a reward or benefit: *Proper tuition will pay great dividends.* **3** in mathematics, a number to be divided by another. [Middle English *divident* from Latin *dividendus*, verbal noun from *dividere*: see DIVIDE[1]]

dividend cover *noun* the proportion of the net profits of a company constituted by the total paid in dividends to its shareholders.

divider *noun* **1** (*in pl*) a compasslike instrument with two pointed ends used for measuring or marking off lines, angles, etc. **2** a partition or screen used to separate parts of a room, hall, etc.

dividing line *noun* **1** a line of demarcation between territories, etc: *The river represents the dividing line between our two counties.* **2** the distinction between two things that shade into each other: *the dividing line between carefreeness and irresponsibility.*

divi-divi /,divi 'divi, ,deevi 'deevi/ *noun* **1** a small tropical American tree of the pea family with twisted pods: *Caesalpinia coriaria.* **2** the pods of this tree, rich in tannin that is used in the tanning of leather. [Spanish *dividivi*, of Carib origin]

divination /divi'naysh(ə)n/ *noun* **1** the art or practice that seeks to foresee the future or discover hidden knowledge, e.g. by using supernatural powers. **2** unusual insight or perception, or an instance of this. ➤➤ **divinatory** /di'vinət(ə)ri/ *adj.* [Middle English *divinacioun* from Latin *divination-, divinatio*, from *divinare*: see DIVINE[3]]

divine[1] /di'vien/ *adj* **1a** being a god or goddess: *a divine presence.* **b** relating to or proceeding from God or a god: *divine inspiration.* **c** devoted to the worship of God or a god; sacred. **2** *informal* delightful or superb. ➤➤ **divinely** *adv, divineness noun.* [Middle English *divin* via French from Latin *divinus* divine: see DIVINE[3]]

divine[2] *noun* a clergyman; *esp* one skilled in theology. [Middle English from late Latin *divinus* soothsayer: see DIVINE[3]]

divine[3] *verb trans* **1** to discover, perceive, or foresee (something) intuitively or by supernatural means: *She somehow divined that I was in trouble.* **2** to discover or locate (water or minerals) by means of a divining rod. ➤ *verb intrans* to practise divination. ➤➤ **divinable** *adj, diviner noun.* [Middle English *divinen* via French from Latin *divinare* to divine, prophesy, from *divinus* soothsayer, noun use of *divinus* holy, from *divus* good]

Divine Liturgy *noun* the form of service used in the Eastern Orthodox celebration of Communion.

Divine Office *noun* the prescribed forms of prayer and ritual for daily worship used by Roman Catholic priests; = BREVIARY.

divine right *noun* **1** the right of a sovereign to rule, held to derive directly from God: *the divine right of kings.* **2** a right which cannot be transferred.

divine service *noun* a service of public Christian worship, *esp* at which there is no celebration of Holy Communion, or other sacrament.

diving beetle *noun* any of numerous species of flesh-eating water beetles that store air under their wing cases for diving, and have fringed back legs for swimming: family Dytiscidae.

diving bell *noun* a bell-shaped metal container open only at the bottom and supplied with compressed air through a tube, in which a person can be let down under water.

diving board *noun* a springboard or platform projecting over a swimming pool, from which people can dive into the water.

diving dress *noun* = DIVING SUIT.

diving duck *noun* any of various ducks, e.g. the pochard or goldeneye, that frequent deep waters and obtain their food by diving.

diving suit *noun* a diver's waterproof suit with a helmet that is supplied with a mixture of gases suitable for breathing pumped through a tube.

divining rod *noun* a forked rod, e.g. a twig, believed to dip downwards when held over ground concealing water or minerals.

divinise /'diviniez/ *verb* see DIVINIZE.

divinity /di'viniti/ *noun* (*pl* **divinities**) **1** the quality or state of being divine. **2a** (**the Divinity**) God. **b** a male or female deity. **3** theology.

divinize *or* **divinise** /'diviniez/ *verb trans* to render (somebody) divine; to deify (them).

divisi /di'veesee/ *adj* used as a musical direction, after a plural noun, as in *cellos divisi* to indicate that the specified instrumental group is further divided into sections playing different parts. [Italian *divisi* divided, from *dividere* to divide, from Latin: see DIVIDE[1]]

divisible /di'vizəbl/ *adj* **1** capable of being divided. **2** said of a number: that can be divided by another without remainder: *20 is divisible by 4.* ➤➤ **divisibility** /-'biliti/ *noun.*

division /di'vizh(ə)n/ *noun* **1a** the action of dividing or process of being divided. **b** distribution: *division of the spoils.* **2** any of the parts or sections into which a whole is divided. **3** (*treated as sing. or pl*). **a** a major army formation having the necessary tactical and administrative services to act independently. **b** a naval unit of men under a single command. **4a** an administrative territorial unit. **b** an administrative or operating unit of an organization. **5** a group of organisms forming part of a larger group; *specif* a primary category of the plant kingdom equivalent to a phylum of the animal kingdom. **6** a competitive class or category, e.g. of a football league. **7** something that divides, separates, or marks off; a dividing line. **8** disagreement or disunity: *division in the ranks.* **9** the physical separation into different lobbies of the members of a parliamentary body voting for and against a question. **10** the mathematical operation of dividing one number by another. ➤➤ **divisional** *adj.* [Middle English via French from Latin *division-, divisio*, from *dividere*: see DIVIDE[1]]

divisionalize *or* **divisionalise** *verb trans* to subdivide (a corporation, etc) into several separate sections.

division bell *noun* a bell rung in the British Parliament to warn that a DIVISION (vote) is about to take place.

divisionism /di'vizh(ə)niz(ə)m/ *noun* = POINTILLISM.

division of labour *noun* the distribution of various parts of the process of production among different people, groups, or machines, each specializing in a particular job, to increase efficiency.

division sign *noun* **1** the symbol (÷) used to indicate division. **2** the oblique stroke (/) used to indicate a fraction.

divisive /di'viesiv, -ziv/ *adj* tending to cause disunity or dissension: *divisive issues.* ➤➤ **divisively** *adv,* **divisiveness** *noun.*

divisor /di'vieza/ *noun* in mathematics, the number by which the number or quantity undergoing division is divided.

divorce[1] /di'vaws/ *noun* **1** a legal dissolution of a marriage, or the decree ratifying this. **2** a separation, dissociation, or severance: *'Leap of faith' denotes a divorce between the intellect and the imagination.* [Middle English *divorse* via French from Latin *divortium,* from *divortere* to leave one's husband, alteration of *divertere:* see DIVERT]

divorce[2] *verb trans* **1** to end marriage with (one's spouse) by divorce. **2** (+ from) to sever (one thing) from another. *Her plots are so divorced from reality.* ➤ *verb intrans* to obtain a divorce. ➤➤ **divorceable** *adj,* **divorcement** *noun.*

divorcé /divaw'say, -'see/ *noun* a divorced man. [French *divorcé,* past part. of *divorcer* to divorce, from Latin *divortium:* see DIVORCE[1]]

divorcée /divaw'say, -'see/ *noun* a divorced woman.

divot /'divət/ *noun* **1** a piece of turf struck out of the ground in making a golf shot. **2** *Scot* a piece of turf, formerly used for roofing. [origin unknown]

divulge /die'vulj, di-/ *verb trans* to make known or reveal (a confidence or secret): *That the secret has not been divulged is the very best proof that it is, in fact, a secret* — Poe. ➤➤ **divulgence** *noun.* [Middle English *divulgen* from Latin *divulgare,* from DIS- + *vulgare* to make known]

divvy[1] /'divi/ *noun* (*pl* **divvies**) *Brit, informal esp* formerly, a DIVI-DEND, *esp* one paid by a cooperative society.

divvy[2] *verb trans* (**divvies, divvied, divvying**) *informal* (*usu* + up) to divide or share (something): *Mother divvied up the sweets.* [by shortening and alteration from *divide*]

divvy[3] /'divi/ *or* **div** /div/ *noun* (*pl* **divvies**) *Brit, informal* a fool.

Diwali /di'wahli/ *or* **Divali** /di'vahli/ *noun* the Hindu or Sikh Festival of Lights, celebrating the end of the monsoon. [Hindi *dīvālī* from Sanskrit *dīpāvali* row of lights]

diwan /di'wahn/ *noun* = DEWAN.

Dixie /'diksi/ *noun informal* the Southern states of the USA. ✳ **whistle Dixie** *NAmer, informal* to be wasting one's time on fantasies.

Word history
name for the Southern states in the song *Dixie* by Daniel Dutch Emmett d.1904, US musician. *Dixie* was a popular marching song among Confederate soldiers in the Civil War; the name may refer to the Mason-Dixon Line, regarded as the boundary between the Northern and Southern states.

dixie *noun* (*pl* **dixies**) a large metal pot in which food and drink is made or carried by soldiers or campers. [Hindi *degcī,* dimin. of *degcā* kettle, pot]

dixieland *noun* jazz music in duple time characterized by collective improvisation.

Editorial note
A style created by the Chicago school of 1920s jazz musicians, dixieland's brash and upbeat manner was an alternative to the more purist associations of traditional New Orleans playing. It has also become familiar as a sometimes disparaging term used to cover any playing within the traditional idiom that is perceived as being created for commercial rather than creative reasons — Richard Cook.

[DIXIE + LAND[1]; from its origin in the Southern states of the USA]

DIY *noun chiefly Brit* **1** amateur repair, maintenance, and building work, *esp* around the home. **2** (*used before a noun*) of or relating to materials and equipment needed for this: *a DIY store.* [from the initials of DO-IT-YOURSELF]

dizygotic /diezie'gotik/ *adj* denoting non-identical twins, born from two simultaneously fertilized ova, as distinct from a single ovum that splits; = FRATERNAL (2). [DI-[1] + *zygotic* (see ZYGOTE) or -ZYGOUS]

dizygous /die'ziegəs/ *adj* = DIZYGOTIC.

dizzy[1] /'dizi/ *adj* (**dizzier, dizziest**) **1a** experiencing a whirling sensation in the head, along with a tendency to lose balance. **b** mentally confused: *You're making me dizzy.* **2** *informal* foolish or silly. ✳ **the dizzy heights** *informal* the pinnacle of power, success, or importance; the top of the ladder. ➤➤ **dizzily** *adv,* **dizziness** *noun.* [Old English *dysig* stupid]

dizzy[2] *verb trans* (**dizzies, dizzied, dizzying**) to make (somebody) dizzy; to bewilder (them). ➤➤ **dizzying** *adj,* **dizzyingly** *adv.*

DJ *noun* (*pl* **DJs**) **1** = DISC JOCKEY. **2** = DINNER JACKET.

djellaba *or* **djellabah** *or* **jellaba** /jə'lahbə, 'jelabə/ *noun* a long loose outer garment with full sleeves and a hood, traditionally worn by Arabs. [French *djellaba* from Arabic *jallabah*]

Djiboutian /ji'boohti-ən/ *noun* a native or inhabitant of Djibouti on the NE coast of Africa. ➤➤ **Djiboutian** *adj.*

djin *or* **djinn** /jin/ *noun* (*pl* **djin** *or* **djinn**) see JINN.

DK *abbr* Denmark (international vehicle registration for Denmark and Greenland).

dkl *abbr NAmer* dekaliter.

dkm *abbr NAmer* dekameter.

dl *abbr* decilitre.

DLitt *abbr* Doctor of Letters. [Latin *Doctor Litterarum*]

DM *abbr* Deutschmark.

dm *abbr* decimetre.

DMA *abbr* in computing, direct memory access.

D-Mark *abbr* Deutschmark.

DMs *pl noun* Doc Martens.

DMus /,dee 'mus/ *abbr* Doctor of Music.

DMZ *abbr NAmer* demilitarized zone.

DNA *noun* any of various nucleic acids that occur chiefly in the nuclei of cells, are the material that makes up genes, and consist of long strands of phosphate groups alternating with deoxyribose groups, from each of which projects a purine or pyrimidine base. The DNA chains typically occur as pairs in a double helix.

Editorial note
DNA constitutes the genetic material within each cell, containing the code on which proteins are synthesized and the information that is transferred between cell generations during reproduction and development. Each strand of the double helix consists of a sequence of nucleotides, adenine, cytosine, guanine, and thymine (ACGT). The order in which they are arranged is the basis for the genetic code — Professor Steven Rose.

[contraction of *deoxyribonucleic acid*]

DNA fingerprinting *noun* genetic fingerprinting.

DNA profiling *noun* = DNA FINGERPRINTING.

DNase /dee-en'ayz/ *noun* the enzyme deoxyribonuclease.

DNB *abbr* Dictionary of National Biography.

D-notice *noun* an official request, e.g. to a newspaper, that certain information be withheld from publication for security reasons. [short for *Defence-notice*]

do[1] /dooh/ *verb* (*third person sing. present tense* **does** /dəz; *strong* duz/, *past tense* **did** /did/, *past part.* **done** /dun/) ➤ *verb trans* **1** to effect, perform, or carry out (an action or activity). **2** to do work on or have work done on (something) to get it in the required state: *I can't do this sum; Shall we do the garden?* **3** to work at (something) for a living or course of study: *She decided to do Chinese.* **4** to make or provide (something): *He does a fine cheesecake; They do a mail-order service.* **5a** to put on or perform (a play, show, etc). **b** to play (a role). **6** to have a specified effect on (sombody): *A rest will do you good.* **7** to perform the expected service for (somebody): *The photographer will do you now.* **8** to travel at (a specified speed) or over (a specified distance): *They were doing at least 90 down the motorway; We did two hundred miles in a single morning.* **9** *informal* to see (a place) as a tourist: *We want to do Prague next.* **10** *informal* to spend (a period of time) doing something, *esp* serving a prison sentence: *He's doing five years for armed robbery.* **11** *informal* to be adequate or suitable for (somebody): *A light salad will do us for lunch.* **12** *chiefly Brit, informal.* **a** to arrest or convict (somebody). **b** to attack or hurt (somebody). **c** to cheat or swindle (somebody). **13** *informal* to burgle and rob (premises). **14** *informal* to have sexual intercourse with (somebody). **15** *informal* to take (drugs). ➤ *verb intrans* **1** to act or behave a certain way: *Do as I say.* **2a** to make progress in a specified way: *They are all doing well at school.* **b** to carry on business or affairs; to manage: *We can do without your help.* **3** *informal* to be happening: *What's doing these days?* **4** (*often* + with) to finish: *Have you done with arguing?* **5** to be adequate or suitable: *Half of that will do.* **6** to be fitting; to conform to custom or propriety: *It won't do to be late.* ➤ *verb aux* **1** used to form questions and negative statements: *I did not agree; Please don't go; Do you like this place?* **2a** used in present and past tenses to emphasize a positive verb: *I do hope you can come; Do be careful; They did ask us to help.* **b** used in legal language and poetry: *to give what she did crave* — Shakespeare; *I do hereby bequeath.* **c** used in declarations with inverted word order: *Fervently do we pray*

— Abraham Lincoln. **3** used as a substitute for a verb already mentioned: *I am earning more than I did last year.* ✳ **could do with** need or would like (something): *I could do with some peace and quiet.* **do away with 1** to put an end to or abolish (something). **2** to put (somebody) to death. **do by** to treat (somebody) in a specified way: *They did very well by her; We felt somewhat hard done by.* **do for 1** *chiefly Brit, informal* to keep house or clean for (somebody). **2** *informal* to wear out or exhaust (somebody). **3** *informal* to bring about the death or ruin of (somebody). **do somebody out of** to cheat or deprive somebody of (something). **do something/nothing for** to enhance or fail to enhance the appearance of (somebody or something). **do without** to manage in spite of not having (something). **have done with** to finish with or have no further concern with (something). **have nothing to do with 1** to refuse to have dealings with (sombody or something). **2** to be no concern of (somebody). **have to do with** to deal with (something or somebody). **to do with** concerned with (something): *a job to do with insurance.* ➤➤ **doable** *adj.* [Old English *dōn*]

do² *noun* (*pl* **dos** *or* **do's** /doohz/) **1** (*usu in pl*) something one ought to do: *I gave her a list of dos and don'ts.* **2** *chiefly Brit, informal* a party or festive occasion.

do³ *or* **doh** /doh/ *noun* in music, the first note of a major scale in the tonic sol-fa system, or the note C in the fixed-doh system. [prob from Latin *Domine* Lord: see also GAMUT]

do. *abbr* ditto.

DOA *abbr* used chiefly in hospitals: dead on arrival.

dob /dob/ *verb trans* (**dobbed, dobbing**) *Aus, informal* (*often* + in) to inform on (somebody): *He'd dob in his workmates if they smoked on the job.* [figurative use of Brit dialect *dob* to set down sharply or throw down]

d.o.b. *abbr* date of birth.

dobbin /'dobin/ *noun* a familiar name for a farm horse. [*Dobbin*, nickname for *Robert*]

Doberman *or* **Dobermann** /'dohbəmən/ *noun* (*in full* **Doberman pinscher** /'pinshə/) a short-haired medium-sized breed of dog originating in Germany, frequently used as a guard dog. [German *Dobermann Pinscher*, from Ludwig *Dobermann*, 19th-cent. German dog-breeder (who bred it) + German *Pinscher*, a breed of terrier]

dobra /'dohbrə/ *noun* the basic monetary unit of São Tomé and Principe, divided into 100 centavos. [Portuguese *dóbra* doubloon]

Dobro /'dohbroh/ *noun* (*pl* **Dobros**) *trademark* an acoustic guitar with steel resonators fitted internally under the bridge. [from *Dopěra Brothers*, the Czech-born inventors]

dobsonfly /'dobsənflie/ *noun* (*pl* **dobsonflies**) a large grey N American fly whose larva is used as fishing bait: *Corydalus cornutus.* [origin unknown]

Dobsonian /dob'sohni·ən/ *adj* denoting a cheaply made Newtonian type of telescope. [named after John *Dobson*, 20th-cent. American amateur astronomer]

DOC *abbr* said of wines: Denominazióne d'Origine Contròllata. [Italian, name of origin controlled]

doc /dok/ *noun* sometimes used as an informal term of address: a doctor.

docent /doh'sent, 'dohs(ə)nt/ *noun* a lecturer in some US colleges and universities. [obsolete German *docent* (now *Dozent*), from Latin *docent-, docens*, present part. of *docēre* to teach]

Docetism /'dohsitiz(ə)m, doh'set-/ *noun* an early Christian heretical belief that Christ seemed to, but did not really, have a human body and suffer and die on the cross. ➤➤ **Docetic** /-'setik/ *adj*, **Docetist** /'dohsitist/ *noun*. [Greek *Dokētai* Docetists, from *dokein* to seem]

DOCG *abbr* said of wines: Denominazióne di Origine Contròllata Garantita. [Italian, name of origin guaranteed controlled]

doch an dorris /,dokh ən 'dorəs/ *noun* SEE DEOCH AN DORIS.

docile /'dohsiel/ *adj* easily led or managed; tractable. ➤➤ **docilely** *adv*, **docility** /doh'siliti/ *noun*. [Latin *docilis* docile, teachable, from *docēre* to teach]

dock¹ /dok/ *noun* a coarse weed, the leaves of which are used to alleviate nettle stings: genus *Rumex*. [Old English *docce*]

dock² *noun* the solid bony part of an animal's tail as distinguished from the hair. [Middle English *dok* from Old English *-docca* (as in *fingirdocca* finger muscle)]

dock³ *verb trans* **1a** to remove part of the tail of (a horse). **b** to cut (a tail) short. **2** to make a deduction from (wages). **3** (*often* + from) to take away (a specified amount) from wages, etc: *He had £1 docked from his pocket money.*

dock⁴ *noun* **1a** an artificially enclosed body of water in a port or harbour, where a ship can moor, e.g. for repair work to be carried out. **b** (**the docks**) the area of such enclosures in a harbour, together with wharves, sheds, etc. **2** *chiefly NAmer* a wharf. ✳ **in dock 1** said of a ship: moored in a harbour. **2** said of a vehicle: in a garage or repair shop: *My car's in dock at the moment.* [prob from early Dutch *docke* dock, ditch]

dock⁵ *verb trans* **1** to haul or guide (a ship) into a dock. **2** to join (two spacecraft) together while in space. ➤ *verb intrans* **1** said of a ship: to come or go into dock. **2** said of spacecraft: to join together while in space.

dock⁶ *noun* the prisoner's enclosure in a criminal court. ✳ **in the dock** on trial. [Flemish *docke* cage]

dockage /'dokij/ *noun* accommodation at a dock for a vessel, or the cost of this.

docker *noun* a person who is employed in loading and unloading ships, barges, etc. [DOCK⁴]

docket¹ /'dokit/ *noun* **1** a brief written summary of a document. **2a** a document recording the contents of a shipment or the payment of customs duties. **b** a label attached to goods bearing identification or instructions. **c** a receipt. **3** *NAmer.* **a** a formal record of legal proceedings. **b** a list of legal causes to be tried. **c** a list of business matters to be acted on. [Middle English *doggette*; earlier history unknown]

docket² *verb trans* (**docketed, docketing**) **1** to put an identifying statement or label on (a consignment, etc). **2** to make an abstract of (legal proceedings, etc). **3** *NAmer* to place (a legal cause) on the docket for action.

docking station *noun* an adapter that converts a laptop computer into a desktop computer, by enabling it to be connected to a monitor, keyboard, and extra disk drives.

dockland *noun* *Brit* (*also in pl*) the district around the docks in a large port.

dockominium /dokə'mini·əm/ *noun* (*pl* **dockominiums**) *NAmer* **1** a condominium on a waterfront, with private mooring facilities. **2** a private landing stage on a marina. [DOCK⁴ + CONDOMINIUM]

dockside *noun* (*often before another noun*) the area beside a dock.

dockyard *noun* a place or enclosure in which ships are built or repaired.

Doc Martens /,dok 'mahtənz/ *pl noun* (*also informal* **Docs**) *trademark* tough-looking laced shoes or boots with thick lightweight rubber soles. [from full form *Doctor Martens*, from the name of Klaus *Maertens*, German inventor of the sole]

doctor¹ /'doktə/ *noun* **1** a person qualified to practise medicine; a physician or surgeon. **2** *NAmer* a licensed dentist or veterinary surgeon. **3** a holder of the highest level of academic degree conferred by a university. **4** *informal* a person who is skilled in repairing or treating a usu specified type of machine, vehicle, etc: *a bicycle doctor.* **5** = DOCTOR OF THE CHURCH. **6** *archaic* a learned or authoritative teacher: *Duns Scotus was known as the Subtle Doctor.* **7** an artificial fishing fly. **8** *Aus, NZ* a cook on board ship or at a station or camp. **9** a cool onshore breeze in certain warm areas. ✳ **go for the doctor** *Aus, NZ* to make a supreme effort. **just what the doctor ordered** just the thing needed. ➤➤ **doctorly** *adj*, **doctorship** *noun*. [Middle English *doctour* teacher, doctor, via French from Latin *doctor* teacher, from *docēre* to teach]

doctor² *verb* (**doctored, doctoring**) ➤ *verb trans* **1a** to give medical treatment to (somebody). **b** to repair or mend (something). **2a** to adapt or modify (something) for a desired end: *The script had to be doctored a bit.* **b** to alter (evidence or statistics) in a dishonest way. **3** *euphem* to castrate or spay (a dog or cat). ➤ *verb intrans informal* to practise medicine. ➤➤ **doctoring** *noun*.

doctoral *adj* relating to a doctorate: *a doctoral thesis.*

doctorate /'doktərət/ *noun* the highest academic degree, awarded by a university for original postgraduate research presented as a thesis.

Doctor of Philosophy *noun* a person who has a doctorate, usu in any subject other than law, medicine, or theology.

Doctor of the Church *noun* any of a small number of particularly revered early theologians in the Christian Church, including St Jerome, St Ambrose, St Augustine of Hippo, and St Gregory the Great, with the later addition of St Thomas Aquinas, St Theresa of Ávila, and St Catherine of Siena.

doctrinaire[1] /ˌdoktriˈneə/ *adj* concerned with abstract theory to the exclusion of practical considerations. [French *doctrinaire*, from *doctrine*: see DOCTRINE]

doctrinaire[2] *noun* a doctrinaire person.

doctrinal /dokˈtrienl/ *adj* relating to or concerned with doctrine: *doctrinal arguments.* ➤➤ **doctrinally** *adv.*

doctrine /ˈdoktrin/ *noun* **1** something that is taught. **2** a principle or the body of principles in a branch of knowledge or system of belief: *Christian doctrine.* [Middle English via French from Latin *doctrina* teaching, from *doctor* see DOCTOR]

docudrama /ˈdokyoodrahmə/ *noun* a play, film, etc in which factual incidents are presented in dramatized form: *Shakespeare's scurrilously inaccurate docudrama Richard III —* The Listener. [DOCUMENTARY[2] + DRAMA]

document[1] /ˈdokyoomənt/ *noun* an original or official paper, or electronic record, that gives information about or proof of something. ➤➤ **documental** /-ˈmentl/ *adj.* [Middle English via French from late Latin *documentum* official paper, earlier lesson, proof, from *docēre* to teach]

document[2] /ˈdokyoomənt/ *verb trans* **1** to record (something) in detail, with the backing of eye-witness reports, photographs, etc. **2** to support (a hypothesis or statement) with authoritative references: *a well-documented thesis with footnotes on every page.* **3** to provide (a ship) with ship's papers for the listing of ownership, cargo, and other details required by law. ➤➤ **documentable** *adj*, **documenter** *noun.*

documentary[1] /ˌdokyooˈment(ə)ri/ *adj* **1** consisting of documents; contained or certified in writing: *documentary evidence.* **2** presenting or based on factual material: *a documentary film.* ➤➤ **documentarily** /-ˈterəli/ *adv.*

documentary[2] *noun* (*pl* **documentaries**) a broadcast or film that presents a factual account of a person or topic using a variety of techniques, e.g. narrative and interview: compare FEATURE[1] (3A). ➤➤ **documentarist** *noun.*

documentation /ˌdokyoomenˈtaysh(ə)n/ *noun* **1** written instructions, plans, specifications, etc. **2** documents provided in evidence or support for a claim, etc. ➤➤ **documentational** *adj.*

documentative /dokyooˈmentətiv/ *adj* said of a presentation, etc: supported by documentation.

document case *noun* a light flat leather or plastic case, usu lockable, for carrying papers.

document reader *noun* a machine for reading documents that are encoded so as to be legible to a person or a machine, such as bank cheques.

docusoap /ˈdokyoosohp/ *noun* a documentary series of television programmes following the lives of a particular group of people, etc, over a period of time. [DOCUMENTARY[2] + SOAP OPERA]

docutainment /dokyooˈtaynmənt/ *noun NAmer* films or other presentations that incorporate documentary material, designed both to inform and entertain. [DOCUMENTARY[2] + ENTERTAINMENT]

dodder[1] /ˈdodə/ *verb intrans* (**doddered, doddering**) **1** to walk feebly and unsteadily. **2** to tremble or shake from weakness or age. ➤➤ **dodderer** *noun.* [Middle English *dadiren*; earlier history unknown]

dodder[2] *noun* a leafless plant of the bindweed family that is wholly parasitic on other plants: genus *Cuscuta.* [Middle English *doder*, of Germanic origin]

doddering *adj* weak, shaky, and slow, *esp* because of old age.

doddery /ˈdodəri/ *adj* = DODDERING.

doddle /ˈdodl/ *noun chiefly Brit, informal* a very easy task. [origin unknown]

dodeca- *or* **dodec-** *comb. form* forming words, with the meaning: twelve: *dodecaphonic.* [Greek *dōdeka-* twelve]

dodecagon /dohˈdekəgən/ *noun* a polygon with twelve angles and twelve sides. ➤➤ **dodecagonal** /dohdeˈkagənl/ *adj.* [Greek *dōdekagōnon*, from *dōdeka-* DODECA- + -*gōnon* -GON]

dodecahedron /ˌdohdekəˈheedrən/ *noun* (*pl* **dodecahedrons** *or* **dodecahedra** /-drə/) a polyhedron with twelve faces. ➤➤ **dodecahedral** *adj.* [Greek *dōdekaedron*, from *dōdeka-* DODECA- + -*edron* -HEDRON]

dodecaphonic /ˌdohdekəˈfonik/ *adj* in music, twelve-tone. ➤➤ **dodecaphonically** *adv*, **dodecaphonist** /dohˈdekəfənist, -ˈkafənist/ *noun*, **dodecaphony** /-ni/ *noun.* [DODECA- + PHON- + -IC[1]]

dodge[1] /doj/ *verb intrans* to shift position suddenly, e.g. to avoid a blow or a pursuer. ➤ *verb trans* **1** to evade (a duty, etc) usu by subterfuge. **2** to avoid (a blow, etc) by a sudden or repeated shift of position. **3** to avoid an encounter with (a person). **4** in photography, to lighten (an area on a print). [origin unknown]

dodge[2] *noun* **1** a sudden movement to avoid something. **2** a clever device to evade something or deceive somebody: *a tax dodge.*

dodgeball *noun* an American game played with a large ball, in which teams of players form circles and try to hit their opponents with it.

dodgem /ˈdojəm/ *or* **dodgem car** *noun* any of a number of small electric cars designed to be steered about and bumped into one another as a funfair amusement. [DODGE[1] + 'EM]

dodger /ˈdojə/ *noun* **1** (*often used in combinations*) a person who uses clever and often dishonest methods, *esp* to avoid payment, e.g. of taxes, or responsibility: *a tax-dodger; a draft-dodger.* **2** a canvas screen on a ship or boat that provides protection against the weather.

dodgy /ˈdoji/ *adj* (**dodgier, dodgiest**) *chiefly Brit, informal* **1** shady or dishonest: *dodgy dealings.* **2** risky or dangerous: *a dodgy plan.* **3** liable to collapse, fail, or break down: *That chair's a bit dodgy.*

dodo /ˈdohdoh/ *noun* (*pl* **dodoes** *or* **dodos**) a large extinct flightless bird that formerly lived on the island of Mauritius: *Raphus cucullatus.* [Portuguese *doudo* fool, simpleton; because of its clumsy movements and lack of fear]

do down *verb trans Brit, informal* to disparage or criticize (somebody).

DOE *abbr Brit* formerly, Department of the Environment.

doe /doh/ *noun* (*pl* **does** *or collectively* **doe**) **1** the adult female fallow deer. **2** the adult female of any of various mammals, e.g. the rabbit, or birds, e.g. the guinea fowl, of which the male is called a buck. [Old English *dā*]

doek /dook/ *noun* a square headscarf worn by S African women. [via Afrikaans from Dutch *doek* cloth]

doer /ˈdooh·ə/ *noun* one who takes action or participates actively in something, rather than theorizing.

does /dəz; *strong* duz/ *verb* third person sing. present tense of DO[1].

doeskin /ˈdohskin/ *noun* **1** the skin of a doe, or leather made from this. **2** a smooth closely woven woollen fabric.

doesn't /ˈduz(ə)nt/ *contraction* does not.

doest /ˈdooh·əst/ *verb* archaic second person sing. present tense of DO[1].

doeth /ˈdooh·əth/ *verb* archaic third person sing. present tense of DO[1].

doff /dof/ *verb trans* **1** to take off (one's hat) in greeting or as a sign of respect. **2** to remove (any item of clothing). [contraction of DO[1] + OFF[2]: compare DON[2]]

dog[1] /dog/ *noun* **1a** a four-legged flesh-eating domesticated mammal occurring in a great variety of breeds and prob descended from the common wolf: *Canis familiaris: Any man who hates dogs and babies can't be all bad —* Leo Rosten. **b** any of a family of carnivores to which the dog belongs, e.g. wolf, jackal, coyote, fox: family Canidae. **c** (*often used before a noun*) a male dog, or the male of members of the dog family: *a dog fox.* **2** any of various usu simple mechanical devices for holding, fastening, etc, that consist of a spike, rod, or bar. **3a** = PARHELION. **b** = FOGBOW. **4** *chiefly NAmer, informal* something inferior of its kind. **5** *informal, dated* a fellow: *You lucky dog!* **6** *derog* an unattractive woman. **7** *NAmer, informal* (*in pl*) feet. **8** (**the dogs**) greyhound racing. ✳ **give a dog a bad name** to cause somebody to gain a bad reputation by slandering them. **go to the dogs** *informal* to decline or deteriorate. **put on the dog** *NAmer, informal* to put on airs [said to come from the popularity in the USA in the 19th cent. of lapdogs carried as fashion accessories]. **turn dog on** *Aus, NZ, informal* to betray or inform on (somebody). ➤➤ **dogdom** *noun*, **doglike** *adj.*

Word history

Old English *docga.* The original term for a dog of any kind was *hund* or *hound. Dog*, which appeared in the 11th cent. but did not become common before the 13th, referred orig to a specific breed of powerful dogs.

dog[2] *verb trans* (**dogged, dogging**) **1** to pursue (somebody) closely like a dog or hound them. **2** said of something unwanted:

to haunt (somebody): *dogged by injury.* **3** to grip (something) with a gripping device. ✳ **dog it** *NAmer, informal* to be lazy. **dog somebody's footsteps** said *esp* of bad luck: to follow somebody around or haunt them.

dog biscuit *noun* a hard dry biscuit for dogs.

dogbox *noun Aus, NZ, informal* a railway compartment without a corridor. ✳ **in the dogbox** in somebody's bad books; in disgrace. [orig a box or bed for a dog, later a compartment for transporting dogs]

dogcart *noun* a light horse-drawn two-wheeled carriage with two seats set back to back. [from its being orig fitted with a box to carry sportsmen's dogs]

dogcatcher *noun chiefly NAmer* a local-government employee whose job is to round up stray dogs.

dog clutch *noun* in mechanics, a clutch in which recesses in one plate are engaged by projections in the other.

dog collar *noun informal* = CLERICAL COLLAR.

dog days *pl noun chiefly poetic* the hottest days in the year: *I am sometimes that dry in the dog days that I could drink a quarter barrel —* Hardy. [from their being reckoned from the heliacal rising of the Dog Star (Sirius)]

doge /dohj/ *noun* the chief magistrate of the former republics of Venice and Genoa. [French *doge* from Venetian dialect *doze,* from Latin *duc-, dux* leader]

dog-ear *noun* the turned-down corner of a page.

dog-eared *adj* **1** said of a book: having dog-ears. **2** worn or shabby.

dog-eat-dog *adj* said of competition in business, etc: marked by ruthless self-interest; cutthroat.

dog-end *noun informal* a cigarette end.

dogface *noun* **1** any of several species of American butterflies with markings on their forewings that resemble a dog's face: genus *Zerene.* **2** *NAmer, informal, dated* a soldier, *esp* an infantryman.

dog fennel *noun* = STINKING MAYWEED.

dogfight *noun* **1** a viciously fought contest. **2** a fight between aircraft, usu at close quarters. ➤➤ **dogfighting** *noun.*

dogfish *noun (pl* **dogfishes** *or collectively* **dogfish)** any of several species of small long-tailed sharks: *Scyliorhinus canicula* and other species.

dog fund *noun* an investment fund that is not providing a good return.

dogged /'dogid/ *adj* **1** stubbornly determined. **2** *archaic* vicious or spiteful: *And dogged Yorke … doth level at my life —* Shakespeare. ➤➤ **doggedly** *adv,* **doggedness** *noun.* [Middle English, in the sense 'doglike, cruel, spiteful', from *dog, dogge* DOG[1] + -ED[1]]

dogger[1] /'dogə/ *noun* formerly, a Dutch two-masted fishing vessel used in the North Sea. [early Dutch *dogger* trawler]

dogger[2] *noun* **1** a type of ironstone found in sedimentary rock, often in the form of spherical concretions. **2** a spherical nodule of this kind. [perhaps related to DOG[1]]

doggerel /'dog(ə)rəl/ *noun* **1** verse that is loosely styled and irregular in measure, *esp* for comic effect. **2** verse that lacks any poetic quality. [Middle English *dogerel* worthless, prob from DOG[1]]

doggie /'dogi/ *noun* see DOGGY[2].

doggie bag *noun* see DOGGY BAG.

doggish /'dogish/ *adj* **1** like a dog in appearance or behaviour. **2** *archaic* surly or vicious: *cruel and doggish hypocrites —* William Tyndale.

doggo /'dogoh/ ✳ **lie doggo** to lie low and stay motionless, to avoid detection. [prob from DOG[1]]

doggone /'dogon/ *adj and adv chiefly NAmer, euphem* damned. [euphemism for GODDAMN]

doggy[1] /'dogi/ *adj* (**doggier, doggiest**) *informal* **1** resembling or suggestive of a dog: *a doggy odour.* **2** concerned with or fond of dogs: *a doggy person.*

doggy[2] *or* **doggie** *noun (pl* **doggies)** used *esp* by or to children: a dog.

doggy bag *or* **doggie bag** *noun* a bag for carrying home leftover food from a meal eaten in a restaurant, etc. [DOGGY[2]; from the giving of such food to a pet dog]

doggy paddle *noun* = DOG PADDLE.

doghouse /'doghaws/ *noun chiefly NAmer* a dog kennel. ✳ **in the doghouse** *informal* in a state of disfavour.

dogie *or* **dogy** /'dohgi/ *noun (pl* **dogies)** *NAmer* a motherless calf, or one abandoned by its mother. [said to be from *doughguts*]

dog in the manger *noun* a person who selfishly deprives others of something of no use to themselves. [from the fable of the dog who prevented an ox from eating hay which he himself did not want]

dog Latin *noun* spurious or debased Latin.

dogleg *noun* **1** a sharp bend, e.g. in a road. **2** an angled fairway on a golf course. ➤➤ **dog-leg** *adj.*

dogma /'dogmə/ *noun* **1** an authoritative tenet or principle. **2** a doctrine or body of doctrines formally and authoritatively stated by a Church. **3** *chiefly derog* a point of view or tenet put forth as authoritative without adequate grounds. [via Latin from Greek *dogma* opinion, from *dokein* to seem or seem good, or think]

dogman *noun (pl* **dogmen)** *Aus, NZ* a person who directs the operator of a crane while riding on the load suspended from it. [from DOG[1], in the sense 'gripping device']

dogmatic /dog'matik/ *or* **dogmatical** *adj* **1** said of statements or opinions: insisted on as if authoritative. **2** said of a person: inclined to make statements or express opinions like this. **3** relating to dogma. ➤➤ **dogmatically** *adv,* **dogmaticalness** *noun.* [via late Latin from Greek *dogmatikos,* from *dogmat-, dogma:* see DOGMA]

dogmatics *pl noun (treated as sing. or pl)* a branch of theology that seeks to interpret the dogmas of a religious faith.

dogmatise /'dogmətiez/ *verb* see DOGMATIZE.

dogmatism /'dogmətiz(ə)m/ *noun* unwarranted assertion of opinion. ➤➤ **dogmatist** *noun.*

dogmatize *or* **dogmatise** /'dogmətiez/ *verb intrans* to speak or write dogmatically. ➤ *verb trans* to state (something) as a dogma or in a dogmatic manner. ➤➤ **dogmatization** /-'zaysh(ə)n/ *noun,* **dogmatizer** *noun.* [French *dogmatiser* via late Latin from Greek *dogmatizein* to lay down as an opinion, from *dogmat-, dogma:* see DOGMA]

do-gooder /,dooh 'goodə/ *noun* often as an unkind label for a charity worker: an earnest, often naive and ineffectual, humanitarian or reformer. ➤➤ **do-goodery** /-ri/ *noun,* **do-goodism** *noun.*

dog paddle *noun* an elementary form of swimming, e.g. for learners, in which the arms paddle and the legs kick.

dog-paddle *verb intrans* to do the dog paddle.

Dogrib /'dogrib/ *noun* **1** a member of a NW Canadian people of the Dene group. **2** the Athabaskan language of this people. ➤➤ **Dogrib** *adj.* [translation of Dogrib *Thlingchadinne* dog's flank, from their claim to be descended from a dog]

dog rose *noun* any of several species of common European wild roses with pink or white flowers: *Rosa canina* and other species. [translation of Latin species name *rosa canina*; because the root of the plant was once placed on a dog-bite to ward off rabies]

dog's age *noun informal, chiefly NAmer* a long time; ages.

dogsbody *noun (pl* **dogsbodies)** *chiefly Brit, informal* a person who carries out routine or menial work at the behest of others. [Brit naval slang *dogsbody,* orig a pudding made of peas, later a junior officer]

dog's breakfast *noun* = DOG'S DINNER.

dog's chance *noun (in negative contexts)* any chance at all: *They don't have a dog's chance of winning the league.*

dog's dinner *noun informal* a horrible mess. ✳ **done up like a dog's dinner** overelaborately dressed or made up.

dog's disease *noun Aus, informal* influenza.

dogshore *noun* either of two wooden blocks fixed on each side of a ship on a slipway, to prevent it sliding before its launch.

dogsled /'dogsled/ *noun* a sledge designed to be pulled by a team of huskies.

dog's life *noun informal* a miserable drab existence.

dog's mercury *noun* a perennial woodland plant of the spurge family: *Mercurialis perennis.* [translation of Latin *Mercurialis canina,* former taxonomic name]

dogstail *noun* any of several species of grasses with spiky flower heads, used as cattle fodder: genus *Cynosurus.*

Dog Star *noun* Sirius, the brightest star in the sky, and the sixth nearest earth. [translation of Greek *kuōn* dog and Latin *canicula* little dog, the star apparently following at the heels of Orion the hunter]

dogstooth check *noun* = HOUNDSTOOTH CHECK.

dog's-tooth violet *noun* any of several species of plants of the lily family with purple flowers and pointed backward-curving leaves: genus *Erythronium*.

dog-tag *noun NAmer, informal* an identification disc for military personnel.

dog-tired *noun informal* extremely tired.

dogtooth *noun* an Early English moulding or architectural ornamentation consisting of a series of four leaves radiating from a raised centre.

dogtooth violet *noun* = DOG'S-TOOTH VIOLET.

dogtrot /'dogtrot/ *noun* a quick easy gait suggesting that of a dog.

dog violet *noun* any of several species of European wild violets with purple or blue flowers: *Viola riviniana* and other species. [translation of Latin species name *viola canina*]

dogwatch *noun* either of two short watches, 4–6 and 6–8 p.m. on a ship.

dog whelk *noun* any of several genera of marine shellfish that prey on other creatures and is found in shallow water or on the shore: genus *Nucella* and other genera.

dogwood *noun* any of several species of trees and shrubs with heads of small flowers, berries, and hard wood: *Cornus sanguinea* and other species. [so called because used to make *dogs*, i.e. skewers]

dogy /'dohgi/ *noun* see DOGIE.

DoH *abbr Brit* Department of Health.

doh /doh/ *noun* see DO³.

doily *or* **doyley** *or* **doyly** /'doyli/ *noun* (*pl* **doilies** *or* **doylies**) a small decorative mat, *esp* of paper, cloth, or plastic openwork, often placed under food, *esp* cakes, on a plate or stand.

Word history ━━━━━
orig the name of a 'cheap and genteel' woollen fabric sold by a 17th-cent. London draper called *Doily* or *Doyley*. The current sense is short for *doily napkin*.

do in *verb trans informal* **1** to kill (somebody). **2** to wear out or exhaust (somebody).

doing /'dooh·ing/ *noun* **1** the result of somebody's activity: *This must be your doing.* **2** (*in pl*) things that are done or that occur; activities: *stories about the children's doings.* ✳ **take some doing** to be difficult to accomplish. [Middle English, verbal noun from DO¹]

doings *noun* (*pl* **doings** *or* **doingses** /-ziz/) *chiefly Brit, informal* (*treated as sing.*) a word used to refer to an unspecified fitting, tool, etc: *Where's the doings?*

doit /doyt/ *noun archaic* (*usu in negative contexts*) the least possible unit of money: *They will not give a doit to relieve a lame beggar* — Shakespeare. [orig a small Dutch coin, equal to half a farthing, from Dutch *duit*]

do-it-yourself *noun* full form of DIY. ➤➤ **do-it-yourselfer** *noun*.

dojo /'dohjoh/ *noun* (*pl* **dojos**) a school for training in various martial arts. [Japanese *dōjō*, from *dō* way, art + *-jō* ground]

dol. *abbr* dollar.

Dolby /'dolbi/ *noun trademark* **1** a sound-recording technique or system that reduces unwanted noise by electronic processing. **2** a stereophonic-sound system used for cinema and television. [named after R *Dolby* b.1933, US inventor]

dolce /'dolchay/ *adj and adv* said of a piece of music: to be performed in a soft sweet manner. [Italian *dolce* sweet, from Latin *dulcis* sweet]

dolce far niente /,dolchay fah 'nyenti/ *noun* carefree idleness. [Italian *dolce far niente*, literally 'sweet doing nothing']

Dolcelatte /dolchə'latay/ *noun trademark* a creamy blue-veined Italian cheese. [Italian *dolce latte* sweet milk]

dolce vita /,dolchi 'veetah/ *noun* a life of indolence and self-indulgence. [Italian *dolce vita* sweet life]

doldrums /'doldrəmz/ *pl noun* (**the doldrums**) an equatorial region of the Atlantic ocean where calms, squalls, and light shifting winds prevail. ✳ **in the doldrums 1** in a state of depression. **2** said of the economy; in a state of stagnation or slump. [18th-cent. *doldrum* a stupid fellow, prob related to Old English *dol* foolish]

dole¹ /dohl/ *noun* **1** *Brit, informal* the government unemployment benefit. **2** *dated* a distribution of food, money, or clothing to the needy. ✳ **on the dole** receiving unemployment benefit. [Old English *dāl* portion; related to Old English *dæl* DEAL²]

dole² *noun archaic* sorrow: *with mirth in funeral, and with dirge in marriage, in equal scale weighing delight with dole* — Shakespeare. [Middle English *dol, doel*, from French *dol* mourning, from Latin *dolere* to grieve]

doleful /'dohlf(ə)l/ *adj* sad or mournful. ➤➤ **dolefully** *adv*, **dolefulness** *noun*. [Middle English *dolful, doelful*, from *dol, doel*: see DOLE²]

dole out *verb trans* to give, distribute, or deliver (something), *esp* in small portions.

dolerite /'doləriet/ *noun* any of various fine- to medium-grained dark igneous rocks, *esp* coarse basalts. ➤➤ **doleritic** /-'ritik/ *adj*. [French *dolerite* from Greek *doleros* deceitful, from *dolos* deceit; because it is easily mistaken for diorite]

doli capax /,doli ka'paks/ *adj* in law, capable of intending to commit a crime, *esp* by being ten years old or more. [Latin *capax doli* capable of evil intent; compare DOLI INCAPAX]

dolichocephalic /,dolikohsi'falik/ *adj* having a relatively long skull; compare BRACHYCEPHALIC. ➤➤ **dolichocephalism** /-'sefaliz(ə)m/ *noun*, **dolichocephaly** /-'sefəli/ *noun*. [Greek *dolichos* long + -CEPHALIC]

doli incapax /,doli in'kapaks/ *adj* in law, incapable of intending to commit a crime, *esp* by being under ten years old. [Latin *doli incapax* incapable of evil intent; compare DOLI CAPAX]

doline /do'leen/ *or* **dolina** /do'leenə/ *noun* a funnel-shaped hollow in a karstic (limestone; see KARST) region. [German *Doline* from Slovene *dolina* valley]

doll /dol/ *noun* **1** a child's toy in the form of a human being, *esp* a child or baby. **2** *derog* a term for a pretty woman, implying brainlessness. **3** *informal* sometimes as a form of address: a complimentary term for an attractive person. ➤➤ **dollish** *adj*, **dollishly** *adv*. [prob from *Doll*, nickname for *Dorothy*]

dollar /'dolə/ *noun* the basic monetary unit of the USA, Canada, Australia, and various other countries, divided into 100 cents. ✳ **bet your bottom dollar** *informal* to be virtually certain: *You can bet your bottom dollar he'll turn up.* [Dutch *daler* dollar, from German *Taler*, short for *Joachimstaler*, named after Sankt *Joachimsthal*, town in Bohemia where talers were first minted]

dollar bird *noun* a bird of SE Asia and Australia with a round white coin-like marking on its wings: *Eurystomus orientalis*.

dollar diplomacy *noun* diplomacy used by a country to promote its financial or commercial interests abroad and hence to strengthen its power.

dollarization *or* **dollarisation** /,dolərie'zaysh(ə)n/ *noun* the linking of the value of a currency to the value of the American dollar.

dollop¹ /'doləp/ *noun* a soft shapeless blob; *esp* a serving of mushy or semiliquid food: *a dollop of mashed potato*. [perhaps of Scandinavian origin]

dollop² *verb trans* (**dolloped, dolloping**) (+ out) to serve out (food) carelessly or clumsily.

doll's house *noun* a child's small-scale toy house.

doll up *verb trans informal* (*usu in passive*) to dress (oneself) prettily or showily: *She was all dolled up for a night out.*

dolly¹ /'doli/ *noun* (*pl* **dollies**) **1** a child's word for DOLL (1). **2** *dated* an attractive young woman. **3** in cricket, an easy catch. **4** a wooden-pronged instrument for beating and stirring clothes while washing them in a tub. **5a** a platform on a roller or on wheels or castors for moving heavy objects. **b** a wheeled platform for a film or television camera.

dolly² *verb intrans* (**dollies, dollied, dollying**) (+ in/out) to move a film or television camera on a dolly towards or away from a subject.

dolly bird *noun chiefly Brit* an attractive, stylish, and lively girl, *esp* an empty-headed one.

dolly mixtures *pl noun* an assortment of miniature sweets, typically in various pastel shades.

dolly tub *noun* a barrel-shaped wash tub of the late 19th cent.

Dolly Varden /,doli 'vahdən/ *noun* **1** a large hat trimmed with flowers, with the brim bent down at one side. **2** a brightly coloured edible CHAR² of the N Pacific: *Salvelinus malma*. [named after *Dolly Varden* in Dickens's *Barnaby Rudge*, who wears this kind of hat]

dolma /'dohlmə/ *noun* (*pl* **dolmas** *or* **dolmades** /dohl'mahdiz/) a vine leaf or cabbage leaf stuffed with a savoury filling. [Turkish *dolma* something stuffed; *dolmades* from modern Greek, pl of *dolmas*, from Turkish *dolma*]

dolman /'dolmən/ *noun* **1** an outer robe traditionally worn by Turks. **2** a wrap or coat made with dolman sleeves. [French *doliman* from Turkish *dolama*, a long robe with sleeves]

dolman sleeve *noun* a sleeve very wide at the armhole and tight at the wrist, often cut in one piece with the bodice.

dolmen /'dolmən/ *noun* a prehistoric monument consisting of two or more upright stones supporting a horizontal slab. [French *dolmen* from Breton *tolmen*, from *tol* table (from Latin *tabula* board, plank) + *men* stone]

dolomite /'doləmiet/ *noun* **1** calcium magnesium carbonate occurring as a mineral. **2** a limestone-like rock consisting mainly of the mineral dolomite. ➤➤ **dolomitic** /-'mitik/ *adj*. [French *dolomite*, named after Déodat de *Dolomieu* d.1801, French geologist, who discovered it]

dolor /'dolə/ *noun NAmer* see DOLOUR.

doloroso /dolə'rohsoh/ *adj and adv* said of a piece of music: to be performed in a sorrowful manner. [Italian *doloroso* grieving, from late Latin *dolorosus*, from Latin *dolor*: see DOLOUR]

dolorous /'dolərəs/ *adj literary* causing or expressing misery or grief. ➤➤ **dolorously** *adv*, **dolorousness** *noun*.

dolos /'dolos/ *noun* (*pl* **dolosse** /də'losə/) *SAfr* a knucklebone used for divination or children's games. [Afrikaans *dolos*, of uncertain derivation]

dolostone /'doləstohn/ *noun* a type of rock consisting of dolomite. [from DOLOMITE + STONE[1]]

dolour (*NAmer* **dolor**) /'dohlə, 'dolə/ *noun* mental suffering or anguish. [Middle English via French from Latin *dolor* pain, grief, from *dolēre* to feel pain, grieve]

dolphin /'dolfin/ *noun* **1** any of several species of small gregarious toothed marine whales with the snout elongated into a beak: family Delphinidae. **2** any of several species of similar freshwater whales: family Platanistidae. **3** a large food fish of warm seas that has spiny fins: *Coryphaena hippurus*. **4** a spar or buoy for mooring boats. [Middle English via Old French *dalfin* and Latin *delphinus* from Greek *delphin-*, *delphis* dolphin]

dolphinarium /dolfi'neəri·əm/ *noun* (*pl* **dolphinariums** *or* **dolphinaria** /-ri·ə/) an establishment where dolphins are trained to perform in public in a large pool. [modelled on words such as OCEANARIUM and AQUARIUM]

dolt /dohlt/ *noun* an extremely dull or stupid person. ➤➤ **doltish** *adj*, **doltishly** *adv*, **doltishness** *noun*. [prob related to Old English *dol* foolish]

DOM *abbr* Dominican Republic (international vehicle registration).

Dom /dom/ *noun* **1** used as a title for Benedictine, Carthusian, and Cistercian monks and some canons regular. **2** used formerly as a title preceding the Christian name of a Portuguese or Brazilian man of rank. [Latin *dominus* master]

dom. *abbr* domestic.

-dom *suffix* forming nouns, denoting: **1a** rank or office: *dukedom*. **b** realm or jurisdiction: *kingdom*; *Christendom*. **2** state: *freedom*; *boredom*. **3** a group or class of people having a specified office, occupation, interest, or character: *officialdom*. [Old English *-dōm*, orig 'judgment']

domain /də'mayn/ *noun* **1** a territory over which control is exercised. **2** a sphere of influence or activity. **3** the set of values to which a variable is limited; *esp* the set of values that the independent variable of a function may take on. **4** in physics, any of the small randomly oriented regions of uniform magnetization in a ferromagnetic substance. **5** in computing, a group of Internet locations having addresses with the same suffix. **6** *Aus, NZ* a public park or recreation ground. ➤➤ **domanial** *adj*. [early French *domaine*, *demaine* from Latin *dominium*, from *dominus* master, owner]

domaine /do'men, do'mayn/ *noun* a French vineyard estate, *esp* one in Burgundy. [French *domaine*: see DOMAIN]

domain name *noun* the combination of letters, words, and punctuation that specifies the location of a website on the Internet.

dome /dohm/ *noun* **1** a hemispherical roof or vault. **2** a dome-shaped geological or other structure. **3** *archaic* a stately building; a

mansion: *a stately pleasure dome*. **4** the top part of the head. ➤➤ **domal** *adj*, **domelike** *adj*. [French *dôme* dome, cathedral, from Italian *duomo* cathedral, from late Latin *domus* church, from Latin, house, home]

domed *adj* **1** said of a building: having a dome. **2** said of somebody's forehead: high and rounded.

Domesday Book /'doohmzday/ *noun* a record of a survey of English lands made by order of William I about 1086. [Middle English, from *domesday* DOOMSDAY]

domestic[1] /də'mestik/ *adj* **1** relating to, belonging to, or devoted to the home or the family: *domestic bliss*; *domestic appliances*. **2** relating to one's own country; not foreign: *domestic politics*. **3** said of an animal: living near or about the habitations of human beings; tame, or bred by human beings for some specific purpose, e.g. food or hunting. ➤➤ **domestically** *adv*. [Middle English via French from Latin *domesticus*, from *domus* house, home]

domestic[2] *noun* a person employed to do household tasks.

domesticate /də'mestikayt/ *verb trans* **1** to bring (an animal or species) under human control for some specific purpose, e.g. for carrying loads, hunting, or food. **2** *humorous* to render (a person) willing to perform household duties and conform to rules of behaviour that make for a civilized home life. ➤➤ **domesticable** *adj*, **domestication** /-'kaysh(ə)n/ *noun*.

domestic fowl *noun* a chicken, turkey, or other bird developed from the jungle fowl, *esp* for meat or egg production.

domestic goddess *noun informal* a woman who is successful and fulfilled in her role as a homemaker.

domestic help *noun* = DOMESTIC[2].

domesticity /domə'stisiti/ *noun* home or family life, or devotion to this.

domestic science *noun dated* instruction in the household arts; = HOME ECONOMICS.

domestic worker *noun* = DOMESTIC[2].

domical /'dohmikl/ *adj* having a dome; = DOMED.

domicile[1] /'domisiel/ *or* **domicil** /-s(i)l/ *noun* a home; *esp* a person's permanent and principal home for legal purposes. [Middle English via French from Latin *domicilium* dwelling, from *domus* house, home]

domicile[2] *verb trans* (*usu in passive*) to establish (somebody) in or provide (them) with a domicile.

domiciliary /domi'sili·əri/ *adj* relating to or taking place in the home: *domiciliary visits*.

dominant[1] /'dominənt/ *adj* **1** commanding, controlling, or prevailing over all others: *a dominant personality*. **2** said of a position: commanding a view from a superior height. **3** denoting the one of a pair of bodily structures that is the more effective or predominant in action: *the dominant eye*. **4** denoting the one of a pair of genes determining contrasting inherited characteristics that predominates: compare RECESSIVE[1]. **5** denoting the species that has the strongest representation in an ecological community. ➤➤ **dominance** *noun*, **dominancy** /-si/ *noun*, **dominantly** *adv*. [via French from Latin *dominant-*, *dominans*, present part. of *dominari*: see DOMINATE]

dominant[2] *noun* **1** a dominant gene or trait. **2** a dominant species in an ecological community. **3** in music, the fifth note of a diatonic scale.

dominate /'dominayt/ *verb trans* **1** to exert controlling influence or power over (a person, a group, a situation, etc). **2** to overlook from a superior height: *The tower dominates the landscape*. **3** to occupy a commanding or preeminent position in: *This corporation dominates the market*. ➤➤ *verb intrans* **1** to have or exert mastery or control. **2** to occupy a higher or superior position. ➤➤ **domination** /-'naysh(ə)n/ *noun*, **dominative** /-tiv/ *adj*, **dominator** *noun*. [Latin *dominatus*, past part. of *dominari* to rule, govern, from *dominus* master]

dominatrix /domi'naytriks/ *noun* (*pl* **dominatrixes** *or* **dominatrices** /-triseez/) a woman who takes an aggressively or sadistically dominant role in sexual interaction. [Latin *dominatrix*, fem of *dominator* a person who dominates, from *dominari*: see DOMINATE]

dominee /'doohmini/ *noun* in S Africa, a minister of the Dutch Reformed Church; used *esp* as a title of address. [Dutch *dominee* from Latin *domine*, vocative of *dominus* master]

domineer /domi'niə/ *verb intrans* to exercise arbitrary or over-bearing control: *a domineering husband.* ⟫⟫ **domineeringly** *adv.* [Dutch *domineren* via French from Latin *dominari*: see DOMINATE]

dominical /də'minikl/ *adj* **1** relating to Jesus Christ. **2** relating to Sunday, as the Lord's day. [late Latin *dominicalis* from *dominicus* relating to the Lord, from *dominus* lord, master]

dominical letter *noun* any of the first seven letters of the alphabet that are used to denote Sundays in a given year in order to determine the dates of various festivals, e.g. Easter, in the Church calendar.

Dominican[1] /də'minik(ə)n/ *noun* a member of a preaching order of mendicant friars founded by St Dominic in 1215. ⟫⟫ **Dominican** *adj.* [named after St *Dominic* (Domingo de Guzman) d.1221, Spanish priest]

Dominican[2] *noun* a native or inhabitant of the Dominican Republic. ⟫⟫ **Dominican** *adj.*

Dominican[3] *noun* a native or inhabitant of Dominica. ⟫⟫ **Dominican** *adj.*

dominie /'domini/ *noun* **1** *esp Scot* a teacher or schoolmaster. **2** *chiefly* a clergyman or minister. [Latin *domine*: see DOMINEE]

dominion /də'minyən/ *noun* **1** the power or right to rule; sovereignty. **2** the territory of a ruler. **3** absolute ownership. **4** (*often* **Dominion**) *esp* formerly, a self-governing nation of the Commonwealth other than the United Kingdom. [Middle English via French from Latin *dominium* ownership, from *dominus* lord, master]

Dominion Day *noun* the former name of CANADA DAY.

domino /'dominoh/ *noun* (*pl* **dominoes** *or* **dominos**) **1a** a flat rectangular block with a face divided into two equal parts that are blank or bear from one to six dots arranged as on dice faces. **b** (*in pl, but usu treated as sing.*) any of several games played with a set of 28 dominoes. **2a** a half mask worn with a masquerade costume. **b** a person wearing a domino. **3** a long loose hooded cloak worn with a mask as a masquerade costume. [French *domino*, orig a monk's hood, prob from Latin *domino* (in the ritual formula *benedicamus Domino* let us bless the Lord), dative of *dominus* lord]

domino effect *noun* a series of causally related events following one after the other, precipitated by some significant initial happening, like a line of dominoes collapsing in sequence.

domino theory *noun* a theory that if one nation in an area, *specif* SE Asia, becomes Communist-controlled, the same thing will happen to the neighbouring nations. [from the fact that if several dominoes are stood on end one behind the other with slight spaces between, a push on the first will make all the others topple]

dom palm *noun* see DOUM PALM.

don[1] /don/ *noun* **1** a university teacher, *esp* a senior member of staff at Oxford or Cambridge. **2a** a Spanish nobleman or gentleman. **b** (**Don**) a title preceding the forename of a Spanish man, *esp* one of rank. **3** *informal* the head of a Mafia family. [Spanish *don* from Latin *dominus* master]

don[2] *verb trans* (**donned, donning**) to put on (an item of clothing). [contraction of DO[1] + ON[2]: compare DOFF]

Doña /'donyə/ *noun* a title preceding the forename of a Spanish woman, *esp* one of rank. [Spanish *doña* from Latin *domina* lady, fem of *dominus* master]

donate /doh'nayt, də-/ *verb trans* **1** to make a gift of (something, e.g. money), *esp* to a public or charitable cause. **2** to give or allow the removal of (blood, semen, organs, etc) for use in the medical treatment of others. ⟫ *verb intrans* to make a donation of, *esp* of money. ⟫⟫ **donator** *noun.* [back-formation from DONATION]

donation /doh'naysh(ə)n, də-/ *noun* **1** the act of donating: *blood donation.* **2** something donated, *esp* money. [Middle English *donatyowne* from Latin *donation-, donatio*, from *donare* to present, from *donum* gift]

donative[1] /'dohnətiv/ *noun* a special gift or donation. [Latin *donativum* gift, from *donare* to give]

donative[2] *adj* **1** of or given as a donation. **2** capable of being donated: *a donative trust.*

done[1] /dun/ *verb* **1** past part. of DO[1]. **2** *chiefly dialect & NAmer* past tense of DO[1].

done[2] *adj* **1** socially acceptable or expected: *It's not done to eat peas off your knife.* **2** arrived at or brought to an end; completed. **3** said of food: cooked sufficiently. **4** physically exhausted; spent. **5** *informal* arrested or imprisoned: *He got done for robbing a bank.* ✳ **done for 1** dead or close to death. **2** doomed to failure or defeat;

ruined. **done in** *informal* physically exhausted. **done with** no longer involved with; through with: *I'm done with the Army.*

done[3] *interj* used in acceptance of a deal or bet.

donee /doh'nee/ *noun* a recipient of a gift or donation. [DONOR + -EE[1]]

doner kebab /'dohnə, 'donə/ *noun* slices of spiced lamb or other meat cut from a large block grilled on a spit, usu served in pitta bread as a fast-food snack. [Turkish *döner* rotating + KEBAB]

dong[1] /dong/ *noun* **1** the deep sound made by a large heavy bell. **2** *coarse slang* a penis. **3** *Aus, NZ, informal* a punch. [imitative]

dong[2] *verb intrans* to make the deep sound of a large heavy bell. ⟫ *verb trans Aus, NZ* to strike or hit (somebody).

dong[3] *noun* the basic monetary unit of Vietnam, divided into 10 hao or 100 xu. [Vietnamese *đông* coin]

donga /'donggə/ *noun SAfr, Aus, NZ* a narrow steep-sided ravine formed by erosion. [Afrikaans *donga*, from Zulu]

dongle /'dongg(ə)l/ *noun* in computing, a security device that, when plugged into a computer, allows a particular program to run, but only on the computer that the device is attached to, and, when unplugged, disables the program. It prevents software from being pirated.

donjon /'dunj(ə)n, 'donj(ə)n/ *noun* a massive inner tower in a medieval castle. [Middle English: see DUNGEON]

Don Juan /don 'jooh-ən, 'wahn (Spanish don xwan)/ *noun* a man who attempts to seduce many women; a lady-killer. [named after *Don Juan*, legendary Spanish nobleman featured in many works of literature]

donkey /'dongki/ *noun* (*pl* **donkeys**) **1** a domesticated animal of the horse family that has long ears and is used to carry loads: *Equus asinus.* **2** a stupid or obstinate person. ✳ **talk the hind leg/legs off a donkey** *Brit, informal* to talk endlessly and often persuasively. [perhaps from DUN[1] + -*key* as in MONKEY[1]]

donkey engine *noun* a small, usu portable, auxiliary engine.

donkey jacket *noun* a thick hip-length hard-wearing jacket, usu dark blue and with a strip of leather or plastic across the shoulders.

donkey's years *pl noun chiefly Brit, informal* a very long time.

donkeywork *noun informal* hard, monotonous, and routine work.

donna /'donə/ *noun* (*pl* **donne** /'donay/) **1** an Italian woman, *esp* one of rank. **2** (**Donna**) a title preceding the forename of an Italian woman. [Italian *donna* from Latin *domina*: see DOÑA]

donnée /'donay/ *noun* a basic fact or assumption, *esp* one essential to the action of a work of fiction or drama. [French *donnée*, fem past part. of *donner* to give, from Latin *donare*]

donnish /'donish/ *adj* characteristic of a university don, *esp* in being pedantic. ⟫⟫ **donnishly** *adv*, **donnishness** *noun.*

donnybrook /'donibrook/ *noun* a chaotic brawl or a heated argument involving many people. [named after *Donnybrook Fair*, an annual fair formerly held at Donnybrook, a suburb of Dublin in the Republic of Ireland, noted for its drunken brawls]

donor /'dohnə/ *noun* **1** somebody who donates blood, organs, etc for use in the medical treatment of others: *a blood donor.* **2** a person who gives, donates, or presents something, *esp* to a public or charitable cause. **3a** in chemistry, an atom that combines with another and provides the two electrons that are shared to make the bond. **b** in physics, an impurity that is added to a semiconductor to increase the number of mobile electrons. [early French *doneur* from Latin *donator*, from *donare* to give]

donor card *noun* a card carried by people who wish to donate organs or other body parts for transplant in the event of their death.

don't[1] /dohnt/ *contraction* **1** do not. **2** *non-standard* does not: *There are simply certain things he don't know* — Ezra Pound.

don't[2] *noun* (*usu in pl*) something that is prohibited: *a list of dos and don'ts.*

donut *noun NAmer* see DOUGHNUT.

doodad /'doohdad/ *noun* **1** *NAmer, informal* a small, trivial, or decorative article. **2** = DOODAH. [origin unknown]

doodah /'doohdah/ *noun Brit, informal* a small article whose name is unknown or forgotten. [origin unknown]

doodle[1] /'doohdl/ *verb trans and intrans* to draw or scribble (something) in a bored or aimless manner. ➤➤ **doodler** *noun.* [perhaps from *doodle* simpleton, from Low German *dudeltopf*]

doodle[2] *noun* an aimless scribble, design, or sketch.

doodlebug /'doohdlbug/ *noun* **1** *Brit, informal* = FLYING BOMB. **2** *NAmer* the larva of an ant lion. **3** *NAmer* a device, e.g. a divining rod, used in attempting to locate underground minerals. [prob from *doodle* fool (see DOODLE[1]) + BUG[1]]

doodly-squat /'doodli,skwot/ *noun* see DIDDLY-SQUAT.

doo-doo /'doodoo/ *noun chiefly NAmer, informal* excrement; poo. [orig baby talk]

doofer /'doofə(r)/ *noun informal* a gadget whose name is unknown or has been forgotten. [perhaps from *do for now*]

doohickey /'dooh-hiki/ *noun* (*pl* **doohickeys**) *chiefly NAmer* = DOODAH.

doolally /'doolali/ *adj informal* crazy; temporarily mad.

Word history

from *doolally tap* Indian army slang for *Deolali tap*, from *Deolali* a town near Bombay + *tap* fever. British soldiers returning home were sent to Deolali to await embarkation and supposedly went mad with boredom.

doom[1] /doohm/ *noun* **1a** destiny, *esp* an unhappy or terrible fate. **b** unavoidable death or destruction. **2a** judgment or condemnation. **b** = JUDGMENT DAY. **3** a law in Anglo-Saxon England. [Old English *dōm* decree, judgment]

doom[2] *verb trans* **1** to cause (somebody or something) to have a bad outcome, *esp* one that results in failure or destruction: *The project was doomed from the start.* **2** *archaic* to give judgment against (somebody); to condemn (them).

doom and gloom *noun* (*treated as sing. or pl*) a feeling of pessimism or dejection: *No doom and gloom, resentment or woeful tales of broken romances, no poses or pontifications here* — M Hamer.

doom palm *noun* see DOUM PALM.

doomsday /'doohmzday/ *noun* **1** = JUDGMENT DAY. **2** some remote point in the future: *You'll have to wait from now till doomsday.*

doomster /'doohmstə/ *noun informal* a person given to forebodings and predictions of impending calamity.

Doona /'doohnə/ *noun Aus, trademark* a duvet or quilt. [prob from Swedish *dun* feathers, down]

door /daw/ *noun* **1a** a hinged or sliding panel by which the entrance to a building, room, or vehicle is closed and opened. **b** a similar part of a piece of furniture, *esp* a sideboard, wardrobe, etc. **2** = DOORWAY. **3** a means of access: *the door to stardom.* **✴ lay something at somebody's door** to charge somebody as being responsible for something: *They laid the blame at our door.* **out of doors** in or into the open air. **show somebody the door** to tell somebody to leave. ➤➤ **doorless** *adj.* [Middle English *dure, dor,* from Old English *duru* door and *dor* gate]

doorbell *noun* a bell at the entrance to a building, rung to summon somebody inside to open the door.

do-or-die *adj* requiring or having the determination to face a danger or challenge without flinching.

door furniture *noun* handles, knobs, knockers, letterboxes, and other fixtures that can be fitted to doors.

doorjamb *noun* = DOORPOST.

doorkeeper *noun* a person who guards the main door to a building and lets people in and out.

doorknob *noun* a knob on a door that when turned releases the latch.

doorknock *noun Aus* a political or charitable campaign in which helpers make door-to-door calls. ➤➤ **doorknocking** *noun.*

doorman *noun* (*pl* **doormen**) a person employed to stand at the entrance to a hotel, theatre, etc and assist people going in or out, e.g. by calling taxis.

doormat *noun* **1** a mat, e.g. of bristles, placed at a doorway for wiping dirt from the shoes before or on entering a building. **2** *informal* a person who submits to bullying and indignities without complaint or resistance.

doornail *noun* a large-headed nail formerly used for the strengthening or decoration of doors. **✴ (as) dead as a doornail** undoubtedly dead.

doorpost *noun* an upright piece forming the side of a door opening.

doorstep[1] *noun* **1** a step in front of an outer door. **2** *Brit, informal* a very thick slice of bread. **✴ on one's/the doorstep** conveniently nearby.

doorstep[2] *verb* (**doorstepped, doorstepping**) ➤ *verb intrans* **1** to go from door to door as a political canvasser, salesperson, etc. **2** said of a journalist: to seek information or photographs by waiting outside somebody's house or by more intrusive tactics. ➤ *verb trans* said of a journalist: to seek out, harass, or accost (somebody) in order to obtain information or photographs. ➤➤ **doorstepper** *noun.*

doorstop *noun* a device for holding a door open or preventing it from opening too far.

door to door *adv* from the precise point of departure to the final point of arrival: *a journey of two hours door to door.*

door-to-door *adj* **1** making an unsolicited call, e.g. for selling, canvassing, etc, at every residence in an area. **2** providing delivery or transport to a specific address.

doorway *noun* an entrance into a building or room that is closed by means of a door.

do over *verb trans* **1** *Brit, informal* to attack and injure (somebody). **2** *informal* to redecorate (a house, room, etc).

doo-wop /'doowop/ *noun* a style of popular music featuring close harmony singing, often using nonsense words made to sound like musical instruments, backed by a stylized form of rhythm and blues, that originated in the USA in the 1950s.

dop /dop/ *noun* (*pl* **dops** *or* **doppe** /'dopə/) **1** *SAfr* a cheap crude brandy. **2** *SAfr* a tot of spirits, *esp* brandy. [Afrikaans *dop*, literally 'husk', from early Dutch, referring to the use of grape skins in its production]

dopa /'dohpə/ *noun* a derivative of PHENYLALANINE, *esp* L-dopa. [contraction of *dihydroxyphenylalanine*]

dopamine /'dohpəmeen/ *noun* a derivative of DOPA that occurs as a neurotransmitter in the brain and as an intermediate compound in the synthesis of adrenalin in body tissue. [DOPA + AMINE]

dopant /'dohp(ə)nt/ *noun* in electronics, a substance, *esp* boron, added in small amounts to a pure semiconductor material to produce a desired electrical effect. [DOPE[2] + -ANT[1]]

dope[1] /dohp/ *noun* **1a** a preparation given illegally to a racing horse, greyhound, etc to make it run faster or slower. **b** *slang* marijuana, opium, or another illegal drug. **2** *informal* a stupid person. **3** (*often* **the dope**) *informal* information, *esp* from a reliable source. **4a** a thick liquid or pasty preparation. **b** a preparation for giving a desired quality to a substance, *esp* a petrol additive. **c** a coating applied to a surface or fabric, e.g. of a balloon, to improve strength, impermeability, or tautness. **5** absorbent material used in various manufacturing processes, e.g. the making of dynamite. [Dutch *doop* sauce, from *dopen* to dip; related to Old English *dyppan* DIP[1]]

dope[2] *verb trans* **1** to administer an illegal or narcotic drug to (a person or animal). **2** to add an impurity to (a semiconductor) so as to give the required electrical properties. **3** to treat (a substance or surface) with dope. ➤ *verb intrans* to take illegal drugs. ➤➤ **doper** *noun.*

dopey *or* **dopy** *adj* (**dopier, dopiest**) **1** stupefied, e.g. by sleep or the effects of a drug: *He was still dopey from the anaesthetic.* **2** *informal* stupid. ➤➤ **dopily** *adv,* **dopiness** *noun.*

dopiaza /'dohpiazə/ *adj* (*used after a noun*) said of an Indian dish: cooked or served in an onion sauce: *chicken dopiaza.* ➤➤ **dopiaza** *noun.* [Hindi *do* two + *pyāz* onion]

doppe /'dopə/ *noun* pl of DOP.

doppelgänger /'doplgengə, -gangə/ *noun* a ghostly counterpart of a living person. [German *doppelgänger*, literally 'double-goer', from *doppel-* double + -*gänger* goer]

Doppler effect /'doplə/ *noun* a change in the apparent frequency of sound, light, or other waves when there is relative motion between the source and the observer: compare SHIFT[2] (3B). [named after Christian *Doppler* d.1853, Austrian scientist and mathematician, who first explained it]

Doppler shift *noun* = DOPPLER EFFECT.

dopy *adj* see DOPEY.

dorado /də'rahdoh/ *noun* (*pl* **dorados** *or collectively* **dorado**) a freshwater game fish, with a golden-coloured body and red fins, that lives in South American rivers: *Salminus maxillosus.* [Spanish *dorado*, literally 'gilded']

dor beetle /daw/ *noun* any of several species of large black European dung beetles that make a droning noise when flying: *Geotrupes stercorarius* and other species.

dorcas gazelle /'dawkəs/ *noun* (*pl* **dorcas gazelles** *or collectively* **dorcas gazelle**) a small gazelle that lives in open arid countryside in parts of northern Africa and western Asia: *Gazella dorcas*. [Greek *dorkas* a gazelle]

Dorian /'dawri·ən/ *noun* a member of an ancient Hellenic people that settled chiefly in the Peloponnesus and Crete. ⇒ **Dorian** *adj*. [via Latin from Greek *dōrios* of *Dōris*, region of ancient Greece]

Doric[1] /'dorik/ *adj* **1** of the Dorians or their language. **2** relating to or denoting the oldest and simplest of the three Greek orders of architecture, characterized by fluted columns and a plain CAPITAL[3] (upper part of a column): compare IONIC[1], CORINTHIAN[2]. **3** said of a dialect: broad or rustic. [via Latin from Greek *Dorikos*, from *dōrios*: see DORIAN]

Doric[2] *noun* **1** a dialect of ancient Greek. **2** a broad rustic dialect of English, *esp* one used in northeast Scotland.

dork /dawk/ *noun chiefly NAmer, slang* a stupid or contemptible person. ⇒ **durky** *adj*. [perhaps alteration of DICK]

dorm /dawm/ *noun informal* = DORMITORY (1).

dormant /'dawmənt/ *adj* **1** asleep or inactive. **2a** temporarily showing no signs of external activity: *a dormant volcano*. **b** temporarily in abeyance: *the plan for visiting Sotherton, which had been started a fortnight before … and had since lain dormant* — Jane Austen; *I am full of dormant good qualities* — Wilkie Collins. **3a** having biological activity suspended, e.g. during hibernation. **b** said of a plant or plant part: not actively growing but protected from the environment. **4** said of a heraldic animal: lying with the head on the forepaws. ⇒ **dormancy** /-si/ *noun*. [Middle English, in the sense 'fixed, stationary', from early French, present part. of *dormir* to sleep, from Latin *dormire*]

dormer *or* **dormer window** /'dawmə/ *noun* **1** a window set vertically in a structure projecting through a sloping roof. **2** (*used before a noun*) having such a window or windows: *dormer bungalow*. [early French *dormeor* dormitory, from Latin *dormitorium*: see DORMITORY]

dormice /'dawmies/ *noun* pl of DORMOUSE.

dormie *or* **dormy** /'dawmi/ *adj* in golf, being ahead by as many holes as remain to be played: *After fourteen holes, Paul was dormie four.* [origin unknown]

dormitory /'dawmit(ə)ri/ *noun* (*pl* **dormitories**) **1** a large room containing a number of beds, e.g. in a boarding school. **2** (*often used before a noun*) a residential community from which the inhabitants commute to their places of employment: *a dormitory town.* **3** *NAmer* = HALL OF RESIDENCE. [Latin *dormitorium*, from *dormire* to sleep]

Dormobile /'dawməbeel/ *noun trademark* a small motorized caravan. [blend of DORMITORY + AUTOMOBILE]

dormouse /'dawmows/ *noun* (*pl* **dormice** /'dawmies/) **1** any of several species of small African and Eurasian rodents that resemble mice with long bushy tails: family Gliridae. **2** a common European rodent of this family: *Muscardinus avellanarius*. [Middle English *dormowse*, perhaps from early French *dormir* to sleep + Middle English *mous* MOUSE[1]]

dormy /'dawmi/ *adj* see DORMIE.

dorp /dawp/ *noun SAfr* a village. [Dutch *dorp* a village]

dors- *or* **dorsi-** *or* **dorso-** *comb. form* forming words, denoting: **1** back: *dorsad.* **2** back and: *dorsolateral.* [late Latin *dors-*, from Latin *dorsum* back]

dorsal /'dawsl/ *adj* relating to or in the region of the back or top surface of something, *esp* an animal or aircraft or any of its parts: compare VENTRAL. ⇒ **dorsally** *adv*. [late Latin *dorsalis*, from Latin *dorsum* back]

dorsal fin *noun* a vertical fin that extends lengthways along the back of a fish, dolphin, etc.

dorsi- *or* **dorso-** *comb. form* see DORS-.

dory[1] /'dawri/ *noun* (*pl* **dories**) a small boat, *esp* a flat-bottomed fishing boat with a high bow and stern. [Miskito *dóri* dugout]

dory[2] *noun* see JOHN DORY.

DOS /dos/ *abbr* disk-operating system.

dosage /'dohsij/ *noun* **1** the amount of a dose of medicine or radiation. **2** the administration of a dose or doses of medicine.

dose[1] /dohs/ *noun* **1a** a measured quantity of medicine to be taken at one time. **b** a quantity of radiation administered or absorbed. **2** a quantity or part of an experience to which one is exposed: *a dose of hard work.* **3** *informal* an infection with a sexually transmitted disease. ✳ **like a dose of salts** *Brit, informal* very quickly. [French *dose* via late Latin from Greek *dosis* act of giving, from *didonai* to give]

dose[2] *verb trans* **1** to give a dose of medicine to (a person or animal). **2** to prescribe, dispense, or administer (medicine) in doses. **3** to adulterate or blend (something, e.g. wine) with an added substance.

do-se-do /dohsee'doh, -zee-/ *noun* see DO-SI-DO.

dosh /dosh/ *noun Brit, informal* money. [origin unknown]

do-si-do *or* **do-se-do** /dohsee'doh, -zee-/ *noun* (*pl* **do-si-dos** *or* **do-se-dos**) a movement in country dancing, *esp* barn dancing, that involves two dancers advancing towards each other, passing back to back, and returning to their own places in the set line. [prob an alteration of French *dos-à-dos* back to back]

dosimeter /doh'simitə/ *noun* a device for measuring doses of X-rays or of radioactivity. ⇒ **dosimetric** /-'metrik/ *adj*, **dosimetry** /-tri/ *noun*.

doss[1] /dos/ *noun chiefly Brit, informal* **1** a crude or makeshift bed, *esp* one in a dosshouse. **2** a short sleep. **3** a very easy task. [perhaps from obsolete *dorse, doss* back, from Latin *dorsum*]

doss[2] *verb intrans* **1** *chiefly Brit, informal* (often + down) to sleep in a makeshift bed: *Can I doss down on your floor tonight?* **2** to sleep rough or sleep somewhere without a bed: *We missed the plane and had to doss in the airport.*

dosser *noun* **1** *chiefly Brit* a person who sleeps in dosshouses; a homeless person. **2** = DOSSHOUSE.

dosshouse /'dos·haws/ *noun chiefly Brit* a hostel for people with no fixed address and little or no money.

dossier /'dosi·ə, 'dosiay/ *noun* a file of papers containing a detailed report or information: *The Special Branch had been watching him, and had accumulated an extensive dossier on his activities.* [French *dossier* bundle of documents labelled on the back, from *dos* back, from Latin *dorsum*]

dost /dust/ *verb archaic* present second person sing. of DO[1].

dot[1] /dot/ *noun* **1** a small spot; a speck. **2** a small mark made with a pointed instrument. **3a** a small round mark used in spelling or punctuation, e.g. over the letter *i* or as a full stop. **b** a decimal point. **c** a point after a note or rest in music increasing the time value by one half. **d** a point over or under a note in music indicating that it is to be played staccato. **e** in Internet addresses, a full stop used to separate the different parts of the domain name: *You can access our website on penguin dot co dot uk.* **4** a very small amount or object. **5** a signal of relatively short duration, e.g. a flash or audible tone, that is one of the two fundamental units of Morse code: compare DASH[2] (2). ✳ **on the dot** exactly; precisely: *She arrived at six on the dot.* **the year dot** *Brit, informal* a very long time ago. [Old English *dott* head of a boil]

dot[2] *verb* (**dotted, dotting**) ➤ *verb trans* **1** to mark or form (something) with a dot or dots. **2** to scatter (something) with small marks, amounts, or objects positioned at random: *a field dotted with poppies.* ➤ *verb intrans* to make a dot or dots. ✳ **dot the i's and cross the t's 1** *informal* to pay minute attention to detail. **2** to put the finishing touches to something.

dot[3] *noun archaic* = DOWRY. [French *dot* from Latin *dot-, dos* dowry]

dotage /'dohtij/ *noun* a state or period of mental decline in old age: *in her dotage.* [Middle English, from *doten* to DOTE]

dotard /'dohtəd/ *noun* a feeble-minded old person.

dotcom /dot'kom/ *noun* = DOT COM COMPANY.

dot com company *noun* (*pl* **dot com companies**) a company that operates exclusively or chiefly on the Internet and that usu has a domain name ending in the suffix .com, which identifies it as a commercial organization.

dot com fever *or* **.com fever** *noun informal* **1** a rush to buy up Internet domain names with the suffix .com in the hope of owning a name that becomes hugely successful as an Internet trading company or owning a name that another company is prepared to buy for vast amounts of money. **2** a rush to buy shares in dot com companies when they are floated on the stock market.

dote /doht/ *verb intrans* **1** (+ on/upon) to show excessive or foolish fondness for (somebody or something). **2** *archaic* to be feeble-minded, *esp* to exhibit mental decline in old age. ≫ **doter** *noun,* **doting** *adj,* **dotingly** *adv.* [Middle English *doten,* of Germanic origin]

doth /duth/ *verb* archaic present third person sing. of DO[1].

dot-matrix printer *noun dated* a printer that uses a MATRIX (rectangular array) of needles for printing and forms each character from dots printed by a particular set of needles in the matrix.

dotted line *noun* a line of dots or short dashes on paper, *esp* to indicate the place where a signature or some other information should be added.

dotterel /'dot(ə)rəl/ *noun* **1** a Eurasian plover with a distinctive white breast band during the summer months and formerly common in Britain, now only rarely found in parts of northern Scotland: *Charadrius morinellus.* **2** *informal* a foolish or gullible person. [Middle English *dotrelle,* from *doten* to DOTE; from its apparent stupidity in being easily caught]

dottle /'dotl/ *noun* unburnt tobacco left in the bowl of a pipe. [Middle English *dottel* plug, from DOT[1]]

dotty /'doti/ *adj* (**dottier, dottiest**) *informal* **1** crazy; mad. **2** eccentric or absurd, often in an endearing way. **3** (*usu* + about) extremely or excessively fond of somebody or something. ≫ **dottily** *adv,* **dottiness** *noun.* [alteration of Scots *dottle* fool, from Middle English *dotel,* from *doten* to DOTE]

Douay Version /'dooh·ay/ *noun* an early 17th-cent. English translation of the Vulgate Bible used by Roman Catholics. [named after *Douay, Douai,* city in France, where it was produced]

double[1] /'dubl/ *adj* **1** twofold; dual: *Mrs Kimble was the Squire's sister, as well as the doctor's wife – a double dignity* — George Eliot. **2** consisting of two, usu combined, similar members or parts: *an egg with a double yolk.* **3** twice as great or as many: *double the number of expected applicants.* **4** of twofold or extra size, strength, or value: *a double Scotch.* **5** designed or intended for two people: *a double room.* **6** folded in two. **7a** marked by duplicity; deceitful: *a double life.* **b** having two interpretations; ambiguous: *a double meaning.* **8** said of a plant or flower: having more than the normal number of petals or sepals: compare SINGLE[1]. **9** said of a musical instrument: sounding an octave lower in pitch: *a double bassoon.* ≫ **doubleness** *noun.* [Middle English via Old French from Latin *duplus,* from *duo* two + *-plus* multiplied by]

double[2] *noun* **1** something twice the usual amount, number, size, etc, *esp* a double measure of spirits. **2a** somebody who closely resembles another person. **b** a ghostly counterpart of a living person; a doppelgänger. **c** a duplicate or counterpart of something. **d** an understudy. **e** somebody who takes the place of an actor in scenes calling for special skills: *a body double.* **3** a sharp turn or twist. **4a** a bet in which the winnings and stake from a first race are bet on a second race. **b** two wins, e.g. in races on the same day or championships in the same year. **5** in bridge, a call that increases the value of tricks won or lost on an opponent's bid. **6** the outermost narrow ring on a dartboard or a throw that lands there, counting double the stated score. ✳ **at the double 1** very quickly; with great haste. **2a** at a fast rate between running and walking. **b** used as a military order to move at this rate.

double[3] *adv* **1** to twice the extent or amount. **2** two together: *seeing double.*

double[4] *verb trans* **1a** to increase (something) by adding an equal amount: *She doubled her fee.* **b** to amount to twice the quantity of (something). **2a** to make (something) into two thicknesses; to fold it. **b** to clench (one's fist). **c** (+ up/over) to stoop or bend over: *He was doubled up in pain.* **3** to make a call in bridge that increases the value of tricks won or lost on (an opponent's bid). **4** to cause (a billiard ball) to rebound. **5** to cause (troops) to move in double time. **6** to sail around (a headland). **7** to reinforce (a musical note or part) with another at the same pitch or at an octave above or below. ≫ *verb intrans* **1** to become twice as much or as many: *The cost has doubled.* **2a** (+ back) to turn back on one's course. **b** to turn sharply or take a circuitous course. **3** (+ up/over) to become bent or folded, usu in the middle. **4a** (+ as) to serve the additional purpose of (something): *The stool doubles as a bedside table.* **b** (+ for) to be an understudy, stand-in, or substitute for (somebody). **c** (*often* + on) to play an additional musical instrument: *The trumpeter doubles on saxophone.* **5a** to hurry along. **b** said of troops: to move in double time. **6** to double a bid (e.g. in bridge). **7** said of a billiard ball: to rebound. ≫ **doubler** *noun.*

double act *noun* an act that involves two performers, *esp* two comedians.

double agent *noun* a spy pretending to serve one government while actually serving another.

double bar *noun* two adjacent vertical lines or a heavy single line marking the end of a principal section of a musical composition.

double-barrelled *adj* **1** said of a firearm: having two barrels. **2** said of a surname: having two parts, usu joined by a hyphen. **3** having a double purpose: *a double-barrelled question.*

double bass *noun* the largest stringed musical instrument of the violin family, tuned a fifth below the cello. Also called CONTRABASS.

double bassoon *noun* a bassoon that is larger than the usual size and pitched an octave lower.

double bed *noun* a bed for two people.

double bill *noun* an entertainment featuring two main acts, bands, etc of equal status.

double bind *noun* a dilemma, *esp* a situation where any choice made will have unpleasant consequences.

double-blind *adj* relating to or denoting an experimental procedure in which neither the subjects nor the experimenters know the make-up of the test group and control group during the actual course of the experiments: compare SINGLE-BLIND.

double bluff *noun* an attempt to deceive somebody who expects to be bluffed by doing the opposite, e.g. by telling the truth instead of lying.

double bogey *noun* in golf, a score of two over par for a particular hole.

double boiler *noun chiefly NAmer* = DOUBLE SAUCEPAN.

double bond *noun* a chemical bond consisting of two covalent bonds (bonds involving shared electrons; see COVALENT BOND) between two atoms in a molecule.

double-book *verb trans* to reserve (the same seat, room, etc) for two different people or groups at the same time.

double-breasted *adj* said of a coat, jacket, etc: having a relatively large overlapping front fastening, usu with two sets of buttons and buttonholes: compare SINGLE-BREASTED.

double-check *verb intrans* to make a careful check, *esp* for a second time. ≫ *verb trans* to subject (something) to such a check.

double chin *noun* a person's chin with a fleshy fold under it. ≫ **double-chinned** *adj.*

double concerto *noun* a concerto with solo parts for two instruments.

double cream *noun* thick heavy cream that contains a relatively high proportion of fat and is suitable for whipping: compare SINGLE CREAM.

double-cross[1] *verb trans* to betray or cheat (somebody) by an act of deceit or duplicity. ≫ **double-crosser** *noun.*

double-cross[2] *noun* an act of betraying or cheating somebody, *esp* an associate.

double dagger *noun* a sign (‡) used in printing as a cross-reference mark, *esp* to a footnote.

double-dealing[1] *noun* underhand or deceitful action. ≫ **double-dealer** *noun.*

double-dealing[2] *adj* given to or marked by deceit or duplicity.

double-decker *noun* something that has two decks, levels, or layers, *esp* a bus with seats on two floors.

double declutch *verb intrans Brit* to change gear in a motor vehicle by disengaging the gear twice, passing first into neutral and then into the desired gear.

double decomposition *noun* a chemical reaction in which two different compounds exchange ions to form two new compounds.

double-density *adj* said of a computer floppy disk, having the capacity of holding twice the amount of data as the previous generation of disks.

double Dutch *noun informal* unintelligible or nonsensical speech or writing; gibberish.

double-edged *adj* **1** said of a knife, sword, etc: having two cutting edges. **2** having two purposes or effects. **3** said of a remark: having two possible and often contradictory interpretations, *esp* seeming innocent but capable of a malicious interpretation.

double entendre /ˌdoohbl on'ton(h)dr (*French* duːbl ātādr)/ *noun* (*pl* **double entendres** /ˌdoohbl on'ton(h)dr (*French* duːbl ātādr)/) an ambiguous word or expression, one of whose meanings is usu risqué. [obsolete French *double entendre* double meaning]

double entry *noun* a method of bookkeeping that records both sides of a business transaction by debiting the amount of the transaction to one account and crediting it to another account.

double exposure *noun* the act of exposing the same section of photographic film twice, resulting in superimposed images, or a photograph produced in this way.

double-faced *adj* **1** two-faced; hypocritical. **2** having two surfaces or sides designed for use: *double-faced fabric*.

double fault *noun* two consecutive service faults in tennis, squash, etc, resulting in the loss of a point or of the service.

double-fault *verb intrans* to serve a double fault.

double feature *noun* a cinema programme consisting of two full-length films.

double figures *pl noun* the range of numbers from 10 to 99: *The next shot took the score into double figures*.

double first *noun Brit* a first-class honours degree in two university examinations or subjects.

double flat *noun* **1** a symbol (♭♭) placed before a note in music indicating a drop in pitch of two semitones. **2** a note with this symbol or that is lowered in this way.

double glazing *noun* **1** a system of glazing windows in which two panes of glass, separated by an air space, are set in a window frame, providing better heat and sound insulation than a single pane. **2** windows or panes of glass used in double glazing. ➤➤ **double-glaze** *verb trans*.

Double Gloucester /'glostə/ *noun* a rich orange-coloured cheese with a firm smooth texture and a flavour that ranges from mellow to sharp as the cheese matures. [named after *Gloucestershire*, county in England where it was orig made]

doubleheader *noun* **1** a train pulled by two locomotives. **2** *chiefly NAmer* two games, contests, or events held consecutively on the same programme.

double helix *noun* two parallel helices arranged round the same axis, *esp* two complementary DNA strands arranged with the bases of each strand pointing inwards and linked by hydrogen bonds.

double indemnity *noun chiefly NAmer* a provision or clause in some types of life insurance policies that twice the face value of the contract will be paid out under certain specified conditions, *esp* in the event of accidental death.

double jeopardy *noun* the act of prosecuting a person for the same offence twice.

double-jointed *adj* having joints that permit an exceptional degree of flexibility in bending. ➤➤ **double-jointedness** *noun*.

double knitting *noun* a type of hand-knitting yarn of medium thickness.

double negative *noun* a syntactic construction containing two negatives and having a negative meaning, e.g. 'I didn't hear nothing' meaning 'I heard nothing'.

Usage note

The use of *not* together with another negative word as in *I don't know nothing* is not standard English. A less glaring error, but still an error, is the use of the second *not* in *It wouldn't surprise me if it didn't rain*. There the second *not* is simply superfluous: *It wouldn't surprise me if it rained* or, with a different emphasis, *It would surprise me if it didn't rain*. Double negative forms may be used when the intention is to express a positive idea: *a not unusual* (quite common) *request*; *not unrelated* (there may be a link); *not infrequently* (quite often); *One simply cannot not be impressed* (one cannot fail to be). The *not un-* construction is often used to express a slight reservation in the speaker's mind (*Let's say that it was not unimpressive.*) and is useful for that purpose. The *cannot not* construction is usually best replaced by something less ungainly: *cannot but be impressed*; *cannot fail to be impressed*. Occasionally more than two negatives in a sequence are encountered: 'This does not imply that sexual relations that don't risk conception are unrelated to personal responsibility and morality' — Margaret Drabble.

double obelisk *noun* in printing, = DOUBLE DAGGER.

double-park *verb trans and intrans* to park (a vehicle) beside a row of vehicles already parked parallel to the kerb.

double pneumonia *noun* pneumonia affecting both lungs.

double-quick¹ *adj* very quick.

double-quick² *adv* very quickly.

double reed *noun* two cane reeds bound and vibrating against each other and used as the mouthpiece of woodwind instruments of the oboe family.

double refraction *noun* = BIREFRINGENCE.

doubles *pl noun* (*treated as sing. or pl*) a game between two pairs of players, e.g. in tennis or badminton.

double salt *noun* a salt regarded as a molecular combination of two simple salts.

double saucepan *noun Brit* two interlocking saucepans, the contents of the upper being cooked or heated by boiling water in the lower: compare BAIN-MARIE.

double sharp *noun* **1** a symbol (×) placed before a note in music indicating a rise in pitch of two semitones. **2** a note with this symbol or that is raised in this way.

double-space *verb trans* to type or print (text) leaving alternate lines blank. ➤ *verb intrans* to type or print on every other line.

doublespeak /'dublspeek/ *noun* = DOUBLE-TALK. [from the novel *1984* by George Orwell d.1950, English writer]

double standard *noun* a principle or code that applies more rigorously to one group than to another.

double star *noun* **1** = BINARY STAR. **2** two stars that appear to be very close together.

double stopping *noun* the simultaneous playing of two strings of a bowed instrument, e.g. a violin.

doublet /'dublit/ *noun* **1** a man's close-fitting jacket, with or without sleeves, worn in Europe, *esp* in the 15th to 17th cents. **2a** a pair of similar or identical things. **b** (*in pl*) two thrown dice showing the same number on the upper face. **3** either of two words in a language having the same derivation but a different meaning, e.g. *guard* and *ward*. [Middle English from early French, from *double*: see DOUBLE¹]

double take *noun* a delayed reaction to a surprising or significant situation: *do a double take*.

double-talk *noun* involved and often deliberately ambiguous language.

doublethink *noun* unconscious acceptance, or cynical propagation, of conflicting principles. [from the novel *1984* by George Orwell d.1950, English writer]

double time *noun* **1** payment of a worker at twice the normal wage rate. **2** a rate of marching of twice the number of steps per minute as the normal slow rate. **3** in music, two beats in the bar.

double tonguing *noun* the use of alternating tongue movements to produce a fast succession of detached notes on a wind instrument.

double twill *noun* a twill weave with intersecting diagonal lines going in opposite directions.

double up *verb intrans* to share accommodation designed for one.

double vision *noun* a disorder of vision in which two images of a single object are seen, e.g. because of unequal action of the eye muscles. Also called DIPLOPIA.

double whammy *noun* two simultaneous blows or setbacks, often resulting from a single action or event.

doubloon /dub'loohn/ *noun* a former gold coin of Spain and Spanish America. [Spanish *doblón*, augmentative of *dobla*, an old Spanish coin, from Latin *dupla*, fem of *duplus*: see DOUBLE¹]

doubly *adv* **1** to twice the degree: *doubly pleased*. **2** in two ways: *doubly mistaken*.

doubt¹ /dowt/ *verb trans* **1** to be uncertain about (something); to feel inclined to disbelieve (it): *The police seemed to doubt my story*.

Editorial note

To doubt a proposition is to suspend judgment on it, to regard it as unsettled. René Descartes's 'method of doubt' required us to suspend judgment on anything that we can doubt: since fallible beliefs are untrustworthy, this is the only way to avoid error. Many recent thinkers urge that fallibility is no obstacle to our making progress in science and in other areas of our knowledge — Professor Christopher Hookway.

2a to consider (something) unlikely: *I doubt that she'll accept our offer*. **b** to lack confidence in (somebody); to distrust (them): *find myself doubting him even when I know that he is honest* — H L Mencken. **3** to fear or suspect (something): *I doubt some foul play* — Shakespeare. ➤ *verb intrans* to be uncertain. ➤➤ **doubtable** *adj*, **doubter** *noun*, **doubtingly** *adv*.

Word history

Middle English *douten* to fear, be uncertain, via Old French from Latin *dubitare* to doubt, from *dubius*: see DUBIOUS. The *b* was introduced in the 14th or 15th cent. to conform with Latin *dubitare*, but has never been pronounced: compare DEBT.

doubt[2] *noun* 1 uncertainty of belief or opinion. 2 an inclination not to believe or accept (something); a reservation. 3 a lack of confidence; distrust. ✳ **in doubt** uncertain. **no doubt** certainly; probably.

doubtful /'dowtf(ə)l/ *adj* 1 causing doubt; open to question: *a doubtful theory*. **2a** lacking a definite opinion; unconvinced: *I'm doubtful about the feasibility of the plan*. **b** uncertain in outcome; not settled. **3** of questionable worth, honesty, or validity. ⟫⟫ **doubtfully** *adv*, **doubtfulness** *noun*.

doubting Thomas /'toməs/ *noun* a person who habitually insists on having some kind of proof before accepting or believing things. [named after *Thomas*, apostle of Jesus who doubted Jesus' resurrection until he had proof of it (John 20:24–9)]

doubtless *adv* 1 without doubt; certainly. 2 probably. ⟫⟫ **doubtlessly** *adv*, **doubtlessness** *noun*.

douche[1] /doohsh/ *noun* 1 a jet or current of water or other fluid, directed against a part or into a cavity of the body, *esp* the vagina. 2 a device for giving a douche. [French *douche* from Italian *doccia* water pipe, from Latin *ducere* to lead]

douche[2] *verb trans and intrans* to clean or treat (something) with a douche.

dough /doh/ *noun* 1 a mixture of flour or meal with milk, water, or another liquid that is stiff enough to knead or roll to make bread, pastry, etc: compare BATTER[2]. 2 *informal* money. [Old English *dãg*]

doughboy *noun* 1 a US infantryman, *esp* in World War I. 2 a dumpling or piece of fried bread dough. [prob from the large round buttons on the US infantry uniform in the Civil War]

doughnut (*NAmer also* **donut**) *noun* 1 a small round or ring-shaped cake that is made with a yeast dough, often filled with jam, and deep-fried. 2 something ring-shaped.

doughnutting *noun* in a televised session of Parliament, the practice of forming a group around a member who is speaking in order to give the impression that the speaker is addressing a large audience.

doughty /'dowti/ *adj* (**doughtier, doughtiest**) *chiefly literary or humorous* bold and resolute. ⟫⟫ **doughtily** *adv*, **doughtiness** *noun*. [Old English *dohtig*]

doughy /'doh·i/ *adj* (**doughier, doughiest**) 1 unhealthily pale; pasty. 2 resembling dough in consistency. ⟫⟫ **doughiness** *noun*.

Douglas fir /'dugləs/ *noun* a tall evergreen US tree of the pine family, with large hanging cones, that is extensively grown for its wood: *Pseudotsuga menziesii*. [named after David *Douglas* d.1834, Scots botanist]

Douglas spruce *noun* = DOUGLAS FIR.

doum palm *or* **doom palm** /doom/ *or* **dom palm** /dom/ *noun* a palm tree that is grown in Egypt and other parts of northeast Africa for its edible oval fruit: *Hyphaene thebaica*. [Arabic *dōm*]

do up *verb trans* 1 to wrap (something). 2 to fasten (clothing or its fastenings) together. 3 *informal* to repair or redecorate (something). ✳ **be done up** to be dressed up for an occasion.

dour /dooə, 'dowə/ *adj* 1 stern, severe, or harsh. 2 gloomy; sullen. ⟫⟫ **dourly** *adv*, **dourness** *noun*. [Middle English, prob from Scottish Gaelic *dùr* and Irish Gaelic *dúr* dull, obstinate, perhaps from Latin *durus* hard]

douroucouli /doohrooh'koohli/ *noun* (*pl* **douroucoulis**) any of several species of nocturnal S American monkeys with large eyes: genus *Aotus*. [native name in S America]

douse *or* **dowse** /dows/ *verb trans* 1 to plunge (something) into or drench (it) with water. 2 to extinguish (a flame, light, etc). 3 to take (a sail) in or down quickly. ⟫⟫ **douser** *noun*. [prob from obsolete *douse* to smite, from *douse* blow, stroke, of Germanic origin]

dove[1] /duv/ *noun* 1 any of several species of birds of the pigeon family that are usu smaller and slenderer than the domestic pigeon: family Columbidae. 2 an advocate of peace, negotiation, or compromise, *esp* an opponent of war: compare HAWK[1]. 3 a light pinkish grey or greyish brown colour. 4 (**the Dove**) in Christianity, the Holy Spirit, *esp* as represented in art or literature. ⟫⟫ **dovelike** *adj*, **dovish** *adj*, **dovishness** *noun*. [Middle English, from (assumed) Old English *dūfe*]

dove[2] /dohv/ *verb NAmer* past tense of DIVE[1].

dovecot *or* **dovecote** /'duvkot/ *noun* a small compartmented raised house or box for domestic pigeons.

dove grey *noun* = DOVE[1] (3).

Dover sole /'dohvə/ *noun* a European marine flatfish highly valued for food: *Solea solea*. [prob named after *Dover*, town and port in England]

dovetail[1] /'duvtayl/ *noun* a TENON[1] (wooden projection) with the flared shape of a dove's tail and the MORTISE[1] (cavity) into which it fits to form a joint.

dovetail[2] *verb trans* 1 to join (pieces of wood etc) by means of dovetails. 2 to fit (things) together skilfully, neatly, or conveniently. ⟫ *verb intrans* to fit together in this way.

dowager /'dowəjə/ *noun* 1 a widow holding property or a title received from her deceased husband: *talking to huge overdressed dowagers and tedious Academicians* — Oscar Wilde. 2 a dignified elderly woman. [early French *douagiere* from *douage* dower, from *douer* to endow, from Latin *dotare*, from *dot-, dos* gift, dower]

dowdy /'dowdi/ *adj* (**dowdier, dowdiest**) 1 old-fashioned or dull in appearance, clothing etc. 2 not neat or smart. ⟫⟫ **dowdily** *adv*, **dowdiness** *noun*. [*dowd* poorly dressed woman, from Middle English *doude*; earlier history unknown]

dowel[1] /'dowəl/ *noun* 1 a wooden or metal pin fitting into holes in adjacent pieces to hold them together. 2 rods of wood or metal for sawing into such pins. [Middle English *dowle*; earlier history unknown]

dowel[2] *verb trans* (**dowelled, dowelling**, *NAmer* **doweled, doweling**) to fasten (adjacent pieces) together by dowels.

dowelling /'dowəling/ *noun* = DOWEL[1] (2).

dower[1] /'dowə/ *noun* 1 a widow's legal share during her life of her deceased husband's property. 2 *archaic* dowry. [Middle English *dowere* via French from medieval Latin *dotarium*, from Latin *dotare*: see DOWAGER]

dower[2] *verb trans* (**dowered, dowering**) to give a dower to (somebody).

dower house *noun* a house provided for a widow, often on the estate of her deceased husband.

Dow-Jones average /,dow 'johnz/ *noun* = DOW-JONES INDEX.

Dow-Jones index /,dow 'johnz/ *noun* an index of the prices of securities in the USA based on the daily average price of selected lists of shares. [named after Charles H *Dow* d.1902 and Edward D *Jones* d.1920, US financial statisticians, whose company compile it]

down[1] /down/ *adv* **1a** at or towards a relatively low level: *down into the cellar*. **b** downwards from the surface of the earth or water. **c** below the horizon. **d** downstream. **e** in or into a lying or sitting position: *lie down*. **f** to or on the ground, surface, or bottom: *The house burned down*. **g** so as to conceal a particular surface: *turn it face down*. **h** downstairs. **2a** in a direction conventionally the opposite of up. **b** in or towards the south. **c** *chiefly Brit* away from the capital of a country or from a university city: *sent down from Cambridge*. **d** to or at the front of a theatrical stage. **e** to leeward: *push the helm down*. **3a** in or into a relatively low condition or status: *The family has come down in the world*. **b** used to express opposition: *Down with the oppressors!* **c** *informal* to prison: *She went down for five years*. **4a** in or into a state of relatively low intensity or activity: *calm down*. **b** into a state of reduced heat, volume, etc: *turn the radio down*. **c** into silence: *They shouted him down*. **d** into a slower pace or lower gear: *change down into second*. **e** to a lower amount, price, figure, or rank: *Prices are coming down*. **f** behind an opponent: *We're three points down*. **5a** so as to be known, recognized, or recorded, *esp* on paper: *scribble it down*. **b** so as to be firmly held in position: *stick down the flap of the envelope; I don't like to feel tied down*. **c** to the moment of catching or discovering: *track the culprits down*. **6** in cash on the spot, *esp* as an initial payment: *I paid £100 down*. **7** from a predecessor or an earlier time: *jewels handed down in the family*. **8a** to a concentrated state: *boil the sauce down*. **b** so as to be flattened, reduced, eroded, or diluted: *water down the gin; heels worn down*. **c** completely from top to bottom: *hose the car down*. ✳ **down to** used to indicate a downward limit or boundary: *from the manager down to the office junior*. [Old English *dūne*, short for *adūne, of dūne* off the hill, from *dūn* DOWN[7]]

down[2] *adj* 1 directed or going downwards: *the down escalator*. **2a** depressed; dejected. **b** ill: *down with flu*. **3** said of a computer system: temporarily out of action. **4** having been finished or dealt with: *eight down and two to go*. **5** *chiefly Brit* bound in a direction regarded as the opposite of up, *esp* travelling away from a large town or city: *the down line*. **6** said of a ship's helm: with the rudder to windward. ✳ **down for** on the list to enter something (e.g. a race or school). **down on** having a low opinion of or grudge against somebody: *She's always down on him*. **down to 1** attributed to: *The company's failure is down to bad management*. **2** the responsibility of: *Sex education used to be down to the parents*.

down³ *prep* **1a** in a downward direction along, through, towards, in, on, etc: *running down the hill*. **b** at the bottom of: *The bathroom is down those stairs*. **c** at or to a position further along: *I drove down the road*. **2** *Brit, informal* down to; to: *I'm going down the shops*.

down⁴ *verb trans* **1** to cause (something or somebody) to go or come down. **2** *informal* to drink or swallow (something) quickly. ✳ **down tools 1** *chiefly Brit* to stop working. **2** *chiefly Brit* to go on strike.

down⁵ *noun* **1** a downward movement. **2** (*also in pl*) a period of depression, ill fortune, etc: *life's ups and downs*. **3** in American football, an attempt to advance the ball. ✳ **have a down on** to have a grudge against (somebody).

down⁶ *noun* **1a** the fine soft feathers that cover a young bird. **b** the finer softer layer of feathers below an adult bird's contour feathers. **c** fine soft feathers used to fill pillows, duvets, etc; eiderdown. **2** fine soft hairs on a person's skin. **3** fine soft hairs on a plant part, e.g. the fuzz on a peach skin. [Middle English *doun* from Old Norse *dūnn*]

down⁷ *noun* (*usu in pl*) a region of undulating treeless usu chalk uplands, *esp* in S England. [Old English *dūn* hill]

down-and-out¹ *adj* destitute and homeless.

down-and-out² *noun* a destitute and homeless person.

downbeat¹ *noun* the principally accented note of a bar of music, usu the first note.

downbeat² *adj* **1** pessimistic; gloomy. **2** relaxed; informal.

downcast¹ *adj* **1** dejected or depressed. **2** directed downwards: *with downcast eyes*.

downcast² *noun* a ventilation shaft in a mine: compare UPCAST¹.

downdraught *noun* a downward movement of air, e.g. in a chimney.

downer *noun* **1** *Informal* a depressing experience or situation. **2** *slang* a depressant drug, *esp* a barbiturate.

downfall *noun* **1** a sudden fall, e.g. from high rank or power, or a cause of such a fall: *Her pride was her downfall*. **2** a heavy fall of rain or snow.

downfield *adv and adj* in various outdoor team sports, in or into the part of the field towards which the attacking team is playing.

downgrade¹ /down'grayd/ *verb trans* **1** to lower (something or somebody) in rank, value, or importance. **2** to alter the status of (an employee or a job) so as to lower the rate of pay.

downgrade² /'downgrayd/ *noun* **1** *chiefly NAmer* a downward slope, e.g. of a road. **2** a descent towards a lower or inferior state or level.

downhearted *adj* discouraged or dejected. ➤➤ **downheartedly** *adv*, **downheartedness** *noun*.

downhill¹ *noun* **1** a descending gradient. **2** a skiing race downhill against time: compare SLALOM.

downhill² *adv* towards the bottom of a hill or slope. ✳ **go downhill** to decline or deteriorate.

downhill³ *adj* going or sloping downhill.

down-home *adj NAmer, informal* **1** from or typical of one's own part of the country. **2** unpretentious, *esp* typical of country life.

Downing Street /'downing/ *noun* the British government, the British prime minister, or a spokesperson for either: *Downing Street is expected to announce cabinet changes soon*. [from *Downing Street*, London, location of the British prime minister's official residence]

downland *noun* undulating countryside, *esp* that of the downs.

downlink *noun* a transmission path for radio signals from a spacecraft, satellite, etc to the earth.

download *verb trans* to transfer (programs or data) from one computer to another, *esp* via a telephone line: *I downloaded the software from the Internet*. ➤➤ **downloadable** *adj*.

down-market¹ *adj* being, producing, selling, or characteristic of goods designed to appeal to the lower end of a market.

down-market² *adv* towards the lower end of a market: *The restaurant seems to have gone down-market*.

down payment *noun* an initial payment for something bought on credit.

downpipe *noun* a pipe for carrying rainwater from a roof or gutter to the ground or into a drain.

downplay *verb trans* to treat (something) as being less significant than it is or might have been.

downpour *noun* a heavy fall of rain.

downright¹ *adv* thoroughly; altogether: *downright careless*.

downright² *adj* **1** absolute; thorough: *There remains nothing of Genesis but an anonymous book of stories, fables … invented absurdities, or … downright lies* — Thomas Paine. **2** plain or blunt: *a downright man*. ➤➤ **downrightly** *adv*, **downrightness** *noun*.

downshift *verb intrans* **1** *NAmer* to put a vehicle into a lower gear; to change down. **2** to adopt a less stressful lifestyle.

downside *noun* **1** a drawback, shortcoming, or undesirable feature. **2** a downward trend, *esp* in economics.

downsize *verb trans* to reduce (something) in size, *esp* to reduce (a workforce) by redundancy.

Down's syndrome /downz/ *noun* a disorder caused by chromosomal abnormality characterized by slanting eyes, a broad short skull, broad hands with short fingers, varying degrees of intellectual impairment, and often heart defects, intestinal malformation, and other physical symptoms such as deafness. See also TRISOMY-21. [named after J L H *Down* d.1896, English physician, who first described it]

downstage *adv and adj* at the front of a theatrical stage, or towards the audience.

downstairs¹ *adv* down the stairs; on or to a lower floor.

downstairs² *adj* situated on the lower or ground floor of a building: *a downstairs bathroom*.

downstairs³ *pl noun* (*treated as sing.*) the lower or ground floor of a building.

downstream *adv and adj* in the direction of the flow of a stream.

downstroke *noun* a stroke made in a downward direction.

downswing /'downswing/ *noun* **1** a downward swing, *esp* of a golf club. **2** a downward trend, *esp* in business activity.

downtime *noun* time during which a computer, machine, etc is inoperative during normal working hours.

down-to-earth *adj* practical or realistic.

downtown¹ *adv and adj chiefly NAmer* of, to, towards, or in the lower part or main business district of a town or city.

downtown² *noun chiefly NAmer* the downtown area of a town or city.

downtrodden *adj* oppressed by those in power.

downturn *noun* a downward turn, *esp* towards diminished economic or commercial activity.

down under¹ *adv informal* in or into Australia or New Zealand.

down under² *noun informal* Australia or New Zealand: *a band from down under*.

downward /'downwəd/ *adj* **1** moving or extending downwards: *the downward path*. **2** descending to a lower pitch, position, etc. **3** descending from a head, origin, or source. ➤➤ **downwardly** *adv*, **downwardness** *noun*.

downwards *adv* **1a** from a higher to a lower place or level; in the opposite direction from up. **b** downstream. **c** so as to conceal a particular surface: *turn it face downwards*. **2a** from a higher to a lower condition. **b** going down in amount, price, figure, or rank: *from £1000 downwards*. **3** from a predecessor or an earlier time.

downwind *adv and adj* in the direction towards which the wind is blowing.

downy *adj* (**downier, downiest**) **1** resembling or covered in soft fluffy feathers or fine hairs. **2** made or filled with the down of birds. **3** *informal* shrewd; sharp-witted. ➤➤ **downily** *adv*, **downiness** *noun*.

dowry /'dowri/ *noun* (*pl* **dowries**) the money, goods, or estate that a woman brings to her husband in marriage. [Middle English *dowarie* via Anglo-French and medieval Latin from Latin *dot-*, *dos* gift, marriage portion]

dowse¹ /dowz/ *verb intrans* to search for hidden water or minerals with a divining rod. ⟫⟫ **dowser** *noun.* [origin unknown]

dowse² /dows/ *verb trans* see DOUSE.

doxology /dok'soləji/ *noun* (*pl* **doxologies**) a liturgical expression of praise to God. ⟫⟫ **doxological** /doksə'lojikl/ *adj.* [medieval Latin *doxologia*, from Greek *doxa* opinion, glory (from *dokein* to seem, seem good) + *-logia* -logy]

doxy /'doksi/ *noun* (*pl* **doxies**) *archaic* **1** a lover or mistress. **2** a prostitute. [perhaps modification of obsolete Dutch *docke* doll]

doyen /'doyən (*French* dwajɛ̃/ *or* **doyenne** /doy'en (*French* dwajɛn/) *noun* the senior or most experienced member of a body or group: *Elizabeth David … doyenne of English cookery writers* — Today. [French *doyen* from late Latin *decanus*: see DEAN¹]

doyley *or* **doyly** /'doyli/ *noun* see DOILY.

doz. *abbr* dozen.

doze¹ /dohz/ *verb intrans* **1** to sleep lightly. **2** (+ off) to fall into a light sleep. ⟫⟫ **dozer** *noun.* [prob of Scandinavian origin]

doze² *noun* a short light sleep.

dozen /'duz(ə)n/ *noun* (*pl* **dozens** *or* **dozen**) **1** a group of twelve. **2** an indefinitely large number: *I've dozens of things to do.* ✳ **talk nineteen to the dozen** *Brit* to talk non-stop and often very quickly. ⟫⟫ **dozen** *adj,* **dozenth** *adj.* [Middle English *dozeine* from Old French *dozaine,* from *doze* twelve, from Latin *duodecim,* from *duo* two + *decem* ten]

dozy /'dohzi/ *adj* (**dozier, doziest**) **1** drowsy; sleepy. **2** *chiefly Brit, informal* stupid and slow-witted. ⟫⟫ **dozily** *adv,* **doziness** *noun.*

DP *abbr* **1** data processing. **2** displaced person.

dpc *abbr* damp-proof course.

DPhil /,dee 'fil/ *abbr* Doctor of Philosophy.

dpi *abbr* in computing, dots per inch.

DPP *abbr* Director of Public Prosecutions.

dpt *abbr* department.

Dr *abbr* **1** doctor. **2** in street names, Drive.

dr *abbr* **1** debtor. **2** drachm. **3** drachma. **4** dram. **5** drawer.

drab¹ /drab/ *adj* (**drabber, drabbest**) **1** dull or cheerless: *a drab existence.* **2** of a dull brown or grey colour. ⟫⟫ **drably** *adv,* **drabness** *noun.* [*drab* kind of undyed cloth, from early French *drap* cloth, from late Latin *drappus*]

drab² *noun* **1** *archaic* a slovenly woman. **2** *archaic* a prostitute. [perhaps from Low German *drabbe* mire, dirt]

drac *noun* see DRACK.

drachm /dram/ *noun* **1a** a unit of measurement equal to one eighth of a fluid ounce. **b** a unit of apothecaries' weight equal to one eighth of an ounce (about 3.89g). **2** = DRACHMA. [alteration of Middle English *dragme*: see DRAM¹]

drachma /'drakmə/ *noun* (*pl* **drachmas** *or* **drachmae** /'drakmee/) **1a** the former basic monetary unit of Greece, divided into 100 lepta (replaced by the euro in 2002). **b** an ancient Greek silver coin equivalent to six obols. **2** any of various ancient Greek units of weight. [via Latin from Greek *drachmē*: see DRAM¹]

drack *or* **drac** /drak/ *adj Aus, informal* said of a woman: unattractive. [origin unknown]

draconian /drə'kohni·ən/ *adj* (*often* **Draconian**) said of laws, measures, etc: extremely severe; drastic: *Could this be he who, of late, with sour visage, and in stuffy habiliments, administered, ferule in hand, the Draconian laws of the Academy?* — Poe.

Word history

Latin *Dracon-, Draco,* from Greek *Drakōn* seventh-cent. BC Athenian law-giver. Draco's code of laws were notorious for their severity; the death penalty was prescribed for the most trivial offences.

draconic /drə'konik/ *adj* = DRACONIAN.

draff /draf/ *noun* **1** the remains of malt left after brewing. **2** *literary* dregs. [Middle English *draf* dregs, draff, from (assumed) Old English *dræf* or Old Norse *draf;* related to Old English *deorc* DARK¹]

draft¹ /drahft/ *noun* **1a** a construction plan or technical drawing. **b** a preliminary sketch, outline, or version: *a rough draft of a book.* **2** the act of drafting something. **3a** an order for the payment of money drawn by one person or bank on another. **b** the act or an instance of drawing from or making demands on something. **4a** a group of individuals selected for a particular job. **b** *Aus, NZ* the selecting of certain animals from a herd or flock, or the animals selected. **5** *chiefly NAmer* conscription for military service: *avoid the draft.* **6** *NAmer* see DRAUGHT¹. [variant of DRAUGHT¹]

draft² *adj* **1** constituting a preliminary version or sketch: *draft copy.* **2** *NAmer* see DRAUGHT².

draft³ *verb trans* **1a** to write a preliminary version or outline of (something, e.g. a letter). **b** to draw a preliminary sketch or plan of (something, e.g. a design). **2a** to select (an individual or group) for a particular job or purpose. **b** *NAmer* to conscript (somebody) for military service. ⟫⟫ **draftable** *adj,* **drafter** *noun.*

draftee /drahf'tee/ *noun NAmer* a person who is conscripted for military service.

draftsman /'drahftsmən/ *noun* (*pl* **draftsmen**) **1** somebody who draws up legal documents or other writings. **2** *NAmer* = DRAUGHTS-MAN (1).

drafty *adj NAmer* see DRAUGHTY.

drag¹ /drag/ *verb* (**dragged, dragging**) ⟫ *verb trans* **1a** to pull (something) along slowly or heavily; to haul (it). **b** to cause (something) to move with painful or undue slowness or difficulty: *dragging his left leg.* **c** to cause (something) to trail along a surface. **d** to move (something) across a computer screen, usu by means of a mouse. **2a** to bring (somebody) by force or compulsion: *She had to drag her husband to the opera.* **b** to obtain (something) by force or with difficulty: *I finally dragged a confession out of them.* **3a** to search (a body of water) with a large net, hook, or other device. **b** to catch (something) with a dragnet. ⟫ *verb intrans* **1** to hang or lag behind. **2** to trail along a surface. **3** to pass, move, or proceed laboriously or tediously: *The book drags.* **4** *informal* (+ on) to draw smoke from (a cigarette, pipe, etc) into the mouth. ✳ **drag one's feet/heels** to act in a deliberately slow, dilatory, or ineffective manner. ⟫⟫ **draggingly** *adv.* [Middle English *draggen,* from Old Norse *draga* or Old English *dragan* DRAW¹]

drag² *noun* **1a** something that retards motion, action, or progress. **b** the retarding force acting on a body, e.g. an aircraft, moving through air, water, or other fluid, parallel and opposite to the direction of motion. **c** a burden or encumbrance. **2a** a drawing along or over a surface with effort or pressure. **b** motion effected with slowness or difficulty. **3** *informal* a drawing into the mouth of cigarette, pipe, or cigar smoke. **4** *informal.* **a** clothing that is generally regarded as appropriate for one sex but worn by somebody of the opposite sex, *esp* woman's clothing worn by a man: *in drag.* **b** (*used before a noun*) relating to or featuring men who dress in women's clothing: *a drag act.* **5** *informal* a dull or boring person or experience. **6** a device that is pulled along under water to search for objects. **7** an object drawn over the ground to leave a scented trail, e.g. for dogs to follow. **8a** = DRAG RACE. **b** (*used before a noun*) relating to or used in drag racing. **9** a coach drawn by four horses. **10** *chiefly NAmer, informal* a street or road: *the main drag.*

dragée /'drazhay (*French* draʒe/) *noun* **1** a sugar-coated nut or fruit. **2** a small silver-coloured sugar ball for decorating cakes. [French *dragée* from early French *dragie*: see DREDGE³]

draggle /'dragl/ *verb trans* to make (something) wet and dirty, *esp* by trailing it on the ground. ⟫ *verb intrans* **1** to trail on the ground. **2** to straggle. [frequentative of DRAG¹]

draggy /'dragi/ *adj* (**draggier, draggiest**) *informal* dull or boring: *I spent a really draggy evening with my relations.*

dragline *noun* an excavating machine in which the bucket is drawn in by cables.

dragnet *noun* **1** a net drawn along the bottom of a body of water or the ground to catch fish or small game. **2** a network of measures designed to lead to capture or discovery, e.g. of a criminal.

dragoman /'dragohmən/ *noun* (*pl* **dragomans** *or* **dragomen**) an interpreter, chiefly of Arabic, Turkish, or Persian, employed *esp* in the Middle Eastern countries. [Middle English *drogman* via French, Old Italian, medieval Greek, and Arabic from Aramaic *tūrgĕmānā* an interpreter]

dragon /'dragən/ *noun* **1** a mythical animal usu represented as a monstrous winged and scaly reptile with a crested head, large claws, and the power to breathe fire. **2** *informal.* **a** a violent, combative, or very strict person. **b** a fierce or formidable woman. **3** any of various lizards, e.g. the Komodo dragon or a small brilliantly coloured tree-dwelling lizard of the E Indies. **4** a newly industrialized and economically successful country in SE Asia. ✳ **chase the dragon** *informal* to take heroin by heating it and inhaling the fumes. [Middle English via Old French from Latin *draco* from Greek *drakōn* serpent]

dragonet /'dragənit/ *noun* any of several species of small marine fishes that are often brightly coloured: *Callionymus lyra* and other species. [DRAGON + -ET]

dragonfly *noun* (*pl* **dragonflies**) any of a suborder of long slender-bodied insects that are often brightly coloured, have two pairs of intricately veined wings held outspread when at rest, and have larvae that live in water: suborder Anisoptera.

dragonnade /dragə'nayd/ *noun* persecution using troops, *esp* any of a series of persecutions of French Protestants under Louis XIV by soldiers who were quartered among them. [French *dragonnade* from *dragon*: see DRAGOON¹]

dragon's blood *noun* a darkened resin from the fruit of a palm tree used for colouring varnish and in photoengraving.

dragoon¹ /drə'goohn/ *noun* **1** a member of a cavalry unit formerly composed of mounted infantrymen armed with carbines. **2** a type of domestic pigeon.

Word history
French *dragon* dragon, carbine, dragoon, from Old French: see DRAGON. So called because the dragoon's carbine appeared to breathe fire like a dragon.

dragoon² *verb trans* **1** to force (somebody) to do something against their will: *We were dragooned into helping.* **2** to force or attempt to force (somebody) into submission by persecution or the harsh use of troops.

drag out *verb trans* to protract or lengthen (something) unnecessarily.

drag queen *noun informal* a man who dresses in women's clothes, *esp* one who wears flamboyant outfits.

drag race *noun* an acceleration contest between cars, motorcycles, etc, usu over a quarter mile course (about 402 metres). >> **drag racer** *noun*, **drag racing** *noun*.

dragster /'dragstə/ *noun* **1** a vehicle, *esp* a motor car, built or modified for use in a drag race. **2** the driver of such a vehicle.

drag up *verb trans* **1** *informal* to bring up (a child) badly or without good manners: *Where were you dragged up?* **2** *informal* to mention (an unpleasant topic) unnecessarily: *He always has to drag up that story about his ex-wife.*

drail /drayl/ *noun* a heavy fishhook dragged behind a moving boat [obsolete *drail* to drag, trail, perhaps alteration of TRAIL²]

drain¹ /drayn/ *verb trans* **1a** to draw off (liquid) gradually or completely. **b** to empty (something) by drawing off liquid: *drain the pond.* **c** to empty (something) by drinking the contents: *He drained his glass.* **d** to carry away the surface water of (something): *The river that drains the area.* **e** to make (something) gradually dry: *drain a swamp.* **2a** to exhaust (somebody) physically or emotionally. **b** to deplete or empty (something) by gradually using up resources etc: *a war that drained the nation of youth and wealth.* >> *verb intrans* **1** to flow off gradually. **2** to become gradually dry. >> **drainer** *noun*. [Old English *drēahnian*]

drain² *noun* **1** a pipe or other means by which usu liquid matter is drained away: *There was a strong smell throughout the house, but whether it was bugs, or rats, or cats, or drains, or a compound of the four, I could not determine* — Samuel Butler. **2** a gradual outflow or withdrawal. **3** something that causes depletion; a burden. ✳ **go down the drain** to be wasted or to come to nothing: *Another week's work went down the drain.*

drainage /'draynij/ *noun* **1a** the act or process of draining. **b** something drained off. **2** a system of drains.

drainer /'draynə/ *noun* **1** a rack where washed dishes are left to dry. **2** = DRAINING BOARD.

draining board *noun Brit* a usu grooved and slightly sloping surface at the side of a sink unit on which washed dishes are placed to drain.

drainpipe *noun* a pipe that carries rainwater from a roof or waste, liquid sewage, etc from a building.

drainpipes *pl noun* = DRAINPIPE TROUSERS.

drainpipe trousers *pl noun* tight trousers with narrow legs.

drake¹ /drayk/ *noun* a male duck, which often has more distinctive or colourful plumage than the female. [Middle English, of Germanic origin]

drake² *noun* a mayfly, *esp* an artificial one used as bait in angling. [Old English *draca* dragon, from a prehistoric Germanic word borrowed from Latin *draco*: see DRAGON]

Dralon /'draylon/ *noun trademark* an acrylic fibre used chiefly in upholstery. [prob a blend of DRAPERY + NYLON]

DRAM /'deeram/ *abbr* dynamic random access memory.

dram¹ /dram/ *noun* **1** a unit of mass equal to one sixteenth of an ounce (about 1.77g). **2** *chiefly Scot* a tot of spirits, usu whisky. [Middle English *dragme* via French and Latin from Greek *drachmē*, literally 'handful', from *drassesthai* to grasp]

dram² *noun* the basic monetary unit of Armenia, divided into 100 luma.

drama /'drahmə/ *noun* **1** a composition in verse or prose intended for performance by actors, *esp* on stage; a play: *Even in an Ibsen drama one must reveal to the audience things that one would suppress before the children or servants* — Saki. **2a** plays or literary works intended to be staged, thought of collectively or as a genre. **b** (*used before a noun*) relating to plays or the theatre: *a drama school.* **3** an exciting or emotionally charged situation or set of events. [via late Latin from Greek *dramat-, drama* deed, drama, from *dran* to do, act]

dramatic /drə'matik/ *adj* **1** of drama, acting, or plays. **2a** characteristic of drama; vivid or exciting. **b** striking in appearance or effect. >> **dramatically** *adv*. [via late Latin from Greek *dramatikos*, from *dramat-, drama*: see DRAMA]

dramatics *pl noun* **1** (*treated as sing. or pl*) the study or practice of theatrical arts, e.g. acting and stage management. **2** dramatic behaviour, *esp* an exaggerated display of emotion.

dramatise /'dramətiez/ *verb trans* see DRAMATIZE.

dramatis personae /,dramətis puh'sohnie/ *pl noun* (*treated as sing. or pl*) the characters or actors in a play, or a list of these: compare PERSONA (2). [Latin *dramatis personae* persons of the drama]

dramatist /'dramətist/ *noun* a writer of plays.

dramatize *or* **dramatise** /'dramətiez/ *verb trans* **1** to adapt (e.g. a novel) for theatrical presentation. **2** to present (something) in a dramatic or exaggerated manner. **3** to exaggerate the significance, seriousness, excitement, etc of (something), *esp* as a means of drawing attention. >> *verb intrans* **1** to be suitable for dramatization. **2** to behave dramatically. >> **dramatization** /-'zaysh(ə)n/ *noun*.

dramaturge /'dramətuhj/ *noun* **1** a writer of plays. **2** (*also* **dramaturg**) a literary adviser attached to a theatrical, operatic, or film company. [German *Dramaturg* and French *dramaturge*, from Greek *dramatourgos*: see DRAMATURGY]

dramaturgy /'dramətuhji/ *noun* the art or technique of dramatic composition and theatrical representation. >> **dramaturgic** /-'tuhjik/ *adj*, **dramaturgical** /-'tuhjikl/ *adj*, **dramaturgically** /-'tuhjikli/ *adv*. [German *Dramaturgie* from Greek *dramatourgia* dramatic composition, from *dramatourgos* dramatist, from *dramat-, drama* (see DRAMA) + -ourgos worker, from *ergon* work]

drank /drangk/ *verb* past tense of DRINK¹.

drape¹ /drayp/ *verb trans* **1** to cover or decorate (something) with folds of cloth. **2** to arrange (cloth, clothing, etc) in flowing lines or folds. **3** to hang or stretch (something) loosely or carelessly: *He draped his legs over the chair.* [Middle English *drapen* to weave, from early French *draper*, from *drap*: see DRAB¹]

drape² *noun* **1a** a piece of drapery. **b** *chiefly NAmer* a curtain. **2** the way in which fabric or clothing hangs.

draper *noun chiefly Brit, dated* a person who deals in or sells cloth and usu also haberdashery and soft furnishings. [Middle English, orig a maker of cloth, from Old French *drapier*, from *drap*: see DRAB¹]

drapery *noun* (*pl* **draperies**) **1a** cloth or clothing arranged or hung gracefully, *esp* in loose folds, or a piece of such cloth or clothing. **b** textile fabrics used *esp* for clothing or soft furnishings. **c** *NAmer* hangings of heavy fabric used as a curtain. **2** *Brit*. **a** the business or shop of a draper. **b** the goods sold by a draper.

drastic /'drastik/ *adj* **1** radical in effect or action; severe: *a drastic solution.* **2** said of a drug, remedy, or treatment: acting rapidly or violently. >> **drastically** *adv*. [Greek *drastikos* effective, from *dran* to do]

drat /drat/ *interj* used to express annoyance. >> **dratted** *adj*. [prob euphemism for *God rot*]

draught¹ (*NAmer* **draft**) /drahft/ *noun* **1** a current of air in an enclosed space. **2a** the act of drinking or inhaling, or the portion drunk or inhaled. **b** a portion poured out or mixed for drinking; a dose. **3** the act of drawing liquid, e.g. from a cask, or a quantity of liquid so drawn. **4** the depth of water a ship or boat requires to float in, *esp* when loaded. **5** a team of animals together with the load they draw. **6** the act of drawing a fishing net, or the quantity of fish so caught. ✳ **on draught** said of beer or cider: ready to be served from the cask or barrel. [Middle English *draght* from Old Norse *drattr*; related to Old English *dragan* DRAW¹]

draught² (*NAmer* **draft**) *adj* **1** used for drawing loads: *draught oxen*. **2** served from the barrel or cask: *draught beer*.

draughtboard *noun* = CHESSBOARD.

draught-proof *verb trans* to plug gaps around (windows, doors, etc) to prevent a draught blowing through: *draught-proof your house for the winter.* ➤➤ **draught-proofing** *noun.*

draughts *pl noun Brit* (*treated as sing. or pl*) a board game for two players each of whom moves twelve disc-shaped pieces according to fixed rules across a chessboard, usu using only the black squares, to capture the opponent's pieces. [Middle English *draghtes*, pl of *draght* draught, move in chess: see DRAUGHT¹]

draughtsman or **draughtswoman** (*NAmer* **draftsman** or **draftswoman**) *noun* (*pl* **draughtsmen** or **draughtswomen**) **1a** a person who draws technical plans and sketches, e.g. of machinery or structures. **b** an artist skilled in drawing. **2** = DRAFTSMAN (1). **3** *Brit* a disc-shaped piece used in draughts. ➤➤ **draughtsmanship** *noun.*

draughty (*NAmer* **drafty**) *adj* (**draughtier, draughtiest**) said of a room, house, etc: having cold draughts blowing through it. ➤➤ **draughtily** *adv,* **draughtiness** *noun.*

Dravidian /drə'vidi·ən/ *noun* **1** a member of a group of indigenous peoples inhabiting S India and Sri Lanka. **2** any of several languages of India, Sri Lanka, and Pakistan spoken by these peoples, including Tamil and Malayalam. ➤➤ **Dravidian** *adj.* [Sanskrit *Drāviḍa* Tamil + -IAN]

draw¹ /draw/ *verb* (*past tense* **drew** /drooh/, *past part.* **drawn**) ➤ *verb trans* **1a** to produce (a picture, diagram, etc) by making lines on a surface, *esp* on paper. **b** to produce a likeness of (a person or thing) in this way. **2a** to pull or haul (a vehicle, load, etc). **b** to cause (somebody or something) to move in a specified direction: *She drew him aside.* **3a** to attract (something or somebody): *Honey draws flies.* **b** to derive (a quality or feeling) from a specified source: *They drew inspiration from their teacher.* **c** to bring (something unwelcome) on oneself; to provoke (an unfavourable result): *draw enemy fire.* **d** to bring (something) out by way of response; to elicit (a reaction): *The display drew cheers from the spectators.* **4** to take in (breath). **5a** to bring or pull (something) out, often with effort: *draw a tooth; draw a sword.* **b** to cause (blood) to flow. **c** to extract the essence from (a herb, flavouring ,etc). **d** to remove the internal organs of (a person or animal); to disembowel. **6** to formulate or arrive at (a conclusion, etc) by reasoning. **7a** (*often* + out) to take (money) from a bank acount or other place of deposit. **b** to receive (money) regularly, *esp* from a particular source: *draw a salary.* **c** to use (a cheque, etc) to make a cash demand. **d** to accumulate or gain (something): *drawing interest.* **8a** to receive or take (something) at random: *draw a winning number.* **b** to take (cards) from a dealer or pack. **c** to be selected randomly to play against (another team). **9** to pull together and close (e.g. curtains). **10a** to stretch or shape (metal) by pulling it through holes in dies. **b** to produce (wire) in this way. **11** to bend (a bow) by pulling back the string. **12** to finish (a contest) with the scores equal or without a winner. **13** said of a ship: require (a specified depth) to float in. **14** to drive game out of (an area). **15** to strike (a ball) so as to impart a curved motion or backspin. ➤ *verb intrans* **1** to make drawings; to sketch. **2** to come or go steadily or gradually: *Night draws near.* **3** to advance as far as a specified position: *draw level.* **4** to finish a competition or contest with the scores equal or neither side winning. **5a** to bring out a weapon. **b** to pull back a bowstring. **6a** to obtain resources, e.g. of information: *drawing from a common fund of knowledge.* **b** to make a written demand for payment of money on deposit. **7a** to produce or allow a draught: *the chimney draws well.* **b** said of a sail: to swell out in a wind. **8** *chiefly NAmer* (+ on) to suck in tobacco smoke from (a pipe, cigarette, etc). **9** to steep or infuse: *give the tea time to draw.* ✳ **draw on/upon** to use (something) as source of supply: *We can draw on our previous experience.* **draw the/a line 1** to fix a boundary or distinction between things that tend to merge: *the difficulty of drawing a line between art and pornography.* **2** (*usu* + at) to fix a boundary excluding what one will not tolerate or engage in: *I draw the line at using that kind of language.* [Old English *dragan*]

draw² *noun* **1** a process of taking names or items randomly, *esp* in a lottery or raffle, or to determine the grouping of opponents in a sports competition. **2** a contest that ends with the scores even; a tie. **3** something that attracts public attention or a large audience.

4a a sucking action on something held between the lips, e.g. a pipe. **b** the removing of a gun from its holster in order to shoot: *quick on the draw.* **5** *NAmer* the movable part of a drawbridge.

drawback *noun* **1** an undesirable feature; a disadvantage: *To have been well brought up is a great drawback now-a-days* — Oscar Wilde. **2** a refund of duties, *esp* on an imported product subsequently exported.

draw back *verb intrans* **1** to avoid an issue or commitment. **2** to retreat.

drawbar *noun* **1a** a beam across the rear of a tractor to which implements are hitched. **b** a railway vehicle coupling. **2** a bar that can be pulled to release something.

drawbridge *noun* a bridge that can be raised, let down, or drawn aside in order to prevent or permit passage, e.g. one over a castle moat.

drawee /draw'ee/ *noun* the person or organization from whose bank, etc account money is taken when a cheque, draft, etc is presented for payment.

drawer *noun* **1** /draw/ an open-topped storage box that slides out of a piece of furniture for access. **2** /'draw·ə/. **a** somebody who draws something. **b** the person or organization to whom money is paid when a cheque, draft, etc is presented for payment. **3** /drawz/ *dated or humorous* (*in pl*) an undergarment for the lower body; knickers or underpants.

draw in *verb intrans* **1** said of a train: to approach a station. **2a** said of successive days: to grow shorter, in autumn and early winter. **b** said of successive nights: to start earlier. ➤ *verb trans* **1** to cause or entice (somebody) to enter or participate. **2** to sketch (something), *esp* roughly.

drawing *noun* **1a** the art or technique of representing an object, figure, or plan by means of lines. **b** a representation formed by drawing. **2** an amount drawn from a fund.

drawing board *noun* **1** a board to which paper is attached for drawing on. **2** a planning stage: *a project still on the drawing board.* ✳ **back to the drawing board** back to the planning stage after failure.

drawing pin *noun Brit* a pin with a broad flat head used *esp* to fasten sheets of paper to boards.

drawing room *noun* **1** a formal reception room. **2** *dated* = LIVING ROOM. [short for *withdrawing room*, a private room into which the family could withdraw from more public parts of the house]

drawknife *noun* (*pl* **drawknives**) a woodworker's tool that has a blade with a handle at each end and is used for shaving off surfaces.

drawl¹ /drawl/ *verb intrans* to speak slowly and often affectedly, with vowels greatly prolonged. ➤ *verb trans* to utter (something) in this way. ➤➤ **drawler** *noun.* [prob frequentative of DRAW¹]

drawl² *noun* a drawling manner of speaking. ➤➤ **drawly** *adj.*

drawn¹ /drawn/ *verb* past part. of DRAW¹.

drawn² *adj* **1** looking strained, tired, or ill: *Her face was drawn with sorrow.* **2** said of a game, competition, etc: ended in a draw.

drawn-thread work *noun* = DRAWN-WORK.

drawn-work *noun* decoration on cloth made by drawing out threads according to a pattern.

draw off *verb trans* to remove (liquid). ➤ *verb intrans* said of troops: to move apart and regroup.

draw on *verb intrans* to approach: *Night draws on.*

draw out *verb trans* **1** to remove or extract (something). **2** to extend (a process) beyond its normal or expected duration. **3** to encourage (somebody) to speak freely. ➤ *verb intrans* said of successive days: to grow longer at the end of winter.

drawstring *noun* a string or tape, usu threaded through a casing, that can be pulled to close an opening, e.g. of a bag, or gather material, e.g. of curtains or clothes.

draw up *verb trans* **1** to produce a version of (a formal document). **2** to straighten (oneself) to an upright posture, *esp* to show dignity or resentment. **3** to bring (somebody or something) to a halt. **4** to bring (fighting troops) into readiness for battle. ➤ *verb intrans* to come to a halt.

dray¹ /dray/ *noun* a strong low cart or wagon without sides, used *esp* by brewers. [Middle English *draye*, a wheelless vehicle, from Old English *drǣge* dragnet; related to Old English *dragan* DRAW¹]

dray² *noun* see DREY.

dread[1] /dred/ *verb trans* **1** to be extremely apprehensive about (something). **2** to fear (something or somebody) greatly. **3** *archaic* to be in great awe of (somebody). ➤ **dreaded** *adj.* [Middle English *dreden*, from Old English *drǣdan*]

dread[2] *noun* **1a** great fear, uneasiness, or apprehension. **b** something that causes this. **2a** *informal* a Rastafarian. **b** (*in pl*) dreadlocks. **3** *archaic* great reverence.

dread[3] *adj* **1** greatly feared. **2** *archaic* held in great reverence. [Middle English *dred*, past part. of *dreden*: see DREAD[1]]

dreadful /'dredf(ə)l/ *adj* **1a** extremely unpleasant or shocking: *What a dreadful thing to say!* **b** very disagreeable, e.g. through dullness or poor quality: *a dreadful film.* **2** extreme: *a dreadful mess.* **3** causing or inspiring dread. ➤ **dreadfully** *adv*, **dreadfulness** *noun*.

dreadlocks /'dredloks/ *pl noun* long matted, plaited, or tightly curled locks of hair worn *esp* by male Rastafarians.

dreadnought /'drednawt/ *noun* **1** a battleship whose main armament consists of big guns of the same calibre. **2** *archaic* a type of heavy overcoat worn *esp* in the 19th cent. **3** *archaic* a brave or fearless person. [(sense 1) *Dreadnought*, Brit battleship, the first of this type, launched in 1906]

dream[1] /dreem/ *noun* **1** a series of thoughts, images, or emotions occurring during sleep. **2** a state of absentmindedness; a daydream: *She walked round in a dream all day.* **3a** a strongly desired goal; an ambition: *His dream of becoming president.* **b** (*used before a noun*) representing the realization of an ambition; perfect: *a dream house.* **4** something notable for its beauty, excellence, or enjoyable quality: *The new car goes like a dream.* ➤ **dreamful** *adj*, **dreamless** *adj*, **dreamlike** *adj.* [Old English *drēam* noise, joy]

dream[2] *verb* (*past tense and past part.* **dreamed** *or* **dreamt** /dremt/) ➤ *verb intrans* **1** to have a dream. **2** to indulge in daydreams or fantasies: *dreaming of a better future.* ➤ *verb trans* **1** to have a dream of (something): *I dreamed I was back at school.* **2** to consider (something) as a possibility; to imagine (it): *She never dreamed he would refuse.* **3** (+ away) to pass (time) in reverie or inaction. ✳ **wouldn't dream of** wouldn't consider even the possibility of (doing something): *We wouldn't dream of disturbing you.* ➤ **dreamer** *noun*.

dreamboat *noun informal, dated* a highly attractive person, *esp* a man.

dreamland *noun* **1** an unreal delightful region existing only in imagination or in fantasy. **2** *informal* sleep.

dreamt /dremt/ *verb* past tense and past part. of DREAM[2].

dreamtime *or* **Dreamtime** *noun* = ALCHERINGA.

dream up *verb trans informal* to devise or invent (something).

dreamy *adj* (**dreamier, dreamiest**) **1** pleasantly abstracted from immediate reality. **2** given to dreaming or fantasy: *a dreamy child.* **3** suggestive of a dream in vague or visionary quality. **4** *informal* delightful; very pleasing or attractive. ➤ **dreamily** *adv*, **dreaminess** *noun*.

drear /driə/ *adj literary* dreary. [short for DREARY]

dreary *adj* (**drearier, dreariest**) causing feelings of cheerlessness or gloom; dull. ➤ **drearily** *adv*, **dreariness** *noun.* [Old English *drēorig* sad, bloody, from *drēor* gore]

dredge[1] /drej/ *noun* **1** a machine for removing earth, mud, etc, usu by buckets on an endless chain or a suction tube. **2** an oblong frame with an attached net for gathering fish, shellfish, etc from the bottom of the sea, a river, etc. [prob from Scots *dreg-*, in *dregbot* dredger, 'dredge boat']

dredge[2] *verb trans* **1** (*often* + up/out). **a** to dig, gather, or remove (something) with a dredge. **b** to deepen (e.g. a waterway) with a dredger or dredge. **2** *informal* (+ up) to bring (something) to light by thorough searching: *dredging up memories.* ➤ *verb intrans* to use a dredge.

dredge[3] *verb trans* to coat (food) by sprinkling with flour, sugar, etc. ➤ **dredger** *noun.* [obsolete *dredge* sweetmeat, from Old French *dragie*, via Latin from Greek *tragēma*, from *trōgein* to gnaw]

dredger *noun* a ship with an apparatus for dredging harbours, waterways, etc.

D region *noun* the lowest part of the ionosphere, occurring between about 40 and 65km (25 and 40mi) above the surface of the earth.

dregs /dregz/ *pl noun* **1** sediment contained in a liquid or deposited by it. **2** the most undesirable part: *the dregs of society.* [Middle English *dreg* from Old Norse *dregg*]

dreich /dreekh/ *adj Scot* bleak or dismal: *a dreich January morning.* [Middle English *dregh, dreich*, of Scandinavian origin]

drench[1] /drench/ *verb trans* **1** to make (something or somebody) thoroughly wet; to soak or saturate (it or them). **2** to administer a drench to (an animal). [Old English *drencan*; related to Old English *drincan* DRINK[1]]

drench[2] *noun* **1** a dose of liquid medicine. **2** *archaic* a poisonous or medicinal drink put down the throat of an animal.

drenched *adj* (*used in combinations*) covered or bathed in the specified substance: *sun-drenched beaches; a violent and blood-drenched movie.*

Dresden /'drezd(ə)n/ *noun* a type of ornate and delicately coloured porcelain made at Meissen near Dresden. ➤ **Dresden** *adj.* [named after *Dresden*, city in SE Germany]

dress[1] /dres/ *verb trans* **1a** to put clothes on (oneself or somebody else). **b** to provide (somebody) with clothing. **2a** to add decorative details or accessories to (something); to embellish (it): *dress a Christmas tree.* **b** to arrange (the hair). **c** to groom and curry (an animal). **d** to arrange goods on a display in (e.g. a shop window). **3a** to apply dressings or medicaments to (e.g. a wound). **b** to apply manure or fertilizer to (soil, land, etc). **c** to finish the surface of (e.g. timber, stone, leather or textiles). **d** to add a dressing to (a salad). **4a** to prepare (something) for use or service. **b** to prepare (a chicken, crab, etc) for cooking or eating. **c** to kill and prepare (an animal) for market. **d** to make (an artificial fishing fly). **5** to arrange (e.g. troops) in the proper alignment. ➤ *verb intrans* **1a** to put on clothing. **b** to put on or wear formal, elaborate, or fancy clothes: *Guests are expected to dress for dinner.* **2** said of troops: to form proper alignment. ✳ **dressed to kill** *informal* wearing clothes that are intended to make a dramatic impact: *In his silver Lurex catsuit and red feather boa, Graham was dressed to kill.* [Middle English *dressen* via Old French *dresser* to arrange, prepare]

dress[2] *noun* **1** a one-piece outer garment including both top and skirt for a woman or girl. **2a** everyday or ornamental covering for the human body; *esp* clothing suitable for a particular purpose or occasion: *in evening dress.* **b** (*used before a noun*) relating to, denoting, or suitable for an occasion requiring or permitting formal dress: *a dress suit.* **3** covering, adornment, or appearance appropriate or peculiar to a specified time: *18th-century dress.*

dressage /'dresahzh/ *noun* **1** the performance by a trained horse of precise movements in response to its rider. **2** the art of riding and training a horse to give such a performance. [French *dressage*, preparation, straightening, training, from Old French *dresser*: see DRESS[1]]

dress circle *noun* the first or lowest curved tier of seats in a theatre. [from the former requirement that its occupants wear evening dress]

dress down *verb trans* to reprove (somebody) severely, often publicly. ➤ *verb intrans* to wear casual or less formal clothes. ➤ **dressing down** *noun.*

dress-down *adj* relating to or denoting a day, *esp* a Friday, when less formal clothes, e.g. jeans and T-shirts, may be worn to work.

dresser[1] *noun* **1** a piece of kitchen furniture resembling a sideboard with a high back that has open shelves for holding or displaying dishes and cooking utensils. **2** *chiefly NAmer* a chest of drawers with a mirror; a dressing table. [Middle English *dressore* sideboard or table for preparing food, from early French *dresseur*, from Old French *dresser*: see DRESS[1]]

dresser[2] *noun* **1** somebody who dresses in a specified way: *a fashionable dresser.* **2** somebody who looks after stage costumes and helps actors to dress. **3** *Brit* somebody who assists a surgeon during an operation, e.g. by passing instruments or dressings.

dressing *noun* **1a** a usu cold sauce for adding to food, *esp* salads. **b** *chiefly NAmer* a seasoned mixture used as stuffing, e.g. for poultry. **2** material applied to cover a wound, sore, etc. **3** manure or compost to improve the growth of plants. **4** a substance used to stiffen fabrics in the finishing process.

dressing gown *noun* a loose robe worn *esp* over nightclothes or when not fully dressed.

dressing room *noun* **1** a room used chiefly for dressing, *esp* a room in a theatre for changing costumes and make-up or a communal room where sports players change into their kit. **2** a small room, often one off a bedroom, where clothes, shoes, etc are kept.

dressing station *noun dated* a place where first aid is given to those wounded in battle.

dressing table *noun* a table usu fitted with drawers and a mirror for use while dressing, applying make-up, combing one's hair, etc.

dressmaker *noun* a person, *esp* a woman, who makes clothes for usu female clients: *If a woman really repents, she has to go to a bad dressmaker, otherwise no one believes in her* — Oscar Wilde. ⧸⧸ **dressmaking** *noun*.

dress parade *noun* a military parade in dress uniform.

dress rehearsal *noun* **1** a full rehearsal of a play in costume and with stage props shortly before the first performance. **2** a full-scale practice; = DRY RUN (1).

dress sense *noun* taste in choosing and wearing clothes that fit well and suit the wearer.

dress shield *noun* a waterproof piece of material attached inside a dress at the armpit to protect it from perspiration.

dress shirt *noun* a man's formal shirt, *esp* for wear with evening dress.

dress uniform *noun* a military uniform worn on formal or ceremonial occasions.

dress up *verb trans* **1a** to dress (oneself or somebody else) in good, formal, or smart clothes. **b** to dress (oneself or somebody else) in clothes suited to a particular assumed role: *The children were dressed up as pirates*. **2** to make (something) suitable for a formal occasion, e.g. by adding accessories. **3** to cause (something) to appear in a more favourable light, e.g. by distortion or exaggeration. ⧸ *verb intrans* to get dressed up.

dressy *adj* (**dressier, dressiest**) **1** said of clothes: stylish, smart, or formal. **2** said of a person: showy in dress. **3** excessively elaborate in appearance. ⧸⧸ **dressiness** *noun*.

drew /drooh/ *verb* past tense of DRAW¹.

drey *or* **dray** /dray/ *noun* (*pl* **dreys** *or* **drays**) a squirrel's nest. [origin unknown]

dribble¹ /'dribl/ *verb intrans* **1** to fall or flow in drops or in a thin intermittent stream; to trickle. **2** to let saliva trickle from the mouth; to drool. **3a** to dribble a ball in football, hockey, basketball, etc. **b** to proceed by dribbling. ⧸ *verb trans* in football, hockey, basketball, etc, to propel (a ball) by successive slight taps or bounces with the foot, stick, or hand. ⧸⧸ **dribbler** *noun*. [frequentative of *drib* to dribble, prob alteration of DRIP¹]

dribble² *noun* **1** a small trickling stream or flow. **2** a tiny or insignificant bit or quantity. **3** an act or instance of dribbling. ⧸⧸ **dribbly** *adj*.

dribs and drabs /ˌdribz ən 'drabz/ *pl noun informal* small usu scattered amounts. [*drib* prob back-formation from DRIBBLE² and *driblet* drop of liquid, trifle; *drab* prob alteration of *drib* by reduplication]

dried *verb* past tense and past part. of DRY².

drier¹ *or* **dryer** /'drie·ə/ *noun* **1** any of various machines for drying something, e.g. the hair or laundry. **2** a substance that accelerates drying, e.g. of oils and printing inks.

drier² *adj* compar of DRY¹.

driest /'drie·əst/ *adj* superl of DRY¹.

drift¹ /drift/ *verb intrans* **1a** to be carried along by a current of water or air. **b** to move or float smoothly and effortlessly. **2a** to move in a random or casual way. **b** to be carried along aimlessly: *The conversation drifted from one topic to another*. **3** said of snow etc: to pile up under the force of wind or water. **4** to deviate from a set course, plan, or adjustment. **5** (*often* + apart) to lose contact or fail to keep in touch: *We used to be close, but lately we've drifted apart*. ⧸ *verb trans* to pile (something) up in a drift.

drift² *noun* **1a** the motion or action of drifting. **b** an easy, moderate, more or less steady flow along a course. **c** an aimless course, with no attempt at direction or control. **d** a gradual shift in attitude, opinion, or emotion. **2a** the lateral motion of an aircraft or ship due to currents of air or water. **b** a slow-moving ocean current. **c** a deviation from a set course, plan, etc. **d** a deviation from a true reproduction, representation, or reading. **e** in motor racing, a controlled skid on a bend taken at high speed. **3a** a mass of snow, sand, rock debris, etc deposited by wind or water. **b** a deposit of clay, sand, gravel, and boulders transported by running water from a glacier. **4** a general underlying tendency or meaning, *esp* of what is spoken or written: *Do you get my drift?* **5** a nearly horizontal mine passage on or parallel to a vein or rock stratum. **6** *SAfr* a ford. **7** the act of driving a group of animals along, or the animals so driven.

drifty *adj*. [Old Norse *drift* snowdrift; related to Old English *drīfan* to DRIVE¹]

drifter *noun* **1** somebody who travels or moves about aimlessly. **2** a coastal fishing boat equipped with drift nets.

drift ice *noun* floating ice masses that drift with the currents in the sea.

drift net *noun* a long shallow fishing net buoyed by floats along its top edge and weighted along its bottom edge so as to hang vertically and drift with the tide. ⧸⧸ **drift netter** *noun*, **drift netting** *noun*.

driftwood *noun* wood floating on water or cast up on a shore or beach.

drill¹ /dril/ *verb trans* **1a** to make (e.g. a hole) by piercing action. **b** to bore or drive a hole in (something) by piercing action, *esp* with a drill. **2a** to fix (something) in the mind or behaviour of somebody by repetitive instruction. **b** to train or exercise (somebody) in military drill. **3** *informal* to hit (e.g. a ball) to make it travel fast and straight. ⧸ *verb intrans* **1** to make a hole with a drill. **2** to engage in drill, *esp* military drill. ⧸⧸ **driller** *noun*. [Dutch *drillen* to bore, whirl]

drill² *noun* **1** a tool with an edged or pointed end for making a hole in a solid substance by revolving or by a succession of blows. **2** military training in marching, parade movements, and the handling of arms. **3** a physical or mental exercise aimed at improving facility and skill by regular practice. **4** *chiefly Brit, informal* the approved or correct procedure for accomplishing something efficiently: *learn the drill*. **5** a marine snail that bores through the shells and eats the flesh of oysters: *Urosalpinx cinerea*.

drill³ *noun* **1a** a shallow furrow into which seed is sown. **b** a row of seed sown in such a furrow. **2** a planting implement that makes holes or furrows, drops in the seed and sometimes fertilizer, and covers them with earth. [perhaps from DRILL¹]

drill⁴ *verb trans* to sow (seeds) by dropping them along a shallow furrow.

drill⁵ *noun* a durable cotton fabric in twill weave. [short for *drilling* from German *drillich* fabric woven with a threefold thread, from Latin *trilic-, trilix*, from TRI- + *licium* thread]

drill⁶ *noun* a W African baboon closely related to the mandrills: *Mandrillus leucophaeus*. [prob native name in W Africa]

drilling rig *noun* the structure, equipment, and machinery used to drill an oil well.

drillmaster *noun* **1** an instructor in military drill, usu a non-commissioned officer. **2** an instructor with a strict manner, *esp* one who stresses trivial points.

drill sergeant *noun* = DRILLMASTER (1).

drily *or* **dryly** /'drieli/ *adv* **1** in a subtly or understatedly ironic or humorous way. **2** in a dry manner or condition.

drink¹ /dringk/ *verb* (*past tense* **drank** /drangk/, *past part.* **drunk** /drungk/) ⧸ *verb trans* **1a** to swallow (a liquid), usu for refreshment or nourishment. **b** to take in or suck up (something); to absorb (it): *drinking air into his lungs*. **c** (+ in) to take in or receive (something) avidly: *She drank in every word of the lecture*. **2** to join in (a toast) by raising one's glass and drinking from it. **3** to bring (oneself or something else) to a specified state by drinking alcohol: *He drank himself into oblivion*; *She tried to drink her troubles away*. ⧸ *verb intrans* **1** to take liquid into the mouth and swallow it. **2** to drink alcohol, *esp* habitually or to excess: *In a few ill-chosen words she told the cook that she drank* — Saki. ✳ **drink like a fish** to drink alcohol habitually to excess. **drink to** to drink a toast to (somebody, a person's health, etc). [Old English *drincan*]

drink² *noun* **1a** liquid suitable for drinking. **b** alcoholic drink. **2** a draught or portion of liquid for drinking. **3** excessive consumption of alcohol. **4** (**the drink**) *informal* the sea or ocean, or any sizable body of water.

drinkable *adj* said *esp* of water: suitable or safe for drinking.

drink-driving *noun Brit* the crime of driving a vehicle while under the influence of alcohol. ⧸⧸ **drink-driver** *noun*.

drinker *noun* **1** somebody who drinks, *esp* one who drinks alcohol to excess. **2** a device that provides water for domestic animals or poultry.

drinking chocolate *noun* **1** a mixture of cocoa powder, dried milk, and sugar. **2** a drink made by adding hot water to this mixture.

drinking fountain *noun* a fixture with a nozzle that delivers a stream of water for drinking.

drinking problem *noun* an inability to consume only moderate amounts of alcohol, sometimes verging on alcoholism.

drinking water *noun* water that is fit for human beings to drink.

drink problem *noun* = DRINKING PROBLEM.

drink up *verb trans and intrans* **1** to finish (a drink): *Let's drink up and go.* **2** to absorb (liquid): *The dry soil drank up the rain in no time.*

drip[1] /drip/ *verb* (**dripped, dripping**) ➤ *verb trans* to let (liquid) fall in drops. ➤ *verb intrans* **1** to let drops of liquid fall: *The tap dripped all night.* **2** to fall in drops. **3** to overflow as if with moisture: *a novel that drips with sentimentality.* [Old English *dryppan*; related to Old English *dropa* DROP[1]]

drip[2] *noun* **1a** a drop of liquid, or liquid that falls in drops. **b** the action or sound of falling in drops. **2** a projection for throwing off rainwater. **3a** a device used in medicine to administer a liquid, e.g. drugs or nutrients in solution, at a slow rate, *esp* into a vein. **b** a substance administered by means of a drip: *a saline drip.* **4** *informal* a dull, weak, or insipid person. ➤➤ **dripless** *adj*.

drip-dry *verb dated* said of a fabric or garment: to dry with few or no creases when hung up dripping wet. ➤➤ **drip-dry** *adj*.

drip-feed[1] *noun* = DRIP[2] (3).

drip-feed[2] *verb trans* to feed (a patient) by means of a drip.

dripping[1] *noun* **1** the fat that runs out from meat during roasting. **2** (*in pl*) liquid that falls in drops, *esp* melted wax, fat, etc.

dripping[2] *adj* extremely wet.

drippy *adj* (**drippier, drippiest**) **1** *informal* weak, insipid, or mawkish. **2** inclined to drip.

dripstone *noun* **1** a stone projection, e.g. over a window, for throwing off rainwater. **2** calcium carbonate in the form of stalactites or stalagmites.

drive[1] /driev/ *verb* (*past tense* **drove** /drohv/, *past part.* **driven** /'driv(ə)n/) ➤ *verb trans* **1a** to control and direct the course of (a vehicle). **b** to convey or transport (somebody or something) in a vehicle. **2a** to set (something) in motion by physical force. **b** to force (something) into position by blows: *drive a nail into the wall.* **c** to cause (something or somebody) to go by force, authority, or influence: *drive the enemy back.* **d** to keep (something) in motion or operation: *drive machinery by electricity.* **3** to cause (draught animals, game, cattle, etc) to move in a desired direction. **4a** to exert inescapable or persuasive pressure on (somebody); to force (them). **b** to compel (somebody) to undergo or suffer a change, e.g. in situation, awareness, or emotional state: *It's driving me crazy.* **c** to urge (somebody) relentlessly to continuous exertion. **5** to transact or execute (something) energetically: *They drove a hard bargain.* **6a** to propel (a ball, shuttlecock, etc) swiftly. **b** to play a drive in cricket or golf at (a ball). **7** to bore (e.g. a tunnel or passage). ➤ *verb intrans* **1** to operate a vehicle. **2** to rush or dash with great speed, force, or momentum, *esp* against an obstruction: *rain driving against the windscreen.* **3** to drive a ball or other object of play. ✳ **be driving at** to imply (something) as an ultimate meaning or conclusion: *I couldn't work out what she was driving at.* ➤➤ **drivable** *adj*, **driveable** *adj*. [Old English *drīfan*]

drive[2] *noun* **1** a journey or trip in a vehicle *esp* a car: *ten minutes' drive from the airport.* **2** a private road giving access from a public right of way to a building, *esp* a surfaced path leading from a public road to a private house. **3a** a motivating instinctual need or acquired desire: *sex drive.* **b** great zeal in pursuing one's ends: *She lacks drive.* **4** a strong systematic group effort; a campaign. **5** a military offensive or expansionist move. **6a** the means for giving motion to a machine or part: *a chain drive.* **b** the means by which or position from which the movement of a motor vehicle is controlled or directed: *a four-wheel drive; a left-hand drive.* **7** = DISK DRIVE. **8a** the act or an instance of driving a ball, shuttlecock, etc. **b** an attacking cricket stroke played conventionally with a straight bat and designed to send the ball in front of the batsman's wicket. **c** a long golf shot, *esp* one played with a driver from the tee. **9** *Brit* a gathering of people to play a specified indoor game: *a whist drive.* **10** a shoot in which the game is driven within the range of the guns.

drive-by[1] *noun* (*pl* **drive-bys**) *informal* the act or an instance of committing a crime, *esp* a shooting, from a moving vehicle.

drive-by[2] *adj* said of a crime: committed from a moving vehicle.

drive-in[1] *adj* relating to or denoting a bank, cinema, restaurant, etc that people can use while remaining in their cars.

drive-in[2] *noun* a drive-in restaurant, cinema, bank, etc.

drivel[1] /'drivl/ *verb intrans* (**drivelled, drivelling,** *NAmer* **driveled, driveling**) **1** to talk foolish or childish nonsense. **2** *archaic* to let saliva dribble from the mouth or mucus run from the nose. ➤➤ **driveller** *noun*. [Old English *dreflian*]

drivel[2] *noun* foolish or childish nonsense: *It was simply a conglomeration of incoherent drivel from beginning to end* — Mark Twain.

driven[1] /'driv(ə)n/ *verb* past part. of DRIVE[1].

driven[2] *adj* **1** influenced chiefly by; geared to: *export-driven; customer-driven.* **2** worked by or responding to a specified type of computer action: *menu-driven software, command-driven programs.*

driver *noun* **1** somebody who drives a vehicle. **2** somebody who drives animals. **3** a golf club with a wooden head and a nearly vertical face used to hit the ball long distances, *esp* from the tee. **4** an implement, e.g. a hammer, for driving. **5** a mechanical piece for imparting motion to another piece. **6** a piece of computer software that controls a piece of hardware: *a printer driver.* ✳ **in the driver's seat** in a position of authority or control. ➤➤ **driverless** *adj*.

driver ant *noun* = ARMY ANT.

drive shaft *noun* = PROPELLER SHAFT.

drive-through *or* **drive-thru** *adj* relating to or denoting a restaurant, bank, etc providing a relatively quick service for customers who remain in their cars.

drive time *noun* either of the periods of time in the morning or the late afternoon when people are driving to or from work.

driveway *noun* = DRIVE[2] (2).

driving *adj* **1** communicating power or force: *a driving wheel.* **2** having great force: *driving rain.* **3** acting with vigour; energetic: *driving ambition.* **4** relating to or used in the driving of a vehicle: *She's just passed her driving test.* ✳ **in the driving seat** in a position of authority or control.

driving range *noun* an area equipped with distance markers, clubs, balls, and tees for practising golf drives.

drizzle[1] /'driz(ə)l/ *verb intrans* to rain in very small drops or very lightly. ➤ *verb trans* to let (liquid) fall in minute drops or a thin stream: *drizzle oil over the salad.* [perhaps ultimately from Old English *dreosan* to fall]

drizzle[2] *noun* a fine misty rain. ➤➤ **drizzly** *adj*.

drogue /drohg/ *noun* **1** a small parachute for stabilizing or decelerating something or for pulling a larger parachute out of stowage. **2** = SEA ANCHOR. [prob alteration of DRAG[2]]

droll /drohl/ *adj* humorous, whimsical, or amusing, *esp* in an odd way. ➤➤ **drollness** *noun*, **drolly** *adv*. [French *drôle*, ultimately from early Dutch *drolle* imp]

drollery *noun* (*pl* **drolleries**) **1** the act or an instance of jesting or droll behaviour. **2** droll humour.

-drome *comb. form* forming nouns, denoting: **1** something that runs in a specified direction: *palindrome; loxodrome.* **2** a place where a specified type of racing is held: *velodrome; hippodrome.* **3** a large place where a specified activity goes on or that has the purpose specified: *aerodrome.* [Greek *-dromos*, from *dromos* course, racecourse, act of running; (senses 2,3) early French *-drome*, from Latin *-dromus*, from Greek *dromos*]

dromedary /'dromǝd(ǝ)ri/ *noun* (*pl* **dromedaries**) a one-humped camel of W Asia and N Africa, *esp* one bred or trained for riding or racing: *Camelus dromedarius: I shall be sitting in a gondola or on a dromedary* — Henry James. [Middle English *dromedarie* via French and late Latin from Greek *dromad-, dromas* running]

drone[1] /drohn/ *noun* **1** the male bee, *esp* a honeybee, that has no sting and whose sole function is to mate with the queen. **2** somebody who lives off others. **3** a remotely-controlled pilotless aircraft, missile, or ship. **4** a droning sound. **5** any of the usu three pipes on a set of bagpipes that sound fixed continuous notes. **6** an unvarying sustained bass note. [Old English *drān*]

drone[2] *verb intrans* **1** to make a sustained deep murmuring or buzzing sound. **2** (*often* + on) to talk persistently and tediously in a monotonous tone. ➤➤ **droning** *adj*, **droningly** *adv*.

drongo[1] /'dronggoh/ *noun* (*pl* **drongos**) any of several species of insect-eating songbirds of tropical India, Africa, and Australia that typically have glossy black plumage and a long forked tail: family Dicruridae. [Malagasy]

drongo² *noun* (*pl* **drongos** *or* **drongoes**) *chiefly Aus, informal* a worthless person; a fool. [perhaps from *Drongo*, name of an unsuccessful Australian racehorse]

drool /droohl/ *verb intrans* **1a** to secrete saliva in anticipation of food. **b** to let saliva dribble from the mouth. **2** (*often* + over) to make an excessive or effusive show of pleasure: *He stood drooling over the cars in the showroom.* [perhaps alteration of DRIVEL¹]

droop¹ /droohp/ *verb intrans* **1** to hang or bend downwards; to sag. **2** to become tired, weakened, or depressed. ➤ *verb trans* to let (something) droop. [Middle English *drupen* from Old Norse *drūpa*; related to Old English *dropa* DROP¹]

droop² *noun* the condition or appearance of drooping. ➤➤ **droopily** *adv*, **droopiness** *noun*, **droopy** *adj*.

drop¹ /drop/ *noun* **1a** a round or pear-shaped mass of falling liquid. **b** the quantity of liquid that falls in such a mass. **2** (*in pl*) a dose of medicine measured or administered by drops. **3a** a minute quantity: *a drop of pity.* **b** the smallest quantity of liquid: *There's not a drop of milk in the house.* **c** a small quantity of drink, *esp* alcohol: *Would you like a drop more?* **4a** an ornament resembling a drop of liquid that hangs from a piece of jewellery, e.g. an earring. **b** a small globular sweet or medicated lozenge: *pear drop.* **5a** the act or an instance of dropping; a fall. **b** a decline in quantity or quality. **6a** the distance from a higher to a lower level or through which something drops. **b** the quantity by which something decreases. **7a** something that drops, hangs, or falls. **b** an unframed piece of cloth stage scenery. **c** a hinged platform on a gallows. **8** a parachute descent, or the people or things dropped by parachute. **9** *NAmer* a central point or depository to which something, e.g. mail, is brought for distribution. **10** *slang* a secret place used for the deposit and collection of letters or stolen or illegal goods. ✳ **a drop in the ocean/a bucket** something much too small to have any effect. **at the drop of a hat** without hesitation; promptly. **have/get the drop on** *chiefly NAmer*, *slang* to have or get an advantage over somebody [orig to be in a position to attack or fire on an opponent from above]. [Old English *dropa*]

drop² *verb* (**dropped, dropping**) ➤ *verb intrans* **1** to fall in drops. **2** to fall vertically. **3a** to become less: *Production has dropped.* **b** said of the voice: to be lowered. **4** to fall in a state of collapse or death: *He'll work until he drops.* **5** to cease to be of concern; to lapse: *let the matter drop.* **6** (+ by/in/over/round) to pay a brief informal visit. ➤ *verb trans* **1** to let (something) fall vertically. **2a** to lower (something) from one level or position to another. **b** to cause (something) to lessen or decrease: *He gradually dropped his speed.* **3a** to set (passengers, cargo, etc) down from a vehicle, ship, or aircraft. **b** to deliver or unload (supplies, troops, etc) by parachute. **4a** to give up or abandon (an idea, charge, etc). **b** to interrupt (an activity or task) for a while: *When I heard the car I dropped what I was doing.* **c** to break off an association or connection with (somebody): *She has dropped all her old friends.* **d** to leave (somebody) out of a team or group. **e** to leave (something) out of a written text. **5a** to utter or mention (something) in a casual way: *Did they drop a hint at all?* **b** to send (an informal message) by post: *Drop us a line soon.* **6a** to bring (something or somebody) down with a shot or blow. **b** in bridge, to play (a high card) without winning the trick, because of having to follow suit. **c** in rugby, to score (a goal) with a drop kick. **d** to hit (a ball, shuttlecock, etc) with a drop shot. **7** to lose (a point or game) in a series. **8** *informal* to take (an illegal drug) orally. **9** said of an animal: to give birth to (young). ✳ **drop a brick** *informal* to make an indiscreet remark. **drop a clanger** *Brit, informal* to make an embarrassing mistake. **drop dead** to die suddenly in the course of ordinary activities. **drop one's aitches** to omit the sound of 'h' at the beginning of a word that is spelt with one. **drop one's guard** to suspend one's vigilance or wariness.

drop back *verb intrans* to move into a position further back, *esp* by moving towards the rear of an advancing line or column.

drop behind *verb intrans* to fail to keep up with the rest of a group.

drop curtain *noun* a stage curtain that can be lowered and raised.

drop-dead *adv informal* impressively or extremely: *drop-dead gorgeous.*

drop-forge *verb trans* to forge (something) between two dies using a drop hammer or similar. ➤➤ **drop forger** *noun*, **drop forging** *noun*.

drop goal *noun* a score in rugby made by drop-kicking the ball over the goal's crossbar.

drop hammer *noun* a power hammer or heavy weight raised and then released to drop on hot metal resting on an anvil or die.

drop handlebars *pl noun* lowered curving handlebars, *esp* on a racing bicycle.

drop kick *noun* **1** a kick made, e.g. in rugby, by dropping a ball to the ground and kicking it at the moment it starts to rebound. **2** in wrestling, martial arts, etc, a kick made after jumping into the air.

drop-kick *verb trans* to kick (something or somebody) with a drop kick.

drop leaf *noun* **1** a hinged flap on the side or end of a table that can be folded down. **2** (*used before a noun*) having such a flap or flaps: *a drop-leaf table.*

droplet /'droplit/ *noun* a small drop of liquid.

drop off *verb intrans* **1** to fall asleep, *esp* unintentionally. **2** to decline or slump: *Demand for souvenir flags dropped off after the royal visit.*

drop-off *noun* **1** a marked dwindling or decline: *a drop-off in attendance.* **2** *NAmer* a very steep or perpendicular descent.

dropout *noun* **1** somebody who rejects or withdraws from participation in conventional society. **2** a student who fails to complete or withdraws from a course, usu of higher education. **3** a spot on a magnetic tape from which data has disappeared. **4** a drop kick awarded to the defending team in rugby, e.g. after an unconverted try.

drop out *verb intrans* **1a** to withdraw from participation. **b** to fail to complete a course of study. **2** to adopt an alternative lifestyle. **3** in rugby, to make a dropout.

dropper *noun* a short usu glass tube fitted with a rubber bulb and used to measure or administer liquids by drops. [DROP² + -ER²]

droppings *pl noun* animal excrement, e.g. from mice, rabbits, or birds.

drop scone *noun* a small round cake made by dropping a spoonful of batter onto a hot griddle. Also called SCOTCH PANCAKE.

drop shot *noun* a delicate shot in tennis, badminton, squash, etc that drops quickly after crossing the net or dies after hitting a wall.

dropsy /'dropsi/ *noun dated* = OEDEMA. ➤➤ **dropsical** *adj*. [Middle English *dropesie*, short for *ydropesie*, via Old French and Latin from Greek *hydrōps*, from *hydōr* water]

droshky /'droshki/ *or* **drosky** /'droski/ *noun* (*pl* **droshkies** *or* **droskies**) a four-wheeled open carriage used *esp* in Russia and Poland in former times. [Russian *drozhki*, from *droga* pole of a wagon; related to Old English *dragan* DRAW¹]

drosophila /dro'sofilə/ *noun* (*pl* **drosophilas** *or* **drosophilae** /-lee/) any of a genus of small two-winged fruit flies extensively used in genetic research: genus *Drosophila.* [Latin *Drosophila*, genus name, from Greek *drosos* dew + scientific Latin *-phila*, fem of *-philus* -PHILE]

dross /dros/ *noun* **1** the scum on the surface of molten metal. **2** waste, rubbish, or foreign matter; impurities. ➤➤ **drossy** *adj*. [Old English *drōs* dregs]

drought /drowt/ *noun* **1** a prolonged period of dryness or lack of rainfall. **2** a prolonged shortage of something. ➤➤ **droughty** *adj*. [Old English *drūgath*, from *drūgian* to dry up; related to Old English *drȳge* DRY¹]

drove¹ /drohv/ *noun* **1** a group of animals driven or moving together. **2** (*also in pl*) a crowd of people moving or acting together: *Bargain hunters arrived in droves.* [Old English *drāf*, from *drīfan* DRIVE¹]

drove² *verb trans* to drive (cattle, sheep, etc) over a long distance, usu to market. ➤ *verb intrans* to work as a drover.

drove³ *verb* past tense of DRIVE¹.

drover *noun* somebody who drives cattle or sheep.

drown /drown/ *verb intrans* to die through suffocation by submersion, *esp* in water. ➤ *verb trans* **1a** to cause (somebody or something) to drown. **b** to submerge (something), *esp* by a rise in the water level: *Prolonged flooding drowned the village.* **c** to wet (something) thoroughly; to drench (it): *She drowned the chips with ketchup.* **2** to engage (oneself) deeply and strenuously: *He drowned himself in work.* **3** (*often* + out) to cause (a sound) not to be heard by making a loud noise: *His speech was drowned out by boos* — New Yorker. ✳ **drown one's sorrows** to attempt to forget or get rid of problems, cares, etc by drinking alcohol. [Middle English *drounen*, prob of Scandinavian origin]

drowse[1] /drowz/ *verb intrans* to sleep lightly; to doze. [back-formation from DROWSY]

drowse[2] *noun* **1** the act or an instance of drowsing. **2** a state of drowsiness.

drowsy *adj* (**drowsier, drowsiest**) **1** sleepy. **2** tending to induce sleepiness: *a drowsy summer afternoon.* **3** lazy or lethargic. **➤➤ drowsily** *adv,* **drowsiness** *noun.* [prob from Old English *drūsian* to be sluggish]

drub /drub/ *verb trans* (**drubbed, drubbing**) **1** to beat (somebody) severely. **2** to defeat (somebody) decisively. **➤➤ drubbing** *noun.* [perhaps from Arabic *ḍaraba*]

drudge[1] /druj/ *noun* a person who does hard, menial, routine, or monotonous work. [Middle English *druggen*; prob related to Old English *drēogan* to work, endure]

drudge[2] *verb intrans archaic* to work as a drudge. **➤➤ drudger** *noun,* **drudgery** /ˈdrujəri/ *noun.*

drug[1] /drug/ *noun* **1** a substance intended for use in the diagnosis, cure, treatment, or prevention of disease. **2** a substance that has a particular effect on the body, e.g. a stimulant or relaxant. **3** something that causes addiction or habituation. **✳ drug on the market** a commodity that will not sell, usu owing to a glut. [Middle English *drogges, drouges,* pl, from Old French *drogue*]

drug[2] *verb trans* (**drugged, drugging**) **1** to adulterate (something, e.g. a drink) with a drug. **2** to administer a drug to (a person or animal). **3** to lull or stupefy (somebody) with or as if with a drug.

drug-driving *noun* the crime of driving a vehicle while under the influence of drugs. **➤➤ drug-driver** *noun.*

drugget /ˈdrugit/ *noun* a coarse durable cloth used chiefly as a floor covering. [early French *droguet,* dimin. of *drogue* trash, drug]

druggie or **druggy** /ˈdrugi/ *noun* (*pl* **druggies**) *informal* a drug addict or frequent user of drugs. **➤➤ druggie** *adj,* **druggy** *adj.*

druggist /ˈdrugist/ *noun* **1** somebody who deals in or dispenses drugs and medicines; a pharmacist. **2** *NAmer* the owner or manager of a drugstore.

druggy *noun* see DRUGGIE.

drug rape *noun* rape carried out while the victim is under the influence of a sedative and often amnesia-inducing drug such as Rohypnol that has been surreptitiously administered to them.

drugstore *noun chiefly NAmer* a chemist's shop, *esp* one that also sells sweets, magazines, and refreshments.

druid /ˈdrooh·id/ or **druidess** /-dis/ *noun* (*often* **Druid** or **Druidess**) a member of an ancient Celtic order of priests, often appearing in legends as magicians, or of a modern movement reviving this cult. **➤➤ druidic** /drooh'idik/ *adj,* **druidical** /drooh'idikl/ *adj,* **druidism** *noun.* [Latin *druides, druidae,* pl, from Gaulish *druides*]

drum[1] /drum/ *noun* **1** a percussion instrument, usu in the form of a hollow cylinder or hemisphere with skin, plastic, or other material stretched over the opening or ends, that is played by beating with a stick, a pair of sticks, or the hands. **2** the sound made by striking a drum, or any similar sound. **3a** something resembling a drum in shape. **b** a cylindrical machine or mechanical device or part; *esp* a metal cylinder coated with magnetic material on which data, e.g. for a computer, may be recorded. **c** a cylindrical container, *esp* a large metal container for liquids, e.g. oil. **d** in architecture, a cylindrical block of stone or circular structure. **4** = EARDRUM. **5** any of several species of spiny-finned fishes that make a drumming noise: family Sciaenidae. **6** *informal* a dwelling; = PAD[1] (5). **7** *Aus, informal* a brothel. **8** *Aus, informal* a piece of information: *Give them the drum.* **9** *archaic* a drummer. **✳ beat/bang the drum for** to support, promote, or publicize (something) with great enthusiasm or vigour. **➤➤ drumlike** *adj.* [prob from Dutch *trom*]

drum[2] *verb* (**drummed, drumming**) **➤** *verb intrans* **1** to beat a drum. **2** to make a succession of strokes, taps, or vibrations that produce drumlike sounds. **3** to throb or sound rhythmically: *Blood drummed in his ears.* **➤** *verb trans* **1a** to strike or tap (something) repeatedly. **b** to produce (rhythmic sounds) by such action. **c** to cause (something) to make such sounds: *drumming her fingers on the desk.* **2** to summon or enlist (somebody), orig by beating a drum: *drum them into service.* **3** (*usu* + into) to instil (an idea or lesson) by constant repetition: *The rules were drummed into us as children.*

drum and bass /ˈdrum ən ˈbays/ *noun* a type of modern dance music characterized by fast insistent drum beats with complex percussion break patterns and low bass lines.

drumbeat *noun* a stroke on a drum or its sound.

drum brake *noun* a brake that operates by the friction of pads pressing against a rotating drum.

drumfire *noun* artillery fire so continuous as to sound like a rapid succession of drumbeats.

drumfish *noun* (*pl* **drumfishes** or *collectively* **drumfish**) = DRUM[1] (5).

drumhead *noun* **1** the material stretched over the end of a drum. **2** the top part of a capstan. **3** a type of cabbage with a flat top.

drum kit *noun* a set of drums and other percussion instruments usu played by a single player, e.g. in a rock band.

drumlin /ˈdrumlin/ *noun* an elongated or oval hill formed from glacial debris. [Irish Gaelic *druim* back, ridge (from Old Irish *druimm*) + English *-lin,* alteration of -LING]

drum major *noun* the marching leader of a band, *esp* a non-commissioned officer in charge of the corps of drums in a military band.

drum majorette *noun* a girl or young woman who twirls a baton while leading or accompanying a procession or marching band.

drummer /ˈdrumə/ *noun* **1** somebody who plays a drum. **2** *chiefly NAmer* a travelling sales representative.

drum'n'bass /drumənˈbays/ *noun* = DRUM AND BASS.

drum out *verb trans* to dismiss (somebody) ignominiously; to expel (them) usu for some misdemeanour: *He was drummed out of the army.*

drum roll *noun* a succession of drum beats played so quickly that they sound like a continuous noise, often used to announce or introduce somebody or something.

drumstick *noun* **1** a stick for beating a drum. **2** the part of a fowl's leg between the thigh and foot when cooked as food.

drum up *verb trans* **1** to obtain (something) by canvassing, soliciting, or persistent effort: *drum up some business.* **2** to invent or originate (something): *drum up a new time-saving method.*

drunk[1] /drungk/ *verb* past part. of DRINK[1].

drunk[2] *adj* **1** under the influence of alcohol. **2** dominated by an intense feeling: *drunk with power.* **3** = DRUNKEN (2B). [Middle English *drunke,* alteration of DRUNKEN]

drunk[3] *noun* **1** a person who is drunk, *esp* habitually. **2** *informal* a bout of drinking alcohol.

drunkard /ˈdrungkəd/ *noun* a person who is habitually drunk: *The rolling English drunkard made the rolling English road — G K Chesterton.*

drunken /ˈdrungk(ə)n/ *adj* **1** = DRUNK[2] (1). **2a** given to habitual excessive use of alcohol. **b** of, characterized by, or resulting from alcoholic intoxication: *a drunken brawl.* **➤➤ drunkenly** *adv,* **drunkenness** *noun.* [Middle English from Old English *druncen,* past part. of *drincan* DRINK[1]]

drupe /droohp/ *noun* a fruit, e.g. a cherry or plum, that has a stone enclosed by a fleshy layer and is usu covered by a thin skin. **➤➤ drupaceous** /drooh'payshəs/ *adj.* [scientific Latin *drupa,* from Latin, overripe olive, from Greek *dryppa* olive]

drupel /ˈdroohpl/ *noun* = DRUPELET.

drupelet /ˈdroohplit/ *noun* any of the small drupes that together form an aggregate fruit such as a raspberry.

Druze or **Druse** /droohz/ *noun* (*pl* **Druzes** or **Druses** or *collectively* **Druze** or **Druse**) a member of a religious sect originating among Muslims and centred in the mountains of Lebanon and Syria. [Arabic *Durūz,* pl, named after Muḥammed ibn-Ismā'īlal-*Darazīy* d.1019, Muslim religious leader who founded the sect]

dry[1] /drie/ *adj* (**drier** or **dryer, driest** or **dryest**) **1a** free from moisture or liquid, *esp* water. **b** not in or under water: *dry land.* **c** having little rainfall or low humidity: *a dry climate.* **2a** characterized by exhaustion of a supply of water or other liquid: *The well is dry.* **b** no longer sticky or damp: *The paint is dry.* **c** lacking natural moisture or lubrication: *a dry mouth; dry hair.* **d** *informal* thirsty. **e** marked by the absence or scantiness of secretions: *a dry cough.* **f** not shedding or accompanied by tears: *There wasn't a dry eye in the room.* **g** said of a mammal: not giving milk: *a dry cow.* **3** said of bread, toast, etc: eaten without butter or other spread. **4** prohibiting the manufacture or sale of alcoholic drinks. **5** said of wine, etc: not sweet. **6** solid as opposed to liquid: *dry goods.* **7a** not showing or communicating warmth, enthusiasm, or feeling; impassive. **b** uninteresting: *dry passages of description.* **c** lacking embellishment, bias, or emotional concern; plain: *the dry facts.* **8** marked by a matter-of-fact, ironic, or terse manner of expression: *dry wit*. **9** functioning without lubrication: *a dry clutch*. **10a** built or constructed without a process which requires water. **b** using no mortar: *dry masonry*. **c** using prefabricated materials, e.g. plasterboard, rather than a construction involving plaster or mortar: *dry wall construction*. ⟫⟫ **dryish** *adj*, **dryness** *noun*. [Old English *drȳge*]

dry² *verb* (**dries, dried, drying**) ⟫ *verb trans* **1** (*often* + out) to cause (something) to become dry. **2** to preserve (something) by removing moisture: *The company dries and cures meats*. ⟫ *verb intrans* (*often* + out) to become dry. ⟫⟫ **dryable** *adj*.

dry³ *noun* (*pl* **dries** *or* **drys**) **1a** a dry place. **b** (**the dry**) *chiefly Aus* the dry season. **2** *Brit, informal* a Conservative politician who holds hard-line or uncompromising views. **3** *NAmer* somebody who supports a ban on the sale of alcoholic drinks; a prohibitionist.

dryad /'driead, 'drie·əd/ *noun* a nymph of the woods in Greek mythology. [via Latin from Greek *dryad-, dryas*, from *drys* tree]

dry battery *noun* an electric battery consisting of a single dry cell or two or more dry cells connected together.

dry bulb *noun* an ordinary exposed thermometer bulb, *esp* as used in conjunction with a wet bulb.

dry cell *noun* a battery cell whose electrolyte is not a liquid: compare WET CELL.

dry-clean *verb trans* to clean (a fabric, garment, etc) with organic solvents rather than water. ⟫⟫ **dry cleaner** *noun*.

dry cleaning *noun* **1** the cleaning of fabrics or garments with organic solvents rather than water. **2** things that have been or are to be dry-cleaned.

dry dock *noun* a dock from which the water can be pumped to allow ships to be repaired.

dryer *noun* see DRIER¹.

dry fly *noun* an artificial angling fly designed to float on the surface of the water.

dry goods *pl noun* **1** solid as opposed to liquid commodities. **2** *NAmer* textiles, clothing, haberdashery, etc, *esp* as distinguished from hardware and groceries.

dry ice *noun* solidified carbon dioxide used *esp* as a refrigerant or to produce the theatrical effect of white mist.

dryly *adv* see DRILY.

dry measure *noun* a series of units for measurement of the capacity of dry goods.

dry out *verb trans* **1** to cause (something) to become dry. **2** *informal* to cause or help (somebody) to overcome an addiction to alcohol or drugs. ⟫ *verb intrans* **1** to become dry. **2** *informal* to overcome an addiction to alcohol or drugs.

drypoint *noun* **1** an engraving made by using a pointed tool, e.g. a needle, directly on a metal plate without the use of acid. **2** a needle or other tool used for this. **3** an engraving produced using this method.

dry riser *noun* a system of pipes in a building with outlets at certain points for distributing water or other extinguishing fluid in the event of a fire.

dry rot *noun* **1a** a decay of seasoned timber in which the cellulose of wood is consumed by fungi leaving it brittle and crumbly. **b** any of various fungi causing dry rot: *Serpula lacrymans* and other species. **2** decay from within, caused e.g. by corruption or by resistance to new forces.

dry run *noun* **1** a practice exercise; a rehearsal or trial. **2** a firing practice without ammunition.

drysalter /'driesawltə/ *noun Brit, dated* a person who sells or deals in dyes, glues, and other chemical products, and sometimes also medicines and dried, cured, or preserved foods.

dry slope *noun* an artificial ski slope covered with matting rather than snow.

drystone *adj* said of a wall: constructed of stone without the use of mortar.

drysuit *noun* a close-fitting waterproof suit worn over other clothing by participants in certain water sports: compare WET SUIT.

dry up *verb intrans* **1** to disappear or cease to yield by evaporation, draining, or the cutting off of a source of supply. **2** to wither or die. **3** to dry washed-up dishes by hand. **4** *informal* to stop talking. ⟫ *verb trans* **1** to cause (something) to dry up. **2** to dry (washed dishes) by hand.

DS *abbr* in music, dal segno. [Italian *dal segno* from the sign]

DSC *abbr Brit* Distinguished Service Cross.

DSc *abbr* Doctor of Science.

DSM *abbr Brit* Distinguished Service Medal.

DSO *abbr Brit* Distinguished Service Order.

dsp *abbr* died without issue. [Latin *decessit sine prole*]

DSS *abbr Brit* formerly, Department of Social Security.

DST *abbr* daylight saving time.

Dt *abbr* Deuteronomy (book of the Bible).

DTI *abbr Brit* Department of Trade and Industry.

DTP *abbr* desktop publishing.

dt's *or* **DT's** /dee 'teez/ *pl noun informal* = DELIRIUM TREMENS.

DTTO *abbr* drug treatment and testing order, an alternative to a custodial sentence for those convicted of drugs-related crime such as theft.

DU *abbr* depleted uranium.

dual¹ /'dyooh·əl/ *adj* **1a** consisting of two parts or elements. **b** having a double character or nature. **2** in grammar, said of a word or word form: denoting two people, things, or instances: compare PLURAL¹ (1), SINGULAR¹ (3B). **3** (*often* + to) said of a mathematical expression: related to another by interchangeable terms. ⟫⟫ **duality** /dyooh'aliti/ *noun*, **dually** *adv*. [Latin *dualis*, from *duo* two]

dual² *noun* **1** in grammar, the dual number, the inflectional form denoting it, or a word in that form. **2** in mathematics, a dual expression.

dual³ *verb trans* (**dualled, dualling**) *Brit* to convert (a road) to a dual carriageway.

dual carriageway *noun chiefly Brit* a road that has traffic travelling in two or more lanes in each direction, usu separated by a central reservation.

dualism *noun* **1** the quality or state of being dual. **2** a theory that considers reality to consist of two independent and fundamental principles, e.g. mind and matter. **3** a doctrine that the universe is ruled by the two opposing principles of good and evil. ⟫⟫ **dualist** *noun*, **dualistic** /-'listik/ *adj*, **dualistically** /-'listikli/ *adv*.

dual-purpose *adj* intended for or serving two purposes.

dual-use *adj* having two possible uses, *esp* able to be used for both non-military and military purposes.

dub¹ /dub/ *verb trans* (**dubbed, dubbing**) **1a** to call (somebody or something) by a descriptive unofficial name or nickname. **b** to confer knighthood on (somebody), *esp* by ceremonial touching on the shoulder with a sword. **2** to dress (a fishing fly). **3** to dress (leather) by rubbing it with grease. [Old English *dubbian*]

dub² *verb trans* **1a** to provide (a film, television broadcast, etc) with a new or altered soundtrack, *esp* one in a different language. **b** to match (a soundtrack) to the pictures of a film. **c** (*often* + in) to add (commentary, sound effects, music, etc) to a film or to a radio or television broadcast. **2a** *chiefly Brit* to construct (a soundtrack) out of two or more different tracks, e.g. music, sound effects, or commentary: compare MIX¹. **b** to transpose (a previous recording) to a new record. ⟫⟫ **dubbing** *noun*. [by shortening and alteration from DOUBLE⁴]

dub³ *noun* **1** the act or an instance of dubbing a soundtrack, sound effects, etc, or the sounds added. **2** a type of popular music that developed from reggae. It is characterized by the use of sparse vocals and instruments that are electronically remixed and brought to prominence and suppressed in a seemingly arbitrary way.

dubbin¹ /'dubin/ *noun* a grease made of oil and tallow used for softening and waterproofing leather. [alteration of DUBBING]

dubbin² *verb trans* (**dubbined, dubbining**) to apply dubbin to (leather).

dubbing /'dubing/ *noun* **1** = DUBBIN¹. **2** material used to make an artificial fishing fly. [DUB¹]

dubiety /dyooh'bieiti/ *noun* (*pl* **dubieties**) *formal* **1** the state of being doubtful. **2** a matter of doubt. [late Latin *dubietas*, from Latin *dubius*: see DUBIOUS]

dubious /'dyoohbi·əs/ *adj* **1** giving rise to doubt; uncertain: *They considered our proposal a little dubious*. **2** unsettled in opinion; undecided: *I'm dubious about this colour scheme*. **3** of uncertain outcome: *a rather dubious experiment*. **4** of questionable value, quality, or origin: *They won by dubious means.* ➤➤ **dubiously** *adv*, **dubiousness** *noun*. [Latin *dubius*, from *dubare* to vacillate]

Dublin Bay prawn /'dublin/ *noun* a large prawn often eaten as scampi. [named after *Dublin Bay* on the E coast of the Republic of Ireland]

dubnium /'dubni·əm/ *noun* an unstable radioactive metallic chemical element of the transactinide group, artificially produced by bombarding plutonium with high-energy atoms: symbol Db, atomic number 105. [named after *Dubna*, town in Russia]

ducal /'dyoohkl/ *adj* of a duke or duchy. ➤➤ **ducally** *adv*. [early French *ducal* from late Latin *ducalis* of a leader, from Latin *duc-, dux*: see DUKE]

ducat /'dukət/ *noun* **1** a usu gold coin formerly used in many European countries. **2** *informal* (*in pl*) money. [Middle English via French from Old Italian *ducato* coin with the doge's portrait on it, from *duca* doge, via late Greek from Latin *duc-, dux*: see DUKE]

Duchenne muscular dystrophy /'doo'shen/ *noun* a form of muscular dystrophy that usu affects only boys and begins to show between three and five years of age. [named after Guillaume *Duchenne* d.1875, French neurologist, who first described it]

duchess /'duchis/ *noun* **1** the wife or widow of a duke. **2** a woman having in her own right the rank of a duke. [Middle English from early French *duchesse*, fem of *duc*: see DUKE]

duchesse potatoes /'duchis, -ches, 'dooshes/ *pl noun* mashed potatoes mixed with egg, butter, and sometimes cream, piped on to a baking sheet and baked or browned under the grill.

duchy /'duchi/ *noun* (*pl* **duchies**) the territory of a duke or duchess; a dukedom. [Middle English *duche* from early French *duché*, from *duc*: see DUKE]

duck¹ /duk/ *noun* (*pl* **ducks** or collectively **duck**) **1a** any of several species of swimming birds that have a short neck, short legs, webbed feet, and a broad flat beak: family Anatidae. **b** the flesh of a duck used as food. **2** a female duck, which often has less distinctive or colourful plumage than the male: compare DRAKE¹. **3** *chiefly Brit, informal* (also *in pl, but treated as sing.*) an affectionate term of address used *esp* by a man to a woman. ✴ **like water off a duck's back** said of a remark, reprimand, etc: having no effect or impact at all. **take to something like a duck to water** to have a natural or instant talent or liking for something. [Old English *dūce*]

duck² *verb trans* **1** to thrust (something or somebody) momentarily under water. **2** to lower (e.g. the head), *esp* quickly as a bow or to avoid being seen or hit. **3** to avoid or evade (something): *duck the issue*. ➤ *verb intrans* **1** to plunge one's head or body under the surface of water. **2a** to lower one's head or body suddenly, e.g. to avoid being seen or hit. **b** to bow or bob. **3** to evade a duty, question, or responsibility. **4** in bridge, to play a low card for tactical reasons. ➤➤ **ducker** *noun*. [Middle English *douken*; related to Old English *dūce* DUCK¹]

duck³ *noun* the act or an instance of ducking, *esp* a sudden lowering of the head.

duck⁴ *noun* a durable usu cotton fabric with a close weave. [Dutch *doek* cloth]

duck⁵ *noun* a score of nought, *esp* in cricket: *Gower was out for a duck*. [short for *duck's egg*; from the egg-shaped number 0]

duck-billed *adj* having a snout or jaws shaped like a duck's bill: *a duck-billed dinosaur.*

duck-billed platypus *noun* = PLATYPUS.

duckboard *noun* (*usu in pl*) a wooden board or slat used to make a path over wet or muddy ground.

ducking stool *noun* a seat attached to a plank that was formerly used to punish offenders by plunging them into water.

duckling /'dukling/ *noun* a young duck.

ducks and drakes *pl noun* (*treated as sing*) the pastime of skimming flat stones along the surface of calm water. ✴ **play ducks and drakes with** to use (e.g. money) recklessly; to squander (it).

duck's arse (*NAmer* **duck's ass**) *noun informal* a hairstyle, often worn by teddy boys, in which the hair is swept back and cut so as to droop at the nape of the neck in the shape of a duck's tail.

duck soup *noun chiefly NAmer, informal* something easy to do; a cinch.

duckweed *noun* any of several genera of small free-floating stemless plants that have small rounded leaves and often cover large areas of the surface of still water: family Lemnaceae.

ducky¹ *adj* (**duckier, duckiest**) *informal* delightful; sweet. [DUCK¹ + -Y⁴]

ducky² *noun* (*pl* **duckies**) *Brit, informal* an affectionate term of address used *esp* by a man to a woman.

duct¹ /dukt/ *noun* **1a** a pipe, tube, or channel that conveys a substance. **b** a pipe or tubular channel for carrying electric power lines, telephone cables, or other conductors. **2** a bodily tube or vessel, *esp* one that carries a glandular secretion. **3** an elongated tubular cavity in plant tissue. ➤➤ **ducting** *noun*. [Latin *ductus* past part. of *ducere* to lead]

duct² *verb trans* to convey (something, e.g. air) through a duct.

ductile /'duktiel/ *adj* **1** said of metals: capable of being drawn out or hammered thin. **2** capable of being easily moulded into a new form. **3** easily led or influenced; tractable: *the ductile masses*. ➤➤ **ductility** /duk'tiliti/ *noun*. [early French *ductile*, from Latin *ductilis*, from *ductus*, past part.]

ductless gland *noun* = ENDOCRINE².

dud¹ /dud/ *noun informal* **1** something that fails to perform as it should; a bomb, missile, etc that fails to explode. **2** a counterfeit or fake. **3** a weak, spiritless, or ineffectual person. **4** (*in pl*) clothes.

Word history

(sense 4) Middle English *dudde* coarse cloak; earlier history unknown. (senses 1,2,3) and DUD² may have evolved via a 16th-cent. meaning 'rags, tatters', or may be a different word of unknown origin.

dud² *adj informal* ineffectual, counterfeit, or valueless: *dud cheques.*

dude /d(y)oohd/ *noun chiefly NAmer, informal* **1** a man: *He's a real cool dude.* **2** a man who wears fashionable or flashy clothes. **3** a city-dweller, *esp* one from the eastern USA holidaying on a ranch in the western USA. ➤➤ **dudish** *adj*, **dudishly** *adv*. [perhaps from German dialect *Dude* fool]

dude ranch *noun* an American cattle ranch converted into a holiday centre, offering activities such as camping and riding.

dudgeon /'dujən/ *noun archaic* great resentment. ✴ **in high dudgeon** in a fit or state of great indignation, resentment, or anger. [origin unknown]

due¹ /dyooh/ *adj* **1a** owed or owing as a debt. **b** payable: *The balance is now due.* **2a** owed or owing as a natural or moral right: *his due reward.* **b** proper or appropriate: *after due consideration.* **3** required or expected in the prearranged or normal course of events: *due to arrive at any time.* **4a** capable of satisfying a need, obligation, or duty. **b** regular or lawful: *due proof of loss.* ✴ **due to 1** ascribable to (somebody or something): *This advance is partly due to a few men of genius* — A N Whitehead. **2** because of (something or somebody): *The flight was delayed due to fog.* **in due course** after a normal passage of time; in the expected or allocated time. [Middle English from early French *deu*, past part. of *devoir* to owe, from Latin *debēre*]

Usage note

due to or owing to? The traditional rule of thumb regarding the use of these two phrases is that *owing to* Owing to means and can be replaced in a sentence by 'because of', while *due to* means and is replaceable by 'caused by': *Owing to circumstances beyond our control, the departure of the train has had to be delayed; The delay is due to circumstances beyond our control.* The basis for this rule is said to be that *due* Due is an adjective and ought either to be attached to a noun (*a mistake due to ignorance*) or to follow a verb such as *to be* or *to seem*: *Her mistakes were mainly due to inexperience. Owing to*, on the other hand, is said to be a compound preposition that can introduce an adverbial phrase: *cancelled owing to rain; Owing to an earlier engagement, I reluctantly had to turn down the invitation.* Most modern authorities recommend that the rule should be remembered, while acknowledging that its grammatical basis is shaky (there is no reason why *due to* should not be seen as a compound preposition if *owing to* is one) and that *due to* is so frequently used in the sense of *because of* that many modern dictionaries show it with that sense.

due² *noun* **1** something due or owed. **2** something that rightfully belongs to somebody. **3** (*in pl*) fees; charges. ✴ **give somebody their due** to give somebody the credit they deserve.

due³ *adv* used before points of the compass: directly or exactly: *due north.*

duel¹ /'dyooh·əl/ *noun* **1** a formal combat with weapons fought between two people in the presence of witnesses in order to settle a quarrel or point of honour. **2** a conflict or contest between usu evenly matched people, ideas, or forces. [medieval Latin *duellum*, from Old Latin, war]

duel² *verb intrans* (**duelled, duelling**, *NAmer* **dueled, dueling**) to fight a duel. ➤➤ **dueller** *noun*, **duellist** *noun*.

duenna /dyooh'enə/ *noun* an older woman serving as governess, companion, or chaperon to the younger ladies in a Spanish or Portuguese family. [Spanish *dueña*, from Latin *domina*: see DOÑA]

due process *noun* (*also* **due process of law**) a course of legal proceedings carried out in accordance with established rules and principles.

duet /dyooh'et/ *noun* **1** a composition for two performers. **2** a performance by two musicians, singers, dancers, etc. ➤➤ **duettist** *noun*. [Italian *duetto*, dimin. of *duo* two musicians, from Latin *duo* two]

duff[1] /duf/ *noun* a boiled or steamed pudding, often containing dried fruit. ✳ **up the duff** *Brit, Aus, informal* pregnant. [northern English dialect variant of DOUGH]

duff[2] *adj Brit, informal* not working; worthless or useless. [perhaps back-formation from DUFFER[1]]

duff[3] *verb trans* **1** *Brit, informal* in golf, to mishit (a shot) by hitting the ground behind the ball. **2** *Aus, informal* to steal and change the brands on (cattle). [perhaps back-formations from DUFFER[1] and DUFFER[2] respectively]

duffel *or* **duffle** /'dufl/ *noun* **1** a coarse heavy woollen material with a thick nap. **2** *NAmer* personal belongings, equipment, or supplies, e.g. for camping or sport. [Dutch *duffel*, named after *Duffel*, town in Belgium where the cloth was made]

duffel bag *noun* a cylindrical canvas bag, closed by a drawstring, used for carrying personal belongings.

duffel coat *noun* a hooded coat made of duffel that is usu thigh-length or knee-length and fastened with toggles.

duffer[1] *noun* **1** *informal* an incompetent, ineffectual, or clumsy person. **2** *Aus, NZ, informal* an unproductive mine. [perhaps from Scots *doofart* stupid person]

duffer[2] *noun Aus, informal* somebody who duffs cattle.

duffle /'dufl/ *noun* see DUFFEL.

duff up *verb trans Brit, informal* to beat (somebody) up.

dug[1] /dug/ *verb* past tense and past part. of DIG[1].

dug[2] *noun* **1** an udder, teat or nipple. **2** *derog* a woman's breast. [perhaps of Scandinavian origin]

dugong /'doohgong/ *noun* a large aquatic plant-eating mammal of shallow tropical waters that has flippers, a broad crescent-shaped tail, and tusks in the male: *Dugong dugon*. [Latin genus name, from Malay and Tagalog *duyong* sea cow]

dugout *noun* **1** a boat made by hollowing out a large log. **2** a shelter dug in the ground or in a hillside, *esp* for troops. **3** a shelter at the side of a sports ground, *esp* one where trainers, managers, substitutes, etc sit during a match.

duiker /'diekə/ *noun* (*pl* **duikers** *or collectively* **duiker**) **1** any of several species of small African antelopes that have short backward-pointing horns: *Sylvicapra Grimmia* and other species. **2** *SAfr* a cormorant. [Afrikaans *duiker* diver, from *duik* to dive, from early Dutch *dūken*; from the antelope's ability to weave and plunge through thick bushland and the bird's swooping and diving flight]

duke /dyoohk/ *noun* **1** a nobleman of the highest hereditary rank, *esp* a member of the highest rank of the British peerage. **2** a sovereign ruler of a European duchy. **3** *informal* (*usu in pl*) a fist. ➤➤ **dukedom** *noun*. [Middle English from Old French *duc*, from Latin *duc-*, *dux*, from *ducere* to lead; (sense 3) rhyming slang *Duke of Yorks* forks, fingers, hands]

dulcet /'dulsit/ *adj* said *esp* of sounds: sweetly pleasant or soothing: *dulcet tones*. [Middle English *doucet* from Old French, from *douz* sweet, from Latin *dulcis*]

dulcimer /'dulsimə/ *noun* a stringed musical instrument having strings of graduated length stretched over a sounding board and played by striking the strings with light hammers. [Middle English *dowcemere* via Old French from Old Italian *dolcimelo*, from *dolce* sweet, from Latin *dulcis*]

dulia /dyoo'li:ə/ *noun* in Roman Catholic theology, reverence accorded to saints and angels: compare LATRIA. [Middle English, via Latin from Greek *douleia* servitude, from *doulos* slave]

dull[1] /dul/ *adj* **1** boring or uninteresting. **2** cloudy or overcast. **3** lacking brilliance, brightness, or intensity: *a dull greenish colour*. **4** not resonant or ringing: *a dull thud*. **5** lacking sharpness of cutting edge or point; blunt. **6a** slow in perception or sensibility. **b** lacking activity or vivacity; listless or sluggish. **7** mentally slow; stupid.

➤➤ **dullish** *adj*, **dullness** *noun*, **dully** *adv*, **dulness** *noun*. [Old English *dol* foolish]

dull[2] *verb trans* to make (something) dull: *Old age had dulled his hearing*. ➤ *verb intrans* to become dull.

dullard /'duləd/ *noun* a stupid or insensitive person.

dulse /duls/ *noun* a coarse edible red seaweed: *Rhodymenia palmata*. [Scottish Gaelic and Irish Gaelic *duileasg*]

duly /'dyoohli/ *adv* in a due manner, time, or degree; properly: *Your suggestion has been duly noted.*

duma /'doohmah/ *noun* a legislative assembly in Russia and some other republics of the former USSR. [Russian *duma*, of Germanic origin; related to Old English *dōm* DOOM[1]]

dumb /dum/ *adj* **1** lacking the power of speech; mute. **2** naturally incapable of speech: *dumb animals*. **3** not expressed in uttered words: *dumb insolence*. **4a** not willing to speak. **b** temporarily unable to speak, e.g. from astonishment: *struck dumb*. **5** devoid of sound: *a dumb piano*. **6** *chiefly NAmer, informal* stupid. **7** said of a computer terminal: able to receive and display data but unable to modify or process it. ➤➤ **dumbly** *adv*, **dumbness** *noun*. [Old English; related to Old English *dēaf* DEAF[1]]

Usage note
The use of *dumb* in the originally American and informal sense of 'stupid' has become so widespread that great care should be taken with the use of the word in its basic sense 'unable to speak'. If there is any risk of misunderstanding or offence, a word such as *mute* or *speech-impaired* should be used instead.

dumbbell *noun* **1** a short bar with adjustable weights at each end used usu in pairs for weight training: compare BARBELL. **2** *NAmer, informal* a stupid person. [orig a piece of exercise equipment resembling that used to ring a church bell, but 'dumb' because it had no bell]

dumb down *verb trans informal* to simplify (something) so as to make it more easily accessible to those with little education or intelligence: *Textbooks were dumbed down to accommodate the least able* — The Economist. ➤ *verb intrans* to become less intellectual or less intellectually challenging.

dumbfound *or* **dumfound** *verb trans* to strike (somebody) dumb with astonishment; to amaze (them). [DUMB + *-found* as in CONFOUND[1]]

dumbo /'dumboh/ *noun* (*pl* **dumbos**) *informal* a foolish or stupid person. [DUMB + -O[1], prob influenced by the cartoon film *Dumbo* featuring a young elephant ridiculed by his elders]

dumb show *noun* **1** movements, signs, and gestures used in place of words. **2** a play or part of a play presented in this way.

dumbstruck *adj* dumbfounded.

dumb waiter *noun* **1** a movable table or stand often with revolving shelves for holding food or dishes. **2** a small lift for conveying food and dishes, e.g. from the kitchen to the dining area of a restaurant.

dumdum /'dumdum/ *noun* a bullet that expands on impact and inflicts a severe wound. [named after *Dum-Dum*, a town near Calcutta, India; the bullets were first produced at the arsenal there]

dum-dum *noun informal* a stupid or silly person. [an alteration and reduplication of DUMB]

dumfound /dum'fownd/ *verb trans* see DUMBFOUND.

dummy[1] /'dumi/ *noun* (*pl* **dummies**) **1** an imitation or copy of something used to reproduce some of the attributes of the original: *The perfume bottles on display are just dummies.* **2a** a model of the human body used e.g. for fitting or displaying clothes. **b** a large puppet, *esp* one in human form, used by a ventriloquist. **3** *chiefly Brit* a rubber or plastic teat given to babies to suck in order to soothe them. **4** a person or corporation that seems to act independently but is in reality acting for another. **5** a pattern for a printing job showing the position of typographic elements, e.g. text and illustrations. **6** *informal* a dull or stupid person. **7** the act or an instance of deceiving an opponent in sports. **8** the exposed hand in bridge played by the declarer in addition to his or her own hand, or the player whose hand is a dummy. [DUMB + -Y[2]; orig meaning 'dumb person']

dummy[2] *adj* **1** resembling or being a dummy. **2a** sham or artificial. **b** existing in name only; fictitious: *bank accounts held in dummy names.*

dummy[3] *verb* (**dummies, dummied, dummying**) ➤ *verb intrans* **1** to deceive an opponent, e.g. in rugby or football, by pretending to pass or release the ball while still retaining possession of it. **2** *NAmer, informal* (+ up) to refuse to talk. ➤ *verb trans* to deceive (an opponent) by dummying.

dummy run *noun* a rehearsal or trial run.

dump¹ /dump/ *verb trans* **1a** to unload or drop (something unwanted, e.g. refuse) in a heap or mass. **b** to deposit or drop (something) carelessly or heavily. **c** to get rid of (something or somebody) unceremoniously or irresponsibly; to abandon (them). **2** to sell (something) in quantity at a very low price, *esp* to sell (it) abroad at less than the market price at home. **3** to copy (data in a computer's internal storage) to an external storage medium. ➤ *verb intrans* **1** to get rid of refuse, etc. **2a** *informal* (+ on) to criticize (somebody) severely. **b** to treat (somebody) badly or without respect. [perhaps from Dutch *dompen* to immerse, topple; related to Old English *dyppan* DIP¹]

dump² *noun* **1a** an accumulation of discarded materials, e.g. refuse. **b** a place where such materials are dumped. **2** an accumulation of *esp* military materials or the place where they are stored: *an arms dump.* **3** an instance of dumping data stored in a computer. **4** *informal* a dirty, unpleasant, or dilapidated place. **5** *chiefly NAmer, informal* an act of defecation: *take a dump.*

dumper *noun* **1** somebody or something that dumps. **2** = DUMPER TRUCK. **3** *chiefly Aus* a powerful wave that breaks suddenly and is impossible for a surfer to ride.

dumper truck *noun* a lorry with a body that can be tilted to empty the contents.

dumpling /'dumpling/ *noun* **1a** a small usu rounded mass of dough cooked by boiling or steaming, often in a stew. **b** a dessert of fruit wrapped in dough and usu baked: *apple dumpling.* **2** *humorous* a short fat person. [perhaps from English dialect *dump* lump + -LING]

dumps *pl noun informal* a gloomy state of mind; despondency: *down in the dumps.* [prob from Dutch *domp* haze, from early Dutch *damp* vapour]

dump truck *noun* = DUMPER TRUCK.

dumpy *adj* (**dumpier, dumpiest**) said of a person: short and thick in build; squat. ➤➤ **dumpily** *adv*, **dumpiness** *noun*. [English dialect *dump* lump + -Y¹]

dun¹ /dun/ *adj* **1** of a brownish grey colour. **2** said of a horse: having a variable colour between brownish grey and yellow and usu black extremities. **3** marked by dullness and drabness. [Old English *dunn*]

dun² *noun* **1** a dun horse. **2** a slightly brownish dark grey. **3a** a mayfly that has not acquired all the typical adult characteristics. **b** an artificial fishing fly tied to imitate this.

dun³ *verb trans* (**dunned, dunning**) to make persistent demands on (somebody) for payment of a debt. [perhaps short for obsolete *dunkirk* privateer, named after *Dunkirk, Dunkerque,* port in France from which they sailed]

dun⁴ *noun* **1** somebody who duns; a persistent creditor or debt collector. **2** an urgent request, *esp* a demand for payment.

dun⁵ *noun* a prehistoric or early medieval Irish or Scottish stronghold protected usu by one or more earthen or stone ramparts. [Scottish Gaelic *dùn* and Irish Gaelic *dún*]

dunce /duns/ *noun* a stupid person or slow learner.

Word history
from the name of John *Duns* Scotus d.1308, Scots theologian whose once accepted writings were ridiculed in the 16th cent. Followers of Duns Scotus, known as *Dunsmen* or *Dunses,* were regarded as dull pedants, and from this the word *dunce* came to mean 'slow learner'.

dunce's cap *or* **dunce cap** *noun* a conical cap that slow learners at school were formerly forced to wear as a punishment or humiliation.

Dundee cake /dun'dee/ *noun* a fruit cake, usu decorated on top with skinned almonds. [named after *Dundee,* city in Scotland]

dunderhead /'dundǝhed/ *noun* a stupid or slow-witted person. ➤➤ **dunderheaded** *adj.* [perhaps from Dutch *donder* thunder + HEAD¹]

dune /dyoohn/ *noun* a hill or ridge of sand piled up by the wind. [French *dune* from early Dutch; related to Old English *dūn* DOWN⁷]

dung¹ /dung/ *noun* the excrement of an animal. ➤➤ **dungy** *adj.* [Old English]

dung² *verb trans* to fertilize or cover with manure. ➤ *verb intrans* said of an animal: to defecate.

dungaree /dungǝ'ree/ *noun* a heavy coarse durable cotton twill woven from coloured yarns, *esp* blue denim. [Hindi *dugrī*]

dungarees *pl noun* a one-piece outer garment, usu made of denim or similar fabric, consisting of trousers and a bib with shoulder straps fastened to the waist at the back.

dung beetle *noun* a beetle that rolls balls of dung in which to lay its eggs and on which the larvae feed.

dungeon /'dunjǝn/ *noun* **1** a dark usu underground prison or vault, *esp* in a castle. **2** = DONJON. [Middle English *donjon* inner tower in a castle, strong prison, via Old French and medieval Latin from Latin *dominus* lord]

dunghill *noun* a heap of dung, e.g. in a farmyard.

dunk¹ /dungk/ *verb trans* **1** to dip (a biscuit, doughnut, a piece of bread, etc) into liquid, e.g. a drink or soup, before eating it. **2** to submerge (somebody or something) temporarily in water. **3** in basketball, to put (the ball) through the hoop from above in a slamming movement, as distinct from scoring from a distance. ➤ *verb intrans* in basketball, to score a goal by dunking. ➤➤ **dunker** *noun.* [Pennsylvania German *dunke,* from early High German *dunken,* from Old High German *dunkon*]

dunk² *noun* **1** the act or an instance of dunking a biscuit, doughnut, etc in liquid. **2** in basketball, a goal scored by dunking.

dunlin /'dunlin/ *noun* (*pl* **dunlins** *or collectively* **dunlin**) a small widely distributed sandpiper with reddish brown upper parts and a white breast marked with a black patch in summer: *Calidris alpina.* [DUN¹ + -*lin,* alteration of -LING]

dunnage /'dunij/ *noun* **1** loose materials or padding used to prevent damage to cargo. **2** *informal* baggage or personal effects. [origin unknown]

dunno /dǝ'noh/ *contraction informal* don't know. [by alteration]

dunnock /'dunǝk/ *noun* a small dull-coloured European bird common in gardens, hedges, and bushy places: *Prunella modularis.* Also called HEDGE SPARROW. [Middle English *dunoke,* from DUN¹ + -OCK]

dunny /'duni/ *noun* (*pl* **dunnies**) *chiefly Aus, NZ, informal* a toilet. [by shortening and alteration from *dunnaken, dannaken* toilet, from *danna* human excrement]

duo /'dyooh·oh/ *noun* (*pl* **duos**) **1** a pair of people or things, *esp* a pair of performers. **2** a composition for two performers; a duet. [via Italian from Latin *duo* two]

duo- *comb. form* forming words, with the meaning: two: *duologue.* [Latin *duo* two]

duodecimal /dyooh·oh'desim(ǝ)l/ *adj* being or belonging to a system of numbers that has twelve as its base. ➤➤ **duodecimally** *adv.* [Latin *duodecim:* see DOZEN]

duodecimo /dyooh·oh'desimoh/ *noun* (*pl* **duodecimos**) a book format in which a folded sheet forms twelve leaves, or a book in this format. [Latin *duodecimo,* ablative of *duodecimus* twelfth, from *duodecim:* see DOZEN]

duoden- *or* **duodeno-** *comb. form* forming words, denoting: duodenum: *duodenitis; duodenogram.* [scientific Latin *duoden-,* from medieval Latin *duodenum:* see DUODENUM]

duodena /dyooh·ǝ'deenǝ/ *noun pl* of DUODENUM.

duodeno- *comb. form* see DUODEN-.

duodenum /dyooh·ǝ'deenǝm/ *noun* (*pl* **duodena** /-nǝ/ *or* **duodenums**) the first part of the small intestine, extending from the stomach to the jejunum. ➤➤ **duodenal** *adj.* [Middle English from medieval Latin, from Latin *duodeni* twelve each, from *duodecim:* see DOZEN; from its length, about twelve fingers' breadth]

duologue /'dyooh·ǝlog/ *noun* **1** a play or part of a play with only two speaking roles. **2** a dialogue between two people.

duomo /'dooh'ohmoh, 'dwohmoh/ *noun* (*pl* **duomos**) an Italian cathedral. [Italian *duomo:* see DOME]

duopoly /dyooh'opǝli/ *noun* (*pl* **duopolies**) a market situation that is controlled by two sellers. ➤➤ **duopolistic** /-'listik/ *adj.* [DUO- + -*poly* as in MONOPOLY]

dup. *abbr* duplicate.

dupe¹ /dyoohp/ *noun* somebody who is easily deceived or cheated. [French *dupe* from early French *duppe,* prob alteration of *huppe* HOOPOE; from the bird's alleged stupidity]

dupe² *verb trans* to cheat or deceive (somebody). ➤➤ **dupable** *adj,* **duper** *noun,* **dupery** /'dyoohpǝri/ *noun.*

dupion /'dyoohpi·ən/ *noun* a rough silk fabric. [French *doupion* from Italian *doppione* double cocoon made by two silkworms, augmentative of *doppio* double, from Latin *duplus*: see DOUBLE[1]]

duple /'dyoohpl/ *adj* **1** having two elements; twofold. **2** said of musical rhythm or time: marked by two, or a multiple of two, beats per bar. [Latin *duplus*: see DOUBLE[1]]

duplex[1] /'dyoohpleks/ *adj* **1** double; twofold. **2** said of a system of communication, computer set-up, etc: allowing transmission of signals in opposite directions simultaneously. [Latin *duplex*, from *duo* two + *-plex* -fold]

duplex[2] *noun* **1** *NAmer.* **a** a house divided into two flats. **b** a flat on two floors. **2** a double strand of a nucleic acid, e.g. DNA or RNA, consisting of two single complementary strands.

duplicate[1] /'dyoohplikət/ *adj* **1** consisting of or existing in two corresponding or identical parts or examples: *duplicate invoices*. **2** being the same as another: *a duplicate key*. [Middle English from Latin *duplicatus*, past part. of *duplicare* to double, from *duplic-*, *duplex*: see DUPLEX[1]]

duplicate[2] *noun* **1** either of two things that exactly resemble each other. **2** a copy. **✳ in duplicate** with an original and one copy, or with two identical copies: *Applications should be typed in duplicate.*

duplicate[3] /'dyoohplikayt/ *verb trans* **1** to make (something) double or twofold. **2** to make an exact copy of (something): *duplicate the document.* **3** to repeat or equal (something). **➤** *verb intrans* to become duplicate; to replicate: *DNA in chromosomes duplicates.* **➤➤ duplicable** *adj,* **duplication** /-'kaysh(ə)n/ *noun.*

duplicator /'dyoohplikaytə/ *noun* a machine for making copies, *esp* by means other than photocopying.

duplicity /dyooh'plisiti/ *noun* (*pl* **duplicities**) malicious deception in thought, speech, or action, or an instance of this. **➤➤ duplicitous** /-təs/ *adj,* **duplicitously** /-təsli/ *adv.* [Old French *duplicite* from late Latin *duplicitas*, from *duplic-*, *duplex*: see DUPLEX[1]]

duppy /'dupi/ *noun* (*pl* **duppies**) a ghost or spirit in W Indian folklore, usu a malevolent one. [Bube *dupe* ghost]

durable /'dyooərəbl/ *adj* able to exist or be used for a long time without significant deterioration. **➤➤ durability** /-'biliti/ *noun,* **durableness** *noun,* **durably** *adv.* [Middle English via Old French from Latin *durabilis*, from *durare*: see DURING]

durables *pl noun* consumer goods, e.g. vehicles and household appliances, that are typically used repeatedly over a period of years without being replaced.

Duralumin /dyoo'ralyoomin/ *noun trademark* an alloy of aluminium, copper, manganese, and magnesium comparable in strength and hardness to soft steel. [either from Latin *durus* hard, or from *Düren*, the name of a German town where such alloys were developed, + ALUMINIUM]

dura mater /ˌdyooərə 'mahtə, 'maytə/ *noun* the tough outermost membrane that envelops the brain and spinal cord. [Middle English from medieval Latin, literally 'hard mother']

duramen /dyoo'raymin, dyoo'rahmin/ *noun* = HEARTWOOD. [Latin *duramen* hardness, from *durare*: see DURING]

durance /'dyooərəns/ *noun archaic* imprisonment: *A convict ... suffered 'durance vile'* — Irish Digest. [early French *durance*, from *durer* to endure, from Latin *durare*: see DURING]

duration /dyoo'raysh(ə)n/ *noun* **1** the time during which something exists or lasts: *for the duration of the war.* **2** continuance in time. **➤➤ durational** *adj.* [medieval Latin *duration-*, *duratio*, from Latin *durare*: see DURING]

durative /'dyooərətiv/ *adj* relating to or denoting a verb or form of a verb expressing continuing action. **➤➤ durative** *noun.*

durbar /'duhbah/ *noun* **1** a reception held in former times by an Indian prince or a British governor or viceroy in India. **2** the court of an Indian prince in former times. [Hindi *darbār* from Persian, from *dar* door + *bār* admission, audience]

duress /dyoo'res/ *noun* **1** compulsion by threat, violence, or imprisonment: *under duress.* **2** forcible restraint or restriction. [Middle English *duresse* via early French *duresce* hardness, severity, from Latin *duritia*, from *durus* hard]

Durex /'dyooəreks/ *noun* (*pl* **Durex** or *informal* **Durexes**) *trademark* a condom. [said to be a blend of *durability, reliability* + *excellence*]

durian /'dyooəri·ən/ *noun* **1** a large oval tropical fruit with a prickly rind and pleasant-tasting but foul-smelling flesh. **2** the Asian tree that bears this fruit: *Durio zibethinus.* [Malay *durian*, from *duri* prickle]

during /'dyooəring/ *prep* **1** throughout the whole duration of: *She went swimming every day during the summer.* **2** at some point in the course of: *He usually takes his holiday during July.* [Middle English, present part. of *duren* to last, via Old French from Latin *durare* to harden, endure, from *durus* hard]

durmast or **durmast oak** /'duhmahst/ *noun* a European oak tree valued *esp* for its dark heavy tough springy wood: *Quercus petraea.* Also called SESSILE OAK. [perhaps alteration of *dun mast*, from DUN[1] + MAST[3]]

durra /'durə/ *noun* any of various grasses of the *Sorghum* genus widely grown in warm dry areas, *esp* for their grain. [Arabic *dhurah*]

durrie /'duri/ *noun* see DHURRIE.

durst /duhst/ *verb archaic* past tense of DARE[1].

durum /'dyooərəm/ *noun* a hard wheat that yields a glutenous flour used *esp* to make pasta: *Triticum durum.* [Latin *durum*, neuter of *durus* hard]

dusk[1] /dusk/ *noun* the darker part of twilight: *She may very well pass for forty-three, in the dusk with the light behind her* — W S Gilbert. [Middle English *dosk, duske* dusky, alteration of Old English *dox*; related to Old English *dunn* DUN[1], *dūst* DUST[1]]

dusk[2] *verb intrans literary* to become dark or dim; to darken.

dusky /'duski/ *adj* (**duskier, duskiest**) **1** somewhat dark in colour, *esp* dark-skinned. **2** shadowy; gloomy. **➤➤ duskily** *adv,* **duskiness** *noun.*

Dussehra /də'sayrə/ *noun* the final day of the Hindu festival of Navaratri. [Hindi *daśahrā* from Sanskrit *daśaharā*]

dust[1] /dust/ *noun* **1a** fine dry particles of any solid matter. **b** the fine particles of waste that settle *esp* on household surfaces. **2** the particles into which something, *esp* the human body, disintegrates or decays. **3** something worthless: *Worldly success was dust to him.* **4** the surface of the ground. **5** a cloud of dust: *The cars raised quite a dust.* **6** the act or an instance of dusting: *I gave the house a quick dust.* **✳ dust and ashes** great disappointment or something very disappointing. **kick up/raise a dust** *informal* to create a disturbance; to cause confusion. **when/after/until the dust settles** when, etc things quieten down or return to normal. **➤➤ dustless** *adj.* [Old English *dūst*]

dust[2] *verb trans* **1** to make (something) free of dust, e.g. by wiping or brushing. **2** (+ down/off) to prepare to use (something) again, *esp* after a long period of disuse. **3a** to sprinkle (something) with fine particles: *dust a cake with icing sugar.* **b** to sprinkle (something) in the form of fine particles: *dusting icing sugar over a cake.* **➤** *verb intrans* to remove dust, e.g. from furniture and household surfaces, *esp* by wiping or brushing.

dust bath *noun* the act or an instance of a bird's working dust into its feathers in order to clean them.

dustbin *noun Brit* a large container for holding household refuse until collection.

dust bowl *noun* a region that suffers from prolonged droughts and dust storms.

dustcart *noun Brit* a vehicle for collecting household refuse.

dustcover *noun* **1** = DUSTSHEET. **2** = DUST JACKET.

dust devil *noun* a small whirlwind containing sand or dust.

duster *noun* **1** a cloth for removing dust from household articles. **2** (*also* **duster coat**) a loose casual lightweight coat for indoor or summer wear.

dusting powder *noun* fine powder used for sprinkling, *esp* talcum powder.

dust jacket *noun* a removable outer paper cover for a book.

dustman *noun* (*pl* **dustmen**) *Brit* somebody employed to remove household refuse.

dustpan *noun* a shovel-like utensil into which household dust and litter is swept.

dustsheet *noun* a large sheet, e.g. of cloth, used as a cover to protect furniture, etc from dust.

dust shot *noun* the smallest size of gunshot.

dust storm *noun* a strong dust-laden wind or whirlwind, *esp* a whirlwind moving across a dry region.

dust-up *noun informal* a quarrel or fight.

dusty /'dusti/ *adj* (**dustier, dustiest**) **1** covered with or full of dust. **2** consisting of dust; powdery. **3** resembling dust, *esp* in consistency or colour. **4** lacking vitality; dry: *dusty scholarship*. * **give/get a dusty answer** to give (somebody) or get an unhelpful or brusque reply. **not so dusty** *informal, dated* fairly good. ➤➤ **dustily** *adv*, **dustiness** *noun*.

dusty miller *noun* any of several species of wild plants of the daisy family with leaves covered in dense white hairs: *Artemisia stellerana* of North America, *Senecio cineraria* of Europe, and other species.

Dutch /duch/ *noun* **1** (**the Dutch**) (*treated as pl*) the people of the Netherlands. **2** the Germanic language of the people of the Netherlands. * **go Dutch** to pay one's own share; to divide expenses equally. ➤➤ **Dutch** *adj*.

Word history
Middle English *Duche* German, from early Dutch *duutsch*. Orig applied to speakers of Low and High German and their language; in the 17th cent. restricted to the people of the Netherlands, as the German-speaking people with whom the British had most contact. Derogatory terms such as *go dutch, Dutch treat, Dutch auction* and *Dutch courage* reflect the rivalry and enmity between the British and the Dutch in the 17th cent. Words borrowed into English from the Dutch language in the 16th and 17th cents reflect the preeminence of the Netherlands in artistic, military, and nautical matters: *beleaguer, cruise, domineer, drill, easel, etch, freebooter, keelhaul, landscape, sketch, sloop, smuggle, splice, stoker, yacht*. Other borrowings of that period include *boss, brandy, frolic, gherkin, isinglass, slim, uproar*, and *wagon*. Quite a few later borrowings resulted from contact between Dutch and English settlers in North America, including *coleslaw, cookie, dope, poppycock, sleigh, spook*, and *waffle*.

dutch *noun Brit, informal* a person's wife, *esp* a Cockney's wife. [by shortening and alteration from DUCHESS]

Dutch auction *noun* an auction in which the auctioneer gradually reduces the bidding price until a bid is received.

Dutch barn *noun* a large barn with a curved roof and open sides used *esp* for storing hay.

Dutch cap *noun* a moulded cap, usu of thin rubber, that fits over the cervix of the womb to act as a contraceptive barrier. [from its resemblance to a cap worn by Dutchwomen in traditional dress]

Dutch courage *noun* confidence or courage induced by drinking alcohol.

Dutch door *noun* = STABLE DOOR.

Dutch elm disease *noun* a fatal disease of elms caused by a fungus, spread from tree to tree by a beetle, and characterized by yellowing and withering of the leaves.

Dutch hoe *noun* a garden hoe that is pushed rather than pulled.

Dutchman or **Dutchwoman** *noun* (*pl* **Dutchmen** or **Dutchwomen**) a native or inhabitant of the Netherlands.

Dutch oven *noun* **1** a heavy pot with a tight-fitting lid used for cooking stews, casseroles, etc. **2** a three-walled metal box used for roasting in front of an open fire. **3** a brick oven in which food is cooked by heat radiating from the prewarmed walls.

Dutch treat *noun* a meal or entertainment for which each person pays their own share.

Dutch uncle *noun informal* somebody who advises, criticizes, or admonishes sternly and bluntly, but in a well-intentioned way.

duteous /'dyoohti-əs/ *adj formal* dutiful; obedient. ➤➤ **duteously** *adv*, **duteousness** *noun*. [irreg from DUTY]

dutiable /'dyoohti-əbl/ *adj* subject to a duty: *dutiable imports*.

dutiful /'dyoohtif(ə)l/ *adj* **1** filled with or motivated by a sense of duty: *a dutiful son*. **2** proceeding from or expressive of a sense of duty: *dutiful affection*. ➤➤ **dutifully** *adv*, **dutifulness** *noun*.

duty /'dyoohti/ *noun* (*pl* **duties**) **1a** a task, service, or function arising from one's position or job, or such tasks etc considered collectively. **b** assigned military or official service or business: *He's just back from a tour of duty in Germany*. **2a** a moral or legal obligation. **b** the force of moral obligation. **3** respectful or obedient conduct due to parents and superiors. **4** a tax, *esp* on imports. **5** *technical* a measure of efficiency expressed in terms of the amount of work done in relation to the energy consumed. * **do duty for** to serve as a substitute for (something): *Barrels did duty for chairs and tables*. **on/off duty** engaged or not engaged in one's usual work. [Middle English *duete* from Anglo-French *dueté*, from Old French *deu*: see DUE¹]

duty-free *adj* **1** exempt from duty: *duty-free cigarettes*. **2** selling goods that are exempt from duty: *a duty-free shop*. ➤➤ **duty-free** *adv*, **duty-free** *noun*.

duty-paid *adj* said of goods: on which duty has been paid in the country of purchase.

duumvir /dyooh'umvə/ *noun* **1** either of two officers or magistrates of ancient Rome constituting a board or court. **2** either of two people having joint authority. [Latin *duumvir*, from *duum* (genitive of *duo* two) + *vir* man]

duumvirate /dyooh'umvirət/ *noun* **1** a board or court in ancient Rome composed of two officers or magistrates who have equal authority. **2** a partnership composed of two people who have equal authority.

duvet /'doohvay/ *noun* a large quilt filled with insulating material, e.g. feathers or synthetic fibre, usu placed inside a removable fabric cover and used in place of an upper sheet and blankets. [French *duvet* down, ultimately from Old Norse *dūnn* DOWN⁶]

dux /duks/ *noun chiefly Scot* the pupil in a class or school with the best academic record. [Latin *dux* leader]

DV *abbr* Deo volente. [Latin *Deo volente*, literally 'God willing']

DVD *abbr* digital videodisc (or digital versatile disc), a disc with a large capacity for storing audio, video, etc information, used *esp* for reproducing feature films in the home with a quality that is close to that of the cinema.

DVLA *abbr Brit* Driver and Vehicle Licensing Agency.

DVT *abbr* deep vein thrombosis.

dwarf¹ /dwawf/ *noun* (*pl* **dwarfs** or **dwarves** /dwawvz/) **1** a person of unusually small stature, *esp* one whose body is not in proportion. **2a** an animal or plant that is much smaller than normal size. **b** (*used before a noun*) related to or denoting such an animal or plant: *dwarf conifers*. **3** in mythology and folklore, a small human-like creature often depicted as ugly, having magical powers, or skilled as a craftsman. **4** = DWARF STAR. ➤➤ **dwarfish** *adj*. [Old English *dweorg, dweorh*]

dwarf² *verb trans* **1** to stunt the growth of (a person, animal, or plant). **2** to cause (somebody or something) to appear smaller or less significant by comparison: *He was dwarfed by the great height of the nave* — Graham Greene.

dwarfism *noun* the condition of unusually small size or stunted growth.

dwarf star *noun* a relatively small star of ordinary or low luminosity.

dwarves /dwawvz/ *noun* pl of DWARF¹.

dweeb /dweeb/ *noun NAmer, informal* a dull or ineffectual person. ➤➤ **dweebish** *adj*, **dweeby** *adj*. [perhaps from Scots *dweeble* weakling]

dwell¹ /dwel/ *verb intrans* (*past tense and past part.* **dwelt** /dwelt/ or **dwelled**) **1** *formal* to live as a resident; to reside. **2** (*often* in + to) to live or exist in a specified condition: *The family dwelt in extreme poverty*. * **dwell on/upon** to think, write, or speak about (something) at length. ➤➤ **dweller** *noun*. [Middle English *dwellen* to delay, pause, stay, from Old English *dwellan* to go astray, hinder]

dwell² *noun technical* a short pause in the action of a machine.

dwelling *noun formal* a place, e.g. a house or flat, in which people live; a home.

dwelling house *noun* in law, a building that is used for residential, as opposed to commercial, purposes.

dwelling place *noun* = DWELLING.

dwelt /dwelt/ *verb* past tense and past part. of DWELL¹.

dwindle /'dwindl/ *verb intrans* to become steadily less in quantity or size; to shrink or diminish. [prob frequentative of English dialect *dwine* to waste away, from Old English *dwīnan*]

DWP *abbr Brit* Department for Work and Pensions.

DY *abbr* Dahomey (international vehicle registration for Benin).

Dy *abbr* the chemical symbol for dysprosium.

dy- or **dyo-** *comb. form* forming words, with the meaning: two: *dyarchy*. [via late Latin from Greek *dy-*, from *dyo*]

dyad /'diead/ *noun* **1** *technical* a pair or couple. **2** a mathematical process indicated by writing the symbols of two vectors with a dot or cross between them. ➤➤ **dyadic** /die'adik/ *adj*. [via late Latin from Greek *dyad-, dyas*, from *dyo* two]

Dyak or **Dayak** /'dieak/ noun (pl **Dyaks** or **Dayaks** or collectively **Dyak** or **Dayak**) **1** a member of a group of indigenous peoples inhabiting the interior of Borneo. **2** a group of Austronesian languages or dialects spoken by these peoples. ➤➤ **Dyak** adj. [Malay dayak up-country]

dyarchy or **diarchy** /'dieahki/ noun (pl **dyarchies** or **diarchies**) a government in which power is held equally by two rulers.

dybbuk /'dibək/ noun (pl **dybbukim** /-kim/ or **dybbuks**) in Jewish folklore, an evil spirit that inhabits the body of a living person. [late Hebrew dibbūq]

dye¹ /die/ noun **1** a soluble or insoluble colouring matter used to colour something. **2** a colour or tint produced by dyeing. [Old English dēah, dēag]

dye² verb trans (**dyes, dyed, dyeing**) to impart a new and often permanent colour to (something, e.g. fabric or hair), esp by impregnation with a dye. ➤➤ **dyeable** adj, **dyer** noun.

dyed-in-the-wool adj thoroughgoing, uncompromising, or unchanging: a dyed-in-the-wool conservative. [because a more permanent colour was obtained by dyeing the wool before spinning]

dyestuff noun = DYE¹ (I).

dying¹ /'dieing/ verb present part. of DIE¹.

dying² adj **1** made or occurring at the point of death: a dying wish. **2** final or last: They equalized in the dying minutes of the game.

dyke¹ or **dike** /diek/ noun **1** a watercourse or ditch. **2** a bank, usu of earth, constructed to control or confine water. **3** a barrier preventing passage. **4** a raised causeway. **5** a wall-like body of rock that has flowed while molten into a fissure and that runs across layers of other rocks. **6** Brit a wall or fence of turf or stone. **7** chiefly Aus, NZ, informal a toilet. [Old English dīc ditch, dyke]

dyke² or **dike** verb trans to surround or protect (land) with a dyke.

dyke³ or **dike** noun informal, derog a female homosexual; a lesbian. ➤➤ **dykey** adj. [origin unknown]

dynamic¹ /die'namik/ adj **1a** of physical force or energy in motion: compare STATIC¹. **b** of dynamics. **2a** marked by continuous activity or change: a dynamic population. **b** energetic and forceful: a dynamic personality. **3** said of computer memory: using devices that require periodic renewal to preserve the stored information. **4** relating to variation in sound intensity or volume in music: dynamic range. ➤➤ **dynamical** adj, **dynamically** adv. [French dynamique from Greek dynamikos powerful, from dynamis power, from dynasthai to be able]

dynamic² noun a dynamic force.

dynamics pl noun (treated as sing. or pl) **1** the branch of mechanics that deals with forces and their relation to the motion of bodies. **2** a pattern of change or growth, or the forces that produce it: population dynamics. **3** variation and contrast in force or intensity, esp in music. ➤➤ **dynamicist** noun.

dynamism /'dienəmiz(ə)m/ noun **1a** a philosophical system that describes the universe in terms of the interplay of forces. **b** = DYNAMICS (2). **2** the quality of being energetic and forceful. ➤➤ **dynamist** noun, **dynamistic** /-'mistik/ adj.

dynamite¹ /'dienəmiet/ noun **1** a blasting explosive that is made of nitroglycerine absorbed in a porous material. **2** informal somebody or something that has a potentially dangerous or spectacular effect: In Victorian and Edwardian politics women were dynamite — Michael Holroyd. [Greek dynamis (see DYNAMIC¹) + -ITE¹]

dynamite² verb trans to blow up or destroy (something) with dynamite. ➤➤ **dynamiter** noun.

dynamo /'dienəmoh/ noun (pl **dynamos**) **1** a machine by which mechanical energy is converted into electrical energy, esp a device that produces direct current, e.g. in a motor vehicle. **2** informal a forceful energetic person. [short for dynamoelectric machine, from Greek dynamis: see DYNAMIC¹]

dynamometer /dienə'momitə/ noun an instrument for measuring power exerted, e.g. by an engine. [French dynamomètre, from Greek dynamis (see DYNAMIC¹) + French -mètre -METER²]

dynast /'dinast, 'dinast/ noun a ruler, esp a hereditary one. [via Latin from Greek dynastēs, from dynasthai to be able, have power]

dynasty /'dinəsti/ noun (pl **dynasties**) **1** a succession of hereditary rulers, or the time during which they rule. **2** a powerful group or family that maintains its position for a considerable time. ➤➤ **dynastic** /di'nastik/ adj, **dynastically** /di'nastikli/ adv.

dyne /dien/ noun a unit of force in the centimetre-gram-second system that would give a mass of one gram an acceleration of one centimetre per second per second, equivalent to 10^{-5} newtons. [French dyne from Greek dynamis: see DYNAMIC¹]

dyo- comb. form see DY-.

dys- prefix forming words, with the meanings: **1** abnormal; impaired: dysfunction; dysplasia. **2** difficult; painful: dysuria; dysmenorrhoea. [Middle English dis- bad, difficult, via French and Latin from Greek dys-]

dysbiosis /,disbie'ohsis/ noun an excess of harmful over beneficial micro-organisms in the gut. [DYS- + SYMBIOSIS]

dyscalculia /diskal'kyooli·ə/ noun difficulty with doing arithmetical calculations caused by brain injury or disease or malfunction of the brain. [scientific Latin, from DYS- + Latin calculare to count]

dyscrasia /dis'krayzi·ə/ noun an abnormal condition of the body or of one of its parts: a blood dyscrasia. ➤➤ **dyscrasic** adj. [from medieval Latin dyscrasia bad mixture (of humours), from Greek dyskrasia, from DYS- + krasis mixture, from kerannynai to mix]

dysentery /'dis(ə)ntri/ noun any of various infectious bacterial or protozoan infections of the intestines characterized by severe diarrhoea, usu with passing of mucus and blood, usu caused by poor sanitation. ➤➤ **dysenteric** /-'terik/ adj. [Middle English dissenterie via Latin from Greek dysenteria, from DYS- + enteron intestine]

dysfunction /dis'fungksh(ə)n/ noun impaired or abnormal functioning.

dysfunctional adj **1** not functioning properly. **2** characterized by or relating to the breakdown of the usual or expected forms of social behaviour, relationships, or interactions: a dysfunctional family. ➤➤ **dysfunctionally** adv.

dysgenic /dis'jenik/ adj detrimental to the hereditary qualities of a people or an animal or plant stock.

dysgenics pl noun (treated as sing.) the study of degeneration of a particular people or species.

dysgraphia /dis'grafi·ə/ noun difficulty in writing intelligibly caused by brain injury or disease or malfunction of the brain. ➤➤ **dysgraphic** adj. [DYS- + Greek graphia writing]

dyslexia /dis'leksi·ə/ noun a general term for difficulties with reading, writing, spelling, and understanding written or printed text, symbols, etc caused by a neurological disorder as opposed to similar learning difficulties exhibited by people with some form of brain injury or disease: compare ALEXIA, APHASIA, APHONIA. ➤➤ **dyslectic** /dis'lektik/ adj and noun, **dyslexic** /-sik/ adj and noun. [scientific Latin dyslexia, from DYS- + Greek lexis word, speech]

dysmenorrhoea (NAmer **dysmenorrhea**) /,dis,menə'ri·ə/ noun a disorder in which menstruation is more painful than normal.

dyspepsia /dis'pepsi·ə/ noun indigestion. [via Latin from Greek dyspepsia, from DYS- + pepsis digestion, from peptein, pessein to cook, digest]

dyspeptic¹ /dis'peptik/ adj **1** relating to or having dyspepsia: One splendid body is worth the brains of a hundred dyspeptic, flatulent philosophers — George Bernard Shaw. **2** ill-tempered. ➤➤ **dyspeptically** adv.

dyspeptic² noun a dyspeptic person.

dysphagia /dis'fayji·ə/ noun difficulty in swallowing, usu a symptom of a physiological disorder. [DYS- + Greek phagia eating]

dysphasia /dis'fayzi·ə/ noun difficulty in using or understanding language caused by brain injury or disease or malfunction of the brain. ➤➤ **dysphasic** /-zik/ noun and adj. [DYS- + Greek phania to utter]

dysphonia /dis'fohni·ə/ noun difficulty in speaking caused by injury to, or disease of, the vocal tract. [DYS- + Latin phonia, from Greek phōē a sound or voice]

dysphoria /dis'fawri·ə/ noun a state of feeling unwell, unhappy, or ill at ease: compare EUPHORIA. ➤➤ **dysphoric** /dis'forik/ adj and noun. [scientific Latin from Greek dysphoria, from dysphoros hard to bear, from DYS- + pherein to bear]

dysplasia /dis'playzi·ə/ noun abnormal growth or development of an organ, cells, tissue, etc. ➤➤ **dysplastic** /dis'plastik/ adj. [DYS- + Greek plasis formation]

dyspnoea (NAmer **dyspnea**) /disp'nee·ə/ noun difficult or laboured breathing. ➤➤ **dyspnoeic** /disp'neeik/ adj. [via Latin from

Greek *dyspnoia*, from *dyspnoos* short of breath, from DYS- + *pnein* to breathe]

dyspraxia /dis'praksi·ə/ *noun* a brain disorder that causes problems with coordination and movement. [DYS- + Greek *praxis* action]

dysprosium /dis'prohzi·əm/ *noun* a silver-white soft metallic chemical element of the rare-earth group that forms highly magnetic compounds, and is used to absorb neutrons in the control rods of a nuclear reactor: symbol Dy, atomic number 66. [scientific Latin *dysprosium* from Greek *dysprositos* hard to get at, from DYS- + *prositos* approachable, from *prosienai* to approach]

dysthymia /dis'thiemi·ə/ *noun* depression, anxiety, and other characteristics associated with introversion. ➤➤ **dysthymic** *adj and noun*. [DYS- + Greek *thymos* mind]

dystopia /dis'tohpi·ə/ *noun* an imaginary place that is depressingly wretched: compare UTOPIA. ➤➤ **dystopian** *adj*. [DYS- + -*topia* as in UTOPIA]

dystrophic /dis'trohfik/ *adj* **1** relating to or affected by dystrophy. **2** said of a lake or other body of water: brownish with dissolved undecomposed organic matter, a scarcity of oxygen and nutrients, and usu little plant or animal life.

dystrophy /'distrəfi/ *noun* **1** any of various disorders of the body characterized by wasting of organs or tissues, e.g. muscles or bones: compare MUSCULAR DYSTROPHY. **2** the state of a body of water being dystrophic. [DYS- + Greek -*trophia* nourishment]

dysuria /dis'yooəri·ə/ *noun* difficult or painful urination. [scientific Latin from Greek *dysouria*, from DYS- + -*ouria* -URIA]

DZ *abbr* Djazir (international vehicle registration for Algeria).

dz *abbr* dozen.

dzo *or* **zo** /zoh/ *noun* (*pl* **dzos** *or* **zos** *or collectively* **dzo** *or* **zo**) an animal of a breed of Tibetan cattle that is a cross between the yak and domestic cattle. [Tibetan *mdzo*]

Dzongkha /'zonggə/ *noun* the dialect of Tibetan spoken by the people of Bhutan. [Tibetan, literally 'language of the fortress']

E¹ *or* **e** *noun* (*pl* **Es** *or* **E's** *or* **e's**) **1a** the fifth letter of the English alphabet. **b** a written character or design denoting this letter. **c** the sound represented by this letter, one of the English vowels. **2** an item designated as E, *esp* the fifth in a series. **3** a mark or grade rating a student's work as poor, usually constituting a low pass or a fail. **4** in music, the third note of the diatonic scale of C major. **5** (*always* **E**) in occupational analysis, a person who is unemployed or without regular employment, or who is not working for health, age, etc reasons, and who therefore depends on the state for his or her income.

E² *abbr* **1** used *esp* on electrical plugs: earth. **2** East. **3** Easterly. **4** Eastern. **5** East (London postcode). **6** electromotive force. **7** (*also* **e**) electronic: *Email*. **8** energy. **9** English. **10** España (international vehicle registration for Spain). **11** European: *E number*; *E322*. **12** exa-.

E³ *noun* (*pl* **Es** *or* **E's**) **1** the drug Ecstasy. **2** a tablet of this drug.

E- *prefix* used before a series of digits, denoting: E number. [short for European, because the system was set up by the European Union]

e¹ *symbol* in mathematics, the base of the system of natural logarithms, having the approximate value 2.71828.

e² *abbr* electron.

e-¹ *prefix* forming words, with the meanings: **1a** to deprive of; to remove (a specified quality or thing): *emasculate*; *eviscerate*. **b** lacking; without: *edentate*; *ecaudate*. **2** outwards; on the outside: *evert*. **3** out: *emanate*; *ejaculate*. [Middle English via Old French from Latin, from EX-¹, out, away]

e-² *prefix* forming words, with the meaning: electronic: *e-commerce*. [ELECTRONIC]

ea. *abbr* each.

each¹ /eech/ *adj* being one of two or more distinct individuals within a pair, group, or number considered separately: *She wiggled each foot in turn*; *They each want something different.* ✶ **each and every** all; every single. [Old English *ǽlc*]

each² *pronoun* each one: *each of us*; *Each is equally attractive*.

each³ *adv* to or for each; apiece: *tickets at £10 each*.

each other *pronoun* (*not used as the subject of a verb*) each of two or more in reciprocal action or relation: *We often wore each other's shirts*; *They looked at each other in surprise*.

Usage note

each other *or* **one another?** The traditional rule states that *each other* refers to a relationship between only two people or things (*We love each other and want to get married*), whereas *one another* refers to a relationship between more than two people (*Christ commanded his disciples to love one another*). Modern authorities point out, however, that there is no basis for this rule except tradition and there can be no objection in principle to sentences such as *Harris and Jones mistrusted their boss even more than they mistrusted one another* or *All members of this organization are expected to help each other*.

each way *adj and adv Brit* said of a bet: backing a horse, dog, etc to win or to finish in the first two, three, or four in a race.

eager /'eegə/ *adj* marked by or showing keen, enthusiastic, or impatient desire or interest: *eager for the fray* — Colley Cibber. ➤➤ **eagerly** *adv*, **eagerness** *noun*. [Middle English *egre* sharp, fierce, via early French *aigre* from Latin *acer* sharp]

eager beaver *noun informal* somebody who is unduly zealous in performing his or her assigned duties and in volunteering for more.

eagle¹ /'eegl/ *noun* **1** any of several species of large birds of prey noted for their strength, size, gracefulness, keenness of vision, and powers of flight: genus *Aquila* and other genera. **2** any of various emblematic or symbolic representations of an eagle, such as the standard of the ancient Romans or the seal or standard of the USA. **3** a former ten-dollar gold coin of the USA. **4** a golf score for one hole of two strokes less than par. [Middle English *egle* via Old French *aigle* from Latin *aquila*]

eagle² *verb trans* to score an eagle at (a hole) in golf. ➤ *verb intrans* to score an eagle.

eagle eye *noun* a close watch; careful attention: *She kept an eagle eye on the students throughout the exam*.

eagle-eyed *adj* **1** having very good eyesight. **2** looking very keenly at something: *He watched eagle-eyed while the cashier counted out the money*. **3** good at noticing details; observant: *He found himself working under an eagle-eyed manager who spotted the smallest mistake*.

eagle hawk *noun* a large brown Australian eagle: *Aquila audax*.

eagle owl *noun* the largest European owl, with prominent ear tufts and large orange eyes: *Bubo bubo*.

eaglet /'eeglit/ *noun* a young eagle.

eagre /'aygə/ *noun* = BORE⁵. [origin unknown]

EAK *abbr* Kenya (international vehicle registration).

ealdorman /'awldəmən/ *noun* (*pl* **ealdormen**) the chief officer in a district, e.g. a shire, in Anglo-Saxon England. [Old English; see ALDERMAN]

-ean *suffix* see -AN¹, -AN².

E and OE *abbr* errors and omissions excepted.

ear¹ /iə/ *noun* **1a** the organ of hearing and equilibrium in humans and other vertebrates. **b** the external part of this organ. **c** any of various organs capable of detecting vibratory motion. **2** the sense or act of hearing. **3** sensitivity to musical tone and pitch. **4a** sympathetic attention: *Give every man thine ear but few thy voice* — Shakespeare; *He eventually gained the ear of the managing director.* **b** (*in pl*) notice or awareness: *It has come to my ears that you are unhappy* *here.* **5** something resembling an ear in shape or position, e.g. a lug or handle. **✳ be all ears** to listen very attentively. **give ear to somebody/something** to listen to somebody or something. **have an ear to the ground** to be in receipt of information not generally known. **have/keep an/one's ear to the ground** to keep oneself informed about news, gossip, etc [from the alleged practice among Native Americans of lying with one ear to the ground to detect vibrations caused by distant horses or bison]. **have somebody's ear** to have access to somebody so that one can give advice, make complaints, etc: *We need to find somebody who has the President's ear.* **in one ear and out the other** straight through one's mind without making an impression. **out on one's ear** thrown out of a job, home, etc with no possibility of returning. **somebody's ears are burning** somebody has a feeling that they are being talked about. **up to one's ears** very busy. [Old English *ēare*]

ear² *noun* the fruiting spike of a cereal, including both the seeds and protective structures. [Old English *ēar*]

earache *noun* an ache or pain in the ear.

eardrum *noun* = TYMPANIC MEMBRANE.

eared *adj (usu used in combinations)* having ears, *esp* ears of a specified kind or number: *a long-eared owl.*

earful /'iəf(ə)l/ *noun informal* **1** an outpouring of news or gossip. **2** a sharp verbal reprimand.

earhole *noun* the ear, *esp* of a person.

earl /uhl/ *noun* a member of the British peerage ranking below a marquess and above a viscount. ➤➤ **earldom** *noun.* [Old English *eorl* warrior, nobleman; related to JARL]

Earl Grey *noun* a black China tea, or blend of China and Indian teas, scented with bergamot oil. [named after Charles, second *Earl Grey* d.1845, English statesman, who is said to have received the recipe from a Chinese Mandarin]

earl marshal *noun* an officer of state in England serving chiefly as a royal attendant on ceremonial occasions, as marshal of state processions, and as head of the College of Arms.

earlobe *noun* the soft, fleshy, lower part of the ear.

earl palatine /'palətin/ *noun* an English earl having in former times royal powers within his county.

early¹ /'uhli/ *adv* (**earlier, earliest**) **1** before the usual, expected, or proper time: *On Friday he got up early.* **2** (*often* + on) at or near the beginning of a period of time, development, or series: *He usually comes early in the morning.* [Old English *ǣrlīce*, from *ǣr* early, soon]

early² *adj* (**earlier, earliest**) **1a** occurring before the usual time. **b** occurring in the near future. **c** maturing or producing sooner than related forms: *an early peach.* **2a** of, at, or occurring near the beginning of a period of time, development, or series. **b** distant in past time. **c** primitive. **✳ at the earliest** not sooner than a specified date or time. **have an early night** to go to bed earlier than usual. **in the early days** during the early part of an activity, etc. **it's early days** it is too soon to be sure of an outcome, to expect a result, etc. ➤➤ **earliness** *noun.*

early³ *noun (pl* **earlies**) **1** a plant, e.g. a potato, that matures more rapidly than average. **2** an early shift.

early bird *noun* somebody who rises or arrives early.

early closing *noun Brit* **1** the closing of shops in a British town or district on one afternoon a week. **2** the day on which shops close early.

Early English *adj* of an early Gothic style of architecture, prevalent in Britain from the late 12th to the late 13th cent., characterized by lancet windows and pointed arches.

early music *noun* medieval and Renaissance music, sometimes also including baroque and early classical music.

early warning *noun* adequate advance notice of something that is going to happen.

early warning system *noun* a network of radar stations which give information in advance of enemy air attack.

earmark¹ *noun* **1** a mark of identification on the ear of an animal. **2** a distinguishing or identifying characteristic.

earmark² *verb trans* **1** to mark (livestock) with an earmark. **2** to designate (e.g. funds) for a specific use or owner.

earmuffs *pl noun* a pair of ear coverings connected by a flexible band and worn as protection against cold or noise.

earn /uhn/ *verb trans* **1** to receive (e.g. money) as return for effort, *esp* for work done or services rendered. **2** to bring in (money) as

income: *My shares earned nothing last year.* **3a** to gain or deserve (a title, reward, etc) because of one's behaviour or qualities: *Alexander earned the title 'the Great' by his victories in war.* **b** to make (somebody or something) worthy of a title, reward, etc; to be the reason for somebody or something getting (a title, reward, etc): *Alexander's victories in war earned him the title 'the Great'.* [Old English *earnian*]

earned income *noun* income from work one is paid for as opposed to income from shares, etc.

earner *noun* **1** somebody who earns wages, etc. **2** *Brit, informal* something profitable: *This deal has been a nice little earner.*

earnest¹ *adj* determined and serious. ➤➤ **earnestly** *adv,* **earnestness** *noun.*

earnest² /'uhnist/ **✳ in earnest** serious or seriously; sincere or sincerely: *At seventy-seven it is time to be in earnest* — Dr Johnson. [Old English *eornost*]

earnest³ *noun* **1** something of value, *esp* money, given by a buyer to a seller to seal a bargain. **2** a token of what is to come; a pledge. [Middle English *ernes, ernest,* from Old French *erres,* pl of *erre* pledge, via Latin and Greek from Hebrew *'ērābhōn*]

earnest money *noun* money given as an EARNEST³.

earnings *pl noun* money or other income earned.

earphone *noun* a device, attached e.g. to a radio, that converts electrical energy into sound waves and is worn over or inserted into the ear.

earpiece *noun* a part of an instrument, e.g. a telephone, to which the ear is applied for listening; an earphone.

earpiercing *adj* distressingly loud and shrill.

ear-piercing *noun* the making of a hole in the lobe of the ear to allow earrings to be worn.

earplug *noun* a device inserted into the outer opening of the ear for protection against water, loud noise, etc.

earring *noun* an ornament for the ear that is attached to the earlobe.

earshot *noun* the range within which something, *esp* the unaided voice, may be heard: *out of earshot.*

earsplitting *adj* distressingly loud.

earth¹ /uhth/ *noun* **1a** (*often* **Earth**) the planet on which we live, third in order from the sun: *I am a passenger on the spaceship, Earth* — R Buckminster Fuller. **b** the people of the planet Earth. **2a** areas of land as distinguished from sea and air. **b** the solid ground. **3a** the loose powdery material on the surface of the planet, in which plants grow; soil. **b** any dry powdery material, e.g. FULLER'S EARTH. **c** the material of which the body consists: *earth to earth, ashes to ashes.* **d** a metallic oxide formerly classed as an element; see RARE EARTH. **4** *chiefly Brit.* **a** an electrical connection to the ground. **b** the terminal, e.g. in a plug, for this connection. **5** (**the earth**) *informal* a huge amount of money: *His suit must have cost the earth!* **6** the lair of a fox, badger, etc. **7** the sphere of mortal or worldly existence as distinguished from spheres of spiritual life: compare HEAVEN, HELL. **8** one of the four elements of the alchemists, the others being fire, air, and water. **✳ back down to earth** to a sense or recognition of the realities of life, a situation, etc. **go to earth** to go into hiding. **on earth** used to intensify an interrogative pronoun: *Where on earth is it?* ➤➤ **earthlike** *adj,* **earthward** /'uhthwəd/ *adj and adv,* **earthwards** /'uhthwədz/ *adv.* [Old English *eorthe*]

earth² *verb trans* **1** *chiefly Brit* to connect (an electrical device) to earth. **2** to drive (e.g. a fox) to hiding in its earth. ➤ *verb intrans* said of a hunted animal: to hide in its lair.

earthbound *adj* **1a** restricted to the earth. **b** heading or directed towards the planet earth: *an earthbound spaceship.* **2a** bound by worldly interests; lacking spiritual quality. **b** pedestrian or unimaginative.

earth closet *noun* a toilet in which earth is used to cover excreta.

earthen /'uhdh(ə)n, 'uhth(ə)n/ *adj* made of earth or baked clay.

earthenware *noun* **1** ceramic ware made of slightly porous opaque clay fired at a low temperature: compare STONEWARE. **2** (*used as before a noun*) made of earthenware: *an earthenware pot.*

earthling /'uhthling/ *noun* an inhabitant of the earth, *esp* as contrasted with inhabitants of other planets, e.g. in science fiction.

earthly¹ *adj* **1a** characteristic of or belonging to the earth. **b** relating to human beings' actual life on this earth; worldly. **2** (*in* *negative or interrogative contexts*) possible: *There is no earthly reason for such behaviour.* ➤ **earthliness** *noun*.

earthly² *noun informal* (*in negative contexts*) a chance of success: *He hasn't an earthly of being elected.*

earthman *noun* (*pl* **earthmen**) a male earthling.

earth mother *noun* **1** (*often* **Earth Mother**) the female principle of fertility. **2** a woman who embodies the earth mother, *esp* in being generously proportioned and maternal.

earthnut *noun* **1a** a plant of the carrot family that has edible tubers (underground stems; see TUBER); = PIGNUT: *Conopodium majus.* **b** a tuber of this plant, used as food. **2a** any of various other plants with roundish edible tubers, roots, or pods growing underground. **b** a tuber, root, or pod of these plants, used as food.

earthquake *noun* a usu violent and often repeated earth tremor caused by volcanic action or processes within the earth's crust.

earth science *noun* any or all of the sciences, such as geology, that deal with one or more parts of the earth.

earthshattering *adj* having tremendous importance or a widespread often violent effect. ➤ **earthshatteringly** *adv.*

earthshine *noun* sunlight reflected by the earth and illuminating the dark part of the moon.

earth sign *noun* in astrology, any of the three signs of the zodiac Taurus, Virgo and Capricorn: compare AIR SIGN, FIRE SIGN, WATER SIGN.

earth up *verb trans* to cover or surround the roots or lower parts of (a plant, e.g. a potato or celery plant) with a raised layer of earth.

earthwoman *noun* (*pl* **earthwomen**) a female earthling.

earthwork *noun* **1** (*also in pl*) an embankment, field fortification, etc made of earth. **2** the construction of such embankments, etc.

earthworm *noun* any of several genera of widely distributed hermaphroditic worms that live in the soil: genus *Lumbricus* and other genera.

earthy /'uhthi/ *adj* (**earthier, earthiest**) **1** consisting of, resembling, or suggesting earth or soil: *an earthy flavour.* **2** crude or coarse: *earthy humour.* ➤ **earthily** *adv,* **earthiness** *noun.*

ear trumpet *noun* a trumpet-shaped device held to the ear to improve hearing.

earwax *noun* the yellow waxy secretion from the glands of the outer ear; = CERUMEN.

earwig¹ *noun* any of numerous species of small insects that have slender many-jointed antennae and a pair of appendages resembling forceps: order Dermaptera.

─────────────────────
Word history
Old English *ēarwicga*, from *ēare* EAR¹ + *wicga* insect. Earwigs were once thought to crawl into people's ears.
─────────────────────

earwig² *verb intrans* (**earwigged, earwigging**) *informal* to eavesdrop.

ease¹ /eez/ *noun* **1a** freedom from pain, discomfort, or anxiety. **b** freedom from labour or difficulty. **c** freedom from embarrassment or constraint; naturalness. **d** freedom from poverty. **e** rest or relaxation. **2** facility or effortlessness. **3** easing or being eased. ✳ **at ease 1** free from pain or discomfort. **2** (*also* **at one's ease**) free from restraint or formality; relaxed: *He's quite at his ease in any kind of company.* **3** used *esp* as a military command: standing with the feet apart and usu one or both hands behind the body. ➤ **easeful** *adj,* **easefully** *adv.* [Middle English *ese* from Old French *aise* convenience, comfort]

ease² *verb trans* **1** to alleviate (pain, suffering, etc); to make (it) less severe or intense. **2** to make (something) less difficult. **3** to manoeuvre (something) gently or carefully in a specified way: *They eased the heavy block into position.* **4** (*often* + off) to lessen the pressure or tension of (a rope, etc), *esp* by slackening, lifting, or shifting. **5** (+ of) to free (somebody) from something that pains, worries, or burdens them. **6** to put the helm of (a ship) towards the lee. ➤ *verb intrans* **1** (*often* + off/up) to decrease in activity, intensity, severity, etc: *The rain is easing off at last.* **2** to manoeuvre oneself gently or carefully: *She eased through a hole in the fence.*

easel /'eezl/ *noun* a frame for supporting something, *esp* an artist's canvas. [Dutch *ezel* ass]

easement *noun* **1** a right in law to the limited use, for access, of another person's ground or property. **2** an act or means of easing or relieving.

easily /'eezəli/ *adv* **1** without difficulty: *My car will do a hundred easily.* **2** without doubt; by far: *easily the best.*

east¹ /eest/ *noun* **1** the direction 90° clockwise from north that is the general direction of sunrise. **2a** (*often* **East**) regions or countries lying to the east of a specified or implied point of orientation. **b** (*usu* **the East**) regions lying to the east of Europe: *East is East, and West is West, and never the twain shall meet* — Kipling. **c** (**the East**) formerly, the bloc of communist countries in eastern Europe. **3** the altar end of a church. [Old English *ēast*]

east² *adj and adv* **1** at, towards, or coming from the east. **2** said of the wind: blowing from the east. ✳ **east by north** in a position or direction between east and east-northeast. **east by south** in a position or direction between east and east-southeast.

eastbound *adj and adv* going or moving east: *the eastbound carriageway.*

East End *noun* (**the East End**) the densely populated inner city area of east London containing industrial areas and docks. ➤ **East Ender** *noun.*

Easter /'eestə/ *noun* a festival celebrated in the Christian Church commemorating Christ's resurrection, observed on the first Sunday after the first full moon following 21 March. [Old English *ēastre*, from the name of a pagan spring festival]

Easter egg *noun* a chocolate or painted and hard-boiled egg given as a present and eaten at Easter.

easterly¹ /'eestəli/ *adj and adv* **1** in an eastern position or direction. **2** said of a wind: blowing from the east.

easterly² *noun* (*pl* **easterlies**) a wind blowing from the east.

Easter Monday *noun* the Monday after Easter, observed as a public holiday.

eastern /'eestə(ə)n/ *adj* **1** in or towards the east; inhabiting the east. **2** (*often* **Eastern**). **a** relating to any region conventionally designated East. **b** steeped in or stemming from Oriental traditions, in contrast with those of Europe or America: *eastern philosophies.* **c** of the former communist countries of Eastern Europe and Asia: *the eastern bloc.* ➤ **easternmost** *adj.*

Eastern Church *noun* **1** (*also* **Eastern Orthodox Church**) the Christian Church or Churches originating in the church of the Eastern Roman Empire and forming the main Christian Churches in Greece, Russia, Serbia, etc. **2** (*also* **Eastern church**) any of the Christian Churches of North Africa and the Middle East professing Monophysitic (holding Christ to be wholly divine; see MONOPHYSITE) theology.

Easterner *noun chiefly NAmer* a native or inhabitant of the East, *esp* the eastern USA.

eastern hemisphere *noun* the half of the earth to the east of the Atlantic Ocean, including Europe, Asia, and Africa.

Eastertide *noun* the period of time around Easter.

easting *noun* **1** distance due east in longitude from the preceding point of measurement. **2** easterly progress.

east-northeast¹ *noun* the direction midway between east and northeast.

east-northeast² *adj and adv* at, towards, or coming from the east-northeast.

east-southeast¹ *noun* the direction midway between east and southeast.

east-southeast² *adj and adv* at, towards, or coming from the east-southeast.

eastward *adj and adv* towards the east; in a direction going east.

eastwards *adv* towards the east; eastward.

easy¹ /'eezi/ *adj* (**easier, easiest**) **1a** causing or involving little difficulty or discomfort: *an easy problem.* **b** not difficult to get, earn, etc: *easy money.* **2a** not severe; lenient. **b** readily prevailed on; compliant. **c** not difficult to deceive or take advantage of: *easy prey.* **d** *informal* readily persuaded to have sexual relations. **3a** marked by peace and comfort: *an easy life.* **b** not hurried or strenuous: *an easy pace.* **c** free from pain, annoyance, or anxiety. **4** marked by social ease: *easy manners.* **5** not burdensome or straitened: *Buy now on easy terms.* **6** marked by ready facility and freedom from constraint: *an easy flowing style of writing.* **7** *chiefly Brit, informal* not having strong preferences on a particular issue. **8** loose; loose-fitting. **9a** plentiful in supply at low or declining interest rates: *easy money.* **b** less in demand and usu lower in price: *Gilts were easier.* ✳ **be easy on** to be lenient with (somebody): *He's too easy on the boy.* **easy does it**

informal doing something slowly and carefully brings success. **easy on the eye/eyes** *informal* attractive. **easy on the ear** *informal* pleasant to listen to. **of easy virtue** *dated* easily persuaded to have sexual relations. ➤➤ **easiness** *noun*. [Middle English *esy*, from Old French *aaisié*, past part. of *aaisier* to ease, from *aise* comfort, convenient, EASE¹]

easy² *adv* **1** easily: *Promises come easy.* **2** without undue speed, stress, or excitement; slowly or cautiously: *We'll take it easy, one step at a time.* ✱ **go easy 1** to be not too lavish with something: *Go easy on the ice, bartender.* **2** (+ on) to deal leniently with somebody: *Go easy on the boy. He meant no harm.* **stand easy** used as a military command to soldiers standing at ease, giving permission to relax further. **take it easy 1** to relax or rest. **2** to remain calm.

easy-care *adj* said of a material or item of clothing: easy to look after, clean, etc.

easy chair *noun* a large usu upholstered armchair designed for comfort and relaxation.

easygoing *adj* **1a** taking life easily. **b** placid and tolerant. **c** indolent and careless. **2** unhurried; comfortable: *an easygoing pace.* ➤➤ **easygoingness** *noun*.

easy listening *noun* music and song that is undemanding and pleasant to listen to. ➤➤ **easy-listening** *adj*.

easy meat *noun chiefly Brit* somebody who is easily duped, imposed upon, or mastered.

easy-peasy /ˈeeziˈpeezi/ *adj Brit, informal* used *esp* by children: very easy. [reduplication of EASY¹]

easy street *noun informal* a position of affluence.

EAT *abbr* Tanzania (international vehicle registration).

eat /eet/ *verb* (*past tense* **ate** /et, ayt/, *past part.* **eaten**) ➤ *verb trans* **1** to put (*esp* food) in the mouth and swallow it, usu after chewing it. **2a** (*also* + *away*) to corrode (something): *Paint had been eaten away by the sea's fine spray.* **b** to cause (damage) by eating or corroding something: *Moths had eaten holes in her jacket.* **c** to devastate (a place) by eating its produce or resources: *Locusts ate the country bare.* **3** *informal* to worry or annoy (somebody): *What's eating them?* ➤ *verb intrans* **1** to take food or a meal: *When shall we eat?* **2** (+ into/through) to cause damage to something by eating: *The fault had been caused by insects eating through the cable.* **3a** (+ into/through) to destroy or corrode (something) gradually: *The acid had started to eat into the metal.* **b** (+ into) to use a great deal of (a limited resource): *Buying a new car will eat into your savings.* ✱ **eat dirt** *informal* to accept insults or humiliation humbly and uncomplainingly. **eat humble pie** see HUMBLE PIE. **eat like a bird** to eat very little. **eat like a horse** to eat a lot. **eat one's hat** used to express one's opinion that something is very unlikely: *If he passes his driving test, I'll eat my hat.* **eat one's heart out** to grieve bitterly, *esp* for something desired but unobtainable. **eat one's words** to retract what one has said, *esp* in an ignominious way. **eat out of somebody's hand** to do everything somebody asks. ➤➤ **eater** *noun*. [Old English *etan*]

eatable *adj* suitable for eating.

Usage note

eatable *or* edible? Both *eatable* and *edible* mean 'reasonably pleasant to eat': *If you put plenty of sauce on it, it's just about eatable or edible.* The primary meaning of *edible*, however, is 'possible to eat', 'nonpoisonous': *Are these berries edible?*

eatables *pl noun* food.

eat away *verb trans* **1** to remove (something) by eating it: *Insects had eaten away the bark.* **2** to destroy or corrode (something) gradually. ➤ *verb intrans* **1** (+ at) to remove part of something by eating it. **2** (+ at) to corrode or destroy part of something.

eaten /ˈeet(ə)n/ *verb* past part. of EAT.

eatery *noun* (*pl* **eateries**) *informal* a restaurant.

eat in *verb intrans* to eat a meal at home, as opposed to in a restaurant, etc.

eating¹ *adj* **1** suitable for eating raw: *an eating apple.* **2** where food is served; where people eat out: *I know a good eating place.*

eating² *noun* the act of eating, *esp* with regard to the quality of the food: *Badly cooked ling doesn't make for good eating.*

eat out *verb intrans* to eat a meal away from home, *esp* in a restaurant.

eats *pl noun informal* food. [Old English *ǣt*; related to Old English *etan* to EAT]

eat up *verb trans* **1** to eat (food) completely. **2a** to use up (money, resources, etc). **b** to travel (a distance) quickly. **3** *informal* to listen attentively to (what somebody says): *The audience ate up every word.* **4** *informal* (*usu in passive*) to absorb or preoccupy (somebody): *He was eaten up by vanity.*

EAU *abbr* Uganda (international vehicle registration).

eau de cologne /ˌoh də kəˈlohn/ *noun* (*pl* **eaux de cologne** /ˌoh/) a variety of TOILET WATER. [French *eau de cologne* literally 'water', from *Cologne*, city in Germany. Eau de cologne was invented by an Italian chemist living in Cologne]

eau-de-nil /ˌoh də ˈneel/ *noun* a pale slightly bluish green. ➤➤ **eau-de-nil** *adj*. [French *eau-de-nil* water from the *Nile*, river in Africa]

eau de toilette /ˌoh də twahˈlet/ *noun* (*pl* **eaux de toilette** /ˌoh/) = TOILET WATER. [French *eau de toilette* toilet water]

eau-de-vie /ˌoh də ˈvee/ *noun* (*pl* **eaux-de-vie** /ˌoh/) = BRANDY. [French *eau-de-vie* water of life, translation of medieval Latin *aqua vitae*]

eaux de cologne /ˌoh/ *noun* pl of EAU DE COLOGNE.

eaux de toilette /ˌoh/ *noun* pl of EAU DE TOILETTE.

eaux-de-vie *noun* pl of EAU-DE-VIE.

eaves /eevz/ *pl noun* the lower border of a roof that overhangs the wall. [Old English *efes*]

eavesdrop *verb intrans* (**eavesdropped, eavesdropping**) to listen secretly to what is said in private. ➤➤ **eavesdropper** *noun*. [orig as *eavesdropper*, literally 'somebody standing where water drips from the eaves']

ebb¹ /eb/ *noun* the flowing out of the tide towards the sea. ✱ **at a low ebb** at a low point; in a poor state: *Relations were at a low ebb.* [Old English *ebba*]

ebb² *verb intrans* **1** said of tidal water: to recede from the highest level. **2** (*often* + *away*) to decline from a higher to a lower level or from a better to a worse state; to disappear gradually.

ebb tide *noun* = EBB¹.

EBCDIC /ˈebsədik, ˈebkədik/ *noun* a computer code consisting of 256 eight-bit characters that is used for representing data and to facilitate the exchange of information between a computer and other data processing equipment. [extended *b*inary *c*oded *d*ecimal *i*nter*c*hange *c*ode]

Ebola fever /eeˈbohlə, ə-/ *noun* an often fatal infectious viral disease characterized by internal bleeding and fever. [named after a river in Zaire (Democratic Republic of Congo), close to which it was first recorded]

e-bomb *noun* **1** = ELECTRONIC BOMB. **2** = ELECTROMAGNETIC BOMB.

ebon /ˈeb(ə)n/ *adj literary* ebony.

ebonise /ˈebəniez/ *verb trans* see EBONIZE.

ebonite /ˈebəniet/ *noun* a hard black vulcanized rubber; = VULCANITE.

ebonize *or* **ebonise** /ˈebəniez/ *verb trans* to colour (wood, furniture, etc) with a black or dark stain in imitation of ebony.

ebony¹ /ˈebəni/ *noun* (*pl* **ebonies**) **1** a hard heavy black wood. **2** any of several species of tropical trees that yield this wood: genus *Diospyros*. **3** a dark brown or black. [Greek *ebenos* from Egyptian *hbnj*]

ebony² *adj* **1** made of or resembling ebony. **2** black or dark brown.

e-book *noun* a text published on a disk, CD-ROM, etc rather than in printed form. [short for *electronic book*]

Ebor. /ˈeebaw/ *abbr* of York, used *esp* in the signature of the Archbishop of York. [Latin *Eboracensis* from *Eboracum* York]

EBRD *abbr* European Bank for Reconstruction and Development.

ebullience /iˈbuli-əns/ *noun* the quality of being full of liveliness and enthusiasm; exuberance.

ebulliency /iˈbuli-ənsi/ *noun* = EBULLIENCE.

ebullient /iˈbuli-ənt/ *adj* **1** characterized by ebullience. **2** *archaic or literary* boiling or agitated. ➤➤ **ebulliently** *adv*. [Latin *ebullient-, ebulliens*, present part. of *ebullire* to bubble out, from EX-¹ + *bullire* to bubble or boil]

ebulliometer /i,buli'omitə/ *noun* an instrument for measuring the boiling point of a solution.

ebullition /ebəˈlish(ə)n/ *noun* **1** the act, process, or state of boiling or bubbling up. **2** *formal* a sudden violent outburst or display.

e-business *noun* = E-COMMERCE.

EC *abbr* **1** East Central (London postcode). **2** Ecuador (international vehicle registration). **3** European Commission. **4** European Community. **5** executive committee.

ec- *or* **eco-** *comb. form* forming words, with the meanings: **1** habitat; environment: *ecospecies; ecophysiology*. **2** ecological: *ecosystem*. [late Latin *oeco-* household, from Greek *oiko-*, from *oikos* house]

e-cash *noun* see E-MONEY. [short for *electronic cash*]

ECB *abbr* **1** English Cricket Board. **2** European Central Bank.

eccentric[1] /ik'sentrik/ *adj* **1** deviating from established convention; odd: *eccentric behaviour*. **2** not having the same centre: *eccentric spheres*. **3a** deviating from a circular path: *an eccentric orbit*. **b** located elsewhere than at the geometrical centre, or having the axis or support so located: *an eccentric wheel*. >>> **eccentrically** *adv*. [via medieval Latin from Greek *ekkentros*, from *ex* out of + *kentron* centre]

eccentric[2] *noun* **1** an eccentric person. **2** a mechanical device using eccentrically mounted parts to transform circular into reciprocating motion.

eccentricity /eksən'trisiti/ *noun* (*pl* **eccentricities**) **1a** being eccentric. **b** eccentric behaviour or an eccentric characteristic: *In the streets of London where beauty goes unregarded, eccentricity must pay the penalty, and it is better not to be very tall, to wear a long blue cloak, or to beat the air with your left hand* — Virginia Woolf. **2** a number that for a given conic section is the ratio of the distances from any point on the curve to the FOCUS[1] (fixed point) and the DIRECTRIX (specified straight line). **3** deviation from a circular path. **4** displacement from the geometrical centre.

Eccl. *or* **Eccles.** *abbr* Ecclesiastes (book of the Bible).

eccl. *or* **eccles.** *abbr* **1** ecclesiastic. **2** ecclesiastical.

ecclesi- *or* **ecclesio-** *comb. form* forming words, denoting: church: *ecclesiology*. [via late Latin from Greek *ekklēsia*: see ECCLESIASTICAL]

ecclesiastic[1] /i,kleezi'astik/ *noun* a member of the clergy.

ecclesiastic[2] *adj* = ECCLESIASTICAL.

ecclesiastical *adj* **1** relating to a church, *esp* as a formal and established institution: *ecclesiastical law*. **2** suitable for use in a church: *ecclesiastical vestments*. >>> **ecclesiastically** *adv*. [late Latin *ecclesiasticus* from Greek *ekklēsiastikos*, from *ekklesia* an assembly of citizens, church, from *ekkalein* to call forth, summon, from *ex* out + *kailein* to call]

ecclesiasticism /i,kleezi'astisiz(ə)m/ *noun* excessive attachment to ecclesiastical forms and practices.

Ecclesiasticus /i,kleezi'astikus/ *noun* a didactic book, written by Ben Sira in the second cent. BC, included in the Protestant Apocrypha and the Roman Catholic Old Testament. [late Latin *ecclesiasticus*: see ECCLESIASTICAL]

ecclesio- *comb. form* see ECCLESI-.

ecclesiology /i,kleezi'oləji/ *noun* **1** the study of church architecture and ornament. **2** theological doctrine relating to the Church. >>> **ecclesiological** /-'lojikl/ *adj*, **ecclesiologist** /-'oləjist/ *noun*.

Ecclus. *abbr* Ecclesiasticus (book of the Apocrypha).

eccrine /'ekrin, 'ekrien, 'ekreen/ *adj* **1** producing a liquid secretion without the loss of CYTOPLASM (jellylike material inside a cell) from the secreting cells: *an eccrine gland*. **2** of or produced by an eccrine gland. [Greek *ekkrinein* to secrete, from *ex* out + *krinein* to sift]

eccrinology /ekri'noləji/ *noun* the branch of medical science that deals with eccrine secretions.

ecdemic /ek'demik/ *adj* not belonging or native to a particular people or region; not endemic or indigenous: *ecdemic diseases*. [Greek *ek* EX-[2] + *-demic* as in ENDEMIC[1]]

ecdysis /'ekdisis/ *noun* (*pl* **ecdyses** /-seez/) the moulting or shedding of an outer layer or skin, e.g. in insects and crustaceans. [Greek *ekdysis*, from *ex* out + *dyein* to put]

ECG *abbr* **1** electrocardiogram. **2** electrocardiograph.

echelon[1] /'eshəlon/ *noun* **1** any of a series of levels or grades, e.g. of authority or responsibility, in some organized field of activity. **2** an arrangement of e.g. troops or ships resembling a series of steps. **3** a particular division of a headquarters or supply organization in warfare. [French *échelon* rung of a ladder, from *échelle* ladder, from Latin *scala*]

echelon[2] *verb* (**echeloned, echeloning**) >> *verb trans* to form or arrange (troops, ships, etc) in an echelon. >> *verb intrans* to form up in an echelon.

echidna /i'kidnə/ *noun* (*pl* **echidnas** *or* **echidnae** /-nee/) either of two species of spiny burrowing nocturnal mammals of Australia, Tasmania, and New Guinea. Echidnas lay eggs, and feed chiefly on ants: *Tachyglossus aculeatus* and *Zaglossus bruijni*. Also called SPINY ANTEATER. [via Latin from Greek *echidna* viper]

echin- *or* **echino-** *comb. form* forming words, denoting: prickle: *echinoderm*. [Latin, from Greek *echinos* sea urchin]

echinacea /eki'naysi-ə/ *noun* **1** a N American plant of the daisy family that has flowers with spiny cone-shaped centres: genus *Echinacea*. **2** a preparation of the leaves and stems of this plant, thought to have medicinal value in strengthening the immune system. [from the Latin genus name, from Greek *echinos* sea urchin]

echini /i'kienie/ *noun* pl of ECHINUS.

echino- *comb. form* see ECHIN-.

echinoderm /i'kienohduhm, i'kin-/ *noun* any of a phylum of radially symmetrical marine animals including the starfishes, sea urchins, and related forms: phylum Echinodermata. >>> **echinodermatous** /-'duhmətəs/ *adj*. [ECHINO- + -*dermata* from Greek *derma* skin, from *derein* to skin]

echinoid /i'kienoyd, i'kinoyd/ *noun* = SEA URCHIN.

echinus /i'kienəs/ *noun* (*pl* **echini** /-nie/) **1** = SEA URCHIN. **2** a convex moulding beneath the abacus of the capital of a classical column. [Middle English via Latin from Greek *echinos* hedgehog, sea urchin, architectural echinus]

echo[1] /'ekoh/ *noun* (*pl* **echoes**) **1a** the repetition of a sound caused by the reflection of sound waves. **b** the repeated sound due to such reflection. **2** somebody or something that repeats or imitates another: *to mistake the echo of a London coffee-house for the voice of the kingdom* — Jonathan Swift. **3a** a repercussion or result. **b** a trace or vestige. **c** a sympathetic response. **d** something that brings back memories. **4a** the reflection by an object of transmitted radar signals. **b** a blip on a radar screen. **5** a soft repetition of a musical phrase. >>> **echoey** *adj*, **echoless** *adj*. [Middle English *ecco* via French and Latin from Greek *ēchō*]

echo[2] *verb* (**echoes, echoed, echoing**) >> *verb intrans* **1** to resound with echoes. **2** to produce an echo. **3** to produce a continual effect. >> *verb trans* **1** to repeat or imitate (somebody or something). **2** to send back or repeat (a sound) as an echo. >>> **echoer** *noun*, **echoing** *adj*.

echocardiography /,ekoh,kahdi'ogrəfi/ *noun* investigation of the action of the heart by means of ultrasound. >>> **echocardiogram** /-'kahdi-əgram/ *noun*, **echocardiograph** /-'kahdi-əgrahf/ *noun*, **echocardiographic** /-'grafik/ *adj*.

echo chamber *noun* a room with sound-reflecting walls used for making acoustic measurements and for producing echoing sound effects, *esp* in radio broadcasting.

echogram /'ekəgram/ *noun* **1** a recording of the information obtained by echo-sounding. **2** a display, e.g. on a screen, of the information obtained by echography. >>> **echograph** /-grahf/ *noun*, **echographic** /-'grafik/ *adj*.

echography /e'kogrəfi/ *noun* investigation of the internal structures of the body by means of ultrasound.

echoic /e'koh-ik/ *adj* **1** relating to an echo. **2** onomatopoeic. >>> **echoically** *adv*, **echoism** /'ekohiz(ə)m/ *noun*.

echolalia /ekoh'layli-ə/ *noun* **1** the pathological echoing of what is said by other people, usu a symptom of mental disorder. **2** the echoing of the words spoken by others by a child who is learning to talk. >>> **echolalic** /-'laylik, -'lalik/ *adj*.

echolocation /'ekohlohkaysh(ə)n/ *noun* the location of distant or invisible objects by means of sound waves reflected back to the sender, e.g. a bat or submarine, by the objects.

echo sounder *noun* an instrument that uses acoustic echolocation to determine depth in water. >>> **echo-sounding** *noun*.

echovirus *or* **ECHO virus** /'ekohvie-ərəs/ *noun* any of a group of viruses found in the gastrointestinal tract and sometimes associated with respiratory ailments and meningitis. [acronym from *enteric cytopathogenic human orphan*, + *virus*. 'Orphan' from the fact that the virus was at first not known to be associated with any disease]

éclair /i'kleə, ay'kleə/ *noun* a small light oblong cake of choux pastry that is split and filled with cream and usu topped with chocolate icing. [French *éclair* literally 'lightning']

eclampsia /i'klampsi·ə/ *noun* an attack of convulsions during pregnancy or childbirth. ➤➤ **eclamptic** /-tik/ *adj*. [Greek *eklampsis* sudden flashing, from *eklampein* to shine out]

éclat /ay'klah (*French* ekla)/ *noun* 1 ostentatious display. 2 brilliant or conspicuous success or distinction. 3 acclaim or applause. [French *éclat* splinter, burst, ostentation, from *éclater* to burst out]

eclectic¹ /i'klektik/ *adj* 1 selecting or using elements from various doctrines, methods, or styles. 2 composed of elements drawn from various sources. ➤➤ **eclectically** *adv*, **eclecticism** /-siz(ə)m/ *noun*. [Greek *eklektikos* from *eklegein* to select, from *ex* out + *legein* to gather]

eclectic² *noun* somebody who uses an eclectic method or approach.

eclipse¹ /i'klips/ *noun* 1a the total or partial obscuring of one celestial body by another, or the time when this happens. b passage into the shadow of a celestial body; compare OCCULTATION, TRANSIT¹. 2 a falling into obscurity or decay; a decline: *His departure was the eclipse of a genius* — Lord Blake. 3 the state of being in ECLIPSE PLUMAGE: *a mallard in eclipse*. [Middle English via Old French and Latin from Greek *ekleipsis*, from *ekleipein* to omit, fail, suffer eclipse, from *ex* out + *leipein* to leave]

eclipse² *verb trans* 1 to cause an eclipse of (a celestial body); to obscure or darken (it). 2 to surpass (a person, achievement, etc).

eclipse plumage *noun* comparatively dull plumage that occurs seasonally in ducks or other birds which adopt a distinct nuptial plumage: compare NUPTIAL PLUMAGE.

eclipsing binary *noun* a BINARY STAR (two stars revolving round each other) whose mutual eclipses cause variations in its observed brightness.

eclipsing variable *noun* = ECLIPSING BINARY.

ecliptic¹ /i'kliptik/ *noun* 1 the plane of the earth's orbit around the sun. 2 the projection of the plane of the earth's orbit on the celestial sphere. [Middle English *ecliptik* from late Latin *ecliptica linea* line of eclipses]

ecliptic² *adj* relating to the ecliptic or an eclipse. ➤➤ **ecliptically** *adv*.

eclogue /'eklog/ *noun* a short poem, *esp* a pastoral dialogue. [Middle English *eclog* from Latin *Eclogae* Selections (title of pastoral poems by Virgil d.19 BC, Roman poet), pl of *ecloga* selection, from Greek *eklogē*, from *eklegein*: see ECLECTIC¹]

eclosion /e'klozh(ə)n/ *noun* the emergence of an insect from the pupal case or of a larva from the egg. [French *éclosion*, from *éclore* to hatch, from Latin EX-¹ + *claudere* to close]

eco- *comb. form* see EC-.

ecocentric /eekoh'sentrik/ *adj* having a strong interest in and concern for environmental issues. [ECO- + -CENTRIC]

ecocide /'eekohsied/ *noun* destruction of the natural environment to the extent that it is unable to support life.

eco-friendly /eekoh'frendli/ *adj* not harmful to the environment.

ecol. *abbr* 1 ecological. 2 ecology.

eco-labelling *noun* the use of labels by manufacturers to identify products that satisfy certain environmental standards. ➤➤ **eco-label** *noun*.

E. coli /'kohlie/ *noun* a bacterium that is found naturally in the intestines of humans and other animals and can sometimes cause severe food poisoning. [short for *Escherichia coli*: see ESCHERICHIA]

ecological /eekə'lojikl, ek-/ *adj* 1 of or relating to ecology. 2 beneficial to or not harmful to the environment. ➤➤ **ecologically** *adv*.

ecology /i'koləji/ *noun* the interrelationship of living organisms and their environments, or the scientific study of this. ➤➤ **ecologist** *noun*. [German *Ökologie*, from Greek *oikos-* house + -LOGY]

e-commerce *noun* the buying and selling of goods and services by computer, *esp* over the Internet. [short for *electronic commerce*]

econ. *abbr* 1 economics. 2 economist. 3 economy.

econometrics /i,konə'metriks/ *pl noun* (*treated as sing.*) the application of statistical methods to the study of economic data and problems. ➤➤ **econometric** *adj*, **econometrical** *adj*, **econo-**

metrically *adv*, **econometrician** /-'trish(ə)n/ *noun*, **econometrist** *noun*. [blend of ECONOMICS and METRIC¹]

economic /ekə'nomik, ee-/ *adj* 1 relating to economics or finance. 2 of or based on the production, distribution, and consumption of goods and services. 3 relating to an economy. 4 having practical or industrial significance or uses; affecting material resources: *economic pests*. 5 profitable. 6 to do with practical or financial necessity. 7 efficient; = ECONOMICAL. ➤➤ **economically** *adv*.

Usage note

economic or economical? *Economic* means 'relating to economics or an economy' (*an economic crisis; economic indicators*), 'reasonably profitable' (*If the price of tin were to rise, it might become economic to reopen the mine*), and 'not wasteful'. This final meaning overlaps with that of *economical* (*an economical or economic use of resources*). *Economical* is, however, far more widely and commonly used in this sense. A person who is thrifty or a machine that uses resources frugally should be described by preference as *economical*: *a very economical little car*.

economical *adj* 1 thrifty. 2 efficient; not wasting money, fuel, etc. 3 relating to economies, finance, or an economy; = ECONOMIC. ✴ **be economical with the truth** to lie, or be less than totally honest or open. ➤➤ **economically** *adv*.

Usage note

economical or economic? See note at ECONOMIC.

economic indicator *noun* a statistic, e.g. the level of prices or production, that gives an indication of the state of part of a national economy.

economic migrant *noun* a person who emigrates from a poor country in order to improve their standard of living.

economic refugee *noun* = ECONOMIC MIGRANT.

economics *pl noun* 1 (*treated as sing. or pl*) a social science concerned chiefly with the production, distribution, and consumption of goods and services.

Editorial note

Given its increasing scope, modern theoretical economics is perhaps best viewed as the study of human decision-taking and its implications, under useful simplifying assumptions, particularly about rational behaviour and human motivation. Indeed, economists have sometimes justly been accused of stretching the simplifying assumptions to explain any observed behaviour, rather than developing more realistic accounts of it — Evan Davis.

2 economic aspect or significance: *We need to consider the economics of the operation*. ➤➤ **economist** /i'konəmist/ *noun*.

economic sanctions *pl noun* measures intended to have an adverse effect on the economy of another nation, often to force it to change some policy or comply with international law.

economize or **economise** /i'konəmiez/ or **-ise** *verb intrans* (*often + on*) to practise economy; to be frugal or not wasteful: *We'll have to economize on electricity*. ➤ *verb trans* to use (something) more economically. ➤➤ **economization** /-'zaysh(ə)n/ *noun*, **economizer** *noun*.

economy¹ /i'konəmi/ *noun* (*pl* **-ies**, *pl* **economies**) 1a thrifty and efficient use of material resources; frugality in expenditure. b an instance or means of economizing: *The government implemented drastic economies*. 2 efficient and sparing use of nonmaterial resources, e.g. effort, language, or motion. 3 the structure of economic life in a country, area, or period; an economic system. 4 a cheaper standard of travel, *esp* by air, than first class. [Middle English *yconomie* via French and Latin from Greek *oikonomia*, from *oikos* house + *nemein* to manage]

economy² *adj* 1 designed to save money: *economy measures*. 2 saving a buyer money by offering a larger than average amount in a pack: *a large economy pack of muesli*. 3 relating to travel in economy class.

economy³ *adv* by economy class: *I always travel economy*.

economy class *noun* = ECONOMY¹ (4).

economy-class syndrome *noun* deep vein thrombosis caused by sitting for long periods of time in cramped conditions on aircraft.

economy of scale *noun* a lowering of average production costs resulting from an increased scale of production.

economy-size or **economy-sized** *adj* saving a buyer money by offering a larger than average amount, e.g. in a pack.

ecospecies /'eekohspeeshiz, 'ekoh-/ *noun* (*pl* **ecospecies**) a taxonomic species regarded as an ecological unit. ➤➤ **ecospecific** /-spə'sifik/ *adj*.

ecosphere /'eekohsfiə, 'ekohsfiə/ *noun* the parts of the universe habitable by living organisms, *esp* the biosphere.

ecossaise /ayko'sez, eko'sez/ *noun* a lively folk dance in duple time, or the music for it. [French *écossaise*, fem of *écossais* Scottish]

ecosystem /'eekohsistəm, 'ekoh-/ *noun* a complex consisting of a community and its environment functioning as a reasonably self-sustaining ecological unit in nature.

ecoterrorist /'eekohterərist/ *noun* a person who uses violence as part of an environmental campaign. >>> **ecoterrorism** *noun.* [ECO- + *terrorist*]

ecotourism /'eekohtooəriz(ə)m, 'ekoh-/ *noun* tourism in unspoiled undeveloped regions, managed in such a way that the environment remains unspoiled and the revenue generated is used towards conservation of the region.

ecotype /'eekohtiep, 'ekohtiep/ *noun* a group equivalent to a taxonomic subspecies and maintained as a distinct population by ecological and geographical factors. >>> **ecotypic** /-'tipik/ *adj,* **ecotypically** /-'tipikli/ *adv.*

ecru /'aykrooh, 'ekrooh/ *noun* a pale fawn colour. >>> **ecru** *adj.* [French *écru* unbleached]

ECSC *abbr* European Coal and Steel Community.

Ecstasy /'ekstəsi/ *noun* an illegal drug, taken recreationally for its strong stimulant and euphoric effects but sometimes with fatal results.

ecstasy *noun* (*pl* **ecstasies**) **1a** a state of very strong feeling, *esp* of joy or happiness. **b** a state of strong emotion. **2** a trance, *esp* a mystic or prophetic one. [Middle English *extasie* via Old French and Latin from Greek *ekstasis*, literally 'standing outside oneself', from *ex* out + *histanai* to stand]

ecstatic[1] /ik'statik/ *adj* **1** extremely happy or enthusiastic. **2** subject to, causing, or in a state of ecstasy. >>> **ecstatically** *adv.* [via medieval Latin from Greek *ekstatikos*, from *ekstasis*: see ECSTASY]

ecstatic[2] *noun* somebody who is prone to ecstatic trancelike states.

ECT *abbr* electroconvulsive therapy.

ect- *or* **ecto-** *comb. form* forming words, with the meaning: outside or external; compare END-, EXO-. [Greek *ekto-*, from *ektos*, from *ex* out]

ectoblast /'ektohblast/ *noun* = EPIBLAST. >>> **ectoblastic** /-'blastik/ *adj.*

ectoderm /'ektohduhm/ *noun* **1** the outer cellular membrane of an animal, such as a jellyfish, having only two germ layers in the embryo. **2** the outermost of the three primary germ layers of an embryo, or a tissue derived from this: compare ENDODERM (1), MESODERM (1). >>> **ectodermal** /-'duhml/ *adj,* **ectodermic** /-'duhmik/ *adj.*

ectogenic /ektə'jenik/ *adj* = ECTOGENOUS.

ectogenous /ek'tojinəs/ *adj* said *esp* of pathogenic bacteria: capable of development apart from the host.

ectomorph /'ektəmawf/ *noun* an ectomorphic person: compare ENDOMORPH, MESOMORPH. [ECTODERM + -MORPH]

ectomorphic /ektə'mawfik/ *adj* having a light slender body build. >>> **ectomorphy** /'ektəmawfi/ *noun.* [ECTODERM + -*morphic* (see -MORPH); from the predominance in such types of structures developed from the ectoderm]

-ectomy *comb. form* forming nouns, denoting: surgical removal of a specified part: *appendectomy.* [medieval Latin -*ectomia*, from Greek *ektemnein* to cut out, from *ex* out + *temnein* to cut]

ectoparasite /ektoh'parəsiet/ *noun* a parasite that lives on the exterior of its host: compare ENDOPARASITE. >>> **ectoparasitic** /-'sitik/ *adj.*

ectopic /ek'topik/ *adj* occurring in an abnormal position or in an unusual manner or form: *ectopic heartbeat; an ectopic pregnancy.* >>> **ectopically** *adv.* [Greek *ektopos* out of place, from *ex-* out + *topos* place]

ectoplasm /'ektəplaz(ə)m, 'ektoh-/ *noun* **1** the outer relatively rigid granule-free layer of the cytoplasm of a cell: compare ENDOPLASM. **2** a substance supposed to emanate from a spiritualist medium in a state of trance as the substance in which a spirit manifests itself. >>> **ectoplasmic** /ektə'plazmik, ektoh-/ *adj.*

ecu *or* **ECU** /ay'kyooh/ *noun* a former money of account within the European Community, used primarily as a standard against which national currencies could float and for transactions between member states: compare EURO. [acronym from *European Currency Unit*]

Ecuadorean /,ekwə'dawriən/ *noun* a native or inhabitant of Ecuador. >>> **Ecuadorean** *adj.*

ecumenical *or* **oecumenical** /ekyoo'menikl, ee-/ *adj* **1** of or representing the whole of a body of Churches: *an ecumenical council.* **2** promoting or tending towards worldwide Christian unity or cooperation: *ecumenical discussions.* >>> **ecumenicalism** *noun,* **ecumenically** *adv,* **ecumenism** /e'kyoohməniz(ə)m/ *noun,* **ecumenist** /e'kyoohmənist/ *noun.* [via late Latin *oecumenicus* from late Greek *oikoumenikos* worldwide, from Greek *oikoumenē* the inhabited world, from *oikos* house]

eczema /'eksimə/ *noun* an inflammatory condition of the skin characterized by itching and oozing blisters. >>> **eczematous** /ek'semətəs/ *adj.* [Greek *ekzema*, from *ekzein* to erupt, from *ex* out + *zein* to boil]

ed. *abbr* **1** edited. **2** edition. **3** editor. **4** education.

-ed[1] *suffix* **1** forming the past participle of regular weak verbs that end in a consonant, a vowel other than *e*, or a final *y* that changes to *i*: *ended; dropped; haloed; cried.* **2** forming adjectives or past participles, with the meanings: **a** having; characterized by; provided with: *polo-necked; two-legged.* **b** wearing; dressed in: *bowler-hatted; jodhpured.* **c** having the characteristics of: *bigoted.* [Old English -*ed*, -*od*, -*ad*]

-ed[2] *suffix* forming the past tense of regular weak verbs that end in a consonant, a vowel other than *e*, or a final *y* that changes to *i*: *resented.* [Old English -*de*, -*ede*, -*ode*, -*ade*]

edacious /i'dayshəs/ *adj formal* voracious. >>> **edacity** /i'dasiti/ *noun.* [Latin *edac-, edax,* from *edere* to eat]

Edam /'eedam/ *noun* a mild yellow cheese of Dutch origin usu made in flattened balls coated with red wax. [named after *Edam,* town in the Netherlands where it is made]

edaphic /i'dafik/ *adj* of the soil. >>> **edaphically** *adv.* [Greek *edaphos* bottom, ground]

EDC *abbr* European Defence Community.

Edda /'edə/ *noun* either of two 13th-cent. Old Norse books, one a collection of mythological and heroic poems, the other a treatise on poetry. >>> **Eddaic** /e'dayik/ *adj,* **Eddic** *adj.* [Old Norse *Edda,* prob from the name of a great-grandmother in a poem]

eddo /'edoh/ *noun* = TARO.

eddy[1] /'edi/ *noun* (*pl* **eddies**) **1** a current of water or air running contrary to the main current, *esp* a small whirlpool. **2** something, e.g. smoke or fog, moving in the manner of an eddy or whirlpool. [Middle English (Scots) *ydy,* prob from Old Norse *itha*]

eddy[2] *verb* (**eddies, eddied, eddying**) >> *verb intrans* to move in or like an eddy: *The crowd eddied about in the marketplace.* >>> *verb trans* to cause (somebody or something) to eddy.

eddy current *noun* an electric current induced by an alternating magnetic field.

edelweiss /'aydlvies/ *noun* a small perennial plant that is covered in dense fine white hairs and grows high in the Alps: *Leontopodium alpinum.* [German *Edelweiss,* from *edel* noble + *weiss* white]

edema /i'deemə/ *noun NAmer* see OEDEMA.

Eden /'eedn/ *noun* **1** the garden where, according to the account in Genesis, Adam and Eve lived before the Fall. **2** = PARADISE (3). >>> **Edenic** /i'denik/ *adj.* [late Latin *Eden,* via Greek from Hebrew *'Edhen*]

edentate[1] /ee'dentayt/ *adj* having few or no teeth. [Latin *edentatus,* past part. of *edentare* to make toothless, from EX-[1] *dent-, dens* tooth]

edentate[2] *noun* any of an order of mammals including the sloths, armadillos, and American anteaters, that have few or no teeth: order Edentata.

edge[1] /ej/ *noun* **1a** the cutting side of a blade. **b** the sharpness of a blade. **c** penetrating power; keenness or intensity: *There was an edge of sarcasm in his voice; Her smile took the edge off her criticism.* **2a** the line where an object or area begins or ends; a border: *The town stands on the edge of a plain.* **b** the narrow part adjacent to a border; the brink or verge. **c** a point that marks a beginning or transition; a threshold: *We stand today on the edge of a new frontier* — J F Kennedy. **d** a line where two planes or two plane faces of a solid body meet or cross. **e** a term used in local place-names in England, *esp* for sharp ridges or cliffs: *Wenlock Edge; Striding Edge.* **3** the edging of a cricket ball. **4** a line or arc in a network joining two nodes. *** have the edge on/over somebody** to have an advantage over somebody. **on edge** anxious or nervous. **on the edge of** just about to have or be in something: *on the edge of a nervous breakdown.* **➤➤ edgeless** *adj.* [Old English *ecg*]

edge² *verb trans* **1** to give or supply an edge to (something). **2** to move or force (somebody or something) gradually in a specified way: *The other car edged him off the road; He edged her out of the leadership.* **3** to incline (a ski) sideways so that one edge cuts into the snow. **4** in cricket, to hit (a ball), or the bowling of (a bowler), with the edge of the bat. **➤** *verb intrans* to advance cautiously, e.g. by short sideways steps: *The climbers edged along the cliff; The car edged round the corner.* **➤➤ edger** *noun.*

edged *adj* (*usu used in combinations*) having an edge, boundary, or border, or the specified kind of edge, boundary or border, or the specified number of edges: *rough-edged; two-edged.*

edge tool *noun* a tool with a sharp cutting edge.

edgeways *adv* **1** with the edge foremost; sideways. **2** on, by, with, or towards the edge: *He balanced the coins edgeways.*

edgewise *adv* = EDGEWAYS.

edging¹ *noun* something that forms an edge or border.

edging² *adj* used for making an edge.

edgy *adj* (**edgier, edgiest**) tense, anxious, or irritable. **➤➤ edgily** *adv,* **edginess** *noun.*

edh /edh/ *noun* see ETH.

EDI *abbr* electronic data interchange.

edible /'edəbl/ *adj* fit to be eaten as food. **➤➤ edibility** /-'biliti/ *noun,* **edibleness** *noun.* [late Latin *edibilis* from Latin *edere* to eat]
Usage note
edible *or* eatable? See note at EATABLE.

edibles *pl noun* things that are eatable; food.

edict /'eedikt/ *noun* **1** an official public decree. **2** the order or command of an authority. **➤➤ edictal** /i'diktl/ *adj.* [Latin *edictum,* neuter past part. of *edicere* to decree]

edification /,edifi'kaysh(ə)n/ *noun formal* the improvement of character or the mind. **➤➤ edificatory** /-t(ə)ri/ *adj.* [EDIFY + -FICA-TION]

edifice /'edifis/ *noun* **1** a building, *esp* a large or massive structure. **2** a large abstract structure or organization: *the keystone which holds together the social edifice* — R H Tawney. [Middle English via French from Latin *aedificium,* from *aedificare:* see EDIFY]

edify /'edifie/ *verb trans* (**edifies, edified, edifying**) to instruct and improve (somebody), *esp* in moral and spiritual knowledge. **➤➤ edifying** *adj,* **edifyingly** *adv.* [Middle English *edifien* from French from late Latin *aedificare* to instruct or improve spiritually, literally 'to erect a house', from Latin *aedes* temple, house + *facere* to make]

edit¹ /'edit/ *verb trans* (**edited, editing**) **1a** to prepare an edition of (a book, article, etc): *He edited Pope's works.* **b** to assemble (e.g. a film or tape recording) by deleting, inserting, and rearranging material. **c** to alter or adapt (e.g. written or spoken words), *esp* to make them consistent with a particular standard or purpose. **2** to direct the publication of (a periodical): *She edits the local newspaper.* **➤➤ editable** *adj.* [back-formation from EDITOR]

edit² *noun* an editorial change or correction.

edit. *abbr* **1** edited. **2** edition. **3** editor.

edition /i'dish(ə)n/ *noun* **1a** the form in which a text is published: *a paperback edition.* **b** the whole number of copies published at one time: *an edition of 50,000.* **c** a number of copies published at one place: *the Kilmarnock edition of Burns's poetry.* **d** one of the copies published at one time, *esp* the first time: *a rare first edition.* **e** the issue of a newspaper or periodical for a specified time or place: *the late edition; the Manchester edition.* **2** the whole number of articles of one style put out at one time: *a limited edition of collectors' pieces.* **3** a copy or version: *She's a friendlier edition of her mother.* [via French from Latin *edition-, editio* publication, edition, from *edere* to bring forth, publish, from EX-¹ + *dare* to give]

editio princeps /i,dishio 'prinseps, ay,ditioh 'prinkeps/ *noun* (*pl* **editiones principes** /-neez 'prinsipeez/) the first printed edition, *esp* of an ancient or medieval text. [Latin *editio princeps* first edition]

editor *noun* **1** a person responsible for the editorial policy and content of a newspaper or periodical or of a section of one: *sports editor.* **2** a person in overall charge of the content of a book containing material by various writers. **3** a person who

commissions written material, etc. **4** somebody who edits written material, films, etc. **5** a person in overall charge of the items included in a radio or television programme. **6** a computer program that allows one to edit data. **➤➤ editorship** *noun.* [Latin *editor* producer, publisher, from *edere:* see EDITION]

editorial¹ /,edi'tawri-əl/ *adj* of or written by an editor: *editorial policy; an editorial statement.* **➤➤ editorially** *adv.*

editorial² *noun* a newspaper or magazine article that gives the opinions of the editors or publishers.

editorialize *or* **editorialise** *verb intrans* **1** to express an opinion in the form of an editorial. **2** to introduce personal opinion into an apparently objective report, e.g. by direct comment or hidden bias. **➤➤ editorialization** /-'zaysh(ə)n/ *noun,* **editorializer** *noun.*

edit out *verb trans* to remove (material) from a book, film, etc while editing it.

EDP *abbr* electronic data processing.

EDT *abbr* Eastern Daylight Time (time zone).

educ. *abbr* **1** education. **2** educational.

educate /'edyookayt, 'ejookayt/ *verb trans* **1** to provide schooling for (somebody). **2** to develop (somebody or something) mentally or morally, *esp* by instruction. **3** to train or improve (a person's faculties, judgment, skills, etc). **➤** *verb intrans* to teach or instruct. **➤➤ educability** /-kə'biliti/ *noun,* **educable** *adj,* **educatability** /-ə'biliti/ *noun,* **educatable** *adj,* **educative** /-kətiv, -kaytiv/ *adj,* **educator** *noun.* [Middle English *educaten* to rear, from Latin *educatus,* past part. of *educare* to rear, educate]

educated *adj* **1** having an education, *esp* one beyond the average. **2a** trained or skilled: *an educated palate.* **b** appropriate to somebody educated: *educated conversation.* **c** based on some knowledge or experience: *an educated guess.* **➤➤ educatedly** *adv,* **educatedness** *noun.*

education /,edyoo'kaysh(ə)n, ejoo-/ *noun* **1a** the action or process of educating or of being educated: *What sculpture is to a block of marble, education is to an human soul* — Joseph Addison; *I can't do with any more education. I was full up years ago* — P G Wodehouse. **b** a stage of such a process, or any kind of process of this type: *tertiary education; I've not had a university education.* **c** instruction in some subject: *religious education.* **2** the knowledge and development resulting from instruction, e.g. in school: *a man of little education.* **3** the field of study that deals mainly with methods of teaching. **4** (**an education**) an experience that causes one to see things in a new way: *That meeting was quite an education.* **➤➤ educational** *adj,* **educationally** *adv.*

educationalist *noun* an educational theorist or administrator.

educational psychology *noun* psychology concerned with human maturation, school learning, and evaluation of aptitude and progress by tests. **➤➤ educational psychologist** *noun.*

educationist *noun* = EDUCATIONALIST.

educe /i'dyoohs, i'joohs/ *verb trans formal* **1** to elicit or develop (something); to bring out (something hitherto unrealized). **2** to arrive at (a conclusion) through a consideration of facts or evidence; to infer (something). **➤➤ educible** *adj,* **eduction** /i'duksh(ə)n/ *noun.* [Latin *educere* to draw out, from EX-¹ + *ducere* to lead]

edutainment /,edyoo'taynmənt, edjoo-/ *noun* entertainment which is designed to include some educational content. [EDUCA-TION + ENTERTAINMENT]

Edwardian¹ /ed'wawdi-ən/ *adj* **1** relating to or characteristic of the reign of Edward VII of England (1901–1910). **2** characteristic of this period.

Edwardian² *noun* a person living in the UK during the reign of Edward VII.

Edwardian car *noun Brit* an old motor car; *specif* one built after 1904 and before 1919: compare VETERAN CAR, VINTAGE CAR.

-ee¹ *suffix* **1** forming nouns from transitive verbs, denoting: a person to whom (a specified action) is done: *appointee; trainee.* **2** forming nouns from nouns, adjectives and verbs, denoting: a person who acts (in a specified way): *escapee; absentee.* [Middle English *-e* from early French *-é,* past part. ending, from Latin *-atus*]

-ee² *suffix* forming nouns from nouns, denoting: a particular, *esp* small, kind of object: *bootee.* [prob alteration of -Y⁴]

EEC *abbr* European Economic Community.

EEG *abbr* **1** electroencephalogram. **2** electroencephalograph.

eel /eel/ *noun* **1** any of several species of long snakelike fishes with a smooth slimy skin and no pelvic fins: order Anguilliformes. **2** any of various similar but unrelated creatures, such as the ELECTRIC EEL. ➤➤ **eel-like** *adj*, **eely** *adj*. [Old English *æl*]

eelgrass *noun* **1** a freshwater plant that has very long narrow leaves and grows underwater: genus *Valisneria*. **2** a marine plant with long grasslike leaves: *Zostera marina*.

eelpout *noun* **1** any of numerous species of eel-like sea fishes resembling blennies: family Zoarcidae. **2** = BURBOT. [EEL + POUT³]

eelworm *noun* any of several species of nematode worms, *esp* one living free in the soil or as a parasite in plants: phylum Nematoda.

e'en /een/ *adv chiefly literary* even.

-een *suffix* forming nouns from nouns, denoting: inferior fabric resembling (a specified fabric): *velveteen*. [prob from *ratteen*, a coarse woollen fabric, from French *ratine*]

EEPROM /'eeprom/ *abbr* electrically erasable programmable read-only memory.

e'er /eə/ *adv chiefly literary* ever.

-eer *suffix* **1** forming nouns from nouns, denoting: a person engaged in (a specified occupation or activity): *auctioneer*. **2** forming verbs from nouns, with the meaning: to be involved in a specified activity: *electioneer; profiteer; racketeer*. [early French *-ier* from Latin *-arius*]

eerie *or* **eery** /'iəri/ *adj* (**eerier, eeriest**) frighteningly strange or gloomy; weird. ➤➤ **eerily** *adv*, **eeriness** *noun*. [Middle English (Northern and Scots) *eri* fearful, from Old English *earg* cowardly, wretched]

EEROM /'eerom/ *abbr* electrically erasable read-only memory.

eery *adj* see EERIE.

eff /ef/ *verb intrans* **1** *Brit, informal* a euphemism for 'fuck': *Eff off!* **2** to say 'fuck': *He was effing and swearing.* ✳ **eff and blind** *euphem* to utter obscenities and swearwords.

efface /i'fays/ *verb trans* **1** to eliminate (something) or make it indistinct by wearing away a surface; to obliterate or erase (it): *The dates on the coins had been effaced by wear.* **2** to make (oneself) modestly or shyly inconspicuous. ➤➤ **effaceable** *adj*, **effacement** *noun*. [early French *effacer*, from EX-¹ + FACE¹]

effect¹ /i'fekt/ *noun* **1a** the result of a cause or agent, or the extent of it. **b** the result of purpose or intention: *She employed her knowledge to good effect.* **2** power to bring about a result; efficacy. **3** (*in pl*) personal movable property; goods: *personal effects*. **4a** a distinctive impression on the human senses: *His use of colour produces a very striking effect.* **b** the creation of an often false desired impression: *Her tears were purely for effect.* **c** (*also in pl*) something designed to produce a distinctive or desired impression: *special lighting effects.* **5** the quality or state of being operative; operation: *The law comes into effect next week.* **6** the basic meaning; intent: *Tell him to get lost, or words to that effect; The company issued a statement to the effect that he would resign.* **7** an experimental scientific phenomenon named usu after its discoverer: *the Doppler effect.* ✳ **in effect** for all practical purposes; actually although not appearing so. **take effect 1** to become operative. **2** to produce a result. [Middle English via Old French from Latin *effectus*, past part. of *efficere* to bring about, from EX-¹ + *facere* to make, do]

Usage note

effect *or* affect? See note at AFFECT¹.

effect² *verb trans* **1** to bring (something) about, often by surmounting obstacles; to accomplish (it): *The arbitrators are hoping to effect a settlement of the dispute.* **2** to put (something) into effect; to carry (it) out: *The duty of the legislature is to effect the will of the citizens.*

effective¹ /i'fektiv/ *adj* **1a** producing or capable of a decided, decisive, or desired effect. **b** impressive or striking. **2** ready for service or action: *effective manpower.* **3** actual or real: *the effective strength of the army.* **4** being in effect; operative: *The tax becomes effective next year.* ➤➤ **effectiveness** *noun*.

effective² *noun* a soldier equipped and fit for duty.

effectively *adv* **1** in an effective manner; impressively. **2** for all practical purposes; in effect: *The scandal effectively led to the fall of the government.*

effector *noun* a gland, muscle, or other bodily organ that becomes active in response to stimulation.

effectual /i'fektyooəl/ *adj* **1** producing or able to produce a desired effect; adequate, effective. **2** said of a legal document: valid or binding; having force in law. ➤➤ **effectuality** /-'aliti/ *noun*, **effectualness** *noun*.

effectually *adv* **1** in an effectual manner; with the desired effect. **2** for all practical purposes; in effect.

effectuate /i'fektyooayt/ *verb trans* to accomplish (something); to carry (it) out or bring it about. ➤➤ **effectuation** /-'aysh(ə)n/ *noun*.

effeminate /i'feminat/ *adj* **1** said of a man: having qualities usu thought of as feminine; not manly in appearance or manner. **2** marked by an unbecoming delicacy or lack of vigour: *effeminate art.* ➤➤ **effeminacy** /-si/ *noun*, **effeminately** *adv*, **effeminateness** *noun*. [Middle English from Latin *effeminatus*, past part. of *effemin-are* to make effeminate, from EX-¹ + *femina* woman]

effendi /e'fendi/ *noun* (*pl* **effendis**) a title of respect for a man of property, authority, or education in an eastern Mediterranean country. [Turkish *efendi* master, from modern Greek *aphentēs*, alteration of Greek *authentēs*: see AUTHENTIC]

efferent¹ /'efərənt/ *adj* conducting outwards from a part or organ; *specif* conveying nervous impulses to an effector: compare AFFERENT. ➤➤ **efference** *noun*, **efferently** *adv*. [French *efférent* from Latin *efferent-, efferens*, present part. of *efferre* to carry outwards, from EX-¹ + *ferre* to carry]

efferent² *noun* an efferent nerve.

effervesce /efə'ves/ *verb intrans* **1a** said of a liquid: to bubble, hiss, and foam as gas escapes. **b** said of a gas: to bubble out of a liquid. **2** to show liveliness or exhilaration. ➤➤ **effervescence** *noun*, **effervescent** *adj*, **effervescently** *adv*. [Latin *effervescere*, from EX-¹ + *fervescere* to begin to boil, from *fervēre* to boil]

effete /i'feet/ *adj* **1** worn out; exhausted. **2** marked by weakness and decadent overrefinement: *an effete civilization.* ➤➤ **effetely** *adv*, **effeteness** *noun*. [Latin *effetus*, from EX-¹ + *fetus* fruitful]

efficacious /efi'kayshəs/ *adj* having the power to produce a desired effect. ➤➤ **efficaciously** *adv*, **efficaciousness** *noun*, **efficacity** /-'kasiti/ *noun*, **efficacy** /'efikəsi/ *noun*. [Latin *efficac-, efficax*, from *efficere*: see EFFECT¹]

efficiency /i'fish(ə)nsi/ *noun* (*pl* **efficiencies**) **1** the quality or degree of being efficient. **2a** efficient operation. **b** the ratio of the useful energy delivered by a dynamic system to the energy supplied to it.

efficient /i'fish(ə)nt/ *adj* **1** said of a person: able and practical; briskly competent. **2** productive of desired effects, *esp* with minimum waste: *an efficient method of generating electricity.* ➤➤ **efficiently** *adv*. [Middle English via Old French from Latin *efficient-, efficiens*, present part. of *efficere*: see EFFECT¹]

effigy /'efiji/ *noun* (*pl* **effigies**) an image or representation, *esp* of a person; *specif* a crude figure representing a hated person. [Latin *effigies*, from *effingere* to fashion or form, from EX-¹ + *fingere* to shape]

effing *adj and adv euphem* fucking.

effleurage /eflə'rahzh/ *noun* a stroking movement in massage.

effloresce /eflaw'res/ *verb intrans* **1** to burst into flower. **2a** to change from crystals to a powder on exposure to air. **b** to form or become covered with a powdery covering: *Bricks may effloresce owing to the deposition of soluble salts.* [Latin *efflorescere*, from EX-¹ + *florescere* to begin to blossom, ultimately from *flor-, flos* FLOWER¹]

efflorescence /eflaw'res(ə)ns/ *noun* **1** the period or state of flowering. **2** the action, process, period, or result of developing and unfolding as if coming into flower; blossoming: *periods of ... intellectual and artistic efflorescence* — Julian Huxley. **3** the process or product of efflorescing chemically. **4** a redness of the skin; an eruption. ➤➤ **efflorescent** *adj*.

effluence /'efloo·əns/ *noun* **1** something that flows out. **2** an action or process of flowing out.

effluent¹ /'efloo·ənt/ *noun* **1** something that flows out. **2a** an outflowing branch of a main stream or lake. **b** smoke, liquid industrial refuse, sewage, etc discharged into the environment, *esp* when causing pollution. **c** the flow of lava from a volcanic fissure. [Latin *effluent-, effluens*, present part. of *effluere* to flow out, from EX-¹ + *fluere* to flow]

effluent² *adj* flowing out; emanating: *an effluent river.*

effluvium /e'floohvi·əm/ *noun* (*pl* **effluvia** /-vi·ə/, **effluviums**) **1** an offensive gas or smell, e.g. from rotting vegetation. **2** a by-product, *esp* in the form of waste. [Latin *effluvium* act of flowing out, from *effluere*: see EFFLUENT²]

efflux /'efluks/ *noun* an effluence, *esp* of liquid or gas. ➤➤ **effluxion** /i'fluksh(ə)n/ *noun*. [Latin *effluxus*, past part. of *effluere*: see EFFLUENT²]

effort /'efət/ *noun* 1 conscious exertion of physical or mental power. 2 a serious attempt; a try. 3 something produced by exertion or trying: *The novel was his most ambitious effort to date.* 4 the force applied, e.g. to a simple machine, as distinguished from the force exerted against the load. ➤➤ **effortful** *adj*, **effortfully** *adv*, **effortless** *adj*, **effortlessly** *adv*, **effortlessness** *noun*. [early French *effort* from Old French *esfort*, from *esforcier* to force, from Latin EX-¹ + *fortis* strong]

effrontery /i'frunt(ə)ri/ *noun* (*pl* **effronteries**) 1 the quality of being shamelessly bold; insolence: *the effrontery to propound three such heresies* — Times Literary Supplement. 2 an instance of insolent behaviour. [French *effronterie* from late Latin *effront-*, *effrons* shameless, barefaced, from Latin EX-¹ + *front-*, *frons* forehead]

effulgence /i'fulj(ə)ns/ *noun* formal radiant splendour; brilliance. ➤➤ **effulgent** *adj*, **effulgently** *adv* [late Latin *effulgentia* from Latin *effulgent-*, *effulgens*, present part. of *effulgēre* to shine forth, from EX-¹ + *fulgere* to shine]

effuse¹ /i'fyoohz/ *verb intrans* formal to flow out or through; to emanate. ➤ *verb trans* formal 1 to pour out (e.g. a liquid). 2 to radiate or emit (e.g. atoms). [Latin *effusus*, past part. of *effundere*, from EX-¹ + *fundere* to pour]

effuse² /i'fyoohs/ *adj* spread out flat without definite form: *effuse lichens*.

effusion /i'fyoohzh(ə)n/ *noun* 1a an act of effusing. b something that is effused or poured out. 2 unrestrained expression of words or feelings. 3 the escape of a fluid from a containing vessel, or the fluid that escapes.

effusive /i'fyoohsiv/ *adj* 1 unduly emotionally demonstrative; gushing. 2 said of rock: characterized or formed by a non-explosive outpouring of lava. ➤➤ **effusively** *adv*, **effusiveness** *noun*.

EFL *abbr* English as a foreign language.

EFT *abbr* electronic funds transfer.

eft /eft/ *noun* a newt. [Middle English *evete, ewte*, from Old English *efete*]

EFTA /'eftə/ *abbr* European Free Trade Association.

EFTPOS /'eftpos/ *abbr* electronic funds transfer at point of sale, a system in which a purchase is made by debit card or credit card in a retail outlet and the funds are transferred directly by computer from the buyer's to the seller's account.

EFTS *abbr* electronic funds transfer system.

e.g. *abbr* for example. [Latin *exempli gratia* for the sake of example]
Usage note
e.g. or *i.e.*? The abbreviation *e.g.* means 'for example' (Latin *exempli gratia*) and usually introduces a brief list of things or people to illustrate a concept: *a computer peripheral, e.g. a printer or a scanner.* The abbreviation *i.e.* means 'that is' (Latin *id est*). It usually introduces a brief amplification or explanation of a concept: *a computer peripheral, i.e. a device such as a printer or scanner that is connected up to a computer.*

egad /ee'gad, i'gad/ *interj* archaic used as a mild oath. [prob euphemism for *oh God*]

egalitarian /i,gali'teəri·ən/ *adj* marked by or advocating egalitarianism. ➤➤ **egalitarian** *noun*. [French *égalitaire* from *égalité* equality, from Latin *aequalitat-*, *aequalitas*, from *aequalis*: see EQUAL¹]

egalitarianism *noun* a belief in or a philosophy advocating social, political, and economic equality among human beings.

egg /eg/ *noun* 1a the hard-shelled reproductive body produced by a bird. b an animal reproductive body consisting of an ovum together with its nutritive and protective envelopes that is capable of developing into a new individual. c = OVUM. 2a the egg of domestic poultry, etc, used as food. b a food prepared with such an egg: *scrambled egg.* 3 something resembling an egg in shape. 4 *dated, informal* a person: *He's a good egg!* ✳ **have egg on one's face** to be made to look foolish. **have/put all one's eggs in one basket** to be relying on one thing for success. ➤➤ **eggy** *adj*. [Middle English *egge* from Old Norse *egg*]

egg and dart *noun* an architectural moulding or ornamentation consisting of alternate egg-shaped figures and arrowheads.

egg-and-spoon race *noun* a race in which the contestants run carrying an egg balanced on a spoon.

eggar or **egger** /'egə/ *noun* any of several species of large moths with brown bodies and wings: *Lasiocampa quercus* and other species. [from EGG + -ER²; from the shape of its cocoon]

eggbeater /'egbeetə/ *noun* 1 a utensil for beating raw eggs; a whisk. 2 *NAmer, informal* a helicopter. [(sense 2) from its rotor blades resembling those of a device used for beating eggs]

eggbound *adj* said of a female bird: unable to lay an egg that she is carrying.

eggcup *noun* a small cup without a handle used for holding a boiled egg.

egger /'egə/ *noun* see EGGAR.

egghead *noun* derog or humorous an intellectual or highbrow. ➤➤ **eggheaded** *adj*.

eggnog /eg'nog/ *noun* a drink consisting of eggs beaten with sugar, milk or cream, and often spirits, e.g. rum or brandy. [EGG + *nog* strong ale, (with which an eggnog was orig made), of unknown origin]

egg on *verb trans* to incite (somebody) to action: *He egged the mob on to riot.* [Middle English *eggen* from Old Norse *eggja*]

eggplant *noun chiefly NAmer* = AUBERGINE¹. [from the shape of the fruit]

eggshell¹ *noun* the hard exterior covering of an egg.

eggshell² *adj* 1 said *esp* of china: thin and fragile. 2 said *esp* of paint: having only a slight sheen.

egg timer *noun* an instrument like a small hourglass in which sand runs for about three minutes and which is used for timing the boiling of eggs.

egg tooth *noun* a prominence on the beak or nose of an unhatched bird or reptile that is used to break through the eggshell.

egg white *noun* the clear viscous material that surrounds an egg yolk; = ALBUMEN.

eglantine /'eglantien, -teen/ *noun* = SWEETBRIER. [Middle English *eglentyn* from early French *aiglent*, ultimately from Latin *acus* needle]

EGM *abbr* extraordinary general meeting.

ego /'eegoh, 'egoh/ *noun* (*pl* **egos**) 1a SELF-ESTEEM (1). b excessive self-esteem: *paranoid-type people with huge egos* — William Burroughs. 2 the one of the three divisions of the mind in psychoanalytic theory that serves as the organized conscious mediator between the person and reality, *esp* in the perception of and adaptation to reality: compare ID, SUPEREGO. 3 the self, *esp* as contrasted with another self or the world. [Latin *ego* I]

egocentric¹ /,eegoh'sentrik, egoh-/ *adj* limited in outlook or concern to one's own activities or needs; self-centred or selfish. ➤➤ **egocentrically** *adv*, **egocentricity** /-'trisiti/ *noun*, **egocentrism** /-'sentriz(ə)m/ *noun*.

egocentric² *noun* an egocentric person.

egoism *noun* 1 a doctrine that individual self-interest is or should be the foundation of morality, or conduct based on this doctrine. 2 = EGOTISM.
Usage note
egoism *or* egotism? The difference between these two words in ordinary use is slight, both being used as equivalents to self-centredness. The more technical uses of the two words give a clue to where the distinction should lie. *Egoism* is also a philosophical belief in selfishness as the only real (and only proper) motive for action: *egoism* is self-obsession, for example the excessive use of *I, me,* and *myself* when speaking. *Egoism* is, therefore, best used for *self-seeking* and *egotism* for *self-importance*.

egoist *noun* 1 a believer in egoism. 2 an egocentric or egotistic person. ➤➤ **egoistic** /-'istik/ *adj*, **egoistical** /-'istikl/ *adj*, **egoistically** /-'istikli/ *adv*.

egomania /,eegoh'mayni·ə, egoh-/ *noun* the quality or state of being extremely egocentric. ➤➤ **egomaniac** /-ak/ *noun*, **egomaniacal** /-mə'nie·əkl/ *adj*.

egotism /'eegətiz(ə)m, 'eg-/ *noun* 1 the practice of talking about oneself too much. 2 an extreme sense of self-importance. ➤➤ **egotist** *noun*, **egotistic** /-'tistik/ *adj*, **egotistical** /-'tistikl/ *adj*, **egotistically** /-'tistikli/ *adv*. [Latin *ego* I + *-t-* + ISM]
Usage note
egotism *or* egoism? See note at EGOISM.

ego trip *noun informal* an act or series of acts that selfishly enhances and satisfies one's ego.

ego-trip *verb intrans* (**ego-tripped, ego-tripping**) to have an ego trip. ⟫⟫ **ego-tripper** *noun*.

egregious /i'greejəs/ *adj* conspicuously or shockingly bad; flagrant: *an egregious mistake.* ⟫⟫ **egregiously** *adv*, **egregiousness** *noun*. [Latin *egregius* extraordinary, distingushed, from EX-[1] + *greg-, grex* herd]

egress[1] /'eegres/ *noun formal* **1** going or coming out; *specif* the emergence of a celestial object from eclipse, transit, or occultation. **2** a place or means of going out; an exit. **3** the right to go or come out. [Latin *egressus*, past part. of *egredi* to go out, from EX-[1] + *gradi* to go]

egress[2] *verb intrans formal* to go out or come out; to emerge. ⟫⟫ **egression** /ee'gresh(ə)n/ *noun*.

egret /'eegrit/ *noun* any of several species of herons that bear long plumes during the breeding season: family Ardeidae. [Middle English via French from Old Provençal *aigreta*, of Germanic origin]

Egyptian[1] /i'jipsh(ə)n/ *adj* of or characteristic of Egypt.

Egyptian[2] *noun* **1** a native or inhabitant of Egypt. **2** the Afro-Asiatic language of the ancient Egyptians to about the third cent. AD.

Word history
Ancient Egyptian words that have passed into English include *gum* (= adhesive), *nitre*, and *pharaoh*.

Egyptology /eejip'toləji/ *noun* the study of Egyptian antiquities. ⟫⟫ **Egyptologist** *noun*.

eh /ay/ *interj* used to ask for confirmation or to express enquiry. [Middle English *ey*]

EHF *abbr* extremely high frequency.

EHT *abbr* extremely high tension.

EI *abbr* emotional intelligence.

Eid /eed/ *noun* **1** = EID-UL-ADHA. **2** = EID-UL-FITR.

eider /'iedə/ *noun* (*pl* **eiders** or *collectively* **eider**) **1** = EIDER DUCK. **2** = EIDERDOWN (1).

eiderdown *noun* **1** the down of the eider duck. **2** *chiefly Brit* a thick warm quilt filled with eiderdown or other insulating material. [prob via German *Eiderdaune* from Icelandic *æthardūnn*, from *æthur* eider duck + *dūnn* down]

eider duck *noun* any of several species of large northern sea ducks having fine soft down that is used by the female to line the nest: genus *Somateria*. [*eider* via Dutch, German, or Swedish from Icelandic *æthur*]

eidetic /ie'detik/ *adj* marked by or involving extraordinarily accurate and vivid recall of visual images: *an eidetic memory.* ⟫⟫ **eidetically** *adv*. [Greek *eidētikos* of a form, from *eidos* form]

eidolon /ie'dohlon/ *noun* (*pl* **eidolons** or **eidola** /-lə/) **1** a phantom or image. **2** an ideal or idealized figure. [Greek *eidōlon* phantom, IDOL]

Eid-ul-Adha /,eed ool 'ahdə/ *noun* a Muslim festival that celebrates the strong faith of Abraham, who had been prepared to sacrifice his son Isaac at Allah's command, and also marking the end of the annual pilgrimage to Mecca. [Arabic *Eid-ul-Adha* Feast of Sacrifice]

Eid-ul-Fitr /,eed ool 'feetə/ *noun* a Muslim festival marking the end of the fast of Ramadan. [Arabic *Eid-ul-Fitr* Feast of Breaking Fast]

eigenvalue /'ieg(ə)nvalyooh/ *noun* the scalar value by which an eigenvector is multiplied under its linear transformation. [part translation of German *Eigenwert*, from *eigen* own, characteristic + *Wert* value]

eigenvector /'ieg(ə)nvektə/ *noun* a non-zero vector that under a given linear transformation becomes a scalar multiple of itself. [German *eigen* own, characteristic + VECTOR[1]]

eight /ayt/ *noun* **1** the number 8, or the quantity represented by it. **2** something having eight parts or members, *esp* an eight-person racing boat or its crew. **3a** the age of 8 years. **b** the hour four hours before midday or midnight. **✲ be/have one over the eight** *informal* to have had too much to drink. ⟫⟫ **eight** *adj*, **eightfold** *adj and adv*. [Old English *eahta*]

eighteen /ay'teen/ *noun* **1** the number 18, or the quantity represented by it. **2** in Britain, a classification of cinema films only suitable for people of 18 years or over. ⟫⟫ **eighteenth** *adj and noun*. [Old English *eahtatīene*, from *eahta* EIGHT + *tīen* TEN]

eighteenmo /ay'teenmoh/ *noun* (*pl* **eighteenmos**) **1** the size of a piece of paper cut 18 from a sheet. **2** a book, a page, or paper of this size.

eighth /ayt·th/ *adj and noun* **1** denoting a person or thing having the position in a sequence corresponding to the number eight. **2** one of eight equal parts of something. **3** in music, = OCTAVE. ⟫⟫ **eighthly** *adv*.

eighth note *noun NAmer* = QUAVER[2] (1).

eights /ayts/ *pl noun* races for eight-oared rowing boats.

eightsome reel /'ayts(ə)m/ *noun* a Scottish reel for eight dancers.

eighty /'ayti/ *adj and noun* (*pl* **eighties**) **1** the number 80, or the quantity represented by it. **2** (*in pl*) the numbers 80 to 89; *specif* a range of temperatures, ages, or dates within a century characterized by these numbers. ⟫⟫ **eightieth** *adj and noun*. [Old English *eahtatig*, short for *hundeahtatig*, group of eighty, from *hund*, literally 'hundred' + *eahta* EIGHT + *-tig* group of ten]

einkorn /'ienkawn/ *noun* a one-grained type of wheat: *Triticum monococcum*. [German *Einkorn* from *ein* one + *Korn* grain]

Einsteinian /ien'stieni-ən/ *adj* relating to Albert Einstein (d.1955) German-born US physicist, or his theories.

einsteinium /ien'stieni-əm/ *noun* a radioactive metallic chemical element artificially produced from plutonium: symbol Es, atomic number 99. [named after Albert *Einstein* d.1955, German-born US physicist and mathematician]

eirenic /ie'reenik, ie'renik/ or **eirenical** /ie'reenikl, ie'renikl/ *adj* see IRENIC.

eisteddfod /ie'stedhvod/ *noun* (*pl* **eisteddfods** or **eisteddfodau** /-die/) a Welsh-language competitive festival of the arts, *esp* music and poetry. ⟫⟫ **eisteddfodic** /-'vodik/ *adj*. [Welsh *eisteddfod* session, from *eistedd* to sit + *bod* being]

Eiswein /'iesvien/ *noun* (*pl* **Eisweine** /-nə/ or **Eisweins**) = ICE WINE. [German *Eiswein*, literally 'ice wine']

either[1] /'iedhə, 'eedhə/ *adj* **1** being the one and the other of two: *There were flowers blooming on either side of the path.* **2** being the one or the other of two: *Take either road.* [Old English *æghwæther* both, each, from *ā* always + *ge-* (collective prefix) + *hwæther* which of two, whether]

Usage note
Both pronunciations ('iedhə or 'eedhə) are acceptable: British English tends to prefer the former, American English, the latter.

either[2] *pronoun* the one or the other: *She could be happy with either of them; I don't want either.*

either[3] *conj* used before two or more sentence elements of the same class or function joined usu by *or* to indicate that what immediately follows is the first of two or more alternatives: *Either that wallpaper goes, or I do* — Oscar Wilde.

Usage note
Either, when it is the subject of a sentence, should be followed by a verb in the singular: *Either of the plans is acceptable*. If both subjects are singular, a singular verb should be used (*Either Peter or Andrew is intending to come*) and if both subjects are plural, a plural verb should be used (*Either relatives or friends are welcome.*) Where there is a combination of singular and plural subjects, it is best to let the form of the second one determine the form of the verb: *Either he or you have to go.*

either[4] *adv* used for emphasis after a negative or implied negation: for that matter; likewise: *I can't drive and I can't ride a bike either.*

either-or *adj* involving an unavoidable choice between only two possibilities: *an either-or situation.* ⟫⟫ **either-or** *noun*.

ejaculate[1] /i'jakyoolayt/ *verb trans* **1** to eject (semen) from the body in orgasm. **2** *formal* to utter (something) suddenly and vehemently. ⟫⟫ **ejaculation** /-'laysh(ə)n/ *noun*, **ejaculative** /-tiv/ *adj*, **ejaculator** *noun*, **ejaculatory** /-lat(ə)ri/ *adj*. [Latin *ejaculatus*, past part. of *ejaculari* to throw out, from EX-[1] + *jaculari* to throw]

ejaculate[2] /i'jakyoolət/ *noun* the semen released by a single ejaculation.

eject /i'jekt/ *verb trans* **1a** to drive (somebody) out, *esp* by physical force: *The hecklers were ejected from the hall.* **b** to throw out or emit (something) forcefully. **2** to evict (somebody) from property. **3** to drive (somebody) out of office. ⟫⟫ *verb intrans* to escape from an aircraft by using the ejector seat. ⟫⟫ **ejectable** *adj*, **ejection** *noun*, **ejective** /-tiv/ *adj*, **ejector** *noun*. [Middle English *ejecten* from Latin *ejectus*, past part. of *eicere*, from EX-[1] + *jacere* to throw]

ejecta /i'jektə/ *pl noun* (*treated as sing. or pl*) material thrown out, e.g. from a volcano. [Latin *ejecta*, neuter pl of *ejectus*: see EJECT]

ejection seat *noun* = EJECTOR SEAT.

ejector seat *noun* an emergency escape seat that propels an occupant out and away from an aircraft by means of an explosive charge.

eke /eek/ *adv archaic* also. [Old English *ēac*]

eke out *verb trans* **1a** to make up for the deficiencies of (something); to supplement (it): *He eked out his income by getting a second job as a barman*. **b** to make (a supply) last longer by using it frugally. **2** to make (e.g. a living) by laborious or precarious means. [*eke* to increase, from Old English *īecan, ēcan*]

ekistics /i'kistiks/ *pl noun* (*treated as sing*.) a science dealing with human settlements and their evolution. >> **ekistic** *adj*. [modern Greek *oikistikē*, from *oikistikos* relating to settlement, from Greek *oikizein* to settle, colonize, from *oikos* house]

elaborate[1] /i'lab(ə)rət/ *adj* **1** planned or carried out with great care and attention to detail: *elaborate preparations*. **2** marked by complexity, wealth of detail, or ornateness; intricate: *a highly elaborate coiffure*. >> **elaborately** *adv*, **elaborateness** *noun*. [Latin *elaboratus*, past part. of *elaborare* to work out, acquire by labour, from EX-[1] + *laborare* to work]

elaborate[2] /i'labərayt/ *verb trans* **1** to work out (e.g. a plan) in detail; to develop (it). **2** to build up (complex organic compounds) from simple ingredients. >> *verb intrans* (*often* + on) to go into detail; to add further information: *Need I elaborate?*; *They urged him to elaborate on his scheme*. >> **elaboration** /-'raysh(ə)n/ *noun*, **elaborative** /-rətiv/ *adj*, **elaborator** *noun*.

élan /ay'lonh, ay'lan (*French* elā)/ *noun* vigorous spirit or enthusiasm; verve. [French *élan* from early French *eslan* rush, ultimately from EX-[1] + *lancer* to hurl]

eland /'eelənd/ *noun* either of two large African antelopes that resemble oxen and have spirally twisted horns: *Tragelaphus oryx* and *Tragelaphus derbianus*. [via Afrikaans from Dutch *eland* elk, ultimately from Lithuanian *elnis*]

elapse /i'laps/ *verb intrans* said of a period of time: to pass by: *Four years elapsed before he returned*. [Latin *elapsus*, past part. of *elabi* to slip away, from EX-[1] + *labi* to slip, slide]

elasmobranch /i'lasməbrangk, i'laz-/ *noun* any of a subclass of fishes, including the sharks, rays, and skates, with a skeleton wholly or largely composed of cartilage: subclass Elasmobranchii. >> **elasmobranch** *adj*. [Greek *elasmos* metal plate + Latin *branchia* gill]

elasmosaur /i'lazməsaw/ *noun* any of various marine reptiles of the Mezozoic era, plesiosaurs with long snake-like necks and small heads. [scientific Latin *Elasmosaurus*, name of the type genus, from Greek *elasmos* beaten metal plate + *sauros* lizard]

elastane /i'lastayn/ *noun* a synthetic stretchy fabric, used for tight-fitting clothing.

elastic[1] /i'lastik/ *adj* **1** made of elastic: *an elastic band*. **2a** said of e.g. a fabric: capable of being easily stretched and resuming its former shape. **b** said of a solid: capable of recovering size and shape after deformation. **c** said of a gas: capable of indefinite expansion. **3a** capable of recovering or rebounding quickly, *esp* from depression or disappointment; buoyant or resilient. **b** able to adapt easily to change. **4** readily changed, expanded, or contracted; flexible or adaptable: *The rules are pretty elastic*. **5** said of supply or demand: affected by prices, etc: *Demand for goods is elastic*. **6** in physics, denoting a collision between particles in which the total kinetic energy of the colliding particles remains unchanged. >> **elastically** *adv*, **elasticity** /eela'stisiti/ *noun*. [Latin *elasticus*, from late Greek *elastos* propelling, from *elaunein* to drive]

elastic[2] *noun* **1** easily stretched rubber, usu prepared in cords, strings, or bands. **2** an elastic fabric usu made of yarns containing rubber.

elasticate /i'lastikayt/ *verb trans* **1** to make (e.g. fabric) stretchy by the insertion or interweaving of elastic. **2** to incorporate elasticated material into (e.g. an item of clothing): *elasticated boots*. >> **elastication** /-'kaysh(ə)n/ *noun*.

elasticated *adj* said of fabric: made stretchy by the insertion or interweaving of elastic.

elastic band *noun Brit* = RUBBER BAND.

elasticize *or* **elasticise** /i'lastisiez/ *verb trans* **1** = ELASTICATE. **2** to make (something) elastic.

elastin /i'lastin/ *noun* a protein similar to collagen that is the chief component of elastic fibres of connective tissue. [from Latin *elasticus*: see ELASTIC[1]]

elastomer /i'lastəmə/ *noun* any of various elastic substances resembling rubber: *polyvinyl elastomers*. >> **elastomeric** /-'merik/ *adj*. [ELASTIC[1] + -O- + Greek *meros* part]

Elastoplast /i'lastəplahst/ *noun trademark* a type of elastic adhesive plaster.

elate /i'layt/ *verb trans* to fill (somebody) with joy or pride; to put (them) in high spirits. >> **elated** *adj*, **elatedly** *adv*, **elatedness** *noun*, **elation** *noun*. [Latin *elatus*, past part. of *efferre* to carry out, from EX-[1] + *ferre* to carry]

elater /'elatə/ *noun* = CLICK BEETLE. [Greek *elatēr* driver, from *elaunein* to drive]

E layer *noun* a layer of the ionosphere occurring at about 95km (about 60mi) above the earth's surface that is capable of reflecting radio waves.

elbow[1] /'elboh/ *noun* **1a** the joint between the human forearm and upper arm. **b** a corresponding joint in the forelimb of a vertebrate animal. **2** the part of a garment that covers the elbow. **3** something resembling an elbow, *esp* an elbow-like pipe fitting. * **get the elbow** *informal* to be dismissed or rejected. **give somebody the elbow** *informal* to dismiss or reject somebody. **out at elbow/elbows** poor; shabbily dressed. **up to the elbows in/with** busily engaged in (something). [Old English *elboga* arm band; related to Old English *eln* ELL and *boga* BOW[3]]

elbow[2] *verb trans* **1** to push or shove (somebody) aside with one's elbow, or in any similar way: *She elbowed him out of the way*. **2** to force (e.g. one's way) rudely or roughly by pushing with one's elbow, or as if with one's elbow: *He's elbowed his way into the best circles*. >> *verb intrans* to advance by elbowing one's way.

elbow grease *noun informal* hard physical effort.

elbowroom *noun* adequate space or scope for movement, work, or operation.

elder[1] /'eldə/ *adj* of earlier birth or greater age, *esp* than another related person or thing: *He doesn't get on with his elder brother*. [Old English *ieldra*, compar of *eald* OLD[1]]

Usage note

elder *or* older? *Elder* is used only in comparing the ages of people, usually within a family group (*my elder brother/sister*), and cannot be followed by *than* (*My brother is two years older – not elder – than I am*). *Older* can be used in place of *elder* and is always used when describing things.

elder[2] *noun* **1** somebody who is older; a senior: *I was brought up to respect my elders*. **2** somebody having authority by virtue of age and experience: *We need the cooperation of the village elders*. **3** an official of the early Christian Church or of a Presbyterian, Quaker, etc congregation. >> **eldership** *noun*.

elder[3] *noun* any of several species of shrubs or small trees of the honeysuckle family: genus *Sambucus*. [Middle English *eldre* from Old English *ellærn*]

elderberry /'eldəb(ə)ri, -beri/ *noun* (*pl* **elderberries**) **1** the edible black or red berry of an elder. **2** an elder shrub or tree.

elderly *adj* rather old: *Obscenity is whatever happens to shock some elderly and ignorant magistrate* — Bertrand Russell. >> **elderliness** *noun*.

elder statesman *noun* an eminent senior or retired member of a group whose advice is often sought unofficially.

eldest /'eldist/ *adj* of the greatest age or seniority; oldest. [Old English *ieldest*, superl of *eald* OLD[1]]

eldest hand *noun* the card player who first receives cards in the deal.

El Dorado /el də'rahdoh/ *noun* a place of fabulous wealth, abundance, or opportunity. [Spanish *el dorado* the gilded man. *El Dorado* was the name of a city or country of fabulous riches believed by 16th-cent. explorers to exist in S America, whose king was said to cover his body in gold dust]

eldritch /'eldrich/ *adj archaic or Scot* weird, uncanny, or unearthly. [perhaps from ELF + *riche* from Old English *rīce* kingdom]

Eleatic[1] /eli'atik/ *adj* relating to a school of Greek philosophers, founded by Parmenides and continued by Zeno, that stressed unity of being and denied the existence of change. >> **Eleaticism** /-siz(ə)m/ *noun*. [via Latin from Greek *Eleatikos*, from *Elea*, ancient town in S Italy where the school was founded]

Eleatic[2] *noun* an Eleatic philosopher.

elec. *abbr* **1** electric. **2** electrical. **3** electricity.

elecampane /ˌelikamˈpayn/ *noun* a large coarse European composite plant with yellow flowers, whose root is used in herbal medicine as an expectorant and digestive: *Inula helenium*. [Middle English *elena campana* from medieval Latin *enula campana*, literally 'field elecampane', from *inula, enula* elecampane + *campana* of the field]

elect[1] /iˈlekt/ *verb trans* **1** to select (somebody) by vote for an office, position, or membership: *the never-ending audacity of elected persons* — Walt Whitman; *He was elected president in 1981.* **2** said of God: to choose or predestine (somebody) to receive salvation. **3** *chiefly NAmer* to select (e.g. a course of study). ➤ *verb intrans formal* to choose or decide to do something. ➤➤ **electable** *adj.* [Latin *electus* choice, past part. of *eligere* to select, from EX-[1] + *legere* to choose]

elect[2] *adj* **1a** picked out in preference to others; elite. **b** of superior value or quality; choice. **c** exclusive. **2** chosen for office or position but not yet installed: *the president-elect.* **3** chosen for salvation through divine mercy.

election /iˈleksh(ə)n/ *noun* **1a** an act or process of electing somebody, e.g. to public office. **b** the period of time during which campaigning for candidates is carried out before this. **c** the fact of being elected. **2** divine choice; *specif* God's electing of certain individuals to salvation.

electioneer[1] /ˌilekshəˈni·ə/ *verb intrans* to work for a candidate or party in an election.

electioneer[2] *noun* somebody who campaigns during an election.

elective[1] /iˈlektiv/ *adj* **1a** chosen or filled by popular election: *an elective office.* **b** relating to election or selection by voting. **c** having the right or power to elect. **2** permitting a choice; optional. ➤➤ **electively** *adv,* **electiveness** *noun.*

elective[2] *noun chiefly NAmer* an elective course or subject of study.

elector /iˈlektə/ *noun* **1** somebody voting or qualified to vote in an election. **2a** (*often* **Elector**) any of the German princes entitled to elect the Holy Roman Emperor. **b** a member of the electoral college in the USA. ➤➤ **electorship** *noun.*

electoral *adj* relating to election, elections, or electors.

electoral college *noun* **1** (*treated as sing. or pl*) a body of electors chosen in each state to elect the president and vice-president of the USA. **2** any body of electors chosen by a larger body.

electoral register *noun* = ELECTORAL ROLL.

electoral roll *noun* the official list of those who are entitled to vote in an election.

electorate /iˈlekt(ə)rət/ *noun* **1** (*treated as sing. or pl*) a body of electors. **2** *Aus, NZ* the area represented by a Member of Parliament. **3** (*often* **Electorate**) the territory, jurisdiction, etc of a German elector.

electr- *or* **electro-** *comb. form* forming words, with the meanings: **1a** of or caused by electricity: *electromagnetism; electrochemistry.* **b** electric: *electrode.* **c** electric and: *electrochemical; electromechanical.* **d** electrically: *electropositive.* **2** electrolytic: *electrodeposition.* **3** electron: *electrophile.* [Latin *electricus*: see ELECTRIC[1]]

Electra complex /iˈlektrə/ *noun* the OEDIPUS COMPLEX when it occurs in a female. [named after *Electra*, character in Greek mythology who incites her brother to avenge their father's death by killing their mother]

electress /iˈlektris/ *noun* (*often* **Electress**) the wife or widow of a German prince having the title of elector.

electret /iˈlektrət, -tret/ *noun* a dielectric body in which a permanent state of electric polarization has been set up. [blend of ELECTRICITY + MAGNET]

electric[1] /iˈlektrik/ *adj* **1a** of, being, supplying, producing, or produced by electricity: *electric current; an electric plug.* **b** operated by or using electricity: *an electric motor.* **2a** producing an intensely stimulating effect; thrilling: *an electric performance.* **b** (*often* + with) tense. **c** said of a musical instrument: electronically producing or amplifying sound: *an electric organ.* [Latin *electricus* from *electrum* amber, alloy of gold and silver, from Greek *ēlektron*. Electricity was first produced by rubbing amber]

Usage note

electric *or* electrical? *Electric* is the adjective generally used to describe specific things that carry or are powered by electricity: *an electric circuit; an electric motor; an electric toothbrush. Electrical* tends to be used with more general or abstract nouns: *an electrical appliance; electrical goods; electrical engineering.* There is, however, a good deal of overlap. *Electric* is the adjective usually used in figurative contexts: *The atmosphere was electric.*

electric[2] *noun* **1** (*in pl*) electrical parts; electric circuitry: *I don't like to tamper with electrics.* **2** an electrically-powered train vehicle. **3** (*in pl*) electric power.

electrical *adj* **1** of or connected with electricity: *electrical output; electrical engineering.* **2** = ELECTRIC[1] (1B): *electrical appliances.* ➤➤ **electrically** *adv.*

Usage note

electrical *or* electric? See note at ELECTRIC[1].

electricals *pl noun* electrical parts or electrical circuitry; electrics.

electric blanket *noun* a blanket containing an electric heating element that is used to warm a bed.

electric blue *adj and noun* harshly bright slightly greenish blue.

electric chair *noun* **1** a chair used in legal electrocution. **2** the penalty of death by electrocution.

electric eel *noun* a large eel-shaped fish of the Orinoco and Amazon rivers that is capable of giving a severe electric shock: *Electrophorus electricus.*

electric eye *noun* = PHOTOELECTRIC CELL.

electric field *noun* a portion of space, e.g. that surrounding an electric charge, in which a perceptible force is exerted on an electric charge.

electric guitar *noun* a guitar with a pickup that converts string vibrations into electrical signals which are then passed through an electrical amplifier.

electrician /elikˈtrish(ə)n, ˌilek-/ *noun* somebody who installs, maintains, operates, or repairs electrical equipment.

electricity /elikˈtrisiti, ˌilek-/ *noun* **1a** any phenomenon due to stationary or moving negatively or positively charged particles. **b** electric current or electric charge. **2** a science that deals with the phenomena and laws governing the behaviour of electric charges. **3** contagious excitement; tension.

electric organ *noun* a specialized tract of tissue, e.g. in the electric eel, in which electricity is generated.

electric ray *noun* any of numerous species of round-bodied rays found in warm seas that can give electric shocks: genus *Torpedo* and other genera.

electric shock *noun* a sudden stimulation of the nerves and convulsive contraction of the muscles caused by the passage of electricity through the body.

electric storm *noun* a violent atmospheric disturbance usu accompanied by thunder and lightning.

electrify /iˈlektrifie/ *verb trans* (**electrifies, electrified, electrifying**) **1a** to charge (something) with electricity. **b** to equip (something) for the use of electric power. **c** to supply (something) with electric power. **2** to excite or thrill (somebody): *But heavens! How that man could talk. He electrified large meetings* — Joseph Conrad. ➤➤ **electrification** /-fiˈkaysh(ə)n/ *noun,* **electrifier** *noun.*

electro /iˈlektroh/ *noun* (*pl* **electros**) **1** = ELECTROPLATE[2]. **2** = ELECTROTYPE[1].

electro- *comb. form* see ELECTR-.

electroacoustic /iˌlektroh-əˈkoohstik/ *adj* said of music: combining acoustic sounds with those generated by computer.

electrocardiogram /iˌlektrohˈkahdi-əgram/ *noun* the tracing made by an electrocardiograph.

electrocardiograph /iˌlektrohˈkahdi-əgrahf/ *noun* an instrument for recording the changes in electrical activity occurring during the heartbeat. ➤➤ **electrocardiographic** /-ˈgrafik/ *adj,* **electrocardiography** /-ˈogrəfi/ *noun.*

electrochemistry /iˌlektrohˈkeməstri/ *noun* the branch of chemistry dealing with the relation of electricity to chemical changes, e.g. in solutions conducting an electric current, and with the interconversion of chemical and electrical energy. ➤➤ **electrochemical** *adj,* **electrochemically** *adv,* **electrochemist** *noun.*

electroconvulsive therapy /iˌlektrohkənˈvulsiv/ *noun* a treatment for serious mental disorder, *esp* severe depression, in which a fit is induced by passing an electric current through the brain.

electrocute /iˈlektrəkyooht/ *verb trans* to execute or kill (somebody) by electric shock. ➤➤ **electrocution** /-ˈkyoohsh(ə)n/ *noun.* [ELECTRO- + -*cute* as in EXECUTE]

electrode /i'lektrohd/ *noun* a conductor used to establish electrical contact with a non-metallic part of a circuit, e.g. the acid in a car battery.

electrodeposit[1] /i'lektrohdipozit/ *noun* a deposit, *esp* of a metal, formed on or at an electrode in contact with a solution by electrolysis.

electrodeposit[2] /i,lektrohdi'pozit/ *verb trans* (**electrodeposited, electrodepositing**) to deposit (e.g. a metal) by electrolysis. ⟫ **electrodeposition** /-depə'zish(ə)n/ *noun*.

electrodynamics /i,lektrohdie'namiks/ *pl noun* (*treated as sing. or pl*) the branch of physics dealing with the effects arising from the interaction of electric currents with magnets or with other electric currents. ⟫ **electrodynamic** *adj*.

electroencephalogram /i,lektroh·in'sef(ə)ləgram/ *noun* the tracing made by an electroencephalograph.

electroencephalograph /i,lektroh·in'sef(ə)ləgrahf, -graf/ *noun* an instrument for detecting and recording the electrical activity of the brain. ⟫ **electroencephalography** /-'lografi/ *noun,* **electroencephalographic** /-'grafik/ *adj*.

electroform /i'lektrəfawm/ *verb trans* to form (an article) by depositing a metal on a mould by electrolysis.

electrokinetics /i,lektrohki'netiks/ *pl noun* (*treated as sing. or pl*) the branch of physics dealing with the movement of particles or liquids resulting from or producing a difference of electric potential. ⟫ **electrokinetic** *adj*.

electrolyse (*NAmer* **electrolyze**) /i'lektrəliez/ *verb trans* to subject (something) to electrolysis. ⟫ **electrolyser** *noun*.

electrolysis /elik'troləsis, ilek-/ *noun* **1** the passage of an electric current through an electrolyte to generate a gas, deposit a metal on an electrode, etc. **2** the destruction of hair roots, warts, moles, etc by means of an electric current.

electrolyte /i'lektrəliet/ *noun* **1** a non-metallic electric conductor, e.g. a solution of a chemical salt, in which current is carried by the movement of ions. **2** a substance that becomes an electrolyte when dissolved in a suitable solvent or melted. **3** the ions of an electrolyte.

electrolytic /i,lektrə'litik/ *adj* relating to electrolysis or an electrolyte. ⟫ **electrolytically** *adv*.

electrolyze /i'lektrəliez/ *verb trans NAmer* see ELECTROLYSE.

electromagnet /i'lektrohmagnit/ *noun* a core of magnetizable material surrounded by a coil of wire through which an electric current is passed to make the core into a magnet.

electromagnetic /i,lektroh·mag'netik/ *adj* of or produced by electromagnetism. ⟫ **electromagnetically** *adv*.

electromagnetic bomb *noun* a type of electronic bomb that produces strong pulses of electromagnetic energy capable of causing destructively high voltage levels in wiring, printed circuits, etc.

electromagnetic radiation *noun* radiation consisting of a series of electromagnetic waves.

electromagnetic spectrum *noun* the entire range of wavelengths or frequencies of electromagnetic radiation extending from gamma rays to the longest radio waves and including visible light.

electromagnetic unit *noun* any of a series of electrical units in the cgs system based primarily on the magnetic properties of electrical currents.

electromagnetic wave *noun* any of the waves that are produced by simultaneous periodic variations in the intensities of electric and magnetic fields and that include radio waves, infrared, visible light, ultraviolet, X-rays, and gamma rays.

electromagnetism /i,lektroh'magnətiz(ə)m/ *noun* **1** magnetism developed, e.g. in an electromagnet, by a current of electricity. **2** the branch of physics dealing with the relations between and the effects resulting from the interaction of electricity and magnetism.

electrometer /elik'tromitə, ilek-/ *noun* any of various instruments for detecting or measuring *esp* voltages or very low currents by means of the forces of attraction and repulsion existing between electrically charged bodies. ⟫ **electrometric** /i,lektroh'metrik/ *adj,* **electrometry** *noun*.

electromotive /i,lektrə'mohtiv/ *adj* producing or relating to an electric current.

electromotive force *noun* the amount of energy derived from an electrical source, e.g. a cell or generator, per unit current of electricity passing round a circuit and through the source.

electromyograph /i,lektrə'mie·əgrahf, -graf/ *noun* an instrument used for recording the electric waves associated with the activity of muscle under voluntary control, used *esp* in diagnosing disorders of the nerves and muscles. ⟫ **electromyographic** /-'grafik/ *adj,* **electromyographically** /-'grafikli/ *adv,* **electromyography** /-'ografi/ *noun*.

electron /i'lektron/ *noun* an elementary particle that carries a single negative electrical charge, that occurs in atoms outside the nucleus, and the overall movement of which constitutes electric current.

electronegative /i,lektroh'negətiv/ *adj* **1** having a negative electric charge. **2** having a tendency to attract electrons. ⟫ **electronegativity** /-'tiviti/ *noun*.

electron gun *noun* the cathode and its surrounding assembly that emits, controls, and focuses a stream of electrons to produce a beam of desired size, e.g. in a cathode-ray tube.

electronic /elik'tronik, ilek-/ *adj* **1a** relating to the methods and principles of electronics. **b** involving or using devices, e.g. transistors or microchips, in which a flow of electrons through a gas, vacuum, or semiconductor is controlled by a voltage. **c** relating to, involving, or using computers or other electronic systems: *electronic commerce; electronic surveillance.* **2** relating to electrons. ⟫ **electronically** *adv*.

electronic bomb *noun* a weapon capable of sending out a powerful beams or pulses of energy that destroy computers and other electrical and electronic systems.

electronic flash *noun* in photography, an electronic device for producing a bright flash of light from a gas-discharge tube.

electronic funds transfer at point of sale *noun* see EFTPOS.

electronic mail *noun* = EMAIL[1] (1).

electronic music *noun* music that consists of sounds electronically generated or modified.

electronic point of sale *noun* see EPOS.

electronic publishing *noun* the publishing of texts on CD-ROMs, etc and in other forms that can be accessed by a computer.

electronics *pl noun* **1** (*treated as sing. or pl*) the branch of physics or technology dealing with the emission, behaviour, and effects of electrons in transistors, microchips, thermionic valves, or other electronic devices. **2** the circuits, devices, etc of a piece of electronic equipment.

electronic tag *noun* an electronic monitoring device attached to somebody or something, *esp* one worn around the wrist or ankle by people convicted of or charged with a crime but not held in custody. ⟫ **electronic tagging** *noun*.

electronic warfare *noun* the use of electromagnetic energy, high-energy lasers, and particle beams for military purposes.

electron lens *noun* a device, e.g. in an electron microscope, for focusing a beam of electrons by means of an electric or magnetic field.

electron microscope *noun* an instrument in which a beam of electrons is used to produce a highly magnified image of an object. ⟫ **electron microscopy** *noun*.

electron optics *pl noun* (*treated as sing. or pl*) the branch of electronics dealing with those properties of beams of electrons that are analogous to the properties of rays of light.

electron tube *noun* an electronic device, e.g. a thermionic valve, consisting of a sealed container in which a controlled flow of electrons takes place through a vacuum or gas.

electron volt *noun* a unit of energy equal to the energy gained by an electron in passing between two points between which there is a voltage difference of one volt.

electrophile /i'lektrohfiel/ *noun* a substance with an affinity for electrons, e.g. a chlorine molecule. ⟫ **electrophilic** /-'filik/ *adj*.

electrophoresis /i,lektrohfə'reesis/ *noun* the movement of particles through a gel or other medium in which particles are suspended under the action of an applied electric field. ⟫ **electrophoretic** /-'retik/ *adj,* **electrophoretically** /-'retikli/ *adv*.

electrophorus /ilek'trofərəs, eelek-/ *noun* (*pl* **electrophori** /-ree/) an instrument for repeatedly generating static electricity in which a plate made of an insulating material is charged by friction and used to induce a charge in a metal plate. [ELECTRO- + scientific Latin *-phorus*: see -PHORE]

electroplate[1] /i'lektrohplayt/ *verb trans* to plate (an object) with a continuous metallic coating by electrolysis. ➤➤ **electroplater** *noun*.

electroplate[2] *noun* articles that have been electroplated, *esp* with silver.

electropositive /i,lektroh'pozətiv/ *adj* **1** having a positive electric charge. **2** having a tendency to release electrons.

electroscope /i'lektrəskohp/ *noun* any of various instruments for detecting the presence of an electric charge, or determining whether it is positive or negative, *esp* as a measure of the intensity of ionizing radiation. ➤➤ **electroscopic** /-'skopik/ *adj*.

electroshock therapy /i,lektroh'shok/ *noun* = ELECTROCONVUL-SIVE THERAPY.

electrostatic /i,lektroh'statik/ *adj* **1** of or producing static electricity: *an electrostatic generator.* **2** relating to electrostatics.

electrostatics *pl noun* (*treated as sing. or pl*) the branch of physics dealing with stationary electric charges, *esp* the phenomena due to attraction between opposite charges and repulsion between identical charges.

electrostatic unit *noun* any of a series of electrical units in the cgs system based primarily on forces of interaction between electric charges.

electrotherapy /i,lektroh'therəpi/ *noun* treatment of disease by the use of electricity, e.g. to generate heat or stimulate muscular activity in tissues. ➤➤ **electrotherapeutic** /-'pyoohtik/ *adj*, **electrotherapist** *noun*.

electrotype[1] /i'lektrətiep/ *noun* a duplicate printing surface made by coating a mould of the original with a thin layer of metal, *esp* copper, by electrolysis.

electrotype[2] *verb trans* to make an electrotype from (a printing surface). ➤➤ **electrotyper** *noun*.

electrovalent /i,lektroh'vaylənt/ *adj* said of a chemical bond: formed between positively and negatively charged ions. ➤➤ **electrovalency** *noun*.

electroweak /i,lektroh'week/ *adj* in physics, relating to both electromagnetic interaction and weak interaction.

electrum /i'lektrəm/ *noun* a pale yellow alloy of gold and silver. [Middle English from Latin: see ELECTRIC[1]]

electuary /i'lektyooəri/ *noun* (*pl* **electuaries**) a medicinal paste that consists of drugs mixed with treacle, sugar, or honey and is administered orally, *esp* in veterinary medicine: *For the rheumatism ... take equal quantities of flour of sulphur, and flour of mustard-seed, make them an electuary with honey or treacle; and take a bolus as big as a nutmeg several times a day* — Dr Johnson. [Middle English *electuarie* via Latin from Greek *ekleikton*, from *ekleichein* to lick up, from *ex* out + *leichein* to lick]

eleemosynary /,eli·ə'mosinəri/ *adj* of, supported by, or giving charity. [medieval Latin *eleemosynarius*, from late Latin *eleemosyna* alms, from Greek *eleēmosynē*: see ALMS]

elegant /'elig(ə)nt/ *adj* **1** gracefully refined or dignified, e.g. in manners, taste, or style. **2** tastefully rich or luxurious, *esp* in design or ornamentation: *elegant furnishings.* **3** said of ideas: simple and ingenious: *an elegant solution.* ➤➤ **elegance** *noun*, **elegantly** *adv*. [via French from Latin *elegant-, elegans* choice]

elegiac /eli'jie·ək/ *adj* **1** relating to or characteristic of an elegy. **2** expressing sorrow, often for something now past. **3** written in or consisting of elegiac couplets or elegiac stanzas. ➤➤ **elegiacally** *adv*. [via late Latin from Greek *elegeiakos*, ultimately from *elegos* song of mourning]

elegiac couplet *noun* a classical verse form consisting of a dactylic hexameter followed by a dactylic pentameter.

elegiacs *pl noun* verse written in elegiac couplets or elegiac stanzas.

elegiac stanza *noun* a stanza consisting of four lines of iambic pentameters with a rhyme scheme of *abab*.

elegize or **elegise** /'eləjiez/ *verb intrans* to write in elegiac style. ➤ *verb trans* to write an elegy on (somebody or something). ➤➤ **elegist** *noun*.

elegy /'eləji/ *noun* (*pl* **elegies**) **1a** a song, poem, or other work expressing sorrow or lamentation, *esp* for a dead person. **b** a pensive or reflective poem that is usu nostalgic or melancholy. **2** a poem in elegiac couplets or elegiac stanzas. [Latin *elegia* poem in elegiac couplets, ultimately from Greek *elegos* song of mourning]

element /'eləmənt/ *noun* **1** in chemistry, any of more than 100 fundamental substances that consist of atoms of only one kind and that singly or in combination constitute all matter. **2** any of the constituent parts that make up a whole. **3** (*in pl*) the simplest principles of a subject of study; the rudiments. **4** (*treated as sing. or pl*) a specified group within a human community: *the criminal element in the city.* **5** any of the factors determining an outcome. **6** something present in a small quantity; a hint: *There is an element of truth in what he said.* **7** the part of an electric device, e.g. a heater or kettle, that contains the heating wire through which an electric current passes. **8a** any of the four substances, air, water, fire, and earth, formerly believed to compose the physical universe. **b** the state or sphere natural or suited to someone or something: *At school she was in her element.* **c** (*in pl*) forces of nature, *esp* violent or severe weather: *We spent a night exposed to the elements.* **9** (*in pl*) the bread and wine used in Communion. **10** a constituent member of a mathematical set or matrix. [Middle English via French from Latin *elementum* principle, rudiment]

elemental[1] /elə'mentl/ *adj* **1** of or being an element. **2** existing as an uncombined chemical element. **3** fundamental, basic, or essential. **4** of or resembling a powerful force of nature: *elemental passions.* ➤➤ **elementalism** *noun*.

elemental[2] *noun* a supernatural being, spirit, or force that is said to be physically manifested.

elementary /elə'ment(ə)ri/ *adj* **1a** of or dealing with the basic elements of something; simple: *He can't handle the most elementary decision-making.* **b** of or dealing with the first principles of something; introductory. **2** = ELEMENTAL[1] (1), (2). ➤➤ **elementarily** *adv*, **elementariness** *noun*.

elementary particle *noun* any of various simple subatomic constituents of matter, e.g. the electron, proton, or photon.

elementary school *noun* **1** *Brit* formerly, a state school for children aged from 5 to 13 or 14. **2** *NAmer* a state school for pupils in the first six or eight years of their education.

elenchus /i'lengkəs/ *noun* (*pl* **elenchi** /-kie/) a logical refutation, *esp* in syllogistic form. [via Latin from Greek *elenchos*, from *elenchein* to shame, cross-examine, refute]

elephant /'elif(ə)nt/ *noun* a very large nearly hairless mammal having the snout prolonged into a muscular trunk and two teeth in the upper jaw developed into long ivory tusks. The African elephant is larger than the Indian elephant of S Asia, which has smaller ears and a humped back: *Loxodonta africana* (African elephant), *Elephas maximus* (Indian elephant). [Middle English via French and Latin from Greek *elephant-, elephas*]

elephantiasis /,elifən'tie·əsis/ *noun* enormous enlargement of tissues, typically those of a limb or the scrotum, caused by lymphatic obstruction, *esp* by filariae (parasitic worms; see FILARIA). [Latin *elephantiasis*, a kind of leprosy, from Greek *elephant-, elephas* ELEPHANT]

elephantine /eli'fantien/ *adj* **1a** huge or massive. **b** clumsy or ponderous. **2** relating to an elephant.

elephant seal *noun* either of two nearly extinct large seals with a long trunklike snout: *Mirounga angustirostris* or *Mirounga leonina*.

Eleusinian mysteries /elyoo'sini·ən/ *pl noun* the secret religious rites celebrated at ancient Eleusis in worship of Demeter and Persephone. [named after *Eleusis*, ancient Greek town near Athens]

elevate /'elivayt/ *verb trans* **1** to lift (something) up; to raise (it). **2** to raise (somebody or something) in rank or status; to exalt (them). **3** to raise the spirits of (somebody); to elate (them). **4** to raise the axis of (a gun) in order to increase its range. [Middle English *elevaten* from Latin *elevare*, from EX-[1] + *levare* to lighten, from *levis* light in weight]

elevated *adj* **1** raised above a surface: *an elevated road.* **2** on a high moral or intellectual plane; lofty: *elevated thoughts.* **3** exhilarated in mood or feeling.

elevation /eli'vaysh(ə)n/ *noun* **1** the height to which something is elevated, e.g.: **a** the height above sea level. **b** the angle at which a gun is aimed above the horizon. **2** the act of elevating or the state of being elevated. **3** a representation drawn to scale of the front, back, or side of a building. **4** an elevated place. **5** the ability of a ballet dancer or skater to leap and be apparently suspended in the air. ➤➤ **elevational** *adj*.

elevator *noun* **1** *chiefly NAmer* = LIFT² (1). **2a** an endless belt or chain conveyor with scoops or buckets for raising grain, liquids, etc. **b** *NAmer* a building for elevating, storing, discharging, and sometimes processing grain. **3** a movable horizontal surface usu attached to the tailplane of an aircraft for controlling climb and descent. **4** a muscle that contracts to raise a part of the body.

eleven /i'lev(ə)n/ *noun* **1** the number 11, or the quantity represented by it. **2** something having eleven parts or members, *esp* a cricket, football, or hockey team. **3a** the age of 11 years. **b** the hour one hour before midday or midnight. ➤➤ **eleven** *adj*, **elevenfold** *adj and adv*. [Old English *endleofan*]

eleven-plus *or* **11-plus** *noun* an examination taken, *esp* formerly, at the age of 10–11 to determine which type of British state secondary education a child should receive.

elevenses *pl noun Brit* (*treated as sing. or pl*) light refreshment taken in the middle of the morning: *What was left for me? Elevenses in the garden, The Times over my face, pension at the end of the month and not a damned thing I wanted to buy with it* — David Marcus. [from *eleven o'clock*]

eleventh *adj and noun* **1** denoting a person or thing having the position in a sequence corresponding to the number eleven. **2** one of eleven equal parts of something. **3** in music, an interval of eleven degrees of a diatonic scale, or the combination of two notes at such an interval.

eleventh hour *noun* (**the eleventh hour**) the latest possible time: *I feel, now, like a man who has redeemed a failing reputation … by a single just deed done at the eleventh hour* — Mark Twain; *as long as they don't make any eleventh-hour alterations.* ➤➤ **eleventh-hour** *adj*.

Word history
from the parable of the vineyard (Matthew 20:1–16). Labourers hired at the eleventh hour of the working day were paid the same as those who started earlier.

ELF *abbr* extremely low frequency.

elf /elf/ *noun* (*pl* **elves** /elvz/) a fairy, *esp* a small mischievous one. ➤➤ **elfish** *adj*, **elfishly** *adv*. [Old English *ælf*]

elfin /'elfin/ *adj* of or resembling an elf, *esp* in being small, delicate, or mischievous.

elf-lock *noun* (*usu in pl*) a tangled lock of hair. [from folklore belief that an elf caused it]

elicit /i'lisit/ *verb trans* (**elicited, eliciting**) **1** (*often* + from) to call forth or draw out (a response or reaction). **2** to evoke (it). **2** to draw forth or bring out (something latent or potential). ➤➤ **elicitation** /-'taysh(ə)n/ *noun*, **elicitor** *noun*. [Latin *elicitus*, past part. of *elicere*, from EX-¹ + *lacere* to allure]

Usage note
elicit *or* illicit? These two words are sometimes confused. *Elicit* is a verb, usually followed by the preposition *from*, meaning 'to call or draw forth (something)': *We managed to elicit from him how he obtained the information. Illicit* is an adjective meaning 'illegal' or 'not allowed': *an illicit love affair.*

elide /i'lied/ *verb trans* to suppress (e.g. a vowel or syllable) by elision. [Latin *elidere* to strike out, from EX-¹ + *laedere* to injure by striking]

eligible /'elijabl/ *adj* **1** qualified to do or receive something: *eligible for promotion; eligible to vote.* **2** worthy or desirable, *esp* as a marriage partner: *an eligible young bachelor.* ➤➤ **eligibility** /-'biliti/ *noun*, **eligibly** *adv*. [Middle English via French and late Latin from Latin *eligere*: see ELECT¹]

eliminate /i'liminayt/ *verb trans* **1a** to get rid of (something) completely; to eradicate (it): *the need to eliminate poverty.* **b** to set (something) aside as unimportant; to ignore (it). **2** to kill (a person), *esp* so as to remove them as an obstacle. **3** to remove (a competitor, team, etc) from a competition, usu by defeat. **4** to expel (e.g. waste) from the living body. ➤➤ **eliminable** *adj*, **elimination** /-'naysh(ə)n/ *noun*, **eliminative** /-nətiv/ *adj*, **eliminator** *noun*. [Latin *eliminatus*, past part. of *eliminare* to turn out of doors, from EX-¹ + *limin-, limen* threshold]

ELISA /i'lieza/ *noun* in biochemistry, an immunological technique for determining the quantity of a substance in a sample. [acronym from *enzyme-linked immunosorbent assay*]

elision /i'lizh(ə)n/ *noun* omission of a vowel or syllable in speech or writing, e.g. *I'm* for *I am*. [late Latin *elision-, elisio*, from Latin *elidere*: see ELIDE]

elite¹ *or* **élite** /i'leet, ay'leet/ *noun* **1** (*treated as sing. or pl*) a relatively small and often powerful group, or a chosen part of a group, that is considered to be intellectually, professionally, or socially superior. **2** a typewriter type producing twelve characters to the inch. [French *élite* from Old French *eslite* chosen, from Latin *eligere*: see ELECT¹]

elite² *or* **élite** *adj* belonging to or suitable for an élite.

elitism *or* **élitism** *noun* **1a** the belief in leadership by an elite. **b** the belief that some people are superior to others and deserve special treatment, or a system based on this belief. **2** consciousness of belonging to an elite. ➤➤ **elitist** *noun and adj*.

elixir /i'liksə, -siə/ *noun* **1** an alchemist's substance supposedly capable of changing base metals into gold. **2a** (*also* **elixir of life**) a substance held to be capable of prolonging life indefinitely. **b** a cure-all. **3** a sweetened liquid, e.g. a syrup, containing a drug or medicine. [Middle English via medieval Latin from Arabic *al-iksīr* the elixir, prob from Greek *xerion* drying powder]

Elizabethan /i,lizə'beeth(ə)n/ *adj* **1** relating to or characteristic of the reign of Elizabeth I of England (1558–1603). **2** denoting styles of art, architecture, and literature associated with this period. ➤➤ **Elizabethan** *noun*.

elk /elk/ *noun* (*pl* **elks** *or collectively* **elk**) **1** the largest existing deer of Europe and Asia, which belongs to the same species as but is smaller than the moose of N America: *Alces alces*. **2** *NAmer* = WAPITI. [prob from Old English *eolh*]

elkhound *noun* a hunting dog of a breed originating in Norway, having a very heavy grey coat tipped with black.

ell /el/ *noun* a former English unit of length equal to 45in. (about 1.14m). [Old English *eln*]

ellipse /i'lips/ *noun* **1** a two-dimensional closed curve generated by a point moving in such a way that the sum of its distances from two fixed points is constant; the intersection of a plane cutting obliquely through a cone: compare HYPERBOLA, PARABOLA. **2** = ELLIPSIS. [Greek *elleipsis*: see ELLIPSIS]

ellipsis /i'lipsis/ *noun* (*pl* **ellipses** /-seez/) **1** the omission of one or more words needed to make a construction grammatically complete, as in *I took flowers, and my sister a book.* **2** marks or a mark (e.g. ... or *** or —), indicating the omission of letters or words. [via Latin from Greek *elleipsis* ellipsis, ellipse, from *elleipein* to leave out]

ellipsoid /i'lipsoyd/ *noun* a solid or surface of which all the plane sections are ellipses or circles: compare HYPERBOLOID, PARABOLOID. ➤➤ **ellipsoidal** /-'soydl/ *adj*.

elliptic /i'liptik/ *adj* = ELLIPTICAL (1), (2A).

elliptical /i'liptikl/ *adj* **1** of or shaped like an ellipse: *on a cloth untrue, with a twisted cue and elliptical billiard balls* — W S Gilbert. **2a** of or marked by ellipsis or an ellipsis. **b** said of speech or writing: extremely or excessively concise, often resulting in obscurity or ambiguity. ➤➤ **elliptically** *adv*, **ellipticity** /elip'tisiti/ *noun*. [Greek *elleiptikos* defective, marked by ellipsis, from *elleipein* to leave out]

elm /elm/ *noun* **1** any of several species of large graceful trees with serrated leaves and small light disc-shaped fruits: genus *Ulmus*. **2** the hard heavy wood of this tree. [Old English]

El Niño /el 'neenyoh/ *noun* a warming of the equatorial Pacific region that occurs every five to eight years, disrupts the climate of the region, and can have severe effects on the weather in other parts of the world. [Spanish *el Niño* the (Christ) Child, because of its original appearance at Christmas time]

elocution /elə'kyoohsh(ə)n/ *noun* the art of effective public speaking, *esp* of good diction. ➤➤ **elocutionary** *adj*, **elocutionist** *noun*. [Middle English *elocucioun* from Latin *elocution-, elocutio*, from *eloqui*: see ELOQUENT]

elongate¹ /'eelonggayt/ *verb trans* to extend the length of (something). ➤ *verb intrans* to grow in length. [late Latin *elongatus*, past part. of *elongare* to withdraw, from Latin EX-¹ + *longus* long]

elongate² *adj* **1** stretched out; lengthened. **2** in botany and zoology, long in proportion to width.

elongated /'eelonggaytid/ *adj* = ELONGATE².

elongation /eelong'gaysh(ə)n/ *noun* **1** the act of elongating or the state of being elongated. **2** the angular distance of one celestial body from another round which it revolves or from a particular point in the sky.

elope /i'lohp/ *verb intrans* to run away secretly with a lover, usu with the intention of getting married or cohabiting. ⏩ **elopement** *noun*, **eloper** *noun*. [Anglo-French *aloper* to run away]

eloquence /'eləkwəns/ *noun* **1** fluent, forceful, and persuasive speech. **2** the art or power of using such speech.

eloquent /'eləkwənt/ *adj* **1** characterized by fluent, forceful, and persuasive use of language. **2** vividly or movingly expressive or revealing: *He put his arm around her in an eloquent gesture of reassurance.* ⏩ **eloquently** *adv*. [Middle English via French from Latin *eloquent-*, *eloquens*, present part. of *eloqui* to speak out, from EX-¹ + *loqui* to speak]

Elsan /'elsan/ *noun trademark* a portable chemical toilet. [from the initials of its manufacturer, *E L Jackson*, + SANITATION]

else /els/ *adv* **1** different from or other than the person, place, manner, or time mentioned or understood: *How else could he have acted?* **2** also; besides: *There's nothing else to eat.* ✳ **or else 1** used to express a threat: *Do what I tell you or else!* **2** if not; otherwise: *I'll go inside or else they might see me.* [Old English *elles*]

elsewhere /els'weə/ *adv* in or to another place: *I'll take my business elsewhere.*

ELT *abbr* English language teaching.

eluant *or* **eluent** /'elyoo-ənt/ *noun* a solvent used in eluting. [Latin *eluent-*, *eluens*, present part. of *eluere*: see ELUTE]

eluate /'elyoo-ət, -ayt/ *noun* the solution obtained by eluting. [Latin *eluere* (see ELUTE) + -ATE¹]

elucidate /i'loohsidayt/ *verb* to make (something) clear, *esp* by explanation. ⏩ **elucidation** /-'daysh(ə)n/ *noun*, **elucidative** /-dətiv/ *adj*, **elucidator** *noun*, **elucidatory** *adj*. [late Latin *elucidatus*, past part. of *elucidare*, from Latin EX-¹ + *lucidus* LUCID]

elude /i'loohd/ *verb trans* **1** to avoid (somebody or something) cunningly or adroitly. **2** to escape the memory, understanding, or notice of (somebody). ⏩ **elusion** /-zh(ə)n/ *noun*. [Latin *eludere*, from EX-¹ + *ludere* to play]

eluent /'elyoo-ənt/ *noun* see ELUANT.

elusive /i'loohsiv/ *adj* **1** difficult to find or catch. **2** difficult to remember or understand. ⏩ **elusively** *adv*, **elusiveness** *noun*. [Latin *elusus*, past part. of *eludere*: see ELUDE]

elute /ee'l(y)ooht/ *verb trans* to remove (adsorbed material) from the surface of a liquid or solid by washing with a solvent. ⏩ **elution** /-sh(ə)n/ *noun*. [Latin *elutus*, past part. of *eluere* to wash out, from EX-¹ + *lavere* to wash]

elutriate /ee'l(y)oohtriayt/ *verb trans* to purify, separate, or remove (a substance) by washing. ⏩ **elutriation** /-'aysh(ə)n/ *noun*. [Latin *elutriatus*, past part. of *elutriare*, irreg from *elutus*: see ELUTE]

eluvium /ee'l(y)oohvi-əm/ *noun* rock debris produced by the weathering and disintegration of rock in situ. ⏩ **eluvial** *adj*. [coined from Latin *eluere*: see ELUTE]

elver /'elvə/ *noun* a young eel. [alteration of dialect *eelfare* (from EEL + FARE²), orig 'migration of young eels upriver', later 'a group of young eels']

elves /elvz/ *noun* pl of ELF.

elvish /'elvish/ *adj* resembling an elf; elfish.

Elysium /i'lizi-əm/ *noun* (*pl* **Elysiums** *or* **Elysia** /-i·ə/) **1** the home of the blessed after death in Greek mythology. **2** a place of bliss, happiness, or delight; a paradise. ⏩ **Elysian** *adj*. [via Latin from Greek *Elysion*]

elytron /'elitron/ *noun* (*pl* **elytra** /-trə/) either of the modified front pair of wings in some insects, e.g. beetles and cockroaches, that cover and protect the hind pair of functional wings. [from Greek *elytron* sheath, wing cover, from *eilyein* to roll, wrap]

em /em/ *noun* **1** in printing, a unit of width equal to the body of a piece of type bearing the letter M or the height of the type size. **2** = PICA¹ (1).

em- *prefix* see EN-¹, EN-².

'em /(ə)m/ *pronoun* used in writing to suggest casual speech: them.

emaciate /i'maysiayt/ *verb trans* to make (somebody or something) excessively thin or feeble. ⏩ *verb intrans* to become excessively thin or feeble. ⏩ **emaciated** *adj*, **emaciation** /-'aysh(ə)n/ *noun*. [Latin *emaciatus*, past part. of *emaciare*, from EX-¹ + *macies* leanness, from *macer* lean]

email¹ *or* **e-mail** /'eemayl/ *noun* **1** a system for transmitting messages from one computer to another via a local area network or through a modem and telephone line. **2** a message or messages sent in this way. [short for *electronic mail*]

email² *or* **e-mail** *verb trans* **1** to send (somebody) an email. **2** to send (a message, document, etc) by email.

emalangeni *noun* pl of LILANGENI.

emanate /'emənayt/ *verb intrans* to come out from a source: *A foul smell emanated from the sewer; Rumours have been emanating from high places.* ➤ *verb trans* to send out or give off (something); to emit (it). [Latin *emanatus*, past part. of *emanare*, from EX-¹ + *manare* to flow]

emanation /emə'naysh(ə)n/ *noun* **1** something that emanates or is produced by emanating. **2** a heavy gaseous element produced by radioactive disintegration: *radium emanation*. **3** the act of emanating. ⏩ **emanational** *adj*, **emanative** /-nətiv/ *adj*.

emancipate /i'mansipayt/ *verb trans* **1** to free (somebody or something) from restraint or control, *esp* from restrictions imposed by society or law. **2** to free (somebody) from slavery. ⏩ **emancipation** /-'paysh(ə)n/ *noun*, **emancipator** *noun*, **emancipatory** /-pətri/ *adj*. [Latin *emancipatus*, past part. of *emancipare*, from EX-¹ + *mancipare* to transfer ownership of, from *mancip-*, *manceps* purchaser]

emasculate /i'maskyoolayt/ *verb trans* **1** to deprive (somebody or something) of strength, vigour, or spirit; to weaken (them). **2** to castrate (a male person or animal). **3** to remove the male representative organs of (a flower) to prevent self-pollination and allow artificial pollination. ⏩ **emasculation** /-'laysh(ə)n/ *noun*, **emasculator** *noun*, **emasculatory** /-lətri/ *adj*. [Latin *emasculatus*, past part. of *emasculare*, from EX-¹ + *masculus* male]

embalm /im'bahm/ *verb trans* **1** to treat (a dead body) in order to protect it against decay. **2** to preserve (something) from oblivion. **3** *literary* to fill (something) with sweet odours; to perfume (it). ⏩ **embalmer** *noun*, **embalmment** *noun*. [Middle English *embaumen* from Old French *embasmer*, from EN-¹ + *basme* BALM]

embank /im'bangk/ *verb trans* to enclose, confine, or protect (something) by an embankment.

embankment *noun* a raised structure to hold back water or to carry a road or railway.

embargo¹ /im'bahgoh/ *noun* (*pl* **embargoes**) **1** a government order prohibiting the departure or entry of commercial ships. **2** a legal prohibition on commerce: *an embargo on arms shipments.* **3** a stoppage, restraint, or impediment, *esp* a prohibition: *I lay no embargo on anybody's words* — Jane Austen. [Spanish *embargo*, from *embargar* to bar, ultimately from IN-² + Latin *barra* bar]

embargo² *verb trans* (**embargoes, embargoed, embargoing**) **1** to place an embargo on (e.g. ships or commerce). **2** to seize (e.g. goods or a ship) for the use or service of the state.

embark /im'bahk/ *verb intrans* **1** to go on board a ship or aircraft. **2** (+ on/upon) to make a start on something: *She embarked on a new career.* ➤ *verb trans* to put or take (somebody or something) on board a ship or aircraft. ⏩ **embarkation** /embah'kaysh(ə)n/ *noun*. [early French *embarquer* from Old Provençal *embarcar*, from EN-¹ + late Latin *barca*: see BARK⁵]

embarrass /im'barəs/ *verb trans* **1** to cause (somebody) to experience a state of self-conscious distress; to disconcert (them): *Smutty stories embarrassed her.* **2** to involve (somebody) in financial difficulties, *esp* debt. **3** *archaic* to hamper the movement of (somebody or something); to hinder or impede (them). ⏩ **embarrassed** *adj*, **embarrassedly** *adv*, **embarrassing** *adj*, **embarrassingly** *adv*, **embarrassment** *noun*. [French *embarrasser* via Spanish from Portuguese *embaraçar*, from *baraço* halter]

Usage note

Embarrass is spelt with two *r*s and two *s*s.

embassy /'embəsi/ *noun* (*pl* **embassies**) **1** the official residence of an ambassador. **2** a diplomatic body headed by an ambassador. **3** the position of an ambassador. **4** an ambassador's official mission abroad. [early French *ambassee*, of Germanic origin]

embattle /im'batl/ *verb trans* **1** to prepare (an army) for battle. **2** to fortify (a town, position, etc) against attack. **3** to provide (a building) with battlements. [Middle English *embatailen* from early French *embatailler*, from EN-¹ + *bataille* to battle; (sense 3) Middle English *embatailen* from EN-¹ + *batailen* to fortify with battlements]

embattled *adj* **1** prepared for or involved in battle: *the embattled defenders of psychoanalytic theory* — David E Stannard. **2** having battlements or other fortifications. **3** hemmed in by adversaries, difficulties, etc.

embay /im'bay/ *verb trans* **1** to enclose or shelter (something) in or as if in a bay: *an embayed fleet.* **2** to form (something) into a bay or bays: *an embayed shoreline.*

embayment *noun* **1** the formation of a bay. **2** a bay or a geographical conformation resembling a bay.

embed *or* **imbed** /im'bed/ *verb trans* (**embedded** *or* **imbedded**, **embedding** *or* **imbedding**) **1** to place or fix (something) firmly or deeply in surrounding matter: *A splinter was embedded in his finger.* **2** to make (something) an integral part of a whole: *embed computer graphics in a document.* **3** to implant (e.g. an idea) in the mind: *Hate was embedded in their hearts.*

embellish /im'belish/ *verb trans* **1** to make (something) beautiful by adding ornaments, to decorate (it). **2** to make (speech or writing) more interesting by adding fictitious or exaggerated detail. ➤➤ **embellish** *noun,* **embellishment** *noun.* [Middle English *embelisshen* from early French *embelir,* from EN-¹ + *bel* beautiful]

ember /'embə/ *noun* **1** a glowing fragment of coal or wood in a dying fire. **2** (*in pl*) the smouldering remains of a fire. **3** (*in pl*) slowly fading emotions, memories, ideas, etc. [Middle English *eymere* from Old Norse *eimyrja*]

ember day *noun* in Anglican and Roman Catholic Churches, any of twelve days set aside for fasting and prayer, which fall on the Wednesday, Friday, and Saturday following the first Sunday in Lent, Whitsunday, 14 September, and 13 December. [Old English *ymbrendæg,* from *ymbrene* circuit, anniversary + *dæg* DAY]

embezzle /im'bezl/ *verb trans* to appropriate (money or property entrusted to one's care) fraudulently to one's own use. ➤➤ **embezzlement** *noun,* **embezzler** *noun.* [Middle English *embesilen* from Anglo-French *embeseiller,* from early French EN-¹ + *besillier* to destroy]

embitter /im'bitə/ *verb trans* (**embittered, embittering**) **1** to make (somebody) bitter. **2** to make (a bad situation or feeling) worse. ➤➤ **embittered** *adj,* **embitterment** *noun.*

emblazon /im'blayz(ə)n/ *verb trans* (**emblazoned, emblazoning**) **1** to display (something) conspicuously. **2** to inscribe or decorate (something) with a heraldic device or other emblem: *vans emblazoned with the company logo.* **3** to deck (something) in bright colours. **4** to celebrate or extol (something): *have his … deeds emblazoned by a poet* — Thomas Nashe. ➤➤ **emblazonment** *noun,* **emblazonry** /-ri/ *noun.*

emblem /'embləm/ *noun* **1** a design, symbol, or figure adopted and used as an identifying mark. **2** an object or a typical representation of an object symbolizing another object or idea. [Middle English via Latin from Greek *emblēmat-, emblēma* inlaid work, from *emballein* to insert, from EN-¹ + *ballein* to throw]

emblematic /emblə'matik/ *adj* of or constituting an emblem; symbolic. ➤➤ **emblematically** *adv.*

emblematical *adj* = EMBLEMATIC.

emblematize *or* **emblematise** /em'blemətiez/ *verb trans* to be an emblem of (something); to symbolize (it).

embody /im'bodi/ *verb trans* (**embodies, embodied, embodying**) **1** to make (e.g. ideas or concepts) concrete and perceptible. **2** (+ in) to make (e.g. connected ideas or principles) a part of a body or system: *Their way of life is embodied in their laws.* **3** to represent (an idea or belief) in human or animal form; to personify (it): *Such men embodied the idealism of the revolution.* **4** to give a body to (a spirit); to incarnate (it). ➤➤ **embodier** *noun,* **embodiment** *noun.*

embolden /im'bohld(ə)n/ *verb trans* (**emboldened, emboldening**) to make (somebody) bold or courageous.

embolectomy /embə'lektəmi/ *noun* (*pl* **embolectomies**) surgical removal of an embolus.

emboli /'embəlie/ *noun* pl of EMBOLUS.

embolic /em'bolik/ *adj* relating to an embolus or an embolism.

embolism /'embəliz(ə)m/ *noun* **1** the sudden obstruction of a blood vessel by an embolus. **2** = EMBOLUS. [Middle English *embolisme* from medieval Latin *embolismus,* from Greek *emballein* to insert, intercalate, from EN-¹ + *ballein* to throw]

embolus /'embələs/ *noun* (*pl* **emboli** /-lie/) a blood clot, air bubble, or other particle likely to cause an embolism. [Greek *embolos* wedge-shaped object, stopper, from *emballein:* see EMBOLISM]

embonpoint /ombom'pwanh (*French* ãbɔ̃pwɛ̃)/ *noun euphem* plumpness or stoutness: *The only fault of the Spanish beauty is that she too soon indulges in the magnificence of en bon point* — Disraeli. [French *en bon point* in good condition]

emboss /im'bos/ *verb trans* **1** to ornament (something) with raised work. **2** to carve, mould, or paint (a design, lettering, etc) in relief on a surface. ➤➤ **embossed** *adj,* **embosser** *noun,* **embossment** *noun.* [Middle English *embosen* from early French *embocer,* from EN-¹ + *boce:* see BOSS⁴]

embouchure /ombooh'shooə/ *noun* in music, the position and use of the lips and tongue in playing a wind instrument. [French *embouchure* from *s'emboucher* to flow into, from EN-¹ + *bouche* mouth]

embower /im'bowə/ *verb trans* (**embowered, embowering**) *literary* to shelter or enclose (somebody or something) in or as if in a bower: *like a rose embowered in its own green leaves* — Shelley.

embrace¹ /im'brays/ *verb trans* **1** to take (somebody) in one's arms and hold them closely as a sign of affection; to hug (them). **2a** to take up (a cause or idea), *esp* readily or eagerly; to adopt (it). **b** to accept (e.g. an opportunity) willingly or welcome (it). **3** to include (something) as an integral part or element of a whole. **4** to encircle or enclose (something). ➤ *verb intrans* said of two people: to embrace or hug one another. ➤➤ **embraceable** *adj,* **embracement** *noun,* **embracer** *noun.* [Middle English *embracen* from Old French *embracier,* from EN-¹ + *brace* two arms: see BRACE¹]

embrace² *noun* the act or an instance of embracing: *a loving embrace.*

embrasure /im'brayzhə/ *noun* **1** a door or window aperture, *esp* one with angled sides that increase the width of the opening on the inside. **2** an opening in a wall or parapet of a fortification through which missiles can be fired. [French *embrasure* from obsolete *embraser* to widen an opening]

embrocate /'embrəkayt/ *verb trans* to moisten and rub (a part of the body) with a lotion or liniment. [late Latin *embrocare,* from part. of *embrocare,* from Greek *embrochē* lotion, from *embrechein* to embrocate, from EN-¹ + *brechein* to wet]

embrocation /embrə'kaysh(ə)n/ *noun* a liquid rubbed into the skin, *esp* to relieve pain; a liniment.

embroider /im'broydə/ *verb trans* (**embroidered, embroidering**) **1a** to ornament (e.g. cloth or a garment) with decorative stitches made by hand or machine. **b** to form (e.g. a design or pattern) in ornamental needlework. **2** to elaborate on (a narrative); to embellish (it) with exaggerated or fictitious details. ➤ *verb intrans* to do or make embroidery. ➤➤ **embroiderer** *noun.* [Middle English *embroideren* from Anglo-French *enbrouder,* from EN-¹ + Old French *brouder* to decorate with embroidery, of Germanic origin]

embroidery *noun* (*pl* **embroideries**) **1** the art or process of embroidering designs. **2** embroidered work. **3** unnecessary additions or embellishments, *esp* to a narrative.

embroil /im'broyl/ *verb trans* **1** to involve (somebody) in conflict or difficulties. **2** to throw (e.g. affairs) into disorder or confusion. ➤➤ **embroilment** *noun.* [French *embrouiller,* from EN-¹ + *brouiller* to broil]

embryo /'embrioh/ *noun* (*pl* **embryos**) **1a** an animal in the early stages of growth before birth or hatching. **b** a developing unborn human during the first eight weeks after conception. **2** a rudimentary plant within a seed. **3** something as yet undeveloped. ✱ **in embryo** in an undeveloped state: *My plans are still in embryo.* [medieval Latin *embryon-, embryo,* from Greek *embryon,* from EN-² + *bryein* to swell]

embryogenesis /embrioh'jenəsis/ *noun* the formation and development of an embryo. ➤➤ **embryogenetic** /-'netik/ *adj.*

embryology /embri'oləji/ *noun* the study of the development of embryos. ➤➤ **embryologic** /-'lojik/ *adj,* **embryological** /-'lojikl/ *adj,* **embryologist** *noun.*

embryonal /em'brie-ənl/ *adj* = EMBRYONIC.

embryonic /embri'onik/ *adj* **1** of or relating to an embryo. **2** in an early stage of development: *Mrs Almond lived much further uptown, in an embryonic street, with a high number – a region where the extension of the city began to assume a theoretic air* — Henry James. ➤➤ **embryonically** *adv.*

emcee¹ /em'see/ *noun informal* a compere or master of ceremonies. [a representation of MC = master of ceremonies]

emcee² *verb trans* (**emcees, emceed, emceeing**) *informal* to act as an emcee of (an event).

-eme *suffix* forming nouns, denoting: a unit of language structure: *phoneme.* [French *-ème,* from *phonème* speech sound, phoneme]

emend /i'mend/ *verb trans* to remove errors or irregularities from (a text). ⫸ **emendable** *adj*. [Middle English *emenden* from Latin *emendare*: see AMEND]

Usage note
emend or amend? See note at AMEND.

emendate /'eemendayt/ *verb trans* = EMEND. ⫸ **emendator** *noun*, **emendatory** /i'mendət(ə)ri/ *adj*.

emendation /eemen'daysh(ə)n/ *noun* **1** an alteration made to a text in the process of emending it. **2** the act of emending a text.

emerald /'em(ə)rəld/ *noun* **1** a bright green variety of the mineral beryl used as a gemstone: compare AQUAMARINE, BERYL. **2** the bright green colour of an emerald. ⫸ **emerald** *adj*. [Middle English *emerallde* from Old French *esmeraud*, ultimately from Greek *smaragdos*, of Semitic origin]

emerge /i'muhj/ *verb intrans* **1** to come out into view. **2** to become manifest or known. **3** to survive a difficult or unpleasant experience. **4** to come into being or develop. ⫸ **emergence** *noun*, **emerging** *adj*. [Latin *emergere*, from EX-[1] + *mergere* to plunge]

emergency /i'muhj(ə)nsi/ *noun* (*pl* **emergencies**) **1a** an unforeseen occurrence or combination of circumstances that is potentially dangerous and calls for immediate action. **b** (*used before a noun*) resulting from or used in such a situation: *an emergency landing*. **2** a patient with a serious injury or medical condition that needs urgent treatment. **3** *Aus, NZ* in sport, a player who has been selected to replace another if the need arises, e.g. through injury. [medieval Latin *emergentia*, literally 'something that emerges', from Latin *emergere*: see EMERGE]

emergent *adj* emerging, *esp* in the early stages of formation or development. [Middle English from Latin *emergent-, emergens*, present part. of *emergere*: see EMERGE]

emeritus /i'meritəs/ *adj* retaining a title on an honorary basis after retirement: *an emeritus professor*. [Latin *emeritus*, past part. of *emereri* to serve out one's term, from EX-[1] + *mereri, merēre* to earn, deserve, MERIT[1]]

emersion /i'muhsh(ə)n/ *noun* **1** the act or an instance of emerging. **2** in astronomy, the reappearance of a celestial body, e.g. after an eclipse. [Latin *emersus*, past part. of *emergere*: see EMERGE]

emery /'em(ə)ri/ *noun* a dark granular mineral that consists mainly of corundum and is used for grinding and polishing. [Middle English via early French *esmeri* from Old Italian *smiriglio*, ultimately from Greek *smyrid-, smyris*]

emery board *noun* a strip of cardboard or wood coated with powdered emery and used as a nail file.

emery paper *noun* paper coated with emery powder for use as an abrasive.

emetic[1] /i'metik/ *noun* something that causes vomiting. [via Latin from Greek *emetikē*, fem of *emetikos* causing vomiting, from *emein* to vomit]

emetic[2] *adj* causing vomiting. ⫸ **emetically** *adv*.

EMF *abbr* European Monetary Fund.

emf *abbr* electromotive force.

-emia *comb. form NAmer* see -AEMIA.

emigrant /'emigrənt/ *noun* a person who emigrates. ⫸ **emigrant** *adj*.

emigrate /'emigrayt/ *verb intrans* to leave one's home or country for permanent residence elsewhere. ⫸ **emigration** /-'graysh(ə)n/ *noun*. [Latin *emigratus*, past part. of *emigrare*, from EX-[1] + *migrare* to migrate]

émigré or **emigré** /'emigray (*French* emigre)/ *noun* a person who emigrates, *esp* for political reasons. [French *émigré*, past part. of *émigrer* to emigrate, from Latin *emigrare*: see EMIGRATE]

eminence /'eminəns/ *noun* **1a** a position of prominence or superiority. **b** (**Eminence**) used as a title of a Roman Catholic cardinal. **2** somebody or something high, prominent, or lofty, e.g.: **a** a person of high rank or attainments. **b** a natural geographical elevation; a height.

éminence grise /ˌayminonhs 'greez (*French* eminãs griz)/ *noun* (*pl* **éminences grises**) a person who exercises power through his or her often unsuspected influence on another person or group of people who have titular authority.

Word history
French *éminence grise*, literally 'grey eminence', nickname of Père Joseph (François du Tremblay) d.1638, French monk and diplomat. He was the confidant of Cardinal Richelieu d.1642, French statesman, who was known

as *Éminence Rouge* red eminence. The names are from the colours of their respective habits.

eminent /'eminənt/ *adj* **1** standing out so as to be readily seen or noted; conspicuous or notable. **2** having or showing eminence, *esp* in position, fame, or achievement; distinguished. ⫸ **eminently** *adv*. [Middle English via French from Latin *eminent-, eminens*, present part. of *eminēre* to stand out, from EX-[1] + *minēre* to stand, project]

eminent domain *noun* in law, a right of a government to take private property for public use, subject to making reasonable compensation.

emir /'emiə, e'miə/ or **ameer** or **amir** *noun* **1** a ruler of a Muslim state. **2** in former times, a Muslim military commander or chief. **3** a male descendant of Muhammad. [Arabic *amīr* commander]

emirate /'emirət/ *noun* **1** the rank or authority of an emir. **2** the territory ruled by an emir.

emissary /'emis(ə)ri/ *noun* (*pl* **emissaries**) **1** an agent or negotiator sent on a mission to represent a government or head of state; an envoy. **2** somebody sent on a secret or spying mission. [Latin *emissarius*, from *emittere*: see EMIT]

emission /i'mish(ə)n/ *noun* **1** the act or an instance of emitting. **2** something emitted, e.g. electromagnetic waves, electrons, fumes, bodily fluids, etc. ⫸ **emissive** /i'misiv/ *adj*.

emissivity /emi'siviti/ *noun* the ability of a surface to emit heat by radiation.

emit /i'mit/ *verb trans* (**emitted, emitting**) **1a** to throw out or give off (e.g. light or radiation). **b** to send (something) out; to discharge (it). **2** to make (a sound); to utter (it): *He emitted a groan*. [Latin *emittere* to send out, from EX-[1] + *mittere* to send]

emitter /i'mitə/ *noun* **1** somebody or something that emits. **2** a region in a transistor that produces charge carriers.

Emmental or **Emmenthal** /'eməntahl/ *noun* a pale yellow Swiss cheese with many holes that form during ripening. [named after *Emmenthal*, valley in Switzerland where it was orig made]

emmer /'emə/ *noun* a hard variety of wheat that is the ancestor of several modern wheats: *Triticum turgidum*. [German *Emmer*, from Old High German *amari* spelt]

emmet /'emit/ *noun chiefly dialect* an ant. [Old English *ǣmete*]

Emmy /'emi/ *noun* (*pl* **Emmys**) in the USA, a statuette awarded annually for notable achievement in television. [alteration of *Immy*, nickname for *image orthicon* a camera tube used in television]

emollient[1] /i'moli·ənt/ *adj* **1** making soft or supple, or giving soothing relief, *esp* to the skin. **2** making a situation calmer. [Latin *emollient-, emolliens*, present part. of *emollire* to soften, from EX-[1] + *mollis* soft]

emollient[2] *noun* an emollient substance, e.g. lanolin.

emolument /i'molyoomənt/ *noun* the returns arising from office or employment; a salary or fee. [Middle English from Latin *emolumentum* miller's fee, from *emolere* to grind up, from EX-[1] + *molere* to grind]

e-money or **e-cash** *noun* money in the form of digitally encoded information that can be used to make payments via the Internet or by specially encoded smart cards. [short for *electronic money*]

emote /i'moht/ *verb intrans* to give expression to emotion, *esp* theatrically. [back-formation from EMOTION]

emoticon /i'mohtikon, i'mot-/ *noun* a representation of a human face that is formed from keyboard characters and used in email to express feelings. [blend of EMOTION and ICON]

emotion /i'mohsh(ə)n/ *noun* **1a** a strong feeling, e.g. anger, fear, or joy, often involving physiological changes, e.g. a rise in the pulse rate. **b** such feelings considered collectively. **2** instinctive feelings or reactions, *esp* as opposed to reason. ⫸ **emotionless** *adj*. [early French *emotion*, from *emouvoir* to stir up, via Old French *esmovoir* from Latin *exmovēre* to move away, disturb, from EX-[1] + *movēre* to MOVE[1]]

emotional *adj* **1** relating to the emotions: *an emotional disorder*. **2** feeling or expressing emotion: *an emotional speech*. **3** inclined to show excessive emotion. **4** = EMOTIVE. ⫸ **emotionality** /-'naliti/ *noun*, **emotionally** *adv*.

Usage note
emotional or emotive? See note at EMOTIVE.

emotional intelligence *noun* the ability to understand and control one's own emotions, to motivate oneself, and to empathize with other people.

emotionalise /i'mohsh(ə)nl·iez/ *verb trans* see EMOTIONALIZE.

emotionalism *noun* the tendency to show or be affected by the emotions too easily. >> **emotionalist** *noun*.

emotionalize *or* **emotionalise** *verb trans* to make (somebody or something) emotional.

emotive /i'mohtiv/ *adj* arousing or appealing to emotion, *esp* as opposed to reason: *Abortion is an emotive issue.* >> **emotively** *adv*, **emotiveness** *noun*, **emotivity** /-'tiviti/ *noun*.

Usage note

emotive or **emotional**? The main meaning of *emotive* is 'arousing strong feelings, appealing to the feelings (rather than reason)': an *emotive* use of language chooses words specifically for their power to produce an *emotional* response. *Emotional* is the commoner word with a broader range of use; its core sense is 'feeling or expressing emotion'. *He made an emotional speech* would mean that the speaker showed in his speech how strongly he himself felt about something. *She made an emotive speech* would suggest that she was more interested in stirring up the crowd than expressing her own feeling.

Emp. *abbr* 1 Emperor. 2 Empire. 3 Empress.

empanel *or* **impanel** /im'panl/ *verb trans* (**empanelled** *or* **impanelled**, **empanelling** *or* **impanelling**, *NAmer* **empaneled** *or* **impaneled**, **empaneling** *or* **impaneling**) to enrol (somebody) on a panel list, *esp* for jury service. >> **empanelment** *noun*.

empathize *or* **empathise** /'empəthiez/ *verb intrans* (*usu* + with) to understand and share the feelings of another person.

empathy /'empəthi/ *noun* 1 the capacity for understanding and sharing another's feelings or ideas. 2 the imaginative re-creation of a mood, feeling or emotional state suggested by a work of art in order to better understand or appreciate it. >> **empathetic** /-'the-tik/ *adj*, **empathetically** *adv*, **empathic** /em'pathik/ *adj*. [Greek *empatheia*, from EN-² + *pathos*: see PATHOS]

emperor /'emp(ə)rə/ *noun* the supreme ruler of an empire. >> **emperorship** *noun*. [Old French *empereor* from Latin *imperator* commander, from *imperare* to command, from IN-² + *parare* to prepare]

emperor penguin *noun* the largest known penguin, found only in the south polar region: *Aptenodytes forsteri*.

emphasis /'emfəsis/ *noun* (*pl* **emphases** /-seez/) **1a** force or intensity of expression that gives special importance to something: *writing with emphasis on the need for reform.* **b** a particular prominence given in speaking or writing to one or more words or syllables. **2** special consideration of or stress on something: *the school's emphasis on examinations.* [via Latin from Greek *emphasis* exposition, emphasis, from *emphainein* to indicate, from EN-¹ + *phainein* to show]

emphasize *or* **emphasise** /'emfəsiez/ *verb trans* **1** to give emphasis to (something); to place emphasis on (it): *He emphasized the need for reform.* **2** to make (something) sharper or clearer in form or outline; to draw attention to (it).

emphatic /im'fatik/ *adj* **1** spoken with or marked by emphasis. **2** tending to express oneself in forceful speech or to take decisive action. **3** clear or definite: *an emphatic victory.* >> **emphatically** *adv*. [Greek *emphatikos*, from *emphainein*: see EMPHASIS]

emphysema /emfi'seemə/ *noun* a disorder characterized by air-filled expansions of body tissues; *specif* such a condition of the lungs involving abnormal enlargement of the air sacs and causing breathlessness. [Greek *emphysēma* bodily inflation]

Empire /'empie·ə/ *adj* of or characteristic of a style, e.g. of furniture or interior decoration, popular during the first French Empire (1804–15). [French *Empire*, short for *le premier Empire* the first Empire of France]

empire *noun* **1a** a large group of countries or peoples under the authority of a single ruler or state: *Fate looks after the Indian Empire because it is so big and so helpless* — Kipling. **b** something resembling such an empire, *esp* an extensive territory or enterprise under single domination or control. **2** imperial sovereignty. **3** the period during which an empire is in existence. **4** (**Empire**) a variety of eating apple with a red skin and crisp juicy flesh. [Middle English via French *empire*, *empirie*, from Latin *imperium* absolute authority, empire, from *imperare*: see EMPEROR]

empire-builder *noun* a person who seeks to extend their power or influence, e.g. within a business organization, by acquiring additional staff or areas of operation. >> **empire-building** *noun*.

empire line *noun* a style of women's dress having a high waistline and a low neckline, first popular in early 19th cent. France.

empiric¹ /im'pirik/ *noun* **1** a person who relies on practical experience rather than theory. **2** *archaic* a quack or charlatan. [Latin *empiricus* doctor relying on experience alone, from Greek *empeirikos*, from *empeiria* experience, from EN-² + *peiran* to attempt]

empiric² *adj* = EMPIRICAL.

empirical /im'pirikl/ *adj* originating in or based on observation, experience, or experiment rather than theory: *empirical data; empirical laws.* >> **empirically** *adv*.

empirical formula *noun* a chemical formula showing the simplest ratio of elements in a compound rather than the total number of atoms in the molecule, e.g. CH_2O rather than $C_2H_{12}O_6$ as the formula for glucose.

empiricism /im'pirisiz(ə)m/ *noun* **1** a theory that all knowledge is dependent on experience of the external world. **2** the practice of discovery by observation and experiment. **3** quackery or charlatanism. >> **empiricist** *noun*.

emplace /im'plays/ *verb trans* to put (something) into position. [back formation from EMPLACEMENT]

emplacement *noun* **1** the situation or location of something. **2** a prepared position for weapons or military equipment: *radar emplacements.* **3** the act of putting something into place. [early French *emplacement* from *emplacer* to emplace, from EN-¹ + *place*]

emplane /im'playn/ *verb intrans* to board an aircraft. > *verb trans* to put (something or somebody) on board an aircraft.

employ¹ /im'ploy/ *verb trans* **1** to pay (somebody) wages or a salary in return for their services, usu on a long-term basis. **2** to give (somebody) a task or occupation; to keep (them) busy. **3** to use (something) in a specified way or for a specific purpose. >> **employability** /-'biliti/ *noun*, **employable** *adj*. [Middle English *emploien* via early French *emploier* from Latin *implicare* to enfold, involve, implicate, from IN-² + *plicare* to fold]

employ² *noun* the state of being employed, *esp* for wages or a salary: *in the government's employ.*

employee (*NAmer* **employe**) /employ'ee, im'ployee/ *noun* somebody employed by another for wages or a salary. [French *employé*, past part. of *employer* to employ, from early French *emploier*: see EMPLOY¹]

employer *noun* a person, company, or other organization that employs people.

employment *noun* **1** the act of employing or the state of being employed: *His letters, which he continually rearranged, and his Will, which he frequently altered, were a source of consolation and employment* — E V Lucas. **2a** paid work. **b** a job or occupation.

employment agency *noun* an agency providing a service for employers seeking workers and for people seeking employment.

employment office *noun Brit* = JOB CENTRE.

emporium /im'pawri·əm/ *noun* (*pl* **emporiums** *or* **emporia** /-ri·ə/) a place of trade, *esp* a large shop or commercial centre. [via Latin from Greek *emporion*, from *emporos* traveller, trader]

empower /im'powə/ *verb trans* (**empowered, empowering**) **1** to give official authority or legal power to (somebody). **2** to give (somebody) the strength and confidence to act on their own initiative: *the word empower ... one of those suspicious New Age buzzwords that always portend a scam or screwball notion* — Guardian. >> **empowerment** *noun*.

empress /'empris/ *noun* **1** the wife or widow of an emperor. **2** a woman having the rank of emperor in her own right. [Middle English *emperesse* from Old French, fem of *empereor*: see EMPEROR]

empty¹ /'empti/ *adj* (**emptier, emptiest**) **1a** containing nothing, *esp* lacking typical or expected contents. **b** not occupied, inhabited, or frequented: *empty streets.* **2a** lacking reality or substance; hollow: *an empty pleasure.* **b** lacking effect, value, or sincerity: *empty threats; an empty gesture.* **c** lacking sense; foolish: *his empty ideas.* **3** *informal* hungry. **4** said of a mathematical set: having no numbers or elements. >> **emptily** *adv*, **emptiness** *noun*. [Old English *æmettig* unoccupied, from *æmetta* leisure]

empty² *verb* (**empties, emptied, emptying**) > *verb trans* **1** to remove the contents of (something); to make (it) empty. **2** to discharge or transfer (contents) by pouring or tipping them out:

She emptied the biscuits onto the plate. **3** (*often* + of) to deprive, divest, or rid (something): *acting emptied of all emotion.* ➤➤ *verb intrans* **1** to become empty. **2** to discharge contents: *The river empties into the ocean.* ➤➤ **emptier** *noun*.

empty³ *noun* (*pl* **empties**) a bottle or other container that has been emptied.

empty-handed *adj* having or bringing nothing, *esp* because nothing has been gained or obtained: *They returned empty-handed.*

empty-headed *adj* foolish or silly.

empty nester *noun informal* a parent whose children have grown up and left home.

empyema /empie'eemǝ/ *noun* (*pl* **empyemata** /-mǝtǝ/ *or* **empyemas**) the presence of pus in a body cavity, *esp* in the chest. ➤➤ **empyemic** /-mik/ *adj.* [via late Latin from Greek *empyēma*, ultimately from EN-² + *pyon* pus]

empyreal /empie'ree·ǝl/ *adj* of the empyrean; celestial or heavenly. [via late Latin from late Greek *empyrios*, from IN-¹ + Greek *pyr* fire]

empyrean¹ /empie'ree·ǝn/ *noun* **1** the highest heavenly sphere in ancient and medieval cosmology. **2** *literary* the heavens; the sky: *The claims which things make are corrupters of manhood, mortgages on the soul, and a drag anchor on our progress towards the empyrean —* William James.

empyrean² *adj* = EMPYREAL.

EMS *abbr* European Monetary System.

EMU *abbr* European monetary union.

emu¹ /'eemyooh/ *noun* a swift-running Australian flightless bird that is related to and smaller than the ostrich: *Dromaius novaehollandiae.* [modification of Portuguese *ema* rhea]

emu² *abbr* electromagnetic unit.

emulate /'emyoolayt/ *verb trans* **1** to imitate (somebody or something) closely, *esp* in order to equal them. **2** to rival or compete with (another). ➤➤ **emulation** /-'laysh(ǝ)n/ *noun*, **emulative** /-lǝtiv/ *adj*, **emulator** *noun*. [Latin *aemulatus*, past part. of *aemulari*, from *aemulus* rivalling, rival]

emulous /'emyoolǝs/ *adj* ambitious or eager to emulate. ➤➤ **emulously** *adv.*

emulsifier /i'mulsifie·ǝ/ *noun* a substance that emulsifies, *esp* a food additive that stabilizes processed foods.

emulsify /i'mulsifie/ *verb* (**emulsifies, emulsified, emulsifying**) ➤ *verb trans* to convert (e.g. an oil) into an emulsion. ➤ *verb intrans* to become an emulsion. ➤➤ **emulsifiable** *adj*, **emulsification** /-fi'kaysh(ǝ)n/ *noun*.

emulsion¹ /i'mulsh(ǝ)n/ *noun* **1** a substance consisting of one liquid dispersed in droplets throughout another liquid. **2** a suspension of a silver compound in a gelatin solution or other solid medium for coating photographic plates, film, etc. **3** a type of paint in which the pigment is dispersed in an oil which forms an emulsion with water. ➤➤ **emulsive** /-siv/ *adj.* [Latin *emulsus*, past part. of *emulgēre* to milk out, from EX-¹ + *mulgare* to milk]

emulsion² *verb trans* to paint (a surface) with emulsion paint.

en /en/ *noun* in printing, a unit of width equal to the body of a piece of type bearing the letter N or half an em.

en-¹ *or* **em-** *prefix* **1** forming verbs from nouns, with the meanings: **a** to put into or onto: *embed; engulf; enthrone.* **b** to provide with: *empower.* **2** forming verbs from nouns and adjectives, with the meaning: to cause to be: *enslave; enable.* **3** forming more intensive forms of verbs: *entangle.* [Middle English via Old French from Latin *in-, im-*, from *in*]

en-² *or* **em-** *prefix* forming nouns, denoting: inclusion or involvement: *energy; empathy.* [Middle English via Latin from Greek, from *en* in]

-en¹ *or* **-n** *suffix* forming adjectives from nouns, with the meaning: made of or consisting of: *earthen; wooden.* [Old English]

-en² *or* **-n** *suffix* forming verbs from adjectives and nouns, with the meaning: to cause to be or have; to become: *sharpen; heighten.* [Middle English *-nen* from Old English *-nian*]

-en³ *or* **-n** *suffix* forming past participles of verbs: *broken; worn.*

enable /i'naybl/ *verb trans* **1** to provide (somebody) with the means or opportunity to do something. **2** to make (something) possible, practical, or easy.

enabling act *noun* in law, an act giving certain legal powers to a person or organization.

enact /i'nakt/ *verb trans* **1** to make (e.g. a bill) into law. **2** to act out or perform (a role, scene, etc). ➤➤ **enactable** *adj*, **enaction** *noun*, **enactment** *noun*, **enactor** *noun*.

enamel¹ /i'naml/ *noun* **1** a usu opaque glassy coating applied to the surface of metal, glass, or pottery. **2** something enamelled, *esp* enamelware. **3** a white substance consisting mainly of calcium that forms a thin hard layer capping the teeth. **4** a paint that dries with a glossy appearance. **5** *chiefly NAmer* an often coloured coating applied to the nails to give them a smooth or glossy appearance; nail varnish.

enamel² *verb trans* (**enamelled, enamelling,** *NAmer* **enameled, enameling**) to cover or decorate (something) with enamel. ➤➤ **enameller** *noun*, **enamellist** *noun*, **enamelwork** *noun.* [Middle English *enamelen* from early French *enamailler*, from EN-¹ + *esmail* enamel, of Germanic origin]

enamelware *noun* metal household or kitchen utensils coated with enamel.

enamour (*NAmer* **enamor**) /i'namǝ/ *verb trans* (*usu in passive*, + of/with) to cause (somebody) to love or like a person or thing: *I'm not enamoured with the colour scheme.* [Middle English *enamouren* from Old French *enamourer*, from EN-¹ + *amour*: see AMOUR]

enantiomer /i'nanti-ǝmǝ/ *noun* = ENANTIOMORPH. ➤➤ **enantiomeric** /-'merik/ *adj.* [Greek *enantios* opposite + -MER]

enantiomorph /i'nanti-ǝmawf/ *noun* either of a pair of chemical compounds or crystals with structures that have a mirror-image relationship to each other. ➤➤ **enantiomorphic** /-'mawfik/ *adj*, **enantiomorphism** /-'mawfizm/ *noun*, **enantiomorphous** /-'mawfǝs/ *adj.* [Greek *enantios* opposite + -MORPH]

en bloc /onh 'blok (*French* ã blɔk)/ *adv and adj* all together; in a mass. [French *en bloc* in a block]

en brosse /onh 'bros (*French* ã brɔs)/ *adv and adj* said of hair: cut short and standing erect; crew-cut: *He was ugly, but what is called distinguished-looking … his hair was cropped en brosse —* Henry James. [French *en brosse*, literally 'in the manner of a brush']

enc. *abbr* **1** enclosed. **2** enclosure.

encamp /in'kamp/ *verb trans* to place or establish (people) in a camp. ➤ *verb intrans* to set up or occupy a camp.

encampment *noun* **1** the place where a group, e.g. a body of troops, is encamped; a camp. **2** the act of encamping or the state of being encamped.

encapsulate /in'kapsyoolayt/ *verb trans* **1** to express (something) in a concise form. **2** to enclose (something) in or as if in a capsule. ➤ *verb intrans* to become encapsulated. ➤➤ **encapsulation** /-'laysh(ǝ)n/ *noun.*

encase *or* **incase** /in'kays/ *verb trans* to enclose (something) in or as if in a case. ➤➤ **encasement** *noun.*

encash /in'kash/ *verb trans Brit, formal* to pay or obtain cash for (e.g. a cheque). ➤➤ **encashable** *adj*, **encashment** *noun.*

encaustic¹ /en'kawstik/ *noun* **1** a paint made from pigment mixed with melted beeswax and resin and fixed by heat after application. **2** a method involving the use of heat to fix or burn a colour onto or into a surface, or a work produced in this way. [via Latin from Greek *enkaustikos*, from *enkaiein* to burn in, from EN-¹ + *kaiein* to burn]

encaustic² *adj* decorated with encaustic.

-ence *suffix* forming nouns, denoting: **1** an action or process: *emergence.* **2** an instance of an action or process: *reference; reminiscence.* **3** a quality or state: *dependence; somnolence.* [Middle English via Old French from Latin *-entia*, from pres parts. ending in *-ent-, -ens*]

enceinte¹ /onh'sant (*French* ãsɛ̃t)/ *adj* = PREGNANT (1). [early French from medieval Latin *incincta* without a girdle, from IN-¹ + *cincta*, fem past part. of *cingere* to gird]

enceinte² *noun* a line of fortification, or the area that it encloses. [Old French *enceinte* enclosing wall, from Latin *incingere* to enclose, from IN-² + *cingere* to gird]

encephal- *or* **encephalo-** *comb. form* forming nouns and their derivatives, denoting: the brain: *encephalitis.* [via French and Latin from Greek *enkephal-*, from *enkephalos*: see ENCEPHALON]

encephala /en'sef(ǝ)lǝ/ *noun* pl of ENCEPHALON.

encephalic /ensi'falik/ *adj* relating to or located in the brain.

encephalin /en'sefalin/ *noun* see ENKEPHALIN.

encephalitis /in,sefǝ'lietis/ *noun* inflammation of the brain, usu caused by infection. ➤➤ **encephalitic** /-'litik/ *adj.*

encephalitis lethargica /li'thahjikə/ *noun* = SLEEPY SICKNESS.

encephalo- *comb. form* see ENCEPHAL-.

encephalogram /en'sef(ə)ləgram/ *noun* **1** an X-ray picture of the brain made by encephalography. **2** = ELECTROENCEPHALOGRAM.

encephalograph /in'sef(ə)ləgrahf/ *noun* **1** = ENCEPHALOGRAM. **2** = ELECTROENCEPHALOGRAPH.

encephalography /in,sef(ə)l'ogrəfi/ *noun* X-ray photography of the brain after some of the cerebrospinal fluid has been replaced by air or oxygen.

encephalomyelitis /in,sef(ə)loh,mie-ə'lietis/ *noun* inflammation of both the brain and spinal cord.

encephalon /en'sef(ə)lon/ *noun* (*pl* **encephala** /-lə/) the brain of a human being or other vertebrate animal. [from Greek *enkephalos*, from EN-² + *kephalē* head]

encephalopathy /in,sef(ə)l'opathi/ *noun* (*pl* **encephalopathies**) a disease of the brain, *esp* one involving alterations of brain structure.

enchain /in'chayn/ *verb trans* to hold or bind (somebody or something) with or as if with chains. ➤➤ **enchainment** *noun*. [Middle English *encheynen* via early French *enchainer* from Old French EN-¹ + *chaeine* CHAIN¹]

enchant /in'chahnt/ *verb trans* **1** to cast a spell on (something or somebody); to bewitch (them): *the enchanted forest.* **2** to attract and move (somebody) deeply; to delight (them). ➤➤ **enchanter** *noun*, **enchantress** *noun*. [Middle English *enchanten* via early French *enchanter* from Latin *incantare*, from IN-² + *cantare*: see CHANT¹]

enchanter's nightshade *noun* a slender European plant of the fuchsia family that bears small whitish pink flowers: *Circaea lutetiana*. [because it was believed to be the plant used by Circe, a witch in Greek mythology who turned Odysseus' crew into pigs]

enchanting *adj* charming; delightful. ➤➤ **enchantingly** *adv*.

enchantment *noun* **1** the act of enchanting or the state of being enchanted. **2** a magic spell. **3** great charm or attraction.

enchase /in'chays/ *verb trans* = CHASE³ (1). [Middle English *enchasen* to emboss, from early French *enchasser* to enshrine, set, from EN-¹ + *chasse* reliquary, from Latin *capsa* case]

enchilada /enchi'lahdə/ *noun* a Mexican dish consisting of a TORTILLA (maize pancake) spread with a meat filling, rolled up, and covered with a chilli sauce. [American Spanish *enchilada* seasoned with chilli]

enchiridion /enkie'ridi·ən/ *noun* (*pl* **enchiridions** *or* **enchiridia** /-di·ə/) a handbook or manual. [via late Latin from Greek *encheiridion*, from EN-² + *cheir* hand]

encipher /in'siefə/ *verb trans* (**enciphered, enciphering**) to convert (a message) into a code. ➤➤ **encipherment** *noun*.

encircle /in'suhkl/ *verb trans* **1** to form a circle round (something); to surround (it). **2** to move or pass completely round (something). ➤➤ **encirclement** *noun*.

encl. *abbr* **1** enclosed. **2** enclosure.

enclave /'enklayv/ *noun* **1** a territorial or culturally distinct unit enclosed within foreign territory: compare EXCLAVE. **2** a distinct social or cultural group surrounded by a larger group: *a male enclave.* [early French *enclaver* to enclose, ultimately from Latin IN-² + *clavis* key]

enclitic¹ /in'klitik/ *adj* said of a word or particle: being without independent accent and forming part of the preceding word, e.g. *not* in *cannot*: compare PROCLITIC¹. ➤➤ **enclitically** *adv*. [via late Latin from Greek *enklitikos*, from *enklinesthai* to lean on, from EN-¹ + *klinein* to lean]

enclitic² *noun* an enclitic word or particle.

enclose *or* **inclose** /in'klohz/ *verb trans* **1** to include (something) in a package or envelope, *esp* along with something else: *We have enclosed a cheque in settlement.* **2** to contain or confine (something). **3** to close in or surround (something) completely: *We enclosed the field with a high fence.* **4** *esp* in former times, to fence off (common land) for private use. [Middle English *enclosen* from early French *enclos*, past part. of *enclore* to enclose, from Latin *includere*: see INCLUDE]

enclosed order *noun* a Christian religious community that avoids or forbids contacts with the outside world.

enclosure *or* **inclosure** /in'klohzhə/ *noun* **1** an area of enclosed ground; *specif* such an area reserved for certain spectators in a sports ground. **2** something included with a letter in the same

envelope or package. **3** *esp* in former times, the fencing in of common land in order to appropriate it for private use.

encode /in'kohd/ *verb trans* to convert (e.g. a body of information) from one system of communication into another; *esp* to convert (a message) into code. ➤➤ **encoder** *noun*.

encomia /en'kohmi·ə/ *noun* pl of ENCOMIUM.

encomiast /en'kohmiast/ *noun* somebody who makes an encomium or encomiums. ➤➤ **encomiastic** /-'astik/ *adj*. [Greek *enkōmiastēs*, from *enkōmiazein* to praise, from *enkōmion*: see ENCOMIUM]

encomium /en'kohmi·əm/ *noun* (*pl* **encomiums** *or* **encomia** /-mi·ə/) a usu formal expression of warm or high praise; a eulogy. [via Latin from Greek *enkōmion*, from EN-¹ + *kōmos* revel, celebration]

encompass /in'kumpəs/ *verb trans* **1** to form a circle round (something); to enclose (it). **2** to include (something), *esp* in a comprehensive manner: *a plan that encompasses a number of aims.* **3** *formal* to cause (something) to occur; to bring (it) about: *plans laid to encompass his downfall.* ➤➤ **encompassment** *noun*.

encore¹ /'ongkaw/ *noun* a performer's reappearance to give an additional or repeated performance at the request of the audience. [French *encore* still, again]

encore² *verb trans* **1** to call for an encore of (a performance). **2** to call for an encore by (a performer).

encore³ *interj* used by an audience to call for an encore.

encounter¹ /in'kowntə/ *verb trans* (**encountered, encountering**) **1a** to meet or come across (somebody), *esp* unexpectedly. **b** to be faced with (something): *We encountered a few problems.* **2a** to meet (somebody) as an adversary or enemy. **b** to engage in conflict with (somebody). [Middle English *encountren* via Old French from medieval Latin *incontrare*, ultimately from Latin IN-² + *contra* against]

encounter² *noun* **1** a chance meeting. **2** a meeting or clash between hostile factions or people.

encounter group *noun* a group of people who meet regularly to develop greater understanding of their own and one another's feelings.

encourage /in'kurij/ *verb trans* **1** to inspire (somebody) with courage, confidence, or hope. **2** to spur (somebody) on: *They were encouraged to paint by their parents.* **3** to give help, support, or approval to (e.g. a process or action): *Many companies encourage union membership.* ➤➤ **encouragement** *noun*, **encourager** *noun*, **encouraging** *adj*, **encouragingly** *adv*. [Middle English *encoragen* from Old French *encoragier*, from EN-¹ + *corage*: see COURAGE]

encroach /in'krohch/ *verb intrans* **1** (+ on/upon) to enter gradually or by stealth into the possessions or rights of another; to intrude or trespass. **2** (*often* + on/upon) to advance beyond the usual or proper limits. ➤➤ **encroacher** *noun*, **encroachment** *noun*. [Middle English *encrochen* to get, seize, from Old French *encrochier*, from EN-² + *croc, croche* hook]

en croûte /ong 'krooht (*French* ã krut)/ *adj* wrapped in pastry: *fillet of beef en croûte.* [French *en croûte*]

encrust *or* **incrust** /in'krust/ *verb trans* to cover, line, or overlay (something) with a hard and decorative layer, e.g. of jewels or precious metal. ➤ *verb intrans* to form a crust. ➤➤ **encrustation** *noun*. [prob from Latin *incrustare*, from IN-² + *crusta* CRUST¹]

encrypt /in'kript/ *verb trans* to convert (a message or other information) into code; to encode (it). ➤➤ **encryption** *noun*.

encumber /in'kumbə/ *verb trans* (**encumbered, encumbering**) **1** to impede or hamper (somebody or something). **2** to weigh (somebody or something) down; to burden (them). **3** to burden (somebody or something) with a debt or legal claim: *encumber an estate.* [Middle English *encombren* from Old French *encombrer*, from EN-¹ + *combre* defensive barrier of felled trees]

encumbrance /in'kumbrəns/ *noun* **1** something that encumbers; an impediment. **2** a mortgage or other claim against property.

-ency *suffix* forming nouns, denoting: a quality or state: *despondency*. [Middle English *-encie* from Latin *-entia*: see -ENCE]

encyclical /en'siklikl/ *noun* in the Roman Catholic Church, a letter from the pope to all bishops or to those in one country. [via late Latin from Greek *enkyklios* circular, general, from EN-² + *kyklos* circle, wheel]

encyclopaedia *noun* see ENCYCLOPEDIA.

encyclopedia or **encyclopaedia** /in‚sieklə'peedi·ə/ noun a work containing general information on all branches of knowledge or comprehensive information on one branch, usu in articles arranged alphabetically by subject. [medieval Latin *encyclopaedia* course of general education, from Greek *enkyklios paideia* general education]

encyclopedic or **encyclopaedic** /in‚sieklə'peedik/ adj **1** of or relating to an encyclopedia or its methods of treating a subject. **2** comprehensive: *an encyclopedic knowledge of silent films.* ⏩ **encyclopedically** adv.

encyclopedism or **encyclopaedism** /in‚sieklə'peediz(ə)m/ noun encyclopedic knowledge.

encyclopedist or **encyclopaedist** /in‚sieklə'peedist/ noun a person who compiles or contributes to an encyclopedia.

encyst /en'sist/ verb trans to enclose (something) in a cyst. ⏵ verb intrans to become enclosed in a cyst. ⏩ **encystation** /-'staysh(ə)n/ noun, **encystment** noun.

end¹ /end/ noun **1a** either of the extreme parts farthest from the middle of something long: *a pencil with a point at each end.* **b** either of the two connected points involved in a telephone call, journey etc: *What's the weather like at your end?* **2a** the point or time at which something stops happening, is completed, or ceases to exist: *the end of the war.* **b** the last part or section of something; the conclusion: *The end of the film was the weakest part.* **c** the farthest point from where one is: *It's at the other end of the garden.* **3** death or destruction. **4** a piece left over; a remnant. **5** an aim, goal, or purpose: *The dog, to gain some private ends, went mad and bit the man* — Goldsmith. **6a** either half of a sports field, pitch, court, etc: *We changed ends at halftime.* **b** in bowls, etc, a period of play in one direction. **7** informal a particular part of an undertaking or organization: *the advertising end of the business.* **8** (**the end**) informal something or somebody extreme of a kind, *esp* something or somebody particularly unpleasant: *I found his rudeness yesterday the absolute end.* ✳ **at an end 1** finished; completed. **2** exhausted; used up. **end on** with the end pointing towards one. **get/have one's end away** *coarse slang* to have sexual intercourse. **in the end** eventually. **keep one's end up** to maintain one's position or perform well in an argument, competition, etc. **make (both) ends meet** to cope financially. **no end 1** exceedingly. **2** a vast amount; a huge quantity: *I had no end of trouble finding her.* **on end 1** in an upright position: *We had to turn the table on end to get it through the door.* **2** without stopping: *It rained for days on end.* [Old English *ende*]

end² verb trans **1** to bring (something) to an end. **2** to destroy (something). ⏵ verb intrans **1** to come to an end. **2** (often + up) to reach a specified ultimate situation, condition, position, or rank: *He ended up as a colonel.* ✳ **end it all** to commit suicide.

end³ adj final or ultimate: *end results; end markets.*

end- or **endo-** comb. form forming words, with the meaning: within or inside: *endoskeleton.* [via French and Latin from Greek *endon* within]

-end suffix forming nouns, denoting: a person or thing treated in the way specified: *reverend; minuend.* [Latin *-endus*]

endanger /in'daynjə/ verb trans (**endangered, endangering**) to put (something) in danger or peril. ⏩ **endangerment** noun.

endangered adj at risk, *esp* threatened with extinction: *endangered species.*

endarterectomy /en‚dahtə'rektəmi/ noun (pl **endarterectomies**) surgical removal of the inner layer of an artery when it is thickened or blocked. [END- + ARTERY + -ECTOMY]

endear /in'diə/ verb trans (often + to) to cause (somebody) to become beloved or admired. ⏩ **endearing** adj, **endearingly** adv.

endearment noun **1** the use of language expressive of affection: *Speak to them [women] the language of truth and soberness, and away with the lullaby strains of condescending endearment* — Mary Wollstonecraft. **2** a word or act expressing affection.

endeavour¹ (*NAmer* **endeavor**) /in'devə/ verb trans formal to attempt (to do something) by exertion or effort: *She endeavoured to control her disgust.* [Middle English *endeveren* to exert oneself, from Old French *deveir* to owe, be obliged, from Latin *debēre*]

endeavour² (*NAmer* **endeavor**) noun **1** serious determined effort: *fields of endeavour.* **2** an instance of endeavouring; an attempt, effort, or undertaking.

endemic¹ /in'demik/ adj **1** belonging to a particular people or native to a particular region; not introduced or naturalized: *endemic diseases; an endemic species of plant.* **2** regularly occurring in or associated with a particular topic, sphere of activity, etc. ⏩ **endemically** adv, **endemicity** /-'misiti/ noun, **endemism** /'endəmiz(ə)m/ noun. [French *endémique* from Greek *endēmos*, from EN-² + *dēmos* people, populace]

endemic² noun an endemic disease or species.

endermic /en'duhmik/ adj acting by direct application to or through the skin.

end game noun the final stage of a game, *esp* the stage of a chess game when only a few pieces remain on the board: compare MIDDLE GAME, OPENING¹ (2A).

ending noun **1** the final part of something, e.g. a book, film, etc. **2** one or more letters or syllables added to a word base, *esp* as an inflection.

endive /'endiev/ noun **1** a plant of the daisy family that resembles a lettuce and is cultivated for its bitter leaves used in salads: *Cichorium endivia.* **2** *NAmer* the developing crown of chicory when blanched, used as a salad plant. [Middle English via French and late Latin from late Greek *entubion*, from Latin *intubus*]

endless adj **1** being or seeming without end. **2** extremely numerous. **3** said of a belt, chain, etc: joined to itself at its ends. ⏩ **endlessly** adv, **endlessness** noun.

endmost adj situated at the very end; farthest.

endo- comb. form see END-.

endocardia /endoh'kahdi·ə/ noun pl of ENDOCARDIUM.

endocarditis /‚endohkah'dietis/ noun inflammation of the lining and valves of the heart. [ENDO- + Greek *kardia* heart + -ITIS]

endocardium /endoh'kahdi·əm/ noun (pl **endocardia** /-di·ə/) a thin membrane lining the cavities of the heart. ⏩ **endocardial** adj. [Latin *endocardium*, from ENDO- + Greek *kardia* heart]

endocarp /'endəkahp/ noun the inner layer of the PERICARP (wall of seed-bearing origin) of a fruit. ⏩ **endocarpal** /-'kahpl/ adj, **endocarpic** /-'kahpik/ adj. [ENDO- + carp as in PERICARP]

endocrine¹ /'endohkrin, -krien/ adj **1** producing secretions that are discharged directly into the bloodstream: compare EXOCRINE (1): *an endocrine gland; the endocrine system.* **2** of an endocrine gland or its secretions: *endocrine hormones.* [ENDO- + Greek *krinein* to separate]

endocrine² noun an endocrine gland, e.g. the thyroid or pituitary.

endocrinology /‚endohkri'noləji/ noun the branch of physiology and medicine dealing with the endocrine glands. ⏩ **endocrinological** /-'lojikl/ adj, **endocrinologist** noun.

endocytosis /‚endohsie'tohsis/ noun the uptake and incorporation of substances into a cell by phagocytosis or pinocytosis. ⏩ **endocytotic** /-'totik/ adj. [Latin *endocytosis*, from ENDO- + -cytosis as in PHAGOCYTOSIS]

endoderm /'endohduhm/ noun **1** the innermost of the three germ layers of an embryo that is the source of the EPITHELIUM (surface lining tissue) of the digestive tract and its derivatives: compare ECTODERM (2), MESODERM (1). **2** any tissue derived from this germ layer. ⏩ **endodermal** /-'duhml/ adj. [French *endoderme*, from ENDO- + Greek *derma*: see EPIDERMIS]

endogamy /en'dogəmi/ noun **1** marriage within a tribe or community: compare EXOGAMY. **2** sexual reproduction between organisms that are closely related, *esp* pollination of a flower by pollen from another flower of the same plant. ⏩ **endogamous** /-məs/ adj.

endogenous /en'dojinəs/ adj **1** developing from or occurring on the inside or below the surface. **2** originating within the body. **3** having no direct or apparent external cause. ⏩ **endogenously** adv, **endogeny** noun.

endolymph /'endohlimf/ noun the watery fluid in the sensory structures of the inner ear.

endometria /endoh'meetri·ə/ noun pl of ENDOMETRIUM.

endometriosis /‚endohmeetri'ohsis/ noun the presence of functioning endometrial tissue in places where it is not normally found, e.g. the ovary, often causing pain and other problems.

endometrium /endoh'meetri·əm/ noun (pl **endometria** /-tri·ə/) the mucous membrane lining the uterus. ⏩ **endometrial** adj. [Latin *endometrium*, from ENDO- + Greek *mētra* uterus, from *mētr-, mētēr* mother]

endomorph /'endəmawf/ noun **1** a person having a heavy rounded build, often with a marked tendency to become fat: compare ECTOMORPH, MESOMORPH. **2** a crystal enclosed in another of a different type. [(sense 1) ENDODERM + -MORPH; from the prominence in such types of structures developed from the endoderm]

endomorphic /ˈendəˈmawfik/ *adj* having a heavy rounded build, often with a marked tendency to become fat. ⟫⟫ **endomorphy** /-fi/ *noun*.

endoparasite /endohˈparəsiet/ *noun* a parasite that lives in the internal organs or tissues of its host: compare ECTOPARASITE. ⟫⟫ **endoparasitic** /-ˈsitik/ *adj*.

endophyte /ˈendohfiet/ *noun* a plant that lives within another plant. ⟫⟫ **endophytic** /-ˈfitik/ *adj*.

endoplasm /ˈendohplaz(ə)m/ *noun* the inner relatively fluid part of the cytoplasm of a cell: compare ECTOPLASM (1). ⟫⟫ **endoplasmic** /-ˈplazmik/ *adj*.

endoplasmic reticulum *noun* a system of interconnected double membranes in the cytoplasm of a cell that functions *esp* in the transport of materials within the cell.

end organ *noun* a structure, e.g. a muscle or sense organ, at the end of a nerve path.

endorphin /enˈdawfin/ *noun* a natural painkiller secreted by the brain that resembles opium derivatives, e.g. morphine or heroin. [ENDO- + MORPHINE]

endorse *or* **indorse** /inˈdaws/ *verb trans* 1 to express approval of or support for (something or somebody), *esp* publicly. 2 to sign the back of (a cheque, bill, etc) as an instruction regarding payment, e.g. to another recipient. 3 to write a (comment) on a document, *esp* on the back. 4 *Brit* to record details of a motoring offence on (a driver's licence). ⟫⟫ **endorsable** *adj*, **endorsee** /indawˈsee, endawˈsee/ *noun*, **endorser** *noun*. [alteration of obsolete *endoss* from Old French *endosser* to put on the back, from EN-¹ + *dos* back, from Latin *dorsum*]

endorsement *or* **indorsement** *noun* 1 the act or an instance of endorsing something or somebody. 2 something that endorses, e.g. a signature. 3 *Brit* a record of a motoring offence entered on a driving licence. 4 a provision added to an insurance contract altering its scope or application.

endoscope /ˈendəskohp/ *noun* a medical instrument for looking inside a hollow organ, e.g. the intestine. ⟫⟫ **endoscopic** /-ˈskopik/ *adj*, **endoscopically** /-ˈskopikli/ *adv*, **endoscopy** /enˈdoskəpi/ *noun*.

endoskeleton /endohˈskelitn/ *noun* an internal skeleton or supporting framework in an animal. ⟫⟫ **endoskeletal** /-itl/ *adj*.

endosperm /ˈendohspuhm/ *noun* a plant tissue that is formed within the seed and provides nutrition for the developing embryo. ⟫⟫ **endospermic** /-ˈspuhmik/ *adj*, **endospermous** /-ˈspuhməs/ *adj*. [French *endosperme*, from ENDO- + Greek *sperma* seed]

endothelium /endohˈtheeli-əm/ *noun* (*pl* **endothelia** /-li-ə/) a tissue composed of a single layer of thin flattened cells that lines internal body cavities. ⟫⟫ **endothelial** *adj*. [Latin *endothelium*, from ENDO- + EPITHELIUM]

endothermal /endohˈthuhml/ *adj* = ENDOTHERMIC.

endothermic /endohˈthuhmik/ *adj* said of a chemical reaction or compound: characterized by or formed with absorption of heat.

endow /inˈdow/ *verb trans* 1 to provide (something or somebody) with a continuing source of income, often by bequest: *endow a hospital*. 2 (+ with) to provide (something or somebody) with an ability or attribute: *She is endowed with a natural grace*. [Middle English *endowen* from Anglo-French *endouer*, from EN-¹ + *douer* to endow, from Latin *dotare*, from *dot-, dos* gift, dowry]

endowment *noun* 1 something endowed; *specif* the part of an institution's income derived from donations. 2 a natural quality with which a person is endowed. 3 (*used before a noun*) of or being a form of life insurance under which an agreed sum is paid to the policyholder at the end of a specified period or to another designated person if the policyholder dies within that period: *an endowment policy*.

endowment mortgage *noun* a mortgage that is paid back by the money received through an endowment policy.

endpaper *noun* a folded sheet of paper pasted to the front or back inside cover and forming the first or last leaf of a book.

end point *noun* a point marking the completion of a process; *specif* the point at which a chemical titration is complete.

end product *noun* the final product of a series of processes or activities, *esp* in manufacturing.

end-stopped *adj* said of verse: having a break in sense, or requiring a pause in delivery, at the end of a line.

endue *or* **indue** /inˈdyooh/ *verb trans formal* (*usu in passive*, + with) to provide (somebody or something) with a quality or attribute: *a prince ... endued with admirable talents for government* — Jonathan Swift. [Middle English *enduen* via early French *enduire* to bring in, introduce, from Latin *inducere*: see INDUCE]

endurance /inˈdyooərəns/ *noun* the ability to withstand hardship, adversity, or stress.

endure /inˈdyooə/ *verb trans* 1 to undergo (e.g. a hardship), *esp* without giving in. 2 to tolerate (something). ⟩ *verb intrans* to continue in the same state; to last. ⟫⟫ **endurable** *adj*. [Middle English *enduren* via early French *endurer* from Latin *indurare* to harden, from IN-² + *durare* to harden, endure]

enduring *adj* lasting or durable. ⟫⟫ **enduringly** *adv*, **enduringness** *noun*.

end user *noun* the final recipient of goods or services produced by a complex process, e.g. somebody who uses a computer program in its completed form.

endways *adv and adj* 1 with the end forwards or towards the observer. 2 in or towards the direction of the ends; lengthways. 3 upright; on end. 4 end to end: *Put the tables together endways*.

endwise *adv and adj* = ENDWAYS.

end zone *noun* in American football, the area at either end of the field in which a touchdown is scored.

ENE *abbr* east-northeast.

-ene *suffix* forming nouns, denoting: an unsaturated carbon compound, *esp* one with a double bond: *benzene*; *ethylene*. [from Greek *-ēnē*, fem of *-ēnos*, adj suffix]

enema /ˈenimə/ *noun* (*pl* **enemas** *or* **enemata** /-ˈmahtə/) 1 injection of liquid into the intestine by way of the anus, e.g. to ease constipation. 2 material for injection as an enema. [via Latin from Greek *enema*, from *enienai* to inject, from EN-¹ + *hienai* to send]

enemy /ˈenəmi/ *noun* (*pl* **enemies**) 1 a person who is antagonistic to somebody or something, *esp* one actively seeking to harm or overthrow an opponent. 2 something harmful or deadly. 3a (*treated as sing. or pl*) a military adversary or hostile military force: *The enemy undertook guerrilla warfare*. b (*used before a noun*) of or belonging to such an adversary or force: *enemy aircraft*. 4 (*treated as sing. or pl*) a hostile nation, organization, etc: *supplying secret information to the enemy*. [Middle English via Old French *enemi* from Latin *inimicus*, from IN-¹ + *amicus* friend]

energetic /enəˈjetik/ *adj* 1 marked by energy, activity, or vigour. 2 operating with power or effect; forceful. 3 relating to energy: *energetic equation*. ⟫⟫ **energetically** *adv*. [Greek *energētikos* from *energein* to be active, from *energos*: see ENERGY]

energetics *pl noun* 1 (*treated as sing. or pl*) a branch of mechanics that deals primarily with energy and its transformations. 2 the total energy relations and transformations of a system, e.g. a chemical reaction or an ecological community.

energize *or* **energise** /ˈenəjiez/ *verb trans* 1 to give energy to (somebody or something); to make (them) energetic or vigorous. 2 to apply voltage to (e.g. an electric motor). ⟫⟫ **energizer** *noun*.

energy /ˈenəji/ *noun* (*pl* **energies**) 1 the capacity of acting or being active: *great intellectual energy*. 2 natural power vigorously exerted: *He devoted all his energies to it*. 3 in physics, the capacity for doing work: *solar energy*. 4 fuel and other sources of power, *esp* electricity. 5 (*used before a noun*) containing nutrients, vitamins, and minerals that enhance or prolong mental and physical energy: *energy bar*; *energy drink*. [via Latin from Greek *energeia* activity, from *energos* active, from EN-² + *ergon* work]

enervate /ˈenəvayt/ *verb trans* to lessen the mental or physical strength or vitality of (somebody); to weaken (them). ⟫⟫ **enervated** *adj*, **enervating** *adj*, **enervation** /-ˈvaysh(ə)n/ *noun*. [Latin *enervatus*, past part. of *enervare*, from EX-¹ + *nervus* sinew, NERVE¹]

en famille /onh faˈmee (*French* ã famiːj)/ *adv* 1 all together as a family. 2 informally. [French *en famille* in the family]

enfant terrible /ˌonfonh teˈreeblə (*French* ãfã tɛribl)/ *noun* (*pl* **enfants terribles** /ˌonfonh teˈreeblə (*French* ãfã tɛribl)/) a person whose outspoken remarks or unconventional actions cause embarrassment or controversy. [French *enfant terrible* terrifying child]

enfeeble /in'feebl/ *verb trans* to make (somebody or something) weak. ➤➤ **enfeeblement** *noun*. [Middle English *enfeblen* from Old French *enfeblir*, from EN-¹ + *feble*: see FEEBLE]

enfeoff /in'feef/ *verb trans* to invest (somebody) with possession of a freehold estate in land, *esp* in exchange for service or homage to a feudal lord. ➤➤ **enfeoffment** *noun*. [Middle English *enfeoffen* from Anglo-French *enfeoffer*, from EN-¹ + Old French *fief* fief, fee, ultimately of Germanic origin]

en fête /on 'fet/ *adv* dressed for or involved in a celebration. [French *en fête* in festival]

enfilade¹ /enfi'layd/ *noun* gunfire directed along the length of an enemy battle line. [French *enfilade* from *enfiler* to thread, enfilade, from EN-¹ + *fil* thread]

enfilade² *verb trans* to direct gunfire along (an enemy battle line).

enfold /in'fohld/ *verb trans* 1 to wrap (something) up; to envelop (it). 2 to clasp (somebody) in one's arms; to embrace (them).

enforce /in'faws/ *verb trans* 1 to cause (a rule or law) to be obeyed or carried out. 2 to give greater force to (e.g. an argument); to reinforce (it). 3 to impose or compel (something). ➤➤ **enforceability** /-'biliti/ *noun*, **enforceable** *adj*, **enforced** *adj*, **enforcedly** /-sidli/ *adv*, **enforcement** *noun*, **enforcer** *noun*. [Middle English *enforcen* from Old French *enforcier*, from EN-¹ + *force* from Latin *fortis* strong]

enfranchise /in'franchiez/ *verb trans* 1 to give the right of voting to (somebody). 2 to set (somebody) free, *esp* from slavery. 3 to admit (a municipality) to political privileges, *esp* the right of having a representative in Parliament. ➤➤ **enfranchisement** /-chizmənt/ *noun*. [Middle English *enfranchisen* from Old French *enfranchir*, from EN-¹ + *franc* free: see FRANK¹]

ENG *abbr* electronic news gathering.

Eng. *abbr* 1 England. 2 English.

engage /in'gayj/ *verb trans* 1 to attract and hold (somebody's) thoughts, attention, affection, etc). 2a to hold the attention of (somebody); to engross (them): *Her work engages her completely.* b to induce (somebody) to participate, *esp* in conversation. 3a to arrange to employ (somebody). b to order (a room, seat, etc) to be kept for one; to reserve (it). 4 said of a mechanical part: to interlock with (another part). 5a to enter into contest with (somebody): *engage the enemy fleet.* b to bring (weapons) together. 6 to pledge or promise (to do something). ➤ *verb intrans* 1 to occupy one's time; to participate or become involved: *At university he engaged in gymnastics.* 2 to enter into conflict: *The fleets engaged in the Atlantic.* 3 to be or become interlocked or meshed.

Word history
Middle English *engagen* from Old French *engagier*, from EN-¹ + *gage*: see GAGE¹. The word originally meant 'to give something as a pledge', later 'to pledge oneself', hence to become involved in something or with somebody.

engagé /ongga'zhay (*French* ɑgaʒe)/ *adj* actively involved in or committed to something, *esp* a political cause. [French *engagé*, past part. of *engager* to engage, from Old French *engagier*: see ENGAGE]

engaged *adj* 1 involved in activity; occupied. 2 pledged to be married. 3 *chiefly Brit*. a in use: *The telephone is engaged.* b reserved; booked: *This table is engaged.* 4 attached to or partly embedded in a wall: *an engaged column.*

engagement *noun* 1 an agreement to marry; a betrothal. 2 a pledge, promise, or other binding obligation. 3a a promise to be present at a certain time and place; an appointment. b employment, *esp* for a limited period, e.g. as a performer. 4 a hostile encounter between military forces. 5 the act of engaging or the state of being engaged.

engaging *adj* attractive or pleasing. ➤➤ **engagingly** *adv*, **engagingness** *noun*.

en garde /on 'gahd/ *interj* in fencing, used to warn one's opponent to assume a defensive position. [French *en garde* on guard]

engender /in'jendə/ *verb trans* (**engendered, engendering**) to cause (something) to exist or develop; to produce (it): *Angry words engender strife.* [Middle English *engendren* via French from Latin *ingenerare*, from IN-² + *generare*: see GENERATE]

engine /'enjin/ *noun* 1 a machine for converting any of various forms of energy into mechanical force and motion. 2 a mechanical tool: *a terrible engine of war.* 3 a railway locomotive. ➤➤ **engineless** *adj*.

Word history
Middle English *engin* ingenuity, via Old French from Latin *ingenium* natural disposition, talent, from IN-² + *gignere* to beget. The word originally meant 'ingenuity, genius', hence the result of ingenuity, a clever device.

engine driver *noun chiefly Brit* a person who drives a railway locomotive.

engineer¹ /enji'niə/ *noun* 1 a person who is trained in or follows as a profession a branch of engineering. 2 a designer or builder of engines. 3 a person who maintains, operates, or supervises an engine or apparatus. 4 a soldier who carries out engineering work. 5 a person who starts or carries through an enterprise, *esp* by skilful or artful contrivance: *the engineer of the agreement.* 6 *NAmer* = ENGINE DRIVER.

engineer² *verb trans* 1 to design or construct (something) as an engineer: *bridges engineered with wonderful invention.* 2 to produce (a product or organism) through biological manipulation: *genetically engineered tomatoes.* 3 to contrive or plan (something), usu with subtle skill and craft: *The flimsy Geneva settlement, engineered by Eden in 1954 to enable the French to withdraw from Indo-China, was breaking down* — Peter Lewis.

engineering *noun* 1 the application of science and mathematics by which the properties of matter and the sources of energy in nature are made useful to human beings in machines, structures, processes, etc. 2 the art of managing engines.

engine room *noun* 1 a room containing engines, *esp* in a ship. 2 *informal* the midfield of a football team.

English¹ /'inglish/ *adj* 1 of or from England. 2 relating or belonging to English: *English grammar.* ➤➤ **Englishness** *noun*. [Old English *englisc*, from *Engle* (pl) Angles]

English² *noun* 1a the Germanic language spoken in Britain, the USA, and most Commonwealth countries. b English language, literature, or composition as an academic subject. 2 (*treated as pl*) the natives or inhabitants of England. 3 *NAmer* sideways spin imparted to a ball in pool or billiards.

English bond *noun* a method of bricklaying in which alternate courses (layers of brickwork see COURSE¹ (9)) consist of all stretchers (bricks laid lengthways; see STRETCHER¹ (3)) or all headers (bricks laid at right angles; see HEADER (3)).

English breakfast *noun* a breakfast typically consisting of cereal, a hot cooked dish such as bacon and eggs, toast and marmalade, and tea or coffee.

English horn *noun chiefly NAmer* = COR ANGLAIS. [translation of Italian *corno inglese*]

Englishman *or* **Englishwoman** *noun* (*pl* **Englishmen** *or* **Englishwomen**) a native or inhabitant of England.

English setter *noun* a gundog of a breed having a moderately long coat of white silky hair with tan or greyish markings.

Englishwoman *noun* see ENGLISHMAN.

engorge /in'gawj/ *verb trans* to fill (e.g. a body organ) with blood, water, etc to the point of congestion. ➤ *verb intrans* to become swollen or congested with blood, water, etc. ➤➤ **engorgement** *noun*. [early French *engorgier* to devour, from EN-¹ + *gorge*: see GORGE¹]

engraft *or* **ingraft** /in'grahft/ *verb trans* 1 to graft (a shoot) onto a stock. 2 to insert or implant (something). ➤➤ **engraftation** /-'taysh(ə)n/ *noun*, **engraftment** *noun*.

engrailed /in'grayld/ *adj* made of or bordered by a circle of small carved indentations or raised dots: *an engrailed coin.* [Middle English *engreled* from early French *engresler* to make thin, from EN-¹ + *gresle* slender, from Latin *gracilis*]

engrain /in'grayn/ *verb trans* see INGRAIN¹.

engrained *adj* see INGRAINED. ➤➤ **engrainedly** *adv*.

engram /'engram/ *noun* a supposed alteration in the tissue of the brain that is held in some theories to be the physical basis of memory. ➤➤ **engrammatic** /-'matik/ *adj*, **engrammic** /en'gramik/ *adj*. [EN-² + Greek *gramma* letter of the alphabet]

engrave /in'grayv/ *verb trans* 1 to cut (a design or lettering) on metal or stone, *esp* with a sharp tool. 2 to cut a design or lettering on (a hard surface), *esp* for printing, or to print from an engraved plate. 3 to impress (something) deeply on somebody's mind: *The incident was engraved in his memory.* ➤➤ **engraver** *noun*. [early French *engraver*, from EN-¹ + *graver* to grave, of Germanic origin]

engraving *noun* an engraved printing surface or a print made from this.

engross /in'grohs/ *verb trans* **1** to occupy all the time and attention of (somebody); to absorb (them): *a scholar engrossed in research; an engrossing problem.* **2a** to copy or write (something) in large clear handwriting. **b** to prepare the final text of (an official document). ➤ **engrosser** *noun,* **engrossment** *noun.* [Middle English *engrossen* from Anglo-French *engrosser,* prob from medieval Latin *ingrossare,* from IN-² + *grossa* large handwriting; (sense 1) French *en gros* wholesale, ultimately from Latin *in* in + *grossus* large]

engulf /in'gulf/ *verb trans* **1** to flow over and completely cover (something): *The mounting seas threatened to engulf the island.* **2** to overwhelm (somebody or something). ➤ **engulfment** *noun.*

enhance /in'hahns/ *verb trans* to improve the value, desirability, or attractiveness of (something). ➤ **enhancement** *noun,* **enhancer** *noun.* [Middle English *enhauncen* to raise, from Anglo-French *enhauncer,* alteration of Old French *enhaucier,* from Latin *inaltiare,* from IN-² + *altus* high]

enharmonic /enhah'monik/ *adj* of or being notes with different names, e.g. A flat and G sharp, that sound the same on keyboard instruments but have a slight difference in pitch on string and wind instruments. ➤ **enharmonically** *adv.* [French *enharmonique* from Greek *enarmonios,* from EN-² + *harmonia* harmony, scale]

enigma /i'nigmə/ *noun* **1** somebody or something hard to understand or explain; a puzzle or mystery. **2** a piece of intentionally obscure speech or writing; a riddle. ➤ **enigmatic** /enig'matik/ *adj,* **enigmatical** /enig'matikl/ *adj,* **enigmatically** /enig'matikli/ *adv.* [via Latin from Greek *ainigmat-, ainigma,* from *ainissesthai* to speak in riddles, from *ainos* fable]

enjambment *or* **enjambement** /in'jam(b)mənt *(French* āʒāˈbmā*)*/ *noun* the running over of a sentence from one verse or couplet into another. [French *enjambement* encroachment, from *enjamber* to straddle, encroach on, from EN-¹ + *jambe* leg]

enjoin /in'joyn/ *verb trans formal* **1** to order (somebody) to do something; to command (them). **2** to impose (a condition or course of action) on somebody. **3** to forbid (somebody) from doing something by law. [Middle English *enjoinen* via Old French from Latin *injungere,* from IN-² + *jungere* to join]

enjoy /in'joy/ *verb trans* **1** to take pleasure or satisfaction in (something). **2a** to have the use or benefit of (something). **b** to experience (something desirable): *He enjoyed good health.* ✳ **enjoy oneself** to take pleasure in what one is doing; to have fun. ➤ **enjoyable** *adj,* **enjoyableness** *noun,* **enjoyably** *adv.* [Old French *enjoier,* from EN-¹ + *joir* to enjoy, from Latin *gaudēre* to rejoice]

enjoyment *noun* **1** the act of deriving pleasure or satisfaction from something. **2** something that gives a person pleasure or satisfaction. **3** the possession or use of something that gives pleasure or satisfaction.

enkephalin /en'kefəlin/ *or* **encephalin** /en'sef-/ *noun* either of two polypeptides that are natural painkillers of the body, are produced by the pituitary gland, and are related to endorphins.

enlace /in'lays/ *verb trans* **1** to encircle (something) with or as if with laces. **2** to entwine or interlace (something). ➤ **enlacement** *noun.* [Middle English *enlacen* from Old French *enlacier,* from EN-¹ + *lacier:* see LACE²]

enlarge /in'lahj/ *verb trans* **1** to make (something) larger. **2** to reproduce (something) in a larger form, *esp* by making a photographic enlargement. ➤ *verb intrans* **1** to grow larger. **2** (*often* + on/upon) to speak or write at length; to elaborate: *The truth is not wonderful enough to suit the newspapers; so they enlarge upon it and invent ridiculous embellishments* — Annie Sullivan. ➤ **enlarger** *noun.* [Middle English *enlargen* from Old French *enlargier,* from EN-¹ + *large:* see LARGE¹]

enlargement *noun* **1** a photographic print that is larger than the negative or larger than an earlier print. **2** the act of enlarging or the state of being enlarged.

enlighten /in'liet(ə)n/ *verb trans* (**enlightened, enlightening**) **1** to give knowledge to (somebody), freeing them from ignorance or prejudice; to cause (them) to understand. **2** to give spiritual insight to (somebody or something).

enlightened *adj* rational, well-informed, and free from prejudice: *the Roman senate, that enlightened body of politically experienced citizens* — Nikolaus Pevsner.

enlightenment *noun* **1** (**the Enlightenment**) an 18th-cent. movement marked by a belief in universal human progress and the importance of reason and the sciences. **2** = NIRVANA (I). **3** the act of enlightening or the state of being enlightened.

enlist /in'list/ *verb trans* **1** to engage (a person) for duty in the armed forces. **2a** to secure the support and aid of (somebody): *We wish to enlist you in a good cause.* **b** to secure and employ (resources, services, etc) in advancing a cause, interest, or venture: *They enlisted the help of local residents in the search.* ➤ *verb intrans* **1** to enrol oneself in the armed forces. **2** to join a movement. ➤ **enlister** *noun,* **enlistment** *noun.*

enlisted man *noun* a member of the US armed forces ranking below a commissioned or warrant officer.

enliven /in'liev(ə)n/ *verb trans* (**enlivened, enlivening**) **1** to make (somebody or something) more lively, active, or interesting. **2** to make (somebody or something) more cheerful or bright. ➤ **enlivenment** *noun.*

en masse /onh 'mas *(French* ā mas*)*/ *adv* in a body; as a whole. [French *en masse* in a mass]

enmesh /in'mesh/ *verb trans* to catch or entangle (something or somebody) in or as if in a net. ➤ **enmeshment** *noun.*

enmity /'enmiti/ *noun* (*pl* **enmities**) a feeling or state of hatred, hostility, or ill will, e.g. between rivals or enemies. [Middle English *enmite* via early French *enemité* from Old French *enemisté,* from *enemi:* see ENEMY]

ennead /'eniad/ *noun* a group of nine. [Greek *ennead-, enneas,* from *ennea* nine]

ennoble /in'nohbl/ *verb trans* **1** to make (something) noble; to elevate (it): *She believes that hard work ennobles the human spirit.* **2** to raise (somebody) to the rank of the nobility. ➤ **ennoblement** *noun.* [Middle English *ennobelen* from Old French *ennoblir,* from EN-¹ + *noble:* see NOBLE¹]

ennui /on'wi *(French* āny*)*/ *noun* weariness and dissatisfaction resulting from lack of interest or boredom: *Animals manifestly enjoy excitement and suffer from ennui* — Darwin. [early French *enui* annoyance, from *enuier* to annoy, from Latin *in odio* in the phrase *mihi in odio est* it is hateful to me]

enology /ee'noləji/ *noun NAmer* see OENOLOGY.

enophile /'eenohfiel/ *noun NAmer* see OENOPHILE.

enormity /i'nawmiti/ *noun* (*pl* **enormities**) **1** the quality or state of being enormous. **2** great wickedness: *the sheer enormity of the crime.* **3** a terribly wicked or evil act.
Usage note
In modern English *enormity* means both 'huge size' (*the enormity of the task*) and 'great wickedness' or 'a wicked act' (*How could such an apparently innocuous person be guilty of these enormities?*). The latter two senses are the older established ones (though probably less common now), and traditionalists think that the meaning 'huge size' should be rendered either by *enormousness* or another word such as *vastness* or *immensity.*

enormous /i'nawməs/ *adj* **1** marked by extraordinarily great size, number, or degree. **2** *archaic* exceedingly wicked; shocking. ➤ **enormously** *adv,* **enormousness** *noun.* [Latin *enormis,* from EX-¹ + *norma* rule]

enosis /'enohsis/ *noun* the union of Cyprus and Greece, which is the aim of various groups of Greek nationalist Cypriots. [modern Greek *henōsis* union, from Greek *henoun* to unite, from *hen-, heis* one]

enough¹ /i'nuf/ *adj* fully adequate in quantity, number, or degree: *not enough beer; He was fool enough to believe her.* [Old English *genōg*]

enough² *adv* **1** to a fully adequate degree; sufficiently: *This hasn't been cooked long enough.* **2** to a tolerable or moderate degree: *He understands well enough.*

enough³ *pronoun* (*pl* **enough**) a sufficient quantity or number: *Enough were present to constitute a quorum; I'd had enough of their foolishness.*

en passant /onh pa'sonh *(French* ā pasā*)*/ *adv* **1** in passing; by the way. **2** used in chess of the capture of a pawn making its first move of two squares by an enemy pawn in a position to take it on the first of these squares. [French *en passant* in passing]

enplane /en'playn/ *verb intrans or trans chiefly NAmer* = EMPLANE.

enprint /'enprint/ *noun* a standard size of photographic print produced from a negative. [short for *enlarged print*]

en prise /onh 'preez *(French* ā priz*)*/ *adj* said of a chess piece: exposed to capture. [French *en prise*]

enquire *or* **inquire** /in'kwie.ə/ *verb intrans* **1** to seek information by questioning; to ask: *They enquired about the cost of accommodation.*

2 (*often* + into) to make an investigation. ➤ *verb trans* to ask (something): *They enquired the way to the station.* ✳ **enquire after** to ask about the health, etc of (somebody). ➤➤ **enquirer** *noun,* **enquiring** *adj,* **enquiringly** *adv.* [Middle English *enquiren* via early French *enquerre* from Latin *inquirere,* from IN-² + *quaerere* to seek]

Usage note
enquire or **inquire?** *Enquire* is the commoner British English spelling; *inquire* is generally used in American English. Some British users distinguish between *enquire* ('ask') and *inquire* (*into*) ('investigate'), but there are no strong grounds for making this distinction.

enquiry or **inquiry** /in'kwie-ǝri/ *noun* (*pl* **enquiries** or **inquiries**) **1** a request for information. **2** a systematic investigation, *esp* of a matter of public concern.

enrage /in'rayj/ *verb trans* to fill (somebody) with rage; to make (them) very angry. [Old French *enragier* to become mad, from EN-¹ + *rage:* see RAGE¹]

en rapport /on ra'paw (*French* ã rapɔːr)/ *adv* in harmony or agreement. [French *en rapport* in agreement]

enrapture /in'rapchǝ/ *verb trans* to fill (somebody) with delight: *My aunt, seeing how enraptured I was with the premises, took them for a month* — Dickens.

enrich /in'rich/ *verb trans* **1** to make (something) rich or richer, *esp* in some desirable quality: *The experience greatly enriched his life.* **2** to adorn or ornament (something): *enriching the ceiling with frescoes.* **3a** to make (soil) more fertile. **b** to add a desirable substance to (something); *specif* to improve (a food) in nutritive value by adding nutrients. **c** to increase the proportion of a valuable or desirable ingredient in (something): *enrich uranium with uranium 235.* **4** to make (somebody) wealthy or wealthier. ➤➤ **enriched** *adj,* **enrichment** *noun.* [Middle English *enrichen* from Old French *enrichir,* from EN-¹ + *riche* rich]

enrol (*NAmer* **enroll**) /in'rohl/ *verb* (**enrolled, enrolling**) ➤ *verb trans* **1** to enter (somebody or something) on a list, roll, etc; *specif* to register (somebody or oneself) as a member. **2** to prepare a final perfect copy of (a bill passed by a legislature) in written or printed form. ➤ *verb intrans* to enrol oneself: *enrol on the history course.* ➤➤ **enrollee** *noun,* **enroller** *noun.* [Middle English *enrollen* from early French *enroller,* from EN-¹ + *rolle* roll, register]

enrolment (*NAmer* **enrollment**) *noun* **1** the act of enrolling or the state of being enrolled. **2** the number of people enrolled, *esp* at a school or college.

en route /on 'rooht (*French* ã rut)/ *adv and adj* on or along the way: *Soon they were en route to the border.* [French *en route* on the way]

Ens. *abbr* ensign.

ENSA /'ensǝ/ *abbr* Entertainments National Service Association.

ensconce /in'skons/ *verb trans* to settle (e.g. oneself) comfortably or snugly: *The cat ensconced itself in the basket.* [EN-¹ + SCONCE²]

ensemble¹ /on'sombl (*French* ãsã:bl)/ *noun* **1** a group that works together as a whole or produces a single effect, e.g.: **a** a complete outfit of matching garments. **b** (*treated as sing. or pl*) a combination of two or more performers or players, *esp* a musical group having only one instrument playing each part. **c** (*treated as sing. or pl*) a group of supporting players, singers, or dancers. **2** the quality of togetherness in performance: *The quartet's ensemble was poor.* [French *ensemble* together, from Latin *insimul* at the same time, from IN-² + *simul* at the same time]

ensemble² *adv* all together.

enshrine /in'shrien/ *verb trans* **1** to enclose (something) in or as if in a shrine. **2** to preserve or cherish (something) as sacred: *They enshrined their leader's memory in their hearts.* ➤➤ **enshrinement** *noun.*

enshroud /in'shrowd/ *verb trans* to cover (something) in or as if in a shroud.

ensign /'ensien, 'ens(ǝ)n/ *noun* **1** /'ensǝn/ a flag that is flown, e.g. by a ship, as the symbol of nationality. **2** a commissioned officer of the lowest rank in the US navy or, formerly, in the British infantry. **3** in former times, a standard-bearer. [Middle English *ensigne* via early French *enseigne* from Latin *insignia:* see INSIGNIA]

ensilage /'ensilij/ *noun* **1** the process of preserving fodder by ensiling. **2** = SILAGE.

ensile /en'siel, 'ensiel/ *verb trans* to prepare and store (fodder made from green crops) for silage in a silo; to convert (it) into silage. [French *ensiler* from Spanish *ensilar,* from EN-¹ + *silo:* see SILO]

enslave /in'slayv/ *verb trans* to reduce (somebody) to slavery; to subjugate (them). ➤➤ **enslavement** *noun,* **enslaver** *noun.*

ensnare /in'sneǝ/ *verb trans* to catch (a person or animal) in or as if in a snare. ➤➤ **ensnarement** *noun.*

ensue /in'syooh/ *verb intrans* (**ensues, ensued, ensuing**) to take place afterwards or as a result. [Middle English *ensuen* from Old French *ensuivre,* from EN-¹ + *suivre* to follow]

en suite /on 'sweet (*French* ã sɥt)/ *adv and adj* said of a room: opening off or into, and forming a single unit with, another room: *a bedroom with an en suite bathroom.* [French *en suite,* literally 'in sequence']

ensure /in'shooǝ, in'shaw/ *verb trans* to make (something) sure or certain; to guarantee (it). [Middle English *ensuren* from Anglo-French *enseurer,* prob alteration of Old French *aseürer,* from medieval Latin *assecurare:* see ASSURE]

Usage note
ensure, assure, or **insure?** See note at ASSURE.

ENT *abbr* ear, nose, and throat.

ent- or **ento-** *comb. form* forming words, with the meaning: inner or within: *entozoa.* [via Latin from Greek *entos* within]

-ent *suffix* **1** forming adjectives, with the meaning: performing a specified action, causing a specified process, or being in a specified condition: *astringent; convenient.* **2** forming nouns, denoting: somebody or something that performs a specified action or causes a specified process: *regent; nutrient.* [Middle English via Old French from Latin *-ent-, -ens*]

entablature /in'tablǝchǝ/ *noun* in classical architecture, the upper section of a wall or storey, usu supported on columns and consisting of an architrave, a frieze, and a cornice. [early French *entablature* from Italian *intavolatura,* from *intavolare* to put on a board or table, from IN-¹ + *tavola* board, table, from Latin *tabula*]

entablement /in'tayb|mǝnt/ *noun* a platform that supports a statue and is placed above the dado. [French *entablement,* from EN-¹ + *table:* see TABLE¹]

entail¹ /in'tayl/ *verb trans* **1** to involve or imply (something) as a necessary accompaniment or result: *The project will entail considerable expense.* **2** to settle (property) so that sale is not permitted and inheritance is limited to a specified category of the owner's heirs. ➤➤ **entailer** *noun,* **entailment** *noun.* [Middle English *entailen, entaillen,* from EN-¹ + *taile, taille:* see TAIL³]

entail² *noun* **1** an instance of entailing property. **2** property that has been entailed. **3** the order of inheritance for entailed property.

entangle /in'tanggl/ *verb trans* **1** to cause (something) to become tangled, complicated, or confused. **2** to involve (somebody) in a difficult situation: *He became entangled in a ruinous lawsuit.* ➤➤ **entanglement** *noun,* **entangler** *noun.*

entasis /'entǝsis/ *noun* (*pl* **entases** /-seez/) a slight convexity in the shaft of a column intended to correct the illusion of concavity created by a straight shaft. [Greek *entasis* distension, stretching, from *enteinein* to stretch tight, from EN-¹ + *teinein* to stretch]

entente /on'tont (*French* ãtã:t)/ *noun* **1** a friendly relationship between two or more countries; an informal international agreement. **2** (*treated as sing. or pl*) the parties of an entente. [French *entente* understanding, from *entendre:* see INTEND]

entente cordiale /kawdi'ahl, -'dyahl (*French* kɔrdjal)/ *noun* (*often* **Entente Cordiale**) the understanding between Britain and France in 1904 or between Britain, France, and Russia in 1908. [French *entente cordiale* cordial understanding]

enter /'entǝ/ *verb* (**entered, entering**) ➤ *verb trans* **1a** to go or come into (a place): *enter a room.* **b** to pierce or penetrate (e.g. flesh): *This is where the bullet entered his brain.* **2** to record (a piece of information) in a diary, account, computer file etc. **3** to become a member of or an active participant in (something): *enter a race; enter politics.* **4** to arrange for (somebody or something) to be received, admitted, or considered: *She entered her story in the competition.* **5** to begin or embark on (something). **6a** to put (something) formally on record: *He entered a complaint against his business partner.* **b** to place (something) in proper form before a court of law: *enter a writ.* ➤ *verb intrans* **1a** to go or come in. **b** to pierce or penetrate: *The bullet entered above the heart.* **2** to gain admission to a group; to join. **3** to register as candidate in a competition: *She decided to enter for the race.* **4** (+ into/on/upon) to begin to embark on something. **5** to come onto the stage in a play. **6** (+ on/upon) in law, to go on or into and take actual possession of land or property. ✳ **enter into**

1 to make oneself a party to or in (e.g. an agreement). **2** to play a part or be a factor in (something): *Money doesn't enter into it.* **3** to participate or share in (something): *He cheerfully enters into the household tasks.* [Middle English *entren* via Old French *entrer* from Latin *intrare*, from *intra* within]

enter- *or* **entero-** *comb. form* forming words, denoting: the intestine: *enteritis.* [via Latin from Greek *enteron* intestine]

enteral /'entərəl/ *adj* = ENTERIC.

enteric /en'terik/ *adj* relating to the intestines.

enteritis /entə'rietis/ *noun* inflammation of the intestines, *esp* the lower part of the small intestine, usu marked by diarrhoea.

entero- *comb. form* see ENTER-.

enteron /'entəron/ *noun* the ALIMENTARY CANAL (digestive tract), *esp* of an embryo. [via Latin from Greek *enteron* intestine]

enterprise /'entəpriez/ *noun* **1** a difficult or complicated project or undertaking. **2** a unit of economic organization or activity, *esp* a business organization. **3** readiness to engage in enterprises; boldness and initiative. ➤➤ **enterpriser** *noun*. [Middle English from early French *entreprise*, from *entreprendre* to undertake, from INTER- + *prendre* to take]

Enterprise Allowance Scheme *noun* in Britain, a scheme in which the government pays a weekly allowance to unemployed people who have started their own business.

enterprise zone *noun* an area, usu in an inner city, in which business enterprises are offered financial incentives by the government to encourage their development.

enterprising *adj* marked by boldness and initiative; ready to engage in enterprises. ➤➤ **enterprisingly** *adv*.

entertain /entə'tayn/ *verb trans* **1** to give enjoyment or amusement to (somebody). **2** to show hospitality to (somebody). **3** to consider or have in one's mind (an idea, doubt, suggestion, etc). **4** to play against (an opposing team) on one's home ground. ➤ *verb intrans* to invite guests, *esp* to one's home. ➤➤ **entertaining** *adj and noun*. [Middle English *entertinen* from early French *entretenir*, from INTER- + *tenir* to hold]

entertainer *noun* a person whose job is to entertain people, e.g. a singer or comedian.

entertainment *noun* **1** something entertaining, diverting, or engaging. **2** a public performance. **3** the act of entertaining somebody or something.

enthalpy /'enthəlpi, en'thalpi/ *noun* a thermodynamic property of a system equal to the sum of its internal energy. [EN-² + Greek *thalpein* to heat]

enthral (*NAmer* **enthrall**) /in'thrawl/ *verb trans* (**enthralled, enthralling**) **1** to hold the complete interest and attention of (somebody); to captivate (them). **2** *archaic* to reduce (somebody) to slavery. ➤➤ **enthralment** *noun*. [Middle English *enthrallen*, from EN-¹ + *thral* THRALL¹]

enthrone /in'throhn/ *verb trans* **1** to place (somebody), *esp* ceremonially, on a throne. **2** to assign supreme virtue or value to (somebody or something); to exalt (them). ➤➤ **enthronement** *noun*.

enthuse /in'thyoohz/ *verb trans* to make (somebody) enthusiastic: *proposals which … shocked the orthodox and enthused the rebellious —* Times Literary Supplement. ➤ *verb intrans* to show enthusiasm. [back-formation from ENTHUSIASM]

enthusiasm /in'thyoohziaz(ə)m/ *noun* **1** keen and eager interest and admiration. **2** an object of enthusiasm. **3** *archaic* excessive display of religious emotion. [Greek *enthousiasmos* from *enthousiazein* to be inspired, from *entheos* inspired, from EN-² + *theos* god]

enthusiast /in'thyoohziast/ *noun* **1** somebody filled with enthusiasm, *esp* somebody ardently attached to a specified cause, object, or pursuit: *a cycling enthusiast.* **2** somebody who is excessively zealous in their religious views. ➤➤ **enthusiastic** /-'astik/ *adj*, **enthusiastically** /-'astikli/ *adv*.

enthymeme /'enthimeem/ *noun* a SYLLOGISM (formal argument) in which one of the premises is implicit rather than stated. [via Latin from Greek *enthymēma*, from *enthymeisthai* to keep in mind, from *en* in + *thumos* mind]

entice /in'ties/ *verb trans* to tempt or persuade (somebody) by arousing hope or desire. ➤➤ **enticement** *noun*, **enticer** *noun*, **enticing** *adj*, **enticingly** *adv*. [Middle English *enticen* via Old French *enticier* from Latin *intitiare*, from IN-² + *titio* firebrand]

entire /in'tie-ə/ *adj* **1** having no element or part left out; whole: *The children were alone the entire day.* **2** complete in degree; total or absolute: *his entire devotion to his family.* **3** intact: *We strove to keep the collection entire.* **4** not castrated. **5** said of a leaf or petal: having the edge continuous; not indented or lobed. ➤➤ **entireness** *noun*. [Middle English via French *entir* from Latin *integer*: see INTEGER]

entirely *adv* **1** wholly or completely: *I entirely agree with you.* **2** in an exclusive manner; solely: *It is his fault entirely.*

entirety /in'tie-əriti/ *noun* **1** the state of being entire or complete. **2** the whole or total.

entitle /in'tietl/ *verb trans* **1** to give a title to (something or somebody). **2** (+ to) to give (somebody) the right to do or have something: *This ticket entitles the bearer to free admission.* ➤➤ **entitlement** *noun*. [Middle English *entitlen* via French from late Latin *intitulare*, from Latin IN-² + *titulus* TITLE¹]

entity /'entiti/ *noun* (*pl* **entities**) **1a** being or existence, *esp* independent, separate, or self-contained existence. **b** the existence of a thing as contrasted with its attributes. **2** something that has separate and distinct existence. [medieval Latin *entitas*, from Latin *ent-, ens* existing thing, from *esse* to be]

ento- *comb. form* see ENT-.

entom- *or* **entomo-** *comb. form* forming words, denoting: an insect: *entomophagous.* [via French from Greek *entomon*]

entomb /in'toohm/ *verb trans* **1** to place (e.g. a body) in a tomb; to bury (it). **2** to cover or hide (something) as if in a tomb. ➤➤ **entombment** *noun*. [Middle English *entoumben* from early French *entomber*, from EN-¹ + *tombe* TOMB]

entomo- *comb. form* see ENTOM-.

entomology /entə'moləji/ *noun* a branch of zoology that deals with insects. ➤➤ **entomological** /-'lojikl/ *adj*, **entomologist** *noun*.

entomophagous /entə'mofəgəs/ *adj* feeding on insects.

entomophilous /entə'mofiləs/ *adj* normally pollinated by insects: compare ZOOPHILOUS. ➤➤ **entomophily** /-li/ *noun*.

entourage /'ontoorahzh (*French* ãtura:ʒ)/ *noun* (*treated as sing. or pl*) a group of attendants or associates, *esp* of a famous or important person. [early French *entourage* from *entourer* to surround, from EN-¹ + *tour* circuit, TOUR¹]

entr'acte /'ontrakt (*French* ãtrakt)/ *noun* **1** the interval between two acts of a play or opera. **2** a dance, piece of music, or dramatic entertainment performed in this interval. [French *entr'acte*, from INTER- + *acte* act]

entrails /'entraylz/ *pl noun* internal parts, *esp* the intestines. [Middle English *entrailes* via French from medieval Latin *intralia*, alteration of Latin *interanea* intestines, internal things, from *inter* between, among]

entrain¹ /in'trayn/ *verb trans* said of a liquid or gas: to draw in and transport (e.g. solid particles). ➤➤ **entrainment** *noun*. [early French *entrainer*, from EN-¹ + *trainer*: see TRAIN²]

entrain² *verb intrans* to board a train. ➤ *verb trans* to put (something or somebody) on board a train. ➤➤ **entrainment** *noun*.

entrance¹ /'entrəns/ *noun* **1** the act or an instance of entering. **2** a means or place of entry. **3** power, right, or permission to enter; admission. **4** an arrival of a performer onto a stage or before film or television cameras.

entrance² /in'trahns/ *verb trans* **1** to fill (somebody) with delight, wonder, or rapture. **2** to put (somebody) into a trance. ➤➤ **entrancement** *noun*, **entrancing** *adj*.

entrant /'entrənt/ *noun* somebody or something that enters or is entered, *esp* somebody who enters a contest, profession, etc.

entrap /in'trap/ *verb trans* (**entrapped, entrapping**) **1** to catch (a person or animal) in or as if in a trap. **2** to lure or trick (somebody) into making a compromising statement or committing a crime. ➤➤ **entrapment** *noun*. [early French *entraper*, from EN-¹ + *trape*: see TRAP¹]

entreat /in'treet/ *verb trans* **1** to ask (somebody) urgently or earnestly; to beg or plead with (them): *He entreated the judge for another chance.* **2** to request (something) urgently or earnestly: *I have come to entreat your help.* **3** *archaic* to treat or deal with (something or somebody). ➤ *verb intrans* to make an urgent or earnest request; to plead. ➤➤ **entreatingly** *adv*, **entreatment** *noun*. [Middle English *entreten* from early French *entraitier*, from EN-¹ + *traitier*: see TREAT¹]

entreaty *noun* (*pl* **entreaties**) an act of entreating; a plea.

entrechat /'onhtrəshah (*French* ātrəʃa)/ *noun* a leap in which a ballet dancer repeatedly crosses his or her feet and beats them together. [French *entrechat* from Italian *capriola intrecciata* intricate caper]

entrecôte /'ontrəkot (*French* ātrəko:t)/ *noun* a steak cut from a boned sirloin of beef. [French *entrecôte*, from INTER- + *côte* rib, from Latin *costa*]

entrée *or* **entree** /'ontray (*French* ātre)/ *noun* **1a** *chiefly Brit* a dish served between the fish and meat courses of a formal dinner or before the main course. **b** the principal dish of a meal. **2** right of entry or access: *She gained an entrée into the highest circles.* [French *entrée* from Old French *entree*: see ENTRY]

entremets /'ontrəmay (*French* ātrəme)/ *noun* (*pl* **entremets**) **1** a light dish served between two courses of a meal, *esp* the main course and dessert. **2** a dessert. [French *entremets* from Old French *entremes*, from INTER- + *mes* dish: see MESS[1]]

entrench *or* **intrench** /in'trench/ *verb trans* **1** to establish (something) firmly and solidly, *esp* so that it is difficult to change. **2a** to surround (something) with a defensive trench. **b** to place (oneself) in a strong defensive position. ➤ *verb intrans* to dig or occupy a defensive trench. ➤➤ **entrenchment** *noun*.

entre nous /ˌontrə 'nooh (*French* ātr nu)/ *adv* between ourselves; confidentially. [French *entre nous* between ourselves]

entrepôt /'ontrəpoh/ *noun* a seaport, warehouse, or other intermediary centre of trade and transshipment. [French *entrepôt* from *entreposer* to put in store, from INTER- + *poser* to put: see POSE[1]]

entrepreneur /ˌontrəprə'nuh (*French* ātrəprɑnœ:r)/ *noun* somebody who organizes, manages, and assumes the risks of a business or enterprise. ➤➤ **entrepreneurial** /-ri·əl/ *adj*, **entrepreneurship** *noun*. [French *entrepreneur* from Old French *entreprendre*: see ENTERPRISE]

entresol /'ontrəsol (*French* ātrəsɔl)/ *noun* = MEZZANINE[1]. [French *entresol* from Spanish *entresuelo*, from *entre* between (from Latin *inter*) + *suelo* storey]

entropy /'entrəpi/ *noun* **1a** a measure of the amount of energy that is unavailable for doing work in a thermodynamic system. **b** the degree to which the particles of a thermodynamic system are randomly arranged, which gives a measure of the amount of disorder in the system. **2** a measure of the amount of information in a message that is based on the logarithm of the number of possible equivalent messages. **3** absence of form, pattern, or differentiation, or the process of decay that leads to this. ➤➤ **entropic** /en'tropik/ *adj*. [German *Entropie*, from Greek *en* in + *tropē* turn, change]

entrust *or* **intrust** /in'trust/ *verb trans* **1** (+ with) to give (somebody) the responsibility to look after or deal with something: *She entrusted the bank with her savings.* **2** (+ to) to put (something) into somebody's care: *He entrusted his savings to the bank.* ➤➤ **entrustment** *noun*.

entry /'entri/ *noun* (*pl* **entries**) **1** the act of entering; entrance. **2** the right or privilege of entering. **3a** a door, gate, hall, vestibule, or other place of entrance. **b** *dialect* an alleyway between buildings. **4a** the act of registering a record. **b** the act of introducing information into a computer. **c** a record made in a diary, account book, index, etc. **d** a headword in a reference book, often with the accompanying definition or article. **5** a person, thing, or group entered in a contest; an entrant. **6** the total of those entered or admitted: *Since then we have doubled the annual entry to our medical schools.* **7** in law, the act of going on land or into property with the intention of taking or declaring possession. **8** in bridge, etc, a card that enables a player to gain or transfer the lead. [Middle English *entre* from Old French *entree*, fem past part. of *entrer*: see ENTER]

entryism *noun* the practice of infiltrating a political party in order to influence its policy from within. ➤➤ **entryist** *noun and adj*.

entry-level *adj* of or being the basic model in a range of products, e.g. computers, designed for new users who may later progress to more sophisticated equipment in the range.

Entryphone *noun trademark* an intercom system at the entrance to a building, which visitors use to identify themselves.

entwine /in'twien/ *verb trans* **1** to twine (things) together. **2** to twine round (something). ➤ *verb intrans* to become twined.

enucleate /i'nyoohkliayt/ *verb trans* **1** to remove a nucleus from (a cell). **2** to remove surgically (e.g. a tumour or an eyeball) from its surrounding capsule without cutting into it. ➤➤ **enucleation** /iˌnyoohkli'aysh(ə)n/ *noun*. [Latin *enucleatus*, past part. of *enucleare* to remove the kernel from, from EX-[1] + *nucleus*: see NUCLEUS]

E number *noun* a number with the letter E in front of it, used in the lists of ingredients on food packaging to denote a particular additive. [*E* short for European, because the system was set up by the European Union]

enumerate /i'nyoohmərayt/ *verb trans* **1** to list or name (a number of items) one by one. **2** to count up (a number of items). ➤➤ **enumerable** *adj*, **enumeration** /iˌnyoohmə'raysh(ə)n/ *noun*, **enumerative** /-rətiv/ *adj*. [Latin *enumeratus*, past part. of *enumerare*, from EX-[1] + *numerare* to count, from *numerus* number]

enumerator *noun Brit* a person employed to issue and collect census forms.

enunciate /i'nunsiayt/ *verb trans* **1** to articulate (words) distinctly, typically by separating the syllables: *'She was the most –' he snapped his fingers noiselessly in the air, enunciating fiercely, 'Kunst – ler – isch!'* — Willa Cather. **2** to state or formulate (something) precisely or systematically: *He enunciated the principles to be followed by the new administration.* ➤ *verb intrans* to articulate or pronounce words clearly. ➤➤ **enunciation** /iˌnunsi'aysh(ə)n/ *noun*, **enunciative** *adj*, **enunciator** *noun*. [Latin *enuntiatus*, past part. of *enuntiare* to report, declare, from EX-[1] + *nuntiare* to report, from *nuntius* messenger]

enure /i'nyooə/ *verb* see INURE.

enuresis /enyoo'reesis/ *noun* an involuntary discharge of urine. ➤➤ **enuretic** /-'retik/ *adj and noun*. [Latin *enuresis* from Greek *enourein* to urinate in, wet the bed, from *en* in + *ourein* to urinate, from *ouron* urine]

envelop /in'veləp/ *verb trans* (**enveloped, enveloping**) **1** to enclose, wrap, or surround (something or somebody) completely with or as if with a covering: *She enveloped him in her arms.* **2** to conceal or obscure (something): *The matter was enveloped in mystery.* ➤➤ **envelopment** *noun*. [Middle English *envolupen* from Old French *envoloper*, from EN-[1] + *voloper* to wrap]

Usage note

envelop *or* envelope? These two words are related and sometimes confused. *Envelop* (always pronounced with the stress on the second syllable *-vel-*) is a verb: *Fog envelops the city; enveloped in a huge black cloak.* *Envelope* (always pronounced with the stress on the first syllable *en-*) is a noun: *She opened the sealed envelope and drew out the winner's name.*

envelope /'envəlohp, 'on-/ *noun* **1** a flat container, usu of folded and gummed paper, e.g. for a letter. **2** something that envelops; a wrapper or covering. **3** a membrane or other natural covering that encloses. **4** in mathematics, a curve tangent to each of a family of curves. **5** the performance limits of a machine, aircraft, etc: *The flight envelope of the prototype fighter was explored.* [French *enveloppe* from Old French *envoloper*: see ENVELOP]

Usage note

envelope *or* envelop? See note at ENVELOP.

envenom /in'venəm/ *verb trans* **1** to put poison into or onto (something): *The point envenomed too? Then, venom, to thy work* — Shakespeare. **2** to fill (somebody) with bitterness. [Middle English *envenimen* from Old French *envenimer*, from EN-[1] + *venim*: see VENOM]

enviable /'envi·əbl/ *adj* worthy of arousing envy; highly desirable. ➤➤ **enviableness** *noun*, **enviably** *adv*.

envious /'envi·əs/ *adj* feeling or showing envy: *envious looks; envious of a neighbour's wealth.* ➤➤ **enviously** *adv*, **enviousness** *noun*.

environ /in'vie(ə)rən/ *verb trans* (**environed, environing**) *formal* to encircle or surround (something). [Middle English *environen* from early French *environner*, from *environ* around, from EN-[2] + *viron* circle, from *virer* to turn, veer]

environment *noun* **1** the circumstances, objects, or conditions by which somebody or something is surrounded. **2** the natural surroundings of or the complex of external factors that acts upon an organism, an ecological community, or plant and animal life in general. ➤➤ **environmental** /-'mentl/ *adj*, **environmentally** /-'ment(ə)li/ *adv*.

environmentalism /inˌvie(ə)rən'ment(ə)liz(ə)m/ *noun* **1** a theory that views environment rather than heredity as the important factor in human development. **2** concern about the protection or quality of the natural environment. ➤➤ **environmentalist** *noun*.

environmentally-friendly *adj* causing or said to cause no harm to the environment: *an environmentally-friendly detergent.*

environment-friendly *adj* = ENVIRONMENTALLY-FRIENDLY.

environs /in'vie(ə)rənz/ *pl noun* the neighbourhood surrounding something, *esp* a town. [early French *environs*, from *environ*: see ENVIRON]

envisage /in'vizij/ *verb trans* **1** to have a mental picture of (something); to visualize (it). **2** to consider (something) as a possibility in the future. [French *envisager*, from EN-¹ + *visage*: see VISAGE]

Usage note

envisage *or* envision? These two words are synonymous in the sense of 'to form a mental picture of (something), *esp* in advance': *The group envisages a future in which all farming will be organic*. *Envisage* is more commonly used in British English; *envision* in American English. The meaning is quite close to that of *expect*, but the distinction should be preserved, and *expect* should be used in place of *envisage* in sentences such as *A further fall in interest rates is expected* not *envisaged* next month.

envision /in'vizh(ə)n/ *verb trans chiefly NAmer* = ENVISAGE.

Usage note

envision *or* envisage? See note at ENVISAGE.

envoy¹ *or* **envoi** /'envoy/ *noun* the concluding words of a poem, essay, or book; *specif* a short fixed final stanza of a BALLADE (poem with three verses). [French *envoi* message, from Old French *envoier* to send on one's way, from Latin *inviare*, from *via* way]

envoy² *noun* **1** a diplomatic agent, *esp* one who ranks immediately below an ambassador. **2** a messenger or representative. [French *envoyé*, past part. of *envoyer* to send, from Old French *envoier*: see ENVOY¹]

envy¹ /'envi/ *noun* (*pl* **envies**) **1** resentful or admiring awareness of an advantage enjoyed by another, accompanied by a desire to possess the same advantage. **2** an object of such a feeling. [Middle English *envie* via Old French from Latin *invidia*, from *invidēre* to look askance at, envy, from IN-² + *vidēre* to see]

envy² *verb trans* (**envies, envied, envying**) to be envious of (somebody or something). ➤➤ **envier** *noun*, **envyingly** *adv*.

enwrap *or* **inwrap** /in'rap/ *verb trans* (**enwrapped** *or* **inwrapped, enwrapping** *or* **inwrapping**) **1** to wrap or envelop (something or somebody): *the coldness of the empty house enwrapped her* — Edith Sitwell. **2** to engross (somebody).

Enzed /en'zed/ *noun Aus, NZ, informal* **1** New Zealand. **2** an inhabitant of New Zealand. [from the pronunciation of the initial letters]

Enzedder /en'zedə/ *noun* = ENZED (2).

enzootic /enzoh'otik/ *adj* said of animal diseases: peculiar to or constantly present in a particular locality.

enzyme /'enziem/ *noun* any of numerous complex proteins that are produced by living cells and that promote specific biochemical reactions without undergoing change themselves. ➤➤ **enzymatic** /-'matik, enzi'matik/ *adj*, **enzymic** /en'ziemik, en'zimik/ *adj*. [German *Enzym* from early Greek *enzymos* leavened, from Greek *en* in + *zymē* leaven]

enzymology /enzie'moləji/ *noun* a branch of science that deals with the nature, activity, and significance of enzymes. ➤➤ **enzymological** /-mə'lojikl/ *adj*, **enzymologist** *noun*.

eo- *comb. form* forming words, with the meaning: earliest or oldest: *eolith*. [Greek *ēō-*, from *ēōs* dawn]

EOC *abbr Brit* Equal Opportunities Commission.

Eocene /'eeohseen/ *adj* relating to or dating from a geological epoch, the second epoch of the Tertiary period, lasting from about 56.5 to about 35.5 million years ago, and marked *esp* by the first appearance of horses and other hoofed animals. ➤➤ **Eocene** *noun*.

eohippus /eeoh'hipəs/ *noun* (*pl* **eohippuses**) an extinct small primitive four-toed ancestor of the horse: genus *Eohippus*.

eolian /ee'ohli-ən/ *adj NAmer* see AEOLIAN.

eolith /'ee-əlith/ *noun* a very crudely chipped flint assumed to be the earliest form of stone tool.

Eolithic /ee-ə'lithik/ *adj* relating to or dating from the early period of the Stone Age, characterized by the use of eoliths.

eon /'eeon, 'ee-ən/ *noun* see AEON.

eosin *or* **eosine** /'ee-əsin, -seen/ *noun* a red fluorescent chemical compound, the salts of which are used as dyes and to stain biological specimens. [Greek *ēōs* dawn + -IN¹, from its colour]

eosinophil /ee-ə'sinəfil/ *or* **eosinophile** /-fiel/ *noun* a white blood cell with granules in the cytoplasm that are readily stained by eosin: compare AGRANULOCYTE, BASOPHIL, GRANULOCYTE. ➤➤ **eosinophilic** /-'filik/ *adj*.

EOT *abbr* **1** end of tape. **2** end of transmission.

-eous *suffix* forming adjectives, with the meaning: having the nature of: *gaseous*. [Latin *-eus*]

EP¹ *noun* a record or compact disc with a playing time greater than a normal single. [short for *extended play*]

EP² *abbr* **1** electroplate. **2** European Parliament.

Ep. *abbr* epistle.

e.p. *abbr* en passant.

ep- *prefix* see EPI-.

EPA *abbr NAmer* Environmental Protection Agency.

epact /'eepakt/ *noun* **1** a period added to harmonize the lunar with the solar calendar; the difference in time between the lunar and solar years. **2** the moon's phase at the start of a calendar year. [early French *epacte* via late Latin from Greek *epaktē*, from *epagein* to bring in, intercalate, from EP- + *agein* to drive]

eparch /'epahk/ *noun* a governor or bishop of a diocese in the Eastern Orthodox Church. ➤➤ **eparchy** *noun*. [Greek *eparchos*, from EP- + *arkhos* ruler]

epaulette (*NAmer* **epaulet**) /epə'let, 'ep-/ *noun* an ornamental strip or pad attached to the shoulder of a garment, *esp* a military uniform. [French *épaulette*, dimin. of *épaule* shoulder, from late Latin *spatula* shoulder blade, spoon]

épée /'epay (*French* epe)/ *noun* a fencing or duelling sword having a bowl-shaped guard and a rigid tapering blade of triangular cross-section with no cutting edge: compare FOIL⁵, SABRE¹. ➤➤ **épéeist** *noun*. [French *épée* via Old French *espee* from Latin *spatha*: see SPADE³]

epeirogenesis /e,pie(ə)roh'jenəsis/ *noun* = EPEIROGENY.

epeirogeny /epie'rojəni/ *noun* the slow deformation of the earth's crust by which continents and their broader features are produced. ➤➤ **epeirogenic** /-'jenik/ *adj*, **epeirogenically** /-'jenikli/ *adv*. [Greek *ēpeiros* mainland, continent + -GENY]

epergne /i'puhn/ *noun* a tiered or branched centrepiece for a dinner table holding fruit, flowers, etc. [prob from French *épargne* saving, ultimately of Germanic origin]

epexegesis /i,peksi'jeesis/ *noun* (*pl* **epexegeses** /-seez/) **1** the addition of a word or words to clarify preceding text or provide additional information. **2** material added in this way. ➤➤ **epexegetic** /-'jetik/ *adj*, **epexegetical** /-'jetikl/ *adj*, **epexegetically** /-'jetikli/ *adv*. [Greek *epexēgēsis*, from EP- + *exēgēsis*: see EXEGESIS]

Eph *abbr* Ephesians (book of the Bible).

ephedra /i'fedrə, 'efədrə/ *noun* any of a large genus of jointed nearly leafless desert shrubs: genus *Ephedra*. [from the Latin genus name, from Latin *ephedra* horsetail plant, from Greek *ephedros* sitting upon, from EP- + *hedra* seat]

ephedrine /i'fedrin, 'efidrin, -dreen/ *noun* an alkaloid drug obtained from Chinese ephedras or made synthetically that is used *esp* to relieve hay fever, asthma, and nasal congestion.

ephemera /i'femərə/ *pl noun* **1** items of short-lived duration, use, or interest, *esp* those that subsequently become collectible. **2** pl of EPHEMERON.

ephemeral /i'femərəl/ *adj* **1** lasting a very short time: *ephemeral pleasures*. **2** lasting one day only: *an ephemeral fever*. ➤➤ **ephemerality** /-'raliti/ *noun*, **ephemerally** *adv*. [Greek *ephēmeros* lasting a day, daily, from EP- + *hēmera* day]

ephemeris /i'feməris/ *noun* (*pl* **ephemerides** /efi'merideez/) a table showing the predicted position of a celestial body at regular intervals. [Latin *ephemeris* diary, ephemeris, from Greek *ephēmeris*, from *ephēmeros*: see EPHEMERAL]

ephemeron /i'feməron/ *noun* (*pl* **ephemera** /-rə/ *or* **ephemerons**) something ephemeral. [from Greek *ephēmeron* mayfly, neuter of *ephēmeros*: see EPHEMERAL]

ephod /'eefod/ *noun* a garment worn by the Jewish high priest in ancient Israel. [Hebrew *ēphōdh*]

ephor /'efaw/ *noun* **1** any of five magistrates of ancient Sparta having power over the king. **2** a government official in modern Greece, *esp* one who supervises public works. ➤➤ **ephorate** /-rət/ *noun*. [via Latin from Greek *ephoros*, from *ephoran* to oversee, from EP- + *horan* to see]

epi- *or* **ep-** *prefix* forming words, with the meanings: **1** outer; external: *epidermis*. **2** besides; in addition: *epilogue*; *epiphenomenon*. **3** over; above: *epigraph*. **4** on; upon: *epiphyte*. **5** after; later: *epigone*.

[Middle English via French and Latin from Greek, from *epi* on, at, besides, after]

epiblast /'epiblast/ *noun* the outer layer of an embryo at a very early stage in its development. ➤➤ **epiblastic** /-'blastik/ *adj.*

epic[1] /'epik/ *adj* **1** characteristic of or relating to an epic. **2a** extending beyond the usual or ordinary, *esp* in size or scope: *His genius was epic* — Times Literary Supplement. **b** heroic. ➤➤ **epical** *adj,* **epically** *adv.* [via Latin from Greek *epikos*, from *epos* word, speech, poem]

epic[2] *noun* **1** a long narrative poem recounting the deeds of a legendary or historical hero. **2** a novel, film, etc that resembles an epic in length, structure, or content. **3** a series of events or body of legend or tradition fit to form the subject of an epic: *that great environmental epic, the wreck of the Torrey Canyon* — The Guardian.

epicanthic fold /epi'kanthik/ *noun* a fold of the skin of the upper eyelid extending over the inner corner of the eye and found among Mongolian peoples. [Latin *epicanthus*, from EPI- + *canthus* corner of the eye]

epicardium /epi'kahdi-əm/ *noun* (*pl* **epicardia** /-di-ə/) the innermost part of the PERICARDIUM (membranous sac) that closely covers the heart. ➤➤ **epicardial** *adj.* [EPI- + Greek *kardia* heart]

epicarp /'epikahp/ *noun* = EXOCARP. [French *épicarpe*, from *épi*- EPI- + *-carpe* -CARP]

epicene /'episeen/ *adj* **1** having characteristics typical of both sexes; hermaphrodite. **2** lacking characteristics typical of either sex; sexless. **3** effeminate. [Middle English via Latin from Greek *epikoinos*, from EPI- + *koinos* common]

epicentre (*NAmer* **epicenter**) /'episentə/ *noun* the part of the earth's surface directly above the place of origin of an earthquake. ➤➤ **epicentral** /-'sentrəl/ *adj.* [EPI- + Latin *centrum*: see CENTRE[1]]

epicontinental /,epi,konti'nentl/ *adj* lying on a continent or continental shelf: *epicontinental seas.*

epicotyl /epi'kotil/ *noun* the part of the stem of a plant embryo or seedling above the cotyledon. [EPI- + COTYLEDON]

epicritic /epi'kritik/ *adj* of or being a nerve or receptor in the skin that responds to and allows accurate discrimination of fine variations in touch, temperature, etc. [Greek *epikritikos* determinative, from *epikrinein* to decide, from EPI- + *krinein* to judge]

epicure /'epikyooə/ *noun* somebody with sensitive and discriminating tastes, *esp* in food or wine. ➤➤ **epicurism** *noun.* [named after *Epicurus* d.270 BC, Greek philosopher]

Epicurean[1] /,epikyoo'ree-ən, -'kyooəri-ən/ *noun* **1** a follower of the doctrine of the materialist Greek philosopher Epicurus (d.270 BC) who taught that pleasure, in the form of mental serenity and freedom from pain, was the highest good. **2** (*often* **epicurean**) an epicure. ➤➤ **Epicureanism** *noun.*

Epicurean[2] *adj* **1** relating to the Greek philosopher Epicurus or his doctrine. **2** (*often* **epicurean**) relating to or suitable for an epicure.

epicycle /'episiekl/ *noun* a circle that itself moves round the circumference of a larger circle. ➤➤ **epicyclic** /-'sieklik/ *adj.* [Middle English *epicicle* via late Latin from Greek *epikyklos*, from EPI- + *kyklos* circle]

epicycloid /epi'siekloyd/ *noun* a curve traced by a point on a circle as it rolls round the outside of a fixed circle. ➤➤ **epicycloidal** *adj.*

epideictic /epi'diektik/ *adj* intended for effect or display, *esp* designed to display the rhetorical skill of a speaker. [Greek *epideiktikos*, from *epideiknynai* to display, show off, from EPI- + *deiknynai* to show]

epidemic[1] /epi'demik/ *noun* **1** an outbreak of a disease affecting many individuals within a population, community, or region at the same time. **2** an outbreak or product of sudden rapid spread, growth, or development. ➤➤ **epidemical** *adj,* **epidemically** *adv.*

epidemic[2] *adj* **1** said of a disease: affecting or tending to affect many individuals within a population, community, or region at the same time. **2** prevalent to an excessive degree: *The practice had reached epidemic proportions.* [French *épidémique* from early French *epidemie* an epidemic, via late Latin *epidemia* from Greek *epidēmia* visit, epidemic, ultimately from EPI- + *demos* the people]

epidemiology /,epideemi'oləji/ *noun* **1** a branch of medicine that deals with the incidence, distribution, and control of disease in a population. **2** the factors controlling the presence or absence of disease. ➤➤ **epidemiological** /-'lojikl/ *adj,* **epidemiologically** /-'lojikli/ *adv,* **epidemiologist** *noun.* [late Latin *epidemia* (see EPIDEMIC[1]) + -LOGY]

epidermis /epi'duhmis/ *noun* **1** the thin outer layer of the external covering of the animal body that is derived from ectoderm; *specif* the outer insensitive layer of the skin of a vertebrate animal that covers the dermis. **2** a thin protective surface layer of cells in higher plants. ➤➤ **epidermal** *adj,* **epidermic** /-mik/ *adj,* **epidermoid** /-moyd/ *adj.* [via Latin from Greek *epidermis*, from EPI- + *dermat-*, *derma* skin, from *derein* to skin]

epidiascope /epi'die-əskohp/ *noun* a projector for producing images of both opaque objects and transparencies.

epididymis /epi'didimis/ *noun* (*pl* **epididymides** /-'dimideez/) a mass of coiled tubes at the back of the testis in which sperm is stored. ➤➤ **epididymal** *adj.* [via Latin from Greek *epididymis*, from EPI- + *didymos* testicle]

epidural[1] /epi'dyooərəl/ *adj* situated on or administered outside the DURA MATER (outermost membrane covering brain and spinal cord): *epidural anaesthesia.*

epidural[2] *noun* an injection of a local anaesthetic into the lower portion of the canal housing the spinal cord, *esp* to reduce the pain of childbirth.

epifauna /epi'fawnə/ *noun* aquatic animals living on a solid surface, *esp* a hard sea floor: compare INFAUNA. ➤➤ **epifaunal** *adj.*

epigamic /epi'gamik/ *adj* in zoology, denoting a feature that attracts the opposite sex. [EPI- + Greek *gamos* marriage]

epigastric /epi'gastrik/ *adj* lying on or over the stomach.

epigastrium /epi'gstri-əm/ *noun* (*pl* **epigastria** /-tri-ə/) the middle region of the upper part of the abdomen above the navel: compare HYPOGASTRIUM. ➤➤ **epigastric** *adj.* [via Latin from Greek *epigastrion*, from EPI- + *gastr-*, *gastēr* belly]

epigeal /epi'jee-əl/ *adj* growing, living, or occurring above the surface of the ground: compare HYPOGEAL. [Greek *epigaios* upon the earth, from EPI- + *gē* earth]

epigene /'epijeen/ *adj* said of rock: formed or occurring on the earth's surface: compare HYPOGENE. [French *épigène* from Greek *epigenēs* growing after, from *epigignesthai*: see EPIGONE]

epigenesis /epi'jenəsis/ *noun* **1** in biology, development of an organism by gradual production of different parts from a single undifferentiated cell, e.g. a fertilized egg. **2** change in the mineral character of a rock owing to outside influences. ➤➤ **epigenetic** /-'netik/ *adj.*

epigeous /epi'jee-əs/ *adj* = EPIGEAL.

epiglottis /epi'glotis/ *noun* a thin plate of flexible cartilage in front of the GLOTTIS (area between vocal cords), at the root of the tongue, that folds back to cover the entrance to the larynx during swallowing. ➤➤ **epiglottal** *adj,* **epiglottic** /-tik/ *adj.*

epigone /'epigohn/ *noun* (*pl* **epigones** *or* **epigoni** /i'pigənie/) an inferior follower or imitator. ➤➤ **epigonic** /-'gonik/ *adj,* **epigonous** /i'pigənəs/ *adj.* [German *Epigone* via Latin from Greek *epigonos* successor, from *epigignesthai* to be born after, from EPI- + *gignesthai* to be born]

epigram /'epigram/ *noun* **1** a short witty or satirical poem: *Has your ladyship heard the epigram he wrote last week on Lady Frizzle's feather catching fire?* — Sheridan. **2** a concise, witty, and often paradoxical remark or saying. ➤➤ **epigrammatic** /-'matik/ *adj,* **epigrammatical** /-'matikl/ *adj,* **epigrammatically** /-'matikli/ *adv.* [Middle English *epigrame* via Latin from Greek *epigramma*, from *epigraphein* to write on, inscribe, from EPI- + *graphein* to write]

epigrammatize *or* **epigrammatise** /epi'gramətiez/ *verb trans* to make or compose an epigram about (something). ➤ *verb intrans* to make or compose epigrams. ➤➤ **epigrammatist** *noun.*

epigraph /'epigrahf/ *noun* **1** an engraved inscription. **2** a quotation at the beginning of a book, chapter, etc, suggesting its theme. [Greek *epigraphē*, from *epigraphein*: see EPIGRAM]

epigraphic /epi'grafik/ *adj* **1** of or being an epigraph. **2** relating to epigraphy. ➤➤ **epigraphically** *adv.*

epigraphical /epi'grafikl/ *adj* = EPIGRAPHIC.

epigraphy /i'pigrəfi/ *noun* **1** epigraphs collectively. **2** the study of inscriptions, *esp* ancient inscriptions. ➤➤ **epigrapher** *noun,* **epigraphist** *noun.*

epigynous /i'pijinəs/ *adj* **1** said of a floral organ, e.g. a petal: attached to the upper surface of the ovary: compare HYPOGYNOUS,

PERIGYNOUS. **2** said of a flower: having epigynous floral organs. ➤➤ **epigyny** /-ni/ *noun*.

epilation /epi'laysh(ə)n/ *noun* the loss or removal of hair. ➤➤ **epilator** /'epilaytə/ *noun*. [French *épilation* from *épiler* to remove hair, from EX-¹ + Latin *pilus* hair]

epilepsy /'epilepsi/ *noun* any of various disorders marked by disturbed electrical rhythms of the brain and typically manifested by convulsive attacks and sometimes loss of consciousness. [early French *epilepsie* via late Latin from Greek *epilēpsia*, from *epilambanein* to seize, from EPI- + *lambanein* to grasp]

epileptic¹ /epi'leptik/ *adj* of or affected with epilepsy. ➤➤ **epileptically** *adv*.

epileptic² *noun* a person who is affected with epilepsy.

epilimnion /epi'limni-ən/ *noun* (*pl* **epilimnia** /-ni-ə/) the warm, less dense, upper layer of water in a lake, which is rich in oxygen: compare HYPOLIMNION. [EPI- + Greek *limnion*, dimin. of *limnē* marshy lake]

epilogue /'epilog/ *noun* **1** a concluding section of a literary or dramatic work that comments on or summarizes the main action or plot. **2** a speech or poem addressed to the audience by an actor at the end of a play. [Middle English *epiloge* via French and Latin from Greek *epilogos*, from *epilegein* to say in addition, from EPI- + *legein* to say]

epinephrine /epi'nefrin, -reen/ *or* **epinephrin** /-rin/ *noun* = ADRENALIN. [EPI- + Greek *nephros* kidney]

epiphany /i'pifəni/ *noun* (*pl* **epiphanies**) **1** (**Epiphany**). **a** the coming of the Magi to see the infant Christ. **b** 6 January, observed as a festival in the Christian Church in commemoration of this. **2** a sudden manifestation or perception of the essential nature or meaning of something. ➤➤ **epiphanic** /epi'fanik/ *adj*. [Middle English *epiphanie* via French and late Latin from Greek *epiphaneia* appearance, manifestation, from *epiphainein* to manifest, from EPI- + *phanein* to show]

epiphenomenon /,epifə'nominən/ *noun* (*pl* **epiphenomena** /-nə/) **1** a secondary phenomenon accompanying another and caused by it. **2** a mental process regarded as an epiphenomenon of brain activity. **3** an unrelated or unexpected symptom occurring during the course of a disease. ➤➤ **epiphenomenal** *adj*.

epiphysis /i'pifisis/ *noun* (*pl* **epiphyses** /-seez/) **1** a part of a bone that develops separately from and later becomes united with the rest, *esp* an end of a long bone of a limb: compare DIAPHYSIS. **2** = PINEAL BODY. [via Latin from Greek *epiphysis* growth, from *epiphyesthai* to grow on]

epiphyte /'epifiet/ *noun* a plant that derives its moisture and nutrients from the air and rain and grows on another plant. ➤➤ **epiphytal** *adj*, **epiphytic** /-'fitik/ *adj*.

episcopacy /i'piskəpəsi/ *noun* (*pl* **episcopacies**) **1** government of the Church by bishops or by a hierarchy. **2** = EPISCOPATE.

episcopal /i'piskəpl/ *adj* **1** of a bishop. **2** having or governed by bishops. **3** (**Episcopal**) Anglican; *esp* of an Anglican Church that is not the official national Church, e.g. in the USA or Scotland. ➤➤ **episcopally** *adv*. [Middle English from late Latin *episcopalis*, from *episcopus*: see BISHOP]

episcopalian¹ /i,piskə'payli-ən/ *adj* **1** of or advocating the episcopal form of Church government. **2** (**Episcopalian**) of or belonging to the Episcopal Church. ➤➤ **episcopalianism** *noun*.

episcopalian² *noun* **1** an adherent of the episcopal form of Church government. **2** (**Episcopalian**) a member of the Episcopal Church.

episcopate /i'piskəpət, -payt/ *noun* **1** the rank, office, or term of a bishop. **2** a body of bishops.

episcope /'episkohp/ *noun* a projector for producing images of opaque objects, e.g. photographs.

episiotomy /i,peezi'otəmi/ *noun* (*pl* **episiotomies**) surgical enlargement of the opening of the vagina during childbirth, to prevent tearing. [Greek *epision* pubic region + -TOMY]

episode /'episohd/ *noun* **1** a distinctive and separate event that is part of a larger series, e.g. in history or in somebody's life. **2** a developed situation or incident that is integral to but separable from a continuous narrative, e.g. a play or novel. **3** an instalment of a serialized literary work, radio or television programme, etc. **4** a digressive subdivision or passage introducing a new theme in a musical composition. **5** the part of an ancient Greek tragedy between two songs from the chorus. [Greek *epeisodion*, neuter of

epeisodios coming in besides, from EPI- + *eisodios* coming in, from *eis* into + *hodos* road, journey]

episodic /epi'sodik/ *adj* **1** made up of separate, *esp* loosely connected, episodes: *an episodic narrative*. **2** limited in duration or significance to a particular episode. **3** occasional or sporadic. ➤➤ **episodically** *adv*.

episodical /epi'sodikl/ *adj* = EPISODIC.

epistasis /i'pistəsis/ *noun* suppression of the effect of a gene by another gene that is not its allele. ➤➤ **epistatic** /epi'statik/ *adj*. [via Latin from Greek *epistasis* act of stopping, from *ephistanai* to stop, from EPI- + *histanai* to cause to stand]

epistaxis /epi'staksis/ *noun* (*pl* **epistaxes** /-seez/) = NOSEBLEED. [via Latin from Greek *epistaxis*, from *epistazein* to drip on, to blood at the nose again, from EPI- + *stazein* to drip]

epistemic /epi'steemik/ *adj* of knowledge or epistemology. ➤➤ **epistemically** *adv*.

epistemology /ip,istə'moləji/ *noun* the study or theory of the nature and limits of experience, belief, and knowledge.

Editorial note
Questions that epistemology concerns itself with include: does all non-trivial knowledge derive from sense-experience? (Empiricism: yes; rationalism: no); can appeal to observation and experience give us any reason for beliefs about other things (the past, the future, the unobservable)? What is the difference between a justified and an unjustified belief? Is knowing like believing, only better? — Professor Jonathan Dancy

➤➤ **epistemological** /-'lojikl/ *adj*, **epistemologically** /-'lojikli/ *adv*, **epistemologist** *noun*. [Greek *epistēmē* knowledge, from *epistanai* to understand, know, from EPI- + *histanai* to stand]

epistle /i'pisl/ *noun* **1** a letter, *esp* a formal or lengthy one. **2** (**Epistle**). **a** any of the letters from the apostles adopted as books of the New Testament. **b** a reading from any of these books at a church service. [Middle English via Old French and Latin from Greek *epistolē* message, letter, from *epistellein* to send to, from EPI- + *stellein* to send]

epistolary /i'pistələri/ *adj* **1** of or appropriate to a letter. **2** carried on by or in the form of letters: *an endless sequence of epistolary love affairs* — Times Literary Supplement. **3** written in the form of a series of letters: *an epistolary novel*.

epistrophe /i'pistrafi/ *noun* repetition of the same word or expression at the end of a series of phrases, sentences, etc, for rhetorical effect: compare ANAPHORA. [Greek *epistrophē*, literally 'turning about', from EPI- + *strophē*: see STROPHE]

epistyle /'epistiel/ *noun* = ARCHITRAVE (1). [French *épistyle* via Latin from Greek *epistylium* on a column, from EPI- + *stylos* column]

epitaph /'epitahf, -taf/ *noun* **1** a commemorative inscription on a tombstone or monument. **2** a brief statement commemorating a deceased person or past event. [Middle English *epitaphe* via French and Latin from Greek *epitaphion* funeral oration, from EPI- + *taphos* tomb, funeral]

epitaxy /'epitaksi/ *noun* the growth of one crystalline substance on another whose structure provides the orientation for that of the overlying layer. ➤➤ **epitaxial** /-'taksi-əl/ *adj*. [French *épitaxie*, from Greek EPI- + *taxis*: see TAXIS]

epithalamium /,epithə'laymi-əm/ *noun* (*pl* **epithalamiums** *or* **epithalamia** /-mi-ə/) a song or poem in celebration of a marriage or in praise of a bride and bridegroom. ➤➤ **epithalamic** /-'lamik/ *adj*. [via Latin from Greek *epithalamion*, from EPI- + *thalamos* room, bridal chamber]

epithelium /epi'theeli-əm/ *noun* (*pl* **epithelia** /-li-ə/) **1** a cellular animal tissue that covers an external or internal surface of the body and serves to enclose and protect other parts, to produce secretions and excretions, and to function in absorption. **2** a thin layer of cells that lines a cavity or tube of a plant. ➤➤ **epithelial** *adj*. [scientific Latin, from EPI- + Greek *thēlē* nipple]

epithet /'epithet/ *noun* **1** a descriptive word or phrase accompanying or occurring in place of the name of a person or thing. **2** a disparaging or abusive word or phrase. ➤➤ **epithetic** /-'thetik/ *adj*, **epithetical** /-'thetikl/ *adj*. [via Latin from Greek *epithetos* added, from *epitithenai* to put on, add, from EPI- + *tithenai* to place]

epitome /i'pitəmi/ *noun* **1** a typical or ideal example; an embodiment: *The British monarchy is the epitome of tradition*. **2** a condensed account or summary, *esp* of a literary work. [Greek *epitomē*, from *epitemnein* to cut short, from EPI- + *temnein* to cut]

epitomize *or* **epitomise** /i'pitəmiez/ *verb trans* **1** to serve as the typical or ideal example of (something); to embody (it). **2** to make an epitome of (something); to summarize (it). ⫸ **epitomist** *noun*, **epitomization** /-'zaysh(ə)n/ *noun*.

epizootic[1] /,epizoh'otik/ *adj* said of a disease: temporarily affecting many animals of one kind at the same time. ⫸ **epizootically** *adv*.

epizootic[2] *noun* an epizootic disease.

EPNS *abbr* electroplated nickel silver.

epoch /'eepok/ *noun* **1a** an extended period of time, usu characterized by a distinctive development or by a memorable series of events. **b** a division of geological time less than a period and greater than an age. **2** a date or time selected as a point of reference, e.g. in astronomy. **3** a memorable event or date; a turning point. ⫸ **epochal** /'epokl/ *adj*. [via late Latin from Greek *epochē* cessation, fixed point, from *epechein* to pause, hold back, from EPI- + *echein* to stay, remain the same]

epoch-making *adj* uniquely or highly significant: *The steam engine was an epoch-making invention.*

epode /'epohd/ *noun* **1** a lyric poem in which a long line is followed by a shorter one. **2** the last part of a Greek ode, following the strophe and the antistrophe. [via Latin from Greek *epōidos* sung or said after, from + EPI- *aidein* to sing]

eponym /'epənim/ *noun* **1** a word or name, e.g. *cardigan* or *Hodgkin's disease*, derived from the name of a real or mythical person. **2** a person after whom something is named or believed to be named.

Word history
Greek *epōnymos* eponym, eponymous, from EPI- + *onyma* name. Many hundreds of English words have been derived from the names of real people. Some, such as *Heaviside layer* and *Hodgkin's disease*, have fairly obviously been formed by this process; less obvious examples include *bloomers*, *bowdlerize*, *boycott*, *cardigan*, *chauvinism*, *derby*, *dunce*, *gerrymander*, *guppy*, *leotard*, *loganberry*, *lynch*, *mackintosh*, *martinet*, *maverick*, *plimsoll*, *sadism*, *salmonella*, *sandwich*, *shrapnel*, *silhouette*, *thespian*, and *volt*.

eponymous /i'poniməs/ *adj* denoting a character in a film, book, etc, whose name is in its title: *the eponymous heroine of 'Jane Eyre'*.

EPOS /'eehpos/ *noun* electronic point of sale, a system of recording every sale made in a shop, by means of bar coding and a laser scanner at the cash desk.

epoxide /i'poksied/ *noun* an epoxy compound.

epoxidize or **epoxidise** /i'poksidiez/ *verb trans* to convert (something) into an epoxy compound: *epoxidized oils.*

epoxy[1] /i'poksi/ *adj* **1** said of a chemical compound: containing a three-membered ring consisting of one oxygen and two carbon atoms. **2** relating to an epoxy compound or epoxy resin. [EPI- + OXY-[2]]

epoxy[2] *verb trans* (**epoxies, epoxied, epoxying**) to glue (something) with epoxy resin.

epoxy resin *noun* a tough resistant resin used *esp* in coatings and adhesives.

EPROM /'eeprom/ *abbr* erasable programmable read-only memory.

eps *abbr* earnings per share.

epsilon /'epsilon/ *noun* the fifth letter of the Greek alphabet (Ε, ε), equivalent to and transliterated as roman e. [Greek *e psilon*, literally 'simple e']

Epsom salts /'eps(ə)m/ *pl noun* hydrated magnesium sulphate used as a laxative. [named after *Epsom*, town in Surrey, England, where the salts occur naturally in the water]

Epstein-Barr virus /,epstien 'bah/ *noun* a virus of the herpes family that causes glandular fever and is associated with a cancer of the lymph nodes. [named after Sir Michael A *Epstein* b.1921, British pathologist, and Yvonne M *Barr* b.1932, Irish pathologist, who discovered it]

EQ *abbr* emotional intelligence. [from *emotional IQ*]

equable /'ekwəbl/ *adj* **1** even-tempered or placid. **2** uniform or even, *esp* free from extremes or sudden changes: *an equable climate.* ⫸ **equability** /-'biliti/ *noun*, **equableness** *noun*, **equably** *adv*. [Latin *aequabilis*, from *aequare* to make level or equal, from *aequus* level, equal]

Usage note
equable or equitable? These two words are sometimes confused. *Equable* means 'even-tempered' or 'free from extremes' and is frequently used to describe a person's character: *He has a very equable temperament. Equitable* means 'fair' or 'just': *an equitable system of taxation.*

equal[1] /'eekwəl/ *adj* **1a** of the same quantity, size, or degree as another. **b** identical in value; equivalent. **2a** of the same quality, nature, or status. **b** identical or equivalent for each member of a group, class, or society: *equal rights.* **3** evenly balanced or matched: *The two opponents were equal.* **4** (+ to) capable of meeting the requirements of (something, e.g. a situation or task): *He is quite equal to the job.* [Middle English from Latin *aequalis*, from *aequus* level, equal]

equal[2] *noun* somebody or something that is equal to another: *She is not your equal.*

equal[3] *verb* (**equalled, equalling**, NAmer **equaled, equaling**) ⫸ *verb trans* **1** to be equal to (something); *esp* to be identical in value to (it). **2** to make or produce something equal to (something); to match (it). ⫸ *verb intrans* (*usu* + out) to become equal or identical.

equalise *verb* see EQUALIZE.

equaliser *noun* see EQUALIZER.

equalitarian /i,kwoli'teəri-ən/ *noun and adj* = EGALITARIAN. ⫸ **equalitarianism** *noun*.

equality /i'kwoliti/ *noun* the quality or state of being equal.

Editorial note
Equality is the ultimate goal of egalitarianism, where all citizens of the state are given equal rights and privileges. Equality affords a comparison without discrimination on grounds of gender, race, creed, age, sexual orientation, disability, or economic background. This can range from equality of opportunity for welfare and/or resources (Dworkin) or is embraced in the notion of justice (Justinian), equal in law. Contemporary debates revolve around equality of outcome and equality of opportunity — Helena Kennedy.

equalize or **equalise** *verb trans* **1** to make (something) equal. **2** to make (something) uniform, *esp* to distribute (it) evenly or uniformly. ⫸ *verb intrans* to make things equal, *esp* to bring the scores level, e.g. in a football match. ⫸ **equalization** /-'zaysh(ə)n/ *noun*.

equalizer or **equaliser** *noun* **1** somebody or something that makes things equal. **2** a goal, point, etc that brings the scores level in a game or match. **3** an electronic device, e.g. in a radio or stereo system, that is designed to reduce distortion by making the frequency response the same for a wide range of frequencies. **4** NAmer, *informal* a weapon, *esp* a gun.

equally *adv* **1** in an equal or uniform manner; evenly. **2** to an equal degree; alike: *She is respected equally by young and old.*

equal opportunity *noun* **1** (*also in pl*) nondiscrimination on the grounds of age, sex, race, etc, *esp* in the workplace. **2** (*used before a noun*) offering or ensuring equal opportunity: *an equal-opportunities employer.*

equals sign or **equal sign** *noun* a sign (=) indicating mathematical equality or logical equivalence.

equal temperament *noun* the division of the musical octave into twelve equal semitones.

Editorial note
Equal temperament is a system devised in the 16th cent. to make each step (semitone) of a chromatic scale the same. Though scientifically this is impossible, the ear gratefully accommodates it. C# and Db on the piano sound the same, but to a string or wind player a C# is actually higher than a Db. Though J S Bach's *Well-Tempered Klavier* celebrates the idea, the system was not fully adopted until the 19th cent. — Amanda Holden.

equanimity /ekwə'nimiti, ee-/ *noun* evenness of mind or temper, *esp* under stress. ⫸ **equanimous** /i'kwaniməs/ *adj*. [Latin *aequa-nimitas*, from *aequo animo* with even mind]

equate /i'kwayt/ *verb trans* **1** to treat, represent, or regard (something) as equal, equivalent, or comparable: *He equates dissension with disloyalty.* **2** to make (things) equal. ⫸ *verb intrans* to be equal or equivalent. ⫸ **equatable** *adj*. [Middle English *equaten* from Latin *aequatus*, past part. of *aequare*: see EQUABLE]

equation /i'kwayzh(ə)n/ *noun* **1** a statement of the equality of two mathematical or logical expressions. **2** an expression representing a chemical reaction quantitatively by means of chemical symbols. **3** a complex of variable factors: *the whole social equation.* **4** the act of equating or the state of being equated. ⫸ **equational** *adj*, **equationally** *adv*.

equator *noun* **1** the notional circle around the earth that is equidistant at all points from the two poles and divides the earth's surface into the northern and southern hemispheres. **2** = CELESTIAL EQUATOR. **3** a circle or circular band dividing the surface of a body into two usu equal and symmetrical parts, sometimes imaginary: *the equator of a dividing cell.* [Middle English from late Latin *aequator*, from *circulus aequator diei et noctis* circle that equalizes day and night]

equatorial[1] /ˌekwə'tawri·əl/ *adj* **1a** of, at, or near the equator of the earth. **b** said of the climate: characterized by consistently high temperatures and rainfall throughout the year. **2** said of a telescope or its mounting: having two axes at right angles to each other and allowing a celestial body to be kept in view as the earth rotates.

equatorial[2] *noun* an equatorial telescope mounting.

equerry /i'kweri, 'ekwəri/ *noun* (*pl* **equerries**) **1** an officer of the British royal household in personal attendance on a member of the royal family. **2** formerly, an officer of a royal or noble household charged with the care of horses. [French *escuirie* office of a squire, stable, from *escuier, esquier*: see ESQUIRE]

equestrian[1] /i'kwestri·ən/ *adj* **1a** of or featuring horses or horse riding: *equestrian skills.* **b** representing a person on horseback. **2** of or composed of knights. ➤➤ **equestrianism** *noun*. [Latin *equestr-, equester* of a horseman, from *eques* horseman, from *equus* horse]

equestrian[2] *noun* a person who rides or performs on horseback.

equi- *comb. form* forming words, with the meanings: **1** equal: *equipoise*. **2** equally: *equiprobable*. [Middle English via French from Latin *aequi-*, from *aequus* equal]

equiangular /ˌeekwi'anggyoolə, ek-/ *adj* having all angles equal or all corresponding angles equal: *equiangular polygons*.

equidistant /ˌeekwi'dist(ə)nt, ek-/ *adj* equally distant. ➤➤ **equidistance** *noun*, **equidistantly** *adv*. [via French or late Latin from Latin *aequi-* EQUI- + *distant-, distans*: see DISTANT]

equilateral /ˌeekwi'lat(ə)rəl, ek-/ *adj* having all sides equal: *an equilateral triangle*. [late Latin *aequilateralis*, from Latin *aequi-* EQUI- + *later-, latus* side]

equilibrant /i'kwilibrənt/ *noun* a force that is capable of balancing out another force.

equilibrate /i'kwilibrayt/ *verb trans* to bring (things) into or keep (things) in equilibrium; to balance (them). ➤ *verb intrans* to come to or be in equilibrium. ➤➤ **equilibration** /-'braysh(ə)n/ *noun*.

equilibria /ˌeekwi'libriə, ek-/ *noun* pl of EQUILIBRIUM.

equilibrist /i'kwilibrist/ *noun* a person who performs balancing tricks, *esp* on a high wire.

equilibrium /ˌeekwi'libri·əm, ek-/ *noun* (*pl* **equilibria** /-bri·ə/) **1** a state of balance between opposing forces, actions, or processes, e.g. in a reversible chemical reaction. **2a** a state of adjustment between opposing or divergent influences or elements: *The introduction of a new and mighty force had disturbed the old equilibrium* — Macaulay. **b** a state of intellectual or emotional balance. **c** the economic condition in which supply and demand are matched. **3** the normal state of the body in relation to its environment that involves adjustment to changing orientation with respect to gravity. [Latin *aequilibrium* from *aequilibris* being in equilibrium, from *aequi-* EQUI- + *libra* weight, balance]

equine[1] /'ekwien/ *adj* of or resembling a horse or other member of the horse family. ➤➤ **equinely** *adv*. [Latin *equinus* from *equus* horse]

equine[2] *noun* a horse or other member of the horse family.

equinoctial[1] /ˌeekwi'noksh(ə)l, ek-/ *adj* **1** relating to or occurring at an equinox: *equinoctial spring tides*. **2** relating to the equator or celestial equator.

equinoctial[2] *noun* **1** = CELESTIAL EQUATOR. **2** an equinoctial storm.

equinoctial circle *noun* = EQUINOCTIAL[2] (1).

equinoctial line *noun* = EQUINOCTIAL[2] (1).

equinoctial point *noun* = EQUINOX (2).

equinoctial year *noun* = SOLAR YEAR.

equinox /'ekwinoks, 'ee-/ *noun* **1** either of the two times each year, around 21 March and 23 September, when the sun crosses the equator and day and night are of equal length everywhere on earth. **2** either of the two points where the apparent path of the sun crosses the celestial equator. [Middle English via French and late Latin from Latin *aequinoctium*, from *aequi-* EQUI- + *noct-, nox* night]

equip /i'kwip/ *verb trans* (**equipped, equipping**) **1** to make (somebody or something) ready for service, action, or use; to provide (them) with appropriate supplies. **2** to provide (somebody) with the necessary abilities, intellectual capacity, emotional resources, etc: *He was not equipped to deal with such a demanding course of study.* **3** *archaic* to dress or array (somebody or something). ➤➤ **equipper**

noun. [early French *equiper*, prob from Old Norse *skipa* to equip a ship, from *skip* ship]

equipage /'ekwipij/ *noun* **1** material or articles used in the equipment and stores of a military unit or other organized group. **2** formerly, a horse-drawn carriage with its servants. **3** *archaic* a set of small useful articles or the case in which they are kept.

equipment *noun* **1** the set of articles, apparatus, or physical, resources serving to equip a person, thing, enterprise, expedition, etc. **2** mental or emotional resources. **3** the act of equipping somebody or something.

equipoise[1] /'ekwipoyz, 'ee-/ *noun* **1** a state of equilibrium. **2** a counterbalance.

equipoise[2] *verb trans* **1** to serve as a counterbalance to (something). **2** to put or hold (something) in equilibrium.

equipollent[1] /ˌeekwi'polənt, ek-/ *adj formal* equal in force, power, validity, or effect. ➤➤ **equipollence** *noun*, **equipollency** /-si/ *noun*. [Middle English via French from Latin *aequipollent-, aequipollens*, from *aequi-* EQUI- + *pollent-, pollens*, present part. of *pollēre* to be able]

equipollent[2] *noun formal* something that is equipollent.

equipotential[1] /ˌeekwipə'tensh(ə)l, ek-/ *adj* having the same or uniform potential, *esp* electrical potential: *an equipotential surface*.

equipotential[2] *noun* an equipotential line or surface.

equiprobable /ˌeekwi'probəbl, ek-/ *adj* having the same degree of logical or mathematical probability: *equiprobable alternatives*.

equisetum /ˌekwi'seetəm/ *noun* (*pl* **equiseta** /-tə/ or **equisetums**) any of a genus of plants that comprises the horsetails: genus *Equisetum*. [Latin *equisaetum* horsetail (plant), from *equus* horse + *saeta* bristle]

equitable /'ekwitəbl/ *adj* **1** fair and just. **2** valid in equity as distinguished from law. ➤➤ **equitability** /-'biliti/ *noun*, **equitableness** *noun*, **equitably** *adv*.

Usage note

equitable *or* equable? See note at EQUABLE.

equitation /ekwi'taysh(ə)n/ *noun formal* the act or art of riding on horseback. [via French from Latin *equitation-, equitatio*, from *equitare* to ride on horseback, from *equit-, eques* horseman, from *equus* horse]

equity /'ekwiti/ *noun* (*pl* **equities**) **1** justice according to natural law or right; fairness. **2** a system of justice orig developed on the basis of conscience and fairness to supplement or override the more rigid common law: compare COMMON LAW, STATUTE LAW. **3** a right, claim, or interest existing or valid in equity. **4** the value of a property, e.g. a mortgaged house, in excess of monetary claims against it. **5** (*usu in pl*) a share that does not bear fixed interest. **6** the value of shares issued by a company. **7** (**Equity**) in Britain, the trade union representing the interests of actors and performers. [Middle English *equite* via French from Latin *aequitat-, aequitas*, from *aequus* equal, fair]

equivalence /i'kwivələns/ *noun* **1** the state or property of being equivalent. **2a** the relation between two statements that are either both true or both false such that each implies the other. **b** a logical function of two statements, which takes the value true if both statements are true or both false and the value false otherwise.

equivalence class *noun* a mathematical set in which an equivalence relation holds between every pair of members of the set.

equivalence relation *noun* a relation between elements of a mathematical set that is symmetric, reflexive, and transitive.

equivalency /i'kwivələnsi/ *noun* (*pl* **equivalencies**) = EQUIVALENCE.

equivalent[1] /i'kwivəl(ə)nt/ *adj* **1** equal in force, amount, or value. **2** corresponding or virtually identical, *esp* in effect, function, or meaning. **3** having the same chemical combining capacity: *equivalent quantities of two elements*. **4** related by an equivalence relation. ➤➤ **equivalently** *adv*. [Middle English via French from late Latin *aequivalent-, aequivalens*, present part. of *aequivalēre* to have equal power, from Latin *aequi-* EQUI- + *valēre* to be strong]

equivalent[2] *noun* **1** something or somebody that is equivalent. **2** the weight of a substance in grams that combines with, displaces, or is otherwise chemically equivalent to 8 grams of oxygen or 1.007 97 grams of hydrogen.

equivalent weight *noun* = EQUIVALENT[2] (2).

equivocal /i'kwivəkl/ *adj* **1** subject to two or more interpretations; ambiguous: *equivocal evidence; And in her ears rang the echo of a boy's laughter, golden and equivocal* — Saki. **2** questionable or suspicious. ➤➤ **equivocality** /-'kaliti/ *noun*, **equivocally** *adv*, **equivocalness** *noun*. [late Latin *aequivocus*, from *aequi-* EQUI- + *voc-*, *vox* voice]

equivocate /i'kwivəkayt/ *verb intrans* to use equivocal or evasive language, *esp* with intent to deceive or to avoid committing oneself. ➤➤ **equivocation** /-'kaysh(ə)n/ *noun*, **equivocator** *noun*, **equivocatory** *adj*.

equivoque or **equivoke** /'ekwivohk, 'ee-/ *noun* an equivocal word or phrase; *specif* a pun. [French *équivoque* from late Latin *aequivocus*: see EQUIVOCAL]

ER *abbr* **1** *NAmer* emergency room. **2** King Edward. **3** Queen Elizabeth. [(sense 2) Latin *Edwardus Rex*, (sense 3) Latin *Elizabetha Regina*]

Er *abbr* the chemical symbol for erbium.

er /uh/ *interj* used to express hesitation or doubt.

-er[1] *suffix* forming the comparative of adjectives and adverbs of one and sometimes two or more syllables: *faster; happier*. [Old English *-ra* (in adjectives), *-or* (in adverbs)]

-er[2] *suffix* forming nouns, denoting: **1a** somebody engaged in the occupation of: *geographer*. **b** somebody or something belonging to or associated with: *sixth-former*. **c** native of; resident of: *cottager; Londoner*. **d** something that has: *three-wheeler; four-poster*. **2a** somebody or something that does or performs (the action specified): *reporter; eye-opener*. **b** something that is a suitable object of (the action specified): *broiler*. **3** somebody or something that is: *foreigner*. [Old English *-ere*, of Germanic origin]

era /'iərə/ *noun* **1** an extended period of years reckoned from a fixed point in time: *the Christian era*. **2a** a historical period begun or typified by some distinctive figure or characteristic feature: *the era of space flight*. **b** a major division of geological time that is subdivided into periods: *the Mesozoic era*. **c** a stage in the development of somebody or something. [late Latin *aera* a number or time used as a basis of reckoning, from Latin, counters, pl of *aer-*, *aes* copper, money]

eradicate /i'radikayt/ *verb trans* **1** to eliminate or do away with (something): *We can try to eradicate ignorance by better teaching*. **2** to pull (something) up by the roots. ➤➤ **eradicable** *adj*, **eradication** /-'kaysh(ə)n/ *noun*, **eradicative** /-tiv/ *adj*, **eradicator** *noun*. [Latin *eradicatus*, past part. of *eradicare*, from EX-[1] + *radic-*, *radix* root]

erase /i'rayz/ *verb trans* **1a** to obliterate or rub out (something written, painted, etc). **b** to remove (recorded matter) from a magnetic tape. **c** to delete (data) from a computer storage device. **2** to remove (something) from existence or memory as if by erasing. ➤ *verb intrans* to yield to being erased: *Pencil erases easily*. ➤➤ **erasable** *adj*. [Latin *erasus*, past part. of *eradere*, from EX-[1] + *radere* to scratch, scrape]

eraser *noun* something, e.g. a piece of rubber or a felt pad, used to erase pencil, ink, chalk, or other marks.

Erastian /i'rasti-ən/ *adj* of or advocating the doctrine of State supremacy over the Church in ecclesiastical affairs. ➤➤ **Erastian** *noun*, **Erastianism** *noun*. [named after Thomas *Erastus* d.1583, Swiss physician and Zwinglian theologian]

erasure /i'rayzhə/ *noun* **1** the act or an instance of erasing. **2** a mark left where something has been erased.

erbium /'uhbi·əm/ *noun* a silver-white soft metallic chemical element of the rare-earth group that occurs in various minerals: symbol Er, atomic number 68. [named after *Ytterby*, town in Sweden where the first rare-earth mineral was found]

ERDF *abbr* European Regional Development Fund.

ere /eə/ *prep and conj literary* before: *I shall see thee, ere I die, look pale with love* — Shakespeare. [Old English *ær*, before, early, soon]

erect[1] /i'rekt/ *adj* **1a** vertical in position; upright. **b** standing up or out from the body: *erect hairs*. **c** characterized by firm or rigid straightness, e.g. in bodily posture: *an erect bearing*. **2** in a state of physiological erection. ➤➤ **erectly** *adv*, **erectness** *noun*. [Middle English from Latin *erectus*, past part. of *erigere* to erect, from EX-[1] + *regere* to lead straight, guide]

erect[2] *verb trans* **1a** to put (something) up by fitting together materials or parts; to build (it): *We erected the tent*. **b** to fix (something) in an upright position: *They erected a statue to the princess*. **2** to establish (something); to set (it) up. **3** to elevate (something) in status: *They erected a few odd notions into a philosophy*. **4** to draw or

construct (a perpendicular, etc) on a given base. ➤➤ **erectable** *adj*, **erector** *noun*.

erectile /i'rektiel/ *adj* **1** capable of being raised to an erect position. **2a** capable of becoming swollen with blood to bring about physiological erection: *erectile tissue*. **b** of or involving the erection of the penis. ➤➤ **erectility** /-'tiliti/ *noun*.

erection /i'reksh(ə)n/ *noun* **1a** the dilation with blood and resulting firmness of a previously limp body part, *esp* the penis, clitoris, or nipples, usu as a result of sexual stimulation. **b** an occurrence of this, *esp* in the penis: *He had an erection*. **2** something erected, *esp* a building. **3** the act of erecting something.

E region *noun* the part of the IONOSPHERE (upper part of the earth's atmosphere) occurring between about 65 and 145km (about 40 and 90mi) above the earth's surface and containing the E layer.

eremite /'erimiet/ *noun* a Christian hermit or recluse. ➤➤ **eremitic** /-'mitik/ *adj*, **eremitical** /-'mitikl/ *adj*. [Middle English: see HERMIT]

erepsin /i'repsin/ *noun* a mixture of protein-digesting enzymes present in the intestinal juice. [*er-* (prob from Latin *eripere* to sweep away) + PEPSIN]

erethism /'erithiz(ə)m/ *noun* **1** abnormal responsiveness or sensitivity, *esp* of human organs and physiological systems, to stimulation. **2** an abnormal tendency to become sexually aroused or irritated in response to verbal or psychic stimulation. ➤➤ **erethismic** /-'thizmik/ *adj*. [French *éréthisme* from Greek *erethismos* irritation, from *erethizein* to irritate]

erewhile /eə'wiel/ or **erewhiles** *adv archaic or literary* some time ago; heretofore: *I am as fair now as I was erewhile* — Shakespeare.

erf /eəf/ *noun* (pl **erven** /'eəvən/) *SAfr* a plot of urban building land, usu large enough for one house. [Afrikaans *erf* from Dutch, plot of land, inheritance]

erg[1] /uhg/ *noun* a unit of work or energy in the centimetre-gram-second system equal to the work done by a force of one dyne moving its point of application through one centimetre, equivalent to 10^{-7} joules. [Greek *ergon* work]

erg[2] *noun* (pl **ergs** or **areg** /ə'reg/) an area of shifting sand dunes in a desert, *esp* the Sahara. [French *erg*, of Hamitic origin]

erg- or **ergo-** *comb. form* forming words, denoting: work: *ergonomics*. [Greek *ergo-* from *ergon* work]

ergative /'uhgətiv/ *adj* of or being the grammatical relationship between two sentences, e.g. *The prisoners marched* and *We marched the prisoners*, such that the subject of the first corresponds to the object of the second, the new subject of which causes rather than performs the action. ➤➤ **ergativity** /-'tiviti/ *noun*. [Greek *ergatēs* worker, from *ergon* work]

ergo /'uhgoh/ *adv* therefore or hence: *The Bishop's views are just as perilous to society. Ergo, to the asylum with him* — Jack London. [Latin *ergo* because of]

ergo- *comb. form* see ERG-.

ergometer /uh'gomitə/ *noun* an apparatus for measuring the work performed by a group of muscles. ➤➤ **ergometric** /-'metrik/ *adj*.

ergonomic /uhgə'nomik/ *adj* designed to maximize productivity by minimizing effort and discomfort. ➤➤ **ergonomically** *adv*.

ergonomics /uhgə'nomiks/ *pl noun* (*treated as sing. or pl*) a science concerned with the relationship between human beings, the machines and equipment they use, and the working environment. ➤➤ **ergonomist** /uh'gonəmist/ *noun*. [ERG- + ECONOMICS]

ergosterol /uh'gostərol/ *noun* a steroid found *esp* in yeast, moulds, and ergot that is converted into vitamin D_2 by ultraviolet light. [ERGOT + STEROL]

ergot /'uhgət, 'uhgot/ *noun* **1a** a black or dark purple club-shaped SCLEROTIUM (hard mass of fungal threads) that develops in place of the seed of a grass, e.g. rye. **b** a fungus bearing such sclerotia: genus *Claviceps*. **2** a disease of rye and other cereals caused by an ergot fungus. **3** the dried sclerotia of an ergot fungus containing ergotamine and other alkaloids, used medicinally. ➤➤ **ergotic** /uh'gotik/ *adj*. [French *ergot*, literally 'cock's spur'; because grain affected by ergot resembles a claw]

ergotamine /uh'gotəmeen/ *noun* a drug obtained from ergot that is used in treating migraine.

ergotism /'uhgətiz(ə)m/ *noun* an abnormal condition produced by eating grain or grain products of cereals infected with ergot fungus and characterized by convulsions and gangrene of the fingers and toes.

erica /'erikə/ *noun* any of a large genus of low evergreen shrubs with many branches, including several species of heather and the heath family: genus *Erica*. [via Latin from Greek *ereikē* heather]

ericaceous /eri'kayshəs/ *adj* **1** of or being a member of the family that includes the heaths, heathers, and rhododendrons. **2** said of compost: suitable for plants that will not grow in limy soil, e.g. heathers and rhododendrons.

erigeron /i'rijərən, i'rig-/ *noun* any of a widely distributed genus of plants of the daisy family with flower heads that resemble asters: genus *Erigeron*. [via Latin from Greek *ērigerōn* groundsel, from *ēri* early | *gerōn* old man, from the hoary down of some species]

Erin /'erin/ *noun* archaic or literary Ireland. [Old Irish *Érinn*, dative of *Ériu* Ireland]

Erinys /i'rinis/ *noun* (*pl* **Erinyes** /-neez/) (*usu in pl*) = FURY (3A). [Greek *Erinys*]

eristic¹ /e'ristik/ *adj* formal employing subtle and usu specious argument. **>> eristically** *adv*. [Greek *eristikos* fond of wrangling, from *erizein* to wrangle, from *eris* strife]

eristic² *noun* formal **1** the art or practice of logical controversial argument. **2** a person who is skilled in this.

eristical /e'ristikl/ *adj* = ERISTIC¹.

Eritrean /eri'trayən/ *noun* a native or inhabitant of Eritrea, NE Africa. **>> Eritrean** *adj*.

erk /uhk/ *noun* Brit, slang a person holding the lowest rank in the air force or navy. [alteration of *airc*, short for *aircraftman*]

Erlenmeyer flask /'əələnmie-ə/ *noun* a flat-bottomed conical laboratory flask. [named after Emil *Erlenmeyer* d.1909, German chemist]

ERM *abbr* exchange-rate mechanism.

ermine /'uhmin/ *noun* (*pl* **ermines** or collectively **ermine**) **1** a stoat or related weasel that has a white winter coat usu with black on the tail. **2** the winter fur of this animal, used to trim ceremonial robes. **3** a heraldic fur consisting of black spots on a white field. [Middle English from Old French *hermine*, prob from medieval Latin *mus Armenius* Armenian mouse]

erne or **ern** /uhn/ *noun* literary an eagle, esp the white-tailed sea eagle. [Old English *earn*]

Ernie /'uhni/ *noun* in Britain, an electronic device used to draw the prizewinning numbers of Premium Bonds. [acronym from *Electronic random number indicator equipment*]

erode /i'rohd/ *verb trans* **1a** to wear (something) away by the action of water, wind, glacial ice, etc. **b** to eat into (something) slowly and destructively. **c** to diminish or destroy (something) by degrees: *He's been eroding her confidence*. **2** to produce or form (something) by eroding. **>** *verb intrans* to be eroded. **>> erodible** *adj*. [Latin *erodere* to eat away, from EX-¹ + *rodere* to gnaw]

erogenic /erə'jenik/ *adj* see EROGENOUS.

erogenous /i'rojənəs/ or **erogenic** /erə'jenik/ or **erotogenic** or **erotogenous** *adj* of or producing sexual excitement when stimulated; sensitive to sexual stimulation: *erogenous zones*. [Greek *erōs* love + -GENOUS, -GENIC]

Eros /'iəros, 'eros/ *noun* **1** sexual love. **2** a desire for self-preservation and uninhibited enjoyment that in Freudian theory is one of two primal instincts: compare THANATOS. [named after *Erōs*, Greek god of love, from *erōs* love]

erosion /i'rohzh(ə)n/ *noun* **1** eroding or being eroded. **2** an instance or product of erosion. **>> erosional** *adj*, **erosive** /-siv/ *adj*. [via French from Latin *erosion-, erosio*, from *erodere*: see ERODE]

erot- or **eroto-** *comb. form* forming words, denoting: eroticism: *erotica*; *erotogenic*. [Greek *erōto*, from *erōt-, erōs* love]

erotic /i'rotik/ *adj* **1** of, concerned with, or tending to arouse sexual desire: *erotic art*. **2** strongly affected by sexual desire. **>> erotically** *adv*. [Greek *erōtikos*, from *erōt-, erōs* love]

erotica /i'rotikə/ *pl noun* (*treated as sing. or pl*) literature or art with an erotic theme or quality. [via Latin from Greek *erōtika*, neuter pl of *erōtikos*: see EROTIC]

eroticise /i'rotisiez/ *verb trans* see EROTICIZE.

eroticism /i'rotisiz(ə)m/ or **erotism** /'erətiz(ə)m/ *noun* **1** an erotic theme, quality, or character. **2** sexual arousal or excitement. **3** sexual impulse or desire. **>> eroticist** *noun*.

eroticize or **eroticise** /i'rotisiez/ *verb trans* to give erotic qualities to (something). **>> eroticization** /-'zaysh(ə)n/ *noun*.

erotism /'erətiz(ə)m/ *noun* see EROTICISM.

eroto- *comb. form* see EROT-.

erotogenic /i,rotə'jenik/ *adj* see EROGENOUS.

erotogenous /erə'tojənəs/ *adj* see EROGENOUS.

erotology /erə'toləji/ *noun* the study and description of sexual love, stimulation, and behaviour.

erotomania /i,rotə'mayni-ə/ *noun* **1** excessive sexual desire. **2** a psychiatric condition in which a person groundlessly believes that another person is in love with them. **>> erotomaniac** /-ak/ *noun*.

err /uh/ *verb intrans* **1** to make a mistake; to be incorrect or inaccurate. **2** to do wrong; to sin. **3** to act with bias, esp towards a better or safer course: *I think we should err on the side of caution*. [Middle English *erren* via early French *errer* from Latin *errare* to stray]

errand /'erənd/ *noun* **1** a short trip taken to attend to some business, often for somebody else. **2** the object or purpose of such a trip. [Old English *ærend* message, business]

errant /'erənt/ *adj* **1** formal doing wrong: *her errant husband*. **2** formal going astray: *an errant lamb*. **3** archaic given to travelling, esp in search of adventure. **>> errancy** /-si/ *noun*, **errantly** *adv*, **errantry** /-tri/ *noun*. [Middle English *erraunt* from early French *errant*, (sense 2) present part. of *errer*: see ERR; (sense 3) present part. of *errer* to travel, from medieval Latin *iterare*, from Latin *iter* road, journey]

errata /i'rahtə/ *noun* pl of ERRATUM.

erratic¹ /i'ratik/ *adj* **1** characterized by lack of consistency, regularity, or uniformity; unpredictable. **2** having no fixed course: *an erratic comet*. **>> erratically** *adv*, **erraticism** /-siz(ə)m/ *noun*. [Middle English via French from Latin *erraticus*, from *errare* to stray]

erratic² *noun* a boulder, rock, etc that has been transported from its original resting place, esp by a glacier.

erratum /i'rahtəm/ *noun* (*pl* **errata** /-tə/) **1** an error in a printed work discovered after printing and shown with its correction on a sheet inserted into the publication. **2** (*in pl, but treated as sing. or pl*) a list of such errors and corrections. [Latin *erratum*, neuter past part. of *errare* to stray]

erroneous /i'rohni-əs/ *adj* containing or characterized by error; incorrect: *erroneous assumptions*. **>> erroneously** *adv*, **erroneousness** *noun*. [Middle English from Latin *erroneus*, from *erron-, erro* wanderer, from *errare* to stray]

error /'erə/ *noun* **1a** a mistake or inaccuracy in speech, writing, thought, or action: *a typing error*. **b** the state of being wrong in behaviour or beliefs: *He realized the error of his ways*. **2** the difference between an observed or calculated value and a true value, e.g. in statistics. *** in error** by mistake. **>> error-free** *adj*, **errorless** *adj*. [Middle English *errour* via Old French from Latin *error*, from *errare* to stray]

ersatz /'eəzatz, 'uhsatz/ *adj* being an artificial and inferior substitute or imitation. [German *Ersatz* a substitute]

Erse /uhs/ *noun* the Irish Gaelic language. **>> Erse** *adj*. [Middle English (Scots) *Erisch*, alteration of IRISH¹]

erst /uhst/ *adv* archaic in the past; formerly. [Middle English *erest* earliest, formerly, from Old English *ærest*, superl of *ær* early]

erstwhile¹ /'uhstwiel/ *adj* former; previous: *her erstwhile students*. [archaic *erst* formerly (from Old English *ærest*, superl of *ær* early) + WHILE¹]

erstwhile² *adv* archaic formerly; previously.

erucic acid /i'roohsik/ *noun* a fatty acid found esp in rapeseed oil: formula $C_{22}H_{42}O_2$. [from Latin *eruca* rocket plant]

eruct /i'rukt/ *verb intrans* formal to belch. **>** *verb trans* said esp of a volcano: to pour or throw out (lava, etc). **>> eructation** /eeruk'taysh(ə)n/ *noun*. [Latin *eructare*, from *e-* + *ructare* to belch, from *-ructus*, past part. of *-rugere* to belch]

erudite /'eroodiet/ *adj* possessing or displaying extensive or profound knowledge; learned: *an erudite scholar*. **>> eruditely** *adv*, **erudition** /-'dish(ə)n/ *noun*. [Middle English *erudit* from Latin *eruditus*, past part. of *erudire* to instruct, from EX-¹ + *rudis* rude, ignorant]

erupt /i'rupt/ *verb intrans* **1a** said of a volcano: to release lava, steam, etc suddenly and usu violently. **b** to burst violently from limits or restraint. **c** said of a tooth: to emerge through the gum. **d** to become suddenly active or violent; to explode: *Will terrorism* *erupt again?* **e** to become violently angry: *He erupted when his son said he had crashed the car.* **2a** said of a rash, spot, etc: to appear on the skin. **b** to break out, e.g. in a rash. ➤ *verb trans* to force out or release (something) suddenly or violently. ➤➤ **eruptive** /-tiv/ *adj.* [Latin *eruptus,* past part. of *erumpere* to burst forth, from EX-¹ + *rumpere* to break]

eruption /i'rupsh(ə)n/ *noun* **1** the act of erupting. **2** a product of erupting, e.g. a rash or spot on the skin.

erven /'eəvən/ *noun* pl of ERF.

-ery *or* **-ry** *suffix* forming nouns, denoting: **1** quality or state of having (a specified trait or mode of behaviour): *snobbery; treachery.* **2** art or practice of: *cookery; archery.* **3** place for doing, keeping, producing, or selling (a specified thing): *fishery; bakery.* **4a** collection or body of: *finery; greenery.* **b** class of (specified goods): *ironmongery; confectionery.* **5** state or condition of: *slavery.* **6** *chiefly derog* all that is concerned with or characteristic of: *popery; tomfoolery.* [Middle English *-erie,* from Old French, from *-ier* -ER¹ + *-ie* -Y²]

erysipelas /eri'sipələs/ *noun* a feverish disease with intense deep red local inflammation of the skin, caused by infection by a streptococcal bacterium. [Middle English *erisipila* via Latin from Greek *erysipelas* red skin]

erythema /eri'theemə/ *noun* abnormal redness of the skin, usu occurring in patches, caused by widening of the blood vessels, e.g. after injury. ➤➤ **erythematous** /-təs/ *adj.* [via Latin from Greek *erythēma,* from *erythainein* to redden, from *erythros* red]

erythr- *or* **erythro-** *comb. form* forming words, with the meanings: **1** red: *erythrocyte.* **2** erythrocyte: *erythrocytic.* [Greek *erythr-,* from *erythros* red]

erythroblast /i'rithrohblast/ *noun* a bone-marrow cell that gives rise to a red blood cell. ➤➤ **erythroblastic** /-'blastik/ *adj.*

erythroblastosis /i,rithrohbla'stohsis/ *noun* (*pl* **erythroblastoses** /-seez/) the abnormal presence of erythroblasts in the circulating blood.

erythrocyte /i'rithrəsiet/ *noun* = RED BLOOD CELL. ➤➤ **erythrocytic** /-'sitik/ *adj.*

erythromycin /i,rithrə'miesin/ *noun* an antibiotic that is produced by a bacterium and is effective against many types of bacteria and some protozoans (single-celled organisms; see PROTOZOAN). [Latin *Streptomyces erythreus,* name of the bacterium that produces it]

erythropoiesis /i,rithrohpoy'eesis/ *noun* the formation of red blood cells. ➤➤ **erythropoietic** /-'etik/ *adj.* [ERYTHR- + Greek *poiēsis* creation]

erythropoietin /i,rithroh'poyitin, -poy'eetin/ *noun* a hormone formed, *esp* in the kidney, in response to reduced oxygen concentration, that stimulates red blood cell formation.

ES *abbr* El Salvador (international vehicle registration).

Es *abbr* the chemical symbol for einsteinium.

-es¹ *suffix* **1** forming the plural of most nouns that end in *s, z, sh, ch,* or a final *y* that changes to *i: glasses; peaches; ladies.* **2** forming the plural of some nouns ending in *o* or in an *f* that changes to *v: tomatoes; loaves.* [Middle English *-es, -s:* see -S¹]

-es² *suffix* forming the third person singular present of most verbs that end in *s, z, sh, ch,* or a final *y* that changes to *i: fizzes; hushes; defies.* [Middle English: see -S²]

ESA *abbr* **1** *Brit* environmentally sensitive area. **2** European Space Agency.

escadrille /'eskədril/ *noun* a small unit of the French air force. [French *escadrille* flotilla, escadrille, from Spanish *escuadrilla,* dimin. of *escuadra* squadron, squad]

escalade /eskə'layd/ *noun* an act of scaling the walls of a fortification with ladders. [French *escalade* from Italian *scalata,* from *scalare* to scale, from late Latin *scala* ladder]

escalate /'eskəlayt/ *verb intrans* **1** to increase in extent, scope, intensity, or seriousness: *The matter has escalated into something like a major scandal — Sunday Times magazine.* **2** to increase in amount or number, usu rapidly: *escalating prices.* ➤ *verb trans* to cause (something) to escalate. ➤➤ **escalation** /-'laysh(ə)n/ *noun.* [back-formation from ESCALATOR]

escalator *noun* a power-driven set of stairs on an endless belt that ascend or descend continuously. [orig a US trademark; blend of ESCALADE + ELEVATOR]

escalator clause *noun* a clause in a contract providing for a proportional upward or downward adjustment, e.g. of prices or wages.

escallonia /eskə'lohni-ə/ *noun* an evergreen shrub of the saxifrage family, grown as a garden ornamental: genus *Escallonia.* [named after *Escallon,* 18th-cent. Spanish traveller who discovered the plants]

escallop¹ /e'skoləp, e'skaləp/ *noun* = SCALLOP¹.

escallop² *verb trans* (**escalloped, escalloping**) = SCALLOP².

escalope /'eskəlop/ *noun* a thin boneless slice of meat, *esp* a slice of veal or pork beaten flat, coated with egg and breadcrumbs, and fried. [French *escalope,* from early French, shell, of Germanic origin]

escapade /'eskəpayd/ *noun* a wild, reckless, and often mischievous adventure, *esp* one that flouts rules or conventions. [French *escapade* from Old Italian *scappata,* from *scappare* to escape, from late Latin EX-¹ + *cappa* cloak]

escape¹ /i'skayp/ *verb intrans* **1a** to get away, *esp* from confinement or restraint: *They escaped from the burning building; He's trying to escape from reality.* **b** said of gases, liquids, etc: to leak out gradually; to seep. **c** said of a plant: to run wild from cultivation. **2** to avoid threatening evil, danger, etc. ➤ *verb trans* **1** to get or stay out of the way of (something or somebody); to avoid (them): *I narrowly escaped death.* **2** to fail to be noticed or recalled by (somebody): *His name escapes me.* **3** to be produced or uttered by (somebody), usu involuntarily: *A cry escaped her lips.* ➤➤ **escapable** *adj,* **escapee** /iskay'pee/ *noun,* **escaper** *noun.* [Middle English *escapen* from Old French *eschaper,* from EX-¹ + late Latin *cappa* head covering, cloak]

escape² *noun* **1** the act or an instance of escaping. **2a** a means of escape. **b** (*used before a noun*) providing a means of escape, release, or avoidance: *an escape hatch; an escape clause.* **3** a key on a computer keyboard that is used e.g. to terminate or interrupt an operation. **4** a cultivated plant run wild.

escape key *noun* = ESCAPE² (3).

escapement *noun* **1** a device in a watch or clock that controls the motion of the cogwheels and through which the energy of the power source is delivered to the regulatory mechanism. **2** a ratchet device, e.g. the spacing mechanism of a typewriter, that permits motion in one direction only in equal steps. **3** a space left between the hammer and the strings of a piano that allows the strings to vibrate.

escape road *noun* a slip road for drivers who are unable to stop or turn safely, e.g. on a steep downward slope.

escape valve *noun* a valve that releases air or steam when it reaches a particular pressure.

escape velocity *noun* the minimum velocity that a moving body, e.g. a rocket, must have to escape from the gravitational field of the earth or of a celestial body.

escape wheel *noun* a notched wheel in the escapement of a watch or clock.

escapism *noun* diversion of the mind to purely imaginative activity or entertainment as an escape from reality or routine. ➤➤ **escapist** *adj and noun.*

escapology /eskə'poləji/ *noun* the art or practice of escaping from confinement or restraint, *esp* as a theatrical performance. ➤➤ **escapologist** *noun.*

escargot /e'skahgoh (*French* ɛskargo)/ *noun* (*pl* **escargots** /e'skahgohz (*French* ɛskargo)/) an edible snail, *esp* when prepared for eating. [French *escargot* from Old Provençal *escaragol*]

escarp¹ /i'skahp/ *noun* = SCARP¹. [French *escarpe* a scarp, from Italian *scarpa*]

escarp² *verb trans* = SCARP².

escarpment *noun* a long cliff or steep slope separating two comparatively level or more gently sloping surfaces. [French *escarpe* (see ESCARP¹) + -MENT]

-escence *suffix* forming nouns, denoting: **1** process of becoming: *obsolescence.* **2** state or condition of being: *alkalescence; effervescence.* [early French *-escence* from Latin *-escentia,* from *-escent-, -escens* (see -ESCENT) + *-ia* -Y²]

-escent *suffix* forming adjectives, with the meanings: **1** being or beginning to be; slightly: *convalescent; incandescent.* **2** reflecting or emitting light (in a specified way): *fluorescent; opalescent.* **3** having the properties of; resembling: *arborescent.* [early French *-escent* from Latin *-escent-, -escens,* present part. suffix of verbs ending in *-escere*]

eschar /'eskah/ *noun* a scab formed *esp* after a burn. [Middle English *escare*: see SCAR[1]]

eschatology /eskə'toləji/ *noun* a branch of theology or religious belief concerned with the ultimate destiny of the universe or of humankind, *esp* the Christian doctrine concerning death, judgment, heaven, and hell. ➤➤ **eschatological** /ˌeskətə'lojikl/ *adj*, **eschatologist** *noun*. [Greek *eschatos* last, farthest + -LOGY]

escheat[1] /is'cheet/ *noun* **1** the reversion of property to a government or sovereign as a result of the owner's dying without having made a will and without heirs. **2** property that has reverted in this way. [Middle English from Old French *eschete* reversion of property, from *escheoir* to fall, devolve, from EX-[1] + Latin *cadere* to fall]

escheat[2] *verb intrans* to revert by escheat. ➤ *verb trans* to cause (property) to revert by escheat. ➤➤ **escheatable** *adj*.

Escherichia /eshə'riki-ə/ *noun* any of a genus of bacteria found in the intestines of humans and other animals, *esp E. coli*, which can cause serious illness and is used in genetic research. [named after Theodor *Escherich* d.1911, German paediatrician]

eschew /is'chooh/ *verb trans formal* to avoid (something) habitually, *esp* on moral or practical grounds; to shun (it). [Middle English *eschewen* from early French *eschiuver*, of Germanic origin]

eschscholtzia /is'kolshə, esh'shohltzi-ə/ *noun* **1** any of a genus of plants of the poppy family with yellow to red flowers: genus *Eschscholtzia*. **2** = CALIFORNIA POPPY. [named after J von *Eschscholtz* d.1831, German botanist]

escort[1] /'eskawt/ *noun* **1** one or more people, cars, ships, etc accompanying somebody or something to give protection or show courtesy. **2** a person who accompanies another person socially, often in return for a fee. [French *escorte* from Italian *scorta*, from *scorgere* to guide, from EX-[1] + Latin *corrigere*: see CORRECT[1]]

escort[2] /i'skawt/ *verb trans* to accompany (somebody or something) as an escort.

escritoire /eskri'twah/ *noun* a writing table or desk. [early French *escritoire* from medieval Latin *scriptorium* room for scribes, from Latin *scribere* to write]

escrow[1] /'eskroh, e'skroh/ *noun* a deed, money, piece of property, etc deposited with somebody to be delivered by them to a designated person only upon the fulfilment of some condition. ❋ **in escrow** in trust as an escrow. [early French *escroue* scroll, of Germanic origin]

escrow[2] *verb trans chiefly NAmer* to deposit (something) in escrow.

escudo /es'koohdoh/ *noun* (*pl* **escudos**) the former basic monetary unit of Portugal and Cape Verde, divided into 100 centavos (in Portugal replaced by the euro in 2002). [Spanish and Portuguese *escudo* shield, from Latin *scutum*; because early coins bore a shield or coat of arms]

esculent[1] /'eskyoolənt/ *adj formal* edible. [Latin *esculentus*, from *esca* food, from *edere* to eat]

esculent[2] *noun* something that is edible.

escutcheon /i'skuch(ə)n/ *noun* **1** a shield on which a coat of arms is displayed. **2** a protective or ornamental shield or plate, e.g. round a keyhole. ❋ **a blot on one's escutcheon** a stain on one's reputation. ➤➤ **escutcheoned** *adj*. [Middle English *escochon* from early French *escuchon*, from Latin *scutum* shield]

Esd. *abbr* Esdras (books of the Apocrypha).

ESE *abbr* east-southeast.

-ese[1] *suffix* forming adjectives from nouns, with the meaning: of or originating in (a specified place or country): *Japanese*; *Viennese*. [Portuguese *-ês* and Italian *-ese*, from Latin *-ensis*]

-ese[2] *suffix* (*pl* **-ese**) forming nouns from nouns, denoting: **1** inhabitant of: *Chinese*. **2a** language of: *Portuguese*; *Cantonese*. **b** *chiefly derog* speech, literary style, or diction peculiar to (the place, person, or group specified): *journalese*; *officialese*.

e-shopping *noun* the purchasing of goods and services via the Internet. [short for *electronic shopping*]

esker *or* **eskar** /'eskə/ *noun* a long narrow ridge of sand and gravel deposited by a stream flowing beneath a retreating glacier or ice sheet. [Irish Gaelic *eiscir* ridge]

Eskimo /'eskimoh/ *noun* (*pl* **Eskimos** *or collectively* **Eskimo**) **1** a member of any of a group of indigenous peoples of N Canada, Greenland, Alaska, and E Siberia. **2** either of the two main languages of these peoples, Inuit and Yupik. ➤➤ **Eskimoan** /-'moh-ən/

adj. [Danish *Eskimo* and French *Esquimau*, of Algonquian origin; related to Cree *askimowew* he eats it raw]

Usage note
Eskimo *or* Inuit? See note at INUIT.

Eskimo dog *noun* = HUSKY[4].

Eskimo roll *noun* a manoeuvre to right a capsized canoe without leaving it.

Esky /'eski/ *noun* (*pl* **Eskies**) *Aus, trademark* a portable insulated container used to keep food and drink cool, e.g. on a picnic. [prob a shortening of ESKIMO]

ESL *abbr* English as a second language.

ESN *abbr* **1** *dated* educationally subnormal. **2** electronic serial number.

esophag- *or* **esophago-** *comb. form NAmer* see OESOPHAG-.

esoteric /eesə'terik, es-/ *adj* **1** designed for, understood by, or restricted to a small group, *esp* of the specially initiated: compare EXOTERIC: *Theoretical linguistics is a rather esoteric subject* — John Lyons. **2** hard to understand. **3** private or confidential: *an esoteric purpose*. ➤➤ **esoterically** *adv*, **esotericism** /-slz(ə)m/ *noun*. [vla Latin from Greek *esōterikos*, from *esōterō* inner, ultimately from *en* in]

ESP *abbr* extrasensory perception.

esp. *abbr* especially.

espadrille /espə'dril/ *noun* a flat sandal that has a canvas upper and a rope sole and is sometimes tied round the ankle or leg with laces. [French *espadrille* from Provençal *espardillo*, from *espart* esparto (from which they were originally made), from Latin *spartum*: see ESPARTO]

espalier[1] /i'spaliay/ *noun* **1** a fruit tree or ornamental shrub trained to grow flat against a railing, trellis, wall, etc. **2** a support on which such plants grow. [French *espalier* via Italian *spalla* shoulder, from late Latin *spatula* shoulder blade: see SPATULA]

espalier[2] *verb trans* (**espaliered**, **espaliering**) to train (a tree or shrub) to grow flat against a railing, trellis, wall, etc.

esparto /i'spahtoh/ *noun* either of two Spanish and Algerian grasses used *esp* to make rope, shoes, and paper: *Stipa tenacissima* or *Lygeum spartum*. [Spanish *esparto* via Latin *spartum* from Greek *sparton* rope]

especial /i'spesh(ə)l/ *adj* **1** distinctively or particularly special. **2** unusually great or significant. **3** distinctly personal: *his especial friend*. [Middle English from early French: see SPECIAL[1]]

especially *adv* **1** in particular: *He hates driving, especially in the dark*. **2** very much: *not especially disappointed*.

Usage note
especially *or* specially? There is some overlap in the meaning of these two words, but there are also areas in which their meanings should be distinguished. *Especially* means both 'very' (*an especially nice surprise*) and 'in particular' (*I was impressed with all the performances, especially Nigel's*). *Specially* means 'in a special way' (*specially cooked using a totally new method*) and, more commonly, 'specifically, for a particular purpose' (*specially trained staff; I specially arranged it so that you would be in the same group as Jean*). In a sentence such as the following, however, either *especially* or *specially* could be used: *I made it especially (or specially) for you*.

Esperanto /espə'rantoh/ *noun* an artificial international language largely based on words common to the chief European languages. ➤➤ **Esperantist** *noun and adj*. [Dr *Esperanto* (from Latin *sperare* to hope), pseudonym of its inventor, Ludwik L Zamenhof d.1917, Polish oculist]

espial /i'spie-əl/ *noun archaic* the act or an instance of espying, observing, or being seen.

espionage /'espi-ənahzh/ *noun* spying or the use of spies to obtain information: *industrial espionage*. [French *espionnage*, from *espionner* to spy, from *espion* spy, from Old Italian *spione*, ultimately of Germanic origin]

esplanade /esplə'nayd, -nahd/ *noun* **1** a level open stretch of paved or grassy ground, *esp* one designed for walking or driving along a shore. **2** an area of clear ground in front of a castle or other fortification. [French *esplanade* from Italian *spianata*, from *spianare* to level, from Latin *explanare*: see EXPLAIN]

espousal /i'spowzl/ *noun* **1** the adoption or support of a cause or belief. **2** *archaic, formal* (*also in pl, but treated as sing.*) a betrothal or marriage.

espouse /i'spowz/ *verb trans* **1** to take up and support (a cause, belief, etc): *For friendship makes us warmly espouse the interest of* *others* — Henry Fielding. **2** *archaic or formal* to marry (somebody): *You shall see what sort of a being I was cheated into espousing* — Charlotte Brontë. ➤➤ **espouser** *noun.* [Middle English *espousen* via Old French from Latin *sponsus*, past part. of *spondēre* to promise, betroth]

espressivo /espre'seevoh/ *adj and adv* said of a musical passage: to be performed with expressive feeling. [Italian *espressivo* from Latin *expressus*: see EXPRESS[1]]

espresso /i'spresoh/ *noun* **1** coffee brewed by forcing steam through finely ground coffee beans. **2** a cup of espresso. **3** an apparatus for making espresso. [Italian *caffè espresso* pressed out coffee]

esprit /e'spree/ *noun* vivacious cleverness or wit. [French *esprit* from Latin *spiritus* SPIRIT[1]]

esprit de corps /də 'kaw/ *noun* the spirit of fellowship, loyalty, and common purpose that unites the members of a group; team spirit: *that esprit de corps which leads him to take a pride in the renown of his general* — William Hickling Prescott. [French *esprit de corps* spirit of the body]

espy /i'spie/ *verb trans* (**espies, espied, espying**) *literary* to catch sight of (something or somebody). [Middle English *espien* from Old French *espier*, of Germanic origin]

Esq. *abbr* Esquire.

-esque *suffix* forming adjectives from nouns, with the meaning: in the manner or style of; like: *statuesque; Kafkaesque.* [French *-esque* from Italian *-esco*, of Germanic origin]

Esquimau /'eskimoh/ *noun* (*pl* **Esquimaux** /-moh/ *or collectively* **Esquimau**) *archaic* = ESKIMO.

esquire /i'skwie·ə/ *noun* **1** *Brit* used instead of Mr as a man's courtesy title and usu placed in its abbreviated form after the surname: *J R Smith, Esq.* **2a** formerly, a member of the English gentry ranking below a knight. **b** formerly, a candidate for knighthood serving as attendant to a knight. **c** formerly, a landed proprietor. [Middle English from early French *esquier* squire, from late Latin *scutarius* shield bearer, from Latin *scutum* shield]

ESRC *abbr Brit* Economic and Social Research Council.

-ess *suffix* forming nouns from nouns, with the meaning: female: *actress; lioness.* [Middle English *-esse* via Old French from late Latin *-issa*, from Greek]

Usage note

As part of the movement to eliminate sexism from language and from people's thinking, the use of the feminizing suffix *-ess* (and similar suffixes such as *-ette* and *-trix*) has, since the late 20th cent., come to be seen as inappropriate and patronizing. The 'male' term is treated as a neutral term with no sexual reference. A woman author should therefore be referred to as an *author*, not an *authoress*, a woman editor as an *editor*, not an *editress* or *editrix*, etc. However a few forms are retained. Female titles of nobility such as *countess* or *baroness* are still correct. *Manageress* is acceptable when referring to a woman who runs a shop, but not when referring to a woman company executive. A *priestess* is a woman priest of a pre-Christian religion, not an ordained Christian minister.

essay[1] /'esay/ *noun* **1** a short piece of prose writing on a specific topic. **2** *formal* an effort or attempt, *esp* an initial or tentative one. **3** a test or trial, e.g. of a design of postage stamp. ➤➤ **essayist** *noun*, **essayistic** /-'istik/ *adj.* [early French *essai* from late Latin *exagium* act of weighing, from EX-[1] + *agere* to drive]

essay[2] /e'say/ *verb trans formal* to attempt (something).

essence /'es(ə)ns/ *noun* **1a** the real or ultimate nature of an individual being or thing, *esp* as opposed to its existence or its accidental qualities. **b** the properties or attributes by means of which something can be categorized or identified. **c** somebody or something that embodies the fundamental nature of an idea, characteristic, etc. **2a** an extract, essential oil, etc possessing the special qualities of a plant, drug, etc in concentrated form, or a preparation containing such a substance. **b** an odour or perfume: *She was the very essence of courtesy.* **3** something that exists, *esp* in an abstract form; an entity. ✻ **in essence** basically, briefly, and most importantly. **of the essence** of the utmost importance; essential: *Time was of the essence.* [Middle English via French from Latin *essentia*, from *essent-, essens*, present part. of *esse* to be]

Essene /'eseen, e'seen/ *noun* a member of a monastic brotherhood of Jews in Palestine from the second cent. BC to the second cent. AD. ➤➤ **Essenian** /e'seeni·ən/ *adj*, **Essenic** /e'senik/ *adj.* [Greek *Essēnos*]

essential[1] /i'sensh(ə)l/ *adj* **1** of the utmost importance; necessary: *Previous experience is desirable but not essential.* **2** of or being the

essence of something; fundamental or inherent. **3** derived from or constituting an essence. **4** said of an amino acid or a fatty acid: required for normal health or growth but manufactured in the body in insufficient quantities or not at all and therefore necessary in the diet. **5** said of a disease: arising from an unknown cause; IDIOPATHIC. ➤➤ **essentiality** /-shi'aliti/ *noun*, **essentially** *adv*, **essentialness** *noun.*

essential[2] *noun* something indispensable or fundamental: *the essentials of astronomy.*

essential element *noun* a chemical element that is required for normal health or growth.

essentialism *noun* a philosophical theory that regards the essence of something as more important than its existence: compare EXISTENTIALISM. ➤➤ **essentialist** *adj and noun.*

essential oil *noun* any of various volatile oils that impart characteristic odours to plants and are used *esp* in perfumes and flavourings: compare FIXED OIL.

Essex girl /'esiks/ *noun informal, derog* a stereotype of a young woman from Essex, SE England, as being vulgar, empty-headed, and promiscuous.

Essex man *noun informal, derog* a stereotype of a man from Essex, SE England, as being affluent, vulgar, and right-wing.

EST *abbr* **1** Eastern Standard Time (time zone). **2** electric-shock treatment.

est. *abbr* **1** established. **2** estate. **3** estimate. **4** estimated.

-est[1] *suffix* forming the superlative of adjectives and adverbs of one and sometimes two or more syllables: *nearest; dirtiest.* [Old English *-st, -est, -ost*]

-est[2] *or* **-st** *suffix* forming the archaic second person singular present of verbs (the form used with *thou*): *goest; canst.* [Old English *-est, -ast, -st*]

establish /i'stablish/ *verb trans* **1** to make (something) firm, stable, secure, or permanent; to set (it) on a firm basis. **2a** to bring (something) into existence; to found (it): *They established a republic.* **b** to bring (something) about; to effect (it): *We established contact with the expedition.* **3a** to enact (something): *This law was established in 1878.* **b** to cause (something) to be accepted: *I don't want to establish a precedent.* **4a** to place (somebody, e.g. oneself) in a permanent or firm position: *He established himself as the leader.* **b** to gain full recognition or acceptance for (something or somebody): *She established her reputation as a novelist.* **5** to put (something) beyond doubt; to prove (it): *He's trying to establish his innocence.* **6** to make (a Church or religion) a national institution supported by civil authority. **7** to cause (a plant) to grow and multiply in a place where it was previously absent. ➤➤ **established** *adj*, **establisher** *noun.* [Middle English *establissen* via early French *establir* from Latin *stabilire*, from *stabilis* stable]

establishment *noun* **1** the act of establishing or the state of being established. **2a** a usu large organization or institution. **b** a place of business or residence with its furnishings and staff. **3** (*treated as sing. or pl*). **a** (**the Establishment**) the group of institutions and people, e.g. the government, the established Church, and the armed forces, held to control public life and to support the existing order of society. **b** a controlling group: *the literary establishment.*

establishmentarian[1] /i,stablishmən'teəri·ən/ *adj* of or favouring the social or political establishment or *esp* the established religion. ➤➤ **establishmentarianism** *noun.*

establishmentarian[2] *noun* a supporter or member of the establishment or the established religion.

estaminet /e'staminay (*French* ɛstaminɛ)/ *noun* (*pl* **estaminets** /-nayz (*French* ɛstaminɛ)/) a small café or bar. [French *estaminet* from Walloon *staminé* cowshed]

estate /i'stayt/ *noun* **1** a large landed property, *esp* in the country, usu with a large house on it. **2** *Brit.* **a** a part of an urban area devoted to a particular type of development: *an industrial estate.* **b** a housing estate: *a council estate.* **3** a property or area of land where wine is produced. **4a** the assets and liabilities left by somebody at death. **b** the whole of somebody's real or personal property. **5** a social or political class, e.g. the nobility, the clergy, or the commons (the three estates). **6** *archaic or literary* a state or condition: *men of low estate.* **7** = ESTATE CAR. [Middle English *estat* via Old French from Latin *status*: see STATE[1]]

estate agent *noun* **1** *chiefly Brit* an agent who is involved in the buying and selling of land and property, *esp* houses and flats. **2**

somebody who manages an estate; a steward. ➤ **estate agency** *noun*.

estate car *noun Brit* a large motor car designed to carry passengers and bulky luggage, with a rear door opening onto the luggage compartment and seats that can be folded down to create more space.

estate duty *noun* = DEATH DUTY.

estate of the realm *noun* = ESTATE (5).

esteem[1] /i'steem/ *verb trans* **1** to regard (something or somebody) highly and prize them accordingly. **2** *formal* to consider or deem (something): *I would esteem it a privilege*. [Middle English *estemen* to estimate, via French from Latin *aestimare*]

esteem[2] *noun* favourable regard: *She is held in high esteem*.

ester /'estə/ *noun* a chemical compound formed by the reaction between an acid and an alcohol, usu with elimination of water. [German *Ester*, from *Essigäther* ethyl acetate, from *Essig* vinegar + *Äther* ether]

Esth. *abbr* Esther (book of the Bible).

esthesia /es'theezyə, -zhyə/ *noun NAmer* see AESTHESIA.

esthete /'eestheet/ *noun NAmer* see AESTHETE.

esthetic /ees'thetik/ *adj NAmer* see AESTHETIC.

estheticism /ees'thetisiz(ə)m, es-/ *noun NAmer* see AESTHETICISM.

esthetics /ees'thetiks, es-/ *pl noun NAmer* see AESTHETICS.

estimable /'estiməbl/ *adj* worthy of esteem. ➤ **estimableness** *noun*, **estimably** *adv*.

estimate[1] /'estimayt/ *verb trans* **1a** to judge approximately the value, worth, or significance of (something). **b** to determine roughly the size, extent, or nature of (something). **c** to produce a statement of the approximate cost of (something). **2** to judge or conclude (something): *We estimated that it would not be feasible.* ➤ **estimative** /-mətiv/ *adj*, **estimator** *noun*. [Latin *aestimatus*, past part. of *aestimare* to value, estimate]

estimate[2] /'estimət/ *noun* **1a** a rough or approximate calculation. **b** a statement of the expected cost of a job. **2** an opinion or judgment of the nature, character, or quality of somebody or something. **3** the act or an instance of appraising, valuing, or estimating.

estimation /esti'maysh(ə)n/ *noun* **1a** the act or an instance of estimating. **b** the value, amount, or size arrived at by estimating. **2** = ESTIMATE[2] (2). **3** = ESTEEM[2].

estival /ee'stievl, 'estivl/ *adj NAmer* see AESTIVAL.

estivate /'eestivayt, 'es-/ *verb intrans NAmer* see AESTIVATE.

estivation /eesti'vaysh(ə)n, est-/ *noun NAmer* see AESTIVATION.

Estonian /i'stohni·ən/ *noun* **1** a native or inhabitant of Estonia, on the Baltic sea. **2** the Finno-Ugric language of Estonia. ➤ **Estonian** *adj*.

estop /i'stop/ *verb trans* (**estopped, estopping**) in law, to impede (something), *esp* by estoppel. [Middle English *estoppen* via early French *estouper* from late Latin *stuppare* to stop up, from Latin *stuppa* oakum]

estoppel /i'stop(ə)l/ *noun* the legal principle that precludes people from denying or disproving facts they have previously stated to be true. [prob from early French *estoupail* bung, from *estouper*: see ESTOP]

estovers /e'stohvəz/ *pl noun Brit esp* formerly, wood etc taken for a necessary purpose from somebody else's land, *esp* by a tenant of that land, or the right to take it. [Anglo-French *estovers* necessities, from *estover* to be necessary, from Latin *est opus* it is necessary]

estr- *or* **estro- comb. form NAmer** see OESTR-.

estradiol /eestra'dieol, estra-/ *noun NAmer* see OESTRADIOL.

estrange /i'straynj/ *verb trans* (*often* + from) to arouse enmity or indifference in (somebody) in place of affection; to alienate (them): *Of my country and family I have little to say. Ill usage and length of years have driven me from the one, and estranged me from the other* — Poe; *Their minds, lately estranged, seemed suddenly to have been drawn closer, one to the other* — James Joyce. ➤ **estranged** *adj*, **estrangement** *noun*. [early French *estranger* from medieval Latin *extraneare*, from Latin *extraneus*: see STRANGE]

estriol /'eestriol, 'estriol/ *noun NAmer* see OESTRIOL.

estro- *comb. form* see ESTR-.

estrogen /'estrəjən, 'ee-/ *noun NAmer* see OESTROGEN.

estrone /'eestrohn, 'estrohn/ *noun NAmer* see OESTRONE.

estrus /'estrəs, 'eestrəs/ *noun NAmer* see OESTRUS.

estuary /'estyooəri/ *noun* (*pl* **estuaries**) a sea inlet at the mouth of a river. ➤ **estuarial** /-'eəri·əl/ *adj*, **estuarine** /-rin, -rien/ *adj*. [Latin *aestuarium* from *aestus* boiling, tide]

Estuary English *noun* a variety of British English used in London and neighbouring counties, containing the speech sounds of standard pronunciation modified by those of cockney and other local accents. [named after the Thames *Estuary*, from which it is perceived to have spread]

esu *abbr* electrostatic unit.

esurient /i'syooəri·ənt/ *adj formal* hungry or greedy. ➤ **esuriently** *adv*. [Latin *esurient-, esuriens*, present part. of *esurire* to be hungry, from *edere* to eat]

ET *abbr* **1** Egypt (international vehicle registration). **2** Employment Training. **3** extraterrestrial.

-et *suffix* forming nouns, denoting: **1** small or lesser kind of: *baronet*; *islet*. **2** group of (the number specified): *octet*. [Middle English from Old French *-et* (masc), *-ete* (fem) from late Latin *-itus*, *-ita*]

ETA *abbr* estimated time of arrival.

eta /'eetə/ *noun* the seventh letter of the Greek alphabet (H, η), equivalent to and transliterated as roman ē. [via late Latin from Greek *ēta*, of Semitic origin]

e-tailer /'eetaylə/ *noun* a company that sells its product through the Internet. ➤ **e-tailing** *noun*.

et al /,et 'al/ *adv* and others. [Latin *et alii* (masc), *et aliae* (fem), *et alia* (neuter)]

etalon /'etəlon/ *noun* an instrument used in physics for studying the fine structure of lines in a spectrum that are produced by the multiple reflection of a beam of light between two half-silvered plates a few millimetres apart. [French *étalon* standard of weights and measures, from early French *estalon, estelon*]

etc /it'setrə/ *abbr* et cetera.

et cetera /it'setrə/ *adv* and other things, *esp* of the same kind; and so forth. [Latin *et cetera* and the rest]

etceteras *pl noun* unspecified additional items.

etch /ech/ *verb trans* **1a** to produce (a picture or letters), *esp* on metal or glass, by the corrosive action of an acid. **b** to subject (metal, glass, etc) to such a process. **2** to delineate or imprint (something) clearly: *scenes that are indelibly etched in our minds.* ➤ *verb intrans* to practise etching. ➤ **etcher** *noun*. [Dutch *etsen* from German *ätzen* to feed, from Old High German *azzen* to eat away]

etching *noun* **1** the art of producing pictures or designs by printing from an etched metal plate. **2** an impression from an etched plate.

ETD *abbr* estimated time of departure.

eternal[1] /i'tuhnl/ *adj* **1** having infinite duration; everlasting: *eternal life*. **2** *informal* incessant or interminable: *their eternal arguments*. **3** timeless: *the eternal truths*. ➤ **eternally** *adv*, **eternalness** *noun*. [Middle English via French from Latin *aeternus*]

eternal[2] *noun* **1** (**the Eternal**) God. **2** something eternal.

eternalize *or* **eternalise** *verb trans* **1** to make (something or somebody) eternal. **2** to make (somebody or something) eternally famous. ➤ **eternalization** /-'zaysh(ə)n/ *noun*.

eternal triangle *noun* a situation of conflict resulting from the emotional or sexual involvement of two people with one other person.

eternity /i'tuhniti/ *noun* (*pl* **eternities**) **1** the quality or state of being eternal. **2** infinite time. **3** the eternal life after death. **4** *informal* a seemingly endless or immeasurable time: *We waited an eternity for the train.* [Middle English *eternite* via Old French from Latin *aeternitat-, aeternitas*, from *aeternus* ETERNAL[1]]

eternity ring *noun* a ring set with gemstones all around, usu given as a symbol of continuing or everlasting affection.

Etesian winds /i'teezhi·ən, -zhən/ *pl noun* annually recurring summer winds that blow over the Mediterranean. [via Latin from Greek *etēsios*, from *etos* year]

ETH *abbr* Ethiopia (international vehicle registration).

eth *or* **edh** /edh/ *noun* a letter ð used in Old English and Icelandic to represent either of the sounds /th/ or /dh/: compare THORN (3). [Icelandic *eth* or Danish *edh*]

eth- *or* **etho- comb. form** forming words, denoting: ethyl: *ethene*.

-eth[1] *or* **-th** *suffix* forming the archaic third person singular present of verbs: *goeth*; *doth*. [Old English *-eth, -ath, -th*]

-eth² *suffix* see -TH¹.

ethanal /'ethənəl/ *noun* = ACETALDEHYDE. [ETHANE + ALDEHYDE]

ethane /'eethayn/ *noun* a colourless, odourless gas that is a member of the alkane series of organic chemical compounds, is obtained from petroleum or natural gas, and is used *esp* as a fuel: formula C_2H_6. [ETHYL + -ANE]

ethanediol /'eethayndie·ol, 'eth-/ *noun* = ETHYLENE GLYCOL. [ETHANE + DI-¹ + -OL¹]

ethanoic acid /ethə'noh·ik, ee-/ *noun* the technical term for ACETIC ACID.

ethanol /'ethənol, 'ee-/ *noun* = ALCOHOL (1).

ethene /'etheen/ *noun* = ETHYLENE.

ether /'eethə/ *noun* **1a** an inflammable liquid that vaporizes readily, used *esp* as a solvent and formerly as a general anaesthetic: formula $C_2H_5OC_2H_5$. **b** any of various organic compounds characterized by an oxygen atom attached to two alkyl groups. **2** *literary* the clear blue sky or upper regions of the atmosphere. **3** a medium formerly held to permeate all space and transmit electromagnetic waves, e.g. light and radio waves. ⠀⠀ **etheric** /ee'therik/ *adj.* [Middle English via Latin from Greek *aithēr*, from *aithein* to ignite, blaze]

ethereal /i'thiəri·əl/ *adj* **1** of the regions beyond the earth: *all the angels and ethereal powers* — Milton. **2a** lacking material substance; intangible. **b** marked by unusual delicacy, lightness, and refinement: *so ethereal a creature that her spirit could be seen trembling through her limbs* — Hardy. **3** /ethə'ree-əl/ of, containing, or resembling a chemical ether. **4** *literary* celestial; heavenly. ⠀⠀ **ethereality** /-'aliti/ *noun*, **ethereally** *adv*, **etherealness** *noun*. [via Latin from Greek *aitherios*, from *aithēr*: see ETHER]

etherealize *or* **etherealise** *verb* **1** to make (something) ethereal. **2** to add a chemical ether to (something). ⠀⠀ **etherealization** /-'zaysh(ə)n/ *noun*.

etherize *or* **etherise** *verb trans* to treat or anaesthetize (somebody) with or as if with ether. ⠀⠀ **etherization** /-'zaysh(ə)n/ *noun*, **etherizer** *noun*.

Ethernet /'eethənet/ *noun trademark* a popular type of local area network connecting a number of computer systems.

ethic¹ /'ethik/ *noun* **1** (*in pl, but treated as sing. or pl*) the principles of conduct governing an individual or a group: *professional ethics.* **2a** a set of moral principles or values: *the current materialistic ethic.* **b** (*in pl*) the moral uprightness of an action, judgment, etc: *I'm not sure of the ethics of this decision.* **3** (*in pl, but treated as sing.*) the study of the nature and basis of moral principles and judgments.

⸻ **Editorial note** ⸻
We speak of ethics in two ways, descriptive and normative. The ethics of a group (Western ethics, business ethics) is the broad pattern of social behaviour and shared self-understanding that in fact knits the group together. When we say that an action would not be ethical, however, we mean that it would be wrong, not just that it is at odds with the ethics of some group. The remark 'We don't do things that way' hovers between these two poles — Professor Jonathan Dancy.
⸻

⠀⠀ **ethicist** /-sist/ *noun.* [Middle English *ethik* via French and Latin from Greek *ēthikē*, from *ēthikos*, from *ethos* custom, character]

ethic² *adj* = ETHICAL.

ethical *adj* **1** conforming to accepted, *esp* professional, standards of conduct or morality. **2** relating to ethics. **3** not invested or not investing in companies whose activities or products, e.g. armaments or tobacco, do not conform to the moral principles of the investor: *an ethical investment fund.* **4** said of a drug: available to the general public only on a doctor's or dentist's prescription. ⠀⠀ **ethicality** /-'kaliti/ *noun*, **ethically** *adv*, **ethicalness** *noun.* [Middle English *ethik*, from Latin *ethicus*, from Greek *ēthikos*: see ETHIC¹]

Ethiopian /eethi'ohpi·ən/ *noun* a native or inhabitant of Ethiopia and Eritrea. ⠀⠀ **Ethiopian** *adj.*

Ethiopic /eethi'opik, -'ohpik/ *noun* **1** a Semitic language formerly spoken in Ethiopia and still used there in Christian services of worship. **2** the group of Semitic languages spoken in Ethiopia, including Amharic and Tigré. ⠀⠀ **Ethiopic** *adj.*

ethmoid /'ethmoyd/ *noun* a bone of the walls and SEPTUM (partition) of the nasal cavity. ⠀⠀ **ethmoid** *adj*, **ethmoidal** /eth'moydl/ *adj.* [French *ethmoïde* from Greek *ēthmoeidēs*, literally 'like a strainer', from *ēthmos* strainer]

ethnic¹ /'ethnik/ *adj* **1a** relating to or involving large groups of human beings classed according to common traits, e.g. race, culture, or language: *ethnic tension; ethnic groups.* **b** belonging to such a group by birth or descent: *ethnic Albanians living in Serbia.* **2** of a traditional, *esp* peasant or non-Western, culture: *ethnic restaurants.* ⠀⠀ **ethnically** *adv*, **ethnicity** /eth'nisiti/ *noun.* [Middle English via late Latin from Greek *ethnikos* national, gentile, from *ethnos* nation]

ethnic² *noun chiefly NAmer* a member of an ethnic minority.

ethnical *adj* = ETHNIC¹.

ethnic cleansing *noun* the systematic and often violent removal of all members of a particular ethnic group from a region or country, usu by killing, expulsion, or intimidation.

ethnic minority *noun* an ethnic group that constitutes a minority of the population of a country or region.

ethno- *comb. form* forming words, denoting: race; people; cultural group: *ethnocentric.* [via French from Greek *ethno-, ethn-*, from *ethnos* nation]

ethnocentric /ethnoh'sentrik/ *adj* **1** characterized by or based on the attitude that one's own race, culture, etc is superior. **2** having race as a central interest. ⠀⠀ **ethnocentrically** *adv*, **ethnocentricity** /-'trisiti/ *noun*, **ethnocentrism** *noun.*

ethnography /eth'nografi/ *noun* the scientific description of races, peoples, cultures, etc; descriptive anthropology. ⠀⠀ **ethnographer** *noun*, **ethnographic** /ethnoh'grafik/ *adj*, **ethnographical** /ethnoh'grafikl/ *adj*, **ethnographically** /ethnoh'grafikli/ *adv.* [French *ethnographie*, from ETHNO- + -*graphie* -GRAPHY]

ethnology /eth'noləji/ *noun* **1** a science that deals with races and peoples and their origin, distribution, relations, and characteristics. **2** = CULTURAL ANTHROPOLOGY. ⠀⠀ **ethnologic** /-'lojik/ *adj*, **ethnological** /-'lojikl/ *adj*, **ethnologically** /-'lojikli/ *adv*, **ethnologist** *noun.*

ethnomusicology /,ethnoh,myoohzi'koləji/ *noun* the study of the music of different, *esp* non-European, cultures. ⠀⠀ **ethnomusicological** /-'lojikl/ *adj*, **ethnomusicologist** *noun.*

etho- *comb. form* see ETH-.

ethology /i'tholəji/ *noun* **1** the study of the formation and evolution of human customs and beliefs. **2** the scientific study of animal behaviour. ⠀⠀ **ethological** /ethə'lojikl/ *adj*, **ethologist** *noun.* [Latin *ethologia* art of depicting character, from Greek *ēthologia*, from *ēthos* custom, character + -*logia* -LOGY]

ethos /'eethos/ *noun* the distinguishing character or guiding beliefs of a person, institution, etc. [via Latin from Greek *ēthos* custom, character]

ethyl /'ethil, 'eethil, 'ethiel, 'eethiel/ *noun* a chemical group derived from ethane: formula CH_3CH_2. [ETHER + -YL]

ethyl acetate *noun* a colourless fragrant inflammable liquid that vaporizes readily and is used *esp* as a solvent and in flavourings: formula $CH_3COOC_2H_5$.

ethyl alcohol *noun* = ALCOHOL (1).

ethylene /'ethileen/ *noun* a colourless inflammable gas found in coal gas and used *esp* in the synthesis of organic chemical compounds: formula $H_2C=CH_2$. Also called ETHENE. ⠀⠀ **ethylenic** /-'lenik/ *adj.*

ethylene glycol *noun* a thick liquid alcohol used *esp* as an antifreeze: formula $C_2H_4(OH)_2$. Also called ETHANEDIOL.

ethyl ether *noun* = ETHER (1A).

ethyne /'eethien, 'ethien/ *noun* = ACETYLENE.

-etic *suffix* **1** = -IC¹: *ascetic.* **2** forming adjectives from nouns ending in -*esis*: *genetic; synthetic.* [via Latin from Greek -*etikos, -ētikos*, from -*etos, -ētos*]

etiolate /'eeti·əlayt/ *verb trans* **1** to bleach and alter the natural development of (a green plant) by excluding sunlight. **2** to make (something or somebody) weak, pale, or sickly. ⠀⠀ **etiolation** /-'laysh(ə)n/ *noun.* [French *étioler* from early French *étieuler* to turn to stubble, from *éteule* stubble, from Latin *stipula* straw]

etiology /eeti'oləji/ *noun NAmer* see AETIOLOGY.

etiquette /'etiket/ *noun* the conventionally accepted standards of proper social or professional behaviour: *medical etiquette.* [French *étiquette*, literally 'ticket', from early French *estiquet*: see TICKET¹; perhaps because rules for behaviour in particular circumstances were sometimes written on cards to be given out]

Eton collar /'eetn/ *noun* a large stiff white collar turned over the edge of a jacket. [named after *Eton* College, public school in England, which has such a collar as part of its uniform]

Eton crop *noun* a very short haircut for women, popular *esp* in the 1920s.

Etonian[1] /i'tohni-ən/ *noun* a pupil of Eton College.

Etonian[2] *adj* of Eton College.

Eton jacket *noun* a waist-length black jacket that is V-shaped at the back and open in front, formerly worn by boys at Eton College.

etrier /'aytriay (*French* etrje)/ *noun* a short rope ladder used in mountaineering, potholing, etc. [French *étrier* stirrup]

Etrurian /i'trooəri-ən/ *noun* = ETRUSCAN.

Etruscan /i'truskən/ *noun* **1** a native or inhabitant of ancient Etruria. **2** the language used by the Etruscans. ⏵⏵ **Etruscan** *adj*. [Latin *Etruscus* of Etruria, ancient country of Italy]

et seq. /ˌet 'sek/ *adv* **1** and the following one. **2** (*also* **et seqq.**) and the following ones. [(sense 1) Latin *et sequens* (masc & fem sing.), (sense 2) *et sequentes* (masc & fem pl), or *et sequentia* (neuter pl)]

-ette *suffix* forming nouns from nouns, with the meanings: **1** small or lesser kind of: *kitchenette; cigarette*. **2** female: *suffragette; usherette*. **3** imitation; substitute: *leatherette; flannelette*. [Middle English, from early French, fem dimin. suffix, from Old French -*ete*: see -ET]

étude /ay'toohd/ *noun* a piece of music written primarily for the practice of a technique. [French *étude* study, from early French *estude, estudie*: see STUDY[1]]

etui /e'twee/ *noun* (*pl* **etuis**) *dated* a small ornamental case, *esp* for needles. [French *étui* from Old French *estuier* to shut up, keep, preserve; related to TWEEZERS]

etyma /'etimə/ *noun* pl of ETYMON.

etymologize *or* **etymologise** /eti'moləjiez/ *verb trans* to discover or give an etymology for (a word or other linguistic form). ⏵ *verb intrans* to study or formulate etymologies.

etymology /eti'moləji/ *noun* (*pl* **etymologies**) **1** the history of the origin and development of a word or other linguistic form. **2** a branch of language study dealing with etymologies. ⏵⏵ **etymological** /-'lojikl/ *adj*, **etymologically** /-'lojikli/ *adv*, **etymologist** *noun*. [Middle English *ethimologie* via Latin from Greek *etymologia*, from *etymon* (see ETYMON) + -*logia* -LOGY]

etymon /'etimon/ *noun* (*pl* **etyma** /-mə/ *or* **etymons**) an earlier linguistic form from which later forms or words are derived. [via Latin from Greek *etymon* literal meaning of a word according to its origin, from *etymos* true]

EU *abbr* European Union.

Eu *abbr* the chemical symbol for europium.

eu- *comb. form* forming words, with the meanings: **1a** well; easily: *euphonious*. **b** good: *eupepsia*. **2** true: *euchromatin*. [Middle English via Latin from Greek *eu-*, from *ey, eu*, neuter of *eys* good]

eucalypt /'yoohkəlipt/ *noun* = EUCALYPTUS.

eucalyptus /yoohkə'liptəs/ *noun* (*pl* **eucalyptuses** *or* **eucalypti** /-tie/) **1** any of a genus of Australasian evergreen trees of the myrtle family that are widely cultivated for their gum, resin, oil, and wood: genus *Eucalyptus*. **2** oil from the leaves of a eucalyptus tree, used medicinally. [Latin genus name, from EU- + Greek *kalyptos* covered, from *kalyptein* to conceal; from the conical covering of the buds]

eucaryote /yooh'karioht/ *noun* see EUKARYOTE.

Eucharist /'yoohkərist/ *noun* **1** the Christian sacrament in which consecrated bread and wine are consumed in accordance with Christ's injunctions at the Last Supper. **2** the consecrated bread and wine consumed in the Eucharist. ⏵⏵ **Eucharistic** /-'ristik/ *adj*, **Eucharistical** /-'ristikl/ *adj*. [Middle English *eukarist* via Old French and late Latin from Greek *eucharistia* Eucharist, gratitude, from *eucharistos* grateful, from EU- + *charizesthai* to show favour or gratitude, from *charis* favour, grace, gratitude]

euchre[1] /'yoohkə/ *noun* a N American card game for two to four players, played with the 32 highest cards, the winner taking at least three out of five tricks. [German dialect *Juckerspiel*]

euchre[2] *verb trans* **1** to prevent (somebody) from winning three tricks in euchre. **2** *NAmer, informal* to cheat, trick, or outwit (somebody).

euchromatin /yooh'krohmətin/ *noun* the major portion of the chromosomes (threadlike genetic material in a cell; see CHROMO-SOME) that contains the active genes. ⏵⏵ **euchromatic** /-'matik/ *adj*. [German *Euchromatin*, from EU- + CHROMATIN]

Euclidean /yooh'klidi-ən/ *adj* (*also* **euclidean**) of the Greek mathematician Euclid (fl.300 BC), his geometry, or the three-dimensional space in which his geometry applies.

eucryphia /yooh'krifi-ə/ *noun* an evergreen shrub or small tree of Australia and S America with large white flowers and dark glossy leaves: genus *Eucryphia*. [Latin genus name, from EU- + Greek *kryphios* covered; because of its joined sepals]

eudemonism *or* **eudaemonism** /yooh'deeməniz(ə)m/ *noun* the philosophical doctrine that the basis of moral and rational action should be its capacity to bring about personal well-being and happiness. ⏵⏵ **eudemonist** *noun*, **eudemonistic** /-'nistik/ *adj*. [Greek *eudaimonia* happiness, from *eudaimōn* happy, from EU- + *daimōn* spirit]

eudiometer /yoohdi'omitə/ *noun* a graduated glass tube used for the analysis and measurement of volumes of gases during chemical reactions. ⏵⏵ **eudiometric** /-'metrik/ *adj*, **eudiometrically** /-'metrikli/ *adv*.

Word history

Italian *eudiometro*, from Greek *eudia* fair weather (from EU- + -*dia* weather) + Italian -*metro* -meter, from Greek *metron* measure. The term was orig applied to an instrument used to measure oxygen, thought to be present in greater amounts in fair weather.

eugenics /yooh'jeniks/ *pl noun* (*treated as sing. or pl*) a science dealing with the improvement of the hereditary qualities of a race or breed, e.g. by control of mating or by careful selection of parents: *Eugenics was a socialist passion before it was a Nazi crime* — Daily Telegraph.

Editorial note

Eugenics is a technique that aims at the improvement of biological and mental standards of human species by the control of heredity, not unlike breeders trying to obtain desirable qualities in animals by artificial selection. The idea of human eugenics was suggested inter alia by Plato, by Campanella in the 17th cent., by Galton in the 19th. Eugenics was discredited as a result of its use by the Nazi regime: slaughtering supposed misfits and 'inferior races'. Whether a voluntary but scientifically organized selection would give better results than the spontaneous one is debatable — Professor Leszek Kołakowski.

⏵⏵ **eugenic** *adj*, **eugenically** *adv*, **eugenicist** /-sist/ *noun*. [Greek *eugenēs* wellborn, from EU- + -*genēs* born]

euglena /yooh'gleenə/ *noun* a green freshwater single-celled organism that manufactures food by photosynthesis and moves by means of a long FLAGELLUM (whiplike appendage): genus *Euglena*. ⏵⏵ **euglenoid** /-noyd/ *adj and noun*. [Latin genus name, from EU- + Greek *glēnē* eyeball, socket of a joint]

eukaryote *or* **eucaryote** /yooh'karioht/ *noun* any of a large group of organisms, characterized by possessing cells having a nucleus, that includes most living things except some minute forms, *esp* bacteria: compare PROKARYOTE. ⏵⏵ **eukaryotic** /-'otik/ *adj*. [EU- + KARY- + -*ote* as in ZYGOTE]

eulogize *or* **eulogise** /'yoohləjiez/ *verb trans* to praise (something or somebody) highly in speech or writing; to extol (them). ⏵⏵ **eulogizer** *noun*.

eulogy /'yoohləji/ *noun* (*pl* **eulogies**) **1** a speech or piece of writing in praise of somebody or something. **2** high praise. ⏵⏵ **eulogist** *noun*, **eulogistic** /-'jistik/ *adj*, **eulogistically** /-'jistikli/ *adv*. [Middle English *euloge* via medieval Latin from Greek *eulogia* praise, from EU- + -*logia* -LOGY]

Eumenides /yooh'menideez/ *pl noun* a group of avenging Greek goddesses; the Furies. [via Latin from Greek *eumenides*, literally 'the well-disposed ones', a euphemistic term used to avoid incurring their wrath]

eunuch /'yoohnək/ *noun* **1** formerly, a castrated man employed as a guard in a harem or as a chamberlain in a palace: *Critics are like eunuchs … They see how it should be done … but they can't do it themselves* — Brendan Behan. **2** a man or boy deprived of the testes or external genitals. **3** *informal* a man lacking effectiveness or vitality. [Middle English *eunuk* via Latin from Greek *eunouchos* bedroom guard, from *eunē* bed + *echein* to have, have charge of]

euonymus /yooh'oniməs/ *noun* any of a genus of evergreen shrubs, small trees, and climbing plants of the spindle tree family typically having red fruits and hard wood: genus *Euonymus*. [Latin genus name, from Greek *euōnymos* spindle tree, from *euōnymos* having an auspicious name, from EU- + *onyma* name]

eupepsia /yooh'pepsi·ə/ *noun formal* **1** good digestion. **2** happiness or optimism. **⟫⟫ eupeptic** /-tik/ *adj*. [EU- + *-pepsia* as in DYSPEPSIA]

euphemise /'yoohfəmiez/ *verb* see EUPHEMIZE.

euphemism /'yoohfəmiz(ə)m/ *noun* **1** a mild, indirect, or vague expression substituted for an offensive or unpleasant one, e.g. *pass away* for *die*. **2** the substitution of such expressions to avoid offence or embarrassment.

Editorial note
Euphemism is the vehicle of language's great escape, rendering the supposedly unpalatable fit for mass consumption. As creative in its efforts to avoid the unacceptable as it is innately deceitful, euphemism can be found across the linguistic spectrum, whether in the rhetorical flourishes of poetic invention or as the underpinning of much sexual and anatomical slang — Jonathon Green.

⟫⟫ euphemistic /-'mistik/ *adj*, **euphemistically** /-'mistikli/ *adv*. [Greek *euphēmismos* from *euphēmos* auspicious, sounding good, from EU- + *phēmē* speech, from *phanai* to say, speak]

euphemize *or* **euphemise** /'yoohfəmiez/ *verb intrans* to use a euphemism or euphemisms. **⟫** *verb trans* to express (something) by euphemisms. **⟫⟫ euphemizer** *noun*.

euphonious /yooh'fohni·əs/ *adj* pleasing to the ear. **⟫⟫ euphoniously** *adv*.

euphonise /'yoohfəniez/ *verb trans* see EUPHONIZE.

euphonium /yooh'fohni·əm/ *noun* a brass musical instrument resembling a tuba but smaller and having a higher range. [Greek *euphōnos* (see EUPHONY) + *-ium* as in HARMONIUM]

euphonize *or* **euphonise** /'yoohfəniez/ *verb trans* **1** to make (something) pleasing to the ear. **2** to alter (a speech sound) for ease of pronunciation.

euphony /'yoohfəni/ *noun* (*pl* **euphonies**) **1** a pleasing or sweet sound, *esp* in speech. **2** the alteration of speech sounds for ease of pronunciation. **⟫⟫ euphonic** /-'fonik/ *adj*, **euphonically** /-'fonikli/ *adv*. [French *euphonie* via late Latin from Greek *euphōnia*, from *euphōnos* sweet-voiced, musical, from EU- + *phōnē* voice]

euphorbia /yooh'fawbiə/ *noun* any of a genus of plants, including the spurges, that have a milky juice and usu green flowers: genus *Euphorbia*. [alteration of Latin *euphorbea*, named after *Euphorbus* first-cent. AD Greek physician, who is said to have discovered it]

euphoria /yooh'fawri·ə/ *noun* an intense or exaggerated feeling of well-being or elation: compare DYSPHORIA. **⟫⟫ euphoric** /yooh'-forik/ *adj*, **euphorically** /yooh'forikli/ *adv*.

Word history
via Latin from Greek *euphoria*, from *euphoros* healthy, from EU- + *pherein* to bear. Orig meaning a false feeling of well-being in a sick person.

euphoriant¹ /yooh'fawri·ənt/ *adj* said of a drug, etc: producing euphoria.

euphoriant² *noun* a euphoriant drug.

euphrasia /yooh'frayzi·ə/ *noun* (*pl* **euphrasias**) = EYEBRIGHT. [via Latin from Greek *euphrasia*, literally 'cheerfulness']

euphrasy /'yoohfrəsi/ *noun* (*pl* **euphrasies**) = EUPHRASIA.

euphuism /'yoohfyooh·iz(ə)m/ *noun* an artificial and ornate style of writing or speaking: *As soon as men begin to write on nature, they fall into euphuism* — Ralph Waldo Emerson. **⟫⟫ euphuist** *noun*, **euphuistic** /-'istik/ *adj*, **euphuistically** /-'istikli/ *adv*. [named after *Euphues*, character who used such a style in prose romances by John Lyly d.1606, English writer]

Eur- *or* **Euro-** *comb. form* forming words, with the meanings: **1** European: *Eurocommunism*. **2** European and: *Eurasian*. **3** European Union: *Eurocrat*.

Eurasian¹ /yoo'rayzh(ə)n/ *adj* **1** of mixed European and Asian origin. **2** of, growing in, or living in Europe and Asia.

Eurasian² *noun* a person of mixed European and Asian origin.

Euratom /yoo'ratom/ *abbr* European Atomic Energy Community.

eureka /yoo'reekə/ *interj* used to express triumph at a discovery.

Word history
Greek *heurēka* I have found, from *heuriskein* to find. The exclamation is attributed to Archimedes d.212 BC, Greek mathematician and inventor, on finding a method for determining the purity of gold.

eurhythmic (*NAmer* **eurythmic**) /yoo'ridhmik/ *adj* **1** harmonious. **2** of eurhythmics.

eurhythmics (*NAmer* **eurythmics**) *pl noun* (*treated as sing. or pl*) the art of harmonious bodily movement, *esp* through expressive timed movements in response to music. [German *Eurhythmie* via Latin from Greek *eurhythmia* rhythmical movement, from EU- + *rhythmos*: see RHYTHM]

eurhythmy /yoo'ridhmi/ *noun* = EURHYTHMICS.

Euro- *comb. form* see EUR-.

euro *noun* (*pl* **euros**) the single European currency used by some member countries of the European Union: compare ECU. [shortening of EUROPEAN¹]

Eurobond /'yooərohbond/ *noun* (*also* **eurobond**) a bond sold outside the country in whose currency it is issued.

euro-cent *noun* a unit of currency used by some member countries of the European Union, worth 100th of a euro.

Eurocentric /yooəroh'sentrik/ *adj* concentrating on European issues, *esp* to the exclusion of those involving the rest of the world.

Eurocheque /'yooərohchek/ *noun* a type of personal cheque that is accepted by banks in most European countries.

Eurocommunism /yooəroh'komyooniz(ə)m/ *noun* the form of Communism advocated by Communist parties of W Europe. **⟫⟫ Eurocommunist** *adj and noun*.

Eurocrat /'yooərəkrat/ *noun* (*also* **eurocrat**) *informal* a member of the administrative commission of the European Union. [EURO- + *-crat* as in BUREAUCRAT]

euro-creep *noun* the gradual increase in the use of the euro in the UK while it is still officially a foreign currency.

Eurocurrency /'yooərohkurənsi/ *noun* (*also* **eurocurrency**) a currency deposit held outside its country of origin.

Eurodollar /'yooərohdolə/ *noun* (*also* **eurodollar**) a US dollar held by a bank or other institution outside the USA, *esp* in Europe.

Euroland /'yooərohland/ *noun* = EURO-ZONE.

Euromarket /'yooərohmahkit/ *noun* **1** (*also* **euromarket**) a financial market backed by the banks of the European Union. **2** (*also* **euromarket**) the European Union treated as a single market for trade or finance.

Euro-MP *noun* a Member of the European Parliament.

European¹ /yooərə'pee·ən/ *adj* **1** of or native to Europe. **2** of European descent or origin. **3a** relating to or affecting the whole of Europe. **b** relating to or affecting mainland Europe. **4** relating or belonging to the European Union. **⟫⟫ Europeanism** *noun*. [via Latin from Greek *Europaios*, from *Europē* Europe]

European² *noun* **1** a native or inhabitant of Europe or the mainland of Europe. **2** a member country of the European Union.

European Commission *noun* the executive body of the European Union, which makes policy proposals and conducts economic relations with other countries or organizations.

European Council *noun* an executive body of the European Union, made up of leaders of the member states, which hold regular summit meetings to decide on the European Commission's proposals.

European Currency Unit *noun* = ECU.

Europeanize *or* **Europeanise** *verb trans* **1** to make (something or somebody) European. **2** to cause (something or somebody) to become European in style, character, etc. **3** to make (a country, etc) part of the European Union. **⟫⟫ Europeanization** /-'zaysh(ə)n/ *noun*.

European Parliament *noun* the parliament of the European Union.

European Union *noun* an economic and political association of European states, including Austria, Belgium, Denmark, Finland, France, Germany, Greece, Ireland, Italy, Luxembourg, the Netherlands, Portugal, Spain, Sweden, and the UK.

Europhile /'yooərohfiel/ *noun* an admirer of Europe or the European Union.

europium /yoo'rohpi·əm/ *noun* a silver-white metallic element of the rare-earth group: symbol Eu, atomic number 63. [scientific Latin, from Latin *Europa* Europe]

Euro-sceptic¹ *noun* a person, *esp* a British politician, who is opposed to the European Union or the increase of its powers.

Euro-sceptic² *adj* being opposed to the European Union.

Eurostar /'yooərohstah/ *noun trademark* a high-speed rail service that links London with mainland Europe via the Channel Tunnel.

Eurotunnel /'yooərohtunl/ *noun trademark* the Channel Tunnel.

euro-zone or **Eurozone** /'yooǝrohzohn/ *noun* the countries of the EU in which the euro is the official currency.

eurythmic /yoo'ridhmik/ *adj NAmer* see EURHYTHMIC.

eurythmics *pl noun NAmer* see EURHYTHMICS.

eurythmy /yooh'ridhmi/ *noun NAmer* = EURYTHMICS.

Eustachian tube /yooh'stayshǝn/ *noun* (*also* **eustachian tube**) a tube connecting the middle ear with the throat, which allows the air pressure on both sides of the eardrum to be equalized. [named after Bartolomeo *Eustachio* d.1574, Italian anatomist, who first described its function]

eustasy /'yoohstǝsi/ *noun* worldwide change of sea level brought about by movements of the sea bed, melting of ice sheets, etc. ⟫⟫ **eustatic** /yooh'statik/ *adj.* [orig as EU- + STATIC[1]]

eutectic /yooh'tektik/ *adj* **1** of or being an alloy or other mixture that has the lowest possible melting or freezing point for a mixture of these constituents. **2** of or being the melting or freezing point of a eutectic alloy or mixture. ⟫⟫ **eutectic** *noun.* [Greek *eutēktos* easily melted, from EU- + *tēktos* melted, from *tēkein* to melt]

euthanasia /yoohthǝ'nayzi-ǝ/ *noun* the act or practice of killing incurably sick or injured individuals for reasons of mercy: *Euthanasia is a long smooth-sounding word, and it conceals its danger as long, smooth words do* — Pearl S Buck. [Greek *euthanasia* easy death, from EU- + *thanatos* death]

euthanize or **euthanise** /'yoohthǝniz/ *verb trans* to practise euthanasia on (somebody).

euthenics /yoo'theniks/ *noun* a science that deals with the development of human well-being by improvement of living conditions, control of the environment, etc. ⟫⟫ **euthenist** *noun.* [Greek *euthenein* to thrive]

eutherian /yooh'thiǝri-ǝn/ *noun* any of a subclass of animals including the mammals whose young are nourished in the womb via a placenta and are born in an advanced stage of development: subclass Eutheria. ⟫⟫ **eutherian** *adj.* [via Latin from EU- + Greek *thērion* wild beast]

euthyroid /yooh'thieroyd/ *adj* characterized by normal function of the thyroid gland.

eutrophic /yooh'trohfik, yooh'trofik/ *adj* said of a body of water: rich in dissolved nutrients, e.g. phosphates, but often shallow and seasonally deficient in oxygen: compare MESOTROPHIC, OLIGO-TROPHIC. ⟫⟫ **eutrophication** /-'kaysh(ǝ)n/ *noun,* **eutrophy** /'yoohtrǝfi, yooh'trohfi/ *noun.* [prob via German from Greek *eutrophos* well nourished, nourishing, from EU- + *trephein* to nourish]

eV *abbr* electron volt.

EVA *abbr* extravehicular activity.

evacuate /i'vakyooayt/ *verb trans* **1a** to remove (a person or people), *esp* from a dangerous place: *The children were evacuated to the countryside.* **b** to vacate (a dangerous place): *They rapidly evacuated the burning building.* **c** to withdraw from military occupation of (a place or area). **2** to empty (something). **3a** to discharge (urine, faeces, etc) from the body as waste. **b** to discharge waste from (the bowels etc). **4** to remove gas, water, etc from (something) *esp* to produce a vacuum in it. ⟩ *verb intrans* **1** to withdraw, *esp* from a dangerous place, in an organized way. **2** to discharge urine or faeces from the body. ⟫⟫ **evacuation** /-'aysh(ǝ)n/ *noun,* **evacuative** /-ǝtiv/ *adj.* [Latin *evacuatus,* past part. of *evacuare,* from EX-[1] + *vacuus* empty]

evacuee /ivakyoo'ee/ *noun* a person evacuated from a dangerous place.

evade /i'vayd/ *verb trans* **1** to get away from or avoid (somebody or something), *esp* by skill or deception. **2a** to avoid facing up to (something): *You are evading the issue.* **b** to fail to pay (taxes, etc). **c** to get around or fail to observe (a law, etc). **3** to baffle or foil (something or somebody): *The problem evades all efforts at solution.* ⟩ *verb intrans* to take refuge by evasion. ⟫⟫ **evadable** *adj,* **evader** *noun.* [via French from Latin *evadere,* from EX-[1] + *vadere* to go, walk]

evaginate /i'vajinayt/ *verb trans* to turn (an organ or other body part) inside out; to evert (it). ⟫⟫ **evagination** /-'naysh(ǝ)n/ *noun.* [Latin *evaginatus,* past part. of *evaginare* to unsheathe, from EX-[1] + *vagina* sheath]

evaluate /i'valyooayt/ *verb trans* to determine the amount, value, or significance of (something), *esp* by careful appraisal and study. ⟫⟫ **evaluation** /-'aysh(ǝ)n/ *noun,* **evaluative** /-ǝtiv/ *adj,* **evaluator** *noun.* [orig as *evaluation,* from French *évaluation,* from *évaluer* to evaluate, from EX-[1] + Old French *value:* see VALUE[1]]

evanesce /evǝ'nes/ *verb intrans chiefly literary* to dissipate or vanish like vapour.

evanescent /evǝ'nes(ǝ)nt/ *adj chiefly literary* tending to dissipate or vanish like vapour; ephemeral: *that love which many waters cannot quench ... beside which the passion usually called by the name is evanescent as steam* — Hardy. ⟫⟫ **evanescence** *noun.* [Latin *evanescent-, evanescens,* present part. of *evanescere:* see VANISH]

evangel /i'vanj(ǝ)l/ *noun* **1** *archaic* the Christian gospel. **2** (*often* **Evangel**) any of the four Gospels. **3** *chiefly NAmer* an evangelist. [Middle English *evangile* via French and late Latin from Greek *euangelion* good news, gospel, from *euangelos* bringing good news, from EU- + *angelos* messenger]

evangelic /eevan'jelik/ *adj* = EVANGELICAL[1].

evangelical[1] /eevan'jelikl/ *adj* **1** of or in accordance with the Christian message as presented in the four Gospels. **2** (*often* **Evangelical**) of or being a Protestant denomination emphasizing salvation by faith in the atoning death of Jesus Christ, personal conversion, and the authority of Scripture. **3a** of, adhering to, or marked by fundamentalism. **b** = LOW CHURCH. **4** evangelistic; zealous: *evangelical ardour.* ⟫⟫ **evangelicalism** *noun,* **evangelically** *adv.*

evangelical[2] *noun* (*often* **Evangelical**) a member of an evangelical denomination.

evangelise *verb* see EVANGELIZE.

evangelism *noun* **1** the spreading of the Christian gospel in an effort to bring about personal conversion. **2** militant or crusading zeal, *esp* in support of a cause.

evangelist *noun* **1** (*often* **Evangelist**) a writer of any of the four Gospels. **2** a person who preaches the Christian gospel; *specif* a Protestant minister or layman who preaches at special services. **3** a person who advocates something or supports a cause with crusading zeal. ⟫⟫ **evangelistic** /-'listik/ *adj,* **evangelistically** /-'listikli/ *adv.*

evangelize or **evangelise** *verb trans* to preach the Christian gospel to (somebody), *esp* with the intention of converting them to Christianity. ⟩ *verb intrans* **1** to preach the Christian gospel. **2** to advocate a cause strongly or insistently, *esp* in an effort to convince others. ⟫⟫ **evangelization** /-'zaysh(ǝ)n/ *noun,* **evangelizer** *noun.*

evaporate /i'vapǝrayt/ *verb intrans* **1a** to change from liquid to vapour. **b** to give out vapour; to lose moisture by evaporation. **2** to pass off or away; to disappear or fade: *His fears evaporated.* ⟩ *verb trans* **1a** to convert (liquid) into vapour. **b** to expel moisture, *esp* water, from (something), leaving a concentrated or solid residue. **2** to cause (something) to disappear or fade. ⟫⟫ **evaporable** *adj,* **evaporation** /-'raysh(ǝ)n/ *noun,* **evaporative** /-rǝtiv/ *adj,* **evaporator** *noun.* [Middle English *evaporaten* from Latin *evaporatus,* past part. of *evaporare,* from EX-[1] + *vapor* steam, VAPOUR[1]]

evaporated milk *noun* unsweetened milk concentrated by partial evaporation, usu sold in tins.

evasion /i'vayzh(ǝ)n/ *noun* the act, an instance, or a means of evading something or somebody: *He was suspected of tax evasion.* [Middle English via Old French from late Latin *evasion-, evasio,* from Latin *evadere:* see EVADE]

evasive /i'vaysiv, -ziv/ *adj* **1** intended to evade or avoid something: *evasive action.* **2** tending to avoid committing oneself; equivocal or indirect: *evasive answers.* ⟫⟫ **evasively** *adv,* **evasiveness** *noun.*

eve /eev/ *noun* **1** the evening or the day before a special day, *esp* a religious holiday: *Christmas Eve.* **2** the period immediately preceding an event: *the eve of the election.* **3** *chiefly literary* the evening. [variant of EVEN[4]]

evection /i'veksh(ǝ)n/ *noun* perturbation of the moon's orbit due to the sun's attraction. [Latin *evection-, evectio* rising, from *evehere* to carry out, raise up, from EX-[1] + *vehere* to carry]

even[1] /'eev(ǝ)n/ *adj* **1a** having a horizontal surface; flat or level: *even ground.* **b** without break or irregularity; smooth. **c** in the same plane or line: *even with the ground.* **2a** without variation; uniform: *an even grey sky.* **b** calm; equable: *an even disposition.* **3a** equal: *The scores were even.* **b** fair: *an even exchange.* **c** in equilibrium; balanced. **4a** exactly divisible by two: *an even number.* **b** marked by an even number: *on the even pages.* **5** exact; precise: *an even pound.* **6** fifty-fifty: *She stands an even chance of winning.* ✳ **be/get even with somebody** to have exacted or exact revenge on somebody. ⟫⟫ **evenly** *adv,* **evenness** *noun.* [Old English *efen*]

even² *verb* (**evened, evening**) ➤ *verb trans* (*often* + up/out) to make (something) even. ➤ *verb intrans* (*often* + up/out) to become even. ➤➤ **evener** *noun*.

even³ *adv* **1** used to emphasize the contrast with a less strong possibility: *I can't even walk, let alone run.* **2** used to emphasize the comparative degree: *even better than last time.* **3** used to express non-fulfilment of expectation: *They didn't even apologize.* **4** *archaic* all the way: *even unto death.* ✳ **even as** at the very time that. **even if** in spite of the possibility or fact that. **even now** 1 at this very moment. **2** in spite of what has happened. **even so** in spite of that. [Old English *efne* from *efen* EVEN¹]

even⁴ *noun archaic or literary* the evening. [Old English *ǣfen*]

evenhanded *adj* fair; impartial. ➤➤ **evenhandedly** *adv*, **even-handedness** *noun*.

evening /'eevning/ *noun* **1a** the latter part of the day and the early part of the night; the time between the end of the afternoon and bedtime. **b** an evening's activity or entertainment. **2** a late period, e.g. of somebody's life; the end. [Old English *ǣfnung* from *ǣfnian* to grow towards evening, from *ǣfen* evening]

evening dress *noun* **1** a dress, *esp* with a floor-length skirt, for wear on formal or semiformal occasions. **2** clothes for formal or semiformal evening occasions.

evening primrose *noun* any of several species of plants with pale yellow flowers that open in the evening and seeds that yield a medicinal oil: genus *Oenothera*.

evenings *adv informal* in the evening repeatedly; on any evening.

evening star *noun* the planet Venus, seen in the western sky at sunset.

even money *noun* odds in betting that give the gambler the opportunity to win the sum staked.

evens *pl noun Brit* = EVEN MONEY.

evensong *noun* **1** (*often* **Evensong**) the daily evening service of the Anglican Church. **2** the daily evening service of the Roman Catholic Church; = VESPERS. [Old English *ǣfensang*, from *ǣfen* evening + *sang* song]

event /i'vent/ *noun* **1a** a happening or occurrence, *esp* a noteworthy or important one. **b** a social occasion or activity. **2** any of the contests in a sporting programme. **3** a contingency or case: *in any event.* ✳ **after the event** after something happens or happened. **at all events** whatever may happen; anyway. **in the event** when something actually happens or happened. **in the event of/that** if the specified thing should happen. ➤➤ **eventless** *adj*. [Latin *eventus*, past part. of *evenire* to happen, from EX-¹ + *venire* to come]

eventful /i'ventf(ə)l/ *adj* marked by noteworthy or exciting occurrences: *We had an eventful journey home.* ➤➤ **eventfully** *adv*, **eventfulness** *noun*.

event horizon *noun* in astronomy, the boundary of a black hole.

eventide *noun chiefly literary* the evening. [Old English *ǣfentīd*, from *ǣfen* evening + *tīd* TIDE¹ in the archaic sense 'space of time']

eventide home *noun euphem* a home for old people.

eventing *noun* the participation of a horse or rider in an equestrian competition, *esp* a three-day event. ➤➤ **eventer** *noun*.

eventual /i'ventyooəl, -chooəl/ *adj* taking place at an unspecified later time; ultimately resulting: *They counted on his eventual success.* ➤➤ **eventually** *adv*. [French *éventuel* relating to or resulting from an event, from Latin *eventus*: see EVENT]

eventuality /i,ventyoo'aliti, -choo'aliti/ *noun* (*pl* **eventualities**) a possible, *esp* unwelcome, event or outcome.

eventuate /i'ventyooayt, -chooayt/ *verb intrans formal* to result. ➤➤ **eventuation** /-'aysh(ə)n/ *noun*.

ever /'evə/ *adv* **1** (*often in negatives and questions*) at any time: *faster than ever; Have you ever met?* **2** (*often in combination*) always: *an ever-growing need.* **3** used as an intensive: *ever since Monday; why ever not?* ✳ **ever and anon/again** *archaic or literary* sometimes. **ever so/such** *chiefly Brit, informal* used as an intensive: *ever such a nice girl; Thanks ever so.* [Old English *ǣfre*]

Usage note
ever and *-ever*. *Whoever, however, whatever, etc* are written as one word when they mean 'any person who', 'in whichever way', or 'no matter what': *However you decide to do it, make sure you get it done quickly.* But when *ever* is used with a word like *who, how,* or *what* in the intensifying sense of 'on earth', the two words are written separately: *Who ever can it be?; What ever did he mean by that?*

evergreen¹ *adj* **1** having leaves that remain green and functional throughout the year: compare DECIDUOUS (IA). **2** always retaining freshness, interest, or popularity: *the evergreen items of the American popular repertoire* — Benny Green.

evergreen² *noun* an evergreen plant.

evergreen fund *noun* a fund that provides capital for the launch and development of new companies.

everlasting¹ *adj* **1** lasting or enduring for all time; eternal. **2** continuing for a long or indefinite time. **3** tediously persistent. **4** said of a plant: retaining its form or colour for a long time when dried. **5** lasting or wearing for a long time; durable. ➤➤ **everlastingly** *adv*, **everlastingness** *noun*.

everlasting² *noun* **1** (**the Everlasting**) God. **2** eternity. **3** a plant of the daisy family that can be dried without loss of form or colour: genus *Helichrysum*.

evermore *adv archaic or literary* always; forever. ✳ **forevermore** *NAmer* forever. **for evermore** *Brit* forever.

evert /i'vuht/ *verb trans* to turn outward or inside out. ➤➤ **eversible** /-səbl/ *adj*, **eversion** /-sh(ə)n/ *noun*. [Latin *evertere*, from EX-¹ + *vertere* to turn]

every /'evri/ *adj* **1** being each member, without exception, of a group larger than two: *I enjoyed every minute; his every word.* **2** each or all possible: *She was given every chance.* **3** once in each: *Change the oil every 5000 miles.* ✳ **every bit** through and through: *She was every bit the film star.* **every bit as** just as; equally: *He is every bit as clever as his sister.* **every now and then/again** at intervals; occasionally. **every other** each alternate: *every other Monday.* **every so often/every once in a while** at intervals; occasionally. [Middle English *everich, every*, from Old English *ǣfre ǣlc*, from *ǣfre* EVER + *ǣlc* EACH¹]

everybody *pronoun* every person.

everyday *adj* encountered or used routinely or typically; ordinary: *clothes for everyday wear.* ➤➤ **everydayness** *noun*.

everyman *noun* the typical or ordinary human being; = MAN IN THE STREET. [from *Everyman*, allegorical character in *The Summoning of Everyman*, 15th-cent. English morality play]

everyone *pronoun* every person.

everything *pronoun* **1a** all that exists. **b** all that is necessary or that relates to the subject: *My new car has everything.* **2** something of the greatest importance; all that counts: *He meant everything to her.*

everywhere *adv* in, at, or to every place or the whole place.

every which way *adv NAmer* in every direction; all over the place. [prob by folk etymology from Middle English *everich way* every way]

evict /i'vikt/ *verb trans* **1a** to remove (a tenant) from rented accommodation or land by a legal process. **b** to recover (property) from somebody by a legal process. **2** to force (somebody) out; to expel (them). ➤➤ **eviction** *noun*, **evictor** *noun*. [Middle English *evicten* from late Latin *evictus*, from Latin *evincere*: see EVINCE]

evidence¹ /'evid(ə)ns/ *noun* **1** an outward sign; an indication. **2** something, *esp* a fact, that gives proof or reasons for believing or agreeing with something; *specif* information used, e.g. by a court, to arrive at the truth. ✳ **in evidence** to be seen; conspicuous. **turn King's/Queen's evidence** *Brit* said of an accomplice: to testify for the prosecution in a court. ➤➤ **evidential** /-'densh(ə)l/ *adj*, **evidentially** /-'densh(ə)li/ *adv*, **evidentiary** /-'denshəri/ *adj*. [Middle English via French from late Latin *evidentia*, from Latin *evident-, evidens*: see EVIDENT]

evidence² *verb trans* to offer evidence of (something); to show (it).

evident /'evid(ə)nt/ *adj* clear to the vision or understanding. [Middle English via French from Latin *evident-, evidens*, from EX-¹ + *vident-, videns*, present part. of *vidēre* to see]

evidently *adv* **1** clearly; obviously: *any style that is ... so evidently bad or second-rate* — T S Eliot. **2** on the basis of available evidence; as seems evident: *Evidently she was away on business at the time.*

evil¹ /'eevl/ *adj* **1a** not good morally; sinful or wicked: *a thoroughly evil doctrine.* **b** arising from bad character or conduct: *a man of evil reputation.* **2a** causing discomfort or repulsion; offensive: *an evil smell.* **b** disagreeable: *an evil temper.* **3a** pernicious or harmful. **b** marked by misfortune: *an evil day.* ➤➤ **evilly** *adv*, **evilness** *noun*. [Old English *yfel*]

evil[2] *noun* **1a** wickedness; sin. **b** the fact of suffering, misfortune, or wrongdoing. **2** something evil; something that brings sorrow, distress, or calamity.

evildoer *noun* somebody who does evil. ➤➤ **evildoing** *noun*.

evil eye *noun* a look believed to be capable of inflicting harm.

evince /i'vins/ *verb trans formal* to show (something) clearly; to reveal (it). ➤➤ **evincible** *adj*. [Latin *evincere* to vanquish, win a point, from EX-[1] + *vincere* to conquer]

eviscerate /i'visərayt/ *verb trans* **1** to disembowel (a person or animal). **2a** to remove an organ from (a patient). **b** to remove the contents of (an organ). **3** *formal* to deprive (something) of vital content or force. ➤➤ **evisceration** /-'raysh(ə)n/ *noun*. [Latin *evisceratus*, past part. of *eviscerare*, from EX-[1] + *viscera* entrails]

evocation /evə'kaysh(ə)n/ *noun* the act or an instance of evoking something.

evocative /i'vokətiv/ *adj* evoking something, e.g. a memory or image, strongly or poignantly. ➤➤ **evocatively** *adv*, **evocativeness** *noun*.

evoke /i'vohk/ *verb trans* **1** to call (something) forth or up: *Her speech evoked a lively response.* **2** to bring (something) to mind or recollection, *esp* imaginatively or poignantly: *This place evokes memories of happier years.* **3a** to summon (a spirit, etc) by invocation. **b** to cite (something), *esp* with approval or for support. ➤➤ **evoker** *noun*. [French *évoquer* from Latin *evocare*, from EX-[1] + *vocare* to call]

evolute /'eevəlooht, 'ev-/ *noun* the curve that passes through the centres of all the circles that touch a given curve on its concave side at each point. [Latin *evolutus*, past part. of *evolvere*: see EVOLVE]

evolution /eevə'loohsh(ə)n/ *noun* **1a** the historical development of a biological group, e.g. a race, species, or higher category. **b** a theory that the various existing types of animals and plants are derived from preexisting types and that the distinguishable differences are due to natural selection.

Editorial note ──────────
Evolution in the biological sense is now an established fact beyond reasonable dispute. All earthly living creatures are cousins, sharing the same genetic code inherited from a remote ancestor which lived some thousands of millions of years ago. More controversial are various theories of how evolution happens, but all biologists accept Darwinian natural selection as at least an important part of the story — Professor Richard Dawkins.

2a a process of change and development, *esp* from a lower or simpler state to a higher or more complex state. **b** a process of gradual and relatively peaceful social, political, economic, etc advance. **3** in chemistry, the action or an instance of forming and giving something off; emission. **4a** a set of prescribed movements, e.g. in a dance. **b** a set of planned manoeuvres, e.g. in a military exercise. ➤➤ **evolutional** *adj*, **evolutionary** *adj*. [Latin *evolution-, evolutio* unrolling, from *evolvere*: see EVOLVE]

evolutionism *noun* the theory of the evolution of animals and plants by natural selection, or belief in this theory. ➤➤ **evolutionist** *noun and adj*.

evolve /i'volv/ *verb trans* **1** to work out or develop (something) gradually. **2** to produce (something, e.g. an organ) by natural evolutionary processes. **3** in chemistry, to give off or emit (gas, heat, etc). ➤ *verb intrans* **1** to undergo evolutionary change. **2** to develop gradually. ➤➤ **evolvable** *adj*, **evolvement** *noun*. [Latin *evolvere* to unroll, from EX-[1] + *volvere* to roll]

evzone /'evzohn/ *noun* a member of an elite Greek infantry unit. [modern Greek *euzōnos*, from Greek, active, well-girt, from EU- + *zōnē* girdle]

ewe /yooh/ *noun* the female of the sheep or a related animal. [Old English *ēowu*]

ewer /'yooh·ə/ *noun* a wide-mouthed pitcher or jug, *esp* one used formerly to hold water for washing. [Middle English via Old French *evier* from Latin *aquarius* of water, from *aqua* water]

Ex. *abbr* Exodus (book of the Bible).

ex[1] /eks/ *prep* **1** from a specified place or source. **2a** said of shares etc: without an indicated value or right: *ex dividend*. **b** free of charges until the time of removal from (a place): *ex dock*. [Latin *ex* out of, from]

ex[2] *noun informal* a former spouse, boyfriend, or girlfriend.

ex-[1] *prefix* forming words, with the meanings: **1** out of; outside: *exclude; exodus*. **2** to cause to be: *exacerbate; exalt*. **3** to deprive of:

expropriate; excommunicate. **4** former: *the ex-president*. [Middle English via Old French from Latin *ex-*, from *ex* out of, from]

ex-[2] *prefix* see EXO-.

exa- *comb. form* forming words, denoting: million million million (10^{18}). [perhaps alteration of HEXA-]

exacerbate /ek'sasəbayt, ig'zas-/ *verb trans* to make (something bad) worse; to aggravate (it). ➤➤ **exacerbation** /-'baysh(ə)n/ *noun*. [Latin *exacerbatus*, past part. of *exacerbare*, from EX-[1] + *acerbus* harsh, bitter, from *acer* sharp]

exact[1] /ig'zakt/ *adj* **1** exhibiting or marked by complete accordance with fact; precise or accurate. **2** marked by thorough consideration or minute measurement of small factual details. ➤➤ **exactness** *noun*. [Latin *exactus*: see EXACT[2]]

exact[2] *verb trans* to demand and obtain (something) by force, threats, etc: *From them has been exacted the ultimate sacrifice* — D D Eisenhower. ➤➤ **exactable** *adj*, **exacter** *noun*, **exactor** *noun*. [Middle English *exacten* from Latin *exactus*, past part. of *exigere* to drive out, demand, measure, from EX-[1] + *agere* to drive]

exacting *adj* making rigorous demands, *esp* requiring careful attention and precise accuracy. ➤➤ **exactingly** *adv*, **exactingness** *noun*.

exaction /ig'zaksh(ə)n/ *noun* **1** the act or an instance of exacting something; extortion. **2** something exacted, *esp* a fee, reward, or contribution demanded or levied with severity or injustice.

exactitude /ig'zaktityoohd/ *noun* the quality of being exact; precision or accuracy.

exactly *adv* **1** altogether; entirely: *not exactly what I had in mind.* **2** used to express complete agreement: *'He must have cheated.' 'Exactly'.*

exaggerate /ig'zajərayt/ *verb trans* **1** to say or believe that (something) is greater, better, more important, etc than it is: *A friend exaggerates a man's virtues* — Joseph Addison. **2** to make (something) greater or more pronounced than normal; to overemphasize (it): *He exaggerated his limp to gain sympathy.* ➤ *verb intrans* to make an overstatement. ➤➤ **exaggeratedly** *adv*, **exaggeration** /-'raysh(ə)n/ *noun*, **exaggerative** /-rətiv/ *adj*, **exaggerator** *noun*, **exaggeratory** /-rət(ə)ri/ *adj*.

Word history ──────────
Latin *exaggeratus*, past part. of *exaggerare* to heap up, from EX-[1] + *agger* heap, from *aggerere* to carry towards. The word originally meant 'to heap up or accumulate', later 'to emphasize praise or blame', hence 'to overstate'.

ex all *adv and adj* in finance, without benefits.

exalt /ig'zawlt/ *verb trans* **1** to raise (something or somebody) high, *esp* in rank, power, or character. **2** to praise (somebody or something) highly; to glorify (them). **3** to enhance the activity of (something); to inspire or stimulate (it): *rousing and exalting the imagination* — George Eliot. ➤➤ **exalter** *noun*. [Middle English *exalten* via French from Latin *exaltare*, from EX-[1] + *altus* high]

exaltation /egzawl'taysh(ə)n/ *noun* **1** an intense or excessive sense of well-being, power, or importance. **2** the act or an instance of exalting.

exam /ig'zam/ *noun* an examination, *esp* one associated with a course of study.

examination /ig.zami'naysh(ə)n/ *noun* **1** the act or an instance of examining: *a medical examination*. **2** an exercise, e.g. a set of questions, designed to test knowledge or proficiency, *esp* during or at the end of a course of study. **3** a formal interrogation, e.g. in a law court. ➤➤ **examinational** *adj*, **examinatorial** /-nə'tawri·əl/ *adj*.

examine /ig'zamin/ *verb trans* **1a** to inspect (something) closely. **b** to investigate the health of (a patient). **2a** to test the knowledge, proficiency, etc of (somebody), *esp* by a set of written or oral questions. **b** to interrogate (a witness, etc) closely. ➤➤ **examinable** *adj*, **examinee** /-'nee/ *noun*, **examiner** *noun*. [Middle English *examinen* via Old French from Latin *examinare*, from *examen* tongue of a balance, examination, from *exigere*: see EXACT[2]]

example[1] /ig'zahmpl/ *noun* **1** something representative of all of the group or type to which it belongs. **2** somebody or something that may be copied by other people: *You have to set an example for your younger brother.* **3** a punishment inflicted as a warning to others, or the recipient of such a punishment: *They decided to make an example of them.* **4** a problem to be solved to illustrate a rule, e.g. in arithmetic. ✳ **for example** as an example or illustration. [Middle

English via Old French from Latin *exemplum* sample, from *eximere* to take out, from EX-[1] + *emere* to take]

example[2] *verb trans* to serve as or give an example of (something); to exemplify (it).

exanthema /eksan'theemə/ *noun* (*pl* **exanthemata** /-tə/) a skin rash that accompanies a disease. ⋙ **exanthematous** /-təs/ *adj.* [via late Latin from Greek *exanthēma*, from *exanthein* to bloom, erupt, from EX-[1] + *anthos* flower]

exarch /'eksahk/ *noun* 1 a bishop in the Eastern Orthodox Church ranking below a PATRIARCH (head of the church) and above a METROPOLITAN[2] (bishop of a province). 2 a viceroy in the Byzantine empire. ⋙ **exarchate** /-kayt/ *noun.* [via late Latin from Greek *exarchos* leader, from *exarchein* to begin, take the lead, from EX-[1] + *archein* to rule, begin]

exasperate /ig'zahspərayt/ *verb trans* to anger or irritate (somebody) intensely. ⋙ **exasperatedly** *adv,* **exasperatingly** *adv,* **exasperation** /-'raysh(ə)n/ *noun.* [Latin *exasperatus,* past part. of *exasperare,* from EX-[1] + *asper* rough]

ex cathedra /ˌeks kə'theedrə/ *adv and adj* 1 with authority: *ex cathedra pronouncements.* 2 in the Roman Catholic Church, with papal authority and therefore infallibly true. [Latin *ex cathedra,* literally 'from the chair']

excavate /'ekskəvayt/ *verb trans* 1 to form a cavity or hole in (something). 2 to form (something, e.g. a hole or tunnel) by hollowing or digging. 3 to dig out and remove (something, e.g. soil or earth). 4 to expose (something) to view by digging away a covering: *They excavated the remains of an ancient settlement.* ⋙ *verb intrans* to make holes or expose things by digging. ⋙ **excavation** /-'vaysh(ə)n/ *noun,* **excavator** *noun.* [Latin *excavatus,* past part. of *excavare,* from EX-[1] + *cavare* to make hollow]

exceed /ik'seed/ *verb trans* 1 to be greater than or superior to (something). 2 to act or go beyond the limits of (something): *You exceeded the speed limit.* 3 to extend beyond (something). [Middle English *exceden* via Old French from Latin *excedere,* from EX-[1] + *cedere* to go]

exceeding[1] *adj archaic or literary* exceptional in amount, quality, or degree: *the exceeding brightness of this early sun* — Wallace Stevens.

exceeding[2] *adv archaic or literary* = EXCEEDINGLY.

exceedingly *adv* very; extremely.

excel /ik'sel/ *verb intrans* (**excelled, excelling**) (*often* + at/in) to be superior to or surpass all others: *She excels at maths.* ✳ **excel oneself** to do something particularly well, *esp* better than ever before. [Middle English *excellen* from Latin *excellere,* from EX-[1] + *-cellere* to rise, project]

excellence /'eks(ə)ləns/ *noun* 1 the state of being excellent. 2 *archaic* an excellent or valuable quality; a virtue. 3 (**Excellence**) = EXCELLENCY (1).

excellency /'eks(ə)lənsi/ *noun* (*pl* **excellencies**) 1 (**Excellency**) used as a title for certain high dignitaries of State, e.g. a governor or ambassador, and Church, e.g. a Roman Catholic archbishop or bishop. 2 *archaic* = EXCELLENCE (2).

excellent /'eks(ə)lənt/ *adj* outstandingly good. ⋙ **excellently** *adv.* [Middle English via Old French from Latin *excellent-, excellens,* present part. of *excellere:* see EXCEL]

excelsior /ik'selsi·aw/ *noun* 1 used to indicate high quality, e.g. in product names. 2 *chiefly NAmer* fine curled wood shavings used *esp* for packing fragile items. [Latin *excelsior* higher, compar. of *excelsus* high, past part. of *excellere:* see EXCEL]

except[1] /ik'sept/ *prep* with the exclusion or exception of (something or somebody): *daily except Sundays; I can do everything except cook.* ✳ **except for 1** with the exception of (something or somebody). 2 but for (something or somebody); were it not for (them): *We couldn't have done it except for your help.* [Latin *exceptus:* see EXCEPT[3]]

except[2] *conj* 1 only; but: *I would go except it's too far.* 2 *archaic* unless: *except you repent.*

except[3] *verb trans* to take or leave out (somebody or something) from a number or a whole; to exclude (them). ⋙ *verb intrans* (*usu* + to/against) *esp* in law, to take exception to something. [Middle English *excepten* via Old French from Latin *exceptare,* from *exceptus,* past part. of *excipere* to take out, from EX-[1] + *capere* to take]

excepting *prep* = EXCEPT[1].

exception /ik'sepsh(ə)n/ *noun* 1 the act or an instance of excepting somebody or something; exclusion: *with the exception of Jack.* 2 somebody or something excepted, *esp* a case to which a rule does not apply. 3 question or objection: *witnesses whose authority is beyond exception* — Macaulay. ✳ **take exception to** to object to (something): *For some reason, she took exception to my remarks.*

exceptionable *adj* likely to cause objection; objectionable. ⋙ **exceptionably** *adv.*

Usage note ———
exceptionable or exceptional? See note at EXCEPTIONAL.

exceptional *adj* 1 forming an exception; unusual: *an exceptional number of rainy days.* 2 not average; superior: *a student of exceptional ability.* ⋙ **exceptionality** /-'naliti/ *noun,* **exceptionally** *adv.*

Usage note ———
exceptional or exceptionable? These two words are sometimes confused. *Exceptional* means 'extremely unusual' (*only under exceptional circumstances*) or 'outstanding' (*an exceptional student*). *Exceptionable* is a formal word meaning 'objectionable', 'offensive': *I was not the only one who found her remarks exceptionable.* See also note at UNEXCEPTIONAL.

excerpt[1] /'eksuhpt/ *noun* a passage taken from a book, musical composition, etc, e.g. for quoting or performing. [Latin *excerptus,* past part. of *excerpere,* from EX-[1] + *carpere* to gather, pluck]

excerpt[2] /ek'suhpt/ *verb trans* to take (a passage) from something for quoting, copying, or performing. ⋙ **excerptible** *adj,* **excerption** *noun,* **excerptor** *noun.*

excess /ik'ses/ *noun* 1a the exceeding of usual, proper, or specified limits. b the amount or degree by which one thing or quantity exceeds another. 2 an amount that is more than normal, prescribed, or desirable. 3 (*also in pl*) undue or immoderate indulgence; intemperance. 4 an amount an insured person agrees to pay towards a claim made on an insurance policy in return for a lower premium. 5a (*used before a noun*) denoting an amount that is more than normal, etc: *excess baggage; excess weight.* b underpaid: *excess postage.* ✳ **in excess of** more than. [Middle English via Old French from Latin *excessus* departure, projection, past part. of *excedere:* see EXCEED]

excessive /ik'sesiv/ *adj* exceeding normal, proper, or desirable limits. ⋙ **excessively** *adv,* **excessiveness** *noun.*

exchange[1] /iks'chaynj/ *noun* 1a the act of giving one thing for another; a swap or transaction: *an exchange of prisoners.* b something given or received in exchange. 2 a brief interchange of words or blows: *I had an acrimonious exchange with the manager.* 3a change or conversion of one currency into another. b = EXCHANGE RATE. c the system of settling debts payable currently, *esp* in a foreign country, usu by bills of exchange rather than money. 4 a place where things or services are exchanged, e.g.: a an organized market for trading in securities or commodities. b a centre or device controlling the connection of telephone calls between many different lines. 5a a system by which students from two different countries spend a period of time studying at institutions in each other's country. b (*used before a noun*) involved in such an exchange: *an exchange student.* [Middle English *exchaunge* from early French *eschange,* from *eschangier* to exchange, ultimately from Latin EX-[1] + *cambiare* to exchange]

exchange[2] *verb trans* 1a to give (something) in return for something received as an equivalent: *exchanging freedom for security.* b said of two parties: to give and receive (things of the same type): *They exchanged blows.* 2 to replace (goods) by other goods: *Will they exchange clothes that don't fit?* ⋙ *verb intrans* 1 to be given or received in exchange. 2 to engage in an exchange. ⋙ **exchangeability** /-jə'biliti/ *noun,* **exchangeable** *adj,* **exchanger** *noun.*

exchange rate *noun* the price at which one currency may be exchanged for another.

exchequer /iks'chekə/ *noun* 1 (*often* **Exchequer**) *Brit* the department of state in charge of the national revenue. 2 a national or royal treasury. 3 (**Exchequer**) *Brit* a former civil court having jurisdiction primarily over revenue and now merged with the Queen's Bench Division.

Word history ———
Middle English *escheker* from Old French *eschequier* chessboard, counting table, from *eschec* check: see CHECK[1]. The connection between the chessboard and the counting table relates to the checked cloth formerly used on such a table.

excise[1] /'eksiez, ek'siez/ *noun* 1 an internal tax levied on the manufacture, sale, or consumption of a commodity within a country. **2** in Britain, a former government department for collecting excise. [early Dutch *excijs*, prob modification of Old French *assise* session, assessment: see ASSIZE]

excise[2] /ek'siez/ *verb trans* to impose an excise on (something or somebody). ⟫⟫ **excisable** *adj*.

excise[3] /ik'siez, eksiez/ *verb trans* **1** to remove (something) by cutting it out, *esp* surgically. **2** to remove or delete (something, e.g. a passage of text). ⟫⟫ **excision** /ik'sizh(ə)n, ek-/ *noun*. [Latin *excisus*, past part. of *excidere*, from EX-[1] + *caedere* to cut]

excise duty *noun* a tax on any of various activities, often levied in the form of a licence that must be bought.

exciseman /ek'siezman, ik-/ *noun* (*pl* **excisemen**) formerly, an officer who inspected and rated articles liable to excise, collected the money payable, and prevented smuggling.

excitable /ik'sietəbl/ *adj* **1** capable of being readily roused into a state of excitement or irritability. **2** capable of being activated by and reacting to stimuli. ⟫⟫ **excitability** /-'biliti/ *noun*, **excitableness** *noun*.

excite /ik'siet/ *verb trans* **1a** to rouse (somebody) to strong, *esp* pleasurable, feeling. **b** to arouse (an emotional response): *Her late arrival excited much curiosity.* **c** to provoke or stir up (action, e.g. a rebellion). **2** to increase the activity of or produce a response in (an organ, tissue, etc); to stimulate (it). **3a** to induce a magnetic field or electric current in (something). **b** to induce (a magnetic field or an electric current). **4** to raise (an atom or a molecule) to a higher energy level. ⟫⟫ **excitant** *noun and adj*, **excitation** /eksi'taysh(ə)n/ *noun*, **excitative** /-tətiv/ *adj*, **excitatory** /-tət(ə)ri/ *adj*, **excitement** *noun*, **exciter** *noun*, **exciting** *adj*, **excitingly** *adv*. [Middle English *exciten* via Old French from Latin *excitare*, from EX-[1] + *citare* to rouse]

excited /is'sietid/ *adj* **1** happy and emotionally aroused. **2** worried or agitated. **3** said of an atom, molecule, etc: raised to a higher energy level. ⟫⟫ **excitedly** *adv*.

exciton /'eksiton/ *noun* a mobile, electrically neutral combination of a high-energy electron bound to a hole in a semiconductor. [*excitation* (see EXCITE) + -ON[2]]

exclaim /ik'sklaym/ *verb trans* to utter (something) sharply, passionately, or vehemently. ⟫ *verb intrans* to cry out or speak in strong or sudden emotion: *She exclaimed in delight.* ⟫⟫ **exclaimer** *noun*. [early French *exclamer* from Latin *exclamare*, from EX-[1] + *clamare* to cry out]

exclamation /eksklə'maysh(ə)n/ *noun* **1** the act or an instance of exclaiming. **2** the words exclaimed. ⟫⟫ **exclamatory** /ik'sklamət(ə)ri/ *adj*.

exclamation mark *noun* a punctuation mark (!) principally used after an interjection or exclamation.

exclamation point *noun NAmer* = EXCLAMATION MARK.

exclave /'eksklayv/ *noun* a portion of a country separated from the main part and surrounded by foreign territory: compare ENCLAVE. [EX-[1] + -*clave* as in ENCLAVE]

exclosure /iks'klohzhə/ *noun* an area from which wild animals or other intruders are excluded, *esp* by fencing. [EX-[1] + -*closure* as in ENCLOSURE]

exclude /ik'skloohd/ *verb trans* **1** to bar (somebody or something) from participation, consideration, or inclusion. **2** to shut (somebody or something) out. **3** to expel (somebody), *esp* from a place or position previously occupied. ⟫⟫ **excludable** *adj*, **excluder** *noun*. [Middle English *excluden* from Latin *excludere*, from EX-[1] + *claudere* to close]

exclusion /iks'kloohzh(ə)n/ *noun* **1** the act or an instance of excluding somebody or something. **2** something that is not covered by a contract, insurance policy, etc.

exclusionist /iks'kloohzh(ə)nist/ *noun* a person who would exclude another from some right or privilege. ⟫⟫ **exclusionist** *adj*.

exclusion order *noun Brit* an official order banning somebody from a particular place, *esp* in order to prevent a crime.

exclusion principle *noun* a principle in physics stating that no two electrons in an atom or molecule will be exactly equivalent in terms of their four quantum numbers.

exclusive[1] /ik'skloohsiv/ *adj* **1a** excluding or having the power to exclude. **b** limiting or limited to possession, control, use, etc by a single individual, group, etc: *an exclusive contract*; *an exclusive interview*. **2a** excluding others, *esp* those considered to be inferior, from participation, membership, or entry: *an exclusive club.* **b** snobbishly

aloof. **3** stylish and expensive. **4a** whole or undivided: *He gave her his exclusive attention.* **b** functioning independently and without assistance or interference; sole: *exclusive jurisdiction.* **5** not inclusive: *Monday to Friday exclusive.* ⟫⟫ **exclusively** *adv*, **exclusiveness** *noun*, **exclusivity** /eksk`looh'siviti/ *noun*. [early French *exclusif* from medieval Latin *exclusivus*, from Latin *excludere*: see EXCLUDE]

exclusive[2] *noun* **1** an interview, article, etc published by only one newspaper or broadcast by only one television channel or radio station. **2** an exclusive right, e.g. to sell a particular product in a certain area.

exclusive disjunction *noun* a complex sentence in logic that is true when one and only one of its constituent sentences is true.

exclusivism /ik'skloohsiviz(ə)m/ *noun* the practice of excluding people or groups from a place or activity.

excogitate /eks'kojitayt/ *verb trans formal* to think (something) out; to devise (it). ⟫⟫ **excogitation** /-'taysh(ə)n/ *noun*. [Latin *excogitatus*, past part. of *excogitare*, from EX-[1] + *cogitare*: see COGITATE]

excommunicate[1] /ekskə'myoohnikayt/ *verb trans* **1** to deprive (somebody) officially of the rights of church membership. **2** to exclude (somebody) from fellowship of a group or community. ⟫⟫ **excommunication** /-'kaysh(ə)n/ *noun*, **excommunicative** /-kətiv/ *adj*, **excommunicator** *noun*, **excommunicatory** /-kət(ə)ri/ *adj*. [Middle English *excommunicaten* from late Latin *excommunicatus*, past part. of *excommunicare*, from EX-[1] + *communicare*: see COMMUNICATE]

excommunicate[2] /ekskə'myoohnikət/ *adj* excommunicated.

excommunicate[3] /ekskə'myoohnikət/ *noun* a person who is excommunicated.

ex-con *noun informal* a former convict.

excoriate /ik'skawriyət/ *verb trans* **1a** to wear away the skin of (somebody or something). **b** to abrade or wear away (skin, etc). **2** *formal* to censure (somebody) scathingly. ⟫⟫ **excoriation** /-'aysh(ə)n/ *noun*. [Middle English *excoriaten* from late Latin *excoriatus*, past part. of *excoriare*, from EX-[1] + *corium* skin, hide]

excrement /'ekskrəmənt/ *noun* faeces or other waste matter discharged from the body. ⟫⟫ **excremental** /-'mentl/ *adj*, **excrementitious** /-'tishəs/ *adj*. [Latin *excrementum* from *excernere*: see EXCRETE]

excrescence /ik'skres(ə)ns/ *noun* **1** an excessive or abnormal outgrowth or enlargement. **2** *literary* an ugly or undesirable thing: *That new building is an excrescence.* ⟫⟫ **excrescent** *adj*. [Middle English via French from Latin *excrescentia*, from *excrescent-*, *excrescens*, present part. of *excrescere* to grow out, from EX-[1] + *crescere* to grow]

excreta /ik'skreetə/ *pl noun* (*treated as sing. or pl*) excrement. ⟫⟫ **excretal** *adj*. [Latin, neuter pl of *excretus*: see EXCRETE]

excrete /ik'skreet/ *verb trans* to separate and discharge (waste) from the body or from living tissue. ⟫⟫ **excreter** *noun*, **excretion** *noun*, **excretive** /-tiv/ *adj*, **excretory** /-t(ə)ri/ *adj*. [Latin *excretus*, past part. of *excernere* to sift out, discharge, from EX-[1] + *cernere* to sift]

excruciate /ik'skroohshiayt/ *verb trans formal* to torment (somebody). [Latin *excruciatus*, past part. of *excruciare*, from EX-[1] + *cruciare* to crucify, from *cruc-*, *crux* cross]

excruciating /ik'skroohshiayting/ *adj* **1** causing great pain or anguish; agonizing or tormenting: *an excruciating headache*; *A neophyte taking a skiing holiday used to spend the first week in excruciating, character-forming exercises* — Economist. **2** very intense; extreme: *excruciating heat.* **3** very bad, irritating, or tedious: *His jokes are excruciating.* ⟫⟫ **excruciatingly** *adv*.

exculpate /'ekskulpayt, ik'skulpayt/ *verb trans* to clear (somebody) from alleged fault, blame, or guilt. ⟫⟫ **exculpation** /ekskul'paysh(ə)n/ *noun*, **exculpatory** /ik'skulpət(ə)ri/ *adj*. [medieval Latin *exculpatus*, past part. of *exculpare*, from Latin EX-[1] + *culpa* blame]

excursion /ik'skuhsh(ə)n/ *noun* **1a** a short pleasure trip, e.g. for sightseeing. **b** (*used before a noun*) of or offered at a reduced rate for such a trip: *an excursion ticket.* **2** a deviation from a direct, definite, or proper course; a digression: *needless excursions into abstruse theory.* **3** *technical* a movement outward and back or from a mean position or axis, or the distance so travelled. ⟫⟫ **excursionist** *noun*. [Latin *excursion-*, *excursio*, from *excurrere* to run out, extend, from EX-[1] + *currere* to run]

excursive /ik'skuhsiv/ *adj formal* digressive. ⟫⟫ **excursively** *adv*, **excursiveness** *noun*.

excursus /ek'skuhsəs/ *noun* (*pl* **excursus** *or* **excursuses**) an appendix or digression that contains further discussion of some point or topic. [Latin *excursus* digression, past part. of *excurrere*: see EXCURSION]

excuse[1] /ik'skyoohz/ *verb trans* **1a** to forgive (somebody) entirely. **b** to overlook (something) as unimportant: *Please excuse my ignorance.* **2a** to seek pardon or make apology for (something). **b** to try to remove blame from (somebody, e.g. oneself): *He excused himself for being so careless.* **3** to be an acceptable reason for (something); to justify (it): *Nothing can excuse their cruelty.* **4** to allow (somebody) to leave; to dismiss (them): *The class was excused.* **5** Brit (*usu in passive*) to free (somebody) from a duty: *The class was excused homework.* ✳ **be excused** *euphem* to go to the toilet. **excuse me** used to attract somebody's attention, to apologize for an interruption or mistake, or to ask to be allowed to pass. **excuse oneself** to announce politely that one is leaving. ➤➤ **excusable** *adj*, **excusably** *adv*, **excusatory** /-zət(ə)ri/ *adj*. [Middle English *excusen* via Old French from Latin *excusare*, from EX-[1] + *causa* cause, explanation]

excuse[2] /ik'skyoohs/ *noun* **1a** something offered as grounds for being excused: *She had a good excuse for being late.* **b** a false reason given in explanation of an action etc: *It's just an excuse for raising the price.* **2** (*in pl*) an expression of regret for failure to do something or *esp* for one's absence: *I phoned Jill to make my excuses for not going to the party.* **3** *informal* a very poor example: *That was an excuse for a meal.*

excuse-me /ik'skyoohzmee/ *noun informal* a dance during which somebody may ask to dance with another person's partner.

ex-directory *adj Brit* intentionally not listed in a telephone directory.

ex div. *abbr* ex dividend.

ex dividend *adj and adv* said of shares: without payment of the next dividend.

exeat /'eksiat/ *noun Brit* a formal leave of absence granted *esp* to a student. [Latin *exeat* let him or her go out, from *exire*: see EXIT[1]]

exec. *abbr* executive.

execrable /'eksikrəbl/ *adj* detestable or appalling: *execrable behaviour; execrable taste; His coats were execrable, his hat not to be handled* — Herman Melville. ➤➤ **execrably** *adv*.

execrate /'eksikrayt/ *verb trans* **1** to detest (something) utterly; to abhor (it). **2** to declare (somebody or something) to be evil or detestable; to denounce (them). ➤➤ **execration** /-'kraysh(ə)n/ *noun*, **execrative** /-krətiv/ *adj*, **execrator** *noun*, **execratory** /-t(ə)ri/ *adj*. [Latin *exsecratus*, past part. of *exsecrari* to put under a curse, from EX-[1] + *sacr-, sacer* sacred]

executant /ig'zekyoot(ə)nt/ *noun formal* **1** somebody who executes something. **2** a performer, *esp* of a musical piece.

execute /'eksikyooht/ *verb trans* **1** to carry (something) out fully; to put (it) completely into effect. **2** to put (somebody) to death as a punishment. **3** to make or produce (a work of art, etc), *esp* by carrying out a design. **4** to do what is required to make (something) legally effective or valid. **5** to play or perform (something, e.g. a musical piece). **6** in computing, to run (a file, program, etc). ➤➤ **executable** *adj*. [Middle English *executen* from early French *executer*, back-formation from *execution*: see EXECUTION]

execution /eksi'kyoohsh(ə)n/ *noun* **1** the act of putting somebody to death as a punishment. **2** a judicial writ directing the enforcement of a judgment. **3** the act, mode, or result of performance: *The execution was perfect but the piece lacked expression.* **4** the act of carrying something out or putting it into effect: *in the execution of her duties.* [Middle English via French from Latin *exsecution-, exsecutio*, from *exsequi* to execute, from EX-[1] + *sequi* to follow]

executioner *noun* a person who puts another person to death; *specif* a person legally appointed to perform capital punishment.

executive[1] /ig'zekyootiv/ *adj* **1a** concerned with making and carrying out laws, decisions, etc. **b** concerned with the detailed application of policy or law rather than its formulation. **2** of, for, or being an executive: *an executive jet.* ➤➤ **executively** *adv*.

executive[2] *noun* **1** a person who holds a position of administrative or managerial responsibility. **2** a person or group that controls or directs an organization. **3** the executive branch of a government.

Executive Council *noun* in Australia and New Zealand, a body of ministers led by the governor or governor general that formally approves cabinet legislation, etc.

executive officer *noun* the officer who is second in command of a military or naval unit.

executor /ig'zekyootə/ *noun* (*pl* **executors**) a person appointed to carry out the provisions of another person's will. ➤➤ **executorial** /igzekyoo'tawri·əl/ *adj*, **executorship** *noun*, **executory** /-t(ə)ri/ *adj*. [Middle English via Old French from Latin *exsecutor*, from *exsequi*: see EXECUTION]

executrix /ig'zekyootriks/ *noun* (*pl* **executrices** /ig,zekyoo'trie-seez/) a female executor.

exegesis /eksi'jeesis/ *noun* (*pl* **exegeses** /-seez/) **1** an explanation or critical interpretation of a text, *esp* a biblical text. **2** an exposition. ➤➤ **exegetic** /-'jetik/ *adj*, **exegetical** /-'jetikl/ *adj*. [via Latin from Greek *exēgēsis*, from *exēgeisthai* to explain, interpret, from EX-[1] + *hēgeisthai* to lead]

exegete /'eksijeet/ *noun* a person who practises exegesis. [Greek *exēgētēs* from *exēgeisthai*: see EXEGESIS]

exempla /ig'zemplə/ *noun* pl of EXEMPLUM.

exemplar /ig'zemplə, -plah/ *noun* **1** somebody or something that serves as a typical or ideal example or model. **2** a copy of a book or text. [Middle English via Old French from late Latin *exemplarium*, from Latin *exemplum*: see EXAMPLE[1]]

exemplary /ig'zempləri/ *adj* **1** deserving imitation; commendable: *His conduct was exemplary.* **2** said of a punishment: serving as a warning. **3** serving as an example, instance, or illustration. ➤➤ **exemplarily** *adv*, **exemplariness** *noun*, **exemplarity** /egzem-'plariti/ *noun*.

exemplary damages *pl noun* in law, a sum awarded in damages that exceeds the compensation required for the actual loss and is intended to punish the guilty party.

exemplify /ig'zemplifie/ *verb trans* (**exemplifies, exemplified, exemplifying**) **1** to show or illustrate (something) by example. **2** to be an instance of or serve as an example of (something); to typify or embody (it). ➤➤ **exemplification** /-fi'kaysh(ə)n/ *noun*. [Middle English *exemplifien* via Old French from medieval Latin *exemplificare*, from Latin *exemplum*: see EXAMPLE[1]]

exemplum /ig'zempləm/ *noun* (*pl* **exempla** /-plə/) **1** an anecdote or story that illustrates a moral point or supports an argument. **2** *chiefly formal* an example or model. [Latin *exemplum*: see EXAMPLE[1]]

exempt[1] /ig'zempt/ *adj* free from some liability or requirement to which others are subject: *exempt from jury service.* [Middle English from Latin *exemptus*, past part. of *eximere*: see EXAMPLE[1]]

exempt[2] *verb trans* to make (somebody or something) exempt; to excuse (them). ➤➤ **exemption** *noun*.

exempt[3] *noun* a person who is exempt, e.g. from paying tax or from duty.

exequy /'eksikwi/ *noun* (*pl* **exequies**) *formal* (*usu in pl*) a funeral ceremony. [Middle English via Old French from Latin *exequiae, exsequiae* (pl), from *exequi, exsequi*: see EXECUTION]

exercise[1] /'eksəsiez/ *noun* **1a** regular or repeated use of a part of the body, the senses, or the powers of the mind. **b** physical exertion for the sake of developing and maintaining bodily fitness: *The doctor said I should take more exercise.* **2** something performed or practised in order to develop, improve, or display a specific power or skill. **3** something done for a particular purpose: *an exercise in crowd control.* **4** a manoeuvre or drill carried out for training and discipline. **5** the use of a specified power or right: *the exercise of his authority.* [Middle English via Old French from Latin *exercitium*, from *exercēre* to drive on, keep busy, from EX-[1] + *arcēre* to enclose, hold off]

exercise[2] *verb intrans* to engage in physical exertion for the sake of fitness. ➤ *verb trans* **1** to make (something) effective in action; to use or exert (it): *She chose to exercise her right to remain silent.* **2a** to use (a part of the body) repeatedly in order to strengthen or develop it. **b** to train (troops, etc) by drills and manoeuvres. **c** to give exercise to (somebody or something): *The grooms are exercising the horses.* **3a** to engage the attention and effort of (somebody or something): *The problem greatly exercised his mind.* **b** to cause anxiety, alarm, or indignation in (somebody): *residents exercised about pollution.* ➤➤ **exercisable** *adj*, **exerciser** *noun*.

exercise bike *noun* a stationary piece of equipment that is pedalled like a bicycle for physical exercise.

exercise book *noun* a booklet of blank, usu lined, pages used for written work in schools.

exercise price *noun* the price at which the owners of traded options on a stock exchange may exercise their right to buy or sell the security.

exert /ig'zuht/ *verb trans* **1** to bring (strength or authority) to bear, *esp* with sustained effort; to employ or wield (it). **2** to take upon (oneself) the effort of doing something: *He never exerts himself to help anyone.* >>> **exertion** *noun*. [Latin *exsertus*, past part. of *exserere* to thrust out, from EX-¹ + *serere* to join]

exeunt /'eksiunt, -oont/ *verb intrans* (*third person pl pres*) used as a stage direction to specify that all or certain named characters leave the stage. [Latin *exeunt* they go out, from *exire*: see EXIT¹]

exeunt omnes /,eksiunt 'omnayz/ *phrase* used as a stage direction: they all go out. [Latin *exeunt omnes* they all go out]

exfoliant /eks'fohli-ənt/ *noun* a gently abrasive skin cream or cleaning device that removes dead skin cells.

exfoliate /eks'fohliayt/ *verb trans* **1** to cast (skin or bark) off in scales, layers, etc. **2** to remove surface cells, layers, etc from (the skin). > *verb intrans* **1** to shed scales, surface body cells, etc. **2** to separate into thin layers or flakes. **3** to come off in a thin piece. >>> **exfoliation** /-'aysh(ə)n/ *noun*, **exfoliative** /-ɒtiv/ *adj*. [late Latin *exfoliatus*, past part. of *exfoliare* to strip of leaves, from EX-¹ + *folium* leaf]

ex gratia /'grayshə/ *adj and adv* as a favour; not compelled by legal right: *ex gratia payments*. [Latin *ex gratia* out of kindness]

exhalation /eks(h)ə'laysh(ə)n/ *noun* **1** the act or an instance of exhaling. **2** something exhaled or given off; an emanation: *the various exhalations which arise from damp cloaks, festering umbrellas, and the coarsest tallow candles* — Dickens.

exhale /iks'hayl, ig'zayl/ *verb trans* **1** to breathe (something) out. **2** to give forth (gas or vapour); to emit (it). > *verb intrans* **1** to emit breath or vapour. **2** to rise or be given off as vapour. >>> **exhalable** *adj*. [Middle English *exalen* from Latin *exhalare*, from EX-¹ + *halare* to breathe]

exhaust¹ /ig'zawst/ *verb trans* **1a** to tire (somebody) out: *exhausted by their efforts*. **b** to consume (something) entirely; to use (it) up: *We exhausted our supplies in two days*. **2a** to develop or deal with (a subject) to the fullest possible extent. **b** to try out the whole number of (possibilities, etc). **3a** to draw off or let out (something) completely. **b** to empty (something) by drawing off the contents; *specif* to create a vacuum in (it). > *verb intrans* to discharge or empty: *The engine exhausts through a silencer*. >>> **exhaustedly** *adv*, **exhauster** *noun*, **exhaustibility** /-'biliti/ *noun*, **exhaustible** *adj*, **exhaustingly** *adv*. [Latin *exhaustus*, past part. of *exhaurire*, from EX-¹ + *haurire* to draw, drain]

exhaust² *noun* **1** used gas or vapour expelled from an engine. **2** the emission of such gases. **3** the pipe or system of parts through which such gases escape.

exhaustion /ig'zawsch(ə)n/ *noun* **1** extreme tiredness. **2** the act or an instance of exhausting.

exhaustive /ig'zawstiv/ *adj* comprehensive; thorough: *an exhaustive investigation*. >>> **exhaustively** *adv*, **exhaustiveness** *noun*.

exhibit¹ /ig'zibit/ *verb* (**exhibited, exhibiting**) > *verb trans* **1** to show (a work of art, etc) publicly, *esp* for purposes of competition, demonstration, or information. **2** to show or display (a feeling, quality, symptom, etc) outwardly, *esp* by visible signs or actions; to reveal or manifest (it): *He exhibited no fear*. > *verb intrans* to display something for public inspection. >>> **exhibitor** *noun*, **exhibitory** /-t(ə)ri/ *adj*. [Middle English *exhibiten* from Latin *exhibitus*, past part. of *exhibēre*, from EX-¹ + *habēre* to have, hold]

exhibit² *noun* **1** something exhibited. **2** something produced as evidence in a court of law.

exhibition /eksi'bish(ə)n/ *noun* **1** a public showing, e.g. of works of art or objects of manufacture. **2** the act or an instance of exhibiting: *an exhibition of ill-temper*. **3** *Brit* a grant awarded, usu on merit, by a school or university to a student. ＊ **make an exhibition of oneself** to behave foolishly in public.

exhibitioner *noun Brit* a student awarded an exhibition.

exhibitionism *noun* **1** the act or practice of behaving so as to attract attention to oneself. **2** a compulsion to commit acts of indecent exposure. >>> **exhibitionist** *noun and adj*, **exhibitionistic** /-'nistik/ *adj*.

exhibitive /ig'zibitiv/ *adj formal* (+ of) illustrative of (something).

exhilarate /ig'zilərayt/ *verb trans* **1** to make (somebody) very happy or cheerful. **2** to enliven or invigorate (somebody).

>>> **exhilarating** *adj*, **exhilaration** /-'raysh(ə)n/ *noun*, **exhilarative** /-'rətiv/ *adj*. [Latin *exhilaratus*, past part. of *exhilarare*, from EX-¹ + *hilarare* to gladden, from *hilarus* cheerful]

exhort /ig'zawt/ *verb trans* to urge or advise (somebody) strongly: *I exhorted them to behave well*. > *verb intrans* to give warnings or advice; to make urgent appeals. >>> **exhortative** /-'tətiv/ *adj*, **exhortatory** /-tət(ə)ri/ *adj*, **exhorter** *noun*. [Middle English *exhorten* via Old French from Latin *exhortari*, from EX-¹ + *hortari* to urge, incite]

exhortation /egzaw'taysh(ə)n/ *noun* **1** the act or an instance of exhorting: *She ignored our exhortations*. **2** language intended to incite, encourage, or inspire.

exhume /eks'syoohm, ig'zyoohm/ *verb trans* **1** to disinter (something buried, *esp* a dead body). **2** to bring (something) back from neglect or obscurity. >>> **exhumation** /-'maysh(ə)n/ *noun*, **exhumer** *noun*. [French *exhumer* from medieval Latin *exhumare*, from EX-¹ + Latin *humus* earth]

ex hypothesi /hie'pothəsie/ *adv* according to the hypothesis. [Latin *ex hypothesi*]

exigence /'eksij(ə)ns/ *noun* = EXIGENCY.

exigency /ig'zij(ə)nsi, 'eksij(ə)nsi/ *noun* (*pl* **exigencies**) *formal* **1** an exigent state of affairs; an emergency: *They must be free to act in any exigency*. **2** (*usu in pl*) such need or necessity as belongs to the occasion; a requirement.

exigent /'eksij(ə)nt, 'egzij(ə)nt/ *adj formal* **1** requiring immediate aid or action. **2** exacting; demanding. >>> **exigently** *adv*. [Latin *exigent-, exigens*, present part. of *exigere*: see EXACT²]

exiguous /ig'zigyoo-əs/ *adj formal* excessively scanty; inadequate; meagre. >>> **exiguity** /eksi'gyooh-iti/ *noun*, **exiguously** *adv*, **exiguousness** *noun*. [Latin *exiguus* from *exigere*: see EXACT²]

exile¹ /'eksiel, 'egziel/ *noun* **1** enforced or voluntary absence from one's country or home: *They are living in exile*. **2** somebody who goes or is sent into exile. >>> **exilic** /ek'silik/ *adj*. [Middle English *exil* via Old French from Latin *exilium*, from *exul* banished person]

exile² *verb trans* to send (somebody) into exile.

exist /ig'zist/ *verb intrans* **1a** to have being in the real world; to be: *Do unicorns exist?* **b** to have being in specified conditions: *Some chemical compounds exist only in solution*. **2a** to have life or the functions of vitality: *One would rather exist, even in pain, than not exist* — Dr Johnson. **b** to live at an inferior level or under adverse circumstances: *starving people existing from one day to the next*. [Latin *exsistere* to come into being, exist, from EX-¹ + *sistere* to stand]

existence *noun* **1a** the state or fact of existing or being: *the existence of such phenomena*. **b** life: *Death is an elementary fact of existence*. **c** the totality of existent things. **2** a manner of living or being: *He pursued a solitary existence*. **3** *archaic* a particular being or entity: *all the fair existences of heaven* — Keats.

existent *adj* having being; existing.

existential /egzi'stensh(ə)l/ *adj* **1** of, affirming, or grounded in existence: *existential propositions*. **2** of or relating to existentialism. >>> **existentially** *adv*. [(sense 2) translation of Danish *eksistentiel* and German *existential*]

existentialism *noun* a philosophical movement characterized by enquiry into human beings' experience of themselves in relation to the world, *esp* with reference to their freedom, responsibility, and isolation: compare ESSENTIALISM.

Editorial note

Existentialism or existential philosophy is a movement that is too varied to be defined by common tenets. It starts with individual human self, experiencing and trying to understand his or her situation in the world; an individual existence can never be properly described in abstract terms or reduced to something 'objective', like 'human nature'. Nor is it ever self-identical, because of its duration in time. 20th-cent. existential thinkers (Heidegger, Sartre, Jaspers, Marcel), some of them atheists, some Christian, often refer to Kierkegaard as their spiritual ancestor — Professor Leszek Kołakowski.

>>> **existentialist** *noun and adj*, **existentialistic** /-'listik/ *adj*.

exit¹ /'eksit, 'egzit/ *verb* (**exited, exiting**) > *verb intrans* **1** (*third person sing. pres*) used as a stage direction to specify that a certain character leaves the stage: *Exit Ophelia*. **2** said of an actor: to leave the stage. **3** to leave or depart. **4** in computing, to terminate a program, process, etc. > *verb trans* in computing, to leave or terminate (a program, process, or system). [Latin *exit* he or she goes out, from *exire* to go out, from EX-¹ + *ire* to go]

exit[2] *noun* **1** a way out of a room, building, or other enclosed space. **2a** the act of going out or away. **b** (*used before a noun*) relating to the right to leave: *an exit visa*. **3** a departure of a performer from the stage. **4** a point at which vehicles can leave a major road, roundabout, etc. **5** *literary or euphem* death. [Latin *exitus* departure, past part. of *exire*: see EXIT[1]]

exit counsellor *noun* a person who offers counselling to people who have left or are attempting to leave a cult.

exit poll *noun* a survey of voting trends conducted by questioning people as they leave a polling station after voting in an election.

ex libris /'leebris/ *noun* (*pl* **ex libris**) a bookplate. [Latin *ex libris* from the books; used before the owner's name on bookplates]

Exmoor /'eksmooə, 'eksmaw/ *noun* a pony of a hardy breed with thick manes native to the Exmoor district. [named after *Exmoor*, area of moorland in SW England]

ex nihilo /'neehiloh/ *adv formal* from or out of nothing: *creation ex nihilo*. [Latin *ex nihilo*]

exo- *or* **ex-** *prefix* forming words, with the meanings: **1** outside: *exogamy*. **2** outer: *exoskeleton*. **3** giving off; releasing: *exocrine*. [Greek *exō* out, outside, from *ex* out of]

exobiology /ˌeksohbie'oləji/ *noun* the study of extraterrestrial plants and animals. ⸺ **exobiological** /-'lojikl/ *adj*, **exobiologist** *noun*.

exocarp /'eksohkahp/ *noun* the outermost layer, e.g. the skin of a cherry, of the tissue surrounding the seeds in a fruit. Also called EPICARP. [EXO- + *carp* as in PERICARP]

exocrine /'eksəkreen, -krin, -krien/ *adj* **1** said of a gland: producing secretions that are discharged through a duct: compare ENDOCRINE[1] (1). **2** of an exocrine gland, e.g. a sweat gland or kidney: *exocrine secretions*. [EXO- + Greek *krinein* to separate]

Exod. *abbr* Exodus (book of the Bible).

exodus /'eksədəs/ *noun* **1** (**Exodus**) the second book of the Old Testament, relating the flight of the Israelites from Egypt. **2** a mass departure; an emigration: *On Saturday at twelve there was a large exodus from barracks* — Evelyn Waugh. [via Latin from Greek *exodos* road out, from *ex* out + *hodos* road]

ex officio /ə'fis(h)ioh/ *adv and adj* by virtue or because of an office: *The president is an ex officio member of the committee*. [late Latin *ex officio*]

exogamy /ek'sogəmi/ *noun* **1** marriage outside a specific group, e.g. a tribe, *esp* as required by custom or law: compare ENDOGAMY. **2** sexual reproduction between organisms that are not closely related. ⸺ **exogamic** /eksoh'gamik/ *adj*, **exogamous** /-məs/ *adj*.

exogenous /ek'sojinəs/ *adj* originating from the outside; due to external causes. ⸺ **exogenously** *adv*. [French *exogène*, from EXO- + *-gène* from Greek *-genēs* born]

exon /'ekson/ *noun* any of four officers of the yeomen of the guard who act as resident commanders. [modification, based on the French pronunciation, of French *exempt* cavalry officer exempt from normal duties]

exonerate /ig'zonərayt/ *verb trans* **1** (*often* + from) to free (somebody) from blame; to exculpate (them). **2** (*often* + from) to relieve (somebody) of a responsibility, obligation, or hardship. ⸺ **exoneration** /-'raysh(ə)n/ *noun*, **exonerative** /-rətiv/ *adj*. [Middle English *exoneraten* from Latin *exoneratus*, past part. of *exonerare* to unburden, from EX-[1] + *oner-*, *onus* load]

exophthalmos /eksof'thalmos, -məs/ *or* **exophthalmus** /-məs/ *noun* abnormal protrusion of the eyeball. ⸺ **exophthalmic** /-mik/ *adj*. [via Latin from Greek *exophthalmos* having prominent eyes, from *ex* out + *ophthalmos* eye]

exorbitant /ig'zawbit(ə)nt/ *adj* said of prices, demands, etc: much greater than is reasonable; excessive. ⸺ **exorbitance** *noun*, **exorbitantly** *adv*. [Middle English, in the sense 'abnormal, irregular', via Old French from late Latin *exorbitant-, exorbitans*, present part. of *exorbitare* to deviate, from EX-[1] + Latin *orbita* track, rut]

exorcize *or* **exorcise** /'eksawsiez/ *verb trans* **1** to expel (an evil spirit) by solemn command, e.g. in a religious ceremony. **2** to free (a person or place) of an evil spirit. **3** to get rid of (an unpleasant thought or emotion) as if by exorcism. ⸺ **exorcism** /-siz(ə)m/ *noun*, **exorcist** *noun*, **exorcizer** *noun*. [Middle English *exorcisen* via French and late Latin from Greek *exorkizein*, from *ex* out + *horkizein* to bind by oath, adjure, from *horkos* oath]

exordium /ek'sawdi·əm/ *noun* (*pl* **exordiums** *or* **exordia** /-di·ə/) *formal* a beginning or introduction, *esp* to a formal speech or

literary work. ⸺ **exordial** *adj*. [Latin *exordium* from *exordiri* to begin, from EX-[1] + *ordiri* to begin]

exoskeleton /eksoh'skelitn/ *noun* **1** a hard external supportive covering of an animal, e.g. a lobster or beetle. **2** a type of powered suit intended for military use, enabling soldiers to carry heavier loads and move and communicate more effectively. ⸺ **exoskeletal** *adj*.

exosphere /'eksohsfiə/ *noun* the outer zone of a planet's atmosphere. ⸺ **exospheric** /-'sferik/ *adj*.

exostosis /ekso'stohsis/ *noun* (*pl* **exostoses** /-seez/) a spur or bony outgrowth from a bone. [via Latin from Greek *exostōsis*, from *ex* out of + *osteon* bone]

exoteric /eksoh'terik/ *adj* **1** designed for, understood by, or suitable for the general public: compare ESOTERIC. **2** not admitted or belonging to the inner circle of enlightened members. ⸺ **exoterically** *adv*. [via Latin from Greek *exōterikos* exoteric, external, from *exōterō*, compar of *exō* outside]

exothermal /eksoh'thuhml/ *adj* = EXOTHERMIC.

exothermic /eksoh'thuhmik/ *adj* said of a chemical reaction or compound: characterized by or formed with the evolution of heat. ⸺ **exothermically** *adv*.

exotic[1] /ig'zotik/ *adj* **1** introduced from another country; not native to the place where found: *an exotic plant*. **2** strikingly or excitingly different or unusual: *an exotic dish*. ⸺ **exotically** *adv*, **exoticism** /-siz(ə)m/ *noun*, **exoticness** *noun*. [Latin *exoticus*, from Greek *exōtikos*, from *exō* outside]

exotic[2] *noun* an exotic plant or animal.

exotica /ig'zotikə/ *pl noun* exotic things, *esp* literary or artistic items with an exotic theme or quality. [Latin *exotica*, neuter pl of *exoticus*: see EXOTIC[1]]

exotic dancer *noun* a striptease dancer or belly dancer.

expand /ik'spand/ *verb trans* **1** to increase the size, extent, number, volume, or scope of (something): *The company has expanded its interests overseas*. **2a** to express (something) in detail or in full: *You will have to expand your argument*. **b** to express (something) in fuller mathematical form, *esp* as the sum of many terms of a series. ▶ *verb intrans* **1** to become larger, greater, etc; to be expanded: *Iron expands when heated*. **2** to unfold or open out. **3** (*often* + on) to speak or write at length; to enlarge: *Please expand on this passage*. **4** to grow genial; to become more sociable: *She only expands among friends*. ⸺ **expandable** *adj*. [Middle English *expaunden* from Latin *expandere*, from EX-[1] + *pandere* to spread]

expanded *adj* said of a plastic, resin, etc: having gas introduced during manufacture to produce a light cellular structure: *expanded polystyrene*.

expanded metal *noun* sheet metal cut and expanded into an open mesh, used e.g. for reinforcement.

expander /ik'spandə/ *noun* somebody or something that expands; *specif* any of several substances, e.g. dextran, used as a blood or plasma substitute for increasing the blood volume.

expanse /ik'spans/ *noun* **1** something spread out, *esp* over a wide area. **2** the extent to which something is spread out. [Latin *expansum*, neuter past part. of *expandere*: see EXPAND]

expansible /ik'spansəbl/ *adj* able to expand or be expanded; expandable. ⸺ **expansibility** /-'biliti/ *noun*.

expansile /ik'spansiel/ *adj* of or capable of expansion.

expansion /ik'spansh(ə)n/ *noun* **1** the act or an instance of expanding: *territorial expansion*. **2** the increase in volume of working fluid, e.g. steam, in an engine cylinder. **3** something expanded, e.g.: **a** an expanded part. **b** a fuller treatment of an earlier theme or work. **4** the expanding of a mathematical expression or function in a series. ⸺ **expansionary** /-n(ə)ri/ *adj*.

expansion bolt *noun* a bolt with an attachment that expands as the bolt is inserted and tightened.

expansionism *noun* a policy of economic or territorial expansion. ⸺ **expansionist** *noun and adj*, **expansionistic** /-'nistik/ *adj*.

expansion joint *noun* a joint that has a gap to allow for thermal expansion of the sections.

expansive /ik'spansiv/ *adj* **1** having a capacity or tendency to expand or cause expansion. **2** freely communicative; genial or effusive: *He grew more expansive after dinner*. **3** having a wide expanse or extent. **4** characterized by extravagance or magnificence of scale: *expansive living.* ➤ **expansively** *adv,* **expansiveness** *noun.*

expansivity /ekspan'siviti/ *noun* the amount that a substance or body expands when its temperature is increased by one degree.

ex parte /'pahti, pahtay/ *adv and adj* said of legal proceedings: from or in the interests of one side only. [medieval Latin *ex parte* from a side]

expat /eks'pat/ *noun and adj informal* = EXPATRIATE².

expatiate /ik'spayshiayt, ek-/ *verb intrans* (*usu* + on/upon) to speak or write at length or in detail on (something, *esp* a single subject): *expatiating on the value of the fabric* — Hardy. ➤ **expatiation** /-'aysh(ə)n/ *noun.* [Latin *exspatiatus,* past part. of *exspatiari* to wander, digress, from EX-¹ + *spatium* space, course]

expatriate¹ /eks'patriayt/ *verb trans* **1** to exile or banish (somebody). **2** to withdraw (oneself) from residence in one's native country. ➤ **expatriation** /-'aysh(ə)n/ *noun.* [medieval Latin *expatriatus,* past part. of *expatriare* to leave one's own country, from EX-¹ + Latin *patria* native country, from *patr-, pater* father]

expatriate² /eks'patri·ət/ *noun* a person who lives outside their native country. ➤ **expatriate** *adj.*

expect /ik'spekt/ *verb trans* **1a** to consider (an event) probable or certain: *She expects to be forgiven.* **b** to consider (something) reasonable, due, or necessary: *He expected respect from his children.* **c** to consider (somebody) bound in duty or obligated: *They expected us to pay for the repair.* **2a** to anticipate, look forward to, or be waiting for (something): *I'm expecting a telephone call.* **b** to be waiting or prepared for the arrival of (somebody). **3** to suppose or think (something): *I expect that's true.* ✳ **be expecting** *informal* to be pregnant. ➤ **expectable** *adj.* [Latin *exspectare* to look forward to, from EX-¹ + *spectare* to look at, from *spectus,* past part. of *specere* to look]

expectance /ik'spekt(ə)ns/ *noun* = EXPECTANCY.

expectancy /ik'spekt(ə)nsi/ *noun* (*pl* **expectancies**) **1** = EXPECTATION (1A), (1B). **2** the expected amount or number, *esp* of years of life, based on statistical probability. **3** the expected length of something: *life expectancy.*

expectant¹ *adj* **1** having, showing, or characterized by expectation: *an expectant hush.* **2** said of a woman· pregnant; expecting the birth of a child. ➤ **expectantly** *adv.*

expectant² *noun* a person, e.g. a candidate for a position, who expects, hopes for, or anticipates something.

expectation /ekspek'taysh(ə)n/ *noun* **1a** the state of expecting something; a mood of anticipation: *Bingley's attentions to your sister had given rise to a general expectation of their marriage* — Jane Austen. **b** hopeful anticipation of a desired event. **c** (*also in pl*) something expected: *The results exceeded our expectations.* **2** *archaic* (*usu in pl*) prospects of inheritance. **3a** = EXPECTANCY (2). **b** = EXPECTED VALUE.

expected frequency *noun* in statistics, the average number of times an event is expected to occur in a given number of trials.

expected value *noun* in statistics, the mean value of a random variable.

expectorant /ik'spektərənt/ *noun* a medicine, drug, or other agent that promotes expectoration. ➤ **expectorant** *adj.*

expectorate /ik'spektərayt/ *verb trans and intrans* **1** to eject (phlegm or similar matter) from the throat or lungs by coughing or spitting. **2** to spit (saliva, etc). ➤ **expectoration** /-'raysh(ə)n/ *noun.* [Latin *expectoratus,* past part. of *expectorare* to cast out of the breast, from EX-¹ + *pector-, pectus* breast, soul]

expedience /ik'speedi·əns/ *noun* = EXPEDIENCY (1).

expediency /ik'speedi·ənsi/ *noun* (*pl* **expediencies**) **1** suitability; fitness. **2** development of or adherence to expedient means and methods. **3** = EXPEDIENT².

expedient¹ /ik'speedi·ənt/ *adj* **1** suitable for achieving a particular end. **2** characterized by concern with what is opportune or advantageous rather than what is right, just, or moral. ➤ **expediently** *adv.* [Middle English via French from Latin *expedient-, expediens,* present part. of *expedire* to extricate, arrange (literally 'to free the feet'), from EX-¹ + *ped-, pes* foot]

Usage note
expedient or **expeditious**? *Expedient* means 'useful or convenient in the circumstances (often disregarding moral considerations)': *It might be expedient to deny any knowledge of the plan.* It is sometimes confused with

expeditious, which is a formal word meaning 'quick and efficient': *the most expeditious method of sending supplies.*

expedient² *noun* a means to an end, *esp* one devised or used in case of urgent need.

expedite /'ekspidiet/ *verb trans formal* **1** to execute (something) promptly. **2** to hasten the process or progress of (something); to facilitate (it). ➤ **expediter** *noun.* [Latin *expeditus,* past part. of *expedire:* see EXPEDIENT¹]

expedition /ekspi'dish(ə)n/ *noun* **1a** a journey or excursion undertaken for a specific purpose, e.g. for war or exploration. **b** (*treated as sing. or pl*) the group of people making such an expedition. **2** *formal* efficient promptness; speed. ➤ **expeditionary** /-n(ə)ri/ *adj.* [Middle English *expedicioun* via Old French from Latin *expedition-, expeditio,* from *expedire:* see EXPEDIENT¹]

expeditious /ekspi'dishəs/ *adj formal* speedy; prompt and efficient. ➤ **expeditiously** *adv,* **expeditiousness** *noun.*
Usage note
expeditious or expedient? See note at EXPEDIENT¹.

expel /ik'spel/ *verb trans* (**expelled, expelling**) **1** to drive or force (something) out: *Air is expelled from the lungs.* **2** to cut (somebody) off from membership of a school, society, etc. **3** to drive (somebody) away; to deport (them). ➤ **expellable** *adj,* **expellee** /ekspe'lee/ *noun,* **expeller** *noun.* [Middle English *expellen* from Latin *expellere,* from EX-¹ + *pellere* to drive]

expend /ik'spend/ *verb trans* **1** to consume (time, care, or attention) by use; to use (it) up: *projects on which he expended great energy.* **2** *formal* to spend or pay out (money). ➤ **expender** *noun.* [Middle English *expenden* from Latin *expendere* to weigh out, expend, from EX-¹ + *pendere* to weigh]

expendable¹ *adj* **1** normally used up in service; not intended to be kept or re-used: *expendable supplies like pencils and paper.* **2** regarded as available for sacrifice or destruction in order to accomplish an objective: *expendable troops.* ➤ **expendability** /-'biliti/ *noun.*

expendable² *noun* (*usu in pl*) something that is expendable.

expenditure /ik'spendichə/ *noun* **1** the act or an instance of spending money. **2** the amount of money spent.

expense /ik'spens/ *noun* **1a** something expended to secure a benefit or bring about a result. **b** financial burden or outlay: *built at considerable expense.* **c** (*in pl*) the charges incurred by an employee in performing their duties. **d** (*also in pl*) an item of business outlay chargeable against revenue in a specific period. **2** a cause or occasion of high expenditure: *A car is a great expense.* ✳ **at somebody's expense** in a manner that causes somebody to be ridiculed: *He made a joke at my expense.* **at the expense of** to the detriment of: *develop a boy's physique at the expense of his intelligence* — Bertrand Russell. [Middle English via Anglo-French from late Latin *expensa,* fem past part. of Latin *expendere:* see EXPEND]

expense account *noun* an account of expenses reimbursable to an employee.

expensive /ik'spensiv/ *adj* **1** commanding a high price; costly. **2** involving great expense: *an expensive hobby.* ➤ **expensively** *adv,* **expensiveness** *noun.*

experience¹ /ik'spiəri·əns/ *noun* **1a** direct participation or observation. **b** the knowledge, skill, or practice derived from such experience, *esp* over a period of time. **2** something personally encountered or undergone: *a terrifying experience.* **3** the sum total of conscious events that make up an individual life or the collective past of a community, nation, etc: *beyond human experience.* [Middle English via Old French from Latin *experientia* act of trying, from *experient-, experiens,* present part. of *experiri* to try out]

experience² *verb trans* to have experience of (something): *She experienced severe hardships as a child.*

experienced *adj* skilful or wise as a result of experience of a particular activity or of life in general: *an experienced driver.*

experiential /ik,spiəri'ensh(ə)l/ *adj* based on or derived from experience; empirical. ➤ **experientially** *adv.*

experiment¹ /ik'sperimənt/ *noun* **1** an operation carried out under controlled conditions in order to test or establish a hypothesis or to illustrate a known law: *a scientific experiment.* **2** a tentative procedure or policy that has not been tried before. **3** the act or an instance of experimenting. [Middle English via Old French from Latin *experimentum,* from *experiri* to try out]

experiment[2] /ik'speriment/ *verb intrans* to carry out an experiment or experiments. ➤➤ **experimentation** /-'taysh(ə)n/ *noun,* **experimenter** *noun.*

experimental /ik,speri'mentl/ *adj* **1** based on or derived from an experiment or experiments. **2** used as a means of or having the characteristics of an experiment: *an experimental school.* **3** innovative: *experimental theatre.* **4** provisional or tentative. **5** *archaic* = EXPERIENTIAL. ➤➤ **experimentalism** *noun,* **experimentally** *adv.*

expert[1] /'ekspuht/ *adj* having or showing special skill or knowledge derived from training or experience. ➤➤ **expertly** *adv,* **expertness** *noun.* [Middle English via French from Latin *expertus,* past part. of *experiri* to try out]

expert[2] *noun* a person who has special skill or knowledge in a particular field.

expertise /ekspuh'teez/ *noun* skill in or knowledge of a particular field: *technical expertise.* [French *expertise* expertness, from *expert:* see EXPERT[1]]

expert system *noun* a computer program that contains specialized knowledge elicited from human experts on a particular subject and can use it to deduce solutions to novel problems.

expiate /'ekspiayt/ *verb trans* **1a** to eradicate the guilt incurred by (a sin, etc). **b** to pay the penalty for (a crime, etc). **2** to make amends for (something). ➤➤ **expiable** *adj,* **expiation** /-'aysh(ə)n/ *noun,* **expiator** *noun,* **expiatory** /ekspi'ayt(ə)ri, 'ekspi-ət(ə)ri/ *adj.* [Latin *expiatus,* past part. of *expiare* to atone for, from EX-[1] + *piare* to atone for, appease]

expiration /ekspi'raysh(ə)n/ *noun* **1** the release of air from the lungs through the nose or mouth. **2** expiry; termination.

expire /ik'spie-ə/ *verb intrans* **1** to come to an end; to cease to be valid: *My passport expires this year.* **2** to breathe out; to exhale. **3** *formal* to die. ➤ *verb trans* to breathe (air) out from the lungs. ➤➤ **expiratory** /-rət(ə)ri/ *adj.* [Middle English *expiren* via Old French from Latin *exspirare,* from EX-[1] + *spirare* to breathe]

expiry /ik'spie-əri/ *noun* (*pl* **expiries**) **1** a termination, *esp* of a time or period fixed by law, contract, or agreement. **2** *archaic* death.

explain /ik'splayn/ *verb trans* **1** to make (something) plain or understandable, *esp* by giving details. **2** to give the reason for or cause of (something): *She was unwilling to explain her conduct.* ➤ *verb intrans* to make something plain or understandable. ✳ **explain oneself** to clarify one's statements or the reasons for one's conduct. ➤➤ **explainable** *adj,* **explainer** *noun.* [Middle English *explanen* from Latin *explanare,* literally 'to make level', from EX-[1] + *planus* level, flat]

explain away *verb trans* to minimize the significance of (errors or unpleasant facts) by making excuses: *He tried to explain away the corruption in his department.*

explanation /eksplə'naysh(ə)n/ *noun* **1** the act or an instance of explaining. **2** something that explains, e.g. a statement, a detailed account, or a reason.

explanative /ik'splanətiv/ *adj* = EXPLANATORY.

explanatory /ik'splanət(ə)ri/ *adj* serving to explain: *explanatory notes.* ➤➤ **explanatorily** *adv.*

explant[1] /eks'plahnt/ *verb trans* to remove (living tissue) from an organism and place it in a nourishing medium for experimental growth. ➤➤ **explantation** /-'taysh(ə)n/ *noun.* [EX-[1] + *-plant* as in IMPLANT[1]]

explant[2] /'eksplahnt/ *noun* a piece of living tissue explanted from an organism.

expletive[1] /ek'spleetiv/ *noun* **1** an exclamatory word or phrase; *specif* one that is obscene or profane. **2** a word, phrase, etc inserted to fill a space, e.g. in a sentence or a line of poetry, without adding to the sense. [late Latin *expletivus* from Latin *expletus,* past part. of *explēre* to fill out, from EX-[1] + *plēre* to fill]

expletive[2] *adj* said of a word or phrase: serving to fill a space.

expletory /ek'spleet(ə)ri/ *adj* = EXPLETIVE[2].

explicable /'eksplikəbl, ik'splikəbl/ *adj* capable of being explained. ➤➤ **explicably** *adv.*

explicate /'eksplikayt/ *verb trans formal* **1** to give a detailed explanation of (something). **2** to develop the implications of (a theory, etc). **3** to analyse (a literary work, etc). ➤➤ **explication** /-'kaysh(ə)n/ *noun,* **explicative** /-tiv, ek'splikətiv/ *adj,* **explicator** *noun,* **explicatory** /-t(ə)ri, ek'splikət(ə)ri/ *adj.* [Latin *explicatus,* past part. of *explicare,* literally 'to unfold', from EX-[1] + *plicare* to fold]

explicit /ik'splisit/ *adj* **1** clear and unambiguous: *explicit instructions.* **2** graphically frank or detailed: *explicit sex scenes.* **3** fully developed or formulated. ➤➤ **explicitly** *adv,* **explicitness** *noun.* [French *explicite* via medieval Latin from Latin *explicitus,* past part. of *explicare:* see EXPLICATE]

explode /ik'splohd/ *verb intrans* **1a** to undergo a rapid chemical or nuclear reaction with the production of noise, heat, and violent expansion of gases: *The bomb exploded.* **b** to burst violently as a result of pressure: *The boiler exploded.* **c** to expand suddenly: *the exploding population.* **2** to give expression to sudden, violent, and usu noisy emotion: *He exploded with anger.* ➤ *verb trans* **1** to cause (something) to explode or burst noisily. **2** to demonstrate the falsity of (a belief or theory) or the non-existence of (a theoretical entity): *explode a rumour; The only small satisfaction I have ... is that your friend Bunbury is quite exploded — Oscar Wilde.* ➤➤ **exploder** *noun.* [Latin *explodere* to drive off the stage by clapping, from EX-[1] + *plaudere* to clap]

exploded *adj* said of a drawing, diagram, etc: showing the parts separated but in correct relationship to each other: *an exploded view of a carburettor.*

exploit[1] /'eksployt/ *noun* a deed or act, *esp* a notable or heroic one. [Middle English in the sense 'outcome, success', via Old French from Latin *explicitum,* neuter past part. of *explicare:* see EXPLICATE]

exploit[2] /ik'sployt/ *verb trans* (**exploited, exploiting**) **1** to use or develop (resources, materials, etc) fully, *esp* for profit or advantage. **2** to take unfair advantage of (somebody) for financial or other gain: *exploiting the workers by paying low wages.* ➤➤ **exploitable** *adj,* **exploitation** /eksploy'taysh(ə)n/ *noun,* **exploitative** *adj,* **exploiter** *noun,* **exploitive** /-tiv/ *adj.*

explore /ik'splaw/ *verb trans* **1** to travel into or through (an unfamiliar place), *esp* for purposes of geographical or scientific discovery. **2** to examine or enquire into (something) thoroughly: *You must explore the possibilities of reaching an agreement.* **3** to examine (something, e.g. a part of the body) minutely, *esp* for diagnostic purposes. ➤ *verb intrans* to explore a place. ➤➤ **exploration** /eksplə'raysh(ə)n/ *noun,* **exploratory** /ik'splorətiv/ *adj,* **exploratory** /ik'splorət(ə)ri/ *adj,* **explorer** *noun.* [Latin *explorare* to search out, from EX-[1] + *plorare* to cry out; prob from the outcry of hunters on sighting game]

explosion /ik'splohzh(ə)n/ *noun* **1** the act or an instance of exploding. **2a** a rapid large-scale expansion, increase, or upheaval: *the population explosion.* **b** a sudden violent outburst of emotion. [Latin *explosion-, explosio* act of driving off by clapping, from *explodere:* see EXPLODE]

explosive[1] /ik'splohsiv/ *adj* **1** capable of exploding or likely to explode: *an explosive substance.* **2** tending or threatening to burst forth with sudden violence or noise: *an explosive situation.* **3** tending to arouse strong reactions; controversial: *the play's explosive topicality.* ➤➤ **explosively** *adv,* **explosiveness** *noun.*

explosive[2] *noun* an explosive substance.

expo /'ekspoh/ *noun* (*pl* **expos**) = EXPOSITION (2).

exponent /ik'spohnənt/ *noun* **1a** (*usu* + of) somebody or something that expounds or interprets. **b** (*usu* + of) somebody or something that advocates or exemplifies something. **c** a skilled performer, artist, etc. **2** a symbol written above and to the right of a mathematical expression to indicate the number of times a quantity is multiplied by itself, e.g. $2^3 = 2 \times 2 \times 2$. [Latin *exponent-, exponens,* present part. of *exponere:* see EXPOSE]

exponential /ekspə'nensh(ə)l/ *adj* **1** involving a variable in an exponent, e.g. 10^x. **2a** expressed in terms of exponential functions. **b** increasing with accelerating rapidity: *exponential growth.*

exponential distribution *noun* in statistics, distribution used to make statements about the length of life of materials or times between events.

exponential function *noun* a mathematical function in which an independent variable appears in an exponent.

export[1] /ik'spawt/ *verb trans* **1** to carry or send (a commodity) to another country for purposes of trade. **2** to take or spread (an idea, custom, etc) abroad. **3** in computing, to transfer (data) from one program or application for use in another. ➤ *verb intrans* to export something abroad. ➤➤ **exportability** /-'biliti/ *noun,* **exportable** *adj,* **exportation** /-'taysh(ə)n/ *noun,* **exporter** *noun.* [Latin *exportare,* from EX-[1] + *portare* to carry]

export[2] /'ekspawt/ *noun* **1** something exported. **2** the act or an instance of exporting.

expose /ik'spohz/ *verb trans* **1** to lay (something) open to view; to uncover or display (it). **2** to deprive (somebody or something) of shelter or protection; to lay (them) open to attack, danger, distress, etc: *exposing himself to ridicule.* **3** to submit or subject (something or somebody) to an action or influence; *specif* to subject (a photographic film, plate, or paper) to the action of light, X-rays, etc. **4** to bring (something shameful) to public notice: *We exposed their trickery.* **5** to reveal the face of (a playing card). **6** to abandon (an infant) in an unsheltered place. ✳ **expose oneself** to engage in indecent exposure. ➤➤ **exposer** *noun.* [Middle English *exposen* via French from Latin *exponere* to set forth, explain, from EX-¹ + *ponere* to put, place]

exposé /ek'spohzay (*French* ɛkspoze)/ *noun* **1** a formal recital or exposition of facts, a statement. **2** an exposure of something discreditable: *a newspaper exposé of organized crime.* [French *exposé*, past part. of *exposer*: see EXPOSE]

exposed *adj* **1** open to view, to inclement weather, etc. **2** vulnerable to danger or criticism.

exposition /ekspə'zish(ə)n/ *noun* **1a** the art or practice of expounding or explaining the meaning or purpose of something, e.g. a text. **b** a detailed explanation or elucidation, *esp* of something that is difficult to understand: *a brilliant exposition of existentialism.* **2** a large, usu international, public exhibition or show, e.g. of industrial products. **3** the first part of a musical composition in which the themes are presented. **4** the act or an instance of exposing. ➤➤ **expositional** *adj.*

expositive /ik'spozətiv/ *adj* descriptive; explanatory.

expositor /ik'spozitə/ *noun* a person who expounds or explains something; a commentator.

expository /ik'spozit(ə)ri/ *adj* = EXPOSITIVE.

ex post facto /'faktoh/ *adj and adv* with retrospective application, action, or effect: *ex post facto approval; ex post facto laws.* [late Latin *ex post facto* from a thing done afterwards]

expostulate /ik'spostyoolayt/ *verb intrans formal (usu* + with) to remonstrate or reason earnestly with (somebody), *esp* in order to dissuade them. ➤➤ **expostulation** /-'laysh(ə)n/ *noun.* [Latin *expostulatus*, past part. of *expostulare* to demand, dispute, from EX-¹ + *postulare*: see POSTULATE¹]

exposure /ik'spohzh(ə)/ *noun* **1a** the act or an instance of being exposed, *esp* to something harmful or unpleasant. **b** the condition arising from lack of protection from cold weather: *She died of exposure.* **c** the specified direction in which a building, room, etc faces: *a house with a western exposure.* **2a** the act or an instance of exposing a sensitized photographic film, plate, or paper, or the product of the light intensity multiplied by the duration of such an exposure. **b** a section of a film with one picture on it. **3** a disclosure, *esp* of a weakness or of something shameful or criminal; an exposé or unmasking: *exposure of electoral frauds.* **4** presentation or exposition, *esp* to the public by means of the mass media.

exposure meter *noun* a device for indicating correct photographic exposure under various light conditions.

expound /ik'spownd/ *verb trans* to set forth (an idea, theory, etc), *esp* in careful or elaborate detail; to state or explain (it). ➤➤ **expounder** *noun.* [Middle English *expounden* via early French *expondre* from Latin *exponere*: see EXPOSE]

express¹ /ik'spres/ *verb trans* **1a** to show or represent (something), *esp* in words; to state (it). **b** to make known the opinions, feelings, etc of (oneself). **c** to represent (something) by a sign or symbol. **2** to force out (the juice of a fruit, etc) by pressure. ➤➤ **expresser** *noun,* **expressible** *adj.* [Middle English *expressen* from Old French *expres* (adj), from Latin *expressus*, past part. of *exprimere* to press out, express, from EX-¹ + *premere* to press]

express² *adj* **1** firmly and explicitly stated: *He disobeyed my express orders.* **2** of a particular sort; specific: *She came for that express purpose.* **3a** travelling at high speed, usu with few stops along the way, or suitable for such travel: *an express train.* **b** *Brit* designated to be delivered without delay by special messenger: *express mail.* [Middle English via early French *expres*: see EXPRESS¹]

express³ *adv* by express.

express⁴ *noun* **1** an express vehicle, *esp* a train. **2** *Brit* an express delivery service.

expression /ik'spresh(ə)n/ *noun* **1a** the act or an instance of expressing something, *esp* in words: *freedom of expression.* **b** a significant word or phrase. **c** an outward manifestation or symbol: *This gift is an expression of my gratitude.* **d** a look on somebody's face that indicates their feelings: *a bored expression.* **e** a mathematical or logical symbol or combination of symbols. **2a** a means or manner of expressing something, *esp* sensitivity and feeling in communicating or performing: *He read the poem with expression.* **b** the quality or fact of being expressive. **3** the act or an instance of squeezing out a liquid. ➤➤ **expressional** *adj,* **expressionless** *adj,* **expressionlessly** *adv,* **expressionlessness** *noun.*

expressionism *noun* a mode of expression in art, literature, or music that attempts to depict subjective emotions and responses to objects and events.

Editorial note ──────────────
In expressionism, what artists aimed to express was generally their own feelings, often through strong colour, emphatic brushwork, and a calculated primitivism. The term was applied – retrospectively – to the German artists belonging to the groups called Die Brücke, and Der Blaue Reiter. it is also sometimes used of the starker German cinema, drama, and architecture of the early 20th cent. — Martin Gayford.

➤➤ **expressionist** *noun and adj,* **expressionistic** /-'nistik/ *adj,* **expressionistically** /-'nistikli/ *adv.*

expressive /ik'spresiv/ *adj* **1** relating to expression: *the expressive function of language.* **2** (+ of) serving to express or represent something: *He used foul and novel terms expressive of rage* — H G Wells. **3** full of expression: *an expressive performance.* **4** full of meaning; significant: *an expressive silence.* ➤➤ **expressively** *adv,* **expressiveness** *noun,* **expressivity** /ekspre'siviti/ *noun.*

expressly *adv* **1** explicitly: *I expressly told you not to do that.* **2** for an express purpose; specially: *a clinic expressly for the treatment of addicts.*

expresso /ik'spresoh/ *noun (pl* **expressos**) = ESPRESSO.

expressway *noun chiefly NAmer* a motorway.

expropriate /eks'prohpriayt/ *verb trans* **1** to deprive (somebody) of possession, occupancy, or owner's rights. **2** to transfer (the property of another) to one's own possession. **3** to take possession of (personal property) for public use: *They expropriated all the land within a ten-mile radius.* ➤➤ **expropriation** /-'aysh(ə)n/ *noun,* **expropriator** *noun.* [medieval Latin *expropriatus*, past part. of *expropriare,* from EX-¹ + *proprius* own]

expulsion /ik'spulsh(ə)n/ *noun* the act or an instance of expelling. ➤➤ **expulsive** /-siv/ *adj.* [Middle English from Latin *expulsion-, expulsio,* from *expellere*: see EXPEL]

expunge /ik'spunj/ *verb trans formal* **1** to delete or erase (words, passages, etc): *Some superfluities I have expunged, and some faults I have corrected* — Dr Johnson. **2** to blot out or obliterate (something): *Nothing can expunge his shame.* ➤➤ **expunction** /ik'spungksh(ə)n/ *noun,* **expunger** *noun.* [Latin *expungere* to mark for deletion by dots, from EX-¹ + *pungere* to prick]

expurgate /'ekspuhgayt/ *verb trans* to rid (something) of something morally offensive, *esp* to remove objectionable parts from (a text) before publication or presentation: *the expurgated version of the story.* ➤➤ **expurgation** /-'gaysh(ə)n/ *noun,* **expurgator** *noun,* **expurgatory** /ik'spuhgət(ə)ri/ *adj.* [Latin *expurgatus,* past part. of *expurgare,* from EX-¹ + *purgare*: see PURGE¹]

exquisite¹ /ik'skwizit, 'ekskwizit/ *adj* **1** marked by flawless, beautiful, and usu delicate craftsmanship. **2** extremely beautiful; delightful: *an exquisite white blossom.* **3** keenly sensitive, *esp* in feeling; discriminating: *exquisite taste.* **4** acute or intense: *exquisite pain.* ➤➤ **exquisitely** *adv,* **exquisiteness** *noun.* [Middle English *exquisit* choice, ingenious, from Latin *exquisitus,* past part. of *exquirere* to search out, from EX-¹ + *quaerere* to seek]

exquisite² *noun dated* a dandy.

ex-serviceman *or* **ex-servicewoman** *noun (pl* **ex-servicemen** *or* **ex-servicewomen**) *chiefly Brit* a former member of the armed forces.

ext. *abbr* **1** extension. **2** exterior. **3** external. **4** extinct.

extant /ek'stant/ *adj* still or currently existing: *extant manuscripts.* [Latin *extant-, exstans,* present part. of *exstare* to stand out, be in existence, from EX-¹ + *stare* to stand]

extemporaneous /ik,stempə'rayni·əs/ *adj* **1** spoken, done, performed, etc on the spur of the moment and without preparation; impromptu: *She gave a witty extemporaneous speech.* **2** provided, made, or put to use as a makeshift. ➤➤ **extemporaneously** *adv,* **extemporaneousness** *noun.* [late Latin *extemporaneus* from Latin *ex tempore*: see EXTEMPORE]

extemporary /ik'stemp(ə)rəri/ *adj* = EXTEMPORANEOUS. ➤➤ **extemporarily** *adv,* **extemporariness** *noun.*

extempore /ik'stempəri/ *adj and adv* spoken or done in an extemporaneous manner: *speaking extempore.* [Latin *ex tempore* out of the moment, from *ex* out of + *tempore*, ablative of *tempus* time]

extemporize *or* **extemporise** /ik'stempəriez/ *verb intrans* to speak or perform something extemporaneously; to improvise. ➤➤ *verb trans* to compose, perform, or utter (something) extemporaneously. ➤➤ **extemporization** /-'zaysh(ə)n/ *noun*, **extemporizer** *noun*.

extend /ik'stend/ *verb trans* **1a** to spread or stretch (something) forth: *She extended both her arms.* **b** to stretch (something) out to its fullest length. **2** to give or offer (something), usu in response to need; to proffer (it): *extending aid to the needy.* **3a** to lengthen or enlarge (something): *The house has been extended.* **b** to prolong (something) in time: *They have extended the deadline.* **c** to increase the scope, meaning, or application of (something); to broaden (it). **4a** to cause (something) to reach the specified place, area, etc: *National authority was extended over the new territories.* **b** to advance or further (something): *extending human knowledge.* **5** to exert (a horse, oneself, etc) to full capacity: *He won the race without extending himself.* ➤➤ *verb intrans* to stretch out in distance, space, time, or scope: *Their jurisdiction extended over the whole area.* ➤➤ **extendable** *adj,* **extendible** *adj.* [Middle English *extenden* via French from Latin *extendere,* from EX-¹ + *tendere* to stretch]

extended family *noun* a family unit that includes three or more generations of near relatives in addition to a nuclear family, *esp* living in one household or close together: compare NUCLEAR FAMILY.

extended-play *noun* = EP¹.

extender *noun* a substance added to a product to increase its bulk or improve its physical properties.

extensible /ik'stensəbl/ *adj* capable of being extended. ➤➤ **extensibility** /-'biliti/ *noun.*

extensile /ik'stensiel/ *adj* = EXTENSIBLE.

extension /ik'stensh(ə)n/ *noun* **1a** the act or an instance of extending. **b** something extended. **2a** a part added to make something longer or larger, e.g. an extra room or rooms added to a building. **b** an extra telephone connected to the principal line. **c** a length of electric cable that enables an appliance to be connected to a distant socket. **3** an increase in length of time, e.g. one that allows extra time to fulfil an obligation. **4** extent or scope. **5** the straightening of a joint between the bones of a limb. **6a** a programme of instruction for students of a university, college, etc who do not attend on a full-time basis. **b** (*used before a noun*) of or being such a programme: *an extension course.* **7** the range of objects, entities, etc to which a term applies, *esp* in logic. **8** the characters following the dot in a filename created by DOS-based software, identifying the type of file. ➤➤ **extensional** *adj.* [Middle English via French from late Latin *extension-, extensio,* from Latin *extendere:* see EXTEND]

extensive /ik'stensiv/ *adj* **1** having wide or considerable extent: *extensive reading.* **2** of or being farming in which large areas of land are used with minimum expenditure and labour. ➤➤ **extensively** *adv,* **extensiveness** *noun.*

extensometer /eksten'somitə/ *noun* an instrument for measuring deformations of test specimens caused by compression, bending, etc. [EXTENSION + -O- + -METER²]

extensor /ik'stensə, -saw/ *noun* a muscle that extends or straightens a part of the body, *esp* a limb: compare FLEXOR.

extent /ik'stent/ *noun* **1** the range or distance over which something extends: *the extent of the forest; the extent of his knowledge.* **2** the point or limit to which something extends: *the extent of our patience.* [Middle English, in the sense 'land valuation, seizure of land', via Anglo-French from Old French *extente* area, surveying of land, ultimately from Latin *extendere:* see EXTEND]

extenuate /ik'stenyooayt/ *verb trans* **1** to lessen the seriousness or extent of (a crime, etc), *esp* by providing a reason or excuses: *extenuating circumstances.* **2** to make (somebody) thin or emaciated. **3** to dilute or weaken (something). ➤➤ **extenuation** /-'aysh(ə)n/ *noun,* **extenuator** *noun,* **extenuatory** /-ət(ə)ri/ *adj.* [Latin *extenuatus,* past part. of *extenuare,* from EX-¹ + *tenuis* thin]

exterior¹ /ik'stiəri·ə/ *adj* **1** on the outside or an outside surface; external. **2** suitable for use on outside surfaces. **3** outdoor. ➤➤ **exteriority** /-'oriti/ *noun,* **exteriorly** *adv.* [Latin *exterior,* compar of *exter, exterus* on the outside, foreign, from *ex* out of]

exterior² *noun* **1a** an exterior part or surface; outside. **b** an outward manner or appearance: *a deceptively friendly exterior.* **2** a representation of an outdoor scene.

exterior angle *noun* the angle outside a polygon formed between a line extending from a side and the adjacent side.

exteriorize *or* **exteriorise** *verb trans* = EXTERNALIZE.

exterminate /ik'stuhminayt/ *verb trans* to destroy (something) completely, *esp* to kill all of (a population of pests, etc): *They exterminated the mice.* ➤➤ **extermination** /-'naysh(ə)n/ *noun,* **exterminator** *noun,* **exterminatory** /-nət(ə)ri/ *adj.* [Latin *exterminatus,* past part. of *exterminare* to banish, expel, from EX-¹ + *terminus* boundary]

external¹ /ik'stuhnl/ *adj* **1** of, on, or intended for the outside or an outer part. **2a** capable of being perceived outwardly: *external signs of a disease.* **b** superficial. **c** not intrinsic or essential: *external circumstances.* **3** situated outside, apart, or beyond. **4a** arising or acting from outside: *an external force.* **b** of dealings with foreign countries. **c** having existence independent of the mind: *external reality.* **5** of or for extramural students. ➤➤ **externally** *adv.* [Middle English from Latin *externus,* from *exter:* see EXTERIOR¹]

external² *noun* **1** (*usu in pl*) an external feature or aspect. **2** *Aus, NZ* an extramural student.

external degree *noun* a degree taken by somebody who does not actually attend the university that awards it.

external ear *noun* the parts of an ear between the eardrum and the exterior, including the parts on the outside of the head.

external examiner *noun* a visiting examiner who ensures impartiality and equality of standards in an examination.

externalise *verb trans* see EXTERNALIZE.

externality /ekstuh'naliti/ *noun* (*pl* **externalities**) **1** the quality or state of being external. **2** something that is external. **3** a long-term incidental consequence of an industrial or technological development.

externalize *or* **externalise** *verb trans* **1** to make (something) external or externally visible. **2** to attribute (a feeling, event, etc) to causes outside the self; to rationalize (it): *He externalizes his failure.* ➤➤ **externalization** /-'zaysh(ə)n/ *noun.*

exteroceptive /,ekstəroh'septiv/ *adj* activated by, relating to, or being stimuli received by an organism from outside. ➤➤ **exteroceptor** *noun.* [Latin *exter* (see EXTERIOR¹) + -O- + -*ceptive* as in RECEPTIVE]

extinct /ik'stingkt/ *adj* **1** no longer existing as a species. **2a** no longer burning; extinguished. **b** no longer active: *an extinct volcano.* **3** having no qualified claimant: *an extinct title.* [Middle English from Latin *exstinctus,* past part. of *exstinguere:* see EXTINGUISH]

extinction /ik'stingksh(ə)n/ *noun* **1** the act or an instance of making extinct: *hunted to extinction.* **2** the act or an instance of extinguishing. **3** in physics, reduction of the intensity of light or of other radiation by absorption, scattering, etc.

extinguish /ik'stinggwish/ *verb trans* **1a** to cause (something) to cease burning; to quench (a flame, fire, etc). **b** to put out (a light). **c** to bring (something) to an end; to destroy (it) completely: *Hope for their safety was slowly extinguished.* **2a** to make (a claim, etc) void. **b** to abolish (a debt) by payment. ➤➤ **extinguishable** *adj,* **extinguisher** *noun,* **extinguishment** *noun.* [Latin *exstinguere* (from EX-¹ + *stinguere* to extinguish) + -*ish* as in ABOLISH]

extirpate /'ekstuhpayt/ *verb trans* **1** to remove or destroy (something) completely as if by uprooting; to annihilate (it): *The present happy union of the states bids fair for extirpating the future use of arms from one quarter of the world —* Thomas Paine. **2** to cut (something) out by surgery. ➤➤ **extirpation** /-'paysh(ə)n/ *noun,* **extirpator** *noun.* [Latin *extirpatus,* past part. of *exstirpare,* from EX-¹ + *stirp-, stirps* trunk, root]

extol (*NAmer* **extoll**) /ik'stohl, ik'stol/ *verb trans* (**extolled, extolling**) to praise (something or somebody) highly; to glorify (them). ➤➤ **extoller** *noun,* **extolment** *noun.* [Middle English *extollen* from Latin *extollere,* from EX-¹ + *tollere* to lift up]

extort /ik'stawt/ *verb trans* to obtain (money or a confession) from somebody by force or threats. ➤➤ **extorter** *noun,* **extortive** /-tiv/ *adj.* [Latin *extortus,* past part. of *extorquēre* to wrench out, extort, from EX-¹ + *torquēre* to twist]

extortion /ik'stawsh(ə)n/ *noun* the act or an instance of extorting; *specif* the unlawful extorting of money. ➤➤ **extortioner** *noun,* **extortionist** *noun.*

extortionate /ik'stawsh(ə)nət/ *adj* **1** said of a price: excessive or exorbitant. **2** using or characterized by extortion. ➤➤ **extortionately** *adv*.

extra¹ /'ekstrə/ *adj* **1** more than is due, usual, or necessary; additional: *extra work*. **2** subject to an additional charge: *Room service is extra*. [prob short for EXTRAORDINARY]

extra² *noun* **1** something extra or additional, e.g. an added charge or an item for which such a charge is made. **2** somebody extra or additional; *specif* somebody hired to act in a group scene in a film or stage production. **3** a specified edition of a newspaper: *the latenight extra*. **4** a run in cricket, e.g. a bye, no-ball, or wide, that is not scored by a stroke of the bat and is not credited to a batsman's individual score: compare BYE¹ (2), LEG BYE.

extra³ *adv* beyond or above the usual size, extent, or amount: *I worked extra hard*; *They charge extra for single rooms*.

extra- *prefix* forming words, with the meaning: outside; beyond: *extrajudicial*; *extramural*. [Middle English from Latin *extra* (adv and prep) outside, except, beyond, from *exter*: see EXTERIOR¹]

extracellular /ekstrə'selyoolə/ *adj* situated or occurring outside a cell or the cells of the body: *extracellular digestion*; *extracellular enzymes*. ➤➤ **extracellularly** *adv*.

extra cover *noun* a fielding position in cricket between mid-off and cover-point and about half-way to the boundary.

extract¹ /ik'strakt/ *verb trans* **1** to pull out, draw forth, or obtain (something), *esp* against resistance or with effort: *The dentist extracted a tooth*; *The police extracted a confession from the suspect*. **2** to withdraw (a juice, etc) or separate (a constituent of a mixture, etc) by a physical or chemical process. **3** to take (a passage) from something for quoting, copying or performing. **4** to find (a mathematical root) by calculation. ➤➤ **extractability** /-'biliti/ *noun*, **extractable** *adj*, **extractive** /-tiv/ *adj*. [Middle English *extracten* from Latin *extractus*, past part. of *extrahere*, from EX-¹ + *trahere* to draw]

extract² /'ekstrakt/ *noun* **1** a passage taken from a book, musical composition, etc, e.g. for quoting or performing. **2** a solution or concentrate of the essential constituents of a complex material, e.g. an aromatic plant, prepared by extraction.

extraction /ik'straksh(ə)n/ *noun* **1** the act or an instance of extracting. **2** ancestry or origin. **3** something extracted.

extractor *noun* **1** a device used to extract something, e.g. juice. **2** = EXTRACTOR FAN.

extractor fan *noun* a type of ventilator, usu electrically driven, designed to expel fumes, stale air, etc.

extracurricular /ˌekstrəkə'rikyoolə/ *adj* **1** not falling within the scope of a regular school or college curriculum: *extracurricular activities*. **2** lying outside one's normal activities.

extraditable /'ekstrədietəbl/ *adj* subject to or warranting extradition: *an extraditable offence*.

extradite /'ekstrədiet/ *verb trans* **1** to hand (somebody) over for extradition. **2** to obtain the extradition of (a criminal suspect or fugitive). [back-formation from EXTRADITION]

extradition /ekstrə'dish(ə)n/ *noun* the surrender of an alleged criminal by one state to another having the power by law to try the charge. [French *extradition*, from EX-¹ + Latin *tradition-*, *traditio* act of handing over, from *tradere*: see TRAITOR]

extrados /ek'straydos/ *noun* in architecture, the convex upper surface of an arch: compare INTRADOS. [French *extrados*, from EXTRA- + *dos* back]

extragalactic /ˌekstrəgə'laktik/ *adj* situated or coming from outside the Milky Way.

extrajudicial /ˌekstrəjooh'dish(ə)l/ *adj* **1** not forming part of regular legal proceedings: *an extrajudicial investigation*. **2** done in contravention of law: *an extrajudicial execution*. ➤➤ **extrajudicially** *adv*.

extramarital /ekstrə'maritl/ *adj* said of sexual relations: occurring outside marriage; adulterous.

extramural /ekstrə'myooərəl/ *adj* **1** outside the walls or boundaries of a place or organization. **2** *chiefly Brit* for students of a university, college, etc who do not attend on a full-time basis: *extramural studies*. ➤➤ **extramurally** *adv*.

extraneous /ik'strayni-əs/ *adj* **1** not forming an essential or vital part; irrelevant: *an extraneous scene that added nothing to the play*. **2** on or coming from the outside. ➤➤ **extraneously** *adv*, **extraneousness** *noun*. [Latin *extraneus*: see STRANGE]

extraordinary /ik'strawdin(ə)ri, ekstrə'aw-/ *adj* **1a** going beyond what is usual, regular, or customary: *extraordinary powers*. **b** highly exceptional; remarkable: *extraordinary beauty*. **2** (*also used after a noun*) on or for a special function or service: *an ambassador extraordinary*; *an extraordinary general meeting*. ➤➤ **extraordinarily** *adv*, **extraordinariness** *noun*. [Middle English *extraordinarie* from Latin *extraordinarius*, from *extra ordinem* out of course, from *extra* outside + *ordinem*, accusative of *ordin-*, *ordo* ORDER¹]

extraordinary general meeting *noun* a meeting of the board of directors or the shareholders of a business company that is held specially to discuss an important matter.

extrapolate /ik'strapəlayt/ *verb trans* **1** in mathematics, to predict (a value of a variable at a given point) by extending a line or curve plotted on a graph from known values at previous points. **2a** to use or extend (known data or experience) in order to surmise or work out something unknown. **b** to predict (something) by extrapolating known data or experience. ➤ *verb intrans* to perform the act or process of extrapolating something. ➤➤ **extrapolation** /-'laysh(ə)n/ *noun*, **extrapolative** /-lətiv/ *adj*, **extrapolator** *noun*. [EXTRA- + *-polate* as in INTERPOLATE]

extrasensory /ekstrə'sens(ə)ri/ *adj* residing beyond or outside the ordinary physical senses.

extrasensory perception *noun* the faculty of perception by means other than the known senses, e.g. by telepathy and clairvoyance.

extraterrestrial¹ /ˌekstrətə'restri-əl/ *adj* originating, existing, or occurring outside the earth or its atmosphere.

extraterrestrial² *noun* an extraterrestrial being.

extraterritorial /ˌekstrəteri'tawri-əl/ *adj* existing or taking place outside the territorial limits of a country etc.

extraterritoriality /ˌekstrəteritawri'aliti/ *noun* exemption from the application or authority of local law or tribunals, *esp* such privileges granted to diplomats serving in a foreign country.

extra time *noun* a period of playing time added to the end of a match, *esp* in certain football competitions, to resolve a draw.

extravagance /ik'stravəg(ə)ns/ *noun* **1** an extravagant act; *specif* an excessive or wasteful outlay of money. **2** something extravagant, e.g. showy or unrestrained behaviour. **3** the quality of being extravagant.

extravagancy /ik'stravəg(ə)nsi/ *noun* (*pl* **extravagancies**) = EXTRAVAGANCE.

extravagant /ik'stravəg(ə)nt/ *adj* **1a** wasteful, *esp* of money. **b** profuse. **2** unreasonably high in price; exorbitant. **3a** lacking in moderation, balance, and restraint; excessive: *extravagant praise*. **b** excessively elaborate or showy. ➤➤ **extravagantly** *adv*. [early French *extravagant* wandering, irregular, from medieval Latin *extravagant-*, *extravagans*, from EXTRA- + Latin *vagant-*, *vagans*, present part. of *vagari* to wander about]

extravaganza /ik,stravə'ganzə/ *noun* **1** a lavish or spectacular show or event. **2** a literary or musical work marked by extreme freedom of style and structure. [Italian *estravaganza* extravagance, from medieval Latin *extravagant-*, *extravagans*: see EXTRAVAGANT]

extravasate /ik'stravəsayt/ *verb trans* to cause (blood or another fluid) to escape from a proper vessel or channel. ➤ *verb intrans* **1** to pass by infiltration from a proper vessel or channel, e.g. a blood vessel, into surrounding tissue. **2** said of lava: to pour out. ➤➤ **extravasation** /-'saysh(ə)n/ *noun*. [EXTRA- + Latin *vas* vessel + -ATE⁴]

extravehicular /ˌekstrəvee'hikyoolə/ *adj* taking place outside a spacecraft in flight: *extravehicular activity*.

extravert /'ekstrəvuht/ *noun and adj* see EXTROVERT.

extra virgin *adj* said of olive oil: extracted by the first cold pressing of the olives and therefore of the highest quality.

extreme¹ /ik'streem/ *adj* **1a** existing in a very high degree: *extreme poverty*. **b** going to great or exaggerated lengths; not moderate: *an extreme right-winger*. **c** exceeding the usual or expected; severe: *extreme measures*. **2** situated at the farthest possible point from a centre or the nearest to an end: *the extreme north of the country*. **3a** most advanced or thoroughgoing: *the extreme avant-garde*. **b** maximum: *the extreme penalty*. ➤➤ **extremely** *adv*, **extremeness** *noun*. [Middle English via Old French from Latin *extremus*, superl of *exter*, *exterus*: see EXTERIOR¹]

extreme² *noun* **1** something situated at or marking a point at one end or the other of a range: *extremes of heat and cold*. **2** (*also in pl*) a very pronounced or extreme degree: *His enthusiasm was carried to extremes.* **3** (*also in pl*) an extreme measure or expedient: *She goes to extremes.* **4** the first or last term of a mathematical proportion or series. ✴ **in the extreme** to the greatest possible extent: *boring in the extreme.*

extreme fighting *noun* = ULTIMATE FIGHTING.

extreme sports *pl noun* sports such as base-jumping, bungee jumping, and canyoning which offer a high level of excitement but which also involve a certain element of danger, sometimes to the point of being life-threatening.

extreme unction *noun* = ANOINTING OF THE SICK.

extremism *noun* advocacy of extreme political measures; radicalism.

extremist[1] /ik'streemist/ *noun* an advocate of extreme measures; a radical.

extremist[2] *adj* advocating extreme measures; radical.

extremity /ik'stremiti/ *noun* (*pl* **extremities**) **1a** the furthest or most extreme part or point. **b** the greatest or most extreme degree. **2** (*also in pl*) a limb or the end of a limb, *esp* a human hand or foot. **3a** extreme misfortune or danger of destruction or death. **b** a moment marked by such misfortune or danger. **4** (*also in pl*) a drastic or desperate act or measure.

extricate /'ekstrikayt/ *verb trans* to disentangle (something, somebody, or oneself), *esp* with considerable effort: *She managed to extricate herself from a tricky situation.* ⋙ **extricable** /-kəbl/ *adj*, **extrication** /-'kaysh(ə)n/ *noun*. [Latin *extricatus*, past part. of *extricare*, from EX-[1] + *tricae* trifles, perplexities]

extrinsic /ek'strinsik, -zik/ *adj* **1** not forming part of or belonging to a thing; extraneous. **2** originating from or on the outside. ⋙ **extrinsically** *adv*. [French *extrinsèque* from Latin *extrinsecus* from without]

extro- *prefix* forming words, with the meaning: outward: *extrovert.* [alteration of EXTRA-]

extrovert *or* **extravert** /'ekstrəvuht/ *noun* **1** a person whose attention and interests are directed wholly or predominantly towards what is outside the self: compare INTROVERT[1]. **2** a sociable, gregarious, or outgoing person: compare INTROVERT[1]. ⋙ **extroversion** /-'vuhsh(ə)n/ *noun*, **extrovert** *adj*, **extroverted** *adj*. [EXTRO- + Latin *vertere* to turn]

extrude /ik'stroohd/ *verb trans* **1** to force or push (something) out. **2** to shape (metal, plastic, etc) by forcing it through a die. ➤ *verb intrans* to become extruded. ⋙ **extrudable** *adj*, **extruder** *noun*. [Latin *extrudere*, from EX-[1] + *trudere* to thrust]

extrusion /ik'stroohzh(ə)n/ *noun* **1** the act or process of extruding, or a form or product produced by this process. **2a** the flowing out of lava onto the earth's surface through vents and fissures in the earth's crust during volcanic eruption. **b** a mass of rock formed by extrusion; an extrusive rock. [medieval Latin *extrusion-, extrusio*, from Latin *extrusus*, past part. of *extrudere*]

extrusive /ik'stroohsiv, -ziv/ *adj* said of a rock: formed by crystallization of lava forced out at the earth's surface. [Latin *extrusus*, past part. of *extrudere*: see EXTRUDE]

exuberant /ig'zyoohb(ə)rənt/ *adj* **1a** joyously unrestrained and enthusiastic: *exuberant high spirits.* **b** lavish and flamboyant: *exuberant metaphors.* **2** great or extreme in degree, size, or extent. **3** abundant or luxuriant: *exuberant vegetation.* ⋙ **exuberance** *noun*, **exuberantly** *adv*. [Middle English via French from Latin *exuberant-, exuberans*, present part. of *exuberare* to be abundant, from EX-[1] + *uber* fruitful, from *uber* udder]

exudate /'eksyoodayt/ *noun* exuded matter.

exude /ig'zyoohd/ *verb intrans* to ooze out: *Moisture exuded from the damp wall.* ➤ *verb trans* **1** to allow or cause (a liquid or smell) to ooze or spread out in all directions. **2** to display (a quality, feeling, etc) in abundance: *She exudes charm.* ⋙ **exudation** /eksyoo'daysh(ə)n/ *noun*. [Latin *exsudare*, from EX-[1] + *sudare* to sweat]

exult /ig'zult/ *verb intrans* (*often* + at/in/over) to be extremely joyful; to rejoice openly: *The captain exulted over his team's victory.* ⋙ **exultancy** /-si/ *noun*, **exultant** *adj*, **exultantly** *adv*, **exultation** /eksəl'taysh(ə)n, egzəl-/ *noun*, **exultingly** *adv*. [early French *exulter*, from Latin *exsultare*, literally 'to leap up', from EX-[1] + *saltare* to leap]

exurb /'eksuhb/ *noun* NAmer a prosperous district outside a city and usu beyond its suburbs. ⋙ **exurban** /ek'suhbən/ *adj*, **exurbanite** /-bəniet/ *noun and adj*. [EX-[1] + *-urb* as in SUBURB]

exurbia /ek'suhbi·ə/ *noun* NAmer exurbs collectively.

exuviae /ig'zyoohviee/ *pl noun* (*treated as sing. or pl*) the natural coverings of animals, e.g. the skins of snakes, after they have been shed. ⋙ **exuvial** /-vi·əl/ *adj*. [Latin *exuviae*, from *exuere* to take off]

exuviate /ig'zyoohviayt/ *verb trans* to moult or shed (skin or a shell). ⋙ **exuviation** /-'aysh(ə)n/ *noun*.

ex-voto /eks'vohtoh/ *noun* (*pl* **ex-votos**) an offering given in fulfilment of a vow or in gratitude or devotion. [Latin *ex voto* according to a vow]

ex-works *adj and adv* Brit direct from the factory.

-ey *suffix* see -Y[1].

eyas /'ee·əs/ *noun* a young hawk, *esp* one reared or taken from the nest for falconry. [Middle English, alteration (by incorrect division of *a neias*) of *neias*, from early French *niais* fresh from the nest, ultimately from Latin *nidus* nest]

eye[1] /ie/ *noun* **1a** an organ of sight; *esp* a nearly spherical liquid-filled organ that is lined with a light-sensitive retina and housed in a bony socket in the skull. **b** the visible parts of the eye with its surrounding structures, e.g. eyelashes and eyebrows. **c** the faculty of seeing with the eyes: *a keen eye for detail.* **d** the faculty of intellectual or aesthetic perception or appreciation: *an eye for beauty.* **e** a gaze or glance: *trying to catch his eye.* **f** view or attention: *in the public eye.* **2** something suggestive of an eye, e.g.: **a** the hole through the head of a needle. **b** a loop, *esp* one of metal into which a hook is inserted or one at the end of a rope. **c** an undeveloped bud, e.g. on a potato. **d** a circular mark, e.g. on a peacock's tail. **e** the centre of a flower, *esp* when differently coloured or marked. **3** a calm area in the centre of a storm, hurricane, etc. **4** the centre or nub: *the eye of the problem* — Norman Mailer. **5** the direction from which the wind is blowing. ✴ **all eyes** watching closely. **an eye for an eye** retaliation in kind [from God's commandments to the Israelites on just retribution (Exodus 21:24)]. **close/shut one's eyes to** to ignore (something) deliberately. **get/keep one's eye in** Brit to get into or keep in practice. **half an eye** less than full attention. **have eyes for** to be interested in (somebody or something): *She only had eyes for her fiancé.* **have one's eye on 1** to watch (somebody or something), *esp* constantly and attentively. **2** to have (something) as an objective. **in the eye/eyes of** in the judgment or opinion of (somebody): *Beauty is in the eye of the beholder.* **keep an/one's eye on** to watch (somebody or something) carefully. **keep one's eyes open/peeled/skinned** to be on the alert; to be watchful. **make eyes at** to ogle (somebody). **more than meets the eye** more than is at first obvious or apparent. **one in the eye for** a disappointment or setback for (somebody). **put somebody's eye/eyes out** to make somebody blind in one or both eyes, e.g. by pushing or poking them. **see eye to eye** to have a common viewpoint; to agree. **set/clap/lay eyes on** to catch sight of (somebody or something); to see (them). **with an eye to** having (something) as an aim or purpose. **with one's eyes open** in a state of full awareness of the problems, difficulties, etc that a situation will present. ⋙ **eyeless** *adj*, **eyelike** *adj*. [Old English *ēage*]

eye[2] *verb trans* (**eyes, eyed, eyeing** *or* **eying**) to fix the eyes on (something or somebody).

eyeball[1] *noun* the more or less spherical capsule of the eye of a vertebrate animal formed by the SCLERA (white outer coat) and the CORNEA (transparent membrane at the front), together with the structures they contain. ✴ **eyeball to eyeball** *informal* face to face, *esp* with hostility.

eyeball[2] *verb trans* chiefly NAmer, *informal* to look at (somebody or something) intently.

eyebath *noun* a small oval cup specially shaped for applying liquid remedies to the eye.

eyebolt *noun* a bolt with a looped head.

eyebright *noun* any of several species of tiny plants of the foxglove family with very small white or violet flowers: genus *Euphrasia*. Also called EUPHRASIA. [from its former use as a remedy for eye ailments]

eyebrow *noun* the ridge over the eye or the line of hair that grows on it: *And then the lover ... with a woeful ballad made to his mistress' eyebrow* — Shakespeare. ✴ **raise an eyebrow** to show surprise. **raise eyebrows** to cause surprise. **up to one's eyebrows** deeply involved.

eyebrow pencil *noun* a cosmetic pencil for defining the eyebrows.

eye-catching *adj* strikingly visually attractive. ➤➤ **eye-catcher** *noun,* **eye-catchingly** *adv.*

eye contact *noun* a meeting of eyes when two people look directly at each other: *They made eye contact.*

eyed *adj (used in combinations)* having an eye or eyes of the kind or number specified: *an almond-eyed woman.*

eyeful /'ief(ə)l/ *noun informal* **1** a pleasing sight; *specif* an attractive person. **2** a look or gaze.

eyeglass *noun* **1** a lens worn to aid vision; *specif* a monocle. **2** *chiefly NAmer (in pl)* glasses; spectacles. **3** = EYEPIECE.

eyehole *noun* = PEEPHOLE.

eyelash *noun* the fringe of hair edging the eyelid or a single hair of this fringe.

eyelet[1] /'ielit/ *noun* **1** a small reinforced hole designed so that a cord, lace, etc may be passed through it. **2** a small typically metal ring to reinforce an eyelet; a grommet. **3** a small hole reinforced with stitching, used decoratively in embroidery. [Middle English *oilet* from early French *oillet,* dimin. of *oil* eye, from Latin *oculus*]

eyelet[2] *verb trans* (**eyeleted, eyeleting**) to make eyelets in (something).

eye level *noun* the height at which the eyes are looking straight ahead.

eyelid *noun* a movable lid of skin and muscle that can be closed over the eyeball.

eyeliner *noun* a cosmetic for emphasizing the outline of the eyes.

eye-opener *noun informal* **1** something surprising and revelatory: *His behaviour was a real eye-opener to me.* **2** *chiefly NAmer* a drink, *esp* of alcohol, intended to stop one feeling sleepy on waking up. ➤➤ **eye-opening** *adj.*

eyepiece *noun* the lens or combination of lenses looked through at the eye end in an optical instrument.

eye rhyme *noun* a rhyme in which two words, e.g. *move* and *love,* appear from their spelling to rhyme but are pronounced differently.

eyeshade *noun* a small shield, usu shaped like the peak of a cap, that shades the eyes from strong light and is fastened to the head with a headband.

eye shadow *noun* a coloured cream or powder applied to the eyelids to accentuate the eyes.

eyeshot /'ieshot/ *noun* the range to which one can see; view.

eyesight *noun* the power of seeing or the ability to see; sight: *You need good eyesight for this job.*

eyesore *noun* something offensive to the sight, *esp* an ugly building.

eyespot /'iespot/ *noun* **1** a simple visual organ of pigment or pigmented cells. **2** a spot of colour, or an eyelike marking, e.g. on the wing of a butterfly.

eyestrain /'iestrayn/ *noun* tiredness or a strained state of the eyes caused by overuse, e.g. with continual close work in poor light, or by neglecting to treat faulty vision.

Eyetie /'ietie/ *noun Brit, informal, offensive* an Italian. ➤➤ **Eyetie** *adj.* [by shortening and alteration]

eyetooth *noun* (*pl* **eyeteeth**) a canine tooth of the upper jaw. ✳ **give one's eyeteeth for** to do anything in order to obtain or achieve (something): *I'd give my eyeteeth for a figure like that!*

eye up *verb trans informal* to look at (somebody) in order to assess their sexual attractiveness: *He was eyeing up the talent.*

eyewash *noun* **1** *informal* deceptive statements or actions; rubbish or nonsense. **2** lotion for the eyes.

eyewitness *noun* a person who sees an occurrence and can bear witness to it, e.g. in a court of law.

eyot /ayt, 'ay·ət/ *noun* see AIT.

eyrie *or* **aerie** /'iəri, 'eəri, 'ie·əri/ *noun* **1** the nest of a bird, *esp* a bird of prey, on a cliff or a mountain top. **2** a room or dwelling situated high up: *in her seventh-floor eyrie in Mayfair.* [medieval Latin *aerea, eyria,* from Old French *aire,* from Latin *area* area: see AREA]

eyrir /'ayriə/ *noun* (*pl* **aurar** /'owrah/) a unit of currency in Iceland, worth 100th of a króna. [Icelandic *eyrir* from Old Norse *aurar* money]

Ezek. *abbr* Ezekiel (book of the Bible).

e-zine /'eezeen/ *noun* a magazine, newsletter, fanzine, etc published on the Internet.

Ezr. *abbr* Ezra (book of the Bible).

F¹ *or* **f** *noun* (*pl* **F's** *or* **Fs** *or* **f's**) **1a** the sixth letter of the English alphabet. **b** a written character or design denoting this letter. **c** the sound represented by this letter, one of the English consonants. **2** an item designated as F, *esp* the sixth in a series. **3** in music, the fourth note of the diatonic scale of C major.

F² *abbr* **1** Fahrenheit. **2** false. **3** farad(s). **4** female. **5** fighter (aircraft type). **6** in genetics, filial generation. **7** *Brit* used on pencils: fine. **8** in physics, force. **9** franc. **10** France (international vehicle registration).

F³ *abbr* the chemical symbol for fluorine.

f¹ *abbr* **1** fathom(s). **2** in grammar, feminine. **3** femto-. **4** folio. **5** following (page). **6** in music, forte. **7** furlong(s).

f² *symbol* **1** focal length. **2** in electronics, frequency. **3** in mathematics, function.

FA *abbr* **1** Fanny Adams. **2** in Britain, Football Association.

fa *or* **fah** /fah/ *noun* in music, the fourth note of a major scale in the tonic sol-fa system, or the note F in the fixed-doh system. [Middle English from Latin: see GAMUT]

FAA *abbr* **1** *NAmer* Federal Aviation Administration. **2** *Brit* Fleet Air Arm.

fab /fab/ *adj informal* fabulous or great.

Fabian¹ /'faybi-ən/ *noun* a member of a socialist society founded in Britain in 1884 to work for the gradual establishment of socialism. ⮞ **Fabianism** *noun,* **Fabianist** *noun.* [Latin *Fabianus* of or like Quintus *Fabius* Maximus d.203 BC, Roman general who wore down his enemies while avoiding open battles]

Fabian² *adj* **1** of or relating to the Fabians. **2** using a cautious, gradual strategy to wear down an enemy.

fable¹ /'faybl/ *noun* **1** a story intended to convey a moral; *esp* one in which animals speak and act like human beings. **2a** a legendary story of supernatural happenings. **b** myths or legendary tales collectively. [Middle English via Old French from Latin *fabula* conversation, story, play, from *fari* to speak]

fable² *verb trans archaic* to talk or write about (a person, event, etc) as if true. ⮞ **fabler** *noun.*

fabled *adj* **1** told or celebrated in fables; legendary. **2** fictitious or imaginary.

fabliau /'fablioh/ *noun* (*pl* **fabliaux** /'fabliohz/) a short verse story, usu a coarsely satirical one, popular in France in the 12th and 13th cents. [French *fabliau* from Old French, dimin. of *fable*: see FABLE¹]

Fablon /'fablon/ *noun trademark* a plastic material with an adhesive backing, used for covering shelves, tables, etc. [prob a blend of FABRIC + NYLON]

fabric /'fabrik/ *noun* **1** a pliable material made by weaving, knitting, etc; cloth. **2a** the basic structure or framework of a building, *esp* the floor, walls, and roof: *The fabric of the theatre is sound.*

b the underlying structure of something abstract, e.g. a society or way of life. [early French *fabrique* from Latin *fabrica* workshop, structure, from *fabr-, faber* smith]

fabricate /'fabrikayt/ *verb trans* **1** to invent or create (e.g. a story), *esp* in order to deceive. **2** to construct or manufacture (a product) from many parts. ⮞ **fabrication** /-'kaysh(ə)n/ *noun,* **fabricator** *noun.* [Middle English *fabricaten* from Latin *fabricatus*, past part. of *fabricari,* from *fabrica*: see FABRIC]

fabulist /'fabyoolist/ *noun* **1** a person who composes fables. **2** a person who tells lies.

fabulous /'fabyooləs/ *adj* **1** resembling things told of in fables, *esp* in incredible or exaggerated quality; extraordinary: *fabulous wealth.* **2** *informal* marvellous or great: *a fabulous party.* **3** told of in or based on fable: *fabulous beasts.* ⮞ **fabulously** *adv,* **fabulousness** *noun.* [Latin *fabulosus* from *fabula*: see FABLE¹]

facade *or* **façade** /fə'sahd/ *noun* **1** a face, *esp* the front or principal face, of a building. **2** a false or superficial appearance: *His confidence was just a facade.* [French *façade* from *face*: see FACE¹]

face¹ /fays/ *noun* **1a** the front part of the human head from the chin to the forehead: *My face looks like a wedding cake left out in the rain* — W H Auden. **b** the part of an animal that corresponds to the human face. **2** a facial expression, *esp* a grimace. **3a** a front, upper, or outer surface. **b** in geometry, each of the plane surfaces of a solid. **c** the side of a mountain or cliff. **d** the exposed working surface of a mine or excavation. **4** one aspect of something: *the ugly face of capitalism.* ✳ **if one's face fits** *Brit* if one is suitable, e.g. for a particular job. **in the face/in face of** in opposition to (something); despite. **on the face of it** at first glance; apparently. **put a bold/brave face on something** to pretend that something unpleasant is tolerable. **set one's face against** to be resolutely opposed to (something). **to somebody's face** in somebody's presence; directly or frankly. [Middle English via French from Latin *facies* make, form, face, from *facere* to make, do]

face² *verb trans* **1** to have the face or front towards (something): *Turn to face the wall; a house facing the park.* **2** to meet or deal with (a situation or problem) firmly and without evasion; to confront. **3** to have (something unpleasant) to come; to have the prospect of: *They were facing ruin.* **4** to cover the front or surface of (something): *a building faced with marble.* ⮞ *verb intrans* **1** to have the face or front turned in a specified direction: *The house faces towards the east.* **2** said of soldiers: to turn the face in a specified direction. ✳ **face the music** to confront and endure the unpleasant consequences of one's actions [said to be from the ceremony of dismissing a disgraced military officer, in which he faces drummers who beat a roll while the insignia are ripped from his uniform and his sword is broken]. **face up to** to confront (a difficulty or problem) without shrinking from it.

face card *noun chiefly NAmer* = COURT CARD.

facecloth noun a cloth for washing the skin, esp the face; a flannel.

faced /fayst/ adj (used in combinations) having a face of the specified kind: hard-faced; two-faced.

face down verb trans to prevail against (somebody) by defiant confrontation.

face flannel noun Brit a facecloth.

faceless adj lacking identity; anonymous: faceless civil servants. ➤➤ **facelessness** noun.

face-lift noun **1** plastic surgery to remove signs of ageing, e.g. wrinkles or sagging skin. **2** an alteration intended to improve appearance or utility; a refurbishment: The kitchen could do with a face-lift.

face mask noun **1** a mask worn over the nose and mouth for protection. **2** a face-pack.

face off verb intrans **1** chiefly NAmer to confront somebody, e.g. before a fight. **2** in lacrosse or ice hockey, to start play with a face-off.

face-off noun **1** chiefly NAmer a confrontation between hostile parties. **2** in lacrosse or ice hockey, a method of putting a ball or puck in play in which two opposing players stand facing each other and on a signal attempt to gain control of the ball or puck.

face-pack noun chiefly Brit a cream, paste, etc applied to the face to improve the complexion and remove impurities.

face paint noun brightly coloured paint for decorating the face. ➤➤ **face-painter** noun, **face-painting** noun.

faceplate noun **1** a disc fixed with its face at right angles to the driven spindle of a lathe, to which the article being worked on is attached. **2** the glass panel at the front of a diving helmet or space helmet. **3** in electronics, the front part of a cathode-ray tube carrying the phosphor screen.

facer noun chiefly Brit, informal **1** an unexpected difficulty for which no solution is immediately apparent. **2** a blow to the face.

face-saving adj serving to preserve one's dignity or reputation. ➤➤ **face-saver** noun.

facet /'fasit/ noun **1** a plane surface, e.g. of a cut gem. **2** one aspect of something. **3** in zoology, the external surface of any of the optical elements of the compound eye of an insect or other arthropod. [French facette, dimin. of face: see FACE¹]

faceted /'fasitid/ adj (used in combinations) having facets of the specified kind: multifaceted.

facetiae /fə'seeshiee/ pl noun dated pornographic items in booksellers' catalogues. [Latin facetiae, pl of facetia jest, from facetus witty]

facetious /fə'seeshəs/ adj **1** inappropriately lacking seriousness; flippant. **2** intended to be amusing. ➤➤ **facetiously** adv, **facetiousness** noun. [early French facetieux from facetie jest, from Latin facetia: see FACETIAE]

face to face adv **1** said of two people: looking directly at each other. **2** in confrontation with somebody or something. ➤➤ **face-to-face** adj.

face value noun **1** the value indicated on the face of a postage stamp, a share certificate, etc, esp when this differs from the actual value. **2** the apparent value or significance of something: The results cannot be taken at face value.

facia¹ /'fayshi·ə/ noun chiefly Brit see FASCIA¹.

facia² /'fashi·ə/ noun see FASCIA².

facial¹ /'faysh(ə)l/ adj relating to or in the region of the face. ➤➤ **facially** adv.

facial² noun a beauty treatment for the face.

-facient comb. form forming adjectives and nouns, with the meaning: causing or bringing about a specified state or quality: abortifacient. [Latin facient-, faciens, present part. of facere to make, do]

facies /'fayshieez/ noun (pl **facies**) **1** in medicine, the facial appearance characteristic of a particular abnormal condition. **2** in geology, the distinguishing characteristics of a rock or rock formation, e.g. its composition, fossil content, and texture. [Latin facies: see FACE¹]

facile /'fasiel/ adj **1** indicating a lack of thought; superficial and glib: a facile solution. **2** easily or readily accomplished, attained, or performed: a facile victory. ➤➤ **facilely** adv, **facileness** noun. [early French facile from Latin facilis, from facere to make, do]

facilitate /fə'silitayt/ verb trans to make (e.g. a task) easier. ➤➤ **facilitation** /-'taysh(ə)n/ noun, **facilitative** /-tətiv/ adj, **facilitator** noun.

facility /fə'siliti/ noun (pl **facilities**) **1** a building, piece of equipment, resource, or feature designed to provide a particular service: leisure facilities; We offer an on-line ordering facility. **2** an ability to do something easily; an aptitude: She has a facility for mathematics. **3** ease in doing or performing something.

facing noun **1a** a lining at the edge of a garment, for stiffening or ornament. **b** (in pl) the collar, cuffs, and trimmings of a uniform coat, of a contrasting colour to the coat itself. **2** an ornamental or protective layer applied to a wall.

facsimile¹ /fak'siməli/ noun an exact copy, esp of printed material. [Latin fac simile make similar]

facsimile² verb trans (**facsimiles, facsimiled, facsimileing**) to make a facsimile of (something).

fact /fakt/ noun **1** an actual event or occurrence. **2** a piece of information. **3** reality; truth. **4** in law, an actual or alleged event or state as distinguished from its legal effect or interpretation. ✳ **after the fact** in law, after a criminal act has been committed. **before the fact** in law, before a criminal act has been committed. **in fact** in reality; actually. **in point of fact** in truth; actually. [Latin factum neuter past part. of facere to make, do]

facticity /fak'tisiti/ noun the quality or condition of being fact; reality or truth.

faction¹ /'faksh(ə)n/ noun **1** a party or minority group within a party, esp one that is seen as divisive. **2** a spirit of dissension within a party or group. ➤➤ **factional** adj, **factionalism** noun, **factionally** adv. [via French from Latin faction-, factio act of making, faction, from facere to make, do]

faction² noun in literature, cinema, etc, the dramatized reconstruction of real historical situations or events: Faction has actually been around for quite some time … Shakespeare was the first great faction writer in his history plays — The Guardian. [blend of FACT and FICTION]

-faction comb. form forming nouns from verbs ending in '-fy', denoting: **1** making: liquefaction. **2** state: satisfaction. [Middle English -faccioun via early French -faction from Latin -faction-, -factio, from facere to make, do]

factionalize or **factionalise** /'fakshənəliez/ verb intrans to break into factions.

factious /'fakshəs/ adj caused by or inclined to dissension. ➤➤ **factiously** adv, **factiousness** noun. [early French factieux from Latin factiosus, from factio: see FACTION¹]

factitious /fak'tishəs/ adj produced artificially; sham or unreal: They created a factitious demand by spreading rumours of shortage. ➤➤ **factitiously** adv, **factitiousness** noun. [Latin facticius from factus, past part. of facere to make, do]

factitive /'faktətiv/ adj in linguistics, denoting a transitive verb that can take an objective complement as well as an object, e.g. paint in paint the town red. [Latin factitivus from factus: see FACTITIOUS]

factive /'faktiv/ adj in linguistics, denoting a verb that gives the status of a fact to its object, e.g. made in I made the party a success: compare CONTRAFACTIVE, NON-FACTIVE.

fact of life noun (pl **facts of life**) **1** something that exists and must be accepted or taken into consideration, esp something unpleasant or undesirable. **2** (**the facts of life**) details of the processes and behaviour involved in sex and reproduction.

factoid /'faktoyd/ noun **1** something that is widely accepted as a fact but is not really true. **2** NAmer a snippet of factual information.

factor¹ /'faktə/ noun **1** a condition, force, or fact that actively contributes to a result. **2** in mathematics, one of two or more numbers or quantities that can be multiplied together to produce a given number or quantity. **3** formerly, in biology, a gene. **4** in physiology, a substance in the blood that causes it to clot. **5a** a person who acts for another; an agent. **b** an organization that purchases a manufacturer's invoices for less than their face value and becomes responsible for collecting payment from customers. **c** chiefly Scot a land agent. [Middle English via French from Latin factor doer, from facere to make, do]

factor² verb trans (**factored, factoring**) **1** to express (a number) as the product of factors. **2** to sell (receivable debts) to a factor.

✳ **factor in/out** to include or exclude (something) as a factor when considering a matter. ⟫ **factorable** adj.

Factor 8 noun a protein in the blood that is involved in clotting. A deficiency of this protein is one of the causes of haemophilia.

factorage /'fakt(ə)rij/ noun the charges made by a factor for his or her services.

factor analysis noun in statistics, a method of analysing a body of data that allows the identification of the various factors that have contributed to the measurements obtained, and the assessment of their contributions.

factorial[1] /fak'tawri-əl/ noun in mathematics, the product of all the integers from one to a given positive integer: *Factorial three (written 3!) is 6 (1 x 2 x 3).*

factorial[2] adj of a factor or a factorial. ⟫ **factorially** adv.

factorize or **factorise** verb trans to calculate the factors of (a number). ⟫ verb intrans said of a number: to be able to be expressed in terms of its factors. ⟫ **factorization** /-'zaysh(ə)n/ noun.

factory /'fakt(ə)ri/ noun (pl **factories**) 1 a building or set of buildings containing machinery used for manufacturing. 2 formerly, a trading settlement or depot, esp one maintained by a European country in Asia or Africa. [early French *factorie* building where factors trade, ultimately from Latin *factor*: see FACTOR[1]]

factory farming noun a system of agriculture, esp in milk, egg, or meat production, that uses intensive production methods. ⟫ **factory farm** noun.

factory floor noun the workers in a factory or company as distinct from the management.

factory outlet noun = FACTORY SHOP.

factory ship noun a large fishing or whaling ship that has the equipment to process its catch.

factory shop noun a shop that sells goods made by a factory directly to the customer, esp surplus goods at a discount.

factotum /fak'tohtəm/ noun (pl **factotums**) a person employed to carry out many types of work. [Latin *fac* do + *totum* everything]

factual /'faktyooəl, -chooəl/ adj restricted to or based on fact. ⟫ **factuality** /-'aliti/ noun, **factually** adv, **factualness** noun.

facture /'fakchə/ noun the manner in which something, esp an artistic work, is made; execution or style. [Middle English via Old French from Latin *factura* action of making, from *facere* to make, do]

facula /'fakyoolə/ noun (pl **faculae** /-lee/) in astronomy, a bright region of the sun's PHOTOSPHERE (luminous surface layer), seen most easily near sunspots. ⟫ **facular** adj. [Latin *facula*, dimin. of *fac-, fax* torch]

facultative /'fakəltətiv/ adj 1 not bound to occur under particular conditions; optional. 2 in biology, said of an organism: able to live under more than one set of environmental conditions: compare OBLIGATE[2]. ⟫ **facultatively** adv.

faculty /'fakəlti/ noun (pl **faculties**) 1 an inherent capability, power, or function of the body: *the faculty of hearing.* 2 a natural aptitude; a talent: *He has a faculty for saying the right things.* 3a chiefly Brit a group of related subject departments in a university. b NAmer (treated as sing. or pl) the staff of an educational institution. 4 power, authority, or prerogative given or conferred by law or a superior, esp a licence from an ecclesiastical authority. [Middle English *faculte* via Old French from Latin *facultat-, facultas* branch of learning or teaching, from *facilis*: see FACILE]

fad /fad/ noun 1 a short-lived but enthusiastically pursued practice or interest; a craze. 2 an idiosyncratic taste or habit. ⟫ **faddish** adj, **faddishly** adv, **faddishness** noun, **faddism** noun, **faddist** noun. [origin unknown]

faddy /'fadi/ adj (**faddier, faddiest**) Brit having idiosyncratic likes and dislikes about food; fussy. ⟫ **faddily** adv, **faddiness** noun.

fade[1] /fayd/ verb intrans 1 to disappear gradually; to vanish: *The smile faded from his face.* 2a to lose freshness or brilliance of colour. b to disappear into obscurity after a period of brilliance: *Oh, the self-importance of fading stars. Never mind, they will all be black holes one day* — Jeffrey Bernard. 3 said of a vehicle brake: to lose power temporarily, esp because of prolonged use. 4a said of an image on a screen: to come gradually into or out of view, e.g. when changing or merging with another. b said of an electronic sound: to increase or decrease in volume or strength. 5 in golf, said of the ball: to deviate from a straight path, usu as a result of spin. ⟫ verb trans 1 to

cause (something) to fade. 2 NAmer, informal in dice, to match the bet of (an opponent). ⟫ **fadeless** adj. [Middle English *faden* via Old French from Latin *fatidus*, alteration of *fatuus* fatuous, insipid]

fade[2] noun 1 the act or an instance of fading. 2 in golf, a shot causing fading.

fade in verb trans and intrans to appear gradually or cause (sound or a picture) to appear gradually.

fade-in noun the gradual appearance of a sound or picture, usu in broadcasting or on film.

fade out verb trans and intrans to disappear gradually or cause (sound or a picture) to disappear gradually.

fade-out noun the gradual disappearance of a sound or picture, usu in broadcasting or on film.

fader /'faydə/ noun a device used to produce fade-in or fade-out of audio or video signals.

fad-surfing noun slang the persistent and often mindless following of the latest trends and gurus, esp in management.

faeces (NAmer **feces**) /'feeseez/ pl noun bodily waste discharged through the anus. ⟫ **faecal** /'feekl/ adj. [Middle English *feces* from Latin *faec-, faex* (sing.) dregs]

faerie or **faery** /'fayəri, 'feəri/ noun literary fairyland. [Old French *faerie*: see FAIRY]

Faeroese or **Faroese** /feəroh'eez/ noun (pl **Faeroese**) 1 a native or inhabitant of the Faeroe Islands. 2 the Germanic language of the Faeroese. ⟫ **Faeroese** adj.

faery /'fayəri, 'feəri/ noun see FAERIE.

faff[1] /faf/ verb intrans Brit, informal (+ about/around) to waste time over trifles; to fuss or dither. [orig to blow about; imitative]

faff[2] noun Brit, informal fuss or dithering.

fag[1] /fag/ noun Brit, informal a cigarette. [shortening of FAG END]

fag[2] noun chiefly Brit, informal 1 a tiring or boring task. 2 a pupil who acts as servant to an older pupil at a public school.

fag[3] verb intrans (**fagged, fagging**) chiefly Brit, informal 1 to work hard; to toil. 2 to act as a fag, esp in a public school. [obsolete *fag* to droop, perhaps from FLAG[3] or from FAG END]

fag[4] noun NAmer, informal, derog a male homosexual. ⟫ **faggy** adj. [shortening of FAGGOT[1]]

fag end noun chiefly Brit, informal 1 a cigarette end. 2 a worn-out end; a remnant. [*fag* end of a piece of cloth or a rope, from Middle English *fagge* flap]

fagged out adj chiefly Brit, informal tired or exhausted.

faggot[1] /'fagət/ noun 1 Brit a round mass of minced meat, e.g. pig's liver, mixed with herbs and usu breadcrumbs. 2 (NAmer **fagot**). a a bundle of sticks used as fuel. b a bundle of pieces of wrought iron to be shaped by hammering or rolling at high temperature. 3 chiefly NAmer, informal, derog a male homosexual. 4 Brit, informal, dated an old woman. [Middle English *fagot* via Old French and Italian from Greek *phakelos* bundle]

faggot[2] (NAmer **fagot**) verb trans (**faggoted, faggoting**, NAmer **fagoted, fagoting**) to ornament (a garment) with faggoting.

faggoting (NAmer **fagoting**) noun embroidery in which some of the threads are tied in the middle to form hourglass shapes.

fag hag noun chiefly NAmer, informal, derog a woman who seeks the company of homosexual men.

fagot /'fagət/ noun NAmer see FAGGOT[1], FAGGOT[2].

fagoting /'fagəting/ noun NAmer see FAGGOTING.

fah /fah/ noun see FA.

Fahr. abbr Fahrenheit.

Fahrenheit /'farənhiet/ adj of or being a scale of temperature on which water freezes at 32° and boils at 212° under standard conditions: *60 degrees Fahrenheit; the Fahrenheit scale.* [named after Gabriel *Fahrenheit* d.1736, German physicist, who invented it]

faience or **faïence** /fie'ahns, fie'onhs (French fajã:s)/ noun tin-glazed decorated earthenware. [*Faïence*, French name of *Faenza*, town in Italy where such pottery was made]

fail[1] /fayl/ verb intrans 1 to be unsuccessful at something: *They failed to reach the summit; Try again. Fail again. Fail better* — Samuel Beckett. 2 to neglect to do something: *The hospital failed to notify the parents.* 3a to stop functioning: *Her kidneys had failed.* b to be or become insufficient or inadequate: *failing schools.* 4a to lose strength; to weaken: *She had to retire because of failing health.* b to fade or die away: *The children were still playing in the failing light.* 5

to become bankrupt or insolvent. ➤ *verb trans* **1a** to be unable to reach the required quality or standard in (a test, examination, interview, inspection, etc). **b** to judge (somebody or something) as having failed an examination, test, etc. **2a** to disappoint the expectations or trust of (somebody): *Her friends had failed her.* **b** to prove inadequate for (somebody): *For once his courage failed him.* [Middle English *failen* via Old French from Latin *fallire*, alteration of *fallere* to deceive, disappoint]

fail² *noun* a mark indicating the failing of an examination. ✳ **without fail** without exception.

failing¹ *noun* a defect in character; a fault or imperfection.

failing² *prep* in absence or default of (something): *Failing specific instructions, use your own judgment.*

faille /fayl/ *noun* a closely woven silk, rayon, or cotton fabric with transverse ribs. [French *faille*, perhaps from early Dutch *falie* scarf]

failsafe *adj* **1** said of a machine: designed to return automatically to a safe condition, e.g. to switch itself off, in the event of failure or breakdown. **2** foolproof.

failure /'faylyə/ *noun* **1a** lack of success. **b** an unsuccessful or disappointing person or thing: *He was a good actor but a complete failure as a director.* **2a** the act or an instance of failing to perform a duty or expected action: *his failure to write to his children.* **b** the act or an instance of failing to function normally: *heart failure; a power failure.* **3** a failing in business; bankruptcy.

fain¹ /fayn/ *adv archaic* with pleasure: *I would fain go to France.* [Old English *fægen*]

fain² *adj archaic* **1** willing. **2** compelled.

fainéant /'fayni·ənt/ *noun archaic* an idle or ineffectual person. [French *fainéant* from early French *fait-nient*, literally, 'does nothing', by folk etymology from *faignant* shirker, from *faindre*, *feindre* to feign, shirk]

faint¹ /faynt/ *adj* **1** lacking distinctness, volume, or brightness; indistinct: *a faint light.* **2** slight: *a faint chance that it might snow.* **3** weak and dizzy as if about to lose consciousness. ✳ **not have the faintest** *informal* to have no idea at all about something. ➤➤ **faintly** *adv*, **faintness** *noun*. [Middle English from Old French *faint*, past part. of *faindre*: see FEIGN]

faint² *verb intrans* to lose consciousness briefly, because of a temporary decrease in the blood supply to the brain, e.g. through exhaustion or shock.

faint³ *noun* a brief loss of consciousness.

faint-hearted *adj* lacking courage or resolution; timid. ➤➤ **faint-heartedly** *adv*, **faint-heartedness** *noun*.

fair¹ /feə/ *adj* **1** free from favouritism or prejudice; honest or just. **2** conforming with the established rules; allowed: *a fair tackle.* **3** said of hair or complexion: light in colour. **4** moderately good or large; adequate: *He showed a fair knowledge of the game; We had to do a fair bit of driving.* **5** *Aus, NZ, informal* complete; utter. **6a** said of weather: fine. **b** said of wind: favourable. **7** *archaic* attractive or beautiful: *a fair maid.* ✳ **fair enough** *informal* used to agree that something is reasonable. **in a fair way to** likely to. **it's a fair cop** *informal* used in admission of guilt and acceptance of punishment. ➤➤ **fairness** *noun*. [Old English *fæger*]

fair² *adv* **1** in a fair way: *Play fair!* **2** *dialect* fairly; completely: *We were fair worn out.*

fair³ *noun* **1** a fun fair. **2** an exhibition designed to acquaint prospective buyers or the general public with products of a particular type: *a book fair.* **3** *esp* formerly, a periodic gathering of buyers and sellers at a particular place and time for trade or a competitive exhibition, usu accompanied by entertainment and amusements: *a sheep fair.* **4** a fete. [Middle English *feire* via Old French from Latin *feria* weekday, fair, sing. of *feriae* holy days, on which fairs were held]

fair⁴ *verb intrans dialect* said of the weather: to clear.

fair⁵ *noun archaic* a woman, *esp* a sweetheart.

fair⁶ *verb trans* to create a smooth outline of (a vehicle); to streamline.

fair and square *adv* **1** in an honest manner: *They won the match fair and square.* **2** exactly or directly: *He hit him fair and square on the nose.*

fair copy *noun* a piece of work written or printed again after corrections have been made.

fair dos /'dooz/ *pl noun Brit, informal* fair treatment. [*dos* treatment, shares, pl of DO²]

fairer sex *noun* = FAIR SEX.

fair game *noun* somebody or something open to legitimate pursuit, attack, or ridicule: *He was fair game for our criticism.*

fairground *noun* an area where outdoor fairs, circuses, or exhibitions are held.

fair-haired *adj* **1** having blond hair. **2** *NAmer* favourite: *He was the office's fair-haired boy.*

fairing¹ *noun* a smooth structure intended to reduce drag or air resistance, e.g. on a car, motorcycle, or aircraft. [FAIR⁶]

fairing² *noun Brit, archaic* a present bought or given at a fair. [FAIR³]

fairish *adj informal* fairly good: *a fairish wage for those days.*

Fair Isle *noun* a style of knitting having horizontal patterned bands worked in two or more colours against a plain background, or a garment or fabric in this style. [named after *Fair Isle*, one of the Shetland Islands, where it originated]

fairlead /'feəleed/ *noun* a block or ring that serves as a guide for a rope or chain on a boat, and keeps it from chafing.

fairly *adv* **1** impartially or honestly. **2** in a proper or legal manner. **3** to a moderate extent or degree: *I was fairly hungry.* **4** positively: *He fairly snatched the newspaper from me.*

fair-minded *adj* just or unprejudiced. ➤➤ **fair-mindedly** *adv*, **fair-mindedness** *noun*.

fair play *noun* equitable or impartial treatment; justice. ✳ **fair play to somebody** used to express approval or support: *Did she throw him out? Fair play to her!*

fair sex *noun* (**the fair sex**) *dated* women.

fair-spoken *adj* pleasant and courteous in speech.

fair trade *noun* trade that supports producers in developing countries by making sure that they receive fair prices.

fairway *noun* **1** the mown part of a golf course between a tee and a green. **2a** a navigable channel in a river, bay, or harbour. **b** a route regularly used by ships.

fair-weather friend *noun* a friend who is present or loyal only in untroubled times.

fairy /'feəri/ *noun* (*pl* **fairies**) **1** a small mythical being in human form with magical powers: *Every time a child says, 'I don't believe in fairies,' there is a fairy somewhere that falls down dead* — J M Barrie. **2** *informal, derog* a male homosexual. **3** a hummingbird of Central and S America: genus *Heliothryx.* ➤➤ **fairylike** *adj*. [Middle English *fairie* fairyland, fairy people, via Old French *faerie* from Latin *Fata*, goddess of fate, from *fatum*: see FATE¹]

fairy cake *noun Brit* an individual sponge cake, usu iced and decorated.

fairy floss *noun Aus* candy floss.

fairy godmother *noun* **1** in fairy stories, a woman who comes to the aid of the heroine or hero. **2** *informal* a benefactor.

fairyland *noun* **1** the land of fairies. **2** a place of magical charm.

fairy lights *pl noun chiefly Brit* small coloured electric lights hung up for decoration, *esp* outdoors or on a Christmas tree.

fairy ring *noun* **1** a ring of dark vegetation on the ground caused by fungi growing outwards in a circle. **2** a ring of mushrooms or toadstools. [from the folk belief that such rings were caused by fairies dancing]

fairy story *noun* **1** a children's story featuring magical or imaginary places and characters. **2** a made-up story, *esp* one designed to mislead; a fabrication.

fairy tale *noun* **1** a fairy story. **2a** (*used before a noun*) marked by apparently magical success or good fortune: *a fairy tale start to his career.* **b** (*used before a noun*) marked by great beauty or perfection: *a fairy tale wedding dress.*

fait accompli /ˌfayt ə'kompli (*French* fɛt akɔ̃pli)/ *noun* (*pl* **faits accomplis** /ˌfayts ə'kompli (*French* fɛz akɔ̃pli)/) something already accomplished and considered irreversible. [French *fait accompli* accomplished fact]

faith /fayth/ *noun* **1** complete confidence or belief in something, *esp* without objective proof. **2a** a particular system of religious beliefs: *the Jewish faith.* **b** belief and trust in God. **c** belief in the traditional doctrines of a religion: *Absolute faith corrupts as absolutely as absolute power* — Eric Hoffer. [Middle English *feith* via Old French from Latin *fides*]

faithful[1] /'faythf(ə)l/ *adj* **1** loyal or steadfast; *specif* having sexual relations only with one's spouse or partner. **2** true to the facts or to an original; accurate: *The portrait is a faithful likeness.* ⟫ **faithfulness** *noun*.

faithful[2] *noun* (*treated as pl*) **1** (**the faithful**) the full members of a church. **2** (**the faithful**) the body of adherents of a religion, e.g. Islam. **3** loyal followers or members: *the party faithful.*

faithfully /'faythf(ə)li/ *adv* in a faithful way. ✳ **yours faithfully** *chiefly Brit* used to end a formal letter when the writer does not know the recipient's name.

faith healing *noun* the cure of illnesses by prayer and faith, rather than by medical treatment. ⟫ **faith healer** *noun*.

faithless *adj* **1** lacking faith; disloyal or untrustworthy, e.g. to a spouse or partner. **2** lacking religious faith. ⟫ **faithlessly** *adv*, **faithlessness** *noun*.

faith school *noun* a school established mainly for pupils belonging to a particular faith or denomination.

faits accomplis /ˌfayts ə'kompli (*French* fɛz akɔ̃pli)/ *noun* pl of FAIT ACCOMPLI.

fajitas /fə'heetəz/ *pl noun* a Mexican dish consisting of small pieces of cooked spiced meat and vegetables, topped with grated cheese and wrapped in a tortilla. [Mexican Spanish *fajitas* little strips]

fake[1] /fayk/ *adj* counterfeit or phoney: *a fake ID card.*

fake[2] *noun* **1** a worthless imitation passed off as genuine. **2** an impostor or charlatan.

fake[3] *verb trans* **1** to forge or counterfeit (something): *He faked the artist's signature.* **2** to feign (an illness or emotion): *Sincerity: if you can fake it, you've got it made* — Daniel Schorr. ⟫ **faker** *noun*, **fakery** *noun*. [prob from German *fegen* to sweep, thrash]

fake[4] *noun* a loop of a coiled rope or cable.

fake[5] *verb trans* to coil (a rope or cable) in fakes. [Middle English *faken*; earlier history unknown]

fakir /'faykiə, 'fakiə/ *noun* **1** a Muslim holy man living off alms. **2** an itinerant Hindu ascetic holy man. [Arabic *faqīr*, literally 'poor man']

falafel *or* **felafel** /fə'lahfl/ *noun* a Middle Eastern snack made of ground chick-peas and spices, formed into balls and deep-fried. [Arabic *falāfil*]

Falangist /fə'lanjist/ *noun* a member of a Spanish fascist party founded in 1933 by José Antonio Primo de Rivera that ruled Spain after the civil war of 1936–39 and was the only legal political party in Spain until the death of General Franco in 1975. ⟫ **Falangism** *noun*, **Falangist** *adj*. [Spanish *Falangista*, from *Falange española* Spanish Phalanx, a fascist organization]

Falasha /fə'lahshə/ *noun* (*pl* **Falashas** *or collectively* **Falasha**) a member of a group of Ethiopian people who follow the Jewish religion. [Amharic *Falasha*, literally 'exile']

falcate /'falkayt/ *adj* in botany or zoology, hooked or curved like a sickle. [Latin *falcatus* from *falc-, falx* sickle, scythe]

falchion /'fawlchən, -sh(ə)n/ *noun* a broad-bladed slightly curved medieval sword. [Middle English *fauchoun* via Old French from Latin *falc-, falx* sickle, scythe]

falciform /'falsifawm/ *adj* = FALCATE. [Latin *falc-, falx* sickle, scythe + -IFORM]

falcon /'fawlkən/ *noun* **1** any of a genus of hawks with long pointed wings: genus *Falco*. **2** in falconry, a female falcon, *esp* a peregrine: compare TERCEL. [Middle English via Old French from late Latin *falcon-, falco*, prob of Germanic origin]

falconer /'fawlkənə/ *noun* a person who hunts with hawks or who breeds or trains hawks for hunting.

falconet /falkə'net/ *noun* **1** a very small cannon used in the 16th and 17th cents. **2** a small falcon, orig from Asia or S America: genus *Microhierax*. [(sense 1) Italian *falconetto*, dimin. of *falcone* falcon, from late Latin *falco*: see FALCON; (sense 2) FALCON + -ET]

falconry /'fawlkənri/ *noun* the art of training falcons or the sport of using falcons to pursue game.

falderal /'faldəral/ *noun* = FOLDEROL.

faldstool /'fawldstoohl/ *noun* **1** a folding stool or chair used by a bishop when officiating away from his throne. **2** a folding stool or small desk at which one kneels to pray. [Old English *fældestōl* and medieval Latin *faldistolium*, both of Germanic origin. More at FOLD[1], STOOL[1]]

fall[1] /fawl/ *verb intrans* (*past tense* **fell** /fel/, *past part.* **fallen** /'fawlən/) **1** to descend freely by the force of gravity. **2** to hang down. **3** to lose one's balance and come down to a prostrate position: *She slipped and fell on the ice.* **4** *euphem* to drop because wounded or dead, *esp* to die in battle. **5** said of the face: to assume a look of disappointment or dismay. **6** said of a place: to be captured in war: *After a long siege the city fell.* **7** to suffer ruin or defeat. **8** in cricket, said of a wicket: to be taken by the bowling side. **9** to become less or lower in level or pitch: *Their voices had fallen to a whisper.* **10** to decline in value: *Shares fell sharply today.* **11** *archaic* to yield to temptation; to sin. **12** to pass, *esp* involuntarily or suddenly, into a new state or condition: *They fell in love; The book fell apart.* **13** (*usu* + on) to occur at a specified time or place: *My birthday falls on a Monday; The accent falls on the second syllable.* **14** (+ on/to/upon) to become the duty or burden of somebody: *It fell to me to break the news.* **15** to come within the limits or scope of something: *The book falls into the category of teenage fiction.* ✳ **fall between two stools** see STOOL[1]. **fall for 1** *informal* to fall in love with (somebody). **2** *informal* to be deceived by (something, e.g. a trick). **fall into place** to begin to seem sensible or coherent. **fall off the back of a lorry** *informal* to be acquired dishonestly. **fall over oneself to do something** *informal* to display almost excessive eagerness to do something. **fall short** to fail to achieve a goal or target. [Old English *feallan*]

fall[2] *noun* **1** the act or an instance of falling. **2** something that falls or has fallen: *a heavy fall of leaves.* **3** *NAmer* autumn. **4** the distance that something falls. **5** a drop in height. **6** (*usu in pl, but treated as sing.*) a large and steep waterfall. **7** a downward slope. **8** a decrease in size, quantity, degree, or value. **9** a loss of greatness or power; a collapse or defeat: *The strikes contributed to the fall of the government.* **10** (**the Fall**) in Jewish and Christian theology, mankind's loss of innocence through the disobedience of Adam and Eve. **11** in wrestling, an act of forcing an opponent's shoulders to the floor for a prescribed time.

fall about *verb intrans* *Brit, informal* to be convulsed with laughter.

fallacy /'faləsi/ *noun* (*pl* **fallacies**) **1** a false idea: *the popular fallacy that scientists are illiterate.* **2** in logic, an argument failing to satisfy the conditions of valid inference. ⟫ **fallacious** /fə'layshəs/ *adj*, **fallaciously** /fə'layshəsli/ *adv*, **fallaciousness** /fə'layshəsnis/ *noun*. [Latin *fallacia*, from *fallac-, fallax* deceitful, from *fallere* to deceive]

fall away *verb intrans* **1** to withdraw friendship or support. **2** to slope down: *The land falls away to the east.*

fallback *noun* **1** something on which one can fall back; a reserve, alternative, or replacement. **2** a falling back; a retreat. **3** a reduction.

fall back *verb intrans* to retreat or recede. ✳ **fall back on/upon** to have recourse to (something): *When facts were scarce he fell back on his imagination.*

fall behind *verb intrans* to fail to keep up with somebody or something: *She had fallen behind with her work.*

fall down *verb intrans* **1** to collapse or drop to the ground. **2** *informal* (*often* + on) to fail to meet expectations or requirements; to be inadequate: *They fell down on the job.*

fallen[1] *verb* past part. of FALL[1].

fallen[2] *adj* **1** *dated* said of a woman: dishonoured from having had sexual relations outside marriage. **2** killed in battle.

faller /'fawlə/ *noun* **1** *Brit* somebody or something that falls, e.g. a racehorse that falls at a fence. **2** *NAmer* a person who fells trees.

fall guy *noun informal* **1** a scapegoat. **2** a person who is easily cheated or tricked.

fallible /'faləbl/ *adj* capable of being or likely to be wrong: *Both men and women are fallible. The difference is, women know it* — Eleanor Bron. ⟫ **fallibility** /-'biliti/ *noun*, **fallibly** *adv*. [Middle English from Latin *fallibilis* from *fallere* FAIL[1]]

fall in *verb intrans* **1** to sink or collapse inwards: *The roof fell in.* **2** said of a soldier: to take one's place in the ranks of a military formation. ✳ **fall in with 1** to concur with (something): *We had to fall in with her wishes.* **2** to begin to associate with (a person or group of people): *He had fallen in with a bad crowd.*

falling-out *noun* a disagreement or quarrel.

falling star *noun* a meteor.

fall line *noun* **1** the natural slope of a hill, e.g. one used for skiing, straight down from top to bottom. **2** in geography, a boundary between a higher region and a plain. Rapids and waterfalls often occur at the point where a river crosses this line.

falloff *noun* a decline, *esp* in quantity or quality: *a falloff in exports.*

fall off *verb intrans* **1** to become detached and drop to the ground. **2** to decline or decrease in quantity or quality.

Fallopian tube /fə'lohpi·ən/ *noun* either of the pair of tubes conducting the egg from the ovary to the uterus in female mammals. [named after Gabriel *Fallopius* d.1562, Italian anatomist who first described them]

fallout *noun* **1** polluting particles, *esp* radioactive particles resulting from a nuclear explosion, descending through the atmosphere. **2** secondary results or products: *The war produced its own literary fallout: a profusion of books* — Newsweek.

fall out *verb intrans* **1** (*often* + with) to have a disagreement; to quarrel. **2** said of a soldier: to leave one's place in the ranks of a military formation. **3** to happen; to come about: *Everything fell out as they had predicted.*

fallow[1] /'faloh/ *adj* **1** said of land: left unsown after ploughing. **2** dormant or inactive: *a fallow period.* **3** said of a sow: not pregnant. ▶▶ **fallowness** *noun.* [Old English *fealg*]

fallow[2] *noun* ploughed and harrowed land that is allowed to lie idle during the growing season.

fallow[3] *verb trans* to allow (land) to lie fallow.

fallow[4] *adj* of a light yellowish brown colour. ▶▶ **fallow** *noun.* [Old English *fealu*]

fallow deer *noun* a small European deer with broad antlers and a pale yellow coat spotted with white in the summer: *Cervus dama.*

fall through *verb intrans* said of a plan or arrangement: to fail to be carried out.

fall to *verb intrans* to begin doing something, e.g. working or eating, *esp* vigorously.

false /fawls/ *adj* **1** not based on reality; untrue or incorrect: *false allegations.* **2** not according to law or rules; invalid. **3a** intended to deceive; artificial: *false eyelashes; a false smile.* **b** illusory: *The weapon gave him a false sense of security.* **4** disloyal or treacherous. **5** used in names of plants, animals, and gems: resembling a more widely known kind: *false oats; false diamond.* ✻ **play somebody false** to deceive somebody; to treat them in a false manner. ▶▶ **falsely** *adv,* **falseness** *noun,* **falsity** *noun.* [Middle English *fals* via Old French from Latin *falsus,* past part. of *fallere* to deceive]

false alarm *noun* a warning that proves to be groundless.

false colour *noun* arbitrary colours added in the production of a photographic or computer image to aid interpretation of the image.

false dawn *noun* light that appears just before sunrise.

false economy *noun* an attempt to save money that actually wastes it.

false friend *noun* a word in one language that looks similar to one in another language, but has a different meaning.

false fruit *noun* in botany, a fruit formed from a part of a flower other than the carpel, e.g. the strawberry, which forms from the RECEPTACLE (end of the stalk).

falsehood *noun* **1** an untrue statement; a lie. **2** absence of truth or accuracy; falsity.

false imprisonment *noun* in law, the unauthorized holding of a person against his or her will.

false memory *noun* an apparent memory of something that did not really happen, e.g. of sexual abuse in childhood, perhaps prompted by suggestion during psychoanalysis.

false pretences *pl noun* acts or appearances intended to deceive: *She got the job under false pretences.*

false rib *noun* = FLOATING RIB.

false start *noun* **1** an early, incorrect start by a competitor in a race. **2** an abortive beginning to an activity or course of action.

false step *noun* **1** a stumble or slip. **2** an unwise action; a mistake.

falsetto /fawl'setoh/ *noun* (*pl* **falsettos**) in music, the technique of artificially producing a high male singing voice that extends above the range of the singer's normal voice. [Italian *falsetto,* dimin. of *falso* false, from Latin *falsus:* see FALSE]

falsework *noun* a temporary erection on which a main work is supported during construction.

falsies /'fawlsiz/ *pl noun informal* pads of foam rubber or other material worn inside a woman's clothing to increase the apparent size of the breasts.

falsify /'fawlsifie/ *verb trans* (**falsifies, falsified, falsifying**) **1a** to make (a document, accounts, etc) false by fraudulent alteration. **b** to represent (something) falsely; to misrepresent. **2** to prove or declare (a statement, etc) false. ▶▶ **falsifiable** *adj,* **falsification** /-fi'kaysh(ə)n/ *noun.* [Middle English *falsifien* via French from Latin *falsificare,* from *falsus:* see FALSE]

Falstaffian /fawl'stahfi·ən/ *adj* fat, jolly, and somewhat disreputable: *An affable Irregular, a heavily-built Falstaffian man, comes cracking jokes* — W B Yeats. [Sir John *Falstaff,* character in Shakespeare's *Henry IV* and *The Merry Wives of Windsor*]

falter /'fawltə/ *verb* (**faltered, faltering**) ▶ *verb intrans* **1a** to hesitate in purpose or action; to waver. **b** to lose strength or effectiveness; to weaken: *The business was faltering.* **2** to walk or move unsteadily or hesitatingly; to stumble. **3** to speak brokenly or weakly; to stammer. ▶ *verb trans* to utter (something) in a hesitant or broken manner. ▶▶ **falterer** *noun,* **faltering** *adj,* **falteringly** *adv.* [Middle English *falteren;* earlier history unknown]

fame /faym/ *noun* the state of being famous; renown or recognition: *Fame will go by and, so long, I've had you, fame* — Marilyn Monroe. [Middle English via Old French from Latin *fama* report, fame]

famed *adj* famous.

familial /fə'mili·əl/ *adj* **1** characteristic of or relating to a family or its members. **2** said of a disease: having a higher than average occurrence among members of a family. [French *familial* from Latin *familia:* see FAMILY]

familiar[1] /fə'milyə/ *adj* **1** frequently seen or experienced; common or well-known: *a familiar sight; familiar faces.* **2** (+ with) having knowledge of something: *She wasn't familiar with the route.* **3a** close or intimate. **b** too intimate and unrestrained; presumptuous. ▶▶ **familiarly** *adv,* **familiarness** *noun.* [Middle English *familier* via Old French from Latin *familiaris,* from *familia:* see FAMILY]

familiar[2] *noun* **1** an intimate associate; a companion. **2** = FAMILIAR SPIRIT. **3** a member of the household of a high official, e.g. a bishop.

familiarise *verb trans* see FAMILIARIZE.

familiarity /fə,mili'ariti/ *noun* (*pl* **familiarities**) **1** (*often* + with) close acquaintance with or knowledge of a thing or a place. **2a** closeness; intimacy. **b** an unduly informal act or expression; an impropriety.

familiarize *or* **familiarise** *verb trans* (+ with) to make (somebody) familiar with something: *Familiarize yourselves with the rules.* ▶▶ **familiarization** /-'zaysh(ə)n/ *noun.*

familiar spirit *noun* a spirit or demon that waits on a witch.

famille /fa'mee/ *noun* a type of Chinese porcelain of the 17th and 18th cents with a background or design of a predominant colour. *Famille jaune* was predominantly yellow, *famille rose* pink or red, *famille verte* green, and *famille noire* black. [French *famille* family, from Latin *familia:* see FAMILY]

family /'faməli/ *noun* (*pl* **families**) **1** (*treated as sing. or pl*). **a** a group of related people living together; *esp* a group comprising one set of parents, or a single parent, and their children. **b** somebody's children. **2** a group of people related by common ancestry, descent, or marriage. **3** a group of related languages descended from a single ancestral language. **4** a group of people united by their common convictions, e.g. of religion or philosophy; a fellowship or brotherhood. **5** in biology, a category in the classification of organisms ranking above genus and below order. **6** a closely related group. **7** (*used before a noun*) of or suitable for a family or all of its members: *family entertainment.* ✻ **in the family way** *informal* pregnant. [Middle English *familie* from Latin *familia* household (including servants as well as kin of the householder), from *famulus* servant]

family balancing *noun* the use of genetic means to determine the sex of children in order to achieve a balanced family.

family credit *noun* in Britain, a state payment for families with a low income and one or more dependent children.

family man *noun* a man who has a wife and children, *esp* one who enjoys spending time with them.

family name *noun* a surname.

family planning *noun* the control of the timing and number of babies born in a family, *esp* with the use of contraception.

family therapy *noun* a form of psychotherapy in which all the members of a family participate, so that they can be helped to understand their relationships and to communicate more effectively.

family tree *noun* a diagram of a genealogy.

family values *pl noun* standards of morality, discipline, etc, thought of as being associated with the traditional family unit.

famine /'famin/ *noun* **1** an extreme scarcity of food. **2** any great shortage. **3** *archaic* a ravenous appetite. [Middle English via Old French from Latin *fames* hunger]

famish /'famish/ *verb trans and intrans archaic* to suffer or cause (somebody) to suffer severely from hunger. [Middle English *famishen* from Old French *afamer*, from AD- + Latin *fames* hunger]

famished /'famishd/ *adj informal* very hungry.

famous /'fayməs/ *adj* **1** well-known. **2** *informal, dated* excellent or first-rate: *famous weather for a walk.* ➤ **famousness** *noun.* [Middle English via Old French from Latin *famosus*, from *fama* FAME]

famously *adv* **1** as is well-known: *He once famously appeared drunk on a chat show.* **2** *informal* very well: *We got on famously together.*

famulus /'famyooləs/ *noun* (*pl* **famuli** /-lie, -lee/) formerly, a private secretary or attendant, e.g. to a scholar. [German *Famulus* assistant to a professor, from Latin *famulus* servant]

fan¹ /fan/ *noun* **1a** a device, usu a series of vanes radiating from a hub rotated by a motor, for producing a current of cool or warm air. **b** a folding circular or semicircular device that is opened and waved to and fro by hand to produce a cooling current of air. **2** something shaped like an open fan. ➤ **fanlike** *adj.* [Old English *fann* from Latin *vannus* winnowing fan]

fan² *verb* (**fanned, fanning**) ➤ *verb trans* **1** to cause a current of air to blow on (somebody or something): *She fanned the child's face with her programme.* **2** to drive (something) away by waving: *He fanned away the smoke, coughing loudly.* **3** to cause (something) to spread out in the shape of an open fan. **4** to increase the intensity of (a fire) by agitating the air around it. **5** to stir up or stimulate (e.g. an emotion). **6** *NAmer* in baseball, to strike out (a batter). ➤ *verb intrans* **1** (*usu* + out) to spread out in the shape of an open fan: *Tanks fanned out across the plain; The bride's train fanned out behind her.* **2** *NAmer* in baseball, to strike out. ➤ **fanner** *noun.*

fan³ *noun* an enthusiastic supporter or admirer, e.g. of a sport, pursuit, or celebrity. [short for FANATIC]

Fanagalo *or* **Fanakalo** /'fanəgəloh, ˌfanəgə'loh/ *noun* a language based on Zulu, Afrikaans, and English that is used as a lingua franca in S Africa, *esp* among the workers in gold mines. [Nguni *fana ka lo* be like this]

fanatic /fə'natik/ *noun* **1** a person who is excessively and often uncritically enthusiastic, *esp* about a religion or cause: *A fanatic is one who can't change his mind and won't change the subject* — Winston Churchill. **2** *informal* a person who is excessively keen on a hobby, sport, etc. ➤ **fanatic** *adj*, **fanatical** *adj*, **fanatically** *adv*, **fanaticism** /-siz(ə)m/ *noun.* [Latin *fanaticus* inspired by a deity, frenzied, from *fanum* temple]

fan belt *noun* in an internal-combustion engine, an endless belt driving a cooling fan for a radiator.

fancier /'fansi·ə/ *noun* somebody with a particular interest in something, *esp* a person who breeds a specified animal or grows a specified plant for points of excellence, e.g. for showing: *a pigeon fancier.*

fanciful /'fansif(ə)l/ *adj* **1** given to or guided by fancy or imagination rather than by reason and experience; unrealistic. **2** existing in fancy only; imaginary. **3** marked by fancy or whim; *specif* elaborate or contrived. ➤ **fancifully** *adv*, **fancifulness** *noun.*

fan club *noun* an organized group of people who are enthusiastic supporters or admirers of the same celebrity, band, sports team, etc.

fancy¹ /'fansi/ *verb trans* (**fancies, fancied, fancying**) **1a** to have a fancy for (somebody or something); to like or desire (them): *How do you fancy going to the pictures?; I really fancy blond men.* **b** to consider (somebody or something) likely to do well: *Which horse do you fancy?* **2** to believe (something) without knowledge or evidence: *I fancy I've seen you somewhere before.* **3** *informal* (*usu in imperative*) to form a conception of (something); to imagine (it): *It's hard to fancy how she thought that would help; Just fancy that! The Queen shopping at Tesco!* ✳ **fancy oneself** *informal* to have a high, usu too high, opinion of one's own worth, ability, etc. ➤ **fanciable** *adj.* [Middle English, contraction of FANTASY²]

fancy² *adj* (**fancier, fanciest**) **1a** not plain or ordinary, and *esp* of a fine quality: *fancy cakes.* **b** ornamental: *fancy goods.* **c** highly decorated or decorative; not plain: *He was all dressed up in his fancy jacket.* **2** based on fancy or the imagination; whimsical. **3** *informal* extravagant or exorbitant: *I don't shop there. I don't like their fancy prices.* **4a** said of an animal or plant: bred *esp* for bizarre or ornamental qualities. **b** said of a flower: of two or more colours: *fancy carnations.* ➤ **fancily** *adv*, **fanciness** *noun.*

fancy³ *noun* (*pl* **fancies**) **1** a liking based on whim rather than reason; an inclination: *He took a fancy to her.* **2a** a notion or whim. **b** a mental image or representation of something. **3a** imagination, *esp* of a capricious or delusive sort. **b** the power of mental conception and representation, used in artistic expression, e.g. by a poet. **4a** (**the fancy**) *archaic* (*treated as sing. or pl*) a group of fanciers or of devotees of a particular sport, *esp* boxing. **b** *informal* somebody or something considered likely to do well, e.g. in a race. **5** a small iced cake: *He bought a box of French fancies.*

fancy dress *noun* unusual or amusing dress, e.g. representing a historical or fictional character, worn for a party or other special occasion.

fancy-free *adj* free to do what one wants, *esp* because not involved in an amorous relationship. ✳ **footloose and fancy-free** see FOOTLOOSE.

fancy goods *pl noun* small decorative goods or novelties.

fancy man *noun* **1** *informal, derog* a woman's, *esp* a married woman's, lover. **2** a pimp.

fancy woman *noun informal, derog* **1** a man's, *esp* a married man's, lover; = MISTRESS. **2** a prostitute.

fancywork *noun* decorative needlework.

fan dance *noun* a solo dance performed by a woman who is or appears to be in the nude and who uses large fans to partially cover herself in a titillating way.

fandangle /fan'dang·gl/ *noun* **1** an elaborate ornament or piece of jewellery. **2** nonsense. [perhaps from FANDANGO]

fandango /fan'danggoh/ *noun* (*pl* **fandangos**) a lively Spanish dance in triple time, usu performed by a couple to the accompaniment of guitar and castanets, or the music for this dance. [Spanish *fandango*]

fane /fayn/ *noun archaic* a church or temple. [Middle English from Latin *fanum* temple]

fanfare /'fanfeə/ *noun* **1** a flourish of brass instruments, *esp* trumpets, usu for a ceremonial occasion. **2** a showy outward display. [French *fanfare*, prob of imitative origin]

fanfaronade /ˌfanfərə'nahd/ *noun formal* empty boasting; bluster. [French *fanfaronnade* from Spanish *fanfarronada*, from *fanfarrón* braggart]

fang /fang/ *noun* **1a** a tooth by which an animal's prey is seized and held or torn. **b** any of the long hollow or grooved teeth of a venomous snake. **c** any of the clawlike structures around the mouthpart of a spider. **2** a projecting tooth or prong. **3** the root of a tooth or any of the prongs into which a root divides. ➤ **fanged** *adj*, **fangless** *adj.*

Word history
Old English *fang* booty, plunder, from Old Norse *fang* capture, grasp; the Old Norse meaning is recorded in English from the 14th to the 17th cent. Current senses probably came from the idea of something that grips, grasps, or snags.

fan heater *noun* an electric heater that blows out warm air by means of a fan.

fan-jet *noun* a jet engine in which some of the air drawn in bypasses the combustion chambers, or an aircraft powered by such an engine.

fanlight *noun* a window, *esp* a semicircular one, with radiating divisions over a door or window.

fanny /'fani/ *noun* (*pl* **fannies**) **1** *Brit, coarse slang* the female genitals. **2** *NAmer, informal* the buttocks. [*Fanny*, nickname for *Frances*]

Fanny Adams *or* **sweet Fanny Adams** /'adəmz/ *noun Brit, informal* absolutely nothing.

Word history
orig a nautical term for tinned meat, named after a murder victim whose body was cut up into small pieces. The current sense is partly a euphemism for *fuck all*.

fanny pack *noun NAmer* a bum bag.

fantail noun **1** a fan-shaped tail or end. **2a** a domestic pigeon having a broad rounded tail often with 30 or 40 feathers. **b** any of numerous species of flycatchers found in SE Asia and Australasia, having fan-shaped tails: genus *Rhipidura*. **3** *chiefly NAmer* the overhanging stern of a vessel; = COUNTER⁴. ➤➤ **fan-tailed** *adj*.

fan-tailed flycatcher /'fantayld/ *noun* = FANTAIL (2B).

fan-tan /'fan tan/ *noun* **1** a Chinese gambling game in which the banker divides a pile of objects into fours and players bet on what number will be left at the end. **2** a card game in which players must build in sequence upon sevens and attempt to be the first one with no cards left. [Chinese (Cantonese), from *faan* chance + *taan* to spread out]

fantasia /fan'tayzi-ə/ *noun* a free instrumental or literary composition not in strict form, comprising familiar tunes. [Italian *fantasia* and German *Fantasie* fancy, fantasy, from Latin *phantasia*: see FANTASY¹]

fantasize *or* **fantasise** /'fantəsiez/ *verb intrans* (*often* + about) to indulge in reverie; to create or develop imaginative and often fantastic views or ideas: *We fantasized about winning the pools.* ➤➤ *verb trans* to indulge in reverie about (something). *He fantasized that he went to the Olympics.* ➤➤ **fantasist** /-sist/ *noun*.

fantastic /fan'tastik/ *adj* **1a** unreal or imaginary. **b** so extreme as to challenge belief; incredible. **c** exceedingly large or great. **2** marked by extravagant fantasy or eccentricity; unrealistic. **3** *informal* wonderful; eccentric: *He looked fantastic in his velvet jacket.* ➤➤ **fantastical** *adj*, **fantasticality** /-'kaliti/ *noun*, **fantastically** *adv*, **fantasticalness** *noun*.

Word history

Middle English *fantastic, fantastical* via French and late Latin from Greek *phantastikos* producing mental images, from *phantazein* to present to the mind and *phantazesthai* to imagine, both from *phantos* visible. In the 16th–19th cent. the spellings *phantastic*, and *phantasy* FANTASY¹, were also used.

fantasy¹ /'fantəsi/ *noun* (*pl* **fantasies**) **1** an extravagant mental image or daydream, or the power or process of creating one, e.g. in response to a psychological need. **2a** a creation of the unrestricted imagination whether expressed or merely conceived, e.g. a fantastic design or idea. **b** a fantasia. **c** imaginative fiction or drama characterized *esp* by strange, unrealistic, or grotesque elements. **3** unrestricted creative imagination; fancy. [Middle English *fantasie* via French from Latin *phantasia* imagination, appearance, ultimately from Greek *phantazein*: see FANTASTIC]

fantasy² *verb trans* (**fantasies**, **fantasied**, **fantasying**) **1** to fantasize (something). **2** to visualize or conceive (something).

Fanti *or* **Fante** /'fanti/ *noun* (*pl* **Fantis** *or* **Fantes** *or collectively* **Fanti** *or* **Fante**) **1** a member of an African people of Ghana. **2** the language of this people, a dialect of Akan.

fan vaulting *noun* an elaborate system of vaulting in which the ribs diverge from a single shaft to resemble the framework of a fan.

fanzine /'fanzeen/ *noun* a magazine for fans, *esp* of a particular sports team, pop star, or literary genre. [FAN³ + MAGAZINE]

FAO *abbr* **1** Food and Agriculture Organization of the United Nations. **2** for the attention of.

FAQ *abbr* in computing, frequently asked question.

far¹ /fah/ *adv* (**farther** /'fahdhə/, **further** /'fuhdhə/, **farthest** /'fah-dhist/, **furthest** /'fuhdhist/) **1** to or at a considerable distance in space: *They wandered far into the woods.* **2a** by a broad interval: *the far distant hills.* **b** (+ from) in total contrast to: *Far from criticizing you, I'm delighted.* **3** to or at an extent or degree: *As far as I know, she won't be coming; I wouldn't go so far as to say you were wrong, but I think you were unwise.* **4a** to or at a considerable distance or degree: *A bright student will go far.* **b** very much: *far too hot.* **5** to or at a considerable distance in time: *I worked far into the night.* ✻ **a far cry from** something totally different to something else: *Life on the island was a far cry from what she had been used to in the city.* **by far** by a considerable margin: *By far the quickest way is through London.* **far and away** by a considerable margin: *They were far and away the best team.* **far and near/wide** in every direction; everywhere; over a large area: *They advertised the event far and wide.* **far be it from me** used to express reluctance, or pretended reluctance, to say or do something: *Far be it from me to interfere, but I do think you are making a big mistake.* **far gone 1** in a very poor or serious state because of drink, injury, etc. **2** said of a period of time: far advanced. **far out 1** *informal, dated* excellent; wonderful. **2** *informal, dated* extremely unconventional; weird: *far-out clothes.* **go too far** to go beyond what is acceptable. **how far** to what extent,

degree, or distance: *They didn't know how far to trust him.* **in so far as** = INSOFAR AS. **so far 1** up to the present: *She has written only one novel so far.* **2** to a given extent, degree, or distance. **thus far** *formal* up to the present. [Old English *feorr*]

far² *adj* (**farther** *or* **further**, **farthest** *or* **furthest**) **1** remote in space, time, or degree: *in the far distance.* **2** long: *a far journey.* **3** being the more distant of two: *the far side of the lake.* **4** said of a political position: extreme: *the far left.*

farad /'farəd/ *noun* the SI unit of electrical capacitance. [named after Michael Faraday: see FARADAY]

faradaic /farə'dayik/ *adj* = FARADIC.

faraday /'farəday/ *noun* the quantity of electrical charge required to remove one gram equivalent of a chemical element from solution when a solution containing the element is broken down by electrolysis; about 96,500 coulombs per mole. [named after Michael *Faraday* d.1867, English physicist and chemist, who discovered the laws of electrolysis]

faradic /fə'radik/ *adj* of an alternating electric current produced by an induction coil. [French *faradique*, from the name of Michael Faraday: see FARADAY]

farandole /farən'dohl (*French* farãdɔl)/ *noun* a Provençal dance in which dancers hold hands forming a chain and follow a leader, or the music for this dance. [French *farandole* from Provençal *farandoulo*]

faraway *adj* **1** situated far away; lying at a great distance; remote. **2** dreamy or abstracted: *There was a faraway look in her eyes.*

farce /fahs/ *noun* **1** a comedy with an improbable plot that is concerned more with situation than characterization. **2** the broad humour characteristic of farce. **3** a ridiculous or nonsensical situation. **4** a travesty; a mockery: *The wine was a farce and the food a tragedy* — Anthony Powell. **5** = FORCEMEAT.

Word history

Middle English *farse* via Old French *farce* from Latin *farsa*, fem past part. of *farcire* to stuff. Senses 1–3 arose from the comic interludes 'stuffed' into religious plays.

farceur /fah'suh (*French* farsœːr)/ *noun* **1** a joker or wag. **2** a writer or actor of farce. [French *farceur* from Old French *farcer*, from *farce*: see FARCE]

farcical /'fahsikl/ *adj* of or resembling a farce, *esp* unintentionally; ludicrous or absurd. ➤➤ **farcicality** /-'kaliti/ *noun*, **farcically** *adv*, **farcicalness** *noun*.

farcy /'fahsi/ *noun* **1** cutaneous glanders, a disease of horses. **2** an ultimately fatal bacterial infection of cattle. [Middle English *farsin, farsi* via French and late Latin from Latin *farcimen* sausage, from *farcire* to stuff; from the swellings the diseases cause]

fardel /'fahdl/ *noun archaic* **1** a bundle. **2** a burden: *Who would fardels bear, to grunt and sweat under a weary life?* — Shakespeare. [Middle English from Old French, prob from Arabic *fardah*]

fare¹ /feə/ *noun* **1a** the price charged to transport somebody. **b** a paying passenger. **2** food provided for a meal: *good simple fare.* [Middle English in the senses 'journey', 'passage', 'supply of food', from Old English *faru, fær* journey, passage; related to Old English *faran* FARE²]

fare² *verb intrans* **1** *formal.* **a** to get along; to succeed or do: *How did you fare in your exam?* **b** to happen. **2** *archaic* to travel. **3** *archaic* to eat. [Old English *faran* to travel]

Far East *noun* the countries in Asia east of India, including China, Japan, Korea, and Indochina. ➤➤ **Far Eastern** *adj*.

fare stage *noun chiefly Brit* **1** any of the stops, e.g. on a bus route, between which a fare is calculated. **2** a distance that can be travelled for a minimum fare or for a single increment in a fare.

farewell¹ *interj archaic* goodbye.

farewell² *noun* **1** a parting wish for good luck; a goodbye. **2** an act of departure or leave-taking. **3** (*used before a noun*) of, for, or before departure or leave-taking: *a farewell drink.*

farfetched *adj* not easily or naturally deduced; improbable: *a farfetched example.* ➤➤ **farfetchedness** *noun*.

far-flung *adj* **1** remote: *a far-flung outpost of the Empire.* **2** widely spread or distributed.

farina /fə'reenə/ *noun* **1** a starchy flour or fine meal of vegetable matter, e.g. cereal grains, used chiefly as a cereal or for making puddings. **2** *archaic* any of various powdery or mealy substances. [Latin *farina* meal, flour, from *far* corn]

farinaceous /fari'nayshəs/ *adj* **1** containing or rich in starch; starchy. **2** having a mealy texture or surface.

farl *or* **farle** /fahl/ *noun Scot* a small thin triangular cake or biscuit sometimes made with oatmeal. [contraction of Scots *fardel* fourth part, from *ferde* fourth + *del* part]

farm[1] /fahm/ *noun* **1a** an area of land devoted to growing crops or raising domestic animals such as cattle and sheep and worked or managed as a single unit. **b** a group of buildings associated with a farm, *esp* a farmhouse: *Milk and eggs can be bought at the farm.* **2a** something resembling a farm, *esp* in housing a large number of individuals under farm-like conditions: *a mink farm.* **b** an area of water used to breed or produce fish, shellfish, etc commercially: *a fish farm.* **3** a place for the processing or storage of something: *a sewage farm.* [Middle English *ferme* rent, lease, via Old French from medieval Latin *firma* fixed payment, ultimately from *firmus* FIRM[1]]

farm[2] *verb intrans* to engage in the production of crops or livestock. ➤ *verb trans* **1a** to cultivate or rear (crops or livestock) on a farm. **b** to manage and cultivate (land) as farmland or as a farm. **2a** formerly, to collect and take the proceeds of (taxation or a business) on payment of a fixed sum. **b** formerly, to give up the proceeds of (an estate or a business) to another on condition of receiving in return a fixed sum of money. ➤ **farmable** *adj*, **farmed** *adj*, **farming** *noun.*

farmer *noun* **1** somebody who cultivates land or crops or raises livestock. **2** formerly, somebody who pays a fixed sum for some privilege or source of income.

farmer's lung *noun* a lung disorder causing breathlessness, fever, coughing, etc, caused by an allergic reaction to dust and spores *esp* from mouldy hay. Also called ASPERGILLOSIS.

farmhand *noun* a farm worker.

farmhouse /'fahmhows/ *noun* **1** a dwelling house on a farm. **2** (*used before a noun*) made on a farm, or of a similar type or quality: *farmhouse Cheddar.*

farm out *verb trans* **1** to turn (work) over to somebody for performance or use, usu on contract. **2** to put (children, etc) into somebody's care in return for a fee. **3** formerly, to give somebody the right to collect and keep the revenue from (a tax) on payment of a fixed sum.

farmstead /'fahmsted/ *noun* the buildings and adjacent areas of a farm.

farmyard *noun* the area round or enclosed by farm buildings.

faro /'feəroh/ *noun* a gambling game in which players bet on the value of the next card to be dealt. [prob alteration of earlier *pharaoh*, translation of French *pharaon* PHARAOH, said to have been a name given to the king of hearts]

Faroese /feəroh'eez/ *noun* see FAEROESE.

far-off *adj* remote in time or space.

farouche /fa'roohsh/ *adj* **1** shy or unpolished. **2** wild. [French *farouche* wild, shy, via late Latin from Latin *foras* outdoors]

farrago /fə'rahgoh/ *noun* (*pl* **farragoes** *or* **farragos**) a confused collection; a hotchpotch. ➤ **farraginous** /fə'rajinəs/ *adj.* [Latin *farragin-, farrago* mixed fodder, mixture, from *far* corn]

far-reaching *adj* having a wide range, influence, or effect.

farrier /'fari-ə/ *noun* **1** a blacksmith who shoes horses. **2** somebody who treats diseases or injuries of horses. ➤ **farriery** *noun.* [Old French *ferrier* from Latin *ferrum* iron]

farrow[1] /'faroh/ *noun* a litter of pigs. [Old English *fearh* young pig]

farrow[2] *verb trans* said of a sow: to give birth to (piglets).

farseeing *adj* = FARSIGHTED (1).

Farsi /'fahsee/ *noun* the modern Persian language, the official language of Iran. [Persian *fārsī*, from *Fārs* Persia]

farsighted *adj* **1** having foresight or good judgment; sagacious. **2** *NAmer* longsighted. ➤ **farsightedly** *adv*, **farsightedness** *noun.*

fart[1] /faht/ *verb intrans informal* to expel wind from the anus. [Old English *feortan*]

fart[2] *noun informal* **1** an expulsion of intestinal wind. **2** a boring or unpleasant person.

fart about *verb intrans chiefly Brit, informal* to spend time in pointless, aimless, or worthless activity.

fart around *verb intrans* = FART ABOUT.

farther[1] /'fahdhə/ *adv* **1** at or to a greater distance or more advanced point: *farther down the corridor.* **2** to a greater degree or extent; = FURTHER[1] (1). [alteration of FURTHER[1]]

Usage note
farther *or* **further**? These two words are sometimes confused. When referring to physical distance, *farther* and *further* are equally correct: *Penzance lies farther* (or *further*) *west than Truro.* In abstract and figurative senses, *further* is the preferred form: *of no further use; closed until further notice.* As a verb, only *further* is used: *to further God's purposes.*

farther[2] *adj* **1a** more distant; remoter. **b** being the more distant of two; = FAR[2] (3): *the farther side.* **2** extending beyond what exists or has happened; = FURTHER[2] (1).

farthermost *adj* most distant; farthest.

farthest[1] /'fahdhist/ *adj* most distant in space or time.

farthest[2] *adv* **1** to or at the greatest distance in space, time, or degree. **2** by the greatest degree or extent; most.

farthing /'fahdhing/ *noun* **1** a former British unit of currency worth a quarter of an old penny, or a coin representing this. **2** something of small value; a mite: *I haven't a farthing to spare.* [Old English *feorthung*, from *feortha* FOURTH]

farthingale /'fahdhinggayl/ *noun* a petticoat consisting of a framework of hoops, worn, *esp* in the 16th cent., to expand a skirt at the hip line. [modification of early French *verdugale* via Old Spanish from Latin *viridis*: see VERDANT]

fasces /'faseez/ *pl noun* (*treated as sing. or pl*) a bundle of rods containing an axe with a projecting blade carried before ancient Roman magistrates as a badge of authority and formerly used as the emblem of the Italian Fascist party. [Latin *fasces*, pl of *fascis* bundle]

fascia[1] (*chiefly Brit* **facia**) /'fayshi-ə/ *noun* **1a** a flat horizontal piece, e.g. of stone or board, under projecting eaves. **b** a nameplate over the front of a shop. **2** *chiefly Brit* the dashboard of a motor car. **3** a broad well-defined band of colour, e.g. on a plant or the wing of an insect. ➤ **fascial** *adj.* [via Italian from Latin *fascia* band, bandage]

fascia[2] *or* **facia** /'fashi-ə/ *noun* (*pl* **fasciae** /'fashi-ee/) a sheet of connective tissue covering or binding together body structures. [Latin *fascia* band, bandage]

fasciation /fashi'aysh(ə)n/ *noun* an abnormal enlargement and flattening of plant stems resulting from the fusion of several separate stems or side branches. ➤ **fasciated** /'fashiaytid/ *adj.*

fascicle /'fasikl/ *noun* **1** a division of a book published in parts. **2** = FASCICULUS. ➤ **fascicled** *adj.* [Latin *fasciculus*, dimin. of *fascis* bundle]

fasciculation /fə,sikyoo'laysh(ə)n/ *noun technical* **1** muscular twitching in which groups of muscle fibres contract simultaneously. **2** the state of being arranged in bundles. [Latin *fasciculus* (see FASCICLE) + -ATION]

fascicule /'fasikyoohl/ *noun* a division of a book published in parts; = FASCICLE (1). [French *fascicule* from Latin *fasciculus*: see FASCICLE]

fasciculus /fə'sikyooləs/ *noun* (*pl* **fasciculi** /-lie/) a slender bundle of anatomical fibres. ➤ **fascicular** *adj*, **fasciculate** /-lət/ *adj.* [Latin *fasciculus*: see FASCICLE]

fascinate /'fasinayt/ *verb trans* **1** to attract (somebody) strongly, *esp* by arousing interest or curiosity; to captivate (them). **2** to transfix (somebody or something) by an irresistible mental power: *Stoats can catch hares by fascinating them.* ➤ *verb intrans* to be irresistibly attractive. ➤ **fascination** /-'naysh(ə)n/ *noun.* [Latin *fascinatus*, past part. of *fascinare*, from *fascinum* witchcraft]

fascinating /'fasinayting/ *adj* **1** very interesting. **2** very attractive. ➤ **fascinatingly** *adv.*

fascinator /'fasinaytə/ *noun* **1** somebody or something that fascinates. **2** a woman's net, lace, or crocheted head covering.

fascine /fa'seen/ *noun* a long bundle of sticks of wood bound together and used for filling ditches, making parapets, etc. [French *fascine* from Latin *fascina*, from *fascis*: see FASCES]

fascism /'fashiz(ə)m/ *noun* **1** a political philosophy, movement, or regime that is aggressively nationalistic and stands for a centralized autocratic government headed by a dictatorial leader, severe regimentation, and forcible suppression of opposition. **2** *informal* brutal dictatorial control. ➤ **fascist** *noun and adj*, **fascistic** /fə'shistik/ *adj.* [Italian *fascismo*, from *fascio* bundle, fasces, group, from Latin *fascis*: see FASCES]

fash /fash/ *verb trans chiefly Scot* to vex (oneself). [early French *fascher* from Latin *fastidium*: see FASTIDIOUS]

fashion[1] /'fash(ə)n/ *noun* **1a** a prevailing and often short-lived custom or style. **b** the prevailing style or custom, *esp* in dress. **c** the business of fashion design and production: *Fashion is really about being naked* — Vivienne Westwood. **d** an affluent and fashionable lifestyle: *women of fashion.* **2** a manner or way: *The people assembled in an orderly fashion.* **3** the make or form of something. * **after a fashion** in an approximate or rough way: *She became an artist after a fashion.* **after/in the fashion of** in a similar way to. **in fashion** fashionable. **out of fashion** not fashionable. [Middle English *facioun, fasoun* shape, manner, via Old French from Latin *faction-, factio*: see FACTION[1]]

fashion[2] *verb trans* (**fashioned, fashioning**) to give shape or form to (something) *esp* by using ingenuity; to mould or construct (it). ▶▶ **fashioner** *noun.*

fashionable *adj* **1** conforming to the latest custom or fashion. **2** of the world of fashion; used or patronized by people of fashion: *fashionable shops.* ▶▶ **fashionability** /-'biliti/ *noun,* **fashionableness** *noun,* **fashionably** *adv.*

fashionista /fashə'histə/ *noun informal* a person who follows or writes about the latest fashions in clothing. [FASHION[1] + Spanish *-ista* -IST[1]]

fashion plate *noun* **1** an illustration of a clothing style, *esp* a new fashion. **2** somebody who dresses as the latest fashion dictates.

fashion victim *noun informal* somebody who dresses according to the latest fashion regardless of suitability or cost.

fast[1] /fahst/ *adj* **1a** moving or able to move rapidly; swift. **b** for rapid movement: *the fast lane of a motorway.* **c** conducive to rapidity of play or action or quickness of motion: *a fast pitch.* **2a** taking a comparatively short time. **b** accomplished quickly. **c** having or being a high photographic speed: *fast film.* **3** said of a suburban train: express. **4** indicating in advance of what is correct: *The clock was fast.* **5a** (*often used in combinations*) resistant to change from destructive action, fading, etc: *colourfast; acid-fast bacteria.* **b** said of a colour: permanently dyed; not liable to fade. **6a** firmly fixed or attached. **b** tightly closed or shut. **7** said of friends: firm; steadfast. **8** quick to learn. **9a** dissipated or wild: *a very fast set.* **b** said *esp* of a woman: forward or promiscuous. **10** *informal* dishonest, shady, or acquired by dishonest means or with little effort: *trying to make a fast buck.*

Word history
Old English *fæst* firm. Senses 1–3 come from the development of the adverb's meaning from 'firmly' to 'steadfastly, diligently, hence 'strongly, vigorously', and eventually 'rapidly'; sense 9 probably from the association of speed with recklessness and excitement.

fast[2] *adv* **1a** in a rapid manner; quickly. **b** in quick succession: *Orders came in thick and fast.* **2** ahead of a correct time or posted schedule. **3** in a firm or fixed manner. **4** sound or deeply: *I fell fast asleep.* **5** in a reckless or dissipated manner. **6** *archaic* close: *The house was fast by the village church.*

fast[3] *verb intrans* to abstain from some or all foods or meals, e.g. for religious reasons. ▶ *verb trans* to deprive (a person or an animal) of food, e.g. for medical reasons: *The animals were fasted for 24 hours before the experiment.* [Old English *fæstan*]

fast[4] *noun* an act or time of fasting.

fastback *noun* a motor car with a roof sloping backward to or nearly to the bumper.

fast breeder reactor *noun* a nuclear reactor in which fast neutrons are used to cause fission with the release of energy, and more fissionable material is produced than is used.

fasten /'fahs(ə)n/ *verb* (**fastened, fastening**) ▶ *verb trans* **1** to attach or secure (somebody or something), *esp* by pinning, tying, or nailing them or it. **2** to fix or direct (something) steadily: *He fastened his eyes on the awful sight.* **3** (+ on) to attach or impose (something) on somebody: *They fastened the blame on me.* ▶ *verb intrans* to become fixed. * **fasten on/upon/onto** **1** to focus attention on (something). **2** to take a firm grip or hold on (something). [Old English *fæstnian* to secure, confirm]

fastener /'fahs(ə)nə/ *noun* somebody or something that fastens, *esp* a means of fastening clothing, etc.

fastening *noun* something that fastens; a fastener.

fast food *noun* **1** take-away food, e.g. hamburgers or fried chicken, usu available on demand rather than being prepared indi-

vidually for each customer. **2** processed, e.g. frozen or packaged, food that can be prepared and served quickly. ▶▶ **fast-food** *adj.*

fast-forward[1] *noun* an operating facility on a video or tape recorder that causes the tape to be wound forward very quickly without being played, or the mechanism controlling this facility.

fast-forward[2] *verb trans* to wind (a video, cassette tape, or other recording) quickly forward. ▶ *verb intrans* to make rapid progress: *The Soviet Union has fast-forwarded into the video age* — Daily Express.

fastidious /fa'stidi·əs/ *adj* **1** excessively difficult to satisfy or please. **2** showing or demanding great delicacy or care. ▶▶ **fastidiously** *adv,* **fastidiousness** *noun.* [Middle English from Latin *fastidiosus,* from *fastidium* disgust, prob from *fastus* arrogance + *taedium* irksomeness]

fastigiate /fa'stijiət/ *adj* **1** said of a plant: having upright, usu clustered, branches. **2** said of body parts or organs: united in a cone-shaped bundle. ▶▶ **fastigiately** *adv.* [Latin *fastigium* gable + -ATE[3]]

fast lane *noun* **1** the lane of a motorway used by vehicles travelling at the highest speed. **2** a place of fast and frenzied activity. **3** a fiercely competitive route to quick promotion or success.

fastness *noun* **1a** the quality of being fixed. **b** the quality of being colourfast. **2** a fortified, secure, or remote place: *He spent the winter in his mountain fastness.*

fast neutron *noun* a neutron with high kinetic energy.

fast-talk *verb trans chiefly NAmer, informal* to influence or persuade (somebody) by fluent, facile, and usu deceptive talk.

fast track *noun* a method or procedure that gets quick results or rapid promotion.

fast-track[1] *adj* **1** rapidly promoting certain employees. **2** rapid; speeded up.

fast-track[2] *verb trans* **1** to deal with (something) as a priority: *We will fast-track your application.* **2** to promote (somebody) rapidly. ▶ *verb intrans* to go or be promoted rapidly: *Fast-track to the top with our graduates' training scheme.* ▶▶ **fast-tracker** *noun.*

fat[1] /fat/ *noun* **1** greasy or oily matter, or animal tissue consisting chiefly of cells distended with greasy or oily matter. **2** fatness; being fat. **3a** any of numerous compounds of carbon, hydrogen, and oxygen that are a major class of energy-rich food and are soluble in organic solvents, e.g. ether, but not in water. **b** a solid or semisolid fat as distinguished from an oil. **4** the best or richest part: *the fat of the land.* * **the fat is in the fire** something has been done which will have serious consequences. ▶▶ **fatless** *adj.*

fat[2] *adj* (**fatter, fattest**) **1** having an unusually large amount of fat; plump or obese: *Imprisoned in every fat man a thin one is wildly signalling to be let out* — Cyril Connolly. **2** said of a farm animal: fattened for market. **3** well filled out; thick or big: *She has written several fat volumes of poetry.* **4a** richly rewarding or profitable; substantial: *He's got a fat part in a new play.* **b** prosperous or wealthy: *They grew fat on the war.* **5** productive or fertile: *1998 was a fat year for crops.* **6** *informal* practically non-existent: *A fat chance you have of becoming Prime Minister!* **7** *informal* foolish or thick: *Get that idea out of your fat head.* ▶▶ **fatly** *adv,* **fatness** *noun,* **fattish** *adj.* [Old English *fætt,* past part. of *fætan* to cram]

fat[3] *verb trans* (**fatted, fatting**) *archaic* to fatten (a person or an animal): *a fatted calf.* * **kill the fatted calf** to put on a celebration: *You can hardly expect them to kill the fatted calf just because he's left Labour and joined the Greens.*

fatal /'faytl/ *adj* **1a** causing death. **b** bringing ruin. **c** *informal* productive of disagreeable or contrary results: *It's fatal to offer him a drink.* **2** fateful or decisive. **3** like fate in proceeding according to a fixed sequence; inevitable. ▶▶ **fatally** *adv.* [Middle English, in the sense 'decided by fate', via Old French from Latin *fatalis,* from *fatum*: see FATE[1]]

Usage note
fatal or **fateful**? These two words are sometimes confused. *Fatal* means 'causing or resulting in death': *a fatal accident* or 'causing ruin; ending in disaster': *a fatal mistake.* *Fateful* means 'momentously important': *their fateful meeting.* In the sense of 'having significant, often unpleasant consequences' either word may be used, although *fateful* is more usual: *that fateful day.* Care should be taken to avoid misinterpretation: *a fateful experiment* may change lives; *a fatal experiment* may lead to death.

fatalism *noun* the belief that all events are predetermined and outside the control of human beings. ▶▶ **fatalist** *noun,* **fatalistic** /-'listik/ *adj,* **fatalistically** /-'listikli/ *adv.*

fatality /fə'taliti/ *noun* (*pl* **fatalities**) **1a** death resulting from a disaster. **b** somebody who experiences or is subject to a fatal outcome, e.g. somebody killed in an accident. **2a** the quality or state of causing death or destruction. **b** the quality or condition of being destined for disaster. **3** something established by fate. **4** destiny; FATE[1].

fata morgana /ˌfahtə mawˈgahnə/ *noun* (*also* **Fata Morgana**) a mirage. [Italian *Fata Morgana* Morgan *le Fay* (Morgan the Fairy), sorceress of Arthurian legend]

fat cat *noun derog* a wealthy, privileged, and usu influential person.

fate[1] /fayt/ *noun* **1** the power beyond human control that determines events; destiny. **2a** an outcome or end, *esp* one that is adverse and inevitable. **b** the expected result of normal development: *the prospective fate of embryonic cells.* **3a** disaster apparently determined by fate. **b** a disaster, *esp* death. [Middle English via Italian from Latin *fatum* what has been spoken, neuter past part. of *fari* to speak]

fate[2] *verb trans* (*usu in passive*) to destine (somebody or something); to doom (them or it): *The plan was fated to fail.*

fateful /ˈfaytf(ə)l/ *adj* **1** having momentous and often unpleasant, catastrophic, or deadly consequences; decisive: *the fateful decision to declare war.* **2** controlled by fate; foreordained. **3** having a quality of ominous prophecy: *a fateful remark.* ➤➤ **fatefully** *adv,* **fatefulness** *noun.*

Usage note
fateful *or* fatal? See note at FATAL.

Fates *pl noun* (**the Fates**) in classical mythology, the three goddesses who determine the course of human life.

fat farm *noun chiefly NAmer, informal* a health farm for people who want to lose weight.

fathead *noun informal* a slow-witted or stupid person; a fool. ➤➤ **fatheaded** /fatˈhedid/ *adj,* **fatheadedness** *noun.*

fat hen *noun* a widely distributed goosefoot that is a common weed: *Chenopodium alba.*

father[1] /ˈfahdhə/ *noun* **1a** a male parent of a child, or the sire of an animal. **b** a man who relates to another in a way suggesting the relationship of father and child, *esp* in receiving filial respect. **2** a forefather. **3a** (*often* **Father**) used as a respectful form of address: an old man. **b** something personified as an old man: *Old Father Time.* **4** (**Father** *or* **the Father**). **a** God. **b** the first person of the Trinity. **5** used *esp* as a title in the Roman Catholic Church: a priest of the regular clergy. **6** (*often* **Father**) an early Christian writer accepted by the Church as authoritative. **7a** somebody who originates or institutes something: *the father of radio.* **b** a source or origin. **8** (*usu in pl*) any of the leading men, e.g. of a city. ➤➤ **fatherhood** *noun,* **fatherless** *adj,* **father-like** *adj and adv.* [Old English *fæder*]

father[2] *verb trans* (**fathered, fathering**) **1a** to beget (offspring). **b** to give rise to (something); to initiate (it). **c** to accept responsibility for (something). **2a** (+ on) to fix the paternity of (somebody) on a man. **b** (+ on) to foist, impose, or attribute responsibility for (something, e.g. a crime, on somebody).

Father Christmas *noun* an old man with a white beard and red suit believed by children to deliver their presents at Christmas time.

father confessor *noun* (*pl* **father confessors**) **1** a priest who hears confessions and gives advice, *esp* spiritual advice. **2** somebody in whom another person confides and who gives them advice.

father-in-law *noun* (*pl* **fathers-in-law**) the father of one's husband or wife.

fatherland *noun* used *esp* with reference to Germany: one's native land.

fatherly *adj* **1** of or characteristic of a father: *fatherly responsibilities.* **2** resembling a father, e.g. in care or affection: *a kind fatherly old man.* ➤➤ **fatherliness** *noun.*

father of the chapel *noun* (*pl* **fathers of the chapel**) a man who is the shop steward in charge of a union branch in the publishing or printing industry.

Father of the House *noun* the man who has been longest a member of the House of Commons.

Father's Day *noun* the third Sunday in June, on which fathers are honoured.

fathom[1] /ˈfadh(ə)m/ *noun* a unit of length used *esp* for measuring the depth of water, equal to 6ft (about 1.83m). [Old English *fæthm* outstretched arms, length of the outstretched arms]

fathom[2] *verb trans* (**fathomed, fathoming**) **1** (*often* + out) to penetrate and come to understand (something). **2** to measure the depth of (water) by a sounding line. ➤➤ **fathomable** *adj.*

Fathometer /fəˈdhomitə/ *noun trademark* a sonic depth finder. [FATHOM[1] + -METER[2]]

fathomless *adj* incapable of being fathomed. ➤➤ **fathomlessness** *noun.*

fatigue[1] /fəˈteeg/ *noun* **1** physical or nervous exhaustion. **2** the tendency of a material to break under repeated stress. **3** inability to respond further to a need, etc because of over-exposure or repeated demands: *It was feared that repeated requests for help for famine victims would lead to compassion fatigue in the general public.* **4a** manual or menial military work. **b** (*in pl*) the uniform or work clothing worn on fatigue. **5** (*used before a noun*) being part of fatigues: *a fatigue cap.* [French *fatigue*, from *fatiguer* to fatigue, from Latin *fatigare*, from *ad fatim* to bursting]

fatigue[2] *verb trans* (**fatigues, fatigued, fatiguing**) **1** to weary or exhaust (somebody). **2** to induce a condition of fatigue in (a material, etc). ➤ *verb intrans* said of a metal, etc: to suffer fatigue. ➤➤ **fatigability** /-ˈbiliti/ *noun,* **fatigable** /ˈfatigəbl/ *adj,* **fatiguability** *noun,* **fatiguable** *adj,* **fatiguingly** *adv.*

fatling /ˈfatling/ *noun* a young animal fattened for slaughter.

fatshedera /fatsˈhedərə/ *noun* a hybrid plant that is a cultivar produced by crossing fatsia with another species of ivy: *Fatsia japonica* × *Hedera helix.* [Latin name, from FATSIA + *Hedera helix*]

fatsia /ˈfatsi·ə/ *noun* a shrub of the ivy family, having deeply lobed leaves and clusters of white flowers: *Fatsia japonica.* [Latin genus name]

fatso /ˈfatsoh/ *noun* (*pl* **fatsoes**) *informal* often used as a derog form of address: a fat person. [prob from *Fats,* nickname for a fat person + -O[1]]

fat-soluble *adj* soluble in fats or in substances, such as ether or chloroform, in which fats dissolve.

fatstock *noun* livestock that is fat and ready for market.

fatten /ˈfat(ə)n/ *verb* (**fattened, fattening**) ➤ *verb trans* **1** (*often* + up) to make (a person or animal) fat, fleshy, or plump, *esp* to feed (a stock animal) for slaughter: *All the things I really like to do are either immoral, illegal, or fattening —* Alexander Woollcott. **2** to make (soil) fertile. ➤ *verb intrans* to become fat.

fattism /ˈfatiz(ə)m/ *noun* discrimination on grounds of fatness. ➤➤ **fattist** *noun and adj.*

fatty[1] /ˈfati/ *adj* (**fattier, fattiest**) **1a** containing large amounts of fat. **b** fat. **2** oily; greasy: *fatty food.* **3** derived from or chemically related to fat. ➤➤ **fattiness** *noun.*

fatty[2] *noun* (*pl* **fatties**) *informal* a fat person or animal.

fatty acid *noun* any of numerous organic acids with one carboxyl group, e.g. acetic acid, including many that occur naturally in fats, waxes, and essential oils.

fatty degeneration *noun* deterioration in an organ of the body such as the heart or liver, caused by accumulation of fat in the cells of the organ.

fatuous /ˈfatyoo·əs/ *adj* complacently or inanely foolish; idiotic. ➤➤ **fatuity** /fəˈtyooh·iti/ *noun,* **fatuously** *adv,* **fatuousness** *noun.* [Latin *fatuus* foolish]

fatwa /ˈfatwah/ *noun* a formal legal opinion delivered by an Islamic religious authority. [Arabic *fatwa,* from *aftā* to decide a point of law]

fauces /ˈfawseez/ *noun* (*pl* **fauces**) (*treated as sing. or pl*) the narrow passage from the mouth to the pharynx situated between the soft palate and the base of the tongue. ➤➤ **faucial** /ˈfawsh(ə)l/ *adj.* [Latin *fauces* (pl), throat, fauces]

faucet /ˈfawsit/ *noun chiefly NAmer* a tap. [Middle English *faucet* bung, faucet, via Old French from Provençal *falset,* from *falser* to bore into, from late Latin *falsare* to corrupt, from Latin *falsus:* see FALSE]

faugh /faw/ *interj* used to express contempt or disgust. [imitative]

fault[1] /fawlt/ *noun* **1a** a failing: *The greatest of faults, I should say, is to be conscious of none —* Thomas Carlyle. **b** an imperfection or defect: *There's a fault in the computer.* **2a** a misdemeanour. **b** a mistake. **c** an action, *esp* a service that does not land in the prescribed area, which loses a rally in tennis, squash, etc. **d** in show-jumping, a penalty point given for a horse hitting or refusing a jump. **3** responsibility for wrongdoing or failure: *The accident was the driver's fault.* **4a** a fracture in the earth's crust accompanied by displacement, e.g. of the strata, along the fracture line. **b** a rupture of rock structures due to strain. * **at fault** in the wrong; liable for blame. **to a fault** to an excessive degree: *Generous to a fault, he is.* ►► **faultless** *adj*, **faultlessly** *adv*, **faultlessness** *noun*. [Middle English *faute* via Old French from Latin *falsus*, past part. of *fallere* to deceive, disappoint]

fault² *verb trans* **1** to find a fault in (somebody or something): *You can't fault his logic.* **2** to produce a geological fault in (the earth's crust). ► *verb intrans* **1** *archaic* to commit a fault; to err. **2** to produce a geological fault.

faultfinding¹ *noun* a predisposition to find fault. ►► **faultfinder** *noun*.

faultfinding² *adj* overinclined to criticize.

faulty *adj* (**faultier, faultiest**) having a fault, blemish, or defect; imperfect. ►► **faultily** *adv*, **faultiness** *noun*.

faun /fawn/ *noun* a figure of Roman mythology similar to the satyr, with a human body and the horns and legs of a goat. [Middle English from Latin *faunus*, named after *Faunus*, Roman god of nature, fertility, and agriculture]

fauna /ˈfawnə/ *noun* (*pl* **faunas** or **faunae** /ˈfawnee/) **1** the animal life of a region, period, or special environment: compare FLORA. **2** a treatise on, or a work used to identify, the animal life of a region, etc. ►► **faunal** *adj*, **faunistic** /fawˈnistik/ *adj*. [scientific Latin *fauna*, named after *Fauna*, sister of *Faunus*: see FAUN]

Faustian /ˈfowstiən/ *adj* of, resembling, or befitting Faust or Faustus, e.g.: **a** sacrificing spiritual values for material gains. **b** striving insatiably for knowledge and mastery. **c** constantly troubled and tormented by spiritual dissatisfaction or spiritual striving. [from Johann *Faust* (Johannes *Faustus*) d. about 1540, German magician and astrologer, said to have sold his soul to the devil in return for knowledge and power]

faute de mieux /ˌfoht də ˈmyuh (*French* fot də mjø)/ *adv* for lack of something more suitable or desirable: *Sherry gave him a headache but he drank it faute de mieux.* [French *faute de mieux* lack of better]

Fauve /fohv/ *noun* an exponent of Fauvism. [French *Fauve*, from *fauve*: see FAUVISM]

Fauvism *noun* a 20th-cent. art movement characterized by pure and vivid colour and a free treatment of form. ►► **Fauvist** *noun and adj*. [French *fauvisme* from *fauve* wild animal, from *fauve* tawny, wild, of Germanic origin]

faux /foh/ *adj* **1** imitation: *faux fox fur.* **2** false; insincere: *faux emotion.* [French *faux* false]

faux-naïf¹ /ˌfoh nahˈeef (*French* fo naif)/ *adj* affecting a childlike innocence or simplicity. [French *faux-naïf* falsely naive]

faux-naïf² *noun* somebody who affects a childlike innocence.

faux pas /ˌfoh ˈpah/ *noun* (*pl* **faux pas** /ˌfoh ˈpahz/) a social blunder. [French *faux pas* false step]

favor /ˈfayvə/ *noun and verb trans NAmer* see FAVOUR¹, FAVOUR².

favorable *adj NAmer* see FAVOURABLE.

favorite /ˈfayv(ə)rit/ *noun and adj NAmer* see FAVOURITE¹, FAVOURITE².

favour¹ (*NAmer* **favor**) /ˈfayvə/ *noun* **1a** approving consideration or attention; approbation: *They looked with favour on our project.* **b** partiality or favouritism. **c** popularity. **2** friendly regard shown towards another, *esp* by a superior. **3** kindness, or an act of kindness beyond what is expected or due. **4a** *archaic* a token of allegiance or love, e.g. a ribbon or badge, usu worn conspicuously: *Hold, Rosaline, this favour shalt thou wear* — Shakespeare. **b** a small gift given to a guest at a party, *esp* at a wedding reception. **5** *archaic* physical, *esp* facial, appearance: *The boy is fair, of female favour* — Shakespeare. **6** *dated* (*usu in pl*) consent to sexual activities, *esp* given by a woman: *She granted her favours freely.* * **in favour** (*often* + with) popular; liked. **in favour of 1** in agreement or sympathy with (something); on the side of (it). **2** to the advantage of (somebody): *John gave up his rights in the house in favour of his wife.* **3** in order to choose (something); out of preference for (it): *He refused a job in industry in favour of an academic appointment.* **in somebody's favour 1** to somebody's advantage: *The odds were in his favour.* **2** liked or esteemed by somebody: *He's doing extra work to get back in his boss's favour.* **out of favour** (*often* + with) unpopular or disliked.

[Middle English via Old French from Latin *favor* from *favēre* to be favourable]

favour² (*NAmer* **favor**) *verb trans* **1a** to regard or treat (somebody) with favour. **b** (+ by/with) to do a favour or kindness for (somebody); to oblige (them): *Wilson favoured them with a kindly smile* — The Listener. **2** to show partiality towards (somebody or something); to prefer (them). **3a** to give support or confirmation to (an idea or theory); to sustain (it): *This evidence favours my theory.* **b** to afford advantages for success to (a plan, etc); to facilitate (it): *Good weather favoured the outing.* **4** *informal* to look like (a relation): *He favours his father.* **5** to treat (*esp* an injured limb) gently or carefully. ►► **favourer** *noun*.

favourable (*NAmer* **favorable**) *adj* **1a** expressing or winning approval, or giving a result in one's favour: *a favourable comparison.* **b** disposed to favour; partial. **2** successful: *a favourable outcome.* ►► **favourably** *adv*.

favoured (*NAmer* **favored**) *adj* **1** (*used in combinations*) having an appearance or features of the kind specified: *an ill-favoured child.* **2** receiving preferential treatment: *the favoured brother.* **3** endowed with special advantages or gifts.

favourite¹ (*NAmer* **favorite**) /ˈfayv(ə)rit/ *noun* **1** somebody or something favoured or preferred above others; *specif* one unduly favoured, *esp* by a person in authority: *Teachers should not have favourites.* **2** the competitor judged most likely to win, *esp* by a bookmaker. [Italian *favorito*, past part. of *favorire* to favour, ultimately from Latin *favor*: see FAVOUR¹]

favourite² (*NAmer* **favorite**) *adj* constituting a favourite; preferred; most liked: *'Gone with the Wind' is my favourite film.*

favouritism (*NAmer* **favoritism**) *noun* the showing of unfair favour; partiality.

fawn¹ /fawn/ *noun* **1** a young deer. **2** a light greyish brown colour. ►► **fawn** *adj*. [Middle English *foun* via French from Latin *fetus* offspring]

fawn² *verb intrans* **1** (+ on/upon) to court favour with somebody by acting in a servilely flattering manner. **2** (+ on/upon) said of a dog, etc: to show affection to somebody. ►► **fawner** *noun*, **fawning** *adj*, **fawningly** *adv*. [Old English *fagnian* to rejoice, from *fægen*, *fagan* glad]

fax¹ /faks/ *noun* **1** a facsimile message. **2** a facsimile machine. [by shortening and alteration]

fax² *verb trans* **1** to send a fax to (somebody). **2** to send (a message) by fax.

fay /fay/ *noun literary* a fairy. [Middle English *faie* via Old French *feie, fee* from Latin *Fata*: see FAIRY]

fayre /feə/ *noun* = FAIR³.

faze /fayz/ *verb trans informal* to disturb the composure of (somebody); to disconcert or daunt (them): *I was fazed by his rudeness.* [alteration of *feeze* to drive away, frighten, from Old English *fēsian* to drive away]

FBA *abbr* Fellow of the British Academy.

FBI *abbr NAmer* Federal Bureau of Investigation.

FC *abbr* **1** Football Club. **2** *Brit* Forestry Commission.

fcap *abbr* foolscap.

FCC *abbr NAmer* Federal Communications Commission.

F clef *noun* = BASS CLEF.

FCO *abbr Brit* Foreign and Commonwealth Office.

FD *abbr* Defender of the Faith. [Latin *Fidei Defensor*]

FDA *abbr NAmer* Food and Drug Administration.

FDR *abbr* Franklin Delano Roosevelt (former US president).

FE *abbr Brit* further education.

Fe *abbr* the chemical symbol for iron. [Latin *ferrum* iron]

fealty /ˈfee-əlti/ *noun* (*pl* **fealties**) formerly, fidelity to one's feudal lord. [alteration of Middle English *feute* via Old French from Latin *fidelitat-, fidelitas*: see FIDELITY]

fear¹ /fiə/ *noun* **1** an unpleasant, often strong, emotion caused by anticipation or awareness of danger, or a state marked by this emotion: *Man's loneliness is but his fear of life* — Eugene O'Neill. **2** anxiety or solicitude. **3** reason for alarm; danger. **4** *archaic* profound reverence and awe, *esp* towards God. * **for fear of/that** because of anxiety about; in case of; lest: *They wouldn't raise taxes for fear of losing electoral support.* **put the fear of God into somebody** to frighten somebody. **without fear or favour** with complete impartiality. ➤➤ **fearless** adj, **fearlessly** adv, **fearlessness** noun. [Old English fær sudden danger]

fear[2] verb trans **1** to be afraid of (somebody or something); to consider or expect (them) with alarm: Let me assert my firm belief that the only thing we have to fear is fear itself — Franklin D Roosevelt. **2** to believe (something) with regret: I fear you are mistaken. **3** archaic to have a reverential awe of (God). ➤ verb intrans (+ for) to be afraid or apprehensive: I fear for your safety. ➤➤ **feared** adj.

fearful /'fiəf(ə)l/ adj **1a** (+ of) full of fear of something; afraid: They were fearful of reprisals. **b** showing or arising from fear: a fearful glance. **c** timid or timorous: a fearful child. **2** causing or likely to cause fear. **3** informal extremely bad, large, or intense: That's a fearful waste of paper. ➤➤ **fearfully** adv, **fearfulness** noun.

fearsome /'fiəs(ə)m/ adj **1** causing fear; = FEARFUL (2). **2** timid; = FEARFUL (1C). **3** awesome. ➤➤ **fearsomely** adv, **fearsomeness** noun.

feasible /'feezəbl/ adj **1** capable of being done or carried out: a feasible plan. **2** informal reasonable or likely. ➤➤ **feasibility** /-'biliti/ noun, **feasibleness** noun, **feasibly** adv. [Middle English faisible from French, from faire to do, from Latin facere]

Usage note

Feasible means 'able to be done or capable of being dealt with': a feasible project. Its use to mean 'likely' or 'probable' (a feasible explanation of the events) is best avoided in formal contexts.

feast[1] /feest/ noun **1a** an elaborate, often public, meal, sometimes accompanied by a ceremony or entertainment; a banquet. **b** something that gives abundant pleasure: a feast for the eyes. **2** a periodic religious observance commemorating an event or honouring a deity, saint, person, or thing. [Middle English feste festival, feast, via Old French feste from Latin festum festival, neuter of festus solemn, festal]

feast[2] verb intrans to have or take part in a feast. ➤ verb trans to give a feast for (somebody). ✳ **feast one's eyes on** to look appreciatively at (something or somebody): Feast your eyes on her beauty. ➤➤ **feaster** noun.

Feast of Dedication noun = HANUKKAH.

Feast of Lights noun = HANUKKAH.

Feast of Lots noun = PURIM.

Feast of Tabernacles noun = SUKKOTH.

Feast of Weeks noun = SHABUOTH.

feat /feet/ noun **1** a notable and esp courageous act or deed. **2** an act or product of skill, endurance, or ingenuity. [Middle English fait act, deed, via French from Latin factum, neuter past part. of facere to make, do]

feather[1] /'fedhə/ noun **1a** any of the light horny outgrowths that form the external covering of a bird's body, consisting of a shaft with two sets of interlocking barbs. **b** the vane of an arrow. **c** (usu in pl) = FEATHERING (2). **2** the act of feathering an oar. ✳ **a feather in one's cap** a deserved honour or mark of distinction in which one can take pride. **in fine feather** in fine condition; in high spirits. ➤➤ **feathery** adj. [Old English fether]

feather[2] verb (**feathered, feathering**) ➤ verb trans **1a** to turn (an oar blade) almost horizontal when lifting it from the water. **b** to change the angle at which (a propeller blade) meets the air so as to have the minimum wind resistance, or to feather the propeller blades attached to (a propeller or engine). **2a** to fit (an arrow, etc) with feathers. **b** to cover, clothe, or adorn (something) with feathers. **3** to cut (air, etc) with or as if with a wing. ➤ verb intrans **1** to feather an oar or an aircraft propeller blade. **2** said of ink or a printed impression: to soak in and spread; to blur. ✳ **feather one's nest** to provide for oneself, esp dishonestly, through a job in which one is trusted. ➤➤ **feathered** adj.

featherbed verb trans (**featherbedded, featherbedding**) **1** to cushion or protect (somebody) from hardship, worry, etc; to pamper (them). **2** to assist (an industry, etc) with government subsidies.

feather bed noun a feather mattress.

featherbrain noun a foolish scatterbrained person. ➤➤ **featherbrained** adj.

featheredge noun a very thin or sharp edge, or a board or plank having such an edge.

feathering noun **1a** plumage. **b** the feathers of an arrow. **2** a fringe of hair, e.g. on the legs of a dog or cart horse.

featherstitch[1] noun an embroidery stitch consisting of a line of loop stitches worked in a zigzag pattern.

featherstitch[2] verb trans to embroider (fabric) with a line of loop stitches worked in a zigzag pattern.

featherweight noun **1a** a weight in boxing of 53.5–57kg (118–126lb) if professional or 54–57kg (119–126lb) if amateur. **b** a weight in amateur wrestling of usu 58–62kg (127–137lb). **2** somebody or something of limited importance or effectiveness.

feature[1] /'feechə/ noun **1** a prominent or distinctive part or characteristic. **2a** a part of the face: Her nose was not her best feature. **b** (in pl) the face: He had an embarrassed look on his features. **3a** a full-length film, esp the main film on a cinema programme. **b** a distinctive article, story, or special section in a newspaper or magazine. **c** a radio documentary, often one about cultural rather than political matters. ➤➤ **featureless** adj. [Middle English feture via Old French faitre form, shape, from Latin factura act of making, from facere to make]

feature[2] verb trans **1** to give special prominence to (a story), e.g. in a performance or newspaper. **2** to have (something or somebody) as a characteristic or feature. ➤ verb intrans (+ in) to play an important part; to be a feature.

featured adj (used in combinations) having facial features of the kind specified: a heavy-featured man.

feature film noun = FEATURE[1] (3A).

Feb. abbr February.

febri- comb. form forming words, denoting: fever: febrifuge. [late Latin, from Latin febris]

febrifuge[1] /'febrifyoohj/ noun a drug that alleviates fever. ➤➤ **febrifugal** /fi'brifyoog(ə)l/ adj. [French fébrifuge from late Latin febrifuga, febrifugia centaury, from FEBRI- + -fuga -FUGE]

febrifuge[2] adj alleviating fever; = ANTIPYRETIC.

febrile /'feebriel/ adj of fever; feverish. ➤➤ **febrility** /fi'briliti/ noun. [medieval Latin febrilis from Latin febris fever]

February /'febrooəri, 'febyooəri/ noun (pl **Februaries**) the second month of the year. [Middle English Februarie from Latin Februarius, from Februa (pl), a Roman feast of purification held during February]

feces /'feeseez/ pl noun NAmer see FAECES.

feckless /'feklis/ adj **1** ineffectual; weak. **2** worthless; irresponsible. ➤➤ **fecklessly** adv, **fecklessness** noun. [Scots, from feck effect, majority, variant of EFFECT[1]]

feculent /'fekyool(ə)nt/ adj formal foul with impurities or excrement. ➤➤ **feculence** noun. [Middle English from Latin faeculentus, from faec-, faex dregs]

fecund /'feekənd, 'fekənd/ adj **1** fruitful in offspring or vegetation; prolific. **2** very intellectually productive or inventive to a marked degree: a fecund imagination. ➤➤ **fecundity** /fi'kunditi/ noun. [Middle English via French fecond from Latin fecundus]

fecundate /'fekəndayt, 'fee-/ verb trans **1** archaic to make (a woman or female animal) fertile; to impregnate (them). **2** literary to make (something) fecund. ➤➤ **fecundation** /-'daysh(ə)n/ noun. [Latin fecundatus, past part. of fecundare, from fecundus fecund]

Fed /fed/ noun **1** (**the Fed**) NAmer the Federal Reserve System. **2** see FED[2].

fed[1] /fed/ verb past tense and past part. of FEED[1].

fed[2] noun (often **Fed**) NAmer, informal a federal agent or officer. [short for FEDERAL]

fed. abbr **1** federal. **2** federation.

fedayee /fidah'yee, fida'yee/ noun (pl **fedayeen** /-yeen/) a member of an Arab commando group operating esp against Israel. [Arabic fidāʾī, literally 'one who sacrifices himself']

Federal /'fed(ə)rəl/ noun a supporter or soldier of the North in the American Civil War.

federal adj **1a** formed by agreement between political units that surrender their individual sovereignty to a central authority but retain limited powers of government, or of or constituting a government so formed. **b** of the central government of a federation as distinguished from those of the constituent units.

Editorial note

Federal government involves a territorial form of power-sharing. More precisely, it refers to a system of government in which power is legally divided between the centre and provincial units, such that neither is legally subordinate to the other. Federalism may be contrasted with a unitary system, such as that in Britain, in which sovereignty remains with Parliament at Westminster — Professor Vernon Bogdanor.

2 of or loyal to the federal government of the USA in the American Civil War. >>> **federalism** noun, **federalist** noun and adj, **federally** adv. [Latin foeder-, foedus compact, league]

federalize or **federalise** /'fed(ə)rəliez/ verb trans **1** to unite (states) in or under a federal system. **2** to bring (something) under the control of a federal government. >>> **federalization** /-'zaysh(ə)n/ noun.

Federal Reserve System noun in the USA, a banking system that consists of twelve Federal Reserve Banks plus their member banks, with the functions of a central bank.

federate /'fedərayt/ verb trans to join (states, etc) in a federation. >>> verb intrans said of states, etc: to join a federation. >>> **federative** /-rətiv/ adj.

federation /fedə'raysh(ə)n/ noun **1** something formed by federating, e.g.: **a** a country formed by the federation of separate states. **b** a union of organizations. **2** the act or an instance of federating, esp the formation of a federal union.

fedora /fi'dawrə/ noun a low felt hat with the crown creased lengthways. [named after Fédora, drama by V. Sardou d.1908, French dramatist]

fed up adj informal (often + with) discontented or bored: I'm fed up with the nine-to-five day.

fee¹ /fee/ noun **1** (also in pl) a sum of money paid esp for entrance or for a professional service. **2** (usu in pl). **a** money paid for education. **b** a gratuity. **3a** formerly, an estate in land held in feudal law from a lord. **b** formerly, an inherited or heritable estate in land. * **in fee** formerly, in absolute and legal possession. [Middle English from Old French feu, fief from medieval Latin feudum, of Germanic origin]

fee² verb trans (**fees, feed, feeing**) to give a fee to (somebody).

feeble /'feebl/ adj **1** lacking in strength or endurance; weak: a feeble old man. **2** deficient in authority, force, or effect: Nothing turns out to be so oppressive and unjust as a feeble government — Edmund Burke. >>> **feebleness** noun, **feebly** adv. [Middle English feble via Old French from Latin flebilis lamentable, wretched, from flēre to weep]

feebleminded adj **1** foolish or stupid. **2** dated mentally deficient. >>> **feeblemindedly** adv, **feeblemindedness** noun.

feed¹ /feed/ verb (past tense and past part. **fed** /fed/) >>> verb trans **1a** (also + on) to give food to (a person or an animal): She fed the baby on puréed carrot. **b** to give (something) to a person or animal as food: She fed puréed carrot to the baby. **c** to produce or provide food for (people). **2** to provide something essential to the growth, sustenance, maintenance, or operation of (something). **3a** to satisfy or gratify (a feeling, etc). **b** to support or encourage (somebody's ambition, dislike, etc). **4** to supply (something) for use, consumption, or processing, esp in a continuous manner: I fed the tape into the machine. **5a** to supply material to (e.g. a machine), esp in a continuous manner. **b** to supply (a signal or power) to an electronic circuit. **6** to act as a feed for (a comedian, etc). **7** to pass or throw a ball or puck to (a teammate). >>> verb intrans **1a** (usu + off/on/upon) to consume food; to eat. **b** (usu + off/on/upon) to prey. **2** (usu + off/on/upon) to become nourished or satisfied as if by food: Ambition if it feeds at all, does so on the ambition of others — Susan Sontag. **3** to be moved into a machine or opening for use, processing, or storage: The grain fed into the silo. [Old English fēdan]

feed² noun **1** the act or an instance of feeding or eating. **2a** a mixture or preparation of food for livestock. **b** the amount given at each feeding. **3a** material supplied, e.g. to a furnace. **b** a mechanism by which the action of feeding is effected. **4** a performer who supplies cues for another performer's, esp a comedian's, lines or actions. **5** informal a large or hearty meal.

feedback noun **1** information about the results of an action or process, usu in response to a request. **2** the return to the input of a part of the output of a machine, system, or process, e.g. noise fed back to a microphone. **3** the modifying influence of the results or effects of a process, esp a biological process, on another stage in the same process.

feeder noun **1** a person or animal that feeds, esp in a stated way: She was a poor feeder for the first couple of weeks after birth. **2** a device or apparatus for supplying food, e.g. to a caged animal or bird. **3** Brit. **a** a baby's bib. **b** a baby's feeding bottle. **4a** a device feeding material into or through a machine. **b** a heavy wire conductor supplying electricity to a point of an electric distribution system. **c** a

transmission line running from a radio transmitter to an antenna. **d** a road, railway, airline, or aircraft that links remote areas with the main transport system.

feeding bottle noun a bottle with a teat, designed to hold milk and used for feeding babies.

feeding frenzy noun **1** a ferocious attack on prey by a group of sharks or piranhas. **2** the insatiable, aggressive, and competitive pursuit of a story by the media. **3** any frenzied or uncontrolled activity: a sexual feeding frenzy.

feedstock noun raw material supplied to a machine or processing plant.

feed up verb trans to fatten (a person or animal) by plentiful feeding.

feel¹ /feel/ verb (past tense and past part. **felt** /felt/) >>> verb trans **1a** to handle or touch (something) in order to examine or explore it. **b** to perceive (something) by a physical sensation, e.g. on the skin or in the muscles: I can feel a draught. **2** to experience (something) actively or passively; to be affected by (an emotion, reaction, etc): He felt my anger. **3a** to be aware of (something) without direct experience or by drawing conclusions from the evidence available: I felt the presence of a stranger in the room. **b** to believe or think (something): It is generally felt that such action is inadvisable. **4** (often + out) to find, ascertain, or explore (something) by cautious trial: They are feeling out the possibilities of starting their own business. >>> verb intrans **1a** to receive or be able to receive the sensation of touch. **b** to search for something by using the sense of touch. **2a** to have or be conscious of a physical condition or state of mind: She feels much better now. **b** to believe oneself to have a particular quality or attribute: I felt rather stupid. **3** (+ for) to have sympathy or pity for (somebody): He really feels for the underprivileged. * **feel like 1** to have a whim or fancy, esp a passing one, for (something). **2** to resemble or seem to be (something) on the evidence of touch. **feel one's way** to make progress or explore a situation cautiously. **feel up to** to be well enough or fit enough to do something. [Old English fēlan]

feel² noun **1** the sense of feeling; touch. **2** sensation or feeling. **3a** the quality of a thing as imparted through touch: The material had a velvety feel. **b** typical or peculiar quality or atmosphere: I like the feel of the place. **4** (+ for) intuitive skill, knowledge, or ability for (something): She has a feel for the music.

feeler noun **1** a tactile appendage, e.g. a tentacle, of an animal. **2** (usu in pl) something, e.g. a proposal, ventured to ascertain the views of others.

feeler gauge noun a set of thin steel strips of various known thicknesses by which small gaps may be measured.

feel-good adj informal inducing a feeling of well-being: a feel-good film.

feeling¹ noun **1a** an emotional state or reaction: a feeling of loneliness. **b** (in pl) susceptibility to impression; sensibility: The remark hurt her feelings. **2** a conscious recognition; a sense: The harsh sentence left him with a feeling of injustice. **3a** an opinion or belief, esp when unreasoned; a sentiment: What are your feelings on the matter? **b** a presentiment: I've a feeling he won't come. **4a** one of the five basic physical senses, by which stimuli, esp to the skin and mucous membranes, are interpreted by the brain as touch, pressure, and temperature, or a sensation experienced through this sense. **b** generalized bodily consciousness, sensation, or awareness: I've lost all feeling in this arm. **5** capacity to respond emotionally, esp with the higher emotions: a man of noble feeling. **6** = FEEL² (3). **7** = FEEL² (4). **8** the quality of a work of art that embodies and conveys the emotion of the artist.

feeling² adj **1** expressing emotion or sensitivity. **2a** having the capacity to feel or respond emotionally; sensitive. **b** easily moved emotionally; sympathetic. >>> **feelingly** adv.

fee simple noun (pl **fees simple**) a FEE¹ (3B) (heritable estate in land) without limitation to any class of heirs.

feet /feet/ noun pl of FOOT¹.

fee tail noun (pl **fees tail**) a FEE¹ (heritable estate in land) limited to a particular class of heirs. [FEE¹ + TAIL³]

feign /fayn/ verb trans **1** to give a false appearance or impression of (something) deliberately: She survived by feigning death. **2** to pretend (something): He feigned innocence. >>> verb intrans to pretend or dissemble. [Middle English feignen via Old French feindre, faindre from Latin fingere to shape, feign]

feijoa /fay'johə/ *noun* **1** a dull-green oblong fruit resembling a guava and tasting somewhat like a pineapple. **2** the S American tree that bears this fruit: genus *Feijoa*. [Latin genus name, named after J. da Silva *Feijó* d.1824, Brazilian naturalist]

feint[1] /faynt/ *noun* something feigned; *specif* a mock blow or attack directed towards a point away from the point one really intends to attack. [French *feinte* from Old French *feint*, past part. of *feindre*: see FEIGN]

feint[2] *verb intrans* to make a feint.

feint[3] *adj* said of rulings on paper: faint or pale. [alteration of FAINT[1]]

feisty /'fiesti/ *adj* (**feistier, feistiest**) *informal* **1** spirited and determined. **2** touchy or quarrelsome. **3** fidgety or agitated. [obsolete *feist fist*, small dog, from obsolete *fisting hound* derogatory term for a lap dog, from obsolete *fist* to break wind; from the behaviour of a pampered dog]

felafel /fə'lahfl/ *noun* see FALAFEL.

feldspar /'fel(d)spah/ *or* **felspar** /'felspah/ *noun* any of a group of minerals that consist of aluminium silicates with either potassium, sodium, calcium, or barium, an essential constituent of nearly all crystalline rocks. ➤➤ **feldspathic** /fel(d)'spathik/ *adj*, **felspathic** *adj*.

Word history
German *Feld* field + obsolete German *Spath*: see SPAR[4]. The variant *felspar* comes from an erroneous association with German *Fels* rock.

felicitate /fə'lisitayt/ *verb trans formal* (+ on/upon) to offer congratulations or compliments to (somebody) on something. ➤➤ **felicitation** /-'taysh(ə)n/ *noun*, **felicitator** *noun*. [late Latin *felicitatus*, past part. of *felicitare* to make happy, from Latin *felic-, felix* happy, fruitful]

felicitous /fə'lisitəs/ *adj formal* **1a** very well suited or expressed; apt: *a felicitous remark*. **b** marked by or given to such expression: *a felicitous speaker*. **2** pleasant or delightful. ➤➤ **felicitously** *adv*, **felicitousness** *noun*.

felicity /fə'lisiti/ *noun* (*pl* **felicities**) *formal* **1** great happiness, or something causing great happiness. **2** a felicitous faculty or quality, *esp* in art or language; aptness. **3** a felicitous expression. [Middle English *felicite* via French from Latin *felicitat-, felicitas*, from *felic-, felix* fruitful, happy]

feline[1] /'feelien/ *adj* **1** of cats or the cat family. **2** resembling a cat; having the characteristics generally attributed to cats, *esp* grace, stealth, or slyness. ➤➤ **felinely** *adv*, **felinity** /fi'lin-/ *noun*. [Latin *felinus* from *felis* cat]

feline[2] *noun* a cat; a member of the cat family.

fell[1] /fel/ *verb* past tense of FALL[1].

fell[2] *verb trans* **1** to cut, beat, or knock (something) down: *felling trees*. **2** to knock down or kill (somebody). **3** = FLAT-FELL[2]. ➤➤ **feller** *noun*. [Old English *fellan*]

fell[3] *noun* **1** a felled seam. **2** *NAmer* an amount of timber felled.

fell[4] *noun* (*also in pl*) a steep rugged stretch of high moorland, *esp* in northern England and Scotland.

Word history
Middle English, hill, mountain, from Old Norse *fell, fjall*. The Old Norse sense became obsolete in English in the 17th cent., but survives in place names such as *Bowfell* and *Scafell* in NW England.

fell[5] *adj literary* **1** fierce or cruel. **2** very destructive; deadly. ✳ **at one fell swoop** all at once, or with a single concentrated effort. [Middle English from Old French *fel*, nominative of *felon*: see FELON[1]]

fell[6] *noun* an animal skin or hide; a pelt. [Old English *fel, fell*]

fellah /'felə/ *noun* (*pl* **fellahin** *or* **fellaheen** /-'heen/) a peasant or agricultural labourer in an Arab country. [Arabic *fallāḥ*, from *falaha* to till the soil]

fellate /fe'layt/ *verb trans* to perform fellatio on (somebody). ➤➤ **fellation** /-sh(ə)n/ *noun*, **fellator** *noun*.

fellatio /fə'layshioh/ *noun* oral stimulation of the penis. [Latin *fellation-, fellatio*, from *fellare, felare* to suck]

feller /'felə/ *noun informal* a fellow or chap: *Do unto the other feller the way he'd like to do unto you, an' do it fust* — Edward Noyes Westcott. [by alteration]

felloe /'feloh/ *or* **felly** /'feli/ *noun* (*pl* **felloes** *or* **fellies**) the exterior rim of a spoked wheel, or a segment of it. [Old English *felg*]

fellow /'feloh/ *noun* **1** *informal* a man or a boy. **2a** an equal in rank, power, or character; a peer. **b** either of a pair; a mate. **3a** (*usu in pl*) a comrade or associate: *She is well respected by her fellows*. **b** (*used before a noun*) being a companion or associate; belonging to the same group: *On the train, we tried to guess the professions of our fellow travellers*. **4** *Brit* a member of an incorporated literary or scientific society. **5** a person appointed to a salaried position allowing for advanced research. **6** an incorporated member of a collegiate foundation. **7** *informal* a boyfriend. [Old English *feolaga* partner, from Old Norse *fēlagi*, from *fēlag* partnership, from *fē* cattle, money + *lag* act of laying]

fellow feeling *noun* a feeling of community of interest or of mutual understanding; *specif* sympathy.

fellowship *noun* **1** the condition of friendly relations between people; companionship. **2a** community of interest, activity, feeling, or experience. **b** the state of being a fellow or associate. **3** (*treated as sing. or pl*) a group of people with similar interests; an association. **4** the position of a fellow, e.g. of a university.

fellow traveller *noun* a non-member who sympathizes with and often furthers the ideals and programme of an organized group, *esp* the Communist party.

felly /'feli/ *noun* (*pl* **fellies**) see FELLOE.

felo-de-se /,feloh day 'say, ,feloh/ *noun* (*pl* **felos-de-se** /,feelohz, ,felohz/) suicide, or somebody who commits suicide. [medieval Latin *felo de se, fello de se*, literally 'evildoer upon himself']

felon[1] /'felən/ *noun* **1** somebody who has committed a felony. **2** *archaic* a whitlow. [Middle English via Old French from medieval Latin *fellon-, fello* evildoer, villain]

felon[2] *adj archaic* cruel or evil.

felony *noun* (*pl* **felonies**) a grave crime, e.g. murder or arson, that was formerly regarded in law as more serious than a misdemeanour and involved forfeiture of property in addition to any other punishment. ➤➤ **felonious** /fə'lohni·əs/ *adj*, **feloniously** /fə'lohni·əsli/ *adv*, **feloniousness** *noun*.

felspar /'felspah/ *noun* see FELDSPAR.

felt[1] /felt/ *noun* **1** a nonwoven cloth made by compressing wool or fur, often mixed with natural or synthetic fibres. **2** a material resembling felt. [Old English]

felt[2] *verb trans* **1** to make (wool, etc) into felt, or to cover (something) with felt. **2** to cause (something) to stick and mat together. ➤ *verb intrans* to become matted.

felt[3] *verb* past tense and past part. of FEEL[1].

felt-tipped pen *noun* = FELT-TIP PEN.

felt-tip pen *noun* a pen with a soft felt tip through which ink flows.

felucca /fe'lukə/ *noun* a narrow lateen-rigged sailing ship, chiefly of the Mediterranean area. [Italian *feluca*, perhaps from Greek *epholkion* small boat]

fem. *abbr* **1** female. **2** used in grammar: feminine.

female[1] /'feemayl/ *adj* **1** relating to or denoting the sex that bears offspring or produces eggs. **2** said of a plant or flower: having an ovary but no stamens. **3** designed with a hollow part for receiving a corresponding male part: *a female electric plug*. ➤➤ **femaleness** *noun*. [Middle English, alteration of *femel, femelle*, via Old French from Latin *femella* girl, dimin. of *femina* woman]

Usage note
female *or* feminine? *Female* is used to describe the sex that bears offspring or produces eggs, and plants or flowers that produce seeds: *a female deer is called a doe*. *Feminine* is used only of human beings, not plants or animals, and describes qualities and behaviour that are traditionally ascribed to women rather than men: *feminine charm*. *Feminine* is also used in some languages to describe certain nouns and adjectives, in contrast to those that are masculine or neuter.

female[2] *noun* a female animal, person, or plant.

female circumcision *noun* the practice, traditional in some ethnic groups, of removing the clitoris of young or adolescent girls, sometimes also involving the removal of the labia and the sewing up of part of the vagina.

female condom *noun* a contraceptive barrier device made of thin rubber, which fits inside the vagina.

female impersonator *noun* a male entertainer whose act involves dressing and performing as a woman on stage.

feminine[1] /'femənin/ *adj* **1** of or being a female person. **2** characteristic of, appropriate to, or peculiar to women; womanly: *The* *feminine mystique has succeeded in burying millions of American women alive* — Betty Friedan. **3** of or belonging to the gender that normally includes most words or grammatical forms referring to females. **4** having or occurring in an extra unstressed final syllable: *feminine rhyme*. ≫ **femininely** *adv*, **feminineness** *noun*, **femininity** /-'niniti/ *noun*. [Middle English via French from Latin *femininus*, from *femina* woman]

Usage note
feminine or female? See note at FEMALE[1].

feminine[2] *noun* the feminine gender, or a word or morpheme of this gender. ✳ **the eternal feminine** the feminine principle in human nature.

feminise /'feminies/ *verb trans* see FEMINIZE.

feminism /'feminiz(ə)m/ *noun* the advocacy or furtherance of women's rights, interests, and equality with men, *esp* in political, economic, and social spheres.

Editorial note
Feminism is a theory which involves women emancipating themselves on their own terms from inequalities and discrimination based on gender. The canon of this political philosophy addresses patriarchal orthodoxies within a male-dominated society. It seeks to bring an end to women's subordination and violence against women by empowering women and giving them control over their own bodies — Helena Kennedy.

≫ **feminist** *noun and adj*.

feminize or **feminise** /'feminiez/ *verb trans* **1** to give a feminine quality to (something). **2** to cause (a male or castrated female) to take on feminine characteristics, e.g. by administration of hormones. ≫ **feminization** /-'zaysh(ə)n/ *noun*.

femme fatale /ˌfam fə'tahl (*French* fam fatal)/ *noun* (*pl* **femmes fatales** /ˌfam fə'tahl (*French* fam fatal)/) a seductive and usu mysterious woman, *esp* one who lures men into dangerous or compromising situations. [French *femme fatale* disastrous woman]

femora /'femərə/ *noun* pl of FEMUR.

femto- *comb. form* forming words, denoting: one thousand million millionth (10^{-15}) part of: *femtoampere*. [Danish or Norwegian *femten* fifteen, from Old Norse *fimmtān*]

femur /'feemə/ *noun* (*pl* **femurs** or **femora** /'femərə/) **1** the bone of the hind or lower limb nearest the body; the thighbone. **2** the third segment of an insect's leg counting from the base. ≫ **femoral** *adj*. [Latin *femor-, femur* thigh]

fen[1] /fen/ *noun* **1a** an area of low marshy or flooded land. **b** such an area when artificially drained. **2** (**the Fens**) a fertile agricultural district of eastern England consisting of land reclaimed from the Wash. ≫ **fenny** *adj*. [Old English *fenn*]

fen[2] *noun* (*pl* **fen**) a unit of currency in China, worth 100th of a yuan. [Chinese (Pekingese) *fen*]

fence[1] /fens/ *noun* **1a** a barrier, e.g. of wire or boards, intended to prevent escape or intrusion or to mark a boundary: *Good fences make good neighbors* — Robert Frost. **b** an upright obstacle to be jumped by a horse, e.g. in showjumping or steeplechasing. **c** a protective guard on a tool or piece of machinery. **2** *informal* a receiver of stolen goods. ✳ **sit on the fence** to adopt a position of neutrality or indecision. ≫ **fenceless** *adj*. [Middle English *fens*, short for *defens* DEFENCE]

fence[2] *verb trans* **1a** (*usu* + in) to enclose (an area) with a fence. **b** (*usu* + off) to separate (an area) off with or as if with a fence. **2** *informal* to receive or sell (stolen goods). ≫ *verb intrans* **1a** to practise fencing. **b** to use tactics of attack and defence, e.g. thrusting and parrying, resembling those of fencing. **2** *informal* to deal in stolen goods. ≫ **fencer** *noun*.

fencible /'fensibl/ *noun* formerly, a soldier belonging to a British militia who signed up for home service only. [Middle English, suitable for defence, shortening of DEFENSIBLE]

fencing *noun* **1** the art of attack and defence with a sword, e.g. the foil, épée, or sabre. **2** fences, or material used for building them.

fend /fend/ *verb intrans* (+ for) to provide a livelihood for somebody, *esp* oneself; to look after oneself. [Middle English, in the sense 'defend', short for *defenden*: see DEFEND]

fender *noun* **1** a cushion, e.g. of rope or wood, hung over the side of a ship to absorb impact. **2** a low metal guard for a fire, used to confine the coals. **3** *NAmer* a wing or mudguard.

fend off *verb trans* to keep or ward (something or somebody) off; to repel (them).

fenestra /fi'nestrə/ *noun* (*pl* **fenestrae** /-tree/) **1a** an oval opening between the middle ear and the vestibule of the inner ear. **b** a round opening between the middle ear and the cochlea of the inner ear. **2** an opening cut in bone. **3** a transparent spot in an insect's wing. **4** a window or opening in a wall. [Latin *fenestra* window]

fenestrate /'fenistrət/ *adj* = FENESTRATED (2).

fenestrated /'fenistraytid/ *adj* **1** provided with or characterized by windows. **2** having one or more openings or pores: *fenestrated blood capillaries*. [Latin *fenestratus*, past part. of *fenestrare* to provide with openings or windows, from *fenestra* window]

fenestration /feni'straysh(ə)n/ *noun* **1** the arrangement of windows in a building. **2** an opening in a surface, e.g. a wall or membrane. **3** the operation of cutting an opening in the bony labyrinth between the inner ear and tympanum as a treatment for deafness.

feng shui /ˌfung 'shway, ˌfeng 'shooh·i/ *noun* in Chinese philosophy, a system of rules governing the placement and arrangement of a building, a room, etc, according to the flow of energy in the environment, so as to bring good fortune. [Chinese *feng shui*, from *feng* wind + *shui* water]

Fenian[1] /'feenyən/ *noun* a member of a secret Irish and Irish-American organization of the 19th cent., dedicated to the overthrow of British rule in Ireland. ≫ **Fenianism** *noun*. [Irish Gaelic *Féinne*, pl of *Fíann*, legendary band of Irish warriors]

Fenian[2] *adj* of the Fenians or Fenianism.

fennec /'fenek/ *noun* a small, pale fawn N African and Arabian fox with large ears: *Vulpes zerda*. [Arabic *fanak, fenek*, from Persian]

fennel /'fenl/ *noun* a European plant of the carrot family cultivated for its aromatic seeds and foliage: *Foeniculum*. [Old English *finule* from Latin *feniculum*, dimin. of *fenum, faenum, foenum* hay]

fennig /'fenig/ *noun* a unit of currency in Bosnia-Herzegovina, worth 100th of a convertible marka.

fenugreek /'fenyoogreek/ *noun* a leguminous Asiatic plant whose aromatic seeds are used as a flavouring: *Trigonella foenum-graecum*. [Middle English via Old French from Latin *fenum, faenum*, or *foenum Graecum* Greek hay]

feoff[1] /fef, feef/ *verb trans* formerly, to grant a fief to (somebody). ≫ **feoffee** /fe'fee, fee'fee/ *noun*, **feoffor** *noun*, **feoffment** *noun*, **feoffor** *noun*. [Middle English via Anglo-French from Old French *feoffer* to invest with a fee, from Old French *fief*: see FEE[1]]

feoff[2] *noun* = FIEF.

-fer *comb. form* (*pl* **-fers** or **-fera**) forming nouns, denoting: somebody or something that bears: *aquifer; conifer*. [French *-fère* from Latin *-fer* bearing, somebody or something that bears, from *ferre* to carry]

feral /'fiərəl/ *adj* **1a** not domesticated or cultivated; = WILD[1]. **b** having escaped from domestication and become wild: *feral pigeons*. **2** of or suggestive of a wild beast; savage. [medieval Latin *feralis* from Latin *fera* wild animal, from fem of *ferus* wild]

fer-de-lance /ˌfeə də 'lahns/ *noun* (*pl* **fers-de-lance** /ˌfeə/ or **fer-de-lances**) a large extremely venomous pit viper of Central and S America: *Bothrops atrox*. [French *fer-de-lance* spearhead, literally 'lance iron']

feretory /'ferit(ə)ri/ *noun* (*pl* **feretories**) **1** a shrine for the relics of a saint, *esp* a portable one for carrying in a procession. **2** a chapel or part of a chapel containing such a shrine. [Middle English via French and medieval Latin from Latin *feretrum* litter, bier, from Greek *pheretron*, from *pherein* to carry]

feria /'fiəri·ə, 'feri·ə/ *noun* (*pl* **ferias** or **feriae** /-i·ee/) a weekday of the Roman Catholic Church calendar on which no feast is celebrated. ≫ **ferial** *adj*. [medieval Latin *feria*: see FAIR[3]]

fermata /fuh'mahtə/ *noun* (*pl* **fermatas** or **fermate** /-tay/) **1** a prolongation of a musical note, chord, or rest beyond its given time value, the length of which is at the discretion of the performer or conductor. **2** the sign denoting this; = PAUSE[1] (2). [Italian *fermata* stop, from *fermare* to stop, from Latin *firmare* to make firm, from *firmus* FIRM[1]]

ferment[1] /fə'ment/ *verb intrans* **1** to undergo fermentation. **2** to be in a state of agitation or intense activity. ≫ *verb trans* **1** to cause (a substance) to undergo fermentation. **2** to cause (a state of agitation). ≫ **fermentable** *adj*, **fermenter** *noun*.

Usage note
ferment or *foment*? Either of these two verbs may be used in the sense 'to rouse or incite a state of agitation': *to ferment/foment rebellion*. In their literal senses, the verbs differ: *foment* means 'to apply a hot moist substance to the body' and *ferment* 'to undergo the chemical process of fermentation'.

ferment² /'fuhment/ *noun* **1** a state of unrest or upheaval; agitation or tumult. **2** *dated* an agent, e.g. an enzyme or organism, capable of bringing about fermentation. [Middle English via Old French from Latin *fermentum* yeast]

fermentation /fuhmen'taysh(ə)n/ *noun* **1a** an enzymatically controlled anaerobic breakdown of an energy-rich compound, e.g. a carbohydrate to carbon dioxide and alcohol, or an enzymatically controlled transformation of an organic compound. **b** a chemical change with effervescence. **2** *archaic* agitation or tumult; = FERMENT² (I). ➤➤ **fermentative** /fə'mentativ/ *adj*.

fermion /'fuhmion/ *noun* a particle, e.g. an electron, that interacts with other particles in a way described by Fermi and Dirac. [named after Enrico *Fermi* d.1954, Italian physicist]

fermium /'fuhmi·əm/ *noun* a radioactive metallic chemical element that is artificially produced: symbol Fm, atomic number 100. [Latin *fermium*, named after Enrico *Fermi*: see FERMION]

fern /fuhn/ *noun* (*pl* **ferns** or collectively **fern**) any of a phylum of flowerless seedless lower plants, *esp* any of an order resembling flowering plants in having a root, stem, and leaflike fronds but differing in reproducing by spores: phylum Filicopsida. ➤➤ **fernery** *noun*, **ferny** *adj*. [Old English *fearn*]

fernbird *noun* a New Zealand bird of the warbler family that has fern-like tail feathers: *Bowdleria punctata*.

ferocious /fə'rohshəs/ *adj* extremely fierce or violent. ➤➤ **ferociously** *adv*, **ferociousness** *noun*, **ferocity** /fə'rositi/ *noun*. [Latin *feroc-*, *ferox*, literally 'fierce looking', from *ferus* wild, fierce]

-ferous or **-iferous** *comb. form* forming adjectives, with the meaning: bearing; yielding; containing: *carboniferous*; *pestiferous*. [Middle English via French from Latin *-fer* producing]

ferrate /'ferayt/ *noun* a compound of a metal with an ion that contains iron and oxygen atoms. [Latin *ferrum* iron + -ATE¹]

ferret¹ /'ferit/ *noun* **1** a partially domesticated European polecat, *esp* an albino, used for hunting small rodents, e.g. rats, or kept as a pet: *Mustela furo*. **2** *informal* an active and persistent search or searcher. ➤➤ **ferrety** *adj*. [Middle English *furet*, *ferret* via Old French from Latin *furittus* little thief, dimin. of *fur* thief]

ferret² *verb* (**ferreted, ferreting**) ➤ *verb intrans* **1** *informal* (+ about/around) to search about or around. **2** to hunt with ferrets. ➤ *verb trans* **1** to hunt (rats, etc) with ferrets. **2** (*usu* + out) to drive (game) out, *esp* from covert or burrows. ➤➤ **ferreter** *noun*.

ferret out *verb trans informal* to find (information) and bring it to light by searching: *They ferreted out the answers.*

ferri- *comb. form* forming words, denoting: **1** iron: *ferriferous*. **2** ferric iron: *ferricyanide*. [Latin, from *ferrum* iron]

ferriage /'feri·ij/ *noun* transport by ferry, or the fare paid for it.

ferric /'ferik/ *adj* of, containing, or being trivalent iron.

ferric oxide *noun* the red or black oxide of iron found in nature as haematite and as rust.

ferricyanide /feri'sie·ənied/ *noun* a complex chemical compound that is used in making blue pigments.

ferriferous /fe'rifərəs/ *adj* containing or yielding iron.

ferrimagnetic /ˌferimag'netik/ *adj* of or being a substance, e.g. ferrite, characterized by magnetization in which one group of magnetic ions is polarized in a direction opposite to the other. ➤➤ **ferrimagnetism** /-'magniti(ə)m/ *noun*.

Ferris wheel /'feris/ *noun chiefly NAmer* = BIG WHEEL. [named after G W *Ferris* d.1896, US engineer, who invented it]

ferrite /'feriet/ *noun* any of several magnetic substances of high magnetic permeability consisting mainly of an iron oxide. ➤➤ **ferritic** /fe'ritik/ *adj*. [Latin *ferrum* iron + -ITE¹]

ferritin /'feritin/ *noun* an iron-containing protein that functions in the storage of iron and is found *esp* in the liver and spleen. [FERRITE + -IN¹]

ferro- *comb. form* forming words, with the meanings: **1** containing iron; iron and: *ferroconcrete*. **2** ferrous iron: *ferrocyanide*. [medieval Latin, from *ferrum* iron]

ferroconcrete /feroh'kongkreet, -'konkreet/ *noun* = REINFORCED CONCRETE.

ferrocyanide /feroh'sie·ənied/ *noun* a complex chemical compound that is used in making blue pigments, *esp* Prussian blue.

ferroelectric /ˌferoh·i'lektrik/ *adj* of or being a crystalline substance having spontaneous electric polarization reversible by an electric field. ➤➤ **ferroelectricity** /ˌferohelik'trisiti, ˌferoh-ˌeelek-/ *noun*.

ferromagnetic /ˌferohmag'netik/ *adj* of or being a substance, *esp* iron, characterized by strong magnetization in which all the magnetic ions are polarized in the same direction. ➤➤ **ferromagnetism** /-'magniti(ə)m/ *noun*.

ferrous /'ferəs/ *adj* of, containing, or being bivalent iron. [Latin *ferrosus*, from *ferrum* iron]

ferrous sulphate *noun* a white or pale green chemical compound containing iron, sulphur, and oxygen, occurring naturally as copperas and used in making inks, in tanning, and in the treatment of anaemia: formula $FeSO_4.7H_2O$.

ferruginous /fe'roohjinəs/ *adj* **1** of or containing iron. **2** resembling iron rust in colour. [Latin *ferrugineus*, *ferruginus*, from *ferrugin-*, *ferrugo* iron rust, from *ferrum* iron]

ferrule /'feroohl/ *noun* **1** a ring or cap, usu of metal, strengthening a cane, tool handle, etc. **2** a short tube or bush for making a tight joint, e.g. between pipes. [alteration of Middle English *virole* via Old French from Latin *viriola*, dimin. of *viria* bracelet]

ferry¹ /'feri/ *verb trans* (**ferries, ferried, ferrying**) **1** to carry (somebody) by boat, hovercraft, etc over a body of water. **2** to convey (somebody) by car, etc from one place to another. **3** to deliver (an aircraft) by air. [Old English *ferian* to carry, convey]

ferry² *noun* (*pl* **ferries**) **1** a boat, etc providing a regular service for carrying passengers, vehicles, or goods across a body of water, e.g. a river. **2** a place where people or things are carried by ferry across a body of water. **3** a ferry service, or the right to operate one.

ferryboat /'feriboht/ *noun* a boat used to ferry passengers, vehicles, or goods.

ferryman /'ferimən, -man/ *noun* (*pl* **ferrymen**) somebody who operates a ferry.

fertile /'fuhtiel/ *adj* **1a** capable of producing or bearing fruit, *esp* in great quantities; productive. **b** capable of sustaining abundant plant growth: *fertile soil*. **c** characterized by great resourcefulness and activity; inventive: *a fertile imagination*. **2a** capable of breeding or reproducing. **b** capable of growing or developing: *a fertile egg*. **c** affording abundant possibilities for development: *a fertile area for research*. **3** said of a substance: capable of being converted into fissile material. ➤➤ **fertilely** *adv*, **fertileness** *noun*, **fertility** /fuh'tiliti/ *noun*. [Middle English via French from Latin *fertilis*, from *ferre* to carry, bear]

Fertile Crescent *noun* (**the Fertile Crescent**) a roughly crescent-shaped region of the Middle East that stretches from the Persian Gulf to the Mediterranean coast and down the Nile valley.

fertilise /'fuhtiliez/ *verb trans* see FERTILIZE.

fertiliser *noun* see FERTILIZER.

fertility drug *noun* a drug which treats infertility in women by stimulating the release of ova from the ovaries.

fertilize or **fertilise** /'fuhtiliez/ *verb trans* **1a** to make (an ovule, egg, etc) capable of developing into a new individual by uniting with a male germ cell. **b** to apply a fertilizer to (soil) or nutrients to (water). **2** to make (something) fertile by insemination, impregnation, or pollination. ➤➤ **fertilizable** *adj*, **fertilization** /-'zaysh(ə)n/ *noun*.

fertilizer or **fertiliser** *noun* **1** somebody or something that fertilizes. **2** a substance, e.g. manure, used to make soil more fertile.

ferula /'feroolə/ *noun* (*pl* **ferulas** or **ferulae** /-lee/) an Old World plant of the carrot family that yields various gum resins: genus *Ferula*. [from Latin *ferula* giant fennel]

ferule /'feroohl/ *noun* a flat ruler used, *esp* formerly, to punish children. [Latin *ferula* giant fennel, ferule; the stalk of the giant fennel was used by the Romans for inflicting corporal punishment]

fervent /'fuhv(ə)nt/ *adj* exhibiting deep sincere emotion; ardent: *He is a fervent believer in free speech.* ➤➤ **fervency** /-si/ *noun*, **fervently** *adv*. [Middle English via Old French from Latin *fervent-*, *fervens*, present part. of *fervēre* to boil, glow]

fervid /'fuhvid/ *adj* passionately intense; ardent: *His fervid manner of lovemaking offended her* — Arnold Bennett. ➤➤ **fervidly** *adv*. [Latin *fervidus*, from *fervēre* to boil, glow]

fervour (*NAmer* **fervor**) /'fuhvə/ *noun* the quality or state of being fervent or fervid. [Middle English *fervour* via Old French from Latin *fervor*, from *fervēre* to boil, glow]

fescue /'feskyooh/ *noun* any of several species of tufted grasses, some of which are important fodder grasses and a few used as lawn grasses: genera *Festuca* and *Vulpia*. [alteration of Middle English *festu* stalk, straw, via Old French and late Latin from Latin *festuca*]

fess *or* **fesse** /fes/ *noun* a broad horizontal bar across the middle of a heraldic shield. [Middle English *fesse* via Old French from Latin *fascia* a band]

fest /fest/ *noun chiefly NAmer* (*often in combination*) a meeting or occasion marked by a specified activity: *a gabfest*. [German *Fest* celebration, from Latin *festum*: see FEAST¹]

festal /'festl/ *adj* = FESTIVE. ⋙ **festally** *adv*. [Latin *festum*: see FEAST¹]

fester¹ /'festə/ *verb* (**festered, festering**) ⊳ *verb intrans* **1** said of a wound: to generate pus. **2** said of food, etc: to putrefy or rot. **3** said of a feeling, etc: to rankle: *It's the things I might have said that fester* — Clemence Dane. **4** said of a problem, situation, etc: to become worse; to intensify. ⊳ *verb trans* to make (a wound) inflamed. [Middle English *festren*, from *fester, festre* suppurating sore: see FESTER²]

fester² *noun* a pus-producing sore; a pustule. [Middle English *fester, festre*, via French from Latin *fistula* pipe, pipe-like ulcer]

festival /'festivl/ *noun* **1a** a time marked by special, e.g. customary, celebration. **b** a religious feast. **2** a programme or season of cultural events or entertainment: *the Edinburgh Festival*. **3** (*used before a noun*) of, appropriate to, or set apart as a festival: *Edinburgh is unbearable during the festival season*. [Middle English via French from Latin *festivus*: see FESTIVE]

festive /'festiv/ *adj* **1** of or suitable for a feast or festival, *esp* Christmas and New Year: *We did a lot of visiting over the festive season*. **2** joyous or merry. ⋙ **festively** *adv*, **festiveness** *noun*. [Latin *festivus*, from *festum*: see FEAST¹]

festivity /fe'stiviti/ *noun* (*pl* **festivities**) **1** (*also in pl*) festive activity; a party or celebration. **2** a festival.

festoon¹ /fe'stoohn/ *noun* a decorative chain or strip hanging between two points, or a carved, moulded, or painted ornament representing this. [French *feston* from Italian *festone*, ultimately from Latin *festa*: see FEAST¹]

festoon² *verb trans* **1** to hang or form festoons round (a room, etc). **2** to cover (something) profusely and gaily with decorations: *Her desk was festooned with balloons and streamers*.

festoon blind *noun* a ruched window blind.

festschrift /'festshrift/ *noun* (*pl* **festschrifts** *or* **festschriften** /-t(ə)n/) a volume of writings by various authors presented as a tribute or memorial, *esp* to a scholar. [German *Festschrift*, from *Fest* festival, celebration + *Schrift* writing]

FET *abbr* field-effect transistor.

feta /'fetə/ *noun* a firm white Greek cheese made of sheep's or goat's milk and cured in brine. [modern Greek (*tyri*) *pheta*, from *tyri* cheese + *pheta* slice, from Italian *fetta*]

fetal /'feetl/ *adj* = foetal (see FOETUS).

fetch¹ /fech/ *verb trans* **1** to go or come after (something or somebody) and bring or take them back. **2a** to cause (somebody) to come; to bring (them). **b** to reach (a specified price) as profit or return. **3** *informal* to strike or deal (a blow, slap, etc). **4** to produce or utter (a sigh, etc). ⊳ *verb intrans* said of a dog: to go after something, e.g. a stick or ball, and bring it back. ✳ **fetch and carry** to perform simple tasks or run errands for somebody. ⋙ **fetcher** *noun*. [Old English *fetian, feccan*]

fetch² *noun* **1a** the distance along open water or land over which the wind blows. **b** the distance traversed by waves without obstruction. **2** the act or an instance of fetching. **3** *archaic* a trick or stratagem.

fetch³ *noun* **1** the ghostly double of a person still alive; = DOPPELGÄNGER. **2** a ghost. [origin unknown]

fetching *adj* attractive or becoming: *She was wearing a very fetching hat*. ⋙ **fetchingly** *adv*.

fetch up *verb intrans informal* to come to rest or arrive: *They eventually fetched up in Paris*. ⊳ *verb trans informal* to vomit (food, etc).

fete¹ *or* **fête** /fayt/ *noun* **1** *Brit* an outdoor bazaar or other entertainment, usu held to raise money for a particular purpose. **2** *chiefly NAmer* a festival. [French *fête* from Old French *feste*: see FEAST¹]

fete² *or* **fête** *verb trans* (*usu in passive*) to honour or commemorate (somebody or something) with or as if with a fete or other ceremony.

fête champêtre /shom'pet(rə) (*French* fɛt ʃɑ̃pɛtr)/ *noun* (*pl* **fêtes champêtres** /,fayt shom'pet(rə) (*French* fɛt ʃɑ̃pɛtr)/) an outdoor entertainment. [French *fête champêtre* rural festival]

feti- *comb. form* see FOETO-.

fetid *or* **foetid** /'fetid, 'feetid/ *adj* having a heavy offensive smell; stinking. ⋙ **fetidly** *adv*, **fetidness** *noun*. [Middle English from Latin *fetidus*, from *fetēre* to stink]

fetish /'fetish/ *noun* **1a** an object believed among a primitive people to have magical power. **b** an object regarded with superstitious trust or reverence. **2** an object or bodily part whose presence in reality or fantasy is psychologically necessary for sexual gratification, or form of sexual desire and gratification related to such an object, etc. **3** an object of irrational reverence or obsessive devotion. [French *fétiche* via Portuguese from Latin *facticius*: see FACTITIOUS]

fetishism *noun* **1** the displacement of erotic interest and satisfaction to a fetish. **2** belief in magical fetishes. ⋙ **fetishist** *noun*, **fetishistic** /-'shistik/ *adj*.

fetlock /'fetlok/ *noun* **1** a projection bearing a tuft of hair on the back of the leg above the hoof of an animal of the horse family. **2** the joint of the limb or tuft of hair at the fetlock. [Middle English *fitlok, fetlak* of Germanic origin; related to FOOT¹]

feto- *comb. form* see FOETO-.

fetor /'feetə/ *noun formal* a strong offensive smell; a stink. [Middle English *fetoure* from Latin *fetor*, from *fetēre* to stink]

fetter¹ /'fetə/ *noun* **1** a shackle for the feet. **2** (*usu in pl*) something that confines; a restraint. [Old English *feter*]

fetter² *verb trans* (**fettered, fettering**) **1** to put fetters on (somebody). **2** to bind (somebody) with or as if with fetters; to shackle or restrain (them).

fettle¹ /'fetl/ *noun* a state of physical or mental fitness or order; condition: *You're in fine fettle today*. [Middle English *fetlen* to shape or prepare, gird oneself, from Old English *fetel* girdle]

fettle² *verb trans* **1** to trim the rough joints or edges of (unfired pottery or a metal casting). **2** to line (a furnace) with loose material, e.g. ore or sand. **3** *dialect* to clean or mend (something).

fettler /'fetlə/ *noun* **1** somebody who fettles. **2** *Aus* a railway maintenance worker.

fettuccine /fetə'cheeni/ *pl noun* (*treated as sing. or pl*) narrow ribbons of egg-enriched pasta. [Italian *fettuccine*, pl of *fettuccina*, dimin. of *fettuccia* small slice, ribbon, dimin. of *fetta* slice]

fetus /'feetəs/ *noun* see FOETUS.

Usage note

foetus *or* fetus? See note at FOETUS.

feu /fyooh/ *noun* a perpetual lease for a fixed rent, or land held under such a lease. [Middle English (Scots) from early French *fé, fief*: see FEE¹]

feud¹ /fyoohd/ *noun* a lasting state of hostilities, *esp* between families or clans, marked by violent attacks for the purpose of revenge. [alteration of Middle English *feide* from Old French, of Germanic origin]

feud² *verb intrans* to carry on a feud.

feudal *adj* **1** of feudalism or a medieval fee. **2** *derog* suggestive of feudalism, usu with reference to the expectation of unquestioning obedience from inferiors, or their servile compliance: *Her old feudal countess of a mother rules the family with an iron hand* — Henry James. ⋙ **feudally** *adv*. [medieval Latin *feodalis, feudalis*, from *feodum, feudum* fee, fief, of Germanic origin]

feudalise *verb trans* see FEUDALIZE.

feudalism *noun* a medieval system of political organization involving the relationship of lord to vassal with all land held in fee, homage, the service of tenants under arms and in court, wardship, and forfeiture. ⋙ **feudalist** *noun*, **feudalistic** /-'listik/ *adj*.

feudality /fyooh'daliti/ *noun* (*pl* **feudalities**) **1** the state of being feudal. **2** a feudal holding.

feudalize *or* **feudalise** /'fyoohdliez/ *verb trans* to make (something) feudal. ⋙ **feudalization** /-'zaysh(ə)n/ *noun*.

feudatory[1] /'fyoohdət(ə)ri/ *adj* **1** formerly, owing feudal allegiance. **2** formerly, under a foreign overlord. [medieval Latin *feudatorius*, from *feudare* to enfeoff, from *feudum*: see FEUDAL]

feudatory[2] *noun* (*pl* **feudatories**) formerly, a person holding lands by feudal tenure; a vassal.

fever /'feevə/ *noun* **1** a rise of body temperature above the normal, or any of various diseases characterized by such a rise in temperature. **2a** a state of intense emotion or activity: *They were in a fever of impatience*. **b** a contagious, usu transient, enthusiasm; a craze: *Football fever raged throughout the world*. [Old English from Latin *febris*]

fevered /'feevəd/ *adj* **1** hot or flushed owing to fever or agitation: *She wiped his fevered brow*. **2** extremely fast or active, and usu agitated or excited: *This story is just a product of a fevered imagination*.

feverfew *noun* a perennial European composite plant with white-yellow flowers: *Tanacetum parthenium*. [Middle English via Anglo-French from late Latin *febrifugia*: see FEBRIFUGE[1]]

feverish *adj* **1a** having the symptoms of a fever. **b** indicating, relating to, or caused by a fever. **c** tending to cause or infect with fever. **2** marked by intense emotion, activity, or instability: *feverish excitement*. >>> **feverishly** *adv*, **feverishness** *noun*.

feverous /'feevərəs/ *adj archaic* = FEVERISH.

fever pitch *noun* a state of intense excitement and agitation: *They raised the crowd to fever pitch*.

few[1] /fyooh/ *adj* **1** amounting to only a small number: *One of his few pleasures is gardening*; *Some few people still believe that the world is flat*. **2** (**a few**) at least some though not many: *He'd had a few drinks*; *I caught a few more fish*. ✸ **few and far between** scarce; rare: *Good days are few and far between*. **not a few** quite a lot. >>> **fewness** *noun*. [Old English *fēawa*]

few[2] *noun* **1** (*pl*) not many: *Few of his stories were true*. **2** (**a few**) at least some though not many: *Only a few of his plans came to fruition*. **3** (**the few**) a select or exclusive group of people; an elite.

fewer *adj* comparative of FEW[1].

Usage note
fewer or less? The general rule is to use *fewer* with plural nouns (*fewer people, fewer books*) and *less* with singular nouns (*less time, less work, less sugar*). More precisely, *fewer* is used with people or things that can be counted (*fewer than 100 people came to the meeting*) and *less* is used with quantities and numbers that give a quantity or size: *less than two years ago*. The use of *less* with plural nouns should be avoided: *fewer opportunities*, not *less opportunities*. This incorrect usage is, however, frequently found in informal contexts.

fey /fay/ *adj* **1a** marked by an otherworldly and irresponsible air. **b** able to see into the future or to see spirits. **2** *chiefly Scot*. **a** fated to die; doomed. **b** marked by an excited or elated state. >>> **feyness** *noun*. [Old English *fǣge* doomed]

fez /fez/ *noun* (*pl* **fezzes**) a red brimless hat shaped like a truncated cone with a tassel, worn by men in southern and eastern Mediterranean countries. [French *fez*, named after *Fez*, city in Morocco where they were orig made]

ff *abbr* **1** folios. **2** following, e.g. pages. **3** fortissimo.

fiacre /fi'ahkrə (*French* fjakr)/ *noun* formerly, a small four-wheeled horse-drawn carriage for hire: *A fiacre was found resting in the shadow of the Arch of Constantine* — Henry James. [French *fiacre*, named after the Hôtel de St *Fiacre* in Paris, where such vehicles were first hired out]

fiancé *or* **fiancée** /fi'onsay/ *noun* a man or woman to whom a person is engaged to be married. [French *fiancé* via Old French from Latin *fidare*, alteration of *fidere* to trust]

fiasco /fi'askoh/ *noun* (*pl* **fiascos**) a complete and ignominious failure. [via French from Italian *fiasco* bottle (from late Latin *flasca*, *flasco*: see FLASK), in the phrase *far fiasco*, literally 'to make a bottle', used in the theatre to mean 'to fail in a performance']

fiat /'feeat, 'fieat/ *noun* an authoritative and often arbitrary order; a decree: *government by fiat*. [Latin *fiat* let it be done, from *fieri* to become, be done]

fib[1] /fib/ *noun informal* a trivial or childish lie. [perhaps by shortening and alteration from FABLE[1]]

fib[2] *verb intrans* (**fibbed, fibbing**) *informal* to tell a trivial or childish lie. >>> **fibber** *noun*.

fiber /'fiebə/ *noun NAmer* see FIBRE.

Fibonacci number /feebə'nahchi/ *noun* a number in the Fibonacci sequence 1, 1, 2, 3, 5, 8, 13, 21, ... [named after Leonardo *Fibonacci* d. about 1250, Italian mathematician]

Fibonacci sequence *noun* an infinite sequence of integers in which every term after the second is the sum of the two preceding terms. [named after Leonardo *Fibonacci*: see FIBONACCI NUMBER]

fibr- *or* **fibro-** *comb. form* forming words, with the meanings: **1** fibre or fibrous tissue: *fibroid*. **2** fibrous and: *fibrovascular*. [Latin *fibra* fibre]

fibre (*NAmer* **fiber**) /'fiebə/ *noun* **1a** an elongated tapering plant cell with thick walls. **b** = NERVE FIBRE. **c** any of the filaments composing most of the intercellular matrix of connective tissue. **d** any of the elongated contractile cells of muscle tissue. **e** a slender natural or manufactured thread or filament, e.g. of wool, cotton, or asbestos. **2** material made of fibres. **3** = DIETARY FIBRE. **4** essential structure or character: *the very fibre of his being*. **5** strength or fortitude: *a man of great moral fibre*. [French *fibre* from Latin *fibra*]

fibreboard *noun* a material made by compressing fibres of wood, etc into stiff boards.

fibreglass *noun* **1** glass in fibrous form used in making various products, e.g. textiles and insulation materials. **2** a combination of synthetic resins and fibreglass.

fibre optics *pl noun* (*treated as sing. or pl*) the use of very thin bundles of glass or plastic fibres that transmit light throughout their length by internal reflections and are used, e.g. for transmitting optical signals. >>> **fibre-optic** *adj*.

fibrescope *noun* a flexible instrument using fibre optics for examining inaccessible areas, e.g. the lining of the stomach.

fibril /'fiebril/ *noun* a small filament or fibre. >>> **fibrillar** *adj*, **fibrillose** /-lohs/ *adj*. [Latin *fibrilla*, dimin. of *fibra* fibre]

fibrillate /'fiebrilayt, 'fib-/ *verb intrans* to undergo fibrillation. >>> *verb trans* to cause (something) to undergo fibrillation.

fibrillation /fiebri'laysh(ə)n/ *noun* **1** the forming of fibres or fibrils. **2** very rapid irregular contractions of muscle fibres of the heart resulting in a lack of synchronization between heartbeat and pulse.

fibrin /'fiebrin/ *noun* a fibrous protein formed from fibrinogen by the action of thrombin, *esp* in the clotting of blood. >>> **fibrinous** /-nəs/ *adj*. [FIBRE + -IN[1]]

fibrinogen /fie'brinəj(ə)n/ *noun* a blood plasma protein that is produced in the liver and is converted into fibrin during clotting of blood.

fibro /'fiebroh/ *noun* (*pl* **fibros**) *Aus* a mixture of asbestos and cement. [short for *fibro-cement*, because of the asbestos fibres that bind the cement]

fibro- *comb. form* see FIBR-.

fibroblast /'fiebrəblast/ *noun* a cell giving rise to connective tissue which secretes collagen. >>> **fibroblastic** /-'blastik/ *adj*.

fibro-cement *noun* = FIBRO.

fibroid[1] /'fiebroyd/ *adj* resembling, forming, or consisting of fibrous tissue.

fibroid[2] *noun* a benign tumour made up of fibrous and muscular tissue that occurs *esp* in the uterine wall.

fibroin /'fiebroh·in/ *noun* an insoluble protein comprising the filaments of the raw silk fibre. [French *fibroïne*, from FIBRO- + -*ine* -IN[1]]

fibroma /fie'brohmə/ *noun* (*pl* **fibromas** *or* **fibromata** /-tə/) a benign tumour consisting mainly of fibrous tissue.

fibrosis /fie'brohsis/ *noun* the abnormal increase of fibrous tissue in an organ or part of the body. >>> **fibrotic** /fie'brotik/ *adj*.

fibrositis /fiebrə'siətəs/ *noun* a painful muscular condition resulting from inflammation of fibrous tissue, e.g. muscle sheaths. [Latin *fibrosus* fibrous + -ITIS]

fibrous /'fiebrəs/ *adj* containing, consisting of, or resembling fibres. >>> **fibrously** *adv*, **fibrousness** *noun*. [French *fibreux* from *fibre* fibre, from Latin *fibra*]

fibrovascular /fiebroh'vaskyoolə/ *adj* said of a plant structure: consisting of fibres and conducting cells.

fibula /'fibyoolə/ *noun* (*pl* **fibulae** /-lee/ *or* **fibulas**) **1** the outer and usu smaller of the two bones of the hind limb of higher vertebrates between the knee and ankle: compare TIBIA. **2** an ornamented clasp used *esp* by the ancient Greeks and Romans. >>> **fibular** *adj*. [Latin *fibula* brooch, clasp; (sense 1) because the shape of the fibula and tibia resembles a clasp]

-fic *suffix* forming adjectives, with the meaning: making or causing: *horrific; pacific.* [French *-fique* from Latin *-ficus*, from *facere* to make]

-fication *comb. form* forming nouns, denoting: action or production: *reification; jollification.* [Middle English *-ficacioun* via French from Latin *-fication-*, *-ficatio*, from verbs ending in *-ficare* to make, from *-ficus*: see -FIC]

fiche /feesh/ *noun* (*pl* **fiche** *or* **fiches**) **1** = MICROFICHE. **2** = ULTRAFICHE.

fichu /'feeshooh (*French* fiʃy)/ *noun* a woman's light triangular scarf draped over the shoulders and fastened at the bosom. [French *fichu*, past part. of *ficher* to stick in, throw on, from Latin *figere* to fasten, pierce]

fickle /'fikl/ *adj* lacking steadfastness or constancy: capricious. ⟫ **fickleness** *noun.* [Old English *ficol* deceitful]

fictile /'fiktiel/ *adj* **1** moulded into shape by a potter. **2** of or relating to pottery. [Latin *fictilis* moulded of clay, from *fingere*: see FICTION]

fiction /'fiksh(ə)n/ *noun* **1a** literature, e.g. novels or short stories, describing imaginary people and events: *I write fiction and I'm told it's autobiography, I write autobiography and I'm told it's fiction* — Philip Roth. **b** something invented by the imagination; *specif* an invented story: *The accused seems to have difficulty distinguishing fact from fiction.* **2** the action of feigning or creating with the imagination. **3** an assumption of a possibility as a fact, irrespective of the question of its truth: *Treating a corporation as a person is a legal fiction.* ⟫ **fictional** *adj,* **fictionality** /-'naliti/ *noun,* **fictionally** *adv,* **fictionist** *noun.* [Middle English *ficcioun* via Old French from Latin *fiction-*, *fictio* act of fashioning, fiction, from *fingere* to shape, fashion, feign]

Usage note
fictional *or* **fictitious?** These two words are sometimes confused. *Fictional* means 'of fiction': *fictional heroes; fictitious* means 'not real or genuine; false': *He gave a fictitious name to the police.*

fictitious /fik'tishəs/ *adj* **1** said of a name: false; assumed. **2** not genuinely felt; feigned. **3** found or described in fiction. ⟫ **fictitiously** *adv,* **fictitiousness** *noun.* [Latin *ficticius* artificial, feigned, from *fingere*: see FICTION]

Usage note
fictitious *or* **fictional?** See note at FICTION.

fictive /'fiktiv/ *adj* **1** not genuinely felt; = FICTITIOUS (2). **2** of or capable of imaginative creation.

fid /fid/ *noun* a tapering wooden pin used in opening the strands of a rope for splicing. [origin unknown]

-fid *comb. form* forming adjectives, with the meaning: divided into parts as specified: *bifid.* [Latin *-fidus*, from *findere* to split]

Fid. Def. *abbr* Defender of the Faith. [Latin *Fidei Defensor*]

fiddle[1] /'fidl/ *noun* **1** *informal* a violin. **2** *Brit, informal* a dishonest practice; a swindle. **3** *Brit, informal* an activity involving intricate manipulation: *It was a bit of a fiddle to get all these wires back in place.* **4** a device to keep objects from sliding off a table on board ship. ✲ **on the fiddle** *Brit, informal* taking part in dishonest practices. [Old English *fithele* violin, prob from medieval Latin *vitula* instrument played at festivals, from *vitulari* to celebrate]

fiddle[2] *verb intrans informal* **1** to play the fiddle. **2a** to move one's hands or fingers restlessly. **b** (*often* + about/around) to spend time in aimless or fruitless activity. ➤ *verb trans Brit, informal* **1** to falsify (accounts, etc), *esp* so as to gain financial advantage. **2** to get or contrive (something) by cheating or deception: *He fiddled an extra ten pounds on his expenses.* ✲ **fiddle with** *informal* to tamper or meddle with (something). ⟫ **fiddler** *noun.*

fiddle-faddle[1] /'fidl fadl/ *noun informal* often used as an exclamation: nonsense. [reduplication of FIDDLE[1] as in FIDDLESTICKS]

fiddle-faddle[2] *verb intrans informal* to waste time; to fuss around.

fiddlehead *noun* ornamentation on a ship's bow curved like a scroll. [from the resemblance to the scroll at the head of a violin]

fiddler crab *noun* a burrowing crab of which the male has one claw much enlarged: genus *Uca.* [from the position in which the enlarged claw is held, resembling the angle of a violinist's arm]

fiddlesticks *pl noun informal* used as an exclamation: nonsense. [*fiddlestick* violin bow; from its small value compared with the fiddle itself]

fiddling *adj informal* **1** trifling or petty: *She made some fiddling excuse.* **2** *Brit* = FIDDLY.

fiddly *adj* (**fiddlier, fiddliest**) *Brit, informal* finicky or intricate.

FIDE *abbr* World Chess Federation. [French *Fédération Internationale des Échecs*]

fideism /'fiedi·iz(ə)m/ *noun* reliance on faith rather than reason, *esp* in metaphysics. ⟫ **fideist** *noun,* **fideistic** /-'istik/ *adj.* [prob from French *fidéisme*, from Latin *fides* faith]

fidelity /fi'deliti/ *noun* (*pl* **fidelities**) **1a** the quality or state of being faithful; loyalty: *Histories are more full of examples of the fidelity of dogs than of friends* — Pope. **b** accuracy in details; exactness. **2** the degree of similarity between some reproduced material and its original source. [Middle English *fidelite* via French from Latin *fidelitat-*, *fidelitas*, from *fidelis* faithful, from *fides* faith]

fidget[1] /'fijit/ *verb* (**fidgeted, fidgeting**) ➤ *verb intrans* to move or act restlessly or nervously. ➤ *verb trans* to cause (somebody) to move or act nervously. ⟫ **fidgeter** *noun,* **fidgetiness** *noun,* **fidgety** *adj.* [*fidge* to fidget, prob alteration of English dialect *fitch*, from Middle English *fichen*]

fidget[2] *noun* **1** somebody who fidgets. **2** (*usu in pl*) uneasiness or restlessness shown by nervous movements: *I've got the fidgets.*

fiducial /fi'd(y)oohsh(ə)l/ *adj* **1** taken as a standard of reference: *a fiducial mark.* **2** founded on faith or trust. **3** having the nature of a trust. [late Latin *fiducialis* from *fiducia*: see FIDUCIARY[1]]

fiduciary[1] /fi'd(y)oohshi·əri/ *adj* **1** of or having the nature of a trust; = FIDUCIAL (3). **2** said of paper money: not backed by gold but depending for its value on securities or public confidence in the issuer. [Latin *fiduciarius* from *fiducia* confidence, trust, from *fidere* to trust]

fiduciary[2] *noun* (*pl* **fiduciaries**) somebody who is entrusted to hold or manage property for another.

fie /fie/ *interj archaic* used to express disgust or shock. [Middle English via Old French from Latin *fi*]

fief /feef/ *noun* **1** formerly, a feudal estate. **2** something over which somebody has rights or exercises control: *He treats the Education Department as his own fief.* ⟫ **fiefdom** *noun.* [French *fief*: see FEE[1]]

field[1] /feeld/ *noun* **1a** an area of open land surrounded by a hedge or fence and used for cultivation or pasture. **b** an area of land containing a natural resource: *a coal field.* **c** the place where a battle is fought, or a battle itself. **d** a large unbroken expanse, e.g. of ice. **e** = AIRFIELD. **2a** an area constructed, equipped, or marked for sports. **b** the part of a sports area enclosed by the running track and used for athletic field events. **3a** an area or division of an activity: *His wife is a lawyer eminent in her field.* **b** an area of knowledge or expertise. **4a** the sphere of practical operation outside a place of work such as a laboratory: *We have a number of geologists working in the field.* **b** an area in which troops are operating, e.g. in an exercise or theatre of war. **c** (*used before a noun*) working or for use in the field: *field operations; field artillery.* **5a** (**the field**) the participants in a sports activity, *esp* with the exception of the favourite or winner. **b** in cricket, the fielders collectively. **6** a space on which something is drawn or projected, *esp* the surface on which a coat of arms is displayed. **7a** a set of mathematical elements that when subject to the two binary operations of addition and multiplication is a COMMUTATIVE (having results independent of the order of the elements involved) group under addition and, excluding zero, is a commutative group under multiplication. **b** a region in which a mathematical quantity, e.g. a scalar or vector, is associated with every point. **c** a region or space in which a given effect, e.g. magnetism, exists. **8** the area visible for observation through an optical instrument. **9** an area, e.g. a region of a computer disk store, in which a particular type of information is recorded. ✲ **take the field 1** said e.g. of a sports team: to go onto a playing field. **2** to enter on a military campaign. [Old English *feld*]

field[2] *verb trans* **1a** to stop and pick up (a batted ball). **b** to deal with (a question) by giving an impromptu answer: *The Minister fielded the reporters' questions.* **2a** to put (a team) into the field of play. **b** to put (troops) into the field of battle. ➤ *verb intrans* to play as a fielder in cricket, baseball, etc.

field artillery *noun* artillery, other than anti-aircraft or antitank guns, used in the field.

field day *noun* **1** a time of unusual pleasure and unrestrained action: *The newspaper had a field day with the scandal.* **2a** a day for military exercises or manoeuvres. **b** an outdoor meeting or social gathering.

field-effect transistor *noun* a transistor in which current is controlled by an applied electric field.

fielder *noun* any of the players whose job is to field the ball in cricket, baseball, etc.

field event *noun* an athletic event, e.g. discus, javelin, or jumping, other than a race: compare TRACK EVENT.

fieldfare *noun* a medium-sized Eurasian thrush with an ash-coloured head and chestnut wings: *Turdus pilaris*. [alteration of Old English *feldeware*, from *feld* field + *-ware* dweller]

field glasses *pl noun* an optical instrument consisting of two telescope-like parts on a single frame with a focusing device.

field goal *noun* 1 in American football, a score made by kicking the ball over the crossbar from ordinary play. 2 in basketball, a goal made while the ball is in play.

field gun *noun* a field artillery cannon.

field hockey *noun chiefly NAmer* hockey.

field hospital *noun* a temporary hospital established for emergency treatment in a combat zone.

field magnet *noun* a magnet for producing and maintaining a magnetic field, *esp* in a generator or electric motor.

field marshal *noun* an officer of the highest rank in the British army.

field mouse *noun* any of several species of mice that inhabit fields: genus *Apodemus*.

field mushroom *noun* the common edible mushroom: *Agaricus campestris*.

field officer *noun* a commissioned army officer of the rank of colonel, lieutenant colonel, or major.

fieldsman *noun* (*pl* **fieldsmen**) = FIELDER.

field sport *noun* an open-air sport, e.g. hunting or shooting, involving the pursuit of animals.

field test *noun* = FIELD TRIAL (2).

field-test *verb trans* to submit (something) to a field test.

field trial *noun* 1 a trial of gun dogs or sheep dogs in actual performance. 2 (*usu in pl*) a test for a new design, invention, variety of plant, etc under authentic working or growing conditions, rather than in the laboratory, workshop, or greenhouse.

field trip *noun* a visit made by students for first-hand observation, e.g. to a farm or a museum.

fieldwork *noun* 1 work done in the field, e.g. by students, to gain practical experience through first-hand observation. 2 the gathering of data in anthropology, sociology, etc through the observation or interviewing of subjects in the field. >> **field-worker** *noun*.

fiend /feend/ *noun* **1a** a demon. **b** (**the Fiend**) the Devil; Satan. **c** a person of great wickedness or cruelty. **2** *informal* somebody greatly or excessively devoted to a specified activity or thing; a fanatic or devotee: *a golf fiend*; *a fresh-air fiend*. **3** *informal* a person who uses immoderate quantities of something specified; an addict: *a dope fiend*. **4** *informal* somebody remarkably clever at a specified activity; = WIZARD[1] (2): *She's a fiend at arithmetic*. [Old English *fiend* enemy]

fiendish *adj* **1** extremely cruel or wicked. **2** *informal* extremely bad, unpleasant, or difficult. **3** *informal* ingeniously clever or complex. >> **fiendishly** *adv*, **fiendishness** *noun*.

fierce /fiəs/ *adj* **1** violently hostile or aggressive; combative or pugnacious. **2a** lacking restraint or control; violent or heated: *a fierce argument*. **b** extremely intense or severe: *fierce pain*. **3** furiously active or determined: *Let's make a fierce effort to finish this project on time*. **4** said of a mechanism: operating with a sharp and powerful action: *These brakes are a bit fierce*. >> **fiercely** *adv*, **fierceness** *noun*. [Middle English *fiers* via Old French from Latin *ferus* wild, savage]

fiery /'fie-əri/ *adj* (**fierier**, **fieriest**) **1a** consisting of fire. **b** burning or blazing: *a fiery cross*. **c** liable to catch fire or explode. **2** said of food: very hot: *a fiery chilli sauce*. **3** of the colour of fire, *esp* red: *fiery red hair*. **4a** full of or exuding strong emotion or spirit; passionate: *a fiery speech*. **b** easily provoked; irascible: *a fiery temper*. >> **fierily** *adv*, **fieriness** *noun*. [Middle English, from *fire*, *fier* FIRE[1]]

fiery cross *noun* **1** a charred and sometimes bloodstained wooden cross formerly used in the Scottish Highlands as a signal to clansmen to rally for battle. **2** a burning cross used, *esp* formerly, as a means of intimidation by the Ku Klux Klan.

fiesta /fi'estə/ *noun* **1** in Spain and Latin America, a saint's day, often celebrated with processions and dances. **2** in Spain and Latin America, a festive occasion; a celebration. [Spanish *fiesta* from Latin *festa*: see FEAST[1]]

FIFA /'feefə/ *abbr* International Football Federation. [French *Fédération Internationale de Football Association*]

fife /fief/ *noun* a small flute used chiefly in military bands. >> **fifer** *noun*. [German *Pfeife* pipe, fife, from Old High German *pfifa*, ultimately via a prehistoric Germanic word from Latin *pipare* to chirp, of imitative origin: compare PIPE[1]]

FIFO /'fiefoh/ *abbr* first in, first out.

fifteen /fif'teen/ *adj and noun* **1** the number 15, or the quantity represented by it. **2** (*treated as sing. or pl*) something having 15 parts or members, *esp* a Rugby Union football team. **3** in Britain, a classification of cinema films only suitable for people of 15 years or over. >> **fifteenth** *adj and noun*. [Old English *fiftēne*]

fifth /fifth/ *adj and noun* **1** denoting a person or thing having the position in a sequence corresponding to the number five. **2** one of five equal parts of something. **3** the fifth and usu highest forward gear of a motor vehicle. **4a** in music, an interval of five degrees of a diatonic scale, or the combination of two notes at such an interval. **b** = DOMINANT[2] (3). >> **fifthly** *adv*. [Old English *fifta*]

Usage note

In careful speech the second *f* is pronounced, but it is commonly omitted.

fifth column *noun* a group within a nation or faction that sympathizes with and works secretly for an enemy or rival. >> **fifth columnist** *noun*. [name applied to rebel sympathizers in Madrid in 1936 when four rebel columns were advancing on the city]

fifth wheel *noun* **1** a spare wheel for a four-wheeled vehicle. **2** *informal* somebody or something superfluous, unnecessary, or burdensome. **3** a coupling between the tractor and trailer of an articulated lorry.

fifty /'fifti/ *adj and noun* (*pl* **fifties**) **1** the number 50, or the quantity represented by it. **2** (*in pl*) the numbers 50 to 59; *specif* a range of temperatures, ages, or dates within a century characterized by these numbers. >> **fiftieth** /'fifti-ith/ *adj and noun*. [Old English *fiftig* group of fifty, from *fif* FIVE + *-tig* group of ten]

fifty-fifty[1] *adv* evenly; equally: *They shared the money fifty-fifty*.

fifty-fifty[2] *adj* half favourable and half unfavourable; even: *a fifty-fifty chance*.

fig[1] /fig/ *noun* **1a** a fleshy pear-shaped or oblong edible fruit with many seeds. **b** the tree that bears this fruit: *Ficus carica*. **2** a contemptibly worthless trifle: *It's not worth a fig*. [Middle English *fige* via Old French from Latin *ficus* fig tree, fig]

fig[2] *noun informal* dress; array: *all belted and plumed, and in full military fig* — De Quincey. [*fig* to adorn, variant of obsolete *feague* to liven up, literally 'to whip', prob from German *fegen* to sweep or burnish]

fig. *abbr* **1** figurative. **2** figuratively. **3** figure.

fight[1] /fiet/ *verb* (*past tense and past part.* **fought** /fawt/) >> *verb intrans* **1a** (*also + for/against*) to contend in battle or physical combat, *esp* to strive to overcome a person by blows or weapons. **b** to disagree verbally; to argue. **c** to take part in the sport of boxing; = BOX[3]. **2** (*often + for/against*) to strive or struggle: *He is fighting for his political life*. >> *verb trans* **1** to contend against (somebody) in or as if in battle or physical combat. **2a** to engage in a boxing match with (somebody). **b** to attempt to prevent the success, effectiveness, or development of (somebody or something): *The company fought the strike for months*. **3a** to wage (a war). **b** to take part in (a boxing match). **c** to stand as a candidate for (a constituency) in an election. **4** to struggle to endure or surmount (a difficulty): *He fought his illness for a year before he died*. **5a** to make (one's way) by fighting, or as if by fighting: *She fought her way through the crowd*. **b** (*usu + back/down*) to control (something) with a struggle: *She fought down her fear*. * **fight shy of** to avoid facing or getting (something): *He fights shy of publicity*. [Old English *feohtan*]

fight[2] *noun* **1a** an act of fighting; a battle or combat. **b** a boxing match. **c** a verbal disagreement; an argument. **2** a protracted struggle for an objective: *a fight for justice*. **3** strength or disposition for fighting; pugnacity: *He is still full of fight*. * **fight or flight** the natural response to stress or threat, in which the body prepares itself to oppose a source of stress or threat or to flee from it.

fight back *verb intrans* to struggle to recover from a losing or disadvantageous position; to resist. >> **fightback** *noun*.

fighter *noun* **1** somebody or something that fights, e.g.: **a** a pugnacious or boldly determined individual. **b** a boxer. **2** a fast manoeuvrable aeroplane designed to destroy enemy aircraft.

fighter-bomber *noun* an aeroplane that combines the functions of fighter and bomber.

fighting chance *noun* (**a fighting chance**) a small chance that may be realized through struggle: *The team has a fighting chance of getting to the final.*

fighting cock *noun* **1** = GAMECOCK. **2** somebody who is always ready for a fight.

fighting fish *or* **Siamese fighting fish** *noun* a small tropical fish the males of which are very aggressive: *Betta splendens.*

fighting fit *adj* very fit; in good health.

fight off *verb trans* to ward (somebody or something) off by fighting, or as if by fighting; to repel (them).

fight out ✳ **fight it out** to settle (an argument) by fighting: *I just left them to fight it out.*

fig leaf *noun* **1** a leaf of a fig tree. **2** a representation of such a leaf positioned so as to conceal the genitals on a statue, etc: *Nobody noticed their [the statues'] nakedness before ... nobody can help noticing it now, the fig-leaf makes it so conspicuous* — Mark Twain. **3** something that conceals or camouflages, usu inadequately or dishonestly: *The opt-out clause is a fig leaf that the Prime Minister is clutching ... to cover the serious disagreements in his party* — Hansard. [from the fig leaves with which Adam and Eve tried to conceal their nakedness (Genesis 3:7)]

figment /'figmənt/ *noun* something fabricated or imagined: *The spy ring was just a figment of the author's imagination.* [Middle English from Latin *figmentum*, from *fingere* to shape]

figurant /'figyoor(ə)nt/ *or* **figurante** /-'ront/ *noun* a male or female ballet dancer who dances only in a group. [French *figurant*, present part. of *figurer* to figure or represent, from Latin *figura*: see FIGURE¹]

figuration /figyoo'raysh(ə)n, figə-/ *noun* **1** the creation or representation of an allegorical or symbolic figure. **2** a form or outline. **3** ornamentation of a musical passage by using musical figures.

figurative /'figyoorətiv, 'figə-/ *adj* **1** characterized by or using figures of speech, *esp* metaphor. **2a** representing by a figure or likeness; emblematic. **b** representational: *figurative sculpture.* ⏵ **figuratively** *adv*, **figurativeness** *noun*.

figure¹ /'figə/ *noun* **1a** a number symbol, *esp* an Arabic one: *She had a salary running into six figures.* **b** (*in pl*) arithmetical calculations: *I'm no good at figures.* **c** a written or printed character. **d** value, *esp* as expressed in numbers: *The house sold at a low figure.* **2** bodily shape or form, *esp* a slim shape: *a slender figure; She lost her figure after her third child was born.* **3a** a personage or personality: *great political figures of the past.* **b** a representative or substitute: *He was very much a father figure to me.* **4a** the graphic representation of a human or animal form. **b** a diagram or pictorial illustration in a text. **c** a geometrical diagram or shape. **5** an appearance made; an impression produced, *esp* a favourable one: *The couple cut quite a figure.* **6a** a series of movements in a dance. **b** an outline representation of a form traced by a series of evolutions, e.g. by a skater on an ice surface. **7** an intentional deviation from the usual form or syntactic relation of words. **8** an often repetitive pattern in a manufactured article, e.g. cloth, or natural substance, e.g. wood. **9** a short musical phrase. **10** in logic, the form of a syllogism with respect to the position of the middle term of the two premises. [Middle English via Old French from Latin *figura*, from *fingere* to form]

figure² *verb trans* **1a** to calculate (a sum, etc). **b** *chiefly NAmer, informal* to conclude or decide (something): *He figured there was no use in further effort.* **c** *chiefly NAmer, informal* to regard or consider (something). **2** to represent (somebody or something) by or as if by a figure or outline; to portray (them or it). **3** to decorate (something, e.g. music) with a pattern. **4** in music, to write figures over or under (the bass) in order to indicate the accompanying chords. ⏵ *verb intrans* **1** (*often* + in) to take an *esp* important or conspicuous part. **2** to calculate. **3** *informal* to seem reasonable or expected. ✳ **figure on** *NAmer, informal* to take (something) into consideration, e.g. in planning: *Figure on $200 a month extra income.*

figured *adj* **1** represented or portrayed. **2** adorned with or formed into a figure: *figured muslin.* **3** indicated by figures.

figured bass *noun* = CONTINUO.

figurehead *noun* **1** an ornamental carved figure on a ship's bow. **2** a head or chief in name only.

figure of eight *noun* something, e.g. a skater's figure, resembling the Arabic numeral eight in form or shape.

figure of speech *noun* a form of expression, e.g. a hyperbole or metaphor, used to convey meaning or heighten effect.

figure out *verb trans informal* **1** to discover or determine (something): *I'll try to figure out a solution.* **2** to solve or fathom (something or somebody): *I just can't figure him out.*

figure skating *noun* skating in which the skater outlines distinctive circular patterns based on the figure eight. ⏵ **figure skater** *noun.*

figurine /'figyooreen/ *noun* a statuette. [French *figurine* from Italian *figurina*, dimin. of *figura* figure, from Latin: see FIGURE¹]

figwort /'figwuht/ *noun* any of several species of chiefly herbaceous plants with an irregular two-lipped corolla: genus *Scrophularia.* [FIG¹ in an obsolete sense 'piles' + WORT¹; from its supposed ability to cure piles]

Fijian /fee'jee·ən/ *noun* **1** a member of the Melanesian people of the Fiji Islands. **2** the Austronesian language of the Fijians. ⏵ **Fijian** *adj* [Fiji Islands, SW Pacific]

filagree¹ /'filəgree/ *noun* see FILIGREE¹.

filagree² *verb trans* see FILIGREE².

filagree³ *adj* see FILIGREE³.

filament /'filəmənt/ *noun* a single thread or a thin flexible thread-like object or part, e.g.: **a** an elongated thin series of attached cells or a very long thin cylindrical single cell, e.g. of some algae, fungi, or bacteria. **b** a slender conductor, e.g. in an electric light bulb, made incandescent by the passage of an electric current. **c** the stalk of a stamen that bears the anther. ⏵ **filamentary** /-'ment(ə)ri/ *adj*, **filamentous** /-'mentəs/ *adj*. [early French *filament* via medieval Latin from late Latin *filare* to spin, from Latin *filum* thread]

filaria /fi'leəri·ə/ *noun* (*pl* **filariae** /-ri·ee/) any of numerous thread-like nematode worms that develop in biting insects and are parasites in the blood or tissues of mammals when adult: superfamily Filarioidea. ⏵ **filarial** *adj*. [scientific Latin *filaria* from Latin *filum* thread]

filariasis /filə'rie·əsis/ *noun* (*pl* **filariases** /-seez/) infestation with or a disease, e.g. elephantiasis, caused by filarial worms. [scientific Latin *filariasis*, from *filaria*: see FILARIA]

filature /'filəchə/ *noun* a place where silk is obtained from cocoons. [French *filature* from late Latin *filatus*, past part. of *filare*: see FILAMENT]

filbert /'filbət/ *noun* **1** a sweet thick-shelled variety of hazelnut. **2** either of two European hazels that bear such nuts: *Corylus avellana pontica* and *Corylus maxima.* [Middle English from Anglo-French *philber*, named after St *Philibert* d.684, Frankish abbot whose feast day falls in the nutting season]

filch /filch/ *verb trans informal* to steal (something of small value); to pilfer (it). ⏵ **filcher** *noun.* [Middle English *filchen*; earlier history unknown]

file¹ /fiel/ *noun* **1** a folder, cabinet, etc in which papers are kept in order. **2** a collection of papers or publications on a subject, usu arranged or classified. **3** a collection of related data records, e.g. for a computer. ✳ **on file** in a file; filed for reference and available for consultation. [Middle English *filen* via Old French from Latin *filum* thread, because documents were formerly hung on strings for easy reference]

file² *verb trans* **1** to arrange (papers, etc) in order, e.g. alphabetically, for preservation and reference. **2** to submit or record (a lawsuit, etc) officially. ⏵ *verb intrans* to place items, *esp* papers, in a file. ⏵ **filer** *noun*, **filing** *noun.*

file³ *noun* **1** a row of people, animals, or things arranged one behind the other. **2** any of the rows of squares that extend across a chessboard from white's side to black's side: compare RANK¹ (5). [early French *file* string, row, from *filer* to spin, via late Latin from Latin *filum* thread]

file⁴ *verb intrans* to march or proceed in file.

file⁵ *noun* a tool, usu of hardened steel, with many cutting ridges for shaping or smoothing objects or surfaces. [Old English *fēol*]

file⁶ *verb trans* to rub or smooth (an object) or cut (it) away with or as if with a file.

filefish *noun* (*pl* **filefishes** *or collectively* **filefish**) any of numerous species of bony tropical fishes with rough granular leathery skins: family *Balistidae.*

file manager *noun* a computer program that allows a user to organize and handle files and directories.

filename *noun* a sequence of characters and/or spaces which identifies a computer file.

file server *noun* the main computer in a network that stores programs and files that are to be accessed by other computers in the network.

filet[1] /'filit, 'filay/ *noun NAmer* see FILLET[1]. [French *filet*: see FILLET[1]]

filet[2] *noun* a lace with a square mesh and geometric designs.

filet mignon /ˌfilay miˈnyon (*French* filɛ miɲɔ̃)/ *noun* (*pl* **filets mignons** /ˌfilay miˈnyon (*French* filɛ miɲɔ̃)/) a small steak cut from the centre of a beef fillet. [French *filet mignon* dainty fillet]

filial /'fili·əl/ *adj* **1** of or befitting a son or daughter, *esp* in his or her relationship to a parent: *But you must know, your father lost a father; that father lost, lost his, and the survivor bound in filial obligation for a while to do obsequious sorrow* — Shakespeare. **2** having or assuming the relation of a child or offspring. ⟫⟫ **filially** *adv.* [Middle English via late Latin from Latin *filius* son]

filial generation *noun* a generation in a breeding experiment that is successive to a parental generation.

filiation /fili'aysh(ə)n/ *noun* **1** filial relationship, *esp* of a son to his father. **2** descent or derivation, *esp* from a culture or language.

filibeg *or* **philibeg** /'filibeg/ *noun archaic* a kilt. [Scottish Gaelic *feileadh-beag*, from *feileadh* kilt + *beag* little]

filibuster[1] /'filibustə/ *noun* **1** *chiefly NAmer* the use of extreme delaying tactics in a legislative assembly. **2** formerly, a military adventurer engaging in unauthorized warfare against a foreign country. [Spanish *filibustero* pirate, from Dutch *vrijbuiter*: see FREE-BOOTER]

filibuster[2] *verb intrans* (**filibustered, filibustering**) **1** *chiefly NAmer* to engage in delaying tactics. **2** formerly, to carry out insurrectionist or revolutionary activities in a foreign country.

filigree[1] *or* **filagree** /'filigree/ *noun* **1** ornamental openwork of delicate or intricate design. **2** a pattern or design resembling such openwork: *a filigree of frost on a window.* [French *filigrane* from Italian, from Latin *filum* thread + *granum* grain]

filigree[2] *or* **filagree** *verb trans* to decorate (something) with filigree. ⟫⟫ **filigreed** *adj.*

filigree[3] *or* **filagree** *adj* of a delicate and intricate design.

filing /'fieling/ *noun* (*usu in pl*) a metal fragment rubbed off in filing: *iron filings.*

Filipino /fili'peenoh/ *or* **Filipina** /-'peenə/ *noun* (*pl* **Filipinos** *or* **Filipinas**) a native or inhabitant of the Philippine Islands. ⟫⟫ **Filipino** *adj.* [Spanish *Filipino, Filipina* from (*Islas*) *Filipinas* Philippine Islands]

fill[1] /fil/ *verb trans* **1a** (*often* + up) to put into (something) as much as can be held or conveniently contained. **b** to supply (something) with a full complement: *The class is already filled.* **c** to cause (something) to swell or billow: *Wind filled the sails.* **d** to trim (a sail) to catch the wind. **e** to repair the cavities of (a tooth). **f** (*often* + up) to stop up or plug (a hole). **2a** to feed or satiate (somebody). **b** to satisfy or fulfil (a need or requirement). **c** *NAmer* to supply the requirements of (an order, prescription, etc). **3a** to occupy the whole of (a place): *Smoke filled the room.* **b** to spread through (a place). **c** to occupy (time): *What do you do to fill your day?* **4a** to hold and perform the duties of (an office). **b** to place a person in (a vacancy). ⟫ *verb intrans* (*often* + up) to become full or obstructed. ✳ **fill somebody's shoes** to take over somebody's job or responsibilities. [Old English *fyllan*]

fill[2] *noun* **1a** as much as one can eat or drink: *Eat your fill.* **b** as much as one can bear: *I've had my fill of them for today.* **c** the quantity needed to fill something: *a fill of pipe tobacco.* **2** material used to fill a receptacle, cavity, passage, or low place.

filler[1] *noun* **1** a substance added to a product, e.g. to increase bulk or strength. **2** a composition or material used to fill holes before painting or varnishing. **3** a piece, e.g. a plate, used to cover or fill a space between two parts of a structure. **4** material, e.g. a brief report, used to fill extra space in a column or page of a newspaper or magazine. **5** an utterance inserted into speech to occupy time.

filler[2] *noun* (*pl* **fillers** *or* **filler**) a unit of currency in Hungary, worth 100th of a forint. [Hungarian *fillér*]

fillet[1] (*NAmer* **filet**) /'filit/ *noun* **1a** a fleshy boneless piece of meat cut from the hind loin or upper hind leg. **b** a long slice of boneless fish. **c** a thin narrow strip of material. **2** a ribbon or narrow strip of material used *esp* as a headband. **3a** a narrow flat architectural moulding, *esp* the raised band between two flutes in a shaft. **b** a plain line, or a narrow line of repeated ornaments, impressed on a book cover. **4a** a junction in which the interior angle is rounded off or partly filled in. **b** a triangular piece that partly fills such an interior. [Middle English from early French *filet* net, fillet, dimin. of *fil* thread, from Latin *filum*]

fillet[2] *verb trans* (**filleted, filleting**) **1a** to remove the bones from (a fish). **b** to cut (meat or fish) into fillets. **2** to bind, provide, or adorn (something) with or as if with a fillet. **3** to remove inessential parts from (something).

fillet steak *noun* a boneless steak fillet.

fill in *verb trans* **1** *Brit* to add what is necessary to complete (a form); = MAKE OUT (2). **2** (*often* + on) to give (somebody) information: *Friends filled him in on the latest news.* **3** to add details to (a drawing or design). ⟫ *verb intrans* (*often* + for) to act as a temporary substitute.

filling *noun* **1** something used to fill a cavity, container, or depression: *a filling for a tooth.* **2** a food mixture used to fill cakes, sandwiches, etc. **3** *chiefly NAmer* = WEFT.

filling station *noun* a retail establishment for selling fuel, oil, etc to motorists.

fillip[1] /'filip/ *noun* something that arouses or boosts; a stimulus: *This should give a fillip to sales.* [orig meaning a blow or gesture made by flipping a finger away from the thumb; prob imitative]

fillip[2] *verb trans* (**filliped, fillipping**) **1** to stimulate (something or somebody). **2** to flick (something) with the fingers.

fill out *verb intrans* to become fatter. ⟫ *verb trans chiefly NAmer* to complete (a form).

filly /'fili/ *noun* (*pl* **fillies**) **1** a young female horse, usu of less than four years. **2** *informal* a young woman; a girl. [Middle English *fyly* from Old Norse *fylja*]

film[1] /film/ *noun* **1a** a roll or strip of plastic coated with a light-sensitive emulsion for taking photographs. **b** a thin flexible transparent sheet, e.g. of plastic, used as a wrapping. **2a** a series of pictures recorded on film for the cinema and projected rapidly onto a screen so as to create the illusion of movement. **b** a representation, e.g. of an incident or story, on film. **c** (*also in pl*) the cinema. **3a** a thin layer or covering: *There was a thin film of ice on the pond.* **b** a thin skin or membranous covering. **c** something that blurs the sight; a fine mist or haze. **d** an abnormal growth on or in the eye, or dimness of sight resulting from this. [Old English *filmen* membrane; related to Old English *fell* FELL[6]]

film[2] *verb trans* **1** to make a film of (something or somebody). **2** (*often* + over) to cover (something) or cause (it) to become covered with a film. ⟫ *verb intrans* **1** to be suitable for photographing. **2** to make a film. **3** (*often* + over) to become covered with a film of something.

filmic /'filmik/ *adj* relating to the cinema. ⟫⟫ **filmically** *adv.*

film noir /ˌfilm 'nwah/ *noun* a style of film-making developed in the 1940s, with a plot involving suspense, mystery, crime, and corruption, and a bleak, often shadowy, setting, or a film in this style.

Editorial note
Film noir begins as the French appreciation of an American genre: the thriller or mystery film with a disillusioned or neurotic hero afraid of the world, the city, the night, and femmes fatales. It covers the period from the mid forties to the late fifties. But we now see Citizen Kane, some films by Marcel Carne, and some German pictures of the twenties as 'noirish' — David Thomson.

[French *film noir* black film]

filmography /fil'mografi/ *noun* (*pl* **filmographies**) a list of films of a prominent film figure or on a particular topic. [FILM[1] + -*ography* as in BIBLIOGRAPHY]

filmset /'filmset/ *verb trans* (**filmsetting**, *past tense and past part.* **filmset**) to set (material to be printed) by photocomposition. ⟫⟫ **filmsetter** *noun.*

filmsetting *noun* = PHOTOCOMPOSITION.

film star *noun* a famous and popular film actor or actress.

filmstrip *noun* a strip of film containing photographs, diagrams, or graphic matter for still projection.

filmy *adj* (**filmier, filmiest**) **1** of, resembling, or composed of film; gauzy. **2** covered with a mist or film; hazy. ⟫⟫ **filminess** *noun.*

filo *or* **phyllo** /'feeloh/ *noun* a flaky pastry made with extremely thin sheets of dough and used *esp* in Mediterranean and Middle Eastern cuisine. [modern Greek *phyllon* leaf, sheet of pastry]

Filofax /'fielәfaks/ *noun trademark* a loose-leaf personal organizer. [phonetic representation of *file of facts*]

fils /fils/ *noun* (*pl* **fils**) a unit of currency in some countries of the Middle East, worth 1000th of a dinar in Bahrain, Iraq, Jordan, and Kuwait; 100th of a dirham in the United Arab Emirates; and 100th of a rial in Yemen. [Arabic]

filter¹ /'filtә/ *noun* **1** a porous article or mass, e.g. of paper, sand, etc, through which a gas or liquid is passed to separate out matter in suspension. **2** an apparatus containing a filter medium, such as a car's oil filter or the filter tip of a cigarette. **3a** a device or material for suppressing or minimizing waves or oscillations of certain frequencies, e.g. of electricity, light, or sound. **b** a transparent material, e.g. coloured glass, that absorbs light of certain colours selectively. **4** Brit a traffic signal at a road junction consisting of a green arrow which, when illuminated, allows traffic to turn left or right when the main signals are red. [Middle English *filtre* from medieval Latin *filtrum* piece of felt used as a filter, of Germanic origin]

filter² *verb* (**filtered, filtering**) ➤ *verb trans* **1** to subject (a substance) to the action of a filter. **2** (*often* + out) to remove (particles, etc) by means of a filter. ➤ *verb intrans* **1** to pass or move through a filter, or as if through a filter. **2** (*often* + in/out/through) to move gradually: *The children filtered out of assembly.* **3** (*often* + in/out/through) said of information: to become known over a period of time: *The news soon filtered through to the public.* **4** Brit said of traffic: to turn left or right in the direction of the green arrow while the main lights are still red.

filterable /'filtәrәbl/ *or* **filtrable** /'filtrәbl/ *adj* **1** said of a substance: capable of being filtered. **2** said of a virus or bacterium: small enough to pass through a fine filter material.

filter bed *noun* a bed of sand or gravel for purifying water or sewage.

filter feeder *noun* an animal, e.g. a blue whale, adapted to filtering minute organisms or other food from water that passes through its system. ➤➤ **filter feeding** *noun*.

filter paper *noun* porous paper used for filtering.

filter tip *noun* a cigarette tip of porous material that filters the smoke before it enters the smoker's mouth, or a cigarette with such a tip. ➤➤ **filter-tipped** *adj*.

filth /filth/ *noun* **1** foul or putrid matter, *esp* dirt or refuse. **2** something loathsome or vile, *esp* obscene or pornographic material. **3** (**the filth**) Brit, *informal, derog* (*treated as sing. or pl*) the police. [Old English *fylth*, from *ful* FOUL¹]

filthy *adj* (**filthier, filthiest**) **1** covered with or containing filth; offensively dirty: *filthy conditions.* **2** vile, evil, or lewd: *That was a filthy trick; He's got some filthy habits.* **3** *dated* used with reference to money: tainted; immoral; corrupt. **4** said of somebody's mood or expression: malevolent: *He gave me a filthy look.* **5** *informal* said of the weather: stormy. **6** *informal* said of books or magazines: pornographic. ✷ **filthy lucre** *literary or humorous* money. **filthy rich** obscenely wealthy. ➤➤ **filthily** *adv,* **filthiness** *noun.*

filtrable /'filtrәbl/ *adj* see FILTERABLE.

filtrate¹ /'filtrayt/ *verb trans* to filter (a fluid). [medieval Latin *filtratus*, past part. of *filtrare* to filter, from *filtrum*: see FILTER¹]

filtrate² *noun* material that has passed through a filter.

filtration /fil'traysh(ә)n/ *noun* **1** the process of passing through, or as if through, a filter. **2** = DIFFUSION (3A): *The kidney produces urine by filtration.*

fimbria /'fimbri-ә/ *noun* (*pl* **fimbriae** /'fimbri-ee/) **1** in anatomy, etc, a fringe-like structure. **2** in anatomy, one of the finger-like projections composing such a structure, *esp* that forming the entrance to each of the Fallopian tubes. ➤➤ **fimbrial** *adj.* [Latin *fimbria* border, fringe]

fimbriate /'fimbri-әt, -ayt/ *adj* having the edge or extremity bordered by long slender projections; fringed: *fimbriate petals.* ➤➤ **fimbriation** /-'aysh(ә)n/ *noun.* [Latin *fimbriatus* fringed, from *fimbria* fringe]

fimbriated /'fimbriaytid/ *adj* = FIMBRIATE.

FIN *abbr* Finland (international vehicle registration).

fin¹ /fin/ *noun* **1** a flattened appendage of an aquatic animal, e.g. a fish or whale, used in propelling or guiding the body. **2** a flattened projecting, often movable, part attached to the underside of a vessel, e.g. a submarine, to give it stability or to improve its controllability. **3** a vertical aerofoil attached to an aircraft for directional stability. **4** = FLIPPER (2). **5** any of the projecting ribs on a radiator or an engine cylinder that improve heat transfer. ➤➤ **finless** *adj,* **finlike** *adj,* **finned** *adj.* [Old English *finn*]

fin² *verb intrans* (**finned, finning**) to lash or move through the water using, or as if using, fins.

finable *or* **fineable** /'fienәbl/ *adj* said of an offence: liable to a fine. ➤➤ **finableness** *noun,* **fineableness** *noun.*

finagle /fi'naygl/ *verb trans informal* **1** to manage to obtain (something) using trickery or persistence. **2** to trick (somebody) into doing what one wants. ➤➤ **finagler** *noun.* [perhaps alteration of English dialect *fainaigue* to cheat]

final¹ /'fienl/ *adj* **1** being the last; occurring at the end: *the final chapter.* **2** not to be altered or undone; conclusive: *The judges' decision is final.* **3** relating to the ultimate object or result of a process: *His final purpose was not altered, though he changed the means* — J Fenimore Cooper. [Middle English via French from Latin *finalis* final, from *finis* boundary, end]

final² *noun* **1a** a deciding match, game, trial, etc in a sport or competition. **b** (*in pl*) a round made up of these: *We were beaten in the finals.* **2** (*in pl*) the last and usu most important series of examinations in an academic or professional course: *She takes her finals in June.* **3** in music, the note on which a modal scale ends.

final cause *noun* in philosophy, the ultimate purpose of an action or process.

final clause *noun* in grammar, a clause expressing purpose, introduced by, e.g., *so that* or *in order that.*

final drive *noun* in a motor vehicle, the last part of the transmission system.

finale /fi'nahli/ *noun* **1a** a final scene or number in a show or an opera, or one of its acts: *in the finale to Act 2.* **b** the last and often most spectacular item in a public performance such as a firework display. **2** the last section of an instrumental musical composition. **3** the last and often climactic event or item in a sequence. [Italian *finale* final, from Latin *finalis*: see FINAL¹]

finalise *verb trans* see FINALIZE.

finalism *noun* the theory that there is a purpose to natural processes such as evolution. ➤➤ **finalistic** /-'listik/ *adj.*

finalist *noun* **1** a contestant in the finals of a competition. **2** a person sitting finals (important college or university exams; see FINAL² (2)).

finality /fie'naliti, fi-/ *noun* **1** the condition of being final, settled, or irrevocable: *The finality of death.* **2** a determined air or tone that admits of no further argument: *'We cannot alter the arrangements,' she said with finality.*

finalize *or* **finalise** *verb trans* **1** to put (plans or arrangements) in final or finished form. **2** to give final approval to (an agreement or transaction). ➤ *verb intrans* to conclude negotiations on a transaction, etc. ➤➤ **finalization** /-'zaysh(ә)n/ *noun.*

finally *adv* **1** after some time, or period of difficulty; eventually: *We finally managed to make a temporary repair and got on our way.* **2** as the last in a series of things: *... whale, yak, and finally zebra.* **3** used to introduce a final point: lastly: *Finally, please remember to collect your free leaflet.*

final solution *noun* (*often* **Final Solution**) the Nazi euphemism for the policy of exterminating all the Jews in Europe during WWII. [translation of German *Endlösung*]

finance¹ /'fienans, fi'nans/ *noun* **1** the system that includes the circulation of money and involves banking, credit, and investment. **2** the science of the management of funds. **3** (*in pl*) resources of money: *My finances are low.* **4** the obtaining of funds: *I'm trying to arrange finance for the expedition.* [Middle English *finance* payment, ransom, settlement, from early French *finance*, from *finer* to end, pay, from *fin* end, from Latin *finis*]

finance² *verb trans* to raise or provide money for (a project or a person).

finance company *noun* a company that specializes in arranging or financing hire purchase.

finance house *noun* = FINANCE COMPANY.

financial /fie'nanshәl, fi'nanshәl/ *adj* **1** relating to finance, finances, or money. **2** *chiefly Aus, NZ, informal* having plenty of money; well-off. ➤➤ **financially** *adv.*

financial futures *pl noun* futures (commodities, etc bought or sold at an agreed price, but not handed over until some specified date in the future; see FUTURE[1] (4)) in currencies or interest rates.

Financial Ombudsman *noun* any of several ombudsmen dealing with finance-related complaints that are made by banking customers, building-society customers, or insurance and unit-trust customers.

Financial Times Stock Exchange 100 Share Index *noun* see FOOTSIE. [because it is published daily in the newspaper, *The Financial Times*]

financial year *noun* in the UK, the tax and accounting year that runs from 6 April of one year to 5 April of the following year.

financier /fi'nansi-ə, fie-/ *noun* a person employed or engaged in large-scale finance or investment.

financing gap *noun* the gap between the amount of money earned by a country through its exports and the foreign exchange it needs to cover its debts and imports.

finback *noun* = FIN WHALE.

finca /'fingkə/ *noun* in Spain or other Spanish-speaking countries, a country property, estate, or ranch. [Spanish *finca*]

finch /finch/ *noun* any of numerous species of songbirds with short stout conical beaks adapted for crushing seeds: *esp* family Fringillidae. [Old English *finc*]

find[1] /fiend/ *verb* (*past tense and past part.* **found** /fownd/) ➤ *verb trans* **1a** to come upon or encounter (something or somebody), *esp* accidentally. **b** to experience or be aware of (something): *We returned to find the windows broken*. **c** to know, discover, or recognize (something) to be present in something or native to an area: *Iodine is found in seaweed*. **2** to meet with (a specified reception): *He was sure of finding a welcome there; Fortunately the idea found favour*. **3a** to seek or provide (a resource such as money or time) for a purpose. **b** to discover or obtain (something) by effort or experiment: *He finally found the courage to speak*. **c** to seek or experience (a feeling such as comfort). **d** to gain or regain the use or power of (e.g. one's voice, tongue, wits) after a surprise, etc. **e** to attain or reach (a level, etc). **4a** to perceive (oneself) to be in a specified place or condition: *He found himself in a dilemma*. **b** to discover (a person or thing) to have a specified quality, attribute, etc: *I found her sympathetic; I don't find that funny*. **c** to discover (a fact): *I found that people stopped noticing*. **d** said of a jury: to pronounce (a defendant) guilty or innocent after deliberation. ➤ *verb intrans* (+ for/against) to determine a case judicially by a verdict: *find for the defendant*. ✳ **all found** *dated* said of wages: with bed and board provided free. **find fault** (*often* + with) to criticize unfavourably: *always finding fault with her son*. **find it in one's heart** to be hard-hearted enough (to do something hurtful). **find one's feet** to gain confidence with experience. **find one's way** to get to a destination without help or direction: *find one's way to the lecture room; The donations found their way into private pockets*. ➤➤ **findable** *adj*. [Old English *findan*]

find[2] *noun* somebody or something found; *esp* a valuable object or talented person discovered.

finder *noun* **1** a person who finds something: *The finder kindly handed in my lost keys*. **2** a small astronomical telescope attached to a larger telescope for finding an object. ✳ **finders keepers (losers weepers)** *informal* the person who finds something has the right to keep it.

fin de siècle /ˌfan də see'eklə (*French* fɛ̃ də sjɛkl)/ *noun* **1** the end of a century, *esp* the 19th cent. **2a** (**fin-de-siècle**) (*used before a noun*) relating to or characteristic of the close of a century, *esp* the 19th cent. and its literary and artistic climate of sophisticated decadence and world-weariness: *Proust, the chronicler of fin-de-siècle society*. **b** decadent. [French *fin de siècle* end of the century]

finding *noun* **1** (*also in pl*) the result of an investigation or piece of research: *the findings of the welfare committee*. **2** the result of a judicial enquiry: *What was the finding of the court?* **3** NAmer (*in pl*) small tools and materials used by a craftsman or dressmaker.

find out *verb trans* **1** to learn or discover (something) by study or inquiry. **2a** to detect (a person) in an offence. **b** to discover the true character or identity of (a person). ➤ *verb intrans* (*often* + about) to discover, learn, or verify something.

fine[1] /fien/ *adj* **1** superior in quality; excellent: *a fine musician*. **2** wonderful; splendid: *The tall ships made a fine show*. **3** dry and usu sunny: *The weather will be fine in all parts of the country*. **4** well; in good health or spirits: *feeling fine*. **5** OK; all right: *'More wine?' 'I'm fine, thanks'*. **6** *ironic* said of something undesirable: splendid: *A fine*

mess we're in! **7** characterized by elegance or refinement: *fine manners*. **8** performed with extreme care and accuracy: *fine workmanship*. **9** said of precious metals: pure in quality: *fine gold*. **10** narrow in gauge or width; not thick or coarse: *fine thread; fine hair; a fine nib*. **11** consisting of relatively small particles: *fine sand*. **12** very small: *fine print*. **13** keen; sharp: *a knife with a fine edge*. **14** having a delicate or subtle quality: *a wine of fine bouquet*. **15** subtle or sensitive in perception or discrimination: *a fine distinction*. **16** in cricket, denoting a fielding position behind the batsman and near an extension of the line between the wickets. ✳ **cut it fine** to leave it dangerously close to the deadline before doing something. **not to put too fine a point on it** to speak bluntly or plainly. **one fine day** one of these days; at some unspecified time. **one's finest hour** one's moment of glory or greatest achievement. **run it fine** to leave only the irreducible margin. ➤➤ **finely** *adv*, **fineness** *noun*.

Word history
Middle English *fin* from Old French, ultimately from Latin *finire*: see FINISH[1]. The underlying sense is 'finished, complete, perfected', hence very good of its kind.

fine[2] *adv* **1** *informal* satisfactorily; well; OK: *doing fine; getting on fine; Everything's going fine*. **2** into small parts; finely: *Chop the chillies fine*.

fine[3] *verb trans* **1** (*often* + down) to purify or clarify (beer or wine). **2** (*often* + down) to make (something) finer in quality or size by paring, trimming, or editing. ➤ *verb intrans* **1** to become pure or clear: *The ale will fine*. **2** (*often* + away/down) to become finer or smaller in lines or proportions; to diminish: *Her features had fined down*.

fine[4] *noun* **1** a sum payable as punishment for an offence. **2** a sum of money paid by a tenant at the start of a tenancy, to reduce subsequent rent. ✳ **in fine** *literary* briefly; in conclusion: *We landed, in fine, more dead than alive* — Poe. [Middle English, in the senses 'end, settlement, compensation', via Old French *fin* from Latin *finis* boundary, end, which in medieval Latin came to mean a sum of money due at the conclusion of a lawsuit]

fine[5] *verb trans* to punish (somebody) by imposing a fine: *The police fined him for speeding*.

fine[6] /feen/ *noun* **1** high-quality French brandy, distilled from wine. **2** = FINE CHAMPAGNE. [French *fine* from Old French *fin*: see FINE[1]]

fine[7] /'feenay/ *noun* a musical direction often occurring in the middle of a composition, indicating the end of a piece of music, where what follows is a repeat of an earlier section. [Italian *fine* end, from Latin *finis*]

fineable *adj* see FINABLE.

fine art /fien/ *noun* (*also in pl*) any of the arts appreciated primarily for aesthetic qualities, such as painting or sculpture. ✳ **have/get something down to a fine art** to reduce effort, expenditure, and performance time on some task, etc to a minimum.

fine champagne /ˌfeen shonh'panhyə/ *noun* brandy from the Champagne district of the Cognac region, more than half the content of which comes from Grande Champagne. [French *fine*, see FINE[6] (I), from Champagne]

fine chemicals /fien/ *pl noun* extremely pure chemicals, e.g. for use in research and industry.

fine-draw /'fien/ *verb trans* to sew (pieces of fabric) together as finely as possible so that the seam is almost imperceptible.

fine-drawn /'fien/ *adj* said of arguments or distinctions: subtle or refined. [from the image of wire drawn out till very fine]

fine-grained /ˌfien/ *adj* said of wood or leather: having a fine even grain.

fine print /ˌfien/ *noun* very small print, typically that on a guarantee or insurance certificate.

finery[1] /'fienəri/ *noun* elaborate, flamboyant, or special clothes, jewellery, or decoration. [FINE[4] + -ERY]

finery[2] *noun* (*pl* **fineries**) formerly, a hearth for converting pig iron into wrought iron. [French *finerie*, from *finer* to refine]

fines /fienz/ *pl noun* ore or coal in the form of a powder or very fine particles. [FINE[1] (II)]

fines herbes /ˌfeenz 'eəb (*French* fin zɛrb)/ *pl noun* a mixture of finely chopped herbs used *esp* as a seasoning. [French *fines herbes* fine herbs]

finespun /'fienspun/ *adj* **1** said of a yarn, fabric, etc: delicate. **2** made or developed with extreme or excessive care or delicacy: *finespun arguments*.

finesse¹ /fi'nes/ *noun* **1** refinement or delicacy of workmanship: *It lacks finesse.* **2a** skilful handling of a situation; adroitness. **b** the subtleties and refinements of any aspect of social intercourse: *Catherine … was not experienced enough in the finesse of love, or the duties of friendship, to know when delicate raillery was properly called for, or when a confidence should be forced* — Jane Austen. **3** in certain card games, *esp* bridge and whist, the withholding of one's highest card in the hope that a lower card will take the trick because the only opposing higher card is in the hand of an opponent who has already played. [Middle English from French, from *fin*: see FINE¹]

finesse² *verb trans* **1a** to bring about (a tricky manoeuvre, etc) by finesse. **b** to avoid blame or trouble by adroit manipulation of (a situation, facts, etc). **2** to play (a card) in a finesse. ➤ *verb intrans* to make a finesse in playing cards.

fine structure /,fien/ *noun* the microscopic structure of an organism or its cells, *esp* as revealed by an electron microscope. ➤➤ **fine structural** *adj*.

fine-tooth comb /,fien/ *noun* a comb with narrow teeth set very close together. ✳ **go over/through something with a fine-tooth comb** to search something very thoroughly. *The police have obviously gone over the crime scene with a fine-tooth comb.*

fine-toothed comb /,fien/ *noun* = FINE-TOOTH COMB.

fine-tune /,fien/ *verb trans* to make minute adjustments to, manipulate, or hone (something) in order to optimize performance or results: *They are still fine-tuning the software prior to its launch; attempts by the Chancellor to fine-tune the economy.* [from the notion of tuning a radio to get the best reception]

finfoot /'finfoot/ *noun* (*pl* **finfoots** or *collectively* **finfoot**) any of three species of tropical and subtropical waterbirds that have long necks, bills, and tails, and are similar to the grebes: family Heliornithidae. [from the flaps on either side of its toes]

finger¹ /'fingga/ *noun* **1** any of the five parts at the end of the hand or forelimb, *esp* one other than the thumb. **2** something that resembles a finger, *esp* in being long, narrow, and often tapering in shape: *a finger of toast.* **3** a part of a glove into which a finger is inserted. **4** the breadth of a finger, *esp* when used as a measure of alcoholic drink. ✳ **be all fingers and thumbs** to be clumsy in handling something. **get one's fingers burned/burn one's fingers** to suffer for one's efforts, enterprise, or temerity. **give somebody the finger** *NAmer, informal* to make an offensive gesture with the middle finger at somebody, *esp* to show contempt or irritation. **have a finger in the/every pie** to be involved or have an interest in something or everything. **have/keep one's finger on the pulse** to ensure one is aware of the latest developments or trends. **keep one's fingers crossed** to hope for the best. **not lay a finger on** to avoid touching or interfering with (a person or thing) in the slightest. **not lift a finger** to make not the slightest effort to help, etc. **pull/take one's finger out** *Brit, informal* to start working hard; to get going. **put one's finger on something** to identify something, *esp* a problem or the cause of a difficulty, etc. **put the finger on somebody** *informal* to identify somebody, *esp* as having committed a crime; to inform on them. **snap/click one's fingers** to make a clicking noise using the middle finger and thumb, *esp* in order to mark a rhythm or attract attention. **twist somebody round one's little finger** to be able to get what one wants from somebody. **work one's fingers to the bone** to wear oneself out with laborious manual work. ➤➤ **fingerless** *adj*, **fingerlike** *adj*. [Old English]

finger² *verb* (**fingered, fingering**) ➤ *verb trans* **1** to touch, feel, or handle (something): *The deep-veined hands fingered many banknotes – one after the other … while Fred leaned back … scorning to look eager* — George Eliot. **2a** *chiefly NAmer, informal* to inform on (somebody): *finger one's associates to the police.* **b** (*often* + for) to select (somebody) for a certain role, etc. **3a** to play (a musical instrument) with the fingers. **b** to mark fingerings (see FINGERING¹) on (a music score) as a guide to playing. **4** *informal* in computing, to obtain information about (another user of the Internet, etc) using a finger program. ➤ *verb intrans* to touch or handle something: *finger through the cards.*

finger alphabet *noun* a sign language using the fingers to make letters and spell out words.

fingerboard *noun* the part of a stringed instrument against which the fingers press the strings to vary the pitch.

finger bowl *noun* a small bowl of water for rinsing the fingers at table.

finger buffet *noun* a meal consisting of FINGER FOOD, typically served at a reception.

finger-dry *verb trans* to dry (hair) by repeatedly running the fingers through it, *esp* in contrast to using a brush or styling tools.

fingered *adj* (*used in combinations*) having fingers of the kind specified or showing a talent for doing the thing specified: *nimble-fingered; green-fingered.*

finger food *noun* canapés, vol-au-vents, small sandwiches, etc that can be picked up in the fingers and eaten easily, served at receptions, drinks parties, etc.

fingering¹ *noun* the use or position of the fingers in sounding notes on an instrument, or the marking indicating this on the score.

fingering² *noun dated* a fine wool yarn for hand knitting. [earlier *fingram*, prob alteration of Old French *fin grain* fine grain: compare GROGRAM]

fingerling /'finggəling/ *noun* a young fish aged up to a year, *esp* the parr of a trout or salmon. [FINGER¹ (from its dark fingerlike markings) + LING]

fingermark *noun* a mark left by a dirty, sticky, or greasy finger, e.g. on a window, wall, or paintwork.

fingernail *noun* the thin horny plate on the upper surface at the tip of a finger.

finger painting *noun* **1** the art or process of painting pictures, designs, etc using the fingers instead of a brush. **2** a picture, etc produced by this.

finger paints *pl noun* a set of thick paints in various colours, used in finger painting.

fingerpick¹ *verb trans* to play (a stringed instrument such as a guitar) with the fingernails, or with plectrums attached to the fingertips. ➤➤ **fingerpicker** *noun*.

fingerpick² *noun* a plectrum worn on a fingertip.

fingerplate *noun* a metal or porcelain plate fastened to a door, usu above the handle, to protect the door surface from finger marks.

fingerpost *noun* a signpost, e.g. at a road junction, that gives directions, distance, etc on signs resembling a pointing finger.

fingerprint¹ *noun* **1a** the impression of a fingertip on any surface. **b** an ink impression of the lines upon the fingertip taken for purposes of identification. **2** any set of characteristics that can be used to identify something.

fingerprint² *verb trans* **1** to take an inked impression of the fingerprints of (somebody), *esp* for identification purposes. **2** to take a sample of blood or tissue from (somebody), *esp* in order to make a DNA record or match.

finger program *noun* (*also* **finger**) an Internet utility that allows somebody to obtain information about other users of various sites, e.g. whether they are currently logged on to a particular site or not.

fingerstall /'finggəstawl/ *noun* a protective cover for an injured finger.

fingertip *noun* **1** the end joint of a finger or the soft part at the end of a finger. **2** (*used before a noun*). **a** activated by the use of a fingertip: *fingertip controls.* **b** using, or as if using, the fingertips; extremely thorough: *a fingertip search.* ✳ **at one's fingertips** said *esp* of information: readily accessible to one. **to one's fingertips** through and through: *a society hostess to her fingertips.*

fingerwave *noun* a wave produced by winding wet hair round the finger.

fingle /'fingg(ə)l/ *verb trans W Indian* to finger, handle, or touch (something) all over. [blend of obsolete *fangle* to trifle and FINGER²]

finial /'fini·əl/ *noun* **1** an ornament forming an upper extremity of a spire, gable, pinnacle, etc, *esp* in Gothic architecture. **2** a crowning ornament or detail, e.g. a decorative knob. [Middle English variant of FINAL¹]

finical /'finikl/ *adj* finicky. ➤➤ **finically** *adv*, **finicalness** *noun*. [prob from FINE¹]

finicking /'finiking/ *adj* finicky. [alteration of FINICAL]

finicky /'finiki/ *adj* **1** excessively exacting or meticulous in taste or standards; fussy. **2** requiring delicate attention to detail: *a finicky job.* ➤➤ **finickiness** *noun*. [alteration of FINICKING]

fining /'fiening/ *noun* (*also in pl*) a substance used for clarifying beer or wine.

finis /'finis/ *noun* used *esp* to mark the end of a book or film: the end. [Middle English from Latin *finis* end]

finish[1] /'finish/ *verb trans* **1** to end (something) or come to the end of it. **2** to stop (doing something). **3** (*often* + off/up) to eat, drink, use, or dispose of (something) entirely. **4** (*also* + off) to complete or perfect (something). **5a** to provide (a product) with a finish; *esp* to put a final coat or surface on (something). **b** to neaten (the raw edge of a piece of sewing) by oversewing or facing, to prevent fraying. **c** to fatten (cattle) before slaughter. **6** *dated* to send (a girl) to finishing school. **7a** to ruin or put an end to (a person, activity, etc): *the scandal that finished his career*. **b** *informal* (*also* + off) to bring about the death of (somebody). **c** *informal* to exhaust (somebody) utterly. ➤ *verb intrans* **1a** to come to an end; to terminate. **b** to come to the end of a course, task, or undertaking in a specified manner: *finish with a song*. **c** to come to the end of a relationship. **2a** (*often* + up) to arrive or end up in a specified place or state. **b** to end a competition, etc in a specified place or order. **3** to complete a manoeuvre in football by scoring. **4** said of a farm animal: to become suitably fat for marketing. ✳ **finish with 1** to have no further need of (something one has been using). **2** to deal fully with (a person). **3** to break off relations with (a person, group, etc): *I've finished with the Greens; finish with one's boyfriend.* [Middle English *finisshen* via French *finir* to finish, from Latin *finire*, from *finis* end]

finish[2] *noun* **1a** the end or final stage of something; the end. **b** the end of a race or the place designated for this. **2a** the final treatment or coating of a surface, or a material such as varnish used for this. **b** the texture or appearance of a surface, *esp* after a coating has been applied. **c** the relative neatness of workmanship on a finished product. **d** polish or refinement. ✳ **fight to the finish** a struggle that ends with the death or total defeat of one of the contestants.

finisher *noun* **1** a person or horse that completes a race: *only five finishers out of a field of fifteen.* **2** a person or machine that does one of the last tasks on a manufactured product. **3** in football, a team member expert at scoring once a goal has been set up by other members. **4** (*often used before a noun*) an animal that is being fattened for slaughter: *finisher cattle.*

finishing line *noun esp* in athletics, the tape or line marking the end of the course.

finishing post *noun esp* in horse racing, the post marking the end of the course.

finishing school *noun* a private school, usu for girls of school-leaving age, that trains its students in social refinement.

finishing touch *noun* (*also in pl*) something done or added as a last detail to enhance the presentation of a piece of work, etc: *Carrie was putting the finishing touches to her toilet* — Theodore Dreiser.

finite /'fieniet/ *adj* **1** having definite or definable limits: *a finite number of possibilities.* **2** subject to limitations, *esp* those imposed by the laws of nature: *finite beings.* **3** completely determinable in theory or in fact by counting, measurement, or thought: *a finite distance; the finite velocity of light.* **4** neither infinite nor infinitesimal. **5** said of a verb form: showing distinction of grammatical person and number, and tense, as distinct from the base form. ➤➤ **finite** *noun,* **finitely** *adv,* **finiteness** *noun,* **finitude** /'finityoohd/ *noun.* [Middle English from Latin *finitus,* past part. of *finire*: see FINISH[1]]

finitism /'fienietiz(ə)m/ *noun* in philosophy and mathematics, the tenet that nothing can be infinite. ➤➤ **finitist** *noun.*

finito /fi'neetoh/ *adj informal* completely finished; all over: *We've broken up again and this time it's finito.* [Italian *finito* finished, from *finire* to finish, from Latin: see FINISH[1]]

fink[1] /fingk/ *noun NAmer, derog* **1** an informer. **2** a strikebreaker. **3** a general term of abuse for a person one dislikes. [perhaps German *Fink* finch, used as a derogatory term for a student not belonging to any of the student corporations]

fink[2] *verb intrans NAmer, informal* **1** (+ on) to inform on somebody. **2** to break a strike. **3** (+ out) to renege on an undertaking or promise: *He said he'd support us, but he finked out.*

Finlandisation /,finləndiezaysh(ə)n/ *noun* see FINLANDIZATION.

Finlandise *verb trans* see FINLANDIZE.

Finlandization *or* **Finlandisation** /,finləndie'zaysh(ə)n/ *noun* the process or outcome of a more powerful nation, *esp* the former Soviet Union, having an influence over a less powerful nation's economic and foreign policies, *esp* an influence that is beneficial to the more powerful nation. [translation of German *Finnlandisierung,* in reference to Finland's relationship with the Soviet Union after 1944]

Finlandize *or* **Finlandise** *verb trans* said of a powerful nation, *esp* the former Soviet Union: to cause (a less powerful nation) to cooperate with the powerful nation, *esp* through economic and foreign policies.

Finn /fin/ *noun* **1** a native or inhabitant of Finland. **2** a member of any people speaking Finnish or a Finnic language. [Swedish *Finne*]

finnan haddie /,finən 'hadi/ *noun chiefly Scot, informal* = FINNAN HADDOCK.

finnan haddock *noun* a haddock that is split and smoked until pale yellow. [*finnan* alteration of *Findon,* fishing village in Scotland, where they were first made]

finnesko /'finəskoh/ *noun* (*pl* **finnesko**) a boot made of reindeer skin, with the hair remaining on it. [Norwegian *finnsko,* from *Finn* Lapp, Finn + *sko* shoe]

Finnic /'finik/ *adj* **1** denoting a group of peoples that includes the Finns. **2** denoting a group of languages that includes Finnish and Estonian.

Finnish *noun* **1** the Finno-Ugric language of the people of Finland, Karelia, and parts of Sweden and Norway. **2** (**the Finnish**) (*treated as pl*) the people of Finland; the Finns. ➤➤ **Finnish** *adj.*

Finno-Ugrian /,finoh 'yoohgri-ən/ *noun and adj* = FINNO-UGRIC.

Finno-Ugric /'yoohgrik/ *noun* **1** a branch of the Uralic family of languages that includes Finnish, Estonian, Lapp, Hungarian, and some other languages of northeastern Europe. **2** a member of any of various peoples who speak one of the Finno-Ugric languages. ➤➤ **Finno-Ugric** *adj.*

finny /'fini/ *adj* (**finnier, finniest**) **1** having fins. **2** *literary or humorous* relating to or denoting fish: *The sportsman had only to cast his line to haul in a bass or some other member of the finny tribe* — J Fenimore Cooper.

fino /'feenoh/ *noun* (*pl* **finos**) a light-coloured dry sherry. [Spanish *fino* fine, ultimately from Latin *finire*: see FINISH[1]]

fin whale *noun* a large common RORQUAL (whale).

fiord *noun* see FJORD.

fioritura /fyori'toorə/ *noun* (*pl* **fioriture** /-'tooray/) a flourish or decoration improvised in a piece of music by a performer, *esp* an opera singer. [Italian *fioritura,* literally 'a flowering', from *fiorire* to flower, ultimately from Latin *florēre*: see FLOURISH[1]]

fipple /'fipl/ *noun* **1** the block fitted into the mouthpiece of a whistle, recorder, or flageolet. **2** the whole mouthpiece of such an instrument. [perhaps related to Old Norse *flipi* horse's lip]

fipple flute *noun* a tubular wind instrument, such as a recorder, flageolet, or whistle, that has a fipple and is played by holding it endwise.

fir /fuh/ *noun* **1** any of numerous species of evergreen trees of the pine family that have flat needle-shaped leaves and erect cones: genus *Abies*: compare PINE[1]. **2** the wood of this tree. [Old English *fyrh*]

fir cone *noun* the fruit of a conifer, covered with overlapping woody scales.

fire[1] /fie-ə/ *noun* **1a** the phenomenon of combustion manifested in light, flame, and heat. **b** one of the four elements of the alchemists or of astrology, the others being earth, air, and water. **2a** burning passion or emotion; ardour: *Perhaps in this neglected spot is laid some heart once pregnant with celestial fire* — Thomas Gray. **b** liveliness of imagination; inspiration: *Anne's character was milder ... she wanted the power, the fire, the originality of her sister* — Charlotte Brontë. **c** enthusiasm or spirit: *I am glad that my weak words have struck but thus much show of fire from Brutus* — Shakespeare; *The leader of the reel ... danced well, and his partner caught his fire* — Edith Wharton. **3** a mass of burning fuel, e.g. in a fireplace or furnace. **4** destructive burning, e.g. of a building or forest, or an instance of this: *insurance against fire; acres of woodland destroyed by a forest fire.* **5** brilliancy or luminosity: *the fire of a diamond.* **6** the discharge of firearms. **7** *Brit* a small domestic heater burning gas or electricity. ✳ **between two fires** under attack from both sides. **catch fire** to begin to burn. **fight fire with fire** to use methods similar to the opposition's tactics, *esp* underhand or distasteful ones. **go on fire** *Scot, Irish* to catch fire. **go through fire and water** to endure great hardship. **hang fire 1** said of a gun: to be slow in exploding. **2** to hesitate or delay, *esp* in expectation of developments. **on fire 1** burning: *The chimney's on fire.* **2** eager or enthusiastic. **open/cease fire** to start or stop firing a gun or other weapon. **play with fire** to take foolhardy risks. **set fire to/set on fire** to start (something) burning, accidentally or maliciously. **set the world on fire** (*chiefly Brit* **set the Thames on fire**) (*usu in negative contexts*) to cause a sensation by achieving something remarkable. **take fire** to start to burn. **under fire 1** being shot at. **2** being harshly criticized. ⋙ **fireless** *adj.* [Old English *fŷr*]

fire² *verb trans* **1a** to discharge (a gun or other firearm). **b** to discharge (a bullet or other projectile) from a gun or other weapon: *The bullet had been fired from an upstairs window; fire poisoned darts at wild animals.* **c** to effect (a salute) with a concerted discharge of guns. **d** to direct (questions, commands, etc) in quick succession at somebody. **2** to dismiss or sack (an employee). **3** to supply (a heating system, furnace, or power station) with fuel: *oil-fired central heating.* **4** to ignite or set fire to (something): *He admitted to firing a number of warehouses.* **5** to bake (pottery, ceramics, or bricks) in a kiln. **6** to kindle or stimulate (somebody's imagination): *the Maori stories that had fired her imagination in childhood.* **7** (*also* + up) to inspire (somebody) or fill them with enthusiasm: *Let's hope you fire them with enthusiasm and they offer to help; We were all fired up for the game and then it was cancelled.* ⋙ *verb intrans* **1** (*often* + at) to discharge a firearm: *She took aim and fired at the intruder.* **2** said of an internal-combustion engine: to burst into life on ignition of its fuel. ✻ **fire away** *informal* go ahead; say what you have to say. **fire on all (four) cylinders** to be in peak functioning form. ⋙ **firer** *noun*, **firing** *noun*.

fire alarm *noun* a device such as a bell, hooter, or siren, that is activated to give warning of a fire.

fire and brimstone *noun* (*treated as sing. or pl*) a terrible fate or punishment. [with allusion to biblical references to the torments of eternal damnation (Psalms 11:7, Revelations 14:10, 20:10, and elsewhere)]

fire ant *noun* any of various ants of tropical America and the southern USA, that build large mounds and can deliver a painful sting: *Solenopsis geminata, Solenopsis saevissima*, and others.

fire appliance *noun* a fire engine.

firearm *noun* a portable gun, *esp* a pistol or rifle.

fireback *noun* **1** the back lining of a furnace or fireplace. **2** any of three species of SE Asian pheasants with grey or blue plumage and a red rump: genus *Lophura*.

fireball *noun* **1** a large brilliant meteor. **2** = BALL LIGHTNING. **3** the bright cloud of vapour and dust created by a nuclear explosion. **4** *informal* a highly energetic person.

fireballer *noun NAmer, informal* in baseball, a pitcher noted for fast and hard delivery of the ball.

fire blanket *noun* a blanket of non-flammable material, *esp* fibreglass, used for smothering flames.

fire blight *noun* a destructive highly infectious disease of apples, pears, and related fruits caused by a bacterium that makes the leaves have a blackened scorched appearance.

fireboat *noun* a motor vessel equipped for fighting fires.

firebomb¹ *noun* an incendiary bomb.

firebomb² *verb trans* to attack or damage (something) with a firebomb.

firebox *noun* a chamber, e.g. of a furnace or steam boiler, where fuel is burned.

firebrand *noun* **1** a piece of burning material, *esp* wood. **2** a person who creates unrest or strife; an agitator or troublemaker.

firebrat *noun* a species of BRISTLETAIL (wingless insect) that inhabits warm places, e.g. bakeries: *Thermobia domestica.*

firebreak *noun* a strip of cleared or unplanted land intended to check a forest or grass fire.

firebrick *noun* a brick that is resistant to high temperatures and is used for lining furnaces, fireplaces, etc.

fire brigade *noun* an organization for preventing or extinguishing fires, *esp* one maintained in Britain by local government.

firebug *noun informal* a pyromaniac; a fire-raiser.

fireclay *noun* clay that is resistant to high temperatures and is used *esp* for firebricks and crucibles.

fire company *noun* **1** *NAmer* = FIRE BRIGADE. **2** an insurance company specializing in policies giving fire cover.

fire control *noun* the planning, preparation, and delivery of gunfire.

fire coral *noun* a HYDROZOAN (type of jellyfish) with a heavy external skeleton, that lives in colonies, forms coral-like reefs, and can inflict a painful sting: genus *Millepora.*

firecracker *noun* a small firework that explodes with a series of bangs and jumps.

firecrest *noun* a small European bird that has a red cap and conspicuous black and white stripes about the eyes: *Regulus ignicapillus.*

firedamp *noun* a combustible mine gas consisting chiefly of methane that forms a highly explosive mixture when combined with air.

fire department *noun NAmer* the department of a local authority in charge of firefighting and fire prevention.

firedog *noun* either of a pair of metal stands for burning logs in a fireplace; = ANDIRON.

fire door *noun* **1** a connecting door inside a building, made of fire-resistant material, designed to prevent the spread of fire. **2** a door to the outside of a building for use as an emergency exit, *esp* one that can easily be opened from inside.

firedrake *noun* a fire-breathing dragon, *esp* in Germanic mythology. [Old English *fyrdraca*, from *fyr* FIRE¹ + *draca* dragon, from Latin *draco*]

fire drill *noun* a practice drill in extinguishing or escaping from fires.

fire-eater *noun* **1** a performer who gives the impression of swallowing fire. **2** *dated* a person who is quarrelsome or violent. ⋙ **fire-eating** *noun and adj.*

fire engine *noun* a vehicle that carries firefighting equipment and a team of firefighters.

fire escape *noun* a device, *esp* an external staircase, for escape from a burning building.

fire-extinguisher *noun* an apparatus for putting out fires with chemicals.

firefight *noun* **1** a fight involving guns as distinct from bombs or other weapons. **2** an often spontaneous exchange of fire between opposing military units.

firefighter *noun* a person trained to fight and extinguish fires. ⋙ **firefighting** *noun.*

firefly *noun* (*pl* **fireflies**) any of several species of night-flying beetles that produce a bright intermittent light: *Luciola lusitanica* and other species.

fireguard *noun* **1** a protective metal framework placed in front of an open fire. **2** *NAmer* = FIREBREAK.

fire hall *noun NAmer, esp Can* = FIRE STATION.

firehouse /'fiə-əhaws/ *noun NAmer* = FIRE STATION.

fire hydrant *noun* a hydrant, *esp* one in the street, for emergency use in fighting fires.

fire insurance *noun* insurance against loss or damage caused by accidental fire or lightning.

fire irons *pl noun* utensils, e.g. tongs, poker, and shovel, for tending a household fire.

firelight *noun* the light of a fire, *esp* of one in a fireplace.

firelighter *noun* a piece of inflammable material used to help light a fire, *esp* in a grate.

fire line *noun* a cleared strip in a forest to check the spread of fire; = FIREBREAK.

firelock *noun* **1a** a gunlock in which a slow match ignites the powder charge. **b** a gun equipped with such a device. **2** a gunlock in which a spark from a flint ignites the powder; = FLINTLOCK (1). **3** an obsolete gunlock in which the powder is ignited by sparks produced by friction between a small steel wheel and a flint; = WHEEL LOCK.

fireman *noun* (*pl* **firemen**) **1** a person trained and employed to extinguish fires. **2** a person who tends or feeds fires or furnaces, e.g. on a steam ship or steam engine.

fire opal *noun* = GIRASOL.

fireplace *noun* a usu framed opening made at the base of a chimney to hold a domestic fire; a hearth.

fireplug *noun NAmer* **1** = HYDRANT. **2** *informal* a person with a short stocky build, *esp* an athlete.

firepower *noun* the capacity, e.g. of a military unit, to deliver effective fire on a target.

fire practice *noun Brit* = FIRE DRILL.

fireproof[1] *adj* able to withstand fire or high temperatures: *fireproof dishes*.

fireproof[2] *verb trans* to make (something) fireproof.

fire-raising *noun Brit* arson. ➤➤ **fire-raiser** *noun*.

fire salamander *noun* a black salamander with red, orange, and yellow markings, found in hilly forest areas in Europe, Africa, and Asia: *Salamandra salamandra*.

fire sale *noun* **1** a sale at bargain prices of goods that have survived a fire on commercial premises. **2** a quick sale of goods at bargain prices, e.g. when the seller faces bankruptcy or closure.

fire screen *noun* **1** a light often ornamental screen placed in front of a fireplace when there is no fire in the grate. **2** *chiefly NAmer* = FIREGUARD (1).

fire ship *noun* a ship carrying combustible materials or explosives sent among the enemy's ships to set them on fire.

fireside *noun* **1** a place near the fire or hearth. **2** (*used before a noun*) taking place at, or having the cosiness and intimacy associated with, the fireside: *a fireside chat*.

fire sign *noun* in astrology, any of the three signs of the Zodiac Aries, Leo, and Sagittarius: compare AIR SIGN, EARTH SIGN, WATER SIGN.

firestarter *noun NAmer* = FIRELIGHTER.

fire station *noun* a building where fire engines and firefighting apparatus are kept and where firefighters are on duty until called to attend a fire or other emergency.

fire step *noun esp* formerly, a step below the edge of a parapet or trench where soldiers can stand when firing.

firestone *noun* a stone that will endure high heat, used to line furnaces, etc.

firestorm *noun* a huge uncontrollable fire that is typically started by bombs and is sustained by its power to draw in strong currents of air from a wide area round about it.

firethorn *noun* = PYRACANTHA.

fire trail *noun* in Australia, a track cleared through the bush to provide access for firefighting.

firetrap *noun* a building that is difficult to escape from in case of fire or that does not have adequate fire escapes, fire-extinguishers, etc.

fire-walking *noun* the activity, *esp* as a religious rite, of walking barefoot over hot stones or ashes. ➤➤ **fire-walker** *noun*.

fire wall *noun* **1** a fireproof wall within a building. **2** a safeguard in place in a financial company to ensure that its banking and share-dealing activities are kept separate. **3** in computing, a software device that protects sensitive areas of a network, etc from unauthorized access.

fire warden *noun* a person appointed to guard against fires, or extinguish those that occur, in a forest, community, campsite, etc.

fire-watcher *noun* somebody who watches for the outbreak of fire, e.g. during an air raid. ➤➤ **fire-watching** *noun*.

firewater *noun informal* strong alcoholic drink.

fireweed *noun* any of various plants that are the first to be seen growing on burned land, *esp* the rosebay willowherb.

firewood *noun* wood used or cut for fuel.

firework *noun* **1a** a device containing explosive material that goes off with dramatic light and sound effects when ignited. **b** (*in pl*) a display of fireworks. **2** (*in pl*). **a** a display of temper or a clash of wills. **b** a sparkling display of brilliance, e.g. in oratory or repartee; pyrotechnics (see PYROTECHNICS (3)).

firing /ˈfīe-əring/ *noun* **1** the process of baking and fusing ceramic products by the application of heat in a kiln. **2** firewood or other fuel. **3** the act or an instance of keeping a fire or furnace burning. **4** the act or an instance of discharging a firearm.

firing line *noun* **1** the troops stationed in the front line of battle. **2** the battle line from which fire is discharged against the enemy. ✳ **in the firing line** in the forefront of an activity, *esp* one involving risk, difficulty, or criticism.

firing party *noun* = FIRING SQUAD.

firing squad *noun* a detachment of soldiers detailed to fire a salute at a military burial or to carry out an execution.

firing step *noun* = FIRE STEP.

firkin /ˈfuhkin/ *noun chiefly dated* **1** a small wooden tub or cask used for storing liquids, butter, or fish. **2** any of various British units of capacity usu equal to 9 imperial gallons (about 41 litres). [Middle English *ferdekyn*, prob from a dimin. of Dutch *vierde* a quarter]

firm[1] /fuhm/ *adj* **1** solidly or securely fixed; stable: *a firm table*. **2** said of a surface or structure: not yielding to pressure; solid and compact: *firm foundations*; *Her arms were slim and firm*. **3** having a sustained strength: *a firm grip*. **4** said of an opinion or principle: unchanging; steadfast. **5** said of friends: having a strong and constant relationship. **6** said of a decision or arrangement: settled or definite. **7** said of a currency, share price, etc: not fluctuating in value; steady or more likely to rise than fall. **8** said of evidence: well-founded. **9** resolute in dealing with people or situations: *You have to be firm with them*. **10** said of the chin, jaw, or mouth: determined-looking. ✳ **a firm hand** strong control or guidance: *The children need a firm hand*. **hold/stand firm** to remain steadfast and unyielding. **on firm ground** sure of one's position in a dispute, etc. ➤➤ **firmish** *adj*, **firmly** *adv*, **firmness** *noun*. [Middle English *ferm* via French from Latin *firmus* firm, durable, steadfast]

firm[2] *verb trans* **1** to make (something) solid, compact, firm, or secure: *Then firm the soil round the plant*; *He firmed his grip on the racket*. **2** (*also* + up) to settle (an agreement, arrangement, etc) or put it into final form: *firm a contract*; *firm up one's plans*. **3** to give additional support to or strengthen (a currency, or the price of a commodity or stock): *A lively stock market helped to firm the pound*. ➤ *verb intrans* said of prices or a market: to recover from a decline; to improve: *At close of trading the market had firmed slightly*.

firm[3] *noun* **1** a business partnership of two or more people. **2** any business unit or enterprise. **3** a group of hospital doctors usu under a particular consultant. **4** (*usu* **The Firm**) a criminal gang or an organized group of troublemakers, *esp* football supporters who look for fights. [Spanish *firma* signature, hence the name or title of a business company, from Latin *firmare* to make firm, confirm, from *firmus* firm, durable]

firmament /ˈfuhməmənt/ *noun* the vault or arch of the sky; the heavens: *this most excellent canopy, the air … this brave o'erhanging firmament* — Shakespeare. ➤➤ **firmamental** /-ˈmentl/ *adj*. [Middle English from late Latin *firmamentum* vault of the sky, earlier 'support', from *firmare*: see FIRM[3]]

firman /ˈfuhman/ *noun* (*pl* **firmans**) formerly, an official command or permit issued by an Oriental ruler. [Turkish *ferman* from Persian *fermān* and Sanskrit *pramāna* authority, literally 'right measure']

firmware *noun* computer programs that are stored in a read-only memory and cannot be altered or erased, constituting permanent software.

firn /fiən/ *noun* permanent but granular snow at the top of a glacier; = NÉVÉ. [German *Firn* from dialect *firn* relating to the previous year, from Old High German *firni* old]

first[1] /fuhst/ *adj* **1** denoting a person or thing having the position in a sequence corresponding to the number one: *Her first novel was her most successful*; *Our first two years were bliss*; *the first baby to be born in the new millennium*. **2** preceding all the rest; earliest: *the first human beings*. **3** in the top or winning place: *be first in maths*. **4** most important and, therefore, taking precedence: *Our first task is to eliminate begging on the streets*. **5** leading or most senior: *Scotland's first minister*. **6** in music, denoting one of two parts for the same instrument or voice, usu higher in pitch and carrying the melody: *the first violins*; *the first sopranos*. **7** denoting the first and lowest forward gear of a motor vehicle. ✳ **first thing** early tomorrow morning or early next day: *I'll see to that first thing*. **first things first** everything in its due order. **not have the first idea/notion** to have not the slightest idea: *They haven't got the first idea what to do*. **of the first order** of the most excellent or outstanding kind: *I really have been an idiot of the first order*. [Old English *fyrst*]

first[2] *adv* **1** before anybody or anything else; at the beginning: *We arrived first and left last*. **2** by way of introduction or preliminary; to start with: *First, let me thank Liz Cooke for arranging this venue*. **3** for the first time: *the men who first landed on the moon*. ✳ **come first** **1** to win or be top. **2** to take precedence: *Passenger safety comes first with us*. **feet/head first** with the feet or head leading: *Lucy slid down the chute head first*. **first and last** always and most importantly: *He was, first and last, a Yorkshireman*. **first come first served** people will be dealt with in the order in which they arrive. **first of all** before doing anything else. **first off** *informal* to start with; firstly: *First off, there's the expense*. **first up** *informal* first of all.

first³ *noun and pronoun* **1a** a person, thing, or group, that is first. **b** a thing that has never happened, been done, or been experienced before: *Who was the first to arrive?*; *He was one of the first to collect Picasso*; *This holiday-camp venture will be a first for us*. **2** the first and lowest forward gear of a motor vehicle; bottom gear: *I couldn't get into first*. **3** in Britain, a first-class honours degree: *He got a first in economics at Manchester University*. * **at first** at the beginning; to start with; initially. **first past the post 1** winning by reaching the finishing post first. **2** (**first-past-the-post**) (*used before a noun*) denoting the electoral system in which the candidate with a simple majority wins. **from first to last** from beginning to end: *He was a devoted friend from first to last*. **from the first** from the very beginning: *We liked her from the first*.

first aid *noun* **1** emergency care or treatment given to an ill or injured person before full medical aid can be obtained. **2** temporary emergency measures taken to alleviate a problem before a permanent solution can be found. ⟫⟫ **first-aider** *noun*.

first base *noun chiefly NAmer* (*usu in negative contexts*) the first step or stage in a course of action: *The plan never got to first base*. [from baseball, the base that must be touched first by a batter making a run]

firstborn *adj* born before all others; eldest: *their firstborn child*. ⟫⟫ **firstborn** *noun*.

first cause *noun* (*also* **First Cause**) in philosophy, the self-created source of all causality: compare PRIME MOVER (3).

first class *noun* **1** the first or highest set or group in a system of classification. **2** *Brit* the highest class in the assessment of the results of a university degree examination. **3a** the highest class of travel accommodation, e.g. on a train, plane, or ship. **b** (**first-class**) (*used before a noun*) relating to or denoting this class of travel: *the first-class lounge*; *a first-class ticket*. **4** *Brit*. **a** the highest class in the assessment of the results of a university degree examination. **b** (**first-class**) (*used before a noun*) relating to or denoting this type of degree: *She gained first-class honours*.

first-class *adv* **1** in the highest quality of accommodation: *travel first-class*. **2** as mail that is delivered as fast as possible: *send a letter first-class*.

first cost *noun* in production, the cost of raw materials and labour; = PRIME COST.

first cousin *noun* a child of one's uncle or aunt; = COUSIN (1). * **first cousin once removed** see REMOVED.

first-day cover *noun* a special envelope with a newly issued postage stamp or a set of postage stamps postmarked on the first day of issue.

first-degree *adj chiefly NAmer* relating to or denoting the most serious form of a particular criminal offence, *esp* murder that is deliberate and premeditated.

first-degree burn *noun* a mild burn characterized by heat, pain, and reddening of the burned surface but without blistering or charring of tissues: compare SECOND-DEGREE BURN, THIRD-DEGREE BURN.

first-degree relative *noun* one's parent, sibling, or child.

first down *noun* in American football, the score resulting from a team keeping possession of the ball by advancing at least ten yards in a series of four downs (chances to advance; see DOWN⁵ (3)).

first finger *noun* the index finger.

first floor *noun* **1** *Brit* the floor immediately above the ground floor. **2** *NAmer* = GROUND FLOOR.

first-foot¹ *noun esp* in Scotland, the first person to cross one's threshold in the New Year.

first-foot² *verb trans* (**first-footed**, **first-footing**) to be the first person to cross the threshold of (somebody) in the New Year. ⟫⟫ **first-footing** *noun*.

first-footer *noun* = FIRST-FOOT¹.

first fruits *pl noun* **1** the first agricultural products of a season, *esp* a selection of these offered to God in thanksgiving. **2** the earliest products or results of an enterprise.

first gear *noun* = BOTTOM GEAR.

first-hand *adj* relating to or coming directly from the original source. * **at first hand** directly; without any intermediary intervention. ⟫⟫ **first-hand** *adv*.

first intention *noun* in medicine, the kind of healing that takes place when parts unite by direct contact without granulation (intermediate formation of new capillaries; see GRANULATE).

first lady *noun* (*often* **First Lady**) the wife or female partner of a US president or other head of state.

first lieutenant *noun* **1** a naval officer in executive charge of a ship. **2** in the US army, air force, or marines, a rank immediately below captain.

firstling /'fuhstling/ *noun archaic* (*in pl*) the first agricultural products or the first offspring of farm animals to be produced in a season.

first-loss policy *noun* an insurance policy that provides cover for less than the full value of the goods in question, because the likelihood of total loss is minimal.

firstly *adv* used to introduce a first point: in the first place; first.

first mate *noun* on a merchant ship, the officer second in command to the master.

First Minister *noun* the chief executive of the Scottish Parliament or the Northern Ireland Assembly.

first mortgage *noun* a mortgage that has priority over all other mortgages on a property except those imposed by law.

first name *noun* the personal or given name that usu stands first in a person's full name. * **on first-name terms** said of two or more people: having an informal relationship.

first night *noun* **1** the first public performance of a play, ballet, show, etc or the day or night this is given. **2** (**first-night**) (*used before a noun*) relating to or denoting a first night: *first-night jitters*.

first offender *noun* a person convicted of an offence for the first time.

first officer *noun* **1** on a merchant ship, = FIRST MATE. **2** on an aircraft, the crew member who is second in command to the captain.

first person *noun* in grammar, the term used to refer to the speaker or speakers, represented by the pronouns *I* or *we*, and to the verb forms appropriate to these: compare PERSON (3), SECOND PERSON, THIRD PERSON.

first position *noun* in ballet, a standing position with the heels together and the toes turned outwards.

first post *noun Brit* the first of two bugle calls that signal the hour of retiring, *esp* in a military camp.

first principles *pl noun* the fundamental principles or assumptions that underlie a theory, set of beliefs, etc: *This distinguished naturalist, like so many other Frenchmen, has not taken the trouble to understand even the first principles of sexual selection* — Darwin.

first-rate *adj* relating to or denoting the best class or the finest quality; excellent; supreme. ⟫⟫ **first-rater** *noun*.

first reading *noun* the first submitting of a bill before a legislative assembly, to allow its introduction.

first refusal *noun* the right of accepting or refusing something before it is offered to others.

first school *noun* a primary school for children between five and eight.

First Secretary *noun* the chief executive of the National Assembly for Wales.

first sergeant *noun* in the US army, the officer of the highest non-commissioned rank.

first-strike *adj* denoting nuclear weapons or an initial nuclear attack designed to destroy the enemy's power to retaliate.

first-string *adj* said of a member of a sports team, group, etc: having a regular place as distinguished from being a substitute.

first water *noun* the purest lustre or highest quality of gemstone: *a diamond of the first water*. * **of the first water** *sometimes ironic* of the most outstanding kind: *a fool of the first water* — Thomas Wolfe.

First World *noun* the industrialized nations of the world, including N America, the countries of W Europe, Japan, Australia, and New Zealand: compare SECOND WORLD, THIRD WORLD (1).

firth /fuhth/ *noun* a sea inlet or estuary, *esp* in Scotland. [Middle English, from Old Norse *fjörthr* FJORD]

fisc /fisk/ *noun* **1** *chiefly NAmer* a public or state treasury. **2** in imperial Rome, the emperor's treasury. [Latin *fiscus* treasury, literally 'rush basket']

fiscal[1] /'fiskl/ *adj* **1** relating to taxation, public revenues, or public debt: *fiscal policy*. **2** *chiefly NAmer* relating to finance generally. ➤➤ **fiscally** *adv*. [Latin *fiscalis* from *fiscus*: see FISC]

fiscal[2] *noun* = PROCURATOR FISCAL.

fiscal year *noun NAmer* = FINANCIAL YEAR.

fish[1] /fish/ *noun* (*pl* **fishes** *or collectively* **fish**) **1a** any of numerous cold-blooded aquatic vertebrates that typically have an elongated scaly body, limbs, when present, in the form of fins, and gills. **b** the flesh of a fish used as food. **2** (*used in combinations*) a term referring generally to any aquatic animal, including invertebrates: *starfish*; *jellyfish*; *shellfish*; *cuttlefish*. **3** (**the Fish**) the constellation and sign of the zodiac Pisces. **4** a person, *esp* one of a specified, often eccentric, nature: *rather a cold fish*. ✳ **a big fish in a little pond** an important person in a small community, therefore not so very important. **a fish out of water** a person who is out of his or her proper sphere or element and therefore seems uneasy or uncomfortable. **have other/bigger fish to fry** to have other, *esp* more important, things to do. **make fish of one and flesh of the other** *Irish* to discriminate between people unjustly. **neither fish, flesh, nor fowl/nor good red herring** of indeterminate character. ➤➤ **fishless** *adj*, **fishlike** *adj*. [Old English *fisc*]

fish[2] *verb intrans* **1** to try to catch fish, e.g. with a hook and line or a net: *go fishing*; *fish for trout*. **2** (*often +* for) to feel about in the interior of a container for something: *fishing in her handbag for her spectacles*. **3** (*often +* for) to try to obtain something, *esp* by using cunning or devious means: *fish for information*; *fish for compliments*; *Stop fishing!* ➤ *verb trans* to go fishing in (a body of water): *He often used to go down to the Borders and fish the Tweed*.

fish[3] *noun* **1** a flat piece of wood or iron fixed lengthways to a beam, etc, or across a joint, to add strength. **2** a curved piece of wood lashed to a split mast or boom, serving as a temporary splint. [French *fiche* from *ficher* to fix, ultimately from Latin *figere*]

fish and chips *noun* a meal of fish fillets coated with batter and deep-fried, accompanied by potato chips, typically bought ready-cooked and wrapped in paper from a take-away restaurant.

fishbowl *noun* **1** a round glass bowl that fish, *esp* pet goldfish, are kept in. **2** *informal* a place or condition that offers little or no privacy.

fishcake *noun* a usu circular portion of flaked fish mixed with mashed potato, coated with breadcrumbs and fried.

fish eagle *noun* any of various eagles that feed mainly on fish: *Haliaetus vocifer* and other species.

fisher *noun* **1** a large brown woodland marten of N America: *Martes pennanti*. Also called PEKAN. **2** *archaic* a fisherman.

fisherfolk *noun* (*treated as pl*) people who live in a community that is dependent on fishing.

fisherman *or* **fisherwoman** *noun* (*pl* **fishermen** *or* **fisherwomen**) **1** a person who engages in fishing as an occupation or for pleasure. **2** (**fisherman**) a ship used in commercial fishing.

fisherman's bat *noun* = BULLDOG BAT.

fisherman's bend *noun* a knot used to secure an anchor to its cable, executed by making a full turn and two half hitches, the first through the turn and the second round the standing part of the rope.

fisherman's knit *noun* = FISHERMAN'S RIB.

fisherman's knot *noun* a knot for tying the ends of two small ropes together, executed by tying each in an overhand knot around the other.

fisherman's rib *noun* a thick ribbed knitting pattern traditionally used for fishermen's pullovers.

fishery *noun* (*pl* **fisheries**) **1** the activity or business of catching fish and other sea animals. **2** a place or establishment for catching fish and other sea animals.

fish-eye *adj* **1** denoting a wide-angle photographic lens that has a highly curved protruding front and covers an angle up to 180°. **2** denoting a camera with such a lens or the photographs taken by it.

fish farm *noun* a tract of water where fish or shellfish are reared and bred commercially.

fish finger *noun* a small oblong of flaked fish coated with breadcrumbs or batter.

fish hawk *noun* = OSPREY (1).

fishhook *noun* a barbed hook used on the end of a line for catching fish.

fishing *noun* **1a** the sport or business of catching fish. **b** (*used before a noun*) relating to, denoting, or used in fishing: *a fishing fly*. **2** a stretch of water, or the facility it provides, for catching fish: *rent the fishing*.

fishing fly *noun* a real or artificial fly used as bait for fishing.

fishing ground *noun* a stretch of a river or area of sea where fish are caught.

fishing line *noun* a strong silk or nylon thread with a baited hook attached to it, used for catching fish.

fishing pole *noun chiefly NAmer* a simple fishing rod without a reel.

fishing rod *noun* a tapering rod with a reel, used with an attached line and hook for catching fish.

fish joint *noun* a joint between two end-to-end sections of timber or railway line, held in position by one or more fishplates.

fish kettle *noun* a usu deep long oval vessel used for cooking fish.

fish knife *noun* a knife with a broad, blunt, usu decorated blade for eating or serving fish.

fish ladder *noun* a series of pools arranged like steps by which fish can pass over a dam or waterfall when going upstream.

fish louse *noun* any of various small crustaceans parasitic on fish: classes Branchiura and Copepoda.

fish meal *noun* ground dried fish used as fertilizer and animal food.

fishmonger /'fishmunggə/ *noun chiefly Brit* a person or shop that sells raw food fish.

fishnet *noun* **1** a coarse open-mesh fabric. **2** (*used before a noun*) made of this fabric: *fishnet tights*.

fish out *verb trans* **1** to draw (something) out of a body of liquid or out of a cavity: *He felt in his pocket and fished out a pencil*. **2** to exhaust the supply of fish in (a body of water) by overfishing.

fishplate *noun* a usu metal plate used to make a joint between consecutive rails on a railway line.

fish slice *noun* a kitchen implement with a broad blade and long handle used *esp* for turning or lifting food in frying.

fishtail[1] *noun* a manoeuvre by a pilot of swinging an aircraft's tail from side to side to reduce speed for landing.

fishtail[2] *verb intrans* **1** to perform a fishtail. **2a** said of a motor vehicle: to swing its rear end from side to side when out of control. **b** said of a driver of a motor vehicle: to cause the vehicle's rear end to swing from side to side.

fishway *noun* = FISH LADDER.

fishwife *noun* (*pl* **fishwives**) **1** *archaic* a woman who sells or guts fish. **2** a vulgar, abusive, or loud-mouthed woman.

fishy *adj* (**fishier, fishiest**) **1** relating to or resembling fish, *esp* in taste or smell. **2** *informal* creating doubt or suspicion; questionable: *It might have struck the officers … that there was 'something fishy' in the affair; but of course they would keep their doubts to themselves —* Joseph Conrad. ➤➤ **fishily** *adv*, **fishiness** *noun*.

fissile /'fisiel/ *adj* **1** said of rock: capable of being easily split. **2** said of an atom or element: capable of undergoing nuclear fission. ➤➤ **fissility** /fi'siliti/ *noun*. [Latin *fissilis*, from *findere* to split]

fission[1] /'fish(ə)n/ *noun* **1** a splitting or breaking up into parts. **2** in biology, a form of asexual reproduction by spontaneous division into two or more parts each of which grows into a complete organism. **3** the splitting of an atomic nucleus with the release of large amounts of energy. ➤➤ **fissional** *adj*. [Latin *fission-, fissio*, from *findere* to split]

fission[2] *verb intrans* said *esp* of an atom: to undergo fission. ➤➤ **fissionability** /-ə'biləti/ *noun*, **fissionable** *adj*.

fission bomb *noun* = ATOM BOMB.

fission-track dating *noun* a means of dating certain minerals by measuring the disruption to their crystal lattice made by uranium nuclei.

fissiparous /fi'sipərəs/ *adj* **1** said of an organism: reproducing by fission. **2a** said of an organization, etc: inclined to division. **b**

inclined to cause division; divisive: *have a fissiparous effect.* ▶▶ **fissiparity** /-'pariti/ *noun,* **fissiparously** *adv,* **fissiparousness** *noun.* [Latin *fissus,* past part. of *findere* to split + -PAROUS]

fissure[1] /'fishə/ *noun* **1** a narrow, long, and deep opening, e.g. in rock, usu caused by breaking or parting. **2** a natural cleft between body parts or in the substance of an organ, e.g. the brain. **3** a division, e.g. within a party or other organization, caused by disagreement; a rift. [Middle English via French from Latin *fissura* cleft, from *findere* to split]

fissure[2] *verb intrans* to break into fissures. ▶▶ **fissured** *adj.*

fist[1] /fist/ *noun* **1** the hand clenched with the fingers doubled into the palm and the thumb across the fingers. **2** *informal* a person's handwriting. *I recognized his fist immediately.* **3** *informal* in printing, a pointing-hand symbol, used for cross references, etc. Also called INDEX[1] (5). ✴ **make a fair/poor fist of/at something** *informal* to make a creditable or ineffectual attempt at something. [Old English *fyst*]

fist[2] *verb trans* **1** to hit (a ball) with the fist: *The goalkeeper fisted the ball clear.* **2** *coarse slang* to penetrate the vagina or anus of (somebody) with one's fist, as a sexual act.

fist-fuck *verb trans taboo* = FIST[2] (2).

fistful /'fistf(ə)l/ *noun* (*pl* **fistfuls**) a handful.

fisticuffs /'fistikufs/ *pl noun dated or humorous* the activity of fighting with the fists. [alteration of *fisty cuff,* from obsolete *fisty* with the fists + CUFF[3]]

fistula /'fistyoolə/ *noun* (*pl* **fistulas** or **fistulae** /-lee/) an abnormal or surgically made passage leading from an abscess or hollow organ to the body surface or between hollow organs: *'What is it ... the King languishes of?' 'A fistula, my lord'* — Shakespeare. [Middle English from Latin *fistula* pipe]

fistular /'fistyoolə/ *adj* = FISTULOUS.

fistulous /'fistyoolǝs/ *adj* **1** relating to or having the form of a fistula: *a fistulous sore.* **2** hollow like a pipe or reed.

fit[1] /fit/ *adj* (**fitter, fittest**) **1** adapted or suited to an end or purpose: *It was a fit punishment for such a crime.* **2** adapted to the environment: *survival of the fittest.* **3** acceptable from a particular viewpoint, e.g. of competence, morality, or qualifications; worthy: *no fitter person for the task; not fit to be a father.* **4** in a suitable state: *The house isn't fit to be seen.* **5** in so advanced a condition, e.g. of exhaustion, as to be about to suffer the extreme result specified: *I was so tired I was fit to drop.* **6** strong and healthy: *Yoga is a good way of keeping fit; looking fit and well.* **7** *informal* said of a person: attractive. ✴ **fit as a fiddle/flea** in excellent health. **fit to be tied** *informal* extremely angry. **fit to bust** *informal* with huge vigour. **see fit** to consider (something) proper or advisable: *They didn't even see fit to warn him of his impending dismissal.* **think fit** to consider it proper or advisable (to do something): *Did nobody think fit to tell his parents?* ▶▶ **fitly** *adv.* [Middle English; earlier history unknown]

fit[2] *verb* (**fitting,** *past tense and past part.* **fitted** or NAmer **fit**) ▶ *verb trans* **1** to be the right size or shape for (somebody or something). **2a** to measure (somebody) for clothes or to try clothes on (somebody) in order to make adjustments in size: *I'm being fitted for a new suit.* **b** to make or find clothes of the right size for (somebody): *It's difficult to fit him because he's so short.* **3** to be suitable for or appropriate to (something): *Make the punishment fit the crime.* **4** to match or correspond to (something): *a theory that fits all the facts.* **5** to render (somebody or something) suitable for a task, purpose, etc: *She had qualities that especially fitted her for leadership.* **6** (often + in) to adjust or adapt (something) in response to needs: *I can fit my plans in with yours.* **7** (often + into) to find time for (something) in the time available: *You can't fit any more activities into the day.* **8a** to insert or adjust (something) until correctly in position. **b** to install (an appliance, etc). **9** to supply (something) with equipment, etc. **10** to adjust (a curve of a specified type) to a given set of points, e.g. to demonstrate a mathematical or *esp* statistical relationship. **11** *archaic* to be seemly or proper for (somebody) to do something; = BEHOVE: *It fits us then to be as provident as fear may teach us* — Shakespeare. ▶ *verb intrans* **1** to be the right size or shape for somebody or something. **2a** said of clothes: to be loose, tight, etc when on: *It's meant to fit snugly.* **b** to be of a correct or suitable size: *The wardrobe won't fit into that space.* **3** said of parts or components: to go together in a certain relationship: *These two parts fit together; One fits inside the other.* **4** to be in accordance with the facts or circumstances: *It all fits.* ✴ **fit like a glove** see GLOVE[1].

fit[3] *noun* **1** the manner in which clothing fits the wearer: *a snug fit.* **2** the degree of closeness with which surfaces are brought together

in an assembly of parts. **3** the conformity between an experimental result and theoretical expectation or between data and an approximating curve.

fit[4] *noun* **1** a sudden violent attack of a disease, e.g. epilepsy, *esp* when accompanied by convulsions or unconsciousness. **2** a spell or attack of something difficult to control: *a coughing fit; a fit of giggles; In a fit of frustration he had attacked his computer with a hammer.* **3** a sudden outburst of a specified activity: *a fit of letter-writing.* ✴ **by/in fits and starts** in an impulsive or irregular manner; with spasmodic bouts of activity: *progress by fits and starts.* **have/throw a fit** to be extremely shocked or horrified. **in fits** *informal* laughing uncontrollably. [Old English *fitt* strife, later 'a position or period of danger']

fit[5] *noun archaic* a division of a poem or song. [Old English *fitt;* perhaps the same word as FIT[4], or related to German *Fitze* skein, in an obsolete sense 'thread used by weavers to mark a day's work']

fitch /fitsh/ *archaic* **1** = POLECAT (1). **2** the fur of a polecat. [Dutch *visse* polecat, from which, via Old French dimin. *ficheau,* also comes *fitchew*]

fitchew /'fitshoo/ *noun* = POLECAT (1).

fitful /'fitf(ə)l/ *adj* having a spasmodic or intermittent character; irregular: *fitful sleep.* ▶▶ **fitfully** *adv,* **fitfulness** *noun.*

fit in *verb trans* to make room, place, or time for (a person or thing). ▶ *verb intrans* to be compatible or in keeping or harmony with an environment.

fitment *noun* **1** a piece of equipment; *esp* an item of built-in furniture. **2** (*also in pl*) a small detachable usu standard part; = FITTING[2] (2): *taps and other fitments.*

fitness *noun* **1a** the condition of being physically strong and healthy, *esp* achieved through regular exercise and eating sensibly: *lack of fitness.* **b** (*used before a noun*) relating to, denoting, or associated with health, exercise, etc: *open a new fitness complex.* **2** (*often* + for) suitability for a particular task, job, role, or post: *Her fitness for office is not in dispute.* **3** in evolutionary biology: **a** an organism's degree of adaptation to its environment, as determined by its genetic make-up and contribution to subsequent generations. **b** an organism's ability to reproduce successfully in its environment.

fit out *verb trans* to supply (somebody or something) with the necessary equipment.

fitted *adj* **1** said of a carpet: cut to the same shape as the floor area of a room. **2a** said of cupboards, kitchen units, etc: built so as to fit a particular space and fixed there. **b** said of a kitchen: having fitted units, shelves, and working surfaces. **3** said of sheets, chair covers, or clothes: made to fit the shape that is to be covered closely: *a fitted jacket.* **4** (+ for/to) suitable, adapted, or qualified for something or to do something: *Some people are not fitted for office life; a creature peculiarly fitted to survive in the harsh Arctic environment.*

fitter *noun* a person who assembles or repairs machinery or appliances: *a gas fitter.*

fitting[1] *adj* **1** appropriate to the situation: *make a fitting answer.* **2** (*used in combinations*) fitting the form of a person or thing in the way specified: *tight-fitting.* ▶▶ **fittingly** *adv,* **fittingness** *noun.*

fitting[2] *noun* **1** the act or an instance of trying on clothes which are in the process of being made or altered. **2** a small often standardized part: *an electrical fitting.* **3** (*in pl*) items, e.g. carpets, curtains, etc, fitted in a property, that the owner is legally entitled to remove should the property be sold: compare FIXTURE (1B). **4** the act or an instance of installing or securing something.

fitting room *noun* a room or cubicle in a shop where one can try on clothes before buying them.

fitting shop *noun* a section of a factory where machine parts are fitted together.

fit up *verb trans* **1** to install all the necessary equipment for the proper functioning of (e.g. an office, shop, or hotel). **2** (*often* + with) to provide (a person) with the equipment they need: *We can soon fit you up with a second computer and a scanner.* **3** *Brit, informal* to incriminate (an innocent person); = FRAME[2] (4).

Fitzgerald contraction /fits'jerəld/ *noun* = FITZGERALD-LORENTZ CONTRACTION.

Fitzgerald-Lorentz contraction /lə'rents/ *noun* the contraction of a moving body in the direction of its movement, *esp* as it approaches the speed of light. [named after G F *Fitzgerald* d.1901, Irish physicist, and H A *Lorentz* d.1928, Dutch physicist, who both, but independently, predicted the phenomenon]

five /fiev/ *noun* **1** the number 5, or the quantity represented by it. **2** something having five parts or members, e.g. a playing card with five pips on it: *the five of clubs*. **3a** the age of 5 years. **b** the hour five hours after midday or midnight. ✳ **take five** *informal* to have a short break or rest. ➤➤ **five** *adj*, **fivefold** *adj and adv*. [Old English *fif*]

five-alarm *adj NAmer, informal* **1** said of a fire: large and extremely serious. **2** said of food: having a fiery or pungent taste.

five-and-dime *noun NAmer* a store selling inexpensive household goods and personal requirements.

five-and-dime store *noun NAmer* = FIVE-AND-DIME.

five-and-ten *noun NAmer* = FIVE-AND-DIME.

five-a-side *noun* a form of football with five players on each side.

five-eighth *noun chiefly Aus, NZ* in rugby, a player positioned between the three-quarters and the scrum half.

five-finger *noun* any of various plants, e.g. the cinquefoil, that have five-petalled flowers or five-lobed leaves.

five hundred *noun* a version of the card game euchre in which making a score of 500 points wins a game.

five-o'clock shadow *noun* a just visible growth of beard. [from the shadow-like appearance of dark beard stubble visible on a man's face by 5 p.m.]

fivepins *pl noun* (*treated as sing.*) a bowling game similar to ninepins, but using only five skittles.

fiver *noun informal* **1** *Brit* a five-pound note. **2** *NAmer* a five-dollar bill.

fives /fievz/ *pl noun* (*treated as sing.*) any of various singles or doubles games in which players use their hands or small bats to hit a ball in a walled court.

five-spice *noun* a powdered blend of five spices, usu cinnamon, cloves, fennel seeds, peppercorns, and star anise, used in Chinese cuisine.

five-star *adj* said of accommodation, etc: of the highest standard or quality: *a five-star hotel; five-star treatment*. [from the number of asterisks used in guidebooks to denote relative excellence]

fivestones *pl noun Brit* (*treated as sing.*) a game similar to jacks (see JACK[1] (5A)), but played with five pieces of stone or metal, usu without a ball.

fix[1] /fiks/ *verb trans* **1** to place (something) somewhere and position or attach it firmly. **2** to make (something) firm or stable. **3a** to change (a substance) into a stable chemical compound or available form: *bacteria that fix nitrogen*. **b** to kill, harden, and preserve (a specimen) for microscopic study. **c** to make the image of (a photographic film) permanent by removing unused sensitive chemicals. **4** to decide upon or establish (a date, price, etc). **5** to fasten (a bayonet) to the muzzle of a rifle. **6** (*often* + with) to gaze intently at (somebody): *He fixed her with an accusing stare*. **7** to direct (one's eyes) steadily somewhere. **8** to set or place (something) conclusively: *That fixes the time of death at around 6.30 a.m.* **9** to assign (blame). **10** to make (something) possible: *I can fix it for you to meet him*. **11** to arrange (to do something): *I've fixed to go into town tomorrow*. **12** *NAmer* to be about to (do something): *We're fixing to leave soon*. **13** to repair or mend (something). **14** to spay or castrate (an animal). **15** *chiefly NAmer* to set (something) in order: *fix one's make-up*. **16** *chiefly NAmer* to get (something) ready, *esp* to prepare (food or drink): *Can I fix you a drink?* **17** *informal* to get even with (somebody). **18** to influence (e.g. a jury or the outcome of something) by illicit means. **19** *informal* to inject oneself with (a narcotic drug). ➤ *verb intrans* (+ on) to agree on something: *The group fixed on George as their leader*. ➤➤ **fixable** *adj*. [Middle English *fixen* from Latin *fixus*, past part. of *figere* to fasten]

fix[2] *noun* **1** *informal* a position of difficulty or embarrassment; a trying predicament: *I'm in a terrible fix*. **2** *informal*. **a** the act or an instance of injecting a narcotic drug. **b** a single dose of a narcotic drug. **c** *chiefly humorous* an intake of a stimulating substance or the exposure to something exciting or pleasurable: *I need my morning fix of strong coffee; He feels deprived if he doesn't have his weekly fix of going to the cinema*. ✳ **get a fix on 1** to determine the position of (a ship, etc) using bearings, observation, radio, etc. **2** *informal* to discover or understand the basic nature of (somebody or something).

fixate /'fiksayt, fik'sayt/ *verb trans* **1** to make (something) fixed, stable, or stationary. **2** to focus or direct one's eyes or attention on or towards (something). ➤ *verb intrans* **1** to become fixed, stable,

or stationary. **2** to focus or direct one's eyes or attention. ✳ **be fixated at** said of a person or somebody's libido: to be arrested at (a specified immature stage of psychosexual development): *He's fixated at the anal stage*. **be fixated on** to have an obsessive preoccupation with (somebody or something): *She has been fixated on one of her colleagues for years*. [Latin *fixus*, past part. of *figere* to fasten + -ATE[4]]

fixation /fik'saysh(ə)n/ *noun* **1** (*also* + on/with) an attachment to or preoccupation with (somebody or something), *esp* if obsessive or unhealthy: *develop a fixation on one's boss; His one fixation was neatness; a mother-fixation*. **2** a concentration of the libido on infantile forms of gratification: *fixation at the oral stage*. **3** concentration of the gaze on something, *esp* words in reading: *Fast readers will take in the sense of words even before fixation*. **4a** *esp* in plant biology, the process of fixing something chemically: *nitrogen fixation*. **b** the use of a chemical to stabilize a specimen, e.g. before examination under a microscope.

fixative /'fiksətiv/ *noun* **1** a substance added to a perfume, *esp* to prevent evaporation occurring too quickly. **2** a varnish used *esp* to protect crayon drawings. **3** a chemical used to fix living tissue, e.g. before examination under a microscope. ➤➤ **fixative** *adj*.

fixed *adj* **1** securely placed or fastened. **2** stationary: *the realization that the earth was a planet, not a fixed body*. **3** formed into a chemical compound: *fixed nitrogen*. **4** not subject to or capable of change or variation; settled: *fixed opinions; The message appears at fixed intervals*. **5a** intent: *a fixed stare*. **b** said of a smile: unvarying and artificial. **6** arranged or determined dishonestly: *a fixed boxing match*. ✳ **how one is fixed** *informal* (*often* + for) what one's position is, *esp* financially: *How are you fixed for cash?* **no fixed abode** no regular home. ➤➤ **fixedly** /'fiksidli/ *adv*, **fixedness** /'fik-sidnis/ *noun*.

fixed assets *pl noun* business assets, such as land, large-scale machinery, buildings, etc, that are put to long-term use and are not readily converted into cash: compare CURRENT ASSETS.

fixed capital *noun* business capital that has been invested in fixed assets.

fixed charge *noun* **1** a regularly recurring expense, e.g. rent, taxes, or interest, that must be met when due. **2** = FIXED COSTS. **3** a loan or liability for which specific assets of the borrowing company serve as security: compare FLOATING CHARGE.

fixed costs *pl noun* costs such as maintenance and rent that do not vary along with product or output: compare OVERHEAD[3], VARIABLE COST.

fixed-doh *adj* in tonic sol-fah, denoting the system of always treating C as doh, D as ray, etc, regardless of the key of the music: compare MOVABLE-DOH.

fixed income *noun* an income that does not vary, e.g. the income from an annuity that is not linked to inflation.

fixed odds *pl noun* in betting, e.g. on the results of football matches, the system of offering a predetermined amount per unit stake for a certain result or combination of results.

fixed oil *noun* a non-volatile oil from a plant or animal: compare ESSENTIAL OIL.

fixed-point *adj* denoting a mathematical notation, e.g. in a decimal system, in which the radix is fixed: compare FLOATING-POINT.

fixed satellite *noun* a satellite that orbits the earth in time with the earth's own rotation, so staying above the same spot on the earth's surface.

fixed star *noun* any of the stars so distant that they appear to remain fixed relative to one another.

fixed-wing *adj* denoting the conventional type of aircraft as distinct from the helicopter type with rotating blades.

fixer *noun* **1** a person who is adept at bringing about a desired result, e.g. by enabling somebody to get round the law or officialdom: *But in LA, man, I tell you, I'm even more of a high-achiever – all fizz and push, a fixer* — Martin Amis. **2** in photography, a substance used to fix a print.

fixings *pl noun* **1** *Brit* the fasteners such as nails, screws, nuts, and bolts, needed for a repair or construction job. **2** *NAmer* trimmings: *a turkey dinner with all the fixings*.

fixity *noun* the quality or state of being fixed or stable: *fixity of expression; fixity of purpose*.

fixture /'fikschə/ *noun* **1a** a household appliance or piece of equipment, e.g. a bath or toilet, that is fixed in position. **b** (*in pl*) items, e.g. sanitary ware, kitchen cupboards, worktops, etc, fixed in a property, that the owner is not legally entitled to remove should the property be sold: compare FITTING² (3). **2** *informal* somebody or something invariably present in a specified setting or long associated with a specified place or activity: *He has become a fixture as the England wicket-keeper.* **3** *chiefly Brit* a sporting event scheduled for a certain date or time. **4** *archaic* the process of fixing or condition of being fixed: *Frights, changes, horrors, divert and crack, rend and deracinate, the unity and married calm of states quite from their fixture* — Shakespeare. [modification of obsolete *fixure*, from late Latin *fixura*, from Latin *fixus*: see FIX¹]

fix up *verb trans* **1** (*often* + with) to provide (somebody) with something. **2** to organize or arrange (something). **3** to adapt, repair, or do up (a place) for a certain purpose.

fizgig /'fizgig/ *noun* **1** *Aus, informal* a police informer. **2** *archaic* a flirtatious young woman. **3** a firework or spinning top that makes a fizzing sound. [alteration of earlier *fisgig*, perhaps from obsolete *fise* intestinal wind + *gig* wanton girl, spinning top]

fizz¹ /fiz/ *verb intrans* **1** to make a hissing or sputtering sound. **2** said of a liquid: to produce bubbles of gas. [imitative]

fizz² *noun* **1** the act or sound of fizzing. **2** spirit or liveliness. **3a** *informal* an effervescent drink, e.g. sparkling wine. **b** the effervescence of sparkling wine, etc: *The fizz has gone out of this lemonade.*

fizzer *noun informal* **1** *Brit* something that is successful or sparkles. **2** *Aus, NZ* something that is a fiasco or dismal failure.

fizzle¹ /'fizl/ *verb intrans* to make a weak fizzing sound. [prob alteration of *fist* to break wind]

fizzle² *noun* the act, an instance, or the sound of fizzling.

fizzle out *verb intrans informal* to fail or end feebly, *esp* after a promising start.

fizzog /fi'zog/ *noun Brit, informal* a person's face; = PHIZOG.

fizzy *adj* (**fizzier, fizziest**) **1** said of a drink: effervescent. **2** said of somebody's personality: exuberant or sparkling. >> **fizzily** *adv*, **fizziness** *noun*.

fjeld /fyeld/ *noun* a barren plateau of the Scandinavian upland. [Norwegian *fjeld*, related to *fjell* mountain, FELL⁴]

FJI *abbr* Fiji (international vehicle registration).

fjord *or* **fiord** /fyawd, 'feeawd/ *noun* a narrow inlet of the sea, *esp* one between steep cliffs that was formed by the action of glaciers, e.g. in Norway or New Zealand. [Norwegian *fjord* from Old Norse *fjörthr*: compare FIRTH]

FL *abbr* **1** Florida (US postal abbreviation). **2** Fürstentum Liechtenstein (international vehicle registration for Liechtenstein). **3** Flight Lieutenant.

fl. *abbr* **1** floor. **2** floruit. **3** fluid.

Fla *abbr* Florida.

flab /flab/ *noun informal* soft loose body tissue. [back-formation from FLABBY]

flabbergast /'flabəgahst/ *verb trans informal* (*usu in passive*) to overwhelm (somebody) with shock or astonishment. [origin unknown]

flabby *adj* (**flabbier, flabbiest**) **1a** said of flesh: lacking resilience or firmness. **b** said of a person or body part: having flesh like this. **2** ineffective or feeble: *flabby reasoning.* >> **flabbily** *adv*, **flabbiness** *noun*. [alteration of *flappy*: see FLAP¹]

flaccid /'flaksid, 'flasid/ *adj* **1a** lacking normal or youthful firmness; flabby: *flaccid muscles.* **b** soft; hanging limply. **2** lacking vigour or force: *a flaccid handshake.* >> **flaccidity** /flak'siditi/ *noun*, **flaccidly** *adv*. [Latin *flaccidus* from *flaccus* flabby]

flack¹ /flak/ *noun NAmer, informal* a person who provides publicity, *esp* a press agent. >> **flackery** *noun*. [origin unknown]

flack² *verb trans NAmer, informal* to promote or publicize (a person or thing). > *verb intrans NAmer, informal* (*often* + for) to provide publicity.

flack³ *noun* see FLAK.

flacon /fla'konh (*French* flakɔ̃)/ *noun* a small, often decorative bottle with a stopper, *esp* one for perfume. [French *flacon* from late Latin *flasca, flasco*: see FLASK]

flag¹ /flag/ *noun* **1** a usu rectangular piece of fabric of distinctive design that is used as an identifying symbol, e.g. of a nation, or as a signalling device, *esp* one flown from a single vertical staff: *flying the Norwegian flag.* **2** a similarly designed device used to give a starting or finishing signal at motorcycle or car races: *and the chequered flag comes down for the winner of the 1997 Grand Prix.* **3** a flag-shaped marker indicating a hole on a golf course, or a smaller device for pinpointing positions on a map. **4** a small paper flag on a pin, given *esp* formerly, as a badge to contributors to a charity on a flag day. **5** something, e.g. a strip of paper inserted into an opening of a book or a piece of coding inserted into a computer file, used as a marker. **6** *NAmer* the name of a newspaper in its front-page typographical form; = MASTHEAD¹ (2). **7** the part of a taximeter that projects upwards when the taxi is for hire. **8** the underside of an upturned tail, *esp* that of a deer. * **fly the flag** said of a ship: to be registered in a specific country and sail under its flag. See also FLAG OF CONVENIENCE. **keep the flag flying** to continue to represent or promote the interests of one's country, organization, etc. **put the flags/flag out** to celebrate. **wave/show/carry the flag** **1** to represent one's country. **2** to support one's organization by representing it in public. **wrap oneself in the flag** *NAmer* to make an ostentatious display of patriotism. [origin uncertain; perhaps related to obsolete *flag* drooping]

flag² *verb trans* (**flagged, flagging**) **1** to mark (a page, word, or passage) with a paper strip or sticker or with a piece of coding. **2** to direct (e.g. the driver of a vehicle, competitor in a race, etc) somewhere by signalling with the hands or a flag: *flag the starters off; He flagged me into the kerb.* **3** to provide or decorate (something) with a flag or flags. **4** to send (a message) using flags, e.g. in semaphore. >> **flagger** *noun*.

flag³ *verb intrans* (**flagged, flagging**) **1** to grow tired; to lose energy: *Some of the marchers were beginning to flag; Our spirits flagged.* **2** to become feeble, less interesting, or less active; to decline: *Conversation flagged; Interest flagged.* [perhaps from obsolete *flag* drooping]

flag⁴ *noun* **1** a hard evenly stratified stone that splits into flat pieces suitable for paving. **2** a slab of this; = FLAGSTONE (1). [Middle English *flagge* sod, flag, from Old Norse *flaga* slab]

flag⁵ *verb trans* (**flagged, flagging**) to lay (e.g. a pavement) with flags: *a stone-flagged passageway.*

flag⁶ *noun* any of various plants that have long bladelike leaves and grow near water or on damp ground: *Iris pseudacorus* and other species. [Middle English *flagge* reed, rush, of Germanic origin]

flag boat *noun* a boat serving as a marker in sailing races.

flag captain *noun* the captain of a flagship.

Flag Day *noun* in the USA, 14 June, the anniversary of the day on which the Stars and Stripes was adopted as the national flag in 1777.

flag day *noun* a collection day held by a charitable concern, when its helpers stand with collection boxes in the street, usu giving contributors paper badges, formerly in the form of flags attached to a pin, to record their contribution.

flag down *verb trans* to direct (a driver or vehicle) to stop by signalling with the hands: *A policeman flagged me down and asked to see my licence.*

flagella *noun* pl of FLAGELLUM.

flagellant /'flajilənt/ *noun* **1** a person who scourges himself or herself as a public penance. **2** a person who responds sexually either to being beaten by somebody or to beating another person. >> **flagellant** *adj*, **flagellantism** *noun*. [Latin *flagellant-, flagellans*, present part. of *flagellare*: see FLAGELLATE¹]

flagellate¹ /'flajilayt/ *verb trans* to whip or flog (somebody), *esp* as a religious punishment or for sexual gratification. >> **flagellation** /-'laysh(ə)n/ *noun*, **flagellator** *noun*, **flagellatory** /-lət(ə)ri/ *adj*. [Latin *flagellatus*, past part. of *flagellare* to whip, from *flagellum* whip, flail, dimin. of *flagrum* scourge]

flagellate² /'flajilət/ *adj* **1** having flagella. **2** shaped like a flagellum. [FLAGELLUM + -ATE³]

flagellate³ /'flajilət/ *noun* any of a group of protozoans (minute single-celled animals; see PROTOZOAN) that swim by means of a FLAGELLUM (thread-like projection) or flagella.

flagellated /'flajilaytid/ *adj* = FLAGELLATE².

flagellum /flə'jeləm/ *noun* (*pl* **flagella** /-lə/ *or* **flagellums**) a thread-like projection of a cell membrane in various organisms, *esp* one of whip-like form by means of which protozoans, spermatozoa, and bacteria swim. >> **flagellar** *adj*. [Latin *flagellum* whip, shoot of a plant]

flageolet[1] /ˈflajəˈlet/ *noun* a small recorder-like instrument with four finger holes and two thumb holes. [French *flageolet* from Old French *flajol* flute, ultimately from Latin *flare* to blow]

flageolet[2] *noun* = FRENCH BEAN. [French *flageolet*, modification of Provençal *faioulet*, prob ultimately from Latin *phaseolus* kidney bean]

flag fall *noun Aus* the minimum hiring charge for a taxi, to which the rate per kilometre is added.

flagitious /fləˈjishəs/ *adj* very wicked, *esp* criminally so; villainous: *The raison d'état, meaning the convenience of the government ... was deemed a sufficient explanation and excuse for the most flagitious crimes* — John Stuart Mill. ⟩⟩ **flagitiously** *adv*, **flagitiousness** *noun*. [Middle English from Latin *flagitiosus*, from *flagitium* something shameful or disgraceful]

flag lieutenant *noun* a naval officer serving an admiral in the capacity of aide-de-camp.

flagman *noun* (*pl* **flagmen**) a person in any of various situations whose job is to make signals with a flag.

flag of convenience *noun* the flag of a country under which a ship is registered in order to avoid the taxes and regulations of the ship-owner's home country.

flag officer *noun* any of the officers in the navy or coast guard above captain. [because they are entitled to display a flag with one or more stars indicating their rank]

flag of truce *noun* a white flag carried or displayed to an enemy as an invitation to conference or parley.

flagon /ˈflagən/ *noun* **1a** a large usu metal or pottery vessel with a handle and spout and often a lid, used *esp* for holding liquids at table. **b** a large squat short-necked bottle, often with one or two ear-shaped handles, in which cider, wine, etc are sold. **2** the contents of or quantity contained in a flagon. [Middle English via French *flascon, flacon* bottle, from late Latin *flascon-, flasco*: see FLASK]

flagpole *noun* a tall pole on which to hoist a flag.

flag rank *noun* the rank of a flag officer.

flagrant /ˈflaygrənt/ *adj* conspicuous; outrageous: *flagrant neglect of duty.* ⟩⟩⟩ **flagrance** *noun*, **flagrancy** /-si/ *noun*, **flagrantly** *adv*. [Latin *flagrant-, flagrans*, present part. of *flagrare* to burn]

Usage note

flagrant or blatant? See note at BLATANT.

flagrante delicto /fləˌgranti diˈliktoh/ *adv* = IN FLAGRANTE DELICTO.

flagship *noun* **1** the ship that carries the commander of a fleet and flies his or her flag. **2** something that is considered the pride of an organization, e.g. a leading product that most of all establishes its public reputation.

flagstaff *noun* (*pl* **flagstaffs** *or* **flagstaves**) = FLAGPOLE.

flagstone *noun* **1** a flat slab of stone used for paving; = FLAG[4] (2). **2** a smooth-textured stratified rock that can be split into slabs. ⟩⟩⟩ **flagstoned** *adj*.

flag-waving *noun informal* a passionate appeal to patriotic or partisan sentiment; jingoism. ⟩⟩⟩ **flag-waver** *noun*.

flail[1] /flayl/ *noun* a threshing implement consisting of a stout short free-swinging stick attached to a wooden handle. [Middle English *fleil, flail*, partly from Old English and partly from early French *flaiel*, ultimately from late Latin *flagellum*: see FLAGELLATE[1]]

flail[2] *verb intrans* **1** (*often* + about/around) to wave one's arms and legs about violently; to flounder or thresh about: *flail around in the water.* **2** said of the arms: to wave about violently. ⟩⟩⟩ *verb trans* **1** to thresh (grain). **2** to strike (something) with a threshing action: *with oars flailing the water.* **3** to swing (one's arms) about wildly: *flailing his arms to ward off the insects.*

flair /fleə/ *noun* **1** (+ for) a natural aptitude, ability, or talent for a certain thing: *have a flair for design.* **2** style, originality, and taste. [French *flair*, literally 'sense of smell', ultimately from Latin *fragrare* to smell sweet]

flak *or* **flack** /flak/ *noun* **1** the fire from anti-aircraft guns. **2** *informal* heavy criticism or opposition. [German *Flak*, contraction of *Fliegerabwehrkanone*, from *Flieger* flyer + *Abwehr* defence + *Kanone* gun]

flake[1] /flayk/ *noun* **1a** a small loose mass or particle. **b** a snowflake. **2a** a thin flattened piece or layer; a chip. **b** a sliver of flint, etc chipped from a core for use as a tool, *esp* one used during the Stone Age. **3** a pipe tobacco of small irregularly cut pieces. **4** *NAmer, informal* a crazy person. [Middle English, of Scandinavian origin]

flake[2] *verb intrans* **1** (+ off) to come away in flakes: *The paint had begun to flake off.* **2** to separate or break up into flakes. ⟩⟩⟩ *verb trans* **1** to separate or chip (something) into flakes: *Flake the fish and combine it with the mashed potato.* **2** to coat or cover (something) with flakes or flaky parts. ⟩⟩⟩ **flaker** *noun.*

flake[3] *noun* a platform, rack, tray, etc for drying fish or produce. [Middle English in the sense 'hurdle', from Old Norse *flaki*]

flake[4] *noun* = FAKE[4].

flake[5] *verb trans* = FAKE[5].

flake out *verb intrans informal* to collapse or fall asleep from exhaustion. [perhaps from obsolete *flake* to become languid, variant of FLAG[3]]

flake white *noun* a pure white pigment made from flakes of white lead and used *esp* in oil painting.

flak jacket /flak/ *noun* a jacket of heavy fabric containing shields, e.g. of metal or plastic, for protection, *esp* against enemy fire.

flaky /ˈflayki/ *adj* (**flakier, flakiest**) **1** consisting of flakes: *of a flaky texture.* **2** tending to flake: *dry, flaky skin.* **3** *chiefly NAmer, informal* eccentric; daft; crazy. ⟩⟩⟩ **flakily** *adv*, **flakiness** *noun.*

flaky pastry *noun* rich pastry composed of numerous very thin layers, used for pies, tarts, etc.

flam /flam/ *noun* a drumbeat of two strokes, the first being a very quick GRACE NOTE (extra decorative note). [prob imitative]

flambé[1] /ˈflombay (*French* flãbe)/ *adj* (*used after a noun*) said of food: sprinkled with brandy, rum, etc and ignited. [French *flambé*, past part. of *flamber* to flame, singe, from Old French *flambe*: see FLAME[1]]

flambé[2] *verb trans* (**flambés, flambéed, flambéing**) to sprinkle (food) with brandy, rum, etc and ignite it.

flambeau /ˈflamboh/ *noun* (*pl* **flambeaux** /ˈflamboh(z)/ *or* **flambeaus** /ˈflambohz/) **1** a flaming torch, e.g. for carrying in a procession. **2** a large ornamental branched candlestick. [French *flambeau* from Old French *flambe*: see FLAME[1]]

flamboyant[1] /flamˈboyənt/ *adj* **1** given to dashing display or ostentatious exuberance: *a flamboyant lifestyle.* **2** said of clothing: colourful or exotic. **3** ornate; florid: *flamboyant handwriting.* **4** (*often* **Flamboyant**) relating to or denoting a style of French Gothic architectural decoration characterized by wavy curves suggesting flames. ⟩⟩⟩ **flamboyance** *noun*, **flamboyancy** /-si/ *noun*, **flamboyantly** *adv*. [French *flamboyant*, present part. of *flamboyer* to flame, from Old French *flambe*: see FLAME[1]]

flamboyant[2] *noun* a Madagascan tree with attractive scarlet flowers, used as a decorative street tree: *Delonix regia.*

flame[1] /flaym/ *noun* **1** a bright mass of burning gas coming from something that is on fire or a single point or tongue of this: *a wall of flame; Flames leaped into the air.* **2** the fierce intensity or ardour of an emotion, etc: *the flame of passion.* **3** a brilliant reddish orange colour. **4** *informal* an abusive message sent by email or appearing on the notice board of a newsgroup, etc: *post a flame on the Internet.* **5** the spirit of something, e.g. a movement, seen as a lamp needing to be tended: *keeping alive the flame of old-style socialism.* ✳ **burst into flames** to start burning fiercely. **go up in flames** to be destroyed by fire. **in flames** on fire; burning. **old flame** *dated* a former admirer or sweetheart. ⟩⟩⟩ **flameless** *adj*, **flamelike** *adj*, **flamy** *adj*. [Middle English *flaume, flaumbe* via Old French *flambe* from Latin *flammula*, dimin. of *flamma* flame]

flame[2] *verb intrans* **1** to burn vigorously; to blaze: *A wood fire flamed in the hearth.* **2** said of an emotion: to be felt or displayed with an intensity: *Their passion flamed but died again.* **3** said of the face or cheeks: to grow fiery red with anger or embarrassment. **4** to send an abusive message by email or other electronic means. ⟩⟩⟩ *verb trans* **1** to apply a flame to (something), e.g. to set alight (spirits used in cooking) or flambé (food). **2** *informal* to send (somebody) an abusive email message or post an abusive message about (somebody) on a computer network.

flame cell *noun* a hollow cell that has a tuft of cilia (small beating hairs; see CILIUM) and is part of the excretory system of various lower invertebrates such as flatworms. [so called because the cilia resemble tongues of flame]

flame gun *noun* a hand-held device that throws out a jet of flame, used *esp* for killing garden weeds.

flamen /'flaymen/ *noun* (*pl* **flamens** *or* **flamines** /'flaymineez/) in ancient Rome, any of 15 priests who each served a particular deity. [Latin *flamen* priest]

flamenco /flə'mengkoh/ *noun* (*pl* **flamencos**) **1** a vivacious style of Spanish guitar music, often accompanied by singing, dancing, and hand clapping. **2** a dance performed to this music. [Spanish *flamenco* like a gypsy, literally 'Flemish', from early Dutch *Vlaminc* Fleming]

flameout /'flaymowt/ *noun* **1** the failure of a jet engine in flight caused by its flame being extinguished and resulting in a loss of power. **2** *chiefly NAmer, informal* any spectacular failure.

flame out *verb intrans* **1** said of a jet engine: to fail during flight as a result of the extinction of its flame. **2** *NAmer, informal* to fail spectacularly.

flameproof[1] *adj* **1** said of fabric: rendered non-flammable by treatment. **2** said of cookware: suitable for use in an oven or on a hob.

flameproof[2] *verb trans* to make (a fabric or cookware) flameproof.

flamer *noun informal* a person who sends abusive messages by email or other electronic means.

flamethrower *noun* a weapon that expels a burning stream of liquid.

flame tree *noun* any of various ornamental trees with vivid scarlet flowers: *Brachychiton acerifolius* (of Australia) and other species.

flamines /'flaymineez/ *noun* pl of FLAMEN.

flaming *adj* **1** emitting flames or on fire; blazing. **2** brilliantly hot or bright: *flaming June*; *flaming red hair*. **3** full of fury or ardour: *a flaming passion*; *We had a flaming row*. **4** *informal* used to express irritation: *That flaming cat's brought in a dead bird.* ⟫ **flamingly** *adv*.

flamingo /flə'minggoh/ *noun* (*pl* **flamingos** *or* **flamingoes**) any of several species of web-footed wading birds with long legs and neck, curved beak, and rosy-white plumage with scarlet and black markings: family Phoenicopteridae. [Portuguese *flamengo* from Spanish *flamenco* Fleming, perhaps in jocular reference to the pink complexion of the Flemings]

flammable /'flaməbl/ *adj* readily combustible; easily set on fire; = INFLAMMABLE[1] (I). ⟫ **flammability** /-'biliti/ *noun*. [Latin *flammare* to flame, set on fire, from *flamma* FLAME[1]]

Usage note
flammable *or* **inflammable?** Although *flammable* and *inflammable* may appear to be opposites, in fact they have the same meaning. Since *inflammable* may seem to mean 'not flammable' (from the prefix *in*- meaning 'not' + *flammable*) and because of the risk of fire and danger to life, use of the word *flammable* is increasingly preferred, especially in technical contexts: *highly flammable solvents*. The preferred negative is *non-flammable*: *non-flammable clothing*.

flan /flan/ *noun* **1** a pastry or cake case containing a sweet or savoury filling. **2** a metal disc from which a coin, medal, etc is made. [French *flan* from Old French *flaon*, from late Latin *fladon-*, *flado* flat cake]

flâneur /fla'nuh (*French* flanœ:r)/ *noun* an aimless person; an idler. [French *flâneur*, from *flâner* to stroll, saunter]

flange /flanj/ *noun* a projecting rib or rim on something for strengthening or guiding it, or for attaching it to another object: *a flange on a pipe*. ⟫ **flanged** *adj*, **flangeless** *adj*. [perhaps alteration of *flanch* a curving device on a heraldic shield, prob ultimately from French *flanc*: see FLANK[1]]

flanger *noun* a device used in electronic sound reproduction to adjust a sound signal so as to alter the sound of an instrument, e.g. in mixing popular music.

flanging *noun* **1** in sound reproduction, the alteration of a sound signal by means of a flanger. **2** the fitting of a flange to an object.

flank[1] /flangk/ *noun* **1a** the side of an animal between the ribs and the hip. **b** a cut of meat from this part. **c** the upper part of a person's buttock. **2** the side of something large, such as a mountain: *the snowy flanks of Ben Alder*. **3** the right or left of a formation of troops or ships: *attack on the left flank*. **4** = WING[1] (7B). [Middle English from Old French *flanc*, of Germanic origin]

flank[2] *verb trans* **1** (*usu in passive*) to be at the side of (a thing or person); to border (it): *a gateway flanked by a tower on either side*; *He stood waiting, flanked by two footmen*. **2** to attack or threaten the flank of (a formation). **3** to protect the flank of (a formation).

flanker *noun* **1** in rugby, an attacking player positioned on the outside of the second row of the scrum. Also called WING FORWARD. **2** in American football, an offensive back at the outside of an end. **3** a military fortification for protecting a flank.

flank forward *noun* = FLANK[1] (4).

flannel[1] /'flanl/ *noun* **1a** a twilled loosely woven wool or worsted fabric with a slightly napped surface. **b** (*used before a noun*) made of flannel: *flannel sheets*. **c** (*in pl*) garments, *esp* trousers, made of flannel: *a pair of flannels*. **2** *Brit* a small square of towelling used for washing, *esp* the face; = FACECLOTH. **3** *chiefly Brit, informal* talk that is intended to deceive or to disguise a lack of knowledge or understanding. ⟫ **flannelly** *adj*. [Middle English *flaunneol* woollen cloth or garment; earlier history unknown]

flannel[2] *verb* (**flannelled, flannelling**, *NAmer* **flanneled, flanneling**) ⟫ *verb intrans chiefly Brit, informal* to speak or write flannel, *esp* with intent to deceive. ⟫ *verb trans* **1** *chiefly Brit, informal* to make (one's way) or persuade (somebody) to one's advantage by flannelling. **2** to clean, polish, or rub (something) using flannel. **3** to cover, wrap, or clothe (something or somebody) in flannel.

flannelette /flanə'let/ *noun* a napped cotton fabric resembling flannel.

flap[1] /flap/ *noun* **1** something broad or flat, flexible or hinged, and usu thin, that hangs loose or projects freely, e.g.: **a** an extended part forming a closure, e.g. of an envelope or carton. **b** a movable control surface on an aircraft wing for increasing lift during takeoff or drag during landing. **2a** the motion of something broad and flexible, e.g. a sail. **b** the up-and-down motion of a wing, *esp* of a bird. **3** *informal* a state of excitement or panicky confusion; an uproar or an instance of this: *They're getting into a terrible flap about the schedule.* **4** a blow or stroke made using a broad flat object; a slap. ⟫ **flappy** *adj*. [Middle English *flappe* blow, slap, prob of imitative origin]

flap[2] *verb* (**flapped, flapping**) ⟫ *verb trans* **1** to shake (e.g. a piece of paper or cloth) up and down or from side to side, usu creating a noise: *flap a towel*. **2** to wave (one's hand) about with a loose wrist. **3** said of a bird or bat: to move (its wings) up and down in flight. ⟫ *verb intrans* **1** said of e.g. a flag, sail, or loose garment: to move to and fro noisily: *Her wet skirt flapped round her ankles*. **2** said of a bird or bat: to beat its wings: *the sound of bats flapping about*. **3** *informal* to get into a panic: *Don't flap*.

flapdoodle /'flapdoohdl/ *noun chiefly NAmer, informal* nonsense. [origin unknown]

flapjack *noun* **1** a thick soft biscuit made with oats and syrup. **2** *NAmer* a pancake. [FLAP[2] + the name *Jack*]

flapper *noun informal* a fashionable young woman of the 1920s, typically with bobbed hair, wearing the cloche hats and knee-length loose-fitting dresses of the period, and flouting the conventions of her mother's generation in her behaviour: *I paid violent and unusual attention to a flapper all through the meal in order to make you jealous. She's probably in her cabin writing reams about me to a fellow-flapper* — Saki.

flap valve *noun* a valve that is opened and closed by a hinged plate.

flare[1] /fleə/ *verb intrans* **1** to shine or blaze with a sudden flame: *a match flared in the darkness*. **2** (*usu* + up) to become suddenly angry: *flare up at the slightest provocation*. **3** (*usu* + up) said of violence, etc: to break out: *Fighting flared up again*. **4** (*usu* + out) said of trousers, a skirt, sleeves, etc: to get wider towards the hem. **5** said of the nostrils: to widen, e.g. as a sign of anger; to dilate. ⟫ *verb trans* **1** to cause (something, *esp* one's nostrils) to widen. **2** to ignite and burn off (waste gas, etc). [origin unknown]

flare[2] *noun* **1** a sudden unsteady glaring light or flame. **2** a fire or blaze of light used to signal, illuminate, or attract attention, or a device used to produce this: *The aircraft dropped flares to illuminate the target*. **3** a sudden outburst, *esp* of anger: *'But I'm in charge!' he snapped, with an uncharacteristic flare of anger*. **4** a temporary outburst of energy, e.g.: **a** from a small area of the sun's surface. Also called SOLAR FLARE. **b** from a star, often amounting to an increase of several magnitudes in its brightness. **5** a flame, usu at the top of a stack, that burns off unwanted gas at an oil refinery or oil well. **6** a gradual widening of a skirt, trouser leg, sleeve, etc towards the hem: *jeans with wide flares*. **7** an area of flushed skin surrounding an inflamed or raised area. **8** in photography, light resulting from reflection, e.g. between lens surfaces, or a fogged area on a negative resulting from this.

flared *adj* said of trousers or a skirt: widening towards the hem.

flarepath *noun* an illuminated area enabling aircraft to land or take off in low visibility.

flares *pl noun* trousers that become wider towards the ankle: *Flares are making a comeback.*

flarestack *noun* a device, e.g. at an oil well, for burning off unwanted material.

flare star *noun* a faint red dwarf star that intermittently brightens suddenly by up to 100 times in a few minutes, prob as a result of intense flares.

flare-up *noun* an instance or renewal of violence, quarrelling, fighting, etc: *another flare-up on the border; a little flare-up at the office today.*

flash[1] /flash/ *verb intrans* **1** to shine briefly with a bright light, once or repeatedly: *Lightning flashed and thunder rolled.* **2** said of the eyes: to widen and brighten with anger or other strong emotion. **3** to appear suddenly: *An error message flashed onto the screen.* **4** to rush or dart: *Cars flashed past; An idea flashed into her head.* **5** (often + by/past) said of time: to pass quickly: *The days flashed by.* **6** *informal* said of a man: to show his genitals in public. ➤ *verb trans* **1** to shine (a bright light) briefly, once or repeatedly: *flash one's headlights.* **2** to display (something) ostentatiously: *flash one's money about; flashing her engagement ring at us.* **3** to direct (a smile or other look or expression) at somebody: *He flashed a smile in my direction.* **4** to broadcast (a message) instantaneously: *News of her death was flashed around the world in seconds.* [Middle English *flasche* to splash, prob imitative]

flash[2] *noun* **1** a sudden burst of light: *a flash of lightning.* **2** a sudden burst of perception, emotion, etc: *have a flash of intuition.* **3** a camera attachment that produces a flash of light for indoor photography. **4** a fleeting glimpse or appearance: *There was a flash of white as the bird swooped.* **5** a quick-spreading flame or momentary intense outburst of radiant heat, e.g. from a nuclear explosion. **6** a brief news report, *esp* on radio or television: *a bad weather flash.* **7** a rush of water released to permit passage of a boat over a weir, etc. **8** a thin ridge on a cast or forged article, resulting from the hot metal, plastic, etc penetrating between the two parts of the mould. **9** a band round a book cover, advertising an attractive selling point. **10** an armband or piece of coloured cloth worn on a uniform as a distinguishing symbol. **11** *archaic* the language of the criminal underworld: *His comrades explained in flash* — Thomas Hood. ✳ **flash in the pan** a sudden success that cannot be repeated [from the firing of the gunpowder in the pan of a musket]. **in a flash** very quickly: *all over in a flash.*

flash[3] *adj* **1** *informal* vulgarly ostentatious: *They consider their neighbours to be rather flash; a flash new sports car.* **2** *archaic* relating to the criminal underworld or its language: *I used all the flash words myself just when I pleased* — Oliver Wendell Holmes. **3** said *esp* of a process such as freezing: carried out very quickly.

flash[4] *noun* a water-filled hollow produced by subsidence, *esp* following mineral extraction. [Middle English from Old French *flache* marshy place, ultimately from early Dutch *vlacke*]

flashback *noun* **1** an interruption of the chronological sequence in a literary, theatrical, or cinematic work by the evocation of earlier events. **2a** a sudden memory of a past event, often of a traumatic experience. **b** a sudden recurrence of the effects of a hallucinogenic drug, *esp* LSD, some considerable time after the drug was taken. **3** a burst of flame back or out to an unwanted position, e.g. in a furnace.

flashboard *noun* one or more boards projecting above the top of a dam to increase its height and therefore capacity.

flashbulb *noun* an electric flash lamp in which metal foil or wire is burned, used e.g. in a flashgun.

flash burn *noun* a burn resulting from momentary exposure to intense radiant heat.

flash card *noun* a card that has a word or words on it, used in some methods of teaching reading.

flashcube *noun* a small cube incorporating four flashbulbs for a camera.

flasher *noun* **1a** a light, e.g. a traffic signal or car light, that catches the attention by flashing. **b** a device for automatically flashing a light. **2** *informal* a person who commits the offence of indecent exposure.

flash flood *noun* a brief but heavy local flood usu resulting from rainfall.

flash-freeze *verb trans* to freeze (food) so rapidly that ice crystals cannot form. ➤➤ **flash-freezing** *noun.*

flashgun *noun* a device for holding and operating a photographic flashlight.

flashing *noun* sheet metal used in waterproofing a roof or the angle between a vertical surface and a roof. [from FLASH[1] in the sense 'to cover with a thin layer']

flash lamp *noun* **1** a portable flashing light. **2** a usu electric lamp for producing flashlight for taking photographs.

flashlight *noun* **1** a usu regularly flashing light used for signalling, e.g. in a lighthouse. **2** a sudden bright artificial light used in taking photographic pictures, or a photograph taken with this. **3** *chiefly NAmer* an electric torch.

flash memory *noun* computer memory that retains data in the absence of a power supply.

flashover *noun* **1** an intense electrical arc produced by an accidental short circuit. **2** a sudden airborne transmission of fire to another object under conditions of intense heat.

flash point *noun* **1** the temperature at which vapour from a volatile substance ignites. **2** a point in a situation or a place at which violence or anger erupts.

flash suit *noun* a suit of protective heatproof clothing.

flashtube *noun* a gas discharge tube that produces very brief intense flashes of light and is used *esp* in photography.

flashy *adj* (**flashier, flashiest**) **1** ostentatious or flamboyant, *esp* beyond the bounds of good taste. **2** superficially brilliant: *a flashy rhetorician* — De Quincey. ➤➤ **flashily** *adv,* **flashiness** *noun.*

flask /flahsk/ *noun* **1** a conical, spherical, etc narrow-necked usu glass container used for wine or in a laboratory. **2** a broad flat bottle, usu of metal or leather-covered glass, used to carry alcohol or other drinks on the person; = HIP FLASK. **3** = VACUUM FLASK. **4** a lead-lined container for nuclear waste. [Middle English *flasce* cask, from late Latin *flasca, flasco,* prob of Germanic origin, the sense 'glass container' arriving in the late 17th cent., influenced by Italian *fiasco* bottle]

flat[1] /flat/ *adj* (**flatter, flattest**) **1** said of a surface: **a** horizontal; not sloping; level. **b** broad and smooth, without raised or hollow areas. **2a** having a broad surface and little thickness: *a flat case.* **b** shallow: *a flat dish.* **3a** said of shoes: without a raised heel. **b** said of shoe heels: low. **4a** clearly unmistakable; downright: *give a flat denial.* **b** fixed or absolute: *charge a flat rate.* **5a** lacking animation; dull or monotonous; inactive: *feeling flat; Trade is a bit flat just now.* **b** having lost effervescence or sparkle: *flat beer.* **6a** said of a tyre: lacking air; deflated. **b** said of a battery: completely or partially discharged. **7a** said of a musical note: lowered a semitone in pitch. **b** said of a key: having one or more flats in the signature: *a piece in B flat.* **c** lower than the proper musical pitch. **8a** having a low trajectory: *throw a fast flat ball.* **b** said of a tennis ball or shot: hit squarely without spin. **9a** uniform in colour. **b** said of a painting: lacking illusion of depth. **c** said of a photograph: lacking contrast. **d** said of lighting for photography: not emphasizing shadows or contours. **e** said *esp* of paint: having a matt finish. ✳ **that's flat** *informal* that's final; there's to be no more argument: *I'm not taking part and that's flat.* ➤➤ **flatness** *noun,* **flattish** *adj.* [Middle English from Old Norse *flatr*]

flat[2] *noun* **1** a flat part or surface: *the flat of one's hand.* **2** (*in pl*). **a** an area of level ground; a plain. **b** mudflats. **3** *chiefly NAmer* (*in pl*) shoes with no heel or a low heel. **4a** a musical note one semitone lower than a specified or particular note. **b** the character (♭) indicating this. **5** a flat piece of theatrical scenery. **6** any of the sides of a nut or bolt head. **7** a flat tyre. **8** (*often* **the Flat**) the flat-racing season: *the end of the Flat.* ✳ **on the flat 1** on level ground; not uphill or downhill. **2** (**on the Flat**) said of a horse race: run on a course without jumps.

flat[3] *adv* **1a** on or against a flat surface: *Keep your feet flat on the ground.* **b** so as to be spread out; at full length: *lie flat; fall flat on the ground.* **c** with the broad surfaces, as distinct from the edges, facing up and down: *lay the tiles flat.* **2** below the proper musical pitch: *sing flat.* **3** *informal.* **a** wholly; completely: *flat broke.* **b** absolutely and emphatically: *turn an offer down flat.* **4** not a moment longer than the time specified; exactly: *do a journey in two hours flat.* ✳ **fall flat** to fail to achieve the intended effect: *The joke fell flat.* **fall flat for** *informal* to fall in love with (somebody). **flat out** as hard or as fast as possible: *working flat out; a flat-out rush to finish his thesis.*

flat[4] *verb trans* (**flatted, flatting**) **1** *NAmer* to lower (a note) by a semitone. **2** *archaic* to flatten (something).

flat[5] *noun* a self-contained set of rooms within a larger building used as a dwelling. *NAmer* Also called APARTMENT (1). ➤➤ **flatlet** /ˈflatlit/ *noun.* [alteration of Scots *flet* floor, dwelling, from Old English]

flatbed *adj* **1** denoting a printing press in which the FORME (assembled type in its frame) is carried on a horizontal surface. **2** *chiefly NAmer* denoting a truck or lorry with a flat sideless load-carrying platform. **3** denoting a scanner or plotter with a flat glass surface that produces digitized images of documents placed on it.

flatboat *noun* any boat with a flat bottom for use in shallow water, *esp* a square-ended one for transporting goods on a canal.

flatbread *noun chiefly NAmer* thin flat usu unleavened bread.

flatcar *noun NAmer* a railway freight car with no sides or roof.

flatette /flaˈtet/ *noun Aus* a very small flat.

flatfeet *noun* pl of FLATFOOT.

flat feet *pl noun* (*treated as pl or sing.*) a condition in which the arches of the insteps of the feet are flattened so that the entire sole rests on the ground and the knees are close together, with the ankles apart and toes turned outwards.

flat-fell[1] *adj* denoting a seam, e.g. on a shirt, whose raw edges are turned under to one side and sewn flat, so that the line of stitching is visible on the outer side of the garment.

flat-fell[2] *verb trans* to turn under and sew down the raw edges of (a seam); = FELL[2] (3). [FLAT[1] + FELL[2] in the sense 'to sew down']

flat-felled *adj* = FLAT-FELL[1].

flat file *noun* **1** a computer file from which all word-processing and formatting characters have been removed, used *esp* for greater portability between different operating systems and for easier transmission by email. **2** a computer file containing records with no embedded or hierarchical structure.

flatfish *noun* (*pl* **flatfishes** *or collectively* **flatfish**) a marine fish, e.g. a flounder or sole, that swims on one side and has both eyes on the upper surface of its horizontally flattened body: order Pleuronectiformes.

flatfoot *noun* (*pl* **flatfoots** *or* **flatfeet**) *informal, dated* a police officer.

flat-footed *adj* **1** affected with flat feet. **2** *informal.* **a** inept; clumsy: *a flat-footed attempt to comfort her.* **b** complete; unequivocal: *a flat-footed refusal.* **c** off guard or unprepared: *His questions caught me flat-footed.* ➤➤ **flat-footedly** *adv,* **flat-footedness** *noun.*

flat-four *adj* denoting an engine that has two pairs of horizontal cylinders, one pair on each side of the crankshaft. ➤➤ **flat four** *noun.*

flathead[1] *noun* (*pl* **flatheads** *or collectively* **flathead**) **1** any of several species of tropical marine fishes with eyes on the top of their flattened heads. They often lie just under the surface of the seabed with only the eyes visible: family Platycephalidae. **2** (**Flathead**) a member of a group of indigenous peoples inhabiting the north-western USA, formerly believed to have flattened their children's heads with weights.

flathead[2] *adj NAmer* **1** denoting a countersunk screw. **2** denoting an engine in which the valves and spark plugs are in the cylinder block rather than the cylinder head.

flatiron *noun* an iron heated in the fire or on a stove, formerly used for pressing laundry.

flatline *verb intrans informal* **1** said of a person: to die. **2** said of a plan, project, etc: to fail or be ineffectual. ➤➤ **flatliner** *noun.* [from the straight line on the heart monitor when cardiac activity ceases]

flatly *adv* **1** emphatically and without compromise: *They flatly refused to listen to our views.* **2** expressionlessly; tonelessly: *'She said he was a god.' Miss Tita gave me this information flatly, without expression* — Henry James.

flatmate *noun Brit* a person who shares a flat with one.

flatpack *noun chiefly Brit* **1a** (*used before a noun*) relating to or denoting furniture or equipment that is sold in pieces packed into a flat box, for assembly by the purchaser: *a flatpack desk.* **b** an item sold or bought in this form. **2** in electronics, a part for an integrated circuit in the form of a small thin rectangular sealed unit. ➤➤ **flatpacked** *adj.*

flat race *noun* a race for horses on a course without jumps: compare HURDLE[1] (2B), STEEPLECHASE (1A). ➤➤ **flat racing** *noun.*

flat spin *noun* **1** an aerial manoeuvre or flight condition consisting of a spin in which the aircraft is roughly horizontal. **2** *informal* a state of extreme agitation: *They always seem to be in a flat spin.*

flat spot *noun* in a machine, engine, etc, an area of poor performance.

flatten *verb* (**flattened, flattening**) ➤ *verb trans* **1** (*also* + out) to make (something) flat or flatter: *Flatten the dough.* **2** to press (oneself) flush against a surface: *She flattened herself against the wall.* **3** to raze (a building) to the ground. **4** to knock (a person) to the ground with a blow. **5** to overcome, subdue, or crush (somebody): *It takes more than a little setback to flatten him.* **6** to lower (a note) in pitch, *esp* by a semitone. ➤ *verb intrans* to become flat or flatter. ➤➤ **flattener** *noun.*

flatten out *verb intrans* **1** said of an increasing rate, etc: to slow down, increase less steeply, or level out. **2** said of an aircraft: to assume a position with the wings and fuselage parallel to the ground.

flatter /ˈflatə/ *verb* (**flattered, flattering**) ➤ *verb trans* **1** to praise (somebody) excessively, *esp* from motives of self-interest or in order to gratify their vanity. **2** (*usu in passive*) to make (somebody) feel valued or sought-after: *I was flattered by the invitation.* **3** said of a painting or photograph: to portray or represent (the subject) over-favourably. **4** to display (a person or thing) to advantage: *Candlelight often flatters the face.* **5** to deceive (oneself), *esp* by believing that something is better or more favourable than it actually is. ➤ *verb intrans* to flatter somebody or something. ➤➤ **flatterer** *noun,* **flatteringly** *adv.* [Middle English *flateren,* prob a back-formation from FLATTERY]

flattery *noun* (*pl* **flatteries**) **1** the act or an instance of flattering. **2** insincere or excessive praise. [Middle English *flaterie* from Old French, from *flater* to stroke, lick, flatter, prob of Germanic origin]

flattie *or* **flatty** /ˈflati/ *noun* (*pl* **flatties**) **1** a low-heeled shoe. **2** *chiefly Aus, NZ, informal* a flatfish. **3** a flatboat.

flat-top *noun* **1** *chiefly NAmer, informal* = AIRCRAFT CARRIER. **2** *informal* a very short hairstyle for men, with the hair standing straight up and cropped level. **3** an acoustic guitar with a flat front.

flatty /ˈflati/ *noun* see FLATTIE.

flatulent /ˈflatyoolənt/ *adj* **1** suffering from or characterized by an excessive accumulation of gas in the alimentary canal. **2** said of a person, speech, piece of writing, etc: pompous or pretentious. ➤➤ **flatulence** *noun,* **flatulency** /-si/ *noun,* **flatulently** *adv.* [Latin *flatulentus,* from *flare* to blow, breathe]

flatus /ˈflaytəs/ *noun* gas generated in the stomach or intestines. [Latin *flatus* blowing, from *flare* to blow, breathe]

flatware *noun* **1** *NAmer* cutlery. **2** relatively flat items of crockery such as plates and saucers: compare HOLLOWARE.

flatways (*NAmer* **flatwise**) *adv* with the broad surfaces, as distinct from the edges, facing up and down: *Lay the plank flatways.*

flatworm *noun* any of various parasitic and free-living worms, e.g. a tapeworm or fluke, that have flattened, as distinct from rounded, bodies: phylum Platyhelminthes.

flatwoven *adj* said of a carpet: woven so as to have no pile.

flaunching /ˈflawnching/ *noun* a slope, e.g. of concrete, round the base of a chimneypot to allow rain to run off. [*flanch, flaunch* to slant, flare, perhaps from French *flanc:* see FLANK[1]]

flaunt /flawnt/ *verb trans* to display or parade (one's possessions, qualities, or oneself) ostentatiously or impudently: *flaunt one's engagement ring; flaunt one's figure; flaunt one's generosity.* ➤ *verb intrans* **1** to parade or display oneself to public notice: *and some, who flaunt amid the throng, shall hide in dens of shame tonight* — W Cullen Bryant. **2** *dated* to wave or flutter proudly: *Hundreds of these handkerchiefs hang dangling from pegs … or flaunting from the doorposts* — Dickens. ✳ **if you've got it, flaunt it** don't be modest about your attributes, *esp* physical ones; put them on display. ➤➤ **flaunter** *noun,* **flauntingly** *adv,* **flaunty** *adj.* [origin unknown]

Usage note

flaunt *or* **flout**? These two words are sometimes confused. To *flaunt* means 'to display ostentatiously': *to flaunt one's superiority; to flaunt one's wealth; flout* means 'to treat with contemptuous disregard': *flout one's parents' wishes; The present laws are widely flouted.* The verb *flaunt* is sometimes incorrectly used for *flout: to flaunt the rules* and *to flaunt convention* are wrong.

flautist /ˈflawtist/ *noun* a person who plays a flute. *NAmer* Also called FLUTIST. [Italian *flautista,* from *flauto* flute]

flavescent /flə'ves(ə)nt/ *adj* slightly yellow; turning yellow. [Latin *flavescent-*, *flavescens*, present part. of *flavescere* to turn yellow, from *flavus* yellow]

Flavian /'flayvi-ən/ *adj* belonging or relating to a dynasty of Roman emperors, including Vespasian and his sons Titus and Domitian, who reigned from AD 69–96. ➤➤ **Flavian** *noun*. [Latin *Flavianus*, from *Flavius*, family name of Vespasian]

flavin /'flayvin/ *noun* any of several yellow pigments occurring as part of the coenzymes (non-protein compounds enabling enzymes to function; see COENZYME) of flavoproteins. [Latin *flavus* yellow + -IN[1]]

flavine /'flayvin/ *noun* acriflavine or a similar yellow dye used as an antiseptic. [Latin *flavus* yellow + -INE[1]]

flavone /'flayvohn/ *noun* 1 a KETONE (type of organic compound) found in the leaves, stems, and seed capsules of many primroses: formula $C_{15}H_{10}O_2$. 2 any of the chemical compounds formed from it, many of which occur as yellow plant pigments and are used as dyestuffs. [Latin *flavus* yellow + -ONE]

flavonoid /'flayvənoyd/ *noun* any of a group of naturally occurring aromatic chemical compounds that are found *esp* as plant pigments. [FLAVONE + -OID]

flavoprotein /flayvoh'prohteen/ *noun* any of various proteins that contain flavin and are involved in biological oxidation reactions. [FLAVIN + PROTEIN]

flavor /'flayvə/ *noun and verb trans NAmer* see FLAVOUR[1], FLAVOUR[2].

flavoring *noun NAmer* see FLAVOURING.

flavour[1] (*NAmer* **flavor**) /'flayvə/ *noun* 1a the blend of taste and smell sensations evoked by a substance in the mouth: *Condiments give flavour to food*. b a flavour of a specified kind: *a lemony flavour*. 2 a characteristic or predominant quality: *The newspaper retains a sporting flavour*. 3 a representative sample of something: *just to give you a flavour of the discussion*. 4 *NAmer* = FLAVOURING. 5 in particle physics, any of the five distinguishing properties of quarks (see QUARK[1]). ✳ **flavour of the month** a person or thing that is currently fashionable. ➤➤ **flavourful** *adj*, **flavourless** *adj*, **flavoursome** /-s(ə)m/ *adj*. [Middle English, in the sense 'aroma', from Old French *flavor*, ultimately from Latin *flare* to blow]

flavour[2] (*NAmer* **flavor**) *verb trans* to give or add flavour to (something). ➤➤ **flavoured** *adj*.

flavour enhancer *noun* something, *esp* monosodium glutamate, that is added to commercially prepared foods and drinks to improve the flavour.

flavouring (*NAmer* **flavoring**) *noun* any substance used to give a stronger, different, or pleasanter flavour to food.

flaw[1] /flaw/ *noun* 1 a blemish or imperfection. 2 a usu hidden defect, e.g. a crack, that may cause failure under stress: *a flaw in a bar of steel*. 3 a weakness in reasoning, etc: *a flaw in his argument*. 4 a fault in a legal paper that may invalidate it. ➤➤ **flawless** *adj*, **flawlessly** *adv*, **flawlessness** *noun*. [Middle English, in the sense 'snowflake, splinter', prob of Scandinavian origin]

flaw[2] *verb intrans and trans* to become or cause (something) to become blemished or imperfect.

flaw[3] *noun* 1 *literary*. a a sudden gust of wind; a squall: *'mid the gust, the whirlwind and the flaw of rain and hail-stones* — Keats. b a spell of stormy weather: *patch a wall to expel the winter's flaw* — Shakespeare. 2 *archaic* a violent attack or outburst of fury: *She … on him ran with furious rage … but he … from that first flaw him selfe right well defended* — Spenser. [Old Norse *flaga* gust, attack]

flawed *adj* spoilt by a flaw or flaws: *a flawed gem; a deeply flawed argument*.

flax /flaks/ *noun* 1 a slender erect blue-flowered plant cultivated for its strong woody fibre and seeds (see LINSEED): *Linum usitatissimum*. 2 the fibre of the flax plant, *esp* when prepared for spinning and used to produce linen. 3 any of various similar plants. 4 = FLAX-LILY. [Old English *fleax*]

flaxen *adj* 1 made of flax. 2 resembling flax, *esp* in being a pale soft straw colour: *flaxen hair*.

flax-lily *noun* a New Zealand plant that yields valuable fibre and is also grown for its ornamental qualities: *Phormium tenax*.

flaxseed *noun* = LINSEED.

flay /flay/ *verb trans* 1 to strip off the skin of (a carcass or a body). 2 to whip (somebody) savagely. 3 to criticize or censure (somebody) harshly. 4 *dated* to strip (somebody) of possessions; = FLEECE[2] (1). ➤➤ **flayer** *noun*. [Old English *flēan*]

F layer *noun* the highest and most densely ionized layer of the ionosphere. [F used arbitrarily]

flea /flee/ *noun* 1 any of numerous species of wingless bloodsucking jumping insects that feed on warm-blooded animals: *esp Pulex irritans* (that lives on humans): order Siphonaptera. 2 = FLEA BEETLE. ✳ **a flea in one's ear** a sharp or embarrassing reprimand: *The boss sent him off with a flea in his ear*. **fit as a flea** see FIT[1]. [Old English *flēa*]

fleabag *noun informal* 1 *chiefly NAmer* an inferior hotel or lodging. 2 a dirty or neglected person or animal. 3 *Brit* a sleeping bag.

fleabane /'fleebayn/ *noun* any of several species of plants of the daisy family that were once supposed to drive away fleas: *Pulicaria dysenterica* and other species.

flea beetle *noun* any of several genera of small jumping beetles that feed on foliage: genus *Phyllotreta* and other genera.

fleabite *noun informal* a trifling problem or expense.

flea-bitten *adj* 1 covered in flea bites or infested with fleas. 2 *informal* shabby; run-down. 3 said of a horse's coat, *esp* if light-coloured: flecked with chestnut or brown.

flea collar *noun* a dog's or cat's collar impregnated with insecticide and worn to kill or repel fleas.

fleadh /flah/ *noun* a festival of Celtic music, dancing, and culture. [Irish and Scottish Gaelic *fleadh* feast, banquet]

flea market *noun* a usu open-air market selling secondhand articles and antiques. [translation of French *Marché aux Puces*, a market in Paris]

fleapit *noun chiefly Brit, informal or humorous* a shabby cinema or theatre.

fleawort *noun* any of various plants related to ragwort that were formerly thought to drive fleas away: *Senecio integrifolius* and others.

flèche /flesh (*French* flɛʃ)/ *noun* a slender usu wooden spire rising from the ridge of a roof. [French *flèche* arrow, of Germanic origin]

flechette *or* **fléchette** /fle'shet/ *noun* a small dart-shaped projectile that can be clustered in an explosive warhead, dropped as a missile from an aircraft, or fired from a hand-held gun. [French *fléchette*, dimin. of *flèche*: see FLÈCHE]

fleck[1] /flek/ *noun* 1 a small spot or mark, *esp* of colour. 2 a grain or particle. [Middle English, prob from Old Norse *flekkr* stain, spot]

fleck[2] *verb trans* to cover (something) with small spots or marks.

flecked *adj* marked with spots or streaks: *the Sun was flecked with bars … as if through a dungeon-grate he peered with broad and burning face* — Coleridge. [Middle English, prob from Old Norse *flekkōttr*, from *flekkr* stain, spot]

flection /'fleksh(ə)n/ *noun* see FLEXION.

fled /fled/ *verb* past tense and past part. of FLEE.

fledge /flej/ *verb trans* 1 to rear (a young bird) until ready for flight or independent activity. 2 see FLETCH. ➤ *verb intrans* said of a young bird: to develop wing feathers ready for flight. ➤➤ **fledged** *adj*. [obsolete *fledge* capable of flying, from Old English *-flycge*]

fledgling *or* **fledgeling** /'flejling/ *noun* 1 a young bird that has just fledged. 2 (*used before a noun*). a relating to or denoting an inexperienced person: *fledgling writers*. b relating to or denoting something in its infancy: *fledgling electronics companies*.

flee /flee/ *verb* (**flees, fleeing**, past tense and past part. **fled** /fled/) ➤ *verb intrans* 1 to run away from danger, evil, etc. 2 to pass away swiftly; to vanish: *mists fleeing before the rising sun*. ➤ *verb trans* to run away from or shun (a person, thing, or place): *Hundreds of people were fleeing the advancing floods*. [Old English *flēon*]

fleece[1] /flees/ *noun* 1a the coat of wool covering a sheep or similar animal. b the wool obtained from a sheep at one shearing: *a pile of fleeces*. 2 a soft bulky deep-piled fabric used chiefly for lining coats. 3 a jacket or pull-on top made of a synthetic fabric with a thick warm pile, used *esp* for outdoor activities. [Old English *flēos*]

fleece[2] *verb trans* 1 *informal* to strip (a person) of money or property, usu by fraud or extortion; *esp* to overcharge (somebody). 2 to remove the fleece from (a sheep); to shear (it). [from FLEECE[1]]

fleecie /'fleesi/ *or* **fleece-oh** /-oh/ *or* **fleece-o** /-oh/ *noun NZ* a person who collects fleeces after shearing and prepares them for baling.

fleecy /'fleesi/ *adj* (**fleecier, fleeciest**) 1 resembling a fleece, *esp* in being soft and fluffy: *fleecy clouds*. 2 made from a natural fleece or from a warm synthetic fabric: *cosy fleecy slippers.* ➤ **fleeciness** noun.

fleer[1] /'flee·ə/ *verb intrans archaic* (*often* + *at*) to mock, *esp* in a crude, coarse manner: *Tush, tush, man! Never fleer and jest at me* — Shakespeare. [prob from Old Norse and related to Norwegian and Swedish *flira* to grin]

fleer[2] *noun archaic* a mocking look or remark.

fleet[1] /fleet/ *noun* **1** a number of warships under a single command. **2** (*often* **the Fleet**) a country's navy. **3** a group of ships, aircraft, lorries, etc operating together or owned or operated under one management: *a fleet of ambulances.* [Old English *flēot* ship, from *flēotan* to float, swim]

fleet[2] *adj* **1** quick and nimble: *Antelopes are fleet of foot.* **2** *archaic or literary* fleeting. ➤ **fleetly** *adv,* **fleetness** *noun.* [prob from FLEET[3]]

fleet[3] *verb intrans chiefly literary* to fly swiftly; to pass rapidly: *clouds fleeting across the sky.* [Old English *flēotan* to float, swim]

fleet[4] *noun dialect* a channel, ditch, or creek in marshland. [Old English *flēot*]

fleet[5] *adj dialect* said of water: shallow. ➤ **fleet** *adv.* [Perhaps related to Dutch *vloot* shallow]

fleet admiral *noun* (*also* **Fleet Admiral**) in the US navy, the highest rank of admiral.

Fleet Air Arm *noun* the branch of the Royal Navy that maintains and operates naval aircraft.

fleet chief petty officer *noun* in the Royal Navy, a noncommissioned officer of equivalence in rank to a warrant officer in the army or the Royal Air Force.

fleeting /'fleeting/ *adj* passing swiftly; transitory: *the fleeting moments; a fleeting glance.* ➤ **fleetingly** *adv,* **fleetingness** *noun.*

fleet rate *noun* a reduced insurance rate offered for a fleet of vehicles, vessels or aircraft.

fleet rating *noun* = FLEET RATE.

Fleet Street *noun* the British press, *esp* newspaper journalism or the people working in the industry. [*Fleet Street*, London, centre of the former newspaper district in London]

Fleming /'fleming/ *noun* **1** a native or inhabitant of Flanders, a region lying on the North Sea coasts of the Netherlands, Belgium, and France. **2** a member of the Flemish speaking people of Belgium: compare WALLOON. [Middle English, from early Dutch *Vlaminc*, from *Vlam-* as in *Vlamland* Flanders]

Flemish /'flemish/ *noun* **1** (**the Flemish**) (*treated as pl*) the people of Flanders. **2** the Germanic language of the people of Flanders. ➤ **Flemish** *adj.*

Flemish bond *noun* a method of laying bricks in which each row consists of alternating headers (bricks with end facing outwards; see HEADER (3)) and stretchers (bricks with long side facing outwards; see STRETCHER[1] (3)).

Flemish horse *noun* a short rope suspended from the end of the yard of a sailing ship, on which a seaman stands when reefing or furling the sails.

flense /flens/ *or* **flinch** /flin(t)sh/ *or* **flench** /flen(t)sh/ *verb trans* to strip (e.g. a whale) of blubber or skin. [Dutch *flensen* or Danish and Norwegian *flense*]

flesh[1] /flesh/ *noun* **1a** the soft, *esp* muscular, parts of the body of an animal, *esp* a vertebrate, as distinguished from visceral structures, bone, hide, etc. **b** excess weight; fat. **2** the edible parts of an animal, *esp* the muscular tissue of any animal usu excluding fish and sometimes fowl. **3** a fleshy part of a plant or fruit, *esp* if edible. **4a** the physical being of humans: *The spirit indeed is willing, but the flesh is weak* — Bible. **b** the physical or sensual aspect of human nature: *pleasures of the flesh.* **5** (**all flesh**). **a** human beings; humankind. **b** living things generally. ✳ **go the way of all flesh** to die. **in the flesh** in bodily form; in person: *I was interested to meet him in the flesh.* **make somebody's flesh creep/crawl** to cause revulsion in somebody. **one's own flesh/flesh and blood** one's own kindred or stock. **press the flesh** *informal* said *esp* of a politician: to meet and shake hands with numerous people, e.g. on an election campaign. **put flesh on/on the bones of something** to fill an idea, etc out or give it substance. ➤ **fleshless** *adj.* [Old English *flǣsc*]

flesh[2] *verb trans* **1a** to feed (e.g. a hawk or hound) with flesh from the kill to encourage interest in the chase. **b** to initiate or habituate (somebody), *esp* by giving them a foretaste of something, e.g. bloodshed or warfare. **2** to remove the flesh from (hides).

flesh and blood *noun* (*treated as sing. or pl*) **1** one's near relations. **2a** human beings as having physical substance: *In spite of which we like to think that we are sound, substantial flesh and blood* — T S Eliot. **b** human nature: *It was more than flesh and blood could stand.* **3** discernible characteristics; substance: *They are merely attempting to give flesh and blood to nebulous ideas.*

flesh-colour *adj* of a pinkish white colour with a slight yellow tint. ➤ **flesh-colour** *noun,* **flesh-coloured** *adj.*

fleshed *adj* (*used in combinations*) having flesh of the kind specified: *pink-fleshed.*

flesher *noun* **1** *chiefly Scot, archaic* a butcher. **2** *NAmer* a knife for removing the flesh from hides.

flesh fly *noun* any of various flies whose maggots feed on flesh: family Sarcophagidae.

fleshings *pl noun* flesh-coloured tights worn by dancers and actors.

fleshly *adj* (**fleshlier, fleshliest**) **1** belonging or relating to the body; carnal; sensual: *the fleshly appetites.* **2** having an actual physical existence or presence: *Then was I born of a virgin pure, of her I took fleshly substance* — traditional carol.

flesh out *verb trans* to develop or expand (something, e.g. an idea, proposal, etc) through fuller treatment or discussion. ➤ *verb intrans* to become fuller or more substantial; to expand.

fleshpot *noun* **1** (*usu in pl*) a place that offers sensual or sexual forms of entertainment: *a tour of the city's fleshpots.* **2** (**the fleshpots**) bodily comfort or good living; luxury. [from the biblical allusion, Exodus 16.3, to Egypt as a place of decadence]

flesh wound *noun* an injury involving penetration of body muscle without damage to bones or internal organs.

fleshy *adj* (**fleshier, fleshiest**) **1a** plump or thickset; corpulent. **b** consisting of or resembling flesh. **2** said of a plant or fruit: succulent or pulpy. ➤ **fleshiness** *noun.*

fletch /flech/ *or* **fledge** /flej/ *verb trans* to fit (an arrow) with feathers. [alteration of FLEDGE or back-formation from FLETCHER]

fletcher *noun* a person who makes arrows, often also selling and repairing them. [Middle English *fleccher* from Old French *flechier,* from *fleche* arrow, of Germanic origin]

fletching *noun* (*also in pl*) the feathers of an arrow.

fletton /'flet(ə)n/ *noun* a mottled yellow and pink brick with sharp edges. [named after *Fletton,* district in Cambridgeshire, England, source of the clay used]

fleur de coin /,fluh də 'kwunh (*French* flœr də kwɛ̃)/ *adj* said of a coin: preserved in mint condition. [French *à fleur de coin,* literally 'with the bloom of the die']

fleur-de-lis *or* **fleur-de-lys** /,fluh də 'lee/ *noun* (*pl* **fleurs-de-lis** *or* **fleurs-de-lys** /lee(z)/) **1** in art and heraldry, a stylized representation of three lily petals, usu bound together at their bases. **2** = IRIS (2). [Middle English *flourdelis* from early French *flor de lis* lily flower]

fleuret *or* **fleurette** /floo·ə'ret/ *noun* a flower-shaped ornament; = FLEURON. [French *fleurette,* dimin. of *fleur* flower, from Old French *flor:* see FLOWER[1]]

fleuron /'flooəron, 'fluh-/ *noun* a flower-shaped ornament used for decorative effect, e.g. in architecture, printing, and cooking. [Middle English from Old French *floron,* from *flor, flour, flur:* see FLOWER[1]]

fleury /'floo·əri/ *adj* see FLORY.

flew /flooh/ *verb* past tense of FLY[1].

flews /floohz/ *pl noun* the drooping side parts of the upper lip of a bloodhound or similar dog. [origin unknown]

flex[1] /fleks/ *verb trans* **1** to bend (something pliable): *He flexed the cane experimentally.* **2a** to bend (a limb or joint). **b** to contract or tense (a muscle or muscles) so as to flex a limb or joint. **3** (*usu in passive*) to bend (a corpse) so that the knees are drawn up under the chin: *Short cists typically contain corpses that have been flexed.* ➤ *verb intrans* **1** said of something pliable: to bend and revert to an original position or shape. **2a** said of a joint: to bend: *Stabilize the ankle so that it cannot flex.* **b** said of a muscle: to contract or tense. **3** *informal* to work flexitime. [Latin *flexus,* past part. of *flectere* to bend]

flex[2] *noun chiefly Brit* a length of flexible insulated electrical cable used in connecting an electrical appliance to a socket. [short for *flexible cord*]

flexible *adj* **1** capable of being bent; pliable: *one of those flexible plastic rulers; flexible disks.* **2** yielding to influence; willing to adapt or fit in with others; tractable. **3** capable of changing in response to new conditions; versatile: *a highly flexible curriculum.* ➤➤ **flexibility** /-'biliti/ *noun,* **flexibly** *adv.*

flexile /'fleksiel, NAmer 'fleksǝl/ *adj archaic* flexible, pliable, or mobile: *a Sicilian … with vehement gestures and flexile features* — Edward Bulwer-Lytton. ➤➤ **flexility** /flek'siliti/ *noun.* [Latin *flexilis* pliant, from *flectere* to bend]

flexion *or* **flection** /'fleksh(ǝ)n/ *noun* the action of flexing *esp* a joint, or the condition or process of being flexed. [Latin *flexion-, flexio,* from *flectere* to bend]

flexitime /'fleksitiem/ *(NAmer* **flextime** /'flekstiem/*) noun* a system whereby employees work a set total of hours per week or month but can choose from a usu limited range of daily starting and finishing times. [FLEXIBLE + TIME[1]]

flexography /flek'sogrǝfi/ *noun* a process of rotary letterpress printing using flexible rubber plates and quick-drying inks, used e.g. for printing on plastic bags and other impervious materials. ➤➤ **flexographic** /-'grafik/ *adj,* **flexographically** /-'grafikli/ *adv.* [FLEXIBLE + -GRAPHY]

flexor /'fleksǝ/ *noun* a muscle that contracts to bend a joint: compare EXTENSOR. [scientific Latin *flexor* from Latin *flectere* to bend]

flextime *noun NAmer* see FLEXITIME.

flexuous /'fleksyoo·ǝs/ *adj* bending and curving; sinuous: *Her flexuous and stealthy figure became an integral part of the scene* — Hardy. ➤➤ **flexuously** *adv.* [Latin *flexuosus* from *flexus* a bend, past part. of *flectere* to bend]

flexure /'flekshǝ/ *noun* **1** the action of flexing; = FLEXION. **2** a turn or fold. ➤➤ **flexural** *adj.*

flex-wing *noun* a flexible, often collapsible wing, *esp* one made of fabric and used in hang-gliding.

flibbertigibbet /,flibǝti'jibit, 'flib-/ *noun informal* a silly, irresponsible person, *esp* one who chatters on or who flits from one thing to another. [Middle English *flepergebet,* perhaps imitative of idle chat]

flic /flik/ *noun* a computer file containing animations. [alteration of FLICK[3]]

flick[1] /flik/ *noun* **1** a light jerky movement or blow: *with a flick of the tail.* **2** a quick-release movement of a finger against the thumb, used for propelling small objects away. ✴ **give somebody the flick** *chiefly Aus, informal* to reject or dismiss somebody in an offhand or insulting way. [imitative]

flick[2] *verb trans* **1a** to strike (something) lightly with a quick sharp motion. **b** (+ away/off) to remove (something) using quick brushing movements. **2** to cause (something) to move with a flick: *The cow flicked its tail from side to side.* ➤ *verb intrans* **1** to move lightly or jerkily; to dart. **2** to direct a flick at something. ✴ **flick through** to look at or read (a book, etc) cursorily, turning the pages quickly.

flick[3] *noun informal* **1** a cinema film; a movie. **2** (**the flicks**) the cinema. [short for FLICKER[2]]

flicker[1] *verb* (**flickered, flickering**) ➤ *verb intrans* **1** said of a light: to vary in intensity. **2** said of a flame or candle: to burn fitfully or with a fluctuating light. **3** to move irregularly or unsteadily; to quiver: *His eyelids flickered.* **4** to appear or be present irregularly or indistinctly: *Interest flickered in his eyes.* ➤ *verb trans* to cause (something, e.g. eyelids) to flicker. ➤➤ **flickering** *noun and adj,* **flickeringly** *adv.* [Old English *flicorian* to flutter]

flicker[2] *noun* **1** the act or an instance of flickering: *a flicker of light.* **2** a momentary quickening or stirring: *a flicker of interest.* ➤➤ **flickery** *adj.*

flicker[3] *noun* any of various American woodpeckers that feed on ants: *Colaptes auratus* and others. [imitative of its call]

flick knife *noun* a pocket knife with a blade that is stored in the handle and springs out when a button is pressed.

flick roll *noun* = SNAP ROLL.

flier *noun* see FLYER.

flight[1] /fliet/ *noun* **1a** a passage through the air using wings. **b** the ability to fly. **2a** a passage or journey through air or space. **b** a journey of this kind made by a scheduled airline. **c** the distance covered in such a journey. **3** the trajectory of a struck or bowled ball, *esp* a relatively high curve imparted to a bowled ball in cricket. **4** swift movement. **5a** a flock of birds flying together. **b** in the airforce, a

unit of six or so aircraft operating together. **6a** a continuous series of stairs from one landing or floor to another. **b** a series of locks taking a canal up an ascent. **c** a set of hurdles across a racetrack. **7** any of the vanes or feathers at the tail of a dart, arrow, etc that provide stability. ✴ **flight of fancy/the imagination** a piece of originality or inventiveness; = JEU D'ESPRIT. **take flight** said of a bird: to leave the ground, a perch, etc and fly off. [Old English *flyht*]

flight[2] *verb trans* **1** to shoot (a bird, *esp* a wild fowl) in flight. **2** to cause (a ball, dart, etc) to move towards a target slowly and often with accuracy. **3** to attach feathers or feather-like parts to (an arrow or dart).

flight[3] *noun* the act or an instance of fleeing. ✴ **put to flight** to cause (somebody) to flee. **take (to) flight** to flee. [Middle English *fluht, fliht,* of Germanic origin; Old English *flēon* FLEE]

flight attendant *noun* a person employed to look after the needs of passengers onboard a commercial aircraft.

flight capital *noun* **1** money transferred from an economically unstable region to a more stable one. **2** money transferred abroad in preparation for emigration or to avoid taxes, inflation, etc.

flight control *noun* **1** the control of an aircraft or spacecraft from a ground station, *esp* by radio. **2** the system of control devices on an aeroplane.

flight deck *noun* **1** the compartment housing the controls and the crew who operate them in an aircraft. **2** the deck of a ship used for the takeoff and landing of aircraft.

flight envelope *noun* in aerodynamics, the range of combinations of variables, such as height, speed, and angle, within which any aircraft or other flying object is stable in flight.

flight feather *noun* any of the large stiff feathers of a bird's wing or tail that are important in providing lift and control for flight.

flightless *adj* said of a bird or insect: naturally unable to fly. ➤➤ **flightlessness** *noun.*

flight lieutenant *noun* in the Royal Air Force, an officer ranking below squadron leader and above flying officer.

flightline *noun* at an airport or military airfield, a parking and servicing area for aircraft.

flight path *noun* the course taken by an aircraft, spacecraft, etc, usu fixed in advance.

flight plan *noun* a statement, usu written, of the details of an intended flight.

flight recorder *noun* a robust device fitted to an aircraft that records details of its flight, *esp* for use in investigating accidents.

flight sergeant *noun* in the Royal Air Force, a non-commissioned officer ranking below warrant officer and above sergeant.

flight simulator *noun* a machine in the form of a cockpit with controls in which conditions in flight can be exactly reproduced, used for training pilots.

flighty *adj* (**flightier, flightiest**) **1** said of a person: irresponsible, silly, flirtatious, or inclined to be restless. **2** said of a horse: easily excited or upset; skittish. ➤➤ **flightily** *adv,* **flightiness** *noun.* [FLIGHT[1]]

flimflam[1] /'flimflam/ *noun informal* **1** deception or trickery. **2** nonsense; humbug. ➤➤ **flimflammery** *noun.* [prob of Scandinavian origin]

flimflam[2] *verb trans* (**flimflammed, flimflamming**) to deceive, cheat, or trick (somebody). ➤➤ **flimflammer** *noun.*

flimsy[1] /'flimzi/ *adj* (**flimsier, flimsiest**) **1a** not built to last; insubstantial: *They put to sea in a flimsy boat.* **b** thin and light: *a flimsy nightgown.* **2** said of an excuse, reason, etc: implausible; unconvincing: *on some flimsy pretext.* ➤➤ **flimsily** *adj,* **flimsiness** *noun.* [perhaps alteration of FILM[1] + -*sy* as in TRICKSY]

flimsy[2] *noun* (*pl* **flimsies**) **1** lightweight paper used *esp* for multiple copies. **2** a document, or a copy of one, printed on this paper.

flinch[1] /flinch/ *verb intrans* **1** to make a nervous shrinking movement, *esp* in response to fear, pain, threats, etc. **2** (+ from) to avoid contact with something or be averse or unwilling to do something. ➤➤ **flinchingly** *adv.* [early French *flenchir* to bend, turn aside, of Germanic origin]

flinch[2] *noun* the act or an instance of flinching.

flinch[3] /flin(t)sh/ *verb trans* see FLENSE.

flinders /'flindǝz/ *pl noun* splinters or fragments. [Middle English *flenderis,* prob of Scandinavian origin]

fling[1] /fling/ *verb* (*past tense and past part.* **flung** /flung/) ➤ *verb trans* **1** to throw, cast, or hurl (something), *esp* with force or recklessness: *fling the books on the table; flinging his arms out.* **2** to send or put (somebody) somewhere unceremoniously: *The authorities flung him in jail.* **3** (+ into) to involve (oneself) energetically in an activity: *She flung herself into her work.* **4** (*often* + at) to throw out (a bad-tempered or confrontational remark) at somebody: *'Stupid cow!' he flung back at her.* ➤ *verb intrans* **1** to move in a hasty or violent manner: *flinging out of the room in a rage.* **2** (+ out) said of an animal: to kick or plunge vigorously: *And Duncan's horses ... turn'd wild in nature, broke their stalls, flung out* — Shakespeare. [Middle English *flingen*, of Scandinavian origin]

fling[2] *noun* **1** a period devoted to self-indulgence: *We've been on a massive shopping fling.* **2** *chiefly informal* a casual attempt; a try: *I thought I'd have a fling at writing a novel.* **3** *informal* a brief sexual relationship with somebody. **4** a vigorous Scottish reel or dance: *the Highland fling.* **5** the act or an instance of flinging.

flint /flint/ *noun* **1** a hard quartz found *esp* in chalk or limestone. **2** a piece of this material chipped or flaked in antiquity to form a tool or weapon. **3** a material, e.g. an alloy of iron and cerium, used for producing a spark, e.g. in a cigarette lighter. ➤➤ **flintlike** *adj.* [Old English]

flint corn *noun* a maize with hard usu rounded kernels.

flint glass *noun* heavy, brilliant, highly refractive glass that contains lead oxide.

flintlock *noun* **1** a gunlock, used in the 17th and 18th cents, in which the charge is ignited by sparks struck from flint. **2** a gun with this kind of lock.

flinty *adj* (**flintier, flintiest**) **1** said of stone or other material: resembling flint. **2** said of a person, facial expression, or attitude: hard, unsympathetic, or unyielding. ➤➤ **flintily** *adv,* **flintiness** *noun.*

flip[1] /flip/ *verb* (**flipped, flipping**) ➤ *verb trans* **1** to toss (something) with a sharp movement, *esp* so that it turns over in the air: *flip a coin.* **2** (+ over) to turn (something) over: *Flip the mattress over.* **3** to propel (something) with a flick of the fingers: *Let's flip a coin to see who goes first.* ➤ *verb intrans* **1** (+ over) to turn over in the air, or lightly and easily. **2** *informal* to lose one's sanity or self-control. * **flip one's lid** (*also NAmer* **flip one's wig**) *informal* to go crazy; to lose one's self-control. **flip through** to turn the pages of (a book, magazine, etc) quickly or casually. [perhaps a contraction of FILLIP[2]]

flip[2] *noun* **1** the act or an instance of flipping. **2** a somersault, *esp* when performed in the air: *a back flip.* **3** an alcoholic drink with beaten eggs added to it.

flip[3] *adj* (**flipper, flippest**) *informal* said of a person, remark, etc: flippant; impertinent.

flip chart *noun* a very large pad of paper mounted on a stand and used as a visual aid during a presentation by a speaker, the sheets being flipped backwards over the top after use or display.

flip-flop[1] /'flip flop/ *noun* **1** *chiefly NAmer* a backward handspring. **2** *NAmer, informal* a sudden about-turn in policy; = VOLTE-FACE (1). **3** a usu electronic device or circuit, e.g. in a computer, capable of assuming either of two stable states. **4** a rubber sandal consisting of a sole and typically two diagonal straps anchored between the big toe and the second toe.

flip-flop[2] *verb intrans* (**flip-flopped, flip-flopping**) **1** to move with repeated flapping sound or movements. **2** *chiefly NAmer, informal* to make an about-turn in opinion, policy, etc.

flippant /'flip(ə)nt/ *adj* said of a person, attitude, remark, etc: not having or showing proper respect or seriousness, *esp* where a solemn response would be expected or appropriate. ➤➤ **flippancy** /-si/ *noun,* **flippantly** *adv.* [prob from FLIP[1]]

flipper *noun* **1** a broad flat limb, e.g. of a seal, adapted for swimming. **2** a flat rubber shoe with the front expanded into a paddle, used for underwater swimming.

flipping *adj informal* used for emphasis or to express irritation: *This is flipping stupid; Where are the flipping painters?* [euphem for FUCKING]

flip side *noun informal* **1** the side of a gramophone record which is not the principal marketing attraction. **2** the less familiar side of a person, situation, etc, *esp* if less acceptable or more sinister: *The facts ... revealed the flip side of the fairytale* — Andrew Morton. [FLIP[1]]

flip-top *adj* denoting a container with a lid that can be flipped open.

flirt[1] /fluht/ *verb intrans* to show sexual interest in or make advances to somebody in a playful way. ➤ *verb trans* said of bird: to flap (its wings) or waggle (its tail). * **flirt with 1** to show superficial or casual interest in or liking for (something): *He flirted with hippiedom for a while.* **2** to risk (danger, death, etc), *esp* deliberately and as a means of obtaining excitement: *Climbers realize they're flirting with death.* ➤➤ **flirty** *adj.* [orig meaning 'to flick or strike'; perhaps imitative]

flirt[2] *noun* **1** a person who flirts, *esp* somebody who flirts regularly or blatantly. **2** the act or instance of flirting.

flirtation /fluh'taysh(ə)n/ *noun* **1** the activity of flirting with somebody, or with an idea, etc. **2** a short-lived romantic or sexual relationship. **3** (*often* + with) a brief foray into some area of activity or thought: *during my flirtation with Existentialism.*

flirtatious /fluh'tayshəs/ *adj* **1** inclined to flirt; coquettish. **2** said of a gesture, etc: indicative of playful sexual intention. ➤➤ **flirtatiously** *adv,* **flirtatiousness** *noun.*

flit[1] /flit/ *verb intrans* (**flitted, flitting**) **1** to pass lightly and quickly or irregularly from one place or condition to another; *esp* to fly in this manner. **2** *chiefly Scot, N Eng* to move house. **3** *Brit* to escape or abscond in order to avoid problems or obligations. [Middle English *flitten*, of Scandinavian origin]

flit[2] *noun* **1** *chiefly Scot, N Eng* the act or an instance of moving house. **2** *Brit* a hurried departure, *esp* in order to avoid problems or obligations: *The company got into debt and did a moonlight flit.* **3** the act or an instance of flitting, *esp* a quick or irregular flying movement.

flitch /flich/ *noun* **1** a salted and often smoked side of pork. **2** a longitudinal section of a log. [Old English *flicce* a cured ham]

flitter[1] /'flitə/ *verb intrans* (**flittered, flittering**) to move about in a random, restless, or agitated way. [frequentative of FLIT[1]]

flitter[2] *noun* the act or an instance of flittering.

flittermouse *noun* (*pl* **flittermice**) *dialect, archaic* = BAT[3].

flixweed /'fliksweed/ *noun* a plant with small yellow flowers formerly believed to cure dysentery: *Descurainia sophia.* [alteration of FLUX[1] (5)]

FLN *abbr* Front de Libération Nationale.

float[1] /floht/ *noun* **1a** a cork or other device used to keep the baited end of a fishing line afloat. **b** a floating platform for swimmers or boats. **c** something, e.g. a hollow ball, that floats at the end of a lever in a cistern, tank, or boiler and regulates the liquid level. **d** a sac containing air or gas and buoying up the body of a plant or animal. **e** a watertight structure enabling an aircraft to float on water. **2** a tool for smoothing a surface of plaster, concrete, etc. **3a** a platform of a lorry supporting an exhibit in a parade. **b** an electrically powered delivery vehicle: *a milk float.* **c** *Aus, NZ* a vehicle for conveying horses. **4** a soft drink with a scoop of ice cream floating in it. **5** a sum of money available for giving change at a stall, in a shop, etc. [Old English *flota* ship]

float[2] *verb intrans* **1** to rest on the surface of or be suspended in a fluid. **2a** to drift on or through a liquid, or move gently in an air current: *Yellow leaves floated down.* **b** to wander aimlessly. **3** to lack firmness of aim or commitment. **4** said of a currency: to find a level in the international exchange market in response to the law of supply and demand, without artificial support or control. ➤ *verb trans* **1a** to cause (something) to float in or on the surface of a liquid. **b** to carry (something) along in this manner. **c** in sport, to send (a ball) on a high smooth flight. **2** to smooth (e.g. plaster) with a float. **3** to present (e.g. an idea) for acceptance or rejection. **4** to cause (currency) to float. **5** to offer the shares of (a company) for the first time for sale on the stock market. * **float somebody's boat** *informal* to excite or interest somebody, *esp* sexually. ➤➤ **floatability** /-'biliti/ *noun,* **floatable** *adj.* [Old English *flotian*]

floatage /'flohtij/ *noun* see FLOTAGE.

floatarium *noun* see FLOTARIUM.

floatation /floh'taysh(ə)n/ *noun* see FLOTATION.

floatation tank *noun* see FLOTATION TANK.

float chamber *noun* the petrol reservoir in a carburettor, in which the level is kept constant by a floating valve.

floatel /floh'tel/ *noun* see FLOTEL.

floater *noun* **1** an employee without a specific job. **2** a spot before the eyes due to dead cells and cell fragments in the vitreous humour and lens. **3** *NAmer* an insurance policy that covers loss of articles without mention of location. **4** *Brit, dated* a gaffe. **5** somebody or something that floats.

float glass *noun* a flat polished glass made by floating a continuous ribbon of molten glass over a liquid metal bath.

floating *adj* **1** located out of the normal position: *a floating kidney.* **2a** continually changing position or abode: *a large floating population.* **b** not presently committed or invested: *floating capital.* **c** short-term and usu not funded: *floating debt.* **3** connected or constructed so as to operate and adjust smoothly: *a floating axle.*

floating charge *noun* a loan or liability for which the total assets of the borrowing company serve as security: compare FIXED CHARGE.

floating debt *noun* a short-term government loan: compare FUNDED DEBT.

floating dock *noun* a floating dry dock that can be partly submerged under a ship and then raised.

floating-point *adj* involving or being a mathematical notation in which a value is represented by a number multiplied by a power of the number base: compare FIXED-POINT: *The value 99.9 could be represented in a floating-point system as* $.999 \times 10^2$.

floating rib *noun* a rib, e.g. any of the lowest two pairs in human beings, that has no attachment to the sternum: compare TRUE RIB.

floating voter *noun* a person who does not always vote for the same party.

floatplane *noun* an aircraft with floats; = SEAPLANE.

floatstone *noun* light porous stone that floats, such as pumice.

float valve *noun* = BALL VALVE.

floaty *adj* (**floatier, floatiest**) said of a fabric: light and flimsy: *floaty voile curtains.*

flob /flob/ *verb intrans* (**flobbed, flobbing**) *Brit, informal* to spit. ➤➤ **flob** *noun.*

floc /flok/ *noun technical* a foamy mass formed by the uniting of fine suspended particles. [short for FLOCCULE]

flocci /ˈfloksie/ *noun* pl of FLOCCUS.

floccinaucinihilipilification /ˌfloksiˌnawsiˌnihiliˌpilifiˈkaysh(ə)n/ *noun chiefly humorous* the act or habit or an instance of contemptuously dismissing something or of treating something as worthless. [facetious combination of the Latin expressions *non flocci facere* to care not a piece of fluff, *non nauci facere* to care not a trifle, *nihili facere* to care nothing, and *non pili facere* to care not a hair, + -FICATION]

floccose /ˈflokohs/ *adj chiefly* said of plant parts: composed of or covered with woolly tufts or hairs. [Latin *floccosus* from *floccus* a flock of wool]

flocculate /ˈflokyoolayt/ *verb trans and intrans technical* to form or cause (a substance) to form a flocculent mass. ➤➤ **flocculant** *noun*, **flocculation** /-ˈlaysh(ə)n/ *noun.*

floccule /ˈflokyoohl/ *noun* a small loosely united mass with a woolly or fluffy texture. [late Latin *flocculus*: see FLOCCULUS]

flocculent /ˈflokyoolənt/ *adj* **1** resembling wool, *esp* in having a loose fluffy texture. **2** made up of flocs or floccules. ➤➤ **flocculence** *noun.* [Latin *floccus* flock of wool + -ULENT]

flocculus /ˈflokyoolǝs/ *noun* (*pl* **flocculi** /-lie/) **1** in anatomy, a small oval lobe of the cerebellum, located below the posterior lobe. **2** a bright or dark patch on the sun. **3** a floccule. [late Latin *flocculus,* dimin. of Latin *floccus* flock of wool]

floccus /ˈflokǝs/ *noun* (*pl* **flocci** /ˈfloksie/) a tuft of wool or other fibre. [Latin *floccus* tuft of wool]

flock¹ /flok/ *noun* **1** (*treated as sing. or pl*) a group of birds or mammals assembled or herded together. **2** (*also in pl*) a large group: *flocks of tourists.* **3** a Christian church congregation, *esp* when considered as being under the charge of a specified minister, priest, etc. [Old English *flocc* crowd, band]

flock² *verb intrans* to gather or move in a crowd: *They flocked to the beach.*

flock³ *noun* **1** a tuft of wool or cotton fibre. **2** woollen or cotton refuse used for stuffing furniture, mattresses, etc. **3** very short or pulverized fibre used *esp* to form a velvety pattern on cloth or paper or a protective covering on metal. **4** = FLOC. ➤➤ **flocky** *adj.* [Middle English via Old French from Latin *floccus* tuft of wool]

flock⁴ *verb trans* to decorate (a fabric, e.g. organdie or wallpaper) with flock. ➤➤ **flocking** *noun.*

flockmaster *noun* the owner or supervisor of a flock of sheep; a sheep farmer or shepherd.

flock wallpaper *noun* wallpaper with a raised pattern produced by dusting powdered wool over the partially sized surface.

floe /floh/ *noun* a sheet of floating ice, *esp* on the sea. [prob from Norwegian *flo* flat layer]

flog /flog/ *verb trans* (**flogged, flogging**) **1** to beat (a person or animal) severely with a rod, whip, etc. **2** to force or drive (oneself, one's memory, etc) into action. **3** *informal* to repeat (something) so frequently as to make it uninteresting: *flog the idea to death.* **4** *Brit, informal* to sell (something) or offer (something) for sale: *I'm hoping to flog my old computer.* ➤ *verb intrans informal* to make one's way with laborious effort. ✳ **flog a dead horse** to waste time or energy on worn-out or previously settled issues. ➤➤ **flogger** *noun.* [perhaps modification of Latin *flagellare*: see FLAGELLATE¹]

flokati /floˈkahti/ *noun* (*pl* **flokatis**) a Greek hand-woven rug with a shaggy pile. [modern Greek *phlokatē* peasant blanket]

flong /flong/ *noun* material made of paper and used for making moulds for stereotyping (form of printing; see STEREOTYPE² (2)). [French *flan* flan, flong: see FLAN]

flood¹ /flud/ *noun* **1a** an overflowing of a body of water, *esp* onto land that is normally dry. **b** (**the Flood**) the biblical flooding of the earth caused by God as a punishment for human wickedness. **2a** the inflow of water associated with a rising tide. **b** (*used before a noun*) relating to or denoting this inflow: *a flood tide.* **3** *literary* a body of water such as a river or the sea: *Darest thou, Cassius, now leap in with me into this angry flood and swim to yonder point?* — Shakespeare. **4** an overwhelming quantity or volume: *a flood of letters; floods of tears.* **5** = FLOODLIGHT¹. [Old English *flōd*]

flood² *verb trans* **1** to cover or inundate (land) with a flood. **2** (+ out) to drive (somebody) out of a house, village, etc by flooding. **3** to fill or supply (a market) to excess: *Strawberries flooded the market and prices dropped.* **4** to supply (a carburettor or engine) with an excess of fuel. **5** to fill or suffuse (a place) throughout with something such as sound or light. ➤ *verb intrans* **1** said of a river: to rise and overflow its banks. **2** to pour forth in a flood: *Suds flooded across the kitchen floor.* **3** to become filled with a flood: *The basement floods whenever the river rises.* **4** said of light, sound, warmth, etc: to flow in an overwhelming mass or wave: *Sunlight flooded into the room.* **5** to arrive in overwhelming quantities: *Offers of help flooded in.* **6** said of a woman: to bleed excessively during menstruation.

floodgate *noun* **1** a gate for shutting out or admitting water. **2** (*also in pl*) something that acts as a barrier to a potentially overwhelming flow.

floodlight¹ *noun* a lamp producing a broad bright beam of light for artificially illuminating e.g. a theatre stage or a sports arena.

floodlight² *verb trans* (*past tense and past part.* **floodlit**) to illuminate (a theatre stage, sports arena, etc) with floodlights. ➤➤ **floodlit** *adj.*

floodplain *noun* a low-lying area beside a river that is composed of sedimentary deposits and is subject to periodic flooding.

flood tide *noun* the tide while flowing in or at its highest point.

floor¹ /flaw/ *noun* **1** the lower surface of a room, hallway, etc. **2a** the bottom inside surface of a hollow structure, e.g. a cave or bodily part. **b** a ground surface: *the ocean floor.* **3** a storey of a building. **4** (**the floor**). **a** the part of a legislative or other assembly in which members sit and speak. **b** the members of an assembly, people attending a meeting, etc: *We'll conclude by calling for questions from the floor.* **5** an area in a stock exchange where trading is done. **6** a lower limit or minimum for wages or prices. ✳ **get/have/be given the floor** to be granted the right to speak in an assembly. **take the floor 1** to stand up, e.g. in a meeting, to make a formal speech. **2** to begin dancing. [Old English *flōr*]

floor² *verb trans* **1** to fit (a room) with a floor. **2a** to knock (somebody) to the floor or ground. **b** said of a question, etc: to confuse or disconcert (somebody) or reduce (them) to silence.

floorboard *noun* a long board or plank forming part of a floor.

floorcloth *noun* **1** *NAmer* a thin mat or rug for the floor. **2** *Brit* a cloth for cleaning floors.

flooring *noun* **1** a floor or base. **2** material for floors: *the disadvantages of softwood flooring.*

floor lamp *noun chiefly NAmer* a lamp that has its base on the floor; = STANDARD LAMP.

floor leader *noun NAmer* a member of a legislative body who directs his or her party's strategy in the assembly.

floor manager *noun* **1** in a store, an overseer of sales staff; = SHOPWALKER. **2** the stage manager of a television programme.

floor show *noun* a series of acts presented in a nightclub.

floorwalker *noun chiefly NAmer* = SHOPWALKER.

floozy *or* **floozie** *or* **floosie** /'floohzi/ *noun* (*pl* **floozies** *or* **floosies**) *informal* a disreputable or promiscuous woman or girl. [perhaps alteration of FLOSSY in the sense 'showy, flashy, fancy']

flop[1] /flop/ *verb intrans* (**flopped, flopping**) **1** to swing or hang loosely but heavily. **2** to fall, move, or drop in a heavy, clumsy, or relaxed manner: *He flopped into the chair with a sigh of relief.* **3** *informal* to relax completely; to slump. **4** *informal* to fail completely: *In spite of good reviews the play flopped.* [alteration of FLAP[2]]

flop[2] *noun* **1** a flopping motion, or the sound of this: *fall with a flop.* **2** *informal* a complete failure.

flop[3] *adv* with a flop.

flop *comb. form* forming words, denoting: a specified number of floating-point operations per second: *a gigaflop processor.*

flophouse *noun chiefly NAmer, informal* a cheap, often run-down, hotel or boarding house, *esp* one used by homeless people. *Brit* Also called DOSSHOUSE.

floppy[1] *adj* (**floppier, floppiest**) limp and tending to hang loosely. >> **floppily** *adv*, **floppiness** *noun*.

floppy[2] *noun* (*pl* **floppies**) *informal* = FLOPPY DISK.

floppy disk *noun* in computing, a flexible disk that is coated with a magnetic substance and is used for storing data. Also called DISKETTE.

flops *abbr* floating-point operations per second, a measure of the speed of a computer processor.

floptical /'floptikl/ *adj* denoting, in computing, a read-write head that is positioned by a laser device or a floppy disk or disk drive using such a head. [blend of FLOPPY[2] and OPTICAL]

flor /flaw/ *noun* a crust of yeast that forms on the surface of sherry as it matures in barrel. [Spanish *flor* mould, flower, from Latin *flor-, flos* flower]

flor. *abbr* floruit.

flora /'flawrə/ *noun* (*pl* **floras** *or* **florae** /'flawree/) **1** the plant life of a region, period, or special environment: compare FAUNA. **2** a treatise on, or a work used to identify, the plants of a region, etc. **3** the bacteria or fungi, whether normal or pathological, occurring in or on a bodily organ. [scientific Latin, named after *Flora*, Roman goddess of flowers]

floral /'flawrəl, 'florəl/ *adj* **1** relating to or composed of flowers: *floral tributes.* **2** relating to a flora. >> **florally** *adv*. [Latin *flor-, flos* FLOWER[1]]

floral leaf *noun* a modified leaf, e.g. a sepal or petal, occurring as part of the inflorescence of a plant.

floreat /'flawriat/ *interj* may (the specified person or thing) flourish!: *Floreat 'EastEnders'!* [Latin *floreat*, third person sing. present subjunctive of *florēre* (see FLOURISH[1]), extracted from *floreat Etona*, motto of Eton college]

Florentine[1] /'florəntien/ *adj* **1** relating or belonging to the Italian city of Florence. **2** (*usu* **florentine**) (*used after a noun*) denoting a dish of food containing spinach or served on a bed of spinach: *eggs florentine.*

Florentine[2] *noun* **1** a native or inhabitant of Florence. **2** (**florentine**) a hard sweet biscuit with a chocolate coated base and topped with nuts and pieces of crystallized fruit.

florescence /flaw'res(ə)ns, flo-/ *noun formal* a state or period of flourishing or flowering. >> **florescent** *adj*. [Latin *florescentia*, from *florescent-, florescens*, present part. of *florescere* to begin to flower, from *florēre*: see FLOURISH[1]]

floret /'florit/ *noun* **1** any of the small flowers forming the head of a composite plant. **2** any small flower. **3** any of the individual flowering stems making up a cauliflower or broccoli head. [Middle English *flourette* from early French *flouret*, dimin. of *flour*: see FLOWER[1]]

flori- *comb. form* forming words, denoting: a flower or flowers: *floriculture; floriferous.* [Latin, from *flor-, flos* FLOWER[1]]

floriated /'flawriaytid, 'flo-/ *adj* in architecture, manuscript illumination, etc, decorated with or shaped like a floral motif: *a floriated initial; floriated capitals.* >> **floriation** /-'aysh(ə)n/ *noun.*

floribunda /flori'bundə/ *noun* a plant, *esp* a hybrid rose, that produces sprays or clusters of flowers, as distinct from single flowers. [Latin *floribunda*, fem of *floribundus* flowering freely]

florican /'flawrikan/ *noun* a S Asian bustard, the male having black plumage and white wings: *Houbaropsis bengalensis* or *Sypheotides indica.* [origin unknown]

floriculture /'flawrikulchə, 'flo-/ *noun* the cultivation and management of ornamental and flowering plants. >> **floricultural** /-'kulch(ə)rəl/ *adj*, **floriculturally** /-'kulch(ə)rəli/ *adv*, **floriculturist** *noun.*

florid /'florid/ *adj* **1** tinged with red; ruddy: *a florid complexion.* **2** excessively flowery or ornate in style: *florid writing.* **3** said of a disease or its symptoms: occurring in fully developed form. >> **floridity** /flo'riditi/ *noun*, **floridly** *adv*, **floridness** *noun.* [Latin *floridus* blooming, flowery, from *florēre*: see FLOURISH[1]]

floriferous /flaw'rifərəs/ *adj* said of a plant: producing or capable of producing flowers, *esp* in abundance. >> **floriferously** *adv*, **floriferousness** *noun.* [Latin *florifer* flower-bearing, from *flor-, flos* FLOWER[1]]

florilegium /flawri'leeji·əm, flo-/ *noun* (*pl* **florilegia** /-jə, -ji·ə/ *or* **florilegiums**) *archaic* an anthology of extracts from various literary texts. [Latin *florilegium*, literally 'bouquet', from *florilegus* culling flowers, from FLORI- + *legere* to gather]

florin /'florin/ *noun* **1** a former British or Commonwealth coin worth two shillings. **2** any of various former gold coins of European countries, *esp* a Dutch guilder. **3** the basic monetary unit of Aruba, divided into 100 cents.

Word history
Middle English via French from Old Italian *fiorino*, from *fiore* flower, from Latin *flor-, flos* FLOWER[1]. The word florin was applied to various European coins, orig to a gold coin issued in Florence in the 13th cent. which had a fleur-de-lis, the city's emblem, on the reverse from the lily on the coins.

florist /'florist/ *noun* **1a** a person who deals in or grows flowers and ornamental plants for sale. **b** a shop that sells cut flowers and floral arrangements. **2** a person who makes floral arrangements. >> **floristry** /-tri/ *noun.*

floristic /flo'ristik/ *adj* relating to flowers or to a flora. >> **floristically** *adv.*

floristics *pl noun* (*treated as sing.*) the scientific study of the types of plant species present in a particular area, *esp* with reference to their relative distribution and interrelationships.

-florous *comb. form* forming adjectives, with the meaning: having or bearing flowers of the type or number specified: *uniflorous.* [late Latin *-florus*, from Latin *flor-, flos* FLOWER[1]]

floruit /'flooroo·it/ *noun* used to indicate the date or period when the person in question, *esp* a historical figure whose birth and death dates are unknown, lived, worked, or was most active or productive. [Latin *floruit* he flourished, from *florēre*: see FLOURISH[1]]

flory /'flawri/ *or* **fleury** /'floo·əri/ *adj* **1** in heraldry, decorated with fleurs-de-lis. **2** said of a cross: with the arms terminating in a trefoil shape. [Old French *florē* from *flour*: see FLOWER[1]]

floss[1] /flos/ *noun* **1** waste or short silk, *esp* from the outer part of a silkworm's cocoon. **2** soft thread of silk or mercerized cotton for embroidery. **3** soft thread, often waxed, for cleaning between the teeth. **4** silky plant fibres, *esp* on maize cobs or cotton bolls. [prob from French *soie floche* floss silk, from Old French *flosche* down, nap]

floss[2] *verb trans* to clean (one's teeth) with dental floss. >> *verb intrans* to use dental floss to clean one's teeth.

flossy /'flosi/ *adj* (**flossier, flossiest**) **1** composed of or resembling floss. **2** *chiefly NAmer, informal* ornate, *esp* in a vulgar, tasteless, or superficial way; flashy.

flotage *or* **floatage** /'flohtij/ *noun* **1** the activity of floating or the ability to float. **2** = FLOTSAM. [FLOAT[2] + -AGE]

flotarium *or* **floatarium** /floh'teəri·əm/ *noun* (*pl* **flotariums** *or* **floatariums**) a commercial establishment where flotation tanks may be hired for short periods. [FLOAT[2] + -ARIUM]

flotation *or* **floatation** /floh'taysh(ə)n/ *noun* **1** the act, process, or state of floating. **2a** the process of launching a company on the stock market by offering shares in the company for the first time. **b** the process of raising a loan or extra capital for a company or business venture by issuing bonds or shares. **3** the separation of particles of a material, e.g. pulverized ore, according to their relative capacity for floating on a liquid. [FLOAT² + -ATION]

flotation tank *or* **floatation tank** *noun* a pod-like chamber containing a small amount of mineral-rich water that a person floats in as a form of stress-relief therapy, often with relaxing background music playing.

flotel *or* **floatel** /floh'tel/ *noun* a platform or vessel with sleeping accommodation and leisure facilities for the workers on an oil rig. [blend of FLOATING and HOTEL]

flotilla /flə'tilə/ *noun* a small fleet of ships, *esp* warships. [Spanish *flotilla*, dimin. of *flota* fleet]

flotsam /'flots(ə)m/ *noun* **1** floating wreckage, *esp* of a ship or its cargo: compare JETSAM. **2** a collective term for vagrants and homeless or destitute people. ✳ **flotsam and jetsam** accumulated odds and ends. [Anglo-French *floteson* from Old French *floter* to float, of Germanic origin]

flounce¹ /flowns/ *verb intrans* (*often* + out/off/about/away) to move in a violent or exaggerated fashion, *esp* to emphasize one's anger: *He flounced out of the room.* ⟫⟫ **flouncy** *adj.* [perhaps of Scandinavian origin]

flounce² *noun* the act or an instance of flouncing.

flounce³ *noun* a wide gathered strip of fabric attached by the gathered edge, e.g. to the hem of a skirt or dress. ⟫⟫ **flounced** *adj*, **flouncy** *adj*. [alteration of Middle English *frounce* fold, plant, from Old French *fronce*, of Germanic origin]

flounder¹ /'flowndə/ *noun* (*pl* **flounders** *or collectively* **flounder**) any of various flatfishes including some marine food fishes: *esp Platichthys flesus*. [Middle English from Old French *flondre*, of Scandinavian origin]

flounder² *verb intrans* (**floundered, floundering**) **1** to stagger or thrash about ineffectually in soft mud or water, trying to maintain one's footing or keep from drowning. **2** to behave or speak in a blundering or incompetent way, as a result of being at a loss. ⟫⟫ **flounder** *noun*. [prob alteration of FOUNDER³, influenced by BLUNDER¹ or FLOUNDER¹]

Usage note

flounder *or* **founder?** *Flounder* means to struggle to move (*floundering in the mud*); *founder* when referring to a ship means 'to sink' and when referring to an animal means 'to go lame'. In their extended senses these two words are sometimes confused, but it is helpful to make the following distinctions: *Founder* implies complete failure: *The plans foundered after attempts to raise money failed*; while someone who *flounders* is struggling awkwardly: *flounder through a speech*.

flour¹ /flowə/ *noun* **1** finely ground meal, *esp* of wheat. **2** a fine soft powder. [Middle English; orig a sense of FLOWER¹ 'best part', that is, the finest grade of ground wheat; the spellings *flour* and *flower* remained undifferentiated till the 18th cent.]

flour² *verb trans* **1** to coat (something) with flour. **2** to make (e.g. grain) into flour.

flourish¹ /'flurish/ *verb intrans* **1** to grow luxuriantly; to thrive. **2** to achieve success; to prosper. **3** to be in good health. **4a** to reach a height of activity, development, or influence: *Unexpectedly the newspaper flourished.* **b** to be at the height of one's career or working most productively at a specified date or during a specified period: *a Venetian painter who flourished circa 1560.* ➤ *verb trans* to wave or brandish (something) with dramatic gestures. ⟫⟫ **flourisher** *noun*. [Middle English *florisshen* from early French *florir*, ultimately from Latin *florēre* to blossom, flourish, from *flor-, flos* FLOWER¹]

flourish² *noun* **1a** a decorative embellishment, *esp* a flowing curve on handwriting, scrollwork, etc. **b** an ostentatious piece of language or passage in a speech or written text. **2** the act or an instance of flourishing or brandishing. **3** an ostentatious or dramatic action: *He removed his hat with a flourish.* **4a** a fanfare on a brass instrument, *esp* a trumpet. **b** an ornate or florid passage in a piece of music.

floury *adj* (**flourier, flouriest**) **1** resembling flour. **2** covered with flour. **3** said of a potato: having a light fluffy texture when cooked. ⟫⟫ **flouriness** *noun*.

flout /flowt/ *verb trans* **1** to treat (something, *esp* a convention or rule of behaviour) with contemptuous disregard: *openly flouting the rules.* **2** *archaic* to mock or insult (somebody or something). ⟫⟫ **flouter** *noun*. [prob from Middle English *flouten* to play the flute, from *floute*: see FLUTE¹]

Usage note
flout *or* **flaunt?** See note at FLAUNT.

flow¹ /floh/ *verb intrans* **1** said of water or other liquid: to move or pour steadily and continuously: *Muddy water flowed along the gutter; Blood flows round our bodies.* **2** said of a river or stream: to move in a certain direction: *The Humber flows into the North Sea.* **3** said of the tide: to move towards the land; to rise: compare EBB¹. **4** said of gas or electricity: to pass along pipes or cables. **5** said of crowds, traffic, etc: to move steadily along: *Traffic is flowing again after an earlier accident.* **6a** said of long hair, loose clothing, etc: to swing or stream gracefully: *long flowing robes.* **b** to have a smooth graceful continuity: *the flowing lines of the new car model.* **7** said of ideas or words: to come easily to one as one speaks or writes. **8** said of conversation: to be animated and lively. **9** to proceed from, or be the result or outcome of something: *the wealth that flows from our labour.* **10** said of rock or other solid material: to deform under stress without cracking or rupturing. ✳ **be flowing with** to have a plentiful supply of (something): *a land flowing with milk and honey.* ⟫⟫ **flowing** *adj*, **flowingly** *adv*. [Old English *flōwan*]

flow² *noun* **1** the action of flowing: *interrupt the flow of the stream.* **2** the action of moving along steadily: *the flow of traffic; the flow of conversation.* **3** the action of issuing forth in a stream: *stop the flow of blood; the flow of ideas.* **4** the rising of the tide: compare EBB¹. **5** *Scot.* **a** a watery swamp or bog. **b** a sea inlet. ✳ **go with the flow** to be content to be carried along by events, current thinking, etc.

flow chart *noun* a diagram consisting of a set of symbols, e.g. rectangles or diamonds, and connecting lines, that shows the step-by-step progression through a usu complicated procedure or system.

flow diagram *noun* = FLOW CHART.

flower¹ /'flowə/ *noun* **1a** a structure in an angiosperm plant that is specialized for reproduction and typically consists of a shortened axis bearing leaves modified to form petals, sepals, carpels (female reproductive structures; see CARPEL) or stamens (male reproductive structures; see STAMEN). **b** a plant that produces a reproductive structure of this kind. **c** a plant that produces any similar type of reproductive structure. **2a** the finest or most perfect part or example of something: *the flower of a nation's youth destroyed in war.* **b** the finest, most vigorous period; the prime: *in the flower of his manhood.* **c** a state of blooming or flourishing: *when most of the plants are in flower.* **3** (*in pl*) a finely divided powder produced *esp* by condensation or sublimation (conversion of a gas directly to a solid; see SUBLIMATE¹ (2)): *flowers of sulphur.* ⟫⟫ **flowerless** *adj*, **flower-like** *adj*. [Middle English *flour* flower, best of anything (see also FLOUR¹) via Old French *flor, flour* from Latin *flor-, flos*]

flower² *verb intrans* (**flowered, flowering**) **1** said of a plant: to produce flowers; to blossom. **2** to develop and flourish: *It was not until his twenties that his creative talent began to flower.* ⟫⟫ **flowerer** *noun*, **flowering** *adj and noun*.

flowered *adj* **1** having a pattern of flowers: *flowered dresses.* **2** (*used in combinations*) producing flowers of the kind specified: *a purple-flowered shrub.*

floweret /'flowərit/ *noun* a floret, *esp* of cauliflower or broccoli.

flower girl *noun* **1** a girl or woman who sells flowers, *esp* in a market or the street. **2** a young girl who is part of the bridal party at a wedding.

flower head *noun* a rounded or flattened cluster of densely packed stalkless flowers at the top of a stem, having the appearance of a single flower; = INFLORESCENCE.

flowering plant *noun* **1** a plant that produces flowers; = ANGIOSPERM. **2** a plant notable and cultivated for its ornamental flowers.

flowerpecker /'flowəpekə/ *noun* any of various species of very small Australasian or SE Asian songbirds that feed on the insects in flowers: family Dicaeidae.

flowerpot *noun* an earthenware or plastic container, typically the shape of a small bucket, in which to grow plants.

flower power *noun* a movement of the late 1960s which promoted peace and love as forces to change the world and used flowers as its symbols.

flowery /'flowəri/ *adj* **1** relating to, full of, or patterned with flowers: *flowery wallpaper; flowery meadows; flowery May.* **2** containing or using highly ornate language: *flowery speeches.* ⟫⟫ **floweriness** *noun*.

flown /flohn/ *verb* past part. of FLY¹.

flow-on *noun Aus* an adjustment in pay that is made to restore differentials or parity of pay following an increase in similar or related occupations: *This could regenerate the wages' spiral and begin flow-ons throughout the work force* — The Age (Melbourne).

flow sheet *noun* = FLOW CHART.

flowstone *noun* a deposit of a calcium mineral, *esp* calcium carbonate, formed by water flowing in a very thin sheet over limestone rocks.

fl oz *abbr* fluid ounce.

Flt Lt *abbr* Flight Lieutenant.

Flt Off *abbr* Flight Officer.

Flt Sgt *abbr* Flight Sergeant.

flu /flooh/ *noun* influenza.

flub[1] /flub/ *verb* (**flubbed, flubbing**) *NAmer, informal* ➤ *verb trans* to botch or bungle (something). ➤ *verb intrans* to blunder. [origin unknown]

flub[2] *noun NAmer, informal* the act or an instance of flubbing.

fluctuant /'fluktyooənt/ *adj* **1** unstable; fluctuating. **2** movable and compressible: *a fluctuant abscess.*

fluctuate /'fluktyooayt/ *verb intrans* **1** to rise and fall; to swing back and forth. **2** to change continually and often irregularly; to waver. ➤ *verb trans* to cause (something) to change continually and often irregularly. ➤➤ **fluctuation** /-'aysh(ə)n/ *noun.* [Latin *fluctuatus*, past part. of *fluctuare* to undulate, from *fluctus* flow, wave, past part. of *fluere* to flow]

flue /flooh/ *noun* **1** a channel in a chimney for flame and smoke. **2** a pipe for conveying heat, e.g. to water in a steam boiler. [origin uncertain]

flue-cured *adj* said of tobacco: cured by heat, usu from flues, without exposure to smoke or fumes.

fluellen /floo'elin/ *noun* either of two species of small creeping plants with purple or yellow flowers, commonly found in cornfields: genus *Kickxia.* [alteration of Welsh *llysiau Llywelyn* Llewelyn's herbs, prob named after *Llewelyn ap Jerweth* or his grandson *Llewelyn ap Gruffud,* 13th-cent. Welsh princes]

fluence /'flooh-əns/ *noun Brit, informal* magical power or influence. [shortening of INFLUENCE[1]]

fluent /'flooh-ənt/ *adj* **1a** able to speak, write, read, etc without difficulty· *Many children rapidly become fluent readers*; *She's fluent in Welsh.* **b** said of somebody's command of a language: effortless and competent: *They speak fluent Italian.* **2** effortlessly smooth and rapid; polished: *a fluent performance.* **3** flowing or capable of flowing; = FLUID[2] (1). ➤➤ **fluency** /-si/ *noun,* **fluently** *adv.* [Latin *fluent-, fluens,* present part. of *fluere* to flow]

flue pipe *noun* an organ pipe whose tone is produced by an air current striking the lip and causing the air within to vibrate: compare REED PIPE.

fluff[1] /fluf/ *noun* **1a** small loose bits of waste material, e.g. hairs and threads, that stick to clothes, carpets, etc. **b** soft light fur, down, etc. **2** *informal* a blunder, *esp* in performance. ✳ **bit of fluff** *informal* an attractive young person, *esp* a young woman considered as being frivolous or as lacking intelligence. [prob alteration of *flue* fluff, from Flemish *vluwe*]

fluff[2] *verb trans* **1** (+ out/up) to make (something) fuller, plumper, or fluffier: *The bird fluffed up its feathers; fluff up the pillows; fluff out one's hair.* **2a** *informal* to fail to perform or achieve (something) successfully; to bungle (it): *He fluffed his exam.* **b** *informal* to do (something) badly, *esp* to forget (one's lines) in a play. ➤ *verb intrans* to make a mistake, *esp* in a performance.

fluffy *adj* (**fluffier, fluffiest**) **1** like or covered with fluff: *fluffy chicks; fluffy clouds.* **2** said of whipped foods, etc: light and soft or airy: *a fluffy sponge cake; fluffy soufflés; fluffy mashed potato.* ➤➤ **fluffily** *adv,* **fluffiness** *noun.*

flugelhorn /'floohglhawn/ *noun* a valved brass musical instrument resembling a cornet. [German *Flügelhorn,* from *Flügel* wing, flank + *Horn* horn; from its use to signal to the outlying beaters in a shoot]

fluid[1] /'flooh-id/ *noun* **1** a substance, *esp* a liquid or gas, that can flow freely, has no fixed shape, yields to pressure, and conforms to the shape of its container. **2** a liquid in the body of an animal or plant: *cerebrospinal fluid.* ➤➤ **fluidal** *adj.* [French *fluide* from Latin *fluidus,* from *fluere* to flow]

fluid[2] *adj* **1** said of liquids, gases, etc: capable of flowing, *esp* in having particles that easily change their relative position without separation of the mass and that yield to pressure. **2** said of a form

or shape: likely or tending to change or move; not fixed. **3** relating to fluids: *fluid mechanics.* **4** said of a coupling or clutch: using a fluid to effect power transmission. **5** said of a style of movement: smooth or easy; effortlessly graceful. **6** said of plans, etc: not yet definite; capable of alteration or adaptation. **7** said of assets: easily converted into cash; = LIQUID[1] (5). ➤➤ **fluidity** /flooh'iditi/ *noun,* **fluidly** *adv,* **fluidness** *noun.*

fluid drachm /dram/ (*NAmer* **fluidram** /'flooh·idram/) *noun* a unit of capacity equal to one eighth of a fluid ounce (about 3.55ml).

fluid drive *noun* a device, e.g. an automatic car gearbox, containing fluid that transmits power from an engine to a driven unit, e.g. the wheels of a car.

fluidics /flooh'idiks/ *pl noun* (treated as *sing.*) the study or use of fluid flow in shaped channels to produce devices, e.g. an amplifier or switch, that function like electronic components. ➤➤ **fluidic** *adj.*

fluidize *or* **fluidise** *verb trans* **1** to cause (something, *esp* a solid) to flow like a fluid. **2** to suspend (e.g. solid particles) in a rapidly moving stream of gas or vapour to induce flowing motion of the whole; *esp* to fluidize the particles of (a loose bed of material) in an upward flow, e.g. of a gas, to increase the rate of a chemical or physical reaction. ➤➤ **fluidization** /-'zaysh(ə)n/ *noun,* **fluidizer** *noun.*

fluid mechanics *pl noun* (treated as *sing.*) the branch of engineering that studies the mechanical properties and flow of liquids; = HYDRAULICS.

fluid ounce (*NAmer* **fluidounce** /flooh·i'downs/) *noun* **1** a British unit of liquid capacity equal to one twentieth of an imperial pint (about 28.4ml). **2** a US unit of liquid capacity equal to one sixteenth of a US pint (about 29.54ml).

fluidram /'flooh·idram/ *noun NAmer* see FLUID DRACHM.

fluke[1] /floohk/ *noun* **1** any of various parasitic flatworms, e.g. a liver fluke: classes Trematoda and Monogenea. **2** *chiefly NAmer* a flatfish, *esp* a flounder. [Old English *flōc*]

fluke[2] *noun* **1** the part of an anchor that digs into the sea, river, etc bottom. **2** a barbed end, e.g. of a harpoon. **3** either of the lobes of a whale's tail. [perhaps from FLUKE[1]; from its flat shape]

fluke[3] *noun* **1** an accidental success, and therefore one unlikely to be repeated: *If I foul up now, they'll all laugh and say Easy Rider was a fluke* — Jack Nicholson. **2** a strange or lucky coincidence: *It was a fluke that we discovered the answer.* [origin unknown]

fluke[4] *verb trans* to achieve or gain (something) by accident or luck.

fluky *or* **flukey** *adj* (**flukier, flukiest**) **1** happening by or depending on chance rather than skill. **2** said *esp* of wind: unsteady; changeable. ➤➤ **flukily** *adv,* **flukiness** *noun.*

flume /floohm/ *noun* **1** an inclined channel for conveying water, e.g. for power generation or for floating logs down. **2** an amusement-park chute with a shallow stream of water flowing down it, or one of tubular design at a swimming pool. **3** a deep gorge with a river or stream running through it. [prob from Middle English *flum* river, via Old French from Latin *flumen,* from *fluere* to flow]

flummery /'fluməri/ *noun* (*pl* **-ies,** *pl* **flummeries**) **1** *informal* pretentious humbug. **2** a sweet dish typically made with flour or oatmeal, eggs, honey, and cream. [Welsh *llymru,* the oatmeal dish]

flummox /'fluməks/ *verb trans* to bewilder or confuse (somebody) completely. [origin uncertain]

flump /flump/ *verb intrans* to move or drop with a dull heavy sound: *flump into a chair.* ➤ *verb trans* to bring (something) down heavily. ➤➤ **flump** *noun.* [imitative]

flung /flung/ *verb* past tense and past part. of FLING[1].

flunk /flungk/ *verb intrans chiefly NAmer, informal* **1** to fail, *esp* in an examination or course. **2** (+ out) to be turned out of a school or college for failure. ➤ *verb trans chiefly NAmer, informal* **1** to give a failing mark to (a candidate). **2** to get a failing mark in (an examination, subject, etc): *The usual crew had flunked the first grade again* — Harper Lee. [perhaps blend of FLINCH[1] and FUNK[2]]

flunky *or* **flunkey** *noun* (*pl* **flunkies** *or* **flunkeys**) **1** a person performing menial duties: *Sam works as a flunky in a cookhouse.* **2** a yesman; a servile follower. **3** a liveried servant. ➤➤ **flunkeyism** *noun.* [Scots, perhaps from FLANKER in the sense 'a person who stands by somebody's side']

fluor- *or* **fluoro-** *comb. form* forming nouns, denoting: **1** fluorine: *fluoride; fluorocarbon.* **2** fluorescence: *fluoroscope.* [French, from *fluor*: see FLUORINE]

fluoresce /flooə'res/ *verb intrans* to glow with fluorescence. ⟫ **fluorescer** *noun.*

fluorescence /flooə'res(ə)ns/ *noun* **1** the emitting of electromagnetic radiation, usu as visible light, as a result of the simultaneous absorption of radiation of shorter wavelength. **2** the light or other radiation emitted in this process.

fluorescent /flooə'res(ə)nt/ *adj* **1** of or having fluorescence. **2** bright and glowing as a result of fluorescence. **3** brightly colourful: *a fluorescent pink.*

fluorescent lamp *noun* a tubular electric lamp with a coating of fluorescent material on its inner surface.

fluori- *comb. form* = FLUOR- (2).

fluoridate /'flooəridayt/ *verb trans* to add a fluoride to (e.g. drinking water) to prevent tooth decay. ⟫ **fluoridation** /-'daysh(ə)n/ *noun.*

fluoride /'flooəried/ *noun* a compound of fluorine, e.g. one added to toothpaste or drinking water to prevent tooth decay.

fluorimeter /flooə'rimitə/ *noun* = FLUOROMETER.

fluorinate /'flooərinayt/ *verb trans* **1** to treat (something) or cause (a chemical) to combine with fluorine or a compound of fluorine. **2** = FLUORIDATE. ⟫ **fluorination** /-'naysh(ə)n/ *noun.*

fluorine /'flooəreen/ *noun* a non-metallic chemical element of the halogen group that normally occurs as a pale yellowish toxic gas: symbol F, atomic number 9. [French *fluor*, a mineral containing fluorine and belonging to a group used as fluxes, now specifically fluorspar, from Latin *fluere* to flow]

fluorite /'flooəriet/ *noun* = FLUORSPAR.

fluoro- *comb. form* see FLUOR-.

fluorocarbon /,flooəroh'kahb(ə)n/ *noun* any of various chemically inert compounds containing carbon and fluorine, used chiefly as lubricants and refrigerants and in making resins and plastics.

fluorometer /flooə'romitə/ *noun* an instrument for measuring fluorescence and related phenomena. ⟫ **fluorometric** /-'metrik/ *adj,* **fluorometry** /-'romitri/ *noun.*

fluoroscope /'flooərəskohp/ *noun* an instrument with a screen coated with a fluorescent substance, used for observing the internal structure of an opaque object, e.g. the living body, by means of X-rays. ⟫ **fluoroscopic** /-'skopik/ *adj,* **fluoroscopically** /-'sko-pikli/ *adv,* **fluoroscopy** /-'roskəpi/ *noun.*

fluorosis /flooə'rohsis/ *noun* an abnormal condition, e.g. mottling of the teeth, caused by excessive intake of fluorine compounds. ⟫ **fluorotic** /-'rotik/ *adj.*

fluorspar /'flooəspah/ *noun* a mineral consisting of calcium fluoride that occurs in a colourless and various coloured forms, the chief source of fluorine and also used in glass-making and as a flux in the manufacture and refining of metals. [FLUOR- + SPAR⁴]

flurry¹ /'fluri/ *noun* (*pl* **flurries**) **1a** a gust of wind. **b** a brief fall of snow or rain, or a quantity of something such as leaves, blown by a light wind. **2** a state of nervous excitement or bustle. **3** a short-lived outburst of trading activity. [prob from obsolete *flurr* to scatter, flutter, of imitative origin]

flurry² *verb* (**flurries, flurried, flurrying**) ⟫ *verb intrans* **1** to become agitated and confused. **2** to come or move in flurries. ⟫ *verb trans* to cause (somebody) to become agitated and confused.

flush¹ /flush/ *noun* **1a** a tinge of red, *esp* in the cheeks; a blush. **b** the act or an instance of flushing. **c** a fresh and vigorous state: *in the first flush of womanhood.* **2** a transitory sensation of extreme heat, e.g. a hot flush. **3a** a surge of emotion: *a flush of anger.* **b** a sudden increase, *esp* of new plant growth. **4a** a sudden flow, *esp* of water. **b** the cleansing of something, e.g. a toilet, with a flow of water. **c** *Brit* a device for flushing toilets or drains. [perhaps modification of Latin *fluxus* flow, from *fluxere* to flow]

flush² *verb intrans* **1a** to glow brightly with a ruddy or rosy colour. **b** to blush. **2** to flow and spread suddenly and freely. **3** to produce new growth: *The plants flushed twice during the year.* ⟫ *verb trans* **1a** to cause liquid to flow over or through (something, e.g. a toilet), *esp* to cleanse it. **b** to cause (something) to flow or be carried along on a stream of liquid. **c** (*often* + away) to dispose of (e.g. waste) in

this way. **2a** to cause (somebody) to blush. **b** to cause (something) to glow with a ruddy or rosy colour. ⟫ **flusher** *noun.*

flush³ *adj* **1a** having or forming a continuous edge or plane surface; not indented, recessed, or projecting: *Make the panelling flush with the wall.* **b** arranged edge to edge so as to fit snugly. **2** *informal* having a plentiful supply of money. **3** *informal* readily available; abundant. **4** filled to overflowing. ⟫ **flushness** *noun.* [origin uncertain; perhaps from or related to FLUSH¹]

flush⁴ *adv* **1** so as to form a level or even surface or edge. **2** squarely: *She hit him flush on the chin.*

flush⁵ *verb trans* to make (something) flush: *Flush the headings on the page.*

flush⁶ *verb trans* **1** to cause (*esp* a game bird) to take flight suddenly. **2** (*often* + out) to force (somebody) to leave a place of concealment: *The gardener flushed the boys from their hiding place.* ⟫ *verb intrans* said *esp* of a game bird: to take flight suddenly. [Middle English *flusshen*, perhaps of imitative origin]

flush⁷ *noun* a hand of playing cards, *esp* in a gambling game such as poker, all of the same suit. [early French *flus, fluz,* from Latin *fluxus*: see FLUSH¹]

flushed *adj* **1** having an abnormal redness in the cheeks: *You're looking a bit flushed. Are you feeling all right?* **2** (+ with) excited or inflamed: *flushed with victory.*

fluster¹ /'flustə/ *verb* (**flustered, flustering**) ⟫ *verb trans* to make (somebody) agitated, nervous, or confused. ⟫ *verb intrans* to become agitated, nervous, or confused. ⟫ **flustered** *adj.* [prob of Scandinavian origin]

fluster² *noun* a state of agitated confusion: *They were in a bit of a fluster.*

flute¹ /flooht/ *noun* **1a** a woodwind musical instrument that consists of a cylindrical tube stopped at one end, held horizontally and played by blowing air across a side hole while closing the other holes with fingers or movable pads. It has a range from middle C upwards for three octaves. **b** any of various similar instruments in which sound is produced by air being blown across a hole. **2a** a grooved pleat or frill on a garment, upholstery, etc. **b** any of the vertical parallel grooves on the shaft of a classical column. **3** a tall narrow wineglass. ⟫ **flutelike** *adj.* [Middle English *floute* via French from Old Provençal *flaut*]

flute² *verb intrans* to produce a flutelike sound. ⟫ *verb trans* **1** to utter (something) with a flutelike sound; to produce (a flutelike sound). **2** to form flutes in (a column, garment, etc). ⟫ **fluter** *noun.*

fluting *noun* a series of parallel grooves or pleats.

flutist *noun chiefly NAmer* = FLAUTIST.

flutter¹ /'flutə/ *verb* (**fluttered, fluttering**) ⟫ *verb intrans* **1** to flap the wings rapidly. **2a** to move or fall with quick wavering or flapping motions: *flags fluttering in the wind.* **b** to beat or vibrate in irregular spasms: *His pulse fluttered.* **3** to move about or behave in an agitated aimless manner. ⟫ *verb trans* to make (something) flutter. ⟫ **flutterer** *noun.* [Old English *floterian,* frequentative of *flotian* FLOAT²]

flutter² *noun* **1** the act or an instance of fluttering. **2a** a state of nervous confusion, excitement, or commotion. **b** abnormal spasmodic fluttering of the heart, etc. **3** a distortion in reproduced sound similar to but at a faster rate than WOW⁴ (distortion heard as slow rise and fall). **4** an unwanted oscillation, e.g. of an aircraft part or bridge, set up by natural forces. **5** *chiefly Brit* a small gamble or bet. ⟫ **fluttery** *adj.*

fluty /'floohti/ *adj* (**flutier, flutiest**) like the sound of a flute; light and clear.

fluvial /'floohvi·əl/ *adj* relating to, found in, or living in or near a stream or river. [Latin *fluvialis* from *fluvius* river, from *fluere* to flow]

fluviatile /'floohvi·ətil, -tiel/ *adj technical* = FLUVIAL. [via French from Latin *fluviatilis* from *fluvius*: see FLUVIAL]

flux¹ /fluks/ *noun* **1a** a continuous flow or flowing: *Beauty halts and freezes the melting flux of nature* — Camille Paglia. **b** an influx. **2** continual change; fluctuation: *The programme was in a state of flux.* **3a** a substance used to promote fusion of metals, e.g. in soldering or brazing. **b** a substance used in smelting ores and refining metals to promote the melting of the ore or metal and to remove impurities. **4a** the rate of transfer of a fluid, particles, or energy across a given surface. **b** the strength or effect of the forces acting in an area of an electric or magnetic field. **5** *archaic* an abnormal flowing of fluid, *esp* excrement, from the body. [Middle English via French from Latin *fluxus* flow, from *fluere* to flow]

flux² *verb trans* **1** to melt (something) so that it becomes fluid. **2** to treat (e.g. metal to be soldered) with a flux. ➤ *verb intrans* to become fluid.

fluxion /'flʌkʃ(ə)n/ *noun* **1** constant change. **2** *archaic.* **a** in calculus, = DERIVATIVE² (2). **b** (*in pl*) = CALCULUS (2A). ➤➤ **fluxional** *adj.* [via French from Latin *fluxion-, fluxio*, from *fluere* to flow]

fly¹ /flie/ *verb* (**flies, flying, flew** /flooh/, **flown** /flohn/) ➤ *verb intrans* **1a** to move in or through the air by means of wings. **b** to move through the air or space. **c** to soar in the air: *Kites flying in the breeze.* **d** to float or wave in the air: *Flags were flying at half-mast.* **2a** to operate or travel in an aircraft or spacecraft. **b** to be transported by air. **3a** to move or pass swiftly: *He flew past me.* **b** to pass suddenly and violently into a specified state: *He flew into a rage.* **c** to seem to pass quickly: *Our holiday simply flew.* **4** *informal* to depart in haste; to dash. **5a** to take flight; to flee: *It is sometimes better not to struggle against temptation. Either fly or yield at once* — F H Bradley. **b** *literary* to fade and disappear; to vanish: *The shadows have flown.* ➤ *verb trans* **1a** to operate (an aircraft or spacecraft) in flight. **b** to transport (somebody or something) by aircraft. **c** to journey over (a specified region) by flying: *fly the Atlantic.* **d** to use (a specified airline) for travelling: *I always fly British Airways.* **e** to cause (something) to fly: *fly a kite.* **2** to flee or escape from (somebody or something). ✳ **fly a kite** *informal* to make information public or set up a rumour, or take some other action, in order to gauge public opinion on some matter. **2** *archaic* to obtain a loan or credit by means of a bill of exchange signed by a guarantor. **fly at** to make a sudden verbal or physical attack on (somebody). **fly high 1** to be ambitious. **2** to be successful. **3** to be elated. **fly in the face of 1** to act in open defiance or disobedience to (e.g. somebody's orders). **2** to be contrary to (a belief, common sense, etc). **fly off the handle** *informal* to become very angry, *esp* without any warning. ➤➤ **flyable** *adj*, **flying** *noun.* [Old English *flēogan*]

fly² *noun* (*pl* **flies**) **1** an act or the process of flying. **2** (*in pl*) the space over a stage where scenery and equipment can be hung. **3a** an opening in a garment, etc concealed by a fold of cloth extending over the fastener. **b** (*usu in pl*) such an opening in the front of a pair of trousers. **4** = FLY SHEET (1). **5a** the outer or loose end of a flag: compare HOIST² (3A). **b** the length of an extended flag from its staff or support. **6** = FLYWHEEL. **7** (*pl also* **flys**) *chiefly Brit* a light covered horse-drawn carriage.

fly³ *noun* (*pl* **flies**) **1** any of a large order of insects having two membranous wings and mouthparts adapted for piercing and sucking: order Diptera. **2** any of various winged insects that are not true flies: *caddis fly; butterfly.* **3** a natural or artificial fly attached to a fishhook for use as bait. ✳ **fly in the ointment** a detracting factor or element. **fly on the wall** somebody who watches others while not being noticed himself or herself. **there are no flies on** there is little or no possibility of deceiving or cheating (him, her, etc). [Old English *flēoge* winged insect]

fly⁴ *adj* (**flier, fliest**) *chiefly Brit, informal* clever and worldly-wise, *esp* in being able to use people or situations to gain advantages. [prob from FLY¹]

fly agaric /'agərik, ə'garik/ *noun* a poisonous toadstool usu with a bright red cap with small white scaly patches: *Amanita muscaria.* [because it was a source of poison for flypaper]

fly ash *noun* fine particles of noncombustible ash carried out of a bed of solid fuel during combustion, *esp* in power stations.

flyaway *adj* **1** lacking practical sense; flighty. **2** said *esp* of the hair: tending not to stay in place.

flyblow *noun* **1** the egg or young larva of a flesh fly or blowfly. **2** infestation, *esp* of meat, with flyblows. [FLY³ + BLOW¹ (10)]

flyblown *adj* **1** infested with flyblows. **2a** impure; tainted. **b** not new; used.

flyby /'fliebie/ *noun* (*pl* **flybys**) a flight of a spacecraft close to a celestial body, *esp* to obtain scientific data.

fly-by-night¹ *adj* **1** given to making a quick profit, usu by disreputable or irresponsible acts; untrustworthy. **2** transitory; passing: *fly-by-night fashions.*

fly-by-night² *noun* **1** an untrustworthy person, *esp* somebody who seeks to evade responsibilities or debts. **2** a shaky business enterprise.

flycatcher *noun* any of various species of small birds that feed on insects caught while flying: *esp* family Muscicapidae.

fly-drive *adj* said *esp* of a holiday: including flights to and from a destination and the hire of a car at that destination.

flyer *or* **flier** /'flie-ə/ *noun* **1** a person or thing that flies or moves very fast. **2a** a passenger on an aircraft. **b** a pilot. **c** an airman. **3** a small leaflet or handbill, *esp* one advertising an event, product, etc. **4** *informal* a fast or auspicious start, *esp* a flying start in athletics. **5** *chiefly NAmer, informal* a daring or speculative business venture or investment. **6** a rectangular step in a straight flight of stairs: compare WINDER (2).

fly-fish *verb intrans* to fish using a rod and artificial flies for bait.

fly-fishing *noun* fishing, e.g. for salmon or trout, using a rod and artificial flies as bait: *If fishing is a religion, fly-fishing is high church* — Tom Brokaw.

fly front *noun* a concealed opening in a garment, *esp* trousers: see FLY² (3).

fly-half *noun* = STAND-OFF HALF. [FLY²]

flying¹ *adj* **1a** moving in the air or capable of doing so. **b** rapidly moving: *flying feet.* **c** very brief; hasty: *a flying visit.* **d** passing quickly. **2** intended or ready for fast movement or instant action: *flying pickets.* **3** of or using an aircraft or of the operation of an aircraft. **4** traversed, or to be traversed, after a flying start. ✳ **with flying colours** with complete or eminent success: *She passed the exam with flying colours.*

flying² *noun* **1** the act or an instance of travelling by air. **2** the operation of an aircraft or spacecraft.

flying boat *noun* a seaplane with a hull adapted for floating.

flying bomb *noun* a pilotless aircraft carrying explosives, *esp* a V-1.

flying bridge *noun* the highest navigational bridge on a ship.

flying buttress *noun* a projecting arched structure that supports a wall or building.

flying doctor *noun* a doctor who visits patients in remote areas by aeroplane, *esp* in Australia.

flying fish *noun* any of several species of tropical fishes that have long pectoral fins and are able to glide some distance through the air: genus *Exocoethus.*

flying fox *noun* any of various fruit-eating bats with foxlike faces, found in Africa, Asia, and Australia: suborder Megachiroptera.

flying gurnard *noun* any of several species of marine fishes with large fins just behind the head that allow them to glide above the water for short distances: family Dactylopteridae.

flying jib *noun* on a ship with two or more triangular sails, the sail set furthest forward.

flying lemur *noun* either of two species of tree-dwelling nocturnal mammals of E India and the Philippines that are about the size of a cat and make long sailing leaps using a broad parachute-like fold of skin that hangs from the neck to the tail: genus *Cynocephalus.*

flying officer *noun* an officer in the Royal Air Force ranking below a flight lieutenant.

flying phalanger *noun* any of several species of nocturnal marsupial mammals of Australia and New Guinea that resemble flying squirrels and have thick fur and a long bushy tail: genera *Petaurus* and *Petauroides.*

flying picket *noun* a person who pickets a place of work other than his or her own, *esp* as part of a group that travels from place to place.

flying saucer *noun* any of various unidentified flying objects reported as being saucer- or disc-shaped and believed by many to come from outer space.

flying squad *noun* (*often* **Flying Squad**) a standby group of people, *esp* police, ready to move or act swiftly in an emergency.

flying squirrel *noun* any of various squirrels with folds of skin connecting the forelegs and hind legs allowing them to make long gliding leaps: *esp* subfamily Pteromyinae.

flying start *noun* **1** a start to a race in which the participants are already moving when they cross the starting line or when they receive the starting signal. **2** a privileged or successful beginning, *esp* one that gives somebody an advantage over others.

flying wing *noun* an aircraft in the shape of a large wing with no fuselage and often no tailplane.

flyleaf *noun* (*pl* **flyleaves**) a blank page at the beginning or end of a book that is fastened to the cover. [FLY² + LEAF¹]

flyover *noun* **1** *Brit* a crossing of two roads, railways, etc at different levels, or the upper level of such a crossing. **2** *chiefly NAmer* = FLY-PAST.

flypaper *noun* paper coated with a sticky, often poisonous, substance that is hung indoors to attract and kill flies.

flypast *noun Brit* a ceremonial usu low-altitude flight by one or more aircraft over an important person or a public gathering.

flyposting *noun* the unauthorized placing of advertising or political material, e.g. posters, in public places. ⟫ **flyposter** *noun.* [FLY²]

fly sheet *noun* **1** an outer protective sheet covering a tent or a flap at the entrance to a tent. **2** a small pamphlet or circular. [FLY²]

fly slip *noun* in cricket, a fielding position behind the conventional slips and about halfway to the boundary. [FLY² + SLIP²]

flyspeck *noun* a tiny spot of fly excrement. ⟫ **flyspecked** *adj.*

flyspray *noun* an aerosol spray for killing flies and other insects.

flyswatter *noun* an implement for killing insects that consists of a flat piece of usu rubber or plastic attached to a handle.

fly-tip *verb trans Brit* to dump (waste) illegally. ⟫ **fly-tipper** *noun*, **fly-tipping** *noun.*

flytrap *noun* **1** = VENUS FLYTRAP. **2** any of various devices for catching and killing flies and other insects.

flyway *noun* an established route used by birds when migrating: *the Atlantic flyway.*

flyweight *noun* **1** a weight in boxing of no more than 51kg (112lb) if professional or between 48–51kg (106–112lb) if amateur. **2** a weight in amateur wrestling of 49–52kg (107–115lb).

flywheel *noun* a wheel with a heavy rim that when revolving can either reduce speed fluctuations in the rotation of an engine or store energy: *Habit is … the enormous fly-wheel of society, its most precious conservative agent* — William James. [FLY²]

FM¹ *adj* relating to or denoting a broadcasting or receiving system using frequency modulation and usu noted for lack of interference.

FM² *abbr* Field Marshal.

Fm *abbr* the chemical symbol for fermium.

fm *abbr* **1** fathom. **2** from.

fml *abbr* formal.

f-number *noun* the ratio of the focal length of a lens to the diameter of the aperture in an optical system, *esp* a camera. [*f* from FOCAL LENGTH]

FO *abbr* **1** Field Officer. **2** Flying Officer. **3** Foreign Office.

fo. *abbr* folio.

foal¹ /fohl/ *noun* a young animal of the horse family. [Old English *fola*]

foal² *verb intrans* said of a mare: to give birth to a foal.

foam¹ /fohm/ *noun* **1a** a light frothy mass of fine bubbles formed in or on the surface of a liquid. **b** any substance in the form of a light frothy mass of bubbles. **c** a chemical froth discharged from fire extinguishers. **d** a frothy mass formed in salivating or sweating. **2** a material in a lightweight cellular form resulting from introduction of gas bubbles during manufacture. **3** (*used before a noun*) existing in the form of a foam: *a foam carpet-cleaner; a foam mattress.* **4** *literary* the sea. ⟫ **foaminess** *noun*, **foamless** *adj*, **foamy** *adj.* [Old English *fām*]

foam² *verb intrans* **1a** to produce or form foam. **b** to froth at the mouth, *esp* in anger. **2** to gush out in foam. **3a** to become covered with foam. **b** to be or become covered with something as if with foam: *streets … foaming with life* — Thomas Wolfe. ⟫ *verb trans* **1** to cause air bubbles to form in (a substance or material). **2** to convert (e.g. a plastic) into a foam. ✳ **foam at the mouth** to be very angry.

foam rubber *noun* fine-textured spongy rubber made by introducing air bubbles before solidification.

fob /fob/ *noun* **1** a tag or tab attached to a key ring. **2** a small pocket on or near the waistband of trousers, orig for holding a watch. **3** a short strap or chain attached to a watch carried in a fob or a waistcoat pocket. **4** any ornament hung on such a strap or chain. [perhaps related to German dialect *Fuppe* pocket]

f.o.b. *abbr* free on board.

fob off *verb trans* (**fobbed**, **fobbing**) **1** (+ with) to put (somebody) off with a trick or excuse. **2** (+ on) to pass or offer (something spurious or inferior) as genuine or perfect. [archaic *fob* to cheat, from Middle English *fobben*; earlier history unknown]

fob pocket *noun* = FOB (2).

fob watch *noun* a large circular watch often with a cover for the face that is usu attached to a strap or chain in e.g. a waistcoat pocket.

FOC *abbr* Father of the Chapel.

f.o.c. *abbr* free of charge.

focaccia /fə'kachə/ *noun* (*pl* **focaccias**) a round flat Italian bread made with olive oil and topped with herbs. [Italian *focaccia*, ultimately from Latin *focus* hearth]

focal /'fohk(ə)l/ *adj* **1** of or having a focus. **2** located at a focus. ⟫ **focally** *adv.*

focal distance *noun* = FOCAL LENGTH.

focalize *or* **focalise** *verb* to focus. ⟫ **focalization** /-'zaysh(ə)n/ *noun.*

focal length *noun* the distance between the optical centre of a lens or mirror and the focal point.

focal plane *noun* a plane that is perpendicular to the axis of a lens or mirror and passes through the focus.

focal point *noun* **1** the focus for a beam of incident rays parallel to the axis of a lens or mirror. **2** a centre of activity or attention: *The fireplace was the focal point of the room.*

foci /'fohkie, 'fohsie/ *noun* pl of FOCUS¹.

fo'c'sle /'fohks(ə)l/ *noun* see FORECASTLE.

focus¹ /'fohkəs/ *noun* (*pl* **focuses** *or* **foci** /'fohkie, 'fohsie/) **1a** a point at which rays of e.g. light, heat, or sound converge or from which they diverge, or appear to diverge, after reflection or refraction. **b** the point at which an object must be placed for an image formed by a lens or mirror to be sharp. **2a** = FOCAL LENGTH. **b** adjustment, e.g. of the eye, necessary for distinct vision. **c** a state in which something must be placed in order to be clearly perceived: *The chairman tried to bring the issues into focus.* **3** a centre of activity or attention: *The focus of the meeting was drug abuse.* **4** a localized area of disease or the chief site of a generalized disease. **5a** a fixed point that together with a straight line forms a reference system for generating a conic section in plane geometry. **b** either of two fixed points used in generating an ellipse or hyperbola. **6** the place of origin of an earthquake. ✳ **in focus** having or giving the proper sharpness of outline due to good focusing. **out of focus** not in focus. [Latin *focus* hearth]

focus² *verb* (**focused** *or* **focussed**, **focusing** *or* **focussing**) ⟫ *verb trans* **1** (*often* + on) to bring (e.g. light rays) to a focus. **2** (*often* + on) to cause (one's thoughts, etc) to be concentrated: *They focused their attention on the most urgent problems.* **3a** to adjust the focus of (e.g. a camera or telescope). **b** to bring (e.g. a view) into focus. ⟫ *verb intrans* **1a** to come to a focus; to converge on a point. **b** to form into a sharp beam, e.g. of light. **2** to bring one's eyes or a camera into focus. ⟫ **focuser** *noun.*

focus group *noun* a number of people gathered together to discuss some topic, such as a new product or service, so that others may get their insights or opinions on the matter concerned.

focus puller *noun* in film-making: the member of a camera crew who keeps the camera in focus while it is tracking.

fodder¹ /'fodə/ *noun* **1** food for cattle, horses, sheep, or other domestic animals, *esp* coarse food such as hay. **2** something used to supply a constant demand: *We spent months collecting data which then became computer fodder.* [Old English *fōdor*; related to Old English *fōda* FOOD]

fodder² *verb trans* (**foddered**, **foddering**) to give fodder to (cattle, horses, sheep, or other domestic animals).

FOE *abbr* (*also* **FoE**) Friends of the Earth.

foe /foh/ *noun literary* an enemy or adversary. [Old English *gefā* enemy, and *fāh* hostile]

foehn /fuhn/ (*German* fø:n) *noun* see FÖHN.

foeti- *comb. form* see FOETO-.

foetid /'feetid/ *adj* see FETID.

foeto- *or* **foeti-** *or* **feto-** *or* **feti-** *comb. form* forming words, with the meanings: **1** foetus: *foeticide.* **2** foetal and: *foetoplacental.*

foetus *or* **fetus** /'feetəs/ *noun* (*pl* **foetuses** *or* **fetuses**) an unborn or unhatched vertebrate; *specif* a developing human from usu seven weeks after conception to birth, from the time of appearance of bone cells in the cartilage. ➤➤ **foetal** *adj*.

Word history
Latin *fetus* act of bearing young, offspring, also erroneously spelt *foetus*. *Foetus* was the usual British spelling until the late 20th cent.; *fetus* being used in American English. *Fetus* is now the only spelling in technical use, and is increasingly found in popular writing in British English, although *foetus* is still more common.

fog[1] /fog/ *noun* **1a** fine particles of water or anything similar suspended in the lower atmosphere causing a lessening of visibility. **b** the atmospheric condition caused by this. **2a** a state of confusion or bewilderment. **b** something that confuses or obscures: *Politicians frequently hide behind a fog of rhetoric.* **3** cloudiness on a developed photograph caused by chemical action or radiation, e.g. from X-rays. [prob of Scandinavian origin]

fog[2] *verb* (**fogged, fogging**) ➤ *verb trans* **1** to envelop or suffuse (something) with fog or anything similar. **2** to make (e.g. an argument) confused or confusing. **3** to produce fog on (e.g. a photographic film) during development. ➤ *verb intrans* **1** to become covered or thick with fog. **2** to become blurred by a covering of fog or mist or anything similar.

fog[3] *noun* **1** a second growth of grass after the first mowing. **2** dead or decaying grass on land in the winter. [Middle English *fog* rank grass; earlier history unknown]

fog bank *noun* a thick mass of fog, *esp* at sea.

fogbound *adj* **1** covered with or surrounded by fog: *a fogbound coast.* **2** unable to move because of fog.

fogbow /'fogboh/ *noun* a dim arc or circle of light sometimes seen in fog.

fogey *or* **fogy** /'fohgi/ *noun* (*pl* **fogeys** *or* **fogies**) a person with old-fashioned ideas: *The world is burdened with young fogies* — Robertson Davies. ➤➤ **fogeyish** *adj*, **fogeyism** *noun*. [origin unknown]

foggy /'fogi/ *adj* (**foggier, foggiest**) **1a** thick with fog. **b** covered or made opaque by moisture or grime. **2** slight; vague; confused: *They hadn't the foggiest notion what they were voting for.* ✳ **not have the foggiest (idea)** *chiefly Brit, informal* to have no idea at all. ➤➤ **foggily** *adv*, **fogginess** *noun*.

foghorn *noun* **1** a horn sounded in a fog to give warning to ships. **2** *informal* a loud deep voice.

fog lamp *noun* an additional headlight for a vehicle, positioned lower on the vehicle than a normal headlight and having a powerful beam used to aid visibility in fog.

fog light *noun* = FOG LAMP.

fog signal *noun* a detonating device placed on a railway track in foggy conditions as a warning to engine drivers.

fogy /'fohgi/ *noun* see FOGEY.

föhn *or* **foehn** /fuhn (*German* fø:n)/ *noun* a warm dry wind that descends the leeward side of a mountain range, *esp* the Alps. [German *Föhn*, from Latin *favonius* warm west wind]

foible /'foybl/ *noun* **1** a minor weakness or shortcoming in personal character or behaviour; a quirk. **2** the part of a sword blade between the middle and point: compare FORTE[1] (2). [French *foible* from Old French *feble*: see FEEBLE]

foie gras /,fwah 'grah (*French* fwa gra)/ *noun* **1** the fatted liver of an animal, *esp* a goose, used in making pâté. **2** *informal* = PÂTÉ DE FOIE GRAS. [French *foie gras* fatted liver]

foil[1] /foyl/ *noun* **1a** very thin sheet metal: *silver foil.* **b** a thin coat of tin or silver laid on the back of a mirror. **c** a thin piece of metal put under a gem or inferior stone to add colour or brilliance. **2** somebody or something that serves as a contrast to another, e.g. in a comedy duo: *He acted as a foil for his partner.* **3** = HYDROFOIL. **4a** a curved recess between cusps, e.g. in Gothic tracery: compare CUSP (2A). **b** any of several arcs that enclose a complex design. [Middle English *foil* leaf, via French from Latin *folium*]

foil[2] *verb trans* **1** to back or cover (e.g. a mirror) with foil. **2** to decorate (something, e.g. a window) with curved recesses.

foil[3] *verb trans* **1a** to prevent (somebody) from attaining an end. **b** to frustrate or defeat (an attempt, etc). **2a** said of a hunted animal: to spoil (a trail or scent) by crossing it or retracing its path. **b** said of hunters, etc: to obliterate (the trail or scent of a hunted animal). [Middle English *foilen* to trample, full cloth, from early French *fouler*]

foil[4] *noun* **1** in hunting, the trail or scent of an animal being hunted. **2** *archaic* a setback or defeat.

foil[5] *noun* a light fencing sword with a circular guard and a flexible blade tipped with a button: compare ÉPÉE, SABRE[1] (2). [origin unknown]

foist /foyst/ *verb trans* **1** (*usu* + off on/on/upon) to force acceptance of (something or somebody unwanted), or to force (somebody) to accept something or somebody they do not want: *Many constituencies don't like to have someone foisted on them* — Jeffrey Archer. **2** (*usu* + off on/on/upon) to deceitfully pass (something or somebody) off as genuine or worthy. **3** (*usu* + in/into) to introduce or insert (something) surreptitiously or without warrant. [prob from early Dutch *vuisten* to take into one's hand, from *vuyst* fist]

fol. *abbr* folio.

folacin /'fohləsin/ *noun* = FOLIC ACID. [from FOLIC ACID + -IN[1]]

fold[1] /fohld/ *verb trans* **1** (*often* + over) to lay one part of (something) over another part. **2** (*often* + up) to reduce the length or bulk of (something) by doubling it over. **3a** to clasp (e.g. one's arms) together. **b** to bring (a part, e.g. wings) to rest close to the body. **4a** to clasp (somebody) closely; to embrace (them): *She folded the child to her breast.* **b** to wrap or envelop (something). **5** (+ in/into) to gently incorporate (a food ingredient) into a mixture without thorough stirring or beating. **6** to bend (e.g. a layer of rock) into folds. ➤ *verb intrans* **1** (*often* + up) to become folded or be capable of being folded. **2** *informal* (*often* + up) to fail completely, *esp* to stop production or operation because of lack of business or capital. **3** *informal* to succumb to fatigue. ➤➤ **foldable** *adj*. [Old English *fealdan*]

fold[2] *noun* **1** a doubling or folding over of e.g. material, or a crease made in this way. **2** a part doubled or laid over another part; a pleat. **3** something that hangs loosely or is loosely folded or draped, or a hollow or sagging part, e.g. of skin, that is formed in this way. **4a** a bend in rock strata produced usu by compression. **b** *chiefly Brit* an undulation in the landscape. **5** a single coil in a rope.

fold[3] *noun* **1a** an enclosure for sheep. **b** a flock of sheep. **2** (**the fold**) (*treated as sing. or pl*) a group of people adhering to a common faith, belief, or enthusiasm. [Old English *falod*]

fold[4] *verb trans* **1** to pen (e.g. sheep) in a fold. **2** to pen sheep for the fertilization of (land).

-fold *suffix* **1** forming adjectives or adverbs, with the meaning: multiplied by the number specified; times: *a twelvefold increase*; *We'll repay you tenfold.* **2** forming adjectives, with the meaning: having a given number of parts: *consider the threefold aspect of the problem.* [Old English *-feald*; related to Old English *fealdan* FOLD[1]]

foldaway *adj* designed to fold out of the way or out of sight: *a foldaway bed.*

folder *noun* **1** a folded cover or large envelope for holding or filing loose papers. **2** a computer directory containing a number of files. **3** *NAmer* a leaflet or brochure.

folderol /'foldərol/ *noun* **1** a useless ornament; a trifle. **2** nonsense. [*fol-de-rol*, a meaningless refrain in old songs]

folding *adj* able to be folded or folded up: *a folding chair.*

folding money *noun informal* money in the form of bank notes.

foldout *noun* a folded insert in a publication larger in size than the page.

foley /'fohli/ *noun* (*pl* **foleys**) in film-making, a person who adds sound effects to a film at the post-production stage. [named after Jack *Foley* d.1967, US technician who invented the process]

foley artist *noun* = FOLEY.

foliaceous /fohli'ayshəs/ *adj* **1** of or resembling a foliage leaf. **2** bearing leaves or leaflike parts. **3** said of a rock, mineral, etc: consisting of thin plates.

foliage /'fohli-ij/ *noun* **1** the leaves of a plant or clump of plants. **2** a cluster of leaves, branches, etc, e.g. for decoration. **3** an ornamental representation of a cluster of leaves. ➤➤ **foliaged** *adj*. [early French *fuellage* from *foille* leaf, from Latin *folium*]

foliage leaf *noun* an ordinary green leaf as distinguished from a floral leaf, scale, or bract.

foliage plant *noun* a plant grown primarily for its decorative foliage.

foliar /'fohli-ə/ *adj technical* of a leaf or leaves.

foliate[1] /'fohli·ət, -ayt/ *adj* **1a** (*often in combination*) having leaves or leaflets: *trifoliate*. **b** leaf-shaped. **2** = FOLIATED. [Latin *foliatus* leafy, from *folium* leaf]

foliate[2] /'fohliayt/ *verb trans* **1** to beat (metal) into a leaf or thin foil. **2** to number the leaves of (e.g. a manuscript): compare PAGINATE. **3** to decorate (e.g. an arch or pedestal) with foils (curved recesses; see FOIL[1] (4A)) or other leaflike designs. ➤ *verb intrans* **1** said of e.g. a mineral: to divide into thin layers or leaves. **2** said of a plant: to produce leaves.

foliated *adj* composed of thin layers, *esp* ones that are easily separable.

foliation /fohli'aysh(ə)n/ *noun* **1a** the process of forming leaves or into a leaf. **b** the state of being in leaf. **c** the arrangement of leaves within a bud. **2** the act of beating a metal into a thin plate or foil. **3a** decoration with foliage. **b** decoration or ornamentation, e.g. of an arch, foils (curved recesses; see FOIL[1] (4A)) or other leaflike designs. **4** the action of numbering the leaves of a book, or the total count of leaves so numbered. **5** the foliated texture of a rock or mineral.

folic acid /'fohlik/ *noun* a vitamin of the vitamin B complex that is found *esp* in green leafy vegetables and liver. A lack of it in the diet results in anaemia. [Latin *folium* leaf]

folie à deux /,foli ah 'duh (*French* fɔli a dø)/ *noun* (*pl* **folies à deux** /foliz ah 'duh (*French* fɔliz a dø)/) the presence of the same or similar delusional ideas in two closely associated people. [French *folie à deux*, literally 'double madness']

folio /'fohlioh/ *noun* (*pl* **folios**) **1a** a sheet of paper folded once, or the size of each of the two leaves so formed. **b** a book printed on pages of this size. **c** a book of the largest size. **d** (*used before a noun*) consisting of folio-size pages: *a folio edition*. **2a** a leaf of a manuscript or book. **b** a page or leaf number. **3** a case or folder for loose papers. **4** a certain number of words taken as a unit in measuring the length of a document. [Middle English from Latin, ablative of *folium*]

folk /fohk/ *noun* **1** *informal*. **a** (*also* **folks**) (*treated as pl*) people; people in general: *Some folk want their luck buttered — Hardy*. **b** (*also* **folks**) (*treated as pl*) a specified kind or class of people: *old folk*. **c** (*also* **folks**) (*treated as pl*) the members of one's own family or community: *It's good to be back among my own folk again*. **d** (*in pl*) used when addressing a group of people: everyone: *That's it, folks! That's all for now*. **2** = FOLK MUSIC. **3** (*treated as pl*) the common people, those who determine the character of a nation or people and preserve its traditions, arts and crafts, legends, etc from generation to generation. **4** (*used before a noun*) relating to or denoting the common people or the study of the common people: *folk culture*. **5** (*used before a noun*) originating from or traditional with the common people: *folk medicine*. **6** *archaic* (*treated as pl*) a group of related tribes. ➤➤ **folkish** *adj*. [Old English *folc*]

folk dance *noun* a traditional dance of a people or region, often one preserved and performed by enthusiasts when no longer generally known. ➤➤ **folk dancer** *noun*, **folk dancing** *noun*.

folk etymology *noun* **1** the transformation of words so as to bring them into an apparent relationship with other more familiar words. One example of folk etymology is the change of Spanish *cucaracha* to *cockroach*. **2** an explanation of the derivation or origin of a word or phrase that is popularly held to be true, but is actually erroneous.

folk hero *noun* **1** a hero of folklore. **2** somebody who enjoys widespread popular esteem.

folkie *or* **folky** /'fohki/ *noun* (*pl* **folkies**) *informal* a folk music enthusiast.

folklore /'fohklaw/ *noun* **1a** the traditional customs and beliefs of a people preserved by oral tradition. **b** the study of the life and spirit of a people through their folklore. **2** the stories, etc attached to a particular place, group, etc: *movie folklore*. ➤➤ **folkloric** /fohk'-lorik/ *adj*, **folklorist** *noun*.

folk medicine *noun* any form of traditional medicine that involves the use of remedies made from herbs, vegetables, etc, *esp* as practised by people in isolated communities.

folk music *noun* the traditional music and songs of a people or region.

folk rock *noun* a type of folk music that incorporates elements of rock, e.g. heavier beats and the use of electric instruments.

folksinger *noun* somebody who sings folk songs, *esp* as a professional or amateur enthusiast. ➤➤ **folksinging** *noun*.

folk song *noun* **1** a traditional song of a people or region. **2** a contemporary song in a similar style.

folksy /'fohksi/ *adj* (**folksier, folksiest**) *informal* **1** informal or familiar in manner or style. **2** having or affecting a lack of sophistication. ➤➤ **folksily** *adv*, **folksiness** *noun*. [FOLK + -Y[1]]

folk tale *noun* an anonymous traditional story that is transmitted orally and in which time and place are rarely specified.

folkway *noun* a traditional social custom.

folkweave *noun* a rough loosely woven fabric.

folky[1] *noun* see FOLKIE.

folky[2] *adj* (**folkier, folkiest**) of or resembling folk music: *Her songs have a folky quality*.

follicle /'folikl/ *noun* **1a** a small anatomical cavity or deep narrow depression, e.g. the tubular sheath surrounding the root of a hair. **b** = GRAAFIAN FOLLICLE. **2** a dry one-celled many-seeded fruit that has a single carpel and opens along one line only. ➤➤ **follicular** /fə'likyoolə/ *adj*, **folliculate** /fə'likyoolət/ *adj*, **folliculated** /fə'likyoolaytid/ *adj*. [Latin *folliculus*, dimin. of *follis* bag]

follicle-stimulating hormone *noun* a hormone produced by the front lobe of the pituitary gland that stimulates the growth of the ovum-containing Graafian follicles and activates sperm-forming cells.

follow /'foloh/ *verb trans* **1a** to go or come after (somebody or something). **b** to go after (somebody or something) in order to observe them or watch their movements. **2a** to accept (somebody) as a guide or leader. **b** to obey or act in accordance with (rules or instructions). **3** to copy or imitate (something or somebody). **4** to walk or proceed along (a path or route). **5a** to engage in (an activity) as a calling or way of life. **b** to undertake (a course of action). **6a** to come or take place after (something) in time or order: *as sure as night follows day*. **b** (+ with) to cause (something) to be followed by something else: *We followed dinner with a walk by the river*. **7** to come into existence or take place as a result or consequence of (something). **8** to watch the progress of (something or somebody): *He followed the animals' movements through binoculars*. **9a** to understand the meaning or significance of (something): *The story was complicated and hard to follow*. **b** to understand the logic of (an argument, or the person making it): *I don't quite follow you*. **10** to keep informed about (something): *She had followed his career with interest*. **11** to be a supporter of (a sport, team, etc). ➤ *verb intrans* **1** to go or come after somebody or something in place, time, or sequence. **2** (*usu* + from) to result or occur as a consequence or inference. **3** *chiefly Brit* to understand the logic of a line of thought. ✳ **follow one's nose 1** to go in a straight or obvious course. **2** to do what one instinctively feels to be right. **follow suit 1** to play a card of the same suit as the card led. **2** to follow an example set. [Old English *folgian*]

follower *noun* **1a** somebody who follows the opinions or teachings of another. **b** somebody who imitates another. **c** a fan or supporter. **2a** a servant, attendant, or henchman. **b** *archaic* a male admirer; a suitor or sweetheart.

following[1] *adj* **1** next after; succeeding: *the following day*. **2** now to be stated: *Trains will leave at the following times this month*. **3** said of a wind: blowing in the direction in which something is travelling.

following[2] *noun* (*treated as sing. or pl*) **1** (**the following**) something that comes immediately after or below in writing or speech. **2** a group of followers, adherents, or partisans.

following[3] *prep* subsequent to (something): *Following the lecture, tea was served*.

Usage note
This use of *following* as a preposition can lead to ambiguity when it comes in the second part of the sentence: *police are looking for a man following a tip-off*. (Did the police have a tip-off or is the man following one?) Here you could either reverse the order (*following a tip-off police are looking for a man*; but this is awkward), or better, use *after* (to express time) or *as a result of* (to express cause and effect).

follow-my-leader *noun Brit* a game in which the actions of a designated leader must be copied by the other players.

follow on *verb intrans* **1** (*often* + from) to continue. **2** (*often* + from) to come as a consequence. **3** said of a side in cricket: to be made to bat again immediately after failing to reach a certain score in the first innings. ➤➤ **follow-on** *noun*.

follow out *verb trans* to implement or adhere to (an instruction, idea, etc).

follow-the-leader *noun NAmer* = FOLLOW-MY-LEADER.

follow through *verb intrans* to continue the movement of a stroke after a cricket, golf, etc ball has been struck. ➤ *verb trans* to pursue or complete (an activity or process).

follow up *verb trans* **1** to continue or enquire into (something) further. **2** to maintain contact with (a person) in order to give them further advice or treatment. ⫸ **follow-up** *noun*.

folly /'foli/ *noun* (*pl* **follies**) **1** a lack of good sense or prudence. **2** a foolish act or idea. **3** foolish actions or conduct. **4** a usu fanciful building built *esp* for scenic effect or to satisfy a whim. **5** (**Follies**) a theatrical revue featuring glamorous female performers in extravagant costumes. [Middle English *folie* from Old French, from *fol*: see FOOL¹]

foment /foh'ment/ *verb trans* **1** to incite or promote the growth or development of (trouble, rebellion, etc). **2** to treat (a part of the body) with moist heat, e.g. for easing pain. ⫸ **fomenter** *noun*. [Middle English *fomenten* from late Latin *fomentare*, from Latin *fomentum* fomentation, from *fovēre* to warm, fondle, foment]

Usage note

foment *or* ferment? See note at FERMENT¹.

fomentation /fohmen'taysh(ə)n/ *noun* **1a** a hot moist substance applied to the body, e.g. to ease pain. **b** the application of such a substance or therapeutic treatment that involves this. **2** the act or an instance of fomenting; inciting trouble, rebellion, etc.

Fon /fon/ *noun* (*pl* **Fons** *or collectively* **Fon**) **1** a member of an indigenous people inhabiting Benin and western parts of Nigeria. **2** the Kwa language of this people. [the local name for this people in several Kwa languages]

fond /fond/ *adj* **1a** (+ of) having an affection or liking for something specified: *fond of music*. **b** (+ of) having an inclination, predisposition, or appetite for something: *fond of arguing*. **2a** affectionate; loving: *Absence makes the heart grow fonder*. **b** foolishly tender; indulgent: *She was completely spoilt by a fond mother*. **3** cherished: *He saw his fondest hopes dashed*. **4** foolish; naive: *I started out on this in the fond belief that one of you would help me*. ⫸ **fondness** *noun*. [Middle English, from *fonne* fool; earlier history unknown]

fondant /'fond(ə)nt/ *noun* a soft creamy preparation of flavoured sugar and water, or a sweet made from this. [French *fondant*, present part. of *fondre* to melt, from Latin *fundere*]

fondle /'fondl/ *verb trans* to handle (something) or to caress (somebody) tenderly and lovingly, sometimes in an erotic or sexually arousing manner. ➤ *verb intrans* to show affection or desire by caressing. ⫸ **fondler** *noun*. [frequentative of obsolete *fond* to be foolish, dote, ultimately from *fonne* fool]

fondly *adv* **1** affectionately. **2** in a naively credulous manner: *The government fondly imagines that cutting taxes will reduce wage demands.*

fondue /'fond(y)ooh (French fɔ̃dy)/ *noun* any of various dishes in which small pieces of food are dipped in a hot liquid, e.g. oil or a sauce of melted cheese, at the table. [French *fondue*, fem past part. of *fondre*: see FONDANT]

font¹ /font/ *noun* **1** a receptacle in a church for holy water, *esp* one used in baptism. **2** a receptacle for oil in a lamp. ⫸ **fontal** *adj*. [Old English, from Latin *font-, fons* FOUNTAIN¹]

font² *noun* = FOUNT².

fontanelle (*NAmer* **fontanel**) /fontə'nel/ *noun* any of the spaces closed by membranous structures between the parietal bones of the skull of an infant or foetus. [Middle English *fontinelle* a bodily hollow or pit, from early French *fontenele*, dimin. of *fontaine*: see FOUNTAIN¹]

food /foohd/ *noun* **1a** material consisting essentially of protein, carbohydrate, and fat, along with minerals, vitamins, etc, taken into the body of a living organism and used to provide energy and sustain processes essential for life. **b** inorganic substances absorbed, e.g. in gaseous form or in solution, by plants. **2** nourishment in solid form: *There is no love sincerer than the love of food —* George Bernard Shaw. **3** something that sustains or supplies: *food for thought*. [Old English *fōda*]

food additive *noun* any of various natural or synthetic substances, e.g. salt, monosodium glutamate, etc, used in the production of commercially processed foods, *esp* something used as a preservative, flavouring, antioxidant, etc.

food chain *noun* a hierarchical arrangement of organisms ordered according to each organism's use of the next as a food source.

foodie *or* **foody** /'foohdi/ *noun* (*pl* **foodies**) *informal* a person who takes a keen interest in food, *esp* in rare or exotic dishes; a gourmet.

food miles *pl noun* the distance in miles that food travels from producer to consumer.

food poisoning *noun* an acute gastrointestinal disorder caused by the toxic products of bacteria or by chemical residues in food.

food processor *noun* an electrical appliance that performs a range of operations in preparing food (such as chopping, shredding, and mixing).

foodstuff *noun* a substance with food value, *esp* the raw material of food before or after processing.

food value *noun* the amount of nourishment that can be obtained from a foodstuff.

food web *noun* all the interacting food chains in an ecological community.

foody *noun* see FOODIE.

fool¹ /foohl/ *noun* **1a** a person lacking in prudence, common sense, or understanding. **b** a person who is victimized or made to appear foolish; a dupe. **2** a jester employed by a royal or noble household. ✳ **act/play the fool** to deliberately behave in an amusingly or irritatingly foolish manner. **be no/nobody's fool** to be wise or shrewd. **make a fool of somebody 1** to trick somebody. **2** to make somebody look foolish. **make a fool of oneself** to behave in a way or do something that leads to embarrassment. **more fool** used to express the opinion that somebody has done, is doing, or is proposing to do something foolish: *More fool you for believing him, then!* ⫸ **foolery** *noun*. [Middle English from Old French *fol*, ultimately from Latin *follis* bellows, bag]

fool² *verb trans* to trick or deceive (somebody or something). ➤ *verb intrans* **1** to say or do something as a joke: *Don't take things so seriously. I was only fooling.* **2** to behave in a silly or irresponsible way. **3a** (+ with) to deal or contend with somebody without serious thought, purpose, or effort: *He's a dangerous man to fool with*. **b** (+ with) to meddle or tamper thoughtlessly or ignorantly with something: *You don't fool with electricity. Call an electrician.*

fool³ *adj NAmer, informal* foolish or silly: *The dog was barking his fool head off.*

fool⁴ *noun chiefly Brit* a cold dessert made from whipped cream or custard and fruit pureé.

fool about *verb intrans* **1** to behave in a silly or irresponsible way. **2** to spend time idly or aimlessly: *He just fools about all day*. **3** *chiefly NAmer* (*often* + with) to have a casual sexual relationship with somebody: *You'd better stop fooling about with my wife.*

fool around *verb intrans* = FOOL ABOUT.

foolhardy *adj* (**foolhardier, foolhardiest**) foolishly adventurous and bold; rash. ⫸ **foolhardily** *adv*, **foolhardiness** *noun*. [Middle English from Old French *fol hardi*, from *fol* foolish + *hardi* bold]

foolish *adj* **1** unwise; silly. **2** absurd; ridiculous. ⫸ **foolishly** *adv*, **foolishness** *noun*.

foolproof *adj* so simple or reliable as to leave no opportunity for error, misuse, or failure: *a foolproof plan*.

foolscap /'foohlskap, 'foolskap/ *noun chiefly Brit* a size of paper usu 17 × 13½in. (432 × 343mm). [from the watermark of a dunce's cap formerly applied to such paper]

fool's cap *noun* **1** a hat with several pointed extensions, usu with bells or tassels attached to them, worn by a court jester. **2** = DUNCE'S CAP.

fool's errand *noun* a needless or fruitless task or activity.

fool's gold *noun* = IRON PYRITES. [because it can be mistaken for gold]

fool's paradise *noun* a state of illusory happiness.

fool's parsley *noun* a poisonous European plant of the carrot family that resembles parsley: *Aethusa cynapium*.

foot¹ /foot/ *noun* (*pl* **feet** /feet/) **1a** the end part of the leg on which an animal or person stands. **b** an organ of locomotion or attachment of an invertebrate animal, *esp* a mollusc or caterpillar. **2** the part of a stocking, sock, tights, etc that covers the human foot. **3** (*pl also* **foot**) a unit of length equal to 0.305m (12in.): *a ten-foot pole; He's over six feet tall.* **4a** the lower edge or lowest part; the bottom: *the foot of a page; the foot of the stairs.* **b** the end of something that is opposite the head or top, or nearest to the human feet: *the foot of the bed.* **c** the lower end of the leg of a chair, table, etc. **5** the basic unit of verse metre consisting of any of various fixed combinations of stressed and unstressed or long and short syllables. **6** the piece on a sewing machine that presses the cloth against the feed. **7** manner or motion of walking or running; step: *fleet of foot.* **8** *chiefly Brit (treated as sing. or pl)* the infantry. * **a foot in the door** a position from which progress may be made. **fall/land on one's feet** to be successful or happy, *esp* after overcoming difficulties. **feet of clay** a flaw or weakness in somebody who is, or is thought to be, otherwise perfect [from a figure that King Nebuchadnezzar of Babylon saw in a dream, which had a head and body made of precious metals but feet of iron and clay, and which subsequently collapsed (Daniel 2:33)]. **get/start off on the right/wrong foot** to start a job, relationship, etc well or badly. **have/keep one's feet on the ground** to have or keep a sensible, practical attitude to life. **keep one's feet** to avoid overbalancing. **my foot** *informal* an expression of disbelief. **not put a foot wrong** to make no mistakes at all. **on/by foot** walking or running, as opposed to using transport. **one foot in the grave** *informal* close to death, *esp* because of old age or illness. **on one's feet 1** in a standing position; not sitting down: *I've been on my feet all day.* **2** having recovered, e.g. after an illness: *We'll soon have you back on your feet again.* **3** established and usu financially sound: *The business is well on its feet now.* **put one's best foot forward** to make every effort; to do one's best. **put one's foot down 1** to take a firm stand. **2** *informal* to press on the accelerator of a vehicle in order to go faster. **put one's foot in it** to make an embarrassing blunder: *Dentopedalogy is the science of opening your mouth and putting your foot in it* — Prince Philip, Duke of Edinburgh. **run/rush somebody off their feet** *(usu in passive)* to keep somebody very busy. **set foot** (+ in/inside/on) to go into (a building or an area), often for the first time. **under foot** on the ground; under a person's feet. **under somebody's feet** in somebody's way. ⨠ **footless** *adj.* [Old English *fōt*]

foot² *verb trans* to pay (e.g. a bill). * **foot it 1** to travel on foot; to walk. **2** to dance.

footage /'footij/ *noun* **1** length or quantity expressed in feet. **2** a length of cinema or television film.

foot-and-mouth *noun* = FOOT-AND-MOUTH DISEASE.

foot-and-mouth disease *noun* a infectious virus disease of cattle, sheep, pigs, and goats, characterized by small ulcers in the mouth, about the hoofs, and on the udder and teats.

football *noun* **1a** any of several games, *esp* Association Football in the UK or American football in the US, that are played between two teams on a usu rectangular field having goalposts at each end and whose object is to get the ball over a goal line or between goalposts by running, passing, or kicking. **b** the inflated round or oval ball used in any of these games. **c** *(used before a noun)* of football: *a football match.* **2** something treated as a basis for contention rather than on its intrinsic merits: *The bill became a political football in Parliament.* ⨠ **footballer** *noun.*

football pools *pl noun* a form of organized gambling based on forecasting the results of football matches.

footbath *noun* a bath for cleaning, warming, or disinfecting the feet.

footboard *noun* **1** a narrow platform on which to stand or brace the feet. **2** a board forming the end of a bed.

foot brake *noun* a brake, e.g. in a motor vehicle, operated by foot pressure.

footbridge *noun* a bridge for pedestrians.

footed *adj (used in combinations)* **1** having the kind or number of feet specified: *a four-footed animal.* **2** having a preference for or greater skill with the foot specified: *left-footed.* **3** having a tread or step of the kind specified: *light-footed.*

footer *noun chiefly Brit, informal, dated* football. [by shortening and alteration from FOOTBALL]

-footer *comb. form* forming nouns, denoting: **1** somebody or something that is a specified number of feet in height, length, or breadth: *a six-footer.* **2** a person who has a preference for or greater skill with the foot specified: *a left-footer.*

footfall *noun* the sound of a footstep.

foot fault *noun* a fault in tennis, squash, etc made when a server's feet are not behind the baseline.

foot-fault *verb intrans* to make a foot fault in tennis, squash, etc.

foothill *noun* a hill at the foot of mountains.

foothold *noun* **1** = FOOTING (1). **2** an established position or basis from which to progress: *The firm eventually secured a foothold in the plastics market.*

footie /'footi/ *noun* see FOOTY.

footing *noun* **1** a stable position or placing of or for the feet. **2a** an established position. **b** a position or rank in relation to others: *They all started off on an equal footing.* **3** a surface, or the condition of a surface, with respect to its suitability for walking or running. **4** *(also in pl)* an enlargement at the lower end of a foundation, wall, pier, or column to distribute the load, or a trench dug to accommodate this: *The footing must be excavated to a minimum depth of 4ft.*

footle /'foohtl/ *verb intrans informal (often + about/around)* to waste time in aimless or fruitless activity. [alteration of *footer* to bungle, from French *foutre* to copulate]

footlights *pl noun* a row of lights set across the front of a stage floor.

footling *adj informal* **1** bungling or inept: *footling amateurs who understand nothing* — E R Bentley. **2a** unimportant or trivial. **b** pettily fussy. [FOOTLE]

footloose *adj* having no ties; free to go or do as one pleases. * **footloose and fancy-free** free to do what one wants, *esp* because of not being involved in a relationship.

footman *noun (pl* **footmen***)* **1** a servant in livery hired chiefly to wait on or receive visitors, etc. **2** *archaic* a foot soldier.

footnote¹ *noun* **1** a note of reference, explanation, or comment typically placed at the bottom of a printed page: *He dreams footnotes, and they run away with all his brains* — George Eliot. **2** something subordinately related to a larger event or work: *Her biography is an illuminating footnote to the history of our times.*

footnote² *verb trans* to supply (e.g. a page, a text, etc) with a footnote or footnotes; to annotate (it).

footpad¹ *noun* a broad foot on the leg of a spacecraft. [FOOT¹ + PAD¹]

footpad² *noun archaic* somebody who robs pedestrians on foot. [FOOT¹ + archaic *pad* a highwayman, from Low German or Dutch *pad* path]

footpath *noun* **1** a narrow path for people on foot, e.g. in the country. **2** a pavement.

footplate *noun Brit* the platform on which the crew stand in a locomotive.

foot-pound *noun (pl* **foot-pounds***)* a unit of work equal to the work done by a force of one pound in moving a body through a distance of one foot, equivalent to about 1.36 joules.

foot-pound-second *adj* of a system of units based upon the foot as the unit of length, the pound as the unit of weight or mass, and the second as the unit of time.

footprint *noun* **1** an impression made by a foot or shoe: *We can make our lives sublime, and, departing, leave behind us footprints on the sands of time* — Longfellow. **2** the area on the earth's surface covered by the transmissions of a communications satellite. **3** the space on a desk occupied by an electronic device such as a computer.

footrest *noun* a support, e.g. a low stool or a rail, for the feet.

foot rot *noun* a bacterial infection that causes progressive inflammation of the feet of sheep, cattle, and other hoofed animals.

footrule *noun* a ruler that is one foot long, or a ruler graduated in feet and inches.

Footsie /'footsi/ *noun* an index showing the prices on the London Stock Exchange of the shares of the hundred largest public companies in Britain. [from *Financial Times Stock Exchange 100 Share Index*]

footsie *noun informal* the act or an instance of surreptitiously and playfully touching, *esp* the feet, as an indication of romantic or sexual interest. * **play footsie 1** *informal* to caress somebody surreptitiously and amorously with the feet. **2** *informal* to have clandestine dealings with somebody. [baby-talk dimin. of FOOT¹]

footslog¹ /'footslog/ *verb intrans (***footslogged, footslogging***)* to march or tramp laboriously. ⨠ **footslogger** *noun.*

footslog² *noun* a long and tiring walk, hike, or march.

foot soldier noun **1** an infantry soldier. **2** a lowly but indispensable worker or member of an organization.

footsore adj having sore or tender feet, esp from much walking. >>> **footsoreness** noun.

footstep noun **1a** the sound of a step or tread. **b** the distance covered by a step. **2** = FOOTPRINT (1). * **follow in somebody's footsteps** to do what another person has done before, e.g. in following in the same career.

footstool noun a low stool used to support the feet.

footwear noun shoes, boots, etc collectively.

footwork noun **1** the control and placing of the feet in sport or dancing. **2** the activity of moving from place to place on foot: The investigation entailed a lot of footwork.

footy /'footi/ or **footie** noun Brit, informal football. [by shortening and alteration of FOOTBALL]

foo yong or **fu yong** /,fooh 'yong/ noun any of various Chinese-style dishes, similar to omelettes, in which eggs are combined with beansprouts and sometimes other vegetables. [Cantonese foo yung, literally 'hibiscus']

fop /fop/ noun a man who is overly concerned about his clothes, hair, appearance, etc; a dandy. >>> **foppish** adj, **foppishly** adv, **foppishness** noun. [Middle English, fool; earlier history unknown]

foppery /'fopəri/ noun the behaviour, dress, or affectations characteristic of a fop.

for[1] /fə; strong faw/ prep **1a** used to indicate purpose or reason: a grant for studying medicine; an operation for cancer; What's this knob for? **b** used to indicate goal or direction, intention, or desire: She left for home an hour ago; He acted for the best; It's getting on for five. **c** used to indicate something that is to be had or gained: Now for a good rest; Run for your life; My wife has an eye for a bargain; The flowers are for you; There's a phone call for you. **2** as being or constituting: Don't take him for a fool; I ate it for breakfast; Take John, for example; I know for a fact he's leaving; I for one don't care. **3a** because of: I cried for joy; You'll feel better for a holiday. **b** because of the hindrance of: They couldn't speak for laughing; If it weren't for you I'd leave. **4a** in place of: Have you got change for a pound; a word-for-word translation. **b** on behalf of; representing: I'm acting for my client; red for danger. **c** in support of; in favour of: He played for England; Who did you vote for? **5** considered as; considering: She's tall for her age; It's cold for April. **6** with respect to; concerning: This region is famous for its scenery; He's a stickler for detail; Eggs are good for you. **7** used to indicate cost, payment, equivalence, or correlation: They were all out for 342 runs; He wouldn't hurt her for the world; There were five duds for every good one; £7 for a hat! **8** used to indicate duration of time or extent of space: Bends for ten miles; The police said it was the worst accident for months. **9** on the occasion or at the time of: She came home for Christmas; We invited them for nine o'clock. **10** used to introduce a clause with a non-finite verb: There's no need for you to worry; It's dangerous for George to hurry. * **for it** chiefly Brit, informal likely to get into trouble: If I'm late again, I'll be for it. **for you** used in exclamations of enthusiasm or exasperation: That's country hotels for you! **Oh for ...** used in expressions of, often exasperated, desire: Oh for a bit of peace and quiet! [Old English]

for[2] conj **1** and the reason is that. **2** because.

for[3] /faw/ adj being in favour of a motion or measure.

for. abbr **1** foreign. **2** forest. **3** forestry.

for- prefix forming verbs, denoting: **1a** prohibition or exclusion: forbid; forfend. **b** omission, refraining, or neglect: forgo; forsake; forget; forswear. **2** destruction: fordo. **3** completion; excess: forspent; forlorn. [Old English; related to FOR[1]]

Usage note

for- or fore-? These two prefixes are sometimes confused. The prefix for- denotes prohibition (forbid) or omission (forsake). The prefix fore- means 'before' (foresee). See also notes at FORBEAR[1] and FORGO.

fora /'fawrə/ noun pl of FORUM.

forage[1] /'forij/ noun **1** food for animals, esp when taken by browsing or grazing, e.g. hay or straw. **2a** the act or an instance of foraging for provisions. **b** a search. [Middle English, from Old French forre fodder, of Germanic origin]

forage[2] verb trans **1** to collect or take provisions or forage from (a place). **2** to obtain (food) by foraging: He foraged a chicken for the feast. **3** to feed (animals), esp with hay or straw. > verb intrans **1** to wander in search of forage or food. **2** (usu + for) to make a search; to rummage. >>> **forager** noun.

forage cap noun a cap worn by infantry soldiers as part of their undress uniform.

foramen /fo'raymin/ noun (pl **foramina** /fo'raminə/ or **foramens**) a small anatomical opening or perforation. >>> **foraminal** /fo'raminəl/ adj. [Latin foramin-, foramen, from forare to bore]

foraminifer /forə'minifə/ noun (pl **foraminifera** /-'nifərə/ or **foraminifers**) any of an order of chiefly marine amoeba-like single-celled organisms usu having hard perforated calcium-containing shells that form the bulk of chalk. The shells have minute holes through which slender pseudopodia (jellylike extensions of the cell used for movement; see PSEUDOPOD) protrude: order Foraminifera. >>> **foraminiferal** /-'nifərəl/ adj, **foraminiferous** /-'nifərəs/ adj. [Latin foramin-, foramen FORAMEN + fera, neuter pl of fer FER]

foraminiferan /forəmi'nifərən/ noun = FORAMINIFER.

forasmuch as /fərəz'much/ conj archaic or formal used e.g. in official proclamations or legal documents: in view of the fact that; since.

foray[1] /'foray/ verb intrans to make a raid or incursion. >>> **forayer** noun. [Middle English forrayen from Old French forrer, from forre; see FORAGE[1]]

foray[2] noun **1** a sudden invasion, attack, or raid. **2** a brief excursion or attempt, esp outside one's accustomed sphere: My father's foray into politics ended in disaster.

forbad /fə'bad/ verb past tense of FORBID.

forbade /fə'bad, fə'bayd/ verb past tense of FORBID.

forbear[1] /faw'beə/ verb (past tense **forbore** /faw'baw/, past part. **forborne** /faw'bawn/) > verb trans (often + from) to hold oneself back from (doing something), esp with an effort of self-restraint: He forbore to answer the slander. > verb intrans **1** (+ from) to hold back or abstain: He forbore from expressing his disagreement. **2** to control oneself when provoked; to be patient. [Old English forberan to endure, do without, from FOR- + beran BEAR[2]]

Usage note

forbear or forebear? The verb that means 'refrain from' is spelt forbear, with bear stressed, (forbore to reply to the accusation); the noun that means 'ancestor' is spelt either forebear or forbear, with for(e) stressed.

forbear[2] /'fawbeə/ noun see FOREBEAR.

forbearance /faw'beərəns/ noun **1** a refraining from the enforcement of something, e.g. a debt, right, or obligation, that is due. **2** patience; self-restraint. **3** leniency.

forbid /fə'bid/ verb trans (**forbidding**, past tense **forbade** /fə'bad, fə'bayd/ or **forbad** /fə'bad/, past part. **forbidden** /fə'bid(ə)n/) **1a** to refuse to allow (something); to refuse to allow (somebody) to do something: The law forbids shops to sell alcohol to minors. **b** to refuse access to (somewhere) or use of (something): Her father forbade him the house. **2** to make (something) impracticable; to hinder or prevent (it): Limited space forbids further treatment of the subject here. * **God/Heaven forbid** used to express a strong wish that something does not happen: Heaven forbid that my daughter inherits her dad's nose! >>> **forbidder** noun. [Old English forbēodan, from FOR- + bēodan to bid]

forbidden adj **1** not allowed. **2** said of quantum phenomena: not conforming to the usual selection principles.

forbidden fruit noun (treated as sing. or pl) something that is very tempting but not allowed. [from the fruit Adam was forbidden by God to eat, Genesis 2:17]

forbidding adj **1** having a menacing or dangerous appearance: forbidding mountains. **2** unfriendly: His father was a stern forbidding figure. >>> **forbiddingly** adv, **forbiddingness** noun.

forbore /faw'baw/ verb past tense of FORBEAR[1].

forborne /faw'bawn/ verb past part. of FORBEAR[1].

force[1] /faws/ noun **1a** strength or energy exerted or brought to bear; active power. **b** moral or mental strength, or somebody showing this. **c** capacity to persuade or convince. **d** legal validity; operative effect. **2a** a body, e.g. of troops or ships, assigned to a military purpose. **b** (in pl) the armed services of a nation or commander. **3a** a body of people or things fulfilling some function: a labour force. **b** (often **the Force**) = POLICE[1] (1). **4** violence or threats of violence, compulsion, or constraint exerted on or against a person or thing. **5a** an agency that if applied to a free body results chiefly in an acceleration of the body and sometimes in elastic deformation and other effects. **b** an agency or influence analogous to a physical force: Reason is a harmonising, controlling force rather *than a creative one* — Bertrand Russell. **c** an individual or group having the power of effective action. **6** the quality of conveying impressions intensely or opinions strongly in writing or speech. **7** (**Force**) a measure of wind strength as expressed by a number on the Beaufort scale. ✷ **by force of** by means of; using. **in force 1** in great numbers. **2** said of a law or rule: valid or operative. [Middle English from Old French, ultimately from Latin *fortis* strong]

force² *verb trans* **1** (*also* + into) to compel (somebody) or produce (a result or action) by physical, moral, or intellectual means. **2** to make (somebody) do something or cause (something) through natural or logical necessity. **3a** (*also* + through) to press, drive, or effect (something) against resistance or inertia. **b** to impose or thrust (oneself, etc) on somebody or something. **4a** to capture or penetrate (a place) by force. **b** to break open or through (a lock, door, etc). **5a** to raise or accelerate (e.g. speed) to the utmost. **b** to produce (e.g. a laugh) only with unnatural or unwilling effort. **c** to strain (e.g. one's voice) by excessive effort. **d** to hasten the growth, onset of maturity, or rate of progress of. **6** to induce (e.g. a particular bid from one's partner) in a card game by some conventional act, bid, etc. **7** said of a batsman in cricket: to play an aggressive shot at (a delivery), *esp* off the back foot. ✷ **force somebody's hand** to cause somebody to act precipitously or reveal their purpose or intention. **force the issue** to compel a decision, action, etc to be taken. ➤➤ **forceable** *adj*, **forcer** *noun*.

force³ *noun* used *esp* in place names in N England: a waterfall: *High Force*. [Middle English from Old Norse *fors*]

forced *adj* **1** unnatural or unwilling and produced only with effort: *a forced smile*. **2** made because of an emergency: *The aircraft had to make a forced landing in a field*. **3** done, or doing something, under pressure or compulsion: *forced labour*. **4** made at great speed without rest: *a forced march*. ➤➤ **forcedly** /'fawsidli/ *adv*.

force-feed *verb trans* (*past tense and past part.* **force-fed**) to feed (somebody, e.g. a person on hunger strike or with an eating disorder) against their will.

force field *noun* chiefly in science fiction stories or films, an invisible barrier that is impermeable to alien life forms, weaponry such as energy beams, etc.

forceful /'fawsf(ə)l/ *adj* possessing or filled with force; intense; effective. ➤➤ **forcefully** *adv*, **forcefulness** *noun*.

force-land *verb trans* to land (an aircraft) involuntarily or in an emergency. [back-formation from *forced landing*]

force majeure /ˌfaws maˈzhuh (*French* fɔrs maʒœːr)/ *noun* **1** a disruptive event or influence, e.g. war or civil disturbance, that cannot be reasonably anticipated or controlled. **2** an unavoidable event that in law excuses a party from fulfilling a contract. **3** overwhelming force or superiority. [French *force majeure*, literally 'superior force']

forcemeat *noun* a savoury highly seasoned stuffing, *esp* of breadcrumbs and meat. [*force* (alteration of FARCE) + MEAT]

force of habit *noun* behaviour made involuntary or automatic by repetition.

forceps /'fawsips, 'fawseps/ *noun* (*pl* **forceps**) **1** (*usu in pl*) an instrument used, e.g. in surgery and watchmaking, for grasping, holding firmly, or pulling: *a pair of forceps*. **2** a large instrument of this type used to clasp a baby's head to assist in its delivery. [Latin *forceps* pincers, from *formus* warm + *capere* to take]

force pump *noun* a pump that can force a liquid, *esp* water, higher than atmospheric pressure could.

force shield *noun* = FORCE FIELD.

forcible *adj* **1** effected by force used against opposition or resistance. **2** powerful; forceful. ➤➤ **forcibleness** *noun*, **forcibly** *adv*.

forcing ground *noun* = HOTBED (2).

ford¹ /fawd/ *noun* a shallow part of a river or other body of water that can be crossed by wading, in a vehicle, etc. [Old English; related to Old English *faran* FARE²]

ford² *verb trans* to cross (a river, stream, etc) at a ford. ➤➤ **fordable** *adj*.

fore¹ /faw/ *adj and adv* situated in, towards, or adjacent to the front, *esp* of a ship. [Old English]

fore² *noun* something that occupies a forward position; a front part. ✷ **to the fore** in or into a position of prominence.

fore³ *interj* used by a golfer to warn anyone in the probable line of flight of the ball. [prob short for BEFORE¹]

fore- *comb. form* **1** forming verbs, with the meaning: occurring, etc earlier or beforehand: *foresee*. **2** forming nouns, with the meanings: **a** situated at the front; in front: *foreleg*. **b** a front part: *forearm*. [Old English *fore-*, from FORE¹, adv]

Usage note
fore- *or* for-? See note at FOR-.

fore and aft *adv* **1** from bow to stern; lengthways. **2** in, at, or towards both the bow and stern of a ship.

fore-and-aft *adj* **1** lying, running, or acting in the general line of the length of a construction, *esp* a ship. **2a** said of a sail: set lengthways in the direction of the bow and stern rather than on a yard set across a ship. **b** said of a ship: having fore-and-aft sails as the principal sails. ➤➤ **fore-and-after** *noun*.

forearm¹ /'fawrahm/ *noun* the human arm between the elbow and the wrist, or the corresponding part of the forelimb of other vertebrates.

forearm² /faw'rahm/ *verb trans* to arm (oneself or others) in advance; to prepare (oneself or others) against attack, etc.

forebear *or* **forbear** /'fawbeə/ *noun* an ancestor or forefather. [Middle English (Scots) *forebear*, from FORE- + *-bear*, *-beer* someone who is, from BE]

Usage note
forebear *or* forbear? See note at FORBEAR¹.

forebode /faw'bohd/ *verb trans archaic or literary* **1** to foretell or portend (something bad that is to happen). **2** to have a premonition of (evil, misfortune, etc). ➤➤ **foreboder** *noun*.

foreboding¹ /faw'bohding/ *noun* an omen, prediction, or presentiment of coming evil.

foreboding² *adj* presaging evil; ominous. ➤➤ **forebodingly** *adv*.

forebrain *noun* the front part of the brain, including the cerebral hemispheres, the thalamus, and the hypothalamus.

forecast¹ *verb* (*past tense and past part.* **forecast** *or* **forecasted**) ➤ *verb trans* **1** to estimate or predict (some future event or condition), *esp* as a result of rational study and analysis of available pertinent data: *I cannot forecast to you the action of Russia* — Winston Churchill. **2** to serve as a forecast of (something that might happen): *Such events may forecast peace*. ➤ *verb intrans* to calculate or predict the future. ➤➤ **forecaster** *noun*. [Middle English *forecasten*, from FORE- + *casten* to cast, contrive, CAST¹]

forecast² *noun* a prophecy, estimate, or prediction of a future happening or condition, *esp* of the weather.

forecastle *or* **fo'c's'le** /'fohks(ə)l/ *noun* **1** a short raised deck at the bow of a ship. **2** a forward part of a merchant ship where the living quarters are situated. [Middle English *forecastel*, from FORE- + *castel* CASTLE¹]

foreclose /faw'klohz/ *verb trans* **1a** to take away the right to redeem (e.g. a mortgage), usu because of nonpayment; to repossess (property) in this way. **b** (*often* + on) to take away the right to redeem a mortgage or other debt from (a person). **2** to rule out (a possible action); to prevent or exclude (it). ➤ *verb intrans* to foreclose a mortgage or other debt. ➤➤ **foreclosure** /faw'klohzhə/ *noun*. [Middle English *forclosen* from Old French *forclos*, past part. of *forclore*, from *fors* outside + *clore* to close, from Latin *claudere*]

forecourt *noun* **1** an open or paved area in front of a building, *esp* the part of a petrol station where the petrol pumps are situated. **2** the part of a court in some racket games lying between the net and the service line.

foredeck *noun* the front part of a ship's main deck.

foredoom *verb trans* (*usu in passive*) to doom (somebody or something) beforehand, *esp* to failure: *The whole project was foredoomed to failure*.

fore-edge *noun* the edge of a book or page opposite the spine.

forefather *noun* **1** an ancestor. **2** a person of an earlier period and common heritage.

forefeet *noun* pl of FOREFOOT.

forefinger *noun* the finger next to the thumb: *I observe from your forefinger that you make your own cigarettes* — Conan Doyle.

forefoot *noun* (*pl* **forefeet**) **1** the front foot of a four-footed animal. **2** the forward part of a ship where the stem and keel meet.

forefront *noun* the foremost part or place; the vanguard: *She was in the forefront of the progressive movement*.

foregather or **forgather** verb intrans (**foregathered** or **for-gathered, foregathering** or **forgathering**) formal to come together or assemble. [Middle English (Scots) forgadder from Dutch vergaderen]

forego[1] verb trans see FORGO.
Usage note
forego or forgo? See note at FORGO

forego[2] verb trans (**foregoes**, past tense **forewent** /faw'went/, past part. **foregone** /faw'gon/) archaic to precede (somebody or something) in time or place. ⟫ **foregoer** noun.

foregoing adj going before; immediately preceding: The foregoing statement is open to challenge. [present part. of FOREGO[2]]

foregone adj archaic previous; past.

foregone conclusion noun an inevitable result; a certainty: Her victory was a foregone conclusion.

foreground[1] noun 1 the part of a picture or view nearest to and in front of the spectator. 2 a position of prominence; the forefront.

foreground[2] verb trans 1 to place (something) in the foreground, e.g. of a picture. 2 to give (something, e.g. a point in an argument) prominence in order to draw attention to it.

forehand[1] noun 1a a stroke in tennis, squash, etc made with the palm of the hand turned in the direction of movement. b the side or part of the court on which such strokes are made. 2 the part of a horse in front of the rider.

forehand[2] adj and adv with the palm of the hand turned in the direction of movement.

forehead /'fawhed, 'forid/ noun the part of the face above the eyes.

foreign /'forən/ adj 1 situated outside a place or country, esp one's own country: a foreign country. 2 born in, belonging to, or characteristic of some place or country other than one's own or the one under consideration: Humour is the first of the gifts to perish in a foreign tongue — Virginia Woolf. 3 concerned with or dealing with other nations: foreign affairs; foreign minister; foreign trade. 4 occurring in an abnormal situation in the living body and commonly introduced from outside: Some foreign body has got into his gut. 5a (usu + to) alien in character; not characteristic of (somebody or something): Such behaviour is foreign to my nature. b (+ to) not connected or relevant. c of or proceeding from some other person or thing than the one under consideration. ⟫ **foreignness** noun. [Middle English forein via Old French from late Latin foranus on the outside, from Latin foris outside]

foreign affairs pl noun political and other newsworthy events happening around the world, esp in terms of how they relate to or affect other countries.

foreign aid noun assistance, esp economic assistance, provided by one nation to another.

foreigner noun 1 a person belonging to or owing allegiance to a foreign country. 2 a stranger or outsider. 3 something, such as a ship, from a foreign country.

foreign exchange noun 1 foreign currency. 2 the buying and selling of foreign currency.

foreign legion noun (also **Foreign Legion**) a body of foreign volunteers serving within a regular national army, esp that of France. [translation of French légion étrangère]

foreign office noun the government department responsible for foreign affairs.

foreign secretary noun (also **Foreign Secretary**) the government minister with responsibility for foreign affairs.

forejudge verb trans to prejudge (something).

foreknow verb trans (past tense **foreknew** /faw'nyooh/, past part. **foreknown** /faw'nohn/) to have previous knowledge of (something); to know (it) beforehand, esp by paranormal means or by revelation. ⟫ **foreknowledge** /faw'nolij/ noun.

foreland noun 1 a promontory or headland. 2 an area of land in front of a body of water or other prominent feature.

foreleg noun a front leg, esp of a quadruped.

forelimb noun an arm, fin, wing, or leg that is a foreleg or homologous to a foreleg.

forelock noun a lock of hair growing just above the forehead. ✳ **touch/tug one's forelock** to make a gesture that indicates one's social inferiority to another person, esp by raising a hand to one's forehead.

foreman noun (pl **foremen**) 1 the chairman and spokesman of a jury. 2 a senior male worker who supervises a group of workers, a particular operation, or a section of a plant.

foremast noun the mast nearest the bow of a ship, or the lower part of it.

foremost[1] adj 1 first in a series or progression. 2 of first rank or position; preeminent. [Old English formest, superl of forma first]

foremost[2] adv most importantly: first and foremost.

forename noun a name that precedes a person's surname.

forenoon noun morning, esp the hours of daylight before midday.

forensic /fə'renzik/ adj 1 relating to or denoting the scientific investigation of crime. 2 belonging to or used in courts of law. ⟫ **forensically** adv. [Latin forensis public, from forum: see FORUM]

forensic medicine noun a science that deals with the application of medical facts and methods to criminal investigations and legal problems.

forensics /fə'renziks/ pl noun 1a scientific tests, methods, etc involved in investigating crime. b (treated as sing. or pl) the department or people involved in this: We'd better call in forensics. 2 (treated as sing. or pl) the practice, art, or study of formal debating.

foreordain verb trans 1 to settle, arrange, or appoint (something) in advance. 2 said of a god, fate, etc: to predestine (somebody or something) to something. ⟫ **foreordination** /,fawrawdi-'naysh(ə)n/ noun.

forepart noun the front part of something.

forepaw noun a front foot of a four-legged mammal that does not have hooves.

foreplay noun erotic stimulation preceding sexual intercourse.

forequarter noun 1 the front half of a side of the carcass of a quadruped. 2 (in pl) the front legs, shoulders, etc of a quadruped.

forerun verb trans (**forerunning**, past tense **foreran**, past part. **forerun**) literary 1 to go before (something). 2 to act as an indication or warning of (something).

forerunner noun 1 a sign or symptom that gives advance warning of something. 2a a predecessor or forefather. b = PROTOTYPE (1).

foresail /'fawsayl, 'faws(ə)l/ noun 1 the lowest square sail on the foremast of a square-rigged ship. 2 the principal fore-and-aft sail set on a schooner's foremast.

foresee /faw'see/ verb trans (past tense **foresaw** /faw'saw/, past part. **foreseen** /faw'seen/) to be aware of (something, e.g. a development or event) beforehand. ⟫ **foreseeable** adj, **foreseeably** adv, **foreseer** noun.

foreshadow verb trans to indicate or suggest beforehand (what is to come); to prefigure or presage (it): Present trends foreshadow future events. ⟫ **foreshadower** noun.

foreshank noun 1 the top part of a four-legged animal's front leg. 2 a cut of meat, esp of beef or lamb, taken from the foreshank.

foresheet noun 1 the SHEET[3] (1) (controlling rope) attached to a foresail. 2 (in pl) the forward part of an open boat.

foreshock noun a small earth tremor that precedes an earthquake.

foreshore noun 1a the part of a seashore between high-tide and low-tide marks. b the land just above the high-water mark. 2 a strip of land bordering a body of water.

foreshorten verb trans (**foreshortened, foreshortening**) 1 to shorten (a detail in a drawing or painting) so as to create an illusion of depth. 2 to make (something) more compact in scale or time.

foreshow verb trans (past tense **foreshowed**, past part. **foreshowed** or **foreshown** /faw'shohn/) archaic to foretell or foreshadow (something).

foresight noun 1 the act of foreseeing or the ability to foresee things; prescience. 2 prudence due to the ability to foresee future events or conditions: He had the foresight to invest his money wisely. 3 the sight nearest the muzzle on a firearm. 4 in surveying, a sighting taken looking forwards. ⟫ **foresighted** adj, **foresightedly** adv, **foresightedness** noun.

foreskin noun the fold of skin that covers the glans of the penis.

forest[1] /'forist/ noun 1 a dense growth of trees and underbrush covering a large tract of land. 2 something resembling a profusion of trees: a forest of TV aerials. 3 a tract of wooded land in Britain formerly owned by the sovereign and used for hunting game.

[Middle English via Old French from medieval Latin *forestis*, from Latin *foris* outside]

forest[2] *verb trans* to cover (a tract of land) with trees or forest. ➤➤ **forestation** /fawri'staysh(ə)n/ *noun*.

forestall *verb trans* **1** to exclude, hinder, or prevent (somebody or something) by taking measures or action in advance. **2** to get ahead of or anticipate (somebody or something). **3** to buy up (goods) in order to create a short supply and thus raise prices, or to affect (a market) in this way. ➤➤ **forestaller** *noun*, **forestalment** *noun*. [Middle English *forstallen* from Old English *foresteall* act of waylaying, from FORE- + *steall* position, stall]

forestay *noun* a stay from the top of the foremast to the bow of a ship.

forester *noun* **1** a person trained in forestry. **2** a person or animal that inhabits forest land. **3** (**Forester**) a member of a friendly society known as the Ancient Order of Foresters. **4** a green-winged day-flying moth found in damp meadows: *Adscita statices*.

forest ranger *noun* an officer charged with the patrolling and guarding of a forest.

forestry /'foristri/ *noun* **1** the scientific study or practice of cultivating or managing forests. **2** forest land.

foretaste *noun* **1** an advance indication or warning. **2** an anticipatory sampling: *It was this marquee that Mr Bambridge was bent on buying, and he appeared to like looking inside it frequently, as a foretaste of its possession* — George Eliot.

foretell *verb trans* (*past tense and past part.* **foretold** /faw'tohld/) to predict (a coming event, etc). ➤➤ **foreteller** *noun*.

forethought *noun* **1** the act or an instance of thinking or planning out in advance. **2** consideration for the future.

foretoken[1] *noun* a premonitory sign.

foretoken[2] *verb trans* (**foretokened, foretokening**) to indicate or warn of (something) in advance.

foretold /faw'tohld/ *verb* past tense and past part. of FORETELL.

foretop *noun* a platform at the top of a ship's foremast.

fore-topgallant /fawtop'galant, fawtə'galənt/ *adj* of the part of the frontmost mast of a ship that is next above the fore-topmast: *a fore-topgallant mast; a fore-topgallant sail.*

fore-topmast /faw'topmast/ *noun* the mast next above the foremast.

fore-topsail /faw'topsayl, -s(ə)l/ *noun* a sail set on a fore-topmast; the sail next above the foresail.

forever[1] /fə'revə/ *adv* **1** (*also* **for ever**) for all future time; indefinitely: *She wants to live for ever.* **2** persistently; incessantly: *He's forever whistling out of tune.* **3** a long time: *The speeches went on forever.*

Usage note

forever or **for ever**? When the meaning is 'for all future time' the spelling as two words is preferred: *I will love you for ever.* When the meaning is 'constantly; with persistence' the spelling as one word is more common: *The children are forever asking me for money.*

forever[2] *noun* a seemingly endless length of time: *It took her forever to find the answer.*

forevermore or **for evermore** *adv* used as a more emphatic form of FOREVER[1].

forewarn *verb trans* to warn (somebody) in advance. ➤➤ **forewarner** *noun*.

forewent /faw'went/ *verb* past tense of FOREGO[1] and FOREGO[2].

forewing *noun* either of the front wings of a four-winged insect.

forewoman *noun* (*pl* **forewomen**) **1** the chairwoman and spokeswoman of a jury. **2** a senior female worker who supervises a group of workers, a particular operation, or a section of a plant.

foreword *noun* a preface, *esp* one written by somebody other than the author of the text. [translation of German *Vorwort*]

forfeit[1] /'fawfit/ *noun* **1** something lost, taken away, or imposed as a penalty. **2** the loss or forfeiting of something, *esp* of civil rights. **3a** (*in pl, but treated as sing. or pl*) a game in which articles are deposited, e.g. for making a mistake, and then redeemed by performing a task such as singing a song. **b** an article deposited or a task performed in the game of forfeits. [Middle English from Old French *forfait*, past part. of *forfaire* to commit a crime, forfeit, from *for-* out (from Latin *foris*) + *faire* to do, from Latin *facere*]

forfeit[2] *verb trans* (**forfeited, forfeiting**) **1** to lose the right to (a privilege, etc) because of some error, offence, or crime. **2** to confiscate (something) as a penalty. ➤➤ **forfeitable** *adj*, **forfeiter** *noun*, **forfeiture** /-chə/ *noun*.

forfeit[3] *adj* forfeited or subject to forfeiture.

forfend /faw'fend/ *verb* **1** *archaic* to forbid (something). **2** *NAmer* to defend, protect, or secure (something). ✳ **Heaven/God forfend** *archaic or humorous* used to express a hope that something does not happen: *Heaven forfend that my daughter inherits a nose like her dad's!* [Middle English *forfenden*, from FOR- + *fenden* to FEND]

forgather /faw'gadhə/ *verb intrans* see FOREGATHER.

forgave /fə'gayv/ *verb* past tense of FORGIVE.

forge[1] /fawj/ *noun* an open furnace where metal, *esp* iron, is heated and worked, or a workshop with such a furnace. [Middle English via Old French from Latin *fabrica*, from *fabr-, faber* smith]

forge[2] *verb trans* **1** to shape (metal or a metal object) by heating and hammering or with a press. **2** to form or bring (something) into being, *esp* by an expenditure of effort: *We made every effort to forge party unity.* **3** to counterfeit (*esp* a signature, document, or bank note). ➤ *verb intrans* to commit forgery. ➤➤ **forgeable** *adj*, **forger** *noun*.

forge[3] *verb intrans* to move forwards slowly and steadily but with effort. [prob alteration of FORCE[2]]

forge ahead *verb intrans* to move with a sudden increase of speed and power: *The horse forged ahead to win the race.*

forgery *noun* (*pl* **forgeries**) **1a** the act or an instance of forging. **b** forging as a crime. **2** a forged document, bank note, etc.

forget /fə'get/ *verb* (**forgetting**, *past tense* **forgot** /fə'got/, *past part.* **forgotten** /fə'got(ə)n/, *or archaic or NAmer* **forgot**) ➤ *verb trans* **1** to be unable to remember (something): *I forget his name.* **2** to fail to give attention to (somebody or something); to disregard (them): *He forgot his old friends.* **3a** to disregard (something) intentionally; to overlook (it): *Women and elephants never forget an injury* — Saki. **b** to reject the possibility of (something): *As for going out tonight, you can forget that!* ➤ *verb intrans* **1** to stop remembering or noticing: *Forgive and forget, that's my motto.* **2** (+ about) to fail to remember something at the proper time: *I forgot about paying the bill.* **3** (+ about) to reject something as a possibility: *Well, you can forget about going out tonight!* ✳ **forget it! 1** reject that possibility or hope. **2** think nothing of it; it's not important. **forget oneself 1** to lose one's dignity, temper, or self-control. **2** to act unsuitably, unworthily, or selfishly. ➤➤ **forgetter** *noun*. [Old English *forgietan*]

forgetful /fə'getf(ə)l/ *adj* **1** likely or apt to forget. **2** (+ of) characterized by negligent failure to remember; neglectful: *Forgetful of his manners, he left without thanking her.* **3** *literary* inducing oblivion: *forgetful sleep.* ➤➤ **forgetfully** *adv*, **forgetfulness** *noun*.

forget-me-not *noun* any of several species of small low-growing plants of the borage family with white or bright blue flowers usu arranged in a spike: genus *Myosotis*. [translation of Old French *ne m'oubliez mye* do not forget me; the flower has associations in legend with remembrance between lovers]

forgettable *adj* deserving to be forgotten, *esp* because of unworthiness or poor quality: *a forgettable performance.*

forgive /fə'giv/ *verb* (*past tense* **forgave** /fə'gayv/, *past part.* **forgiven** /fə'giv(ə)n/) ➤ *verb trans* **1** to stop feeling angry about (something) or to stop feeling resentful towards (somebody): *I find it hard to forgive an insult; One should forgive one's enemies.* **2** to pardon (somebody) for doing something; to pardon (something done): *Forgive us our trespasses, as we forgive them that trespass against us* — Prayer Book. **3a** to cancel or write off (a debt or other obligation). **b** to absolve or free (somebody) from paying a debt or discharging an obligation, etc. ➤ *verb intrans* to grant forgiveness. ➤➤ **forgivable** *adj*, **forgivably** *adv*, **forgiver** *noun*. [Old English *forgifan*, from FOR- + *gifan* to give]

forgiveness *noun* forgiving or being forgiven; pardon.

forgiving *adj* willing or able to forgive. ➤➤ **forgivingly** *adv*.

forgo or **forego** /fə'goh, faw'goh/ *verb trans* (**forgoes** or **foregoes, forgoing** or **foregoing**, *past tense* **forwent** or **forewent** /faw'went/, *past part.* **forgone** or **foregone** /faw'gon/) to abstain or refrain from (something desirable): *Children learn to forgo immediate gratification for the sake of future gains.* [Old English *forgān* to pass by, forgo, from FOR- + *gān* to go]

Usage note ─────────

forgo or **forego**? *Forgo*, more rarely spelt *forego*, means 'to refrain from': *The country decided to forgo its right to intervene.* The spelling *forego*, in the sense 'to go before', is usually only found in the forms *foregoing* (*The foregoing remarks apply in all instances*) and *foregone* (*The victory was a foregone conclusion*).

forgot /fə'got/ *verb* **1** past tense of FORGET. **2** *archaic or NAmer* past part. of FORGOT.

forgotten /fə'got(ə)n/ *verb* past part. of FORGOT.

forint /'forint/ *noun* the basic monetary unit of Hungary, divided into 100 fillers. [Hungarian *forint* from Italian *fiorino* florin, literally 'little flower', ultimately from Latin *flor-, flos* FLOWER[1]]

fork[1] /fawk/ *noun* **1** a tool or implement with two or more prongs set on the end of a handle, e.g.: **a** an agricultural or gardening tool for digging, carrying, etc. **b** a small implement for eating or serving food. **2a** a forked part, or piece of equipment. **b** either of two forked supports for a bicycle or motorcycle wheel. **3a** a division into branches, or a place where this happens. **b** any of the branches into which something forks. **4** an attack by a chess piece, e.g. a knight, on two pieces simultaneously. ➤ **forkful** (*pl* **forkfuls**) *noun*. [Old English *forca* from Latin *furca*]

fork[2] *verb intrans* **1** to divide into two or more branches: *You'll find the garage just where the road forks.* **2** to make a turn into one of the branches of a fork: *We forked left at the inn.* **3** *informal* (+ out/up) to make a payment or contribution. ➤ *verb trans* **1** to raise, pitch, dig, or work (something) with a fork: *We watched them fork hay in the traditional way.* **2** to attack (two chessmen) simultaneously. **3** *informal* (+ out/over/up) to pay or contribute (a specified amount): *He's forked out half of his salary for a new car.*

forked *adj* having one end divided into two or more branches or points.

forked lightning *noun* lightning that is seen as a branching or zigzag line in the sky: compare SHEET LIGHTNING.

forklift *noun* a vehicle for hoisting and transporting heavy objects by means of steel prongs inserted under the load.

forklift truck *noun* = FORKLIFT.

forlorn /fə'lawn/ *adj* **1** sad and lonely because of isolation or desertion; desolate. **2** in poor condition; miserable or wretched: *forlorn tumbledown buildings.* **3** nearly hopeless: *a forlorn attempt.* **4** (+ of) without; bereft of (something): *forlorn of hope.* ➤ **forlornly** *adv*, **forlornness** *noun*. [Old English *forloren*, past part. of *forlēosan* to lose, from FOR- + *lēosan* to LOSE]

forlorn hope *noun* **1** a desperate or extremely difficult enterprise. **2** a hope or desire that persists despite the knowledge that it is unlikely to materialize. [by folk etymology from Dutch *verloren hoop*, literally 'lost troop', a band of soldiers who led an attack and were not expected to survive]

form[1] /fawm/ *noun* **1a** the shape and structure of something as distinguished from its material or content. **b** a body, e.g. of a person, *esp* in its external appearance or as distinguished from the face. **2** the essential nature of a thing as distinguished from the matter in which it is embodied. **3a** an established or correct method of proceeding or behaving; formality: *I must ask for your name as a matter of form.* **b** a prescribed and set order of words: *We will follow the form of the traditional marriage service.* **4** a printed or typed document, *esp* one with blank spaces for insertion of required or requested information: *income-tax forms.* **5a** conduct regulated by external controls, e.g. custom or etiquette; ceremony: *He found the rigid form of the imperial court stifling.* **b** manner or conduct of a specified sort, as tested by a prescribed or accepted standard: *Rudeness is simply bad form.* **6** a long seat without a back; a bench. **7** something, e.g. shuttering, that holds, supports, and determines the shape of something. **8a** the way in which something is arranged, exists, or shows itself: *The novel is written in the form of a letter.* **b** a kind or variety: *Writing is a socially acceptable form of schizophrenia* — E L Doctorow. **9a** orderly method of arrangement, e.g. in the presentation of ideas, a way of coordinating elements, as, for example, in an artistic production or line of reasoning: *His work lacks form.* **b** the structural element, plan, or design of a work of art: compare CONTENT[4] (3). **10** *chiefly Brit* (*treated as sing. or pl*) a school class organized for the work of a particular year. **11a** the past performances of a competitor, racehorse, greyhound, etc considered as a guide to future performance. **b** known ability to perform: *What we hear is a singer at the top of his form.* **c** (*often* + in/out of/off) condition suitable for performing, *esp* in sports: *She was out of form all season.* **12** *Brit, informal* a criminal

record. **13** any of the ways in which a word may be written or spoken as a result of inflection or change of spelling or pronunciation: *Some dictionaries prefer the hyphenated forms.* **14** the bed or nest of a hare. **15** *NAmer* = FORME. ➤ **formless** *adj*, **formlessly** *adv*, **formlessness** *noun*. [Middle English via Old French *forme* from Latin *forma*]

form[2] *verb trans* **1a** to give form, shape, or existence to (something or somebody): *The pots were formed from clay; It's hard to form a judgment.* **b** to join together as (a group): *We formed a pressure group.* **2a** to give a particular shape to (something); to shape or mould (it) into a certain state or after a particular model: *The children formed the dough into various shapes; It's a state formed along the lines of the Roman Republic.* **b** to arrange or be arranged in (a shape): *The women formed a line outside the shop.* **c** to arrange (somebody or something) in order: *The battalion advanced as soon as the lines were formed.* **d** to model or train (a person, a person's mind, etc) by instruction and discipline: *There is nothing finer than a mind formed by classical education.* **3** to develop or acquire (e.g. a habit). **4** to serve to make up or constitute (e.g. a dish); to be a usu essential or basic element of (it): *Yogurt forms the basis for this sauce.* **5a** to produce (e.g. a tense) by inflection: *All these verbs form the past in -ed.* **b** to combine to make (a compound word). **6** to articulate (a sound, etc): *She's unable to form a 'sh'.* ➤ *verb intrans* **1** to become formed or shaped: *A scab had formed over the wound.* **2** to take a definite form; to come into existence: *Thunderclouds were forming over the hills.* ➤ **formability** /-'biliti/ *noun*, **formable** *adj*.

form- *comb. form* forming words, denoting: formic acid: *formaldehyde.*

-form or **-iform** *comb. form* forming adjectives, with the meaning: having the form or shape of; resembling: *cruciform.* [early French *-forme* from Latin *-formis*, from *forma* form]

formal /'fawml/ *adj* **1a** following established form, custom, rule, or convention: *We'll have to do this in a more formal way than we would like.* **b** based on or observing conventional or prescribed forms and rules: *a formal reception.* **c** characterized by punctilious respect for form or correct procedure: *He's very formal in all his dealings.* **d** rigidly ceremonious; prim. **2** suitable for or expected on formal occasions: *formal dress.* **3a** characteristic of speech and writing in solemn, official, and learned contexts: *formal language.* **b** said of a second-person pronoun in some languages: used in addressing a person formally or in referring to a person one respects or a person of higher social standing, greater age, etc: *In French, 'vous' is used as the formal pronoun.* **4** having a normal or recognizable structure: *There are no formal qualifications for the job.* **5** official: *She made a formal complaint to the directors.* **6a** having the appearance without the substance; nominal: *He is especially critical of formal Christians who only go to church at Christmas and Easter.* **b** relating to the outward form or appearance of something as distinguished from its content. **7** having a symmetrical or orderly arrangement of elements: *a formal garden.* **8** involving logical or mathematical reasoning: *a formal proof.* **9** determining or being the essential constitution or structure of something. ➤ **formally** *adv*, **formalness** *noun*. [Middle English from Latin *formalis*, from *forma* FORM[1]]

formaldehyde /fə'maldihied/ *noun* a pungent irritating gas used chiefly as a disinfectant and preservative and in chemical synthesis. [a blend of FORMIC ACID + ALDEHYDE]

formalin /'fawməlin/ *noun* a clear aqueous solution of formaldehyde. [orig a trademark: from FORMALDEHYDE + -IN[1]]

formalise *verb trans* see FORMALIZE.

formalism *noun* **1** strict or excessive adherence to prescribed or external forms, structures, or techniques, e.g. in religion or art, often without regard to their content, inner significance, moral value, etc.

Editorial note ─────────

Formalism privileges form (style, structure, genre) over thematic content or historical specificity in the analysis or evaluation of works of art and literature. In the 1920s the Russian Formalists believed that art should make strange the familiar by representing it in new ways — Professor Catherine Belsey.

2 the structure of a logical, mathematical, or scientific argument as opposed to its content. ➤ **formalist** *noun and adj*, **formalistic** *adj*, **formalistically** /-'listikli/ *adv*.

formality /faw'maliti/ *noun* (*pl* **formalities**) **1** the quality or state of being formal. **2** compliance with or observance of formal or conventional rules; ceremony. **3a** an established form or procedure that is required or conventional. **b** something required by rule or custom but which has little real significance: *Don't worry about the interview. It's just a formality.*

formalize *or* **formalise** *verb trans* **1** to make (an arrangement, etc) formal. **2** to give formal status or approval to (something). **3** to give (something) a definite shape. ➤➤ **formalization** /-'zaysh(ə)n/ *noun.*

formal logic *noun* a system of logic that examines the form of propositions and means of deductive reasoning, rather than their content.

formant /'fawmənt/ *noun* a characteristic resonance band of a vowel sound or musical instrument. [German *Formant* from Latin *formant-, formans,* present part. of *formare*: see FORMAT[1]]

format[1] /'fawmat/ *noun* **1** the shape, size, and general make-up, e.g. of a book. **2** the general plan of organization or arrangement. **3** in computing, the structure of data e.g. held on a disk or displayed on a screen. [via French and German from Latin *formatus,* past part. of *formare* to form, from *forma* FORM[1]]

format[2] *verb trans* (**formatted, formatting**) **1** to arrange (material, e.g. a book or data) in a particular format or style. **2** in computing, to prepare (a floppy disk, etc) to receive data. ➤➤ **formatting** *noun.*

formation /faw'maysh(ə)n/ *noun* **1** giving form or shape to something, or taking form; development: *I am convinced that ... an unhappy childhood is essential for the formation of exceptional gifts —* Thornton Wilder. **2** something formed: *new word formations.* **3** the manner in which a thing is formed; structure. **4** a body or series of rocks represented as a unit in geological mapping. **5a** an arrangement of a group of people or things in some prescribed manner or for a particular purpose. **b** (*treated as sing. or pl*) such a group. **c** (*used before a noun*) done in a pattern or arrangement: *formation dancing.* ➤➤ **formational** *adj.*

formative[1] /'fawmətiv/ *adj* **1a** giving or capable of giving form to something, *esp* having a significant influence on the growth or development of somebody or something: *a formative influence.* **b** of or characterized by formation or development or by formative effects: *Certain emotional responses develop subconsciously during a child's formative years.* **2** used in word formation or inflection: *'-ing' is a formative affix.* **3a** said of a cell, tissue, etc: capable of alteration by growth and development. **b** producing new cells and tissues. ➤➤ **formatively** *adv,* **formativeness** *noun.* [Middle English via French from Latin *formativus,* from *formare*: see FORMAT[1]]

formative[2] *noun* **1** a word-forming element. **2** a formative affix.

form class *noun* **1** *dated* = PART OF SPEECH. **2** a group of words that share some grammatical feature or features, e.g. a common pattern of inflections.

forme (*NAmer* **form**) /fawm/ *noun* a frame enclosing metal type or blocks ready for printing. [Old French *forme*: see FORM[1]]

former[1] /'fawmə/ *adj* **1** of or occurring in the past: *in former times.* **2** having been previously or once: *the former Prime Minister.* **3** denoting the first of two things mentioned or understood. [Old English *forma* first]

former[2] *noun* (*pl* **former**) the first mentioned: *Of puppies and kittens, the former are the harder to train.*

Usage note
former and *latter.* The *former* refers back to the first of two previously mentioned things or people, the *latter* to the second. They are used to avoid tedious or awkward repetition: *Given the choice of being vilified by a newspaper or being ignored by it,* I would instinctively opt for the former. They should never be used when more than two things are listed. In that case use *first, first-named, second, last* etc. They should also be avoided when it is not absolutely and immediately clear what they refer to.

former[3] *noun chiefly Brit* (*usu in combination*) a member of a specified school form or year: *a sixth-former.* [FORM[1] + -ER[2]]

former[4] *noun* **1** somebody or something that forms something. **2** a frame or core on which an electrical coil is wound. [FORM[2] + -ER[2]]

formerly *adv* at an earlier time; previously.

Formica /faw'miekə/ *noun trademark* any of various laminated plastics used to make heat-resistant surfaces, *esp* for worktops, tables, etc. [said to be from its development as a substitute *for mica* as an insulation material]

formic acid /'fawmik/ *noun* a pungent corrosive liquid acid naturally produced by ants: formula HCOOH. [Latin *formica* ant]

formidable /fə'midəbl, 'fawmidəbl/ *adj* **1** causing fear, dread, or apprehension: *a formidable prospect.* **2** difficult to overcome: *The most formidable weapon against errors of every kind is reason —*

Thomas Paine. **3** said of a person: tending to inspire respect or awe; discouraging approach by others. ➤➤ **formidableness** *noun,* **formidably** *adv.* [Middle English from Latin *formidabilis,* from *formidare* to fear]

Usage note
Nowadays in British English *formidable* is usually pronounced with the stress on the second syllable *-mid-.* The older pronunciation, in which the stress falls on the first syllable *for-,* is preferred in American English and is the standard pronunciation in British English.

form letter *noun* a letter in a standardized format, to which pertinent details such as people's names and addresses can be added for sending to a usu large number of people.

form of address *noun* a correct title or expression of politeness to be used to somebody.

formula /'fawmyoolə/ *noun* (*pl* **formulas** *or* **formulae** /-lee, -lie/) **1a** a set form of words for use in a ceremony or ritual. **b** a truth, principle, or procedure, *esp* as a basis for negotiation or, often conventionalized, as a recommended basis for action: *The two sides worked out a peace formula; There is no set formula for a good marriage.* **c** a prescribed or set form or method, e.g. of writing, often followed uncritically; an established rule or custom: *They just churn out unimaginative television programmes written to a formula.* **2a** a fact, rule, or principle expressed in symbols, e.g. in mathematics. **b** a symbolic expression of the chemical composition of a substance. **c** a group of numerical symbols used to express a single concept. **3a** a recipe or the list of ingredients in it. **b** liquid baby food made from milk or soya. **4a** (**Formula**) a classification of racing cars (Formula One, Two, etc) specifying *esp* size, weight, and engine capacity. **b** (*used before a noun*) relating to or denoting one of these classifications: *Formula One cars.* ➤➤ **formulaic** /-'layik/ *adj,* **formulaically** /-'layikli/ *adv.* [Latin *formula,* dimin. of *forma* FORM[1]]

formularize *or* **formularise** /'fawmyoolariez/ *verb trans* to state (something) as a formula or reduce it to a formula; = FORMULATE (1). ➤➤ **formularization** /-'zaysh(ə)n/ *noun.*

formulary[1] /'fawmyoolari/ *noun* (*pl* **formularies**) **1** a book or other collection of stated and prescribed forms, e.g. of prayers. **2** a book containing a list of medicinal substances and formulas: *the British National Formulary.* **3** a prescribed form or model; a formula.

formulary[2] *adj* relating to or denoting a formula.

formulate /'fawmyoolayt/ *verb trans* **1** to state (something) as a formula or reduce it to a formula. **2** to devise or develop (a policy, plan, product, etc): *The company claims to have formulated a new soap.* ➤➤ **formulation** /-'laysh(ə)n/ *noun,* **formulator** *noun.*

form up *verb intrans* to take one's place in a pattern, shape, line-up, etc. ➤ *verb trans* to make (e.g. soldiers, Scouts) arrange themselves in a particular pattern or shape: *They were formed up for inspection in rows of ten.*

formwork *noun* a wooden structure that holds concrete in place and in shape while it hardens.

fornicate /'fawnikayt/ *verb intrans formal or humorous* to commit fornication. ➤➤ **fornicator** *noun.* [late Latin *fornicatus,* past part. of *fornicare,* from Latin *fornic-, fornix* arch, vault, brothel]

fornication /fawni'kaysh(ə)n/ *noun formal or humorous* voluntary sexual intercourse outside marriage.

forsake /fə'sayk/ *verb trans* (**forsaking,** past tense **forsook** /fə'sook/, past part. **forsaken** /fə'sayk(ə)n/) **1** to renounce (e.g. something once cherished), often for ever: *She forsook her family ties.* **2** to desert or abandon (somebody): *False friends forsake us in adversity.* [Old English *forsacan,* from FOR- + *sacan* to dispute]

forsaken *adj* **1** said of a place: completely deserted. **2** said of a person: left absolutely alone or helpless. ➤➤ **forsakenly** *adverb,* **forsakenness** *noun.*

forsook /fə'sook/ *verb* past tense of FORSAKE.

forsooth /fə'soohth/ *adv archaic or humorous* indeed; actually; no less: *Her family owns a castle in the Scottish Highlands, forsooth.* [Old English *forsōth,* from FOR[1] + SOOTH[1]]

forswear /faw'swea/ *verb* (*past tense* **forswore** /faw'swaw/, past part. **forsworn** /faw'swawn/) ➤ *verb trans* **1a** to reject or deny (something) under oath. **b** to solemnly renounce (something). **2** to perjure (oneself). ➤ *verb intrans* to swear to something falsely; to commit perjury. [Old English *forswerian,* from FOR- + *swerian* to SWEAR]

forsworn /faw'swawn/ *adj* guilty of perjury; having lied under oath.

forsythia /faw'siethi·ə/ *noun* any of a genus of ornamental shrubs of the olive family with bright yellow bell-shaped flowers appearing in early spring before the leaves: genus *Forsythia*. [named after William *Forsyth* d.1804, Brit botanist, who is said to have introduced the plant from China]

fort /fawt/ *noun* a fortified building, *esp* one built in former times for defence, or any strongly fortified place maintained for defence. ✳ **hold the fort** to cope with problems for somebody, or look after their work, while they are temporarily absent [from a signal sent by General Sherman during the American Civil War urging General Corse to hold the fort at Allatoona Pass until reinforcements arrived; the message, misquoted as *hold the fort, for I am coming*, was later incorporated in a popular gospel song]. [Middle English *forte* via French from Latin *fortis* strong]

forte[1] /fawt, 'fawtay/ *noun* 1 /'fawtay/ something at which a person excels; a person's strong point: *Grammar is George's forte.* 2 the strongest part of a sword blade, being between the middle and the hilt: compare FOIBLE (2). [French *fort* strong, from Latin *fortis*]

forte[2] /'fawti, 'fawtay/ *adv and adj* said of a piece of music: to be performed in a loud and often forceful manner. ➤➤ **forte** *noun*. [Italian *forte* strong, from Latin *fortis*]

Fortean /'fawti·ən/ *adj* relating to or denoting the paranormal or paranormal phenomena. [named after Charles H *Fort* d.1932, US student of the paranormal]

forte-piano /fawti'pyahnoh/ *adj and adv* said of a piece of music: to be performed in a manner that is loud then immediately soft. ➤➤ **forte-piano** *noun*. [Italian *forte-piano* loud-soft]

forth /fawth/ *adv chiefly archaic* 1 onwards in time, place, or order; forwards: *And from that day forth, he was never seen again.* 2 out; into notice or view: *The trees will put forth leaves.* 3 away from a centre; abroad: *He went forth to preach.* ✳ **and so forth** and so on; and other related things: *Here are the baby's nappies, cream, and so forth.* [Old English]

forthcoming *adj* 1 approaching; about to occur or appear. 2a made available: *New funds will be forthcoming next year.* b willing to give information; responsive. [obsolete *forthcome* to come forth]

forthright[1] *adj* going straight to the point without ambiguity or hesitation: *the difference between open forthright bigotry and the shamefaced kind that works through unwritten agreements* — Shirley Chisholm. ➤➤ **forthrightly** *adv*, **forthrightness** *noun*

forthright[2] *adv* 1 directly and candidly. 2 at once.

forthwith *adv* immediately.

fortification /,fawtifi'kaysh(ə)n/ *noun* 1a the act or an instance of fortifying. b the science or art of providing defensive works. 2 something that fortifies, defends, or strengthens, *esp* works erected to defend a place or position.

fortified wine /'fawtified/ *noun* a wine to which alcohol has been added during or after fermentation.

fortify /'fawtifie/ *verb trans* (**fortifies, fortified, fortifying**) to make (somebody or something) strong, e.g.: a to strengthen and secure (a place, etc) by military defences. b to give strength, courage, or endurance to (somebody); to strengthen (them). c to add (e.g. alcohol to wine or vitamins to food) to strengthen or enrich it. ➤ *verb intrans* to erect fortifications. ➤➤ **fortifiable** *adj*, **fortifier** *noun*. [Middle English *fortifien* via French from late Latin *fortificare*, from Latin *fortis* strong]

fortissimo /faw'tisimoh/ *adj and adv* said of a piece of music: to be performed in a very loud manner. [Italian *fortissima*, superl of *forte*: see FORTE[2]]

fortitude /'fawtityoohd/ *noun* courage or endurance, *esp* in the face of pain or adversity. [Middle English from Latin *fortitudin-, fortitudo*, from *fortis* strong]

fortnight /'fawtniet/ *noun chiefly Brit* two weeks. [Middle English *fourtenight*, alteration of *fourtene night* fourteen nights]

fortnightly[1] *adj* occurring or appearing once a fortnight.

fortnightly[2] *adv chiefly Brit* once in a fortnight; every fortnight.

fortnightly[3] *noun* (*pl* **fortnightlies**) a publication issued fortnightly.

Fortran /'fawtran/ *noun* a high-level computer language, primarily for mathematical and scientific applications. [contraction of *formula translation*]

fortress /'fawtris/ *noun* a fortified place, *esp* a large and permanent fortification, sometimes including a town. [Middle English *forteresse*, from early French *forteresce*, from Latin *fortis* strong]

fortuitous /faw'tyooh·itəs/ *adj* 1 occurring by chance. 2 *informal* fortunate; lucky. ➤➤ **fortuitously** *adv*, **fortuitousness** *noun*, **fortuity** *noun*. [Latin *fortuitus* from *forte* by chance, from *fort-, fors* chance, luck]

Usage note

fortuitous *or* fortunate? Primarily, and from its origins, *fortuitous* means 'occurring by chance': *I had no idea she was going to be there; our meeting was entirely fortuitous.* In modern writing and speech *fortuitous* has also come to refer to things that happen by good fortune, not simply by chance (*The event could not have happened at a more fortuitous time*), but this is a usage that traditionalists seek to avoid. *Fortunate*, by contrast, means 'lucky' or 'auspicious'.

fortunate /'fawch(ə)nət/ *adj* 1 unexpectedly bringing something good; auspicious. 2 lucky. ➤➤ **fortunateness** *noun*.

Usage note

fortunate *or* fortuitous? See note at FORTUITOUS.

fortunately *adv* 1 in a fortunate manner. 2 having or being a fortunate outcome; luckily: *Fortunately I got back in time.*

fortune /'fawchoohn, 'fawchən/ *noun* 1a a large quantity of material possessions or wealth: *A single man in possession of a good fortune must be in want of a wife* — Jane Austen. b (*often* **small fortune**) *informal* a very large sum of money: *He won a fortune on the pools.* 2a luck. b prosperity attained partly through luck. c (*in pl*) the favourable or unfavourable events that accompany the progress of an individual or thing: *In this story, we find ourselves tracing the fortunes of a rags-to-riches hero; the declining fortunes of the film industry.* 3 destiny or fate: *He asked her to tell his fortune with Tarot cards.* 4 (*often* **Fortune**) a supposed power, sometimes personified, that unpredictably determines events and issues. [Middle English via French from Latin *fortuna* luck]

fortune cookie *noun NAmer* a biscuit containing a slip of paper with a prediction, proverb, or joke printed on it.

fortune-hunter *noun* a person who seeks wealth, *esp* by marriage. ➤➤ **fortune-hunting** *noun*.

fortune-teller *noun* a person who claims to foretell future events. ➤➤ **fortune-telling** *noun and adj*.

forty /'fawti/ *adj and noun* (*pl* **forties**) 1 the number 40, or the quantity represented by it. 2 (*in pl*) the numbers 40 to 49; *specif* a range of temperatures, ages, or dates within a century characterized by these numbers. ➤➤ **fortieth** /'fawti·əth/ *adj and noun*. [Old English *feowertig* group of forty, from *feower* FOUR + *-tig* group of ten]

Forty-five *noun* (*also* **the Forty-five**) the Jacobite rebellion that took place in the United Kingdom in 1745 to 1746.

forty-five *noun* (*usu* **45**) a gramophone record that plays at 45 revolutions per minute.

forty-niner /-'nienə/ *noun* a person who took part in the gold rush in California during 1849.

forty winks *pl noun informal* (*treated as sing. or pl*) a short sleep; a nap.

forum /'fawrəm/ *noun* (*pl* **forums** *or* **fora** /'fawrə/) 1a a public meeting place for open discussion. b a public meeting or lecture involving audience participation. c a radio or television programme broadcasting discussions of public concern. d a medium, such as a newspaper, an Internet newsgroup, etc, where views may be aired and debated. 2 *chiefly NAmer* a court or tribunal. 3 the marketplace or public place of an ancient Roman city which formed the centre for judicial and public business. [Latin *forum*, literally 'a place outside']

forward[1] /'faw·wəd/ *adj* 1 in or towards the direction in which one is facing or moving. 2 (*also* + of) located at, near, or nearer to the front, *esp* of a ship or aircraft. 3a lacking modesty or reserve; brash, assertive, or impudent. b advanced in physical or mental development; precocious. 4 advanced in what is being or needs to be done. 5 from the original point of departure; outward: *the forward journey.* 6a of or getting ready for the future: *forward planning.* b for the future: *Forward bookings are accepted.* 7a moving, tending, or leading towards a position in front: *England need some new forward players.* b in cricket: occupying a fielding position in front of the batsman's wicket. ➤➤ **forwardly** *adv*, **forwardness** *noun*. [Old English *foreweard*, from FORE- + *-weard* -WARD]

forward[2] *adv* 1a to or towards what is ahead or in front: *She moved slowly forward through the crowd.* b into the future: *from that time forward.* 2 to or towards an earlier time: *Can we bring the date of the meeting forward?* 3 into prominence or open view.

forward[3] *noun* **1** in hockey, football, etc, an attacking player stationed at or near the front of his or her side or team. **2** (*usu* **forwards**) in commerce, an arrangement to trade specified assets at an agreed price at a particular date in the future.

forward[4] *verb trans* **1a** to send (something): *We will forward the goods on payment.* **b** to send (something) onwards from an intermediate point in transit. **2** to help (something) onwards; to promote (it). ▶▶ **forwarder** *noun*.

forwards *adv* = FORWARD[2] (1A).

forwent /faw'went/ *verb* past tense of FORGO.

foss /fos/ *noun* see FOSSE.

fossa /'fosə/ *noun* (*pl* **fossae** /'fosee, 'fosie/) an anatomical pit or depression. ▶▶ **fossate** /'fosayt/ *adj*. [Latin *fossa* ditch, from *fodere* to dig]

fosse *or* **foss** /fos/ *noun* a ditch or moat, *esp* one that forms part of a fortification. [Middle English *fosse* via Old French from Latin *fossa*: see FOSSA]

fossick /'fosik/ *verb intrans* **1** *Aus, NZ* to search for gold, *esp* by picking over abandoned workings. **2** (*usu* + about/around/for) to search or rummage for something. ▶▶ **fossicker** *noun*. [English dialect *fussick, fussock* to potter]

fossick out *verb trans Aus, NZ* to look for or find (something) by rummaging, or as if by rummaging.

fossil /'fosl/ *noun* **1** a relic or the remains of an animal or plant of a past geological age, preserved in the earth's crust. **2a** a person with outmoded views. **b** something such as an outdated viewpoint or custom that has become rigidly fixed. **3** an obsolete word or word element that only occurs in an idiom, such as *fro* in *to and fro*. [Latin *fossilis* dug up, from *fossus*, past part. of *fodere* to dig]

fossil fuel *noun* a fuel, e.g. coal, that is extracted from the earth and derived from the remains of living things.

fossiliferous /fosil'ifərəs/ *adj* containing fossils.

fossilize *or* **fossilise** /'fosiliez/ *verb trans* **1** to convert (e.g. a plant or animal) into a fossil. **2** to make (a custom, etc) outmoded, rigid, or fixed. ▶ *verb intrans* to become fixed in an outmoded state. ▶▶ **fossilization** /-'zaysh(ə)n/ *noun*.

fossorial /fo'sawri-əl/ *adj* **1** said of an animal: burrowing. **2** said of an animal's limbs: used for or adapted to digging. [medieval Latin *fossorius*, from Latin *fodere* to dig]

foster[1] /'fostə/ *verb trans* (**fostered, fostering**) **1** to promote the growth or development of (friendship, trade, etc); to encourage or promote (it). **2a** to rear or give parental care to (a child with whom one has no blood or legal ties) in one's home. **b** *Brit* to place (a child) in a foster home. **3** to cherish (a hope, etc). ▶▶ **fosterer** *noun*, **fostering** *noun*. [Old English *fōstor-*, from *fōstor* food, feeding]

foster[2] *adj* providing, receiving, or sharing care in a family home though not related by blood or legal ties: *a foster home; a foster child*.

fosterage /'fostərij/ *noun* **1** the act or an instance of fostering. **2** the state of being fostered. **3** the act or an instance of encouraging or promoting something.

fosterling /'fostəling/ *noun archaic* a foster child.

fouetté /fooh'etay (*French* fwɛte)/ *noun* in ballet, a quick whipping movement of the raised leg in a pirouette. [French *fouetté*, from past part. of *fouetter* to whip, from *fouet* whip]

fought /fawt/ *verb* past tense and past part. of FIGHT[1].

foul /fowl/ *adj* **1a** offensive to the senses; evil-smelling; loathsome or repugnant. **b** impure; polluted; rotten. **2** morally or spiritually evil; detestable: *But he that hides a dark soul and foul thoughts benighted walks under the midday sun* — Milton. **3** particularly unpleasant, disagreeable, or distressing: *The boss was in a foul temper*. **4** obscene or abusive: *foul language*. **5** wet and stormy: *foul weather*. **6** unfair, treacherous, or dishonourable: *I'll have my way by fair means or foul*. **7** infringing the rules, *esp* in a game or sport: *a foul punch*. **8a** filled or covered with dirty or offensive matter; soiled: *foul linen*. **b** full of dirt or mud: *a foul drain*. **c** (*often* + with) encrusted, clogged, or choked with a foreign substance: *The chimney was foul and smoked badly*. **9** obstructive to navigation: *a foul tide*. **10** marked up or defaced by changes: *a foul copy of a manuscript*. **11** placed in a situation that blocks or obstructs movement; entangled: *a foul anchor*. ✳ **fall/run foul of 1** to come into conflict with (somebody or something): *Inevitably he fell foul of the law*. **2** to collide with (something): *Just outside the harbour, we ran foul of a hidden reef*. ▶▶ **foully** *adv*, **foulness** *noun*. [Old English *fūl*]

foul[2] *noun* **1** an infringement of the rules in a game or sport. **2** an entanglement or collision in angling, sailing, etc.

foul[3] *verb trans* **1** to make (something) dirty; to pollute (it): *Do not allow your dog to foul the pavement or grass verges*. **2** in sport, to commit a foul against (e.g. an opposing player). **3a** to obstruct or block (e.g. a drain). **b** to entangle or collide with (e.g. a boat). **c** to cover (e.g. the bottom of a ship) so as to adversely affect its speed: *Barnacles had fouled the ship's bottom*. **4** to discredit or disgrace (somebody or something). ▶ *verb intrans* **1** to commit a foul in a sport or game. **2** to become or be foul, e.g.: **a** to decompose or rot. **b** to become filled, obstructed, or covered with a foreign substance. **c** to become entangled or come into collision: *The ropes have fouled*.

foulard /'foohlah(d)/ *noun* a lightweight plain-woven or twilled silk, or silk and cotton, fabric, usu decorated with a printed pattern. [French *foulard*]

foulbrood *noun* a bacterial disease of honeybee larvae.

foulmouthed *adj* using or given to using obscene, profane, or abusive language.

foul play *noun* **1** violence, *esp* murder. **2** play that infringes the rules in a game or sport.

foul up *verb trans* **1** to spoil or confuse (something) by making mistakes or using poor judgment. **2** to entangle or block (something): *Bad weather fouled up the communications*. **3** *chiefly NAmer* to contaminate (something). ▶ *verb intrans* **1** to do something badly; to bungle it. **2** to become entangled or blocked.

foul-up *noun informal* **1** a state of confusion caused by ineptitude, carelessness, or mismanagement. **2** a mechanical difficulty.

found[1] /fownd/ *verb* past tense and past part. of FIND[1].

found[2] *adj* **1** equipped: *The boat is fully found and ready to go*. **2** *Brit* including meals, heating, and/or other services: *The rent is £60 a week all found*. **3** said of an object: taken from a place where it occurs naturally, often for use in a work of art.

found[3] *verb trans* **1** to establish (e.g. an institution), often with provision for continued financial support. **2** (*often* + on/upon) to set or ground (e.g. a plan, a system of thought) on something sure or solid. **3** to take the first steps in building (something). [Middle English *founden* via Old French from Latin *fundare*, from *fundus* bottom]

found[4] *verb trans* **1** to melt (metal) and pour it into a mould. **2** to cast (metal) in this way. **3** to make or shape (something metal) in this way. [early French *fondre* to pour, melt, from Latin *fundere*]

foundation /fown'daysh(ə)n/ *noun* **1** the act or an instance of establishing something, e.g. an institution or colony. **2** the basis on which something stands or is supported, a reason or justification: *Your fears are without foundation*. **3a** an organization or institution established by endowment with provision for future maintenance. **b** the endowment on which an organization or institution is established. **4** (*also in pl*) an underlying natural or prepared base or support, *esp* the masonry substructure on which a building rests. **5** a cream, lotion, etc applied to the face as a base for other make-up. ▶▶ **foundational** *adj*, **foundationally** *adv*, **foundationless** *adj*.

foundation course *noun* a basic general course, e.g. as taught in the first year at certain universities.

foundation garment *noun* a girdle, corset, or other supporting undergarment.

foundation stone *noun* **1** a stone in the foundation of a building, *esp* when laid with public ceremony. **2** something that underpins or forms a basis.

founder[1] /'fowndə/ *noun* a person who establishes an institution, colony, etc. [FOUND[3]]

founder[2] *noun* a person who owns, manages, or works in a foundry. [FOUND[4]]

founder[3] *verb* (**foundered, foundering**) ▶ *verb intrans* **1** said of a ship: to sink. **2** said of e.g. a plan, project, or arrangement: to fail. **3** to collapse or give way. **4** said of a horse: to stumble or go lame. ▶ *verb trans* to disable or lame (e.g. a horse), *esp* by overwork. [Middle English *foundren* to send to the bottom, collapse, from early French *fondrer*, ultimately from Latin *fundus* bottom] **Usage note** founder *or* flounder? See note at FLOUNDER[2].

founding father *noun* **1** a founder. **2** (**Founding Father**) a member of the American Constitutional Convention of 1787.

foundling /'fowndling/ *noun* an infant found abandoned by unknown parents.

found object *noun* = OBJET TROUVÉ.

foundry /'fowndri/ *noun* (*pl* **foundries**) a place for casting metals. [FOUND⁴]

fount¹ /fownt/ *noun* 1 *literary* a fountain or spring. 2 a source. [early French *font* from Latin *font-, fons* fountain]

fount² *or* **font** /font/ *noun* in printing: a complete set of characters for printing in one style. [orig meaning 'the process of melting or founding'; French *fonte* from early French *fondre*: see FOUND⁴]

fountain¹ /'fowntən/ *noun* 1 an artificially produced jet of water, or the structure providing this. 2 anything that streams out like a fountain: *A film is a petrified fountain of thought* — Jean Cocteau. 3 a spring of water issuing from the ground. 4 a source. 5 a reservoir containing a supply of liquid, e.g. in a lamp or printing press. [Middle English from early French *fontaine*, ultimately from Latin *fontanus* of a spring, from *font-, fons* fountain]

fountain² *verb intrans* to flow or spout like or in a fountain.

fountainhead *noun* 1 a spring that is the source of a stream. 2 a principal source.

fountain pen *noun* a pen with a reservoir or cartridge that automatically feeds the nib with ink: *the small agitated figures ... decorated with fountain pens, and burdened with despatch boxes* — Virginia Woolf.

four /faw/ *noun* 1 the number 4, or the quantity represented by it. 2 something having four parts or members, *esp* a four-person racing boat or its crew. 3a the age of 4 years. b the hour four hours after midday or midnight. 4 a shot in cricket that crosses the boundary after having hit the ground and so scores four runs: compare SIX. ⪢ **four** *adj*, **fourfold** *adj and adv*. [Old English *fēower*]

four-by-four *or* **4x4** *noun* a motor vehicle equipped with a transmission system that sends power directly to all four wheels.

four-dimensional *adj* relating to or denoting something that has or exists in four dimensions, usu length, breadth, and depth, plus time or a fourth spatial dimension.

four-eyes *noun* (*pl* **four-eyes**) *informal, derog* a person who wears glasses. ⪢ **four-eyed** *adj*.

four flush¹ *noun* a poker hand of four cards of the same suit and one card of a different suit. It has little intrinsic value, but can be useful in bluffing.

four-flush² *verb intrans informal* 1 to use a poor poker hand, *esp* a four-flush, to bluff. 2 *chiefly NAmer* to act in a blatantly misleading way. ⪢ **four-flusher** *noun*.

four-handed *adj* 1 designed for four hands. 2 engaged in by four people.

Four Hundred *noun* (**the Four Hundred** *or* **the 400**) *NAmer* the exclusive social set of a community. [arbitrary smallish number]

Fourierism /'foori·əriz(ə)m, 'foori·ayiz(ə)m/ *noun* a system for reorganizing society into cooperative communities. ⪢ **Fourierist** *noun and adj*. [French *fouriérisme*, named after F M C *Fourier* d.1837, French social reformer]

Fourier series /'foori·ə, 'fooriay/ *noun* an infinite series in which the terms are constants multiplied by sine or cosine functions of integer multiples of the variable and which is used in the analysis of periodic functions such as simple harmonic motion. [named after Baron J B J *Fourier* d.1830, French geometrician and physicist, who devised it]

four-in-hand *noun* 1 a team of four horses driven by one person, or a vehicle drawn by such a team. 2 *NAmer* a necktie tied loosely and with the two ends dangling, a style that was popular at the end of the 19th cent.

four-leaf clover *noun* a clover leaf that has four leaflets instead of three and is believed to bring good luck.

four-leaved clover *noun* = FOUR-LEAF CLOVER.

four-letter word *noun* any of a group of vulgar or obscene words typically relating to sexual intercourse or excretion and often made up of four letters: *Good authors who once knew better words now only use four-letter words* — Cole Porter.

four-o'clock *noun* a tropical American plant with trumpet-shaped flowers that open in the late afternoon: *Mirabilis jalapa*. Also called MARVEL OF PERU.

four-o'clock plant *noun* = FOUR-O'CLOCK.

fourpenny one *noun Brit, informal, dated* a sharp blow. [prob from rhyming slang *fourpenny bit* hit]

four-poster *noun* a bed with four tall often carved corner posts designed to support curtains or a canopy.

fourscore *noun and adj dated* eighty.

foursome /'faws(ə)m/ *noun* 1 a group of four people or things. 2 a golf match between two pairs of partners in which each pair plays one ball.

foursquare¹ *adj* 1 bold and resolute. 2 solid; squarely based. 3 square.

foursquare² *adv* 1 in a solidly based and steady way. 2 resolutely.

four-star *adj* of a superior standard or quality: *a four-star restaurant*. [from the number of asterisks used in guidebooks to denote relative excellence]

four-stroke *adj* 1 relating to or denoting an internal-combustion engine with a cycle of four strokes, usu intake, compression, combustion, and exhaust. 2 said of a vehicle: powered by a four-stroke engine.

fourteen /faw'teen/ *adj and noun* the number 14, or the quantity represented by it. ⪢ **fourteenth** *adj and noun*. [Old English *fēowertiene*, from *fēower* FOUR + *tien, tēn* TEN]

fourth /fawth/ *adj and noun* 1 denoting a person or thing having the position in a sequence corresponding to the number four. 2 one of four equal parts of something. 3 the fourth and sometimes highest forward gear of a motor vehicle. 4a in music, an interval of four degrees of a diatonic scale, or the combination of two notes at such an interval. b = SUBDOMINANT. ⪢ **fourthly** *adv*. [Old English *fēortha, fēowertha*, from *fēower* FOUR + -TH¹]

fourth dimension *noun* 1 a dimension in addition to length, breadth, and depth; *specif* a fourth spatial coordinate in addition to three rectangular coordinates, or the time coordinate in a space-time continuum. 2 something outside the range of ordinary experience. ⪢ **fourth-dimensional** *adj*.

fourth estate *noun* (**the Fourth Estate**) journalists; the press. [orig humorous; from its status as a rival to the three groups (clergy, nobility, commons) traditionally holding political power]

fourth official *noun* in football, a match official additional to the referee and two assistant referees (linesmen), having various ancillary duties and able to stand in for any of the main officials.

Fourth World *noun* (*treated as sing. or pl*) the poorest and most underdeveloped nations of the world: compare THIRD WORLD.

four-way *adj* 1 allowing passage in any of four directions. 2 including four participants.

four-wheel *adj* having four wheels.

four-wheel drive *noun* 1 a transmission system in a motor vehicle that sends power directly to all four wheels. 2 a vehicle equipped with this type of transmission system.

four-wheeled *adj* = FOUR-WHEEL.

fovea /'fohvi·ə/ *noun* (*pl* **foveae** /'fohvi·ee, 'fohviie/) a small anatomical pit, e.g. in the retina of the eye. ⪢ **foveal** *adj*, **foveate** /'fohviayt/ *adj*, **foveiform** /foh'vee·ifawm/ *adj*. [Latin *fovea*, literally 'small pit']

fowl¹ /fowl/ *noun* (*pl* **fowls** *or collectively* **fowl**) 1a a domestic bird such as a chicken, turkey, or duck, *esp* an adult hen. b any similar or related bird hunted for food; = WILDFOWL. c the flesh of a fowl used as food. 2 *archaic* (*or in combination*) a bird: *the fowls of the air*; *waterfowl*. [Old English *fugel* bird]

fowl² *verb intrans* to hunt, catch, or kill wildfowl. ⪢ **fowler** *noun*, **fowling** *noun*.

fowling piece *noun* a light gun for shooting birds or small animals.

fowl pest *noun* a fatal infectious virus disease of domestic poultry.

Fox /foks/ *noun* (*pl* **Fox**) 1 a member of an indigenous North American people inhabiting parts of Oklahoma and Illinois. 2 the Algonquian language spoken by this people.

fox¹ /foks/ *noun* (*pl* **foxes** *or collectively* **fox**) 1a any of several species of flesh-eating mammals of the dog family with a pointed muzzle, large erect ears, and a long bushy tail: *Vulpes vulpes* (the red fox) and other species. b the fur of a fox. 2 a clever crafty person. 3 *NAmer, informal* a physically attractive woman. ⪢ **foxlike** *adj*. [Old English]

fox² *verb trans* to outwit or baffle (somebody).

foxed *adj* said of a document, book, etc: discoloured with foxing. [see FOXING]

foxfire *noun chiefly NAmer* a phosphorescent glow emitted by certain fungi growing on rotting wood.

foxglove *noun* any of numerous species of common tall European wild or garden plants that have attractive white or purple tubular flowers and are a source of digitalis: genus *Digitalis*.

foxhole *noun* a pit dug, usu hastily, for individual cover against enemy fire.

foxhound *noun* a hound of a breed developed to hunt foxes, having a short-haired, often brindled, coat.

fox-hunting *noun* the practice of hunting foxes usu on horseback, with a pack of hounds. ➤ **fox hunt** *noun*, **fox-hunter** *noun*.

foxing *noun* discoloration, *esp* brownish spots, on old paper. [from its resemblance to the colour of a fox's fur]

foxtail *noun* any of several species of grasses with spikes resembling the tail of a fox: genera *Alopecurus*, *Hordeum*, and *Setaria*.

fox terrier *noun* a small terrier of a breed formerly used to dig out foxes, having a short-haired or wire-haired coat.

foxtrot¹ *noun* a ballroom dance that includes slow walking and quick running steps.

foxtrot² *verb intrans* (**foxtrotted, foxtrotting**) to dance a foxtrot.

foxy *adj* (**foxier, foxiest**) **1** cunningly shrewd. **2** warmly reddish brown. **3** *NAmer, informal* said of a woman: physically attractive. **4** foxlike. **5** said of paper: foxed. ➤ **foxily** *adv*, **foxiness** *noun*. [FOX¹ + -Y¹]

foyer /'foyay, 'foyə (*French* fwaje)/ *noun* an anteroom or lobby, e.g. of a theatre, or an entrance hallway. [orig meaning 'the centre of attention or activity'; French *foyer* fireplace, via medieval Latin from Latin *focus* hearth]

FP *abbr* former pupil or former pupils.

fp *abbr* **1** in music, forte-piano. **2** (*also* **f.p.**) freezing point.

FPA *abbr Brit* Family Planning Association.

fpm *abbr* feet per minute.

fps *abbr* **1** feet per second. **2** foot-pound-second. **3** frames per second.

FR *abbr* Faeroe Islands (international vehicle registration).

Fr *abbr* the chemical symbol for francium.

Fr. *abbr* **1** Father. **2** French. **3** Friar.

fr. *abbr* **1** from. **2** franc(s).

Fra /frah/ *noun* used as a title preceding the name of an Italian monk or friar: brother: *Fra Angelico*. [Italian *Fra*, short for *frate* brother, from Latin *frater*]

fracas /'frakah, *NAmer* 'fraykəs/ *noun* (*pl* **fracas** /'frakahz/, *NAmer* **fracases** /'fraykəsiz/) a noisy quarrel; a brawl. [French *fracas* din, row, from Italian *fracasso*, from *fracassare* to shatter]

fractal /'frakt(ə)l/ *noun* an irregular geometric shape or pattern that can be successively subdivided into parts which are smaller copies of the whole. Fractals are often used to produce computer models of the shapes of naturally occurring objects that cannot be successfully reproduced using standard geometric forms.

fraction /'fraksh(ə)n/ *noun* **1a** a number that is not a whole number, most often a number less than one, e.g. ¾, ⅝, 0.234, that is expressed as the result of dividing one quantity into another and usu shown as one figure placed over another or a series of figures after a decimal point. **b** a small portion, amount, or section: *We had to sell the house at a fraction of its value.* **2** (**a fraction**) a tiny bit; a little: *The cat crept a fraction closer.* **3** in chemistry, any of several portions, e.g. of a distillate, separable by fractionation. **4** (*usu* **the Fraction**) the breaking of the bread by a priest in the Eucharist. [Middle English *fraccioun* via late Latin from Latin *fractus*, past part. of *frangere* to break]

fractional *adj* **1** relating to or being a fraction. **2** relatively small; inconsiderable. **3** in chemistry, relating to or being a process for separating components of a mixture through differences in physical or chemical properties: *fractional distillation*. ➤ **fractionally** *adv*.

fractional distillation *noun* a distillation process in which a mixture of substances with different boiling points is heated and its various components are condensed as they vaporize.

fractionalize *or* **fractionalise** *verb trans* to divide (something) into separate parts. ➤ **fractionalization** /-'zaysh(ə)n/ *noun*.

fractionate /'frakshənayt/ *verb trans* to separate (a compound mixture) into its different components. ➤ **fractionation** /-'naysh(ə)n/ *noun*.

fractious /'frakshəs/ *adj* irritable and restless; hard to control. ➤ **fractiously** *adv*, **fractiousness** *noun*. [FRACTION, in an obsolete sense 'discord' + -OUS]

fracture¹ /'frakchə/ *noun* **1a** a break in or the breaking of something, *esp* hard tissue such as bone. **b** a split, division, or breach. **2** the appearance of the surface of a mineral or rock that has been recently broken. **3** in phonetics, the substitution of a diphthong for a simple vowel, *esp* under the influence of a following consonant. [Middle English from Latin *fractura*, from *frangere* to break]

fracture² *verb trans* **1** to cause a fracture in (e.g. a bone). **2** to damage or destroy (something) as if by breaking it apart. ➤ *verb intrans* **1** to undergo fracture. **2** to break up or split into separate parts.

frae /fray/ *prep Scot* from. [Middle English (northern) *fra, frae*, from Old Norse *frā*]

fraenulum /'frenyooləm/ *noun* see FRENULUM.

fraenum *or* **frenum** /'freenəm/ *noun* (*pl* **frena** /'freenə/) a connecting fold of membrane that supports or retains a body part, e.g. the tongue. [Latin *fraenum, frenum* bridle]

frag¹ /frag/ *noun NAmer, slang* a fragmentation grenade.

frag² *verb trans* (**fragged, fragging**) *NAmer, slang* to injure or kill (a soldier) deliberately by means of a grenade.

fragile /'frajiel/ *adj* **1** easily broken, cracked, or shattered; flimsy; brittle. **2** not secure or firmly founded; vulnerable: *a fragile peace*. **3** light or delicate. **4a** physically weak or weakened. **b** *informal* unwell, *esp* hung over. ➤ **fragilely** *adv*, **fragility** /frə'jiliti/ *noun*. [via French from Latin *fragilis*: see FRAIL]

fragile X syndrome *noun* a hereditary condition causing mental disability, resulting from a weakness of the X chromosome.

fragment¹ /'fragmənt/ *noun* an incomplete, broken off, or detached part; a bit or scrap. [Middle English from Latin *fragmentum*, from *frangere* to break]

fragment² /frag'ment/ *verb intrans* to fall to pieces. ➤ *verb trans* to break (something) up or apart into fragments. ➤ **fragmental** *adj*, **fragmentation** /-'taysh(ə)n/ *noun*.

fragmentary /'fragmənt(ə)ri/ *adj* being only a fragment, or consisting of fragments; incomplete. ➤ **fragmentarily** *adv*.

fragmentation bomb *noun* a bomb or shell that, when it explodes, sprays deadly fragments of its casing in all directions.

fragmentation grenade *noun* = FRAGMENTATION BOMB.

fragrance /'fraygrəns/ *noun* **1** a sweet or pleasant smell. **2** a perfume or aftershave; the smell of this. ➤ **fragranced** *adj*. [French *fragrance* or Latin *fragrantia*, from *fragrant-, fragrans*, present part. of *fragrare* to be fragrant]

fragrant /'fraygrənt/ *adj* smelling sweet or pleasant. ➤ **fragrantly** *adv*.

frail /frayl/ *adj* **1** physically weak; delicate. **2** easily broken or destroyed. **3** morally weak. ➤ **frailly** *adv*, **frailness** *noun*. [Middle English via French from Latin *fragilis* fragile, from *frangere* to break]

frailty /'fraylti/ *noun* (*pl* **frailties**) **1** being frail. **2** a moral or physical fault due to weakness: *Thou seest I have more flesh than another man, and therefore more frailty* — Shakespeare.

framboesia (*NAmer* **frambesia**) /fram'beezi·ə/ *noun* = YAWS. [scientific Latin from French *framboise* raspberry; from the appearance of the lesions]

frame¹ /fraym/ *noun* **1a** something composed of parts fitted together and joined. **b** a structure that gives shape or strength, e.g. to a building. **2a** an open case or structure made for admitting, enclosing, or supporting something: *a window frame*. **b** a rigid surrounding structure in which a painting, photograph, etc is placed for display. **3** a framework covered with glass or plastic, used for plants growing outside. **4a** the rigid part of a bicycle or other vehicle. **b** (*in pl*) the outer structure of a pair of glasses that holds the lenses. **5** the physical structure of the human body; the physique. **6a** an enclosing border. **b** a box of a strip cartoon. **7a** a single picture of the series on a length of film. **b** a single complete television picture made up of lines. **8** a limiting, typical, or *esp* appropriate set of circumstances; a framework: *within the frame of* *our society and culture.* **9a** in snooker or bowling, one round of play. **b** in snooker, the triangular piece of wood used to place the balls on the table. **10** *informal* a frame-up. ✳ **in the frame 1** under consideration for a particular purpose, appointment, etc. **2** wanted or suspected by the police.

frame² *verb trans* **1** to place (a picture) in a frame. **2a** to plan or work (something) out; to formulate (it): *A committee is already at work framing a bill to legalize cannabis.* **b** to shape or construct (something). **3** to fit or adjust (something) for a purpose; to arrange (it). **4** *informal* to make up evidence against (an innocent person); to incriminate (them) falsely: *He insisted he had been framed.* ➤ **framed** *adj,* **frameless** *adj,* **framer** *noun.* [Old English *framian* to benefit, make progress]

frame house *noun* a house with a wooden framework

frame of mind *noun* a particular mental or emotional state.

frame of reference *noun* **1** a set or system of facts or ideas serving to orient or give particular meaning to a statement, a point of view, etc. **2** an arbitrary set of axes used as a reference to describe the position or motion of something or to formulate physical laws.

frame up *noun informal* a conspiracy to incriminate somebody falsely.

framework *noun* **1** a skeletal, openwork, or structural frame. **2** a basic structure, e.g. of ideas: *Language is not simply a reporting device for experience but a defining framework for it* — Benjamin Whorf.

franc /frangk/ *noun* the former basic monetary unit of France, Belgium, Switzerland, Luxembourg, and certain other French-speaking countries, divided into 100 centimes (in France, Belgium, and Luxembourg replaced by the euro in 2002). [French *franc* from Latin *Rex Francorum* king of the Franks, used on 14th-cent. coins]

franchise¹ /'franchiez/ *noun* **1** (*usu* **the franchise**) the right to vote. **2a** the right granted to an individual or group to market a company's goods or services in a particular territory. **b** a business or service to which such a right has been granted. **3** any special privilege or right. ➤ **franchisee** /-'zee/ *noun,* **franchiser** *noun.* [Middle English from Old French, from *franchir* to free, from *franc* free: see FRANK¹]

franchise² *verb trans* to grant a franchise to (a person or company).

Franciscan /fran'sisk(ə)n/ *noun* a member of the order of missionary friars founded by St Francis of Assisi in 1209. ➤ **Franciscan** *adj.* [late Latin *Franciscus* Francis]

francium /'fransi·əm/ *noun* a radioactive metallic chemical element of the alkali metal group that occurs naturally in uranium and thorium ores, and is artificially produced by bombarding thorium with protons: symbol Fr, atomic number 87. [scientific Latin, from the country *France* + -IUM]

Franco- *comb. form* forming words, with the meanings: **1** the French nation, people, or culture: *Francophile.* **2** French and: *Franco-German.* [late Latin, from *Francus* Frenchman, Frank]

francolin /'frangkohlin/ *noun* any of various species of game birds of S Asia and Africa resembling partridges: genus *Francolinus.* [French *francolin* from Italian *francolino*]

Francophile /'frangkəfiel/ *noun* somebody who is markedly friendly to France or French culture. ➤ **Francophile** *adj,* **Francophilia** /-'filiə/ *noun,* **Francophilic** /-'filik/ *adj.*

Francophobe /'frangkəfohb/ *noun* a person with a strong dislike or fear of France or French culture, customs, or people. ➤ **Francophobe** *adj,* **Francophobia** /-'fohbiə/ *noun,* **Francophobic** /-'fohbik/ *adj.*

Francophone¹ /'frangkəfohn/ *adj* French-speaking, or having a French-speaking population.

Francophone² *noun* somebody who speaks French.

frangible /'franjəbl/ *adj formal* readily or easily broken; fragile. ➤ **frangibility** /-'biliti/ *noun.* [Middle English via French from Latin *frangibilis,* from *frangere* to break]

frangipane /'franjipayn/ *noun* an almond-flavoured pastry or cream.

Word history ————
French *frangipane* from Italian *frangipani:* see FRANGIPANI. The perfume of the frangipani plant was used as a flavouring.

frangipani /franji'pahni/ *noun* (*pl* **frangipanis** *or* **frangipani**) **1** any of several species of tropical American shrubs or small trees of the periwinkle family: genus *Plumeria.* **2** a perfume derived from or imitating the odour of the flower of the red jasmine. [Italian

frangipani, named after Marquis Muzio Frangipani, 16th-cent. Italian nobleman who invented the perfume]

franglais /'frongglay/ *noun* French with a considerable number of words borrowed from English. [French *franglais,* blend of *français* French and *anglais* English]

Frank /frangk/ *noun* a member of a W Germanic people who established themselves in the Netherlands, Gaul, and on the Rhine in the third and fourth cents. ➤ **Frankish** *adj.* [Old English *Franca* and Old French *Franc* from late Latin *Francus,* of Germanic origin; perhaps from the name of a weapon]

frank¹ *adj* **1** marked by free, forthright, and sincere expression: *a frank reply.* **2** undisguised: *frank admiration.* ➤ **frankness** *noun.* [Middle English in the senses 'free', 'generous' via Old French from medieval Latin *francus,* from late Latin *Francus* FRANK: because only the Franks in Gaul had full political freedom]

frank² *verb trans* **1a** to mark (a piece of mail) with an official signature or sign indicating that the postal charges need not be paid. **b** to send (a piece of mail) without charge. **2** to enable (somebody or something) to pass unhindered: *The delegates will frank the policy.* ➤ **franker** *noun,* **franking** *noun.* [FRANK¹ in an obsolete sense 'free from obligation']

frank³ *noun* a signature or mark used to frank a piece of mail.

franked investment income *noun* dividends that one British company receives from another, with the corporation tax being paid by the company paying the income.

Frankenstein food *noun slang* food consisting of or containing genetically modified substances. [from FRANKENSTEIN'S MONSTER]

Frankenstein's monster /'frangkənstien/ *noun* a creation that ruins its creator.

Word history ————
named after Baron *Frankenstein,* hero of the novel *Frankenstein* by Mary Shelley d.1851, English novelist. In the novel Frankenstein creates a human monster who destroys him.

frankfurter /'frangkfuhtə/ *noun* a cured cooked sausage usu made from beef and pork. [German *Frankfurter* of *Frankfurt* (Frankfurt am Main), a city in Germany: compare HAMBURGER]

frankincense /'frangkinsens/ *noun* a fragrant gum resin chiefly from E African or Arabian trees which is burned as incense: *Boswellia sacra.* [Middle English from Old French *frank encens,* from *frank* pure, free (see FRANK¹) + *encens* INCENSE¹]

franklin /'frangklin/ *noun* a medieval English landowner of free but not noble birth. [Middle English *frankeleyn* from Anglo-French *fraunclein,* from Old French *franc* free: see FRANK¹]

frankly *adv* **1** to tell the truth; actually: *Frankly, I couldn't care less.* **2** in a frank manner.

frantic /'frantik/ *adj* **1** emotionally out of control: *She was frantic with anger and frustration.* **2** marked by fast and nervous, disordered, or anxiety-driven activity: *He made a frantic search for the lost toddler.* ➤ **frantically** *adv,* **franticly** *adv,* **franticness** *noun.* [Middle English *frenetik, frantik* insane: see FRENETIC]

frap /frap/ *verb trans* (**frapped, frapping**) to draw (e.g. a sail) tight, e.g. with ropes or cables. [Middle English *frapen* to strike, beat, from early French *fraper*]

frappé¹ /'frapay (*French* frape)/ *noun* a drink that is chilled or partly frozen. [French *frappé,* past part. of *frapper* to strike, chill, from early French *fraper* to strike]

frappé² *adj* said of a drink: chilled or partly frozen.

Frascati /fra'skahti/ *noun* a usu white wine of the Frascati region of Italy.

frat /frat/ *noun NAmer, informal* a college fraternity. [short for FRATERNITY]

frater /'fraytə/ *noun* a dining hall in a monastery; a refectory. [Middle English from Old French *fraitur,* short for *refraitur,* from medieval Latin *refectorium* refectory]

fraternal /frə'tuhnl/ *adj* **1a** relating to or involving brothers; brotherly. **b** relating to or being a fraternity or society. **2** said of twins: derived from two ova: compare IDENTICAL (3). ➤ **fraternalism** *noun,* **fraternally** *adv.* [Middle English from late Latin *fraternalis,* from Latin *frater* brother]

fraternise /'fratəniez/ *verb intrans* see FRATERNIZE.

fraternity /frə'tuhniti/ *noun* (*pl* **fraternities**) **1** (*treated as sing. or pl*) a group of people associated or formally organized for a common purpose, interest, or pleasure, e.g.: **a** a guild or religious order of brothers. **b** a club for male students in some US universities: compare SORORITY. **2** brotherliness. [Middle English via Old French from Latin *fraternitas*, from *frater* brother]

fraternize or **fraternise** /'fratəniez/ *verb intrans* (*usu* + with) to associate or mingle on friendly terms. >>> **fraternization** /-'zaysh(ə)n/ *noun*, **fraternizer** *noun*.

fratricide /'fratrisied, 'fray-/ *noun* **1** the act of killing one's brother or sister. **2** somebody who does this. >>> **fratricidal** /-'siedl/ *adj*. [Middle English via French from Latin *fratricida* and *fratricidium*, from *fratr-*, *frater* brother + *-cida* and *-cidium*: see -CIDE]

Frau /frow (*German* frau)/ *noun* (*pl* **Frauen** /'frowən/) used as a title equivalent to Mrs: a German-speaking married woman or widow. [German *Frau* woman, wife, from Old High German *frouwa* mistress, lady]

fraud /frawd/ *noun* **1a** deception, *esp* for unlawful gain. **b** an act of deception; a trick. **2a** a person who is not what he or she pretends to be; an impostor. **b** something that is not what it seems or is represented to be. [Middle English *fraude* via Old French from Latin *fraud-*, *fraus* deception]

fraudster /'frawdstə/ *noun* somebody who commits a fraud.

fraudulent /'frawdyoolənt/ *adj* characterized by or involving fraud; dishonest. >>> **fraudulence** *noun*, **fraudulently** *adv*.

Frauen /'frowən/ *noun* pl of FRAU.

fraught /frawt/ *adj* **1** (+ with) filled or charged with (something specified): *The situation is fraught with danger*. **2** characterized by anxieties and tensions: *fraught and complex relationships*. [Middle English, past part. of *fraughten* to load, from *fraught*, *freight*: see FREIGHT[1]]

Fräulein /'frawlien (*German* frɔɪlaɪn)/ *noun* used as a title equivalent to Miss: an unmarried German-speaking woman. [German *Fräulein*, dimin. of *Frau*: see FRAU]

Fraunhofer lines /'frownhohfə (*German* fraʊnhofə)/ *pl noun* the dark lines seen in spectra of the sun or stars. [named after Joseph von *Fraunhofer* d.1826, Bavarian optician and physicist, who observed and mapped the lines]

fraxinella /fraksi'nelə/ *noun* = GAS PLANT. [Latin *fraxinella*, dimin. of *fraxinus* ash tree]

fray[1] /fray/ *verb intrans* **1** said of fabric or rope: to become worn, *esp* to start showing loose ragged threads at the edges. **2** said *esp* of a person's temper: to become strained so that one has difficulty maintaining self-control. >>> *verb trans* **1** to separate the threads at the edge of (e.g. fabric). **2** to strain or irritate (the temper or nerves). [early French *froyer*, *frayer* to rub, from Latin *fricare*]

fray[2] *noun* **1** (**the fray**) a dispute or competition: *Two more candidates had decided to enter the fray*. **2** a brawl or fight. [Middle English *fraien* to quarrel, from *affraien*: see AFFRAY]

frazil /'frazl, frə'zil/ *noun* NAmer ice crystals formed in turbulent water and often piling up on the shore. [Canadian French *frazil* from French *fraisil* cinders]

frazzle[1] /'frazl/ *verb trans informal* to put (somebody) in a state of extreme physical or nervous fatigue; to upset (them). [alteration of English dialect *fazle* to tangle, fray]

frazzle[2] ✳ **to a frazzle** *informal* completely; utterly: *By Sunday evening I was worn to a frazzle*; *The sausages were burned to a frazzle*.

freak[1] /freek/ *noun* **1** a person, animal, or plant with a physical abnormality. **2** a person seen as being highly unconventional, *esp* in dress or ideas. **3a** a highly unusual, rare, and unforeseeable event or phenomenon. **b** (*used before a noun*) occurring unexpectedly and under most unusual circumstances: *a freak accident*. **4** *informal* an ardent enthusiast: *a sci-fi freak*. **5** *slang* (*usu in combination*) a person who uses an illegal drug, usu of a type specified: *an acid freak*. **6** *archaic* a sudden and odd or seemingly pointless idea or whim. >>> **freakish** *adj*, **freakishly** *adv*, **freakishness** *noun*. [origin unknown]

freak[2] *verb trans and intrans informal* = FREAK OUT.

freak out *verb intrans informal* to behave in an irrational, uncontrolled, or unconventional manner as if under the influence of drugs. >>> *verb trans informal* to put (somebody) into a state of intense excitement or agitation.

freaky *adj* (**freakier, freakiest**) *informal* very or disturbingly strange: *The way she knew what I had been thinking was freaky*. >>> **freakily** *adv*, **freakiness** *noun*.

freckle[1] /'frekl/ *noun* a small brownish spot on the skin increasing in number and intensity on exposure to sunlight: *Four be the things*

I'd been better without: love, curiosity, freckles, and doubt — Dorothy Parker. >>> **freckly** *adj*. [Middle English *freken*, *frekel*, from Old Norse *freknur* (pl)]

freckle[2] *verb intrans* to become marked with freckles or small spots. >>> *verb trans* to mark (a surface) with freckles or small spots.

free[1] /free/ *adj* (**freer, freest**) **1a** not subject to the control or domination of another. **b** not bound, confined, or detained by force: *The prisoner was now free*. **2** exempt, relieved, or released, *esp* from an unpleasant or unwanted condition or obligation: *free from pain*. **3a** enjoying civil and political liberty. **b** politically independent. **4a** having no trade restrictions. **b** not subject to government regulation or official control. **5a** having no obligations or commitments: *I'll be free this evening*. **b** not taken up with obligations or commitments: *Have you got a free half-hour today?* **6a** not obstructed or impeded; clear. **b** not being used or occupied: *I found a free changing cubicle*; *She waved with her free hand*. **7a** not hampered or restricted; unfettered. **b** not fastened: *the free end of the rope*. **8** not costing or charging anything. **9a** (*usu* + with) lavish or unrestrained: *She was very free with her praises*. **b** outspoken or too familiar. **10a** not determined by external influences: *a free agent*. **b** voluntary or spontaneous. **11a** said of a translation: not literal or exact. **b** said of jazz: not restricted by or conforming to conventional forms. **12** in physics and chemistry: not permanently united with, attached to, or combined with something else; separate: *free oxygen*. **13** said of the wind: blowing in a direction favourable to the course one is sailing. **14** (*used in combinations*) free from: *duty-free*; *trouble-free*. ✳ **for free** *informal* at no charge; for nothing. **free and easy** marked by informality and lack of constraint; casual. **give somebody a free hand** to give somebody complete freedom of action. **make free with** to make use of (something) without restraint and usu without respecting the wishes of the person it actually belongs to: *They're making very free with your whisky in there!* >>> **freely** *adv*, **freeness** *noun*. [Old English *frēo*]

free[2] *adv* **1** in a free manner. **2** without charge: *We were admitted free*. **3** not against the wind: *sailing free*.

free[3] *verb trans* (**frees, freed, freeing**) **1** to cause (somebody or something) to be free; to release (them). **2** to relieve or rid (somebody) of something confining or restricting: *She worked hard to free her husband from debt*; *Try to free your mind of all thoughts*. **3** to disentangle or clear (something). **4** (*often* + up) to make (something) available: *We want to free up more resources for childcare*.

free alongside ship *adj and adv* said of goods: delivered free of charge to the docks, though the cost of loading must be met by the buyer.

free association *noun* a psychoanalytical technique used to reveal unconscious mental processes, in which the patient expresses the thoughts or responses spontaneously elicited by key words used by the psychoanalyst.

freebase[1] *noun* purified cocaine produced by mixing with ether or ammonia, heating, and evaporation. [because the process 'frees' the cocaine from impurities]

freebase[2] *verb trans* **1** to purify (cocaine) by mixing with ether or ammonia, heating, and evaporation. **2** to smoke (freebased cocaine). >>> *verb intrans* to take cocaine produced by freebasing.

freebie /'freebi/ *noun informal* **1** a gift provided with a magazine or other purchase, or a free service offered to customers: *a freebie joystick*; *Banks are offering more perks than ever. But don't be fooled by the freebies*. **2** a free holiday, restaurant meal, theatre seat, etc. typically offered to somebody expected to write a favourable report for a newspaper: *My description of a week … in Spain, horrified the features editor. He saw a lifetime of freebies turning to ashes if he dared to publish it* — Punch. [obsolete slang *freeby* gratis, from FREE[1]]

freeboard *noun* the vertical distance between the waterline and the deck of a ship.

freebooter *noun* a pirate or plunderer. [Dutch *vrijbuiter* from *vrijbuit* plunder, from *vrij* free + *buit* booty]

freeborn *adj* not born in slavery.

Free Church *noun chiefly Brit* a British Nonconformist Church.

free climbing *noun* rock or mountain climbing without the use of aids such as pitons, though usu with ropes.

freedman *noun* (*pl* **freedmen**) a man freed from slavery.

freedom /'freedəm/ *noun* **1** being free, e.g.: **a** the absence of necessity or constraint in choice or action. **b** liberation from slavery, bondage, imprisonment, or restraint.

Editorial note
Freedom is a state of liberty, guaranteed by the law to the extent that it bestows personal freedoms (of thought, speech, assembly etc) on the individual and protects physical freedom from assault by others or by agents of the state. Freedom of the individual exists within society when the only restraints serve to prevent harm to other individuals — Geoffrey Robertson.

2 (+ from) being exempt or released from something (onerous): *freedom from care.* **3a** (+ of) unrestricted use of: *They gave him the freedom of their home.* **b** the full rights and privileges of a citizen of a city, granted as an honour to a distinguished person. **4** a right or privilege, *esp* political. **5** ease or facility: *the freedom of the artist's brushstrokes.* **6** frankness, openness, or outspokenness: *You can speak with complete freedom here.* **7** boldness of conception or execution.

freedom fighter *noun* somebody engaged in militant action against established rule, *esp* against a government seen as illegal or repressive.

freedwoman *noun* (*pl* **freedwomen**) a woman freed from slavery.

free energy *noun* in physics, the capacity that a system has to perform work under certain conditions.

free enterprise *noun* an economic system that relies on private business operating competitively for profit to satisfy consumer demands and in which government action is restricted.

free fall *noun* **1** unrestrained motion in a gravitational field. **2** the part of a parachute jump before the parachute opens.

free-fall *verb intrans* to fall in a fast or uncontrolled way, *esp* during a parachute jump before the parachute opens.

free flight *noun* the time during an aircraft or spacecraft's flight when it is travelling without using the engine's thrust.

free-floating *adj* relatively uncommitted to a particular course of action, party, etc.

free-for-all *noun* **1** a fight or competition open to all comers and usu with no rules. **2** an often vociferous quarrel or argument involving several participants.

free-form *adj* said of an art form: not having a fixed outline or structure; spontaneous.

freehand *adj and adv* done without the aid of drawing or measuring instruments.

free-handed *adj* openhanded or generous. ➤➤ **free-handedly** *adv.*

freehold[1] *noun* **1** a form of ownership of land or property that gives owners the unconditional right to dispose of it as they will. **2** a property held by this form of tenure. ➤➤ **freeholder** *noun.*

freehold[2] *adj and adv* in a state of freehold: *I've seen a weekend cottage near Dorking that I should rather like to buy … Six hundred and eighty, freehold* — Saki.

free house *noun* a public house in Britain that is entitled to sell drinks supplied by more than one brewery.

free kick *noun* in football or rugby, an unhindered kick awarded because of a breach of the rules by an opponent.

freelance[1] *noun* a person who pursues a profession without long-term contractual commitments to any one employer. ➤➤ **freelance** *adj and adv.* [a *free lance* was a mercenary knight in medieval Europe]

freelance[2] *verb intrans* to act as a freelance.

freelancer *noun* = FREELANCE[1].

free-living *adj* **1** said of a living organism: neither parasitic nor symbiotic. **2** living for pleasure. ➤➤ **free-liver** *noun.*

freeload *verb intrans informal* to take advantage of somebody else's generosity or hospitality without sharing in the cost or responsibility involved. ➤➤ **freeloader** *noun.*

free love *noun* the concept or practice of sexual relations without being faithful or committed to one partner: *But I draw the line at anarchism and free love and that sort of thing* — George Bernard Shaw.

freeman *noun* (*pl* **freemen**) **1** somebody enjoying civil or political liberty, *esp,* formerly, somebody who is no longer a slave. **2** somebody who has the full rights of a citizen, *esp* somebody who has been granted the freedom of a city.

free market *noun* an economic market operating by free competition. ➤➤ **free marketeer** *noun.*

freemartin *noun* a sexually imperfect usu sterile female calf born as a twin with a male. [origin unknown]

Freemason *noun* a member of an ancient and widespread secret fraternity called Free and Accepted Masons who offer each other support and friendship.

freemasonry *noun* **1** (**Freemasonry**) the principles, institutions, or practices of Freemasons. **2** natural or instinctive fellowship or sympathy.

free on board *adj and adv* said of goods: delivered on board, e.g. a ship, without additional charge to the buyer.

free port *noun* **1** a port that can be used by ships of all nations on equal terms. **2** an enclosed port or port area where goods can be received and re-exported free of customs duty.

freepost *noun Brit* a system whereby the charge for a posted item is paid by the recipient.

free radical *noun* an atom or a group of atoms having at least one unpaired electron and participating in various reactions.

free-range *adj* **1** said of farm animals, *esp* poultry: reared in the open air and allowed to move about. **2** said of eggs: produced by free-range hens.

freesia /'freez(y)ə, -zh(y)ə/ *noun* a sweet-scented African plant of the iris family with red, white, yellow, or purple flowers: genus *Freesia.* [Latin genus name, named after Friedrich H T *Freese* d.1876, German physician]

free skating *noun* the part of a competitive figure-skating event that features artistic interpretation of steps and movements to music.

free space *noun* in physics, space that can be used as a standard because it contains no electromagnetic or gravitational fields.

free-spoken *adj archaic* outspoken.

freestanding *adj* standing alone, not attached to or supported by something else: *a freestanding column.*

freestone *noun* **1** a stone that can be cut without splitting, *esp* sandstone or limestone. **2** a fruit with a stone to which the flesh does not cling.

freestyle *noun* **1** (*often used before a noun*) a competition in which a contestant uses a style of his or her choice: *freestyle swimming.* **2** all-in wrestling. **3** = CRAWL[2] (2).

freethinker *noun* a person who forms opinions on the basis of reason; *esp* one who rejects religious dogma. ➤➤ **freethinking** *adj and noun.*

free throw *noun* in basketball, an unhindered shot at the basket awarded because of a foul by an opponent.

free-to-air *adj* denoting a television service for which the viewer does not have to pay a subscription.

free trade *noun* trade based on the unrestricted international exchange of goods.

Editorial note
Free trade is a controversial but important doctrine in economics, typically promoted as enabling countries to specialize in the production of items they can produce with the least sacrifice. Trade theory developed in an era when some countries made manufactured goods, while others provided raw materials. The term has now lasted into an era when most manufactured trade is actually between similar countries in similar products. It can also now refer to low levels of government regulation of so-called invisible trade, in services and cross-border financial flows — Evan Davis.

free verse *noun* verse without rhyme or a fixed metrical form.

free vote *noun chiefly Brit* a vote in Parliament not subject to party instructions.

freeware *noun* computer software that is available for people to use without charge.

freeway *noun NAmer* a motorway or highway without tolls.

freewheel[1] *noun* a device fitted to a vehicle wheel allowing it to move freely when the motive power is removed, e.g. when a cyclist stops pedalling.

freewheel[2] *verb intrans* to coast freely without power from the pedals of a bicycle or engine of a vehicle. ➤➤ **freewheeler** *noun.*

freewheeling *adj* moving, living, or drifting along freely or irresponsibly.

free will *noun* the power of choosing, *esp* of making moral choices, independently of divine necessity or causal law.

free world *noun* (**the free world**) the non-Communist countries of the world.

freeze[1] /freez/ *verb* (*past tense* **froze** /frohz/, *past part.* **frozen** /'frohz(ə)n/) ➤ *verb intrans* **1** to become congealed into a solid, e.g. ice, by cold. **2** to become chilled with cold: *We almost froze to death.* **3** to stick solidly by or as if by freezing. **4** to become clogged with ice: *The water pipes froze.* **5** to be capable of undergoing freezing for preservation: *Do strawberries freeze well?* **6a** to become fixed or motionless; *esp* to abruptly cease acting or speaking. **b** to become coldly formal or hostile in manner. **7** said of a computer screen: to stop working temporarily due to a fault, lack of memory, or other problem. ➤ *verb trans* **1** to convert (e.g. water) from a liquid to a solid by cold. **2a** to make (something) extremely cold. **b** to act on (something), usu destructively, by frost. **3** to anaesthetize (a part of the body) by or as if by cold: *The injection froze her gum.* **4** to preserve (e.g. food) by freezing the water content and maintaining at a temperature below 0°C. **5** to cause (somebody or something) to become fixed, immovable, or unalterable, as if paralysed. **6** to immobilize the expenditure, withdrawal, or exchange of (foreign-owned bank balances) by government regulation. ➤➤ **freezable** *adj.* [Old English *frēosan*]

freeze[2] *noun* **1** freezing cold weather. **2** an act or period of freezing something, *esp* wages or prices at a certain level.

freeze-dry *verb trans* (**freeze-dries, freeze-dried, freeze-drying**) to dehydrate (e.g. food) while in a frozen state in a vacuum, *esp* for preservation. ➤➤ **freeze-dried** *adj.*

freeze-frame *noun* **1** a frame of a film that is repeated so as to give the illusion of a static picture. **2a** a static picture produced from a videodisc or videotape recording. **b** the function on a video camera or recorder that enables a static picture to be produced.

freeze out *verb trans informal* to deliberately ignore or fail to respond to (somebody).

freezer *noun* an apparatus that freezes or keeps cool; *esp* an insulated cabinet or room for storing frozen food or for freezing food rapidly.

freezing *adj* **1** *informal* very cold. **2** below 0°C.

freezing point *noun* the temperature at which a liquid solidifies.

freezing works *noun Aus, NZ* an abattoir where the carcasses are frozen ready for export.

freight[1] /frayt/ *noun* **1** goods transported commercially. **2a** the transport of goods commercially, *esp* at the ordinary or comparatively slower rate. **b** the charge for this. [Middle English from early Dutch or Middle Low German *vracht, vrecht* cargo]

freight[2] *verb trans* to load (*esp* a ship) with goods for transport.

freightage /'fraytij/ *noun* = FREIGHT[1].

freighter *noun* **1** a ship or aircraft used chiefly to carry freight. **2** a person or company that charters or loads a ship.

Freightliner *noun Brit, trademark* a train designed for carrying containerized cargo.

frena /'freenə/ *noun* pl of FRENUM.

French[1] /french/ *adj* relating to France, its people, or their language. ➤➤ **Frenchness** *noun.* [Old English *frencisc*, from *Franca*: see FRANK]

French[2] *noun* **1** the Romance language of the people of France and parts of Belgium, Switzerland, Canada, and Africa. **2** (**the French**) (*treated as pl*) the people of France. ✳ **excuse/pardon my French** excuse these swear words: *I wish we'd never heard of the bugger, pardon my French* — Alan Coren.

Word history
It has been estimated that over 10,000 French words had been adopted in English by 1500 (see note at ANGLO-NORMAN). Since then, the rate of borrowing has decreased but the contribution of French to the English vocabulary has remained significant. In the 16th and 17th cents French loanwords included *grotesque, liaison, ravine, pioneer, platoon, role,* and *vase.* In the 18th cent., when French was above all the language of diplomacy and polite society, it gave English *boutique, bureau, corps, debut, envelope, espionage, etiquette, police, regime,* and *terrain.* Borrowings in the 19th cent. include *chauffeur, coupon, gourmet, menu, milieu, mirage, prestige, repertoire,* and *restaurant;* and in the 20th cent. *brassiere, camouflage, compere, discotheque, fuselage,* and *garage.*

French bean *noun* **1** *chiefly Brit* a common bean plant often cultivated for its slender edible green pods: *Phaseolus vulgaris.* **2** a pod of this plant, used as a vegetable.

French bread *noun* crusty white bread made in long thin loaves.

French Canadian *noun* a French-speaking Canadian, *esp* one of French descent. ➤➤ **French Canadian** *adj.*

French chalk *noun* a soft white granular variety of soapstone used for drawing lines on cloth and as a dry lubricant.

French cricket *noun* a children's game in which one player has a bat, and any other player may bowl at the batter's legs from the point at which the ball was fielded.

French cuff *noun* a wide band turned back to make a cuff of double thickness.

French doors *pl noun chiefly NAmer* = FRENCH WINDOWS.

French dressing *noun* a salad dressing of oil, vinegar, and seasonings.

french fries *pl noun chiefly NAmer* chips. [short for *French fried potato*]

French horn *noun* a spiral-shaped brass musical instrument with valves to vary the pitch, a funnel-shaped mouthpiece, and a convoluted tube that flares outwards at the end.

frenchify /'frenchifie/ *verb trans* (**frenchifies, frenchified, frenchifying**) (*also* **Frenchify**) to make (somebody or something) French in qualities, traits, or typical practices. ➤➤ **frenchification** /-fi'kaysh(ə)n/ *noun.*

French kiss *noun* a kiss made with open mouths and usu with tongue-to-tongue contact.

French knickers *pl noun* wide-legged underpants for women.

French leave *noun dated* leave taken without permission. [from an 18th-cent. French custom of leaving a reception without taking leave of the host or hostess]

French letter *noun Brit, informal* a condom.

Frenchman *noun* (*pl* **Frenchmen**) a native or inhabitant of France.

French mustard *noun Brit* mustard that has been mixed with vinegar.

French polish *noun* a solution of shellac used as a wood polish.

French-polish *verb trans* to apply French polish to (wood or furniture) in order to obtain a high gloss finish.

French seam *noun* a double seam sewn on first the right, then the wrong side of a piece of fabric to enclose the raw edges.

French stick *noun* a long thin loaf of French bread.

French toast *noun* **1** sliced bread dipped in a mixture of egg and milk and fried. **2** *Brit* sliced bread buttered on one side and toasted on the other.

French windows *pl noun Brit* a pair of doors with full length glazing, often opening onto a garden.

Frenchwoman *noun* (*pl* **Frenchwomen**) a female native or inhabitant of France.

frenetic /frə'netik/ *adj* frenzied or frantic: *He lives life at a frenetic pace.* ➤➤ **frenetically** *adv.* [Middle English *frenetik, frantik* insane, via Old French from Latin *phreneticus*, modification of Greek *phrenitikos*, from *phrenitis* inflammation of the brain, from *phren-, phrēn* diaphragm, mind + -ITIS; compare FRANTIC]

frenulum *or* **fraenulum** /'frenyooləm/ *noun* (*pl* **frenula** /-lə/) **1** = FRAENUM. **2** a bristle or group of bristles on the front edge of a moth's hind wing that keeps the hind wing and forewing together in flight. [Latin *frenulum* dimin. of *frenum* FRAENUM]

frenum /'freenəm/ *noun* see FRAENUM.

frenzied /'frenzid/ *adj* marked by uncontrolled activity or emotion or wild haste; frantic: *The dog's frenzied barking was getting on my nerves.* ➤➤ **frenziedly** *adv.*

frenzy /'frenzi/ *noun* (*pl* **frenzies**) **1a** a state of extreme agitation or intense uncontrolled emotion. **b** a temporary madness. **2** a spell of wild, compulsive, or agitated behaviour. [Middle English *frenesie* via French from Latin *phrenesis*, from *phreneticus*: see FRENETIC]

Freon /'freeon/ *noun trademark* any of various non-flammable gaseous and liquid fluorinated hydrocarbons used as refrigerants and as propellants for aerosols.

freq. *abbr* **1** frequent. **2** frequentative. **3** frequently.

frequency /'freekwənsi/ *noun* (*pl* **frequencies**) **1** the fact or condition of occurring frequently. **2** the number of repetitions of an event over a particular period of time. **3a** the number of complete alternations per second of an alternating current of electricity. **b** the number of complete oscillations per second of an electromagnetic wave. **4** the number of sound waves per second produced by a sounding body. **5a** in statistics, the number of individuals in a class, *esp* considered as a proportion of the whole.

b in ecology, the number of individuals of a particular species living within a particular area.

frequency distribution *noun* in statistics, an arrangement of data showing the frequency of the occurrence of the values of a variable.

frequency modulation *noun* a modulation of the frequency of a wave, *esp* a radio carrier wave, in accordance with the instantaneous value of some signal waveform: compare AMPLITUDE MODULATION, PHASE MODULATION.

frequency response *noun* in electronics, the ability of a device, e.g. an audio amplifier, to deal with the various frequencies applied to it.

frequent[1] /'freekwant/ *adj* **1** often repeated or occurring. **2** habitual or persistent. ➤➤ **frequently** *adv*. [Middle English via French from Latin *frequent-, frequens* crowded, full]

frequent[2] /fri'kwent/ *verb trans* to be in or visit (a place) often or habitually. ➤➤ **frequentation** /freekwen'taysh(ə)n/ *noun*, **frequenter** *noun*.

frequentative[1] /fri'kwentativ/ *adj* said of a verb or verbal form: denoting repeated or recurrent action.

frequentative[2] *noun* a frequentative verb or verb form.

fresco /'freskoh/ *noun* (*pl* **frescoes** *or* **frescos**) a painting made by the application of watercolours to moist plaster: *the high living rooms where the ... pompous frescoes of the sixteenth century looked down on the familiar commodities of the age of advertisement* — Henry James. [Italian *fresco* fresh, of Germanic origin; because the paint is applied to fresh plaster]

fresh[1] /fresh/ *adj* **1** new or recent: *Fresh footprints led to the door; There hadn't been any fresh developments.* **2** original or different: *a fresh approach.* **3a** said of food: not tinned or frozen: *fresh green peas.* **b** not stale, sour or decayed: *fresh milk; fresh bread.* **4** said of water: not salty. **5** free from taint; clean and pure: *fresh air.* **6a** said of weather: cool and windy. **b** said of wind: rather strong; invigorating. **7** refreshed and alert. **8a** said of a complexion: clear and healthy-looking. **b** said of colours: not faded; bright. **9** not worn or rumpled; clean: *a fresh white shirt.* **10a** newly come or arrived: *fresh from college.* **b** inexperienced. **11** *informal* too forward or disrespectful; presumptuous, *esp* in a sexual way: *He got fresh with me so I slapped his face.* ➤➤ **freshly** *adv*, **freshness** *noun*. [Old English *fersc* and Old French *freis*, of Germanic origin]

fresh[2] *adv* **1** just recently; newly: *a fresh laid egg.* **2** *informal* as of a very short time ago: *We're fresh out of tomatoes.*

fresh[3] *noun* **1** the fresh part of something, *esp* the cool part of the day. **2** = FRESHET.

fresh breeze *noun* a wind having a speed of 29 to 38km/h (about 19 to 24mph).

freshen *verb* (**freshened, freshening**) ➤ *verb intrans* **1** to become fresh or fresher. **2** said of wind: to increase in strength. ➤ *verb trans* **1** (**freshen up**) to make (oneself) fresher or more comfortable, *esp* by washing, changing one's clothes, etc. **2** to refresh (e.g. a drink).

fresher *noun chiefly Brit, informal* a student in the first year at college or university. [from FRESHMAN]

freshet /'freshit/ *noun* **1** a stream of fresh water flowing into salt water. **2** a great rise or overflowing of a stream caused by heavy rains or melted snow. [*fresh* a stream of fresh water + -ET]

freshman *noun* (*pl* **freshmen**) a student in the first year at college or university.

freshwater *adj* **1** relating to or living in fresh water. **2** accustomed to sailing usually only on fresh water, hence comparatively unskilled: *a freshwater sailor.*

fresnel lens /fray'nel, 'fraynel/ *noun* a lens that has a surface consisting of a series of simple lens sections together constituting a single thin lens, used *esp* for spotlights. [named after Augustin Fresnel d.1827, French physicist who invented it]

fret[1] /fret/ *verb* (**fretted, fretting**) ➤ *verb intrans* **1** to be vexed or worried. **2a** to chafe. **b** to eat into something; to corrode or fray. **3** said of running water: to become agitated. ➤ *verb trans* **1** to torment (somebody) with anxiety or worry; to vex (them). **2a** to eat or gnaw into (something); to corrode (it). **b** to rub or chafe (something). **3** to make (e.g. a channel) by wearing away the earth or other surface material. [Old English *fretan* to devour]

fret[2] *noun* a state of mental agitation or irritation.

fret[3] *noun* in art or architecture, an ornamental pattern or decoration consisting of small straight bars intersecting usu at right angles.

fret[4] *verb trans* (**fretted, fretting**) to decorate (e.g. a ceiling) with embossed or carved patterns. [Middle English *fretten* from Old French, from *frete* trellis work]

fret[5] *noun* any of a series of ridges fixed across the fingerboard of a stringed musical instrument, e.g. a guitar. ➤➤ **fretless** *adj*. [origin unknown]

fretboard *noun* a fingerboard of a stringed musical instrument with frets.

fretful /'fretf(ə)l/ *adj* tending to fret; in a fret. ➤➤ **fretfully** *adv*, **fretfulness** *noun*.

fretsaw *noun* a fine-toothed saw with a narrow blade held under tension in a frame and used for cutting intricate patterns in thin wood.

fretwork *noun* ornamental openwork, *esp* in thin wood.

Freudian[1] /'froydi·ən/ *adj* relating or conforming to the psychoanalytic theories or practices of the Austrian neurologist Sigmund Freud (d.1939).

Editorial note ────────────────
Freud held that our motives are largely unconscious. This belief changes the moral basis of blame and praise. His insistence on sexually based libido as the spring of human motivation produced consternation; yet it liberated behaviour, especially for women, for the modern world — Professor Richard Gregory.

Freudian[2] *noun* somebody who believes in or uses the ideas of Sigmund Freud. ➤➤ **Freudianism** *noun*.

Freudian slip *noun* a slip of the tongue that is held to reveal some unconscious aspect of the speaker's mind.

Fri. *abbr* Friday.

friable /'frie·əbl/ *adj* easily crumbled. ➤➤ **friability** /-'biliti/ *noun*, **friableness** *noun*. [via French from Latin *friabilis*, from *friare* to crumble]

friar /'frie·ə/ *noun* a member of a religious order combining monastic life with outside religious activity and orig owning neither personal nor community property. [Middle English *frere, fryer* via Old French from Latin *fratr-, frater* brother]

friar's balsam *noun* a solution of BENZOIN (a chemical compound like camphor) in alcohol, used mixed with hot water as an inhalant for the relief of cold symptoms.

friary *noun* (*pl* **friaries**) a building housing a community of friars.

fricandeau /'frikandoh/ *noun* (*pl* **fricandeaus** *or* **fricandeaux** /-doh(z)/) larded veal braised or roasted and glazed in its own juices. [French *fricandeau*, irreg from early French *fricasser* to fricassee]

fricassee[1] /'frikəsee, frikə'see/ *noun* a dish of small pieces of stewed chicken, rabbit, etc served in a white sauce. [early French *fricassee*, fem past part. of *fricasser* to fricassee]

fricassee[2] *verb trans* (**fricassees, fricasseed, fricasseeing**) to stew (chicken, etc) in white sauce.

fricative /'frikativ/ *noun* a consonant, e.g. *f, th, sh*, made by forcing air through a narrow opening formed by placing the tongue or lip close to another part of the mouth, or by constricting the pharynx. ➤➤ **fricative** *adj*. [scientific Latin *fricativus*, from Latin *fricare* to rub]

friction /'friksh(ə)n/ *noun* **1a** the rubbing of one body against another. **b** resistance to relative motion between two bodies in contact. **2** disagreement between two people or parties of opposing views. ➤➤ **frictional** *adj*, **frictionless** *adj*. [via French from Latin *friction-, frictio*, from *fricare* to rub]

Friday /'frieday, 'friedi/ *noun* the sixth day of the week, following Thursday.

Word history ────────────────
Old English *frīgedæg*, named after *Frigga*, Norse goddess of married love and wife of Odin (see WEDNESDAY). *Friday* was based on the Latin name *Veneris dies* day of *Venus*, Roman goddess of love.

fridge /frij/ *noun chiefly Brit* a refrigerator. [by shortening and alteration]

fridge-freezer *noun* a unit consisting of a separate refrigerator and freezer, usu one above the other.

fried /fried/ *verb* past tense and past part. of FRY[1].

friend /frend/ *noun* **1a** a person whose company, interests, and attitudes one finds sympathetic and to whom one is not closely related: *Restrain yourself to … genuine and authorised tea-table talk – such as mending fashions, spoiling reputations, railing at absent friends, and so forth* — Congreve. **b** an acquaintance. **2a** somebody or something not hostile; an ally. **b** somebody or something of the same nation, party, or group. **3** somebody or something that favours or encourages something, e.g. a charity: *a friend of the poor.* **4 (Friend)** a Quaker. **✳ friend at court** somebody who can use their influence to help one. **make friends 1** to acquire friends. **2** to become friendly. ⟫⟫ **friendless** *adj*, **friendship** *noun*. [Old English *frēond*]

friendly[1] *adj* (**friendlier, friendliest**) **1** like a friend; kind. **2** not hostile: *friendly nations.* **3** inclined to be favourable. **4** (*used in combinations*) adapted to the needs of; helpful to: *a user-friendly software manual; child-friendly restaurants.* ⟫⟫ **friendliness** *noun*.

friendly[2] *noun* (*pl* **friendlies**) *chiefly Brit* a match played for practice or pleasure and not as part of a competition.

friendly fire *noun* in warfare, weapon fire that injures or kills one's own soldiers.

friendly society *noun Brit* a mutual insurance association providing its subscribers with benefits during sickness, unemployment, and old age.

frier /'frie-ə/ *noun* = FRYER.

fries /friez/ *pl noun chiefly NAmer* chips, *esp* thin ones.

Friesian /'freezh(ə)n/ *noun Brit* an animal of a breed of large black-and-white dairy cattle originating in N Holland and Friesland and producing relatively low-fat milk. [variant of FRISIAN]

frieze[1] /freez/ *noun* **1** a sculptured or ornamented band, e.g. on a building. **2** in architecture, the part of an entablature between the architrave and the cornice. [early French *frise*, perhaps from late Latin *phrygium, frisium* embroidered cloth, from *Phrygia* ancient country of Asia Minor whose people were famous for their craftsmanship]

frieze[2] *noun* a heavy coarse fabric made of wool. [Middle English *frise* via French from Dutch *vriese*]

frig /frig/ *verb* (**frigged, frigging**) ⟩ *verb trans coarse slang* to have sexual intercourse with or masturbate (somebody). ⟩ *verb intrans coarse slang* to have sexual intercourse or masturbate. [prob from Middle English *friggen* to rub, from Latin *fricare*]

frigate /'frigət/ *noun* **1a** *Brit* a warship smaller than a destroyer. **b** *NAmer* a warship larger than a destroyer. **2** formerly, a square-rigged warship next in size below a ship of the line. **3** a general-purpose naval escort vessel. [early French from Old Italian *fregata*]

frigate bird *noun* any of several species of strong-winged seabirds with a forked tail and a long bill, noted for their habit of snatching food from other birds: genus *Fregata*.

fright[1] /friet/ *noun* **1** fear excited by sudden danger or shock. **2** *informal* something unsightly, strange, ugly, or shocking: *She looks a fright.* [Old English *fyrhto, fryhto*]

fright[2] *verb trans archaic or literary* to frighten (somebody).

frighten *verb* (**frightened, frightening**) ⟩ *verb trans* **1** to make (somebody) afraid; to scare (them). **2** to force (somebody) by frightening (them): *I frightened them into confessing; The cat frightened the robin away.* ⟩ *verb intrans* to become frightened: *He doesn't frighten easily.* ⟫⟫ **frightened** *adj*, **frightening** *adj*, **frighteningly** *adv*.

frightener *noun* somebody or something frightening. **✳ put the frighteners on** *Brit, informal* to intimidate (somebody).

frightful /'frietf(ə)l/ *adj* **1** causing intense fear, shock, or horror. **2** *informal* unpleasant or difficult: *I had a frightful time getting to work.* ⟫⟫ **frightfully** *adv*, **frightfulness** *noun*.

frigid /'frijid/ *adj* **1a** intensely cold. **b** *formal* unenthusiastic or unfriendly. **2** said *esp* of a woman: abnormally averse to sexual contact, *esp* intercourse. ⟫⟫ **frigidity** /fri'jiditi/ *noun*, **frigidly** *adv*, **frigidness** *noun*. [Latin *frigidus* from *frigēre* to be cold]

frigid zone *noun* either of the two regions between the poles of the earth and the polar circles.

frill[1] /fril/ *noun* **1** a gathered or pleated fabric edging used on clothing or as ornament. **2** a ruff of hair, skin, or feathers round the neck of an animal or bird. **3** something decorative but not essential; a luxury. ⟫⟫ **frilled** *adj*, **frilliness** *noun*, **frilly** *adj*. [perhaps from Flemish *frul*]

frill[2] *verb trans* to provide or decorate (something) with a frill.

frilled lizard *noun* a large Australian lizard with a broad fold of skin on each side of the neck: *Chlamydosaurus kingii*.

fringe[1] /frinj/ *noun* **1** an ornamental border, e.g. on a curtain or garment, consisting of straight or twisted threads or tassels. **2a** something resembling a fringe; a border. **b** *chiefly Brit* the hair that falls over the forehead. **3** something marginal, additional, or secondary. **4** (*treated as sing. or pl*) an unconventional or extremist group: *Every reform movement has a lunatic fringe* — Theodore Roosevelt. **5 (the Fringe)** a part of the British professional theatre featuring small-scale experimental productions. **6** in physics, any of the alternating light or dark bands produced by interference or diffraction of light. ⟫⟫ **fringeless** *adj*. [Middle English *frenge* from French, ultimately from Latin *fimbriae* (pl) fibres]

fringe[2] *verb trans* **1** to provide or decorate (e.g. material) with a fringe. **2** to serve as a fringe for (something): *a clearing fringed with trees.*

fringe benefit *noun* a benefit, e.g. a pension, granted by an employer to an employee in addition to basic wages.

fringing reef *noun* a coral reef close to a shoreline.

frippery /'fripəri/ *noun* (*pl* **fripperies**) **1** non-essential ornamentation, *esp* of a showy kind. **2** affected elegance; ostentation. [early French *friperie* from Old French *frepe* rag, old clothes]

Frisbee /'frizbi/ *noun trademark* a plastic disc thrown between players by a flip of the wrist. [said to be from the name of the *Frisbie* bakery, Connecticut, whose pie tins could be thrown in this way]

frisée /'freezay/ *noun* curly endive. [French *chicorée frisée* curled chicory, from *frisé*, past part. of *friser*: see FRIZZ[1]]

Frisian /'freezh(ə)n/ *noun* **1** a native or inhabitant of Friesland or the Frisian islands. **2** the Germanic language of the Frisian people. ⟫⟫ **Frisian** *adj*. [Latin *Frisii* Frisians]

frisk[1] /frisk/ *verb trans informal* to search (a person) for something, *esp* a hidden weapon, by running the hand over their clothing and through their pockets. ⟩ *verb intrans* to leap, skip, or dance in a lively or playful way. ⟫ *frisker noun*. [obsolete *frisk* lively, from Old French *frisque*, prob of Germanic origin]

frisk[2] *noun* **1** *informal* an act of frisking (somebody). **2** a gambol or romp.

frisky *adj* (**friskier, friskiest**) lively or playful. ⟫⟫ **friskily** *adv*, **friskiness** *noun*.

frisson /'freesonh (*French* fris5)/ *noun* (*pl* **frissons** /'freesonh(z) (*French* fris5)/) a shudder or thrill. [French *frisson*, ultimately from Latin *frigere* to be cold]

frit[1] /frit/ *noun* **1** the wholly or partly fused materials of which glass is made. **2** ground-up glass used as a basis for glaze or enamel. [Italian *fritta*, fem of *fritto* from *friggere* to fry: see FRITTATA]

frit[2] *verb trans* (**fritted, fritting**) to prepare (materials for glass) by heat; to fuse (them).

frit fly *noun* a minute fly whose larva is a pest of cereals: *Oscinella frit*. [Latin *frit* speck on an ear of corn + FLY[3]]

fritillary /fri'tiləri/ *noun* (*pl* **fritillaries**) **1** any of a genus of plants of the lily family with mottled or chequered bell-shaped flowers: genus *Fritillaria*. **2** any of numerous species of butterflies that are usu orange with black spots: genus *Argynnis* and other genera. [Latin genus name, from *fritillus* dice-cup; from the markings on the wings and petals]

frittata /fri'tahtə/ *noun* an unfolded omelette usu containing vegetables, cheese, and seasonings. [Italian *frittata* from *fritto*, past part. of *friggere* to fry, from Latin *frigere*]

fritter[1] /'fritə/ *noun* a piece of fried batter containing fruit, meat, etc. [Middle English *fritour* from French *friture*, ultimately from Latin *frigere* to fry]

fritter[2] *verb trans* (**frittered, frittering**) (*usu* + away) to waste (e.g. money or time) bit by bit: *She fritters away all her money on clothes.* [from obsolete *fritters* fragments, alteration of *fitters* rags, fragments, from Middle English *fiteres*; earlier history unknown]

fritto misto /ˌfreetoh 'meestoh/ *noun* a dish of mixed foods, e.g. seafood, fried in batter. [Italian *fritto misto* mixed fried food]

frivolous /'frivələs/ *adj* **1** lacking in seriousness; irresponsibly self-indulgent. **2** lacking practicality or serious purpose; unimportant. ⟫⟫ **frivolity** /fri'voliti/ *noun*, **frivolously** *adv*, **frivolousness** *noun*. [Middle English from Latin *frivolus* worthless, silly]

frizz[1] /friz/ *verb intrans* said of hair: to form a mass of tight curls. ⟩ *verb trans* to form (e.g. hair) into small tight curls. [French *friser* to shrivel up, curl, prob from *fris-*, stem of *frire*: see FRY[1]]

frizz[2] *noun* hair in a mass of small tight curls.

frizzle¹ /'frizl/ *verb intrans* to cook with a sizzling noise. ➤ *verb trans* to fry (e.g. bacon) until crisp and curled. [FRY¹, prob influenced by *sizzle*]

frizzle² *verb trans* to frizz or curl (the hair). ➤➤ **frizzly** *adj.* [from FRIZZ²]

frizzle³ *noun* a tight curl in the hair.

frizzy *adj* (**frizzier, frizziest**) said of hair: in small tight curls. ➤➤ **frizziness** *noun.*

fro /froh/ *adv* see TO².

frock /frok/ *noun* **1** *Brit* a woman's or girl's dress. **2** a loose garment, *esp* a monk's or friar's habit. ➤➤ **frocked** *adj.* [Middle English *frok* from early French *froc*, of Germanic origin]

frock coat *noun* a usu double-breasted coat with knee-length skirts worn by men, *esp* in the 19th cent.

frog¹ /frog/ *noun* **1** any of various species of tailless largely aquatic leaping amphibians with a smooth skin and webbed feet, *esp* a common European frog: *Rana temporaria* and other species. **2** (**Frog**) *informal, derog* a French person. ✲ **have a frog in one's throat** to have a hoarse voice. ➤➤ **froggy** *adj.* [Old English *frogga*; (sense 2) from the reputation of the French for eating frogs' legs]

frog² *noun* **1a** a loop attached to a belt to hold a weapon or tool. **b** a usu ornamental braiding, consisting of a button and a loop, for fastening the front of a garment. **2** a device with spikes, used to hold flowers in a flower arrangement. **3** a shallow hollow in the face of a brick to take the mortar. **4** a steel plate enabling the wheels of a train on one rail of a track to cross an intersecting rail. ➤➤ **frogged** *adj*, **frogging** *noun.* [perhaps from Latin *floccus* a lock of hair, or from FROG¹]

frog³ *noun* the triangular elastic horny pad in the middle of the sole of a horse's foot. [perhaps from FROG¹, influenced by Italian *forchetta* small fork, because of its shape]

frogfish *noun* (*pl* **frogfishes** or *collectively* **frogfish**) any of numerous species of angler fishes with warty skin that gives them camouflage on the bottom of the sea: *Antennaria hispidus* and other species.

froghopper *noun* any of numerous species of leaping insects whose larvae secrete froth: family Cercopidae.

frogman *noun* (*pl* **frogmen**) a person equipped with face mask, flippers, rubber suit, etc and an air supply for swimming underwater for extended periods.

frogmarch *verb trans* to force (a person) to move forwards by holding his or her arms firmly from behind. [orig to carry someone face downwards with one person holding each limb, so that the person carried resembled a frog]

frogmouth *noun* any of several species of SE Asian and Australian nocturnal birds resembling nightjars: *Podargus strigoides* and other species. [from the wide mouth of these birds]

frogspawn *noun* a gelatinous mass of frogs' eggs.

frog spit *noun* **1** an alga that forms green slimy masses on quiet water. **2** = CUCKOO SPIT.

frolic¹ /'frolik/ *verb intrans* (**frolicked, frolicking**) to play and run about happily. [Dutch *vroolijk* merry, from early Dutch *vrolijc*, from *vro* happy]

frolic² *noun* **1** a playful expression of high spirits; gaiety. **2** a light-hearted entertainment or game. ➤➤ **frolicsome** /-s(ə)m/ *adj*, **frolicsomely** /-s(ə)mli/ *adv.*

from /frəm; *strong* from/ *prep* **1** used to indicate a starting point, e.g.: **a** a place where a physical movement or action begins: *They came here from the city.* **b** a starting point in measuring or reckoning: *These cost from £5 to £10; There were from 60 to 80 people; Come a week from today.* **2** used to indicate separation or removal: *They live miles from anywhere; Take a glass from the cupboard.* **3** used to indicate a source, cause, or basis: *He suffers from gout; The pudding is made from simple ingredients.* [Old English]

fromage frais /ˌfromahzh 'fray/ *noun* a soft smooth fresh cheese that is low in fat, sometimes with a fruit flavouring added. [French *fromage frais* fresh cheese]

frond /frond/ *noun* a leaf, *esp* of a palm or fern. ➤➤ **fronded** *adj.* [Latin *frond-, frons* foliage]

front¹ /frunt/ *noun* **1** the part or surface of something that usually faces forward, e.g.: **a** the part of the human body opposite to the back. **b** the part of a garment covering the chest. **2** a face of a building, *esp* the side that contains the main entrance; a frontage. **3a** a

line of battle. **b** (*often* **Front**) a zone of conflict between armies: *the Western Front.* **4** a movement linking divergent elements to achieve certain common objectives; *esp* a political coalition: *a popular democratic front.* **5** a particular situation or sphere of activity: *He's making progress on the educational front; Have you heard anything from them on the marriage front?* **6** in meteorology, the boundary between two dissimilar air masses. **7** the beach promenade at a seaside resort. **8a** a person, group, or thing used to mask the identity or true character of something, *esp* something illegal. **b** a person who serves as the nominal head or spokesman of an enterprise or group; a figurehead. **9** demeanour or bearing, *esp* in the face of a challenge or danger: *She put up a brave front.* **10** *archaic* the forehead, or the whole face. ✲ **in front of 1** directly ahead of. **2** in the presence of: *Don't swear in front of the children.* **out front** *chiefly NAmer* at the front, *esp* in the audience. **up front** as payment in advance: *The star demanded $1 million up front.* ➤➤ **frontless** *adj.* [Middle English via Old French *front-, frons*]

front² *verb intrans* **1** (*often* + on/onto) to face: *A garden fronting onto a lake.* **2** (*often* + for) to serve as a front. **3** *Aus, NZ* (*often* + up) to appear; to turn up. ➤ *verb trans* **1** to be in front of (something). **2a** to lead (e.g. a band or group). **b** to present (a television programme). **3** to face towards: *The house fronts the street.* **4a** to act as a front for (something). **b** to supply a front for (something): *The building was fronted with bricks.* **5** in phonetics, to articulate (a sound) with the tongue farther forward. **6** *archaic* to confront (somebody).

front³ *adj* **1** of or situated at the front. **2** said of a speech sound: articulated at or towards the front of the mouth.

frontage /'fruntij/ *noun* **1** the front face of a building. **2** the land between the front of a building and the street.

frontal¹ *adj* **1** relating to, situated at, or showing the front: *full frontal nudity.* **2** relating or adjacent to the forehead: *the frontal bone.* ➤➤ **frontally** *adv.* [Latin *frontalis*, from *front-, frons* front]

frontal² /'fruntl/ *noun* a cloth hanging over the front of an altar. [FRONTAL¹]

frontal lobe *noun* the front lobe of either cerebral hemisphere.

front bench *noun Brit* either of two rows of benches in the House of Commons on which party leaders sit. ➤➤ **frontbencher** *noun.*

front-end¹ *adj* **1** required or provided at the beginning of a project: *High front-end costs are a feature of solar energy systems.* **2** said of a computer program: relating to the user interface of the system.

front-end² *noun* the software or hardware of a computer that takes in and processes the raw data.

frontier /frun'tiə/ *noun* **1** a border between two countries. **2** *NAmer* a region that forms the margin of settled or developed territory. **3** (*also in pl*) the boundary between the known and the unknown: *the frontiers of medicine.* [Middle English *fronter* front, from French *frontière* vanguard, ultimately from Latin *front-, frons* FRONT¹]

frontiersman or **frontierswoman** *noun* (*pl* **frontiersmen** or **frontierswomen**) a man or woman living on the frontier, *esp* of settled territory.

frontispiece /'fruntispees/ *noun* **1** an illustration preceding and usu facing the title page of a book or magazine. **2** in architecture, the main façade of a building. **3** a pediment over a door or window. [French *frontispice* from late Latin *frontispicium* view of the front, from Latin *front-, frons* FRONT¹ + *-i-* + *specere* to look at]

front line *noun* **1** a military front. **2** the most advanced, responsible, or significant position in a field of activity. **3** (**frontline**) (*used before a noun*) of or relating to a front line: *frontline states.*

front loader *noun* a washing machine with the door for loading the clothes into the drum at the front.

front man *noun* a person serving as a front or figurehead.

front office *noun chiefly NAmer* the head office or administrative headquarters of a company or other organization.

front of house *noun* the parts of a theatre accessible to the public, e.g. the auditorium and foyer.

front-page *adj* featuring or worth featuring on the front page of a newspaper; very newsworthy.

front-runner *noun* **1** the leading contestant in a competition. **2** a contestant who runs best when in the lead.

front-running *noun* on the Stock Exchange, the practice of using information from investment analysts before it is given to clients.

frost¹ /frost/ *noun* **1** a covering of minute ice crystals formed on a cold surface when the temperature falls below freezing. **2** a period of freezing weather. **3** coldness of attitude or manner. **4** (**a frost**) *informal* a failure or fiasco: *The party was a total frost*. [Old English]

frost² *verb trans* **1a** to cover (something) with or as if with frost. **b** to produce a fine-grained slightly roughened surface on (metal, glass, etc). **2a** to cover (e.g. a cake or grapes) with sugar. **b** *chiefly NAmer* to ice (a cake). **3** to injure or kill (e.g. plants) by frost. ➤ *verb intrans* (*often* + over) to freeze.

frostbite *noun* gangrene or other local damage caused by a partial freezing of some part of the body.

frosted *adj* **1** covered with frost. **2** said of glass: having a slightly roughened surface, making it hard to see through. **3** having a frosty or sparkling sheen: *frosted lipstick*. **4** said of a cake: covered with frosting.

frosting *noun* **1** a dull or roughened finish on metal or glass. **2a** *Brit* thick fluffy cooked icing. **b** *chiefly NAmer* icing.

frosty *adj* (**frostier, frostiest**) **1** marked by or producing frost; freezing. **2** covered with frost; hoary. **3** marked by coolness or extreme reserve in manner. ➤➤ **frostily** *adv*, **frostiness** *noun*.

froth¹ /froth/ *noun* **1a** a mass of bubbles formed on or in a liquid; foam. **b** a foamy saliva sometimes accompanying disease, e.g. rabies. **2** something insubstantial or of little value. [Middle English from Old Norse *frotha*]

froth² *verb trans* (*often* + up) to cause (a liquid) to foam. ➤ *verb intrans* (*often* + up) to produce or emit froth. ➤➤ **frothily** *adv*, **frothy** *adj*.

frottage /'frotahzh/ *noun* **1** in art, the technique or process of creating an image of an object by rubbing, e.g. with a pencil, on a sheet of paper placed over it. **2** the practice of rubbing against somebody in a crowd as a way of getting sexual pleasure. [French *frottage* from *frotter* to rub]

froufrou /'froohfrooh/ *noun* **1** a rustling sound, *esp* of a woman's dress. **2** frilly ornamentation, *esp* in women's clothing. [French *froufrou*, of imitative origin]

froward /'frohəd/ *adj archaic* habitually disobedient or contrary. ➤➤ **frowardly** *adv*, **frowardness** *noun*. [Middle English, literally 'turned away', from *fro* from + -WARD]

frown¹ /frown/ *verb intrans* **1** to contract the brow in a frown. **2** (*often* + on/upon) to give evidence of displeasure or disapproval. ➤ *verb trans* to express (disapproval) by frowning. ➤➤ **frowner** *noun*, **frowningly** *adv*. [Middle English *frounen* from early French *froigner* to snort, frown, ultimately of Celtic origin]

frown² *noun* **1** a wrinkling of the brow in displeasure, concentration, or puzzlement. **2** an expression of displeasure.

frowst¹ /frowst/ *verb intrans chiefly Brit, informal* to remain indoors in a hot airless room: *The cure for this ill is not to sit still, or frowst with a book by the fire* — Kipling. [back-formation from FROWSTY]

frowst² *noun chiefly Brit, informal* a stuffy atmosphere.

frowsty *adj* (**frowstier, frowstiest**) *chiefly Brit* lacking fresh air; stuffy. ➤➤ **frowstiness** *noun*. [alteration of FROWZY]

frowzy *or* **frowsy** /'frowzi/ *adj* (**frowzier** *or* **frowsier, frowziest** *or* **frowsiest**) **1** having a slovenly or uncared-for appearance. **2** musty or stale. [origin unknown]

froze /frohz/ *verb* past tense of FREEZE¹.

frozen¹ *adj* **1a** treated, affected, solidified, or crusted over by freezing. **b** said of a region: subject to long and severe cold. **2** said of food: preserved by freezing. **3** said of assets: not available for present use. **4** said of e.g. wages or prices: incapable of being changed or moved. ➤➤ **frozenly** *adv*.

frozen² *verb* past part. of FREEZE¹.

frozen shoulder *noun* a medical condition in which the shoulder is stiff and painful.

FRS *abbr Brit* Fellow of the Royal Society.

fructify /'fruktifie/ *verb* (**fructifies, fructified, fructifying**) ➤ *verb intrans formal* to bear fruit. ➤ *verb trans formal* to make (something) fruitful or productive: *Social philosophy fructified the political thinking of liberals* — Times Literary Supplement. [Middle English *fructifien* via French from Latin *fructificare*, from *fructus*: see FRUIT¹]

fructose /'fruktohz, 'fruktohs/ *noun* a very sweet sugar that occurs in fruit juices and honey. [Latin *fructus* (see FRUIT¹) + -OSE²]

frugal /'froohg(ə)l/ *adj* **1** economical in the expenditure of resources; sparing. **2** small in quantity or involving little cost; meagre: *a frugal meal*. ➤➤ **frugality** /frooh'galiti/ *noun*, **frugally**

adv. [via French from Latin *frugalis* virtuous, frugal, from *frug-, frux* fruit, value]

frugivore /'froohjivaw/ *noun* an animal that feeds on fruit. ➤➤ **frugivorous** /frooh'jivərəs/ *adj*. [Latin *frug-, frux* fruit + -*vore* eater, from -VOROUS]

fruit¹ /frooht/ *noun* **1** the usu edible reproductive body of a seed plant; *esp* one having a sweet pulp associated with the seed, e.g. an apple or pear. **2** in botany, a product of fertilization in a plant with its modified skins or attached structures; *specif* the ripened ovary of a flowering plant together with its contents. **3** a harvestable product of plant growth, e.g. grain, vegetables, or cotton. **4** (*also in pl*) the effect or consequence of an action or operation, *esp* a favourable one: *He admired the fruits of his labour*. **5** *chiefly NAmer, informal, offensive* a male homosexual. **6** (**old fruit**) *Brit, informal, dated* a friendly form of address by one man to another. **7** *archaic* offspring or progeny. [Middle English via Old French from Latin *fructus* fruit, use, past part. of *frui* to enjoy, have the use of]

fruit² *verb intrans* to bear fruit.

fruitarian /frooh'teəri·ən/ *noun* somebody whose diet consists of fruit.

fruit bat *noun* any of numerous species of large fruit-eating bats found in warm regions of Africa and Eurasia: family *Pteropodidae*.

fruitcake *noun* **1** a rich usu dark cake typically containing nuts, dried fruit, cherries, and spices. **2** *Brit, informal* a crazy or eccentric person.

fruit cup *noun* **1** *Brit* a drink made of a mixture of fruit juices and often containing pieces of fruit. **2** *NAmer* = FRUIT SALAD.

fruit drop *noun* **1** the premature shedding by a tree of its fruit while still unripe. **2** a boiled sweet with a fruit flavouring.

fruiterer *noun chiefly Brit* a person who sells fruit.

fruit fly *noun* a small fly whose larvae feed on fruit or decaying vegetable matter: families Drosophilidae and Tephritidae.

fruitful /'froohtf(ə)l/ *adj* **1** yielding or producing a great deal of fruit; fertile. **2** having beneficial results; productive: *a fruitful meeting*. ➤➤ **fruitfully** *adv*, **fruitfulness** *noun*.

fruiting body *noun* a plant organ, e.g. in lichens and mosses, specialized for producing spores.

fruition /frooh'ish(ə)n/ *noun* **1** the realization or fulfilment of a project. **2** bearing fruit. [Middle English *fruicioun* via French from Latin *fruitus*, alteration of *fructus*: see FRUIT¹]

fruitless *adj* **1** useless or unsuccessful. **2** lacking or not bearing fruit. ➤➤ **fruitlessly** *adv*, **fruitlessness** *noun*.

fruit machine *noun Brit* a coin-operated gambling machine that pays out according to different combinations of symbols, e.g. different types of fruit, visible on wheels.

fruit salad *noun* a dessert consisting of a mixture of chopped pieces of fruit, served in a juice or syrup.

fruit sugar *noun* = FRUCTOSE.

fruit tree *noun* a tree known or grown especially for the fruit it bears.

fruity *adj* (**fruitier, fruitiest**) **1** resembling or having the flavour of fruit: *a fruity wine*. **2** said of a voice: marked by richness and depth; mellow. **3** *chiefly Brit, informal* amusing in a sexually suggestive way. **4** *NAmer, informal* homosexual. **5** *NAmer, informal* eccentric. ➤➤ **fruitily** *adv*, **fruitiness** *noun*.

frumenty /'froohmənti/ *noun Brit* wheat boiled in milk and usu flavoured with sugar and spices. [Middle English via French from Latin *frumentum*, from *frui* to enjoy]

frump /frump/ *noun chiefly informal* a dowdy unattractive girl or woman. ➤➤ **frumpish** *adj*, **frumpy** *adj*. [prob from Middle English *frumple* to wrinkle, from early Dutch *verrompelen*]

frusemide /'froohzəmied/ *noun* a powerful synthetic diuretic used in the treatment of oedema and high blood pressure. [alteration of *fursemide*, from *furfural* (a liquid aldehyde made of plant materials; from Latin *furfur* bran) + -*emide*, prob alteration of AMIDE]

frusta /'frustə/ *noun* pl of FRUSTUM.

frustrate /fru'strayt/ *verb trans* **1a** to prevent (somebody) from carrying out a plan or intention; to foil (them). **b** to prevent (e.g. a plan) from being carried out or (e.g. a hope) from being realized. **2** to induce feelings of discouragement and vexation in (somebody). ➤➤ **frustrated** *adj*, **frustrating** *adj*, **frustratingly** *adv*, **frustration** *noun*. [Middle English *frustraten* from Latin *frustratus*, past part. of *frustrare* to deceive, frustrate, from *frustra* in error, in vain]

frustule /'frustyoohl/ *noun* in botany, the hard silica-containing shell of a DIATOM (single-celled alga). [French *frustule* from Latin *frustulum*, dimin. of *frustum* piece]

frustum /'frustəm/ *noun* (*pl* **frustums** *or* **frusta** /'frustə/) **1** the part of a cone or pyramid left after cutting off the top at a plane parallel to the base. **2** the part of a solid intersected between two usu parallel planes. [Latin *frustum* piece, bit]

fry[1] /frie/ *verb* (**fries, fried, frying**) ➤ *verb trans* **1** to cook (food) in hot oil or fat, *esp* in a pan over direct heat. **2** *NAmer, slang* to execute (somebody) by electric chair. ➤ *verb intrans* **1** said of food: to cook in hot oil or fat. **2** *informal* said of a person: to feel very hot or to burn in the sun. **3** *NAmer, slang* to be executed by electric chair. [Middle English *frien* via Old French *frire* from Latin *frigere*]

fry[2] *noun* (*pl* **fries**) **1** a dish of fried food, *esp* offal. **2** *NAmer* a social gathering, e.g. a picnic, at which food is fried and eaten.

fry[3] *pl noun* **1** recently hatched fishes. **2** the young of other animals, *esp* when occurring in large numbers. [Middle English from Old French *frier, froyer* to rub, spawn, from Latin *fricare* to rub]

fryer *noun* **1** a deep vessel for frying foods. **2** *NAmer* a young chicken suitable for frying.

frying pan *noun* a shallow metal pan with a handle, used for frying food. ✱ **out of the frying pan into the fire** clear of one difficulty only to fall into a greater one.

fry-up *noun Brit, informal* a dish or a simple *esp* impromptu meal consisting of fried food.

FSA *abbr Brit* Fellow of the Society of Antiquaries.

FSH *abbr* follicle-stimulating hormone.

f-stop *noun* a camera lens aperture setting indicated by an f-number.

FT *abbr* Financial Times.

ft *abbr* **1** feet. **2** foot.

fth *or* **fthm** *abbr* fathom.

FTP *abbr* in computing, file transfer protocol.

FTSE index /'footsi/ *noun* an index of relative share prices on the London Stock Exchange, published in the *Financial Times*. [abbr of *Financial Times Stock Exchange*]

fuchsia /'fyoohshə/ *noun* **1** any of a genus of decorative shrubs with hanging flowers with flared petals usu in deep pinks, reds, and purples: genus *Fuchsia*. **2** a vivid reddish purple. [Latin genus name, named after Leonhard *Fuchs* d.1566, German botanist]

fuchsin /'foohksin/ *or* **fuchsine** /'foohkseen/ *noun* a brilliant bluish red dye. [French *fuchsine*, prob from Latin *fuchsia* (see FUCHSIA); from its colour]

fuci /'fyoohsie/ *noun* pl of FUCUS.

fuck[1] /fuk/ *verb trans and intrans taboo* **1** to have sexual intercourse with (somebody). **2** to spoil or ruin (something).

Editorial note
Whatever the truth of its still debatable etymology, fuck remains the best-known example of the large vocabulary of slang words equating sexual intercourse with striking or hitting. Briefly acknowledged as standard English in the 16th cent., the word is still primarily taboo, although a growing erosion of linguistic prissiness has rendered such exclusion almost equally honoured in its ever-widening breach — Jonathon Green.

➤➤ **fucker** *noun*. [perhaps of Scandinavian origin]

fuck[2] *noun taboo* **1** an act of sexual intercourse. **2** a sexual partner. **3** the slightest amount: *He didn't care a fuck.*

fuck[3] *interj taboo* used to express annoyance or impatience.

fuck about *verb intrans taboo* to waste time; to mess about. ➤ *verb trans taboo* to treat (somebody) badly; to mess (them) about.

fuck all *noun Brit, taboo* nothing at all.

fuck around *verb intrans taboo* = FUCK ABOUT.

fucking /fuking/ *adj taboo* **1** used to intensify disgust, irritation, anger, etc: *It's fucking ridiculous to make mistakes like these; Don't be so fucking stupid.* **2** used by some without adding much to an existing sense: *And then he took these six fucking balls out of his pocket and started fucking juggling with them.*

fuck off *verb intrans taboo* **1** to go away. **2** *NAmer* to fuck about.

fuck up *verb trans and intrans taboo* **1** to spoil or ruin (something). **2** to do psychological damage to (somebody): *They fuck you up, your mum and dad. They may not mean to, but they do.* — Philip Larkin.

fucus /'fyoohkəs/ *noun* (*pl* **fuci** /'fyoohsie/) a seaweed with greenish brown leathery fronds used in the kelp industry: genus *Fucus*. ➤➤ **fucoid** /'fyoohkoyd/ *adj.* [Latin genus name, from Greek *phykos* seaweed, orchil, rouge, of Semitic origin]

fuddle[1] /'fudl/ *verb trans* to make (somebody) drunk or confused. [origin unknown]

fuddle[2] *noun* a confused or intoxicated state.

fuddy-duddy /'fudi dudi/ *noun* (*pl* **fuddy-duddies**) *informal* a person who is old-fashioned, pompous, unimaginative, or concerned about trifles. [perhaps alteration of FUSSY + DUD[1]]

fudge[1] /fuj/ *noun* **1** a soft creamy sweet made of sugar, milk, butter, and flavouring. **2** a decision, agreement, or statement that evades the central and most difficult issues. **3** the stop-press box or column of a newspaper. [from an early sense of FUDGE[2] 'to merge or meld']

fudge[2] *verb trans* **1** to present (e.g. facts or figures) in a misleading way. **2** to fail to come to grips with (a problem or issue). [prob alteration of *fadge* to fit, adjust, of unknown origin]

fudge[3] *interj informal* used to express mild annoyance.

fuehrer /'fyooərə (*German* fyrə)/ *noun* see FÜHRER.

fuel[1] /'fyooh·əl/ *noun* **1a** a material used to produce heat or power by combustion. **b** a material from which atomic energy can be liberated, *esp* in a nuclear reactor. **2a** a source of sustenance, strength, or encouragement: *fuel for their passions.* **b** material providing nutrition; food. [Middle English *fewel* from Old French *fouaille*, from Latin *focus* hearth]

fuel[2] *verb* (**fuelled, fuelling**, *NAmer* **fueled, fueling**) ➤ *verb trans* **1** to provide (e.g. a machine or vehicle) with fuel. **2** to support or stimulate (e.g. an emotion or activity): *Inflation is being fuelled by massive wage awards.* ➤ *verb intrans* (*often* + up) to take in fuel.

fuel cell *noun* a cell that continuously changes chemical energy to electrical energy.

fuel injection *noun* the introduction of liquid fuel under pressure directly into the cylinders of an internal-combustion engine, without using a carburettor. ➤➤ **fuel-injected** *adj.*

fuel oil *noun* an oil that is used for fuel, *esp* in furnaces and engines.

fug /fug/ *noun Brit, informal* the stuffy atmosphere of a poorly ventilated space. ➤➤ **fuggy** *adj.* [prob alteration of FOG[1]]

fugacious /fyoo'gayshəs/ *adj formal* lasting a short time; fleeting. ➤➤ **fugacity** /fyoo'gasiti/ *noun.* [Latin *fugac-, fugax*, from *fugere* to flee]

fugal /'fyoohgl/ *adj* in the style of a musical fugue. ➤➤ **fugally** *adv.*

-fuge *comb. form* forming nouns, denoting: something that drives another thing away: *febrifuge.* [French *-fuge* from late Latin *-fuga*, from Latin *fugare* to put to flight, from *fuga* flight]

fugitive[1] /'fyoohjətiv/ *noun* a person who flees or tries to escape, *esp* from danger, justice, or oppression. [Middle English via French from Latin *fugitivus*, from *fugere* to flee]

fugitive[2] *adj* **1** running away or trying to escape. **2** elusive or fleeting; ephemeral.

fugleman /'fyoohglmən/ *noun* (*pl* **fuglemen**) **1** a leader of a group. **2** formerly, a trained soldier copied by others during drill exercises. [modification of German *Flügelmann*, from *Flügel* wing + *Mann* man]

fugu /'foohgooh/ *noun* a poisonous pufferfish eaten as a delicacy in Japan.

fugue /fyoohg/ *noun* **1** a musical composition in which one or two themes are repeated or imitated by successively entering voices, instruments, or parts and are developed by a continuous interweaving.

Editorial note
The origins of fugue are found in choral motets by 15th-cent. Flemish composers; slowly the typical features of fugue evolved and three hundred years later J S Bach, in his last work, The Art of Fugue, took this most sophisticated form of imitative counterpoint to its limits. Composers have continued to find its challenge irresistible; Verdi failed his entrance test to music school with an early fugue, but the ten-part finale of his last opera Falstaff is one of the most remarkable examples of the genre — Amanda Holden.

2 in psychiatry, a disturbed state characterized by loss of memory and by the patient's disappearance from home. [prob from Italian *fuga* flight, fugue, from Latin *fuga* flight, from *fugere* to flee]

führer *or* **fuehrer** /'fyooərə (*German* fyrə)/ *noun* a leader exercising tyrannical authority, *esp* Hitler, leader of the Nazis in Germany. [German *Führer* leader, guide, from Old High German *fuoren* to lead]

-ful¹ *suffix* **1** forming adjectives from nouns, with the meaning: full of: *eventful; colourful.* **2** forming adjectives from nouns, with the meaning: characterized by: *peaceful; boastful.* **3** forming adjectives from nouns, with the meaning: having the qualities of: *masterful.* **4** forming adjectives from verbs, with the meaning: tending to or able to: *mournful.* [Old English, from FULL¹]

-ful² *suffix* forming nouns from nouns, denoting: number or amount that (the thing specified) holds or can hold: *a roomful; a handful.*

Usage note

The standard modern way of forming the plural of nouns ending in *-ful* is simply to add *-s* to the end of the word: *handfuls, pocketfuls, spoonfuls.* It is generally preferable to the alternative way, where *-s* is added to the end of the first element (*handsful, pocketsful*), which may seem quaint or pedantic, except where measurements for cooking are involved (*cupsful, spoonsful*).

fulcrum /'foolkrəm, 'fulkrəm/ *noun* (*pl* **fulcrums** *or* **fulcra** /'foolkrə, 'fulkrə/) the support about which a lever turns. [orig in the general sense 'prop, support'; Latin *fulcrum* bedpost, from *fulcire* to prop]

fulfil (*NAmer* **fulfill**) /fool'fil/ *verb trans* (**fulfilled, fulfilling**) **1a** to cause (something) to happen as appointed or predicted: *And so the prophecy was fulfilled.* **b** to put (e.g. an order) into effect; to carry (it) out. **2** to measure up to (a requirement or condition); to satisfy (it). **3** to develop the full potential of (somebody or something): *She never fulfilled her early promise.* ➤➤ **fulfilled** *adj*, **fulfilling** *adj*, **fulfilment** *noun*. [Old English *fullfyllan*, from FULL¹ + *fyllan* FILL¹]

fulgent /'fulj(ə)nt/ *adj formal or literary* dazzlingly bright. [Middle English from Latin *fulgent-, fulgens*, present part. of *fulgēre* to shine]

fulgurite /'fulgyooriet/ *noun* a glasslike crust produced by the fusion of sand or rock by lightning. [Latin *fulgur* lightning, from *fulgēre* to shine + -ITE¹]

fuliginous /fyooh'lijinəs/ *adj formal* sooty, murky, or dark. [late Latin *fuliginosus* from Latin *fuligin-, fuligo* soot]

full¹ /fool/ *adj* **1** containing as much or as many as is possible or normal. **2a** complete, *esp* in detail, number, or duration: *a full report; She did her full share.* **b** not lacking in any essential; perfect: *in full control of his senses.* **3** (+ of) possessing or containing a great number or amount of: *a room full of pictures.* **4a** at the highest or greatest degree; maximum: *full speed.* **b** at the height of development: *in full bloom.* **5** said of a member of an organization: enjoying all rights and privileges. **6a** said of somebody's figure or face: rounded in outline; plump. **b** said of a garment: having an abundance of material. **7a** said of a sound: having volume or depth. **b** said of a colour: rich and strong. **8** rich in experience: *a full life.* **9** (*often* + up) satisfied, *esp* with food or drink. **10a** (*often* + of) with the attention completely occupied by something: *full of gloomy thoughts.* **b** (*often* + of) filled with and expressing excited anticipation or pleasure: *full of his holiday plans.* ✳ **full of oneself** self-satisfied and conceited. **full up** completely full. **in full flight 1** fleeing as fast as possible. **2** in top operating form: *You've obviously never seen her in full flight.* **in full flow** speaking fluently and animatedly: *interrupted in full flow.* **in full swing** at a high level of activity. ➤➤ **fullness** *noun*, **fulness** *noun*. [Middle English from Old English]

full² *adv* **1** very: *You knew full well he had lied.* **2** exactly or squarely: *The ball hit him full in the face.*

full³ *noun* (**the full**) the highest or fullest state, extent, or degree: *He enjoyed life to the full.* ✳ **in full** completely or entirely: *repaid in full.*

full⁴ *verb intrans* said of the moon: to become full. ➤ *verb trans* in sewing, to make a (garment) full by gathering or pleating the material.

full⁵ *verb trans* to cleanse and finish (woollen cloth) by moistening, heating, and pressing. ➤➤ **fuller** *noun*. [Middle English *fullen* via French from Latin *fullo* one who fulls cloth]

fullback *noun* a primarily defensive player in football, rugby, etc, usu stationed nearest the defended goal.

full-blooded *adj* **1** of unmixed ancestry; purebred. **2** forceful or vigorous; hearty. ➤➤ **full-bloodedness** *noun*.

full-blown *adj* **1** fully developed or mature; complete: *The riots escalated into full-blown civil war.* **2** said of a flower: at the height of bloom.

full board *noun Brit* accommodation at a guest house or hotel with all meals included.

full-bodied *adj* marked by richness and fullness, *esp* of flavour: *a full-bodied wine.*

full-court press *noun* in basketball, the strategy of attacking an opposing player who has the ball anywhere on the court, not just near the basket.

full dress *noun* **1** the style of dress prescribed for ceremonial or formal social occasions. **2** (*used before a noun*) requiring full dress; formal: *a full-dress occasion.*

fullerene /'fooləreen/ *noun* = BUCKMINSTERFULLERENE.

fuller's earth *noun* a clayey substance used in fulling cloth and as a catalyst.

full-face *adj* **1** covering the whole face: *a full-face crash helmet.* **2** showing the whole face: *a full-face photograph.*

full-fledged *adj NAmer* see FULLY-FLEDGED.

full-frontal *adj* **1** exposing the whole front of the body, including the genitals. **2** without concealment or restraint: *a full-frontal approach to life.*

full house *noun* **1** a full theatre or other venue. **2** in poker, a hand containing three of a kind and a pair. **3** in bingo, a winning set of numbers.

full-length *adj* **1** showing or adapted to the entire length, *esp* of the human figure. **2** having a normal or standard length; unabridged.

full monty /'monti/ *noun* (**the full monty**) *Brit, informal* everything needed or wanted; the whole thing or the whole lot. [origin unknown, perhaps a reference to a complete suit of clothes available from *Montague Burton's*, a popular British chain of men's outfitters]

full moon *noun* the moon when its whole apparent disc is illuminated.

full nelson *noun* a wrestling hold in which both arms are thrust under the corresponding arms of an opponent and the hands clasped behind the opponent's head: compare HALF NELSON.

full-on *adj informal* unrestrained or intense; explicit.

full point *noun* = FULL STOP.

full-scale *adj* **1** identical to an original in proportion and size. **2** involving full use of available resources: *He wrote a full-scale biography.*

full stop *noun* a punctuation mark (.) used to mark the end of a sentence or abbreviation.

full time¹ *noun* **1** the amount of time considered the normal or standard amount for working during a given period, *esp* a week. **2** the end of e.g. a football match.

full time² *adv* on a full-time basis.

full-time *adj* employed for or involving full time: *full-time employees.* ➤➤ **full-timer** *noun*.

full toss *noun* in cricket, a bowled ball that has not hit the ground by the time it reaches the batsman.

fully *adv* **1** completely. **2** at least: *Fully nine tenths of us voted for it.*

fully-fashioned *adj* said of clothing: shaped and seamed so that it fits the body.

fully-fledged (*NAmer* **full-fledged**) *adj* **1** said of a bird: having fully developed feathers and able to fly. **2** having attained complete status: *a fully-fledged lawyer.*

fulmar /'foolmə/ *noun* a grey and white seabird of colder regions closely related to the petrels: *Fulmarus glacialis.* [ultimately from Old Norse *fúll* foul + *már* gull; because it regurgitates its stomach contents when threatened]

fulminant /'foolminənt, 'ful-/ *adj* = FULMINATING (2).

fulminate¹ /'foolminayt, 'ful-/ *verb intrans* **1a** (*usu* + against/at) to criticize or denounce something vehemently. **b** to be furiously indignant; to feel enraged: *He fulminated in silence.* **2** to make a sudden loud noise; to explode. ➤➤ **fulmination** /-'naysh(ə)n/ *noun*, **fulminator** *noun*. [Middle English *fulminaten* via late Latin from Latin *fulminare* to flash with lightning, strike with lightning, from *fulmin-, fulmen* lightning]

fulminate[2] *noun* an often explosive salt, e.g. of mercury, containing the radical CNO. [Latin *fulmin-, fulmen* lightning + -ATE[1]]

fulminating *adj* **1** exploding with a vivid flash. **2** said of a disease or infection: coming on suddenly with great severity.

fulsome /'fools(ə)m/ *adj* **1** unnecessarily effusive or obsequious: *fulsome praises*. **2** overabundant or copious: *described in fulsome detail*. >>> **fulsomely** *adv*, **fulsomeness** *noun*. [Middle English *fulsom* copious, cloying, from FULL[1] + *-som* -SOME[1]]

Usage note

In its standard modern meaning, *fulsome* is a strongly uncomplimentary word. *Fulsome praise* is embarrassingly excessive or insincerely flattering. Though *fulsome* derives originally from a word meaning 'abundant', its use in a positive sense to mean 'copious', 'very full', or 'lavish' should be avoided for fear of misunderstanding.

fulvous /'fulvəs/ *adj* dull brownish yellow. [Latin *fulvus*; perhaps related to Latin *flavus* yellow]

fumaric acid /fyooh'marik/ *noun* an acid that has two carboxyl groups in its molecular structure, is found in various plants, and is used in making resins: formula $C_4H_4O_4$. [Latin *Fumaria*, genus of herbs, from late Latin *fumaria* fumitory, from Latin *fumus* smoke, FUME[1]]

fumarole /'fyoomərohl/ *noun* a hole in a volcanic region from which hot vapours are emitted. >>> **fumarolic** /-'rolik/ *adj*. [Italian *fumarola* from late Latin *fumariolum*, from Latin *fumarium* smoke chamber for ageing wine, from *fumus* smoke, FUME[1]]

fumble[1] /'fumbl/ *verb intrans* **1** to grope for or handle something clumsily or awkwardly. **2** (*often* + about/around) to make awkward attempts to do or find something: *I fumbled in my pocket for a pound coin.* > *verb trans* **1** to feel or handle (e.g. a ball) clumsily. **2** to deal with (something) awkwardly or clumsily. >>> **fumbler** *noun*, **fumblingly** *adv*. [Middle English from Low German *fommeln* or Dutch *fommelen*]

fumble[2] *noun* an act of fumbling.

fume[1] /fyoohm/ *noun* (*also in pl*) an irritating or offensive smoke, vapour, or gas. >>> **fumy** *adj*. [Middle English via Old French from Latin *fumus* smoke]

fume[2] *verb intrans* **1** to emit fumes. **2** to be in a state of excited irritation or anger: *She fretted and fumed over the delay.* > *verb trans* to expose (e.g. wood) to or treat (something) with fumes: *fumed oak*. >>> **fuming** *adj*, **fumingly** *adv*.

fumigate /'fyoohmigayt/ *verb trans* to apply smoke, vapour, or gas to (an area), *esp* in order to disinfect it or destroy pests. >>> **fumigant** *noun*, **fumigation** /-'gaysh(ə)n/ *noun*, **fumigator** *noun*. [Latin *fumigatus*, past part. of *fumigare*, from *fumus* smoke]

fumitory /'fyoohmit(ə)ri/ *noun* (*pl* **fumitories**) an erect or climbing plant with purple or white flowers: genus *Fumaria*. [Middle English *fumeterre* via French from Latin *fumus terrae* smoke of the earth; because of its greyish leaves]

fun[1] /fun/ *noun* **1a** amusement or enjoyment. **b** a cause of this. **2** good humour. **3** derisive amusement; ridicule: *a figure of fun.* **4** violent or excited activity or amusement: *They let a snake loose in the classroom; then the fun began.* ✳ **fun and games** confused activity, or trouble and difficulty. **in fun** not intending harm or to be taken seriously. **make fun of/poke fun at** to make (somebody or something) an object of amusement or ridicule. [dialect *fun* to hoax, perhaps alteration of Middle English *fonnen*, from *fonne* dupe; earlier history unknown]

fun[2] *adj chiefly NAmer, informal* providing entertainment, amusement, or enjoyment: *a fun person to be with.*

funambulism /fyooh'nambyooliz(ə)m/ *noun formal* tightrope walking. >>> **funambulist** *noun*. [Latin *funambulus* ropewalker, from *funis* rope + *ambulare* to walk]

function[1] /'fungksh(ə)n/ *noun* **1** the purpose of a person or thing, or for which a thing exists, or what a person or thing characteristically does: *We will be examining the function of poetry in modern society.* **2** an impressive, elaborate, or formal ceremony or social gathering. **3** a mathematical relationship between each element of one set and at least one element of the same or another set. **4** a quality, trait, or fact dependent on and varying with another: *The time they arrive is a function of how far they have to travel.* **5** a facility on a computer or similar device that carries out a particular operation: *Using the Copy function allows you to place text into the Clipboard.* >>> **functionless** *adj*. [Latin *function-, functio* performance, from *fungi* to perform]

function[2] *verb intrans* **1** to have a function; to serve: *An attributive noun functions as an adjective.* **2** to operate: *The government functions through numerous divisions.*

functional *adj* **1** designed or developed for practical use without ornamentation. **2** designed for performing a function. **3** connected with or being a function. **4** said of disease: affecting physiological or psychological functions but not organic structure. >>> **functionally** *adv*.

functionalism *noun* **1** a theory or practice that emphasizes practical utility or functional relations to the exclusion of ornamentation. **2** a theory that stresses the interdependence of the institutions of a society. >>> **functionalist** *noun and adj*.

functionary *noun* (*pl* **functionaries**) somebody who serves in a certain function; an official or bureaucrat.

function key *noun* a keyboard key, e.g. on a calculator or computer, which controls a command or action sequence.

function word *noun* a word, e.g. a preposition or conjunction, chiefly expressing grammatical relationship rather than meaning.

functor /'fungktə/ *noun* in logic and mathematics, = FUNCTION[1].

fund[1] /fund/ *noun* **1** a sum of money whose principal or interest is set apart for a specific objective. **2** (*in pl*) an available supply of money. **3** an available quantity of material or intangible resources: *a fund of knowledge.*

Word history

Latin *fundus* bottom, basis, or piece of landed property. The word was orig used in the Latin senses 'bottom, basis', later 'source of supply', perhaps from the idea of landed property as the basis or source of wealth, although *fund* has never had the meaning 'landed property'.

fund[2] *verb trans* to provide funds for (something): *research funded by the government.*

fundament /'fundəmənt/ *noun euphem* the buttocks. [Middle English via Old French from Latin *fundamentum*, from *fundare* to found, from *fundus* bottom]

fundamental[1] /fundə'mentl/ *adj* **1** of central importance; principal: *fundamental purpose.* **2** of the essential structure, function, or facts of something; radical: *fundamental change.* **3** belonging to one's innate or ingrained characteristics; deep-rooted: *You couldn't disturb his fundamental good humour.* >>> **fundamentality** /-'taliti/ *noun*, **fundamentally** *adv*.

fundamental[2] *noun* **1** a minimum constituent without which a thing or system would not be what it is. **2** in music, the prime tone of a harmonic series. **3** in music, the lowest note of a chord in normal position.

fundamentalism *noun* **1a** a belief in the literal truth of the Bible. **b** (*often* **Fundamentalism**) a movement in 20th-cent. Protestantism emphasizing such belief. **2** a movement stressing strict adherence to a set of basic principles or beliefs, *esp* in religion.

Editorial note

Fundamentalism is the general attempt to get to the basics, or fundamentals, of belief, setting aside any sophisticated theological argument or doctrines. In Christianity it has generally come to be used for an approach based on a literal interpretation of the Bible. In Islam it applies to those who claim to take an uncompromising approach to applying the Shariah, or religious law — Dr Mel Thompson.

>>> **fundamentalist** *noun and adj*.

fundamental particle *noun* = ELEMENTARY PARTICLE.

fundamental unit *noun* a basic unit in a system of measurement, e.g. the metre, kilogram, or second.

funded debt *noun* the part of Britain's national debt that does not have to be repaid by a fixed date: compare FLOATING DEBT.

fundholding *noun* a system formerly used in Britain in which general practitioners controlled their own budgets. >>> **fundholder** *noun*.

fundi /'fundee, 'fundie/ *noun* pl of FUNDUS.

fund-raiser *noun* **1** somebody who works to raise funds for a cause. **2** an event held to raise funds for a cause. >>> **fund-raising** *noun*.

fundus /'fundəs/ *noun* (*pl* **fundi** /'fundee, 'fundie/) the bottom, or part opposite the opening, of the stomach, uterus, or other hollow organ. [Latin *fundus* bottom]

funeral /'fyoohn(ə)rəl/ *noun* **1** a formal and ceremonial disposing of a dead body, *esp* by burial or cremation. **2** a procession of people at a funeral. ✳ **be somebody's funeral** *informal* to be somebody's own problem or fault. [Middle English *funerelles* (pl) via French from late Latin *funeralia* funeral rites, ultimately from Latin *funer-, funus* funeral]

funeral director *noun* = UNDERTAKER.

funeral parlour *noun* an undertaker's establishment.

funerary /'fyoohnərəri/ *adj* used for or associated with burial: *a pharaoh's funerary chamber*. [Latin *funerarius*, from *funer-, funus* FUNERAL]

funereal /fyooh'niəri·əl/ *adj* gloomy or solemn: *The supper-party … was remarkable for the unrestrained gaiety of two of the participants and the funereal mirthlessness of the remaining guests* — Saki. ⟫⟫ **funereally** *adv*. [Latin *funereus*, from *funer-, funus* FUNERAL]

fun fair *noun chiefly Brit* a usu outdoor show offering amusements, e.g. sideshows, rides, or games of skill.

fungi /'fungie, 'funggee/ *noun* pl of FUNGUS.

fungible¹ /'funjəbl/ *adj* in law, said of movable goods: such that one specimen may be used in place of another in the fulfilment of a contract. ⟫⟫ **fungibility** /-'biliti/ *noun*. [Latin *fungibilis* from *fungi* to perform]

fungible² *noun* (*usu in pl*) something fungible, e.g. food or fuel.

fungicide /'funjisied, 'funggisied/ *noun* a substance used for destroying or preventing fungus. ⟫⟫ **fungicidal** /-'siedl/ *adj*.

fungoid /'funggoyd/ *adj* resembling a fungus.

fungous /'funggəs/ *adj* **1** relating to or like a fungus or fungi. **2** caused by a fungus.

fungus /'funggəs/ *noun* (*pl* **fungi** /'fungie, 'funggee/ *or* **funguses**) any of a major group of saprotrophic and parasitic organisms lacking chlorophyll and including moulds, rusts, mildews, smuts, mushrooms, and toadstools; reproduction involves minute spores. ⟫⟫ **fungal** *adj*. [Latin *fungus*, perhaps modification of Greek *spongos* sponge]

funicular¹ /fyooh'nikyoolə/ *noun* a cable railway on a steep slope in which an ascending carriage counterbalances a descending carriage. [Latin *funiculus* small rope, dimin. of *funis* rope]

funicular² *adj* **1** said of a railway: dependent on a rope or cable to draw the carriages. **2** *formal* relating to or associated with a rope.

funk¹ /fungk/ *noun informal* **1** a state of paralysing fear. **2** a fit of inability to face difficulty. [prob from obsolete Flemish *fonck*]

funk² *verb trans informal* to avoid doing or facing (something) because of lack of determination.

funk³ *noun* funky music. [back-formation from FUNKY]

funky *adj* (**funkier, funkiest**) **1** *informal* having an earthy unsophisticated style and feeling, as in the blues; soulful. **2** *informal* said of clothes: original and stylish. **3** *NAmer* smelling mouldy or musty. ⟫⟫ **funkily** *adv*, **funkiness** *noun*. [*funk* offensive smell, perhaps from French dialect *funquer* to emit smoke]

funnel¹ /'funl/ *noun* **1** a utensil usu having the shape of a hollow cone with a tube extending from the smaller end, designed to direct liquids or powders into a small opening. **2** a shaft, stack, or flue for ventilation or the escape of smoke or steam. [Middle English *fonel*, ultimately from Latin *infundibulum*, from *infundere* to pour in, from IN-² + *fundere* to pour]

funnel² *verb* (**funnelled, funnelling,** *NAmer* **funneled, funneling**) ⟫ *verb intrans* **1** to pass through or as if through a funnel: *The crowd funnelled out of the football ground*. **2** to have or take the shape of a funnel. ⟫ *verb trans* to move (something) to a focal point or into a central channel: *Contributions were funnelled into one account*.

funnel web *noun* any of various spiders that build tube-shaped webs; *esp* an extremely poisonous large black Australian spider: *Atrax robustus*.

funny¹ /'funi/ *adj* (**funnier, funniest**) **1** causing amusement and laughter; seeking or intended to amuse. **2** peculiar, strange, or odd. **3** involving trickery, deception, or dishonesty: *They told the prisoner not to try anything funny*. **4** unwilling to be helpful; difficult: *At first he was a bit funny about it but in the end he agreed*. **5a** *informal* slightly unwell. **b** slightly mad. ⟫⟫ **funnily** /'funəli/ *adv*, **funniness** *noun*.

funny² *noun* (*pl* **funnies**) **1** *informal* (*usu in pl*) a comic strip or comic section in a periodical. **2** *informal* a joke.

funny bone *noun* the place at the back of the elbow where the nerve supplying the hand and forearm rests against the bone. [from the tingling felt when it is struck, with a pun on HUMERUS]

funny farm *noun informal* a psychiatric hospital.

fun run *noun informal* a long-distance run, *esp* to raise money for charity.

fur¹ /fuh/ *noun* **1** the hairy coat of a mammal, *esp* when fine, soft, and thick. **2a** a piece of the dressed pelt of an animal used to make, trim, or line garments. **b** an article of clothing made of or with fur. **3** a coating resembling fur, e.g.: **a** a coating of dead cells on the tongue of somebody who is unwell. **b** the thick pile of a fabric, e.g. chenille. **4** a coating formed in vessels, e.g. kettles or pipes, by deposition of scale from hard water. **5** any of the heraldic representations of animal pelts or their colours that have a stylized pattern of tufts or patches. ✳ **make the fur fly** to cause an argument or a scene. ⟫⟫ **furless** *adj*, **furred** *adj*.

fur² *verb* (**furred, furring**) ⟫ *verb trans* **1** to trim or line (a garment) with fur. **2** (*often* + up) to coat or clog (e.g. a pipe) with, or as if with, fur. **3** to apply strips of wood, brick, etc to (floor or wall timbers). ⟫ *verb intrans* (*often* + up) to become coated or clogged with, or as if with, fur. [Middle English *furren* to line or trim with fur, from Old French *forrer* to line or encase, from *fuerre* sheath, of Germanic origin]

fur. *abbr* furlong.

furbelow /'fuhbiloh/ *noun* **1** a pleated or gathered piece of material; *specif* a flounce on women's clothing. **2** something that suggests a furbelow, *esp* in being showy or superfluous: *frills and furbelows*. [by folk etymology from French dialect *farbella* a frill]

furbish /'fuhbish/ *verb trans* **1** to give a new look to (e.g. a building); to renovate (it). **2** to polish (e.g. a weapon). ⟫⟫ **furbisher** *noun*. [Middle English *furbisshen* from early French *fourbir*, of Germanic origin]

furcate¹ /'fuhkayt, 'fuhkət/ *adj technical* divided into two or more branches; forked. ⟫⟫ **furcately** *adv*. [late Latin *furcatus* from Latin *furca* FORK¹]

furcate² /'fuhkayt, fuh'kayt/ *verb trans and intrans* to divide (something) into branches. ⟫⟫ **furcation** /fuh'kaysh(ə)n/ *noun*.

furcula /'fuhkyoolə/ *noun* (*pl* **furculae** /-lee, -lie/) a wishbone or other forked part. ⟫⟫ **furcular** *adj*. [Latin *furcula* forked prop, dimin. of *furca* FORK¹]

furfuraceous /fuhf(y)ə'rayshəs/ *adj* covered with scales that resemble bran; scurfy.

furfural /'fuhf(y)oorəl/ *noun* a liquid aldehyde with a penetrating smell that is usu made from plant materials, used *esp* in making synthetic plastics and as a solvent. [Latin *furfur* bran]

furioso /fyooəri'ohsoh/ *adj and adv* said of a piece of music: to be performed with great force or vigour. [Italian *furioso* from Latin *furiosus*: see FURIOUS]

furious /'fyooəri·əs/ *adj* **1** exhibiting or goaded by uncontrollable anger. **2a** having a stormy or turbulent appearance: *furious bursts of flame from the fire*. **b** marked by noise, excitement, or activity. **3** intense: *the furious growth of tropical vegetation*. ⟫⟫ **furiously** *adv*, **furiousness** *noun*. [Middle English via French from Latin *furiosus*, from *furia*: see FURY]

furl /fuhl/ *verb trans* to fold or roll (e.g. a sail or umbrella) close to or round something. ⟫ *verb intrans* to curl or fold as in being furled. ⟫⟫ **furl** *noun*, **furlable** *adj*, **furled** *adj*. [early French *ferler*, from Old French *fer, ferm* tight (from Latin *firmus* FIRM¹) + *lier* to tie, from Latin *ligare*]

furlong /'fuhlong/ *noun* a unit of length equal to 220 yards (about 0.2km). [Old English *furlang*, from *furh* FURROW¹ + *lang* LONG¹]

furlough¹ /'fuhloh/ *noun* a leave of absence from duty granted *esp* to a soldier. [Dutch *verlof* permission, from early Dutch *ver*- for- + *lof* permission]

furlough² *verb trans chiefly NAmer* to grant a furlough to (e.g. a soldier).

furmety /'fuhmiti/ *noun* = FRUMENTY.

furnace /'fuhnis/ *noun* an enclosed apparatus in which heat is produced, e.g. for heating a building or reducing ore. [Middle English *furnas* via Old French from Latin *fornac-, fornax* oven]

furnish /'fuhnish/ *verb trans* **1a** to provide, supply, or give (something). **b** to provide or supply (somebody) with what they need. **2** to equip (a room, flat, etc) with furniture. ⟫⟫ **furnished** *adj*, **furnisher** *noun*. [Middle English *furnisshen* from early French *fournir* to complete, equip, of Germanic origin]

furnishing *noun* **1** (*in pl*) articles of furniture and fittings used to make a room comfortable. **2** (*used before a noun*) denoting material used for carpets, cushions, etc.

furniture /'fuhnichǝ/ *noun* **1** the movable articles, e.g. tables, chairs, and beds, that make an area suitable for living in or use. **2** accessories: *door furniture*. **3** the whole movable equipment of a ship, e.g. rigging, sails, anchors, and boats. **4** pieces of wood, metal, or plastic placed in an arrangement of printing type to make blank spaces and secure the type in its frame. **5** *archaic* the trappings of a horse. [early French *fourniture*, from *fournir*: see FURNISH]

furniture beetle *noun* a small beetle whose larva is a wood-worm: *Anobium punctatum*.

furore /fyoo'rawri/ (*NAmer* **furor** /'fyooǝraw/) *noun* an outburst of general excitement or indignation. [Italian *furore* from Latin *furor*, from *furere* to rage]

furphy /'fuhfi/ *noun* (*pl* **furphies**) *Aus, informal* an unlikely or absurd rumour. [named after the *Furphy* family, who supplied sanitation carts in Australia during World War I]

furred /fuhd/ *furred wall*.

furrier /'furi·ǝ/ *noun* a fur dealer. [Middle English *furrer* from Old French *forreor*, from *forrer*: see FUR²]

furring strip /'fuhring/ *noun* a thin strip of wood, brick, or metal fixed to walls, floors, or ceilings to form a level surface, e.g. for plastering, or an air space.

furrow¹ /'furoh/ *noun* **1** a trench in the earth made by a plough. **2** a groove. **3** a deep wrinkle. [Old English *furh*]

furrow² *verb trans* to make a furrow or line in (a surface). ⪢ *verb intrans* to become grooved or wrinkled.

furry /'fuhri/ *adj* (**furrier, furriest**) like, made of, or covered with fur. ⪢⪢ **furriness** *noun*.

fur seal *noun* any of several species of eared seals that has a double coat with a dense soft underfur, which is used for clothing and trimmings: *Callorhinus ursinus* and other species.

further¹ /'fuhdhǝ/ *adv* **1** to a greater degree or extent: *She was further annoyed by a second interruption*. **2** moreover. **3** = FARTHER (1). [Old English *furthor*]

Usage note ──────────
further *or* farther? See note at FARTHER¹.
──────────────────────────

further² *adj* **1** extending beyond what exists or has happened; additional: *There are two further volumes*. **2** coming after the one referred to: *closed until further notice*. **3** = FARTHER² (1).

further³ *verb trans* (**furthered, furthering**) to bring (something) closer to fulfilment, realization, or success; to help or advance (it): *This will further your chances of success*. ⪢⪢ **furtherance** *noun*, **furtherer** *noun*.

further education *noun Brit* vocational, cultural, or recreational education for people who have left school.

furthermore *adv* in addition to what precedes; moreover.

furthermost *adj* most distant.

further to *prep formal* in response to and following on from: *Further to your letter of the fourth July*.

furthest¹ /'fuhdhist/ *adj* most distant in space or time.

furthest² *adv* **1** to or at the greatest distance in space, time, or degree. **2** by the greatest degree or extent; most.

furtive /'fuhtiv/ *adj* expressive of or done by stealth; surreptitious or sly. ⪢⪢ **furtively** *adv*, **furtiveness** *noun*. [via French from Latin *furtivus* hidden, stolen, from *furtum* theft, from *fur* thief]

furuncle /'fyooǝrungkl/ *noun* a boil on the skin. ⪢⪢ **furuncular** /fyoo'rungkoolǝ/ *adj*, **furunculous** /fyoo'rungkyoolǝs/ *adj*. [Latin *furunculus* petty thief, sucker, furuncle, ultimately from *fur* thief]

furunculosis /fyoo,rungkyoo'lohsis/ *noun* **1** a medical condition characterized by the occurrence of boils on the skin. **2** a highly infectious bacterial disease of trout, salmon, and related fishes. [Latin *furunculosis*, from *furunculus* (see FURUNCLE) + -OSIS]

fury /'fyooǝri/ *noun* (*pl* **furies**) **1a** intense, disordered, and often destructive rage. **b** a fit of intense rage. **2** wild disordered force or activity. **3a** (**Fury**) any of the three avenging deities who in Greek mythology punished crimes. **b** an angry or vengeful woman: *There is no fury like an ex-wife searching for a new lover* — Cyril Connolly. [Middle English *furie* via French from Latin *furia*, from *furere* to rage]

furze /fuhz/ *noun* = GORSE. ⪢⪢ **furzy** *adj*. [Old English *fyrs*]

fuscous /'fuskǝs/ *adj* dark brownish grey. [Latin *fuscus* dusky]

fuse¹ /fyoohz/ *noun* **1** a combustible substance enclosed in a cord or cable for setting off an explosive charge by transmitting fire to it. **2** (*NAmer* **fuze**) the detonating device for setting off the charge in a projectile, bomb, etc. [orig the tube or casing of an explosive device; Italian *fuso* spindle, from Latin *fusus*]

fuse² (*NAmer* **fuze**) *verb trans* to equip (a bomb) with a fuse.

fuse³ *verb trans* **1** to blend (two things) thoroughly, e.g. by melting together. **2** to reduce (a material) to a liquid or plastic state by heat; to melt (it). **3** to cause (e.g. a light bulb) to fail by fusing. **4** to equip (e.g. a plug) with an electrical fuse. ⪢ *verb intrans* **1** to become fluid with heat. **2** to become blended by, or as if by, melting together. **3** said of an electrical appliance: to fail because of the melting of a fuse. [Latin *fusus*, past part. of *fundere* to pour, melt]

fuse⁴ *noun* **1** an electrical safety device that includes a wire or strip of fusible metal that melts and interrupts the circuit when the current exceeds a particular value. **2** = CIRCUIT BREAKER.

fusee *or* **fuzee** /fyooh'zee/ *noun* **1** a conical spirally grooved pulley or wheel, *esp* in a watch or clock. **2** a match with a large head. **3** *NAmer* a red flare used as a warning signal. [French *fusée*, literally 'spindleful of yarn', ultimately from Latin *fusus* spindle]

fuselage /'fyoohzǝlahzh/ *noun* the central body portion of an aeroplane designed to accommodate the crew and the passengers or cargo. [French *fuselage* from *fuselé* spindle-shaped, ultimately from Latin *fusus* spindle]

fusel oil /'fyoohzl/ *noun* an acrid oily poisonous liquid consisting chiefly of amyl alcohol and used as a source of alcohols and as a solvent. [German *Fusel* bad liquor]

fusible /'fyoohzibl/ *adj* able, or easily able, to be fused or melted.

fusiform /'fyoohzifawm/ *adj* tapering towards each end: *fusiform bacteria*.

fusil /'fyoohzil/ *noun* a light flintlock musket. [French *fusil* steel for striking fire, from Old French *foisil*, from late Latin *focus* fire]

fusilier (*NAmer* **fusileer**) /fyoohzǝ'liǝ/ *noun* a member of a British regiment formerly armed with fusils. [French *fusilier* from *fusil*: see FUSIL]

fusillade¹ /fyoohzǝ'layd/ *noun* **1** a number of shots fired simultaneously or in rapid succession. **2** a spirited outburst, *esp* of criticism. [French *fusillade* from *fusiller* to shoot, from *fusil*: see FUSIL]

fusillade² *verb trans archaic* to attack (a place) or shoot down (a person) by a fusillade.

fusilli /fyooh'zili/ *pl noun* (*treated as sing. or pl*) spiral-shaped pasta. [Italian *fusilli* little spindles, ultimately from Latin *fusus* spindle]

fusion /'fyoohzh(ǝ)n/ *noun* **1** the act or process of fusing. **2** the union of light atomic nuclei to form heavier nuclei, resulting in the release of enormous quantities of energy. **3** a union formed when two things fuse; a merging. **4** a blend of two or more styles, e.g. in music, cookery, or design.

Editorial note ──────────
When jazz musicians began applying rock rhythms to their work, around 1970, the hybrid term jazz-rock was used to describe the results, but this subsequently gave way to the more all-embracing term 'fusion'. Besides this generic application, it has grown into a widely used epithet for virtually any amalgamation, induced or otherwise, of popular instrumental forms — Richard Cook.
──────────────────────────

[Latin *fusion-, fusio*, from *fundere* to pour, melt]

fusion bomb *noun* a bomb in which nuclei of a light chemical element, e.g. hydrogen, unite to form nuclei of heavier elements, e.g. helium, with a release of energy; *esp* a hydrogen bomb.

fuss¹ /fus/ *noun* **1** needless or useless bustle or excitement. **2a** a state of agitation, *esp* over a trivial matter. **b** an objection or protest. [perhaps imitative]

fuss² *verb intrans* **1** to pay close or undue attention to small details. **2** (*usu* + with) to keep touching or moving something anxiously or unnecessarily: *She fussed with her hair*. **3** to become upset; to worry. ⪢ *verb trans* to agitate or upset (somebody). ✳ **not fussed** *Brit, informal* with no strong feelings about something, *esp* a choice of alternatives; not bothered. ⪢⪢ **fusser** *noun*.

fusspot *noun informal* a person who fusses about trifles.

fussy *adj* (**fussier, fussiest**) **1a** showing too much concern over details. **b** fastidious: *not fussy about food*. **2** having too much or too detailed ornamentation. ⪢⪢ **fussily** *adv*, **fussiness** *noun*.

fustanella /fustǝ'nelǝ/ *noun* a white pleated skirt worn by Greek and Albanian men. [Italian *fustanella*, prob from *fustagno* fustian]

fustian /'fusti·ǝn, 'fuschǝn/ *noun* **1** a strong cotton or linen fabric, e.g. corduroy or moleskin, usu having a pile face and twill weave.

2 pretentious and banal writing or speech; bombast. ➤➤ **fustian** *adj*. [Middle English via Old French and medieval Latin from Latin *fustis* club]

fustic /'fustik/ *noun* **1** a tropical American tree of the fig family: *Maclura tinctoria*. **2** a yellow dye yielded by the wood of this tree. **3** the European sumac, which also yields dye: *Cotinus Coggygria*.

Word history
Middle English *fustik* via French and Arabic from Greek *pistakē* pistachio tree. Greek *pistakē* was transferred to the sumac, to which the pistachio is related, and thus to other plants yielding dye.

fusty /'fusti/ *adj* (**fustier, fustiest**) **1** stale or musty from being left undisturbed for a long time. **2** rigidly old-fashioned or reactionary. ➤➤ **fustily** *adv*, **fustiness** *noun*. [Middle English via French from Latin *fustis* cub]

futhark /'foohthahk/ *or* **futhorc** /'foothawk/ *or* **futhork** /'foohthawk/ *noun* the alphabet of runes used by early Germanic peoples. [from the first six letters, f, u, þ (th), o (or a), r, c (=k)]

futile /'fyoohtiel/ *adj* completely ineffective; pointless: *Our speculations are futile until we have all the facts* — Conan Doyle. ➤➤ **futilely** *adv*, **futility** /fyooh'tiliti/ *noun*. [via French from Latin *futilis* that pours out easily, leaky, useless, prob from *fundere* to pour]

futon /'foohton/ *noun* a thick padded quilt that is laid on the floor or on a frame to serve as a bed. [Japanese *futon*]

futtock /'futək/ *noun* any of the usu four or five curved timbers joined together to form the lower part of the compound ribs of a ship. [prob alteration of *foothook*]

future[1] /'fyoohchə/ *noun* **1a** (**the future**) time that is to come. **b** that which is going to occur. **2** a likelihood of success: *He didn't have any future as a cricketer*. **3a** in grammar, the future tense of a language. **b** a verb form in this tense. **4** (*in pl*) something, e.g. a bulk commodity, bought for future acceptance or sold for future delivery. ✳ **in future** from now on. ➤➤ **futureless** *adj*. [Middle English via Old French from Latin *futurus* about to be]

future[2] *adj* **1** that is to be. **2** of or constituting the future tense.

future perfect *noun* a verb tense, e.g. *will have finished*, expressing completion of an action at or before a future time.

futurism *noun* **1** (*often* **Futurism**) a movement in art, music, and literature begun in Italy about 1910 and seeking to express the dynamic energy and movement of mechanical processes. **2** a point of view that finds meaning or fulfilment in the future rather than in the past or present. ➤➤ **futurist** *noun and adj*.

futuristic /fyoohchə'ristik/ *adj* to do with a vision of the future; *esp* in being revolutionary or technologically advanced. ➤➤ **futuristically** *adv*.

futurity /fyooh'tyooəriti/ *noun* (*pl* **futurities**) **1** the future. **2** a future event or prospect. **3** *chiefly NAmer* a competition, *esp* a horse race, for which entries are made well in advance of the event.

futurology /fyoohchə'roləji/ *noun* the forecasting of the future from current trends in society. ➤➤ **futurologist** *noun*. [German *Futurologie*, from *futur* future + -O- + -*logie* -LOGY]

fu yong /,fooh 'yong/ *noun* see FOO YONG.

fuze /fyoohz/ *noun and verb trans NAmer* see FUSE[1] (2) and FUSE[2].

fuzee /fyooh'zee/ *noun* see FUSEE.

fuzz[1] /fuz/ *noun* **1** fine light particles or fibres, e.g. of down or fluff. **2** a blur. **3** a distortion in sound, e.g. on a radio. [prob back-formation from FUZZY]

fuzz[2] *verb intrans* said of hair: to become fuzzy or frizzy. ➤ *verb trans* to make (e.g. a picture) fuzzy or blurred.

fuzz[3] *noun* (**the fuzz**) *informal* the police.

fuzzy *adj* (**fuzzier, fuzziest**) **1** marked by or giving a suggestion of fuzz: *a fuzzy covering of felt*. **2** not clear; indistinct: *He had moved the camera and the photo was fuzzy*. ➤➤ **fuzzily** *adv*, **fuzziness** *noun*. [perhaps from Low German *fussig* loose, spongy]

fuzzy logic *noun* a system of logic that allows for degrees of uncertainty, rather than depending on absolute truth-values, and that is used to make human thought processes or imprecise information accessible to computers.

fuzzy-wuzzy /'wuzi/ *noun Brit, offensive* **1** a Sudanese soldier or tribesman encountered in the wars of the late 19th cent. **2** a black African. [reduplication of FUZZY; from the appearance of the hair]

FWD *or* **f.w.d.** *abbr* **1** four-wheel drive. **2** front-wheel drive.

fwd *abbr* forward.

f-word *noun euphem* the word 'fuck'.

FX *abbr* used in film-making: special effects.

-fy *or* **-ify** *suffix* forming verbs, with the meanings: **1** to become or cause to be: *purify*. **2** to fill with: *horrify*. **3** to give the characteristics of; to make similar to: *countrify*. **4** to engage in (a specified activity): *speechify*. [Middle English -*fien* via Old French from Latin -*ficare*, from -*ficus*: see -FIC]

fylfot /'filfot/ *noun* a swastika. [Middle English, denoting a device used to fill the lower part of a painted glass window, from *fillen* to fill + *fot* foot]

G¹ *or* **g** *noun (pl* **G's** *or* **Gs** *or* **g's*)* **1a** the seventh letter of the English alphabet. **b** a written character or design denoting this letter. **c** the sound represented by this letter, one of the English consonants. **2** an item designated as G, *esp* the seventh in a series. **3** in music, the fifth note of the diatonic scale of C major.

G² *abbr* **1** Gabon (international vehicle registration). **2** gauss. **3** German. **4** giga-. **5** *NAmer, informal* grand ($1000). **6** gravitational constant. **7** Gulf.

g *abbr* **1** gallon(s). **2** gas. **3** gauge. **4** gelding. **5** gram(s). **6** gravity, or acceleration due to gravity.

GA *abbr* **1** General Assembly. **2** Georgia (US postal abbreviation).

Ga¹ *abbr* Georgia (USA).

Ga² *abbr* the chemical symbol for gallium.

gab¹ /gab/ *verb intrans* (**gabbed, gabbing**) *informal* to chatter or blab. [prob short for GABBLE¹]

gab² *noun informal* idle talk.

gabardine /gabə'deen, 'gabədeen/ *noun* see GABERDINE.

gabble¹ /'gabl/ *verb intrans* to talk rapidly or unintelligibly; to jabber. ➤➤ **gabbler** *noun*. [prob imitative]

gabble² *noun* rapid or unintelligible talk.

gabbro /'gabroh/ *noun (pl* **gabbros**) a coarse-grained, dark-coloured igneous rock composed of a calcium-containing feldspar and iron and magnesium minerals. ➤➤ **gabbroic** /ga'broh·ik/ *adj*. [Italian *gabbro*, prob from Latin *glaber* smooth]

gabby /'gabi/ *adj* (**gabbier, gabbiest**) *informal* talkative or garrulous.

gaberdine *or* **gabardine** /gabə'deen, 'gabədeen/ *noun* **1** a firm durable fabric, e.g. of wool or rayon, woven with diagonal ribs on the right side. **2** *chiefly Brit* a waterproof coat made of gaberdine. **3** a coarse long coat or smock worn chiefly by Jews in medieval times: *You call me misbeliever, cut-throat dog, and spit upon my Jewish gaberdine* — Shakespeare. [early French *gaverdine*]

gabfest /'gabfest/ *noun* **1** *NAmer, informal* an informal gathering for conversation: *political gabfests*. **2** a prolonged conversation. [GAB² + FEST]

gabion /'gaybi·ən/ *noun* a hollow cylinder of wickerwork, iron, etc filled with earth and used in building fieldworks or as a support in mining. [early French via Old Italian from Latin *cavea*: see CAGE¹]

gable /'gaybl/ *noun* **1** the vertical triangular section of wall between two slopes of a pitched roof. **2** a triangular part used as a decoration over a window or door. ➤➤ **gabled** *adj*. [Middle English via Old French from Old Norse *gafle*]

gable end *noun* an end wall that has a gable at the top.

Gabonese /gabə'neez/ *noun (pl* **Gabonese**) a native or inhabitant of Gabon in West Africa. ➤➤ **Gabonese** *adj*.

gaboon /gə'boon/ *noun* a dark hardwood from a W African tree. [an alteration of *Gabon*, a republic in W central Africa]

gaboon viper *noun* a large venomous African snake: *Bitis gabonica*.

gaby /'gaybi/ *noun (pl* **gabies**) *chiefly Eng dialect* a person lacking common sense; a simpleton. [perhaps of Scandinavian origin]

gad¹ /gad/ *verb intrans* (**gadded, gadding**) (+ about/around) to go or travel in an aimless or restless manner or in search of pleasure. [Old English *gædeling* vagabond]

gad² ✴ **on the gad** *archaic* travelling about, especially in search of pleasure.

gad³ *interj archaic* used as a mild oath. [euphemism for GOD¹]

gadabout *noun informal* a person who goes from place to place in search of pleasure.

Gadarene /'gadəreen/ *adj* headlong or precipitate: *a Gadarene rush to the cities*. [from the demon-possessed *Gadarene* swine (Matthew 8:28) that rushed into the sea]

gadfly *noun (pl* **gadflies**) **1** any of various flies, e.g. a horsefly or botfly, that bite or annoy livestock. **2** a usu intentionally annoying person who stimulates or provokes others, *esp* by persistent irritating criticism. [obsolete *gad* metal spike, goad, rod, from Old Norse *gaddr* spike, sting]

gadget /'gajit/ *noun* a usu small and often novel mechanical or electronic device. ➤➤ **gadgetry** /-tri/ *noun*. [perhaps from French *gâchette* catch of a lock, trigger, dimin. of *gâche* staple, hook]

gadoid /'gaydoyd/ *noun* any of an order of soft-finned fishes including the cod and hake: order Gadiformes. ➤➤ **gadoid** *adj*. [Latin *Gadus*, genus of fishes, from Greek *gados* cod]

gadolinite /'gadəliniet/ *noun* a black or brown mineral that is a silicate of iron, beryllium, yttrium, and cerium. [German *Gadolinit*, named after Johann *Gadolin* d.1852, Finnish chemist who first identified it]

gadolinium /gadə'lini·əm/ *noun* a silvery metallic chemical element of the rare-earth group: symbol Gd, atomic number 64. [Latin *gadolinium*, named after J *Gadolin*: see GADOLINITE]

gadroon /gə'droohn/ *noun* an elaborately notched or indented convex moulding used in architecture and as a decoration on silverware. ➤➤ **gadrooning** *noun*. [French *godron* round plait, gadroon, from early French *goderon*, perhaps dimin. of Old French *godet* drinking cup]

gadwall /'gadwawl/ *noun (pl* **gadwalls** *or collectively* **gadwall**) a greyish brown duck about the size of a mallard: *Anas strepera*. [origin unknown]

gadzooks /gad'zooks/ *interj archaic* used as a mild oath. [perhaps alteration of *God's hooks*, i.e. the nails by which Christ was fixed to the cross]

Gael /gayl/ *noun* a Gaelic-speaking inhabitant of Scotland or Ireland. [Scottish Gaelic *Gaidheal* and Irish Gaelic *Gaedheal*]

Gaelic /'gaylik; *Scot* 'galik; *Irish* 'galik/ *noun* the Celtic languages of Ireland, the Isle of Man, and Scotland. ➤➤ **Gaelic** *adj.* [Scottish Gaelic *Gàidhlig*, Irish Gaelic *Gaeilge*, and Manx Gaelic *Gaelg*]

Gaelic coffee *noun* = IRISH COFFEE.

Gaelic football *noun* a football game played between teams of 15 players using a round football and a low net slung between rugby posts, in which the players score by kicking, punching, or bouncing the ball over the bar or into the net.

Gaeltacht /'gayltahkh/ *noun* the part of Ireland where native speakers of Irish Gaelic live. [Irish Gaelic *Gaedhealtacht*, from *Gaedheal* Gaelic]

gaff¹ /gaf/ *noun* **1a** a pole with a hook for holding or landing heavy fish. **b** a spear or spearhead for killing fish or turtles. **2** a spar on which the head of a fore-and-aft sail is extended. [French *gaffe* boat-hook, blunder, from Provençal *gaf* hook, from *gafar* to seize]

gaff² *verb trans* to strike or secure (e.g. a fish) with a gaff.

gaff³ *noun Brit, informal* a house, flat, or other dwelling place. [origin unknown]

gaff⁴ ✳ **blow the gaff** see BLOW¹. [origin unknown]

gaffe /gaf/ *noun* a social or tactical blunder; a faux pas: *A gaffe is when a politician tells the truth* — Michael Kinsley, US journalist. [French *gaffe*: see GAFF¹]

gaffer /'gafə/ *noun* **1** *Brit* the chief lighting electrician in a film or television studio. **2** *Brit, informal* a foreman or overseer. **3** *Brit, informal* an old man. [prob alteration of GODFATHER: compare GAMMER]

gag¹ /gag/ *verb* (**gagged, gagging**) ➤ *verb trans* **1** to apply a gag to or put a gag in the mouth of (somebody) to prevent speech. **2** to prevent (somebody) from having free speech or expression. ➤ *verb intrans* **1** to heave or retch. **2** to tell jokes. [Middle English *gaggen* to strangle, of imitative origin]

gag² *noun* **1** something thrust into the mouth to keep it open or prevent speech or outcry. **2** a joke or humorous story. **3** a check to free speech. **4** = CLOSURE¹ (3).

gaga /'gahgah/ *adj informal* **1** senile. **2** slightly mad. **3** (+ about) infatuated. [French *gaga*, imitating mumbled or incoherent speech]

gage¹ /gayj/ *noun archaic* **1** a token of defiance; *specif* a glove, cap, etc thrown on the ground in former times as a challenge to a fight. **2** something deposited as a pledge of performance. [Middle English from Old French, of Germanic origin]

gage² *verb trans archaic* to pledge (something) as a gage.

gage³ *noun NAmer* see GAUGE¹.

gage⁴ *verb trans NAmer* see GAUGE².

gage⁵ *noun* a greengage.

gaggle¹ /'gagl/ *noun* **1** a flock of geese. **2** *informal* a typically noisy or talkative group or cluster. [Middle English *gagyll*, from *gagelen* to cackle, of imitative origin]

gaggle² *verb intrans* said of geese: to cackle.

Gaia /'gie·ə/ *noun* the earth and all living things on it considered as an organic whole, with the different parts interacting to promote survival and stability. [Greek *gaia* earth, named after *Gaia*, the Greek goddess of the earth]

gaiety /'gayiti/ *noun* (*pl* **gaieties**) **1** the quality of being cheerful, merry, or bright. **2** merrymaking; festive activity. [French *gaieté* from *gai* GAY¹]

gaillardia /gay'lahdi·ə/ *noun* a plant of the daisy family with showy flowers that have a purple centre surrounded by yellow, reddish orange, or white: genus *Gaillardia*. [Latin genus name, named after *Gaillard* de Marentonneau, 18th-cent. French botanist]

gaily /'gayli/ *adv* **1** cheerfully or merrily. **2** with bright colours.

gain¹ /gayn/ *verb trans* **1** to get possession of or win (something good), usu by industry, merit, or craft. **2a** to increase a lead over or catch up a rival by (*esp* time or distance): *He gained 35 metres on the third lap*. **b** to get (something) by a natural development or process: *I began to gain strength*. **c** to acquire (something): *You won't gain any friends that way*. **d** to arrive at (a place): *We gained the river that night*. **3** to increase in (e.g. speed): *You gain momentum as you come down the hill*. **4** said of a watch or clock: to run too fast by (an amount): *The clock gains a minute a day*. ➤ *verb intrans* **1** to get advantage; to

profit: *He hoped to gain from his crime*. **2** to increase, *esp* in weight. **3** said of a watch or clock: to run fast.

gain² *noun* **1** resources or advantage acquired or increased; a profit. **2** the obtaining of profit or possessions. **3a** an increase in amount, magnitude, or degree: *a gain in efficiency*. **b** the ratio of output power to input power in an amplifier. [Middle English *gayne* from Old French *gaaigne, gaaing*, from *gaaignier* to till, earn, gain, of Germanic origin]

gainer *noun* **1** a person or thing that gains. **2** a type of dive in which the diver leaves the board facing forwards, does a backward somersault, and enters the water feet first.

gainful /'gaynf(ə)l/ *adj* profitable: *gainful employment*. ➤➤ **gainfully** *adv*.

gainsay *verb trans* (*third person sing. present* **gainsays,** *past tense and past part.* **gainsaid**) *formal* to deny or dispute (e.g. an allegation). ➤➤ **gainsayer** *noun*. [Middle English *gainsayen*, from *gain-* against (from Old English *gēan-*) + *sayen* to SAY¹]

'gainst *or* **gainst** /gaynst/ *prep literary* against. [short for AGAINST¹]

gait¹ /gayt/ *noun* **1** a manner of walking or moving on foot. **2** a sequence of foot movements, e.g. a walk, trot, or canter, by which a horse moves forwards. [Scots variant of Middle English *gate* path, way, way of doing something, from Old Norse *gata*]

gait² *verb trans* to train (a horse) to use a particular gait or set of gaits.

gaiter *noun* (*usu in pl*) **1** formerly, a cloth or leather legging worn by men to protect the hose from mud splashes, etc, usu buttoned on the outside, retained only in certain types of formal wear, e.g. that of bishops: *Mr Knightley was hard at work upon the lower buttons of his thick leather gaiters* — Jane Austen; *I see already his muscular calves encased in the gaiters episcopal* — Somerset Maugham. **2** formerly, an ankle boot or overshoe for women, with a fabric upper. **3** a climber's legging of tough nylon canvas for the lower leg and boot upper, for preventing snow from getting into the top of the boots. [French *guêtre* from early French *guestre, guiestre*, prob of Germanic origin]

gaiter boot *noun* = GAITER (2).

Gal. *abbr* Galatians (book of the Bible).

gal¹ /gal/ *noun informal* a girl. [by alteration]

gal² *noun* a unit of acceleration equivalent to one centimetre per second per second. [named after *Galileo* Galilei d.1642, Italian astronomer and physicist]

gal. *abbr* see GALL.

gala /'gahlə/ *noun* **1** a festive gathering, *esp* one that marks a special occasion. **2** *Brit* a special sports meeting: *a swimming gala*. **3** (*used before a noun*) marking or being a special occasion: *a gala performance*. [Italian *gala* from early French *gale* merrymaking, festivity, pleasure]

galactic /gə'laktik/ *adj* of a galaxy, *esp* the Milky Way galaxy. [from Greek *galakt-, gala* milk]

galactic equator *noun* the circle of the celestial sphere lying in the plane that bisects the band of the Milky Way.

galactic halo *noun* in astronomy, an almost spherical mass of stars, globular clusters, dust, and gas surrounding a galaxy.

galactose /gə'laktohz, -tohs/ *noun* a sugar that is less soluble and less sweet than glucose. [French *galactose*, ultimately from Greek *gala, galaktos* milk]

galago /gə'laygoh/ *noun* (*pl* **galagos**) = BUSH BABY. [Latin genus name, perhaps from Wolof *golokh* monkey]

galah /gə'lah/ *noun* **1** an Australian cockatoo with a rose-coloured breast and a grey back, kept as a cage bird but seen as a pest in wheat-growing areas: *Eulophus roseicapillus*. **2** *Aus, informal* a fool or simpleton. [from Yuwaalaraay (an Aboriginal language) *gilaa*]

Galahad /'galəhad/ *noun* a noble or chivalrous person. [named after Sir *Galahad*, one of King Arthur's knights]

galangal /'galənggal/ *or* **galingale** /'galinggayl/ *noun* a plant of the ginger family with an aromatic rhizome used in Asian cookery: genera *Alpinia* and *Kaempferia*. [Middle English *galingale* via Old French from Arabic *kalanjān*, perhaps from Chinese *gaoliangjiang*, from *Gaoliang*, a Chinese district + *jiang* ginger]

galantine /'galənteen/ *noun* a cold dish of boned and usu stuffed cooked meat glazed with aspic. [French *galantine* via Old French from late Latin *galatina*, prob from Latin *gelatus*, past part. of *gelare* to freeze, congeal]

Galatian /gəˈlaysh(ə)n/ *noun* a native or inhabitant of Galatia, an ancient Roman province in Asia Minor. ▶▶ **Galatian** *adj*.

galaxy /ˈgaləksi/ *noun* (*pl* **galaxies**) **1a** a system composed chiefly of stars, dust, and gas. **b** (**the Galaxy**) the Milky Way. **2** an assemblage of brilliant or notable people or things. [Middle English *galaxie, galaxias* via late Latin from Greek *galaxia* milky, from *galakt-, gala* milk]

galbanum /ˈgalbənəm/ *noun* a yellowish aromatic gum resin obtained from any of several Asian plants, formerly used for medicinal purposes and in incense. [Middle English via Latin from Greek *chalbanē*, from Hebrew *ḥelbēnāh*]

gale /gayl/ *noun* **1** a strong wind; *specif* a wind having a speed of 50 to 102km/h (32 to 63mph). **2** a noisy outburst of laughter. [origin unknown]

galea /ˈgayli·ə/ *noun* (*pl* **galeae** /ˈgayli·ee/ *or* **galeas**) a botanical or anatomical part shaped like a helmet. ▶▶ **galeate** /-ayt/ *adj*, **galeated** /-aytid/ *adj*. [Latin *galea* helmet]

galena /gəˈleenə/ *noun* lead sulphide occurring as a bluish grey mineral: formula PbS. [Latin *galena* lead ore]

Galenic /gəˈlenik/ *adj* of or being the medical methods or principles of Galen, a Greek physician and writer of the second cent. ▶▶ **Galenical** *adj*.

galette /gəˈlet/ *noun* a type of savoury pancake. [French *galette* from Old French *galete*, from *galet* pebble]

Galibi /gəˈleebi/ *noun* (*pl* **Galibis** *or collectively* **Galibi**) **1** a member of a Carib people inhabiting French Guiana. **2** the language spoken by these people. [Carib *galibi* strong man]

Galician /gəˈlishən/ *noun* **1** a native or inhabitant of Galicia, a region of Spain. **2** the Romance language of the Spanish Galicians. **3** a native or inhabitant of Galicia, a region now in Poland and the Ukraine. ▶▶ **Galician** *adj*.

Galilean /galəˈlayən, -ˈlee·ən/ *adj* of or developed by Galileo Galilei. [from *Galileo* Galilei d.1642, Italian physicist and astronomer]

galilee /ˈgalilee/ *noun* a chapel or porch at the entrance of a church. [via Anglo-French from late Latin *galilaea* Galilee; so called because it was at the furthest point from the altar, as Galilee was the furthest province from Jerusalem]

galingale /ˈgalinggayl/ *noun* **1** a sedge with an aromatic root: *Cyperus longus*. **2** see GALANGAL. [Middle English, in the sense 'a kind of ginger': see GALANGAL]

galiot /ˈgali·ət/ *noun* see GALLIOT.

galipot /ˈgalipot/ *noun* a crude turpentine oleoresin obtained from a S European pine. [French *galipot*]

gall[1] /gawl/ *noun* **1** brazen and insolent audacity; impudence. **2a** *archaic* bile. **b** something bitter to endure. **c** rancour or bitterness. [Old English *gealla* bile]

gall[2] *noun* **1** a cause or state of exasperation. **2** a skin sore caused by rubbing. [Old English *gealla* and early Low German *galle* sore]

gall[3] *verb trans* **1** to cause feelings of mortification and irritation in (somebody); to vex (them) acutely: *a great mind like his, cramped and galled by narrow circumstances* — James Boswell. **2** to wear (something) away by rubbing; to chafe (it).

gall[4] *noun* a diseased swelling of plant tissue produced by infection with fungi, insect parasites, etc. [Middle English via French *galle* from Latin *galla*]

gall. *or* **gal.** *abbr* gallon(s).

gallant[1] /ˈgalənt/ *adj* **1** nobly chivalrous and brave. **2** /ˈgalənt, gəˈlant/ courteously and elaborately attentive, *esp* to women. **3** splendid or stately: *a gallant ship*. **4** *archaic* showy in dress. ▶▶ **gallantly** *adv*. [Middle English *galaunt* from early French *galant*, present part. of *galer* to have a good time, from *gale* pleasure, of Germanic origin]

gallant[2] /ˈgalənt, gəˈlant/ *noun* a man of fashion who is particularly attentive to women.

gallant[3] /ˈgalənt, gəˈlant/ *verb trans archaic* said of a man: to flirt with (a woman).

gallantry /ˈgaləntri/ *noun* (*pl* **gallantries**) **1** spirited and conspicuous bravery. **2a** an act of marked courtesy. **b** courteous attention to a lady. **3** (*in pl*) gallant words or actions.

gall bladder *noun* a membranous muscular sac in which bile from the liver is stored.

galleass /ˈgalias/ *noun* a large fast warship equipped with both oars and sails and used *esp* in the 16th and 17th cents. [early French *galeasse* via Old Italian *galeazza* from late Greek *galea* galley]

galleon /ˈgali·ən/ *noun* a heavy square-rigged sailing ship of the 15th cent. to early 18th cent. used for war or commerce. [Old Spanish *galeón* via Old French from medieval Latin *galea*: see GALLEY]

gallery /ˈgaləri/ *noun* (*pl* **galleries**) **1a** a room or building devoted to the exhibition of works of art. **b** an institution or business exhibiting or dealing in works of art. **2** a balcony projecting from one or more interior walls of a hall, auditorium, or church, to accommodate additional people, or reserved for musicians, singers, etc. **3** the occupants of a balcony, e.g. in a theatre. **4** the spectators at a golf or tennis tournament match. **5** a long and narrow passage, room, or corridor: *a shooting gallery*. **6** a horizontal subterranean passage in a cave or military mining system. ✳ **play to the gallery** to act in a way calculated to win popular support or approval. ▶▶ **galleried** *adj*. [early French *galerie* from late Latin *galeria*, prob alteration of *galilea, galilaea* GALILEE]

galley /ˈgali/ *noun* (*pl* **galleys**) **1** a large low usu single-decked ship propelled by oars and sails and used in the Mediterranean in the Middle Ages and in classical antiquity. **2** a large rowing boat. **3** a kitchen on a ship or aircraft. **4** in printing: **a** a long oblong tray with upright sides for holding set type. **b** a proof in the form of a long sheet taken from type on a galley. [Middle English *galeie* via Old French from medieval Latin *galea*, from early Greek]

galley proof *noun* = GALLEY (4B).

galley slave *noun* **1** a slave or criminal forced to act as an oarsman on a galley ship. **2** somebody who has to do menial work; a drudge.

gallfly *noun* (*pl* **gallflies**) any of several insects that produce galls by laying their eggs in plant tissues.

galliard /ˈgalyəd/ *noun* a lively dance in triple time that was popular in the 16th cent. [Old French *gaillarde*, fem of *gaillard* lively, valiant, prob of Celtic origin]

Gallic /ˈgalik/ *adj* of or characteristic of Gaul or France. [Latin *Gallicus*, from *Gallia*: see GAUL]

gallic acid /ˈgalik/ *noun* an acid found widely in plants and used in dyes, inks, and as a photographic developer: formula $C_7H_6O_5$. [French *gallique*, from *galle*: see GALL[4]]

Gallicise /ˈgalisiez/ *verb trans* see GALLICIZE.

Gallicism /ˈgalisiz(ə)m/ *noun* a characteristic French word or expression occurring in another language.

Gallicize *or* **Gallicise** /ˈgalisiez/ *verb trans* to cause (somebody or something) to conform to a French mode or idiom.

galligaskins /galiˈgaskinz/ *pl noun Brit* loose wide trousers or breeches, worn formerly by men. [prob modification of early French *garguesques* via Old Spanish or Italian from Latin *Graecus*: see GREEK[1]]

gallimaufry /galiˈmawfri/ *noun* (*pl* **gallimaufries**) a medley or jumble. [early French *galimafree* hash]

gallinacean /galiˈnayshən/ *noun* a gallinaceous bird.

gallinaceous /galiˈnayshəs/ *adj* of an order of birds including the pheasants, turkeys, grouse, and the common domestic fowl, which have heavy bodies and live mainly on the ground: order Galliformes. [Latin *gallinaceus* of domestic fowl, from *gallina* hen, from *gallus* cock]

galling /ˈgawling/ *adj* markedly irritating or vexing; deeply mortifying. ▶▶ **gallingly** *adv*.

gallinule /ˈgalinyoohl/ *noun* **1** any of several species of aquatic birds of the rail family with dark plumage and long thin toes; *esp* the purple gallinule: *Porphyrula martinica* and other species. **2** *NAmer* a moorhen: *Gallinula chloropus* and other species. [Latin *Gallinula* genus name, literally 'little hen', from *gallina*: see GALLINACEOUS]

galliot *or* **galiot** /ˈgali·ət/ *noun* **1** a small swift galley ship formerly used in the Mediterranean. **2** a long narrow Dutch merchant sailing ship that can be floated in shallow water. [Middle English *galiote* via French or Dutch from late Latin *galeota*, dimin. of *galea*: see GALLEY]

gallipot /ˈgalipot/ *noun* a small usu ceramic vessel formerly used to hold medicines, e.g. ointments. [Middle English *galy pott*, prob from *galy, galeie* galley + *pott* pot; because they were imported in galleys]

gallium /'gali·əm/ *noun* a rare bluish white metallic chemical element that is soft and melts just above room temperature, and occurs naturally in zinc and aluminium ores and in germanite: symbol Ga, atomic number 31. [Latin *gallium* from *gallus* cock, intended as translation of Paul *Lecoq* de Boisbaudran d.1912, French chemist, who first discovered it]

gallivant /'galivant/ *verb intrans* to travel energetically or roam about for pleasure. [perhaps alteration of GALLANT² used to mean 'to act like a gallant, flirt']

galliwasp /'galiwosp/ *noun* any of several species of lizards found in the Caribbean and Central America: *Diploglossus monotropis* and other species. [origin unknown]

gall mite *noun* any of various tiny four-legged mites that form galls on plants: family Eriophyidae.

gallnut *noun* a plant gall that has a rounded shape resembling a nut.

Gallo- *comb. form* forming words, denoting: France or the French: *Gallophile.* [Latin *Gallus* a Gaul]

gallon /'galən/ *noun* **1** a unit of liquid capacity equal to eight pints (about 4.546l). **2** a unit of liquid capacity in the USA equal to 0.83 imperial gallon (3.79l). **3** *informal* (*in pl*) large quantities. ⨠ **gallonage** /-nij/ *noun.* [Middle English *galon* via French from late Latin *galeta* pail, a liquid measure]

galloon /gə'loohn/ *noun* a narrow lace or braid trimming for dresses. [French *galon* from Old French *galonner* to adorn with braid]

gallop¹ /'galəp/ *noun* **1** a fast bounding gait of a quadruped; *specif* the fastest natural four-beat gait of the horse. **2** a ride or run at a gallop. **3** *Brit* a stretch of grass where racehorses are exercised. [early French *galop* variant of *walop*: see WALLOP¹]

gallop² *verb* (**galloped, galloping**) ⨠ *verb intrans* **1** to go or ride at a gallop. **2** to read, talk, or proceed at great speed. ⨠ *verb trans* to make (a horse) ride at a gallop. ⨠ **galloper** *noun,* **galloping** *adj.*

Galloway /'galəway/ *noun* an animal of a breed of hardy chiefly black beef cattle native to SW Scotland. [named after *Galloway*, district of SW Scotland]

gallows /'galohz/ *noun* (*pl* **gallows** *or* **gallowses**) **1** a frame, usu of two upright posts and a crosspiece, for hanging criminals. **2** (**the gallows**) the punishment of hanging. [Old English *gealga*]

gallows bird *noun archaic, informal* a person who deserves hanging.

gallows humour *noun* grim humour that makes fun of a very serious or terrifying situation.

gallows tree *noun* = GALLOWS (1).

gallsickness *noun* a disease affecting the livers of cattle and sheep.

gallstone *noun* a rounded solid mass of cholesterol and calcium salts formed in the gall bladder or bile ducts.

Gallup poll /'galəp/ *noun* a survey of public opinion used as a means of forecasting something, e.g. an election result. [named after George *Gallup* d.1984, US public opinion statistician, who devised it]

gall wasp *noun* any of various wasps whose larvae produce plant galls in which they feed: family Cynipidae.

galoot /gə'looht/ *noun NAmer, informal* somebody who is foolish or uncouth. [origin unknown]

galop /'galəp/ *noun* a lively dance in duple time. [French *galop*: see GALLOP¹]

galore /gə'law/ *adj* (*used after a noun*) abundant or plentiful: *bargains galore.* [Irish Gaelic *go leor* enough]

galosh /gə'losh/ *noun* a rubber overshoe. [Middle English *galoche* clog, patten, via Old French from late Latin *gallicula*, dimin. of Latin *gallica solea* Gaulish shoe]

galumph /gə'lumf/ *verb intrans informal* to stride along or bound around with exuberant din: *He left it dead, and with its head he went galumphing back* — Lewis Carroll. ⨠ **galumphing** *adj.* [prob from GALLOP² + TRIUMPHANT; coined by Lewis Carroll d.1898, English writer]

galvanic /gal'vanik/ *adj* **1** of, being, or producing a direct current of electricity resulting from chemical action. **2** having an electric effect; stimulating vigorous activity or vitality. ⨠ **galvanically** *adv.*

galvanise /'galvəniez/ *verb trans* see GALVANIZE.

galvanism /'galvəniz(ə)m/ *noun* **1** direct electric current produced by chemical action. **2** the therapeutic use of such a current, e.g. in the removal of birthmarks. [French *galvanisme* from Italian *galvanismo*, named after Luigi *Galvani* d.1798, Italian physician and physicist, who first described it]

galvanize *or* **galvanise** /'galvəniez/ *verb trans* **1** to stimulate, rouse, or excite (somebody) as if by the action of an electric current: *The candidate galvanized his supporters into action.* **2** to coat (iron or steel) with zinc as a protection from rust. ⨠ **galvanization** /-'zaysh(ə)n/ *noun,* **galvanizer** *noun.*

galvanized iron *noun* iron coated with a protective layer of zinc.

galvanometer /galvə'nomitə/ *noun* an instrument for detecting or measuring a small electric current. ⨠ **galvanometric** /-'metrik/ *adj.*

gam /gam/ *noun informal* a leg. [prob from early French *gambe* from late Latin *gamba*: see GAMBIT]

Gamay /'gamay/ *noun* **1** a variety of grape used in the production of red wine, *esp* Beaujolais. **2** a wine produced from this grape. [named after *Gamay*, village in E France]

Gambian /'gambi·ən/ *noun* a native or inhabitant of Gambia, a country in W Africa. ⨠ **Gambian** *adj.*

gambier /'gambi·ə/ *noun* an astringent substance from a Malayan woody climbing plant, used in tanning. [Malay *gambir*]

gambit /'gambit/ *noun* **1** a calculated move; a stratagem. **2** a remark intended to start a conversation or make a telling point. **3** a chess opening, *esp* one in which a player risks minor pieces to gain an advantage. [Italian *gambetto* act of tripping someone, from *gamba* leg, via late Latin *gamba, camba* from Greek *kampē* bend]

gamble¹ /'gambl/ *verb* ⨠ *verb intrans* **1a** to play a game of chance for money or property. **b** to bet or risk something on an uncertain outcome: *Women's total instinct for gambling is satisfied by marriage* — Gloria Steinem. **2** to take on a business risk with the expectation of gain; to speculate. ⨠ *verb trans* **1** to risk (e.g. money) by gambling; to wager (it). **2** to venture or hazard (something). ⨠ **gambler** *noun.* [obsolete *gamel* to play, or its source, GAME²]

gamble² *noun* **1** something involving an element of risk. **2** the playing of a game of chance for stakes.

gamboge /gam'bohj, gam'boozh/ *noun* a gum resin from some SE Asian trees, used as a yellow pigment. [Latin *gambogium*, alteration of *cambugium*, named after *Cambodia*, country of SE Asia from which it was obtained]

gambol¹ /'gambl/ *verb intrans* (**gambolled, gambolling,** *NAmer* **gamboled, gamboling**) to skip or leap about in play. [modification of early French *gambade* spring of a horse, gambol, prob via Old Provençal from late Latin *gamba, camba*: see GAMBIT]

gambol² *noun* a skipping or leaping about in play.

gambrel /'gambrəl/ *noun* **1** *Brit* a roof that has sloping ends and sides, and a ridge in a small vertical triangular gable at each end. **2** *NAmer* a roof that has two sides with a double slope, with the lower slope steeper than the upper one. **3** the hock of an animal. [early French *gamberel* crooked stick used to hang animal carcasses, from *gambe* leg, from late Latin *gamba*: see GAMBIT]

gambrel roof *noun* = GAMBREL (1), (2).

game¹ /gaym/ *noun* **1** an activity engaged in for diversion or amusement. **2** a physical or mental competition conducted according to rules with the participants in direct opposition to each other. **3** a division of a larger contest. **4** the number of points necessary to win a game. **5** (*often* **Games**) organized sports, *esp* athletics. **6** the equipment used for a particular game. **7** a computer game. **8a** a course or plan consisting of manoeuvres directed towards some end: *They're playing a waiting game.* **b** a specified type of activity seen as competitive or governed by rules, and pursued for financial gain: *the newspaper game.* **9** a situation that involves contest, rivalry, or struggle: *I got into microelectronics early in the game.* **10** *Brit* (*in pl*) a school lesson in which a sport is taught or played. **11a** animals under pursuit or taken in hunting; *esp* wild mammals, birds, and fish hunted for sport or food. **b** the edible flesh of game animals, e.g. deer and pheasant. ✳ **on the game** *Brit, informal* working as a prostitute. **the game is up** the crime, plot, etc has been discovered or exposed. [Old English *gamen* amusement, fun]

game² *verb intrans* **1** to play for money; to gamble. **2** to play computer games. [Old English *gamenian* to play, from *gamen* GAME¹]

game³ *adj* **1** ready to take risks or try something new: *She was game for anything.* **2** having a resolute unyielding spirit: *He was game to the end.* ⟫⟫ **gamely** *adv*, **gameness** *noun*. [GAME¹]

game⁴ *adj* said of somebody's leg: injured, crippled, or lame. [orig in the sense of 'bad, false'; perhaps from GAME³]

gamecock *noun* a male domestic fowl of a strain developed for cockfighting.

game fish *noun* any fish sought by anglers for sport, e.g. salmon, trout, and whitefish.

gamekeeper *noun* somebody who has charge of the breeding and protection of game animals or birds on a private estate.

gamelan /'gamilan/ *noun* a flute, string, and percussion orchestra of SE Asia. [Javanese *gamelan*]

game laws *pl noun* laws dealing with the protection and hunting of game.

game plan *noun* **1** *NAmer* the strategy adopted by a team in a match. **2** a strategy for winning a game or achieving an objective by a series of steps, e.g. in politics.

game point *noun* a situation in tennis, badminton, etc in which one player or side will win the game by winning the next point.

gamesmanship *noun* the art or practice of winning games by means other than superior skill without actually violating the rules.

gamesome /'gayms(ə)m/ *adj* merry or frolicsome. ⟫⟫ **gamesomely** *adv*, **gamesomeness** *noun*.

gamester /'gaymstə/ *noun* somebody who plays games, *esp* a gambler.

gamet- *or* **gameto-** *comb. form* forming words, denoting: gamete: *gametophyte.* [Latin, from *gameta*: see GAMETE]

gametangium /gami'tanji·əm/ *noun* (*pl* **gametangia** /-ji·ə/) a plant organ in which gametes are developed. [scientific Latin *gametangium*, from GAMET- + Greek *angeion* vessel]

gamete /'gameet, gə'meet/ *noun* a mature germ cell with a single set of chromosomes, capable of fusing with another gamete of the other sex to form a zygote from which a new organism develops. ⟫⟫ **gametic** /gə'metik/ *adj*. [Latin *gameta* from Greek *gametēs* husband, from *gamein* to marry, from *gamos* marriage]

gamete intrafallopian transfer *noun* a technique for the treatment of infertile women, in which eggs and sperm from the prospective parents are injected, by means of a catheter, into the fallopian tubes where fertilization can occur naturally.

game theory *noun* the rigorous analysis of strategy, e.g. in a business or military situation, where there is a conflict of interest.

gameto- *comb. form* see GAMET-.

gametocyte /gə'meetohsiet/ *noun* a cell that divides to produce gametes.

gametogenesis /,gamitoh'jenəsis/ *noun* the production of gametes. ⟫⟫ **gametogenic** *adj*, **gametogeny** /-'tojəni/ *noun*.

gametophyte /gə'meetohfiet/ *noun* the haploid phase of a plant of a species that exhibits alternation of generations, e.g. a moss or fern, which develops from asexual spores and bears sex organs that produce the gametes. ⟫⟫ **gametophytic** /-'fitik/ *adj*.

gamey *adj* see GAMY.

gamin /'gamin (*French* gamɛ̃)/ *noun* a street urchin. [French *gamin* urchin]

gamine /'gameen (*French* gamin)/ *noun* a girl or woman having an elfin impish appeal. ⟫⟫ **gamine** *adj*. [French *gamine*, fem of *gamin* urchin]

gaming /'gayming/ *noun* **1** the practice of gambling. **2** the playing of games that simulate actual conditions, e.g. of business or war, *esp* for training or testing purposes.

gamma /'gamə/ *noun* **1** the third letter of the Greek alphabet (Γ, γ), equivalent to and transliterated as roman g. **2** the third item in a series. [Middle English via late Latin from Greek, of Semitic origin; related to Hebrew *gīmel*, third letter of the Hebrew alphabet]

gamma globulin *noun* any of several immunoglobulins in blood or serum including most antibodies.

gamma radiation *noun* radiation composed of gamma rays.

gamma rays *pl noun* streams of high-energy electromagnetic radiation that have a shorter wavelength than X-rays and are emitted in the radioactive decay of some unstable atomic nuclei.

gammer /'gamə/ *noun dialect, archaic* an old woman. [prob alteration of GODMOTHER: compare GAFFER]

gammon¹ /'gamən/ *noun* **1** ham that has been smoked or cured. **2** the lower end of a side of bacon, removed from the carcass after curing with salt: compare HAM¹. [early French *gambon* ham, augmentative of *gambe* leg, from late Latin *gamba*: see GAMBIT]

gammon² *noun* in backgammon, the winning of a game before the loser removes any men from the board. [perhaps alteration of Middle English *gamen* GAME¹]

gammon³ *verb trans* (**gammoned, gammoning**) in backgammon, to beat (an opponent) by scoring a gammon.

gammon⁴ *noun Brit, informal, dated* nonsense or humbug: *Hold your peace, and don't bother our game with your gammon* — Scott. [obsolete *gammon* to talk, perhaps from Middle English *gamen* GAME¹]

gammon⁵ *verb trans* (**gammoned, gammoning**) *Brit, informal, dated* to deceive or fool (somebody).

gammy /'gami/ *adj* (**gammier, gammiest**) *Brit, informal* said of somebody's leg: injured or lame. [prob irreg from GAME⁴ + -Y¹]

gamopetalous /gamoh'petələs/ *adj* said of a flower: having petals that are united to form a tube, as in the primrose or primula. [Latin *gamopetalus*, from Greek *gamos* marriage + *petalus* PETALOUS]

-gamous *comb. form* see -GAMY.

gamp /gamp/ *noun Brit, informal* a large umbrella. [named after Sarah *Gamp*, a nurse with a large umbrella in the novel *Martin Chuzzlewit* by Charles Dickens d.1870, English writer]

gamut /'gamət/ *noun* **1** an entire range or series: *She ran the whole gamut of the emotions from A to B* — Dorothy Parker. **2** the whole series of recognized musical notes.

Word history

late Latin *gamma ut*, lowest note in medieval scale of music, from *gamma*, applied to the lowest note G on the bass clef + *ut*, applied to the first note of a hexachord, the notes of which were named after syllables of a Latin hymn: Ut *queant laxis resonare fibris* Mira *gestorum* famuli tuorum, Solve polluti labii reatum, Sancte Johannes. In the 18th cent. DOH replaced *ut*, SOH replaced *sol*, and another note, named *si* from the initials of *Sancte Johannes*, was added to the scale; *si* was later changed to TE to avoid having two notes with the same initial letter. In the 20th cent. *me* became a common spelling for MI¹, reflecting its pronunciation.

gamy *or* **gamey** /'gaymi/ *adj* (**gamier, gamiest**) having the strong flavour or smell of game that has been hung until high. ⟫⟫ **gaminess** *noun*.

-gamy *comb. form* forming nouns, denoting: marriage: *polygamy*. ⟫⟫ **-gamous** *comb. form*. [Middle English *-gamie* via late Latin from Greek, from *gamos* marriage]

ganache /gə'nash/ *noun* a creamy chocolate-flavoured cake filling or icing. [French *ganache*, literally 'jaw', ultimately from Greek *gnathos*]

gander¹ /'gandə/ *noun* an adult male goose. [Old English *gandra*]

gander² *noun informal* a look or glance: *talking and taking ganders at the girls* — Life. [prob from GANDER¹; from the outstretched neck of a person craning to look at something]

Gandhian /'gandi·ən/ *adj* of or relating to the Indian leader Mahatma Gandhi (d.1948) or his principle of nonviolent protest.

gang¹ /gang/ *noun* **1** a group of people associating for criminal or disreputable ends. **2** a group of people working together, e.g. as labourers. **3** a group of adolescents who spend leisure time together. **4** a series of switches or devices arranged to act together. [Old English *gang* a journey, going, from Old Norse *gangr, ganga*. The current sense comes from the idea of people going around together]

gang² *verb intrans* (+ together) to move or act as a gang: *The children ganged together and made the new boy feel left out.* ⟫ **verb trans** to assemble or operate (e.g. mechanical parts) simultaneously as a group.

gang³ *verb intrans Scot* to go. [Old English *gangan*; related to Old English *gang* GANG¹]

gang-bang *noun coarse slang* **1** the rape of somebody by a succession of men on one occasion. **2** sexual intercourse involving several people; an orgy.

ganger *noun Brit* the foreman of a gang of labourers.

gangland *noun* the world of organized crime; the criminal underworld.

ganglia /'ganggli·ə/ *noun* pl of GANGLION.

gangling /'ganggling/ *adj* tall, thin, and awkward in movement: *a gangling gawky child*. [perhaps irreg from Scot *gangrel* vagrant, lanky person]

ganglion /'ganggli·ən/ *noun* (*pl* **ganglia** /-gli·ə/ *or* **ganglions**) **1a** a small cyst on a joint membrane or tendon sheath. **b** a mass of nerve cells outside the brain or spinal cord. **2** a focus of strength, energy, or activity. ⟫ **ganglionic** /-'onik/ *adj*. [late Latin from Greek *ganglion* tumour, nerve centre]

ganglioside /'ganggliəsied/ *noun* any of a group of sugar-containing fatty chemical compounds found in nerve tissue. [GANGLION + -OSE² + -IDE]

gangly /'ganggli/ *adj* = GANGLING.

gangplank *noun* a movable board or plank used to board a ship from a quay or another ship.

gangrene¹ /'ganggreen/ *noun* death of soft tissues in a localized area of the body, due to loss of blood supply. ⟫ **gangrenous** /'ganggrinəs/ *adj*. [via Latin from Greek *gangraina*]

gangrene² *verb intrans* to become gangrenous.

gang saw *noun* a saw with several blades fitted in a frame, used in a timber mill.

gangsta /'gangstə/ *noun NAmer, slang* **1** a member of a black street gang. **2** a kind of rap music, often with lyrics about gang warfare and fighting. [alteration of GANGSTER]

gangster /'gangstə/ *noun* a member of a criminal gang. ⟫ **gangsterism** *noun*.

gangue /gang/ *noun* the worthless part of an ore. [French *gangue* from German *Gang* course, vein of metal, from Old High German *gang* act of going]

gang up *verb intrans* (*often* + on/against) to combine as a group for a specific purpose, *esp* a disreputable one.

gangway¹ *noun* **1** a passageway; *esp* a temporary way constructed from planks. **2a** the opening in a ship's side or rail through which the ship is boarded. **b** a gangplank. **c** a ladder or stairway slung over a ship's side, used for boarding. **3** *Brit* a narrow passage between sections of seats in a theatre, storage bays in a warehouse, etc.

gangway² *interj* used when trying to make one's way round an obstacle: make way!

ganister *or* **gannister** /'ganistə/ *noun* a fine-grained quartz used for furnace linings. [origin unknown]

ganja /'ganjə/ *noun* cannabis. [Hindi *gāmjā* from Sanskrit *gañjā*]

gannet /'ganit/ *noun* **1** any of several species of large white fish-eating seabirds, breeding in large colonies mainly on offshore islands: *Morus bassanus* and other species. **2** *Brit, informal* a greedy person; a scavenger. [Old English *ganot*]

gannister /'ganistə/ *noun* see GANISTER.

ganoid /'ganoyd/ *adj* said of the scales of fish: hard and bony, covered with a substance like enamel: compare CTENOID, PLACOID. [French *ganoïde* from Greek *ganos* brightness]

gantlet /'gantlit, 'gawntlit/ *noun chiefly NAmer* a gauntlet.

gantry /'gantri/ *noun* (*pl* **gantries**) **1** a frame structure raised on side supports that spans over or round something and is used for railway signals, as a travelling crane, for servicing a rocket before launching, etc. **2** a frame for supporting barrels. **3** a structure on which bottles are displayed in a bar. [perhaps modification of early French *gantier* from Latin *cantherius* trellis]

gaol /jayl/ *noun and verb Brit* see JAIL¹, JAIL².

gap /gap/ *noun* **1** a break in a barrier, e.g. a wall or hedge. **2** an empty space between two objects or two parts of an object. **3** a break in continuity; an interval. **4** a disparity or difference: *the gap between imports and exports*. **5a** a mountain pass. **b** a ravine. **6** = SPARK GAP. ⟫ **gapped** *adj*, **gappy** *adj*. [Middle English from Old Norse *gap* chasm, hole]

gape¹ /gayp/ *verb intrans* **1a** to open the mouth wide. **b** to open or part widely: *Holes gaped in the pavement*. **2** to gaze stupidly or in openmouthed surprise or wonder. ⟫ **gaping** *adj*, **gapingly** *adv*. [Middle English *gapen* from Old Norse *gapa*]

gape² *noun* **1** an act of gaping; *esp* an openmouthed stare. **2** the average width of the open mouth or beak. **3** (**the gapes**) a disease of young birds characterized by constant gaping, caused by gapeworms infesting the windpipe.

gaper /'gaypə/ *noun* a large edible burrowing clam: genus *Mya*.

gapeworm *noun* a nematode worm that causes the gapes in birds.

gap year *noun* a year's break that somebody takes between leaving school and starting further education.

gar /gah/ *noun* = GARFISH (2).

garage¹ /'garahzh, 'garij/ *noun* **1** a building for the shelter of motor vehicles. **2** an establishment for providing essential services, e.g. the supply of petrol or repair work to motor vehicles. **3** a style of house music with a soul influence. [French *garage* act of docking, garage, from *garer* to dock, shelter, ultimately of Germanic origin]

garage² *verb trans* to keep or put (a car) in a garage.

garage band *noun* an amateurish or unsophisticated rock group. [from the idea of such bands rehearsing in garages]

garage sale *noun* a sale of secondhand furniture and household goods, held in the seller's garage or house.

garam masala /,garəm mə'sahlə/ *noun* an aromatic mixture of ground coriander, cumin, cinnamon, etc used *esp* in curries. [Hindi *garam masālā*, from *garam* hot, pungent + *masālā* spice]

garb¹ /gahb/ *noun* a style of clothing; dress: *a figure in priestly garb*. [early French *garbe* elegance, grace from Old Italian *garbo*, of Germanic origin]

garb² *verb trans* to dress (somebody); to attire (them).

garbage /'gahbij/ *noun* **1** *chiefly NAmer* rubbish or waste. **2** worthless writing or speech. ✻ **garbage in, garbage out** *informal* invalid or poor data put in to a computer will produce equally poor output. [Middle English, in the sense 'animal entrails', from early French]

garble¹ /'gahbl/ *verb trans* to distort or confuse (a message), giving a false impression of the facts. ⟫ **garbler** *noun*.

Word history
Middle English *garbelen* to sift, select, via Old Italian and Arabic from late Latin *cribellum*, dimin. of Latin *cribum* sieve. The current meaning of *garble*, which suggests mixing things together confusedly, seems to be at odds with its etymology. The notion originally underlying the metaphorical sense was, however, that of distorting the facts by deliberately selecting those that supported one's case and screening out those that were disadvantageous.

garble² *noun* the act of garbling, or a garbled message.

garboard /'gahbawd/ *noun* the plank next to a ship's keel. [obsolete Dutch *gaarboord*]

garboard strake *noun* = GARBOARD.

garbology /gah'boləji/ *noun* the study of people's rubbish as a method of analysing their culture and lifestyle. ⟫ **garbologist** *noun*.

garçon /gah'sonh (*French* garsɔ̃)/ *noun* a waiter in a French restaurant. [French *garçon* boy, servant]

garda /'gahdə/ *noun* (*pl* **garda** /'gahdee, 'gahdie/) **1** (*often* **Garda**) (*treated as sing. or pl*) the Irish police. **2** a member of the garda. [shortening of Irish Gaelic *Garda Síochána* Civic Guard, literally 'guard of peace']

garden¹ /'gahd(ə)n/ *noun* **1** *Brit* a plot of ground where herbs, fruits, vegetables, or typically flowers are cultivated. **2a** a public recreation area or park: *a botanical garden*. **b** an open-air eating or drinking place: *a beer garden*. **3** (*used before a noun*) found in, or suitable for, a garden: *garden furniture*. ✻ **lead somebody up the garden path** to mislead or deceive somebody. [Middle English *gardin* from early French, of Germanic origin]

garden² *verb intrans* (**gardened**, **gardening**) to work in, cultivate, or lay out a garden. ⟫ **gardener** *noun*, **gardening** *noun*.

garden centre *noun* an establishment selling equipment for gardens or gardening, e.g. tools, furniture, plants, and seeds.

garden city *noun* a planned town with spacious residential areas including public parks and considerable garden space.

gardenia /gah'deeni·ə/ *noun* any of a genus of Old World tropical trees and shrubs with showy fragrant white or yellow flowers: genus *Gardenia*. [Latin genus name, named after Alexander *Garden* d.1791, Scottish naturalist]

garden leave *or* **gardening leave** *noun* paid leave that an employee is obliged to take between the time when they notify their employer, or are given notice by their employer, that they are leaving their post of employment and the time of leaving it.

garden party *noun* a usu formal party held on the lawns of a garden.

garderobe /'gahdrohb/ *noun* **1** a part of a medieval building used as a privy. **2** a wardrobe or private room in a medieval building.

[Middle English from early French, from *garder* to keep + *robe* robe, dress: compare WARDROBE]

garfish *noun* (*pl* **garfishes** *or collectively* **garfish**) **1** any of several species of fishes of European and N Atlantic waters with a long body and elongated jaws: family Belonidae. **2** *NAmer* a similar freshwater fish: genus *Lepisosteus*. [Middle English *garfysshe*, prob from *gar, gare* spear + *fysshe* FISH[1]]

garganey /'gahgəni/ *noun* (*pl* **garganeys** *or collectively* **garganey**) a small European duck the male of which has a broad white stripe over the eye: *Anas querquedula*. [Italian dialect *garganei*, of imitative origin]

gargantuan /gah'gantyooən/ *adj* (*often* **Gargantuan**) gigantic or colossal: *a gargantuan meal*. [from *Gargantua*, gigantic king in the novel *Gargantua* by François Rabelais d.1553, French humorist and satirist]

gargle[1] /'gahgl/ *verb intrans* to cleanse one's mouth or throat by blowing through a liquid held in the mouth. [Old French *gargouiller* from *gargouille* throat]

gargle[2] *noun* **1** a liquid used in gargling. **2** a bubbling liquid sound produced by gargling.

gargoyle /'gahgoyl/ *noun* **1** a spout in the form of a grotesque human or animal figure projecting from a roof gutter to throw rainwater clear of a building. **2** a person of grotesque appearance. [Middle English *gargoyl* from Old French *gargouille* throat]

gargoylism *noun* = HURLER'S SYNDROME.

garibaldi /gari'bawldi/ *noun* (*pl* **garibaldis**) *Brit* a biscuit with a layer of currants in it. [named after Giuseppe *Garibaldi* d.1882, Italian patriot]

garish /'geərish/ *adj* excessively and gaudily bright or vivid. ⋙ **garishly** *adv*, **garishness** *noun*. [origin unknown]

garland[1] /'gahlənd/ *noun* **1** a wreath of flowers or leaves worn as an ornament or sign of distinction. **2** *archaic* an anthology or collection of verse or prose. [Middle English from Old French *garlande*]

garland[2] *verb trans* to crown or deck (somebody) with a garland.

garlic /'gahlik/ *noun* **1** a bulbous plant of the lily family, widely cultivated for its bulbs: *Allium sativum*. **2** the pungent compound bulb of this plant, used as a flavouring in cookery: *And, most dear actors, eat no onions or garlic, for we are to utter sweet breath —* Shakespeare. ⋙ **garlicky** *adj*. [Old English *gārlēac*, from *gār* spear + *lēac* LEEK]

garment[1] /'gahmənt/ *noun* an article of clothing. [Middle English from French *garnement* equipment from *garnir*: see GARNISH[1]]

garment[2] *verb trans* (*usu in passive*) to clothe (somebody).

garner[1] /'gahnə/ *noun* **1** *archaic* a granary or grain bin. **2** a store. [Middle English via Old French from Latin *granarium*, from *granum* GRAIN[1]]

garner[2] *verb trans* (**garnered, garnering**) **1** to collect (e.g. evidence or information): *The facts you have garnered with such infinite trouble invariably fail you at a pinch —* Helen Keller. **2** *archaic* to gather or store (e.g. grain).

garnet /'gahnit/ *noun* a hard brittle silicate mineral used as an abrasive, and in its transparent deep red form as a gem. [Middle English *garnet* from early French *grenat* red like a pomegranate, from *pomme grenate* pomegranate]

garnish[1] /'gahnish/ *verb trans* **1** to decorate or embellish (*esp* food). **2** to garnishee (somebody). [Middle English *garnishen* from early French *garnir* to warn, equip, garnish, of Germanic origin]

garnish[2] *noun* an embellishment, *esp* an edible savoury or decorative addition to a dish.

garnishee[1] /gahni'shee/ *noun* in law, somebody served with a garnishment.

garnishee[2] *verb trans* (**garnishees, garnisheed, garnisheeing**) **1** to serve (somebody) with a garnishment. **2** to take (money owed) by legal authority following a garnishment.

garnishment *noun* **1** a garnish. **2** a judicial warning to a debtor not to pay his or her debt to anyone other than the appropriate third party. [GARNISH[1], in the sense 'to serve notice, to warn']

garniture /'gahnichə/ *noun* an embellishment or trimming. [early French *garniture* equipment, alteration of Old French *garnesture*, from *garnir*: see GARNISH[1]]

garotte /gə'rot/ *noun and verb NAmer* see GARROTTE[1], GARROTTE[2].

garpike *noun* = GARFISH.

garret /'garit/ *noun* a small room just under the roof of a house. [Middle English *garette* watchtower, from Old French *garite*, from *garir* to protect, of Germanic origin]

garrison[1] /'garis(ə)n/ *noun* **1** a body of troops stationed in a fortified town or place to defend it. **2** a town or place in which troops are stationed. [Middle English *garisoun* protection, from Old French *garison*, from *garir*: see GARRET]

garrison[2] *verb trans* (**garrisoned, garrisoning**) **1** to station troops in (a place). **2** to assign (troops) as a garrison.

garrison cap *noun NAmer* a visorless folding cap worn as part of a military uniform.

garron /'garən/ *noun Scot, Irish* a small sturdy workhorse. [Irish Gaelic *gearrán* and Scottish Gaelic *gearran* gelding]

garrotte[1] (*NAmer* **garotte** *or* **garrote**) /gə'rot/ *noun* **1** a Spanish method of execution using an iron collar for strangling somebody. **2** an iron collar or a wire or cord used for strangling somebody. [Spanish *garrote* cudgel, garrotte, prob from early French *garrot* heavy wooden projectile]

garrotte[2] (*NAmer* **garotte** *or* **garrote**) *verb trans* to execute or kill (somebody) with a garrotte.

garrulous /'garooləs/ *adj* excessively talkative, *esp* about trivial things. ⋙ **garrulity** /ga'roohliti/ *noun*, **garrulously** *adv*, **garrulousness** *noun*. [Latin *garrulus* from *garrire* to chatter]

garryowen /gari'oh·in/ *noun* in rugby, an offensive tactic consisting of a high kick upwards followed by a charge from the forward players. [named after *Garryowen* R.F.C., a rugby club in Co. Limerick, Ireland]

garter[1] /'gahtə/ *noun* **1** a band, usu of elastic, worn to hold up a stocking or sock. **2** *NAmer* = SUSPENDER (1). **3a** (**Garter**) the Order of the Garter. **b** the blue velvet garter that is a badge of the Order. **c** membership of the Order. [Middle English from early French *gartier*, from *garet* bend of the knee, of Celtic origin]

garter[2] *verb trans* (**gartered, gartering**) to fasten or support (something) with or as if with a garter.

garter snake *noun* **1** any of several species of harmless longitudinally striped American snakes: genus *Thamnophis*. **2** any of several species of venomous African snakes: genus *Elapsoidea*.

garter stitch *noun* the ribbed pattern formed by using only a plain knit stitch.

garth /gahth/ *noun* **1** the open space bounded by a cloister. **2** *archaic* a small yard or enclosure. [Middle English from Old Norse *garthr* yard]

gas[1] /gas/ *noun* (*pl* **gases** *or* **gasses**) **1** a fluid substance, e.g. air, that has neither independent shape nor volume and tends to expand indefinitely. **2a** a gas or gaseous mixture used to produce general anaesthesia, as a fuel, etc. **b** a substance, e.g. tear gas or mustard gas, that can be used to produce a poisonous, asphyxiating, or irritant atmosphere. **3** *NAmer, informal* petrol. **4** *informal* empty talk. **5** *informal* an enjoyable or amusing person or thing: *The party was a real gas*. **6** *NAmer* flatulence. [Latin *gas*, alteration of Greek *chaos* space, CHAOS; (sense 3) short for GASOLINE]

gas[2] *verb* (**gassed, gassing**) ⋗ *verb trans* **1** to poison or otherwise affect (a person or animal) adversely with gas. **2** *NAmer, informal* (+ up) to fill the tank of (a motor vehicle) with petrol. ⋗ *verb intrans* **1** said of a battery or cell: to give off gas. **2** *informal* to talk idly. **3** *NAmer, informal* (+ up) to fill the tank of a motor vehicle with petrol.

gasbag *noun informal* an idle talker.

gas chamber *noun* a chamber in which prisoners are executed or animals killed by poison gas.

gas chromatography *noun* = GAS-LIQUID CHROMATOGRAPHY.

gascon /'gaskən/ *noun* **1** (**Gascon**) a native or inhabitant of Gascony in France. **2** *archaic* a braggart. ⋙ **Gascon** *adj*. [Middle English *Gascoun* via French from Latin *vascon-, vasco* BASQUE]

gasconade[1] /gaskə'nayd/ *noun* bravado or boasting. [French *gasconnade* from *gasconner* to boast, from *gascon* Gascon, boaster]

gasconade[2] *verb intrans* to boast or brag. [French *gasconnade* from *gasconner* to boast, from *gascon* Gascon, boaster]

gas constant *noun* the constant of proportionality in the equation describing the relation of the pressure and volume of a gas to its absolute temperature: 8.314 joule kelvin^{-1} mole^{-1}.

gas-cooled reactor *noun* a nuclear reactor that uses gas, usu carbon dioxide, as a coolant.

gas-discharge tube *noun* a tube in which an electrical discharge takes place through a gas.

gaseous /'gasiəs, 'gay-/ *adj* having the form or nature of a gas. ▶▶ **gaseousness** *noun*.

gas equation *noun* the equation of state for one mole of an IDEAL GAS (a hypothetical gas that obeys the gas laws).

gas gangrene *noun* gangrene marked by impregnation of the dying tissue with gas, caused by infection with a clostridial bacterium.

gas guzzler *noun chiefly NAmer, informal* a large motor car that has a high consumption of petrol.

gash[1] /gash/ *verb trans* to injure (somebody or something) with a deep long cut or cleft. [Middle English *garsen* via French from late Latin *charaxare* to sharpen, from Greek *charassein* to scratch, engrave]

gash[2] *noun* a deep long cut, *esp* in flesh.

gasholder *noun* = GASOMETER.

gasify /'gasifie, 'gay-/ *verb* (**gasifies, gasified, gasifying**) ▶ *verb trans* to change (a solid or liquid) into gas: *gasify coal.* ▶ *verb intrans* to become a gas. ▶▶ **gasification** /-fi'kaysh(ə)n/ *noun.*

gasket /'gaskit/ *noun* **1** a specially shaped piece of sealing material for ensuring that a joint, *esp* between metal surfaces, does not leak liquid or gas. **2** *archaic* a line or band used to tie a furled sail to a beam on a ship's mast. [prob alteration of French *garcette* thin rope, literally 'little girl', dimin. of Old French *garce* girl]

gaskin /'gaskin/ *noun* a part of the hind leg of a quadruped between the stifle and the hock. [obsolete *gaskin* hose, breeches, prob short for GALLIGASKINS]

gaslight *noun* light from a gas flame or gas lighting fixture. ▶▶ **gaslit** *adj.*

gas-liquid chromatography *noun* a technique for analysing a mixture of volatile chemical substances in which the mixture is carried by an inert gas, e.g. argon, through a column of a stationary liquid or solid. The components are separated according to their relative velocities through the column and are identified by a detector as each leaves the column.

gasman /'gasman/ *noun* (*pl* **gasmen**) a man whose job is fitting and repairing gas appliances or reading household gas meters.

gas mantle *noun* a small cap or tube of chemically treated fibres fitted to the flame of a gas lamp to give out a brilliant glowing white light.

gas mask *noun* a mask connected to a chemical air filter and used as a protection against noxious fumes or gases.

gas meter *noun* a device for measuring and recording the amount of gas used by a domestic customer.

gasoline *or* **gasolene** /gasə'leen, 'gasəleen/ *noun NAmer* petrol. [GAS[1] + -OL[1] + -INE[1] *or* -ENE]

gasometer /ga'somitə/ *noun* a large cylindrical storage container for gas.

gasp[1] /gahsp/ *verb intrans* **1** to catch the breath suddenly and audibly, e.g. with shock. **2** to breathe laboriously. **3** (+ for) to crave: *He was gasping for a glass of water.* ▶ *verb trans* (+ out) to utter (words) with gasps: *He gasped out his message.* [Middle English *gaspen* from Old Norse *geispa* to yawn]

gasp[2] *noun* an audible catching of the breath.

gasper *noun Brit, informal, dated* a cigarette.

gas plant *noun* a Eurasian plant with showy white flowers and leaves that give off a flammable vapour: *Dictamnus albus.* Also called BURNING BUSH, DITTANY, FRAXINELLA.

gas ring *noun* a perforated metal ring through which jets of gas issue and over which food is cooked: compare RING[1] (3).

gassy *adj* (**gassier, gassiest**) **1** full of, containing, or like gas: *gassy beer.* **2** *informal* full of boastful or insincere talk. ▶▶ **gassiness** *noun.*

Gastarbeiter /'gastahbietə/ *noun* (*pl* **Gastarbeiter** *or* **Gastarbeiters**) a foreign worker, *esp* in a German-speaking country. [German *Gastarbeiter* guest worker]

gasteropod /'gast(ə)rəpod/ *noun* = GASTROPOD.

gas thermometer *noun* a device for measuring temperature by determining the volume of a gas at constant pressure or the pressure of a gas at constant volume.

gastr- *or* **gastro-** *comb. form* forming words, with the meanings: **1** belly: *gastropod.* **2** stomach: *gastritis.* **3** gastric and: *gastrointestinal.* [Greek, from *gastr-, gastēr* stomach]

gastric /'gastrik/ *adj* to do with or in the region of the stomach. [scientific Latin *gastricus* from Greek *gastr-, gastēr* stomach]

gastric juice *noun* a thin acidic digestive liquid secreted by glands in the lining of the stomach.

gastric ulcer *noun* an ulcer in the mucous membrane lining the stomach.

gastrin /'gastrin/ *noun* a polypeptide hormone secreted by the stomach lining that induces secretion of gastric juice.

gastritis /ga'strietis/ *noun* inflammation of the membrane lining the stomach.

gastro- *comb. form* see GASTR-.

gastrocolic /gastroh'kolik/ *adj* relating to the stomach and colon.

gastroenteritis /,gastroh-entə'rietəs/ *noun* inflammation of the lining of the stomach and the intestines, usu causing painful diarrhoea.

gastrointestinal /,gastroh-in'testinl/ *adj* to do with or in the region of both the stomach and intestine.

gastrolith /'gastrohlith/ *noun* a hard solid mass in the stomach, *esp* one formed around a stone that has been swallowed.

gastronome /'gastrənohm/ *noun* an epicure or gourmet. [French *gastronome,* back-formation from *gastronomie:* see GASTRONOMY]

gastronomist /ga'stronəmist/ *noun* = GASTRONOME.

gastronomy /ga'stronəmi/ *noun* the art or science of good eating. ▶▶ **gastronomic** /-'nomik/ *adj,* **gastronomical** /-'nomikl/ *adj,* **gastronomically** /-'nomikli/ *adv.* [French *gastronomie* from Greek *Gastronomia,* title of a fourth-cent. BC poem, from *gastr-, gaster* stomach + *-nomia* -NOMY]

gastropod /'gastrəpod/ *noun* any of a large class of molluscs including the snails, usu with a distinct head bearing sensory organs: class Gastropoda. ▶▶ **gastropod** *adj,* **gastropodan** /ga'stropədən, -'pohdən/ *adj and noun.* [Latin class name, from Greek *gastr-, gastēr* stomach + *pod-, pous* foot]

gastroporn /'gastrohpawn/ *noun* sensuous or erotic depictions of or references to food in literature or broadcasting.

gastropub /'gastrohpub/ *noun* a pub that serves fine food.

gastroscope /'gastrəskohp/ *noun* an instrument for looking at the interior of the stomach. ▶▶ **gastroscopic** *adj,* **gastroscopist** *noun,* **gastroscopy** *noun.*

gastrula /'gastroolə/ *noun* (*pl* **gastrulas** *or* **gastrulae** /-li/) the embryo of a multicellular animal at the stage in its development succeeding the BLASTULA (early) stage and consisting of a hollow two-layered cellular cup: compare BLASTULA, MORULA. [scientific Latin *gastrula,* from GASTR-]

gas turbine *noun* an internal-combustion engine in which turbine blades are driven by hot gases, the pressure and velocity of which are intensified by compressed air introduced into the combustion chamber.

gasworks *noun* (*pl* **gasworks**) (*treated as sing.*) a plant for manufacturing gas.

gat[1] /gat/ *verb archaic* past tense of GET[1].

gat[2] *noun informal* a firearm, *esp* a handgun. [short for GATLING GUN]

gate[1] /gayt/ *noun* **1** the usu hinged frame or door that closes an opening in a wall or fence. **2** a city or castle entrance, often with defensive structures. **3a** a means of entrance or exit; *specif* a numbered exit from an airport building to the airfield. **b** a mountain pass. **c** a mechanically operated barrier used as a starting device for a race. **d** either of a pair of barriers that let water in and out of a lock or close a road at a level crossing. **4** an electronic device, e.g. in a computer, that produces a defined output for every combination of input conditions: *a logic gate.* **5** the set of notches in a manually worked gearbox into which the gear lever is pushed to select the gears. **6** the total admission receipts or the number of spectators at a sporting event. **7** the part of a film camera or projector that holds the film flat behind the lens. [Old English *geat*]

gate[2] *verb trans Brit* to punish (a student) by confinement to the premises of a school or college.

-gate *comb. form* forming nouns, denoting: political or economic scandal: *Irangate.* [*Watergate,* name given to a US political scandal in the early 1970s involving burglary of the Democratic Party headquarters in the Watergate building in Washington, DC]

gateau /'gatoh/ *noun* (*pl* **gateaux** *or* **gateaus** /'gatohz/) a rich often filled elaborate cream cake. [French *gâteau* cake, from Old French *gastel*, prob of Germanic origin]

gate-crash *verb trans* to enter or attend (a party) without a ticket or invitation: *the trauma of walking endlessly up and down Glasgow's Byres Road with a bottle of Hirondelle looking for a party to gatecrash* — Muriel Gray. ➤➤ **gate-crasher** *noun*.

gatefold *noun* a large folded page inserted in a book, journal, etc; *esp* one with a single fold.

gatehouse /'gayt·hows/ *noun* **1** a structure above or beside a gate, e.g. of a city wall or castle, often used in former times as a guard-room or prison. **2** a lodge at the entrance to the grounds of a large house.

gatekeeper *noun* **1** somebody who or something that tends or guards a gate. **2** a butterfly with orange and brown wings: *Pyronia tithonus*.

gateleg table *noun* a table with drop leaves supported by two movable legs.

gatepost *noun* the post on which a gate is hung or against which it closes.

gateway *noun* **1** an opening for a gate. **2** in computing, a piece of hardware or software used to connect networks. **3** a point of entry or access: *gateway to the North*.

gather[1] /'gadhə/ *verb* (**gathered**, **gathering**) ➤ *verb trans* **1** to bring (things) together; to collect (them). **2** to pick or harvest (flowers, crops, etc). **3a** to summon up (e.g. nerves or courage). **b** to accumulate (speed). **c** to prepare (e.g. oneself) for an effort: *She gathered herself for her first entrance*. **4a** to clasp (somebody), e.g. to oneself, in an embrace: *He gathered her into his arms*. **b** to draw (e.g. a garment) about or close to something: *She gathered her cloak about her*. **c** to pull (fabric) together, *esp* along a line of stitching, to create small tucks. **5** to reach a conclusion intuitively from hints or through inferences: *I gather you're ready to leave*. ➤ *verb intrans* to come together in a body: *A crowd had gathered*. ➤➤ **gatherer** *noun*. [Old English *gaderian*]

gather[2] *noun* something gathered; *esp* a tuck in cloth made by gathering.

gathering *noun* **1** an assembly or meeting. **2** a gather or series of gathers in cloth. **3** in printing, a sheet of printed pages forming a unit in a book.

Gatling gun /'gatling/ *noun* an early machine gun with a revolving cluster of barrels fired once each per revolution. [named after R J *Gatling* d.1903, US inventor]

GATT /gat/ *abbr* General Agreement on Tariffs and Trade.

gauche /gohsh/ *adj* lacking social experience or grace. ➤➤ **gauchely** *adv*, **gaucheness** *noun*. [French *gauche* left, left-handed, from *gauchir* to turn aside]

gaucherie /'gohsh(ə)ri/ *noun* tactless or awkward manner or behaviour, or an instance of this. [French *gaucherie* from *gauche*: see GAUCHE]

gaucho /'gowchoh/ *noun* (*pl* **gauchos**) a cowboy of the pampas regions in S America. [American Spanish *gaucho*, prob from Quechua *wáhcha* poor person, orphan]

gaud /gawd/ *noun archaic* a gaudy ornament or trinket: *Sir Walter Scott ... sets the world in love with ... sham grandeurs, sham gauds, and sham chivalries of a brainless and worthless long-vanished society* — Mark Twain. [Middle English *gaude* trick, toy, prob via Old French from Latin *gaudēre* to rejoice]

gaudy[1] *adj* (**gaudier**, **gaudiest**) ostentatiously or tastelessly and brightly ornamented. ➤➤ **gaudily** *adv*, **gaudiness** *noun*.

gaudy[2] *noun* (*pl* **gaudies**) *Brit* a feast, *esp* a dinner for ex-students, in some universities. [prob from Latin *gaudium* joy]

gauge[1] (*NAmer* **gage**) /gayj/ *noun* **1** an instrument for measuring or testing, e.g. a dimension or quantity. **2a** the thickness of a thin sheet of metal, plastic, film, etc. **b** the diameter of wire, a hypodermic needle, a screw, etc. **3** a measure of the size of the bore of a shotgun. **4** the distance between the rails of a railway, wheels on an axle, etc. **5** *archaic* the relative position of a ship with reference to another ship and the wind. [Middle English *gauge* from early French, prob of Germanic origin]

gauge[2] (*NAmer* **gage**) *verb trans* **1** to measure exactly the size, dimensions, capacity, or contents of (something). **2** to estimate or

judge (something): *Can you gauge his reaction?* **3** to check (something) for conformity to specifications or limits. ➤➤ **gaugeable** *adj*, **gaugeably** *adv*.

gauge theory *noun* a theory in physics that describes the interaction between particles.

Gaul /gawl/ *noun* a native or inhabitant of ancient Gaul, ancient region of Europe including most of what is now France. [via French from Latin *Gallia*, prob of Celtic origin]

Gauleiter /'gowlietə/ *noun* **1** an official in charge of a district in Nazi Germany. **2** (*also* **gauleiter**) an arrogant henchman or subordinate. [German *Gauleiter*, from *Gau* district, region + *Leiter* leader]

Gaulish /'gawlish/ *noun* the Celtic language of the ancient Gauls. ➤➤ **Gaulish** *adj*.

Gaullism /'gawliz(ə)m/ *noun* the political principles and policies of the French political leader Charles de Gaulle (d.1970). ➤➤ **Gaullist** *adj and noun*.

gaunt /gawnt/ *adj* **1** excessively thin and angular, *esp* from hunger or suffering. **2** said of a place: barren or desolate. ➤➤ **gauntly** *adv*, **gauntness** *noun*. [Middle English, perhaps of Scandinavian origin]

gauntlet[1] /'gawntlit/ *noun* **1** a strong protective glove with a wide extension above the wrist, used *esp* for sports and in industry. **2** a glove to protect the hand, formerly worn with medieval armour. ✳ **take up the gauntlet** to accept a challenge. **throw down the gauntlet** to issue a challenge. ➤➤ **gauntleted** *adj*. [Middle English from early French *gantelet*, dimin. of *gant* glove, of Germanic origin]

gauntlet[2] *noun* **1** a double file of men armed with weapons with which to strike at somebody made to run between them, used formerly as a military punishment. **2** criticism or an ordeal or test. ✳ **run the gauntlet 1** to have to suffer criticism or a testing experience. **2** formerly, to have to run through a gauntlet as a punishment. [by folk etymology from *gantelope*, modification of Swedish *gatlopp*, from Old Swedish *gata* road, lane + *lop* course, run]

gaur /'gowə/ *noun* a large E Indian wild ox with a broad forehead and short thick horns: *Bibos gaurus*. [Hindi *gaur* from Sanskrit *gaura*]

gauss /gows/ *noun* (*pl* **gauss** *or* **gausses**) a unit of magnetic induction equal to 10^{-4} tesla. [named after K F *Gauss* d.1855, German mathematician and astronomer]

Gaussian distribution /'gowsi·ən/ *noun* = NORMAL DISTRIBUTION. [named after K F *Gauss* (see GAUSS), who first described it]

gauze /gawz/ *noun* **1a** a thin often transparent fabric used chiefly for clothing or draperies. **b** a loosely woven cotton surgical dressing. **c** a fine mesh of metal or plastic filaments. **2** a thin haze or mist. ➤➤ **gauzily** *adv*, **gauziness** *noun*, **gauzy** *adj*. [early French *gaze*, prob from *Gaza*, a town in Palestine known for the production of fine fabrics]

gavage /'gavahzh, 'gavij/ *noun* introduction of material, *esp* food, into the stomach by a tube. [French *gavage* from *gaver* to stuff, feed forcibly]

gave /gayv/ *verb* past tense of GIVE[1].

gavel /'gavl/ *noun* a small mallet with which a chairman, judge, or auctioneer commands attention or confirms a vote, sale, etc. [origin unknown]

gavial /'gayvi·əl/ *noun* a large Indian crocodile: *Gavialis gangeticus*. [French *gavial*, modification of Hindi *ghariyāl*]

gavotte /gə'vot/ *noun* **1** an 18th-cent. dance in which the feet are raised rather than slid. **2** a composition or movement of music in quadruple time. [French *gavotte* from Old Provençal *gavoto*, from *Gavot* inhabitant of the Alps]

gawk[1] /gawk/ *verb intrans* to gawp. ➤➤ **gawker** *noun*. [perhaps alteration of obsolete *gaw* to stare, from Old Norse *gā* to heed, mark]

gawk[2] *noun* a clumsy awkward person. ➤➤ **gawkish** *adj*. [prob from English dialect *gawk* left-handed]

gawky *adj* (**gawkier**, **gawkiest**) awkward and lanky: *a gawky child*. ➤➤ **gawkily** *adv*, **gawkiness** *noun*. [GAWK[2] + -Y[1]]

gawp /gawp/ *verb intrans Brit, informal* to gape or stare stupidly. ➤➤ **gawper** *noun*. [alteration of GAPE[1]]

gay[1] /gay/ *adj* **1** homosexual. **2** for or relating to homosexuals: *a gay bar*. **3** *dated* bright or attractive: *a room with gay curtains at the windows*. **4** *dated* happily excited; carefree. ➤➤ **gayness** *noun*.

[Middle English from early French *gai* happy, prob of Germanic origin]

Usage note ─────────────

The primary meaning of *gay* in contemporary English is 'homosexual'. As an adjective or a noun, it is the standard term used by homosexuals to describe themselves and as such has become part of the standard vocabulary of world English. This development has only occurred since the 1960s. Before then, in standard usage, *gay* was an adjective meaning 'cheerful' or 'bright'. These senses are still sometimes used, but care should be taken when using the word with these meanings to avoid misunderstanding.

gay² *noun* a homosexual; *esp* a man: *In future, all movie gays will be law-abiding citizens with healthy relationships … and a glitter-free wardrobe* — New Statesman.

gazania /gə'zayni·ə/ *noun* a S African herbaceous plant with large orange or yellow flowers: genus *Gazania*. [Latin genus name, named after Theodore of *Gaza* d.1478, Greek scholar]

gaze¹ /gayz/ *verb intrans* to fix the eyes in a steady and intent look. ⯈⯈ **gazer** *noun*. [Middle English *gazen*, prob of Scandinavian origin]

gaze² *noun* a fixed intent look.

gazebo /gə'zeeboh/ *noun* (*pl* **gazebos** *or* **gazeboes**) a freestanding structure, e.g. a summerhouse, placed to command a view. [perhaps from GAZE¹ + Latin *-ebo* as in *videbo* I shall see]

gazelle /gə'zel/ *noun* (*pl* **gazelles** *or collectively* **gazelle**) any of several species of small, graceful, and swift African and Asian antelopes noted for their soft lustrous eyes: genus *Gazella* and other genera. [French *gazelle*, ultimately from Arabic *ghazāl*]

gazette¹ /gə'zet/ *noun* **1** a newspaper or journal, *esp* an official one. **2** an official journal containing announcements of honours and government appointments. [French *gazette* via Italian from Italian dialect *gazeta* small copper coin (the price of the newspaper)]

gazette² *verb trans Brit* to publish or report (news, military appointments, etc) in an official gazette: *M.P.'s baronetted, sham colonels gazetted, and second-rate aldermen knighted* — W S Gilbert.

gazetteer /gazə'tiə/ *noun* a dictionary of place names. [orig denoting a journalist; the current sense comes from *The Gazetteer's or Newsman's Interpreter*, a geographical index edited by Laurence Echard d.1730, English historian]

gazpacho /gəz'pachoh, gəs-/ *noun* (*pl* **gazpachos**) a Spanish cold soup containing tomatoes, olive oil, garlic, peppers, and usu breadcrumbs. [Spanish *gazpacho*]

gazump /gə'zump/ *verb trans Brit* to thwart (a would-be house purchaser) by raising the price after agreeing to sell at a certain price. ⯈⯈ **gazumper** *noun*. [earlier *gezumph, gazoomph, gazumph* to swindle, perhaps from Yiddish]

gazunder /gə'zundə/ *verb trans* (**gazundered, gazundering**) *Brit* to attempt to force an unreasonably low offer upon (the seller of a house) by reducing a previous offer at the latest possible stage of the transaction. ⯈⯈ **gazunderer** *noun*. [blend of GAZUMP and UNDER¹]

GB *abbr* **1** (*also* **Gb**) gigabyte(s). **2** Great Britain (international vehicle registration).

GBA *abbr* Alderney (international vehicle registration).

GBE *abbr* Knight or Dame Grand Cross of the Order of the British Empire.

GBG *abbr* Guernsey (international vehicle registration).

GBH *abbr Brit* grievous bodily harm.

GBJ *abbr* Jersey (international vehicle registration).

GBM *abbr* Isle of Man (international vehicle registration).

Gbyte *abbr* gigabyte(s).

GBZ *abbr* Gibraltar (international vehicle registration).

GC *abbr* George Cross.

GCA *abbr* Guatemala Central America (international vehicle registration for Guatemala).

GCB *abbr Brit* Knight or Dame Grand Cross of the Order of the Bath.

GCE *abbr Brit* formerly, General Certificate of Education.

GCHQ *abbr Brit* Government Communications Headquarters.

G clef *noun* = TREBLE CLEF.

GCMG *abbr Brit* Knight or Dame Grand Cross of the Order of St Michael and St George.

GCSE *abbr Brit* General Certificate of Secondary Education.

GCVO *abbr Brit* Knight or Dame Grand Cross of the Royal Victorian Order.

Gd *abbr* the chemical symbol for gadolinium.

g'day /gə'day/ *interj Aus, informal* used as a greeting. [*good day*]

Gdns *abbr* in street names, gardens.

GDP *abbr* gross domestic product.

GDR *abbr* German Democratic Republic.

GE *abbr* Georgia (international vehicle registration).

Ge *abbr* the chemical symbol for germanium.

gean /geen/ *noun* **1** a wild sweet cherry. **2** the tree that bears this fruit: *Prunus avium*. [early French *guisne, guine*]

gear¹ /giə/ *noun* **1** a toothed wheel that is one of a set of interlocking wheels. **2a** any of two or more adjustments of a transmission, e.g. of a bicycle or motor vehicle, that determine direction of travel or ratio of engine speed to vehicle speed. **b** working relation, position, or adjustment: *out of gear; She put the car in gear*. **3** a mechanism that performs a specific function in a complete machine: *the steering gear*. **4** a set of equipment usu for a particular purpose: *fishing gear*. **5a** *informal* clothing or garments: *motorcycle gear*. **b** movable property; goods. **6** *slang* drugs, *esp* illegal ones. [Old English *gearwe* equipment]

gear² *verb trans* **1** to provide (machinery) with gears or connect it by gearing. **2** (+ to) to adjust (something) so as to match, blend with, or satisfy something: *an institution geared to the needs of the blind*. ⯈ *verb intrans* said of machinery: to be in or come into gear.

gearbox *noun* a protective casing enclosing a set of *esp* car gears, or the gears so enclosed.

gearing *noun* **1** a series of gear wheels. **2** *Brit* the advantage gained by the use of extra capital, e.g. borrowed money, to increase the returns on invested equity capital.

gear lever *noun* a control, *esp* a rod, on a gear-changing mechanism, e.g. a gearbox, used to engage the different gears.

gearshift *noun NAmer* = GEAR LEVER.

gearstick *noun* = GEAR LEVER.

gear train *noun* a system of two or more gear wheels that transmit motion from one shaft to another.

gear up *verb trans* **1** to make (something) ready for effective operation. **2** to put (e.g. oneself) into a state of anxious excitement or nervous anticipation.

gearwheel *noun* a toothed wheel that engages another piece of a mechanism; a cogwheel.

gecko /'gekoh/ *noun* (*pl* **geckos** *or* **geckoes**) any of numerous species of small chiefly tropical lizards able to walk on vertical or overhanging surfaces: family Gekkonidae and other families. [Malay *ge'kok*, of imitative origin]

gee /jee/ *interj NAmer, informal* used as an exclamation of surprise or enthusiasm. [euphemism for JESUS²]

geebung /'jeebung/ *noun* **1** a small green edible but rather tasteless fruit. **2** the Australian tree or shrub with hard narrow leaves and long-lasting yellow or white flowers that bears this fruit: genus *Persoonia*. [from Dharuk, an Aboriginal language]

gee-gee /'jee jee/ *noun Brit, informal* used by or to children: a horse. [reduplication of *gee* as in GEE-UP]

geek /geek/ *noun informal* **1** somebody who is unfashionable or socially awkward. **2** somebody who is obsessively interested in computers and technology. ⯈⯈ **geeky** *adj*. [prob from English dialect *geck, geek* fool]

geese /gees/ *noun* pl of GOOSE¹.

gee up *verb trans informal* **1** to stir (somebody) to greater activity. **2** to encourage (e.g. a horse) to go faster.

gee-up *interj* used as a direction, *esp* to a horse: move ahead; go faster. [origin unknown]

gee whiz /wiz/ *interj chiefly NAmer, informal* gee. [euphemism for *Jesus Christ*]

geezer /'geezə/ *noun informal* a man. [prob alteration of Scot *guiser* one in disguise, mummer]

gefilte fish /gə'filtə/ *noun* a dish consisting of fish, breadcrumbs, eggs, and seasoning shaped into balls or ovals and boiled in a fish stock. [Yiddish *gefilte* filled, stuffed]

gegenschein /'gaygənshien/ *noun* a faint patch of light usu in the ECLIPTIC¹ (apparent path of the sun among the stars) opposite the sun. [German *Gegenschein*, from *gegen* against, counter- + *Schein* shine]

Gehenna /gə'henə/ *noun* hell: *Down to Gehenna or up to the Throne, he travels fastest who travels alone* — Kipling. [late Latin *Gehenna*, via Greek from Hebrew *Gê' Hinnōm* valley of Hinnom, a valley outside Jerusalem where the Israelites sacrificed their children to Baal (Jeremiah 19:5–6)]

Geiger counter /'giegə/ *noun* an electronic instrument for detecting the presence and intensity of ionizing radiations, e.g. particles from a radioactive substance. [named after Hans *Geiger* d.1945, German physicist]

geisha /'gayshə/ *noun* (*pl* **geisha** *or* **geishas**) a Japanese girl who is trained to provide entertaining and light-hearted company, *esp* for a man or a group of men. [Japanese *geisha*, from *gei* art + *-sha* person]

Geissler tube /'gieslə/ *noun* a glass or quartz tube filled with vapour that produces a luminous electrical discharge, used e.g. in spectroscopy. [named after Heinrich *Geissler* d.1879, German mechanic and glassblower, who invented it]

gel[1] /jel/ *noun* **1** a jelly-like substance, e.g. a hair gel or shaving gel. **2** a COLLOID (non-crystalline substance) composed of a liquid evenly dispersed in a solid: compare SOL[3]. [shortening of GELATIN]

gel[2] *verb* (**gelled, gelling**) ➤ *verb intrans* **1** to change into a gel; to set. **2** (*NAmer* **jell**) said of an idea, plan, etc: to take shape or become definite. **3** (*NAmer* **jell**) said of a group of people: to get on well together. ➤ *verb trans* to put gel on (the hair).

gelati /jə'lahti/ *noun* pl of GELATO.

gelatin *or* **gelatine** /'jelatin, -teen/ *noun* a glutinous material obtained from animal tissues by boiling; *esp* a protein used in food, e.g. to set jellies, and photography. [French *gélatine* edible jelly, gelatin, via Italian from Latin *gelare* to freeze, congeal]

gelatinize /ji'latiniez/ *or* **gelatinise** *verb trans* **1** to convert (a substance) into a jelly or jelly-like form. **2** to coat or treat (something) with gelatine. ➤ *verb intrans* to become jelly-like in consistency or change into a jelly. ➤ **gelatinization** /-'zaysh(ə)n/ *noun*.

gelatinous /ji'latinəs/ *adj* resembling gelatin or jelly, *esp* in consistency; viscous. ➤ **gelatinously** *adv*, **gelatinousness** *noun*.

gelation[1] /ji'laysh(ə)n/ *noun* the action or process of freezing. [Latin *gelation-, gelatio*, from *gelare* to freeze]

gelation[2] *noun* the action or process of forming into a gel.

gelato /jə'lahtoh/ *noun* (*pl* **gelati** /jə'lahti/) an Italian ice cream. [Italian *gelato* ice cream]

geld /geld/ *verb trans* to castrate (a male animal). [Middle English *gelden* from Old Norse *gelda*]

gelding *noun* a castrated male horse. [Middle English from Old Norse *geldingr*, from *gelda* to GELD]

gel-filler *noun* a substance injected into a part of the body to remove wrinkles.

gelid /'jelid/ *adj* extremely cold; icy. ➤ **gelidity** /ji'liditi/ *noun*. [Latin *gelidus* from *gelu* frost, cold]

gelignite /'jeligniet/ *noun* a dynamite in which the adsorbent base is a mixture of potassium or sodium nitrate usu with wood pulp. [GELATIN + Latin *ignis* fire + -ITE[1]]

gem[1] /jem/ *noun* **1** a precious or sometimes semiprecious stone, *esp* when cut and polished for use in jewellery. **2** somebody or something highly prized or much beloved. [Middle English *gemme* via French from Latin *gemma* bud, gem]

gem[2] *verb trans* (**gemmed, gemming**) to adorn (something) with gems. ➤ **gemmed** *adj*.

Gemara /ge'mahrə/ *noun* in Judaism, the commentary on the Mishnah forming most of the Talmud. [Aramaic *gĕmārā* completion]

Gemeinschaft /gə'mienshaft, -shahft/ *noun* a social relationship or community characterized by solidarity based on loyalty and kinship: compare GESELLSCHAFT. [German *Gemeinschaft* community, from *gemein* common, general + *-schaft* -ship]

geminate[1] /'jeminat/ *adj* arranged in pairs; doubled. ➤ **geminately** *adv*. [Latin *geminatus*, past part. of *geminare* to double, from *geminus* twin]

geminate[2] /'jeminayt/ *verb trans* in phonetics, to make (a speech sound) paired or doubled. ➤ **gemination** /-'naysh(ə)n/ *noun*.

Gemini /'jemini, -nie/ *noun* **1** in astronomy, a constellation (the Twins) depicted as the twins Castor and Pollux. **2a** in astrology, the

third sign of the zodiac. **b** a person born under this sign. ➤ **Geminian** /-'nee-ən, -'nie-ən/ *adj and noun*. [Latin *gemini* the twins (Castor and Pollux)]

gemma /'jemə/ *noun* (*pl* **gemmae** /'jemee/) **1** a plant bud, *esp* one that develops a leaf. **2** an asexual reproductive body that occurs in mosses, liverworts, etc. **3** an outgrowth of an animal, produced by asexual reproduction and capable of developing into a new animal. ➤ **gemmate** /'jemayt/ *adj*. [Latin *gemma* bud, gem]

gemmation /je'maysh(ə)n/ *noun* asexual reproduction in plants and animals by budding.

gemmiparous /je'mipərəs/ *adj* said of plants and animals: reproducing by budding; gemmate.

gemmology /je'moləji/ *noun* the study of gems. ➤ **gemmological** /-'lojikl/ *adj*, **gemmologist** *noun*.

gemmule /'jemyoohl/ *noun* an internal reproductive bud, e.g. of a sponge, with a resistant case. ➤ **gemmulation** /-'laysh(ə)n/ *noun*. [French *gemmule* from Latin *gemmula*, dimin. of *gemma* bud]

gemsbok /'gemzbok/ *noun* (*pl* **gemsboks** *or collectively* **gemsbok**) a large and strikingly marked oryx with long straight horns, formerly abundant in southern Africa: *Oryx gazella*. [via Afrikaans from Dutch *gemsbok* male chamois, from *gems* chamois + *bok* buck]

gemstone *noun* a mineral or petrified material used as a gem.

Gen. *abbr* **1** General. **2** Genesis (book of the Bible).

gen /jen/ *noun Brit, informal* the correct or complete information. [World War II army slang; short for *general information*]

gen. *abbr* **1** general. **2** genitive. **3** genus.

-gen *comb. form* forming nouns, denoting: **1** something that produces something: *androgen; carcinogen*. **2** something that is produced: *cultigen*. [French *-gène* from Greek *-genēs* born]

gendarme /'zhondahm (*French* ʒɑ̃darm)/ *noun* **1** a member of a corps of armed police, *esp* in France. **2** a pinnacle of rock on a mountain ridge. [French *gendarme* back-formation from *gens-darmes*, pl of *gent d'armes* armed man]

gendarmerie *or* **gendarmery** /'zhondahməri, zhon'dah- (*French* ʒɑ̃darməri)/ *noun* (*treated as sing. or pl*) a body of gendarmes, or their headquarters. [early French *gendarmerie*, from *gendarme*: see GENDARME]

gender /'jendə/ *noun* **1a** a system of subdivision within a grammatical class of a language, e.g. noun or verb, partly based on sexual characteristics, that determines agreement with and selection of other words or grammatical forms. **b** a subclass within such a system. **c** membership of such a subclass. **2** sex; the state of being male or female: *black divinities of the feminine gender* — Dickens. ➤ **gendered** *adj*. [Middle English *gendre* via French from Latin *gener-, genus* birth, race, kind, gender]

Usage note

gender and **sex**. Efforts have been made in recent years to enforce a distinction between *gender* and *sex*, using *gender* to refer to femaleness or maleness in cultural, social, and linguistic contexts and *sex* in biological ones. This distinction is far from being universally applied or accepted, and it is still perfectly in order to speak of 'sex roles' or 'sexual stereotypes'. *Gender* should, however, be used where there is a risk of *sex* being misunderstood to mean 'sexual activity' rather than maleness or femaleness. *Gender* is the correct term to use in language contexts when classifying nouns as masculine, feminine, or neuter.

gender apartheid *noun* discriminatory treatment of a person on account of his or her sex.

gender-bender *noun informal* a person whose appearance and behaviour are sexually ambiguous or do not conform to expected norms.

gendering *noun* discrimination in assessing men and women in similar activities.

gene /jeen/ *noun* a unit of inheritance that is carried on a chromosome, controls transmission of hereditary characters, and consists of DNA or, in some viruses, RNA.

Editorial note

Gregor Mendel (1822–84) discovered that inheritance comes in discrete particles, each from one parent or the other, rather than as substances blended from both parents. His idea was rediscovered in 1900, and the word gene coined thereafter. But genes not only assort independently as strings of particles. DNA itself is made up of strings of digits – particles again — Professor Richard Dawkins.

[German *Gen*, short for *Pangen*, from Greek *pan-* all + *-gen*, from *genos* race]

genealogy /jeeni'aləji/ *noun* (*pl* **genealogies**) **1a** the descent of a person, family, or group from an ancestor or from older forms. **b** an account of this. **2** the study of family pedigrees. ➤➤ **genealogical** /-'lojikl/ *adj*, **genealogically** /-'lojikli/ *adv*, **genealogist** *noun*. [Middle English *genealogie* via French and late Latin from Greek *genealogia*, from *genea* race, family + *-logia* -LOGY]

gene bank *noun* a collection of living organisms kept as a store of genetic material, to be used for genetic engineering, breeding crops, etc.

gene pool *noun* the whole body of genes in an interbreeding population.

genera /'jenərə/ *noun* pl of GENUS.

general[1] /'jen(ə)rəl/ *adj* **1** of, involving, or applicable to every member of a class, kind, or group. **2a** applicable to or characteristic of the majority of individuals involved; prevalent. **b** concerned or dealing with universal rather than particular aspects. **3** holding superior rank or taking precedence over others similarly titled: *the general manager*. **4** approximate rather than strictly accurate: *a general resemblance*. **5** not confined by specialization or careful limitation: *a general amnesty*. ✳ **in general** usually; for the most part. [Middle English via French from Latin *generalis*, from *gener-*, *genus* kind, class]

general[2] *noun* **1** an officer in the British and US armies and the US air force ranking below a field marshal, general of the army, or general of the air force. **2** the chief of a religious order or congregation. **3** (**the general**) *archaic* the general public.

General American *noun* nonregional US pronunciation.

general anaesthetic *noun* an anaesthetic that causes loss of consciousness and lack of sensation over the whole body.

general assembly *noun* (*often* **General Assembly**) the highest governing body of a religious denomination, e.g. the Presbyterian Church.

general average *noun* in marine insurance, voluntary partial loss that is shared proportionally by all parties: compare PARTICULAR AVERAGE.

General Certificate of Education *noun* a British national examination in any of many subjects taken at three levels. The first (Ordinary level) was taken at about the age of 16 and was replaced in England and Wales by the General Certificate of Secondary Education in 1988. The second and third (Advanced and Scholarship levels), which serve as university entrance qualifications, are taken at about 18.

General Certificate of Secondary Education *noun* a British Certificate of Education which replaced the Ordinary Level General Certificate of Education and the Certificate of Secondary Education in 1988. It is taken by pupils of all levels of ability, in any of many subjects, and may involve a final examination, assessment of work done during a two-year course, or a combination of the two.

general election *noun* an election in which candidates are elected in all constituencies of a nation or state.

generalisation /,jen(ə)rəlie'zaysh(ə)n/ *noun* see GENERALIZATION.

generalise /jen(ə)rəliez/ *verb intrans* see GENERALIZE.

generalissimo /,jen(ə)rə'lisimoh/ *noun* (*pl* **generalissimos**) the supreme commander of several armies acting together or of a nation's armed forces. [Italian *generalissimo*, from *generale* general + *-issimo*, superl suffix]

generalist *noun* somebody whose skills, interests, etc extend to several different fields or activities.

generality /jenə'raliti/ *noun* (*pl* **generalities**) **1** a generalization. **2** total applicability. **3** the quality or state of being general. **4** (**the generality**) the greatest part; the bulk; the majority: *The generality … are content to jog on in the safe trammels of national orthodoxy —* Charles Lamb.

generalization *or* **generalisation** /,jen(ə)rəlie'zaysh(ə)n/ *noun* **1** a general statement, law, principle, or proposition that does not take adequate account of the facts. **2** the act or process of generalizing.

generalize *or* **generalise** /'jen(ə)rəliez/ *verb intrans* to make generalizations or vague or indefinite statements. ➤ *verb trans* **1** to make (something) more general or widespread. **2** to derive or induce (a general conception or principle) from particulars; to infer (it). **3** to give general applicability to (e.g. a law). ➤➤ **generalizable** *adj*, **generalizer** *noun*.

generally *adv* **1** without regard to specific instances: *generally speaking*. **2** usually; as a rule: *He generally drinks tea*. **3** collectively; as a whole: *The book should be of interest to children generally*.

general of the air force *noun* an officer of the highest rank in the US air force.

general of the army *noun* an officer of the highest rank in the US army.

general practitioner *noun* a medical doctor who treats all types of disease and is usu the first doctor consulted by a patient. ➤➤ **general practice** *noun*.

general-purpose *adj* suitable to be used for two or more basic purposes.

generalship *noun* **1** the office of a general. **2** military skill in a high commander.

general staff *noun* (*treated as sing. or pl*) a group of officers who aid a commander in administration, training, supply, etc.

general strike *noun* a strike in all or many of the industries of a region or country.

General Synod *noun* the governing body of the Church of England, composed of the bishops and elected members of the clergy and laity.

generate /'jenərayt/ *verb trans* **1** to bring (something) into existence; to create (it). **2** to originate (e.g. energy) by a physical process: *a machine to generate electricity*. **3** in mathematics, to define (a set) by the application of one or more rules or operations to given quantities; *esp* to trace out (a curve) by a moving point or trace out (a surface) by a moving curve. **4** in linguistics, to produce (a structure) by the applications of rules or operations to given items. **5** to be the cause of (a situation, action, or state of mind): *The stories generated a good deal of suspense*. ➤➤ **generable** *adj*. [Latin *generatus*, past part. of *generare*, from *gener-*, *genus* birth]

generation /jenə'raysh(ə)n/ *noun* **1a** (*treated as sing. or pl*) a group of individuals born and living at the same time. **b** (*treated as sing. or pl*) a group of individuals sharing a usu specified status for a limited period: *the next generation of students*. **c** a group of living organisms constituting a single step in the line of descent from an ancestor. **d** a type or class of objects usu developed from an earlier type: *a new generation of computers*. **2** the average time between the birth of parents and that of their offspring, usu considered to be about 30 years. **3a** the producing of offspring; procreation. **b** the process of coming or bringing into being; production or origination: *generation of income*; *generation of electricity*. ➤➤ **generational** *adj*. [Middle English *generacioun* via French from Latin *generation-*, *generatio*, from *generare*: see GENERATE]

generation gap *noun* the difference in ideas, feelings, and interests between older and younger people, *esp* considered as causing a mutual lack of understanding.

generation X *noun* the generation of people who were born between the mid 1960s and the mid 1970s, seen as being well-educated but having no direction in life. ➤➤ **Generation Xer** *noun*.

generative /'jen(ə)rətiv/ *adj* having the power or function of generating, originating, producing, reproducing, etc.

generative grammar *noun* an ordered set of rules for producing the grammatical sentences of a language.

generator *noun* **1** a machine by which mechanical energy is changed into electrical energy. **2** an apparatus for producing a vapour or gas. **3** a person or thing that generates.

generatrix /jenə'raytriks/ *noun* (*pl* **generatrices** /-'raytrəseez, -rə'triseez/) a point, line, or surface whose motion generates a line, surface, or solid. [scientific Latin *generatrix* from Latin, fem of *generator*]

generic /ji'nerik/ *adj* **1** characteristic of or applied to a whole group or class; general. **2** not having a trademark: *generic drugs*. **3** having the rank of a biological genus. ➤➤ **generically** *adv*. [French *générique* from Latin *gener-*, *genus* birth, kind, class]

generic advertising *noun* advertising that is designed to promote a broad class of product rather than an individual brand.

generous /'jen(ə)rəs/ *adj* **1** liberal in giving e.g. money or help. **2** magnanimous and kindly. **3** marked by abundance, ample proportions, or richness. **4** said of wine: rich in alcohol. ➤➤ **generosity** /-'rositi/ *noun*, **generously** *adv*, **generousness** *noun*. [French *genereux* from Latin *generosus* of noble birth, noble, from *gener-*, *genus* birth, family]

geneses /'jenəseez/ *noun* pl of GENESIS.

Genesis /'jenəsis/ *noun* the first book of the Old Testament. [via Latin from Greek, from *gignesthai* to be born]

genesis *noun* (*pl* **geneses** /-seez/) the origin or coming into being of something.

-genesis *comb. form* forming nouns, denoting: origin or generation: *parthenogenesis*.

genet /'jenit/ *noun* any of a genus of small African and European flesh-eating cat-like mammals related to the civets: genus *Genetta*. [Middle English *genete* via French from Arabic *jarnayṭ*]

gene technology *noun* the techniques and equipment used in the study, identification, and modification of genes.

gene therapy *noun* the correction of genetic defects by the replacement or supplementation of affected cells with genetically corrected cells, or with normal genes.

genetic /jə'netik/ *adj* **1a** of or involving genetics. **b** of or involving genes. **2** of or determined by the origin or development of something. ⟩⟩ **genetical** *adj*, **genetically** *adv*. [GENESIS]

-genetic *comb. form* forming adjectives, with the meanings: **1** producing: *psychogenetic*. **2** produced by: *spermatogenetic*.

genetic code *noun* the triplet sequences of bases in DNA or RNA strands that form the biochemical basis of heredity and determine the specific amino acid sequences in proteins.

genetic counselling *noun* advice given to prospective parents about the chances of their conceiving children with hereditary disorders.

genetic engineering *noun* the artificial manipulation of the genetic constitution of living things for experimental or industrial purposes.

genetic fingerprint *noun* a unique pattern of repeated DNA sequences in the genetic make-up of an individual that can be used to identify that individual. ⟩⟩ **genetic fingerprinting** *noun*.

genetic map *noun* the arrangement of genes on a chromosome.

genetics *pl noun* **1** (*treated as sing.*) a branch of biology that deals with the mechanisms and structures involved in the heredity and variation of organisms. **2** (*treated as sing. or pl*) the genetic make-up of an organism, type, group, or condition. ⟩⟩ **geneticist** /-sist/ *noun*.

genetic trespass *noun* the acquisition of a sample of a person's DNA without their permission.

genetic use restriction technology *noun* genetic modification of seeds that renders the subsequent generation of seeds infertile.

Geneva bands /je'neevə/ *pl noun* two strips of white cloth suspended from the front of the collar of some ecclesiastical robes. [named after *Geneva*, a city in Switzerland; from their use by the Calvinist clergy of Geneva]

Geneva Convention *noun* any of a series of agreements, first made at Geneva, concerning the treatment of prisoners of war and of the sick, wounded, and dead in battle.

Geneva gown *noun* a loose large-sleeved black gown worn by academics and some Protestant clergymen. [from its use by the Calvinist clergy of Geneva]

Genevan *noun* a Calvinist. ⟩⟩ **Genevan** *adj*.

genial[1] /'jeeni·əl/ *adj* **1** cheerfully good-tempered; kindly. **2** *literary* said of the weather: favourable to growth or comfort; mild: *genial sunshine*. ⟩⟩ **geniality** /-'aliti/ *noun*, **genially** *adv*. [Latin *genialis* from *genius*: see GENIUS]

genial[2] /jə'nee·əl/ *adj* to do with or in the region of the chin. [Greek *geneion* chin, from *genys* jaw]

genic /'jeenik, 'jenik/ *adj* of or being a gene.

-genic *comb. form* forming adjectives, with the meanings: **1** producing; forming: *erotogenic*. **2** produced by; formed from: *phytogenic*. **3** well-suited to or suitable for: *photogenic*; *telegenic*. [from -GEN + -IC[1]]

genie /'jeeni/ *noun* (*pl* **genies** or **genii** /'jeeniie/) a jinn or spirit in stories who can be summoned to grant wishes. [French *génie* from Arabic *jinnīy*]

genii /'jeeniie/ *noun* **1** pl of GENIE. **2** pl of GENIUS.

genii loci /'lohsie/ *noun* pl of GENIUS LOCI.

genista /ji'nistə/ *noun* any of a genus of leguminous shrubs with yellow flowers, related to broom: genus *Genista*. [Latin]

genital /'jenitl/ *adj* **1** to do with or in the region of the genitalia. **2** in psychoanalysis, of or characterized by the final stage of sexual development in which oral and anal impulses are replaced by gratification obtained from sexual relationships: compare ANAL, ORAL[1]. ⟩⟩ **genitally** *adv*. [Middle English from Latin *genitalis*, from *gignere* to beget]

genital herpes *noun* a sexually transmitted disease caused by the herpes simplex virus and characterized by blisters in the genital region.

genitalia /jeni'tayli·ə/ *pl noun* the external reproductive and sexual organs. [Latin *genitalia*, neuter pl of *genitalis*: see GENITAL]

genitals *pl noun* the genitalia.

genitive[1] /'jenitiv/ *adj* denoting a grammatical case expressing a relationship of possessor or source. ⟩⟩ **genitival** /-'tievl/ *adj*, **genitivally** /-'tievəli/ *adv*. [Middle English from Latin *genitivus* of birth, from *gignere* to beget]

genitive[2] *noun* the genitive case or a word in this case.

genitourinary /ˌjenitoh'yoo·ərin(ə)ri/ *adj* to do with the genital and urinary organs.

genius /'jeenyəs/ *noun* (*pl* **geniuses**) **1** a person endowed with extraordinary intellectual power; *specif* a person of a very high intelligence. **2** extraordinary intellectual power, *esp* as displayed in creative activity: *Mediocrity knows nothing higher than itself, but talent instantly recognizes genius* — Conan Doyle. **3** a single strongly marked capacity or aptitude: *He had a genius for teaching maths*. **4** (*pl* **genii** /'jeeniie/) a spirit, *esp* in Arabic folklore. **5** a special, distinctive, or identifying character or spirit: *Optimism was the genius of the Victorian era*. [Latin *genius* tutelary spirit, fondness for social enjoyment, from *gignere* to beget]

genius loci /'lohsie/ *noun* (*pl* **genii loci**) the pervading spirit or atmosphere of a place. [Latin *genius loci* spirit of a place]

genizah /ge'neezə/ *noun* a storeroom in a synagogue, for discarded books, papers, and sacred objects. [Hebrew *gĕnīzāh* hiding place]

genoa /'jenoh·ə/ *noun* a large jib which partly overlaps a ship's mainsail. [named after *Genoa*, a city in Italy]

genocide /'jenəsied/ *noun* the deliberate murder of a racial or cultural group. ⟩⟩ **genocidal** /-'siedl/ *adj*. [Greek *genos* race + -CIDE]

genome /'jeenohm/ *noun* **1** the complete single or basic set of chromosomes characteristic of a particular kind of organism. **2** a single set of an organism's chromosomes with the genes they contain.

Editorial note
An organism's genome is its complete set of DNA. It contains all the genetic instructions to build and maintain the organism. The DNA of different individuals is not the same, and strictly speaking there is no such thing as 'the' human genome. But the DNA of all humans is sufficiently similar, as compared with other life forms, that we can reasonably talk of the human genome — Dr Mark Ridley.

⟩⟩ **genomic** /ji'nomik/ *adj*. [German *Genom*, from GENE + *Chromosom* chromosome]

genotoxin /jeenoh'toksin/ *noun* a substance that damages or alters the DNA in the cells of living organisms, causing gene mutations, chromosomal aberrations, or cancer. ⟩⟩ **genotoxic** /-'toksik/ *adj*, **genotoxicity** /-tok'sisiti/ *noun*. [GENE + TOXIN]

genotype /'jenohtiep/ *noun* the genetic constitution of an individual or group: compare PHENOTYPE. ⟩⟩ **genotypic** /-'tipik/ *adj*.

-genous *comb. form* forming adjectives, with the meanings: **1** producing or yielding: *erogenous*. **2** produced by or originating in: *endogenous*. [-GEN + -OUS]

genre /'zhonhrə (*French* ʒɑ̃:r)/ *noun* **1** a sort or type. **2** a category of artistic, musical, or literary composition characterized by a particular style, form, or content. [French *genre* kind, gender, from Latin *gener-*, *genus*]

genre painting *noun* painting that depicts scenes or events from everyday life.

gens /jenz/ *noun* (*pl* **gentes** /'jenteez/) **1** an ancient Roman clan embracing the families of the same stock in the male line, with the members having a common name and being united in worship of their common ancestor. **2** in anthropology, a clan; *esp* one formed through the male line of descent. [Latin *gent-*, *gens* class, nation]

gent /jent/ *noun informal* a gentleman.

genteel /jen'teel/ *adj* **1** of or appropriate to the status or manners of the gentry or upper class. **2** free from vulgarity or rudeness;

polite. ⟫ **genteelly** adv, **genteelness** noun. [Old French gentil: see GENTLE[1]]

gentes /'jenteez/ noun pl of GENS.

gentian /'jensh(ə)n/ noun any of several related plants with smooth leaves and showy usu blue flowers found esp in mountainous regions: genera Gentiana and Gentianella. [Middle English gencian via French from Latin gentiana, perhaps named after Gentius, second-cent. BC Illyrian king said to have discovered its medicinal properties]

gentian violet noun a violet dye used as a biological stain and as a skin disinfectant in the treatment of boils, ulcers, etc.

gentile[1] /'jentiel/ noun **1a** (often **Gentile**) a person of a non-Jewish nation or of non-Jewish faith. **b** a person who is not a Mormon. **2** a heathen or pagan. [Middle English via late Latin from Latin gentilis (see GENTLE[1]), applied in the Vulgate to non-Jews]

gentile[2] adj **1** (often **Gentile**) of the nations at large as distinguished from the Jews. **2** heathen or pagan. **3** of a nation, tribe, or clan.

gentility /jen'tiliti/ noun **1a** genteel attitudes, behaviour, or activity. **b** superior social status or prestige indicated by manners, possessions, etc. **2** (treated as sing. or pl) the members of the upper class. [Middle English gentilete via French from Latin gentilitat-, gentilitas state of belonging to the same clan, from gentilis: see GENTLE[1]]

gentle[1] /'jentl/ adj (**gentler, gentlest**) **1** said of a person: kind and mild; not harsh or violent. **2** soft or delicate: I heard a gentle knock on the door. **3** said of a breeze: moderate. **4** said of a slope: gradual. **5** archaic honourable, distinguished; specif of or belonging to a gentleman. ⟫ **gentleness** noun, **gently** adv. [Middle English gentil via Old French gentil from Latin gentilis of a clan, of the same clan, from gent-, gens clan, nation]

gentle[2] noun a maggot, esp when used as bait for fish. [GENTLE[1], in the sense 'soft']

gentle[3] verb trans to make (e.g. an animal) mild, docile, soft, or moderate. ~ verb intrans to become docile or calm.

gentle breeze noun a wind having a speed of 12 to 19km/h (8 to 12mph).

gentlefolk or **gentlefolks** pl noun archaic people of good family and breeding.

gentleman noun (pl **gentlemen**) **1a** a man who is chivalrous, well-mannered, and honourable. **b** a man belonging to the landed gentry or nobility. **c** a man of independent wealth who does not work for gain. **2** in polite or formal reference: a man: ladies and gentlemen; Show this gentleman to a seat. ⟫ **gentlemanliness** noun, **gentlemanly** adj.

gentleman-at-arms noun (pl **gentlemen-at-arms**) any of a bodyguard of 40 gentlemen who attend the British sovereign on state occasions.

gentleman farmer noun (pl **gentlemen farmers**) a wealthy man who farms mainly for pleasure rather than for basic income.

gentleman's agreement noun an unwritten agreement that is secured only by the honour of the participants and is not legally enforceable.

gentleman's gentleman noun a valet.

gentlemen's agreement noun = GENTLEMAN'S AGREEMENT.

gentlewoman noun (pl **gentlewomen**) **1** archaic. **a** a woman of noble or gentle birth. **b** a woman attendant on a lady of rank. **2** dated a woman of refined manners; a lady.

gentrification /,jentrifi'kaysh(ə)n/ noun the purchase and renovation, by middle-class people, of urban and run-down properties that are traditionally inhabited by working-class people.

gentrify /'jentrifie/ verb trans (**gentrifies, gentrified, gentrifying**) to change (a property or area) by gentrification. ⟫ **gentrifier** noun.

gentry /'jentri/ noun **1** (treated as sing. or pl) the upper class, or those regarded as constituting it in local society: Mr Brooke ... was in this case brave enough to defy the world – that is to say, Mrs Cadwallader the Rector's wife, and the small group of gentry with whom he visited — George Eliot. **2** derog or humorous (treated as pl) people of a specified kind or class: You can't trust these academic gentry. [Middle English gentrie from Old French genterise, gentelise, from gentil: see GENTLE[1]]

gents /jents/ noun (pl **gents**) Brit, informal a public lavatory for men. [short for gentlemen's]

genuflect /'jenyooflekt, -'flekt/ verb intrans to bend the knee, esp in worship or as a gesture of respect to sacred objects. ⟫ **genuflection** /-'fleksh(ə)n/ noun, **genuflector** noun, **genuflexion** /-'fleksh(ə)n/ noun. [late Latin genuflectere, from Latin genu knee + flectere to bend]

genuine /'jenyooin/ adj **1** actually produced by or proceeding from the alleged source or author or having the reputed qualities or character: The signature is genuine; This is a genuine antique. **2** free from pretence; sincere. ⟫ **genuinely** adv, **genuineness** noun. [Latin genuinus native, genuine, from genu knee; from the Roman custom of a father putting a child on his knee to acknowledge paternity]

gen up /jen/ verb intrans (**genned, genning**) Brit, informal (+ on) to find information; to learn about something: She's genning up on the company before her interview. [GEN]

genus /'jeenəs/ noun (pl **genera** /'jenərə/) **1** a category in the classification of living things ranking between family and species. **2** a class divided into several subordinate classes. [Latin gener-, genus birth, race, kind]

-geny comb. form forming nouns, denoting: origin, development, or mode of production: biogeny; ontogeny. [Greek -geneia act of being born, from -genēs born]

geo- comb. form forming words, with the meanings: **1** ground or soil: geophyte; geophagy. **2** earth, or the earth's surface: geophysics; geodesic. **3** geographical; geography and: geopolitics. [Middle English geo- via French and Latin from Greek gē-, gēo-, from gē earth]

geocentric /jeeoh'sentrik/ adj **1** having or relating to the earth as centre: compare HELIOCENTRIC. **2** measured from or observed as if from the earth's centre. ⟫ **geocentrically** adv, **geocentrism** noun.

geochronology /,jeeohkrə'noləji/ noun the chronology of the past as indicated by geological data. ⟫ **geochronological** /-kronə'lojikl/ adj, **geochronologist** noun.

geode /'jeeohd/ noun **1** a cavity lined with crystals or mineral matter. **2** a rounded stone having such a cavity. ⟫ **geodic** /ji'odik/ adj. [via Latin from Greek geōdēs earthlike, from gē earth]

geodesic[1] /jeeoh'deesik/ adj **1** made of light straight structural elements mostly in tension: a geodesic dome. **2** geodetic.

geodesic[2] noun the shortest line on a given surface between two points.

geodesy /ji'odəsi/ noun a branch of applied mathematics that determines the exact positions of points and the shape and area of large portions of the earth's surface. ⟫ **geodesist** noun. [Greek geōdaisia, from gē earth + daiesthai to divide]

geodetic[1] /jeeoh'detik/ adj **1** of or determined by geodesy. **2** relating to the geometry of geodetic lines. ⟫ **geodetically** adv. [Greek geōdaitēs land surveyor, from geōdaisia: see GEODESY]

geodetic[2] noun a geodesic on the earth's surface.

geodetic line noun = GEODETIC[2].

geog. abbr **1** geographic. **2** geographical. **3** geography.

geographical /jee-ə'grafikl/ adj **1** to do with geography. **2** belonging to or characteristic of a particular region. ⟫ **geographic** adj, **geographically** adv.

geographical mile noun a nautical mile (1853.2m).

geographic profiling or **geographical profiling** noun computer-based analysis of the circumstances of related crimes to help determine the likely social environment of the offender. ⟫ **geographical profiler** noun, **geographic profiler** noun.

geography /ji'ografi/ noun **1** a science that deals with the earth and its life; esp the description of land, sea, air, and the distribution of plant and animal life including human beings and their industries. **2** the geographical features of an area. ⟫ **geographer** noun. [via Latin from Greek geōgraphia, from geōgraphein to describe the earth's surface, from gē earth + graphein to write]

geoid /'jeeoyd/ noun the shape of the surface that the earth would have if all parts of the earth had the same height as the mean sea level of the oceans. [German Geoid from Greek geoeidēs earthlike, from gē earth]

geol. abbr **1** geologic. **2** geological. **3** geology.

geology /ji'oləji/ noun **1** a science that deals with the origin, structure, composition, and history of the earth, esp as recorded in rocks. **2** the geological features of an area. ⟫ **geologic** /jee-ə'lojik/ adj,

geological /jee-ə'lojikl/ adj, **geologically** /jee-ə'lojikli/ adv, **geologist** noun. [Latin geologia, from Greek gē earth + -logia -LOGY]

geom. abbr **1** geometric. **2** geometrical. **3** geometry.

geomagnetism /jeeoh'magnitiz(ə)m/ noun **1** the magnetic field of the earth. **2** the branch of geology that deals with this. ➤➤ **geomagnetic** /-'netik/ adj, **geomagnetically** /-'netikli/ adv.

geomancy /'jee-əmansi/ noun **1** divination by means of configurations of earth or by dots jotted down hastily at random. **2** the supposed discovery and mystical interpretation of the disposition and alignment of prominent landscape features and sacred sites. ➤➤ **geomantic** /-'mantik/ adj. [Middle English geomancie via French and late Latin from late Greek gēomanteia, from Greek gē earth + -manteia -MANCY]

geometer /ji'omitə/ noun **1** a specialist in geometry. **2** a geometrid moth or caterpillar. [via late Latin from Greek geōmetrēs, from gē earth + metrēs measurer]

geometric /jee-ə'metrik/ adj **1a** of or according to geometry or its laws. **b** increasing in a geometric progression: geometric population growth. **2a** using, being, or decorated with patterns formed from straight and curved lines. **b** (**Geometric**) of or being a style of ancient Greek pottery decorated with geometric patterns. ➤➤ **geometrical** adj, **geometrically** adv.

geometric mean noun the nth root of the product of n numbers, e.g. the square root of two numbers: The geometric mean of nine and four is six.

geometric progression noun a sequence, e.g. one, ½, ¼, in which the ratio of any term to its predecessor is constant.

geometric series noun a series (e.g. $1 + x + x^2 + x^3 + ...$) whose terms form a geometric progression.

geometrid /ji'omətrid/ noun any of a family of moths with large wings and larvae that move by looping the body: family Geometridae. [Greek geōmetrēs (see GEOMETER) + -ID[1]]

geometry /ji'omətri/ noun (pl **geometries**) **1a** a branch of mathematics that deals with the measurement, properties, and relationships of points, lines, angles, surfaces, and solids. **b** a particular type or system of geometry. **2** a surface shape, e.g. of a crystal. **3** an arrangement of objects or parts that suggests geometrical figures. ➤➤ **geometrician** /-'trish(ə)n/ noun. [Middle English geometrie via French and Latin from Greek geōmetria, from geōmetrein to measure the earth, from gē earth + metron measure]

geomorphic /jeeoh'mawfik/ adj of or concerned with the form or solid surface features of the earth.

geomorphology /,jeeohmaw'folәji/ noun the geology of the structure and formation of the features of the surface of the earth. ➤➤ **geomorphological** /-'lojikl/ adj, **geomorphologist** noun.

geophysics /jeeoh'fiziks/ pl noun (treated as sing.) the physics of the earth including meteorology, oceanography, seismology, etc. ➤➤ **geophysical** adj, **geophysicist** /-sist/ noun.

geopolitics /jeeoh'politiks/ pl noun **1** (treated as sing.) the study of the influence of geography, economics, and demography on politics. **2** (treated as sing.) worldwide politics. **3** the combination of geographical and political factors that affect a region or country. ➤➤ **geopolitical** /-'litikl/ adj, **geopolitically** /-'litikli/ adv, **geopolitician** /-'tish(ə)n/ noun.

Geordie /'jawdi/ noun Brit, informal **1** a native or inhabitant of Tyneside in NE England. **2** the English dialect spoken in Tyneside. ➤➤ **Geordie** adj. [Scots and northern dialect Geordie, nickname for George]

georgette /jaw'jet/ noun a thin strong crepe fabric of silk or of other material with a dull pebbly surface. [named after Georgette de la Plante fl.c.1900, French dressmaker]

Georgian[1] /'jawj(ə)n/ adj **1** relating to or characteristic of the reigns of the first four King Georges of Britain (1714–1830). **2** relating to or characteristic of the reign of King George V of Britain (1910–36). **3** denoting a style of architecture associated with this period, characterized by neoclassicism. **4** denoting a style of British pastoral poetry of 1910 to 1920.

Georgian[2] noun **1** a native or inhabitant of Georgia in the Caucasus. **2** the national language of the people of Georgia. ➤➤ **Georgian** adj.

Georgian[3] noun a native or inhabitant of the US state of Georgia. ➤➤ **Georgian** adj.

geostatics /jeeoh'statiks/ pl noun (treated as sing.) the branch of physics concerned with the balance of forces within the earth.

geostationary /jeeoh'stayshən(ə)ri/ adj said of an artificial satellite: travelling above the equator at the same speed as the earth rotates, so remaining above the same place.

geostrophic /jeeoh'strofik/ adj of or caused by the rotation of the earth: geostrophic wind. ➤➤ **geostrophically** adv. [GEO- + Greek strophikos turned, from strophē turning]

geosynchronous /jeeoh'singkrənəs/ adj = GEOSTATIONARY.

geosyncline /jeeoh'singklien/ noun a great downward fold of the earth's crust consisting of an elongated basin that becomes filled with sediment. ➤➤ **geosynclinal** adj.

geothermal /jeeoh'thuhml/ adj of or produced by the heat of the earth's interior. ➤➤ **geothermally** adv.

geothermic /jeeoh'thuhmik/ adj GEOTHERMAL.

geotropism /jee-ə'trohpiz(ə)m/ noun tropism, e.g. in the downward growth of roots, in which gravity is the orienting factor. ➤➤ **geotropic** /-'tropik/ adj.

geranium /jə'rayni-əm/ noun **1** any of a widely distributed genus of plants with radially symmetrical pinkish to blue flowers: genus Geranium. **2** a pelargonium. [Latin genus name, from Greek geranion, dimin. of geranos crane; from the long narrow fruit of some species, thought to resemble a crane's beak: compare CRANESBILL, PELARGONIUM]

gerbera /'juhbərə, 'guh-/ noun any of a genus of African and Asian plants of the daisy family, with tufted leaves and showy yellow, pink, or orange flowers: genus Gerbera. [Latin genus name, named after Traugott Gerber d.1743, German naturalist]

gerbil /'juhbil/ noun any of numerous species of African and Asian burrowing desert rodents with long hind legs adapted for leaping: genus Gerbillus and other genera. [French gerbille from Latin genus name Gerbillus, dimin. of JERBOA]

gerfalcon /juh'fawlkən/ noun = GYRFALCON.

geriatric[1] /jeri'atrik/ adj **1** of or for geriatrics, the aged, or the process of ageing. **2** informal, derog aged or decrepit. [Greek gēras old age + -IATRIC]

geriatric[2] noun an elderly person.

geriatrics pl noun (treated as sing. or pl) a branch of medicine that deals with old age and the diseases associated with old age. ➤➤ **geriatrician** /-'trish(ə)n/ noun.

germ /juhm/ noun **1** a micro-organism, esp one that causes disease. **2** a small mass of cells capable of developing into an organism or one of its points. **3** the embryo of a cereal grain that is usu separated from the starchy endosperm during milling: wheat germ. **4** the rudimentary state from which something develops: the germ of an idea. ➤➤ **germy** adj. [Middle English via Old French from Latin germin-, germen seed, sprout, from gignere to beget]

German /'juhmən/ noun **1** a native or inhabitant of Germany. **2** the Germanic language of the people of Germany, Austria, and parts of Switzerland. ➤➤ **German** adj.

Word history

late Latin Germanus, a member of the Germanic peoples. Most of the obvious similarities between the German and English languages result from their common descent from a Germanic language spoken in prehistoric times, which in turn was a descendant of the prehistoric Indo-European language. Although the Norman Conquest of Britain in 1066 introduced many French words into English, a significant number of these were actually of Germanic origin: cramp, crush, flatter, feud, fresh, frock, garden, helmet, roast, scale, stout, and so on. Borrowings from German that have passed into English since the 16th cent. include hamster, lager, marzipan, meerschaum, plunder, poltergeist, poodle, quartz, seminar, spanner, veneer, and zinc. Events in the first half of the 20th cent. produced further borrowings such as blitz, flak, führer, putsch, and strafe.

german /juh'mən/ adj archaic germane. [Middle English germain via French from Latin germanus having the same parents, from gignere to beget]

germander /juh'mandə/ noun **1** any of several species of plants of the mint family: genus Teucrium. **2** a blue-flowered speedwell: Veronica chamaedrys. [Middle English germaunder via French and Latin from Greek chamaidrys, from chamai on the ground + drys oak, tree; because the leaves of some species resemble oak leaves]

germane /juh'mayn/ adj relevant and appropriate. ➤➤ **germanely** adv, **germaneness** noun. [variant of GERMAN]

Germanic[1] /juh'manik/ adj **1** relating to Germanic. **2** characteristic of the Germanic-speaking peoples. **3** characteristic of the German people.

Germanic[2] *noun* **1** a branch of the Indo-European language family containing English, German, Dutch, Afrikaans, Flemish, Frisian, the Scandinavian languages, and Gothic. **2** Proto-Germanic, the unrecorded early language from which these languages developed.

germanium /juh'mayni·əm/ *noun* a greyish white metalloid chemical element that resembles silicon, occurs naturally in sulphide ores, and is used as a semiconductor: symbol Ge, atomic number 32. [Latin *germanium*, from late Latin *Germania* Germany; named by C A Winkler d.1904, German chemist who discovered it]

German measles *pl noun* (*treated as sing.*) = RUBELLA.

Germano- *comb. form* forming words, with the meanings: **1** the German nation, people, or culture: *Germanophile*. **2** German and: *Germano-Russian*.

German shepherd *noun* = ALSATIAN (1).

German silver *noun* = NICKEL SILVER.

germ cell *noun* an egg or sperm cell, or any of the cells from which they develop.

germicide /'juhmisied/ *noun* a substance that kills germs. ⟫ **germicidal** /-'siedl/ *adj.*

germinal /'juhminl/ *adj* **1** of or having the characteristics of a germ cell or early embryo. **2a** in the earliest stage of development. **b** creative or seminal. ⟫ **germinally** *adv.* [French *germinal* from Latin *germin-*, *germen*: see GERM]

germinate /'juhminayt/ *verb intrans* **1** to begin to grow; to sprout. **2** to come into being; to evolve. ⟫ *verb trans* to cause (a seed or spore) to sprout or develop. ⟫ **germination** /-'naysh(ə)n/ *noun*, **germinative** /-nətiv/ *adj*, **germinator** *noun*. [Latin *germinatus*, past part. of *germinare* to sprout, from *germin-*, *germen*: see GERM]

germ layer *noun* any of the three primary layers of cells, endoderm, ectoderm, or mesoderm, differentiated early in the development of most embryos.

germ plasm *noun* the hereditary material of the germ cells; the genes.

germ warfare *noun* the use of germs to spread disease as a form of warfare.

gerontocracy /jeron'tokrəsi/ *noun* (*pl* **gerontocracies**) **1** a society in which a group of old men or a council of elders dominates or exercises control. **2** rule by old men: *An … important antidote to American democracy is American gerontocracy* — J K Galbraith. ⟫ **gerontocratic** /-'kratik/ *adj.* [French *gérontocratie*, from Greek *geront-* old man + *-cratie* -CRACY]

gerontology /jeron'toləji/ *noun* the biology and medicine of ageing and the problems of the aged. ⟫ **gerontological** /-'lojikl/ *adj*, **gerontologist** *noun*.

-gerous *comb. form* forming adjectives, with the meaning: bearing or producing: *dentigerous*. [Latin *-ger* bearing, from *gerere* to bear]

gerrymander[1] /'jerimandə/ *verb trans* (**gerrymandered, gerrymandering**) **1** to divide (an area) into election districts to give one political party an electoral advantage. **2** to manipulate or alter (something) to give oneself an advantage. ⟫ **gerrymanderer** *noun*, **gerrymandering** *noun*.

gerrymander[2] *noun* gerrymandering, or the pattern of districts resulting from this.

Word history
named after Elbridge *Gerry* d.1814, US statesman + SALAMANDER; from the shape of an election district formed during Gerry's governorship of Massachusetts, which favoured his own party. A map of the district, with wings, claws, and teeth added, was published in a Boston newspaper in 1812.

gerund /'jerənd/ *noun* **1** a verbal noun in Latin that expresses generalized or uncompleted action and is used in all cases but the nominative. **2** any of several linguistic forms similar in function to the Latin gerund in languages other than Latin; *esp* the English verbal noun ending in *-ing* that has the function of a noun and at the same time shows certain verbal features, e.g. *singing* in *He likes singing* and in *Singing chorales is fun*. [late Latin *gerundium* from Latin *gerundus*, verbal noun from *gerere* to bear, carry on]

gerundive[1] /ji'rundiv/ *noun* **1** the Latin future passive participle that expresses the desirability or necessity of an action and has the same suffix as the gerund. **2** a linguistic form in another language that has a similar function.

gerundive[2] *adj* of or similar to the gerund or gerundive.

Gesellschaft /gə'zelshaft, -shahft/ *noun* a social relationship or society characterized by mechanistic associations based on division of labour, utility, and self-interest: compare GEMEINSCHAFT. [German *Gesellschaft* companionship, society, from *Gesell* companion + *-schaft* -ship]

gesso /'jesoh/ *noun* (*pl* **gessoes**) **1** plaster of Paris or gypsum mixed with glue for use in painting or making bas-reliefs. **2** a paste used as a basis for painting or gilding on wood or occasionally canvas. [Italian *gesso* gypsum, from Latin *gypsum*: see GYPSUM]

gest or **geste** /jest/ *noun* a tale of adventures; *esp* a romance in verse. [Middle English *geste*: see JEST[1]]

gestalt /gə'shtalt/ *noun* (*pl* **gestalten** /-tn/ or **gestalts**) a structure, pattern, etc, e.g. a melody, that as an object of perception constitutes a functional unit with properties not derivable from the sum of its parts. [German *Gestalt* shape, form]

Gestalt psychology *noun* the study of perception and behaviour using the theory that perceptions, reactions, etc are gestalts.

Gestapo /gə'shtahpoh, gə'stahpoh/ *noun* the secret police organization operating against suspected traitors in Nazi Germany. [German *Gestapo*, from *Geheime Staatspolizei* secret state police]

gestate /jə'stayt, 'jestayt/ *verb trans* to carry (a foetus) in gestation. ⟫ *verb intrans* said of a foetus: to be in the process of gestation. [back-formation from GESTATION]

gestation /jə'staysh(ə)n/ *noun* **1** the carrying of young in the uterus; pregnancy. **2** conception and development, *esp* in the mind. [Latin *gestation-*, *gestatio*, from *gestare* to bear, from *gestus* action, bearing, past part. of *gerere* to bear]

geste /jest/ *noun* see GEST.

gesticulate /jə'stikyoolayt/ *verb intrans* to make expressive gestures, *esp* when speaking: *He gesticulated to the waiter for the bill*. ⟫ **gesticulation** /-'laysh(ə)n/ *noun*, **gesticulative** /-lətiv/ *adj*, **gesticulator** *noun*, **gesticulatory** /-lət(ə)ri/ *adj.* [Latin *gesticulatus*, past part. of *gesticulari*, from *gesticulus*, dimin. of *gestus*: see GESTATION]

gesture[1] /'jeschə/ *noun* **1a** a movement, usu of the body or limbs, that expresses or emphasizes an idea, sentiment, or attitude. **b** the use of gestures. **2** something said or done for its effect on the attitudes of others or to convey a feeling, e.g. friendliness. ⟫ **gestural** *adj.* [late Latin *gestura* mode of action, from Latin *gestus*: see GESTATION]

gesture[2] *verb intrans* to make a gesture. ⟫ *verb trans* to express (something) with a gesture.

get[1] *verb* (**getting**, past tense **got** /got/, past part. **got** or NAmer or archaic **gotten** /'gotn/) ⟫ *verb trans* **1a** to receive or gain possession of (something). **b** to seek out and fetch or provide (something): *Get me a pencil*. **c** to obtain (permission, approval, etc) by concession or entreaty. **d** to seize or capture (something or somebody). **2a** to receive (something unpleasant) as a return; to earn: *She got a reputation for carelessness*; *He got the sack*. **b** to become affected by (an illness or other unwelcome condition). **c** to suffer a specified injury to (a part of the body): *He got his fingers burned*. **3** to cause (something), e.g.: **a** to cause (somebody or something) to come, go, or move: *Get him out of the house*. **b** to bring (something) into a specified condition by direct action: *I must get my shoes mended*. **c** to prevail on or induce (somebody): *Get your Dad to pick you up*. **4** to catch (e.g. a train). **5** to make (e.g. a meal) ready; to prepare (something). **6a** *informal* to punish or harm (somebody). **b** *informal* to hit (somebody). **c** *informal* to puzzle (somebody): *You've got me there!* **7a** to hear (something): *I didn't quite get that*. **b** to establish communication with (somebody). **8** *informal* to irritate (somebody). **9** *informal* to understand (somebody or something): *Don't get me wrong*. **10** *informal* used as an exclamation of scorn: to look at (somebody): *Get you in your mother's high heels!* **11** *archaic* to beget (a child). ⟫ *verb intrans* **1** to reach or enter into the specified condition or activity; to become: *get lost*; *get drunk*; *You're getting a big girl now*. **2** used as a verbal auxiliary instead of *be* to form the passive: *They didn't want to take the slightest risk of getting trapped inside*. **3a** to reach or arrive: *Where's my pen got to?* **b** to succeed in coming or going: *At last we're getting somewhere*; *I finally got to sleep after midnight*. **c** to contrive by effort, good fortune, or permission: *She never gets to drive the car*. **4** *informal* to leave immediately. ✱ **get cracking/weaving** *informal* to make a start; to get going. **get at 1** to reach (something) or gain access to it. **2** to bribe or corrupt (somebody). **3** *Brit, informal* to criticize or tease (somebody). **4** *informal* to mean or imply (something): *What's he getting at?* **get it** to be scolded or punished. **get it together 1** *informal* to become organized. **2** *informal* to achieve peace of mind. **get one's** *informal* to be killed. **get one's own back** *informal* to revenge oneself. **get somebody with child** *archaic* to make a woman pregnant. **get through 1** to reach the end of (an ordeal or difficulty). **2** *chiefly Brit* to use up or consume (a supply, etc). **get to 1** to influence or have an effect on (somebody). **2** *informal* to annoy or anger (somebody). **have got** to have or possess. **have got to** to be obliged to or find it necessary to do something. ➤➤ **gettable** *adj*.

get² *noun* **1** the offspring of a male animal. **2** *Brit, informal or dialect* a git.

get about *verb intrans* **1** to be up and about; to be well enough to walk. **2** *said of information*: to become circulated, *esp* orally.

get across *verb trans* to make (something) clear or convincing.

get ahead *verb intrans* to achieve success.

get along *verb intrans* **1** to manage. **2** to be or remain on congenial terms.

get around *verb intrans* **1** = GET ABOUT. **2** *NAmer* = GET ROUND.

getaway *noun* **1** a departure or escape. **2** *informal* a short holiday.

get away¹ *verb intrans* to escape, *esp* from the scene of a crime or from getting caught. ✳ **get away with murder** to behave badly with impunity. **get away with something** to escape blame or punishment for a wrongdoing.

get away² *interj* used to express disbelief or shock.

get back *verb intrans* to return or revert. ✳ **get back at somebody** to retaliate against them.

get by *verb intrans* **1** to manage with difficulty or limited resources. **2** to be barely acceptable.

get down *verb intrans* to leave or descend, e.g. from a vehicle. ➤ *verb trans* **1** to make (somebody) dejected. **2** to swallow (something unpleasant). **3** to record (something) in writing. ✳ **get down to something** to start to give attention to (an activity).

get in *verb intrans* **1** to be admitted to a place, *esp* an educational institution. **2** to be elected to office or come to power. **3** *said of a train, etc*: to arrive at its destination. ➤ *verb trans* **1** to collect or buy a supply of (something). **2** to call (somebody) to one's home for help. **3** to submit or deliver (something expected). **4** to interpose (a remark) during a conversation.

get off *verb intrans* **1** to start or leave. **2** to escape danger or punishment. **3** to finish work. **4** to fall asleep. ➤ *verb trans* **1** *informal* to secure the release or acquittal of (an accused person). **2** to write and send (e.g. a letter). **3** to leave (work). ✳ **get off on something** *informal* to enjoy something, *esp* to be stimulated by it. **get off with somebody** *Brit, informal* to start a sexual relationship with somebody.

get on *verb intrans* **1** = GET ALONG. **2** to succeed. ✳ **be getting on for** to be approaching (a specified age, time, distance, etc).

get out *verb intrans* **1** to emerge or escape. **2** *of a secret, etc*: to become known. ➤ *verb trans* to cause (somebody or something) to emerge or escape. ✳ **get out of something** to escape responsibility for doing something.

get-out *noun* a means of escaping or avoiding something.

get over *verb trans* **1** to overcome (a difficulty). **2** to recover from (something unpleasant). **3** to succeed in communicating (an idea, etc).

get round *verb trans* **1** to persuade (somebody) to do what you want. **2** to evade (a law or responsibility). ✳ **get round to something** to make a start eventually on (a task, etc).

getter *noun* a substance introduced into a vacuum tube, electric lamp, etc to remove traces of gas. [GET¹ + -ER²]

get through *verb intrans* **1** to reach somebody, *esp* by telephone. **2** to make oneself understood; to convey one's feelings.

get together *verb intrans* to assemble or come together for a social purpose or to cooperate.

get-together *noun* an informal social gathering or meeting.

get up *verb intrans* **1** to rise from a sitting or lying position. **2** to rise from bed in the morning. **3** *said of the wind*: to become stronger. ➤ *verb trans* **1** to improvise (something). **2** to arrange the external appearance of (somebody). ✳ **get up to something** *Brit, informal* to be involved in something mischievous, wrong, etc.

get-up *noun informal* an outfit or costume.

get-up-and-go *noun informal* energy or drive.

geum /'jee·əm/ *noun* any of a genus of plants of the rose family including the avens: genus *Geum*. [scientific Latin *geum*, from Latin *gaeum* herb bennet, a member of this family]

GeV *abbr* gigaelectronvolt.

gewgaw /'gyoohgaw/ *noun* something showy but worthless; a bauble or trinket. [origin unknown]

Gewürztraminer /gə'vooətstrəmeenə (*German* gəvyrtstraminər), gə'vooatstrəmeenə/ *noun* **1** a variety of grape used in the production of white wine. **2** a wine produced from this grape, typically a medium-dry white wine with a spicy bouquet. [German *Gewürz* spice + *Traminer*, a variety of grape, named after *Tramin* in S Tyrol]

geyser /'geezə, *NAmer* 'giezə/ *noun* **1** a spring that intermittently throws out jets of heated water and steam. **2** *Brit* an apparatus with a boiler in which water, e.g. for a bath, is rapidly heated by a gas flame and may be stored. [Icelandic *Geysir*, literally 'gush', name of a hot spring in Iceland, from *geysa* to gush, from Old Norse]

G-force *noun* the force of gravity.

GH *abbr* Ghana (international vehicle registration).

Ghanaian /gah'nayən/ *noun* a native or inhabitant of Ghana, country in W Africa. ➤➤ **Ghanaian** *adj*.

gharial /'geəri·əl/ *noun* = GAVIAL. [Hindi *ghariyāl*]

gharry *or* **gharri** /gari/ *noun* (*pl* **gharries**) a horse-drawn Indian taxi. [Hindi *gāṛī*]

ghastly /'gahstli/ *adj* (**ghastlier, ghastliest**) **1a** terrifyingly horrible: *a ghastly crime*. **b** *informal* intensely unpleasant, disagreeable, or objectionable: *Such a life seems ghastly in its emptiness and sterility* — Aldous Huxley. **2** pale and wan. ➤➤ **ghastliness** *noun*.

Word history

Middle English *gastly*, from *gasten* to terrify, from Old English *gǣstan*. The *h* was added in the 17th cent. by association with GHOST¹, to which ghastly is related.

ghat /gawt/ *noun* **1** a broad flight of steps providing access to an Indian river. **2** a level place next to a river where Hindus are cremated. **3** a mountain pass, *esp* in India. [Hindi *ghāṭ*]

Ghazi /'gahzi/ *noun* (*pl* **Ghazis**) a Muslim soldier fighting a non-Muslim adversary. [Arabic *ghāzī*]

ghee /gee/ *noun* a clarified butter, *esp* in India, used for cooking. [Hindi *ghī*, from Sanskrit *ghṛtá*]

gherkin /'guhkin/ *noun* **1** a slender annual climbing plant of the cucumber family that bears a small prickly fruit used for pickling: *Cucumis anguria*. **2** the small immature fruit of the cucumber, used for pickling. [Dutch *gurken*, pl of *gurk* cucumber, ultimately via Low German and Polish from medieval Greek *agouros* watermelon, cucumber]

ghetto /'getoh/ *noun* (*pl* **ghettos** *or* **ghettoes**) **1** an area of a city, *esp* a slum area, in which a minority group live because of social, legal, or economic pressures. **2** part of a city in which Jews formerly lived. [Italian *ghetto*, perhaps from *getto* foundry, from a ghetto established on the site of a foundry in Venice in 1516]

ghetto blaster *noun informal* a large portable radio, usu incorporating a cassette or CD player.

ghettoize *or* **ghettoise** *verb trans* **1** to force (a group of people) to live in a ghetto, or as if in a ghetto because of their customs, beliefs, or social class; to segregate (them). **2** to cause (an area) to become a ghetto. ➤➤ **ghettoization** /-'zaysh(ə)n/ *noun*.

Ghibelline /'gibilien/ *noun* a member of a political party in medieval Italy supporting the German emperors: compare GUELF. [Italian *Ghibellino*, prob from the name of *Waibeling* castle, seat of the Hohenstauffen dukes of Swabia who supported the German emperors]

ghillie /'gili/ *noun* see GILLIE.

ghost¹ /gohst/ *noun* **1** a disembodied soul; *esp* the soul of a dead person haunting the living. **2a** a faint shadowy trace: *a ghost of a smile*. **b** the least bit: *I didn't have a ghost of a chance*. **3** a false image in a photographic negative or on a television screen. ✳ **give up the ghost** to die. ➤➤ **ghostlike** *adj*.

Word history

Old English *gāst*. The *h* was added in the 16th cent., prob from Flemish *gheest*: see GHASTLY.

ghost² *verb trans* to ghostwrite (e.g. a book). ➤ *verb intrans* to move like a ghost; to glide.

ghostly *adj* (**ghostlier, ghostliest**) of, like, or being a ghost; spectral. ➤➤ **ghostliness** *noun*.

ghost town *noun* a once-flourishing but now deserted town.

ghost word *noun* a word that appears in dictionaries, or has come into the language, because of an error or misunderstanding.

ghostwrite *verb trans* (*past tense* **ghostwrote**, *past part.* **ghostwritten**) to write (e.g. a speech) for another person, who is the presumed author. [back-formation from GHOSTWRITER]

ghostwriter *noun* a person who ghostwrites articles, books, etc.

ghoul /goohl/ *noun* **1** an evil being of Arabic legend, *esp* one that robs graves and feeds on corpses. **2** an evil spirit or ghost. **3** a person who enjoys the macabre. ➤ **ghoulish** *adj*, **ghoulishly** *adv*, **ghoulishness** *noun*. [Arabic *ghūl*, from *ghāla* to seize]

GHQ *abbr* General Headquarters.

ghyll /gil/ *noun* see GILL³.

GI *noun* (*pl* **GI's** *or* **GIs**) a member of the US army, *esp* a private. [orig abbr for *galvanized iron* used in listing articles such as rubbish bins, but taken as abbr for *government issue* or *general issue*]

gi. *abbr* gill.

giant¹ /ˈjie-ənt/ *noun* **1** a legendary being, like a human in shape, but having great size and strength. **2** an extraordinarily large person, animal, or plant. **3** a person of extraordinary powers: *a literary giant*. ➤ **giantlike** *adj*. [Middle English *giaunt* via French from Latin *gigant-*, *gigas*, from Greek]

giant² *adj* extremely large.

giantess /ˈjie-əntes/ *noun* a female giant.

giant hogweed *noun* a plant that is a close relative of cow parsley but grows to more than 3m (10ft) tall: *Heracleum mantegazzianum*.

giantism *noun* gigantism.

giant-killer *noun* a person or team, *esp* a football team, that defeats an apparently far superior opponent.

giant panda *noun* = PANDA.

giant slalom *noun* a long slalom course with obstacles that are far apart.

giant star *noun* a star of great brightness and enormous size that is reaching the end of its life.

giaour /ˈjow-ə/ *noun archaic, derog* a person outside the Muslim faith, *esp* a Christian; an infidel. [Turkish *gâvur*, prob ultimately from Arabic *kāfir*: see KAFFIR]

gib¹ *noun* a metal or wooden plate machined to hold other parts in place, to afford a bearing surface, or to provide means for taking up wear. [origin unknown]

gib² *verb trans* (**gibbed**, **gibbing**) to fasten (something) with a gib.

gibber¹ /ˈjibə/ *verb intrans* (**gibbered**, **gibbering**) to make rapid, inarticulate, and usu incomprehensible utterances: *The graves stood tenantless and the sheeted dead did squeak and gibber in the Roman streets* — Shakespeare. [imitative]

gibber² *noun Aus* **1** a level gravel-covered plain in the arid parts of Australia. **2** a stone or pebble. [from Dharuk, an Aboriginal language]

gibberellin /jibəˈrelin/ *noun* any of several plant hormones that promote shoot growth. [Latin *Gibberella fujikoroi*, fungus from which it was first isolated]

gibberish *noun* unintelligible or meaningless language. [prob from GIBBER¹ + *-ish* as in SPANISH]

gibbet¹ /ˈjibit/ *noun* **1** a gallows. **2** an upright post with an arm, used formerly for hanging the bodies of executed criminals as a warning. [Middle English *gibet* from Old French, prob of Germanic origin]

gibbet² *verb trans* (**gibbeted**, **gibbeting**) **1** to hang (somebody) on a gibbet. **2** to execute (somebody) by so hanging.

gibbon /ˈgib(ə)n/ *noun* any of several species of small tailless tree-dwelling apes of SE Asia: genus *Hylobates*. [French *gibbon*, prob from an Indian dialect word]

gibbous /ˈgibəs/ *adj* **1** said of the moon or a planet: seen with more than half but not all of the apparent disc illuminated. **2** swollen on one side; convex or protuberant. **3** *formal* having a hump; humpbacked. ➤ **gibbosity** /giˈbositi/ *noun*, **gibbously** *adv*, **gibbousness** *noun*. [Middle English via French and late Latin from Latin *gibbus* hump]

gibe /jieb/ *verb and noun* see JIBE¹, JIBE².

giblets /ˈjiblits/ *pl noun* a fowl's heart, liver, or other edible internal organs: compare HASLET. [Middle English *gibelet* entrails, garbage, from early French *gibelet* stew of wildfowl]

Gibraltarian /jibrawlˈteəri-ən/ *noun* a native or inhabitant of Gibraltar. ➤ **Gibraltarian** *adj*.

gid /gid/ *noun* a disease, *esp* of sheep, caused by the larva of a tapeworm developing in the brain. [back-formation from GIDDY¹]

giddy¹ /ˈgidi/ *adj* (**giddier**, **giddiest**) **1a** feeling a sensation of unsteadiness and lack of balance as if everything is whirling round; dizzy. **b** causing dizziness: *a giddy height*. **2** lightheartedly frivolous. ➤ **giddily** *adv*, **giddiness** *noun*. [Old English *gydig* possessed, mad]

giddy² *verb trans* (**giddies**, **giddied**, **giddying**) to make (somebody) feel giddy.

gidgee /ˈgidji/ *noun Aus* a small Australian acacia tree: *Acacia cambagei*. [from Wirachuri, an Aboriginal language]

gie /gee/ *verb trans and intrans* (**gies**, **gi'ed**, **gi'ing**) *chiefly Scot* to give. [by alteration]

GIF /gif/ *abbr* graphic interchange format.

GIFT *abbr* gamete intrafallopian transfer.

gift¹ /gift/ *noun* **1** something freely given by one person to another; a present or donation. **2** a natural capacity or talent. **3** the act, right, or power of giving: *The job is not in his gift*. **4** *Brit, informal* something obtained easily: *That pass in front of the goal was an absolute gift*. ✳ **gift of the gab** *informal* the ability to talk glibly and persuasively. [Middle English from Old Norse *gipt* something given, talent]

gift² *verb trans* **1** to give (something) as a gift. **2** to present (somebody) with a gift.

gifted *adj* **1** having or revealing great natural ability. **2** highly intelligent: *gifted children*. ➤ **giftedly** *adv*, **giftedness** *noun*.

gift of tongues *noun* the practice of ecstatic speaking in usu incomprehensible language, *esp* in evangelical Christianity; GLOSSOLALIA.

gift token *noun Brit* a voucher redeemable for merchandise to the stated amount.

gift voucher *noun* = GIFT TOKEN.

gift wrap *noun* decorative wrapping paper.

gift-wrap *verb trans* (**gift-wrapped**, **gift-wrapping**) to wrap (a gift) decoratively.

gig¹ /gig/ *noun* **1** a light two-wheeled carriage pulled by a horse. **2** a long light ship's boat propelled by oars, sails, etc. [Middle English *gigg* spinning top, perhaps of Scandinavian origin]

gig² *noun informal* a musician's engagement for a specified time; *esp* such an engagement for one performance. [origin unknown]

gig³ *verb intrans* (**gigged**, **gigging**) *informal* to perform a gig.

gig⁴ *noun* a pronged spear for catching fish. [short for *fizgig*, *fishgig*, of unknown origin]

gig⁵ *verb trans* (**gigged**, **gigging**) to catch (fish) with a gig.

gig⁶ *abbr informal* gigabyte.

giga- *comb. form* forming words, denoting: **1** a factor of one thousand million (10^9): *gigavolt*. **2** in computing, a factor of 2^{30}: *gigabyte*. [from Greek *gigas* GIANT¹]

gigabyte /ˈgigəbiet/ *noun* in computing, a quantity of data equal to one thousand million (10^9) or (more accurately) 2^{30} bytes.

gigaflop /ˈgigəflop/ *noun* in computing, a unit of speed equal to one thousand million flops.

gigantic /jieˈgantik/ *adj* unusually great or enormous. ➤ **gigantically** *adv*.

gigantism /ˈjiegantiz(ə)m, jieˈgan-/ *noun* development of a plant or animal to abnormally large size.

giggle¹ /ˈgigl/ *verb intrans* to laugh with repeated short catches of the breath or in a silly manner. ➤ **giggler** *noun*. [imitative]

giggle² *noun* **1** an act or instance of giggling. **2** *Brit, informal* something that amuses or diverts: *We did it for a giggle*. ➤ **giggly** *adj*.

GIGO /ˈgiegoh/ *abbr* in computing, garbage in, garbage out.

gigolo /ˈzhigəloh/ *noun* (*pl* **gigolos**) **1** a man paid by a usu older woman for companionship or sex. **2** a professional dancing partner or male escort. [French *gigolo*, back-formation from *gigolette* girl who frequents public dances, prostitute, from *giguer* to dance]

gigot /'zhigoh, 'jigət/ *noun* a leg of meat, e.g. lamb. [early French *gigot*, dimin. of *gigue* fiddle; from its shape]

gigot sleeve *noun* a leg-of-mutton sleeve.

gigue /zheeg/ *noun* a lively dance movement with compound triple rhythm and consisting of two sections, each of which is repeated: compare JIG¹ (1A). [French *gigue* jig]

Gila monster /'heelə/ *noun* a large orange and black venomous lizard of SW USA: *Heloderma suspectum*. [named after *Gila*, a river in Arizona, USA, where they are found]

gilbert /'gilbət/ *noun* the unit of magnetomotive force in the centimetre-gram-second system equivalent to 10/4π ampere-turn. [William *Gilbert* d.1603, English physicist]

gild¹ /gild/ *verb trans* (*past tense and past part.* **gilded** or **gilt** /gilt/) **1** to overlay (something) with a thin covering of gold. **2** to give an attractive but often deceptive appearance to (something). ✳ **gild the lily** to add unnecessary ornamentation to something already beautiful. ⟫⟫ **gilder** *noun*. [Old English *gyldan*]

gild² *noun archaic* a guild.

gilding *noun* **1** the art or process of applying gilt to a surface. **2** the surface produced by this.

gilet /'zheelay/ *noun* a loose waistcoat. [French *gilet* via Spanish and Arabic from Turkish *yelek* waistcoat]

gill¹ /gil/ *noun* **1** an organ, *esp* of a fish, for oxygenating blood using the oxygen dissolved in water. **2** any of the radiating plates forming the undersurface of the cap of some fungi, e.g. mushrooms. **3** (*in pl*) the flesh under or about the chin or jaws: *We were full up to the gills.* ⟫⟫ **gilled** *adj*. [Middle English *gile, gille*, from Old Norse]

gill² /jil/ *noun* a unit of liquid capacity equal to a quarter of a pint. [Middle English *gille* via Old French from late Latin *gille* water pot]

gill³ or **ghyll** *noun* **1** *Brit* a ravine. **2** a narrow mountain stream or rivulet.

Word history
Middle English *gille* from Old Norse *gil*. The spelling *ghyll* was apparently introduced by Wordsworth.

gill⁴ or **jill** /jil/ *noun* a female ferret: compare HOB² (1).

gill cover /gil/ *noun* the flap of skin that protects a fish's gills; = OPERCULUM.

gillie or **gilly** or **ghillie** /'gili/ *noun* **1** an attendant to somebody who is hunting or fishing in Scotland. **2** formerly, a male attendant of a Scottish Highland chief. [Scottish Gaelic *gille* and Irish Gaelic *giolla* boy, servant]

gilliflower /'jiliflowə/ *noun* see GILLYFLOWER.

gill net /gil/ *noun* a flat net suspended vertically in the water with meshes for entangling fishes' gills.

gillyflower or **gilliflower** /'jiliflowə/ *noun* any of several plants having clove-scented flowers, e.g. a wallflower or stock. [by folk etymology from Middle English *gilofre* clove, via French and Latin from Greek *karyophyllon*, from *karyon* nut + *phyllon* leaf]

gilt¹ /gilt/ *adj* covered with gold or gilt; of the colour of gold. [Middle English, past part. of *gilden* to gild, from Old English *gyldan*]

gilt² *noun* **1** gold leaf or gold paint laid on a surface. **2** superficial brilliance; surface attraction. **3** (*in pl*) gilt-edged securities. ✳ **take the gilt off the gingerbread** to make something less attractive; to take away the part that makes the whole thing attractive [because gingerbread was traditionally sold at fairs decorated with 'Dutch gold', an alloy of copper and bronze].

gilt³ *noun* a young female pig. [Middle English *gylte* from Old Norse *gyltr*]

gilt⁴ *verb* past tense and past part. of GILD¹.

gilt-edged *adj* **1** said of government securities: traded on the Stock Exchange and having a guaranteed fixed interest rate. **2** of the highest quality or reliability.

gimbal /'jimbl, 'gimbl/ *noun* (*also* **gimbals**) (*treated as sing.*) a device that allows a ship's compass, stove, etc to remain level when its support is tipped. [alteration of obsolete *gemel*, *gimmal* double ring, ultimately from Latin *geminus* twin]

gimcrack¹ /'jimkrak/ *adj* showy but unsubstantial; shoddy. ⟫⟫ **gimcrackery** *noun*. [perhaps alteration of Middle English *gibecrake*, of uncertain meaning]

gimcrack² *noun* a showy unsubstantial object of little use or value.

gimlet¹ /'gimlit/ *noun* **1** a tool for boring small holes in wood, usu consisting of a crosswise handle fitted to a tapered screw: compare AUGER. **2** a cocktail consisting of lime juice, gin or vodka, and soda water. [Middle English from early French *guimbelet*, dimin. of *guimble* anger, of Germanic origin]

gimlet² *adj* said of eyes: piercing or penetrating: *She gave him a gimlet-eyed stare.*

gimmick /'gimik/ *noun* a scheme, device, or object devised to gain attention or publicity. ⟫⟫ **gimmickry** /-kri/ *noun*, **gimmicky** *adj*. [origin unknown]

gimp¹ /gimp/ *noun* **1** an ornamental flat braid or round cord used as a trimming. **2** the thread used to fill in ornamental details, e.g. flowers, in lace. [Dutch *gimp*]

gimp² *verb intrans NAmer, informal* to walk with a limp. [origin unknown]

gimp³ *noun NAmer, informal* **1** a person with a limp or other physical handicap. **2** a limp.

gin¹ /jin/ *noun* **1** a spirit made by distilling grain flavoured with juniper berries: *'But it can't have been right . . . to pour spirits down her throat like that. It might have killed her.' 'Not her. Gin was mother's milk to her.'* — George Bernard Shaw. **2** a glass or measure of gin. [by shortening and alteration from *geneva*, modification of obsolete Dutch *genever* juniper, ultimately from Latin *juniperus*]

gin² *noun* **1** = COTTON GIN. **2** a machine for raising or moving heavy weights. **3** a snare or trap for game. [Middle English *gin*, modification of Old French *engin*: see ENGINE]

gin³ *verb trans* (**ginned**, **ginning**) **1** to separate (cotton fibre) from seeds and waste material. **2** to snare (game) in a gin. ⟫⟫ **ginner** *noun*.

gin⁴ *noun Aus, derog* a female Aborigine. [from Dharuk]

ginger /'jinjə/ *noun* **1a** a widely cultivated tropical plant with pungent aromatic rhizomes that supply most of the ginger used commercially: *Zingiber officinale*. **b** the dried and ground rhizome of this plant, used as a spice. **c** the rhizome itself, which has a strong hot taste and is used in cooking, candied as a sweet, or preserved in syrup. **2** a reddish brown or yellowish brown colour. **3** high spirit; vigour. ⟫⟫ **gingery** *adj*. [Middle English via Old French and late Latin from Greek *zingiberis*, from Pali *singivera*]

ginger ale *noun* a sweet yellowish carbonated non-alcoholic drink flavoured with ginger.

ginger beer *noun* **1** a weak alcoholic effervescent drink of milky appearance, made by the fermentation of ginger and syrup. **2** a similar non-alcoholic commercial preparation.

gingerbread *noun* a thick biscuit or cake made with treacle or syrup and flavoured with ginger. ✳ **take the gilt off the gingerbread** see GILT². [Middle English *gingerbreed*, by folk etymology from *gingebras* ginger paste, from Old French *gingembraz*, from *gimgibre* GINGER]

ginger group *noun Brit* a pressure group, e.g. within a political party, urging stronger action.

gingerly¹ *adv* very cautiously or carefully. [perhaps from early French *gensor, genzor*, compar of *gent* well-born, dainty, delicate, from Latin *genitus*, past part. of *gignere* to beget]

gingerly² *adj* very cautious or careful. ⟫⟫ **gingerliness** *noun*.

ginger nut *noun* a hard biscuit flavoured with ginger.

ginger snap *noun* = GINGER NUT.

ginger up *verb trans* to stir (somebody or something) to activity; to vitalize (them or it): *ginger up boardroom attitudes.* [from the practice of putting ginger in a horse's rectum to make it seem lively]

gingham /'ging·əm/ *noun* a lightweight fabric usu woven from dyed cotton yarn to give a checked design. [Dutch *gingang* from Malay *genggang* striped cloth]

gingili /'jinjili/ *noun* sesame, or the oil obtained from sesame seeds, *esp* as used in Indian cookery. [Hindi *jingalī*]

gingiva /jin'jievə/ *noun* (*pl* **gingivae** /-vee/) *technical* = GUM¹. ⟫⟫ **gingival** *adj*. [Latin *gingiva* gum]

gingivitis /jinji'vietəs/ *noun* inflammation of the gums.

gingko /'gingkoh/ *noun* see GINKGO.

ginglymus /'ging·gliməs, 'jing-/ *noun* (*pl* **ginglymi** /-mie/) in anatomy, a hinge joint, e.g. the elbow or knee. [scientific Latin from Greek *ginglymos* hinge]

gink /gingk/ *noun slang* a person, *esp* one viewed with contempt. [origin unknown]

ginkgo /'gingkgoh/ *or* **gingko** /'gingkoh/ *noun* (*pl* **ginkgoes** *or* **gingkoes**) a showy Chinese tree that has fan-shaped leaves and yellow fruit and is often grown for ornament: *Ginkgo biloba.* [via Latin from Japanese *ginkyo*]

ginormous /jie'nawməs/ *adj Brit, informal* exceptionally large. [GIANT¹ + ENORMOUS]

gin rummy *noun* a form of rummy for two players in which both are dealt ten cards and may end play when the value of their unmatched cards is less than ten. [GIN¹]

ginseng /'jinseng/ *noun* **1** the aromatic root, widely valued as a tonic, of a Chinese or N American plant. **2** the plant, belonging to the ivy family, that yields this root: genus *Panax.* [Chinese (Pekingese) *renshen*]

gip /jip/ *noun* see GYP¹.

gippy tummy /'jipi/ *noun informal* indigestion and diarrhoea, *esp* that affecting visitors to hot countries. [*gippy* by shortening and alteration from EGYPTIAN¹]

gipsy /'jipsi/ *noun* see GYPSY.

gipsy moth *noun* see GYPSY MOTH.

giraffe /ji'raf, ji'rahf/ *noun* (*pl* **giraffes** *or collectively* **giraffe**) a large African ruminant mammal, the tallest living four-legged animal, that has a very long neck and a fawn or cream coat marked with brown or black patches: *Giraffa camelopardalis.* [Italian *giraffa* from Arabic *zirāfah*]

girandole /'jirəndohl/ *noun* **1** an ornamental branched candle holder. **2** a radiating display of fireworks. [French *girandole* from Italian *girandola*, from *girare* to turn, ultimately from Latin *gyrus* circle, spiral]

girasol *or* **girasole** /'jirəsol, -sohl/ *noun* an opal that gives out reddish reflections in bright light. [Italian *girasole* literally 'sunflower' from *girare* to turn + *sole* sun, from Latin *sol*]

gird¹ /guhd/ *verb* (*past tense and past part.* **girded** *or* **girt** /guht/) ➤ *verb trans* **1a** to encircle or bind (something) with a flexible band, e.g. a belt. **b** to surround (something). **2** to prepare (oneself) for action. ➤ *verb intrans* to prepare for action. ✻ **gird (up) one's loins** to prepare for action; to muster one's resources. [Old English *gyrdan*]

gird² *verb trans and intrans N Eng dialect or archaic* to make sarcastic remarks or sneer at (somebody or something). [Middle English *girden* to strike, thrust]

gird³ *noun N Eng dialect or archaic* a sarcastic remark.

girder *noun* a horizontal main structural member, e.g. in a building or bridge, that supports vertical loads. [from GIRD¹, in the sense 'to brace, strengthen']

girdle¹ /'guhdl/ *noun* **1** something that encircles or confines something, e.g.: **a** a belt or cord encircling the body, usu at the waist. **b** a woman's tightly fitting undergarment that extends from the waist to below the hips. **c** a ring made by the removal of the bark round a tree trunk. **2** the edge of a cut gem that is grasped by the setting. [Old English *gyrdel*]

girdle² *verb trans* **1** to encircle (something or somebody) with or as if with a girdle. **2** to cut a girdle round (a tree), usu in order to kill it.

girdle³ *noun Scot, N Eng dialect* = GRIDDLE¹. [Middle English (Scots) *girdill, girdil*, alteration of Middle English *gredil*: see GRIDDLE¹]

girl /guhl/ *noun* **1a** a female child. **b** a young unmarried woman. **2a** a girlfriend. **b** a daughter. **c** a female employee or servant. **3** *informal* a woman. ➤➤ **girlhood** *noun*, **girlish** *adj*, **girlishness** *noun*. [Middle English *gurle, girle* young person of either sex; earlier history unknown]

girlfriend *noun* **1** a frequent or regular female companion with whom somebody is romantically or sexually involved. **2** a female friend.

Girl Guide *noun chiefly Brit* = GUIDE¹ (4).

girlie¹ *or* **girly** /'guhli/ *adj* **1** featuring nude or scantily clothed young women: *girlie magazines.* **2** of or for girls or women. **3** *chiefly derog* suitable for or like a young girl, *esp* affectedly so: *The room was decorated in an awful girlie pink.*

girlie² *or* **girly** *noun* (*pl* **girlies**) *informal* a girl or young woman.

girl scout *noun NAmer* = GUIDE¹ (4).

girly¹ *adj* = GIRLIE¹.

girly² *noun* = GIRLIE².

girn *or* **gurn** /guhn/ *verb intrans* **1** *Brit* to pull a grotesque face: *the one who girned to the judge's greatest satisfaction being declared the winner* — M F Wakelin. **2** *chiefly Scot dialect* to be peevish or fretful: *The bairn's been girning all day.* ➤➤ **girner** *noun*. [Middle English *girnen*, alteration of *grinnen*: see GRIN¹]

giro /'jie(ə)roh/ *noun* (*pl* **giros**) **1** a computerized low-cost system of money transfer comparable to a current account. **2** *informal* a giro cheque or payment, *esp* a social security benefit. [German *Giro* from Italian *giro* turn, transfer, from Latin *gyrus* circle, spiral]

Girondin /ji'rondin *(French* ʒirɔ̃dɛ̃*)/ noun* = GIRONDIST.

Girondist /ji'rondist *(French* ʒirɔ̃dist*)/ noun* a member of a political group in revolutionary France that advocated republicanism through non-violent means. [from *Gironde*, the name of the department where the group's leaders were deputies]

girt¹ /guht/ *verb* past tense and past part. of GIRD¹.

girt² *noun dated* = GIRTH¹.

girth¹ /guhth/ *noun* **1** a measurement round something, e.g. a tree trunk or somebody's waist. **2** a strap that passes under the body of a horse or other animal to fasten *esp* a saddle on its back. [Middle English from Old Norse *gjörth*; related to Old English *gyrdan* GIRD¹]

girth² *verb trans archaic* **1** to encircle (something). **2** to bind or fasten (something) with a girth.

gismo /'gizmoh/ *noun* see GIZMO.

gist /jist/ *noun* the main point of a matter; essence: *the gist of the argument.* [Anglo-French *gist* it lies (from early French *gesir* to lie, from Latin *jacēre*), in the phrase *cest action gist* this action lies, used to mean that there were sufficient grounds to proceed; hence the grounds themselves]

git /git/ *noun chiefly Brit, informal* a worthless, contemptible, or foolish person. [variant of GET² in the sense 'offspring, bastard']

gîte /zheet/ *noun* a furnished house in France that is rented to holidaymakers. [French *gîte* lodging, from early French *gesir*: see GIST]

gittern /'gituhn/ *noun* a medieval guitar. [Middle English *giterne* from early French *guiterne*, modification of Old Spanish *guitarra*: see GUITAR]

give¹ /giv/ *verb* (*past tense* **gave** /gayv/, *past part.* **given** /'giv(ə)n/) ➤ *verb trans* **1a** to transfer the possession of (something that one owns or has a right to) to another; to cause somebody to have (something). **b** to commit or entrust (something) to another. **c** to yield possession of (something) as payment or in exchange. **d** to devote (something) or make it available: *I can give you ten minutes*; *They gave their lives for their country.* **2a** to cause somebody to experience or feel (something): *You gave me a fright*; *Digging gives me backache.* **b** to inflict (something) as punishment: *She gave the child a rebuke.* **3** to offer or present (something) for another to use or act on: *He gave me his hand.* **4a** to offer (something) to another: *Let me give you some advice.* **b** to agree to act in accordance with (a promise, undertaking, etc): *I give you my word.* **5a** to utter (a sound): *The boy gave a shout.* **b** to communicate or express (something): *to give a signal*; *to give a reason.* **6** to make (a movement): *The ship gave a lurch.* **7a** to provide (something) by way of entertainment: *to give a party.* **b** to perform or present (something) in public: *to give a concert.* **8** to yield (something) as a product or effect: *Cows give milk*; *84 divided by 12 gives 7.* **9** to grant or bestow (something) by formal action: *to give a judgement.* **10** in games, to make a specified ruling on the status of (a player or action): *Bowles was given offside*; *The referee gave the goal.* **11** to allow or concede (something): *I'll give you that game*; *It's late, I give you that.* **12** to cause (somebody) to think something: *I was given to understand that he was ill.* **13** to care to a specified extent: *They don't give a damn.* **14** to propose (somebody or something) as a toast: *I give you the Queen.* ➤ *verb intrans* **1** to make gifts or donations. **2** to yield or collapse in response to pressure: *The fence gave under his weight.* **3** to afford a view or passage: *The door gives directly on to the garden.* ✻ **give as good as one gets** to counterattack with equal vigour. **give or take** allowing for a specified imprecision: *three hours, give or take a few minutes either way.* **give way 1** to concede a right of way. **2** to be overcome by an emotion or reaction: *to give way to tears.* **3** to yield to physical stress: *The snow caused the roof to give way.* **4** to withdraw before superior force; to retreat. **5** to yield to entreaty or insistence; to give a point. **6** (+ to) to be superseded by (something). **what gives?** *informal* what is happening? ➤➤ **giver** *noun*. [Old English *giefan*]

give² *noun* the capacity or tendency to yield to pressure; resilience or elasticity: *There's no give in this mattress.*

give-and-take noun **1** the practice of making mutual concessions. **2** the good-natured exchange of ideas or words.

giveaway noun **1** an unintentional revelation or betrayal. **2** something given free or at a reduced price.

give away verb trans **1** to make a present of (something). **2** to hand over (a bride) ceremonially to the bridegroom at a wedding. **3a** to betray (somebody). **b** to disclose or reveal (something). **4** to concede (an advantage) to an opponent: *He was giving away four years to the junior champion.* * **give the game/show away** to reveal plans or a secret, usu by mistake.

give in verb trans to submit or deliver (something). ➤ verb intrans to yield under insistence or entreaty; to surrender.

given[1] verb past part. of GIVE[1].

given[2] adj **1** prone; disposed: *given to swearing.* **2a** fixed; specified: *at a given time.* **b** assumed as actual or hypothetical: *given that all are equal before the law.* **3** said of an official document: executed on the date specified.

given[3] noun a known or accepted fact.

given name noun chiefly NAmer = FORENAME

give off verb trans to emit (something): *The drains give off an unpleasant smell.*

give out verb trans **1** to issue or distribute (something). **2** to emit (something). **3** to declare or publish (something): *giving out that the doctor … required a few days of complete rest — Dickens.* ➤ verb intrans to come to an end; to fail: *Their patience finally gave out.*

give over verb trans **1** to set (something) apart for a particular purpose or use. **2** to deliver (something) to somebody's care. ➤ verb intrans informal to bring an activity to an end; to stop or desist: *told him to give over and let me alone* — Brendan Behan.

give up verb trans **1** to surrender (oneself or somebody else), esp as a prisoner. **2** to desist from (something). **3** to renounce or cease. **4** to abandon (oneself) to a particular feeling, influence, or activity. **5** to declare (somebody) incurable or (something) insoluble: *The doctors gave her up for dead.* **6** to stop having a relationship with (somebody). ➤ verb intrans to abandon an activity or course of action, esp to stop trying. * **give up the ghost** see GHOST[1].

gizmo or **gismo** /'gizmoh/ noun (pl **gizmos** or **gismos**) informal a gadget, esp one whose name is unknown or has been forgotten or one whose function is complicated. [origin unknown]

gizzard /'gizəd/ noun **1** an enlargement of the digestive tract of birds, immediately following the CROP[1] (pouchlike part of the gullet), that has thick muscular walls and usu contains small stones or grit for breaking up and grinding food. **2** a thickened or enlarged part of the digestive tract in some invertebrate animals, e.g. an insect or earthworm, that is similar in function to the gizzard of a bird. [alteration of Middle English *giser* from early French *guisier*, from Latin *gigeria* giblets]

Gk abbr Greek.

GLA abbr Greater London Authority.

glabella /glə'belə/ noun (pl **glabellae** /-lee/) the smooth part of the forehead between the eyebrows. ➤➤ **glabellar** adj. [scientific Latin *glabella*, fem of Latin *glabellus* hairless, dimin. of *glaber* smooth, bald]

glabrous /'glaybrəs/ adj technical having a surface without hairs or projections; smooth. [Latin *glabr-*, *glaber* smooth, bald + -OUS]

glacé /'glasay/ adj **1** said of a food, esp fruit: coated with a glaze; candied: *glacé cherries.* **2** said of fabric, leather, etc: finished with a smooth glossy surface: *glacé silk.* [French *glacé*, past part. of *glacer* to freeze, ice, glaze, from Latin *glaciare*, from *glacies* ice]

glacial /'glaysiəl, 'glayshəl/ adj **1a** extremely cold: *a glacial wind.* **b** lacking warmth or cordiality: *a glacial smile.* **2a** of or produced by glaciers. **b** relating to or denoting a period of geological time when much of the earth was covered by glaciers. **3** resembling ice in appearance, esp when frozen: *glacial acetic acid.* ➤➤ **glacially** adv. [Latin *glacialis*, from *glacies* ice]

glacial period noun any period of the earth's history when the surface of the planet was extensively covered with ice sheets.

glaciate /'glaysiayt/ verb trans **1a** to cover (land, etc) with ice or a glacier. **b** to subject (rock, etc) to the action or effects of glaciers. **2** to freeze (something). ➤➤ **glaciation** /-'aysh(ə)n/ noun.

glacier /'glasi·ə, 'glaysi·ə/ noun a large body of ice moving slowly down a slope or spreading outwards on a land surface. [French dialect, from early French *glace* ice, from Latin *glacies*]

glaciology /glasi'oləji, glay-/ noun the study of glaciers and their effects. ➤➤ **glaciological** /-'lojikl/ adj, **glaciologist** noun.

glacis /'glasis, 'glaysis/ noun (pl **glacis** /'glasiz, 'glaseez, 'glaysiz, 'glayseez/) a slope that runs downwards from a fortification and offers no protection for attackers. [French *glacis*, from *glacer* to freeze, slide: see GLACÉ]

glad[1] /glad/ adj (**gladder, gladdest**) **1** expressing or experiencing pleasure, joy, or delight. **2** very willing: *glad to help.* **3** causing happiness and joy: *glad tidings.* **4** (+ of) grateful for; pleased to have: *glad of a chance to sit down.* ➤➤ **gladly** adv, **gladness** noun. [Old English *glæd* shining, joyful, happy]

glad[2] verb trans (**gladded, gladding**) literary or archaic to make (somebody or something) glad.

gladden verb trans (**gladdened, gladdening**) to make (somebody or something) glad: *The news gladdened her heart.*

glade /glayd/ noun an open space in a wood or forest. [Middle English perhaps from GLAD[1]]

glad eye noun informal an amorous or sexually inviting look: *giving her the glad eye.*

glad hand noun informal a warm welcome or greeting, often prompted by ulterior motives.

glad-hand verb trans to extend a glad hand to (somebody): *parliamentary candidates glad-handing everyone they meet.* ➤ verb intrans to extend a glad hand. ➤➤ **glad-hander** noun.

gladiator /'gladiaytə/ noun **1** a man trained to fight another man or wild animals in a public arena for the entertainment of ancient Romans. **2** somebody engaging in a public fight or controversy. ➤➤ **gladiatorial** /ˌgladi·ə'tawri·əl/ adj. [Latin *gladiator* from *gladius* sword, of Celtic origin]

gladiolus /gladi'ohləs/ noun (pl **gladioli** /-lie/ or **gladioluses**) any of a genus of chiefly African plants of the iris family with erect sword-shaped leaves and spikes of brilliantly coloured irregular flowers: genus *Gladiolus*. [Latin *gladiolus*, dimin. of *gladius*: see GLADIATOR]

glad rags pl noun informal smart clothes worn for a party or special occasion.

gladsome /'glads(ə)m/ adj chiefly literary giving or showing joy; cheerful. ➤➤ **gladsomely** adv, **gladsomeness** noun.

Gladstone bag /'gladstən/ noun a travelling bag with flexible sides on a hinged frame that opens flat into two equal compartments. [named after W E *Gladstone* d.1898, British statesman, who did an unusual amount of travelling during election campaigns]

Glagolitic /glagə'litik/ adj relating to or denoting an alphabet formerly used for some Slavic languages. [via Latin from Serbo-Croat *glagolica* the Glagolitic alphabet]

glair or **glaire** /gleə/ noun **1** a liquid filler or adhesive made from egg white. **2** a thick sticky substance resembling egg white. ➤➤ **glairy** adj. [Middle English *gleyre* egg white, from early French *glaire*, ultimately from Latin *clarus* CLEAR[1]]

Glam. abbr Glamorgan.

glam[1] /glam/ adj informal glamorous.

glam[2] noun informal **1** glamour. **2** = GLAM ROCK.

glam[3] verb trans (**glammed, glamming**) (often + up) to dress or decorate (somebody, oneself, or something) in a glamorous way.

glamor /'glamə/ noun NAmer see GLAMOUR.

glamorize or **glamorise** or **glamourize** or **glamourise** /'glaməriez/ verb trans **1** to make (something or somebody) glamorous: *glamorize the living room.* **2** to romanticize (something): *The novel glamorizes war.* ➤➤ **glamorization** /-'zaysh(ə)n/ noun.

glamour (NAmer **glamor**) /'glamə/ noun **1a** a romantic, exciting, and often illusory attractiveness: *the glamour of the film industry.* **b** alluring or fascinating beauty. **2** archaic a magic spell: *The girls appeared to be under a glamour* — Llewelyn Powys. ➤➤ **glamorous** adj, **glamorously** adv.

Word history

Scot *glamour*, alteration of GRAMMAR, influenced in spelling by medieval Latin *glomeria* grammar. Glamour is first recorded in the 18th cent. in the phrase *to cast the glamour over* 'to put a spell on'. In the 19th cent. the word came to mean 'enchantment, a magical or deceptive beauty or charm'; the sense of physical or sexual attractiveness originated in the USA in the early 20th cent. The association of grammar with magic probably arose because grammar was used in connection with the study of Latin, the language of scholarship in the Middle Ages. The uneducated, who did not understand Latin, tended to regard it and learning expressed in it with suspicion. While the English word *grammar* has never explicitly been linked with magic, a related Middle English word *gramarye*, which originally meant 'grammar', was later applied to learning in general and by the 15th cent. specifically to knowledge of astrology and the occult.

glamourize *or* **glamourise** *verb trans* see GLAMORIZE.

glam rock *noun* a style of popular music, prominent in the UK during the 1970s, characterized by sing-along tunes performed by bands and singers wearing outrageous clothes and flamboyant, often glittery, make-up. ⨠ **glam-rock** *adj.*

glance[1] /glahns/ *verb intrans* **1a** (*usu* + at) to take a quick look: *I glanced at my watch.* **b** said of the eyes: to move swiftly from one thing to another. **2** (*often* + off) to strike a surface obliquely in such a way as to go off at an angle: *The bullet glanced off the wall.* **3a** to flash or gleam with intermittent rays of reflected light: *brooks glancing in the sun.* **b** to make sudden quick movements: *dragonflies glancing over the pond.* **4** to touch on a subject or refer to it briefly or indirectly: *The study glances at the customs of ancient cultures.* ⨠ *verb trans* to cause (something) to glance off a surface. [Middle English *glencen, glenchen,* perhaps alteration of *glenten* to move quickly, slide, ultimately from French *glacer:* see GLACÉ]

glance[2] *noun* **1a** a quick or cursory look. **b** a swift movement of the eyes. **2** a quick intermittent flash or gleam. **3a** a deflected impact or blow. **b** a stroke in cricket that barely deflects the ball from its line of flight. **4** an allusion. ✳ **at first glance** on first consideration: *At first glance, it seemed easy enough.*

glance[3] *noun* any of several usu dark minerals with a metallic lustre. [German *Glanz* lustre, glance]

glancing *adj* having a slanting direction; deflected: *a glancing blow.* ⨠ **glancingly** *adv.*

gland[1] /gland/ *noun* **1a** an organ of the body that selectively removes materials from the blood, alters them, and secretes them for further use or for elimination. **b** a bodily structure that resembles a gland but does not secrete, e.g. a lymph node. **2** any of various plant organs that secrete oil, nectar, resin, etc. ⨠ **glandless** *adj.* [French *glande,* from Old French *glandre:* see GLANDERS]

gland[2] *noun* a device for preventing leakage of fluid past a joint or moving part in machinery. [origin unknown]

glanders /'glandəz/ *pl noun* (*treated as sing. or pl*) a contagious bacterial disease, *esp* of horses, in which mucus is discharged profusely from the nostrils. [Old French *glandre* glandular swelling on the neck, gland, from Latin *glandula,* dimin. of *gland-, glans* acorn]

glandes /'glandeez/ *noun* pl of GLANS.

glandular /'glandyoolə/ *adj* relating to, denoting, affecting, or produced by a gland or glands. ⨠ **glandularly** *adv.*

glandular fever *noun* = INFECTIOUS MONONUCLEOSIS.

glans /glanz/ *noun* (*pl* **glandes** /'glandeez/) the rounded mass of tissue at the end of the penis or clitoris. [Latin *gland-, glans,* literally 'acorn']

glare[1] /gleə/ *verb intrans* **1** to stare angrily or fiercely. **2** to shine with a harsh uncomfortably brilliant light. ⨠ *verb trans* to express (e.g. hostility) by staring fiercely. [Middle English *glaren* from early Dutch or early Low German; related to Old English *glæs* GLASS[1]]

glare[2] *noun* **1** an angry or fierce stare. **2a** a harsh uncomfortably bright light; *specif* painfully bright sunlight. **b** garishness.

glaring *adj* obtrusively evident: *a glaring error.* ⨠ **glaringly** *adv,* **glaringness** *noun.*

glasnost /'glaznost, 'glasnost/ *noun* the willingness of an organization, orig the government of the former USSR, to be open about its affairs and invite public scrutiny and debate. [Russian *glasnost* publicity, openness, from *glas* voice]

glass[1] /glahs/ *noun* **1a** a hard brittle usu transparent or translucent substance formed by melting sand or some other form of silica with metallic oxides and other ingredients and cooling the mixture rapidly. **b** a substance resembling glass, *esp* in hardness and transparency. **c** (*used before a noun*) relating to or made of glass: *a glass door.* **2** something made of glass, e.g.: **a** a glass drinking vessel. **b** a mirror. **c** a barometer. **d** an optical instrument, e.g. a magnifying glass, for viewing objects not easily seen. **3** articles made of glass; glassware. **4** the quantity held by a glass drinking vessel. ⨠ **glassful** (*pl* **glassfuls**) *noun,* **glassless** *adj,* **glasslike** *adj.* [Old English *glæs*]

glass[2] *verb trans* **1** to enclose, cover, or fit (something) with glass: *It cost over £100 to glass the broken window.* **2** *chiefly Brit, informal* to smash a drinking glass in the face of (somebody), *esp* in a pub brawl.

glass-blowing *noun* the art or process of shaping a mass of semimolten glass by blowing air into it through a tube. ⨠ **glass-blower** *noun.*

glass ceiling *noun* a hypothetical barrier, *esp* one caused by sexism or racism, denying people access to a goal that seems to be within their reach, *esp* such a barrier to career advancement.

glasses *pl noun* a pair of glass lenses in a frame worn in front of the eyes to correct defects of vision or for protection: *A celebrity is a person who works hard all his life to become well known, and then wears dark glasses to avoid being recognized* — Fred Allen.

glass fibre *noun* = FIBREGLASS.

glass harmonica *noun* a set of glass bowls with graduated pitches used as a musical instrument and played by rubbing their moistened rims with the finger or by using a keyboard mechanism to strike them.

glasshouse /'glahs·hows/ *noun chiefly Brit* **1** a greenhouse. **2** *informal* a military prison or place of detention.

glassine /'glaseen/ *noun* a glazed transparent paper that is highly resistant to air and grease and used for book jackets, food wrappers, etc.

glass lizard *noun* = GLASS SNAKE.

glasspaper *noun* paper to which a thin layer of powdered glass has been glued for use as an abrasive.

glass snake *noun* **1** a limbless snakelike lizard of the southern USA with a fragile tail that readily breaks into pieces: *Ophisaurus ventralis.* **2** any of various similar Eurasian and N American lizards.

glassware *noun* articles made of glass, *esp* drinking glasses or glass ornaments.

glass wool *noun* glass fibres in a mass resembling wool used for insulation, filtering, packing, etc.

glasswort *noun* any of several species of salt-marsh plants with jointed fleshy stems and leaves reduced to fleshy sheaths: genus *Salicornia.* [from its former use in the manufacture of glass]

glassy *adj* (**glassier, glassiest**) **1** resembling glass. **2** dull or lifeless: *There was a fatuous and glassy squint in his eyes* — Evelyn Waugh. ⨠ **glassily** *adv,* **glassiness** *noun.*

Glaswegian /glaz'weej(ə)n/ *noun* a native or inhabitant of Glasgow. ⨠ **Glaswegian** *adj.* [irreg from *Glasgow,* city in Scotland]

Glauber's salt /'glowbəz/ *noun* (*also in pl*) hydrated sodium sulphate, *esp* when used as a laxative. [named after Johann *Glauber* d.1668, German chemist, who produced it]

glaucoma /glaw'kohmə/ *noun* increased pressure within the eyeball causing damage to the retina and gradual impairment or loss of vision. ⨠ **glaucomatous** *adj.* [via Latin from Greek *glaukōma,* from *glaukos* GLAUCOUS; from the greyish haze on the pupil]

glaucous /'glawkəs/ *adj* **1** said *esp* of plants or plant parts: of a dull blue or bluish green colour. **2** said of a leaf or fruit: having a powdery or waxy coating giving a frosted appearance: *glaucous grapes.* ⨠ **glaucousness** *noun.* [Latin *glaucus* silvery grey, from Greek *glaukos*]

glaze[1] /glayz/ *verb trans* **1** to provide or fit (e.g. a window frame) with glass. **2** to coat (e.g. food or pottery) with a glaze. **3** to give a smooth glossy surface to (something). ⨠ *verb intrans* **1** (*often* + over) to become dull or lifeless: *His eyes glazed over.* **2** to form a glaze. ⨠ **glazer** *noun,* **glazing** *noun.* [Middle English *glasen,* from GLASS[1]]

glaze[2] *noun* **1a** a liquid preparation that sets or hardens to give a glossy coating to food. **b** a vitreous coating made chiefly from a mixture of oxides and used to seal or decorate pottery. **c** a transparent or translucent colour applied to a painted or printed surface to modify its tone. **d** a smooth glossy or lustrous surface or finish. **2** *chiefly NAmer* a smooth slippery coating of thin ice.

glazier /'glayzi·ə/ *noun* a person who fits glass, *esp* into windows and doors, as an occupation.

GLC *abbr* **1** gas-liquid chromatography. **2** formerly, Greater London Council.

gleam[1] /gleem/ *noun* **1a** a short-lived appearance of reflected, subdued, or partly obscured light. **b** a small bright light. **2** a brief or faint indication of emotion, etc: *a gleam of anticipation in his eyes.*

3 a brief or faint appearance or occurrence: *a gleam of hope*. >>> **gleamy** *adj*. [Old English *glǣm*]

gleam² *verb intrans* **1** to shine, *esp* with reflected light. **2** to appear briefly or faintly. >>> **gleaming** *adj*, **gleamingly** *adv*.

glean /gleen/ *verb intrans* **1** to gather produce, *esp* grain, left by reapers. **2** to gather material, e.g. information, bit by bit. > *verb trans* **1** to pick up (e.g. grain) after a reaper. **2** to gather (e.g. information) bit by bit. >>> **gleaner** *noun*. [Middle English *glenen* via French from late Latin *glennare*, of Celtic origin]

gleanings *pl noun* things acquired by gleaning.

glebe /gleeb/ *noun* **1** in former times, land belonging or yielding revenue to a church or clergyman. **2** *archaic* land; *specif* a plot of cultivated land. [Latin *gleba* clod, land]

glee /glee/ *noun* **1** a feeling of merry high-spirited joy or delight. **2** an unaccompanied song for three or more usu male solo voices. [Old English *glēo* entertainment]

glee club *noun* a choir, *esp* in N America, organized for singing usu short secular pieces.

gleeful /'gleef(ə)l/ *adj* full of glee; merry or triumphant. >>> **gleefully** *adv*, **gleefulness** *noun*.

gleeman *noun* (*pl* **gleemen**) *archaic* a professional entertainer, *esp* a travelling singer; a minstrel.

glen /glen/ *noun* a narrow valley, *esp* in Scotland or Ireland. [Middle English (Scots), valley, from Scottish Gaelic and Irish Gaelic *gleann*]

glengarry /glen'gari/ *noun* (*pl* **glengarries**) a straight-sided woollen cap with a crease in the crown from front to back and two short ribbons hanging down behind, worn *esp* as part of Highland military uniform. [named after *Glengarry*, valley in Scotland]

gley /glay/ *noun* a sticky clay formed under the surface of some waterlogged soils. [Russian *glei* clay]

glia /'glie-ə, 'glee-ə/ *noun* = NEUROGLIA. >>> **glial** *adj*. [via Latin from Greek *glia* glue]

glib /glib/ *adj* (**glibber, glibbest**) **1** showing little forethought or preparation; lacking depth and substance: *glib solutions to problems.* **2** marked by ease and fluency in speaking or writing, often to the point of being superficial or dishonest. >>> **glibly** *adv*, **glibness** *noun*. [prob modification of Low German *glibberig* slippery]

glide¹ /glied/ *verb intrans* **1** to move noiselessly in a smooth, continuous, and effortless manner. **2** to pass gradually and imperceptibly. **3a** said of an aircraft: to fly without the use of engines. **b** to fly in a glider. > *verb trans* to cause (something) to glide. >>> **gliding** *adj and noun*, **glidingly** *adv*. [Old English *glīdan*]

glide² *noun* **1** the act or an instance of gliding. **2** in music, = PORTAMENTO. **3** a transitional sound produced by the vocal organs passing from one articulatory position to another.

glide path *noun* the path of descent of an aircraft in landing, *esp* as marked by ground radar or radio.

glider *noun* **1** an aircraft similar to an aeroplane but without an engine. **2** a person or thing that glides.

glimmer¹ /'glimə/ *verb intrans* (**glimmered, glimmering**) **1** to shine faintly or unsteadily. **2** to appear indistinctly with a faintly luminous quality. >>> **glimmering** *adj and noun*, **glimmeringly** *adv*. [Middle English *glimeren*, prob of Scandinavian origin]

glimmer² *noun* **1** a feeble or unsteady light. **2a** a dim perception or faint idea. **b** a small sign or amount: *a glimmer of intelligence.*

glimpse¹ /glimps/ *verb trans* to see (something) briefly or partially. [Middle English *glimsen*, of Germanic origin]

glimpse² *noun* a brief or partial view or look.

glint¹ /glint/ *verb intrans* **1** to shine with tiny bright flashes; to sparkle or glitter, *esp* by reflection. **2** said of rays of light: to strike a reflecting surface obliquely and dart out at an angle. > *verb trans* to cause (something) to glint. [Middle English *glinten* to dart obliquely, glint, of Scandinavian origin]

glint² *noun* **1** a tiny bright flash of usu reflected light; a sparkle. **2** a brief or faint manifestation: *a glint of recognition in her expression.*

glioma /glie'ohmə/ *noun* (*pl* **gliomas** *or* **gliomata** /-tə/) a tumour of the brain and spinal cord arising from the NEUROGLIA (tissue supporting nerve cells and fibres). [GLIA + -OMA]

glissade¹ /gli'sahd, gli'sayd/ *noun* **1** a slide down a snow- or ice-covered slope, usu in a standing or squatting position. **2** a gliding step in ballet. [French *glissade* slide, from *glisser* to slide, ultimately of Germanic origin]

glissade² *verb intrans* to perform a glissade.

glissando /gli'sandoh/ *noun* (*pl* **glissandi** /-dee/ *or* **glissandos**) in music, a rapid sliding up or down the scale. [prob modification of French *glissade*: see GLISSADE¹]

glisten¹ /'glis(ə)n/ *verb intrans* (**glistened, glistening**) to shine, usu by reflection, with a sparkling radiance or with the lustre of a wet or oily surface. [Old English *glisnian*]

glisten² *noun* a sheen or sparkle, *esp* a reflected light given off by something wet or oily.

glister¹ /'glistə/ *verb intrans* (**glistered, glistering**) *chiefly literary* = GLITTER¹. [Middle English *glistren*, prob from early Dutch *glisteren* or early Low German *glistern*]

glister² *noun chiefly literary* = GLITTER¹.

glitch /glich/ *noun* **1** *informal* a technical hitch; a temporary malfunction or setback. **2** in astronomy, a brief irregularity or change in the rotation of a pulsar. [prob from German *glitschen* to slide, slip]

glitter¹ /'glitə/ *verb intrans* (**glittered, glittering**) **1a** to shine by reflection in bright flashes or with a metallic lustre: *The sequins on her dress glittered in the moonlight.* **b** to shine with a glassy brilliance: *His eyes glittered with anger.* **2** to have an enticing brilliance: *The world continues to offer glittering prizes to those who have stout hearts and sharp swords* — F E Smith. >>> **glitteringly** *adv*. [Middle English *gliteren* from Old Norse *glitra*]

glitter² *noun* **1** bright shimmering reflected light or metallic lustre. **2** small glittering particles used for ornamentation. **3** something that is brilliantly attractive, sometimes in a superficial way: *the glitter of a showbiz career.* >>> **glittery** *adj*.

glitterati /glitə'rahti/ *pl noun informal* celebrated and fashionable people, *esp* those in the world of entertainment. [blend of GLITTER¹ and LITERATI]

glitz /glits/ *noun informal* superficial glamour: *an award ceremony with all the expected glitz.* [Yiddish *glitz* glitter]

glitzy /'glitsi/ *adj* (**glitzier, glitziest**) *informal* glamorous, *esp* in a superficial, overstated, or ironic way: *a glitzy Hollywood party.* >>> **glitzily** *adv*, **glitziness** *noun*.

gloaming /'glohming/ *noun* (**the gloaming**) *literary* twilight or dusk. [Middle English (Scots) *gloming*, from Old English *glōmung*, from *glōm* twilight]

gloat¹ /gloht/ *verb intrans* (*often* + over) to think or talk about something, *esp* one's own achievements or another person's misfortunes or failures, with great and often malicious satisfaction, gratification, or relish. >>> **gloater** *noun*, **gloatingly** *adv*. [prob of Scandinavian origin]

gloat² *noun* the act or an instance of gloating.

glob /glob/ *noun chiefly informal* a blob, *esp* of a semiliquid substance. [perhaps blend of GLOBE¹ and BLOB¹]

global /'glohbl/ *adj* **1** of or involving the entire world. **2** general; comprehensive. **3** operating on, applying to, or affecting the whole of a computer file or program. **4** spherical. >>> **globally** *adv*.

globalize *or* **globalise** *verb trans* to make (something, e.g. a company, business, social trend, etc) international or worldwide in scope or application.

Editorial note

Globalize is an umbrella term which contains several disparate concepts: the rapid growth of international trade in finished goods and services; the extension of free international markets in private capital able to flow across borders; growth of large, multinational enterprises organizing production across national boundaries; and the slow convergence of consumer tastes in different countries around certain global standards — Evan Davis.

>>> **globalization** /-'zaysh(ə)n/ *noun*.

Global Positioning System *noun* a system of satellites orbiting the earth that enables an appropriate receiver to establish an exact geographical location, altitude, and speed and direction of travel.

global village *noun* the world viewed as a totally integrated system in which all the constituent parts are interdependent and linked.

global warming *noun* an increase in the average temperature of the earth's atmosphere that is believed to be caused by the GREENHOUSE EFFECT.

globe¹ /glohb/ *noun* **1a** a spherical representation of the earth or a heavenly body. **b** (**the globe**) the world; the earth. **2** something spherical or rounded, e.g. a glass bowl or light. **3** = ORB (1).

➤➤ **globe-like** *adj,* **globoid** /'glohboyd/ *adj,* **globose** /'glohbohs/ *adj.* [via French from Latin *globus* ball, sphere]

globe² *verb intrans* to become spherical or rounded. ➤ *verb trans* to form (something) into a globe.

globe artichoke *noun* = ARTICHOKE (1B).

globefish *noun* (*pl* **globefishes** *or collectively* **globefish**) **1** any of several species of chiefly tropical marine fishes that can distend themselves to a globular form, *esp* as a form of defence: family Tetraodontidae. Also called BLOWFISH, PUFFER. **2** = PORCUPINE FISH.

globeflower *noun* a plant of the buttercup family with spherical yellow flowers: genus *Trollius*.

globetrotter *noun informal* somebody who travels widely. ➤➤ **globetrotting** *noun and adj.*

globigerina /gloh,bijə'rienə/ *noun* (*pl* **globigerinas** *or* **globigerinae** /-nee/) a minute single-celled marine animal that has a chalky shell and lives in the surface waters of the sea: genus *Globigerina.* [Latin genus name, from *globus* GLOBE¹ (from the spherical chambers in its shell) + *gerere* to carry, bear]

globular /'globyoolə/ *adj* **1** having the shape of a globe or globule: *globular proteins.* **2** having or consisting of globules. ➤➤ **globularity** /-'lariti/ *noun,* **globularly** *adv.* [partly from Latin *globus* GLOBE¹ + -ULAR; partly from Latin *globulus* GLOBULE + -AR¹]

globule /'globyoohl/ *noun* a tiny globe or ball, e.g. of liquid or melted solid. ➤➤ **globulous** *adj.* [via French from Latin *globulus,* dimin. of *globus* GLOBE¹]

globulin /'globyoolin/ *noun* any of a class of widely occurring proteins that are soluble in dilute salt solutions.

glockenspiel /'glokənspeel, -shpeel/ *noun* a percussion instrument consisting of a series of graduated metal bars played with two hammers. [German *Glockenspiel,* from *Glocke* bell + *Spiel* play]

glomerule /'gloməroohl/ *noun* a compact clustered flower head like that of a daisy or thistle. [scientific Latin *glomerulus*: see GLOMERULUS]

glomerulus /glo'meryoolas/ *noun* (*pl* **glomeruli** /-lie/) a small coiled or intertwined mass of blood vessels, nerve fibres, etc, *esp* a knot of capillaries (tiny blood vessels; see CAPILLARY¹) at the point of origin of each NEPHRON (urine-secreting unit in a kidney). ➤➤ **glomerular** *adj.* [scientific Latin *glomerulus,* dimin. of Latin *glomer-, glomus* ball]

gloom¹ /gloohm/ *noun* **1** partial or total darkness. **2a** depression of a person's spirits. **b** an atmosphere of despondency.

gloom² *verb trans and intrans* to become or cause (somebody or something) to become gloomy. [Middle English *gloumen* to look gloomy; earlier history unknown]

gloomy *adj* (**gloomier, gloomiest**) **1** partially or totally dark, *esp* dismally or depressingly dark: *gloomy weather.* **2a** low in spirits. **b** causing despondency: *a gloomy story.* ➤➤ **gloomily** *adv,* **gloominess** *noun.*

gloop /gloop/ (*NAmer* **glop** /glop/) *noun informal* a sticky or messy semiliquid substance or mixture. ➤➤ **gloopy** *adj.* [prob imitative]

Gloria /'glawri·ə/ *noun* a hymn or DOXOLOGY (text giving praise to God) that begins with the word *Gloria,* used in Christian services of worship. [Latin *gloria* GLORY¹]

glorified /'glawrified/ *adj* appearing or made to appear more special, important, valuable, etc than is really the case: *He calls her his research assistant, but glorified dogsbody is more like it.*

glorify /'glawrifie/ *verb trans* (**glorifies, glorified, glorifying**) **1a** to bestow honour, praise, or admiration on (somebody or something). **b** to elevate (somebody or something) to heavenly glory. **2** to give glory to (God), e.g. in worship. **3** to shed radiance or splendour on (something). ➤➤ **glorification** /-fi'kaysh(ə)n/ *noun,* **glorifier** *noun.*

glorious /'glawri·əs/ *adj* **1a** possessing or deserving glory. **b** conferring glory: *a glorious victory.* **2** marked by great beauty or splendour. **3** delightful; wonderful: *glorious weather.* ➤➤ **gloriously** *adv,* **gloriousness** *noun.*

glory¹ /'glawri/ *noun* (*pl* **glories**) **1a** praise, honour, or distinction granted by common consent; renown. **b** worshipful praise, honour, and thanksgiving: *giving glory to God.* **2a** something that secures praise or renown. **b** a highly commendable asset: *Her hair was her crowning glory.* **3a** resplendence or magnificence: *the glory that was Greece and the grandeur that was Rome* — Poe. **b** the splendour, blessedness, and happiness of heaven; eternity. **4** a state of

great gratification or exaltation. **5** a ring or spot of light, e.g. one round a representation of a holy figure or around a heavenly body. **✳ glory be!** *informal* used to express great surprise or enthusiastic piety. **in (all) its/his/her/their glory** *informal* in a state of great pride, satisfaction, happiness, etc. [Middle English *glorie* via French from Latin *gloria*]

glory² *verb intrans* (**glories, gloried, glorying**) **1** (*often* + in) to rejoice proudly: *They were glorying in their youth and vigour.* **2** *informal* (*often* + in) to have or take great pride or pleasure: *He glories in the name of Ben Pink Dandelion!*

glory box *noun Aus, NZ* = BOTTOM DRAWER.

glory hole *noun informal* a cupboard or small room used for storage, *esp* one that is often untidy.

Glos. *abbr* Gloucestershire.

gloss¹ /glos/ *noun* **1a** surface lustre, sheen, or brightness. **b** something that gives this: *lip gloss.* **2** a deceptively attractive outer appearance. **3a** paint to which varnish has been added to give a shiny finish. **b** (*used before a noun*) relating to or denoting such paint: *gloss paint; gloss finish.* [prob of Scandinavian origin]

gloss² *verb trans* to give a gloss to (something), *esp* to varnish (it) or paint (it) with gloss paint. ➤➤ **glosser** *noun.*

gloss³ *noun* **1a** a brief explanation, e.g. in the margin of a text, of a difficult word or expression. **b** an interlinear translation. **c** a continuous commentary accompanying a text. **2** a deliberately false or misleading interpretation, e.g. of a text. **3** = GLOSSARY. [Middle English *glose* via Old French from Latin *glossa* unusual word requiring explanation, from Greek *glōssa, glōtta* tongue, language]

gloss⁴ *verb trans* to supply a gloss or glosses for (a word, text, etc).

gloss- *or* **glosso-** *comb. form* forming words, denoting: **1** tongue: *glossal; glossitis.* **2** tongue and: *glossopharyngeal.* **3** language: *glossology.* [via Latin from Greek *glōss-, glōsso-,* from *glōssa* tongue, language]

glossary /'glosəri/ *noun* (*pl* **glossaries**) a list of terms, e.g. those used in a particular text or in a specialized field, usu with their meanings. ➤➤ **glossarial** /glo'seəri·əl/ *adj,* **glossarist** *noun.* [Middle English from medieval Latin *glossarium,* from Latin *glossa*: see GLOSS³]

glossitis /glo'sietis/ *noun* inflammation of the tongue.

glosso- *comb. form* see GLOSS-.

glossolalia /glosə'layli·ə/ *noun* the phenomenon of ecstatic speaking in usu incomprehensible language, *esp* in evangelical Christianity or as a symptom of a psychiatric or psychological disorder. [Greek *glossa* tongue, language + *lalia* chatter, from *lalein* to chatter, talk]

gloss over *verb trans* **1** to make (something wrong) appear right and acceptable. **2** to veil or hide (something undesirable) by rapid or superficial treatment: *glossing over humiliations, gilding small moments of glory* — Times Literary Supplement.

glossy¹ /'glosi/ *adj* (**glossier, glossiest**) **1** said of a surface: having a lustre, sheen, or brightness. **2** superficially attractive in an opulent, sophisticated, or smoothly captivating manner: *a glossy musical.* ➤➤ **glossily** *adv,* **glossiness** *noun.*

glossy² *noun* (*pl* **glossies**) *informal* **1** *chiefly Brit* a magazine expensively produced on glossy paper with many colour photographs and often having a fashionable or sophisticated content. **2** a photograph, *esp* of somebody famous, printed on expensive glossy paper.

glottal /'glot(ə)l/ *adj* of or produced by the glottis: *glottal constriction.*

glottal stop *noun* a speech sound produced by closure and sudden reopening of the glottis, as heard between the two syllables in a Cockney pronunciation of *butter.*

glottis /'glotis/ *noun* (*pl* **glottises** *or* **glottides** /'glotideez/) **1** *technical* the slit-like space between the two vocal cords in the larynx. **2** *not in technical use* all of the anatomical structures of the voice box involved in producing speech sounds. [Greek *glōttid-, glōttis,* from *glōtta* tongue]

glove¹ /gluv/ *noun* **1** a close-fitting covering for the hand having separate sections for each of the fingers and the thumb and often extending above the wrist, worn for warmth, fashion, or protection. **2** = BOXING GLOVE. **✳ fit like a glove** said of clothes: to be a perfect fit. [Old English *glōf*]

glove² *verb trans* to cover (something) with or as if with a glove.

glove box *noun* **1** a sealed compartment that has holes with gloves attached for handling dangerous materials inside the compartment. **2** *chiefly Brit* = GLOVE COMPARTMENT.

glove compartment *noun* a small storage compartment in the dashboard of a motor vehicle.

glove puppet *noun* a puppet, usu a fabric representation of a person, animal, cartoon character, etc, worn on the hand and animated by moving the fingers.

glover *noun* a person who makes or sells gloves.

glow[1] /gloh/ *verb intrans* **1** to shine with the steady light produced by intense heat: *The coals were glowing in the grate.* **2a** to have or experience a sensation of or as if of heat: *Her eyes glowed with rage.* **b** said of the complexion, etc: to have or show a strong, healthy *esp* red, colour: *After hours of playing in the snow, the children's cheeks were glowing.* **c** to show great pleasure or satisfaction: *The winning athletes were glowing with pride.* ⪢ **glowingly** *adv.* [Old English *glōwan*]

glow[2] *noun* **1a** the state of glowing with heat and light. **b** steady light from or as if from something burning without flames or smoke. **2** brightness or warmth of colour: *the glow of his cheeks.* **3a** a sensation of warmth. **b** warmth of feeling or emotion.

glow discharge *noun* a luminous discharge of electricity in a gas at low pressure.

glower[1] /'glowə/ *verb intrans* (**glowered, glowering**) to look or stare with sullen annoyance or anger. ⪢ **gloweringly** *adv.* [Middle English (Scots) *glowren*, perhaps of Scandinavian origin]

glower[2] *noun* a sullen or angry look or stare.

glow-worm *noun* any of several species of luminescent wingless insects, *esp* a larva or wingless female of a beetle, that emits light from the abdomen: *Lampyris noctiluca* and other species.

gloxinia /glok'sini·ə/ *noun* any of several species of tropical plants widely cultivated for their attractive white or purple bell-shaped flowers: genera *Gloxinia* and *Sinningia*. [named after B P *Gloxin* 18th-cent. German botanist, who first described it]

gloze /glohz/ *verb trans archaic* **1** to explain (something) away. **2** to gloss or comment on (a word, text, etc). ⪢ *verb intrans archaic* to use flattering or fawning language. [Middle English *glosen* to gloss, flatter, from *glose*: see GLOSS[3]]

glucagon /'gloohkəgon, -gən/ *noun* a hormone produced in the pancreas that responds to low sugar content in the blood by increasing the rate at which glycogen in the liver is broken down to glucose. [GLUCOSE + Greek *agōn*, present part. of *agein* to lead, drive]

glucocorticoid /gloohkoh'kawtikoyd/ *noun* any of several corticosteroid hormones or drugs, e.g. cortisol, that affect metabolic processes and are used in medicine, e.g. in treating rheumatoid arthritis, because they suppress inflammation and inhibit the activity of the immune system.

glucose /'gloohkohz, 'gloohkohs/ *noun* **1** a simple sugar that occurs widely in nature and is the usual form in which carbohydrate is absorbed and used in the body by animals: formula $C_6H_{12}O_6$. **2** a light-coloured syrup obtained by partial breakdown of starch. [French *glucos* from Greek *gleukos* must, sweet wine]

glucoside /'gloohkəsied/ *noun* a glycoside that yields glucose on hydrolysis. ⪢ **glucosidic** /-'sidik/ *adj.*

glue[1] /glooh/ *noun* **1** any of various strong adhesives, *esp* a gelatinous protein substance obtained by boiling animal hides, bones, etc. **2** a solution of glue used for sticking things together. ⪢ **glue-like** *adj,* **gluey** *adj.* [Middle English *glu* via French from late Latin *glut-, glus*, from Latin *gluten*]

glue[2] *verb trans* (**glues, glued, gluing** *or* **glueing**) **1** to cause (something) to stick tightly with glue: *I glued the handle back onto the jug.* **2** to fix (something, e.g. the eyes, one's attention, etc) steadily or with deep concentration: *She glued her eyes on the TV as the news unfolded.*

glue ear *noun* a condition in which an accumulation of a sticky substance in the middle ear impairs hearing, *esp* of children, often corrected or alleviated by the surgical insertion of a GROMMET (2).

glue-sniffing *noun* the practice of breathing in the fumes from various kinds of glue as an intoxicant. ⪢ **glue-sniffer** *noun.*

glug[1] /glug/ *verb trans* (**glugged, glugging**) **1** to pour (something) in such a way as to make a gurgling noise. **2** to drink (something) quickly and often noisily: *We spent the evening chatting and glugging loads of wine.*

glug[2] *noun* **1** the act or an instance of glugging. **2** the noise of glugging.

gluggable *adj informal* said of a drink, *esp* an alcoholic one: capable of being consumed in quantity with ease and enjoyment: *It's a relatively cheap but eminently gluggable burgundy.*

gluhwein *or* **Glühwein** /'gloohvien, German 'gly:vain/ *noun* warmed red wine to which sugar and spices have been added; mulled red wine. [German *Glühwein*, from *glühen* to glow, heat + *Wein* wine]

glum /glum/ *adj* (**glummer, glummest**) **1** broodingly morose. **2** dreary; gloomy. ⪢ **glumly** *adv,* **glumness** *noun.* [from GLOOM[2]]

glume /gloohm/ *noun* either of the two dry scale-like bracts (specialized leaves: see BRACT) at the base of the SPIKELET (flower cluster) in grasses. ⪢ **glumaceous** /glooh'mayshəs/ *adj.* [Latin *gluma* hull, husk]

gluon /'glooh·on/ *noun* an elementary particle held to be responsible for the force that binds quarks together. [GLUE[1] + -ON[2]]

glut[1] /glut/ *noun* an excessive supply of something, e.g. a harvested crop, that exceeds market demand.

glut[2] *verb trans* (**glutted, glutting**) **1** to fill or feed (something or somebody) beyond capacity. **2** to flood (the market) with goods so that supply exceeds demand. [Middle English *glouten, glotten* to fill to excess, prob from early French *glotir, gloutir* to swallow, from Latin *gluttire*]

glutamate /'gloohtəmayt/ *noun* **1** a salt or ester of glutamic acid. **2** *informal* = MONOSODIUM GLUTAMATE. [GLUTAMIC ACID + -ATE[1]]

glutamic acid /glooh'tamik/ *noun* an acidic amino acid found in most proteins. [GLUTEN + AMINO + -IC[1]]

glutamine /'gloohtəmeen, -min/ *noun* an amino acid found in many proteins that breaks down to yield glutamic acid and ammonia. [GLUTEN + AMINE]

glutei /'gloohtiie/ *noun* pl of GLUTEUS.

gluten /'gloohtin/ *noun* a tough sticky protein substance, *esp* of wheat flour, that gives dough its cohesive and elastic properties. ⪢ **glutenous** /-nəs/ *adj.* [Latin *glutin-, gluten* glue]

gluteus /'gloohti·əs/ *noun* (*pl* **glutei** /'gloohtiie/) any of the three large muscles of the buttock. ⪢ **gluteal** *adj.* [via Latin from Greek *gloutos* buttock]

glutinous /'gloohtinəs/ *adj* resembling glue; sticky. ⪢ **glutinously** *adv,* **glutinousness** *noun.* [early French *glutineux* from Latin *glutinosus*, from *glutin-, gluten* glue]

glutton /'glut(ə)n/ *noun* **1a** a habitually greedy and voracious eater and drinker. **b** somebody who has a great liking for something: *He's a glutton for horror movies.* **2** *dated* = WOLVERINE. ✳ **a glutton for punishment** a person who is keen to take on difficult or unpleasant tasks, etc. ⪢ **gluttonous** /-nəs/ *adj,* **gluttonously** *adv,* **gluttonousness** /-nəsnis/ *noun.* [Middle English *glotoun* via Old French from Latin *glutton-, glutto*]

gluttony *noun* habitual greed or excess in eating or drinking: *Gluttony is an emotional escape, a sign something is eating us* — Peter de Vries.

glyc- *or* **glyco-** *comb. form* forming words, denoting: sugar: *glycoside.* [Greek *glyk-* from *glykys* sweet]

glyceride /'glisəried/ *noun* an ester of glycerol, *esp* one formed by combination with a fatty acid.

glycerin /'glisərin/ *or* **glycerine** /-reen, -rin/ *noun* = GLYCEROL. [French *glycérine* from Greek *glykeros* sweet]

glycerol /'glisərol/ *noun* a sweet syrupy alcohol usu obtained from fats and used *esp* as a solvent and plasticizer: formula $CH_2OHCHOHCH_2OH$. [GLYCERIN + -OL[1]]

glycine /'glieseen/ *noun* a sweet amino acid found in most proteins. [GLYC- + -INE[2]]

glyco- *comb. form* see GLYC-.

glycogen /'gliekəjen/ *noun* a POLYSACCHARIDE that is the chief form in which carbohydrate is stored in the body tissue of animals. ⪢ **glycogenic** /-'jenik/ *adj.*

glycogenesis /gliekə'jenəsis/ *noun* the formation of glycogen, or the formation of sugar from glycogen.

glycol /'gliekol/ *noun* = ETHYLENE GLYCOL.

glycolic acid /glie'kolik/ *noun* a colourless crystalline soluble biodegradable acid found in unripe grapes, sugar beet, and sugar cane and also produced by oxidation of glycol, which has a wide range of industrial uses and is also used cosmetically in acid peels: formula $CH_2OHCOOH$.

glycolysis /glie'kolǝsis/ *noun* the partial oxidation of a carbohydrate, e.g. glucose, by enzymes, releasing a little energy as ATP in the cell. >> **glycolytic** /-'litik/ *adj*.

glycoprotein /gliekoh 'prohteen/ *noun* a protein containing one or more carbohydrate groups.

glycoside /'gliekǝsied/ *noun* any of numerous chemical compounds in which a sugar is attached by an oxygen or nitrogen atom to a nonsugar group and that break down to yield a sugar. >> **glycosidic** /-'sidik/ *adj*.

glycosuria /gliekoh'syooǝri-ǝ/ *noun* the presence of abnormal amounts of sugar in the urine, a symptom of diabetes or a disorder of the kidneys. >> **glycosuric** *adj*. [French *glycosurie*, from *glucos* (see GLUCOSE) + -*uria*]

glyph /glif/ *noun* 1 a symbolic figure or character usu incised or carved in relief. 2 a symbol, e.g. on a road sign or in computer graphics, that conveys information without using words. 3 an ornamental vertical groove in architecture. >> **glyphic** *adj*. [Greek *glyphē* carved work, from *glyphein* to carve]

glyptic /'gliptik/ *adj* relating to carving or engraving, *esp* on gems. [prob via French *glyptique* from Greek *glyptikē*, from *glyphein* to carve]

glyptodont /'gliptǝdont/ *noun* any of various extinct mammals related to the armadillos and having the body covered with horny armour: genus *Glyptodon*. [Greek *glyptos* carved (from *glyphein* to carve) + -ODONT tooth]

GM *abbr* 1 general manager. 2 genetically modified. 3 George Medal. 4 in chess, grandmaster. 5 *Brit* said of a school: grant-maintained. 6 guided missile.

gm *abbr* gram.

G-man *noun informal* 1 *NAmer* a special agent of the Federal Bureau of Investigation. 2 *Irish* a political detective. [prob short for *government man*]

GMO *abbr* genetically modified organism.

GMT *abbr* Greenwich Mean Time.

GMWU *abbr Brit* General and Municipal Workers Union.

gnarl /nahl/ *noun* a hard knotty lump, *esp* on a tree; a knot. [back-formation from GNARLED]

gnarled *adj* 1 said *esp* of a tree: full of or covered with knots or lumps. 2 said of hands, etc: rough and twisted, *esp* with age. [prob alteration of *knurled*: see KNURL]

gnarly /'nahli/ *adj* (**gnarlier, gnarliest**) 1 gnarled. 2 *chiefly NAmer, informal* said of an undertaking, problem, etc: difficult or tricky.

gnash /nash/ *verb trans* to strike or grind (the teeth) together. [alteration of Middle English *gnasten*, prob of imitative origin]

gnashers /'nashǝz/ *pl noun Brit, informal* teeth.

gnat /nat/ *noun* any of various small two-winged flies many of which are biting: *Trichocera annulata*, *Culex pipiens*, and many others. [Old English *gnætt*]

gnathic /'nathik/ *adj* relating to the jaw. [Greek *gnathos* jaw]

gnaw /naw/ *verb trans* 1a to bite or chew on (something) with the teeth, *esp* to wear (it) away by persistent biting or nibbling: *The dog was gnawing a bone*. **b** to make (e.g. a hole) by gnawing. 2 to affect (something) as if by continuous eating away. 3 to erode or corrode (something). > *verb intrans* 1 to bite or nibble persistently. 2 to destroy or reduce something by or as if by gnawing: *Waves had gnawed away at the cliffs*. >> **gnawer** *noun*. [Old English *gnagan*]

gnawing *adj* persistently worrying or distressing: *gnawing doubts*; *gnawing pain*.

gneiss /nies/ *noun* a metamorphic rock usu composed of light bands of feldspar and quartz alternating with dark bands of mica or hornblende. >> **gneissic** *adj*, **gneissoid** /'niesoyd/ *adj*, **gneissose** /'niesohs/ *adj*. [German *Gneis*, prob alteration of early High German *gneiste*, *ganeiste* spark, from Old High German *gneisto*]

gnocchi /'n(y)oki/ *pl noun* small dumplings made from flour, semolina, or potatoes. [Italian *gnocchi*, pl of *gnocco*, alteration of *nocchio* knot in wood]

gnome /nohm/ *noun* 1 in folklore, a dwarf who lives under the earth and guards treasure. 2 a garden ornament in the form of a gnome. >> **gnomish** *adj*.

Word history

via French from modern Latin *gnomus*. The word *gnome* was apparently coined by the 16th-cent. Swiss scientist Paracelsus. He may have derived it from a hypothetical Greek form *gēnomos* meaning 'earth-dweller', but it is more probably a purely fanciful coinage.

Gnome of Zurich /'zyooǝrikh/ *noun* (*pl* **Gnomes of Zurich**) *informal* (*usu pl*) an international banker usu considered to have great power over the financial sector of national economies. [*Zurich*, city in Switzerland famous for banking]

gnomic /'nohmik, 'nomik/ *adj* characterized by APHORISM (short wise sayings): *She claimed to be in love with her brother, whom nobody had ever seen, and went in for gnomic utterances and baroque clutter* — Margaret Drabble. >> **gnomically** *adv*. [via late Latin from Greek *gnōmikos*, from *gnōmē* maxim, from *gignōskein* to know]

gnomon /'nohmon/ *noun* 1 a fixed projecting part that casts a shadow on the face of a sundial, allowing the time to be told. 2 in geometry, the remainder of a parallelogram after the removal of a similar parallelogram containing one of its corners. >> **gnomonic** /noh'monik/ *adj*. [via Latin from Greek *gnōmōn* interpreter, pointer on a sundial, from *gignōskein* to know]

gnosis /'nohsis/ *noun* secret knowledge of spiritual truth available only to the initiated, *esp* as held by the ancient Gnostics to be essential to salvation. >> **gnostic** /'nostik/ *adj*. [Greek *gnōsis* knowledge, from *gignōskein* to know]

-gnosis *comb. form* (*pl* **-gnoses**) forming nouns, denoting: knowledge; recognition: *prognosis*. >> **-gnostic** *comb. form*. [via Latin from Greek *gnōsis*: see GNOSIS]

Gnosticism /'nostisiz(ǝ)m/ *noun* a religious outlook or system, *esp* of various cults of the late pre-Christian and early Christian era, distinguished by the conviction that matter is evil and that emancipation comes through esoteric spiritual knowledge.

Editorial note

Gnosticism is the term used for a range of religious and philosophical beliefs that claim secret knowledge, conferring power and/or salvation. Gnostic influences were found both in Judaism and in early Christianity. It tended to devalue the physical and to promote speculation about, or mystical union with, spiritual beings or levels of reality — Dr Mel Thompson.

>> **Gnostic** *noun and adj*. [via late Latin from Greek *gnōstikos* of knowledge, from *gignōskein* to know]

gnotobiotic /ˌnohtohbie'otik/ *adj* relating to or denoting a controlled environment, e.g. a germ-free culture, containing no unknown organisms. >> **gnotobiotically** *adv*. [Greek *gnōtos* known (from *gignōskein* to know) + *biotē* life, way of life]

GNP *abbr* gross national product.

gnu /nooh/ *noun* (*pl* **gnus** *or collectively* **gnu**) a large African antelope with an oxlike head, a short mane, a long tail, and horns that curve downward and outward: *Connochaetes gnou* and *Connochaetes taurinus*. [Khoikhoi *t'gnu* (Khoikhoi is an indigenous language of Southern Africa)]

GNVQ *abbr Brit* General National Vocational Qualification.

go¹ /goh/ *verb* (*past tense* **went** /went/, *past part.* **gone** /gon/) > *verb intrans* 1 to proceed on a course; to travel: *I must go; The ferry goes every hour*. **b** used with a further verb to express purpose: *I went to see them; I'll go and look*. **c** to make an expedition for a specified activity: *to go shopping*. 3a to pass by means of a specified process or according to a specified procedure: *Your suggestion will go before the committee*. **b** to extend: *It's true as far as it goes*. **c** to speak, proceed, or develop in a specified direction or up to a specified limit: *You've gone too far; Don't let's go into details*. 4 (*often* + and) used to intensify a complementary verb: *Don't go saying that; He went and won first prize*. 5 to be, *esp* habitually: *to go barefoot*. 6a to come or arrive at a specified state or condition: *to go to sleep; to go to waste*. **b** to join a specified institution professionally or attend it habitually: *to go on the stage*. **c** to come to be; to turn: *The tyre went flat*. **d** to become voluntarily: *He went absent without leave*. **e** to change to a specified system or tendency: *The company went public*. **f** to continue to be; to remain: *to go hungry*. 7a to become lost, consumed, or spent: *My pen's gone; Half their income goes in rent*. **b** to die. **c** to elapse: *only three weeks to go*. **d** to be got rid of, e.g. by sale or removal: *These slums must go*. **e** to fail: *His hearing started to go*. **f** to give way: *At last the dam went*. 8a (*often* + on) to happen or progress: *Let's find out what's going on; How are things going?* **b** to be in general or on an average: *The cook was a good cook, as cooks go, and as cooks go, she went* — Saki. **c** to pass or be granted by award, assignment, or lot: *The prize went to a French girl*. **d** to turn out, *esp* in a specified manner: *The party went well.* **9** to put or subject oneself: *They went to unnecessary expense.* **10a** to begin an action, motion, or process: *Ready, steady, go!* **b** to maintain or perform an action or motion: *Go like this with your left foot.* **c** to function in a proper or specified way: *trying to get the car to go; I felt ill but kept going.* **d** to make a characteristic noise: *The doorbell went.* **11a** to be known or identified as specified: *She now goes by another name.* **b** to be in phrasing or content: *as the saying goes.* **c** to be sung or played in a specified manner: *The song goes to the tune of 'Greensleeves'.* **12a** to act or occur in accordance or harmony: *a good rule to go by.* **b** to contribute to a total or result: *taxes that go for education.* **13** (+ an infinitive) to be about, intending, or destined: *Is it going to rain?* **14** (+ with) to be compatible or harmonize with (something): *a wine that goes with beef.* **15a** to be capable of passing, extending, or being contained or inserted: *It won't go round my waist; Three into two won't go.* **b** to belong: *These books go on the top shelf.* **16a** to carry authority: *What she said went.* **b** to be acceptable, satisfactory, or adequate: *In America everything goes and nothing matters, while in Europe nothing goes and everything matters —* Philip Roth. **c** to be the case; to be valid: *and that goes for you too.* **17** *informal* to empty the bladder or bowels: *I've been needing to go for ages.* ➤ **verb trans 1** to proceed along or according to (a way, course, etc): *to go one's own way.* **2** to pass through (a distance): *to go ten miles.* **3** to undertake (e.g. an errand) by travelling. **4** to emit (a sound). **5** to participate to the extent of (something): *to go halves.* **6** to perform or effect (something): *to go the limit.* **7** *Brit, informal* to say: *So she goes 'Don't you ever do that again!'* * **go about 1** to undertake or begin to tackle (something). **2** in sailing, to change tack. **go after** to seek or pursue (something or somebody). **go against 1** to act in opposition to (e.g. somebody's wishes or principles). **2** to turn out unfavourably for (somebody). **go ahead 1** to begin. **2** to continue; to advance or proceed. **go all the way** *informal* to engage in full sexual intercourse. **go at 1** to attack (somebody or something). **2** to undertake (e.g. a task) energetically. **go back on 1** to fail to keep (e.g. a promise). **2** to be disloyal to (somebody or something); to betray (them). **go for 1** to serve or be accounted as (something): *It all went for nothing.* **2** to try to secure (something): *He went for the biggest slice.* **3** to choose, favour, or accept (something). **4** to have an interest in or liking for (somebody or something): *She went for him in a big way.* **5** to attack (somebody or something). **go into 1** said of a number: to be contained in (another number): *5 goes into 60 12 times.* **2** to investigate (something). **3** to explain (something) in depth: *The book doesn't go into the moral aspects.* **go it 1** to behave in a reckless, excited, or impulsive manner. **2** to proceed rapidly or furiously. **go it alone** to act alone, *esp* courageously. **go missing** *chiefly Brit* to disappear. **go off** *informal* to stop liking or begin to dislike (something or somebody). **go on** to be enthusiastic about or have a liking for (something) to the specified degree: *We don't go much on cars —* Len Deighton. **go one better** to outdo or surpass another. **go out of one's way** to take extra trouble. **go over 1** to examine, inspect, or check (something). **2** to repeat (something). **3** to study or revise (something). **go through 1** to subject (something) to thorough examination, study, or discussion. **2** to experience or undergo (something difficult or unpleasant). **3** to spend, use, or exhaust (something). **go west** *informal* to die or become destroyed or expended [sometimes said to refer to the gallows at Tyburn, at the west end of Oxford Street in London, but prob from the fact that the sun goes down in the west]. **go with 1** to accompany (something): *the responsibility that goes with parenthood.* **2** to be the social, romantic, or sexual companion of (somebody). **go without** to be deprived of (something). **leave/let go** to stop holding. **to go** *chiefly NAmer, informal* said of prepared food and drink: to be taken away for consumption off the premises. [Old English *ga*, first person singular present tense of *gan; went* was orig the past tense of WEND]

go² *noun* (*pl* **goes**) **1** the act or manner of going. **2a** a turn in an activity, e.g. a game. **b** an attempt, a try: *have a go at painting.* **c** a chance; an opportunity: *a fair go at work for everyone.* **3a** energy; vigour: *full of go.* **b** vigorous activity: *It's all go!* **4** a spell of activity: *We finished the job at one go.* **5** *chiefly informal* an often unexpected or awkward turn of affairs: *It's a rum go.* * **all the go** *informal, dated* the height of fashion; the rage. **have a go at (somebody)** to attack (somebody), *esp* verbally; to criticize (them). **make a go of (something)** to make a success of (e.g. a business venture); to be successful in (it). **no go** *informal* to no avail; useless. **on the go** *informal* constantly or restlessly active.

go³ *adj* (*used after a noun*) functioning properly: *declared all systems go for the rocket launch.*

go⁴ *noun* a Japanese board game of capture and territorial domination played by two players with counters on a board covered in a grid. [Japanese *go*]

goad¹ /gohd/ *noun* **1** a pointed rod used to urge on an animal. **2** something that pricks, urges, or stimulates somebody into action. [Old English *gād* spear, goad]

goad² *verb trans* **1** to drive (e.g. cattle) with a goad. **2** to incite, rouse, or urge (somebody) by nagging or persistent annoyance.

go-ahead¹ *adj* energetic and progressive.

go-ahead² *noun* (**the go-ahead**) a signal, authority, or permission to proceed: *They finally gave us the go-ahead.*

goal /gohl/ *noun* **1a** an area or object into which players in various games attempt to put a ball, etc against the defence of the opposing side. **b** the act or instance of putting a ball, etc into a goal. **c** the position of a player defending a goal: *in goal.* **2** an end towards which effort is directed; an aim or objective. **3** the end or destination of a journey. ➤➤ **goalless** *adj.* [Middle English *gol* boundary, limit; earlier history unknown]

goalball *noun* a team game played by blindfolded or visually impaired people using a large ball that makes a sound when it is thrown.

goalie /'gohli/ *noun informal* a goalkeeper.

goalkeeper *noun* a player who defends the goal in football, hockey, lacrosse, etc. ➤➤ **goalkeeping** *noun.*

goal kick *noun* **1** a free kick in football awarded to the defending side when the ball is sent over the goal line by an opposing player. **2** in rugby, an attempt to kick a goal. ➤➤ **goal-kicker** *noun,* **goal-kicking** *noun.*

goal line *noun* a line at either end and usu running the width of a playing area on which a goal or goal post is situated.

go along *verb intrans* **1** to move along; to proceed. **2** to go or travel as a companion: *I went along for the ride.* * **go along with** to agree or cooperate with (something).

goalpost *noun* either of usu two vertical posts with or without a crossbar that constitute the goal in football, rugby, etc. * **move the goalposts** to change the rules, conditions, parameters, etc that pertain to something, *esp* in order to gain a personal advantage or affect the outcome of something.

goanna /goh'anə/ *noun* any of several species of large Australian lizards: genus *Varanus.* [alteration of IGUANA]

goat /goht/ *noun* **1** any of various species of long-legged agile ruminant mammals that are related to the sheep and have backward-curving horns, a short tail, and usu straight hair: genus *Capra.* **2** *informal* a lecherous man. **3** *informal* a foolish person. **4** (**the Goat**) the constellation and sign of the zodiac Capricorn. * **get somebody's goat** *informal* to annoy or irritate somebody. ➤➤ **goatish** *adj,* **goaty** *adj.* [Old English *gāt*]

goatee /'gohtee/ *noun* a small pointed beard covering only the bottom of the chin. [from its resemblance to the beard of a male goat]

goatfish *noun* (*pl* **goatfishes** *or collectively* **goatfish**) *chiefly NAmer* = RED MULLET. [from the barbels under its mouth]

goatherd *noun* somebody who tends goats.

goat's beard *noun* **1** a Eurasian plant of the daisy family with grasslike leaves and yellow flower heads that close at about midday: *Tragopogon pratensis.* **2** a plant of the rose family with dense clusters of tiny white flowers: *Aruncus dioicus.*

goatskin *noun* **1** the skin of a goat or the leather made from this. **2** a container or other article made from goatskin.

goatsucker *noun* = NIGHTJAR. [from the belief that it sucks the milk from goats]

gob¹ /gob/ *noun* **1** a shapeless or sticky lump. **2** *NAmer* (*usu in pl*) a large amount: *gobs of money.* [Middle English *gobbe* from early French *gobe* large piece of food, mouthful, from *gober* to swallow, prob of Celtic origin]

gob² *verb intrans* (**gobbed, gobbing**) *chiefly Brit, informal* to spit.

gob³ *noun Brit, informal* the mouth: *Shut your gob!* [Irish Gaelic and Scottish Gaelic *gob* beak, protruding mouth]

gobbet /'gobit/ *noun* a piece or portion. [Middle English *gobet* from early French, dimin. of *gobe*: see GOB¹]

gobble¹ /'gobl/ *verb trans* **1** to swallow or eat (something) greedily or noisily. **2** (*often* + up) to take, use, or read (something) quickly or eagerly. [prob from GOB¹]

gobble² *verb intrans* to make the guttural sound of a male turkey or a similar sound. [imitative]

gobble³ *noun* a gobbling sound.

gobbledygook *or* **gobbledegook** /ˈgobldigoohk/ *noun* wordy and generally unintelligible jargon. [prob imitating a turkey gobbling]

gobbler *noun informal* a male turkey.

go-between *noun* an intermediary or agent.

goblet /ˈgoblit/ *noun* 1 a drinking vessel that has a rounded bowl, a foot, and a stem and is used *esp* for wine. 2 the part of a liquidizer in which food is liquidized or ground by means of rotating blades. [Middle English from early French *gobelet* dimin. of *gobel* cup]

goblet cell *noun* a mucus-secreting cell that is shaped like a goblet and found in mucous membranes, e.g. those of the intestines.

goblin /ˈgoblin/ *noun* a grotesque mischievous elf. [Middle English *gobelin* via Old French from medieval Latin *gobelinus*, perhaps from Greek *kobalos* rogue]

gobo /ˈgohboh/ *noun* (*pl* **gobos** *or* **goboes**) any of various shielding devices used in theatre, television, or film productions, e.g. a screen used to shape a beam of light or a piece that shields a microphone from unwanted sounds. [origin unknown]

gobshite *noun chiefly Irish, coarse slang* a stupid or contemptible person.

gobsmacked *adj Brit, informal* utterly taken aback; overwhelmed with astonishment: *Aghast, concussed and altogether gobsmacked I find myself this week, having just listened to an extraordinary documentary* — The Listener.

gobstopper *noun* a large round hard sweet.

goby /ˈgohbi/ *noun* (*pl* **gobies** *or collectively* **goby**) any of numerous species of small spiny-finned fishes often with the pelvic fins united to form a sucking disc: family Gobiidae. [Latin *gobius* gudgeon, from Greek *kōbios*]

go by *verb intrans* to pass: *as time goes by.*

go-by *noun informal* an act of avoidance; a snub: *We gave them the go-by.*

GOC *abbr Brit* General Officer Commanding.

go-cart *noun* see GO-KART.

god¹ /god/ *noun* 1 (**God**) the supreme or ultimate reality; the being perfect in power, wisdom, and goodness whom people worship as creator and ruler of the universe.

Editorial note
God is a word that can apply to whatever is worshipped, and to which power and holiness are ascribed. Eastern religions acknowledge a multiplicity of gods, each representing an aspect of reality, but in the West 'God' is thought of primarily as a personal, loving creator, all-powerful and present everywhere, as taught in the monotheistic religions of Judaism, Christianity, and Islam — Dr Mel Thompson.

2 a being or object believed to have more than natural attributes and powers, e.g. the control of a particular aspect of reality, and to require human worship. 3 a very influential person. 4 somebody or something of supreme value. 5 (**the gods**) the highest gallery in a theatre, usu with the cheapest seats. ➤➤ **godlike** *adj.* [Old English]

god² *or* **God** *interj* used to express astonishment, exasperation, etc.

god-awful *adj informal* extremely unpleasant: *god-awful explosions of violence* — Playboy.

godchild *noun* (*pl* **godchildren**) somebody for whom another person becomes godparent at baptism.

goddamn *or* **goddam** *or* **goddamned** *adj and adv* damned.

goddamned /ˈgoddamd/ *adj and adv* see GODDAMN.

goddaughter *noun* a female godchild.

goddess /ˈgodes, ˈgodis/ *noun* 1 a female deity. 2 a woman whose great charm or beauty arouses adoration.

godet /goh'det, ˈgohday/ *noun* an inset, usu triangular in shape, inserted into a garment to give fullness or flare, e.g. at the bottom of a skirt. [French *godet*, literally 'drinking cup, mug' prob of Germanic origin]

godetia /gə'deeshə/ *noun* an American plant of the fuchsia family widely grown for its attractive white, pink, or red flowers: genus *Godetia*. [named after C H *Godet* d.1879, Swiss botanist]

godfather *noun* 1 a male godparent at baptism. 2 somebody having a relation to another or others like that of a godfather to his godchild: *the godfather of a whole generation of rebels* — Times Literary Supplement. 3 the leader of a criminal organization, *esp* the Mafia.

God-fearing *adj* devout.

godforsaken *adj* 1 remote; desolate. 2 neglected or miserable.

godhead *noun* 1 divine nature or essence. 2 (**the Godhead**). a the supreme being; God. b the nature of God. [Middle English *godhed*, from GOD¹ + *-hed* -hood]

godless *adj* 1 not acknowledging a deity; impious. 2 wicked. ➤➤ **godlessness** *noun.*

godly *adj* (**godlier, godliest**) 1 divine. 2 pious; devout. ➤➤ **godliness** *noun.*

godmother *noun* a female godparent.

godown /ˈgohdown/ *noun* a warehouse in an Asian country, *esp* India. [Malay *gudang*]

go down *verb intrans* 1a to decrease. b to undergo a decline or decrease: *The market is going down.* 2 said of the sun: to go below the horizon. 3a said of a ship or aircraft: to sink or crash. b to undergo defeat. c said of a computer system or program: to become inoperative; to crash. 4 to be capable of being swallowed. 5a to be received in a specified way: *The plan won't go down well with the farmers.* b to come to be remembered, *esp* by posterity: *He will go down in history as a great general.* 6 (*often* + with) to become ill: *He went down with flu.* 7 *Brit* to leave a university. 8 *informal* to be sent to prison. ✳ **go down on** *coarse slang* to perform fellatio or cunnilingus on (somebody).

godparent *noun* somebody who undertakes responsibility for the religious education and spiritual welfare of another person at baptism.

God's acre *noun archaic, literary* a churchyard.

godsend /ˈgodsend/ *noun* a desirable or needed person, thing, or event, *esp* one that comes unexpectedly or at just the right time.

God's gift *noun informal, chiefly ironic* somebody or something that is the best of their or its kind, or somebody that considers himself or herself to be so, *esp* in terms of sexual attractiveness.

godson *noun* a male godchild.

Godspeed /god'speed/ *noun dated* a prosperous journey; success: *They bade him Godspeed.* [Middle English *god speid*, from the phrase *God spede you* may God prosper you]

godsquad /ˈgod,skwod/ *noun chiefly derog* any religious, usu Christian, group that is thought to be overly pious or to be acting in a zealously evangelical way, often to the extent of being intrusive.

godwit *noun* any of several species of wading birds with long upward-curving bills, related to the sandpipers and curlews: genus *Limosa*. [origin unknown]

goer /ˈgoh-ə/ *noun* 1 (*usu in combination*) a regular attender of something specified: *a theatregoer*. 2 *informal* somebody or something that moves or does things fast. 3 *informal* a lively, *esp* sexually active, person. 4 *Aus* a proposal or idea that is acceptable or feasible.

goes *verb* third person present sing. of GO¹.

goest *verb* archaic second person present sing. of GO¹.

goeth *verb* archaic third person present sing. of GO¹.

gofer /ˈgohfə/ *noun informal* somebody who runs errands or carries messages for others. [alteration of *go for*]

goffer¹ /ˈgohfə, ˈgofə/ *verb trans* (**goffered, goffering**) 1 to crimp, wave, or flute (e.g. a lace edging), *esp* with a heated iron. 2 to emboss (the edges of a book). [French *gaufrer* to stamp with a decorative tool, from *gaufre* honeycomb, ultimately from Dutch or early Low German *wafel* WAFFLE¹]

goffer² *noun* an iron or other tool used for goffering lace etc.

go-getter *noun* an aggressively enterprising person. ➤➤ **go-getting** *adj.*

goggle /ˈgogl/ *verb intrans* to stare with wide or bulging eyes. [Middle English *gogelen* to squint; earlier history unknown]

goggle-box *noun Brit, informal* a television set.

goggle-eyed *adj and adv* with the eyes wide or bulging, in amazement or fascination.

goggles *pl noun* protective glasses set in a flexible frame that fits snugly against the face.

go-go *noun* a style of popular music that originated in Washington, DC, and is characterized by strong percussion, jazz and African elements, and chanting with audience response.

go-go dancer *noun* a female dancer employed to entertain by dancing in a modern usu erotic style, e.g. in a disco, pub, or nightclub. ➤➤ **go-go dance** *noun*, **go-go dancing** *noun*. [alteration (influenced by GO¹) of A GOGO, from *Whisky à Gogo*, the name of a café and disco in Paris, from French *à gogo* galore]

Goidelic /goy'delik/ *noun* the group of Celtic languages comprising Irish Gaelic, Scottish Gaelic, and Manx: compare BRYTHONIC. ➤➤ **Goidelic** *adj*. [early Irish *Góidel* Gaelic]

go in *verb intrans* **1** to enter. **2** said of the sun, etc: to become obscured by a cloud. **3** (*often* + with) to form a union or alliance: *They asked us to go in with them on the project.* ✳ **go in for 1** to engage in (an activity), *esp* as a hobby or for enjoyment. **2** to enter and compete in (e.g. a test or race).

going¹ *noun* **1** (*often in combination*) the act or instance of going: *comings and goings; theatregoing*. **2** the condition of the ground, e.g. for horse racing. **3** advance; progress: *I found the going too slow*.

going² *adj* **1a** living; existing: *the best novelist going*. **b** available, to be had: *She asked if there were any jobs going*. **2a** current; prevailing: *the going price*. **b** profitable or thriving: *a going concern*. ✳ **going for** favourable to: *He had everything going for him*.

going-over *noun* (*pl* **goings-over**) **1** a thorough examination or investigation. **2** a severe scolding or beating.

goings-on *pl noun* **1** actions or events: *sundry goings-on*. **2** irregular or reprehensible happenings or conduct: *tales of scandalous goings-on in high circles*.

goitre (*NAmer* **goiter**) /'goytə/ *noun* an abnormal enlargement of the thyroid gland visible as a swelling of the front of the neck. ➤➤ **goitred** *adj*, **goitrous** /'goytrəs/ *adj*. [early French *goitre*, backformation from *goitron* throat, ultimately from Latin *guttur* throat, crop of a bird]

go-kart *or* **go-cart** *noun* a tiny racing car with small wheels used in karting. [GO¹ + *kart*, alteration of CART¹]

Golconda /gol'kondə/ *noun* a source of great wealth, happiness, or good fortune. [named after *Golconda*, city in India famous for its diamonds]

gold /gohld/ *noun* **1a** a yellow precious metallic chemical element that is soft and easily worked, occurs chiefly uncombined or in a few minerals, and is used *esp* in jewellery and as a currency reserve: symbol Au, atomic number 79. **b** (*used before a noun*) made of or containing gold: *a gold ring*. **2a** gold coins. **b** money. **c** = GOLD STANDARD. **d** gold as a commodity. **3** = GOLD MEDAL: *another gold for the French team*. **4** a deep metallic yellow colour. **5** something valued as excellent or the finest of its kind: *a heart of gold*. **6** the gold-coloured or yellow centre spot of an archery target, or a shot that hits it. [Old English]

goldbrick¹ *noun* **1** *informal* something that appears to be valuable but is actually worthless. **2** *chiefly NAmer*, *informal* a person who shirks assigned work. [from a confidence trick in which an ordinary brick is passed off as solid gold]

goldbrick² *verb trans informal* to swindle or cheat (somebody). ➤ *verb intrans chiefly NAmer*, *informal* to shirk assigned work. ➤➤ **goldbricker** *noun*.

goldcrest *noun* a very small olive-green European bird that has a bright yellow crown with a black border: *Regulus regulus*.

gold digger *noun informal* a woman who uses her charms and sexual attraction to extract money or gifts from men.

gold disc *noun* a music award in the form of a framed gold record given to an artist, group, etc, in Britain for selling 250,000 copies of an album or 500,000 copies of a single, and in the USA for selling 500,000 copies of an album or one million copies of a single.

gold dust *noun* gold in the form of very fine particles. ✳ **like gold dust** very rare or valuable.

golden *adj* **1** consisting of, relating to, or containing gold. **2a** of the colour of gold. **b** said of hair: having a colour between blond and ginger. **3** prosperous; flourishing: *golden days*. **4** favourable; advantageous: *a golden opportunity*. **5** of or marking a 50th anniversary: *golden wedding*. ➤➤ **goldenly** *adv*, **goldenness** *noun*.

golden age *noun* **1** a period of great happiness, prosperity, or achievement. **2** a period of time when a particular art form, type of music, literature, etc was flourishing. **3** a period of time in a country's history when its arts, empire, etc flourished.

golden boy *noun* **1** a man or boy who is very successful or who possesses talents that promise success: *the golden boy of snooker*. **2** a man or boy who is highly favoured or popular.

Golden Delicious *noun* a variety of eating apple with a greenish yellow skin and sweet juicy flesh.

golden eagle *noun* a large eagle of the northern hemisphere with brownish yellow tips on the head and neck feathers: *Aquila chrysaetos*.

goldeneye *noun* (*pl* **goldeneyes** *or collectively* **goldeneye**) either of two species of large-headed swift-flying diving duck of northern regions, the male of which is strikingly marked in black and white and has yellow eyes: genus *Bucephala*.

golden girl *noun* **1** a woman or girl who is very successful or who possesses talents that promise success. **2** a woman or girl who is highly favoured and popular.

golden goal *noun* **1** in certain football matches, a system operating in extra time under which the first team to score wins the match. **2** a goal scored under this system.

golden goose *noun* a source of continuing prosperity that must be handled with restraint. [from the phrase *kill the goose that lays the golden eggs*, from a fable in which a goose that lays a golden egg every day is killed for the gold thought to be inside her]

golden hamster *noun* a small tawny hamster widely kept as a pet: *Mesocricetus auratus*.

golden handcuffs *pl noun informal* a series of payments or other benefits given to an employee as an inducement to remain with a company.

golden handshake *noun informal* a large sum of money given to an employee on leaving a company, *esp* on retirement.

golden hello *noun informal* a substantial one-off payment given to a person after they have agreed to join a company as a new employee, often used to induce a person to leave a rival organization.

golden mean *noun* **1** the medium between extremes; moderation. **2** = GOLDEN SECTION.

golden number *noun* a number marking a year in the Metonic cycle of 19 years that is used in calculating the date of Easter.

golden oldie *noun informal* a hit song from the past that is still popular.

golden parachute *noun informal* a substantial payment contractually guaranteed to a business executive in the event of dismissal or demotion, *esp* following a takeover or merger.

golden plover *noun* either of two plovers whose brownish upper parts are speckled with golden yellow and white in summer: *Pluvialis apricaria* and *Pluvialis dominica*.

golden retriever *noun* a medium-sized retriever of a breed with a silky gold-coloured coat.

golden rice *noun* a form of rice genetically modified to produce yellow grains containing beta-carotene in order to counteract vitamin-A deficiency.

goldenrod *noun* a plant of the daisy family with heads of small yellow flowers often clustered in branching spikes: genus *Solidago*.

golden rule *noun* **1** a moral principle, derived from Matthew 7:12 and Luke 6:31, requiring that one treat others as one would wish to be treated by them. **2** a guiding principle.

golden section *noun* the proportion of a geometrical figure or a divided line such that the ratio of the smaller part to the greater is the same as that of the greater to the whole.

golden share *noun* a share in a company that is sufficient to prevent a takeover, *esp* such a share held by the government in a company considered to be of national importance.

golden syrup *noun* a pale yellow syrup derived from cane sugar refining and used in cooking.

goldfield *noun* a district in which gold-bearing minerals occur.

goldfinch *noun* a small red, black, yellow, and white European finch: *Carduelis carduelis*.

goldfish *noun* (*pl* **goldfishes** *or collectively* **goldfish**) a small usu golden-yellow or orange-red fish related to the carps and widely kept in aquariums and ponds: *Carassius auratus*.

goldfish bowl *noun chiefly Brit* **1** a small usu spherical tank for keeping goldfish in, *esp* in the home. **2** *informal* any place or situation that affords little or no privacy.

gold leaf *noun* gold beaten into very thin sheets and used *esp* for gilding.

gold medal *noun* a medal of gold awarded to somebody who comes first in a competition or race.

gold mine *noun* **1** an extremely profitable enterprise, business, etc. **2** a rich source of something desired. **3** a place where gold is mined. ➤➤ **gold miner** *noun*.

gold plate *noun* **1** a thin coating of gold on another metal. **2** articles that are made of or plated with gold.

gold-plate *verb trans* to cover (metal, etc) with a thin layer of gold.

gold reserve *noun* gold held by a central bank, e.g. to protect a nation's currency or to meet international payments.

gold rush *noun* a rush of people to newly discovered goldfields in pursuit of riches.

goldsmith *noun* somebody who makes or deals in articles of gold.

gold standard *noun* a monetary system in which the basic unit of currency is defined by a stated quantity of gold of a fixed purity.

golem /'gohləm/ *noun* **1** a clay figure of Hebrew folklore supernaturally endowed with life. **2** something, e.g. a robot, resembling a golem. [Yiddish *goylem* from Hebrew *gōlem* shapeless mass]

golf /golf/ *noun* a game in which a player using long-shafted clubs attempts to hit a small ball into each of the 9 or 18 successive holes on a course with the object of taking as few strokes as possible: *If you watch a game, it's fun. If you play it, it's recreation. If you work at it, it's golf*— Bob Hope. [Middle English (Scots), perhaps from early Dutch *colf, colve* club, bat]

golf ball *noun* **1** a small hard usu white ball used in playing golf: *If you think it's hard to meet new people, try picking up the wrong golf ball*— Jack Lemmon. **2** a spherical ball that carries the characters in some electric typewriters.

golf club *noun* **1** any of a set of clubs with long shafts and shaped metal or wooden heads used to strike the ball in the game of golf. **2** an association of golf players, often having their own course, clubhouse, and other facilities.

golf course *noun* an area of land laid out for playing golf consisting of a series of 9 or 18 holes, each with a tee, fairway, and putting green, and usu various natural or artificial hazards.

golfer *noun* somebody who plays golf.

golfing *noun* the sport or practice of playing golf.

golf links *pl noun* (*treated as sing. or pl*) a golf course, *esp* one near the sea.

Golgi apparatus *noun* a specialized organelle in the CYTOPLASM (jellylike material) of a eukaryote cell that appears in electron microscopy as a series of parallel membranes and is concerned with secretion of cell products. [named after Camillo *Golgi* d.1926, Italian physician, who first described it]

Golgi body *noun* **1** a separate particle of the Golgi apparatus. **2** = GOLGI APPARATUS.

goliath beetle /gə'lie·əth/ *noun* a very large African beetle that has a black body marked with white stripes: *Goliathus giganteus*. [named after *Goliath*, biblical giant of the Philistines killed by David (I Samuel 17)]

golliwog /'goliwog/ *noun* a soft doll with a black face, often dressed in colourful clothes. [named after *Golliwogg*, an animated doll in children's books by Bertha Upton d.1912, US writer]

gollop[1] /'goləp/ *verb trans* (**golloped, golloping**) *informal* to gulp (food or drink). [by alteration]

gollop[2] *noun* a gulp of food or drink.

golly[1] /'goli/ *interj* used to express surprise. [euphemism for GOD[2]]

golly[2] *noun* (*pl* **gollies**) = GOLLIWOG. [by shortening and alteration]

golosh /gə'losh/ *noun chiefly Brit* = GALOSH.

gombeen /gom'been, 'gombeen/ *noun Irish* **1** usury. **2** (*used before a noun*) of or involved in usury: *gombeen man*. [Irish Gaelic *gaimbín*]

-gon *comb. form* forming nouns, denoting: a geometrical figure having the number of angles specified: *decagon*. [via Latin from Greek *-gōnon*, from *gōnia* angle]

gonad /'gohnad/ *noun* any of the primary sex glands in which the egg or sperm cells are produced, e.g. the ovaries or testes. ➤➤ **gonadal** /goh'nadl, goh'naydl/ *adj*. [scientific Latin *gonad-,*

gonas, from Greek *gonos* procreation, seed, from *gignesthai* to be born]

gonadotrophic /ˌgonədoh'trohfik/ *adj* acting on or stimulating the gonads.

gonadotrophin /ˌgonədoh'trohfin/ *noun* a gonadotrophic hormone, e.g. a follicle-stimulating hormone.

gonadotropic /ˌgonədoh'tropik/ *adj* = GONADOTROPHIC.

gonadotropin /gonədoh'trohpin/ *noun* = GONADOTROPHIN.

gondola /'gondələ/ *noun* **1** a long narrow flat-bottomed boat used on the canals of Venice. **2a** an enclosure suspended from a balloon for carrying passengers or instruments. **b** a cabin suspended from a cable and used for transporting passengers, e.g. up a ski slope. **3** a fixture approachable from all sides used in self-service retail shops to display merchandise. **4** *NAmer* an open railway goods wagon with a flat bottom and fixed sides. [Italian *gondola* from medieval Latin *gondula*, dimin. of (assumed) vulgar Latin *condua*]

gondolier /gondə'liə/ *noun* somebody who propels a gondola. [via French from Italian *gondoliere* from *gondola*: see GONDOLA]

gone[1] /gon/ *verb* past part. of GO[1].

gone[2] *adj* **1a** past; ended. **b** lost; ruined. **c** used up. **2a** involved; absorbed. **b** intoxicated with drugs, alcohol, etc. **c** *informal* (*usu + on*) infatuated (with somebody): *I was really gone on that man*. **3** pregnant by a specified length of time: *She's six months gone*. **4** *euphem* dead.

gone[3] *adv Brit* later or older than; turned: *It's gone three o'clock*.

goner *noun informal* **1** somebody or something whose case or state is hopeless or lost. **2** a dead person.

gonfalon /'gonfalən/ *or* **gonfanon** /-nən/ *noun* a flag or banner that hangs from a crosspiece or frame. [Italian *gonfalone* from Old French *gonfanon, gonfalon*, of Germanic origin]

gong[1] /gong/ *noun* **1** a disc-shaped percussion instrument that produces a resounding tone when struck, usu with a padded hammer. **2** a flat saucer-shaped bell. **3** *Brit, informal* a medal or decoration. [Malay and Javanese *gong*, of imitative origin]

gong[2] *verb intrans* **1** to strike a gong. **2** to make the resonant sound of a gong.

goniometer /gohni'omitə/ *noun* an instrument for measuring angles. ➤➤ **goniometric** /-'metrik/ *adj*, **goniometry** /-tri/ *noun*. [French *goniomètre* from Greek *gōnia* angle + -METER[2]]

gonna /'gonə, 'gənə/ *contraction informal* going to: *I'm gonna wash that man right out of my hair*— Oscar Hammerstein II.

gonococcus /gonoh'kokəs/ *noun* (*pl* **gonococci** /-'kok(s)ie, -'kok(s)ee/) the pus-producing bacterium that causes gonorrhoea: *Neisseria gonorrhoeae*. ➤➤ **gonococcal** *adj*. [blend of GONORRHOEA and COCCUS]

gonorrhoea (*NAmer* **gonorrhea**) /gonə'ri·ə/ *noun* a sexually transmitted disease in which there is inflammation of the mucous membranes of the genital tracts caused by gonococcal bacteria. ➤➤ **gonorrhoeal** *adj*. [via late Latin from Greek *gonorrhoia*, from *gonos* semen + *-rrhoia* -RRHOEA]

-gony *comb. form* forming nouns, denoting: origin; reproduction; manner of coming into being: *sporogony; cosmogony*. [via Latin from Greek *-gonia*, from *gonos* procreation, seed]

gonzo /'gonzoh/ *adj NAmer, informal* **1** bizarre; crazy. **2** relating to or denoting a highly subjective or eccentric style of journalism. [Italian *gonzo* dupe, simpleton]

goo /gooh/ *noun informal* **1** a sticky substance. **2** cloying sentimentality. [perhaps alteration of GLUE[1]]

good[1] /good/ *adj* (**better** /'betə/, **best** /best/) **1a** of a favourable or desirable character or tendency: *good news*. **b** agreeable; pleasant. **c** amusing: *That's a good one!* **d** (+ for) beneficial to the health or character of (somebody): *Spinach is good for you*. **2a** morally commendable; virtuous: *a good man*. **b** well-behaved; obedient. **3** (*often + at*) competent; skilful: *a good doctor*. **4a** suitable; fit: *It's a good day for planting roses*. **b** free from injury or disease; whole: *one good arm*. **c** not rotten; fresh. **d** bountiful; fertile: *good land*. **e** not depreciated: *bad money drives out good*. **f** commercially sound: *a good risk*. **5a** (+ for) certain to last or live for (a specified time): *good for another year*. **b** (+ for) certain to pay or contribute (a specified sum): *good for a few quid*. **c** (+ for) certain to elicit (a specified result): *always good for a laugh*. **6a** kind; benevolent: *good intentions*. **b** reputable; *specif* upper-class: *a good family*. **c** deserving of respect; honourable: *in good standing*. **d** loyal: *a good Catholic*. **7a** well-founded; true: *good reasons*. **b** correct; conforming to a standard: *good English*. **c** legally valid: *good title*. **d** choice; discriminating: *good taste*. **8a** adequate; satisfactory. **b** strong; robust. **c** ample; full: *have a good look*. **9** suitable for smart or formal wear: *my good trousers*. **10a** at least: *a good hour later*. **b** said of an amount: large or fairly large: *There were a good number of people at the meeting*. **11** used in expressions of greeting and farewell: *good day*. * **as good as** virtually; in effect: *as good as dead*. **as good as gold** extremely well-behaved. **good and** *informal* very; entirely: *It should be good and ready by now*. **good for/on you!** well done! **in good faith** with honest or sincere intentions. **make good 1** to be successful in life. **2** *chiefly Brit* to repair (something). **3** to provide compensation for (a loss, damage, expense, etc). **4** to fulfil (a promise, etc). >> **goodish** *adj*. [Old English *gōd*]

good² *noun* **1a** something good; merit or use: *It's no good complaining*. **b** the quality of being good: *know good from evil*. **c** a good element or portion: *recognize the good in others*. **2** benefit; advantage: *for the good of the community*. **3a** (*usu in pl*) something that has economic utility or satisfies an economic want. **b** (*usu in pl*) personal property having intrinsic value but usu excluding money, securities, etc. **c** (*usu in pl*) wares; merchandise: *tinned goods*. **d** (*in pl, used before a noun*) relating to the transport of merchandise, *esp* by rail: *goods train*. **4** *informal* (*in pl, but treated as sing. or pl*) the desired or necessary article: *They came up with the goods*. **5** *chiefly NAmer, informal* (*in pl*) proof of wrongdoing: *The police have got the goods on him*. * **do somebody/something good** to be beneficial to somebody or something. **for good** forever; permanently. **to the good 1** for the best; beneficial: *This rain is all to the good*. **2** in a position of net gain or profit: *We ended up £10 to the good*.

good book *noun* (*often* **the Good Book**) the Bible.

goodbye¹ (*NAmer* **goodby**) /good'bie/ *interj* used to express farewell. [alteration of *God be with you*]

goodbye² (*NAmer* **goodby**) *noun* (*pl* **goodbyes** or *NAmer* **goodbys**) a concluding remark or gesture at parting: *It's time to say our goodbyes*.

goodfella /'goodfelə/ *noun* (*pl* **goodfellas**) *chiefly NAmer, informal* a gangster, *esp* a member of the Mafia or a person involved in organized crime.

good-for-nothing¹ *adj* of no value; worthless.

good-for-nothing² *noun* an idle worthless person.

Good Friday *noun* the Friday before Easter Sunday, observed in the Christian Church as the anniversary of the crucifixion of Christ. [from its special sanctity]

good-hearted *adj* having a kindly generous disposition. >> **good-heartedness** *noun*.

good-humoured *adj* good-natured; cheerful. >> **good-humouredly** *adv*.

goodie /'goodi/ *noun* see GOODY¹.

goodies *pl noun* = GOODY¹ (1A).

good-looking *adj* having a pleasing or attractive appearance. >> **good-looker** *noun*.

goodly *adj* (**goodlier, goodliest**) **1** significantly large in amount; considerable: *a goodly number*. **2** *archaic* pleasantly attractive; handsome. >> **goodliness** *noun*.

goodman *noun* (*pl* **goodmen**) *archaic* **1** a husband. **2** a title or form of address for a man who is not of noble birth. **3** *chiefly Scot* a male head of a household.

good-natured *adj* said of a person or animal: having a pleasant, cheerful, and cooperative disposition. >> **good-naturedly** *adv*, **good-naturedness** *noun*.

goodness¹ *noun* **1** the quality or state of being good. **2** the nutritious or beneficial part of something: *Don't boil all the goodness out of the meat*.

goodness² *interj* used to express surprise. [euphem for GOD²]

goodness of fit *noun* in statistics, the extent to which observed values match those predicted theoretically.

goodnight or **good night** *interj* used to express good wishes when leaving somebody at night or when going to bed.

good-o /'goodoh/ *interj* see GOOD-OH.

good offices *pl noun* power or action that helps somebody out of a difficulty: *Through the good offices of the policeman, I found my way to the station*. [OFFICE in an old sense 'service, attention']

good-oh or **good-o** /'goodoh/ *interj dated* used as an expression of approval or pleasure.

Good Samaritan *noun* = SAMARITAN (2A).

goods and chattels *pl noun* all the things belonging to a person.

good-tempered *adj* having an even temper; not easily annoyed. >> **good-temperedly** *adv*, **good-temperedness** *noun*.

good-time *adj* said of a person, *esp* a young woman: devoted to the pursuit of pleasure.

goodwife *noun* (*pl* **goodwives**) *archaic* **1** a title or form of address for a woman who is not of noble birth. **2** *chiefly Scot* a female head of a household.

goodwill *noun* **1** a kindly feeling of approval and support; benevolent interest or concern. **2a** cheerful consent. **b** willing effort. **3** the favour or prestige that a business has acquired beyond the mere value of what it sells.

goodwives *noun* pl of GOODWIFE.

good word *noun* a favourable statement: *Would you put in a good word for me?*

goody¹ or **goodie** *noun* (*pl* **goodies**) *informal* **1a** (*usu in pl*) something particularly attractive, pleasurable, or desirable. **b** (*used before a noun*) relating to or containing goodies: *a party goody bag*. **2** a good person or hero, *esp* in a film or book.

goody² *interj informal* used, *esp* by children, to express pleasure or delight.

goody³ *noun* (*pl* **goodies**) *archaic* used as a title preceding a surname of a married woman of lowly station. [alteration of GOODWIFE]

goody-goody¹ *noun* (*pl* **goody-goodies**) *informal* somebody who is affectedly or ingratiatingly prim or virtuous.

goody-goody² *adj* relating to or characteristic of a goody-goody.

gooey /'gooh·i/ *adj* (**gooier, gooiest**) **1** soft and sticky. **2** cloyingly sentimental.

goof¹ /goohf/ *noun informal* **1** a ridiculous or stupid person. **2** *chiefly NAmer* a blunder. [prob alteration of English dialect *goff* simpleton]

goof² *verb intrans* **1** (*often* + about/around) to fool around. **2** *chiefly NAmer, informal* to make a foolish mistake; to blunder. **3** *chiefly NAmer, informal* (*usu* + off) to play truant from work, school, etc; to shirk a duty. >> *verb trans chiefly NAmer, informal* (*often* + up) to make a mess of (something); to bungle (it).

goofball *noun* **1** *NAmer, informal* a stupid or gullible person. **2** a barbiturate sleeping pill.

go off *verb intrans* **1** to go forth or away; to depart. **2** to explode. **3** said of food: to begin to decompose. **4** to follow a specified course; to proceed: *The party went off well*. **5** to make a characteristic noise; to sound: *The alarm went off*. **6** to fall asleep.

goofy *adj* (**goofier, goofiest**) *informal* **1** *chiefly NAmer* silly; foolish. **2** *chiefly Brit* said of teeth: protruding. >> **goofily** *adv*, **goofiness** *noun*.

goog /goohg/ *noun Aus, NZ, informal* an egg. [perhaps from Dutch *oog* or from a Scottish dialect word for an egg]

googly /'goohgli/ *noun* (*pl* **googlies**) in cricket, a slow ball that is apparently bowled with an action that would make it turn one way on bouncing but that actually turns the other way. [origin unknown]

googol /'goohgol/ *noun* the figure 1 followed by 100 zeros; 10^{100}. [said to have been coined by the nine-year-old nephew of E Kasner d.1955, US mathematician]

goo-goo /'gooh gooh/ *adj informal* sentimentally amorous: *make goo-goo eyes at each other*. [prob alteration of *goggle* staring, squinting, from Middle English *gogelen*: see GOGGLE]

gook /gook/ *noun chiefly NAmer, informal* a foreigner, *esp* somebody from southeast Asia or of southeast Asian descent. [origin unknown]

gooly or **goolie** /'goohli/ *noun* (*pl* **goolies**) *informal* **1** *Brit* a testicle. **2** *Aus, NZ* a stone. [Hindi *goli* ball, bullet]

goon /goohn/ *noun informal* **1** somebody who behaves in a silly or foolish manner. **2** *chiefly NAmer* somebody hired to terrorize or eliminate opponents; a bully or thug. [partly short for English dialect *gooney* simpleton; partly from Alice the Goon, comic-strip character created by E C Segar d.1938, US cartoonist]

go on *verb intrans* **1** to continue; to carry on. **2a** to proceed by or as if by a logical step: *He went on to explain why*. **b** said of time: to pass. **3** to take place; to happen: *What's going on?* **4** to be capable of being put on: *Her gloves wouldn't go on*. **5a** to talk, *esp* in an effusive manner. **b** (*often* + *at*) to criticize or nag somebody constantly. **6a** to come into operation, action, or production: *The lights went on at sunset.* **b** to appear on the stage. **7** *Brit* to manage; to get along: *How did you go on for money?* ✳ **go on! 1** used to encourage somebody. **2** used to express disbelief.

gooney bird /'goohni/ *noun chiefly NAmer, informal* = ALBATROSS. [origin unknown]

goop[1] /goohp/ *noun chiefly NAmer, informal* a stupid or useless person. ⟫⟫ **goopiness** *noun,* **goopy** *adj.* [coined by G Burgess d.1951, US humorist]

goop[2] *noun chiefly NAmer, informal* = GLOOP. ⟫⟫ **goopiness** *noun,* **goopy** *adj.* [origin unknown]

goosander /gooh'sandə/ *noun* (*pl* **goosanders** *or collectively* **goosander**) a sawbill duck of the northern hemisphere, the male of which has a black back, pinkish white underparts, and a greenish black head: *Mergus merganser*. [alteration of earlier *goosander,* prob from *gos-* as in GOSLING + *-ander* as in dialect *bergander* shelduck, which the male goosander resembles in colouring]

goose[1] /goohs/ *noun* (*pl* **geese** /gees/) **1a** any of several genera of large water birds with long necks and webbed feet: family Anatidae. **b** the female of such a bird: compare GANDER[1]. **c** the flesh of a goose used as food. **2** *informal* a foolish person; a simpleton. **3** (*pl* **gooses**) a tailor's smoothing iron with a gooseneck handle. [Old English *gōs*]

goose[2] *verb trans informal* to poke (somebody) on the bottom.

gooseberry /'goozb(ə)ri/ *noun* (*pl* **gooseberries**) **1a** a small round edible green or yellow fruit with soft usu prickly skin and acid flesh. **b** the thorny shrub that bears this fruit: *Ribes grossularia.* **2** an unwanted companion to two lovers: *play gooseberry.* [*goose* perhaps from GOOSE[1], or perhaps an alteration of Old French *groseille* redcurrant; the connection with the bird is unexplained]

goose bumps *pl noun chiefly NAmer* = GOOSEFLESH.

gooseflesh *noun* a bristling rough or bumpy condition of the skin accompanying erection of its hairs, usu caused by cold or fear. [prob from the resemblance to a plucked fowl]

goosefoot *noun* (*pl* **goosefoots**) a plant with small green flowers that grow *esp* on disturbed or cultivated land: genus *Chenopodium*. [from the shape of its leaves]

goosegog /'goozgog/ *noun Brit, informal* = GOOSEBERRY (1A). [GOOSEBERRY + *gog*, of unknown origin]

goosegrass *noun* = CLEAVERS.

gooseneck *noun* something, e.g. a joint or pipe, that is curved like the neck of a goose or U-shaped.

goose pimples *pl noun* = GOOSEFLESH.

gooseskin *noun* = GOOSEFLESH.

goose step *noun* a straight-legged marching step with the legs swung high.

goose-step *verb intrans* to march with straight legs swung high.

goosey *adj* (**goosier, goosiest**) *informal* having gooseflesh: *I went all goosey when they said the house was haunted.*

go out *verb intrans* **1a** to leave a room, house, country, etc. **b** to go to social events, entertainments, etc: *We don't go out much.* **c** (+ *with*) to spend time regularly with somebody in a romantic relationship. **2a** to become extinguished: *The lamps are going out all over Europe* — Viscount Grey of Falloden. **b** to become obsolete or unfashionable. **c** to play the last card of one's hand. **3** to be broadcast: *The programme went out at nine o'clock.*

go over *verb intrans* **1** to become converted, e.g. to a religion or political party. **2** to be received in a specified way: *The play should go over well in Scotland.*

gopak /'gohpak/ *or* **hopak** /'hohpak/ *noun* a Ukrainian folk dance featuring high leaps and performed by men. [via Russian from Ukrainian *hopak,* from *hop,* interj used in lively dances, from German *hopp*]

gopher /'gohfə/ *noun* **1** any of several species of American burrowing rodents that are the size of a large rat and have large cheek pouches: family Geomyidae. **2** any of various small ground squirrels of the N American prairies, closely related to the chipmunks: genus *Spermophilus* and other genera. **3** any of several species of American burrowing tortoises: genus *Gopherus*. **4** in computing, an early form of Internet search engine. [perhaps from Canadian French *gaufre* honeycomb (see GOFFER[1]), from the network of burrows the rodents make; (sense 5) prob an alteration of GOFER]

gopher wood *noun* in the Bible, the wood that was used to build Noah's ark. [Hebrew *gōper*]

gopik /'gohpik/ *noun* (*pl* **gopik** *or* **gopiks**) a unit of currency in Azerbaijan, worth 100th of a manat.

goral /'gawrəl/ *noun* either of two E Asian mammals that resemble small antelopes: *Naemorhaedus goral* or *Naemorhaedus cranbrooki*. [perhaps derivative of Sanskrit *gaura* GAUR]

gorblimey /gaw'bliemi/ *interj Brit, informal* used to express surprise or indignation. [euphemism for *God blind me*]

Gordian knot /'gawdi·ən/ *noun* an intricate problem, *esp* one insoluble in its own terms: *cut the Gordian knot*. [named after *Gordius*, King of Phrygia, who tied an intricate knot that supposedly could be undone only by the future ruler of Asia, and which Alexander the Great cut with his sword]

gore[1] /gaw/ *noun* thick or clotted blood, *esp* blood that has been shed as a result of violence. [Old English *gor* filth]

gore[2] *verb trans* said of an animal, *esp* a bull: to pierce or wound (somebody or something) with a horn or tusk. [Middle English *goren,* prob from Old English *gār* spear]

gore[3] *noun* a tapering or triangular piece of material used to give shape to something, e.g. a garment or sail. [Old English *gāra* wedge-shaped piece of land]

gore[4] *verb trans* to give shape to (something, *esp* a garment or sail) by inserting a gore or gores. ⟫⟫ **gored** *adj.*

gorge[1] /gawj/ *noun* **1** a narrow steep-walled valley, often with a stream flowing through it. **2** the contents of the stomach. **3** *archaic* the throat. **4** the narrow rear entrance into an outwork of a fort. ✳ **one's gorge rises** one is disgusted, sickened, or nauseated. [Middle English via early French *gorge* throat, ultimately from Latin *gurges* throat, whirlpool]

gorge[2] *verb intrans* to eat hungrily or greedily. ⟫ *verb trans* **1a** to swallow (food) greedily. **b** to stuff (oneself) with food. **2** to fill completely or to the point of swelling: *veins gorged with blood.* ⟫⟫ **gorger** *noun.*

gorgeous /'gawjəs/ *adj* **1** splendidly beautiful or magnificent. **2** *informal* very fine or pleasant: *a gorgeous day for a picnic.* ⟫⟫ **gorgeously** *adv,* **gorgeousness** *noun.* [Middle English *gorgayse* from early French *gorgias* elegant, perhaps from *gorgias* neckerchief, from *gorge*: see GORGE[1]]

gorget /'gawjit/ *noun* **1** a piece of armour protecting the throat. **2** a part of a wimple covering the throat and shoulders. **3** a band or patch of colour on a bird's or other animal's throat. [Middle English from early French *gorge*: see GORGE[1]]

gorgio /'gawji·oh/ *noun* (*pl* **gorgios**) used *esp* by gypsies: somebody who is not a gypsy. [Romany *gorjo*]

gorgon /'gawgən/ *noun* **1** (**Gorgon**) any of three sisters in Greek mythology who had live snakes in place of hair and who could turn anybody who looked at them to stone. **2** a repulsive or formidable woman: *I don't really know what a Gorgon is like, but I am quite sure Lady Bracknell is one* — Oscar Wilde. [Latin *Gorgon-, Gorgo,* from Greek *Gorgōn,* from *gorgos* terrible]

gorgonian /gaw'gohni·ən/ *noun* any of an order of corals that live in colonies and typically have a horny branching or treelike skeleton: order Gorgonacea. ⟫⟫ **gorgonian** *adj.* [Latin *gorgonia* coral, from *Gorgon-, Gorgo*: see GORGON]

Gorgonzola /gawgən'zohlə/ *noun* a blue-veined strongly flavoured Italian cheese. [named after *Gorgonzola,* town in Italy where it was orig made]

gorilla /gə'rilə/ *noun* **1** an anthropoid ape of western equatorial Africa that is related to the chimpanzee but less upright and much larger: *Gorilla gorilla.* **2** *informal* an ugly, heavily-built, or brutal man. [Greek *Gorillai,* a mythical African tribe of hairy women]

gormandize *or* **gormandise** /'gawməndiez/ *verb intrans* **1** to eat voraciously. **2** to enjoy good food. ⟫ *verb intrans* to eat (food) voraciously. ⟫⟫ **gormandizer** *noun.* [*gormand,* alteration of GOURMAND]

gormless /'gawmlis/ *adj Brit, informal* lacking understanding and intelligence; stupid. ⟫⟫ **gormlessly** *adv,* **gormlessness** *noun.* [alteration of English dialect *gaumless,* from *gaum* attention, understanding (from Old Norse *gaum, gaumr*) + -LESS]

go round *verb intrans* **1** to spread or circulate: *There's a rumour going round.* **2** to satisfy demand; to meet the need: *There are not enough jobs to go round.*

gorse /gaws/ *noun* any of several species of evergreen European shrubs of the pea family that have yellow flowers and green spines in place of leaves: *Ulex europaeus* and other species. ➤➤ **gorsy** *adj.* [Old English *gorst*]

Gorsedd /'gawsedh/ *noun* (*pl* **Gorseddau** /gaw'sedhie/ *or* **Gorsedds**) **1** the institution of bards and druids governing a Welsh EISTEDDFOD (festival of music, poetry, etc) and assembling twice a year to confer bardic degrees and titles. **2** the daily assembly of bards and druids during the course of an eisteddfod. [Welsh *gorsedd* mound, court, throne]

gory /'gawri/ *adj* (**gorier, goriest**) **1** full of violence and bloodshed: *a gory film*. **2** covered with gore; bloodstained: *Thou canst not say I did it; never shake thy gory locks at me* — Shakespeare. ✳ **(all) the gory details** *informal, often humorous* the explicit or most intimate details of something. ➤➤ **gorily** *adv*, **goriness** *noun*.

gosh /gosh/ *interj* used to express surprise. [euphemism for GOD[2]]

goshawk /'gos·hawk/ *noun* any of several species of long-tailed hawks with short rounded wings: genus *Accipiter*. [Old English *gōshafoc*, from *gōs* GOOSE[1] + *hafoc* HAWK[1]]

gosling /'gozling/ *noun* a young goose. [Middle English, from *gōs* GOOSE[1] + -LING]

go-slow *noun Brit* a deliberate slowing down of production by workers as a means of forcing management to comply with their demands.

gospel /'gospl/ *noun* **1a** (*often* **Gospel**) the teachings of Jesus Christ or the message of the life, death, and resurrection. **b** (*usu* **Gospel**) any of the first four books of the New Testament relating these teachings and this message. **c** (**Gospel**) a reading from any of these books as part of a church service. **2** the message or teachings of a religious teacher or movement. **3a** something accepted as a guiding principle: *the gospel of hard work*. **b** something so authoritative as not to be questioned: *I took it as gospel that she was leaving*. **4a** a type of religious music that has its roots in black American culture, *esp* in the folk and spiritual songs of the southern states, and is associated with fervent Christian evangelism. **b** (*used before a noun*) relating to or denoting this type of music: *gospel singing; a gospel choir*. [Old English *gōdspel*, from *gōd* GOOD[1] + *spell* tale]

gospel music *noun* = GOSPEL (4A).

gospel truth *noun* = GOSPEL (3B).

goss /gos/ *noun Brit, informal* gossip: *What's been going on since I've been away? Gimme all the goss!*

gossamer /'gosəmə/ *noun* **1** a film of cobwebs floating in the air in calm clear weather. **2** very fine gauze or silk. **3** (*used before a noun*) light, delicate, insubstantial, or tenuous. ➤➤ **gossamery** *adj*.

Word history

Middle English *gossomer*, from *gos* GOOSE[1] + *somor* SUMMER[1]. Gossamer is most often seen in autumn, around the time of year when geese are ready for eating.

gossip[1] /'gosip/ *noun* **1** somebody who habitually reveals facts concerning other people's actions or lives, *esp* sensational or unsubstantiated facts. **2a** the facts related by a gossip or an act or an instance of reporting of such facts. **b** a chatty talk. ➤➤ **gossipy** *adj*.

Word history

Old English *godsibb* godparent, baptismal sponsor, from *god* + *sibb* kinsman, from *sibb* related. Because of the close relationship between parent and godparent, or between the baptismal sponsor and the person baptised, the word gossip came to mean 'close friend' in the 14th cent. and in the late 16th cent. 'person with whom one shares news and idle talk'. The extension of the word to the idle talk itself is first recorded in the early 19th cent.

gossip[2] *verb intrans* (**gossiped, gossiping**) **1** to relate gossip. **2** to engage in casual conversation. ➤➤ **gossiper** *noun*.

gossip column *noun* a column in a newspaper relating gossip about well-known people. ➤➤ **gossip columnist** *noun*.

gossipmonger /'gosip,munggə/ *noun* = GOSSIP[1] (I).

gossypol /'gosipol/ *noun* a poisonous plant pigment present in cottonseed oil. [Latin *gossypion* cotton + -OL[1]]

got /got/ *verb* **1** past tense and past part. of GET[1]. **2** *non-standard* have; have got: *I got news for you; We got to go.*

gotcha /'gochə/ *interj informal* **1** used to indicate that one has understood something somebody has said. **2** used in triumph when seizing somebody or something or succeeding in an attempt. [alteration of *got you*]

Goth /goth/ *noun* **1** a member of a Germanic people that invaded parts of the Roman Empire between the third and fifth cent. AD. **2** (*often* **goth**). **a** a style of rock music that evolved from PUNK ROCK in the 1980s and is characterized by guitar-based rhythms, dark lyrics, and references to the occult. **b** a person who dresses mainly in black clothes, often with dyed jet black hair and starkly white and black make-up, and who enjoys this type of music. [Old English *Gotan* and late Latin *Gothi* (pl), of Germanic origin]

Gothic[1] *adj* **1** relating to the Goths, their culture, or language. **2** relating to or denoting a style of architecture prevalent from the middle of the 12th to the early 16th cent. characterized by vaulting and pointed arches.

Editorial note

Gothic was originally associated with the concept of the barbarian Goths as assailants of classical civilization. From the 18th cent. it was used to define western European architecture and art from the later 12th cent. to the Renaissance. Gothic style is characterized by the pointed arch, an often skeletal masonry structure for churches, combined with large glazed windows, and, generally, a formalized treatment of the human figure in sculpture and painting — Bridget Cherry.

3 (*often* **gothic**). **a** denoting or resembling a class of novels of the late 18th and early 19th cent. dealing with macabre or mysterious events in remote and desolate settings. **b** (*also* **Gothick**) relating to the macabre or supernatural. **4** relating to or denoting a form of type or lettering with a heavy thick face and angular outlines used *esp* by the earliest European printers. ➤➤ **Gothically** *adv*, **Gothicism** /-siz(ə)m/ *noun*.

Gothic[2] *noun* **1** the extinct E Germanic language spoken by the ancient Goths. **2** the Gothic architectural style. **3a** Gothic type or lettering. **b** = SANS SERIF.

Gothick *adj* **1** see GOTHIC[1] (3B). **2** relating to or denoting a genre of modern literature, a type of film, video game, etc featuring the macabre or eerily supernatural events.

Gothic Revival *noun* an artistic and architectural style of the 18th and 19th cent. largely imitative of Gothic style.

Gothic Rock *noun* = GOTH (2A).

go through *verb intrans* **1** said of a plan or proposal: to receive approval or sanction. **2** to come to a desired or satisfactory conclusion. ✳ **go through with** to continue resolutely with (something): *Are you able to go through with the plan?*

gotta /'gotə/ *contraction non-standard* **1** have got a: *I gotta horse*. **2** have got to: *We gotta go.*

gotten /'gotn/ *verb NAmer* past part. of GET[1].

Götterdämmerung /guhtə'deməroong/ *noun* in Germanic mythology, the final destruction of the gods and the world. [German *Götterdämmerung* twilight of the gods]

gouache /goo'ahsh (*French* gwaʃ)/ *noun* **1** a method of painting with opaque watercolours that have been ground in water and mixed with a gum preparation. **2** paint mixed with gouache. [French *gouache* from Italian *guazza*, prob ultimately from Latin *aqua* water]

Gouda /'gowdə/ *noun* a mild cheese of Dutch origin that is similar to Edam but contains more fat, usu in the form of a disc coated in yellow wax. [named after *Gouda*, town in the Netherlands where it is made]

gouge[1] /gowj/ *verb trans* **1** to make (an uneven hole, dent, etc) in a surface: *I dropped the iron and gouged a hole in the wooden floor*. **2** (+ out) to force (something) out roughly or violently; *specif* to force (a person's eye) out using one's thumb. **3** *chiefly NAmer, informal* to subject (somebody) to extortion; to overcharge (them) deliberately. ➤➤ **gouger** *noun*. [Middle English *gowge* via early French *gouge* from Latin *gulbia* a chisel, of Celtic origin]

gouge[2] *noun* **1** a chisel with a curved cross section and a sharpened edge on the concave side of the blade. **2** a groove, cavity, or mark made by gouging something. **3** *chiefly NAmer, informal* the act or an instance of overcharging; extortion.

goujon /'goohzhonh/ *noun* a small strip of fish, chicken, etc, often coated in batter or breadcrumbs and deep-fried. [French *goujon*: see GUDGEON[2]]

goulash /'goohlash/ *noun* **1** a meat stew of Hungarian origin made usu with beef or veal and highly seasoned with paprika. **2** a round in bridge played with cards dealt several at a time from a pack formed by the unshuffled hands from a previous deal. [Hungarian *gulyás* herdsman's stew]

go under *verb intrans* to be destroyed or defeated; to fail.

go up *verb intrans* **1** to increase. **2** to burst into flames. **3** *Brit* to enter or return to a university.

gourami /'gooərəmi/ *noun* (*pl* **gouramis** *or collectively* **gourami**) **1** a large freshwater food fish of SE Asia: *Osphronemus goramy*. **2** any of several families of small brightly coloured fishes often kept in aquariums: family Anabantidae and other families. [Malay *gurami*]

gourd /gooəd/ *noun* **1a** any of various tendril-bearing climbing plants of the marrow family, including the melon, squash, and pumpkin: genus *Cucurbita* and other genera. **b** the fleshy fruit of such a plant, *esp* an inedible fruit with a hard rind used for ornament or to make vessels and utensils. **2** a cup, bottle, or other article made from a gourd. [Middle English *gourde* via Old French from Latin *cucurbita*]

gourde /gooəd/ *noun* the basic monetary unit of Haiti, divided into 100 centimes. [American French *gourde* from French *gourd* numb, dull, heavy, from Latin *gurdus* dull, stupid]

gourmand /'gawmənd, 'gooəmənd (*French* gurmã)/ *noun* somebody who is excessively fond of or heartily interested in food and drink. ⟫ **gourmandism** *noun*. [early French *gourmant* glutton]

Usage note

gourmand *or* **gourmet**? These two words are often confused. A *gourmand* is somebody who eats large or excessive amounts of food. It is not a complimentary word. A *gourmet*, on the other hand, is a complimentary word that refers to somebody with a refined taste in food, whose interest is in quality not quantity.

gourmet /'gawmay, 'gooəmay (*French* gurme)/ *noun* **1** a connoisseur of food and drink. **2** (*used before a noun*) suitable for a gourmet: *a gourmet dinner*. [French *gourmet*, alteration (influenced by *gourmant* GOURMAND) of early French *gromet* boy servant, vintner's assistant, from Middle English *grom* GROOM[1]]

Usage note

gourmet *or* **gourmand**? See note at GOURMAND.

gout /gowt/ *noun* **1** a metabolic disorder that results in crystals of uric acid compounds being deposited in the joints, *esp* that of the big toe, causing painful inflammation. **2** *archaic, literary* a blob or splash, e.g. of blood. ⟫ **goutiness** *noun*, **gouty** *adj*. [Middle English from Old French *goute*, gout, drop, from Latin *gutta* drop. Gout was formerly thought to be caused by drops of diseased matter in the blood]

gov. *abbr* **1** government. **2** governor.

govern /'guv(ə)n/ *verb trans* **1** to control and direct the making and administration of policy in (a state, organization, etc). **2a** to control, determine, or strongly influence (something): *Availability often governs choice*. **b** to hold (something) in check; to restrain (it). **c** to serve as a precedent or deciding principle for (something): *habits and customs that govern human decisions*. **3** said of a word: to require (another word or group of words) to be in a specified grammatical case. ⟩ *verb intrans* to prevail or rule; to exercise authority. ⟫ **governability** *noun*, **governable** *adj*. [Middle English *governen* via Old French from Latin *gubernare* to steer, govern, from Greek *kyberan*]

governance *noun formal* the action or manner of governing or being governed.

governess /'guv(ə)nis/ *noun* a woman entrusted with the teaching and often supervision of a child in a private household: *The few employments open to women ... are menial; and when a superior education enables them to take charge of children as governesses they are not treated like the tutors of sons* — Mary Wollstonecraft.

government /'guv(ə)nmənt, 'guvəmənt/ *noun* **1** (*treated as sing. or pl*) the body of people that governs a state, nation, or other political unit. **2a** the act or process of governing. **b** the direction and supervision of public affairs: *local government*. **c** the political function of policy-making. **3** the office, authority, or function of a governing body. **4** the form or system of rule by which a political unit is governed. **5** the governing of a word in grammar. ⟫ **governmental** /guv(ə)n'mentl/ *adj*, **governmentally** /guv(ə)n'mentəli/ *adv*.

governor /'guv(ə)nə/ *noun* **1a** a ruler, chief executive, or nominal head of a political unit. **b** a commanding officer. **c** the most senior officer or administrator of an institution or organization, e.g. a prison. **d** a member of a group, e.g. the governing body of a school, that controls an institution. **e** the representative of the British Crown in a colony. **2** *informal*. **a** somebody, e.g. a father or employer, in a position of authority. **b** used as an informal term of address to a man. **3** a device giving automatic control of pressure, fuel, steam, etc, *esp*

to regulate speed. ⟫ **governorate** /-rət, -rayt/ *noun*, **governorship** *noun*.

governor general *noun* (*pl* **governors general** *or* **governor generals**) a governor of high rank, *esp* one representing the British Crown in a Commonwealth country. ⟫ **governor generalship** *noun*.

govt *abbr* government.

gowan /'gowən/ *noun chiefly Scot* any wild white or yellow flower, *esp* the oxeye daisy. [prob alteration of Middle English *gollan* buttercup, of Scandinavian origin]

gowk /gowk/ *noun chiefly Scot and N Eng, informal* **1** a foolish or ridiculous person. **2** a cuckoo. [Middle English *goke, gowke*, from Old Norse *gaukr* cuckoo]

gown[1] /gown/ *noun* **1a** a loose flowing robe worn *esp* by a professional or academic person when acting in an official capacity. **b** a woman's dress, *esp* one that is elegant or worn on formal occasions. **c** a protective outer garment worn in an operating theatre. **2** the body of students and staff of a college or university: *We try to foster good relations between town and gown*. [Middle English via French from late Latin *gunna*, a fur or leather garment]

gown[2] *verb trans* (*usu in passive*) to dress (somebody or oneself) in a gown.

goy /goy/ *noun* (*pl* **goyim** /'goyim/ *or* **goys**) *offensive* used by Jews to refer to somebody who is not a Jew; a Gentile. ⟫ **goyish** *adj*. [via Yiddish from Hebrew *gōy* people, nation]

GP *abbr* **1** general practitioner. **2** Grand Prix.

Gp Capt *abbr* Group Captain.

GPO *abbr Brit, dated* general post office.

GPRS *abbr* General Packet Radio Service, an always-on packet-switching service that enables data to be transmitted and received at high speeds by mobile phone.

GPS *abbr* Global Positioning System.

GR *abbr* **1** Greece (international vehicle registration). **2** King George. [(sense 2) Latin *Georgius Rex*]

Gr. *abbr* Greek.

gr. *abbr* **1** grade. **2** grain. **3** gram. **4** gravity. **5** gross.

Graafian follicle /'grahfi-ən/ *noun* a small liquid-filled capsule in the ovary of a mammal enclosing a developing egg. [named after Regnier de *Graaf* d.1673, Dutch anatomist, who discovered the capsules]

grab[1] /grab/ *verb* (**grabbed, grabbing**) ⟩ *verb trans* **1** to take or seize (something) hastily or by a sudden snatching motion. **2** to obtain (something) unscrupulously, illegally, or opportunistically. **3** *informal* to forcefully engage the attention of (somebody); to impress (them): *It doesn't really grab me*. ⟩ *verb intrans* to make a sudden snatch. ⟫ **grabber** *noun*. [early Dutch or Low German *grabben*]

grab[2] *noun* **1a** a sudden snatch. **b** an unlawful or unscrupulous seizure. **2** (*used before a noun*) intended to be grabbed: *a grab rail*. **3** a mechanical device for clutching an object. ✳ **up for grabs** *informal* available for anyone to take or win.

grab bag *noun chiefly NAmer* = LUCKY DIP.

grabby *adj* **1** *informal* grasping; greedy. **2** forcefully attracting attention.

graben /'grahb(ə)n/ *noun* (*pl* **graben** *or* **grabens**) = RIFT VALLEY. [German *Graben* ditch]

grace[1] /grays/ *noun* **1a** ease and suppleness of movement or bearing. **b** an elegant appearance or effect. **c** a charming trait or accomplishment. **2a** an act of or disposition to kindness or clemency. **b** a special favour; a privilege: *Each in his place, by right, not grace, shall rule his heritage* — Kipling. **c** a temporary exemption; a reprieve: *three days' grace*. **d** (*also in pl*) approval; favour: *in his good graces*. **3a** unmerited divine assistance given to human beings for their regeneration or sanctification. **b** a state of being pleasing to God. **4** a short prayer at a meal asking a blessing or giving thanks. **5** (**Her/His/Your Grace**) used as a title for a duke, duchess, or archbishop. **6** consideration; decency: *She had the grace to blush*. ✳ **with bad/good grace** unwillingly or unhappily, or willingly or happily: *He took his defeat with good grace*. [Middle English via Old French from Latin *gratia* favour, charm, thanks, from *gratus* pleasing, grateful]

grace² *verb trans* **1** (+ with) to favour (somebody or an event) with one's presence. **2** to confer dignity or honour on (somebody or something). **3** to adorn or embellish (something).

grace-and-favour *adj Brit* denoting a house, flat, etc in which somebody is allowed to live rent-free as a special privilege granted by the sovereign or government.

graceful /'graysf(ə)l/ *adj* having or displaying grace in form, action, or movement. ➤➤ **gracefully** *adv*, **gracefulness** *noun*.

graceless *adj* **1** lacking a sense of propriety. **2** devoid of elegance; awkward. ➤➤ **gracelessly** *adv*, **gracelessness** *noun*.

grace note *noun* a musical note added as an ornament.

Graces *pl noun* (**the Graces, the Three Graces**) in Greek mythology, the three sister goddesses believed to personify and endow charm, grace, and beauty.

gracile /'grasiel/ *adj* **1** *technical* said of a hominid species: slender or slight in build. **2** *formal* graceful. ➤➤ **gracility** /grə'siliti/ *noun*. [Latin *gracilis*]

gracious¹ /'grayshəs/ *adj* **1a** marked by kindness and courtesy. **b** marked by tact and delicacy. **c** having those qualities, e.g. comfort and elegance, made possible by wealth: *gracious living*. **2** used conventionally of royalty and high nobility: merciful; compassionate. ➤➤ **graciously** *adv*, **graciousness** *noun*. [Middle English *gracious* via early French *gracieus* from Latin *gratiosus* enjoying favour, agreeable, from *gratia*: see GRACE¹]

gracious² *interj* used to express surprise.

grackle /'grakl/ *noun* **1** any of several genera of Asian starlings or mynahs: genus *Gracula* and other genera. **2** any of several species of American songbirds with shiny black plumage: *Quiscalus quiscula* and other species. [Latin *graculus* jackdaw]

grad. *abbr* **1** gradient. **2** graduate. **3** graduated.

gradable /'graydəbl/ *adj* said of an adjective: capable of being used in the comparative and superlative and with a word that intensifies or modifies the sense. ➤➤ **gradability** /-'biliti/ *noun*.

gradate /grə'dayt/ *verb intrans* to pass by small changes into the next colour, note, or stage. ➤ *verb trans* to arrange (items) in a progression, scale, or series. [back-formation from GRADATION]

gradation /grə'daysh(ə)n/ *noun* **1a** a series forming successive stages. **b** a step or place in such a series. **2** a gradual passing from one shade or tone to another, e.g. in a painting. **3** in linguistics, = ABLAUT. ➤➤ **gradational** *adj*, **gradationally** *adv*. [via French from late Latin *gradation-*, *gradatio* making steps from *gradus* step, GRADE¹]

grade¹ /grayd/ *noun* **1** a position in a scale of ranks or qualities. **2** a mark indicating a degree of accomplishment at school. **3** a class of things of the same stage or degree. **4** *NAmer* a group of pupils at the same level; a school form, class, or year. **5** a stage in a process. **6** a gradient. **7** a domestic animal with one parent purebred and the other of inferior breeding. ✳ **make the grade** to reach the expected standard or an acceptable level; to succeed. [via French from Latin *gradus* step, degree]

grade² *verb trans* **1a** to sort (things) according to quality etc. **b** to arrange (things) in a scale or series. **2** to assign a grade to (something or somebody). **3** (*often* + up) to improve (e.g. cattle) by breeding with purebred animals. **4** to level off (a road etc) to a smooth horizontal or sloping surface. ➤ *verb intrans* to pass from one stage or level to another, often by scarcely perceptible degrees.

-grade *comb. form* forming adjectives, with the meanings: **1** walking: *plantigrade*. **2** moving: *retrograde*. [via French, from Latin *-gradus*, from *gradi*: see GRADIENT]

grade crossing *noun chiefly NAmer* = LEVEL CROSSING.

gradely *adj* (**gradelier, gradeliest**) *NW Eng* proper or fitting; *broadly* excellent. [Middle English *greithly*, *graithly* ready, prompt, excellent, from Old Norse *greithligr*, from *greithr* ready, free]

grader /'graydə/ *noun* **1** a person or thing that grades. **2** a machine for levelling something, *esp* one used in constructing roads. **3** (*used in combination*) a student in a specified school grade: *a fifth grader*.

grade school *noun NAmer* a primary or elementary school.

gradient /'graydi-ənt/ *noun* **1a** the degree of inclination, *esp* of a road or slope. **b** a sloping road or railway. **2** change in the value of a quantity with respect to the change in another quantity: *a steep temperature gradient at sunrise*. **3** In mathematics, the slope of the tangent at any point on a curve with respect to the horizontal. [Latin *gradient-, gradiens*, present part. of *gradi* to step, go, from *gradus* step, GRADE¹]

gradin /'graydin/ *or* **gradine** /grə'deen/ *noun* **1** any of a series of steps or seats arranged in rows on a slope, e.g. in an amphitheatre. **2** a ledge at the back of an altar. [French *gradin*, derivative of Latin *gradus* step, GRADE¹]

gradual¹ /'gradyooəl, 'grajooəl/ *adj* **1** proceeding or happening by small steps or degrees, usu over a long period. **2** said of a slope: not steep. ➤➤ **gradually** *adv*, **gradualness** *noun*. [medieval Latin *gradualis* from Latin *gradus* step, GRADE¹]

gradual² *noun* **1** a pair of verses, usu from the Psalms, sung or said after the Epistle in the Mass. **2** a book containing the choral parts of the Mass. [medieval Latin *graduale*, alteration of late Latin *gradale*, from Latin *gradus* step, GRADE¹; from its being sung on the steps of the altar]

gradualism *noun* the policy of approaching a desired end by gradual stages. ➤➤ **gradualist** *noun and adj*, **gradualistic** /-'listik/ *adj*.

graduand /'gradyooand, 'grajooand/ *noun Brit* somebody who is about to receive an academic degree. [medieval Latin *graduandus*, verbal noun from *graduare* to graduate]

graduate¹ /'gradyoo-ət, 'grajoo-ət/ *noun* **1** the holder of a first academic degree. **2** *chiefly NAmer* somebody who has been awarded a high school diploma. [Middle English *graduat* from medieval Latin *graduatus*, past part. of *graduare* to graduate, from *gradus* step, GRADE¹]

graduate² /'gradyooayt, 'grajooayt/ *verb trans* **1** to mark (e.g. an instrument or vessel) with degrees of measurement. **2** to divide (something) into grades or intervals. ➤ *verb intrans* **1a** to receive an academic degree. **b** *NAmer* to receive a high school diploma. **2** to move up to a higher stage of experience, proficiency, or prestige. **3** to change gradually. ➤➤ **graduator** *noun*.

graduate school /'gradyoo-ət, 'grajoo-ət/ *noun NAmer* a place or period of postgraduate study.

graduation /gradyoo'aysh(ə)n, grajoo-/ *noun* **1** a mark, e.g. on an instrument or vessel, indicating degrees of measurement. **2a** the award or acceptance of an academic degree, or a ceremony at which this takes place. **b** *NAmer* the award or acceptance of a high school diploma, or a ceremony at which this takes place.

Graecism (*NAmer* **Grecism**) /'greesiz(ə)m/ *noun* **1** a Greek idiom, *esp* one occurring in another language. **2a** the spirit or style of Greek culture or art. **b** a quality or feature imitative or suggestive of Greek culture or art. [medieval Latin *Graecismus* from *Graecus*: see GREEK¹]

Graeco- (*NAmer* **Greco-**) *comb. form* forming words, with the meanings: **1** the Greek nation, people, or culture. **2** Greek and: *Graeco-Roman*. [Latin *Graeco-* from *Graecus*: see GREEK¹]

Graeco-Roman /,greekoh/ *adj* **1** relating to the ancient Greeks and Romans. **2** denoting a style of wrestling in which holds below the waist are disallowed.

graffiti /grə'feeti/ *pl noun* (*treated as sing. or pl*) drawings or writing painted in a public place, *esp* on a wall. [pl of Italian *graffito*: see GRAFFITO]

Usage note
Graffiti is a plural noun and should, theoretically, always be followed by a plural verb. It comes from Italian and has a regular Italian singular form, *graffito*. In English, however, the singular form is rare and its use tends to sound pedantic. The form *graffiti* is therefore commonly used with a singular verb to refer to a single drawing (*a graffiti*) or to drawings collectively (*Graffiti is a good way of telling people your message*).

graffito /grə'feetoh/ *noun* (*pl* **graffiti** /-ti/) **1** in archaeology, a drawing or writing scratched on a surface, e.g. a rock. **2** an item of graffiti. [Italian *graffito*, dimin. of *graffio* scratch, from *graffiare* to scratch]

graft¹ /grahft/ *verb trans* **1a** to cause (a plant cutting) to unite with a growing plant. **b** to propagate (a plant) by this method. **2** to attach or add (something). **3** to implant (living tissue) surgically. ➤ *verb intrans* **1** to become grafted. **2** to use one's position improperly to one's own advantage. ➤➤ **grafter** *noun*. [Middle English via Old French and Latin from Greek *grapheion* stylus (because of the tapered tip of the cutting) from *graphein* to write]

graft² *noun* **1a** a grafted plant or cutting. **b** the point of insertion of a cutting on a growing plant. **2a** a surgical operation in which living tissue is grafted. **b** the living tissue so grafted. **3a** the improper use of one's position, e.g. public office, to one's private, *esp* financial, advantage. **b** something, *esp* money, acquired in this way.

graft[3] *verb intrans Brit, informal* to work hard. ➤➤ **grafter** *noun*. [English dialect *graft* to dig, alteration of GRAVE[3]]

graft[4] *noun Brit, informal* hard work.

graham /'grayəm/ *adj NAmer* denoting wholemeal flour or something made from it. [named after Sylvester *Graham* d.1851, US dietary reformer]

Graham's law *noun* in chemistry, a law that states that the rate of diffusion or effusion of a gas is inversely proportional to the square root of the density of the gas. [named after Thomas *Graham* d.1869, British physicist]

Grail /grayl/ *noun* = HOLY GRAIL. [Middle English *graal* from early French *grael* bowl, grail, from medieval Latin *gradalis* dish]

grain[1] /grayn/ *noun* **1a** a seed or fruit of a cereal grass. **b** the seeds or fruits of cereal grasses considered collectively. **c** cereal grasses or similar food plants considered collectively. **2a** a discrete small hard particle or crystal, e.g. of sand, salt, or a metal. **b** the least amount possible: *There's not a grain of truth in what he said.* **3a** a granular surface, nature, or appearance. **b** the outer side of a skin or hide from which the hair has been removed. **4a** the arrangement of the fibres in wood. **b** the direction, alignment, or texture of the constituent particles, fibres, or threads of rock, fabric, etc. **5** natural disposition or character; temper. **6** a particle of photographic emulsion. **7** a unit of weight based on the weight of a grain of wheat, equal to approximately 0.065 gram. **8** in former times, a brilliant scarlet dye made from either kermes or cochineal. ✳ **be/go against the grain** to be contrary to one's inclination, disposition, or feeling. [Middle English; partly from early French *grein* cereal grain partly from early French *graine* seed, kermes, both from Latin *granum* seed, grain of corn]

grain[2] *verb trans* **1** to form (something) into grains; to granulate (it). **2** to paint (something) in imitation of the grain of wood and stone. **3** to give (something) a roughened texture or surface. **4** to remove the hair from (a hide or skin). ➤ *verb intrans* to become granular; to granulate. ➤➤ **grainer** *noun*.

grain alcohol *noun* alcohol that has been made by fermenting a cereal such as wheat or maize.

grainy *adj* (**grainier, grainiest**) **1** consisting of or resembling grains; granular. **2** having or resembling the grain of wood. **3** said of a photograph: having poor definition because the particles of emulsion are large and visible. ➤➤ **graininess** *noun*.

gram[1] *or* **gramme** /gram/ *noun* a metric unit of mass equal to 1000th of a kilogram (about 0.04oz). [French *gramme* via late Latin from Greek *grammat-, gramma*: see GRAMMAR]

gram[2] *noun* **1** any of various plants of the pea family, e.g. the chickpea, grown for their edible seeds. **2a** the seed or seeds of such a plant used as food. **b** (*used before a noun*) denoting a food made from these seeds: *gram flour.* [early Portuguese *gram* (now *grão*) grain, from Latin *granum*]

gram. *abbr* **1** grammar. **2** grammatical.

-gram *comb. form* forming nouns, denoting: **1** drawing; writing; record: *ideogram; telegram.* **2** a jocular greeting delivered on a special occasion by a messenger who wears the costume specified or performs the action specified: *kissogram; gorillagram.* [Latin *-gramma* from Greek *gramma*: see GRAMMAR]

gram atom *or* **gram-atomic weight** *noun no longer in technical use* a quantity of an element in grams with a weight numerically equal to its atomic weight. Now called MOLE[5].

graminaceous /grami'nayshəs/ *adj* = GRAMINEOUS.

gramineous /grə'mini·əs/ *adj* **1** relating to or resembling a grass. **2** belonging to the grass family. ➤➤ **gramineousness** *noun*. [Latin *gramineus*, from *gramin-, gramen* grass]

graminivorous /grami'nivərəs/ *adj* said of an animal: feeding on grass. [Latin *gramin-, gramen* grass + -VOROUS]

grammalogue /'graməlog/ *noun* = LOGOGRAM. [Greek *gramma* (see GRAM[1]) + -LOGUE]

grammar /'gramə/ *noun* **1** the study of the classes of words, their inflections, and their functions and relations in the sentence; *broadly* this study when taken to include that of phonology and sometimes of usage. **2** the characteristic system of inflections and syntax of a language. **3** a grammar textbook. **4** speech or writing evaluated according to its conformity to grammatical rules: *No one in the world speaks blemishless grammar* — Mark Twain. **5** the principles or rules of an art, science, or technique. [Middle English *gramere* from early French *gramaire*, modification of Latin *grammatica*, ultimately from Greek *grammatikos, grammat-, gramma* letter of the alphabet, writing, a small weight, from *graphein* to write]

grammarian /grə'meari·ən/ *noun* a person who studies, writes about, or has expert knowledge of grammar.

grammar school *noun* **1** *Brit* a secondary school providing an academic type of education from the age of 11 to 18. **2** in former times, a secondary school that emphasized the study of the classics. **3** *NAmer* a primary or elementary school.

grammatical /grə'matikl/ *adj* **1** relating to grammar. **2** conforming to the rules of grammar. ➤➤ **grammaticality** /-'kaliti/ *noun*, **grammatically** *adv*, **grammaticalness** *noun*.

gramme *noun* see GRAM[1].

gram-molecular weight *noun* = MOLE[5].

gram molecule *noun* = MOLE[5].

Grammy /'grami/ *noun* (*pl* **Grammys**) a statuette presented annually by the American National Academy of Recording Arts and Sciences for notable achievement in the recording industry. [GRAMOPHONE + -*my* (as in EMMY)]

gram-negative *adj* said of bacteria: not holding the purple dye when stained by Gram's method.

gramophone /'graməfohn/ *noun* **1** any device for reproducing sounds from the vibrations of a stylus resting in a spiral groove on a rotating disc, *esp* an old-fashioned device with an acoustic horn instead of modern speakers. **2** *Brit, dated* a record player. [alteration of PHONOGRAM]

gram-positive *adj* said of bacteria: holding the purple dye when stained by Gram's method.

gramps /gramps/ *noun informal* **1** an affectionate name for one's grandfather. **2** used as a form of address to any elderly man. [by shortening and alteration from *grandpa*]

grampus /'grampəs/ *noun* **1** a marine animal that looks like a dolphin but has the bulbous head of the pilot whale: *Grampus griseus.* **2** the killer whale or any small whale. **3** *Brit, dated* someone who breathes or snores loudly. [alteration of Middle English *graspey, grapay*, from early French *graspeis*, from *gras* fat (from Latin *crassus*) + *peis* fish (from Latin *piscis*)]

Gram's method /gramz/ *noun* a method of establishing to which broad class of bacteria a particular bacterium belongs, in which it is stained with a solution of iodine and potassium iodide after staining with gentian violet. [named after Hans *Gram* d.1938, Danish physician, who developed it]

gran /gran/ *noun chiefly Brit, informal* = GRANDMOTHER.

grana /'graynə/ *noun* pl of GRANUM.

granadilla /granə'dilə/ *noun* the egg-shaped, purple-skinned, many-seeded edible fruit of a passionflower; a passion fruit. [Spanish *granadilla*, dimin. of *granada* pomegranate]

granary /'granəri/ *noun* (*pl* **granaries**) **1** a storehouse for threshed grain. **2** a region producing grain in abundance. **3** *trademark* (*used before a noun*) denoting bread and other bakery products that contain malted wheat grains. [Latin *granarium* from *granum* GRAIN[1]]

grand[1] /grand/ *adj* **1a** large and striking in size, extent, or conception: *a grand design.* **b** characterized by magnificence or opulence; sumptuous: *a grand celebration.* **2** extremely dignified and proud; imposing. **3a** intended to impress: *a man of grand gestures and pretentious statements.* **b** elevated in character or style, sometimes self-consciously so; lofty: *writing in the grand style.* **4** having more importance than others; principal. **5** including or made up of a number of lesser items; complete: *the grand total of all money paid out.* **6** *Brit, informal* very good; wonderful: *a grand time.* ➤➤ **grandly** *adv*, **grandness** *noun*. [early French *grand* large, great, grand, from Latin *grandis* fully-grown, large, great]

grand[2] *noun* **1** = GRAND PIANO. **2** *informal.* **a** *Brit* a thousand pounds. **b** *NAmer* a thousand dollars.

grandad *or* **granddad** /'grandad/ *noun* **1** *informal* an affectionate term for one's grandfather. **2** used as a form of address to any elderly man.

grandam /'grandam, 'grandəm/ *or* **grandame** /'grandaym, 'grandəm/ *noun archaic* **1** = GRANDMOTHER. **2** an old woman. [Middle English *graundam* from Anglo-French *graund dame* great lady]

grandaunt *noun* = GREAT-AUNT.

grandchild /'granchield/ *noun* a child of one's son or daughter.

granddad /'grandad/ *noun* see GRANDAD.

granddaughter /'grandawtə/ *noun* a daughter of one's son or daughter.

grand duchess *noun* **1** the wife or widow of a grand duke. **2** a woman who has the rank of a grand duke in her own right.

grand duchy *noun* the territory of a grand duke or grand duchess.

grand duke *noun* **1** the sovereign ruler of any of various European states. **2** a son or male descendant of a Russian tsar in the male line.

grande dame /,grond 'dahm (*French* grãd dam)/ *noun* **1** the most eminent and experienced woman in a particular field: *She is the grande dame of American ballet.* **2** a usu elderly and dignified woman of high rank or standing. [French *grande dame*, literally 'great lady']

grandee /gran'dee/ *noun* **1** a Spanish or Portuguese nobleman of the highest rank. **2** any senior or high-ranking man. [Spanish and Portuguese *grande*, ultimately from Latin *grandis* GRAND¹]

grandeur /'granjə, 'grandyə/ *noun* **1** the quality of being large or impressive; magnificence: *The immense plains ... possess, in some degree, the grandeur of the ocean* — Washington Irving. **2** personal greatness marked by nobility, dignity, or power. [Middle English from early French, from *grand*: see GRAND¹]

grandfather /'gran(d)fahdhə/ *noun* **1** the father of one's father or mother. **2** a male ancestor. ⟫⟫ **grandfatherly** *adj*.

grandfather clock *noun* a tall pendulum clock standing directly on the floor. [from the song *My Grandfather's Clock* by Henry C Work d.1884, US songwriter]

Grand Guignol /,gronh gee'nyol (*French* grã ginɔl)/ *noun* a type of sensational or melodramatic entertainment featuring the gruesome or horrible. ⟫⟫ **Grand Guignol** *adj*. [named after *Le Grand Guignol*, literally 'The Great Punch', small theatre in Paris specializing in such plays]

grandiloquence /gran'diləkwəns/ *noun* high-sounding or pompously eloquent speech or writing; bombast. ⟫⟫ **grandiloquent** *adj*, **grandiloquently** *adv*. [prob via French from Latin *grandiloquus* using lofty language, from *grandis* GRAND¹ + *loqui* to speak]

grandiose /'grandiohs, -ohz/ *adj* **1** characterized by the affectation of grandeur or by absurd exaggeration. **2** impressive because of uncommon largeness, scope, or ambitiousness. ⟫⟫ **grandiosely** *adv*, **grandioseness** *noun*, **grandiosity** /-'ositi/ *noun*. [French *grandiose* from Italian *grandioso*, from Latin *grandis* GRAND¹]

grand jury *noun* a jury in the USA that examines accusations and decides whether a case will go to trial.

grand larceny *noun NAmer* theft of property of a value greater than a sum specified by US law: compare PETTY LARCENY.

grandma /'granmah, 'grammah/ *noun* **1** *informal* an affectionate name for one's grandmother. **2** used as a form of address to any elderly woman.

grand mal /,gronh 'mal (*French* grã mal)/ *noun* the severe form of epilepsy involving muscle spasms and prolonged unconsciousness, or an attack of it: compare PETIT MAL. [French *grand mal* great illness]

grand master *noun* **1** a chess player who has consistently scored higher than a standardized score in international competition. **2** (**Grand Master**) a title given to the head of various societies and orders, e.g. the Freemasons, and to senior exponents of some martial arts.

grandmother /'gran(d)mudhə/ *noun* **1** the mother of one's father or mother. **2** a female ancestor. ⟫⟫ **grandmotherly** *adj*.

grandmother clock *noun* a smaller version of a grandfather clock.

Grand National *noun* the major British steeplechase for horses that is run annually at Aintree near Liverpool.

grandnephew *noun* = GREAT-NEPHEW.

grandniece *noun* = GREAT-NIECE.

grand opera *noun* opera with a serious dramatic plot and with all the dialogue sung, not spoken.

grandpa /'granpah, 'grampah/ *noun informal* = GRANDFATHER.

grandparent /'gran(d)peərənt/ *noun* a parent of one's father or mother. ⟫⟫ **grandparental** /-pə'rentl/ *adj*, **grandparenthood** *noun*.

grand piano *noun* a large piano with a horizontal frame and strings.

grand prix /,gronh 'pree (*French* grã pri)/ *noun* (*pl* **grands prix** /'pree(z)/) **1** (*often* **Grand Prix**) any of a series of long-distance races for FORMULA (4A) cars (cars conforming to specifications laid down by rules), held consecutively in different countries. **2** (*often* **Grand Prix**) a major competitive event in various other sports. [French *Grand Prix de Paris*, literally 'grand prize of Paris', an international horse race established in 1863]

grandsire /'gran(d)sie·ə/ *noun* **1** *archaic* = GRANDFATHER. **2** *literary* = FOREFATHER.

grand slam *noun* **1** the winning of all the major tournaments in a particular sport in a given year, or of all the games in a tournament. **2** in bridge, the winning of all 13 tricks by one player or side. **3** in baseball, a home run scored when there is a batter waiting at each of the three other bases, so that four runs are scored in all.

grandson /'gran(d)sun/ *noun* a son of one's son or daughter.

grandstand¹ *noun* **1** a usu roofed stand for spectators at a racecourse, stadium, etc in the best position for viewing the contest. **2** (*used before a noun*) giving an ideal viewing position: *a grandstand seat.*

grandstand² *verb intrans NAmer, informal* to behave or perform in such a way as to attract the attention of and impress onlookers. ⟫⟫ **grandstander** *noun*.

grandstand finish *noun* a particularly exciting end to a race or competition because the winner is in doubt until the last possible moment.

grand tour *noun* **1** (**the grand tour**) an extended tour of the cultural sites of Europe, formerly a usual part of the education of young British gentlemen. **2** an extensive and usu educational tour.

grand tourer *adj* a full form of GT, denoting a saloon car with a sporty appearance and performance but with enough comfort to make it suitable for long journeys.

granduncle *noun* = GREAT-UNCLE.

grand unified theory *noun* in physics, any of various theories that seek to represent the numerous interactions between subatomic particles in terms of a single mathematical structure.

grange /graynj/ *noun* **1** a large country house, often with many outbuildings. **2** *archaic* a barn or granary. [Middle English, granary, farmhouse, via French from medieval Latin *granica*, from Latin *granum* GRAIN¹]

grani- *comb. form* forming words, denoting: grain or seeds: *granivorous*. [Latin *grani-* from *granum* GRAIN¹]

granite /'granit/ *noun* **1** a very hard granular igneous rock formed of quartz, feldspar, and mica and used *esp* for building. **2** unyielding firmness or endurance. ⟫⟫ **granitelike** *adj*, **granitic** /gra'nitik/ *adj*, **granitoid** /-toyd/ *adj*. [Italian *granito*, past part. of *granire* to granulate, ultimately from Latin *granum* GRAIN¹]

graniteware *noun* **1** ironware covered with mottled enamel usu in two tones of grey. **2** pottery with a speckled granitelike appearance.

granivorous /gra'nivərəs/ *adj* said of animals: feeding on seeds or grain.

granny *or* **grannie** /'grani/ *noun* (*pl* **grannies**) **1a** *informal* an affectionate name for one's grandmother. **b** an elderly woman. **2** *informal* a fussy person. **3** = GRANNY KNOT. [by shortening and alteration]

granny bond *noun Brit* a savings bond, formerly available only to those over a certain age, which is guaranteed to maintain its value in line with the rate of inflation.

granny flat *noun Brit* a part of a large house converted into a more-or-less independent dwelling, usu to accommodate an elderly relative.

granny knot *noun* a reef knot with the ends crossed the wrong way and therefore liable to slip.

Granny Smith *noun* a large green variety of dessert apple. [named after Maria Ann ('Granny') *Smith* d.1870, Australian gardener who first grew them]

granny specs *pl noun informal* glasses with small circular lenses and metal frames.

granola /grə'nohlə/ *noun NAmer* a breakfast dish that consists of rolled oats mixed with dried fruit and nuts and covered with brown sugar; muesli. [orig a trademark: based on GRAIN¹ or GRANULAR]

granolith /'granəlith/ *noun* an artificial stone consisting of crushed granite and cement. >>> **granolithic** /-'lithik/ *adj.* [*grano*-granite (via German from Italian *granito*: see GRANITE) + -LITH]

grant[1] /grahnt/ *verb trans* **1a** to consent to carry out or fulfil (e.g. a wish or request). **b** to give (something) as a right, privilege, or favour. **2** to bestow or transfer (something, e.g. a title or property) formally. **3a** to be willing to concede (something): *I grant you it was a rather rash decision.* **b** to assume (something) to be true. * **take somebody or something for granted 1** to assume (something) as true, real, or certain to occur. **2** to value (somebody or something) too lightly. >>> **grantable** *adj*, **grantee** *noun*, **granter** *noun*, **grantor** /grahn'taw/ *noun*. [Middle English *granten* via early French *creanter*, *graanter* to guarantee, assure from Latin *credent-*, *credens*, present part. of *credere* to believe]

grant[2] *noun* **1** an amount of money given by a government or other body for a particular purpose, e.g. paying for a course of study. **2a** the act or an instance of granting. **b** a transfer of property or the property so transferred.

grant-in-aid *noun* (*pl* **grants-in-aid**) **1** a grant or subsidy paid by a central to a local government to fund a public project. **2** a grant to a school or individual for a project.

grant-maintained *adj* denoting a British state school funded directly by the Department of Education and run by its governors and head teacher rather than by a local education authority.

gran turismo /,gran too'rizmoh/ *adj* a full form of GT, denoting a saloon car with a sporty appearance and performance but with enough comfort to make it suitable for long journeys. [Italian *gran turismo* great touring]

granular /'granyoolə/ *adj* consisting of granules, or having a grainy texture or appearance. >>> **granularity** /-'lariti/ *noun*, **granularly** *adv*.

granulate /'granyoolayt/ *verb trans* **1** to form or crystallize (something) into grains or granules: *granulated sugar.* **2** to give (something) a roughened or granular appearance or texture. >>> *verb intrans* **1** to become rough or granular in appearance or texture. **2** said of a wound: to form minute grainy particles laced with tiny blood vessels as part of the process of healing. >>> **granulation** /-'laysh(ə)n/ *noun*, **granulative** /- lətiv/ *adj*, **granulator** *noun*.

granule /'granyoohl/ *noun* a small hard particle. [late Latin *granulum*, dimin. of Latin *granum* GRAIN[1]]

granulocyte /'granyooləsiet/ *noun* any of various white blood cells that have cytoplasm containing large numbers of conspicuous stainable granules and a nucleus with many lobes: compare AGRANULOCYTE, BASOPHIL, EOSINOPHIL. >>> **granulocytic** /-'sitik/ *adj*.

granum /'graynəm/ *noun* (*pl* **grana** /'graynə/) any of the stacks of thin layers of chlorophyll-containing material in plant chloroplasts. [Latin *granum* GRAIN[1]]

grape /grayp/ *noun* **1a** a smooth-skinned juicy greenish white to deep red or purple berry that grows in clusters on a grapevine, eaten as a fruit or fermented to produce wine. **b** = GRAPEVINE (1). **2** (**the grape**) *informal* wine: *Don't mix the grape and the grain.* **3** = GRAPE-SHOT. >>> **grapy** *adj*. [Middle English from early French *grape* bunch of grapes, grape, prob from *grap* hook (used in gathering grapes) of Germanic origin]

grapefruit *noun* **1** a large round citrus fruit with a bitter yellow rind and a somewhat acid juicy pulp. **2** the tropical or subtropical evergreen tree that bears this fruit: *Citrus paradisi*. [because the fruit grows in clusters like grapes]

grape hyacinth *noun* a small plant of the lily family with clusters of usu blue flowers: genus *Muscari*.

grapeshot *noun* ammunition for cannons, in the form of small iron balls fixed in clusters, for use against personnel.

grape sugar *noun* = DEXTROSE.

grapevine *noun* **1** any vine on which grapes grow: genus *Vitis*. **2** (**the grapevine**) *informal* a secret or unofficial means of circulating information or gossip, *esp* word of mouth.

graph[1] /grahf, graf/ *noun* **1** a diagram expressing a relation between quantities or variables, typically a line joining points plotted in relation to a vertical and a horizontal axis. **2** in mathematics, the collection of all points whose coordinates satisfy a given relation (e.g. the equation of a function). [short for *graphic formula*]

graph[2] *verb trans* to plot (something) on a graph, or represent (something) using a graph.

graph[3] *noun* in linguistics, a written symbol representing a single unit of sound. [prob from *-graph*]

-graph *comb. form* forming nouns, denoting: **1** something written or represented: *monograph*; *pictograph*. **2** an instrument for recording or transmitting something specified or by a specified means: *seismograph*; *telegraph*. [(sense 1) early French *-graphe* via Latin *-graphum* from Greek *-graphos* written, from *graphein* to write; (sense 2) French *-graphe* via late Latin *-graphus* writer, from Greek *-graphos*]

grapheme /'grafeem/ *noun* any set of units in a writing system that can represent a phoneme, such as the *f* of *fin*, the *ph* of *phantom*, and the *gh* of *laugh*. >>> **graphemic** /gra'feemik/ *adj*, **graphemically** /gra'feemikli/ *adv*.

-grapher *comb. form* forming nouns, denoting: **1** a person with expertise in a particular field or area of study: *geographer*. **2** a person involved or skilled in a particular kind of writing: *calligrapher*; *biographer*.

graphic[1] /'grafik/ *or* **graphical** *adj* **1** formed by writing, drawing, or engraving. **2** marked by clear and vivid description; explicit. **3a** relating to or employing methods of producing pictures, such as engraving, etching, lithography, and photography. **b** relating to the pictorial arts. **4** said of a rock or mineral surface: having marks resembling written characters. **5** represented by a graph. **6** relating to writing. >>> **graphically** *adv*, **graphicness** *noun*. [via Latin from Greek *graphikos*, from *graphein* to write]

graphic[2] *noun* **1** a picture, map, or graph used for illustration or demonstration. **2** a graphic representation displayed by a computer (e.g. on a VDU). **3** any product of graphic art.

-graphic *or* **-graphical** *comb. form* forming adjectives, with the meanings: **1** written, represented, or transmitted in a particular way: *ideographic*. **2** relating to writing on a specified subject: *autobiographic*. [via late Latin from Greek *-graphikos*, from *graphikos*: see GRAPHIC[1]]

graphicacy /'grafikəsi/ *noun* the ability to design and interpret graphics.

graphical *adj* = GRAPHIC[1].

-graphical *comb. form* see -GRAPHIC.

graphical user interface *noun* any visual means by which a computer user gives instructions to the computer (e.g. icons on the screen), particularly as distinct from voice-recognition systems.

graphic arts *pl noun* the fine and applied arts of representation, decoration, and writing or printing on flat surfaces.

graphic design *noun* the art of combining text, illustration, and decoration in the design of printed matter. >>> **graphic designer** *noun*.

graphic equalizer *noun* an electronic device for adjusting the level of certain frequencies in a recording system, built into most standard systems.

graphic novel *noun* a work of literature in the form of a comic strip.

graphics *pl noun* **1a** (*treated as sing. or pl*) the art or science of drawing an object on a two-dimensional surface according to mathematical rules of projection. **b** designs (e.g. advertising posters) containing both typographical and pictorial elements. **2** (*treated as sing. or pl*). **a** = GRAPHIC ARTS. **b** = GRAPHIC DESIGN. **3a** the images on a computer screen. **b** (*treated as sing. or pl*) the use of computers to create and manipulate images, e.g. in television and films.

graphite /'grafiet/ *noun* a soft black lustrous form of carbon that conducts electricity and is also used in lead pencils, as a lubricant, and in lightweight sports equipment. >>> **graphitic** /gra'fitik/ *adj*. [German *Graphit* from Greek *graphein* to write]

grapho- *comb. form* forming words, denoting: writing: *graphologist*. [French *grapho-*, ultimately from Greek *graphein* to write]

graphology /gra'foləji/ *noun* **1** the study of handwriting, *esp* for the purpose of character analysis. **2** the study of writing systems and the symbols used in them. >>> **graphological** /-'lojik/ *adj*, **graphologist** *noun*. [French *graphologie*, from GRAPHO- + -logie -LOGY]

graph paper *noun* paper printed with small squares for drawing graphs and diagrams.

-graphy *comb. form* forming nouns, denoting: **1** writing or representation in a particular manner, on a particular subject, or by a specified means: *calligraphy*; *biography*. **2** the art or science of: *choreography*. [via Latin from Greek *-graphia*, from *graphein* to write]

grapnel /'grapnəl/ *noun* **1** a device, like a small anchor with several claws or hooks radiating from a central stem and bent backwards, that is hurled with a line attached in order to hook onto a ship, the top of a wall, etc. **2** a small anchor with several hooks used for anchoring small boats. [Middle English *grapenel*, ultimately from early French *grap*: see GRAPE]

grappa /'grapə/ *noun* an Italian spirit distilled from the fermented remains of grapes after the juice has been extracted for making wine. [Italian *grappa* grape stalk, of Germanic origin]

grapple[1] /'grapl/ *verb intrans* **1** (*often* + with) to engage in hand-to-hand fighting; to wrestle. **2** (+ with) to struggle to deal successfully with something: *She has spent the last three hours grappling with a mathematical problem.* ➤ *verb trans* **1** to seize and wrestle with (somebody). **2** to seize (something) with, or as if with, a grapnel. **3** *archaic or literary* to lay hold of (something) and attach it firmly with or as if with a grapnel: *Those friends thou hast … grapple them unto thy soul with hoops of steel* — Shakespeare. ➤➤ **grappler** *noun*.

grapple[3] *noun* **1** a hand-to-hand struggle. **2** a grapnel. [early French *grappelle*, dimin. of *grap*: see GRAPE]

grappling iron *noun* a device with claws, attached to a line and designed to hook into a surface when thrown; a grapnel.

graptolite /'graptəliet/ *noun* any of numerous extinct fossil marine animals from the Palaeozoic era.

Word history ──
Greek *graptos* painted (from *graphein* to write, paint) + -LITE. So called because the fossils leave pencil-like markings on the rocks.

grasp[1] /grahsp/ *verb trans* **1** to take hold of (something or somebody) eagerly with the fingers or arms. **2** to take advantage of (something) enthusiastically: *You must grasp this wonderful opportunity.* **3** to succeed in understanding (something); to comprehend (it). ➤ *verb intrans* (*often* + at) to make the motion of seizing; clutch. ➤➤ **graspable** *adj*, **grasper** *noun*. [Middle English *graspen*, of Germanic origin]

grasp[2] *noun* **1** a firm hold. **2** control or power: *He is entirely in her grasp.* **3** the ability or opportunity to seize and hold or to attain something: *Success was just beyond his grasp.* **4** understanding or ability to understand: *a firm grasp of the subject.*

grasping *adj* eager for material possessions; greedy. ➤➤ **graspingly** *adv*, **graspingness** *noun*.

grass[1] /grahs/ *noun* **1** any of a large family of plants with slender leaves and green flowers in small spikes or clusters, including bamboo, wheat, rye, and corn: family Gramineae. **2** an area covered in growing grass: *Keep off the grass*. **3a** vegetation suitable or used for grazing animals. **b** land on which animals are grazed; pasture. **4** grass leaves or plants collectively. **5** *slang* marijuana. **6** *Brit, slang* a police informer. ✳ **let the grass grow under one's feet** to delay before taking action. **put/send out to grass** to cause (somebody) to enter usu enforced retirement [from the practice of putting a horse out to pasture at the end of its working life]. ➤➤ **grasslike** *adj*. [Old English *græs*; (sense 6) rhyming slang *grass(hopper)* copper (policeman)]

grass[2] *verb trans* **1** to feed (livestock) on grass. **2** to cover or seed (an area) with grass. **3** *Brit, slang* (*usu* + up) to inform against or betray (somebody) to the authorities, *esp* the police. ➤ *verb intrans* *Brit, slang* (*often* + on) to inform the police or some other person or people in authority about wrongdoing committed by somebody.

grasshopper *noun* any of numerous species of plant-eating insects with hind legs that are adapted for leaping and produce a chirping noise when rubbed together: family Acrididae: compare LOCUST.

grassland *noun* **1** farmland used for grazing. **2** land on which the natural dominant plant forms are grasses.

grass of Parnassus /pah'nasəs/ *noun* a marsh plant with a single small whitish flower: *Parnassia palustris*. [named after *Parnassus*, mountain in Greece]

grass roots *pl noun* (*treated as sing. or pl*) **1** society at the local level as distinguished from the centres of political leadership. **2** the fundamental level or source. ➤➤ **grass-roots** *adj*.

grass ski *noun* a small board mounted on a set of wheels with a caterpillar track, strapped to the feet to simulate the movements of skiing on grass-covered slopes.

grass snake *noun* a nonpoisonous European snake with two yellow or orange patches forming a collar behind its head: *Natrix natrix*.

grass tree *noun* any of several species of Australian plants of the lily family with a thick woody trunk bearing a cluster of stiff leaves resembling blades of grass and a spike of small flowers: genus *Xanthorrhoea*. Also called BLACKBOY.

grass widow *noun* a woman whose husband is temporarily away from her, often or for long periods.

grass widower *noun* a man whose wife is temporarily away from him.

grassy *adj* (**grassier, grassiest**) **1** consisting of or covered with grass. **2** having the texture or smell of grass.

grat /grat/ *verb* past tense of GREET[2].

grate[1] /grayt/ *noun* **1a** a frame or bed of metal bars that holds the fuel in a fireplace, stove, or furnace. **b** a fireplace. **2** = GRATING[1]. [Middle English via medieval Latin *crata*, *grata* from Latin *cratis* hurdle]

grate[2] *verb trans* **1** to reduce (something, *esp* a hard food) to small particles by rubbing it on something rough. **2a** to gnash or grind (teeth) noisily. **b** to cause (something) to make a rasping sound. ➤ *verb intrans* **1** to rub or rasp noisily. **2** to cause irritation; to jar: *His way of talking grates on my nerves.* ➤➤ **grater** *noun*. [Middle English *graten* from early French *grater* to scratch, of Germanic origin]

grateful /'graytf(ə)l/ *adj* **1** feeling or expressing thanks. **2** *archaic* pleasing or comforting. ➤➤ **gratefully** *adv*, **gratefulness** *noun*. [obsolete *grate* pleasing, thankful, from Latin *gratus*]

graticule /'gratikyoohl/ *noun* **1** a network or scale visible on the eyepiece of a telescope, microscope, etc and used in locating or measuring objects. **2** the network of latitude and longitude lines on which a map is drawn. [French *graticule* from Latin *craticula* fine latticework, dimin. of *cratis* wickerwork]

gratification /ˌgratifi'kaysh(ə)n/ *noun* **1** the act or an instance of gratifying or being gratified. **2** a source of satisfaction or pleasure.

gratify /'gratifie/ *verb trans* (**gratifies, gratified, gratifying**) **1** to give pleasure or satisfaction to (someone). **2** to give in to (something); to satisfy (it): *gratify a whim*. ➤➤ **gratifyingly** *adv*. [early French *gratifier* from Latin *gratificari* to make oneself pleasing, from *gratus* pleasing, thankful]

gratin /'gratanh (French gratẽ)/ *noun* a dish cooked with a topping of breadcrumbs or grated cheese that has formed a brown crust. [French *gratin*, from *grater*: see GRATE[2]]

grating[1] *noun* **1** a framework of parallel bars or crossbars, e.g. covering a window. **2** a set of close parallel lines or bars ruled on a polished surface to produce optical spectra by diffraction. **3** the action of rubbing something against a rough surface or, *esp*, the sound produced by this. [GRATE[1] + -ING[2]]

grating[2] *adj* said of sounds: with an annoyingly or unnervingly harsh quality; rasping. [GRATE[2] + -ING[1]]

gratis /'gratis, 'grah-/ *adv and adj* without charge, interest, or recompense: *This is the fool that lent out money gratis* — Shakespeare. [Middle English from Latin *gratiis*, *gratis*, from *gratia*: see GRACE[1]]

gratitude /'gratityoohd/ *noun* the state or feeling of being grateful; thankfulness. [Middle English via French from medieval Latin *gratitude*, from Latin *gratus* pleasing, grateful]

gratuitous /grə'tyooh·itəs/ *adj* **1** not called for by the circumstances; unwarranted: *scenes of gratuitous violence*. **2a** costing nothing; free. **b** not involving a return benefit or compensation. ➤➤ **gratuitously** *adv*, **gratuitousness** *noun*. [Latin *gratuitus* given freely, from *gratus* grateful, pleasing]

gratuity /grə'tyooh·iəti/ *noun* (*pl* **gratuities**) **1** a small sum of money given in return for or in anticipation of some service; a tip. **2** a sum of money given to someone when they retire, *esp* from the armed services. [Old French *gratuité* or medieval Latin *gratuitas* gift, from Latin *gratus* pleasing, grateful]

gravadlax /'gravədlaks/ *noun* = GRAVLAX.

gravamen /grə'vaymen, -mən/ *noun* (*pl* **gravamens** or **gravamina** /grə'vaminə/) the most significant part of a complaint or legal grievance; the substance. [late Latin *gravamen* burden, from Latin *gravare*: see GRIEVE[1]]

grave[1] /grayv/ *noun* **1a** a pit excavated for the burial of a body or bodies. **b** a tomb. **2** (**the grave**) *literary* death. **3** the end or destruction of something, the place where it ended, or the thing that caused it to end: *the grave of all my hopes.* ✳ **turn in one's grave** used to suggest that a dead person would strongly disapprove of something if he or she knew about it: *After what they did to the symphony, Beethoven must be turning in his grave.* [Old English *græf*]

grave[2] *adj* **1a** requiring serious consideration; important: *grave problems.* **b** likely to produce great harm or danger: *a grave mistake.* **2** serious and dignified. **3** drab in colour; sombre. **4** said of a sound: low in pitch. ⟫⟫ **gravely** *adv*, **graveness** *noun.* [early French *grave* from Latin *gravis* heavy, serious]

grave[3] *verb trans* (*past part.* **graven** *or* **graved**) *archaic* to engrave (something). [Old English *grafan*]

grave[4] *verb trans* to clean and then tar (e.g. a ship's bottom). [Middle English *graven*, perhaps from Old French *grave, greve* shore, because orig the ship would have been beached]

grave[5] /grahv/ *noun* a mark (ˋ) placed over a vowel in some languages to show that it is pronounced with a fall of pitch (e.g. in ancient Greek) or has a particular tone quality (e.g. *è* in French). ⟫⟫ **grave** *adj.* [early French *grave*: see GRAVE[2]]

gravel[1] /'gravl/ *noun* **1** loose fragments of rock or small stones, often used to surface roads and paths. **2** a sandy deposit of small stones in the kidneys and urinary bladder. [Middle English from Old French *gravele*, dimin. of *grave, greve* pebbly ground, beach]

gravel[2] *verb trans* (**gravelled, gravelling**, NAmer **graveled, graveling**) **1** to cover or spread (a surface, e.g. a road) with gravel. **2** to perplex or confuse (somebody).

gravel[3] *adj* harsh-sounding; gravelly.

gravel-blind *adj* having very weak vision. [suggested by SAND-BLIND]

gravelly *adj* **1** like, containing, or covered with gravel. **2** harsh-sounding; grating: *a gravelly voice.*

graven image /'grayv(ə)n/ *noun* an idol, usu carved from wood or stone.

graver /'grayvə/ *noun* any of various tools (e.g. a burin) used in engraving.

Graves /grahv/ *noun* (*pl* **Graves** /grahv/) a dry white or occasionally red wine produced in the Graves district of the Bordeaux region of France.

Graves' disease /grayvz/ *noun* a medical condition in which there is enlargement of the thyroid gland and abnormal protrusion of the eyeball. [Robert J *Graves* d.1853, Irish physician, one of the first people to describe it]

gravestone /'grayvstohn/ *noun* a stone over or at one end of a grave, usu inscribed with the name and details of the dead person.

graveyard /'grayvyahd/ *noun* **1** an area of ground used for burials, usu beside a church. **2** a condition of final disappointment or failure: *the graveyard of their hopes.*

graveyard shift *noun* NAmer, *informal* the working shift that starts late at night and finishes early in the morning; the night shift.

gravi- *comb. form* forming words, with the meaning: heavy or weight: *gravimeter.* [via French from Latin *gravi-*, from *gravis* heavy]

gravid /'gravid/ *adj* = PREGNANT. ⟫⟫ **gravidity** /grə'viditi/ *noun*, **gravidly** *adv.* [Latin *gravidus* from *gravis* heavy, serious]

gravimeter /grə'vimitə, 'gravimeetə/ *noun* **1** a weighing instrument for measuring variations in gravity on the earth, moon, etc. **2** a device similar to a hydrometer for determining relative intensity. [French *gravimètre*, from GRAVI- + *-mètre* -METER[2]]

gravimetric /gravi'metrik/ *adj* **1** relating to the measurement of density or weight. **2** relating to the measurement of a gravitational field using a gravimeter. ⟫⟫ **gravimetrically** *adv*, **gravimetry** /grə'vimətri/ *noun.*

graving dock /'grayving/ *noun* = DRY DOCK.

gravitas /'gravitas/ *noun* a solemn and serious quality or manner: *the gravitas of Oxford marmalade with its acerbic subtext* — The Economist. [Latin *gravitas* from *gravis* heavy, serious]

gravitate /'gravitayt/ *verb intrans* to move under the influence of gravitation. ✳ **gravitate towards** to move or be drawn gradually and steadily towards.

gravitation /gravi'taysh(ə)n/ *noun* the natural force of mutual attraction between objects or particles, or the movement caused by this force. ⟫⟫ **gravitational** *adj*, **gravitationally** *adv*, **gravitative** /-tiv/ *adj.*

gravitational constant /gravi'taysh(ə)nl/ *noun* in Newton's law of gravity, the factor that relates gravity to the mass of and distance between bodies under the influence of the force of gravity.

gravitational field *noun* a property of the region of space surrounding a body (e.g. a planet) that exerts a force of attraction on nearby bodies: *The rocket entered the gravitational field of Saturn.*

gravitational wave *noun* **1** a hypothetical wave by means of which gravitational attraction is effected. **2** a wave on the surface of a liquid that is under the influence of gravity.

graviton /'graviton/ *noun* a hypothetical elementary particle with zero electric charge and no mass, held to be responsible for gravitational interactions. [GRAVITY + -ON[2]]

gravity /'graviti/ *noun* **1** the force that attracts objects towards the earth, or towards any body that has mass. **2** the quality of being heavy; weight. **3a** dignity or sobriety of bearing. **b** significance, *esp* seriousness: *He couldn't comprehend the gravity of the situation.* ⟫⟫ **gravity** *adj.* [early French *gravité* from Latin *gravitat-, gravitas*, from *gravis* heavy]

gravity feed *noun* any system that causes a material to flow by the action of gravity alone.

gravity wave *noun* a wave of gravitational force that is held to be produced when a body is accelerating under the influence of the force of gravity.

gravlax /'gravlaks/ *noun* filleted salmon which has been seasoned and pressed, and is usu eaten raw. [Norwegian *gravlaks* from *grav* buried + *laks* salmon; because orig the salmon was buried in salt in a trench]

gravure /grə'vyooə/ *noun* **1** the process of printing from an engraved plate made of copper or wood. **2** = PHOTOGRAVURE. [French *gravure* from *graver* to engrave, of Germanic origin]

gravy /'grayvi/ *noun* **1** the fat and juices from cooked meat, thickened and seasoned and used as a sauce. **2** *informal* something of benefit that is obtained easily and sometimes unexpectedly. [Middle English *gravey* from early French *gravé*, of unknown origin]

gravy boat *noun* a small boat-shaped vessel used for pouring gravy or other sauces.

gravy train *noun informal* a much exploited source of easy money.

gray[1] /gray/ *adj, noun, and verb* NAmer = GREY[1], GREY[2], and GREY[3].
Usage note
gray or grey? See note at GREY[1].

gray[2] *noun* the SI unit of ionizing radiation equal to an absorbed dose of one joule per kilogram. [named after L H *Gray* d.1965, English physicist]

grayling /'grayling/ *noun* (*pl* **graylings** *or collectively* **grayling**) **1** any of several species of silvery freshwater fishes that resemble the trout: genus *Thymallus.* **2** a common European butterfly with greyish wings: *Hipparchia semele.* [Middle English, from GRAY[1] + -LING]

graze[1] /grayz/ *verb intrans* **1** to feed on growing grass and other green plants. **2** *informal* to eat snacks frequently, instead of eating meals at regular times. **3** *informal* to sample things casually and irregularly, *esp* to switch television channels frequently without watching any programme fully. **4** NAmer, *informal* to take things from supermarket shelves and eat them while shopping, often without paying for them. ⟫ *verb trans* **1a** to crop and eat (growing grass). **b** to feed on the grass in (e.g. a particular field). **2** to put (animals) out to graze: *They grazed the cows on the meadow.* ⟫⟫ **grazable** *adj*, **grazer** *noun.* [Old English *grasian*, from *græs* grass]

graze[2] *verb trans* **1** to touch (something) lightly in passing. **2** to abrade or scratch (something), usu by glancing contact: *She grazed her elbow on the wall.* ⟫ *verb intrans* to touch or rub against something in passing: *Our bumpers just grazed.* [perhaps from GRAZE[1]]

graze[3] *noun* an abrasion, *esp* of the skin, made by a scraping along a surface.

grazier /'grayzi·ə/ *noun* **1** somebody who grazes cattle, usu for beef production. **2** *Aus* a sheep farmer.

grazing /'grayzing/ *noun* **1** the act of feeding, or of setting animals to feed, on grass and other vegetation: *Heavy grazing will kill off some plant species.* **2** vegetation or land for grazing.

grazioso /gratsi'ohzoh/ *adj and adv* said of a piece of music: to be performed in a light and graceful manner. [Italian *grazioso* graceful]

grease[1] /grees/ *noun* **1** any thick oily substance used as a lubricant. **2** any oily substance. **3** animal fat used in cooking, or produced when meat is cooked. **4** oily wool as it comes from the sheep. ✱ **in the grease** said of wool or fur: in the natural uncleaned condition. ➤➤ **greaseless** *adj.* [Middle English *grese* via early French *craisse, graisse* from Latin *crassus* fat]

grease[2] *verb trans* **1** to smear or lubricate (something) with grease. **2** to hasten or ease the process or progress of (something). ✱ **grease somebody's palm** to bribe somebody.

grease gun *noun* a motor mechanic's tool for releasing a controlled amount of lubricant.

grease monkey *noun informal* a mechanic.

grease nipple *noun* a small projection with a hole in it through which grease can be squirted into a mechanism using a grease gun.

greasepaint *noun* theatrical make-up.

greaseproof paper *noun* paper resistant to penetration by grease, oil, or wax and used *esp* for wrapping food.

greaser /'greesa/ *noun* **1** somebody whose work involves greasing machinery, *esp* a motor mechanic. **2** *informal* a long-haired man belonging to a motorcycle gang. **3** *NAmer, informal, offensive* a Mexican or other person of Latin American origin.

greasy *adj* (**greasier, greasiest**) **1a** smeared or soiled with grease. **b** oily in appearance or texture. **2** containing an unusual or unpalatable amount of grease: *greasy food.* **3** insincerely polite or fawning in a distasteful way. **4** = SLIPPERY. ➤➤ **greasily** *adv*, **greasiness** *noun.*

great[1] /grayt/ *adj* **1** notably large in size or number. **2a** extreme in amount, degree, or effectiveness: *great bloodshed.* **b** of importance; significant: *a great day in European history.* **3a** eminent or distinguished: *There just aren't that many great figures around now* — Martin Amis. **b** aristocratic or grand: *great ladies.* **4** denoting the largest or most important of several; main or principal: *a reception in the great hall.* **5** used in plant and animal names: of a relatively large kind: *great crested grebe.* **6** (*chiefly in combination*) removed in a family relationship by at least three stages directly or two stages indirectly: *great-grandfather.* **7a** remarkably skilled: *a great organizer.* **b** enthusiastic: *a great film-goer.* **8** *informal* used as a generalized term of approval: *We all had a great time.* ➤➤ **great** *adv*, **greatly** *adv*, **greatness** *noun.* [Old English *grēat*]

great[2] *noun* (*pl* **great** *or* **greats**) **1** (*usu in pl*) somebody who is eminent in a particular field: *the greats of the stage.* **2** = GREAT ORGAN.

great auk *noun* an extinct large flightless auk formerly abundant along N Atlantic coasts: *Pinguinus impennis.*

great-aunt *noun* an aunt of one's father or mother.

Great Bear *noun* = URSA MAJOR.

great circle *noun* a circle formed on the surface of a sphere, e.g. the earth, by the intersection of a plane that passes through the centre of the sphere.

greatcoat *noun* a heavy overcoat.

great crested grebe *noun* a large diving water bird found in Europe, Africa, and Asia that has black projecting ear tufts in the breeding season: *Podiceps cristatus.*

Great Dane *noun* a dog of a massive powerful smooth-coated breed with long legs.

great divide *noun* **1** a significant point of division, e.g. between nations, generations, or cultures. **2** (**the great divide**) *euphem* death, or the boundary between life and death. [named after the *Great Divide*, watershed in N America]

greater *adj* (*often* **Greater**) consisting of a central city together with adjacent areas that are geographically or administratively connected with it: *Greater London.* [compar of GREAT[1]]

greater celandine *noun* = CELANDINE (2).

greathearted *adj* generous in spirit; magnanimous. ➤➤ **greatheartedly** *adv*, **greatheartedness** *noun.*

great horned owl *noun* = HORNED OWL.

great-nephew *noun* a grandson of one's brother or sister.

great-niece *noun* a granddaughter of one's brother or sister.

great organ *noun* the principal keyboard of an organ together with its stops, usu the loudest on the organ.

great power *noun* (*often* **Great Power**) any of the nations that figure most decisively in international affairs.

Great Russian *noun* **1** a member of the Russian-speaking people of the central and NE region of the former Soviet Union. **2** the Russian language itself, as distinct from the other languages of the former Soviet Union.

Greats *pl noun* the course and final BA examination in classics at Oxford University.

great seal *noun* the official seal of a nation or monarch that is used *esp* for the authentication of state documents.

great skua *noun* a large stocky SKUA (large seabird) with dusky plumage and broad rounded wings, which breeds chiefly along Arctic and Antarctic shores and forages over cold and temperate seas: *Stercorarius skua.*

great tit *noun* a large common black, white, and yellow Eurasian and N African tit: *Parus major.*

great-uncle *noun* an uncle of one's father or mother.

Great War *noun* the first World War, 1914 to 1918.

great white shark *noun* a large predatory shark with white underparts that is widespread in warm and tropical seas and sometimes attacks humans: *Carcharodon carcharias.*

greave /greev/ *noun* a piece of armour for the leg below the knee. [Middle English *greve* from Old French *greve* shin, greave]

grebe /greeb/ *noun* any of several species of swimming and diving birds closely related to the divers but with lobed instead of webbed toes: family Podicipedidae. [French *grèbe*]

Grecian /'greesh(ə)n/ *adj* relating to ancient Greece. ➤➤ **Grecian** *noun.* [Latin *Graecia* Greece]

Grecism /'greesiz(ə)m/ *noun NAmer* see GRAECISM.

Greco- *comb. form chiefly NAmer* see GRAECO-.

greed /greed/ *noun* **1** excessive desire for or consumption of food. **2** excessive desire to acquire or possess things; avarice. [back-formation from GREEDY]

greedy *adj* (**greedier, greediest**) **1** consuming something, *esp* food, in excessive amounts. **2** (+ for) having a great or excessive desire or need for something. ➤➤ **greedily** *adv*, **greediness** *noun.* [Old English *grǣdig*]

greedy-guts *noun* (*pl* **greedy-guts**) *chiefly Brit, informal* somebody who eats too much; a glutton.

greegree /'greegree/ *noun* see GRIS-GRIS.

Greek[1] /greek/ *noun* **1** a native or inhabitant of Greece. **2** the Indo-European language of the people of ancient Greece or the modern language derived from it currently used in Greece. **3** *informal* something unintelligible: *It's all Greek to me.*

Word history

Old English *Grēca* via Latin *Graecus* from Greek *Graikos*; (sense 3) translation of Latin *Graecum* in the medieval phrase *Graecum est; non potest legi* it is Greek; it cannot be read. Numerous English words and word-elements derive from the ancient Greek language, but few of them have been borrowed directly (*amnesty, idiosyncrasy, myth,* and *pathos* are exceptions). Many came by way of Latin during the revival of classical learning in the 16th and 17th cents (*chaos, climax, crisis, dilemma, drama, energy, enigma, epoch, irony, system, theory, zone*). Even more have entered English as part of the Latin- and Greek-based international scientific vocabulary of modern times. A few words from modern Greek (New Greek) have also entered English, mostly terms relating to food and drink (*moussaka, ouzo, pitta, retsina, taramasalata*).

Greek[2] *adj* relating to Greece, the Greeks, or the Greek language.

Greek cross *noun* a cross with four equal arms intersecting at right angles.

Greek fire *noun* an incendiary substance used in ancient sea warfare and said to have burst into flame on contact with water.

Greek Orthodox Church *noun* the branch of the Orthodox Church that uses Greek in its liturgy and is the national Church of Greece.

green[1] /green/ *adj* **1** of the colour of grass, between blue and yellow in the spectrum. **2a** covered by grass or other green growth or foliage: *green fields.* **b** said *esp* of food: consisting of green plants: *a green salad.* **3a** said of fruit: not ripe. **b** said of wood, leather, etc: not matured or seasoned. **4** lacking experience or sophistication; naive. **5** said of a person: **a** appearing pale, sickly, or nauseated. **b** affected by intense envy or jealousy. **6a** relating to or beneficial to the natural environment: *green issues.* **b** (*often* **Green**) concerned about environmental issues and supporting policies aimed at protecting the environment. **7** in the EU, denoting an exchange unit that has a differential rate of exchange in relation to the specified currency and is used for paying agricultural producers: *the green pound.* **8** said of meat: not cured or smoked: *green bacon.* ⮞ **greenness** *noun.* [Old English *grēne*, related to Old English *grōwan* to GROW]

green² *noun* **1** the colour of grass, between blue and yellow in the spectrum. **2** (*in pl*) green leafy vegetables, e.g. spinach and cabbage, the leaves and stems of which are cooked for food. **3a** an area of open grass for public use in a town or village. **b** a smooth area of grass for a special purpose, *esp* bowling or putting. **4** (*often* **Green**) somebody who is a member or supporter of an environmentalist party or group. **5** *NAmer, informal* money, *esp* paper money. **6** a green traffic light meaning go.

green³ *verb trans* **1** to make (something) green. **2a** to make (somebody or something) more environmentally aware. **b** to make (something) less harmful to the environment. ⮞ *verb intrans* to become green.

green alga *noun* an alga in which the chlorophyll is not masked by other pigments.

greenback *noun NAmer, informal* a dollar.

green bean *noun* **1** the narrow green edible pod of any of various beans, e.g. the French bean or the runner bean. **2** a plant that bears green beans.

green belt *noun* an area of parks, farmland, etc encircling an urban area and usu subject to restrictions on new building.

green card *noun* **1** an international certificate of motor insurance for UK drivers. **2** a permit allowing a foreign person to settle permanently and work in the USA.

Green Cross Code *noun* a British code of safety for the use of people, *esp* children, crossing roads.

greenery *noun* green foliage or plants.

green-eyed *adj* = JEALOUS.

green-eyed monster *noun* jealousy: *O, beware, my lord, of jealousy! It is the green-eyed monster, which doth mock the meat it feeds on* — Shakespeare. [from Shakespeare's *Othello* (3:3)]

greenfield *adj* **1** consisting of land not previously built on: *The companies with most chance of success are those setting up on greenfield sites* — The Economist. **2** not previously developed or exploited: *a greenfield area in medical research.* **3** breaking new ground; innovative: *greenfield development in communications technology.*

greenfinch *noun* a common European finch with green and yellow plumage: *Carduelis chloris.*

green fingers *pl noun* an unusual ability to make plants grow. ⮞ **green-fingered** *adj.*

greenfly *noun* (*pl* **greenflies** *or collectively* **greenfly**) *Brit* any of various green aphids that are destructive to plants, or an infestation of them.

greengage *noun* **1** any of several small rounded greenish cultivated plums. **2** the tree that bears this fruit: *Prunus domestica.* [GREEN¹ + Sir William *Gage* d.1820, English botanist who introduced it to England]

greengrocer *noun chiefly Brit* a retailer of fresh vegetables and fruit. ⮞ **greengrocery** *noun.*

greenheart *noun* **1** a tropical S American evergreen tree of the laurel family: *Ocotea rodiaei.* **2** the durable, greenish-coloured wood of this tree that is widely used in boatbuilding.

greenhorn *noun* **1** an inexperienced or unsophisticated person, *esp* somebody who is easily cheated. **2** *chiefly NAmer* a newcomer (e.g. to a country) unacquainted with local manners and customs. [orig in the sense 'animal with young horns']

greenhouse /'greenhows/ *noun* a building or enclosure with glass walls and a glass roof for the cultivation or protection of tender plants.

greenhouse effect *noun* the warming of the lower layers of the atmosphere by absorption and reradiation of solar radiation that cannot escape through the build-up of carbon dioxide and other pollutants in the atmosphere.

greenhouse gas *noun* a gas, *esp* carbon dioxide or methane, that contributes to the greenhouse effect.

greenie /'greeni/ *noun Aus, informal derog* somebody with an interest in environmental issues.

greening *noun* any of several apples that have a green skin when ripe.

greenish *adj* rather green. ⮞ **greenishness** *noun.*

greenkeeper /'greenkeepə/ *noun* somebody who is responsible for the maintenance of a golf course or a bowling green.

green light *noun* authority or permission to undertake a project. [from the green traffic light which signals permission to proceed]

greenmail¹ *noun* **1** the business tactic whereby a company buys a substantial block of shares in another company and threatens to make a takeover, so forcing the threatened company to repurchase the shares at a higher price. **2** the payment made to repurchase the shares. ⮞ **greenmailer** *noun.* [GREEN² in the sense 'money' + -*mail* as in BLACKMAIL¹]

greenmail² *verb trans* to subject (a company) to greenmail.

green manure *noun* a herbaceous crop (e.g. clover) ploughed under while green to enrich the soil.

green monkey disease *noun* an often fatal virus disease that causes high fever and internal bleeding and is transmitted to humans by the green monkey, a small W African species.

Green Paper *or* **green paper** *noun chiefly Brit* a set of proposals issued by the government for public comment. [from the colour of its cover]

green pepper *noun* a green unripe fruit of the sweet pepper plant, eaten raw or cooked as a vegetable.

green revolution *noun* a process of rapid development and improvement in agriculture due to extensive use of artificial fertilizers and high-yielding plant strains leading to greatly increased crop yields.

greenroom *noun* a room in a theatre or concert hall where performers can relax when not on stage. [prob because it was orig painted green]

greensand *noun* a greenish form of sandstone coloured by the dull green silicates of iron and potassium.

greenshank *noun* a European wading bird of the sandpiper family with olive-green legs and feet: *Tringa nebularia.*

greensick *adj* said of plants: suffering from chlorosis. ⮞ **greensickness** *noun.*

greenstick fracture *noun* a fracture in a young person in which the bone is partly broken and partly bent.

greenstone *noun* **1** any of numerous dark green compact rocks (e.g. diorite). **2** a variety of jade found in New Zealand and used *esp* in Maori jewellery.

greenstuff *noun* green vegetation or green vegetables.

greensward /'greenswawd/ *noun archaic or literary* turf that is green with growing grass: *We had broken suddenly into a lovely glade of greensward surrounded by ancient trees* — Conan Doyle.

green tea *noun* tea that is light in colour from incomplete fermentation of the leaf before firing.

green thumb *noun NAmer* the ability to grow plants well; green fingers. ⮞ **green-thumbed** *adj.*

green turtle *noun* a large edible sea turtle: *Chelonia midas.*

green vitriol *noun* = FERROUS SULPHATE.

green-wellie *adj Brit, informal, humorous* belonging to or supposedly characteristic of the stratum of upper-class British society that is especially fond of outdoor pursuits of the hunt-following and horse-riding variety. [from their supposed preference for green wellington boots over the more workaday black ones]

Greenwich Mean Time /'grenich/ *noun* the mean solar time of the meridian of Greenwich used as the primary point of reference for standard time throughout the world. [named after *Greenwich*, borough of London]

greenwood *noun archaic or literary* a forest with trees that are in full leaf.

greet¹ /greet/ *verb trans* **1a** to acknowledge the presence or arrival of (somebody) with gestures or words. **b** to send greetings to (somebody). **2** to meet or react to (somebody or something) in a specified manner: *The proposal was greeted with derision.* **3** to be perceived by (somebody): *A surprising sight greeted her eyes.* ⮞ **greeter** *noun.* [Old English *grētan*]

greet² *verb intrans* (*past tense* **grat** /grat/, *past part.* **grutten** /'grutn/) *Scot* to weep or lament. [Old English *grǣtan*]

greeting *noun* **1** a phrase or gesture expressing welcome or recognition on meeting. **2** (*usu in pl*) an expression of good wishes; regards: *birthday greetings.*

greetings card *noun* a card containing a message of goodwill usu sent or given on some special occasion (e.g. an anniversary).

gregarious /gri'geəri·əs/ *adj* **1** said of people: marked by or indicating a liking for companionship; sociable: *But the gregarious men and women who have no home-life flee to the bright and clattering public house in a vain attempt to express their gregariousness* — Jack London. **2a** said of animals: tending to associate with others of the same kind: *a gregarious gull*. **b** said of a plant: growing in a cluster or a colony. ➤➤ **gregariously** *adv*, **gregariousness** *noun*. [Latin *gregarius* of a flock or herd, from *greg-*, *grex* flock, herd]

Gregorian calendar /gri'gawri·ən/ *noun* a revision of the Julian Calendar now in general use, that was introduced in 1582 by Pope Gregory XIII and adopted in Britain and the American colonies in 1752. It restricts leap years to every fourth year except for those centenary years not divisible by 400.

Gregorian chant *noun* a rhythmically free liturgical chant in unison practised in the Roman Catholic Church. [named after Pope *Gregory* I d.604, who is said to have introduced it]

Gregorian telescope *noun* a reflecting telescope in which light that has been reflected from a secondary concave mirror passes through a perforation in the primary mirror to the eye-piece. [named after James *Gregory* d.1675, Scottish mathematician and astronomer, who invented it]

greisen /'griez(ə)n/ *noun* a light-coloured rock consisting chiefly of quartz and mica that is common in Cornwall and Saxony. [German *Greisen*]

gremlin /'gremlin/ *noun* a mischievous creature said to cause the unexplained malfunctioning of machinery or equipment. [perhaps modification of Irish Gaelic *gruaimín* ill-humoured little fellow]

Grenache /grə'nash/ *noun* **1** a variety of grape used in the production of red and rosé wine. **2** a wine produced from this grape, *esp* a sweet dessert wine. [French *grenache*]

grenade /grə'nayd/ *noun* **1** a small bomb that contains explosive, gas, incendiary chemicals, etc and is thrown by hand or fired from a launcher. **2** a glass container of chemicals that bursts when thrown, releasing a fire extinguishing agent, tear gas, etc. [early French *grenade* pomegranate, because of the shape of early grenades]

Grenadian /gri'naydiən/ *noun* a native or inhabitant of Grenada. ➤➤ **Grenadian** *adj*.

grenadier /grenə'diə/ *noun* **1** a member of a regiment or corps formerly specially trained in the use of grenades. **2** (*often* **Grenadier**) in Britain, a member of the Grenadier Guards, the first regiment of the royal household infantry. **3** any of numerous species of deep-sea fishes related to the cod that have long tapering bodies and pointed tails: family Macrouridae.

grenadine[1] /'grenədeen/ *noun* a syrup flavoured with pomegranates and used in mixed drinks. [French *grenadine*, from *grenade* pomegranate]

grenadine[2] /grenə'deen, 'gren-/ *noun* a plain or patterned fabric, e.g. of silk or wool, in an open weave like that of gauze.

Gresham's law /'gresh(ə)mz/ *noun* the observation in economics that a currency of lower value will tend to remain in circulation while a currency of higher value will tend to be hoarded or exported, often described using the maxim 'bad money drives out good'. [named after Sir Thomas *Gresham* d.1579, English financier]

grew /grooh/ *verb* past tense of GROW.

grey[1] (*NAmer* **gray**) /gray/ *adj* **1** of a colour that is intermediate between black and white, like that of ash or a rain cloud. **2a** lacking light, sunshine, or brightness; dull or dismal: *a grey day*. **b** intermediate or unclear in position, condition, or character: *a grey area*. **3a** having grey hair, *esp* hair that is turning white with age. **b** relating to or involving elderly people: *the grey vote* — The Economist. **4** unexciting or without colour or character; nondescript. **5** said of a textile: in an unbleached undyed state as taken from the loom. **6** said of a horse: having white hair but dark skin. ➤➤ **greyness** *noun*. [Old English *grǽg*]

Usage note ──────────────
grey or **gray**? *Grey* is the correct spelling in British English; *gray* is the correct spelling for the same word in American English.

grey[2] (*NAmer* **gray**) *noun* **1** a neutral colour between black and white like that of ash or a rain cloud. **2** a grey horse.

grey[3] (*NAmer* **gray**) *verb trans and intrans* to become grey or make (something, e.g. hair) grey.

grey area *noun* **1** an intermediate zone between two clearly defined ones that has some of the qualities of each. **2** a subject or situation that is imprecisely defined or difficult to categorize.

greybeard *noun* **1** an old man. **2** a large earthenware jug used for alcoholic spirits.

grey eminence *noun* = ÉMINENCE GRISE.

Grey Friar *noun* a Franciscan friar. [from the colour of his habit]

greyhound *noun* a dog of a tall slender smooth-coated breed, characterized by swiftness and keen sight and used for coursing game and racing. [Old English *grīghund*, from *grīg-* (related to Old Norse *grey* bitch) + *hund* HOUND[1]]

greylag /'graylag/ *noun* a common grey Eurasian wild goose with pink legs: *Anser anser*. [GREY[1] + LAG[2] one who lags or is last; prob from its late migration]

grey market *noun* **1** trade in goods or commodities that is underhand and usu involves profiteering, but is not illegal. **2** trade in newly issued equities before official dealing has begun.

grey matter *noun* **1** brownish grey nerve tissue, *esp* in the brain and spinal cord, containing nerve-cell bodies as well as nerve fibres. **2** *informal* brains or intellect.

grey squirrel *noun* a common light grey to black squirrel that causes severe damage to deciduous trees: *Sciurus carolinensis*.

greywacke /'graywakə/ *noun* a coarse usu dark grey sandstone or conglomerate of cemented rock fragments. [partial translation of German *Grauwacke*]

grey water *noun* in conservation terms, used water (e.g. water from domestic baths) that is not too dirty to be reused, for example for watering plants.

grid /grid/ *noun* **1** a framework of parallel metal bars covering an opening, *esp* a drain; a grating. **2a** a network of uniformly spaced horizontal and perpendicular lines, e.g. for locating points on a map. **b** a layout (e.g. of streets) with intersecting horizontal and perpendicular elements. **3** a network of conductors for the distribution of electricity. **4** the starting positions of vehicles on a racetrack. **5** an ELECTRODE (structure that conducts an electric current) in a thermionic valve or other electronic device that usu has the form of a wire mesh and controls the flow of electrons between the cathode and the anode. ➤➤ **gridded** *adj*. [back-formation from GRIDIRON]

griddle[1] /'gridl/ *noun* **1** a flat metal pan on which food is cooked by dry heat. **2** a metal plate set into the top of an old-fashioned stove, for cooking food in the same way. [Middle English *gredil* gridiron, via late Latin from Latin *craticula*, dimin. of *cratis* wickerwork]

griddle[2] *verb trans* to cook (food) on a griddle.

gridiron /'gridie·ən/ *noun* **1** a framework of metal bars on which food is placed to be cooked; a grill. **2** any arrangement of horizontal and perpendicular lines or elements; a grid. **3** *informal*. **a** an American football field. **b** the game of American football. [Middle English *gredire*, perhaps alteration of *gredil*: see GRIDDLE[1]]

gridlock /'gridlok/ *noun* **1a** a severe traffic jam affecting the traffic over a whole area with intersecting streets. **b** a state in which traffic is obstructed and unable to move over a wide area. **2a** a complete halting or breakdown of an overloaded system or organization. **b** a point in a dispute or negotiations where the positions adopted by the parties involved make further progress impossible. ➤➤ **gridlocked** *adj*.

grief /greef/ *noun* **1** deep distress, *esp* that caused by bereavement. **2a** a cause of deep distress. **b** *archaic* = GRIEVANCE. **3** *informal* trouble of any kind. ✳ **come to grief** to end badly; to fail. **good grief!** an exclamation of surprise, annoyance, or alarm. ➤➤ **griefless** *adj*. [Middle English *gref* via French from Latin *gravis* heavy, serious]

grievance /'greev(ə)ns/ *noun* **1** a cause of resentment: *Stephen had not forgotten the trifling grievance that Elfride had known earlier admiration than his own* — Hardy. **2** a cause of dissatisfaction, e.g. at poor working conditions, constituting grounds for protest or complaint. **3** the formal expression of a grievance; a complaint.

grieve[1] /greev/ *verb intrans* (*often* + for) to feel or express grief, *esp* over a bereavement. ➤ *verb trans* to cause (somebody) to suffer grief: *It grieves me to hear that*. ➤➤ **griever** *noun*. [Middle English *greven* via early French *grever* from Latin *gravare* to burden, from *gravis* heavy, serious]

grieve² *noun Scot* a farm or estate manager or overseer. [Old English *græfa* governor, sheriff; related to Old English *gerēfa* REEVE¹]

grievous /'greevəs/ *adj* **1** causing or characterized by severe pain, suffering, or sorrow: *a grievous loss*. **2** of great seriousness; grave: *grievous fault*. ⟫⟫ **grievously** *adv*, **grievousness** *noun*.

grievous bodily harm *noun* serious physical harm done to a person in an attack, for which the attacker may be charged in a court of law.

griffin /'grifin/ *or* **griffon** /'grifən/ *or* **gryphon** *noun* a mythical animal with the head and wings of an eagle and the body and tail of a lion. [Middle English *griffon* via French and Latin from Greek *grypos* curved]

griffon /'grifən/ *noun* **1** see GRIFFIN. **2** = GRIFFON VULTURE. **3** a dog of a small, wire-haired terrier breed orig from Belgium. [French *griffon*: see GRIFFIN]

griffon vulture *noun* any of several species of large vultures of Europe, Asia, and Africa with brown plumage: genus *Gyps*.

grift /grift/ *verb intrans NAmer, slang* to engage in petty crime, *esp* swindling or illegal gambling. ⟫⟫ **grift** *noun*, **grifter** *noun*. [*grift* a petty swindle, alteration of GRAFT⁴]

grigri /'greegree/ *noun* (*pl* **grigris** /'greegreez/) see GRIS-GRIS.

grike *or* **gryke** /griek/ *noun* a cleft in a horizontal limestone surface: compare CLINT. [alteration of Middle English *crike* from Old Norse *criki* crack, bend]

grill¹ /gril/ *noun* **1** a cooking utensil consisting of a set of parallel bars on which food is exposed to heat (e.g. from burning charcoal). **2** *Brit* an apparatus on a cooker under which food is cooked or browned by radiant heat. **3** an article or dish of grilled food. **4** a *usu* informal restaurant or dining room, *esp* in a hotel. **5** see GRILLE. [French *gril* from late Latin *craticula*: see GRIDDLE¹]

grill² *verb trans* **1a** to cook (food) on or under a grill by radiant heat. **b** to subject (somebody or something) to intense or painful heat. **2** *informal* to subject (somebody) to intense and *usu* long periods of questioning. ⟫ *verb intrans* to become grilled. ⟫⟫ **griller** *noun*.

grillage /'grilij/ *noun* a framework of timber or metal beams used as a foundation for something built on soft or marshy ground. [French *grillage* from *griller* to supply with grilles, from *grille*: see GRILLE]

grille *or* **grill** /gril/ *noun* **1** a grating forming a barrier or screen; *specif* an ornamental metal one at the front end of a motor vehicle. **2** an opening covered with a grille. [French *grille* from Latin *craticula*: see GRIDDLE¹]

grillroom *noun* = GRILL¹ (4).

grilse /grils/ *noun* (*pl* **grilse**) a young mature salmon returning from the sea to spawn for the first time. [Middle English *grills*, perhaps from early French *grisel*: see GRIZZLED]

grim /grim/ *adj* (**grimmer, grimmest**) **1** fierce or forbidding in disposition or appearance. **2** not flinching from a plan or intention; unyielding: *grim determination*. **3** ghastly or sinister in character. **4** *informal* unpleasant in some way; nasty: *I had a pretty grim afternoon at the dentist's*. ⟫⟫ **grimly** *adv*, **grimness** *noun*. [Old English *grimm*]

grimace¹ /'griməs, gri'mays/ *noun* a distorted facial expression, *usu* of disgust, anger, or pain. [French *grimace* from Spanish *grimazo* caricature, prob of Germanic origin]

grimace² *verb intrans* to express pain, disapproval, or disgust by twisting one's face. ⟫⟫ **grimacer** *noun*.

grimalkin /gri'malkin/ *noun* **1** *archaic* an old cat, *esp* a female cat. **2** a spiteful or bad-tempered old woman. [alteration of *grey malkin*, from GREY¹ + English dialect *malkin* female cat]

grime¹ /griem/ *noun* dirt, *esp* when sticking to or ingrained in a surface. ⟫⟫ **griminess** *noun*, **grimy** *adj*. [Flemish *grijm* from early Dutch *grime* soot, mask]

grime² *verb trans* to cover or soil (something) with grime.

Grimm's law /grimz/ *noun* in historical linguistics, the theory that the Germanic languages are related to Proto-Indo-European by a regular system of consonantal changes. [named after Jacob Grimm d.1863, German philologist]

grin¹ /grin/ *verb intrans* (**grinned, grinning**) **1** to smile broadly, *usu* in a self-satisfied or silly way. **2** to smile in a fierce or sinister way, showing the teeth. ✳ **grin and bear it** to put up with an unpleasant experience in a stoical way. ⟫⟫ **grinner** *noun*. [Middle English *grinnen* from Old English *grennian* to snarl, bare the teeth]

grin² *noun* **1** a broad smile. **2** a sinister smile.

grind¹ /griend/ *verb* (*past tense and past part.* **ground** /grownd/) ⟫ *verb trans* **1** to reduce (something) to powder or small fragments by crushing it between hard surfaces. **2** to polish, sharpen, or wear (something) down by friction: *grind an axe*. **3a** to rub, press, or twist (something) harshly: *He ground his fist into his opponent's stomach*. **b** to press (things) together with a rotating motion: *grind the teeth*. **4** to operate or produce (something) by turning a crank: *grind a hand organ*. ⟫ *verb intrans* **1** to perform the operation of grinding. **2** to become pulverized, polished, or sharpened by friction. **3** to move with difficulty or friction, *esp* so as to make a grating noise: *grinding gears*. **4** (*often* + away) to work monotonously, *esp* to study hard: *She's grinding away at her history*. **5** to rotate the hips in an erotic manner. **6** in skateboarding, in-line skating etc, to slide along a surface or rail rather than on the wheels, e.g. on the edge of a skate. ✳ **grind to a halt** to stop in a noisy, jarring, or disconcerting way. ⟫⟫ **grindingly** *adv*. [Old English *grindan*]

grind² *noun* **1** dreary monotonous labour or routine. **2** a particular degree of fineness of grinding. **3a** the act of rotating the hips in an erotic manner: compare BUMP². **b** *Brit, dated coarse slang* an act of sexual intercourse. **4** *chiefly NAmer, informal* a swot.

grind down *verb trans* to subject (someone) to domineering treatment; to oppress (them).

grinder *noun* **1** a machine for sharpening tools by means of an abrasive revolving wheel; a grindstone. **2** a molar tooth.

grind out *verb trans derog* to produce (something, *esp* something of inferior quality) in a mechanical way: *grinding out potboilers*.

grindstone *noun* **1** = MILLSTONE (1). **2** a flat circular stone that revolves on an axle and is used for grinding, shaping, etc.

gringo /'gringgoh/ *noun* (*pl* **gringos**) an English-speaking foreigner in Spain or Latin America. [Spanish *gringo*, prob alteration of *griego* Greek, stranger, from Latin *Graecus*: see GREEK¹]

grip¹ /grip/ *verb* (**gripped, gripping**) ⟫ *verb trans* **1** to seize or hold (something) firmly. **2** to attract and hold the interest of (somebody): *It's a story that really grips the reader*. ⟫ *verb intrans* to take firm hold. ⟫⟫ **gripper** *noun*, **grippingly** *adv*. [Old English *grippan*]

grip² *noun* **1a** a strong or tenacious grasp. **b** a particular manner or style of gripping. **2a** control, mastery, or power: *He kept a good grip on his pupils*. **b** understanding or the ability to understand: *She has a good grip of the situation*. **3** a part or device that grips: *a hair grip*. **4** a part by which something is grasped, *esp* a handle. **5** somebody who handles scenery, props, lighting, or camera equipment in a theatre or film or television studio. **6** a travelling bag; a holdall. ✳ **come/get to grips with 1** to set about dealing with a problem or situation. **2** to grapple or wrestle with somebody. **get a grip** *informal* to pull oneself together: *But if the Prime Minister does not get a grip soon … there is no alternative but for him to go — Liverpool Daily Post*. **get a grip on** to take control of a situation. **lose one's grip** to be unable any longer to deal with things effectively.

gripe¹ /griep/ *verb intrans* **1** to experience sharp intestinal pains. **2** *informal* to complain persistently. ⟫ *verb trans* to cause (somebody) to feel sharp intestinal pain. ⟫⟫ **griper** *noun*. [Old English *grīpan* to grasp, seize]

gripe² *noun* **1** (*usu in pl*) a stabbing spasmodic intestinal pain. **2** *informal* a grievance or complaint, *esp* one regarded as unjustified. **3** *archaic* grasp or grip: *Just one glance and down you grovel, hand and foot in Belial's gripe — Browning*.

gripe water *noun* a liquid preparation given to babies to aid digestion.

grippe /grip/ *noun dated* influenza. ⟫⟫ **grippy** *adj*. [French *grippe*, from *gripper* to seize, of Germanic origin]

grisaille /gri'zayl (*French* grizaj)/ *noun* **1a** a method of decorative painting in tones of grey, designed to produce a three-dimensional effect. **b** a painting done using this method. **2** grey-coloured, patterned stained glass. [French *grisaille*, from *gris*: see GRIZZLED]

griseofulvin /ˌgrizioh'foolvin, -'fulvin/ *noun* an antibiotic given orally to treat fungal infections, *esp* of the hair and skin. [from *Penicillium griseofulvum*, the mould from which it is obtained]

grisette /gri'zet/ *noun dated* a young French working-class woman. [French *grisette* (dress made of) cheap grey cloth, from *gris*: see GRIZZLED]

gris-gris *or* **gri-gri** *or* **greegree** /'gree gree/ *noun* (*pl* **gris-gris** *or* **gri-gris** *or* **greegrees** /'gree greez/) an African amulet or spell. [French *gris-gris*, of African origin]

grisly /'grizli/ *adj* (**grislier, grisliest**) inspiring horror, intense fear, or disgust; forbidding: *houses that were dark and grisly under the blank, cold sky* — D H Lawrence. ⋙ **grisliness** *noun*. [Old English *grislic*]

grison /'gries(ə)n, 'griz(ə)n/ *noun* either of two species of S American carnivorous mammals that resemble large weasels: genus *Galictis*. [French *grison* grey, from *gris*: see GRIZZLED]

grissini /gri'seeni/ *pl noun* thin, Italian-style breadsticks.

grist /grist/ *noun* **1a** grain for grinding. **b** a batch of grain ground at one time. **2** crushed malt used to make a brewing mash. ✲ **grist to the mill** something that can be put to use or profit. [Old English *grist*, related to Old English *grindan* GRIND¹]

gristle /'grisl/ *noun* cartilage, *esp* tough cartilaginous or fibrous matter in cooked meat. ⋙ **gristliness** *noun*, **gristly** *adj*. [Old English]

grit¹ /grit/ *noun* **1** small hard particles of stone or coarse sand, often used as a road surface or, mixed with salt, as a means of making icy roads manageable. **2** the structure or texture of a stone that adapts it to grinding. **3** *informal* firmness of mind or spirit; determination. [Old English *grēot*]

grit² *verb* (**gritted, gritting**) ➤ *verb trans* **1** to cover or spread (*esp* a road surface) with grit. **2** to clench (one's teeth) as a sign of determination or stoical firmness. ➤ *verb intrans* to produce a grating sound.

grits *pl noun* (*treated as sing. or pl*) **1** grain, *esp* oats, husked and usu coarsely ground. **2** *NAmer* coarsely ground maize with the husks removed, boiled with water or milk and eaten as a breakfast dish, usu with butter. [Old English *grytt* bran, chaff]

gritty *adj* (**grittier, grittiest**) **1** courageously persistent or determined. **2** not flinching from dealing with unpleasantness; uncompromising: *gritty realism*. ⋙ **grittily** *adv*, **grittiness** *noun*.

grizzle /'grizl/ *verb intrans informal* **1** *Brit, dated* said of a child: to cry quietly and fretfully. **2** (*often* + about) to complain in a self-pitying way. [origin unknown]

grizzled *adj* sprinkled or streaked with grey: *a grizzled beard*. [Middle English *griseled* from early French *gris, grisel* grey, of Germanic origin]

grizzly¹ *adj* (**grizzlier, grizzliest**) streaked with grey; grizzled. [Middle English *grisel* grey, from early French *grisel*: see GRIZZLED]

grizzly² *noun* (*pl* **grizzlies**) a very large bear that lives in the highlands of western N America and has brownish fur streaked with white on its back. [from GRIZZLY¹, from the grey or white tips of its fur]

grizzly bear *noun* = GRIZZLY².

Gro. *abbr* in street names, grove.

gro. *abbr* gross.

groan¹ /grohn/ *verb intrans* **1** to utter a deep moan. **2** to creak under strain: *The boards groaned under our weight*. ➤ *verb trans* to say (something) with a groan. ⋙ **groaner** *noun*. [Old English *grānian*]

groan² *noun* **1** a deep moaning sound. **2** a creaking sound.

groat /groht/ *noun* a former British coin worth four old pence. [Middle English *groot*, from early Dutch *groot* or early Low German *grote* thick, thick penny: compare GROSCHEN, GROSZ]

groats *pl noun* hulled grain broken into fragments larger than grits. [Old English *grotan*]

grocer /'grohsə/ *noun* a dealer in staple foodstuffs, household supplies, and usu fruit, vegetables, and dairy products. [Middle English from early French *grossier* wholesaler, from *gros* coarse, wholesale, from Latin *grossus* GROSS¹]

groceries /'grohs(ə)riz/ *pl noun* foodstuffs and other general items sold by a grocer.

grocery /'grohs(ə)ri/ *noun* a grocer's shop.

grockle /'grok(ə)l/ *noun Brit, informal, derog* a tourist or other visitor to the West Country of England, as viewed disparagingly by the locals.

grog /grog/ *noun* **1** an alcoholic spirit, usu rum, mixed with water, *esp* as a sailor's traditional drink. **2** *informal* alcohol in general, *esp* spirits. [from *Old Grog*, nickname of Edward Vernon d.1757,

English admiral responsible for diluting the sailors' rum; the nickname came from the grogram coat he usu wore]

groggy /'grogi/ *adj* (**groggier, groggiest**) weak and dazed, *esp* owing to illness or tiredness. ⋙ **groggily** *adv*, **grogginess** *noun*.

grogram /'grogrəm/ *noun* a coarse loosely woven fabric of silk, silk and mohair, or silk and wool: compare GROSGRAIN. [early French *gros grain* coarse texture; compare FINGERING²]

groin /groyn/ *noun* **1a** the fold marking the join between the lower abdomen and the inner part of the thigh. **b** *euphem* the male genitals. **2** the line along which two intersecting vaults meet in a vaulted roof or ceiling. **3** *chiefly NAmer* = GROYNE. [Old English *grynde* abyss; related to Old English *grund* GROUND¹]

grommet /'gromit/ *noun* **1** an eyelet of firm material to strengthen or protect an opening, e.g. a hole that rope or cable passes through. **2** a small plastic tube inserted in the ear to drain off fluid, e.g. in glue ear and other medical conditions. [perhaps from obsolete French *gormette* curb of a bridle]

gromwell /'gromwəl/ *noun* any of several species of hard-seeded plants of the borage family with white or blue flowers: genus *Lithospermum*. [Middle English *gromil*, from early French]

groom¹ /groohm/ *noun* **1** somebody who is in charge of the feeding, care, and stabling of horses. **2** a bridegroom. **3** *archaic* a manservant. [Middle English *grom* boy, man, manservant]

groom² *verb trans* **1** to clean and care for (e.g. a horse). **2** to make (oneself or one's clothes or appearance) neat or attractive: *an impeccably groomed woman*. **3** to get (somebody) ready for a specific role or task; to prepare (them): *She was being groomed as a Tory candidate*. **4** said of a paedophile: to develop a friendship with (a child) in order to entice them into a sexual relationship. ➤ *verb intrans* to groom oneself. ⋙ **groomer** *noun*, **grooming** *noun*.

groomsman *noun* (*pl* **groomsmen**) a male friend who attends a bridegroom at his wedding.

groove¹ /groohv/ *noun* **1a** a long narrow channel or depression, e.g. one cut into a length of wood. **b** the continuous spiral track on a record, whose irregularities correspond to the recorded sounds. **2** a fixed routine; a rut. **3** *informal* the state of performing at one's peak; top form: *He's a great talker when he is in the groove*. **4** *dated, informal* an enjoyable or exciting experience. [Middle English *groof* mine, mineshaft, from Dutch *groeve* pit; related to Old English *grafan* GRAVE³]

groove² *verb trans* **1** to make a groove in (something, e.g. a length of wood). **2** *dated, informal* to excite (someone). ➤ *verb intrans* **1** to form a groove. **2** *dated, informal*. **a** to enjoy oneself. **b** to get on well together. ⋙ **groover** *noun*.

groovy *adj* (**groovier, grooviest**) *informal* **1** *dated* fashionably attractive or exciting. **2** laughably outdated.

grope¹ /grohp/ *verb intrans* **1** to feel about blindly or uncertainly with the hands. **2** to search blindly or uncertainly: *I was groping for the right words*. ➤ *verb trans* **1** to touch or fondle the body of (a person) for sexual pleasure. **2** to find (e.g. one's way) by groping. ⋙ **groper** *noun*. [Old English *grāpian*; related to Old English *grīpan* GRIPE¹]

grope² *noun* **1** a feeling around blindly. **2** a fondling of somebody, or a session of mutual fondling.

groper /'grohpə/ *noun* = GROUPER.

grosbeak /'grohsbeek/ *noun* any of several species of finches or songbirds of Europe or America that have large thick conical beaks: families Fringillidae and Emberizidae. [partial translation of French *grosbec*, from *gros* thick + *bec* BEAK]

groschen /'grohsh(ə)n/ *noun* (*pl* **groschen**) **1** a former unit of currency in Austria, worth 100th of a schilling (up to the introduction of the euro in 2002). **2** a German coin worth ten pfennigs. [German *Groschen*, ultimately from medieval Latin *denarius grossus* thick penny: compare GROAT, GROSZ]

grosgrain /'grohgrayn/ *noun* a strong closely woven corded fabric, usu of silk or rayon and with crosswise ribs: compare GROGRAM. [French *gros grain* coarse texture]

gros point /'groh poynt/ *noun* **1** a large cross-stitch or tent stitch. **2** needlepoint embroidery worked on canvas across double threads in gros point: compare NEEDLEPOINT, PETIT POINT. [French *gros point* large point]

gross¹ /grohs/ *adj* **1** glaringly noticeable, usu because excessively bad or objectionable; flagrant: *gross error*. **2a** constituting an overall total before deductions (e.g. for taxes) are made: compare NET³:

gross income. **b** said of weight: including both the object in question and any incidentals, e.g. the container and packaging or, in the case of a vehicle, the load. **3** coarse or vulgar: *crowflowers, nettles, daisies, and long purples, that liberal shepherds give a grosser name* — Shakespeare. **4** *informal* disgustingly unpleasant; repulsive. **5a** big or bulky, *esp* excessively overweight. **b** said of vegetation: dense or luxuriant. **6** *archaic* made up of material or perceptible elements; corporal: *the grosser part of human nature.* ⫸ **grossly** *adv*, **grossness** *noun*. [Middle English via early French *gros* thick, coarse, from Latin *grossus*]

gross² *noun* an overall total exclusive of deductions.

gross³ *verb trans* **1** to earn or bring in (an overall total) exclusive of deductions. **2** *informal* (+ out) to make (somebody) feel disgusted or repelled. ⫸ **grosser** *noun*.

gross⁴ *noun* (*pl* **gross**) a group of twelve dozen things: *a gross of pencils.* [Middle English *groce* from early French *grosse*, fem of *gros*: see GROSS¹]

gross domestic product *noun* the total value of the goods and services produced in a country during a specified period, usu a year, excluding income from possessions and investments abroad: compare GROSS NATIONAL PRODUCT.

gross national product *noun* the total value of the goods and services produced in a country during a specified period, usu a year: compare GROSS DOMESTIC PRODUCT.

grosso modo /ˌgrosoh ˈmohdoh/ *adv formal* as an approximation; roughly. [Italian *grosso modo*]

gross ton *noun* a unit of capacity, e.g. of a merchant ship, equal to 100ft³ (about 2.83m³).

grosz /grosh/ *noun* (*pl* **groszy**) a unit of currency in Poland, worth 100th of a zloty. [Polish *grosz* from medieval Latin *denarius grossus*: compare GROAT, GROSCHEN]

grot¹ /grot/ *noun informal* something unpleasant, *esp* dirt. [back-formation from GROTTY]

grot² *noun archaic, literary* = GROTTO.

grotesque¹ /grohˈtesk, grəˈtesk/ *adj* **1** amusingly or repellently unnatural in appearance, usu tending towards ugliness. **2** absurdly incongruous or inappropriate. **3** of the grotesque style in art. ⫸ **grotesquely** *adv*, **grotesqueness** *noun*.

Word history

early French *crotesque* from Old Italian *pittura grottesca*, literally 'cave painting', from *grotta*: see GROTTO. *Grotta* in this case prob referred to excavated Roman buildings which had paintings in the grotesque style.

grotesque² *noun* **1** a style of decorative art in which incongruous or fantastic human and animal forms are interwoven with natural motifs (e.g. foliage). **2** somebody who is grotesque in appearance: *All who have passed the age of thirty are joyless grotesques … staying alive without, so far as the child can see, having anything to live for* — George Orwell. **3** a family of 19th-cent. sans serif typefaces.

grotesquerie *or* **grotesquery** *noun* (*pl* **grotesqueries**) **1** something grotesque. **2** the quality of being grotesque; grotesqueness.

grotto /ˈgrotoh/ *noun* (*pl* **grottoes** *or* **grottos**) **1** a small cave, *esp* one in a picturesque setting. **2** an excavation or structure made to resemble a natural cave. [Italian *grotta, grotto* from Latin *crypta* cavern: see CRYPT]

grotty /ˈgroti/ *adj* (**grottier, grottiest**) *Brit, informal* **1** unpleasant in some way; nasty. **2** cheaply made or of poor quality generally. **3** not healthy; unwell. ⫸ **grottily** *adv*. [by shortening and alteration from GROTESQUE¹]

grouch¹ /growch/ *noun* **1** a bad-tempered complaint. **2** a habitually irritable or complaining person; a grumbler. ⫸ **grouchy** *adj*. [prob alteration of *grutch* grudge, from Old French *groucier*: see GRUDGE¹]

grouch² *verb* to complain annoyingly or habitually.

ground¹ /grownd/ *noun* **1a** the surface of the earth. **b** soil or earth. **2** land or an area of land of a particular type: *high ground; marshy ground.* **3** an area of land used for a particular purpose: *parade ground; football ground.* **4** (*in pl*) the area around and belonging to a house or other building. **5a** an area of knowledge or special interest: *She covered a lot of ground in her lecture.* **b** an area to be won or defended in or as if in battle. **6** (*also in pl*) a basis for belief, action, or argument: *grounds for complaint.* **7a** a surrounding area; a background. **b** a prepared underlying surface on which something (e.g. paint or a road) is to be added or applied. **8** (*in pl*) ground coffee beans after brewing. **9** the bottom of a body of water; the bed. **10**

NAmer an electrical earth. ✳ **cut the ground from under somebody's feet** to do something that makes somebody's actions or arguments unnecessary or superfluous. **gain ground** to become more popular or widely accepted. **gain ground on** to begin to catch up on or overtake. **give ground** to withdraw before superior force; to retreat. **go to ground 1** to go into hiding. **2** said of a fox: to enter its burrow. **lose ground** to fall behind in a contest of some kind or become less popular or widely accepted. **off the ground** started and in progress: *The programme never got off the ground.* **on the ground** in the area or at the level where practical work takes place and from which those who manage or theorize are remote. **run into the ground** to tire out or use up with heavy work. [Old English *grund*]

ground² *verb trans* **1** to bring (something) to or place (something) on the ground. **2a** (*usu in passive*) to provide a reason or justification for (something). **b** to instruct (somebody) in the fundamentals, e.g. of a subject. **3a** to forbid (a pilot or aircraft) to fly. **b** *informal* to give (a child) the punishment of having to stay indoors. **4** *NAmer* to earth (an electrical appliance). ⫸ *verb intrans* said of a ship: to run aground.

ground³ *verb* past tense and past part. of GRIND¹.

groundbait *noun* bait scattered on the water so as to attract fish.

ground bass /bays/ *noun* in music, a short bass passage continually repeated below constantly changing melody and harmony.

ground-breaking *adj* introducing entirely new developments or methods; pioneering: *Beatty sealed his reputation by funding a ground-breaking movie where the violence is shockingly off-hand* — New Musical Express.

ground control *noun* **1** (taking *sing*. or *pl verb*) the machinery (e.g. computers) and operators that control or communicate with aircraft from the ground. **2** a system for directing from the ground the landing of an aircraft whose vision is obscured.

ground cover *noun* low-growing plants that grow in a spreading fashion and are often planted to help suppress weeds.

ground effect *noun* **1** an aircraft's gaining of added buoyancy when close to the ground. **2** a similar but intentionally produced effect (e.g. in a hovercraft). ⫸ **ground-effect** *adj*.

ground elder *noun* a coarse European plant of the carrot family that has creeping white underground stems and is commonly found growing as a weed on cultivated ground: *Aegopodium podagraria.*

ground floor *noun* the floor of a house on a level with the ground. ✳ **get in on the ground floor** to be involved in an enterprise, *esp* a profitable scheme, at the outset.

ground frost *noun* a temperature below freezing on the ground, harmful to low-growing vegetation.

ground glass *noun* **1** glass that is translucent but not transparent through having a light-diffusing surface produced by etching or grinding. **2** glass ground into a powder, for use as a coating on abrasives.

groundhog *noun NAmer* a small N American marmot; a woodchuck.

grounding *noun* fundamental training in a field of knowledge.

ground ivy *noun* a trailing plant of the mint family with bluish purple flowers: *Glechoma hederacea.*

groundless *adj* having no basis in fact or reason; unjustified: *groundless fears.* ⫸ **groundlessly** *adv*, **groundlessness** *noun*.

groundling /ˈgrowndling/ *noun* **1a** a spectator who stood in the pit of an Elizabethan theatre: *O, it offends me to the soul to hear … a fellow tear a passion to tatters, to very rags, to split the ears of the groundlings* — Shakespeare. **b** somebody regarded as being of low status. **2** an animal or plant that stays or grows close to the ground, or a fish that lives on or near the bottom of the water. **3** a person who works on the ground as opposed to in the air or on water.

groundnut *noun* **1a** a N American leguminous plant with an edible tuberous root: *Apios tuberosa.* **b** the tuber produced by this plant. **2** *chiefly Brit* = PEANUT.

ground pine *noun* **1** a European yellow-flowered plant of the mint family with a resinous smell: *Ajuga chamaepitys.* **2** any of several species of N American club mosses with long creeping stems: genus *Lycopodium.*

ground plan *noun* **1** a plan of the ground floor of a building. **2** a first or basic plan.

ground rent *noun* the rent paid by the owner of a building to the owner of the land that it is built on.

ground rule *noun* a basic rule of procedure.

groundsel /'grown(d)zl, 'grown(d)sl/ *noun* any of several species of European plant of the daisy family that are common weeds and have small yellow flower heads: genus *Senecio*. [Old English *grundeswelge*, from *grund* GROUND[1] + *swelgan* SWALLOW[2]]

groundsheet *noun* a waterproof sheet placed on the ground (e.g. in a tent).

groundsman *noun* (*pl* **groundsmen**) somebody who tends a playing field, *esp* a cricket pitch.

ground speed *noun* the speed of an aircraft relative to the ground.

ground squirrel *noun* any of several genera of burrowing N American rodents including the chipmunk and the suslik: genus *Spermophilus* and other genera.

groundstaff *noun* the people who maintain a sports ground.

ground state *noun* the lowest possible energy level of a system of interacting elementary particles.

ground stroke *noun* a stroke made (e.g. in tennis) by hitting a ball that has rebounded from the ground: compare VOLLEY[1].

groundswell /'growndswel/ *noun* **1** a sea swell caused by an often distant gale or ground tremor. **2** a rapid and spontaneous build-up of public opinion.

groundwater *noun* underground water that supplies wells and springs, *esp* water that has saturated surface soil and rocks.

groundwork *noun* work done to provide a foundation or basis.

ground zero *noun* **1** the point on the surface of the earth at or directly below or above the centre of a nuclear explosion. **2** (*often* **Ground Zero**) *chiefly NAmer* the site of a destroyed building, *esp* the former World Trade Centre in New York, destroyed in a terrorist attack on 11 September 2001.

group[1] /groohp/ *noun* **1** (*treated as sing. or pl*) a number of people or things gathered together or regarded as forming a single unit. **2** a small band of musicians, *esp* playing pop music. **3** an operational and administrative unit in an air force consisting of two or more squadrons. **4** two or more figures or objects forming a distinct unit in a painting or other artistic work. **5** a number of business companies under the ultimate ownership of a single individual or association. **6a** an assemblage of atoms forming part of a molecule; a radical: *a methyl group*. **b** all the chemical elements forming one of the vertical columns of the periodic table. **7** a mathematical set that is closed under a binary associative operation, has an identity element, and has an inverse for every element. [French *groupe* from Italian *gruppo*, of Germanic origin]

group[2] *verb trans* **1** to combine (people or things) in a group. **2** (*often* + under/with) to assign (somebody or something) to a group; to classify (them). ➤ *verb intrans* to form or belong to a group. ➤➤ **groupable** *adj*.

group captain *noun* in the RAF and some other air forces, an officer who is senior to a wing commander and junior to an air commodore.

group dynamics *pl noun* the relationships that exist or establish themselves between individuals in a group, or the processes involved in the formation of these relationships.

grouper *noun* (*pl* **groupers** *or collectively* **grouper**) any of numerous species of large fishes of the sea bass family, found in tropical seas: genera *Epinephelus*, *Mycteroperca*, and other genera. [Portuguese *garoupa*]

groupie /'groohpi/ *noun* an ardent female fan of a famous person, *esp* a rock star, who follows the object of admiration on tour, *esp* in the hope of striking up a sexual relationship with them. [GROUP[1] (2) + -IE]

grouping *noun* a set of individuals or objects combined in a group.

group practice *noun* a medical practice run by a group of associated general practitioners.

group therapy *noun* the treatment of several individuals with similar psychological problems simultaneously through group discussion and mutual aid.

groupuscule /'groohpəskyoohl/ *noun* a small group that forms a faction; a splinter group. [French *groupuscule*, dimin. of *groupe*: see GROUP[1]]

groupware *noun* computer software that enables a network of users (e.g. within an organization) to share information and other resources.

grouse[1] /grows/ *noun* (*pl* **grouse**) any of several species of birds with a plump body and strong feathered legs, *esp* the red grouse, which is a popular game bird: genus *Lagopus*. [origin unknown]

grouse[2] *verb intrans informal* to complain, *esp* annoyingly or without reason; to grumble. ➤➤ **grouser** *noun*. [perhaps from Old French *groucier*: see GRUDGE[1]]

grouse[3] *noun informal* a complaint.

grouse[4] *adj Aus, NZ, informal* excellent or attractive. [origin unknown]

grout[1] /growt/ *noun* **1a** (*also* **grouting**) a thin mortar used for filling spaces, *esp* the gaps between wall or floor tiles. **b** plaster that can be applied to the outside of buildings or as a thin finishing coat on ceilings. **2** (*usu in pl*) sediment of any kind at the bottom of a container. [Old English *grūt* coarse meal]

grout[2] *verb trans* to fill up the spaces between (tiles) with grout. ➤➤ **grouter** *noun*.

grove /grohv/ *noun* a small wood, group, or planting of trees. [Old English *grāf*]

grovel /'grovl/ *verb intrans* (**grovelled, grovelling,** *NAmer* **groveled, groveling**) **1** to lie or creep with the body prostrate to show subservience or abasement. **2** to abase or humble oneself, e.g. in order to earn forgiveness or favour. ➤➤ **groveller** *noun*, **grovellingly** *adv*. [back-formation from obsolete *groveling* prone, from Middle English *on gruf* on the face, from Old Norse *á grúfu*]

grow /groh/ *verb* (*past tense* **grew** /grooh/, *past part.* **grown** /grohn/) ➤ *verb intrans* **1a** said of an organism: to increase in size and develop to maturity. **b** to take on a particular appearance or assume a particular position through a process of natural growth: *two tree trunks grown together*. **2a** to increase in size by the addition of new parts or elements: *The business just grew and grew*. **b** to increase or expand: *Her confidence grew daily*. **3** (+ from/out of) to develop from a parent source: *The book grew out of a series of lectures*. **4** to become gradually: *She grew pale*. ➤ *verb trans* **1** to cause (a plant or the fruit or vegetables it yields) to grow; to cultivate (them): *He grows roses*. **2** to develop (something) as a natural product of growing: *They don't start to grow wings until several weeks later*. **3** to cause (something, e.g. a business) to increase in size or expand. ➤➤ **grower** *noun*, **growingly** *adv*. [Old English *grōwan*]

growbag *noun* a large bag of compost designed to be laid flat and used as a container for planting.

growing pains *pl noun* **1** pains felt in the muscles and joints of growing children, *esp* in the legs, that have no known cause. **2** the problems that are commonly experienced in the early stages of a new project or development.

grow into *verb trans* **1** to become big enough to fit (something, *esp* a piece of clothing) that is currently too large. **2** to become mature or skilled enough to deal with (something, e.g. a job) successfully.

growl[1] /growl/ *verb intrans* **1a** to utter a deep sound in the throat that expresses hostility. **b** to speak in an angry or hostile way. **2** to make a continuous low sound that suggests hostility or impending doom: *Thunder growled in the dark sky*. ➤ *verb trans* to say (something) in an angry or hostile way. [prob imitative]

growl[2] *noun* a growling sound or way of talking.

growler *noun* **1** a small iceberg. **2** *archaic* a four-wheeled hansom cab.

grown[1] /grohn/ *adj* fully developed; mature: *grown men*.

grown[2] *verb past part.* of GROW.

grown-up *adj* fully mature; adult. ➤➤ **grown-up** *noun*.

grow on *verb trans* **1** to become gradually more pleasing or likeable to (somebody). **2** to become gradually more apparent to (somebody): *The feeling's been growing on me that we aren't particularly welcome here*.

grow out of *verb trans* **1** to become too big to fit in (something, *esp* a piece of clothing). **2** to become too mature or too accomplished to get enjoyment or satisfaction from (something).

growth /grohth/ *noun* **1a** the process of growing. **b** progressive development. **2a** an increase or expansion. **b** the degree to which something has grown or increased. **3a** something that grows or has grown. **b** a tumour or other abnormal growth of tissue.

growth factor *noun* a substance stimulating a cell to divide, move, differentiate, or continue living.

growth hormone *noun* 1 a polypeptide growth-regulating hormone of vertebrates that is secreted by the front lobe of the pituitary gland. 2 any of various plant substances (e.g. an auxin or gibberellin) that promote growth.

growth ring *noun* a layer of wood, shell, etc produced by a plant or animal during a particular period of growth.

grow up *verb intrans* 1 said of a person: to develop towards or arrive at a mature state. 2 to arise and develop: *The movement grew up in the 60s.* 3 (*usu in imperative*) to begin to act sensibly.

groyne (*NAmer* **groin**) /groyn/ *noun* a rigid wall-like structure built out from a shore, *esp* to check erosion of the beach; a breakwater. [alteration of obsolete *groin* snout, via Old French from late Latin *grunium* pig's snout, from Latin *grunnire* to grunt]

GRP *abbr* glass-reinforced plastic.

grub[1] /grub/ *verb* (**grubbed, grubbing**) ➤ *verb intrans* 1 to dig in the ground, *esp* for something that is difficult to find or extract. 2 to search about; to rummage. 3 to do hard, boring, or demeaning work in an effort to achieve something. ➤ *verb trans* 1 (*usu* + up) to dig (something) up or out by, or as if by, the roots. 2 to clear (an area) by digging up roots and stumps. ➤➤ **grubber** *noun*. [Middle English *grubben*, of Germanic origin]

grub[2] *noun* 1 a soft thick wormlike larva of an insect. 2 *informal* food. [Middle English *grubbe*, prob from *grubben* GRUB[1]]

grubby *adj* (**grubbier, grubbiest**) 1 unpleasantly or extremely dirty; grimy: *grubby hands*. 2 disreputable or sordid: *I'm not interested in your grubby little schemes.* ➤➤ **grubbily** *adv*, **grubbiness** *noun*.

grub-screw *noun* a headless screw-bolt.

grubstake[1] *noun* *NAmer* 1 supplies or funds given to a mining prospector in return for a share in his or her discoveries. 2 any material assistance provided to an organization or individual. [GRUB[2] + STAKE[1]]

grubstake[2] *verb trans* *NAmer* to provide (somebody) with a grubstake. ➤➤ **grubstaker** *noun*.

Grub Street *noun* the world or lifestyle of struggling journalists and literary hacks. [*Grub Street*, London, formerly inhabited by literary hacks]

grudge[1] /gruj/ *verb trans* 1 to be unwilling or reluctant to give or admit (something); to begrudge (it): *She grudged the money they took in taxes.* 2 to feel resentful towards (somebody) who has something that you are envious of: *I don't grudge him his success.* ➤➤ **grudger** *noun*. [Middle English *grucchen, grudgen* to grumble, complain, from Old French *groucier*, of Germanic origin]

grudge[2] *noun* a feeling of deep-seated resentment or ill will.

grudging *adj* offered or given only unwillingly; reluctant. ➤➤ **grudgingly** *adv*.

gruel /'grooh·əl/ *noun* thin porridge. [Middle English *grewel* from early French *gruel*, of Germanic origin; related to Old English *grūt* GROUT[1]]

gruelling (*NAmer* **grueling**) *adj* trying or taxing to the point of causing exhaustion; punishing: *a gruelling race*. [present part. of obsolete *gruel* to punish, from the phrase *get one's gruel* get one's punishment]

gruesome /'groohs(ə)m/ *adj* inspiring horror or repulsion; ghastly: *gruesome scenes of torture*. ➤➤ **gruesomely** *adv*, **gruesomeness** *noun*. [alteration of *growsome* (from English dialect *grow, grue* to shiver, prob from early Dutch *grūwen*) + -SOME[1]]

gruff /gruf/ *adj* 1 brusque or stern in manner or speech: *a gruff reply*. 2 deep and harsh: *a gruff voice*. ➤➤ **gruffly** *adv*, **gruffness** *noun*. [Dutch *grof* rough, harsh]

grumble[1] /'grumbl/ *verb intrans* 1 to mutter discontentedly or in complaint. 2 to rumble. ➤ *verb trans* to express (something) in a moaning or discontented way. ➤➤ **grumbler** *noun*, **grumblingly** *adv*, **grumbly** *adj*. [prob from early French *grommeler*, derivative of early Dutch *grommen*]

grumble[2] *noun* 1 the sound of grumbling. 2 a complaint or cause of complaint.

grumbling *adj* causing intermittent pain or discomfort: *a grumbling appendix*.

grummet /'grumit/ *noun* = GROMMET.

grump[1] /grump/ *noun* 1 (*usu in pl*) a fit of ill humour or sulkiness. 2 a grumpy person. [obsolete *grumps* snubs, slights, prob of imitative origin]

grump[2] *verb intrans* to be bad-tempered or show one's displeasure by grumbling and being unsociable; to sulk.

grumpy *adj* (**grumpier, grumpiest**) moodily cross; surly. ➤➤ **grumpily** *adv*, **grumpiness** *noun*.

Grundyism /'grundiiz(ə)m/ *noun* excessive attachment to conventional standards, *esp* in sexual matters; prudery.

Word history
named after *Mrs Grundy*, a character frequently alluded to in the play *Speed the Plough* by Thomas Morton d.1838, English lawyer and playwright. The phrase 'What would Mrs Grundy say?' became a popular catchphrase, used to refer to something slightly shocking.

grunge /grunj/ *noun* 1 *informal* dirt. 2 a style of rock music that developed in North America in the 1980s and features markedly discordant guitar and a sneering and listless vocal style. 3 a fashion style in which layers of clothing give a deliberately careless and uncoordinated appearance. [back-formation from GRUNGY]

grungy *adj* (**grungier, grungiest**) 1 *informal* dilapidated, dirty, or sordid. 2 typical of grunge music or the grunge fashion style. [perhaps a blend of GRUBBY and DINGY]

grunion /'grunyən/ *noun* a small marine fish found off the coast of California, where it comes ashore in large numbers to spawn: *Leuresthes tenuis*. [prob from Spanish *gruñón* grunter]

grunt[1] /grunt/ *verb intrans* 1 to utter the deep short guttural sound typical of a pig. 2 to utter a similar sound when suffering from the effects of exertion. ➤ *verb trans* to say (something) with a deep voice and in a muted way that suggest irritation, disgust, or unwillingness to speak openly. ➤➤ **grunter** *noun*. [Old English *grunnettan*, frequentative of *grunian*, of imitative origin]

grunt[2] *noun* 1 the deep short guttural sound of a pig. 2 a muted speech sound that expresses irritation, disgust, or reserve. 3 a low sound produced as a result of exertion. 4 *NAmer, informal*. **a** an infantryman in the US Army or Marines. **b** a person who does unskilled or routine work. 5 a tropical seafish that makes a grunting sound when taken out of the water: family Pomadasyidae.

gruntled /'gruntld/ *adj informal* made contented or satisfied: *I could see that, if not exactly disgruntled, he was far from being gruntled* — P G Wodehouse. [back-formation from DISGRUNTLED]

grutten /'grutn/ *verb* past part. of GREET[2].

Gruyère /'groohyeə (*French* gryjɛːr)/ *noun* a Swiss cheese with smaller holes and a slightly fuller flavour than Emmenthal. [named after *Gruyère*, district of Switzerland where it was orig made]

gr wt *abbr* gross weight.

gryke /griek/ *noun* = GRIKE.

gryphon /'grifən/ *noun* see GRIFFIN.

grysbok /'griesbok/ *noun* either of two species of small SW African antelopes with small erect horns, seen mainly at night: genus *Raphicerus*. [Afrikaans *grysbok* grey buck]

GS *abbr* 1 General Secretary. 2 General Staff.

Gs *abbr* gauss.

GSM *abbr* 1 Global System for Mobile Communications, an international digital mobile telephone system. 2 Global Standard for Mobile Communications.

GSOH *abbr* good sense of humour.

G spot *noun* a small area near the front of the vagina that is highly erogenous in some women. [shortening of *Grafenberg spot*, named after Ernst *Grafenberg* d.1957, German gynaecologst who identified it]

G-string *noun* a small piece of cloth, leather, etc covering the genitalia and held in place by thongs, elastic, etc passed round the hips and between the buttocks. [origin unknown]

G suit *noun* a suit designed to counteract the physiological effects of high acceleration in an aircraft or spacecraft. [short for *gravity suit*]

GSVQ *abbr* General Scottish Vocational Qualification.

GT *abbr* grand tourer or gran turismo, denoting a saloon car with a sporty appearance and performance but enough comfort to make it suitable for long journeys.

gt *abbr* great.

gtd *abbr* guaranteed.

guacamole /gwahkə'mohli/ *noun* a dip or hors d'oeuvre made of seasoned avocado, mashed or sieved with tomato and chilli. [Spanish *guacamole* from Nahuatl *ahuacamolli*, literally 'avocado sauce']

guaiac /'g(w)ieak/ *noun* the resin from the guaiacum tree; guaiacum. [Latin *Guaiacum*: see GUAIACUM]

guaiacum /'g(w)ie·əkəm/ *noun* 1 either of two species of tropical American and Caribbean trees that produce an oily greenish brown wood: genus *Guaiacum*. 2 the brownish resin produced by this tree, which has a faint balsamic smell and is used in varnishes. 3 the wood of this tree. [Latin genus name, via Spanish *guayaco* from Taino *guayacan*]

guanaco /gwah'nahkoh/ *noun* (*pl* **guanacos** *or collectively* **guanaco**) a S American mammal that has a soft thick fawn-coloured coat and resembles a llama: *Lama guanicoe*. [Spanish *guanaco* from Quechua *huanacu*]

guanine /'gwahneen/ *noun* a chemical compound that is one of the four bases whose order in a DNA or RNA chain codes genetic information: compare ADENINE, CYTOSINE, THYMINE, URACIL. [GUANO + -INE², from its being found *esp* in guano]

guano /'gwahnoh/ *noun* a phosphate-rich substance consisting chiefly of the excrement of seabirds and used as a fertilizer, or an artificial fertilizer that resembles it, usu made from fish. [Spanish *guano* from Quechua *huanu* dung]

guanosine /'gwahnəseen/ *noun* a NUCLEOSIDE (chemical compound found in DNA and RNA) containing guanine. [blend of GUANINE and RIBOSE]

guarani /gwahrə'nee/ *noun* 1 (**Guarani**) a member of a Native South American people inhabiting Bolivia, Paraguay, and S Brazil. 2 (**Guarani**) the language of the Guarani people. 3 the basic monetary unit of Paraguay, divided into 100 centimos. ⟩⟩ **guaranian** /-'nee·ən/ *noun and adj*. [Spanish *guaraní*]

guarantee¹ /garən'tee/ *noun* 1a an assurance of the quality of, or the length of use to be expected from, a product offered for sale, accompanied by a promise to replace the product or pay the customer back if it proves defective. b a certificate or document containing an assurance of this kind. 2 an agreement by which one person accepts responsibility for another's obligations, *esp* debts, in case of default. 3 a written undertaking to answer for the payment of a debt or the performance of a duty of another in case of the other's default. 4 somebody who offers a guarantee; a guarantor. 5 something given as security; a pledge. [prob alteration of GUARANTY]

guarantee² *verb trans* (**guaranteed, guaranteeing**) 1 to provide a guarantee of replacement, repayment, etc with respect to (a product sold or work carried out). 2a to undertake to do or secure (something): *She guaranteed delivery of the goods.* b to give an assurance relating to (something): *I can guarantee that he'll be there.* 3 to undertake to answer for the debt or default of (somebody).

guarantor /garən'taw/ *noun* somebody who makes or gives a guarantee.

guaranty /'garənti/ *noun* 1 = GUARANTEE¹ (3). 2 something offered as security by a person making a guaranty. 3 the act or an instance of pledging something as security. [early French *garantie*, from *garant* warrant, of Germanic origin: compare WARRANTY]

guard¹ /gahd/ *noun* 1 the act or duty of protecting or defending. 2a a person or group whose duty is to watch over and protect a place, people, etc. b a person or group whose duty is to control (somebody) or prevent (them) from escaping. 3 (*in pl*) = HOUSEHOLD TROOPS. 4 a protective or safety device, e.g. a device on a machine for protecting the operator against injury. 5a a defensive position in boxing, fencing, etc. b in cricket, the position of the batsman and his bat relative to the wicket he is defending when waiting to receive the ball. 6 a state of readiness to deal with or ward off adverse events: *You let your guard slip.* 7 *Brit* the person in charge of the carriages, wagons, and any passengers in a railway train. ✳ **be off (one's) guard** to be relaxed and unwary, unprepared to deal with a threat. **be on (one's) guard** to be alert and vigilant, ready to deal with a threat. **stand guard** to act as a guard or sentry. [Middle English *garde* from early French *garder* to guard, defend, of Germanic origin]

guard² *verb trans* 1 to protect (somebody or something) from danger, *esp* by watchful attention; to make (them) secure: *The duty of police officers is to guard our cities.* 2 to watch over (somebody or something) so as to prevent escape, entry, theft, etc. 3 to keep (something) in check; to restrain (it): *Guard your tongue.* 4 in

basketball, to remain close beside (an opponent) to prevent them receiving or passing the ball. ⟩ *verb intrans* to watch by way of caution or defence; stand guard. ✳ **guard against** to attempt to prevent (something) by taking precautions. ⟩⟩ **guarder** *noun*.

guard cell *noun* either of the two crescent-shaped cells that border and open and close a plant stoma.

guarded *adj* marked by caution: *a guarded reply*; *a guarded look*. ⟩⟩⟩ **guardedly** *adv*, **guardedness** *noun*.

guard hair *noun* any of the long coarse hairs forming a protective coating over the underfur of a mammal.

guardhouse /'gahdhows/ *noun* a building used by soldiers on guard duty or as a prison.

guardian /'gahdi·ən/ *noun* 1 somebody or something that guards or protects. 2 somebody who has the care of the person or property of another, *specif* somebody entrusted by law with the care of somebody who is of unsound mind, not of age, etc. ⟩⟩ **guardianship** *noun*.

guardian angel *noun* 1 somebody who is regarded as a person's special protector. 2 an angel who is thought to watch over a particular person.

guardrail *noun* a railing that protects people from falling from a high place.

guard ring *noun* 1 a ring worn to prevent another ring from slipping off one's finger. 2 a circular electrode used to limit or define the extent of a magnetic field.

guardroom *noun* a room serving as a guardhouse.

guardsman *noun* (*pl* **guardsmen**) a member of a military body called *guard* or *guards*, *esp* a soldier in the Household Troops in the British Army or a member of the US National Guard.

guard's van *noun Brit* a railway wagon or carriage attached usu at the rear of a train for the use of the guard.

Guatemalan /,gwahtə'mahlən/ *noun* a native or inhabitant of Guatemala. ⟩⟩ **Guatemalan** *adj*.

guava /'gwahvə/ *noun* 1 a sweet acid yellow edible fruit with pink aromatic flesh. 2 the tropical American tree that bears this fruit: genus *Psidium*. [modification of Spanish *guayaba*, of Arawakan origin]

guayule /gwə'yoohli/ *noun* a silvery-leaved shrub with many branches that belongs to the daisy family, is found in Mexico and SW USA, and is cultivated as a source of rubber: *Parthenium argentatum*. [American Spanish *guayule* from Nahuatl *cuauhuli* tree gum]

gubbins /'gubinz/ *pl noun Brit, informal* 1 (*treated as sing.*) an object the name of which you do not know or have forgotten; a thingamajig. 2 (*treated as sing. or pl*) a miscellaneous or disorganized group or collection of objects, often associated with something specified: *He received the catalogue and all the other marketing gubbins.* 3 (*treated as sing.*) a silly person. [pl of obsolete *gubbin* fragment, scrap, from Old French *gobbon*]

gubernatorial /,gyoohbənə'tawri·əl/ *adj* relating to or belonging to a governor, *esp* a governor of a US state. [Latin *gubernator* governor, from *gubernare*: see GOVERN]

guddle¹ /'gudl/ *verb chiefly Scot* to catch (fish) by groping with the hands (e.g. under stones or banks of streams). [prob imitative]

guddle² *noun Scot* a mess or muddle.

gudgeon¹ /'guj(ə)n/ *noun* 1 a pivot or spindle. 2 the socket into which the pins of a hinge fit. 3 a socket into which the rudder of a boat fits. [Middle English *gudyon* from early French *goujon*, dimin. of *gouge*: see GOUGE¹]

gudgeon² *noun* (*pl* **gudgeons**) 1 (*pl esp collectively* **gudgeon**) a small European freshwater fish used *esp* for food or bait: *Gobio gobio*. 2 *archaic* somebody who is easily fooled; a dupe: *The bait is so palpably artificial that the most credulous gudgeon turns away —* Hardy. [Middle English *gojune* via French *goujon* from Latin *gobion-, gobio*, alteration of *gobius*: see GOBY]

gudgeon pin *noun* a metal pin linking the piston and connecting rod in an internal-combustion engine.

guelder rose /'geldə/ *noun* a shrub of the honeysuckle family with clusters of fragrant white flowers: *Viburnum opulus*. [Dutch *geldersche roos* rose of *Gelderland*, province of the Netherlands]

Guelf *or* **Guelph** /gwelf/ *noun* a member of a political party in medieval Italy which opposed the German emperors: compare GHIBELLINE. [Italian *Guelfo* from German *Welf*, name of one of the major dynasties of the Holy Roman Empire who opposed the German emperors]

guenon /gə'non (*French* gɛn5/ *noun* (*pl* **guenons** or *collectively* **guenon**) any of several species of long-tailed tree-dwelling African monkeys: genus *Cercopithecus*. [French *guenon*]

guerdon /'guhd(ə)n/ *noun literary* a reward or recompense. ➤➤ **guerdon** *verb trans*. [Middle English via French from Old High German *widarlōn* repayment]

guerilla /gə'rilə/ *noun* see GUERRILLA.

guernsey /'guhnzi/ *noun* **1** (*often* **Guernsey**) a breed of fawn and white dairy cattle larger than the jersey. **2** a thick knitted tunic or jersey traditionally worn by sailors. [named after *Guernsey*, Channel islands, where both originated]

guerrilla *or* **guerilla** /gə'rilə/ *noun* a member of a small independent fighting force which engages in sabotage, unexpected assaults, etc, usu with a political objective.

Word history
Spanish *guerrilla*, dimin. of *guerra* war, of Germanic origin. This word entered English from Spanish during the Peninsular War fought in Spain and Portugal from 1808 to 1814; its first recorded use appears in the writings of the Duke of Wellington, commander of the British forces. It was originally applied to Spanish and Portuguese groups who harassed the French troops and played a significant role in expelling them from the Peninsula.

guess[1] /ges/ *verb trans* **1** to form an opinion of or estimate (something) without having sufficient knowledge or information for an accurate assessment. **2** to arrive at a correct conclusion about (something) by conjecture, chance, or intuition: *She guessed the answer*. **3** *chiefly NAmer, informal* to believe or suppose (something): *I guess you're right*. ➤ *verb intrans* to make a guess. ➤➤ **guessable** *adj*, **guesser** *noun*. [Middle English *gessen*, prob of Scandinavian origin]

guess[2] *noun* an opinion or estimate arrived at by chance or on the basis of inadequate knowledge or information; a conjecture or surmise. ✱ **be anybody's guess** to be impossible to judge or estimate with any chance of accuracy.

guesstimate[1] /'gestimət/ *noun informal* an estimate made without adequate information. [blend of GUESS[1] and ESTIMATE[1]]

guesstimate[2] *verb trans* to make a guesstimate of (something).

guesswork *noun* the act of guessing, or a judgment based on a guess.

guest[1] /gest/ *noun* **1a** a person entertained in one's home: *Guests can be, and often are, delightful, but they should never be allowed to get the upper hand* — Elizabeth von Arnim. **b** a person taken out, entertained, and paid for by another. **2** a person who pays for the services of an establishment (e.g. a hotel). **3** somebody who is present by invitation: *a guest star on a TV programme*. [Middle English *gest* from Old Norse *gestr*]

guest[2] *verb intrans* to appear as a guest, for example in a TV show.

guest beer *noun* a draught beer that is on sale in a pub for a limited period only and is not normally sold there.

guesthouse /'gest·hows/ *noun* a private house used to accommodate paying guests.

guest rope *noun* a rope that hangs over the side of a boat for the use of other boats drawing alongside or as a supplementary towing rope.

guest worker *noun* an immigrant worker who is a temporary resident of a country, *esp* in the EU, and is usu employed in an unskilled job. [translation of German GASTARBEITER]

guff /guf/ *noun informal* foolish talk or ideas; nonsense. [prob imitative]

guffaw[1] /gə'faw/ *noun* a loud or boisterous laugh. [imitative]

guffaw[2] *verb intrans* to laugh loudly or boisterously.

GUI /'gooh·i/ *abbr* graphical user interface.

guidance /'gied(ə)ns/ *noun* **1** advice or instructions on how to do something. **2** the process of controlling the course of something as it moves.

guide[1] /gied/ *noun* **1a** somebody who leads or directs another person or people. **b** somebody who shows and explains places of interest to travellers, tourists, etc. **2a** (*often* + to) something, *esp* a guidebook, that provides somebody with information about a place, activity, etc. **b** something or somebody that directs a person in his or her conduct or course of life: *Always let your conscience be your guide*. **3** a bar, rod, etc for steadying or directing the motion of

something. **4** (*often* **Guide**) *chiefly Brit* a member of a worldwide movement of girls and young women founded with the aim of forming character and teaching good citizenship through outdoor activities and domestic skills, *specif* a member of the intermediate section for girls aged from ten to 15. [Middle English via French from Old Provençal *guida*, of Germanic origin]

guide[2] *verb trans* **1** to lead or direct (somebody) along a route or to a place. **2** to control and direct the movement of (something). **3** to give advice or instructions to (somebody) as regards their behaviour, an appropriate course of action, etc. **4** to supervise (somebody), *esp* during their training. ➤ *verb intrans* to act or work as a guide; give guidance. ➤➤ **guidable** *adj*, **guider** *noun*.

guidebook *noun* a handbook, *esp* a book of information for travellers.

guided missile *noun* a missile whose course in flight is controlled electronically from the ground or by an inbuilt device, e.g. one that causes it to seek heat.

guide dog *noun* a dog trained to lead a blind or partially sighted person.

guideline *noun* a recommendation as to policy or conduct.

guidepost *noun archaic* a signpost.

Guider *noun* (*often* **guider**) an adult leader of a Guide company or Brownie pack.

guideway *noun* a channel or track that dictates the course of something.

guiding *noun chiefly Brit* the activities of the Guide movement.

guidon /'gied(ə)n/ *noun* a triangular or forked pennant (e.g. a standard of a regiment of dragoons). [early French *guidon* from Italian *guidone*, from *guida* guide, of Germanic origin]

guild /gild/ *noun* (*treated as sing. or pl*) **1** an association of people with similar interests or pursuits. **2** a medieval association of merchants or craftsmen. ➤➤ **guildship** *noun*. [Middle English *gilde* from Old Norse *gildi* payment, guild]

guilder *or* **gulden** /'goold(ə)n/ *noun* the former basic monetary unit of the Netherlands and Surinam, divided into 100 cents (in the Netherlands replaced by the euro in 2002). [modification of Dutch *gulden*: see GULDEN]

guildhall *noun* **1** a hall where a guild or corporation assembles, or used to assemble. **2** in some British towns, the town hall.

guild socialism *noun* an early socialist theory advocating state ownership of industry with control by guilds of workers.

guile /giel/ *noun* deceitful cunning; duplicity. ➤➤ **guileful** *adj*, **guilefully** *adv*, **guileless** *adj*, **guilelessly** *adv*. [Middle English via Old French from Old Norse]

guillemot /'gilimot/ *noun* (*pl* **guillemots** or *collectively* **guillemot**) any of several species of sea birds of the auk family that have black and white plumage and are found mainly in northern seas: genus *Uria*. [French *guillemot*, dimin. of the name *Guillaume* William]

guilloche /gi'losh/ *noun* an architectural decoration in the form of interlaced bands. [French *guillochis*]

guillotine[1] /'giləteen/ *noun* **1** a machine for beheading consisting of a heavy blade that slides down between grooved posts. **2** an instrument (e.g. a paper cutter) that works like a guillotine. **3** limitation of the discussion of legislative business by the imposition of a time limit: compare CLOSURE[1].

Word history
French *guillotine*, named after Joseph *Guillotin* d.1814, French physician. Contrary to what some people have believed, Joseph Guillotin did not invent the guillotine; similar machines had been used in Scotland, Italy, and elsewhere for centuries before their use in the French revolution. He was, however, the leading advocate in the National Assembly of this method of execution; partly on humanitarian grounds, but more importantly on egalitarian grounds, since previously decapitation had been a privileged method of execution for nobles. The design of the guillotine is attributed to Antoine Louis, a French surgeon, and originally the machine was named after him *Louison* or *Louisette*. The name *guillotine* caught on, however, and was in use in English as early as 1793.

guillotine[2] *verb trans* to execute (somebody) on a guillotine.

guilt /gilt/ *noun* **1** the fact of having committed an offence, *esp* a criminal offence in law. **2a** responsibility for a criminal or other offence. **b** feelings of being at fault or to blame, *esp* for imagined offences or from a sense of inadequacy: *How extraordinary it is that one feels most guilt about the sins one is unable to commit* — V S Pritchett. [Old English *gylt* an offence, delinquency, guilt]

guiltless /'giltlis/ *adj* not to blame for a crime or offence; innocent. ➤ **guiltlessly** *adv*, **guiltlessness** *noun*.

guilt trip *noun informal* a period of suffering strong, but sometimes unwarranted feelings of guilt, or a self-indulgent display of guilt and remorse.

guilty *adj* (**guiltier, guiltiest**) **1a** responsible for an offence or wrongdoing and deserving punishment. **b** found to have committed a criminal offence by a judge, jury, etc after a trial. **2a** suggesting or involving guilt: *a guilty deed*. **b** feeling guilt: *their guilty consciences*. ➤ **guiltily** *adv*, **guiltiness** *noun*.

guimpe /gimp/ *noun* **1** a high-necked blouse of a kind formerly worn under a pinafore. **2** = GIMP¹. [French *guimpe* from early French *guimple*, of Germanic origin; related to Old English *wimpel* WIMPLE¹]

guinea /'gini/ *noun* **1** a former British gold coin worth 21 shillings. **2** a modern money unit worth £1 and five new pence, used *esp* in setting professional fees and in the auction trade. [named after *Guinea*, region of W Africa, source of the gold from which it was orig made]

guinea fowl *noun* any of several species of W African birds with white-speckled slaty plumage, related to the pheasants and widely kept for food: genus *Numida*.

guinea hen *noun* a female guinea fowl.

Guinean /'giniən/ *noun* a native or inhabitant of Guinea, country in W Africa. ➤ **Guinean** *adj*.

guinea pig *noun* **1** a small stout-bodied short-eared nearly tailless rodent often kept as a pet: *Cavia porcellus*. **2** somebody or something used as a subject of research or experimentation. [erroneously named after *Guinea*, region of W Africa (the guinea pig originated in S America); (sense 2) because it is frequently used as a laboratory animal]

guinea worm *noun* a very long slender nematode worm of warm climates that lives under the skin of human beings and other mammals: *Dracunculus medinensis*.

guipure /gi'pyooə/ *noun* a heavy large-patterned decorative lace on a fabric foundation. [French *guipure*, of Germanic origin]

guise /giez/ *noun* **1** assumed appearance; semblance: *Criticism in the guise of advice*. **2** external appearance; aspect. [Middle English from early French *guise*, of Germanic origin]

guiser *noun Scot* a child in fancy dress who visits houses at Halloween and offers to tell a joke, sing a song, etc in return for a gift of sweets. ➤ **guising** *noun*.

guitar /gi'tah/ *noun* a flat-bodied stringed musical instrument with a long fretted neck and six or twelve strings, plucked with a plectrum or the fingers. ➤ **guitarist** *noun*. [French *guitare* via Spanish *guitarra* and Arabic *qītār* from Greek *kithara* CITHARA]

Gujarati *or* **Gujerati** /gooja'rahti/ *noun* **1** a member of a people of the state of Gujarat in W India. **2** the Indic language spoken by the people of Gujarat. ➤ **Gujarati** *adj*. [Hindi *gujarātī*]

gulab jamun /goo,lab ja'moon/ *noun* an Indian dessert consisting of a deep-fried ball of curd cheese served in syrup.

Gulag /'goohlag/ *noun* **1** the penal system of labour camps in the former Soviet Union. **2** a prison camp or forced labour camp, *esp* in the former Soviet Union. [Russian *Gulag*, acronym from *Glavnoe Upravlenie Ispravitel'no-trudovykh Lagerei*, Chief Directorate of Labour Camps]

gulch /gulch/ *noun chiefly NAmer* a ravine, *esp* with a fast-flowing river running through it. [perhaps from English dialect *gulch* to swallow, from Middle English *gulchen*, of imitative origin]

gulden /'goold(ə)n/ *noun* (*pl* **guldens** *or* **gulden**) see GUILDER. [Middle English from early Dutch *gulden florijn* golden florin]

gules /gyoohlz/ *noun* the colour red when it appears on coats of arms and other heraldic emblems. [Middle English *goules* from Old French *goles, goules* red fur neck ornament, pl of *gole, goule* throat, from Latin *gula*]

gulf¹ /gulf/ *noun* **1** a partially landlocked part of the sea, usu larger than a bay. **2** a deep chasm; an abyss. **3** an unbridgeable gap: *the gulf between theory and practice*. [Middle English *goulf* via early French *golfe* and late Latin *colpus* from Greek *kolpos* bosom, gulf]

gulf² *verb trans* to swallow up or absorb (something) completely; to engulf (it).

Gulf Stream *noun* (**the Gulf Stream**) a warm ocean current flowing from the Gulf of Mexico northeast along the coast of the USA

to Nantucket island and from there across the N Atlantic to the British Isles and NW Europe as the North Atlantic Drift.

Gulf War Syndrome *noun* a medical condition that affects some veterans of the 1991 Gulf War, with symptoms of chronic fatigue, recurrent headaches, and skin disorders.

gulfweed *noun* = SARGASSUM. [named after the *Gulf* of Mexico]

gull¹ /gul/ *noun* any of numerous species of sea birds with long wings and webbed feet, which are largely white, grey, or black: family Laridae. [Middle English, of Celtic origin]

gull² *verb trans dated* to trick, cheat, or deceive (somebody): *They had been gulled into parting with their savings*. [obsolete *gull* gullet, from Middle English *golle*]

gull³ *noun archaic* a person who is easily deceived or cheated; a dupe.

Gullah /'gulə; *also* 'goolə/ *noun* **1** a member of a people of African descent living mainly on the sea islands and coast of S Carolina, Georgia, and NE Florida. **2** the English dialect of the Gullahs, heavily influenced by W African languages. ➤ **Gullah** *adj*. [perhaps by shortening from Angola, country in SW Africa]

gullet /'gulit/ *noun* **1** the oesophagus. **2** the throat. [Middle English *golet* via early French *goulet* from Latin *gula* throat]

gulley /'guli/ *noun* see GULLY¹.

gullible /'guləbl/ *adj* easily deceived or cheated. ➤ **gullibility** /-'biliti/ *noun*.

gull-wing *adj* **1** said of a car door: hinged at the top and opening upwards. **2** said of an aircraft wing: slanting upwards from the fuselage for a short distance with a long horizontal outer section.

gully¹ *or* **gulley** /'guli/ *noun* (*pl* **gullies** *or* **gulleys**) **1** a trench worn in the earth by running water. **2** a deep gutter or drain. **3** in cricket, a fielding position close to the batsman on the off side and between point and the slips, or the fielder in this position. [prob alteration of Middle English *golet*: see GULLET]

gully² *verb trans* (**gullies, gullied, gullying**) to make gullies in (the earth).

gulp¹ /gulp/ *verb trans* (*often* + down) to swallow (something) hurriedly, greedily, or in one swallow. ➤ *verb intrans* to make a sudden swallowing movement as if surprised or nervous. [Middle English *gulpen*, from an early Dutch *gulpen* to bubble forth, drink deep, of imitative origin]

gulp² *noun* **1** a swallowing sound or action. **2** the amount swallowed in a gulp.

gulp back *verb trans* to keep back (tears) by or as if by swallowing; to suppress (them).

gum¹ /gum/ *noun* the parts of the jaws from which the teeth grow, or the tissue that surrounds the teeth. [Old English *gōma* palate]

gum² *noun* **1a** any of numerous polysaccharide plant substances that are gelatinous when moist but harden on drying: compare MUCILAGE. **b** any of various substances (e.g. a mucilage or gum resin) that exude from plants. **2** any sticky substance or deposit resembling a plant gum. **3** any soft glue used for sticking paper and other lightweight materials. **4** *informal* chewing gum. **5** *Aus* a eucalyptus tree. [Middle English *gomme* from early French, via Latin *gummi*, and Greek *kommi* from Egyptian *kernai*]

gum³ *verb* (**gummed, gumming**) ➤ *verb trans* to smear or stick (something) with or as if with gum. ➤ *verb intrans* to exude or form gum. ➤ **gummer** *noun*.

gum⁴ ✳ **by gum** *dated, informal* a mild oath. [euphemism for *God*]

gum arabic *noun* a water-soluble gum obtained from several acacia plants and used *esp* in the manufacture of adhesives and in pharmacy.

gumbo /'gumboh/ *noun* **1** a meat and vegetable soup thickened with okra pods, a popular dish in Cajun cooking. **2** *NAmer* = OKRA (1). **3** a type of soil found in the central USA that becomes very muddy and sticky when wet. **4** *NAmer, informal* a mixture of miscellaneous things. **5** (**Gumbo**) a regional language based on French and incorporating W African elements, spoken in parts of Louisiana and the French West Indies. [American French *gombo*, of Bantu origin]

gumboil *noun* an abscess in the gum.

gumboot *noun* a strong waterproof rubber boot reaching usu to the knee.

gumdrop *noun* a hard jellylike sweet, originally one made of flavoured gum arabic.

gumma /'gumə/ *noun* (*pl* **gummas** *or* **gummata** /'gumətə/) a rubbery tumour characteristic of the latter stages of syphilis. ➤➤ **gummatous** /-təs/ *adj.* [Latin *gummi*: see GUM²]

gummy¹ /'gumi/ *adj* (**gummier, gummiest**) **1a** consisting of or containing gum. **b** covered with gum. **2** viscous or sticky. ➤➤ **gumminess** *noun.*

gummy² *adj* (**gummier, gummiest**) with gums showing clearly, usu because of the absence of teeth: *a gummy smile.*

gumption /'gumpsh(ə)n/ *noun* **1** the intelligence and courage to take action; initiative. **2** shrewd practical common sense. [origin unknown]

gum resin *noun* a mixture of gum and resin (e.g. myrrh), usu obtained by making an incision in a plant and allowing the juice that exudes to solidify.

gumshoe *noun chiefly NAmer, informal* a detective. [*gumshoe* in the sense 'rubber shoe', suggesting somebody who walks stealthily]

gum tree *noun* any tree that exudes a gum, *esp* a eucalyptus tree. ✳ **up a gum tree** *informal* in a difficult situation.

gum turpentine *noun* = TURPENTINE¹ (IA).

gum up *verb trans informal* to prevent or impede the proper working of (something).

gun¹ /gun/ *noun* **1a** any weapon that discharges a bullet or shell through a metal tube; a firearm: *My, my. Such a lot of guns around town and so few brains* — Humphrey Bogart. **b** a piece of artillery with a high muzzle velocity and a comparatively flat trajectory. **2** a discharge of a gun; gunfire. **3a** somebody who carries a gun in a shooting party. **b** *NAmer* somebody who is skilled with a gun, *esp* a hired killer. **4** a device that releases a controlled amount of something, e.g. grease or glue, and is operated broadly like a firearm. ✳ **go great guns** to be working at great speed or very effectively. **jump the gun 1** to start in a race before the starting signal. **2** to move or act before the proper time. **stick to one's guns** to refuse to change one's decision, intentions, or opinion in spite of opposition. ➤➤ **gunned** *adj.* [Middle English *gonne, gunne,* prob of Scandinavian origin]

gun² *verb trans* (**gunned, gunning**) *informal* **1** to press hard on the accelerator of (a vehicle) so as to increase its speed. **2** to use the accelerator to make (an engine) run faster. ✳ **be gunning for 1** to be intent on finding somebody in order to criticize, punish, or kill them. **2** to be trying very hard to obtain or achieve something.

gunboat *noun* a relatively heavily armed ship of shallow draught.

gunboat diplomacy *noun* the high-handed threat or use of naval or military power.

guncotton *noun* an explosive chemical compound consisting of cellulose nitrate with a high nitrogen content.

gundog *noun* a dog trained to locate or retrieve game for hunters.

gun down *verb trans* to kill (somebody) by shooting them, usu in cold blood.

gunfight *noun* a duel with guns. ➤➤ **gunfighter** *noun.*

gunfire *noun* the firing of guns, or the noise they make.

gunge /gunj/ *noun Brit, informal* any unpleasant, dirty, or sticky substance. ➤➤ **gunged** *adj,* **gungy** *adj.* [origin unknown]

gung ho /ˌgung 'hoh/ *adj* extremely or excessively enthusiastic, *esp* for fighting or warfare. [*Gung ho!*, motto of certain US marine raiders in World War II, from Chinese (Pekingese) *gong he* work together]

gunk /gungk/ *noun informal* any unpleasant, dirty, or sticky substance; gunge. [orig the trade name of a detergent used for cleaning oily machinery etc]

gunlayer *noun* a soldier with the task of aiming a large gun.

gunlock *noun* the mechanism for igniting the charge of a firearm.

gunman *noun* (*pl* **gunmen**) a man armed with a gun, *esp* a professional killer.

gunmetal *noun* **1** a greyish form of bronze formerly used for cannons. **2** a bluish grey colour. ➤➤ **gunmetal** *adj.*

gunnel¹ /'gunl/ *noun* see GUNWALE.

gunnel² *noun* any of several species of small long N Atlantic fishes that resemble an eel and belong to the blenny family: family Pholidae. [origin unknown]

gunner *noun* **1** a soldier or airman who operates a gun, *specif* a private in the Royal Artillery. **2** somebody who hunts with a gun.

3 formerly, a warrant officer who supervised naval ordnance and ordnance stores.

gunnery *noun* the science of the flight of projectiles and of the effective use of guns.

gunnery sergeant *noun* a non-commissioned officer in the US Marines, ranking below a master sergeant.

gunny /'guni/ *noun* a coarse heavy material, usu of jute, used *esp* for sacking. [Hindi *ganī*]

gunpoint ✳ **at gunpoint** while threatening somebody, or being threatened, with the use of a gun.

gunpowder *noun* an explosive mixture of potassium nitrate, charcoal, and sulphur formerly used in firearms and still used in blasting.

gun room *noun* **1** a room in which firearms are stored, usu in locked cabinets. **2** *dated* quarters on a British warship used by junior officers.

gunrunner *noun* somebody who carries or deals in contraband arms and ammunition. ➤➤ **gunrunning** *noun.*

gunship *noun* a heavily armed helicopter used to attack targets on the ground.

gunshot *noun* **1** a shot or projectile fired from a gun. **2** the range of a gun: *out of gunshot.*

gun-shy *adj* said *esp* of a dog: afraid of the sound of a gun.

gunslinger *noun informal* somebody who carries a gun, *esp* a cowboy in the Wild West who was notoriously quick to settle disputes with his gun.

gunsmith *noun* somebody who designs, makes, or repairs firearms.

gunwale *or* **gunnel** /'gunl/ *noun* the upper edge of a ship's or boat's side. [Middle English *gonnewale,* from *gonne* GUN¹ + WALE, from its former use as a support for guns]

gunyah /'gunyə/ *noun Aus* a hut built by Australian aboriginals in the bush. [native name in Australia]

guppy /'gupi/ *noun* (*pl* **guppies** *or collectively* **guppy**) a small fish that is native to the W Indies and S America and is a popular aquarium fish: *Poecilia reticulata.* [named after R J L *Guppy* d.1916, Trinidadian amateur naturalist who sent the first specimen to the British Museum]

gurdwara /'guhrdwahra/ *noun* a Sikh place of worship. [Punjabi *gurduārā,* from Sanskrit *guru* (see GURU) + *dvāra* door]

gurgle /'guhgl/ *verb* (**gurgling**) ➤ *verb intrans* **1a** to make the sound of unevenly flowing water. **b** to flow or move with such a sound. **2** to make a low-pitched bubbling sound from the throat. ➤ *verb trans* to utter (something) with a gurgling sound. ➤➤ **gurgle** *noun.* [Middle English, ultimately from Latin *gurgulio* gullet]

Gurkha /'guhkə/ *noun* **1** a member of any of several Nepalese peoples. **2** a Gurkha serving in the British or Indian army. [Sanskrit *goraska* protector of cattle, an epithet of their deity]

gurn /guhn/ *verb intrans* see GIRN.

gurnard /'guhnəd/ *noun* (*pl* **gurnards** *or collectively* **gurnard**) any of several species of fishes with large armoured heads and three pairs of pectoral fins used like feet to walk along the sea floor: family Triglidae. [Middle English, ultimately from Latin *grunnire* to grunt, from the sound it makes when taken from the water]

gurney /'guhni/ *noun NAmer* a wheeled stretcher of the kind used in hospitals to transport patients. [orig denoting a kind of cab, later a similar vehicle used as an ambulance: prob named after J T Gurney, US inventor, who patented a new design of cab in 1883]

guru /'goohrooh, 'goorooh/ *noun* (*pl* **gurus**) **1** a Hindu or Sikh personal religious teacher and spiritual guide. **2a** any spiritual and intellectual guide; a mentor. **b** *informal* an acknowledged leader or chief proponent (e.g. of a cult or idea): *the guru of modern philosophical thought.* [Hindi *gurū* from Sanskrit *guru,* from *guru* weighty, venerable]

gush¹ /gush/ *verb intrans* **1** to flow out copiously or violently. **2** to emit a sudden copious flow: *The wound was gushing.* **3** to make an effusive often affected display of sentiment or enthusiasm: *They were all gushing over the baby.* ➤ *verb trans* to emit (something) in a copious free flow. [Middle English *guschen,* prob of imitative origin]

gush² *noun* **1** a sudden outpouring. **2** an effusive and usu affected display of sentiment or enthusiasm.

gusher *noun* 1 an oil well with a copious natural flow. 2 somebody or something that gushes, *esp* somebody who talks effusively.

gushy *adj* (**gushier, gushiest**) marked by effusive often affected sentiment or enthusiasm. ⟫ **gushily** *adv*.

gusset /'gusit/ *noun* 1 a piece of material inserted in a seam (e.g. the crotch of an undergarment) to provide reinforcement or allow for movement. 2 a plate or bracket for strengthening a join in a timber or metal framework. [Middle English in the sense 'piece covering the joints in a suit of armour', from early French *gousset*, dimin. of *gousse* pod, shell]

gust[1] /gust/ *noun* 1 a sudden brief rush of wind. 2 a sudden outburst; a surge: *a gust of emotion*. ⟫ **gustily** *adv*, **gustiness** *noun*, **gusty** *adj* [Old Norse *gustr*]

gust[2] *verb intrans* to blow in gusts: *winds gusting up to 40 mph*.

gustation /gu'staysh(ə)n/ *noun formal* the action of tasting, or the sense of taste.

gustative /'gustətiv/ *adj* = GUSTATORY.

gustatory /'gustət(ə)ri/ *adj* of, associated with, or denoting the sense of taste. ⟫ **gustatorily** *adv*. [Latin *gustatus*, past part. of *gustare* to taste, from *gustus* taste, liking]

gusto /'gustoh/ *noun* enthusiastic and vigorous enjoyment or vitality: *He sang with great gusto*. [Spanish *gusto* from Latin *gustus* taste]

gut[1] /gut/ *noun* 1 (*also in pl*). **a** the belly or abdomen. **b** the intestine: *A king may go a progress through the guts of a beggar* — Shakespeare. 2 (*often used before a noun*) the basic emotionally or instinctively responding part of a person: *a gut feeling*. 3 = CATGUT. 4 the sac of silk taken from a silkworm and drawn out into a thread for use in attaching a fish hook to a fishing line. 5 *informal* (*in pl*) the inner essential parts: *the guts of a car*. 6 *informal* (*in pl*) courage or determination. 7 a narrow water passage; a strait. ✳ **bust a gut** *informal* to exert oneself or make a great effort. **hate somebody's guts** *informal* to hate somebody with great intensity. [Middle English from Old English *guttas* (pl)]

gut[2] *verb trans* (**gutted, gutting**) 1 to remove the intestines of (*esp* an animal); to disembowel (it). 2a to destroy the inside of (something, *esp* a building). **b** to destroy the essential power or effectiveness of (something): *Inflation had gutted their economy.* 3 to extract the essentials of (a piece of writing) and present them in summary form.

Guthrie test /'guthri/ *noun* a blood test that is routinely carried out on newborn babies, to test for PHENYLKETONURIA, which can result in brain and nerve damage. [named after Robert *Guthrie* b.1916, American microbiologist]

gutless *adj informal* lacking courage; cowardly. ⟫ **gutlessness** *noun*.

gutsy /'gutsi/ *adj* (**gutsier, gutsiest**) *informal* 1 courageous. 2 expressing or appealing strongly to the physical passions; lusty: *They belted out a string of gutsy rock numbers.* ⟫ **gutsiness** *noun*.

gutta-percha /ˌgutə 'puhchə/ *noun* a tough plastic substance obtained from the latex of several Malaysian trees and used in golfballs, waterproofing materials, and electrical insulation. [Malay *gĕtah-pĕrcha*, from *gĕtah* sap, latex + *pĕrcha* tree producing gutta-percha]

guttate /'gutayt/ *adj* said of plants: having small coloured spots. [Latin *guttatus* from *gutta* drop]

gutted *adj Brit, informal* deeply disappointed or disheartened.

gutter[1] /'gutə/ *noun* 1a a trough just below the eaves of a roof or at the side of a street to catch and carry off rainwater, surface water, etc. **b** a trough or groove to catch or direct something, e.g. at the side of a bowling alley. 2 a white space between two pages of a book, two postage stamps on a sheet, etc. 3 (**the gutter**) the lowest or most vulgar level or condition of human life. [Middle English *goter* via early French *goutiere* from Latin *gutta* drop]

gutter[2] *verb* (**guttered, guttering**) ▷ *verb intrans* 1 to flow in rivulets. 2a said of a candle: to burn unevenly so that melted wax runs down one side. **b** said of a flame: to burn fitfully or feebly, frequently being on the point of going out. ▷ *verb trans* to cut or wear gutters in.

guttering *noun* 1 the gutters on the roof of a building collectively. 2 metal or plastic channels for use as gutters.

gutter press *noun* that section of the national press that is marked by extreme vulgarity or cheapness.

guttersnipe *noun dated* a deprived child living in poverty and usu dressed in ragged clothes. [orig denoting someone who lived by picking saleable refuse from street gutters: GUTTER[1] + SNIPE[1]]

guttural[1] /'gut(ə)rəl/ *adj* 1 relating to the throat. 2a formed or pronounced in the throat: *guttural sounds*. **b** featuring guttural sounds prominently. **c** velarized. ⟫ **gutturally** *adv*. [via French from medieval Latin *gutturalis*, from Latin *guttur* throat]

guttural[2] *noun* a guttural consonant or speech sound, e.g. the *l* sound in *milk*.

guv /guv/ *noun Brit, informal* sir, used as a form of address.

guvnor /'guvnə/ *noun informal* = GUV.

GUY *abbr* Guyana (international vehicle registration).

guy[1] /gie/ *noun* a rope, chain, rod, etc attached to something (e.g. a tent or the boom of a yacht) as a brace or guide. [prob from Dutch *gei* brail]

guy[2] *verb trans* to secure (something, e.g. a tent or a yacht) with guys.

guy[3] *noun* 1 *informal* a person, *esp* a man. 2 (*often* **Guy**) a humorous effigy of a man burned in Britain on Guy Fawkes Night. 3 *chiefly Brit, dated, informal* a person whose appearance is grotesque or ridiculous: *The lady from the provinces who dresses like a guy and who doesn't think she dances but would rather like to try* — W S Gilbert. [named after *Guy* Fawkes d.1606, English conspirator: see GUY FAWKES NIGHT]

guy[4] *verb trans dated* to make fun of (somebody or something); to ridicule (them).

Guyanese /gieə'neez/ *noun* a native or inhabitant of Guyana. ⟫ **Guyanese** *adj*.

Guy Fawkes Night /'fawks/ *noun* 5 November, observed in Britain with fireworks and bonfires in commemoration of the arrest of Guy Fawkes in 1605 for attempting to blow up the Houses of Parliament.

guzzle /'guzl/ *verb* (**guzzling**) to consume (something) greedily, continually, or habitually. ⟫ **guzzler** *noun*. [origin unknown]

gwyniad /'gwiniad/ *noun* a whitefish found in Lake Bala in N Wales. [Welsh *gwyniad*, from *gwyn* white]

Gy *abbr* the symbol for the gray, the SI unit for the absorbed dose of ionizing radiation.

gybe (*NAmer* **jibe**) /jieb/ *verb intrans* 1 to change a ship's course greatly, taking the stern of the ship through the wind, as when rounding a buoy, a headland, etc. 2 said of a fore-and-aft sail: to swing suddenly and violently from one side to the other of a boat when running before the wind. ▷ *verb trans* to cause (a ship) to gybe. [obsolete Dutch *gijben*]

gym /jim/ *noun* 1 a gymnasium. 2 development of the body by games, exercises, etc, *esp* in school.

gymkhana /jim'kahnə/ *noun* a local sporting event featuring competitions and displays relating to horse riding.

▶ **Word history**
Urdu *gend-khāna* racket court, from Hindi *gemd* ball + Persian *khanah* house. The word was used in Indian in the mid 19th cent. to refer to a public sports facility; later, particularly by Europeans, to an athletics display or contest, which might include horsemanship, and by the late 19th cent. to mounted games.

gymn- *or* **gymno-** *comb. form* forming words, with the meaning: naked; bare: *gymnosperm*. [Greek *gymno-*, from *gymnos* naked]

gymnasium /jim'nayzi·əm/ *noun* (*pl* **gymnasiums** *or* **gymnasia** /-zi·ə/) 1 a large room or separate building used for indoor sports and gymnastic activities. 2 a German or Scandinavian secondary school that prepares pupils for university. [Latin *gymnasium* from Greek *gymnasion*, exercise ground, school, from *gymnazein* to exercise naked, from *gymnos* naked; (sense 2) German *Gymnasium* from Latin *gymnasium*]

gymnast /'jimnast/ *noun* somebody trained in gymnastics. [early French *gymnaste* from Greek *gymnastēs* trainer, from *gymnazein*: see GYMNASIUM]

gymnastics /jim'nastiks/ *pl noun* 1 (*treated as sing.*) physical exercises developing or displaying bodily strength and coordination, often performed in competition. 2 (*treated as pl*) exercises in intellectual or physical dexterity: *verbal gymnastics*. ⟫ **gymnastic** /jim'nastik/ *adj*.

gymno- *comb. form* see GYMN-.

gymnosperm /'jimnohspuhm/ *noun* any of a group of woody plants (e.g. conifers) that produce naked seeds not enclosed in an ovary: compare ANGIOSPERM. ⋙ **gymnospermous** /-'spuhməs/ *adj,* **gymnospermy** /-mi/ *noun.* [GYMN- + Greek *sperma* seed]

gym shoe *noun* = PLIMSOLL.

gymslip *noun chiefly Brit* **1** a girl's tunic or pinafore dress worn, *esp* formerly, as part of a school uniform. **2** *dated, informal* (used before a noun) relating to schoolgirls or girls of school age: *a gymslip pregnancy.*

gyn- *or* **gyno-** *comb. form* forming words, denoting: **1** woman: *gynocracy.* **2** female reproductive organ; ovary: *gynophore.* **3** pistil: *gynoecium.* [Greek *gyn-,* from *gynē* woman]

gynaec- *or* **gynaeco-** (*NAmer* **gynec-** *or* **gyneco-**) *comb. form* forming words, denoting: woman, or the reproductive organs of women: *gynaecology.* [Greek *gynaik-, gynaiko-,* from *gynaik-, gynē* woman]

gynaecology (*NAmer* **gynecology**) /gienə'kolǝji/ *noun* a branch of medicine that deals with diseases and disorders of women, *esp* of the female reproductive system. ⋙ **gynaecological** /-'lojikl/ *adj,* **gynaecologist** *noun.*

gynandromorph /jie'nandrǝmawf/ *noun* an abnormal individual, *esp* an insect, having characters of both sexes in different parts of the body. ⋙ **gynandromorphic** /-'mawfik/ *adj,* **gynandromorphism** /-'mawfiz(ǝ)m/ *noun,* **gynandromorphous** /-'mawfǝs/ *adj,* **gynandromorphy** /-fi/ *noun.* [Greek *gynandros* (see GYNANDROUS) + -MORPH]

gynandrous /ji'nandrǝs, jie-, gie-/ *adj* said of a flower, *esp* an orchid: having the male and female parts united in a column. [Greek *gynandros* of doubtful sex, from *gynē* woman + *andr-, anēr* man]

-gyne *comb. form* forming nouns, with the meaning: woman or female: *pseudogyne.* [Greek *gynē*]

gynec- *or* **gyneco-** *comb. form NAmer* see GYNAEC-.

gyno- *comb. form* see GYN-.

gynoecium /jie'neesi-ǝm, gie-/ *noun* (*pl* **gynoecia** /-si-ǝ/) all the female parts of a flower collectively. [scientific Latin from Greek *gynaikeion* women's apartments, from *gynaik-, gynē* woman]

gynophobia /jienǝ'fohbi-ǝ/ *noun* extreme fear of women.

gynophore /'jienǝfaw/ *noun* an elongation of a flower stalk in some plants, e.g. a caper, that bears the gynoecium at its tip.

-gynous *comb. form* forming adjectives, with the meaning: having females or female parts or organs of the kind or number specified: *heterogynous.* ⋙ **-gyny** *comb. form.* [Latin *-gynus* from Greek *-gynos,* from *gynē* woman]

gyp¹ *or* **gip** /jip/ ✳ **give somebody gyp** *Brit, informal* to cause (somebody) pain or discomfort. [alteration of GEE UP]

gyp² *verb trans and intrans* (**gypped, gypping**) *NAmer, informal* to cheat, or cheat (somebody).

gyp³ *noun* **1** *Brit* a college servant at Cambridge and Durham universities: compare SCOUT¹ (5). **2** *NAmer, informal.* **a** a cheat or swindler. **b** a fraud or swindle. [prob short for GYPSY]

gypsophila /jip'sofilǝ/ *noun* any of a genus of plants of the pink family that are native to the Mediterranean and have clusters of small delicate flowers: genus *Gypsophila.* [Latin genus name, from Greek *gypsos* (see GYPSUM) + *-philos* (see -PHILE)]

gypsum /'jipsǝm/ *noun* hydrated calcium sulphate occurring as a mineral and used *esp* in plaster of Paris. ⋙ **gypseous** /'jipsi-ǝs/ *adj,* **gypsiferous** /jip'sif(ǝ)rǝs/ *adj.* [via Latin from Greek *gypsos,* of Semitic origin]

gypsy *or* **gipsy** /'jipsi/ *noun* (*pl* **gypsies** *or* **gipsies**) **1** (*often* **Gypsy**) a member of the Romany people, a largely nomadic people who migrated from India to Europe in about the ninth cent. and retain an itinerant lifestyle in modern societies. **2** the Romany language, which is related to Hindi. **3** somebody with an unconventional or nomadic way of life.

Word history
by shortening and alteration from EGYPTIAN². When gypsies first came to Europe they claimed to be from a country called 'Little Egypt'.

gypsy moth *or* **gipsy moth** *noun* a large European moth that is brown in the male and white in the female: *Lymantria dispar.*

gyr- *or* **gyro-** *comb. form* forming words, denoting: **1** ring; circle; spiral; rotation: *gyromagnetic.* **2** gyroscope: *gyrocompass.* [prob from early French via Latin from Greek *gyr-,* from *gyros* circle]

gyrate /jie'rayt/ *verb intrans* to revolve or move with a circular or spiral motion: *The stripper gyrated slowly upon the tiny square of painted hardboard at the end of the bar* — Len Deighton. ⋙ *verb trans* to cause (something) to revolve or move with a circular or spiral motion. ⋙ **gyration** /jie'raysh(ǝ)n/ *noun,* **gyrational** /jie'raysh(ǝ)nǝl/ *adj,* **gyrator** *noun,* **gyratory** /'jierǝt(ǝ)ri, jie'rayt(ǝ)ri/ *adj.*

gyre¹ /jieǝ/ *verb intrans literary* to move with a swirling or rotating motion; to gyrate. [Middle English *giren* from late Latin *gyrare,* from *gyrus* circle, from Greek *gyros*]

gyre² *noun literary* a swirling or rotating motion. ⋙ **gyral** *adj.*

gyrfalcon /'juhfawlkǝn/ *noun* a large and powerful Arctic falcon: *Falco rusticolus.*

Word history
Middle English *gerfaucun* from early French *girfaucon,* of Germanic origin. The current spelling arose in the 19th cent. from the mistaken belief that the first syllable came from Latin *gyrare* to gyrate; its real meaning is not known.

gyro /'jie·(ǝ)roh/ *noun* (*pl* **gyros**) *informal* **1** a gyroscope. **2** a gyrocompass.

gyro- *comb. form* see GYR-.

gyrocompass *noun* a compass in which the horizontal axis of a constantly spinning gyroscope always points to true north.

gyromagnetic /,jie·ǝrohmag'netik/ *adj* relating to the magnetic properties of a rotating electrical particle.

gyroplane *noun* an aircraft supported by rapidly rotating horizontal aerofoils.

gyroscope *noun* a device containing a wheel that is mounted to spin rapidly about an axis and is free to turn in any direction so that it maintains the same orientation. ⋙ **gyroscopic** /-'skopik/ *adj,* **gyroscopically** /-'skopikli/ *adv.* [French *gyroscope,* from GYRO- + -SCOPE; from its original use to illustrate the rotation of the earth]

gyrostabilizer *noun* a stabilizing device (e.g. for a ship or aeroplane) in which a constantly spinning gyroscope opposes sideways motion.

gyve /jiev/ *noun* a fetter or shackle. [Middle English; earlier history unknown]

H¹ *or* **h** *noun* (*pl* **H's** *or* **Hs** *or* **h's**) **1a** the eighth letter of the English alphabet. **b** a written character or design denoting this letter. **c** the sound represented by this letter, one of the English consonants. **2** an item designated as H, *esp* the eighth in a series.

H² *abbr* **1** harbour. **2** used on lead pencils: hard. **3** *informal* heroin. **4** henry. **5** hospital. **6** Hungary (international vehicle registration).

H³ *abbr* the chemical symbol for hydrogen.

h¹ *abbr* **1** hect-. **2** height. **3** high. **4** hour. **5** husband.

h² *symbol* in physics, Planck's constant.

ha¹ *abbr* hectare.

ha² *or* **hah** /hah/ *interj* used to express surprise, joy, triumph, etc. [Middle English]

haar /hah/ *noun* a cold fog on the E coast of Britain. [prob from a Low German or Dutch dialect word]

Hab. *abbr* Habakkuk (book of the Bible).

habanera /habə'neərə/ *noun* a Cuban dance in slow duple time, or a piece of music for this dance. [Spanish *danza habanera* Havanan dance, from La *Habana* (Havana), capital city of Cuba]

Habdalah /hav'dahlə/ *noun* a Jewish domestic ceremony marking the close of a Sabbath or holy day. [Hebrew *habhdālāh* separation]

habeas corpus /ˌhaybi-əs 'kawpəs/ *noun* a judicial writ requiring a detained person to be brought before a court so that the legality of their detention may be examined. [Middle English from medieval Latin *habeas corpus* you should have the body, the opening words of the writ]

haberdasher /'habədashə/ *noun* **1** *Brit* a dealer in buttons, thread, ribbon, and other small articles used in making clothes. **2** *NAmer* a dealer in shirts, ties, and other minor articles of menswear. [Middle English *haberdassher*, prob a modification of Anglo-French *hapertas* petty merchandise]

haberdashery *noun* (*pl* **haberdasheries**) **1** goods sold by a haberdasher. **2** a haberdasher's shop.

habergeon /'habəjən/ *noun* formerly, a hauberk, or a sleeveless chain-mail jacket shorter than a hauberk. [Middle English *haubergeoun* from early French *haubergeon*, dimin. of *hauberc*: see HAUBERK]

Haber process /'hahbə/ *noun* an industrial process for producing ammonia by causing atmospheric nitrogen to react at high temperature and pressure with hydrogen, in the presence of a catalyst. [named after Fritz *Haber* d.1934, German chemist]

habiliment /hə'bilimənt/ *noun archaic or literary* (*usu in pl*) an article of clothing: *Toad is busy arraying himself in those singularly hideous habiliments so dear to him* — Kenneth Grahame. [early French *habillement* from *habiller* to dress, alteration of *abiller* to trim a log, from *bille* log]

habilitate /hə'bilitayt/ *verb intrans* to qualify, e.g. as a teacher in a German university. ⟫ **habilitation** /-'taysh(ə)n/ *noun.* [Late Latin *habilitatus*, past part. of *habilitare*, from Latin *habilitas*: see ABILITY]

habit¹ /'habit/ *noun* **1a** a settled tendency or usual manner of behaviour. **b** an acquired pattern or mode of behaviour. **2** an addiction: *a cocaine habit.* **3** characteristic mode of growth, occurrence, or appearance, e.g. of a plant or crystal. **4** *archaic* a person's bodily or mental make-up: *a cheerful habit of mind.* **5** a costume characteristic of a calling, rank, or function: *a monk's habit; a riding habit.* [Middle English via Old French from Latin *habitus* condition, character, past part. of *habēre* to have, hold]

habit² *verb trans* (**habited, habiting**) *archaic* (*often as past part.*) to clothe or dress (somebody, *esp* oneself): *The three charming Miss Foresters … had come habited all in green* — Charles Lamb.

habitable *adj* capable of being lived in: *They loved restoring dilapidated properties and making them habitable.* ⟫ **habitability** /-'biliti/ *noun*, **habitableness** *noun*, **habitably** *adv.*

habitant *noun* **1** /abitonh/ a French settler in Louisiana or Quebec, or a descendant of French settlers. **2** /'habitənt/ *archaic* an inhabitant or resident: *If only I were a habitant of Campagna* — Mark Twain.

habitat /'habitat/ *noun* **1** the place or type of place where a plant or animal naturally grows or lives: *People are conditioned to prefer heathers in gardens to those in their natural habitat* — New Scientist. **2** one's preferred surroundings: *a strange place to find somebody whose normal habitat was the pub.* [Latin *habitat* it inhabits, from *habitare*: see HABITATION]

habitation /habi'taysh(ə)n/ *noun* **1** the inhabiting of a place; occupancy: *dwellings unfit for habitation.* **2** *formal or literary* a dwelling place; a residence or home: *There was no serious objection raised, except in one habitation, the Vicarage* — Jane Austen. [Middle English *habitacioun* via French from Latin *habitation-, habitatio,* from *habitare* to inhabit, from *habitus,* past part. of *habēre* to have, hold]

habit-forming *adj* said of a drug, etc: addictive.

habitual /hə'bityooəl/ *adj* **1** having the nature of a habit: *my habitual laziness.* **2** by force of habit: *not that he was an habitual liar.* **3** in accordance with habit; customary: *one's habitual morning routine.* ⟫ **habitually** *adv*, **habitualness** *noun.*

habituate /hə'bityooayt/ *verb trans* (+ to) to make (somebody, *esp* oneself) used to something: *habituate oneself to rising early.* ⟫ *verb intrans* to become used to something. ⟫⟫ **habituation** /-'aysh(ə)n/ *noun.*

habitude /'habityoohd/ *noun archaic or literary* **1** disposition or cast of mind: *There was something of the habitude of the wild animal in the unreflecting instinct with which she rambled on* — Hardy. **2** habit; habituation: *the white girl who took to the trees with the ability of long habitude* — Edgar Rice Burroughs.

habitué /hə'bityooay/ *noun* a person who frequents a specified place: *habitués of the theatre*. [French *habitué*, past part. of *habituer* to frequent, ultimately from Latin *habitus*: see HABITATION]

habitus /'habitəs/ *noun* (*pl* **habitus** or **habituses**) a person's physical constitution or physique. [Latin *habitus* deportment, appearance, nature]

haboob /hə'boohb/ *noun* in N Africa, a sandstorm. [Arabic *habūb* violent wind]

Habsburg /'hapsbuhg/ *noun and adj* see HAPSBURG.

háček /'hahchek/ *noun* a diacritic mark (ˇ) placed over a letter in some languages, e.g. over *c* in Czech and other Slavic languages, to modify the sound of the letter. [Czech *háček* little hook]

hachure /ha'shyooə/ *noun* **1** (*in pl*) short parallel lines used on a map to indicate sloping land. **2** the shading produced by such lines. [French *hachure*, from *hacher*: see HATCH⁴]

hacienda /hasi'endə/ *noun* in a Spanish-speaking country, a large estate or plantation, or the main house of such an estate or plantation. [Spanish *hacienda* from Latin *facienda* things to be done, from *facere* to make, do]

hack¹ /hak/ *verb trans* **1a** to cut (something) with or as if with repeated irregular or unskilful blows. **b** to sever (something) with repeated blows: *hack off branches*. **2** to clear (a path) by cutting away vegetation. **3a** in football or rugby, to commit the foul of kicking (an opposing player) on the shins. **b** to kick (e.g. a ball) somewhere. **4** *informal* (*used with a negative*) to bear or tolerate (something): *He gave up the course because he just couldn't hack it*. ➤ *verb intrans* **1** to make cutting blows or rough cuts. **2** *dated* to cough repeatedly in a short dry manner: *He was troubled from time to time with a dry hacking cough* — Wilkie Collins. **3** (+ into) to gain unauthorized access to a computer system. [Old English *haccian*]

hack² *noun* **1** a hacking blow. **2a** a wound or gash. **b** a kick on the shins in rugby or football. **c** a painful split in the skin caused e.g. by the cold. **3** a mattock, pick, etc. **4** *informal* an act or instance of computer hacking.

hack³ *noun* **1** a person who produces mediocre work for financial gain; *esp* a commercial writer. **2a** a riding horse let out for hire. **b** a vicious or worn-out old horse; = JADE² (1). **c** a light easy saddle horse. **3** an act of hacking; a ride. **4** *NAmer* a taxi. ➤➤ **hackery** *noun*. [see HACKNEY¹]

hack⁴ *adj* **1** performed by, suited to, or characteristic of a hack: *hack writing*. **2** hackneyed; trite.

hack⁵ *verb trans* to ride (a horse) at an ordinary pace, *esp* over roads. ➤ *verb intrans* to go horse-riding in this way.

hack⁶ *noun* the board on which a falcon's meat is served. ✳ **at hack** in the state of partial liberty in which a young hawk is kept before training. [blend of HATCH¹ and *heck*, in the senses 'hatch', 'rack']

hackamore /'hakəmaw/ *noun* a bridle with a loop capable of being tightened about a horse's nose and used in place of a bit. [alteration of Spanish *jáquima* headstall, from Arabic *shakīmah*]

hackberry /'hakb(ə)ri/ *noun* (*pl* **hackberries**) **1** a purple cherry-like edible berry. **2** the N American tree with nettle-like leaves that bears this berry (*Celtis occidentalis*), or another species of *Celtis*. [alteration of *hagberry* a type of wild cherry, from Old Norse *heggr* wild cherry]

hacked off *adj informal* annoyed or bored; fed up.

hacker /'hakə/ *noun* **1** *informal* a computer enthusiast or fanatic, *esp* one who uses a personal computer to gain unauthorized access to data, e.g. that stored in the system of a company or organization.

Editorial note
Hackers seek to gain unauthorized access to a computer or network by trying to guess passwords using programs that try millions of permutations. Alternatively they set traps to capture passwords from legitimate users — Dick Pountain.

2 a person who cuts or slashes. **3** a person who goes horse-riding along ordinary roads.

hacking jacket *noun* a tweed jacket with slits at the side, often worn for riding.

hackle /'hakl/ *noun* **1a** (*in pl*) the erectile hairs along the neck and back of *esp* a dog. **b** any of the long narrow feathers on the neck of a domestic cock or other bird. **2** an artificial fishing fly made from a cock's hackles. **3** a bunch of feathers worn as part of a military headdress. **4** a steel comb with long teeth for dressing flax or hemp. [Middle English *hakell*, *heckle* of Germanic origin]

hackney¹ /'hakni/ *noun* any of an English breed of rather compact English horses with a high leg action.

Word history
Middle English *hakeney*, prob from *Hakeneye* Hackney, borough of London, where many horses were formerly pastured. The word orig denoted an ordinary riding horse, later shortened to *hack* (see HACK³ (2C)); such horses were often hired out for riding or driving, hence HACKNEY², HACK³ (2A), and HACKNEYED (from the idea of being used by all and sundry). From the 17th cent. a vehicle available for hire became known as a *hackney coach* or *hackney carriage*; the latter is still the official term for a taxi (compare HACK³ (4)); this usage prob led to the current sense, the hackney being chiefly used for driving.

hackney² *adj esp* formerly, kept for public hire: *a hackney cab*; *hackney coaches*; *hackney chairs*.

hackneyed *adj* lacking in freshness or originality; meaningless because used or done too often: *But that expression of 'violently in love' is so hackneyed* — Jane Austen.

hacksaw¹ *noun* a fine-toothed saw, *esp* for cutting metal.

hacksaw² *verb trans* to cut (metal) with a hacksaw.

had /d, əd, had; *strong* had/ *verb* past tense and past part. of HAVE¹.

haddock /'hadək/ *noun* (*pl* **haddocks** or collectively **haddock**) a silver-grey food fish of the N Atlantic, usu smaller than the related common cod: *Melanogrammus aeglefinus*. [Middle English *haddok* from Old French *hadot*]

hade¹ /hayd/ *noun* the angle made by the plane of a rock fault or vein with the vertical. [origin unknown]

hade² *verb intrans* to incline from the vertical.

Hades /'haydeez/ *noun* **1** in Greek mythology, the underground abode of the dead. **2** (*often* **hades**) *euphem* hell. [Greek *Haidēs*]

Hadith /hə'deeth/ *noun* the body of traditions relating to Muhammad and his companions. [Arabic *ḥadīṯ* tradition]

hadj /haj/ *noun* see HAJJ.

hadji /'haji/ *noun* see HAJJI.

hadn't /'hadnt/ *contraction* had not.

hadron /'hadron/ *noun* an elementary particle that takes part in strong interactions. ➤➤ **hadronic** /ha'dronik/ *adj*. [Greek *hadros* thick, heavy + -ON²]

hadrosaur /'hadrəsaw/ *noun* a duck-billed herbivorous dinosaur of the Cretaceous period. [Latin genus name *Hadrosaurus* from Greek *hadros* thick, stout + *sauros* lizard]

hadst /hadst/ *verb* archaic second person sing. past tense of HAVE¹.

haecceity /hek'seeiti, heek-/ *noun* in philosophy, the property a thing has of being individual and identifiable, such that it can be referred to as 'this' or 'this one'; individuality; uniqueness. [medieval Latin *haecceitas* from Latin *haec*, fem of *hic* this]

haem (*NAmer* **heme**) /heem/ *noun* a deep red compound containing iron, which occurs *esp* as the oxygen-carrying part of haemoglobin. [shortened from HAEMATIN]

haem- or **haemo-** (*NAmer* **hem-** or **hemo-**) *comb. form* forming words, denoting: blood: *haemodialysis*; *haemophilia*. [early French *hemo-* via Latin from Greek *haim-*, *haimo-*, from *haima* blood]

haemal (*NAmer* **hemal**) /'heeml/ *adj* **1** relating to the blood. **2** relating to or situated on the same side of the spinal cord as that on which the heart is placed: compare NEURAL, VENTRAL.

haemat- or **haemato-** (*NAmer* **hemat-** or **hemato-**) *comb. form* = HAEM-: *haematoma*. [Latin *haemat-*, *haemato-*, from Greek *haimat-*, *haimato-*, from *haimat-*, *haima* blood]

haematic (*NAmer* **hematic**) /hee'matik/ *adj dated* relating to or affecting the blood.

haematin (*NAmer* **hematin**) /'heemətin/ *noun* a brownish black or bluish black derivative of oxidized haem.

haematite (*NAmer* **hematite**) /'heemətiet/ *noun* iron oxide occurring as a crystalline or red earthy mineral. [via Latin from Greek *haimatitēs* bloodlike, from *haimat-*, *haima* blood]

haemato- *comb. form* see HAEMAT-.

haematocrit (*NAmer* **hematocrit**) /'heemətohkrit/ *noun* **1** the ratio of the volume of red blood cells to the total volume of blood. **2** an instrument used for determining this. [HAEMATO- + Greek *kritēs* judge, from *krinein* to judge]

haematology (*NAmer* **hematology**) /heemə'toləji/ *noun* the biology and medicine of diseases of the blood and blood-forming organs. ➤➤ **haematologic** /-'lojik/ *adj*, **haematological** /-'lojikl/ *adj*, **haematologist** *noun*.

haematoma (*NAmer* **hematoma**) /heemə'tohmə/ *noun* (*pl* **haematomas** *or* **haematomata** /-tə/) a tumour or swelling containing blood; = BRUISE¹ (1).

haematuria (*NAmer* **hematuria**) /heemə'tyooəri·ə/ *noun* the abnormal presence of blood or blood cells in the urine.

-haemia *comb. form* = -AEMIA.

haemo- *comb. form* see HAEM-.

haemocoele *or* **haemocoel** (*NAmer* **hemocoele** *or* **hemocoel**) /'heeməseel/ *noun* a body cavity in arthropods (phylum including insects and spiders; see ARTHROPOD) or some other invertebrates that normally contains blood and functions as part of the circulatory system.

haemocyanin (*NAmer* **hemocyanin**) /heemoh'sieɪənin/ *noun* a colourless respiratory pigment containing copper, found in the blood of various arthropods and molluscs. [HAEMO- + CYAN + -IN¹]

haemocytometer (*NAmer* **hemocytometer**) /ˌheemohsie'to mitə/ *noun* an instrument for counting blood cells suspended in a liquid, usu when viewed under a microscope.

haemodialysis (*NAmer* **hemodialysis**) /ˌheemohdie'aləsis/ *noun* (*pl* **haemodialyses** /-seez/) the purification of the blood by dialysis, in cases of kidney failure.

haemoglobin (*NAmer* **hemoglobin**) /heemoh'glohbin/ *noun* a protein containing iron that occurs in the red blood cells of vertebrates and is the means of oxygen transport from the lungs to the body tissues; found in haemolymph of some invertebrates. [short for earlier *haematoglobulin*]

haemolymph (*NAmer* **hemolymph**) /'heemohlimf/ *noun* a circulatory fluid in various invertebrate animals that is functionally comparable to the blood and lymph of vertebrates.

haemolysis (*NAmer* **hemolysis**) /hee'molisis/ *noun* the dissolution of red blood cells with release of haemoglobin. ⯈ **haemolytic** /-'litik/ *adj.*

haemophilia (*NAmer* **hemophilia**) /heemə'fili·ə/ *noun* delayed clotting of the blood with consequent difficulty in controlling bleeding even after minor injuries, occurring as a hereditary defect, usu in males. ⯈ **haemophiliac** /-ak/ *noun and adj*, **haemophilic** *adj.*

haemopoiesis (*NAmer* **hemopoiesis**) /ˌheemohpoy'eesis/ *noun* the formation of blood cells and platelets in the vertebrate bone marrow and lymphoid tissue, and of plasma in the liver. ⯈ **haemopoietic** /-'etik/ *adj.* [scientific Latin *haemopoiesis*, from HAEMO- + Greek *poiēsis* making]

haemoptysis (*NAmer* **hemoptysis**) /heeməp'tiesis/ *noun* the coughing up of blood from some part of the respiratory tract. [scientific Latin *haemoptysis* from HAEMO- + Greek *ptysis* act of spitting, from *ptyein* to spit]

haemorrhage¹ (*NAmer* **hemorrhage**) /'hemərij/ *noun* 1 a loss of blood from a ruptured blood vessel. 2 a continuous and severe depletion of a certain resource. ⯈ **haemorrhagic** /-'rajik/ *adj.* [French *hémorrhagie* via Latin from Greek *haimorrhagia*, from HAEMO- + -*rrhagia* a bursting forth, from *rhēgnynai* to burst]

haemorrhage² (*NAmer* **hemorrhage**) *verb intrans* to bleed profusely from a ruptured blood vessel; to suffer a haemorrhage. ⯈ *verb trans* 1 to expend or lose (a resource) at a disastrous rate: *We were haemorrhaging money on the new hospital wing.* 2 to disappear rapidly: *They watched helplessly as their support haemorrhaged.*

haemorrhoid (*NAmer* **hemorrhoid**) /'heməroyd/ *noun* (*usu in pl*) a mass of dilated veins in swollen tissue round or near the anus. ⯈⯈ **haemorrhoidal** /-'roydl/ *adj.* [early French *hemorrhoides* (pl) via Latin from Greek *haimorrhoides*, from *haimorrhoos* flowing with blood, from HAEMO- + *rhein* to flow]

haemostasis (*NAmer* **hemostasis**) /heemoh'staysis/ *noun* the arrest of bleeding. ⯈⯈ **haemostatic** /-'statik/ *adj.*

haemostat (*NAmer* **hemostat**) /'heemə stat/ *noun* an instrument for compressing a bleeding vessel. ⯈⯈ **haemostatic** /-'statik/ *adj.*

haeremai /hierə'mie/ *interj NZ* welcome. [Maori *haeremai*, literally 'come here']

hafiz /'hahfiz/ *noun* used as a title: a Muslim who knows the Koran by heart. [Persian *ḥafiẓ* from Arabic *ḥāfiẓ* guardian, from *ḥāfiẓa* to know by heart]

hafnium /'hafni·əm/ *noun* a silvery metallic transition chemical element that occurs naturally in zirconium ores, and is used in tungsten alloys for filaments: symbol Hf, atomic number 72. [Latin

hafnium from *Hafnia*, Latinized form of Danish *Havn*, former name of Copenhagen, city in Denmark]

haft¹ /hahft/ *noun* the handle of a weapon or tool. [Old English *hæft*]

haft² *verb trans* to fit (a weapon or tool) with a haft.

Hag. *abbr* Haggai (book of the Bible).

hag¹ /hag/ *noun* 1 a witch. 2 an ugly or ill-natured old woman. 3 = HAGFISH. ⯈⯈ **haggish** *adj.* [Middle English *hagge*, prob of Germanic origin]

hag² *noun Scot, N Eng* a bog, or a firm spot in a bog. [English dialect *hag* felled timber, of Scandinavian origin]

hagfish *noun* (*pl* **hagfishes** *or collectively* **hagfish**) any of several genera of jawless marine eel-like vertebrates with a sucking mouth surrounded with barbels, that feeds on dead or dying fishes by boring into their bodies: family Myxinidae. [HAG¹]

Haggadah /hə'gahdə/ *noun* (*pl* **Haggadoth** *or* **Haggadot** /-doht/) in Judaism: **a** ancient Jewish lore forming the nonlegal part of the TALMUD (body of Jewish law): compare HALAKAH. **b** the narrative read at the Passover SEDER (feast and ritual). ⯈⯈ **Haggadic** /hə'gadik/ *adj.* [Hebrew *haggādhāh* a tale]

haggard¹ /'hagəd/ *adj* 1 having a worn or gaunt appearance, *esp* through anxiety, illness, or lack of sleep. 2 said of a hawk: already mature before being caught and trained; untamed. ⯈⯈ **haggardly** *adv*, **haggardness** *noun.* [early French *hagard*, untamed]

haggard² *noun* an adult hawk caught wild.

haggis /'hagis/ *noun* (*pl* **haggis** *or* **haggises**) a traditional Scottish dish that consists of minced sheep's or calf's offal with suet, oatmeal, and seasonings, and traditionally boiled in the stomach of the animal. [Middle English *hagese*, perhaps from *haggen* to hack, chop, from Old Norse *haggva*]

haggle /'hagl/ *verb intrans* (**haggling**) to bargain or wrangle. ⯈⯈ **haggler** *noun.* [frequentative of English dialect *hag* to hew, from Old Norse *hoggva*]

hagi- *or* **hagio-** *comb. form* forming words, with the meanings: 1 holy: *hagioscope.* 2 saints: *hagiography.* [via late Latin from Greek, from *hagios* holy]

Hagiographa /hagi'ogrəfə/ *noun* the third part of the Jewish scriptures. [late Latin *Hagiographa* from late Greek, from *hagio-* (see HAGI-) + *graphein* to write]

hagiographer /hagi'ogrəfə/ *noun* 1 one of the compilers of the Hagiographa. 2 a person who writes the lives of saints.

hagiography /hagi'ogrəfi/ *noun* (*pl* **hagiographies**) 1 biography of saints or venerated people. 2 an idealizing or idolizing biography. ⯈⯈ **hagiographic** /-'grafik/ *adj*, **hagiographical** /-'grafikl/ *adj.*

hagiolatry /hagi'olətri/ *noun* 1 the worship of saints. 2 excessive veneration of any celebrated person. ⯈⯈ **hagiolater** *noun*, **hagiolatrous** *adj.*

hagiology /hagi'oləji/ *noun* 1 literature dealing with venerated people or writings. 2 a list of venerated figures. ⯈⯈ **hagiological** *adj*, **hagiologically** *adv.*

hagioscope /'hagiəskohp/ *noun* in a church, a narrow opening in a wall or column to give a view of the altar from a side aisle; = SQUINT² (2).

hagridden *adj* said of a facial expression: harassed or tormented.

hah /hah/ *interj* see HA².

ha-ha¹ /hah 'hah/ *interj* 1 used to express or represent laughter. 2 an exclamation of triumph. [Old English]

ha-ha² /'hah hah/ *noun* a fence or retaining wall sunk into a ditch and used as a boundary to a park or grounds, so as to give an uninterrupted view. [French *haha*, prob from *haha*, interj of surprise]

hahnium /'hahni·əm/ *noun* the name formerly proposed both for the synthetic radioactive chemical element HASSIUM (atomic number 108) and for another synthetic element, DUBNIUM (atomic number 105). [suggested in honour of Otto *Hahn* d.1968, German chemist, joint discoverer of nuclear fission]

HAI *abbr* 1 healthcare-associated infection. 2 hospital-acquired infection.

haik *or* **haick** /hayk, 'hah·ik/ *noun* an outer wrap for the head and body, of traditional Arabian design, worn in N Africa. [Arabic *hā'ik*]

haiku /'hiekooh/ *noun* (*pl* **haiku** *or* **haikus**) an unrhymed Japanese verse form of three lines containing five, seven, and five syllables respectively, or a poem written in this form: compare TANKA. [Japanese *haiku*]

hail¹ /hayl/ *noun* **1** precipitation in the form of small particles of clear ice or compacted snow. **2** used figuratively for a shower of things coming at one fast and furiously: *a hail of bullets*; *a hail of obscenities*; *facing a hail of questions*. [Old English *hægl*]

hail² *verb intrans* **1** to precipitate hail: *It's hailing.* **2** to pour down or strike like hail: *Bullets hailed down on all sides.*

hail³ *verb trans* **1a** to salute or greet (somebody). **b** to greet (somebody or something) with enthusiastic approval; to acclaim (them) as something: *He has been hailed as the new John Lennon.* **2** to summon (a taxi) by calling. ✳ **hail from** to be or have been a native or resident of (a place). ➤➤ **hailer** *noun*. [Middle English from Old Norse *heill*, literally 'healthy']

hail⁴ *interj archaic* (*also* **all hail**) used as a respectful salutation, sometimes by way of acclamation: *Hail, King, for so thou art* — Shakespeare; *So Judas kissed his master and cried 'All hail!' when as he meant all harm* — Shakespeare. [Old Norse *heill* healthy, as HAIL³, prob with the sense 'Be healthy!']

hail⁵ *noun* a call to attract attention: *Suddenly there came a hail from the edge of the clearing* — Edgar Rice Burroughs. ✳ **within hail** within earshot; within shouting distance.

hail-fellow-well-met *adj* heartily and often excessively informal from the first moment of meeting. [from the archaic greeting 'Hail, fellow! Well met!']

Hail Mary /'meəri/ *noun* (*pl* **Hail Marys**) a Roman Catholic prayer to the Virgin Mary that consists of salutations and a plea for her intercession. [translation of medieval Latin *Ave, Maria*, the first words of the prayer]

hailstone *noun* a pellet of hail.

hair /heə/ *noun* **1a** a slender threadlike outgrowth on the surface of an animal; *esp* any of the many pigmented hairs that form the characteristic coat of a mammal. **b** a structure resembling a hair, e.g. on a plant. **c** the coating of hairs on the human head or other body part, or on an animal. **2** haircloth. **3** a hair's breadth: *They won by a hair.* ✳ **hair of the dog** an alcoholic drink taken to cure a hangover [orig *a hair of the dog that bit you*, believed to cure the bite of a mad dog]. **in somebody's hair** persistently annoying or distracting somebody. **keep your hair on!** *Brit, informal* calm down! **let one's hair down** to relax and enjoy oneself. **make somebody's hair stand on end** to give them a fright. **not turn a hair** to give not the least indication of surprise or alarm: *She did not turn a hair when told of the savage murder.* ➤➤ **hairless** *adj*, **hairlike** *adj*. [Old English *hær*]

hair ball *noun* a compact mass of hair formed in the stomach of *esp* a hair-shedding animal, e.g. a cat, that cleans its coat by licking.

hairbrush *noun* a brush for the hair.

haircloth *noun* a stiff wiry fabric, *esp* of horsehair or camel hair, used for upholstery or for stiffening in garments.

haircut *noun* a cutting and shaping of the hair, or the style in which hair is cut.

hairdo /'heədooh/ *noun* (*pl* **hairdos**) *informal* a hairstyle.

hairdresser *noun* a person whose occupation is cutting, dressing, and styling people's hair. ➤➤ **hairdressing** *noun*.

hairdryer *or* **hairdrier** *noun* an electrical appliance for drying the hair by blowing it with warm air.

haired *adj* (*used in combinations*) having hair of the kind specified: *curly-haired*; *long-haired*; *dark-haired*.

hair extensions *pl noun* pieces of hair attached to a person's hair to make it look longer or fuller.

hair gel *noun* a jellylike substance used to hold a hairstyle.

hairgrip *noun Brit* a flat hairpin with prongs that close together.

hairline *noun* **1** the line above the forehead beyond which hair grows. **2** (*often used before a noun*) a very fine line; *esp* a fine crack in a surface: *a hairline crack*; *a hairline fracture*.

hairnet *noun* a loosely woven net, usu of hair, nylon, or silk, that is worn over the hair to keep it in place.

hairpiece *noun* a section of false hair worn to enhance a hairstyle or make a person's natural hair seem thicker or more plentiful.

hairpin *noun* **1** a two-pronged U-shaped pin of thin wire for holding the hair in place. **2** (*often used before a noun*) a sharp bend in a road: *a hairpin bend*; *approaching the hairpin*.

hair-raising *adj* causing terror, astonishment, or horror: *hair-raising adventures*; *hair-raising accounts of mistaken amputations.*

hair's breadth *noun* a very small distance or margin: *He was within a hair's breadth of losing the fight.*

hair shirt *noun* a shirt of haircloth formerly worn next to the skin as a penance by sinners, or in self-denial by ascetics.

hair-slide *noun Brit* a decorative clip for the hair.

hairsplitting *noun* **1** argument over unimportant differences and points of detail; quibbling. **2** (*used before a noun*) concerned with unimportant details; quibbling: *a hairsplitting distinction.* ➤➤ **hairsplitter** *noun*.

hairspray *noun* **1** a substance sprayed onto the hair to hold a style. **2** a flexible tubular apparatus, with tap attachments and a nozzle, for washing the hair.

hairspring *noun* a slender spiral spring that regulates the motion of the balance wheel of a watch.

hairstreak *noun* any of several species of small butterflies with striped markings or a row of dots on the underside of the wings and thin threadlike projections from the hind wings: *esp Callophrys rubi*, family Lycaenidae.

hairstyle *noun* a way of wearing or arranging the hair. ➤➤ **hairstyling** *noun*, **hairstylist** *noun*.

hair trigger *noun* a trigger so adjusted that very slight pressure will fire the gun.

hair-trigger *adj* immediately responsive to or disrupted by the slightest stimulus: *a hair-trigger temper.*

hairweaving *noun* the process of weaving a hairpiece into a person's hair, *esp* to cover a bald patch. ➤➤ **hair weave** *noun*.

hairy *adj* (**hairier, hairiest**) **1** covered with hair or material like hair: *Behold, Esau my brother is a hairy man, and I am a smooth man* — Bible. **2** *informal*. **a** frighteningly dangerous: *a hairy crossing through mountainous waves.* **b** alarmingly difficult. ➤➤ **hairiness** *noun*.

Haitian /'haysh(ə)n, hie'eeshən/ *noun* **1** a native or inhabitant of Haiti, a country in the Caribbean. **2** (*also* **Haitian Creole**) the language of Haiti, based on French and various W African languages. ➤➤ **Haitian** *adj*.

hajj *or* **hadj** /haj/ *noun* the pilgrimage to Mecca prescribed as a religious duty for Muslims. [Arabic *ḥajj* pilgrimage]

hajji *or* **hadji** /'haji/ *noun* **1** used as a title: a Muslim who has made a pilgrimage to Mecca. **2** a Christian, *esp* from Greece or the Near East, who has visited the Holy Sepulchre in Jerusalem. [Arabic *ḥajjī* from *ḥajj* pilgrimage]

haka /'hahkə/ *noun* **1** a ceremonial Maori chant and war dance. **2** a ritual imitating this, performed by New Zealand rugby teams as a preliminary to a match. [Maori *haka*]

hake /hayk/ *noun* (*pl* **hakes** *or collectively* **hake**) any of several species of large marine food fishes related to the common Atlantic cod: genera *esp Merluccius* and *Urophycis*. [Middle English, perhaps from old English *haca* hook]

hakea /'hahkiə, 'haykiə/ *noun* an Australian tree bearing hard woody fruits, important for its timber: genus *Hakea*. [scientific Latin *hakea*, named after C L von *Hake* d.1818, German botanist]

Hakenkreuz /'hahkənkroyts/ *noun* the clockwise swastika used as a Nazi symbol. [German *Hakenkreuz*, from *Haken* hook + *Kreuz* cross]

hakim¹ /'hakeem/ *noun* a Muslim physician trained in traditional medicine. [Arabic *ḥakīm* wise one]

hakim² /'hahkim/ *noun* a Muslim ruler, governor, or judge. [Arabic *ḥākim*]

hal- *or* **halo-** *comb. form* forming words, denoting: salt: *halophyte*. [Greek *hal-, hals* salt]

Halakah /halə'khah, hə'lahkə/ *noun* the body of Jewish law supplementing the scriptural law and forming the legal part of the TALMUD (body of Jewish law): compare HAGGADAH (A). ➤➤ **halakic** /-kik/ *adj*. [Hebrew *halākhāh* way]

halal¹ *or* **hallal** /hə'lahl/ *noun* **1** meat from an animal slaughtered according to Islamic law. **2** (*used before a noun*) relating to meat prepared in this way: *a halal butcher.* [Arabic *halāl* that which is lawful]

halal² *or* **hallal** *verb trans* (**halalled, halalling**) to slaughter (animals) for meat according to Islamic law.

halala or **halalah** /hə'lahlə/ noun (pl **halala** or **halalas**) a unit of currency in Saudi Arabia, worth 100th of a riyal. [Arabic *halala*]

halation /hə'laysh(ə)n/ noun the spreading of light beyond its proper boundaries, e.g. in a faulty photographic image. [HALO¹]

halberd /'halbəd/ or **halbert** noun a long-handled weapon combining a spear and battle-axe, used *esp* in the 15th and 16th cents. ➤➤ **halberdier** /-'diə/ noun. [Middle English *halberd* via French from early High German *helmbarde*, from *helm* handle + *barte* axe]

halcyon¹ /'halsi-ən/ noun **1** *literary* a kingfisher. **2** a mythical bird believed to breed at sea and calm the waves. [Middle English *alceon* via Latin from Greek *alkyōn, halkyōn*]

halcyon² adj **1** calm; peaceful: *the blue sky and halcyon sunshine of the genial spring weather* — Charlotte Brontë. **2** denoting a time, *esp* past, of idyllic tranquillity: *Journalists arriving in Beirut would invariably be told of the halcyon days which had just ended, of the peaceful Phoenician land in which Christians and Muslims ... could live in peace* — Robert Fisk.

hale¹ /hayl/ adj free from defect, disease, or infirmity; sound: *a hale and hearty old man*. [partly from Old English *hāl* whole, healthy; partly via Middle English *hail* from Old Norse *heill* healthy]

hale² verb trans archaic to haul or drag (something or somebody): *He ... saw six tall men haling a seventh along* — Tennyson; *Evil and good run strong in me, haling me both ways* — Stevenson; *The young Shakespeare poached upon Sir Thomas Lucy's deer preserves and got haled before the magistrate for it* — Mark Twain. [Middle English *halen* via early French *haler* from old Norse *hala*]

haler /'hahlə/ noun (pl **halers** or **haleru** /'hahlərooh/) a unit of currency in the Czech Republic and Slovakia, worth 100th of a koruna. [Czech *haler*]

half¹ /hahf/ noun (pl **halves** /hahvz/) **1** the fraction ½ or 0.5: *two and a half; a pound and a half; an hour and a half*. **2** either of two equal parts into which something is divisible, or a part of a thing approximately equal to a half: *the first half of the 20th century*. **3a** either of two equal periods of a match or performance: *Madrid were dominant during the second half*. **b** used *esp* at some British public schools, reflecting the old division of the school year into two: a school term: *This half, all my friends had returned to Whitminster* — A R Hope. **4** something of approximately half the value or quantity, e.g.: **a** *Brit, informal* half a pint, *esp* of beer. **b** *informal* a child's ticket: *one and two halves to Marble Arch*. **5** = HALFBACK. **6** a golfing score for a hole that equals one's opponent's. **✳ and a half** *informal* of remarkable quality: *That was a party and a half!* **by half** by a great deal: *increase profits by half; reduce costs by half*. **go halves** *informal* to pay half each. **in half** into two equal, or nearly equal, parts: *cut in half*. **not do things by halves** *informal* to go in for things with enthusiasm: *She was never one to do things by halves*. **one's other half** *informal* one's marital or other partner. **too clever, etc, by half** *informal* too clever, etc for one's own good; far too clever, etc: *You're too suspicious by half*. [Old English *healf*]

half² adj **1a** denoting half, or one of two equal parts, of a quantity: *a half share; half a dozen; half an hour; another half hour; a half pint*. **b** amounting to approximately half, or even a major proportion: *half the class; half my life; I was up half the night with the baby*. **c** stopping, or falling short, of the full or complete thing: *a half-volley; a half smile*. **2** extending over or covering only half: *a half door; half sleeves*.

half³ adv **1** in an equal part or degree: *I'm half Scots and half English; She was half crying, half laughing*. **2a** to the extent of a half: *a half-full glass; when the performance was half over*. **b** incompletely: *half cooked; half-remembered stories from her childhood*. **c** almost: *I half expected her to break into Russian*. **✳ half a chance** *informal* the slightest opportunity: *He'd appropriate the main bedroom, given half a chance*. **half as much again** one-and-a-half times as much. **half past two/three, etc** thirty minutes past two, three, etc. **half two/ three, etc** *informal* half past two, three, etc. **not half 1** *dated, informal*. **a** used as an emphatic positive, often as an interjection: *She wasn't half mad at us; 'Did he yell?' 'Not half!'* **b** not at all: *The orchestra aren't half bad*. **2** not nearly: *not half finished*. **not know the half of it** *informal* to be unaware of the major issue.

half-a-crown noun = HALF CROWN.

half a dozen noun **1** a set of six. **2** several.

half-and-half¹ noun something that is approximately half one thing and half another; *specif* a mixture of two beers, e.g. mild and bitter.

half-and-half² adj and adv approximately half one thing and half another: *The voting was split half-and-half; a half-and-half result*.

half-arsed adj *coarse slang* ineffectual or incompetent: *a half-arsed attempt to cover up the evidence*.

halfback noun a player in rugby, football, hockey, etc positioned immediately behind the forward line.

half-baked adj showing a lack of forethought or judgment; foolish: *a half-baked scheme for making money*.

halfbeak noun any of several species of small slender marine fishes with a long protruding lower jaw: esp *Euleptorhamphus viridus*, family Exocoetidae.

half-binding noun a type of bookbinding using two materials, with the better-quality or stronger material, e.g. leather, on the spine and corners. ➤➤ **half-bound** adj.

half blood noun **1a** the relationship between people having only one parent in common. **b** a person so related to another. **2** *offensive* a half-breed. ➤➤ **half-blooded** adj.

half-board noun *Brit* provision of bed, breakfast, and evening meal, e.g. by a hotel.

half boot noun a boot reaching up to mid calf.

half bottle noun a wine bottle that is half the size of a standard bottle: *In each of the guest rooms was a half bottle of spumante and a local guide book*.

half-breed noun *offensive* a person with parents of different races. ➤➤ **half-breed** adj.

half brother noun a brother related through one parent only.

half-butt noun a billiard cue that is longer than an ordinary cue.

half-caste noun *offensive* a person with parents of different races. ➤➤ **half-caste** adj.

half-century noun (pl **half-centuries**) **1** a period of 50 years. **2** *esp* in cricket, a score of 50.

half cock noun the position of the hammer of a firearm when about half retracted and held by the safety catch so that it cannot be operated by a pull on the trigger. **✳ go off at half cock** to move into action without adequate preparation, and risk failure.

half-cocked adj lacking adequate preparation or forethought.

half crown noun **1** a former British silver coin worth two shillings and sixpence. **2** this amount: *Entry to the castle was a half crown*.

half-cut adj *Brit, informal* somewhat drunk.

half-dozen noun = HALF A DOZEN.

half gainer noun a dive incorporating half a backward somersault, so that the diver enters the water headfirst, facing the diving board.

half-hardy adj said of a plant: able to withstand a moderately low temperature but injured by severe frost.

halfhearted adj lacking enthusiasm or effort: *halfhearted attempts to start a conversation*. ➤➤ **halfheartedly** adv, **halfheartedness** noun.

half hitch noun a type of simple knot made so as to be easily unfastened.

half-holiday noun a holiday of half a day, *esp* an afternoon.

half hour noun **1** a period of 30 minutes: *It was checked every half hour*. **2** the middle point of an hour: *The bus leaves on the half hour*. ➤➤ **half-hourly** adv and adj.

half-hunter noun a pocket watch that has a hinged metal cover with a small opening so that the approximate time can be read.

half-inch¹ noun a unit of length equal to half an inch.

half-inch² verb trans *Brit, slang* to steal (something): *She left her purse on the bar and somebody half-inched it*. [rhyming slang *half inch* to pinch]

half-landing noun a landing halfway up a flight of stairs.

half-length noun a portrait showing only the upper half of the body. ➤➤ **half-length** adj.

half-life noun **1** the time required for half of the atoms of a radioactive substance to become disintegrated. **2** the time required for the concentration of a drug or other substance in an organism to be reduced to half by natural processes.

half-light noun dim greyish light, e.g. at dusk.

half-mast noun **1** the position of a flag lowered halfway down the staff as a mark of mourning. **2** *humorous* the position of a garment when not fully pulled up: *A child appeared in the doorway with his shorts at half-mast.*

half measures *pl noun* (*in negative contexts*) a partial, half-hearted, or weak line of action: *I want your best efforts, no half measures.*

half-moon *noun* **1** the figure of the moon when half its disc is illuminated. **2** the first or last quarter of the moon's phases, the time corresponding to this appearance. **3** something like a half-moon in shape: *push down the cuticle to reveal the half-moon.*

half nelson *noun* a wrestling hold in which one arm is thrust under the corresponding arm of an opponent and the hand placed on the back of the opponent's neck: compare FULL NELSON.

half note *noun chiefly NAmer* a minim.

halfpenny *or* **ha'penny** /'haypni/ *noun* (*pl* **halfpennies** *or* **half-pence** /'hayp(ə)ns/ *or* **ha'pennies**) **1** a former British bronze coin representing one half of a penny. **2** a small amount.

halfpennyworth /'haypniwuhth/ *noun* **1** formerly, as much as could be bought for one halfpenny. **2** *Brit, informal* (*in negative contexts*) the least amount: *not a halfpennyworth of sense.*

half-pie *adj NZ, informal* inadequately planned or carried out. [*pie* possibly from Maori *pai* good]

half-pint *noun informal* a small or inconsequential person.

half-plate *noun* a photographic plate measuring 16.5 by 10.8 centimetres (6½ by 4¼ inches).

half seas over *adj Brit, informal, dated* somewhat drunk.

half sister *noun* a sister related through one parent only.

half size *noun* a size of clothing, *esp* in shoes, e.g. 5½, 6½ that is intermediate between two sizes.

half sole *noun* the part of the sole of a shoe from the central shank to the toe.

half sovereign *noun* a former British gold coin worth ten shillings.

half step *noun* in music, a semitone.

half term *noun Brit* a short holiday taken at a period about half-way through a school term.

half-timbered *adj* said of a building: constructed of timber framework with spaces filled in by brickwork or plaster. ➤➤ **half-timbering** *noun.*

halftime *noun* an intermission marking the completion of half of a game or contest.

half-title *noun* **1** the title of a book standing alone on a right-hand page immediately preceding the title page. **2** the title of a section of a book, printed on the right-hand page preceding it.

halftone *noun* **1** a photoengraving made from an image photographed through a screen and then etched so that the details of the image are reproduced in dots. **2** *chiefly NAmer* in music, a semitone.

half-track *noun* a vehicle with a drive system of an endless chain or track at the back and wheels at the front.

half-truth *noun* a statement that is only partially true; *esp* one intended to deceive.

half-volley *noun* **1** a shot in tennis made at a ball just after it has bounced. **2** an easily hit delivery of the ball in cricket that bounces closer than intended to the batsman.

halfway *adj and adv* **1** midway between two points: *at the halfway point; We were halfway home.* **2** (*usu in negative contexts*) in the least; minimally: *They're desperate for teachers and anyone whose English is halfway decent will get a job.*

halfway house *noun* **1** a halfway point or place; *esp* a compromise. **2** a house, hostel, etc for former residents of institutions, e.g. psychiatric patients, that is designed to help them readjust to living in the community. **3** formerly, a place, e.g. an inn, to stop midway on a journey.

half-wit *noun informal* a foolish or stupid person. ➤➤ **half-witted** *adj,* **half-wittedness** *noun.*

half year *noun* a six-month period: *profits in the first half year after the takeover.* ➤➤ **half-yearly** *adj and adv.*

halibut /'halibət/ *noun* (*pl* **halibuts** *or collectively* **halibut**) a large, dark green flatfish of the N Atlantic, used as food: *Hippoglossus hippoglossus.* [Middle English *halybutte,* from *haly* holy + *butte* flatfish, from early Dutch or early Low German *but;* from its being eaten on holy days]

halide /'haylied/ *noun* a binary compound of a halogen and another element or radical. [blend of HALOGEN + -IDE]

halite /'haliet/ *noun* the mineral sodium chloride; = ROCK SALT.

halitosis /hali'tohsis/ *noun* the condition of having offensive-smelling breath. [Latin *halitus* breath, from *halare* to breathe]

hall /hawl/ *noun* **1** the entrance room or passage of a building. **2** *NAmer* a corridor or passage in a building. **3** a large room for public assembly or entertainment. **4** (**the halls**) music hall as a form of entertainment, or the venues used for it: *play the halls.* **5a** the common dining room of a college or university, or a meal served there: *dine in hall.* **b** a building used by a college or university for some special purpose: *a hall of residence.* **6** the chief living room in a medieval house or castle. **7** *Brit* the manor house of a landed proprietor. [Old English *heall*]

hallal[1] /hə'lahl/ *noun* see HALAL[1].

hallal[2] *verb trans* (**hallalled, hallalling**) see HALAL[2].

hallelujah[1] /hali'loohyə/ *or* **alleluia** /ali'looh·yə/ *interj* used to express praise, joy, or thanks. [Hebrew *halălūyāh* praise (ye) the Lord]

hallelujah[2] *or* **alleluia** *noun* a shout or song used to express praise, joy, etc.

halliard /'halyəd/ *noun* see HALYARD.

hallmark[1] /'hawlmahk/ *noun* **1** in Britain, an official mark stamped on gold and silver articles after an assay test to testify to their purity. **2** a distinguishing characteristic or object: *Infantilism is possibly the hallmark of our generation* — John Wells. [named after Goldsmiths' *Hall,* London, where gold and silver articles were assayed and stamped]

hallmark[2] *verb trans* **1** to stamp (a gold or silver article) with a hallmark. **2** to characterize: *the discipline that hallmarks their teamwork.* ➤➤ **hallmarked** *adj.*

hallo[1] /hə'loh/ *noun* (*pl* **hallos**) see HELLO.

hallo[2] *or* **halloa** /hə'loh(ə)/ *interj, noun, and verb* (**halloing** *or* **halloaing, halloed** *or* **halloaed,** *pl* **hallos** *or* **halloas**) = HOLLO[1], HOLLO[2].

Hall of Fame *noun chiefly NAmer* a group of famous or illustrious individuals in a particular field.

hall of residence *noun* (*also* **halls of residence**) a building on a university or college campus with living, sleeping, and often eating facilities for students.

halloo /hə'looh/ *interj, noun, and verb* (**hallooing, hallooed,** *pl* **halloos**) = HOLLO[1], HOLLO[2].

hallow /'haloh/ *verb trans* **1** to make (something) holy or set it apart for holy use: *We cannot dedicate, we cannot consecrate, we cannot hallow this ground* — Abraham Lincoln. **2** (*usu as past part.*) to revere or venerate (a person, thing, place, etc): *the hallowed precincts of the quarter-deck* — Herman Melville. [Middle English *halowen* from Old English *hālgian,* from *hālig* HOLY]

Halloween *or* **Hallowe'en** /haloh'een/ *noun* 31 October, the eve of All Saints' Day, observed by dressing up in disguise, party turns, etc. [short for *All Hallow Even* All Saints' Eve]

Hallstadt /'halshtat/ *adj* see HALLSTATT.

hallstand *noun* a piece of furniture with pegs for holding coats, hats, and umbrellas.

Hallstatt *or* **Hallstadt** /'halshtat/ *adj* belonging to a central European early Celtic culture of the late Bronze Age and early Iron Age, lasting roughly 1200–600 BC and preceding the LA TÈNE culture. [*Hallstatt,* village in Austria, the site of remains associated with the culture]

hall tree *noun NAmer* = HALLSTAND.

halluces /'haləseez/ *noun pl* of HALLUX.

hallucinate /hə'loohsinayt/ *verb intrans* to have hallucinations. ➤➤ **hallucinator** *noun.* [Latin *hallucinatus,* past part. of *hallucinari* to prate or dream]

hallucination /hə,loohsi'naysh(ə)n/ *noun* the perception of something apparently real to the perceiver but which has no objective reality, or the image, object, etc perceived. ➤➤ **hallucinatory** /hə'loohsinət(ə)ri/ *adj.*

hallucinogen /hə'loohsinəjən/ *noun* a substance, e.g. LSD, that induces hallucinations. ➤➤ **hallucinogenic** /-'jenik/ *adj.*

hallux /'halǝks/ *noun* (*pl* **halluces** /'halǝseez/) **1** the big toe. **2** the innermost digit of the hind limb of vertebrates. [Latin *hallus, hallux*]

hallway *noun* an entrance hall or corridor.

halma /'halmǝ/ *noun* a board game played on a chequered board by two or four players with 19 or 13 pieces respectively. [Greek *halma* leap, from *hallesthai* to leap]

halo[1] /'hayloh/ *noun* (*pl* **haloes** *or* **halos**) **1a** in art, a circle of light surrounding the head or placed over it, in depictions of Christ or the saints. **b** something resembling this: *his sweet face with its halo of blond curls*. **c** the aura of glory or veneration surrounding an idealized person or thing: *European writers … pass before our imaginations like superior beings … surrounded by a halo of literary glory* — Washington Irving. **2a** a circle of light appearing to surround the sun or moon and resulting from refraction or reflection of light by ice particles in the earth's atmosphere. **b** any appearance resembling this: *the blurred haloes of the gas-lamps* — Conan Doyle. [via Latin from Greek *halōs* threshing floor, disc, halo]

halo[2] *verb trans* (**haloes, haloed, haloing**) to surround (somebody or something) with a halo, or as if with a halo: *haloed by steaming breath* — Robert W Service.

halo- *comb. form* see HAL-.

halogen /'halǝjǝn/ *noun* **1** any of the five elements fluorine, chlorine, bromine, iodine, and astatine, that form group VII B of the periodic table. **2** (*used before a noun*) denoting a lamp or a heat source that has a filament surrounded by halogen vapour. ⋙ **halogenous** /hǝ'lojǝnǝs/ *adj*. [HALO- + -GEN, because these elements easily form salts when combined with metals]

halogenate /'halǝjinayt/ *verb trans* to treat (a compound, etc) with a HALOGEN or cause it to combine with one. ⋙ **halogenation** *noun*.

haloid /'haloyd/ *noun* a compound whose molecules contain HALOGEN atoms. ⋙ **haloid** *adj*.

halon /'haylon/ *noun* any of several bromine-based chemical compounds, e.g. bromochlorodifluoromethane, that were formerly widely used in fire extinguishers but are now banned because they cause damage to the ozone layer when released into the atmosphere. [HALOGEN + -ON[3]]

halothane /'halǝthayn/ *noun* a nonexplosive general anaesthetic that is inhaled. [blend of HALO- + ETHANE]

halt[1] /hawlt/ *verb intrans* (*usu in imperative*) to come to a stop: *Company, halt!*; *She halted before another large canvas*. ⋗ *verb trans* **1** to bring (something) to a stop: *The strike has halted tubes and buses*. **2** to cause (a practice, etc) to stop; to end (it): *Halt the slaughter of seals*.

halt[2] *noun* **1** a stop or interruption, *esp* a temporary one: *We made the journey in five hours, with just one halt for refreshments*; *Traffic came to a halt*. **2** *Brit* a railway stopping place, without normal station facilities, for local trains. ✳ **call a halt to** to demand a stop to (an activity, etc): *It's time to call a halt to these arguments*. [German *Halt* from early High German *haltan* to hold]

halt[3] *adj archaic* lame: *Bring in hither the poor, and the maimed, and the halt, and the blind* — Bible. [Old English *healt*]

halt[4] *verb intrans archaic or literary* **1** to walk with a limp: *Halting on crutches of unequal size* — Cowper. **2** said of argumentation or versification: to proceed lamely or inadequately. **3** to hesitate between alternative courses; to waver: *halt between good and evil*.

halter[1] /'hawltǝ/ *noun* **1a** a rope or strap for leading or tying an animal. **b** a band round an animal's head to which a lead may be attached. **2** a U-shaped strap passing behind the neck, holding up the bodice of a woman's dress; = HALTER NECK. **3** *archaic* a noose for hanging criminals: *'What mercy can you offer him, Antonio?' 'A halter gratis; nothing else, for God's sake!'* — Shakespeare. [Old English *hælftre*]

halter[2] *verb trans* (**haltered, haltering**) to put a halter on (an animal) or catch it with or as if with a halter.

halterbreak *verb trans* (*past tense* **halterbroke**, *past part.* **halterbroken**) to accustom (a colt, etc) to wearing a halter.

haltere /'haltiǝ/ *noun* (*pl* **halteres** /hal'tiǝreez/) either of a pair of club-shaped sensory organs in a two-winged fly that maintain equilibrium in flight. [Greek *haltēres* weights held in the hand to give impetus when jumping, from *hallesthai* to leap]

halter neck /'hawltǝ/ *noun* a neckline formed by a strap passing from the front of a garment round the neck and leaving the shoulders and upper back bare, or a garment having such a neckline.

halting *adj* **1** hesitant or faltering: *People seldom see the halting and painful steps by which the most insignificant success is achieved* — Annie Sullivan, teacher of Helen Keller. **2** limping: *a halting gait*. **3** said of verse: scanning imperfectly: *For here's a paper written in his hand, a halting sonnet … fashioned to Beatrice* — Shakespeare. ⋙ **haltingly** *adv*.

halvah *or* **halva** /'halvah/ *noun* a sweet confection of crushed sesame seeds mixed with honey. [Yiddish *halva* via Romanian and Turkish from Arabic *ḥalwā* sweetmeat]

halve /hahv/ *verb trans* **1a** to divide (something) into two equal parts. **b** to share (something) equally: *We halved the proceeds*. **c** to reduce (an amount) to a half. *halving the present cost*. **2** to play (a hole or match in golf) in the same number of strokes as one's opponent. [Middle English *halven*, from HALF[1]]

halves /hahvz/ *noun* pl of HALF[1].

halyard *or* **halliard** /'halyǝd/ *noun* a rope or tackle for hoisting or lowering a sail, etc. [alteration of Middle English *halier*, from *halen*: see HAUL[1]]

ham[1] /ham/ *noun* **1** the meat of the rear end of a bacon pig, *esp* the thigh, when removed from the carcass before curing with salt: compare GAMMON[1]. **2** (*usu in pl*) a buttock with its associated thigh. [Old English *hamm*]

ham[2] *noun* **1** an inexpert though showy performer, *esp* an actor who overplays clumsily. **2** an amateur radio operator. [short for *hamfatter* a third-rate actor, minstrel, or other performer, prob from *The Hamfat Man*, a negro minstrel song; influenced by AMATEUR[1]]

ham[3] *verb intrans* (**hammed, hamming**) *informal* to overplay a part. ✳ **ham it up** to perform with exaggerated speech or gestures; to overact. [HAM[2]]

hamadryad /hamǝ'drieǝd, -ad/ *noun* **1** in classical mythology, a nymph who inhabits a tree and dies when it dies. **2** = KING COBRA. [via Latin from Greek *hamadryad-, hamadryas* from *hama* together with + *dryad- dryas* DRYAD]

hamadryas /hamǝ'drie-ǝs/ *noun* a large baboon of N Africa and Arabia, with a silvery-grey cape of fur and a red face and rump, worshipped by the ancient Egyptians: *Papio hamadryas*. [Latin *hamadryas*: see HAMADRYAD]

hamba /'hambǝ/ *interj S Afr, usu offensive* go away! beat it! [Nguni (Bantu language group) *ukuttamba* to go away]

hamburger *noun* **1** (*also* **beefburger**) a round flat cake of minced beef, fried or grilled. **2** a bread roll containing one of these. [German *Hamburger* of *Hamburg*, city in Germany: compare FRANKFURTER]

hame /haym/ *noun* either of two curved projections on the collar of a draught horse to which the traces are attached. [Middle English from early Dutch]

ham-fisted *adj informal* lacking dexterity with the hands; clumsy. ⋙ **ham-fistedly** *adv*, **ham-fistedness** *noun*.

ham-handed *adj* = HAM-FISTED.

hamlet /'hamlit/ *noun* a small village, *esp*, in Britain, one without its own church. [Middle English from early French *hamelet*, dimin. of *ham* village, of Germanic origin]

hammer[1] /'hamǝ/ *noun* **1a** a hand tool consisting of a solid head set crosswise on a handle, used to strike a blow, e.g. to drive in a nail. **b** a power tool that substitutes a metal block or a drill for the hammerhead. **2a** a lever with a striking head for ringing a bell or striking a gong. **b** the part of the mechanism of a modern gun whose action ignites the cartridge. **c** in a mammal, the outermost of three bones that transmit sound to the inner ear; = MALLEUS. **d** an auctioneer's mallet; = GAVEL. **e** a padded mallet in a piano action for striking a string. **f** a hand mallet for playing various percussion instruments. **3a** a metal sphere weighing about 7.3kg (16lb), attached by a flexible wire to a handle and thrown as far as possible, as an athletic contest. **b** an athletic field event in which the hammer is thrown. ✳ **come/go under the hammer** to be sold by auction. **hammer and tongs** with determination and vigour: *They argued hammer and tongs*. [Old English *hamor*]

hammer[2] *verb* (**hammered, hammering**) ⋗ *verb intrans* **1** to strike blows, *esp* repeatedly, with, or as if with, a hammer; to pound: *hammer on the door*. **2a** (+ away at) to reiterate an opinion or attitude: *hammer away at the same points*. **b** to apply oneself vigorously to something: *hammer away at revision*. ⋗ *verb trans* **1** to beat or drive (something) with repeated blows of a hammer: *hammer in a nail.* **2** (*often* + *into*) to force (somebody) into compliance by repeated threats, etc: *They wanted to hammer him into submission.* **3a** *informal* to beat (a person or team) decisively: *We hammered them at football.* **b** to condemn (a person or their work) roundly: *get hammered by the critics.* **4** to declare formally (a member of the Stock Exchange) to be insolvent and therefore forbidden to trade. ✳ **hammer into shape** to make (a thing or person) conform to a desired pattern by persistent effort: *We'll soon hammer the text into shape.* **hammer something into** to make (somebody) learn or remember something by continual repetition: *He had grammar hammered into him at school.*

hammer and sickle *noun* an emblem consisting of a crossed hammer and sickle used chiefly as a symbol of Communism.

hammer beam *noun* either of the short horizontal beams or cantilevers to support either end of an arch or principal rafter in a roof truss.

hammerhead *noun* **1** the striking part of a hammer. **2** any of several species of medium-sized sharks with eyes at the ends of bulging projections on each side of the flattened head, so as to have the appearance of a double-headed hammer: genus *Sphyrna*. **3** an African wading bird related to the stork, with a backward-pointing crest: *Scopus umbretta*. **4** an African fruit bat with a hammer-shaped muzzle: *Hypsignathus monstrosus*.

hammering *noun informal* a decisive defeat: *Our team took a terrible hammering in the final.*

hammerlock *noun* a wrestling hold in which an opponent's arm is held bent behind their back.

hammer out *verb trans* to produce (something) or bring it about through lengthy discussion: *The committee hammered out a new policy.*

hammertoe *noun* a deformity of the toe, giving it the appearance of an inverted V, usu resulting from ill-fitting footwear.

hammock /'hamək/ *noun* a hanging bed, usu made of netting or canvas and suspended by cords at each end. [Spanish *hamaca* from Taino *hamaka*]

hammy *adj* (**hammier, hammiest**) *informal* **1** characterized by clumsy overacting: *a hammy performance.* **2** said of a bodily part, *esp* the thighs, hands, or upper arms: large and solid. ➤➤ **hammily** *adv,* **hamminess** *noun.*

hamper[1] /'hampə/ *verb trans* (**hampered, hampering**) **1** to restrict the movement or operation of (somebody); to hinder (them): *hampered by the baby's paraphernalia.* **2** to interfere with the progress of (something): *Our investigations were severely hampered by his refusal to cooperate.* [Middle English *hamperen,* prob of Germanic origin]

hamper[2] *noun* essential though cumbersome tackle on board ship.

hamper[3] *noun* **1** a large basket with a cover for packing, storing, or transporting food, etc: *a picnic hamper.* **2** to restrict fare contained in a hamper, presented as a gift: *a Christmas hamper.* [Middle English *hampere,* alteration of *hanaper* case to hold goblets from early French *hanap* goblet, of Germanic origin]

hamster /'hamstə/ *noun* any of several species of small Eurasian rodents with very large cheek pouches, often kept as pets: genus *Cricetus* and other genera. [German *Hamster* from Old High German *hamustro,* of Slavonic origin]

hamstring[1] *noun* **1** any of the five tendons at the back of the human knee. **2** a large tendon above and behind the hock of a horse or other four-legged animal.

hamstring[2] *verb trans* (*past tense and past part.* **hamstrung**) **1** to cripple (a person or animal) by cutting the leg tendons. **2** to restrict (somebody) severely or render them powerless: *We were hamstrung by our lack of local knowledge.*

hamulus /'hamyooləs/ *noun* (*pl* **hamuli** /-lie/) in biology, a hook or hooked part, e.g. those linking the fore- and hindwings in a bee or wasp. [Latin *hamulus,* dimin. of *hamus* hook]

Han /han/ *noun* the Chinese people; ethnic Chinese, as distinct from Mongolians, Manchus, etc. [Chinese (Pekingese) *Han,* the name of a Chinese dynasty 206 BC–AD 220]

hand[1] /hand/ *noun* **1** the end of the forelimb of human beings, monkeys, etc when modified as a grasping organ, or the segment of the forelimb of vertebrate animals corresponding to this. **2** something resembling a hand, e.g.: **a** an indicator or pointer on a

dial. **b** a stylized figure of a hand used as a pointer or marker. **c** a group of usu large leaves, e.g. of tobacco, reaped or tied together or of bananas growing together. **d** a foreleg of pork. **3** (*in pl*). **a** possession: *The documents fell into the hands of the enemy.* **b** control or supervision: *I'll leave the matter in your capable hands.* **4** a side; a direction: *on my right hand; sailing along the canal with fields of cattle on either hand; New buildings were going up on every hand.* **5** a pledge, *esp* of betrothal or marriage: *He asked for her hand in marriage.* **6** handwriting: *She wrote a small neat hand.* **7** a unit of measure equal to about 102mm (4in.) used *esp* for the height of a horse: *horses under fourteen hands.* **8a** a player in a card or board game, or the cards or pieces held by them. **b** a single round in a game: *a hand of bridge.* **c** the force or solidity of one's position, e.g. in negotiations: *strengthen one's hand.* **d** a turn to serve in a game, e.g. squash, in which only the server may score points and which lasts as long as the server can win points. **9a** a person who performs or executes a particular work: *two portraits by the same hand.* **b** a worker or employee: *They employed over 100 hands.* **c** a person employed at manual labour or general tasks: *a field hand.* **d** a member of a ship's crew: *She sank with all hands.* **10a** handiwork. **b** style of execution; workmanship: *the hand of a master.* **11** (*used before a noun*). **a** for use in the hand: *a hand grenade.* **b** for carrying personally: *hand luggage.* **c** operated by hand: *the hand brake; a hand drill.* ✳ **all hands on deck!** a summons to all crew members or, more generally, to all personnel, to participate urgently in a joint effort. **an old hand at something** a person who has had plenty of experience at it: *She's an old hand at compromising.* **at first/second hand** directly, or through an intermediary: *hear news at second hand.* **at hand** near in time or place. **at the hand(s) of** by the act or instrumentality of (somebody). **by hand** with the hands, rather than mechanically. **do a hand's turn** (*in negative contexts*) to do the least scrap of work: *people who have huge incomes and never do a hand's turn.* **fight hand to hand** to fight in single combat or with close physical contact. **give/lend a hand** to help: *In the end everybody lent a hand to get the job finished; Can you give me a hand?* **give somebody a big hand** *informal* to give them a hearty clap. **go hand in hand** to be closely linked: *Poverty and crime go hand in hand.* **hand in glove** in close collaboration or cooperation: *the days when the unions and Labour worked hand in glove; They were hand in glove with the racketeers.* **hand in hand 1** holding hands. **2** in close cooperation: *working hand in hand with MI5.* **have one's hands tied** to be prevented from acting. **have one's hands full** *informal* to be fully occupied: *What with the triplets, six goldfish, three dogs, and the mushroom farm, he's got his hands full most days.* **have/take a hand in something** to have an instrumental part in it: *I suspect her of having had a hand in this; Then Fate took a hand.* **hold hands** to hold each other's inside hand. **hold somebody's hand** to give them guidance and reassurance. **in hand 1** not used up or lost and at one's disposal: *They have a game in hand.* **2** said of a horse: being led rather than being ridden. **3** under way: *She has the work in hand.* **keep one's hand in** to remain in practice. **keep one's hands clean** to avoid becoming involved in underhand, immoral, or illegal activities. **know something like the back of one's hand** to be intimately acquainted with it: *She knows his poetry like the back of her hand.* **lay hands/get one's hands on** to locate or get hold of (a person or thing): *Wait till I get my hands on him!* **live hand to mouth** to lead an existence in which one satisfies one's immediate needs only, having no resources for more. **make/lose/spend money hand over fist** to do so very rapidly. **off hand** without checking or investigating: *I can't say off hand how many members we have.* **off somebody's hands** out of somebody's care or charge. **on hand 1** ready to use. **2** in attendance; present. **on one's hands** in one's possession, care, or management. **on the one hand ... on the other hand** a formula for presenting contraries: *On the one hand I could do with a break, on the other I can't just let things go.* **out of hand 1** out of control: *That child has got quite out of hand.* **2** without delay; without reflection or consideration: *He refused it out of hand.* **put one's hands together** to clap or applaud. **put one's hands up** to raise one's hands e.g. to show surrender when being threatened with a firearm. **set one's hand to** to become engaged in (a task, etc). **take somebody/something in hand 1** to undertake something. **2** to embark on the control or reform of somebody or something. **to hand** available and ready for use; *esp* within reach. **turn one's hand to** to try doing (something, *esp* a practical task). **wait on somebody hand and foot** to attend to their every need. **win hands down** *informal* to win with ease. [Old English]

hand[2] *verb trans* **1** to give or pass (something) to somebody with the hand or hands. **2** to lead or assist (somebody) somewhere with the hand: *He handed her out of the car.* **3** to furl (a sail). ✳ **hand it**

to to give credit to (somebody): *You have to hand it to them, they did a good job.*

hand- *comb. form* forming words, with the meanings: **1** used or carried in, worn on, or operated by, the hand: *handset; handcuffs; handcart.* **2** by hand; by human skill as distinct from machine: *hand-operated; handcrafted.* **3** personally as distinct from randomly: *handpicked.*

-hand *comb. form* forming adjectives, denoting: **1** intermediate users or intermediaries of the number specified: *a second-hand car; third-hand information.* **2** side: *the top lefthand drawer.*

handbag *noun Brit* a bag designed for carrying small personal articles and money, carried usu by women.

handball *noun* **1** a game resembling fives and played in a walled court or against a single wall, or the small rubber ball used in this game. **2** an amateur indoor or outdoor game between two teams of seven or eleven players the object of which is to direct a football into the opponent's goal by throwing and catching. **3** the offence of handling the ball in football.

handbarrow *noun* a flat rectangular frame with handles at both ends for carrying loads.

handbill *noun* a small printed sheet to be distributed, e.g. for advertising, by hand.

handbook *noun* a short reference book, *esp* on a particular subject.

hand brake *noun* a hand-operated brake in a motor vehicle, used to hold a vehicle that is already stationary.

handbrake turn *noun* a sharp U-turn in a vehicle caused by speedy application of the hand brake while turning the steering wheel.

handbreadth *or* **hand's breadth** *noun* any of various units of length varying from about 2½ to 4in. (63.5 to 102mm) based on the breadth of a hand.

h and c *abbr Brit* said of water: hot and cold.

handcart *noun* a cart drawn or pushed by hand.

handcraft¹ *noun* = HANDICRAFT.

handcraft² *verb trans* to fashion (an object) by handicraft.

handcuff *verb trans* to apply handcuffs to (somebody); to manacle (them).

handcuffs *pl noun* a pair of metal rings, usu connected by a chain or bar, for locking round prisoners' wrists.

hand down *verb trans* **1** to transmit (a possession, skill, etc) in succession, e.g. from father to son; to bequeath (something). **2** to give (an outgrown article of clothing) to a younger member of one's family. **3** to deliver (a judgment) in court.

handed *adj* (*used in combinations*) **1** having or using the kind of hand or number of hands specified: *right-handed; a two-handed shot; four-handed cribbage.* **2** with the hands in the specified state: *She returned empty-handed.* ➤➤ **handedness** *noun.*

-hander *comb. form* forming nouns, denoting: **1** a play, film, etc having a specified number of leading roles: *The new musical was a spectacular two-hander.* **2** a person tending to use the specified hand: *a left-hander.*

handful /'handf(ə)l/ *noun* (*pl* **handfuls**) **1** an amount held in the hand, or as much or as many as the hand will grasp. **2** a small quantity or number: *only a handful of applicants.* **3** *informal* somebody or something, e.g. a child or animal, that is difficult to control: *That boy is a real handful.*

handgrip *noun* a handle.

handgun *noun* a firearm held and fired with one hand.

hand-held *adj* said of a computer, camera, etc: small enough to be used while held in the hand.

handhold *noun* something to hold onto for support, e.g. in mountain climbing.

handicap¹ /'handikap/ *noun* **1** a disability or disadvantage that makes achievement unusually difficult. **2a** an artificial advantage or disadvantage given to contestants so that all have a more equal chance of winning, or a race or contest with such an advantage or disadvantage. **b** the number of strokes by which a golfer on average exceeds par for a course. **c** the extra weight assigned to a racehorse as a handicap. [orig in the sense 'a game in which forfeits were held in a cap', from *hand in cap*]

handicap² *verb trans* (**handicapped, handicapping**) **1** to assign handicaps to (people or horses); to impose handicaps on (them). **2** to put (somebody) at a disadvantage.

handicapped *adj* **1** *dated, sometimes offensive.* **a** affected by physical or mental disability: *the physical strain of looking after her handicapped husband.* **b** (**the handicapped**) (*used as a pl noun*) people with physical or mental disabilities: *organizations offering holidays for the handicapped.* **2** said of a golfer or other participant in a competition: assigned a disadvantage at the start of play, a race, etc.

handicapper *noun* **1** somebody who assigns handicaps. **2** (*usu in combination*) somebody who competes, *esp* in golf, with a specified handicap: *a five-handicapper.*

handicraft /'handikrahft/ *noun* **1** manual skill, or an occupation requiring it. **2** an article or articles fashioned by handicraft. [Middle English *handi-crafte*, alteration of HANDCRAFT¹]

handiwork /'handiwuhk/ *noun* **1** work done personally: *She was standing and admiring her handiwork.* **2** work done by the hands, or the product of such work. [Old English *handgeweorc*, from HAND¹ + *geweorc*, from *ge-* (collective prefix) + *weorc* WORK¹]

handkerchief /'hangkəchif/ *noun* (*pl* **handkerchiefs** *or* **handkerchieves** /-cheevz/) a small piece of cloth used for various purposes, e.g. blowing the nose or wiping the eyes, or as a clothing accessory.

handle¹ /'handl/ *noun* **1** a part that is designed to be grasped by the hand. **2** the feel and quality of a textile, evident from touching it. **3** *informal.* **a** one's name or nickname. **b** a title of rank or nobility, or double-barrelled name: *have a handle to one's name.* **4** *informal* any means of coming to grips with something: *get a handle on the situation.* ➤➤ **handleless** *adj.* [Old English]

handle² *verb trans* **1a** to try or examine (something), e.g. by touching or moving, with the hand: *You have to handle silk to judge its weight.* **b** to manage (a horse, etc) with the hands. **2a** to deal with (a subject, idea, etc) in speech or writing, or as a work of art. **b** to manage or be in charge of (something): *A solicitor handles all my affairs.* **3** to deal with (somebody or something): *She handled the clients very well.* **4** to engage in the buying, selling, or distributing of (a commodity). ➤ *verb intrans* said of a vehicle, etc: to respond to the controls in a specified way: *a car that handles well.* ➤➤ **handleable** *adj,* **handling** *noun.*

handlebar *noun* (*also in pl*) a bar, *esp* on a cycle or scooter, for steering.

handlebar moustache *noun* a long heavy moustache that curves upwards at each end.

handler *noun* **1** (*usu in combination*) a person who handles or deals with a specified thing: *the baggage-handlers; food-handlers.* **2** a person who is in immediate physical charge of an animal: *a police-dog handler.* **3a** a boxer's personal trainer, also acting as a second. **b** *informal* a performer's manager or publicity agent.

handlist *noun* a short list for circulation, e.g. of items on display at a sale or exhibition, or of books and articles constituting the required reading for a course.

handmade *adj* made by hand rather than by machine.

handmaid *noun* = HANDMAIDEN.

handmaiden *noun* **1** *archaic* a personal maid or female servant. **2** something whose essential function is to serve or assist: *good sense ... which is the indispensable handmaiden of the critical art* — Carlos Baker.

hand-me-down *noun* a garment or other possession that has been passed on to one, *esp* by an older sibling; = REACH-ME-DOWN¹.

handoff *noun* in rugby, the act or an instance of pushing away an opponent with the palm of the hand.

hand off *verb trans* in rugby, to push off (an opposing player) with the palm of the hand so as to avoid a tackle.

hand on *verb trans* to transmit (something) to the next person in a succession.

hand organ *noun* a barrel organ operated by a hand crank.

handout *noun* **1** something, e.g. food, clothing, or money, distributed free, *esp* to people in need. **2** a folder or circular of information for free distribution.

hand out *verb trans* **1** to give (something) freely to a group of people. **2** to administer (a punishment).

handover *noun* an act of transferring something, *esp* power or responsibility, from one person or group to another.

hand over *verb trans* to yield control or possession of (something or somebody).

handpick *verb trans* to select (somebody or something) personally and carefully. ➤➤ **handpicked** *adj*.

handrail *noun* a narrow rail for grasping with the hand as a support, *esp* near stairs.

handsaw *noun* a saw, usu operated with one hand.

hand's breadth *noun* see HANDBREADTH.

handsel[1] *or* **hansel** /'hansl/ *noun archaic* a gift made as a token of good wishes or luck, *esp* at the beginning of a new year. [Middle English *hansell*, prob from Old Norse *handsal* promise or bargain confirmed by a handshake, from *hand-, hond* hand + *sal* payment]

handsel[2] *or* **hansel** *verb trans* (**handselled**, **handselling** *or* NAmer **handseled, handseling**) 1 to give a handsel to (somebody). 2 to inaugurate or make ceremonial first use of (something): *handsel the new premises.*

handset *noun* 1 the part of a telephone that contains the mouth-piece and earpiece; = RECEIVER (1B). 2 the remote-control device for a television set, video recorder, etc.

hands-free *adj* said of a telephone, etc: able to be used without being held in the hands.

handshake *noun* a clasping and shaking of each other's usu right hand by two people, e.g. in greeting or agreement.

hands-off *adj* 1 said of a mechanical device, etc: not requiring the use of the hands: *a hands-off cellular telephone.* 2 said of management style: encouraging a degree of autonomy and keeping free of involvement as far as possible.

handsome /'hansəm/ *adj* 1a said of a man: having a pleasing appearance; good-looking. b said of a woman: attractive in a dignified statuesque way. 2 said of a building, room, etc: well-proportioned; stately. 3 considerable or sizable: *a painting that commanded a handsome price.* 4 generous, gracious, magnanimous, or liberal: *handsome contributions to charity; That's very handsome of you.* ➤➤ **handsomely** *adv*, **handsomeness** *noun*. [Middle English *handsom* easy to manipulate, from HAND[1] + -SOME[1]]

hands-on *adj* involving direct personal participation or practical experience: *hands-on computer courses.*

handspike *noun* formerly, an iron-tipped bar used as a lever, chiefly by sailors and gunners. [by folk etymology from Dutch *handspaak*, from *hand* hand + *spaak* pole]

handspring *noun* an acrobatic movement in which one turns one's body forward or backward in a full circle from a standing position and lands first on the hands and then on the feet.

handstand *noun* an act of supporting and balancing the body upside down on the hands with the legs in the air.

hand-to-hand *adj* involving physical contact; very close: *hand-to-hand fighting.*

hand-to-mouth *adj* having or providing only just enough for immediate needs; precarious: *a hand-to-mouth existence.*

handwork *noun* work done with the hands rather than by machine.

handwriting *noun* writing done by hand; *esp* the style of writing peculiar to a particular person.

handwritten *adj* said of a letter, etc: written by hand. [back-formation from HANDWRITING]

handy *adj* (**handier, handiest**) 1a convenient for use; useful. b said of a vessel or vehicle: easily handled. 2 conveniently near. 3 clever in using the hands, *esp* in a variety of practical ways. ➤➤ **handily** *adv*, **handiness** *noun*.

handyman *noun* (*pl* **handymen**) 1 a man who does odd jobs. 2 a man who is competent in a variety of skills or repair work.

hang[1] /hang/ *verb* (*past tense and past part.* **hung** /hung/) ➤ *verb trans* 1a to fasten (something) to an elevated point by the top so that the lower part is free; to suspend (something). b (*past tense and past part.* **hanged**) to suspend (somebody) by the neck until dead, usu as a form of capital punishment: *Few believe it certain they are ... to die, and those who do, set themselves to behave with resolution, as a man does who is going to be hanged: he is not the less unwilling to be hanged* — Dr Johnson. c to fasten (a door, window, etc) on a point of suspension so as to allow free motion within given limits. d to suspend (meat, *esp* game) before cooking to make the flesh tender and develop the flavour. 2 to decorate, furnish, or cover (a place) by hanging something up, e.g. draperies or bunting: *a room hung with tapestries.* 3 to hold or bear (the head) in a suspended or inclined position: *He hung his head in shame.* 4 to fasten (something, *esp* wallpaper) to a wall, e.g. with paste. 5 to display (a picture), e.g. in a gallery. ➤ *verb intrans* 1a to remain fastened at the top so that the lower part is free; to dangle. b (*past tense and past part.* **hanged**) to die by hanging. 2 to remain poised or stationary in the air: *The bird hung for a minute before swooping.* 3 to stay on; to persist: *The smell of the explosion hung in the afternoon air.* 4 (+ over) to be imminent; to impend; to be a threat to somebody: *The threat of redundancy hung over the workforce.* 5 to fall or droop from a tense or taut position: *His mouth hung open.* 6 (+ up/upon) to depend on something: *The result of the election hangs on one vote.* 7 to lean, incline, or jut over or downward. 8 to fall in flowing lines: *Your coat hangs well.* ✱ **can go hang** *informal* used in contemptuous dismissal: *They can all go hang for all I care.* **hang a left/right** *NAmer, informal* to take a right or left turn. **hang fire** see FIRE[1]. **hang heavily** said of time: to pass slowly and tediously. **hang in the balance** to be uncertain or at stake. **hang it/hang it all!** an expression of annoyance or frustration. **hang on every word** to listen attentively to what somebody is saying. **hang tough** *NAmer, informal* to remain obdurate or firmly resolved. [partly from Old English *hon* (verb trans); partly from Old English *hangian* (verb intrans and verb trans)]

Usage note

hanged *or* **hung**? *Hung* is the correct form of the past tense and past participle of *to hang*, except in the sense 'to execute by hanging'. In this sense the form *hanged* (*was hanged at Tyburn*) is preferable, although *hung* is often found (*hung, drawn and quartered*). *Hanged* is the form used in the mild, rather dated oath: (*I'll be*) *hanged if I know!*

hang[2] *noun* 1 the manner in which a thing hangs. 2 a downward slope, or a droop. ✱ **get the hang of** *informal* to learn how to use, or deal with (something); to get the knack of (it).

hang[3] ✱ **not care/give a hang** *informal* not to care in the least; not to give a damn.

hang about *verb intrans Brit* 1 to wait or stay, usu without purpose or activity. 2 (+ with) to associate or be friendly with somebody.

hangar /'hangə/ *noun; esp* a large shed for housing aircraft. [French *hangar* shelter, prob of Germanic origin]

hang around *verb intrans* = HANG ABOUT.

hang back *verb intrans* to be reluctant to move or act; to hesitate.

hangdog *adj* ashamed or abject: *a hangdog expression.*

hanger[1] *noun* 1 a loop, strap, peg, or other device on or by which something can be hung. 2 a piece of shaped wire, plastic, or wood, surmounted by a hook, for hanging clothes on; = COAT HANGER. 3 (*usu in combinations*) a person who hangs something: *a paper-hanger.* 4 a short sword or dagger: *I made him a belt ... such as in England we wear hangers in* — Defoe.

hanger[2] *noun Brit* a wood growing on a steeply sloping hillside. [Old English *hangra* from *hangian* to hang]

hanger-on *noun* (*pl* **hangers-on**) a sycophantic follower or associate of a person, group, etc.

hang-glider *noun* a glider that resembles a kite and is controlled by the body movements of the harnessed person suspended beneath it. ➤➤ **hang-gliding** *noun*.

hangi /'hahngi/ *noun* (*pl* **hangis**) *NZ* 1 a Maori oven in the form of an open-air cooking pit. 2 the food produced in such an oven. 3 a social gathering for such a meal. [Maori *hangi*]

hang in *verb intrans chiefly NAmer, informal* to refuse to be discouraged or intimidated; to persist.

hanging[1] *noun* 1 execution by suspension from a noose. 2a a covering, e.g. a tapestry, for a wall. b a curtain.

hanging[2] *adj* 1 situated or lying on steeply sloping ground: *hanging gardens.* 2 jutting out; overhanging: *a hanging rock.* 3 adapted for sustaining a hanging object: *a hanging rail.* 4 deserving hanging: *a hanging matter.* 5 said of a judge: inclined to inflict the death sentence. [(senses 1 and 2) present part. of HANG[1]; (senses 3, 4, and 5) verbal noun from HANG[1]]

hanging valley *noun* a valley ending in a steeply descending cliff face.

hangman *noun* (*pl* **hangmen**) a man who hangs a condemned person; a public executioner.

hangnail *noun* a bit of skin hanging loose at the side or root of a fingernail. [by folk etymology from AGNAIL]

hang on *verb intrans* **1** to keep hold; to hold onto something. **2** *informal* to persist tenaciously: *a cold that hung on all spring.* **3a** *informal* to wait for a short time. **b** to remain on the telephone.

hangout *noun informal* a place where one is often to be seen.

hang out *verb intrans* **1** to protrude, *esp* downward. **2** *informal* to spend time in a leisurely or idle way: *The kids hang out on street corners.* ✳ **let it all hang out** *informal* to relax and enjoy oneself, without inhibitions.

hangover *noun* **1** the disagreeable physical effects following heavy consumption of alcohol, e.g. headache and nausea. **2** something, e.g. a custom, that remains from the past.

Hang Seng index /hang 'seng/ *noun* a figure representing an indication of share prices on the Hong Kong Stock Exchange, based on 33 selected stocks. [named after the *Hang Seng* Bank, Hong Kong]

hang together *verb intrans* **1** said of people: to be united or supportive. **2** said of ideas, statements, etc: to fit together; to be consistent.

hang up *verb trans* **1** to place (e.g. a garment) on a hook or hanger. **2** to end a telephone conversation by replacing (the receiver). ➤ *verb intrans* to end a telephone conversation, often abruptly.

hang-up *noun informal* a source of mental or emotional difficulty.

hank /hangk/ *noun* **1a** a coil or loop of yarn, rope, hair, or wire. **b** a unit of measurement for yarn, equal to 840yd (767m) in the case of cotton yarn, and 560yd (512m) in the case of worsted yarn. **2** a ring attaching a jib or staysail to a stay. [Middle English, of Scandinavian origin]

hanker *verb intrans* (**hankered, hankering**) (+ after/for) to desire something strongly or persistently: *You know how men have always hankered after unlawful magic* — William James. ➤ **hankering** *noun.* [prob from Flemish *hankeren,* frequentative of *hangen* to hang]

hankie *or* **hanky** /'hangki/ *noun* (*pl* **hankies**) *informal* a hand-kerchief.

hanky-panky /,hangki 'pangki/ *noun informal* mildly improper or deceitful behaviour. [prob alteration of HOCUS-POCUS]

Hanoverian /hanə'viəri·ən/ *noun* any of a line of monarchs belonging to the British royal house that reigned from 1714 to 1901. ➤ **Hanoverian** *adj.*

Word history ────────────
named after *Hanover,* former province of Germany. George Louis, Elector of Hanover, became George I, the first Hanoverian monarch of Great Britain, and the British monarch also governed Hanover until Queen Victoria came to the throne: continental Salic law prohibited rule by a woman.

Hansard /'hansahd/ *noun* the official report of Parliamentary proceedings. [named after Luke *Hansard* d.1828, English printer whose company first produced it]

Hanse /hans/ *noun* **1** (*treated as sing. or pl*) a medieval merchant guild. **2** = HANSEATIC LEAGUE. **3** the entrance fee to a Hanse. ➤ **Hanseatic** /hansi'atik/ *noun and adj.* [Middle English via French from old High German *hansa* troop, company]

Hanseatic League *noun* (*treated a sing. or pl*) a commercial association of N German cities formed in the mid 14th cent. to control and protect trade.

hansel[1] /'hansl/ *noun* = HANDSEL[1].

hansel[2] *verb trans* see HANDSEL[2].

hansom /'hansəm/ *noun* a light two-wheeled covered carriage for hire, seating two, with the driver's seat high up at the back: *We are ashamed to walk, ashamed to ride in an omnibus, ashamed to hire a hansom instead of keeping a carriage* — George Bernard Shaw. [named after Joseph *Hansom* d.1882, English architect who patented a similar cab]

hansom cab *noun* = HANSOM.

hantavirus /'hantəvie·ərəs/ *noun* (*pl* **hantaviruses**) any of a genus of viruses carried by rodents that can be transmitted to humans, causing fever, haemorrhage, and kidney or respiratory damage: genus *Hantavirus.* [named after the River *Hantaan* in Korea, where the virus was first isolated]

Hants /hants/ *abbr* Hampshire. [Old English *Hantescire,* variant of *Hamtunscir* Hampshire]

Hanukkah *or* **Chanukah** /'hanookə, -'khah/ *noun* an eight-day Jewish festival falling in December and commemorating the

rededication of the Temple of Jerusalem in 165 BC after its defile-ment by Antiochus of Syria. [Hebrew *ḥănukkāh* dedication]

hanuman /hanoo'mahn, 'han-/ *noun* **1** a long-tailed Asian monkey considered sacred by Hindus: *Presbytis entellus.* **2** (**Hanuman**) the Hindu monkey-god, noted for his devotion to Rama. [Hindi *Hanumān* from Sanskrit *hanumant* possessing (large) jaws, from *hanu* jaw]

haoma /'howmə/ *noun* see HOM.

hap[1] /hap/ *noun archaic* **1** a happening or occurrence: *certain ill haps.* **2** chance or fortune: *Wish me partaker of thy happiness when thou dost meet good hap* — Shakespeare. [Middle English from Old Norse *happ* good luck]

hap[2] *verb intrans* (**happed, happing**) *archaic* to happen: *And what-soever else shall hap tonight, give it an understanding but no tongue* — Shakespeare; *Ah, if thou issueless shall hap to die* — Shakespeare.

hapax legomenon /,hapaks li'gominon/ *noun* (*pl* **hapax legomena** /-nə/) a word or form which occurs only once. [Greek *hapax legomenon* something said once, from *hapax* once, *legein* to say]

ha'penny /'haypni/ *noun* (*pl* **ha'pennies**) a halfpenny.

haphazard /hap'hazəd/ *adj* lacking any method, organization, plan, or order; aimless: *lead a haphazard existence.* ➤➤ **haphazardly** *adv,* **haphazardness** *noun.* [*haphazard* (noun) chance, accident from HAPPY + HAZARD[1]]

hapl- *or* **haplo-** *comb. form* forming words, with the meaning: single; simple: *haploid.* [Latin from Greek, from *haploos,* from *ha-* one + *-ploos* multiplied by]

hapless *adj* luckless; unfortunate: *the hapless porker whose fate I have just rehearsed* — Herman Melville; *the terrific gale which beat down upon the hapless vessel* — Edgar Rice Burroughs. ➤➤ **haplessly** *adv,* **haplessness** *noun.*

haplo- *comb. form* see HAPL-.

haplography /hap'logrəfi/ *noun* a written haplology, e.g. *repetive* for *repetitive.*

haploid[1] /'haployd/ *adj* having a single and unpaired set of chromosomes: compare DIPLOID[1], POLYPLOID[1]. ➤➤ **haploidy** *noun.* [Greek *haploeidēs* single, from *haploos:* see HAPL-]

haploid[2] *noun* a cell or organism having a single set of chromo-somes; i.e. chromosomes that are unpaired.

haplology /hap'loləji/ *noun* contraction of a word by the omission of one or more similar sounds or syllables in pronunciation, e.g. /'liebri/ for 'library'.

haply /'hapli/ *adv archaic or literary* by chance; perhaps: *Haply a woman's voice may do some good* — Shakespeare; *But in his distress he bethought himself of Johnson's persuasive power of writing, if haply it might avail to obtain for him the Royal Mercy* — James Boswell.

ha'p'orth *or* **haporth** /'haypəth/ *noun* = HALFPENNYWORTH: *It doesn't make a ha'p'orth of difference.* [by contraction]

happen[1] /'hapn/ *verb intrans* (**happened, happening**) **1** to take place; to occur: *How did it happen?* **2** to occur or do something by chance: *He happened to overhear the plotters; It happened to be a Wednesday.* **3** to be the case: *It happened that both fire doors were locked; It so happens I'm going your way.* ✳ **happen on/upon** *literary* to encounter (something or somebody) by chance: *I happened upon an old acquaintance last week.* [Middle English *happenen* from HAP[1]]

happen[2] *adv N Eng, dialect* perhaps; it may be: *'How far is it from this?' 'Happen fourteen miles o'er the hills.'* — Emily Brontë; *They'd happen be a bit better if they did get a good hiding* — D H Lawrence.

happening[1] *noun* **1** something that happens; an occurrence. **2** an unscripted or improvised public performance in which the audi-ence participates.

happening[2] *adj informal* exciting and fashionable; = COOL[1] (7): *the happening place to be.*

happenstance /'hapnstans/ *noun NAmer* a circumstance regarded as due to chance: *The crow means nothing by crowing, that he crows at this moment is mere happenstance* — T A Shippey. [blend of HAPPENING[1] and CIRCUMSTANCE]

happy /'hapi/ *adj* (**happier, happiest**) **1a** enjoying or expressing pleasure and contentment. **b** glad; pleased: *I was very happy to hear from you.* **2** favoured by luck or fortune; fortunate: *the happy pair; on this happy day; in the happy position of being able to choose.* **3** well adapted or fitting; felicitous: *a happy choice.* **4** (*usu in combination*) impulsively quick or overinclined to use something: *trigger-happy.*

5 (*usu in combination*) characterized by a dazed irresponsible state: *a punch-happy boxer*. **6** *euphem* tipsy. ➤➤ **happily** *adv*, **happiness** *noun*. [Middle English, from HAP¹]

happy-clappy *adj derog* denoting an unrestrained type of Christian worship characterized by pop-style hymns and clapping in time with the music.

happy event *noun slightly humorous* the birth of a baby.

happy-go-lucky *adj* blithely unconcerned; carefree.

happy hour *noun* a limited period of the day during which drinks are sold in a bar, pub, etc at reduced prices.

happy hunting ground *noun informal* a choice or profitable area of activity.

happy medium *noun* an acceptable compromise; a course judiciously steered between extremes: *I was ... divided between my desire to appear to advantage, and my apprehensions of putting on anything that might impair my severely practical character in the eyes of the Misses Spenlow. I endeavoured to hit a happy medium between these two extremes* — Dickens.

Hapsburg or **Habsburg** /'hapsbuhg/ *noun* any of a line of monarchs belonging to a princely German house that reigned in Austria from 1278 to 1918 and in Spain from 1516 to 1700. ➤➤ **Hapsburg** *adj*. [named after *Habsburg*, castle in Aargau, Switzerland built by ancestors of the house]

hapten /'hapt(ə)n/ *noun* a small separable part of an antigen that reacts specifically with an antibody. [German *Hapten* from Greek *haptein* to fasten]

haptic /'haptik/ *adj technical* relating to or based on the sense of touch. [Greek *haptikos* relating to touch, from *haptesthai* to touch]

hapuka or **hapuku** /hə'pukə, 'hahpookə/ *noun* a tropical fish of the bass family; = GROUPER. [Maori *hapuka*]

hara-kiri /,harə 'keeri/ *noun* suicide by ritual disembowelment, formerly practised by the Japanese samurai when disgraced, as an honourable alternative to execution. [Japanese *harakiri*, from *hara* belly + *kiri* cutting]

harangue¹ /hə'rang/ *noun* a lengthy, ranting, censorious speech or piece of writing. [Middle English *arang* via French from Old Italian *aringa*]

harangue² *verb trans* to lecture (somebody) at length in a sententious or censorious manner. ➤➤ **haranguer** *noun*.

harass /'harəs, hə'ras/ *verb trans* to annoy or worry (somebody) persistently. ➤➤ **harassed** *adj*, **harasser** *noun*, **harassment** *noun*. [French *harasser* from Old French *hare*, interj used to incite dogs, of Germanic origin]

Usage note

harass *and* harassment. The traditional and still predominant British pronunciation of these words places the stress on the first syllable *ha-*. In modern American English the stress has moved to the second syllable. This pronunciation is gaining ground in Britain, but is disliked by some traditionalists as an example of the Americanization of British English.

harbinger¹ /'hahbinjə/ *noun literary* a person or thing that signals or heralds a future event, change, etc; a precursor or forerunner: *the cuckoo ... that harbinger of summer and plenty* — Edmund Burke; *I am afraid I am not altogether a harbinger of good* — Henry James.

Word history

Middle English from Old French *herbergere* host, from *herberge* hostelry, of Germanic origin. Orig meaning someone who provided lodgings, later a person sent ahead to find accommodation, hence a herald; current senses date from the 16th cent.

harbinger² *verb trans* (**harbingered, harbingering**) *literary* to give warning of or foreshadow (what is to come).

harbour¹ (*NAmer* **harbor**) /'hahbə/ *noun* **1** a port or coastal inlet providing shelter and safe anchorage for ships, usu with jetties or other artificial structures giving protection from rough water. **2** a place of security and comfort; a refuge: *in the safe harbour of the family home*. [Old English *hereborg* shelter]

harbour² (*NAmer* **harbor**) *verb trans* **1** to have or keep (thoughts or feelings) in the mind: *harbour a grudge against one's neighbour; harbour doubts about the value of such research*. **2** to give shelter or refuge to (somebody): *They had been harbouring a criminal unawares*. **3** to be the home or habitat of (something); to contain (it): *These cracks can harbour dangerous bacteria*. ➤ *verb intrans* to take shelter in or as if in a harbour.

harbourage /'hahbərij/ *noun* shelter or harbour.

harbourmaster *noun* the officer who regulates the use of a harbour.

hard¹ /hahd/ *adj* **1** not easily penetrated or yielding to pressure; firm. **2a** physically fit; able to cope with stress; tough: *The hard men ran 100 miles a week*. **b** revealing no weakness: *her hard unyielding will*. **3a** consisting of metal as distinct from paper: *hard money*. **b** said of currency: stable in value, or soundly backed and readily convertible into foreign currencies without large discounts. **c** said of share prices or commodity prices: high and firm. **d** said of money or credit: available to borrowers in limited supply and at high interest rates. **4** firmly and closely twisted: *hard yarns*. **5a** demanding energy or stamina: *hard work*. **b** expending great energy or effort: *a hard worker*. **c** oppressive or exacting: *a hard taskmaster*. **d** harsh or severe: *She said some hard things*. **e** said of the weather or a season: inclement: *a hard winter*. **f** forceful or violent: *hard blows*. **g** resentful: *There were hard feelings on both sides*. **h** lacking consideration or compassion: *a hard heart*. **6** difficult to endure: *hard times*. **7a** not speculative or conjectural; factual: *hard evidence*. **b** close or searching: *We'll be taking a long hard look at these statistics*. **8a** difficult to understand, explain, or answer: *Some questions are harder than others*. **b** said of iron: difficult to magnetize or demagnetize. **9** firm or definite: *They reached a hard agreement*. **10a** said of a drink: containing a high percentage of alcohol. **b** said of water: containing salts of calcium, magnesium, etc that inhibit lathering with soap. **11a** said of a drug: addictive and gravely detrimental to health: *such hard drugs as heroin*. **b** said of pornography: hard-core. **12a** denoting radiation of relatively high penetrating power: *hard X-rays*. **b** having or producing relatively great photographic contrast: *a hard negative*. **13a** sharply defined; stark: *a hard outline*. **b** jarring to the senses: *His voice had a hard quality*. **c** not used technically, said of c and g: pronounced /k/ and /g/ respectively. **14** said of a chemical, e.g. a pesticide or a detergent: breaking down only slowly; = PERSISTENT (2). **✲ hard as nails** having no finer feelings; totally without compassion. **hard going 1** arduous: *The course was hard going to start with*. **2** difficult to understand: *People make the mistake of thinking Shakespeare is hard going*. **hard lines** an expression of sympathy or condolence; hard luck (see LUCK). **hard of hearing** rather deaf. **hard on/upon** inequitably harsh in respect of (a certain person or group): *It was hard on girls, watching their brothers going off to be educated; Don't be too hard on first offenders*. **learn the hard way** to learn by making mistakes and suffering, rather than at second hand. **no hard feelings** no offence taken. **put the hard word on** *NZ, informal* to ask (somebody) a favour. ➤➤ **hardness** *noun*. [Old English *heard*]

hard² *adv* **1a** with great or maximum effort or energy; strenuously: *work hard; They were hard at work*. **b** in a violent manner; fiercely: *She hit him hard*. **c** used in nautical directions: to the full extent: *Steer hard aport*. **d** in a searching or concentrated manner: *She stared hard at him*. **2a** in such a manner as to cause hardship, difficulty, or pain; severely. **b** with bitterness or grief: *He took his defeat hard*. **3** in a firm manner; tightly: *Grip it hard*. **4** to the point of hardness: *The water froze hard*. **✲ be hard put to it** to have difficulty: *One would be hard put to it to find a better example*. **feel hard done by** to think oneself unfairly treated. **go hard with somebody** *archaic* to cause them suffering. **hard by** *archaic* close to a place; close by: *We found lodgings hard by; They lived hard by the church*. **hard on/upon** immediately after (something): *'My Lord, I came to see your father's funeral.' '... I think it was to see my mother's wedding.' 'Indeed, my lord, it followed hard upon.'* — Shakespeare; *The killing ... the mutilation ... the blowing up ... the murder ... all followed hard upon one another* — Conan Doyle. **hard up** *informal* short of something, *esp* money: *his hard-up relations; I'm hard up for summer clothes*.

hard³ *noun Brit* a firm artificial foreshore or landing place. [HARD¹]

hard-and-fast *adj* fixed or strict: *no hard-and-fast rules*.

hardback *noun* a book bound in stiff covers: compare PAPERBACK. ➤➤ **hardback** *adj*.

hard-bitten *adj* steeled by difficult experience; tough.

hardboard *noun* composition board made by compressing shredded wood chips.

hard-boil *verb trans* to cook (an egg) in the shell until both white and yolk have solidified.

hard-boiled *adj* said of a person: devoid of sentimentality; tough.

hard case *noun Brit, informal* a tough or hardened person.

hard cash *noun* money in the form of coin or bank notes as opposed to cheques or credit.

hard coal *noun* anthracite.

hard copy *noun* a paper copy of data held on computer: compare SOFT COPY.

hardcore *noun* **1** *Brit* compacted rubble or clinker used *esp* as a foundation for roads, paving, or floors. **2** a revived form of punk rock originating in the 1980s.

hard core *noun* (*treated as sing. or pl*) the unyielding or uncompromising members that form the nucleus of a group.

hard-core *adj* **1** constituting a hard core: *hard-core Conservative supporters*. **2** said of pornography: extremely explicit; *esp* showing real rather than simulated sexual acts.

hard disk *noun* a rigid magnetic disk permanently installed in a computer, with a large storage capacity for data.

hard drive *noun* = HARD DISK.

harden *verb* (**hardened, hardening**) ➤ *verb trans* **1** to make (something) hard or harder. **2** to make (a person, their heart, attitude, etc) more inflexible or unyielding: *The government has hardened its heart towards street beggars; Bitter experience had hardened him against her entreaties; The setback served only to harden their resolve.* **3a** to toughen or inure (somebody): *hardened troops*. **b** (*often + off*) to inure (plants) to cold or other unfavourable environmental conditions. ➤ *verb intrans* **1** to become hard or harder. **2a** to become confirmed or strengthened: *Opposition began to harden*. **b** to assume an appearance of harshness: *Her face hardened at the word*. **3** to become higher or less subject to fluctuations downward: *Prices hardened quickly*. ➤➤ **hardened** *adj*, **hardener** *noun*.

hard hat *noun* **1** a protective hat made of rigid material, e.g. metal or fibreglass, and worn *esp* by construction workers. **2** *chiefly NAmer, informal* a construction worker.

hardhead *noun* **1** *Brit* (*usu in pl, treated as sing.*) = KNAPWEED. **2** a diving duck of Australasia with brown plumage: *Aythya australis*. **3** an Atlantic catfish, the male of which incubates eggs in its mouth: *Arius felis*.

hardheaded *adj* sober or realistic: *hardheaded common sense*. ➤➤ **hardheadedly** *adv*, **hardheadedness** *noun*.

hardhearted *adj* lacking in sympathetic understanding; unfeeling. ➤➤ **hardheartedly** *adv*, **hardheartedness** *noun*.

hard-hitting *adj* vigorous or effective: *a hard-hitting series of articles*.

hardihood /'hahdihood/ *noun* **1** resolute courage and fortitude. **2** boldness marked by firm determination and often disdainful insolence: *No historian will have the hardihood to maintain that he commands this view* — A J Toynbee.

hard labour *noun* compulsory labour as part of prison discipline.

hard landing *noun* **1** a rough, uncomfortable landing by an aircraft. **2** a crash landing by a space vehicle or rocket, in which the craft is destroyed on impact. **3** a drastic way of dealing with an economic or other problem that involves hardship.

hard-line *adj* advocating or involving a persistently firm course of action; unyielding: *a hard-line policy on unemployment*. ➤➤ **hard-liner** *noun*.

hardly *adv* **1a** not in the least: *That news is hardly surprising*. **b** used as a response: certainly not!: *'You won't change your mind?' 'Hardly!'* **2** only just; barely: *I hardly knew her; Hardly had he noticed the approaching tornado when it struck*. **3** with difficulty; painfully: *I could hardly walk*. **4** *archaic* in a severe manner; harshly: *We ... use thee not so hardly* — Shakespeare.

Usage note
Hardly should not be used as the adverbial form of *hard*; *hard* itself performs this function (*hit someone hard; be hard pressed*). *Hardly* means the same as *barely* or *scarcely* and, like them, has an in-built negative effect, so that *I can hardly see* and *hardly anything* are correct, and *I can't hardly see* and *nothing hardly* are incorrect. When *hardly* begins a sentence, the usual order of auxiliary verb and subject is reversed: *Hardly had the meeting begun, when trouble erupted*. Note that the clause following this construction should begin with *when* or *before*, not *than*.

hard-nosed *adj informal* **1** sober or realistic; = HARDHEADED: *hard-nosed budgeting*. **2** hard-bitten; stubborn.

hard-on *noun* (*pl* **hard-ons**) *coarse slang* an erection of the penis.

hard pad *noun* a frequently fatal virus disease of dogs related to distemper.

hard palate *noun* the bony front part of the palate forming the roof of the mouth.

hardpan *noun* a hard compact soil layer.

hard paste *noun* = PORCELAIN (1A).

hard-paste porcelain *noun* = PORCELAIN (1A).

hard-pressed *adj* **1** in difficulties; hard put to it: *hard-pressed town-hall employees; They were hard pressed to find sufficient volunteers*. **2** said of troops, etc: closely pursued or under fire.

hard rock *noun* basic rock music played with a heavy beat.

hard sauce *noun* a creamed mixture of butter and sugar, usu flavoured with brandy or rum and served *esp* with Christmas puddings.

hard science *noun* any of the physical or natural sciences, e.g. physics, chemistry, astronomy, geology.

hard sell *noun* aggressive high-pressure salesmanship: compare SOFT SELL.

hard-shell *adj* **1** uncompromising or confirmed: *a hard-shell conservative*. **2** said of an animal: having a hard thick shell or carapace: *a hard-shell clam*. **3** having a rigid outer casing: *a hard-shell briefcase*.

hardship *noun* suffering, privation, or an instance of this.

hard shoulder *noun* *Brit* either of two surfaced strips alongside a motorway, on which stopping is allowed only in an emergency.

hardstanding *noun* *Brit* a hard-surfaced area on which vehicles, e.g. cars, caravans, or aeroplanes, may park.

hardtack *noun* *archaic* a ship's biscuit.

hardtop *noun* a motor car with a rigid top.

hardware *noun* **1** the physical components, e.g. electronic and electrical devices, of a computer or other electronically controlled device: compare SOFTWARE. **2** items sold by an ironmonger such as household tools and gardening equipment. **3** tape recorders, closed-circuit television, etc used as instructional equipment. **4a** heavy military equipment such as tanks and missiles. **b** *informal* a gun.

hard-wired *adj* in computing: **a** denoting an electronic circuit whose functions and operations are determined by its physical construction rather than by programming. **b** controlled by such a circuit. ➤➤ **hard-wiring** *noun*.

hardwood *noun* **1** a broad-leaved as distinguished from a coniferous tree. **2** the wood of such a tree.

hardy *adj* (**hardier, hardiest**) **1a** inured to fatigue or hardships; tough; robust. **b** said of a plant: capable of withstanding adverse conditions; *esp* capable of living outdoors over winter without artificial protection. **2** *archaic* = FOOLHARDY. ➤➤ **hardily** *adv*, **hardiness** *noun*. [Middle English *hardi* from Old French *hardir* to make hard, of Germanic origin]

hare[1] /heə/ *noun* **1** any of several species of swift long-eared mammals like large rabbits with long hind legs: genus *Lepus* and other genera. **2** an electrically driven dummy hare propelled before the dogs in greyhound racing. **✳ run with the hare and hunt with the hounds** to remain on good terms with both sides. **start a hare** to introduce a topic that generates discussion. [Old English *hara*]

hare[2] *verb intrans informal* to run fast: *I hared over to Mabel's with the news*.

hare and hounds *noun* (*treated as sing.*) a paper chase.

harebell *noun* a slender plant with blue bell-shaped flowers that grows *esp* on heaths and in open woodlands: *Campanula rotundifolia*.

harebrained *adj* flighty or foolish.

Hare Krishna /ˌhari 'krishnə/ *noun* **1** a missionary Hindu cult characterized *esp* by the public chanting of a psalm taken from the sacred writings of Hinduism and beginning 'Hare Krishna'. **2** a member of this cult. [Sanskrit *Hare Krsna* O Lord Krishna, from *Hari* Vishnu, Lord + *Krsna* Krishna]

harelip *noun* a split in the upper lip like that of a hare occurring as a congenital deformity, often in association with a CLEFT PALATE. Also called CLEFT LIP. ➤➤ **harelipped** *adj*.

harem /hah'reem, 'heərəm/ *noun* **1a** a secluded part of a house allotted to women in a Muslim household. **b** (*treated as sing. or pl*) the women occupying a harem. **2** used with reference to polygamous animals: a group of females associated with one male. [Arabic *ḥarīm* something forbidden, and *ḥaram* sanctuary]

hare's-foot *noun* a type of clover growing in sandy soils, whose white or pink flowers are covered with downy hair: *Trifolium arvense*.

haricot /'harikoh/ *noun* a type of French bean with white edible seeds that can be dried and stored. [French *haricot*, prob from Nahuatl *ayacotli*]

Harijan /'hurij(ə)n, 'harijan/ *noun* an Indian untouchable. [Sanskrit *harijana* a person belonging to the god Vishnu, from *Hari* Vishnu + *jana* person]

hari-kari /,hari 'kahri/ *noun* = HARA-KIRI.

hark /hahk/ *verb intrans* archaic or literary (*usu in imperative*) to listen: *Hark! A drum!* ✳ **hark at so-and-so!** used disparagingly to draw attention to a foolish or pompous comment, etc: *Hark at him, telling us our duty!* [Middle English *herken*, of Germanic origin]

hark back *verb intrans* (+ to) to return to an earlier topic or circumstance: *He kept harking back to 'the good old days'.* [orig a term in hunting, referring to hounds called back to retrace a scent they had lost]

harken *verb intrans* see HEARKEN.

harl /hahl/ *verb trans Scot* to finish (exterior walls) with a covering of cement mixed with small stones; = ROUGHCAST². ≫ **harling** *noun*. [orig meaning 'to drag'; ultimate origin unknown]

harlequin¹ or **Harlequin** /'hahlikwin/ *noun* 1 a mute character in traditional pantomime, in mask and lozenge-patterned costume. 2 formerly, a stock character in the Italian commedia dell'arte, a quick-witted servant. [Italian *arlecchino* from early French *Helquin*, a demon]

harlequin² *adj* said of a pattern: consisting of coloured lozenges, or simply, brightly variegated.

harlequinade /,hahlikwi'nayd/ *noun* 1 a part of a play or pantomime in which Harlequin has a leading role. 2 buffoonery.

harlequin duck *noun* a small N American and Icelandic diving sea duck the male of which is bluish with black, white, and chestnut markings: *Histrionicus histrionicus.* [referring to Harlequin's multicoloured costume]

harlot /'hahlət/ *noun archaic* a female prostitute. ≫ **harlotry** /-tri/ *noun.* [Old French *herlot* rogue]

harm¹ /hahm/ *noun* 1 physical or mental damage; injury: *Spanking children does them more harm than good; Your precious glassware will come to no harm if it's properly packed; No harm will come to you if you cooperate.* 2 mischief or wrong: *I didn't mean any harm.* ✳ **it will do so-and-so no harm** it will be good for so-and-so (to do something): *It will do him no harm to lose some weight.* **out of harm's way** safe from danger. **there's no harm in** it's at least worth (doing something): *There's no harm in trying.* ≫ **harmful** *adj,* **harmfully** *adv,* **harmfulness** *noun.* [Middle English from Old English *hearm*]

harm² *verb trans* 1 to damage (something) or injure (somebody). 2 to have a deleterious effect on (something): *A long absence from the workplace will harm your chances of promotion.*

harmattan /hah'mat(ə)n/ *noun* a dry dust-laden wind that blows off the desert onto the Atlantic coast of Africa from December to February. [Twi *haramata*]

harmless *adj* 1 lacking capacity or intent to injure: *harmless insects; a bit of harmless fun.* 2 *rather derog* said of a person: inoffensive to the point of ineffectuality. 3 *archaic or legal* free from harm, liability, or loss. ≫ **harmlessly** *adv,* **harmlessness** *noun.*

harmonic¹ /hah'monik/ *adj* 1 relating to musical harmony, a harmonic, or harmonics. 2 pleasing to the ear; harmonious. 3 in mathematics, expressible in terms of sine or cosine functions: *harmonic function.* ≫ **harmonically** *adv.* [Latin *harmonicus* from Greek *harmonikos,* from *harmonia*: see HARMONY]

harmonic² *noun* 1a a tone in a harmonic series. b a flutelike overtone produced on a stringed instrument by touching a vibrating string at a point, e.g. the midpoint, which divides it into halves, thirds, etc. 2 in physics, a component frequency of a harmonic motion that is an integral multiple of the fundamental frequency.

harmonica /hah'monikə/ *noun* a small rectangular wind instrument with free reeds recessed in air slots from which notes are sounded by breathing out and in. [Italian *armonica,* fem of *armonico* harmonious]

harmonic analysis *noun* in mathematics, the expression of a PERIODIC FUNCTION (function whose value repeats itself at regular intervals) as a sum of sines and cosines, *esp* by means of a FOURIER SERIES.

harmonic mean *noun* the reciprocal of the arithmetic mean of the reciprocals of a finite set of numbers: *The harmonic mean of 2, 4, 6, and 8 is 4/½ + ¼ + ⅙ + ⅛ = 96/23.*

harmonic minor scale *noun* a musical scale that has semitones between the second and third, fifth and sixth, and seventh and

eighth steps, with tones for the other intervals: compare MELODIC MINOR SCALE.

harmonic motion *noun* = SIMPLE HARMONIC MOTION.

harmonic progression *noun* 1 in music, the sequence of chord changes that represents the harmonic structure of a composition, etc. 2 in mathematics, a sequence whose terms are the reciprocals of an arithmetic progression.

harmonics *pl noun* 1 (*treated as sing.*) the study of the physical characteristics of musical sounds. 2 (*treated as pl*) the set of overtones of a fundamental note.

harmonic series *noun* 1 a set of tones consisting of a fundamental and all the overtones whose frequency ratio to it can be expressed in whole numbers. 2 in mathematics, a series of terms whose reciprocals are in arithmetic progression.

harmonious /hah'mohni·əs/ *adj* 1 musically concordant. 2 having the parts arranged so as to produce a pleasing effect: *The patterns blended into a harmonious whole.* 3 said of relations between people: characterized by mutual respect and amicable cooperation. ≫ **harmoniously** *adv,* **harmoniousness** *noun.*

harmonise /'hahməniez/ *verb* see HARMONIZE.

harmonist /'hahmənist/ *noun* a person who is skilled in musical harmony.

harmonium /hah'mohni·əm/ *noun* a musical instrument of the reed organ family in which pedals operate a bellows that forces air through free reeds. [French *harmonium* from early French *harmonie, armonie*: see HARMONY]

harmonize or **harmonise** /'hahməniez/ *verb intrans* 1 to play or sing in harmony. 2 (*often* + with) to be in harmony or keeping: *The newer supermarkets attempt to harmonize with their surroundings.* ➤ *verb trans* 1 to provide (a tune) with harmony. 2 to bring (differing things) into consonance or accord: *The sets of rules should be harmonized.* ≫ **harmonization** /-'zaysh(ə)n/ *noun.*

harmony /'hahməni/ *noun* (*pl* **harmonies**) 1a the pleasant-sounding combination of simultaneous musical notes in a chord. b the structure of music with respect to the composition and progression of chords, or the science of the structure of music in this respect. 2a pleasing or congruent arrangement of parts: *a painting exhibiting harmony of colour and line.* b agreement or accord: *live in harmony with one's neighbours.* 3 an arrangement of parallel literary passages, e.g. of the Gospels. [Middle English *armony* via French and Latin from Greek *harmonia* joining, harmony, from *harmos* joint]

harness¹ /'hahnis/ *noun* 1a the gear of a draught animal other than a yoke. b *archaic* military equipment for a knight. 2 something that resembles a harness, e.g. in holding or fastening something: *a safety harness.* 3 the part of a loom that holds and controls the heddles (wires with eyes through which the warp threads pass; see HEDDLE). ✳ **in harness** 1 in one's usual work, surroundings, or routine: *back in harness after a long illness.* 2 in close association: *working in harness with a group of colleagues.* [Middle English *herneis* baggage, gear, from Old French *harneis,* ultimately from old Norse *herr* army + *nest* provisions]

harness² *verb trans* 1a to put a harness on (a horse, etc). b to attach (a wagon, etc) by means of a harness. 2 to utilize (something); *esp* to convert (a natural force) into energy: *harness wave power; harness the sun's energy.* ≫ **harnesser** *noun.*

harness racing *noun* the sport of trotting.

harp¹ /hahp/ *noun* a stringed musical instrument with strings stretched across an open triangular frame, plucked with the fingers. ≫ **harper** *noun,* **harpist** *noun.* [Old English *hearpe*]

harp² *verb intrans* 1 (+ on) to dwell on or return to a subject tediously or monotonously. 2 *archaic* to play a harp.

harpoon¹ /hah'poohn/ *noun* a barbed spear used *esp* in hunting large fish or whales. ≫ **harpooner** *noun.* [prob from Dutch *harpoen* from Old French *harpon* brooch, ultimately from Greek *harpē* sickle]

harpoon² *verb trans* to spear (a large fish or whale) with a harpoon. ≫ **harpooner** *noun.*

harp seal *noun* an arctic seal with a black saddle-shaped mark on the back: *Phoca groenlandica.*

harpsichord /'hahpsikawd/ *noun* a keyboard musical instrument with one or two manuals, having a horizontal frame and strings and producing notes by the action of quills or leather points plucking the strings. ⟫ **harpsichordist** *noun*. [modification of Italian *arpicordo*, from *arpa* harp + *corda* string]

harpy /'hahpi/ *noun* (*pl* **harpies**) **1** (**Harpy**) a rapacious creature of Greek mythology with the head of a woman and the body of a bird. **2** *derog* a rapacious woman. [Latin *Harpyia*, from Greek]

harquebus /'hahkwibəs/ *noun* see ARQUEBUS.

harridan /'harid(ə)n/ *noun* an ill-tempered unpleasant woman. [perhaps modification of French *haridelle* old horse, gaunt woman]

harried /'harid/ *adj* beset by worrying problems; harassed.

harrier[1] /'hari·ə/ *noun* **1** a hunting dog resembling a small foxhound and used for hunting hares. **2** (**Harrier**) used in naming cross-country teams: *the Altrincham Harriers*. [irreg from HARE[1]]

harrier[2] *noun* any of several species of slender hawks with long angled wings: genus *Circus*. [alteration of *harrower*, from HARROW[2] (2) in an archaic sense 'to rob, plunder']

Harris tweed /'haris/ *noun trademark* a loosely woven tweed made in the Outer Hebrides, chiefly on the island of Lewis and Harris.

Harrovian /ha'rohvi·ən/ *noun* a pupil of Harrow School. ⟫ **Harrovian** *adj*. [Latin *Harrovia* Harrow, district of London where the school is situated]

harrow[1] /'haroh/ *noun* a cultivating implement set with spikes, spring teeth, or discs and drawn over the ground *esp* to pulverize and smooth the soil. [Middle English *harwe* from Old Norse *herfi*]

harrow[2] *verb trans* **1** to cultivate (ground or land) with a harrow. **2** to cause distress to (somebody): *a harrowing experience*. ✳ **the harrowing of Hell** in medieval theology, the descent of Christ into hell between his death and resurrection, to rescue the souls of the righteous. ⟫ **harrower** *noun*. [(sense 2) variant of HARRY]

harrumph[1] /ha'rumf/ *verb intrans* to make a guttural sound as if clearing the throat, *esp* as a sign of disapproval. [imitative]

harrumph[2] *noun* a guttural sound made as if to clear the throat.

harry /'hari/ *verb trans* (**harries**, **harried**, **harrying**) **1** to make a destructive raid on (enemy territory), or ravage it. **2** to harass or torment (somebody) by or as if by constant attack. ⟫ **harrier** *noun*. [Middle English *harien* from Old English *hergian*]

harsh /hahsh/ *adj* **1** disagreeable or painful to the senses: *like sweet bells jangled, out of tune and harsh* — Shakespeare. **2** lacking in aesthetic appeal or refinement; crude: *harsh colours; a harsh white light*. **3** unduly exacting; severe: *a harsh punishment*. **4** said of a climate, conditions, etc: unpleasant; difficult to endure: *a harsh environment*. **5** said of facts, etc: unpalatable; difficult to face: *harsh reality*. **6** having too strong or rough an effect: *harsh soaps*. ⟫ **harshen** *verb*, **harshly** *adv*, **harshness** *noun*. [Middle English *harsk*, of Scandinavian origin]

hart /haht/ *noun* the male of the red deer, *esp* when over five years old: compare HIND[2]. [Old English *heort*]

hartal /'hahtahl/ *noun* in the Indian subcontinent, a general strike called for a political purpose. [Hindi *hartāl*, from *hāt* shop + *tālā* lock]

hartebeest /'hahtibeest/ *noun* any of several species of large African antelopes with ridged horns that project upward and outward: genus *Alcelaphus*. [obsolete Afrikaans (now *hartbees*) from Dutch, from *hart* deer + *beest* beast]

hartshorn /'hahts·hawn/ *noun archaic* ammonium carbonate. [from the earlier use of hart's horns as the chief source of ammonia]

hart's-tongue *noun* a Eurasian fern with undivided fronds: *Phyllitis scolopendrium*.

harum-scarum[1] /,heərəm 'skeərəm/ *adj informal* usu said of a person: reckless or irresponsible. ⟫ **harum-scarum** *noun*. [perhaps alteration of HELTER-SKELTER[1]]

harum-scarum[2] *adv informal* recklessly or irresponsibly.

haruspex /hə'ruspeks/ *noun* (*pl* **haruspices** /-piseez/) in ancient Rome, a diviner who based his predictions on the entrails of animals. [Latin *haruspex*]

harvest[1] /'hahvist/ *noun* **1** the gathering in of agricultural crops, or the season when this is done. **2** a mature crop, or the yield of a crop, of grain, fruit, etc. **3** the product or fruit of exertion. [Old English *hærfest*]

harvest[2] *verb trans* **1** to gather in (a crop); to reap (it). **2** to gather (a natural product) as if by harvesting: *harvesting bacteria*. ⟩ *verb intrans* to gather in a food crop. ⟫ **harvestable** *adj*, **harvester** *noun*.

harvester /'hahvistə/ *noun* **1** a person who harvests. **2** = COMBINE HARVESTER.

harvest home *noun* **1** the gathering in of the harvest, or the time of this. **2** a festival at the close of harvest.

harvestman *noun* (*pl* **harvestmen**) any of numerous species of arachnids with a small rounded body and very long slender legs: order Opiliones.

harvest mite *noun* a six-legged mite larva that sucks the blood of vertebrates and causes intense irritation: genus *Trombicula*.

harvest moon *noun* the full moon nearest the time of the September equinox.

harvest mouse *noun* a small European field mouse that nests *esp* in cornfields: *Micromys minutus*.

has /s, z, əz, həz; *strong* haz/ *verb* third person sing. present of HAVE[1].

has-been *noun informal* somebody or something that has passed the peak of effectiveness, success, or popularity.

hash[1] /hash/ *noun* **1** a dish consisting chiefly of reheated cooked chopped food, *esp* meat. **2** *informal* a rehash. **3** *informal* a muddle; a jumble. ✳ **make a hash of something** *informal* to do it incompetently. **settle somebody's hash** *informal* to deal summarily with (an opponent, etc).

hash[2] *verb trans* to chop (meat, potatoes, etc) into small pieces. [French *hacher* from Old French *hache* battle-axe, of Germanic origin]

hash[3] *noun informal* hashish.

hash browns *pl noun* cooked potatoes that have been chopped or mashed and fried in hot oil or fat until browned.

hashish /'hasheesh/ *noun* the resin from the flowering tops of the female hemp plant, smoked, chewed, etc for its intoxicating effect. [Arabic *ḥashīsh*]

hash out *verb trans informal* to come to agreement on (a matter) after much discussion.

Hasid /'hasid/ *noun* (*pl* **Hasidim** /-dim/) **1** a member of a Jewish sect of the second cent. BC opposed to the influence of ancient Greek culture and devoted to the strict observance of Jewish ritual forms. **2** a member of a Jewish mystical sect founded in Poland about 1750 in opposition to formalistic ritualism. ⟫ **Hasidic** /hə'sidik/ *adj*, **Hasidism** *noun*. [Hebrew *ḥāsīdh* pious]

haslet /'hazlit/ *noun* the edible entrails, e.g. the liver, of an animal, *esp* a pig, cooked and compressed into a meat loaf: compare GIBLETS. [Middle English from early French *hastelet* piece of meat roasted on a spit]

hasn't /'haznt/ *contraction* has not.

hasp[1] /hasp/ *noun* a device for fastening; *esp* a hinged metal strap that fits over a metal loop and is secured by a pin or padlock. [Old English *hæsp*]

hasp[2] *verb trans* to fasten (something) with a hasp.

hassium /'hasi·əm/ *noun* a very unstable chemical element artificially produced by high-energy atomic collisions: symbol Hs, atomic number 108. [Latin *hassium* from *Hassias* Hesse, the German state where it was discovered]

hassle[1] /'hasl/ *noun informal* **1** a trying problem; a struggle: *It's such a hassle getting across London*. **2** a heated often protracted argument; a wrangle. [perhaps from HAGGLE + TUSSLE[2]]

hassle[2] *verb trans informal* to subject (somebody) to persistent harassment. ⟩ *verb intrans informal* to argue or fight: *The player hassled with the referee*.

hassock /'hasək/ *noun* **1** *chiefly Brit* a cushion for kneeling on, *esp* in church. **2** a clump of grass; = TUSSOCK. [Old English *hassuc*]

hast /hast/ *verb archaic* present second person sing. of HAVE[1].

hastate /'hastayt/ *adj* said of a leaf: having a triangular shape like a spearhead. [Latin *hastatus* from *hasta* spear]

haste[1] /hayst/ *noun* **1** rapidity of motion; swiftness. **2** rash or headlong speed; precipitateness: *Marry in haste, repent at leisure*. ✳ **make haste** to act quickly; to hurry. [Middle English from Old French, of Germanic origin]

haste[2] *verb intrans archaic* to move or act swiftly: *Let us haste to hear it* — Shakespeare.

hasten /'hays(ə)n/ *verb* (**hastened**, **hastening**) ⟩ *verb trans* **1** to accelerate (something): *They had to hasten the tests; hasten one's steps; Sorrow hastened his end*. **2** to cause (somebody) to hurry: *He hastened her to the door*. ⟩ *verb intrans* to move or act quickly; to hurry: *I was hastening to greet her with one of my best considered bows* — Poe. ⟫⟫ **hastener** *noun*.

hasty /'haysti/ *adj* (**hastier, hastiest**) **1** done or made in a hurry: *hasty preparations; a hasty meal*. **2** precipitate; rash: *She later regretted her hasty words*. **3** said of somebody's temper: too readily roused. **4** *archaic* prone to or showing anger; irritable. ⟫⟫ **hastily** *adv*, **hastiness** *noun*.

hat /hat/ *noun* **1** a covering for the head, *esp* one with a shaped crown and brim. **2** *informal* used to specify a particular role of somebody who has more than one: *wearing his ministerial hat*. ✱ **first out of the hat** the first name, etc to be selected at random. **hat in hand** in a deferential manner; cap in hand. **keep something under one's hat** to keep it a secret. **take one's hat off to somebody** to give them due credit. **talk through one's hat** *informal* to voice irrational or erroneous ideas, *esp* in attempting to appear knowledgeable. **throw one's hat into the ring** to offer to take up a challenge. ⟫⟫ **hatless** *adj*. [Old English *hæt*]

hatband *noun* a band made of fabric, leather, etc round the crown of a hat just above the brim.

hatbox *noun* a large cylindrical box for storing a hat.

hatch[1] /hach/ *noun* **1** a small door or opening, e.g. in a wall or aircraft. **2a** an opening in the deck of a ship or in the floor or roof of a building, or a cover over such an opening. **b** = HATCHWAY. **3** a sluice in a dyke or dam. **4** = HATCHBACK. ✱ **down the hatch!** *informal* an expression of encouragement to drink up; bottoms up! **under hatches** below decks. [Old English *hæc*]

hatch[2] *verb intrans* **1** said of young: to emerge from an egg or pupa. **2** said of an egg: to open and release young. **3** said of a female bird: to incubate eggs; to brood. ⟩ *verb trans* **1a** to incubate (an egg). **b** to cause (young) to emerge from an egg. **2** to devise or originate (a plot or plan), usu conspiratorially. [Middle English *hacchen*, of Scandinavian origin]

hatch[3] *noun* a brood of young produced by hatching.

hatch[4] *verb trans* to mark (a drawing, map, or engraving) with fine closely spaced parallel lines to show eminences and depressions. ⟫⟫ **hatching** *noun*. [Middle English *hachen* from early French *hacher* to inlay, chop up, from *hache*: see HATCHET]

hatchback *noun* **1** an upward-opening hatch giving entry to the luggage and passenger compartment of a motor car. **2** a car with a hatchback.

hatchery *noun* (*pl* **hatcheries**) a place for hatching eggs, *esp* fish eggs.

hatchet /'hachit/ *noun* **1** a short-handled axe. **2** (*used before a noun*) said of a person's face: grimly sharp-featured. [Middle English *hachet* from early French *hachette*, dimin. of *hache* battle-axe, or Germanic origin]

hatchet job *noun informal* a vicious or damaging attack on a person or their work, delivered either verbally or in writing.

hatchet man *noun informal* **1** a person hired for murder, coercion, or attack. **2** a vicious or merciless critic.

hatchling /'hachling/ *noun* a recently hatched animal.

hatchment *noun* a square panel set cornerwise bearing the coat of arms of a deceased person for display outside a house or in a church. [perhaps an alteration of ACHIEVEMENT (4), or from obsolete French *hachement*, from Old French *acesmement* adornment]

hatchway *noun* **1** a passage giving access, e.g. to a lower deck in a ship. **2** an opening in a ship's deck, etc, or a covering over such an opening.

hate[1] /hayt/ *verb trans* to feel extreme enmity or aversion towards (somebody or something): *He hated her sufficiently to murder her* — D H Lawrence. ⟩ *verb intrans* to feel enmity or aversion. ✱ **hate somebody's guts** see GUT[1]. ⟫⟫ **hatable** *adj*, **hateable** *adj*, **hater** *noun*. [Old English *hatian*]

hate[2] *noun* **1** intense hostility or dislike; loathing. **2** *informal* an object of hatred: *one of my pet hates*. [Old English *hete*]

hate crime *noun* a crime that is committed against somebody because the perpetrator disapproves of their race, sexuality, religion, etc. It usu takes the form of physical violence, verbal abuse or threats, or damage to property, etc.

hateful /'hayt**f**(ə)l/ *adj* **1** deserving or arousing hate: *'My name's Macbeth.' 'The devil himself could not pronounce a title more hateful to mine ear.'* — Shakespeare. **2** *archaic* full of hate; malicious: *See how the giddy multitude do point … Ah, Gloucester, hide thee from their hateful looks* — Shakespeare. ⟫⟫ **hatefully** *adv*, **hatefulness** *noun*.

Word history

As its form suggests, *hateful* orig meant 'full of hate'. Probably because hatred is often a reciprocal act, the focus of the word soon came to be transferred from the person hating to the object of hatred. The two meanings have coexisted for more than six centuries, but the first meaning given above is now so prevalent that the second is liable to be misunderstood.

hath /hath/ *verb archaic* third person sing. present of HAVE[1].

hatha yoga /'hutə, 'hathə/ *noun* a system of yoga consisting of physical exercises and breath control designed to keep the body healthy and thus leave the mind free from its demands. [Sanskrit *haṭha* force, persistence + YOGA]

hatred /'haytrid/ *noun* intense dislike or hate. [Middle English, from HATE[2] + Old English *rǣden* condition]

hatstand *noun* an upright post with hooks for hanging hats on.

hatter *noun* a person who makes and sells hats.

hat trick *noun* three successes by one person or side, usu in a sporting activity; *specif* the dismissing of three batsmen with three consecutive balls by a bowler in cricket. [prob from a former practice of rewarding the feat by the gift of a hat]

hauberk /'hawbuhk/ *noun* a tunic of chain mail worn as defensive armour, *esp* from the 12th to the 14th cent. [Middle English from Old French *hauberc*, of Germanic origin]

haughty /'hawti/ *adj* (**haughtier, haughtiest**) disdainfully proud; arrogant. ⟫⟫ **haughtily** *adv*, **haughtiness** *noun*. [Middle English *haught* proud, via French from Latin *altus* high]

haul[1] /hawl/ *verb trans* **1a** to pull (something) with effort; to drag (it). **b** to transport (goods) in a vehicle, *esp* a lorry. **2** *informal* (+ up) to bring (somebody) before an authority for judgment: *He was hauled up before the magistrate for a traffic offence*. ⟩ *verb intrans* **1** to pull or drag: *They hauled on the rope*. **2** said of the wind: to shift: *The wind had hauled round to a point more to the northward* — Poe. **3** to steer a ship in a certain direction: *We hauled out into the stream* — R H Dana. ✱ **haul somebody over the coals** to give them a severe reprimand. [Middle English *halen* to pull, from Old French *haler*, of Germanic origin]

haul[2] *noun* **1** the act or process of hauling. **2a** an amount gathered or acquired, *esp* illegally; booty or spoils: *The burglars had abandoned their haul of jewellery and antiques and fled*. **b** a seizure by the authorities of illicit goods: *a drugs haul; an arms haul*. **c** the fish taken in a single draught of a net. **3a** transport by hauling or the load transported. **b** the distance or route to be travelled, or over which a load is to be transported: *a long haul*.

haulage /'hawlij/ *noun* **1** the act or process of hauling. **2** a charge made for hauling.

haulier /'hawli·ə/ (*NAmer* **hauler** /'hawlə/) *noun* **1** a person or commercial establishment whose business is transport by lorry. **2** a mineworker responsible for transporting coal from the face to the shaft.

haulm /hawm/ *noun* **1** a plant stem. **2** the stems or tops of potatoes, peas, beans, etc, after the crop has been gathered. [Old English *healm*]

haunch /hawnch/ *noun* **1** the human hip. **2a** (*in pl*) the back legs of a four-legged animal; the hindquarters. **b** the back half of the side of a slaughtered animal; a hindquarter. **3** the lower half of either of the sides of an arch. ✱ **on one's haunches** in a squatting position. [Middle English *haunche* from Old French *hanche*, of Germanic origin]

haunt[1] /hawnt/ *verb trans* **1** said of a ghost: **a** to visit (a person). **b** to inhabit (a place): *The building is said to be haunted*. **2a** said of a person: to visit (a place) often; to frequent (it): *She had managed to furnish the house by haunting boot sales and craft fairs*. **b** said of a clinging acquaintance: to continually seek the company of (somebody) or run after them. **3a** to recur constantly and spontaneously to (somebody): *The tune haunted her all day; Memories of the scene never ceased to haunt me*. **b** to reappear continually in (something); to pervade (it): *a sense of loss that haunts his writing*. ⟩ *verb intrans* **1** said of a ghost: to appear habitually. **2** to stay around or persist; to linger. ⟫⟫ **haunter** *noun*. [Middle English *haunten* from Old French *hanter*, of Germanic origin]

haunt[2] *noun* a place habitually frequented: *The bar was a favourite haunt of the legal fraternity*.

haunted *adj* **1** said of a building: inhabited by a ghost. **2** worried or anguished: *a haunted expression*.

haunting *adj* **1** said of concerns, memories, etc: constantly recurring to one; persistent. **2** poignantly evocative: *a haunting melody*. ➤➤ **hauntingly** *adv*.

Hausa /'howsə/ *noun* (*pl* **Hausas** *or collectively* **Hausa**) **1** a member of a people inhabiting N Nigeria and S Niger. **2** the language of this people, one of the national languages of Nigeria, and widely used in W Africa as a lingua franca. ➤➤ **Hausa** *adj*. [the Hausa name]

hausfrau /'howsfrow/ *noun* a German housewife. [German *Hausfrau*, from *Haus* house + *Frau* woman, wife]

haustellum /haw'steləm/ *noun* (*pl* **haustella** /-lə/) a mouth part, e.g. of an insect, adapted to suck blood, plant juices, etc. ➤➤ **haustellate** /'hawstəlit/ *adj*. [Latin *haustellum* from *haustus*, past part. of *haurire* to drink, draw]

hautbois *or* **hautbois** /'ohboy/ *noun* **1** *archaic* an oboe. **2a** a large strawberry of central Europe and Asia. **b** the plant bearing this: *Fragaria moschata*. [early French *hautbois*, from *haut* high + *bois* wood]

haute couture /,oht kooh'tyooə/ *noun* the designing and making of highly fashionable or fashion-setting clothes by leading fashion houses. [French *haute couture*, literally 'high sewing']

haute cuisine /kwi'zeen/ *noun* cooking of a high standard, *esp* following French methods. [French *haute cuisine*, literally 'high cooking']

haute école /ay'kol/ *noun* a highly stylized form of classical horse-riding; advanced dressage. [French *haute école*, literally 'high school']

hauteur /oh'tuh (*French* otœr)/ *noun* arrogance or haughtiness: *He did not take fits of chilling hauteur* — Charlotte Brontë. [French *hauteur* from *haut* high, from Latin *altus*]

haut monde /,oh 'mon(h)d/ *noun* high society. [French *haut monde*, literally 'high world']

Havana /hə'vanə/ *noun* a cigar made in Cuba or from tobacco of the type grown in Cuba. [named after *Havana*, capital city of Cuba]

have¹ /v, əv, hav; *strong* hav/ *verb* (*third person sing. present tense* **has** /s, z, əz, həz; *strong* haz/, *past tense and past part.* **had** /d, əd, həd; *strong* had/) ➤ *verb trans* **1a** to own or possess (something) as property: *They have three houses*. **b** to possess (something or somebody) as an attribute or asset: *She has red hair; They have many friends*. **2** to exercise or display (a feeling or quality): *He has a lot of courage; They had the nerve to ask for more money*. **3** to be able to speak (a language): *I have a little French*. **4a** to purchase or obtain (something). **b** to receive (something): *I've had no news of my brother for weeks*. **5a** to accept or admit (somebody). **b** *coarse slang* to have sexual intercourse with (somebody). **6a** to be affected by (a disease): *Have you had mumps?* **b** to experience (something), *esp* by undergoing or suffering it: *I've already had one bicycle stolen*. **c** to engage in an activity: *I'm going to have a bath; Have a look at that*. **d** to hold or organize (an event, etc). **e** to partake of (food, drink, etc): *We're about to have dinner*. **f** to entertain (a feeling, emotion, etc) in the mind: *You must have an opinion*. **7a** to tell or persuade (somebody) to do something: *Have the children form a line*. **b** to get (something) done: *I'll soon have it finished; We'd better have this gas leak seen to*. **8** to give birth to or be the parents of (a baby or young animal). **9** to invite or entertain (somebody) as a guest: *Thanks for having me*. **10** (*in negative contexts*) to allow or permit (something): *I'm not having any more of that*. **11** *informal*. **a** to hold (somebody) in a position of disadvantage or certain defeat: *We have them now*. **b** to perplex or floor (somebody): *You have me there*. ➤ *verb aux* used with a past part. to form perfect, pluperfect, and future perfect tense of verbs: *She has gone home; They had already eaten; We will have finished dinner by then*. ✳ **be had** *informal* to be the victim of a fraud or deception: *I think you've been had*. **have had it 1** *informal* to have missed one's chance. **2** *informal* to be useless or past one's best. **have/have got to** to be obliged to or find it necessary to do something. **have it away/off** *coarse slang* (*usu* + *with*) to have sexual intercourse with somebody. **have it in for somebody** *informal* to be noticeably bent on harming them. **have it in one** to have the capacity (to do something). **have it out** *informal* to settle a point at issue with somebody. **have it that** to allege that (something is the case): *Rumour has it that they're splitting up*. **have nothing on** *informal* to be negligible in comparison with (something): *Today's groups have nothing on those thirties dance bands*. **have something on somebody** *informal* to know something compromising about somebody that could be useful. **never had it so good/easy** *informal* never been in such easy circumstances before. [Old English *habban*]

have² ✳ **the haves and have-nots** *informal* wealthy people and poor people.

have-a-go *adj Brit, informal* said of a member of the public: actively attempting to stop somebody who is committing a crime, *esp* one involving violence: *a have-a-go hero*.

havelock /'havlok/ *noun* a light-coloured cover for an army cap with a flap hanging down at the back to protect the neck from the sun. [named after Sir H *Havelock* d.1857, British general serving in India]

haven /'hayv(ə)n/ *noun* chiefly literary **1** a place of safety or refuge: *She found the art gallery a haven of peace*. **2** a harbour or port: *a land-locked haven for all manner of ships* — Stevenson. [Old English *hæfen*]

have-not *noun* see HAVE².

haven't /'havnt/ *contraction* have not.

have on *verb trans* **1** to be wearing (something). **2** to have planned (something) for a particular time: *What do you have on for tomorrow?* **3** *chiefly Brit, informal* to deceive or tease (somebody): *She was just having you on*.

haver /'hayvə/ *verb intrans* (**havered**, **havering**) **1** *Scot* to talk nonsense. **2** *chiefly Brit* to be indecisive; to hesitate. [origin unknown]

haversack /'havəsak/ *noun* a knapsack. [French *havresac* from German *Habersack* bag for oats, from *Haber* oats + *Sack* bag]

haversine /'havəsien/ *noun* in mathematics, half of a VERSED SINE. [shortening of HALF¹ + VERSED SINE]

have up *verb trans Brit, informal* to bring (somebody) before the authorities to answer a charge, etc: *He was had up in court for dangerous driving*.

havildar /'havldah/ *noun* a non-commissioned officer in the Indian army, equivalent to a sergeant. [Hindi *hawāldār*, from Arabic *hawāla* charge + Persian *dār* having]

havoc /'havək/ *noun* **1** widespread destruction; devastation. **2** great confusion and disorder; chaos: *It's amazing the havoc even a few children can create in a house*. ✳ **cry havoc** *archaic* to give an army the signal to plunder. **play havoc with something** to disrupt it: *The flu epidemic has played havoc with the teaching schedule*. [Middle English *havok* from Anglo-French, modification of Old French *havot* plunder]

haw¹ /haw/ *noun* **1** the red berry of the hawthorn. **2** = HAWTHORN. [Middle English *hawe* from Old English *haga*]

haw² *noun* the NICTITATING MEMBRANE (inner eyelid) of certain animals. [origin unknown]

haw³ ✳ **hum and haw** see HUM¹.

Hawaiian /hə'wie-ən/ *noun* **1** a native or inhabitant of the US state of Hawaii, group of islands in Pacific Ocean. **2** the Austronesian language of Hawaii. ➤➤ **Hawaiian** *adj*.

Hawaiian guitar *noun* an electric stringed musical instrument consisting of a long soundboard and six to eight steel strings that are plucked while being pressed with a movable steel bar.

hawfinch *noun* any of several species of large Eurasian finches with a large heavy bill: genus *Coccothraustes*. [HAW¹ + FINCH]

hawk¹ /hawk/ *noun* **1** any of numerous species of medium-sized birds of prey with short rounded wings and a long tail, that hunt during the day: genus *Accipiter* and other genera. **2** a person who takes a militant attitude; a supporter of a warlike policy: compare DOVE¹ (2). **3** a small board with a handle on the underside for holding mortar or plaster. ➤➤ **hawkish** *adj*, **hawkishly** *adv*, **hawkishness** *noun*. [Middle English *hauk* from Old English *hafoc*]

hawk² *verb intrans* **1** to hunt game with a trained hawk. **2** to soar and strike like a hawk: *birds hawking after insects*. ➤ *verb trans* to hunt (game) on the wing like a hawk.

hawk³ *verb trans* to offer (goods) for sale in the street: *hawking newspapers*. [back-formation from HAWKER¹]

hawk⁴ *verb intrans* to utter a harsh guttural sound in or as if in clearing the throat. ➤ *verb trans* to raise (phlegm) by hawking. [imitative]

hawk⁵ *noun* an audible effort to force up phlegm from the throat.

hawkbit *noun* a plant of the daisy family, similar to a dandelion, with yellow flowers and leaves arranged in a rosette: genus *Leontodon*, family Compositae. [blend of HAWKWEED and *devil's bit*, a scabious]

hawker¹ *noun* a person who hawks wares. [Low German *höker* from early Low German *höken* to peddle]

hawker² *noun* a falconer.

hawk-eyed *adj* **1** having sharp sight. **2** watchful; vigilant.

hawkmoth *noun* any of numerous species of stout-bodied moths with long narrow forewings: family Sphingidae.

hawksbill *noun* a flesh-eating sea turtle whose shell yields a valuable tortoiseshell: *Eretmochelys imbricata*. [from the shape of its jaws, thought to resemble a hawk's bill]

hawkweed *noun* a plant of the daisy family with red, orange, or yellow dandelion-like heads: genus *Hieracium*.

hawse /hawz/ *noun* **1** a hawsehole. **2a** the part of a ship's bow that contains the hawseholes. **b** the distance between the bow and the anchor. [Middle English *halse* from Old Norse *hals* neck, hawse]

hawsehole *noun* a hole in the bow of a ship through which the anchor cable passes.

hawsepipe /'hawzpiep/ *noun* a metal pipe on either side of a ship's bow, through which the anchor cable passes.

hawser *noun* a large rope, *esp* one used on a ship. [Middle English via French from Latin *altiare*, from *altus* high]

hawser-laid *adj* = CABLE-LAID.

hawthorn *noun* any of numerous species of spiny shrubs of the rose family with white or pink flowers and small red fruits: genus *Crataegus*. [Middle English *hawethorn* from Old English *hagathorn*, from *haga* HAW¹ + THORN]

hay¹ /hay/ *noun* **1** grass that has been mown and dried for fodder. **2** *NAmer, informal* (*in negative contexts*) a negligible amount: *You can earn up to fifty grand, and that ain't hay*. ✳ **hit the hay** *informal* to go to bed. **make hay of** to make a mess or nonsense of (something): *new evidence that makes hay of his theories*. **make hay while the sun shines** to utilize an opportunity fully while it lasts. **roll in the hay** *informal, dated* to make love. [Old English *hīeg*]

hay² *verb intrans* to cut, cure, and store grass for hay.

haybox *noun* formerly, a well-insulated airtight box used to keep a previously heated vessel hot and allow slow cooking to continue.

haycock *noun* a small conical pile of hay in a field.

hay fever *noun* nasal catarrh and conjunctivitis occurring usu in the spring and summer through allergy to pollen.

haymaker *noun* **1** a person who tosses and spreads hay to dry after cutting. **2** *informal* a powerful swinging blow, e.g. in boxing. **3** a machine that breaks or bends hay so that it dries more rapidly. ⋙ **haymaking** *noun*.

haymow /'haymoh/ *noun* **1** a stack or store of hay. **2** the part of a barn where hay is stored.

hayrick *noun* a haystack.

hayseed *noun* **1** grass seed from hay. **2** *chiefly NAmer, informal* a bumpkin or yokel.

haystack *noun* a large, constructed pile of hay, usu protected by thatch.

haywire *adj informal* out of control; erratic; crazy: *Her blood pressure's gone haywire – she needs hospital care; Your emotions are bound to be a bit haywire just now; The computer's gone completely haywire*. [from the use of baling wire for makeshift repairs]

hazard¹ /'hazəd/ *noun* **1a** a risk or peril: *the hazards of skiing*. **b** a source of danger: *These piles of paper constitute a fire hazard*. **c** *chiefly archaic or literary* chance; accident; uncertainty: *You therein ... give up yourself merely to chance and hazard from their security* — Shakespeare. **2** a golf-course obstacle, e.g. a bunker. **3** a game of chance played with two dice. **4** in billiards, a stroke that pockets a ball, a *winning hazard* being the pocketing of the object ball, and a *losing hazard* the pocketing of the cue ball off another ball. **5** in real tennis, each of the winning openings in a court: *We will in France ... play a set shall strike his father's crown into the hazard* — Shakespeare. [Middle English via French from Arabic *az-zahr* the die]

hazard² *verb trans* **1** to venture (an estimate, guess, etc): *Would you care to hazard a guess?; 'About two hundred miles?' I hazarded*. **2** to expose (something) to danger: *They are forced to take arms and hazard their young lives; a captain guilty of hazarding his ship*.

hazard lights *pl noun* a vehicle's right and left indicator lights when flashing simultaneously, operated to warn that the vehicle is stationary or very slow-moving, and temporarily obstructing traffic.

hazardous /'hazədəs/ *adj* **1** involving or exposing one to risk, e.g. of loss or harm: *a hazardous occupation*. **2** depending on hazard

or chance: *such hazardous affirmations* — Charlotte Brontë. ⋙ **hazardously** *adv*, **hazardousness** *noun*.

haze¹ /hayz/ *noun* **1** vapour, dust, smoke, etc causing a slight decrease in the air's transparency: *a summer haze*. **2** vagueness or confusion of mental perception: *Through an alcoholic haze he was dimly aware that guests were departing*. [prob back-formation from HAZY]

haze² *verb intrans* (+ over) to become hazy or cloudy: *Later on the sky hazed over*. [prob back-formation from HAZY]

haze³ *verb trans chiefly NAmer* **1** to harass (a new student or recruit) with ridicule, humiliating tricks, etc. **2** to drive (cattle) while on horseback: *haze the calves into a pen*. [origin unknown]

hazel /'hayzl/ *noun* **1** any of several species of small trees of the birch family, bearing edible nuts in autumn and catkins in spring: *Corylus avellana* and other species. **2** the wood of these trees. **3** = HAZELNUT. **4** a yellowish light to strong brown, *esp* as an eye colour. ⋙ **hazel** *adj*. [Old English *hæsel*]

hazel hen *noun* a European woodland grouse with speckled plumage: *Tetrastes bonasia*.

hazelnut *noun* the small round hard-shelled edible nut of the hazel.

hazy *adj* (**hazier, haziest**) **1** obscured or cloudy: *a hazy view of the mountains*. **2** vague or indefinite: *I had only a hazy recollection of what happened*. ⋙ **hazily** *adv*, **haziness** *noun*. [origin unknown]

HB *abbr* used as a designation of medium grade on lead pencils: hard black.

Hb *abbr* haemoglobin.

hb *abbr* hardback.

HBM *abbr* His or Her Britannic Majesty.

H-bomb *noun* a hydrogen bomb.

HC *abbr* **1** Holy Communion. **2** *Brit* House of Commons. **3** hydrocarbon.

HCF *abbr* highest common factor.

HCG *abbr* human chorionic gonadotrophin, a hormone manufactured by the placenta during pregnancy, its presence in the urine being a standard indication of pregnancy.

hcp *abbr* handicap.

HD *abbr* heavy duty.

HDL *abbr* high-density lipoprotein.

HDTV *abbr* high-definition television.

HE *abbr* **1** high explosive. **2** His Eminence. **3** His or Her Excellency.

He *abbr* the chemical symbol for helium.

he¹ /(h)i, ee; *strong* hee/ *pronoun* **1** used to refer to a male person or creature, previously mentioned, who is neither speaker nor hearer: *He is my father*. **2** used in a generic sense or when the sex of the person is unspecified: **a** *archaic or literary* to mean 'anyone', followed by a relative clause: *He that hath ears to hear, let him hear* — Bible; *Tell me he that knows* — Shakespeare. **b** *dated* to refer back to an indefinite pronoun or common-gender noun (now superseded by *he or she* or *they*): *Nobody may act just as he pleases; A doctor must give the treatment he judges best*. **3** (**He**) *esp* formerly, used to refer to God. [Old English *hē*]

he² *noun* **1** (*also in combination*) a male person or creature: *a he-goat; Is the parrot a he or a she?* **2** in children's games, the player who tries to catch the others; = IT² (I).

head¹ /hed/ *noun* **1** the upper or foremost division of the human body containing the brain, the chief sense organs, and the face, also clearly demarcated in most other animals, although only certain mammals have the musculature for facial expression. **2** the seat of the intellect; the mind: *Use your head; Two heads are better than one; Surely you can work it out in your head?* **3** *informal* a headache: *What a head I had in the morning!* **4** (*in pl, but treated as sing. or pl*) the obverse of a coin, typically bearing the head of the monarch or president: compare TAIL¹ (5): *It came down heads; Heads you win*. **5a** a person or individual: *The cost is £20 per head; take a head count; count heads*. **b** (*with pl meaning*) used in counting livestock: *500 head of cattle*. **6a** the end that is upper, higher, or opposite the foot: *the head of the table*. **b** the source of a stream, river, etc. **c** the end of a lake or inlet into which a river flows. **d** (*used in place names*) a headland: *Worms Head*. **e** either end of something, e.g. a cask or drum, whose two ends need not be distinguished. **7** a director or leader, e.g.: **a** a school principal. **b** a person in charge of a department in an institution: *the head of the English department*. **8a** a rounded or flattened cluster of flowers; = CAPITULUM (1). **b** the foliaged part of a plant, *esp* when consisting of a compact mass of leaves or fruits. **9** the leading part of a military column, procession, etc. **10a** the uppermost extremity or projecting part of an object; the top. **b** the striking or operational part of a weapon, tool, implement, etc. **c** the flattened or rounded end of a nail, tack, screw, etc. **11a** a body of water kept in reserve at a height. **b** a mass of water in motion. **12a** the difference in height between two points in a body of liquid, or the pressure resulting from this. **b** the pressure of a fluid: *a good head of steam*. **13** *Brit* (*usu in pl*) a toilet, *esp* a ship's toilet. **14** a measure of length equivalent to a head: *The horse won by a head*. **15** the place of leadership, honour, or command: *at the head of his class*. **16a** a word often in larger letters placed above a passage in order to introduce or categorize it; = HEADING (1). **b** a separate section or topic: *matters discussed under various heads*. **17** the foam or froth that rises on a fermenting or effervescing liquid, *esp* beer. **18** the part of a boil, pimple, etc at which it is likely to break. **19a** a part of a machine or machine tool containing a device, e.g. a cutter or drill, or the part of an apparatus that performs the chief or a particular function. **b** any of at least two electromagnetic components which bear on the magnetic tape in a tape recorder, such that one can erase recorded material if desired and another may either record or play back. ✳ **above/over somebody's head** said of intellectual material: to be too difficult for them to understand. **bang/knock people's heads together** to deal summarily with people who persist in arguing and refusing to cooperate with each other. **come to a head** to arrive at a culminating point or crisis: *Things came to a head, with street riots and attacks on private property*. **do somebody's head in** *informal* to be more than they can cope with emotionally or intellectually: *This income tax form is doing my head in*. **from head to foot/toe** so as to cover the body completely: *clad from head to foot in orange*. **get a head start** to secure an advantage for oneself at the outset of a competition, etc. **get one's head round/around something** *informal* to manage to understand it. **get one's head down 1** *informal* to get some sleep. **2** *informal* to start concentrating on a task, *esp* a mental one. **give a horse its head** to allow it to gallop. **give somebody head** *coarse slang* to perform oral sex on them. **give somebody their head** to give them scope to act on their own initiative. **go over somebody's head** to ignore the person immediately senior to one in a hierarchy and appeal, complain, etc to somebody in higher authority. **go to somebody's head 1** said of alcohol: to make them intoxicated or dizzy. **2** said of fame or success: to make them conceited or overconfident. **have a head/good head for something** to have an aptitude for, or an ability to cope with, it: *She has a good head for legal issues*; *He had no head for heights*. **have something hanging over one's head** to be constantly under its threat. **head over heels 1** so as to execute a somersault: *The impact sent him head over heels*. **2** helplessly: *fall head over heels in love*. **heads will roll** there will be serious trouble with the possibility of dismissals. **keep one's head** to keep emotionally and intellectually cool, and act the more effectively as a result. **keep one's head above water** to remain solvent; *broadly* to stay out of difficulty. **knock an idea/rumour on the head** to dismiss it at a stroke. **laugh/talk/shout/bawl one's head off** to laugh, talk, etc with inordinate vigour and vociferousness. **lose one's head** to panic or behave irrationally. **not make head or tail of something** to make no sense of it; to fail to understand it. **off one's head** *informal* crazy or mad. **on your own head be it** you are responsible for whatever unwanted results your conduct, etc brings. **put our/your/their heads together** to think something out jointly. **stand head and shoulders above** to be noticeably superior to (others). **stand/turn an argument, etc on its head** to reverse it, or apply it the other way round. **take it into one's head** to conceive a sudden notion, wish, or resolve: *She's taken it into her head that she's fat and needs to diet*; *He took it into his head to try paragliding*. **turn heads** to draw the gaze of passers-by. **turn somebody's head** to make them conceited: *Success had not turned his head*. **with one's head in the clouds** in a dreamy state of mind. ⋙ **headless** *adj*. [Old English *hēafod*]

head² *adj* principal or chief: *the head teacher*; *the head office*.

head³ *verb trans* **1** to be at the head of (a movement, etc); to lead (it): *head a revolt*; *head a procession*. **2a** to put something as the heading to (a list, article, paragraph, etc): *a paragraph headed 'pitfalls'*. **b** to stand as the first or leading member or item of (a list, catalogue, etc): *He heads the list of heroes*. **3** to drive (a football, etc) with the head. **4** to cut back or off the upper growth of (a plant). **5** to set the course of (a vessel): *The ship was headed northwards*. **6** to go round

the head of (a stream). ⋙ *verb intrans* **1** to move in a specified direction: *He was heading towards Doncaster*; *The children headed for the nearest McDonalds*; *You're heading for disaster*. **2** to form a head: *This cabbage heads early*.

-head *comb. form* forming words, denoting: **1** the tip, end, or point of something: *arrowhead*; *spearhead*. **2** *derog* a person with the specified substitute for brains: *airhead*; *dickhead*. **3** *informal* a person addicted to the specified drug: *acidhead*; *crackhead*.

headache *noun* **1** a sustained pain in the head. **2** *informal* something that causes worry or difficulty: *Finding babysitters was a bit of a headache*. ⋙ **headachy** *adj*.

headband *noun* **1** a band, typically of stretch fabric, worn round the head, *esp* to keep hair or sweat out of the eyes. **2** a narrow coloured band attached to the top of a book spine for reinforcement and decoration.

headbanger *noun Brit, informal* **1** a person who shakes their head violently and rhythmically to the beat of loud rock music, *esp* heavy metal. **2** an insane or violent person; a maniac.

headboard *noun* a board forming the head of a bed.

headbutt¹ *verb trans* to strike (somebody) with the head.

headbutt² *noun* a blow with the head.

head case *noun informal* a mad person; an eccentric.

headcheese *noun NAmer* meat from a pig's or calf's head moulded in aspic; = BRAWN (2).

headdress *noun* any elaborate covering for the head, e.g. one worn ceremonially.

headed *adj* **1** said of writing paper: having a heading, typically consisting of the name and address of the writer. **2** (*used in combinations*) having a head or heads of the kind or number specified: *a coolheaded businessman*; *a roundheaded screw*; *a two-headed monster*.

header *noun* **1** a shot or pass in football made by heading the ball. **2** *informal* a headfirst fall or dive. **3** a brick or stone laid in a wall with its end towards the face of the wall: compare STRETCHER¹ (3). **4** a person or device that forms or removes heads, e.g. a grain-harvesting machine that cuts off grain heads. **5** a raised water tank that maintains fluid pressure in a plumbing system, etc. **6** a line of text appearing at the top of each page of a book, etc.

header tank *noun* = HEADER (5).

headfirst *adv and adj* with the head foremost; headlong.

headgear *noun* clothing for the head, *esp* hats.

headguard *noun* a protective helmet of various designs worn for certain sports, e.g. by batsmen in cricket.

headhunter *noun* **1** a member of a people that collects the decapitated heads of defeated enemies. **2** a person who identifies and recruits personnel to fill business positions, *esp* at senior levels and from other firms. ⋙ **headhunting** *noun*.

heading *noun* **1** an inscription, headline, or title standing at the top or beginning of a letter, chapter, etc. **2** the compass direction in which a ship or aircraft points. **3** in mining, a horizontal tunnel; = DRIFT² (5). **4** the top edge of a curtain, extending above the hooks suspending it.

headlamp *noun* a headlight.

headland /'hedlənd/ *noun* **1** a point of high land jutting out into the sea. **2** unploughed land near an edge of a field.

headlight *noun* the main light mounted on the front of a motor vehicle.

headline¹ *noun* **1** a title printed in large type above a newspaper story or article. **2** *Brit* (*in pl*) a summary given at the beginning or end of a news broadcast.

headline² *verb trans* **1** to provide (an article or story) with a headline: *a piece headlined 'The bad news is …'*. **2** to be a star performer in (a show). ⋙ *verb intrans* to be a star performer.

headlong *adv and adj* **1** headfirst: *fall headlong*. **2** without pause or delay: *rush headlong*; *in headlong flight*. **3** without deliberation: *plunging in rather a headlong manner into talk with strangers* — Wilkie Collins. **4** *archaic* precipitous: *headlong cliffs*. [Middle English *hedlong*, alteration of *hedling*, from *hed* HEAD¹]

headman *noun* (*pl* **headmen**) a chief of a tribe or community.

headmaster *or* **headmistress** *noun chiefly Brit* a head teacher.

headmost *adj archaic* said of a ship, etc: most advanced; leading.

head off *verb trans* to stop the progress of (a person, animal, or developing crisis, etc), block them, or turn them aside by taking preventive action: *We'll head them off at the pass.*

head of state *noun* the titular head of a state, e.g. a monarch, as distinguished from the head of government, e.g. a prime minister.

head-on *adv and adj* **1** with the head or front making the initial contact: *The cars collided head-on; a head-on collision.* **2** in direct opposition: *a head-on confrontation; What happens when primitive and civilized man meet head-on?*

headphones *pl noun* a pair of earphones held over the ears by a band worn on the head.

headpiece *noun* **1** an ornamental printed device *esp* at the beginning of a chapter. **2** a protective covering, e.g. a helmet, for the head. **3** the part of a halter or bridle that fits over a horse's head behind its ears.

headpin /'hedpin/ *noun* the pin that stands nearest the bowler when the pins are arranged in tenpin bowling.

headquarters *noun* (*pl* **headquarters**) (*treated as sing. or pl*) **1** a place from which a military commander exercises command. **2** the administrative centre of an enterprise.

headrace *noun* a channel taking water to a mill wheel or turbine.

head register *noun* = HEAD VOICE.

headrest *noun* a support for the head; *esp* a cushioned pad supporting the head in a vehicle.

headroom *noun* vertical space, e.g. beneath a bridge, sufficient to allow passage or unrestricted movement.

headscarf *noun* (*pl* **headscarves** *or* **headscarfs**) a scarf worn on the head.

headset *noun* an attachment for holding earphones and a microphone to one's head.

headship *noun* the position or office of a head, e.g. a head teacher; leadership.

headshrinker *noun* **1** *chiefly NAmer, informal* a psychiatrist. **2** a headhunter who shrinks the heads of slaughtered victims.

headsman *noun* (*pl* **headsmen**) formerly, an executioner.

headspring *noun* a fountainhead or source.

headstall *noun* the part of a bridle or halter that encircles the horse's head.

headstock *noun* **1** a bearing or pedestal for a revolving or moving part, e.g. in a lathe. **2** on a guitar, the part at the end of the neck to which the tuning pegs are fixed.

headstone *noun* a memorial stone placed at the head of a grave.

headstrong *adj* wilful or obstinate: *violent headstrong actions.*

head teacher *noun chiefly Brit* the teacher in charge of a school.

head-to-head *adj and adv* said of competition, disputes, etc: involving direct confrontation between parties: *head-to-head rivalry; battling head-to-head.* >>> **head-to-head** *noun.*

head-up *adj* said of an instrument display in an aircraft or vehicle: visible without the pilot or driver having to lower their eyes, usu by being projected on to the windscreen or visor.

head voice *noun* the high register of a human voice, in which the vibrations are apparent in the head.

headwater *noun* the upper part or source of a river.

headway *noun* **1a** advance or progress. **b** motion in a forward direction. **2** the time interval between two vehicles travelling in the same direction on the same route, *esp* trains or buses. **3** headroom.

headwind /'hedwind/ *noun* a wind blowing in a direction opposite to a course, *esp* that of a ship or aircraft.

headword *noun* a word or term placed at the beginning of a chapter, an encyclopedia or dictionary entry, etc.

headwork *noun* mental effort; thinking.

heady *adj* (**headier, headiest**) **1a** said of alcoholic drinks: tending to make one giddy or exhilarated; intoxicating. **b** exciting or exhilarating: *in my heady university days.* **2** *archaic* violent or impetuous: *his heady rage* — Dr Johnson. >>> **headily** *adv,* **headiness** *noun.*

heal /heel/ *verb trans* **1a** to restore (somebody) to health. **b** to make (a wound, etc) sound or whole. **2a** to make (pain or sorrow) less acute. **b** to mend (a breach between friends, etc). > *verb intrans* to return to a sound or healthy state. >>> **healer** *noun,* **healing** *adj and noun.* [Old English *hælan*]

health /helth/ *noun* **1a** soundness of body, mind, or spirit. **b** the general condition of the body: *in poor health.* **2** condition or state generally: *the economic health of the country.* **3** used in toasts to people's health or prosperity: *Your health!* [Old English *hælth,* from *hāl* HALE[1]]

health care *noun* the provision of services designed to promote health and prevent, cure, or alleviate disease.

healthcare-associated infection *noun* an infection that originates in a hospital or other medical facility and is acquired by a patient or a healthcare worker in that facility.

health centre *noun Brit* an establishment providing a variety of local medical services.

health farm *noun* a residential establishment that provides treatments and regimes for people wishing to improve their health by losing weight, exercising, etc.

health food *noun* organically grown untreated food containing no synthetic ingredients and eaten for the health-giving properties credited to it: compare JUNK FOOD, WHOLEFOOD.

healthful /'helthf(ə)l/ *adj* **1** beneficial to the health of body or mind: *My pulse as yours doth temperately keep time and makes as healthful music* — Shakespeare. **2** enjoying good health.

health salts *pl noun* (*treated as pl or sing.*) any of various medicinal preparations, e.g. Epsom Salts or Glauber's salt, used as a laxative.

health visitor *noun Brit* a nurse employed by a local authority to visit elderly people, new parents, etc and advise them on health matters.

healthy /'helthi/ *adj* (**healthier, healthiest**) **1** enjoying or showing health and vigour of body, mind, or spirit. **2** conducive to good health. **3** prosperous or flourishing. **4** said of one's bank balance, profits, etc: reassuringly substantial. >>> **healthily** *adv,* **healthiness** *noun.*

heap[1] /heep/ *noun* **1** a collection of things lying one on top of another; a pile. **2** *informal* (*in pl*) a great number or large quantity; a lot: *There are heaps of jobs left; I had heaps more to say.* **3** *informal* an old or dilapidated car or building. [Old English *hēap*]

heap[2] *verb trans* **1a** (*often* + up) to throw or lay (things) in a heap; to accumulate (them): *His sole object was to heap up riches.* **b** to form or round (something) into a heap: *He heaped the earth into a mound.* **2a** (*often* + with) to supply (somebody) abundantly with something: *He retired eventually, heaped with awards and honours.* **b** to bestow (things) lavishly or in large quantities on somebody: *She persisted in heaping gifts on him.*

hear /hiə/ *verb* (*past tense and past part.* **heard** /huhd/) > *verb trans* **1** to perceive (sound) with the ear. **2** to learn (something) by hearing: *I heard you were leaving.* **3a** (*also* + out) to listen to (somebody) with attention; to heed (them): *Hear me out.* **b** to attend (mass). **4** to give a legal or official hearing to (a case, complaint, etc). > *verb intrans* **1** to have the ability to perceive sound. **2** (+ of/about) to gain information; to learn: *I've heard about what you did; We'd never heard of Aids before about 1982.* *** hear from** to receive a communication from (somebody). **hear! hear!** an expression indicating approval, e.g. during a speech. **hear of** (*in negative contexts*) to entertain the idea of (something): *I offered to run them home, but they wouldn't hear of it.* >>> **hearer** *noun.* [Old English *hīeran*]

hearing *noun* **1a** the one of the five basic physical senses by which waves received by the ear are interpreted by the brain as sounds varying in pitch, intensity, and timbre. **b** earshot: *Don't mention the party in his hearing.*

Editorial note
Hearing is one of the five senses. Waves received by the ear are interpreted by the brain as sounds varying in pitch, intensity and timbre. The external protrusion, or 'auricle', of the ear directs sound waves into the external auditory canal, where they travel towards the tympanic membrane and cause it to vibrate. The vibrations are transmitted to the oral window by three small bones in the middle ear before reaching the cochlea. These movements are then conveyed to the brain via the vestibulocochlear nerve to be interpreted — Dr John Cormack.

2a an opportunity to be heard. **b** a trial in court.

hearing aid *noun* an electronic device worn by a person with defective hearing for amplifying sound before it reaches the ears.

hearing dog *noun* a dog kept by a deaf person that is trained to alert them to any sound such as the telephone, doorbell, or an alarm.

hearken or **harken** /'hahk(ə)n/ verb intrans (**hearkened** or **harkened, hearkening** or **harkening**) archaic (usu + to) to listen. [Old English heorcnian]

hearsay noun something heard from somebody else; rumour.

hearsay evidence noun in law, evidence based not on a witness's personal knowledge but on information received from others.

hearse /huhs/ noun a vehicle for transporting a coffin at a funeral. [Middle English herse candelabrum, catafalque, via early French herce harrow, frame for holding candles, from Latin hirpic-, hirpex harrow]

heart /haht/ noun **1** a hollow muscular organ that uses rhythmic contractions to maintain the circulation of the blood. **2** the essential or most vital part, the heart of the matter. **3** something resembling a heart in shape; specif a conventionalized representation of a heart. **4a** a playing card marked with one or more red heart-shaped figures. **b** (in pl) the suit comprising cards identified by this figure. **c** (in pl) a card game in which the object is to avoid winning tricks containing a heart or the queen of spades. Also called BLACK MARIA. **5a** tenderness or compassion: Have you no heart? **b** love or affections. He lost his heart to her. **c** courage or spirit. She did not have the heart for the task. **d** one's innermost character or feelings: a man after my own heart; She's a country girl at heart. **6** the central or inner-most part of a lettuce, cabbage, etc. **7** the fertility of agricultural land. ✳ **by heart** by rote or from memory. **have a heart of gold** to be very kind or generous. **have one's heart in one's mouth** to be very worried, frightened, or excited. **have one's heart in the right place** to mean well; to have good intentions. **in one's heart of hearts** deep within one's innermost feelings. **one's heart bleeds** used, sometimes ironically, as an expression of sympathy. **set one's heart on** to want (something) very much. **take heart** to gain courage or confidence. **take something to heart** to be deeply affected by (something, e.g. criticism). **wear one's heart on one's sleeve** to show one's feelings and emotions. **with one's heart in one's boots** feeling very depressed or apprehensive. [Old English heorte]

heartache noun mental anguish; great sorrow.

heart attack noun = CORONARY THROMBOSIS.

heartbeat noun **1** a single complete pulsation of the heart. **2** a driving impulse.

heart block noun lack of coordination of the heartbeat in which the upper and lower chambers of the heart beat independently, marked by decreased output of blood from the heart.

heartbreak noun intense grief or distress. ⧉ **heartbreaker** noun.

heartbreaking adj causing intense sorrow or distress: a heart-breaking waste of talent. ⧉ **heartbreakingly** adv.

heartbroken adj overcome by sorrow.

heartburn noun a burning pain behind the lower part of the breastbone, usu caused by regurgitation of acid from the stomach into the gullet.

hearted adj (used in combinations) having a heart or disposition of a specified kind: hard-hearted; gentle-hearted.

hearten verb trans (**heartened, heartening**) to cheer or encour-age (somebody). ⧉ **heartening** adj, **hearteningly** adv.

heart failure noun **1** a condition in which the heart is unable to pump blood at an adequate rate or in adequate volume. **2** sudden stopping of the heartbeat causing death.

heartfelt adj deeply felt; earnest or sincere.

hearth /hahth/ noun **1** an area, e.g. of brick or stone, in front of the floor of a fireplace, often used as a symbol representing home and family life. **2** the lowest section of a metal-processing furnace. [Old English heorth]

hearthrug noun a rug placed in front of a fireplace.

hearthstone noun the stone forming a hearth.

heartily /'hahtili/ adv **1** in a hearty manner; wholeheartedly or vigorously. **2** thoroughly: I'm heartily sick of all this talk.

heartland noun a central or important region: The move was designed to appeal to voters in Labour's heartlands.

heartless adj unfeeling or cruel. ⧉ **heartlessly** adv, **heartless-ness** noun.

heart-lung machine noun a mechanical pump used during heart surgery to divert the blood away from the heart and maintain the circulation and respiration.

heart-rending adj causing great sorrow. ⧉ **heart-rendingly** adv.

heart-searching noun close examination of one's motives or feelings.

heartsease /'hahtseez/ noun a wild European pansy with small variously coloured flowers, often violet and yellow: Viola tricolor.

heartsick adj deeply disappointed or despondent, esp from loss of love. ⧉ **heartsickness** noun.

heartsore adj = HEARTSICK.

heart-stopping adj tense or thrilling. ⧉ **heart-stoppingly** adv.

heartstrings pl noun the deepest emotions or affections: Her words tugged at his heartstrings.

heart-throb noun informal a good-looking man who arouses infatuation.

heart-to-heart[1] adj sincere and intimate: heart-to-heart confidences.

heart-to-heart[2] noun a frank or intimate talk.

heart-warming adj inspiring sympathetic feeling; cheering or uplifting.

heartwood noun the nonliving central wood in a tree, which is usu darker and denser than the surrounding sapwood.

hearty[1] adj (**heartier, heartiest**) **1** vigorous or enthusiastic: a hearty laugh. **2** sincere; heartfelt: hearty congratulations. **3** robustly healthy: hale and hearty; a hearty appetite. **4** said of food: substantial or abundant: a hearty meal. ⧉ **heartiness** noun.

hearty[2] noun (pl **hearties**) **1** used by and to sailors: a brave fellow; a comrade. **2** Brit, informal a sporty outgoing person: rugger hearties.

heat[1] /heet/ noun **1a** the state of being hot; warmth. **b** in physics, the form of energy associated with the random motions of the molecules, atoms, etc of which matter is composed, transmitted by conduction, convection, or radiation. **c** excessively high bodily temperature. **d** hot weather. **e** a source or level of heat: Take the pan off the heat. **2a** intensity of feeling or reaction: the heat of passion. **b** the height or stress of an action or condition: in the heat of battle. **3** informal pressure or criticism: The police turned the heat on him. **4** a single round of a contest; specif any of several preliminary con-tests in which the winners proceed to the final. ✳ **in the heat of the moment** while angry, excited, etc; without thinking. **on/in heat** said of a female mammal: ready for sexual intercourse; in oestrus. [Old English hætu]

heat[2] verb trans (often + up) to make (something) warm or hot. **2** archaic to excite (somebody). ⧉ verb intrans **1** (often + up) to become warm or hot. **2** (+ up) to become more exciting or intense. [Old English hætan]

heat barrier noun = THERMAL BARRIER.

heat capacity noun the heat required to raise the temperature of something by one unit.

heat death noun a state in which energy is uniformly distributed throughout a closed system, leaving no energy available. It is some-times suggested that the universe is tending towards this state.

heated adj marked by anger or passion: a heated debate. ⧉ **heatedly** adv.

heat engine noun a mechanism, e.g. an internal-combustion engine, for converting heat energy into mechanical energy.

heater noun **1** a device that gives off heat, esp an apparatus for heating air or water. **2** NAmer, informal, dated a gun.

heat exchanger noun a device, e.g. in a nuclear power station, that transfers heat from one liquid or gas to another without allow-ing them to mix.

heat exhaustion noun a condition marked by weakness, sick-ness, dizziness, and profuse sweating, resulting from physical exertion in a hot environment.

heath /heeth/ noun **1** chiefly Brit a large area of level uncultivated land, usu with poor peaty soil and plants such as heather and gorse. **2** a small evergreen shrub that thrives on barren soil, with needle-like leaves and small pink or purple flowers: Erica tetralix and other species. ⧉ **heathy** adj. [Old English hæth]

heathen /'heedh(ə)n/ noun (pl **heathens** or collectively **heathen**) derog **1** somebody who does not acknowledge the God of Judaism, Christianity, or Islam. **2** informal an uncivilized or immoral person. ⧉ **heathen** adj, **heathendom** noun, **heathenish** adj, **heathen-ism** noun. [Old English hæthen]

heather /'hedhə/ *noun* **1** a common northern heath with purplish pink flowers: *Calluna vulgaris*. Also called LING². **2** *informal* any of several plants of the heath family: family Ericaceae. [Old English *hadre*, *hedre*; the spelling altered by association with *heath*, where it grows]

heathery /'hedhəri/ *adj* **1** of or resembling heather. **2** having flecks of various colours: *a soft heathery tweed*.

Heath Robinson /,heeth 'robins(ə)n/ *adj Brit* said of a mechanical device: impractically complicated in design. [named after W. *Heath Robinson* d.1944, English cartoonist famous for his drawings of absurdly ingenious machines]

heating *noun* **1** a system for supplying heat to a building. **2** the heat supplied by such a system.

heat pump *noun* an apparatus for transferring heat by mechanical means to a place of higher temperature, e.g. for heating or cooling a building.

heat rash *noun* = PRICKLY HEAT.

heat-seeking *adj* said of a missile: having a guiding apparatus that homes in on heat, *esp* the hot exhaust gases from an aircraft or rocket.

heat shield *noun* a part of the hull of a spacecraft designed to prevent excessive heating during re-entry into the earth's atmosphere.

heat sink *noun* a device or substance for absorbing or dissipating unwanted heat.

heatstroke *noun* overheating of the body resulting from prolonged exposure to high temperature and leading in serious cases to collapse or death.

heat-treat *verb trans* to treat (a metal or alloy) by heating and cooling in a way that will produce desired properties, e.g. hardness. ➤➤ **heat treatment** *noun*.

heat wave *noun* a prolonged period of unusually hot weather.

heave¹ /heev/ *verb* (*past tense and past part.* **heaved** *or* **hove** /hohv/) ➤ *verb trans* **1** to lift or pull (something heavy), *esp* with great effort. **2** *informal* to throw (something heavy). **3** to utter (a sigh). ➤ *verb intrans* **1** to rise and fall rhythmically: *His chest was heaving with sobs*. **2** to retch. ✳ **heave in sight/into view** to come into view. ➤➤ **heaver** *noun*. [Old English *hebban*]

heave² *noun* **1a** an effort to heave something. **b** a throw. **2** an upward motion, *esp* a rhythmical rising: *the heave of the sea*. **3** (*in pl*) = BROKEN WIND. **4** in geology, a horizontal displacement, e.g. of rock layers, caused by a fracture in the earth's crust.

heave-ho¹ *interj* used as a cry when lifting something heavy. [orig a sailors' cry when heaving up the anchor]

heave-ho² *noun* (**the heave-ho**) *informal* dismissal, *esp* from a job.

heaven /'hev(ə)n/ *noun* **1** in some beliefs, the dwelling place of God or the gods; the place where good people go when they die: compare EARTH¹, HELL. **2** (**the heavens**) *literary* the expanse of space that surrounds the earth like a dome; the sky. **3** *informal* a place or condition of complete happiness. **4** (*also in pl*) used in exclamations in place of 'God': *for heaven's sake*; *Good heavens!* ✳ **move heaven and earth** to do everything that one can: *They moved heaven and earth to get him a place at the school*. **stink/smell to high heaven** *informal* to smell terrible. **the heavens opened** it suddenly began to pour with rain. [Old English *heofon*]

heavenly *adj* **1a** relating to heaven or the sky. **b** suggesting the blessed state of heaven; divine: *heavenly peace*. **2** *informal* delightful: *What a heavenly idea!* ➤➤ **heavenliness** *noun*.

heavenly body *noun* a planet, star, or other body in space.

heaven-sent *adj* timely or providential.

heavenward /'hev(ə)nwəd/ *adj and adv* directed towards heaven or the sky. ➤➤ **heavenwards** *adv*.

heave to *verb trans and intrans* to bring (a ship) to a stop by adjusting the sails against the wind, or to stop in this way.

heaving /'heeving/ *adj Brit, informal* said of a place: extremely crowded.

Heaviside-Kennelly layer /'hevisied 'kenəli/ *noun* = E LAYER. [named after Oliver *Heaviside* d.1925, English physicist, and Arthur E *Kennelly* d.1939, US electrical engineer, who both predicted it]

Heaviside layer /'hevisied/ *noun* = E LAYER.

heavy¹ /'hevi/ *adj* (**heavier**, **heaviest**) **1a** having great weight; difficult to carry, move, or lift. **b** large or heavy of its kind: *a heavy fabric*. **c** having great density; thick or solid. **d** in physics, said of an isotope or compound: having, being, or containing atoms of

greater than normal mass: *heavy hydrogen*. **2** said of food: digested with difficulty, usu because of excessive richness. **3** said of ground or soil: full of clay and inclined to hold water. **4** not delicate: *heavy features*. **5** slow or sluggish; clumsy: *heavy movements*. **6** falling with force; powerful: *a heavy blow*. **7** loud and dull in sound: *a heavy thud*. **8** said of a smell: very strong. **9a** of an unusually large amount, degree, or force: *heavy traffic*; *a heavy drinker*. **b** (+ on) using something in large quantities: *My car is heavy on petrol*. **10** said of industry: producing heavy goods, e.g. coal, steel, or machinery. **11** said of rock music: loud and having a strong rhythm. **12a** needing physical effort and strength: *Gardening can be heavy work*. **b** demanding or oppressive: *a heavy burden*. **c** needing considerable mental effort to read or understand: *a heavy novel*. **d** of weighty import; serious or dull. **13** *informal*. **a** emotionally difficult: *a heavy scene with his parents*. **b** strict or severe: *Was I too heavy with her?* ✳ **heavy going** difficult to understand or deal with. ➤➤ **heavily** *adv*, **heaviness** *noun*, **heavyish** *adj*. [Old English *hefig*]

heavy² *adv* in a heavy manner; heavily: *Time hangs heavy on us*.

heavy³ *noun* (*pl* **heavies**) **1** *informal* somebody hired to compel or deter by means of threats or physical violence. **2** *informal* somebody of importance or significance. **3** a villain in a film or play. **4** *informal* (*in pl*) serious newspapers. **5** *Scot* bitter beer.

heavy breathing *noun* deep and noisy breathing, e.g. from sexual excitement. ➤➤ **heavy breather** *noun*.

heavy-duty *adj* **1** able or designed to withstand unusual strain or wear. **2** *informal* more substantial or intensive than usual.

heavy-handed *adj* **1** clumsy or awkward. **2** oppressive or harsh. ➤➤ **heavy-handedly** *adv*, **heavy-handedness** *noun*.

heavy-hearted *adj* despondent or melancholy.

heavy hydrogen *noun* = DEUTERIUM.

heavy metal *noun* **1** a metal with a high relative density or high relative atomic weight. **2** a type of highly amplified rock music.

heavy petting *noun* sexual contact between two people that involves touching the genitals but not intercourse.

heavy spar *noun* = BARYTES.

heavy water *noun* water enriched *esp* with deuterium, used to slow down nuclear reactions.

heavyweight¹ *noun* **1a** a weight in boxing of more than 79kg (about 175lb) if professional or more than 81kg (about 178lb) if amateur. **b** a weight in wrestling of more than 95kg (about 209lb) if professional or more than 100kg (about 220lb) if amateur. **2** *informal* an important or influential person: *an intellectual heavyweight*.

heavyweight² *adj* **1** of above average weight. **2** *informal* important or influential.

Heb. *abbr* **1** Hebrew. **2** Hebrews (book of the Bible).

hebdomadal /heb'domədl/ *adj formal* weekly. [via Latin from Greek *hebdomad-*, *hebdomas* the number seven, seven days, from *hepta* seven]

hebe /'heebi/ *noun* any of a genus of evergreen shrubs, mostly native to New Zealand, cultivated for their decorative leaves and usu white or purplish flowers: genus *Hebe*. [Latin genus name, named after *Hebe*, Greek goddess of youth]

hebephrenia /heebi'freeni-ə/ *noun* schizophrenia characterized by delusions, seemingly foolish behaviour, and regression to a childish state. ➤➤ **hebephrenic** /-'frenik/ *adj and noun*. [Latin *hebephrenia*, from Greek *hēbē* youth + *phren* mind]

Hebraic /hi'brayik/ *adj* relating to the Hebrews or the Hebrew language. ➤➤ **Hebraically** *adv*. [Middle English *Ebrayke* via late Latin from Greek *Hebraikos*, from *Hebraios*: see HEBREW]

Hebraism /'heebrayiz(ə)m/ *noun* **1** a characteristic feature of the Hebrew language, *esp* one occurring in another language. **2** the religion or culture of the Jews.

Hebraist /'heebrayist/ *noun* a specialist in Hebrew and Hebraic studies.

Hebraistic /heebray'istik/ *adj* = HEBRAIC.

Hebrew /'heebrooh/ *noun* **1** a member or descendant of any of a group of ancient N Semitic peoples, *esp* an Israelite. **2** the Semitic language of the ancient Hebrews, or the revived form of it spoken in modern Israel. **3** *offensive* a Jew. ➤➤ **Hebrew** *adj*.

Word history
Middle English *Ebreu* via Old French and Latin from Greek *Hebraios*, from Aramaic *'Ebrai*. Words from the ancient Hebrew language that have passed into English, mostly through their use in the Bible, include *amen*, *cherub*, *jubilee*, *manna*, *rabbi*, *sabbath*, and *shibboleth*. Modern Hebrew has

provided a few loanwords, such as *kibbutz*. Other words of Hebrew origin have entered English by way of Yiddish (e.g. *chutzpah* and *kosher*).

Hebridean /'hebridiən/ *noun* a native or inhabitant of the Hebrides off NW Scotland. ➤➤ **Hebridean** *adj*.

hecatomb /'hekətoohm/ *noun* **1** an ancient Greek and Roman sacrifice of 100 oxen or cattle. **2** the sacrifice or slaughter of many victims. [via Latin from Greek *hekatombē*, from *hekaton* hundred + *bous* cow]

heck /hek/ *interj* used to express annoyance, surprise, etc, or as an intensive: *a heck of a lot of money*; *What the heck!* [euphemistic alteration of HELL]

heckelphone /'heklfohn/ *noun* a woodwind musical instrument similar to an oboe, but larger and about an octave lower in range. [named after William *Heckel* d.1909, German instrument-maker who invented it]

heckle[1] /'hekl/ *verb trans* to interrupt and try to disconcert (e.g. a speaker) with questions, comments, or jeers. ➤➤ **heckler** *noun*. [Middle English *hekelen*, from *heckele*: see HACKLE. The word orig meant 'to comb with a hackle'; the current sense dates from the 17th cent.]

heckle[2] *noun* a heckling comment or jeer.

hect- *or* **hecto-** *comb. form* forming words, with the meaning: hundred: *hectogram*. [French, irreg from Greek *hekaton*]

hectare /'hektah/ *noun* a metric unit of area equal to 10,000 square metres (2.471 acres). [French *hectare*, from HECT- + *are* ARE[2]]

hectic[1] /'hektik/ *adj* **1** filled with excitement or feverish activity. **2** *archaic* denoting or affected by a fluctuating fever, e.g. in tuberculosis. ➤➤ **hectically** *adv*. [Middle English *etyk* via French and late Latin from Greek *hektikos* habitual, consumptive, from *echein* to have]

hectic[2] *noun archaic* a hectic fever.

hecto- *comb. form* see HECT-.

hectogram *or* **hectogramme** /'hektəgram/ *noun* a metric unit of mass equal to 100g.

hectolitre (*NAmer* **hectoliter**) /'hektəleetə/ *noun* a metric unit of capacity equal to 100l.

hectometre (*NAmer* **hectometer**) /'hektəmeetə/ *noun* a metric unit of length equal to 100m.

hector /'hektə/ *verb trans* (**hectored, hectoring**) to intimidate (somebody) by bullying or blustering. ➤➤ **hectoring** *adj*, **hectoringly** *adv*. [from the name *Hector*, a Trojan warrior in Homer's *Iliad*]

he'd /id, hid; *strong* heed/ *contraction* **1** he had. **2** he would.

heddle /'hedl/ *noun* one of the sets of parallel cords or wires that with their mounting compose the harness used to guide warp threads in a loom. [prob from Old English *hefeld*]

heder *or* **cheder** /'khaydə, 'khedə/ *noun* (*pl* **hedarim** *or* **heders** *or* **chedarim** *or* **cheders**) an elementary Jewish school in which children are taught to read prayers, parts of the Bible, and other material in Hebrew. [Yiddish *kheyder* from Hebrew *ḥedher* room]

hedge[1] /hej/ *noun* **1** a boundary formed by a dense row of shrubs or low trees: *You know you would rather dine under the hedge than with Casaubon alone* — George Eliot. **2** a means of protection or defence, e.g. an asset held as protection against financial loss. **3** a deliberately non-committal or evasive use of language. ➤➤ **hedging** *noun*. [Old English *hecg*]

hedge[2] *verb trans* **1** to enclose or protect (an area) with a hedge. **2** to limit or qualify (e.g. a statement): *a promise hedged with ifs and buts*. **3** to protect oneself against losing (e.g. an investment), *esp* by making counterbalancing transactions. ➤ *verb intrans* to avoid committing oneself, *esp* by making evasive statements. ✳ **hedge one's bets** to cover oneself by supporting two sides, courses of action, etc. ➤➤ **hedger** *noun*.

hedgehog *noun* any of several species of small spine-covered mammals that eat insects and are active at night: genus *Erinaceus*.

hedgehop *verb intrans* (**hedgehopped, hedgehopping**) to fly an aircraft close to the ground and rise over obstacles as they appear. ➤➤ **hedgehopper** *noun*. [earliest as *hedgehopper*]

hedgerow /'hejroh/ *noun* a row of shrubs or trees surrounding a field: *There is more violence in an English hedgerow than in the meanest streets of a great city* — P D James.

hedge sparrow *noun* = DUNNOCK.

hedonic /hee'donik/ *adj* **1** of or characterized by pleasure. **2** relating to hedonism.

hedonism /'heedəniz(ə)m, 'hed-/ *noun* **1** the pursuit of personal pleasure, *esp* sensual pleasure. **2** in philosophy, the doctrine that personal pleasure is the sole or chief good. ➤➤ **hedonist** *noun*, **hedonistic** /-'nistik/ *adj*, **hedonistically** /-'nistikli/ *adv*. [Greek *hēdonē* pleasure + -ISM]

-hedra *comb. form* pl of -HEDRON.

-hedral *comb. form* forming adjectives, with the meaning: having the type of surface or number of surfaces specified: *dihedral*.

-hedron *comb. form* (*pl* **-hedrons** *or* **-hedra**) forming nouns, denoting: a crystal or geometrical figure having the type of surface or number of surfaces specified: *pentahedron*. [Greek *-edron*, from *hedra* seat]

heebie-jeebies /,heebi 'jeebiz/ *pl noun* (**the heebie-jeebies**) *informal* a state of nervousness or anxiety. [coined by Billy DeBeck d.1942, US cartoonist]

heed[1] /heed/ *verb trans* to pay close attention to (somebody or something). [Old English *hēdan*]

heed[2] *noun* careful attention; notice: *Take heed of what I say.*

heedful /'heedf(ə)l/ *adj* paying close attention; taking notice. ➤➤ **heedfully** *adv*, **heedfulness** *noun*.

heedless *adj* **1** inconsiderate or thoughtless. **2** (*often* + of) without thinking or paying attention; reckless: *heedless of the risk*. ➤➤ **heedlessly** *adv*, **heedlessness** *noun*.

hee-haw[1] /'hee haw/ *noun* the bray of a donkey. [imitative]

hee-haw[2] *verb intrans* to make the sound of a donkey braying.

heel[1] /heel/ *noun* **1a** the back of the human foot below the ankle. **b** the back part of a vertebrate's hind limb corresponding to this. **2** the part of the palm of the hand nearest the wrist. **3** the part of an article of footwear that covers or supports the heel. **4** the crusty end of a loaf of bread. **5** a lower or bottom part, e.g. the lower end of a mast or the end of a violin bow that the violinist holds. **6** the base of a tuber or cutting of a plant used for propagation. **7** *informal, dated* a contemptible person. ✳ **down at heel** in or into a run-down or shabby condition. **on/hot on the heels of** immediately following; closely behind. **take to one's heels** to run away. **to heel 1** used in training a dog: close behind. **2** into agreement or line; under control. **turn on one's heel** to turn abruptly to face or go in the opposite direction: *She turned on her heel and stormed out.* ➤➤ **heeled** *adj*, **heelless** *adj*. [Old English *hēla*]

heel[2] *verb trans* **1** to supply (e.g. a shoe) with a heel, *esp* to replace its heel. **2** to strike (something) with the heel; *specif* to kick (a rugby ball) with the heel, *esp* out of a scrum. **3** in golf, to strike (the ball) with the part of the club nearest the shaft. ➤ *verb intrans* said of a dog: to walk close behind the person in charge of it. ➤➤ **heeler** *noun*.

heel[3] *verb intrans* said of a ship: to tilt to one side. [alteration of Middle English *hield* from Old English *hieldan* to lean; the *d* disappeared in the 16th cent. when *hield* was taken to be a past part.]

heel[4] *noun* a tilt to one side, or the extent of this.

heel[5] *verb trans* (+ in) to plant (cuttings or plants) temporarily before setting in the final growing position. [alteration of English dialect *hele, heal* to cover over, from Old English *helian* to hide, conceal]

heelball *noun* a mixture of wax and lampblack used to polish the heels of footwear and to take brass or shoe rubbings.

heel bar *noun* a small shop or counter where shoes can be taken to be repaired.

heeltap *noun* **1** a layer, e.g. of leather, forming the heel of a shoe. **2** *dated* a small quantity of alcoholic drink remaining in a glass after drinking.

heft[1] /heft/ *noun Brit dialect and NAmer* weight or heaviness. [from HEAVE[1], on the pattern of *cleave, cleft*]

heft[2] *verb trans* **1** to heave (something) up; to hoist. **2** to test the weight of (something) by lifting.

hefty *adj* (**heftier, heftiest**) large, heavy, or powerful: *a hefty blow*; *a hefty pay rise*. ➤➤ **heftily** *adv*, **heftiness** *noun*.

Hegelian /hay'geeli-ən/ *adj* relating to Hegel or his philosophy equating mind and nature. ➤➤ **Hegelian** *noun*, **Hegelianism** *noun*. [Georg *Hegel* d.1831, German philosopher]

hegemony /hi'gemani, hi'jemani/ *noun* (*pl* **hegemonies**) domination or leadership of one nation, group, etc over others.

>> **hegemonic** /ˌhegəˈmonik, ˌhejə-/ *adj.* [Greek *hēgemonia*, from *hēgemōn* leader, from *hēgeisthai* to lead]

hegira *or* **hejira** /ˈhejirə/ *or* **hijra** /ˈhijrə/ *noun* 1 (**Hegira**) the flight of Muhammad from Mecca to Medina in AD 622, marking the beginning of the Muslim era: compare ANNO HEGIRAE. 2 a journey, *esp* when undertaken to escape from a dangerous or undesirable situation. [medieval Latin *hegira* from Arabic *hijrah* flight]

heifer /ˈhefə/ *noun* a young cow, *esp* one that has not had more than one calf. [Old English *hēahfore*]

heigh-ho /ˈhay hoh/ *interj* used to express boredom, weariness, or happiness: *'Tis but a little word – 'heigho!' … an idle breath – yet life and death may hang upon a maid's 'heigho!'* — W S Gilbert. [*heigh* (variant of HEY) + HO[1]]

height /hiet/ *noun* 1 the distance from the bottom to the top of something or somebody standing upright. 2 the elevation above a level. 3 the quality of being tall or high. 4a (*usu in pl*) a piece of land, e.g. a hill or plateau, rising to a considerable degree above the surrounding country. b a high point or position. 5 the highest or most extreme point; the zenith: *at the height of his powers*. [Old English *hīehthu* the highest point]

heighten *verb* (**heightened, heightening**) >> *verb trans* 1 to increase the amount or degree of (something); to augment: *Recent reports have heightened our awareness of the problem.* 2 to deepen or intensify (something): *Her colour was heightened by emotion.* 3 to make (something) higher; to elevate: *The building was heightened by another storey.* >> *verb intrans* to become greater in amount, degree, extent, or intensity.

height of land *noun NAmer* a watershed.

Heimlich manoeuvre /ˈhiemlikh/ *noun* = HEIMLICH PROCEDURE.

Heimlich procedure /ˈhiemlikh/ *noun* an emergency technique for saving somebody from choking by pressing hard on the diaphragm to compress the air in the lungs, forcing the obstruction out of the windpipe. [named after Henry J *Heimlich* b.1920, US physician]

heinous /ˈhaynəs, ˈheenəs/ *adj* hatefully or shockingly evil; abominable: *a heinous crime.* >> **heinously** *adv*, **heinousness** *noun*. [Middle English from early French *haineus*, from *haine* hate, from *hair* to hate, of Germanic origin]

heir /eə/ *noun* 1 a person who inherits property or is entitled to succeed to an estate or rank. 2 a person who receives some position, role, or quality passed on from a parent or predecessor. >> **heirdom** *noun*, **heirless** *adj*, **heirship** *noun*. [Middle English via Old French from Latin *hered-, heres*]

heir apparent *noun* (*pl* **heirs apparent**) 1 an heir who cannot be displaced so long as he or she outlives the person from whom he or she is to inherit: compare HEIR PRESUMPTIVE. 2 a person whose succession, *esp* to a position or role, appears certain under existing circumstances.

heiress /ˈeəris/ *noun* a female heir, *esp* to great wealth: *Marriageable heiresses … are not to be had for nothing* — Henry James.

heirloom *noun* a piece of valuable property handed down within a family for generations. [Middle English *heirlome*, from HEIR + *lome* LOOM[1], in an obsolete sense 'implement']

heir presumptive *noun* (*pl* **heirs presumptive**) an heir who can be displaced only by the birth of a child with a superior claim: compare HEIR APPARENT.

heist[1] /hiest/ *noun chiefly NAmer, informal* a robbery. [alteration of HOIST[1]]

heist[2] *verb trans chiefly NAmer, informal* to steal (something).

hejira /ˈhejirə/ *noun* see HEGIRA.

HeLa cells /ˈheelə/ *pl noun* a particular strain of human cells kept continuously in tissue culture, used for research. [named after Henrietta *Lacks* d.1951, whose cervical cancer provided the original cells]

held /held/ *verb* past tense and past part. of HOLD[1].

heldentenor /ˈheldntenə/ *noun* (*often* **Heldentenor**) a powerful tenor voice suited to heroic roles, or a singer with this voice. [German *Heldentenor*, from *Held* hero + *Tenor* tenor]

helenium /heˈleeniəm/ *noun* a plant of the daisy family, orig from N America, that has bold red, gold, or yellow flowers with notched petals: genus *Helenium*. [Latin genus name, from Greek *helenion* the herb elecampane]

heli-[1] *or* **helio-** *comb. form* forming words, denoting: sun: *heliocentric*. [Latin from Greek *hēli-, hēlio-*, from *hēlios*]

heli-[2] *comb. form* forming words, denoting: helicopter: *heliport*.

heliacal /hiˈlie-əkl/ *adj* in astronomy, relating to the last setting of a star before and its first rising after invisibility due to alignment with the sun. [via late Latin from Greek *hēliakos*, from *hēlios* sun]

helianthemum /heeliˈanthəməm/ *noun* a low shrub with brightly coloured flowers: genus *Helianthemum*. [Latin genus name, from Greek *hēlios* sun + *anthemon* flower; because the flowers turn to follow the sun's path]

helianthus /heeliˈanthəs/ *noun* (*pl* **helianthuses**) any of several species of large daisy-like plants including the sunflower: genus *Helianthus*. [Latin genus name, from Greek *hēlios* sun + *anthos* flower; because the flowers turn to follow the sun's path]

helic- *or* **helico-** *comb. form* forming words, denoting: helix or spiral: *helical*. [Greek *helik-, heliko-*, from *helik-, helix* spiral]

helical /ˈhelikl/ *adj* having the form of a helix; spiral. >> **helically** *adv*.

helices /ˈheeliseez, heliseez/ *noun* pl of HELIX.

helichrysum /heliˈkriesəm/ *noun* a plant of the daisy family grown for its flowers, which retain their shape and colour when dried: genus *Helichrysum*. [Latin genus name, from Greek *helikhrusos* from *helix* spiral + *khrusos* gold]

helico- *comb. form* see HELIC-.

helicoid[1] /ˈhelikoyd/ *adj* forming or arranged in a spiral.

helicoid[2] *noun* a helicoid object or surface.

helicoidal /heliˈkoydl/ *adj* = HELICOID[1].

helicon /ˈhelikən/ *noun* a large circular tuba similar to a sousaphone. [prob from Greek *helik-, helix* spiral + *-on*; because its tube forms a spiral encircling the player's body]

helicopter /ˈhelikoptə/ *noun* an aircraft which derives both lift and propulsive power from a set of horizontally rotating rotors or vanes and is capable of vertical takeoff and landing. [French *hélicoptère*, from HELICO- + Greek *pteron* wing]

helio- *comb. form* see HELI-[1].

heliocentric /ˌheelioh'sentrik/ *adj* 1 having or relating to the sun as a centre: compare GEOCENTRIC. 2 in astronomy, referred to, measured from, or as if observed from the sun's centre. >> **heliocentrically** *adv*.

heliograph /ˈheeli-əgrahf/ *noun* 1 an apparatus for signalling using the sun's rays reflected from a mirror. 2 a telescope adapted for photographing the sun. 3 an early photographic engraving. >> **heliographic** /-ˈgrafik/ *adj*, **heliography** /-ˈogrəfi/ *noun*.

heliometer /heeliˈomitə/ *noun* a refracting telescope used for measuring the angular distances between stars.

heliopause /ˈheeli-əpawz/ *noun* in astronomy, the outer edge of the heliosphere.

heliosphere /ˈheeli-əsfiə/ *noun* in astronomy, the region of space around the sun through which the effect of the solar wind extends. >> **heliospheric** /-ˈsferik/ *adj*.

heliostat /ˈheeli-əstat/ *noun* an instrument consisting of a mirror moved on an axis so that it can reflect a sunbeam steadily in one direction.

heliotrope /ˈheeli-ətrohp/ *noun* 1 any of a genus of plants of the borage family, *esp* a S American variety cultivated for its fragrant purplish flowers: genus *Heliotropium*. 2 = BLOODSTONE. [Latin genus name, from Greek *hēliotropion*, from *hēlios* sun + *tropos* turning, from *trepein* to turn]

heliotropism /heeliˈotrəpiz(ə)m/ *noun* the growth or movement of a plant in response to the stimulus of sunlight. >> **heliotropic** /-ˈtropik/ *adj*.

helipad /ˈhelipad/ *noun* a place where helicopters can land and take off, e.g. on the top of a high building.

heliport /ˈhelipawt/ *noun* an airport for helicopters.

helium /ˈheeli-əm/ *noun* a gaseous chemical element of the noble gas group found in natural gases, and used *esp* for inflating balloons and in low-temperature research: symbol He, atomic number 2. [Greek *hēlios* sun, because its emission line in the sun's spectrum led to its discovery]

helix /ˈheeliks/ *noun* (*pl* **helices** /ˈheeliseez, ˈheliseez/ *or* **helixes**) 1 something spiral in form. 2 in architecture, a spiral scroll-shaped ornament. 3 in anatomy, the curved rim of the external ear. 4 in biochemistry, a chain of atoms in a spiral form. [via Latin from Greek *helic-, helix* spiral]

hell /hel/ *noun* **1** a place regarded in some beliefs as a place of torment and punishment for the dead, and as the abode of devils and demons: compare EARTH[1], HEAVEN: *'How comes it then that thou art out of hell?' 'Why, this is hell, nor am I out of it.'* — Marlowe. **2** a place or state of torment, misery, or wickedness. **3** used in exclamations or for emphasis: *one hell of a mess; Oh hell!* ✳ **all hell broke loose** *informal* there was great commotion or uproar. **come hell or high water** regardless of opposition or difficulties. **for the hell of it** *informal* for the fun of it. **get hell** *informal* to be severely scolded. **give somebody hell 1** *informal* to scold somebody severely. **2** *informal* to make somebody's life difficult. **hell to pay** *informal* serious trouble. *If he's late there'll be hell to pay.* **like hell 1** *informal* very hard or much: *We worked like hell to get the job done on time.* **2** *informal* used to intensify denial or contradiction: *'I did four hours overtime.' 'Like hell you did!'* **not a hope/chance in hell** no hope or chance at all. **play (merry) hell** *informal* to cause disruption or damage. **what the hell** it doesn't matter. **when hell freezes over** never. [Old English *hel*]

he'll /il, hil; *strong* heel/ *contraction* **1** he shall. **2** he will.

hellacious /he'layshəs/ *adj* *NAmer, informal* excellent, exceptional, or immense. [HELL + -*acious* as in AUDACIOUS]

Helladic /he'ladik/ *adj* of or relating to the Bronze Age culture on the mainland of Greece (c.3000–1050 BC). [Greek *Helladikos* from *Hellas* Greece]

hell-bent *adj* stubbornly and often recklessly determined: *Civilization is hell-bent on self-destruction* — R F Delderfield.

hellcat *noun* a spiteful ill-tempered woman.

hellebore /'helibaw/ *noun* any of a genus of showy-flowered plants of the buttercup family having poisonous parts: genus *Helleborus*. [via Latin from Greek *helleboros*]

helleborine /'helibərin, -rien/ *noun* any of several species of plants of the orchid family found mainly in woodland: genera *Epipactis* and *Cephalanthera*. [via Latin from Greek *helleborine* a plant resembling the hellebore, from *helleboros* HELLEBORE]

Hellene /'heleen/ *noun* a Greek. [Greek *Hellēn*]

Hellenic[1] /hə'lenik, hə'leenik/ *adj* **1** Greek. **2** in archaeology, of or relating to Greek culture between the Iron Age and the Classical period (1050–323 BC).

Hellenic[2] *noun* the Greek language in its classical or modern form.

Hellenise /'heliniez/ *verb trans and intrans* see HELLENIZE.

Hellenism /'heliniz(ə)m/ *noun* the culture and ideals associated with ancient Greece, or devotion to the imitation of these.

Hellenist /'helinist/ *noun* somebody who studies or admires ancient Greek civilization.

Hellenistic /heli'nistik/ *adj* relating to Greek history, culture, or art from the death of Alexander the Great in 323 BC to the defeat of Antony and Cleopatra in 31 BC.

Hellenize *or* **Hellenise** /'heliniez/ *verb trans and intrans* to conform or make (something) conform to Greek or Hellenistic form or culture. ⟫ **Hellenization** /-'zaysh(ə)n/ *noun*.

hellfire *noun* **1** punishment in hell, imagined as eternal fire. **2** (*used before a noun*) denoting preaching that emphasizes eternal punishment: *a hellfire sermon*.

hell-for-leather *adv and adj* at full speed: *We pelted hell-for-leather down the street.* [perhaps alteration of *all of a lather*]

hellhole *noun* a place of extreme discomfort, squalor, or evil.

hellhound *noun* a fiend in the form of a dog.

hellion /'helyən/ *noun* *NAmer, informal* a troublesome or mischievous person. [prob alteration of dialect *hallion* scamp, by association with HELL]

hellish[1] *adj* of or resembling hell; diabolical. ⟫ **hellishly** *adv*, **hellishness** *noun*.

hellish[2] *adv* *Brit, informal* extremely: *It was a hellish cold day.*

hello *or* **hallo** *or* **hullo** /hə'loh, he'loh/ *interj* **1** used as a greeting or in answering the telephone. **2** *Brit* used to express surprise or to attract attention. [alteration of HOLLO[1]]

hellraiser *noun* a person who acts in a loud, wild, or drunken manner. ⟫ **hellraising** *noun and adj*.

Hell's Angel *noun* a member of a motorcycle gang associated with lawless and sometimes violent behaviour.

hell's bells *interj* *informal* used to express irritation or impatience.

helluva /'heləvə/ *adj* *informal* used as an intensive: great or terrific: *a helluva din*. [alteration of *hell of a*]

helm[1] /helm/ *noun* **1** a tiller or wheel controlling the steering of a ship. **2** (**the helm**) the position of control; the head: *The medical school has a new dean at the helm*. [Old English *helma*]

helm[2] *verb trans* **1** to steer (a ship). **2** to manage or direct (e.g. a company).

helm[3] *noun* *archaic* a helmet. [Old English]

helmet /'helmit/ *noun* **1** any of various protective head coverings, *esp* made of a hard material to resist impact. **2** a covering or enclosing headpiece of ancient or medieval armour. **3** a hood-shaped petal or sepal of a plant. **4** a mollusc with a thick ridged shell, found in tropical or temperate seas and preying on sea urchins: family Cassidae. ⟫ **helmeted** *adj*. [early French *helmet*, dimin. of *helme* helmet, of Germanic origin]

helminth /'helminth/ *noun* a parasitic worm, *esp* one living in the intestines of an animal. ⟫ **helminthic** /hel'minthik/ *adj*. [Greek *helminth-, helmis*]

helminthiasis /helmin'thie-əsis/ *noun* infestation with parasitic worms.

helmsman *noun* (*pl* **helmsmen**) a person steering a ship.

helot /'helət/ *noun* **1** (**Helot**) a serf in ancient Sparta. **2** a serf or slave. ⟫ **helotism** *noun*, **helotry** *noun*. [Latin *Helotes* (plural) from Greek *Heilōtes*]

help[1] /help/ *verb trans* **1** to give assistance or support to (somebody). **2a** to be of use to (somebody or something); to benefit. **b** to further the advancement of (something); to promote: *Comments like that will not help our cause*. **3a** to refrain from (doing something): *I couldn't help laughing*. **b** to keep (something) from occurring; to prevent: *They couldn't help the accident*. **c** to restrain (oneself) from taking action: *I tried not to say anything, but couldn't help myself*. **4** to remedy, relieve, or improve (something). **5** to serve (somebody or oneself) with food or drink, *esp* at a meal: *Let me help you to some salad*. **6** to enable (somebody) to move in a specified direction: *The nurse helped him into the chair*. **7** to appropriate something for (oneself), *esp* dishonestly: *He helped himself to my pen*. ✳ **so help me (God)** used to show that one is sincere and determined. ⟫ **helper** *noun*. [Old English *helpan*]

help[2] *noun* **1** aid or assistance. **2** something that provides assistance: *A map would be a help*. **3a** somebody hired to do work, *esp* housework. **b** the services of a paid worker or the workers providing such services: *The family advertised for help in the house*. **4** in computing, a system that provides information about a particular choice or action. ✳ **no help for it** no way of avoiding something; no alternative or remedy: *There was no help for it, we had to sell the house*.

helpful /'helpf(ə)l/ *adj* of service or assistance; useful. ⟫ **helpfully** *adv*, **helpfulness** *noun*.

helping *noun* a serving of food.

helping hand *noun* help or assistance.

helpless *adj* **1** lacking protection or support; defenceless. **2** lacking strength or effectiveness; powerless. **3** lacking control or restraint: *They collapsed into helpless giggles*. ⟫ **helplessly** *adv*, **helplessness** *noun*.

helpline *noun* a telephone service provided by an organization offering advice and information, e.g. on personal problems, financial matters, or technical queries.

helpmate *noun* a companion and helper, *esp* a spouse. [by folk etymology from HELPMEET]

helpmeet *noun* *archaic* = HELPMATE. [HELP[2] + MEET[3]; from a misunderstanding of Genesis 2:18, in which God says He will make Adam 'an help meet for him']

help out *verb trans* to give assistance or aid to (somebody), *esp* when they are in difficulty: *She helped me out when my mother was in hospital*.

helter-skelter[1] /,heltə 'skeltə/ *adj and adv* in a hurried and disorderly manner: *We ran helter-skelter down the stairs*. [perhaps based on Middle English *skelten* to hurry]

helter-skelter[2] *noun* *Brit* a spiral slide at a fairground.

helve /helv/ *noun* the handle of a weapon or tool. [Old English *hielfe*]

Helvetian /hel'veesh(ə)n/ *adj* Swiss. ⟫ **Helvetian** *noun.* [Latin *Helvetii,* ancient people of Switzerland]

hem[1] /hem/ *noun* the border of a cloth article when turned back and stitched down, *esp* the bottom edge of a garment finished in this manner. [Old English]

hem[2] *verb trans* (**hemmed, hemming**) **1a** to finish (e.g. a skirt) with a hem. **b** to border or edge (something). **2** (+ in/about) to enclose or confine (somebody or something): *We were hemmed in by enemy troops.*

hem[3] *interj* used to indicate a pause in speaking, or the sound made by clearing the throat. [imitative]

hem[4] *verb intrans* (**hemmed, hemming**) *archaic* to utter the sound represented by *hem, esp* in hesitation. ✳ **hem and haw** to equivocate.

hem- or **hemo-** *comb. form NAmer* see HAEM-.

hemal /'heeml/ *adj NAmer* see HAEMAL.

he-man /'hee/ *noun* (*pl* **he-men**) *informal* a strong masculine man.

hemat- or **hemato-** *comb. form NAmer* see HAEMAT-.

heme /heem/ *noun NAmer* see HAEM.

hemerocallis /,heməroh'kalis/ *noun* (*pl* **hemerocallis**) any of a genus of plants that comprises the day lilies: genus *Hemerocallis.* [Greek *hēmerokalles,* from *hēmera* day + *kallos* beauty]

hemi- *prefix* forming words, denoting: half: *hemisphere.* [Middle English via Latin from Greek *hēmi-*]

-hemia *comb. form NAmer* see -AEMIA.

hemicellulose /hemi'selyoolohs, -lohz/ *noun* any of various polysaccharides (complex sugars; see POLYSACCHARIDE) of plant cell walls that form the matrix in which cellulose fibres are embedded.

hemidemisemiquaver /,hemidemi'semikwayvə/ *noun chiefly Brit* a musical note with the time value of half a demisemiquaver. *NAmer* Also called SIXTY-FOURTH NOTE.

hemihedral /hemi'heedrəl/ *adj* said of a crystal: having half the surfaces required by complete symmetry: compare HOLOHEDRAL.

hemiola /hemi'ohlə/ *noun* a musical rhythmic alteration consisting of three beats in place of two or two beats in place of three. [via late Latin from Greek *hēmiolia* ratio of 1.5 to 1, from *hēmi-* half + *holos* whole]

hemiplegia /hemi'pleejə/ *noun* paralysis of one side of the body: compare PARAPLEGIA, QUADRIPLEGIA. ⟫ **hemiplegic** /-jik/ *adj and noun.* [scientific Latin from Greek *hēmiplēgia* from *hēmi-* half + *-plēgia* -PLEGIA]

hemipode /'hemipohd/ *noun* = BUTTON QUAIL. [scientific Latin from Greek *hēmi-* half + *pous, pod-* foot; because the bird has only three toes on each foot]

hemipteran /hi'miptərən/ *noun* any of a large order of insects that have piercing and sucking mouthparts and usu two pairs of wings. They include many pests, e.g. aphids: order Hemiptera. ⟫ **hemipteran** *adj,* **hemipterous** *adj.* [scientific Latin from Greek *hēmi-* half + *pteron* wing]

hemisphere /'hemisfiə/ *noun* **1** a half sphere. **2a** the northern or southern half of the earth divided by the equator or the eastern or western half divided by a MERIDIAN (imaginary circle passing through both poles). **b** a half of the celestial sphere when divided by the horizon, the celestial equator, or the ECLIPTIC[1] (apparent path of the sun). **3** = CEREBRAL HEMISPHERE. ⟫ **hemispheric** /-'sferik/ *adj,* **hemispherical** /-'sferikl/ *adj,* **hemispherically** *adv.* [Middle English *hemispere* via Latin from Greek *hēmisphairion,* from *hēmi-* half + *sphairion,* dimin. of *sphaira* SPHERE[1]]

hemistich /'hemistik/ *noun* half of a line of verse, usu divided from the other half by a CAESURA (break or pause). [via Latin from Greek *hēmistichion,* from *hēmi-* half + *stichos* line, verse]

hemline *noun* the line formed by the lower hemmed edge of a garment, *esp* a skirt or dress.

hemlock *noun* **1** a poisonous plant of the parsley family with small white flowers: *Conium maculatum.* **2** a poisonous drink made from this plant: *My heart aches, and a drowsy numbness pains my sense, as though of hemlock I had drunk* — Keats. **3a** any of several species of evergreen coniferous trees of the pine family: genus *Tsuga.* **b** the soft light wood of this tree. [Old English *hemlic*]

hemo- *comb. form NAmer* see HAEM-.

hemp /hemp/ *noun* **1a** a tall widely cultivated Asiatic plant: *Cannabis sativa.* Also called INDIAN HEMP. **b** the fibre of hemp, used

for making rope and fabrics. **c** the intoxicating drug cannabis, obtained from hemp. **2** a fibre, e.g. jute, from a plant similar to hemp, e.g. Manila hemp. [Old English *hænep*]

hemp nettle *noun* any of several species of hairy Eurasian plants of the mint family: genus *Galeopsis.*

hemstitch[1] *noun* decorative needlework that consists of open spaces and embroidered groups of cross threads, used on or next to the stitching line of hems.

hemstitch[2] *verb trans* to decorate (e.g. a border) with hemstitch.

hen /hen/ *noun* **1** a female bird, *esp* a domestic fowl. **2** (*in pl*) domestic fowls of both sexes. **3** used in the names of other birds, e.g. moorhen. **4** a female lobster, crab, fish, or other aquatic animal. **5** *Scot* used as a familiar form of address to a girl or woman. [Old English *henn*]

hen and chickens *noun* any of several plants, e.g. the houseleek, that multiply by producing shoots from the base or flowers: *Jovibarba sobilifera* and other species.

henbane *noun* a poisonous foul-smelling African and Eurasian plant of the nightshade family having sticky hairy toothed leaves and yielding the drugs hyoscyamine and scopolamine: *Hyoscyamus niger.* [HEN + BANE; from its poison being fatal *esp* to fowl]

hence /hens/ *adv* **1** because of a preceding fact; for this reason: *He was born at Christmas, hence the name Noel.* **2** from this time; later than now: *three days hence.* **3** (also **from hence**) *archaic* from here; away. [Middle English *hennes, henne* from Old English *heonan*]

henceforth *adv* from this time or point on.

henceforward *adv* = HENCEFORTH.

henchman /'henchmən/ *noun* (*pl* **henchmen**) a follower or supporter, *esp* one who is willing to be unscrupulous or dishonest.

Word history ─────────────
Middle English *hengestman* groom, from Old English *hengest* stallion + MAN[1]. About 200 years after its original senses 'groom' or 'squire' had fallen out of use, *henchman* was reintroduced by Sir Walter Scott in the early 19th cent. to mean the principal attendant of a Highland chief. As its meaning broadened to refer to a follower of any important person, so it quickly acquired derogatory suggestions of an obsequious or self-serving follower. Its frequent connotations of thuggery and gangsterism in current use perhaps come from association with *hatchet man.*

hendeca- *comb. form* forming words, denoting: eleven: *hendecagon.* [Greek *hendeka*]

hendecagon /hen'dekəgən/ *noun* a polygon with eleven angles and eleven sides. ⟫ **hendecagonal** /-'kagənl/ *adj.*

hendecasyllable /,hendekə'siləbl/ *noun* a line of verse consisting of eleven syllables. ⟫ **hendecasyllabic** /hen,dekəsi'labik/ *adj.*

hendiadys /hen'die-ədis/ *noun* the expression of an idea by the use of two independent words connected by *and,* e.g. *nice and cool* instead of *nicely cool* or *grace and favour* instead of *gracious favour.* [late Latin *hendiadys, hendiadyoin,* modification of Greek *hen dia dyoin* one through two]

henequen /'henikin/ *noun* **1** a strong hard fibre obtained from the leaves of a tropical American agave plant and used for making ropes and twine. **2** the plant from which this fibre is obtained: *Agave fourcroydes.* [Spanish *henequén*]

henge /henj/ *noun* a prehistoric monument consisting of a circular structure made of wood or stones. [back-formation from *Stonehenge,* a prehistoric stone monument near Salisbury in England]

hen harrier *noun* a common Eurasian hawk found on moors and marshes. The male is pale grey with black wingtips, and the female is brown with a white rump: *Circus cyaneus.*

hen house *noun* a chicken coop.

Henle's loop /'henleez/ *noun* = LOOP OF HENLE.

henna[1] /'henə/ *noun* **1** a reddish brown dye obtained from the leaves of a tropical shrub and used to colour the hair or as a body decoration. **2** the tropical shrub or small tree from which this dye is obtained: *Lawsonia inermis.* [Arabic *ḥinnā*]

henna[2] *verb trans* (**hennas, hennaed, hennaing**) to dye or tint (*esp* hair) with henna.

hen night *noun Brit, informal* a party for women, held for a woman who is about to get married: compare STAG NIGHT.

henotheism /'henoh·thiiz(ə)m/ *noun* the belief that one's family, clan, etc have a special relationship with one god in particular, without denying the existence of other gods. [German *Henotheismus,* from Greek *hen-, heis* one + *theos* god]

hen party *noun informal* a party for women only.

henpecked *adj* persistently nagged by a woman: *a henpecked husband*.

henry /'henri/ *noun* (*pl* **henrys** *or* **henries**) the SI unit of electrical inductance equal to the self-inductance of a closed circuit in which the variation in current of one amp per second results in an induced electromotive force of one volt. [named after Joseph *Henry* d.1878, US physicist]

hentai /'hentie/ *noun* (*pl* **hentai**) erotic or pornographic animation. [Japanese *hentai* pervert]

hep /hep/ *adj* (**hepper, heppest**) *dated* = HIP⁴.

heparin /'heparin/ *noun* a POLYSACCHARIDE (complex sugar) found in the liver and other tissues that is injected to slow the clotting of blood, *esp* in the treatment of thrombosis. [Greek *hēpar* liver + -IN¹]

hepat- *or* **hepato-** *comb. form* forming words, denoting: the liver: *hepatitis; hepatocyte*. [via Latin from Greek *hēpat-, hēpato-*, from *hēpat-, hēpar* liver]

hepatic /hi'patik/ *adj* relating to or in the region of the liver. [Latin *hepaticus* from Greek *hēpatikos*, from *hēpat-, hēpar* liver]

hepatica /hi'patikə/ *noun* a plant of the buttercup family found in N temperate regions, with lobed leaves and delicate flowers: genus *Hepatica*. [Latin genus name, from medieval Latin *hepatica* liverwort, fem of *hepaticus*: see HEPATIC]

hepatitis /hepə'tietəs/ *noun* a disease marked by inflammation of the liver.

hepatitis A *noun* a form of viral hepatitis transmitted by contaminated food and drink, causing jaundice, fever, and nausea.

hepatitis B *noun* a severe and sometimes fatal form of viral hepatitis usu transmitted through infected blood or contaminated hypodermic syringes, causing jaundice, fever, and debility.

hepatitis C *noun* a severe form of viral hepatitis transmitted through infected blood, causing chronic liver disease.

hepato- *comb. form* see HEPAT-.

hepatocyte /'hepətohsiet, hi'patohsiet/ *noun* a cell of the liver; *specif* one forming part of the distinctive functional tissue of the liver and specialized to carry out various chemical activities.

hepatoma /hepə'tohmə/ *noun* (*pl* **hepatomas** *or* **hepatomata** /-tohmətə/) a cancer of the liver cells.

hepatotoxic /,hepətoh'toksik, he'patoh-/ *adj* capable of causing injury to the liver: *hepatotoxic drugs*. >> **hepatotoxicity** /-tok'sisiti/ *noun*.

Hepplewhite /'heplwiet/ *adj* of or being a late 18th-cent. English furniture style characterized by lightness, elegance, and graceful curves. [named after George *Hepplewhite* d.1786, English cabinet-maker]

hepta- *or* **hept-** *comb. form* forming words, with the meanings: **1** seven: *heptameter*. **2** containing seven atoms, groups, or chemical equivalents in the molecular structure: *heptane*. [Greek, from *hepta* seven]

heptad /'heptad/ *noun technical* a group or series of seven. [Greek *heptad-, heptas*, from *hepta* seven]

heptagon /'heptəgən/ *noun* a polygon with seven angles and seven sides. >> **heptagonal** /hep'tagənl/ *adj*. [Greek *heptagonon*, neuter of *heptagōnos* heptagonal, from *hepta* seven+ *gōnia* angle]

heptahedron /heptə'heedrən/ *noun* (*pl* **heptahedrons** *or* **heptahedra** /-drə/) a polyhedron with seven faces. >> **heptahedral** *adj*.

heptameter /hep'tamitə/ *noun* a line of verse consisting of seven metrical feet.

heptane /'heptayn/ *noun* a colourless liquid that is a member of the alkane series of organic chemical compounds, occurs in petroleum, and is used *esp* as a solvent and in determining octane numbers: formula C_7H_{16}.

heptarchy /'heptahki/ *noun* (*pl* **heptarchies**) **1** a country or state divided into seven regions. **2** government by seven rulers. >> **heptarchic** /-'tahkik/ *adj*, **heptarchical** /-'tahkik(ə)l/ *adj*.

Heptateuch /'heptətyoohk/ *noun* the first seven books of the Old Testament. [via late Latin from Greek *heptateuchos*, from *hepta* seven + *teuchos* book]

heptathlon /hep'tathlən/ *noun* an athletic contest for women in which each contestant takes part in seven events: the 100m

hurdles, the shot put, the javelin, the high jump, the long jump, the 200m sprint, and the 800m race. >> **heptathlete** *noun*. [Greek *hepta* seven + *athlon* contest]

heptavalent /heptə'vaylənt/ *adj* having a valency of seven.

her¹ /ə, hə; *strong* huh/ *adj* **1** belonging to or associated with her: *her house; her children; her being chosen; her rescue*. **2** used in titles: *Her Majesty*. [Old English *hiere*, genitive of *hēo* she]

her² *pronoun* used as the objective case: she: *I'm bigger than her; He spoke to her*.

her. *abbr* heraldry.

herald¹ /'herəld/ *noun* **1** formerly, an official crier or messenger. **2** formerly, a person who officiated at tournaments. **3** somebody or something that is a sign of the arrival of something: *It was the lark the herald of the morn* — Shakespeare. **4** an officer responsible for recording names, pedigrees, and armorial bearings or tracing genealogies. **5** in Britain, an officer of arms ranking above a pursuivant and below a king of arms. **6** a moth of N Europe with brown mottled wings: *Scoliopteryx libatrix*. [Middle English from early French *hiraut*, of Germanic origin]

herald² *verb trans* **1** to announce or give notice of (something). **2** to be a sign of the arrival of (something). **3** to greet or hail (something).

heraldic /hi'raldik/ *adj* relating to a herald or heraldry. >> **heraldically** *adv*.

heraldry /'herəldri/ *noun* **1** the system of identifying individuals by hereditary insignia, e.g. coats of arms, or the practice of granting, classifying, and creating these. **2** the study of the history, display, and description of heraldry and heraldic insignia, or the heraldic symbols themselves.

herb /huhb/ *noun* **1** any aromatic plant used to flavour food or in medicine or perfume, e.g. thyme, lavender, or mint. **2** in botany, a plant that bears seeds, does not develop permanent woody tissue, and dies down at the end of a growing season. >> **herby** *adj*. [Middle English *herbe* via Old French from Latin *herba*]

herbaceous /huh'bayshəs/ *adj* of, being, or having the characteristics of a herb (in the botanical sense).

herbaceous border *noun* a permanent border of hardy, usu perennial, flowering plants.

herbage /'huhbij/ *noun* **1** herbaceous plants, e.g. grass, *esp* when used for grazing. **2** the succulent parts of these plants. **3** *esp* formerly, the right of pasture on somebody's land.

herbal¹ *adj* relating to or made of herbs, *esp* aromatic herbs: *herbal tea; herbal remedies*.

herbal² *noun* a book about plants, *esp* describing their medicinal qualities.

herbalist *noun* somebody who grows or sells herbs, *esp* for medicines.

herbarium /huh'beəri-əm/ *noun* (*pl* **herbaria** /-ri-ə/) a collection of dried plant specimens usu mounted and systematically arranged for reference.

herb bennet /'benit/ *noun* = WOOD AVENS. [Middle English *herb beneit* via Old French from medieval Latin *herba benedicta* blessed herb (from its medicinal properties)]

herb Christopher /'kristəfə/ *noun* = BANEBERRY. [translation of medieval Latin *herba Christophori*, from St *Christopher*, third-cent. Christian martyr]

herbicide /'huhbisied/ *noun* a chemical used to destroy or inhibit plant growth. [Latin *herba* HERB + -I- + -CIDE]

herbivore /'huhbivaw/ *noun* a plant-eating animal. >> **herbivorous** /huh'bivərəs/ *adj*. [scientific Latin *Herbivora*, group of mammals, neuter pl of *herbivorus* plant-eating, from Latin *herba* HERB + -I- + -VOROUS]

herb Paris /'paris/ *noun* a Eurasian woodland plant of the lily family that has a whorl of four leaves and a single green flower: *Paris quadrifolia*. [medieval Latin *herba paris* herb of a pair (because the four leaves on the stalk resemble a lovers' knot)]

herb Robert /'robət/ *noun* a common geranium with small pink flowers: *Geranium robertianum*. [prob named after *Robertus* (St Robert) d.1067, French ecclesiastic]

herculean /huhkyoo'lee-ən/ *adj* (*often* **Herculean**) requiring immense effort or strength, or showing such strength: *a herculean task*. [from *Hercules*, Greco-Roman mythological hero]

Hercules beetle /'huhkyooleez/ *noun* a very large S American beetle, the male of which has two projecting horns: *Dynastes hercules*.

herd[1] /huhd/ *noun* **1** a number of animals of one kind kept together or living as a group, *esp* cattle. **2** *derog* (*treated as sing. or pl*) a large group of people: *the common herd*. [Old English *heord*]

herd[2] *verb intrans* to assemble or move in a herd or group. ➤ *verb trans* **1** to keep or move (animals) together. **2** to gather, lead, or drive (people) as if in a herd: *He herded his pupils into the hall.* ➤ **herder** *noun*.

herd instinct *noun* the tendency of people or animals to follow the behaviour of the majority.

herdsman *noun* (*pl* **herdsmen**) a manager, breeder, or tender of livestock.

here[1] /hiə/ *adv* **1** in or at this place or position: *Turn here.* **2** to this place or position: *Come here.* **3** used when introducing, offering, or drawing attention to something: *Here she comes; Here is the news; Here, take it.* **4** at or in this point or particular: *Here we agree.* ✳ **here, there, and everywhere** scattered profusely about. **here goes** used to express resolution at the outset of a bold act. **here's to** used when drinking a toast. **neither here nor there** of no consequence; irrelevant. [Old English *hēr*]

here[2] *adj* **1** used for emphasis: *this book here; Ask my son here.* **2** *nonstandard* used for emphasis between a demonstrative and the following noun: *this here book.*

here[3] *noun* this place or point: *I'm full up to here.*

here[4] *interj* **1** used in answering a roll call. **2** used to attract attention: *Here, what's all this?*

hereabouts *or* **hereabout** *adv* in this vicinity.

hereafter[1] *adv formal* **1** after this. **2** in some future time or state. **3** after death.

hereafter[2] *noun* (**the hereafter**) life after death.

here and now *adv* at the immediate present: *I can't give you an answer here and now.*

here and there *adv* in various places.

hereat /hiə'rat/ *adv archaic* because of this.

hereby /hiə'bie/ *adv formal* by this means or pronouncement: *I hereby declare her elected.*

hereditable /hə'reditəbl/ *adj* = HERITABLE. [early French *hereditable* from late Latin *hereditare*: see HERITAGE]

hereditament /heri'ditəmənt/ *noun dated* in law, an item of property that can be inherited. [medieval Latin *hereditamentum* from late Latin *hereditare*: see HERITAGE]

hereditary /hi'redit(ə)ri/ *adj* **1** received by, based on, or relating to inheritance. **2** having title through inheritance: *a hereditary peer.* **3** genetically transmitted or transmissible from parent to offspring: *a hereditary disease.* ➤➤ **hereditarily** *adv*, **hereditariness** *noun*.

heredity /hi'rediti/ *noun* **1** the transmission of qualities from ancestor to descendant primarily through the genes. **2** the sum of the qualities genetically derived from one's ancestors. [early French *heredité* from Latin *hereditat-, hereditas*, from *hered-, heres* HEIR]

Hereford /'herifəd/ *noun* an animal of an English breed of red hardy beef cattle with white faces and markings. [named after *Herefordshire*, county of England where the breed originated]

herein /hiə'rin/ *adv formal* in this document, matter, etc.

hereinafter *adv formal* in the following part of this writing or document.

hereof /hiə'rov/ *adv formal* of this document.

heresiarch /hi'reeziahk/ *noun* the originator or chief advocate of a heresy. [via late Latin from late Greek *hairesiarchēs*, from *hairesis* (see HERESY) + Greek *-archēs* -ARCH]

heresy /'herəsi/ *noun* (*pl* **heresies**) **1** a religious belief or doctrine contrary to or incompatible with an explicit Church dogma, *esp* Christian doctrine.

Editorial note
Heresy arises because organized religion tends to define its experience in terms of creeds or accepted statements of belief. Such statements set the boundaries of each religious group, within which those who reject the formal doctrines, or who hold beliefs deemed contrary to them, are termed heretics, and may be expelled or persecuted from the group. What counts as heresy may change, if what is accepted as orthodoxy is redefined — Dr Mel Thompson.

2 adherence to an opinion or doctrine contrary to generally accepted belief. [Middle English *heresie* via Old French and late Latin from Greek *hairesis* action of taking, choice, sect, from *hairein* to take]

heretic /'herətik/ *noun* a person who dissents from established Church dogma, or from an accepted belief. ➤➤ **heretical** /hi'retikl/ *adj*, **heretically** /hi'retikli/ *adv*. [Middle English *(h)eretik* via French and late Latin from Greek *hairetikos* able to choose, from *hairein* to take]

hereto /hiə'tooh/ *adv formal* to this matter or document.

heretofore /hiətoo'faw/ *adv formal* up to this time; hitherto.

hereunder *adv formal* under or in accordance with this writing or document.

hereunto *adv formal or archaic* to this document.

hereupon *adv archaic* **1** on this matter: *if all are agreed hereupon.* **2** immediately after this: *Let us hereupon adjourn.*

herewith *adv formal* with this; enclosed in this.

heriot /'heriət/ *noun* under English law in medieval times, a duty or tribute due to a lord on the death of a tenant, orig the return of military equipment. [Old English *heregeatwe* military equipment, from *here* army + *geatwe* equipment]

heritable /'heritəbl/ *adj* capable of being inherited. ➤➤ **heritability** /-'biliti/ *noun*, **heritably** *adv*.

heritage /'heritij/ *noun* **1** property that descends to an heir; an inheritance. **2** something valuable transmitted by or acquired from a predecessor or predecessors; *specif* a country's history and traditions. **3** (*used before a noun*) being a part of a country's history and traditions that is considered worthy of preservation: *a heritage site.* **4** (*used before a noun*) presenting a country's history and traditions, *esp* in an attractive and nostalgic way: *a heritage centre.* [Middle English from early French *heriter* to inherit, from late Latin *hereditare*, from Latin *hered-, heres* HEIR]

heritor /'heritə/ *noun* **1** an inheritor. **2** in Scot law, the owner of an object that can be inherited.

herl /huhl/ *noun* a barb of a feather used in tying an artificial fishing fly. [Middle English *herle*, prob of Germanic origin]

herm /huhm/ *noun* a square stone pillar surmounted by a bust or head, *esp* of the god Hermes, that is used as an ornament in classical architecture. [Latin *herma, hermes* from Greek *hermēs* statue of Hermes, herm, from *Hermēs* Hermes]

hermaphrodite /huh'mafrədiet/ *noun* **1** a person or animal having both male and female reproductive organs and secondary sexual characteristics. **2** in botany, a plant with both male and female organs (stamens and pistils) in the same flower. **3** *archaic* something that is a combination of two usu opposing elements. ➤➤ **hermaphrodite** *adj*, **hermaphroditic** /-'ditik/ *adj*, **hermaphroditical** /-'ditikl/ *adj*, **hermaphroditism** *noun*. [Middle English *hermofrodite* via Latin from Greek *hermaphroditos*, named after *Hermaphroditos*, mythological son of Hermes and Aphrodite who became joined in body with the nymph Salmacis]

hermaphrodite brig *noun* a two-masted vessel with square sails on the foremast and a fore-and-aft mainsail on the rear mast.

hermeneutic /huhmə'nyoohtik/ *adj* relating to the interpretation of literary texts or the Bible; interpretative. ➤➤ **hermeneutical** *adj*, **hermeneutically** *adv*. [Greek *hermēneutikos* from *hermēneuein* to interpret, from *hermēneus* interpreter]

hermeneutics *pl noun* (*treated as sing. or pl*) **1** the study of the principles and methodology of interpretation, *esp* of the Bible or literary texts. **2** in philosophy, the study and interpretation of human behaviour in society. **3** in existentialist philosophy, the study of the meaning of life.

hermetic /huh'metik/ *adj* **1** said of a seal: airtight. **2** impervious to external influences. **3** (*often* **Hermetic**) of or relating to the Gnostic and alchemical writings attributed to Hermes Trismegistus. **4** (*often* **Hermetic**) abstruse or recondite. ➤➤ **hermetically** *adv*, **hermeticism** *noun*. [via Latin from *Hermes Trismegistus* (from Greek *Hermēs trismegistos*, literally 'Hermes thrice-greatest'), legendary author of mystical and alchemical works; (sense 1) from the belief that Hermes Trismegistus invented a magic seal to keep vessels airtight]

hermit /'huhmit/ *noun* **1** a person who retires from society and lives in solitude, *esp* for religious reasons. **2** a reclusive person. ➤➤ **hermitic** /huh'mitik/ *adj*. [Middle English *eremite* via Old French and late Latin from Greek *erēmitēs* living in the desert, from *erēmia* desert, from *erēmos* lonely]

hermitage /'huhmitij/ *noun* **1** a place where a hermit lives. **2** a secluded residence or private retreat; a hideaway.

hermit crab *noun* any of numerous chiefly marine ten-legged crustaceans that have soft abdomens and occupy the empty shells of gastropod molluscs: families Paguridae and Parapaguridae.

hernia /'huhni·ə/ *noun* (*pl* **hernias** *or* **herniae** /'huhni·ee/) a protrusion of part of an organ, usu the intestine, through a wall of its enclosing cavity. ➤➤ **hernial** *adj*, **herniated** *adj*, **herniation** /huhni'aysh(ə)n/ *noun*. [Latin *hernia*]

hero /'hiəroh/ *noun* (*pl* **heroes**) **1** a person, *esp* a man, admired for special courage, nobility, or great achievements: *Indolence and inability have too large a share in your composition, ever to suffer you to be anything more than the hero of little villainies and unfinished adventures* — Thomas Paine. **2** the principal male character in a literary or dramatic work. **3** a mythological or legendary figure, often of divine descent, endowed with great strength or ability. **4** = HERO SANDWICH. [via Latin from Greek *hērōs*]

heroic /hi'roh·ik/ *adj* **1** showing great courage. **2** of heroes or heroines. **3** said of language: grand; impressive. **4** said of a work of art, *esp* a sculpture: larger than life-size: compare COLOSSAL (2). ➤➤ **heroically** *adv*.

heroic age *noun* the period in history, *esp* Greek history, when legendary heroes were supposed to have lived.

heroic couplet *noun* two rhyming lines of verse, each of which consists of five iambic feet.

heroics *pl noun* **1** extravagantly grand behaviour or language. **2** = HEROIC VERSE.

heroic verse *noun* the verse form employed in epic poetry, e.g. the heroic couplet in English.

heroin /'heroh·in/ *noun* a strongly addictive narcotic drug made from morphine. It is used in medicine to relieve severe pain: formula $C_{21}H_{23}NO_5$. [German *Heroin*, prob from HERO, because of its effects on the self-esteem of the user]

heroine /'heroh·in/ *noun* **1** a woman admired for special courage, nobility, or great achievements. **2** the principal female character in a literary or dramatic work. **3** a mythological or legendary woman, often of divine descent, endowed with great strength or ability. [via Latin from Greek *hērōinē*, fem of *hērōs* HERO]

heroism /'heroh·iz(ə)m/ *noun* heroic conduct or qualities, *esp* extreme courage: *What attracts and impresses us … is … the heroism of daring to be the enemy of God* — George Bernard Shaw.

heron /'herən/ *noun* (*pl* **herons** *or collectively* **heron**) any of numerous species of long-necked long-legged wading birds with a long tapering bill and large wings: family Ardeidae. [Middle English *heiroun* from early French *hairon*, of Germanic origin]

heronry /'herənri/ *noun* (*pl* **heronries**) a breeding colony of herons.

hero sandwich *noun* chiefly NAmer a long roll split and filled with meat, cheese, salad, etc. Also called HOAGIE.

hero worship *noun* **1** veneration of a hero. **2** foolish or excessive admiration for somebody.

hero-worship *verb* *trans* (**hero-worshipped, hero-worshipping**, NAmer **hero-worshiped, hero-worshiping**) to feel or show great or excessive admiration for (somebody). ➤➤ **hero-worshipper** *noun*.

herpes /'huhpeez/ *noun* an inflammatory viral disease of the skin, *esp* herpes simplex. ➤➤ **herpetic** /huh'petik/ *adj*. [via Latin from Greek *herpēs*, from *herpein* to creep]

herpes simplex /'simpleks/ *noun* a viral disease marked by groups of watery blisters on the skin or mucous membranes, e.g. of the mouth, lips, or genitals: compare COLD SORE. [scientific Latin, literally 'simple herpes']

herpesvirus /'huhpeezvie·ərəs/ *noun* any of a group of viruses that reproduce in cell nuclei and that cause herpes.

herpes zoster /'zostə/ *noun* = SHINGLES. [scientific Latin, literally 'girdle herpes']

herpetology /huhpi'toləji/ *noun* the branch of zoology dealing with reptiles and amphibians. ➤➤ **herpetological** /-'lojikl/ *adj*, **herpetologist** *noun*.

Herr /hea/ *noun* (*pl* **Herren** /'heərən, 'herən/) used of or to a German-speaking man as a title equivalent to *Mr*. [German *Herr* master, from Old High German *hēr* exalted]

Herrenvolk /'herənfolk/ *noun* a master race; *specif* the German people as regarded by the Nazis. [German *Herrenvolk*, from *Herr* (see HERR) + *Volk* people, folk]

herrerasaurus /erayrə'sawrəs/ *noun* any of a group of large flesh-eating reptiles of the Triassic period that evolved into the dinosaurs. [named after V *Herrera*, a member of the expedition that found the first specimen in Argentina in the mid-20th cent. + Greek *sauros* lizard]

herring /'hering/ *noun* (*pl* **herrings** *or collectively* **herring**) any of several species of valuable silvery food fishes that are abundant in the N Atlantic: *Clupea harengus* and other species. [Old English *hæring*]

herringbone[1] *noun* **1** a pattern made up of rows of parallel lines slanting in opposite directions on adjacent rows, *esp* on fabric. **2** in skiing, the ascent of a slope by walking with the toes of the skis pointing outwards.

herringbone[2] *verb* *trans* to make a herringbone pattern on (something). ➤ *verb intrans* in skiing, to ascend a slope using the herringbone method.

herringbone stitch *noun* a needlework stitch that forms a zigzag pattern.

herring gull *noun* a large gull of the northern hemisphere that is largely white with a blue-grey MANTLE[1] (back and wing feathers) and dark wing tips: *Larus argentatus*.

hers /huhz/ *pronoun* the one or ones that belong to her or are associated with her: *The book is hers; Hers are on the table; My house is older than hers*. ✳ **of hers** belonging to or associated with her: *friends of hers*.

herself /hə'self/ *pronoun* **1** used reflexively to refer to a female person or animal that is the subject of the clause: *The girl has hurt herself*. **2** used for emphasis: *She herself said it*. ✳ **be herself** to be fit or healthy as normal: *She isn't quite herself today*.

Herts /hahts/ *abbr* Hertfordshire.

hertz /huhts/ *noun* (*pl* **hertz**) the SI unit of frequency, equal to one cycle per second. [named after Heinrich *Hertz* d.1894, German physicist]

Hertzian wave /'huhtsi·ən/ *noun* a radio wave of wavelength ranging from less than 1mm to more than 1km. [named after Heinrich *Hertz*: see HERTZ]

Hertzsprung-Russell diagram /'huhtssproong'rusl/ *noun* a graph on which the temperatures of stars are plotted against their absolute magnitudes. From a star's position on the diagram an astronomer can tell its mass and how far it has reached in its evolution. [named after Ejnar *Hertzsprung* d.1967, Danish astronomer and H N *Russell* d.1957, US astronomer]

he's /eez, iz; *strong* heez/ *contraction* **1** he has. **2** he is.

hesitant /'hezit(ə)nt/ *adj* tending to hesitate; irresolute. ➤➤ **hesitance** *noun*, **hesitancy** *noun*, **hesitantly** *adv*.

hesitate /'hezitayt/ *verb intrans* **1** to pause or hold back, *esp* in doubt or indecision: *Trust the man who hesitates in his speech and is quick and steady in action* — George Santayana. **2** to be reluctant or unwilling to do something: *She hesitated to take such a drastic step*. ➤➤ **hesitater** *noun*, **hesitating** *adj*, **hesitatingly** *adv*, **hesitation** /-'taysh(ə)n/ *noun*. [Latin *haesitatus*, past part. of *haesitare* to stick fast, hesitate]

Hesperian /hes'piəri·ən/ *adj* **1** in Greek mythology, of or relating to the Hesperides, the Daughters of Night who lived on a western island and guarded a tree bearing golden apples. **2** *literary* western. [via Latin from Greek *Hesperia* the west, from fem of *hesperios* of the evening, western, from *hesperos* evening]

hesperidium /hespə'ridi·əm/ *noun* (*pl* **hesperidia** /-di·ə/) in botany, a fruit with a leathery rind and a pulp divided into sections, e.g. an orange or lime. [scientific Latin, named after the *Hesperides*: see HESPERIAN]

Hesperus /'hespərəs/ *noun* literary the planet Venus. [via Latin from Greek *Hesperos* evening, the evening star]

hessian /'hesi·ən/ *noun* **1** a coarse heavy plain-weave fabric, usu of jute or hemp, used *esp* for sacking. **2** a lightweight material resembling hessian and used in interior decoration. [named after *Hesse*, region or state in SW Germany]

Hessian fly *noun* a small fly that is destructive to wheat in the USA: *Mayetiola destructor*. [so called because it was wrongly thought to have been introduced to the USA by troops from Hesse in SW Germany during the American War of Independence]

hest /hest/ *noun archaic* behest. [Old English *hǣs*]

hetaera /hi'tee-ərə/ *or* **hetaira** /hi'tierə/ *noun* (*pl* **hetaeras** *or* **hetaerae** /-ree/ *or* **hetairas** *or* **hetairai** /-rie/) a courtesan, *esp* in ancient Greece. [Greek *hetaira*, fem of *hetairos* companion]

heter- *or* **hetero-** *comb. form* forming words, with the meaning: other or different: *heteromorphic*. [early French via late Latin from Greek, from *heteros*]

hetero /'hetəroh/ *noun* (*pl* **heteros**) a heterosexual.

heterocercal /hetəroh'suhkl/ *adj* **1** said of the tail fin of a fish: having the upper lobe larger than the lower with the end of the spinal column prolonged and somewhat upturned in the upper lobe: compare HOMOCERCAL. **2** of or having a heterocercal tail fin.

heterochromatic /,hetərohkroh'matik/ *adj* **1** of or having different colours. **2** in physics, made up of various wavelengths or frequencies.

heteroclite[1] /'hetəroh,kliet/ *adj formal* deviating from common forms or rules; abnormal. ⋙ **heteroclitic** *adj.* [early French via late Latin from Greek *heteroklitos*, from HETER- + *klinein* to lean, inflect]

heteroclite[2] *noun formal* **1** somebody or something unusual or abnormal. **2** a word that is irregular in inflection; *esp* a noun that is irregular in DECLENSION (addition of word parts for different grammatical cases).

heterocyclic /,hetəroh'siklik, -'sieklik/ *adj* in chemistry, of or being a ring composed of atoms of more than one kind.

heterodox /'hetərə,doks/ *adj* **1** contrary to or different from established doctrines or opinions, *esp* in matters of religion: *a heterodox sermon.* **2** holding opinions or doctrines that are not orthodox. ⋙ **heterodoxy** *noun.* [via late Latin from Greek *heterodoxos*, from HETER- + *doxa* opinion]

heterodyne[1] /'hetərohdien/ *adj* said of a radio signal, receiver, etc: combining two similar radio frequencies to produce a lower frequency or beat.

heterodyne[2] *verb trans* in electronics, to combine (a wave) with a wave of a different frequency so that a beat is produced.

heterogamete /het(ə)roh'gameet/ *noun* either of a pair of gametes (reproductive cells; see GAMETE) that differ in form, size, or behaviour and occur typically as large nonmoving female gametes, e.g. eggs, and small moving male gametes, e.g. sperm.

heterogametic /,hetərohgə'metik/ *adj* in biology, forming two kinds of germ cells of which one produces male offspring and the other female offspring.

heterogamy /hetə'rogəmi/ *noun* **1** sexual reproduction involving fusion of unlike gametes (reproductive cells; see GAMETE) often differing in size, structure, and physiology. **2** the occurrence of different types of reproduction, e.g. sexual and asexual, in successive generations. **3** in botany, the presence of both male and female flowers in one plant: compare HOMOGAMY (1A). **4** marriage between people who come from different backgrounds: compare HOMOGAMY (2C). ⋙ **heterogamous** *adj.*

heterogeneous /,hetərə'jeeni-əs/ *adj* **1** consisting of dissimilar ingredients or constituents; disparate. **2** in chemistry, said of a system: containing more than one PHASE[1] (physical state). ⋙ **heterogeneity** /-rohjə'neeiti/ *noun,* **heterogeneously** *adv,* **heterogeneousness** *noun.* [medieval Latin *heterogeneus, heterogenus* from Greek *heterogenēs*, from HETER- + *genos* kind]

heterogenesis /,hetərə'jenəsis/ *noun* = ALTERNATION OF GENERATIONS. ⋙ **heterogenetic** /-'netik/ *adj.*

heterograft /'hetərohgrahft/ *noun* = XENOGRAFT.

heterologous /hetə'roləgəs/ *adj* derived from a different species: *heterologous transplants.* ⋙ **heterology** *noun.*

heteromerous /hetə'romərəs/ *adj* in biology, having parts that differ, *esp* in number. [HETER- + -MEROUS]

heteromorphic /,hetəroh'mawfik/ *adj* in biology, exhibiting diversity of form or forms: *heteromorphic pairs of chromosomes.* ⋙ **heteromorph** *noun,* **heteromorphism** *noun,* **heteromorphy** *noun.*

heteromorphous /hetəroh'mawfəs/ *adj* = HETEROMORPHIC.

heteronomous /hetə'ronəməs/ *adj* **1** subject to the law or domination of another. **2** in biology, subject to different laws of growth, development, and specialization.

heteronomy /hetə'ronəmi/ *noun* subjection to the law or domination of another; *esp* a lack of moral freedom or self-determination.

heteronym /'hetərohnim/ *noun* any of two or more words spelt alike but different in meaning and pronunciation, e.g. *sow* (noun) and *sow* (verb). ⋙ **heteronymic** /-'nimik/ *adj,* **heteronymous** /-'roniməs/ *adj.*

heteropteran /hetə'roptərən/ *noun* a heteropterous insect. ⋙ **heteropteran** *adj.*

heteropterous /hetə'roptərəs/ *adj* of or being a bug of a group having forewings with a thick base and membranous tip: suborder Heteroptera. [HETER- + Greek *pteron* wing]

heterosexism /het(ə)rə'seksiz(ə)m/ *noun* discrimination against a person on the grounds of his or her homosexuality. ⋙ **heterosexist** *noun and adj.*

heterosexual[1] /,hetəroh'seksh(ə)l/ *adj* **1** having a sexual preference for members of the opposite sex: compare HOMOSEXUAL: *From birth we are relentlessly socialized into a heterosexual identity that we may later choose to reject but which remains an always familiar landscape* — Screen. **2** said of a relationship: between a man and a woman. ⋙ **heterosexuality** /-shoo'aliti/ *noun,* **heterosexually** *adv.*

heterosexual[2] *noun* a person who is heterosexual.

heterosis /hetə'rohsis/ *noun technical* a marked vigour or capacity for growth often shown by crossbred animals or plants. ⋙ **heterotic** /-'rotik/ *adj.*

heterostyly /'hetərohstieli/ *noun* in botany, the condition of having two or more different lengths of STYLE[1] (part of ovary) on different individuals of a plant species, e.g. the primrose, to promote cross-pollination. ⋙ **heterostylous** *adj.*

heterotrophic /,hetəroh'trohfik/ *adj* said of an organism: needing complex organic compounds for essential metabolic processes: compare AUTOTROPHIC. ⋙ **heterotroph** /'hetərohtrohf/ *noun,* **heterotrophy** *noun.*

heterozygote /,hetəroh'ziegoht/ *noun* an animal, plant, or cell in which the members of at least one pair of genes that code for a particular inheritable characteristic are different versions of each other: compare HOMOZYGOTE. ⋙ **heterozygosity** /-'gositi/ *noun,* **heterozygous** *adj.*

hetman /'hetmən/ *noun* (*pl* **hetmen**) a Polish or Cossack leader. [Polish *hetman* commander in chief, from German *Hauptmann* headman]

het up *adj informal* angry, agitated, or upset. [*het*, dialect past part. of HEAT[1]]

heuchera /'hoykərə, 'hyook-/ *noun* any of a genus of N American plants with tiny red or pink flowers and heart-shaped leaves: genus *Heuchera.* [named after Johann H von *Heucher* d.1747, German botanist]

heuristic[1] /hyooə'ristik/ *adj* **1** allowing people to learn for themselves: *heuristic teaching methods.* **2** denoting problem-solving techniques that proceed by trial and error: *a heuristic computer program.* ⋙ **heuristically** *adv.* [German *heuristisch* from Latin *heuristicus*, from Greek *heuriskein* to discover]

heuristic[2] *noun* a heuristic method or procedure.

heuristics *pl noun* (*treated as sing. or pl*) the study or practice of heuristic methods or procedures.

HEW *abbr NAmer* (Department of) Health, Education, and Welfare.

hew /hyooh/ *verb* (*past part.* **hewed** *or* **hewn** /hyoohn/) ⋗ *verb trans* **1** to strike, chop, or fell (e.g. wood) with blows of a heavy cutting instrument: *I hewed off a lump of coal; We hewed down the tree.* **2** (*often* + out) to give form or shape to (something) with heavy cutting blows. ⋗ *verb intrans NAmer* (+ to) to conform to something: *hewing to the official line.* ⋙ **hewer** *noun.* [Old English *hēawan*]

hex[1] /heks/ *verb trans chiefly NAmer* to cast a spell on (somebody); to bewitch. [Pennsylvania German *hexe* from German *hexen*, from *Hexe* witch]

hex[2] *noun chiefly NAmer* **1** a magic spell or jinx. **2** a witch.

hex[3] *adj* = HEXADECIMAL.

hexa- *or* **hex-** *comb. form* forming words, with the meanings: **1** six: *hexagon.* **2** containing six atoms, groups, or chemical equivalents in the molecular structure: *hexane; hexavalent.* [Greek, from *hex* six]

hexachord /'heksəkawd/ *noun* in medieval music, a scale of six notes based on C, F, or G, from which SOLMIZATION (using syllables to represent notes) developed.

hexad /'heksad/ *noun technical* a group or series of six. [Greek *hex* six]

hexadecimal /heksə'desiml/ *adj* of or being a number system with a base of 16, using the letters A to F as well as the digits 0 to 9, and used in computing. ➤➤ **hexadecimally** *adv*.

hexagon /'heksəgən/ *noun* a polygon with six angles and six sides. ➤➤ **hexagonal** /hek'sagənl/ *adj*. [Greek *hexagōnon*, neuter of *hexagōnos* hexagonal, from HEXA- + *gōnia* angle]

hexagram /'heksəgram/ *noun* **1** a six-pointed star drawn by extending the sides of a regular hexagon. **2** any of a set of 64 different figures used in the Chinese I Ching, each consisting of six parallel lines.

hexahedron /,heksə'heedrən/ *noun* (*pl* **hexahedrons** or **hexahedra** /-drə/) a polyhedron with six faces. ➤➤ **hexahedral** *adj*. [via late Latin from Greek *hexaedron*, neuter of *hexaedros* of six surfaces, from HEXA- + *hedra* seat]

hexameter /hek'samitə/ *noun* a line of verse consisting of six metrical feet. [via Latin from Greek *hexametron*, neuter of *hexametros* having six measures, from HEXA- + -METER[1]]

hexane /'heksayn/ *noun* a volatile liquid that is a member of the alkane series of organic chemical compounds and is found in petroleum: formula C_6H_{14}. [HEXA- + -ANE]

hexapla /'heksəplə/ *noun* an edition of the Old Testament with six versions of the text in parallel columns. [Greek *hexapla*, neuter pl of *hexaploos* sixfold, from *hexa* six]

hexapod /'heksəpod/ *noun* an animal with six feet; an insect. [Greek *hexapod-*, *hexapous* having six feet, from HEXA- + *pod-*, *pous* foot]

hexavalent /heksə'vaylənt/ *adj* in chemistry, having a valency of six.

hexose /'heksohs, 'heksohz/ *noun* a MONOSACCHARIDE (simple sugar), e.g. glucose, containing six carbon atoms in the molecule.

hexyl /'heks(ə)l/ *noun* a group, C_6H_{13}, derived from a hexane.

hey /hay/ *interj* used to attract attention or to express enquiry, surprise, or exultation. [Middle English]

heyday *noun* the period of one's greatest vigour, prosperity, or fame. [archaic *heyday*, exclamation of joy or exultation, from *heyda*, alteration of HEY]

hey presto /,hay 'prestoh/ *interj* used as an expression of triumph or satisfaction on completing or demonstrating something, *esp* used by conjurers about to reveal the outcome of a trick.

HF *abbr* high frequency.

Hf *abbr* the chemical symbol for hafnium.

hf *abbr* half.

HG *abbr* **1** His/Her Grace. **2** Home Guard.

Hg *abbr* the chemical symbol for mercury.

hg *abbr* hectogram(s).

HGH *abbr* human growth hormone.

HGV *abbr* Brit heavy goods vehicle.

HH *abbr* **1** used on lead pencils: double hard. **2** His/Her Highness. **3** His Holiness.

HI *abbr* Hawaii (US postal abbreviation).

hi /hie/ *interj informal* used to attract attention or as a greeting. [Middle English *hy*]

hiatal hernia /hie'aytəl/ *noun* = HIATUS HERNIA.

hiatus /hie'aytəs/ *noun* (*pl* **hiatuses**) **1** a break or gap in continuity. **2** in prosody or grammar, the occurrence of two separate vowel sounds together without pause or without an intervening consonantal sound, as in *the egg*. ➤➤ **hiatal** *adj*. [Latin *hiatus*, past part. of *hiare* to yawn]

hiatus hernia *noun* a hernia in which part of the stomach protrudes through the oesophageal opening of the diaphragm.

hibachi /hi'bahchi, hi'bachi/ *noun* (*pl* **hibachis**) a portable charcoal-burning brazier or barbecue, used for cooking food at a table or for heating. [Japanese *hibachi* from *hi* fire + *bachi* bowl]

hibernal /hie'buhnl/ *adj* of or occurring in winter; wintry. [Latin *hibernalis* from *hibernus* wintry]

hibernate /'hiebənayt/ *verb intrans* said of an animal or plant: to pass the winter in a dormant or resting state: compare AESTIVATE. ➤➤ **hibernation** /-'naysh(ə)n/ *noun*, **hibernator** *noun*. [Latin *hibernatus*, past part. of *hibernare* to pass the winter, from *hibernus* of winter]

Hibernian /hie'buhni·ən/ *adj* used *esp* in names: of or characteristic of Ireland. ➤➤ **Hibernian** *noun*. [Latin *Hibernia* Ireland]

Hibernicism /hie'buhnisiz(ə)m/ *noun* a characteristic expression, idiom, etc of Irish English.

Hiberno- *comb. form* forming words, denoting: **1** Irish. **2** Irish and: *Hiberno-English*.

hibiscus /hi'biskəs/ *noun* any of a genus of herbaceous plants, shrubs, or small trees of the mallow family with large showy flowers: genus *Hibiscus*. [Latin genus name, from Greek *hibiskos* marshmallow]

hic /hik/ *interj* used to express the sound made by somebody hiccuping. [imitative]

hiccup[1] or **hiccough** /'hikup/ *noun* **1** a spasmodic involuntary inhalation with closure of the GLOTTIS (opening between the throat and windpipe) accompanied by a characteristic sharp sound. **2** (*in pl*) an attack of hiccuping. **3** a brief interruption or breakdown; a hitch: *a mistake due to a hiccup in the computer system*. [imitative: *hiccough* influenced by *cough*]

hiccup[2] or **hiccough** *verb intrans* (**hiccuped** or **hiccupped**, **hiccuping** or **hiccupping**) to make the sound of a hiccup, or be affected with hiccups.

hic jacet /,hik 'yaket/ *noun literary* an epitaph. [Latin *hic jacet* here lies]

hick /hik/ *noun chiefly NAmer, informal* an unsophisticated provincial person. [*Hick*, nickname for *Richard*]

hickey /'hiki/ *noun* (*pl* **hickeys**) **1** *NAmer, informal* a gadget or unspecified object. **2** *NAmer, informal* a lovebite. **3** in printing, a blemish. [origin unknown]

hickory /'hikəri/ *noun* (*pl* **hickories** or collectively **hickory**) **1** any of several species of N American hardwood trees of the walnut family, often having sweet edible nuts: genus *Carya*. **2** the usu tough pale wood of this tree. **3** a stick of this wood. [short for obsolete *pokahickory*, from Algonquian *pawcohiccora* food prepared from pounded nuts]

hid /hid/ *verb* past tense of HIDE[1].

hidalgo /hi'dalgoh/ *noun* (*pl* **hidalgos**) a member of the lower nobility of Spain. [Spanish *hidalgo*, from *hijo de algo* son of something]

hidden[1] /'hid(ə)n/ *verb* past part. of HIDE[1].

hidden[2] *adj* **1** out of sight; concealed. **2** obscure or unexplained.

hidden agenda *noun* a concealed motive behind the ostensible purpose of an action.

hide[1] /hied/ *verb* (*past tense* **hid** /hid/, *past part.* **hidden** /'hid(ə)n/) ➤ *verb trans* **1** to put (something) out of sight; to conceal. **2** to keep (something) secret: *He hid the news from his parents.* ➤ *verb intrans* to conceal oneself. ✱ **hide one's light under a bushel** to be modest about one's own talent or success. ➤➤ **hider** *noun*. [Old English *hȳdan*]

hide[2] *noun Brit* a camouflaged hut or other shelter used for observation, *esp* of wildlife or game.

hide[3] *noun* the raw or dressed skin of an animal. ✱ **hide or hair** the least vestige or trace: *We haven't seen hide or hair of her for months.* [Old English *hȳd*]

hide[4] *noun* any of various former units of land area based on the amount that would support one family, *esp* a unit of 120 acres (about $0.5km^2$). [Old English *hīgid*]

hide-and-seek *noun* a children's game in which one player covers his or her eyes while the other players hide, and then hunts for them.

hideaway *noun* a retreat or hideout.

hidebound *adj* narrow or inflexible in character, outlook, etc: *the hidebound humour which he calls his judgment* — Milton.

Ⓦ**ord history**

HIDE[3] + BOUND[4]. The original meaning was 'emaciated, thin', hence 'narrow, cramped'.

hideous /'hidi·əs/ *adj* **1** exceedingly ugly; repulsive. **2** very unpleasant; disgusting. **3** terrifying. ➤➤ **hideously** *adv*, **hideousness**

noun. [alteration of Middle English *hidous*, from Old French, from *hisde, hide* terror]

hideout *noun* a place of refuge or concealment, *esp* a hiding place used by a criminal.

hidey-hole *or* **hidy-hole** /'hiedi/ *noun informal* a hiding place. [alteration of *hiding-hole*]

hiding[1] /'hieding/ *noun* **1** a beating or thrashing. **2** *informal* a severe defeat. **✳ be on a hiding to nothing** *Brit* to be engaged in an enterprise that can only end in failure. [HIDE[3]]

hiding[2] *noun* a state, act, or place of concealment.

hidrosis /hi'drohsis/ *noun technical* sweat or perspiration. **➤➤ hidrotic** /hi'drotik/ *adj.* [Greek *hidrōsis* from *hidrōs* sweat]

hidy-hole /'hiedi/ *noun* see HIDEY-HOLE.

hie /hie/ *verb intrans* (**hies, hied, hying** *or* **hieing**) *archaic* to hurry. [Old English *higian* to strive, hasten]

hier- *or* **hiero-** *comb. form* forming words, with the meaning: sacred or holy: *hieratic.* [via late Latin from Greek, from *hieros* sacred]

hierarch /'hie-ərahk/ *noun* **1** a religious leader in a position of authority, e.g. an archbishop. **2** a person with a high position in a hierarchy. [early French via medieval Latin from Greek *hierarchēs*, from HIER- + *-archēs* -ARCH]

hierarchy /'hie-ərahki/ *noun* (*pl* **hierarchies**) **1a** a system in which people or groups are ranked according to their status or authority: *In a hierarchy, every employee tends to rise to his level of incompetence* — Laurence J Peter. **b** (**the hierarchy**) people in authority; the people at the top of a hierarchy: *This won't go down well with the hierarchy.* **c** a system in which things are ranked according to importance, e.g. the arrangement of plants into classes, species, etc. **2** (**the hierarchy**) the clergy in the Catholic Church or an episcopal Church organized according to rank; *specif* the bishops of a province or nation. **3** in theology, the organization of heavenly beings, e.g. angels, into ranks. **➤➤ hierarchic** /hie-ə'rahkik/ *adj,* **hierarchical** /-'rahkikl/ *adj,* **hierarchically** /-'rahkikli/ *adv.*

Word history ⸺
Middle English *ierarchie* via French and medieval Latin from late Greek *hierarchia,* from Greek *hierarchēs:* see HIERARCH. The word originally referred to the hierarchy of angels in heaven.

hieratic /hie-ə'ratik/ *adj* **1** of or characteristic of a priest, *esp* in dignity or stateliness of manner. **2** of or written in a simplified form of ancient Egyptian hieroglyphics used by priests. **3** said of Egyptian or Greek art: following certain religious traditions; fixed or stylized. **➤➤ hieratically** *adv.* [via Latin from Greek *hieratikos* priestly, from *hieros* sacred]

hiero- *comb. form* see HIER-.

hieroglyph /'hie-ərəglif/ *noun* a pictorial character used in hieroglyphics. [French *hiéroglyphe,* back-formation from *hiéroglyphique:* see HIEROGLYPHIC]

hieroglyphic /'hie-ərəglifik/ *adj* **1** relating to or using a system of writing mainly in hieroglyphs. **2** difficult to decipher. **➤➤ hieroglyphical** *adj,* **hieroglyphically** *adv.* [early French *hiéroglyphique* via late Latin from Greek *hieroglyphikos,* from HIERO- + *glyphein* to carve]

hieroglyphics *pl noun* (*treated as sing. or pl*) **1** a system of hieroglyphic writing; *specif* the picture script of various ancient peoples such as the Egyptians. **2** something like hieroglyphics, *esp* in being difficult to decipher.

hierophant /'hie-ərəfant/ *noun* **1** a priest in ancient Greece responsible for initiation rites to sacred mysteries. **2** an interpreter of esoteric knowledge. **➤➤ hierophantic** /-'fantik/ *adj.* [via late Latin from Greek *hierophantēs,* from HIERO- + *phainein* to show]

hi-fi /'hie fie/ *noun* (*pl* **hi-fis**) *informal* **1** a set of equipment for the high-fidelity reproduction of sound. **2** (*used before a noun*) of or for high fidelity: *hi-fi equipment.*

higgledy-piggledy /,higldi 'pigldi/ *adv and adj* in confusion; disordered. [origin unknown]

high[1] /hie/ *adj* **1a** extending upwards for a considerable or above average distance: *The rooms all have high ceilings.* **b** situated at a considerable height above the ground or above sea level: *The town was on a high plateau.* **c** having a specified elevation; tall: *six metres high.* **d** relatively far from the equator: *high latitudes.* **2** of greater degree, amount, value, or content than average: *high prices; food high in iron.* **3a** foremost in rank, dignity, or standing: *high officials.* **b** critical or climactic: *The high point of the novel is the escape.* **c** marked by sublime or heroic events or subject matter: *high tragedy.* **4** at the

period of culmination or fullest development: *high summer; high Gothic.* **5a** exalted in character; noble: *high principles.* **b** good or favourable: *We have a very high opinion of you.* **6** near the upper end of a sound range: *a high note.* **7** forceful or strong: *high winds.* **8a** said of food: beginning to go bad. **b** said of meat, *esp* game: slightly decomposed and ready to cook. **9** *informal* elated or excited, *esp* as an effect of drugs or alcohol. **10** advanced in complexity, development, or elaboration: *higher animals and plants; high technology.* **11** in phonetics, said of a vowel: produced with the tongue close to the palate. **12** rigidly traditionalist: *a high Tory.* **13** relating to the High Church. **✳ high days and holidays** *informal* special occasions. **high time** time for something that should have happened already: *It's high time the system was changed.* **on one's high horse** stubbornly or disdainfully proud. **the high ground** a position of advantage or superiority: *She likes to occupy the moral high ground.* [Old English *hēah*]

high[2] *adv* **1** at or to a high place or altitude: *Throw the ball high in the air.* **2** highly: *A sense of humour ranks high on my list of priorities.* **3** said of a sound: at or to a high pitch.

high[3] *noun* **1** a high point or level: *Sales have reached a new high.* **2** a region of high atmospheric pressure. **3** *informal* a state of ecstasy or euphoria, *esp* one produced by a drug. **4** *chiefly NAmer, informal* high school. **✳ on high** in or to a high place, *esp* a position of authority or heaven.

high altar *noun* the principal altar in a church.

high and dry *adv* **1** stranded by the sea; out of the water. **2** in a helpless or abandoned situation; without recourse.

high and low *adv* everywhere: *We hunted high and low but could not find the ring.*

high-and-mighty *adj informal* arrogant or imperious.

highball *noun NAmer* a drink of spirits, e.g. whisky, and water or a carbonated beverage, served with ice in a tall glass.

highborn *adj* of noble birth.

highboy *noun NAmer* = TALLBOY (1).

highbrow *adj* having or showing refined intellectual and cultural interests: *a highbrow radio programme.* **➤➤ highbrow** *noun.*

high chair *noun* a child's chair with long legs, a footrest, and usu a feeding tray.

High Church *noun* a movement or tendency in the Anglican Church that favours aspects of Roman Catholicism in liturgy, ceremonial, and dogma: *Gladstone's Oxford training and High Church illusions … caused wild eccentricities in his judgment* — Henry Adams. **➤➤ High Churchman** *noun.*

high-class *adj* superior or first-class.

high-coloured *adj* said of the complexion: ruddy or florid.

high comedy *noun* comedy employing subtle characterizations and witty dialogue: compare LOW COMEDY.

high command *noun* the commander-in-chief and high-ranking officers of a country's army, navy, and air force.

high commissioner *noun* a principal commissioner, *esp* an ambassador of one Commonwealth country stationed in another.

high court *noun* **1** a supreme judicial court. **2** (**High Court**) the lower branch of the Supreme Court of England and Wales, consisting of the Queen's Bench Division, the Chancery Division, and the Family Division. **3** (**High Court**) the superior criminal court of Scotland, dealing with cases of treason, murder, rape, etc.

High Court of Justice *noun* = HIGH COURT (2).

high-definition television *noun* an advanced television system that has many more horizontal lines per frame than the conventional system and produces a much sharper and clearer image.

High Dutch *noun* **1** = HIGH GERMAN. **2** Dutch of the Netherlands rather than Afrikaans.

high-energy *adj* in biology, said of phosphate compounds: yielding a relatively large amount of energy when undergoing HYDROLYSIS (chemical breakdown due to reaction with water).

Higher *noun* in Scotland, the advanced level of the Scottish Certificate of Education, or an examination at this level.

higher criticism *noun* the critical study of biblical writings, *esp* to determine their sources: compare LOWER CRITICISM.

higher education *noun* education beyond the secondary level, at a college or university.

higher mathematics *pl noun* (*usu treated as sing.*) mathematics involving advanced abstract ideas such as number theory and topology.

higher-up *noun informal* a person occupying a superior rank or position.

highest common factor *noun* the largest integer that can be divided exactly into each of two or more integers.

high explosive *noun* a powerful explosive, e.g. TNT.

highfalutin /hiefə'loohtin/ *or* **highfaluting** /-'looting/ *adj informal* pretentious or pompous. [perhaps from HIGH¹ + alteration of *fluting*, present part. of FLUTE¹]

high fashion *noun* = HAUTE COUTURE.

high fidelity *noun* sound reproduction that is very close to the original.

high finance *noun* large and complex financial operations.

high-five *noun chiefly NAmer, informal* a gesture of greeting or triumph in which two people hold their hands high and slap each other's palms.

high-flier *or* **high-flyer** *noun* a person who shows extreme ambition or outstanding promise.

high-flown *adj* 1 excessively ambitious or extravagant: *high-flown plans*. 2 said of language: excessively elaborate or inflated; pretentious: *high-flown rhetoric*.

high-flyer *noun* see HIGH-FLIER.

high-flying *adj* 1 rising to a considerable height. 2 marked by or showing excessive ambition or outstanding promise.

high frequency *noun* a radio frequency between 3 and 30 megahertz.

high gear *noun* a gear used for a high speed of travel.

High German *noun* German as orig spoken in S Germany and now in standard use throughout the country.

high-grade *adj* of superior grade or quality.

high-handed *adj* overbearing or inconsiderate. ➤➤ **high-handedly** *adv*, **high-handedness** *noun*.

high-hat¹ *noun* 1 (*also* **hi-hat**) a pair of cymbals on a stand, forming part of a drum kit. 2 (**high hat**) a top hat. 3 (**high hat**) *NAmer, informal* a supercilious or snobbish person.

high-hat² *adj NAmer, informal* supercilious or snobbish.

high-hat³ *verb trans* (**high-hatted, high-hatting**) *NAmer, informal* to treat (somebody) in a supercilious manner.

High Holiday *or* **High Holy Day** *noun* either of two important Jewish holidays, Rosh Hashanah or Yom Kippur.

high hurdles *pl noun* (*treated as sing.*) a race in which competitors jump over hurdles 107cm high.

high-impact *adj* said of physical exercise, *esp* aerobics: making stressful demands on the body.

high-jack¹ /'hiejak/ *verb trans* see HIJACK¹.

high-jack² *noun* see HIJACK².

high jinks /jingks/ *pl noun* high-spirited fun and games.

high jump *noun* an athletic field event in which contestants jump over a high bar suspended between uprights. ✳ **for the high jump** *Brit, informal* about to receive a severe reprimand or punishment. ➤➤ **high jumper** *noun,* **high jumping** *noun.*

high-key *adj* said of a photograph, print, etc: having or composed of mainly light tones with little contrast.

high-keyed *adj* = HIGH-KEY.

highland *noun* 1 (*also in pl*) high or mountainous land. 2 (**the Highlands**) the northwest mountainous part of Scotland. ➤➤ **highlander** *noun,* **highlandman** *noun.*

Highland cattle *pl noun* animals of a Scottish breed of shaggy-haired beef cattle with long horns.

Highland dress *noun* the traditional clothing of the Scottish Highlands, including the kilt, plaid, and sporran.

Highland fling *noun* a lively solo Scottish folk dance.

Highland Games *pl noun* (*treated as sing. or pl*) a meeting held in the Scottish Highlands for competitions in sports events, bagpipe-playing, and traditional dancing.

high-level *adj* 1 occurring, done, or placed at a high level. 2 of high importance or rank: *high-level diplomats*. 3 said of a computer

language: having each word equal to several machine code instructions so as to be more easily understood by humans.

high life *noun* 1 luxurious living associated with the rich. 2 (*usu* **highlife**) a style of West African music incorporating elements of jazz.

highlight¹ *noun* 1 an event or detail of special significance or interest: *one of the highlights of the tour*. 2 the lightest spot or area, e.g. in a painting or photograph. 3 (*usu in pl*) a contrasting brighter part in the hair produced by tinting some of the strands.

highlight² *verb trans* 1a to emphasize or focus attention on (something). b to emphasize or draw attention to (e.g. a figure) with light tones in painting, photography, etc. c to mark (part of a text) with a highlighter. 2 to give highlights to (hair).

highlighter *noun* 1 a fluorescent marker pen used to draw attention to part of a text with transparent colour. 2 white or sparkling cosmetic cream or powder used to emphasize the cheeks, eyes, etc.

high living *noun* = HIGH LIFE (1).

highly *adv* 1 to a high degree; extremely: *We were highly delighted with our prize*. 2 with approval; favourably: *Your boss speaks highly of you*.

highly-strung *adj Brit* extremely nervous or sensitive.

High Mass *noun* in the Roman Catholic and Anglican Churches, an elaborate sung mass: compare LOW MASS.

high-minded *adj* having or marked by elevated principles and feelings. ➤➤ **high-mindedly** *adv,* **high-mindedness** *noun.*

Highness /'hienis/ *noun* 1 used as a title for a person of exalted rank, e.g. a king or prince: *Your Highness*. 2 (**highness**) the quality or state of being high: *the highness of his voice*.

high-octane *adj* 1 said of petrol: having a high octane number and hence good antiknock properties. 2 intense or dynamic.

high-pitched *adj* 1 having a high pitch: *a high-pitched voice*. 2 marked by or exhibiting strong feeling: *a high-pitched election campaign*.

high polymer *noun* a polymer, e.g. polystyrene, of high molecular weight.

high-powered *adj informal* having great drive, energy, or capacity; dynamic: *high-powered executives*.

high-pressure *adj* 1 having or involving high pressure, *esp* greatly exceeding that of the atmosphere. 2a using or involving aggressive and insistent sales techniques. b imposing or involving severe strain or tension: *high-pressure occupations*.

high priest *noun* 1 a chief priest, *esp* of the ancient Jewish Levitical priesthood traditionally traced from Aaron. 2 the head or chief exponent of a movement. ➤➤ **high priesthood** *noun.*

high priestess *noun* 1 a chief priestess. 2 the female head or chief exponent of a movement.

high profile *noun* a deliberately conspicuous presence or position: *She keeps a high profile through her many TV appearances.*

high-profile *adj* tending to attract attention; conspicuous: *She has taken on the high-profile task of restoring the Tories' battered image.*

high relief *noun* sculptural relief in which at least half of the circumference of the design stands out from the surrounding surface: compare BAS-RELIEF.

high-rise *adj* having a large number of storeys. ➤➤ **high rise** *noun.*

highroad *noun* 1 *chiefly Brit* a main road. 2 the easiest course: *the highroad to success.*

high roller *noun chiefly NAmer, informal* 1 a person who spends extravagantly on luxurious living. 2 a person who gambles recklessly or for high stakes.

high school *noun* 1 in the USA, a secondary school. 2 in Britain, *usu* in names: an independent or grammar school.

high seas *pl noun* (**the high seas**) the part of a sea or ocean outside territorial waters.

high season *noun Brit* a time of high profitability, *esp* a period of the year when the number of visitors to a holiday resort is at a peak and prices are higher.

high-sounding *adj* said of language: pompous or high-flown.

high-speed *adj* 1 operated at high speed. 2 relating to the production of photographs by very short exposures.

high-spirited *adj* characterized by a bold or lively spirit. ➤➤ **high-spiritedness** *noun.*

high spirits *pl noun* a cheerful state of mind or lively behaviour.

highspot *noun* the most important or enjoyable feature of something: *The cabaret was the highspot of the evening.*

high-stepping *adj* said of a horse: lifting the feet high. ➤ **high-stepper** *noun.*

high street *noun* Brit **1** a main or principal street of a town, *esp* containing shops and other businesses. **2** *(used before a noun)* having branches in many towns: *Most of the high street banks offer this service.*

high-strung *adj* NAmer = HIGHLY-STRUNG.

high table *noun (often* **High Table***) Brit* a table in a dining hall, usu on a platform, used by people of high rank, *esp* the masters and fellows of a college.

hightail *verb intrans chiefly NAmer, informal (often + it)* to move away at full speed.

high tea *noun Brit* a fairly substantial early evening meal at which tea is served.

high tech /tek/ *noun* = HIGH TECHNOLOGY.

high-tech *or* **hi-tech** /tek/ *adj* **1** using or requiring high technology. **2** said of a style of interior decoration: involving the use of industrial building materials, fittings, etc.

high technology *noun* advanced technological processes, *esp* in electronics.

high-tension *adj* having a high voltage, or relating to apparatus to be used at high voltage.

high tide *noun* **1** the tide when the water reaches its highest level, or the time of this. **2** the culminating point; the climax: *It was the high tide of the independence movement.*

high-tops *pl noun* sports shoes with a soft sole and an upper that extends above the ankle.

high treason *noun* see TREASON (1).

high-up *noun informal* a person of high rank or status.

high water *noun* = HIGH TIDE (1): compare LOW WATER, WATER[1] (8).

high-water mark *noun* **1** a mark showing the highest level reached by the surface of a body of water. **2** the highest point, stage, or value.

highway *noun* **1** a public road. **2** *chiefly NAmer* a main road.

Highway Code *noun* in Britain, the official code of rules and advice for the safe use of roads.

highway contract route *noun NAmer* a mail-delivery route served by a private contractor.

highwayman *noun (pl* **highwaymen***)* formerly, a robber of travellers on a road, *esp* one on horseback.

high wire *noun* a tightrope high above the ground.

HIH *abbr Brit* His/Her Imperial Highness.

hi-hat *noun* see HIGH-HAT[1] (1).

hijack[1] *or* **high-jack** /'hiejak/ *verb trans* **1** to seize control of (a vehicle or aircraft) by force while it is in transit. **2** to steal, rob, or kidnap (something or somebody) as if by hijacking. ➤ **hijacker** *noun.*

Word history
origin unknown. This word first achieved wide currency in the USA in the 1920s, when it was applied to stealing bootleg alcohol in transit, but there is some evidence that it was earlier used by hoboes to mean 'to rob a sleeping person'. It has been conjectured that the word derives from *High, Jack!,* i.e. a command to the victim to put his hands up, or possibly from *Hi, Jack!,* i.e. a menacing greeting to the victim, but neither explanation is very convincing.

hijack[2] *or* **high-jack** *noun* the act or an instance of hijacking.

hijra /'hijrə/ *noun* see HEGIRA.

hike[1] /hiek/ *noun* **1** a long walk in the country, *esp* for pleasure or exercise. **2** a big increase or rise, *esp* in prices or wages. ✳ **take a hike** *chiefly NAmer, informal (usu in imperative)* to go away. [origin unknown]

hike[2] *verb intrans* to go on a hike. ➤ *verb trans* **1** *(usu + up)* to pull or lift (something) up: *She hiked up her skirt.* **2** *(usu + up)* to raise (prices, wages, etc). ➤ **hiker** *noun.*

hila /'hielə/ *noun* pl of HILUM.

hilar /'hielə/ *adj* in botany, of, relating to, or located near a HILUM (scar on a seed).

hilarious /hi'leəri-əs/ *adj* extremely funny. ➤ **hilariously** *adv.* [irreg from Latin *hilarus, hilaris* cheerful, from Greek *hilaros*]

hilarity /hi'lariti/ *noun* mirth or merriment.

Hilary term /'hiləri/ *noun* in some British universities, the term beginning in January. [named after St *Hilary* d.367, French bishop, whose feast day is 13 January]

hili /'hielie/ *noun* pl of HILUS.

hill[1] /hil/ *noun* **1** a usu rounded natural rise of land lower than a mountain. **2** a heap or mound, e.g. of earth. **3** a slope. ✳ **over the hill** *informal* past one's prime; too old. ➤ **hilly** *adj.* [Old English *hyll*]

hill[2] *verb trans* **1** to draw earth round the roots or base of (plants). **2** to form (something) into a heap.

hillbilly /'hilbili/ *noun (pl* **hillbillies***) NAmer, informal* a person from a remote or culturally unsophisticated area, e.g. the Appalachian mountains. [HILL[1] + *Billy,* nickname for *William*]

hill climb *noun* a race for cars, motorcycles, etc up a steep hill.

hill figure *noun* a design cut into a hillside, e.g. a horse cut into chalk.

hillfort *noun* a fortified hilltop characteristic of Iron Age settlements in W Europe.

hillock /'hilək/ *noun* a small hill. ➤ **hillocky** *adj.*

hill station *noun* a town or settlement in the low mountains of N India, *esp* one orig established by the British as a place for officials and their families to stay during the hot season.

hilt /hilt/ *noun* the handle of a sword, dagger, or knife. ✳ **to the hilt** completely. [Old English]

hilum /'hieləm/ *noun (pl* **hila** /'hielə/) **1** in botany, a scar on a seed, e.g. a bean, marking the point of attachment of the ovule to its stalk. **2** = HILUS. [Latin *hilum* trifle]

hilus /'hieləs/ *noun (pl* **hili** /'hielie/) in anatomy, a notch or opening in a body part, usu where a vessel, nerve, etc enters. [Latin *hilus,* alteration of HILUM]

HIM *abbr* His/Her Imperial Majesty.

him /əm; *strong* him/ *pronoun* used as the objective case: he: *Don't talk to him; I can run faster than him.* [Old English, dative of *hē* HE[1]]

Himalayan /himə'layən, hi'mahli-ən/ *adj* of or relating to the Himalayas.

himation /hi'mation/ *noun* an ancient Greek garment comprising a rectangle of cloth draped about the body and over the left shoulder. [Greek *himation* from *hennynai* to clothe]

himself /him'self/ *pronoun* **1** used reflexively to refer to a male person or animal that is the subject of the clause: *The boy has hurt himself.* **2** used for emphasis: *He himself said it.* **3** *chiefly Irish* an important man, *esp* the master of the house. ✳ **be himself** to be fit or healthy as normal: *He isn't quite himself today.*

Hinayana /heenə'yahnə/ *noun* an early form of Buddhism, *esp* Theravada. [Sanskrit *hinayāna,* literally 'lesser vehicle']

hind[1] /hiend/ *adj* situated at the back or behind; rear: *a hind leg.* [Middle English, prob back-formation from Old English *hinder* (adv) behind]

hind[2] *noun (pl* **hinds** *or collectively* **hind***)* a female deer, *esp* a red deer: compare HART. [Old English]

hind[3] *noun archaic* **1** a farm worker. **2** a peasant. [Middle English *hine* servant, farmhand, from Old English *hīna,* genitive of *hīwan* (pl), members of a household]

hindbrain *noun* **1** the rearmost part of the embryonic vertebrate brain. **2** the parts of the adult brain, including the cerebellum, pons, and medulla oblongata, that develop from the hindbrain. Also called RHOMBENCEPHALON.

hinder[1] /'hində/ *verb trans (***hindered, hindering***)* to retard or obstruct the progress of (something or somebody); to hamper: *She was hindered by her long skirt.* [Old English *hindrian*]

hinder[2] /'hində/ *adj* situated behind or at the rear; posterior: *the hinder end of its body.* [Old English *hinder* (adv)]

Hindi /'hindi/ *noun* the Indic language of N India, used as an official language of India. ➤ **Hindi** *adj.*

Word history
Hindi *hindī* from *Hind* India, from Persian. British involvement in India – trading from the early 17th cent., and controlling most of the subcontinent from the mid-18th cent. to 1947 with a large army and civil service – has resulted in a considerable number of words being borrowed from Hindi into English. Words in general use include *bangle, bungalow, chutney, cot,*

cummerbund, dungaree, gymkhana, juggernaut, jungle, jute, khaki, loot, pundit, pyjamas, shampoo, thug, and veranda. British slang has also been enriched by Hindi words picked up by British soldiers serving in India, such as blighty, cushy, dekko, and gooly; doolally, based on an Indian place name, is another memento of their service. All these words, unlike many borrowings from non-European languages, have become so anglicized that their origin is rarely recognized. Other Hindi loanwords, which probably still betray their origin, include guru, pukka, purdah, puttee, and topee. See also usage note at HINDU.

hindmost adj furthest back; last.

hindquarter noun **1** the back half of a side of the carcass of a quadruped. **2** (in pl) the hind legs and adjoining parts of a quadruped.

hindrance /'hindrəns/ noun **1** the act of hindering. **2** an impediment or obstacle.

hindsight noun understanding of a situation, or realization of what is required, only after the event.

Hindu /'hindooh, hin'dooh/ noun an adherent of Hinduism. ➤➤ **Hindu** adj. [Persian Hindū inhabitant of India, from Hind India]

Usage note

Hindu or Hindi? These two words are sometimes confused. Hindi is a language spoken in northern India and one of India's two official languages. A Hindu is a follower of Hinduism, the main religion of India.

Hinduism /'hindoohiz(ə)m/ noun a major religious faith of the Indian subcontinent, which involves belief in cycles of reincarnation and the worship of many gods.

Editorial note

Hinduism is a term of relatively recent coinage used to refer to Hindus, those South Asians who are not Muslims, Jains, Buddhists, or Christians. Although derived from a Persian name for the Indus river, Hinduism is currently used as a term of self-reference and is counted as one of the 'world religions' — Professor Donald Lopez.

Hindustani¹ /hindooh'stahni/ noun **1** a group of Indic dialects of N India and Pakistan of which Hindi and Urdu are considered the main written forms. **2** the dialect of Hindi spoken in Delhi, used throughout India as a lingua franca. [Hindi Hindūstānī, from Persian Hindūstān country of the Indians, from Hindū: see HINDU]

Hindustani² adj relating to Hindustan (N India), its people, or the Hindustani language.

hinge¹ /'hinj/ noun **1a** a device that attaches a swinging part, e.g. a door or lid, and enables it to turn. **b** a flexible joint in which bones are held together by ligaments. **c** a small piece of thin gummed paper used to fasten a postage stamp in an album. **2** a point or principle on which something turns or depends. [Middle English heng, of Germanic origin]

hinge² verb (**hingeing** or **hinging**) ➤ verb trans to attach (something) by or as if by a hinge. ➤ verb intrans **1** to hang or turn on a hinge: The door hinges outwards. **2** (+ on) to depend or turn on a single consideration or point: The whole trip hinges on whether we can borrow the car.

hinnie /'hinj/ noun see HINNY².

hinny¹ /'hini/ noun (pl **hinnies**) a hybrid offspring of a stallion and a female ass: compare MULE¹. [via Latin from Greek hinnis]

hinny² or **hinnie** noun (pl **hinnies**) Scot, N Eng used as a term of endearment. [English dialect, variant of HONEY]

hint¹ /hint/ noun **1** a brief practical suggestion or piece of advice: hints for home decorators. **2** an indirect or veiled statement; an insinuation: His hint about having to get up early reminded us that it was getting late. **3** (+ of) a slight indication or trace; a suggestion: There was a hint of irony in her voice. [prob alteration of obsolete hent to grasp]

hint² verb trans and intrans (often + at) to indicate (something) indirectly or by allusion; to suggest: The Chancellor hinted that there might be further tax cuts.

hinterland /'hintəland/ noun **1** a region lying inland from a coast or away from a major river. **2** a region remote from urban or cultural centres. **3** an unknown or unseen side of something or somebody. [German Hinterland, from hinter hinder + Land land]

hip¹ /hip/ noun **1a** the projecting region at each side of the lower or rear part of the body, formed by the pelvis and upper thigh: He tells you when you've got on too much lipstick, and helps you with your girdle when your hips stick — Ogden Nash. **b** the joint between the femur and the hipbone. **2** an external angle between two adjacent sloping sides of a roof. [Old English hype]

hip² noun the ripened fruit of a rose. Also called ROSEHIP. [Old English hēope]

hip³ interj used to begin a cheer: Hip hip hooray. [origin unknown]

hip⁴ adj (**hipper, hippest**) informal **1** conforming to or interested in the latest trends or fashions. **2** (+ to) aware of what is happening. ➤➤ **hipness** noun. [origin unknown]

hip bath noun a portable bath in which one sits rather than lies.

hipbone noun the large bone composed of the ilium, ischium, and pubis that forms half of the pelvis in mammals.

hip flask noun a flat flask for spirits, which can be carried in a hip pocket.

hip hop noun **1** a style of popular music in which spoken words are accompanied by music with a regular heavy beat, and effects are produced by manipulating records on turntables. **2** the fashions and slang associated with devotees of hip hop music. [reduplication of HIP⁴]

hipp- or **hippo-** comb. form forming words, denoting: horse: hippodrome. [via Latin from Greek, from hippos]

hipped¹ adj **1** (usu used in combinations) having hips of a specified kind: broad-hipped. **2** said of a roof: having a hip or hips.

hipped² adj chiefly NAmer, informal (+ on) obsessed or infatuated with something: He's hipped on meditation.

hippie or **hippy** /'hipi/ noun (pl **hippies**) a person who rejects established values, advocates non-violence, and dresses unconventionally. In the 1960s hippies were associated with free love, communal living, and the use of psychedelic drugs. ➤➤ **hippiedom** noun, **hippiness** noun, **hippyish** adj. [HIP⁴ + -IE]

hippo /'hipoh/ noun (pl **hippos** or collectively **hippo**) informal a hippopotamus.

hippo- comb. form see HIPP-.

hippocampus /hipoh'kampəs/ noun (pl **hippocampi** /-pie/) in anatomy, a curved elongated ridge of nervous tissue inside each hemisphere of the brain. It is part of the limbic system, the structures of the brain concerned with emotion and motivation. [via Latin from Greek hippokampos sea horse, from HIPPO- + kampos sea monster]

hippocras /'hipohkras/ noun a drink of wine flavoured with spices that was popular in medieval times. [Middle English ypocras from Old French, named after Hippocrates fl fourth cent. BC, Greek physician who is said to have invented the filter used to strain it]

Hippocratic oath /hipə'kratik/ noun an oath embodying a code of medical ethics. [named after Hippocrates: see HIPPOCRAS]

hippodrome /'hipədrohm/ noun **1** usu in names: a music hall, theatre, etc. **2** an arena for equestrian performances or chariot races in ancient Greece or Rome. [early French via Latin from Greek hippodromos, from HIPPO- + dromos racecourse]

hippogriff or **hippogryph** /'hipohgrif/ noun a mythological creature with a griffin's wings, claws, and head and a horse's body. [French hippogriffe from Italian ippogrifo, from Greek hippos horse + Italian grifo griffin]

hippopotamus /hipə'potəməs/ noun (pl **hippopotamuses** or **hippopotami** /-mie/) a large chiefly aquatic mammal with an extremely large head and mouth, thick hairless skin, and short legs: Hippopotamus amphibius. [via Latin from Greek hippopotamos, from HIPPO- + potamos river]

hippy¹ noun (pl **hippies**) see HIPPIE.

hippy² adj said of a woman: having large hips.

hipster /'hipstə/ noun informal somebody who is keenly aware of and interested in new trends and unconventional patterns, esp in jazz. [HIP⁴]

hipsters /'hipstəz/ pl noun Brit trousers that start at the hips rather than the waist. [HIP¹]

hircine /'huhsien/ adj archaic of or resembling a goat, esp in smell. [Latin hircinus, from hircus he-goat]

hire¹ /hie-ə/ verb trans **1** to obtain the temporary use of (something) or the services of (somebody) for a fixed sum. **2** (+ out) to grant the services of (somebody) or the temporary use of (something) for a fixed sum: They hired themselves out as labourers. ➤➤ **hireable** adj, **hirer** noun.

hire² noun **1** payment for the temporary use of something. **2** hiring or being hired. **3** NAmer somebody who has been hired. **4** (used before a noun) available to be hired: a hire car. * **for/on hire** available to be hired. [Old English hȳr]

hireling /'hie-əling/ *noun derog* a person who works for payment, *esp* for purely mercenary motives.

hire purchase *noun Brit* a system whereby a customer may take possession of goods after paying an initial deposit and then pay the remainder of the price in regular instalments over a specific period.

hirsute /huh'syooht/ *adj formal* very hairy. ➤➤ **hirsuteness** *noun*. [Latin *hirsutus*]

hirsutism *noun* excessive growth of hair.

his[1] /iz; *strong* hiz/ *adj* **1** belonging to or associated with him: *his house; his children; his being chosen; his acquittal.* **2** used in titles: *His Majesty.* [Old English, genitive of *hē* HE[1]]

his[2] /hiz/ *pronoun* the one or ones that belong to him or are associated with him: *Is this house his?; His are on the table; children younger than his.* ✳ **of his** belonging to or associated with him: *friends of his.*

Hispanic[1] /hi'spanik/ *adj* characteristic of or relating to Spain, Portugal, or Latin America, or to Spanish-speaking people. ➤➤ **Hispanicist** /-sist/ *noun*, **Hispanist** /'hispənist/ *noun*. [Latin *hispanicus*, from *Hispania* Iberian peninsula, Spain]

Hispanic[2] *noun* a Spanish-speaking person of Latin American descent living in the USA.

hispid /'hispid/ *adj* covered with bristles or stiff hairs: compare PUBESCENT (2): *a hispid plant.* ➤➤ **hispidity** /hi'spiditi/ *noun*. [Latin *hispidus*]

hiss[1] /his/ *verb intrans* to make a sharp voiceless sound like a prolonged *s*, *esp* in disapproval. ➤ *verb trans* **1** to show disapproval of (somebody or something) by hissing. **2** to utter (something) with a hiss. [Middle English *hissen*, of imitative origin]

hiss[2] *noun* **1** a hissing sound. **2** electrical interference; noise.

hist /hist/ *interj archaic* used to attract attention. [origin unknown]

hist. *abbr* **1** historian. **2** historical. **3** history.

hist- *or* **histo-** *comb. form* forming words, denoting: tissue: *histology.* [via French from Greek *histos* mast, loom beam, web, from *histanai* to cause to stand]

histamine /'histəmin, -meen/ *noun* a chemical compound that transmits nerve impulses in the autonomic nervous system. The release of this compound, usu after injury or in the presence of an allergen, causes an allergic reaction. ➤➤ **histaminic** /-'minik/ *adj*. [blend of HISTIDINE + AMINE]

histidine /'histədeen/ *noun* an amino acid that is a chemical base and is found in most proteins. [HIST- + -IDE + -INE[2]]

histiocyte /'histi-əsiet/ *noun* a MACROPHAGE (large cell) that is not capable of independent movement. ➤➤ **histiocytic** /-'sitik/ *adj*. [Greek *histion* web (dimin. of *histos*: see HIST-) + -CYTE]

histo- *comb. form* see HIST-.

histochemistry /histoh'kemistri/ *noun* the branch of science dealing with the use of chemical techniques in making the structure of tissues and cells visible for examination under a microscope. ➤➤ **histochemical** /-'kemikl/ *adj*.

histocompatibility /,histohkəmpatə'biliti/ *noun* in medicine, a state of mutual tolerance that allows some tissues to be grafted effectively onto others.

histogram /'histəgram/ *noun* in statistics, a diagram consisting of a series of adjacent rectangles, the height and width of which represent each of two variables.

histology /hi'stoləji/ *noun* the branch of anatomy that deals with the organization and microscopic structure of animal and plant tissues. ➤➤ **histological** /-'lojikl/ *adj*, **histologist** *noun*. [French *histologie*, from HISTO- + *-logie* -LOGY]

histolysis /hi'stolisis/ *noun* in biology, the breakdown of body tissues. ➤➤ **histolytic** /-'litik/ *adj*. [scientific Latin, from HISTO- + -LYSIS]

histone /'histohn/ *noun* any of various basic proteins that are found associated with DNA in the chromosomes (strands of gene-carrying material; see CHROMOSOME) of cells.

histopathology /,histohpə'tholəji/ *noun* the branch of pathology concerned with the tissue changes accompanying disease. ➤➤ **histopathological** /-pathə'lojikl/ *adj*, **histopathologist** *noun*.

historian /hi'stawri-ən/ *noun* a student of or expert in history.

historic /hi'storik/ *adj* **1** famous or important in history, or likely to be so: *a historic occasion.* **2** *archaic* of the past; historical: *historic battlefields.* **3** in grammar, said of a tense: expressive of past time.

historical *adj* **1** relating to history and past events: *The writer was not too concerned about historical accuracy.* **2** belonging to the past: *historical figures.* **3** dealing with or representing the events of history: *a historical novel.* **4** relating to changes over a period of time: *historical linguistics.* ➤➤ **historically** *adv*.

historicism /hi'storisiz(ə)m/ *noun* **1** a theory that emphasizes the importance of history in judging or determining events. **2** the belief that events in history are governed by natural laws. **3** excessive emphasis on past styles, e.g. in art and architecture. ➤➤ **historicist** *adj and noun*.

historicity /histə'risiti/ *noun* historical authenticity.

historic present *noun* in grammar, the present tense used to relate past events.

historiographer /,histori'ogrəfə/ *noun* a writer of history; a historian. [early French *historiographeur* via late Latin from Greek *historiographos*, from *historia* (see HISTORY) + *graphein* to write]

historiography /hi,stori'ogrəfi/ *noun* **1** the writing of history. **2** the principles of historical writing. ➤➤ **historiographic** /-ə'grafik/ *adj*, **historiographical** /-ə'grafikl/ *adj*.

history /'histəri/ *noun* (*pl* **histories**) **1** a branch of knowledge that records and interprets past events. **2** past events as a whole: *Does history repeat itself, the first time as tragedy, the second time as farce?* — Julian Barnes. **3** an account of past events: *a history of the university.* **4** a person's medical, sociological, etc background: *a history of schizophrenia in the family.* **5** an unusual or interesting past: *This goblet has a curious history.* **6** a treatise presenting systematically related natural phenomena: *a history of British birds.* [via Latin from Greek *historia* enquiry, history, from *histōr, istōr* knowing, learned]

histrionic /histri'onik/ *adj* **1** deliberately affected; theatrical. **2** *formal* of actors, acting, or the theatre. ➤➤ **histrionically** *adv*. [late Latin *histrionicus* from Latin *histrion-, histrio* actor, alteration of *hister*, from Etruscan]

histrionics *pl noun* (*treated as sing. or pl*) the deliberate display of emotion for effect.

hit[1] /hit/ *verb* (**hitting**, *past tense and past part.* **hit**) ➤ *verb trans* **1a** to aim a blow at (somebody or something) with the hand or with a weapon or implement. **b** to bring (part of the body) into violent contact with something, *esp* accidentally. **c** said of something moving: to make sudden forceful contact with (something stationary). **d** *informal* to press (a button or switch). **2a** to have a detrimental effect or impact on (something or somebody): *The region was hit by floods.* **b** to discover or meet (e.g. a problem). **3a** to cause a propelled object to reach or strike (e.g. a target). **b** in cricket, said of a batsman: to score (a specified number of runs). **c** *informal* to reach or attain (e.g. a specified level). **d** *informal* to arrive at (a place). **4** *chiefly NAmer, informal* to rob or kill (somebody). **5** to be suddenly obvious to (somebody): *It hit her that the man was someone she knew.* ➤ *verb intrans* said of a substance, e.g. a drug: to take effect. ✳ **hit it off** *informal* to get along well. **hit on 1** to discover or arrive at (a solution or answer) by chance. **2** *NAmer* to make sexual advances towards (somebody). **hit the deck** *informal* to fall or throw oneself to the ground. **hit the road** *informal* to start on a journey. **hit the roof** *informal* to give vent to a burst of anger. **hit the sack** *informal* to go to bed. **hit the trail** *NAmer, informal* to start on a journey. ➤➤ **hitter** *noun*. [Middle English *hitten* from Old Norse *hitta* to meet with, hit]

hit[2] *noun* **1** a blow, *esp* one that meets its target. **2a** something that enjoys great success: *a hit musical.* **b** a person who is popular. **3a** in computing, a successful match when a database is being searched for a particular item. **b** a visit to a site on the Internet. **4** *chiefly NAmer, informal* a murder carried out by a criminal. **5** in baseball, a base hit. **6** *informal* a dose of a substance, e.g. a drug.

hit-and-miss *adj* = HIT-OR-MISS.

hit-and-run *adj* **1** said of a road accident: involving a driver who does not stop after causing damage or injury. **2** said of an attack: involving rapid action and immediate withdrawal: *hit-and-run raids on coastal towns.*

hitch[1] /hich/ *verb trans* **1** to move (something) by jerks. **2** to catch or fasten (something) by a hook or knot: *He hitched a plough to the tractor.* **3** *informal* to request and obtain (a free lift) in a passing vehicle. ➤ *verb intrans informal* to hitchhike. ✳ **get hitched** *informal* to get married. [Middle English *hytchen*; earlier history unknown]

hitch[2] *noun* **1** a sudden halt or obstruction; a stoppage: *a hitch in the proceedings.* **2** a knot used for a temporary fastening. **3** *NAmer* a device used to connect two things. **4** *informal* an act of hitchhiking. **5** *NAmer* a period of service, e.g. in the armed forces.

hitcher /'hichə/ *noun* a hitchhiker.

hitchhike /'hichhiek/ *verb intrans* to travel by obtaining free lifts in passing vehicles. ➤➤ **hitchhiker** *noun.*

hi tech /hie 'tek/ *adj see* HIGH TECH.

hither[1] /'hidhə/ *adv archaic or literary* to or towards this place. [Old English *hider*]

hither[2] *adj archaic* nearer: *the hither side of the hill.*

hither and thither *adv* in all directions; to and fro.

hitherto /hidhə'tooh/ *adv* up to this time; until now.

Hitler /'hitlə/ *noun* an autocratic or dictatorial person. ➤➤ **Hitlerian** /hit'liəri-ən/ *adj.* [named after Adolf *Hitler* d.1945, German political leader]

Hitlerism *noun* the nationalistic and totalitarian principles and policies of Adolf Hitler. ➤➤ **Hitlerite** *noun and adj.*

hit list *noun* a list of people to be killed, organizations to be eliminated, etc.

hitman *noun* (*pl* **hitmen**) *informal* a hired assassin.

hit-or-miss *adj* lacking method or consistency of procedure; unreliable; haphazard: *Documenting such unwritten languages was a hit-or-miss affair* — New Internationalist.

hit out *verb intrans* (*often* + at) to act or speak violently or aggressively.

hit parade *noun dated* a listing of pop records ranked in order of the number sold each week.

Hittite /'hitiet/ *noun* **1** a member of a people that established an empire in Asia Minor and Syria in the second millennium BC. **2** the Anatolian language of this people. ➤➤ **Hittite** *adj.* [Hebrew *Ḥittīm*, from Hittite *hatti*]

HIV *abbr* human immunodeficiency virus, a RETROVIRUS (virus containing ribonucleic acid) that breaks down the human body's immune system and is the cause of Aids.

hive[1] /hiev/ *noun* **1** a beehive. **2** a place full of busy occupants: *a hive of industry.* [Old English *hȳf*]

hive[2] *verb trans* to collect (bees) into a hive. ➤ *verb intrans* said of bees: to enter and take possession of a hive.

hive off *verb trans chiefly Brit* to separate (something) from a group or larger unit; *specif* to assign (e.g. assets or responsibilities) to a subsidiary company or agency.

hives *pl noun* (*treated as sing. or pl*) = URTICARIA. [origin unknown]

HIV-positive *adj* having been tested for and found to be infected with HIV.

hiya /'hieyə/ *interj* used as an informal greeting. [shortened from *how are you?*]

HK *abbr* Hong Kong (international vehicle registration).

HKJ *abbr* Hashemite Kingdom of Jordan (international vehicle registration for Jordan).

HL *abbr Brit* House of Lords.

hl *abbr* hectolitre(s).

HM *abbr* **1** headmaster or headmistress. **2** heavy metal (music). **3** His/Her Majesty.

hm *abbr* hectometre(s).

h'm /həm/ *interj see* HMM.

HMG *abbr Brit* His/Her Majesty's Government.

HMI *abbr Brit* formerly, His/Her Majesty's Inspector (of Schools).

hmm *or* **h'm** /həm/ *interj* used to express hesitation, doubt, etc.

HMS *abbr* His/Her Majesty's Ship.

HMSO *abbr Brit* formerly, His/Her Majesty's Stationery Office.

HNC *abbr Brit* Higher National Certificate.

HND *abbr Brit* Higher National Diploma.

Ho *abbr* the chemical symbol for holmium.

ho[1] /hoh/ *interj* **1** used to express surprise or triumph. **2** used *esp* by sailors to attract attention to something specified: *Land ho!* [Middle English]

ho[2] *or* **hoe** *noun* (*pl* **hos** *or* **hoes**) **1** *NAmer, slang* a prostitute. **2** a girlfriend or woman. [black or dialect pronunciation of WHORE[1]]

ho. *abbr* house.

hoagie /'hohgi/ *noun chiefly NAmer* = HERO SANDWICH. [origin unknown]

hoar[1] /haw/ *noun archaic or literary* = HOARFROST.

hoar[2] *adj archaic or literary* grey with age; hoary. [Old English *hār*]

hoard[1] /hawd/ *noun* **1** an often secret supply, e.g. of money or food, stored up for preservation or future use. **2** a cache of valuable archaeological remains. **3** a store of useful information or facts. [Old English]

Usage note

hoard or **horde**? These two words are pronounced the same but have different meanings. A *hoard* is a store or collection, often of valuable things (*a pirate's hoard*). A *horde* is a large and sometimes unruly group of people (*resorts overrun by hordes of tourists*).

hoard[2] *verb trans* to accumulate (a hoard).

hoarding *noun Brit* **1** a large board designed to carry outdoor advertising. **2** a temporary fence put round a building site. [obsolete *hourd, hoard,* prob from Old French *hourt* scaffold, platform]

hoarfrost *noun* a covering of minute ice crystals that forms on the ground, trees, etc.

hoarhound *noun see* HOREHOUND.

hoarse /haws/ *adj* **1** said of a voice: rough or harsh in sound. **2** having a hoarse voice, *esp* temporarily because of overuse or illness: *She was hoarse with shouting.* ➤➤ **hoarsely** *adv,* **hoarseness** *noun.* [Old English *hās*]

hoarsen *verb trans and intrans* (**hoarsened, hoarsening**) to make (somebody or their voice) hoarse or become hoarse.

hoary *adj* (**hoarier, hoariest**) **1a** grey or white with age. **b** having greyish or whitish hair, down, or leaves. **2** impressively or venerably old; ancient. **3** hackneyed: *a hoary old joke.* ➤➤ **hoariness** *noun.*

hoatzin /hoh'atsin/ *noun* a crested olive-coloured S American bird with claws on the first and second fingers of the wing: *Opisthocomus hoazin.* [American Spanish *hoatzin* from Nahuatl *uatzin*]

hoax[1] /hohks/ *noun* an act of deception; a trick or practical joke: *The bomb warning turned out to be a hoax.*

hoax[2] *verb trans* to deceive or play a trick on (somebody). ➤➤ **hoaxer** *noun.* [prob contraction of HOCUS]

hob[1] /hob/ *noun* **1** *Brit* a horizontal surface, either on a cooker or installed as a separate unit, that contains heating areas on which pans are placed. **2** a ledge near a fireplace on which something may be kept warm. **3** a cutting tool used to make gear wheels or screw threads. [origin unknown]

hob[2] *noun* **1** a male ferret: compare GILL[4]. **2** *archaic or dialect* a hobgoblin. [Middle English from *Hobbe,* nickname for *Robert*]

hobbit /'hobit/ *noun* a member of an imaginary race of genial hole-dwellers that resemble small human beings. [figure in novels by J R R Tolkien d.1973, English writer]

hobble[1] /'hobl/ *verb intrans* to walk along unsteadily or with difficulty. ➤ *verb trans* **1** to cause (a person or animal) to limp. **2** to fasten together the legs of (a horse) to prevent it from straying; to fetter. **3** to impede or hamper the progress of (somebody or something). ➤➤ **hobbler** *noun.* [Middle English *hoblen,* prob from Low German or Dutch]

hobble[2] *noun* **1** a hobbling movement. **2** something, e.g. a rope, used to hobble a horse.

hobbledehoy /,hobldi'hoy/ *noun informal, dated* an awkward gawky youth. [origin unknown]

hobby[1] /'hobi/ *noun* (*pl* **hobbies**) **1** a leisure activity or pastime engaged in for interest or recreation. **2** *archaic* a small horse. **3** an early type of bicycle without pedals. [short for HOBBYHORSE]

hobby[2] *noun* (*pl* **hobbies**) a small falcon of Asia, Africa, and Europe that catches small birds while in flight: *Falco subbuteo.* [Middle English *hoby* from early French *hobet,* dimin. of *hobe* falcon]

hobbyhorse *noun* **1** a toy consisting of an imitation horse's head attached to one end of a stick on which a child can pretend to ride. **2** a rocking horse. **3** in morris dancing, a model of a horse attached to the waist of a performer. **4** a favourite topic or preoccupation. [archaic *hobby* small light horse, from Middle English *hoby, hobyn*, prob from *Hobbin*, nickname for *Robin*]

hobbyist *noun* a person with a particular hobby.

hobgoblin /'hob'goblin/ *noun* **1** a mischievous goblin. **2** a bugbear or bogey.

hobnail /'hobnayl/ *noun* a short large-headed nail for studding the soles of shoes or boots. ⟫⟫ **hobnailed** *adj.* [HOB², in the archaic sense 'peg or stake used as a target in games']

hobnob /'hobnob/ *verb intrans* (**hobnobbed, hobnobbing**) *informal* (+ with) to socialize or chat with somebody. [from the obsolete phrase *drink hobnob* to drink alternately to one another]

hobo /'hohboh/ *noun* (*pl* **hoboes** or **hobos**) **1** *NAmer* a tramp or vagrant. **2** *chiefly NAmer* a migratory worker. [perhaps from *ho, bo*, assumed to be a form of greeting between tramps]

Hobson's choice /'hobs(ə)nz/ *noun* an apparently free choice that offers no real alternative. [prob named after Thomas *Hobson* d.1631, English liveryman, who required every customer to take the first available horse]

hock¹ /hok/ *noun* **1** the joint of the hind limb of a horse or related quadruped that corresponds to the ankle in human beings. **2** a knuckle of meat. [Old English *hōh* heel]

hock² *noun* *Brit* a dry to medium-dry or sometimes sweet white table wine produced in the Rhine valley. [modification of German *Hochheimer*, named after *Hochheim*, town in Germany]

hock³ *verb trans* *informal* to pawn (something). [from HOCK⁴]

hock⁴ * **in hock 1** said of an object: having been pawned. **2** said of a person: in debt. [Dutch *hok* pen, prison]

hockey /'hoki/ *noun* **1** a field game played between two teams of eleven players who hit a small hard ball with a long hooked stick that has a flat-faced blade at the lower end. **2** *NAmer* = ICE HOCKEY. [perhaps from early French *hoquet* shepherd's crook, dimin. of *hoc* hook, of Germanic origin]

hocus /'hohkəs/ *verb trans* (**hocussed** or **hocused, hocussing** or **housing**) **1** *archaic* to deceive or trick (somebody). **2** to drug (e.g. an animal or its drink). [orig meaning obsolete *hocus* 'to deceive'; trickery, deceit, short for HOCUS-POCUS]

hocus-pocus /,hohkəs 'pohkəs/ *noun* **1** deliberately nonsensical words, e.g. uttered by a conjurer, usu intended to obscure or deceive. **2** the use of trickery in order to deceive. [modification of *hax pax max Deus adimax*, imitation Latin phrase used by conjurers]

hod /hod/ *noun* **1** a trough mounted on a pole handle for carrying mortar, bricks, etc. **2** a coal scuttle, *esp* a tall one used to shovel fuel directly onto a fire. [prob from early Dutch *hodde*]

hodgepodge /'hojpoj/ *noun* *NAmer* see HOTCHPOTCH. [by alteration]

Hodgkin's disease /'hojkinz/ *noun* a malignant disease characterized by progressive anaemia with enlargement of the lymph glands, spleen, and liver. [named after Thomas *Hodgkin* d.1866, English physician who first described it]

hodograph /'hodəgrahf/ *noun* in mathematics, a curve having a RADIUS VECTOR (line joining fixed point to variable point) that represents the velocity of a moving point. [Greek *hodos* way, path + -GRAPH]

hoe¹ /hoh/ *noun* an implement with a long handle and a flat blade, used for tilling, weeding, etc. [Middle English *howe* from early French *houe*, of Germanic origin]

hoe² * *verb trans and intrans* **1** to weed or cultivate (land or a crop) with a hoe. **2** to remove (weeds) with a hoe. ⟫⟫ **hoer** *noun*.

hoe³ *noun* see HO².

hoedown *noun* *NAmer* a square dance, or a gathering that features square dances. [from the idea of putting down the hoe, i.e. stopping work]

hog¹ /hog/ *noun* **1a** *Brit* a castrated male pig raised for slaughter. **b** *chiefly NAmer* a domestic pig. **2** a warthog or other wild pig. **3** *informal* a selfish, gluttonous, or filthy person. **4** = HOGG. * **go the whole hog** *informal* to do something thoroughly: *We might as well go the whole hog and hire a limousine.* ⟫⟫ **hog-like** *adj.* [Old English *hogg*]

hog² *verb trans* (**hogged, hogging**) **1** *informal* to appropriate a selfish or excessive share of (something); to monopolize (something): *She hogged the discussion.* **2** to cut (a horse's mane) off or short. **3** to cause (something) to arch. ⟫⟫ **hogger** *noun*.

hogan /'hohgən/ *noun* a building usu made of posts and branches covered with mud and used as a dwelling by the Navaho Indians of N New Mexico and Arizona. [Navaho *hogan*]

hogback *noun* see HOGSBACK.

hogfish *noun* (*pl* **hogfishes** or *collectively* **hogfish**) a colourful fish of the W Atlantic, the male of which has a long snout and bristles on its head: *Lachnolaimus maximus*.

hogg /hog/ *noun* *dialect* a young unshorn sheep. [variant of HOG¹]

hogget /'hogit/ *noun* **1** *Brit* a young sheep. **2** *NZ* a lamb that has been weaned but not yet shorn.

hoggish *adj* grossly selfish, gluttonous, or filthy.

Hogmanay /'hogmənay, hogmə'nay/ *noun* in Scotland, New Year's Eve. [prob from Norman French *hoguiné*, alteration of Old French *accuiellis l'an neuf* welcome the new year]

hognose snake *noun* any of several species of N American non-venomous snakes that have upturned snouts and inflate their bodies when disturbed: genus *Heterodon*.

hogsback or **hogback** *noun* a ridge with a sharp summit and steeply sloping sides.

hogshead *noun* **1** a large cask or barrel. **2** any of several measures of capacity, *esp* a measure of 52½ imperial gallons (about 238l).

hog-tie *verb trans* (**hog-ties, hog-tied, hog-tying**) *NAmer* **1** to tie together all four feet of (an animal) or the hands and feet of (a person). **2** to impede or thwart (somebody).

hogwash *noun* **1** *informal* nonsensical talk. **2** pigswill.

hogweed *noun* any of several species of tall foul-smelling plants of the carrot family, with large leaves and broad heads of white or pinkish flowers: genus *Heracleum*. [because it used to be fed to pigs]

ho-ho /,hoh 'hoh/ *interj* used to express laughter or triumph. [imitative]

ho hum /,hoh 'hum/ *interj* used to express weariness, boredom, or disdain. [imitative]

hoick¹ /hoyk/ *verb trans* *Brit, informal* to lift or pull (something) abruptly; to yank: *I hoicked my case out of the rack.* [prob alteration of HIKE²]

hoick² *noun* a jerk.

hoiden /'hoydn/ *noun* see HOYDEN.

hoi polloi /,hoy pə'loy/ *pl noun* (**the hoi polloi**) the common people; the masses. [Greek *hoi polloi* the many]

hoisin sauce /'hoy'sin/ *noun* a thick dark red sauce used in Chinese cookery as a sweet and spicy flavouring in savoury dishes. [prob from Chinese (Cantonese) *hoishin*, from *hoi* sea + *shin* food, delicacy]

hoist¹ /hoyst/ *verb trans* to raise (something) into position, *esp* by means of tackle. ⟫⟫ **hoister** *noun*. [alteration of *hoise*, perhaps from early Dutch *hischen*]

hoist² *noun* **1** an apparatus for hoisting something. **2** the act of hoisting; a lift. **3a** the end of a flag next to the staff: compare FLY² (5A). **b** the distance a flag extends along its staff or support. **c** a group of flags used as a signal.

hoity-toity /,hoyti 'toyti/ *adj* **1** haughty or self-important. **2** *archaic* frivolous or foolish. [reduplication of English dialect *hoit* to play the fool]

hokey /'hohki/ *adj* (**hokier, hokiest**) *NAmer, informal* mawkishly sentimental or contrived. [HOKUM + -Y¹]

hokey cokey /'kohki/ *noun* a dance performed by a large group of people in a circle, who sing a song with lyrics that specify the actions. [origin unknown]

hokey-pokey /'pohki/ *noun* *NAmer* = HOKEY COKEY. [origin unknown]

hoki /'hohkee/ *noun* a food fish of the waters south of New Zealand, related to the hake: *Macruronus novaezeelandiae*. [Maori *hoki*]

hokonui /'hokənooee/ *noun* *NZ* illicit spirits, *esp* whisky. [*Hokonui*, Maori place name]

hokum /'hohkəm/ *noun* *informal* **1** pretentious nonsense. **2** a technique, e.g. the use of sentimentality, designed to captivate the audience of a play, film, etc. [prob from HOCUS-POCUS + BUNKUM]

hol- or **holo-** *comb. form* forming words, with the meanings: **1** complete or total: *holocaust.* **2** completely or totally: *holographic.* [Middle English via Old French and Latin from Greek, from *holos* whole]

Holarctic /ho'lahktik/ *adj* relating to the biogeographical area that includes the northern parts of the Old World and New World.

hold¹ /hohld/ *verb* (*past tense and past part.* **held** /held/) ➤ *verb trans* **1a** to have, keep, or support (something) in the hands or arms. **b** to embrace (somebody). **2** to support or sustain (something): *The roof won't hold your weight.* **3a** to keep (somebody) in confinement or under restraint. **b** to keep (something) in a specified position or state: *A wedge will hold the door open.* **c** to keep possession of (something): *Cars don't hold their value; The troops are still holding the ridge; He held the children's attention for a full hour.* **d** said of a ship or aircraft: to continue to follow (a course). **4** to keep (an opponent) from full success: *We held them to a draw.* **5a** to contain or be capable of containing (an amount). **b** to be capable of drinking (a large amount of alcohol), *esp* without becoming drunk. **6a** to have (a distinction or qualification): *They hold the world record.* **b** to occupy (a position or job): *Is he fit to hold office?* **c** to sustain (a musical note). **d** to have (something) in store: *What does the future hold?* **e** to have (a belief, view, etc). **f** said of a court: to rule or decide (something): *The judge held that there was no case to answer.* **g** to consider (somebody) to be to blame for something: *He held me responsible for the mix-up.* **7a** to set (something) aside or reserve it. **b** to delay or stop the action of (something). **8** to keep (a telephone connection). **9** *NAmer, informal* to refrain from using or adding (something). **10a** to organize (a meeting, party, etc). **b** to take part in (a conversation). ➤ *verb intrans* **1** to withstand strain without breaking or giving way: *The anchor should hold.* **2** to continue unchanged; to last: *I hope the good weather will hold.* **3** to remain valid; to apply: *I will stay overnight, if your offer still holds.* **4** *NAmer, informal* to have illegal drugs in one's possession: *She was arrested for holding.* * **be left holding the baby** to be left to bear alone a responsibility that should have been shared by others. **hold forth** to speak at great length. **hold good** to be true or valid. **hold it** *informal* to wait. **hold one's own** to maintain one's position in the face of competition or adversity. **hold somebody to something** to make somebody honour a promise, commitment, etc. **hold something against somebody** to have a grudge against somebody. **hold something dear** to value something greatly. **hold the fort** see FORT. **hold to** to remain steadfast or faithful to (a principle). **hold with** *informal* to agree with or approve of (something). ➤➤ **holdable** *adj.* [Old English *healdan*]

hold² *noun* **1** a manner of grasping something or somebody; a grip. **2** something that may be grasped as a support. **3** influence or control: *His father had a strong hold over him.* **4** *archaic* a fortress. * **get hold of 1** to grasp or grip (something). **2** to obtain (something). **3** to contact (somebody). **no holds barred** with no restrictions. **on hold** held in a state of postponement or temporary inactivity: *She had put her career on hold while she wrote the novel.* **take hold 1** (*often* + *of*) to grasp, grip, or seize something. **2** to become attached or established; to take effect.

hold³ *noun* a space or compartment for the storage of cargo in a ship or aircraft. [alteration of HOLE¹ by association with HOLD¹]

holdall *noun Brit* a bag or case for miscellaneous articles.

hold back *verb trans* **1** to impede the progress of (somebody). **2** to inhibit (somebody) or prevent them from doing something: *Don't let shyness hold you back.* **3** to keep (tears or laughter) in check. **4** not to give (information, etc) to somebody who needs it. ➤ *verb intrans* to hesitate before doing something, or be reluctant to do it.

hold down *verb trans* **1** *informal* to possess and perform (a job) satisfactorily. **2** to prevent (prices, costs, etc) from rising.

holder *noun* **1** a stand or other device designed to contain, grip, or support an object or set of objects: *a pencil-holder; a cigarette in an amber holder.* **2** the possessor of something, e.g.: **a** a ticket, qualification, etc: *Ticket-holders this way; holders of membership cards.* **b** an estate or property as owner or tenant, or a financial investment: *the leaseholder; shareholders.* **c** a title, record, etc: *the current record-holder.* **3** a person in possession of a PROMISSORY NOTE or BILL OF EXCHANGE on which they can legally enforce payment.

holdfast *noun* **1** a hook, clamp, or other device for securing an object to a surface, wall, etc. **2** a part by which a seaweed or other organism clings to a surface.

hold in *verb trans* to repress or keep (one's feelings, etc) in check.

holding¹ *noun* **1** a piece of land held by somebody *esp* as a tenant. **2** (*in pl*) one's financial assets, *esp* in the form of land or securities.

holding² *adj Aus* not short of money; in funds.

holding company *noun* a company whose primary business is holding a controlling interest in the shares of other companies: compare INVESTMENT COMPANY.

holding operation *noun* a ploy or procedure designed to keep the status quo going.

holding paddock *noun Aus, NZ* a paddock in which animals are kept temporarily, e.g. one for sheep before shearing.

holding pattern *noun* the circling flightpath around an airport that an aircraft keeps to while waiting for permission to land.

hold off *verb trans* **1** to keep (an attacker or a challenge) at a distance. **2** to delay (doing something of a final nature): *I held off signing the contract.* ➤ *verb intrans* **1** said of expected bad weather: not to occur after all. **2** to defer or delay action: *They hold off from arresting him in spite of all the evidence.* **3** to fail to give needed support; to remain at a distance: *If you love me hold me off* — Shakespeare.

hold on *verb intrans* **1** to persevere in difficult circumstances. **2** used as an instruction to a telephone caller: to wait a minute; = HANG ON. * **hold on to** to keep possession of (something).

hold out *verb trans* to proffer (a hope, etc) or present it as likely or realizable. ➤ *verb intrans* **1** to keep functioning in spite of difficulty. **2** to refuse to yield or give way. * **hold out for** to insist on (higher wages, etc) as the price for an agreement. **hold out on** *informal* to withhold something, e.g. information, from (somebody who might expect to receive it).

hold over *verb trans* **1** to postpone or defer (an event, or action on something). **2** *chiefly NAmer* to prolong (a theatre engagement, etc).

hold together *verb intrans* to remain intact; not to disintegrate.

holdup *noun* **1** an armed robbery. **2** a delay, or the cause of this: *a traffic holdup; What's the holdup?* **3** (*in pl*) a stocking with an elasticated top for gripping the thigh that stays up without suspenders.

hold up *verb trans* **1** to delay (something or somebody). **2** to rob (people, a bank, etc) at gunpoint. **3** to present (somebody or something) as an example. ➤ *verb intrans* to remain strong: *The defence held up well throughout the match.*

hole¹ /hohl/ *noun* **1** a hollow in something solid; a pit or cavity: *He dug a hole; a hole in my tooth.* **2** a gap or opening right through something: *I found out that the big toe always ends up making a hole in a sock; so I stopped wearing socks* — Einstein. **3** a small animal's underground home; a burrow. **4a** in various games played with a ball or balls, a cavity into which a ball must be struck. **b** in golf, a lined cylindrical cavity in a putting green into which the ball is to be played. **c** in golf, the section of the course, or the unit of play, from the tee to the hole: *The sixth hole is the longest on the course; I'd only played four holes when down came the rain.* **5** *informal* an unpleasant place; a dump. **6** a deep place in a body of water. **7** a vacant position in a substance, *esp* a semiconductor such as silicon, that was formerly occupied by an electron and can be regarded as equivalent to a positively charged particle. * **blow a hole in** to spoil or wreck (a theory or a scheme). **hole in one** in golf, a shot from a tee that lands in the hole. **hole in the heart** a congenital heart defect in the form of an abnormal opening in the SEPTUM (partition) dividing the left and right sides of the heart, resulting in inadequate oxygenation of the blood. **hole in the wall 1** *informal* a poky little establishment, *esp* the premises of a tiny business concern. **2** *Brit* an automatic cash machine set into the external wall of a bank, etc. **in a hole** in difficulties, *esp* of a financial kind. **in holes** *informal* said of a garment, etc: so worn as to be full of holes. **in the hole** *NAmer, informal* in debt. **make a hole in** to use up a lot of (a supply of money, food, or other resource): *That must have made a hole in their savings.* [Old English *hol*, neuter *hol* hollow, and *holh* hole]

hole² *verb trans* **1** to make a hole in (something); *specif* to pierce the side of (a vessel): *The yacht was holed below the waterline.* **2** in golf, to putt (the ball) into a hole. ➤ *verb intrans* in golf, to play one's ball into the hole, usu in a specified number of shots: *She holed in one at the sixth.*

hole-and-corner *adj* clandestine; underhand.

hole card *noun* **1** in the game of STUD POKER, a card that is dealt face down. **2** *chiefly NAmer, informal* a secret asset.

hole out *verb intrans* in golf, to putt one's ball into the hole, usu in a specified number of shots: *She holed out in three.*

hole saw *noun* a saw for making circular holes, in the form of a metal cylinder with a serrated edge.

hole up *verb intrans informal* (*usu* + in) to hide oneself in a confined place: *I holed up in a rented room.* ➤ *verb trans informal* (*usu in passive*) to confine (somebody) in a small space: *I didn't want to spend this glorious weather holed up in my bedsit.*

Holi /'hohli/ *noun* a Hindu festival celebrated in the spring in honour of Krishna, an incarnation of the god Vishnu as a cowherd. [via Hindi from Sanskrit *holī*]

-holic *or* **-aholic** *or* **-oholic** *comb. form* forming adjectives and nouns, with the meaning: addicted to or addict of the substance, activity, etc specified: *chocoholic; workaholic.* [from ALCOHOLIC²]

holiday¹ /'holiday/ *noun* 1 *chiefly Brit* a period taken as leave or a break from one's normal occupation, *esp* if spent away from home: *a two-day holiday; a holiday in Turkey.* 2 *chiefly Brit* (*in pl*) a period of the year between academic or legal terms, or a period of scheduled leave from one's job: *You're expected to do a lot of reading in the holidays; I'm going to Madeira for my holidays.* 3 an official day of leave from work, such as a religious festival or a day of celebration: *a bank holiday.* [Old English *hāligdæg*, from *hālig* HOLY + *dæg* DAY]

holiday² *verb intrans* to take or spend a holiday: *holidaying in Ibiza.*

holiday camp *noun* an establishment for holidaymakers at the seaside or in the countryside, usu with accommodation in chalets and facilities for a variety of sports and entertainments.

holidaymaker *noun* a person who is going somewhere for a holiday, or is on holiday in a particular resort.

holier-than-thou /'hohli-ə/ *adj* having an air of superior piety or morality; sanctimonious; self-righteous.

holily /'hohlili/ *adv* 1 in a holy manner. 2 not using dishonest means: *What thou wouldst highly, that wouldst thou holily; wouldst not play false, and yet wouldst wrongly win* — Shakespeare.

holiness /'hohlinis/ *noun* 1 the quality of being holy. 2 (**His/Your Holiness**) a title for the Pope, Orthodox patriarchs, and the Dalai Lama: *His Holiness Pope John Paul II.* 3 (*often* **Holiness**) a US religious movement related to Methodism, teaching the doctrine of sanctification (purification of believers by the Holy Spirit; see SANCTIFY).

holism /'hohliz(ə)m/ *noun* 1 a view of the universe, and *esp* living nature, as being composed of interacting wholes that are more than simply the sum of their parts. 2 in alternative medicine, the practice of trying to treat the whole person, not merely their symptoms. ➤➤ **holistic** /hoh'listik/ *adj.*

holla¹ /'holə/ *interj and noun* (*pl* **hollas**) *archaic* a cry used to attract attention; = HOLLO¹.

holla² *verb intrans* (**hollas, holla'd, hollaing**) to shout 'holla!'; = HOLLO², HALLOO: *Don't holla till you are out of the wood* — Charles Kingsley. [French *holà*, from *ho!* + *là* there]

holland *or* **Holland** /'holənd/ *noun* a cotton or linen fabric in plain weave, usu heavily sized or glazed, that is used for window blinds, bookbinding, and clothing: *The waiter had helped him on with a thin holland overcoat* — Hardy. [Middle English *holand*, named after *Holand* Holland, province of the Netherlands, where it was first made]

hollandaise sauce /holən'dayz/ *noun* a rich sauce made with butter, egg yolks, and lemon juice or vinegar, served with salmon, trout, etc. [French *sauce hollandaise* Dutch sauce]

Hollands *noun archaic* Dutch gin. [Dutch *Hollandsche genever*]

holler /'holə/ *verb* (**hollered, hollering**) ➤ *verb intrans NAmer* 1 to shout: *Holler when you're ready.* 2 to yell or howl. 3 to complain. ➤ *verb trans* to shout (something): *He hollered my name.* [alteration of HOLLO²]

hollo¹ *or* **holloa** /'holoh/ *interj and noun* (*pl* **hollos** *or* **holloas**) *archaic* a cry used to attract attention or as a call of encouragement: *The Albatross did follow, and every day, for food or play, came to the mariners' hollo!* — Coleridge. [prob variant of HOLLA¹]

hollo² *or* **holloa** *verb intrans* (**hollos** *or* **holloas, holloed** *or* **holloa'd, holloing** *or* **holloaing**) to shout 'hollo!'

hollow¹ /'holoh/ *adj* 1 having a recessed surface; curved inwards; concave; sunken: *hollow cheeks.* 2 having a cavity within: *a hollow tree.* 3 echoing like a sound made in or by beating on an empty container; muffled: *speaking in a hollow voice.* 4a said of an achievement: deceptively lacking in real value or significance: *a hollow victory.* b said of a vow or promise: insincere; not to be trusted. ✳ **beat somebody hollow** *humorous* to defeat somebody thoroughly. ➤➤ **hollowly** *adv,* **hollowness** *noun.* [Old English *holh* hole]

hollow² *verb trans* 1 (*usu* + out) to make a cavity in (something): *canoes made from hollowed-out tree trunks.* 2 (*usu* + out) to make (a cavity) in something: *They hollowed out a shelter in the snow.*

hollow³ *noun* 1 a depressed or hollow part of a surface; *esp* a small valley or basin: *a wooded hollow.* 2 an unfilled space; a cavity: *in the hollow of one's hand.*

hollowware *or* **holloware** *noun* domestic vessels that have a significant depth and volume, e.g. pots, pans, and jugs: compare FLATWARE (2).

holly /'holi/ *noun* (*pl* **hollies**) any of numerous species of trees and shrubs with thick glossy spiny-edged leaves and bright red berries: *Ilex aquifolium* and other species. [Old English *holen, holegn*]

hollyhock /'holihok/ *noun* a tall plant of the mallow family with large coarse rounded leaves and tall spikes of showy flowers: *Alcea rosea.* [Middle English *holihoc* orig referring to the marsh mallow, which has medicinal uses; from *holi* holy + Old English *hoc* mallow]

Hollywood *noun* 1 the American film industry.

Editorial note
Hollywood is a district of Los Angeles where much early film-making took place. It is now an area where few studios are found. But the name has become synonymous with the manufacture of entertainment movies in America (and even other countries). Thus, 'Hollywood' extends to TV, advertising, and other media and exists in opposition to American 'independent' film-making (cheaper, less glamorous, more personal) — David Thomson.

2 (*used before a noun*) of or relating to the American film industry: *a Hollywood star.* [*Hollywood*, district of Los Angeles, California, USA, centre of the industry]

holm¹ /hohm, hohm/ *noun Brit* 1 a small inshore island. 2 an area of flat low-lying land near a river; a flood plain. [Old English, from Old Norse *hōlmr* islet, river meadow]

holm² /hohm/ *noun* 1 = HOLM OAK. 2 *Brit dialect* = HOLLY. [Old English *holen* HOLLY]

holmium /'holmi-əm/ *noun* a silver-white metallic chemical element of the rare-earth group that occurs naturally in various rare-earth minerals and forms highly magnetic compounds: symbol Ho, atomic number 67. [Latin *holmium*, named after *Holmia* Stockholm, capital city of Sweden]

holm oak /hohm/ *noun* a S European evergreen oak with glossy dark-green leaves: *Quercus ilex.* [Middle English *holm* holly, alteration of *holin*]

holo- *comb. form* see HOL-.

holocaust /'holəkawst/ *noun* 1 an instance of wholesale destruction or loss of life: *the nuclear holocaust.* 2 (**the Holocaust**) the genocidal persecution of European Jewry by Hitler and the Nazi party during World War II. 3 formerly, in Jewish religious practice, a sacrificial offering wholly consumed by fire on the altar; = BURNT OFFERING (1). [Middle English via Old French and late Latin from Greek *holokauston*, neuter of *holokaustos* burned whole, from HOLO- + *kaustos* burned, from *kaiein* to burn]

Holocene /'holəseen/ *adj* relating to the present geological epoch, the second epoch of the Quaternary period, which began 10,000 years ago and followed the Pleistocene epoch. ➤➤ **Holocene** *noun.* [French *holocène*, from HOLO- + Greek *kainos* new]

holoenzyme /holoh'enziem/ *noun* a complete active enzyme consisting of a protein component combined with a COENZYME (non-protein activating component).

hologram /'holəgram/ *noun* 1 a pattern produced by the interference between one part of a split beam of coherent light, e.g. from a laser, and the other part of the same beam reflected off an object. 2 a photographic reproduction of this pattern that when suitably illuminated produces a three-dimensional picture.

holograph /'holəgrahf, -graf/ *noun* 1 a document wholly in the handwriting of its author. 2 the handwriting itself, or autograph. ➤➤ **holographic** /-'grafik/ *adj.* [via late Latin from Greek *holographos* written entirely in the same hand, from HOLO- + Greek *graphein* to write]

holography /ho'logrəfi/ *noun* the technique of making or using a hologram. ➤➤ **holographic** /-'grafik/ *adj,* **holographically** /-'grafikli/ *adv.*

holohedral /holə'heedrəl/ *adj* said of a crystal: having all the faces required for complete symmetry: compare HEMIHEDRAL.

holophrastic /holoh'frastik/ *adj* said of a language, or of telescoped utterances, *esp* those of children, e.g. *more!, up!, down!*:

expressing a complex of ideas in a single word. [HOLO- + -*phrastic* from Greek *phrazein* to point out, declare]

holophytic /holoh'fitik/ *adj* said of a green plant: obtaining food by photosynthetic activity.

holothurian /holə'thyooəri-ən/ *noun* any of a class of echinoderms including the sea cucumbers: class Holothuroidea. ⋙ **holothuroid** /-'thyooəroyd/ *adj.* [via Latin from Greek *holothourion* water polyp]

holotype /'holətiep/ *noun* the single specimen of an organism designated as the type of a species, subspecies, or variety, either by an author at the time the species is established or at a later date by another person. ⋙ **holotypic** /-'tipik/ *adj.*

holozoic /holoh'zoh·ik/ *adj* said of an animal: obtaining food by ingesting complex organic matter.

hols /holz/ *pl noun* (**the hols**) *chiefly Brit, informal* holidays.

holstein /'holstien/ *noun chiefly NAmer* a Friesian cow or bull. [short for *holstein-friesian*, from *Holstein*, region of Germany + FRIESIAN]

holster /'hohlstə/ *noun* a leather holder for a pistol, usu worn on a belt. [Dutch *holster*]

holt[1] /hohlt/ *noun* **1** a den or lair, *esp* of an otter. **2** *NAmer* a grip or grasp; = HOLD². [Middle English, alteration of HOLD²]

holt[2] *noun archaic or literary* a wood or wooded hill. [Old English]

holus-bolus /,hohləs 'bohləs/ *adv chiefly Canadian or archaic* all together in one lump; all at once: *making a sudden snatch at the heap of silver, put it back, holus-bolus, in her pocket* — Wilkie Collins. [prob mock rhyming Latin based on *whole bolus* whole lump (see BOLUS)]

holy /'hohli/ *adj* (**holier, holiest**) **1** set apart to the service of God or a god; sacred: *holy water; the Holy Bible.* **2** characterized by perfection and transcendence; commanding absolute adoration and reverence: *the holy child; the holy Trinity.* **3** spiritually pure; godly: *a holy man; leading a holy life.* **4** *derog* overtly religious. **5** *dated, informal* used with certain other words as a mild expletive: *Holy Moses!; He's a holy terror.* [Old English *hālig*]

Holy City *noun* **1** any city considered sacred by members of a particular religion, *esp* Jerusalem as a city at the heart of Judaism, Christianity, and Islam. **2** heaven; the City of God.

Holy Communion *noun* the celebration of the Eucharist; = COMMUNION (1).

holy day *noun* a day set aside for special religious observance.

Holy Family *noun* the infant Jesus, Mary, and Joseph, as depicted in paintings, etc, sometimes accompanied by St Anne, the mother of Mary, or by John the Baptist, second cousin of Jesus.

Holy Father *noun* (**the Holy Father**) a designation for the pope.

Holy Ghost *noun* (**the Holy Ghost**) = the HOLY SPIRIT.

Holy Grail *noun* the cup or platter used, according to medieval legend, by Christ at the Last Supper, which became the object of knightly quests.

holy hour *noun* **1** (**Holy Hour**) in the Roman Catholic Church, an hour of prayer and meditation before the Eucharist. **2** *Irish, informal* an afternoon period during which public houses close in Ireland.

Holy Innocents' Day *noun* 28 December, kept by churches in memory of the children killed by Herod according to Matthew 2:16.

Holy Joe /joh/ *noun informal* **1** a pious person. **2** a parson or chaplain.

Holy Land *noun* (**the Holy Land**) the area occupied by modern Israel and Palestine, containing sites associated with the ministry and death of Christ.

holy of holies /'hohliz/ *noun* **1** in Jewish history, the innermost and most sacred chamber of the Jewish tabernacle and temple. **2** any place or thing considered sacred. [translation of late Latin *sanctum sanctorum*, itself translating Hebrew *qōdhesh haq-qŏdhāshīm*]

holy orders *pl noun* the office of a Christian minister.

Holy Roller *noun derog* a member of any of several ecstatic Protestant fundamentalist sects.

Holy Roman Empire *noun* a loose confederation of mainly German and Italian territories, representing the western part of the Roman Empire, as revived by Charlemagne in 800, that existed until 1806.

Holy Saturday *noun* the Saturday before Easter.

Holy Scripture *noun* the sacred writings pertaining to Christianity embodied in the Bible.

Holy See *noun* (**the Holy See**) the papacy.

Holy Spirit *noun* (**the Holy Spirit**) the third person of the Trinity.

holystone[1] *noun* a piece of soft sandstone formerly used for scrubbing a ship's decks. [said to be so called because it is used while kneeling]

holystone[2] *verb trans* to scrub (a ship's deck) with a holystone.

Holy Synod *noun* (**the Holy Synod**) the governing body of a national Eastern Orthodox Church.

Holy Thursday *noun* **1** *dated* in the Anglican Church, ASCENSION DAY. **2** in the Roman Catholic Church, MAUNDY THURSDAY.

holy war *noun* a war that is undertaken in the name of religion, either to defend or to promote a religious cause.

holy water *noun* water that has been blessed by a priest for symbolic use in purification rituals.

Holy Week *noun* the week before Easter during which the last days of Christ's life are commemorated.

holy writ *noun* **1** (*often* **Holy Writ**) = HOLY SCRIPTURE. **2** a writing or utterance of unquestionable authority: *Trifles light as air are to the jealous confirmations strong as proofs of holy writ* — Shakespeare.

holy year *noun* in the Roman Catholic Church, a JUBILEE year (during which remission from punishment for sin is granted), held at intervals of 25 years.

hom /hohm/ *or* **homa** /'hohmə/ *or* **haoma** /'howmə/ *noun* the sacred plant of the Parsis (followers of Zoroastrianism; see PARSI), perhaps of the leafless-vine genus *Sarcostemma*, or the sacred intoxicating drink prepared from it; = SOMA¹. [Persian *hūm* or Avestan *haoma*]

hom- *or* **homo-** *comb. form* forming words, with the meanings: **1** one and the same; similar; alike: *homograph.* **2** relating to homosexual love: *homophobia.* **3** containing one more CH_2 group than the specified compound: *homocysteine.* [Greek *homos* same]

homa /'hohmə/ *noun* see HOM.

homage /'homij/ *noun* **1a** reverential regard; deference: *the shrine where the villagers paid homage to their patron saint.* **b** flattering attention: *She was used to this kind of homage from her admirers.* **2** in a feudal society: **a** a ceremony by which a man acknowledges himself the vassal of a lord. **b** an act done or payment made by a vassal. [Middle English from Old French *hommage*, from *homme* man, vassal]

hombre /'hombray/ *noun chiefly NAmer, informal* a man; a fellow: *a tough-looking hombre.* [Spanish *hombre* man, from Latin *homin-, homo*]

homburg /'hombuhg/ *noun* a felt hat with a stiff curled brim and a high crown creased lengthways. [named after *Homburg*, town in Germany, where such hats were first worn]

home[1] /hohm/ *noun* **1** the place where one lives permanently, *esp* with one's family, or as a member of a household. **2** a house, flat, apartment, etc. **3** the social unit constituted by a family living together: *She comes from a broken home.* **4** one's native region or country: *I regard the Midlands as home.* **5** the social or professional environment to which one belongs: *The stage was my home from an early age.* **6** the place where a certain object is kept: *I must find a home for the new picture.* **7** the place of origin of something: *Welcome to Oxford, the home of pressed steel.* **8** an establishment providing residence and care, *esp* for children, the elderly, or those physically or mentally unfit to look after themselves. **9** the finishing point in a race. **10** in board games, etc, a place where one is safe from attack. **11** (**Home**) in computing, the beginning of the line or file one is in. ✳ **a home from home** a place other than one's own home where one is welcome or belongs. **at home** relaxed and comfortable: *Make yourself at home.* **close/near to home** said of a comment, etc: too accurate for comfort. ⋙ **homelike** *adj.* [Old English *hām* village, home]

home[2] *adv* **1** to or at the place where one lives: *I usually get home at six.* **2** to one's family or residence from somewhere else: *She's writing home.* **3** to one's ultimate objective, e.g. a finishing line: *Our horse romped home well ahead of the field.* **4** into place; into position: *Drive the nail home.* ✳ **bring home to somebody** to make somebody aware of (a fact or circumstance). **come home** in golf, to play the last nine holes. **come home to roost** said of past misdeeds: to rebound upon the perpetrator. **come home to one** said of a fact or circumstance: to enter one's awareness. **drive/hammer home**

to express (a point) forcibly, so as to convince one's hearers. **hit/strike home 1** said of somebody's words: to have the effect intended by the speaker. **2** said of the point or significance of a situation: to be truly understood. **home and hosed** *Aus, NZ* having reached one's objective. **home and dry** *chiefly Brit* having reached one's objective [from horse-racing, when the winner is so far ahead that it can be rubbed down before the other runners finish]. **home free** *NAmer* having reached one's objective. **nothing to write home about** *informal* of no special merit or interest.

home³ *adj* **1a** relating to one's home; domestic: *home comforts*. **b** done, used, etc in the home: *a home computer*. **2** denoting the headquarters or centre of operations: *the home base*. **3a** said of a team or player: belonging to the ground where a sporting fixture is held. **b** said of a match: played on a team's own ground. **4** relating to or belonging to one's own country; domestic: *the home market*.

home⁴ *verb intrans* said of a bird or animal: to return to its base by means of instinct. ➤ *verb trans* to provide (a domestic pet) with a home. ✱ **home in on 1** (*also* **home on to**) said of a missile: to find (its target) automatically by electronic programming, automatic navigational aids, etc. **2** to concentrate one's critical attention on (particular weaknesses in an opponent's argument, etc).

home-alone *adj chiefly NAmer, informal* **1** said of a child: left alone in the house while its parents are away from home. **2** relating to this situation: *home-alone parents*.

home banking *noun* the management of one's bank account from home, using a computer with a modem to access information at the bank and to pay in or withdraw funds electronically.

homebird *noun informal* a homebody.

homebody *noun* a person whose life centres round the home.

homebound¹ *adj* confined to the home; housebound: *homebound invalids*. [BOUND⁴]

homebound² *adj* on one's way home. [BOUND¹]

home boy *noun NAmer, SAfr, informal* a man from one's own neighbourhood or home town.

homebred *adj* **1** produced at home; indigenous: *hereditary transmission of homebred virtues* — Washington Irving. **2** unsophisticated or uneducated: *School-taught men and boys looked down on home-bred boys* — Henry Adams.

home brew *noun* an alcoholic drink, e.g. beer, made at home. ➤➤ **home-brewed** *adj*.

homecoming *noun* **1** a returning home. **2** *NAmer* an annual reunion of former students at a high school or college.

home economics *pl noun* (*treated as sing. or pl*) a school subject teaching the skills needed for running a household. ➤➤ **home economist** *noun*.

home farm *noun* a farm attached to and supplying produce to a large country house.

home fries *pl noun NAmer* fried sliced potatoes.

home front *noun* the sphere of civilian activity in war.

home girl *noun NAmer, SAfr, informal* a woman from one's own neighbourhood or home town.

homegrown *adj* produced in, coming from, or characteristic of the home country or region: *homegrown vegetables*; *homegrown footballers*.

Home Guard *noun* the volunteer citizen army recruited early in World War II to defend the UK against invasion.

home help *noun Brit* a person employed by a local authority to carry out certain household chores for the sick, elderly, or disabled.

home key *noun* **1** in music, the key in which a piece is basically composed. **2** in touch-typing, the key corresponding to a certain finger when the hands are in the starting or base position.

homeland *noun* **1** one's native land. **2** in S Africa, formerly, an area reserved for black people.

homeless¹ /'hohmlis/ *adj* said of a person: having no place to live. ➤➤ **homelessness** *noun*.

homeless² *pl noun* (**the homeless**) homeless people.

homely *adj* (**homelier, homeliest**) **1** commonplace; familiar: *She explained the problem in homely terms*. **2** said *esp* of a woman: having a warm, affectionate, kindly, and sympathetic personality. **3** simple; unpretentious: *plain homely furniture*. **4** *chiefly NAmer* not good-looking; plain. ➤➤ **homeliness** *noun*.

homemade *adj* **1** made in the home, on the premises, or by one's own efforts: *homemade cakes*. **2** made in crude or amateurish fashion.

homemaker *noun* the member of a household who takes the chief responsibility for its housekeeping. ➤➤ **homemaking** *noun*.

home movie *noun* an amateur film made with a video camera or a cinecamera.

homeo- *or* **homoeo-** *or* **homoio-** *comb. form* forming words, with the meaning: like; similar: *homeomorphism*. [Latin *homoeo-* from Greek *homoi-, homoio-*, from *homoios* similar, from *homos* same]

homeobox *or* **homoeobox** /,homi·ə'boks, ,hoh-/ *noun* a sequence of nucleotides (chemical compounds forming the structural units of RNA and DNA; see NUCLEOTIDE) present in homeotic genes (those regulating structural development; see HOMEOTIC GENE) in a wide range of organisms, e.g. fruit flies and humans.

Home Office *noun* the government office concerned with internal affairs.

homeomorphism *or* **homoeomorphism** /,homi-ə'mawfiz(ə)m, ,hoh-/ *noun* a near-similarity of crystalline forms between different chemical compounds.

homeopath *or* **homoeopath** /'homi·apath/ *noun* somebody who practises homeopathy.

homeopathy *or* **homoeopathy** /homi-'opathi/ *noun* a system of complementary medicine in which diseases are treated by administering minute doses of substances that produce symptoms like those of the disease. ➤➤ **homeopathic** /-'pathik/ *adj*, **homeopathically** /-'pathikli/ *adv*, **homeopathist** /-'opəthist/ *noun*. [HOMEO- + -PATH, coined first in German as *Homöopath*]

homeosis *or* **homoeosis** /homi'ohsis, hoh-/ *noun* (*pl* **homeoses** *or* **homoeoses** /-seez/) in a segmented insect or other segmented animal, the replacement of part of one segment by a part characteristic of a different segment, by a process of mutation. ➤➤ **homeotic** /-'otik/ *adj*.

homeostasis *or* **homoeostasis** /,homioh'staysis, ,hoh-/ *noun* the physiological maintenance of relatively constant conditions, e.g. constant internal temperature, within the body in the face of changing external conditions. ➤➤ **homeostatic** /-'statik/ *adj*, **homeostatically** /-'statikli/ *adv*.

homeotherm *or* **homoiotherm** /'homi·əthuhm, hohmi-/ *noun* an organism that maintains its body temperature approximately constant despite changes in external temperature; a warm-blooded organism. ➤➤ **homeothermal** /-'thuhm(ə)l/ *adj*, **homeothermic** *adj*, **homeothermy** *noun*.

homeotic gene *or* **homoeotic gene** /homi'otik, hohmi-/ *noun* a gene that is responsible for regulating the structural development of an organism, such that a mutation within that gene causes radical alterations in appearance.

homeowner *noun* a person who owns the house in which they live.

home page *noun* on the World Wide Web, a first page of information designed to introduce an individual or a concern and to advertise their product, services, interests, etc.

home plate *noun* in baseball, a rubber slab at which a batter stands.

homer *noun* = HOMING PIGEON.

Homeric /hoh'merik/ *adj* **1** relating to or characteristic of Homer, his age, or his writings. **2** of epic proportions; heroic: *a Homeric feat of endurance*. [Greek *Homērikos*, from *Homēros* Homer, ninth- or eighth-cent. BC author of the *Iliad* and the *Odyssey*]

home room *noun NAmer* the room in a school assigned to a particular class or set of students as their base for administrative purposes, presided over by their particular teacher.

home rule *noun* limited self-government by the people of a dependent political unit: compare SELF-GOVERNMENT.

Editorial note
Home Rule was the name given in the late 19th cent. to Gladstone's proposals to grant Ireland its own parliament within the United Kingdom. Twice defeated at Westminster, Home Rule was brought forward a third time in 1912–14 but thwarted by the outbreak of the First World War. Today similar measures for Scotland and Wales are known as devolution — Professor Peter Clarke.

home run *noun* in baseball, a hit that enables the batter to make a complete circuit of the bases and score a run.

Home Secretary *noun* a government minister for internal affairs.

homesick *adj* longing for home and family while absent from them. ➤➤ **homesickness** *noun*. [earliest as *homesickness*]

home signal *noun* a railway signal that controls the movement of trains into a section of track.

homespun[1] *adj* **1** made of HOMESPUN[2] or from cloth spun or woven at home: *clad in sombre homespun garments* — Conan Doyle. **2** lacking sophistication; simple: *There is not that in Eustacia Vye which will make a good homespun wife* — Hardy.

homespun[2] *noun* a loosely woven woollen or linen fabric orig made from yarn spun at home: *lean brown guides in baggy homespun* — Henry James.

homestead *noun* **1** a house and adjoining land occupied by a family. **2** in N America, an area of land formerly granted to a settler. **3** *Aus, NZ* the owner's living quarters on a sheep or cattle station. ➤➤ **homesteader** *noun*, **homesteading** *noun*.

homestead law *noun* any of several US or Canadian legislative acts authorizing the sale of public lands to settlers.

home straight *noun* (**the home straight**) straight final part of a racecourse, usu opposite the grandstand.

home stretch *noun* **1** (**the home stretch**) *chiefly NAmer* = HOME STRAIGHT. **2** (**the home stretch**) the final triumphant stage of a project, etc.

homestyle *adj NAmer* said *esp* of food: prepared and served in a simple unsophisticated way.

home truth *noun* (*also in pl*) an unpleasant but true fact that somebody undertakes to tell one about one's character or situation: *He had quarrelled with all his friends … He developed a talent for telling them home truths* — Somerset Maugham.

home unit *noun Aus, NZ* a self-contained owner-occupied flat or unit of accommodation that is one of several within a building.

home video *noun* **1** commercial videotapes for viewing at home. **2** an amateur film made with a video camera.

homeward /ˈhohmwəd/ *adj* heading towards home: *the homeward march*.

homewards (*NAmer* **homeward**) *adv* towards home: *heading homewards*. ➤➤ **homeward-bound** *adj*.

homework *noun* **1** school work that a pupil is given to do at home. **2** work done in one's own home for pay. **3** preparatory reading or research, e.g. for a discussion: *She's done her homework on the subject.*

homeworker *noun* a person who earns their living taking in work to complete at home.

homey[1] *adj* see HOMY.

homey[2] *noun NAmer* = HOME BOY, HOME GIRL.

homicide /ˈhomisied/ *noun* **1** the illegal killing of one person by another; murder. **2** a person who kills another illegally; a murderer. ➤➤ **homicidal** /-ˈsiedl/ *adj*. [Middle English via French from Latin *homicida* murderer, and *homicidium* murder, from *homin-, homo* man and *-cida, -cidium*: see -CIDE]

homie /ˈhohmi/ *noun NAmer* = HOME BOY, HOME GIRL.

homiletics *pl noun* (*treated as sing. or pl*) the art of writing sermons and preaching.

homily /ˈhomili/ *noun* (*pl* **homilies**) **1** a sermon intended for spiritual guidance: *If need were, he could preach a homily on the fragility of life* — Charles Lamb. **2** a talking-to on moral conduct. ➤➤ **homilist** *noun*. [Middle English *omelie* via French and ecclesiastical Latin from Greek *homilia* conversation, discourse, from *homilein* to consort with, address, from *homilos* crowd, assembly]

homing *adj* **1a** denoting a bird, etc that can find its way home after travelling long distances. **b** relating to this ability: *the homing instinct*. **2** denoting, or relating to, a missile that is capable of locating its target electronically.

homing pigeon *noun* a domesticated pigeon bred for its homing instinct, often used as a racer.

hominid /ˈhominid/ *noun* any of a family of two-legged primate mammals comprising humans and their extinct immediate ancestors: family Hominidae. ➤➤ **hominid** *adj*. [Latin *Hominidae* (pl) from *homin-, homo* man]

hominoid[1] /ˈhominoyd/ *adj* **1** resembling or related to man. **2** relating to or belonging to the primates, comprising humans and the anthropoid apes: superfamily Hominoidea.

hominoid[2] *noun* a hominoid mammal.

hominy /ˈhomini/ *noun* crushed or coarsely ground husked maize, *esp* when boiled with water or milk to make GRITS. [prob from Algonquian *uskatahomen*, perhaps meaning 'that which is ground']

hominy grits *pl noun NAmer* = GRITS (2).

Homo /ˈhohmoh/ *noun* a genus of primate mammals including recent man, *Homo sapiens*, and various extinct ancestors. [Latin *homo* man]

homo *noun* (*pl* **homos**) *informal, chiefly derog* a homosexual.

homo- *comb. form* see HOM-.

homocentric[1] /hohoh'sentrik, hoh-/ *adj* = ANTHROPOCENTRIC. [from Latin *homo* man + -CENTRIC]

homocentric[2] *adj* having the same centre; concentric: *homocentric spheres*. [HOMO- + -CENTRIC]

homocercal /homə'suhkl, hoh-/ *adj* **1** said of the tail fin of a fish: having the upper and lower lobes approximately symmetrical and the spinal column ending at or near the middle of the base: compare HETEROCERCAL. **2** relating to or having a homocercal tail fin. [HOMO- + Greek *kerkos* tail]

homocyclic /homə'sieklik, hoh-/ *adj* said of a chemical compound: having a closed ring of atoms of the same chemical element, e.g. carbon.

homocysteine /ˌhomə'sisti·een, hoh-, -'sistayn/ *noun* an organic amino acid occurring in the body as an INTERMEDIATE[2] (compound formed by one reaction and involved in another) in the metabolism of methionine and cysteine.

homoeo- *comb. form* see HOMEO-.

homoeobox *noun* see HOMEOBOX.

homoeomorphism *noun* see HOMEOMORPHISM.

homoeopath *noun* see HOMEOPATH.

homoeopathy *noun* see HOMEOPATHY.

homoeosis *noun* see HOMEOSIS.

homoeostasis *noun* see HOMEOSTASIS.

homoeotic gene *noun* see HOMEOTIC GENE.

homoerotic /ˌhohoh·ə'rotik, ˌhoh-/ *adj* relating to or denoting sexual desire aroused by or centred on a person of one's own sex. ➤➤ **homoeroticism** /-siz(ə)m/ *noun*.

homogametic /ˌhoməgə'metik, ˌhoh-/ *adj* denoting the sex that has two similar sex chromosomes, as the human female sex (with two X-chromosomes) does, and as the male sex does in birds. [HOMO- + *gametic*: see GAMETE]

homogamy /hə'mogəmi/ *noun* **1a** uniformity of sex in all the flowers of an inflorescence: compare HETEROGAMY (3). **b** the maturing of the stamens and ovaries of a flower at the same time so that self-pollination can take place. **2a** reproduction within an isolated group that results in the preservation of qualities which distinguish that group from a larger one of which it is a part. **b** the mating of like with like; inbreeding. **c** marriage between people who come from similar backgrounds: compare HETEROGAMY (4). ➤➤ **homogamic** /homə'gamik/ *adj*, **homogamous** /-məs/ *adj*.

homogenate /hə'mojinayt/ *noun* a product of homogenizing.

homogeneity /ˌhomojə'nee·ti, -'nayiti/ *noun* the quality or state of being homogeneous.

homogeneous /homə'jeeni·əs/ *adj* **1** of the same or a similar kind or nature. **2** of uniform structure or composition throughout: *a culturally homogeneous neighbourhood.* **3** said of an equation, fraction, etc: having each term of the same degree when all variables are taken into account, as in $x^2 + xy + y^2 = 0$. ➤➤ **homogeneously** *adv*, **homogeneousness** *noun*. [via late Latin from Greek *homogenēs* of the same kind, from HOMO- + *genos* race, kind]

homogenize *or* **homogenise** /hə'mojəniez/ *verb trans* **1a** to reduce the particles of (a substance) so that they are uniformly small and evenly distributed. **b** to break up the fat globules of (milk) into fine particles, so that the cream does not rise. **2** to render (something) uniform throughout, or make (different things) similar: *The two societies and cultures are utterly different. It is to noone's advantage that they should be homogenised* — The Scotsman. ➤➤ *verb intrans* to become homogenized. ➤➤ **homogenization** /-'zaysh(ə)n/ *noun*, **homogenized** *adj*, **homogenizer** *noun*.

homogeny /həˈmojəni/ *noun* correspondence between parts or organs due to descent from the same ancestral type. ⟫ **homogenous** *adj*.

homograft /ˈhohməgrahft, ˈhom-/ *noun* a graft of tissue taken from a donor of the same species as the recipient.

homograph /ˈhoməgrahf, -graf/ *noun* any of two or more words spelt alike but different in meaning, derivation, or pronunciation, e.g. the noun *conduct* and the verb *conduct*. ⟫ **homographic** /-ˈgrafik/ *adj*.

homoio- *comb. form* see HOMEO-.

homoiotherm /ˈhomoy-əhthuhm/ *noun* see HOMEOTHERM.

homoiousian /homoyˈoohzi·ən/ *noun* in the history of Christian belief, an adherent of the doctrine that God the Father and God the Son are of similar but not identical substance: compare HOMOOUSIAN. ⟫ **homoiousian** *adj*. [Greek *homoios* similar + *ousia* essence, substance]

homolog /ˈhoməlog/ *noun NAmer* see HOMOLOGUE.

homologate /hoˈmoləgayt/ *verb trans* 1 to sanction, allow, or approve (something) *esp* officially: *Saint Paul homologates this doctrine* — Bishop John Maxwell. 2 to approve (an engine or vehicle) for sale or for a certain class of racing. ⟫ **homologation** /-ˈgaysh(ə)n/ *noun*. [late Latin *homologatus*, past part. of *homologare* to agree, from Greek *homologein*, from *homologos*: see HOMOLOGOUS]

homologous /hoˈmoləgəs/ *adj* 1 said of geometrical figures or their parts: having the same relative position, value, or structure. 2 said of organs: exhibiting biological homology. 3 said of chromosomes: joining together with each other in pairs at meiotic cell division and having the same or corresponding sequence of genetic loci. 4 said of chemical compounds: belonging to or consisting of a chemical series, e.g. the alkanes, whose members exhibit homology. 5 said of a tissue graft: derived from an organism of the same species. ⟫ **homologize** /-jiez/ *verb*. [Greek *homologos* agreeing, from HOMO- + *legein* to say]

homologue (*NAmer* **homolog**) /ˈhoməlog/ *noun* a homologous organ, chromosome, element, chemical compound, or geometrical figure: compare ANALOGUE[1]: *The vesicula prostatica, which has been observed in many male mammals, is now universally acknowledged to be the homologue of the female uterus* — Darwin.

homology /hoˈmoləji/ *noun* (*pl* **homologies**) 1 correspondence in structure and embryological origin but not necessarily in function: compare ANALOGY: **a** between different parts of the same individual. **b** between parts of different organisms due to evolutionary differentiation from a common ancestor. 2 the relation existing: **a** between chemical compounds in a series whose successive members have a regular difference in composition. **b** between elements in the same group of the periodic table. 3 *formal or literary* a similarity often attributable to common origin: *the plain law of homology, which declares that like must be compared with like* — Oliver Wendell Holmes. ⟫ **homologic** /-ˈlojik/ *adj*, **homological** /-ˈlojik/ *adj*, **homologically** /-ˈlojikli/ *adv*.

homolosine projection /hoˈmoləsien/ *noun* a map projection of the world that distorts the oceans, the more accurately to represent the continents. [Greek *homologos* (see HOMOLOGOUS) + SINE]

homomorphy /ˈhoməmawfi/ *noun* similarity of biological form, sometimes with different fundamental structure or origin. ⟫ **homomorphic** /-ˈmawfik/ *adj*, **homomorphism** *noun*.

homonym /ˈhomənim/ *noun* 1 any of two or more words that have the same spelling and pronunciation but different meanings and origins, as with the noun and the verb *bear*. 2 in taxonomy, a species or genus name that has been used for two or more different organisms. ⟫ **homonymic** /-ˈnimik/ *adj*, **homonymous** /hoˈmoniməs/ *adj*, **homonymously** /hoˈmoniməsli/ *adv*, **homonymy** /hoˈmonimi/ *noun*. [via Latin from Greek *homōnymon*, neuter of *homōnymos* having the same name, from HOM- + *onyma, onoma* name]

homoousian /ˈhomoh·oohziən, hoh-/ *or* **homousian** /hoˈmoohzi·ən, hoh-/ *noun* in the history of Christian belief, an adherent of the doctrine that God the Father and God the Son are identical in substance: compare HOMOIOUSIAN. ⟫ **homoousian** *adj*. [Greek *homos* same + *ousia* essence, substance]

homophobia /homəˈfohbi·ə, hoh-/ *noun* intense and unreasoning hatred of homosexuality and homosexuals. ⟫ **homophobe** /ˈhoməfohb, ˈhoh-/ *noun*, **homophobic** *adj*.

homophone /ˈhoməfohn/ *noun* 1 any of two or more words pronounced alike but different in meaning, derivation, or spelling, e.g.

to, too, and *two*. 2 any of two or more characters or groups pronounced the same, e.g. *ph* and *f*. ⟫ **homophonous** /hoˈmofənəs/ *adj*.

homophonic /homəˈfonik/ *adj* relating to or denoting music in which the parts move rhythmically in step with one another. ⟫ **homophonically** *adv*, **homophony** /hoˈmofəni/ *noun*.

homopolar /homohˈpohlə, hoh-/ *adj* denoting a chemical bond in which there is an equal distribution of electric charge between atoms; = COVALENT (denoting a chemical bond formed by shared electrons).

homopterous /hohˈmoptərəs/ *adj* denoting a large suborder of true bugs that have wings of a uniform texture and sucking mouthparts, including the aphids and cicadas. ⟫ **homopteran** *noun and adj*. [HOMO- + Greek *pteron* wing]

homorganic /homawˈganik/ *adj* said of sets of consonantal sounds such as *k*, *g*, and *ng*: articulated using the same part of the vocal tract.

Homo sapiens /ˌhohmoh ˈsapi·enz, ˌhomoh/ *noun* the species of primate that comprises human beings, the only extant species of the genus *Homo*. [Latin *homo sapiens*, literally 'wise man']

homosexual /homəˈseksyoo(ə)l, -ˈseksh(ə)l, hoh-/ *noun* a person who has a sexual preference for members of their own sex: compare HETEROSEXUAL[1]. ⟫ **homosexual** *adj*, **homosexuality** *noun*, **homosexually** *adv*.

homosocial /homəˈsohsh(ə)l, hoh-/ *adj* relating to interaction between members of the same sex, *esp* between men.

homotransplant /homohˈtransplahnt, hoh-/ *noun* = HOMOGRAFT (tissue transplant between individuals of the same species). ⟫ **homotransplantation** /-ˈtaysh(ə)n/ *noun*.

homousian /hoˈmoohzi·ən/ *noun* see HOMOOUSIAN.

homozygote /homohˈziegoht, homoh-/ *noun* an animal, plant, or cell having identical alleles (forms of a gene; see ALLELE) of a particular gene and so breeding true for that character: compare HETEROZYGOTE. ⟫ **homozygosis** /-ˈgohsis/ *noun*, **homozygosity** /-ˈgositi/ *noun*, **homozygous** /-ˈziegəs/ *adj*.

homunculus /həˈmungkyoolas/ *noun* (*pl* **homunculi** /-lie/) a little man; a manikin or dwarf. [Latin *homunculus*, dimin. of *homin-, homo* man]

homy *or* **homey** /ˈhohmi/ *adj* (**homier, homiest**) *informal* 1 cosy, comfortable, and homelike. 2 unpretentious or unsophisticated.

Hon. *abbr* used as a title: Honourable.

hon /hun/ *noun chiefly NAmer, informal* used as a form of address: short for HONEY.

hon. *abbr* 1 honorary. 2 honour. 3 honourable.

honcho /ˈhonchoh/ *noun* (*pl* **honchos**) *chiefly NAmer, informal* an important man; a boss. [Japanese *hanchō*, from *han* squad + *chō* chief]

Honduran /honˈdyooərən/ *noun* a native or inhabitant of Honduras, a country in central America. ⟫ **Honduran** *adj*.

hone[1] /hohn/ *verb trans* 1 to sharpen (a blade, tool, etc) with a whetstone. 2 (*usu in passive*). **a** to make (something) keener or give (it) a sharper focus: *wit honed to a sharp edge*. **b** to shape (something) as if by whittling: *finely honed phrases*. **c** (*also* + down) to reduce as though by whittling: *costs honed to the bone*.

hone[2] *noun* a whetstone, *esp* a fine one for sharpening razors. [Old English *hān* stone]

honest /ˈonist/ *adj* 1 free of deceit: *You haven't been quite honest with me*. 2 frank; sincere; truthful: *an honest opinion*. 3 trustworthy; of dependable integrity: *an honest trader*. 4 worthy; wholehearted: *making an honest effort*. 5 earned fairly, through hard work: *earning an honest living*. 6 morally right: *Do the honest thing and return it*. 7 *archaic* said of a woman: chaste: *Those that she [Fortune] makes fair she scarce makes honest; and those she makes honest she makes very ill-favouredly* — Shakespeare. ✳ **earn/turn an honest penny** to earn an honest living. **honest to God** *informal* truly; honestly: *I tried not to forget. Honest to God I did, George* — John Steinbeck. **make an honest woman of** *dated or humorous* to save the reputation of (a woman, *esp* an unmarried pregnant woman) by marrying her. **to be honest** used to introduce a candid statement, admission, etc: *To be honest, I was bored stiff*. [Middle English via Old French from Latin *honestus* honourable, from *honor* HONOUR[1]]

honest broker *noun* a neutral mediator.

honestly *adv* **1** with honesty or integrity. **2** used for emphasis in averring something: frankly: *Honestly, I don't know why I bother.*

honest-to-God *adj informal* real, genuine, or authentic.

honest-to-goodness *adj* simple, ordinary, or straightforward.

honesty *noun* **1a** upright and straightforward conduct; integrity. **b** sincerity; truthfulness. **2** a European plant of the mustard family with large broad smooth translucent seed pods: genus *Lunaria*.

honewort *noun* either of two species of a plant of the parsley family, the American and Asian *Cryptotaenia canadensis* and the European *Trinia glauca*, once thought effective against swellings. [obsolete *hone* swelling + WORT¹]

honey /'huni/ *noun* **1a** a sweet viscous sticky pale golden liquid formed from the nectar of flowers in the HONEY SAC of various bees. **b** this in processed form, whether liquid or solid, used as a food. **c** a sweet liquid resembling honey that is collected or produced by various insects. **2** something sweet or agreeable; sweetness: *and I ... that suck'd the honey of his music vows* — Shakespeare. **3** chiefly *NAmer* used in affectionate address: sweetheart; dear. **4** *informal* a superlative example: *a honey of a girl* — Philip Roth. [Old English *hunig*]

honey ant *noun* any of several genera of ants that supply their fellows with nectar and honeydew that they have stored in their abdomen and regurgitated: genus *Myrmecocystus* and other genera.

honey badger *noun* = RATEL.

honeybee *noun* any of several species of honey-producing bees that live in more or less organized communities, *esp Apis mellifera*, a European bee kept for its honey and wax: genus *Apis*.

honey bird *noun* any of three species of African birds of the HONEY GUIDE family: genus *Prodotiscus*.

honey bucket *noun NAmer, informal* a waterless non-flushing outdoor toilet that must be emptied manually.

honeybun *noun* (*also* **honeybunch**) *NAmer, informal* used as a form of address: sweetheart; darling.

honey buzzard *noun* any of several species of a Eurasian and African hawk that feeds on the larvae of wasps and bees: *Pernis apivorus* and other species.

honeycomb¹ *noun* **1** a mass of six-sided wax cells built by honeybees in their nest to contain their brood and stores of honey. **2** any cellular structure resembling this, or one riddled with cavities: *The whole rock was a honeycomb of sepulchres* — H Rider Haggard. **3** the second stomach of a cow or other ruminant mammal, or tripe prepared from it.

honeycomb² *verb trans* (*usu in passive*) **1** to cause (a structure) to be chequered or full of cavities like a honeycomb. **2** to burrow or penetrate into every part of (a structure) or riddle it with holes: *The government is honeycombed with spies* — T H White.

honeycreeper *noun* **1** either of several species of tropical American TANAGER (type of songbird) that have long curved beaks and feed on nectar and insects: genera *Chlorophanes* and *Cyanerpes*. **2** any of several species of Hawaiian songbirds: family Drepanididae.

honeydew *noun* a sweet deposit secreted on the leaves of plants usu by aphids.

honeydew melon *noun* a pale smooth-skinned MUSKMELON with pale greenish sweet flesh.

honey-eater *noun* any of several species of songbirds with a long tongue for extracting nectar and small insects from flowers: family Meliphagidae.

honeyed *or* **honied** *adj literary* said of words or tone: sweet and agreeable or soft and soothing.

honey fungus *noun* a honey-coloured fungus that grows round the base of trees, *esp* decaying ones, and is lethal to most plant life: *Armillaria mellea*. Also called BOOTLACE FUNGUS, HONEY MUSHROOM.

honey guide *noun* any of several species of small plainly coloured birds that inhabit Africa, the Himalayas, and the E Indies, and feed on beeswax and bee grubs: family Indicatoridae.

honey locust *noun* a tall spiny N American tree with very hard durable wood and long flattened pods containing a sweet edible pulp and seeds that resemble beans: *Gleditsia triacanthos*.

honeymoon¹ *noun* **1** the period immediately following marriage, *esp* when taken as a holiday by the married couple. **2** a period of unusual harmony following the establishment of a new relationship, e.g. that of a new government with the public.

Word history

HONEY + MOON¹. Orig with reference to its phases, the *honey moon* being the full moon of intense married bliss; later *moon* was understood in its other sense 'month', Dr Johnson's definition being: 'the first month after marriage, when there is nothing but tenderness and pleasure'.

honeymoon² *verb intrans* said of a newly married couple: to have a honeymoon: *They are honeymooning in Paris.* ⋙ **honeymooner** *noun.*

honey mushroom *noun* = HONEY FUNGUS.

honey parrot *noun Aus* = LORIKEET.

honey possum *noun* a small marsupial of SW Australia, with a long snout and prehensile tail, which feeds on pollen and nectar: *Tarsipes rostratus.*

honeypot *noun* **1** a jar of or for honey. **2** a place of rich tourist attractions that draws visitors in large numbers, or one of financial possibilities that draws investors, etc.

honey sac *noun* a distension of the oesophagus of a bee in which honey is produced.

honeysuckle *noun* any of numerous species of climbing shrubs usu with showy yellow and pink sweet-smelling flowers rich in nectar: genus *Lonicera*. [Old English *hunisūce*, from *hunig* HONEY + *sūcan* to SUCK¹]

honeytrap *noun informal* a stratagem for luring somebody to a compromising sexual assignation, *esp* with a view to blackmailing them.

honeywort *noun* a Mediterranean plant with tubular purple or yellow flowers that contain nectar: *Cerinthe major* and other species.

hongi /'hong-i/ *noun NZ* amongst the Maoris, the action of pressing noses together as a form of greeting. [Maori *hongi*]

honied /'hunid/ *adj* see HONEYED.

Honiton lace /'honit(ə)n, 'hun-/ *noun* lace made by hand-sewing floral sprigs onto fine net, or by linking them up with lace work. [named after *Honiton*, the Devon town where the lace was first made]

honk¹ /hongk/ *verb trans* said of a driver: to sound (one's horn). ⋗ *verb intrans* **1** to make the characteristic cry of a goose. **2** said of a driver or vehicle: to give a honk. **3** *Brit, informal* to vomit. ⋙ **honker** *noun.* [imitative]

honk² *noun* a honking sound.

honkie *or* **honky** /'hongki/ *noun* (*pl* **honkies**) *chiefly NAmer, derog* used by Blacks: a white man. [origin unknown]

honky-tonk /'hongki tongk/ *noun* **1** a form of ragtime piano playing. **2** *chiefly NAmer, informal* a cheap nightclub or dance hall. ⋙ **honky-tonk** *adj.* [origin unknown]

honnête homme /,onet 'om/ *noun literary* a cultivated civilized decent man; a gentleman. [French *honnête homme* honest man]

honor¹ /'onə/ *noun NAmer* see HONOUR¹.

honor² *verb trans NAmer* see HONOUR².

honorable *adj NAmer* see HONOURABLE.

honorand /'onərand/ *noun* a person being honoured or recognized in some ceremonial way, *esp* somebody receiving an honorary degree. [Latin *honorandus* to be honoured, from *honorare* to honour, from *honor* HONOUR¹]

honorarium /onə'reəri-əm/ *noun* (*pl* **honorariums** *or* **honoraria** /-ri-ə/) a payment in recognition of professional services that are nominally given free. [Latin *honorarium* a gift made on being admitted to public office, neuter of *honorarius*: see HONORARY]

honorary /'on(ə)rəri/ *adj* **1a** said of a degree, doctorate, etc: conferred in recognition of achievement, without the usual obligations. **b** awarded a degree in this manner: *an honorary doctor of laws.* **2** said of an office-bearer: unpaid or voluntary: *an honorary chairman.* **3** depending on honour for fulfilment: *an honorary obligation.* ⋙ **honorarily** *adv.* [Latin *honorarius* conferring honour, honorary, from *honor* HONOUR¹]

honorific¹ /onə'rifik/ *adj* **1** conferring or conveying honour: *honorific titles.* **2** belonging to or constituting a class of grammatical forms, e.g. in Chinese and Japanese, used in speaking to or about a social superior. ⋙ **honorifically** *adv.*

honorific² *noun* **1** an honorific expression. **2** a respectful title or form of address, such as *Your/His Excellence.*

honoris causa /ˌɒnawris ˈkowzə/ *adv* used *esp* in relation to the awarding of an honorary degree: as a mark of honour. [Latin *honoris causa* for the sake of honour]

honour[1] (*NAmer* **honor**) /ˈɒnə/ *noun* 1 one's good name or reputation: *My honour was at stake.* 2 *dated* chastity or purity, *esp* that of a woman: *Thou didst seek to violate the honour of my child* — Shakespeare. 3 one's sense of morality and justice: *men of honour.* 4 a privilege: *since I last had the honour of welcoming you to our establishment.* 5 public recognition or fame: *The football team brought honour to the school.* 6 a person who brings credit or recognition: *an honour to her profession.* 7 an award or distinction conferred for achievement or excellence: *the Queen's Birthday honours.* 8 (*in pl*) the highest academic standard in a degree course or examination: *She passed with first-class honours.* 9 (*in pl*) ceremonial rites performed in official respect or recognition: *He was buried with full military honours.* 10a in whist, an ace, king, queen, or jack of the trump suit. b (*in pl*) in bridge, these cards and the ten, or the four aces when there are no trumps. 11 in golf, the privilege of playing first from the tee in golf awarded to the player who won the previous hole. 12 (**Your/His Honour**) used as a title of respectful address or reference to a holder of high office, *esp* a judge in court. ✳ **do the honours** *informal or humorous* to perform a social duty, *esp* to serve guests with food or drink. **honours of war** privileges conceded to a defeated force by the victors, *specif* that of marching out fully armed with all colours flying. **in honour bound** (*also* **honour bound**) morally obliged to do or not do something; on one's honour. **in honour of** as a mark of respect for (a person or occasion): *a dinner held in her honour.* **on one's honour 1** morally obliged to do or not do something; in honour bound: *We were on our honour not to reveal her whereabouts.* 2 used to emphasize one's sincerity: *I promise on my honour not to tell.* [Middle English via Old French from Latin *honor*]

honour[2] (*NAmer* **honor**) *verb trans* 1 to regard (somebody or something) with deep respect. 2 *archaic* to treat (one's wife, husband, parents, etc) with respect: *Honour thy father and thy mother* — Bible. 3 to confer honour on (an event or the people holding it) by being present: *if you would honour us with your presence.* 4 (*in passive*) to be conscious of an honour done to one: *I would be honoured to be invited.* 5 to confer a distinction such as an honorary degree on (somebody): *She was honoured with a doctorate by her own university.* 6 to fulfil the terms of (an agreement) or follow up (a commitment). 7 to recognize and respect (an arrangement), or accept (it) as right or appropriate: *The lorry-drivers were honouring the picket line.* 8 to accept and make payment in respect of (a bill, debt, cheque, etc). 9 to salute (one's partner) with a bow in a country dance.

honourable (*NAmer* **honorable**) *adj* 1 characterized by a sense of honour: *For Brutus is an honourable man; so are they all, all honourable men* — Shakespeare. 2 worthy of respect: *an honourable contribution.* 3 noble; illustrious: *of honourable descent.* 4 (*often* **Honourable**) used as a title for the children of certain British noblemen and for various government officials, and as a respectful epithet for fellow Members of Parliament: *the honourable Member for Maidstone.* 5 consistent with an untarnished reputation: *an honourable discharge from the army.* 6 *dated or humorous* said of the intentions of a suitor: involving marriage.

honourable mention *noun* a distinction awarded, e.g. in a contest or exhibition, for work of exceptional merit that has not obtained a prize.

honour point *noun* the centre point of the upper half of a heraldic shield.

honours list *noun* a list produced twice yearly of people who are to be honoured by the British sovereign in recognition of their public service.

honour system *noun* the system of relying on honesty as the only form of control available, e.g. where services or goods are to be paid for, or examinations to be sat, without supervision.

Hons *abbr Brit* honours.

Hon. Sec. *abbr Brit* Honorary Secretary.

hooch *or* **hootch** /hoohch/ *noun NAmer, informal* spirits, *esp* inferior or illicitly made or obtained. [short for *hoochinoo*, spirits made by the Hoochinoo Indians of Alaska]

hood[1] /hood/ *noun* 1 a loose, *esp* protective, covering for the top and back of the head and neck that is usu attached to the neckline of a garment. 2 a usu leather covering for a hawk's head and eyes. 3 an ornamental scarf worn over an academic gown that indicates by its colour or border the wearer's university and degree. 4 a

hoodlike marking, crest, or expansion on the head of an animal, e.g. a cobra or seal. 5 a folding waterproof top cover for an open car, pram, etc. 6 a cover or canopy, e.g. over a cooker, for carrying off fumes, smoke, etc. 7 *NAmer* = BONNET (3). ➤➤ **hoodless** *adj*, **hoodlike** *adj*. [Old English *hōd*]

hood[2] *verb trans* to cover or protect (somebody or something) with or as if with a hood; *specif* to drop one's eyelids halfway over (one's eyes).

hood[3] *noun NAmer, informal* a hoodlum or gangster. [short for HOODLUM]

-hood *suffix* forming nouns from nouns or adjectives, denoting: 1 the state or condition of (a certain class of person): *priesthood*; *manhood.* 2 a state (of a certain character): *likelihood.* 3 the time or period of (a certain stage in life): *childhood.* 4 an instance of something (or a specified quality or condition): *a falsehood.* 5 (*treated as sing. or pl*) a body or class of people sharing (a specified character or state): *brotherhood*; *priesthood.* [Old English *-hād*]

hooded *adj* 1 covered by, or as if by, a hood: *a hooded figure; hooded eyes.* 2 said of a plant: shaped like a hood. 3 said of a bird or animal: having a part, or contrasting coloration, on the head suggestive of a hood.

hooded crow *noun* a black and grey Eurasian crow closely related to the carrion crow: *Corvus corone cornix.*

hooded seal *noun* a large seal of the N Atlantic, the male having a large sac on its head that inflates during display: *Cystophora cristata.*

hoodie /ˈhoodi/ *noun chiefly Scot* = HOODED CROW.

hoodie crow *noun chiefly Scot* = HOODED CROW.

hoodlum /ˈhoohdləm/ *noun* 1 a thug. 2 a young rowdy. ➤➤ **hoodlumish** *adj*. [origin unknown]

hoodman-blind *noun archaic* blind man's buff: *What devil was't that thus hath cozen'd you at hoodman-blind?* — Shakespeare.

hood mould *noun* = HOOD MOULDING.

hood moulding *noun* a stone projection to throw off rainwater over a door or window.

hoodoo[1] /ˈhoohdooh/ *noun* (*pl* **hoodoos**) 1 voodoo. 2 a malign influence that haunts one, *esp* that prevents one achieving winning form in a sport. 3 *NAmer* a pillar of rock, *esp* of a weird shape. ➤➤ **hoodooism** *noun*. [variant of VOODOO[1]]

hoodoo[2] *verb trans* (**hoodoos, hoodooed, hoodooing**) *chiefly NAmer* to cast an evil spell on (somebody) or bring (them) bad luck.

hoodwink *verb trans chiefly informal* to deceive or delude (somebody). ➤➤ **hoodwinker** *noun*. [HOOD[1] + WINK[1] in the sense 'to close the eyes']

hooey /ˈhooh·i/ *noun informal* nonsense. [origin unknown]

hoof[1] /hoohf, hoof/ *noun* (*pl* **hooves** /hoohvz/ *or* **hoofs**) 1 a curved horny casing that protects the ends of the digits of a horse, cow, or similar mammal and that corresponds to a nail or claw. 2 the whole foot of such a mammal. ✳ **on the hoof 1** said in reference to a meat animal before being butchered: while still alive: *50p a pound on the hoof.* 2 *informal* while moving around and doing other things. 3 *informal* quickly or extempore; without much thought. ➤➤ **hoofed** *adj*. [Old English *hōf*]

hoof[2] *verb trans informal* to kick (a ball, etc). ✳ **hoof it 1** *informal* to go somewhere on foot. 2 *informal* to dance.

hoofbeat *noun* the sound of a hoof striking a hard surface.

hoofed *adj* (*usu used in combinations*) having hoofs, *esp* of the type or number specified: *cloven-hoofed.*

hoofer *noun NAmer, informal* a professional dancer.

hoo-ha /ˈhooh hah/ *noun chiefly informal* a fuss; a to-do. [prob imitative]

hook[1] /hook/ *noun* 1 a curved or bent metal or plastic device for hanging things on, attaching things to, or gripping. 2 a bent and barbed metal device for catching fish. 3 part of a presentation, e.g. a television documentary, that serves to gain the attention and interest of the audience. 4 a repeated melodic phrase in a popular musical composition. 5 a sickle. 6a in golf, the flight of a ball that deviates from a straight course in a direction opposite to the dominant hand of the player propelling it: compare SLICE[1]. b in cricket, an attacking stroke played with a horizontal bat aimed at a ball of higher than waist height and intended to send the ball on the leg side. 7 in boxing, a short blow delivered with a circular motion while the elbow remains bent and rigid. ✳ **by hook or by crook**

by any possible means [prob from a feudal custom by which tenants were entitled to as much firewood as they could cut with a billhook or pull down with a shepherd's crook]. **get one's hooks into** *informal* to grab or get hold of (somebody or something). **get the hook** *NAmer, informal* to be sacked. **give somebody the hook** *NAmer, informal* to sack somebody. **hook, line, and sinker** completely: *She swallowed all his lies hook, line, and sinker.* **off the hook 1** *informal* freed from a difficulty or embarrassment. **2** said of a telephone receiver: not on its base. **on the hook for** *NAmer, informal* committed to paying (a certain sum). **sling one's hook** *Brit, informal* to leave. ➤➤ **hooklike** *adj.* [Old English *hōc*]

hook² *verb trans* **1** to attach (one thing to another) by means of a hook or hooks. **2** (+ round/over) to crook or bend (an arm or leg) round something. **3** to get hold of (something) with a hook or hooked implement. **4** to catch (a fish) with a line and hook. **5** to hit or throw (a ball) so that a hook results. **6a** in cricket, to play a hook at (a ball). **b** in cricket, to play a hook at the bowling of (the bowler). **7** in boxing: to hit (one's opponent) with a short swinging blow. **8** *informal* to steal (something). ➤ *verb intrans* **1** to be linked or attached by a hook or hooks: *The baby seat hooks over the back of an ordinary chair.* **2** in cricket or golf, to play a hook.

hookah /'hookə/ *noun* an oriental pipe for smoking tobacco, marijuana, etc, consisting of a flexible tube attached to a container of water, through which cooled smoke is inhaled; = WATER PIPE (2), HUBBLE-BUBBLE: compare NARGHILE. [Arabic *ḥuqqah* bottle of a water pipe]

hook and eye *noun* a fastening device used chiefly on garments that consists of a hook that links with a bar or loop.

hooked *adj* **1** shaped like a hook: *a hooked nose.* **2** fitted with a hook: *a hooked pole.* **3** denoting a rug, etc made by pulling loops of yarn through it with a hook. **4** *informal.* **a** (*often* + on) addicted to drugs: *hooked on crack cocaine.* **b** (*often* + on) very enthusiastic or compulsively attached to something specified: *hooked on skiing.*

hooker¹ *noun* **1a** in rugby, a player stationed in the middle of the front row of the scrum. **b** this position. **2** *informal* a woman prostitute.

Word history ——————
Two popular theories are proposed about the origin of *hooker* meaning 'prostitute'. First, it is alleged to have referred originally to women thronging the camp of Joseph Hooker, a Federal general in the US Civil War, whose headquarters in Washington, DC, had an unsavoury reputation. This theory is disproved by the appearance of the word in 1845, predating the Civil War by more than a decade. Secondly, it supposedly derives from Corlear's Hook, a red-light district of New York City in the 19th cent. There is no firm evidence to support this suggestion. More likely, the word simply suggested a woman 'hooking' or catching hold of a man.

hooker² *noun* **1** a one-masted sailing boat used in the west of Ireland, formerly for cargo, now for racing or recreative sailing. **2** a boat engaged in commercial fishing but using lines and hooks rather than nets. **3** *informal* an old boat. [Dutch *hoeker*, from *hoek* hook, short for *hoekboot* a two-masted fishing vessel]

hooker³ *noun NAmer* a glass of neat spirits, e.g. whisky or brandy. [origin unknown]

hookey /'hooki/ *noun* see HOOKY¹.

hook nose *noun* a nose with a prominent, angled bridge; an aquiline nose.

hookup *noun* a temporary linking up of broadcasting stations for a special broadcast, or of electronic equipment for a particular purpose.

hook up *verb trans* to connect or link (radio stations or electronic equipment). ➤ *verb intrans* said of radio stations or electronic equipment: to be linked up.

hookworm *noun* **1** any of several parasitic nematode worms that have strong mouth hooks for attaching to the host's intestinal lining: *Ancylostoma, Uncinaria, Necator*, and other genera. **2** infestation by one of these.

hooky¹ *or* **hookey** ✳ **play hooky** *NAmer, Aus, NZ, informal* to play truant: *He ... took his flogging ... for playing hooky the day before —* Mark Twain. [prob from slang *hook, hook it* to make off]

hooky² *adj* (**hookier, hookiest**) *informal* said of a tune: catchy; memorable.

hooley /'hoohli/ *noun* (*pl* **hooleys**) *Irish* a wild party. [origin unknown]

hooligan /'hoohlig(ə)n/ *noun* a young ruffian or hoodlum. ➤➤ **hooliganism** *noun.* [perhaps named after Patrick *Hooligan* fl 1898, Irish criminal in London]

hoon /hoohn/ *noun Aus, NZ, informal* **1** a procurer or manager of prostitutes. **2** a lout. [origin unknown]

hoop¹ /hoohp/ *noun* **1** a large circular strip of rigid material, used: **a** for holding together the staves of a barrel. **b** for bowling along the ground or exercising with: *a hula hoop.* **c** formerly, for expanding a woman's skirt. **d** typically paper-covered, for animals to jump through in a circus. **2** a circular figure or object: *'What's the matter?' 'About a hoop of gold, a paltry ring that she did give me.'* — Shakespeare. **3** an arch through which balls must be hit in croquet. **4** a horizontal band of contrasting colour round a cap or sports shirt. **5** *Aus, informal* a jockey (from the band round his shirt). ✳ **be put/go through the hoops** to undergo a demanding series of tests. [Old English *hōp*]

hoop² *verb trans* to encircle, bind, or fasten (something) with or as if with a hoop. ➤➤ **hooped** *adj,* **hooper** *noun.*

hoop-la /'hoohp lah/ *noun* **1** *Brit* a game, *esp* at a fairground, in which prizes are won by tossing rings over them. **2** *NAmer.* **a** a fuss; noise. **b** nonsense. [partly from HOOP¹; partly from French *houp-là* ups-a-daisy!]

hoopoe /'hoohpooh, 'hoohpoh/ *noun* a Eurasian and N African bird with pale pinkish brown plumage, a long erectile crest, and a slender downward-curving bill: *Upupa epops.* [alteration of obsolete *hoop*, via French *huppe* from Latin *upupa*, of imitative origin]

hoop pine *noun* an Australian pine tree noted for fast growth and for the hoop-like divisions in its rough bark: *Araucaria cunninghamii.*

hooray /hoo'ray/ *interj* = HURRAY.

Hooray Henry *or* **Hooray** *noun* (*pl* **Hooray Henries** *or* **Henrys**) *informal* a well-off upper-class young man who behaves in a noisy insensitive way. [alteration of Damon Runyon's term *Hurrah Henry* of 1936]

hoosegow /'hoohsgow/ *noun chiefly NAmer, informal* a jail. [Mexican Spanish *juzgado* jail, in Spanish 'court of justice', past part. of *juzgar* to judge, from Latin *judicare*: see JUDGE¹]

Hoosier /'hoohzi-ə/ *noun NAmer* **1** a native or inhabitant of the US state of Indiana. **2** (**hoosier**) *derog* an uncultivated person; a rustic or hick. [origin unknown]

hoot¹ /hooht/ *verb intrans* **1a** to make the characteristic cry of an owl. **b** to sound the horn, whistle, etc of a motor car or other vehicle: *The driver hooted at me as he passed.* **2** to utter a loud derisive shout. **3** *informal* to laugh loudly. ➤ *verb trans* **1a** to jeer (an actor, speaker, etc). **b** (+ down/off) to shout down (a speaker) or jeer (an actor, performer, etc) off the stage. **2** to express (one's disapproval, etc) by hooting. **3** to say (something) in a hearty carrying voice. [Middle English *houten*, of imitative origin]

hoot² *noun* **1** a hooting sound. **2** *informal* a source of laughter or amusement: *The play was an absolute hoot.* ✳ **not care/give a hoot/two hoots** not to care in the least.

hootch /hoohch/ *noun* see HOOCH.

hootenanny /'hoohtənani/ *or* **hootnanny** /,hooht'nani/ *noun* (*pl* **hootenannies** *or* **hootnannies**) an informal gathering with entertainment by folksingers, usu with the audience singing along. [orig meaning 'thingummy, whatsit'; origin unknown]

hooter *noun* **1** *chiefly Brit* a device, e.g. the horn of a car, for producing a loud hooting noise. **2** *dated, informal* the nose.

hootnanny /,hooht'nani/ *noun* see HOOTENANNY.

Hoover /'hoohvə/ *noun trademark* a vacuum cleaner. [named after W H *Hoover* d.1932, US manufacturer]

hoover *verb* (**hoovered, hoovering**) **1** to clean (a carpet, room, etc) using a vacuum cleaner. **2** (+ up) to suck up (dust, debris, etc) with a vacuum cleaner.

hooves /hoohvz/ *noun* pl of HOOF¹.

hop¹ /hop/ *verb* (**hopped, hopping**) ➤ *verb intrans* **1a** said of a frog, etc: to move by a quick springy leap or in a series of leaps. **b** said of a human being: to jump on one foot. **c** said of a bird: to jump with both feet. **2** to make a quick trip, *esp* by air: *We hopped over to France.* **3** to board or leave a vehicle. ➤ *verb trans informal* **1** to jump over (something). **2** *NAmer* to ride on (some form of transport), *esp* without authorization: *We hopped a train downtown.* **3** to cross (an ocean) by air. ✳ **hop it!/hop off!** *Brit, informal* go away! **hop the twig/stick** *Brit, informal* to depart or to die. [Old English *hoppian*]

hop² *noun* **1** a short leap, *esp* on one leg. **2** a short or long flight between two landings: *We flew to Bangkok in three hops.* **3** *informal* a dance. ✲ **catch somebody on the hop** *informal* to find somebody unprepared. **hop, skip/step, and jump** formerly, the triple jump.

hop³ *noun* **1** a climbing plant of the hemp family with inconspicuous green flowers of which the female ones are in cone-shaped catkins: *Humulus lupulus.* **2a** (*in pl*) the ripe dried catkins of a hop used *esp* in the brewing process to impart a bitter flavour to beer. **b** *Aus, NZ, informal* beer. **3** *NAmer, informal* opium or some other narcotic. ⋙ **hoppy** *adj.* [Middle English *hoppe* from early Dutch or Low German]

hop⁴ *verb trans* (**hopped, hopping**) to impregnate (beer) with hops. ✲ **be hopped up** *informal* to be in a state of intoxication from or as if from a narcotic drug.

hopak /ˈhohpak/ *noun* see GOPAK.

hope¹ /hohp/ *verb trans* **1** to desire or trust that (something is or may be the case): *I hope I didn't disturb you.* **2** to desire and expect (to do something): *I hope to see you soon.* ➤ *verb intrans* **1** to have faith in the possibility of something: *We must keep hoping.* **2** (+ for) to be eager for (something): *We're hoping for plenty of snow.* ✲ **hope against hope** to hope for something when there is virtually no possibility of it. [Old English *hopian*]

hope² *noun* **1** (*also in pl*) the feeling that what one wants to happen can happen: *Don't give up hope.* **2** a chance that the desired thing may happen: *There's little hope of her regaining consciousness.* **3** (*in pl*) the things one wants to happen: *our hopes for the new millennium.* **4** a person or thing that one is depending on for something: *The china shop was our last hope.* **5** *archaic* religious faith or trust: *All our hope is in God.*

hope chest *noun NAmer* a chest in which a woman accumulates household linen, etc in preparation for marriage; = BOTTOM DRAWER.

hopeful¹ /ˈhohpf(ə)l/ *adj* **1** full of hope: *I'm hopeful he'll come.* **2** inspiring hope: *The situation looks hopeful.* ⋙ **hopefulness** *noun.*

hopeful² *noun* a person who hopes to, or is likely to, succeed: *young hopefuls.*

hopefully *adv* **1** in a hopeful manner. **2** *informal* it is hoped; I hope: *Hopefully he will arrive in time.*

Usage note

Though the use of *hopefully* as a sentence adverb in the sense, 'it is to be hoped (that); let us hope' in sentences such as *Hopefully, they'll be home before it gets dark* is still decried by traditionalists in Britain and America, it has generally established itself as part of normal usage. It is interesting to note, however, that opposition to such words as *frankly* and *regretfully* with a similar function has not been expressed. So while it may appear unnecessarily restrictive to reserve the use of the word to such constructions as *She eyed the plate of jam tarts hopefully* it is probably better to limit the sentence adverb use of *hopefully* to informal or spoken contexts.

hopeless *adj* **1** having no expectation of success; despairing. **2** giving no grounds for hope: *a hopeless case.* **3** incapable of solution, management, or accomplishment: *a hopeless task.* **4** *chiefly informal* incompetent or useless: *I'm hopeless at sums.* ⋙ **hopelessly** *adv,* **hopelessness** *noun.*

hophead *noun informal* **1** a drug addict, *esp* one taking heroin or opium. **2** *Aus, NZ* a heavy drinker. [HOP³]

Hopi /ˈhohpi/ *noun* (*pl* **Hopis** or *collectively* **Hopi**) **1** a member of a Native American people of NE Arizona. **2** the language of the Hopis. ⋙ **Hopi** *adj.* [Hopi *hópi* good, peaceful]

hoplite /ˈhoplit/ *noun* a heavily armed infantry soldier of ancient Greece. [Greek *hoplitēs*, from *hoplon* tool, weapon]

hopper¹ *noun* **1** somebody or something that hops. **2** a leaping insect; *specif* an immature hopping form of an insect. **3** a receptacle, *esp* funnel-shaped, for the discharging or temporary storage of grain, coal, etc. **4** a goods wagon with a floor through which bulk materials may be discharged. **5** a barge that can discharge dredged material through an opening bottom. [(sense 3) from the shaking motion of hoppers used to feed grain into a mill]

hopper² *noun* a person who picks hops.

hopping *adj NAmer, informal* very busy: *Keep them hopping.* ✲ **hopping mad** *informal* absolutely furious.

hopple¹ /ˈhopl/ *verb trans* to fasten together the legs of (a horse) to prevent it straying; = HOBBLE¹ (2). [prob of Low Germanic origin]

hopple² *noun* a strap or rope for tying together a horse's legs.

hopsack *noun* **1** a coarse material for making sacks. **2** a firm rough-surfaced clothing fabric woven in basket weave. [Middle English *hopsak* sack for hops, from *hoppe* HOP³ + *sak* SACK¹]

hopsacking *noun* = HOPSACK (1).

hopscotch *noun* a children's game in which a player tosses an object, e.g. a stone, into areas of a figure outlined on the ground and hops through the figure and back to regain the object. [HOP¹ + SCOTCH⁴]

hora *or* **horah** /ˈhawrə/ *noun* a Romanian or Israeli dance performed in a circle. [Romanian *horă* and Hebrew *hōrāh*]

horary¹ /ˈhawrəri/ *noun* (*pl* **horaries**) *archaic* **1** a book of prayers for the canonical hours (see CANONICAL HOUR); BOOK OF HOURS. **2** a timetable or schedule. [late Latin *horarium* dial, book of hours, neuter of *horarius*: see HORARY²]

horary² *adj archaic* **1** relating to or showing the hours: *the horary spaces on a dial.* **2** hourly: *the horary motion of the earth.* [late Latin *horarius* relating to hours, from Latin *hora*: see HOUR]

Horatian /həˈrayshi-ən/ *adj* relating to or characteristic of Horace or his poetry. [Latin *Horatianus*, from *Horatius* Horace (Quintus Horatius Flaccus) d.8 BC, Roman poet]

horde /hawd/ *noun* **1** *usu derog* (*also in pl*) a crowd or swarm: *hordes of tourists; hordes of flies.* **2** a nomadic tribe or army, *esp* of Asian origin. **3** an anthropological term for a loose social unit of five or so families. [Polish *horda* from Turkish *ordu* camp, royal camp]

Usage note

horde *or* **hoard**? See note at HOARD¹.

horehound *or* **hoarhound** /ˈhawhownd/ *noun* a strong-smelling plant of the mint family with downy leaves and bitter juice, used medicinally. [Old English *hārhūne*, from *hār* hoary + *hūne* horehound]

horizon /həˈrʌɪz(ə)n/ *noun* **1a** the apparent junction of earth and sky. **b** the plane that is parallel to and passes through the earth's surface at an observer's position. **c** the circle formed by the intersection of this plane with the CELESTIAL SPHERE (imaginary sphere surrounding the earth). **d** the plane parallel to the plane of the apparent horizon but passing through the earth's centre. **e** the circle formed by the intersection of this plane with the CELESTIAL SPHERE. **2** (*also in pl*) one's range of perception, experience, or knowledge: *It's time you widened your horizons.* **3a** a planar surface between two beds of rock; a time plane of no thickness. **b** an archaeological layer of a particular time, usu identified by distinctive fossils or artefacts. **c** any of the reasonably distinct soil or subsoil layers in a vertical section of land. ✲ **on the horizon** said of an event: due shortly. [Middle English *orizon* via late Latin from Greek *horizont-, horizōn*, present part. of *horizein* to bound, define, from *horos* boundary]

horizontal¹ /horiˈzontl/ *adj* **1** at right angles to the vertical; parallel to the plane of the horizon; level. **2** at or near the horizon: *the horizontal moon.* **3** *humorous* lying flat in bed: *I was horizontal for a week with flu.* **4** said of a mechanism: having the main part lying or working in the horizontal plane, as is the piston in a *horizontal engine.* **5** relating to people or positions of the same status in separate hierarchies; compare VERTICAL¹: *horizontal promotion.* **6** applying uniformly to all members of a group: *a horizontal bonus.* **7** said of a merger: combining businesses involved in the same kind or stage of production. ⋙ **horizontality** /-ˈtaliti/ *noun,* **horizontally** *adv.*

horizontal² *noun* a horizontal line or structure.

horizontal bar *noun* **1** a steel bar supported in a horizontal position 2.5 metres (about eight feet) above the floor and used for swinging exercises in gymnastics. **2** a gymnastics event, usu for men, in which the horizontal bar is used.

hormone /ˈhawmohn/ *noun* **1** a product of living cells that usu circulates in body liquids, e.g. the blood or sap, and produces a specific effect on the activity of cells remote from its point of origin: compare CHALONE. **2** a synthetic substance that imitates the action of a natural hormone. ⋙ **hormonal** /hawˈmohnl/ *adj,* **hormonally** /hawˈmoh-/ *adv.* [Greek *hormōn*, present part. of *horman* to stir up, from *hormē* impulse, assault]

hormone replacement therapy *noun* the treatment of menopausal women with the hormone oestrogen to counteract such adverse effects of the menopause as hot flushes and lethargy, and to help prevent OSTEOPOROSIS (bone thinning).

horn¹ /hawn/ *noun* **1** any of the usu paired bony projecting parts on the head of cattle, giraffes, deer, and similar hoofed mammals and some extinct mammals and reptiles. **2** a permanent solid pointed part consisting of keratin that is attached to the nasal bone of a rhinoceros. **3** a natural projection from an animal, e.g. a snail or owl, resembling or suggestive of a horn. **4** *archaic* (*in pl*) in ribald imagery, a pair of horns traditionally believed to grow from the head of a cuckold: *There will the devil meet me like an old cuckold with horns on his head* — Shakespeare. **5** the tough fibrous material consisting chiefly of keratin that covers or forms the horns and hooves of cattle and related animals, or other hard parts, e.g. claws or nails. **6** a hollow horn used as a container: *a powder horn.* **7** something resembling or suggestive of a horn, e.g.: **a** either of the curved ends of a crescent. **b** a horn-shaped body of land or water. **8a** an animal's horn used as a wind instrument. **b** = HUNTING HORN. **c** = FRENCH HORN. **d** a wind instrument used in a jazz band; *esp* a trumpet. **e** a device, e.g. on a motor car, for making loud warning noises: *a fog horn.* **9** *Brit, coarse slang* an erect penis. ✴ **draw in one's horns** to reduce one's activities or spending. **on the horn** *NAmer, informal* on the telephone. **on the horns of a dilemma** faced with two equally undesirable alternatives. **toot/blow one's own horn** *NAmer, informal* to sing one's own praises; to blow one's own trumpet. ➤➤ **horned** *adj,* **hornist** *noun,* **hornless** *adj,* **hornlike** *adj.* [Old English]

horn² *verb trans* **1** *chiefly literary* to give a cuckold's horns to (*esp* one's husband) through an adulterous liaison; = CUCKOLD². **2** said of a bull or other horned animal: to butt or gore (a person or another animal) with the horns.

hornbeam *noun* any of several species of trees of the hazel family with smooth grey bark and hard white wood: genus *Carpinus.* [HORN¹ + BEAM¹; from its hard smooth wood]

hornbill *noun* any of numerous species of large Old World birds with enormous bills: family Bucerotidae.

hornblende /'hawnblend/ *noun* a dark mineral that consists chiefly of silicates of calcium, magnesium, and iron and is a major constituent of many igneous and metamorphic rocks. ➤➤ **hornblendic** /hawn'blendik/ *adj.* [German *Hornblende,* from *Horn* horn + *Blende* (see BLENDE)]

hornbook *noun* formerly, a child's learning aid that consisted of a sheet of parchment or paper, usu with the alphabet and sometimes also the Lord's Prayer, mounted on a wooden tablet and protected by a sheet of transparent horn: *He teaches boys the hornbook* — Shakespeare.

horned lizard *noun* = HORNED TOAD.

horned owl *noun* an owl of N and S America that has horn-like ear tufts: *Bubo virginianus.*

horned poppy *noun* any of several species of poppies with a long curved seed capsule: *Glaucium flavum* and other species.

horned toad *noun* any of several species of small lizards of W USA and Mexico that have hornlike spines and eat insects: *Phrynosoma cornutum* and other species.

horned viper *noun* a poisonous snake of the desert areas of N Africa and SW Asia that has a hornlike spine above each eye and moves similarly to a SIDEWINDER¹: *Cerastes cerastes.*

hornero *noun* (*pl* **horneros**) any of several species of OVENBIRD of tropical America that tend to construct their oven-like nests on top of fence posts: genus *Furnarius.* [Spanish *hornero* baker]

hornet /'hawnit/ *noun* any of several species of large wasps with black and yellow bands on the abdomen and a powerful sting: *Vespa crabro* and other species. ✴ **stir up a hornets' nest** to provoke an angry reaction. [Old English *hyrnet*]

hornfels /'hawnfelz/ *noun* a hard fine-grained rock formed by the alteration of slate, shale, or a similar clay rock subjected to high temperature, and commonly containing small crystals of garnet and mica. [German *Hornfels,* from *Horn* horn + *Fels* cliff, rock]

horn in *verb intrans informal* (*often* + on) to intrude on something: *He horned in on the discussion.*

horn-mad *adj archaic* mad with rage: *If he had found the young man he would have been horn-mad* — Shakespeare. [with reference to a bull or other horned animal]

horn of plenty *noun* **1** a cornucopia. **2** an edible mushroom with a trumpet-shaped cap: *Craterellus cornucopioides.*

hornpipe *noun* a lively British folk dance typically associated with sailors, or a piece of music for dancing it to. [Middle English,

denoting a wind instrument made partly of horn for accompanying dancing]

horn-rims *pl noun* glasses with horn rims. ➤➤ **horn-rimmed** *adj.*

hornswoggle /'hawnswogl/ *verb trans informal* to hoax or outwit (somebody). [origin unknown]

hornworm *noun NAmer* the caterpillar of any of many species of HAWKMOTH, having a spike on the tail, some species of which damage certain types of crop: *Manduca sexta* (tobacco hornworm), *Manduca quinquemaculata* (tomato hornworm) and other species.

hornwort *noun* any of several species of rootless thin-stemmed submerged water plants: genus *Ceratophyllum.*

horny *adj* (**hornier, horniest**) **1** composed of or resembling horn. **2** *informal* sexually aroused; randy. ➤➤ **horniness** *noun.* [(sense 2) HORN¹ meaning 'erect penis']

horologe /'horəloj/ *noun* a timekeeping device. [Middle English via French and Latin from Greek *hōrologion,* from *hōra* hour + *legein* to gather]

horology /ho'roləji/ *noun* **1** the science of measuring time. **2** the art of constructing instruments for indicating time. ➤➤ **horologer** *noun,* **horologic** /-'lojik/ *adj,* **horological** /-'lojikl/ *adj,* **horologist** *noun.* [Greek *hōra* HOUR + -LOGY]

horoscope /'horəskohp/ *noun* **1** a diagram of the relative positions of planets and signs of the zodiac at a specific time, *esp* somebody's birth, used by astrologers to infer individual character and personality traits and to foretell events in a person's life. **2** an astrological forecast based on this, made for a particular person, or one presented, e.g. in a newspaper column, for people born under a certain zodiac sign. [via French and Latin from Greek *hōroskopos* caster of nativities, horoscope, from *hōra* HOUR + *skopein* to look at]

horrendous /ho'rendəs/ *adj* dreadful or horrible. ➤➤ **horrendously** *adv.* [Latin *horrendus* from *horrēre* to bristle, tremble]

horrible /'horəbl/ *adj* **1** causing, or of a nature to cause, horror: *a horrible accident.* **2** *chiefly informal* extremely unpleasant or disagreeable: *horrible weather.* ➤➤ **horribleness** *noun,* **horribly** /-bli/ *adv.* [Middle English via French from Latin *horribilis,* from *horrēre* to bristle, tremble]

horrid /'horid/ *adj* **1** horrible; shocking. **2** *informal* repulsive; nasty. ➤➤ **horridly** *adv,* **horridness** *noun.* [Latin *horridus* rough, shaggy, bristling, from *horrēre* to bristle, tremble]

horrific /ho'rifik/ *adj* arousing horror; horrifying: *a horrific account of the tragedy.* ➤➤ **horrifically** *adv.*

horrify /'horifie/ *verb trans* (**horrifies, horrified, horrifying**) **1** to cause (somebody) to feel horror. **2** to shock (somebody) or fill them with distaste. ➤➤ **horrification** /-fi'kaysh(ə)n/ *noun,* **horrified** *adj,* **horrifiedly** *adv,* **horrifying** *adj,* **horrifyingly** *adv.* [Latin *horrificare,* ultimately from *horrēre* to bristle, tremble]

horripilation /,horipi'laysh(ə)n/ *noun* the raising of hairs on the skin as a result of cold, fear, etc; GOOSEFLESH. [late Latin *horripilation-, horripilatio,* from Latin *horripilare* to bristle, be shaggy, from *horrēre* to bristle, tremble + *pilus* hair]

horror /'horə/ *noun* **1a** intense fear, dread, or dismay. **b** intense aversion or repugnance. **2a** the quality of inspiring horror: *contemplating the horror of their lives* — Liam O'Flaherty. **b** *informal* an unpleasant or ugly person or thing: *That child is a perfect horror.* **3** (**the horrors**) *informal* a state of horror, depression, or apprehension. [Middle English via French from Latin *horror* from *horrēre* to tremble]

horror-stricken *adj* = HORROR-STRUCK.

horror-struck *adj* filled with horror.

horror vacui /'vakyooie/ *noun* in painting, a compulsive need to fill every corner of the picture with detail. [Latin *horror vacui* dislike of an empty space]

hors concours /,aw konh'kooə (*French* ɔːr kɔ̃kur)/ *adj* **1** *literary* without equal; unrivalled; peerless. **2** said of an exhibit or exhibitor: not competing for an award. [French *hors concours* out of competition]

hors de combat /,aw də 'kombah (*French* ɔːr də kɔ̃ba)/ *adv and adj* out of the fight; disabled. [French *hors de combat* outside the fighting]

hors d'oeuvre /,aw 'duhv (*French* ɔːr dœvr)/ *noun* (*pl* **hors d'oeuvres** *or* **hors d'oeuvre** /'duhv(z) (*French* dœvr)/) any of various savoury foods usu served as appetizers. [French *hors-d'œuvre,* literally 'outside the work']

horse[1] /haws/ *noun* (*pl* **horses** *or collectively* **horse**) **1** a large solid-hoofed four-footed mammal that eats plants and has been, domesticated by humans since prehistoric times and used as a beast of burden, a draught animal, or for riding: *Equus caballus* and other species. **2** a racehorse. **3** a male horse; a stallion or gelding. **4** a four-legged frame for supporting something, e.g. planks. **5a** = POMMEL HORSE. **b** = VAULTING HORSE. **6** (*treated as sing. or pl*) cavalry: *two regiments of horse.* **7** *informal* short for HORSEPOWER. **8** a mass of wall rock occurring in a vein. **9** a rope suspended from the yard of a sailing ship, on which the seamen stand when working on the sails. **10** *slang* heroin. ✳ **a horse of another/a different colour** a completely different thing. **from the horse's mouth** said of information: from the original source; first-hand. **hold one's horses** to postpone action; to restrain oneself. **horses for courses** different people or things to suit different needs. **to horse!** *archaic* a command to mount. >> **horseless** *adj*, **horselike** *adj*. [Old English *hors*]

horse[2] *verb intrans informal* (*usu* + around/about) to engage in horseplay. >> *verb trans* to provide (a person or vehicle) with a horse.

horse-and-buggy *adj NAmer, informal* **1** belonging to an era before the advent of certain modern inventions such as the motor car. **2** outdated; old-fashioned.

horseback[1] ✳ **on horseback** mounted on a horse.

horseback[2] *adj and adv* mounted on a horse; on horseback.

horsebean *noun* = BROAD BEAN. [*horse* large, coarse (in names of plants and animals), from HORSE[1]]

horsebox *noun* a lorry or closed trailer for transporting horses.

horse brass *noun* a brass ornament attached orig to a horse's harness.

horsebreaker *noun* a person who breaks in or trains horses.

horse chestnut *noun* **1** any of several species of large trees with five-lobed leaves and erect conical clusters of showy flowers: *Aesculus hippocastanum* and other species. **2** the large glossy brown nut of this tree, enclosed in a spiny case; = CONKER.

horse-coper /'kohpə/ *noun archaic* a dealer in horses. [obsolete *cope* to trade, deal, exchange, from Middle English *copen* to buy, of Germanic origin]

horseflesh *noun* **1** horses collectively: *carts, carriages everywhere, the most astonishing miscellany of conveyances and horseflesh* — H G Wells. **2** horse meat.

horsefly *noun* (*pl* **horseflies**) any of numerous species of large swift flies, the females of which suck blood: *Haematopota pluvialis* and other species. Also called CLEG.

horsehair *noun* **1** the hair of a horse, *esp* from its mane or tail. **2** padding made from this, used in upholstery.

horsehide *noun* the hide of a horse, or leather prepared from it.

horse latitudes *pl noun* either of two high-pressure belts in the latitudes 30°–35°N and 30°–35°S with weather characterized by calms and light changeable winds. [origin unknown]

horse laugh *noun* a loud boisterous laugh.

horseleech *noun* **1** a large carnivorous freshwater leech that feeds on small invertebrates or on carrion: genus *Haemopis*. **2** *archaic* a veterinary surgeon.

horseless carriage *noun archaic* a motor car.

horse mackerel *noun* a large mackerel-like edible fish of the E Atlantic, with a row of bony spikes along its sides: *Trachurus trachurus*.

horseman *noun* (*pl* **horsemen**) **1** a rider on horseback. **2** a breeder, tender, or manager of horses, *esp* a skilled one. >> **horsemanship** *noun*.

horse mushroom *noun* a large edible mushroom with a creamy-white cap and greyish gills: *Agaricus arvensis*.

horse mussel *noun* a large marine mussel widely distributed on the shores of N Europe and America: *Modiolus modiolus*.

horse opera *noun NAmer, informal* = WESTERN[2].

horse pistol *noun* formerly, a large pistol carried by a horseman at the pommel of his saddle.

horseplay *noun* rough or boisterous play.

horsepower *noun* an imperial unit of power equal to about 746 watts.

horse racing *noun* the sport of racing horses, either over a flat course or on one with fences or hurdles. >> **horse race** *noun*.

horseradish *noun* **1** a tall coarse white-flowered plant of the mustard family: *Armoracia rusticana*. **2** the pungent root of the horseradish or a condiment prepared from it.

horse sense *noun* = COMMON SENSE.

horseshit *noun chiefly NAmer, coarse slang* = BULLSHIT[1].

horseshoe *noun* **1** a shoe for horses, usu consisting of a narrow U-shaped plate of iron fitting the rim of the hoof, traditionally a lucky symbol. **2** something resembling this, such as a bend in a road or river.

horseshoe bat *noun* any of several species of bat with a horseshoe-shaped pad on the muzzle: genus *Rhinolophus*.

horseshoe crab *noun* any of several species of marine invertebrate animals that are related to spiders and scorpions, have a horseshoe- or crescent-shaped CEPHALOTHORAX (combined head and central region of the body) and an abdomen ending in a long spike: *Limulus polyphemus* and other species. Also called KING CRAB.

horse's neck *noun informal* a cocktail consisting of spirits, *esp* brandy, with ginger ale and a twist of lemon.

horsetail *noun* a flowerless plant with a hollow jointed stem, related to the ferns: genus *Equisetum*.

horse-trading *noun* negotiation accompanied by hard bargaining and reciprocal concessions. >> **horse-trader** *noun*.

horsewhip[1] *noun* a long whip used for controlling horses.

horsewhip[2] *verb trans* (**horsewhipped, horsewhipping**) to flog (a person or animal) with or as if with a horsewhip.

horsewoman *noun* (*pl* **horsewomen**) **1** a female rider on horseback. **2** a female breeder, tender, or manager of horses, *esp* a skilled one. >> **horsewomanship** *noun*.

horsey *or* **horsy** /'hawsi/ *adj* (**horsier, horsiest**) **1** relating to or resembling a horse: *a long-nosed horsey face.* **2** very interested in horses, horse-riding, or horse racing: *Her friends are very horsey.* >> **horsily** *adv*, **horsiness** *noun*.

horst /hawst/ *noun* a geological term denoting a block of the earth's crust higher than and separated by faults from adjacent blocks. [German *Horst* heap]

horsy /'hawsi/ *adj* see HORSEY.

hortative /'hawtətiv/ *or* **hortatory** /'hawtət(ə)ri/ *adj formal* giving encouragement. >> **hortatively** *adv*. [late Latin *hortativus* from Latin *hortari* to urge]

horticulture /'hawtikulchə/ *noun* the science and art of growing fruits, vegetables, and flowers. >> **horticultural** /'kulch(ə)rəl/ *adj*, **horticulturally** /-'kulch(ə)rəli/ *adv*, **horticulturist** /-'kulch(ə)rist/ *noun*. [Latin *hortus* garden + CULTURE[1]]

hortus siccus /,hawtəs 'sikəs/ *noun* (*pl* **horti sicci** /,hawtie 'sikie/) = HERBARIUM. [Latin *hortus siccus* dry garden]

Hos. *abbr* Hosea (book of the Bible).

hosanna /hoh'zanə/ *interj and noun* a cry of acclamation and adoration. [Middle English *osanna* via late Latin from Greek *hōsanna*, from Hebrew *hōshī'āh-nnā* pray, save (us)!]

hose[1] /hohz/ *noun* **1** (*pl* **hose, hosen** /'hohzən/) (*usu in pl*) till the late 16th cent., close-fitting covering for the leg and foot: *his youthful hose, well saved, a world too wide for his shrunk shank* — Shakespeare. **2** (*pl* hose) (*usu in pl*) from the mid 16th cent., short pouched breeches reaching to the knee. **3** (*pl* hose) *NAmer* (*in pl*) tights or stockings: *pantihose.* **4** (*pl* hoses) a flexible tube for conveying fluids, e.g. from a tap, or in a car engine. [Old English *hosa* husk]

hose[2] *verb trans* (*often* + down) to spray, water, or wash (something) with a hose: *Hose down the stable floor.*

hosel /'hohz(ə)l/ *noun* on a golf club, the socket into which the head fits. [dimin. of HOSE[1]]

hosen /'hohz(ə)n/ *noun archaic* pl of HOSE[1].

hosepipe *noun* a length of hose for conveying water, e.g. for watering plants or putting out fires.

hosier /'hohzi-ə/ *noun* a person or business that sells socks, stockings, and tights. [HOSE[1] + -IER]

hosiery /'hohzyəri/ *noun* a collective term for socks, stockings, and tights.

hospice /'hospis/ *noun* **1** *Brit* a nursing home, *esp* for terminally ill patients. **2** formerly, a place of shelter for travellers or the destitute, often run by a religious order. [French *hospice* from Latin *hospitium* inn, lodging, hospitality, from *hospit-, hospes* HOST¹]

hospitable /ho'spitəbl, 'hos-/ *adj* **1** offering a generous and cordial welcome to guests or strangers. **2** offering a pleasant or sustaining environment: *a hospitable climate.* **3** readily receptive: *hospitable to new ideas.* ➤➤ **hospitably** *adv.*

hospital /'hospitl/ *noun* **1** an institution where the sick or injured are given medical care: *The injured were taken to hospital.* **2** a repair shop for specified small objects: *a dolls' hospital.* **3** formerly, a charitable institution, e.g. for the needy, aged, infirm, or young; HOME¹ (8). [Middle English via Old French from late Latin *hospitale* hospice, guest room from Latin *hospitalis* of a guest, from *hospit-, hospes* guest, HOST¹]

hospital acquired infection *noun* an infection acquired by a patient during a stay in hospital.

hospital corner *noun* in bed-making, a way of securing the sheet round the corner of the mattress with a neat diagonal fold, used in hospitals.

hospitaler /'hospitələ/ *noun NAmer* see HOSPITALLER.

hospital fever *noun* louse-borne typhus, with which hospital patients easily became infected in the unhygienic conditions of former times.

hospitalise *verb trans* see HOSPITALIZE.

hospitality /hospi'taliti/ *noun* hospitable treatment or reception.

hospitality suite *noun* at a conference, etc, a room or suite where guests or delegates are entertained and usu offered free drinks.

hospitalize *or* **hospitalise** *verb trans* to place (somebody) in a hospital as a patient. ➤➤ **hospitalization** /-'zaysh(ə)n/ *noun.*

Hospitaller (*NAmer* **Hospitaler**) *noun* a member of a military religious order founded in Jerusalem at the time of the first Crusade.

hospitaller (*NAmer* **hospitaler**) *noun* a person, *esp* a member of a charitable religious order devoted to hospital or ambulance services. [Middle English *hospitaller* via French from late Latin *hospitalarius* hospitaller, innkeeper, from late Latin *hospitale*: see HOSPITAL]

hospital ship *noun* a ship equipped as a hospital; *esp* one built or specifically assigned to assist the wounded, sick, and shipwrecked in time of war.

hospital trust *noun* in Britain, an autonomous trust within the National Health Service, established to run a hospital or group of hospitals that has withdrawn from local-authority management.

host¹ /hohst/ *noun* **1a** a person who receives or entertains guests socially or officially. **b** an innkeeper: *mine host.* **c** a person or establishment, etc that provides facilities for an event or function: *Our college served as host for the chess tournament.* **2a** a living animal or plant on or in which a parasite or smaller organism lives. **b** an individual into which a tissue or part is transplanted from another. **3** a compere on a radio or television programme. **4** a computer that provides services to others linked up to it, e.g. access to the databases stored in it. [Middle English *hoste* host, guest, via Old French from Latin *hospit-, hospes*]

host² *verb trans* **1** to act as host at or of (a reception, etc). **2** to act as compere of (a broadcast show, etc): *He hosted a talent show in the '70s.*

host³ *noun* (*also in pl*) **1** (*often* + of) a very large number; a multitude: *hosts of friends; a host of suggestions.* **2** *chiefly literary or archaic* an army: *the captains of the hosts* — Bible. [Middle English via Old French from Latin *hostis* stranger, enemy]

host⁴ *or* **Host** *noun* the bread consecrated in the Eucharist. [Middle English *hoste* via French from Latin *hostia* Eucharist, earlier 'sacrifice']

hosta /'hostə/ *noun* an Asian perennial herbaceous plant of the lily family that is cultivated for its variegated foliage and spikes of lilac, mauve, or white flowers: genus *Hosta.* Also called PLANTAIN LILY. [Latin genus name, named after Nicolaus *Host* d.1834, Austrian botanist]

hostage /'hostij/ *noun* a person held by one party as a pledge that promises will be kept or terms met by another party: *The hijackers took three hostages.* ✱ **hostage to fortune** a commitment that lays one open to the risk of failure, attack, etc, if things go the wrong way: *The Good Friday deadline was bound to be a hostage to fortune.* [Middle English from Old French, from *hoste*: see HOST¹]

hostel /'hostl/ *noun* **1** *chiefly Brit* a supervised residential home, e.g.: **a** an establishment providing accommodation for nurses, students, etc. **b** an institution for junior offenders, ex-offenders, etc, encouraging social adaptation. **2** = YOUTH HOSTEL. **3** *literary or archaic* an inn. [Middle English, lodging, inn, via Old French from late Latin *hospitale*: see HOSPITAL]

hostelling (*NAmer* **hosteling**) *noun* the holidaying activity of travelling from place to place staying in youth hostels. ➤➤ **hosteller** *noun.*

hostelry /'hostlri/ *noun* (*pl* **hostelries**) an inn; a hotel.

hostess /'hohstes/ *noun* **1** a woman who entertains socially or acts as host. **2a** a female employee on a ship, aeroplane, etc who manages the provisioning of food and attends to the needs of passengers; STEWARDESS. **b** a woman who acts as a companion to male patrons, *esp* in a nightclub; *also* a prostitute.

hostile /'hostiel/ *adj* **1** relating to or constituting an enemy: *hostile tanks.* **2** antagonistic; unfriendly: *a hostile glance.* **3** not hospitable: *a hostile environment.* **4** said of a takeover: not endorsed by the company being bought. ➤➤ **hostilely** *adv.* [via French from Latin *hostilis*, from *hostis* enemy]

hostile witness *noun* in a legal action, a witness whose evidence is detrimental to the case of the party calling them.

hostility /ho'stiliti/ *noun* (*pl* **hostilities**) **1** (*in pl*) overt acts of warfare. **2** antagonism, opposition, or resistance.

hostler /'oslə/ *noun* see OSTLER.

hot¹ /hot/ *adj* (**hotter, hottest**) **1** having a relatively high temperature. **2** capable of burning or scalding: *Watch! The plates are hot.* **3** said of food: cooked in the oven etc and served immediately. **4** uncomfortable because of surrounding heat, thick clothes, etc: *You must be hot in those clothes.* **5** having a higher than normal body temperature: *hot from running.* **6** said of somebody's temper: easily provoked. **7** sexually aroused or sexually arousing. **8** denoting a heavily rhythmic style of jazz. **9** pungent, peppery, or spicy. **10** very recent; fresh: *This article's hot off the press.* **11** of intense and immediate interest: *hot gossip.* **12** said of colours: strong and bright; suggestive of heat or flames. **13** said of a process: performed on a heated material: *Steel ingots can be formed into tubing by hot rolling.* **14** said of an atom: having a higher than normal energy level due usu to nuclear processes. **15** *informal* radioactive; *also* dealing with dangerously radioactive material. **16** *chiefly NAmer, informal* electrically live: *a hot terminal.* **17** *esp* in children's games, close to something sought: *Guess again, you're getting hot.* **18** said of the scent of a quarry: fresh and strong. **19** (+ on) knowledgeable about (something): *She's pretty hot on car maintenance.* **20** (+ on) strict about rules, standards, etc: *They tend to be hot on drink-driving.* **21** fancied by everyone to win: *the hot favourite.* **22** currently popular or retailing fast: *a hot seller.* **23** *informal.* **a** recently stolen and too easily identifiable to dispose of easily: *These jewels are hot.* **b** said of a person: wanted by the police. ✱ **have the hots for** *informal* to desire (somebody) sexually. **hot on the trail of** eagerly tracking (somebody or something) down. **hot under the collar** *informal* angry or irritated. **in hot pursuit** following closely. **in hot water** in trouble. **make it/things hot for** *informal* to create trouble for (somebody). **not so hot/not very hot** *informal* not very good: *He's not so hot at French.* ➤➤ **hotness** *noun*, **hottish** *adj.* [Old English *hāt*]

hot² *verb* (**hotted, hotting**) ➤ *verb trans* **1** *informal* (+ up) to heat (food, etc): *He hotted up the remains of last night's meal for lunch.* **2** *W Indian* to heat (something) up: *Hot some water for washing.* ➤ *verb intrans* **1** (+ up) to get more intensive, faster, more exciting, etc: *Air raids began to hot up about the beginning of February* — George Orwell. **2** *W Indian* to become hot.

hot air *noun informal* empty talk.

hotbed *noun* **1** a bed of soil heated *esp* by fermenting manure and used for forcing or raising seedlings. **2** an environment that favours rapid growth or development, *esp* of something specified: *a hotbed of crime.*

hot-blooded *adj* excitable; ardent. ➤➤ **hot-bloodedness** *noun.*

hot button *noun NAmer, informal* a highly sensitive issue.

hotchpot /'hochpot/ *noun* the legal procedure of combining properties into a common lot to ensure equality of division among heirs, e.g. where a parent dies intestate. [via Anglo-French from Old French *hochepot*, from *hocher* to shake + *pot* pot]

hotchpotch /'hochpoch/ (*NAmer* **hodgepodge** /'hojpoj/) *noun* a mixture composed of many unrelated parts; a jumble. [Middle English variant of HOTCHPOT]

hot cross bun *noun* a spicy bun leavened with yeast, with a pastry cross on top, eaten *esp* on Good Friday.

hot desking *noun* in an office, etc, the system of assigning desks on a temporary or rotation system, rather than allocating them on a permanent basis to particular employees.

hotdog *verb intrans* (**hotdogged, hotdogging**) *NAmer, informal* to perform stunts, *esp* while skiing, surfing, or skateboarding. ➤ **hotdogger** *noun*.

hot dog[1] *noun* **1** a frankfurter or other sausage heated and served in a bread roll. **2** *NAmer, informal* a performer of skiing, surfing, or skateboarding stunts.

hot dog[2] *interj NAmer, informal* an expression of admiring approval.

hotel /hoh'tel/ *noun* an establishment that provides meals and temporary accommodation for the public, *esp* for people travelling away from home, usu equipped with a public bar. [French *hôtel*, from Old French *hostel*: see HOSTEL]

hotelier /hoh'teli-ə, -iay/ *noun* the proprietor or manager of a hotel. [French *hôtelier* from Old French *hostelier*, from *hostel*: see HOSTEL]

hotel ship *noun* an accommodation vessel moored alongside an oil rig.

hot flash *noun NAmer* = HOT FLUSH.

hot flush *noun* a sudden brief flushing and sensation of heat, usu associated with an imbalance of endocrine hormones occurring *esp* at the menopause.

hotfoot[1] *adv* in haste: *He had come hotfoot from the railway station.*

hotfoot[2] ✻ **hotfoot it** *informal* to hurry.

hot gospel *noun informal* zealous evangelism or revivalism, *esp* now in the form of fervent preaching with communal praying and singing. ➤➤ **hot-gospeller** *noun*, **hot-gospelling** *noun*.

hothead *noun* a hotheaded person.

hotheaded *adj* fiery; impetuous. ➤➤ **hotheadedly** *adv*, **hotheadedness** *noun*.

hothouse[1] /'hothows/ *noun* **1** a heated greenhouse, *esp* for tropical plants. **2** an environment that promotes rapid, *esp* over-rapid growth or development.

hothouse[2] *verb trans* to speed up the education of (particular children), advancing them intellectually beyond the normal level for their age.

hot key *noun* in computing, a key or combination of keys that has been programmed to carry out a certain series of commands.

hot line *noun* a direct telephone line kept in constant readiness for immediate communication, e.g. between heads of state.

hot link *noun* in computing, a HYPERLINK (shortcut to additional information in another file) in a HYPERTEXT document.

hotly *adv* in a hot or fiery manner: *a hotly debated issue.*

hot metal *noun* a method of printing using type cast directly from molten metal.

hot money *noun* capital that is frequently transferred from one financial institution to another in order to maximize the interest or profit that attaches to it.

Hotol /'hohtol/ *abbr* horizontal takeoff and landing.

hotpants *pl noun* women's very brief tight-fitting shorts, typically with a bib, that were fashionable *esp* in the early 1970s.

hot pepper *noun* **1** a small thin-walled pungent capsicum fruit. **2** the plant that bears this fruit: *Capsicum frutescens.*

hot plate *noun* a metal plate or spiral, usu on an electric cooker, on which food can be heated and cooked.

hot pot *noun Brit* a stew of mutton, lamb, or beef and potato cooked in a casserole.

hot potato *noun informal* a controversial or sensitive question or issue.

hot press *noun* a machine that applies heat and pressure to paper or cloth by means of hot metal plates, in order to give a smooth glossy finish.

hot-press *verb trans* to press (paper or cloth) with a hot press.

hot rod *noun* a motor vehicle rebuilt or modified for high speed and fast acceleration.

hot-rod *verb* (**hot-rodded, hot-rodding**) ➤ *verb trans* to modify (a motor vehicle) for high speed and fast acceleration. ➤ *verb intrans* to drive a hot rod.

hot seat *noun informal* **1** (**the hot seat**) a position involving risk, embarrassment, or responsibility for decision-making: *in the hot seat at the interview.* **2** *chiefly NAmer* = ELECTRIC CHAIR.

hot shoe *noun* a socket in a camera for accessories, through which there is direct electrical contact with a flashgun, for flash synchronization.

hotshot *noun informal* a showily successful or important person. ➤➤ **hotshot** *adj*.

hot spot *noun* **1** an area of potential danger, where violence may break out; a trouble spot. **2** *informal* a much-frequented nightclub or disco. **3** a local area of greater heat or greater activity, e.g.: **a** in a petrol engine, part of the manifold that is heated by the exhaust gases it receives from the cylinders to vaporize the fuel. **b** in molecular biology, a region of DNA that is particularly prone to spontaneous mutation, or RECOMBINATION (combination of genes in an offspring not found in the parents). **c** in electronics, a small region of an electrode where the temperature is raised above the average. **d** in geology, an area of greater heat deep within the earth's mantle that is associated with increased volcanic activity at the earth's surface. **e** in nuclear engineering, a highly radioactive area in a plant or reactor. **f** in image technology, a point in an interactive video image that can be clicked on to access information from elsewhere.

hot spring *noun* a spring of naturally hot water.

hotspur *noun archaic* a person who rushes precipitately into dangerous activity or involvement; a rash or impetuous person. [from the idea of a spur hot with constant use by a horseman, occurring first and most notably as the nickname of Sir Henry Percy, son of the Earl of Northumberland, killed at the battle of Shrewsbury in 1403]

hot stuff *noun informal* **1** a description used of somebody or something of outstanding ability or quality. **2** somebody or something that is sexually exciting.

hot swap *noun* the replacement of a major computer part, such as the hard drive or CD-ROM drive, while the computer is switched on. ➤➤ **hot-swappable** *adj*, **hot swapping** *noun*.

hotsy-totsy /ˌhotsi 'totsi/ *adj NAmer* **1** *dated slang* as near perfect as can be. **2** = HOITY-TOITY. [reputedly coined by Billie de Beck d.1942, US cartoonist]

hot-tempered *adj* inclined to lose one's temper easily.

Hottentot /'hot(ə)ntot/ *noun offensive* see KHOIKHOI. [Dutch *Hottentot*]

hotting /'hoting/ *noun Brit, informal* the act or an instance of performing dangerous manoeuvres in a stolen car.

hot-water bottle *noun* a flattish rubber container that is filled with hot water and used *esp* to warm a bed.

hot-wire *verb trans* to start (a vehicle) by bypassing the ignition switch.

houbara bustard /hooh'bahrə/ *noun* a threatened species of bustard found in arid country or semi-desert, *esp* in N Africa and S Asia: *Chlamydotis undulata.* [*houbara* via Latin from Arabic *hubārā*]

Houdini /hooh'deeni/ *noun* a term for somebody who is adroit at escaping from confinement or from desperate situations: *The hamster had done a Houdini – bitten through its cage and disappeared.* [named after Harry *Houdini* (born Erich Weiss) d.1926, US magician and escape artist]

hough /hok/ *noun* **1** *Brit* = HOCK[1]. **2** a joint of meat including the hock. [Old English *hōh* heel]

hoummos /'hoomas/ *noun* see HUMMUS.

hound[1] /hownd/ *noun* **1a** a dog; *esp* one of any of various hunting breeds typically with large drooping ears and a deep bark that track their prey by scent. **b** (*used in combinations*) used in the names of hunting dog breeds: *deerhound; foxhound.* **2** a dismissive term for a domestic dog: *Better take the hound for a walk.* **3** a mean or despicable person, *esp* a man. **4** an untiring enthusiast for something: *an autograph hound.* [Old English *hund* dog]

hound[2] *verb trans* **1** to pursue (a person) as if with hounds: *She was hounded by reporters.* **2** to harass (somebody) persistently. ➤➤ **hounder** *noun*.

hound's-tongue *noun* a coarse plant of the borage family with tongue-shaped leaves and dull reddish purple flowers: *Cynoglossum officinale*. [translation of the Greek name *kynoglōssos*, from *kyn-*, *kyōn* dog + *glōssa* tongue, from the leaf shape]

houndstooth check *or* **hound's-tooth check** *noun* a small broken-check textile pattern.

houngan *or* **hungan** /'hoohng·gǝn/ *noun* a voodoo priest *esp* of Haiti: *Persistent failure to achieve cures will lose a hungan his reputation and his practice* — M J Herskovits. [Fon (W African language) *hun* deity associated with a fetish + *ga* chief]

hour /owǝ/ *noun* **1** the 24th part of a day; a period of 60 minutes: *He puts in two hours' practice every day; a half-hour programme.* **2** the time reckoned in hours and minutes by the clock; *esp* the beginning of each full hour. *The clock had just struck the hour.* **3** (*in pl*) the time reckoned in one 24-hour period from midnight to midnight: *We attack at 0900 hours.* **4** *archaic or literary* the time of day: *'What hour is it?' 'It lacks of twelve'* — Shakespeare. **b** a time late at night: *Sorry to telephone you at this hour.* **5** a fixed or customary period of time set aside for a specified purpose: *the lunch hour.* **6** (*in pl*) the period during which a business, etc is operational: *outside office hours.* **7** the work done or distance travelled at normal rate in an hour: *Chicago is only one hour away.* **8** *literary* a moment in one's life of peculiar significance: *He deserted her in her hour of need.* **9** *literary* the time for action of some kind: *The hour has come to prove your loyalty.* **10** in astronomy, a unit used to measure the position of a celestial body, e.g. a star or planet, that is equal to an angle of 15° in an east–west direction from a reference point (the VERNAL EQUINOX) and that represents the distance that the celestial body has travelled in one hour. **11** any of the canonical hours (times for worship or the prayers or services prescribed for them; see CANONICAL HOUR) in the Roman Catholic Church. * **after/out of hours** outside normal working hours. **keep early/late hours** to get up and go to bed early or late. **on the hour** at an exact hour, *esp* every hour: *Trains leave on the hour.* **the early/small hours** the period between midnight and dawn. **the story, etc of the hour** the story, etc, that everyone is talking about. **till all hours** until very late at night: *He stays out drinking till all hours.* **within the hour** in less than one hour. [Middle English via Old French *heure* and Latin *hora* from Greek *hōra*]

hourglass *noun* **1** an instrument for measuring time consisting of two glass bulbs joined by a narrow neck from the uppermost of which a quantity of sand runs into the lower in the space of an hour. **2** (*used before a noun*) describing a shapely female silhouette, with a narrow waist: *an hourglass figure.*

hour hand *noun* the short hand that marks the hours on the face of a watch or clock.

houri /'hooǝri/ *noun* (*pl* **houris**) **1** any of the female virgin attendants of the blessed in the Muslim paradise. **2** a voluptuously beautiful young woman. [French *houri* via Persian *ḥūri* from Arabic *ḥūrīyah*]

hourly[1] *adv* **1** at or during every hour: *Buses pass hourly.* **2** any time now: *We're expecting him hourly.* **3** by the hour: *hourly-paid workers.*

hourly[2] *adj* **1** occurring or done every hour: *an hourly check.* **2** constant: *in hourly expectation of a call from the hospital.* **3** reckoned by the hour: *hourly wages.*

house[1] /hows/ *noun* (*pl* **houses** /'howziz/) **1** a building designed for people to live in. **2** (*used in combinations*) a building in which animals live or things are stored: *the henhouse; the boathouse.* **3** (*used in combinations*) a building or establishment with a particular purpose: *a public house; an opera house.* **4** (*used in combinations*) a specific type of business company: *a publishing house.* **5a** a legislative or deliberative assembly, *esp* as one of two chambers: *the lower house of the Manx parliament.* **b** the building or room where such an assembly meets. **c** a quorum in such an assembly. **6** a community of monks or nuns, or the building they live in: *one of the Cistercian houses.* **7** any of several units into which a large school may be divided for social purposes, internal competitions, etc. **8** a family, *esp* an important or ancient one: *the House of Windsor.* **9** a household: *the woman of the house.* **10** the area occupied by the audience in a theatre or cinema, or the audience itself: *a full house.* **11** in astrology, any of the twelve equal sectors into which the CELESTIAL SPHERE (imaginary sphere surrounding earth on whose surface the stars appear to be placed) is divided. **12** in the game of curling, the circular area three yards (about 2.7 metres) in diameter surrounding the mark at which a stone is aimed and within which the stone must rest in order to count. **13** (**House**) = HOUSE MUSIC. * **bring the house down** to receive rapturous applause from an audience. **get on like a house on fire** *informal* to get on very well with somebody. **go round the houses** to go by a long indirect route. **keep house** to run a household. **on the house** at the expense of an establishment or its management: *Drinks are on the house.* **put/set one's house in order** to put one's affairs straight. ⋙ **houseful** *noun,* **houseless** *adj.* [Old English *hūs*]

house[2] /howz/ *verb trans* **1a** to provide (a person) with accommodation. **b** to provide (things) with storage space: *We had to house the printing press in the garage.* **2** to contain (something): *The library houses a large collection of oriental literature.*

house agent *noun Brit* = ESTATE AGENT.

house arrest *noun* confinement in one's place of residence instead of prison.

houseboat *noun* a moored boat that is fitted out as a home.

housebound *adj* confined to the house, e.g. because of illness.

housebreak *verb trans chiefly NAmer* = HOUSETRAIN. ⋙ **housebroken** *adj.*

housebreaking *noun* an act of breaking into and entering somebody's house with a criminal purpose. ⋙ **housebreaker** *noun.*

housecarl *or* **housecarle** /'howskahl/ *noun* a member of the bodyguard of a Danish or early English king or noble. [Old English *hūscarl* from Old Norse *hūskarl*, from *hūs* house + *karl* man]

house church *noun* **1** a charismatic Church (fundamentalist Church emphasizing the gifts of the Holy Spirit; see CHARISMATIC MOVEMENT) outside the control of the established denominations. **2** a meeting of Christians for worship in a private house.

housecoat *noun* **1** a woman's light dressing gown for wear round the house. **2** a short overall.

housecraft *noun* skill in running a household.

house cricket *noun* a cricket native to N Africa and SW Asia, but found in or near dwellings elsewhere, that warbles like a bird: *Acheta domesticus.*

housefather *noun* a man in charge of a group of young people living in care, e.g. in a children's home.

house finch *noun* a common brown finch of NW America, with a red breast: *Carpodacus mexicanus.*

housefly *noun* (*pl* **houseflies**) a fly found in most parts of the world that frequents houses and carries disease: *Musca domestica.*

houseguest *noun* a person who is staying as a guest in somebody's house.

household /'howshohld/ *noun* (*treated as sing. or pl*) a dwelling and all the people who live together in it, considered as a unit.

household cavalry *noun* a cavalry regiment appointed to guard a sovereign or his or her residence.

householder *noun* a person who occupies a dwelling as owner or tenant.

household god *noun* (*also in pl*) any of the gods that protect the home, *esp* one of the LARES and PENATES that were guardians of the ancient Roman household.

household name *or* **household word** *noun* a person or thing that everyone has heard of: *Filboid Studge had become a household word* — Saki.

household troops *pl noun* troops appointed to guard a sovereign or his or her residence.

household word *noun* see HOUSEHOLD NAME.

house-hunting *noun* the activity of looking for a house or flat to buy or rent. ⋙ **house-hunter** *noun.*

house husband *noun* a man who lives with his wife or partner and himself performs the household tasks traditionally done by the housewife or the woman of the house.

housekeep /'howskeep/ *verb intrans dated* to run a household.

housekeeper *noun* somebody employed to take charge of the running of a house.

housekeeping *noun* **1a** the day-to-day running of a house and household affairs. **b** money allotted or used for this. **2** the general management of an organization which ensures its smooth running, e.g. the provision of equipment, keeping of records, etc. **3** the routine tasks that have to be done in order for something to function properly.

houseleek *noun* any of several species of Eurasian plants with pink flowers that grow *esp* on walls and roofs: *Sempervivum tectorum* and other species.

house lights *pl noun* the lights that illuminate the auditorium of a theatre.

housemaid *noun* a female servant employed to do housework.

housemaid's knee *noun* a swelling over the knee due to an enlargement of the BURSA (fluid-filled sac) in the front of the knee-cap. [from its frequent occurrence among servants who often work on their knees]

houseman *noun* (*pl* **housemen**) *Brit* a resident junior doctor in a hospital; = HOUSE OFFICER.

house martin *noun* a European martin with blue-black plumage and white rump that nests on cliffs and under the eaves of houses: *Delichon urbica*.

housemaster *or* **housemistress** *noun* a teacher in charge of a school house.

housemother *noun* a woman in charge of a group of young people living in care, e.g. in a children's home.

house mouse *noun* a common grey-brown mouse that lives and breeds in and around buildings and is found in most parts of the world: *Mus musculus*.

house music *noun* pop music with a strong fast beat which is chiefly instrumental with occasional repeated phrases of song or speech. [prob named after *The Warehouse*, a club in Chicago]

house of assembly *noun* a legislative body or the lower house of such a body in various British colonies, protectorates, countries of the Commonwealth, etc.

house of cards *noun* a precarious structure or situation.

House of Commons *noun* the lower house of the British and Canadian parliaments.

house of correction *noun* formerly, an institution for the confinement of minor offenders, where they were given work to do.

house officer *noun Brit* a newly qualified doctor resident in a hospital, usu receiving training from a senior physician or surgeon by working as a member of their team.

house of God *noun* a church or other place of religious worship.

house of ill fame *noun* = HOUSE OF ILL REPUTE.

house of ill repute *noun euphem* a brothel.

House of Keys *noun* in the Isle of Man, the lower, elected house of TYNWALD (the Manx parliament), with 24 members. [origin of *Keys* uncertain; perhaps alteration of Manx *kiare-as-feed* four and twenty]

House of Lords *noun* **1** in Britain, the upper house of Parliament. **2** in Britain, the body of Law Lords that constitutes the highest court of appeal.

House of Representatives *noun* the lower house of the US Congress or Australian Parliament.

houseparent *noun* a housemother or housefather.

house party *noun* a party lasting for a day or more, held typically at a large country house.

houseplant *noun* a plant grown or kept indoors.

house-proud *adj* careful about the management and appearance of one's house.

houseroom ✳ **not give something houseroom** *Brit* not to want or not to be interested in something at all.

house-sit *verb intrans* (**house-sat, house-sitting**) to live in somebody's house and look after it while they are away. ➤ **house-sitter** *noun*.

house sparrow *noun* a brown Eurasian sparrow that lives in or near human settlements: *Passer domesticus*.

house style *noun* the rules for punctuation, spelling, etc followed by a particular publishing house, journal, etc.

house-to-house *adj* said of enquiries or searches: systematically including every house in an area; = DOOR-TO-DOOR (I).

housetop *noun* a roof. ✳ **from the housetops** for all to hear; publicly: *shouting their grievances from the housetops*.

housetrain *verb trans chiefly Brit* to train (a pet) to defecate and urinate outdoors, or in the indoor receptacle provided. ➤ **housetrained** *adj*.

housewarming *noun* a party to celebrate moving into a new house or premises.

housewife *noun* (*pl* **housewives**) **1** a woman, usu married, who runs a house. **2** /'huzif/ a small container for needlework articles,

e.g. thread. ➤ **housewifely** *adj*, **housewifery** /'howswif(ə)ri/ *noun*.

house wine *noun* a wine that appears unnamed on a restaurant's wine list and is sold at a lower price than those that are named.

housework *noun* the work, e.g. cleaning, involved in maintaining a house.

housey-housey /howsi 'howsi/ *noun Brit, dated* = BINGO². [reduplication of *house*, earlier name for BINGO²]

housing¹ /'howzing/ *noun* **1a** houses or dwelling-places collectively. **b** the provision of these. **2** a protective cover for machinery, sensitive instruments, etc.

housing² *noun* (*also in pl*) a cloth covering for a horse: *the Baron of Bradwardine, mounted on an active and well-managed horse … with deep housings to agree with his livery* — Scott. [via Old French *houce* from late Latin *hultia*, of Germanic origin]

housing association *noun Brit* a non-profitmaking society that constructs, renovates, and helps tenants to rent or buy housing.

housing estate *noun Brit* a planned area of housing, *esp* one that is self-contained, with its own shops and other amenities.

housing project *noun NAmer* see PROJECT¹ (3A).

houting /'howting/ *noun* a European sea fish related to the salmon that ascends rivers to spawn in the autumn and is an important food fish: *Coregonus oxyrhinchus*. [Dutch *houting* from early Dutch *houtic*, of unknown origin]

hove /hohv/ *verb* past tense and past part. of HEAVE¹.

hovel /'hovl/ *noun* **1** a small squalid dwelling, *esp* in a poor state of repair. **2** formerly, a conical building enclosing a kiln. [Middle English, perhaps of Low German origin]

hover¹ /'hovə/ *verb intrans* (**hovered, hovering**) **1** said of a bird, insect, or helicopter: to keep itself in one place in the air. **2** to hang in the air: *His fingers hovered over the doorknob*. **3** to linger or wait restlessly around a place. **4** to be in a state of uncertainty, irresolution, or suspense, or on the borderline between two states: *hovering between life and death*. ➤ **hoverer** *noun*. [Middle English *hoveren*, frequentative of *hoven* to hover, of unknown origin]

hover² *noun* the act or an instance of hovering.

hovercraft *noun* (*pl* **hovercraft**) a vehicle supported on a cushion of air provided by fans and designed to travel over both land and sea.

hoverfly *noun* (*pl* **hoverflies**) any of numerous species of brightly coloured flies that hover in the air: family Syrphidae.

hoverport *noun* a place where passengers embark on and disembark from hovercraft. [blend of HOVERCRAFT + PORT¹]

hovertrain *noun* a train that travels on a cushion of air along a special concrete track.

how¹ /how/ *adv* **1** in what way or manner, or by what means: *Let's see how it works; How do you spell dahlia?* **2** used in challenging or confronting: *How do you account for the discrepancy?* **3** used to express incredulity: *How could you be so rude!* **4** used to enquire about the state of somebody's health or the state or progress of something: *How are you?; How's the market today?* **5** (*used before an adverb or adjective*) to what extent or degree: *How seriously hurt is she?* **6** (*used before an adverb or adjective*) used intensively in exclamations: *How nice you look!* **7** (*used before an adjective or adverb*) used to enquire about age, measurements, etc: *How old is Peter now?* ✳ **and how** *informal* used for emphasis: *'Were you scared?' 'And how!'* **how about** used to make suggestions: *How about a drink?* **how come** how does it happen; why is it?: *How come we never meet?* **how do you do** used as a formal greeting between people meeting for the first time. **how ever** used to ask emphatically: *How ever could you have thought that?* **how much** used to ask about cost or other amounts: *How much are the artichokes?* **how now** *archaic* used to summon, greet, or challenge: *How now, ambitious Humphry! What means this?* — Shakespeare. **how's that 1** used to call attention or invite comment: *How's that for enterprise?* **2** = HOWZAT. [Old English *hū*]

how² *conj* **1** introducing a clause after asking or telling verbs, etc: **a** in what manner, state, to what degree, etc: *I know how much you care; Did you ask how his wife was?* **b** that: *She kept telling me how nobody understood her*. **2** as; however: *Do it how you like*.

how³ *noun* the manner in which something is done: *the how and the why of it*.

how⁴ *interj* used as a greeting by Native Americans, or in humorous imitation of them. [Sioux or Dakota *háo*, or Omaha *hau*]

howbeit[1] /how'bee-it/ *adv archaic* however: *Howbeit the hair of his head began to grow again after he was shaven* — Bible.

howbeit[2] *conj archaic* although: *The Moor, howbeit that I endure him not, is of a constant, loving, noble nature* — Shakespeare.

howdah /'howdə/ *noun* a canopied seat on the back of an elephant or camel. [Urdu *haudah* from Arabic *hawdaj* litter]

how-do-you-do *or* **how d'ye do** /,how dyə 'dooh/ *noun informal* a confused or embarrassing situation. [from the phrase *how do you do?*]

howdy /'howdi/ *interj chiefly NAmer, informal* hello. [alteration of *how do (you do)*]

how d'ye do /,how dyə 'dooh/ *noun* see HOW-DO-YOU-DO.

howe[1] /how, hoh/ *noun Scot* a hollow or valley. [Middle English (northern) *how, holl*, from Old English *hol* hollow]

howe[2] /how/ *noun* **1** *N Eng* a barrow or tumulus. **2** used in place names: a hill. [Middle English from Old Norse *haugr* mound]

however[1] *conj* **1** in whatever manner or way; as: *Dress however you want to.* **2** (*used esp before adjectives, adverbs, or pronouns*) no matter how: *It's worth it, however much you have to pay.*

however[2] *adv* **1** be that as it may; nevertheless: *I'd like to; however, I think I'd better not.* **2** used emphatically: = HOW[1]; how ever: *However many times must I tell you?*

howff *or* **howf** /howf, hohf/ *noun Scot* a haunt or resort; *esp* a pub. [from the name of Dundee's main burial ground, hence any burial ground, meeting place, or haunt]

howitzer /'how-itsə/ *noun* a short cannon usu with a medium muzzle velocity and a relatively high trajectory. [Dutch *houwitser* from Czech *houfnice* ballista]

howk /howk/ *verb trans chiefly Scot* (*usu* + out) to dig (something) out.

howl[1] /howl/ *verb intrans* **1** to yell or shriek long and loud e.g. with pain or laughter. **2** to cry or sob loudly and without restraint. **3** said *esp* of dogs, wolves, etc: to make a loud sustained doleful cry. **4** said of wind: to make a sustained wailing sound. ➤ *verb trans* to utter (something) with a loud sustained cry. [Middle English *houlen*, of imitative origin]

howl[2] *noun* **1** a howling sound. **2** in electronics, a high-pitched sound in a loudspeaker caused by feedback.

howl down *verb trans* to express one's disapproval of (a speaker or their views) by shouting in order to prevent them from being heard.

howler *noun informal* a stupid and comic blunder.

howler monkey *noun* any of several species of S and Central American monkeys that have long prehensile tails and a loud howling cry: genus *Alouatta.*

howling *adj informal* great or extreme: *a howling success.*

howsoever[1] *adv formal or archaic* to whatever extent: *His mother's eye was an evil eye to the rest of the world ... howsoever affectionate to him* — Dickens.

howsoever[2] *conj formal or archaic* in whatever way: *But, howsoever thou pursuest this act, taint not thy mind, nor let thy soul contrive against thy mother aught* — Shakespeare.

how-to *adj* denoting a book of basic instruction in some skill, etc: *The How-to Book of Computing.*

howzat /how'zat/ *interj* used in cricket as an appeal to the umpire to give the batsman out; how's that.

hoy[1] /hoy/ *interj* used in attracting attention or in driving animals. [Middle English]

hoy[2] *noun* a small fore-and-aft rigged coaster. [Middle English from Middle Dutch *hoei*]

hoya /'hoyə/ *noun* a climbing evergreen plant with waxy flowers, native to SE Asia and cultivated as a greenhouse plant: genus *Hoya.* [Latin genus name, named after Thomas *Hoy* d.1821, English gardener]

hoyden *or* **hoiden** /'hoydn/ *noun* a boisterous girl. ➤➤ **hoydenish** *adj.* [perhaps from obsolete Dutch *heiden* country lout, heathen]

Hoyle /hoyl/ ✳ **according to Hoyle** exactly in accordance with the rules or regulations. [named after Edmond *Hoyle*, d.1769, British writer on card games]

HP *abbr* **1** (*also* **hp**) high pressure. **2** (*also* **hp**) hire purchase. **3** (*also* **hp**) horsepower. **4** Houses of Parliament.

HPV *abbr* human papilloma virus.

HQ *abbr* headquarters.

HR *abbr* **1** Croatia (international vehicle registration). **2** human resources.

hr *abbr* hour.

HRH *abbr* His/Her Royal Highness.

HRT *abbr* hormone replacement therapy.

hryvna /'hrivnə/ *noun* the basic monetary unit of Ukraine, divided into 100 kopiykas.

Hs *abbr* the chemical symbol for hassium.

HSH *abbr* His/Her Serene Highness.

HSO *abbr* Higher Scientific Officer.

HST *abbr* high-speed train.

HT *abbr* high-tension.

ht *abbr* height.

HTLV *abbr* human T-cell lymphotropic virus, any of a family of retroviruses (viruses containing RNA; see RETROVIRUS) associated with certain leukaemias and immune-system deficiencies.

HTML *abbr* hypertext markup language, a system for presenting text for use on a network, e.g. the Internet, with provision, through hot links or hypertext links, for accessing related material in other parts of the network.

HTTP *abbr* hypertext transfer protocol, the system for transferring hypertext documents over the Internet.

huarache /wa'rahchi/ *noun* a sandal held on by leather thongs, traditionally the footwear of Mexican Indians. [Mexican Spanish *huarache*]

hub /hub/ *noun* **1** the central part of a wheel, propeller, or fan, through which the axle passes. **2** the focal point of activity. [prob alteration of HOB[1]]

hub and spoke *noun* a system of organizing air-traffic routes in which major airports act as centres to and from which all flights from outlying airports operate.

hubba hubba /,hubə 'hubə/ *interj NAmer, dated slang* an expression of enthusiastic appreciation, orig *esp* used by World-War-II GIs in admiration of an attractive girl. [origin unknown]

hubble-bubble /'hubl bubl/ *noun* **1** an oriental tobacco- or marijuana-smoking device; = HOOKAH, WATER PIPE (2). **2** a flurry of noise or activity; a commotion or hubbub. [reduplication of BUBBLE[1]]

Hubble's constant /'hublz/ *noun* the ratio between the speed of a galaxy's recession and its distance from the observer: see HUBBLE'S LAW. [named after E P *Hubble*: see HUBBLE'S LAW]

Hubble's law *noun* a law stating that as the universe expands, the RED SHIFT in the spectrum of a distant galaxy (representing its speed of recession) is proportional to its distance from the observer. [named after E P *Hubble* d.1953, US astronomer, who discovered the relationship]

Hubble space telescope *noun* = HUBBLE TELESCOPE.

Hubble telescope *noun* an astronomical observatory launched into orbit round the earth in 1990. [named after E P *Hubble*: see HUBBLE'S LAW]

hubbub /'hubub/ *noun* a noisy confusion; uproar. [prob of Celtic origin and connected with Scottish Gaelic *ub ub*, interj of contempt]

hubby /'hubi/ *noun* (*pl* **hubbies**) *informal* one's husband.

hubcap *noun* a removable metal cap placed over the hub of a wheel.

hubris /'hyoohbris/ *noun* overweening pride, usu leading to retribution. ➤➤ **hubristic** /hyooh'bristik/ *adj.* [Greek *hybris* insolence, violation, outrage]

huckaback /'hukəbak/ *noun* an absorbent durable fabric of cotton, linen, or both, used chiefly for towels. [origin unknown]

huckleberry /'huklb(ə)ri/ *noun* (*pl* **huckleberries**) **1a** an American shrub of the heath family: genus *Gaylussacia.* **b** the edible dark blue or black berry that grows on this shrub. **2** = BLUEBERRY. [perhaps alteration of *hurtleberry* whortleberry, huckleberry]

huckster[1] /'hukstə/ *noun* **1** a hawker or pedlar. **2** *chiefly NAmer.* **a** a person who uses aggressive methods to sell or publicize something. **b** a person who writes advertising material, *esp* for radio or television. ➤➤ **hucksterism** *noun.* [Middle English *hukster* from Dutch *hokester*, from *hoeken* to peddle]

huckster² *verb* (**huckstered, huckstering**) *chiefly NAmer* ➤ *verb intrans chiefly NAmer* to haggle. ➤ *verb trans chiefly NAmer* **1** to deal in or bargain over (dubious commodities). **2** to promote or advertise (something), *esp* in an aggressive or underhand manner.

huddle¹ /'hudl/ *verb trans* (*usu in passive*) **1** to crowd (people or animals) together. **2** to draw or curl (oneself) up: *She was huddled up in an armchair.* ➤ *verb intrans* **1** (*often* + together) to gather in a closely-packed group. **2** to curl up or crouch. [prob from or related to Middle English *hoderen* to huddle, of Low German origin]

huddle² *noun* **1** a closely-packed group; a bunch. **2** a secretive or conspiratorial meeting: *He went into a huddle with his colleagues.*

hue /hyooh/ *noun* **1a** the attribute of colours that permits them to be classed as red, yellow, green, blue, or an intermediate between any adjacent pair of these colours. **b** a colour having this attribute. **c** a shade of a colour. **2** a complexion or aspect: *political factions of every hue.* ➤➤ **hueless** *adj.* [Old English *hīw*]

hue and cry *noun* **1** formerly, a cry used when in pursuit of a criminal. **2** a clamour of alarm or protest; an outcry. [*hue* shout, outcry from Middle English *hew, hu,* from Old French *hue,* from *huer* to shout, from *hu* (interj)]

hued *adj* (*usu used in combinations*) coloured: *green-hued.*

huff¹ /huf/ *verb intrans* **1** to emit loud puffs, e.g. of breath or steam. **2** to make empty threats: *Management huffed and puffed about the chances of a lockout.* ➤ *verb trans* **1** in draughts, to take (an opponent's piece) as a penalty for failing to make a compulsory capture. **2** *archaic* to treat (somebody) with contempt; to bully (them). ✴ **huffing and puffing** bluster. [imitative]

huff² ✴ **in a huff** in a piqued and resentful mood.

huffish /'hufish/ *adj* = HUFFY.

huffy /'hufi/ *adj* (**huffier, huffiest**) **1** sulky or petulant. **2** easily offended; touchy. ➤➤ **huffily** *adv,* **huffiness** *noun.*

hug¹ /hug/ *verb trans* (**hugged, hugging**) **1** to hold or embrace (somebody) tightly in one's arms. **2** to feel very pleased with (oneself): *He was hugging himself with delight.* **3** to cling to (something) or cherish (it): *He hugged his miseries like a sulky child* — John Buchan. **4** to move parallel to and in close proximity to (something): *The trawler was hugging the shoreline.* ➤➤ **huggable** *adj.* [perhaps of Scandinavian origin]

hug² *noun* a tight clasp or embrace.

huge /hyoohj/ *adj* great in size, scale, degree, or scope; enormous. ➤➤ **hugely** *adv,* **hugeness** *noun.* [Middle English from Old French *ahuge,* of unknown origin]

hugely *adv* very much; enormously: *hugely excited.*

hugger-mugger¹ /,hugə 'mugə/ *noun* **1** secrecy: *and we have done but greenly in hugger-mugger to inter him* — Shakespeare. **2** confusion or muddle. [origin unknown]

hugger-mugger² *adj and adv* **1** in secrecy. **2** in confusion.

Hughie /'hyooh·i/ ✴ **send it/her down, Hughie!** *Aus, NZ* a plea for the rain to come down good and hard, addressed as though to a rain god. [of 20th-cent. origin. *Hughie* is said to be a dimin. of the given name *Hugh,* but could represent a facetious use of Greek *huei* it's raining]

Huguenot /'hyoohgənoh/ *noun* a member of the French Protestant Church, *esp* of the 16th and 17th cents. ➤➤ **Huguenot** *adj,* **Huguenotic** /-'notik/ *adj,* **Huguenotism** /-notiz(ə)m/ *noun.* [French dialect *huguenot* adherent of a Swiss political movement, alteration (influenced by Besançon *Hugues* d.1532, Swiss political leader) of *eidgnot* from Swiss German *Eidgnoss* confederate, from *Eid* oath and *Genoss* associate]

huh /huh, hah/ *interj* used to express surprise, disapproval, or enquiry.

huhu /'hoohhooh/ *noun* a large dark-brown beetle of New Zealand that bores into wood: *Prionoplus reticularis.* [Maori *huhu*]

hui /'hooh·i/ *noun* **1** *NZ* a large social or ceremonial gathering of Maoris. **2** *informal* a party. **3** in Hawaii, a club or association. [Maori and Hawaiian *hui*]

huia /'hooi·ə/ *noun* an extinct black bird of New Zealand, the female having a long curved beak, whose striking tail feathers were prized by the Maoris: *Heteralocha acutirostris.* [Maori *huia*]

hula /'hoolə/ *or* **hula-hula** /,hoohlə 'hoohlə/ *noun* a Polynesian dance involving swaying of the hips. [Hawaiian *hula*]

hula hoop *noun* a light plastic or cane hoop that can be made to spin round the waist by gyrating the body.

hula-hula *noun* see HULA.

hula skirt *noun* a long grass skirt of the kind worn by a hula dancer.

hulk /hulk/ *noun* **1a** the hull of a ship that is no longer seaworthy and is used as a storehouse or, *esp* formerly, as a prison. **b** an abandoned wreck or shell, *esp* of a vessel. **2** a person, creature, or thing that is bulky or unwieldy: *a big hulk of a man.* [Old English *hulc* fast ship, via late Latin from Greek *holkas* cargo ship, merchantman]

hulking *adj informal* bulky; massive.

hull¹ /hul/ *noun* **1** the main frame or body of a ship, flying boat, airship, etc. **2a** the outer covering of a fruit or seed; = HUSK¹. **b** the calyx that surrounds some fruits, e.g. the strawberry. **3** a covering or casing. [Old English *hulu* husk, pod, hull]

hull² *verb trans* **1** to remove the hulls of (fruit, seeds, etc). **2** to hit or pierce the hull of (a ship). ➤➤ **huller** *noun.*

hullabaloo /,hulǝbǝ'looh/ *noun* (*pl* **hullabaloos**) *informal* a confused noise; uproar. [perhaps from HALLO¹ + Scots *balloo* (interj) used to hush children]

hullo /hu'loh, hǝ'loh/ *interj chiefly Brit* see HELLO.

hum¹ /hum/ *verb intrans* (**hummed, humming**) **1** to utter a prolonged /m/ sound. **2** to make the characteristic droning noise of an insect in motion or a similar sound. **3** to sing with the lips closed and without articulation. **4** *informal* to be lively or active: *The place was humming.* **5** *informal* to have an offensive smell. ➤ *verb trans* to sing (a tune) with the lips closed and without articulation. ✴ **hum and haw/ha** to equivocate. ➤➤ **hummable** *noun,* **hummer** *noun.* [imitative]

hum² *noun* **1** a humming sound. **2** in electronics, an obtrusive low vibrating sound in an amplifier.

hum³ *interj* used to express hesitation, uncertainty, disagreement, etc.

human¹ /'hyoohmən/ *adj* **1** relating to, belonging to, or characteristic of people. **2** denoting a person; consisting of people. **3** denoting the faults that we as people have, possessed neither of divine perfection nor a machine's accuracy: *human failings.* **4** having the good attributes, e.g. kindness and compassion, thought to be characteristic of people: *She seems austere but she's really very human.* ➤➤ **humanness** *noun.* [Middle English *humain* via French from Latin *humanus,* from *homo* man, human being; compare HUMANE]

Usage note

human *or* humane? *Human* means 'belonging or relating to human beings as a race' (*human nature; human society*). *Humane* has a more limited use. It means 'showing compassion or kindness' (*humane treatment of animals*) or, more rarely, 'culturally broad and liberal' (*a humane education*).

human² *noun* a man, woman, or child; a person.

human being *noun* = HUMAN².

human chain *noun* a large number of people forming a line stretching between two sites, for the purpose of passing things quickly by hand from one site to the other.

humane /hyooh'mayn/ *adj* **1a** marked by compassion or consideration for other human beings or animals. **b** causing the minimum pain possible: *humane killing of animals.* **2** characterized by broad humanistic culture; liberal: *humane studies.* ➤➤ **humanely** *adv,* **humaneness** *noun.* [Middle English *humain:* see HUMAN¹. *Humane* was a common earlier spelling of *human* in all its meanings, but since the 18th cent. has been restricted to its current senses, referring to the better aspects of human nature]

Usage note

humane *or* human? See note at HUMAN¹.

human engineering *noun chiefly NAmer* = ERGONOMICS.

human interest *noun* the aspect of a news story that concerns the personal experiences and feelings of individual people, readily exploitable by the media.

humanise *verb trans* see HUMANIZE.

humanism *noun* **1a** a cultural movement dominant during the Renaissance that was characterized by a revival of classical learning and a shift of emphasis from religious to secular concerns. **b** literary culture. **2** humanitarianism. **3** a doctrine, attitude, or way of life based on human interests or values; *esp* a philosophy that asserts the intrinsic worth of human beings and that usu rejects religious belief. ➤➤ **humanist** *noun and adj,* **humanistic** /-'nistik/ *adj,* **humanistically** /-'nistikli/ *adv.*

humanitarian[1] /hyooh,mani'teəri·ən/ *adj* **1** relating to the promotion of human welfare, or the relief of human suffering: *humanitarian aid*. **2** said of a disaster: involving human suffering on a large scale.

humanitarian[2] *noun* a person who promotes human welfare and social reform; a philanthropist. ➤➤ **humanitarianism** *noun*.

humanity /hyooh'maniti/ *noun* (*pl* **humanities**) **1** humankind. **2** the quality or state of being human. **3** the quality of being humane. **4** (*in pl*) the cultural branches of learning.

humanize *or* **humanise** *verb trans* **1** to give (something) a human quality or character: *Something is wanting to science until it has been humanized* — Ralph Waldo Emerson. **2** to make (a person) humane: *She wanted ... a grief that should deeply touch her, and thus humanise her and make her capable of sympathy* — Nathaniel Hawthorne. ➤➤ **humanization** /-'zaysh(ə)n/ *noun*.

humankind *noun* (*treated as sing. or pl*) human beings collectively.

humanly *adv* **1a** from a human viewpoint. **b** within the range of human capacity: *as much as is humanly possible*. **2a** in a manner characteristic of human beings, *esp* in showing emotion or weakness. **b** with humaneness.

human nature *noun* the nature of human beings; the innate and acquired behavioural patterns, motives, attitudes, ideas, etc characteristic of human beings.

humanoid[1] /'hyoohmənoyd/ *adj* having human form or characteristics.

humanoid[2] *noun* in science fiction, a being with human form or characteristics.

human papilloma virus *noun* any of a class of viruses that cause warts and tumours in humans, certain strains of which infect the cervix and are thought to be a cause of cervical cancer.

human resources *pl noun* **1** (*used with a pl verb*) = PERSONNEL (1). **2** (*used with a sing. verb*) = PERSONNEL (2).

human rights *pl noun* the rights to which all human beings are entitled, including the rights to liberty, freedom of speech, and equality.

humble[1] /'humbl/ *adj* **1** having a low opinion of oneself; unassertive. **2** marked by deference or submission: *a humble apology*. **3** ranking low in a hierarchy or scale: *people of humble origins*. **4** modest or unpretentious: *a humble dwelling*. ✳ **in my humble opinion** used in mock humility to preface one's own views. ➤➤ **humbleness** *noun*, **humbly** *adv*. [Middle English via Old French from Latin *humilis* low, humble, from *humus* earth]

humble[2] *verb trans* **1** to humiliate (somebody) or render (them) humble in spirit or manner. **2** to defeat (somebody) decisively; to destroy the power, independence, or prestige of (them). **3** to sacrifice one's pride and abase (oneself).

humble-bee *noun* = BUMBLEBEE. [Middle English *humbylbee*, prob from Low German *hummelbē*, from *hummel* to buzz + *bē* bee]

humble pie ✳ **eat humble pie** to abase oneself by apologizing. [*humple pie* from a pun on UMBLES, deer's offal, a lowly food]

humbug[1] /'humbug/ *noun* **1** pretence or deception, *esp* of a hypocritical kind: *There's no imaginative sentimental humbug about me. I call a spade a spade* — Dickens. **2** a hypocritical impostor or sham. **3** drivel or nonsense. **4** *Brit* a hard peppermint-flavoured striped sweet made from boiled sugar. ➤➤ **humbuggery** *noun*. [origin unknown]

humbug[2] *verb trans* (**humbugged, humbugging**) to deceive (somebody) with a hoax.

humdinger /hum'ding·ə/ *noun informal* an excellent or remarkable person or thing. [origin unknown]

humdrum[1] /'humdrum/ *adj* monotonous or dull. [reduplication of HUM[1]]

humdrum[2] /'humdrum/ *noun* (**the humdrum**) monotonous or dull people or situations.

humectant[1] /hyoo'mektənt/ *noun* a substance, such as glycerin, that promotes retention of moisture and lends itself to use in skin preparations or as a food additive. [Latin *humectant-, humectans*, present part. of *humectare* to moisten, from *humectus* moist, from *humēre* to be moist]

humectant[2] *adj* promoting retention of moisture.

humeral /'hyoohmərəl/ *adj* **1** relating to or in the region of the humerus or shoulder. **2** in the Roman Catholic Church, denoting a vestment worn round the shoulders for administering the sacrament.

humerus /'hyoohmərəs/ *noun* (*pl* **humeri** /-rie/) the long bone of the upper arm or forelimb extending from the shoulder to the elbow. [Latin *humerus* upper arm, shoulder]

humic /'hyoohmik/ *adj* relating to or derived from humus.

humid /'hyoohmid/ *adj* containing or characterized by perceptible moisture: *a humid climate*. ➤➤ **humidly** *adv*. [French *humide* from Latin *(h)umidus* moist, from *humēre* to be moist]

humidex /'hyoohmideks/ *noun Can* an index of the level of discomfort likely from combined temperature and humidity. [blend of HUMIDITY and INDEX[1]]

humidifier /hyooh'midifie·ə/ *noun* a device for supplying or maintaining humidity, e.g. in a centrally heated room.

humidify /hyooh'midifie/ *verb trans* (**humidifies, humidified, humidifying**) (*usu in passive*) to make (air) humid. ➤➤ **humidification** /-fi'kaysh(ə)n/ *noun*.

humidity /hyooh'miditi/ *noun* moisture or dampness, or the degree of this, *esp* in the atmosphere: compare RELATIVE HUMIDITY.

humidor /'hyoohmidaw/ *noun* a case or room in which cigars or tobacco can be kept moist. [HUMID + -*or* as in CUSPIDOR]

humify /'hyoohmifie/ *verb* (**humifies, humified, humifying**) ➤ *verb trans* to convert (plant remains) into humus. ➤ *verb intrans* said of plant remains: to form humus. ➤➤ **humification** /-fi'kaysh(ə)n/ *noun*.

humiliate /hyooh'miliayt/ *verb trans* to cause (somebody) to feel humble or lower their dignity or self-respect. ➤➤ **humiliation** /-'aysh(ə)n/ *noun*. [late Latin *humiliatus*, past part. of *humiliare*, from Latin *humilis*: see HUMBLE[1]]

humility /hyooh'militi/ *noun* the quality or state of being humble.

hummingbird *noun* any of numerous species of tiny brightly coloured tropical American birds related to the swifts, having a slender bill and narrow wings that beat rapidly making a humming sound: family Trochilidae.

hummock /'humək/ *noun* **1** a hillock. **2** a ridge of ice. ➤➤ **hummocky** *adj*. [alteration of *hammock*, of unknown origin]

hummus *or* **houmous** /'hoohməs, 'hooməs/ *noun* a puree made from chick-peas and sesame seed paste, served as an appetizer or salad. [Turkish *humus* mashed chick-peas]

humongous *or* **humungous** /hyooh'mung·gəs/ *adj chiefly NAmer, informal* very large; huge. ➤➤ **humongously** *adv*. [prob based on HUGE and TREMENDOUS]

humor /'hyoohmə/ *noun and verb trans NAmer* see HUMOUR[1], HUMOUR[2].

humoral /'hyoohmərəl/ *adj* **1** relating to a bodily fluid or secretion, e.g. an endocrine hormone, or *esp* to blood serum and the antibodies circulating in it. **2** relating to the four humours of medieval physiology (see HUMOUR[1] (7)). [late Latin *humoralis* from *(h)umor*: see HUMOUR[1]]

humoresque /hyooma'resk/ *noun* a musical composition that is whimsical or fanciful in character. [German *Humoreske*, ultimately from HUMOUR[1]]

humorist /'hyoohmərist/ *noun* a person specializing in or noted for humour in speech, writing, or acting. ➤➤ **humoristic** /-'ristik/ *adj*.

humorous /'hyoohmərəs/ *adj* full of, characterized by, or expressing humour. ➤➤ **humorously** *adv*, **humorousness** *noun*.

humour[1] (*NAmer* **humor**) /'hyoohmə/ *noun* **1** a comic or amusing quality: *He failed to see the humour of his predicament*. **2** the faculty of expressing or appreciating the comic or amusing: *She has no sense of humour*. **3** things that are intended to be comic or amusing; wit: *books classified as 'humour'*. **4** *formal or literary* temperament: *a man of cheerful humour*. **5** a state of mind; temper: *He was in no humour to listen to further argument*. **6** *archaic* an inclination; a whim: *You'll ask me why I rather choose to have a weight of carrion flesh than to receive three thousand ducats. I'll not answer that, but say it is my humour* — Shakespeare. **7** *dated or archaic* a liquid or secretion in an animal or plant body, *esp* any of the four fluids, that is, bile or choler, black bile or melancholy, blood, and phlegm, regarded in medieval physiology as entering into the constitution of the body and determining by their relative proportions a person's health and temperament: *right as the humour of malencolie causeth ful many a man in sleepe to cry* — Chaucer. ✳ **out of humour** in a bad temper. ➤➤ **humourless** *adj*, **humourlessness** *noun*. [Middle English via

French *humeur* from Latin *(h)umor* moisture, from *humere* to be moist]

humour[2] (*NAmer* **humor**) *verb trans* to indulge (somebody); to comply with the mood or wishes of (them).

hump[1] /hump/ *noun* **1** a humped or crooked back. **2** a fleshy protuberance on the back of a camel, bison, etc. **3** a mound or knoll. ✳ **get the hump** *Brit, informal* to have a fit of sulking or depression. **over the hump** *informal* past the most difficult phase. ⪢ **humped** *adj*, **humpless** *adj*. [prob related to Low German *hump* bump]

hump[2] *verb trans* **1** to form or curve (the back) into a hump. **2** *chiefly Brit* to carry (something cumbersome) with difficulty: *humping suitcases around.* **3** *coarse slang* to have sexual intercourse with (somebody). ⪢ *verb intrans* **1** to rise in a hump. **2** *Aus, informal* to travel around or go on foot. **3** *coarse slang* to have sexual intercourse.

humpback *noun* **1** = HUNCHBACK. **2** a large whale related to the rorquals (see RORQUAL) but having very long flippers: *Megaptera novaeangliae.* ⪢ **humpbacked** *adj*.

humpback bridge *noun Brit* a narrow bridge rising and falling steeply from a central hump.

humph /hum(p)f/ *interj and noun* a gruntlike sound used to express doubt or contempt. [imitative]

humpty-dumpty /ˌhumpti ˈdumpti/ *noun* (*pl* **humpty-dumpties**) **1** *Brit, informal* a short fat person. **2** something that once damaged can never be repaired or made operative again. [*Humpty-Dumpty*, egg-shaped nursery-rhyme character who fell from a wall and broke into bits]

humpy[1] *adj* (**humpier, humpiest**) **1** full of or covered in humps. **2** having the form of a hump. **3** *informal* irritable or irascible. ⪢ **humpiness** *noun*.

humpy[2] *noun* (*pl* **humpies**) *Aus* a small or primitive hut. [Aboriginal *yumbi*]

humungous /hyooh'mung-gəs/ *adj* see HUMONGOUS.

humus /ˈhyoohməs/ *noun* a brown or black organic soil material resulting from partial decomposition of plant or animal matter. [Latin *humus* earth]

Humvee /ˈhumvee/ *noun chiefly NAmer, trademark* a modern military vehicle; a jeep. [phonetic representation of initials of *high-mobility multi-purpose vehicle*]

Hun /hun/ *noun* **1** a member of a nomadic Mongolian people who overran a large part of central and E Europe under Attila during the fourth and fifth cents AD. **2** (*often* **hun**) a person who is wantonly destructive or barbarically cruel. **3** (*also collectively* **the Hun**) *derog* a German; *esp* a German soldier in World War I or II. ⪢ **Hunnish** *adj*. [Old English *Hūne* via late Latin *Hunni* (pl) from Greek *Hounnoi*, of Iranian origin]

hunch[1] /hunch/ *verb intrans* to assume a bent or crooked posture. ⪢ *verb trans* **1** to arch (one's shoulders). **2** (*usu in passive*) to bend (oneself) into a cramped position: *He was hunched in a corner.* [orig in the sense 'push, shove', unknown origin]

hunch[2] *noun* **1** a strong intuitive feeling. **2** a hump or protuberance. **3** *archaic* a large lump of something.

hunchback *noun* **1** a humped back. **2** *offensive* a person with a humped back. ⪢ **hunchbacked** *adj*.

hundred /ˈhundrəd/ *noun* (*pl* **hundreds** *or* **hundred**) **1** (**a/one hundred**) the number 100, or the quantity represented by it. **2** (*in pl*) the numbers 100 to 999: *The death toll is likely to rise into the hundreds*; *He reckons his sexual partners in hundreds.* **3** (*usu in pl*) the number occupying the position three to the left of the decimal point in Arabic notation, or this position in a number or sum. **4** 100 units or digits; *specif* 100 pounds: *That outfit must have cost hundreds.* **5** in cricket, a score of 100 or more runs made by a batsman. **6** something, e.g. a bank note, having a denomination of 100. **7** a historical subdivision of some English and American counties, with its own court: *the Chiltern Hundreds.* **8** (**the sixteen hundreds, etc**) (*in pl*) the hundred years of a specified century: *from the late eighteen hundreds to the early nineteen hundreds.* **9** the first nine years of a specified century: *The Labour Party was founded in the nineteen hundreds.* **10** *informal* (*in pl*) a very large number: *I've got hundreds of letters to write.* ✳ **a hundred to one** in all probability: *A hundred to one he's married.* **in their hundreds** in great quantities: *Applications were arriving in their hundreds.* **not a hundred miles from here** *informal* not far off; in this very place. **one/a-hundred-per-cent** with complete conviction; wholeheartedly:

I'm one-hundred-per-cent behind you. **twenty, etc hundred hours 1** a verbal representation of 20.00, etc, that is, 8.00 p.m., etc, in the 24-hour system. **2** *archaic* six score, or 120. ⪢ **hundred** *adj*, **hundredfold** *adj and adv*, **hundredth** *adj and noun*. [Old English *hund*; (sense 7) prob because it consisted of 100 hides of land]

hundreds and thousands *pl noun* tiny strips of sugar of assorted bright colours, used *esp* for cake decoration.

hundredweight *noun* (*pl* **hundredweights** *or* **hundredweight**) **1** a British unit of weight equal to 112lb (about 50.80kg). **2** *NAmer* a US unit of weight equal to 100lb (about 45.36kg). **3** a unit of weight equal to about 50kg.

hung /hung/ *verb* past tense and past part. of HANG[1]. ✳ **hung up** *informal* in a state of anxiety, *esp* of an emotional nature. **hung up on** *informal* obsessed with (somebody or something).

Usage note

hung *or* hanged? See note at HANG[1].

hungan /ˈhoohng-gən/ *noun* see HOUNGAN.

Hungarian /hung'geəri-ən/ *noun* **1** a native or inhabitant of Hungary. **2** the Finno-Ugric language of Hungary. ⪢ **Hungarian** *adj*.

Word history

Words from Hungarian that have passed into English include *coach*, *goulash*, *hussar*, *paprika*, and *shako*.

hunger[1] /ˈhunggə/ *noun* **1a** a craving or urgent need for food. **b** the unpleasant sensation or weakened condition arising from this. **2** a strong desire; a craving: *a hunger for affection.* [Old English *hungor*]

hunger[2] *verb intrans* (**hungered, hungering**) **1** to feel or suffer hunger. **2** (+ for/after) to have an eager desire for something: *He hungered for fame and recognition.*

hunger march *noun* a march undertaken as a protest against unemployment or poverty, *esp* in the 1920s and 1930s. ⪢ **hunger-marcher** *noun*.

hunger strike *noun* refusal, as an act of protest, to eat enough to sustain life. ⪢ **hunger-striker** *noun*.

hung jury *noun* a jury that fails to reach a verdict.

hung over *adj* suffering from a hangover.

hung parliament *noun* a parliament in which no party holds an overall majority.

hungry /ˈhunggri/ *adj* (**hungrier, hungriest**) **1** feeling hunger. **2** characterized by or indicating hunger or longing: *a hungry look.* **3** (+ for) eager or avid for something: *hungry for power.* **4** said of land: not rich or fertile; barren. **5** *Aus, NZ* mean, grasping, or greedy. **6** *NZ* said of timber: parched and bare. ⪢ **hungrily** *adv*, **hungriness** *noun*. [Old English *hungrig*]

hunk /hungk/ *noun* **1** a large lump or piece of something: *a hunk of cheese.* **2** *informal* a sexually attractive, usu muscular man. ⪢ **hunky** *adj*. [Flemish *hunke* piece of food]

hunker *verb intrans* (**hunkered, hunkering**) **1** (*usu* + down) to squat or crouch. **2** to sit in a hunched position: *hunkering over the table.* **3** (*usu* + down) to take refuge or hide somewhere: *hunkering down in a cave.* ⪢ **hunkered** *adj*. [prob related to Old Norse *hūka* to squat]

hunkers *pl noun informal* the haunches. [HUNKER]

hunky-dory /ˌhungki ˈdawri/ *adj informal* perfectly satisfying; as one would wish. [obsolete English dialect *hunk* home base in games, from Dutch *honk*; origin of *-dory* uncertain]

hunt[1] /hunt/ *verb trans* **1a** to pursue (a quarry) for food or enjoyment: *hunt foxes.* **b** said of an animal: to chase and kill (prey): *Cats hunt birds as well as mice.* **c** to use (hounds) in the search for game. **2** said of the police: to pursue (a suspect, etc) with intent to capture. **3** (+ out) to search out or seek (something): *I'll hunt out a copy for you.* **4** to traverse (wild country, etc) in search of prey. ⪢ *verb intrans* **1** to take part in a hunt, *esp* regularly. **2** (+ for) to attempt to find something: *I'm hunting for a replacement for the vase I broke.* **3** said of a device, machine, etc: to run alternately fast and slowly. ✳ **hunt up/down** used with reference to change-ringing: to alter the place of a bell in systematic progression. [Old English *huntian*]

hunt[2] *noun* **1** the act or an instance of hunting: *We're on the hunt for a new manager.* **2a** (*treated as sing. or pl*) a group of mounted hunters and their hounds. **b** the area hunted.

huntaway *noun NZ* a dog trained to drive sheep forward a long way from the shepherd.

hunt down *verb trans* to pursue (somebody) in order to capture, attack, or kill them: *He was hunted down by his enemies and murdered.*

hunted *adj* said of somebody's look or expression: suggestive of being harried or persecuted.

hunter *noun* **1a** somebody who hunts game, *esp* with hounds. **b** a fast strong horse used in hunting. **2** (*used in combinations*) a person who hunts or seeks something, *esp* over-eagerly: *a fortune-hunter.* **3** a watch with a hinged metal cover to protect it.

hunter-gatherer *noun* in anthropology, a member of a nomadic people living by hunting, fishing, and gathering fruit, etc, as distinct from staying in one place and cultivating the soil.

hunter-killer *adj* denoting a submarine or other vessel equipped to locate and destroy enemy vessels.

hunter's moon *noun* the first full moon after harvest moon.

hunting *noun* the pursuit of game on horseback with hounds.

hunting crop *noun* a short riding whip with an angled handle and looped thong, used by foxhunters.

hunting dog *noun* (*also* **Cape hunting dog**) a wild dog of Africa that hunts in packs, having a dark coat with paler markings and a white-tipped tail: *Lycaon pictus.*

hunting ground *noun* an area of fruitful search or exploitation: *The British Empire is now a favourite hunting ground for historians.*

hunting horn *noun* a signal horn used in the chase, usu consisting of a long coiled tube with a flared bell.

hunting pink *noun* the red colour of the coats worn by fox-hunters.

Huntington's chorea /'huntingt(ə)nz/ *noun* a hereditary fatal brain disorder that develops usu in middle age and is characterized by CHOREA (spasmodic movement with lack of coordination) and nervous degeneration. [named after George *Huntington* d.1916, US neurologist, who first described it]

Huntington's disease *noun* = HUNTINGTON'S CHOREA.

huntress /'huntris/ *noun esp* in mythology, a woman or goddess that hunts: *Diana the huntress.*

hunt saboteur *noun* a person who tries to disrupt fox hunts.

huntsman *noun* (*pl* **huntsmen**) **1** a person who hunts. **2** a person who trains and looks after the hounds of a hunt.

Huon pine /'hyooh·on/ *noun* a large conifer of Tasmania with aromatic red timber and yew-like berries: *Dacrydium franklinii.* [named after the *Huon* River in S Tasmania]

hurdle¹ /'huhdl/ *noun* **1a** a portable framework, usu of interlaced branches and stakes, used *esp* for enclosing land or livestock. **b** a frame formerly used for dragging traitors to execution. **2a** a light barrier jumped by athletes, horses, dogs, etc in certain races. **b** (*in pl, but treated as sing. or pl*) any of various races over hurdles: compare FLAT RACE, STEEPLECHASE (1A). **3** a barrier, obstacle, or testing experience: *a number of hurdles to surmount.* [Old English *hyrdel*]

hurdle² *verb trans* to jump over (a barrier, etc), *esp* while running. ➤ *verb intrans* to run in hurdle races. ➤➤ **hurdler** *noun*, **hurdling** *noun.*

hurdy-gurdy /,huhdi'guhdi/ *noun* (*pl* **hurdy-gurdies**) **1** a BARREL ORGAN or other musical instrument in which the sound is produced by turning a crank. **2** a medieval stringed instrument on which music was produced by turning a wheel and pressing keys. [prob imitative]

hurl¹ /'huhl/ *verb trans* **1** to throw, drive, or thrust (something) violently somewhere. **2** (*usu* + at) to utter or shout (abuse, etc) violently at somebody: *She hurled insults at him.* ➤ *verb intrans* to rush or hurtle somewhere. ➤➤ **hurler** *noun.* [Middle English *hurlen*, prob of imitative origin]

hurl² *noun* **1** an act of hurling something somewhere. **2** *Scot* a ride in a car.

Hurler's syndrome /'huhləz/ *noun* a serious inherited disorder resulting from an enzyme deficiency and causing dwarfism, severe mental retardation, overgrowth of the skull, and other skeletal and constitutional defects. Also called GARGOYLISM. [named after Gertrud *Hurler* d.1965, Austrian paediatrician, who first described it]

hurley /'huhli/ *noun* **1** a stick for playing the game of hurling. **2** = HURLING. [HURL¹]

hurling *noun* an Irish field game resembling hockey played between two teams of 15 players each. [verbal noun from HURL¹]

hurly-burly /,huhli'buhli/ *noun* an uproar or commotion: *when the hurly-burly's done, when the battle's lost and won* — Shakespeare. [prob alteration and reduplication of *hurling*, verbal noun from HURL¹]

hurrah /hoo'rah/ *interj* = HURRAY. [alteration of the obsolete cheer *Huzza!*]

hurray *or* **hooray** /hoo'ray/ *interj* used as a cheer to express joy, approval, or encouragement. [see HURRAH]

Hurrian /'uri·ən/ *noun* **1** a member of a people who entered Syria and Mesopotamia and flourished between 4000 and 2000 BC, eventually becoming absorbed into the Assyrian and Hittite populations. **2** the language of these people, not belonging to any known language group, or the cuneiform script in which it was written. ➤➤ **Hurrian** *adj.* [Assyrian and Hittite *hurri, hurli*]

hurricane /'hurik(ə)n/ *noun* **1** a usu tropical cyclone with a wind having a speed of greater than 117km/h (73mph). **2** (*used before a noun*) denoting this wind velocity: *hurricane-force gales.* [Spanish *huracán* from Taino *hurakán* god of the storm]

hurricane deck *noun* an upper covered deck of a ship.

hurricane lamp *noun* a candlestick or oil lamp equipped with a glass chimney to protect the flame.

hurricane tape *noun* heavy-duty adhesive tape for securing window panes in their frames during severe storms.

hurried /'hurid/ *adj* done in a hurry: *a hurried search.* ➤➤ **hurriedly** *adv*, **hurriedness** *noun.*

hurry¹ /'huri/ *verb* (**hurries, hurried, hurrying**) ➤ *verb intrans* (*often* + up) to go somewhere, or do something, as quickly as possible. ➤ *verb trans* **1** (*often* + up) to make (a person or process) go faster: *Don't try to hurry the recuperation period; Can't somebody hurry her up?* **2** to rush (somebody) somewhere: *He was hurried to the doctor's.* ➤➤ **hurrier** *noun.* [prob of imitative origin]

hurry² *noun* haste or rush: *in my hurry to answer the phone.* ✳ **in a hurry** in haste; rushed. **in no hurry** not needing to hurry: *I'll wait; I'm in no hurry.* **2** *informal* reluctant to do something: *I'm in no hurry to get involved with the police again.* **not do something in a hurry** *informal* to be unlikely or reluctant to do something: *I won't sample his cooking again in a hurry.* **there's no hurry** there is no urgency: *There's no hurry for the report.* **what's the hurry?** stop trying to rush things.

hurry-up *adj* NAmer, informal requiring or executed in haste: *a hurry-up meal; a hurry-up call.*

hurst /huhst/ *noun archaic* **1** a hillock. **2** a sandbank. [Old English *hyrst*, of Germanic origin]

hurt¹ /huht/ *verb* (**hurting**, *past tense and past part.* **hurt**) ➤ *verb trans* **1** to do something that causes injury to (oneself or a part of one's body): *Have you hurt yourself?; I've hurt my wrist.* **2** to injure (somebody) or cause them to feel pain. **3** to offend or upset (a person or their feelings). **4** to damage the interests of (a person or group): *The new regulations will hurt the small investor most.* ➤ *verb intrans* **1** to be painful. **2** to inflict distress: *What I have to say is going to hurt.* ✳ **hurt for** NAmer, informal to need (something) urgently: *They're not hurting for cash.* [Middle English *hurten* to strike, injure, from Old French *hurter* to collide with, of Germanic origin]

hurt² *adj* **1** injured: *not badly hurt.* **2** upset or offended.

hurt³ *noun* **1** the emotional distress caused by an unpleasant experience or somebody's cruelty. **2** *archaic* harm: *My name is Caius Martius, who hath done to thee particularly … great hurt and mischief* — Shakespeare. **3** *archaic* a wound: *This gentleman … hath got this mortal hurt in my behalf* — Shakespeare.

hurtful /'huhtf(ə)l/ *adj* said of words or behaviour: causing pain or distress; intended to hurt feelings: *hurtful comments.* ➤➤ **hurtfully** *adv*, **hurtfulness** *noun.*

hurtle /'huhtl/ *verb intrans* to move somewhere rapidly or precipitately: *hurtling along the motorway.* [Middle English *hurtlen* to collide, frequentative of *hurten*: see HURT¹]

husband¹ /'huzbənd/ *noun* the man to whom a woman is married. ➤➤ **husbandhood** *noun*, **husbandless** *adj*, **husbandly** *adj.* [Old English *hūsbonda* master of a house, from Old Norse *hūsbōndi*, from *hūs* house + *bōndi* householder]

husband² *verb trans* to conserve or make the most economical use of (a resource, etc): *Husband your strength.* ➤➤ **husbander** *noun.*

husbandman /'huzbəndmən/ *noun* (*pl* **husbandmen**) *archaic* a person who ploughs and cultivates land; a farmer.

husbandry /'huzbəndri/ *noun* **1** the judicious management of resources. **2** farming, *esp* of domestic animals.

hush[1] /hush/ *verb trans* to quieten (a crying baby, etc). ➤ *verb intrans* often used as an exclamation: to stop making a noise: *Hush, everyone!* ➤ **hushed** *adj.* [back-formation from *husht* hushed, from Middle English *hussht* (interj), used to enjoin silence]

hush[2] *noun* a silence or calm, *esp* following noise.

hushaby *or* **hushabye** /'hushəbie/ *interj archaic* used to lull a baby to sleep. [from HUSH[1] + -*by* as in BYE-BYE]

hush-hush *adj informal* secret or confidential.

hush money *noun* money paid secretly to prevent disclosure of damaging information.

hush up *verb trans* to keep secret or suppress (facts).

husk[1] /husk/ *noun* **1** a dry or membranous outer covering, e.g. a shell or pod, of a seed or fruit. **2** a useless outer layer of something. [Middle English *husk, huske*, prob modification of early Dutch *huuskijn*, dimin. of *huus* house, cover]

husk[2] *verb trans* to strip the husk from (a fruit, seed, etc).

husky[1] *adj* (**huskier, huskiest**) hoarse; breathy: *a husky voice.* ➤➤ **huskily** *adv*, **huskiness** *noun.* [prob from obsolete *husk* to have a dry cough, prob of imitative origin]

husky[2] *adj* (**huskier, huskiest**) of, resembling, or containing husks.

husky[3] *adj* (**huskier, huskiest**) *informal* burly or hefty. [prob from HUSK[1]]

husky[4] *noun* (*pl* **huskies**) a powerful sledge dog with a broad chest and a shaggy outer coat, native to Greenland and Labrador. Also called ESKIMO DOG. [prob by alteration from ESKIMO]

huss /hus/ *noun Brit* a dogfish, *esp* the NURSEHOUND: genus *Scyliorhinus.* [alteration of Middle English *husk*, of unknown origin]

hussar /hoo'zah/ *noun* **1** a Hungarian horseman of the 15th cent. **2** (*often* **Hussar**) a member of any of various European cavalry regiments. [Hungarian *huszár* hussar, formerly 'highway robber', from Serbian *husar* pirate, from medieval Latin *cursarius*: see CORSAIR]

Hussite /'husiet/ *noun* a member of the Bohemian religious movement led by John Huss. ➤➤ **Hussite** *adj*, **Hussitism** *noun.* [Latin *Hussita*, named after John *Huss* d.1415, Bohemian religious reformer]

hussy /'husi/ *noun* (*pl* **hussies**) *derog* an impudent or promiscuous woman or girl. [alteration of HOUSEWIFE]

hustings /'hustingz/ *pl noun* (*treated as sing. or pl*) **1** a place where election speeches are made. **2** the proceedings of an election campaign. **3** formerly, a raised platform used for the nomination of candidates for Parliament and for election speeches.

Word history

Old English *hūsting* deliberative assembly, from Old Norse *hūsthing*, formed from *hūs* house + *thing* assembly. From the 12th cent. onwards *husting* or *hustings* referred to a court held in the Guildhall, London by the Lord Mayor and the Aldermen, hence to the platform on which these dignitaries sat; the current senses date from the 18th cent.

hustle[1] /'husl/ *verb trans* **1** to push or convey (somebody) roughly, forcibly, or hurriedly somewhere: *They hustled him into a taxi.* **2** (+ into) to impel or force (somebody) into doing something: *They hustled her into accepting.* **3** *informal* (+ out of) to swindle or cheat (somebody) out of something. ➤ *verb intrans* **1** to hasten or hurry. **2** *chiefly NAmer* to make strenuous, often dishonest, efforts to secure money or business. **3** *chiefly NAmer* to engage in prostitution; to solicit. ➤➤ **hustler** *noun.* [Dutch *husselen* from early Dutch *hutselen*, frequentative of *hutsen* to shake]

hustle[2] *noun* the act or an instance of hustling.

hut[1] /hut/ *noun* **1** a small, often temporary, dwelling of simple construction. **2** in mountain-climbing areas, e.g. the Alps, a building with dormitories, etc for the accommodation of walkers and climbers. ➤➤ **hutlike** *adj.* [early French *hutte*, of Germanic origin]

hut[2] *verb* (**hutted, hutting**) ➤ *verb trans* to accommodate (troops, etc) in huts. ➤ *verb intrans* said of military personnel: to construct huts for accommodation.

hutch /huch/ *noun* **1** a pen or cage for a small animal, e.g. a rabbit. **2** *informal, derog* a shack or shanty. [Middle English *huche* via Old French from medieval Latin *hutica*]

hutment *noun* an encampment of huts.

hutted *adj* said of accommodation or an encampment: consisting of huts.

Hutterite /'hutəriet/ *noun* **1** a member of a 16th-cent. sect of Anabaptists established in Moravia. **2** a member of a N American group still adhering to the beliefs of this sect, and following an old-style way of life, including common ownership of property. ➤➤ **Hutterite** *adj.* [named after Jacob *Hutter*, 16th-cent. Moravian Anabaptist]

Hutu /'hoohtooh/ *noun* (*pl* **Hutus** *or collectively* **Hutu** *or* **Bahutu** /bə-/) a member of the Bantu-speaking people that constitute the majority of the population of Rwanda and Burundi: compare TUTSI. ➤➤ **Hutu** *adj.* [the Bantu name of the people]

huzzah *or* **huzza** /hə'zah/ *interj* = HURRAY.

HV *abbr* **1** high velocity. **2** high-voltage.

HWM *abbr* high-water mark.

hwyl /'hooh·il/ *noun* Welsh emotional intensity or passion, e.g. in speaking or recitation. [Welsh *hwyl* mood]

hyacinth /'hie·əsinth/ *noun* **1** any of a genus of common garden plants with fragrant blue, pink, or white flowers that grow in spikes: genus *Hyacinthus.* **2** a colour varying from light violet to mid-purple. **3** = JACINTH. ➤➤ **hyacinth** *adj*, **hyacinthine** /-sinthien/ *adj.* [via Latin from Greek *hyakinthos* a precious stone, a flowering plant, in reference to the myth of the youth Hyacinthus, killed accidentally by Apollo, from whose blood grew a flower]

hyaena /hie'eena/ *noun* see HYENA.

hyal- *or* **hyalo-** *comb. form* forming words, with the meaning: glass; glassy: *hyaline.* [Greek *hyalos* glass]

hyalin /'hie·əlin/ *noun* a clear glassy substance found in degenerating body tissues. [via Latin from Greek *hyalinos* glassy, from *hyalos* glass]

hyaline[1] /'hie·əlin/ *adj* **1** belonging to or relating to glass. **2** said of biological materials or structures: transparent or nearly so; consisting of HYALIN. **3** said of a mineral: glassy; vitreous. [via Latin from Greek *hyalinos*: see HYALIN]

hyaline[2] *noun literary* something glassy or transparent, e.g. a clear sky: *the clear hyaline, the glassy sea … with stars numerous* — Milton.

hyaline cartilage *noun* translucent bluish white cartilage that is present in joints and respiratory passages and forms most of the foetal skeleton.

hyalite /'hie·əliet/ *noun* a colourless or translucent opal. [German *Hyalit*, from Greek *hyalos* glass]

hyalo- *comb. form* see HYAL-.

hyaloid /'hie·əloyd/ *adj* said of biological materials or structures: glassy or transparent.

hyaloid membrane *noun* a thin transparent membrane that encloses the vitreous humour of the eye.

hyaloplasm /'hie·əlohplaz(ə)m/ *noun* the clear, fluid, apparently homogeneous basic substance of cytoplasm.

hybrid /'hiebrid/ *noun* **1** an offspring of two animals or plants of different races, breeds, varieties, etc, e.g. a mule. **2** something heterogeneous in origin or composition. **3** a word, e.g. *television*, made up of elements from different languages. ➤➤ **hybridism** *noun*, **hybridist** *noun*, **hybridity** /hie'briditi/ *noun.* [Latin *hybrida* offspring of a mixed union]

hybridize *or* **hybridise** /'hiebridiez/ *verb intrans* to produce hybrids; to interbreed. ➤ *verb trans* to cause (animals or plants) to produce hybrids; to interbreed (them). ➤➤ **hybridization** /-'zaysh(ə)n/ *noun*, **hybridizer** *noun.*

hybridoma /hiebri'dohmə/ *noun* (*pl* **hybridomas** *or* **hybridomata** /-tə/) a hybrid cell or clone of cells formed by the fusion of a tumour cell with a normal LYMPHOCYTE (antibody-producing cell).

hybrid vigour *noun* = HETEROSIS.

hydantoin /hie'dantoh·in/ *noun* a crystalline compound found in sugar beet and used in the preparation of certain anticonvulsant drugs. [Greek *hydat-, hydōr* water + *allantoic*: see ALLANTOIS]

hydatid /'hiedatid/ *noun* **1** a fluid-filled sac produced by and containing a tapeworm larva. **2** the larva itself. [Greek *hydatid-, hydatis* watery cyst, from *hydat-, hydōr* water]

hydatidiform mole /hiedə'tidifawm/ *noun* a cluster of fluid-filled sacs resembling a bunch of grapes, that forms in the womb as the CHORION (membrane around the foetus) degenerates during abortion.

hydr- *or* **hydro-** *comb. form* forming words, denoting: **1a** water: *hydrous; hydroelectric.* **b** liquid: *hydrokinetics; hydrometer.* **2**

hydrogen; containing or combined with hydrogen: *hydrocarbon*; *hydrochloride*. [Middle English *ydr-*, *ydro-* via Old French and Latin from Greek, from *hydōr* water]

hydra /'hiedrə/ *noun* **1** a small tubular freshwater polyp with a mouth surrounded by tentacles: genus *Hydra*. **2** a persistent evil that is not easily overcome. [named after *Hydra*, a serpent in Greek mythology with many heads, which regrew when cut off]

hydrangea /hie'draynjə/ *noun* any of several species of shrubs that produce large clusters of white, pink, or pale blue flowers: *Hydrangea macrophylla* and other species. [Latin *hydrangea*, literally 'water pot', from HYDR- + Greek *angeion* vessel; because of its cap-shaped seed pod]

hydrant /'hiedrənt/ *noun* a discharge pipe with a valve and nozzle from which water may be drawn from a main.

hydrate[1] /'hiedrayt/ *noun* a compound or complex ion formed by the union of water with another substance.

hydrate[2] /hie'drayt, 'hiedrayt/ *verb trans* to cause (a substance) to take up or combine with water or its constituent elements. ⟫ **hydratable** *adj*, **hydration** /hie'draysh(ə)n/ *noun*, **hydrator** *noun*.

hydraulic /hie'drawlik, hie'drolik/ *adj* **1** operated, moved, or effected by means of liquid, *esp* water. **2** relating to hydraulics: *a hydraulic engineer*. **3** relating to liquid, *esp* water, in motion: *hydraulic erosion*. **4** operated by the transmission of pressure in a liquid being forced through pipes, tubes, etc: *hydraulic brakes*; *a hydraulic press*. **5** hardening or setting under water: *hydraulic cement*. ⟫ **hydraulically** *adv*. [via Latin from Greek *hydraulikos*, from *hydraulis* hydraulic organ, from HYDR- + *aulos* pipe]

hydraulic coupling *noun* = TORQUE CONVERTER.

hydraulic ram *noun* a pump that forces running water to a higher level by using the kinetic energy of a descending flow.

hydraulics *pl noun* (*treated as sing.*) a branch of physics that deals with the practical applications of liquid in motion.

hydrazine /'hiedrəzeen, -zin/ *noun* a colourless liquid that acts as a reducing agent and is used *esp* in rocket fuels. [HYDR- (2) + AZO- + -INE[2]]

hydria /'hiedri-ə/ *noun* (*pl* **hydriae** /'hiedri-ee/ *or* **hydriai**) an ancient Greek three-handled water pot. [Greek *hydria* water pot, from *hydōr* water]

hydric /'hiedrik/ *adj* **1** containing or requiring moisture: compare MESIC[1], XERIC: *a hydric habitat*; *a hydric plant*. **2** relating to hydrogen.

-hydric *comb. form* forming adjectives, with the meaning: containing a specified number of acid hydrogens: *monohydric*.

hydride /'hiedried/ *noun* a compound of hydrogen usu with a less electronegative element or radical.

hydriodic acid /hiedri'odik/ *noun* a solution of hydrogen iodide in water that is a strong acid and reducing agent: formula HI. [HYDR- (1) + IODIC]

hydro[1] /'hiedroh/ *noun* (*pl* **hydros**) *Brit* a hotel or establishment formerly providing facilities for hydropathic treatment. [short for *hydropathic establishment*]

hydro[2] *adj* hydroelectric.

hydro[3] *abbr* hydroelectricity.

hydro- *comb. form* see HYDR-.

hydrobromic acid /hiedroh'brohmik/ *noun* a solution of hydrogen bromide in water that is a strong acid and a weak reducing agent: formula HBr.

hydrocarbon /hiedroh'kahb(ə)n, 'hie-/ *noun* an organic compound, e.g. benzene, containing only carbon and hydrogen. ⟫ **hydrocarbonaceous** /-'nayshəs/ *adj*, **hydrocarbonic** /-'bonik/ *adj*, **hydrocarbonous** /-nəs/ *adj*.

hydrocele /'hiedrohseel/ *noun* an accumulation of watery liquid in a body cavity, e.g. the scrotum.

hydrocephalus /hiedroh'sefələs/ *or* **hydrocephaly** /-li/ *noun* an abnormal increase in the amount of cerebrospinal fluid within the brain cavity accompanied by enlargement of the skull and brain atrophy. ⟫ **hydrocephalic** /-'falik/ *adj*. [scientific Latin, from Greek *hydōr* water + *kephalē* head]

hydrochloric acid /hiedrə'klorik/ *noun* a solution of hydrogen chloride in water that is a strong corrosive acid and is naturally present in the gastric juice: formula HCl.

hydrochloride /hiedrə'klawried/ *noun* a compound of hydrochloric acid, *esp* with an organic chemical base, e.g. an alkaloid.

hydrocortisone /hiedroh'kawtizohn, -sohn/ *noun* a steroid hormone that is produced by the cortex of the adrenal gland and used *esp* in the treatment of rheumatoid arthritis. Also called CORTISOL.

hydrocyanic acid /hiedrohsie'anik/ *noun* a solution of hydrogen cyanide in water that is a highly poisonous weak acid: formula HCN. Also called HYDROGEN CYANIDE.

hydrodynamics /,hiedrohdie'namiks, -di'namiks/ *pl noun* (*treated as sing. or pl*) a science that deals with the motion of fluids and the forces acting on solid bodies immersed in them. ⟫ **hydrodynamic** *adj*, **hydrodynamicist** /-die'naməsist/ *noun*.

hydroelectric /,hiedroh'lektrik/ *adj* relating to or denoting the production of electricity by waterpower. ⟫ **hydroelectrically** *adv*, **hydroelectricity** /-ilek'trisiti, elik'trisiti/ *noun*.

hydrofluoric acid /,hiedrohflooh'orik/ *noun* a solution of hydrogen fluoride in water that is a poisonous weak acid, used *esp* in etching glass: formula HF.

hydrofoil /'hiedrəfoyl/ *noun* **1** a ship or boat fitted with an aerofoil like device that lifts the hull out of the water at speed. **2** the aerofoil-like device itself. [blend of HYDRO- + AEROFOIL]

hydroforming /'hiedrohfawming/ *noun* **1** a process by which hydrogen, with other catalysts, causes certain hydrocarbons to rearrange themselves into aromatic or cyclic forms, used to produce high-octane petrol. **2** in engineering, a hydraulic forming process in which sheet metal is shaped between a punch and the flexible surface of a fluid-filled bag.

hydrogel /'hiedrohjel/ *noun* a gel whose liquid component is water.

hydrogen /'hiedrəj(ə)n/ *noun* the simplest and lightest of the chemical elements, normally occurring as a highly flammable gas: symbol H, atomic number 1: compare DEUTERIUM, PROTIUM, TRITIUM. ⟫ **hydrogenous** /hie'drojinəs/ *adj*. [French *hydrogène*, from HYDRO- + *-gène* -GEN; because water is generated by its combustion]

hydrogenase /hie'drojinayz/ *noun* an enzyme of various anaerobic micro-organisms, e.g. some bacteria, that promotes the oxidation of hydrogen atoms or the uptake and release of gaseous hydrogen.

hydrogenate /hie'drojinayt/ *verb trans* to combine or treat (an unsaturated organic compound, etc) with hydrogen. ⟫ **hydrogenation** /-'naysh(ə)n/ *noun*.

hydrogen bomb *noun* a bomb whose violent explosive power is due to the sudden release of atomic energy resulting from the nuclear fusion of hydrogen initiated by the explosion of an atom bomb.

hydrogen bond *noun* an electrostatic chemical bond consisting of a hydrogen atom bonded to two small electronegative atoms, e.g. oxygen or nitrogen.

hydrogen bromide *noun* a colourless pungent gas that dissolves in water to form hydrobromic acid and is used *esp* in the synthesis of organic chemical compounds that are bromides: formula HBr.

hydrogen chloride *noun* a colourless pungent poisonous gas that dissolves in water to form hydrochloric acid and is used *esp* in the synthesis of organic chemical compounds that are chlorides: formula HCl.

hydrogen cyanide *noun* **1** a poisonous gaseous compound that has the smell of bitter almonds: formula HCN. **2** = HYDROCYANIC ACID.

hydrogen fluoride *noun* a colourless corrosive poisonous gaseous chemical compound that dissolves in water to form hydrofluoric acid and is used *esp* as a catalyst in the petroleum industry and in the synthesis of organic chemical compounds that are fluorides: formula HF.

hydrogen iodide *noun* an acrid colourless gas that dissolves in water to form hydriodic acid and is used *esp* in the synthesis of organic chemical compounds that are iodides: formula HI.

hydrogen ion *noun* **1** the positively charged ion, H+, characteristic of acids, that consists of a hydrogen atom that has lost an electron; a proton. **2** a hydrogen ion combined with water that is present in solutions of acids; = HYDRONIUM.

hydrogen peroxide *noun* an unstable compound used *esp* as an oxidizing and bleaching agent, an antiseptic, and a rocket propellant: formula H_2O_2.

hydrogen sulphide *noun* an inflammable poisonous gas that has a smell of rotten eggs and is formed in putrefying matter: formula H_2S.

hydrogeology /,hiedrohji'oləji/ *noun* the branch of geology dealing with underground water and with the geological aspects of surface water.

hydrography /hie'drogrəfi/ *noun* the description, measurement, and mapping of bodies of water, e.g. seas. ➤ **hydrographer** *noun*, **hydrographic** /-'grafik/ *adj*, **hydrographically** /-'grafikli/ *adv*.

hydroid /'hiedroyd/ *noun* any of an order of coelenterates, *esp* one that is a polyp: order Hydroida. ➤ **hydroid** *adj*.

hydrokinetic /,hiedrohki'netik/ *adj* relating to the motions of liquids or the forces that produce or affect such motions. ➤ **hydrokinetically** *adv*, **hydrokinetics** *pl noun*.

hydrokinetical /hiedrohki'netikl/ *adj* = HYDROKINETIC.

hydrolase /'hiedrohlayz/ *noun* an enzyme that promotes HYDROLYSIS (chemical breakdown in combination with water). [HYDROLYSIS + -ASE]

hydrology /hie'droləji/ *noun* a science dealing with the properties, distribution, and circulation of the water of the earth's surface. ➤ **hydrologic** /-'lojik/ *adj*, **hydrological** /-'lojikl/ *adj*, **hydrologically** /-'lojikli/ *adv*, **hydrologist** *noun*.

hydrolyse (*NAmer* **hydrolyze**) /'hiedrəliez/ *verb trans* to subject (a substance) to hydrolysis: *hydrolysed protein*. ➤ **hydrolysable** *adj*. [back-formation from HYDROLYSIS on the model of ANALYSE]

hydrolysis /hie'droləsis/ *noun* chemical breakdown involving splitting of a bond and addition of the elements of water. ➤ **hydrolytic** /-'litik/ *adj*, **hydrolytically** /-'litikli/ *adv*.

hydrolyze /'hiedrəliez/ *verb trans NAmer* see HYDROLYSE.

hydromagnetic /,hiedroh·mag'netik/ *adj* = MAGNETOHYDRODYNAMIC. ➤ **hydromagnetics** *pl noun*.

hydromassage /'hiedrohmasahzh/ *noun* massage performed using jets of water.

hydromechanics /,hiedrohmi'kaniks/ *pl noun* (*treated as sing. or pl*) the mechanics of fluids; = HYDRODYNAMICS.

hydromel /'hiedrəmel/ *noun* a mixture of honey and water; *esp* mead. [Middle English *ydromel* via French and Latin from Greek *hydromeli*, from HYDRO- + *meli* honey]

hydrometer /hie'dromitə/ *noun* an instrument for determining relative densities of solutions and hence their strength. ➤ **hydrometric** /hiedroh'metrik/ *adj*, **hydrometrical** /hiedroh'-metrikl/ *adj*, **hydrometry** /-tri/ *noun*.

hydronaut /'hiedrənawt/ *noun NAmer* a person trained to work in or operate deep-sea vessels used for research or rescue. [HYDRO- and -*naut* as in AERONAUT]

hydronic /hie'dronik/ *adj* denoting a heating or cooling system that uses circulating water.

hydronium /hie'drohni·əm/ *noun* a hydrated hydrogen ion H_3O^+. [German *Hydronium*, contraction of *hydroxonium*: see HYDROXONIUM ION]

hydropathy /hie'dropəthi/ *noun* the use of water in treating diseases; = HYDROTHERAPY. ➤ **hydropathic** /hiedroh'pathik/ *adj*, **hydropathically** /hiedroh'pathikli/ *adv*.

hydrophane /'hiedrəfayn/ *noun* a semitranslucent opal that becomes transparent in water. ➤ **hydrophanous** /hie'drofənəs/ *adj*. [HYDRO- + Greek *phanos* bright, clear, from *phanein* to show]

hydrophilic /hiedrə'filik/ *adj* relating to or having a strong affinity for water. ➤ **hydrophilicity** /-'lisiti/ *noun*.

hydrophobia /hiedrə'fohbi·ə/ *noun* **1** abnormal dread of water. **2** = RABIES. [(sense 2) because fear of water is a symptom]

hydrophobic /hiedrə'fohbik/ *adj* **1** characteristic of or suffering from hydrophobia. **2** lacking affinity for water. ➤ **hydrophobicity** /-'bisiti/ *noun*.

hydrophone /'hiedrəfohn/ *noun* an instrument for listening to sound transmitted through water.

hydrophyte /'hiedrohfiet/ *noun* a plant that grows in water or waterlogged soil. ➤ **hydrophytic** /-'fitik/ *adj*.

hydroplane¹ /'hiedrəplayn/ *noun* **1** a speedboat fitted with hydrofoils or a stepped bottom so that the hull is raised wholly or partly

out of the water when moving at speed. **2** a horizontal surface on a submarine's hull, used to control movement upward or downward.

hydroplane² *verb intrans* **1** to skim over the water with the hull largely clear of the surface. **2** to ride in a hydroplane. **3** *chiefly NAmer* = AQUAPLANE² (2). ➤ **hydroplaner** *noun*.

hydroponics /hiedrə'poniks/ *pl noun* (*treated as sing. or pl*) the growing of plants in liquid, sand, or gravel containing nutrient solutions rather than soil. ➤ **hydroponic** *adj*, **hydroponically** *adv*. [HYDRO- + Greek *ponos* labour, *ponein* to toil]

hydropower /'hiedrohpowə/ *noun* hydroelectric power.

hydroquinone /,hiedrohkwi'nohn/ *noun* a phenol that is a reducing agent and is used *esp* as a photographic developer.

hydrospeed /'hiedrohspeed/ *or* **hydrospeeding** *noun* the sport of jumping into white water with a float for buoyancy, and being carried along at speed.

hydrosphere /'hiedrəsfiə/ *noun* all the waters (liquid or frozen) at the earth's surface, including soil and ground water. ➤ **hydrospheric** /-'sferik/ *adj*.

hydrostatic /hiedrə'statik/ *adj* relating to or denoting liquids at rest, or the pressure exerted by them. ➤ **hydrostatically** *adv*.

hydrostatical /hiedroh'statikl/ *adj* = HYDROSTATIC.

hydrostatics *pl noun* (*treated as sing. or pl*) physics dealing with the characteristics of liquids at rest, *esp* the pressure in or exerted by a liquid.

hydrotherapeutics /,hiedrohtherə'pyoohtiks/ *pl noun* (*treated as sing. or pl*) the branch of medicine dealing with hydotherapy.

hydrotherapy /hiedrə'therəpi/ *noun* the use of water in the treatment of disease; *esp* treatment using exercise in heated water.

hydrothermal /hiedrə'thuhml/ *adj* relating to or caused by the action of hot water, *esp* on the earth's crust. ➤ **hydrothermally** *adv*.

hydrothorax /hiedroh'thawraks/ *noun* an excess of watery fluid in the pleural cavity, usu resulting from failing circulation.

hydrotropism /hie'drotrəpiz(ə)m/ *noun* a TROPISM (twisting tendency) e.g. in plant roots, in which water or water vapour is the orienting factor. ➤ **hydrotropic** /hiedroh'tropik/ *adj*, **hydrotropically** /hiedroh'tropikli/ *adv*.

hydrous /'hiedrəs/ *adj* containing water (chemically combined with other atoms or molecules).

hydroxide /hie'droksied/ *noun* a compound of hydroxyl with an element or radical.

hydroxonium ion /hiedrok'sohni·əm/ *noun* the ion H_3O^+, found in all aqueous acids; = HYDRONIUM. [blend of HYDRO-, OXY-² + AMMONIUM]

hydroxy /hie'droksi/ *adj* (*often used in combinations*) hydroxyl; *esp* containing hydroxyl, *esp* in place of hydrogen: *hydroxyacetic acid*. [from HYDROXYL]

hydroxyl /hie'droksil, -siel/ *noun* the univalent group or radical OH consisting of one hydrogen atom and one oxygen atom that is characteristic of hydroxides, alcohols, etc. ➤ **hydroxylic** /-'silik/ *adj*. [HYDR- + OX- + -YL]

hydroxytryptamine /hie,droksi'triptəmeen/ *noun* = SEROTONIN.

hydrozoan /hiedrə'zoh·ən/ *noun* any of a class of coelenterates that includes simple and compound polyps and jellyfishes: class Hydrozoa. ➤ **hydrozoan** *adj*. [HYDR- + Greek *zōion* animal]

hyena *or* **hyaena** /hie'eenə/ *noun* any of three species of doglike nocturnal carnivorous mammals of Asia and Africa, with front legs longer than the rear legs, and an erect mane: family Hyaenidae. [via Latin from Greek orig fem. of *hys* hog; because the stiff hairs of the mane resemble a hog's bristles]

hygiene /'hiejeen/ *noun* conditions or practices, *esp* cleanliness, conducive to the establishment and maintenance of health. [via French *hygiène* and Latin *hygieina* from Greek *hygieinē technē* the art relating to health, from *hygiēs* healthy]

hygienic /hie'jeenik/ *adj* clean and conducive to the establishment and maintenance of health. ➤ **hygienically** *adv*.

hygienics /hie'jeeniks/ *pl noun* (*treated as sing. or pl*) = HYGIENE.

hygienist /hie'jeenist/ *noun* **1** a person who is trained in the theory and practice of hygiene. **2** = DENTAL HYGIENIST.

hygr- *or* **hygro-** *comb. form* forming words, denoting: humidity; moisture: *hyroscope*; *hygrometer*. [Greek *hygros* wet]

hygrometer /hie'gromitə/ *noun* an instrument for measuring the humidity of the atmosphere. ➤➤ **hygrometric** /-'metrik/ *adj*, **hygrometry** /-tri/ *noun*.

hygrophilous /hie'grofiləs/ *adj* said of a plant: living or growing in moist places.

hygrophyte /'hiegrəfiet/ *noun* any plant that grows in wet or waterlogged ground. ➤➤ **hygrophytic** /-'fitik/ *adj*.

hygroscope /'hiegrəskohp/ *noun* an instrument that shows changes in humidity, e.g. of the atmosphere.

hygroscopic /hiegrə'skopik/ *adj* said of a substance: readily taking up and retaining moisture, e.g. from the air. ➤➤ **hygroscopically** *adv*, **hygroscopicity** /-'pisiti/ *noun*. [from the use of such materials in the hygroscope]

hying /'hie·ing/ *verb* present part. of HIE.

Hyksos /'hiksos/ *pl noun* a mixed Semitic and Asian dynasty that ruled Egypt from about the 18th to 16th cent. BC. [Greek *Hyksōs*, the 'shepherd-king' dynasty, from Egyptian *heqa khoswe* ruler of the country of the nomads]

hyl *or* **hylo** *comb. form* forming words, denoting: matter; material. *hylozoism*. [Greek *hulē* matter]

hyla /'hielə/ *noun* any of a genus of tree frogs: genus *Hyla*. [Latin genus name, from Greek *hylē* wood]

hylo- *comb. form* see HYL-.

hylomorphism /hieloh'mawfiz(ə)m/ *noun* the philosophical doctrine that matter is the first cause of the universe and that physical objects are the product of a combination of matter and form.

hylozoism /hieloh'zoh·iz(ə)m/ *noun* a doctrine held *esp* by early Greek philosophers that all matter has life. ➤➤ **hylozoist** *noun*, **hylozoistic** /-'istik/ *adj*. [HYL- + *zōos* alive, living]

hymen /'hiemen, 'hiemən/ *noun* a fold of mucous membrane partly closing the opening of the vagina until it is ruptured, usu on the first occurrence of sexual intercourse. ➤➤ **hymenal** *adj*. [via late Latin from Greek *hymēn* membrane]

hymeneal /hiemə'nee·əl/ *adj literary* nuptial: *when I was myself in a state of celibacy, and Mrs Micawber had not yet been solicited to plight her faith at the Hymeneal altar* — Dickens. [via Latin *hymenaeus* wedding song, wedding, named after Greek *hymenaios*, formed from *Hymēn*, god of marriage]

hymenium /hie'meeni·əm/ *noun* (*pl* **hymenia** /-ni·ə/ *or* **hymeniums**) a spore-bearing layer in fungi. ➤➤ **hymenial** *adj*. [via Latin from Greek *hymenion*, dimin. of *hymēn* membrane]

hymenopteran *or* **hymenopteron** /hiemi'noptərən/ *noun* any of an order of highly specialized usu stinging insects including the bees, wasps, or ants, that often associate in large colonies and have usu four membranous wings: order Hymenoptera. ➤➤ **hymenopteran** *adj*, **hymenopterous** /-rəs/ *adj*. [via Latin from Greek *hymenopteron*, neuter of *hymenopteros* membrane-winged, from *hymēn* membrane + *pteron* wing]

hymn[1] /him/ *noun* **1** a song of praise to God; *esp* a metrical composition that can be included in a religious service. **2** a song of praise or joy. ➤➤ **hymnic** /'himnik/ *adj*. [Middle English *ymne* via Old French and Latin from Greek *hymnos* song of praise]

hymn[2] *verb trans* to praise or worship (somebody, *esp* God, or something) in hymns: *Give me one lonely hour to hymn the setting day* — W Cullen Bryant. ➤ *verb intrans* to sing a hymn.

hymnal[1] /'himnəl/ *noun* a book or a collection of church hymns.

hymnal[2] *adj* of or relating to hymns.

hymnary /'himnəri/ *noun* (*pl* **hymnaries**) = HYMNAL[1].

hymnbook *noun* = HYMNAL[1].

hymnody /'himnədi/ *noun* (*pl* **hymnodies**) **1** the singing or writing of hymns. **2** collectively, the hymns of a time, place, or church. ➤➤ **hymnodist** *noun*. [via late Latin from Greek *hymnōidia*, from *hymnos* HYMN[1] + *aeidein* to sing]

hymnography /him'nogrəfi/ *noun* the writing of hymns. ➤➤ **hymnographer** *noun*.

hymnology /him'noləji/ *noun* **1** the writing of hymns. **2** the study of hymns. ➤➤ **hymnological** /-'lojikl/ *adj*, **hymnologist** *noun*. [Greek *hymnologia* the singing of hymns, which was the sense in English until mid 19th cent.]

hyoid /'hie·oyd/ *adj* relating to the hyoid bone.

hyoid bone *noun* a complex of joined bones situated at the base of the tongue and supporting the tongue and its muscles. [via Latin

from Greek *hyoeidēs* shaped like the letter upsilon (ϒ, υ), denoting the hyoid bone, formed from *y, hy* upsilon]

hyoscine /'hie·əseen/ *noun* an alkaloid found in various plants of the nightshade family that has effects on the nervous system similar to those of atropine. [HYOSCYAMINE + -INE[2]]

hyoscyamine /hie·ə'sie·əmeen, -min/ *noun* the laevorotatory form of atropine found *esp* in deadly nightshade and henbane. [via Latin from Greek *hyoskyamos* henbane, literally 'swine's bean', from *hys* swine + *kyamos* bean]

hyp- *prefix* see HYPO-.

hypabyssal /hipə'bisl/ *adj* relating to or denoting igneous rock representing magma that has solidified close to the earth's surface, occurring as minor intrusions in the form of dykes and sills.

hypaesthesia (*NAmer* **hypesthesia**) /hiepees'theezyə, -zh(y)ə/ *noun* an abnormally low capacity for physical sensation. ➤➤ **hypaesthetic** /-'thetik/ *adj*.

hypaethral *or* **hypethral** /hie'peethrəl, hi-/ *adj* open to the sky: *a hypaethral temple*. [via Latin from Greek *hypaithros* exposed to the open air, from HYPO- + *aithēr* ether, air]

hypallage /hie'paləji/ *noun* transposition of the natural relations between elements in a sentence, etc, *esp* the transferring of an adjective from the more natural to the less natural noun for rhetorical effect, as in *slain by a rival's envious hand* or *Tarquin's ravishing strides* — Shakespeare. [via late Latin from Greek *hypallagē* interchange, from *hypallassein* to interchange, from HYPO- + *allassein* to exchange, from *allos* other]

hype[1] /hiep/ *verb trans informal* (*also* + up) to publicize or promote (a new product, forthcoming event, etc) intensively, *esp* making extravagant or exaggerated claims for it: *It was being hyped as the show of the decade*. [orig NAmer, in the sense 'to cheat, short-change', of uncertain origin]

hype[2] *noun informal* **1** intensive advertising or publicity used in the promotion of a product, forthcoming event, etc, *esp* making exaggerated or misleading claims for it: *They produce a botched job and rely on hype to sell it*. **2** a swindle, deception, or hoax.

hype[3] *noun informal* **1** a hypodermic needle or injection. **2** a drug addict. [shortening of HYPODERMIC[2]]

hype[4] *verb trans informal* (+ up) to stimulate or excite (a person or group), *esp* artificially: *The kids were hyped up to fever pitch by the time the band appeared on stage*. ➤➤ **hyped-up** *adj*.

hyper /'hiepə/ *adj informal* over-excited; overwrought. [HYPER-]

hyper- *prefix* forming words, with the meanings: **1a** excessively: *hypersensitive; hyperactive*. **b** excessive: *hyperaemia; hypertension*. **2** above; beyond; super-: *hyperphysical*. **3** existing in, or denoting a space of, more than three dimensions: *hypercube; hyperspace*. [Greek *hyper* over, beyond]

Usage note

hyper- or hypo-? These two prefixes are easily confused. *Hyper-* means 'excessively' or 'higher than normal': *hypercritical, hypersensitive, hyperinflation; hypertension* is abnormally high blood pressure. *Hypo-* means 'below' or 'less than normal': a *hypodermic* needle pierces beneath the skin, *hypotension* is abnormally low blood pressure. Note that someone who is exposed to extreme cold suffers from *hypothermia*. The word *hyperthermia* also exists, but refers to a condition in which the body temperature is abnormally high.

hyperacid /hiepər'asid/ *adj* said *esp* of the stomach: secreting more acid than is normal. ➤➤ **hyperacidity** /-'siditi/ *noun*.

hyperactive /hiepər'aktiv/ *adj* **1** said of a child: persistently active and disinclined to rest, sometimes behaving disruptively. **2** excessively or abnormally active: *a hyperactive gland; a hyperactive imagination*. ➤➤ **hyperactivity** /-'tiviti/ *noun*.

hyperaemia *or* **hyperemia** /hiepə'reemi·ə/ *noun* excess of blood in a body part.

hyperaesthesia *or* **hyperesthesia** /,hiepərees'theezyə, -zh(y)ə/ *noun* a pathologically increased sensitivity to sensory stimuli, e.g. touch.

hyperalgesia /,hiepərəl'jeezi·ə/ *noun* an abnormally high sensitivity to pain. ➤➤ **hyperalgesic** /-zik/ *adj*.

hyperbaric /hiepə'barik/ *adj* of or using greater than normal pressure, *esp* of oxygen: *hyperbaric oxygen chambers*. ➤➤ **hyperbarically** *adv*. [HYPER- + BAR- + -IC[1]]

hyperbaton /hie'puhbətən/ *noun* an inversion of word order for emphatic effect, as in *Temper tantrums I can do without*. [via Latin from Greek *hyperbaton*, neuter of *hyperbatos* transposed, from *hyper-bainein* to step over, from HYPER- + *bainein* to step, walk]

hyperbola /hie'puhbələ/ *noun* (*pl* **hyperbolas** or **hyperbolae** /-lee/) a plane curve generated by a point so moving that the difference of its distances from two fixed points is a constant; the intersection of a double right circular cone with a plane that cuts both halves of the cone: compare ELLIPSE, PARABOLA. [Greek *hyperbolē*: see HYPERBOLE]

hyperbole /hie'puhbəli/ *noun* deliberate extravagant exaggeration, used for effect, as in: *I knew him, Horatio ... He hath borne me on his back a thousand times* — Shakespeare. ➤➤ **hyperbolist** *noun*. [Greek *hyperbolē* excess, hyperbole, hyperbola, from *hyperballein* to exceed, from HYPER- + *ballein* to throw]

hyperbolic[1] /hiepə'bolik/ *adj* relating to, characterized by, or given to hyperbole. ➤➤ **hyperbolically** *adv*.

hyperbolic[2] *adj* relating to or analogous to a hyperbola.

hyperbolical /hiepə'bolikl/ *adj* = HYPERBOLIC[1], HYPERBOLIC[2].

hyperbolic function *noun* any of a set of six functions related to the hyperbola in a way similar to that in which the trigonometric functions are related to a circle: compare SECH.

hyperboloid /hie'puhbəloyd/ *noun* a surface, some plane sections of which are hyperbolas and no plane sections of which are parabolas: compare ELLIPSOID, PARABOLOID. ➤➤ **hyperboloidal** /-'loydl/ *adj*.

hyperborean[1] /hiepə'bawri·ən/ *adj* **1** relating to an extreme northern region. **2** relating to any of the Arctic peoples.

hyperborean[2] *noun* **1** an inhabitant of a cool northern climate. **2** (**Hyperborean**) in Greek mythology, a member of a people who worshipped Apollo and lived in a sunny land beyond the north wind. [Greek *Hyperboreoi*, from HYPER- + *Boreas* the North Wind]

hypercalcaemia (*NAmer* **hypercalcemia**) /hiepəkal'seemyə/ *noun* an excess of calcium in the blood: compare HYPOCALCAEMIA. ➤➤ **hypercalcaemic** *adj*.

hypercholesterolaemia /,hiepəkəlest(ə)ro'leemi·ə/ *noun* the presence of excess cholesterol in the blood.

hyperconscious /hiepə'konshəs/ *adj* more than usually aware or sensitive.

hypercorrection /,hiepəkə'reksh(ə)n/ *noun* a mistake in speech or writing resulting from wrong analogy with a form dimly apprehended as correct or well-bred, e.g. the wrong use of the subject form in *between you and I* where the object form *you and me* is needed, as in *between you and I*. ➤➤ **hypercorrect** *adj*.

hypercritical /hiepə'kritikl/ *adj* gratuitously faultfinding or captious.

hypercube /'hiepəkyoohb/ *noun* a hypothetical geometrical solid in four or more dimensions with all sides equal and all angles right angles.

hyperemia /hiepə'reemi·ə/ *noun* see HYPERAEMIA.

hyperesthesia /,hiepərees'theezyə, -zh(y)ə/ *noun* see HYPER-AESTHESIA.

hyperextend /,hiepərik'stend/ *verb trans* to extend (part of the body, e.g. a joint, a limb, or the back) beyond its normal range of movement.

hyperfocal distance /hiepə'fohkl/ *noun* the limit of the region of sharp focus for a lens focused at infinity.

hypergamy /hie'puhgəmi/ *noun* marriage into an equal or higher caste or social group.

hyperglycaemia or **hyperglycemia** /,hiepəglie'seemi·ə/ *noun* excess of sugar in the blood, e.g. in diabetes mellitus. ➤➤ **hyperglycaemic** *adj*.

hypergolic /hiepə'golik/ *adj* **1** said of rocket fuel: igniting spontaneously on contact with an oxidizing agent without external means of ignition such as a spark. **2** relating to or using hypergolic fuel: *a hypergolic engine*. ➤➤ **hypergolically** *adv*. [German *Hypergol* perhaps from HYPER- + Greek *ergon* work + -OL[1]]

hypericum /hie'perikəm/ *noun* any of a genus of shrubs with yellow five-petalled flowers, including SAINT JOHN'S WORT and ROSE OF SHARON: genus *Hypericum*. [Latin genus name, from Greek *hyperikon*, from HYPER- + *ereikē* heath, heather]

hyperinflation /,hiepərin'flaysh(ə)n/ *noun* very rapid growth in the rate of inflation in an economy. ➤➤ **hyperinflationary** *adj*.

hyperkeratosis /,hiepəkerə'tohsis/ *noun* overgrowth and abnormal thickening of the outer layer of the skin.

hyperkinetic /,hiepəki'netik/ *adj* relating to or characterized by abnormally increased, usu uncontrollable, muscular movement. ➤➤ **hyperkinesis** /-'neesis/ *noun*.

hyperlink /'hiepəlingk/ *noun* a link to another file or location from a HYPERTEXT document, that is activated by clicking on a highlighted word, icon, etc in the document; = HOT LINK, HYPERTEXT LINK.

hypermarket /'hiepəmahkit/ *noun* a very large self-service retail store selling a wide range of household and consumer goods and usu situated on the outskirts of a major town or city.

hypermedia /'hiepəmeedi·ə/ *noun* hypertext software that enables the user to combine text and graphics with audio and video on a computer.

hypermetropia /,hiepəmi'trohpi·ə/ or **hypermetropy** /-'metrəpi/ *noun* a condition in which visual images come to a focus behind the retina of the eye and vision is better for distant than for near objects; longsightedness: compare MYOPIA. ➤➤ **hypermetropic** /-'tropik/ *adj*, **hypermetropical** /-'tropikl/ *adj*. [Greek *hypermetros* beyond measure (from HYPER- + *metron* measure, metre) + -OPIA]

hypermnesia /hiepə'mneezyə, -zh(y)ə/ *noun* an unusually strong capacity for recall, *esp* as enhanced by trauma, hypnosis, or drug use. [HYPER- + -*mnēsia* as in AMNESIA]

hyperon /'hiepəron/ *noun* any of a group of unstable elementary particles that are greater in mass than the proton or neutron and belong to the baryon group. [prob from HYPER- + -ON[2]]

hyperopia /hiepə'rohpi·ə/ *noun* = HYPERMETROPIA. ➤➤ **hyperopic** /-'ropik/ *adj*.

hyperparasite /hiepə'parəsiet/ *noun* a parasite living on or in another parasite. ➤➤ **hyperparasitic** /-'sitik/ *adj*, **hyperparasitism** /-sitiz(ə)m/ *noun*.

hyperparathyroidism /,hiepəparə'thieroydiz(ə)m/ *noun* **1** an excess of parathyroid hormone in the body. **2** the resulting abnormal state marked by an excess of calcium in the blood and urine and the withdrawal of calcium from bones: compare HYPO-PARATHYROIDISM. ➤➤ **hyperparathyroid** *adj*.

hyperphysical /hiepə'fizikl/ *adj* supernatural. ➤➤ **hyperphysically** *adv*.

hyperpituitarism /,hiepəpi'tyooh·itəriz(ə)m/ *noun* excessive production of hormones, e.g. growth hormone, by the pituitary gland: compare HYPOPITUITARISM. ➤➤ **hyperpituitary** *adj*.

hyperplasia /hiepə'playzyə, -zh(y)ə/ *noun* an abnormal or unusual increase in the elements, e.g. the cells of a tissue composing a body part: *cervical hyperplasia*. ➤➤ **hyperplastic** /-'plastik/ *adj*.

hyperpower /'hiepəpowə/ *noun* a large and powerful state which dominates other states politically, militarily, economically, and culturally. [French *hyperpuissance*, coined by the French politician Hubert Védrine, referring specifically to the USA]

hyperpyrexia /,hiepəpie'reksi·ə/ *noun* a very high fever, with a body temperature of 41°C (106°F) or more, e.g. in cases of heatstroke. ➤➤ **hyperpyrexial** *adj*.

hyperreal /hiepə'riəl/ *adj* **1** arrestingly or startlingly real. **2** said of a simulation, etc: imitating reality in an exaggerated way. **3** said of art: extremely realistic. ➤➤ **hyperrealism** *noun*, **hyperrealistic** /-'listik/ *adj*, **hyperreality** /-ri'aliti/ *noun*.

hypersensitive /hiepə'sensətiv/ *adj* abnormally susceptible, e.g. to a drug or antigen. ➤➤ **hypersensitiveness** *noun*, **hypersensitivity** /-'tiviti/ *noun*.

hypersonic /hiepə'sonik/ *adj* relating to or denoting a speed five times that of the speed of sound, or in excess of this: compare SONIC (2). ➤➤ **hypersonically** *adv*.

hyperspace /'hiepəspays/ *noun* **1** space of more than three dimensions. **2** in science fiction, a hypothetical space-time continuum allowing faster-than-light travel. ➤➤ **hyperspatial** /-'spaysh(ə)l/ *adj*.

hypersthene /'hiepəstheen/ *noun* iron magnesium silicate occurring as a green to black mineral in igneous rocks. ➤➤ **hypersthenic** /-'thenik/ *adj*. [French *hypersthène*, from Greek HYPER- + *sthenos* strength]

hypertension /hiepə'tensh(ə)n/ *noun* abnormally high blood pressure, or the physiological condition accompanying it. ➤➤ **hypertensive** /-siv/ *adj and noun*.

hypertext /'hiepətekst/ *noun* **1** a type of computerized document that contains active cross-references, called hyperlinks, which, when activated by a mouse, transfer the reader to another part of the document or to another document. **2** (*used before a noun*) of or relating to hypertext: *a hypertext document.*

hypertext link *noun* a link to another file or location from a hypertext document; = HYPERLINK, HOT LINK.

hyperthermia /hiepə'thuhmi·ə/ *noun* very high body temperature. ▶▶ **hyperthermic** /-mik/ *adj.*

hyperthyroidism /hiepə'thieroydiz(ə)m/ *noun* excessive activity of the thyroid gland, or the condition of increased metabolic and heart rate, enlargement of the thyroid gland, nervousness, etc resulting from it: compare HYPOTHYROIDISM. ▶▶ **hyperthyroid** *adj.*

hypertonic /hiepə'tonik/ *adj* **1** having excessive muscular tone or tension. **2** having a higher concentration than a surrounding medium or a liquid under comparison: compare HYPOTONIC, ISOTONIC. ▶▶ **hypertonia** /-'tohni·ə/ *noun,* **hypertonicity** /-toh'nisiti/ *noun.*

hypertrophy /hie'puhtrəfi/ *noun* excessive increase in bulk of an organ or part. ▶▶ **hypertrophic** /hiepə'trofik/ *adj,* **hypertrophied** *adj.*

hyperventilate /hiepə'ventilayt/ *verb intrans* to breathe excessively fast and deep, often leading to dizziness.

hyperventilation /,hiepəventi'laysh(ə)n/ *noun* excessive breathing leading to abnormal loss of carbon dioxide from the blood.

hypesthesia /hiepees'theezyə, -zh(y)ə/ *noun NAmer* see HYP-AESTHESIA.

hypethral /hie'peethrəl/ *adj* see HYPAETHRAL.

hypha /'hiefə/ *noun* (*pl* **hyphae** /'hiefee/) any of the threads that make up the MYCELIUM (vegetative part) of a fungus. ▶▶ **hyphal** *adj.* [Greek *hyphē* web]

hyphen¹ /'hief(ə)n/ *noun* a punctuation mark (-) used to join words to show that they are to be understood as a combination, or that they have a syntactic relationship, or to divide a word at a line end. [Greek *hyph' hen* under one, together, from *hypo* under + *hen,* neuter of *heis* one]

hyphen² *verb trans* (**hyphened, hyphening**) = HYPHENATE.

hyphenate /'hiephənayt/ *verb trans* to join or separate (words or word elements) with a hyphen. ▶▶ **hyphenation** /-'naysh(ə)n/ *noun.*

hypn- *or* **hypno-** *comb. form* forming words, denoting: **1** sleep: *hypnopaedia.* **2** hypnotism: *hypnogenesis.* [Greek *hypnos* sleep]

hypnagogic *or* **hypnogogic** /hipnə'gojik/ *adj* relating to or associated with the drowsiness preceding sleep: compare HYPNOPOMPIC.

hypno- *comb form* see HYPN-.

hypnogenesis /hipnoh'jenəsis/ *noun* the induction of a hypnotic state. ▶▶ **hypnogenetic** /-'netik/ *adj,* **hypnogenetically** /-'netikli/ *adv.*

hypnogogic /hipnə'gojik/ *adj* see HYPNAGOGIC.

hypnopaedia (*NAmer* **hypnopedia**) /hipnoh'peedi·ə/ *noun* earning or conditioning during sleep. [HYPNO- + Greek *paideia* education]

hypnopompic /hipnoh'pompik/ *adj* relating to or associated with the semiconsciousness preceding waking: compare HYPNAGOGIC. [HYPNO- + Greek *pompē* act of sending away, from *peimpein* to send]

hypnosis /hip'nohsis/ *noun* (*pl* **hypnoses** /-seez/) **1** any of various conditions that resemble sleep, at least superficially; *specif* one induced by a person to whose suggestions the subject is then markedly susceptible. **2** = HYPNOTISM.

hypnotherapy /hipnoh'therəpi/ *noun* the treatment of mental or physical disease, compulsive behaviour, etc using hypnosis. ▶▶ **hypnotherapist** *noun.*

hypnotic¹ /hip'notik/ *adj* **1** tending to produce sleep; soporific. **2** relating to hypnosis or hypnotism. ▶▶ **hypnotically** *adv.* [Greek *hypnōtikos* causing sleep, from *hypnoun* to put to sleep, from *hypnos* sleep]

hypnotic² *noun* **1** a drug or other substance that induces sleep. **2** a person or animal that is or can be hypnotized.

hypnotise /'hipnətiez/ *verb trans* see HYPNOTIZE.

hypnotism /'hipnətiz(ə)m/ *noun* the act of inducing hypnosis. ▶▶ **hypnotist** *noun.*

hypnotize *or* **hypnotise** /'hipnətiez/ *verb trans* **1** to induce hypnosis in (a subject). **2** to dazzle or overcome (somebody) as if

by suggestion; to mesmerize (a person or animal): *drivers hypnotized by speed.* ▶▶ **hypnotizable** *adj,* **hypnotization** /-'zaysh(ə)n/ *noun.*

hypo¹ /'hiepoh/ *noun* sodium thiosulphate, used as a fixing agent in photography. [short for HYPOSULPHITE]

hypo² *noun* (*pl* **hypos**) *informal* = HYPODERMIC².

hypo³ *noun* (*pl* **hypos**) *informal* an attack of HYPOGLYCAEMIA (abnormally low blood sugar).

hypo⁴ *adj informal* said of a diabetic: suffering from HYPO-GLYCAEMIA; hypoglycaemic.

hypo- *or* **hyp-** *prefix* forming words, with the meanings: **1** under; beneath: *hypoblast; hypodermic.* **2** less than normal or normally: *hypaesthesia; hypotension.* **3** in a lower state of oxidation: *hypochlorous acid.* [Greek *hypo* under]

Usage note
hypo- *or* hyper-? See note at HYPER-.

hypoallergenic /,hiepoh·alə'jenik/ *adj* said of cosmetics: specially formulated so as to be unlikely to cause an allergic reaction: compare NON-ALLERGENIC.

hypoblast /'hiepəblast/ *noun* the ENDODERM (inner layer) of an embryo. ▶▶ **hypoblastic** /-'blastik/ *adj.*

hypocalcaemia (*NAmer* **hypocalcemia**) /,hiepohkal'seemi·ə/ *noun* a deficiency of calcium in the blood: compare HYPER-CALCAEMIA. ▶▶ **hypocalcaemic** /-mik/ *adj.*

hypocaust /'hiepəkawst/ *noun* an ancient Roman central heating system with an underground furnace and flues. [via Latin from Greek *hypokauston,* from *hypokaiein* to light a fire under, from HYPO- + *kaiein* to burn]

hypochlorite /hiepə'klawriet/ *noun* a salt or ester of hypochlorous acid.

hypochlorous acid /hiepə'klawrəs/ *noun* an unstable weak acid that is a strong oxidizing agent and is used *esp* as a bleach or disinfectant: formula HOCl.

hypochondria /hiepə'kondri·ə/ *noun* morbid concern about one's health.

Word history
via late Latin from Greek *hypochondria,* neuter pl of *hypochondrios* relating to the soft parts below the lower, cartilaginous ribs, from HYPO- + *chondros* cartilage. This area was formerly thought to be the seat of melancholy and anxiety.

hypochondriac /hiepə'kondriak/ *noun* a person who is affected by hypochondria. ▶▶ **hypochondriac** *adj,* **hypochondriacal** /-'drie·əkl/ *adj.*

hypochondriasis /,hiepəkon'drie·əsis/ *noun* = HYPOCHONDRIA.

hypocorism /hie'pokəriz(ə)m/ *noun* **1** a pet name. **2** the practice of using pet names. ▶▶ **hypocoristic** /,hiepəkaw'ristik/ *adj.* [Greek *hypokorisma* pet name, from *hypokorizesthai* to call by pet names, play the child, from HYPO- + *koros* boy, *korē* girl]

hypocotyl /hiepə'kotil/ *noun* the part of a plant embryo or seedling below the COTYLEDON (embryonic leaf or group of leaves, being the first to appear).

hypocrisy /hi'pokrəsi/ *noun* (*pl* **hypocrisies**) **1** the pretence of possessing virtues, beliefs, or qualities that one does not really have, *esp* in matters of religion or morality. **2** an instance of this behaviour. [Middle English *ypocrisie* via Old French and late Latin from Greek *hypokrisis* acting on the stage, hypocrisy, from *hypokrinesthai* to act on the stage, pretend, feign]

hypocrite /'hipəkrit/ *noun* a person given to hypocrisy: *My dear fellow, you forget that we are in the native land of the hypocrite* — Oscar Wilde. ▶▶ **hypocritical** /-'kritikl/ *adj,* **hypocritically** /-'kritikli/ *adv.* [Middle English *ypocrite* via Old French and late Latin from Greek *hypokritēs* actor, hypocrite, from *hypokrinesthai:* see HYPOCRISY]

hypocycloid /hiepoh'siekloyd/ *noun* a curve traced by a point on the circumference of a circle that rolls round the inside of a fixed circle.

hypodermic¹ /hiepə'duhmik/ *adj* **1** relating to the parts immediately beneath the skin. **2** said of a syringe or needle: used to inject drugs beneath the skin. **3** said of a drug: injected beneath the skin. ▶▶ **hypodermically** *adv.* [HYPO- + Greek *dermis* skin]

hypodermic² *noun* a hypodermic syringe, hypodermic needle, or hypodermic injection.

hypodermic needle *noun* **1** the hollow needle used in a hypodermic syringe. **2** a hypodermic syringe.

hypodermic syringe *noun* a small syringe used with a hollow needle for injection or withdrawal of material beneath the skin.

hypodermis /hiepə'duhmis/ *noun* **1** the layer of tissue immediately beneath the EPIDERMIS of a plant, *esp* when modified to serve as a supporting and protecting or water-storing layer. **2** the layer of cells that underlies and secretes the material of the CUTICLE (outer protective cover) of an insect, crab, etc. ➤➤ **hypodermal** *adj*.

hypogastrium /hiepə'gastri·əm/ *noun* (*pl* **hypogastria** /-tri·ə/) the middle region of the lower part of the abdomen beneath the navel: compare EPIGASTRIUM. ➤➤ **hypogastric** /-trik/ *adj*. [via Latin from Greek *hypogastrion* lower abdomen, from HYPO- + *gastr-, gastēr* belly]

hypogea /hiepə'jee·ə/ *noun* pl of HYPOGEUM.

hypogeal /hiepə'jee·əl/ *adj* growing, remaining, or occurring below the surface of the ground: compare EPIGEAL: *hypogeal cotyledons*. [via late Latin from Greek *hypogeios* subterranean, from HYPO- + *gē* earth]

hypogean /hiepə'jee·ən/ *adj* = HYPOGEAL.

hypogene /'hiepəjeen/ *adj* said of rock: formed or occurring at depths below the earth's surface: compare EPIGENE. [HYPO- + Greek *-genēs* born, produced]

hypogeous /hiepə'jee·əs/ *adj* = HYPOGEAL.

hypogeum /hiepə'jee·əm/ *noun* (*pl* **hypogea** /-'jee·ə/) an underground vault or chamber, e.g. one hollowed out in prehistoric times for burials. [via Latin, from Greek *hypogeion* underground chamber, neuter of *hypogeios* subterranean, from HYPO- + Greek *gē* earth]

hypoglossal nerve /hiepə'glosl/ *noun* either of the twelfth and final pair of cranial nerves that supply the muscles of the tongue in higher vertebrates.

hypoglycaemia *or* **hypoglycemia** /,hiepohglie'seemi·ə/ *noun* an abnormally low amount of sugar in the blood, or the condition resulting from this, involving confusion, headache, and sometimes convulsion and coma. ➤➤ **hypoglycaemic** *adj*.

hypogonadism /hiepoh'gonədiz(ə)m/ *noun* diminution or absence of functional activity in the gonads (testes or ovaries; see GONAD), resulting in retarded growth and sexual development. ➤ **hypogonadal** *adj*, **hypogonadic** /-'nadik/ *adj*.

hypogynous /hie'pojinəs/ *adj* **1** said of a floral organ, e.g. a petal or sepal: attached to the receptacle or stem below the ovary, and free from it. **2** said of a flower: having hypogynous floral organs: compare EPIGYNOUS, PERIGYNOUS. ➤➤ **hypogyny** /-ni/ *noun*.

hypoid gear /'hiepoyd/ *noun* a system of two gears with the PINION[3] (smaller gear) not intersecting the axis of the main gear. [short for *hyperboloidal*: see HYPERBOLOID]

hypokalaemia (*NAmer* **hypokalemia**) /,hiepohkə'leemi·ə/ *noun* a deficiency of potassium in the blood. ➤➤ **hypokalaemic** /-mik/ *adj*. [HYPO- + scientific Latin *kalium* potassium (from ALKALI) + -AEMIA]

hypolimnion /hiepoh'limni·ən/ *noun* (*pl* **hypolimnia** /-ni·ə/) the cold lower layer of water in a lake, usu rich in nutrients and low in oxygen: compare EPILIMNION. [HYPO- + Greek *limnion*, dimin. of *limnē* lake]

hypomagnesaemia (*NAmer* **hypomagnesemia**) /,hiepoh-magni'zeemi·ə/ *noun* a deficiency of magnesium in the blood.

hypomania /hiepə'mayni·ə/ *noun* a mild form of mania, often characterized by hyperactivity, overexcitement, or excessive optimism. ➤➤ **hypomanic** /-'manik/ *adj*.

hypoparathyroidism /,hiepohparə'thieroydiz(ə)m/ *noun* **1** a deficiency of parathyroid hormone in the body. **2** the resulting abnormal state marked by abnormally low amounts of calcium in the blood, often resulting in TETANY (involuntary prolonged muscular contraction): compare HYPERPARATHYROIDISM.

hypophosphate /hiepoh'fosfayt/ *noun* any salt or ester of hypophosphoric acid.

hypophosphoric acid /,hiepohfos'forik/ *noun* a TETRABASIC (having four hydrogen atoms) acid produced as phosphorous oxidizes in moist air: formula $H_4P_2O_6$.

hypophosphorous acid /hiepoh'fosfərəs/ *noun* a MONOBASIC (having one hydrogen atom) acid, acting as a reducing agent: formula H_3PO_2.

hypophysis /hie'pofəsis/ *noun* (*pl* **hypophyses** /-seez/) = PITUITARY[2]. ➤➤ **hypophyseal** /-'see·əl/ *adj*, **hypophysectomy** /-'sektəmi/ *noun*, **hypophysial** /-'fizi·əl/ *adj*. [Greek *hypophysis* attachment underneath, from *hypophyein* to grow beneath, from HYPO- + *phyein* to grow, produce]

hypopituitarism /,hiepohpi'tyooh·itəriz(ə)m/ *noun* deficient production of hormones, e.g. growth hormone, by the pituitary gland: compare HYPERPITUITARISM. ➤➤ **hypopituitary** *adj*.

hypoplasia /hiepə'playzyə, -zh(y)ə/ *noun* arrested development in which an organ or part remains below the normal size or in an immature state. ➤➤ **hypoplastic** /-'plastik/ *adj*.

hyposensitize *or* **hyposensitise** /hiepoh'sensətiez/ *verb trans* to reduce the sensitivity of (somebody), *esp* to something that causes an allergic reaction; to desensitize (a person). ➤➤ **hyposensitization** /-'zaysh(ə)n/ *noun*.

hypospadias /hiepoh'spaydi·əs/ *noun* an abnormality in the male body in which the opening of the URETHRA (urine canal) is on the underside of the penis. [HYPO- + prob Greek *span* to draw]

hypostasis /hie'postəsis/ *noun* (*pl* **hypostases** /-seez/) **1** the settling of blood in the lower parts of an organ or body, *esp* due to impaired circulation or death. **2** the substance or essential nature of an individual. **3** in Christian theology: **a** any of the three persons of the Trinity. **b** the person of Christ, combining divine and human nature. [via Latin from Greek *hypostasis* support, foundation, substance, sediment, from *hyphistasthai* to stand under, support, from HYPO- + *histasthai* to be standing]

hypostasize *or* **hypostasise** /hie'postəsiez/ *verb trans* to think of (a concept) as having concrete reality, or reify it. ➤➤ **hypostasization** /-'zaysh(ə)n/ *noun*. [from HYPOSTASIS]

hypostatic /hiepoh'statik/ *adj* relating to HYPOSTASIS. ➤➤ **hypostatical** *adj*, **hypostatically** *adv*.

hypostatize *or* **hypostatise** /hie'postətiez/ *verb trans* chiefly *NAmer* = HYPOSTASIZE. ➤➤ **hypostatization** /-'zaysh(ə)n/ *noun*.

hypostyle /'hiepohstiel/ *noun* a building that has the roof resting on a grid of columns. ➤➤ **hypostyle** *adj*. [Greek *hypostylos*, from HYPO- + *stylos* pillar]

hyposulphite /hiepoh'sulfiet/ *noun* THIOSULPHATE, *esp* as used as a fixing agent in photography.

hyposulphurous acid /hiepoh'sulfərəs/ *noun* an unstable acid found only in solution and acting as a powerful reducing agent: formula $H_2S_2O_4$.

hypotaxis /hiepoh'taksis/ *noun* in grammar, the subordination of one clause to another, *esp* by use of a conjunction. ➤➤ **hypotactic** /-'taktik/ *adj*. [via Latin from Greek *hypotaxis* subordination, from *hypotassein* to append or arrange under, from HYPO- + *tassein* to arrange]

hypotension /hiepoh'tensh(ə)n/ *noun* abnormally low blood pressure. ➤➤ **hypotensive** /-siv/ *adj and noun*.

hypotenuse /hie'pot(ə)nyoohz/ *noun* the side of a right-angled triangle that is opposite the right angle. [via Latin from Greek *hypoteinousa*, fem present part. of *hypoteinein* SUBTEND]

hypothalamus /hiepoh'thaləməs/ *noun* (*pl* **hypothalami** /-mie/) a part of the brain that lies beneath the thalamus and includes centres that regulate body temperature, appetite, and other autonomic functions. ➤➤ **hypothalamic** /-'lamik/ *adj*.

hypothec /hie'pothik/ *noun* used in Roman and Scots law: a legal right in favour of a creditor over the property of their debtor. [French *hypothèque* via French from late Latin from Greek *hypothēkē* deposit, pledge, from *hypotithenai*: see HYPOTHESIS]

hypothecate /hie'pothikayt/ *verb trans* to pledge (property) by law as security for a debt. ➤➤ **hypothecation** /-'kaysh(ə)n/ *noun*. [Latin *hypothecat-, hypothecare* to give as a pledge]

hypothermia /hiepoh'thuhmi·ə/ *noun* abnormally low body temperature. ➤➤ **hypothermic** /-mik/ *adj*.

hypothesis /hie'pothəsis/ *noun* (*pl* **hypotheses** /-seez/) **1** a proposed possible explanation for a phenomenon, set of circumstances, etc; a theory. **2** a proposition assumed for the sake of argument. [Greek *hypothesis* proposal, assumption from *hypotithenai* to deposit, submit, or suggest, from HYPO- + *tithenai* to put]

hypothesize *or* **hypothesise** /hie'pothəsiez/ *verb trans* to propose or assume (something) as a hypothesis. ➤ *verb intrans* to form hypotheses.

hypothetical /hiepə'thetikl/ *adj* **1** *esp* in logic, involving hypothesis or a condition: *hypothetical questions*. **2** relating to or depending on supposition; conjectural: *Forelimbs evolving into wings would probably become awkward for climbing or grasping long before they became very useful for gliding, thus placing the hypothetical intermediate creature at a serious disadvantage* — Phillip E Johnson. ⟫ **hypothetically** *adv*.

hypothyroidism /hiepoh'thieroydiz(ə)m/ *noun* deficient activity of the thyroid gland, or the condition of lowered metabolic rate, lethargy, etc resulting from this: compare HYPERTHYROIDISM. ⟫ **hypothyroid** *adj*.

hypotonic /hiepə'tonik/ *adj* **1** having deficient muscular tone or tension. **2** having a lower concentration than a surrounding medium or a liquid under comparison: compare HYPERTONIC, ISOTONIC. ⟫ **hypotonia** /-'tohni·ə/ *noun*, **hypotonically** *adv*, **hypotonicity** /-'nisiti/ *noun*.

hypoventilation /,hiepohventi'laysh(ə)n/ *noun* an abnormally slow rate of breathing, with a resultant accumulation of carbon dioxide in the blood.

hypovolaemia (*NAmer* **hypovolemia**) /,hiepohvə'leemi·ə/ *noun* an abnormally low volume of blood circulating in the body. [HYPO- + VOLUME + -AEMIA]

hypoxia /hie'poksi·ə, hi-/ *noun* a deficiency of oxygen reaching the tissues of the body. ⟫ **hypoxic** /-sik/ *adj*. [HYPO- + OX- + -IA¹]

hyps- *or* **hypsi-** *or* **hypso-** *comb. form* forming words, denoting: height; altitude: *hypsography*. [Greek *hypsos* height]

hypsilophodont /hipsi'lofədont/ *noun* a small bipedal swift-running herbivorous dinosaur of the Jurassic and Cretaceous periods. [Greek *hypsilophos* high-crested + -ODONT]

hypso- *comb. form* see HYPS-.

hypsography /hip'sogrəfi/ *noun* the measurement and mapping of the earth's surface with reference to elevation. ⟫ **hypsographic** /-'grafik/ *adj*, **hypsographical** /-'grafikl/ *adj*.

hypsometer /hip'somitə/ *noun* **1** an apparatus for estimating altitudes in mountainous regions from the boiling points of liquids. **2** any of various instruments for determining the height of trees by TRIANGULATION (calculation of distances by the measurement of angles).

hyraces /'hierəseez/ *noun* pl of HYRAX.

hyracotherium /,hierəkoh'thiəri·əm/ *noun* (*pl* **hyracotheria** /-ri·ə/) the earliest ancestor of the horse, a small woodland animal of the Eocene period, with four-toed front legs and three-toed back legs. [Latin genus name, from *hyrac-*, *hyrax* HYRAX + Greek *therion* wild animal]

hyrax /'hieraks/ *noun* (*pl* **hyraxes** *or* **hyraces** /'hierəseez/) any of several species of small thickset short-legged mammals having feet with soft pads and broad nails: family Procaviidae. [via Latin from Greek *hyrak-*, *hyrax* shrewmouse]

hyssop /'hisəp/ *noun* **1** a Eurasian plant of the mint family with aromatic leaves: *Hyssopus officinalis*. **2** in biblical references, a plant used in purificatory rites by the ancient Hebrews. [Old English *ysope* via Latin from Greek *hyssōpos*, of Semitic origin]

hyster- *or* **hystero-** *comb. form* forming words, denoting: womb: *hysterectomy*. [Greek *hystera* womb]

hysterectomy /histə'rektəmi/ *noun* (*pl* **hysterectomies**) surgical removal of the uterus.

hysteresis /histə'reesis/ *noun* a delay in the production of an effect by a cause; *esp* an apparent lag in the values of resulting magnetization in a magnetic material due to a changing magnetizing force. ⟫ **hysteretic** /-'retik/ *adj*. [Greek *hysterēsis* shortcoming, from *hysterein* to be late, fall short, from *hysteros* later]

hysteria /hi'stiəri·ə/ *noun* **1** a mental disorder marked by emotional excitability and disturbances, e.g. paralysis, of the normal bodily processes. **2** unmanageable emotional excess, *esp* fits of laughing or weeping. [from HYSTERIC¹]

hysteric¹ /hi'sterik/ *noun* **1** a person who suffers from hysteria. **2** (*in pl, but treated as sing. or pl*) an attack of hysteria, *esp* with uncontrollable laughing or crying. ✳ **in hysterics** *informal* laughing vociferously.

Word history

Greek *hysterikos* relating to the womb, hysterical, from *hystera* womb. Hysteria was once thought to be a woman's disorder, caused by malfunction of the womb.

hysteric² *adj* = HYSTERICAL.

hysterical *adj* **1** relating to or associated with hysteria: *a hysterical fit; hysterical crying*. **2** suffering from or as if from hysteria. **3** *informal* very funny.

hystero- *comb. form* see HYSTER-.

hysteron proteron /,histəron 'protəron/ *noun* a figure of speech consisting of the reversal of a natural or rational order, as in Virgil's *Let us die and rush into the midst of the battle* (*Moriamur et in media arma ruamus*). [Greek *hysteron proteron* the later earlier, from *hysteron* later, *proteron* earlier]

hystricomorph /'histrikəmawf/ *noun* any of the suborder Hystricomorpha of rodents, that includes porcupines, chinchillas, and guinea pigs. [Latin *hystic-*, *hystrix* porcupine + -MORPH]

Hz *abbr* hertz.

I¹ *or* **i** *noun* (*pl* **I's** *or* **Is** *or* **i's**) **1a** the ninth letter of the English alphabet. **b** a written character or design denoting this letter. **c** the sound represented by this letter, one of the English vowels. **2** an item designated as I, *esp* the ninth in a series. **3** the Roman numeral for one.

I² *pronoun* the word used by a person who is speaking or writing to refer to himself or herself. [Old English *ic*]

I³ *abbr* **1** Independent. **2** inductance. **3** Institute or Institution. **4** International. **5** Island or Isle. **6** Italy (international vehicle registration).

I⁴ *abbr* the chemical symbol for iodine.

I⁵ *symbol* electric current.

i *symbol* in mathematics, the symbol used to represent the imaginary number equal to the square root of minus one, represented in electrical engineering and electronics by J.

-i- *suffix* used as a connective vowel to join word elements, *esp* of Latin origin: *matrilinear.* [Middle English, from Old French, from Latin, stem vowel of most nouns and adjectives in combination]

-i¹ *suffix* **1** used to form the plural of nouns adopted from Latin that end in *-us*: *radii.* **2** used to form the plural of nouns adopted from Italian that end in *-e* or *-o*: *panettoni; graffiti.*

-i² *suffix* **1** forming adjectives, with the meaning: relating to or denoting a specified place, *esp* a country of the Middle or Near East: *Afghani.* **2** forming nouns, denoting: a person who is a native or inhabitant of a specified place: *Iraqi.*

IA *abbr* Iowa (US postal abbreviation).

Ia *abbr* Iowa.

-ia¹ *suffix* forming nouns, denoting: **1** a pathological condition: *hysteria; anaemia.* **2** a genus of plants or animals: *Fuchsia.* **3** a territory, world, or society: *suburbia; Australia.* **4** a state or condition: *utopia.* [Latin and Greek suffix forming feminine nouns]

-ia² *suffix* forming pl nouns, denoting: **1** things derived from or relating to something: *regalia; juvenilia.* **2** a higher taxon, e.g. class or order, of plants or animals: *Amphibia.* [Latin and Greek neuter pl adj ending]

-ia³ *suffix* **1** forming the plural of nouns of Latin and Greek origin ending in *-e*, *-ion*, and *-ium*: *maria; criteria; emporia.* **2** forming the pl of technical nouns ending in *-ium*: see -IUM.

IAA *abbr* indoleacetic acid.

IAEA *abbr* International Atomic Energy Agency.

-ial *suffix* **1** forming adjectives, with the meaning: of or having the character of: *bestial; manorial; spatial.* **2** forming nouns, denoting: something done by or involving somebody: *editorial; tutorial.* [Middle English via French from Latin *-ialis*]

iamb /'ieam(b)/ *or* **iambus** /ie'ambəs/ *noun* (*pl* **iambs** *or* **iambuses** *or* **iambi** /ie'ambie/) a metrical foot consisting of one short or unstressed syllable followed by one long or stressed syllable. [via Latin from Greek *iambos*, from *iaptein* to attack in words; because the iamb was first used by Greek satirists]

iambic¹ /ie'ambik/ *noun* **1** an iamb. **2** (*in pl*) verse written in iambs.

iambic² *adj* **1** relating to or denoting an iamb. **2** relating to or denoting verse or metre that is predominantly in iambs.

iambus /ie'ambəs/ *noun* see IAMB.

-ian *suffix* see -AN¹, -AN².

-iana *suffix* see -ANA.

IAP *abbr* Internet access provider.

-iasis *or* **-asis** *suffix* forming nouns, denoting: a disease or diseased condition: *elephantiasis; psoriasis.* [Latin and Greek *-asis*, suffix of action]

IATA /ie'ahtə/ *abbr* International Air Transport Association.

-iatric *comb. form* forming adjectives, denoting: the medical treatment specified: *paediatric.* [see IATRO-, -IATRY]

-iatrical *comb. form* = -IATRIC.

-iatrics *comb. form* forming nouns, denoting: the medical treatment specified: *paediatrics.*

iatro- *comb. form* forming words, with the meaning: medical or healing: *iatrogenic.* [Greek *iatros* physician]

iatrogenic /ie,atroh'jenik/ *adj* said of a disease or condition: induced inadvertently by medical treatment: *an iatrogenic rash.* ➤➤ **iatrogenesis** /-nəsis/ *noun*, **iatrogenically** *adv*, **iatrogenicity** /-'nisiti/ *noun*.

-iatry *comb. form* forming nouns, denoting: a specified medical treatment: *psychiatry.* [French *-iatrie* via Latin from Greek *iatreia* art of healing, from *iatros* physician]

ib. /ib/ *abbr* = IBIDEM.

IBA *abbr* Independent Broadcasting Authority.

I-beam *noun* an iron or steel beam or girder that is I-shaped in cross-section.

Iberian /ie'biəri-ən/ *noun* **1a** a native or inhabitant of Spain or Portugal. **b** a member of any of the peoples that, in ancient times, inhabited Spain and Portugal. **2** either of the extinct Romance or Celtic languages of the ancient Iberians. ➤➤ **Iberian** *adj.* [*Iberia*, the former name of the Iberian Peninsula, via Latin from Greek *Ibēres* Spaniards]

Iberian Peninsula *noun* (**the Iberian Peninsula**) the peninsula comprising Portugal and Spain.

iberis /ie'biəris/ *noun* (*pl* **iberis**) any of a genus of low-growing plants belonging to the cabbage family that are grown in gardens for their white, pink, red, or purple flowers, *esp* candytuft: genus *Iberis*. [Latin genus name, prob from Greek]

ibex /'iebeks/ *noun* (*pl* **ibexes** *or* **ibices** /'iebiseez/ *or collectively* **ibex**) any of several wild goats living chiefly in high mountain areas of Europe, Asia, and N Africa and having large ridged backward-curving horns: *Capra ibex* (of Europe, Asia, and N Africa) and *Capra pyrenaica* (of the Pyrenees). [Latin *ibex*]

ibid. /i'bid/ *abbr* = IBIDEM.

ibidem /i'biedem, 'ibidem/ *adv* in the same book, chapter, passage, etc, used to reference a work that has been previously mentioned. [Latin *ibidem*, literally 'in the same place']

-ibility *suffix* see -ABILITY.

ibis /'iebis/ *noun* (*pl* **ibises** *or collectively* **ibis**) any of several species of long-legged wading birds with long necks and a long slender downward-curving bill: genera *Threskiornis*, *Plegadis*, and other genera. [via Latin from Greek *ibis*, from Egyptian *hby*]

-ible *suffix* see -ABLE.

IBM *abbr* International Business Machines.

Ibo /'eeboh/ *noun* see IGBO.

IBRD *abbr* International Bank for Reconstruction and Development.

IBS *abbr* irritable bowel syndrome.

ibuprofen /iebjooh'prohfen/ *noun* a synthetic drug that is used to relieve pain and reduce inflammation. [from the chemical name of the drug, *isobutylphenyl propionic* acid]

IC *noun* **1** integrated circuit. **2** internal-combustion.

i/c *abbr* **1** in charge (of). **2** internal-combustion.

-ic[1] *suffix* forming adjectives from nouns, with the meanings: **1** having the character or form of; being: *panoramic*; *runic*. **2a** characteristic of or associated with: *Homeric*; *quixotic*. **b** related to, derived from, or containing: *alcoholic*; *oleic*. **3** utilizing: *atomic*; *electric*. **4** exhibiting: *historic*; *nostalgic*. **5** affected with: *allergic*. **6** characterized by; producing: *analgesic*. **7** having a valency relatively higher than in compounds or ions named with an adjective ending in *-ous*: *ferric*; *mercuric*. ➤➤ **-ically** *suffix*. [Middle English from Old French *-ique*, Latin *-icus*, or Greek *-ikos*]

-ic[2] *suffix* forming nouns, denoting: **1** a person having a given character or nature: *fanatic*. **2** something belonging to or associated with a specified thing: *epic*. **3** a person affected by something: *alcoholic*. **4** something that produces an effect: *emetic*.

-ical *suffix* forming adjectives from nouns with meanings similar to those of -IC[1]: *electrical*; *geological*; *historical*; *symmetrical*. ➤➤ **-ically** *suffix*. [Middle English from late Latin *-icalis*]

-ically *suffix* see -IC[1], -ICAL.

ICAO *abbr* International Civil Aviation Organization.

ICBM *abbr* intercontinental ballistic missile.

ICC *abbr* **1** International Cricket Council. **2** International Chamber of Commerce. **3** *NAmer* Interstate Commerce Commission.

ICE *abbr* **1** Institution of Civil Engineers. **2** internal-combustion engine.

ice[1] /ies/ *noun* **1a** frozen water: *as chaste as ice, as pure as snow* — Shakespeare. **b** a sheet, stretch, or covering of ice: *Ice formed on the butler's upper slopes* — P G Wodehouse. **c** a substance reduced to a solid state by cold: *There is ammonia ice in the rings of Saturn.* **2a** a frozen dessert such as ICE CREAM or WATER ICE. **b** a serving or portion of such a dessert. **3** *informal* a diamond or diamonds. **4** *informal* a stimulant drug consisting of powdered smokable crystals of methamphetamine. ✳ **on ice** in abeyance; in reserve for later use: *The directors kept their plans on ice for the time being.* **on thin ice** perilously close to doing or saying something that will lead to trouble, danger, etc. ➤➤ **iceless** *adj*. [Old English *īs*]

ice[2] *verb trans* **1** to cover (e.g. a cake) with icing or with something similar. **2a** to coat (something) with ice. **b** to convert (something) into ice. **c** to supply or chill (e.g. a drink) with ice. **3** *chiefly NAmer, informal* to kill (somebody), *esp* to murder (them). ➤ *verb intrans* **1** (*often* + over/up) to become covered or clogged with ice: *The carburettor iced up.* **2** to become ice-cold.

ice age *noun* **1** a time of widespread glaciation. **2** (**the Ice Age**) the Pleistocene glacial epoch.

ice axe *noun* a combination pick and adze with a spiked handle used in climbing on snow or ice.

ice bag *noun* = ICE PACK (2).

ice beer *noun* a type of lager that is brewed by using very low temperatures and removing some of the ice that forms during the process, so increasing the alcohol content.

iceberg /'iesbuhg/ *noun* **1** a large floating mass of ice detached from a glacier. **2** *chiefly NAmer, informal* an emotionally cold person. ✳ **the tip of an/the iceberg** the small visible or known part of something much larger, *esp* something that is potentially troublesome, problematic, etc. [prob part translation of Danish or Norwegian *isberg* or Dutch *ijsberg* ice mountain]

iceberg lettuce *noun* a variety of lettuce with a round head of crisp close-packed leaves.

iceblink *noun* a glare in the sky over a sheet of ice, caused by the reflection of light.

iceboat *noun* **1** a boat or frame on runners propelled on ice, usu by sails. **2** = ICEBREAKER (1).

icebound *adj* surrounded or obstructed by ice so as to be unable to move.

icebox *noun* **1** *Brit* the freezing compartment of a refrigerator. **2** *NAmer* a refrigerator. **3** a container that is chilled by means of ice, used for keeping food and drink, etc cold.

icebreaker *noun* **1** a ship equipped to make and maintain a channel through ice. **2** something or somebody that breaks down feelings of reserve, awkwardness, or formality in a social situation.

ice cap *noun* a permanent cover of ice over an area of land such as the peak of a mountain or a polar region of a planet.

ice cream *noun* **1** a sweet flavoured frozen food made from milk, cream, or custard: *My advice to you is to just enjoy your ice cream while it's on your plate* — Thornton Wilder. **2** a serving or portion of ice cream.

ice cube *noun* a small block of ice, e.g. for chilling a drink.

ice dancing *noun* a form of ice skating with movements based on those of ballroom dancing. ➤➤ **ice dance** *noun*, **ice dancer** *noun*.

icefall *noun* a steeply descending part of a glacier that looks like a frozen waterfall.

ice field *noun* **1** an extensive sheet of sea ice; a large ice floe. **2** a flat expanse of ice covering an area of land; = ICE CAP.

ice floe *noun* a sheet of floating ice, *esp* on the sea.

ice hockey *noun* a game played on an ice rink by two teams of six players on skates who try to drive a PUCK[1] into the opposing side's goal with a stick that resembles an elongated hockey stick.

ice house *noun* *esp* formerly, a building in which ice is made or stored.

Icelander /'ieslandə/ *noun* a native or inhabitant of Iceland, an island in the North Atlantic. [Danish *Islænder*, from *Island* Iceland]

Icelandic *noun* the N Germanic language of the people of Iceland. ➤➤ **Icelandic** *adj*.

Word history
Words from the modern Icelandic language that have passed into English include *auk*, *eider*, and *geyser*. (For the contribution of the older Icelandic vocabulary, see note at OLD NORSE).

Iceland moss /'iesland/ *noun* an edible lichen of mountainous and arctic regions that yields an extract used *esp* as a sizing agent: *Cetraria islandica*.

Iceland poppy *noun* a poppy orig of subarctic regions, which in the wild has large fragrant usu yellow or white flowers, but which exists in cultivated varieties with fairly small flowers in usu pastel shades of e.g. pink, orange, yellow, and scarlet: *Papaver nudicaule*.

Iceland spar *noun* a doubly refracting transparent form of calcite.

ice lolly *noun* *Brit* a shaped portion of ice cream or, more usually, a flavoured piece of ice on a stick.

iceman *noun* (*pl* **icemen**) **1** a man who sells or delivers ice, *esp* in the USA. **2** *chiefly NAmer, informal* a contract killer.

ice pack *noun* **1** an expanse of PACK ICE (masses of compacted ice floating on the sea, *esp* in polar regions). **2** a bag of ice for applying cold to a part of the body, e.g. to reduce swelling or lower temperature.

ice pick *noun* a spiked hand tool for chipping ice off a larger block. **2** a small pick used by mountaineers for splitting ice.

ice plant *noun* **1** a southern African plant that has fleshy leaves covered with glistening blister-like swellings and pink or white flowers: *Mesembryanthemum crystallinum*. **2** an orig Chinese plant with flattish flower heads, pink in the wild form but in brighter shades of red in cultivated varieties: *Sedum spectabile.*

ice sheet *noun* a thick and long-lasting expanse of ice over an area of land; = ICE CAP.

ice shelf *noun* a mass of ice attached to land but extending out over the adjacent area of sea.

ice show *noun* an entertainment consisting of various acrobatic, dance, etc routines by ice skaters, *esp* to musical accompaniment.

ice skate *noun* a shoe with a metal runner attached for skating on ice.

ice-skate *verb intrans* to glide over ice wearing ice skates, e.g. in an ice rink or on a frozen expanse of outdoor water, often performing dancing or gymnastic movements, *esp* as a sport or pastime. ⟫ **ice skater** *noun,* **ice skating** *noun.*

ice wine *noun* any of various sweet wines made from grapes that have been allowed to become partially decayed and completely or partly frozen on the vine before being picked and pressed while still frosted, a process that results in high concentrations of grape sugar. [translation of German *Eiswein,* from *Eis* ice + *Wein* wine]

IChemE *abbr* Institute of Chemical Engineers.

I Ching /ˌee ˈching/ *noun* an ancient Chinese book that is a source of Confucian and Taoist philosophy. It is mainly used for divination by means of 64 hexagrams (symbolic six-line figures; see HEXAGRAM) that are believed to provide information that can be interpreted to give advice and answer questions relevant to everyday life and future events. [Chinese (Pekingese) *I Ching,* also written *Yi Jing* literally 'classic (book) of changes']

ichn- *or* **ichno-** *comb. form* forming words, denoting: footprint; track; trace: *ichnography.* [Greek, from *ichnos* track]

ichneumon /ikˈnyoohmən/ *noun* 1 any of numerous species of four-winged insects with long antennae, whose larvae are parasites of other insect larvae, *esp* caterpillars: family Ichneumonidae. 2 a large mongoose that lives in Africa and southern Europe and has grey fur with black tail tufts: *Herpestes ichneumon.* [via Latin from Greek *ichneumōn* tracker, from *ichneuein* to track, from *ichnos* track]

ichno- *comb. form* see ICHN-.

ichnography /ikˈnogrəfi/ *noun* (*pl* **ichnographies**) 1 a ground plan of a building. 2 the process or art of making ground plans.

ichor /ˈiekaw/ *noun* 1 *archaic* a thin watery or blood-tinged discharge. 2 a fluid that flowed like blood in the veins of the ancient Greek gods. ⟫ **ichorous** /-rəs/ *adj.* [Greek *ichōr*]

ichthy- *or* **ichthyo-** *comb. form* forming words, denoting: fish: *ichthyology.* [via Latin from Greek, from *ichthys* fish]

ichthyology /ikthiˈoləji/ *noun* the branch of zoology that deals with fish; the scientific study of fish. ⟫ **ichthyological** /-ˈlojikl/ *adj,* **ichthyologically** /-ˈlojikli/ *adv,* **ichthyologist** *noun.*

ichthyophagous /ikthiˈofəgəs/ *adj* eating or subsisting on fish.

ichthyosaur /ˈikthiˌəsaw/ *or* **ichthyosaurus** /-ˈsawrəs/ *noun* any of various extinct marine reptiles with fish-shaped bodies, paddle-like flippers, and long snouts. ⟫ **ichthyosaurian** /-ˈsawri·ən/ *adj and noun.* [scientific Latin *ichthyosaurus,* ICHTHY- + Greek *sauros* lizard]

ichthyosis /ikthiˈohsis/ *noun* a rare congenital skin disease in which the skin becomes dry, hard, and scaly. ⟫ **ichthyotic** /-ˈotik/ *adj.*

ICI *abbr* Imperial Chemical Industries.

-ician *suffix* forming nouns, denoting: a specialist in or practitioner of a specified subject or occupation: *beautician; technician.* [Middle English via Old French *-icien* from Latin *-ica* (as in *rhetorica* rhetoric), Old French *-ien* -IAN]

icicle /ˈiesikl/ *noun* a hanging tapering mass of ice formed by the freezing of dripping water. [Middle English *isikel,* from *is* ICE¹ + *ikel* icicle, from Old English *gicel*]

icing /ˈiesing/ *noun* 1 *chiefly Brit* a sweet, creamy or hard decorative coating for cakes, biscuits, etc, usu made with icing sugar and water, butter, or egg white, sometimes with added flavouring or colouring. *NAmer* Also called FROSTING. 2 the formation of ice, e.g. on a ship in freezing conditions. ✱ **the icing on the cake** a desirable but inessential addition.

icing sugar *noun chiefly Brit* finely powdered sugar used in making icing and sweets.

icky /ˈiki/ *adj* (**ickier, ickiest**) *informal* 1 disgustingly sticky. 2 cloying; sentimental. ⟫ **ickiness** *noun.* [perhaps baby-talk alteration of STICKY]

icon /ˈiekon/ *noun* 1 (*also* **ikon**) a religious image, e.g. of Christ, the Virgin Mary, or a saint, typically painted on a small wooden panel and used as an aid to devotion in the Eastern Orthodox churches. 2 a pictorial representation; an image or symbol. 3 somebody who is an object of uncritical devotion; an idol. 4 in computing, a picture or symbol displayed on a VDU or a monitor to show a program option or a facility available to the user. ⟫ **iconic** /ieˈkonik/ *adj,* **iconically** /ieˈkonikli/ *adv,* **iconicity** /-ˈnisiti/ *noun.* [via Latin from Greek *eikōn* likeness, image from *eikenai* to resemble]

icon- *or* **icono-** *comb. form* forming words, denoting: 1 image; symbol: *iconology.* 2 icon: *iconoclast.* [Greek *eikon-, eikono-,* from *eikon-, eikōn:* see ICON]

iconoclast /ieˈkonəklast/ *noun* 1 a person who attacks established beliefs or institutions. 2 a person who destroys religious images or opposes their veneration. ⟫ **iconoclasm** /-klaz(ə)m/ *noun,* **iconoclastic** /-ˈklastik/ *adj,* **iconoclastically** /-ˈklastikli/ *adv.* [via late Latin from Greek *eikonoklastēs* image destroyer, from *eikōn* (see ICON) + *klan* to break]

iconography /iekəˈnogrəfi/ *noun* (*pl* **iconographies**) 1 pictorial material relating to or illustrating a subject; a pictorial record of a subject. 2 the traditional or conventional images or symbols associated with a subject, *esp* a religious or legendary subject. 3 the imagery or symbolism of a work of art, an artist, or a body of art, or the use of such imagery or symbolism. 4 the study of imagery or symbolism; = ICONOLOGY. 5 a published work dealing with or featuring iconography. ⟫ **iconographer** *noun,* **iconographic** /ˌiekonəˈgrafik/ *adj,* **iconographical** /ˌiekonəˈgrafikl/ *adj,* **iconographically** /ˌiekonəˈgrafikli/ *adv.* [Greek *eikonographia* sketch, description, from *eikonographein* to describe, from *eikōn* (see ICON) + *graphein* to write]

iconolatry /iekəˈnolətri/ *noun* the worship of images or icons.

iconology /iekəˈnoləji/ *noun* the study of icons or of artistic symbolism. ⟫ **iconological** /ˌiekonəˈlojikl/ *adj,* **iconologist** *noun.* [French *iconologie,* from *icono-* ICON- + *-logie* -LOGY]

iconostasis /iekəˈnostəsis/ *noun* (*pl* **iconostases** /-seez/) a screen or partition with doors and tiers of icons separating the sanctuary from the nave in Eastern churches. [Greek *eikonostasis,* from *eikōn* (ICON) + *stasis* standing, from *histanai* to stand]

icosahedron /ˌiekəsəˈheedrən/ *noun* (*pl* **icosahedrons** *or* **icosahedra** /-drə/) a polyhedron with 20 faces, *esp* one with equal triangular faces. ⟫ **icosahedral** /-drəl/ *adj.* [Greek *eikosaedron,* from *eikosi* twenty + *-edron* -HEDRON]

-ics *suffix* forming plural nouns, denoting: 1 a branch of study, knowledge, skill, or practice: *linguistics; electronics.* 2 actions, activities, or mode of behaviour: *histrionics; acrobatics.* 3 qualities, operations, or phenomena relating to something: *mechanics; acoustics.* [-IC² + -S¹; translation of Greek *-ika,* neuter pl of *-ikos* -IC¹]

ICT *abbr* information and communications technology.

icterus /ˈiktərəs/ *noun technical* = JAUNDICE. ⟫ **icteric** /ikˈterik/ *adj.* [via Latin from Greek *ikteros*]

ictus /ˈiktəs/ *noun* (*pl* **ictuses** *or* **ictus**) 1 rhythmic or metrical stress. 2 in medicine, a stroke, seizure, or sudden attack. ⟫ **ictal** *adj.* [Latin *ictus,* past part. of *icere* to strike]

ICU *abbr* intensive care unit.

icy /ˈiesi/ *adj* (**icier, iciest**) 1a covered with, full of, or consisting of ice. b intensely cold. c resembling ice. 2 characterized by personal coldness; hostile: *an icy stare.* ⟫ **icily** *adv,* **iciness** *noun.*

ID¹ *abbr* 1 Idaho (US postal abbreviation). 2 identification. 3 identity: *ID card.*

ID² /eiˈdee/ *verb trans* (**IDs, IDed, IDing**) *informal* to identify (somebody) or check the identity of (somebody): *The police IDed him from footage taken by closed-circuit TV; Forensics examined the bloodstains to try to ID the culprit.*

Id *abbr* Idaho (US postal abbreviation).

I'd /ied/ *contraction* 1 I had. 2 I should. 3 I would.

id /id/ *noun* in psychoanalytic theory, the division of the mind that is completely unconscious and is the source of psychic energy derived from instinctual needs and drives: compare EGO, SUPER-EGO. [Latin *id* it]

id. *abbr* = IDEM.

-id¹ *suffix* 1 forming nouns and adjectives, denoting: membership of a specified zoological family: *arachnid.* 2 forming nouns, denoting: a body, particle, or structure of a given type. 3 forming nouns, denoting: a meteor associated with the comet specified: *Perseid.* 4

forming nouns, denoting: a member of a dynasty: *Seleucid*. [via Latin from Greek *-idēs*, suffix denoting offspring]

-id² *suffix* see -IDE.

IDA *abbr* International Development Association.

Ida. *abbr* Idaho.

-idae *suffix* forming pl nouns, denoting: names of specified zoological families: *Felidae*. [Latin from Greek *-idai*, pl of *-idēs* -ID¹]

IDD *abbr* international direct dialling.

ide /ied/ *noun* = ORFE. [Swedish *id*]

-ide *or* **-id** *suffix* forming nouns, denoting: **1** a binary chemical compound: *hydrogen sulphide*. **2** a chemical compound derived from a specified compound: *glucoside*. **3** a member of a class of related compounds or elements *lanthanide*. [German *-id* from French *-ide* as in OXIDE]

idea /ie'di·ə/ *noun* **1a** a thought, concept, or image actually or potentially present in the mind. **b** a formulated thought or opinion. **2** whatever is known or supposed about something; a belief. **3** an indefinite or vague impression: *I'd an idea you were coming*. **4** a plan of action. **5** an individual's conception of the perfect or typical example of something specified: *My idea of an agreeable person is a person who agrees with me* — Disraeli. **6** the central meaning or aim of a particular action or situation: *The idea of the game is to score goals*. **7** (*often* **Idea**) *esp* in the philosophy of Plato, a transcendent entity of which existing things are imperfect representations. ✳ **get ideas** to begin to have inappropriate, undesirable, or unrealistic thoughts, desires, or expectations. **give somebody ideas** to cause somebody to get ideas. **have no idea** not to know at all. **that's an idea** that's a worthwhile suggestion. **that's the idea** *informal* that's right. **the very idea!** *informal* that is ridiculous, unreasonable, etc. ⯮ **idealess** *adj*. [Latin from Greek *idea* form, pattern, from *idein* to see]

ideal¹ /ie'di·əl/ *noun* **1** a standard of morality, perfection, beauty, or excellence. **2** a person looked up to as embodying an ideal or as a model for imitation. **3** something that exists only as an idea. **4** an ultimate object or aim. [French *idéal* from late Latin *idealis*, from *idea*: see IDEA]

ideal² *adj* **1a** perfect: *This is an ideal spot for a picnic*. **b** embodying an ideal: *an ideal beauty*. **2** existing only in the mind, *esp* as an ideal that cannot be found in real life: *In an ideal world perhaps no one would have to work*. **3** relating to or constituting mental images, ideas, or conceptions. ⯮ **idealness** *noun*.

ideal gas *noun* a hypothetical gas that would obey the laws pertaining to the behaviour of gases at all temperatures and pressures.

idealise *verb trans* see IDEALIZE.

idealism *noun* **1** the practice of living according to one's ideals. **2** in philosophy: **a** a theory that the essential nature of reality lies in consciousness or reason. **b** a theory that only what is immediately perceived, e.g. sensations or ideas, is real. **3a** the representation of things in ideal forms. **b** a literary or artistic theory or practice that values imagination and the representation of ideal types rather than a faithful copying of nature.

idealist *noun* **1** somebody guided by ideals, *esp* one who places ideals before practical considerations. **2** somebody who advocates or practises idealism in art, philosophy, or writing. ⯮ **idealist** *adj*, **idealistic** /-'listik/ *adj*, **idealistically** /-'listikli/ *adv*.

ideality /iedi'aliti/ *noun* (*pl* **idealities**) *formal* **1** the quality or state of being ideal. **2** something imaginary or idealized.

idealize *or* **idealise** *verb trans* **1** to attribute qualities of excellence or perfection to (somebody or something). **2** to represent (somebody or something) in an ideal form. ⯮ *verb intrans* to form ideals. ⯮ **idealization** /-'zaysh(ə)n/ *noun*, **idealizer** *noun*.

ideally *adv* **1** in accordance with an ideal; perfectly: *She's ideally suited for the job*. **2** for best results: *Ideally, we should eat less sugar*.

ideate /'iediayt/ *verb trans* to form an idea of (something). ⯮ *verb intrans* to imagine. ⯮ **ideation** /-'aysh(ə)n/ *noun*, **ideational** /-'aysh(ə)nəl/ *adj*, **ideationally** *adv*.

idée fixe /,eeday 'feeks (*French* ide fiks)/ *noun* (*pl* **idées fixes** /,eeday 'feeks/) a fixed or obsessive idea. [French *idée fixe*, literally 'fixed idea']

idem /'idem, 'iedem/ *pronoun* the same, used in citations to indicate that a book, author, etc is the same as the one just mentioned. [Latin *idem* same]

identical /ie'dentikl/ *adj* **1** (*often* + to) being the same: *We found ourselves in the identical place we had stopped in before*. **2** (*often*

+ to/with) being very similar or exactly alike: *The copy was identical to the original*. **3** said of twins, triplets, etc: derived from a single ovum and therefore very similar in appearance: compare FRATERNAL (2). ⯮ **identically** *adv*. [prob from late Latin *identicus*, from *identitas*: see IDENTITY]

identification /ie,dentifi'kaysh(ə)n/ *noun* **1a** the act or process of identifying or being identified. **b** evidence of identity: *Employees must carry identification at all times*. **c** (*used before a noun*) serving to identify somebody: *an identification card*. **2a** (*often* + with) the act or an instance of putting oneself mentally in the position of another. **b** the conscious or unconscious attribution of the characteristics of another to oneself in order to attain gratification, emotional support, etc.

identification parade *noun chiefly Brit* a line up of people arranged by the police to see whether a witness can identify a suspect.

identify /ie'dentifie/ *verb* (**identifies, identified, identifying**) ⯮ *verb trans* **1a** to establish the identity of (somebody or something): *They identified the murderer by his fingerprints*. **b** to determine the taxonomic category, e.g. the species, to which (a plant or animal) belongs. **2a** (+ with) to consider (oneself) as sharing the same qualities or experiences as somebody else: *He could identify himself with the hero of the play*. **b** (+ with) to equate or link (somebody, oneself, or something) with another person or thing: *Groups such as these are closely identified with the conservation movement*. **3** to consider (two or more things) to be identical. ⯮ *verb intrans* (*usu* + with) to consider that one shares the same qualities or experiences as somebody else: *He could identify with the hero of the play*. ⯮ **identifiable** *adj*, **identifiably** *adv*, **identifier** *noun*. [early French *identifier* from late Latin *identificare* to make the same, from Latin *idem* same + *facere* to make]

Identikit¹ /ie'dentikit/ *noun* **1** *trademark* a set of alternative facial features used by the police to build up a likeness, *esp* of a suspect, using witnesses' descriptions. **2** a likeness constructed in this way.

Identikit² *adj* **1** said of a picture of a suspect, etc: produced by Identikit. **2** (*usu* **identikit**) like many others of the same type: *the type of bland, middlebrow, identikit novel … with which the market is flooded* — Paul Bailey.

identity /ie'dentiti/ *noun* (*pl* **identities**) **1a** who or what somebody or something is: *The police are trying to establish the identity of the murder victim*. **b** the individual characteristics that define a person or thing or by which a person or thing can be recognized: *The police accused me of the theft, but it was a case of mistaken identity*. **2** the condition of being exactly alike; sameness: *identity of interests*.

Editorial note

We speak of two or more distinct objects being 'identical' in the sense that they are indistinguishable from one another (five-pence coins, identical twins), even though we know that their similarity is not absolute. In the strict sense identity consists in being the same object, and the question is: when an object that changes in time ceases to be the same. To a person, to keep one's own identity implies memory — Professor Leszek Kołakowski.

3a the distinguishing character or personality of an individual: *She has a distinct identity, even though she's only two years old*. **b** the fact of having such individuality. **4a** an algebraic equation that remains true whatever values are substituted for the symbols, e.g. $(x + y)^2 = x^2 + 2xy + y^2$. **b** = IDENTITY OPERATION. **c** = IDENTITY ELEMENT. **5** *Aus, NZ* a personality or character: *He was a well-known television identity*. **6** *Aus, NZ* an eccentric. [early French *identité* from late Latin *identitat-, identitas*, from Latin *idem* same]

identity card *noun* a card bearing information that establishes the identity of the holder.

identity element *noun* in mathematics, an element that leaves any element of the set to which it belongs unchanged when combined with it by a specified mathematical operation: *0 is the identity element in the group of numbers under addition*.

identity operation *noun* a mathematical operation involving the combination of an identity element with another element in the same set.

identity parade *noun* = IDENTIFICATION PARADE.

identity theft *n* the fraudulent use of another person's personal data, such as bank details, PIN number, or telephone number: compare SHOULDER SURFING.

ideo- *comb. form* forming words, denoting: an idea or ideas: *ideogram*. [French *idéo-* from Greek *idea*: see IDEA]

ideogram /'idi-əgram/ *noun* **1** a symbol used to represent a thing or idea, e.g. (&) or (+). **2** in writing systems such as hieroglyphics, a stylized picture or symbol used instead of a word to represent a thing or idea: compare LOGOGRAM, PICTOGRAPH. ➤➤ **ideogrammatic** /-'matik/ *adj*, **ideogrammic** /-'gramik/ *adj*.

ideograph /idi·əgrahf, -graf/ *noun* = IDEOGRAM. ➤➤ **ideographic** /-'grafik/ *adj*, **ideographically** /-'grafikli/ *adv*.

ideography /idi'ogrəfi/ *noun* the use of ideograms.

ideologue /'ieedee·əlog/ *noun* **1** a strong advocate or adherent of a particular ideology. **2** a theorist, *esp* one who shows little concern for practicalities. [French *idéologue*, back-formation from *idéologie*: see IDEOLOGY]

ideology /iedi'oləji/ *noun* (*pl* **ideologies**) **1** a systematic body of concepts. **2** a manner of thinking characteristic of an individual, group, or culture: *medical ideology.* **3** the ideas behind a social, political, or cultural programme. **4** the study of the origin and nature of ideas. ➤➤ **ideological** /-'lojikl/ *adj*, **ideologically** /-'lojikli/ *adv*, **ideologist** *noun*. [French *idéologie*, from *idéo-* IDEO- + *-logie* -LOGY]

ides /iedz/ *pl noun* (*treated as sing. or pl*) in the ancient Roman calendar, the 15th day of March, May, July, or October or the 13th day of any other month, or the week preceding any of these dates: compare CALENDS, NONES: *'The ides of March are come.' 'Ay, Caesar, but not gone.'* — Shakespeare. [via French, from Latin *idus*]

-idia *suffix* pl of -IDIUM.

idio- *comb. form* forming words, with the meaning: one's own; personal; distinct: *idiolect; idiosyncrasy.* [Greek, from *idios* one's own, private]

idiocy /'idi·əsi/ *noun* (*pl* **idiocies**) **1** foolishness. **2** something notably stupid or foolish. **3** *dated* extreme mental deficiency.

idiolect /'idi·əlekt/ *noun* the language or speech pattern of an individual. ➤➤ **idiolectal** /-'lektl/ *adj*, **idiolectic** /-'lektik/ *adj*. [IDIO- + *-lect* as in DIALECT]

idiom /'idi·əm/ *noun* **1** an expression that has become established in a language and that has a meaning that cannot be derived from the meanings of its individual elements, e.g. *have bats in one's belfry* meaning to be mad or eccentric. **2a** the language peculiar to a people or to a district, community, or class. **b** the syntactic, grammatical, or structural form peculiar to a language. **3** a characteristic style or form of artistic expression: *the modern jazz idiom.* [French *idiome* via Latin from Greek *idiōma* individual peculiarity of language, from *idios* one's own, private]

idiomatic /idi·ə'matik/ *adj* denoting, relating, or conforming to idioms or an idiom. ➤➤ **idiomatically** *adv*, **idiomaticity** /-'tisiti/ *noun*.

idiopathic /idi·ə'pathik/ *adj* said of a disease: arising spontaneously or from an unknown cause. ➤➤ **idiopathically** *adv*.

idiopathy /idi'opəthi/ *noun* (*pl* **idiopathies**) an idiopathic disease.

idiosyncrasy /ˌidioh'singkrəsi/ *noun* (*pl* **idiosyncrasies**) **1** a characteristic of thought or behaviour peculiar to an individual or group; an eccentricity. **2** characteristic peculiarity of habit or structure. **3** an individual's allergic sensitivity or reaction to a drug, food, etc. ➤➤ **idiosyncratic** /-'kratik/ *adj*, **idiosyncratically** /-'kratikli/ *adv*. [Greek *idiosynkrasia*, from IDIO- + *synkerannynai* to blend, from SYN- + *kerannynai* to mingle, mix]

idiot /'idi·ət/ *noun* **1** a silly or foolish person. **2** *dated* a person afflicted with idiocy, *esp* from birth. ➤➤ **idiotic** /-'otik/ *adj*, **idiotically** /-'otikli/ *adv*. [Middle English from Latin *idiota* ignorant person, from Greek *idiōtēs* private person, layman, ignorant person, from *idios* one's own, private]

idiot board *noun informal* a device that displays a continually rolling version of a script and is used to prompt a performer on television.

idiot box *noun chiefly NAmer, informal* television or a television set.

idiot savant /ˌidi·ət 'savənt* (*French* idjo savã)/ *noun* (*pl* **idiots savants** /ˌidi·ət 'savənt/ *or* **idiot savants**) a person who is considered to have a psychological or psychiatric disorder or some form of learning difficulty but who also exhibits exceptional skill or brilliance in some field. [French *idiot savant* learned idiot]

-idium *suffix* (*pl* **-idiums** *or* **-idia**) forming nouns, denoting: small or lesser kind of: *antheridium.* [from Greek *-idion*, dimin. suffix]

idle¹ /'iedl/ *adj* (**idler, idlest**) **1a** not occupied or employed: *Young people ought not to be idle* — Margaret Thatcher. **b** not in use or operation: *The factory machines were idle because of the strike.* **c** not turned to appropriate use: *idle funds.* **2** lazy. **3** having no particular purpose or value: *idle curiosity.* **4** groundless: *idle rumour.* **5** without

force or effect: *idle threats.* ➤➤ **idleness** *noun*, **idly** /'iedli/ *adv*. [Old English *īdel* empty, useless]

idle² *verb intrans* **1a** to spend time in idleness. **b** to move idly or aimlessly. **2** said *esp* of an engine: to run without being connected to the part, e.g. the wheels of a car, that is driven, so that no useful work is done. ➤ *verb trans* **1** (*often* + away) to pass (time) in idleness. **2** to cause (something, e.g. an engine) to idle.

idle pulley *noun* a guide or tightening pulley for a belt or chain.

idler *noun* **1** a lazy or idle person. **2** = IDLE PULLEY. **3** = IDLE WHEEL.

idler pulley *noun* = IDLE PULLEY.

idler wheel *noun* = IDLE WHEEL.

idle wheel *noun* a wheel, gear, or roller used to transfer motion or to guide or support something.

idol /'iedl/ *noun* **1a** an image or representation, e.g. of a god, used as an object of worship. **b** a false god. **2** an object of passionate or excessive devotion: *a pop idol.* [Middle English via Old French and Latin from Greek *eidōlon* phantom, idol]

idolater /ie'dolətə/ *noun* **1** a worshipper of idols. **2** a passionate and often uncritical admirer. [Middle English *idolatrer* via French and Latin from Greek *eidōlolatrēs*, from *eidōlon* IDOL + *-latrēs* worshipper]

idolatry /ie'dolətri/ *noun* **1** the worship of an idol or idols. **2** excessive attachment or devotion to something. ➤➤ **idolatrous** /-trəs/ *adj*, **idolatrously** /-trəsli/ *adv*, **idolatrousness** /-trəsnis/ *noun*.

idolize *or* **idolise** /'ied(ə)liez/ *verb trans* **1** to love or admire (somebody or something) to excess. **2** to worship (something) idolatrously. ➤ *verb intrans* to practise idolatry. ➤➤ **idolization** /-'zaysh(ə)n/ *noun*, **idolizer** *noun*.

idyll *or* **idyl** /'idl/ *noun* **1** a time or situation of peace and happiness. **2a** a simple work in poetry or prose describing peaceful rustic life or pastoral scenes. **b** an episode suitable for this. **3** a pastoral or romantic musical composition. ➤➤ **idyllic** /i'dilik/ *adj*, **idyllically** /i'dilikli/ *adv*. [via Latin from Greek *eidyllion*, from *eidos* form, picture]

IE *abbr* Indo-European.

i.e. *abbr* that is to say. [Latin *id est*]

Usage note

i.e. or e.g.? See note at E.G.

-ie *suffix* see -Y⁴.

IEE *abbr* Institution of Electrical Engineers.

IEEE *abbr* Institute of Electrical and Electronic Engineers.

-ier *suffix* = -ER².

IF *abbr* intermediate frequency.

if¹ /if/ *conj* **1a** in the event that: *If she phones, let me know.* **b** supposing: *If you'd listened, you'd know.* **c** on condition that: *I'll lend you my laptop if you can get it back to me by Friday.* **2** whether: *She asked if the mail had come.* **3** used to introduce an exclamation expressing a wish: *If it would only rain!* **4** even if; although: *That's an interesting if irrelevant point.* **5** used after expressions of emotion: that: *I don't care if she is cross!; It's not surprising if you're annoyed.* **6** used to introduce expressions, usu in the negative, of surprise, dismay, etc: *Blow me if he didn't hand in his notice right there and then.* ✳ **if anything** used to suggest tentatively or tactfully that something is or could be the case: *If anything, you ought to apologize.* **if not 1** if that is not so. **2** perhaps to the point of being: *It was unwise, if not downright idiotic.* [Old English *gif*]

Usage note

if *and* whether. If and whether can often be used interchangeably: *He asked if (or whether) he could come too; I doubt whether (or if) we'll have time.* Whether should be preferred in more formal writing, however, and where there is a danger that using if could be ambiguous. Let me know if he calls could mean 'tell me that he's calling, when and if he calls' or 'tell me (afterwards) whether he called or not'.

if² *noun* **1** a condition or stipulation: *The question depends on too many ifs.* **2** a supposition: *a theory full of ifs.*

IFA *abbr* independent financial adviser.

IFC *abbr* International Finance Corporation.

-iferous *comb. form* see -FEROUS.

iff /if/ *abbr* in mathematics and logic, if and only if. [an arbitrary extension of IF¹]

iffy /'ifi/ *adj* (**iffier, iffiest**) *informal* **1** full of contingencies and uncertainties: *The situation is far too iffy for any predictions.* **2** of doubtful probability, legality, or morality. >> **iffiness** *noun*. [IF[1] + -Y[1]]

-iform *comb. form* see -FORM.

IFS *abbr* Institute for Fiscal Studies.

-ify *suffix* see -FY.

Igbo /'eeboh/ *noun* (*pl* **Igbos** *or collectively* **Igbo**) **1** a member of an indigenous people inhabiting southeastern Nigeria. **2** (*usu* **Igbo**) the Kwa language spoken by this people. >> **Igbo** *adj*. [the name in various local languages for this people]

igloo /'iglooh/ *noun* (*pl* **igloos**) **1** an Inuit dwelling, usu made of snow blocks and in the shape of a dome. **2** a structure shaped like a dome. [Inuktitut *iglu, igldu* house]

igneous /'igni·əs/ *adj* **1** said of rocks: formed by the flow or solidification of molten rock from the earth's core. **2** *formal* relating to fire; fiery. [Latin *igneus*, from *ignis* fire]

ignis fatuus /,ignis 'fatyoo·əs/ *noun* (*pl* **ignes fatui** /,igneez 'fatyooie/) = WILL-O'-THE-WISP (1). [late Latin *ignis fatuus*, literally 'foolish fire'; from its erratic movements]

ignite /ig'niet/ *verb trans* **1a** to set fire to (something). **b** to cause (a fuel mixture) to burn. **c** to arouse (an emotion, *esp* passion). **2** to cause or start (e.g. a riot or protest), *esp* suddenly. >> *verb intrans* **1** to catch fire. **2** to begin to glow. **3** said of a volatile situation, etc: to burst forth suddenly into violence or conflict. >> **ignitability** /-'biliti/ *noun*, **ignitable** *adj*, **igniter** *noun*, **ignitibility** /-'biliti/ *noun*, **ignitible** *adj*, **ignitor** *noun*. [Latin *ignitus*, past part. of *ignire* to ignite, from *ignis* fire]

ignition /ig'nish(ə)n/ *noun* **1** the act or an instance of igniting or the state of being ignited. **2a** the process of igniting a fuel mixture, e.g. in an internal-combustion engine. **b** a device that effects this.

ignitron /ig'nietron, 'ignitron/ *noun* a RECTIFIER (electrical device for converting alternating current to direct current) in which the electric current passes as an arc between the cathode, which is a pool of mercury, and the anode. [IGNITE or IGNITION + -TRON]

ignoble /ig'nohbl/ *adj* **1** base; dishonourable. **2** *formal* of low birth or humble origin. >> **ignobility** /-'biliti/ *noun*, **ignobleness** *noun*, **ignobly** *adv*. [Latin *ignobilis*, from IN-[1] + *nobilis* (earlier *gnobilis*): see NOBLE[1]]

ignominious /ignə'mini·əs/ *adj* **1** marked by or causing disgrace or discredit. **2** humiliating; degrading: *He suffered an ignominious defeat in the last election*. >> **ignominiously** *adv*, **ignominiousness** *noun*.

ignominy /'ignəmini/ *noun* (*pl* **ignominies**) **1** deep personal humiliation and disgrace, or a cause of this. **2** disgraceful or dishonourable conduct or quality, or an example of this. [early French *ignominie* from Latin *ignominia*, from IN-[1] + a variant of *nomen* name, repute]

ignoramus /ignə'rayməs/ *noun* (*pl* **ignoramuses**) an ignorant or stupid person. [named after *Ignoramus*, the ignorant lawyer in *Ignoramus*, play by George Ruggle d.1622, English dramatist, from Latin *ignoramus* we do not know]

ignorant /'ignərənt/ *adj* **1** having or showing a lack of knowledge or of education in things in general: *I do not pretend to know where many ignorant men are sure* — Clarence Darrow. **2** (*often* + of) uninformed about or unaware of a specified subject, etc: *Being ignorant of the law is no excuse*. **3** *chiefly informal* lacking social training; impolite. >> **ignorance** *noun*, **ignorantly** *adv*. [Middle English via Old French from Latin *ignorant-, ignorans*, present part. of *ignorare*: IGNORE]

ignore /ig'naw/ *verb trans* to refuse or fail to take notice of (something or somebody); to disregard (them) deliberately. >> **ignorable** *adj*, **ignorer** *noun*. [Middle English, in the sense 'to be ignorant of', via French from Latin *ignorare* not to know, from IN-[1] + *gnoscere* to know]

iguana /igyoo'ahnə, i'gwahnə/ *noun* either of two species of large plant-eating, usu dark-coloured, tropical American lizards with a serrated or spiny crest on their backs: family Iguanidae. >> **iguanian** *adj*, **iguanid** *noun*. [Spanish *iguana* from Arawak *iwana*]

iguanodon /igyoo'ahnədon, i'gwah-/ *noun* any of various large long-tailed plant-eating dinosaurs from the late Jurassic and early Cretaceous periods, fossils of which have been found in Europe, Asia, and N Africa. [IGUANA + -*odon* from Greek *odont-, odous* tooth]

IHS *abbr* used as a Christian symbol and monogram to indicate Jesus. [late Latin, part transliteration of Greek IHΣ, abbr for IHΣOYΣ *Iēsous* Jesus]

ikat /'eekaht/ *noun* **1** a fabric, traditionally made in Asia, in which the warp or weft threads, or both, are tied and dyed before weaving, so that a distinctive blurred pattern is produced. **2** the technique of producing such fabric. [Malay *ikat* tying]

ikebana /ikay'bahnə, iki-/ *noun* the Japanese art of flower-arranging that emphasizes form and balance in accordance with strict rules. [Japanese *ikebana*, literally 'living flowers', from *ikeru* to keep alive, arrange + *hana* flower]

ikon /'iekon/ *noun* see ICON (1).

IL *abbr* **1** Illinois (US postal abbreviation). **2** Israel (international vehicle registration).

il- *prefix* see IN-[1], IN-[2].

-il *suffix* see -ILE.

ilang-ilang /,eelang 'eelang/ *noun* see YLANG-YLANG.

ile- *or* **ileo-** *comb. form* forming words, denoting: ileum: *ileitis*.

-ile *or* **-il** *suffix* **1** forming adjectives and nouns, denoting: a part or relationship: *percentile*. **2** forming adjectives, with the meaning: denoting, relating to, capable of, etc: *penile; audile*. [Middle English via French from Latin -*ilis*]

ilea *noun* pl of ILEUM.

ileitis /ili'ietəs/ *noun* inflammation of the ileum.

ileo- *comb. form* see ILE-.

ileostomy /ili'ostəmi/ *noun* (*pl* **ileostomies**) the surgical formation of an opening through the abdominal wall into the ileum, that acts as an artificial anus. [ILE- + -*stomy* from STOMA]

ileum /'ili·əm/ *noun* (*pl* **ilea** /'ili·ə/) the last division of the small intestine extending between the jejunum and the caecum. >> **ileac** /-ak/ *adj*, **ileal** *adj*. [Latin *ileum* groin, viscera]

ileus /'ili·əs/ *noun* obstruction of the bowel. [Latin *ileus* from Greek *eileos*, from *eilyein* to roll]

ilex /'ieleks/ *noun* (*pl* **ilexes**) **1** = HOLM OAK. **2** any of a genus of trees or shrubs including the holly: genus *Ilex*. [Latin *ilex* holm oak]

ilia /'ili·ə/ *noun* pl of ILIUM.

iliac /'iliak/ *adj* relating to or in the region of the ilium. [late Latin *iliacus*, from Latin *ilium, ileum* groin, viscera]

ilial /'ili·əl/ *adj* = ILIAC.

ilium /'ili·əm/ *noun* (*pl* **ilia** /'ili·ə/) the uppermost and largest of the three principal bones that form either half of the pelvis. [Latin *ilium, ileum* groin, viscera]

ilk /ilk/ *noun* sort or kind: *I hate politicians and others of that ilk*. ✳ **of that ilk** *chiefly Scot, dated* from or of the place or landed estate of the same name (as that of the person mentioned): *McDonald of that ilk*. [Old English *ilca* same]

Ill. *abbr* Illinois.

I'll /iel/ *contraction* I will or I shall.

ill[1] /il/ *adj* **1a** not in good health. **b** nauseated: *I do feel ill. I shouldn't have eaten as much*. **c** *chiefly Brit* not fully recovered, e.g. after an accident; hurt. **d** said of a person's health: not normal or sound. **2** causing discomfort or inconvenience; disagreeable: *ill effects*. **3a** malevolent; hostile: *ill feeling*. **b** attributing evil or an objectionable quality: *He held an ill opinion of his neighbours*. **c** morally evil: *He never repented of his ill deeds*. **4** unlucky or disadvantageous: *an ill omen; ill fortune*. **5** harsh: *ill treatment*. **6** socially improper: *ill breeding*. ✳ **ill at ease** uneasy or uncomfortable. **take it ill** to resent something: *I take it rather ill that she didn't tell me first*. [Middle English from Old Norse *illr* evil, difficult]

ill[2] *adv* (**worse, worst**) (*often used in combinations*) **1** hardly; scarcely: *I can ill afford such extravagances*. **2a** in an unfortunate manner; badly or unluckily: *ill-fated*. **b** in a faulty, imperfect, or unpleasant manner: *ill-equipped*. **3a** with displeasure or hostility. **b** in a harsh manner: *She has used him ill*. **c** unfavourably; critically: *He never spoke ill of his neighbours*. **4** in a reprehensible, harsh, or deficient manner: *They fared ill; ill-adapted to city life*.

ill[3] *noun* **1a** something that disturbs or afflicts: *There must be a cure for the country's economic and social ills*. **b** an ailment or illness. **c** misfortune or trouble, or a misfortune or trouble: *We can only hope no more ills befall him*. **2** the opposite of good; evil. **3** something that reflects unfavourably; criticism: *She spoke no ill of him*.

ill-advised *adj* **1** unwise. **2** showing lack of proper thought or planning or sound advice: compare ADVISED, UNADVISED, WELL-ADVISED. ⫸ **ill-advisedly** *adv*.

ill-assorted *adj* not matching or not well matched; incompatible.

illative¹ /i'laytiv/ *adj* **1a** relating to or having the quality of inference. **b** proceeding by inference; inferential. **2** denoting a grammatical case, in certain languages, e.g. Finnish, expressing motion into something. ⫸ **illatively** *adv*. [late Latin *illativum* conclusion, neut of *illativus* inferential, from Latin *illatus*, past part. of *inferre*: see INFER]

illative² *noun* **1** a word, e.g. *therefore*, or phrase, e.g. *as a consequence*, introducing an inference. **2** the illative case or a word in this case.

ill-bred *adj* having or showing bad upbringing; impolite. ⫸ **ill-breeding** *noun*.

ill-considered *adj* showing a lack of proper thought or planning; ill-advised.

ill-disposed *adj* (*often* + to/towards) unfriendly; unsympathetic.

illegal¹ /i'leegl/ *adj* **1** not authorized by law. **2** contrary to established rules, e.g. of a game: *an illegal move*. ⫸ **illegality** /ili'galiti/ *noun*, **illegally** *adv*. [French *illégal* from late Latin *illegalis*, from Latin IN-¹ + *legalis*: see LEGAL]

illegal² *noun chiefly NAmer* an illegal immigrant.

illegible /i'lejəbl/ *adj* said of handwriting, printed text, etc: unable to be read or deciphered. ⫸ **illegibility** /-'biliti/ *noun*, **illegibly** *adv*.

illegitimate /ili'jitimət/ *adj* **1** illegal; not allowed by law or rules. **2a** said of a child: born to parents who are not lawfully married to each other. **b** occurring out of wedlock. **3** wrongly deduced or inferred. **4** departing from the regular; abnormal. ⫸ **illegitimacy** /-məsi/ *noun*, **illegitimately** *adv*.

ill-fated *adj* suffering, leading to, or destined for misfortune; unlucky: *an ill-fated expedition*.

ill-favoured (*NAmer* **ill-favored**) *adj* **1** unattractive in physical appearance. **2** offensive; objectionable.

ill-gotten *adj* acquired by illicit or improper means: *ill-gotten gains*.

ill-humoured *adj* surly; irritable; bad-tempered. ⫸ **ill humour** *noun*.

illiberal /i'libərəl/ *adj* **1** said of a person, views, attitude, etc: **a** not broad-minded; bigoted. **b** opposed to liberalism. **2** not generous; mean. **3** *archaic* having or showing a lack of culture or refinement. ⫸ **illiberalism** *noun*, **illiberality** /-'raliti/ *noun*, **illiberally** *adv*, **illiberalness** *noun*. [via French from Latin *illiberalis* ignoble, stingy, from IN-¹ + *liberalis*: see LIBERAL¹]

illicit /i'lisit/ *adj* not permitted by law, rules, or custom: *illicit love affairs*. ⫸ **illicitly** *adv*, **illicitness** *noun*. [Latin *illicitus*, from IN-¹ + *licitus*: see LICIT]

Usage note
illicit or elicit? See note at ELICIT.

illimitable /i'limitəbl/ *adj* without limits; measureless. ⫸ **illimitability** /-'biliti/ *noun*, **illimitableness** *noun*, **illimitably** *adv*.

illiterate¹ /i'litərət/ *adj* **1** unable to read or write. **2** showing a lack of education, e.g. by the use of poor grammar and spelling. **3** showing a lack of knowledge in a particular field: *economically illiterate*. ⫸ **illiteracy** /-si/ *noun*, **illiterately** *adv*, **illiterateness** *noun*. [Latin *illiteratus*, from IN-¹ + *litteratus*: see LITERATE¹]

illiterate² *noun* an illiterate person.

ill-mannered *adj* having bad manners. ⫸ **ill-manneredly** *adv*, **ill-manneredness** *noun*.

ill-natured *adj* having or showing a disagreeable disposition; surly. ⫸ **ill-naturedly** *adv*, **ill-naturedness** *noun*.

illness *noun* **1** a disease, period of sickness, or other indisposition. **2** an unhealthy condition of the body or mind: *Illness is the night-side of life* — Susan Sontag.

illogical /i'lojikl/ *adj* **1** contrary to the principles of logic. **2** devoid of logic; senseless. ⫸ **illogicality** /-'kaliti/ *noun*, **illogically** *adv*, **illogicalness** *noun*.

ill-starred *adj* ill-fated; unlucky.

ill-tempered *adj* bad-tempered; surly. ⫸ **ill-temperedly** *adv*, **ill-temperedness** *noun*.

ill-timed *adj* badly timed; inopportune.

ill-treat *verb trans* to treat (somebody or something) cruelly or improperly. ⫸ **ill-treatment** *noun*.

illuminance /i'l(y)oohminəns/ *noun* the amount of light per unit area of a surface on which it falls. [from ILLUMINATE]

illuminant¹ /i'l(y)oohminənt/ *noun* an illuminating device or substance. [Latin *illuminant-, illuminans*, present part. of *illuminare*: see ILLUMINATE]

illuminant² *adj* illuminating; providing light.

illuminate /i'l(y)oohminayt/ *verb trans* **1a** to cast light on (something); to fill (e.g. a place) with light. **b** to decorate (e.g. a building) with lights. **c** to brighten (something). **2** to decorate (a manuscript) with elaborate initial letters or marginal designs in gold, silver, and brilliant colours. **3a** to elucidate or clarify (something). **b** to enlighten (somebody) spiritually or intellectually. ⫸ **illuminating** *adj*, **illuminatingly** *adv*, **illuminative** /-nətiv/ *adj*, **illuminator** *noun*. [Latin *illuminatus*, past part. of *illuminare*, from IN-² + *luminare* to light up, from *lumin-, lumen* light]

illuminati /i,l(y)oohmi'nahtee/ *pl noun* (*sing.* **illuminato** /-toh/) **1** people who are or claim to be unusually enlightened. **2** (**Illuminati**) any of various groups claiming special religious enlightenment. [via Italian from Latin *illuminati*, pl of *illuminatus* enlightened person, past part. of *illuminare*: see ILLUMINATE]

illumination /i,l(y)oohmi'naysh(ə)n/ *noun* **1** the act or an instance of illuminating or the state of being illuminated. **2** spiritual or intellectual enlightenment. **3** (*also in pl*) decorative lighting or lighting effects: *the Blackpool illuminations*. **4** decoration of a manuscript by the art of illuminating. **5** any of the decorative features used in the art of illuminating or in decorative lighting. **6** = ILLUMINANCE.

illuminato /,il(y)oohmi'nahtoh/ *noun* sing. of ILLUMINATI.

illumine /i'l(y)oohmin/ *verb trans literary* to illuminate. ⫸ **illuminable** *adj*. [Middle English *illuminen* via French from Latin *illuminare*: see ILLUMINATE]

ill-use *verb trans* to treat (somebody or something) harshly or unkindly. ⫸ **ill-usage** or **ill-use** *noun*.

illusion /i'l(y)oohzh(ə)n/ *noun* **1a** a false impression or notion: *I have no illusions about my ability*. **b** something that deceives or misleads intellectually. **2a** a misleading image presented to the vision. **b** perception of an object in such a way that it presents a misleading image: *an optical illusion*. **c** = HALLUCINATION. ✱ **be under the illusion that** to have the mistaken belief that (something is the case). ⫸ **illusional** *adj*. [Middle English via French from Latin *illusion-, illusio* action of mocking, from *illudere* to mock at, from IN-¹ + *ludere* to play]

illusionism *noun* the use of perspective or shading to create the illusion of reality, *esp* in a work of art.

illusionist *noun* **1** a conjuror or magician, *esp* one who performs tricks depending on the production of illusions rather than on sleight of hand. **2** an artist who practises illusionism. ⫸ **illusionistic** /-'nistik/ *adj*.

illusive /i'l(y)oohsiv/ *adj chiefly literary* deceptive; illusory. ⫸ **illusively** *adv*, **illusiveness** *noun*.

illusory /i'l(y)oohsəri, -zəri/ *adj* deceptive; unreal: *illusory hopes*. ⫸ **illusorily** *adv*, **illusoriness** *noun*.

illustrate /'iləstrayt/ *verb trans* **1** to provide (e.g. a book) with pictures or other visual material. **2** to clarify, explain, or demonstrate (something), *esp* by using examples, analogy, etc. **3** to be an example of (something). ⫸ *verb intrans* to give an example or instance. ⫸ **illustrator** *noun*. [Latin *illustratus*, past part. of *illustrare*, from IN-² + *lustrare* to purify, make bright, shine]

illustration /ilə'straysh(ə)n/ *noun* **1a** a picture or diagram that helps to make something clear or attractive. **b** something such as an example, analogy, etc that explains or clarifies something. **2** the act or an instance of illustrating or the fact of being illustrated. ⫸ **illustrational** *adj*.

illustrative /'iləstrativ, -straytiv/ *adj* serving or intended to illustrate: *illustrative examples*. ⫸ **illustratively** *adv*.

illustrious /i'lustri-əs/ *adj* **1** said of somebody: admired and well-known, *esp* for something done in the past; eminent. **2** said of an action, etc: impressive and publicly acclaimed. ⫸ **illustriously** *adv*, **illustriousness** *noun*. [Latin *illustris* famous, prob back-formation from *illustrare*: see ILLUSTRATE]

ill will *noun* unfriendly feeling; animosity or enmity.

Illyrian /i'liri-ən/ *noun* **1** a native or inhabitant of Illyria, an ancient region lying along the eastern coast of the Adriatic Sea. **2** the extinct Indo-European language of the Illyrians, possibly related to modern Albanian. ➤➤ **Illyrian** *adj*.

ILO *abbr* International Labour Organization.

ILP *abbr* Independent Labour Party.

I'm /iem/ *contraction* I am.

im- *prefix* see IN-¹, IN-².

image¹ /'imij/ *noun* **1a** exact likeness: *So God created man in his own image* — Bible. **b** a person who strikingly resembles another specified person: *He's the image of his father.* **2a** a reproduction, e.g. a portrait or statue, of the form of a person or thing. **b** an idol. **3a** the optical counterpart of an object produced by a lens, mirror, etc or an electronic device. **b** a likeness of an object produced on a photographic material. **c** the pattern of light that enters the eye from an external subject. **4** a typical example or embodiment, e.g. of a quality: *She's the image of goodness.* **5a** a mental picture of something not actually present. **b** an idea or concept. **6** a conception created in the minds of people, *esp* the general public: *He's very worried about his public image.* **7** a figure of speech, *esp* a metaphor or simile. **8** an element in the range of a mathematical function that corresponds to a particular element in the domain. ➤➤ **imageless** *adj*. [Middle English via Old French from Latin *imagin-, imago* representation, copy]

image² *verb trans* **1** to reflect or mirror (somebody or something). **2** to describe or portray (somebody or something) in language, *esp* vividly. **3** to form an image of (somebody or something) in one's mind. **4a** to create a representation of (somebody or something). **b** to represent (something) symbolically. **5** to exemplify or typify (something). ➤➤ **imageable** *adj*.

image converter *noun* an electronic device in which a visible image of electromagnetic radiation, e.g. infrared light or X-rays, is produced on a fluorescent screen.

image enhancement *noun* a method of improving the definition of a picture by means of a computer program which detects and amplifies strong changes in contrast, so making images sharper.

image intensifier *noun* a device used to increase the brightness of an optical image.

image orthicon *noun* a highly sensitive television camera tube in which electrons emitted from a surface in proportion to the intensity of light are focused onto a target from which greater numbers of electrons are emitted, leaving the target with an intensified pattern of electrostatic charge which is then scanned by an electron beam. [*orthicon* from ORTH- + *iconoscope*, a kind of television camera tube, from ICON- + -SCOPE]

imagery /'imij(ə)ri/ *noun* (*pl* **imageries**) **1a** figurative language. **b** descriptive language, *esp* in a literary work. **2** mental images, *esp* the products of imagination. **3** the art of making images. **4** the mental images characteristic of a particular person.

image tube *noun* **1** = IMAGE CONVERTER. **2** = IMAGE INTENSIFIER.

imaginable /i'majinəbl/ *adj* capable of being thought of or believed. ➤➤ **imaginably** *adv*.

imaginal¹ /i'majinl/ *adj* of imagination, images, or imagery. [IMAGINE + -AL¹]

imaginal² *adj* of the insect imago. [IMAGO + -AL²]

imaginary /i'majin(ə)ri/ *adj* **1** existing only in imagination; lacking factual reality. **2** in mathematics, expressed in terms of or relating to the square root of minus one. ➤➤ **imaginarily** *adv*, **imaginariness** *noun*.

imaginary number *noun* = COMPLEX NUMBER.

imagination /i,maji'naysh(ə)n/ *noun* **1** the act or power of forming a mental image of something not present to the senses or never before wholly perceived in reality: *Cowardice ... is almost always simply a lack of ability to suspend the functioning of the imagination* — Hemingway. **2a** creative ability. **b** resourcefulness; inventiveness. **3** a fanciful or empty notion.

imaginative /i'maj(i)nətiv/ *adj* **1** of or characterized by imagination. **2a** creative. **b** resourceful; inventive. **3** given to imagining; having a lively imagination. **4** showing a command of imagery. ➤➤ **imaginatively** *adv*, **imaginativeness** *noun*.

imagine /i'maj(ə)n/ *verb trans* **1** to suppose or think (something): *I imagine it will rain.* **2** to believe (something) without sufficient basis: *He imagines himself to be indispensable.* **3** to form a mental image of (something not present). ➤ *verb intrans* to use one's imagination. ➤➤ **imaginer** *noun*. [Middle English *imaginen* via French from Latin *imaginari*, from *imagin-, imago* IMAGE¹]

imagines /i'mayjineez, i'mah-, -gineez/ *noun* pl of IMAGO.

imagism *or* **Imagism** /'imijiz(ə)m/ *noun* a 20th-cent. movement in poetry advocating the expression of ideas and emotions through clear precise images. ➤➤ **imagist** *noun and adj*, **imagistic** /-'jistik/ *adj*, **imagistically** /-'jistikli/ *adv*.

imago /i'maygoh/ *noun* (*pl* **imagoes** *or* **imagines** /i'mayjineez, i'mah-, -gineez/) **1** an insect in its final mature state. **2** in psychoanalysis, a subconscious idealized mental image of a person, *esp* a parent, seen as having an influence on a person's behaviour. [Latin *imago* IMAGE¹]

imam /i'mahm, 'imahm/ *noun* **1** the leader of prayer in a mosque: compare MUEZZIN. **2** (**Imam**) a leader held by Shiite Muslims to be a divinely appointed successor of Muhammad. **3** a caliph, or any of various Islamic doctors of law or theology. ➤➤ **imamate** /-mət, -mayt/ *noun*. [Arabic *imām* leader]

IMAX /'iemaks/ *noun* **1** *trademark* a system for projecting cinematic film that gives images approximately ten times larger than those of standard 35mm film, often using an enormous curved screen that sweeps round the front of the auditorium. **2** (*used before a noun*) relating to, denoting, or used in this system: *The new multiplex has an IMAX screen.* [prob from *i* a phonetic realization of EYE¹ + *max* a contraction of MAXIMUM¹]

imbalance /im'baləns/ *noun* **1** lack of functional balance in a physiological system: *hormonal imbalance.* **2** lack of balance between segments of a country's economy. **3** a lack of proportion or numerical balance.

imbecile¹ /'imbəseel/ *noun* **1** *informal* a fool or idiot. **2** *dated* a person of very low intelligence, usu having an IQ of between 25 and 50 and a mental age of under 7 years. ➤➤ **imbecilic** /-'silik/ *adj*, **imbecilically** /-'silikli/ *adv*, **imbecility** /imbə'siliti/ *noun*. [French *imbécile* weak, weak-minded, from Latin *imbecillus* feeble, literally 'without a supporting stick', from IN-¹ + *baculum* stick, staff]

imbecile² *adj* **1** *informal* very stupid. **2** *dated* relating to or denoting an IMBECILE¹ (2). ➤➤ **imbecilely** *adv*.

imbed /im'bed/ *verb* see EMBED.

imbibe /im'bieb/ *verb trans* **1** *chiefly formal or humorous*. **a** to drink (*esp* alcohol). **b** to take in (something) as if drinking it. **2** to take in (e.g. water); to absorb or assimilate (something): *A sponge imbibes moisture.* **3** to receive (e.g. ideas) into the mind and retain them; to assimilate (something): *Children imbibe moral principles from their parents.* ➤ *verb intrans* to drink alcohol. ➤➤ **imbiber** *noun*. [Latin *imbibere* to drink in, conceive, from IN-² + *bibere* to drink]

imbricate¹ /'imbrikət, -kayt/ *adj* **1** having scales, sepals, etc that overlap each other in regular order: compare VALVATE (3). **2** overlapping. ➤➤ **imbricately** *adv*. [late Latin *imbricatus*, past part. of *imbricare* to cover with pantiles, from Latin *imbrex* pantile]

imbricate² /'imbrikayt/ *verb intrans* to overlap, *esp* in regular order. ➤ *verb trans* **1** to arrange (e.g. roof tiles) in an overlapping pattern. **2** to decorate (something) with objects that overlap. ➤➤ **imbrication** /-'kaysh(ə)n/ *noun*.

imbricated /'imbrikaytid/ *adj* = IMBRICATE¹.

imbroglio /im'brohlioh/ *noun* (*pl* **imbroglios**) **1a** an intricate or complicated situation, e.g. in a drama. **b** a confused or complicated misunderstanding or disagreement. **2** *archaic* a confused mass or heap. [Italian *imbroglio*, from *imbrogliare* to entangle, from IN-² + *brogliare* to mix up]

imbrue /im'brooh/ *verb trans* (**imbrues, imbrued, imbruing**) *chiefly formal* to stain or drench (something), *esp* with blood. [Middle English *enbrewen*, prob from early French *abrevrer, embevrer* to soak, drench, ultimately of Germanic origin]

imbue /im'byooh/ *verb trans* (**imbues, imbued, imbuing**) **1** said of a feeling, ideal, principle, etc: to be a pervasive presence in (somebody): *A strong sense of duty imbues him.* **2** to tinge or dye (something) deeply. [Latin *imbuere* to saturate, stain]

IMechE /,ie mek 'ee/ *abbr* Institution of Mechanical Engineers.

IMF *abbr* International Monetary Fund.

IMHO *abbr* in my humble opinion, used *esp* in email messages, newsgroup postings on the Internet, etc to indicate that something is merely a personal view and not an established fact.

imidazole /imi'dazohl, imi'day-, i'midəzohl/ *noun* an organic compound that is a chemical base with a characteristic heterocyclic structure or any of various derivations of it. [IMIDE + AZOLE]

imide /'imied/ *noun* a compound that is derived from ammonia by replacement of two hydrogen atoms by a metal or by acid radicals: compare AMIDE. ➤➤ **imidic** /i'midik/ *adj.* [alteration of AMIDE]

imit. *abbr* **1** imitation. **2** imitative.

imitate /'imitayt/ *verb trans* **1** to follow (somebody or something) as a pattern, model, or example. **2** to mimic (somebody or something), *esp* for humorous effect. **3** to resemble or simulate (something). **4** to reproduce or duplicate (something). ➤➤ **imitable** *adj*, **imitator** *noun*. [Latin *imitatus*, past part. of *imitari* to copy]

imitation /imi'taysh(ə)n/ *noun* **1** the act or an instance of imitating: *Imitation is the sincerest form of flattery* — Charles Colton. **2a** something produced as a copy; a counterfeit. **b** (*used before a noun*) relating to or denoting something that is not genuine; fake: *imitation leather*. **3** the repetition in one musical part of the melodic theme, phrase, or motive previously found in another musical part: compare OSTINATO, SEQUENCE¹ (6). ➤➤ **imitational** *adj.*

imitative /'imitətiv/ *adj* **1a** marked by or given to imitation; imitating: *Acting is an imitative art.* **b** said of a word: reflecting the sound it represents; onomatopoeic (see ONOMATOPOEIA). **2** imitating something superior. ➤➤ **imitatively** *adv*, **imitativeness** *noun.*

immaculate /i'makyoolət/ *adj* **1** spotlessly clean and very tidy. **2** free from flaw or error. **3** without blemish; pure. **4** free from sin. **5** said of petals, wings, etc: without spots or other markings. ➤➤ **immaculacy** /-si/ *noun*, **immaculately** *adv*, **immaculateness** *noun.* [Middle English *immaculat* from Latin *immaculatus*, from IN-¹ + *maculatus*, past part. of *maculare* to stain, from *macula* spot, stain]

Immaculate Conception *noun* **1** in the Roman Catholic Church, the doctrine that, from the moment she was conceived, the Virgin Mary was without taint of original sin. **2** a feast commemorating the Immaculate Conception, observed on 8 December.

immanent /'imənənt/ *adj* **1** existing within something; indwelling; inherent. **2** said e.g. of God: always present in nature or the universe: compare TRANSCENDENT. ➤➤ **immanence** *noun*, **immanency** /-si/ *noun*, **immanently** *adv.* [late Latin *immanent-, immanens*, present part. of *immanēre* to remain in place, from Latin IN-² + *manēre* to remain]

immanentism *noun* a belief in God's immanence. ➤➤ **immanentist** *noun.*

immaterial /imə'tiəri·əl/ *adj* **1** unimportant or not relevant. **2** not consisting of matter; incorporeal; spiritual, *esp* as distinct from being physical. ➤➤ **immateriality** /-'aliti/ *noun*, **immaterially** *adv*, **immaterialness** *noun.* [Middle English *immateriel* via French from late Latin *immaterialis*, from IN-¹ + Latin *materialis*: see MATERIAL²]

immaterialism *noun* in philosophy, the belief or theory that the reality of matter consists in its being conceived by the mind. ➤➤ **immaterialist** *noun.*

immature /imə'tyooə/ *adj* **1** lacking complete growth, differentiation, or development; not yet fully developed. **2a** exhibiting less than an expected degree of maturity, wisdom, sense, etc: *emotionally immature adults.* **b** not having arrived at a definitive form or state: *a vigorous but immature school of art.* ➤➤ **immaturely** *adv*, **immatureness** *noun*, **immaturity** *noun.* [Latin *immaturus*, from IN-¹ + *maturus* MATURE¹]

immeasurable /i'mezh(ə)rəbl/ *adj* unable to be measured, *esp* because of extreme size or extent; indefinitely extensive. ➤➤ **immeasurability** /-'biliti/ *noun*, **immeasurableness** *noun*, **immeasurably** *adv.*

immediacy /i'meedi·əsi/ *noun* (*pl* **immediacies**) **1** the quality or state of being immediate. **2** (*usu in pl*) something requiring immediate attention: *People here have no time for anything but the immediacies of life.*

immediate /i'meedi·ət/ *adj* **1a** occurring at once or likely to occur very shortly: *There's no immediate danger.* **b** current; most in need of attention or action: *Our immediate problem is lack of funds.* **2** next in line or relationship: *Only the immediate family was present.* **3** in close or direct physical proximity: *The police searched the immediate neighbourhood.* **4** acting or being without any intervening agency or factor: *The immediate cause of death was a blow to the head.* **5** directly touching or concerning a person or thing. **6a** directly known or intuited. **b** involving or derived from a single premise:

an immediate inference. ➤➤ **immediateness** *noun.* [late Latin *immediatus*, from IN-¹ + *mediatus*: see MEDIATE¹]

immediately¹ *adv* **1** without delay. **2** in direct relation or proximity; directly: *The Government agreed to talks with all parties immediately involved.*

immediately² *conj chiefly Brit* as soon as.

immemorial /imi'mawri·əl/ *adj* extending beyond the reach of memory, record, or tradition: *These paths have existed from time immemorial.* ➤➤ **immemorially** *adv.* [prob via French *immémorial* from Latin *immemorialis*, from IN-¹ + *memorialis* relating to memory, from *memoria*: see MEMORY]

immense /i'mens/ *adj* **1** very great, *esp* in size, degree, or extent: *It is of immense importance to learn to laugh at ourselves* — Katherine Mansfield. **2** *informal* very good. ➤➤ **immensely** *adv*, **immenseness** *noun*, **immensity** *noun.* [early French *immense* from Latin *immensus* immeasurable, from IN-¹ + *mensus*, past part. of *metiri* to MEASURE¹]

immerse /i'muhs/ *verb trans* **1** (*usu* + in) to plunge (somebody or something) completely into a fluid. **2** (*usu* + in) to engross or absorb (oneself) in something: *She completely immersed herself in her work.* **3** to baptize (somebody) by complete submergence. ➤➤ **immersible** *adj.* [Latin *immersus*, past part. of *immergere*, from IN-² + *mergere* to dip, MERGE]

immerser *noun* = IMMERSION HEATER.

immersion /i'muhsh(ə)n/ *noun* **1** the act or an instance of immersing or being immersed. **2** *chiefly NAmer* a method of teaching a foreign language by placing the student in a situation where only the foreign language is spoken. **3** in astronomy, the disappearance of a celestial body behind or into the shadow of another.

immersion heater *noun* an electrical apparatus for heating a liquid in which it is immersed, *esp* an electric water-heater fixed inside a domestic hot-water storage tank.

immigrant /'imigrənt/ *noun* **1a** a person who comes to a country to take up permanent residence. **b** (*used before a noun*) relating to, denoting, or involving immigrants: *immigrant labour.* **2** a plant or animal that becomes established in an area where it was previously unknown. [IMMIGRATE + -ANT]

immigrate /'imigrayt/ *verb intrans* **1** to come into a country of which one is not a native to take up permanent residence. **2** said of a plant or animal: to become established in an area where it was previously unknown. ➤➤ **immigration** /-'graysh(ə)n/ *noun*, **immigrational** /-'graysh(ə)nəl/ *adj.* [Latin *immigratus*, past part. of *immigrare* to go in, from IN-² + *migrare* to MIGRATE]

imminent /'iminənt/ *adj* **1** about to take place; impending *esp* in a threatening way. **2** *archaic* overhanging. ➤➤ **imminence** *noun*, **imminently** *adv.* [Latin *imminent-, imminens*, present part. of *imminēre* to project, threaten, from IN-² + *minēre* to overhang]

immiscible /i'misəbl/ *adj* said of two or more different liquids: incapable of being thoroughly mixed together. ➤➤ **immiscibility** /-'biliti/ *noun*, **immiscibly** *adv.*

immobile /i'mohbiel/ *adj* **1** incapable of being moved. **2** motionless: *You must keep the patient immobile.* ➤➤ **immobility** /imoh'bil·iti/ *noun.* [Middle English via French from Latin *immobilis*, from IN-¹ + *mobilis*: see MOBILE¹]

immobilize *or* **immobilise** /i'mohbiliez/ *verb trans* **1** to prevent (somebody or something) from moving freely, effectively, or normally: *The shock had completely immobilized him; The traffic warden immobilized the illegally parked cars.* **2** to prevent or restrict (somebody or a body part) from moving by mechanical means or by strict bed rest, as a treatment to encourage healing. **3** to withhold (money or capital) from circulation. ➤➤ **immobilization** /-'zaysh(ə)n/ *noun*, **immobilizer** *noun.*

immoderate /i'mod(ə)rət/ *adj* lacking moderation; excessive. ➤➤ **immoderately** *adv*, **immoderateness** *noun*, **immoderation** /-'raysh(ə)n/ *noun.* [Middle English *immoderat* from Latin *immoderatus*, from IN-¹ + *moderatus*, past part. of *moderare*: see MODERATE¹]

immodest /i'modist/ *adj* **1** not conforming to the accepted or expected standards, *esp* of sexual propriety. **2** bold; shameless. ➤➤ **immodestly** *adv*, **immodesty** *noun.* [Latin *immodestus*, from IN-¹ + *modestus* MODEST]

immolate /'imohlayt/ *verb trans* **1** to kill or offer (somebody, oneself, or something) as a sacrificial victim, *esp* by burning. **2** *literary* to relinquish or sacrifice (something highly valued). ➤➤ **immolation** /-'laysh(ə)n/ *noun*, **immolator** *noun.* [Latin *immolatus*, past part. of *immolare*, from IN-² + *mola* meal; from the Roman custom of sprinkling sacrificial victims with meal]

immoral /i'morəl/ *adj* **1** not conforming to conventional or expected moral standards, e.g. in sexual matters or business: compare AMORAL. **2** gained by corrupt or immoral means: *immoral earnings*. ➤ **immorally** *adv*.

Usage note
immoral *or* amoral? See note at AMORAL.

immorality /imə'raliti/ *noun* (*pl* **immoralities**) **1** the quality or state of being immoral. **2** an immoral act or immoral behaviour, *esp* in sexual matters or business.

immortal¹ /i'mawtl/ *adj* **1** living for ever: *the immortal gods*. **2** enduring for ever; imperishable: *immortal love*. **3** having enduring fame. ➤ **immortality** /-'taliti/ *noun*, **immortally** *adv*. [Middle English from Latin *immortalis*, from IN-¹ + *mortalis*: see MORTAL¹]

immortal² *noun* **1a** a person or being that lives for ever. **b** (*often* **Immortal**) (*usu in pl*) any of the gods of classical Greece and Rome. **2** a person of lasting fame.

immortalize *or* **immortalise** *verb trans* to give everlasting fame or notoriety to (somebody or something), *esp* through a work of art, film, or literary work, etc: *New York's criminal underworld is immortalized in the Godfather trilogy of films*. ➤ **immortalization** *noun*.

immortelle /imaw'tel/ *noun* = EVERLASTING² (3). [French *immortelle*, from fem of *immortel* immortal, from Latin *immortalis*: see IMMORTAL¹]

immovable *or* **immoveable** /i'moohvəbl/ *adj* **1** not moving, not able to be moved, or not intended to be moved. **2a** steadfast; unyielding. **b** incapable of being moved emotionally. **c** unchanging or unchangeable. **3** said of a religious festival such as Christmas: always occurring on the same date every year. **4** in law, denoting property, such as land and buildings, that cannot be moved. ➤ **immovability** /-'biliti/ *noun*, **immovableness** *noun*, **immovably** *adv*.

immovables *or* **immoveables** *pl noun* in law, immovable property.

immun- *comb. form* see IMMUNO-.

immune¹ /i'myoohn/ *adj* **1a** (*often* + to) not susceptible to something, *esp* having high resistance to a disease: *immune to diphtheria*. **b** (*often* + to/from) not liable to be affected by something bad: *No science is immune to the infection of politics and the corruption of power* — Jacob Bronowski. **2a** having or producing antibodies to a corresponding antigen: *an immune serum*. **b** concerned with or involving immunity: *the immune system*. **3** (*often* + from) free or exempt: *He would only testify if he was himself immune from prosecution*. [Latin *immunis*, from IN-¹ + *munia* services, obligations]

immune² *noun* an immune person or animal.

immune response *noun* an integrated bodily response to the presence of foreign matter, *esp* a disease-causing antigen, that results in the production of lymphocytes. In certain disorders, such as Aids, the immune response can be severely compromised.

immune system *noun* the various cells and tissues in humans and other vertebrate animals which enable them to mount a specific protective response to invading micro-organisms, parasites, etc and, protecting the body from infection and often setting up a long-lasting immunity to reinfection.

immunise /'imyooniez/ *verb trans* see IMMUNIZE.

immunity /i'myoohniti/ *noun* (*pl* **immunities**) **1** (*often* + from/to) the state of being immune. **2** (*often* + against/to) the ability to resist the effects or development of a disease-causing parasite, *esp* a micro-organism.

immunize *or* **immunise** /'imyooniez/ *verb trans* to make (a person, animal, etc) immune, *esp* by inoculation. ➤ **immunization** /-'zaysh(ə)n/ *noun*, **immunizer** *noun*.

immuno- *or* **immun-** *comb. form* forming words, denoting: immunity: *immunochemistry*.

immunoassay /,imyoonoh·ə'say, ,imyoonoh'asay/ *noun* the identification and measurement of the concentration of a substance, e.g. a protein, through its capacity to act as an antigen in the presence of specific antibodies that react with it. ➤ **immunoassayable** *adj*.

immunochemistry /,imyoonoh'keməstri/ *noun* a branch of chemistry that deals with the chemical aspects of immunology and immunological products such as antibodies.

immunocompetent /i,myoonoh'kompitənt/ *adj* having an immune system that responds normally. ➤ **immunocompetence** *noun*.

immunocompromised /,imyoonoh'komprəmiezd/ *adj* having an impaired immune system that has been damaged e.g. by disease.

immunodeficiency /,imyoonoh·di'fish(ə)nsi/ *noun* (*pl* **immunodeficiencies**) any deficiency in the body's ability to mount an effective immune response, often resulting in infections. ➤ **immunodeficient** *adj*.

immunogenesis /,imyoonoh'jenəsis/ *noun* the production of immunity. ➤ **immunogenic** /-nik/ *adj*, **immunogenically** /-nikli/ *adv*, **immunogenicity** /-'nisiti/ *noun*.

immunoglobulin /,imyoonoh'globyoolin/ *noun* a protein antibody that is made up of light and heavy amino acid chains and usu binds specifically to a particular antigen.

immunology /imyoo'noləji/ *noun* the branch of biology that deals with the phenomena and causes of immunity. ➤ **immunologic** /-'lojik/ *adj*, **immunological** /-'lojikl/ *adj*, **immunologically** /-'lojikli/ *adv*, **immunologist** *noun*.

immunoreaction /,imyoonohri'aksh(ə)n/ *adj* the reaction between an antigen and an antibody.

immunosuppression /,imyoonohsə'presh(ə)n/ *noun* suppression, e.g. by drugs, of natural immune responses, *esp* when deliberately induced to help to prevent rejection of a transplanted organ. ➤ **immunosuppressant** /-'pres(ə)nt/ *noun and adj*, **immunosuppressed** *adj*.

immunosuppressive¹ /i,myoonohsə'presiv/ *adj* said of a drug or treatment: having the ability to suppress the body's natural response to attack any foreign matter that is introduced to the body and used *esp* to help to prevent rejection of a transplanted organ.

immunosuppressive² *noun* an immunosuppressive drug.

immunotherapy /,imyoonoh'therəpi/ *noun* treatment of or preventive measures against disease by stimulating or altering the immune response.

immure /i'myooə/ *verb trans* **1** to enclose (somebody or something) within walls or as if within walls; to imprison (them). **2** to shut (oneself) away from other people. **3a** to entomb (somebody) in a wall. **b** to build (something, *esp* a shrine) into a wall. ➤ **immurement** *noun*. [medieval Latin *immurare*, from IN-² + Latin *murus* wall]

immutable /i'myoohtəbl/ *adj* not capable of or susceptible to change. ➤ **immutability** /-'biliti/ *noun*, **immutableness** *noun*, **immutably** *adv*. [Middle English, from Latin *immutabilis*, from IN-¹ + *mutabilis*: see MUTABLE]

IMO *abbr* International Maritime Organization.

imp¹ /imp/ *noun* **1** a small demon. **2** a mischievous child; a scamp. [Old English *impa* graft, shoot, offspring, child from *impian* to graft: see IMP²]

imp² *verb trans archaic* to graft or repair (e.g. a falcon's wing or tail) with a feather to improve flight. [Old English *impian*, ultimately from Greek *emphyein* to implant, from EN-² + *phyein* to plant]

imp. *abbr* **1** imperative. **2** imperfect. **3** imperial. **4** import. **5** importer.

impact¹ /'impakt/ *noun* **1a** a striking of one body against another. **b** a violent contact or collision or the impetus produced by this. **c** force or impetus. **2** a strong or powerful effect or impression: *It is hard to overestimate the impact of modern science on our society*.

impact² /im'pakt/ *verb trans* to fix or press (something) firmly e.g. by packing or wedging. ➤ *verb intrans* **1** to make contact, *esp* forcefully. **2** (*usu* + on) to have a strong effect or make a great impression on somebody or something. ➤ **impactive** /-tiv/ *adj*. [Latin *impactus*, past part. of *impingere*: see IMPINGE]

Usage note
Many traditionalists dislike the use of the verb *impact on* in figurative contexts – *Higher interest rates have impacted on consumer spending* – preferring the use of such verbs as *affect* or *influence* instead. *Impact* is pronounced differently depending on whether it is used as a verb or a noun. The stress in *impact* the noun (*braced themselves for the impact*) is on the first syllable *im-* (see IMPACT¹). The stress in verbal use (*How will this impact on our plans for expansion?*) is on the second syllable.

impacted /im'paktid/ *adj* **1** said of a tooth: not able to grow into its proper position because of a lack of space in the jaw or obstruction by bone or other teeth. **2** said of a fracture: with the broken ends of the bone wedged together. **3** said of faeces: lodged in a body passage.

impaction /im'paksh(ə)n/ *noun* the act or an instance of becoming or being impacted.

impair /im'peə/ *verb trans* to diminish (something) in quality, strength, or amount. ➤➤ **impairer** *noun*, **impairment** *noun*. [Middle English *empeiren* from early French *empeier*, ultimately from Latin IN-² + late Latin *pejorare*: see PEJORATIVE]

impaired *adj* **1** suffering from an impairment: *visually impaired*. **2** *Can* said of a driver or driving: under the influence of alcohol or narcotics.

impala /im'pahlə/ *noun* (*pl* **impalas** *or collectively* **impala**) a large brownish African antelope noted for its ability to make long graceful leaps, the male of which has slender horns that grow in the shape of a lyre: *Aepyceros melampus*. [Zulu *i-mpala*]

impale /im'payl/ *verb trans* **1a** to pierce (somebody, oneself, or something) with something pointed. **b** to torture or kill (somebody) by piercing (them) with a sharp stake. **2** in heraldry, to put (two coats of arms) together on a shield with a PALE³ (a broad vertical band) between them. ➤➤ **impalement** *noun*. [early French *empaler* from medieval Latin *impalare*, from IN-² + Latin *palus* stake]

impalpable /im'palpəbl/ *adj* **1** incapable of being sensed by the touch; intangible. **2** not easily discerned or grasped by the mind. ➤➤ **impalpability** /-'biliti/ *noun*, **impalpably** *adv*.

impanel /im'panl/ *verb trans* see EMPANEL. ➤➤ **impanelment** *noun*.

impart /im'paht/ *verb trans* **1** to make known or disclose (information, etc). **2** to give or bestow (something): *John disliked the flavour imparted by the herbs*. ➤➤ **impartable** *adj*, **impartation** /-'taysh(ə)n/ *noun*, **impartment** *noun*. [early French *impartir* from Latin *impartire*, from IN-² + *partire*: see PART²]

impartial /im'pahsh(ə)l/ *adj* not having or showing any favouritism, *esp* towards rivals; not biased. ➤➤ **impartiality** /-shi'aliti/ *noun*, **impartially** *adv*, **impartialness** *noun*.

impartible /im'pahtəbl/ *adj* said of property, an estate, etc: not divisible: *an impartible inheritance*. ➤➤ **impartibility** /-'biliti/ *noun*, **impartibly** *adv*. [late Latin *impartibilis*, from IN-¹ + *partibilis* divisible, from Latin *partire*: see PART²]

impassable /im'pahsəbl/ *adj* said of a road, etc: incapable of being passed, traversed, or surmounted. ➤➤ **impassability** /-'biliti/ *noun*, **impassableness** *noun*, **impassably** *adv*.

impasse /'ampas (*French* ɛ̃pas)/ *noun* **1** a deadlock or stalemate. **2** a predicament from which there is no obvious escape. [French *impasse*, from IN-¹ + *passer*: see PASS¹]

impassible /im'pasəbl/ *adj formal* incapable of suffering or feeling emotion or of experiencing pain or injury. ➤➤ **impassibility** /-'biliti/ *noun*, **impassibleness** *noun*, **impassibly** *adv*. [Middle English via French from late Latin *impassibilis*, from IN-¹ + *passibilis* capable of feeling, from Latin *pati* to suffer]

impassion /im'pash(ə)n/ *verb trans* to arouse the feelings or passions of (somebody). [Italian *impassionare*, from *in-* (from Latin, expressing intensity) + *passione* passion from late Latin *passion-*, *passio*: see PASSION]

impassioned *adj* filled with passion or zeal; showing great warmth or intensity of feeling: *He made an impassioned appeal for peace*.

impassive /im'pasiv/ *adj* **1** incapable of or not susceptible to emotion. **2** showing no feeling or emotion. ➤➤ **impassively** *adv*, **impassiveness** *noun*, **impassivity** /-'siviti/ *noun*.

impasto /im'pastoh/ *noun* (*pl* **impastos**) **1** in art, the technique or process of applying paint so thickly that it stands out from the canvas, etc, often deliberately leaving visible brush or palette knife strokes. **2** paint that has been applied in this way. ➤➤ **impastoed** *adj*. [Italian *impasto*, from *impastare* to make into a paste, from IN-² + *pasta*: see PASTA]

impatiens /im'paysh(ə)nz/ *noun* any of various plants, including the BUSY LIZZIE, that have exploding seed pods: genus *Impatiens*. [Latin *impatiens*: see IMPATIENT; from the bursting of its ripe seed pods when touched]

impatient /im'paysh(ə)nt/ *adj* **1a** lacking patience; quickly roused to anger or exasperation by delays, incompetence, incomprehension, etc. **b** (+ of) intolerant: *Impatient of delay, Sally ran to the station*. **2** showing or caused by a lack of patience: *an impatient reply*. **3** (*often* + to/for) eagerly desirous; anxious: *She was impatient to see*

her boyfriend. ➤➤ **impatience** *noun*, **impatiently** *adv*. [Middle English *impacient* via French from Latin *impatient-*, *impatiens*, from IN-¹ + *patient-*, *patiens*: see PATIENT¹]

impeach /im'peech/ *verb trans* **1a** to bring a criminal accusation against (somebody). **b** *Brit* to charge (somebody) with a serious crime against the state. **c** *NAmer* to charge (a serving public official) with misconduct. **2** to cast doubt on or challenge the credibility or validity of (e.g. a person's honesty): *The only way out is to impeach the testimony of the witnesses*. ➤➤ **impeachable** *adj*, **impeachment** *noun*. [Middle English *empechen* from early French *empeechier* to hinder, from late Latin *impedicare* to fetter, from IN-² + *pedica* fetter, from *ped-*, *pes* foot]

impeccable /im'pekəbl/ *adj* **1** free from fault or blame; flawless. **2** incapable of sinning. ➤➤ **impeccability** /-'biliti/ *noun*, **impeccably** *adv*. [Latin *impeccabilis*, from IN-¹ + *peccare* to sin]

impecunious /impi'kyoohni·əs/ *adj* having very little or no money. ➤➤ **impecuniosity** /-'ositi/ *noun*, **impecuniously** *adv*, **impecuniousness** *noun*. [IN-¹ + obsolete *pecunious* rich, from Latin *pecuniosus*, from *pecunia* money]

impedance /im'peed(ə)ns/ *noun* **1** the opposition in an electrical circuit to the flow of an alternating current that is analogous to the opposition of an electrical resistance to the flow of a direct current. **2** the ratio of the sound pressure to the rate of volume displacement at a given surface in a sound-transmitting medium that is vibrating to produce the sound. **3a** the act or an instance of impeding. **b** something that impedes.

impede /im'peed/ *verb trans* to interfere with or retard the progress of (somebody or something). ➤➤ **impeder** *noun*. [Latin *impedire* to shackle, from IN-² + *ped-*, *pes* foot]

impediment /im'pedimənt/ *noun* **1** (*often* + to) something that impedes: *There is no greater impediment to the advancement of knowledge than the ambiguity of words* — Thomas Reid. **2** a physiological speech defect, e.g. a stammer or lisp. **3** (*pl* **impediments** *or* **impedimenta**) in law, something that obstructs the making or finalizing of a contract, *esp* a marriage contract.

impedimenta /im,pedi'mentə/ *pl noun* **1** unwieldy baggage or equipment. **2** things that impede; encumbrances. [Latin *impedimenta*, pl of *impedimentum* impediment]

impel /im'pel/ *verb trans* (**impelled**, **impelling**) **1** to urge (somebody) forward or force (them) into action: *The blatant injustice impelled him to speak out*. **2** to propel (something); to put (it) into motion or drive (it) forward. [Latin *impellere*, from IN-² + *pellere* to drive]

impeller *or* **impellor** *noun* **1a** a rotor or the blade of a rotor. **b** a disc of angled blades which impart motion to a gas or liquid by rotating, e.g. in a pump, compressor, etc. **2** somebody or something that impels.

impend /im'pend/ *verb intrans* **1a** to be about to happen. **b** to hover threateningly; to menace. **2** *archaic* to be suspended; to hang. [Latin *impendēre*, from IN-² + *pendēre* to hang]

impending *adj* about to happen: *a brooding sense of impending annihilation* — David Lehman.

impenetrable /im'penitrəbl/ *adj* **1a** incapable of being penetrated or pierced. **b** not open to intellectual influences or ideas. **2** incapable of being comprehended. **3** said of matter: unable to occupy the same space as other matter at the same time. ➤➤ **impenetrability** /-'biliti/ *noun*, **impenetrableness** *noun*, **impenetrably** *adv*. [Middle English *impenetrabel* via French from Latin *impenetrabilis*, from IN-¹ + *penetrabilis* penetrable, from *penetrare* to PENETRATE]

impenitent /im'penit(ə)nt/ *adj* feeling or showing no regret or shame, e.g. about a wicked deed, bad behaviour, etc; unrepentant. ➤➤ **impenitence** *noun*, **impenitency** /-si/ *noun*, **impenitently** *adv*. [late Latin *impaenitent-*, *impaenitens*, from IN-¹ + Latin *paenitens*: see PENITENT¹]

imper. *abbr* imperative.

imperative¹ /im'perətiv/ *adj* **1** very urgent or important; not to be avoided: *It is our imperative duty to stop the killing*. **2a** commanding; showing authority. **b** expressive of a command, entreaty, or exhortation. **c** having the power to restrain, control, and direct. **3** relating to or denoting the grammatical mood that expresses command, e.g. the verb *stop* in *Stop that at once!* ➤➤ **imperatively** *adv*, **imperativeness** *noun*. [late Latin *imperativus*, from Latin *imperare* to command, from IN-² + *parare* to make ready]

imperative[2] *noun* **1a** an obligatory, necessary, or urgent act or duty. **b** a command or order. **c** a judgment, principle, or proposition that leads to a particular action. **2** the imperative mood or a verb form expressing this mood.

imperator /impə'rahtaw/ *noun* in ancient Rome, a title of respect given to victorious generals and later to emperors. ➤➤ **imperatorial** /im,perə'tawri-əl/ *adj,* **imperatorship** *noun.* [Latin *imperator* from *imperare:* see IMPERATIVE[1]]

imperceptible /impə'septəbl/ *adj* **1** extremely slight, gradual, or subtle: *We could feel an imperceptible change in her attitude.* **2a** not perceptible by the mind or senses. **b** too small to be perceptible. ➤➤ **imperceptibility** /-'biliti/ *noun,* **imperceptibly** *adv.* [early French from late Latin *imperceptibilis,* from IN-[1] + *perceptibilis* perceptible, from Latin *percipere:* see PERCEIVE]

imperceptive /impə'septiv/ *adj* lacking the ability to see or understand things; not perceptive. ➤➤ **imperception** *noun,* **imperceptively** *adj,* **imperceptiveness** *noun.*

impercipient /impə'sipi-ənt/ *adj* failing to see or understand something. ➤➤ **impercipience** *noun.*

imperfect[1] /im'puhfikt/ *adj* **1** flawed, defective, or incomplete; not perfect. **2** relating to or denoting a verb tense expressing a continuing state or an incomplete action, *esp* in the past. **3** said of a flower: having only stamens or a pistil. **4** said of a cadence in music: ending on a dominant chord. **5** not legally enforceable. ➤➤ **imperfectly** *adv,* **imperfectness** *noun.* [Middle English *imperfit* via French from Latin *imperfectus,* from IN-[1] + *perfectus:* see PERFECT[1]]

imperfect[2] *noun* the imperfect tense or a verb form expressing it.

imperfection /impə'feksh(ə)n/ *noun* **1** the quality or state of being imperfect. **2** a fault or blemish.

imperfective[1] /impə'fektiv/ *adj* relating to or denoting an aspect of verbs in Slavic languages that indicates that an action is in progress but does not refer to its completion: compare PERFECTIVE.

imperfective[2] *noun* the imperfective aspect or a verb form in this aspect.

imperforate /im'puhf(ə)rət/ *adj* **1** said e.g. of a stamp or a sheet of stamps: lacking perforations. **2** lacking a normal anatomical opening. ➤➤ **imperforation** /-'raysh(ə)n/ *noun.*

imperial[1] /im'piəri-əl/ *adj* **1a** of or befitting an empire, emperor, or empress. **b** of the former British Empire. **2a** sovereign; royal. **b** regal, imperious, or majestic. **3** belonging to an official nonmetric British series of weights and measures such as the pound and the pint. **4** said of a product: of a superior size or quality. ➤➤ **imperially** *adv,* **imperialness** *noun.* [Middle English via French from late Latin *imperialis,* from Latin *imperium* command, empire, from *imperare:* see IMPERATIVE[1]]

imperial[2] *noun* **1** a size of paper measuring 762 x 559mm (30 x 22in.) in the UK, slightly more in the USA. **2** a small pointed beard growing below the lower lip, so called from the style of beard worn as a young man by Napoleon III, Emperor of France. **3** something of unusual size or excellence, e.g. a wine bottle holding the equivalent of eight standard bottles.

imperial gallon *noun* = GALLON (I).

imperialism *noun* **1a** the policy, practice, or advocacy of extending the power and dominion of a nation, *esp* by territorial acquisition. **b** any unacceptable extension or attempted extension of power or influence. **2a** government by an emperor or empress. **b** the spirit or character of empire or an empire. ➤➤ **imperialist** *noun and adj,* **imperialistic** /-'listik/ *adj,* **imperialistically** /-'listikli/ *adv.*

imperil /im'perəl/ *verb trans* (**imperilled, imperilling,** *NAmer* **imperiled, imperiling**) to put (somebody or something) in danger or at risk of harm. ➤➤ **imperilment** *noun.*

imperious /im'piəri-əs/ *adj* marked by arrogant assurance; domineering: *I hate his imperious arbitrariness.* ➤➤ **imperiously** *adv,* **imperiousness** *noun.* [Latin *imperiosus,* from *imperium:* see IMPERIAL[1]]

imperishable[1] /im'perishəbl/ *adj* **1** not subject to decay or deterioration; not perishable. **2** enduring permanently: *imperishable fame.* ➤➤ **imperishability** /-'biliti/ *noun,* **imperishableness** *noun,* **imperishably** *adv.*

imperishable[2] *noun* (*usu in pl*) something that is imperishable.

imperium /im'piəri-əm/ *noun* absolute or supreme power; sovereignty. [Latin *imperium:* see IMPERIAL[1]]

impermanent /im'puhmənənt/ *adj* transient; not permanent or lasting. ➤➤ **impermanence** *noun,* **impermanency** /-si/ *noun,* **impermanently** *adv.*

impermeable /im'puhmi-əbl/ *adj* said of a substance, membrane, etc: not permitting something, *esp* a fluid, to pass through. ➤➤ **impermeability** /-'biliti/ *noun,* **impermeableness** *noun,* **impermeably** *adv.* [late Latin *impermeabilis,* from IN-[1] + *permeabilis* permeable, from *permeare:* see PERMEATE]

impersonal /im'puhsənl/ *adj* **1a** not showing, influenced by, or involving personal feelings or opinions; objective or unbiased. **b** cold, formal, or detached: *He spoke in a flat impersonal tone.* **c** not having human characteristics: *an impersonal deity.* **2a** said of a verb: used to express an action that has no definite subject, the subject in English usu being *it,* e.g. *rained* in *it rained.* **b** said of a pronoun: not referring to a particular person, e.g. *it* in *it rained.* ➤➤ **impersonality** /-'naliti/ *noun,* **impersonally** *adv.* [late Latin *impersonalis,* from IN-[1] + *personalis:* see PERSONAL]

impersonalize *or* **impersonalise** *verb trans* to make (something) impersonal, objective, unbiased, lacking in warmth or human emotion, etc. ➤➤ **impersonalization** /-'zaysh(ə)n/ *noun.*

impersonate /im'puhsənayt/ *verb trans* to pretend to be (somebody), either for entertainment or as an act of deception. ➤➤ **impersonation** /-'naysh(ə)n/ *noun,* **impersonator** *noun.* [IN-[2] + Latin *persona:* see PERSON]

impertinent /im'puhtinənt/ *adj* **1** rude; insolent. **2** not restrained within due or proper bounds: *impertinent curiosity.* **3** *formal* irrelevant; lacking pertinence. ➤➤ **impertinence** *noun,* **impertinency** /-si/ *noun,* **impertinently** *adv.* [Middle English via French from late Latin *impertinent-, impertinens,* from IN-[1] + Latin *pertinent-, pertinens,* present part. of *pertinēre:* see PERTAIN]

imperturbable /impə'tuhbəbl/ *adj* marked by great calm and composure. ➤➤ **imperturbability** /-'biliti/ *noun,* **imperturbableness** *noun,* **imperturbably** *adv.* [Middle English from late Latin *imperturbabilis,* from IN-[1] + *perturbare:* see PERTURB]

impervious /im'puhvi-əs/ *adj* **1** (+ to) not capable of being affected or disturbed by something: *He is quite impervious to criticism.* **2** (*often* + to) not allowing a fluid to pass through; impermeable: *This coat is impervious to rain.* ➤➤ **imperviously** *adv,* **imperviousness** *noun.* [Latin *impervius,* from IN-[1] + *pervius:* see PERVIOUS]

impetigo /impə'tiegoh/ *noun* a contagious bacterial skin disease characterized by blisters and pustules. ➤➤ **impetiginous** /-'tijinəs/ *adj.* [Latin *impetigo,* from *impetere* to attack]

impetuous /im'petyoo-əs/ *adj* **1a** acting or done with impulsiveness or rashness. **b** impulsive or rash by nature: *a youth to whom was given ... such impetuous blood* — Wordsworth. **2** *literary* marked by forceful and violent movement. ➤➤ **impetuosity** /-'ositi/ *noun,* **impetuously** *adv,* **impetuousness** *noun.* [Middle English via French from late Latin *impetuosus,* from Latin *impetus:* see IMPETUS]

impetus /'impitəs/ *noun* **1a** a driving force. **b** an incentive or stimulus: *The changes in taxation were intended to give a new impetus to the ailing economy.* **2** in physics, the energy possessed by a moving body. [Latin *impetus* assault, impetus, from *impetere* to attack]

impi /'impi/ *noun* (*pl* **impis**) formerly in South Africa, a band or regiment of Zulu warriors. [Zulu *impi*]

impiety /im'pieiti/ *noun* (*pl* **impieties**) a lack of reverence or an irreverent act.

impinge /im'pinj/ *verb intrans* **1** (+ on/upon) to encroach or infringe on something: *We mustn't impinge on other people's rights.* **2** (+ on/upon) to make an impression. **3** (+ on/upon/against) to strike or collide with something or somebody. ➤➤ **impingement** *noun,* **impinger** *noun.* [Latin *impingere,* from IN-[2] + *pangere* to fasten, drive in]

impious /'impi-əs/ *adj* lacking in reverence or proper respect, e.g. for God; irreverent. ➤➤ **impiously** *adv,* **impiousness** *noun.* [Latin *impius,* from IN-[1] + *pius* PIOUS]

impish *adj* mischievous. ➤➤ **impishly** *adv,* **impishness** *noun.*

implacable /im'plakəbl/ *adj* **1** not capable of being appeased or pacified: *an implacable enemy.* **2** unrelenting; never stopping, weakening, or changing. ➤➤ **implacability** /-'biliti/ *noun,* **implacableness** *noun,* **implacably** *adv.* [via French from Latin *implacabilis,* from IN-[1] + *placabilis* easy to appease, from *placare* to PLACATE]

implant[1] /im'plahnt/ *verb trans* **1** to set (e.g. an idea or principle) permanently in consciousness or habit patterns. **2** to insert (something, e.g. artificial tissue, a hormone, etc) in a living organism. **3** to fix or set (something) securely or deeply. ➤ *verb intrans* said of a fertilized egg: to become attached to the wall of the uterus or, abnormally, the Fallopian tube. **≫ implantable** *adj,* **implantation** /-'taysh(ə)n/ *noun,* **implanter** *noun.*

implant² /'implahnt/ *noun* something, e.g. a graft or hormone pellet, implanted in the tissue of a living organism.

implausible /im'plawzəbl/ *adj* said of a story, excuse, etc: unlikely to be true; liable not to be believed; not plausible. **≫ implausibility** /-'biliti/ *noun,* **implausibleness** *noun,* **implausibly** *adv.*

implement¹ /'implimənt/ *noun* **1** a utensil or tool, *esp* one with a specified purpose: *gardening implements.* **2** a means of achieving an end; an agent: *bombs and other implements of destruction.* **3** in Scots law, the act or an instance of carrying out an obligation. [Middle English from late Latin *implementum* action of filling up, from Latin *implēre* to fill up, later 'to employ' from IN-² + *plere* to fill]

implement² /'impliment/ *verb trans* to put (plans, orders, etc) into effect: *These plans have not yet been implemented due to lack of funds.* **≫ implementation** /-'taysh(ə)n/ *noun,* **implementer** *noun.*

implicate /'implikayt/ *verb trans* **1a** (*often* + in) to show that (somebody, oneself, or something) has a connection with something, *esp* to show that (a person) is involved in a crime, wrongdoing, etc. **b** to involve (something) in the way something else is or operates. **2** to involve (something) as a consequence, corollary, or inference; to imply (it). **3** *archaic* to entwine (something). [Latin *implicatus,* past part. of *implicare* to involve, from IN-² + *plicare* to fold]

implication /impli'kaysh(ə)n/ *noun* **1a** the act or an instance of implicating or being implicated. **b** (*usu* + in) incriminating involvement. **2a** the act or an instance of implying or being implied. **b** a logical relation between two propositions such that, if the first is true, the second must be true. **3** something implied. **≫ implicative** /im'plikətiv/ *adj,* **implicatively** /im'plikətivli/ *adv.*

implicit /im'plisit/ *adj* **1a** implied rather than directly stated: *an implicit assumption.* **b** (+ in) present but underlying rather than explicit. **2** unquestioning; absolute: *He demands implicit obedience.* **≫ implicitly** *adv,* **implicitness** *noun.* [Latin *implicitus,* later form of *implicatus:* see IMPLICATE]

implode /im'plohd/ *verb intrans* to collapse inwards suddenly. **≫ verb trans** to cause (something) to do this. **≫ implosion** /-'plohzh(ə)n/ *noun.* [IN-² + -*plode* as in EXPLODE]

implore /im'plaw/ *verb trans* **1** to beg (somebody) to do something. **2** *archaic* to beg for (something) earnestly. **≫ imploration** /-'raysh(ə)n/ *noun,* **imploratory** /im'plorət(ə)ri/ *adj,* **imploring** *adj,* **imploringly** *adv.* [via French from Latin *implorare,* from IN-² + *plorare* to cry out]

imply /im'plie/ *verb* (**implies, implied, implying**) **≫ verb trans** **1** to express (something) indirectly; to hint at (it): *His silence implied consent.* **2** to involve (something) as a necessary or potential consequence. **≫ impliedly** /im'plieidli/ *adv.* [Middle English *emplien* via early French *emplier* from Latin *implicare:* see IMPLICATE]

Usage note

imply *or* **infer?** These two words are sometimes confused, though they are in fact opposite in meaning. To *imply* something is to suggest it by what you say without stating it explicitly: *She implied that I was untrustworthy.* To *infer* something is to deduce it from what someone says, even though they have not explicitly said as much: *I inferred from her remark that she thought me untrustworthy.* That said, the use of *infer* to mean the same as *imply* has become increasingly common.

impolite /impə'liet/ *adj* not having or showing good manners; not polite. **≫ impolitely** *adv,* **impoliteness** *noun.*

impolitic /im'polətik/ *adj* unwise or ill-advised. **≫ impoliticly** *adv.*

imponderable¹ /im'pond(ə)rəbl/ *adj* incapable of being precisely evaluated or assessed. **≫ imponderability** /-'biliti/ *noun,* **imponderableness** *noun,* **imponderably** *adv.* [late Latin *imponderabilis,* from IN-¹ + *ponderabilis* able to be weighed up, from Latin *ponderare:* see PONDER]

imponderable² *noun* something whose effect is hard or impossible to calculate: *We can't be sure of the outcome because there are just too many imponderables.*

import¹ /im'pawt/ *verb trans* **1** to bring (something) in from a foreign or external source, *esp* to bring (e.g. merchandise) in from abroad. **2** in computing, to transfer (a file, data, etc) from one computer, database, or package to another. **3** *formal or archaic* to signify (something). **≫ importable** *adj,* **importation** /-'taysh(ə)n/ *noun,* **importer** *noun.* [Middle English *importen* from Latin *importare* to

bring into, later 'to imply, be significant', from IN-² + *portare* to carry]

import² /'impawt/ *noun* **1** something imported, *esp* merchandise from abroad. **2** the act or an instance of importing, *esp* merchandise from abroad. **3** *formal* meaning or significance. **4** *formal* importance: *We should not underestimate the import of this decision.*

importance /im'pawt(ə)ns/ *noun* **1** consequence; significance. **2** high rank or social standing.

important /im'pawt(ə)nt/ *adj* **1** of considerable significance or consequence: *The little things are infinitely the most important —* Conan Doyle. **2** having high rank or social standing. **≫ importantly** *adv.* [via French and Old Italian from Latin *important-, importans,* present part. of *importare:* see IMPORT¹]

importunate /im'pawtyoonət/ *adj* **1** very persistent in making requests or demands. **2** made persistently. **≫ importunately** *adv.*

importune /im'pawtyoohn/ *verb trans* **1a** to make persistent demands of (somebody). **b** to be troublesomely persistent in asking for (something). **2** to solicit (somebody) for purposes of prostitution. **≫ verb intrans** to beg, urge, or solicit with troublesome persistence. **≫ importuner** *noun,* **importunity** /-'tyoohniti/ *noun.* [early French *importuner* from medieval Latin *importunare,* from Latin *importunus* unfit, troublesome, from IN-¹ + -*portunus* as in *opportunus:* see OPPORTUNE]

impose /im'pohz/ *verb trans* **1a** (*often* + on/upon) to establish or apply (something, e.g. a tax, fine, rule, etc) as compulsory. **b** (*often* + on/upon) to establish (something) by force. **2** to force (oneself) into the company or on the attention of another. **3** (+ on/upon) to pass off (something fake) on somebody: *He made a career of imposing fake antiques on the public.* **4** to arrange (typeset pages) in the required order for printing. **≫ verb intrans** **1** (*usu* + on/upon) to take unwarranted advantage of something: *I felt we were imposing on his good nature.* **2** (*often* + on/upon) to be an excessive requirement or burden. **≫ imposable** *adj,* **imposer** *noun.* [early French *imposer* from Latin *impositus,* past part. of *imponere* to put upon, from IN-² + *ponere* to put]

imposing *adj* impressive because of size, bearing, dignity, or grandeur. **≫ imposingly** *adv,* **imposingness** *noun.*

imposition /impə'zish(ə)n/ *noun* **1** the act or an instance of imposing. **2a** a levy or tax. **b** an excessive or unwarranted requirement or burden. **c** a task, e.g. a written exercise, given as a punishment in school. **d** the arrangement of pages to be printed so that they will be in the correct order in the finished work.

impossible /im'posəbl/ *adj* **1a** incapable of being or occurring; not possible. **b** seemingly incapable of being done, attained, or fulfilled; insuperably difficult: *an impossible task.* **c** difficult to believe: *an impossible story.* **2** extremely undesirable or difficult to put up with or deal with: *Life became impossible because of lack of money.* **≫ impossibility** /-'biliti/ *noun,* **impossibly** *adv.* [Middle English via French from Latin *impossibilis,* from IN-¹ + *possibilis:* see POSSIBLE¹]

impost¹ /'imposht/ *noun* **1** a tax. **2** in horse-racing, the weight that a horse must carry as a handicap. [early French from Latin *impositum,* neuter of *impositus:* see IMPOSE]

impost² *noun* a bracket, the top part of a pillar, or a moulding that supports an arch. [Italian *imposta* from Latin *impositus:* see IMPOSE]

impostor *or* **imposter** /im'postə/ *noun* a person who assumes a false identity or title for fraudulent purposes. [late Latin *impostor,* from Latin *imponere:* see IMPOSE]

imposture /im'poschə/ *noun* fraud or deception, or an instance of this. [late Latin *impostura,* from Latin *imponere:* see IMPOSE]

impotent /'impət(ə)nt/ *adj* **1** lacking in efficacy, strength, or vigour. **2** said of an adult male: unable to perform sexual intercourse through an inability to attain or maintain an erection of the penis. **≫ impotence** *noun,* **impotency** /-si/ *noun,* **impotent** *noun,* **impotently** *adv.* [Middle English via French from Latin *impotent-, impotens,* from IN-¹ + *potent-, potens:* see POTENT¹]

impound /im'pownd/ *verb trans* **1a** to shut up (e.g. an animal) in a pound; to confine (somebody or something) as if in a pound. **b** to take legal possession of (something, e.g. evidence from a crime scene, an illegally parked vehicle, etc). **2** to collect and confine (water) in or as if in a reservoir. **≫ impoundable** *adj,* **impoundage** /-dij/ *noun,* **impounder** *noun,* **impoundment** *noun.*

impoverish /im'pov(ə)rish/ *verb trans* **1** to make (somebody) poor. **2** to deprive (somebody or something) of strength, richness, or fertility; to lower the quality or value of (something). **⋙ impoverisher** noun, **impoverishment** noun. [Middle English *enpoverisen* from early French *empovrir*, from EN-[1] + *povre*: see POOR]

impracticable /im'praktikəbl/ adj **1** incapable of being put into effect or carried out. **2** not suitable or fit for use or for a particular use. **⋙ impracticability** /-'biliti/ noun, **impracticableness** noun, **impracticably** adv.

Usage note —————
impracticable or impractical? See note at IMPRACTICAL.

impractical /im'praktikl/ adj **1a** incapable of dealing sensibly with practical matters, *esp* financial matters. **b** not good at doing practical things, *esp* manual tasks. **2** not able to be put into effect or carried out: *an impractical pipe dream* — James Laughlin. **⋙ impracticality** /-'kaləti/ noun, **impractically** adv.

Usage note —————
impractical or impracticable? These two words are very close in meaning, but it is useful to distinguish between them. A plan that is *impractical* may be fine in theory but is difficult to carry out or of little use in practice. An *impracticable* plan is, quite simply, impossible to carry out. A person can be described as *impractical* ('not good at ordinary tasks' or 'not down to earth'), but not as *impracticable*.

imprecate /'imprikayt/ verb trans **1** to utter (a curse). **2** to invoke (evil) against somebody or something. **➤ verb intrans** to curse. **⋙ imprecatory** /impri'kaytəri/ adj. [Latin *imprecari* to invoke, from IN-[2] + *precari* to pray: see PRAY[1]]

imprecation /impri'kaysh(ə)n/ noun a curse.

imprecise /impri'sies/ adj inexact, vague, or inaccurate; not precise. **⋙ imprecisely** adv, **impreciseness** noun, **imprecision** /-'sizh(ə)n/ noun.

impregnable[1] /im'pregnəbl/ adj **1** incapable of being taken by assault: *an impregnable fortress*. **2** beyond criticism or question: *an impregnable social position*. **3** strong; firm; unbeatable; unassailable: *He has an impregnable belief in his own ability*. **⋙ impregnability** /-'biliti/ noun, **impregnably** adv. [Middle English *imprenable* from early French, from IN-[1] + *prenable* vulnerable to capture, from *prendre* to take, from Latin *prehendere*: see PREHENSILE]

impregnable[2] adj capable of being impregnated.

impregnate[1] /'impregnayt/ verb trans **1a** to make (a female person or animal) pregnant; to fertilize (her). **b** to introduce sperm cells into (an ovum). **2a** (+ with) to soak or saturate (something) with something: *paper impregnated with perfume*. **b** said of a quality, emotion, etc: to fill or be a dominant presence in (speech or writing): *Awe and wonder impregnated his articles*. **⋙ impregnation** /-'naysh(ə)n/ noun, **impregnator** noun. [late Latin *impraegnatus*, past part. of *impraegnare*, from IN-[2] + Latin *praegnas*: see PREGNANT]

impregnate[2] /im'pregnit, -nayt/ adj **1** (often + with) filled or saturated. **2** pregnant.

impresario /impri'sahrioh/ noun (pl **impresarios**) a person who organizes, puts on, finances, or sponsors a public entertainment, *esp* an opera, ballet, or concert. [Italian *impresario*, literally 'one who undertakes something', from *impresa* undertaking, from *imprendere* to undertake, from IN-[2] + Latin *prehendere*: see PREHENSILE]

imprescriptible /impri'skriptəbl/ adj in law, denoting rights, etc that cannot be taken away or revoked; inalienable. [early French *imprescriptible*, from IN-[1] + *prescriptible* subject to prescription, from late Latin *praescriptibilis*, from *praescribere* to claim by right of prescription: see PRESCRIBE]

impress[1] /im'pres/ verb trans **1a** (often + by/with) to produce a deep and usu favourable impression on (somebody). **b** (*usu* + on) to fix (e.g. an idea or thought) strongly or deeply in the mind or memory; to emphasize (it) strongly: *He impressed on them the need for secrecy*. **2a** to apply (something) with pressure so as to imprint it on something. **b** to mark (something) by, or as if by, pressure or stamping. **3** to transmit (force or motion) by pressure. **➤ verb intrans** to produce a usu favourable impression: *The orchestra has given a number of performances that have failed to impress*. **⋙ impresser** noun, **impressible** adj. [Middle English *impressen* from Latin *impressus*, past part. of *imprimere*, from IN-[2] + *premere* to press]

impress[2] /'impres/ noun **1** the act of impressing. **2** a mark made by pressure. **3** an impression or effect.

impress[3] /im'pres/ verb trans dated **1a** to force (a man) into service in the army or navy. **b** to take (something) forcibly for public use. **2** to procure or enlist (somebody) to do something by forcible per-

suasion: *They had impressed a small school to assist in the performances* — Dickens. **⋙ impressment** noun. [IN-[2] + PRESS[1]]

impress[4] /'impres/ noun dated **1** the act or an instance of forcing somebody to do something, *esp* to join the army or navy. **2** the act or an instance of forcibly taking something for public use.

impression /im'presh(ə)n/ noun **1a** (often + on) an influence or effect, *esp* a marked one, on the mind or senses: *Unfortunately, I made a very bad impression at my interview*. **b** (often + on) a favourable effect: *The new singer made quite an impression*. **2a** (also in pl) a thought or opinion: *What were your first impressions of Greece?* **b** (also in pl) a telling image impressed on the mind or senses. **c** a notion or recollection, *esp* one that is vague, intuitive, or subjective: *I had the impression she was trying to leave*. **3a** (often + on) an effect produced by some action or effort: *All our hard work made little impression on the garden*. **b** a characteristic, trait, or feature resulting from some influence: *One must not underestimate the impression on behaviour produced by the social milieu*. **4** an imitation of a person, animal, etc; *esp* an imitation in caricature of a noted personality as a form of entertainment: *He does a fantastic impression of Elvis; Her cat impressions kept the kids amused*. **5** the act or process of impressing. **6** the effect produced by impressing: e.g. **a** a stamp, form, or figure produced by physical contact. **b** an imprint of the teeth and adjacent portions of the jaw for use in dentistry. **7a** in printing, the amount of pressure with which an inked printing surface deposits its ink on the paper. **b** a single instance of the meeting of a printing surface and the material being printed. **c** a print or copy so made. **d** all the copies of a publication, e.g. a book, printed for issue at a single time. **⋙ impressional** adj, **impressionally** adv.

impressionable adj **1** easily influenced: *Give me a girl at an impressionable age and she is mine for life* — Muriel Spark. **2** easily moulded. **⋙ impressionability** /-'biliti/ noun, **impressionableness** noun, **impressionably** adv.

impressionism noun **1** (often **Impressionism**) an art movement, begun in late 19th-cent. France, that tries to convey the visual effects of actual reflected light on natural usu outdoor subjects.

Editorial note —————
Like many artistic movements, impressionism was named not by its exponents but by its enemies. It applies most accurately to those who, like Monet in his Impression: Sunrise, which gave rise to the name, painted mainly outdoors, and used broad-brush-strokes with a disregard for conventional 'finish'. More loosely, it has been used of writers and composers, such as Debussy, who created an analogous mood — Martin Gayford.

2 literary depiction that seeks to convey a general subjective impression rather than a detailed re-creation of reality. **3** a style of musical composition designed to create impressions and moods through rich and varied harmonies and tones. **⋙ Impressionist** noun and adj, **impressionist** noun and adj.

impressionistic /im,preshə'nistik/ adj **1** based on or involving subjective impression as distinct from knowledge, fact, or systematic thought. **2** (usu **Impressionistic**) relating to or denoting impressionism, *esp* in art. **⋙ impressionistically** adv.

impressive /im'presiv/ adj making a marked impression; stirring deep feelings, *esp* of awe or admiration. **⋙ impressively** adv, **impressiveness** noun.

imprest /'imprest/ noun **1** in a business, etc, a cash fund from which small expenses are paid and which is topped up periodically from the organization's central funds; petty cash. **2a** a loan from a government for public business. **b** an advance of money, *esp* formerly, advance wages given to a soldier or sailor. [obsolete *imprest* to lend, prob from Italian *imprestare*, from IN-[2] + Latin *praestare* to pay]

imprimatur /impri'mahtə, -'maytə/ noun **1** a licence granted, *esp* by Roman Catholic episcopal authority, to print or publish. **2** sanction or approval. [Latin *imprimatur* let it be printed, from *imprimere* to print: see IMPRESS[1]]

imprint[1] /'imprint/ noun **1** a mark or depression made by pressure: *the fossil imprint of a dinosaur's foot*. **2a** a publisher's name printed at the foot of a title-page, or a printer's name on any publication. **b** a brand name under which a range of books are published. **3** an indelible distinguishing mark, effect, or influence: *Their work bears a sort of regional imprint* — Malcolm Cowley. [early French *empreinte*, fem past part. of *empreindre* to imprint, from Latin *imprimere*: see IMPRESS[1]]

imprint[2] /im'print/ verb trans **1a** to make (a mark) on something by pressure. **b** to make a mark on (something) by pressure. **2** to fix (an image, etc) indelibly or permanently in the mind, memory, etc. **3** to cause (a young animal, chick, etc) to undergo imprinting. ➤ *verb intrans* (*usu* + on) said of a young animal, chick, etc: to undergo imprinting.

imprinting /im'printing/ *noun* a behaviour pattern rapidly established early in the life of an animal that involves attachment to an object or other animal, *esp* the animal's mother, seen just after birth or hatching.

imprison /im'priz(ə)n/ *verb trans* (**imprisoned, imprisoning**) **1** to put (somebody) in prison. **2** to confine (somebody or something) as if in a prison: *He has an active mind imprisoned in a shrivelled body.* ➤➤ **imprisonment** *noun.* [Middle English *imprisonen* from Old French *emprisoner*, from EN-¹ + *prison*: see PRISON]

improbable /im'probəbl/ *adj* unlikely to be true or to occur. ➤➤ **improbability** /-'biliti/ *noun*, **improbableness** *noun*, **improbably** *adv.* [early French *improbable* from Latin *improbabilis*, from IN-¹ + *probabilis*: see PROBABLE¹]

improbity /im'prohbiti/ *noun* (*pl* **improbities**) *formal* lack of integrity; dishonesty; wickedness. [early French *improbité* from Latin *improbitas*, from *improbus* bad, dishonest, from IN-¹ + *probus* good, honest]

impromptu¹ /im'promptyooh/ *adj* made, done, composed, or uttered on the spur of the moment; unplanned or not rehearsed: *We had an impromptu change of plan.* ➤➤ **impromptu** *adv.* [French *impromptu* extemporaneously, from Latin *in promptu* in readiness]

impromptu² *noun* (*pl* **impromptus**) **1** something impromptu. **2** a musical composition suggesting improvisation.

improper /im'propə/ *adj* **1** not in accordance with propriety or modesty; indecent. **2** not suitable or appropriate. **3** not in accordance with fact, truth, or normal or correct procedure: *That would be an improper inference from the evidence we have seen.* ➤➤ **improperly** *adv*, **improperness** *noun.* [early French *impropre* from Latin *improprius*, from IN-¹ + *proprius* proper]

improper fraction *noun* a fraction whose numerator is larger than the denominator.

impropriate¹ /im'prohpriayt/ *verb trans* to transfer (Church land, property, etc) to lay ownership. [Latin *impropriare* to make one's own, from IN-² + *propriare* to appropriate]

impropriate² *adj* said of former Church land, property, etc: having been transferred to lay ownership.

impropriety /imprə'prieiti/ *noun* (*pl* **improprieties**) **1** an absence of accepted standards of decency. **2** an improper act or remark, *esp* an unacceptable use of a word. [French *impropriété* from late Latin *improprietat-, improprietas*, from Latin *improprius*: see IMPROPER]

improve /im'proohv/ *verb trans* **1** to enhance (something) in value or quality; to make (it) better. **2** to increase the value of (land or property), *esp* by cultivation or the erection of buildings. ➤ *verb intrans* **1** to advance or make good progress: *Her health is steadily improving.* **2** (*usu* + on/upon) to produce or achieve something better than a previous version, result, etc: *We must try to improve on last week's score.* ➤➤ **improvability** /-'biliti/ *noun*, **improvable** *adj*, **improver** *noun.* [Anglo-French *emprouer* to invest profitably, from Old French EN-¹ + *prou* advantage, from late Latin *prode*: see PROUD]

improvement *noun* **1** the act or an instance of improving or being improved. **2** an increase in value or excellence, or something that brings this about: *improvements to an old house.*

improvident /im'provid(ə)nt/ *adj* lacking foresight, *esp* in not providing for the future. ➤➤ **improvidence** *noun*, **improvidently** *adv.* [late Latin *improvident-, improvidens*, from IN-¹ + Latin *provident-, providens*: see PROVIDENT]

improvise /'imprəviez/ *verb* **1** to make or provide (something) using what is available: *We improvised a stretcher from branches and a jacket.* **2** to compose or perform (music, poetry, drama, etc) impromptu or without a set script or musical score. ➤➤ **improvisation** /-'zaysh(ə)n/ *noun*, **improvisatory** /-'zayt(ə)ri, -'viezət(ə)ri/ *adj*, **improviser** *noun.* [French *improviser* from Italian *improvvisare*, from *improvviso* sudden, from Latin *improvisus* unforeseen, from IN-¹ + *provisus*, past part. of *providēre*: see PROVIDE]

imprudent /im'proohd(ə)nt/ *adj* lacking discretion or caution. ➤➤ **imprudence** *noun*, **imprudently** *adv.* [Middle English from Latin *imprudent-, imprudens*, from IN-¹ + *prudent-, prudens*: see PRUDENT]

impudent /'impyood(ə)nt/ *adj* showing contemptuous or cocky boldness or disrespect. ➤➤ **impudence** *noun*, **impudently** *adv.*

[Middle English from Latin *impudent-, impudens*, from IN-¹ + *pudent-*, present part. of *pudēre* to feel shame]

impugn /im'pyoohn/ *verb trans* to call into question or dispute the validity or integrity of (something said or done). ➤➤ **impugnable** *adj*, **impugner** *noun.* [Middle English *impugnen* via French from Latin *impugnare*, from IN-² + *pugnare* to fight]

impulse /'impuls/ *noun* **1** a sudden spontaneous inclination or desire to do something. **2a** a force that produces motion suddenly. **b** inspiration or stimulus: *the creative impulse.* **3a** an impelling or driving force. **b** a wave of electrical energy transmitted through tissues, *esp* nerve fibres and muscles, that results in physiological activity or inhibition. **4a** in physics, the product of the average value of a force and the time during which it acts, being a quantity equal to the change in momentum produced by the force. **b** = PULSE¹ (4A). [Latin *impulsus*, past part. of *impellere*: see IMPEL]

impulse buying *noun* the act of making an unplanned purchase or purchases on the spur of the moment. ➤➤ **impulse buy** *noun*, **impulse buyer** *noun.*

impulsion /im'pulsh(ə)n/ *noun* **1** a strong urge, desire, or inclination. **2** a motivating factor. **3** an impelling or driving force. **4** the act of impelling or the state of being impelled.

impulsive /im'pulsiv/ *adj* **1a** acting or inclined to act on the basis of a sudden whim or desire. **b** done spontaneously on such a basis: *an impulsive gesture.* **2** having the power of driving or propelling. **3** acting or lasting only momentarily. ➤➤ **impulsively** *adv*, **impulsiveness** *noun.*

impunity /im'pyoohniti/ *noun* exemption or freedom from punishment, harm, loss, or retribution: *trespassing with impunity.* [early French *impunité* from Latin *impunitat-, impunitas*, from *impune* without punishment, from IN-¹ + *poena*: see PAIN¹]

impure /im'pyooə/ *adj* **1** not pure, *esp* as a result of contamination. **2** morally wrong. **3** ritually unclean. **4** mixed, *esp* adulterated or tainted. ➤➤ **impurely** *adv*, **impureness** *noun.* [French *impure* from Latin *impurus*, from IN-¹ + *purus* PURE]

impurity /im'pyooəriti/ *noun* (*pl* **impurities**) **1** the quality or state of being impure. **2** something that is impure or that makes something else impure. **3** in electronics, a minute amount of an element added to a semiconductor to control its conductive properties.

impute /im'pyooht/ *verb trans* **1** to attribute (*esp* something bad) to somebody, often unjustly. **2** to attribute (something) to a specified source or cause. **3** to assign (a notional value) to something of unknown value. ➤➤ **imputable** *adj*, **imputation** /-'taysh(ə)n/ *noun*, **imputative** /-'tətiv/ *adj.* [Middle English *inputen* from Latin *imputare*, from IN-² + *putare* to think, consider]

IN *abbr* Indiana (US postal abbreviation).

In *abbr* the chemical symbol for indium.

in¹ /in/ *prep* **1** used to indicate location within or inside something three-dimensional: *You'll find it in the cupboard.* **2** used to indicate location more generally: *in reach; in the garden; in London; wounded in the leg.* **3** used to indicate location in time: *in the summer; in 1959; They will come in an hour.* **4** = INTO (1A): *She went in the house.* **5a** used to indicate a means, instrument, or medium of expression: *drawn in pencil; written in French; drink your health in champagne.* **b** used to describe a person's clothing: *a child in dungarees; a girl in red.* **6** used to indicate qualification, manner, circumstance, or condition: *in public; in a hurry; in pain; broken in pieces.* **7** used to indicate occupation or membership: *a job in insurance; everybody in the team.* **8** used to indicate relevance or reference: *equal in distance; weak in arithmetic; said in reply; the latest thing in shoes.* **9a** used to indicate division, arrangement, or quantity: *standing in a circle; arrived in their thousands.* **b** used to indicate the larger member of a ratio: *One in six is eligible; a tax of 40p in the £.* **10** said of an animal: pregnant with (young): *in calf.* **11** used to introduce indirect objects: *rejoicing in their good fortune.* **12** used to form adverbial phrases: *in fact.* ✲ **in it** of advantage, e.g. between competitors or alternatives: *There's not much in it between them; What's in it for me?* **in that** for the reason that; because: *It's of limited use in that it has no lid.* [Old English]

in² *adv* **1** used to indicate: **a** movement to or towards the inside or centre: *come in out of the rain.* **b** incorporation: *mix in the flour.* **c** movement to or towards home, the shore, a destination, etc: *Three ships came sailing in.* **d** presence at a particular place, *esp* at one's home or business: *be in for lunch.* **e** concealment: *The sun went in.* **2** used to indicate: **a** addition or inclusion: *fit a piece in.* **b** tenure of an office or political power: *vote them in.* **c** being on good terms: *in with the boss.* **d** a state of efficiency or proficiency: *work a horse in.* **e** vogue or fashion: *Platform shoes are in again.* **f** a central position or point of control: *letters pouring in; after the harvest is in; He went in to bat.* ✳ **be in for** to be certain to experience (usu something undesirable): *If you're late again, you'll be in for trouble.* **in on** having a share in or knowledge of something: *They were all in on the secret; Are you in on this deal?*

in³ *adj* **1** extremely fashionable: *the in place to go.* **2** shared only by a certain group: *an in joke.*

in. *abbr* inch.

in-¹ *or* **il-** *or* **im-** *or* **ir-** *prefix* **1** forming adjectives, with the meaning: not: *inaccurate; illegal; impractical; irresponsible.* **2** forming nouns, denoting: a lack of something: *incivility; illiteracy; imbalance; irregularity.* [Middle English via French from Latin; related to Old English UN-]

in-² *or* **il-** *or* **im-** *or* **ir-** *prefix* forming words, with the meanings: **1** in; within; into; towards; on: *influx; immerse; irradiance.* **2** a causative or intensifying effect or action: *imperil; illuminate; inspirit.* [Middle English via French from Latin, from *in* in, into]

-in¹ *suffix* forming nouns, denoting: **1** a chemical compound: *pepsin.* **2** an antibiotic: *streptomycin.* [French *-ine* from Latin *-ina*, fem of *-inus* of or belonging to]

-in² *comb. form* forming nouns, denoting: **1** an organized public protest by means of the specified action; a demonstration: *sit-in.* **2** a group activity: *teach-in.* [IN² as in SIT-IN]

inability /inə'biliti/ *noun* lack of sufficient power, resources, or capacity: *He was hampered by his inability to do maths.* [Middle English *inabilite* from early French *inhabilité*, from IN-¹ + *habilité* ABILITY]

in absentia /,in ab'senti·ə/ *adv* in the absence of the specified person: *She was elected treasurer in absentia.* [Latin *in absentia*]

inaccessible /inak'sesəbl/ *adj* **1** difficult or impossible to reach. **2** difficult or impossible to understand: *an inaccessible book.* ⋙ **inaccessibility** /-'biliti/ *noun*, **inaccessibly** *adv.*

inaccuracy /in'akyoorəsi/ *noun* (*pl* **inaccuracies**) **1** lack of accuracy. **2** a mistake; an error.

inaccurate /in'akyoorət/ *adj* faulty or imprecise. ⋙ **inaccurately** *adv.*

inaction /in'aksh(ə)n/ *noun* lack of action or activity.

inactivate /in'aktivayt/ *verb trans* **1** to cause (something, *esp* a machine) to stop operating. **2** to render (something) chemically or biologically inactive. ⋙ **inactivation** *noun.*

inactive /in'aktiv/ *adj* **1** not given to action or effort. **2** out of use; not functioning. **3** relating to members of the armed forces who are not performing or available for military duties. **4** said of a disease: quiescent or dormant. **5** chemically or biologically inert, *esp* because of the loss of some quality. ⋙ **inactively** *adv*, **inactivity** /-'tiviti/ *noun.*

inadequate /in'adikwət/ *adj* **1** not adequate; lacking the required or expected quantity or quality. **2** not capable; unable to cope: *Her remarks left him feeling totally inadequate.* ⋙ **inadequacy** /-si/ *noun*, **inadequately** *adv*, **inadequateness** *noun.*

inadmissible /inəd'misəbl/ *adj* said *esp* of evidence in a court of law: invalid. ⋙ **inadmissibility** /-'biliti/ *noun.*

inadvertence /inəd'vuht(ə)ns/ *noun* (*pl* **inadvertences** *or* **inadvertencies**) **1** the act or an instance of being inadvertent. **2** a result of heedlessness or inattention; an oversight or slip. [medieval Latin *inadvertentia*, from IN-¹ + Latin *advertent-, advertens*, present part. of *advertere*: see ADVERT¹]

inadvertency /inəd'vuht(ə)nsi/ *noun* (*pl* **inadvertencies**) = INADVERTENCE.

inadvertent /inəd'vuht(ə)nt/ *adj* **1** heedless, inattentive, or lacking in care or consideration. **2** unintentional. ⋙ **inadvertently** *adv.* [back-formation from INADVERTENCE]

inadvisable /inəd'viezəbl/ *adj* said *esp* of a course of action: likely to have unpleasant or unpleasant consequences; unwise: *'Do you, in England, allow no friendship to exist between a young man and a young girl?' 'We think it very inadvisable.'* — Oscar Wilde.

-inae *suffix* forming plural nouns, denoting: members of a subfamily: *Felinae.* [Latin *-inae*, fem pl of *-inus* of or belonging to]

inalienable /in'ayliənəbl/ *adj* incapable of being removed or surrendered: *an inalienable right to a fair trial.* ⋙ **inalienability** /-'biliti/ *noun*, **inalienably** *adv.* [prob from French *inaliénable*, from IN-¹ + *aliénable* alienable, ultimately from Latin *alienare*: see ALIENATE]

inalterable /in'awltərəbl, in'ol-/ *adj* not able to be changed. ⋙ **inalterability** /-'biliti/ *noun*, **inalterably** *adv.*

inamorata /i,namə'rahtə/ *noun* a female romantic or sexual partner: *His inamorata adjusted her garter and lifted her voice in duet* — Flanders. [Italian *innamorata*, fem past part. of *innamorare* to inspire with love, from *in-* (from IN-¹) +*amore* love, from Latin *amor*, from *amare* to love]

inamorato /i,namə'rahtoh/ *noun* a male romantic or sexual partner. [Italian *innamorato*, past part. of *innamorare*: see INAMORATA]

inane /i'nayn/ *adj* senseless or unintelligent: *inane comments.* ⋙ **inanely** *adv*, **inaneness** *noun.* [Latin *inanis* empty, insubstantial]

inanimate /in'animət/ *adj* **1** without life or spirit, *esp* in contrast to living things. **2** lacking consciousness or power of motion. ⋙ **inanimately** *adv*, **inanimateness** *noun.* [late Latin *inanimatus*, from Latin IN-¹ + *animatus*, past part. of *animare*: see ANIMATE¹]

inanition /inə'nish(ə)n/ *noun formal* **1** exhaustion due to lack of food. **2** the absence or loss of social, spiritual, or intellectual vitality or vigour. [Middle English from medieval Latin *inanition-, inanitio*, from *inanire* to make empty, from *inanis* empty, insubstantial]

inanity /i'naniti/ *noun* (*pl* **inanities**) **1** the quality or state of being inane. **2** an inane action, remark, etc.

inapplicable /inə'plikəbl/ *adj* not appropriate or relevant. ⋙ **inapplicability** /-'biliti/ *noun*, **inapplicably** *adv.*

inapposite /in'apəzit/ *adj* not suitable or pertinent. ⋙ **inappositely** *adv*, **inappositeness** *noun.*

inappreciable /inə'preesh(y)əbl/ *adj* too small or slight to be perceived or to make a difference. ⋙ **inappreciably** *adv.*

inappropriate /inə'prohpri·ət/ *adj* not appropriate or suitable. ⋙ **inappropriately** *adv*, **inappropriateness** *noun.*

inapt /in'apt/ *adj* **1** not suitable or appropriate. **2** lacking skill or ability. ⋙ **inaptitude** /-tityoohd/ *noun*, **inaptly** *adv*, **inaptness** *noun.*

inarch /in'ahch/ *verb trans* to graft (a plant) by connecting a shoot or branch that is still attached to its parent plant.

inarticulate /inah'tikyoolət/ *adj* **1a** unable to speak or to express one's ideas or feelings coherently, clearly, or effectively. **b** not coherently, clearly, or effectively expressed: *an inarticulate speech.* **c** not understandable as spoken words: *inarticulate cries.* **2** not jointed or hinged. ⋙ **inarticulacy** *noun*, **inarticulately** *adv*, **inarticulateness** *noun.* [late Latin *inarticulatus*, from Latin IN-¹ + *articulatus*, past part. of *articulare*: see ARTICULATE²; (sense 3) scientific Latin *inarticulatus*, from IN-¹ + Latin *articulatus*: see ARTICULATE¹]

inartistic /inah'tistik/ *adj* **1** not conforming to the principles of art. **2** not appreciative of art. **3** lacking in artistic skill. ⋙ **inartistically** *adv.*

inasmuch as /inəz'much əz/ *conj* **1** = INSOFAR AS. **2** in view of the fact that; because.

inattention /inə'tensh(ə)n/ *noun* failure to pay attention; disregard. ⋙ **inattentive** /-tiv/ *adj.*

inaudible /in'awdəbl/ *adj* unable to be heard. ⋙ **inaudibly** *adv.*

inaugural¹ /in'awgyoorəl/ *adj* **1** marking a beginning. **2** first in a projected series. **3** relating to an inauguration. [French *inaugural* from *inaugurer* to inaugurate, from Latin *inaugurare*: see INAUGURATE]

inaugural² *noun* an address given at an inauguration.

inaugurate /in'awgyoorayt/ *verb trans* **1a** to induct (somebody) ceremonially into office. **b** to open (e.g. a new building) ceremonially. **2** to mark the beginning or introduction of (a new system, project, etc). ⋙ **inauguration** /-'raysh(ə)n/ *noun*, **inaugurator** *noun*, **inauguratory** /-rət(ə)ri/ *adj.* [Latin *inauguratus*, past part. of *inaugurare* to practise augury, later 'to induct after observing the omens', from IN-² + *augurare* to augur]

inauspicious /inaw'spishəs/ *adj* not promising future success.

in between *adv* = BETWEEN².

in-between *adj* intermediate. ⋙ **in-betweener** *noun.*

inboard /in'bawd/ *adj and adv* within or towards the centre line of a ship, aircraft, etc. [IN¹ + BOARD¹ in the sense 'ship's side']

inborn /in'bawn/ *adj* **1** forming part of the natural make-up of somebody or something: *that inborn craving which undermines some women's morals almost more than unbridled passion – the craving to attract and captivate* — Hardy. **2** existing from birth; congenital.

inbred /in'bred/ *adj* **1** rooted and deeply ingrained in the nature of somebody or something. **2** subjected to or produced by inbreeding.

inbreed /in'breed/ *verb* (*past tense and past part.* **inbred** /-bred/) **1** to cause (closely related individuals) to breed with each other, *esp* over a number of generations, usu with the intention or result of preserving or fixing certain characteristics. **2** to produce (offspring) in this way. ⋙ **inbreeder** *noun,* **inbreeding** *noun.*

inbuilt /in'bilt/ *adj* built-in; inherent or integral.

Inc. *abbr chiefly NAmer* incorporated.

Inca /'ingkə/ *noun* **1** a member of an indigenous South American people who lived in the region of the central Andes before the Spanish conquest. **2** a ruler or member of the ruling family of this people. ⋙ **Incaic** /ing'kayik/ *adj,* **Incan** *adj.* [Spanish *Inca* from Quechua *inka* king, prince]

incalculable /in'kalkyooləbl/ *adj* **1** too great or numerous to be calculated. **2** unable to be predicted or estimated. ⋙ **incalculability** /-'biliti/ *noun,* **incalculably** *adv.*

incandesce /inkan'des/ *verb intrans* said of a light: to glow with heat.

incandescent /inkan'des(ə)nt/ *adj* **1** white, glowing, or luminous with intense heat. **2** *informal* extremely angry. ⋙ **incandescence** *noun,* **incandescently** *adv.* [prob via French from Latin *incandescent-, incandescens,* present part. of *incandescere* to become hot, from IN-[2] + *candescere* to become white or bright, from *candidus:* see CANDID]

incandescent lamp *noun* a lamp in which an electrically heated filament gives off light.

incantation /inkan'taysh(ə)n/ *noun* **1** the use of spoken or sung spells in magic ritual. **2** a formula used in incantation. ⋙ **incantatory** /in'kantət(ə)ri/ *adj.* [Middle English *incantacioun* via French from late Latin *incantation-, incantatio,* from Latin *incantare:* see ENCHANT]

incapable /in'kaypəbl/ *adj* **1** (*usu* + of) lacking the capacity, ability, etc to do or admit of something: *He's incapable of making decisions; The distance is incapable of precise measurement.* **2** unfit, *esp* because of illness or the effects of alcohol or drugs. **3** *archaic* (+ of) having no understanding or awareness of something; unable to take it in: *She chanted snatches of old tunes, as one incapable of her own distress* — Shakespeare. ⋙ **incapability** /-'biliti/ *noun,* **incapably** *adv.* [via French from late Latin *incapabilis,* from IN-[1] + *capabilis:* see CAPABLE]

incapacitate /inkə'pasitayt/ *verb trans* **1** to prevent (somebody or something) from functioning or operating properly; to disable (them). **2** to disqualify (somebody) legally. ⋙ **incapacitation** /-'taysh(ə)n/ *noun.*

incapacity /inkə'pasiti/ *noun* (*pl* **incapacities**) **1** lack of ability or power. **2** legal disqualification. [French *incapacité* from Latin *incapacitas,* from IN-[1] + *capacitas:* see CAPACITY]

incarcerate /in'kahsərayt/ *verb trans* to imprison or confine (somebody). ⋙ **incarceration** /-'raysh(ə)n/ *noun,* **incarcerator** *noun.* [Latin *incarceratus,* past part. of *incarcerare,* from IN-[2] + *carcer* prison]

incarnadine[1] /in'kahnədien/ *adj literary* **1** flesh-coloured. **2** blood red. [early French *incarnadin* from Old Italian *incarnadino,* from *incarnato* flesh-coloured, from late Latin *incarnatus:* see INCARNATE[1]]

incarnadine[2] *verb trans* to give a red or pinkish colour to (something): *Will all great Neptune's ocean wash this blood clean from my hand? No, this my hand will rather the multitudinous seas incarnadine, making the green one red* — Shakespeare.

incarnate[1] /in'kahnət, -nayt/ *adj* (*used after a noun*) **1** invested with bodily, *esp* human, nature and form: *the devil incarnate.* **2** personified, typified, or represented in extreme form: *evil incarnate.* [Middle English *incarnat* from late Latin *incarnatus,* past part. of *incarnare,* from IN-[2] + *carn-, caro* flesh]

incarnate[2] /'inkahnayt/ *verb trans* **1** to give (e.g. a deity) bodily or human form. **2** to be a representative or typical example of (an abstract concept or quality).

incarnation /inkah'naysh(ə)n/ *noun* **1** the embodiment of a deity or spirit in an earthly form. **2** somebody or something that is a representative or typical example of an abstract concept or quality. **3** (**Incarnation**) in Christian belief, the manifestation of Christ in human form: compare ADVENT (2). **4** any of several successive bodily manifestations or lives.

incase /in'kays/ *verb* see ENCASE.

incautious /in'kawshəs/ *adj* lacking care or caution; rash. ⋙ **incaution** *noun,* **incautiously** *adv,* **incautiousness** *noun.*

incendiary[1] /in'sendi-əri/ *adj* **1** relating to the deliberate burning of property. **2** tending to inflame or stir up trouble. **3** said of a device or substance: able or designed to ignite spontaneously on contact. ⋙ **incendiarism** *noun.* [Latin *incendiarius,* from *incendium* conflagration, from *incendere:* see INCENSE[1]]

incendiary[2] *noun* (*pl* **incendiaries**) **1a** somebody who deliberately sets fire to property; an arsonist. **b** an incendiary substance or device, e.g. a bomb. **2** somebody who inflames or stirs up factions, quarrels, or sedition; an agitator.

incense[1] /'insens/ *noun* **1** a substance, such as aromatic spices, gum, etc, used to produce a fragrant smell when burned, *esp* in a religious ceremony. **2** the perfume this gives off when burned. **3** any pleasing aromatic scent. [Middle English *encens* via Old French and late Latin from Latin *incensum,* neuter of *incensus,* past part. of *incendere* to set on fire, from IN-[2] + *-cendere* to burn]

incense[2] /'insens/ *verb trans* to perfume (something) with incense.

incense[3] /in'sens/ *verb trans* to arouse (a person or group) to extreme anger or indignation. [Middle English *encensen* via French from Latin *incensus:* see INCENSE[1]]

incensory /in'sensəri/ *noun* (*pl* **incensories**) = CENSER.

incentive /in'sentiv/ *noun* **1** something that motivates somebody or spurs them on. **2** an extra payment to encourage employees to greater productivity. [Middle English from late Latin *incentivum,* neuter of *incentivus* stimulating, setting the tune, from Latin *incinere* to set the tune, from IN-[2] + *canere* to sing]

incentivize or **incentivise** /in'sentiviez/ *verb trans* to stimulate or motivate (e.g. employees) by offering an incentive or incentives.

incept /in'sept/ *verb trans* said of an organism: to ingest (food). ⋙ *verb intrans Brit* in former times, to take a higher degree at university. ⋙ **inceptor** *noun.* [Latin *inceptus,* past part. of *incipere:* see INCEPTION]

inception /in'sepsh(ə)n/ *noun* the act or an instance of beginning a process or undertaking: *She has worked on the project since its inception.* [Latin *inception-, inceptio,* from *incipere* to begin, from IN-[2] + *capere* to take]

inceptive[1] /in'septiv/ *adj* **1** initial, beginning, or first. **2** said of a verb: expressing the beginning of an action. Also called INCHOATIVE[1]. ⋙ **inceptively** *adv.*

inceptive[2] *noun* an inceptive verb.

incertitude /in'suhtityoohd/ *noun* uncertainty; doubt. [early French *incertitude* from late Latin *incertitudo,* from Latin IN-[1] + *certitudo:* see CERTITUDE]

incessant /in'ses(ə)nt/ *adj* usu said of something unpleasant or undesirable: continuing without interruption: *I've had enough of your incessant complaints.* ⋙ **incessancy** /-si/ *noun,* **incessantly** *adv.* [Middle English *incessaunt* from late Latin *incessant-, incessans,* from IN-[1] + Latin *cessant-, cessans,* present part. of *cessare:* see CEASE[1]]

incest /'insest/ *noun* sexual intercourse between people so closely related that they are forbidden by law to marry. [Middle English from Latin *incestum,* neuter of *incestus* impure, from IN-[1] + *castus* pure]

incestuous /in'sestyooəs/ *adj* **1** relating to, guilty of, or involving incest. **2** excessively or unhealthily close to or shut off from outside influences. ⋙ **incestuously** *adv,* **incestuousness** *noun.*

inch[1] /inch/ *noun* **1** a unit of length equal to one twelfth of a foot (about 2.54cm). **2** a small amount, distance, or degree: *They came within an inch of scoring.* **3** (*in pl*) stature or height. **4** a fall of rain, snow, etc enough to cover a level surface to the depth of one inch. **5** a unit of pressure that can support a mercury column one inch high in a barometer. ✳ **every inch** to the utmost degree: *He looks every inch a winner.* **inch by inch** slowly and gradually. **(to) within an inch of one's life** almost to the point of death; very thoroughly or soundly: *They thrashed him within an inch of his life.* [Old English *ynce* from Latin *uncia:* see OUNCE[1]]

inch[2] *verb intrans* to move slowly: *The train inched forward to the buffers.* ⋙ *verb trans* to move (something) by small degrees.

inch[3] *noun chiefly Scot* usu in place names: an island. [Middle English from Scottish Gaelic *innis*]

inchoate /'inkoh·ayt/ *adj* **1** only partly in existence or operation, *esp* imperfectly formed or formulated: *an inchoate longing.* **2** said of a criminal offence: liable to lead to another crime. ➤➤ **inchoately** *adv*, **inchoateness** *noun*. [Latin *inchoatus*, past part. of *inchoare* to begin, literally 'to hitch up', from IN-² + *cohum* strap fastening a plough beam to the yoke]

inchoative¹ /in'koh·ətiv/ *adj* = INCEPTIVE¹ (2).

inchoative² *noun* an inchoative verb.

inchworm *noun* = LOOPER (I). [because its movement resembles that of measuring something with a tape measure]

incidence /'insid(ə)ns/ *noun* **1** the rate of occurrence or the extent of influence that something has: *a high incidence of crime.* **2** the arrival of something, e.g. a projectile or a ray of light, at a surface.

incident¹ /'insid(ə)nt/ *noun* **1** something that happens; an event or occurrence, considered either on its own or as part of a series. **2a** an occurrence that is a cause of conflict or disagreement: *a serious border incident.* **b** a violent act or exchange. [Middle English via French from Latin *incident-, incidens*, present part. of *incidere* to fall into, from IN-² + *cadere* to fall]

incident² *adj* **1** (*usu* + to) relating to, accompanying, or resulting from something: *the confusion incident to moving house.* **2** (*usu* + to) dependent on another thing in law. **3** said *esp* of light: falling on or striking a surface.

incidental¹ /insi'dentl/ *adj* **1** occurring merely by chance. **2** (*often* + to) occurring or likely to ensue as a minor consequence or accompaniment: *social obligations incidental to his job.*

incidental² *noun* something incidental, *esp* a minor expense or an insignificant event.

incidentally *adv* **1** by the way; as a digression: *Incidentally, did you know they were getting divorced?* **2** by chance.

incidental music *noun* background music in a play, film, etc, often reflecting the current action or mood.

incinerate /in'sinərayt/ *verb trans* to burn (something) to ashes. ➤➤ **incineration** /-'raysh(ə)n/ *noun*. [medieval Latin *incineratus*, past part. of *incinerare*, from IN-² + Latin *ciner-, cinis* ashes]

incinerator *noun* a furnace or container for incinerating waste materials.

incipient /in'sipi·ənt/ *adj* just beginning to come into being or to become apparent. ➤➤ **incipience** *noun*, **incipiency** /-si/ *noun*, **incipiently** *adv*. [Latin *incipient-, incipiens*, present part. of *incipere*: see INCEPTION]

incise /in'siez/ *verb trans* **1** to cut into (something). **2a** to carve letters, designs, etc into (something). **b** to carve (e.g. an inscription) into a surface. [early French *inciser* from Latin *incisus*, past part. of *incidere*, from IN-² + *caedere* to cut]

incision /in'sizh(ə)n/ *noun* **1** a cut, *esp* one made in a surgical operation. **2** the act or process of cutting into something.

incisive /in'siesiv/ *adj* **1** having or showing sharp intelligence: *an incisive mind.* **2** impressively direct and decisive: *an incisive move to attract new business.* **3** hurtfully sarcastic: *incisive remarks.* **4** having a sharp edge. ➤➤ **incisively** *adv*, **incisiveness** *noun*.

incisor *noun* a cutting tooth, *esp* one of the front teeth in mammals.

incite /in'siet/ *verb trans* **1** to move (a person or group) to action. **2** to encourage (violence, unlawful behaviour, etc). ➤➤ **incitation** /-'taysh(ə)n/ *noun*, **incitement** *noun*, **inciter** *noun*. [early French *inciter* from Latin *incitare*, from IN-² + *citare*: see CITE]

incivility /insi'viliti/ *noun* (*pl* **incivilities**) **1** rudeness or discourtesy. **2** a rude or discourteous act. [early French *incivilité* from late Latin *incivilitat-, incivilitas*, from *incivilis* impolite, from IN-¹ + Latin *civilis*: see CIVIL]

incl. *abbr* **1** included. **2** including. **3** inclusive.

inclement /in'klemənt/ *adj* **1** said of the weather: unpleasant, *esp* cold and wet. **2** unmerciful. ➤➤ **inclemency** /-si/ *noun*, **inclemently** *adv*. [Latin *inclement-, inclemens*, from IN-¹ + *clement-, clemens* CLEMENT]

inclination /inkli'naysh(ə)n/ *noun* **1** a particular tendency, propensity, or urge, *esp* a liking: *She had little inclination for housekeeping.* **2a** a deviation from the vertical or horizontal, or the degree of this. **b** a slope. **c** the angle between two lines or planes. **d** = MAGNETIC DIP. **3a** the act or an instance of bending or inclining. **b** a bow or nod. ➤➤ **inclinational** *adj*.

incline¹ /in'klien/ *verb trans* **1** to influence or dispose (somebody) to a specified action or way of thinking. **2** to cause (something) to lean or slope; to move (it) into a position that is neither horizontal nor vertical. **3** to drop, nod, or bend (the head), e.g. as a gesture of agreement. ➤ *verb intrans* **1** to slope or slant; to deviate from the horizontal or vertical: *The road inclines gently for about a mile.* **2** to bend the head or upper body forward. ✳ **inclined to 1** having a tendency to (do or be something): *They are inclined to be late.* **2** in favour of (doing something); willing to (do it): *I'm inclined to believe him.* ➤➤ **incliner** *noun*. [Middle English *inclinen* via French from Latin *inclinare*, from IN-² + *clinare* to lean]

incline² /'inklien/ *noun* an inclined surface; a slope.

inclined plane /'inkliend/ *noun* a plane surface that makes an angle with the horizontal.

inclinometer /inkli'nomitə/ *noun* **1** an apparatus for determining the direction of the earth's magnetic field with reference to the plane of the horizon. **2** an instrument for indicating the inclination to the horizontal, *esp* of an aircraft.

inclose /in'klohz/ *verb trans* see ENCLOSE.

inclosure /in'klohzhə/ *noun* see ENCLOSURE.

include /in'kloohd/ *verb trans* **1** to take in, contain, or consider (something or somebody) as a part of a larger group or whole: *The price includes VAT.* **2** to add or put in (something or somebody): *You need to include more detail to strengthen your argument.* ➤➤ **includable** *adj*, **includible** *adj*. [Middle English *includen* from Latin *includere*, from IN-² + *claudere* to close]

include out *verb trans informal* to leave (somebody) out of a group or activity, usu at their suggestion: *If you're planning to travel overland, you can include me out!*

inclusion /in'kloohzh(ə)n/ *noun* **1** the act or process of including or being included. **2** something or somebody that is included. **3** a foreign body enclosed in a mass, *esp* a mineral. [Latin *inclusion-, inclusio*, from *includere*: see INCLUDE]

inclusive /in'kloohsiv, -ziv/ *adj* **1** including or intended to include all or the specified items, costs, or services: *inclusive of VAT.* **2** including the stated limits or extremes: *Monday to Friday inclusive.* **3** broad in orientation or scope. **4** said of language: avoiding the use of gender-specific words. ➤➤ **inclusively** *adv*, **inclusiveness** *noun*.

inclusive disjunction *noun* a complex sentence in logic that is true when either or both of its constituent sentences are true.

inclusivism *noun* the practice or theory of including or accepting diverse things, *esp* the tendency in some religions to advocate greater unity between denominations. ➤➤ **inclusivist** *noun and adj*.

incognito¹ /inkog'neetoh/ *adv and adj* with one's identity concealed; in disguise or under a false name: *The celebrity arrived incognito.* [Italian *incognito* from Latin *incognitus* unknown, from IN-¹ + *cognitus*, past part. of *cognoscere*: see COGNITION]

incognito² *noun* (*pl* **incognitos**) the disguise or false name of somebody who is incognito.

incognizant /in'kogniz(ə)nt/ *adj* (*often* + of) lacking awareness or consciousness: *incognizant of all the relevant details.* ➤➤ **incognizance** *noun*.

incoherent /inkoh'hiərənt/ *adj* **1** not clearly intelligible; inarticulate: *incoherent with rage.* **2** lacking in logical connection: *an incoherent account.* **3** in physics, denoting waves of the same frequency that are different in phase. ➤➤ **incoherence** *noun*, **incoherency** /-si/ *noun*, **incoherently** *adv*.

incombustible /inkəm'bustəbl/ *adj* incapable of being ignited or burned. ➤➤ **incombustibility** /-'biliti/ *noun*. [Middle English from medieval Latin *incombustibilis*, from IN-¹ + *combustibilis* combustible, from Latin *comburere*: see COMBUST]

income /'inkəm, 'ingkəm/ *noun* money received from work, property, or investment, *esp* regularly or over a specified time: *Elton is … not at all likely to make an imprudent match. He knows the value of a good income as well as any body* — Jane Austen.

incomer /'inkumə/ *noun* a person who moves into an area, *esp* as contrasted with those who have lived there for all or most of their lives.

income support *noun Brit* a social security payment made to people on low incomes.

income tax *noun* a tax levied on personal income.

incoming[1] /'inkuming/ *noun* **1** the act or an instance of coming in; arrival or entrance. **2** (*in pl*) an amount received; income or revenue.

incoming[2] *adj* **1** arriving, coming in, or being received: *an incoming message; the incoming tide.* **2** taking on a role or office: *the incoming president.*

incommensurable[1] /inkə'mensh(ə)rəbl/ *adj* **1** lacking a common basis of comparison; incapable of being compared. **2** in mathematics, having no common factor: *√2 and 3 are incommensurable.* ➤➤ **incommensurability** /-'biliti/ *noun,* **incommensurably** *adv.*

incommensurable[2] *noun* something that is incommensurable.

incommensurate /inkə'menshərət/ *adj* **1** (*usu* + with) disproportionate to something, *esp* in being more or less than is expected or appropriate. **2** = INCOMMENSURABLE[1] (I). ➤➤ **incommensurately** *adv,* **incommensurateness** *noun.*

incommode /inkə'mohd/ *verb trans formal* to inconvenience or trouble (somebody). [early French *incommoder* from Latin *incommodare,* from *incommodus* inconvenient, from IN-[1] + *commodus:* see COMMODE]

incommodious /inkə'mohdi-əs/ *adj formal* inconvenient or uncomfortable, *esp* from being too small. ➤➤ **incommodiously** *adv,* **incommodiousness** *noun.*

incommunicado /,inkəmyoohni'kahdoh/ *adv and adj* without means of communication, e.g. while in solitary confinement or voluntary seclusion. [Spanish *incomunicado,* past part. of *incomunicar* to deprive of communication, from *in-* (from IN-[1]) + *comunicar* to communicate, from Latin *communicare:* see COMMUNICATE]

incommutable /inkə'myoohtəbl/ *adj* **1** not interchangeable. **2** unchangeable. ➤➤ **incommutably** *adv.* [Middle English from Latin *incommutabilis,* from IN-[1] + *commutabilis* commutable, from *commutare:* see COMMUTE]

incomparable /in'komp(ə)rəbl/ *adj* **1** beyond comparison; matchless. **2** not suitable for comparison. ➤➤ **incomparability** /-'biliti/ *noun,* **incomparableness** *noun,* **incomparably** *adv.* [Middle English via French from Latin *incomparabilis,* from IN-[1] + *comparabilis* comparable, from *comparare:* see COMPARE[1]]

incompatible /inkəm'patəbl/ *adj* **1** said of two or more people: unable to live or work together, *esp* because of opposing views, temperaments, etc. **2** unable to exist together: *incompatible beliefs.* **3** unsuitable for use together: *incompatible blood types.* **4** in logic, denoting two propositions that cannot both be true at the same time. ➤➤ **incompatibility** /-'biliti/ *noun,* **incompatibly** *adv.* [via French from medieval Latin *incompatibilis,* from IN-[1] + *compatibilis:* see COMPATIBLE]

incompetent[1] /in'kompit(ə)nt/ *adj* **1** lacking the qualities, skill, experience, etc needed for effective action. **2** not legally qualified: *an incompetent witness.* **3** inadequate to or unsuitable for a particular purpose. ➤➤ **incompetence** *noun,* **incompetency** /-si/ *noun,* **incompetently** *adv.* [early French *incompétent,* from IN-[1] + *compétent:* see COMPETENT]

incompetent[2] *noun* an incompetent person.

incomplete /inkəm'pleet/ *adj* **1** unfinished. **2** lacking one or more parts: *an incomplete set.* ➤➤ **incompletely** *adv,* **incompleteness** *noun,* **incompletion** *noun.* [Middle English *incompleet* from late Latin *incompletus,* from IN-[1] + Latin *completus:* see COMPLETE[1]]

incomprehensible /in,kompri'hensəbl/ *adj* impossible to understand; unintelligible. ➤➤ **incomprehensibility** /-'biliti/ *noun,* **incomprehensibleness** *noun,* **incomprehensibly** *adv.* [Middle English from Latin *incomprehensibilis,* from IN-[1] + *comprehensibilis* comprehensible, from *comprehendere:* see COMPREHEND]

incomprehension /in,kompri'hensh(ə)n/ *noun* lack of understanding; inability to understand.

incompressible /inkəm'presəbl/ *adj* resistant to compression. ➤➤ **incompressibility** /-'biləti/ *noun.*

inconceivable /inkən'seevəbl/ *adj* unimaginable or unbelievable. ➤➤ **inconceivability** /-'biliti/ *noun,* **inconceivableness** *noun,* **inconceivably** *adv.*

inconclusive /inkən'kloohsiv/ *adj* leading to no conclusion or definite result: *The evidence was inconclusive.* ➤➤ **inconclusively** *adv,* **inconclusiveness** *noun.*

incongruent /in'konggrooənt/ *adj* **1** = INCONGRUOUS. **2** said of some chemical processes involving melting or dissolution: affecting different alloys or other substances in different ways. **3** in geometry, not congruent.

incongruous /in'konggrooəs/ *adj* out of place; not in keeping with what is appropriate or expected. ➤➤ **incongruity** /-'grooh-iti/ *noun,* **incongruously** *adv,* **incongruousness** *noun.* [late Latin *incongruus,* from IN-[1] + Latin *congruus:* see CONGRUOUS]

inconnu /in'konyoo, in'konoo/ *noun* **1** an unknown person or thing. **2** an edible freshwater fish that lives in the waters of northern Canada: genus *Stenodus.* [French *inconnu,* literally 'unknown']

inconsequent /in'konsikwənt/ *adj* **1** lacking reasonable sequence; illogical. **2** irrelevant. ➤➤ **inconsequence** *noun,* **inconsequently** *adv.* [late Latin *inconsequent-, inconsequens,* from IN-[1] + Latin *consequent-, consequens:* see CONSEQUENT[2]]

inconsequential /in,konsi'kwensh(ə)l/ *adj* **1** irrelevant. **2** of no significance; unimportant. ➤➤ **inconsequentiality** /-shi'aliti/ *noun,* **inconsequentially** *adv.*

inconsiderable /inkən'sid(ə)rəbl/ *adj* **1** insignificant or trivial: *They exercised no inconsiderable influence.* **2** small in size, amount, etc: *sold for a not inconsiderable sum.* ➤➤ **inconsiderableness** *noun,* **inconsiderably** *adv.* [early French *inconsidérable* from medieval Latin *inconsiderabilis,* from IN-[1] + *considerabilis* considerable, from Latin *considerare:* see CONSIDER]

inconsiderate /inkən'sid(ə)rət/ *adj* having or showing a lack of care for others; thoughtless. ➤➤ **inconsiderately** *adv,* **inconsiderateness** *noun,* **inconsideration** /-'raysh(ə)n/ *noun.* [Latin *inconsideratus,* from IN-[1] + *consideratus* considerate, from *considerare:* see CONSIDER]

inconsistent /inkən'sist(ə)nt/ *adj* **1** containing conflicting or contradictory elements: *an inconsistent argument.* **2** not consistent in thought, action, behaviour, quality, etc; changeable. ➤➤ **inconsistency** /-si/ *noun,* **inconsistently** *adv.*

inconsolable /inkən'sohləbl/ *adj* incapable of being consoled; brokenhearted. ➤➤ **inconsolability** /-'biliti/ *noun,* **inconsolably** *adv.* [Latin *inconsolabilis,* from IN-[1] + *consolabilis* consolable, from *consolari:* see CONSOLE[1]]

inconsonant /in'kons(ə)nənt/ *adj* not in harmony or agreement. ➤➤ **inconsonance** *noun,* **inconsonantly** *adv.*

inconspicuous /inkən'spikyooəs/ *adj* not readily noticeable: *He looked about as inconspicuous as a tarantula on a slice of angel food —* Raymond Chandler. ➤➤ **inconspicuously** *adv,* **inconspicuousness** *noun.* [Latin *inconspicuus,* from IN-[1] + *conspicuus:* see CONSPICUOUS]

inconstant /in'konst(ə)nt/ *adj* **1** likely to change frequently without apparent reason. **2** *dated* unfaithful: *an inconstant lover.* ➤➤ **inconstancy** /-si/ *noun,* **inconstantly** *adv.* [Middle English via French from Latin *inconstant-, inconstans,* from IN-[1] + *constant-, constans:* see CONSTANT[1]]

incontestable /inkən'testəbl/ *adj* not contestable; indisputable: *For where is the man that has incontestable evidence of the truth of all he holds, or of the falsehood of all he condemns? —* John Locke. ➤➤ **incontestability** /-'biliti/ *noun,* **incontestably** *adv.* [French *incontestable,* from IN-[1] + *contestable* contestable, from *contester:* see CONTEST[1]]

incontinent /in'kontinənt/ *adj* **1** suffering from a lack of control over urination or defecation. **2** lacking self-restraint, *esp* sexually. **3** not under control or restraint. ➤➤ **incontinence** *noun,* **incontinently** *adv.* [Middle English via French from Latin *incontinent-, incontinens,* from IN-[1] + *continent-, continens:* see CONTINENT[2]]

incontrovertible /in,kontrə'vuhtəbl/ *adj* not able to be denied, disputed, or challenged. ➤➤ **incontrovertibly** *adv.*

inconvenience[1] /inkən'veenyəns/ *noun* **1** the state of being inconvenient; difficulty, trouble, discomfort, or annoyance. **2** a cause or instance of inconvenience.

inconvenience[2] *verb trans* to cause (somebody or something) inconvenience: *I hope postponing our meeting won't inconvenience you too much.*

inconvenient /inkən'veenyənt/ *adj* not convenient, *esp* in causing difficulty, trouble, discomfort, or annoyance. ➤➤ **inconveniently** *adv.* [Middle English via French from Latin *inconvenient-, inconveniens,* from IN-[1] + *convenient-, conveniens:* see CONVENIENT]

incoordination /,inkoh-awdi'naysh(ə)n/ *noun* lack of coordination, *esp* of muscular movements.

incorporate[1] /in'kawpərayt/ *verb trans* **1a** to make (something) a *usu* indistinguishable part of a larger whole. **b** to admit (an organization) to membership of a corporate body. **2a** to combine (parts) thoroughly to form a consistent whole. **b** to form (a company, organization, etc) into a legal corporation. ➤ *verb intrans* **1** to unite in or as one body. **2** to form a legal corporation. ➤➤ **incorporation** /-'raysh(ə)n/ *noun*, **incorporative** *adj*, **incorporator** *noun*. [Middle English *incorporaten* from late Latin *incorporatus*, past part. of *incorporare*, from IN-² + Latin *corpor-*, *corpus* body]

incorporate² /in'kawpərit/ *adj* **1** united in one body. **2** formed into a legal corporation.

incorporated /in'kawpəraytid/ *adj* = INCORPORATE².

incorporeal /inkaw'pawri-əl/ *adj* **1** having no material body or form. **2** in law, based on property, e.g. copyrights or patents, with no physical existence. ➤➤ **incorporeality** /-'aliti/ *noun*, **incorporeally** *adv*, **incorporeity** /-'rayiti/ *noun*. [Latin *incorporeus*, from IN-¹ + *corporeus*: see CORPOREAL]

incorrect /inkə'rekt/ *adj* **1** inaccurate; factually wrong. **2** not in accordance with an established norm; improper. ➤➤ **incorrectly** *adv*, **incorrectness** *noun*. [Middle English via French from Latin *incorrectus*, from IN-¹ + *correctus*: see CORRECT¹]

incorrigible /in'korijəbl/ *adj* **1** incapable of being corrected or improved, *esp* incurably bad. **2** unwilling or unlikely to change. ➤➤ **incorrigibility** /-'biliti/ *noun*, **incorrigibly** *adv*. [Middle English from late Latin *incorrigibilis*, from Latin IN-¹ + *corrigere*: see CORRECT¹]

incorruptible /inkə'ruptəbl/ *adj* **1** incapable of being bribed or morally corrupted. **2** not subject to decay or dissolution. ➤➤ **incorruptibility** /-'biliti/ *noun*, **incorruptibly** *adv*.

increase¹ /in'krees/ *verb intrans* to become progressively greater in size, amount, number, or intensity. ➤ *verb trans* to make (something) greater. ➤➤ **increasable** *adj*, **increasingly** *adv*. [Middle English *encresen* via French from Latin *increscere*, from IN-² + *crescere* to grow]

increase² /'inkrees/ *noun* **1** the act or an instance of increasing. **2** the amount by which something increases: *a 5% increase in profits*. ✳ **on the increase** becoming greater, more common, or more frequent.

incredible /in'kredəbl/ *adj* **1a** too extraordinary and improbable to be believed. **b** hard to believe; amazing or astonishing. **2** *informal* excellent; outstanding: *We found this incredible new club near the railway station*. ➤➤ **incredibility** /-'biliti/ *noun*, **incredibly** *adv*. [Middle English from Latin *incredibilis*, from IN-¹ + *credibilis*: see CREDIBLE]

incredulous /in'kredyooləs/ *adj* unwilling or unable to believe something, or expressing such disbelief. ➤➤ **incredulity** /inkri'dyoohliti/ *noun*, **incredulously** *adv*, **incredulousness** *noun*. [Latin *incredulus*, from IN-¹ + *credulus*: see CREDULOUS]

increment /'ingkrimənt/ *noun* **1** an increase, *esp* in quantity or value, or the amount of this. **2** a regular increase in pay resulting from an additional year's service. **3** any of a series of regular consecutive increases or additions. **4** a usu small negative or positive change in the value of a mathematical variable or function. ➤➤ **incremental** /-'mentl/ *adj*, **incrementally** /-'mentəli/ *adv*. [Middle English from Latin *incrementum*, from *increscere*: see INCREASE¹]

incriminate /in'kriminayt/ *verb trans* **1** to suggest or demonstrate that (somebody) is guilty of a crime or other wrongdoing. **2** to charge (somebody) with a crime or other wrongdoing. ➤➤ **incrimination** /-'naysh(ə)n/ *noun*, **incriminatory** /-nət(ə)ri/ *adj*. [late Latin *incriminatus*, past part. of *incriminare*, from IN-² + Latin *crimin-*, *crimen* CRIME]

in-crowd *noun* (**the in-crowd**) *informal* people who are considered to be, or who consider themselves to be, particularly popular, fashionable, or knowledgeable.

incrust /in'krust/ *verb* see ENCRUST.

incubate /'ingkyoobayt/ *verb trans* **1a** said of a bird: to sit on (eggs) so as to hatch them by the warmth of the body. **b** to maintain (something) under conditions favourable for hatching, development, growth, reaction, etc. **c** to develop (a disease), *esp* without any noticeable symptoms. **2** to cause (e.g. an idea) to develop. ➤ *verb intrans* to incubate something or be incubated. ➤➤ **incubation** /-'baysh(ə)n/ *noun*, **incubative** /-tiv/ *adj*, **incubatory** /-t(ə)ri/ *adj*. [Latin *incubatus*, past part. of *incubare*, from IN-² + *cubare* to lie]

incubation period *noun* the time between exposure to a disease or a pathogenic organism and the appearance of the first symptoms.

incubator /'ingkyoobaytə/ *noun* **1** an apparatus in which a premature or sick baby is kept under controlled conditions until it is able to survive independently. **2** an apparatus in which eggs are hatched artificially. **3** an apparatus in which bacteria etc are grown under controlled conditions.

incubus /'ingkyoobəs/ *noun* (*pl* **incubuses** *or* **incubi** /-bie/) **1** a male demon believed to have sexual intercourse with women in their sleep: compare SUCCUBUS. **2** *archaic* a nightmare. **3** somebody or something that oppresses or burdens like a nightmare. [Middle English from late Latin *incubus* nightmare, from Latin *incubare*: see INCUBATE]

incudes /in'kyoodeez/ *noun* pl of INCUS.

inculcate /'inkulkayt/ *verb trans* to teach or instil (something) by frequent repetition or warning: *She inculcated a sense of social responsibility in her children*. ➤➤ **inculcation** /-'kaysh(ə)n/ *noun*, **inculcator** *noun*. [Latin *inculcatus*, past part. of *inculcare* to press or tread in, from IN-² + *calcare*: see CAULK]

inculpate /'inkulpayt/ *verb trans* to incriminate, blame, or accuse (somebody). ➤➤ **inculpation** /-'paysh(ə)n/ *noun*, **inculpatory** /in'kulpət(ə)ri/ *adj*. [late Latin *inculpatus*, from IN-² + Latin *culpatus*, past part. of *culpare*: see CULPABLE]

incumbency /in'kumb(ə)nsi/ *noun* the sphere of action or period of office of an incumbent.

incumbent¹ /in'kumb(ə)nt/ *noun* the holder of an office; *specif* the holder of an Anglican benefice. [Middle English from Latin *incumbent-*, *incumbens*, present part. of *incumbere* to lie down on, from IN-² + *-cumbere* to lie down]

incumbent² *adj* **1** (+ on/upon) imposed as a duty or obligation on somebody: *Johnson was by no means of the opinion, that every man of a learned profession should consider it as incumbent upon him, or as necessary to his credit, to appear as an author* — James Boswell. **2** holding a specified office: *the incumbent caretaker*.

incunabulum /inkyoo'nabyooləm/ *noun* (*pl* **incunabula** /-lə/) **1** a book printed before 1501. **2** the beginning or the early stages of something. [Latin *incunabula* (pl) swaddling clothes, cradle, source, from IN-² + *cunae* cradle]

incur /in'kuh/ *verb trans* (**incurred**, **incurring**) to become liable or subject to (something unpleasant or unwanted); to bring (it) upon oneself: *They incurred several new debts*. ➤➤ **incurrable** *adj*, **incurrence** *noun*. [Latin *incurrere*, literally 'to run into', from IN-² + *currere* to run]

incurable¹ /in'kyooərəbl/ *adj* said *esp* of a disease: not able to be cured or treated. ➤➤ **incurability** /-'biliti/ *noun*, **incurably** *adv*.

incurable² *noun* a person with an incurable disease.

incurious /in'kyooəri-əs/ *adj* lacking curiosity; uninterested: *a blank incurious stare*. ➤➤ **incuriosity** /-'ositi/ *noun*, **incuriously** *adv*, **incuriousness** *noun*. [Latin *incuriosus*, from IN-¹ + *curiosus*: see CURIOUS]

incursion /in'kuhsh(ə)n/ *noun* a sudden usu brief invasion into another's territory. ➤➤ **incursive** /-siv/ *adj*. [Middle English via French from Latin *incursion-*, *incursio*, from *incurrere*: see INCUR]

incus /'ingkəs/ *noun* (*pl* **incudes** /in'kyoohdeez/) a small anvil-shaped bone, the middle of the chain of three small bones that transmit sound to the inner ear of mammals; the anvil: compare MALLEUS, STAPES. [Latin *incus* anvil, from *incudere*: see INCUSE¹; from the shape of the bone]

incuse¹ /in'kyoohz/ *noun* a design or impression stamped on a coin. [Latin *incusus*, past part. of *incudere* to stamp, strike, from IN-² + *cudere* to beat]

incuse² *verb trans* to stamp (a coin) with a design or impression.

IND *abbr* India (international vehicle registration).

Ind. *abbr* **1** Independent. **2** India. **3** Indian. **4** Indiana.

ind. *abbr* **1** independent. **2** indicative. **3** indirect. **4** industrial. **5** industry.

indaba /in'dahbə/ *noun* **1** *chiefly SAfr* a conference. **2** a problem or a topic under discussion. [Zulu *in-daba* affair]

indebted /in'detid/ *adj* **1** owing gratitude or recognition to another: *Virgil was indebted to Homer for the whole invention of the structure of an epic poem* — Dr Johnson. **2** owing money. ➤➤ **indebtedness** *noun*. [Middle English *indetted* from Old French *endeté*, past part. of *endeter* to involve in debt, from EN-¹ + *dette*: see DEBT]

indecent /in'dees(ə)nt/ *adj* **1** improper or unseemly: *He remarried with indecent haste.* **2** morally offensive. ⟫⟫ **indecency** /-si/ *noun*, **indecently** *adv.* [early French *indécent* from Latin *indecent-*, *indecens*, from IN-[1] + *decent-*, *decens*: see DECENT]

indecent assault *noun* a criminal offence of sexual assault that does not involve rape.

indecent exposure *noun* the criminal offence of publicly exposing one's genitals.

indecipherable /indi'sief(ə)rəbl/ *adj* **1** said of handwriting: impossible to read. **2** said of a code: unable to be solved or understood.

indecision /indi'sizh(ə)n/ *noun* wavering between two or more possible courses of action; irresolution. [French *indécision*, from *indécis* undecided, ultimately from Latin IN-[1] + *decisus*, past part. of *decidere*: see DECIDE]

indecisive /indi'siesiv/ *adj* **1** marked by or prone to indecision. **2** giving an uncertain result: *an indecisive battle.* ⟫⟫ **indecisively** *adv*, **indecisiveness** *noun.*

indeclinable /indi'klienəbl/ *adj* said of a noun, pronoun, or adjective: having no grammatical inflections. [via French from late Latin *indeclinabilis*, from IN-[1] + *declinabilis* capable of being inflected, from Latin *declinare*: see DECLINE[1]]

indecorum /indi'kawrəm/ *noun* failure to conform to acceptable standards of behaviour, taste, etc; impropriety. ⟫⟫ **indecorous** /in'dekərəs/ *adj.* [Latin *indecorum*, neuter of *indecorus* improper, from IN-[1] + *decorus*: see DECOROUS]

indeed /in'deed/ *adv* **1a** without any question; truly: *It is indeed remarkable.* **b** used to indicate agreement: *Indeed I will.* **c** used as an intensifier or for emphasis: *It has been very cold indeed.* **2** often used to introduce additional information: actually: *I don't mind, indeed I'm pleased; if indeed they come at all.* **3** used to express irony, contempt, disbelief, or surprise: *Does she indeed!* [Middle English *in dede*, from IN[1] + *dede* DEED[1]]

indefatigable /indi'fatigəbl/ *adj* tireless or unflagging: *that indefatigable and unsavoury engine of pollution, the dog* — John Sparrow. ⟫⟫ **indefatigability** /-'biliti/ *noun*, **indefatigably** *adv.* [via French from Latin *indefatigabilis*, from IN-[1] + *defatigare* to fatigue, from *de* down + *fatigare* to FATIGUE[1]]

indefeasible /indi'feezəbl/ *adj* not capable of being legally annulled or forfeited: *an indefeasible right.* ⟫⟫ **indefeasibility** /-'biliti/ *noun*, **indefeasibly** *adv.*

indefensible /indi'fensəbl/ *adj* **1** not capable of being justified or excused: *Your behaviour was indefensible.* **2** said e.g. of a military position: impossible to defend against an enemy attack. ⟫⟫ **indefensibility** /-'biliti/ *noun*, **indefensibly** *adv.*

indefinable /indi'fienəbl/ *adj* incapable of being precisely described or analysed. ⟫⟫ **indefinable** *noun*, **indefinably** *adv.*

indefinite /in'definət/ *adj* **1** not precise; vague or unsettled: *The meeting was postponed until some indefinite date next month.* **2** having no exact limits. **3** said of a word, phrase, etc: not identifying any particular person or thing. ⟫⟫ **indefinitely** *adv*, **indefiniteness** *noun.* [Latin *indefinitus*, from IN-[1] + *definitus*: see DEFINITE]

indefinite article *noun* in grammar, a word, e.g. *a*, *an*, or *some* in English, that refers to an unspecified person or thing: compare DEFINITE ARTICLE.

indefinite integral *noun* a mathematical function whose derivative is a given function: compare DEFINITE INTEGRAL.

indefinite pronoun *noun* in grammar, a pronoun, e.g. *somebody* or *anything* in English, that refers to an unspecified person or thing.

indehiscent /indi'his(ə)nt/ *adj* said of a fruit, pod, etc: not opening to release seeds at maturity. ⟫⟫ **indehiscence** *noun.*

indelible /in'deləbl/ *adj* **1a** said of a mark, stain, etc: incapable of being removed or erased. **b** said of ink: designed to make marks that cannot be removed or erased. **2** said e.g. of a memory: not able to be forgotten. ⟫⟫ **indelibility** /-'biliti/ *noun*, **indelibly** *adv.* [medieval Latin *indelibilis*, alteration of Latin *indelebilis*, from IN-[1] + *delēre*: see DELETE]

indelicate /in'delikət/ *adj* **1** said e.g. of a remark: almost indecent or offensive. **2** lacking in good manners, taste, or sensitivity. ⟫⟫ **indelicacy** /-si/ *noun*, **indelicately** *adv.*

indemnify /in'demnifie/ *verb trans* (**indemnifies, indemnified, indemnifying**) **1** to secure (somebody or something) against harm, loss, damage, or liability. **2** to compensate (somebody) for

harm, loss, or damage. ⟫⟫ **indemnification** /-fi'kaysh(ə)n/ *noun.* [Latin *indemnis* unharmed, from IN-[1] + *damnum* DAMAGE[1]]

indemnity /in'demniti/ *noun* (*pl* **indemnities**) **1** security against harm, loss, damage, or liability. **2** exemption from incurred penalties or liabilities. **3** compensation for harm, loss, or damage. [Middle English *indempnyte* via French from Latin *indemnitat-*, *indemnitas*, from *indemnis*: see INDEMNIFY]

indemonstrable /indi'monstrəbl/ *adj* not able to be proved.

indene /'indeen/ *noun* a colourless organic liquid obtained from petroleum and coal tar and used in the manufacture of synthetic resins: formula C_9H_8. [INDOLE + -ENE]

indent[1] /in'dent/ *verb trans* **1** to set (a line of text, a paragraph, etc) in from the margin. **2** to notch the edge of (something). **3a** to draw up (a legal document) in two or more exact copies. **b** in former times, to cut or divide (a document drawn up in duplicate, triplicate, etc) to produce two or more copies with edges that can be lined up to ensure their authenticity. **4** *chiefly Brit* to make an official requisition or order for (something). ⟩ *verb intrans* **1** to form an indentation. **2** *chiefly Brit* (*often* + on/for) to make an official requisition or order. ⟫⟫ **indenter** *noun.* [Middle English *indenten* from early French *endenter*, from EN-[1] + *dent* tooth, from Latin *dent-*, *dens*]

indent[2] /'indent/ *noun* **1** = INDENTATION. **2** = INDENTURE[1]. **3** *chiefly Brit* an official requisition or order.

indent[3] /in'dent/ *verb trans* to make a dent or depression in (a surface). ⟫⟫ **indenter** *noun.* [Middle English *endenten*, from EN-[1] + *denten* to dent]

indent[4] /'indent/ *noun* a dent or depression.

indentation /inden'taysh(ə)n/ *noun* **1a** an angular cut or series of cuts in an edge. **b** a deep recess in a coastline. **2** the blank space produced by indenting a line of text, etc. **3** the act of indenting or the state of being indented.

indenture[1] /in'denchə/ *noun* **1a** an indented document, *esp* an agreement, contract, etc. **b** (*also in pl*) a contract binding somebody, *esp* an apprentice, to work for another. **2a** a formal certificate, e.g. an inventory or voucher, prepared for purposes of control. **b** a document stating the terms under which a security is issued. ⟫⟫ **indentureship** *noun.*

indenture[2] *verb trans* to bind (an apprentice) by an indenture.

independent[1] /indi'pend(ə)nt/ *adj* **1a** not affiliated with a larger controlling unit: *an independent bookshop.* **b** not connected with or relying on something else: *an independent conclusion.* **c** not committed to a political party: *standing as an independent candidate.* **d** not requiring or relying on others, or allowing oneself to be controlled by them: *a very independent child.* **e** having or providing enough money to live on, *esp* without working: *people of independent means.* **2** said of a country: self-governing and free of external control. **3** in logic, unrelated to another statement: *independent postulates.* **4** (**Independent**) in former times, relating or belonging to the Congregational Church. ⟫⟫ **independence** *noun*, **independency** *noun*, **independently** *adv.*

independent[2] *noun* **1** somebody who is independent, *esp* of any political party. **2** (**Independent**) in former times, a member of the Congregational Church.

independent school *noun* a school providing full-time education without support from government or local authority funds.

independent variable *noun* a mathematical variable whose value determines that of another variable in an equation or statement.

in-depth *adj* **1** comprehensively detailed and thorough: *an in-depth study.* **2** searching: *in-depth questions.*

indescribable /indi'skriebəbl/ *adj* **1** unable to be put into words: *an indescribable sensation.* **2** beyond adequate description: *indescribable joy; a scene of indescribable horror.* ⟫⟫ **indescribability** /-'biliti/ *noun*, **indescribably** *adv.*

indestructible /indi'struktəbl/ *adj* impossible to destroy. ⟫⟫ **indestructibility** /-'biliti/ *noun*, **indestructibly** *adv.*

indeterminable /indi'tuhminəbl/ *adj* incapable of being definitely decided or ascertained.

indeterminate /indi'tuhminət/ *adj* **1** not definitely or precisely determined or fixed; vague. **2a** said of mathematical equations: having an infinite number of solutions. **b** being a mathematical expression of undefined value. ⟫⟫ **indeterminacy** /-si/ *noun*, **indeterminately** *adv*, **indeterminateness** *noun*, **indetermination** /-'naysh(ə)n/ *noun.* [Middle English *indeterminat* from late

Latin *indeterminatus*, from IN-¹ + Latin *determinatus*, past part. of *determinare*: see DETERMINE]

indeterminism /indi'tuhminiz(ə)m/ *noun* a theory that actions and choices are not determined by previous physical or mental events. ➤➤ **indeterminist** *noun,* **indeterministic** /-'nistik/ *adj.*

index¹ /'indeks/ *noun (pl* **indexes** *or* **indices** /'indiseez/) **1a** an alphabetical list of names, topics, etc mentioned in a printed work indicating the page number or numbers where the items appear. **b** = CARD INDEX. **c** any systematic guide or list to aid reference, e.g. a catalogue of publications. **2** a device, e.g. a pointer on a scale, that indicates a value or quantity. **3** something that indicates or demonstrates a fact or circumstance: *The strength of a currency is an index of economic performance.* **4** a mathematical figure, letter, or expression, esp an exponent. **5** in printing, a character in the form of a pointing hand that directs a reader to a note, cross-reference, etc. **6a** a number derived from a series of observations and used as an indicator or measure: *the cost-of-living index.* **b** = INDEX NUMBER. [Latin *indic-, index* forefinger, informer, guide, from *indicare*: see INDICATE]

Usage note
indexes *or* **indices**? The plural of *index* in its common sense of an alphabetical list or catalogue is *indexes* (*a book with two indexes; card indexes*). In technical uses, e.g. in mathematics and economics, the plural is more commonly *indices: indices of economic progress.*

index² *verb trans* **1a** to provide (e.g. a book) with an index. **b** to list (an item) in an index. **2** to serve as an index of (something). **3** to cause (something, e.g. a pension) to be index-linked. **4** to cause (a machine or machine part) to move from one position to another in a sequence of repeated operations. ➤ *verb intrans* to prepare an index. ➤➤ **indexer** *noun.*

indexation /indek'saysh(ə)n/ *noun* the act or process of making something, e.g. a pension, index-linked.

index finger *noun* = FOREFINGER.

index futures *pl noun* on the stock exchange, futures (commodities bought or sold for future delivery at an agreed price: see FUTURE¹ (4)) based on projections of prices given in an index of shares.

indexical /in'deksikl/ *adj* **1** relating to or arranged in an index. **2** *dated* = DEICTIC.

index-linked *adj* increasing or decreasing in proportion to a rise or fall in an index, *esp* the cost-of-living index: *an index-linked pension.*

index number *noun* a number used to indicate a change in value, price, etc as compared with the value, price, etc usu taken to be 100, at some earlier time.

India ink /'indi-ə/ *noun NAmer* see INDIAN INK.

Indiaman *noun (pl* **Indiamen**) a ship, *esp* a sailing ship, used in trade with India or the E Indies in former times.

Indian *noun* **1** a native or inhabitant of India. **2** *dated, offensive.* **a** a member of any of the indigenous peoples of N, Central, or S America. **b** any of the languages of these peoples. ➤➤ **Indian** *adj.* [(sense 2) because early explorers of the New World thought they had reached India by a new route]

Indian club *noun* a club shaped like a large bottle that is swung, often in pairs, for gymnastic exercise.

Indian corn *noun chiefly NAmer* = MAIZE.

Indian file *noun* = SINGLE FILE. [from the Native American practice of going through woods in single file]

Indian hemp *noun* = HEMP (1A).

Indian ink (*NAmer* **India ink**) *noun Brit* an ink made from a solid black pigment and used in drawing and lettering: *that part of Anthea's desk where she had long pretended that an arrangement of gum and cardboard painted with Indian ink was a secret drawer* — E Nesbit. [from a belief that it was made in India]

Indian meal *noun* = CORNMEAL.

Indian rope trick *noun* a feat in which somebody supposedly climbs up an unsupported rope.

Indian summer *noun* **1** a period of warm weather in late autumn or early winter. **2** a happy or flourishing period occurring towards the end of a person's life or career. [said to be because it was first noted in areas of North America still inhabited by Native Americans]

Indian wrestling *noun NAmer* = ARM WRESTLING.

India paper *noun* a thin soft opaque paper, used *esp* for proofs of engravings.

India rubber *noun* = RUBBER¹ (1A).

Indic /'indik/ *noun* the branch of the Indo-European languages that includes Sanskrit and related modern languages, e.g. Hindi and Gujarati, spoken in parts of India, Pakistan, and elsewhere. ➤➤ **Indic** *adj.* [via Latin from Greek *indikos* Indian]

indicate /'indikayt/ *verb trans* **1** to point to or point out (something or somebody). **2** to be a sign or symptom of (something). **3** to show or register (something) with or as if with a pointer: *The fuel gauge indicated half-full.* **4** (*usu in passive*) to demonstrate or suggest the necessity or advisability of (something): *Surgery is indicated in extreme cases.* **5** to state or express (something) briefly or indirectly: *to suggest (it).* ➤ *verb intrans* said of a vehicle or its driver: to show an intention to change direction by flashing an indicator. [Latin *indicatus,* past part. of *indicare,* from IN-² + *dicare* to proclaim, dedicate]

indication /indi'kaysh(ə)n/ *noun* **1** a sign, suggestion, etc that serves to indicate something. **2** the degree, quantity, etc indicated on a graduated instrument, a reading. **3** something indicated as advisable or necessary. **4** the action of indicating.

indicative¹ /in'dikətiv/ *adj* **1** (*usu* + of) serving to indicate: *His actions were indicative of fear.* **2** in grammar, of or being the mood that represents the denoted act or state as an objective fact. ➤➤ **indicatively** *adv.*

indicative² *noun* the indicative mood or a verb form expressing this.

indicator *noun* **1a** a hand or needle on a graduated instrument. **b** an instrument for giving visual readings attached to a machine or apparatus. **c** a flashing light or other device on a vehicle that is used to show the driver's intention to change direction. **d** a screen at a railway station or airport showing details of arrivals and departures. **2a** a substance that shows, *esp* by change of colour, the condition of a solution, the presence of a particular material, or the end point of a chemical reaction: *Litmus is an indicator of acidity or alkalinity.* **b** = TRACER (2). **3** something that gives an indication, e.g. a statistic that indicates the state of a national economy. **4** a plant or animal species that is known to prefer particular environmental conditions and therefore indicates the existence of those conditions by its presence. ➤➤ **indicatory** /in'dikət(ə)ri/ *adj.*

indices /'indiseez/ *noun* pl of INDEX¹.

Usage note
indices *or* **indexes**? See note at INDEX¹.

indicia /in'dishi·ə/ *pl noun formal* distinctive marks; indications. [Latin *indicia,* pl of *indicium* sign, from *indicare*: see INDICATE]

indict /in'diet/ *verb trans* to charge (somebody) with an offence, *esp* a serious crime. ➤➤ **indictable** *adj,* **indictee** /-'ee/ *noun,* **indicter** *noun,* **indictor** *noun.*

Word history
alteration of *indite,* from Middle English *inditen* via Anglo-French *enditer* from Latin *indictus*: see INDITE. The *c* was added in the 17th cent. to conform with the Latin spelling, but has never been pronounced.

indictable offence *noun* a serious crime that must be tried before a jury.

indictment *noun* **1** a formal written accusation by a prosecuting authority. **2** (+ of) grounds for severe censure or condemnation of something: *The number of young children left to fend for themselves is a searing indictment of contemporary society.*

indie /'indi/ *noun informal* **1a** a small independent film or record company, *esp* one that produces films or music considered more avant-garde than those of the main commercial companies. **b** (*used before a noun*) relating to or produced by such a film or record company. **2a** a type of melodic guitar-based popular music. **b** (*used before a noun*) relating to this type of music or the culture, clothes, etc associated with it. [short for INDEPENDENT²]

indifference /in'dif(ə)rəns/ *noun* **1** the state of being indifferent: *The opposite of love is not hate, it's indifference* — Elie Wiesel. **2** absence of interest or importance: *It's a matter of complete indifference to me.*

indifferent /in'dif(ə)rənt/ *adj* **1** mediocre or poor: *We ate cheese and drank an indifferent wine.* **2** (*often* + to) not interested or concerned: *I'm completely indifferent to the outcome.* **3** making little or no difference one way or the other. ➤➤ **indifferently** *adv.* [Middle English via French from Latin *indifferent-, indifferens* neither good nor bad, from IN-¹ + *different-, differens*, present part. of *differre*: see DIFFER]

indifferentism *noun* the belief that all religions are equally valid. ⟫ **indifferentist** *noun*.

indigenous /in'dijənəs/ *adj* **1** originating, growing, or living naturally in a particular region or environment; native: *A bird that is indigenous to Australia; indigenous moorland plants.* **2** innate; inborn. ⟫ **indigenously** *adv,* **indigenousness** *noun.* [late Latin *indigenus* from Latin *indigena* a native, from Old Latin *indu, endo* in, within + Latin *gignere* to beget]

indigent¹ /'indij(ə)nt/ *adj* very needy or poor. ⟫ **indigence** *noun.* [Middle English via French from Latin *indigent-, indigens,* present part. of *indigēre* to need, from Old Latin *indu* in, within + Latin *egēre* to need]

indigent² *noun* an indigent person.

indigestible /indi'jestəbl/ *adj* **1** not able to be digested or difficult to digest. **2** difficult to understand, read, take in, etc: *an indigestible mass of facts.* ⟫ **indigestibility** /-'biliti/ *noun,* **indigestibly** *adv.* [late Latin *indigestibilis,* from IN-¹ + *digestibilis* digestible, from Latin *digerere*: see DIGEST²]

indigestion /indi'jeschən/ *noun* difficulty in digesting something, or the pain or discomfort resulting from this.

indignant /in'dignənt/ *adj* filled with or marked by indignation. ⟫ **indignantly** *adv.* [Latin *indignant-, indignans,* present part. of *indignari* to be indignant, from *indignus* unworthy, from IN-¹ + *dignus* worthy]

indignation /indig'naysh(ə)n/ *noun* anger aroused by something judged unjust, unworthy, or mean.

indignity /in'digniti/ *noun* (*pl* **indignities**) **1** an act that causes a loss of dignity or self-respect. **2** humiliating treatment. [Latin *indignitat-, indignitas,* from *indignus*: see INDIGNANT]

indigo /'indigoh/ *noun* (*pl* **indigos** or **indigoes**) **1** a dark greyish blue colour, between blue and violet in the spectrum. **2a** a dark blue dye formerly obtained from plants and now made artificially. **b** any of a genus of tropical plants of the pea family that yield this dye: genus *Indigofera.* ⟫ **indigo** *adj.* [Italian dialect *indigo* via Latin *indicum* from Greek *indikon,* neuter of *indikos*: see INDIC]

indirect /indi'rekt, indie'rekt/ *adj* **1a** deviating from a direct line or course; circuitous: *We took an indirect route.* **b** not going straight to the point: *Your essay is flawed by an indirect approach to the question.* **2** not being a direct cause or consequence of something: *indirect benefits.* **3** not straightforward or open; evasive or deceitful. **4** said of a free kick in football: not permitting the direct scoring of a goal. ⟫ **indirection** *noun,* **indirectly** *adv,* **indirectness** *noun.* [Middle English from medieval Latin *indirectus,* from IN-¹ + Latin *directus*: see DIRECT¹]

indirect costs *pl noun* = FIXED COSTS.

indirect object *noun* a grammatical object representing a person or thing that is indirectly affected by the action of a transitive verb, e.g. *her* in *I gave her the book.*

indirect question *noun* in grammar, a question in indirect speech, e.g. *He asked if I'd ever been to New York before.*

indirect speech *noun* in grammar, the reporting of something previously said with appropriate changes of tense, person, etc, e.g. *I told him I'd never been to New York before*: compare DIRECT SPEECH. Also called REPORTED SPEECH.

indirect tax *noun* a tax levied on goods, services, etc and paid indirectly by a person or organization purchasing these goods or services at an increased price: compare DIRECT TAX.

indiscernible /indi'suhnəbl/ *adj* **1** not able to be perceived or recognized. **2** not recognizable as separate or distinct. ⟫ **indiscernibly** *adv.*

indiscipline /in'disiplin/ *noun* lack of discipline. ⟫ **indisciplined** *adj.*

indiscreet /indi'skreet/ *adj* not discreet, *esp* in revealing secret or private things. ⟫ **indiscreetly** *adv.* [Middle English *indiscrete* via French and late Latin from Latin *indiscretus* indistinguishable, from IN-¹ + *discretus*: see DISCREET]

indiscrete /indi'skreet/ *adj* not separated into distinct parts. [Latin *indiscretus*: see INDISCREET]

indiscretion /indi'skresh(ə)n/ *noun* lack of discretion, or an act or remark that shows this.

indiscriminate /indi'skriminət/ *adj* **1** not marked by careful distinction; random. **2** lacking in discrimination and discernment. **3** not differentiated; confused. ⟫ **indiscriminately** *adv,* **indiscriminateness** *noun,* **indiscrimination** /-'naysh(ə)n/ *noun.*

indispensable¹ /indi'spensəbl/ *adj* essential; not able to be done without. ⟫ **indispensability** /-'biliti/ *noun,* **indispensableness** *noun,* **indispensably** *adv.*

indispensable² *noun* something or somebody indispensable.

indispose /indi'spohz/ *verb trans* **1** to make (somebody or something) unfit. **2** (*usu* + to) to make (somebody or something) averse or unwilling to do something. [prob back-formation from INDISPOSED]

indisposed *adj* **1** slightly ill. **2** (*usu* + to) averse or unwilling to do something: *He seems indisposed to help.* ⟫ **indisposition** /-'zish(ə)n/ *noun.* [Middle English in the senses 'not prepared for, unfitted' from IN-¹ + DISPOSED]

indisputable /indi'spyoohtəbl/ *adj* incontestable; not able to be denied or called into question. ⟫ **indisputability** /-'biliti/ *noun,* **indisputableness** *noun,* **indisputably** *adv.* [late Latin *indisputabilis,* from IN-¹ + Latin *disputabilis* disputable, from *disputare*: see DISPUTE¹]

indissoluble /indi'solyoobl/ *adj* incapable of being dissolved, undone, or annulled. ⟫ **indissolubility** /-'biliti/ *noun,* **indissolubly** *adv.*

indistinct /indi'stingkt/ *adj* **1** not sharply outlined; not clearly seen: *The host with someone indistinct converses at the door apart* — T S Eliot. **2** not clearly understandable: *indistinct mutterings.* **3** vague or uncertain: *an indistinct recollection.* ⟫ **indistinctly** *adv,* **indistinctness** *noun.* [Latin *indistinctus,* from IN-¹ + *distinctus*: see DISTINCT]

indistinctive /indi'stingktiv/ *adj* lacking distinctive qualities or features.

indistinguishable /indi'stinggwishəbl/ *adj* (*usu* + from) incapable of being clearly identified as different; identical. ⟫ **indistinguishably** *adv.*

indite /in'diet/ *verb trans* **1** *archaic* to put (something) down in writing. **2** to compose (e.g. a poem). [Middle English *enditen* from Old French *enditer* to write down, proclaim, ultimately from Latin *indictus,* past part. of *indicere* to proclaim, from IN-² + *dicere* to say]

indium /'indi-əm/ *noun* a rare silvery soft metallic chemical element that occurs naturally in zinc blendes, and is used in electroplating and as a semi-conductor: symbol In, atomic number 49. [INDIGO + -IUM; from the two indigo-blue lines in its spectrum]

individual¹ /indi'vidyooəl/ *adj* **1** relating to or intended for a single person or thing: *an individual serving.* **2** existing as a distinct entity; separate: *An itemized phone bill lists individual calls.* **3** having unusual or distinguishing features, traits, etc: *an individual style.* ⟫ **individually** *adv.* [medieval Latin *individualis* from Latin *individuus* indivisible, from IN-¹ + *dividuus* divided, from *dividere*: see DIVIDE¹]

individual² *noun* **1a** a particular person or thing, *esp* as distinguished from a group or from others in a group. **b** a single plant or animal, *esp* as distinguished from a species. **2a** a person: *an odd individual.* **b** a person who has unusual or distinguishing characteristics: *She's a real individual.*

individualise *verb trans* see INDIVIDUALIZE.

individualism *noun* **1a** independent self-reliance. **b** self-centredness; egoism. **2a** a doctrine that bases morality on the interests of the individual. **b** a social theory maintaining the political and economic independence of the individual and stressing individual initiative. ⟫ **individualist** *noun and adj,* **individualistic** /-'listik/ *adj.*

individuality /,individyoo'aliti/ *noun* (*pl* **individualities**) **1** the general character or a particular characteristic that distinguishes one person or thing from others: *The twins are beginning to assert their individuality.* **2** the quality of being distinctive or unique. **3** separate or distinct existence.

individualize or **individualise** *verb trans* to make (something) individual; to adapt (it) to a purpose. ⟫ **individualization** /-'zaysh(ə)n/ *noun.*

individuate /indi'vidyooayt/ *verb trans* to give individuality or individual form to (somebody or something); to differentiate or distinguish (them). ⟫ **individuation** /-'aysh(ə)n/ *noun.*

indivisible /indi'vizəbl/ *adj* **1** not able to be separated or divided. **2** said of a number: not able to be divided by another number without leaving a remainder: *Five is indivisible by two.*

Indo- *comb. form* forming words, with the meanings: **1** Indian: *Indo-British.* **2** Indian and: *Indo-African.*

Indo-Aryan /,indoh/ *noun* **1** any of the peoples of India of Indo-European language and Caucasian physique. **2** any of the early Indo-European invaders of Persia, Afghanistan, and India. **3** = INDIC. ⋙ **Indo-Aryan** *adj.*

Indo-Chinese *noun* (*pl* **Indo-Chinese**) **1** a native or inhabitant of Indochina. **2** = SINO-TIBETAN. ⋙ **Indo-Chinese** *adj.*

indoctrinate /in'doktrinayt/ *verb trans* **1** to teach (a person or group) to accept a view, ideology, etc uncritically, *esp* by systematic repetition. **2** *archaic* to instruct (somebody). ⋙ **indoctrination** /-'naysh(ə)n/ *noun,* **indoctrinator** *noun.* [prob from Middle English *endoctrinen* from Old French *endoctriner,* from EN-¹ + *doctrine:* see DOCTRINE]

Indo-European *noun* **1** a family of languages spoken in most of Europe, Asia as far as N India, and N and S America. **2** = PROTO-INDO-EUROPEAN. ⋙ **Indo-European** *adj.*

Indo-Iranian *noun* a subfamily of the Indo-European languages comprising the Indic and the Iranian branches. ⋙ **Indo-Iranian** *adj.*

indole *or* **indol** /'indohl/ *noun* **1** a chemical compound that is present in some plant oils and coal tar and occurs in the faeces as a product of the decomposition of some proteins: formula C_8H_7N. **2** a derivative of such a compound. [INDIGO + Latin *oleum* oil]

indoleacetic acid /,indohlə'setik/ *noun* a plant hormone that promotes growth and rooting of plants.

indolent /'indələnt/ *adj* **1a** averse to activity, effort, or movement; lazy. **b** conducive to laziness: *indolent weather.* **2a** causing little or no pain. **b** slow to develop or heal: *an indolent ulcer.* ⋙ **indolence** *noun,* **indolently** *adv.* [late Latin *indolent-, indolens* insensitive to pain, from IN-¹ + Latin *dolent-, dolens,* present part. of *dolēre* to feel pain]

indomitable /in'domitəbl/ *adj* incapable of being subdued: *indomitable courage.* ⋙ **indomitability** /-'biliti/ *noun,* **indomitably** *adv.* [late Latin *indomitabilis,* from IN-¹ + Latin *domitare* to tame]

Indonesian /ində'neezh(ə)n, -zi-ən/ *noun* **1** a native or inhabitant of Indonesia or the Malay archipelago. **2** the Austronesian language of the Indonesians. ⋙ **Indonesian** *adj.*

indoor /in'daw/ *adj* **1** relating to the interior of a building. **2** done, situated, or belonging indoors: *an indoor sport; indoor plants.* [alteration (influenced by IN¹) of obsolete *within-door* (adj), from the phrase *within door* in a building]

indoors /in'dawz/ *adv* inside or into a building.

indorse /in'daws/ *verb trans* see ENDORSE.

indorsement *noun* see ENDORSEMENT.

indraught (*NAmer* **indraft**) /'indrahft/ *noun* **1** the act or process of drawing or pulling in. **2** an inward flow or current, *esp* of air or water.

indrawn /in'drawn/ *adj* **1** drawn in. **2** aloof, reserved, or introspective.

indri /'indri/ *noun* (*pl* **indris**) a large Madagascan lemur with black and white markings and a short tail: *Indri indri.*

Word history

French *indri* from Malagasy *indry* look!. It is reported, apparently reliably, that this name arose from a misapprehension by the French naturalist Pierre Sonnerat, who visited Madagascar in the 1780s. When the animal came into sight, Sonnerat's Malagasy escorts cried *indry!* (= look!), which he mistook for the name of the animal. The true Malagasy name is *babakoto.*

indubitable /in'dyoohbitəbl/ *adj* too evident to be doubted or called into question: *This evening I had not proceeded a hundred yards, before finding indubitable signs of the recent presence of the tiger —* Darwin. ⋙ **indubitability** /-'biliti/ *noun,* **indubitably** *adv.* [via French from Latin *indubitabilis,* from IN-¹ + *dubitabilis* open to doubt, from *dubitare* to DOUBT¹]

induce /in'dyoohs/ *verb trans* **1** to persuade or influence (somebody) to do something: *My being charming ... is not enough to induce me to marry; I must find other people charming – one other person at least —* Jane Austen. **2a** to cause or bring about (something). **b** to cause (labour) to begin, *esp* by the use of drugs. **c** to produce (an electric charge, magnetism, etc) by induction. **3** to establish

(something) by logical induction; *specif* to infer (a general principle) from particular cases: compare DEDUCE. ⋙ **inducer** *noun,* **inducible** *adj.* [Middle English *inducen* from Latin *inducere,* from IN-² + *ducere* to lead]

inducement *noun* **1a** something that induces, *esp* a motive or consideration that encourages somebody to do something. **b** *euphem* a bribe. **2** in law, introductory statements outlining the case in a dispute.

induct /in'dukt/ *verb trans* **1** to install (somebody) formally into office. **2** to introduce or initiate (somebody). **3** *NAmer* to enrol (somebody) for military training or service. **4** = INDUCE (2C). [Middle English *inducten* from medieval Latin *inductus,* past part. of Latin *inducere:* see INDUCE]

inductance *noun* **1a** a property of an electric circuit by which an electromotive force is induced in it by a variation of current, either in the circuit itself or in a neighbouring circuit. **b** the amount of inductance of an electric circuit. **2** a circuit or device possessing or producing inductance.

induction /in'duksh(ə)n/ *noun* **1a** the act or process of inducting, *esp* of installing somebody formally into office. **b** an initial experience or initiation; *specif* preparatory training or a formal introduction, e.g. for new employees. **2a** the act or an instance of reasoning from particular premises to a general conclusion, or a conclusion reached by such reasoning. **b** mathematical demonstration of the validity of a law concerning all the positive integers, by proving that if it holds for all the integers preceding a given integer, it must hold for the given integer. **3** the act or process of inducing something, *esp* labour. **4a** the production of an electric charge, magnetism, or an electromotive force in an object by the proximity of, but not contact with, a similarly energized body. **b** the process of drawing the fuel-air mixture from the carburettor into the combustion chamber of an internal-combustion engine.

induction coil *noun* a transformer, used *esp* in the ignition systems of road vehicles, that produces intermittent pulses of high-voltage alternating current from low-voltage direct current.

induction heating *noun* **1** the process of creating heat in a conducting material by inducing electrical currents within it. **2** the heat produced by doing this.

induction loop system *or* **induction loop** *noun* in public buildings, *esp* theatres, cinemas, etc, a system of sound distribution within a designated area encircled by a loop of wire that sends out electromagnetic signals which are picked up by people wearing hearing aids or earphones.

inductive /in'duktiv/ *adj* **1** relating to or employing logical or mathematical induction. **2** relating to or involving electrical or magnetic induction. **3** bringing about, causing, or inducing. ⋙ **inductively** *adv,* **inductiveness** *noun.*

inductor *noun* a component that is included in an electrical circuit to provide inductance, *esp* one that consists of a coiled conductor. Also called CHOKE².

indue /in'dyooh/ *verb trans* see ENDUE.

indulge /in'dulj/ *verb trans* **1a** to give free rein to (a taste, desire, etc): *She now has the money to indulge her passion for antiques.* **b** to allow (oneself) to do or have something pleasurable or gratifying. **2** to treat (somebody) with great or excessive leniency, generosity, etc; to pamper or spoil (them): *He tends to indulge the kids.* ⋙ *verb intrans* (*often* + in) to allow oneself to do or have something enjoyable. ⋙ **indulger** *noun.* [Latin *indulgēre* to be complaisant]

indulgence *noun* **1** the act or an instance of indulging. **2** something indulged in; a luxury: *Cream cakes are such an indulgence.* **3** leniency or tolerance. **4** in the Roman Catholic Church, remission of all or part of the punishment that is due, *esp* in purgatory, for pardoned sins.

indulgent *adj* indulging or characterized by indulgence. ⋙ **indulgently** *adv.* [Latin *indulgent-, indulgens,* present part. of *indulgēre* to be complaisant]

induna /in'doohnə/ *noun* in South Africa, a black African working as a supervisor in a factory, mine, etc. [Zulu *in-duna* official, councillor, chief]

indurate /'indyooərayt/ *verb trans* **1** to make (somebody) unfeeling or obdurate. **2** to make (e.g. a plant) hardy. **3** to make (something) hard. ⋙ *verb intrans* to become hard or hardened. ⋙ **induration** /-'raysh(ə)n/ *noun,* **indurative** /in'dyooərətiv/ *adj.* [Latin *induratus,* past part. of *indurare,* from IN-² + *durare* to harden, from *durus* hard]

indusium /in'dyoohzi·əm/ *noun* (*pl* **indusia** /-zi·ə/) **1** in plants, a covering outgrowth or membrane, *esp* over a cluster of fern spores. **2** in animals, an enveloping layer or membrane. [Latin *indusium* tunic]

industrial[1] /in'dustri·əl/ *adj* **1** relating to, involved in, or derived from industry. **2** characterized by highly developed industries: *an industrial nation*. **3** used in industry: *industrial diamonds*. **4** *informal* very large: *She goes through industrial quantities of coffee and breakfast cereals.* ⟫ **industrially** *adv*.

industrial[2] *noun* (*usu in pl*) a share or bond issued by an industrial enterprise.

industrial action *noun* a strike, go-slow, work-to-rule, etc by a body of workers, *esp* in industry.

industrial archaeology *noun* the scientific study of the products and remains of past industrial activity.

industrial diamond *noun* a small diamond of inferior quality, often synthetically produced, used in cutting tools, drills, abrasives, etc.

industrial espionage *noun* acquiring or attempting to acquire secret information about the products or processes of a rival company, e.g. by infiltrating the workforce with spies.

industrial estate *noun chiefly Brit* an area, often on the edge of a city or town, designed for a community of industries and businesses.

industrialise /in'dustri·əliez/ *verb trans* see INDUSTRIALIZE.

industrialism *noun* an economic or social organization in which manufacturing industries, *esp* large-scale mechanized industries, are dominant.

industrialist *noun* somebody who is engaged in the management of an industry.

industrialize *or* **industrialise** *verb trans* to cause (something) to become industrial; to introduce industry to (a region). ⟫ *verb intrans* to become industrialized. ⟫ **industrialization** /-'zaysh(ə)n/ *noun*.

industrial park *noun NAmer* = INDUSTRIAL ESTATE.

industrial relations *pl noun* the dealings or relationships between the management of a business or industrial enterprise and the employees or their trade unions.

Industrial Revolution *noun* (**the Industrial Revolution**) the transformation from a mainly agricultural economy to one based on industrial production that took place in Britain and other countries during the 18th and 19th cents. [coined by Arnold Toynbee d.1883, English academic and historian]

industrial-strength *adj* very strong or powerful; suitable for use in industry: *industrial-strength cleaning fluid*.

industrial tribunal *noun* an official tribunal set up to handle legal disputes, e.g. allegations of unfair dismissal, between employers and employees.

industrious /in'dustri·əs/ *adj* conscientious and hard-working. ⟫ **industriously** *adv*, **industriousness** *noun*.

industry /'indəstri/ *noun* (*pl* **industries**) **1a** economic activity that is concerned with the manufacture of goods, the processing of raw materials, construction work, etc. **b** a specified branch of this: *the car industry*. **c** any activity that generates employment: *the tourist industry*. **2** hard-working diligence: *The boss praised their accuracy and industry*. [early French *industrie* skill, employment involving skill, from Latin *industria* diligence, from *industrius* diligent, from Old Latin *indostruus*, from *indu* in + -*struus* building]

indwell /in'dwel/ *verb trans* (*past tense and past part.* **indwelt** /-'dwelt/) said of a spirit, force, principle, etc: to exist within (a person or group). ⟫ **indweller** /'in-/ *noun*.

Indy /'indi/ *noun* a type of high-speed motor racing that involves specially adapted cars doing many laps of a regular oval track with steeply banked sides. [named after *Indianapolis*, US city where the first race of this kind was held in 1911 and which continues to host the most famous race in this class]

-ine[1] *suffix* forming adjectives, denoting: **1** resemblance: *feminine*; *saturnine*. **2** membership of a group, *esp* a genus or family of animals: *canine*; *passerine*. **3** composition: *crystalline*. [Middle English -*in*, -*ine* from early French -*in* and from Latin -*īnus*, from Greek -*inos*]

-ine[2] *suffix* forming nouns, denoting: **1a** a chemical compound: *gasoline*. **b** a carbon compound, e.g. an amino acid or alkaloid, that

is a chemical base and contains nitrogen: *atropine*; *morphine*; *leucine*; *glycine*. **c** a mixture of compounds, e.g. of hydrocarbons: *kerosine*. **d** a usu gaseous hydride: *arsine*. **2** a feminine form: *heroine*. [Middle English -*ine*, -*in* from early French -*ine* from Latin -*īna*, fem of -*inus* of or belonging to]

inebriate[1] /in'eebriayt/ *verb trans* said *esp* of alcohol: to intoxicate (somebody). ⟫ **inebriated** *adj*, **inebriation** /-'aysh(ə)n/ *noun*, **inebriety** /ini'brieiti/ *noun*. [Latin *inebriatus*, past part. of *inebriare*, from IN-[2] + *ebriare* to intoxicate, from *ebrius* drunk]

inebriate[2] /in'eebri·ət/ *adj* drunk, *esp* habitually.

inebriate[3] /in'eebri·ət/ *noun* somebody who is drunk, *esp* habitually.

inedible /in'edəbl/ *adj* not fit to be eaten. ⟫ **inedibility** /-'biliti/ *noun*.

ineducable /in'edyookəbl/ *adj* incapable of being educated, *esp* because of low intelligence or disruptive behaviour. ⟫ **ineducability** /-'biliti/ *noun*.

ineffable /in'efəbl/ *adj* **1a** too great or intense to be expressed; inexpressible: *At Oxford he distinguished himself, to his father's ineffable satisfaction* — Henry James. **b** unspeakable: *What ineffable twaddle!* — Conan Doyle. **2** too sacred to be uttered: *His ineffable effable effanineffable deep and inscrutable singular name* — T S Eliot. ⟫ **ineffability** /-'biliti/ *noun*, **ineffably** *adv*. [Middle English via French from Latin *ineffabilis*, from IN-[1] + *effabilis* capable of being expressed, from *effari* to speak out, from EX-[1] + *fari* to speak]

ineffective /ini'fektiv/ *adj* **1** not producing an effect or the intended effect. **2** not capable of performing efficiently or achieving results. ⟫ **ineffectively** *adv*, **ineffectiveness** *noun*.

ineffectual /ini'fektyooəl/ *adj* **1** unable to get things done; weak in character: *a very ineffectual person*. **2** not producing or not able to produce an effect or the proper or intended effect. ⟫ **ineffectuality** /-'aliti/ *noun*, **ineffectually** *adv*, **ineffectualness** *noun*.

inefficacy /in'efikəsi/ *noun* lack of power to produce a desired effect. ⟫ **inefficacious** /-'kayshəs/ *adj*. [late Latin *inefficacia*, from Latin *inefficac-, inefficax* ineffective, from IN-[1] + *efficac-, efficax*: see EFFICACIOUS]

inefficient /ini'fish(ə)nt/ *adj* failing to work, operate, etc in a capable or economical way. ⟫ **inefficiency** /-si/ *noun*, **inefficiently** *adv*.

inelastic /ini'lastik/ *adj* **1** inflexible; unyielding. **2** said of supply or demand: slow to react or respond to changing economic conditions. **3** in physics, denoting a collision between particles in which part of the kinetic energy of the colliding particles changes into another form of energy. ⟫ **inelasticity** /-'stisiti/ *noun*.

inelegant /in'eligənt/ *adj* lacking in refinement, grace, or good taste. ⟫ **inelegance** *noun*, **inelegantly** *adv*. [via French from Latin *inelegant-, inelegans*, from IN-[1] + *elegant-, elegans* ELEGANT]

ineligible /in'elijəbl/ *adj* not qualified or able to receive or do something. ⟫ **ineligibility** /-'biliti/ *noun*. [French *inéligible*, from IN-[1] + *éligible*: see ELIGIBLE]

ineluctable /ini'luktəbl/ *adj formal* unavoidable; inescapable. ⟫ **ineluctability** /-'biliti/ *noun*, **ineluctably** *adv*. [Latin *ineluctabilis*, from IN-[1] + *eluctari* to struggle out, from EX-[1] + *luctari* to struggle]

inept /i'nept/ *adj* **1** incompetent or clumsy. **2** not suitable or appropriate to the time, place, or occasion. **3** lacking sense or reason. ⟫ **ineptitude** /-'tityoohd/ *noun*, **ineptly** *adv*, **ineptness** *noun*. [French *inepte* from Latin *ineptus*, from IN-[1] + *aptus*: see APT]

inequality /ini'kwoliti/ *noun* (*pl* **inequalities**) **1** the state or an instance of being unequal; lack of equality. **2a** social or economic disparity. **b** disparity of distribution or opportunity. **3** in mathematics: **a** a formal statement of inequality between two expressions. **b** a symbol denoting inequality, e.g. (≠) meaning 'is not equal to', (<) meaning 'is less than', or (>) meaning 'is greater than'. **4** *archaic* lack of evenness, smoothness, or regularity. [early French *inequalité* from Latin *inaequalitat-, inaequalitas*, from *inaequalis* unequal, from IN-[1] + *aequalis*: see EQUAL[1]]

inequitable /in'ekwitəbl/ *adj* unfair or unjust. ⟫ **inequitably** *adv*.

inequity /in'ekwiti/ *noun* (*pl* **inequities**) injustice or unfairness, or an instance of this.

ineradicable /ini'radikəbl/ *adj* incapable of being eradicated. ⟫ **ineradicably** *adv*.

inert /i'nuht/ *adj* **1** lacking the power to move. **2** lacking active chemical or biological properties. **3** not moving; inactive or indolent. **⋙ inertly** *adv*, **inertness** *noun*. [Latin *inert-, iners* unskilled, idle, from IN-¹ + *art-, ars* skill, ART¹]

inert gas *noun* = NOBLE GAS.

inertia /i'nuhshə/ *noun* **1** a tendency to resist motion, exertion, or change. **2a** in physics, a property of matter by which it remains at rest or in uniform motion in the same straight line unless acted on by some external force. **b** an analogous property of other physical quantities, e.g. electricity. **⋙ inertial** *adj*. [Latin *inertia*, from *inert-, iners*: see INERT]

inertial guidance /i'nuhshəl/ *noun* a means of controlling the flight path of a missile, spacecraft, or aircraft, using equipment that measures inertial forces within the craft.

inertial navigation *noun* = INERTIAL GUIDANCE.

inertia-reel seat belt *noun* a seat belt that allows steady unwinding to accommodate slow body movements but resists a sudden sharp jerk by locking the drum.

inertia selling *noun chiefly Brit* the illegal practice of sending unsolicited goods to people with the intention of demanding payment if the goods are not returned.

inescapable /ini'skaypəbl/ *adj* incapable of being avoided, ignored, or denied. **⋙ inescapably** *adv*.

inessential¹ /ini'sensh(ə)l/ *adj* not absolutely necessary.

inessential² *noun* something that is not absolutely necessary.

inestimable /in'estiməbl/ *adj* **1** too great in number or amount to be estimated. **2** too valuable or excellent to be measured. **⋙ inestimably** *adv*. [Middle English via French from Latin *inaestimabilis*, from IN-¹ + *aestimabilis* estimable, from *aestimare* to ESTIMATE¹]

inevitable¹ /in'evitəbl/ *adj* incapable of being avoided; bound to happen. **⋙ inevitability** /-'biliti/ *noun*, **inevitableness** *noun*, **inevitably** *adv*. [Middle English from Latin *inevitabilis*, from IN-¹ + *evitabilis* avoidable, from *evitare* to avoid]

inevitable² *noun* (**the inevitable**) something that is unavoidable or bound to happen.

inexact /iniq'zakt/ *adj* not precisely correct or true. **⋙ inexactitude** /-tityoohd/ *noun*, **inexactly** *adv*, **inexactness** *noun*.

inexcusable /inik'skyoohzəbl/ *adj* too bad to be excused or justified. **⋙ inexcusableness** *noun*, **inexcusably** *adv*. [Latin *inexcusabilis*, from IN-¹ + *excusabilis* excusable, from *excusare*: see EXCUSE¹]

inexhaustible /inig'zawstəbl/ *adj* **1** said of a supply: incapable of being used up. **2** said of a person: tireless. **⋙ inexhaustibility** /-'biliti/ *noun*, **inexhaustibly** *adv*.

inexorable /in'eks(ə)rəbl/ *adj* **1** not to be persuaded or moved by entreaty. **2** continuing inevitably; unable to be averted: *the inexorable march of time*. **⋙ inexorability** /-'biliti/ *noun*, **inexorably** *adv*. [Latin *inexorabilis*, from IN-¹ + *exorabilis* pliant, from *exorare* to prevail upon, from EX-¹ + *orare* to speak]

inexpedient /inik'speedi·ənt/ *adj* said of a plan or undertaking: difficult or impractical to implement; inadvisable. **⋙ inexpediency** *noun*.

inexpensive /inik'spensiv/ *adj* reasonable in price; cheap. **⋙ inexpensively** *adv*, **inexpensiveness** *noun*.

inexperience /inik'spiəri·əns/ *noun* lack of experience or of the skill or knowledge gained from experience. **⋙ inexperienced** *adj*. [via French from late Latin *inexperientia*, from IN-¹ + Latin *experientia*: see EXPERIENCE¹]

inexpert /in'ekspuht/ *adj* unskilled or lacking knowledge. **⋙ inexpertly** *adv*, **inexpertness** *noun*. [Middle English via French from Latin *inexpertus*, from IN-¹ + *expertus*: see EXPERT¹]

inexpiable /in'ekspi·əbl/ *adj* said of an offence or sin: impossible to atone for; not able to be pardoned.

inexplicable /inik'splikəbl, in'eks-/ *adj* incapable of being explained, interpreted, or accounted for. **⋙ inexplicability** /-'biliti/ *noun*, **inexplicably** *adv*. [via French from Latin *inexplicabilis*, from IN-¹ + *explicabilis* explicable, from *explicare*: see EXPLICATE]

inexpressible /inik'spresəbl/ *adj* not able to be expressed, *esp* in words. **⋙ inexpressibly** *adv*.

inexpressive /inik'spresiv/ *adj* lacking expression or meaning. **⋙ inexpressively** *adv*, **inexpressiveness** *noun*.

in extenso /in ik'stensoh/ *adv* at full length or in full: *The conference report contained every contributor's paper in extenso*. [medieval Latin *in extenso* at a stretch]

inextinguishable /inik'stinggwishəbl/ *adj* unable to be extinguished or suppressed: *inextinguishable bush fires; an inextinguishable thirst to learn*. **⋙ inextinguishably** *adv*.

in extremis /in ik'streemis/ *adv* **1** in extremely difficult circumstances. **2** at the point of death. [Latin *in extremis* in the extremes]

inextricable /in'ekstrikəbl, -'strikəbl/ *adj* **1** said of a difficult situation: impossible to escape from. **2** incapable of being disentangled, untied, or separated: *an inextricable knot*. **⋙ inextricably** *adv*. [via French from Latin *inextricabilis*, from IN-¹ + *extricabilis* extricable, from *extricare*: see EXTRICATE]

INF *abbr* intermediate-range nuclear force or forces.

inf. *abbr* **1** infantry. **2** infinitive. **3** informal.

infallible /in'faləbl/ *adj* **1a** incapable of error. **b** said of the pope: incapable of error in defining dogma.

Editorial note

Infallible in religious contexts denotes the claim made by the Roman Catholic Church to be inspired by the Holy Spirit, such that, even if individual members are mistaken, the Church as a whole is able to define what counts as orthodox belief. As its head, the pope (bishop of Rome) therefore claims as infallible a limited number of formal statements of Catholic belief, issued with the full authority of his office — Dr Mel Thompson.

2 not liable to fail; known to be effective: *an infallible remedy for a hangover*. **⋙ infallibility** /-'biliti/ *noun*, **infallibly** *adv*. [medieval Latin *infallibilis*, from IN-¹ + *fallibilis*: see FALLIBLE]

infamous /'infəməs/ *adj* **1** having a bad reputation; notorious: *an infamous criminal*. **2** disgraceful: *infamous behaviour*. **⋙ infamously** *adv*. [Middle English from Latin *infamis*, from IN-¹ + *fama* FAME]

infamy /'infəmi/ *noun* (*pl* **infamies**) **1** disrepute brought about by something grossly criminal, shocking, or brutal. **2** an extreme and publicly known criminal or evil act.

infancy /'inf(ə)nsi/ *noun* (*pl* **infancies**) **1** early childhood: *Heaven lies about us in our infancy* — Wordsworth. **2** a beginning or early period of existence: *The computer industry was in its infancy*. **3** the legal status of being a minor.

infant /'inf(ə)nt/ *noun* **1** a child in the first period of life: *Lord knows what incommunicable small terrors infants go through* — Margaret Drabble. **2** *Brit* a child at school between the ages of five and seven or eight. **3** somebody who is legally a minor. **4** (*used before a noun*) in an early stage of development: *infant technology*. [Middle English *enfaunt* via French from Latin *infant-, infans* incapable of speech, young, from IN-¹ + *fant-, fans*, present part. of *fari* to speak]

infanta /in'fantə/ *noun* a daughter of a Spanish or Portuguese monarch. [Spanish and Portuguese *infanta*, fem of *infante*: see INFANTE]

infante /in'fanti/ *noun* a younger son of a Spanish or Portuguese monarch. [Spanish and Portuguese *infante* infant, from Latin *infant-, infans*: see INFANT]

infanticide /in'fantisied/ *noun* **1** the act of killing an infant. **2** somebody who does this. **3** the practice in some societies of killing unwanted newborn babies. **⋙ infanticidal** /'siedl/ *adj*. [late Latin *infanticidium* and *infanticida*, from Latin *infant-, infans* (see INFANT) + -I- + -*cidium* and -*cida*: see -CIDE]

infantile /'inf(ə)ntiel/ *adj* **1** relating to or suitable for infants or infancy. **2** *derog* childish or immature: *infantile behaviour*. **3** in an early stage of development. **⋙ infantility** /-'tiliti/ *noun*.

infantile paralysis *noun dated* = POLIOMYELITIS.

infantilism /in'fantiliz(ə)m/ *noun* **1** the persistence or retention of childish physical, mental, or emotional qualities in adult life. **2** a childish act or expression, *esp* one taken to indicate lack of maturity.

infant mortality *noun* the death of a child under the age of one year.

infantry /'inf(ə)ntri/ *noun* (*treated as sing. or pl*) soldiers trained, armed, and equipped to fight on foot. [early French *infanterie* from Old Italian *infanteria*, from *infante* boy, foot soldier, from Latin *infant-, infans*: see INFANT]

infantryman *noun* (*pl* **infantrymen**) an infantry soldier.

infant school *noun Brit* a school for children aged from five to seven or eight.

infarct /in'fahkt, 'infahkt/ *noun* an area of dead tissue, e.g. in the heart or other organ, resulting from obstruction of the blood circulation in that area by a clot, air bubble, etc. ➤➤ **infarcted** *adj.* [Latin *infarctus*, past part. of *infarcire* to stuff in, from IN-² + *farcire* to stuff]

infarction /in'fahksh(ə)n/ *noun* the development of an infarct: *Myocardial infarction can sometimes follow a coronary thrombosis.*

infatuate /in'fatyooayt/ *verb trans* to inspire (somebody) with powerful but often superficial or short-lived feelings of love, desire, etc. ➤➤ **infatuated** *adj*, **infatuation** /-'aysh(ə)n/ *noun.* [Latin *infatuatus*, past part. of *infatuare*, from IN-² + *fatuus* FATUOUS]

infauna /'infawnə/ *noun* aquatic animals living on the bottom, *esp* in a soft sea bed: compare EPIFAUNA. ➤➤ **infaunal** *adj.*

infect /in'fekt/ *verb trans* **1** to contaminate (e.g. air or food) with an agent that causes disease. **2a** to pass on a disease or an agent that causes disease to (somebody or something). **b** said of a pathogenic organism: to invade (an individual or organ) and cause a disease. **3** (*usu* + with) to transmit or pass on to (somebody) an emotion, laughter, etc: *He infected us with his enthusiasm.* **4** said of a computer virus: to invade and damage (a system, program, file, etc). **5** to corrupt or taint (something). ➤➤ **infector** *noun.* [Middle English *infecten* from Latin *infectus*, past part. of *inficere* to stain, from IN-² + *facere* to make, do]

infection /in'feksh(ə)n/ *noun* **1** a contagious or infectious disease, or an agent that causes this. **2a** the act of infecting or the state of being infected. **b** an instance of infecting or being infected. **3** the communication of emotions or qualities through example or contact.

infectious /in'fekshəs/ *adj* **1a** said of a disease: caused and communicable by infection with a micro-organism, e.g. a bacterium or virus: compare CONTAGIOUS. **b** said of a micro-organism: capable of causing disease. **2** readily spread or communicated to others: *infectious excitement.* ➤➤ **infectiously** *adv*, **infectiousness** *noun.*
Usage note
infectious or contagious? See note at CONTAGIOUS.

infectious hepatitis *noun* a highly infectious liver inflammation caused by a virus.

infectious mononucleosis *noun* an acute infectious disease characterized by fever, swollen and painful lymph glands, and an increase in the number of lymphocytes in the blood. Also called GLANDULAR FEVER.

infective /in'fektiv/ *adj* said of a micro-organism: capable of causing or likely to cause disease.

infelicitous /infə'lisitəs/ *adj* not apt; not suitably chosen for the occasion. ➤➤ **infelicitously** *adv.*

infelicity /infə'lisiti/ *noun* (*pl* **infelicities**) **1** an infelicitous act or remark. **2** *archaic* misfortune; unhappiness. [Middle English *infelicite* from Latin *infelicitas*, from *infelic-*, *infelix* unhappy, from IN-¹ + *felic-*, *felix* fruitful, happy]

infer /in'fuh/ *verb* (**inferred, inferring**) ➤ *verb trans* **1** to derive (something) as a conclusion from evidence or premises as opposed to what is explicitly stated. **2** *informal* to suggest or imply (something). ➤ *verb intrans* to draw inferences. ➤➤ **inferable** *adj*, **inferrable** *adj.* [early French *inferer* from Latin *inferre* to carry or bring into, from IN-² + *ferre* to carry]
Usage note
infer or imply? See note at IMPLY.

inference /'inf(ə)rəns/ *noun* **1** the act or process of inferring. **2** something inferred, *esp* a conclusion arrived at by considering the available evidence or premises.

inferential /infə'rensh(ə)l/ *adj* deduced or deducible by inference. ➤➤ **inferentially** *adv.* [medieval Latin *inferentia* inference, from Latin *inferent-, inferens*, present part. of *inferre*: see INFER]

inferior¹ /in'fiəri-ə/ *adj* **1** of low or lower degree or rank. **2** of little or less importance, value, or merit. **3** situated at a lower position. **4a** said of an animal or plant part: situated below, behind, or at the base of another often corresponding part. **b** said of a plant ovary: lying below the petals or sepals. **5** said of a letter or other character: positioned below the line; subscript. **6** said of a planet: nearer the sun than the earth is. ➤➤ **inferiority** /-'oriti/ *noun*, **inferiorly** *adv.* [Middle English from Latin *inferior*, compar of *inferus* low]

inferior² *noun* **1** a person who is lower in rank, standing, ability, intelligence, etc than another or others. **2** in printing, a letter or other character that is positioned below the line, e.g. the number ₂ in H_2O.

inferiority complex *noun* a sense of personal inferiority, either actual or imagined, often resulting in timidity or aggressiveness.

infernal /in'fuhnl/ *adj* **1** of or relating to hell. **2** characteristic of hell or the devil. **3** *informal* dreadful; awful: *an infernal nuisance.* ➤➤ **infernally** *adv.* [Middle English *infernal* from late Latin *infernalis*, from Latin *infernus* hell, literally 'below, underground']

inferno /in'fuhnoh/ *noun* (*pl* **infernos**) **1** a place or a state that resembles or suggests hell, *esp* in intense heat or raging fire. **2** (*often* **the Inferno**) hell. [Italian *inferno* hell, from Latin *infernus*: see INFERNAL]

infertile /in'fuhtiel/ *adj* **1** not capable of producing offspring; sterile. **2** said of land: not capable of sustaining vegetation, *esp* crops; barren. ➤➤ **infertility** /infə'tiliti/ *noun.* [via French from late Latin *infertilis*, from IN-¹ + Latin *fertilis*: see FERTILE]

infest /in'fest/ *verb trans* **1** to spread or swarm in or over (something) in a troublesome or undesirable manner: *Sharks infest these waters.* **2** to live in or on (a host) as a parasite. ➤➤ **infestation** /-'staysh(ə)n/ *noun.* [early French *infester* from Latin *infestare* to attack, from *infestus* hostile]

infeudation /infyooh'daysh(ə)n/ *noun* the act of granting possession of a fief to a vassal under a feudal system.

infibulate /in'fibyoolayt/ *verb trans* to partially close the vagina, the labia majora, or the foreskin by means of a clasp, stitches, etc. ➤➤ **infibulation** /-'laysh(ə)n/ *noun.* [Latin *infibulatus*, past part. of *infibulare*, from IN-² + *fibula* clasp]

infidel /'infidl/ *noun* **1** somebody who opposes or does not believe in a particular religion, *esp* Christianity or Islam. **2** somebody who acknowledges no religious belief. ➤➤ **infidel** *adj.* [early French *infidele*, from Latin *infidelis* unbelieving, unfaithful, from IN-¹ + *fidelis*: see FIDELITY]

infidelity /infi'deliti/ *noun* (*pl* **infidelities**) **1** unfaithfulness or disloyalty, *esp* in marital or sexual matters. **2** lack of belief in a religion.

infield¹ /'infeeld/ *noun* **1** the area of a cricket or baseball field near the wickets or bounded by the bases, or the fielding positions stationed there. **2** a field near a farmhouse. ➤➤ **infielder** *noun.*

infield² /in'field/ *adv* away from the edge of a playing field.

infighting /'infieting/ *noun* **1** prolonged and often bitter dissension among members of a group or organization. **2** fighting or boxing at close quarters. ➤➤ **infighter** *noun.*

infill¹ /'infil/ *verb trans* **1** to fill in (a gap). **2** to build houses between (houses already standing). ➤➤ **infilling** *noun.*

infill² *noun* **1** the act or an instance of infilling. **2a** material used to fill a gap. **b** houses built between those already standing.

infiltrate¹ /'infiltrayt/ *verb trans* **1** to enter or become established in (e.g. an organization) gradually or unobtrusively, often with a hostile intention. **2** said of a fluid: to pass into or through (a substance) by filtering or permeating. ➤➤ **infiltration** /-'traysh(ə)n/ *noun*, **infiltrative** /-tiv/ *adj*, **infiltrator** *noun.*

infiltrate² *noun* something that infiltrates.

infin. *abbr* infinitive.

infinite¹ /'infinət/ *adj* **1** subject to or having no limitations or boundaries in time, space, number, etc: *Some scientists believe the universe to be infinite; He seems to have infinite reserves of energy.* **2** great, immense, or extreme: *Her new boyfriend is an infinite improvement on the last one.* **3a** said e.g. of a mathematical series: able to continue or be continued forever. **b** said of a quantity: too large to have a numerical value assigned to it; unquantifiable. ➤➤ **infiniteness** *noun.* [Middle English *infinit* via French from Latin *infinitus*, from IN-¹ + *finitus*: see FINITE]

infinite² *noun* (**the infinite**) divineness; sublimity.

infinitely *adv* **1** greatly; extremely: *This wine is infinitely better than the previous one.* **2** in a limitless, unrestricted, or immeasurable way: *The new technology offers enormous and infinitely varied possibilities.*

infinitesimal¹ /'infini'tesiml/ *adj* **1** having values arbitrarily close to zero. **2** immeasurably or incalculably small. ➤➤ **infinitesimally** *adv.* [scientific Latin *infinitesimus* infinite in rank, from Latin *infinitus*: see INFINITE¹]

infinitesimal² *noun* an infinitesimal variable or quantity.

infinitesimal calculus *noun* = CALCULUS (2A).

infinitive /in'finətiv/ *noun* the base form of a verb, without inflection, in English sometimes preceded by the particle *to* (e.g. *go, take, to go, to take*): *Would you convey my compliments to the purist who reads your proofs and tell him or her that … when I split an infinitive, God* *damn it, I split it so it will stay split* — Raymond Chandler. **▶▶ infinitival** /in‚fini'tievl/ *adj,* **infinitivally** /infini'tievl·i/ *adv.* [late Latin *infinitivus* unlimited, indefinite, from Latin *infinitus*: see INFINITE[1]]

infinitude /in'finityoohd/ *noun* **1** the quality or state of being infinite. **2** something infinite, *esp* in extent or quantity.

infinity /in'finiti/ *noun* (*pl* **infinities**) **1a** the quality of being infinite. **b** unlimited extent of time, space, etc. **2** a very great number or amount. **3** in mathematics, a value greater than that of any finite quantity. **4** a distance so great that the rays of light from a point or source at that distance may be regarded as parallel.

infirm /in'fuhm/ *adj* **1** physically feeble, *esp* from age. **2** weak in mind, will, or character. **3** not solid or stable; insecure. **▶▶ infirmly** *adv.* [Middle English from Latin *infirmus*, from IN-[1] + *firmus* FIRM[1]]

infirmary /in'fuhməri/ *noun* (*pl* **infirmaries**) usu in proper names: a hospital: *the Royal Infirmary.*

infirmity /in'fuhmiti/ *noun* (*pl* **infirmities**) **1** the state of being infirm. **2** a disease or malady. **3** a moral weakness or defect of character: *Fame is the spur that the clear spirit doth raise (that last infirmity of noble mind) to scorn delights and live laborious days* — Milton.

infix[1] /in'fiks/ *verb trans* **1** to fasten or fix (something) by piercing or thrusting in. **2** to instil or inculcate (a lesson, moral values, etc). **3** in grammar, to insert (an affix) in the middle of a word or root. **▶▶ infixation** /-'saysh(ə)n/ *noun.* [Latin *infixus*, past part. of *infigere*, from IN-[2] + *figere* to fasten]

infix[2] /'infiks/ *noun* an affix inserted in the middle of a word or root: compare PREFIX[1], SUFFIX[1].

in flagrante delicto /in flə'granti di'liktoh/ *adv* in the very act of committing a misdeed; red-handed. [medieval Latin *in flagrante delicto,* literally 'in blazing crime']

inflame /in'flaym/ *verb trans* **1** to set (something) on fire. **2a** to excite or arouse passion or strong feeling in (a person or group). **b** to make (e.g. an emotion or dispute) more heated or violent; to intensify (it). **3** to cause (something) to redden or grow hot: *cheeks inflamed by rage.* **4** to cause inflammation in (body tissue). **▶▶ verb intrans 1** to burst into flame. **2** to become excited or angered. **3** to become affected with inflammation. **▶▶ inflamer** *noun.* [Middle English *enflame* via French from Latin *inflammare,* from IN-[2] + *flamma* FLAME[1]]

inflammable[1] /in'flaməbl/ *adj* **1** capable of being easily ignited and of burning rapidly; flammable. **2** easily excited or angered. **▶▶ inflammability** /-'biliti/ *noun.* [via French from medieval Latin *inflammabilis,* from Latin *inflammare:* see INFLAME]

Usage note ─────────
inflammable *or* **flammable**? See note at FLAMMABLE.

inflammable[2] *noun* something that is inflammable.

inflammation /inflə'maysh(ə)n/ *noun* **1** a response to injury or infection of body tissues marked by local redness, heat, swelling, and pain. **2** the act of inflaming or the state of being inflamed.

inflammatory /in'flamət(ə)ri/ *adj* **1** tending to arouse strong feeling, *esp* anger, indignation, outrage, etc: *inflammatory speeches.* **2** accompanied by or tending to cause inflammation.

inflatable[1] /in'flaytəbl/ *adj* capable of being inflated.

inflatable[2] *noun* an inflatable boat, toy, etc.

inflate /in'flayt/ *verb trans* **1** to swell or distend (something, e.g. a balloon or the lungs) with air or gas. **2** to expand or increase (something) abnormally or excessively. **3** to cause inflation in (e.g. prices or the economy). **▶▶ verb intrans** to become inflated. **▶▶ inflater** *noun,* **inflator** *noun.* [Latin *inflatus,* past part. of *inflare* to blow into, from IN-[2] + *flare* to blow]

inflated *adj* **1** said of speech, writing, opinions, etc: bombastic, exaggerated, or puffed up. **2** expanded or increased to an abnormal or excessive volume or level: *inflated prices.* **3** swollen or distended.

inflation /in'flaysh(ə)n/ *noun* **1** a substantial and continuing rise in the general level of prices, caused by or causing an increase in the supply of money and credit or an expansion of the economy. **2** the act of inflating or the state of being inflated. **3** in some theories of the universe, a sudden period of rapid expansion immediately following the BIG BANG (explosion from which the universe originated). **▶▶ inflationary** *adj.*

inflationary spiral *noun* a continuous rise in prices that is sustained by the tendency of wage increases and cost increases to react on each other.

inflationism /in'flayshəniz(ə)m/ *noun* the policy of economic inflation, *esp* through expansion of currency or bank deposits. **▶▶ inflationist** *noun and adj.*

inflect /in'flekt/ *verb trans* **1** to change the form or ending of (a word) by inflection. **2** to vary the pitch of (a voice or note). **3** *technical* to bend (a line, etc) from a normal or straight course. **▶▶ verb intrans** to become modified by inflection. **▶▶ inflective** /-tiv/ *adj.* [Middle English *inflecten* from Latin *inflectere* to bend, modulate, from IN-[2] + *flectere* to bend]

inflection *or* **inflexion** /in'fleksh(ə)n/ *noun* **1a** in grammar, a change in the form of a word to show its case, gender, number, tense, etc. **b** a form or element, *esp* a suffix, showing such variation. **2** variation in pitch or loudness of the voice. **3** in mathematics, change of curvature from concave to convex or vice versa. **▶▶ inflectional** *adj,* **inflectionally** *adv,* **inflectionless** *adj.*

inflexed /in'flekst/ *adj technical* bent or turned abruptly inwards, downwards, or towards the axis. [Latin *inflexus,* past part. of *inflectere:* see INFLECT]

inflexible /in'fleksəbl/ *adj* **1a** incapable of or resistant to change: *an inflexible attitude.* **b** not variable to suit a particular circumstance: *an inflexible rule.* **2** rigidly firm; not able to be bent. **▶▶ inflexibility** /-'biliti/ *noun,* **inflexibly** *adv.* [Middle English from Latin *inflexibilis,* from IN-[1] + *flexibilis* flexible, from *flectere* to bend]

inflexion /in'flekshən/ *noun Brit* see INFLECTION.

inflict /in'flikt/ *verb trans* (*usu* + on) to force or impose (something unpleasant or painful) on somebody. **▶▶ inflicter** *noun,* **infliction** /-sh(ə)n/ *noun,* **inflictor** *noun.* [Latin *inflictus,* past part. of *infligere,* from IN-[2] + *fligere* to strike]

in-flight *adj* done, occurring, or provided during flight in an aircraft: *in-flight refuelling; in-flight meals.*

inflorescence /inflaw'res(ə)ns/ *noun* **1a** a flower-bearing stem, including stalks and branches, or the arrangement of flowers on a stem. **b** a flower cluster or a solitary flower. **2** the budding and unfolding of blossoms; flowering. **▶▶ inflorescent** *adj.* [scientific Latin *inflorescentia* from late Latin *inflorescent-, inflorescens,* present part. of *inflorescere* to begin to bloom, from IN-[2] + Latin *florescere:* see FLORESCENCE]

inflow /'infloh/ *noun* **1** the act or process of flowing in: *a pipe taking the maximum rate of inflow.* **2** something, e.g. liquid, money, or traffic, that flows, moves, or comes in.

influence[1] /'infloo-əns/ *noun* **1** the act, power, or capacity of causing or producing an effect on somebody or something, *esp* in indirect or intangible ways, or the effect itself. **2** the power to achieve something desired by using wealth or position. **3** somebody or something that has or exerts influence, *esp* in matters of morality and behaviour. **4** an ethereal fluid supposed to flow from the stars and to affect the actions of human beings. **✳ under the influence** *informal* affected by alcohol; drunk: *She was arrested for driving under the influence.* [Middle English via French from medieval Latin *influentia,* from Latin *influent-, influens,* present part. of *influere* to flow in, from IN-[2] + *fluere* to flow]

influence[2] *verb trans* to affect (somebody or something), *esp* by indirect or intangible means.

influent[1] /'inflooh-ənt/ *noun* **1** a tributary stream. **2** an organism that directly affects other flora or fauna in an ecological community. [Middle English *influent* flowing in, from Latin *influent-, influens:* see INFLUENCE[1]]

influent[2] *adj* said e.g. of a tributary: flowing into a river, lake, or sea.

influential /infloo'ensh(ə)l/ *adj* exerting or possessing influence: *Your badinage so airy, your manner arbitrary, are out of place when face to face with an influential fairy* — W S Gilbert. **▶▶ influentially** *adv.*

influenza /infloo'enzə/ *noun* a highly infectious viral disease characterized by sudden onset, fever, severe aches and pains, and inflammation of the mucous membranes lining the respiratory passages; flu. **▶▶ influenzal** *adj.* [Italian *influenza,* literally 'influence', from medieval Latin *influentia:* see INFLUENCE[1]; from the belief that epidemics were due to the influence of the stars]

influx /'influks/ *noun* **1** an arrival of people or things in large numbers. **2** an inflow, *esp* of water into a sea, lake, or river, or the mouth of a tributary where this occurs. [late Latin *influxus,* from Latin, past part. of *influere:* see INFLUENCE[1]]

info /'infoh/ *noun informal* information.

infobahn *noun* = INFORMATION SUPERHIGHWAY. [INFORMATION + AUTOBAHN]

infold /in'fohld/ *verb trans* = ENFOLD.

infomercial /infoh'muhsh(ə)l/ *noun* a television or video commercial in the form of a short documentary. [INFORMATION + COMMERCIAL²]

inform /in'fawm/ *verb trans* **1** to communicate knowledge or information to (somebody). **2** to impart an essential quality or character to (something): *A sense of the absurd informs most of his writing.* ⟩ *verb intrans* **1** to give information or knowledge. **2** (*usu* + against/on) to give the police or other authorities information about a criminal or crime. [Middle English *informen* via French from Latin *informare* to give shape to, from IN-² + *forma* FORM¹]

informal /in'fawml/ *adj* **1** marked by an absence of formality or ceremony: *an informal meeting; informal dress.* **2** said of language: relating or belonging to a style appropriate to conversation rather than formal writing. ⟩⟩ **informality** /-'maliti/ *noun*, **informally** *adv*.

informal vote *noun Aus, NZ* a spoiled or invalid ballot paper.

informant *noun* **1** a person who gives somebody information about something. **2** = INFORMER (1).

information /infə'maysh(ə)n/ *noun* **1a** knowledge obtained from investigation, study, or instruction: *I was brought up to believe that the only thing worth doing was to add to the amount of accurate information in the world* — Margaret Mead. **b** facts or data, *esp* pertaining to a particular subject or regarded as significant. **c** news. **d** a signal or sequence of symbols, e.g. in a radio transmission or computing, that represents data. **2** the communication or reception of facts or ideas. **3** a formal accusation presented to a magistrate. ⟩⟩ **informational** *adj*.

information explosion *noun* the creation and availability of many different sources of information brought about by innovations such as the Internet.

information retrieval *noun* the process of finding and displaying information that is stored electronically, *esp* by accessing it from a computer database or the Internet.

information science *noun* the collection, classification, storage, retrieval, and distribution of recorded knowledge, e.g. on computers or in libraries, or the formal study of this.

information superhighway *noun* an electronic network of information such as the Internet.

information technology *noun* the use of computers, telecommunications, etc in electronically processing, storing, retrieving, and sending information.

information theory *noun* a collection of theories dealing statistically with information, the measurement of its content, and the efficiency of processes by which it is communicated between human beings and machines.

informative /in'fawmətiv/ *adj* conveying information; instructive. ⟩⟩ **informatively** *adv*, **informativeness** *noun*.

informatory /in'fawmət(ə)ri/ *adj* = INFORMATIVE.

informed *adj* **1** possessing or based on possession of information: *an informed opinion.* **2** knowledgeable about matters of contemporary interest.

informer *noun* **1** a person who gives information about a criminal or crime to the police, often for a financial or other reward. **2** = INFORMANT (1).

infotainment /infoh'taynmənt/ *noun* a genre of television broadcasting in which educational or serious topics are presented in an accessible and entertaining format. [INFORMATION + ENTERTAINMENT]

infra /'infrə/ *adv* lower on the same or a following page. [Latin *infra* below]

infra- *prefix* forming words, with the meaning: below: *infrasonic; infrastructure.* [Latin *infra*]

infraction /in'fraksh(ə)n/ *noun* a violation or infringement, *esp* of a law or a person's rights. [Latin *infraction-, infractio,* from *infringere*: see INFRINGE]

infra dig *adj informal* beneath one's dignity; demeaning or humiliating. [short for Latin *infra dignitatem*]

infrangible /in'franjəbl/ *adj formal* **1** not capable of being broken or separated. **2** said of a rule, right, etc: not to be infringed or violated. ⟩⟩ **infrangibility** /-'biliti/ *noun*, **infrangibly** *adv*. [via

French from late Latin *infrangibilis*, from IN-¹ + Latin *frangere* to break]

infrared /infrə'red/ *noun* electromagnetic radiation lying outside the visible spectrum, with a wavelength between red light and microwaves, and commonly perceived as heat. ⟩⟩ **infrared** *adj*.

infrasonic /infrə'sonik/ *adj* relating to, denoting, using, or produced by sound waves or vibrations with a frequency below the lower threshold of human hearing.

infrasound *noun* infrasonic sound waves or vibrations.

infrastructure /'infrəstrukchə/ *noun* **1** the permanent features, e.g. road and rail networks, power supplies, educational institutions, manufacturing outlets, etc, necessary for a country's economic well-being. **2** an underlying foundation or basic framework.

infrequent /in'freekwənt/ *adj* **1** not occurring often; rare. **2** not habitual or persistent. ⟩⟩ **infrequency** /-si/ *noun*, **infrequently** *adv*. [Latin *infrequent-, infrequens,* from IN-¹ + *frequent-, frequens* FREQUENT¹]

infringe /in'frinj/ *verb trans* **1** to encroach on (a right or privilege). **2** to violate (a law, agreement, etc). ⟩ *verb intrans* (*usu* +on/upon) to encroach or trespass on something. ⟩⟩ **infringement** *noun*, **infringer** *noun*. [Latin *infringere,* literally 'to break off', from IN-² + *frangere* to break]

infundibula /infun'dibyoolə/ *noun* pl of INFUNDIBULUM.

infundibular /infun'dibyoolə/ *adj* funnel-shaped.

infundibulum /infun'dibyooləm/ *noun* (*pl* **infundibula** /-lə/) a funnel-shaped body part or cavity, *esp* the mass of tissue that connects the pituitary gland to the brain. [Latin *infundibulum* funnel, from *infundere*: see INFUSE]

infuriate /in'fyooəriayt/ *verb trans* to make (a person or animal) furious; to anger or enrage (them). ⟩⟩ **infuriating** *adj*, **infuriatingly** *adv*. [medieval Latin *infuriatus,* past part. of *infuriare,* from IN-² + Latin *furia*: see FURY]

infuse /in'fyoohz/ *verb trans* **1** to steep (tea, herbs, etc) in liquid without boiling so as to extract the flavour, soluble properties, etc. **2** to imbue or pervade (something): *A pink tinge infused the evening sky.* **3** to instil (a quality or value) in somebody or something. **4** in medicine, to cause (a liquid, *esp* blood or plasma) to flow gradually into a person, vein, etc. ⟩⟩ **infuser** *noun*. [Middle English *infusen* via French from Latin *infusus,* past part. of *infundere* to pour in, from IN-² + *fundere* to pour]

infusible *adj* very difficult or impossible to fuse or melt. ⟩⟩ **infusibility** /-'biliti/ *noun*.

infusion /in'fyoohzh(ə)n/ *noun* **1** the process of infusing. **2** in medicine, the continuous slow introduction of a solution, *esp* blood or plasma, into a person, vein, etc. **3** an extract obtained by infusing: *an infusion of camomile tea.*

-ing¹ *suffix* forming the present participle of verbs, or participial adjectives: *making; gruelling.* [Middle English, alteration of Old English *-ende,* from *-e-,* verb stem vowel + *-nde,* present part. suffix]

-ing² *suffix* forming nouns, denoting: **1** an action or process, or a result of it: *running; a meeting; earnings.* **2** an activity or occupation: *banking; skiing.* **3** materials used in an activity: *scaffolding.* **4** a collection of things: *housing; shipping.* [Old English, suffix forming nouns from verbs]

-ing³ *suffix* forming nouns, denoting: something or somebody of a specified kind: *sweeting.* [Old English; related to Old High German *-ing* belonging to, of thing]

ingenious /in'jeenyəs/ *adj* marked by originality, resourcefulness, and cleverness: *an ingenious solution.* ⟩⟩ **ingeniously** *adv*. [early French *ingenieux* from Latin *ingeniosus,* from *ingenium*: see ENGINE]

Usage note

ingenious *or* ingenuous? These two words are easy to confuse. *Ingenious* means 'clever' or 'effective', especially in an original or surprising way: *an ingenious method of recycling household waste.* *Ingenuous* means 'innocent', 'artless', or 'guileless': *too ingenuous to imagine that they might not mean what they said.*

ingenue *or* **ingénue** /anzhay'nooh (*French* ɛ̃ʒeny)/ *noun* **1** a naive or artless young woman. **2** a female stage role characterized by artless naivety, or a person playing this kind of role. [French *ingénue,* fem of *ingénu* ingenuous, from Latin *ingenuus*: see INGENUOUS]

ingenuity /inji'nyooh·iti/ *noun* **1** resourcefulness, cleverness, or inventiveness. **2** *archaic* ingenuousness. [Latin *ingenuitas* ingenuousness, from *ingenuus*: see INGENUOUS; afterwards influenced in meaning by *ingenious*]

ingenuous /in'jenyoo-əs/ *adj* **1** showing innocent or childlike simplicity. **2** frank; candid. >> **ingenuously** *adv*, **ingenuousness** *noun*. [Latin *ingenuus* native, inborn, from IN-² + *gignere* to beget]
Usage note
ingenuous *or* ingenious? See note at INGENIOUS.

ingest /in'jest/ *verb trans* **1** to take (food or drink) into the body. **2** to absorb (e.g. information). >> **ingestible** *adj*, **ingestion** /-chən/ *noun*, **ingestive** /-tiv/ *adj*. [Latin *ingestus*, past part. of *ingerere* to carry in, from IN-² + *gerere* to bear]

ingle /'ingg(ə)l/ *noun archaic or dialect* an open fire in a room, or the area around an open fireplace. [Scottish Gaelic *aingeal* light, fire]

inglenook /'ingg(ə)lnook/ *noun* an alcove by a large open fireplace, or a seat situated there.

inglorious /in'glawri·əs/ *adj* shameful; ignominious. >> **ingloriously** *adv*. [Latin *inglorius*, from IN-¹ + *gloria* GLORY¹]

ingoing /'ingohing/ *adj* entering.

ingot /'inggət/ *noun* a mass of cast metal, often in the shape of a bar or brick. [Middle English in the sense 'mould for casting metal', prob from IN-² + Old English *goten*, past part. of *gēotan* to pour, cast in metal]

ingraft /'ingrahft/ *verb* see ENGRAFT.

ingrain¹ *or* **engrain** /in'grayn/ *verb trans* **1** to work (something) indelibly into a fibre, fabric, etc. **2** to implant (an idea, moral value, etc) in a person's mind.

ingrain² /'ingrayn/ *adj* said e.g. of fabric: made of fibres that are dyed before being spun into yarn.

ingrained *or* **engrained** *adj* **1** said e.g. of a habit, moral value, etc: firmly and deeply implanted; deep-rooted. **2** said of dirt, stains, etc: thoroughly worked into something: *The carpet was covered in ingrained mud.* **3** having a firmly established attitude or belief: *He's an ingrained pacifist.* >> **ingrainedly** /-nidli/ *adv*.

ingrate¹ /'ingrayt/ *noun formal* an ungrateful person. [Latin *ingratus*, from IN-¹ + *gratus* grateful]

ingrate² /in'grayt/ *adj archaic* ungrateful.

ingratiate /in'grayshiayt/ *verb trans* to gain favour for (e.g. oneself) by deliberate effort: *The politicians tried to ingratiate themselves with the public.* >> **ingratiatingly** *adv*, **ingratiation** /-'aysh(ə)n/ *noun*, **ingratiatory** /-shi·ət(ə)ri/ *adj*. [Latin *in gratiam* into favour, from *in* into + *gratia*: see GRACE¹]

ingratitude /in'gratityoohd/ *noun* forgetfulness or scant recognition of kindness received; lack of gratitude: *Blow, blow, thou winter wind, thou art not so unkind as man's ingratitude* — Shakespeare. [Middle English via French from medieval Latin *ingratitudo*, from IN-¹ + Late Latin *gratitudo*: see GRATITUDE]

ingredient /in'greedi·ənt/ *noun* something that forms a component part of a compound, combination, or mixture, *esp* any of the edible substances that are combined in the preparation of food. [Middle English from Latin *ingredient-*, *ingrediens*, present part. of *ingredi* to go into, from IN-² + *gradi* to go]

ingress /'ingres/ *noun* **1** the act or an instance of entering, e.g. the entering of a substance into a place where it is not wanted. **2** the right of entrance or access. **3** a way in; an entrance. **4** the entering of the sun, moon, or other celestial body into a particular state, e.g. eclipse, or a particular part of the sky. [Middle English from Latin *ingressus*, past part. of *ingredi*: see INGREDIENT]

in-group *noun* a select group within a larger unit, which does not readily admit outsiders.

ingrowing /'ingrohing/ *adj* said *esp* of a toenail: having the free tip or edge embedded in the flesh.

ingrown /'in·grohn/ *adj* **1** inward-looking in activities or interests; withdrawn. **2** having developed naturally: *an ingrown habit.* **3** said *esp* of a toenail: ingrowing. >> **ingrownness** *noun*.

ingrowth /'ingrohth/ *noun* **1** the act or an instance of growing inwards. **2** something that grows in or into a space.

inguinal /'inggwinl/ *adj* relating to or in the region of the groin. [Latin *inguinalis*, from *inguin-*, *inguen* groin]

ingulf /in'gulf/ *verb trans* = ENGULF.

ingurgitate /in'guhjitayt/ *verb trans* to swallow (something) greedily or in large quantities. >> **ingurgitation** /-'taysh(ə)n/ *noun*. [Latin *ingurgitatus*, past part. of *ingurgitare*, from IN-² + *gurgit-*, *gurges* gulf, whirlpool]

inhabit /in'habit/ *verb trans* (**inhabited, inhabiting**) **1** to occupy (a place) permanently; to live (there). **2** to be present in (something): *Who can understand the hopes and fears that inhabit the human mind?* >> **inhabitability** /-'biliti/ *noun*, **inhabitable** *adj*, **inhabitancy** /-si/ *noun*, **inhabitant** *noun*, **inhabitation** /-'taysh(ə)n/ *noun*. [Middle English *enhabiten* via French from Latin *inhabitare* to dwell in, from IN-² + *habitare*: see HABITATION]

inhalant¹ /in'haylənt/ *noun* something, e.g. a medication, that is inhaled.

inhalant² *adj* **1** said of a medication, etc: taken by inhaling. **2** inhaling or for inhaling.

inhalation /inhə'laysh(ə)n/ *noun* **1** the act or an instance of inhaling. **2** an inward breath.

inhalator /'inhəlaytə/ *noun* = RESPIRATOR (2).

inhale /in'hayl/ *verb intrans* to breathe in. >> *verb trans* to breathe (something, e.g. a perfume) in. [IN-² + *-hale* as in EXHALE]

inhaler *noun* **1** somebody who inhales. **2** a device used for inhaling a medication, e.g. to relieve asthma or congestion in the nose.

inharmonious /inhah'mohni·əs/ *adj* **1** not harmonious; discordant. **2** not congenial or compatible; conflicting. >> **inharmoniously** *adv*.

inhere /in'hiə/ *verb intrans* (+ in) to be inherent; to reside: *Power to make laws inheres in the state.* [Latin *inhaerēre*, from IN-² + *haerēre* to adhere]

inherent /in'herənt, in'hiərənt/ *adj* forming an essential and indivisible part of something; innate. >> **inherence** *noun*, **inherently** *adv*. [Latin *inhaerent-*, *inhaerens*, present part. of *inhaerēre*: see INHERE]

inherit /in'herit/ *verb* (**inherited, inheriting**) >> *verb trans* **1** to receive (property) from an ancestor at his or her death, either by succession or under the terms of a will. **2** to receive (something, e.g. a physical attribute) by genetic transmission: *She's inherited her father's good looks.* **3** to come to possess (something) because it was left by a predecessor. >> *verb intrans* to receive something by inheritance. >> **inheritor** *noun*. [Middle English *enheriten* to make heir, inherit, via French from late Latin *inhereditare* to appoint as heir, from IN-² + *hered-*, *heres* HEIR]

inheritable *adj* **1** capable of being inherited. **2** capable of inheriting. >> **inheritability** /-'biliti/ *noun*.

inheritance *noun* **1a** the act or an instance of inheriting property. **b** property that is or may be inherited. **2** the transmission of genetic qualities from parent to offspring, or the offspring's acquisition of them. **3** something acquired or derived from the past, e.g. from a predecessor.

inheritance tax *noun* in the UK, a tax levied on inherited property and money above a certain value: compare CAPITAL TRANSFER TAX, DEATH DUTY.

inhibit /in'hibit/ *verb* (**inhibited, inhibiting**) >> *verb trans* **1** to discourage (somebody) from free or spontaneous activity, *esp* by psychological or social controls. **2** (+ from) to prohibit (somebody) from doing something. **3** to restrain (e.g. an impulse). **4** to prevent or lessen (a chemical reaction). >> *verb intrans* to cause inhibition. >> **inhibitive** /-tiv/ *adj*, **inhibitory** *adj*. [Middle English *inhibiten* from Latin *inhibitus*, past part. of *inhibēre* to hinder, from IN-² + *habēre* to hold]

inhibiter /in'hibitə/ *noun* see INHIBITOR.

inhibition /in(h)i'bish(ə)n/ *noun* **1** a psychological restraint on the way somebody thinks or behaves: *sexual inhibitions.* **2a** the act or an instance of inhibiting or being inhibited. **b** something that forbids, debars, or restricts. **3** a restraining of a function, e.g. of a bodily organ or enzyme.

inhibitor *or* **inhibiter** *noun* **1** somebody or something that inhibits. **2** something that slows or interferes with a chemical reaction or a physiological process.

inhospitable /inho'spitəbl/ *adj* **1** said of a person: not friendly or welcoming. **2** said of a place, climate, etc: providing no shelter or means of support; hard to live in. >> **inhospitableness** *noun*, **inhospitably** *adv*.

inhospitality /inhospi'taliti/ *noun* the quality of being inhospitable.

in-house¹ *adj* of or carried on within a group or organization, *esp* without the help of freelancers.

in-house² *adv* within a group or organization.

inhuman /in'hyoohmən/ *adj* **1** failing to conform to basic human needs; austere: *inhuman living conditions*. **2** extremely cruel; barbarous. **3** not human in nature or quality. ➤➤ **inhumanly** *adv.* [early French *inhumain* from Latin *inhumanus*, from IN-¹ + *humanus* HUMAN¹]

Usage note ⸺
inhuman or **inhumane**? These are both words of condemnation: *inhuman* is, however, a considerably stronger one than *inhumane*. *Inhumane* means 'lacking compassion or kindness' (*inhumane treatment of animals*). To describe someone's treatment of animals or other people as *inhuman*, however, suggests that it is deliberately cruel or shockingly neglectful and shows none of the qualities that are desirable in a human being: *inhuman torture of prisoners*.

inhumane /inhyooh'mayn/ *adj* completely lacking in kindness or compassion; cruel. ➤➤ **inhumanely** *adv.* [early spelling of INHUMAN; cf HUMANE]

Usage note ⸺
inhumane or **inhuman**? See note at INHUMAN.

inhumanity /inhyooh'maniti/ *noun* (*pl* **inhumanities**) **1** pitiless or cruel nature or behaviour: *Man's inhumanity to Man makes countless thousands mourn* — Burns. **2** a cruel or barbarous act.

inhume /in'hyoohm/ *verb trans formal* to bury (a body). ➤➤ **inhumation** /inhyooh'maysh(ə)n/ *noun.* [prob via French *inhumer* from Latin *inhumare* to put in the ground, from IN-² + *humus* ground]

inimical /i'nimik(ə)l/ *adj* **1** hostile or indicating hostility: *a voice apparently cold and inimical* — Arnold Bennett. **2** adverse in tendency, influence, or effects; harmful. ➤➤ **inimically** *adv.* [late Latin *inimicalis* from Latin *inimicus*: see ENEMY]

inimitable /i'nimitəbl/ *adj* so good or extraordinary that no others can match it; unique. ➤➤ **inimitability** /-'biliti/ *noun,* **inimitableness** *noun,* **inimitably** *adv.* [via French from Latin *inimitabilis*, from IN-¹ + *imitabilis* imitable, from *imitare* to IMITATE]

iniquity /i'nikwiti/ *noun* (*pl* **iniquities**) **1** lack of justice or moral rectitude; wickedness. **2** a wicked act; a sin. ➤➤ **iniquitous** /-təs/ *adj.* [Middle English *iniquite* via French from Latin *iniquitat-, iniquitas,* from *iniquus* uneven, from IN-¹ + *aequus* equal, just]

initial¹ /i'nish(ə)l/ *adj* **1** existing at the beginning: *the initial symptoms of a disease.* **2** placed at the beginning; first: *the initial number of a code.* ➤➤ **initially** *adv.* [early French *initial* from Latin *initialis,* from *initium* beginning, from *inire* to go in, from IN-² + *ire* to go]

initial² *noun* **1a** the first letter of a name. **b** (*in pl*) the first letter of each word in a full name. **2** a cell, or group of cells, giving rise to new tissues or structures.

initial³ *verb trans* (**initialled, initialling,** *NAmer* **initialed, initialing**) to put initials on (something), usu as an indication of ownership or authorization.

initialize or **initialise** *verb trans* to prepare (computer hardware or software) for operation by setting its configuration to a known state.

Initial Teaching Alphabet *noun* a 44-character phonetic alphabet designed for teaching children to read English.

initiate¹ /i'nishiayt/ *verb trans* **1** to cause or allow (something) to begin; to start (it). **2** to teach (somebody) the rudiments or principles of something complex or obscure. **3** to grant (somebody) membership of an organization or society, traditionally by formal rites. ➤➤ **initiatory** *adj.* [late Latin *initiatus,* past part. of *initiare* to begin, from *initium*: see INITIAL¹]

initiate² /i'nishi·ət/ *noun* **1** somebody who is undergoing or has undergone initiation. **2** somebody who is instructed or proficient in a complex or specialized field.

initiate³ /i'nishi·ət/ *adj* **1** initiated or properly admitted, e.g. to membership or an office. **2** instructed in some secret knowledge.

initiation /ˌinishi'aysh(ə)n/ *noun* **1** the ceremony or formal procedure with which somebody is made a member of a sect or society. **2** the act or an instance of initiating or being initiated.

initiative¹ /i'nish(y)ətiv/ *noun* **1** energy or resourcefulness displayed in being the first to act or in acting without being prompted; enterprise. **2a** a first or new step, *esp* in the attainment of an end or goal: *a peace initiative.* **b** the right to take the first step or to act first. **3** in certain countries, a procedure enabling voters to propose a law by petition. ✳ **on one's own initiative** without being prompted; independently of outside influence or control.

initiative² *adj* introductory or preliminary.

initiator /i'nishiaytə/ *noun* **1** somebody or something that initiates. **2** a chemical that starts a chain reaction. **3** an explosive used in detonators.

inject /in'jekt/ *verb trans* **1a** to force a fluid into the body of (somebody) using a syringe. **b** to force (a fluid) in in this way. **c** to throw, drive, or force (something) somewhere: *Fuel is injected into the engine.* **2** to introduce (something) as an element or factor: *She managed to inject a lighter tone into the proceedings.* ➤➤ **injector** *noun.* [Latin *injectus,* past part. of *inicere,* from IN-² + *jacere* to throw]

injection /in'jeksh(ə)n/ *noun* **1** something, e.g. a medication, that is injected into a person's body using a syringe. **2a** the act or an instance of injecting or being injected. **b** = FUEL INJECTION. **3** the placing of an artificial satellite or a spacecraft into an orbit or on a trajectory.

injection moulding *noun* the manufacture of rubber or plastic articles by injecting heated material into a mould. ➤➤ **injection-moulded** *adj.*

in-joke *noun* a joke that is understood only by people who belong to a particular clique.

injudicious /injooh'dishəs/ *adj* showing a lack of judgment; unwise. ➤➤ **injudiciously** *adv,* **injudiciousness** *noun.*

Injun /'injən/ *noun dated, offensive* a Native American, *esp* in the Wild West. [alteration of *Indian*]

injunction /in'jungksh(ə)n/ *noun* **1** a court order requiring somebody to do or refrain from doing a particular act. **2** a firm warning or an order. ➤➤ **injunctive** /-tiv/ *adj.* [early French *injonction* from late Latin *injunction-, injunctio,* from Latin *injungere*: see ENJOIN]

injure /'injə/ *verb trans* **1a** to inflict bodily harm on (somebody, a part of the body, etc). **b** to impair the soundness of (e.g. somebody's health). **c** to inflict damage or loss on (something): *The Opposition said the new taxes would injure small business.* **2** *archaic* to do (somebody) an injustice. [back-formation from INJURY]

injurious /in'jooəri·əs/ *adj* **1** inflicting or tending to inflict injury. **2** said of language: abusive or insulting: *Speak not injurious words* — George Washington. ➤➤ **injuriously** *adv,* **injuriousness** *noun.*

injury /'injəri/ *noun* (*pl* **injuries**) **1** a physical hurt caused to somebody. **2** damage or loss sustained. **3** *archaic* a wrong done to somebody. [Middle English *injurie* from Latin *injuria* a wrong, from IN-¹ + *jur-, jus* right, law]

injury time *noun* time added onto the end of a match in football, rugby, etc to compensate for time lost through injuries to players.

injustice /in'justis/ *noun* **1** the absence of justice, *esp* as apparent in the violation of somebody's rights; unfairness. **2** an unjust act or state of affairs. [Middle English via French from Latin *injustitia,* from *injustus* unjust, from IN-¹ + *justus*: see JUST¹]

ink¹ /ingk/ *noun* **1** a coloured liquid used for writing and printing. **2** the black secretion of a squid or similar cephalopod mollusc that hides it from a predator or prey. ➤➤ **inkiness** *noun,* **inky** *adj.* [Middle English *enke* via French and Latin from Greek *enkauston* purple ink, from *enkaustos* burned in, from *enkaiein*: see ENCAUSTIC¹]

ink² *verb trans* **1** to apply ink to (something, e.g. a printing plate). **2** to write (something) in ink.

inkblot test *noun* = RORSCHACH TEST.

ink cap *noun* any of several species of toadstools whose cap melts into an inky fluid after the spores have matured: genus *Coprinus.*

inked *adj Aus, NZ, informal* drunk. [INK¹ in the sense 'cheap wine']

inkhorn¹ *noun* a small portable bottle formerly used for holding ink, orig one made from horn.

inkhorn² *adj dated* ostentatiously pedantic: *inkhorn terms.*

ink in *verb trans* **1** to go over (the pencil lines of a drawing, etc) in ink. **2** to apply ink to (e.g. a printing plate). **3** to write (something) in ink.

ink-jet printer *noun* a computer printer that prints by means of droplets of ink released from a bank of tiny jets.

inkling /'ingkling/ *noun* **1** a slight knowledge or vague idea; a suspicion. **2** a faint indication; a hint. [Middle English *yngkiling,* prob from *inclen* to hint at, related to Old English *inca* suspicion]

inkstand *noun dated* a stand with fittings for holding ink, pens, and other items of stationery.

inkwell *noun* a container for ink, *esp* one set into a hole in the desktop of a schoolchild.

INLA *abbr* Irish National Liberation Army.

inlaid[1] /in'layd/ *verb* past tense and past part. of INLAY[1].

inlaid[2] *adj* **1** set into a surface in a decorative design: *tables with inlaid marble.* **2** decorated with a design or material set into a surface: *a table with an inlaid top.*

inland[1] /'inland, 'inlənd/ *adv* into or towards the interior part of a country, away from the coast.

inland[2] /'inlənd/ *adj* **1** of the interior of a country. **2** *chiefly Brit* not foreign; domestic.

inland[3] /'inland, 'inlənd/ *noun* the interior of a country.

inlander /'inləndə/ *noun* somebody who lives inland.

Inland Revenue *noun* the government department responsible for collecting taxes in Britain.

in-law *noun informal* a relative by marriage: *All her in-laws turned up.* [back-formation from *mother-in-law*, etc]

inlay[1] /in'lay/ *verb* (*past tense and past part.* **inlaid**) **1** to set (something) into a surface for decoration or reinforcement. **2** (*usu* + with) to decorate (something) with inlaid material.

inlay[2] /'inlay/ *noun* **1** inlaid work or a decorative inlaid pattern. **2** a dental filling shaped to fit a cavity.

inlet /'inlet/ *noun* **1** a usu long and narrow recess in a shoreline, or a water passage between two land areas. **2** a means of entry, *esp* an opening for fluid to enter: *a fuel inlet.* **3** something set in, e.g. a piece of material inserted into clothing. [from its letting e.g. water in]

inlier /'inlie·ə/ *noun* an outcrop of rock surrounded by rock of younger age. [IN[1] + *-lier* as in OUTLIER]

in-line skates *pl noun* roller skates on which the wheels are fixed in line with each other along the length of the boot; Rollerblades.

in loc. cit. /in ˌlok 'sit/ *abbr* in the place cited. [Latin *in loco citato*]

in loco parentis /in ˌlohkoh pə'rentis/ *adv* in the place of and *esp* having the responsibilities of a parent, as, for example, teachers are and have while children are in their care. [Latin *in loco parentis* in the place of a parent]

inly /'inli/ *adv literary* inwardly or intimately.

inmate /'inmayt/ *noun* any of a group of people occupying an institution, *esp* a prison or hospital.

in medias res /in ˌmeedias 'rayz/ *adv* in or into the middle of a narrative or plot, with no introduction or preamble. [Latin *in medias res* into the middle of things]

in memoriam /in mi'mawriam/ *prep and adv* in memory of (somebody). [Latin *in memoriam*]

inmost /'inmohst/ *adj* **1** furthest within. **2** most intimate. [Old English *innemest*, superl of *inne* (adv) in, within]

inn /in/ *noun* **1a** a pub, *esp* one that can or used to provide accommodation. **b** any small establishment providing lodging and food for travellers. **2** a residence formerly provided for students in London.

Word history ───────
Old English *inn* dwelling, lodging. In the 13th cent. *inn* was used to translate Latin *hospitium* hospice, in the sense 'residence for students', surviving in the names of buildings formally used as students' hostels, notably *Gray's Inn* and *Lincoln's Inn*, two of the four INNS OF COURT. From the 14th cent. an inn was a public house obliged by the terms of its licence to provide food and accommodation for travellers; in modern use there is no practical difference between a public house and one calling itself an inn.

innards /'inədz/ *pl noun informal* **1** the internal organs of a human being or animal, *esp* the intestines. **2** the internal parts of a structure or mechanism. [alteration of INWARDS]

innate /i'nayt/ *adj* **1a** existing in or belonging to an individual from birth. **b** existing as a basic and inseparable part; inherent. **c** originating in the mind before and independently of experience; instinctive; unlearned. **2** = ENDOGENOUS (2). ⟫ **innately** *adv*, **innateness** *noun*. [Middle English *innat* from Latin *innatus*, past part. of *innasci* to be born in, from IN-[2] + *nasci* to be born]

inner[1] /'inə/ *adj* **1a** situated inside something; internal: *an inner chamber.* **b** situated near to a centre, *esp* of influence: *an inner circle of government ministers.* **2** relating to the mind or soul: *a person's inner life.* **3** unexpressed; private: *inner thoughts.* [Old English *innera*, compar of *inne* within]

inner[2] *noun* the ring on a target next to the bull's-eye, or a shot that hits this ring.

inner bar *noun* (**the inner bar**) all the barristers who collectively form the Queen's or King's counsel, as distinct from ordinary barristers.

inner child *noun* (*pl* **inner children**) that part of an adult's personality that arises from and is influenced by their experiences and treatment in childhood.

inner city *noun* a usu older and more densely populated central section of a city, *esp* such an area that suffers social and economic problems. ⟫ **inner-city** *adj*.

inner ear *noun* the innermost part of the ear from which sound waves are transmitted to the brain as nerve impulses.

inner light *or* **Inner Light** *noun* a divine influence held, *esp* in Quaker doctrine, to enlighten and guide the soul.

inner man *noun* **1** the soul or the mind of a man. **2** *humorous* the stomach or the appetite.

innermost /'inəmohst/ *adj* **1** most inward or central. **2** most secret and private: *Her diary revealed her innermost thoughts.*

inner planet *noun* any of the planets Mercury, Venus, Earth, and Mars that as a group have orbits nearer the sun than the outer planets.

inner space *noun* **1a** the region of space that exists at or near the earth's surface, as distinct from outer space. **b** the part of the earth under the sea. **2** the unconscious mind.

inner tube *noun* an inflatable tube inside the casing of a pneumatic tyre.

innervate /'inəvayt/ *verb trans* **1** to supply (an organ) with nerves. **2** to stimulate the nerves in (a part of the body). ⟫ **innervation** /-'vaysh(ə)n/ *noun*.

inner woman *noun* **1** the soul or the mind of a woman. **2** *humorous* the stomach or the appetite.

inning /'ining/ *noun* a baseball team's turn at batting, or a division of a baseball game consisting of a turn at batting for each team. [IN[2] + -ING[2]]

innings *noun* (*pl* **innings**) **1a** any of the alternating divisions of a cricket match during which one side bats and the other bowls. **b** the turn of one player to bat, or the runs that the player scores. **c** an unplayed innings of a side: *They won by an innings and 32 runs.* **2a** a period in which somebody has the opportunity for action or achievements. **b** *chiefly Brit, informal* the duration of somebody's life: *He had a good innings.*

innkeeper *noun* the landlord or landlady of an inn.

innocence /'inəs(ə)ns/ *noun* **1** freedom from guilt or sin through being unacquainted with evil; blamelessness. **2** freedom from legal guilt of a particular crime or offence. **3** freedom from guile or sophistication; artlessness. **4** lack of knowledge; ignorance: *written in entire innocence of English grammar.* **5** *archaic* chastity.

innocent[1] /'inəs(ə)nt/ *adj* **1a** free from guilt or sin; pure: *innocent children.* **b** harmless in effect or intention: *an innocent conversation.* **c** (*often* + of) free from legal guilt: *found innocent of all charges.* **2a** not aware; ignorant. **b** not crafty or scheming in nature; ingenuous. **3** *literary* (+ of) lacking or deprived of something: *a face innocent of make-up.* ⟫ **innocently** *adv*. [Middle English via French from Latin *innocent-*, *innocens*, from IN-[1] + *nocent-*, *nocens* wicked]

innocent[2] *noun* somebody who is innocent, *esp*: **a** a child regarded as free from all sin or blame. **b** somebody who lacks sophistication or is ignorant of the evil ways of the world.

innocuous /i'nokyoo·əs/ *adj* **1** having no harmful effects; harmless. **2** unlikely to provoke or offend; inoffensive. ⟫ **innocuously** *adv*, **innocuousness** *noun*. [Latin *innocuus*, from IN-[1] + *nocuus*: see NOCUOUS]

innominate bone *noun* = HIPBONE. [late Latin *innominatus*, from Latin IN-[1] + *nominatus*, past part. of *nominare*: see NOMINATE[1]]

innovate /'inəvayt/ *verb intrans* to make changes by introducing something new, e.g. new practices or ideas. ⟫ **innovation** /-'vaysh(ə)n/ *noun*, **innovative** /-vətiv/ *adj*, **innovator** *noun*, **innovatory** *adj*. [Latin *innovatus*, past part. of *innovare* to alter, renew, from IN-[2] + *novus* new]

Inns of Court *pl noun* **1** four societies of students and barristers in London which have the exclusive right of admission to the English Bar. **2** the four buildings that house these societies.

innuendo /inyoo'endoh/ *noun* (*pl* **innuendos** *or* **innuendoes**) an obliquely worded comment, typically suggestive or subtly disparaging, or the use of such comments: *Above all study innuendo. Hint* *everything – assert nothing* — Poe. [Latin *innuendo* by hinting, from *innuere* to hint, from IN-² + *nuere* to nod]

Innuit /'inyooh-it/ *noun* see INUIT.

innumerable /i'nyoohmərəbl/ *adj* too many to be counted; countless. ➤➤ **innumerably** *adv.* [Middle English from Latin *innumerabilis*, from IN-¹ + *numerabilis* numerable, ultimately from *numerus* NUMBER¹]

innumerate¹ /i'nyoohmərət/ *adj Brit* having no knowledge even of basic arithmetic and not able to use numbers effectively. ➤➤ **innumeracy** /-si/ *noun.*

innumerate² *noun* an innumerate person.

inobservance /inəb'zuhvəns/ *noun* **1** lack of attention. **2** failure to observe a custom, rule, etc. ➤➤ **inobservant** *adj.* [French *inobservant* from Latin *inobservantia*, from IN-¹ + *observantia* observance, from *observare*: see OBSERVE]

inocula /i'nokyoolə/ *noun* pl of INOCULUM.

inoculant /i'nokyoolənt/ *noun* = INOCULUM.

inoculate /i'nokyoolayt/ *verb trans* **1a** to introduce a disease-causing organism into the body of (somebody) in order to induce immunity; to vaccinate (them). **b** to introduce a micro-organism into (an animal) for testing purposes: *The experiment involves inoculating mice with anthrax.* **c** to introduce (e.g. a micro-organism) into a culture, animal, etc. **2** to introduce something into the mind of (somebody); to imbue (them) with it. ➤➤ **inoculation** /-'laysh(ə)n/ *noun,* **inoculative** /-lətiv/ *adj,* **inoculator** *noun.* [Middle English *inoculaten* to insert a bud in a plant, from Latin *inoculatus*, past part. of *inoculare* to graft on, from IN-² + *oculus* eye, bud]

inoculum /i'nokyooləm/ *noun* (*pl* **inocula** /-lə/) a substance used for inoculation. [Latin *inoculare*: see INOCULATE]

in-off *noun* the potting of one ball after it has touched another in billiards, snooker, etc. [from the phrase *in off (the red ball* or *the white ball)*]

inoffensive /inə'fensiv/ *adj* **1** not causing any harm; innocuous. **2** not objectionable. ➤➤ **inoffensively** *adv,* **inoffensiveness** *noun.*

inoperable /in'op(ə)rəbl/ *adj* **1** not suitable for treatment by surgery. **2** not likely to work or be successful; impracticable. ➤➤ **inoperability** /-'biliti/ *noun,* **inoperableness** *noun,* **inoperably** *adv.*

inoperative /in'op(ə)rətiv/ *adj* not functioning, or having no effect. ➤➤ **inoperativeness** *noun.*

inopportune /in,opə'tyoohn/ *adj* happening at an awkward or unwelcome time; inconvenient. ➤➤ **inopportunely** *adv,* **inopportuneness** *noun.* [Latin *inopportunus*, from IN-¹ + *opportunus*: see OPPORTUNE]

inordinate /in'awdinət/ *adj* **1** going beyond reasonable limits; excessive. **2** *archaic* not controlled or disciplined in behaviour; disorderly. ➤➤ **inordinately** *adv.* [Middle English *inordinat* from Latin *inordinatus*, from IN-¹ + *ordinatus*, past part. of *ordinare* to put in order, arrange, from *ordin-, ordo* ORDER¹]

inorganic /inaw'ganik/ *adj* **1a** being or composed of matter other than plant or animal; mineral. **b** relating to or dealt with by a branch of chemistry concerned with inorganic substances. **2** not arising through natural growth; artificial. **3** without an ordered structure or system. ➤➤ **inorganically** *adv.*

inosculate /i'noskyoolayt/ *verb intrans* to join by contact; to become a continuous unit or blended substance. ➤ *verb trans* to join (things) in this way. ➤➤ **inosculation** /-'laysh(ə)n/ *noun.* [IN-² + Latin *osculare* to provide with a mouth or outlet, from *osculum*, dimin. of *os* mouth]

inositol /i'nohsitol/ *noun* any of several alcohols that occur in micro-organisms, plants, and animals including humans, *esp* in the vitamin B complex. [Greek *inos*, genitive of *is* sinew, + -ITE¹ + -OL¹]

inotropic /ienə'trohpik, eenə-, -'tropik/ *adj* relating to or influencing the force of contraction of heart muscle. [*ino-* (from Greek *in-, is* sinew) + -TROPIC]

inpatient /'inpaysh(ə)nt/ *noun* a hospital patient who lives at a hospital while undergoing treatment there: compare OUTPATIENT.

in perpetuum /in puh'petyooəm/ *adv* forever. [Latin *in perpetuum*]

input¹ /'inpoot/ *noun* **1a** something, e.g. energy, material, or data, supplied to a machine or system. **b** an amount of anything coming or put in. **c** in economics, a component of production, e.g. land, labour, or raw materials. **2** work, suggestions, advice, etc that somebody contributes; a contribution. **3** the point in a system, machine, etc at which an input, e.g. of energy, material, or data, is made. **4** the act or an instance of putting something in.

input² *verb trans* (**input** *or* **inputted, inputting**) to enter (data) into a computer.

input/output *noun* the passage of information into and out of a computer, or the data that passes in and out.

inquest /'inkwest, 'ingkwest/ *noun* **1** a judicial enquiry, *esp* by a coroner, into the cause of a death. **2** an enquiry or investigation, *esp* into something that has failed. [Middle English from early French *enqueste* from Latin *inquirere*: see ENQUIRE]

inquietude /in'kwie-ətyoohd/ *noun* physical restlessness or mental unease. [Middle English via French from Latin *inquietus* disturbed, from IN-¹ + *quietus*: see QUIET²]

inquiline¹ /'inkwilien/ *noun* an animal that uses or lives habitually in the home of some other species, as does the cuckoo, for example, which lays its eggs in other birds' nests. ➤➤ **inquilinism** /in'kwiliniz(ə)m/ *noun,* **inquilinous** /-'lienəs/ *adj.* [Latin *inquilinus* tenant, lodger, from IN-² + *colere* to cultivate, dwell]

inquiline² *adj* relating to inquilines or inquilinism.

inquire *verb intrans and trans* see ENQUIRE.

Usage note

inquire *or* enquire? See note at ENQUIRE.

inquiry *noun* see ENQUIRY.

inquiry agent *noun Brit, dated* a private detective.

inquisition /inkwi'zish(ə)n/ *noun* **1a** (**the Inquisition**) a former Roman Catholic tribunal for the discovery and punishment of heresy. **b** a ruthless investigation or examination. **2** *formal* a judicial or official enquiry. **3** *formal* the act or an instance of enquiring. ➤➤ **inquisitional** *adj.* [Middle English *inquisicioun* via French from Latin *inquisition-, inquisitio*, from Latin *inquirere*: see ENQUIRE]

inquisitive /in'kwizətiv/ *adj* **1** fond of making enquiries, *esp* unduly curious about the affairs of others. **2** eager for knowledge or understanding; enquiring. ➤➤ **inquisitively** *adv,* **inquisitiveness** *noun.*

inquisitor /in'kwizitə/ *noun* somebody who makes enquiries or asks questions, *esp* harshly or with hostility.

inquisitorial /in,kwizi'tawri-əl/ *adj* **1** investigating or asking questions with the ruthlessly searching zeal of an inquisitor. **2** said of a system of criminal procedure: in which the judge is also the prosecutor: compare ACCUSATORIAL. ➤➤ **inquisitorially** *adv.*

inquorate /in'kwawrət, -rayt/ *adj formal* not having a quorum; not quorate.

in re /,in 'ray/ *prep* in the matter of. [Latin *in re*]

INRI *abbr* Jesus of Nazareth, King of the Jews. [Latin *Iesus Nazarenus Rex Iudaeorum*]

inro /'inroh/ *noun* (*pl* **inro** *or* **inros**) a set of decorated boxes worn hanging from the belt as part of traditional Japanese dress, formerly containing medicines and seals. [Japanese *inrō*, from *in* seal + *rō* basket]

inroad /'inrohd/ *noun* **1** a serious or forcible encroachment or intrusion: *A long illness made inroads on his savings.* **2** a raid.

inrush /'inrush/ *noun* a crowding or flooding in. ➤➤ **inrushing** *noun and adj.*

INS *abbr* **1** inertial navigation system, a system of navigational guidance. **2** International News Service.

ins. *abbr* **1** inches. **2** insurance.

insalubrious /insə'loohbri-əs/ *adj* not conducive to good health; unhealthy: *an insalubrious climate.* ➤➤ **insalubriously** *adv,* **insalubrity** *noun.* [Latin *insalubris*, from IN-¹ + *salubris*: see SALUBRIOUS]

ins and outs *pl noun* characteristic peculiarities and complexities; ramifications.

insane /in'sayn/ *adj* **1** *dated, offensive* suffering from a mental illness or psychological disorder. **2** *dated, offensive* intended for mentally ill people: *an insane asylum.* **3** utterly absurd: *an insane suggestion.* ➤➤ **insanely** *adv,* **insanity** /in'saniti/ *noun.* [Latin *insanus*, from IN-¹ + *sanus* SANE]

insanitary /in'sanit(ə)ri/ *adj* very dirty, *esp* unclean enough to endanger health.

insatiable /in'saysh(y)əbl/ *adj* incapable of being satisfied: *He had an insatiable desire for wealth.* ➤➤ **insatiability** /-'biliti/ *noun,* **insatiably** *adv.* [Middle English *insaciable* via French from Latin *insatiabilis,* from IN-¹ + *satiare:* see SATIATE]

inscape /'inskayp/ *noun* a unity perceived in natural objects or in somebody's mind and expressed in literature. [IN-² + -SCAPE; orig coined by Gerard Manley Hopkins d.1889, English poet]

inscribe /in'skrieb/ *verb trans* **1a** to write, engrave, or print (something), *esp* as a lasting record. **b** to write, engrave, or print on (something). **2** to address or dedicate (*esp* a book) to somebody by a handwritten note on the inside. **3** in geometry, to draw (a figure) within a figure, usu so that they touch but do not intersect: *a regular polygon inscribed in a circle.* **4** to enter the name of (somebody) on a list; to enrol (them). ➤➤ **inscriber** *noun.* [Latin *inscribere,* from IN-² + *scribere* to write]

inscription /in'skripsh(ə)n/ *noun* **1** a handwritten dedication in a book or on a work of art. **2** any written or engraved form of words, e.g. on a statue or a coin. **3** the act or an instance of inscribing. **4** the entering of a name on a list. ➤➤ **inscriptional** *adj,* **inscriptive** /-tiv/ *adj.* [Middle English *inscripcioun* from Latin *inscription-, inscriptio,* from *inscribere:* see INSCRIBE]

inscrutable /in'skroohtəbl/ *adj* hard to interpret or understand; enigmatic. ➤➤ **inscrutability** /-'biliti/ *noun,* **inscrutableness** *noun,* **inscrutably** *adv.* [Middle English from late Latin *inscrutabilis,* from Latin IN-¹ + *scrutari:* see SCRUTINY]

insect /'insekt/ *noun* **1** any of a large class of invertebrate animals with a well-defined head, thorax, and abdomen, three pairs of legs, and typically one or two pairs of wings: class Insecta: *A fly, sir, may sting a stately horse and make him wince; but the one is but an insect, and the other a horse still — Dr Johnson.* **2** loosely, any of various small invertebrate animals that do not belong to the insect class but that superficially resemble insects, e.g. woodlice and spiders. **3** a worthless or insignificant person. [Latin *insectum,* neuter of *insectus,* past part. of *insecare* to cut up, from IN-² + *secare* to cut; because of the insect's segmental body]

insectarium /insek'teəri.əm/ *noun* (*pl* **insectariums** or **insectaria** /-ri.ə/) a place where insects are kept or reared.

insectary /in'sektəri/ *noun* (*pl* **insectaries**) = INSECTARIUM.

insecticide /in'sektisied/ *noun* a substance that destroys insects. ➤➤ **insecticidal** /-'siedl/ *adj.*

insectile /in'sektiel/ *adj* resembling an insect.

insectivore /in'sektivaw/ *noun* **1** any of an order of mammals including the moles, shrews, and hedgehogs that are mostly small, nocturnal, and eat insects: order Insectivora. **2** an insect-eating plant or animal. ➤➤ **insectivorous** *adj.* [Latin *insectum* (see INSECT)+ -*vorus* -VOROUS]

insecure /insi'kyooə/ *adj* **1a** lacking in self-confidence. **b** feeling afraid or anxious. **2** lacking adequate protection or guarantee: *an insecure job.* **3** not firmly fixed or supported: *The hinge is insecure.* **4** not stable or well-adjusted: *an insecure marriage.* ➤➤ **insecurely** *adv,* **insecurity** *noun.* [medieval Latin *insecurus,* from IN-¹ + Latin *securus:* see SECURE¹]

inselberg /'ins(ə)lbuhg/ *noun* a single steep-sided hill on a plateau. [German *Inselberg,* from *Insel* island + *Berg* mountain]

inseminate /in'seminayt/ *verb trans* **1** to introduce semen into (a woman or female animal). **2** *formal* to introduce ideas, principles, etc into the mind of (somebody). ➤➤ **insemination** /-'naysh(ə)n/ *noun,* **inseminator** *noun.* [Latin *inseminatus,* past part. of *inseminare* to sow seed, from IN-² + *semin-, semen* seed, SEMEN]

insensate /in'sensayt, -sət/ *adj* **1** not capable of feeling; insentient. **2** lacking in human feeling; insensitive. **3** senseless; foolish. ➤➤ **insensately** *adv,* **insensateness** *noun.* [late Latin *insensatus,* from IN-¹ + *sensatus:* see SENSATE]

insensible /in'sensəbl/ *adj* **1** bereft of feeling or sensation, e.g.: **a** having lost consciousness; unconscious: *She was knocked insensible by the blow.* **b** lacking or deprived of sensory perception: *He was struggling with the lock with hands insensible from cold.* **2** lacking concern or awareness; indifferent: *She was completely insensible to fear.* **3** incapable of being felt or sensed; imperceptible: *an insensible change.* ➤➤ **insensibility** /-'biliti/ *noun,* **insensibly** *adv.* [Middle English via French from Latin *insensibilis,* from IN-¹ + *sensibilis:* see SENSIBLE]

insensitive /in'sensətiv/ *adj* **1** failing to respond to or sympathize with the needs or feelings of others; callous. **2** (+ to) not physically

or chemically sensitive: *insensitive to light.* ➤➤ **insensitively** *adv,* **insensitiveness** *noun,* **insensitivity** /-'tiviti/ *noun.*

insentient /in'senshi.ənt/ *adj* not endowed with the capacity to perceive; inanimate. ➤➤ **insentience** *noun.*

inseparable /in'sep(ə)rəbl/ *adj* **1** incapable of being separated: *the pettiness and sneakiness and cowardice inseparable from villainy —* David Graham Phillips. **2** always seen or found together: *At school, we were inseparable.* ➤➤ **inseparability** /-'biliti/ *noun,* **inseparably** *adv.* [Middle English from Latin *inseparabilis,* from IN-¹ + *separabilis* separable, from *separare:* see SEPARATE¹]

insert¹ /in'suht/ *verb trans* **1** to put or thrust (something) in through an opening: *Insert a coin into the slot.* **2** to introduce (something) into the body of something, e.g. text: *She decided to insert an advertisement in the local paper.* **3** to set (something) into a position between two parts, e.g. by sewing it. ➤ *verb intrans technical* said of a muscle: to be attached to a specified part: *muscles inserting on bone.* ➤➤ **inserter** *noun.* [Latin *insertus,* past part. of *inserere* to join in, from IN-² + *serere* to join]

insert² /'insuht/ *noun* something inserted, e.g.: **a** a piece of written or printed material placed between the pages of a book or magazine. **b** = INSET¹ (2).

insertion /in'suhsh(ə)n/ *noun* **1** the act or an instance of inserting. **2** the mode or place of attachment of an organ or part. **3** embroidery or needlework inserted as a decoration between two pieces of fabric. **4** a single appearance of an advertisement in a newspaper or magazine. ➤➤ **insertional** *adj.*

in-service *adj* said of training: undertaken during the course of work, *esp* during the hours of work, as distinct from in the evening or at weekends.

insessorial /inse'sawri.əl/ *adj* **1** said of a bird's claws: adapted for perching. **2** said of a bird: having such claws. [Latin *insessus,* past part. of *insidēre* to sit on, from IN-² + *sedēre* to sit]

inset¹ /'inset/ *noun* **1** a small illustration set within a larger one. **2** a piece of cloth set into a garment for decoration, shaping, etc. **3** = INSERT² (A).

inset² /in'set/ *verb trans* (**insetting,** *past tense and past part.* **inset** or **insetted**) to insert (something) as an inset.

inshallah /in'shala/ *interj* if Allah wills it. [Arabic *in ša' Allāh* if Allah wills]

inshore /in'shaw/ *adj and adv* towards the shore, or operating near the shore.

inside¹ /in'sied/ *noun* **1** an inner side or surface. **2a** an interior or internal part: *Fire destroyed the inside of the house.* **b** inward nature, thoughts, or feelings. **3** (*usu in pl*) the stomach or the intestines. **4** a position of confidence or of access to confidential information: *We have a man working on the inside.* **5a** the side of a pavement farthest from the road. **b** the side of a double seat on a bus nearer the window. **6** the downstairs part of a double-decker bus. **7** *dated* the middle portion of a playing area. ✳ **inside out 1** with the inner surface on the outside: *He turned his socks inside out.* **2** in a very thorough manner: *She knows her subject inside out.*

inside² *adj* **1** of, on, near, or towards the inside: *an inside toilet.* **2** on the inner side of a curve or near the side of the road nearest the kerb or hard shoulder: *the inside lane.* **3** coming from, carried out by, etc somebody within an organization or with access to personal information: *The police reckon the theft was an inside job.*

inside³ *prep* **1a** in or into the interior of: *They told us to go inside the house.* **b** on the inner side of. **c** closer to the centre than. **2** within: *inside an hour.*

inside⁴ *adv* **1** to or on the inner side. **2** in or into the interior. **3** indoors. **4** within somebody's body or mind. **5** *chiefly Brit, informal* in or into prison.

inside-left *noun* an attacking player to the left of the centre-forward in a traditional football line-up.

inside leg *noun* **1** the leg from the crotch to the inside of the ankle. **2** the length of this.

inside of *prep informal* **1** in less time than. **2** *chiefly NAmer* inside.

insider *noun* somebody recognized or accepted as a member of a group, category, or organization, *esp* somebody who has access to confidential information or is in a position of power.

insider dealing *noun* the illegal exploitation of confidential information, e.g. about the prospective takeover of a company, in buying or selling securities at a price which would have been materially affected if that information had been made public. ➤➤ **insider dealer** *noun.*

inside-right *noun* an attacking player to the right of the centre-forward in a traditional football line-up.

insider trading *noun* = INSIDER DEALING.

insidious /in'sidi-əs/ *adj* **1a** acting gradually and imperceptibly but with very harmful consequences. **b** said of a disease: developing so gradually as to be well established before becoming apparent. **2** harmful but enticing. ➤➤ **insidiously** *adv,* **insidiousness** *noun.* [Latin *insidiosus,* from *insidiae* ambush, from *insidēre* to sit in, sit on, from IN-² + *sedēre* to sit]

insight /'insiet/ *noun* **1** the ability to discern the true or underlying nature of something. **2** an explanation or understanding that displays this ability: *Her book provides us with some valuable insights into human nature.* **3** in psychiatry, a patient's understanding that their thoughts, impulses, and other mental experiences are not based on reality. ➤➤ **insightful** *adj.*

insignia /in'signi-ə/ *noun* (*pl* **insignia, insignias**) **1** a badge of authority or honour. **2** *literary* a sign or token of something. [Latin *insignia* mark, badge, neuter pl of *insignis* marked, distinguished, from IN-² + *signum* mark, SIGN¹]

insignificant /insig'nifikənt/ *adj* **1** too unimportant to be worth consideration; inconsequential. **2** very small in size, amount, or number. ➤➤ **insignificance** *noun,* **insignificancy** /-si/ *noun,* **insignificantly** *adv.*

insincere /insin'siə/ *adj* not expressing feelings or opinions honestly; hypocritical. ➤➤ **insincerely** *adv,* **insincerity** /-'seriti/ *noun.* [Latin *insincerus,* from IN-¹ + *sincerus* SINCERE]

insinuate /in'sinyooayt/ *verb trans* **1** to introduce (an idea) or suggest (something unpleasant) in a subtle or oblique manner: *My liveliness and your solidity would produce perfection. – Not that I presume to insinuate, however, that some people may not think you perfection already* — Jane Austen. **2** (+ into) to gain acceptance for (e.g. oneself) by crafty or stealthy means: *He insinuates himself into the favour of the chief.* **3** to insert or squeeze in (oneself, a remark, etc) somewhere: *Fagin walked straight up the stairs … and softly insinuating himself into the chamber, looked anxiously about* — Dickens; *I will insinuate a few remarks at this point* — William James. ➤➤ **insinuative** /-tiv/ *adj,* **insinuator** *noun.* [Latin *insinuatus,* past part. of *insinuare* to bend inwards, from IN-² + *sinuare:* see SINUATE]

insinuation /in,sinyoo'aysh(ə)n/ *noun* **1** the act or an instance of insinuating. **2** a sly and usu derogatory reference.

insipid /in'sipid/ *adj* **1** lacking flavour; tasteless. **2** with no interesting or stimulating qualities; dull: *We see so many insipid beauties made wives of, that could not have caught the particular fancy of any man that had any fancy at all* — Charles Lamb. ➤➤ **insipidity** /-'piditi/ *noun,* **insipidly** *adv.* [French *insipide* from late Latin *insipidus,* from IN-¹ + Latin *sapidus:* see SAPID]

insist /in'sist/ *verb intrans* **1** (*usu* + on/upon) to state wishes or requirements forcefully, accepting no refusal or compromise: *They insisted on coming.* **2** (*usu* + on/upon) to take a resolute stand: *She insisted on her innocence.* ➤ *verb trans* to maintain (something) persistently: *He insisted that he was not involved.* [early French *insister* from Latin *insistere* to stand upon, persist, from IN-² + *sistere* to stand]

insistent *adj* **1** insisting forcefully or repeatedly; emphatic. **2** demanding attention: *the insistent ring of the doorbell.* ➤➤ **insistence** *noun,* **insistently** *adv.* [Latin *insistent-, insistens,* present part. of *insistere:* see INSIST]

in situ /in 'sityooh/ *adv and adj* in the natural, original, or permanent position. [Latin *in situ* in position]

insobriety /insə'brieiti/ *noun* lack of moderation, *esp* in drinking.

insofar as /insə'fah, insoh'fah/ *conj* to the extent or degree that: *I'll help you insofar as I can.*

insolation /insə'laysh(ə)n/ *noun* **1** the amount of solar radiation that has been received on a given surface. **2** exposure to the sun's rays. **3** sunstroke. [French *insolation* exposure to the sun, ultimately from Latin *insolare* to place in the sunlight, from IN-² + *sol* sun]

insole /'insohl/ *noun* **1** a strip the shape of the sole that is placed inside a shoe or boot for warmth or comfort. **2** a fixed inside sole of a shoe or boot.

insolent /'insələnt/ *adj* showing disrespectful rudeness; impudent. ➤➤ **insolence** *noun,* **insolently** *adv.* [Middle English from Latin

insolent-, insolens immoderate, arrogant, from IN-¹ + *solent-, solens,* present part. of *solēre* to be accustomed]

insoluble /in'solyoobl/ *adj* **1** incapable of being dissolved in liquid. **2** impossible to solve or explain. ➤➤ **insolubility** /-'biliti/ *noun,* **insolubleness** *noun,* **insolubly** *adv.* [Middle English *insolible* from late Latin *insolubilis,* from IN-¹ + *solubilis:* see SOLUBLE]

insolvable /in'solvəbl/ *adj chiefly NAmer* impossible to solve; insoluble: *an apparently insolvable problem.* ➤➤ **insolvably** *adv.*

insolvent¹ /in'solvənt/ *adj* **1** unable to pay debts as they fall due, *esp* having liabilities in excess of the value of assets held; bankrupt. **2** relating to or for the relief of people or companies that are insolvents. ➤➤ **insolvency** /-si/ *noun.*

insolvent² *noun* somebody who is insolvent.

insomnia /in'somni-ə/ *noun* prolonged inability to obtain adequate or uninterrupted sleep. ➤➤ **insomniac** /-ak/ *adj and noun.* [Latin *insomnia,* from *insomnis* sleepless, from IN-¹ + *somnus* sleep]

insomuch as /insə'much, insoh'much/ *conj* to such a degree that.

insomuch that *conj* = INSOMUCH AS.

insouciance /in'soohsi-əns (*French* ɛ̃su:sjɑ̃:s)/ *noun* light-hearted unconcern; nonchalance. ➤➤ **insouciant** *adj,* **insouciantly** *adv.* [French *insouciance,* from IN-¹ + *soucier* to trouble, disturb, from Latin *sollicitare:* see SOLICIT]

insp. *abbr* inspector.

inspan /in'span/ *verb trans* (**inspanned, inspanning**) *SAfr* **1** to yoke or harness (an animal). **2** to bring (something) or force (somebody) into service. [Afrikaans *inspan* from Dutch *inspannen,* from *in* in + *spannen* to stretch, yoke]

inspect /in'spekt/ *verb trans* **1** to examine (something or somebody) closely and critically; to scrutinize (them). **2** to view or examine (something) officially. ➤➤ **inspection** /-sh(ə)n/ *noun,* **inspective** /-tiv/ *adj.* [Latin *inspectus,* past part. of *inspicere* to look into, from IN-² + *specare* to look at]

inspector *noun* **1a** an official who carries out examinations in order to assess whether standards are being met or established rules and practices followed, e.g. in schools. **b** an official of a railway or bus company who checks passengers' tickets for validity. **2** a police officer ranking immediately above a sergeant. ➤➤ **inspectorate** /-rət/ *noun,* **inspectorship** *noun.*

inspiration /inspi'raysh(ə)n/ *noun* **1** the action or power of stimulating the intellect or emotions: *Genius is one per cent inspiration, ninety-nine per cent perspiration* — Thomas Edison. **2** an inspiring agent or influence: *She's been an inspiration to generations of schoolchildren.* **3** an inspired idea: *I've had an inspiration. Let's go to the seaside.* **4a** a divine influence or action on a person which qualifies him or her to receive and communicate sacred revelation, *esp* in the writing of the Bible. **b** a similar divine or supernatural action believed by some, *esp* formerly, to underlie the artistic creativity of e.g. poets. **5** the drawing of air into the lungs; inhalation. ➤➤ **inspirational** *adj,* **inspirationally** *adv,* **inspiratory** /in'spirət(ə)ri, in'spie-/ *adj.*

inspire /in'spie-ə/ *verb trans* **1** to have an animating or uplifting influence on (somebody): *She was particularly inspired by the Impressionists; inspiring music.* **2** to act as a stimulus for (somebody or something): *Threats don't necessarily inspire people to work harder; This piece of music was inspired by a trip to Venice.* **3** (+ with) to cause (somebody) to feel a particular emotion: *Seeing the old room again inspired him with nostalgia.* **4a** to communicate (something) to somebody supernaturally: *He believed his writings to be inspired by God.* **b** to influence or guide (somebody) by divine or supernatural inspiration. **5** *formal* to inhale (something). ➤ *verb intrans formal* to breathe in. ➤➤ **inspirer** *noun,* **inspiring** *adj,* **inspiringly** *adv.* [Middle English *inspiren* via French from Latin *inspirare* to blow or breathe upon, from IN-² + *spirare* to breathe]

inspired *adj* **1a** outstanding or brilliant in a way that suggests divine inspiration: *She gave an inspired rendering of the piano sonata.* **b** given or created by inspiration. **2** having been inhaled.

inspirit /in'spirit/ *verb trans* (**inspirited, inspiriting**) to motivate or encourage (somebody). ➤➤ **inspiriting** *adj,* **inspiritingly** *adv.*

inspissate /in'spisayt/ *verb trans* to make (something) thick or thicker, *esp* by condensation. ➤➤ **inspissation** /-'saysh(ə)n/ *noun.* [late Latin *inspissatus,* past part. of *inspissare* to thicken, from IN-² + *spissus* thick]

inst. *abbr* **1** formerly used in business letters: instant. **2** institute. **3** institution.

instability /instə'biliti/ *noun* (*pl* **instabilities**) lack of stability, *esp* emotional or mental stability.

install (*NAmer* **instal**) /in'stawl/ *verb trans* **1** to place (something) in position for use or service: *They had a shower installed in the bathroom.* **2** to establish (somebody) in a specified place, condition, or status. **3** to induct (somebody) into an office, rank, or order, *esp* with ceremonies or formalities: *Once a new chairman had been installed, the company's fortunes began to improve.* ➤➤ **installer** *noun.* [early French *installer* from medieval Latin *installare* to put in a stall, from IN-² + *stallum* place, stall]

installation /instə'laysh(ə)n/ *noun* **1** the act or an instance of installing or being installed. **2** a device or piece of equipment fitted in place to perform some specified function: *a new gas central-heating installation.* **3** a military base or establishment: *US installations in Europe.* **4** a large-scale work of art that is assembled in the gallery where it is exhibited.

instalment (*NAmer* **installment**) /in'stawlmənt/ *noun* **1** any of the parts into which a debt is divided when payment is made at intervals. **2a** any of several parts, e.g. of a publication, presented at intervals. **b** a single part of a serial story. [alteration of earlier *estallment* payment by instalment, from early French *estaler* to place, fix]

instance[1] /'inst(ə)ns/ *noun* **1** an example cited as an illustration or proof: *the justice ... full of wise saws and modern instances —* Shakespeare. **2** a situation viewed as one stage in a process or series of events: *The author prefers, in this instance, to remain anonymous.* **3** the institution of a legal action: *a court of first instance.* **4** *formal* a request: *I am writing to you at the instance of my client.* ✳ **for instance** as an example.

Word history
Middle English *instaunce* via French from Latin *instantia* presence, urgency, from *instare* to be present, from IN-² + *stare* to stand. The word originally meant 'urgency, an urgent entreaty'; in medieval Latin *instantia* was used to translate Greek *enstasis* objection, example to the contrary, hence the current sense 'example', which dates from the 16th cent.

instance[2] *verb trans* **1** to serve as an example of (something). **2** to put (something) forward as a case or example; to cite (it).

instancy /'inst(ə)nsi/ *noun archaic* urgency or insistence.

instant[1] /'inst(ə)nt/ *noun* **1** a very brief period of time; a second. **2** a precise point in time, *esp* separating two states: *at the instant of death.* **3** *formal, dated* used in business correspondence: the present or current month: compare PROXIMO, ULTIMO. [Middle English ultimately from Latin *instant-, instans,* present part. of *instare*: see INSTANCE[1]]

instant[2] *adj* **1** immediate: *The play was an instant success.* **2** premixed, precooked, or otherwise prepared for easy final preparation: *instant coffee.* **3** appearing in or as if in ready-to-use form: *updating your image with instant beards, moustaches and sideburns —* Playboy. **4a** existing in the present; current: *previous felonies not related to the instant crime.* **b** *formal, dated* used in business correspondence: of or occurring in the present month. **5** *formal* demanding or urgent.

instantaneous /inst(ə)n'tayni·əs/ *adj* **1** occurring or acting instantly; immediate: *Death was instantaneous.* **2** occurring or present at a particular instant: *instantaneous velocity.* ➤➤ **instantaneity** /-'neeiti, -'nayiti/ *noun,* **instantaneously** *adv,* **instantaneousness** *noun.* [medieval Latin *instantaneus,* from *instant-, instans*: see INSTANT[1]]

instanter /in'stantə/ *adv archaic or formal* instantly. [Latin *instanter* earnestly, vehemently, from *instant-, instans*: see INSTANT[1]]

instantiate /in'stanshiayt/ *verb trans* to represent (something abstract) by a concrete example. ➤➤ **instantiation** /-'aysh(ə)n/ *noun.* [Latin *instantia*: see INSTANCE[1]]

instantly *adv* at once; immediately.

instar /'instah/ *noun* an insect or similar arthropod in a particular stage between successive moults, or the stage itself. [Latin *instar* equivalent, figure]

instate /in'stayt/ *verb trans* to establish (somebody) in a rank or office. ➤➤ **instatement** *noun.*

instauration /instaw'raysh(ə)n/ *noun formal* the restoration of something after decay or a lapse. [Latin *instauration-, instauratio,* from *instaurare* to renew, restore]

instead /in'sted/ *adv* as a substitute or alternative: *I was going to write but called instead; He sent his son instead.*

instead of *prep* as a substitute for or alternative to. [Middle English *in sted of* in place of]

instep /'instep/ *noun* **1** the arched middle portion of the human foot, or the upper surface of it. **2** the part of a shoe, sock, etc over the instep.

instigate /'instigayt/ *verb trans* **1** to initiate (a course of action or procedure, e.g. a legal investigation). **2** to provoke or incite (somebody) to do something. ➤➤ **instigation** /-'gaysh(ə)n/ *noun,* **instigative** *adj,* **instigator** *noun.* [Latin *instigatus,* past part. of *instigare* to urge, incite, from IN-² + *stigare* to prick]

instil (*NAmer* **instill**) /in'stil/ *verb trans* (**instilled, instilling**) **1** (+ in/into) to impart (something) gradually: *She was a gifted teacher, instilling in children a love of learning.* **2** to cause (something) to enter drop by drop: *Instil the medication into the infected eye.* ➤➤ **instillation** /-'laysh(ə)n/ *noun,* **instilment** *noun.* [early French *instiller* from Latin *instillare* to drip, from IN-² + *stillare* to drop, from *stilla* a drop]

instinct[1] /'instingkt/ *noun* **1** a natural or inherent way of acting or thinking: *She had an instinct for the right word.* **2** an animal's largely inheritable tendency to respond in a particular way without reason.

Editorial note
Instinct is inherited behaviour patterns, or skills, with motivations for rewards and fears for avoiding danger, though it is not in consciousness. It might be described as knowledge, gradually discovered by natural selection and stored in the genetic code. Although individual learning is not transmitted for inheritance, instinctive knowledge is — Professor Richard Gregory.

➤➤ **instinctual** /in'stingkchooəl/ *adj.* [Middle English from Latin *instinctus* impulse, from *instinguere* to incite, from IN-² + *stinguere* to sting, goad]

instinct[2] *adj formal* (+ with) imbued or infused with something: *writing instinct with patriotism.*

instinctive /in'stingktiv/ *adj* **1** relating to or prompted by instinct: *instinctive behaviour.* **2** arising spontaneously and being independent of judgment or will: *an instinctive doubt of their honesty.* ➤➤ **instinctively** *adv.*

institute[1] /'instityooht/ *noun* **1a** an organization for the promotion of a particular cause or for the carrying on of research or education in a particular field. **b** the premises of such an organization. **2a** *formal* an elementary principle recognized as authoritative. **b** (*usu in pl*) a treatise of principles, *esp* of law.

institute[2] *verb trans* **1** to originate and establish (something): *She instituted many social reforms.* **2** *archaic* to appoint (somebody) to an official position; to install (them). [Middle English from Latin *institutus,* past part. of *instituere* to establish, from IN-² + *statuere*: see STATUTE]

institution /insti'tyoohsh(ə)n/ *noun* **1** an established organization or body, e.g. a university or hospital. **2** an established practice in a culture: *the institution of marriage.* **3** a familiar activity or object: *His bow tie is something of an institution.* **4** *dated* a psychiatric hospital or unit. ➤➤ **institutional** *adj.*

institutionalise /insti'tyoohsh(ə)nliez/ *verb trans* see INSTITUTIONALIZE.

institutionalism *noun* emphasis on organization, e.g. in religion, at the expense of other factors.

institutionalize *or* **institutionalise** *verb trans* **1** to establish (something) as a custom or regular practice: *institutionalized racism.* **2a** to put or keep (somebody) in an institution, *esp* a psychiatric hospital. **b** to cause (somebody) to acquire personality traits typical of people in an institution, *esp* a lack of independent thought or action. ➤➤ **institutionalization** /-'zaysh(ə)n/ *noun.*

instruct /in'strukt/ *verb trans* **1** to teach (somebody), *esp* in a non-academic discipline. **2** to direct (somebody) authoritatively; to command (them). **3** to engage (a lawyer, *specif* a barrister) for a case. **4** to inform (somebody) of something. ➤ *verb intrans* to teach. [Middle English *instructen* from Latin *instructus,* past part. of *instruere* to construct, equip, instruct, from IN-² + *struere* to build, pile up]

instruction /in'struksh(ə)n/ *noun* **1** (*usu in pl*). **a** an order or command: *They had instructions not to admit strangers.* **b** advice on how to do something, or a manual outlining the procedure for doing it.

2 a code that tells a computer to perform a particular operation. **3** teaching or training. ⟫ **instructional** *adj*.

instructive /in'struktiv/ *adj* giving useful information or advice; enlightening. ⟫ **instructively** *adv*, **instructiveness** *noun*.

instructor *noun* **1** a teacher, *esp* of a technical or practical subject: *a swimming instructor*. **2** *NAmer* a college teacher below professorial rank. ⟫ **instructorship** *noun*.

instructress /in'struktris/ *noun dated* a female instructor.

instrument[1] /'instrəmənt/ *noun* **1** an implement, tool, or device designed *esp* for delicate work or measurement: *scientific instruments*. **2** a device used to produce music. **3** an electrical or mechanical device used in navigating an aircraft, ship, or vehicle. **4** a formal legal document. **5a** a means whereby something is achieved, performed, or furthered. **b** somebody who is used by a person to achieve their usu dishonourable ends; a dupe. [Middle English from Latin *instrumentum*, from *instruere*: see INSTRUCT]

instrument[2] *verb trans* **1** to orchestrate (a piece of music). **2** to equip (e.g. a vehicle) with instruments.

instrumental[1] /instrə'mentl/ *adj* **1** (+ in) serving as an instrument, means, agent, or tool: *She was instrumental in organizing the strike*. **2** relating to, composed for, or performed on a musical instrument, *esp* as distinct from the human voice. **3** said of a grammatical case: expressing means or agency. ⟫ **instrumentality** /-'taliti/ *noun*, **instrumentally** *adv*.

instrumental[2] *noun* a musical composition or passage for instruments but not voice.

instrumentalist *noun* a player of a musical instrument.

instrumentation /,instrəmən'taysh(ə)n, 'instrəmen-/ *noun* **1** the instruments specified for the performance of a musical composition. **2** the set of navigation instruments on an aeroplane, ship, etc.

instrument panel *noun* a panel on which instruments are mounted, *esp* a dashboard.

insubordinate[1] /insə'bawdinət/ *adj* unwilling to submit to authority; disobedient. ⟫ **insubordinately** *adv*, **insubordination** /-'naysh(ə)n/ *noun*.

insubordinate[2] *noun* somebody who is insubordinate.

insubstantial /insəb'stansh(ə)l/ *adj* **1** lacking firmness or solidity; flimsy. **2** lacking substance or material nature; imaginary or unreal. ⟫ **insubstantiality** /-shi'aliti/ *noun*. [prob via French *insubstantiel* from late Latin *insubstantialis*, from IN-[1] + Latin *substantia*: see SUBSTANCE]

insufferable /in'suf(ə)rəbl/ *adj* too bad or unpleasant to put up with; intolerable: *an insufferable bore*. ⟫ **insufferably** *adv*.

insufficiency /insə'fish(ə)nsi/ *noun* **1** the quality of being insufficient. **2** the inability of an organ or body part, e.g. the heart or kidneys, to function normally.

insufficient /insə'fish(ə)nt/ *adj* deficient in power, capacity, or competence; inadequate. ⟫ **insufficiently** *adv*. [Middle English via French from late Latin *insufficient-, insufficiens*, from IN-[1] + Latin *sufficient-, sufficiens*: see SUFFICIENT]

insufflate /'insuflayt/ *verb trans formal* **1** to blow (something) on or into something. **2** to blow (e.g. a medicinal powder or gas) into a body cavity. ⟫ **insufflation** /-'flaysh(ə)n/ *noun*, **insufflator** *noun*. [late Latin *insufflatus*, past part. of *insufflare* to blow in, from IN-[2] + *sufflare*: see SOUFFLÉ]

insular /'insyoolə/ *adj* **1** relating to islands or in the form of an island. **2a** cut off from other people or the wider community. **b** lacking in breadth of outlook or in liberalism; narrow-minded. **3** in medicine, relating to an island of cells or tissue. ⟫ **insularism** *noun*, **insularity** /-'lariti/ *noun*, **insularly** *adv*. [late Latin *insularis* from Latin *insula* island]

insulate /'insyoolayt/ *verb trans* **1** to separate (something) from conducting bodies by means of nonconductors so as to prevent the transfer or loss of electricity, heat, or sound. **2** to place or confine (somebody) in a situation that is detached from the wider world, *esp* to protect them from harsh realities. [Latin *insula* island + -ATE[4]]

insulating tape *noun* a form of adhesive tape that can be wrapped around exposed electrical wires or connections to insulate them.

insulation /insyoo'laysh(ə)n/ *noun* **1** material used in insulating. **2** the act or an instance of insulating or being insulated.

insulator *noun* any material that is a poor conductor of electricity, heat, or sound.

insulin /'insyoolin/ *noun* a pancreatic hormone that is essential for regulating the level of glucose in the blood, and a deficiency of which leads to diabetes mellitus. [Latin *insula* island + -IN[1], referring to the ISLETS OF LANGERHANS]

insult[1] /in'sult/ *verb trans* to treat (somebody or something) with insolence, indignity, or contempt, usu causing offence: *These are arguments that insult the reader's intelligence*. ⟫ **insultingly** *adv*. [early French *insulter* from Latin *insultare*, literally 'to spring upon', ultimately from IN-[2] + *salire* to leap]

insult[2] /'insult/ *noun* **1** a remark, gesture, etc that insults. **2** in medicine, injury to the body or one of its parts, or something that causes such an injury.

insuperable /in's(y)oohpərəbl/ *adj* incapable of being surmounted, overcome, or passed over: *insuperable difficulties*. ⟫ **insuperability** /-'biliti/ *noun*, **insuperably** *adv*. [Middle English via French from Latin *insuperabilis*, from IN-[1] + *superare* to surmount, from *super* over, above]

insupportable /insə'pawtəbl/ *adj* **1** impossible to tolerate; unendurable: *insupportable pain*. **2** incapable of being supported or sustained: *insupportable charges*. ⟫ **insupportably** *adv*. [early French *insupportable* from late Latin *insupportabilis*, from IN-[1] + *supportare*: see SUPPORT[1]]

insurance /in'shooərəns, in'shawrəns/ *noun* **1a** a contract whereby one party undertakes to indemnify another against loss by a particular contingency or risk, or the protection offered by such a contract. **b** the premium demanded under such a contract. **c** the sum for which something is insured. **2** the business of insuring people or property. **3** the act or an instance of insuring somebody or something.

Usage note
insurance *or* **assurance**? See note at ASSURANCE.

insure /in'shooə, in'shaw/ *verb trans* **1** to give, take, or procure insurance on (a property, etc) or for (an owner). **2** (+ against) to protect (somebody) from something unpleasant. **3** *chiefly NAmer* to ensure (something). ⟫ *verb intrans* to contract to give or take insurance, *specif* to act as underwriter. ⟫ **insurability** /-'biliti/ *noun*, **insurable** *adj*, **insurer** *noun*. [Middle English *insuren*, prob alteration of *assuren*: see ASSURE]

Usage note
insure, **ensure**, *or* **assure**? See note at ASSURE.

insured *noun* (*pl* **insured**) (**the insured**) somebody whose life or property is insured.

insurgence /in'suhj(ə)ns/ *noun* = INSURGENCY.

insurgency /in'suhj(ə)nsi/ *noun* (*pl* **insurgencies**) a condition of revolt against a government that is less than an organized revolution and is not recognized as warfare.

insurgent[1] /in'suhj(ə)nt/ *noun* somebody who revolts against civil authority or an established government. [Latin *insurgent-, insurgens*, present part. of *insurgere* to rise up, from IN-[2] + *surgere*: see SURGE[1]]

insurgent[2] *adj* rising in opposition to civil authority or established leadership; rebellious. ⟫ **insurgently** *adv*.

insurmountable /insə'mowntəbl/ *adj* too great or difficult to conquer; insuperable: *insurmountable problems*. ⟫ **insurmountability** /-'biliti/ *noun*, **insurmountably** *adv*.

insurrection /insə'reksh(ə)n/ *noun* a revolt against civil authority or established government. ⟫ **insurrectional** *adj*, **insurrectionary** *adj and noun*, **insurrectionist** *noun*. [Middle English via French from late Latin *insurrection-, insurrectio*, from *insurgere*: see INSURGENT[1]]

inswing /'inswing/ *noun* the swing of a bowled cricket ball from the off to the leg side: compare OUTSWING. ⟫ **inswinger** *noun*.

int. *abbr* **1** integral. **2** interior. **3** intermediate. **4** internal. **5** international. **6** interpreter. **7** intransitive.

intact /in'takt/ *adj* **1** not harmed, damaged, or diminished; whole. **2a** being a virgin. **b** not castrated. [Middle English *intacte* from Latin *intactus*, from IN-[1] + *tactus*, past part. of *tangere* to touch]

intaglio /in'tahlioh/ *noun* (*pl* **intaglios**) **1a** an incised or engraved design made in hard material, *esp* stone, and sunk below the surface of the material. **b** the process of producing such designs. **c** printing done from a plate engraved in intaglio. **2** something, e.g. a gem, carved in intaglio. ⟫ **intaglioed** *adj*, **intaglioed** *adj*. [Italian *intaglio*, from *intagliare* to engrave, from *in-* (from Latin IN-[2]) + *tagliare* to cut]

intake /'intayk/ *noun* **1** an opening through which liquid or gas enters an enclosure or system; an inlet. **2a** (*treated as sing. or pl*) an amount or number taken in: *This year's intake of students are not as bright as last year's*. **b** the act or an instance of taking in.

intangible[1] /in'tanjəbl/ *adj* **1** not able to be perceived by touch; impalpable. **2** not clear or definite; vague: *The unknown never ceased to press upon him with its mysteries and terrors, intangible and ever-menacing* — Jack London. **3** said of assets such as patents or goodwill: having no physical form but having a value and able to be bought and sold. ➤➤ **intangibility** /-'biliti/ *noun*, **intangibly** *adv*. [French *intangible* from medieval Latin *intangibilis*, from IN-[1] + late Latin *tangibilis*: see TANGIBLE[1]]

intangible[2] *noun* something intangible.

intarsia /in'tahsi-ə/ *noun* **1** elaborate inlaid mosaic work in wood. **2** a geometric knitting pattern resembling intarsia, or a method of knitting that produces this. [German *Intarsia*, modification of Italian *intarsio*, ultimately from Latin IN-[2] + Arabic *tarṣī* mosaic inlay]

integer /'intijə/ *noun* the number 1 or any number, e.g. 6, 0, –23, obtainable by once or repeatedly adding one to or subtracting one from the number one. [Latin *integer*, literally 'untouched', from IN[1] + *tangere* to touch]

integrable /'intigrəbl/ ➤➤ /-'biliti/.

integral[1] /'intigrəl, in'tegrəl/ *adj* **1** essential to completeness; constituent: *Timing is an integral part of the plan*. **2** lacking nothing essential; whole. **3** formed as a unit with another part. **4** relating to a mathematical integer, integral, or integration. ➤➤ **integrality** /inti'graliti/ *noun*, **integrally** *adv*. [late Latin *integralis*, from Latin *integer*: see ENTIRE]

Usage note
Modern dictionaries of both British and American English accept two ways of pronouncing *integral*: with the stress on the first syllable *in-*, or, less commonly, with the stress on the second syllable *-teg-*.

integral[2] /'intigrəl/ *noun* **1** a mathematical expression which is essentially the sum of a large number of infinitely small quantities, and one form of which can be used to find the area under a given curve. **2** a solution of a differential equation.

integral calculus /'intigrəl/ *noun* a branch of mathematics dealing with methods of finding integrals and with their applications, e.g. to the determination of lengths, areas, and volumes and to the solution of differential equations.

integrand /'intigrand/ *noun* a mathematical expression to be integrated. [Latin *integrandus*, verbal noun from *integrare*: see INTEGRATE]

integrate /'intigrayt/ *verb trans* **1** to form or blend (separate elements) into a whole. **2a** to combine (things) together or (one thing) with something else. **b** (+ into) to incorporate (somebody or something) into a larger unit. **3** to end the segregation of (peoples, groups, etc), bringing them together to form a single community. **4** in mathematics, to find the integral of (e.g. a function or differential equation). ➤ *verb intrans* **1** to become integrated. **2** in mathematics, to calculate an integral. ➤➤ **integrability** /-'biliti/ *noun*, **integrable** *adj*, **integrative** /-'tiv/ *adj*. [Latin *integratus*, past part. of *integrare* to make whole, from *integer*: see INTEGER]

integrated circuit *noun* an electronic circuit formed in or on a single tiny piece of semiconductor material, e.g. silicon. ➤➤ **integrated circuitry** *noun*.

integrated services digital network *noun* a telecommunications network that allows both voice and computer data to be transmitted as digital signals.

integration /inti'graysh(ə)n/ *noun* **1** the act or an instance of integrating or being integrated, *esp* the bringing together of different peoples, groups, etc as equals in a single community. **2** in mathematics: **a** the operation of finding a function whose derivative is known. **b** the operation of solving a differential equation. **3** in psychology, coordination of mental processes into an effective personality.

integrationist[1] *noun* an advocate of social, *esp* racial, integration.

integrationist[2] *adj* advocating or producing social, *esp* racial, integration.

integrator *noun* **1** somebody or something that integrates. **2** a device, e.g. in a computer, whose output is the value of a mathematical integral.

integrity /in'tegriti/ *noun* **1** uncompromising adherence to a code of *esp* moral or artistic values. **2** the quality or state of being complete or undivided: *The integrity of the Empire was threatened*. **3** *formal* an unimpaired condition; wholeness. [Middle English via French from Latin *integritas*, from *integer*: see INTEGER]

integument /in'tegyoomənt/ *noun* a skin, membrane, husk, or other covering or enclosure, *esp* of an animal or plant, or part of it. ➤➤ **integumental** /-'mentl/ *adj*, **integumentary** /-'ment(ə)ri/ *adj*. [Latin *integumentum*, from *integere* to cover up, from IN-[2] + *tegere* to cover]

intellect /'int(ə)lekt/ *noun* **1** the capacity for intelligent thought, *esp* when highly developed. **2** *informal* a highly intelligent person; a brain. [Middle English via French from Latin *intellectus*, past part. of *intellegere*: see INTELLIGENT]

intellection /int(ə)'leksh(ə)n/ *noun* *formal* thought or reasoning. ➤➤ **intellective** /-tiv/ *adj*.

intellectual[1] /int(ə)'lektyoo-əl, -chəl/ *adj* **1a** of the intellect. **b** developed or chiefly guided by the intellect rather than by emotion or experience: *a coldly intellectual artist*. **2** given to or requiring the use of the intellect. ➤➤ **intellectuality** /-tyoo'aliti/ *noun*, **intellectually** *adv*.

intellectual[2] *noun* an intellectual person: *To the man-in-the-street … the word 'Intellectual' suggests straight away a man who's untrue to his wife* — W H Auden.

intellectualise /intə'lektyoo-əliez, -'lekchəliez/ *verb trans and intrans* see INTELLECTUALIZE.

intellectualism *noun* **1** devotion to the exercise of intellect or to intellectual pursuits, *esp* excessively and to the detriment of the emotions. **2** the doctrine that knowledge comes from the use of reasoning. ➤➤ **intellectualist** *noun*.

intellectualize or **intellectualise** /intə'lektyoo-əliez, -'lekchəliez/ *verb trans* **1** to make (something) intellectual or more intellectual. **2** to consider (something) in a intellectual way. ➤ *verb intrans* to think or reason. ➤➤ **intellectualization** /-'zaysh(ə)n/ *noun*.

intellectual property *noun* in law, property that is the product of the creative imagination and cannot therefore be touched but may still be owned, such as a copyright.

intelligence /in'telij(ə)ns/ *noun* **1** the ability to learn, apply knowledge, or think abstractly. **2a** information concerning an enemy, or an organization or group with the task of gathering such information. **b** news or information of any kind. **3** *formal* the act of understanding. **4** an intelligent being: *He believed he'd been contacted by alien intelligences*. [Middle English via French from Latin *intelligentia*, from *intelligent-*, *intelligens*: see INTELLIGENT]

intelligence quotient *noun* a number expressing the ratio of somebody's intelligence as determined by a test to the average for his or her age: compare MENTAL AGE.

intelligencer *noun* *archaic* somebody who brings news; a reporter.

intelligence test *noun* a test designed to determine relative mental capacity.

intelligent /in'telij(ə)nt/ *adj* **1** having or indicating intelligence, *esp* high intelligence. **2** said of electronic equipment: able to respond to change and to initiate action based on that response: *intelligent weapons systems*. ➤➤ **intelligently** *adv*. [Latin *intelligent-*, *intelligens*, present part. of *intelligere*, *intellegere* to understand, from INTER- + *legere* to choose]

intelligentsia /in,teli'jentsi-ə/ *noun* (*treated as sing. or pl*) the intellectuals who form an artistic, social, or political class or vanguard. [Russian *intelligentsiya* from Latin *intelligentia* intelligence, from *intelligent-*, *intelligens*: see INTELLIGENT]

intelligible /in'telijəbl/ *adj* **1** capable of being understood. **2** in philosophy, able to be apprehended by the intellect only. ➤➤ **intelligibility** /-'biliti/ *noun*, **intelligibly** *adv*. [Middle English from Latin *intelligibilis*, from *intelligere*: see INTELLIGENT]

intemperate /in'temp(ə)rət/ *adj* **1** going beyond the bounds of reasonable behaviour; unrestrained: *an intemperate outburst*. **2** marked by lack of moderation; excessive: *intemperate drinking*. **3** said of a climate: extreme, *esp* harsh. ➤➤ **intemperately** *adv*, **intemperateness** *noun*. [Middle English *intemperat* from Latin *intemperatus*, from IN-[1] + *temperatus*: see TEMPERATE]

intend /in'tend/ *verb trans* **1a** to have (something) in mind as a purpose or goal. **b** to design (something) for a specified use or future: *His poems are intended for reading aloud*. **2** to mean or signify (something): *What do you intend by that remark?* ⟫ **intender** *noun*. [Middle English *entenden, intenden* via French from Latin *intendere* to purpose, extend, attend from IN-² + *tendere* to stretch]

intendant *noun* **1** a senior administrator, *esp* in the arts. **2** an administrative official, *esp* under the French, Spanish, or Portuguese monarchies. ⟫ **intendancy** *noun*. [French *intendant*, ultimately from Latin *intendent-, intendens*, present part. of *intendere*: see INTEND]

intended¹ *adj* planned; future. ⟫ **intendedly** *adv*.

intended² *noun* (*pl* **intendeds**) *informal* somebody's future spouse: *He was walking arm in arm with his intended.*

intendment *noun* the true meaning or intention of something, *esp* a law.

intense /in'tens/ *adj* **1a** feeling emotion deeply, *esp* by nature or temperament. **b** said of an emotion: deeply felt. **2** highly concentrated; intensive. **3a** existing or occurring in an extreme degree: *intense heat.* **b** having or showing a usual characteristic in extreme degree: *an intense sun.* ⟫ **intensely** *adv*, **intenseness** *noun*. [Middle English via French from Latin *intensus*, past part. of *intendere*: see INTEND]

Usage note
intense *or* intensive? These two words, though similar in form and meaning, have different areas of use. *Intense* means 'extreme': *intense heat*; *under intense pressure to find a solution*. It can also be used to describe people who are serious and feel emotion deeply (*a very intense young man*) and, when used in connection with people and their activities, usually suggests a high degree of personal commitment or emotional involvement: *an intense effort to stave off bankruptcy*. *Intensive*, on the other hand, is used more objectively and means 'highly concentrated', suggesting organized effort more than personal involvement: *conducted an intensive search of the area*.

intensifier /in'tensifie-ə/ *noun* **1** a word or form, e.g. *very*, that gives force or emphasis. **2** in photography, a chemical used to improve the RESOLUTION (clarity of image) of a negative.

intensify /in'tensifie/ *verb* (**intensifies, intensified, intensifying**) ➤ *verb trans* to make (something) intense. ➤ *verb intrans* to become intense. ⟫ **intensification** /-fi'kaysh(ə)n/ *noun*.

Word history
This word was first used by S T Coleridge in his *Biographia Literaria* (1817): 'the will itself by confining and intensifying the attention may arbitrarily give vividness or distinctness to any object whatsoever'. Coleridge added a footnote to justify his coinage, asserting that the earlier use of *intend* in this sense had become confusingly ambiguous, and that the periphrastic *render intense* would ruin the beautiful harmony of his sentence, although he admits that the new word sounds 'uncouth to my own ear'. The word was well established by the middle of the 19th cent.

intension /in'tensh(ə)n/ *noun* **1** intensity. **2** in philosophy, the set of characteristics that belong to the thing that a word refers to; a connotation. ⟫ **intensional** *adj*.

intensity *noun* (*pl* **intensities**) **1** extreme degree of strength, force, or energy. **2** the magnitude of force or energy per unit, e.g. of surface, charge, or mass. **3** the purity of a colour; saturation.

intensive¹ /in'tensiv/ *adj* **1** highly concentrated: *an intensive bombardment of the enemy positions.* **2** dealing very thoroughly with a subject and at a fast pace: *intensive training.* **3** (*usu in combination*) using a specified factor of production to a greater extent than others: *labour-intensive.* **4** constituting or relating to a method designed to increase productivity by the expenditure of more capital and labour rather than by increase in the land or raw materials used: *intensive farming.* ⟫ **intensively** *adv*.

Usage note
intensive *or* intense? See note at INTENSE.

intensive² *noun* in grammar, an intensifier.

intensive care *noun* the continuous care and treatment of a seriously ill patient, usu in a special section of a hospital: *an intensive-care unit.*

intent¹ /in'tent/ *noun* **1** *chiefly archaic, literary, or formal.* **a** the fact of intending; intention: *I hope you have no intent to turn husband, have you?* — Shakespeare; *First there was the broad statement of intent in the policy review document* — Independent. **b** the state of mind with which an act is done: *I did not do it of an evil intent* — Bunyan; *It's only dirty play if there is intent there* — Independent. **2** criminal intention; the intention of committing a crime: *loitering with intent.* **3** meaning or significance. ✴ **to all intents and purposes** in every practical or important respect; virtually. [Middle English *entent* via French from Latin *intentus*, from *intendere*: see INTEND]

intent² *adj* **1** (+ on/upon) having the mind, attention, or will concentrated on something or some end or purpose: *He was already intent on stirring up trouble.* **2** directed with strained or eager attention; concentrated: *an intent gaze.* ⟫ **intently** *adv*, **intentness** *noun*.

intention /in'tensh(ə)n/ *noun* **1** what somebody intends to do or bring about; an aim. **2** a determination to act in a certain way; a resolve. **3** in philosophy, a concept. **4** the object for which a prayer or other religious devotion is offered. **5** (*in pl*) purpose with respect to proposal of marriage. **6** in medicine, the healing process of a wound.

intentional *adj* done by intention or design; deliberate. ⟫ **intentionally** *adv*.

inter /in'tuh/ *verb trans* (**interred, interring**) to place (usu a dead body) in the earth or a tomb. [Middle English *enteren* from early French *enterrer*, from IN-² + Latin *terra* earth]

inter. *abbr* intermediate.

inter- *prefix* forming words, with the meanings: **1** between, among, or in the midst: *intercity; interpenetrate; interstellar.* **2a** reciprocal: *interrelation.* **b** reciprocally: *intermarry.* **3** located between: *interface.* **4** carried on between: *international.* **5** occurring between: *interglacial.* **6** with intensity: *internecine.* [Middle English *inter-, enter-* via French from Latin *inter-*]

Usage note
inter-, intra-, *or* intro-? These three prefixes are easily confused. *Inter-* means 'between': *international; intermarriage*. *Intra-* means 'within': *an intrauterine device*. *Intro-* means 'inwards': *introspection; an introvert*. The *Internet* is the system of (or between) computer networks throughout the world; an *intranet* is a private network of computer communications within an organization.

interact /intə'rakt/ *verb intrans* to act upon each other. ⟫ **interactant** *noun*, **interaction** /-sh(ə)n/ *noun*.

interactive /intə'raktiv/ *adj* characterized by interaction; *specif* involving the exchange of information between a computer and user while a program is being run.

inter alia /,intər 'ayli-ə, 'ahli-ə/ *adv* among other things. [Latin *inter alia*]

interbreed /intə'breed/ *verb* (*past tense and past part.* **interbred** /-'bred/) ➤ *verb intrans* **1** to crossbreed. **2** to breed within a single family or other closed population. ➤ *verb trans* to cause (*esp* animals) to interbreed.

intercalary /in'tuhkəl(ə)ri/ *adj* **1a** inserted in a calendar to resynchronize it with some objective time-measure, e.g. the solar year, as is February 29 in the Gregorian calendar. **b** said of a year: containing an intercalary period. **2** inserted between other elements or layers; interpolated. [Latin *intercalarius* from *intercalare*: see INTERCALATE]

intercalate /in'tuhkəlayt/ *verb trans* **1** to insert (something) between or among existing items, elements, or layers. **2** to insert (an intercalary period) into a calendar. ⟫ **intercalation** /-'laysh(ə)n/ *noun*. [Latin *intercalatus*, past part. of *intercalare* to state to have been inserted, from INTER- + *calare* to proclaim]

intercede /intə'seed/ *verb intrans* to beg or plead on behalf of another person with a view to reconciling differences. [Latin *intercedere*, from INTER- + *cedere* to go]

intercellular /intə'selyoolə/ *adj* occurring between cells: *intercellular spaces.*

intercensal /intə'sensl/ *adj* relating to a period of time between censuses.

intercept¹ /intə'sept/ *verb trans* **1** to stop, seize, or interrupt (something or somebody) in progress, course, or movement, *esp* from one place to another. **2** in mathematics, to intersect (e.g. a curve). ⟫ **interception** /-sh(ə)n/ *noun*. [Latin *interceptus*, past part. of *intercipere* to catch between, from INTER- + *capere* to take]

intercept² /'intəsept/ *noun* **1a** an interception, *esp* the interception of a missile by an interceptor or of a target by a missile. **b** *NAmer* in sport, the intercepting of an opponent's pass. **2** the distance from the origin to a point where a graph crosses a coordinate axis, or the point itself.

interceptor *or* **intercepter** /intə'septə, 'intə-/ *noun* **1** somebody or something that intercepts. **2** a high-speed fast-climbing fighter plane or missile designed for defence against raiding bombers or missiles.

intercession /intə'sesh(ə)n/ *noun* the act or an instance of interceding, *esp* by prayer, petition, or entreaty. ➤➤ **intercessional** *adj*, **intercessor** /-'sesə/ *noun*, **intercessory** /-'sesəri/ *adj*. [via French from Latin *intercession-*, *intercessio*, from *intercedere*: see INTERCEDE]

interchange[1] /intə'chaynj/ *verb trans* **1** to put each of (two things) in the place of the other. **2** to give (one thing in return for another), to exchange (them). ➤ *verb intrans* to change places reciprocally. ➤➤ **interchangeability** /-'biliti/ *noun*, **interchangeable** *adj*, **interchangeably** *adv*. [Middle English *entrechaungen* from early French *entre-* INTER- + *changier* to change]

interchange[2] /'intəchaynj/ *noun* **1** a junction of two or more roads having a system of separate levels that permit traffic to pass from one to another without the crossing of traffic streams. **2** the act or an instance of interchanging. **3** alternation.

intercity /intə'siti/ *adj* **1** existing or travelling between cities. **2** (**Intercity**) *trademark* in Britain, a fast rail service, mostly between main towns and cities.

intercollegiate /,intəkə'leeji-ət/ *adj* between colleges: *intercollegiate athletics competitions*.

intercolumniation /,intəkə,lumni'aysh(ə)n/ *noun* **1** the system of spacing the columns in a structure such as an ancient Greek or Roman temple or a building of a similar style. **2** the space between columns. [Latin *intercolumnium* space between two columns, from INTER- + *columna* column]

intercom /'intəkom/ *noun* an internal communication system, e.g. in a ship or building, with a microphone and loudspeaker at each station. [short for *intercommunication (system)*]

intercommunicate /,intəkə'myoohnikayt/ *verb intrans* to communicate with each other, e.g. **a** to have free passage from one to another: *The two rooms intercommunicate.* **b** to hold a conversation or exchange information. ➤➤ **intercommunication** /-'kaysh(ə)n/ *noun*.

intercommunion /,intəkə'myoohnyən/ *noun* the practice between denominations of the Christian faith of admitting one another's members to Communion.

interconnect /,intəkə'nekt/ *verb intrans* to connect with one another. ➤ *verb trans* to connect (one thing with another). ➤➤ **interconnection** /-'neksh(ə)n/ *noun*.

intercontinental /,intəkonti'nentl/ *adj* extending among continents, carried on between continents, or capable of travelling between continents: *an intercontinental ballistic missile*.

intercostal[1] /intə'kostl/ *adj* said of a body part: situated between the ribs. [Latin *intercostalis*, from INTER- + Latin *costa* rib]

intercostal[2] *noun* an intercostal muscle or other body part.

intercourse /'intəkaws/ *noun* **1a** = SEXUAL INTERCOURSE. **b** physical sexual contact between individuals that involves the genitals of at least one person: *oral intercourse*. **2** *formal* communication or dealings between people or groups. **3** *formal* exchange, *esp* of thoughts or feelings. [Middle English *intercurse* communication, commerce, via Old French from Latin *intercursus*, from *intercurrere* to run between, from INTER- + *currere* to run]

intercrop[1] /'intəkrop/ *verb* (**intercropped, intercropping**) ➤ *verb trans* to grow a crop in between rows, plots, etc of (another crop). ➤ *verb intrans* to grow two or more crops simultaneously on the same plot.

intercrop[2] *noun* a crop grown in between rows, plots, etc of another crop.

intercross[1] /'intəkros/ *noun* a product of crossbreeding; a hybrid.

intercross[2] /intə'kros/ *verb trans and intrans* = CROSSBREED[1].

intercurrent /intə'kurənt/ *adj* **1** said of a disease: occurring during the course of another disease. **2** *formal* occurring between things or in the middle of something; intervening. ➤➤ **intercurrently** *adv*. [Latin *intercurrent-*, *intercurrens*, present part. of *intercurrere*: see INTERCOURSE]

intercut /intə'kut/ *verb* (**intercutting**, *past tense and past part.* **intercut**) ➤ *verb trans* to insert shots from (one cinematic scene) alternately with shots from another, *esp* contrasting scene. ➤ *verb intrans* to alternate usu contrasting camera shots by cutting.

interdenominational /,intədinomi'naysh(ə)nl/ *adj* occurring between or involving different denominations, *esp* denominations of the Christian Church. ➤➤ **interdenominationalism** *noun*, **interdenominationally** *adv*.

interdepartmental /,intədeepaht'mentl/ *adj* carried on between or involving different departments, e.g. of a firm or an educational institution. ➤➤ **interdepartmentally** *adv*.

interdepend /,intədi'pend/ *verb intrans* to depend on each other.

interdependent /intədi'pend(ə)nt/ *adj* depending one on the other. ➤➤ **interdependence** *noun*.

interdict[1] /'intədikt/ *noun* **1** a prohibition, *esp* a court order forbidding something. **2** a Roman Catholic disciplinary measure withdrawing most sacraments and Christian burial from a person or district. [Middle English *entredit* via French from Latin *interdictum* prohibition, from past part. of *interdicere* to interpose, from INTER- + *dicere* to say]

interdict[2] /intə'dikt/ *verb trans* **1** to forbid (something) in a formal or authoritative manner. **2** to destroy, cut, or damage (e.g. an enemy line of supply) by firepower in order to stop or hamper the enemy. ➤➤ **interdiction** /-sh(ə)n/ *noun*, **interdictory** *adj*.

interdisciplinary /,intədisə'plinəri/ *adj* involving two or more disciplines or fields of study.

interest[1] /'int(ə)rest, -rəst/ *noun* **1a** readiness to be concerned with, moved by, or have one's attention attracted by something; curiosity. **b** the quality in a thing that arouses interest, or the thing itself: *Sport doesn't hold much interest for me; She has many interests*. **2a** a charge for borrowed money, generally a percentage of the amount borrowed. **b** something added above what is due. **3** benefit or advantage to somebody: *It is to your interest to speak first*. **4** a right, title, or legal share in something. **5** a person or group with a financial stake. **6** a business in which somebody has a financial stake. ✳ **declare one's interest** to disclose a personal, *esp* financial, connection with a subject under discussion, e.g. in Parliament. **in the interest/interests of** for the sake of something; for the benefit of something. [Middle English via Anglo-French from Latin *interesse* to be between, make a difference, concern, from INTER- + *esse* to be]

interest[2] *verb trans* **1** to engage the attention or arouse the interest of (somebody). **2** to induce or persuade (somebody) to have or do something.

interested *adj* **1** having the interest aroused or attention engaged. **2** affected or involved; not impartial. ➤➤ **interestedly** *adv*, **interestedness** *noun*.

interest-free *adj* not incurring interest charges: *interest-free credit*.

interesting *adj* holding the attention. ➤➤ **interestingly** *adv*, **interestingness** *noun*.

interface[1] /'intəfays/ *noun* **1** the place at which independent systems meet and act on or communicate with each other, *esp* a piece of computer hardware or software that allows a user to communicate with a computer. **2** a surface forming a common boundary between two bodies, regions, or phases: *an oil–water interface*. ➤➤ **interfacial** /-'faysh(ə)l/ *adj*.

interface[2] *verb trans* **1** to connect (things) by means of an interface: *This allows you to interface the production line with the computers*. **2** to serve as an interface for (something). ➤ *verb intrans* **1** to become interfaced. **2** to serve as an interface. **3** to interact.

interfacing *noun* stiffening material attached between two layers of fabric.

interfere /intə'fiə/ *verb intrans* **1** (+ with) to get in the way or be a hindrance: *Noise interferes with my work*. **2** (*often* + in) to enter into or take a part in matters that do not concern one: *I've told you not to interfere*. **3** said of sound, light, etc waves: to act so as to augment, diminish, or otherwise affect one another. **4** (+ with) in sport, to hinder illegally an attempt of a player to catch or hit a ball or puck. **5** *informal* (+ with) to carry out a sexual assault, *esp* one that falls short of rape. **6** to claim priority for an invention. **7** said of a horse: to hit a hoof against the opposite leg when walking. [early French *s'entreferir* to strike one another, ultimately from Latin INTER- + *ferire* to strike]

interference *noun* **1a** the act or an instance of interfering. **b** unwelcome meddling in the affairs of others. **2** something that produces the confusion of received radio signals by unwanted signals or noise, or the signals or noises themselves. **3** the illegal hindering of an opponent in hockey, ice hockey, etc. **4** the phenomenon resulting from the meeting of two wave trains (successions of waves: see WAVE TRAIN), e.g. of light or sound, with an increase in intensity at some points and a decrease at others. ➤➤ **interferential** /-fə'rensh(ə)l/ *adj*.

interferometer /ˌintəfəˈromitə/ *noun* an instrument that uses light interference phenomena for precise determination of wavelength, distance, etc. ➤➤ **interferometric** /-fiərəˈmetrik/ *adj*, **interferometry** /-tri/ *noun*.

interferon /intəˈfiəron/ *noun* a protein that inhibits the development of viruses and is produced by cells in response to infection by a virus. [INTERFERENCE + -ON¹]

interfuse /intəˈfyoohz/ *verb trans* to cause (two or more things) to blend. ➤ *verb intrans* to blend. ➤➤ **interfusion** /-zh(ə)n/ *noun*. [Latin *interfusus*, past part. of *interfundere* to pour between, from INTER- + *fundere* to pour]

intergalactic /intəgəˈlaktik/ *adj* existing, carried on, or operating between galaxies.

interglacial¹ /intəˈglays(h)iəl/ *adj* occurring or formed between two periods of glacial activity when much of the earth was covered by ice sheets.

interglacial² *noun* an interglacial period of relatively mild climate marked by a temporary retreat or shrinking of the ice.

intergovernmental /ˌintəguvə(n)ˈment(ə)l/ *adj* existing or occurring between two or more governments.

intergrade¹ /intəˈgrayd/ *verb intrans* to merge gradually one with another through a continuous series of intermediate forms. ➤➤ **intergradation** /-grəˈdaysh(ə)n/ *noun*.

intergrade² /ˈintəgrayd/ *noun* an intermediate or transitional form.

interim¹ /ˈintərim/ *noun* an intervening time: *Nothing will change in the interim.* [Latin *interim* (adv) meanwhile, from *inter* between]

interim² *adj* **1** temporary or provisional. **2** in finance, relating to something given or declared part way through the financial year.

interior¹ /inˈtiəri-ə/ *adj* **1** lying, occurring, or functioning within or inside something. **2** away from the border or shore. **3** relating to the domestic affairs of a country; internal. **4** of the mind or soul. ➤➤ **interiority** /-ˈoriti/ *noun*, **interiorly** *adv*. [Latin *interior* inner, comparative of *inter* between, within]

interior² *noun* **1** the internal or inner part of a thing. **2** the part of a country that lies away from the border or the shore. **3** the internal affairs of a country: *She was recently appointed Minister of the Interior.* **4** a representation of the interior of a building or room.

interior angle *noun* **1** the angle between two sides of a polygon. **2** any of the angles contained within two parallel lines and an intersecting line.

interior decoration *noun* the decorating and furnishing of the interiors of rooms, or the art or practice of planning it. ➤➤ **interior decorator** *noun*.

interior design *noun* = INTERIOR DECORATION.

interiorize *or* **interiorise** /inˈtiəriəriez/ *verb trans* to make (something) interior, *esp* to make (something) into a part of one's own inner being or personality; to internalize (it): *The whole problem is women interiorizing at a young age a culturally suggested inferiority.* ➤➤ **interiorization** /-ˈzaysh(ə)n/ *noun*.

interior monologue *noun* a literary device presenting a character's thoughts and feelings in the form of a monologue.

interior-sprung *adj* having springs within a padded casing: *interior-sprung mattress.*

interj. *abbr* interjection.

interject /intəˈjekt/ *verb trans* to throw in (e.g. a remark) abruptly among or between other things. ➤➤ **interjector** *noun*, **interjectory** *adj*. [Latin *interjectus*, past part. of *intericere* to throw between, from INTER- + *jacere* to throw]

interjection /intəˈjeksh(ə)n/ *noun* **1** an abruptly uttered word or phrase that expresses emotion; an exclamation. **2** the act or an instance of interjecting. ➤➤ **interjectional** *adj*, **interjectionally** *adv*.

interlace /intəˈlays/ *verb trans* **1** to join (things) by or as if by lacing them together. **2** to intersperse (something) with other things: *His narrative was interlaced with anecdotes.* ➤ *verb intrans* to cross one another intricately. ➤➤ **interlacement** *noun*. [Middle English *entrelacen* from early French *entrelacier*, from *entre-* INTER- + *lacier*: see LACE²]

interlard /intəˈlahd/ *verb trans* to intersperse (something) with something else, *esp* with something very different or irrelevant: *There was matter for a smile in that honest sermon, interlarded, as it was, with scraps of Greek and Hebrew, which no one understood, but*

every one expected as their right — Charles Kingsley. [early French *entrelarder*, from *entre* INTER- + *larder* to lard, from *lard*: see LARD¹]

interleaf /ˈintəleef/ *noun* a usu blank leaf inserted between two leaves of a book.

interleave /intəˈleev/ *verb trans* to provide (something) with interleaves, e.g. to supply (a book) with blank pages for notes or with sheets to protect colour plates, etc.

interleukin /intəˈl(y)oohkin/ *noun* any of various proteins produced by cells of the immune system that act on other cells of the immune system. [INTER- + *leuk-* + -IN¹]

interline¹ /intəˈlien/ *verb trans* to provide (a garment) with an interlining. [Middle English *interlinen*, from INTER- + *linen*: see LINE³]

interline² *verb trans* to insert something between written or printed lines of (a document, text, etc). ➤➤ **interlineation** /-liniˈaysh(ə)n/ *noun*. [Middle English *enterlinen* from medieval Latin *interlineare*, from Latin INTER- + *linea*: see LINE¹]

interlinear /intəˈlini-ə/ *adj* inserted between lines already written or printed. [Middle English *interliniare*, from Latin INTER- + *linea*: see LINE¹]

interlining /ˈintəliening/ *noun* a lining, e.g. of a coat, sewn between the ordinary lining and the outside fabric to give additional warmth or bulk.

interlock¹ /intəˈlok/ *verb intrans* to become firmly connected or related to each other, usu by parts designed to fit together. ➤ *verb trans* **1** to lock (things) together. **2** to connect (things) so that motion of any part is constrained by another. ➤➤ **interlocker** *noun*, **interlocking** /ˈin-/ *adj*.

interlock² /ˈintəlok/ *noun* **1** something that is interlocked. **2** a mechanism for synchronizing or coordinating the operation of other parts. **3** a fabric knitted with interlocking stitches.

interlocutor /intəˈlokyootə/ *noun formal* somebody who takes part in dialogue or conversation. ➤➤ **interlocution** /-ˈkyoohsh(ə)n/ *noun*. [Latin *interlocutus*, past part. of *interloqui* to speak between, from INTER- + *loqui* to speak]

interlocutory *adj* said of a judgment, etc: pronounced during a legal action and having only provisional status: *an interlocutory decree.* [medieval Latin *interlocutorius*, from late Latin *interlocutus*, past part. of *interloqui* (see INTERLOCUTOR) in the sense 'to pronounce a provisional sentence']

interlope /intəˈlohp/ *verb intrans* **1** to be an interloper. **2** to intrude or interfere. **3** to encroach on the rights, e.g. in trade, of others.

interloper /ˈintəlohpə/ *noun* somebody who interferes or encroaches; an intruder. [INTER- + *-loper* as in obsolete *landloper* vagabond, from early Dutch *landlooper*, from *land* land + *loopen* to run]

interlude /ˈintəloohd/ *noun* **1** an intervening period, space, or event, *esp* of a contrasting character; an interval. **2** a break between parts of a play or other performance. **3** a musical composition inserted between the parts of a longer composition, a drama, or a religious service. [Middle English *enterlude* from medieval Latin *interludium*, from INTER- + Latin *ludus* play]

intermarriage /intəˈmarij/ *noun* **1** marriage between members of different families, peoples, etc. **2** marriage between close relations; endogamy.

intermarry /intəˈmari/ *verb intrans* (**intermarries, intermarried, intermarrying**) **1** to marry somebody from the same group. **2** to become connected by marriage with another group: *The different races intermarry freely.*

intermediary¹ /intəˈmeedi-əri/ *noun* (*pl* **intermediaries**) somebody or something acting as a mediator or go-between.

intermediary² *adj* **1** intermediate. **2** acting as a mediator.

intermediate¹ /intəˈmeedi-ət/ *adj* being or occurring at the middle place, level, or degree or between two others or extremes. ➤➤ **intermediacy** /-si/ *noun*, **intermediately** *adv*, **intermediateness** *noun*. [medieval Latin *intermediatus*, from Latin *intermedius*, from INTER- + *medius* mid, middle]

intermediate² *noun* **1** somebody or something intermediate. **2** a chemical compound formed as an intermediate step in a reaction.

intermediate³ /intəˈmeediayt/ *verb intrans* to act as an intermediary; to mediate or intervene. ➤➤ **intermediation** /-ˈaysh(ə)n/ *noun*, **intermediator** *noun*. [medieval Latin *intermediatus*, past part. of *intermediare*, from INTER- + late Latin *mediare* to mediate]

intermediate technology *noun* technology that makes the best use of local resources, e.g. labour, for maximum economic and environmental benefit, in use particularly in developing countries but not necessarily economic for use in developed countries.

interment /in'tuhmənt/ *noun* the placing of a corpse in a grave; burial: *We enjoy an interment* — W S Gilbert.

Usage note
interment *or* internment? These two words are sometimes confused. *Interment* is a formal word for 'burial'; *internment* is the confinement of people who have not committed a crime but are thought to constitute a possible danger to the state, especially in wartime.

intermezzo /intə'metsoh/ *noun* (*pl* **intermezzi** /-see/ *or* **intermezzos**) **1** a movement that comes between the major sections of an extended musical work, e.g. an opera. **2** a short independent instrumental composition. [Italian *intermezzo*, from Latin *intermedius*: see INTERMEDIATE[1]]

interminable /in'tuhminəbl/ *adj* having or seeming to have no end, *esp* wearisomely long. ➤➤ **interminability** /-'biliti/ *noun*, **interminableness** *noun*, **interminably** *adv*. [Middle English from late Latin *interminabilis*, from Latin IN-[1] + *terminare*: see TERMINATE]

intermingle /intə'minggl/ *verb trans* to mix or mingle (things) together or combine (something) with something else. ➤ *verb intrans* to be mixed or mingled together.

intermission /intə'mish(ə)n/ *noun* **1** a break between acts of a performance. **2** an intervening period between attacks of a disease. **3** the act or an instance of intermitting or being intermitted. [Latin *intermission-*, *intermissio*, from *intermittere* to put between]

intermit /intə'mit/ *verb* (**intermitted**, **intermitting**) ➤ *verb intrans* to cease for a time or at intervals. ➤ *verb trans* to cause (something) to cease in this way. [Latin *intermittere* to put between: see INTERMITTENT]

intermittent *adj* coming and going at intervals; not continuous: *intermittent rain*. ➤➤ **intermittence** *noun*, **intermittently** *adv*. [Latin *intermittent-*, *intermittens*, present part. of *intermittere* to put between, from INTER- + *mittere* to send]

intermix /intə'miks/ *verb intrans* to mix together. ➤ *verb trans* to cause (diverse things) to mix together. ➤➤ **intermixture** *noun*. [back-formation from obsolete *intermixt* intermingled, from Latin *intermixtus*, past part. of *intermiscēre* to intermix, from INTER- + *miscēre* to mix]

intermolecular /,intəmə'lekyoolə/ *adj* existing or acting between molecules. ➤➤ **intermolecularly** *adv*.

intern[1] /in'tuhn/ *verb trans* to confine (somebody) e.g. in prison or a concentration camp, *esp* during a war. ➤➤ **internment** *noun*. [French *interner*, from *interne* internal, ultimately from Latin *internus*, inward, INTERNAL[1]]

Usage note
internment *or* interment? See note at INTERMENT.

intern[2] *or* **interne** /'intuhn/ *noun* **1** *chiefly NAmer* a graduate in medicine who is gaining supervised practical experience in a hospital. **2** a graduate who is receiving practical training in the workplace. ➤➤ **internship** *noun*. [French *interne*: see INTERN[1]]

intern[3] /'intuhn/ *verb intrans chiefly NAmer* to act as an intern.

internal[1] /in'tuhnl/ *adj* **1** existing or situated within the limits or surface of something; inside. **2** present within the body or an organism: *an internal organ*; *an internal stimulus*. **3** applied through the stomach by swallowing: *an internal medicine*. **4** within a state; domestic: *internal strife*; *internal affairs*. **5** of or existing within the mind. **6** depending only on the properties of the thing under consideration without reference to things outside it: *internal evidence of forgery in a document*. ➤➤ **internality** /-'naliti/ *noun*, **internally** *adv*. [Latin *internalis*, from *internus*]

internal[2] *noun informal* a medical examination of the vagina, uterus, or adjacent parts.

internal-combustion engine *noun* an engine in which the combustion that generates the heat energy takes place inside the engine, e.g. in a cylinder, as opposed to in a separate furnace.

internalize *or* **internalise** *verb trans* **1** to incorporate (e.g. learned values) within the self and use them as guiding principles. **2** to learn or digest (something) thoroughly. ➤➤ **internalization** /-'zaysh(ə)n/ *noun*.

internal market *noun* **1** a system in which different departments within an organization, *esp* a local council or other public body, purchase goods and services from each other. **2** the market

for labour, capital, goods, and services existing between countries of the European Union.

internal rhyme *noun* rhyme between a word within a line and another either at the end of the same line or within another line.

international[1] /intə'nash(ə)nl/ *adj* **1** affecting or involving two or more nations: *international trade*; *an international movement*. **2** known, recognized, or renowned in more than one country: *an international celebrity*. **3** open to all nations; not belonging to a particular country: *international waters*. ➤➤ **internationality** /-'naliti/ *noun*, **internationally** *adv*.

international[2] *noun* **1** a sporting or other contest between two national teams. **2** a player who has taken part in such a contest. **3** (*often* **International** *or* **Internationale** /,intə,nasha'nahl/) any of several socialist or communist organizations of international scope. [(sense 3) French *internationale*, fem of *international*]

International Baccalaureate *noun* an international qualification which allows students holding it to enter higher education in any of various countries, or the examinations for this qualification.

International Date Line *noun* an arbitrary line approximately along the 180th meridian, east and west of which the date differs by one calendar day.

Internationale /,intənasha'nahl/ *noun* **1** (**the Internationale**) a socialist revolutionary song widely adopted as an anthem by socialist organizations. **2** see INTERNATIONAL[2] (3). [French *(chanson) internationale* international song]

internationalise /intə'nash(ə)nəliez/ *verb trans and intrans* see INTERNATIONALIZE.

internationalism *noun* **1** international character, interests, or outlook. **2** cooperation among nations, or support for such cooperation. ➤➤ **internationalist** *noun and adj*.

internationalize *or* **internationalise** *verb intrans* **1** to become international. **2** to come under international control. ➤ *verb trans* **1** to make (something) international. **2** to place (something) under international control. ➤➤ **internationalization** /-'zaysh(ə)n/ *noun*.

international law *noun* a body of rules accepted as governing relations between nations.

International Phonetic Alphabet *noun* an alphabet designed to represent each human speech sound with a unique symbol.

International Scientific Vocabulary *noun* a set of international specialized or technical terms adapted to the structure of the individual languages in which they are used.

international style *noun* functional architectural design employing modern materials and avoiding regional and traditional influences.

international unit *noun* an internationally agreed unit of a vitamin, hormone, etc that produces a standard biological effect.

interne /'intuhn/ *noun* see INTERN[2].

internecine /intə'neesien/ *adj* **1** of or involving conflict within a group. **2** mutually destructive.

Word history
Latin *internecinus* deadly, from *internecare* to destroy, exterminate, from INTER- + *necare* to kill, from *nex* death. The original sense was 'with great slaughter'; current senses come from the interpretation of Latin *inter*, which in *internecare* is used simply for emphasis, in its more usual sense 'between'.

internee /intuh'nee/ *noun* an interned person; a prisoner.

Internet /'intanet/ *noun* (**the Internet**) the worldwide computer network that can link all smaller networks via telephone lines and satellite links, allowing individual users to communicate with each other via email and to gain access to information sites on the World Wide Web and to other electronic archives.

Editorial note
Created by the US government as a decentralized and resilient communications network that could not be destroyed by nuclear attack, the Internet at first connected only government defence laboratories, but was eventually opened to the public and now permits email to be sent to and from anywhere in the world and supports interactive services such as the World Wide Web — Dick Pountain.

Internet banking *noun* a banking system in which customers can view the status of their account, transfer funds, make payments, etc, by entering instructions at the appropriate website on the Internet.

internist /in'tuhnist, 'in-/ *noun NAmer* a doctor who specializes in the treatment of internal diseases and disorders, *esp* by nonsurgical means.

internode /'intənohd/ *noun* an interval or part between two nodes, e.g. of a plant stem. ⋙ **internodal** /-'nohdl/ *adj.* [Latin *internodium*, from INTER- + *nodus* NODE]

internuclear /intə'nyoohkliə/ *adj* situated or occurring between atomic or biological nuclei.

internuncial /intə'nunsh(ə)l/ *adj* serving to link sensory and motor neurons. ⋙ **internuncially** *adv.* [Italian *internunzio* go-between, from Latin *internuntius*, *internuncius*, from INTER- + *nuntius, nuncius* messenger]

interoceptive /,intəroh'septiv/ *adj* of or being stimuli arising within the body, *esp* in the intestine. [INTERIOR[1] + RECEPTIVE]

interpellate /in'tuhpilayt/ *verb trans* to question (e.g. a minister) formally concerning an action or policy, *esp* during the order of parliamentary business. ⋙ **interpellation** /-'laysh(ə)n/ *noun*, **interpellator** *noun.* [Latin *interpellatus*, past part. of *interpellare* to interrupt, from INTER- + *pellere* to drive]

interpenetrate /intə'penitrayt/ *verb trans* to penetrate (something) thoroughly. ➤ *verb intrans* to penetrate mutually. ⋙ **interpenetration** /-'traysh(ə)n/ *noun*, **interpenetrative** /-trətiv/ *adj.*

interpersonal /intə'puhs(ə)nl/ *adj* involving or dealing with relations between people: *interpersonal skills.* ⋙ **interpersonally** *adv.*

interphase /'intəfayz/ *noun* in cell division, the interval between the end of one division and the beginning of another.

interplanetary /intə'planət(ə)ri/ *adj* existing, carried on, or operating between planets.

interplay /'intəplay/ *noun* the effect that two or more things have on each other; interaction.

interpleader /'intəpleedə/ *noun* a legal proceeding by which two parties making the same claim against a third party determine between themselves which is the rightful claimant. [Anglo-French *enterpleder* to plead together, from *entre-* INTER- + *pleder*, from Old French *plaidier*: see PLEAD]

Interpol /'intəpol/ *noun* an international police organization for liaison between national police forces, based in France. [short for *international police*]

interpolate /in'tuhpəlayt/ *verb trans* **1** to insert (something) between other things or parts, *esp* to insert (words) into a text or conversation. **2** to alter or corrupt (e.g. a text) by inserting new, false, or misleading matter. **3** in mathematics, to estimate values of (a function) between two known values. ⋙ **interpolation** /-'laysh(ə)n/ *noun*, **interpolative** /-lətiv/ *adj*, **interpolator** *noun.* [Latin *interpolatus*, past part. of *interpolare* to refurbish, alter, interpolate]

interpose /intə'pohz/ *verb trans* **1** to place (something) between two things or in an intervening position. **2** to introduce (something) by way of interference or intervention: *The chairman prevented a decision by interposing a veto.* **3** to interrupt with (words) during a conversation or argument. ➤ *verb intrans* **1** to be or come in an intervening position. **2** to interrupt. ⋙ **interposer** *noun*, **interposition** /-pə'zish(ə)n/ *noun.* [early French *interposer*, from Latin *interponere* to put between, from INTER- + *ponere* to put]

interpret /in'tuhprit/ *verb* (**interpreted, interpreting**) ➤ *verb trans* **1** to understand the meaning of (something), often in the light of one's beliefs, judgments, or circumstances; to construe the meaning of (it). **2** to explain the meaning of (something): *Daniel interpreted the king's dream.* **3** to give an oral translation of (somebody's words). **4** to represent (something) by means of art, bringing to realization one's understanding of it or one's feelings about it. ➤ *verb intrans* to act as an interpreter. ⋙ **interpretable** *adj*, **interpretative** /-tətiv/ *adj*, **interpretatively** /-tətivli/ *adv*, **interpretive** /-tiv/ *adj.* [Middle English *interpreten* via French from Latin *interpretari* to explain]

interpretation /in,tuhpri'taysh(ə)n/ *noun* **1a** the act or an instance of interpreting. **b** the result of interpreting: *Freud's interpretations of dreams.* **2** the act or an instance of artistic interpreting in performance or adaptation. ⋙ **interpretational** *adj.*

interpreter *noun* **1** somebody who translates orally for people speaking in different languages. **2** somebody who interprets something, e.g. artistically. **3** a computer program that translates another program, one instruction at a time, into machine language for immediate execution.

interregnum /intə'regnəm/ *noun* (*pl* **interregnums** *or* **interregna** /-nə/) **1** the time during which: **a** a throne is vacant between reigns. **b** the normal functions of government are suspended. **2** any lapse or pause in a continuous series: *upon a dim, warm, misty day, toward the close of November ... during the strange interregnum of the seasons which in America is termed the Indian Summer* — Poe. [Latin *interregnum*, from INTER- + *regnum*: see REIGN[1]]

interrelate /,intəri'layt/ *verb intrans* to be in a relationship where each one person or thing depends upon or is acting upon another. ➤ *verb trans* to bring (people or things) into such a relationship. ⋙ **interrelation** /-sh(ə)n/ *noun*, **interrelationship** /-sh(ə)nship/ *noun.*

interrog. *abbr* **1** interrogation. **2** interrogative. **3** interrogatively.

interrogate /in'terəgayt/ *verb trans* **1** to question (somebody) formally, exhaustively, or aggressively. **2** to give or send out a signal to (e.g. a computer) to trigger a response. ⋙ **interrogation** /-'gaysh(ə)n/ *noun*, **interrogational** /-'gaysh(ə)nl/ *adj*, **interrogator** *noun.* [Latin *interrogatus*, past part. of *interrogare* to question, from INTER- + *rogare* to ask]

interrogation mark *noun* = QUESTION MARK.

interrogative[1] /intə'rogətiv/ *adj* **1** questioning. **2a** used in a question. **b** of the grammatical mood that expresses a question. ⋙ **interrogatively** *adv.*

interrogative[2] *noun* **1** a word, *esp* a pronoun, used in asking questions. **2** the interrogative mood of a language.

interrogatory[1] /intə'rogət(ə)ri/ *noun* (*pl* **interrogatories**) a formal question, *esp* a written question to be answered under direction of a court.

interrogatory[2] *adj* = INTERROGATIVE[1].

interrupt[1] /intə'rupt/ *verb trans* **1** to break the flow or action of (a speaker or speech). **2** to break the uniformity or continuity of (something). ➤ *verb intrans* to interrupt an action or somebody's words. ⋙ **interruptible** *adj*, **interruptive** /-tiv/ *adj.* [Middle English *interrupten* from Latin *interruptus*, past part. of *interrumpere* to break in, from INTER- + *rumpere* to break]

interrupt[2] *noun* a signal to a computer that halts a program while a higher-priority program is carried out, or the circuit that conveys the signal.

interrupter *or* **interruptor** /intə'ruptə/ *noun* **1** somebody or something that interrupts. **2** an automatic device for periodically interrupting or breaking an electric current.

interruption /intə'rupsh(ə)n/ *noun* **1** something that interrupts what somebody is doing or saying. **2** a break or interval of any kind.

interruptor /intə'ruptə/ *noun* see INTERRUPTER.

inter se /,intə 'say/ *adv and adj* among or between themselves. [Latin *inter se*]

intersect /intə'sekt/ *verb trans* to pierce or divide (e.g. a line or area) by passing through or across it. ➤ *verb intrans* said of lines, roads, etc: to meet and cross at a point. [Latin *intersectus*, past part. of *intersecare* to cut between, from INTER- + *secare* to cut]

intersection /'intəseksh(ə)n/ *noun* **1** the act or an instance of intersecting. **2** a place where two or more things, e.g. streets, roads, etc, intersect. **3a** in mathematics, the set of elements common to two sets, or the process by which this set is established. **b** the set of points common to two geometric configurations. ⋙ **intersectional** *adj.*

intersex /'intəseks/ *noun* an intersexual individual or its intersexual nature.

intersexual /intə'seksyooəl, -sh(ə)l/ *adj* **1** intermediate in sexual character between a typical male and a typical female. **2** existing between the sexes. ⋙ **intersexuality** /-syoo'aliti, -shoo'aliti/ *noun*, **intersexually** *adv.*

interspace[1] /intə'spays/ *verb trans* to separate (e.g. printed letters) by spaces.

interspace[2] /'intəspays/ *noun* an intervening space; an interval.

interspecies *adj* = INTERSPECIFIC.

interspecific /,intəspə'sifik/ *adj* existing or arising between different species.

intersperse /intə'spuhs/ *verb trans* **1** to insert (things) at intervals among other things: *You'd need to intersperse drawings throughout the text.* **2** (+ with) to diversify or vary (something) with scattered things: *You'd need to intersperse the text with drawings.*

⋙ **interspersion** /-sh(ə)n/ *noun.* [Latin *interspersus*, past part. of *interspergere* to scatter between, from INTER- + *spargere* to scatter]

interstate¹ /intə'stayt/ *adj* between two or more states, *esp* of the USA or of Australia: *an interstate highway.*

interstate² /'intəstayt/ *noun NAmer* a wide road allowing for fast travel between states.

interstate³ *adv Aus* to or in another state: *They went interstate to live.*

interstellar /intə'stelə/ *adj* existing, carried on, or operating between the stars.

interstice /in'tuhstis/ *noun formal* a small space between adjacent things. [French *interstice* from late Latin *interstitium*, from Latin *intersistere* to stand still in the middle, from INTER- + *sistere* to stand]

interstitial /intə'stishl/ *adj* **1** of or situated in interstices. **2** of or being a crystalline compound in which small atoms or ions occupy holes between larger metal atoms or ions in the crystal lattice. ⋙ **interstitially** *adv.*

intertextuality /,intətekstyoo'aliti/ *noun* in literary criticism, reference made in one text to a different text, whether overtly or by the choice of similar subject matter, style, etc.

intertidal /intə'tiedl/ *adj* of the part of a seashore between high and low watermarks. ⋙ **intertidally** *adv.*

intertrigo /intə'triegoh/ *noun* inflammation of the skin caused when one area of skin chafes another. [Latin *intererere* to rub together, from INTER- + *terere* to rub, grind]

intertwine /intə'twien/ *verb trans* to join (things) by wrapping or twisting them round each other. ⋙ *verb intrans* to twine about one another. ⋙ **intertwinement** *noun.*

interval /'intəv(ə)l/ *noun* **1** an intervening space, e.g.: **a** a time between events or states; a pause. **b** a distance or gap between objects, units, or states: *The lamp posts were placed at regular intervals.* **c** the difference in pitch between two notes. **2** *Brit* a break in the presentation of an entertainment, e.g. a play. **3** in mathematics, a set of real numbers between two numbers, or the set of real numbers greater or less than some number. ⋙ **intervallic** /intə'valik/ *adj.* [Middle English *intervalle* via French from Latin *intervallum* space between ramparts, interval, from INTER- + *vallum* rampart]

intervene /intə'veen/ *verb intrans* **1** to occur or come between two things, *esp* points of time or events. **2** to come in or between things so as to hinder or modify them. **3** to enter or appear as something irrelevant or extraneous. **4a** to enter a lawsuit as a third party. **b** to interfere in another nation's internal affairs. ⋙ **intervenor** *noun.* [Latin *intervenire* to come between, from INTER- + *venire* to come]

intervention /intə'vensh(ə)n/ *noun* **1** the act or an instance of intervening. **2** action taken when intervening, *esp*: **a** government influence brought to bear on the economy, usu for political reasons. **b** medical treatment. **3a** the purchasing by the EU of a commodity from the producer when the market price falls to a specified level. **b** (*used before a noun*) purchased in this way: *intervention butter.*

interventionism *noun* **1** action taken by a government to influence the domestic economy, usu in order to bring about a political objective. **2** interference in the political affairs of another country. ⋙ **interventionist** *noun and adj.*

intervertebral disc /intə'vuhtibrəl/ *noun* any of the tough elastic discs between the bodies of adjoining vertebrae.

interview¹ /'intəvyooh/ *noun* **1** a formal consultation usu to evaluate qualifications, e.g. of a prospective student or employee. **2** a meeting at which information is obtained, e.g. by a journalist, from somebody, or a written or filmed report of such a meeting. ⋙ **interviewee** /-ee/ *noun,* **interviewer** *noun.* [early French *entrevue,* from *s'entrevoir* to see one another, from *entre-* INTER- + *voir* to see, from Latin *vidēre*]

interview² *verb trans* to invite or subject (somebody) to an interview. ⋙ *verb intrans* to hold interviews.

inter vivos /,intə 'veevohs/ *adv and adj* between living people, *esp* as distinct from under the terms of a will: *property transferred inter vivos.* [late Latin *inter vivos*]

interwar /intə'waw/ *adj* occurring or falling between wars, *esp* World War I and World War II.

interweave /intə'weev/ *verb* (*past tense* **interwove** /-'wohv/, *past part.* **interwoven** /-'wohv(ə)n/) ⋙ *verb trans* **1** to weave (things) together. **2** to blend (things). ⋙ *verb intrans* **1** to become woven together. **2** to become blended. ⋙ **interwoven** *adj.*

intestate¹ /in'testayt, -tət/ *adj* having made no valid will. ⋙ **intestacy** /-təsi/ *noun.* [Middle English from Latin *intestatus,* from IN-¹ + *testatus*: see TESTATE¹]

intestate² *noun* somebody who dies intestate.

intestinal /in'testinl/ *adj* affecting or occurring in the intestine. ⋙ **intestinally** *adv.*

intestine /in'testin/ *noun* (*also in pl*) the tubular part of the alimentary canal that extends from the stomach to the anus. [early French *intestin* from Latin *intestinum,* neuter of *intestinus,* from *intus* within]

intifada /inti'fahdə/ *noun* a resistance movement, originating in the late 1980s, among Palestinian Arabs of the West Bank and the Gaza Strip against Israeli occupation. [Arabic *intifada* uprising]

intimacy /'intiməsi/ *noun* (*pl* **intimacies**) **1** the state of being intimate; familiarity. **2** an intimate remark. **3** *euphem* sexual intercourse.

intimate¹ /'intimət/ *adj* **1** belonging to or characterizing one's deepest nature: *He shared his intimate thoughts.* **2a** marked by a warm friendship developing through long association: *We're not exactly on intimate terms.* **b** suggesting informal warmth or privacy: *an intimate atmosphere.* **3** of a very personal or private nature: *an intimate diary.* **4** marked by very close association, contact, or familiarity: *an intimate knowledge of the law.* **5** *euphem* involved in a sexual relationship, *esp* engaging in an act of sexual intercourse: *They were intimate six times in the car and twice on a mountainside —* News of the World. ⋙ **intimately** *adv.* [alteration of obsolete *intime,* from Latin *intimus* innermost]

intimate² /'intimayt/ *verb trans* **1** to make (something) known, e.g. by announcing it formally. **2** to hint at or imply (something). ⋙ **intimation** /-'maysh(ə)n/ *noun.* [late Latin *intimatus,* past part. of *intimare* to put in, announce, from *intimus* innermost]

intimate³ /'intimət/ *noun* a close friend or confidant.

intimidate /in'timidayt/ *verb trans* **1** to frighten or unnerve (somebody). **2** to compel or deter (somebody) with or as if with threats. ⋙ **intimidation** /-'daysh(ə)n/ *noun,* **intimidator** *noun,* **intimidatory** /-'dayt(ə)ri/ *adj.* [medieval Latin *intimidatus,* past part. of *intimidare* to make timid, from *timidus*: see TIMID]

intinction /in'tingksh(ə)n/ *noun* the administration of Communion by dipping the bread in the wine and giving both together to the communicant. [late Latin *intinction-, intinctio* immersion, from Latin *intingere* to dip in, from IN-² + *tingere* to dip, moisten]

intitule /in'tityoohl/ *verb trans Brit* to give a title to (*esp* a parliamentary act). [early French *intituler* from late Latin *intitulare*: see ENTITLE]

intnl *abbr* international.

into /'intə *before consonants, otherwise* 'intooh/ *prep* **1a** so as to be inside: *Come into the house.* **b** so as to be: *One day she'll grow into a woman.* **c** so as to be in (a state): *Don't get into trouble.* **d** so as to be expressed in: *Translate it into French.* **e** so as to be dressed in: *He changed into his uniform.* **f** so as to be engaged in: *He went into farming.* **g** so as to be a member of: *The Government was not willing to enter into an alliance.* **2** used in division as the inverse of *by* or *divided by*: *Divide 35 into 70.* **3** used to indicate a partly elapsed period of time or a partly traversed extent of space: *far into the night; deep into the jungle.* **4** in the direction of: *Don't look into the sun without protecting your eyes; I'll enquire into the matter.* **5** to a position of contact with; against: *The car ran into a wall.* **6** *informal* involved with: *They were into hard drugs.* **7** *informal* keen on: *Are you into meditation?* [Old English *intō*]

intolerable /in'tol(ə)rəbl/ *adj* too bad or unpleasant to endure; unbearable. ⋙ **intolerableness** *noun,* **intolerably** *adv.* [Middle English from Latin *intolerabilis,* from IN-¹ + *tolerabilis* tolerable, from *tolerare* to TOLERATE]

intolerant /in'tolərənt/ *adj* **1** unwilling to grant or share social, professional, political, or religious rights; bigoted. **2** (+ of) unable or unwilling to endure: *a plant intolerant of direct sunlight.* ⋙ **intolerance** *noun,* **intolerantly** *adv.*

intonation /intə'naysh(ə)n/ *noun* **1** the rise and fall in pitch of the voice in speech. **2** performance of music with respect to correctness of pitch. **3** the act or manner of intoning something. **4** something that is intoned; *specif* the opening notes of a Gregorian chant.

intone /in'tohn/ *verb* **1** to say (something) in a monotonous tone that suggests solemnity. **2** to recite (something) in singing tones or in a monotone: *The lama, both hands raised, intoned a final blessing in ornate Chinese* — Kipling. ➤➤ **intoner** *noun*. [Middle English *entonen* via French from medieval Latin *intonare*, from IN-² + Latin *tonus*: see TONE¹]

in toto /in 'tohtoh/ *adv* totally or entirely. [Latin *in toto*]

intoxicant /in'toksik(ə)nt/ *noun* something that intoxicates, *esp* an alcoholic drink.

intoxicate /in'toksikayt/ *verb trans* **1a** to excite or stupefy (somebody) with alcohol or drugs, *esp* to the point where physical and mental control is markedly diminished. **b** to cause (somebody) to lose self-control through excitement or elation. **2** *esp* in medicine, to poison (somebody). ➤➤ **intoxicatedly** *adv*, **intoxication** /-'kaysh(ə)n/ *noun*. [medieval Latin *intoxicatus*, past part. of *intoxicare* to poison, from IN-² + *toxicum*: see TOXIC]

intoxicating *adj* causing or producing intoxication: *intoxicating drinks; intoxicating beauty*.

intra- *prefix* forming adjectives, with the meaning: inside; within: *intrauterine*. [Latin *intra*]

Usage note
intra-, inter-, *or* intro-? See note at INTER-.

intracellular /intrə'selyoolə/ *adj* situated, occurring, or functioning within a living cell: *intracellular enzymes*.

intracranial /intrə'krayni·əl/ *adj* within the skull, or affecting things within the skull. ➤➤ **intracranially** *adv*.

intractable /in'traktəbl/ *adj* **1** not easily solved or dealt with. **2** not easily influenced or directed; stubborn. **3** not easily relieved or cured: *intractable pain*. ➤➤ **intractability** /-'biliti/ *noun*, **intractableness** *noun*, **intractably** *adv*. [Latin *intractabilis*, from IN-¹ + *tractabilis*: see TRACTABLE]

intrados /in'traydos/ *noun* in architecture, the underside of an arch: compare EXTRADOS. [French *intrados*, from Latin *intra* within + French *dos* back]

intramural /intrə'myooərəl/ *adj* **1** within the limits of a community or institution, *esp* within a college or university or between students of a single college or university rather than between different institutions. **2** inside a cell or a hollow organ. ➤➤ **intramurally** *adv*.

intramuscular /intrə'muskyoolə/ *adj* in or going into a muscle. ➤➤ **intramuscularly** *adv*.

intranet /'intrənet/ *noun* an internal computer network that operates by using Internet protocols.

intransigent¹ /in'tranzij(ə)nt, -sij(ə)nt/ *adj* refusing to compromise or to abandon a position or attitude, *esp* in politics; uncompromising. ➤➤ **intransigence** *noun*, **intransigently** *adv*. [French *intransigent* from Spanish *los intransigentes*, literally 'the uncompromising ones', the name adapted by an extreme left-wing party in the Cortes of 1873–4, ultimately from Latin IN-¹ + *transigere*: see TRANSACT]

intransigent² *noun* an intransigent person.

intransitive /in'transitiv/ *adj* said of a verb or a sense of a verb: not having a direct object. ➤➤ **intransitively** *adv*, **intransitively** *adv*. [late Latin *intransitivus*, from IN-¹ + *transitivus*: see TRANSITIVE]

intrapreneur /,intrəprə'nuh/ *noun* somebody who initiates or manages a new business or division within a company or organization. ➤➤ **intrapreneurial** *adj*. [INTRA- + *-preneur* as in ENTREPRENEUR]

intraspecific /,intrəspə'sifik/ *adj* occurring within a species, or involving members of one species. ➤➤ **intraspecifically** *adv*.

intrauterine /intrə'yoohtərin, -rien/ *adj* situated, used, or occurring in the uterus.

intrauterine device *noun* a contraceptive device inserted and left in the uterus, e.g. a coil.

intravascular /intrə'vaskyoolə/ *adj* situated or occurring in a blood vessel. ➤➤ **intravascularly** *adv*.

intravenous /intrə'veenəs/ *adj* situated in a vein, or entering by way of a vein. ➤➤ **intravenously** *adv*.

in tray *noun* a receptacle for mail, memos, and other items yet to be dealt with.

intrench /in'trench/ *verb trans and intrans archaic* see ENTRENCH.

intrepid /in'trepid/ *adj* fearless, bold, and resolute. ➤➤ **intrepidity** /-'piditi/ *noun*, **intrepidly** *adv*. [Latin *intrepidus*, from IN-¹ + *trepidus* alarmed]

intricacy /'intrikəsi/ *noun* (*pl* **intricacies**) **1** the quality of being intricate. **2** something intricate: *I was unable to follow the intricacies of the plot*.

intricate /'intrikət/ *adj* **1** having many complexly interrelating parts or elements. **2** difficult to resolve or analyse. ➤➤ **intricately** *adv*. [Middle English from Latin *intricatus*, past part. of *intricare* to entangle, from IN-² + *tricae* complications, tricks]

intrigue¹ /in'treeg/ *verb trans* **1** to arouse the interest or curiosity of (somebody). **2** to occupy the attention of (somebody) fully; to captivate (them): *Her beauty intrigues me*. ➤ *verb intrans* to develop or execute a secret scheme. ➤➤ **intriguer** *noun*. [French *intriguer* via Italian *intrigare* from Latin *intricare*: see INTRICATE]

intrigue² *noun* **1** the quality of arousing interest or curiosity. **2a** a secret scheme or plot. **b** the practice of engaging in or using scheming or underhand plots. **3** a clandestine love affair.

intriguing *adj* engaging the interest to a great degree; fascinating. ➤➤ **intriguingly** *adv*.

intrinsic /in'trinzik/ *adj* **1** belonging to the essential nature or constitution of something: *an ornament of no intrinsic worth but of great sentimental value*. **2** originating or situated within the body or a particular part of it. ➤➤ **intrinsically** *adv*. [early French *intrinsèque* internal, ultimately from Latin *intrinsecus* inwardly]

intro /'introh/ *noun* (*pl* **intros**) *informal* an introduction, *esp* the opening passage of a piece of pop music.

intro- *prefix* forming words, with the meaning: **1** in or into: *introjection*. **2** inwards or within: *introvert*. [Middle English via French from Latin *intro* inside, to the inside]

Usage note
intro-, intra-, *or* inter-? See note at INTER-.

introduce /intrə'dyoohs/ *verb trans* **1** to bring (something) in, *esp* for the first time: *Horses were introduced into North America in the 16th century*. **2a** to bring (something) into play: *They introduced a new line of approach into the argument*. **b** to bring (something) into practice or use; to institute (it). **3** to make (somebody) known, e.g.: **a** to cause (somebody or oneself) to be acquainted with another person. **b** to present (somebody) formally, e.g. at court or into society. **c** to make preliminary explanatory or laudatory remarks about (e.g. a speaker). **4** to announce (something, e.g. a piece of legislation) formally or by an official reading. **5** to give (somebody) knowledge of something: *I introduced him to the works of Byron*. **6** to place or insert (something) somewhere: *There is a risk of introducing harmful substances into the body*. **7** to start (something): *I'd like to introduce this evening's entertainment with a song*. **8** to present (a radio or television programme). [Latin *introducere*, from INTRO- + *ducere* to lead]

introduction /intrə'duksh(ə)n/ *noun* **1a** the act or an instance of introducing or being introduced. **b** a formal presentation of one person to another. **c** a letter, etc introducing one person to another. **2** something that introduces, e.g.: **a** a part of a book, lecture, etc that is preliminary to the main part. **b** a course of study that gives a basic grounding in a subject. **c** a book that teaches the basics of a subject. **d** a short introductory musical passage. **3** something introduced; *specif* a plant or animal new to an area. [Middle English *introduccioun* via French from Latin *introduction-, introductio*, from *introducere*: see INTRODUCE]

introductory /intrə'dukt(ə)ri/ *adj* of or being a first step that sets something going or puts it into proper perspective; preliminary. ➤➤ **introductorily** *adv*.

introit *or* **Introit** /'introyt/ *noun* a piece of music sung or played at the beginning of a church service; *specif* the antiphon or psalm sung as the priest approaches the altar to celebrate Mass or Holy Communion. [early French *introite*, ultimately from Latin *introitus*, past part. of *introire* to go in, from INTRO- + *ire* to go]

introject /intrə'jekt/ *verb trans* to incorporate (attitudes or ideas) unconsciously into one's personality. ➤➤ **introjection** /-'jeksh(ə)n/ *noun*. [INTRO- + *-ject* as in PROJECT²]

intromission /intrə'mish(ə)n/ *noun* the act or an instance of intromitting, *esp* the insertion of the penis in the vagina in intercourse. [French *intromission* from Latin *intromission-, intromissio* from *intromittere*: see INTROMIT]

intromit /intrǝ'mit/ *verb trans* (**intromitted, intromitting**) to put (something) in; to insert (it). ➤➤ **intromittent** *adj*. [Latin *intromittere*, from INTRO- + *mittere* to send]

introspect /intrǝ'spekt/ *verb intrans* to examine the contents of one's mind, e.g. thoughts and feelings, reflectively. [Latin *introspectus*: see INTROSPECTION]

introspection /intrǝ'speksh(ǝ)n/ *noun* the examining of one's own mind or its contents reflectively. ➤➤ **introspective** /-tiv/ *adj*, **introspectively** *adv*. [Latin *introspectus*, past part. of *introspicere* to look inside, from INTRO- + *specere* to look]

introvert[1] /'intrǝvuht/ *noun* **1** somebody whose attention and interests are directed towards his or her own mental life: compare EXTROVERT. **2** somebody who is uneasy in company, a shy person. compare EXTROVERT.

introvert[2] *adj* of or being an introvert.

introvert[3] /intrǝ'vuht/ *verb trans* to turn inwards or in on itself or oneself, e.g.: **a** to draw in (a tubular part), usu by INVAGINATION (making the outer surface the inner one). **b** to concentrate or direct (the mind, thoughts, or emotions) on oneself. ➤➤ **introversion** /-'vuhsh(ǝ)n/ *noun*, **introverted** *adj*. [scientific Latin *introvertere*, from INTRO- + Latin *vertere* to turn]

intrude /in'troohd/ *verb intrans* **1** to thrust oneself into a situation or a place without invitation, permission, or welcome: *It is rude, madam, to intrude, madam, with your brood, madam, brazen-faced —* W S Gilbert. **2** to enter as a geological intrusion. ➤ *verb trans* **1** to force (something) in or on something, *esp* without permission, welcome, or suitable reason: *She decided to intrude a trite moral into her lecture.* **2** to cause (e.g. rock) to intrude. [Latin *intrudere* to thrust in, from IN-[2] + *trudere* to thrust]

intruder *noun* somebody who intrudes, *esp* a burglar.

intrusion /in'troohzh(ǝ)n/ *noun* **1** the act or an instance of intruding or an action that intrudes: *Forgive this intrusion into your privacy.* **2a** something that intrudes. **b** rock or magma forced while molten into or between other rock formations, or its forcible entry. [Middle English via French and medieval Latin from Latin *intrusus*, past part. of *intrudere*: see INTRUDE]

intrusive /in'troohsiv, -ziv/ *adj* **1** constituting an intrusion, or tending to intrude. **2** said of a rock: being an intrusion. **3** said of a speech sound: inserted where there is no corresponding letter in spelling or etymology: *an intrusive r.* ➤➤ **intrusively** *adv*.

intrust /in'trust/ *verb trans* see ENTRUST.

intubate /'intyoobayt/ *verb trans* to introduce a tube into a hollow organ, e.g. the windpipe. ➤➤ **intubation** /-'baysh(ǝ)n/ *noun*.

intuit /in'tyooh·it/ *verb trans* (**intuited, intuiting**) to apprehend (something) by intuition. ➤➤ **intuitable** *adj*.

intuition /intyooh'ish(ǝ)n/ *noun* **1a** quick and ready insight. **b** a hunch. **2a** the power of attaining direct knowledge without evident rational thought or the drawing of conclusions from evidence available. **b** knowledge gained by this power. ➤➤ **intuitional** *adj*. [late Latin *intuition-, intuitio* act of contemplating, from Latin *intueri* to look at, contemplate, from IN-[2] + *tueri* to look]

intuitionism /intyooh'ishǝniz(ǝ)m/ *noun* **1** a doctrine that knowledge rests on basic truths that can be known intuitively. **2** a doctrine that moral values and principles can be discerned intuitively. ➤➤ **intuitionist** *adj or noun*.

intuitive /in'tyooh·itiv/ *adj* **1** known or perceived by intuition; directly apprehended: *He had an intuitive awareness of his sister's feelings.* **2** possessing or given to intuition or insight: *an intuitive mind.* **3** of intuition: *the intuitive faculty.* ➤➤ **intuitively** *adv*, **intuitiveness** *noun*.

intumesce /intyoo'mes/ *verb intrans* to become enlarged or swollen. ➤➤ **intumescence** *noun*, **intumescent** *adj*. [Latin *intumescere* to swell up, from IN-[2] + *tumescere* to begin to swell, from *tumēre* to swell]

intussusception /ˌintǝsǝ'sepsh(ǝ)n/ *noun* **1** a drawing in of something from outside, *esp* the slipping of a length of intestine into an adjacent portion, usu producing obstruction. **2** in botany, the increase of the area of a cell wall by particles being deposited between existing particles of the wall. ➤➤ **intussusceptive** /-tiv/ *adj*. [Latin *intussuscipere* to cause to turn inwards, from Latin *intus* within + *suscipere*: see SUSCEPTIBLE]

Inuit or **Innuit** /'inyooh·it/ *noun* (pl **Inuits** or **Innuits** or collectively **Inuit** or **Innuit**) **1** a member of the indigenous peoples inhabiting N Canada, Alaska, and Greenland. **2** the language spoken by these peoples. ➤➤ **Inuit** *adj*. [Inuit *inuit*, pl of *inuk* person]

Usage note

Inuit or Eskimo? The indigenous peoples of the Arctic prefer to be known as the *Inuit* rather than *Eskimos*. The term *Eskimo* is still sometimes used, but *Inuit* should be preferred.

Inuktitut /i'nooktitoot/ *noun* the form of Inuit spoken in Quebec and Labrador. [Inuit *inuktitut* literally 'The Inuit way']

inunction /in'ungksh(ǝ)n/ *noun* the act or an instance of anointing with or applying oil or ointment. [Middle English from Latin *inunction-, inunctio*, from *inunguere* to anoint, from IN-[2] + *unguere* to smear]

inundate /'inundayt/ *verb trans* **1** to cover or overwhelm (an area) with water; to flood (it). **2** to overwhelm (somebody) with demands, offers, etc. ➤➤ **inundation** /-'daysh(ǝ)n/ *noun*. [Latin *inundatus*, past part. of *inundare* to flood, from IN-[2] + *undare* to flow, from *unda* a wave]

inure or **enure** /i'nyooǝ/ *verb trans* (+ to) to accustom (somebody) to something undesirable. ➤ *verb intrans* in law, to come into use or operation. ➤➤ **inurement** *noun*. [Middle English *enuren*, from EN-[1] + *ure* use, custom, from Old French *euvre* work, from Latin *opera*]

in utero /in 'yoohtǝroh/ *adv and adj* in the uterus. [Latin *in utero*]

in vacuo /in 'vakyoo·oh/ *adv* in a vacuum, *esp* without being related to practical application, relevant facts, etc. [Latin *in vacuo*]

invade /in'vayd/ *verb trans* **1** to enter (e.g. a country) for hostile purposes. **2** to encroach on (something): *The noise invaded his privacy.* **3a** to spread over or into (something) as if invading it. **b** to affect (a part of the body) injuriously and progressively: *Gangrene invades healthy tissue.* ➤➤ **invader** *noun*. [Middle English *invaden* from Latin *invadere*, from IN-[2] + *vadere* to go]

invaginate /in'vajinayt/ *verb trans* **1** to fold in (something) so that an outer surface becomes an inner surface. **2** to enclose or sheathe (something). ➤ *verb intrans* to become folded in on itself. [medieval Latin *invaginatus*, past part. of *invaginare*, from Latin IN-[2] + *vagina* sheath]

invagination /in,vaji'naysh(ǝ)n/ *noun* **1** the act or an instance of invaginating. **2** an invaginated part.

invalid[1] /'invǝlid/ *noun* somebody who is unwell or disabled.

invalid[2] /'invǝlid/ *adj* **1** suffering from disease or disability: *She gave up work to look after her invalid mother.* **2** designed for use by disabled people: *an invalid chair.* ➤➤ **invalidity** /-'liditi/ *noun*. [from INVALID[3], influenced by French *invalide*]

invalid[3] /in'valid/ *adj* **1** without legal force: *an invalid passport.* **2** logically inconsistent: *an invalid argument.* ➤➤ **invalidity** /-'liditi/ *noun*, **invalidly** *adv*, **invalidness** *noun*. [Latin *invalidus* weak, from IN-[1] + *validus*: see VALID]

invalid[4] /in'valid/ *verb trans* (**invalided, invaliding**) (*usu* + out) to remove (somebody) from active duty by reason of sickness or disability: *He was invalided out of the army.* [from INVALID[2]]

invalidate /in'validayt/ *verb trans* to make (something) invalid, *esp* to weaken or destroy the convincingness of (e.g. an argument or claim). ➤➤ **invalidation** /-'daysh(ǝ)n/ *noun*.

invaluable /in'valyooǝbl/ *adj* **1** valuable beyond estimation; priceless. **2** very useful. ➤➤ **invaluably** *adv*.

Invar /'invah/ *noun trademark* an alloy of iron and nickel with a low coefficient of thermal expansion. [shortening of INVARIABLE[1]]

invariable[1] /in'veǝri·ǝbl/ *adj* not changing; constant. ➤➤ **invariability** /-'biliti/ *noun*, **invariableness** *noun*, **invariably** *adv*.

invariable[2] *noun* an invariable quantity or thing; a constant.

invariant[1] /in'veǝri·ǝnt/ *adj* unchanging; *specif* unaffected by a particular mathematical operation: *invariant under rotation of the coordinate axes.* ➤➤ **invariance** *noun*.

invariant[2] *noun* something that remains constant and unchanging.

invasion /in'vayzh(ǝ)n/ *noun* **1** a hostile attack on a foreign territory by an army. **2** *informal* a visit by a large number of people, *esp* when unwelcome: *the tourist invasion.* **3** the incoming or spread of something harmful, e.g. a tumour. ➤➤ **invasive** /-siv, -ziv/ *adj*. [Middle English *invasioune* via French from late Latin *invasion-, invasio*, from Latin *invadere*: see INVADE]

invective[1] /in'vektiv/ *noun* abusive or insulting language. [Middle English *invectif* abusive, via French from Latin *invectivus* attacking, from *invehere* to carry in, from IN-[2] + *vehere* to carry]

invective[2] *adj* abusive or insulting. >> **invectively** *adv*.

inveigh /in'vay/ *verb intrans* (+ against) to speak or protest bitterly or vehemently: *The 'monopoly' of the Civil Service, so much inveighed against, is like the monopoly of judicial offices by the bar* — J S Mill. [Latin *invehi* to attack, inveigh, passive of *invehere*: see INVECTIVE[1]]

Usage note
inveigh *or* **inveigle**? These two words are sometimes confused. *Inveigh* is always followed by the preposition *against*. To *inveigh against* someone or something is to speak or write about them in a very bitter, hostile and condemnatory way: *inveighed against the enemies of the working class. Inveigle* is followed by a direct object and means 'to use cunning or deceitful methods in order to get someone to do something': *inveigled her into parting with most of her savings.*

inveigle /in'vaygl/ *verb trans* (*usu* + into) to win (somebody or something) over by ingenuity or flattery: *The woman took advantage of a slight amorous propensity that may be a weakness in my disposition ... and inveigled me into a contract* — J Fenimore Cooper. >> **inveiglement** *noun*. [modification of early French *aveugler* to blind, hoodwink, from medieval Latin *ab oculis* lacking eyes]

Usage note
inveigle *or* **inveigh**? See note at INVEIGH.

invent /in'vent/ *verb trans* **1** to produce (e.g. a device or machine) for the first time. **2** to think (something) up, *esp* in order to deceive: *He'll invent an excuse.* >> **inventor** *noun*. [Middle English *inventen* to find, discover, from Latin *inventus*, past part. of *invenire* to come upon, find, from IN-[2] + *venire* to come]

invention /in'vensh(ə)n/ *noun* **1** something invented, e.g. a device or process devised as a result of prolonged study and experiment. **2** something thought up, *esp* to deceive: *The story was pure invention.* **3** productive imagination; inventiveness: *Necessity is the mother of invention.* **4** a short keyboard composition, usu contrapuntal. **5** the act or an instance of inventing. **6** *archaic* the act or an instance of finding something.

inventive /in'ventiv/ *adj* **1** showing evidence of original thought or ingenuity; creative. **2** good at inventing things. >> **inventively** *adv*, **inventiveness** *noun*.

inventory[1] /'invəntri/ *noun* (*pl* **inventories**) **1a** an itemized list, e.g. of the contents of a building or stock in a warehouse. **b** a list of traits, preferences, attitudes, etc used to evaluate personal characteristics or skills. **2a** the items listed in an inventory. **b** *NAmer* the quantity of goods, components, or raw materials on hand; stock. **3** the taking of an inventory. [medieval Latin *inventorium*, alteration of late Latin *inventarium* list of things found, from Latin *invenire*: see INVENT]

inventory[2] *verb trans* (**inventories, inventoried, inventorying**) to make an inventory of (things); to catalogue (them).

inverse[1] /'invuhs/ *adj* **1** opposite in order, direction, nature, or effect. **2a** said of a mathematical function: expressing the same relationship as another function but from the opposite viewpoint. **b** relating to an inverse function: *an inverse sine.* >> **inversely** *adv*. [Latin *inversus*, past part. of *invertere* to turn inside out or upside down, from IN-[2] + *vertere* to turn]

inverse[2] *noun* **1** a direct opposite. **2** in mathematics: **a** an inverse function or operation: *Addition is the inverse of subtraction.* **b** a reciprocal.

inverse proportion *noun* the relation between two quantities, one of which increases proportionally as the other decreases: compare DIRECT PROPORTION.

inversion /in'vuhsh(ə)n/ *noun* **1** the act or an instance of inverting something. **2** a reversal of position, order, form, or relationship, e.g. a change in normal word order, *esp* the placement of a verb before its subject. **3** in music, the process or result of inverting the relative positions of the elements of an interval, chord, or phrase. **4** in mathematics, the operation of forming the inverse of a magnitude, operation, or element. **5** in biochemistry, a conversion of a substance showing dextrorotation into one showing laevorotation or vice versa: *inversion of sucrose.* **6** a conversion of direct current into alternating current. **7** (*also* **temperature inversion**) a reversal of the normal atmospheric temperature gradient, in which the layer of air nearest the earth is cooler than the layer above it. **8** *archaic, derog* homosexuality. >> **inversive** /-siv/ *adj*.

invert[1] /in'vuht/ *verb trans* **1a** to turn (something) inside out or upside down. **b** to turn (e.g. a foot) inwards. **2a** to reverse the position, order, or relationship of (things). **b** to subject (a chord, etc) to musical inversion. **c** to subject (a substance) to chemical inversion. **d** to express the mathematical inverse, *esp* the reciprocal, of (a magnitude, etc). >> **invertible** *adj*. [Latin *invertere*: see INVERSE[1]]

invert[2] /'invuht/ *noun* **1** something characterized by inversion. **2** *archaic, derog* a homosexual.

invertase /in'vuhtayz, -tays/ *noun* an enzyme capable of converting sucrose into invert sugar.

invertebrate[1] /in'vuhtibrət, -brayt/ *noun* **1** any animal that does not have a spinal column, including insects, molluscs, and worms. **2** *informal* somebody lacking in strength or vitality of character. [scientific Latin *invertebratus*, from IN-[1] + *vertebratus*: see VERTEBRATE[1]]

invertebrate[2] *adj* **1a** said of an animal: lacking a backbone. **b** relating to invertebrate animals. **2** lacking in strength, vitality, or character; weak or spineless.

inverted comma /in'vuhtid/ *noun* = QUOTATION MARK.

inverted pleat *noun* a pleat made by forming two folded edges which are secured to face each other on the right side of the fabric.

inverted snob *noun* somebody who sneers indiscriminately at people and things associated with wealth and high social status.

inverter /in'vuhtə/ *noun* a device for converting direct current into alternating current.

invert sugar /'invuht/ *noun* a mixture of glucose and fructose found in fruits or produced artificially from sucrose.

invest[1] /in'vest/ *verb trans* **1** (*often* + in) to commit (money) to a particular use, e.g. buying shares or new capital outlay, in order to earn a financial return. **2** (*often* + in) to devote (e.g. time or effort) to something for future advantages. >> *verb intrans* to make an investment: *We decided to invest in a new car.* >> **investable** *adj*, **investor** *noun*. [Italian *investire* to clothe, invest money, from Latin *investire*: see INVEST[2]]

invest[2] *verb trans* **1a** (+ in) to confer authority, office, or rank on (somebody), *esp* ceremonially. **b** to dress (somebody) in a robe, etc, *esp* ceremonially. **c** *literary* (+ with) to adorn (something) with something. **2** (+ with) to endow (something) with something: *The whole affair was invested with an air of mystery.* **3** *archaic* to surround a place with troops or ships so as to prevent escape or entry; to besiege (it). [Latin *investire* to clothe, surround, from IN-[2] + *vestis* clothing]

investigate /in'vestigayt/ *verb trans* **1** to make a systematic examination or study of (something or somebody). **2** to conduct an official enquiry into (something or somebody). >> *verb intrans* to conduct an investigation. >> **investigator** *noun*, **investigatory** *adj*. [Latin *investigatus*, past part. of *investigare* to track, investigate, from IN-[2] + *vestigium* footprint]

investigation /in,vesti'gaysh(ə)n/ *noun* **1** a systematic examination or an official enquiry. **2** the act or an instance of investigating something or somebody.

investigative /in'vestigətiv/ *adj* **1** having the duty to investigate or the function of investigating. **2** said of journalism: enquiring searchingly into issues and uncovering wrongdoings, anomalies, etc.

investiture /in'vestichə/ *noun* a formal ceremony conferring an office or honour on somebody. [Middle English, ultimately from Latin *investire*: see INVEST[2]]

investment[1] *noun* **1** a sum of money invested for income or profit. **2** an asset, e.g. property, purchased. **3a** the act or an instance of investing something other than money, e.g. time or effort. **b** something that is invested for this. [INVEST[1]]

investment[2] *noun archaic* a siege or blockade. [INVEST[2]]

investment bond *noun* a form of life assurance designed for long-term growth, linked to a unit trust and with a single lump sum paid in.

investment company *noun* a company whose primary business is acquiring shares or securities of other companies purely for investment purposes: compare HOLDING COMPANY.

investment trust *noun* an investment company that purchases securities on behalf of its investors: compare UNIT TRUST.

inveterate /in'vet(ə)rət/ *adj* **1** firmly, obstinately, and persistently established: *He had an inveterate tendency to back off from arguments.*

2 confirmed in a habit; habitual: *an inveterate liar.* ⟫⟫ **inveteracy** /-si/ *noun,* **inveterately** *adv.* [Latin *inveteratus,* past part. of *inveterare* to age, from IN-² + *veter-, vetus* old]

invidious /in'vidi-əs/ *adj* **1** tending to cause discontent, ill will, or envy: *Marriage ... is a monopoly, and not of the least invidious sort —* Charles Lamb. **2** said of a comparison: objectionable because of discriminating unfairly. ⟫⟫ **invidiously** *adv,* **invidiousness** *noun.* [Latin *invidiosus* envious, invidious, from *invidia:* see ENVY¹]

invigilate /in'vijilayt/ *verb* **1** *Brit.* **a** to supervise (candidates) at an examination. **b** to supervise (an examination). **2** *archaic* to keep watch over (something or somebody). ⟫⟫ **invigilation** /-'laysh(ə)n/ *noun,* **invigilator** *noun.* [Latin *invigilatus,* past part. of *invigilare* to keep watch, from IN-² + *vigilare* to watch, from *vigil* watchful]

invigorate /in'vigərayt/ *verb trans* to give fresh life and energy to (somebody or something). ⟫⟫ **invigoratingly** *adv,* **invigoration** /-'raysh(ə)n/ *noun,* **invigorator** *noun.* [Middle English via Old French from medieval Latin *invigorare,* from IN-² + Latin *vigorare* to make strong, from *vigor:* see VIGOUR]

invincible /in'vinsəbl/ *adj* incapable of being overcome: *He is a fellow of a most arrogant and invincible dullness* — Ben Jonson. ⟫⟫ **invincibility** /-'biliti/ *noun,* **invincibleness** *noun,* **invincibly** *adv.* [Middle English via French from late Latin *invincibilis,* from Latin IN-¹ + *vincere* to conquer]

in vino veritas /in ,veenoh 'veritas/ *phrase humorous* people speak the truth when they are drunk. [Latin, literally 'truth in wine']

inviolable /in'vie-ələbl/ *adj* that cannot or must not be violated or degraded: *an inviolable right.* ⟫⟫ **inviolability** /-'biliti/ *noun,* **inviolably** *adv.* [via French from Latin *inviolabilis,* from IN-¹ + *violabilis* from *violare* to VIOLATE]

inviolate /in'vie-ələt, -layt/ *adj* not violated or profaned. ⟫⟫ **inviolacy** /-si/ *noun,* **inviolately** *adv,* **inviolateness** *noun.*

invisible¹ /in'vizəbl/ *adj* **1** incapable of being seen, whether by nature or because of concealment: *An atheist is a man who has no invisible means of support* — John Buchan. **2a** not appearing in published financial statements: *invisible assets.* **b** not reflected in statistics: *invisible earnings.* **c** of or being trade in services, e.g. insurance or tourism, rather than goods: compare VISIBLE. **3** too small or unobtrusive to be seen or noticed; inconspicuous. ⟫⟫ **invisibility** /-zə'biliti/ *noun,* **invisibleness** *noun,* **invisibly** *adv.* [Middle English via French from Latin *invisibilis,* from IN-¹ + *visibilis:* see VISIBLE]

invisible² *noun* (*usu in pl*) an invisible asset, earning, export, etc.

invisible ink *noun* an ink that remains invisible on paper until it is given some special treatment.

invitation /invi'taysh(ə)n/ *noun* **1** the act or an instance of inviting, *esp* an often formal request to be present or participate. **2** something that incites or induces somebody to behave in a particular way: *The bell is not an invitation to go wild.* **3** (*used before a noun*) to which participants are invited.

invitational /invi'taysh(ə)n)l/ *adj chiefly NAmer* limited to invited participants: *an invitational lecture.*

invite¹ /in'viet/ *verb trans* **1** to request (something), or the presence of (somebody), *esp* formally or politely. **2** to increase the likelihood of (something), often unintentionally: *His actions invite trouble.* ⟫⟫ **invitatory** /in'vitət(ə)ri/ *adj,* **invitee** /-'tee/ *noun,* **inviter** *noun.* [early French *inviter* from Latin *invitare*]

invite² /'inviet/ *noun informal* an invitation.

inviting /in'vieting/ *adj* attractive or tempting. ⟫⟫ **invitingly** *adv.*

in vitro /in 'veetroh/ *adv and adj* outside the living body and in an artificial environment such as a test tube. [Latin *in vitro,* literally 'in glass']

in vivo /in 'veevoh/ *adv and adj* in the living body of a plant or animal. [Latin *in vivo,* literally 'in the living']

invocation /invə'kaysh(ə)n/ *noun* **1** the act or an instance of petitioning somebody for help or support. **2** a prayer asking God for help or support. **3** the performance of magical rites in order to summon spirits, or a formula or incantation used for this. ⟫⟫ **invocational** *adj,* **invocatory** /in'vokət(ə)ri/ *adj.* [Middle English *invocacioun* via French from Latin *invocation-, invocatio,* from *invocare:* see INVOKE]

invoice¹ /'invoys/ *noun* **1** an itemized list of goods or services provided, together with a note of the sum of money the recipient

owes. **2** a consignment of merchandise. [modification of early French *envois,* pl of *envoi* message, from *envoier:* see ENVOY¹]

invoice² *verb trans* **1** to submit an invoice to (somebody) for goods or services provided. **2** to submit an invoice for (goods or services provided).

invoke /in'vohk/ *verb trans* **1a** to petition (e.g. a deity) for help or support. **b** to appeal to (an arbitrator or other authority) for help, a judgment, confirmation of an opinion, etc. **2** to call forth (e.g. a spirit) by uttering a spell or magical formula. **3** to make an earnest request for (something); to solicit (it): *We invoked their forgiveness.* **4** to put (something) into effect: *They will invoke economic sanctions.* ⟫⟫ **invocable** *adj,* **invoker** *noun.* [Middle English *invoken* via French from Latin *invocare,* from IN-² + *vocare* to call]

involucre /invə'loohkə/ *noun* one or more whorls (circular arrangements: see WHORL) of bracts (thin leaflike or spiny parts: see BRACT) situated below and close to a flower or flower cluster. ⟫⟫ **involucral** *adj.* [French *involucre* from Latin *involucrum* sheath, from *involvere:* see INVOLVE]

involuntary /in'volənt(ə)ri/ *adj* **1** not subject to conscious control; reflex: *an involuntary muscle.* **2** done contrary to or without choice. ⟫⟫ **involuntarily** *adv,* **involuntariness** *noun.*

involute¹ /'invəlooht/ *adj* **1** *technical.* **a** said of e.g. a shell: curled spirally. **b** said of e.g. a leaf: curled or curved inwards, *esp* at the edge. **c** having the form of an involute: *a gear with involute teeth.* **2** *formal* very intricate or complex; convoluted. ⟫⟫ **involutely** *adv.* [Latin *involutus,* past part. of *involvere:* see INVOLVE]

involute² *noun* a curve traced by a point on a thread kept taut as it is unwound from another curve.

involute³ /invə'looht/ *verb intrans* **1** to become involute. **2** in medicine, said of e.g. a part of the body: to return to a former condition: *After pregnancy the uterus involutes.*

involution /invə'loohsh(ə)n/ *noun* **1** *formal or technical* a part curving inwards, or its inward curvature. **2** in medicine, a shrinking or return to a former size, e.g. of the uterus following pregnancy. **3** *formal* the complicated nature of something. **4** the act or an instance of raising a mathematical quantity to a particular power. [Latin *involution-, involutio,* from *involvere:* see INVOLVE]

involve /in'volv/ *verb trans* **1a** to cause (somebody) to be associated or take part. **b** to occupy (oneself) absorbingly or to commit (oneself) emotionally. **2** to require (something) as a necessary accompaniment: *The kind of job that involves dealing with the public.* **3** to relate (something) closely: *This problem is closely involved with another.* **4** *archaic* to envelop (something). ⟫⟫ **involvement** *noun,* **involver** *noun.* [Middle English *involven* to roll up, wrap, from Latin *involvere* to roll in, enfold, from IN-² + *volvere* to roll]

involved *adj* **1** complex, *esp* needlessly or excessively so. **2a** taking part: *I was one of the workers involved in building the dam.* **b** connected with something, *esp* emotionally. ⟫⟫ **involvedly** /-vidli/ *adv.*

invulnerable /in'vulnərəbl/ *adj* **1** incapable of being injured or harmed. **2** immune to or protected against attack. ⟫⟫ **invulnerability** /-'biliti/ *noun,* **invulnerableness** *noun,* **invulnerably** *adv.* [late Latin *invulnerabilis,* from IN-¹ + *vulnerabilis:* see VULNERABLE]

inward¹ /'inwəd/ *adj* **1** situated within or directed towards the inside; interior. **2** of or relating to the mind or spirit; inner: *inward peace.* **3** said of investment: coming into a country or region from outside it. ⟫⟫ **inwardness** *noun.* [Old English *inweard*]

inward² *adv NAmer* see INWARDS.

inwardly *adv* **1** beneath the surface; internally: *The hungry sheep look up, and are not fed ... rot inwardly, and foul contagion spread* — Milton. **2** to oneself, or in one's private thoughts.

inwards (*NAmer* **inward**) *adv* **1** towards the inside, centre, or interior. **2** towards the inner being.

inwrap *verb trans* see ENWRAP.

in-wrought *adj* **1** said of a fabric: decorated with a pattern woven or worked in. **2** said of a pattern: woven or worked in, e.g. to a fabric.

inyala /in'yahlə/ *noun* (*pl* **inyalas** *or collectively* **inyala**) = NYALA. [Zulu *inxala*]

in-your-face *adj informal* consciously frank, aggressive, or controversial: *in-your-face programming.*

i/o *abbr* input/output.

IOC *abbr* International Olympic Committee.

iod- or **iodo-** comb. form forming words, denoting: iodine: *iodize*; *iodoform*. [French *iode*: see IODINE]

iodic /ie'odik/ adj of or containing iodine, esp with a valency of 5. ➤➤ **iodate** /'ie·ədayt/ noun. [French *iodique*, from *iode*: see IODINE]

iodide /'ie·ədied/ noun a compound of iodine with an element or radical, esp a salt or ester of hydriodic acid.

iodine /'ie·ədeen/ noun **1** a blackish grey non-metallic chemical element of the halogen group, used in various compounds in medicine and photography: symbol I, atomic number 53. **2** a solution of iodine in alcohol, used as an antiseptic. [French *iode* from Greek *ioeidēs* violet-coloured, from *ion* violet]

iodize or **iodise** /'ie·ədiez/ verb trans to treat (something) with iodine or a compound of iodine: *iodized salt*.

iodo- comb. form see IOD-.

iodoform /ie'odəfawm/ noun a yellow solid compound that has a penetrating smell and is a mild disinfectant. [IODO- + -form as in CHLOROFORM[1]]

iodopsin /ie·ə'dopsin/ noun a light-sensitive pigment in the retinal cones of the eye that is important in the perception of colour, esp in daylight vision. [IOD- + Greek *opsis* sight, vision + -IN[1]]

iodous /ie'ədəs/ adj of or containing iodine, esp in its trivalent form.

IOM abbr Isle of Man.

ion /'ie·ən/ noun **1** an atom or group of atoms that carries a positive or negative electric charge as a result of having lost or gained one or more electrons. **2** a free electron or other charged subatomic particle. [Greek *iōn*, present part. of *ienai* to go]

-ion suffix forming nouns, denoting: **1a** the act or process of: *validation*. **b** the result of a specified act or process: *regulation*. **2** the quality or condition of: *hydration*; *ambition*. [Middle English *-ioun*, *-ion* via French *-ion* from Latin *-ion-*, *-io*]

ion exchange noun a reversible reaction, used esp for softening or removing dissolved substances from water, in which one kind of ion is interchanged with another of similar charge. ➤➤ **ion exchanger** noun.

Ionic[1] /ie'onik/ adj **1** relating to or denoting one of the three Greek orders of architecture, characterized esp by fluted columns and a scroll-shaped CAPITAL[3] (upper part of a column): compare CORINTHIAN[2], DORIC[1]. **2a** belonging to the ancient Greek region of Ionia, or the dialect of ancient Greek used there. **b** belonging to the modern Ionian islands. [early French *ionique* via Latin from Greek *iōnikos*, from *Iōnia* Ionia, an ancient region on the Aegean coast colonized by the Greeks c.1000 BC]

Ionic[2] noun a dialect of ancient Greek used in Ionia.

ionic /ie'onik/ adj **1** of, existing as, or characterized by ions: *ionic gases*. **2** functioning by means of ions: *ionic conduction*. ➤➤ **ionicity** /ie·ə'nisiti/ noun.

ionic bond noun an electrovalent chemical bond.

ionise /'ie·əniez/ verb trans and intrans see IONIZE.

ionium /ie'ohni·əm/ noun a natural radioactive isotope of thorium with a mass number of 230. [from its ionizing action]

ionize or **ionise** verb trans to convert (something) wholly or partly into ions. ➤ verb intrans to become converted wholly or partly into ions. ➤➤ **ionizable** adj, **ionization** /-'zaysh(ə)n/ noun, **ionizer** noun.

ionophore /ie'onəfaw/ noun a compound that increases the transport of ions across a lipid barrier, e.g. a cell membrane, by reversibly combining with the ions and by increasing the permeability of the barrier to them.

ionosphere /ie'onəsfiə/ noun the layer of the earth's atmosphere that extends from an altitude of about 60km (about 40mi), through the MESOSPHERE and THERMOSPHERE to at least 480km (about 300mi) and consists of several distinct regions containing free ions, atoms, and electrons. ➤➤ **ionospheric** /-'sferik/ adj.

iota /ie'ohtə/ noun **1** the ninth letter of the Greek alphabet (Ι, ι), equivalent to and transliterated as roman i. **2** an infinitesimal amount; a bit: *It makes not one iota of a difference*. [via Latin from Greek *iōta*, of Semitic origin; (sense 2) because iota is the smallest Greek character]

IOU /,ie oh 'yooh/ noun a written acknowledgment of a debt. [prob from the pronunciation of *I owe you*]

-ious suffix forming adjectives, with the meaning: full of: *cautious*. [Middle English, partly from Old French -ious, -ieux, from Latin -iosus, partly from Latin -ius, adj suffix]

IOW abbr Isle of Wight.

IPA abbr International Phonetic Alphabet.

ipecacuanha /,ipikakyoo'ahnə/ noun **1** the underground stem and root of a S American plant, formerly used dried as a purgative and emetic. **2** the plant that it is obtained from, a S American creeping plant of the madder family: *Cephaelis ipecacuanha*. [Portuguese *ipecacuanha* from Tupi *ipekaaguéne*, from *ipe* small + *kaâ* leaves + *guéne* to vomit]

ippon /'ipon/ noun in judo, karate, and other competitive martial arts, a full point awarded for a move executed with admirable technique. [Japanese *ippon* one point]

ipse dixit /,ipsay 'diksit/ noun something stated dogmatically but without evidence or proof to support it. [Latin *ipse dixit* he himself said it]

ipsilateral /ipsi'lat(ə)rəl/ adj situated or appearing on or affecting the same side of the body: compare CONTRALATERAL. ➤➤ **ipsilaterally** adv. [Latin *ipse* self, himself + *later-*, *latus* side]

ipso facto /,ipsoh 'faktoh/ adv by that very fact, or by the very nature of the case. [Latin *ipso facto* by the fact itself]

IQ abbr intelligence quotient.

IR abbr **1** infrared. **2** Inland Revenue. **3** Iran (international vehicle registration).

Ir abbr the chemical symbol for iridium.

Ir. abbr Irish.

ir- prefix see IN-[1], IN-[2].

IRA abbr Irish Republican Army.

Iranian /i'rayni·ən, i'rah-/ noun **1** a native or inhabitant of Iran in SW Asia. **2** a branch of the Indo-European family of languages that includes Persian. ➤➤ **Iranian** adj.

Iraqi /i'rahki, i'raki/ noun (pl **Iraqis**) **1** a native or inhabitant of Iraq in SW Asia. **2** the dialect of Modern Arabic spoken in Iraq. ➤➤ **Iraqi** adj. [Arabic *'irāqīy*, from *'Irāq* Iraq]

irascible /i'rasibl/ adj having an easily provoked temper; irritable: *Rach can be so irascible at times*. ➤➤ **irascibility** /-'biliti/ noun, **irascibleness** noun, **irascibly** adv. [early French *irascible* from late Latin *irascibilis*, from Latin *irasci* to be or become angry, from *ira* anger]

irate /ie'rayt/ adj extremely angry or arising from anger. ➤➤ **irately** adv, **irateness** noun. [Latin *iratus*, from *ira* anger]

IRBM abbr intermediate range ballistic missile.

ire /ie·ə/ noun literary intense and usu openly displayed anger. ➤➤ **ireful** adj. [Middle English via French from Latin *ira*]

irenic or **eirenic** /ie'reenik, ie'renik/ or **irenical** or **eirenical** /ie'reenikl, ie'renikl/ adj conducive to or operating towards peace or conciliation. ➤➤ **irenically** adv. [Greek *eirēnikos*, from *eirēnē* peace]

irid- or **irido-** comb. form forming nouns and adjectives, denoting: **1** rainbow: *iridescent*. **2** iris of the eye: *iridectomy*. **3** iridium; iridium and: *iridic*. **4** the iris flower: *iridaceous*. [Latin *irid-*, *iris*: see IRIS]

iridaceous /iri'dayshəs/ adj relating or belonging to the iris family.

irides /'ierideez/ noun pl of IRIS.

iridescent /iri'des(ə)nt/ adj displaying a shimmering shift of colours such as is seen in a soap bubble, bird's plumage, etc. ➤➤ **iridescence** noun, **iridescently** adv.

iridium /i'ridi·əm/ noun a silver-white metallic chemical element of the platinum group: symbol Ir, atomic number 77. ➤➤ **iridic** /-ik/ adj. [scientific Latin *iridium* from Latin *irid-*, *iris* rainbow, from the colours produced when it is dissolved in hydrochloric acid]

irido- comb. form see IRID-.

iris /'ieris/ noun **1a** (pl **irises** or **irides** /'ierideez/) the opaque contractile diaphragm perforated by the pupil that forms the coloured portion of the eye. **b** an adjustable diaphragm of thin opaque plates that can be moved to control the size of an aperture. **2** (pl **irises** or collectively **iris**) any of a large genus of plants with long straight leaves and large showy flowers: genus *Iris*. [via Latin from Greek *iris* rainbow, iris plant, iris of the eye]

iris diaphragm noun = IRIS (IB).

Irish[1] /'ierish/ adj **1** of Ireland, the people of Ireland, or the Celtic language of Ireland. **2** offensive amusingly illogical. ➤➤ **Irishman**

noun, **Irishness** noun, **Irishwoman** noun. [Old English *Īras* Irish-men, of Celtic origin]

Irish² noun **1** (*treated as pl*) the people of Ireland. **2** (*also* **Irish Gaelic**) the Celtic language of the people of Ireland.

Word history
Words from Irish Gaelic that have passed into common use in English include *brogue, galore, leprechaun, shamrock, smithereens,* and *whiskey.*

Irish coffee noun hot sugared coffee with Irish whiskey and whipped cream.

Irish moss noun = CARRAGEEN.

Irish setter noun a gundog of a chestnut-brown or mahogany-red breed with a long silky coat.

Irish stew noun a stew consisting chiefly of meat, traditionally mutton, potatoes, and onions in a thick gravy.

Irish terrier noun a terrier of an active medium-sized breed with a dense usu reddish wiry coat.

Irish whiskey noun whisky made in Ireland, chiefly of barley.

Irish wolfhound noun a hound of a very large tall breed that broadly resemble the greyhound but are much larger and stronger and have a shaggy coat.

iritis /ie'rietis/ noun inflammation of the iris of the eye.

irk /uhk/ verb trans to make (somebody) weary, irritated, or angry. [Middle English *irken* to be weary, prob from Old Norse *yrkja* to work]

irksome /'uhks(ə)m/ adj troublesome or annoying. >>> **irksomely** adv, **irksomeness** noun.

IRL abbr Ireland (international vehicle registration).

IRO abbr **1** Inland Revenue Office. **2** International Refugee Organization.

iron¹ /'ie·ən/ noun **1** a silver-white magnetic metallic chemical element that is heavy and malleable, readily rusts in moist air, occurs in most igneous rocks, and is vital to biological processes: symbol Fe, atomic number 26. **2** a metal implement with a smooth flat typically triangular base that is heated, now usu by electricity, and used to smooth or press clothing. **3** a heated metal implement used for branding, cauterizing, or soldering. **4** (*usu in pl*) a device, *esp* fetters, used to bind or restrain. **5** any of a numbered series of usu nine golf clubs with metal heads of varying angles for hitting the ball to various heights and lengths. **6** any of various tools, implements, or devices made of iron: *a grappling iron*. **7** great strength or hardness. ✳ **iron in the fire** a prospective course of action, or a plan not yet realized [from the days when smoothing irons for pressing clothes were heated in the fire; as one cooled with use another would be in the fire heating up]. [Old English *īsern, īren*]

iron² adj **1** made of iron. **2** resembling iron, e.g. in appearance, strength, solidity, or durability: *an iron will.* >>> **ironness** noun.

iron³ verb (**ironed, ironing**) > verb trans **1** to smooth (something) with a heated iron: *He ironed his shirt.* **2** (*often* + out) to remove (e.g. wrinkles) by ironing. > verb intrans to be capable of being ironed: *This skirt irons well.*

Iron Age noun (**the Iron Age**) the period of human culture characterized by the widespread use of iron for making tools and weapons and dating from before 1000 BC.

Editorial note
The Iron Age was the period of antiquity in the Old World in which iron metallurgy superseded the use of bronze for tools and weapons. Iron was a far more accessible and plentiful metal, it could be produced more cheaply, it was more readily available and produced far tougher implements. In Europe the earliest iron appeared around 1100 BC, and the period lasts until the arrival of the Romans. In the Far East and North Africa, iron usage arose around 500 BC, while in southern Africa the Iron Age spans a period from about AD 200 to the 19th cent. — Dr Paul Bahn.

ironbark noun any of several species of Australian eucalyptus trees with thick bark and dense wood: genus *Eucalyptus.*

ironbound adj **1** rugged or harsh: *an ironbound coast.* **2** stern or rigorous: *ironbound traditions.*

ironclad¹ adj said *esp* of warships: sheathed in iron or steel armour.

ironclad² noun an ironclad naval vessel, *esp* in the 19th and early 20th cents.

Iron Curtain noun (**the Iron Curtain**) a political and ideological barrier between the Communist countries of E Europe and the non-Communist countries of W Europe and those friendly to them.

iron grey adj dark greenish grey. >>> **iron grey** noun.

iron hand noun stern or rigorous control: compare VELVET GLOVE: *She ruled her family with an iron hand.* >>> **ironhanded** adj and adv.

iron horse noun NAmer, archaic an early locomotive engine.

ironic /ie'ronik/ adj **1** containing or constituting irony: *an ironic situation.* **2** tending to use irony. >>> **ironically** adv, **ironicalness** noun.

ironical /ie'ronikl/ adj = IRONIC.

ironing noun clothes and other items of laundry that are ironed or are to be ironed.

ironing board noun a narrow flat board on which clothes, etc are ironed, mounted on collapsible and adjustable legs.

ironist /'ierənist/ noun somebody who uses irony, *esp* in the development of a literary work or theme.

iron lung noun a device, formerly used for artificial respiration, in the form of a rigid metal case that fits over the patient's chest and forces air into and out of the lungs.

iron maiden noun a medieval instrument of torture consisting of a box or hollow statue lined with iron spikes which impaled the victim.

iron man noun **1** a man of outstanding strength or athletic prowess. **2** any of various sporting contests that demand outstanding athletic prowess.

ironmonger /'ie·ənmunggə/ noun Brit a dealer in hardware. >>> **ironmongery** noun.

iron out verb trans to put right or correct (e.g. a problem or defect).

iron pyrites noun iron disulphide occurring as a lustrous pale brass-yellow mineral; pyrite.

iron rations pl noun emergency food rations, *esp* for a soldier. [because it orig consisted mainly of tinned food]

Ironsides noun (**the Ironsides**) the cavalry regiment of the Parliamentary side in the English Civil War, or the entire Parliamentary army.

ironstone noun a hard sedimentary iron ore, *esp* a siderite.

ironware noun articles, *esp* pots, pans, and implements for domestic use, made of iron.

ironwood noun any of numerous trees and shrubs with exceptionally tough or hard wood, or the wood itself.

ironwork noun **1** articles made of iron. **2** (*in pl, but treated as sing. or pl*) a mill or building where iron or steel is smelted or heavy iron or steel products are made.

irony¹ /'ierəni/ noun (*pl* **ironies**) **1a** the use of words to express a meaning other than the literal meaning, and *esp* the opposite of it. **b** an expression or utterance using irony. **2a** incongruity between actual circumstances and the normal, appropriate, or expected result. **b** an event or situation showing such incongruity. **c** incongruity between a situation developed in a play and the accompanying words or actions that is understood by the audience but not by the characters. **d** = SOCRATIC IRONY. **3** an attitude of detached awareness of incongruity: *She viewed with irony the craze for individuality.* [Latin *ironia* from Greek *eirōneia,* from *eirōn* dissembler]

irony² /'ie·əni/ adj like iron: *It's a sort of irony colour.*

Iroquoian /irə'kwoyən/ noun a language family of eastern N America including Cherokee, Erie, and Mohawk. >>> **Iroquoian** adj.

Iroquois /'irəkwoy(z)/ noun (*pl* **Iroquois** /'irəkwoy(z)/) **1** (*in pl*) a confederation of Native American tribes of the western USA. **2** a member of any of these tribes. **3** any of the languages of these tribes. >>> **Iroquois** adj. [French *Iroquois* from Algonquin *Irina-khoiw,* literally 'real adders']

IRQ abbr Iraq (international vehicle registration).

irradiate /i'raydiayt/ verb trans **1** to expose (food) to electromagnetic radiation in order to kill bacteria and prolong its shelf life. **2** to cast rays of light on (something). **3** to emit (something that can be likened to rays of light). **4** literary to give intellectual or spiritual insight to (somebody). >>> **irradiance** noun, **irradiative** /-tiv/ adj, **irradiator** noun. [Latin *irradiatus,* past part. of *irradiare* to shine upon, from IN-² + *radiare:* see RADIATE¹]

irradiation /i,raydi'aysh(ə)n/ noun **1** the act or an instance of irradiating or being irradiated. **2** exposure to radiation, e.g. the electromagnetic radiation used to treat some foods.

irrational[1] /i'rash(ə)nl/ *adj* **1a** not governed by or according to reason; illogical. **b** not capable of reasoning. **2** having a value that is an irrational number: *an irrational root of an equation*. ➤➤ **irrationalism** *noun,* **irrationalist** *noun,* **irrationality** /-'naliti/ *noun,* **irrationally** *adv.* [Middle English from Latin *irrationalis,* from IN-[1] + *rationalis*: see RATIONAL[1]]

irrational[2] *noun* a number, e.g. π, that cannot be expressed exactly as the result of dividing one integer by another: compare RATIONAL[2], SURD[2].

irrational number *noun* = IRRATIONAL[2].

irreclaimable /iri'klayməbl/ *adj* incapable of being reclaimed. ➤➤ **irreclaimably** *adv.*

irreconcilable[1] /i'rekənsieləbl/ *adj* impossible to reconcile; incompatible. ➤➤ **irreconcilability** /-lə'biliti/ *noun,* **irreconcilableness** *noun,* **irreconcilably** *adv.*

irreconcilable[2] *noun* **1** an opponent of compromise or collaboration. **2** something that cannot be reconciled with others or with something larger.

irrecoverable /iri'kuv(ə)rəbl/ *adj* not capable of being recovered or retrieved. ➤➤ **irrecoverably** *adv.*

irrecusable /iri'kyoohzəbl/ *adj* said of evidence, etc: not able to be questioned or rejected. ➤➤ **irrecusably** *adv.* [late Latin *irrecusabilis,* ultimately from IN-[1] + Latin *recusare*: see RECUSANT]

irredeemable /iri'deeməbl/ *adj* **1** too bad to be saved or improved; beyond remedy. **2** said of bonds, etc: without a specified date for repayment. ➤➤ **irredeemably** *adv.*

irredentism /iri'dentiz(ə)m/ *noun* advocacy of the restoration of territories to the countries to which they are historically or ethnically related. ➤➤ **irredentist** *noun and adj.* [Italian *irredentismo,* from *Italia irredenta,* literally 'unredeemed Italy', Italian-speaking territory not incorporated in Italy]

irreducible /iri'dyoohsəbl/ *adj* **1** impossible to be brought into a desired, normal, or simpler state: *an irreducible matrix*. **2** said of a mathematical expression: not capable of being split up into factors whose variables have lower powers than those in the expression. ➤➤ **irreducibility** /-'biliti/ *noun,* **irreducibly** *adv.*

irrefragable /i'refrəgəbl/ *adj* **1** *formal* impossible to deny or refute: *irrefragable arguments*. **2** impossible to break or alter: *irrefragable rules*. ➤➤ **irrefragability** /-'biliti/ *noun,* **irrefragably** *adv.* [late Latin *irrefragabilis,* ultimately from IN-[1] + Latin *refragari* to oppose]

irrefrangible /iri'franjəbl/ *adj* not capable of being refracted.

irrefutable /iri'fyoohtəbl/ *adj* not able to be denied or disproved; incontrovertible. ➤➤ **irrefutability** /-'biliti/ *noun,* **irrefutably** *adv.* [late Latin *irrefutabilis,* ultimately from IN-[1] + Latin *refutare*: see REFUTE]

irregardless[1] /iri'gahdlis/ *adj* = REGARDLESS[1]. ✳ **irregardless of** = REGARDLESS OF.

Usage note ───────────────────────────
Irregardless is a non-standard word that means 'regardless'. It was probably formed from *irrespective* and *regardless*.

irregardless[2] *adv* = REGARDLESS[2].

irregular[1] /i'regyoolə/ *adj* **1** lacking continuity or regularity, *esp* of occurrence or activity: *irregular bowel movements*. **2** lacking symmetry or evenness: *an irregular shape*. **3** contrary to rules, customs, or moral principles: *a most irregular practice*. **4** said of a word: not inflected in the normal manner. **5** said of troops: not belonging to the regular army organization. ➤➤ **irregularly** *adv.* [Middle English *irreguler* via French from late Latin *irregularis* not in accordance with rule, from IN-[1] + *regularis*: see REGULAR[1]]

irregular[2] *noun* **1** an irregular soldier. **2** *NAmer* a substandard item sold at a reduced price; a second.

irregularity /i,regyoo'lariti/ *noun* (*pl* **irregularities**) **1** something irregular, e.g. contrary to accepted professional or ethical standards. **2** the irregular nature of something.

irrelevance /i'reliv(ə)ns/ *noun* **1** the quality or state of being irrelevant. **2** something irrelevant.

irrelevancy /i'reliv(ə)nsi/ *noun* (*pl* **irrelevancies**) = IRRELEVANCE.

irrelevant /i'reliv(ə)nt/ *adj* not relevant; inapplicable. ➤➤ **irrelevantly** *adv.*

irreligion /iri'lij(ə)n/ *noun* hostility to or disregard of religion. ➤➤ **irreligionist** *noun,* **irreligious** /-jəs/ *adj,* **irreligiously** /-jəsli/ *adv.* [early French *irreligion* from Latin *irreligion-, irreligio,* from IN-[1] + *religion-, religio*: see RELIGION]

irremediable /iri'meedi·əbl/ *adj* impossible to remedy; incurable: *the worst and most irremediable of all evils – a connection for life with an unprincipled man* — Jane Austen. ➤➤ **irremediableness** *noun,* **irremediably** *adv.* [Latin *irremediabilis,* from IN-[1] + *remediabilis* curable, from *remedium*: see REMEDY[1]]

irremissible /iri'misəbl/ *adj* **1** too bad to forgive; unpardonable. **2** not to be avoided or abandoned; obligatory. ➤➤ **irremissibly** *adv.* [early French *irremissible* from late Latin *irremissibilis,* ultimately from Latin IN-[1] + *remittere*: see REMIT[1]]

irremovable /iri'moohvəbl/ *adj* not able to be removed, *esp* from an official position.

irreparable /i'rep(ə)rəbl/ *adj* not able to be restored to a previous condition. ➤➤ **irreparableness** *noun,* **irreparably** *adv.* [Middle English via French from Latin *irreparabilis,* from IN-[1] + *reparabilis* reparable, from *reparare*: see REPAIR[1]]

irreplaceable /iri'playsəbl/ *adj* having no adequate substitute. ➤➤ **irreplaceably** *adv.*

irrepressible /iri'presəbl/ *adj* impossible to restrain or control. ➤➤ **irrepressibility** /-'biliti/ *noun,* **irrepressibly** *adv.*

irreproachable /iri'prohchəbl/ *adj* offering no foundation for blame or criticism; above reproach. ➤➤ **irreproachability** /-'biliti/ *noun,* **irreproachably** *adv.*

irresistible /iri'zistəbl/ *adj* too attractive or enticing to resist. ➤➤ **irresistibility** /-'biliti/ *noun,* **irresistibleness** *noun,* **irresistibly** *adv.*

irresolute /i'rezəl(y)ooht/ *adj* lacking decisiveness or a firm aim and purpose. ➤➤ **irresolutely** *adv,* **irresoluteness** *noun,* **irresolution** /-'l(y)oohsh(ə)n/ *noun.*

irrespective /iri'spektiv/ *adv* regardless. ✳ **irrespective of** without regard or reference to; in spite of. ➤➤ **irrespectively** *adv.*

irresponsible /iri'sponsəbl/ *adj* **1** showing no regard for the consequences of one's actions; reckless. **2** unable to bear responsibility. ➤➤ **irresponsibility** /-'biliti/ *noun,* **irresponsibly** *adv.*

irresponsive /iri'sponsiv/ *adj* not responsive, *esp* not able, ready, or inclined to respond. ➤➤ **irresponsiveness** *noun.*

irretrievable /iri'treevəbl/ *adj* not retrievable; irrecoverable. ➤➤ **irretrievability** /-'biliti/ *noun,* **irretrievably** *adv.*

irreverence /i'rev(ə)rəns/ *noun* lack of respect, or something done or said that shows a lack of respect. ➤➤ **irreverent** *adj,* **irreverently** *adv.*

irreversible /iri'vuhsəbl/ *adj* unable to be changed back into a previous state or condition: *irreversible brain damage*. ➤➤ **irreversibility** /-'biliti/ *noun,* **irreversibly** *adv.*

irrevocable /i'revəkəbl/ *adj* incapable of being revoked or altered. ➤➤ **irrevocability** /-'biliti/ *noun,* **irrevocably** *adv.* [Middle English from Latin *irrevocabilis,* from IN-[1] + *revocabilis,* from *revocare*: see REVOKE[1]]

irrigate /'irigayt/ *verb trans* **1** to supply (land) with water by artificial means, e.g. canals or channels. **2** to flush (e.g. an eye or wound) with a stream of liquid. ➤➤ **irrigation** /-'gaysh(ə)n/ *noun,* **irrigator** *noun.* [Latin *irrigatus,* past part. of *irrigare* to add water, from IN-[2] + *rigare* to moisten]

irritable /'iritəbl/ *adj* **1** easily angered or exasperated. **2** abnormally sensitive to stimuli. **3** capable of responding to stimuli such as light, heat, etc. ➤➤ **irritability** /-'biliti/ *noun,* **irritableness** *noun,* **irritably** *adv.*

irritable bowel syndrome *noun* any of various abnormal or unusual conditions of the intestines that are accompanied by discomfort and pain and have no apparent organic cause.

irritant[1] /'irit(ə)nt/ *noun* something that irritates.

irritant[2] *adj* causing irritation. ➤➤ **irritancy** *noun.*

irritate /'iritayt/ *verb trans* **1** to make (somebody) impatient or angry. **2** to cause (a part of the body) to become tender or inflamed. **3** in biology, to stimulate (a cell, etc) so that it produces a response. ➤➤ **irritating** *adj,* **irritatingly** *adv,* **irritative** /-tətiv/ *adj.* [Latin *irritatus,* past part. of *irritare*]

irritation /iri'taysh(ə)n/ *noun* **1** an irritated state. **2** something that makes somebody irritated. **3** a cause or condition of soreness, roughness, or inflammation of a body part.

irrupt /i'rupt/ *verb intrans* **1** to rush in forcibly or violently. **2a** said *esp* of birds: to migrate into an area in abnormally large numbers. **b** said of a natural population: to undergo a sudden upsurge in numbers, *esp* when natural ecological balances and checks are disturbed. ⟫ **irruption** /-sh(ə)n/ *noun*, **irruptive** /-tiv/ *adj*, **irruptively** *adv*. [Latin *irruptus*, past part. of *irrumpere* to break in, from IN-² + *rumpere* to break]

IS *abbr* Iceland (international vehicle registration).

is /z; *strong* iz/ *verb* third person sing. present tense of BE. [Old English]

is. *abbr* island or isle.

is- *or* **iso-** *comb. form* forming words, with the meanings: **1** equal, homogeneous, or uniform: *isodynamic*. **2** isomeric with (the compound or radical specified): *isoleucine*. [via late Latin from Greek *is-*, from *isos* equal]

ISA /'iesə/ *noun* an individual savings account, a tax-free savings scheme.

Isa *abbr* Isaiah (book of the Bible).

isagogics /isə'gojiks/ *pl noun* (*treated as sing. or pl*) the study of the Bible that precedes exegesis. ⟫ **isagogic** *adj*. [Greek *eisagogē* introduction, from *eis* into + *agein* to lead]

isatin /'iesətin/ *noun* an orange-red compound used in the manufacture of dyes. [Greek *isatis* woad + -IN¹]

ISBN *abbr* International Standard Book Number.

ischaemia (*NAmer* **ischemia**) /is'keemi-ə/ *noun* deficiency of blood in a part of the body due to decreased arterial flow. [Latin *ischaemus* styptic, from Greek *ischaimos*, from *ischein* to restrain + *haima* blood]

ischium /'iski-əm/ *noun* (*pl* **ischia** /'iski-ə/) the rearmost and lowest of the three principal bones composing either half of the pelvis. ⟫ **ischial** *adj*. [via Latin from Greek *ischion* hip joint]

ISDN *abbr* integrated services digital network.

-ise *suffix* see -IZE.

isentropic /iesen'tropik/ *adj* in physics, of equal or constant ENTROPY (amount of disorder in a system). ⟫ **isentropically** *adv*.

-ish *suffix* **1** forming adjectives from nouns, with the meaning: of or belonging to (a specified country or ethnic group): *Finnish*. **2** forming adjectives from nouns and adjectives, with the meanings: **a** having a trace of: *summerish*. **b** slightly: *purplish*; *biggish*. **3** forming adjectives from nouns, with the meanings: **a** having the approximate age of: *fortyish*. **b** being or occurring at the approximate time of: *eightish*. **c** having the characteristics of: *boyish*; *mulish*. [Old English *-isc*]

isinglass /'iezingglahs/ *noun* **1** a very pure gelatin prepared from the air bladders of sturgeons and other fish and used *esp* in jellies and glue. **2** *chiefly NAmer* mica or a similar substance. [prob by folk etymology from obsolete Dutch *huizenblas*, from early Dutch *huusblase* sturgeon's bladder, from *huus* sturgeon + *blase* bladder]

isl. *abbr* island.

Islam /'izlahm, 'izlam/ *noun* **1** the religious faith of Muslims including belief in Allah as the sole deity and in Muhammad as his prophet.

Editorial note
Islam means submission to the will of Allah (God), the supreme reality. Muslims (those who practise Islam) believe that all creatures do this naturally, and that every child is therefore born Muslim, even if he or she later follows another path. Islam is the community of those who accept that there is no God but Allah, and that Muhammad is his prophet — Dr Mel Thompson.

2 the civilization or culture based on Islam. ⟫ **Islamic** /iz'lamik/ *adj*. [Arabic *islām* submission (to the will of God)]

Islamise /'izləmiez/ *verb trans* see ISLAMIZE.

Islamist /'izlamist/ *noun* **1a** a Muslim who espouses a militant and politicized form of Islam. **b** somebody who upholds the faith, doctrine, or cause of Islam. **2** somebody who studies Islam, Islamic culture, etc. ⟫ **Islamism** *noun*.

Islamize *or* **Islamise** /'izləmiez/ *verb trans* **1** to make (something) Islamic; to make (it) conform to Islamic law, etc. **2** to convert (people, a country, etc) to Islam. ⟫ **Islamization** *noun*.

island /'ieland/ *noun* **1** an area of land surrounded by water and smaller than a continent: *This island is made mainly of coal and surrounded by fish. Only an organizing genius could produce a shortage of coal and fish at the same time* — Aneurin Bevan. **2** something that is isolated or surrounded, like an island is by water: *No man is an island, entire of itself; every man is a piece of the continent, a part of the main* — John Donne. **3** = TRAFFIC ISLAND. **4** an isolated superstructure on the deck of a ship, *esp* an aircraft carrier. **5** in anatomy, a body part or group of cells that is structurally different from its

surroundings. ⟫ **islander** *noun*. [alteration, by association with ISLE, of earlier *iland* from Old English *īgland*, from *īg* island + LAND¹]

isle /iel/ *noun* an island, *esp* a small one. [Middle English via French from Latin *insula*]

islet /'ielit/ *noun* **1** a little island. **2** in anatomy, a small isolated mass of one type of tissue.

islets of Langerhans /'langəhanz/ *pl noun* any of the groups of endocrine cells in the pancreas that secrete insulin. [named after Paul *Langerhans* d.1888, German physician who first described them]

ism /'iz(ə)m/ *noun often derog* a distinctive doctrine, cause, theory, or practice. [-ISM]

-ism *suffix* forming nouns from adjectives, verbs, and nouns denoting: **1a** the act, practice, or process of: *plagiarism*. **b** a mode of behaviour characteristic of (the person or thing specified): *cannibalism*. **2a** the state, condition, or property of: *magnetism*. **b** a pathological state or condition resulting from excessive use of (the drug specified): *alcoholism*. **c** a pathological state or condition marked by resemblance to (the person or thing specified): *gigantism*. **3a** a doctrine, theory, or cult of: *Buddhism*. **b** adherence to (the doctrine or system specified): *stoicism*. **c** prejudice on grounds of: *sexism*. **4** a characteristic or peculiar feature of (the language or variety of language specified): *colloquialism*; *anglicism*. [Middle English *-isme* from early French, partly from Latin *-isma* and partly from Latin *-ismus*, from Greek *-ismos*]

Ismaili /izmah'eelee, iz'mielee/ *noun* (*pl* **Ismailis**) **1** one of the branches of Shiite Islam, whose members believe that Ismail, the eldest son of the sixth imam Jafar, d.765, was the rightful seventh imam. **2** a member of this branch.

isn't /'iznt/ *contraction* is not.

ISO *abbr* **1** Imperial Service Order. **2a** International Organization for Standardization. **b** in photography, used in classifications of film speeds.

iso- *comb. form* see IS-.

isobar /'iesohbah, 'iesəbah/ *noun* **1** a line on a chart connecting places where the atmospheric pressure is the same. **2** any of two or more atoms or elements having the same atomic weights or mass numbers but different atomic numbers. ⟫ **isobaric** /-'barik/ *adj*. [Greek *isobaros* of equal weight, from ISO- + *baros* weight]

isobutylene /iesoh'byoohtileen/ *noun* a gaseous chemical compound used *esp* in making a synthetic rubber: formula C_4H_8. [IS- + BUTYL + -ENE]

isocheim /'iesohkiem/ *noun* a line on a chart connecting places with the same average temperature in winter. [ISO- + Greek *cheima* winter weather]

isochron /'iesəkron/ *noun* a line on a chart connecting points at which an event occurs simultaneously or which represents the same time or time difference. [Greek *isochronos*, from ISO- + *chronos* time]

isochronal /ie'sokrənl/ *adj* **1** having equal duration. **2** recurring at regular intervals. ⟫ **isochronally** *adv*, **isochronism** *noun*. [Greek *isochronos*: see ISOCHRON]

isochronous /ie'sokrənəs/ *adj* = ISOCHRONAL.

isocline /'iesohklien/ *noun* **1** a fold of rock so closely compressed that the two sides are parallel or nearly parallel. **2** = ISOCLINIC LINE. ⟫ **isoclinal** /-'klienl/ *adj*, **isoclinic** /-'klinik/ *adj*.

isoclinic line *noun* a line on a map or chart joining points on the earth's surface at which a magnetic needle has the same inclination to the vertical.

isodynamic /,iesohdie'namik/ *adj* connecting points at which the magnetic intensity is the same: *isodynamic line*.

isoelectric /,iesohi'lektrik/ *adj* having or representing no difference of electric potential.

isoenzyme /iesoh'enziem/ *noun* = ISOZYME. ⟫ **isoenzymatic** /-zi'matik/ *adj*, **isoenzymic** /-'ziemik/ *adj*.

isogenic /iesoh'jenik/ *adj* characterized by essentially identical genes: *Identical twins are isogenic*.

isogeotherm /iesoh'jeeohthuhm/ *noun* a line on a chart joining points within the earth having the same temperature.

isogloss /'iesohglos/ *noun* a line on a chart dividing places or regions that differ in a particular linguistic feature. ⟫ **isoglossal** /-'glosl/ *adj*. [ISO- + Greek *glōssa* language]

isogonal /ie'sogənl/ *adj* = ISOGONIC.

isogonic /iesə'gonik/ *adj* **1** of or having equal angles. **2** of, having, or indicating equality of magnetic dip. [ISO- + Greek *gōnia* angle]

isohel /'iesohhel, 'iesəhel/ *noun* a line on a chart connecting places of equal duration of sunshine. [ISO- + Greek *hēlios* sun]

isohyet /'iesoh'hie·ət/ *noun* a line on a chart connecting areas of equal rainfall. ➤➤ **isohyetal** /-'hie·ətl/ *adj.* [ISO- + Greek *hyetos* rain]

isolate[1] /'ies(ə)layt/ *verb trans* **1** to set (somebody or something) apart from others. **2** to quarantine (a person or animal) in order to prevent the spread of infection. **3** to separate (a substance) from another substance so as to obtain in a pure form. **4** to break the electrical connection between (an appliance) and a supply or network. ➤➤ **isolable** *adj,* **isolatable** *adj,* **isolator** *noun.* [back-formation from *isolated* set apart, ultimately from Latin *insula* island]

isolate[2] /'iesələt, -layt/ *noun* **1** a product of isolating; something that has become isolated or cut off; an individual or kind obtained by selection or separation. **2** a language that is the only surviving representative of its family.

isolating /'iesəlayting/ *adj* said of a language: not using changes in the form of words to express grammatical relationships; = ANALYTICAL (4).

isolation /iesə'laysh(ə)n/ *noun* **1** the act or an instance of isolating or being isolated. **2** an isolated state.

isolationism *noun* a policy of national isolation by refraining from engaging in international relations. ➤➤ **isolationist** *noun and adj.*

isoleucine /iesoh'loohseen, -sin/ *noun* an amino acid found in most proteins and an essential constituent of the human diet.

isomer /'iesəmə/ *noun* a chemical compound that has the same chemical formula as one or more others but has different properties and a different arrangement of atoms. [back-formation from *isomeric,* from Greek *isomerēs* equally divided, from ISO- + *meros* a share]

isomerise /ie'soməriez/ *verb trans and intrans* see ISOMERIZE.

isomerism /ie'soməriz(ə)m/ *noun* **1** the relation of two or more chemical compounds, radicals, or ions that contain the same numbers of atoms of the same elements but differ in structural arrangement and properties. **2** the relation of two or more types of atom with the same mass number and atomic number but different energy states and rates of radioactive decay. **3** the condition of being isomerous. ➤➤ **isomeric** /iesoh'merik/ *adj.*

isomerize *or* **isomerise** /ie'soməriez/ *verb intrans* to become changed into an isomeric form. ➤ *verb trans* to cause (something) to isomerize. ➤➤ **isomerization** /-'zaysh(ə)n/ *noun.*

isomerous /ie'somərəs/ *adj* having an equal number of parts, e.g. on each flower on a plant.

isometric /iesə'metrik/ *adj* **1** having equal dimensions or measurements. **2** denoting a crystal that has three axes of equal length each at 90° to the other; cubic. **3** of or involving isometrics. **4** denoting a representation of an object in which three mutually perpendicular axes are equally inclined to the drawing surface. ➤➤ **isometrically** *adv.*

isometric line *noun* a line representing changes of pressure or temperature under conditions of constant volume.

isometrics *pl noun* (*treated as sing. or pl*) physical exercise in which opposing muscles are contracted so that there is little shortening but great increase in tone of muscle fibres involved.

isomorphic /iesə'mawfik/ *adj* having or involving structural similarity or identity. ➤➤ **isomorph** /'iesəmawf/ *noun,* **isomorphically** *adv,* **isomorphism** *noun,* **isomorphous** /-fəs/ *adj.*

isophote /'iesohfoht, 'iesəfoht/ *noun* a line on a chart joining points of equal light intensity from a given source. ➤➤ **isophotal** /-'fohtl/ *adj.* [ISO- + Greek *phōt-, phōs* light]

isopleth /'iesohpleth, 'iesə-/ *noun* a line on a map connecting points at which a given variable, e.g. humidity, has a constant value. ➤➤ **isoplethic** /-'plethik/ *adj.* [ISO- + Greek *plēthos* quantity]

isopod /'iesəpod/ *noun* any of a large order of small crustaceans with eyes that are not borne on stalks and seven pairs of similar legs: order Isopoda. ➤➤ **isopodous** /ie'sopədəs/ *adj.* [ISO- + Greek *pod-, pous* foot]

isoprene /'iesohpreen/ *noun* an inflammable liquid compound used *esp* in synthetic rubber. [prob from ISO- + PROPYLENE]

isopteran /ie'soptərən/ *noun* a termite. [ISO- + Greek *pteron* wing]

isosceles /ie'sosəleez/ *adj* said of a triangle: having two equal sides. [via late Latin from Greek *isoskelēs,* from ISO- + *skelos* leg]

isoseismal /iesoh'siezməl/ *adj* relating to, having, or indicating equal intensity of earthquake shock.

isostasy /ie'sostəsi/ *noun* the condition of equilibrium in the earth's crust maintained by a yielding flow of sub-surface rock material under gravitational stress. ➤➤ **isostatic** /iesoh'statik, iesə-/ *adj.* [ISO- + Greek -*stasia* condition of standing]

isothere /'iesothee·ə/ *noun* a line on a chart connecting places with the same average temperature in summer. [French *isothère,* from Greek ISO- + *theros* summer]

isotherm /'iesohthuhm, 'iesə-/ *noun* **1** a line on a chart connecting points having the same temperature at a given time or the same mean temperature for a given period. **2** a line on a chart representing changes of volume or pressure under conditions of constant temperature. ➤➤ **isothermal** /-'thuhml/ *adj.* [French *isotherme,* from Greek ISO- + *thermē* heat]

isotonic /iesə'tonik/ *adj* **1** having the same concentration as a surrounding medium or a liquid under comparison: compare HYPERTONIC, HYPOTONIC. **2** said of a drink: containing minerals and essential salts in the body's natural properties and designed to replace those lost as a result of strenuous exercise. **3a** relating to the contraction of muscles under fairly constant tension. **b** said of two or more muscles: exhibiting equal tension. ➤➤ **isotonicity** /-'nisiti/ *noun.*

isotope /'iesətohp/ *noun* any of two or more forms of a chemical element that have the same atomic number and nearly identical chemical behaviour but differ in atomic mass or mass number and physical properties. ➤➤ **isotopic** /-'topik/ *adj,* **isotopically** /-'topikli/ *adv,* **isotopy** /ie'sotəpi, 'iesətohpi/ *noun.* [ISO- + Greek *topos* place]

isotropic /iesoh'tropik, iesə-/ *adj* having physical properties with the same values in all directions: *an isotropic crystal.* ➤➤ **isotropy** /ie'sotrəpi/ *noun.*

isozyme /'iesohziem/ *noun* any of two or more chemically distinct but functionally similar enzymes. ➤➤ **isozymic** /-'ziemik/ *adj.*

ISP *abbr* an Internet service provider, a commercial company providing individual users with an Internet connection and usually a portfolio of Internet-related services.

I-spy /,ie 'spie/ *noun* a children's game in which a visible object is guessed from the initial letter of its name.

Israel /'izrayəl, 'izrayl/ *noun* **1** the Jewish people. **2** the people chosen by God: *Many Christians claim that the church is the true Israel.* [Old English via late Latin from Greek *Israēl,* from Hebrew *Yiśrā'ēl*]

Israeli /iz'rayli/ *noun* (*pl* **Israelis**) a native or inhabitant of modern Israel. ➤➤ **Israeli** *adj.* [New Hebrew *yiśrĕ'ēlī*]

Israelite /'izr(i)əliet/ *noun* a descendant of the Hebrew patriarch Jacob, or Israel, e.g.: **a** a member of any of the twelve tribes descended from Jacob's sons. **b** after the establishment of separate kingdoms of Israel and Judah, a native or inhabitant of the northern kingdom of Israel. **c** a Jew. ➤➤ **Israelite** *adj.* [Middle English via late Latin *Israelita* from Greek *Israēlitēs,* from *Israēl:* see ISRAEL]

issei /'eesay, ee'say/ *noun* (*pl* **issei, isseis**) a Japanese immigrant to the USA. [Japanese *issei* first generation, from *is* first + *sei* generation]

ISSN *abbr* International Standard Serial Number.

issue[1] /'ish(y)ooh, 'isyooh/ *noun* **1** a matter that is in dispute between two or more parties; a controversial topic. **2a** the thing or the whole quantity of things given out, published, or distributed at one time: *Read the latest issue.* **b** the act or an instance of publishing something, giving it out, or making it available: *I'm waiting for the next issue of commemorative stamps.* **3** *formal* the action or an instance of going, coming, or flowing out. **4** *formal* a means or place of going out. **5** *formal* offspring: *He died without issue.* **6** *formal* something coming out from a usu specified source. **7** *formal* an outcome that usu resolves or decides a problem. **✳ at issue** under discussion or consideration; in dispute. **join/take issue** to take an opposing or conflicting stand, *esp* to disagree or engage in argument on a point of dispute: *Her nose and chin are the only parties likely to join issue* — Sheridan. ➤➤ **issueless** *adj.* [Middle English, in the sense 'exit, proceeds', via French from Latin *exire* to go out, from EX-[1] + *ire* to go]

issue² *verb trans* **1** to send (e.g. a newspaper or magazine) out for sale or circulation. **2** to give (something, e.g. a statement) out or provide it officially. ➤ *verb intrans* **1a** to go, come, or flow out. **b** to emerge. **2** to descend from a specified parent or ancestor. **3** (+ in) to be a consequence; to result. **4** to appear or become available through being given out, published, or distributed. ➤ **issuance** *noun*, **issuer** *noun*.

-ist¹ *suffix* forming nouns, denoting: **1** somebody who performs (the action specified): *cyclist*. **2** somebody who makes or produces (the thing specified): *novelist*. **3** somebody who plays (the musical instrument specified): *harpist*. **4** somebody who operates (the mechanical instrument or device specified): *motorist*. **5** somebody who specializes in or practises (the art, science, skill, or profession specified): *geologist; ventriloquist*. **6** somebody who adheres to or advocates (the doctrine, system, or code of behaviour specified): *socialist; royalist; hedonist; Calvinist*. **7** somebody who is prejudiced on grounds of: *sexist*. [Middle English *-iste* via French and Latin from Greek *-istēs*, from verbs ending in *-izein* -IZE]

-ist² *suffix* forming adjectives, with the meanings: **1** relating to, or characteristic of: *dilettantist; obscurantist*. **2** showing prejudice on grounds of: *racist*.

-ista *suffix* forming nouns, denoting: **1** a person who is involved in some sphere or activity: *fashionista*. **2** a supporter of a person or cause: *Portillista*.

isthmian /'isthmi·ən/ *adj* **1** of or occurring on or near an isthmus. **2** of the Isthmus of Corinth in Greece or the games held there in ancient times.

isthmus /'isməs, 'isthməs/ *noun* **1** a narrow strip of land connecting two larger land areas. **2** a narrow part of the body connecting two larger parts. [via Latin from Greek *isthmos*]

istle /'istli/ *noun* a strong fibre made from various tropical American plants, *esp* agaves and yuccas, used e.g. for basketry and to make ropes. [American Spanish *ixtle* from Nahuatl *ichtli*]

ISV *abbr* International Scientific Vocabulary.

IT *abbr* **1** Information Technology. **2** Intermediate Technology.

it¹ /it/ *pronoun* **1** used as subject or object: **a** that thing, creature, or group: *I saw the house and noticed that it was very old; She had a baby but lost it*. **b** the person in question: *Who is it?* **2** used as subject of an impersonal verb: *It's raining; It's not far to London*. **3** used as anticipatory subject or object of a verb: *It's no fun being a secretary; I take it that you refuse*. **4** used to highlight part of a sentence: *It was the President who arrived yesterday*. **5** used with many verbs and prepositions as a meaningless object: *Run for it; We legged it back to camp*. **6** used to refer to an explicit or implicit state of affairs: *How's it going?* **7** that which is available: *We have one boiled egg and that's it*. **8** the important thing: *Yes, that's just it*. **9** the appropriate thing: *A bit tighter; that's it*. [Old English *hit*]

it² *noun* **1** the player in a children's game who performs a unique role, e.g. trying to catch others in a game of tag. **2** *informal* sex appeal or sexual intercourse.

it³ *noun informal* Italian vermouth, a bitter-sweet vermouth originally made in Italy: *gin and it*.

ITA *abbr* Initial Teaching Alphabet.

ital. *abbr* italic.

Italian /i'talyən/ *noun* **1** a native or inhabitant of Italy. **2** the Romance language of Italy. ➤ **Italian** *adj*, **Italianate** /-nət, -nayt/ *adj*.

Word history
Middle English via Latin from Greek *Italia* Italy, country in southern Europe. The substantial Italian contribution to the English vocabulary is perhaps most distinguished by words in music (*opera, solo, soprano, trill, tuba, violin*, and the large number of Italian terms used in musical scores), art (*cartoon, profile, scenario, studio, virtuoso*), and literature (*canto, sonnet, stanza*). Other notable groups are those referring to food (*broccoli, salami, semolina, spaghetti*), to martial pursuits (*infantry, salvo, squadron, stiletto*), and to festivities (*carnival, confetti, gala, masquerade, regatta*). The many other loanwords from Italian include *balcony, fiasco, ghetto, granite, inferno, influenza, malaria, motto, portfolio, replica, umbrella, volcano*, and *zebra*.

italic¹ /i'talik/ *noun* **1** a printed character that slants upwards to the right, as the labels *noun, adj*, etc do in this dictionary. **2** (**Italic**) the branch of the Indo-European language family that includes Latin and some ancient Italian languages. [Middle English via Latin from Greek *Italikos*, from *Italia* Italy; (sense 1) because this form of writing originated in Italy]

italic² *adj* **1** said of a printed character: in italic. **2** (**Italic**) of ancient Italy or Italic.

italicize *or* **italicise** /i'talisiez/ *verb trans* to print (something) in italics. ➤ **italicization** /-'zaysh(ə)n/ *noun*.

Italo- *comb. form* forming words, with the meanings: **1** the Italian nation, people, or culture: *Italophile*. **2** Italian and: *Italo-Austrian*.

ITC *abbr* Independent Television Commission.

itch¹ /ich/ *verb intrans* **1** to have or produce an itch. **2** *informal* to have a restless desire: *Perhaps she knew … that the chains she forged only aroused his instinct for destruction, as the plate-glass window makes your fingers itch for half a brick* — Somerset Maugham. ➤ *verb trans* to cause (an area of the body) to itch. [Middle English *icchen* from Old English *giccan*]

itch² *noun* **1a** an irritating sensation in the upper surface of the skin that makes one want to scratch. **b** a skin disorder characterized by such a sensation. **2** *informal* a restless desire: *A love of the theatre is so general, an itch for acting so strong among young people* — Jane Austen. ➤ **itchiness** *noun*, **itchy** *adj*.

itchy feet *pl noun informal* a restless desire for travel or change of circumstances.

it'd /'itəd/ *contraction* it had or it would.

-ite¹ *suffix* forming nouns, denoting: **1** somebody who belongs to (the place, group, etc specified): *Israelite; socialite; Hittite*. **2** an adherent or follower of (the doctrine or movement specified): *Pre-Raphaelite; Thatcherite*. **3** a product of: *metabolite*. **4** a commercially manufactured product: *ebonite*. **5** a fossil: *ammonite*. **6** a mineral: *bauxite*. **7** a segment or constituent part of (the body or organ specified): *somite; dendrite*. [Middle English via French and Latin from Greek *-itēs*]

-ite² *suffix* forming adjectives relating to nouns ending in -ITE¹.

-ite³ *suffix* forming nouns, denoting: salt or ester of (a specified acid with a name ending in *-ous*): *sulphite*. [French *-ite*, alteration of *-ate* -ATE¹, from scientific Latin *-atum*]

item¹ /'ietəm/ *noun* **1** a separate piece of news or information. **2** a separate unit in an account or series. **3** (**an item**) *informal* two people in a romantic or sexual relationship.

item² *adv archaic* and in addition, used to introduce each article in a list: *I will give out divers schedules of my beauty. It shall be inventoried … as — item, two lips indifferent red; item, two grey eyes with lids to them; item, one neck, one chin, and so forth* — Shakespeare. [Middle English from Latin *item*, likewise, also, from *ita* thus]

itemize *or* **itemise** *verb trans* to set (things) down in the form of a list of individual items: *She itemized all expenses*. ➤ **itemization** /-'zaysh(ə)n/ *noun*.

iterate /'itərayt/ *verb trans* to say or do (something) again or repetitively. ➤ **iteration** /-'raysh(ə)n/ *noun*. [Latin *iteratus*, past part. of *iterare* to repeat, from *iterum* again]

iterative /'itərətiv/ *adj* **1** in grammar, FREQUENTATIVE¹ (marking a repeated action or state of affairs). **2** relating to successive repetition of a mathematical process, using the result of one stage as the input for the next. ➤ **iteratively** *adv*.

ithyphallic /ithi'falik/ *adj* said of figures in pictures or statues: having an erect penis. [via late Latin from Greek *īthyphallikos*, from *īthyphallos* erect phallus, from *īthos* straight + *phallos* PHALLUS]

itinerancy /ie'tinərənsi, i-/ *noun* a system, e.g. in the Methodist Church, of rotating ministers among several congregations.

itinerant¹ /ie'tinərənt, i-/ *adj* travelling from place to place: *an itinerant preacher*. [late Latin *itinerant-, itinerans*, present part. of *itinerari* to journey, from Latin *itiner-, iter* road, journey]

itinerant² *noun* **1** somebody who moves from place to place. **2** *formal, dated* a homeless person who moves around.

itinerary /ie'tinərəri, i-/ *noun* (*pl* **itineraries**) **1** the proposed route of a journey, sometimes including a list of stops to be made and sights to see on the way. **2** a travel diary. **3** a traveller's guidebook. [Middle English from late Latin *itinerarius*, from Latin *itiner-, iter* road, journey]

itinerate /ie'tinərayt, i-/ *verb intrans* to travel from place to place, *esp* on a preaching or judicial circuit. ➤ **itineration** /-'raysh(ə)n/ *noun*.

-itious *suffix* forming adjectives, with the meaning: relating to or having the characteristics of: *fictitious; superstitious*. [Latin *-icius, -itius*]

-itis *suffix* (*pl* **-itises** *or* **-itides**) forming nouns, denoting: **1** disease or inflammation of: *bronchitis*. **2** *humorous*. **a** suffering caused by a surfeit or excess of: *electionitis*. **b** infatuation or obsession with: *jazzitis*. [via Latin from Greek *-itis*, fem of *-itēs* -ITE¹]

it'll /'itl/ *contraction* it will or it shall.

ITN *abbr* Independent Television News.

ITO *abbr* International Trade Organization.

-itol *suffix* forming nouns, denoting: an alcohol containing two or more hydroxyl groups, usu related to a sugar: *mannitol*. [-ITE¹ + -OL¹]

its /its/ *adj* belonging to or associated with it: *its tail*; *a child and its parents*; *its being late*; *its rejection*.

Usage note
its *or* it's? Note the difference between these two forms. *Its* is the possessive form of *it* (*The bottle has lost its top*; *my car is in for its MOT*): it has no apostrophe *s*, but neither has *his* or *ours*. *It's* is a shortened form of *it is* or *it has*: *it's raining*; *it's been an awful day*.

it's /its/ *contraction* it is or it has.

Usage note
it's *or* its? See note at ITS.

itself /it'self/ *pronoun* **1** used reflexively to refer to a thing, animal, etc that is the subject of the clause: *The cat was washing itself*. **2** used for emphasis: *The letter itself was missing*. ✳ **be itself** to be fit or healthy as normal: *The dog isn't quite itself today*. **in itself** intrinsically considered: *not dangerous in itself*.

itsy-bitsy /ˌitsi 'bitsi/ *or* **itty-bitty** /ˌiti 'biti/ *adj informal* tiny. [prob from baby talk for *little bit*]

ITU *abbr* International Telecommunication Union.

ITV *abbr* Independent Television.

-ity *suffix* forming nouns, denoting: **1** the quality or state of: *authority*; *theatricality*. **2** an instance of (the quality or state specified): *an obscenity*. **3** the amount or degree of: *humidity*; *salinity*. [Middle English *-ite* via French *-ité* from Latin *-itat-*, *-itas*]

IU *abbr* international unit.

IUD *abbr* intrauterine device.

-ium *suffix* (*pl* **-iums** *or* **-ia** /-i·ə/) forming nouns, denoting: **1a** a chemical element: *sodium*. **b** a positive ion: *ammonium*. **2** in botanical terms, a small kind of or a mass of: *pollinium*. **3** a biological part, or a part or region of the body: *epithelium*; *hypogastrium*. [Latin *-ium* from Greek *-ion*]

IV *abbr* **1** intravenous. **2** intravenously.

I've /iev/ *contraction* I have.

-ive¹ *suffix* forming adjectives, with the meanings: **1** tending to, or disposed to: *corrective*; *sportive*. **2** performing (the function specified): *descriptive*; *generative*. [Middle English *-if*, *-ive* via French from Latin *-ivus*]

-ive² *suffix* forming nouns, denoting: **1** somebody or something that performs or serves to accomplish (a specified action): *sedative*; *detective*. **2** somebody who is in or affected by (a specified state or condition): *captive*; *consumptive*.

IVF *abbr* in vitro fertilization.

ivied /'ievid/ *adj literary* overgrown with ivy: *ivied walls*.

Ivorian /ie'vawri·ən/ *noun* a native or inhabitant of Côte d'Ivoire. ➤➤ **Ivorian** *adj*.

ivory¹ /'ievəri/ *noun* (*pl* **ivories**) **1** the hard creamy-white form of dentine of which the tusks of elephants and other tusked mammals are made. **2** a creamy slightly yellowish white colour. **3** *informal* (*in pl*) things, e.g. dice or piano keys, made of ivory or something resembling ivory. [Middle English *ivorie* via French *ivoire* from Latin *eboreus* of ivory, from *ebor-*, *ebur* ivory]

ivory² *adj* made of ivory.

ivory black *noun* a fine black pigment made by calcining orig ivory but now bone.

ivory nut *noun* the nutlike seed of a S American palm tree that is the source of vegetable ivory.

ivory tower *noun* **1** remoteness from everyday life or practical concerns. **2** a place encouraging such an attitude or position. [translation of French *tour d'ivoire*, first used by Charles-Augustin Sainte-Beuve d.1869, French writer and critic]

ivorywood *noun* **1** the creamy white wood of an Australian tree. **2** the tree itself: *Siphonodon australe*.

IVR *abbr* International Vehicle Registration.

ivy /'ievi/ *noun* any of several species of very common and widely cultivated Eurasian woody climbing plants with evergreen leaves, small yellowish flowers, and black berries: genus *Hedera*: *ivy-covered professors in ivy-covered halls* — Tom Lehrer. [Old English *īfig*]

Ivy League *noun* a group of long-established prestigious eastern US colleges that includes Harvard, Princeton, Yale, Cornell, Brown, Columbia, Dartmouth, and the University of Pennsylvania. [prob from the ivy growing on the older college buildings]

IW *abbr* **1** inside width. **2** isotopic weight.

IWC *abbr* International Whaling Commission.

IWW *abbr* Industrial Workers of the World.

ixia /'iksi·ə/ *noun* any of a genus of plants of the iris family that are native to southern Africa, with large ornamental flowers: genus *Ixia*. [Latin genus name, from Greek *ixos* mistletoe, birdlime]

IYHF *abbr* International Youth Hostels Federation.

izard /'izəd/ *noun* a chamois found in the Pyrenees. [French *isard*]

-ize *or* **-ise** *suffix* forming verbs, with the meanings: **1** to cause to be, conform to, or resemble: *liquidize*; *popularize*. **2** to subject to (the action specified): *plagiarize*; *criticize*. **3a** to impregnate, treat, or combine with: *oxidize*. **b** to treat like or make into: *lionize*; *proselytize*. **c** to treat according to the method of: *bowdlerize*. **4a** to become, or become like: *crystallize*. **b** to engage in (the activity specified): *philosophize*. [Middle English *-isen* via French and late Latin from Greek *-izein*]

Usage note
-ize *or* -ise? Either spelling is correct, in British English, for verbs that end with this suffix: *criticize* or *criticise*; *privatise* or *privatize*. The *-ize* form reflects the original Greek spelling *-ize*, whereas the *-ise* form reflects an intermediate spelling in French, from which many of these words are derived. Many British people, British newspapers, and British English spellcheckers prefer the *-ise* form. The *-ize* form is, however, standard in American English and totally acceptable in British English, so that it has come to be regarded as the world English norm and, as such, has been adopted by most modern dictionaries and many British publishers. There are, however, a number of verbs which must end in *-ise*, either because they are related to other words with *-ise* spelling (such as *advertisement*) or because the ending is not the active suffix *-ize*/*-ise* at all but a longer element such as *-cise* (typically meaning 'cut') or *-vise* (typically meaning 'see'): for example, *advertise*, *advise*, *chastise*, *comprise*, *compromise*, *despise*, *devise*, *enfranchise*, *excise*, *exercise*, *franchise*, *improvise*, *merchandise*, *revise*, *supervise*, *surmise*, *surprise*, and *televise*.

J¹ *or* **j** *noun* (*pl* **J's** *or* **Js** *or* **j's**) **1a** the tenth letter of the English alphabet. **b** a written character or design denoting this letter. **c** the sound represented by this letter, one of the English consonants. **2** an item designated as J, *esp* the tenth in a series.

J² *abbr* **1** Japan (international vehicle registration). **2** joule. **3** Judge. **4** Justice.

j *symbol* in electrical engineering and electronics, the symbol used to represent the imaginary number equal to the square root of minus one, represented in mathematics by ı.

JA *abbr* Jamaica (international vehicle registration).

jab¹ /jab/ *verb* (**jabbed, jabbing**) ➤ *verb trans* **1a** to pierce (something or somebody) with a sharp object. **b** to poke (something or somebody) quickly or abruptly. **2** to strike (somebody) with a short straight blow. ➤ *verb intrans* to make quick or abrupt thrusts with a sharp or pointed object. [alteration of Middle English *job* to prod or strike]

jab² *noun* **1** a short straight punch in boxing delivered with the leading hand. **2** a quick or abrupt poke. **3** *informal* a hypodermic injection, *esp* a vaccination.

jabber¹ /'jabə/ *verb intrans* (**jabbered, jabbering**) to talk rapidly and unintelligibly. ➤➤ **jabberer** *noun*. [Middle English *jaberen*, of imitative origin]

jabber² *noun* rapid or unintelligible talk or chatter.

jabberwocky /'jabəwoki/ *noun* nonsensical speech or writing. [*Jabberwocky*, nonsense poem in *Through the Looking-Glass* by Lewis Carroll (C L Dodgson) d.1898, English writer]

jabiru /'jabirooh/ *noun* **1** a large tropical stork found in Central and S America, with white plumage, a dark-coloured naked head, and a dark bill: *Jabiru mycteria*. **2** a large Australian stork with black and white colouring: *Xenorhynchus asiaticus*. [Portuguese *jabiru* from Tupi and Guarani *jabirú*]

jaborandi /jabə'randi/ *noun* **1** the dried leaves of either of two S American shrubs of the rue family that are a source of the drug pilocarpine. **2** either of the two shrubs from which these leaves come: *Pilocarpus jaborandi* and *Pilocarpus microphyllus*. [Portuguese *jaborandi* from Tupi *yaborandi*]

jabot /'zhaboh/ *noun* a decorative lace or cloth frill extending from the centre of the neckpiece down the front of a blouse or shirt: *He took a delicate pinch of snuff, then, having dusted his dainty lace jabot, he rubbed his thin, bony hands contentedly together* — Baroness Orczy. [French *jabot* bird's crop, shirt frill]

jacana *or* **jaçana** /zhahsə'nah, jas-/ *noun* any of several species of long-legged and long-toed wading birds, able to walk on floating plants, that frequent coastal freshwater marshes and ponds in warm regions: family Jacanidae. [Portuguese *jaçanã* from Tupi and Guarani *jasanã*]

jacaranda /jakə'randə/ *noun* a tropical American tree with showy blue flowers: genus *Jacaranda*. [Latin genus name, from Portuguese *jacaranda* a tree of this genus, from Tupi and Guarani *jakara'nda*]

jacinth /'jasinth/ *noun* a reddish orange transparent variety of zircon used as a gem. [Middle English *iacinct* via Old French *jacinthe* from Latin *hyacinthus*: see HYACINTH; in early use both *hyacinth* and *jacinth* also denoted a bluish gemstone]

jack¹ /jak/ *noun* **1** any of various portable mechanisms for lifting a heavy object a short distance: *a car jack*. **2** a playing card marked with a stylized figure of a soldier or servant and ranking usu below the queen. **3a** = JACK PLUG. **b** = JACK SOCKET. **4** a small target ball in the game of bowls. **5a** (*in pl, but treated as sing.*) a game in which players toss and pick up small plastic or metal objects between throws of a ball. **b** a small six-pointed object used in the game of jacks. **6** a male donkey or ass. **7** a small national flag flown at the bow of a ship. **8** part of the mechanism of a harpsichord to which the plectrum is fixed. **9** a device for turning a spit. **10a** any of numerous species of tropical seafishes similar to the perch: family Carangidae. **b** a young pike. **11** *NAmer, informal* money. ✳ **every man jack** everybody. [Middle English, from *Jack*, nickname for John]

jack² *verb trans* **1** (*usu* + up) to move or lift (something) by a jack. **2** (+ up) to raise the level or quality of (something).

jackal /'jakl/ *noun* **1** any of several species of wild dogs from Africa, Asia, and Europe, smaller than the related wolves. Jackals hunt in packs and are scavengers: genus *Canis*. **2** somebody who performs routine or menial tasks for another person. [Turkish *çakal* via Persian *shagāl* from Sanskrit *sṛgāla*]

jackanapes /'jakənayps/ *noun* **1a** an impudent or conceited person. **b** a mischievous child. **2** *archaic* a monkey or ape. [perhaps alteration of *Jack Napes*, name given to a pet ape, perhaps from *Jack an ape*]

jackaroo *or* **jackeroo** /jakə'rooh/ *noun Aus* a young inexperienced worker on a cattle or sheep station. [JACK¹ + *-aroo* as in KANGAROO]

jack around *verb trans NAmer, informal* to cause inconvenience or trouble to (somebody).

jackass *noun* **1** a male ass. **2** a stupid person; a fool.

jackboot *noun* **1** a leather military boot reaching to the knee. **2** (**the jackboot**) political repression effected by military or paramilitary force. ➤➤ **jackbooted** *adj*.

jackdaw /'jakdaw/ *noun* a black and grey Eurasian bird that is related to but smaller than the common crow: *Corvus monedula*.

jackeroo /jakə'rooh/ *noun* see JACKAROO.

jacket¹ /'jakit/ *noun* **1** an outer garment for the upper body opening down the full length of the centre front. **2** a thermally insulating cover, e.g. for a hot-water tank. **3** = DUST JACKET. **4** the framework, attached to the seabed, that supports an oil rig. **5** the skin of a baked potato. [Middle English *jaket* via early French *jaquet* short jacket, from *jacque* peasant, from the name *Jacques* James]

jacket² *verb trans* (**jacketed, jacketing**) to put a jacket on (something or somebody); to enclose in or with a jacket.

jacket potato *noun* (*pl* **jacket potatoes**) *Brit* a potato baked and served with the skin on.

jackfish *noun* (*pl* **jackfishes** *or collectively* **jackfish**) = JACK¹ (IOB).

Jack Frost *noun* frost or frosty weather personified.

jackfruit *noun* **1** a large tropical tree of the fig family, closely related to the breadfruit, that yields a fine-grained yellow wood and immense fruits containing an edible pulp and nutritious seeds: *Artocarpus heterophyllus*. **2** the edible fruit of this tree. [Portuguese *jaca* jackfruit (from Malayalam *cakka*) + English *fruit*]

jackhammer *noun* *NAmer* = PNEUMATIC DRILL.

jack in *verb trans* *informal* to give (something) up; to abandon (something): *I was fed up with the job so I jacked it in.*

jack-in-office *noun* a self-important minor official.

jack-in-the-box *noun* (*pl* **jack-in-the-boxes** *or* **jacks-in-the-box**) a toy consisting of a small box out of which a figure springs when the lid is raised.

jackknife¹ *noun* (*pl* **jackknives**) **1** a large pocket knife with a folding blade. **2** a dive in which the diver bends from the waist, touches the ankles without bending the knees, and straightens out before hitting the water.

jackknife² *verb trans* to cause (something) to double up like a jackknife. ➤ *verb intrans* **1** to double up like a jackknife. **2** said of an articulated lorry: to go out of control so that the trailer swings round and ends up at an angle of 90 degrees or less to the tractor.

jack-of-all-trades *noun* (*pl* **jacks-of-all-trades**) a handy versatile person.

jack off *verb trans and intrans* *NAmer, coarse slang* = MASTURBATE.

jack-o'-lantern *noun* **1** a lantern made from a hollowed-out pumpkin with holes cut in it to look like a human face. **2** = WILL-O'-THE-WISP.

jack plane *noun* a plane used in the first stages of smoothing wood.

jack plug *noun* a single-pronged electrical plug that can be inserted into a jack socket.

jackpot *noun* **1** the largest prize, e.g. in a lottery or on a fruit machine. **2** a large accumulated stake in a gambling game. ✳ **hit the jackpot** *informal* to have a big success or a piece of very good fortune. [JACK¹ (2) + POT¹ (6A); from a form of poker in which a player requires two jacks or better to open]

jackrabbit *noun* any of several species of large hares of western N America that have long ears and long hind legs: genus *Lepus*. [JACKASS + RABBIT¹, from its long ears]

Jack Russell terrier /'rusl/ *noun* a dog of a breed of small pugnacious terriers orig bred to hunt rats. [named after *Jack* (John) *Russell* d.1883, English clergyman and fox-hunter, who bred a similar kind of terrier to dig out foxes that had gone to earth]

jacksie *or* **jacksy** /'jaksi/ *noun* (*pl* **jacksies**) *Brit, informal* a person's bottom. [dimin. of the name *Jack*]

jacksnipe *noun* a SNIPE¹ (wading bird) from Africa, Asia, and Europe that is smaller and more highly coloured than the common snipe: *Lymnocryptes minimus*.

jack socket *noun* an electrical socket, e.g. on sound equipment, that is designed to receive a jack plug.

jackstone *noun* = JACK¹ (5B).

jackstraw *noun* **1** = SPILLIKIN (2). **2** (*in pl, but treated as sing.*) spillikins (see SPILLIKIN (I)).

jacksy /'jaksi/ *noun* see JACKSIE.

jack tar *noun* *informal* a sailor.

Jack the lad *noun* a brashly self-confident, stylish, and mischievous young man. [orig the nickname of *Jack* Sheppard d.1724, a notorious English robber]

jack up *verb trans* = JACK². ➤ *verb intrans* *slang* to inject oneself with a drug.

Jacobean /jakə'bee-ən/ *adj* **1** relating to or characteristic of the reign of James I of England (1603–25). **2** denoting a style of art or architecture associated with this period. [Latin *Jacobaeus*, from *Jacobus* James]

Jacobin /'jakəbin/ *noun* **1** a member of a radical democratic political group that seized power during the French Revolution and instituted the Reign of Terror: *Napoleon … knew, as well as any Jacobin in France, how to philosophize on liberty and equality* — Ralph Waldo Emerson. **2** an extremist radical. ➤➤ **Jacobinism** *noun*.

Word history
French *Jacobin*, orig in the sense 'Dominican'. The group was formed in the Dominican convent in the rue St-Jacques in Paris.

Jacobite /'jakəbiet/ *noun* a supporter of James II of England or of the Stuarts after 1688: *A Jacobite, sir, believes in the divine right of kings … A Jacobite believes in the divine right of bishops … Therefore, sir, a Jacobite is neither an atheist nor a deist. That cannot be said of a Whig; for Whiggism is the negation of all principle* — Dr Johnson. ➤➤ **Jacobitism** *noun*. [from Latin *Jacobus* James]

Jacob's ladder /'jaykəbz/ *noun* **1** a plant of the phlox family that has bell-shaped white or blue flowers: *Polemonium caeruleum*. **2** a ladder, *esp* on a ship, that has rungs fitted between ropes or chains and rolls up for storage. [from the ladder seen in a dream by Jacob in Genesis 28:12; (sense 1) because it has divided leaves that resemble a ladder]

Jacobson's organ /'jaykəbs(ə)nz/ *noun* a scent-detecting organ in the form of a pair of sacs or tubes, situated in the roof of the mouth in snakes, lizards, and some other vertebrates. [named after Ludwig *Jacobson*, d.1843, Dutch anatomist]

Jacob's staff *noun* an instrument formerly used for measuring heights and distances.

jaconet /'jakənit/ *noun* a lightweight cotton cloth used for clothing and bandages. [modification of Urdu *jagannāthī*, from *Jagannath* (*Puri*), former name of Puri, city in E India, where it was first produced]

jacquard /'jakahd/ *noun* **1** (*often* **Jacquard**) an apparatus for a loom holding punched cards that enable decorated and patterned fabrics to be woven. **2** a fabric with an intricate variegated weave or pattern. [named after Joseph *Jacquard* d.1834, French inventor of the loom]

jacquerie /'zhakəri (*French* ʒakri)/ *noun* (*often* **Jacquerie**) a peasants' revolt. [French *jacquerie*, referring to the French peasants' revolt in 1358, from early French *jacque*: see JACKET¹]

jactitation /jakti'taysh(ə)n/ *noun* a tossing to and fro or jerking and twitching of the body. [late Latin *jactitation-, jactitatio*, from *jactare* to throw]

Jacuzzi /jə'koohzi/ *noun* trademark a large bath fitted with a system of underwater jets that massage the body. [named after Candido *Jacuzzi* d.1986, Italian-born US engineer, who invented it for his son who suffered from rheumatoid arthritis]

jade¹ /jayd/ *noun* **1** either of two typically green hard gemstones: **a** = JADEITE. **b** = NEPHRITE. **2** a light bluish green colour. ➤➤ **jade** *adj*. [French *jade* from obsolete Spanish *piedra de ijada*, literally 'loin stone', from the belief that jade cures renal colic]

jade² *noun* **1** a worn-out old horse. **2** *archaic* a disreputable woman. [Middle English; earlier history unknown]

jaded *adj* **1** weary, bored, or dulled, *esp* by a surfeit of something: *the jaded morning countenance of the debauchee* — Charles Lamb; *the ideal pick-me-up for a jaded palate*. **2** overused: *outworn, jaded language*. [past part. of *jade* to wear out by overwork, from JADE²]

jadeite /'jaydiet/ *noun* a green or white mineral, the more valuable variety of jade, that is a silicate of sodium and aluminium.

j'adoube /zha'doohb/ *interj* used in chess to indicate that one is touching a piece merely to adjust it rather than to move it. [French *j'adoube* I adjust]

jaeger /'yaygə/ *noun* = SKUA. [German *Jäger* hunter]

Jaffa /'jafə/ *noun* a type of large thick-skinned orange grown *esp* in Israel. [named after *Jaffa*, port in Israel, near which it was first grown]

jag¹ /jag/ *verb trans* (**jagged, jagging**) **1** to cut or tear (something) unevenly or raggedly. **2** *Scot* to prick or pierce (something). [Middle English *jaggen* to stab, slash]

jag² *noun* **1** a sharp projecting part. **2** *Scot*. **a** a prick with a sharp object. **b** an injection with a needle.

jag³ *noun* *informal* a period of indulgence in an activity: *a crying jag*. [origin unknown]

jagged /'jagid/ *adj* having a sharply indented or uneven edge or surface. ➤➤ **jaggedly** *adv*, **jaggedness** *noun*.

jaggy /'jagi/ *adj* (**jaggier, jaggiest**) **1** jagged or notched. **2** *Scot* prickly.

jaguar /'jagyooə/ *noun* a large wild animal of the cat family found in Central and S America that is stockier than the leopard and is typically brownish yellow with black spots: *Panthera onca*. [Spanish *yaguar* and Portuguese *jaguar*, from Guarani *yaguara* and Tupi *jaguara*]

jaguarundi /jagwə'roondi/ *noun* (*pl* **jaguarundis**) a slender long-tailed greyish wildcat of Central and S America: *Felis yagouaroundi*. [American Spanish and Portuguese *yagouaroundi*, from Tupi *jaguarundi* and Guarani *yagouarundi*, literally 'dark jaguar']

jai alai /,khay ah'lay/ *noun* a court game similar to pelota for two or four players who use a long curved wicker basket strapped to the wrist to catch and hurl a ball against a wall. [Spanish *jai alai*, from Basque *jai* festival + *alai* merry]

jail¹ (*Brit* **gaol**) /jayl/ *noun* a place where people are confined while awaiting trial or for punishment after conviction; prison: *No man will be a sailor who has the contrivance to get himself into jail … A man in jail has more room, better food, and commonly better company* — Dr Johnson.

Word history ━━━━━
Middle English *jaiole* from Old French, and *gayole* from Anglo-French *gaole*, both ultimately from Latin *cavea*: see CAGE¹. Middle English *gayole* survives in *gaol*, the usual spelling in British official use, which was pronounced with a hard *g* (as in *goat*) at least until the 17th cent.

jail² (*Brit* **gaol**) *verb trans* to confine (somebody) in a jail.

jailbait *noun informal* a girl considered sexually attractive but below the age of consent.

jailbird *noun* a person who is or has frequently been confined in jail.

jailbreak *noun* an escape from jail.

jailer *or* **jailor** *noun* **1** a person in charge of the prisoners in a jail. **2** somebody or something that restricts another's liberty by or as if by imprisonment.

jailhouse /'jaylhows/ *noun* *NAmer* a prison.

jailor *noun* see JAILER.

Jain /jayn, jien/ *noun* an adherent of Jainism. [Hindi *Jain*, from Sanskrit *Jaina* of a *Jina*, literally 'victor', a title given to great Jain teachers]

Jainism /'jayniz(ə)m, 'jie-/ *noun* a religion originating in India in the sixth cent. BC that emphasizes the perfectibility of man and teaches liberation of the soul, *esp* by the practice of self-denial and AHIMSA (non-violence).

Editorial note ━━━━━
Jainism is the religion of the Jains, the followers of the Jinas ('Conquerors'), revered as enlightened beings who taught the path to liberation from rebirth. One of the Jinas was Mahavira, a contemporary of the Buddha. Although it has many influential doctrines and practices, Jainism is particularly known among Indian religions for ahimsa (non-violence) toward humans, animals, and plants — Professor Donald Lopez.

jake /jayk/ *adj NAmer, Aus, informal* all right or satisfactory. [origin unknown]

jakes *noun* (*pl* **jakes**) *archaic* a lavatory, *esp* an outdoor one. [perhaps from French *Jacques* James]

jalap /'jaləp/ *noun* a purgative drug prepared from the root of a Mexican plant. [French *jalap* from Spanish *jalapa*, from *Jalapa*, city in Mexico]

jalapeño /halə'paynyoh/ *noun* (*pl* **jalapeños**) a short thick green chilli, often used in Mexican cooking. [Mexican Spanish *jalapeño* of *Jalapa*, city in Mexico]

jalopy /jə'lopi/ *noun* (*pl* **jalopies**) *informal* a dilapidated old vehicle or aircraft. [origin unknown]

jalousie /'zhaləzi, 'zhaloozee/ *noun* a blind with adjustable horizontal slats for admitting light and air while excluding sun and rain. [French *jalousie*, literally 'jealousy', prob with reference to the eastern practice of keeping women out of sight]

Jam. *abbr* **1** Jamaica. **2** *esp* in biblical references, James.

jam¹ /jam/ *verb* (**jammed, jamming**) ➤ *verb trans* **1** to cause (e.g. a door or part of a machine) to become stuck so that it does not work or move. **2** to fill (e.g. a street) so that passage along it is blocked: *Crowds jammed the streets.* **3a** to squeeze or pack (something) closely or tightly into a space. **b** to fill (something), sometimes to excess: *a book jammed with facts.* **4** to send out interfering signals in order to make (a radio signal) unintelligible. **5** (+ on) to

apply (the brakes) suddenly and violently. ➤ *verb intrans* **1a** to become blocked or wedged. **b** to become unable to work or move through the jamming of a part. **2** to crowd or squash tightly together: *They all jammed into the room.* **3** *informal* to take part in a jam session. [perhaps imitative]

jam² *noun* **1a** a crowd or mass that impedes or blocks something: *a traffic jam.* **b** the pressure or congestion of a crowd. **2** an instance of jamming. **3** *informal* a difficult or awkward situation: *I'm in a bit of a jam.* **4** = JAM SESSION.

jam³ *noun* **1** a preserve made by boiling fruit and sugar to a thick consistency. **2** *Brit, informal* something agreeable or easy: *money for jam.* ✳ **jam on it** *Brit, informal* a situation wherever everything is very easy or just as one would want it to be. **jam tomorrow** a promise of something desirable that is never fulfilled. [prob from JAM³]

Jamaican /jə'maykən/ *noun* a native or inhabitant of Jamaica, an island in the Caribbean. ⟫⟫ **Jamaican** *adj*.

jamb /jam/ *noun* a straight vertical post or surface forming the side of an opening for a door, window, etc. [Middle English *jambe* from early French *jambe* leg, from late Latin *gamba*]

jambalaya /jambə'lie-ə/ *noun* a dish of rice cooked with ham, sausage, chicken, shrimp, or oysters and seasoned with herbs. [Louisiana French *jambalaya*, from Provençal *jambalaia*]

jamboree /jambə'ree/ *noun* **1** a large festive gathering. **2** a large gathering of scouts or guides in a camp. [origin unknown]

jammy *adj* (**jammier, jammiest**) *informal* **1** *Brit* having good luck; lucky: *He had not been able to find any really cheering quotations on the subject of death … the trouble was, he found, one became almost too jolly at Donald's expense, the implication being that he, the jammy bastard, was well off out of it* — Nigel Williams. **2** covered in or filled with jam.

jam-packed *adj* full to overflowing.

jam session *noun* an impromptu jazz performance that features group improvisation. [JAM¹]

Jan. *abbr* January.

Jandal /'jandl/ *noun* *NZ, trademark* a type of flip-flop sandal. [prob alteration of *sandal*]

jangle¹ /'janggl/ *verb intrans and trans* **1** to make or cause (something) to make a harsh or discordant ringing noise: *like sweet bells jangled out of tune and harsh* — Shakespeare. **2** to be or cause (the nerves) to be in a state of tense irritation. ⟫⟫ **jangly** *adj*. [Middle English *janglen* from Old French *jangler*, of Germanic origin]

jangle² *noun* **1** a discordant ringing noise. **2** a noisy quarrel.

janissary /'janisəri/ *or* **janizary** /-zəri/ *noun* (*pl* **janissaries** *or* **janizaries**) **1** (*often* **Janissary**) a soldier of an elite corps of Turkish troops organized in the 14th cent. and abolished in 1826. **2** a loyal or subservient official or supporter. [Italian *giannizzero* from Turkish *yeniçeri*]

janitor /'janitə/ *noun* *NAmer, Scot* a caretaker, *esp* of a school. ⟫⟫ **janitorial** /-'tawri·əl/ *adj*. [Latin *janitor* door-keeper, from *janua* door, from *janus* arch, gate]

janizary *noun* (*pl* **janizaries**) see JANISSARY.

jankers /'jankəz/ *pl noun* *Brit, slang* (*treated as sing.*) punishment, *esp* confinement, for military offences committed by service personnel.

Jansenism /'jansəniz(ə)m/ *noun* the doctrine of a 17th- and 18th-cent. movement, *esp* among French Roman Catholics, holding that one would be saved less because of one's good deeds than because God had chosen one for salvation. ⟫⟫ **Jansenist** *noun and adj*. [French *jansénisme*, named after Cornelis *Jansen* d.1638, Dutch theologian, on whose writings the movement was based]

January /'janyoo(ə)ri/ *noun* the first month of the year. [Middle English *Januarie* from Latin *Januarius*, first month of the ancient Roman year, from *Janus*, god of doors, gates, and beginnings]

Jap /jap/ *noun offensive* a Japanese person. ⟫⟫ **Jap** *adj*.

japan¹ /jə'pan/ *noun* **1** a black varnish giving a hard brilliant finish. **2** work, e.g. lacquer ware, finished and decorated in the Japanese manner. [*Japan*, country in E Asia where it originated]

japan² *verb trans* (**japanned, japanning**) **1** to cover (something) with a coat of japan. **2** to give a high gloss to (something).

Japanese /japə'neez/ *noun* (*pl* **Japanese**) **1** a native or inhabitant of Japan. **2** the language of the Japanese. ⟫⟫ **Japanese** *adj*.

Word history
Since Japan began to open its borders to Europeans in the 1850s, many Japanese words have appeared in English, but nearly all are restricted to specialized fields such as food and drink (*sake, soy, sukiyaki*), martial arts (*judo, karate*), and practices, activities, and titles (*kamikaze, bonsai, origami*) of unmistakably Japanese origin. *Tycoon* is a rare example of a Japanese word (ultimately from Chinese) which has become thoroughly anglicized; and the more recent borrowing *honcho*, picked up by US servicemen during the Korean War (1950–3), is fast establishing itself in English.

jape[1] /'jayp/ *noun* a jest or joke.

Word history
Middle English *japen* to trick, copulate with, jest, from Old French *japer* to yelp, influenced in meaning by Old French (*gaber* to mock. The word came to be regarded as coarse in the 16th cent. and was virtually obsolete by the 17th; it was revived in the 19th cent. by, among others, Sir Walter Scott and Charles Lamb.

jape[2] *verb intrans* to jest or joke. ➤➤ **japery** *noun*.

Japlish /'japlish/ *noun* a variety of Japanese incorporating many English words, sometimes spoken in Japan. [blend of JAPANESE + ENGLISH[2]]

japonica /jə'ponikə/ *noun* any of several species of hardy ornamental shrubs of the rose family with clusters of scarlet, white, or pink flowers: *Chaenomeles speciosa* and other species. [scientific Latin *japonica*, fem of *Japonicus* Japanese, from *Japonia* Japan]

jar[1] /jah/ *noun* **1a** a short-necked and wide-mouthed container, usu cylindrical and made of glass. **b** the contents of a jar. **2** *informal* a glass of an alcoholic drink, *esp* beer. ➤➤ **jarful** *noun*. [early French *jarre* via Old Provençal *jarra* from Arabic *jarrah* earthen water vessel]

jar[2] *verb* (**jarred, jarring**) ➤ *verb intrans* **1** (*usu* + on/upon) to have a harshly disagreeable effect. **2** (*often* + with) to appear unpleasant, incongruous, or out of keeping with something. **3** to make a harsh or discordant noise. **4** to jolt or vibrate. ➤ *verb trans* **1** to give (something or somebody) a shock, shake, or jolt. **2** to have a harshly disagreeable effect on (somebody or something). ➤➤ **jarringly** *adv*. [prob imitative]

jar[3] *noun* **1a** a sudden or unexpected jolt or shake. **b** an unsettling shock (e.g. to nerves or feelings). **2** a jarring noise.

jar[4] * **on the jar** said of a door: slightly open; ajar. [alteration of earlier *char* turn, from Middle English: see CHORE]

jardinière /zhahdi'nyeə (*French* ʒardinjɛːr)/ *noun* **1** an ornamental stand or large pot for plants or flowers. **2** a garnish consisting of several vegetables arranged in groups round meat. [French *jardinière*, literally 'female gardener']

jargon /'jahg(ə)n/ *noun* **1** the terminology or idiom of a particular activity or profession: *scientific jargon*. **2** obscure and often pretentious language.

Editorial note
Based on the French for 'the twittering of birds', jargon works on two levels: the deliberate obfuscations of governments, business and similar institutions, and what might be described as 'professional slang', the 'in' vocabularies of given occupations. Such jargons confer twin benefits: the affirmation of the group identity and the exclusion of those outside the initiated — Jonathon Green.

➤➤ **jargonistic** /-'nistik/ *adj*. [Middle English from early French]

jarl /yahl/ *noun* in medieval Scandinavia, a nobleman ranking immediately below the king. [Old Norse *jarl*]

jarrah *or* **jarra** /'jarə/ *noun* **1** an Australian eucalyptus tree with rough bark and oval leaves: *Eucalyptus marginata*. **2** the tough wood of this tree. [from Nyungar, an Aboriginal language of SW Australia]

Jas *abbr* James (book of the Bible).

jasmine /'jazmin/ *noun* **1a** any of numerous plants, often climbing shrubs, with very fragrant yellow or white flowers: genus *Jasminum*. **b** = WINTER JASMINE. **c** = YELLOW JASMINE. **2** a light yellow colour. **3** a scent made from oil extracted from a variety of jasmine. [French *jasmin* via Arabic from Persian *yāsamīn*]

jaspé /'jaspay/ *adj* variegated or mottled like jasper. [French *jaspé*, past part. of *jasper* to mottle]

jasper /'jaspə/ *noun* an opaque quartz which is usu reddish brown, yellow, or dark green, used as a gemstone. [Middle English *jaspre* via French and Latin from Greek *iaspis*, of Semitic origin]

jasperware *noun* a fine-grained unglazed stoneware developed by Josiah Wedgwood, usu decorated with raised white classical motifs on a coloured ground.

Jat /jaht/ *noun* a member of an Indo-Aryan people living *esp* in the Punjab and Uttar Pradesh. [Hindi *Jāt*]

jato /'jaytoh/ *noun* (*pl* **jatos**) **1** an auxiliary power unit that is used for assisting the takeoff of an aircraft and consists of one or more jet engines to provide temporary extra thrust. **2** a takeoff assisted in this way. [acronym from *jet-assisted takeoff*]

jaundice /'jawndis/ *noun* **1** an abnormal condition marked by yellowish pigmentation of the skin, tissues, and body fluids caused by the deposition of bile pigments. **2** a state of bitterness, envy, or resentment. [Middle English *jaundis* from French *jaunisse* yellowness, from Latin *galbinus* yellowish green, from *galbus* yellow]

jaundiced *adj* **1** affected with jaundice. **2** bitter, envious, or resentful.

jaunt[1] /jawnt/ *noun* a short journey for pleasure. [origin unknown]

jaunt[2] *verb intrans* to go on a jaunt.

jaunty *adj* (**jauntier, jauntiest**) **1** having or showing airy self-confidence. **2** smart or stylish. ➤➤ **jauntily** *adv*, **jauntiness** *noun*. [modification of French *gentil* genteel, elegant, from Latin *gentilis*: see GENTLE[1]]

Java /'jahvə/ *noun trademark* a computer programming language used to add interactivity to web pages.

java *noun NAmer, informal* coffee, *esp* filter or similar coffee rather than instant coffee. [from *Java*, a variety of rich coffee grown on the Indonesian island of Java]

Java man *noun* either of two types of small-brained prehistoric humans (*Homo erectus* and *Homo robustus*) who lived during the Palaeolithic era: compare PITHECANTHROPUS. [named after *Java*, island in Indonesia, where skull fragments were found]

Javanese /jahvə'neez/ *noun* (*pl* **Javanese**) **1** a member of an Indonesian people inhabiting the island of Java. **2** the Austronesian language of the inhabitants of Java. ➤➤ **Javanese** *adj*.

Word history
Javanese words that have passed into English include *batik, gong, junk* (= ship), and *muntjac*.

javelin /'jav(ə)lin/ *noun* **1** a light spear thrown in an athletic field event or as a weapon. **2** (**the javelin**) the sport of throwing the javelin. [early French *javeline*, alteration of *javelot*, of Celtic origin]

jaw[1] /jaw/ *noun* **1a** either of two cartilaginous or bony structures that in most vertebrates form a framework above and below the mouth in which the teeth are set. **b** any of various organs of invertebrates that perform the function of the vertebrate jaw. **2** (*in pl*) the two parts of a machine, tool, etc between which something may be clamped or crushed: *the jaws of a vice*. **3** (*in pl*) the imminent prospect of something unpleasant, imagined as a pair of open jaws about to seize or swallow a victim: *He has stared into the jaws of death*. **4** *informal*. **a** continual talk. **b** a friendly chat. [Middle English, prob from Old French *joe* cheek]

jaw[2] *verb intrans informal* to talk for a long time.

jawbone *noun* the bone of a jaw, *esp* a lower jaw.

jawbreaker *noun* **1** *informal* a word that is difficult to pronounce. **2** *chiefly NAmer* = GOBSTOPPER.

jawed *adj* (*usu used in combinations*) having jaws, *esp* of a specified type or shape: *square-jawed*.

jawline *noun* the outline of the lower jaw.

jay /jay/ *noun* any of several species of Eurasian and African birds of the crow family with strongly patterned plumage: *Garrulus glandarius* and other species. [Middle English via early French *jai* from late Latin *gaius*, perhaps from the male first name *Gaius*]

jaywalk *verb intrans* to cross a street carelessly so that one is endangered by traffic. ➤➤ **jaywalker** *noun*. [JAY, in the sense 'simpleton, yokel' + WALK[1]]

jazz /jaz/ *noun* **1** music developed *esp* from ragtime and blues and characterized by syncopated rhythms and improvisation around a basic theme or melody.

Editorial note
Although originally developed by African-Americans from musical strands drawn from both African and European-American sources, jazz has grown into a global idiom of expression. It remains based on principles of musical improvisation, within or without a structure, and its inherent freedoms fed into all 20th-cent. music — Richard Cook.

2 *informal* empty pretentious talk: *He got up and spouted a lot of scientific jazz*. * **and all that jazz** *informal* and other similar things. [origin unknown]

jazz up *verb trans informal* **1** to make (something) more lively or interesting. **2** to make (something) bright, *esp* in a vivid or garish way. **3** to play (a piece of music) in the style of jazz.

jazzy *adj* (**jazzier, jazziest**) **1** having the characteristics of jazz. **2** *informal* colourful, garish, or gaudy. ➤ **jazzily** *adv,* **jazziness** *noun.*

JC *abbr* **1** Jesus Christ. **2** Julius Caesar.

JCB *noun trademark* a type of mechanical earth-mover with a shovel at the front end and a digging bucket on an extendable arm at the rear. [from the initials of the designer and manufacturer *J C Bamford*]

JCL *abbr* Job Control Language.

JCR *abbr* Junior Common Room.

JCS *abbr* Joint Chiefs of Staff.

jct. *abbr* junction.

jealous /'jeləs/ *adj* **1** apprehensive and suspicious of rivalry, *esp* in sexual love. **2** (+ of) resentful and envious of an advantage, possession, etc that somebody else has or is believed to have. **3** vigilant in guarding a possession, right, etc: *He was jealous of his honour.* **4** intolerant of rivalry or unfaithfulness: *The Lord your God is a jealous God* — Bible. ➤ **jealously** *adv,* **jealousness** *noun.* [Middle English *jelous* via Old French from late Latin *zelus* zeal, from Greek *zēlos*]

jealousy *noun* (*pl* **jealousies**) **1** the state or quality of being jealous. **2** an instance of jealousy.

jean /jeen/ *noun* a durable twilled cotton cloth used *esp* for work clothes. [short for *jean fustian*, from Middle English *Gene* Genoa, city in Italy + FUSTIAN]

jeans *pl noun* casual usu close-fitting trousers, made *esp* of blue denim. [plural of JEAN]

jeep /jeep/ *noun trademark* a small rugged general-purpose motor vehicle with four-wheel drive, used *esp* by the armed forces. [alteration of *gee pee,* short for *general-purpose*]

jeepers *interj chiefly NAmer, informal* used to express surprise. [euphemism for JESUS²]

jeepers creepers *interj informal* = JEEPERS.

jeer¹ /jiə/ *verb intrans* (*often* + at) to laugh mockingly or make rude and mocking comments. ➤➤ **jeerer** *noun,* **jeeringly** *adv.* [origin unknown]

jeer² *noun* a jeering remark; a taunt.

jehad /ji'hahd/ *noun* = JIHAD.

Jehovah /ji'hohvə/ *noun* = GOD¹ (1): *In the Lord Jehovah is everlasting strength* — Bible. [medieval Latin *Jehouah,* erroneous transliteration of Hebrew YHWH (see YAHWEH) incorporating vowels taken from ADONAI]

Jehovah's Witness *noun* a member of a fundamentalist sect practising personal evangelism, rejecting the authority of the secular state, and preaching that the end of the present world is imminent.

jejune /ji'joohn/ *adj* **1** lacking maturity; puerile. **2** lacking interest or significance. ➤➤ **jejunely** *adv,* **jejuneness** *noun.* [Latin *jejunus* barren, fasting]

jejunum /ji'joohnəm/ *noun* the section of the small intestine between the duodenum and the ileum. ➤➤ **jejunal** *adj.* [Latin *jejunum,* neuter of *jejunus* fasting; because the jejunum was believed to be empty after death]

Jekyll and Hyde /,jekəl ənd 'hied/ *noun* a person having a split personality, one side of which is good and the other evil. ➤➤ **Jekyll-and-Hyde** *adj.* [named after Dr *Jekyll* and Mr *Hyde,* the two sides of the split personality of the protagonist of R L Stevenson's *The Strange Case of Dr Jekyll and Mr Hyde* (1886)]

jell /jel/ *verb chiefly NAmer* see GEL² (2), (3).

jellaba /jə'lahbə/ *noun* see DJELLABA.

jello /'jeloh/ *noun NAmer* a fruit jelly made from a commercially manufactured powder.

jelly¹ /'jeli/ *noun* (*pl* **jellies**) **1a** a soft fruit-flavoured transparent dessert set with gelatin, characterized by an elastic texture and a tendency to wobble. **b** a savoury food product of similar consistency, made *esp* from meat stock and gelatin. **c** any non-food substance resembling jelly in consistency. **2** a clear fruit preserve made by boiling sugar and the juice of fruit. **3** *informal* = JELLY SHOE. [Middle English *gelly* from French *gelee,* from *geler* to freeze, congeal, from Latin *gelare*]

jelly² *verb* (**jellies, jellied, jellying**) ➤ *verb intrans* to set like a jelly. ➤ *verb trans* **1** to bring (something) to the consistency of jelly; to cause (something) to set. **2** to set (something) in a jelly: *jellied beef.*

jelly³ *noun Brit, informal* = GELIGNITE. [shortening of GELIGNITE]

jelly baby *noun* (*pl* **jelly babies**) a small soft gelatinous sweet in the shape of a baby.

jelly bean *noun* **1** a small bean-shaped sweet with a hard sugar coating and a gelatinous filling. **2** *NAmer, slang* a stupid or contemptible person.

jellyfish *noun* (*pl* **jellyfishes** *or collectively* **jellyfish**) **1** a free-swimming invertebrate sea animal that has a nearly transparent saucer-shaped body and tentacles covered with stinging cells: classes Scyphozoa and Cubozoa. **2** a person lacking firmness of character.

jelly shoe *noun* a light plastic sandal or slipper for beach or casual wear.

jemmy¹ /'jemi/ (*NAmer* **jimmy** /'jim-/) *noun* (*pl* **jemmies** *or NAmer* **jimmies**) a short steel crowbar, used *esp* by burglars. [*Jemmy,* nickname for *James*]

jemmy² (*NAmer* **jimmy**) *verb trans* (**jemmies, jemmied, jemmying,** *NAmer* **jimmies, jimmied, jimmying**) to force open (e.g. a door or window) with a jemmy.

je ne sais quoi /,zhə nə say 'kwah (*French* ʒə nə sɛ kwa)/ *noun* a quality that cannot be adequately described or expressed, *esp* one that makes somebody or something more attractive or interesting. [French *je ne sais quoi* I know not what]

jennet /'jenit/ *noun* **1** a small Spanish riding horse. **2** a female donkey. [Middle English *genett* via French from Catalan *ginet, genet* light horseman, from Arabic *Zenāta,* a Berber people renowned for their horsemanship]

jenny /'jeni/ *noun* (*pl* **jennies**) **1** a female donkey or ass. **2** = SPINNING JENNY. [from the name *Jenny*]

jeon /jun/ *noun* (*pl* **jeon**) a unit of currency in South Korea, worth 100th of a won. [Korean *jeon*]

jeopardize *or* **jeopardise** /'jepədiez/ *verb trans* to put (somebody or something) in danger.

jeopardy /'jepədi/ *noun* **1** exposure to or risk of death, loss, injury, etc; danger. **2** liability to conviction faced by a defendant in a criminal trial. [Middle English *jeopardie* via Anglo-French *juparti* from Old French *jeu parti* alternative, literally 'divided game']

jequirity bean /ji'kwiriti/ *noun* **1** the poisonous scarlet and black seed of an Asian climbing plant of the pea family, often used as a bead in necklaces and rosaries. **2** the plant bearing these seeds: *Abrus precatorius.* [Portuguese *jequiriti* from Tupi and Guarani *jekiriti*]

Jer. *abbr* Jeremiah (book of the Bible).

jerboa /juh'boh·ə/ *noun* any of several species of nocturnal mouse-like African and Eurasian desert rodents with long back legs adapted for jumping: family Dipodidae. [Arabic *yarbū*]

jeremiad /jerə'mie·əd/ *noun* a prolonged lamentation or complaint. [French *jérémiade* from *Jérémie* Jeremiah, ultimately from Hebrew *Yirmĕyāh;* referring to the lamentations of the prophet Jeremiah in the Old Testament]

Jeremiah /jerə'mie·ə/ *noun* somebody who is mournfully pessimistic about the present and foretells a calamitous future: *Roddick ... refused to listen to the Jeremiahs who predicted she would have to change her operating style once her company came under the scrutiny of the Stock Exchange* — Derek Ezra, David Oates. [named after the prophet Jeremiah: see JEREMIAD]

jerk¹ /juhk/ *verb trans* **1** to move (something) with a short sudden pull, push, twist, or jolt: *She jerked her head out of the way.* **2** (*often* + out) to say (something) in an abrupt or explosive manner. ➤ *verb intrans* **1** to make a sudden spasmodic motion: *They jerked to attention.* **2** to move in a series of short abrupt motions. ➤➤ **jerker** *noun.* [prob alteration of English dialect *yerk* to thrash, attack, excite, from Middle English *yerken* to bind tightly, to lash; earlier history unknown]

jerk² *noun* **1** a single quick forceful motion, e.g. a pull, twist, or jolt. **2** an involuntary spasmodic muscular movement. **3** in weightlifting, the pushing of a weight from shoulder height to a position above the head. **4** *chiefly NAmer, informal* a stupid, foolish, or naive person.

jerk³ *verb trans* to preserve (e.g. beef or venison) by cutting it into long slices or strips and drying it in the sun. [back-formation from JERKY²]

jerk⁴ *noun* = JERKY².

jerk around *verb trans NAmer, informal* to treat (somebody) badly or without consideration.

jerkin /'juhkin/ *noun* **1** a man's or woman's sleeveless jacket. **2** a close-fitting hip-length sleeveless jacket, made *esp* of leather, worn by men in the 16th and 17th cents. [origin unknown]

jerk off *verb trans and intrans chiefly NAmer, coarse slang* = MASTURBATE.

jerky¹ *adj* (**jerkier, jerkiest**) **1** marked by irregular or spasmodic movements. **2** marked by abrupt or awkward changes. ➤➤ **jerkily** *adv*, **jerkiness** *noun*.

jerky² *noun* raw meat cut into strips and dried in the sun; jerked meat. [from American Spanish *charqi*, from Quechua *ch'arki* sun-dried meat]

jeroboam /jerə'boh·əm/ *noun* a wine bottle holding four times the amount of a standard bottle. [named after *Jeroboam* 11th cent. BC, king of the northern kingdom of Israel, a mighty man who 'did sin, and who made Israel to sin' (I Kings 14:16)]

jerrican *noun* see JERRY CAN.

Jerry /'jeri/ *noun* (*pl* **Jerries**) *chiefly Brit, dated* **1** a German, *esp* a German soldier in World War II. **2** the Germans or the German armed forces collectively in World War II. [by shortening and alteration]

jerry *noun* (*pl* **jerries**) *Brit, informal, dated* = CHAMBER POT. [prob by shortening and alteration from JEROBOAM]

jerry-build *verb trans* (*past tense and past part.* **jerry-built**) to build (e.g. houses) cheaply and flimsily. ➤➤ **jerry-builder** *noun*, **jerry-built** *adj*. [back-formation from *jerry-built*, of uncertain origin; perhaps referring to the walls of Jericho, a town in Palestine whose walls fell when the Israelites blew their trumpets (Joshua 6:20)]

jerry can *or* **jerrican** *noun* a narrow flat-sided container for carrying liquids, *esp* petrol or water, with a capacity of about 25l (about 5gall). [JERRY + CAN²; from its German design]

jersey /'juhzi/ *noun* **1** a knitted garment with or without sleeves that is worn on the upper body; a jumper. **2** a shirt worn by a footballer or other sports player. **3** a knitted, slightly elastic fabric made of cotton, wool, nylon, etc and used *esp* for clothing. **4** (*often* **Jersey**) an animal belonging to a breed of small short-horned cattle noted for their rich milk. [named after *Jersey*, one of the Channel islands]

Jerusalem artichoke /jə'roohsələm/ *noun* a perennial N American sunflower cultivated for its edible sweet-tasting tubers: *Helianthus tuberosus*.

Ⅾord history

This plant has nothing to do with Jerusalem, nor is it closely related to the artichoke. Soon after its introduction from America to Europe in the early 17th cent., it was apparently imported to Britain from Italy, probably under the name *girasole articiocco* meaning 'sunflower artichoke'. Folk etymology changed *girasole* to *Jerusalem*, while a supposed similarity of flavour to the artichoke produced the second part of the name.

jess /jes/ *noun* a short strap made *esp* of leather that is secured to the leg of a hawk and usu has a ring on the other end for attaching a leash. [Middle English *ges* from early French *gies*, from *jeter*: see JET¹]

jessamine /'jesəmin/ *noun* = JASMINE.

jessie /'jesi/ *noun Brit, derog* an effeminate man. [*Jessie*, nickname for *Janet*]

jest¹ /jest/ *noun* **1** an amusing or mocking act or utterance; a joke. **2** a way of behaving, speaking, etc that is not intended to be taken seriously: *He said it in jest*.

Ⅾord history

Middle English *geste* deed, exploit, via Old French from Latin *gesta* deeds, from *gerere* to do. In the 13th cent. the word denoted a romantic tale of heroic exploits, hence an entertaining or funny story.

jest² *verb intrans* **1** to speak or act without seriousness: *What is truth? said jesting Pilate, and would not wait for an answer* — Bacon. **2** to make a witty remark.

jester *noun* a clown formerly employed in royal or noble households to provide casual amusement and commonly dressed in a brightly coloured costume.

Jesu /'jeezyooh/ *noun literary* = JESUS¹.

Jesuit /'jezyoo·it/ *noun* a member of the Society of Jesus, a Roman Catholic order founded by St Ignatius Loyola in 1534 that is devoted to missionary and educational work. [Latin *Jesuita*, from late Latin JESUS¹]

jesuitical /jezyoo'itikl/ *adj* **1** (*often* **Jesuitical**) relating to the Jesuits. **2** *derog* given to subtle, hair-splitting argumentation or deception. ➤➤ **jesuitic** *adj*, **jesuitically** *adv*.

Jesus¹ /'jeezəs/ *or* **Jesus Christ** *noun* the Jewish religious teacher whose life, death, and resurrection as reported in the New Testament are the basis of the Christian religion.

Jesus² *or* **Jesus Christ** *interj informal* used to express surprise, dismay, annoyance, etc.

Jesus freak *noun informal* a member of an evangelical Christian group, *esp* a deeply committed and demonstrative one.

jet¹ /jet/ *noun* **1a** a stream of liquid or gas forced out under pressure from a narrow opening or a nozzle. **b** a nozzle or other narrow opening for emitting a jet of liquid or gas. **2a** = JET ENGINE. **b** an aircraft powered by one or more jet engines. [early French *jeter* to throw, from Latin *jactare* to throw repeatedly, from *jacere* to throw]

jet² *verb intrans* (**jetted, jetting**) **1** to spurt out. **2** to travel by jet aircraft: *They're jetting off to New York for the weekend*.

jet³ *noun* **1** a hard black form of coal that is often polished and used for jewellery. **2** an intense black colour. [Middle English via French *jaiet* and Latin *gagates* from Greek *gagatēs*, from *Gagas*, town and river in Asia Minor where it was found]

jet-black *adj* of a very dark black colour.

jeté /zhə'tay (*French* ʒəte)/ *noun* a high arching leap in ballet in which the dancer has one leg stretched forwards and the other backwards. [French *jeté*, past part. of *jeter*: see JET¹]

jet engine *noun* an engine that produces motion in one direction as a result of the discharge of a jet of fluid in the opposite direction; *specif* an aircraft engine that discharges the hot air and gases produced by the combustion of a fuel to produce propulsion or lift.

jet lag *noun* a temporary disruption of a person's normal bodily rhythms after a long flight, *esp* due to differences in local time.

jet-propelled *adj* moving by jet propulsion.

jet propulsion *noun* propulsion of a body produced by the discharge of a jet of fluid; *specif* propulsion of an aeroplane by jet engines.

jetsam /'jetsəm/ *noun* goods thrown overboard from a ship and washed up on shore: compare FLOTSAM. [alteration of JETTISON²]

jet set *noun* (*treated as sing. or pl*) wealthy people who frequently travel by air to fashionable resorts anywhere in the world. ➤➤ **jetsetter** *noun*, **jet-setting** *adj, noun*. [JET¹]

jet-ski¹ *noun* a small motorized vessel, consisting of a platform with a prow, steering column, and handlebars, that is ridden as a form of water sport.

jet-ski² *verb intrans* (**jet-skied, jet-skiing**) to ride over water on a jet-ski.

jet stream *noun* **1** a current of strong winds high in the atmosphere usu blowing from a westerly direction. **2** the exhaust from a jet engine.

jettison¹ /'jetis(ə)n/ *verb trans* (**jettisoned, jettisoning**) **1** to cast (something) off as superfluous or encumbering; to abandon. **2a** to throw (e.g. goods or cargo) overboard to lighten the load of a ship in distress. **b** to drop (e.g. unwanted material) from an aircraft or spacecraft in flight. ➤➤ **jettisonable** *adj*. [Middle English via Old French *getaison*, from Latin *jactation-, jactatio*, from *jactare*: see JET¹]

jettison² *noun* **1** the act of jettisoning cargo, etc. **2** abandonment or rejection of something or somebody.

jetton /'jetən/ *noun* a counter used as a chip in gambling games. [French *jeton* from *jeter* to throw, calculate: see JET¹]

jetty /'jeti/ *noun* (*pl* **jetties**) **1** a small landing pier. **2** a structure, e.g. a pier or breakwater, extending into a sea, lake, or river to influence the current or to protect a harbour. [Middle English *jette* from early French *jetee*, from past part. of *jeter*: see JET¹]

jeu d'esprit /,zhuh de'spree (*French* ʒø dɛspri)/ *noun* (*pl* **jeux d'esprit** /,zhuh de'spree (*French* ʒø dɛspri)/) a witty comment or composition. [French *jeu d'esprit*, literally 'play of the mind']

jeunesse dorée /zhuh,nes daw'ray (*French* ʒønɛs dɔre)/ *noun* young people of wealth and fashion. [French *jeunesse dorée* gilded youth]

jeux d'esprit /,zhuh de'spree/ *noun* pl of JEU D'ESPRIT.

Jew /jooh/ *noun* **1** a member of a Semitic people existing as a nation in Palestine from the sixth cent. BC to the first cent. AD, and now living in Israel and other countries throughout the world. **2** a person whose religion is Judaism. [Middle English via French and Latin from Greek *Ioudaios*, from Hebrew *Yĕhūdhī*, from *Yĕhūdhāh* Judah, Jewish kingdom]

jewel /'jooh·əl/ *noun* **1** a precious stone, such as a diamond, ruby, or emerald. **2** an ornament of precious metal often set with stones and worn as an accessory; a piece of jewellery. **3** a bearing for a watch or compass made of crystal, precious stone, or glass. **4** somebody or something highly valued or esteemed. ⟫ **jewelled** *adj.* [Middle English from Old French *juel*, dimin. of *jeu* game, play, from Latin *jocus* game, JOKE¹]

jeweler *noun* NAmer see JEWELLER.

jewelfish *noun* (*pl* **jewelfishes** *or collectively* **jewelfish**) a scarlet and green tropical freshwater fish: *Hemichromis bimaculatus*.

jeweller (NAmer **jeweler**) *noun* somebody who deals in, makes, or repairs jewellery and often watches, silverware, etc.

jeweller's rouge *noun* a fine powder of ferric oxide used as a metal polish.

jewellery (NAmer **jewelry**) /'jooh·əlri, 'jooləri/ *noun* articles, *esp* personal ornaments such as rings and necklaces, made of precious stones or precious metals.

Jewess /'jooh·es, 'jooh·is/ *noun dated or offensive* a Jewish woman or girl.

jewfish *noun* (*pl* **jewfishes** *or collectively* **jewfish**) any of various large fish of the sea bass family with dark spots living in tropical or subtropical seas: *esp Epinephelus itajara*.

Jewish *adj* **1** relating to or characteristic of Jews. **2** being a Jew. ⟫ **Jewishly** *adv*, **Jewishness** *noun*.

Jewry /'joohri/ *noun* **1** the Jewish people collectively. **2** a Jewish quarter of a town.

Jew's ear *noun* an edible brown fungus that grows on dying trees: *Auricularia auricula-judae*.

Jew's harp *noun* a small lyre-shaped musical instrument that is placed between the teeth and sounded by striking a metal tongue with the finger.

Jezebel /'jezəbel/ *noun* (*often* **jezebel**) a shameless or immoral woman. [*Jezebel*, wife of a King of Israel, known for her wicked conduct (I Kings 16:31ff)]

JHVH *noun* = YHWH.

jiao /jow/ *noun* a unit of currency in China, worth a tenth of a yuan. [Chinese *jiao*]

jib¹ /jib/ *noun* a triangular sail set on a stay extending from the top of the foremast to the bow. ✳ **the cut of somebody's jib** somebody's general appearance and manner. [origin uncertain; perhaps the same word as JIB³]

jib² *verb intrans* (**jibbed, jibbing**) said *esp* of a horse: to refuse to proceed further. ✳ **jib at** to take fright at (something) or balk at it: *The ready-made tailors quote me as their great double-barrel … I allow them to do so, though Robinson Crusoe would jib at their wearing apparel* — W S Gilbert. ⟫ **jibber** *noun*. [prob from ‼LINK‼]

jib³ *noun* the projecting arm of a crane. [prob by shortening and alteration from GIBBET¹]

jib-boom *noun* a spar that forms an extension of the BOWSPRIT (pole projecting from the bow of a ship). [JIB¹ + BOOM³]

jibe¹ *or* **gibe** /jieb/ *verb* to make scornful, taunting, or insulting remarks. [perhaps from Old French *giber* to handle roughly]

jibe² *or* **gibe** *noun* a scornful, taunting, or insulting remark.

jibe³ *verb chiefly* NAmer see GYBE.

jibe⁴ *verb intrans* NAmer, *informal* (+ with) to be in accord; to agree: *His account of the accident jibes pretty well with other accounts.* [origin unknown]

jiffy /'jifi/ *or* **jiff** /jif/ *noun informal* a moment or instant: *I'll be ready in a jiffy.* [origin unknown]

Jiffy bag *noun trademark* a padded envelope: *Only the most conscientious … dutifully plough through everything that flops out of a jiffy bag and on to their desk* — Norton York.

jig¹ /jig/ *noun* **1a** any of several lively dances with springing movements in triple time: compare GIGUE. **b** a piece of music for such a dance. **2** a fishing lure that jerks up and down in the water. **3** a device used to hold a piece of work in position, e.g. during machining or assembly, and to guide the tools working on it. **4** a device in which crushed ore or coal is separated from waste by shaking in water. [prob from early French *giguer* to dance, from *gigue* fiddle, of Germanic origin]

jig² *verb* (**jigged, jigging**) ⟫ *verb intrans* **1** to move along or move up and down in a rapid and jerky fashion. **2** to dance a jig. **3** to fish using a jig as a lure. ⟫ *verb trans* **1** to make (something) move up and down with a rapid jerky movement. **2** to separate (a mineral) from waste material with a jig. **3** to machine (something) using a jig to guide the cutting or drilling tool.

jigger¹ /'jigə/ *noun* **1a** a variable measure of spirits used *esp* in preparing mixed drinks. **b** a small container or glass for measuring this. **2** chiefly NAmer, *informal* something, *esp* a gadget, the correct name for which is temporarily forgotten. **3** a small sail set at the stern of a boat. **4** a mechanical device or part of a mechanism that operates with a jerky movement. **5** in billiards, a cue rest. **6** dated a metal golf club with a narrow face, equivalent to a number 4 iron. [JIG² + -ER²]

jigger² *noun* = CHIGOE.

jiggered *adj Brit, informal* damaged, broken, or exhausted. ✳ **I'll be jiggered** *informal* used to express astonishment. [perhaps euphemism for *buggered*]

jiggery-pokery /ˌjigəri 'pohkəri/ *noun Brit, informal* dishonest underhand dealings or scheming. [alteration of Scots *joukery-pawkery*, from *jouk* to cheat + *pawk* trick]

jiggle /'jigl/ *verb trans and intrans informal* to move or cause (something) to move with quick short jerks. ⟫ **jiggle** *noun*. [frequentative of JIG²]

jigsaw *noun* **1** a puzzle consisting of small irregularly cut pieces, *esp* of wood or card, that are fitted together to form a picture. **2** a power-driven fretsaw. **3** something composed of many disparate parts or elements.

jigsaw puzzle *noun* = JIGSAW (1).

jihad /ji'had/ *noun* **1** a holy war waged on behalf of Islam as a religious duty or a personal striving against evil. **2** a crusade for a principle or belief. ⟫ **jihadi** /-di/ *noun and adj*, **jihadist** *noun and adj*. [Arabic *jihād*]

jill /jil/ *noun* see GILL⁴.

jilt¹ /jilt/ *verb trans* to break off a romantic relationship with (somebody) suddenly. [from JILT²]

jilt² *noun* a person, usu a woman, who jilts a lover. [prob alteration of English dialect *jillet*, from *Jill*, diminutive form of the girl's name *Gillian*]

jim crow /jim/ *noun* NAmer **1** (*often* **Jim Crow**) (*often used before a noun*) racial discrimination, *esp* against black Americans: *jim crow laws*. **2** *offensive* a black person. **3** an implement used for bending iron bars or rails. [named after *Jim Crow*, stereotype Negro in a 19th-cent. song-and-dance act]

jimjams¹ /'jimjamz/ *pl noun informal* **1** = DELIRIUM TREMENS. **2** a state of extreme nervousness. [perhaps alteration of DELIRIUM TREMENS]

jimjams² *pl noun informal* = PYJAMAS.

jimmy¹ /'jimi/ *noun and verb* NAmer see JEMMY¹, JEMMY². [*Jimmy*, nickname for *James*]

jimmy² *noun* **1** chiefly Scot used as a term of address to a man. **2** *informal* an act of urination. [*Jimmy*, nickname for *James*]

jimsonweed *or* **Jimsonweed** /'jims(ə)nweed/ *noun* NAmer = THORN APPLE. [*jimson* alteration of *Jamestown*, site of first permanent English settlement in USA]

jingle¹ /'jinggl/ *verb trans and intrans* to make, or cause (something) to make, a light clinking or tinkling sound. [Middle English *ginglen*, of imitative origin]

jingle² *noun* **1** a light clinking or tinkling sound. **2** a short catchy song, rhyme, or tune used *esp* in advertising. ⟫ **jingly** *adj*.

jingo /'jinggoh/ *noun* (*pl* **jingoes**) *dated* a belligerently patriotic person, a jingoist. ✳ **by jingo** used to express surprise, or to express determination or add emphasis. [prob euphemism for JESUS²]

jingoism *noun* belligerent patriotism; chauvinism. ⟫ **jingoist** *noun*, **jingoistic** /-'istik/ *adj*, **jingoistically** /-'istikli/ *adv*. [from the occurrence of *by jingo* in the refrain of a 19th-cent. English chauvinistic song]

jink¹ /jingk/ *noun* a quick turn or sidestep while running, *esp* to avoid being caught. [origin unknown]

jink² *verb intrans* to move quickly with sudden turns and shifts, *esp* in order to dodge something or somebody.

jinker *noun Aus* a wheeled vehicle for transporting timber. [alteration of Scots *janker*, of unknown origin]

jinn *or* **djinn** *or* **djin** /jin/ *noun* (*pl* **jinns** *or* **jinn**) **1** any of a class of spirits that according to Muslim demonology inhabit the earth, assume various forms, and exercise supernatural power. **2** a spirit, often in human form, that serves whoever summons it; a genie. [Arabic *jinnīy* demon]

jinni *or* **jinnee** /ji'nee, 'jini/ *noun* = JINN.

jinx¹ /jingks/ *noun informal* somebody or something, usu an intangible force akin to a curse or spell, that brings bad luck. [prob alteration of *jynx* wryneck; from the use of this bird in witchcraft]

jinx² *verb trans* to put a jinx on (somebody) or bring them bad luck.

JIT *abbr* just-in-time.

jitney /'jitni/ *noun* (*pl* **jitneys**) *NAmer, informal* **1** a small bus that carries passengers over a regular route according to a flexible timetable. **2** = NICKEL¹ (2A). [origin unknown]

jitter¹ /'jitə/ *noun* **1** (**the jitters**) panic or extreme nervousness. **2** an irregular random movement. ➤ **jittery** *adj*. [origin unknown]

jitter² *verb intrans* (**jittered, jittering**) **1** to be nervous or act in a nervous way. **2** to make continuous fast repetitive movements.

jitterbug¹ *noun* a fast athletic dance popular in the 1940s, a jazz variation of the two-step in which couples swing and twirl.

jitterbug² *verb* (**jitterbugged, jitterbugging**) to dance the jitterbug.

jiu-jitsu /jooh 'jitsooh/ *noun* = JU-JITSU.

jive¹ /jiev/ *noun* **1** a style of energetic dancing, popular from the 1940s to the early 1960s, performed to fast jazz or swing music and later to rock and roll. **2** *NAmer.* **a** a type of slang used *esp* by black Americans. **b** glib or deceptive talk. [origin unknown]

jive² *verb intrans* **1** to dance the jive. **2** *NAmer, informal* to engage in good-humoured deception; to kid. ➤ *verb trans NAmer, informal* to cajole or tease (somebody).

jizz /jiz/ *noun informal* the distinguishing features of a particular species of animal or plant. [origin unknown]

Jn *abbr* John (books of the Bible).

jnr *abbr* junior.

Jo. *abbr* Joel (book of the Bible).

jo /joh/ *noun* (*pl* **joes**) *chiefly Scot* a sweetheart. [alteration of JOY¹]

joanna /joh'anə/ *noun Brit, informal* a piano. [rhyming slang]

job¹ /job/ *noun* **1** a regular paid position of employment or occupation. **2a** a piece of work. **b** a set of operations to be done by a computer. **3** a task. **4** a specific duty, role, or function. **5** something difficult: *We had a job persuading her.* **6** *informal* an object, occasion, etc of a usu specified type: *The party was a black-tie job.* **7** a crime, *esp* a robbery. **8** a piece of plastic surgery to improve one's appearance: *a nose job.* ✳ **a good job** a fortunate state of affairs: *It's a good job she was wearing a seat belt.* **jobs for the boys** *Brit* lucrative employment for friends, associates, etc, or a system of patronage or favouritism involving this. **just the job** exactly what is needed. **on the job 1** engaged in doing something; at work. **2** *coarse slang* having sexual intercourse. ➤ **jobless** *adj*. [perhaps from Middle English *jobbe* lump, later 'cartload', possibly an alteration of *gobbe* GOB¹]

job² *verb* (**jobbed, jobbing**) ➤ *verb intrans* **1** to do odd or occasional pieces of work, usu at a stated rate: *a jobbing gardener.* **2** to carry on public business for private gain. **3a** to carry on the business of a middleman or wholesaler. **b** to work as a stockjobber. ➤ *verb trans* **1** to buy and sell (e.g. shares) for profit. **2** to get, deal with, or effect (something) by jobbery.

jobber *noun* **1** *dated* = STOCKJOBBER. **2** somebody who does odd jobs or occasional work.

jobbery *noun* the use of a public office for personal gain; corruption.

jobbie /'jobi/ *noun informal* **1** a product or gadget of a particular kind: *one of those laptop jobbies.* **2** a piece of excrement.

Job Centre *or* **Jobcentre** *or* **jobcentre** *noun* a government office where unemployed people can look at job vacancies on display and arrange interviews with prospective employers.

Job Club *or* **job club** *noun* an organization that gives advice and support to unemployed people trying to find work.

job description *noun* a precise written description of the duties belonging to a particular job.

job lot *noun* **1** a miscellaneous collection of goods sold as one item. **2** any miscellaneous collection of articles.

Job's comforter /johbz/ *noun* somebody whose attempts to encourage or comfort a sufferer have the opposite effect. [from the tone of the speeches made to Job in the Old Testament by his friends (Job 15–16)]

jobseeker's allowance *noun* in Britain, a state payment for the unemployed.

job share¹ *noun* **1** an arrangement by which the work and responsibilities of a full-time employee are divided between two or more part-time employees. **2** a part-time job created by such an arrangement.

job share² *verb intrans* to work part-time in a job share arrangement. ➤ **jobsharer** *noun*, **jobsharing** *noun*.

Job's tears /johbz/ *pl noun* (*treated as sing.*) an Asiatic grass whose seeds grow inside white pear-shaped cases often used as beads: *Coix lacryma-jobi.* [named after the patriarch *Job* in the Old Testament]

jobsworth /'jobzwuhth/ *noun Brit, informal* (*sometimes used before a noun*) a minor official who follows procedures rigidly and is unhelpful to the public: *We stop at a war memorial for … 'a photo opportunity', only to be chased away by a jobsworth demanding a permit* — New Musical Express. [from the saying 'I'd like to help you, but it's more than my job's worth']

Jock /jok/ *noun Brit, informal* a Scotsman. [Scots form of *Jack*, nickname for *John*]

jock¹ *noun NAmer, informal* **1** a male athlete. **2** = JOCKSTRAP. [back-formation from JOCKSTRAP]

jock² *noun informal* **1** = JOCKEY¹. **2** = DISC JOCKEY.

jockey¹ /'joki/ *noun* (*pl* **jockeys**) **1** somebody who rides a horse in races, *esp* as a professional. **2** *NAmer* somebody who operates a specified vehicle, device, or object: *a truck jockey.* [*Jockey*, Scots nickname for *John*]

jockey² *verb* (**jockeys, jockeyed, jockeying**) ➤ *verb trans* **1** to ride (a horse) as a jockey. **2** to manoeuvre or manipulate (somebody) by adroit or devious means: *He jockeyed me into handing over the money.* **3** *chiefly NAmer* to drive or operate (something). ➤ *verb intrans* **1** to ride as a jockey. **2** to manoeuvre for advantage: *A group of photographers jockeyed for position.*

jockstrap *noun* a support for the genitals worn by men taking part in strenuous *esp* sporting activities. [obsolete *jock* penis + STRAP¹]

jocose /jə'kohs/ *adj formal* given to or characterized by joking. ➤ **jocosely** *adv*, **jocoseness** *noun*, **jocosity** /jə'kositi/ *noun*. [Latin *jocosus*, from *jocus* JOKE¹]

jocular /'jokyoolə/ *adj* **1** given to joking; habitually jolly. **2** characterized by joking; playfully humorous. ➤ **jocularity** /-'lariti/ *noun*, **jocularly** *adv*. [Latin *jocularis*, from *joculus*, dimin. of *jocus* JOKE¹]

jocund /'jokənd/ *adj literary* cheerful and good-humoured. ➤ **jocundity** /joh'kunditi, jə-/ *noun*, **jocundly** *adv*. [Middle English from late Latin *jocundus*, alteration of *jucundus* pleasant, from *juvare* to help, please]

jodhpurs /'jodpəz/ *pl noun* riding trousers cut full at the hips and close-fitting from knee to ankle. [named after *Jodhpur*, city in India, where men wear similar trousers as part of formal dress]

joe /joh/ *noun NAmer, informal* a fellow or guy. [*Joe*, nickname for *Joseph*]

Joe Bloggs /blogz/ *noun Brit, informal* any ordinary male member of the public; an average man.

Joe Blow /bloh/ *noun NAmer, informal* = JOE BLOGGS.

Joe Public *noun Brit, informal* the general public.

joey /'joh·i/ *noun* (*pl* **joeys**) *Aus* **1** a young kangaroo. **2** any young animal or a young child. [native name in Australia]

jog¹ /jog/ *verb* (**jogged, jogging**) ➤ *verb trans* **1** to give a slight shake or push to (something); to nudge. **2** to prompt (the memory). ➤ *verb intrans* **1** to run at a slow steady pace, *esp* to keep fit. **2** said of a horse or rider: to run or ride at a slow trot. **3** to go or progress at a slow, steady, or monotonous pace. **4** to move up and down with a short heavy motion. [variant of JAG¹]

jog² *noun* **1** a slight nudge or shake. **2** a period of running, or a distance run, at a slow, steady pace. **3** a jogging movement or pace.

jogger *noun* somebody who regularly jogs to keep fit.

joggle[1] /'jogl/ *verb trans and intrans informal* to move or shake slightly, or cause (something) to do so. ⟫⟫ **joggle** *noun.* [frequentative of JOG[1]]

joggle[2] *noun* **1** a notch or tooth in the surface of a piece of wood, building material, etc to join it to a neighbouring piece. **2** a peg or dowel for joining two neighbouring blocks of stone. [dimin of *jog* projecting part, prob alteration of JAG[2]]

joggle[3] *verb trans* to join (two things) with a joggle.

jog trot *noun* **1** a slow regular trot, e.g. of a horse. **2** a routine or monotonous progression.

john *noun* **1** *NAmer, informal* = TOILET (1). **2** *chiefly NAmer, informal* a prostitute's client. [from the name *John*]

John Barleycorn /'bahlikawn/ *noun* alcoholic liquor personified.

John Bull *noun* **1** the English nation personified. **2** a typical Englishman, *esp* regarded as truculently insular. [named after *John Bull*, character typifying the English nation in *The History of John Bull* by John Arbuthnot d.1735, Scots physician and writer]

John Doe *noun* **1** a person involved in legal proceedings or a crime whose true name is unknown or withheld. **2** *chiefly NAmer* an average man. [arbitrary name]

John Dory *noun* (*pl* **John Dories** *or collectively* **John Dory**) **1** a common European food fish, ranging in colour from yellow to olive, with an oval compressed body, long spines on its back, and a dark spot on each side: *Zeus faber*. **2** a closely related fish widely found in southern seas: *Zeus capensis*. [earlier *dory*, from Middle English *dorre*, from early French *doree* gilded one]

johnny /'joni/ *noun* (*pl* **johnnies**) *Brit, informal* **1** (*often* **Johnny**) a fellow or guy. **2** a condom. [*Johnny*, nickname for *John*]

Johnny-come-lately *noun* (*pl* **Johnny-come-latelies** *or* **Johnnies-come-lately**) a late or recent arrival; a newcomer.

Johnsonian /jon'sohni·ən/ *adj* relating to or characteristic of Samuel Johnson, his works, or his style of writing; *esp* having balanced phraseology and Latinate vocabulary. ⟫⟫ **Johnsonese** /jonsə'neez/ *noun.* [Samuel *Johnson* d.1784, English lexicographer and writer]

John Thomas /'toməs/ *noun Brit, euphem* a penis. [from the names *John* and *Thomas*]

joie de vivre /,zhwah də 'veevrə (*French* ʒwa də viːvr)/ *noun* keen enjoyment of life. [French *joie de vivre* joy of living]

join[1] /joyn/ *verb trans* **1a** to put or bring (two or more things) together so that they form a unit. **b** (*often* + up) to connect (e.g. points) by a line. **c** said of a river, road, etc: to meet or merge into (something): *where the river joins the sea.* **2** to put or bring (two people or things) into close association or relationship: *joined in marriage.* **3a** to enter into the company of (somebody): *Will you join us for lunch?* **b** (*usu* + in) to associate oneself with (somebody) in doing something: *My wife joins me in sending sincere thanks for your hospitality.* **c** to become a member or employee of (a club, organization, etc). ⟫ *verb intrans* **1** to come together so as to be connected. **2** to become a member of a group. **3** (*often* + in/with) to take part or associate oneself in an activity with other people. ✷ **join battle** to engage in battle or conflict. **join forces** to form an alliance, or to combine one's efforts to do something with those of somebody else. ⟫⟫ **joinable** *adj.* [Middle English *joinen* via Old French *joindre* from Latin *jungere*]

join[2] *noun* a place where two things or parts are joined.

joinder /'joyndə/ *noun* a joining in a legal action. [French *joindre*: see JOIN[1]]

joined up *adj* providing a coherent, integrated, and effective service: *joined up government.*

joiner *noun* **1** somebody who constructs or repairs wooden articles, *esp* furniture or fittings: compare CARPENTER[1]. **2** *informal* a gregarious person who joins many organizations.

joinery *noun* **1** the craft or trade of a joiner. **2** woodwork done or made by a joiner.

joint[1] /joynt/ *noun* **1** a place where two things or parts are joined. **2** a point of contact between two or more bones together with the surrounding and supporting parts. **3** a large piece of meat cut from a carcass and suitable for roasting. **4** a point on a plant stem at which a leaf or branch emerges. **5** a crack in rock not accompanied by dislocation. **6** the hinge of the binding of a book along the back edge of each cover. **7** *informal* a shabby or disreputable place of entertainment, café, etc. **8** *slang* a cannabis cigarette. **9** (**the joint**) *NAmer, slang* = PRISON. ✷ **out of joint 1** said of a bone: dislocated.

2 disordered or disorganized. ⟫⟫ **jointed** *adj,* **jointedly** *adv,* **jointedness** *noun.* [Middle English *jointe* from Old French *joindre*: see JOIN[1]]

joint[2] *adj* **1** united or combined: *a joint effort.* **2** common to, held by, shared by, or affecting two or more: *joint custody of the children.* **3** sharing with another: *joint heirs.* **4** being a function of or involving two or more random variables: *a joint probability density function.* [Middle English from early French, past part. of *joindre*: see JOIN[1]]

joint[3] *verb trans* **1** to provide (something) with a joint. **2** to fit (two things) together with a joint. **3** to prepare (e.g. a board) for joining by planing the edge. **4** to cut (e.g. meat) into joints.

joint account *noun* a bank account held by more than one person, e.g. a husband and wife.

joint and several *adj* said of a legal obligation: involving two or more people, each of whom is individually liable for the performance of the whole obligation.

jointer *noun* any of various tools used in making joints.

jointly *adv* sharing or in conjunction with one another; together.

joint stock *noun* capital held jointly and usu divided into shares between the owners.

joint-stock company *noun* a company consisting of individuals who own shares representing a joint stock of capital.

jointure /'joynchə/ *noun* property settled on a wife as provision for her widowhood. [Middle English via French from Latin *junctura*, from *jungere* to JOIN[1]]

join up *verb intrans* **1** to enlist in the armed forces. **2** to come together or link with something else. ⟫ *verb trans* = JOIN[1] (1A), (1B).

joist /joyst/ *noun* any of the parallel small timbers or metal beams that support a floor or ceiling. [Middle English *giste* from early French, from Latin *jacēre* to lie]

jojoba /hə'hohbə/ *noun* a shrub or small tree of the box family, native to N America, with edible seeds that yield a valuable wax similar in properties to sperm oil: *Simmondsia chinensis*. [Mexican Spanish *jojoba*]

joke[1] /johk/ *noun* **1a** something said or done to provoke laughter, *esp* a brief story with a humorous twist: compare PRACTICAL JOKE. **b** the humorous or ridiculous element in something. **c** an instance of joking or making fun: *She can't take a joke.* **d** = LAUGHING STOCK. **2** something of little difficulty or seriousness; a trifling matter: *That exam was a joke.* ✷ **be no joke** to be a serious matter. ⟫⟫ **jokey** *adj,* **joky** *adj.* [Latin *jocus* a jest or pun]

joke[2] *verb intrans* **1** to make jokes. **2** to speak facetiously. ⟫⟫ **jokingly** *adv.*

joker *noun* **1** somebody given to joking. **2** a playing card with a picture of a jester, added to a pack usu as a wild card. **3** *chiefly NAmer* an unsuspected minor clause in a document that greatly alters it. **4** *informal* an insignificant, obnoxious, or incompetent person. ✷ **the joker in the pack** a person or factor whose effect is unpredictable.

jolie laide /,zholi 'led (*French* ʒɔli lɛd)/ *noun* (*pl* **jolies laides** /,zholi 'led(z)/) a woman who, though not good-looking, has a manner and charm that make her attractive. [French *jolie laide*, literally 'pretty' ugly (woman)]

jollification /,jolifi'kaysh(ə)n/ *noun* merrymaking; a party, celebration, or other jolly occasion.

jollity /'joliti/ *noun* the quality or state of being jolly; merriment.

jolly[1] /'joli/ *adj* (**jollier, jolliest**) **1** cheerful, lively, and good-humoured. **2** expressing, suggesting, or inspiring gaiety. **3** *informal* extremely pleasant or agreeable: *I fancy I do like slang. I think it's awfully jolly to talk about things being jolly* — Trollope. **4** *Brit, euphem* slightly drunk. ⟫⟫ **jolliness** *noun.* [Middle English *jolif, joli* from Old French]

jolly[2] *adv informal* very: *It's jolly cold for the time of year.*

jolly[3] *verb trans* (**jollies, jollied, jollying**) **1** (+ along) to put (somebody) in good humour, *esp* in order to gain an objective. **2** *informal* (+ up) to make (somebody or something) more cheerful and lively.

jolly[4] *noun* (*pl* **jollies**) *chiefly Brit* an enjoyable excursion or a jollification: *rumbustious Australians out for a jolly* — Edward Heath. ✷ **get one's jollies** *informal* to derive pleasure from something.

jolly boat *noun* a ship's boat of medium size used for general work. [origin unknown]

Jolly Roger *noun* a pirate's black flag with a white skull and crossbones. [prob from JOLLY¹ + the name *Roger*, formerly a slang word for a thief]

jolt¹ /johlt/ *verb trans* **1** to make (something) move with a sudden jerky motion. **2** to give a sudden knock or blow to (something). **3** to disturb abruptly the composure of (somebody): *crudely jolted out of that mood* — Virginia Woolf. ➤ *verb intrans* to move with a jerky motion. [prob blend of obsolete *joll* to strike, and *jot* to bump, both of unknown origin]

jolt² *noun* an unsettling blow, movement, or shock. ➤➤ **jolty** *adj*.

Jon. *abbr* Jonah (book of the Bible).

Joneses /'johnziz/ ✱ **keep up with the Joneses** to compete with and attempt to impress one's friends and neighbours, *esp* by spending lavishly. [from a series 'Keeping up with the Joneses – by Pop' (pseudonym of cartoonist A Momand) which appeared in the *New York Globe* in 1913]

jongleur /zhong'gluh (*French* ʒɔ̃glœːr)/ *noun* a wandering medieval minstrel. [French *jongleur* from Old French *jogleour*: see JUGGLER]

jonquil /'jongkwil/ *noun* a Mediterranean plant of the narcissus family that is widely cultivated for its yellow or white fragrant flowers: *Narcissus jonquilla*. [French *jonquille* from Spanish *junquillo*, dimin. of *junco* reed, from Latin *juncus*]

Jordanian /jaw'dayniən/ *noun* a native or inhabitant of Jordan. ➤➤ **Jordanian** *adj*.

jorum /'jawrəm/ *noun* a large drinking vessel or its contents. [perhaps from *Joram* in the Bible who 'brought with him vessels of silver' (II Sam 8:10)]

Josh. *abbr* Joshua (book of the Bible).

josh¹ /josh/ *verb trans chiefly NAmer* to tease or make fun of (somebody). ➤ *verb intrans* to engage in banter; to joke. ➤➤ **josher** *noun*. [origin unknown]

josh² *noun chiefly NAmer* a good-humoured joke.

Joshua tree /'josh(y)ooə/ *noun* a tall yucca tree of the SW USA with sword-shaped leaves and clusters of greenish white flowers: *Yucca brevifolia*. [prob named after *Joshua* in the Old Testament, because the tree's branching shape resembles a man brandishing a spear (Joshua 8:18)]

joss /jos/ *noun* a Chinese religious statue or idol. [Javanese *dejus*, from Portuguese *deus* god, from Latin]

joss house *noun* a Chinese temple or shrine.

joss stick *noun* a slender stick of incense.

jostle /'josl/ *verb intrans* **1** to push and shove roughly against other people. **2** to make one's way by pushing and shoving. **3** to vie or compete with other people to gain an objective. ➤ *verb trans* **1** to push and shove (somebody) roughly. **2** to vie or compete with (somebody) to gain an objective. ➤➤ **jostle** *noun*. [alteration of *justle*, frequentative of JOUST²]

jot¹ /jot/ *noun* the least bit: *not a jot of evidence*. [Latin *iota, jota*: see IOTA]

jot² *verb trans* (**jotted, jotting**) (*usu* + down) to write (something) briefly or hurriedly: *You might want to jot this name down*.

jota /'khota/ *noun* a Spanish folk dance in fast triple time. [Spanish *jota*]

jotter *noun* a small book or pad for notes or memoranda.

jotting *noun* a brief note.

joual /zhooh'al/ *noun* a non-standard Canadian dialect of French. [from Canadian French dialect *joual* horse, alteration of French *cheval*]

joule /'joohl/ *noun* the SI unit of work or energy equal to the work done when a force of one newton moves its point of application through a distance of one metre. [named after James *Joule* d.1889, English physicist]

jounce /jowns/ *verb intrans* to jolt or bounce. ➤ *verb trans* to cause (something) to jolt or bounce. ➤➤ **jounce** *noun*. [Middle English *jouncen*; earlier history unknown]

journ. *abbr* journalistic.

journal /'juhnl/ *noun* **1a** a periodical dealing *esp* with specialist subjects: *a medical journal*. **b** a daily newspaper. **2** a daily record of business transactions. **3a** a private record of experiences, ideas, or reflections kept regularly; a diary. **b** a record of the transactions of a public body, learned society, etc. **c** = LOG¹ (2), (4). **4** the part of a rotating shaft, axle, roll, or spindle that turns in a bearing. [Middle English, in the sense 'service book containing the day hours', via early French *journal* daily, from Latin *diurnalis*, from *dies* day]

journal box *noun* a metal housing to support and protect a journal bearing.

journalese /juhn'leez/ *noun* a style of writing supposed to be characteristic of newspapers; *specif* loose or cliché-ridden writing.

journalise *verb trans and intrans* see JOURNALIZE.

journalism *noun* **1** the profession or activity of collecting and editing material of current interest for presentation through news media. **2** written material for publication in a newspaper or magazine.

journalist *noun* a person who works in journalism, *esp* one working for a newspaper or magazine. ➤➤ **journalistic** /-'listik/ *adj*.

journalize *or* **journalise** *verb trans and intrans* to record (information) in or keep a journal. ➤➤ **journalizer** *noun*.

journey¹ /'juhni/ *noun* (*pl* **journeys**) **1** an act of travelling from one place to another; a voyage or trip. **2** the distance involved in a journey, or the time taken to cover it. [Middle English *iournee* a day's journey, a day's work, via Old French from late Latin *diurnum* a day's portion, from Latin *dies* day]

journey² *verb intrans* (**journeys, journeyed, journeying**) to make a journey; to travel. ➤➤ **journeyer** *noun*.

journeyman *noun* (*pl* **journeymen**) **1** a worker who has learned a trade and is employed by another person, *usu* by the day. **2** an experienced and reliable worker or performer, as distinguished from one who is outstanding. [Middle English *iournee* (see JOURNEY¹) + MAN¹]

journo /'juhnoh/ *noun* (*pl* **journos**) *informal* a journalist. [by shortening and alteration]

joust¹ /jowst/ *noun* a combat on horseback between two knights armed with lances.

joust² *verb intrans* **1** to fight in a joust or tournament: *There are princes and knights come from all parts of the world to joust and tourney for her love* — Shakespeare. **2** (*often* + with) to engage in a contest or argument with somebody. ➤➤ **jouster** *noun*. [Middle English *jousten* from Old French *juster* to bring together, engage, ultimately from Latin *juxta* near]

Jove /johv/ ✱ **by Jove** used to express surprise or strong agreement. [*Jove*, a name for the Roman god Jupiter, from Latin *Jovis*]

jovial /'johvi·əl/ *adj* very or habitually good-humoured and cheerful. ➤➤ **joviality** /-'aliti/ *noun*, **jovially** *adj*. [via French from late Latin *jovialis* Jovian, from Latin *Jovis* Jupiter; because those born under the influence of the planet Jupiter were believed to have a cheerful nature]

Jovian /'johvi·ən/ *adj* characteristic of or relating to the god or planet Jupiter.

jowl¹ /jowl/ *noun* **1** the jaw; *esp* the lower jaw. **2** either of the cheeks. [Old English *ceafl*]

jowl² *noun* **1** (*also in pl*) usu slack and drooping flesh associated with the lower jaw or throat. **2** the dewlap of an animal or the wattle of a bird. [Old English *ceole* throat]

joy¹ /joy/ *noun* **1** a feeling of great happiness, pleasure, or delight. **2** a source or object of delight. **3** *Brit, informal* success or satisfaction: *We had no joy at the first shop we went into*. ➤➤ **joyless** *adj*, **joylessly** *adv*, **joylessness** *noun*. [Middle English via Old French *joie* from Latin *gaudium*, from *gaudēre* to rejoice]

joy² *verb intrans literary* (*usu* + in) to experience joy; to rejoice.

joyful /'joyf(ə)l/ *adj* filled with, causing, or expressing joy. ➤➤ **joyfully** *adv*, **joyfulness** *noun*.

joyous /'joyəs/ *adj* filled with, causing, or expressing joy; joyful. ➤➤ **joyously** *adv*, **joyousness** *noun*.

joyride *noun* a ride taken for pleasure in a car, *esp* one in a stolen car involving reckless driving. ➤➤ **joyrider** *noun*, **joyriding** *noun*.

joystick *noun* **1** a hand-operated lever that controls an aeroplane's elevators and ailerons. **2** a lever for controlling the image on a computer screen, *esp* in computer games. [perhaps from slang *joystick* penis]

JP *abbr* Justice of the Peace.

Jr *abbr* Junior.

jube /joohb/ *noun Aus, NZ, informal* a fruit-flavoured chewy sweet. [by shortening of JUJUBE]

jubilant /'joohbilənt/ *adj* filled with or expressing great joy or triumph. ➤➤ **jubilance** *noun*, **jubilantly** *adv*. [Latin *jubilant-, jubilans*, present part. of *jubilare* to rejoice]

Jubilate /joohbi'lahti/ *noun* the 100th Psalm sung liturgically in Catholic and Anglican churches, beginning *Jubilate deo*. [Latin *jubilate*, imperative of *jubilare* to rejoice]

jubilation /joohbi'laysh(ə)n/ *noun* a feeling or the expression of great joy and satisfaction; rejoicing. [Middle English *jubilacioun* from Latin *jubilation-, jubilatio*, from *jubilare* to rejoice]

jubilee /joohbi'lee, 'jooh-/ *noun* **1a** a special anniversary of an event such as a sovereign's accession, *esp* a 25th, 50th, or 60th anniversary. **b** a celebration of such an anniversary. **2** (*often* **Jubilee**) a year of emancipation and restoration provided by ancient Hebrew law to be kept every 50 years. **3** a period of time, proclaimed by the pope ordinarily every 25 years, during which a special INDULGENCE (exemption from the penalties of sin) is granted to Catholics who perform certain works of repentance and piety. [early French *jubilé* from late Latin *jubilaeus annus* jubilee year, ultimately from Hebrew *yōbhēl* ram's horn, jubilee; the beginning of Jubilee year was announced by blowing ram's-horn trumpets]

Jud. *abbr* Judith (book of the Apocrypha).

Judaean *or* **Judean** /jooh'deeən/ *noun* a native or inhabitant of Judaea, the ancient kingdom and Roman province forming the southern part of Palestine. ➤➤ **Judaean** *adj*.

Judaic /jooh'day·ik/ *adj* relating to or characteristic of Jews or Judaism. [via Latin from Greek *ioudaikos*, from *Ioudaios*: see JEW]

Judaical /jooh'day·ikl/ *adj* = JUDAIC.

Judaise /'joohdayiez/ *verb trans and intrans* see JUDAIZE.

Judaism /'joohdayiz(ə)m/ *noun* **1** the religious faith developed among the ancient Jews and characterized by belief in one God and by a religious life in accordance with scriptures and rabbinic traditions.

> **Editorial note**
> Judaism is a practical religion based on the belief that God has revealed through the written and oral law (the Torah) ways of obeying his commandments in every aspect of daily life. Within modern Judaism groups such as Reformed Judaism lay stress on carrying out the spirit of the commandments rather than their literal observance — Professor John Rogerson.

2 the cultural, social, and religious beliefs and practices of the Jews. [via late Latin from Greek *ioudaismos*, from *Ioudaios*: see JEW]

Judaize *or* **Judaise** /'joohdayiez/ *verb intrans* to adopt the customs, beliefs, or character of a Jew. ➤ *verb trans* to convert (somebody) to Judaism. ➤➤ **Judaization** /-'zaysh(ə)n/ *noun*.

Judas /'joohdəs/ *noun* somebody who betrays another, *esp* under the guise of friendship. [named after *Judas* Iscariot, the apostle who betrayed Christ (Matthew 26:47–50)]

judas *noun* a peephole in a door.

judas hole *noun* = JUDAS.

Judas tree *noun* a Eurasian tree of the pea family with purplish pink flowers that open before the leaves: *Cercis siliquastrum*. [from the belief that Judas Iscariot hanged himself from such a tree (Matthew 27:3–5)]

judder[1] /'judə/ *verb intrans* (**juddered, juddering**) *chiefly Brit* to vibrate jerkily. [prob alteration of SHUDDER[1]]

judder[2] *noun* a sharp vibration or jerky movement.

Judean /jooh'deeən/ *noun* see JUDAEAN.

Judg. *abbr* Judges (book of the Bible).

judge[1] /juj/ *verb trans* **1** to form an opinion about (something) through careful weighing of evidence. **2** to sit in judgment on (somebody), *esp* in a court of law. **3** to decide the result of (a competition or contest). **4** to determine or pronounce (something) after deliberation: *The film was judged to be unsuitable for children.* **5** to form an estimate or evaluation of (something): *It's difficult to judge the distance.* ➤ *verb intrans* **1** to form a judgment or opinion. **2** to act as a judge. [Middle English *juggen* via Old French from Latin *judicare*, from *judic-, judex* a judge, from *jus* right, law + *dicere* to decide, say]

judge[2] *noun* **1** a public official authorized to decide cases brought before a court. **2** somebody appointed to decide the winner of a competition or contest. **3** somebody who is qualified to give an opinion: *a good judge of character; a poor judge of modern art.* **4** (*often* **Judge**) a Hebrew tribal leader in the period after the death of

Joshua. ➤➤ **judgeship** *noun*. [Middle English *juge* via French from Latin *judex*: see JUDGE[1]]

judge advocate *noun* an officer appointed to superintend the trial and advise on law at a court martial.

judge advocate general *noun* the senior civil legal officer in control of court martials.

judgement *noun* see JUDGMENT.

judgemental /juj'mentl/ *adj* see JUDGMENTAL.

Judges' Rules *pl noun* formerly, in English law, the rules governing police interrogation of suspects.

judgment *or* **judgement** *noun* **1** the capacity for forming an opinion about something, or reaching a wise decision, through careful consideration of relevant facts. **2** an opinion or evaluation based on examining and comparing. **3a** a formal decision by a court or judge. **b** an obligation, e.g. a debt, created by a court decision. **4a** (**the Judgment/Last Judgment**) the final judging of humankind by God. **b** a calamity held to be sent by God as a punishment. ✱ **against one's better judgment** in spite of one's feeling that something is unwise.

> **Usage note**
> judgment *or* judgement? Either spelling is acceptable in all varieties of English. In British English, however, *judgement* is often used (with *judgment* in legal contexts), whereas in American English *judgment* is employed in all contexts.

judgmental *or* **judgemental** /juj'mentl/ *adj* **1** given to making moral judgments about other people's behaviour. **2** relating to the use of judgment.

Judgment Day *noun* the day of God's judgment of humankind at the end of the world, according to various theologies.

judicature /'joohdikəchə/ *noun* **1** the administration of justice. **2** = JUDICIARY (2). **3** the office or function of a judge. ➤➤ **judicatory** /-t(ə)ri/ *adj*. [early French via medieval Latin *judicatura* from Latin *judicatus*, past part. of *judicare*: see JUDGE[1]]

judicial /jooh'dish(ə)l/ *adj* **1** relating to a judgment, judging, justice, or the judiciary. **2** ordered by a court: *judicial separation.* **3** of, characterized by, or expressing judgment. ➤➤ **judicially** *adv*. [Middle English from Latin *judicialis*, from *judicium* judgment, from *judex*: see JUDGE[1]]

> **Usage note**
> judicial *or* judicious? These two words are sometimes confused. A *judicial* decision is one made by a court of law or by a judge; a *judicious* decision is one that shows wisdom and good judgment. A person can be described as *judicious* but not as *judicial*. *Judicial* is typically used in phrases such as *a judicial enquiry, judicial proceedings*, and *the British judicial system*.

judiciary /jooh'dishəri/ *noun* (*pl* **judiciaries**) **1** the branch of government concerned with the administration of justice. **2** the judges collectively who preside over a country's courts. **3** a system of courts of law. ➤➤ **judiciary** *adj*. [from Latin *judiciarius* judicial, from *judicium*: see JUDICIAL]

judicious /jooh'dishəs/ *adj* having, exercising, or characterized by sound judgment: *The learned, yet judicious research of etymology, the various, yet accurate display of definition, and the rich collection of authorities, were reserved for the superior mind of our great philologist* — James Boswell. ➤➤ **judiciously** *adv*, **judiciousness** *noun*.

> **Usage note**
> judicious *or* judicial? See note at JUDICIAL.

judo /'joohdoh/ *noun* a martial art developed from ju-jitsu and emphasizing the use of quick movement and leverage to throw an opponent. ➤➤ **judoist** *noun*. [Japanese *jūdō*, from *jū* weakness, gentleness + *dō* art]

Judy /'joohdi/ *noun* (*pl* **Judies**) *informal* a girl or young woman. [*Judy*, nickname for *Judith*]

jug[1] /jug/ *noun* **1** *chiefly Brit* a vessel for holding and pouring liquids that typically has a handle and a lip or spout. **2** *chiefly NAmer* a large deep earthenware or glass vessel for liquids that usu has a handle and a narrow mouth often fitted with a cork. **3** the contents of or quantity contained in a jug; a jugful. **4** *informal* prison: *He spent three years in jug.* **5** *coarse slang* (*in pl*) a woman's breasts. ➤➤ **jugful** *noun*. [perhaps from *Jug*, nickname for *Joan*]

jug[2] *verb trans* (**jugged, jugging**) **1** to stew (e.g. a hare) in an earthenware vessel. **2** *informal* to imprison (somebody).

juggernaut /'jugənawt/ *noun* **1** *chiefly Brit* a very large, usu articulated, lorry. **2** an inexorable force or object that crushes anything in its path.

Word history

Hindi *Jagannāth*, title of the God Vishnu, literally 'lord of the world'. It was formerly believed that devotees of Vishnu threw themselves beneath the wheels of a cart bearing his image in procession.

juggins /'juginz/ *noun (pl* **juggins** *or* **jugginses)** *informal or humorous, dated* a naive or simpleminded person; a simpleton. [prob from the name *Juggins*: compare MUGGINS]

juggle[1] /'jugl/ *verb* **(juggling)** ➤ *verb intrans* **1** to perform the tricks of a juggler. **2** to engage in manipulation, *esp* in order to achieve a desired end. ➤ *verb trans* **1** to toss and catch (things) in the manner of a juggler. **2** to deal with (several activities) at the same time through skilful organization. **3** to manipulate (e.g. facts or figures), *esp* in order to achieve a desired end. **4** to hold or balance (something) precariously. [Middle English *jogelen* via early French *jogler* from Latin *joculari* to joke, from *joculus*, dimin. of *jocus* JOKE[1]]

juggle[2] *noun* an act of juggling.

juggler *noun* a person skilled in keeping several objects in motion in the air at the same time by alternately tossing and catching them. ➤➤ **jugglery** *noun*. [Old English *geogelere* via Old French *jogleour* from Latin *joculator*, from *joculari*: see JUGGLE[1]]

jugular[1] /'jugyoolə/ *adj* **1a** relating to the throat or neck. **b** relating to the jugular vein. **2** said of a ventral fin of a fish: located on the throat. [late Latin *jugularis* from Latin *jugulum* collarbone, throat, dimin. of *jugum* yoke]

jugular[2] *noun* = JUGULAR VEIN.

jugular vein *noun* any of several veins of each side of the neck that return blood from the head.

juice[1] /joohs/ *noun* **1a** the liquid or moisture contained in something, *esp* in a fruit or vegetable. **b** a drink made from fruit or vegetable juice. **2a** the extractable fluid contents of cells or tissues. **b** (*in pl*) the natural fluids of the body. **3** *informal* a source of power, such as electricity or petrol. **4** the inherent quality of something, *esp* the basic force or strength of something. ➤➤ **juiceless** *adj*. [Middle English *jus* via Old French from Latin *jus* broth, juice]

juice[2] *verb trans* to extract the juice from (e.g. a fruit).

juice fasting *noun* a form of diet restricted to liquidized fruit and vegetables.

juicer *noun* an appliance for extracting juice from fruit or vegetables.

juice up *verb trans NAmer, informal* to liven (something) up.

juicy *adj* **(juicier, juiciest) 1** succulent; full of juice. **2** *informal* rich in interest, *esp* because of titillating content: *a juicy scandal*. **3** *informal* financially rewarding or profitable. ➤➤ **juicily** *adv*, **juiciness** *noun*.

ju-jitsu *or* **jiu-jitsu** /jooh 'jitsooh/ *noun* a martial art using holds, throws, and paralysing blows to subdue or disable an opponent. [Japanese *jūjutsu*, from *jū* weakness, gentleness + *jutsu* art]

juju /'joohjooh/ *noun* **1** a charm or FETISH (object believed to have magical power), of W African peoples. **2** the magic attributed to jujus. [of W African origin]

jujube /'joohjoohb/ *noun* **1a** a tree of the buckthorn family with small yellow flowers and dark red edible fruits: *Ziziphus jujuba*. **b** the edible berry-like fruit from this tree. **2** a fruit-flavoured gum or lozenge. [Middle English via medieval Latin *jujuba*, alteration of Latin *zizyphum*, from Greek *zizyphon*]

jukebox /'joohkboks/ *noun* a coin-operated machine that automatically plays records or CDs chosen from a restricted list. [Gullah *juke* disorderly, of W African origin]

Jul. *abbr* July.

julep /'joohlip/ *noun chiefly NAmer* a drink consisting of a spirit and sugar poured over crushed ice and garnished with mint. [Middle English, in the sense 'syrupy liquid', via French and Arabic from Persian *gulāb*, from *gul* rose + *āb* water]

Julian calendar /'joohli-ən/ *noun* a calendar introduced in Rome in 46 BC establishing the twelve-month year of 365 days with an extra day every fourth year: compare GREGORIAN CALENDAR. [named after Gaius *Julius* Caesar d.44 BC, Roman general and statesman, who introduced it]

julienne[1] /joohli'en/ *noun* **1** vegetables cut into long thin strips used as a garnish. **2** a clear soup containing julienne vegetables. [French *julienne*, prob from the name *Jules, Julien*]

julienne[2] *adj* cut into long thin strips: *julienne potatoes; green beans julienne*.

juliet cap /'joohli-ət, -et/ *noun* a woman's small close-fitting brimless cap worn *esp* by brides. [named after *Juliet*, heroine of Shakespeare's tragedy *Romeo and Juliet*]

July /joo'lie/ *noun* the seventh month of the year. [Old English *Julius* from Latin, named after Gaius *Julius* Caesar (see JULIAN CALENDAR), whose birthday fell in this month]

jumble[1] /'jumbl/ *verb trans* (*often* + up) to mix (things) up in a confused or disordered manner. [perhaps imitative]

jumble[2] *noun* **1** a mass or collection of things mingled together without order or plan. **2** *Brit* articles for a jumble sale.

jumble sale *noun Brit* a sale of donated secondhand articles, usu to raise money for some charitable purpose.

jumbo /'jumboh/ *noun (pl* **jumbos) 1** a very large specimen of its kind. **2** a jumbo jet. ➤➤ **jumbo** *adj*. [prob from MUMBO JUMBO, influenced in meaning by *Jumbo*, the name of a huge elephant exhibited in London and the USA in the late 19th cent.]

jumbo jet *noun* a large jet aeroplane capable of carrying several hundred passengers.

jumbuck /'jumbuk/ *noun Aus, informal* = SHEEP. [origin unknown]

jump[1] /jump/ *verb intrans* **1** to spring into the air, *esp* using the muscular power of the feet and legs. **2** to move quickly or energetically, e.g. in getting on or off a vehicle. **3** to move suddenly or involuntarily from shock, surprise, etc. **4** to pass rapidly or abruptly from one point or state to another. **5** said of prices, etc: to undergo a sudden sharp increase. **6** to parachute from an aircraft. **7** (+ on/upon) to make a sudden verbal or physical attack. **8** to bustle with activity. ➤ *verb trans* **1a** to leap over (something). **b** to make (e.g. a horse) leap over an obstacle. **c** to support or catch (somebody who is jumping): *The ladies ... were contented to pass quietly and carefully down the steep flight [of steps], excepting Louisa; she must be jumped down them by Captain Wentworth* — Jane Austen. **d** to pass over (something), *esp* to a point beyond; to skip or bypass (something): *You've jumped a couple of lines*. **e** to move over (a piece) in a board game such as draughts or chess. **2a** to act, move, or begin before (e.g. a signal). **b** to fail to stop at (a traffic light). **3** to become dislodged from (e.g. a track or groove): *The train jumped the rails*. **4** to make a sudden or surprise attack on (somebody). **5a** to fail to honour (an obligation, e.g. bail). **b** *chiefly NAmer* to leave or escape from (a place) hastily. **6a** to usurp (a claim to land) without proper legal rights. **b** *chiefly NAmer* to leap aboard (e.g. a train), *esp* so as to travel illegally. **7** *NAmer, coarse slang* to have sexual intercourse with (somebody). **8** in bridge, to raise (a partner's bid) by more than is necessary, usu to indicate a strong hand. ✷ **jump at something** to accept (e.g. a chance) eagerly. **jump down somebody's throat** to speak, *esp* to reply, to somebody in a very angry or hostile way. **jump ship** said of a crew member: to leave a ship in violation of one's contract of employment. **jump the queue 1** to move in front of others in a queue. **2** to obtain an unfair advantage over others who have been waiting longer. **jump to it 1** to make an enthusiastic start. **2** to hurry. [origin unknown]

jump[2] *noun* **1a** an act of jumping; a leap. **b** a height or distance cleared by a jump. **2** a sports contest involving a jump: *the long jump*. **3** an obstacle to be jumped over, e.g. in a horse race. **4** a sudden involuntary movement; a start. **5** a descent by parachute from an aircraft. **6** a sudden sharp increase, e.g. in amount, price, or value. **7a** a sudden change or transition, *esp* one that leaves a break in continuity. **b** any of a series of moves from one place or position to another; a move. **8** (**the jumps**) *informal* extreme nervousness or restlessness. ✷ **be one jump ahead of somebody** to preempt somebody or gain an advantage over them. **get the jump on somebody** to get somebody at a disadvantage by acting quickly. **take a running jump** used as a rude way of indicating that one is totally unconcerned about somebody.

jumped-up *adj derog* recently risen in wealth, rank, or status.

jumper[1] /'jumpə/ *noun* **1** *Brit* a usu knitted garment worn on the upper body. **2** *NAmer* = PINAFORE (2). [prob from English dialect *jump* loose jacket, perhaps alteration of Scots *jupe* via Old French from Arabic *jubbah*]

jumper[2] *noun* **1** a jumping animal, *esp* a horse trained to jump obstacles. **2** a short wire used to close a break in or bypass part of a circuit. **3** a heavy power drill or drilling bit that works with a hammer action, used *esp* in quarrying for drilling blast holes.

jumping bean *noun* a seed of any of several Mexican shrubs of the spurge family that tumbles about because of the movements of the larva of a small moth inside it.

jumping jack *noun* a firework that jumps about when lit.

jumping-off place *noun* a place or point from which an enterprise is launched.

jumping-off point *noun* = JUMPING-OFF PLACE.

jump-jet *noun chiefly Brit* a jet aircraft able to take off and land vertically.

jump jockey *noun Brit, informal* a jockey who rides in steeplechases.

jump leads /'leedz/ *pl noun* two lengths of thick cable used to start a motor vehicle with a flat battery by connecting its terminals to those of another battery, usu in another vehicle.

jump-off *noun* the final round, *esp* an extra deciding round, of a showjumping competition.

jump seat *noun* a folding seat for temporary use in a vehicle or aircraft.

jump start *noun* the starting of a motor vehicle's engine using jump leads.

jump-start *verb trans* to start (a motor vehicle or its engine) with jump leads.

jumpsuit *noun* a one-piece garment combining top and trousers or shorts.

jumpy *adj* (**jumpier, jumpiest**) **1** nervous or jittery. **2** having jumps or sudden variations. ➤➤ **jumpiness** *noun*.

Jun. *abbr* June.

jun /jun/ *noun* (*pl* **jun**) a unit of currency in North Korea, worth 100th of a won. [Korean *jun*]

junco /'jungkoh/ *noun* (*pl* **juncos** *or* **juncoes**) any of a genus of small widely distributed American finches with grey and brown plumage: genus *Junco*. [Latin genus name, from Spanish *junco* reed]

junction /'jungksh(ə)n/ *noun* **1** the act of joining or being joined. **2a** an intersection of roads or railway lines, *esp* where one terminates by joining the other. **b** a point on a motorway where traffic joins or leaves it. **3** a place where things meet or join. **4** a point of contact or interface between dissimilar metals or semiconductor regions. ➤➤ **junctional** *adj*. [Latin *junction-, junctio,* from *jungere* to JOIN¹]

junction box *noun* a box containing connections between separate electric circuits.

juncture /'jungkchə/ *noun* **1** a point of time, *esp* a critical one: *'We have perfect confidence in you, Mr Micawber,' ... 'Mr Copperfield,' returned Mr Micawber, 'your confidence is not, at the existing juncture, ill-placed.'* — Dickens. **2** an instance or place of joining; a connection or joining part.

June /joohn/ *noun* the sixth month of the year. [early French *Juin* from Latin *Junius mensis* month of June, named after the goddess Juno]

june bug *noun* = CHAFER.

Jungian /'yoongi-ən/ *adj* relating to or characteristic of the psychoanalytical psychology of Carl Jung.

Editorial note
Jungian denotes the theories of Carl Jung who was initially a follower of Freud. However, Jung questioned Freud's emphasis on sexual libido, and developed his own more metaphysical account of mind – with the 'collective unconscious', seeing 'archetype' symbols, especially of alchemy, as significant. At a more down to earth level, he described extraversion–introversion personality types — Professor Richard Gregory.

➤➤ **Jungian** *noun*. [Carl *Jung* d.1961, Swiss psychologist]

jungle /'junggl/ *noun* **1** an area overgrown with thickets or masses of trees and other vegetation, *esp* in the tropics. **2a** a confused, disordered, or complex mass: *the jungle of tax laws.* **b** a place of ruthless struggle for survival. **3** a type of fast electronic dance music derived from ragga, popular in the 1990s. ➤➤ **jungly** *adj*. [Hindi *janṅgal* wasteland, from Sanskrit *jāṅgala* dry]

jungle fever *noun* a severe malarial fever.

jungle fowl *noun* any of several species of Asian wild birds from which domestic fowls are thought to have descended: genus *Gallus*.

jungle juice *noun informal* alcoholic liquor, *esp* strong or crude homemade liquor.

junior¹ /'joohnyə/ *noun* **1** a person who is younger than another: *She is three years my junior.* **2a** a person holding a lower or subordinate rank. **b** a member of a younger form in a school, sports team, etc. **3** in England and Australia, a barrister who is not a Queen's Counsel, *esp* one who is assisting a senior barrister in the conduct of a case. **4** *NAmer* a student in the penultimate year before graduating. **5** *NAmer, informal* a male child; a son. [Latin *junior*: see JUNIOR²]

junior² *adj* **1** used, *esp* in the USA, to distinguish a son with the same name as his father. **2** lower in standing or rank. **3a** for children aged from seven to eleven: *a junior school.* **b** of, for, or comprising younger pupils, players, etc: *the junior team.* [Latin *junior,* compar of *juvenis* young]

junior college *noun* a US college that offers two years of studies corresponding to the first two years of a four-year college course.

Junior Common Room *noun* a common room for students, pupils, etc.

junior lightweight *noun* a weight in professional boxing of 57.1–59.0kg (126–130lb).

junior middleweight *noun* a weight in professional boxing of 66.7–69.9kg (147–154lb).

junior school *noun* a primary school for children aged from seven to eleven.

junior technician *noun* a member of the Royal Air Force ranking below a corporal.

junior welterweight *noun* a weight in professional boxing of 61.0–63.5kg (135–140lb).

juniper /'joohnipə/ *noun* any of a genus of evergreen shrubs or trees of the cypress family with small purple cones resembling berries that are sometimes used to flavour gin and in cooking: genus *Juniperus*. [Middle English *junipere* from Latin *juniperus*]

junk¹ /jungk/ *noun* **1a** secondhand or discarded articles or material; rubbish. **b** something of little value or inferior quality. **2** *slang* narcotics, *esp* heroin. ➤➤ **junky** *adj*. [Middle English *jonke*; earlier history unknown]

junk² *verb trans informal* to get rid of (something) as worthless.

junk³ *noun* a sailing ship used in the Far East with a high poop and overhanging stem, usu no keel, and lugsails often stiffened with horizontal battens. [Portuguese *junco* from Javanese *jonṅ*]

junk bond *noun* a high-yield speculative security, *esp* one issued to finance an intended takeover.

Junker /'yoongkə/ *noun* a member of the Prussian landed aristocracy. ➤➤ **Junkerdom** *noun*. [German *Junker,* ultimately from Old High German *junc* young + *herre* lord]

junket¹ /'jungkit/ *noun* **1** a dessert of sweetened flavoured milk curdled with rennet. **2** *chiefly informal* a trip made by an official, business person, etc at public or a firm's expense.

Word history
Middle English *ioncate* rush basket, ultimately from Latin *juncus* rush. In the 15th cent. the word referred to a kind of cream cheese made in a rush basket or served on a rush mat, later to other dishes made with cream; (sense 2) from a 16th-cent. sense 'feast, banquet'.

junket² *verb intrans* (**junketed, junketing**) *informal* to go on a junket. ➤➤ **junketeer** /-'tiə/ *noun,* **junketer** *noun*.

junk food *noun* processed food that typically has a high carbohydrate content but overall low nutritional value: compare HEALTH FOOD, WHOLEFOOD.

junkie *or* **junky** /'jungki/ *noun* (*pl* **junkies**) *informal* a drug addict. [JUNK¹ (2) + -IE, -Y¹]

junk mail *noun* unsolicited mail, e.g. advertising material.

junk shop *noun* a shop selling secondhand articles or usu inferior antique goods.

junky /'jungki/ *noun* see JUNKIE.

Junoesque /joohnoh'esk/ *adj* said of a woman: tall, stately, and imposing in appearance: *She seldom ran – it did not suit her style, she thought, for, being tall, the stately and Junoesque was more appropriate than the sportive or piquante* — Louisa M Alcott. [*Juno,* ancient Roman goddess, wife of Jupiter]

junta /'juntə/ *noun* (*treated as sing. or pl*) **1** a political council or committee, *esp* a group controlling a government after a revolution. **2** = JUNTO. [Spanish *junta,* fem of *junto* joined, from Latin *jungere* to JOIN¹]

junto /'juntoh/ *noun* (*pl* **juntos**) (*treated as sing. or pl*) a group of people joined for a common purpose. [prob alteration of JUNTA]

jural /'jooərəl/ *adj* relating to law, rights, or obligations. ➤➤ **jurally** *adv.* [Latin *jur-, jus* law]

Jurassic /joo'rasik/ *adj* relating to or dating from a geological period, the second period of the Mesozoic era, lasting from about 208 million to about 146 million years ago, and marked by the dominance of large reptiles and the first appearance of birds. ➤➤ **Jurassic** *noun.* [French *jurassique*, from the *Jura* mountain range between France and Switzerland, largely formed during this period]

jurat /'jooərat/ *noun* **1** a certificate added to an AFFIDAVIT (sworn declaration in writing) stating when, before whom, and where it was made. **2** *Brit.* **a** an officer, *esp* of the Cinque Ports of the SE coast of England, similar in function to an ALDERMAN (member of English borough or county council). **b** a magistrate in the Channel Islands. [(sense 2) Middle English *jurate* from medieval Latin *juratus*, past part. of *jurare* to swear; (sense 1) short for Latin *juratum est* it has been sworn]

juridical /joo'ridikl/ *adj* **1** = JUDICIAL (1). **2** relating to jurisprudence; legal: *juridical terms.* ➤➤ **juridically** *adv.* [Latin *juridicus*, from *jur-, jus* law + *dicere* to say]

jurisconsult /jooəris'konsult/ *noun* = JURIST. [Latin *jurisconsultus*, from *jur-, jus* of law + *consultus*, past part. of *consulere* to CONSULT]

jurisdiction /jooəris'diksh(ə)n/ *noun* **1** the power, right, or authority to apply the law. **2** the authority of a sovereign power. **3** the limits within which authority may be exercised. ➤➤ **jurisdictional** *adj*, **jurisdictionally** *adv.* [Middle English *jurisdiccioun* via Old French from Latin *jurisdiction-, jurisdictio*, from *jur-, jus* law + *diction-, dictio* act of saying, from *dicere* to say]

jurisprudence /jooəris'proohd(ə)ns/ *noun* **1** the science or philosophy of the law: *criminal jurisprudence.* **2** a branch or body of law. ➤➤ **jurisprudential** /-prooh'densh(ə)l/ *adj.* [late Latin *jurisprudentia*, from Latin *jur-, jus* law + *prudentia* knowledge]

jurist /'jooərist/ *noun* **1** somebody with a thorough knowledge of law. **2** *NAmer* a lawyer or a judge. [early French *juriste* from medieval Latin *jurista*, from *jur-, jus* law]

juristic /joo'ristik/ *adj* relating to a jurist, jurisprudence, or law. ➤➤ **juristically** *adv.*

juristical /joo'ristikl/ *adj* = JURISTIC.

juror /'jooərə/ *noun* **1** a member of a jury. **2** a person who takes an oath.

jury¹ /'jooəri/ *noun* (*pl* **juries**) **1** a body of usu twelve people who hear evidence in court and give a verdict, *esp* of guilty or not guilty, based on this evidence. **2** a committee for judging a contest or exhibition. ✳ **the jury is still out (on something)** a decision has not yet been reached, *esp* as to the correctness or worth of something. [Middle English *jure* from Old French *jurer* to swear, ultimately from Latin *jur-, jus* law]

jury² /'jooəri/ *adj* improvised for temporary use, *esp* in an emergency: *a jury rig for a sailing boat.* [origin unknown]

jury box *noun* the part of a courtroom where the jury sits during a trial.

juryman *noun* (*pl* **jurymen**) = JUROR (1).

jury-rigged *adj* **1** improvised for temporary use. **2** said of a ship: with an improvised mast, spars, and tackle.

jurywoman *noun* (*pl* **jurywomen**) a female member of a jury.

jussive /jusiv/ *noun* a word, form, case, or mood expressing command. ➤➤ **jussive** *adj.* [Latin *jussus*, past part. of *jubēre* to order]

just¹ /just/ *adj* **1** acting or being in conformity with what is morally upright or equitable; honest and impartial. **2a** being what is merited; deserved. **b** legally correct. **3a** conforming to fact or reason; well-founded. **b** conforming to a standard of correctness; proper. ➤➤ **justly** *adv*, **justness** *noun.* [Middle English via French from Latin *justus*, from *jus* right, law]

just² *adv* **1** exactly or precisely: *The temperature is just right; This is just the thing for your cold.* **2** at the moment in question or within a very short time before or after: *He's only just arrived; I'm just coming.* **3** by a very small margin; barely: *We arrived just too late; This is only just possible.* **4** only or simply: *just a short note.* **5** quite: *not just yet.* **6** *informal* very or completely: *just wonderful.* **7** *informal* expressing ironic agreement: *didn't he just!* ✳ **just about 1** almost. **2** not more than: *There's just about room in here to cook.* **just in case** as a precaution. **just now 1** at this moment. **2** a moment ago. **just so 1** tidily

arranged: *Everything in the room was just so.* **2** used to express agreement. **just the same** nevertheless; even so.

justice /'justis/ *noun* **1** the quality or principle of being just, impartial, or fair. **2a** the maintenance or administration of what is just: *Though justice be thy plea, consider this – that in the course of justice, none of us should see salvation; we do pray for mercy* — Shakespeare. **b** the administration of law in accordance with established principles: *court of justice.*

Editorial note ───────────────────
Justice is the right result, a seemly or appropriate end, especially to litigation (for example, by conviction of the guilty or acquittal of the innocent). It is a compassionate decision – hence Portia's 'mercy seasons justice' speech in The Merchant of Venice – but always preceded by accurate determination of facts. Justice cannot be predetermined: in court, it is the result of a game, played fairly according to the rules of law — Geoffrey Robertson.

3 conformity to truth, fact, or reason. **4a** a judge or magistrate. **b** *Brit* used as a title for a judge: *Mr Justice Smith.* ✳ **bring to justice** to arrest (somebody) and try them in a court of law. **do justice to 1** to treat (somebody or something) fairly or adequately. **2** to show due appreciation for (somebody or something). **3** to show (something or somebody, *esp* oneself) in the best light: *I hope he did himself justice in the interview.* [Middle English via Old French from Latin *justitia*, from *justus*: JUST¹]

justice of the peace *noun* a lay magistrate empowered chiefly to administer summary justice in minor cases.

justiciable /ju'stishi-əbl/ *adj* **1** liable to trial: *a justiciable offence.* **2** able to be decided legally: *a justiciable issue.* ➤➤ **justiciability** /-'biliti/ *noun.*

justiciar /ju'stishiah/ *noun* the chief political and judicial officer of the Norman and later kings of England until the 13th cent. [Middle English from medieval Latin *justitiarius*, from Latin *justitia*: see JUSTICE]

justiciary¹ /ju'stishi-əri/ *noun* (*pl* **justiciaries**) **1** an administrator of justice. **2** the administration of justice.

justiciary² *adj* relating to the administration of justice.

justifiable /'justifie-əbl, -'fie-əbl/ *adj* capable of being justified; defensible. ➤➤ **justifiability** /-'biliti/ *noun*, **justifiably** *adv.*

justifiable homicide *noun* an act of killing a person, e.g. in self-defence or in carrying out a judicial death sentence, to which no legal blame attaches.

justify /'justifie/ *verb trans* (**justifies, justified, justifying**) **1** to prove or show (something) to be just, right, or reasonable. **2** to space out (e.g. a line of printed text) so that it is flush with a margin. **3** to extend freedom from the consequences of sin to (somebody), e.g. by Christ's righteousness. ➤➤ **justification** /-fi'kaysh(ə)n/ *noun*, **justificatory** /-fi'kayt(ə)ri/ *adj*, **justifier** *noun.* [Middle English *justifien* via French from late Latin *justificare* from Latin *justus* (see JUST¹) + *facere* to make, do]

just-in-time *noun* a technique of inventory management that enables industrial production to be keyed precisely to demand, rather than building up large stocks in advance of orders. ➤➤ **just-in-time** *adj.*

jut¹ /jut/ *verb intrans* (**jutted, jutting**) (*often* + out) to extend out, up, or forwards; to project or protrude. [partly variant of JET², in the sense 'to project'; partly short for obsolete *jutty* to project, from Middle English *jutteyen*]

jut² *noun* something that juts out.

Jute /jooht/ *noun* a member of a Germanic people that invaded England, *esp* Kent, along with the Angles and Saxons in the fifth cent. AD. ➤➤ **Jutish** *adj.* [Middle English from medieval Latin *Jutae* Jutes, of Germanic origin]

jute *noun* the glossy fibre of either of two E Indian plants of the linden family used chiefly for sacking and twine. [Hindi and Bengali *jūt*]

juvenescence /joohvə'nes(ə)ns/ *noun formal* the state of being or becoming youthful. ➤➤ **juvenescent** *adj.* [Latin *juvenescent-, juvenescens*, present part of *juvenescere* to reach the age of youth, become young again, from *juvenis* young, young person]

juvenile¹ /'joovəniel/ *adj* **1** characteristic of or suitable for children or young people. **2** physiologically immature or undeveloped. ➤➤ **juvenilely** *adv*, **juvenility** /-'niliti/ *noun.* [French *juvénile* from Latin *juvenilis*, from *juvenis* young, young person]

juvenile² *noun* **1** a young person. **2** a young individual resembling an adult of its kind except in size and reproductive activity. **3** an actor who plays youthful parts.

juvenile court *noun* a court with special jurisdiction over young people.

juvenile delinquent *noun* a child or young person below a particular age who has committed a criminal offence or who habitually commits criminal offences. ➤➤ **juvenile delinquency** *noun*.

juvenile hormone *noun* an insect hormone that controls the maturation of the IMAGO (final state of an insect's development) and plays a role in reproduction.

juvenilia /joohvə'nili·ə/ *pl noun* artistic or literary works produced in an artist's or author's youth: *Had [Mary] Leapor survived she might have burned some of her unpublished verses as she did her juvenilia —* Richard Greene. [Latin *juvenilia*, neuter pl of *juvenilis*: see JUVENILE[1]]

juxtapose /jukstə'pohz/ *verb trans* to place (two or more things) side by side: *Between the mother ... and the daughter ... there was a gap of two hundred years as ordinarily understood. When they were together, the Jacobean and Victorian ages were juxtaposed —* Hardy. ➤➤ **juxtaposition** /-pə'zish(ə)n/ *noun*, **juxtapositional** /-pə'zish(ə)nl/ *adj.* [French *juxtaposer*, from Latin *juxta* near + French *poser*: see POSE[1]]

K¹ *or* **k** *noun* (*pl* **K's** *or* **Ks** *or* **k's**) **1a** the eleventh letter of the English alphabet. **b** a written character or design denoting this letter. **c** the sound represented by this letter, one of the English consonants. **2** an item designated as K, *esp* the eleventh in a series.

K² *abbr* **1** Kampuchea (international vehicle registration for Cambodia). **2** kelvin. **3** kilobit. **4** kilobyte. **5** in chess or card games, king. **6** Köchel (number). **7** *informal* thousand. [(sense 7) KILO-]

K³ *abbr* the chemical symbol for potassium. [scientific Latin *kalium*]

k *abbr* **1** carat. **2** kilo-.

ka /kah/ *noun* the spirit of an individual, believed by the ancient Egyptians to survive after death: compare BA². [Egyptian *ka*]

Kaaba *or* **Caaba** /'kahbə/ *noun* a small building in the court of the Great Mosque at Mecca that contains a black stone and is a focus of Islamic pilgrimage. [Arabic *ka'bah* square building]

kabaddi /kə'bahdi/ *noun* a team game of Indian origin that involves chasing and trying to touch opponents without being captured by them. [Tamil *kabaddi*]

kabala *or* **kabbala** *or* **kabbalah** /kə'bahlə/ *noun* see CABALA.

Kabinett /kabi'net/ *noun* a high-quality German wine with no added sugar, usu a light dry white table wine. [German *Kabinett-wein*, literally 'chamber wine'; from the cellar in which the wine was orig kept]

kabuki /kə'boohki/ *noun* traditional Japanese popular drama with singing and dancing performed in a highly stylized manner by males only. [Japanese *kabuki* art of singing and dancing, from *ka* song + *bu* dance + *ki* art, skill]

Kabyle /kə'biel/ *noun* **1** a member of a Berber people of the mountainous coastal area E of Algiers. **2** the language of this people. [Arabic *qabā'il*, pl of *qabīlah* tribe]

kaddish /'kadish/ *noun* (*often* **Kaddish**) a Jewish prayer recited in the daily ritual of the synagogue and by mourners after the death of a close relative. [Aramaic *qaddīsh* holy]

kadi /'kahdi, 'kaydi/ *noun* see QADI.

Kaffir *or* **Kafir** /'kafə/ *noun* (*often* **kaffir**) *chiefly SAfr, derog, offensive* a black S African. [Arabic *kāfir* infidel, from *kafara* to disbelieve]

kaffirboom /'kafəboom/ *noun* a S African deciduous flowering tree. [KAFFIR + Afrikaans *boom* tree]

kaffir corn *noun* a variety of sorghum grown in southern Africa for its grain and as fodder: *Sorghum caffrorum*.

Kaffir lily *noun* **1** a plant of the iris family with fleshy strap-shaped leaves and showy usu red funnel-shaped flowers: *Schizo-stylis coccinea*. **2** a plant of the daffodil family with strap-shaped fleshy leaves and showy funnel-shaped flowers: *Clivia miniata*.

kaffiyeh /kə'fee(y)ə/ *noun* see KEFFIYEH.

Kafir /'kafə/ *noun* **1** a member of a people of the Hindu Kush mountain range in NE Afghanistan. **2** see KAFFIR. [Arabic *kāfir*: see KAFFIR]

Kafkaesque /kafkə'esk/ *adj* suggestive of the writings of Franz Kafka, *esp* in expressing the anxieties of 20th-cent. people and their sense of isolation and unreality. [Franz *Kafka* d.1924, Austrian writer]

kaftan *or* **caftan** /'kaftan/ *noun* a loose ankle-length garment with long sleeves, traditionally worn in Arab countries. [Russian *kaftan* via Turkish from Persian *qaftān*]

kagoul /kə'goohl/ *noun* see CAGOULE.

kahawai /'kah·həwie, 'kah·wie/ *noun* (*pl* **kahawais** *or collectively* **kahawai**) a marine food fish of the perch family found in New Zealand and Australia: *Arripis trutta*. [Maori *kahawai*]

kai /kie/ *noun* NZ food. [Maori *kai*]

kail /kayl/ *noun* see KALE.

kailyard /'kaylyahd/ *noun* see KALEYARD.

kainite /'kieniet, 'kayniet/ *noun* a white mineral containing magnesium sulphate and potassium chloride that is used as a fertilizer. [German *Kainit*, from Greek *kainos* new]

kaiser /'kieza/ *noun* **1** an emperor of Germany during the period from 1871 to 1918. **2** in former times, the emperor of Austria or the head of the Holy Roman Empire. [German *Kaiser*, from Old High German *keisur* emperor, ultimately from Latin *Caesar*, cognomen of Roman emperors]

kaizen /kie'zen/ *noun* in business and industry, a Japanese philosophy of continuous improvement in quality, efficiency, productivity, etc. [Japanese *kaizen* improvement]

kaka /'kahkə/ *noun* an olive brown New Zealand parrot with grey and red markings: *Nestor meridionalis*. [Maori *kaka*]

kakapo /'kahkəpoh/ *noun* (*pl* **kakapos**) a chiefly nocturnal burrowing New Zealand parrot with green and brown plumage: *Strigops habroptilus*. [Maori *kakapo* night kaka]

kakemono /kaki'mohnoh/ *noun* (*pl* **kakemonos**) a Japanese painting or inscription on a silk or paper scroll designed to be hung on a wall. [Japanese *kakemono*, literally 'hanging thing']

kala-azar /,kahlə ə'zah, ,kalə/ *noun* a severe infectious disease, chiefly of Asia, marked *esp* by fever and enlargement of the spleen and liver and caused by a protozoan transmitted by the bite of sand flies. [Hindi *kālā-āzār* black disease, from *kālā* black + Persian *āzār* disease]

kalanchoe /kalən'koh·i/ *noun* a tropical succulent plant with clusters of small brightly coloured tubular flowers that is widely grown as a pot plant: genus *Kalanchoe*. [via Latin and French from Chinese *galancai*]

Kalashnikov /kə'lashnikof/ *noun* a type of automatic rifle made in Russia: *Mogadishu ... a trigger-happy city where children as young as 10 roam the streets brandishing Kalashnikovs* — Robert Fisk. [named after Mikhail *Kalashnikov* b.1919, its Russian designer]

kale *or* **kail** /kayl/ *noun* a hardy cabbage with curled often finely cut leaves that do not form a dense head: *Brassica oleracea acephala*. [Scots *kale*, from Old English *cāl*: see COLE]

kaleidoscope /kə'liedəskohp/ *noun* **1** a tubular instrument containing loose chips of coloured glass between flat plates and mirrors so placed that an endless variety of symmetrical patterns is produced as the instrument is rotated. **2** something that is continually changing, *esp* a variegated pattern or scene or a succession of events: *the kaleidoscope of European affairs*. ➤➤ **kaleidoscopic** /-'skopik/ *adj*, **kaleidoscopically** /-'chopikli/ *adv* [Greek *kalos* beautiful + *eidos* form + -SCOPE]

kalends /'kaləndz/ *pl noun* see CALENDS.

kaleyard *or* **kailyard** *noun* **1** *Scot* a cabbage patch or vegetable garden. **2** a late 19th-cent. literary movement specializing in a parochial and sentimentalized depiction of Scottish Lowland life: *It certainly wasn't dull: old Thingmyjig up from Bloomsbury trailing a kaleyard scribbler* — Scottish Field. [Scots]

kaleyard school *noun* = KALEYARD (2).

kalied /'kaylied/ *adj NW England, informal* drunk.

kalmia /'kalmi-ə/ *noun* an evergreen shrub of the heather family with showy clusters of flowers: genus *Kalmia*. [Latin genus name, named after Peter *Kalm* d.1779, Swedish botanist]

Kalmuck /'kalmuk/ *or* **Kalmyk** /'kalmik/ *noun* (*pl* **Kalmucks** *or collectively* **Kalmuck** *or* **Kalmyks** *or collectively* **Kalmyk**) **1** a member of a group of Mongolian peoples inhabiting a region stretching from W China to the Caspian Sea. **2** the Mongolian language of these peoples. [Russian *Kalmyk*]

kalong *noun* a fruit-eating bat of SE Asia: *Pteropus vampyrus*. [Javanese *kalong*]

kalpa /'kalpə/ *noun* a period in which, according to Hindu belief, the universe undergoes a cycle of creation and destruction. [Sanskrit *kalpa*]

Kamasutra /kahmə'soohtrə/ *noun* (**the Kamasutra**) an ancient treatise on erotic love and sexual technique. [Sanskrit *kāma* love + *sūtra* thread]

kame /kaym/ *noun* a mound of sand and gravel deposited by water from a melting glacier. [Scots *kame*, from Old English *camb* COMB[1]]

kameez /kə'meez/ *noun* a long-sleeved tunic or long shirt, traditionally worn above trousers, e.g. the SALWAR, by women in north India, Pakistan, and Bangladesh. [Arabic *gamīs* from late Latin *camisia*: see CHEMISE]

kami /'kahmi/ *noun* (*pl* **kami**) a divinity or god in the Shinto religion. [Japanese *kami*]

kamikaze[1] /kami'kahzi/ *noun* **1** in World War II, a member of the Japanese air force who volunteered to crash an aircraft laden with explosives suicidally on a target. **2** an aircraft used in such an attack.

Word history
Japanese *kamikaze*, literally 'divine wind'. The word *kamikaze* was originally applied to a providential storm that destroyed a Mongol fleet attacking Japan in 1281; the name was revived in 1944 when Japan resorted to desperate measures to hold off the advancing US fleet.

kamikaze[2] *adj* extremely reckless or foolhardy; self-defeating or self-destructive: *the city's kamikaze taxi drivers*.

Kamilaroi /kə'miləroy, 'kamə-/ *noun* (*pl* **Kamilaroi**) **1** a member of a group of Australian Aboriginal peoples of New South Wales. **2** the extinct language of these peoples. ➤➤ **Kamilaroi** *adj*. [the Kamilaroi name]

kampong *or* **campong** /'kampong, kam'pong/ *noun* a hamlet or village in a Malay-speaking country. [Malay *kampong*]

Kampuchean /kampoo'chee-ən/ *noun and adj* = CAMBODIAN. [*Kampuchea*, a former name of Cambodia, country in SE Asia]

Kan. *abbr* Kansas.

kana /'kahnə/ *noun* any of various Japanese syllabaries (sets of characters representing the syllables of a language: see SYLLABARY). [Japanese *kana*, from *ka* temporary, false + *na* name]

kanaka /kə'nakə/ *noun* **1** (*often* **Kanaka**) an islander of the S Pacific; *specif* a member of the native people of Hawaii. **2** (*also* **Kanaka**) in former times, an islander of the S Pacific employed in forced labour on Australian sugar plantations. [Hawaiian *kanaka* person, human being]

Kanarese *or* **Canarese** /kanə'reez/ *noun* (*pl* **Kanarese** *or* **Canarese**) **1** a member of a Kannada-speaking people of Kanara, district in S India. **2** = KANNADA. ➤➤ **Kanarese** *adj*.

kanban /'kanban/ *noun* **1** in manufacturing industry, a Japanese stock-control system in which the parts and materials required for each stage of a production process are recorded on cards so that they can be ordered and supplied at the appropriate time. **2** any of the cards used in this system. [Japanese *kanban* billboard, poster, sign]

kanga *or* **khanga** /'kang·gə/ *noun* a woman's dress of African origin, consisting of a length of cloth wound round the body and usu printed with colourful patterns. [Swahili *kanga*]

kangaroo /kanggə'rooh/ *noun* (*pl* **kangaroos**) any of several species of plant-eating marsupial mammals of Australia, New Guinea, and adjacent islands that hop on their long powerful hind legs and have a long thick tail: genus *Macropus*.

Word history
native name in an Aboriginal language. In their journals of their voyage to Australia in 1770, both Captain James Cook and his companion Joseph Banks recorded *kangooroo* or *kanguru* as the aboriginal name for this animal. Later travellers, failing to find the word in use among various aboriginal tribes, suggested that Cook and Banks misheard the word, or misapplied an aboriginal name for an emu, or even mistook some irrelevant expression for the animal's name (compare note at INDRI). They were not mistaken, however; the word belongs to the Gungu Yimidhirr language of Northern Queensland.

kangaroo court *noun* an unofficial or irregular court, *esp* one in which justice is disregarded or perverted.

kangaroo paw *noun* any of several species of Australian plants with long thin leaves and tubular hairy flowers: genera *Anigozanthos* and *Macropidia*.

kangaroo rat *noun* any of several species of pouched nocturnal burrowing rodents of NW America that hop on well-developed hind legs rather than run: genus *Dipodomys*.

kangaroo vine *noun* an Australian evergreen vine with glossy green leaves, widely grown as a house plant: *Cissus antarctica*.

kanji /'kanji/ *noun* a set of characters derived from Chinese writing used to represent the syllables of the Japanese language. [Japanese *kanji*, from *kan* Chinese + *ji* character, letter]

Kannada /'kanədə/ *noun* the Dravidian language of Karnataka, a state in S India. ➤➤ **Kannada** *adj*. [Kannada *kannaḍa*]

Kans. *abbr* Kansas.

Kantian /'kanti-ən/ *adj* relating to Immanuel Kant or his philosophy. ➤➤ **Kantianism** *noun*. [Immanuel *Kant* d.1804, German philosopher]

KANU /'kahnooh/ *abbr* Kenya African National Union.

kaolin /'kayəlin/ *noun* a fine usu white clay formed from decomposed feldspar and used *esp* in ceramics and medicine. [French *kaolin*, named after *Gaoling*, also written *Kao-ling*, hill in SE China where it was orig obtained]

kaon /'kayon/ *noun* an unstable heavy elementary particle of the meson family that exists in positive, negative, and neutral forms. [*ka* K (from *K-meson*) + -ON[2]]

kapellmeister /ka'pelmiestə/ *noun* the director of a choir or orchestra, *esp* in German-speaking royal households of the 18th cent. [German *Kapellmeister*, from *Kapelle* choir, orchestra + *Meister* master]

kapok /'kaypok/ *noun* a mass of silky fibres that surround the seeds of a tropical tree and are used *esp* as a soft filling for mattresses, cushions, sleeping bags, etc. [Malay *kapok*]

Kaposi's sarcoma /kə'pohsiz/ *noun* a cancer of the skin and connective tissue that is characterized by brown or purple patches, *esp* on the feet and hands, and often occurs in people affected by Aids. [M K *Kaposi* d.1902, Hungarian dermatologist, who first described it]

kappa /'kapə/ *noun* the tenth letter of the Greek alphabet (K, κ), equivalent to and transliterated as roman k. [Greek *kappa*, of Semitic origin]

kaput /kə'poot/ *adj informal* no longer able to function; broken or useless: *The German economy is kaput; the French are morally bankrupt; racism is becoming endemic; America's had it; Britain's in for five years of total chaos and the middle-classes will soon be taking to the* *streets* — Punch. [German *kaputt*, from French *être capot* to be without a trick at piquet]

karabiner or **carabiner** /karə'beenə/ *noun* an oblong ring with an openable side that is used in mountaineering to hold freely running rope. [German *Karabiner*]

karahi /ku'rie/ *noun* a two-handled frying pan shaped like a bowl, used for cooking Indian balti dishes. [Hindi *karahi*]

karakul or **caracul** /'karəkl/ *noun* **1** an animal of a breed of hardy fat-tailed sheep from Bukhara. **2** the tightly curled glossy black coat of karakul lambs, valued as fur. [named after *Karakul*, region in Bukhara, Uzbekistan]

karaoke /karə'ohki/ *noun* **1** a machine designed to play recorded music that a singer can use as accompaniment. **2** the practice of singing to such an accompaniment, *esp* as a form of social recreation or entertainment. [Japanese *karaoke*, literally 'empty orchestra']

karat /'karət/ *noun NAmer* see CARAT (2).

karate /kə'rahti/ *noun* a martial art in which the hands and feet are used to deliver crippling blows. [Japanese *karate*, literally 'empty hand']

karateka *noun* an expert in or practitioner of karate. [Japanese *karateka*]

Karelian /kə'reeli-ən/ *noun* **1** a native or inhabitant of Karelia in NE Europe. **2** the Finno-Ugric language of Karelia, often considered as a dialect of Finnish. ➤➤ **Karelian** *adj*.

Karen /kə'ren/ *noun* (*pl* **Karens** or collectively **Karen**) **1a** a group of peoples of E and S Myanmar (formerly Burma). **b** a member of any of these peoples. **2a** a group of languages spoken by the Karen peoples. **b** a language of this group.

karma /'kahmə/ *noun* **1** the force generated by a person's actions that is believed in Hinduism and Buddhism to influence their destiny.

Editorial note
Karma (a Sanskrit word meaning 'action') is a law of cause and effect whereby virtuous actions result in happiness in the future (of this lifetime or a future lifetime) and unvirtuous actions result in suffering. Much of the practice of Hinduism, Buddhism, and Jainism is directed towards accumulating good karma and avoiding bad karma. In common English parlance, karma has come to mean fate — Professor Donald Lopez.

2 fate or destiny. **3** an aura or spirit felt to emanate from a person, place, or thing. ➤➤ **karmic** /'kahmik/ *adj*. [Sanskrit *karma* action, effect, work]

kaross /kə'ros/ *noun* a simple garment or rug of animal skins used *esp* by native tribesmen of southern Africa. [Afrikaans *karos*]

karri /'kahri/ *noun* (*pl* **karris**) **1** an Australian eucalyptus tree: *Eucalyptus diversicolor*. **2** the hard dark red wood of this tree. [Nyungar, an Aboriginal language of W Australia]

karst /kahst/ *noun* an irregular limestone region with underground streams, caverns, and potholes. ➤➤ **karstic** /'kahstik/ *adj*. [German *Karst*, the name of a limestone plateau in Slovenia]

kart /kaht/ *noun* = GO-KART.

karting *noun* the sport of racing go-karts.

kary- or **karyo-** *comb. form* forming words, denoting: the nucleus of a cell: *karyokinesis*. [via Latin from Greek *karyon* nut, kernel]

karyokinesis /ˌkariohki'neesis/ *noun* (*pl* **karyokineses** /-seez/) the division of the nucleus and other phenomena that occur in MITOSIS (cell division producing two new cells) and in meiosis. ➤➤ **karyokinetic** /-'netik/ *adj*.

karyotype /'kariohtiep/ *noun* the specific characteristics, e.g. number, size, and shape, of the chromosomes of a cell. ➤➤ **karyotypic** /-'tipik/ *adj*.

kasbah or **casbah** /'kazbah/ *noun* **1** the older Arab section of a N African city. **2** a market in such a N African city. [French *casbah* from Arabic dialect *qaṣbah*]

kasha /'kashə/ *noun* a type of porridge of E European origin made from boiled or baked buckwheat or other grain. [Russian *kasha*]

Kashmiri /kash'miəri/ *noun* (*pl* **Kashmiris** or collectively **Kashmiri**) **1** a native or inhabitant of Kashmir, a region of the Indian subcontinent. **2** the Indic language of Kashmir. ➤➤ **Kashmiri** *adj*.

kashruth or **kashrut** /kash'root/ *noun* the Jewish laws concerning food. [Hebrew *kashrūth*, literally 'fitness']

kat or **khat** /kaht, kat/ *noun* **1** a shrub of the spindle tree family cultivated by the Arabs for its leaves and buds that have addictive stimulant properties when chewed or used as a tea: *Catha edulis*. **2** the leaves and buds of this shrub used as an addictive stimulant drug. [Arabic *qāt*]

kata /'kahtah/ *noun* a formal training exercise in a martial art, e.g. karate. [Japanese *kata*, literally 'model, pattern']

katabatic /katə'batik/ *adj* said of a wind: moving downwards as air cools and sinks: compare ANABATIC. [late Greek *katabatikos* of descent, from Greek *katabainein* to descend, from *kata-* CATA- + *bainein* to go]

katabolism /kə'tabəliz(ə)m/ *noun* see CATABOLISM.

katana /kə'tahnə/ *noun* a long sword used by Japanese samurai. [Japanese *katana*]

Kathak /'kathək, 'kutək/ *noun* a form of N Indian classical dance including passages of mime. [Bengali *kathak*, literally 'storyteller', from Sanskrit *kathaka*]

Kathakali /kahthə'kahli/ *noun* a form of S Indian classical drama, using stylized and elaborate costumes and make-up, in which stories from Hindu mythology are enacted in mime and dance. [Malayalam *kathakali*, from *katha* story + *kalī* play]

Katharevusa /kahthə'revəsah/ *noun* modern Greek conforming to classical Greek usage. [modern Greek *kathareuousa* from Greek, fem of *kathareuōn*, present part. of *kathareuein* to be pure, from *katharos* pure]

katsura /kat'soorə/ *noun* a type of Japanese wig worn *esp* by women. [Japanese *katsura*]

katydid /'kaytidid/ *noun* any of several genera of large green long-horned grasshoppers of N America, the males of which have organs on the forewings that produce a loud shrill sound when rubbed together: genus *Microcentrum* and other genera. [imitative]

kauri /'kowri/ *noun* (*pl* **kauris**) **1** a tall coniferous timber tree of New Zealand: *Agathis australis*. **2** the fine white straight-grained wood of this tree. **3** a brown resin obtained from this tree and used *esp* in varnishes and linoleum. [Maori *kawri*]

kava /'kahvə/ *noun* **1** an Australasian shrubby pepper plant: *Piper methysticum*. **2** an intoxicating beverage made from the crushed root of this plant. **3** (**kava kava**) the ground root of the plant or an extract prepared from it, taken in the form of capsules, tinctures, etc or as a drink. [Tongan and Marquesan *kava* bitter]

Kawasaki disease /kahwə'sahki/ *noun* a disease of children that is characterized by a rash, fever, and glandular swelling and sometimes causes heart damage. [named after T *Kawasaki*, 20th-cent. Japanese physician]

kayak /'kie(y)ak/ *noun* **1** an Eskimo canoe made of a frame covered with skins except for a small opening in the centre and propelled by a double-bladed paddle. **2** a similar canvas-covered or fibreglass boat used chiefly for sport or recreation. ➤➤ **kayaking** *noun*. [Inuit *qajaq*]

kayo[1] /'kay'oh/ *noun* (*pl* **kayos**) *informal* = KNOCKOUT (1B). [pronunciation of KO[1], initials of *knock out*]

kayo[2] *verb trans* (**kayoes** or **kayos**, **kayoed**, **kayoing**) *informal* to knock out (a boxing opponent).

Kazakh /kə'zak, 'kazak/ *noun* **1** a member of a people living in or originating from Kazakhstan in central Asia. **2** the Turkic language of Kazakhstan. ➤➤ **Kazakh** *adj*.

kazoo /kə'zooh/ *noun* (*pl* **kazoos**) a musical instrument consisting of a tube into which the player hums to vibrate a thin skin covering a hole, which adds a buzzing or nasal quality to the sound. [imitative]

KB *abbr* **1** kilobyte. **2** King's Bench.

KBE *abbr Brit* Knight Commander of the Order of the British Empire.

kbyte *abbr* kilobyte.

KC *abbr* **1** Kennel Club. **2** King's Counsel.

kc *abbr* kilocycle.

kcal *abbr* kilocalorie.

KCB *abbr Brit* Knight Commander of the Order of the Bath.

KCMG *abbr Brit* Knight Commander of the Order of St Michael and St George.

kc/s *abbr* kilocycles per second.

KCVO *abbr Brit* Knight Commander of the Royal Victorian Order.

KE *abbr* kinetic energy.

kea /'kee·ə/ *noun* a large green New Zealand parrot that normally eats insects but sometimes destroys sheep by slashing the back to feed on the kidney fat: *Nestor notabilis*. [Maori *kea*, of imitative origin]

kebab /ki'bab/ *noun* **1** cubes of meat, vegetables, etc, grilled on a skewer. **2** = DONER KEBAB. [Persian and Hindi *kabāb* via Arabic from Turkish *kebap*]

kecks /keks/ *pl noun NEng, informal* trousers. [prob alteration of *kicks, kicksies*, from KICK²]

kedge¹ /kej/ *verb* to pull (a boat or ship) along by means of a line attached to an anchor. [Middle English *caggen* to tie; earlier history unknown]

kedge² *noun* a small anchor used *esp* in kedging.

kedgeree /keja'ree, 'kej-/ *noun* a dish containing rice, flaked smoked fish, and chopped hard-boiled eggs. [Hindi *khichṛī*, from Sanskrit *khiccā*]

keek¹ /keek/ *verb intrans chiefly Scot* to peep or look surreptitiously. ⮞⮞ **keeker** *noun*. [Middle English *kiken*, prob from early Dutch *kiken*]

keek² *noun* a surreptitious look or peep.

keel¹ /keel/ *noun* **1a** a structure that runs lengthways along the centre of the bottom of a ship or boat, from which the framework of the hull is built up, and that often projects downward to improve stability. **b** the main load-bearing member, e.g. in an airship or aeroplane. **2** a projection or ridge suggesting a keel, e.g. the breastbone of a bird or a pair of linked flower petals. ✳ **on an even keel** without any sudden changes or trouble; steady; calm. ⮞⮞ **keeled** *adj*, **keelless** *adj*. [Middle English *kele* from Old Norse *kjölr*]

keel² *verb intrans* **1** (*usu* + over) to turn over; to capsize. **2** *informal* (+ over) to fall over in or as if in a faint; to collapse. ⮞ *verb trans* (*often* + over) to cause (something) to turn over.

keel³ /keel/ *noun* a flat-bottomed ship, *esp* a barge formerly used on the river Tyne to carry coal. [Middle English *kele* from early Dutch *kiel* ship]

keelhaul *verb trans* **1** to drag (somebody) under the keel of a ship as punishment. **2** to rebuke (somebody) severely. [Dutch *kielhalen*, from *kiel* KEEL¹ + *halen* to haul]

keelie /'keeli/ *noun Scot* an urban thug, *esp* in Glasgow. [prob modif of Scottish Gaelic *gille* lad]

keelson /'kelsən, 'kelsən/ *or* **kelson** /'kelsən/ *noun* a structural beam fastened to the keel of a ship for strength and to support the flooring. [prob of Scandinavian origin]

keen¹ /keen/ *adj* **1a** enthusiastic; eager: *a keen swimmer*. **b** said of emotion or feeling: intense: *take a keen interest*. **2a** having a fine edge or point; sharp. **b** affecting one as if by cutting or piercing: *a keen wind*. **3** intellectually alert or shrewdly astute: *a keen awareness of the problem*. **4a** sharply contested; competitive. **b** *Brit* said of prices: low in order to be competitive. **c** extremely sensitive in perception: *keen eyesight*. ✳ **keen on** interested in, attracted to, or fond of (something or somebody). ⮞⮞ **keenly** *adv*, **keenness** *noun*. [Old English *cēne* brave]

keen² *verb intrans* to utter a loud wailing lamentation, *esp* for the dead. ⮞⮞ **keener** *noun*. [Irish Gaelic *caoinim* I lament]

keen³ *noun* a lamentation for the dead uttered in a loud wailing voice, *esp* at Irish funerals.

keep¹ /keep/ *verb* (*past tense and past part.* **kept** /kept/) ⮞ *verb trans* **1** to retain possession or control of (something). **2a** to cause (somebody or something) to remain in a specified place or condition: *Keep the door closed*. **b** (*often* + on) to retain possession or use of (something): *Should we keep the apartment on over the summer?* **c** to store (something) habitually for use: *Where do you keep the butter?* **d** to preserve (food) in an unspoilt condition. **e** to have (goods) customarily in stock for sale. **f** to record (accounts, events, etc) by entries in a book. **3a** to watch over, defend, or guard (somebody or something): *Keep us from harm*. **b** to take care of (something), *esp* as an owner. **c** to support or provide for (somebody). **d** to maintain (something) in a specified condition: *a well-kept garden*. **e** to continue to maintain (order, etc). **f** to manage or run (a shop, household, etc). **4a** to obey or honour (a law, promise, etc). **b** to act fittingly in relation to (a festival, ceremony, etc): *to keep the Sabbath*. **c** to conform to (something) in habits or conduct: *to keep late hours*. **d** to stay in accord with (a beat or rhythm): *to keep step*. **5** to stay or remain on or in (a place, position, etc) often against opposition: *Will you keep my place?* **6a** to delay or detain (somebody): *What kept you?* **b** to hold back or restrain (somebody): *Try to keep him from*

going. **c** to save or reserve (something): *I'll keep some for later*. **d** to refrain from revealing or releasing (something secret or confidential). ⮞ *verb intrans* **1a** to maintain a specified course: *Keep right at the junction*. **b** to continue or persist in doing something: *Just keep talking; She would keep bothering them*. **2a** to stay or remain in a specified usu desirable place, situation, or condition: *We must keep calm; Keep out of the way*. **b** to remain in good condition: *Knowledge doesn't keep any better than fish* — A N Whitehead. **c** to be or remain with regard to health: *How are you keeping?* **d** to call for no immediate action: *The matter will keep till morning*. ✳ **keep at** to persevere in doing (something). **keep from** to refrain from (doing something): *I couldn't keep from laughing*. **keep one's shirt/hair on** *informal* to remain calm or not lose one's temper. **keep to 1** to stay in or on (a place, path, etc): *Please keep to the path*. **2** not to deviate from (a schedule, promise, etc): *We have to keep to the rules*. **keep to oneself 1** to keep (information) secret. **2** (*also* **keep oneself to oneself**) to remain solitary or apart from other people. **you, he, etc can keep it** used in rejection of something distasteful. [Old English *cēpan*]

keep² *noun* **1** a castle, fortress, or fortified tower. **2** the essentials of living, *esp* food; maintenance or support: *earn one's keep*. ✳ **for keeps 1** *informal* with the provision that one may retain possession of what one wins or receives: *He gave it to me for keeps*. **2** permanently: *come home for keeps*.

keep back *verb trans* **1** to prevent (somebody or something) from moving forward: *Police kept the crowds back*. **2** to prevent (something) from making progress. **3a** to conceal or refuse to disclose (information). **b** to keep (some of something) in one's possession.

keep down *verb trans* **1** to keep (something) in control or within limits. **2** to prevent (something) from growing, advancing, or succeeding. **3** to prevent (food) from being vomited.

keeper *noun* **1a** a protector, guardian, or custodian. **b** somebody who looks after animals, *esp* in a zoo. **c** a curator. **d** a goalkeeper or wicketkeeper. **2** any of various devices for keeping something in position. **3** = ARMATURE (2).

keep fit *noun* physical exercises designed to keep one's body healthy and supple.

keeping *noun* **1** custody; care: *in my keeping*. **2** conformity or accordance with something implied or specified: *in keeping with accepted standards; The new building is out of keeping*.

keepnet *noun* a large net suspended in the water in which an angler keeps caught fish alive.

keep on *verb intrans* **1** to continue to do something. **2** (*often* + about) to talk persistently about something. **3** (*often* + at) to harass or nag somebody. ⮞ *verb trans* **1** to continue to employ (somebody). **2** to continue to use (something).

keepsake *noun* something kept as a memento, *esp* of the giver. [KEEP¹ + -*sake* as in NAMESAKE]

keep up *verb trans* **1** to persist or persevere in (an activity). **2** to preserve (something) from decline: *to keep up appearances*. **3** to prevent (somebody) from going to bed. ⮞ *verb intrans* **1** to continue without interruption: *The rain kept up all night*. **2** (*often* + with) to maintain an equal pace or level of activity, progress, or knowledge: *We must keep up with developments in technology*.

keeshond /'kays·hond, 'kees·hond/ *noun* an animal of a breed of small grey dogs with a heavy coat, pointed ears, and a foxlike face. [Dutch *keeshond*, from *Kees* (nickname for *Cornelius*) + *hond* dog; said to have been named after *Cornelis* de Glyselaer, leader of the Dutch Patriots Party in the 18th cent., who owned a keeshond]

kef /kef/ *noun* see KIF.

keffiyeh *or* **kaffiyeh** /kə'fee(y)ə/ *noun* a cotton head covering worn by Arabs. [Arabic *keffiyya*]

keftedes /kef'tedheez, kef'tedhes/ *pl noun* a Greek dish of meatballs with herbs and onions. [Greek *kephtedes*, pl of *kephtes*, via Turkish from Persian *koftah* KOFTA]

keg /keg/ *noun* **1** *Brit* a small barrel having a capacity of 10gall (about 45.5l) or less; *specif* a metal barrel from which beer is pumped by pressurized gas. **2** beer from a keg. [Middle English *kag* from Old Norse *kaggi*]

kelim /ki'leem, 'keelim/ *noun* see KILIM.

keloid /'keeloyd/ *noun* a thick scar resulting from excessive growth of fibrous tissue at the point of injury. [French *kiloïde*, from Greek *chēlē* claw]

kelp /kelp/ *noun* **1** any of various large brown seaweeds: family Laminariaceae. **2** the ashes of seaweed used *esp* as a source of iodine. [Middle English *culp*; earlier history unknown]

kelpie[1] /'kelpi/ *noun* a water sprite of Scottish folklore, usu in the form of a horse, that is said to bring about the drowning of travellers. [prob of Celtic origin; perhaps from Scottish Gaelic *cailpeach* colt]

kelpie[2] *noun* a dog bred in Australia from British collies and used there as a sheepdog. [*Kelpie*, name of an early specimen of this breed]

kelson /'kelsən/ *noun* see KEELSON.

Kelt /kelt/ *noun* see CELT.

kelt *noun* a salmon or sea trout after spawning. [Middle English (northern), prob from Scottish Gaelic *cealt*]

kelter /'keltə/ *noun chiefly Brit* = KILTER.

Keltic *adj and noun* see CELTIC[1], CELTIC[2].

Kelvin /'kelvin/ *adj* of or being a scale of temperature on which absolute zero is at 0° and water freezes at 273.16° under standard conditions. [named after William Thomson, Lord *Kelvin* d.1907, Scots physicist, who introduced it]

kelvin *noun* the basic SI unit of temperature defined by the Kelvin scale.

kempt /kem(p)t/ *adj* neatly kept; trim or tidy. [Middle English, past part. of *kemben* to comb, from Old English *cemban*]

ken[1] /ken/ *verb trans* (**kenned** or **kent, kenning**) *chiefly Scot* to know or recognize (something or somebody). [Old English *cennan* to make known and Old Norse *kenna* to perceive]

ken[2] *noun* range of perception, understanding, or knowledge: *beyond our ken.*

kenaf /kə'naf/ *noun* **1** the fibre of an E Indian hibiscus plant, used *esp* for ropes. **2** the plant from which this fibre is obtained: *Hibiscus cannabinus.* [Persian *kenaf*]

kendo /'kendoh/ *noun* a Japanese martial art of fencing with bamboo sticks. [Japanese *kendō*, from *ken* sword + *dō* art]

kennel[1] /'kenl/ *noun* **1a** a shelter for a dog. **b** (*also in pl*) an establishment for the breeding or boarding of dogs. **2** a pack of dogs. [Middle English from Anglo-French *kenel*, ultimately from Latin *canis* dog]

kennel[2] *verb trans* (**kennelled, kennelling,** *NAmer* **kenneled, kenneling**) to put or keep (a dog) in a kennel.

Kennelly-Heaviside layer /,kenəli 'hevisied/ *noun* = E LAYER. [see HEAVISIDE-KENNELLY LAYER]

kenning /'kening/ *noun* a metaphorical compound word or phrase used *esp* in Old English and Old Norse poetry, e.g. *swan-road* for *ocean.* [Old Norse *kenning*, from *kenna* to perceive]

kenspeckle /'kenspekl/ *adj chiefly Scot* conspicuous or well-known; easy to recognize. [prob of Scandinavian origin]

kent /kent/ *verb* past tense and past part. of KEN[1].

Kentish /'kentish/ *adj* of or from the county of Kent in SE England.

Kenyan /'kenyən/ *noun* a native or inhabitant of Kenya in E Africa. ➤➤ **Kenyan** *adj.*

kepi /'kaypee (*French* kepi)/ *noun* a round French military cap with a flat top and a horizontal peak. [French *képi* from German dialect *käppi*, dimin. of *kappe* cap, ultimately from late Latin *cappa* head covering, cloak]

kept[1] /kept/ *verb* past tense and past part. of KEEP[1].

kept[2] ✳ **a kept man/woman** a lover or mistress who is supported financially by somebody.

kerat- or **kerato-** *comb. form* forming words, with the meanings: **1** cornea: *keratitis.* **2** horn; horny: *keratin.* [Greek *kerat-, kerato-*, from *keras* horn]

keratin /'kerətin/ *noun* any of various fibrous proteins that form the chemical basis of nails, claws, hooves, horns, feathers, and hair. ➤➤ **keratinous** /ki'ratinəs/ *adj.*

keratinize or **keratinise** /'kerətiniez, ki'ratiniez/ *verb trans* to make (something) into keratin or keratinous tissue. ➤ *verb intrans* to become keratinous. ➤➤ **keratinization** /-'zaysh(ə)n/ *noun.*

kerato- *comb. form* see KERAT-.

keratoplasty /'kerətəplasti/ *noun* surgery carried out on the cornea.

keratose /'kerətohs, -tohz/ *adj* having a horny skeleton.

keratosis /kerə'tohsis/ *noun* (*pl* **keratoses** /-seez/) a horny growth on the skin, e.g. a wart; a condition that produces this.

kerb (*NAmer* **curb**) /kuhb/ *noun* an edging, *esp* of stone or concrete, to a pavement, path, etc. ➤➤ **kerbing** *noun.* [alteration of CURB[1]]

kerb crawling *noun* the act of driving slowly close to a pavement with the intention of enticing a potential sexual partner into the car. ➤➤ **kerb crawler** *noun.*

kerb drill *noun Brit* a sequence of actions, *esp* looking to right and left, performed before crossing a road.

kerbstone (*NAmer* **curbstone**) *noun* a block of stone or concrete forming a kerb.

kerchief /'kuhchif/ *noun* (*pl* **kerchiefs** /'kerchifs/ or **kerchieves** /'kerchifs, 'kercheevz/) **1** a square or triangle of cloth used as a head covering or worn as a scarf around the neck. **2** = HANDKERCHIEF. ➤➤ **kerchiefed** *adj.* [Middle English *courchef* from Old French *cuevrechief*, from *covrir* to cover + *chief* head]

kerf /kuhf/ *noun* a slit or notch made *esp* by a saw or cutting torch. [Old English *cyrf* action of cutting, a cut]

kerfuffle /kə'fufl/ *noun chiefly Brit, informal* a fuss or commotion. [Scots *curfuffle* disorder, agitation]

kermes /'kuhmiz/ *noun* the dried bodies of female scale insects that are found on the kermes oak, used as a red dyestuff. [French *kermès* from Arabic *qirmiz*]

kermes oak *noun* a dwarf often shrubby Mediterranean oak tree: *Quercus coccifera.* [from its use as a host plant for kermes insects]

kermis /'kuhmis/ *noun* **1** an annual outdoor festival, *esp* in the Netherlands. **2** *NAmer* a fair held usu for charitable purposes. [Dutch *kermis* from early Dutch *kercmisse*, from *kerc* church + *misse* mass, church festival]

kern[1] /kuhn/ *noun* a part of a letter that overhangs the piece of type on which it is cast. [French *carne* corner, from Latin *cardin-, cardo* hinge]

kern[2] *verb trans* to provide (a printed character) with a kern: *kerned letters.*

kern[3] or **kerne** *noun* **1** a lightly-armed medieval Irish foot soldier. **2** *archaic* a peasant or yokel. [Middle English *kerne* from early Irish *cethern* band of soldiers]

kerne /kuhn/ *noun* see KERN[2].

kernel /'kuhnl/ *noun* **1** the inner, softer, and often edible part of a seed, fruit stone, or nut. **2** a whole seed of a cereal. **3** a central or essential part; the core of something. [Old English *cyrnel*, dimin. of *corn* seed, CORN[1]]

kerosene or **kerosine** /'kerəseen/ *noun chiefly NAmer, Aus, NZ* = PARAFFIN. [Greek *kēros* wax + -ENE]

kerria /'keri-ə/ *noun* a Chinese shrub of the rose family with solitary yellow flowers: genus *Kerria.* [scientific Latin, genus name, from William *Kerr* d.1814, English gardener]

kerry /'keri/ *noun* (*pl* **kerries**) (*often* **Kerry**) an animal of an Irish breed of small black dairy cattle. [named after County *Kerry* in SW Ireland, where the breed originated]

Kerry blue *noun* a terrier of an Irish breed, having a silky bluish coat.

kersey /'kuhzi/ *noun* a heavy compact ribbed woollen cloth with a short nap: *Taffeta phrases, silken terms precise ... I do forswear them ... Henceforth my wooing mind shall be expressed in russet yeas and honest kersey noes* — Shakespeare. [Middle English, prob named after *Kersey*, village in Suffolk, England where woollen cloth was made]

kerseymere /'kuhzimiə/ *noun* a fine woollen fabric made in fancy twill weaves. [alteration (influenced by KERSEY) of *cassimere* cashmere, from obsolete *Cassimere* Kashmir]

kestrel /'kestrəl/ *noun* a small common Eurasian and N African falcon that is noted for its habit of hovering in the air against the wind: *Falco tinnunculus.* [Middle English *castrel*, from early French *crecerelle* from *crecelle* rattle, prob of imitative origin]

ketamine /'keetəmeen/ *noun* a synthetic chemical compound used as an anaesthetic and analgesic drug and sometimes illegally to induce hallucinations. [KETONE + AMINE]

ketch /kech/ *noun* a fore-and-aft rigged sailing vessel with two masts, the forward mast being taller than the after mast, which is located ahead of the rudder. [Middle English *cache*, prob from *cacchen*: see CATCH[1]]

ketchup /'kechəp, 'kechup/ (*NAmer* **catchup** /'kechəp, 'kachəp/) *noun* any of several sauces made with vinegar and seasonings and used as a relish, *esp* a sauce made from seasoned tomato puree. [Malay *kĕchap* spiced fish sauce, from Chinese (Cantonese) *ke tsiap* tomato juice, sauce]

ketone /'keetohn/ *noun* an organic compound, e.g. acetone, with a carbonyl group attached to two carbon atoms. ➤➤ **ketonic** /ki'tonik/ *adj*. [German *Keton*, alteration of *Aketon* acetone]

ketone body *noun* a ketone or related compound found in the blood and urine in abnormal amounts in conditions of impaired metabolism, e.g. diabetes mellitus.

ketonuria /keetə'nooriə/ *noun* the presence of abnormally large amounts of ketone bodies in the urine. [KETONE + -URIA]

ketosis /ki'tohsis/ *noun* an abnormal increase of ketone bodies in the body. ➤➤ **ketotic** /ki'totik/ *adj*. [KETONE + -OSIS]

kettle /'ketl/ *noun* **1** a metal or plastic vessel used *esp* for boiling water, usu having a lid, handle, and spout and heated on top of a stove or cooker or by an internal electric element. **2** a steep-sided hollow in a glacial deposit, caused by the melting of a mass of underlying ice. * **a different/another kettle of fish** *informal* an altogether different matter. **a pretty/fine kettle of fish** *informal* a muddled or awkward state of affairs [*a kettle of fish* was an old Scottish term for a picnic at which a freshly caught salmon was boiled and eaten; the practical difficulties of catching the fish and cooking it on the river bank leading to the idea of muddle]. [Middle English *ketel* from Old Norse *ketill* and Old English *cietel*, both ultimately from Latin *catillus*, dimin. of *catinus* bowl]

kettledrum *noun* a percussion instrument that consists of a hollow metal hemisphere with a covering of parchment or plastic stretched across it, the tension of which can be changed to vary the pitch.

kettle hole *noun* = KETTLE (2).

KeV *abbr* kilo-electron volt.

Kevlar /'kevlah/ *noun trademark* a fibre-reinforced composite material with great tensile strength.

Kewpie /'kyoohpi/ *noun trademark* a small chubby doll with a topknot of hair.

key[1] /kee/ *noun* **1a** a usu metal instrument by which the bolt of a lock is turned. **b** something having a similar form or function, e.g. a device used to wind a clock. **2** a small button or knob on a keyboard, e.g. of a computer or typewriter, that is pushed down by a finger to work the machine. **3a** any of the levers of a keyboard instrument, e.g. a piano, that is pressed to operate the mechanism and produce the notes. **b** a lever that controls an air hole in a woodwind instrument or a valve in a brass instrument. **4** a small switch for opening or closing an electric circuit. **5** a small piece of wood or metal used as a wedge or for preventing motion between parts. **6a** a means of gaining or preventing entrance, possession, or control. **b** an instrumental or deciding factor: *the key to success*. **7a** something that gives an explanation or identification or provides a solution. **b** a list of words or phrases explaining symbols or abbreviations. **c** a piece of secret information used to unlock encrypted messages. **8** in music, a system of seven notes based on their relationship to the first and lowest note, providing the overall tonal framework for a piece of music: *in the key of A minor*. **9** a characteristic style or tone. **10** a dry usu single-seeded fruit, e.g. of an ash or elm tree. **11** the indentation, roughness, or roughening of a surface to improve adhesion of plaster, paint, glue, etc. ➤➤ **keyed** *adj*, **keyless** *adj*. [Old English *cæg*]

key[2] *verb trans* **1** to secure or fasten (something) by a key. **2** to roughen (a surface) to provide a key for plaster, paint, etc. **3** to bring (something) into harmony or conformity; to make (it) appropriate. **4** (*often* + in) to enter (e.g. data or text) by means of a keyboard or keypad. **5** to provide (something) with a key, *esp* to provide it with identifying or explanatory cross-references or symbols. * **be keyed up** to be nervous, tense, or excited: *She was keyed up about the interview*. ➤➤ **keyer** *noun*.

key[3] *adj* of great importance; fundamental.

key[4] *noun* a low island or reef, *esp* in the Caribbean area. [Spanish *cayo*, from Lucayo]

keyboard[1] *noun* **1a** a set of keys on a musical instrument, e.g. a piano, typically having seven white and five black keys in each octave. **b** (*also in pl*) any musical instrument having such a keyboard, *esp* an electronic instrument used in rock or pop music. **2** a set of systematically arranged keys by which a machine, e.g. a computer or typewriter, is operated.

keyboard[2] *verb intrans* to operate a machine, *esp* a computer, by means of a keyboard. ➤ *verb trans* to enter or typeset (e.g. data or text) by means of a keyboard. ➤➤ **keyboarder** *noun*.

key card *noun* a plastic card containing a magnetic strip encoded with information which can be read by an electronic device, used instead of a door key.

key grip *noun* the chief GRIP[2] (person who handles and manoeuvres cameras) in a film or television studio.

keyholder *noun* a person who keeps the keys to business or industrial premises.

keyhole *noun* a hole in a lock into which the key is put.

keyhole surgery *noun* surgery performed through a very small incision using techniques such as fibre optics and specially designed instruments.

key money *noun* a payment made by a tenant to secure occupancy of a rented property.

Keynesianism /'kaynzi-əniz(ə)m/ *noun* the economic theories of J M Keynes and his followers; *specif* the theory that the monetary and taxation policies of a government directly affect actual demand, inflation, and employment. ➤➤ **Keynesian** *adj and noun*. [J M *Keynes* d.1946, English economist]

keynote[1] *noun* **1a** the fundamental or central fact, principle, idea, or mood. **b** (*used before a noun*) said of a speech: presenting the issues of primary interest to an assembly. **2** the first note of a musical scale considered as the base note for purposes of harmony.

keynote[2] *verb trans* **1** to set the keynote of (something). **2** *NAmer* to deliver the keynote address at (e.g. a rally or conference). ➤➤ **keynoter** *noun*.

keypad *noun* **1** a small keyboard or set of buttons for operating something, e.g. a telephone, calculator, or security system. **2** a separate section on a computer keyboard with a restricted range of keys, e.g. one used for inputting numbers.

keypunch[1] *noun* a machine with a keyboard used to transfer data by cutting holes or notches in punched cards.

keypunch[2] *verb trans* to transfer (data) by means of a keypunch. ➤➤ **keypuncher** *noun*.

key signature *noun* the sharps or flats placed on the musical staff to indicate the key in diatonic music.

Key Stage *noun* in Britain, any of the four divisions of the National Curriculum, studied by pupils aged 5–7, 7–11, 11–14, and 14–16 respectively.

keystone *noun* **1** the wedge-shaped piece at the highest point of an arch that locks the other pieces in place. **2** something on which associated things depend for support: *collective bargaining – the keystone of industrial democracy* — Adlai Stevenson.

keystroke *noun* a single instance of pressing down a key on a typewriter or computer keyboard.

KG *abbr Brit* Knight of the Order of the Garter.

kg *abbr* **1** keg. **2** kilogram.

KGB *noun* the secret police of the former USSR. [abbr of Russian *Komitet Gosudarstvennoye Bezopastnosti* State Security Committee]

Kgs *abbr* Kings (books of the Bible).

khadi /'kahdi/ *or* **khaddar** /'kadə, 'kahdə/ *noun* Indian cotton cloth woven in the home. [Hindi *khādī, khādar*]

khaki /'kahki/ *noun* **1** a dull yellowish brown colour. **2** a khaki-coloured cloth made usu of cotton or wool and used *esp* for military uniforms. ➤➤ **khaki** *adj*. [Hindi *khākī* dust-coloured, from *khāk* dust, from Persian]

Khalkha /'kalkə/ *noun* **1** a member of a people forming the majority of the population of Mongolia. **2** the official language of Mongolia, a dialect of Mongolian. ➤➤ **Khalkha** *adj*. [origin unknown]

Khalsa /'kalsə, 'kulsə/ *noun* an order of orthodox Sikhs. [via Urdu from Persian, ultimately from Arabic *Kālis* pure]

khamsin /'kamsin, kam'seen/ *noun* a hot southerly Egyptian wind coming from the Sahara. [Arabic *rīh al-khamsīn* the wind of the fifty (days between Easter and Pentecost, when it usually blows)]

khan[1] /kahn/ *noun* **1a** a medieval supreme ruler over the Turkish, Tartar, and Mongol peoples. **b** a medieval sovereign of China. **2** a local chieftain or person of rank in some countries of Central Asia. ➤➤ **khanate** /'kahnayt/ *noun*. [Middle English *caan* via early French *chan* from Turkic *kān* lord, ruler]

khan² *noun* = CARAVANSERAI. [Arabic *khān*]

khanga /'kang·gə/ *noun* see KANGA.

khat /kaht, kat/ *noun* see KAT.

khazi /'kahzi/ *noun* (*pl* **khazies**) *Brit, informal* a toilet. [from Italian *casa* house]

khedive /ki'deev/ *noun* a ruler of Egypt during the period from 1867 to 1914, governing as a viceroy for the sultan of Turkey. ⟩⟩ **khedival** *adj,* **khedivial** *adj.* [French *khédive,* from Turkish *hidiv*]

Khmer /kmeə/ *noun* (*pl* **Khmer** *or* **Khmers**) **1** a member of the majority ethnic group of Cambodia; *broadly* a Cambodian. **2** the language of Cambodia. ⟩⟩ **Khmer** *adj,* **Khmerian** *adj.* [the Khmer name for the people and language]

Khoikhoi /'koykoy/ *noun* **1** a member of a people of southern Africa apparently of mixed Bushman and Bantu origin. **2** the Khoisan language of this people. ⟩⟩ **Khoikhoi** *adj.* [Nama *khoikhoi,* literally 'men of men']

Khoisan /'koysahn, koy'sahn/ *noun* a group of African languages including Nana, San, and others. ⟩⟩ **Khoisan** *adj.* [blend of KHOIKHOI + *San* Bushman, Bushman language, from Nama *sān*]

khoum /khoom/ *noun* a unit of currency in Mauritania, worth one fifth of an ouguiya. [Arabic *kums* one fifth]

kHz *abbr* kilohertz.

kiang /ki'ang/ *noun* an Asiatic wild ass usu with a reddish back and sides and white underparts, muzzle, and legs: *Equus hemionus.* [Tibetan *rkyanň*]

kia ora /ˌki·ə 'awrə/ *interj* NZ used as a greeting or to express good wishes. [Maori *kia ora,* literally 'be well']

kibble¹ /'kibl/ *verb trans* to grind (e.g. grain) coarsely. [origin unknown]

kibble² *noun* a bucket used for hoisting in mines or wells. [German *Kübel* from medieval Latin *cupellus,* dimin. of Latin *cuppa:* see CUP¹]

kibbutz /ki'boots/ *noun* (*pl* **kibbutzim** /-'seem/) a farm or settlement in Israel run as a cooperative. [modern Hebrew *qibbūṣ* gathering]

kibbutznik /ki'bootsnik/ *noun* a member of a kibbutz.

kibe /kieb/ *noun archaic* an ulcerated chilblain, *esp* on the heel. [Middle English, prob from Welsh *cibi, cibwst*]

kibitz /'kibits/ *verb intrans chiefly NAmer, informal* to look on and often offer unwanted advice or comment, *esp* at a card game. ⟩⟩ **kibitzer** *noun.* [Yiddish *kibitsen* from German *kiebitzen,* from *kiebitz* lapwing, busybody, from early High German *gibitz* lapwing, of imitative origin]

kiblah /'kiblə, 'kiblah/ *noun* the direction of Mecca, or of the Kaaba at Mecca, to which Muslims turn when praying. [Arabic *kibla* that which is opposite]

kibosh *or* **kybosh** /'kiebosh/ ✳ **put the kibosh on** to put an end to (a plan, etc); to ruin (it): *Worse, the wife does the one thing absolutely guaranteed to put the kibosh on the whole matter. She says she'll forgive him* — Daily Mirror. [origin unknown]

kick¹ /kik/ *verb trans* **1** to strike (something or somebody) forcefully with the foot. **2** in rugby, to score (a goal) by kicking a ball. **3** *informal* to free oneself of (a habit or addiction). ⟩⟩ *verb intrans* **1a** to strike out with the foot or feet. **b** to make a kick in football. **2** to show opposition; to rebel: *kicking against authority.* **3** said of a gun: to recoil when fired. ✳ **kick oneself** to reprove oneself for a failure or shortcoming. **kick one's heels 1** to be kept waiting. **2** to be idle. **kick over the traces** to cast off restraint or control. **kick the bucket** *informal, humorous* to die. **kick upstairs** to promote (somebody) to a higher but less influential position. ⟩⟩ **kickable** *adj.* [Middle English *kiken;* earlier history unknown]

kick² *noun* **1a** a blow or sudden forceful thrust with the foot; *specif* one that propels something, e.g. a ball. **b** the power to kick. **c** a repeated motion of the legs used in swimming. **d** a sudden burst of speed, *esp* in a running race. **2** the recoil of a gun. **3** power or strength to resist; *broadly* resilience: *He still has some kick in him.* **4a** a stimulating effect or quality: *This drink has quite a kick.* **b** (*also in pl*) a stimulating or pleasurable experience or feeling: *They did it for kicks.* **c** an absorbing or obsessive new interest: *on a health food kick.* ✳ **kick in the teeth** *informal* a sharp rebuff or harsh disappointment.

kick³ *noun* an indentation in the base of a glass vessel, *esp* a bottle. [origin unknown]

kick about *verb* = KICK AROUND.

kick around *verb trans informal* **1** to treat (somebody) inconsiderately or high-handedly. **2** to consider or discuss (an idea, problem, etc) among a number of people in a casual or desultory way. ⟩⟩ *verb intrans informal* **1** to wander aimlessly or idly. **2** to lie unused or unwanted: *There's a spare blanket kicking around in a cupboard.*

kick-ass *adj chiefly NAmer, informal* forceful and aggressive.

kickback *noun* **1** a sharp violent reaction. **2** money received, often secretly or illicitly, because of help or favours given.

kick back *verb intrans* **1** said of a gun: to recoil unexpectedly. **2** to pay a kickback to somebody.

kickboxing *noun* a martial art in which contestants are allowed both to punch with gloved hands and to kick with bare feet. ⟩⟩ **kickboxer** *noun.*

kickdown *noun* a method of changing gear by pressing the accelerator down to the floor in a vehicle with automatic transmission.

kicker /'kikə/ *noun* someone or something that kicks; *esp* a horse with a habit of kicking.

kick in *verb intrans* **1** to start functioning. **2** to begin to take effect. ⟩⟩ *verb trans Aus, NZ, informal* to contribute (e.g. money).

kickoff *noun* **1** a kick that puts the ball into play in football, rugby, etc, *esp* at the beginning of a game. **2** an act or instance of starting or beginning.

kick off *verb intrans* **1** in ball games, to start or resume play with a kickoff. **2** *informal* to start or begin proceedings.

kick out *verb trans informal* to dismiss or eject (somebody or something) forcefully or unceremoniously.

kick pleat *noun* a short pleat consisting of a layer of fabric sewn under an opening at the lower edge of a narrow skirt to allow freedom of movement.

kickshaw /'kikshaw/ *noun archaic* **1** a fancy dish; a delicacy: *Some pigeons, Davy, a couple of short-legged hens, a joint of mutton, and any pretty tiny kickshaws, tell William cook* — Shakespeare. **2** a bauble or trinket of little value. [modification of French *quelque chose* something]

kickstand *noun* a swivelling stand attached to a two-wheeled vehicle that can be kicked into position to hold it upright when stationary.

kick-start¹ *verb* **1** to operate the kick-start of (an engine or motorcycle). **2** to cause (something) to start, restart, or become more active or productive, *esp* by sudden or forceful action: *kick-start the economy.*

kick-start² *noun* **1** the act of kick-starting something. **2** a lever that can be kicked down to start an engine, *esp* of a motorcycle.

kick starter *noun* = KICK-START² (2).

kick up *verb trans* **1** to cause (something) to rise upwards: *clouds of dust kicked up by passing cars.* **2** *informal* to stir up (a row, a fuss, trouble, etc). ✳ **kick up one's heels** *informal* to enjoy oneself in a lively uninhibited manner.

kid¹ /kid/ *noun* **1** the young of a goat or related animal. **2** = KIDSKIN. **3a** *informal* a child or young person. **b** (*used before a noun*) younger: *my kid sister.* ✳ **with kid gloves** with great care or special consideration. ⟩⟩ **kiddish** *adj.*

Word history
Middle English *kide* from Old Norse *kith* young goat. The use of *kid* to mean 'child' goes back at least to the 17th cent. Although probably originating in slang or cant, by the 19th cent. it was current among reputable users in informal contexts.

kid² *verb intrans* (**kidded, kidding**) said of a goat or antelope: to give birth to young.

kid³ *verb* (**kidded, kidding**) ⟩⟩ *verb trans informal* **1a** to deceive (somebody) as a joke. **b** to convince (oneself) of something untrue or improbable. **2** to tease or make fun of (somebody) in a playful manner. ⟩⟩ *verb intrans informal* to engage in good-humoured deception or horseplay. ⟩⟩ **kidder** *noun,* **kiddingly** *adv.* [prob from KID¹]

Kidderminster /'kidəminstə/ *noun* a type of carpet made from yarn that is dyed before being woven. [named after *Kidderminster,* town in England, where such carpets were produced]

kiddie *or* **kiddy** /'kidi/ *noun* (*pl* **kiddies**) *informal* a small child.

kiddush /'kidoosh, ki'doohsh/ *noun* a ceremonial blessing pronounced over wine or bread in a Jewish home or synagogue on the Sabbath or another holy day. [Hebrew *qiddūsh* sanctification]

kiddy /'kidi/ *noun* see KIDDIE.

kid-glove *adj* using or involving gentle, considerate, or tactful methods: *kid-glove diplomacy.*

kidnap /'kidnap/ *verb trans* (**kidnapped, kidnapping**, NAmer **kidnaped, kidnaping**) to seize and detain (a person) by force and often for ransom: compare ABDUCT. ⟫⟫ **kidnap** *noun,* **kidnapper** *noun.* [earliest as *kidnapper,* from KID¹ + obsolete *napper* thief, from dialect *nap* to steal, NAB]

kidney /'kidni/ *noun* (*pl* **kidneys**) **1** either of a pair of organs situated in the body cavity near the spinal column that excrete waste products of metabolism in the form of urine. **2** the kidney of an animal eaten as food. **3** sort, kind, or type, *esp* with regard to temperament: *The South Seas were getting too hot to hold gentlemen of his kidney* — Joseph Conrad. [Middle English; earlier history unknown]

kidney bean *noun* any of the kidney-shaped seeds of the French bean, *esp* when mature and dark red in colour.

kidney machine *noun* a machine that artificially purifies the blood of somebody whose kidneys do not function properly.

kidney stone *noun* **1** a hard stony mass that forms abnormally in the kidney, requiring surgical removal; = CALCULUS (1A). **2** = NEPHRITE.

kidology /ki'dolǝji/ *noun chiefly Brit, informal* playful deception or teasing. [KID³ + -OLOGY]

kidskin *noun* a soft pliant leather made from the skin of a young goat or related animal.

kids' stuff (NAmer **kid stuff**) *noun informal* something befitting or appropriate to children; *specif* something extremely simple or easy.

kidstakes /'kidstayks/ *pl noun Aus, NZ, informal* nonsense. [prob humorous formation based on *kid* nonsense, deception, from KID³]

kid stuff *noun NAmer* see KIDS' STUFF.

kiekie /'keekee/ *noun* a climbing plant of New Zealand that has edible bracts (specialized leaves; see BRACT): *Freycinetia banksii.* [Maori *kiekie*]

Kierkegaardian /kiǝkǝ'gahdi·ǝn/ *adj* relating to the philosopher Kierkegaard or his work. [S A *Kierkegaard* d.1855, Danish philosopher]

kieselguhr *or* **kieselgur** /'keezlgooǝ/ *noun* loose or porous DIATOMITE (silica-containing material) used for polishing, filtering, and in the manufacture of dynamite. [German *Kieselgur,* from *Kiesel* gravel + dialect *Guhr,* literally 'yeast', used for a loose deposit of earth found in rocks]

kif /kif, keef/ *or* **kef** /kef/ *noun* **1** a state of drowsy tranquillity. **2** a substance, e.g. marijuana, that is smoked to produce such a state. [Arabic *kayf* pleasure]

kike /kiek/ *noun chiefly NAmer, offensive* a Jew. [prob alteration of *kiki,* reduplication of -*ki,* common ending of names of Jews who lived in Slavic countries]

Kikuyu /ki'kooh·yooh/ *noun* (*pl* **Kikuyus** *or collectively* **Kikuyu**) **1** a member of a Bantu-speaking people of Kenya in E Africa. **2** the language of this people. ⟫⟫ **Kikuyu** *adj.*

kilderkin /'kildǝkin/ *noun* a small cask having a capacity of 16 or 18gall (about 73 or 82l). [Middle English from early Dutch *kindekijn* dimin., from medieval Latin *quintale:* see QUINTAL]

kilim *or* **kelim** /ki'leem, 'keelim/ *noun* a pileless woven rug from Turkey or Iran. [Turkish *kilim* from Persian *kilīm*]

kill¹ /kil/ *verb trans* **1** to deprive (somebody or something) of life. **2a** to put an end to (something): *It killed her hopes of becoming a doctor.* **b** to defeat or veto (e.g. a bill). **3a** to destroy the vital, active, or essential quality of (something): *kill the pain with drugs.* **b** to spoil, subdue, or neutralize the effect of (something): *That colour kills the room.* **4** to pass or occupy (time), e.g. while waiting. **5a** to hit (a shot) so hard in a racket game that a return is impossible. **b** in football, etc, to stop or control (the ball). **6** *informal.* **a** to cause (e.g. an engine) to stop. **b** to turn off (e.g. lights). **7** *informal.* **a** to cause extreme pain to (somebody): *My feet are killing me.* **b** to exhaust (somebody) almost to the point of collapse: *Don't kill yourself to meet the deadline.* **8** *informal* to overwhelm (somebody), e.g. with amusement. **9** in journalism, to discard or abandon further investigation of (a story). ⟫ *verb intrans* to destroy life. ✳ **kill the**

goose that lays the golden eggs to destroy a regular source of income or profit, *esp* by using it too much [from a Greek fable in which the owner of a goose that laid golden eggs killed the bird to get at the gold inside it]. **kill two birds with one stone** to deal with two matters with the same means. [Middle English *killen, cullen* to strike, beat, kill; related to QUELL]

kill² *noun* **1** an act or the moment of killing: *move in for the kill.* **2** something killed, e.g.: **a** animals killed in a shoot, hunt, season, or particular period of time. **b** an enemy aircraft, submarine, etc destroyed by military action. ✳ **in at the kill** present at the usu triumphant or successful conclusion of an undertaking.

killdeer *noun* (*pl* **killdeers** *or collectively* **killdeer**) a plover of temperate N America with a mournful penetrating cry: *Charadrius vociferus.* [imitative]

killer /'kilǝ/ *noun* **1** a person or thing that kills. **2** = KILLER WHALE. **3** *informal* something that is extremely arduous or exhausting. **4** *informal* a highly amusing joke.

killer cell *noun* any of certain white blood cells that can destroy foreign or sometimes host cells.

killer whale *noun* a flesh-eating black-and-white toothed whale found in most seas of the world: *Orcinus orca.*

killick /'kilik/ *noun* a small anchor, *esp* of stone. [origin unknown]

killifish /'kilifish/ *noun* (*pl* **killifishes** *or collectively* **killifish**) any of numerous small fishes resembling minnows that are used as bait and to control mosquitoes, whose larvae they eat: families Cyprinodontidae and Poeciliidae. [*kill* channel, river, stream (from early Dutch *kille*) + -IE + FISH¹]

killing¹ *noun* **1** an act of causing death. **2** *informal* a sudden notable gain or profit: *make a killing on the stock exchange.*

killing² *adj* **1** causing death. **2** *informal.* **a** extremely exhausting or difficult to endure. **b** highly amusing. ⟫⟫ **killingly** *adv.*

killing bottle *noun* a bottle containing poisonous vapour for killing insects caught as specimens.

killing field *noun* a place where a large number of people have been killed or massacred.

killjoy *noun* somebody who spoils the pleasure of others.

kill off *verb trans* to destroy (something) totally or in large numbers.

kiln /kiln/ *noun* an oven, furnace, or heated enclosure used for processing a substance, e.g. clay, by burning, firing, or drying. [Old English *cyln* from Latin *culina* kitchen, from *coquere* to cook]

Kilner jar /'kilnǝ/ *noun trademark* a wide glass jar that has an airtight lid and is used for preserving foods, *esp* fruit and vegetables.

kilo /'keeloh/ *noun* (*pl* **kilos**) **1** a kilogram. **2** a kilometre.

kilo- *comb. form* forming words, denoting: **1** thousand: *kilojoule.* **2** in some computing contexts, 1024: *kilobyte.* [French *kilo-* from Greek *chilioi* thousand]

kilobit /'kilǝbit/ *noun* in computing, a unit of memory or information equal to 1024 bits.

kilobyte /'kilǝbiet/ *noun* in computing, a unit of memory or information equal to 1024 bytes.

kilocalorie /'kilohkalǝri/ *noun* = CALORIE (1B).

kilocycle /'kilohsiekl/ *noun* a former unit of frequency equal to one kilohertz.

kilogram /'kilǝgram/ *noun* the basic metric SI unit of mass equal to that of an international standard kept near Paris, and approximately equal to the weight of one litre of water (about 2.205lb). [French *kilogramme,* from KILO- + *gramme:* see GRAM¹]

kilohertz /'kilǝhuhts/ *noun* a unit of frequency equal to 1000 hertz.

kilojoule /'kilǝjoohl/ *noun* a unit of work or energy equal to 1000 joules.

kilolitre (NAmer **kiloliter**) /'kilǝleetǝ/ *noun* a metric unit of volume equal to 1000 litres (about 220gall).

kilometre (NAmer **kilometer**) /'kilǝmeetǝ, ki'lomitǝ/ *noun* a metric unit of length equal to 1000m (about 0.62mi). [French *kilomètre,* from KILO- + *mètre:* see METRE¹]

Usage note

Modern dictionaries of British English accept two ways of pronouncing *kilometre* – with the stress on the first syllable *kil-*, or with the stress on the second syllable -*om*-. The first is the traditional way and accords with the usual pronunciation of other metric measurements such as *centimetre* and *kilohertz.* The second is the standard American pronunciation.

kiloton /'kilətun/ *noun* a unit of explosive force equivalent to that of 1000 tons of TNT.

kilovolt /'kiləvohlt/ *noun* a unit of potential difference equal to 1000 volts.

kilowatt /'kiləwot/ *noun* a unit of electrical power equal to 1000 watts.

kilowatt-hour *noun* a unit of work or energy equal to that expended by one kilowatt in one hour.

kilt[1] /kilt/ *noun* a skirt traditionally worn by Scotsmen that is formed usu from a length of tartan, is pleated at the back and sides, and is wrapped round the body and fastened at the front. [Middle English *kilten* to gather up (a skirt), of Scandinavian origin]

kilt[2] *verb trans* **1** to pleat (fabric or a garment). **2** (*often* + up) to tuck up (e.g. a skirt): *Her slateblue skirts were kilted boldly about her waist and dovetailed behind her* — James Joyce.

kilter ✳ **out of kilter** not in proper working order. [origin unknown]

kimberlite /'kimbəliet/ *noun* a coarse-grained igneous rock that is found chiefly in South Africa and often contains diamonds. [*Kimberley*, city and diamond-mining centre in South Africa + -ITE[1]]

kimono /ki'mohnoh/ *noun* (*pl* **kimonos**) a loose robe with wide sleeves and a broad sash traditionally worn by the Japanese. ⟫ **kimonoed** *adj*. [Japanese *kimono* clothes, from *ki* wearing + *mono* thing]

kin[1] /kin/ *noun* **1** a group of people of common ancestry. **2** (*treated as sing. or pl*) one's relatives. [Old English *cyn*]

kin[2] *adj* kindred; related.

-kin *suffix* forming nouns, denoting: a small kind of something: *catkin*; *manikin*. [Middle English, from early Dutch *-kijn* or Low German *-kin*]

kina /'keenə/ *noun* the basic monetary unit of Papua New Guinea, divided into 100 toeas. [native name in Papua]

kinaesthesia (*NAmer* **kinesthesia**) /kinis'theezi-ə, kie-/ *noun* the sense of the position and movement of the parts of the body. ⟫ **kinaesthetic** /-'thetik/ *adj*. [via Latin from Greek *kinein* + *aisthēsis* perception]

kinase /'kienayz, -ays/ *noun* an enzyme that speeds up the transfer of phosphate groups from the energy-storing chemical compounds ATP or ADP to another substance involved in the chemical reaction. [KINETIC + -ASE]

kincob /'kingkob/ *noun* a richly brocaded silk fabric with gold or silver embroidery, usu made in India. [Urdu *kimkhāb*, ultimately of Chinese origin]

kind[1] /kiend/ *noun* **1** fundamental nature or quality. **2a** a group united by common features or interests: *characteristic of their kind*. **b** a specific or recognized variety: *What kind of car do you drive?* **c** a doubtful or barely admissible member of a category: *a kind of grey*. ✳ **in kind 1** in goods, commodities, or natural produce as distinguished from money. **2** in a similar way or with the equivalent of what has been offered or received: *They repaid his generosity in kind*. **kind of 1** to a moderate degree; somewhat: *It's kind of late to begin*. **2** in a manner of speaking: *You have to kind of twist it*. **3** roughly or approximately. **nothing of the kind** not at all like the thing mentioned; completely the opposite. **one of a kind** unique. [Old English *cynd* nature, natural order or group; related to *cyn* KIN[1]]

Usage note
kind, sort, and **type.** Though quite common in casual speech, constructions such as *these kind of things, those type of people* are ungrammatical and should be avoided in careful speech or writing. *This sort of thing* is a perfectly acceptable phrase; problems arise when a plural form is required because the singular form does not seem inclusive enough. *These sorts of thing* or *those types of books* are grammatically correct. Understood strictly, however, these phrases imply that there are several different categories of thing or book involved. Probably the best and most elegant way of overcoming the difficulty is to reverse the construction: *books of that kind* (many books, all of the same type) or *books of those kinds* (many books of several different types).

kind[2] *adj* **1a** disposed to be helpful and benevolent. **b** of a considerate or compassionate nature. **2** showing sympathy, benevolence, or forbearance: *kind words*. **3** cordial; friendly. **4** not harmful; mild or gentle.

kinda /'kiendə/ *contraction* kind of: *I kinda like it*. [by alteration]

kindergarten /'kindəgahtn/ *noun* a school or class for young children. [German *Kindergarten*, from *Kinder* children + *Garten* garden]

kindhearted *adj* marked by a sympathetic nature. ⟫ **kindheartedly** *adv*, **kindheartedness** *noun*.

kindle[1] /'kindl/ *verb trans* **1** to produce (a spark) or light (a fire), or start (wood, etc) burning: *In short, if you'd kindle the spark of a swindle, lure simpletons into your clutches ... you cannot do better than trot out a Duke or a Duchess* — W S Gilbert. **2** to arouse or stir up (e.g. emotion). ⟫ *verb intrans* **1** to catch fire. **2** to become animated or aroused. ⟫⟫ **kindler** *noun*. [Middle English *kindlen* from Old Norse *kynda*]

kindle[2] *verb intrans and trans* said of a hare or rabbit: to give birth. [Middle English *kindlen*, prob from *kinde* kind]

kindling *noun* material, e.g. dry wood and leaves, for starting a fire.

kindly[1] /'kiendli/ *adj* (**kindlier, kindliest**) **1** sympathetic; generous. **2** agreeable; beneficial: *a kindly climate*. ⟫⟫ **kindliness** *noun*.

kindly[2] *adv* **1a** in a kind manner. **b** in an appreciative or sincere manner: *He didn't take our criticism kindly*. **2a** used to add politeness or emphasis to a request: *Kindly fill in the attached questionnaire*. **b** used to convey irritation or anger in a command: *Will you kindly shut that door*. ✳ **not take kindly to** to react with displeasure to (e.g. a request or suggestion).

kindness /'kiendnis/ *noun* **1** the quality or state of being kind. **2** a kind deed or kind behaviour.

kindred[1] /'kindrid/ *noun* **1** (*treated as sing. or pl*) one's relatives. **2** family relationship. [Middle English, from KIN[1] + Old English *rǣden* condition, from *rǣdan* to advise, read]

kindred[2] *adj* **1** similar in nature or character. **2** related.

kindred spirit *noun* somebody with interests, opinions, etc that are similar to one's own.

kine /kien/ *pl noun archaic* cows; cattle.

kinematics /kini'matiks, kie-/ *pl noun* (*treated as sing.*) a branch of physics that deals with aspects of motion without consideration of mass or force. ⟫⟫ **kinematic** *adj*, **kinematically** *adv*. [Greek *kinēmat-, kinēma* motion, from *kinein* to move]

kinematograph /kini'matəgrahf/ *noun* = CINEMATOGRAPH.

kineses /ki'neeseez, kie-/ *noun* pl of KINESIS.

kinesics /ki'neesiks, kie-/ *pl noun* (*treated as sing.*) a systematic study of the relationship between bodily cues or movements, e.g. blushes, or shrugs, and communication. [Greek *kinēsis* (see KINESIS) + -ICS]

kinesis /ki'neesis, kie-/ *noun* (*pl* **kineses** /-seez/) a movement made by an organism in response to the intensity rather than the direction of a stimulus, in which the organism moves at random until a better environment is reached. [via Latin from Greek *kinēsis* motion, from *kinein* to move]

-kinesis *comb. form* (*pl* **-kineses**) forming nouns, denoting: **1** movement: *telekinesis*. **2** division: *karyokinesis*. [via Latin from Greek *kinēsis*: see KINESIS]

kinesthesia /kinəs'theezi-ə, kie-/ *noun chiefly NAmer* see KINAESTHESIA.

kinet- or **kineto-** *comb. form* forming words, denoting: movement or motion: *kinetogenic*; *kinetoscope*. [Greek *kinētos*: see KINETIC]

kinetic /ki'netik/ *adj* relating to motion. [Greek *kinētikos* from *kinētos* moving, from *kinein* to move]

kinetic art *noun* art, e.g. sculpture, depending for its effect on the movement of surfaces or volumes.

kinetic energy *noun* energy that a body or system has by virtue of its motion.

kinetics /ki'netiks/ *pl noun* **1** (*treated as sing. or pl*) a branch of science that deals with the effects of forces on the motions of material bodies or with changes in a physical or chemical system. **2** the mechanism by which a physical or chemical change is effected.

kinetic theory *noun* any of several theories in physics based on the fact that constituent particles of a substance are in vigorous motion.

kineto- *comb. form* see KINET-.

kinfolk *pl noun chiefly NAmer* = KINSFOLK.

king[1] /king/ *noun* **1** a male monarch of a state, country, etc, *esp* one who inherits his position and rules for life. **2** the holder of a preeminent position, *esp* among competitors within a particular area or sphere: *the king of jazz*. **3** in chess, the principal piece of each colour, which can move one square in any direction and must be protected against check. **4** a playing card marked with a stylized figure of a king and ranking usu below the ace. **5** a draughtsman that has reached the opposite side of the board and can therefore move both forwards and backwards. **6** (*used before a noun*) of the largest variety: *king cobra*. ✳ **a king's ransom** a large amount of money. ➤➤ **kinghood** *noun*, **kingliness** *noun*, **kingly** *adj*, **kingship** *noun*. [Old English *cyning*; related to *cyn* KIN¹]

king² *verb trans archaic* to make (somebody) a king. ✳ **king it** to behave in an overbearing, superior, or arrogant manner.

kingbird *noun* any of several species of American tyrant fly-catchers: genus *Tyrannus*.

kingbolt *noun* a large or major bolt.

King Charles spaniel *noun* a spaniel of a small breed with a well-rounded upper skull and a short turned-up nose. [named after *King Charles* II of England d.1685, who popularized the breed]

king cobra *noun* a large brownish venomous cobra of SE Asia and the Philippines: *Ophiophagus hannah*.

king crab *noun* = HORSESHOE CRAB.

kingcraft *noun* the art of governing as a king.

kingcup *noun* = MARSH MARIGOLD.

kingdom *noun* **1** a territorial unit with a monarchical form of government. **2** an area or sphere in which somebody or something holds a preeminent position: *in the untroubled kingdom of reason* — Bertrand Russell. **3** (*often* **Kingdom**). **a** the eternal kingship of God. **b** the realm in which God's will is fulfilled. **4** any of the primary divisions into which natural objects are commonly classified: *the animal kingdom*.

kingdom come *noun informal* **1** the next world: *blown to kingdom come*. **2** the end of the world: *wait till kingdom come*.

King Edward *noun* a variety of potato with a white skin mottled with red. [named after King *Edward* VII]

kingfish *noun* (*pl* **kingfishes** *or collectively* **kingfish**) **1** = OPAH. **2** any of various other large fishes valued for food.

kingfisher *noun* **1** any of numerous small brightly-coloured fish-eating birds with a short tail, a large head, and a long stout sharp bill: family Alcedinidae. **2** a kingfisher of Eurasia and N Africa that has cobalt blue, green, and chestnut plumage: *Alcedo atthis*.

King James Version /jaymz/ *noun* = AUTHORIZED VERSION. [named after *King James* I of England d.1625, who commissioned this translation of the Bible]

kingklip /kingklip/ *noun* an edible eel-like marine fish. [short for *kingklipfish*, translation of Afrikaans *koningklipvis*, from *King* king + *klip* rock + *vis* fish]

kinglet /'kinglit/ *noun* **1** *chiefly derog* a weak or insignificant king, *esp* one who rules over a small territory. **2** *chiefly NAmer* any of several species of small birds related to the warblers, e.g. the gold-crest or firecrest: genus *Regulus*.

kingmaker *noun* somebody having influence over the choice of candidates for office.

king of arms *noun* in heraldry, an officer of arms of the highest rank; a chief herald.

King of Kings *noun* in the Christian church, God.

king of the castle *noun* a children's game in which one child beats others to the top of a mound and tries to prevent them from taking his or her place.

king penguin *noun* a large Antarctic penguin: *Aptenodytes patagonica*.

kingpin *noun* **1** the key person or thing in a group or undertaking. **2a** = KINGBOLT. **b** a pin connecting two pivoting parts, e.g. on a hinge joint. **3** the pin which stands at the front of the triangle of pins to be aimed at in tenpin bowling.

king post *noun* a centrally placed vertical post rising to the apex of a triangular framework supporting a roof or other structure.

king prawn *noun* a large prawn found in Australian waters: genus *Penaeus*.

Kings *pl noun* (*treated as sing.*) either of two or, in the Roman Catholic Bible, any of four narrative and historical books of the Old Testament.

King's Bench *noun* used when the British monarch is a king: = QUEEN'S BENCH.

King's Counsel *noun* used when the British monarch is a king: = QUEEN'S COUNSEL.

King's English *noun* used when the British monarch is a king: = QUEEN'S ENGLISH.

King's evidence *noun* used when the British monarch is a king: = QUEEN'S EVIDENCE.

king's evil *or* **the king's evil** *noun* = SCROFULA. [from the former belief that it could be healed by a king's touch]

King's Guide *noun* used when the British monarch is a king: = QUEEN'S GUIDE.

King's highway *noun* used when the British monarch is a king: = QUEEN'S HIGHWAY.

king-size *or* **king-sized** *adj* larger or longer than the regular or standard size.

King's Scout *noun* used when the British monarch is a king: = QUEEN'S SCOUT.

King's speech *noun* used when the British monarch is a king: = QUEEN'S SPEECH.

kinin /'kienin/ *noun* **1** any of various hormones that are formed locally in the tissues and chiefly affect smooth muscle. **2** = CYTOKININ. [Greek *kinein* to move, stimulate + -IN¹]

kink¹ /kingk/ *noun* **1** a short tight twist or curl: *a kink in the wire*. **2** an eccentricity or quirk, *esp* such eccentricity in sexual behaviour or preferences. **3** an imperfection likely to cause difficulties, e.g. in the operation of something. [Dutch *kink*]

kink² *verb intrans* to become twisted, curled, or bent. ➤ *verb trans* to cause (wire, rope, hair, etc) to kink.

kinkajou /'kingkəjooh/ *noun* a slender nocturnal tree-dwelling mammal of Mexico and Central and South America that has a long prehensile tail, large lustrous eyes, and soft woolly yellowish brown fur: *Potos flavus*. [French *kinkajou*, of Algonquian origin]

kinky *adj* (**kinkier, kinkiest**) **1** closely twisted or curled. **2** *informal*. **a** sexually perverted or deviant. **b** idiosyncratic, unusual, or bizarre. ➤➤ **kinkily** *adv*, **kinkiness** *noun*.

kinnikinnick *or* **kinnikinic** /'kinikinik/ *noun* a mixture of dried leaves and bark and sometimes tobacco smoked by the American Indians and pioneers, *esp* in the Ohio valley; *also* a plant, e.g. a sumach or dogwood, used in it. [of Algonquian origin; related to Natick *kinukkinuk* mixture]

kino /'keenoh/ *noun* a red gum obtained from various trees of the pea family, used in tanning and in medicine for its astringent properties. [of West African origin]

-kins *suffix* forming nouns, denoting: a small kind of something, *esp* to express endearment: *bunnikins*.

kin selection *noun* a form of natural selection in which individuals risk death in order to increase the chance of survival of related animals.

kinsfolk *pl noun* one's relatives.

kinship *noun* **1** blood relationship. **2** similarity.

kinsman *noun* (*pl* **kinsmen**) a male relative.

kinswoman *noun* (*pl* **kinswomen**) a female relative.

kiosk /'keeosk/ *noun* **1** a small stall or stand used *esp* for the sale of newspapers, cigarettes, and sweets. **2** *Brit* a public telephone box. **3** in Turkey or Iran, an open summerhouse or pavilion. [French *kiosque* from Turkish *köşk*, from Persian *kūshk* portico]

kip¹ /kip/ *noun chiefly Brit, informal* **1** a period of sleep. **2** a place to sleep. [perhaps from Danish *kippe* cheap tavern]

kip² *verb intrans* (**kipped, kipping**) *chiefly Brit, informal* **1** to sleep. **2** (*often* + down) to lie down to sleep.

kip³ *noun* (*pl* **kip** *or* **kips**) the basic monetary unit of Laos, divided into 100 at. [Thai *kip*]

kip⁴ *noun* a bundle of untreated hides of young or small animals, or a hide from such a bundle. [Middle English from early Dutch *kip, kijp*]

kipper¹ /'kipə/ *noun* **1** a fish, *esp* a herring, that has been split open, cleaned out, salted, and dried, usu in smoke. **2** a male salmon or sea trout during or after the spawning season. [Old English *cypera* male salmon]

kipper² *verb trans* (**kippered, kippering**) to cure (a split cleaned fish) by salting and drying, usu in smoke.

kipper tie *noun* a very wide tie worn *esp* during the 1960s. [partly from its kipper-like shape; partly suggested by the name of Michael *Fish fl.* 1966, English clothes designer]

kir /kiə/ *noun* a drink consisting of white wine mixed with CASSIS (blackcurrant liqueur). [Felix *Kir* d.1968, mayor of Dijon in France, its alleged inventor]

Kirby grip /'kuhbi/ *noun trademark* a hairgrip made from a thin strip of metal folded in two, usu with one straight and one ridged side. [named after its original manufacturers, *Kirby*, Beard & Co. Ltd., Birmingham, England]

Kirghiz /'kuhgiz/ *noun* see KYRGYZ.

kirk /kuhk/ *noun* **1** *chiefly Scot* a church. **2** (**the Kirk**) the national Church of Scotland as distinguished from the Church of England or the Episcopal Church in Scotland. [Middle English (northern), from Old Norse *kirkja*, from Old English *cirice*: see CHURCH¹]

Kirk session *noun* the ruling body of a Church of Scotland congregation, consisting of the minister and the elders.

kirsch /kiəsh/ *noun* a dry colourless spirit distilled from the fermented juice of the black morello cherry. [German *Kirschwasser*, from *Kirsche* cherry + *Wasser* water]

kirtle /'kuhtl/ *noun archaic* **1** a man's tunic or coat. **2** a woman's long gown or dress. [Old English *cyrtel*, ultimately from Latin *curtus* shortened]

kismet /'kizmit, 'kismit/ *noun* (*often* **Kismet**) fate or destiny. [Turkish *kismet* from Arabic *qismah* portion, lot]

kiss¹ /kis/ *verb trans* **1** to touch (somebody or something) with the lips, *esp* as a mark of affection or greeting. **2** to touch (something) gently or lightly. ➤ *verb intrans* **1** to touch one another with the lips, *esp* as a mark of love or sexual desire. **2** to come into gentle contact. ➤➤ **kissable** *adj*. [Old English *cyssan*]

kiss² *noun* an act or instance of kissing.

kissagram *or* **kissogram** /'kisəgram/ *noun* **1** a surprise greeting, usu on a special occasion, accompanied by a kiss from the person employed to deliver it. **2** somebody, often an attractive young person, who delivers kissagrams.

kiss-and-tell *adj* said of a book, article, interview etc: revealing intimate secrets about former associates or famous people with whom the writer or interviewee has had a sexual relationship: *Kiss-and-tell books have been composed about other administrations* — The Economist.

kiss-curl *noun* a small curl of hair falling on the forehead or cheek.

kisser *noun* **1** somebody who kisses, *esp* in the specified way. **2** *informal* the mouth or face.

kissing gate *noun Brit* a gate swinging in a V- or U-shaped enclosure so that only one person can pass through at a time.

kiss of death *noun informal* an act or relationship bound to cause ruin or failure. [from the kiss with which Judas betrayed Jesus (Mark 14:44–6)]

kiss of life *noun* **1** artificial respiration in which the rescuer blows air into the victim's lungs by mouth-to-mouth contact. **2** an action or occurrence that restores or revitalizes something.

kiss of peace *noun* a ceremonial kiss, embrace, or handclasping used in Christian services of worship, *esp* the Eucharist.

kissogram /'kisəgram/ *noun* see KISSAGRAM.

kist¹ /kist/ *noun chiefly SAfr* a large chest or trunk, *esp* one used for storing a bride's trousseau. [Afrikaans *kis* from Dutch *kist*, from early Dutch *kiste*]

kist² *noun* see CIST¹.

kit¹ /kit/ *noun* **1a** a set of tools or implements. **b** a set of equipment, supplies, etc for use in a specified situation: *a first-aid kit*. **2** a set of parts ready to be assembled: *a model aeroplane kit*. **3** a set of clothes and equipment for a particular use, *esp* that equipment carried by a member of the armed forces. ✳ **get one's kit off** *informal* to undress.

▬▬ **Word history** ▬▬▬▬▬▬▬▬▬▬▬▬▬▬▬
Middle English *kitt, kyt* wooden tub, prob from Middle Dutch *kitte, kit* jug, vessel. Current senses, of which sense 3 is the earliest (18th cent.) probably come from the idea of a collection of items packed in a container.

kit² *verb trans* (**kitted, kitting**) *chiefly Brit* (+ out/up) to equip or clothe (somebody), usu for a specified situation or activity: *all kitted out for camping*.

kit³ *noun* a kitten.

kitbag *noun* a large cylindrical bag carried over the shoulder and used by soldiers, travellers, etc to carry their kit.

kitchen /'kichin/ *noun* a room or other place where food is prepared and cooked. [Old English *cycene* from a prehistoric Germanic word, from late Latin *coquina*, from Latin *coquere* to cook]

kitchen cabinet *noun* an informal group of advisers to the head of a government, often considered to have more influence than the official cabinet.

kitchenette /kichi'net/ *noun* a small kitchen or part of a room containing cooking facilities.

kitchen garden *noun* a garden in which vegetables are grown.

kitchen midden *noun* a domestic refuse heap usu including food remains; *specif* a refuse mound marking the site of a prehistoric settlement.

kitchen paper *noun* absorbent paper used chiefly in the kitchen, e.g. for draining food cooked in fat.

kitchen roll *noun* = KITCHEN PAPER.

kitchen-sink *adj Brit* said *esp* of drama: portraying modern daily life in a realistic and often sordid manner.

kitchen tea *noun Aus, NZ* a party at which a bride-to-be receives presents of kitchen equipment.

kitchenware *noun* utensils and equipment for use in a kitchen.

kite¹ /kiet/ *noun* **1** a light frame covered with thin material, e.g. paper or cloth, designed to be flown in the air at the end of a long string. **2** any of various hawks with long narrow wings, a deeply forked tail, and feet adapted for taking insects and small reptiles as prey: family Accipitridae. **3** *informal*. **a** a spinnaker or similar lightweight sail. **b** an aircraft. **4** *informal* a fraudulent worthless cheque or bill of exchange. **5** *archaic* somebody who preys on others. **6** a quadrilateral with two pairs of equal adjacent sides. [Old English *cȳta*, denoting the bird]

kite² *verb intrans* **1** to move rapidly or in a carefree manner. **2** *chiefly NAmer* to rise rapidly; to soar: *The prices of necessities continue to kite*. ➤ *verb trans* **1** to cause (something) to move or rise rapidly. **2** *chiefly NAmer, informal* to write, issue, or use (a fraudulent cheque or bill of exchange).

kite-flying *noun* **1** the act of gauging public opinion on some matter, e.g. by making information public. **2** the act of obtaining a loan or credit by means of a bill of exchange signed by a guarantor.

Kite-mark *noun* a kite-shaped mark on goods approved by the British Standards Institution.

kith /kith/ ✳ **kith and kin** one's friends and relations. [Old English *cȳthth*, from *cūth* familiar, known]

kitsch¹ /kich/ *noun* artistic or literary material that is pretentious or inferior and is usu designed to appeal to popular or sentimental taste. ➤➤ **kitschy** *adj*. [German *Kitsch*]

kitsch² *adj* having the characteristics of kitsch.

kitten¹ /'kitn/ *noun* the young of a cat or any of various other small mammals, e.g. the beaver. ✳ **have kittens** *Brit, informal* to be extremely worried or upset. [Middle English *kitoun*, from Old French *chitoun*, dimin. of *chat* cat, from late Latin *cattus*]

kitten² *verb intrans* (**kittened, kittening**) to give birth to kittens.

kitten heel *noun* a short narrow heel on a woman's shoe.

kittenish *adj* coyly playful or flirtatious.

kittiwake /'kitiwayk/ *noun* a gull with mainly white plumage and black-tipped wings: genus *Rissa*. [imitative]

kittle /'kitl/ *adj chiefly Scot, archaic* difficult or risky to deal with; unpredictable. [dialect *kittle* to tickle, from Middle English (northern) *kytyllen*, prob from Old Norse *kitla*]

kitty¹ /'kiti/ *noun* (*pl* **kitties**) used chiefly as a pet name or calling name: a cat or kitten.

kitty² *noun* (*pl* **kitties**) **1** a jointly held fund of money, e.g. for household expenses. **2** a fund in a card game, e.g. poker. **3** in bowls, the jack. [KIT¹ + -Y⁴]

kitty-cornered *adj* = CATERCORNER.

kiwi /'keewee/ *noun* (*pl* **kiwis**) **1** any of several species of flightless New Zealand birds with stout legs, a long bill, and greyish brown hairlike plumage: genus *Apteryx*. **2** (**Kiwi**) *chiefly informal* a New Zealander. **3** = KIWI FRUIT. [Maori *kiwi*, of imitative origin]

kiwi fruit *noun* the edible oval fruit of an Asian climbing plant (*Actinidia chinensis*), which has a brown hairy skin, green flesh, and black seeds. Also called CHINESE GOOSEBERRY. [because the fruit is commercially exported from New Zealand]

kJ *abbr* kilojoule.

KKK *abbr* Ku Klux Klan.

KL *abbr* Kuala Lumpur.

kl *abbr* kilolitre.

Klan /klan/ *noun* = KU KLUX KLAN. ⟫ **Klanism** *noun,* **Klansman** *noun,* **Klanswoman** *noun.*

klatch /klatsh/ *noun NAmer* a social gathering. [German *Klatsch* gossip]

Klaxon /'klaks(ə)n/ *noun trademark* a powerful electrically operated horn or warning signal. [from the name of the original manufacturer]

klebsiella /klebzi'olə/ *noun* any of a genus of plump nonmobile frequently encapsulated rod-shaped bacteria that can cause disease, e.g. pneumonia: genus *Klebsiella*. [scientific Latin, genus name, from Edwin *Klebs* d.1913, German pathologist]

Kleenex /'kleeneks/ *noun trademark* a paper handkerchief. [invented name based on *clean*]

Klein bottle /klien/ *noun* a one-sided surface that is formed by passing the narrow end of a tapered tube through the side of the tube and flaring it out to join the other end. [Felix *Klein* d.1925, German mathematician, who first described it]

klepht /kleft/ *noun* (*often* **Klepht**) a Greek belonging to any of several independent guerrilla communities after the Turkish conquest of Greece in the 15th cent. [modern Greek *klephtēs*, literally 'robber', from Greek *kleptēs*, from *kleptein* to steal]

kleptomania /kleptə'mayni·ə/ *noun* an irresistible and recurrent desire to steal, *esp* when not accompanied by economic or other motives. ⟫ **kleptomaniac** /-ak/ *noun.* [Greek *kleptein* to steal + -MANIA]

klezmer /'klezmə/ *noun* (*pl* **klezmorim** /-rim/) traditional Jewish music of E Europe, or a musician who plays it. [via Yiddish from Hebrew *kĕlē zemer* musical instruments]

klieg light /kleeg/ *noun* a powerful arc lamp used in film studios. [John H *Kliegl* d.1959 and Anton T *Kliegl* d.1927, German-born US lighting experts, who invented it]

Klinefelter's syndrome /'klienfeltəz/ *noun* an abnormal condition in males that is caused by the presence of an extra X chromosome and results in infertility and smallness of the testicles. [named after Harry F *Klinefelter* b.1912, US physician, who first described it]

klipspringer /'klipspringə/ *noun* a small agile African antelope that lives in rocky regions: *Oreotragus oreotragus*. [Afrikaans *klipspringer*, from *klip* cliff, rock + *springer* springer, leaper]

kloof /kloohf/ *noun SAfr* a deep glen; a ravine. [Afrikaans *kloof*, from early Dutch *clove* cleft]

klutz /kluts/ *noun chiefly NAmer, informal* a foolish, clumsy, or awkward person. [Yiddish *klotz, klutz*, from German *Klotz* block of wood]

klutzy /'klutsi/ *adj chiefly NAmer, informal* **1** stupid. **2** clumsy or awkward. **3** bulky or unwieldy: *klutzy recording equipment.*

klystron /'klistron, 'kliestron/ *noun* an electronic device in which the speed of a beam of electrons is regulated by electric fields and that is used for the generation and amplification of ultrahighfrequency current. [Greek *kluzein* to wash over + -TRON]

km *abbr* kilometre.

K-meson *noun* = KAON.

kn. *abbr* knot.

knack /nak/ *noun* **1** a special capacity or skill that enables something difficult to be done with ease: *Skating is easy once you've got the knack.* **2** a tendency or aptitude: *She has a knack for saying the wrong thing.* [Middle English *knak, knakke* trick, prob from *knak* sharp blow or sound, of imitative origin]

knacker[1] *noun* **1** *Brit* somebody who buys and slaughters worn-out horses for use *esp* as animal food or fertilizer: *a knacker's yard.* **2** somebody who buys old ships, houses, or other structures for their constituent materials. ⟫ **knackery** *noun.* [orig in the sense 'saddlemaker'; prob from KNACK]

knacker[2] *verb trans* (**knackered, knackering**) *chiefly Brit, informal* to exhaust (somebody): *After working all night I felt knackered.*

knacker[3] *noun coarse slang* a testicle. [prob from English dialect *knack* to make a cracking noise, strike]

knacker's yard *noun* **1** *Brit* a slaughterhouse for horses. **2** *informal* a place for someone who has been discarded as no longer useful; the scrap heap: *I'm not ready for the knacker's yard yet.*

knag /nag/ *noun* **1** a knot in wood. **2** a wooden peg. [Low German *knagge*]

knap /nap/ *verb trans* (**knapped, knapping**) to hit or break (something) with a quick blow, or to shape (flints) by breaking off pieces. ⟫ **knapper** *noun.* [Middle English *knappen*, of imitative origin]

knapsack /'napsak/ *noun* a bag, usu of canvas or leather, strapped on the back and used *esp* by a soldier for carrying supplies or personal belongings. [Low German *knappsack* or Dutch *knapzak*, from Low German and Dutch *knappen* to make a snapping noise, eat + Low German *sack* or Dutch *aak anah*, ultimately from Latin *saccus*: see SACK[1]]

knapweed /'napweed/ *noun* any of several species of thistle-like European plants of the daisy family, typically with tough wiry stems and knobby heads of purple flowers: *Centaurea nigra* and other species. Also called HARDHEAD. [Middle English *knopwed*, from *knop* knob + *wed* WEED[1]]

knar /nah/ *noun* = KNUR.

knave /nayv/ *noun* **1** *archaic* a wicked or unprincipled man; a scoundrel: *The same ambition can destroy or save, and makes a patriot, as it makes a knave* — Pope. **2** = JACK[1] (2). **3** *archaic* a male servant. ⟫ **knavery** /'nayv(ə)ri/ *noun,* **knavish** *adj,* **knavishly** *adv.* [Old English *cnafa* boy, male servant]

knead /need/ *verb trans* **1** to work and press (something soft, e.g. dough) with the hands. **2** to manipulate (something) by or as if by kneading: *knead the idea into shape.* ⟫ **kneadable** *adj,* **kneader** *noun.* [Old English *cnedan*]

knee[1] /nee/ *noun* **1a** a joint in the middle part of the human leg that is the articulation between the FEMUR (thighbone), TIBIA (shinbone), and kneecap. **b** the part of the leg that includes this joint. **c** the upper surface of the thigh of a seated person; the lap. **2** the part of an article of clothing that covers the knees: *He's gone through the knees of his trousers.* **3** something, e.g. a piece of wood or iron, shaped like the human knee in its angular bent form. ✳ **bend/bow the knee** to submit. **bring (somebody) to their knees** to cause (somebody) to submit or accept defeat or failure. [Old English *cnēow*, related to *cnēowlian* to KNEEL]

knee[2] *verb trans* to strike (somebody or something) with the knee.

kneecap[1] *noun* a thick flat triangular movable bone, developing inside tendon, that forms the front point of the knee and protects the front of the joint; = PATELLA.

kneecap[2] *verb trans* (**kneecapped, kneecapping**) to smash or shoot the kneecap of (somebody) as a punishment or torture.

knee-deep *adj* **1** = KNEE-HIGH. **2a** immersed up to the knees: *knee-deep in mud.* **b** deeply engaged or occupied: *knee-deep in work.*

knee-high *adj* high or deep enough to reach up to the knees.

kneehole *noun* a space, e.g. under a desk, for the knees.

knee jerk *noun* an involuntary forward kick produced by a light blow on the tendon below the kneecap.

knee-jerk *adj* occurring as a conditioned response; automatic: *knee-jerk radicalism.*

kneel /neel/ *verb intrans* (*past tense and past part.* **knelt** /nelt/ *or* **kneeled**) to fall or rest on the knee or knees. [Old English *cnēowlian*; related to *cnēow* KNEE[1]]

knee-length *adj* said *esp* of a garment: reaching down or up to the knees.

kneeler *noun* **1** somebody who kneels. **2** something for kneeling on, e.g. a cushion or a low stool.

knees-up *noun* (*pl* **knees-ups**) *chiefly Brit, informal* **1** a party dance in which alternate knees are raised in time with the increasing tempo of the music. **2** a boisterous celebration, usu with dancing.

knee-trembler *noun Brit, informal* an act of sexual intercourse between two standing people.

knell[1] /nel/ *verb intrans* **1** said of a bell: to ring, *esp* for a death, funeral, etc. **2** to sound ominously. ⟫ *verb trans* to announce or proclaim (something) by or as if by a knell. [Old English *cnyllan*]

knell[2] *noun* **1** the sound of a bell rung slowly, e.g. for a funeral or disaster. **2** an indication of the end or failure of something.

knelt /nelt/ *verb* past tense and past part. of KNEEL.

Knesset /'knesit/ *noun* the legislative assembly of Israel. [modern Hebrew *kĕneseth* gathering, assembly, from Hebrew *kānas* to gather]

knew /nyooh/ *verb* past tense of KNOW[1].

Knickerbocker /'nikəbokə/ *noun* a descendant of the early Dutch settlers of New York. [named after Diedrich *Knickerbocker*, fictitious author of *History of New York* by Washington Irving d.1859, US writer]

knickerbocker glory *noun* an elaborate dessert, typically consisting of layers of fruit, jelly, ice cream, and cream served in a tall glass.

knickerbockers *pl noun* short baggy trousers gathered on a band at the knee. [from the knee-breeches worn by KNICKERBOCKER, in George Cruikshank's illustrations to Irving's *History of New York*]

knickers /'nikəz/ *pl noun* **1** *Brit* women's or girls' pants. **2** *NAmer* = KNICKERBOCKERS. ✳ **get one's knickers in a twist** *Brit, informal* to become agitated or angry. [short for KNICKERBOCKERS]

knick-knack or **nicknack** /'niknak/ *noun informal* a small trivial ornament or trinket. [reduplication of KNACK]

knife[1] /nief/ *noun* (*pl* **knives** /nievz/) **1a** a cutting implement consisting of a blade fastened to a handle. **b** such an instrument used as a weapon. **2** a sharp cutting blade or tool in a machine. ✳ **have/get one's knife into** to behave in a hostile way towards (somebody). **under the knife** having a surgical operation. ➤➤ **knifelike** *adj*. [Old English *cnīf*]

knife[2] *verb trans* **1** to cut, slash, or stab (somebody or something) with a knife. **2** to mark or spread (something) with a knife. **3** *chiefly NAmer, informal* to try to defeat (somebody) by underhand means.

knife-edge *noun* **1** the cutting edge of a knife. **2** an uncertain or precarious position or condition: *on a knife-edge*. **3** something sharp and narrow, e.g. a ridge of rock, resembling the edge of a knife. **4** a sharp wedge of hard material, e.g. steel, used as a fulcrum or pivot in a pair of scales, a pendulum, etc.

knife pleat *noun* a narrow flat pleat, *esp* any of a series of such pleats that overlap and fall in the same direction.

knifepoint *noun* the point of a knife. ✳ **at knifepoint** under a threat of death or injury by being knifed.

knight[1] /niet/ *noun* **1** in medieval times, a mounted armed soldier serving a feudal superior, *esp* a man ceremonially inducted into special military rank as page and squire. **2** in Britain, a man honoured by a sovereign for merit, ranking below a baronet. **3a** somebody equivalent to a knight in rank. **b** a man devoted to the service of a lady or cause, e.g. as their champion. **4** in chess, either of two pieces of each colour, usu in the shape of a horse's head, that move diagonally from one corner to another of a rectangle of three by two squares. **5** in ancient Rome, a member of the class below the senators. ➤➤ **knighthood** *noun*, **knightliness** *noun*, **knightly** *adj and adv*. [Old English *cniht* boy, youth, male servant]

knight[2] *verb trans* to make a knight of (somebody).

knight-errant *noun* (*pl* **knights-errant**) **1** a knight travelling in search of chivalrous adventures. **2** a quixotic or chivalrous person. ➤➤ **knight-errantry** *noun*.

knight of the road *noun informal* **1** a tramp. **2a** a commercial traveller. **b** a truck driver. **3** a courteous driver of a motor vehicle.

Knight Templar /'templə/ *noun* (*pl* **Knights Templars** or **Knights Templar**) = TEMPLAR.

kniphofia /ni'fohfi-ə/ *noun* = RED-HOT POKER. [named after J H *Kniphof* d.1763, German botanist]

knish /knish/ *noun* a piece of dough with a potato or other filling, baked or fried. [Yiddish, from Russian *knish, knysh*]

knit[1] /nit/ *verb* (**knitted** or **knit, knitting**) ➤ *verb trans* **1a** to form (e.g. a fabric or garment) by working yarn into a series of interlocking loops using knitting needles or a knitting machine: *If she does but send her aunt the pattern of a stomacher, or knit a pair of garters for her grandmother, one hears of nothing else for a month* — Jane Austen. **b** to work (e.g. a specified number of stitches or rows) in this way, *specif* using knit stitch: *knit one, purl one*. **2a** to link (things) firmly or closely. **b** to unite (people) intimately. **3a** to cause (e.g. bone) to grow together. **b** to contract (e.g. one's brow) into wrinkles. ➤ *verb intrans* **1a** to make knitted fabrics or articles. **b** to work yarn in a knitting stitch, *specif* knit stitch. **2a** to grow together. **b** to become joined or drawn together. ➤➤ **knitter** *noun*. [Old English *cnyttan* to tie with a knot; related to *cnotta* KNOT[1]]

knit[2] *noun* **1** a basic knitting stitch that produces a raised pattern on the front of the work: compare PURL[1] (1). **2** a fabric or garment made by knitting.

knit stitch *noun* = KNIT[2] (1).

knitting *noun* **1** work that has been or is being knitted. **2a** the action or process of producing this. **b** (*used before a noun*) of or used to produce knitting: *a knitting machine*.

knitting needle *noun* either of a pair of long thin pointed rods, usu of metal or plastic, around which yarn is looped in knitting.

knitwear *noun* knitted clothing, *esp* jumpers and cardigans.

knives *noun* pl of KNIFE[1].

knob /nob/ *noun* **1a** a rounded protuberance or ornament. **b** a small rounded handle or control for pushing, pulling, or turning. **2** a small piece or lump, e.g. of coal or butter. **3** *chiefly NAmer* a rounded usu isolated hill or mountain. **4** *Brit, coarse slang* the penis. ✳ **with knobs on** *informal* to an even greater degree. ➤➤ **knobbed** *adj*, **knobby** *adj*. [Middle English *knobbe* from early Low German]

knobble /'nobl/ *noun* a small knob or lump. ➤➤ **knobbly** *adj*. [Middle English *knoble*, from *knobbe* (see KNOB) + *-le* (dimin. suffix)]

knobkerrie /'nobkeri/ *noun* a short wooden club with a knobbed head used *esp* by S African tribesmen. [Afrikaans *knopkierie*, from *knop* knob + *kierie* club]

knock[1] /nok/ *verb trans* **1** to strike (a surface) sharply with the knuckles or a hard object. **2** to drive, force, make, or remove (something) by striking: *to knock a hole in the wall*. **3** to remove or subtract (an amount) from a larger total: *Her earnings would be knocked off her mother's benefit* — The Times. **4** to cause (one thing) to collide with another or (things) to collide with each other. **5** *informal* to find fault with (something or somebody): *always knocking those in authority*. **6** *informal* to have sexual intercourse with (somebody). ➤ *verb intrans* **1** to strike a surface with a sharp audible blow, *esp* to strike a door seeking admittance. **2** to collide. **3a** to make a sharp pounding noise. **b** said of an internal-combustion engine: to make a metallic rapping noise because of a mechanical defect. **4** *informal* to find fault. ✳ **knock (something) on the head** *informal* to put an end to or prevent the development of (an idea, plan, etc). **knock spots off** *informal* to surpass or outdo (something or somebody) with ease. **knock together** to make or assemble (something), *esp* hurriedly or in a makeshift way. [Old English *cnocian*]

knock[2] *noun* **1a** a sharp blow or collision. **b** the sound made by a sharp blow on a hard surface. **c** the sound of knocking in an internal-combustion engine. **2** a piece of bad luck or misfortune. **3** a harsh and often petty criticism. **4** *informal* = INNINGS.

knockabout *adj* **1** suitable for rough use: *knockabout clothes*. **2** boisterous or characterized by boisterous antics: *a knockabout comedy*.

knock about *verb trans informal* to treat (somebody or something) roughly or violently. ➤ *verb intrans informal* **1** to be present by chance. **2a** to travel or wander about. **b** to associate or keep company: *They've been knocking about together for years*.

knock around *verb trans and intrans* = KNOCK ABOUT.

knock back *verb trans informal* **1** *chiefly Brit* to drink (something, *esp* an alcoholic drink) rapidly. **2** to involve a cost to (somebody): *It must have knocked them back a few thousand*. **3** to surprise or disconcert (somebody).

knock-back *noun* a setback or refusal.

knockdown *adj* **1** having such force as to strike down or overwhelm somebody: *a knockdown argument*. **2** said of furniture etc: easily assembled or dismantled. **3** said of a price: very low or substantially reduced, *esp* being the lowest acceptable to the seller.

knock down *verb trans* **1** to strike (somebody or something) to the ground. **2** to dispose of (an item for sale at an auction). **3** to take (something) apart. **4** *informal*. **a** to make a reduction in (a price). **b** to cause (somebody) to make such a reduction: *I knocked him down to £500*. **5** *Aus, NZ, informal* to spend (*esp* a pay cheque).

knocker *noun* **1** a metal ring or object hinged to a door for use in knocking. **2** *informal* somebody who finds fault; a critic. ✳ **on the knocker** *informal* promptly or immediately: *pay on the knocker*.

knockers *pl noun coarse slang* a woman's breasts.

knocker-up *noun* (*pl* **knockers-up**) *Brit* formerly, a person whose job was to wake people up for work by knocking on their doors or windows.

knock-for-knock *adj* of or being an agreement between insurance companies whereby each company indemnifies its own policyholder regardless of legal liability.

knocking copy *noun* advertising material which disparages or criticizes competitors' products.

knocking shop *noun Brit, coarse slang* a brothel.

knock-knees *pl noun* a condition in which the legs curve inward at the knees. ➤➤ **knock-kneed** *adj.*

knock off *verb intrans* to stop doing something, *esp* work. ➤ *verb trans* **1** to do (something) hurriedly or routinely: *She knocked off one painting after another.* **2** to stop (*esp* work). **3** to deduct (an amount): *He offered to knock £50 off.* **4** *informal* to kill (somebody), *esp* to murder (them). **5** *informal.* **a** to steal (something), **b** to rob (e.g. a shop or bank). **6** *Brit, coarse slang* to have sexual intercourse with (somebody). * **knock it off** often used as a command: to stop doing something.

knock on *verb trans* in rugby, to knock (the ball) towards the opponents' goal line with the hand or arm in violation of the rules. ➤ *verb intrans informal* to grow old: *She's knocking on a bit.*

knock-on *noun* **1** any or all of a series of events, actions, etc, each caused by the preceding one: *a knock-on effect throughout industry.* **2** in rugby, an instance of knocking on.

knockout *noun* **1a** knocking out or being knocked out. **b** in boxing, a blow that knocks an opponent down for longer than a particular time, usu a count of ten, and results in the termination of the match. **c** = TECHNICAL KNOCKOUT. **2a** a competition or tournament with successive rounds in which losing competitors are eliminated until a winner emerges in the final. **b** (*used before a noun*) being such a contest: *a knockout competition.* **3** *informal* somebody or something that is sensationally striking or attractive.

knock out *verb trans* **1a** to make (somebody) unconscious. **b** to defeat (a boxing opponent) by a knockout. **2** to exhaust (somebody). **3** to eliminate (an opponent) from a knockout competition. **4** *informal* to overwhelm (somebody) with amazement or pleasure. **5** to make or produce (something) quickly or hastily: *knock out an essay.* **6** to make (e.g. equipment) inoperative or useless: *The storm knocked out the telephone system.*

knockout drops *pl noun* drops of liquid containing a drug, e.g. chloral hydrate, put into a drink, *esp* surreptitiously, to produce unconsciousness or stupefaction.

knock up *verb trans* **1** to make or arrange (something) hastily or in a makeshift way. **2** to exhaust (somebody). **3** *Brit, informal* to rouse or awaken (somebody), *esp* by knocking at their door. **4** *chiefly NAmer, informal* to make (a woman) pregnant. **5** to achieve a total of (the specified amount or number, e.g. of runs in cricket). ➤ *verb intrans* to practise a racket game informally before a match.

knock-up *noun* a period of informal practice before a match in tennis, badminton, squash, etc.

knoll /nol/ *noun* a small round hill; a mound. [Old English *cnoll*]

knop /nop/ *noun* a usu ornamental knob. ➤➤ **knopped** *adj.* [Old English *-cnoppa* knob]

knot¹ /not/ *noun* **1a** a looping or interlacing of string, thread, etc pulled tight to form a fastening or lump. **b** a tangled mass, e.g. of hair. **c** a piece of ribbon, braid etc tied as an ornament. **d** a sense of tight constriction: *a knot in his stomach.* **2** something hard to solve. **3** a bond of union, *esp* the marriage bond. **4** a protuberant lump or swelling in tissue. **5a** the base of a woody branch enclosed in the stem from which it arises. **b** the cross-section of the base of a branch that appears in timber as a rounded usu cross-grained area. **6** a cluster of people or things. **7** a unit of speed equal to one nautical mile per hour. * **at a rate of knots** *informal* very fast. **tie (somebody) in knots** to confuse (somebody) utterly; to bewilder (them). **tie the knot** to get married. ➤➤ **knotless** *adj.* [Old English *cnotta*; related to *cnyttan* KNIT¹]

knot² *verb* (**knotted, knotting**) ➤ *verb trans* **1** to tie (something) in or with a knot. **2** to cause (something, e.g. hair) to become tangled. **3** to cause (something, e.g. muscles) to become tense or constricted. **4** to make (e.g. a carpet) by tying knots. ➤ *verb intrans* to form a knot or knots. ➤➤ **knotter** *noun.*

knot³ *noun* (*pl* **knots** *or collectively* **knot**) a sandpiper with grey plumage that breeds in the Arctic and winters in temperate or warm parts of the world: *Calidris canutus.* [Middle English *knott*; earlier history unknown]

knot garden *noun* a formal garden with plants arranged to form intricate knot-like patterns.

knotgrass *noun* **1** a widely occurring plant of the dock family with jointed stems and minute green flowers: *Polygonum aviculare.* **2** any of several species of related plants.

knothole *noun* a hole in a board or tree trunk where a knot or branch has come out.

knotty *adj* (**knottier, knottiest**) **1** full of knots. **2** complicated or difficult to solve: *a knotty problem.* ➤➤ **knottiness** *noun.*

knout /nowt/ *noun* a whip formerly used in Russia for flogging criminals. [Russian *knut* from Old Norse *knútre*]

know¹ /noh/ *verb* (*past tense* **knew** /nyooh/, *past part.* **known** /nohn/) ➤ *verb trans* **1** to be aware of or have information about (something); to perceive or understand (it). **2a** to be aware of the truth or factual nature of (something); to be convinced or certain of (it). **b** to have a practical understanding of (how to do something): *We want better reasons for having children than not knowing how to prevent them* — Dora Russell. **3a** to recognize or identify (somebody or something): *I would know him again.* **b** to be acquainted or familiar with (somebody or something): *Do you know my sister?* **c** to have experience of (something): *He has known suffering.* **4** *archaic* to have sexual intercourse with (somebody). ➤ *verb intrans* **1** to have knowledge. **2** (+ of/about) to be aware of or have information about (something). * **know no bounds** to be unlimited or unconfined. **know what's what** to be competent, experienced, or knowledgeable. **not know somebody from Adam** to have no idea who somebody is. **you know** used for adding emphasis to a statement: *You'll have to try harder, you know, if you want to succeed.* ➤➤ **knowable** *adj,* **knower** *noun.* [Middle English *knowen* from Old English *cnāwan*]

know² * **in the know** in possession of confidential or otherwise exclusive knowledge or information.

know-all *noun* somebody who behaves as if they know everything.

know-how *noun* expertise in a particular field.

knowing¹ *adj* **1** implying knowledge of a secret: *a knowing look.* **2** shrewd or astute. **3** deliberate or conscious. ➤➤ **knowingly** *adv,* **knowingness** *noun.*

knowing² *noun* the fact or condition of being aware of or understanding something: *There's no knowing what will happen.*

know-it-all *noun* = KNOW-ALL.

knowledge /'nolij/ *noun* **1** information, understanding, or skills, acquired through learning or experience: *the pursuit of knowledge; I had some knowledge of first aid.* **2** the total body of known facts, or those associated with a particular subject: *First come I; my name is Jowett. There's no knowledge but I know it. I am the master of this college: what I don't know isn't knowledge* — H C Beeching. **3** in philosophy, justified or verifiable belief, as distinct from opinion. **4** awareness of something: *If he left the house this afternoon he did so without my knowledge.* * **to one's knowledge** as far as one knows or is able to judge: *not to my knowledge.* [Middle English *knowlege,* from *knowlechen* to acknowledge, irreg from *knowen*: see KNOW¹]

knowledgeable *adj* having or exhibiting knowledge or intelligence; well-informed. ➤➤ **knowledgeably** *adv.*

known¹ /nohn/ *verb* past part. of KNOW¹.

known² *adj* **1** generally recognized: *a known authority on this topic.* **2** identified: *a known thief.*

knuckle¹ /'nukl/ *noun* **1** the rounded prominence formed by the ends of the two bones at a joint; *esp* any of the joints between the hand and the fingers or the finger joints closest to these. **2** a cut of meat consisting of the lowest leg joint of a pig, sheep, etc with the adjoining flesh. * **near the knuckle** almost improper or indecent. ➤➤ **knuckly** *adj.* [Middle English *knokel* from early Low German *knökel* or early Dutch *knökel,* dimin. of *knoke* bone]

knuckle² *verb trans* to hit, press, or rub (something) with the knuckles. ➤ *verb intrans* to place the knuckles on the ground in shooting a marble.

knucklebone *noun* **1** either of the bones forming a knuckle. **2** an animal's knucklebone formerly used in the game of jacks or in divination. **3** (*in pl, but treated as sing.*) the game of jacks (see JACK¹ (5A)).

knuckle down *verb intrans* to apply oneself earnestly.

knuckle-duster *noun* a metal device worn over the front of the doubled fist for protection and use as a weapon.

knucklehead *noun informal* a stupid person. ➤➤ **knuckle-headed** *adj.*

knuckle under *verb intrans* to give in; to submit: *They refused to knuckle under to any dictatorship.*

knur *or* **knurr** /nuh/ *noun* a hard lump or knot, e.g. on a tree trunk. [Middle English *knorre* from early Dutch or early Low German]

knurl /nuhl/ *noun* a small knob or protuberance, *esp* any of a series of small ridges, beads, etc on a surface to aid in gripping. ➤➤ **knurled** *adj.* [prob alteration of KNUR]

knurr /nuh/ *noun* see KNUR.

KO¹ *noun* (*pl* **KOs**) *informal* = KNOCKOUT (1B). [initials of *knock out*]

KO² *verb trans* (**KO's, KO'ing, KO'd**) *informal* to knock out (a boxing opponent).

koa /'koh·ə/ *noun* **1** a Hawaiian tree grown for its wood: *Acacia koa*. **2** the fine-grained red wood of this tree, used *esp* for furniture. [Hawaiian *koa*]

koala /koh'ahlə/ *noun* an Australian tree-dwelling marsupial mammal that has large hairy ears, grey fur, and sharp claws and feeds on eucalyptus leaves: *Phascolarctos cinereus*. [from Dhoruk, an Aboriginal language of Southern Australia]

koala bear *noun* = KOALA.

koan /'koh·ahn/ *noun* a paradox to be meditated upon, used by Zen Buddhist monks to gain enlightenment. [Japanese *kōan*, from *kō* public + *an* proposition]

kobo /'kohboh/ *noun* (*pl* **kobo**) a unit of currency in Nigeria, worth 100th of a naira. [corruption of COPPER¹]

kobold /'kobohld/ *noun* **1** a gnome in German folklore that inhabits underground places, e.g. mines. **2** an often mischievous domestic spirit of German folklore. [German *Kobold*: see COBALT]

Köchel number /'kuhkh(ə)l/ *noun* any of a group of numbers used as a cataloguing system for Mozart's works. [named after Ludwig von *Köchel* d.1877, Austrian naturalist and cataloguer of Mozart's works, who devised the system]

kodiak bear /'kohdiak/ *noun* a brown bear of Alaska: *Ursus middendorffi*. [named after *Kodiak* Island, S Alaska]

koel /'koh·əl/ *noun* a cuckoo with dark-coloured plumage, native to Asia and Australasia: *Eudynamys scolopacea*. [Hindi *koël* from Sanskrit *kokila*]

kofta /'koftə/ *noun* an Indian dish of minced meat or vegetables formed into small balls and fried. [Hindi *koftā*]

kohl /kohl/ *noun* a black powder, or a cosmetic preparation made from it, used to darken the eyelids, orig chiefly by Asian women. [Arabic *kuḥl*]

kohlrabi /kohl'rahbi/ *noun* (*pl* **kohlrabies**) a cabbage with a greatly enlarged fleshy edible stem resembling a turnip: *Brassica oleracea caulorapa*. [German *Kohlrabi* from Italian *cavoli rape*, pl of *cavolo rapa* kohlrabi, from *cavolo* cabbage + *rapa* turnip]

koi /koy/ *noun* any of several very colourful breeds of common carp that originated in Japan and other parts of eastern Asia and are kept as aquarium or pond fish: *Cyprinus carpio*. [Japanese *koi* carp]

koine /'koyni/ *noun* **1** (**Koine**) the Greek language as used in E Mediterranean countries in the Hellenistic and Roman periods. **2** a language or dialect that has become the lingua franca of a large area of shared culture. [Greek *koinē*, fem of *koinos* common]

kokanee /'kohkani, koh'kani/ *noun* (*pl* **kokanees** *or collectively* **kokanee**) a salmon of the sockeye family found in landlocked lakes of W North America. [from Shuswap, a Native American language of SE British Columbia]

kola /'kohlə/ *noun* see COLA.

kola nut *or* **cola nut** *noun* the bitter caffeine-containing seed of any of several trees of the cocoa family that is chewed *esp* as a stimulant and used in beverages. [from Temne, a W African language]

kolinsky /kə'linski/ *noun* (*pl* **kolinskies**) **1** an Asiatic mink with dark brown fur: *Mustela sibirica*. **2** the fur or pelt of this animal. [Russian *kolinskiĭ* of *Kola*, town and peninsula in NW Russia]

kolkhoz /kol'hawz, kol'khoz, 'kolkoz/ *noun* (*pl* **kolkhozy** /-zee/ *or* **kolkhozes**) a collective farm of the former USSR. [Russian *kolkhoz*, short for *kollektivnoe khozyaĭstvo* collective farm]

Kol Nidre /ˌkol 'nidray/ *noun* in Judaism, a formula for the annulment of private vows chanted in the synagogue on the eve of Yom Kippur. [Aramaic *kol nidhrē* all the vows; the opening phrase of the prayer]

komatik /'kohmətik/ *noun* *chiefly Can* an Eskimo dogsled. [Inuit *qamutik*]

komodo dragon /kə'mohdoh/ *noun* an Indonesian monitor lizard that is the largest of all known lizards, reaching 3m (10ft) in length: *Varanus komodoensis*. [named after *Komodo* Island, Indonesia, where it is chiefly found]

Komsomol /'komsə'mol, 'komsəmol/ *noun* a Communist youth organization of the former USSR. [Russian *Komsomol*, short for *Kommunisticheskiĭ Soyuz Molodezhi* Communist Union of Youth]

Kongo /'konggoh/ *noun* (*pl* **Kongos** *or collectively* **Kongo**) **1** a member of a people of the lower Congo river. **2** a Bantu language of the lower Congo river and northern Angola. ➤➤ **Kongo** *adj.*

koodoo /'koohdooh/ *noun* see KUDU.

kook /koohk/ *noun* *NAmer, informal* an eccentric or crazy person. ➤➤ **kookie** /'koohki/ *adj*, **kookiness** *noun*, **kooky** *adj.* [by shortening and alteration from CUCKOO¹]

kookaburra /'kookəburə/ *noun* a large Australian kingfisher that has a call resembling loud laughter: *Dacelo gigas*. [from Wiradhuri, an Aboriginal language of SE Australia]

kop *noun* **1** *Brit* a bank of terracing at a football ground, or the supporters who stand or sit there. **2** *SAfr* a prominent peak or hill. [from Afrikaans *kopjea* little head, from Dutch *kop* head]

kopeck *or* **copeck** *or* **kopek** /'kohpek/ *noun* a unit of currency in Russia and Belarus, worth 100th of a rouble. [Russian *kopeĭka*]

kopiyka /ko'piekə/ *noun* a unit of currency in Ukraine, worth 100th of a hryvna.

kopje *or* **koppie** /'kopi/ *noun* *SAfr* a small hill. [Afrikaans *koppie* from Dutch *kopje*, dimin. of *kop* head]

kora /'kawrə/ *noun* a lute-shaped stringed musical instrument of West Africa that has 21 strings and is played like a harp. [from a West African language]

Koran /kaw'rahn, kə'rahn/ *or* **Qur'an** /koo'rahn/ *noun* the sacred book of Islam, composed of writings accepted by Muslims as revelations made to Muhammad by Allah through the angel Gabriel. ➤➤ **Koranic** /-nik/ *adj.* [Arabic *qur'ān*, from *qara'a* to read, recite]

Korean /kə'ree·ən/ *noun and adj* **1** a native or inhabitant of North or South Korea. **2** the language of the Koreans. ➤➤ **Korean** *adj.*

korfball /'kawfbawl/ *noun* a game played by two mixed teams of twelve who try to shoot a ball into a high net. [Dutch *korfbal*, from *korf* basket + *bal* ball]

korma /'kawmə/ *noun* an Indian dish of meat, fish, or vegetables braised in water, stock, yogurt, or cream. [Urdu *kormā* braised meat, from Turkish *kavurma*]

Korsakoff's psychosis /'kawsəkofs/ *noun* = KORSAKOFF'S SYNDROME.

Korsakoff's syndrome *noun* a mental illness that is characterized by failure to remember recent events and is associated with alcoholism. [S *Korsakoff* d.1900, Russian psychiatrist]

koruna /ko'roohnə/ *noun* (*pl* **koruny** /-nee/ *or* **korunas**) the basic monetary unit of the Czech Republic and Slovakia, divided into 100 haleru. [Czech *koruna* crown, from Latin *corona*]

kosher¹ /'kohshə/ *adj* **1a** said of food: prepared according to Jewish law. **b** selling kosher food: *a kosher butcher.* **2** *informal.* **a** proper or legitimate. **b** genuine or authentic: *Vic says the lab report on yesterday's scuffle wasn't too kosher* — Julian Barnes. [Yiddish *kosher* from Hebrew *kāshēr* fit, proper]

kosher² *verb trans* (**koshered, koshering**) to prepare (food) according to Jewish law.

Kosovar /'kosəvah/ *noun* a native or inhabitant of Kosovo, region of SW Serbia. ➤➤ **Kosovan** /-vən/ *adj.*

koto /'kohtoh/ *noun* (*pl* **kotos**) a Japanese plucked stringed musical instrument with a long rectangular wooden body and 13 silk strings. [Japanese *koto*]

koulibiac *noun* see COULIBIAC.

koumiss *or* **kumiss** /'koohmis/ *noun* an alcoholic drink of fermented mare's milk made orig by the nomadic peoples of central Asia. [Russian *kumys* from Tartar *kumiz*]

kouprey /'koohpray/ *noun* (*pl* **koupreys**) a rare wild animal of the cattle family that is dark brown or grey in colour and lives in the forests of SE Asia: *Bos sauveli*. [Cambodian *kouprey*, from Pali *gō* cow + Khmer *brai* forest]

kowhai /'kohwie/ *noun* a golden-flowered shrub or small tree of the pea family found in Australasia and Chile: *Sophora tetraptera*. [Maori *kowhai*]

kowtow[1] /kow'tow/ *noun* a former Chinese gesture of deep respect in which one kneels and touches the ground with one's forehead. [Chinese (Pekingese) *ke tou*, from *ke* to bump + *tou* head]

kowtow[2] *verb intrans* **1** to make a kowtow. **2** to show obsequious deference: *She likes to patronize and be kowtowed to* — David Graham Phillips.

kph *abbr* kilometres per hour.

Kr *abbr* the chemical symbol for krypton.

kr *abbr* **1** krona. **2** krone.

kraal[1] /krahl/ *noun* **1** a village of southern African tribesmen, often enclosed by a fence. **2** an enclosure for domestic animals in southern Africa. [Afrikaans *kraal*, from Portuguese *curral* pen for cattle, enclosure]

kraal[2] *verb trans* to pen (animals) in a kraal.

kraft /krahft/ *noun* a strong paper made from wood pulp boiled in an alkaline solution. [Swedish *kraft* or German *Kraft*, literally 'strength']

krait /kriet/ *noun* any of several species of brightly coloured extremely venomous E Asian snakes that are active at night: genus *Bungarus*. [Hindi *karait*]

kraken /'krahkən/ *noun* a mythical Scandinavian sea monster. [Norwegian dialect *kraken*]

krans *or* **krantz** /krahns/ *noun* SAfr a steep overhanging cliff. [Afrikaans *krans*, from Dutch]

kraut /krowt/ *noun* (*often* **Kraut**) *offensive* a German. [German *Kraut* cabbage; from the idea that Germans lived mainly on sauerkraut]

Krebs cycle /krebz/ *noun* a sequence of respiratory reactions in the living cell that releases energy for storage in phosphate bonds. Also called CITRIC ACID CYCLE. [Sir Hans (Adolf) *Krebs* d.1981, German-born British biochemist, who discovered it]

kremlin /'kremlin/ *noun* **1** a citadel within a Russian town or city. **2a** (**the Kremlin**) the building in Moscow that houses the national government offices. **b** the government of Russia. **c** in former times, the government of the USSR. [prob from early German *kremelin*, from Russian *kreml'* citadel]

kreplach /'kreplahkh/ *pl noun* in Jewish cookery, triangular noodles with a meat or cheese filling, served with soup. [Yiddish from German dialect *Kräppel* fritter]

krill /kril/ *pl noun* small marine invertebrate animals that resemble shrimps and constitute the principal food of many sea animals, e.g. whalebone whales: order Euphausiacea. [Norwegian *kril* fry of fish]

krimmer /'krimə/ *noun* tightly curled fur with grey or black wool made from the skins of Crimean lambs. [German *Krimmer*, from *Krim* Crimea]

kris /krees/ *noun* a Malay or Indonesian dagger with a scalloped blade. [Malay *kĕris*]

Krishna /'krishnə/ *noun* a god of Hinduism worshipped as an incarnation of Vishnu. ➤➤ **Krishnaism** *noun*. [Sanskrit *Kṛṣṇa*]

krona /'krohnə/ *noun* (*pl* **kronor** /'krohnə/) the basic monetary unit of Sweden, divided into 100 öre. [Swedish *krona* crown]

króna /'krohnə/ *noun* (*pl* **krónur** /'krohnə/) the basic monetary unit of Iceland, divided into 100 auras. [Icelandic *krōna* crown]

krone /'krohnə/ *noun* (*pl* **kroner** /'krohnə/) the basic monetary unit of Denmark and Norway, divided into 100 øre. [Danish *krone* crown]

kronor /'krohnə/ *noun* pl of KRONA.

krónur /'krohnə/ *noun* pl of KRÓNA.

kroon /kroohn/ *noun* (*pl* **kroon** *or* **kroons**) the basic monetary unit of Estonia, divided into 100 senti. [Estonian *kroon* crown]

Kru /krooh/ *noun* (*pl* **Krus** *or collectively* **Kru**) **1** a member of a people of the Liberian coast. **2** the language of this people. ➤➤ **Kru** *adj*. [the name in a W African language]

Krugerrand /'kroohgərand/ *noun* a gold coin of S Africa weighing one ounce (28.35g). [S J J P *Kruger* d.1904, South African statesman whose portrait the coin bears + RAND[1]]

krummholz /'kroomholts/ *noun* stunted forest characteristic of the timberline. [German, from *krumm* crooked + *Holz* wood]

krummhorn *or* **crumhorn** /'kroomhawn, 'krumhawn/ *noun* a Renaissance woodwind musical instrument with a DOUBLE REED (two flat pieces of cane that vibrate to make the sound when blown across) and a hooked tube. [German *Krummhorn*, from *krumm* crooked + *Horn* horn]

krypton /'kript(ə)n/ *noun* a colourless gaseous chemical element of the noble gas group found in very small amounts in air, and used *esp* in fluorescent lights: symbol Kr, atomic number 36. [Greek *krypton*, neuter of *kryptos* hidden]

KS *abbr* **1** Kansas (US postal abbreviation). **2** Kyrgyzstan (international vehicle registration).

Kshatriya /'kshatri-ə/ *noun* a Hindu of an upper caste traditionally assigned to military occupations: compare BRAHMAN, SUDRA, VAISYA. [Sanskrit *kṣatriya*, from *kṣatra* rule]

KStJ *abbr* Brit Knight of the Order of St John.

KT *abbr* **1** Brit Knight of the Order of the Thistle. **2** Knight Templar.

Kt *abbr* knight.

kt *abbr* **1** karat. **2** knot.

kudos /'kyoohdos/ *noun* renown and prestige, *esp* resulting from an act or achievement: *A lifetime of debauchery somehow loses its romantic kudos once it winds down to a respectable job and keep-fit classes* — Esquire. [Greek *kydos* praise]

kudu *or* **koodoo** /'koohdooh/ *noun* (*pl* **kudus** *or* **koodoos** *or collectively* **kudu** *or* **koodoo**) either of two greyish brown African antelopes with large spirally twisted horns: *Tragelaphus strepsiceros* and *Tragelaphus imberbis*. [Afrikaans *koedoe* from Xhosa *inqudu*]

kudzu /'kudzooh/ *noun* a climbing plant with clusters of reddish-purple flowers: *Pueraria lobata*. [Japanese *kudzu*]

Kufic *or* **Cufic** /'koohfik, 'kyoohfik/ *noun* an early form of Arabic lettering, used *esp* in manuscripts of the Koran and inscriptions. ➤➤ **Kufic** *adj*. [*Kufa, Cufa*, ancient city in SW Asia]

Ku Klux Klan /,kooh kluks 'klan/ *noun* **1** a secret society in the USA that opposed the right of black people to vote after the US Civil War. **2** a secret political organization in the USA that confines its membership to white American-born Protestants and is hostile to black people. [perhaps from Greek *kyklos* circle + CLAN]

kukri /'kookri/ *noun* (*pl* **kukris**) a short curved knife used *esp* by Gurkhas. [Hindi *kukrī* from Nepalese *khukuri*]

kulak /'koohlak/ *noun* **1** a prosperous peasant farmer in pre-revolutionary Russia. **2** in Marxist literature, a member of a class of peasant-proprietors working for individual profit. [Russian *kulak*, literally 'fist, tight-fisted person']

kulfi /'koolfi/ *noun* an Indian dessert resembling ice cream that is flavoured with nuts and usu cone-shaped. [Hindi *kulfi*]

Kulturkampf /kool'tooəkampf/ *noun* conflict between civil and religious authorities, *esp* over control of education; *specif* the conflict between the German government and the Catholic Church in the late 19th cent. [German *Kulturkampf*, from *Kultur* culture + *Kampf* conflict]

kumara /'koomərə/ *noun* NZ = SWEET POTATO. [Maori *kumara*]

Kumbh Mela /koom 'maylə/ *or* **Kumbha Mela** *noun* the Pitcher Festival, a major Hindu festival held every three years in one of four towns (Allahabad, Hardwar, Ujjain and Nashik), the cycle culminating in the Maha Kumbh Mela or Great Pitcher Festival held in Allahabad every twelve years, with a particularly important festival taking place every 144 years. [Sanskrit *kumbha* pot, pitcher + *mela* festival; from the pitcher or pot containing nectar of immortality, from which according to Hindu tradition drops of nectar were spilt in the four places in which the festivals are now held]

kumiss /'koohmis/ *noun* see KOUMISS.

kumkum /'kumkum/ *noun* a red powder used by Hindu women to make a small mark on the forehead. [from Sanskrit *kunkuma* saffron]

kümmel /'kooml/ *noun* a colourless aromatic liqueur flavoured with caraway seeds. [German *Kümmel* caraway seed, from Old High German *kumīn* cumin]

kumquat *or* **cumquat** /'kumkwot/ *noun* **1** any of several small orange citrus fruits with sweet spongy rind and rather acid pulp that are used chiefly for preserves. **2** any of several trees or shrubs of the orange family that bear this fruit: genus *Fortunella*. [Chinese (Cantonese) *gam gwat*, from *gam* gold + *gwat* orange]

kuna /'koohnə/ *noun* the basic monetary unit of Croatia, divided into 100 lipas.

Word history
Serbo-Croat *kuna* marten. The fur of the marten was formerly used as currency.

kung fu /ˌkung 'fooh/ *noun* a Chinese martial art resembling karate. [Chinese (Pekingese) *gongfu* skill, from *gong* work, merit + *fu* man]

kunzite /ˈkoontsiet/ *noun* in mineralogy, a spodumene that occurs in pinkish lilac crystals and is used as a gem. [named after G F *Kunz* d.1932, US gem expert]

Kurd /kuhd/ *noun* a member of a pastoral and agricultural people who chiefly inhabit adjoining parts of Turkey, Iran, and Iraq. ⟫ **Kurdish** *adj.*

Kurdish *noun* the Iranian language of the Kurds. ⟫ **Kurdish** *adj.*

kurgan /ˈkooəgən/ *noun* a prehistoric burial mound found in E Europe and *esp* S Russia. [Russian, of Turkic origin]

kuri /ˈkoori/ *noun* (*pl* **kuris**) 1 *NZ* a mongrel dog. 2 *NZ, informal* an unpopular man or woman. 3 *Aus, derog* a Maori. [Maori *kuri*]

kurrajong /ˈkurəjong/ *noun* any of several Australian trees or shrubs yielding strong woody fibre: *Brachychiton populneum* and others. [Dharuk (an Aboriginal language of S Australia) *garrajung* fibrous fishing line]

kursaal /ˈkooəsahl, ˈkuhz(ə)l/ *noun* the part of a spa or health resort where visitors are entertained. [German *Kursaal*, from *Kur* cure + *Saal* room]

kurta /ˈkertə/ *noun* a loose-fitting collarless shirt worn by Hindu men and women. [from Urdu and Persian *kurtah*]

kurtosis /kuh'tohsis/ *noun* the peakedness or flatness of the graph of a frequency distribution, *esp* as determining the concentration of values near the mode. [Greek *kyrtōsis* convexity, from *kyrtos* convex]

kuru /ˈkoorooh/ *noun* a fatal disease of the nervous system that occurs among tribespeople of eastern New Guinea. [native name in New Guinea, literally 'trembling']

kurus /koo'roohsh/ *noun* (*pl* **kurus**) a unit of currency in Turkey, worth 100th of a lira. [Turkish *kuruş*]

Kuwaiti /k(y)oo'wayti/ *noun* a native or inhabitant of Kuwait in SW Asia. ⟫ **Kuwaiti** *adj.*

kV *abbr* kilovolt.

kvass /kvahs/ *noun* a slightly alcoholic beverage made in E Europe usu by fermenting mixed cereals and adding flavouring. [Russian *kvas*]

kvetch /kvech/ *verb intrans NAmer, informal* to complain persistently. [Yiddish *kvetshn* to squeeze, complain]

kW *abbr* kilowatt.

Kwa /kwah/ *noun* a branch of the Niger-Congo language family that includes Igbo and Yoruba. ⟫ **Kwa** *adj.* [the Kwa name]

kwacha /ˈkwahchə/ *noun* (*pl* **kwacha**) the basic monetary unit of Zambia and Malawi. [native name in Zambia, literally 'dawn'; previously used as a nationalist slogan in Zambia, referring to a 'new dawn of freedom', and adopted as the name of the currency of the newly independent state]

kwanza /ˈkwanzə/ *noun* (*pl* **kwanza** or **kwanzas**) the basic monetary unit of Angola, divided into 100 lwei. [of Bantu origin]

kwashiorkor /kwashi'awkə/ *noun* severe malnutrition in babies and children that is caused by a diet high in carbohydrate and low in protein. [native name in Ghana, literally 'red boy', because the condition turns the hair red]

kWh *abbr* kilowatt-hour.

KWIC /kwik/ *abbr* keyword in context.

KWOC /kwok/ *abbr* keyword out of context.

KWT *abbr* Kuwait (international vehicle registration).

KY *abbr* Kentucky (US postal abbreviation).

Ky *abbr* Kentucky.

kyanise /ˈkie-əniez/ *verb trans* see KYANIZE.

kyanite /ˈkie-əniet/ *noun* a mineral containing aluminium, silicon, and oxygen that occurs in blue crystals and crystalline masses and is sometimes used as a gemstone. [German *zyanit*, from Greek *kyanos* dark blue enamel, lapis lazuli]

kyanize or **kyanise** /ˈkie-əniez/ *verb trans* to treat (timber) with a substance such as mercuric chloride to protect it from decay. ⟫ **kyanization** /-'zaysh(ə)n/ *noun.* [named after J H *Kyan* d.1850, Irish inventor who patented the process]

kyat /ki'aht/ *noun* (*pl* **kyat** or **kyats**) the basic monetary unit of Myanmar (formerly Burma), divided into 100 pyas. [Burmese *kyat*]

kybosh /ˈkiebosh/ *noun* see KIBOSH.

kyle /kiel/ *noun Scot* often in place names: a narrow channel between islands or between an island and the mainland. [Scottish Gaelic *caol* narrow]

kylie /ˈkieli/ *noun Aus* a type of boomerang. [native name in Australia]

kylix /ˈkieliks/ *noun* (*pl* **kylixes** or **kylikes** /ˈkielikeez/) a two-handled drinking cup with a shallow bowl and a tall stem, used in ancient Greece. [from Greek *kulix*]

kyloe /ˈkieloh/ *noun Scot* an animal of a breed of long-horned long-haired Highland cattle. [Scottish Gaelic *gaidhealach* Gaelic, Highland]

kymograph /ˈkieməgrahf/ *noun* a rotating cylindrical device that graphically records motion or pressure, e.g. heartbeat or muscle contraction. ⟫ **kymographic** /-'grafik/ *adj.* [Greek *kyma* wave + -GRAPH]

kyphosis /kie'fohsis/ *noun* an abnormal curvature of the spine resulting in a humped back: compare LORDOSIS, SCOLIOSIS. ⟫ **kyphotic** /-'fotik/ *adj.* [via Latin from Greek *kyphōsis*, from *kyphos* humpbacked]

Kyrgyz /ˈkiəgiz, kiə'geez/ or **Kirghiz** /ˈkuhgiz/ *noun* (*pl* **Kyrgyz** or **Kirghiz**) 1 a member of a Mongolian people inhabiting chiefly the Central Asian steppes. 2 the Turkic language of this people. ⟫ **Kyrgyz** *adj.* [the Kyrgyz name for the people and language]

Kyrie /ˈkiriay, 'kee-/ *noun* a short prayer, often set to music as the first section of the mass, that begins with or consists of these words or their English translation. [via late Latin from Greek *kyrie eleēson* Lord, have mercy]

Kyrie eleison /i'lay(i)son, -zon/ *noun* = KYRIE.

kyu /kyooh/ *noun* in judo and other martial arts, a grade of proficiency for novices. [Japanese *kyu* class]

KZ *abbr* Kazakhstan (international vehicle registration).

L¹ *or* **l** *noun* (*pl* **L's** *or* **Ls** *or* **l's**) **1a** the twelfth letter of the English alphabet. **b** a written character or design denoting this letter. **c** the sound represented by this letter, one of the English consonants. **2** an item designated as L, *esp* the twelfth in a series. **3** the Roman numeral for 50.

L² *abbr* **1** Lady. **2** Large (clothing size). **3** Latin. **4** *Brit* learner driver. **5** Liberal. **6** Linnaeus. **7** lost (used in tables of match results). **8** Luxembourg (international vehicle registration). **9** live (used on electrical plugs).

l *abbr* **1** lake. **2** left. **3** length(s). **4** lightning. **5** line. **6** liquid. **7** litre(s). **8** little. **9** long. **10** low. **11** *archaic* pound(s).

LA *abbr* **1** Library Association. **2** *Brit* local authority. **3** Los Angeles. **4** Louisiana (US postal abbreviation).

La¹ *abbr* **1** in street names, lane. **2** Louisiana.

La² *abbr* the chemical symbol for lanthanum.

la *or* **lah** /lah/ *noun* in music, the sixth note of a major scale in the tonic sol-fa system, or the note A in the fixed-doh system. [Middle English: see GAMUT]

laager¹ /'lahgə/ *noun* *SAfr* **1** formerly, an encampment protected by a circle of wagons. **2** an entrenched position or point of view. [obsolete Afrikaans *lager* (now *laer*), from German *Lager* or Dutch *leger*]

laager² *verb trans* *SAfr* formerly, to arrange (wagons) in a laager.

Lab. *abbr* **1** *Brit* Labour. **2** Labrador.

lab /lab/ *noun* *informal* a laboratory.

labarum /'labərəm/ *noun* (*pl* **labara** /-rə/) an imperial standard or banner of the later Roman emperors, *esp* the standard adopted by Constantine after his conversion to Christianity. [late Latin *labarum*]

labdanum /'labdənəm/ *or* **ladanum** /'lad-/ *noun* a fragrant OLEORESIN (a mixture of oil and plant resin) derived from various rockroses and used in perfumery. [medieval Latin *lapdanum* via Latin from Greek *ladanon*, *lēdanon*, from *lēdon* rockrose]

label¹ /'laybl/ *noun* **1** a slip, e.g. of paper or cloth, attached to something to give information about it. **2** a brand name, *esp* the name of a fashion house or a record company. **3** a descriptive or identifying word or phrase, e.g.: **a** an epithet. **b** a word or phrase used with a dictionary definition to provide additional information, e.g. level of usage. **4** in chemistry or biology, a radioactive ISOTOPE (form in which an atom can occur), a fluorescent dye, or an enzyme used to follow through a chemical reaction or biological process. **5** in computing, a number or word that identifies a location within a computer program. **6** in heraldry, a CHARGE² (heraldic figure) consisting of a narrow horizontal band with usu three pendants. **7** in architecture, a dripstone. [Middle English, in the sense 'narrow band, strip', from early French, prob of Germanic origin]

label² *verb trans* (**labelled, labelling,** *NAmer* **labeled, labeling**) **1** to fasten a label to (an item). **2** to describe or categorize (somebody or something), *esp* unfairly or sweepingly: *She had been labelled disruptive at the age of five.* **3** to make (a chemical compound, atom, cell, etc) traceable using a label. ➤ **labeller** *noun*.

labia /'laybi-ə/ *noun* pl of LABIUM.

labial¹ *adj* **1** relating to or in the region of the lips or labia. **2** in phonetics, said of a speech sound: articulated using one or both lips: *the labial sounds /f/, /p/, and /ooh/.* ➤ **labially** *adv.* [medieval Latin *labialis* from Latin *labium* lip]

labial² *noun* in phonetics, a labial sound.

labialize *or* **labialise** /'laybi-əliez/ *verb trans* to pronounce (a sound) using the lips. ➤ **labialization** /-lie'zaysh(ə)n/ *noun*.

labia majora /mə'jawrə/ *pl noun* the thick outer folds of the vulva. [Latin *labia majora* larger lips]

labia minora /mi'nawrə/ *pl noun* the thin inner folds of the vulva. [Latin *labia minora* smaller lips]

labiate /'laybiayt, -ət/ *adj* **1** belonging or relating to the family of plants that have a COROLLA (petals) or CALYX (sepals) arranged in two unequal portions that project one over the other like lips, e.g. mint, thyme, and sage: family Labiatae. **2** in botany and zoology, having a lip or labium. [Latin *labiatus* from *labium* lip]

labile /'laybil, 'laybiel/ *adj* **1** in chemistry, liable to break down; unstable: *a labile mineral.* **2** apt to change: *an emotionally labile person.* ➤ **lability** /lə'biliti/ *noun*. [Middle English, in the sense 'prone to err', via French from late Latin *labilis*, from Latin *labi* to slip]

labio- *comb. form* forming adjectives, with the meaning: labial and: *labiodental.* [Latin *labium* lip]

labiodental¹ /laybioh'dentl/ *adj* said of a speech sound: articulated using the bottom lip and the teeth: *the labiodental sounds /f/ and /v/.*

labiodental² *noun* a labiodental consonant.

labium /'laybi-əm/ *noun* (*pl* **labia** /'laybi-ə/) **1** a lower mouthpart of an insect. **2** the lower lip of a flower that has projecting parts resembling lips. **3** (*in pl*) the labia majora or labia minora. [Latin *labium* lip]

labor¹ /'laybə/ *noun* *NAmer*, *Aus* see LABOUR¹.

labor² *verb trans and intrans* *NAmer*, *Aus* see LABOUR².

laboratory /lə'borətri/ *noun* (*pl* **laboratories**) **1** a place equipped for scientific experiment, testing, or analysis. **2** a place where chemicals and chemical products are developed. [medieval Latin *laboratorium* from Latin *laborare* to labour, from *labor* LABOUR¹]

labored *adj* *NAmer* see LABOURED.

laborer /'layb(ə)rə/ *noun* *NAmer* see LABOURER.

laborious /lə'bawri·əs/ *adj* **1** requiring a lot of time or effort. **2** said of writing: lacking ease of expression; laboured. ➤➤ **laboriously** *adv*, **laboriousness** *noun*. [Middle English via early French *laborieux* from Latin *laboriosus*, from *labor* LABOUR[1]]

laborism /'laybərizm/ *noun NAmer* see LABOURISM.

laborite /'laybəriet/ *noun NAmer* see LABOURITE.

labour[1] (*NAmer, Aus* **labor**) /'laybə/ *noun* **1** work, *esp* when difficult or done for wages; toil: *Once you are a showman you are plumb ruined for manual labour again* — Will Rogers. **2** workers collectively. **3** (**Labour**) (*treated as sing. or pl*) the Labour Party. **4** the process of childbirth, usu regarded as beginning at the time of the first regular contractions of the uterus, and ending at delivery. [Middle English via French from Latin *labor*]

labour[2] (*NAmer, Aus* **labor**) *verb intrans* **1a** to work hard. **b** to do unskilled manual work. **2a** to struggle to do something difficult: *I was labouring over the application form*. **b** said of an engine: to work noisily. **3a** to move with difficulty: *He laboured up the steps with his cases*. **b** said of a ship: to pitch or roll heavily. **4** (+ under) to be misled by (something): *She was labouring under the misapprehension that we had already gone*. **5** to be in the process of giving birth. ➤ *verb trans* **1** to deal with or explain (something) in laborious detail: *He always has to labour the point*. **2** *archaic* to cultivate (the ground).

labour camp *noun* a prison camp in which inmates are forced to work.

Labour Day *noun* a public holiday in recognition of working people, held in some countries on 1 May, and in the USA and Canada on the first Monday in September.

laboured (*NAmer* **labored**) *adj* **1** showing signs of effort; lacking natural grace or easy fluency: *Blanche Boveal retired early, leaving the room in a series of laboured leaps that she hoped might be recognized as a tolerable imitation of Pavlova* — Saki. **2** performed with great effort: *Her breathing was laboured*.

labourer (*NAmer* **laborer**) *noun* a person who does unskilled manual work, *esp* outdoors.

labour exchange *noun* (*often* **Labour Exchange**) *dated* = JOB CENTRE.

labour-intensive *adj* using a high proportion of labour in the process of production: compare CAPITAL-INTENSIVE.

labourism (*NAmer* **laborism**) /'laybərizm/ *noun* the principles and policies of the labour movement. ➤➤ **labourist** *noun and adj*.

labourite (*NAmer* **laborite**) /'laybəriet/ *noun* (*often* **Labourite**) a member or supporter of a Labour party.

labour of love *noun* a task performed for the pleasure it yields rather than for personal gain.

Labour Party *noun* **1** in Britain, a political party founded in 1900 to represent working people, based on socialist principles. **2** a similar political party in various other countries.

labour-saving *adj* designed to replace or decrease manual labour: *a labour-saving domestic appliance*.

labour union *noun chiefly NAmer* a trade union.

labra /'labrə, 'laybrə/ *noun* pl of LABRUM.

Labrador /'labrədaw/ *noun* a retriever of a breed originating in Newfoundland, having a short thick golden or black coat and a broad head and chest. [named after the *Labrador* peninsula, Canada, where the breed originated]

labradorite /labrə'dawriet/ *noun* a mineral that is a variety of feldspar occurring in igneous rocks. It is characterized by a play of several colours due to light diffraction. [named after the *Labrador* peninsula, Canada, where it was found]

Labrador retriever *noun* = LABRADOR.

labret /'laybret/ *noun* an ornament, e.g. a piece of shell, worn in a perforation of the lip. [Latin *labrum* lip + -ET]

labrum /'labrəm, 'laybrəm/ *noun* (*pl* **labra** /'labrə, 'laybrə/) an upper or front mouthpart of a crustacean, insect, or other arthropod. [Latin *labrum* lip, edge]

laburnum /lə'buhnəm/ *noun* any of a small genus of Eurasian shrubs and trees of the pea family with bright yellow flowers that hang in clusters and pods of poisonous seeds: genus *Laburnum*. [Latin genus name, of unknown origin]

labyrinth /'labərinth/ *noun* **1** a place that is a network of intricate passageways, tunnels, blind alleys, etc. **2** something perplexingly complex or tortuous in structure, arrangement, or character. **3** in anatomy, the complex network of twisting bony cavities that forms the inner ear. ➤➤ **labyrinthian** *adj*. [Middle English *laborintus* via Latin from Greek *labyrinthos*, orig with reference to the maze in Greek mythology in which the Minotaur was kept]

labyrinthine /labə'rinthien/ *adj* of, like, or forming a labyrinth; intricate or involved.

LAC *abbr* Leading Aircraftman.

lac[1] /lak/ *noun* a resinous substance secreted by a scale insect and used to make varnishes, including shellac. [Persian *lak* and Hindi *lākh*, from Sanskrit *lākṣā*]

lac[2] *noun* see LAKH.

Lacanian /lə'kayniən/ *adj* relating to the work of Jacques Lacan, *esp* his reinterpretation of Freud's theories in terms of structural linguistics and anthropology. ➤➤ **Lacanian** *noun*. [Jacques *Lacan* d.1981, French psychoanalyst and writer]

laccolith /'lakəlith/ *noun* a mass of igneous rock that is forced up between beds of existing rock and produces domed bulging of the overlying strata. [Greek *lakkos* cistern + -LITH]

lace[1] /lays/ *noun* **1** a fine decorative cotton or silk fabric made by twisting or looping thread in symmetrical patterns and figures, used for trimming and for garments. **2** a cord or string used for drawing together two edges, e.g. of a garment or shoe. **3** an ornamental braid used for trimming, *esp* on military dress uniforms. [Middle English via early French *laz* from Latin *laqueus* noose, snare]

lace[2] *verb trans* **1** to fasten (something, e.g. a shoe) by means of a lace passed through eyelets. **2** to squeeze in the waist of (a woman) by tightening the laces of a corset. **3** to trim (e.g. a garment) with lace or laces. **4** to entwine or interlace (*esp* the fingers). **5** to add a dash of an alcoholic drink to (*esp* another drink): *a trifle laced with sherry*. **6** to give savour or variety to (something): *a mundane story laced with witty repartee*. **7** (*usu* + with) to mark (something) with streaks of colour: *a red sky laced with gold*. **8** *informal* (+ into) to tackle or make an assault on (somebody or something). ➤ *verb intrans* (+ up) to be fastened or tied with a lace. [Middle English *lacen* via early French *lacier* from Latin *laqueare* to ensnare, from *laqueus* noose, snare]

Lacedaemonian /ˌlasidi'mohni·ən/ *noun* a native or inhabitant of Lacedaemon, a name given to the area around the ancient Greek city of Sparta. ➤➤ **Lacedaemonian** *adj*.

lacerate /'lasərayt/ *verb trans* to tear or cut (skin or flesh) roughly. ➤➤ **laceration** /lasə'raysh(ə)n/ *noun*. [Latin *laceratus*, past part. of *lacerare* to tear, from *lacer* torn, mangled]

lace-up *noun chiefly Brit* a shoe or boot that is fastened with laces.

lacewing *noun* any of various insects that have wings with a fine network of veins, long antennae, and very bright eyes. They prey on aphids and other pests: order Neuroptera.

laches /'lachiz/ *noun* (*pl* **laches** /'lacheez/) in law, negligence in carrying out a legal duty or unreasonable delay in making a legal claim. [Middle English *lachesse* from early French *laschesse*, from *lasche* lax, from Latin *laxus*]

lachrymal *or* **lacrimal** *or* **lacrymal** /'lakriməl/ *adj* **1** *formal or literary* causing tears to be shed or marked by the shedding of tears. **2** (**lacrimal**) relating to or in the region of the glands that produce tears. [early French *lacrymal* from medieval Latin *lacrimalis*, *lachrymalis*, from Latin *lacrima* tear]

lachrymation *or* **lacrimation** *or* **lacrymation** /lakri'maysh(ə)n/ *noun* **1** *literary* the shedding of tears. **2** in medicine, abnormal or excessive secretion of tears. [Latin *lacrimation-*, *lacrimatio*, from *lacrimare* to weep, from *lacrima* tear]

lachrymator *or* **lacrimator** /'lakrimaytə/ *noun* a tear-producing substance, e.g. a tear gas.

lachrymatory[1] *or* **lacrimatory** /'lakrimət(ə)ri/ *adj* **1** *literary* prompting tears. **2** in medicine, relating to tears or the shedding of tears. [medieval Latin *lachrymatorius* from late Latin *lacrimatorius*, from Latin *lacrimare*: see LACHRYMATION]

lachrymatory[2] *noun* (*pl* **lachrymatories**) a small bottle found in ancient tombs, formerly believed to hold the tears of mourners.

lachrymose /'lakrimohs/ *adj formal or literary* **1** given to weeping; tearful. **2** tending to cause tears; sad or mournful. ➤➤ **lachrymosely** *adv*. [Latin *lacrimosus* from *lacrima* tear]

lacing /'laysing/ *noun* **1** something that laces, *esp* a laced fastening or a lace trimming. **2** something added to give flavour or spice, *esp* a dash of spirits added to food or drink. **3** a course usu of brick added to a wall of stone or rubble to increase strength. **4** *informal* a beating or thrashing.

laciniate /lə'siniayt, -ət/ *adj* cut into deep irregular segments; fringed or lobed: *a laciniate petal.* >>> **lacination** /-'aysh(ə)n/ *noun.* [Latin *lacinia* flap + -ATE³]

laciniated /lə'siniaytid/ *adj* = LACINIATE.

lack¹ /lak/ *verb trans* to suffer from the absence or deficiency of (something): *The script lacks sparkle.* > *verb intrans* **1** (*often* + in) to be deficient in something: *The only thing lacking was a decent wine*; *He's not lacking in intelligence.* **2** (*usu* + for) to be short of or have need of something: *She will not lack for advisers.* [Middle English *laken* from early Dutch]

lack² *noun* an absence or shortage of something: *Power corrupts, but lack of power corrupts absolutely* — Adlai Stevenson.

lackadaisical /lakə'dayzikl/ *adj* **1** lacking enthusiasm or zest. **2** reprehensibly casual or negligent; lax. >>> **lackadaisically** *adv.* [archaic *lackadaisy*, exclamation of regret (alteration of earlier *lackaday, alack the day*) + -ICAL]

lackey¹ /'laki/ *noun* (*pl* **lackeys**) **1** a servant, *esp* a liveried footman. **2** a servile follower; a toady. **3** a European moth. Its caterpillars have stripes resembling a footman's livery and live in silken tents in trees: *Malacosoma neustria.* [early French *laquais*]

lackey² *verb trans archaic* to act as a servant for (somebody); to wait on (them).

lacklustre (*NAmer* **lackluster**) *adj* **1** lacking in vitality, enthusiasm, or interest; uninspired. **2** lacking in sheen or radiance; dull: *His eyes had assumed the vacant, lack-lustre expression which showed mental abstraction* — Conan Doyle.

Laconian /lə'kohni·ən/ *noun* a native or inhabitant of Laconia, an ancient Greek region with Sparta as its capital. >>> **Laconian** *adj.*

laconic /lə'konik/ *adj* using a minimum of words; terse or concise. >>> **laconically** *adv*, **laconicism** /-siz(ə)m/ *noun.* [Latin *laconicus* Spartan, from Greek *lakōnikos*; from the Spartan reputation for terseness of speech]

lacquer¹ /'lakə/ *noun* **1** a clear or coloured varnish obtained by dissolving a substance, e.g. shellac, in a solvent, e.g. alcohol. **2** the sap of the lacquer tree, used as a wood varnish. **3** *Brit* a substance sprayed onto the hair to fix it in place; hair lacquer. **4** decorative wooden articles that have been coated with lacquer. [Portuguese *lacré* sealing wax, via Arabic *lakk* from Persian *lak*: see LAC¹]

lacquer² *verb trans* (**lacquered, lacquering**) **1** to coat (e.g. wooden furniture) with lacquer. **2** to spray (hair) with hair lacquer. >>> **lacquerer** *noun.*

lacquer tree *noun* an E Asian tree of the sumach family, with a sap from which a hard-wearing varnish is obtained: *Rhus verniciflua.*

lacrimal¹ /'lakriml/ *adj* see LACHRYMAL.

lacrimal² *noun* = LACRIMAL BONE.

lacrimal bone *noun* a small bone in the eye socket.

lacrimation /lakri'maysh(ə)n/ *noun* see LACHRYMATION.

lacrimator /'lakrimaytə/ *noun* see LACHRYMATOR.

lacrimatory /'lakrimətri/ *adj* see LACHRYMATORY¹.

lacrosse /lə'kros/ *noun* a field game played between two teams of ten players who try to throw a ball into the opposing side's goal with a long-handled stick that has a triangular head with a loose mesh pouch for catching and carrying the ball. [Canadian French *la crosse* the crosse: see CROSSE]

lacrymal /'lakriml/ *adj* see LACHRYMAL.

lacrymation /lakri'maysh(ə)n/ *noun* see LACHRYMATION.

lact- *or* **lacti-** *or* **lacto-** *comb. form* forming words, denoting: **1** milk: *lacto-vegetarian.* **2** lactic acid: *lactobacillus.* **3** lactose: *lactase.* [French *lact-* from Latin *lact-, lac* milk]

lactam /'laktam/ *noun* an organic chemical compound that contains an amide group —NHCO—.

lactase /'laktayz, -ays/ *noun* an enzyme that breaks down certain sugars, e.g. lactose, and occurs in the intestines of young mammals and in yeasts.

lactate¹ /'laktayt/ *verb intrans* said of a female mammal: to produce or secrete milk. [Latin *lactatus*, past part. of *lactare*, from *lact-, lac* milk]

lactate² /'laktayt/ *noun* any of various chemical salts or esters formed by combination between lactic acid and a metal atom, an alcohol, or another chemical group.

lactation /lak'taysh(ə)n/ *noun* **1** the production of milk by the mammary glands. **2** the period during which milk is produced and the young are suckled. >>> **lactational** *adj.*

lacteal¹ /'lakti·əl/ *adj* **1** consisting of, producing, or resembling milk. **2** conveying or containing a milky fluid, e.g. CHYLE (type of lymph). [Latin *lacteus* of milk, from *lact-, lac* milk]

lacteal² *noun* any of the lymphatic vessels that convey CHYLE (type of lymph) to the thoracic duct.

lactescent /lak'tes(ə)nt/ *adj* said of plants or insects: secreting a milky juice. **2** milky. >>> **lactescence** *noun* [Latin *lactescent-, lactescens*, present part. of *lactescere* to turn to milk, ultimately from *lact-, lac* milk]

lacti- *comb. form* see LACT-.

lactic /'laktik/ *adj* of, relating to, or obtained from milk.

lactic acid *noun* an organic acid formed in the muscles during strenuous exercise and found in sour milk: formula $CH_3CH(OH)COOH$.

lactiferous /lak'tifərəs/ *adj* **1** secreting or conveying milk. **2** yielding a milky juice. [French *lactifère* from late Latin *lactifer*, from Latin *lact-, lac* milk + -FER]

lacto- *comb. form* see LACT-.

lactobacillus /,laktohbə'siləs/ *noun* (*pl* **lactobacilli** /-'silie/) any of a genus of rod-shaped bacteria that form lactic acid by fermentation: genus *Lactobacillus.*

lactose /'laktohz, 'laktohs/ *noun* a sugar that is present in milk and consists of glucose and galactose. It yields lactic acid when fermented: formula $C_{12}H_{22}O_{11}$.

lacto-vegetarian /'laktoh/ *noun* a vegetarian who eats dairy products such as milk and cheese, sometimes including eggs: compare VEGETARIANISM.

lacuna /lə'kyoohnə/ *noun* (*pl* **lacunae** /-nee/ *or* **lacunas**) **1** a blank space or a missing part. **2** in anatomy, a small cavity in a bone or other body part. >>> **lacunal** *adj*, **lacunar** *adj*, **lacunary** *adj*, **lacunate** /-nət/ *adj*, **lacunose** *adj.* [Latin *lacuna* pool, pit, gap, from *lacus* LAKE¹]

lacustrine /lə'kustrien/ *adj technical or literary* of or occurring in lakes. [from French or Italian *lacustre*, from Latin *lacus* LAKE¹]

LACW *abbr* Leading Aircraftwoman.

lacy /'laysi/ *adj* (**lacier, laciest**) resembling or consisting of lace. >>> **lacily** *adv*, **laciness** *noun.*

lad /lad/ *noun* **1** *informal* a boy or young man. **2** *chiefly Brit, informal* a man with whom other men socialize: *He's one of the lads.* **3** *Brit, informal* a boisterous or macho man. **4** *Brit* a person who works in a stable, whether male or female; a stable lad. [Middle English *ladde*; earlier history unknown]

ladanum /'ladənəm/ *noun* see LABDANUM.

ladder¹ /'ladə/ *noun* **1** a structure for climbing up or down that has two long sidepieces of metal, wood, rope, etc joined at intervals by crosspieces on which one steps. **2** a hierarchy seen as having steps or stages allowing for advancement, e.g. to a higher status or rank. **3** *Brit* a vertical line in hosiery or knitting caused by stitches becoming unravelled. [Old English *hlǣder*]

ladder² *verb trans and intrans* (**laddered, laddering**) *Brit* to cause a ladder to develop in (e.g. tights), or to become damaged by a ladder.

ladder-back *noun* a chair with a back consisting of two upright posts connected by horizontal slats.

ladder gang *noun* roofing contractors who prey on vulnerable customers such as the elderly by carrying out unnecessary, nonexistent, or shoddy repairs to roofs at exorbitant prices.

ladder stitch *noun* an embroidery stitch consisting of transverse bars worked between raised often parallel lines.

laddie /'ladi/ *noun chiefly Scot, informal* a boy or young man.

laddish *adj* characteristic of some young men, *esp* irritatingly rowdy or macho. >>> **laddishness** *noun.*

lade /layd/ *verb trans* (*past tense* **laded**, *past part.* **laden**) **1** *archaic* to put a load on or in (a ship); to load (it). **2** to put or place (goods) as a load, *esp* for shipment. [Old English *hladan*]

laden /'layd(ə)n/ *adj* carrying a heavy load: *trees laden with apples.*

ladette /la'det/ *noun informal* a young woman who has an independent, liberated lifestyle and is seen as flouting the conventional ideas of femininity.

la-di-da *or* **lah-di-dah** /,lah di 'dah/ *adj informal* affectedly refined, *esp* in voice and pronunciation: *Nobody can afford to be so la-di-bloody-da, in a bar on the Piccola Marina* — Noël Coward. [prob imitative of affected speech]

ladies /'laydiz/ *pl noun Brit* (*treated as sing.*) a public lavatory for women. [short for *ladies' room, ladies' lavatory*, etc]

ladies' fingers *pl noun* see LADY'S FINGERS.

ladies' man *or* **lady's man** *noun informal* a man who enjoys flirting with women.

ladies' room *noun chiefly NAmer* a room in a public building equipped with toilets for use by women.

ladies' tresses *or* **lady's tresses** *pl noun* (*usu treated as sing.*) any of a genus of orchids with slender, often twisted spikes of irregular white flowers: genus *Spiranthes*.

Ladin /la'deen/ *noun* a language spoken in some parts of the Italian Alps, belonging to the Rhaeto-Romanic group. [Rhaeto-Romanic *Ladin* from Latin *latinus*: see LATIN¹]

lading /'layding/ *noun* cargo or freight. [from LADE]

Ladino /la'deenoh/ *noun* (*pl* **Ladinos**) **1** a language spoken by some Sephardic Jews, a descendant of medieval Spanish; Judaeo-Spanish. **2** a Spanish-American of mixed descent.

Word history
Spanish *ladino* learned, literally 'Latin', from Latin *latinus*: see LATIN¹. First recorded in Latin America in the 19th cent. in the sense 'cunning, learned', later applied to a stray or unruly animal and to a Spanish-speaking person of mixed descent. Sense 1 is an independent formation.

ladle¹ /'laydl/ *noun* **1** a deep-bowled long-handled spoon used for serving liquids or semiliquid foods, e.g. soup. **2** a vessel for carrying molten metal in a foundry. ➤➤ **ladleful** (*pl* **ladlefuls**) *noun*. [Old English *hlædel*]

ladle² *verb trans* to serve (something) with a ladle.

ladle out *verb trans* to distribute (something) lavishly or effusively.

lad-lit *noun* a genre of literature dealing with the lives of young city-based men and their social or romantic problems and aspirations.

lady /'laydi/ *noun* (*pl* **ladies**) **1** a woman of refinement or superior social position. **2** used in courteous or formal reference: a woman: *Show the lady to a seat.* **3** (**Lady**) a title given to a marchioness, countess, viscountess, baroness, or to the wife of a knight, baronet, or member of the peerage. **4** *dated* a wife: *the captain and his lady.* **5** formerly, a woman receiving the homage or devotion of a knight or lover. ✳ **My Lady** used as a form of address to women judges and noblewomen.

Word history
Old English *hlæfdīge*, from *hlāf* bread + *-dīge*, related to *dæge* kneader of bread; compare with LORD¹. In origin, *lady* (a compound peculiar to English, and literally meaning 'kneader of bread') was the female counterpart of *lord* ('keeper of bread'), and in Old English the word was applied to the female head of a household or a female ruler. By the 13th cent. its meaning had extended to any woman of superior social position, the female counterpart of *gentleman*, and it was thus distinguished from the more general term *woman*.

ladybird *noun* any of numerous small beetles of temperate and tropical regions, *esp* any of several species that have red wing cases with black spots: family Coccinellidae. [named after Our *Lady*, the Virgin Mary, prob because it preys on aphids which are harmful to plants]

lady bountiful *noun* a woman noted for patronizing and interfering generosity. [named after *Lady Bountiful*, a character in the play *The Beaux' Stratagem* by George Farquhar d.1707, Irish dramatist]

ladybug *noun NAmer* a ladybird.

lady chapel *noun* (*often* **Lady Chapel**) a chapel dedicated to the Virgin Mary that is usu part of a larger church.

Lady Day *noun* the feast of the Annunciation, observed on 25 March.

lady-in-waiting *noun* (*pl* **ladies-in-waiting**) a woman appointed to wait on a queen or princess.

lady-killer *noun informal* a man who captivates women.

ladylike *adj* resembling or befitting a well-bred woman or girl; refined and dignified.

Lady Mayoress *noun* **1** a title given to the wife of a Lord Mayor. **2** a woman who holds the position of mayor in the City of London or another large city.

lady's bedstraw *noun* a common Eurasian plant that is a variety of bedstraw and has bright yellow flowers: *Galium verum*. [named after Our *Lady*, the Virgin Mary, because it is believed to discourage fleas]

lady's fingers *or* **ladies' fingers** *pl noun Brit* = OKRA.

ladyship *noun* (*usu* **Your/Her Ladyship**) a title used to women with the rank of Lady: *Never had the general loved his daughter so well ... as when he first hailed her 'Your Ladyship'* — Jane Austen.

lady's man *noun* see LADIES' MAN.

lady's mantle *noun* a perennial plant with broad flat leaves and clusters of delicate greenish flowers: *Alchemilla vulgaris*. [named after Our *Lady*, the Virgin Mary, because of its medicinal properties]

lady's slipper *noun* any of several species of orchid with flowers that have a shape that suggests a slipper: genus *Cypripedium*.

lady's-smock *noun* = CUCKOOFLOWER.

lady's tresses *pl noun* see LADIES' TRESSES.

laev- *or* **laevo-** (*NAmer* **lev-** *or* **levo-**) *comb. form* forming words, with the meaning: to the left: *laevorotatory*. [Latin *laevus* left]

laevonorgestrel *or* **levonorgestrel** /,leevohnaw'jestral/ *noun* a synthetic hormone similar in action to progesterone, used in oral contraceptives. [LAEV- + *norgestrel* a synthetic steroid hormone]

laevorotary /leevoh'rohtari/ *adj* = LAEVOROTATORY.

laevorotatory (*NAmer* **levorotatory**) /leevoh'rohtat(a)ri, -'tayt(a)ri/ *adj* turning towards the left or anticlockwise, *esp* rotating the plane of polarization of light to the left: compare DEXTRO-ROTATORY. ➤➤ **laevorotation** /-'taysh(a)n/ *noun*.

laevulose (*NAmer* **levulose**) /'levyoolohs, -lohz/ *noun* = FRUCTOSE. [LAEV- + -OSE²]

Laffer curve /'lafa/ *noun* a theory of the relationship between taxation rates and economic activity, which maintains that lower taxes lead to greater productivity and eventually to higher government revenue. [named after Arthur B *Laffer* b.1940, US economist]

LAFTA *abbr* Latin American Free Trade Association, former name of Latin American Integration Association.

lag¹ /lag/ *verb intrans* (**lagged, lagging**) **1** (*often* + behind). **a** to stay or fall behind, *esp* to fail to keep pace. **b** to advance or develop with comparative slowness. **2** *NAmer* in billiards, to determine the order of play by hitting the cue ball against the end rail. The player whose ball rebounds closest to the head rail shoots first. [prob of Scandinavian origin]

lag² *noun* an interval between two events; a time lag or delay.

lag³ *verb trans* (**lagged, lagging**) to cover or provide (e.g. pipes) with lagging. ➤➤ **lagger** *noun*. [from *lag* barrel stave, later 'board forming part of an insulating cover for a boiler or steam engine', prob of Scandinavian origin]

lag⁴ *noun Brit, informal* a convict or ex-convict.

lag⁵ *verb trans* (**lagged, lagging**) *archaic* **1** to send (somebody) to prison. **2** to arrest (somebody). [origin unknown]

lagan /'lagan/ *noun archaic* in law, wreckage or goods lying on the seabed. [early French *lagan* or medieval Latin *laganum* debris washed up from the sea, prob of Germanic origin]

lager /'lahga/ *noun* **1** a light beer brewed by slow fermentation and usu served chilled. **2** a glass or measure of lager. [German *Lagerbier* beer made for storage, from *Lager* storehouse + *Bier* beer]

lager lout *noun Brit, informal* a drunken hooligan.

laggard¹ /'lagad/ *noun* a person who lags or lingers. ➤➤ **laggardly** *adv and adj*, **laggardness** *noun*.

laggard² *adj* slow or reluctant.

lagging *noun* material for thermal insulation, e.g. wrapped round pipes or laid in a roof.

lagomorph /'lagamawf/ *noun* any of an order of mammals including the rabbits and hares, that have double incisor teeth: order Lagomorpha. [Greek *lagōs* hare + -MORPH]

lagoon /la'goohn/ *noun* **1** a shallow channel or pool usu separated from a larger body of water by a sand bank, reef, etc. **2** *NAmer, Aus, NZ* a freshwater lake near a larger body of water. **3** a shallow artificial pool, e.g. for the processing of sewage. [French *lagune* via Italian *laguna* from Latin *lacuna*: see LACUNA]

Lagrangian point /lə'gronhzhi-ən/ *noun* in astronomy, a point in the orbital plane of two massive objects circling about their centre of gravity where a smaller mass can remain in equilibrium.

Editorial note

There are five Lagrangian points but only two, 60° either side of the less massive body and in the same orbit, can be stable. The two groups of Trojan asteroids, which share the orbit of Jupiter, are trapped at the two stable Lagrangian points in the Sun-Jupiter system — Dr Jacqueline Mitton.

[named after Joseph Louis *Lagrange* d.1813, French mathematician and astronomer]

lah /lah/ *noun* see LA.

lahar /'lahhah/ *noun* a mudflow that develops on the side of a volcano from the combined effects of the eruption and heavy rain or snow. It can travel many kilometres and cause catastrophic destruction.

lah-di-dah /,lah di 'dah/ *adj* see LA-DI-DA.

Lahnda /'lahndə/ *noun* an Indic language of the W Punjab.

LAIA *abbr* Latin American Integration Association.

laic /'layik/ *adj formal* of the laity; secular. >>> **laically** *adv*, **laicity** *noun*. [via late Latin from late Greek *laïkos* of the people, from *laos* people]

laical /'layikl/ *adj* = LAIC.

laicise /'layisiez/ *verb trans* see LAICIZE.

laicism /'layisiz(ə)m/ *noun* a political movement or programme that has secularization as its principal aim.

laicize or **laicise** /'layisiez/ *verb trans formal* to remove the religious or ecclesiastical element from (something); to secularize (it). >>> **laicization** /-'zaysh(ə)n/ *noun*.

laid /layd/ *verb* past tense and past part. of LAY[1].

laid back *adj informal* relaxed or casual.

laid paper *noun* paper watermarked with fine lines running across the grain: compare WOVE[2].

lain /layn/ *verb* past part. of LIE[1].

lair[1] /leə/ *noun* **1** the resting or living place of a wild animal. **2** a refuge or place for hiding; a den. [Old English *leger*]

lair[2] *noun Aus, NZ, informal* a showily dressed young man. >>> **lairy** *adj*. [*leary*, *lairy* artful, flash in dress or manners; orig British slang, perhaps from LEER[2]]

lair[3] *verb intrans Aus, NZ, informal* to behave or dress in a showy way.

laird /leəd/ *noun Scot* a person who owns a large country estate. [Middle English (northern) form of LORD[1]]

laissez-faire /,lesay 'feə/ *noun* see LAISSEZ-FAIRE.

laissez-aller /,lesay 'alay (*French* lese ale)/ *noun* lack of constraint. [French *laissez aller* let (someone) go]

laissez-faire or **laisser-faire** /,lesay 'feə (*French* lese fɛːr)/ *noun* **1** a doctrine opposing government interference in economic affairs. **2** a deliberate refraining from interfering in the freedom and choices of others. [French *laissez faire*, imperative of *laisser faire* to let (people) do (as they choose)]

laissez-passer /,lesay pa'say (*French* lese pase)/ *noun* a permit or pass. [French *laissez-passer*, from *laissez passer* let (someone) pass]

laity /'layiti/ *noun* (**the laity**) (*usu treated as pl*) lay people: *All professions are conspiracies against the laity* — George Bernard Shaw. [LAY[4] + -ITY]

lake[1] /layk/ *noun* **1** a large inland body of water. **2** a surplus of a liquid product: *a wine lake*. [Middle English via early French *lac* from Latin *lacus*]

lake[2] *noun* **1a** a deep purplish red pigment orig prepared from lac or cochineal. **b** any of numerous usu bright pigments composed essentially of a soluble dye absorbed in or combined with an inorganic carrier. **2** a vivid red colour; carmine. [French *laque* lac, via Old Provençal *laca* from Arabic *lakk*: see LACQUER[1]]

lake dwelling *noun* a prehistoric dwelling built on piles in a lake. >>> **lake dweller** *noun*.

Lakeland terrier /'layklənd/ *noun* a terrier of a breed having stiff wiry hair. [*Lakeland*, another name for the Lake District, area in NW England where the breed was developed]

lake trout *noun* a large char found in the Great Lakes of N America: *Salvelinus namaycush*.

lakh or **lac** /lak/ *noun* in India, the number 100,000. [Hindi *lākh* from Sanskrit *lakṣa*, literally 'mark, sign']

laksa /'lahksə/ *noun* a SE Asian dish of noodles served in a sauce or soup. [Malay *laksa*]

-lalia *comb. form* forming nouns, denoting: a speech disorder of the kind specified: *echolalia*. [Greek *lalia* chatter, from *lalein* to chat]

Lallans /'lalənz/ *noun* a literary form of the Scottish dialect spoken in the Lowlands of Scotland. >>> **Lallans** *adj*. [Scottish variant of *Lowlands*]

lallation /la'laysh(ə)n/ *noun* a speech fault whereby /r/ is pronounced as /l/. [Latin *lallare* to sing a lullaby]

Lam. *abbr* Lamentations (book of the Bible).

lam[1] /lam/ *verb* (**lammed, lamming**) >>> *verb trans informal* to hit (somebody) hard. >>> *verb intrans informal* (*usu* + into) to strike something with great force. [prob of Scandinavian origin]

lam[2] *noun NAmer, informal* a sudden or hurried flight, *esp* from the law. * **on the lam** *NAmer, informal* running away to avoid arrest. [LAM[1] in the obsolete sense 'to depart hurriedly']

lama /'lahmə/ *noun* **1** a title given to a Tibetan Buddhist spiritual leader. **2** a Tibetan or Mongolian Buddhist monk. [Tibetan *blama*, literally 'superior one']

Lamaism /'lahmeiz(ə)m/ *noun* the Buddhism of Tibet, marked by a dominant monastic hierarchy headed by the Dalai Lama. >>> **Lamaist** *noun and adj*, **Lamaistic** /-'istik/ *adj*.

Lamarckism /lah'mahkiz(ə)m/ *noun* a theory of evolution asserting that changes in the environment of plants and animals cause changes in their structure that are transmitted to their offspring. >>> **Lamarckian** *noun and adj*. [named after J B de Monet *Lamarck* d.1829, French botanist and zoologist]

lamasery /'lahməsəri/ *noun* (*pl* **lamaseries**) a monastery of lamas. [French *lamaserie*, from *lama* (see LAMA) + Persian *sarāi* palace]

lamb[1] /lam/ *noun* **1a** a young sheep, *esp* one that is less than a year old or without permanent teeth. **b** the flesh of a lamb used as food. **2** a gentle, meek, or innocent person. [Old English]

lamb[2] *verb intrans* said of a ewe: to give birth to lambs. >>> *verb trans* to tend (ewes) at lambing time. >>> **lamber** *noun*, **lambing** *noun*, **lamblike** *adj*.

lambada /lam'bahdə/ *noun* a fast ballroom dance of Brazilian origin in which couples dance in very close contact with each other. [Portuguese *lambada*, literally 'a beating', from *lambar* to beat]

lambaste or **lambast** /lam'bast/ *verb trans* to attack (somebody) verbally; to censure (them). [prob from LAM[1] + BASTE[3]]

lambda /'lamdə/ *noun* **1** the eleventh letter of the Greek alphabet (Λ, λ), equivalent to and transliterated as roman l. **2** in anatomy, the point at the back of the cranium between the occipital bone and the parietal bones, resembling the Greek letter in shape. [Greek *lambda*, of Semitic origin; related to Hebrew *lāmedh*, twelfth letter of the Hebrew alphabet]

lambent /'lamb(ə)nt/ *adj literary* **1** playing lightly on or over a surface; flickering: *lambent flames*. **2** softly bright or radiant: *eyes lambent with love*. **3** marked by lightness or brilliance, *esp* of expression: *a lambent wit*. >>> **lambency** /-si/ *noun*, **lambently** *adv*. [Latin *lambent-, lambens*, present part. of *lambere* to lick]

lambert /'lambət/ *noun* formerly, a unit of surface brightness equal to one lumen per square centimetre. [named after Johann Heinrich *Lambert* d.1777, German physicist and philosopher, because of his work in the measurement of light]

Lamb of God *noun* (**the Lamb of God**) a title given to Jesus Christ.

lambrequin /'lamb(r)əkin/ *noun* **1** *NAmer* a short decorative piece of drapery, e.g. for the top of a window or door. **2** a scarf used to cover a knight's helmet. [French *lambrequin*, ultimately from Dutch *lamper* veil]

Lambrusco /lam'broohskoh/ *noun* **1** a variety of grape grown in N Italy and used in the production of red and white wine. **2** a slightly sparkling wine produced from this grape. [Italian *lambrusco* grape of the wild vine]

lambskin *noun* the skin of a lamb or small sheep with the wool still on it, or a garment made from this.

lamb's lettuce *noun* a plant of the valerian family with small green leaves that are eaten raw in salads: *Valerianella locusta*. Also called CORN SALAD.

lamb's tails *pl noun Brit* the catkins that grow on a hazel tree.

lame[1] /laym/ *adj* **1** having a leg or foot so disabled as to impair freedom of movement. **2** said of a story or excuse: weak and unconvincing. **3** *informal* socially inept and lacking in street credibility. ⟩⟩ **lamely** *adv*, **lameness** *noun*. [Old English *lama*]

lame[2] *verb trans* to make (a person or animal) lame.

lamé /'lahmay/ *noun* a brocaded clothing fabric interwoven with metallic gold or silver threads. [French *lamé* from Latin *lamina* thin plate, leaf]

lamebrain *noun informal* a dull-witted person. ⟩⟩ **lamebrained** *adj*.

lame duck *noun* **1** somebody or something, e.g. a person or business, that is weak or incapable. **2** *NAmer* an elected officer or group continuing to hold office in the period before the inauguration of a successor.

lamell- *or* **lamelli-** *comb. form* forming words, denoting: lamella: *lamellibranch*.

lamella /lə'melə/ *noun* (*pl* **lamellae** /-lee/ *or* **lamellas**) a thin flat scale, membrane, or part, e.g. a thin plate composing the gills of an oyster, or a gill of a mushroom. ⟩⟩ **lamellar** *adj*, **lamellate** /'lamilayt, 'lamelayt, -lət/ *adj*, **lamelliform** *adj*, **lamellose** *adj*. [Latin *lamella*, dimin. of *lamina* thin plate]

lamelli- *comb. form* see LAMELL-.

lamellibranch /lə'melibrangk/ *noun* a bivalve. [LAMELLI- + Latin *branchia* gill]

lamellicorn /lə'melikawn/ *adj* denoting or belonging to a group of large beetles, e.g. the stag beetle, with antennae that have flat ends: superfamily Scarabaeoidea or Lamellicornia. ⟩⟩ **lamellicorn** *noun*. [LAMELLI- + Latin *cornu* horn]

lament[1] /lə'ment/ *noun* **1** an expression of grief; a wail. **2** a song or poem expressing grief; a dirge or elegy.

lament[2] *verb trans* to feel or express grief or sorrow for (a person's loss or death); to mourn (them). ⟩ *verb intrans* (+ for/over) to express regret, disappointment, or sorrow over something. ⟩⟩ **lamentation** /lamən'taysh(ə)n/ *noun*, **lamenter** *noun*. [early French *lamenter* from Latin *lamentari*, from *lamentum* a lament]

lamentable /'lamantəbl/ *adj* **1** that is to be regretted; regrettable. **2** woefully bad or inadequate; deplorable. **3** *archaic* expressing grief; mournful: *a faint and lamentable cry* — Walter de la Mare. ⟩⟩ **lamentably** *adv*.

lamia /'laymi-ə/ *noun* (*pl* **lamias** *or* **lamiae** /-miee/) a female demon in classical mythology, *esp* one who preyed on human beings and sucked their blood. [Middle English via Latin from Greek *lamia* devouring monster]

lamin- *or* **lamini-** *or* **lamino-** *comb. form* forming words, denoting: lamina or laminae: *laminar; laminitis*.

lamina /'lamina/ *noun* (*pl* **laminae** /-nee/ *or* **laminas**) *technical* a thin plate, scale, layer, or flake. ⟩⟩ **laminose** *adj*. [Latin *lamina*]

laminar /'lamina/ *adj* arranged in, consisting of, or resembling laminae.

laminar flow *noun* a smooth nonturbulent flow of gases or liquids passing over or near a solid usu streamlined surface.

laminate[1] /'laminayt/ *verb trans* **1** to overlay (something) with a thin sheet or sheets of material, e.g. metal or plastic. **2** to make (e.g. a building material) by uniting superimposed layers of one or more materials. **3** to separate (a substance) into layers. **4** to roll or compress (e.g. metal) into a thin plate or plates. ⟩⟩ **laminable** *adj*, **lamination** /-'naysh(ə)n/ *noun*, **laminator** *noun*.

laminate[2] /'laminət, -nayt/ *noun* a product made by laminating.

laminate[3] *adj* covered with or consisting of a lamina or laminae.

laminated /'laminaytid/ *adj* = LAMINATE[3].

lamington /'lamingtən/ *noun* a cake made by dipping a cube of sponge cake in chocolate and coconut, popular in Australia. [prob named after Charles Baillie, Lord *Lamington* d.1940, Governor of Queensland]

lamini- *comb. form* see LAMIN-.

laminitis /lami'nietəs/ *noun* painful inflammation of the lining of a hoof, *esp* of a horse.

lamino- *comb. form* see LAMIN-.

Lammas /'laməs/ *noun* **1** 1 August, formerly celebrated in England as a harvest festival. **2** the time of the year around Lammas. [Old English *hlāfmæsse*, from *hlāf* loaf, bread + *mæsse* mass, from the fact that loaves from the first ripe grain were consecrated on this day]

Lammas Day *noun* = LAMMAS (1).

Lammastide *noun* = LAMMAS (2).

lammergeier *or* **lammergeyer** /'lamǝgie-ǝ/ *noun* a large vulture that lives in mountain regions from the Pyrenees to northern China: *Gypaetus barbatus*. [German *Lämmergeier*, from *Lämmer*, pl of *Lamm* lamb + *Geier* vulture]

lamp /lamp/ *noun* **1** any of various devices for producing visible light, e.g.: **a** a container filled with an inflammable substance, e.g. oil or gas, that is burned to give out artificial light. **b** a usu portable electric device containing a light bulb. **2** any of various light-emitting devices, e.g. a sunlamp, that produce electromagnetic radiation, e.g. heat radiation. [Middle English via French and Latin from Greek *lampas*, from *lampein* to shine]

lampblack *noun* a pigment made from finely powdered black soot. [from the black soot deposited by the flame of a smoking oil lamp]

lamp chimney *noun* the glass cylinder that encloses and protects the wick in an oil lamp.

lamplighter *noun* formerly, a person whose job was to light and extinguish street gas lamps.

lampoon[1] /lam'poohn/ *verb trans* to make (somebody or something) the subject of a satire; to ridicule (them). ⟩⟩ **lampooner** *noun*, **lampoonery** *noun*, **lampoonist** *noun*. [from LAMPOON[2]]

lampoon[2] *noun* a satirical attack on a person, literary work, etc. [French *lampon*, prob from *lampons* let's drink, a common refrain in drinking songs, from *lamper* to drink, guzzle]

lamp post *noun* a post, usu of metal or concrete, supporting a light that illuminates a street or other public area.

lamprey /'lampri/ *noun* (*pl* **lampreys**) any of several eel-like aquatic vertebrates that have a large sucking mouth with no jaws: family Petromyzonidae: *We must also admit that there is a much wider interval in mental power between one of the lowest fishes, as a lamprey or lancelet, and one of the higher apes, than between an ape and man* — Darwin. [Middle English via early French *lampreie* from medieval Latin *lampreda*]

lampshade *noun* a decorative translucent cover placed round an electric light bulb to reduce glare.

lampshell *noun* a marine shellfish that has tentacles with which it feeds: phylum Brachiopoda. [from the resemblance of the shell and its protruding stalk to an ancient oil lamp with the wick protruding]

lamp standard *noun* a lamp post.

LAN /lan/ *abbr* local area network.

lanai /lə'nie/ *noun* (*pl* **lanais**) a porch or veranda that serves, *esp* in summer, as an open-air living room. [Hawaiian *lanai*]

Lancashire /'langkashǝ/ *noun* a whitish yellow crumbly-textured cheese with a high fat content and a flavour that ranges from mild to tangy as the cheese matures. [*Lancashire*, English county where it was orig made]

Lancashire hotpot *noun* a meat and vegetable stew with a topping of sliced potatoes.

Lancastrian /lang'kastri-ǝn/ *noun* **1** a native or inhabitant of Lancashire or Lancaster in NW England. **2** an adherent of the English royal house of Lancaster that ruled from 1399 to 1461. ⟩⟩ **Lancastrian** *adj*.

lance[1] /lahns/ *noun* **1** a weapon with a long shaft and a sharp steel head, carried by horsemen for use when charging. **2** a spear or harpoon for killing whales. **3** a metal pipe or tube through which oxygen is directed, e.g. to pierce a hot metal surface. [Middle English via French from Latin *lancea*]

lance[2] *verb trans* **1** to open (e.g. a boil) with a lancet or other sharp instrument. **2** to pierce (something) with a lance or other sharp weapon or instrument. ⟩ *verb intrans* to move forward as if by cutting one's way. [Middle English *launcen* via early French *lancer* from late Latin *lanceare*, from Latin *lancea* LANCE[1]]

lance corporal *noun* a non-commissioned officer of the lowest rank in the British army, Royal Marines, and US Marines. [*lance* from obsolete *lancepesade* lance corporal, ultimately from early Italian *lancia spezzata* experienced soldier, literally 'broken lance']

lancelet /'lahnslit/ *noun* any of various small translucent marine animals that live buried in sand: subphylum Cephalochordata.

lanceolate /'lahnsi·əlayt, -lət/ *adj technical* tapering to a point at the apex and sometimes at the base, in a shape that loosely resembles a lance head: *a lanceolate leaf.* [late Latin *lanceolatus* from Latin *lanceola*, dimin. of *lancea* LANCE¹]

lancer *noun* **1** a soldier who carries a lance. **2** (**Lancer**) a member of a regiment armed with lances. **3** (*in pl, but treated as sing.*) a set of five quadrilles each danced to music in a different time, or the music for them.

lancet /'lahnsit/ *noun* **1** a sharp-pointed and usu two-edged surgical instrument used to make small incisions. **2** = LANCET ARCH. **3** = LANCET WINDOW. [Middle English *lancette* from early French *lancette*, dimin. of *lance*: see LANCE¹]

lancet arch *noun* a sharply pointed arch.

lancet window *noun* a high window composed of one or more narrow pointed openings.

lancewood *noun* **1** any of various hardwood trees, *esp* one found in the Caribbean: *Oxandra lanceolata* and one found in New Zealand: *Pseudopanax crassifolius.* **2** the tough elastic wood of these trees, used for fishing rods and bows

Lancs /langks/ *abbr* Lancashire.

Land /land (*German* lant)/ *noun* (*pl* **Länder** /'lendə (*German* 'lɛndər)/) any of the provinces of Germany or Austria. [German *Land* land, country, province]

land¹ /land/ *noun* **1** the solid part of the earth's surface, as distinct from seas, lakes, rivers, etc. **2** ground owned as property or attached to a building. **3** *SAfr* a field. **4** a particular country, region, or state. **5** an area of a surface that is left between holes or grooves, e.g. the space between the grooves of a rifle bore. ✳ **how the land lies** how things are in a particular situation. **in the land of the living** alive; conscious. ➤➤ **landless** *adj.* [Old English]

land² *verb trans* **1** to bring (e.g. an aeroplane) to a surface from the air. **2** to set or put (somebody or something) on shore from a ship. **3** to catch and bring in (a fish). **4** *informal* to gain or secure (something): *She landed the job.* **5** *informal* (+ in) to put (somebody) in a specified place, position, or condition: *His carelessness landed him in trouble.* **6** *informal* to cause (a blow) to hit somebody: *He didn't land a single punch.* **7** *informal* (+ with) to present or burden (somebody) with something unwanted: *I was landed with the job of clearing up.* ➤ *verb intrans* **1a** said of an aircraft, bird, etc: to alight on a surface. **b** to go ashore from a ship; to disembark. **c** said of a boat, ship, etc: to come to shore. **d** to arrive in a ship, aircraft, etc. **2** to strike or come to rest on a surface, e.g. after a fall: *He landed on his head.*

land agent *noun* **1** *Brit* the manager of a large country estate. **2** a person who buys and sells land on behalf of clients. ➤➤ **land agency** *noun.*

landau /'landaw, 'landow/ *noun* a four-wheeled carriage with a folding top divided into two sections. [named after *Landau*, town in Rhineland-Palatinate (pre-1945 Bavaria), Germany, where it was first made]

landaulet /landə'let/ *noun* **1** a small landau. **2** an early type of car with a folding hood over the back seats.

land breeze *noun* a breeze blowing seawards from the land, generally at night: *A land-breeze shook the shrouds and she was overset; down went the Royal George with all her crew complete — Cowper.*

land bridge *noun* a piece of land connecting two areas of land, e.g. continents, that are now separate.

land crab *noun* any of various crabs that live mostly on land and breed in the sea: family Gecarcinidae.

landed *adj* **1** owning land, *esp* through inheritance: *the landed gentry.* **2** consisting of or including land: *landed property.*

Länder /'lendə (*German* 'lɛndər)/ *noun* pl of LAND.

lander /'landə/ *noun* a space vehicle that is designed to land on the moon, a planet, etc.

landfall *noun* **1a** the act or an instance of sighting or reaching land after a voyage or flight. **b** the land sighted or reached. **2** the collapse of a mass of land, *esp* one that causes a route to be blocked.

landfill *noun* **1** the disposal of rubbish by burying it in a pit or natural depression and then covering it with earth. **2** rubbish that is disposed of in this way.

landform *noun* a natural feature of the earth's surface, e.g. a mountain.

landgirl *noun* *Brit* a woman working on a farm in wartime as a replacement for a man on military duty; *specif* a member of the Women's Land Army during the two World Wars.

landgrave /'landgrayv/ *noun* **1** a title given to certain German princes. **2** formerly, a German count who ruled over a particular territory. [Middle English from early Low German *Landgrave*, from *Land* land + *grave* count]

landholder *noun* the owner or occupier of an area of land. ➤➤ **landholding** *noun.*

landing *noun* **1** the act of coming or bringing something to land. **2** a place for discharging and taking on passengers and cargo. **3** a level space at the end of a flight of stairs or between two flights of stairs.

landing craft *noun* a naval craft designed for putting troops and equipment ashore.

landing gear *noun* the undercarriage of an aircraft.

landing stage *noun* a platform for landing passengers or cargo from a ship.

landing strip *noun* a runway or airstrip.

landlady *noun* (*pl* **landladies**) **1** a woman who owns land, buildings, or accommodation for lease or rent. **2** a woman who keeps a guesthouse, lodging house, or pub.

ländler /'lendlə/ *noun* an Austrian folk dance in triple time, a forerunner of the waltz. [German *Ländler*, from *Landl* Upper Austria]

land-line *noun* a telecommunications link using cables as opposed to radio transmission.

landlocked *adj* completely or almost completely enclosed by land.

landlord *noun* **1** a person, usu a man, who owns land, buildings, or accommodation for lease or rent. **2** a person, usu a man, who keeps a guesthouse, lodging house, or pub.

landlubber /'landlubə/ *noun informal* a person unacquainted with the sea or seamanship.

landmark *noun* **1** a conspicuous object that can be used to identify a locality. **2** an object, e.g. a stone, that formerly marked a boundary. **3** an event that marks a turning point or new development: *a landmark in the history of aviation.*

landmass *noun* a continent or other large mass of land.

landmine *noun* an explosive mine hidden just below the surface of the ground so that it is detonated by the weight of a person or vehicle passing over it.

landowner *noun* a person who owns large areas of land. ➤➤ **landownership** *noun*, **landowning** *adj and noun.*

land rail *noun* a corncrake.

landscape¹ *noun* **1** an expanse of natural inland scenery. **2a** a picture, drawing, etc of a landscape. **b** the genre of landscape painting. **3** the distinctive features of a situation or area of intellectual activity: *The results changed the political landscape completely.* **4** (*used before a noun*) denoting a printed format in which the object or text is wider than it is high: compare PORTRAIT. [Dutch *landschap*, from *land* land + *-schap* -ship]

landscape² *verb trans* to improve (a natural landscape). ➤➤ **landscaper** *noun.*

landscape architect *noun* a person who designs the features of the outdoor environment in a particular area of land, seeking to create sympathy between these features and the buildings, bridges, roads, and other structures that inhabit the space. ➤➤ **landscape architecture** *noun.*

landscape gardener *noun* a person who designs and arranges the layout of gardens and grounds. ➤➤ **landscape gardening** *noun.*

landside *noun* **1** the part of an airport terminal to which the general public has access, with its boundary marked by the areas beyond which only passengers are allowed to progress, such as passport control and security: compare AIRSIDE. **2** the flat part of a plough that guides it along a furrow and takes the side pressure when the earth is turned.

landslide *noun* **1** a usu rapid movement of rock, earth, etc down a slope, or the moving mass of rock, earth, etc itself. **2** an overwhelming victory in an election.

landslip *noun chiefly Brit* a small landslide.

Landsmål /'lahntsmawl/ *noun* = NYNORSK. [Norwegian *Landsmål*, literally 'language of the country']

landsman *noun* (*pl* **landsmen**) a person who knows little or nothing of the sea or seamanship.

land up *verb intrans* to end up at or in a place or situation: *We took the wrong bus and landed up on the other side of town; These children often land up homeless and living on the streets.*

landward[1] /'landwəd/ *or* **landwards** /-wədz/ *adv* to or towards the land.

landward[2] *adj* lying or being towards the land or on the side towards the land.

landwards *adv* see LANDWARD[1].

land yacht *noun* a lightweight wheeled vehicle with sails, designed for use on beaches.

lane /layn/ *noun* **1a** a narrow passageway or road, *esp* between fences or hedges. **b** usu in proper names: a street. **2** a strip of road for a single line of vehicles, e.g. on a motorway. **3** any of several marked parallel courses to which a competitor must keep during a race, e.g. in running or swimming. **4** a fixed route used by ships or aircraft. **5** in tenpin bowling, a narrow hardwood surface down which the ball is bowled towards the pins. [Old English *lanu*]

laneway *noun chiefly Can* a lane or mews running between or behind houses.

lang. *abbr* language.

langlauf /'lang·lowf/ *noun* cross-country running or racing on skis. ➤➤ **langlaufer** *noun*. [German *Langlauf*, from *lang* long + *Lauf* race, run]

langouste /'longgoohst/ *noun* a spiny lobster, *esp* when cooked. [French *langouste* via Old Provençal *lagosta* from Latin *locusta* lobster, crustacean, LOCUST]

langoustine /'longgoosteen/ *noun* a Norway lobster. [French *langoustine*, dimin. of *langouste*: see LANGOUSTE]

lang syne /,lang 'sien, 'zien/ *noun Scot, archaic* times long ago. ➤➤ **lang syne** *adv*. [Scottish, from *lang* long + *syne* since]

language /'langgwij/ *noun* **1a** the ability to make and use audible, articulate, and meaningful sound by the action of the vocal organs. **b** a systematic means of communicating ideas or feelings by the use of conventionalized signs, sounds, gestures, or marks that have understood meanings. **c** the suggestion by objects, actions, or conditions of associated ideas or feelings: *body language; the language of flowers*. **2a** the words, their pronunciation, and the methods of combining them that are used and understood by a particular community: *I am always sorry when any language is lost, because languages are the pedigrees of nations* — Dr Johnson. **b** the specialized vocabulary and phraseology belonging to a particular group or profession: *legal language*. **c** a formal system of signs and symbols, e.g. for use in programming a computer, together with rules for their use.

Editorial note
There are two major dimensions of language study. The first focuses on specific languages, along with their varieties and styles; the second focuses on the general properties of language. The research task facing linguists is to establish how a common biological faculty has given rise to the enormous diversity of the world's languages, currently numbering around 6000 — Professor David Crystal.

3a a particular form or manner of verbal expression; *specif* style: *The letter was written in formal language*. **b** abusive, impolite, or irreligious speech: *The programme contains strong language*. ✳ **speak the same language** to have the same interests, ideas, etc; to get on well together. [Middle English from early French *langage*, ultimately from Latin *lingua* tongue]

language laboratory *noun* a room, usu divided into booths equipped with tape recorders, where foreign languages are learned by listening and speaking.

langue /longg (*French* lãːg)/ *noun* language regarded as a system of elements or a set of habits common to a community of speakers: compare PAROLE[1]. [French *langue* language, from Latin *lingua* tongue]

langue de chat /longg də 'shah (*French* lãːg də sha)/ *noun* a long thin finger-shaped piece of chocolate or crisp biscuit. [French *langue de chat*, literally 'cat's tongue']

langue d'oc /,longg 'dok (*French* lãːg dɔk)/ *noun* **1** the medieval dialects that formed the basis of modern Provençal. **2** the modern dialects of S France. [French *langue d'oc* language of *oc*, from the Provençal use of the word *oc* for 'yes']

langue d'oïl /do'eel (*French* dɔil)/ *noun* the medieval French dialects of N France which formed the basis of modern French. [French *langue d'oïl* language of *oïl*, from the medieval French use of the word *oïl* for 'yes']

languid /'langgwid/ *adj* **1** without energy; spiritless or apathetic. **2** drooping or flagging from fatigue or exhaustion; weak. ➤➤ **languidly** *adv*, **languidness** *noun*. [early French *languide* from Latin *languidus*, from *languēre* to LANGUISH]

languish /'langgwish/ *verb intrans* **1** to be or become feeble. **2** to suffer hardship or neglect: *She languished in prison for two years*. **3** *archaic* (*often* + for) to become dispirited or depressed; to pine. ➤➤ **languishment** *noun*. [Middle English *languishen* from early French *languir*, ultimately from Latin *languēre*]

languor /'langgə/ *noun* **1** weakness or weariness of body or mind. **2** a feeling or mood of wistfulness or dreaminess. **3** heavy or soporific stillness of the air. ➤➤ **languorous** /-rəs/ *adj*, **languorously** /-rəsli/ *adv*. [Middle English via French from Latin *languor*, from *languēre* to LANGUISH]

langur /lung'gooə/ *noun* any of various slender long-tailed monkeys native to Asia, with a very loud cry: family Colobidae. [Hindi *lāgūr*]

laniard /'lanyəd/ *noun* see LANYARD.

lank /langk/ *adj* **1** said of hair: straight and limp. **2** thin and unhealthy-looking; gaunt. ➤➤ **lankly** *adv*, **lankness** *noun*. [Old English *hlanc*]

lanky *adj* (**lankier**, **lankiest**) tall, thin, and ungraceful. ➤➤ **lankily** *adv*, **lankiness** *noun*.

lanner /'lanə/ *noun* **1** a falcon of S Europe, SW Asia, and Africa: *Falco biarmicus*. **2** in falconry, the female of this bird. [Middle English *laner* from early French *lanier*]

lanneret /'lanəret/ *noun* in falconry, a male lanner.

lanolin *or* **lanoline** /'lanəlin/ *noun* wool grease, *esp* when refined for use in ointments and cosmetics. [Latin *lana* wool + -OL[1] + -IN[1]]

lantern /'lantən/ *noun* **1** a portable protective case with transparent windows that houses a light, e.g. a candle. **2** the chamber in a lighthouse containing the light. **3** a structure above an opening in a roof which has glazed or open sides for light or ventilation. [Middle English *lanterne* via French and Latin from Greek *laptēr*, from *lampein* to shine]

lantern fly *noun* any of several large brightly marked insects that have a hollow structure at the front of the head once thought to emit light: family Fulgoridae.

lantern jaw *noun* a long narrow lower jaw that projects beyond the upper jaw, *esp* one that gives the cheeks and face a hollow appearance. ➤➤ **lantern-jawed** *adj*.

lantern slide *noun* a transparency, *esp* of glass, formerly used for projecting pictures with a magic lantern.

lanthanide /'lanthənied/ *noun* any one of a series of chemical elements of increasing atomic numbers beginning with lanthanum (atomic number 57) and ending with lutetium (atomic number 71). [LANTHANUM + -IDE]

lanthanum /'lanthənəm/ *noun* a silver-white metallic chemical element of the rare-earth group that is soft and malleable, and is used in alloys: symbol La, atomic number 57. [Greek *lanthanein* to escape notice, because it was long undiscovered in cerium oxide]

lanthorn /'lant·hawn, 'lantən/ *noun chiefly Brit, archaic* a lantern. [by alteration, influenced by *horn*, from which lanterns were formerly made]

lanugo /lə'nyoohgoh/ *noun* soft downy hair, *esp* that covering the foetus of some mammals including humans. [Latin *lanugo* down, from *lana* wool]

lanyard *or* **laniard** /'lanyəd/ *noun* **1** a piece of rope or line for fastening something on board ship or for extending or tightening rigging. **2** a cord worn round the neck as a decoration or to hold something, e.g. a knife or whistle. **3** a cord used in firing certain types of cannon. [alteration of Middle English *lanyer* from early French *laniere* strap]

LAO *abbr* Laos (international vehicle registration).

Lao /low/ *noun* (*pl* **Laos** *or collectively* **Lao**) **1** a member of a people living in Laos and adjacent parts of NE Thailand. **2** a Tai language of Laos and N Thailand. ➤➤ **Lao** *adj*. [the Lao name]

Laodicean /,layohdi'see·ən/ *adj archaic* lukewarm or indifferent, *esp* with regard to religion or politics. ➤➤ **Laodicean** *noun*.

[*Laodicea* (now Latakia), ancient city in Asia Minor; from the reproach to the church of the Laodiceans in Rev 3:15–16]

Laotian /lay'ohsh(ə)n, 'lowsh(ə)n/ *noun* a native or inhabitant of Laos. ⟫⟫ **Laotian** *adj.* [prob from French *laotien*, from LAO]

lap¹ /lap/ *noun* **1** the front part of the lower trunk and thighs of a seated person. **2** the part of a garment covering the lap. **3** *archaic* a loose panel or hanging flap, e.g. on a garment. **✳ drop/fall into somebody's lap** to come to somebody easily or effortlessly. **drop something in somebody's lap** to cause something to become somebody's responsibility. **in the lap of luxury** in an environment of great ease, comfort, and wealth. **in the lap of the gods** beyond human influence or control. ⟫⟫ **lapful** (*pl* **lapfuls**) *noun*. [Old English *læppa* flap or fold in a garment, later the front of a skirt when held up to hold something, hence the corresponding part of the body as a place on or in which to hold something]

lap² *noun* **1a** one circuit round a closed course or track. **b** one length of a straight course, e.g. a swimming pool. **2** one stage of a journey. **3a** a part of an object that overlaps another. **b** the amount by which one object overlaps or projects beyond another. **4** one complete turn, e.g. of a rope round a drum. **5** a layer of a flexible substance, e.g. a layer of cotton or wool wound round something, *esp* a roller, before spinning. **6** a smoothing and polishing tool, e.g. for metal or precious stones, usu comprising a piece of wood, leather, felt, or soft metal covering a rotating disc. [from LAP³]

lap³ *verb* (**lapped, lapping**) ⟫ *verb trans* **1** to overtake and thereby lead or increase the lead over (another contestant in a race) by a full circuit of a track. **2** *literary* (+ in) to hold or wrap (somebody or something) protectively in something; to swathe (them) in it. **3** to smooth or polish (e.g. a metal surface) to a high degree of refinement or accuracy. ⟫ *verb intrans* **1** to overlap or project beyond something: *Her mantle laps over my lady's wrist too much* — Robert Browning. **2** said of somebody in a race: to complete a lap. [Middle English *lappe* to coil, fold, or wrap, from LAP¹]

lap⁴ *verb* (**lapped, lapping**) ⟫ *verb trans* **1** said of an animal: to take in (liquid) with the tongue. **2** said of water: to flow or splash against (something) in little waves. ⟫ *verb intrans* to move in little waves, usu making a gentle splashing sound: *The sea lapped gently against the edge of the quay*. [Old English *lapian*]

lap⁵ *noun* the act or sound of lapping.

laparoscopy /lapə'roskəpi/ *noun* (*pl* **laparoscopies**) a surgical procedure in which a fine fibre-optic tube is inserted into the abdomen or other bodily cavity to allow direct observation of the contents. ⟫⟫ **laparoscope** /'lapərəskohp/ *noun*, **laparoscopic** /ˌlapərə'skopik/ *adj.* [Greek *lapara* flank (from *laparos* slack, soft) + -SCOPY]

laparotomy /lapə'rotəmi/ *noun* (*pl* **laparotomies**) a surgical incision through the abdominal wall. [Greek *lapara* (see LAPAROSCOPY) + -TOMY]

lap dancing *noun* erotic dancing performed by a dancer who circulates among members of the audience, dancing closely to each in turn. ⟫⟫ **lap dance** *noun*, **lap dancer** *noun*.

lapdog *noun* **1** a small pet dog, *esp* one that is docile. **2** somebody who is completely controlled by or under the influence of somebody else.

lapel /lə'pel/ *noun* a fold of the top front edge of a coat or jacket that is continuous with the collar. [dimin. of LAP¹]

lapelled /lə'peld/ *adj* (*used in combinations*) having lapels of a specified kind: *narrow-lapelled*.

lapidary¹ /'lapidəri/ *adj* **1** of or relating to the cutting, polishing, and engraving of stones and gems: *In lapidary inscriptions a man is not upon oath* — Dr Johnson. **2** said of a literary style: having the elegance and dignity associated with monumental inscriptions. [Latin *lapidarius* of stone, from *lapid-, lapis* stone]

lapidary² *noun* (*pl* **lapidaries**) a person who cuts, polishes, or engraves stones and gems.

lapillus /lə'piləs/ *noun* (*pl* **lapilli** /-lie/) (*usu in pl*) a small fragment of lava ejected in a volcanic eruption. [Latin *lapillus*, dimin. of *lapis* stone]

lapis lazuli /ˌlapis 'lazyoolie, -lee/ *noun* **1** a rich blue semiprecious stone, used in making jewellery. **2** = ULTRAMARINE¹ (I). [Middle English, ultimately from Latin *lapis* stone + medieval Latin *lazuli*, genitive of *lazulum* lapis lazuli, from Arabic *lāzaward*: see AZURE²]

lap joint *noun* a joint made by overlapping two ends or edges and fastening them together. ⟫⟫ **lap-jointed** *adj*.

Laplander /'laplandə/ *noun* a native or inhabitant of Lapland.

lap of honour *noun Brit* a celebratory circuit of a track performed by a winning runner, driver, etc.

Lapp /lap/ *noun* **1** a member of a nomadic people of Lapland, a region of N Europe that covers N Scandinavia and the Kola peninsula of N Russia. **2** the Finno-Ugric language of the people of Lapland. ⟫⟫ **Lapp** *adj.* [Swedish *Lapp*]

lappet /'lapit/ *noun* **1** a flat overlapping or hanging piece, *esp* of flesh or membrane, e.g. the wattle of a bird. **2** a fold or flap on a garment or headdress. **3** any of several species of purplish brown moths. Their furry caterpillars have flaps along their sides: *Gastropacha quercifilia* and other species. [LAP¹ + -ET]

Lappish *noun* = LAPP (2).

lapsang souchong /ˌlapsang 'soohshong/ *noun* a variety of Chinese tea that has a distinctive smoky flavour. [*lapsang* an invented name + SOUCHONG]

lapse¹ /laps/ *noun* **1** a slight error, e.g. of memory or in manners: *a security lapse*. **2** a fall or decline, *esp* a moral fall or decline. **3** a continuous passage or elapsed period; an interval: *They returned after a lapse of several years*. **4** in law, the termination of a right or privilege through failure to exercise it. **5** an abandonment of religious faith. [Latin *lapsus*, past part. of *labi* to slip]

lapse² *verb intrans* **1** to go out of existence or use; to cease: *Our friendship lapsed when we left college*. **2** to become invalid, e.g. because of omission or negligence: *She had let her membership lapse*. **3** to abandon a religion or doctrine: *Nelly Mahone, who had lapsed from her native religion on religious grounds* — Muriel Spark. **4a** to fall from a high level, e.g. of morals or manners, to one much lower. **b** (+ into) to return to a particular state, way of behaving, etc: *The guests lapsed into silence when the speech began; The children lapsed into their local dialect.* **5** said of time: to run its course; to pass.

lapse rate *noun* the rate of change of temperature, humidity, or pressure with changing height.

lapsus calami /ˌlapsəs 'kaləmie/ *noun* (*pl* **lapsus calami**) *formal* a slip of the pen. [Latin *lapsus calami*]

lapsus linguae /ˌlapsəs 'linggwee/ *noun* (*pl* **lapsus linguae**) a slip of the tongue. [Latin *lapsus linguae*]

laptop *noun* a portable computer with an integral keyboard and a flat screen that folds down to form a lid.

lap up *verb trans* **1** to drink (a liquid). **2** to take (something) in eagerly or uncritically; to enjoy (it): *The crowd lapped up every word he spoke.*

lapwing *noun* a crested plover that is native to Europe, Africa, and Asia, noted for its shrill wailing cry: *Vanellus vanellus*. [Middle English, by folk etymology from Old English *hlēapewince*, related to Old English *hlēapan* to leap, *wincian* to wink; because as it flies it shows its dark back and white front alternately, appearing to 'wink']

LAR *abbr* Libyan Arab Republic (international vehicle registration for Libya).

larboard /'lahbəd/ *noun archaic* the left side of a boat or ship; port. [Middle English *ladeborde* loading side, altered by association with STARBOARD¹]

larceny /'lahsəni/ *noun* (*pl* **larcenies**) *dated* theft of personal property. [Middle English via early French *larcin* from Latin *latrocinium* robbery, from *latron-, latro* mercenary soldier, later 'robber', from Greek *latron* pay]

larch /lahch/ *noun* **1** any of a genus of trees of the pine family with short deciduous needles: genus *Larix*. **2** the tough wood of this tree. [prob from German *Lärche*, from Latin *laric-, larix*]

lard¹ /lahd/ *noun* a soft white solid fat obtained by rendering the abdominal fat of a pig, used in cooking. ⟫⟫ **lardy** *adj.* [Middle English via French from Latin *lardum* bacon, lard]

lard² *verb trans* **1a** to dress (e.g. meat) for cooking by inserting or covering with fat, bacon, etc. **b** to cover (food) with grease. **2** (+ with) to intersperse or embellish (speech or writing) with something; to garnish (it): *The book is well larded with anecdotes.*

lardass /'lahdas/ *noun NAmer, informal* a fat person, *esp* somebody who is thought to be lazy.

larder /'lahdə/ *noun* a room or cupboard where food is stored; a pantry. [Middle English from early French *lardier*, from *lard* bacon, from Latin *lardum* bacon, lard]

lardon /'lahd(ə)n/ *or* **lardoon** /lah'doon/ *noun* a strip, e.g. of pork fat or bacon, with which meat is larded: compare BARD². [French *lardon* piece of fat pork, from *lard*: see LARDER]

lardy cake *noun Brit* a sweet cake made with yeast dough, dried fruit, and lard.

lares /'lahreez/ *pl noun* the ancient Roman gods charged with watching over crossroads and domestic property: compare PENATES. [Latin *lares*, pl of *lar*, a Roman household god]

large¹ /lahj/ *adj* **1** great or relatively great in size, quantity, extent, etc. **2** dealing in great numbers or quantities or operating on an extensive scale: *a large business.* **3** having more than usual power, capacity, or scope; comprehensive. ✳ **have it large** (*also* **large it**) *informal* to enjoy oneself, *esp* partying and clubbing. ➤➤ **largeness** *noun,* **largish** *adj.* [Middle English via French from Latin *largus* large, abundant]

large² ✳ **at large 1** not imprisoned or restrained; at liberty. **2** as a whole: *among the population at large.*

large calorie *noun* = CALORIE (1B).

large intestine *noun* the rear division of the vertebrate intestine that is divided into the caecum, colon, and rectum, and concerned *esp* with the resorption of water and formation of faeces.

largely *adv* to a large extent; mostly.

large-scale *adj* **1** involving great numbers or quantities. **2** said of a map: showing great detail.

largesse *or* **largess** /lah'jes/ *noun* **1** generosity, *esp* to people regarded as occupying an inferior position. **2** something, e.g. money, given generously as a gift. [Middle English *largesse* from early French *largesse*, from *large*: see LARGE¹]

larghetto /lah'getoh/ *adj and adv* said of a piece of music: to be performed more slowly than andante but not as slowly as largo. [Italian *larghetto* somewhat slow, dimin. of *largo*: see LARGO]

largo /'lahgoh/ *adj and adv* said of a piece of music: to be performed in a very slow and broad manner. [Italian *largo* slow, broad, from Latin *largus* abundant]

lari /'lahri/ *noun* (*pl* **lari** *or* **laris**) **1** the basic monetary unit of Georgia, divided into 100 tetri. **2** a unit of currency in the Maldives, worth 100th of a rufiyaa. [Persian *lārī*]

lariat /'lari-ət/ *noun* a rope used as a lasso or for tethering animals. [American Spanish *la reata* the lasso, from Spanish *reatar* to tie again, from *re-* again (from Latin) + *atar* to tie, from Latin *aptare*: see ADAPT]

lark¹ /lahk/ *noun* **1** any of numerous brown singing birds mostly of Europe, Asia, and northern Africa, e.g. a skylark: family Alaudidae. **2** used in the names of birds of other families, e.g. the meadowlark. [Old English *lāwerce*]

lark² *noun informal* **1** a prank or light-hearted adventure. **2** *Brit* a type of activity, *esp* one regarded as misguided or foolish: *I'm really getting into this acting lark.* ➤➤ **larky** *adj.*

lark³ *verb intrans informal* (+ about/around) to have fun in a playful or mischievous way. [prob alteration of English dialect *lake* to frolic, via Middle English *laiken* from Old Norse *leika* to play, dance]

larkspur *noun* any of various plants related to the delphinium, *esp* a cultivated annual delphinium grown for its bright irregular flowers: genus *Consolida.* [from the spur-shaped calyx, thought to resemble a lark's claw]

larn /lahn/ *verb trans and intrans dialect* = LEARN.

larrikin /'larikin/ *noun Aus, NZ* **1** a hooligan or lout. **2** a maverick. [perhaps from *Larry*, nickname for *Lawrence* + -KIN]

larrup /'larəp/ *verb trans* (**larruped, larruping**) *informal* to beat (somebody) soundly. [perhaps imitative]

larva /'lahvə/ *noun* (*pl* **larvae** /'lahvee/) **1** the immature, wingless, and often wormlike feeding form that hatches from the egg of many insects and is transformed into a pupa or chrysalis from which the adult emerges. **2** the early form of an animal that undergoes metamorphosis before becoming an adult, e.g. a tadpole. ➤➤ **larval** *adj.* [Latin *larva* spectre, mask]

larvicide /'lahvisied/ *noun* an agent for killing larval pests.

laryng- *or* **laryngo-** *comb. form* forming words, denoting: the larynx: *laryngitis.* [Greek *laryng-, larynx*]

laryngeal /larin'jee-əl, lə'rinji-əl/ *adj* **1** relating to or in the region of the larynx. **2** said of a speech sound: formed in the larynx and with the vocal cords narrowed and partly vibrating.

laryngectomy /larin'jektəmi/ *noun* (*pl* **laryngectomies**) surgical removal of the larynx or part of it.

larynges /lə'rinjeez/ *noun* pl of LARYNX.

laryngitis /larin'jietəs/ *noun* inflammation of the larynx. ➤➤ **laryngitic** /-'jitik/ *adj.*

laryngo- *comb. form* see LARYNG-.

laryngoscope /lə'ring-gəskohp/ *noun* an instrument for examining the interior of the larynx. ➤➤ **laryngoscopy** /laring'goskəpi/ *noun.*

laryngotomy /laring'gotəmi/ *noun* (*pl* **laryngotomies**) surgical incision into the larynx to help the patient to breathe.

larynx /'laringks/ *noun* (*pl* **larynges** /lə'rinjeez/ *or* **larynxes**) the upper part of the trachea of air-breathing vertebrates. In human beings, most other mammals, and a few lower forms it contains the vocal cords. [Greek *larynx*]

lasagne /lə'zanyə/ *noun* **1** pasta in the form of broad flat sheets. **2** a baked dish of minced meat or vegetables in tomato sauce layered with lasagne, white sauce, and cheese. [Italian *lasagne*, via Latin *lasanum* cooking pot, from Greek *lasanon* chamber pot]

lascar /'laskə/ *noun* (*often* **Lascar**) *dated* an E Indian sailor. [Hindi *lashkar* army, influenced in meaning by Hindi *lashkarī* soldier, sailor]

lascivious /lə'sivi-əs/ *adj* showing or expressing an unseemly or offensive sexual interest. ➤➤ **lasciviously** *adv,* **lasciviousness** *noun.* [Latin *lascivia* wantonness, from *lascivus* wanton]

lase /layz/ *verb intrans* to function as a laser by emitting coherent light. [back-formation from LASER]

laser *noun* a device that generates an intense narrow beam of light or other electromagnetic radiation of a single wavelength by using the natural oscillations of atoms or molecules. [acronym based on *light amplification by stimulated emission of radiation*]

laserdisc *noun* a multimedia storage medium that looks like a large compact disc. Laser discs can carry video data, e.g. a film.

laser printer *noun* a high-quality computer printer in which a laser writes a pattern of electrostatically charged dots that transfer a powdered pigment called toner onto paper.

lash¹ /lash/ *verb trans* **1** to strike (something or somebody) with a whip or similar object. **2** to beat hard against (something): *Rain lashed the forecourt.* **3** (+ into) to drive or incite somebody into a (particular state): *She lashed the crowd into a frenzy.* **4** said of an animal: to flick (the tail) quickly or sharply. ➤ *verb intrans* **1** said of rain: to beat against something. **2** said of an animal's tail: to flick. ➤➤ **lasher** *noun.* [Middle English *lashen,* perhaps of imitative origin]

lash² *noun* **1** a stroke or blow with a whip. **2** the flexible part of a whip. **3** an eyelash.

lash³ *verb trans* to bind or fasten (something) with a cord, rope, etc. ➤➤ **lasher** *noun.* [Middle English *lasschen* to lace, from early French *lacier*: see LACE²]

lashed /lasht/ *adj* (*used in combinations*) having lashes of a specified kind: *long-lashed.*

lashing¹ *noun* a physical or verbal beating. [LASH¹]

lashing² *noun* a cord used for binding, wrapping, or fastening. [LASH³]

lashings *pl noun Brit, informal* (+ of) an abundance of something: *And now chips … four plates … and lashings of tomato ketchup —* Maeve Binchy. [verbal noun from LASH¹]

lash out *verb intrans* **1** to make a sudden violent or physical attack; to hit out. **2** said of a horse: to kick. **3** *Brit, informal* to spend money freely or recklessly.

lash-up *noun chiefly Brit, informal* something improvised or makeshift. ➤➤ **lash-up** *adj.*

lass /las/ *noun chiefly Scot, N Eng* a girl or young woman. [Middle English *las,* from or related to Old Norse *laskura* unmarried]

Lassa fever /'lasə/ *noun* an acute severe virus disease of tropical countries that is often fatal. [named after *Lassa,* village in northern Nigeria where the first cases were reported]

lassi /'lasi/ *noun* a refreshing Indian drink made from natural yogurt blended with fruit or herbs. [Hindi *lassī*]

lassie /'lasi/ *noun* = LASS.

lassitude /'lasityoohd/ *noun* physical or mental fatigue; weariness. [early French *lassitude* from Latin *lassitudo,* from *lassus* weary]

lasso[1] /la'sooh, 'lasoh/ *noun* (*pl* **lassos** *or* **lassoes**) a rope or long thong of leather with a running noose that is used *esp* in N America for catching horses and cattle. [Spanish *lazo* from Latin *laqueus* noose, snare]

lasso[2] *verb trans* (**lassoes** *or* **lassos**, **lassoed**, **lassoing**) to catch (something) with a lasso. ⟫ **lassoer** *noun*.

last[1] /lahst/ *adj* **1** following all the rest; final in time or place: *He was the last child to get dressed; It's the last house in the street.* **2** least suitable or likely: *She was the last person you would think of asking.* **3** most up-to-date; latest: *How did you get on at your last visit to the hospital?* **4** next before the present: *They came last week; I preferred her last book.* **5** being the only remaining: *He had eaten his last sandwich.* * **last but one 1** second most recent. **2** penultimate. **on one's last legs** near the end of one's resources; on the verge of failure, exhaustion, etc. [Old English *latost*, superl of *læt* LATE[1]]

last[2] *adv* **1** on the most recent occasion: *When did we last meet?* **2** after all others; at the end: *He came last and left first.* **3** (*used in combinations*) denoting the last or latest thing: *the last-born child.* **4** in conclusion; lastly: *And last, I'd like to thank my family.*

last[3] *noun* (*pl* **last**) **1** somebody or something that is last. **2** (**the last**) the final moments of something, *esp* of somebody's life. * **at last/at long last** after everything; after much delay. **the last of** the remaining part, amount, etc of something: *Is this the last of the bread?* **to the last** till the end.

last[4] *verb intrans* **1** to continue in time; to go on: *How long does the film last?* **2** to continue to live: *He won't last much longer.* **3** to remain in good or adequate condition, use, or effectiveness; to endure: *Things nowadays just aren't built to last.* **4** to continue to be available or unexhausted; to be sufficient or enough: *The money should last until the end of the month.* ⟫ *verb trans* to be enough for the needs of (somebody) during a length of time: *The supplies will last them a week.* [Old English *læstan* to last, follow]

last[5] *noun* a shoemaker's metal model of the human foot, over which a shoe is shaped or repaired. [Old English *læste*, from *lāst* footprint]

last-ditch *adj* made as a final effort, *esp* to avert disaster: *a last-ditch attempt.*

last-gasp *adj informal* done at the very last moment; last-minute.

lasting *adj* existing or continuing for a long while; enduring. ⟫ **lastingly** *adv*, **lastingness** *noun*. [present part. of LAST[4]]

Last Judgment *noun* the final judgment of humankind before God at the end of the world.

lastly /'lahstli/ *adv* at the end; last.

last minute *noun* the moment just before a climactic, decisive, or disastrous event. ⟫ **last-minute** *adj*.

last name *noun* a surname.

last offices *pl noun* the preparation and laying out of a dead body.

last out *verb intrans* **1** to be sufficient: *The coal might not last out.* **2** to survive: *We weren't sure that she could last out until the ambulance came.*

last post *noun* **1** the second of two bugle calls sounded at the hour for retiring in a military camp. **2** a bugle call sounded at a military funeral or tattoo.

last rites *pl noun* rites performed by a Roman Catholic priest for somebody who is about to die.

last straw *noun* (**the last straw**) the last of a series, e.g. of events or indignities, stretching one's patience beyond its limit. [from the fable of the last straw that broke the camel's back when added to his burden]

Last Supper *noun* the supper eaten by Jesus and his disciples on the night of his betrayal, in which he initiated the celebration of the Eucharist.

last thing *adv* as the final action, *esp* before going to bed: *He always has a cup of cocoa last thing at night.*

Last Things *pl noun* events, e.g. the resurrection and divine judgment of all humankind, marking the end of the world; *specif* death, judgment, Heaven, and Hell in Catholic theology. [translation of medieval Latin *Novissima*]

last word *noun* **1** the definitive statement or treatment of something: *This study will surely be the last word on the subject for many years.* **2** the power of final decision. **3** the most up-to-date or fashionable example of its kind: *This is the last word in sports cars.*

4 the final remark in a verbal exchange: *I hate posterity – it's so fond of having the last word* — Saki.

Lat. *abbr* Latin.

lat[1] /lat/ *noun informal* = LATISSIMUS.

lat[2] /lat/ *noun* (*pl* **lati** /'lati/ *or* **lats**) the basic monetary unit of Latvia, divided into 100 santims. [from the first syllable of *Latvia*]

lat. *abbr* latitude.

latakia /latə'kiə/ *noun* (*often* **Latakia**) a highly aromatic oriental tobacco. [*Latakia*, seaport in Syria from which it was exported]

latch[1] /lach/ *noun* **1** any of various devices in which mechanical parts engage to fasten but usu not to lock something, e.g.: **a** a fastener, e.g. for a gate, with a pivoted bar that falls into a notch on the gatepost. **b** a fastener, e.g. for a door, in which a spring slides a bolt into a hole. **2** in electronics, a circuit that is held in a particular state until a time signal is given which may change its state.

latch[2] *verb trans* to fasten (e.g. a door) with a latch. ⟫ *verb intrans* said of an electronic device: to be held in a particular position. [Old English *læccan* to seize]

latchkey *noun* a key to an outside door, *esp* the front door of a house.

latchkey child *noun* a child whose parents are at work all day and who has to let himself or herself into the house after school.

latch on *verb intrans* **1** to understand something: *We didn't know the rules at first but we soon latched on.* **2** to take up something enthusiastically: *People are latching on to the idea of shopping on-line.* **3** to attach oneself to somebody or something: *He had latched onto the group of older boys.*

late[1] /layt/ *adj* **1** occurring or arriving after the expected time: *a late spring.* **2** happening or belonging far on in a particular time or period: *the late Middle Ages; We scored a late hat trick.* **3** far on in the day or night: *It was getting late.* **4a** recently deceased: *the late James Scott; his late wife.* **b** former: *the late government.* **5** very recent: *Here is some late news.* * **late in the day** at a late stage. ⟫ **lateness** *noun*. [Old English *læt*]

late[2] *adv* **1** after the usual or proper time: *He always arrived late.* **2** at or near the end of a period of time or of a process: *We bought the house late in 1995.* **3** far on in the day or night: *We stayed up late.* **4** (+ of) until lately: *Dr Evans, late of Birmingham, now lectures at Durham.* * **of late** in the period shortly or immediately before; recently: *We have not seen him of late.*

latecomer *noun* somebody who arrives late.

lateen /lə'teen/ *adj* denoting a rig characterized by a triangular sail hung from a long spar set at an angle on a low mast. [French *voile latine* lateen sail, ultimately from Latin *latinus* (see LATIN[1]), from its use in the Mediterranean]

Late Greek *noun* the Greek language as used in the third cent. to eighth cent. AD.

Late Latin *noun* the Latin language as used in the third cent. to sixth cent. AD.

lately *adv* recently; of late: *She has been friendlier lately.*

latency /'layt(ə)nsi/ *noun* the quality or state of being latent; dormancy.

latency period *noun* in Freudian psychology, a stage of personality development observed in W Europe, N America, and some other cultures, that extends from about the age of five to puberty. During this period, sexual urges appear to lie dormant.

La Tène /lah 'ten (*French* la tɛn)/ *adj* belonging or relating to the later period of the Iron Age in Europe dating from the fifth cent. BC to the Roman conquests. [named after *La Tène*, shallows of the Lake of Neuchâtel, Switzerland, where remains of it were first discovered]

latent /'layt(ə)nt/ *adj* present but not manifest or active: *a latent infection; His desire for success remained latent.* ⟫ **latently** *adv*. [Latin *latent-, latens*, present part. of *latēre* to lie hidden]

latent heat *noun* heat given off or absorbed in a change of phase, e.g. from a solid to a liquid, without a change in temperature.

latent image *noun* the invisible image first produced on photographic film, paper, etc by a reaction with light which is then made visible, usu by chemical developers.

latent period *noun* the incubation period of a disease.

later /'laytə/ *adv* **1** afterwards. **2** at a time in the future.

-later *comb. form* forming nouns, denoting: worshipper: *idolater.* [Greek *-latrēs* worshipper]

lateral[1] /'lat(ə)rəl/ *adj* **1** situated on, directed towards, or coming from the side. **2** said of a speech sound: made by allowing air to escape on either or both sides of the tongue: */l/ is a lateral consonant.* ➤➤ **laterally** *adv.* [Latin *lateralis*, from *later-, latus* side]

lateral[2] *noun* **1** a lateral part of something, e.g. a side branch or root. **2** a lateral consonant. **3** in American football, a pass, usu underhand, thrown sideways or backwards.

lateral line *noun* a sense organ along the side of a fish that is sensitive to low vibrations.

lateral thinking *noun chiefly Brit* thinking that concentrates on unexpected aspects of a problem or that proceeds by seemingly illogical methods: *Dorothy Sayers did it by having the victim ... actively painting when in fact he was dead, and it is by using some such piece of lateral thinking ... that the trick is probably most easily brought off —* H R F Keating. [concept defined by Edward de Bono b.1933, British writer on thought processes]

laterite /'latəriet/ *noun* a usu red clay formed from rock decay and consisting *esp* of iron oxides and aluminium hydroxides. ➤➤ **lateritic** /-'ritik/ *adj.* [Latin *later* brick + -ITE[1]]

latest /'laytist/ *noun* the most recent news or style. ✳ **at the latest** no later than the specified time: *Be home by one at the latest.*

latex /'layteks/ *noun* (*pl* **latices** /'latəseez/ *or* **latexes**) **1** a milky usu white fluid that is produced by various flowering plants, e.g. of the spurge and poppy families, and is the source of rubber and chewing gum. **2** a water emulsion of a synthetic rubber or plastic, used in paints and other liquid preparations. [Latin *latex* fluid]

lath[1] /lahth, lath/ *noun* a thin narrow strip of wood, *esp* for nailing to woodwork, e.g. rafters or studding, as a support for tiles or plaster. [Old English *lætt*]

lath[2] *verb trans* to cover or line (a wall or ceiling) with laths.

lathe[1] /laydh/ *noun* a machine for shaping wood or metal. The work is rotated about a horizontal axis and shaped by a fixed tool. [prob from Middle English *lath* supporting stand, prob of Scandinavian origin]

lathe[2] *noun* a former administrative district of Kent. [Old English *læth* estate]

lather[1] /'lahdhə/ *noun* **1** a foam or froth formed when a detergent, e.g. soap, is agitated in water. **2** foam or froth on a horse's skin from profuse sweating. **3** *informal* an agitated or overwrought state. ➤➤ **lathery** *adj.* [Old English *lēathor*]

lather[2] *verb* (**lathered, lathering**) ➤ *verb trans* **1** to cause (soap) to form a lather. **2** to spread lather over (something). **3** (+ with) to spread something with (a substance): *She lathered the bread with jam.* **4** *informal* to beat or defeat (somebody); to thrash (them). ➤ *verb intrans* to form a lather.

lathi /'lahti/ *noun* a heavy stick often of bamboo bound with iron used in India as a weapon, *esp* by police. [Hindi *lāṭhī*]

latices /'latəseez/ *noun* pl of LATEX.

latifundium /lati'fundi·əm/ *noun* (*pl* **latifundia** /-di·ə/) a large landed estate, *esp* one in ancient Italy or modern Latin America, with workers who are slaves or peasants. [Latin *latifundium*, from *latus* wide + *fundus* piece of landed property]

latimeria /lati'miəri·ə/ *noun* any of a genus of living coelacanth fishes found in deep seas off southern Africa: genus *Latimeria.* [Latin genus name; named after Marjorie Courtenay-*Latimer* b.1907, SAfr museum director who brought the first known live specimen to scientific attention]

Latin[1] /'latin/ *noun* **1** the Italic language of ancient Rome and the Roman Empire. **2** a member of any of the peoples whose language developed from Latin. **3** *chiefly NAmer* a native or inhabitant of Latin America. **4** a member of the people of ancient Latium in W central Italy.

Word history
Old English from Latin *latinus* from *Latium*, an ancient province of Italy which included Rome. The Roman occupation of most of Britain from AD 43 until the early fifth cent. left no certain traces in the English language, apart from a few place-names, although some loanwords of Latin origin occurring early in the Old English period (such as *candle*) may have survived in Celtic and thence come into English. The large Latin element in English comes from five main sources. (1) The West Germanic language spoken by the Anglo-Saxon invaders of England in the fifth cent., which developed into English, contained some words borrowed from Latin in prehistoric times: *belt, butter, chalk, cheese, copper, cup, pillow, street,* and so on. (2) The activities of Latin-speaking missionaries from the end of the sixth cent. were responsible for the adoption of *altar, disciple,* and some other words mainly of a religious nature. (3) The Norman Conquest in 1066 led to the intro-

duction of many words which were ultimately of Latin origin, but which came to English by way of French (see note at FRENCH[2]). (4) The large-scale adoption of Latinate vocabulary in English began with the revival of classical learning in the 16th cent., and continued strongly throughout the Tudor and Stuart periods; words introduced at this time include *acumen, apparatus, appendix, area, candidate, census, estimate, focus, obscene, series, specimen,* and *vacuum.* (5) The Latin- and Greek-based international scientific vocabulary of modern times has further increased the Latin element in English with words such as *appendicitis, arboretum,* and *circadian;* but the basic vocabulary of English, as well as its grammar, is distinctively Germanic.

Latin[2] *adj* **1** of or relating to Latin. **2** of the peoples or countries using Romance languages. **3** *chiefly NAmer* of the peoples or countries of Latin America. **4** relating to the Romance languages. **5** relating to those branches of the Christian Church that use a Latin liturgy; *specif* Roman Catholic. **6** of ancient Latium, the people of ancient Rome, or the people of the Roman Empire.

Latina /la'teenə/ *noun* (*pl* **Latinas**) *NAmer* a girl or woman of Latin American or Spanish American descent. [American Spanish *Latina,* fem of *Latino* Latin]

Latin American *noun* a native or inhabitant of a part of the American continent where Spanish or Portuguese is spoken. ➤➤ **Latin American** *adj.*

Latinate /'latinət, -nayt/ *adj* of, resembling, or derived from Latin.

Latin cross *noun* a plain cross consisting of a long upright bar crossed near the top by a shorter transverse bar.

latinise *verb trans* see LATINIZE.

Latinism *noun* **1** a characteristic feature of Latin occurring in another language. **2** a Latin quality, character, or mode of thought.

latinize *or* **latinise** *verb trans* **1** to give a Latin form to (a word). **2** *archaic* to translate (something) into Latin. **3** to make (something) Latin in doctrine, ideas, or traits; *specif* to cause (something) to conform to the Roman Catholic Church. ➤➤ **latinization** /-'za-ysh(ə)n/ *noun,* **latinizer** *noun.*

Latino /la'teenoh/ *noun* (*pl* **Latinos**) *NAmer* a person of Latin American or Spanish American descent. [American Spanish *Latino* Latin]

Latin Quarter *noun* a section of the Left Bank in Paris historically frequented by students and artists. [translation of French *Quartier Latin*]

Latin square *noun* a square array of symbols in which each symbol appears once and once only in each row and column. It is used in the design of statistical experiments.

latish /'laytish/ *adj* rather late.

latissimus /lah'tisimas/ *noun* (*pl* **latissimi** /lah'tisimie, lah'tisimi/) either of a pair of large triangular muscles in the upper back. [shortened from scientific Latin *musculus latissimus dorsi,* literally 'broadest muscle of the back']

latissimus dorsi /'dawsie, 'dawsi/ *noun* = LATISSIMUS.

latitude /'latityoohd/ *noun* **1** the angular distance of a point on the surface of the earth measured North or South from the equator: compare LONGITUDE. **2** (*in pl*) regions as marked by their latitude: *in northern latitudes.* **3** freedom of action or choice. ➤➤ **latitudinal** /-'tyoohdinl/ *adj,* **latitudinally** /-'tyoohdinəli/ *adv.* [Middle English from Latin *latitudin-, latitudo,* from *latus* wide]

latitudinarian /,latityoohdi'neəri·ən/ *adj* liberal in standards of religious belief and conduct; *specif* favouring freedom of doctrine and practice within the Church of England. ➤➤ **latitudinarian** *noun,* **latitudinarianism** *noun.*

latke /'latkə/ *noun* a fried pancake that is a Jewish speciality, *esp* one made from grated potato. [Yiddish *latke* from Russian *latka* earthenware cooking pot]

latria /lə'trie·ə, 'latri·ə/ *noun* in Roman Catholic theology, the adoration that may be offered only to God: compare DULIA. [via Latin from Greek *latreia* worship]

latrine /lə'treen/ *noun* a small pit used as a toilet, *esp* in a military camp or barracks. [French *latrine* from Latin *latrina,* contraction of *lavatrina,* from *lavere* to wash]

-latry *comb. form* forming nouns, denoting: worship: *heliolatry; idolatry.* [Middle English *-latrie* via French and late Latin from Greek *-latria*]

latte /'lahtay/ *noun* a caffè latte.

latten *or* **lattin** /'lat(ə)n/ *noun* a yellow alloy identical to or resembling brass typically hammered into thin sheets, and formerly much used for church utensils. [Middle English *laton* metal resembling brass, from early French *laton*]

latter[1] /'latə/ *adj* **1** near the end; later: *the latter stages of a process; She suffered from Alzheimer's in her latter years.* **2** recent or present: *In latter years the company has expanded.* **3** second of two things mentioned or understood: *Of ham and beef the latter meat is cheaper.* [Old English *lætra*, compar of *læt* LATE[1]]

latter[2] *noun* (*pl* **latter**) the second mentioned.

Usage note
latter *and* former. See note at FORMER[2].

latter-day *adj* of present or recent times, *esp* referring to somebody resembling somebody in the past: *a latter-day Joan of Arc.*

Latter-Day Saint *noun* a Mormon. [from Mormons' name for themselves, the Church of Jesus Christ of *Latter-Day Saints*]

latterly *adv* **1** recently. **2** towards the end or latter part of a period.

lattice /'latis/ *noun* **1** a framework or structure of crossed wooden or metal strips with open spaces between. **2** a network or design like a lattice. **3a** a regular geometrical arrangement of points or objects over an area or in space. **b** the geometrical arrangement of the atoms or ions in a crystal. ⯈⯈ **latticed** *adj.* [Middle English *latis* from early French *lattis*, from *latte* lath, of Germanic origin]

lattice window *noun* a window with very small panes fitted in leaded, diamond-shaped panels.

latticework *noun* a design or structure made of lattices.

lattin /'lat(ə)n/ *noun* see LATTEN.

Latvian /'latvi-ən/ *noun* **1** a native or inhabitant of Latvia, country in central Europe. **2** the Baltic language of the people of Latvia. ⯈⯈ **Latvian** *adj.*

laud[1] /lawd/ *verb trans formal* to praise (somebody or something) enthusiastically or generously. ⯈⯈ **laudation** *noun.* [Latin *laudare* from *laud-, laus* praise]

laud[2] *noun archaic* praise. [Middle English *laude* via Old French from Latin *laud-, laus* praise]

laudable *adj* worthy of praise; commendable. ⯈⯈ **laudability** /-'biliti/ *noun,* **laudably** *adv.*

laudanum /'lawdənəm/ *noun* **1** any of various preparations of opium formerly used in medicine, *esp* as painkillers. **2** a tincture of opium. [perhaps an alteration of *ladanum* LABDANUM; the name was given by Paracelsus to a costly medicine believed to contain opium]

laudatory /'lawdət(ə)ri/ *adj* expressing praise.

lauds *pl noun* a religious service usu immediately following matins and forming with it the first of the canonical hours.

laugh[1] /lahf/ *verb intrans* to make the explosive vocal sounds characteristically expressing amusement, mirth, joy, or derision. ⯈ *verb trans* **1** to influence or bring (somebody) to a specified state by laughter: *We laughed him out of his fears; They laughed themselves silly.* **2** (+ at) to ridicule (somebody or something); to make fun of (them). ✱ **be laughing** *informal* to be successful or fortunate: *If you do that well in the exam, you'll be laughing.* **laugh on the other side of one's face** to be embarrassed after feeling confident or proud. **laugh up one's sleeve** to be secretly amused. ⯈⯈ **laugher** *noun,* **laughing** *adj,* **laughingly** *adv.* [Old English *hliehhan*]

laugh[2] *noun* **1** the act or an instance of laughing. **2** (*also in pl*) a means of entertainment; a diversion. **3** *informal* a cause for derision or merriment; a joke: *Swim in that current? That's a laugh.* ✱ **have the last laugh** to be proved right, successful, etc.

laughable *adj* provoking laughter or derision; ridiculous. ⯈⯈ **laughably** *adv.*

laughing gas *noun* = NITROUS OXIDE.

laughing jackass *noun Aus* the kookaburra. [from its call, which resembles loud laughter]

laughing stock *noun* an object of ridicule.

laugh off *verb trans* to minimize or dismiss (something) by treating it as amusingly trivial: *He laughed off the injury, saying it wasn't serious.*

laughter /'lahftə/ *noun* **1** the sound of laughing. **2** the action of laughing. [Old English *hleahtor*, related to Old English *hliehhan* to laugh]

launch[1] /lawnch/ *verb trans* **1** to set (a boat or ship) afloat. **2** to release or send off (e.g. a rocket). **3** to start or set (something or somebody) in motion, e.g. on a course or career: *I take any lady whose conduct is shady ... and launch her in first-rate society* — W S Gilbert. **4** to introduce (a new product) onto the market: *a party to*

launch a new book. **5** to throw (oneself) forward: *She launched herself at the player's legs.* ⯈ *verb intrans* (+ into) to begin to do something energetically and with commitment: *He launched into a rendition of his favourite pop song.* [Middle English *launchen* to hurl a missile, via French *lancher* from late Latin *lanceare* to wield a lance]

launch[2] *noun* an act or an instance of launching something.

launch[3] *noun* **1** a large motorboat. **2** formerly, the largest boat carried by a warship. [Spanish *lancha* from Portuguese *lancha*, perhaps ultimately from Malay *lanchar* swift]

launcher *noun* a device for launching rockets, missiles, etc.

launching pad *noun* = LAUNCH PAD.

launch pad *noun* **1** a platform from which a rocket can be launched. **2** a base from which something is set in motion: *The programme was an effective launch pad for his career.*

launch vehicle *noun* the rocket power source or sources used to launch a spacecraft.

launder /'lawndə/ *verb trans* (**laundered, laundering**) **1** to make (clothes) ready for use again by washing and ironing. **2** *informal* to pass (money obtained illegally) through a bank or legal business. ⯈⯈ **launderer** *noun.* [Middle English *launder* launderer, from Old French *lavandier*, ultimately from Latin *lavare* to wash]

launderette *or* **laundrette** /lawnd(ə)'ret/ *noun* a self-service laundry providing coin-operated machines. [formerly a trademark: from LAUNDER + -ETTE]

laundress /'lawndrəs/ *noun* a woman who launders clothes and linen as a job.

laundrette /lawnd(ə)'ret/ *noun* see LAUNDERETTE.

Laundromat /'lawndrəmat/ *noun chiefly NAmer, trademark in US* a self-service laundry providing coin-operated machines. [blend of LAUNDRY + AUTOMATIC[1]]

laundry /'lawndri/ *noun* (*pl* **laundries**) **1** clothes and linen that have been or are to be washed and dried. **2** a place where laundering is done, *esp* a commercial laundering establishment.

laureate[1] /'lawri-ət/ *noun* **1** a person specially honoured for achievement in an art or science. **2** a Poet Laureate. ⯈⯈ **laureateship** *noun.* [Latin *laureatus* crowned with laurel, from *laurea* laurel wreath, from *laurus* LAUREL]

laureate[2] *adj literary* crowned with laurel as a token of pre-eminence or honour.

laurel /'lorəl/ *noun* **1** any of several species of evergreen trees or shrubs that have smooth shiny leaves, small flowers, and oval-shaped berries: family Lauraceae. **2** a tree or shrub that resembles the true laurel, such as the cherry laurel or mountain laurel. **3a** (*in pl*) a crown of laurel awarded as a token of victory or preeminence. **b** distinction or honour. ✱ **look to one's laurels** to take care that one's position is not lost to a rival. **rest on one's laurels** to become complacent or uninspired in the wake of previous successes or achievements. [Middle English *lorel* via French from Latin *laurus*]

laurustinus /lawrə'stienəs/ *noun* an evergreen plant with glossy green leaves and white or pink flowers borne in winter: *Viburnum tinus.* [Latin *laurus* LAUREL + *tinus* wild laurel]

lav /lav/ *noun informal* a lavatory.

lava /'lahvə/ *noun* molten rock that flows from a volcano or from a crack in the earth's surface. [Italian dialect *lava* lava stream, orig 'stream caused by a sudden downpour' from Latin *lavare* to wash]

lavabo /lə'vayboh/ *noun* (*pl* **lavabos**) **1** (*often* **Lavabo**) the ritual washing of the celebrant's hands after the OFFERTORY (offering of unconsecrated bread and wine to God) at a Catholic Mass. **2** the towel or basin used for this. **3** a trough used for washing in a monastery or convent. **4** *archaic* a washbasin. [Latin *lavabo* I shall wash, from *lavare* to wash]

lavage /'lavij (*French* lava:ʒ)/ *noun* the medical washing out of an organ, e.g. the colon. [French *lavage* from *laver* to wash, from Latin *lavare*]

lava lamp *noun* an electric lamp containing a viscous liquid in which a lump of a coloured waxy substance stretches and forms blobs as the lamp warms up.

lavatorial /lavə'tawri-əl/ *adj* **1** relating to lavatories. **2** characterized by excessive reference to lavatories and bodily functions.

lavatory /'lavətri/ *noun* (*pl* **lavatories**) a toilet or a room containing one or more toilets.

Word history

Middle English *lavatorie* washbasin, bath, piscina, from late Latin *lavatorium*, from Latin *lavare* to wash. The sense 'washroom' dates from the 17th cent., 'washroom with a toilet' from the mid-19th cent., and 'toilet' from the early 20th cent.

lavatory paper *noun Brit* = TOILET PAPER.

lave /layv/ *verb trans literary* to wash or bathe (somebody or something). [Old English *lafian*]

lavender /'lavində/ *noun* **1** any of a genus of Mediterranean plants of the mint family widely cultivated for their narrow aromatic leaves and spikes of lilac or purple flowers which are traditionally dried and used in perfume sachets: genus *Lavandula*. **2** a pale purple colour. **3** lavender oil. ➤➤ **lavender** *adj.* [Middle English *lavendre* via Anglo-French from medieval Latin *lavandula*]

lavender oil *noun* a fragrant oil distilled from lavender flowers.

lavender water *noun* a perfume consisting of lavender oils and alcohol.

laver¹ /'layvə/ *noun* **1** a large basin used for ceremonial ablutions in ancient Jewish worship. **2** *archaic or literary* a basin used for washing. [Middle English *lavour* via French from late Latin *lavatorium*: see LAVATORY]

laver² /'lahvə/ *noun* any of several mostly edible reddish purple seaweeds: genus *Porphyra*. [Latin *laver* a water plant]

laver bread *noun* a flattened cake made from seaweed and eaten in Wales.

lavish¹ /'lavish/ *adj* **1** spent, given, or produced in abundance. **2** giving or spending profusely. ➤➤ **lavishly** *adv*, **lavishness** *noun*. [Middle English *lavas* abundance, from early French *lavasse* downpour of rain, ultimately from Latin *lavare* to wash]

lavish² *verb trans* to spend or give (something) with profusion.

law /law/ *noun* **1a** a rule of conduct formally recognized as binding or enforced by authority. **b** the whole body of such rules, comprising common law, civil law, and statute law: *'The law supposes that your wife acts under your direction.' 'If the law supposes that … the law is a ass – a idiot.'* — Dickens.

Editorial note

Law is a rule (or body of rules) routinely enforced by officials, and (unlike ethical and other rules) backed by sanctions if disobeyed. Laws may be criminal (threatening punishment for anti-social acts), civil (permitting suits between civilians, for example for damages or injunctions or divorce), or constitutional, enabling a citizen to challenge the state. Law aims to provide justice but does not always succeed: at best, it serves to reduce the level of grievance in society — Geoffrey Robertson.

2 the science or philosophy of law; jurisprudence. **3** control or authority: *Her word was law.* **4** (**the law**) *informal* the police. **5a** a statement of an order or relation of natural phenomena: *the first law of thermodynamics.* **b** a necessary relation between mathematical or logical expressions. **6** a rule of action or procedure in a sport: *the laws of cricket.* **7a** (*often* **Law**) the revelation of the will of God set out in the Old Testament. **b** (**the Law**) the first part of the Jewish scriptures; the Pentateuch. **c** the precepts of the Pentateuch. * **be a law unto oneself** to be unconventional. **in/at law** according to the law. **lay down the law** to give orders or express one's opinions with great force. **take the law into one's own hands** to do something, e.g. as an act of revenge, justice, or self-defence, that is not strictly legal or can by law only be done by   the police or other authorized people. [Old English *lagu*, of Scandinavian origin]

law-abiding *adj* abiding by or obedient to the law.

law agent *noun* a solicitor in Scotland.

lawbreaker *noun* somebody who violates the law. ➤➤ **lawbreaking** *adj and noun*.

law centre *noun* in Britain, a publicly funded centre dispensing free legal advice to members of the public.

lawful /'lawf(ə)l/ *adj* constituted, authorized, or allowed by law; rightful or legal. ➤➤ **lawfully** *adv*, **lawfulness** *noun*.

lawgiver *noun* a person who makes or gives laws.

lawks /lawks/ *interj Brit, dated* an expression of surprise. [euphemism for LORD²]

lawless *adj* **1** not regulated by or based on law. **2** not restrained or controlled by law; unruly. ➤➤ **lawlessly** *adv*, **lawlessness** *noun*.

Law Lord *noun* in Britain, a member of the House of Lords qualified to take part in its judicial proceedings.

lawmaker *noun* a legislator. ➤➤ **lawmaking** *noun*.

lawman *noun* (*pl* **lawmen**) in the USA, a law-enforcement officer, e.g. a sheriff or police officer.

law merchant *noun* (*pl* **laws merchant**) the legal rules formerly applied to commercial transactions. [Middle English *lawe marchaund*, translation of medieval Latin *lex mercatoria*]

lawn¹ /lawn/ *noun* an area of ground, e.g. around a house or in a garden or park, that is covered with mown grass. [Middle English *launde* from early French *lande* heath, of Celtic origin]

lawn² *noun* a fine sheer linen or cotton fabric of plain weave that is thinner than cambric. ➤➤ **lawny** *adj.* [Middle English, named after *Laon*, town in France known for its fine linens]

lawn mower *noun* a machine for cutting grass on lawns.

lawn tennis *noun dated or formal* tennis played on a grass court.

law of averages *noun* the principle that one extreme will always be cancelled out by its opposite at some future time, and the balance redressed.

law officer *noun* an official appointed to administer and interpret the law; *specif* a British attorney general or solicitor general.

law of nations *noun* = INTERNATIONAL LAW.

lawrencium /law'rensi-əm, lo-/ *noun* a radioactive metallic chemical element that is short-lived and artificially produced: symbol Lr, atomic number 103. [named after Ernest O *Lawrence* d.1958, US physicist who founded the laboratory that first produced it]

lawsuit *noun* a non-criminal case in a court of law.

lawyer /'lawyə, 'loyə/ *noun* a person whose profession is to conduct lawsuits or to advise on legal matters.

lax /laks/ *adj* **1** not strict or stringent; negligent: *lax morals*; *He had been lax in his duties.* **2** not tense, firm, or rigid; relaxed or slack: *lax muscles.* **3** said of a speech sound: articulated with the muscles in a relatively relaxed state, as is the vowel /i/ in contrast with the vowel /ee/: compare TENSE¹. ➤➤ **laxity** *noun*, **laxly** *adv*, **laxness** *noun*. [Middle English from Latin *laxus* loose]

laxative /'laksətiv/ *noun* a medicinal preparation that loosens or relaxes the bowels to relieve constipation. ➤➤ **laxative** *adj.* [Middle English *laxatif* from medieval Latin *laxativus*, from Latin *laxare* to loosen, from *laxus* loose]

lay¹ /lay/ *verb* (**laid** /layd/) ➤ *verb trans* **1** to put (something) down on a surface, especially gently or with care. **2** to spread (something or somebody) over a surface. **3a** to set (something) in order or position for use: *Lay the table for dinner.* **b** to put (strands) in place and twist them to form a rope, hawser, or cable. **4** said of a female, bird, reptile, etc: to produce (an egg). **5a** (*often* + on/upon) to put or impose (something) as a duty, burden, or punishment. **b** (*often* + on/upon) to advance (a charge or accusation) against somebody. **c** to assign (blame) to a particular person or group. **d** (+ on/upon) to assign (importance) to something: *We lay great stress on grammar.* **6a** to assert or allege (a claim, etc). **b** to submit (a case, argument, etc) for examination and judgment. **c** to prepare or contrive (a plan, scheme, etc). **7a** to bring (something) into position or against or into contact with something. **b** to bring (something) to a specified condition: *They blow laid the bone bare.* **8** to put (a stake) on an outcome: *I'd lay my life on it.* **9** *coarse slang* to have sexual intercourse with (somebody). **10** *archaic* to exorcize (a ghost). **11** *archaic* to bury (a dead person). ➤ *verb intrans* said *esp* of a hen: to produce eggs. * **lay about one** to deal blows indiscriminately, lashing out on all sides. **lay hands on 1** to seize (somebody or something) forcibly. **2** to find (something). **lay into** *informal* to attack or criticize (somebody) fiercely. **lay it on 1** to exaggerate, *esp* in order to flatter or convince somebody: *That was really laying it on a bit thick.* **2** to charge an exorbitant price. **lay low 1** to knock or bring (somebody) down. **2** to cause (somebody) to be ill or physically weakened. **lay on the table** to make (something) public; to disclose (information). **lay open** to expose (something), e.g.: **a** to cut it: *a blow that laid his head open.* **b** to explain it or make it known: *the facts of the case were laid wide open.* [Middle English *leyen, leggen* from Old English *lecgan*, related to Old English *licgan* LIE¹]

Usage note

lay *or* **lie**? These two words are sometimes confused, especially since the past tense of *lie* is *lay*. To *lay* (past tense and past participle *laid*) usually takes a direct object and describes the action of putting something down: *to lay a carpet*; *to lay an egg*; *she laid herself down on the bed*. To *lie* (past tense *lay*, past participle *lain*) never takes a direct object and describes the state of resting on something: *I think better lying down*; *he lay groaning on the sofa*; *the stones had lain undisturbed for centuries*.

lay² *noun* **1** the position or situation in which something lies or has been laid: *the lay of the land.* **2** *coarse slang* an act of sexual intercourse or a sexual partner. **3** the laying of eggs by a bird, etc.

lay³ *verb* past tense of LIE¹.

lay⁴ *adj* **1** not belonging to the clergy; not ecclesiastical. **2** denoting domestic or manual workers in a religious community: *a lay brother.* **3** not belonging to a particular profession: *lay members serving on the appeals panel.* [Middle English via French and late Latin from Greek *laikos* of the people, from *laos* people]

lay⁵ *noun* **1** a simple narrative poem intended to be sung; a ballad. **2** *literary* a song. [Middle English from early French *lai*]

layabout *noun* a lazy shiftless person.

lay aside *verb trans* **1** to reserve (something) for future use. **2** to dismiss or reject (something, e.g. an objection).

layaway /'layəway/ *noun NAmer* a system of reserving a purchase by paying a deposit on it.

lay by *verb trans* to reserve (something) for future use; to lay (something) aside.

lay-by *noun* (*pl* **lay bys**) **1** an area at the side of a road to allow vehicles to stop without obstructing traffic. **2** *Aus, NZ, SAfr* = LAY-AWAY.

lay day *noun* a day allowed for loading or unloading a vessel.

lay down *verb trans* **1** to place (something) down. **2** to sacrifice (one's life). **3** to formulate (e.g. a rule). **4** to store (wine) in a cellar. **5** to begin to build (ship or railway). **6** to pay or bet (money). **7** *informal* to record (music) in a studio.

layer¹ /'layə/ *noun* **1a** a single thickness of some substance spread or lying over or under another. **b** any of a series of gradations or depths: *layers of meaning.* **2a** a branch or shoot of a plant tied or staked so as to induce rooting while still attached to the parent plant. **b** a plant developed by layering. **3** somebody or something that lays. [Middle English, in the sense 'stone-layer, mason', from LAY¹ + -ER². Current senses date from the 17th cent.]

layer² *verb* (**layered, layering**) ➤ *verb trans* **1** to arrange (something) in layers: *potato slices layered with cheese.* **2** to cut (hair) in layers. **3** to propagate (a plant) by means of layers. ➤ *verb intrans* said of a plant: to form roots where a stem comes in contact with the ground.

layette /lay'et/ *noun* a complete outfit of clothing and equipment for a newborn baby. [French *layette*, ultimately from early Dutch *laege* drawer, box]

lay figure *noun* **1** a jointed model of the human body used by artists, *esp* to show the arrangement of drapery. **2** a person likened to a dummy or puppet. [obsolete *layman* lay figure, from Dutch *leeman*, from *lid* limb + *man* man]

lay in *verb trans* to accumulate a supply of (something) and reserve it for future use.

layman *noun* (*pl* **laymen**) a male layperson.

layoff *noun* **1** the laying off of an employee or workforce. **2** a period of unemployment, inactivity, or idleness.

lay off *verb trans* **1** to cease to employ (a worker) because of a shortage of work. **2** *informal.* **a** to let (something or somebody) alone. **b** to avoid (something); to give (something) up. ➤ *verb intrans informal* to stop or desist, *esp* from an activity causing annoyance.

lay on *verb trans* **1** to supply or organize (something). **2** *chiefly Brit* to supply (e.g. water or gas) to a building.

layout *noun* **1** the plan, design, or arrangement of something laid out, e.g. rooms in a building or material to be printed. **2** something laid out: *a model train layout.*

lay out *verb trans* **1** to arrange (something on the ground) according to a plan. **2** *informal* to make (somebody) unconscious. **3** *informal* to spend (an amount of money). **4** to prepare (a body) for a funeral.

layover *noun NAmer* = STOPOVER.

layperson *noun* (*pl* **laypeople**) **1** a person who is not a member of the clergy. **2** a person without special, e.g. professional, knowledge of some field.

lay reader *noun* in the Anglican Church, a layperson authorized to conduct parts of church services but not to celebrate the Eucharist.

lay shaft *noun* an intermediate shaft that receives and transmits power, *esp* in a gearbox. [prob from LAY¹]

lay up *verb trans* **1** to put (something) in storage; to have or keep (something) for future use. **2** to take (a vehicle or ship) out of active service. ✳ **be laid up** to be incapacitated by an illness or injury.

laywoman *noun* (*pl* **laywomen**) a female layperson.

lazar /'lazə/ *noun archaic* a person who has a disfiguring disease; *specif* a leper. [Middle English via medieval Latin from late Latin *Lazarus*, a beggar with sores mentioned in Luke 16:20]

lazaret /lazə'ret/ *noun* = LAZARETTO. [French *lazaret* from Italian dialect *lazareto*: see LAZARETTO]

lazaretto /lazə'retoh/ *noun* (*pl* **lazarettos**) **1** in former times, a hospital for people with infectious or contagious diseases. **2** a storeroom or storage locker on a ship or boat. [Italian dialect *lazareto*, partly from *lazar* leper, from late Latin *Lazarus* (see LAZAR), partly an alteration of *nazareto*, from *Santa Maria di Nazaret* St Mary of Nazareth, church in Venice that maintained a hospital]

laze¹ /layz/ *verb intrans* to act or rest lazily; to idle. ➤ *verb trans* (+ away) to pass (time) in idleness or relaxation. [back-formation from LAZY]

laze² *noun* an instance of being lazy or idling.

lazy *adj* (**lazier, laziest**) **1a** disinclined or averse to activity; indolent. **b** not energetic or vigorous: *a lazy movement.* **c** encouraging inactivity or indolence: *a lazy afternoon.* **2** said of a river: moving slowly. ➤ **lazily** *adv,* **laziness** *noun.* [perhaps from Middle Low German *lasich* feeble]

lazybones *noun* (*pl* **lazybones**) *informal* a lazy person.

lazy Susan /'soohz(ə)n/ *noun* a revolving tray placed on a dining table for serving food, condiments, or relishes. [from the forename *Susan*]

LB *abbr* Liberia (international vehicle registration).

lb *abbr* **1** in cricket, leg bye. **2** pound. [(sense 2) Latin *libra* scales, pound]

LBO *abbr* leveraged buyout.

lbw *abbr* in cricket, leg before wicket.

LC *abbr* left centre.

l.c. *abbr* **1** in the place cited. **2** letter of credit. **3** in printing, lower case. [(sense 1) Latin *loco citato*]

LCD *abbr* **1** liquid crystal display. **2** (*also* **lcd**) lowest (or least) common denominator.

LCJ *abbr* Lord Chief Justice.

LCM *abbr* (*also* **lcm**) lowest (or least) common multiple.

LCpl *abbr* lance corporal.

LD *abbr* lethal dose.

Ld *abbr* Lord.

Ldg *abbr* used chiefly in titles: Leading.

LDL *abbr* low-density lipoprotein.

L-dopa /,el 'dohpə/ *noun* the laevorotatory form of the chemical compound dopa that occurs naturally in plant and animal cells and is used in the treatment of Parkinson's disease. Also called LEVODOPA.

LDS *abbr* **1** Latter-Day Saints. **2** Licentiate in Dental Surgery.

LEA *abbr Brit* Local Education Authority.

lea /lee/ *noun chiefly literary* an area of grassland or pasture. [Old English *lēah*]

leach¹ /leech/ *verb trans* **1** to separate the soluble components from (e.g. soil or other mixed material) by the action of a liquid, *esp* water, passing through it. **2** to remove (something soluble) in this way. ➤ *verb intrans* to pass out or through by or as if by percolation: *Harmful chemicals leached into the river.* ➤➤ **leacher** *noun.* [Old English *leccan* to moisten]

leach² *noun* **1** a perforated vessel used in leaching, *esp* one used to hold wood ashes through which water is passed to extract the LYE (alkaline liquid used in making soap). **2** a solution or product obtained by leaching. **3** the act or process of leaching.

lead¹ /leed/ *verb* (*past tense and past part.* **led** /led/) ➤ *verb trans* **1a** to guide (a person or an animal) along a way, *esp* by going in front. **b** to cause (somebody) to go with one, *esp* under duress: *The guards led the condemned man to the scaffold.* **c** to direct or guide (somebody) on a course or to a state or condition; to influence (somebody): *Reflection led her to a better understanding of the problem.* **d** to serve as a channel or route for (something): *A pipe leads water to the house.* **2a** to go or be at the head of (something): *The mayor led the* *procession.* **b** to act as or be a leader in or of (a group, activity, etc). **c** to direct the operations, activity, or performance of (an undertaking); to have charge of: *The investigation was led by a senior police officer.* **d** to be ahead of (a rival or rivals), e.g. in a race. **3** to experience (a specified kind of life or existence). **4** in card games, to begin play with (a card). ➤ *verb intrans* **1a** to guide somebody or something along a way. **b** to lie or run in a specified place or direction: *The path leads uphill.* **c** to serve as an entrance or passage: *This door leads to the garden.* **d** to tend or be directed towards a specified result: *study leading to a degree.* **2a** to act as or be a leader. **b** to be first or ahead. **3a** (*often* + off) to begin or open: *She led off with a joke about her hotel room.* **b** to play the first card of a trick, round, or game. **c** (+ with) to direct the first of a series of blows at an opponent in boxing with the specified hand: *He led with his right.* ✳ **lead somebody a merry dance** to cause somebody a lot of trouble. **lead somebody astray** to encourage somebody to behave badly. **lead up to** to prepare the way for (something), *esp* by using a gradual or indirect approach. [Old English *lǣdan*]

lead² *noun* **1a** a position at the front or ahead: *in the lead.* **b** a margin or position of advantage or superiority. **c** guidance, direction, or example: *I followed her lead.* **d** an indication or clue. **2** the act or privilege of leading in cards, or the card or suit led. **3** a principal role in a dramatic production, or an actor who plays a principal role. **4** a news story of chief importance. **5** *Brit* a line or strap for leading or restraining a dog. **6** an insulated wire or cable that conducts an electrical current. **7** a channel of water leading to a mill or through an ice field.

lead³ /led/ *noun* **1** a bluish white metallic chemical element that is heavy and soft, and is used in pipes, batteries, shields against radioactivity, etc: symbol Pb, atomic number 82. **2** a thin stick of graphite or crayon in or for a pencil. **3a** the lead weight on a sounding line. **b** (*in pl*) lead framing for panes in windows. **c** in printing, a space between lines of type, or a thin strip of metal used to create this. **d** bullets or similar projectiles: *The lead was flying.* **e** *Brit* (*in pl*) a flat roof covered with thin lead sheets, or the lead sheets themselves. **4a** = WHITE LEAD. **b** = TETRAETHYL LEAD. [Old English *lēad*]

leaded /'ledid/ *adj* **1** said of windows: made up of small panes fixed in position with leads: *leaded lights.* **2** said of type: having lines separated by leads. **3** said of petrol: containing tetraethyl lead. **4** covered or weighted with lead.

leaden /'led(ə)n/ *adj* **1a** oppressively heavy: *leaden limbs; a leaden silence.* **b** lacking spirit or animation; sluggish: *leaden prose.* **2a** *archaic* made of lead. **b** dull grey. ➤➤ **leadenly** *adv,* **leadenness** *noun.*

leader /'leedə/ *noun* **1a** somebody or something that ranks first, precedes others, or holds a principal position. **b** somebody who has commanding authority or influence: *the leader of the rebellion.* **c** the principal officer of a political party, trade union, etc: *the leader of the opposition.* **d** *Brit* either of two government ministers in charge of initiating business in Parliament: *the Leader of the House of Commons.* **e** somebody who guides or inspires others: *a spiritual leader.* **2a** the principal first violinist of an orchestra. **b** *NAmer* the conductor of an orchestra. **3** *Brit* a newspaper editorial; a leading article. **4a** (*in pl*) in printing, dots or dashes used to lead the eye horizontally, e.g. across a table. **b** a blank section at the beginning or end of a reel of film or recording tape. **c** a main or end shoot of a plant. **d** a short length of material for attaching the end of a fishing line to a lure or hook. **5** a horse or dog placed in advance of the other or others of a pair or team. ➤➤ **leaderless** *adj,* **leadership** *noun.*

leader board *noun* a board or other display that shows the scores of the leading competitors, e.g. in a golf tournament.

lead-free /led/ *adj* = UNLEADED.

lead glass /led/ *noun* glass containing lead monoxide, *esp* a tough brilliant high-quality glass containing 30% or more lead monoxide.

lead-in /leed/ *noun* **1** introductory matter. **2** the cable that runs from an aerial to a transmitter or receiver.

leading¹ /'leeding/ *adj* coming or ranking first; foremost, principal: *the leading role.*

leading² /'leding/ *noun* in printing, the space between lines of type.

leading aircraftman *or* **leading aircraftwoman** /'leeding/ *noun* a member of the Royal Air Force ranking below a senior aircraftman or senior aircraftwoman.

leading article /'leeding/ *noun Brit* a newspaper editorial; a leader.

leading edge /'leeding/ *noun* **1** the foremost edge of an aerofoil, e.g. a wing or propeller blade. **2** the most advanced position or group in a particular field of activity, *esp* technology. **3** in electronics, the part of a pulse that has increasing amplitude.

leading lady /'leeding/ *noun* a female actor who plays a principal role in a film, play, etc.

leading light /'leeding/ *noun* a prominent and influential person in a particular sphere.

leading man /'leeding/ *noun* a male actor who plays a principal role in a film, play, etc.

leading note /'leeding/ *noun* = SUBTONIC.

leading question /'leeding/ *noun* a question so phrased as to suggest the desired answer.

leading rein /'leeding/ *noun* **1** a rein used for leading a horse, *esp* one for controlling the horse of a pupil. **2** (*in pl*) straps by which young children are supported when beginning to walk.

leading seaman /'leeding/ *noun* a member of the Royal Navy ranking below a petty officer.

lead-off /leed/ *noun* a beginning or leading action; a start.

lead on /leed/ *verb trans* **1** to entice or induce (somebody) to proceed in a mistaken or unwise course. **2** to cause (somebody) to believe something that is untrue.

lead pencil /led/ *noun* a pencil containing a graphite lead.

lead replacement petrol /led/ *noun* a form of petrol in which non-lead-containing additives replace the tetraethyl lead of leaded petrol.

leadscrew /'leedskrooh/ *noun* a screw that moves the carriage of a lathe.

lead tetraethyl /led/ *noun* = TETRAETHYL LEAD.

lead time /leed/ *noun* **1** the period between the initiation and the completion of a new production process. **2** the period between the placing of an order and the delivery of the goods.

leaf¹ /leef/ *noun* (*pl* **leaves** /leevz/) **1a** any of the flat, usu green, and typically broad-bladed outgrowths from the stem of a plant that function primarily in food manufacture by photosynthesis. **b** foliage, or the state of having foliage: *in leaf.* **2a** a part of a book or folded sheet of paper containing a page on each side. **b** a part of a window shutter, folding door, or table that slides or is hinged. **c** a section that can be inserted into a tabletop to extend it. **d** metal, e.g. gold or silver, in sheets that are usu thinner than foil. ✳ **take a leaf out of somebody's book** to copy or imitate somebody's behaviour. **turn over a new leaf** to make a change for the better, *esp* in one's way of living [from the practice of making a pupil who had spoilt a page of their copybook turn over and write the exercise out again]. ➤➤ **leafless** *adj,* **leaflike** *adj.* [Old English *lēaf*]

leaf² *verb intrans* said of a plant: to produce leaves. ✳ **leaf through** to turn over the pages of (a book, magazine, etc) quickly while only glancing at the contents.

leafage /'leefij/ *noun* = FOLIAGE (1).

leafhopper *noun* a small leaping insect that sucks the juices of plants: family Cicadellidae.

leaf insect *noun* any of various insects of S Asia with flat green bodies and flaps on the legs that closely resemble plant leaves: family Phyllidae.

leaflet¹ /'leeflit/ *noun* **1** a single sheet of paper or small pamphlet containing printed matter, e.g. an advertisement or public information. **2a** a small or young foliage leaf. **b** any of the divisions of a compound leaf.

leaflet² *verb trans and intrans* (**leafleted, leafleting**) to distribute leaflets to (people).

leaf miner *noun* any of various small insects that as larvae burrow in and eat the internal tissues of leaves.

leaf mould *noun* **1** a compost or soil layer composed chiefly of decayed vegetable matter. **2** a mould or mildew that affects leaves.

leaf spring *noun* a spring made of superimposed metal strips.

leafstalk *noun* = PETIOLE (1).

leafy *adj* (**leafier, leafiest**) **1** having abundant trees or foliage: *the leafy avenues of middle-class suburbia, among the … Guardian readers, the teachers and social workers* — The Guardian. **2** consisting chiefly of leaves: *green leafy vegetables.* ➤➤ **leafiness** *noun.*

league¹ /leeg/ *noun* **1a** an association of nations, groups, or people for a common purpose or to promote a common interest. **b** an association of people or sports clubs that organizes a competition for an overall title, in which each person or team plays all the others at least once. **2** a class or category: *the top league*. ✲ **in league** in alliance or conspiracy. [Middle English (Scots) *ligg* via French from Old Italian *lega*, from *legare* to bind, from Latin *ligare*]

league² *verb trans* to form (nations, groups, or people) into a league. ➤ *verb intrans* to be formed into a league.

league³ *noun* a former unit of distance equal to about 3mi (5km). [Middle English *leuge, lege*, from late Latin *leuga, leuca*, of Gaulish origin]

leaguer¹ *noun chiefly NAmer* a member of a league, *esp* a sports league or a major league.

leaguer² *noun* = LAAGER¹. [Dutch *leger*]

leaguer³ *verb trans* = LAAGER².

league table *noun* **1** a table showing the relative positions of competitors in a league. **2** a list in order of merit.

leak¹ /leek/ *verb intrans* **1a** said of a liquid, gas, etc: to enter or escape through a crack or hole, usu accidentally. **b** said of a container: to let something enter or escape in this way. **2** (*often* + out) said of information: to become known despite efforts at concealment. ➤ *verb trans* **1** to permit (a liquid, gas, etc) to enter or escape through or as if through a crack or hole. **2** to give out (information) surreptitiously: *He leaked the story to the press.* ➤➤ **leakage** /'leekij/ *noun*, **leaker** *noun*. [Middle English *leken* from Old Norse *leka*]

leak² *noun* **1a** a crack or hole through which something, e.g. a liquid or gas, enters or escapes, usu accidentally. **b** a means by which information becomes known despite efforts at concealment. **2a** an instance of leaking or something that leaks out. **b** a loss of electricity due to faulty insulation. **3** *informal* an act of urinating: *He's gone to take a leak.* ✲ **spring a leak** said of a vessel or container: to develop a leak.

leaky *adj* (**leakier, leakiest**) permitting something to leak in or out; not watertight: *a leaky pipe.* ➤➤ **leakiness** *noun*.

leal /leel/ *adj chiefly Scot, archaic* loyal; true. ➤➤ **leally** *adv*. [Middle English *leel* from Old French *leial, leel*, earlier form of *loial*: see LOYAL]

lean¹ /leen/ *verb* (*past tense and past part.* **leaned** /leend, lent/ *or* **leant** /lent/) ➤ *verb intrans* **1a** to incline or bend from a vertical position: *I leant forward to look.* **b** (+ on/against) to rest supported on or against something. **2** (+ on/upon) to rely on somebody for support or inspiration. **3** (+ towards) to incline in a particular direction in opinion, taste, etc: *She leans towards socialism.* **4** *informal* (+ on) to exert pressure on somebody to do something. ➤ *verb trans* (+ on/against) to place (something) on or against something for support. [Old English *hleonian*]

lean² *noun* an instance or degree of leaning.

lean³ *adj* **1a** said of a person or animal: lacking or deficient in flesh or bulk; thin. **b** said of meat: containing little or no fat. **2** lacking richness, sufficiency, or value: *a lean harvest.* **3a** deficient in an essential or important quality or ingredient: *a lean ore.* **b** said of a fuel mixture: low in the combustible component. ➤➤ **leanly** *adv*, **leanness** *noun*. [Old English *hlǣne*]

lean⁴ *noun* the part of meat that consists principally of fat-free muscular tissue.

lean-burn *adj* said of an internal-combustion engine: using a reduced proportion of fuel in the fuel-air mixture, thus lessening fuel consumption and pollution from exhaust fumes.

leaning *noun* an attraction, tendency, or partiality: *a leaning towards the bizarre.*

leant /lent/ *verb* past tense and past part. of LEAN¹.

lean-to *noun* (*pl* **lean-tos**) a small building with a roof that rests on the side of a larger building or wall.

leap¹ /leep/ *verb* (*past tense and past part.* **leaped** /leept, lept/ *or* **leapt** /lept/) ➤ *verb intrans* **1** to jump in or through the air: *leaping from rock to rock.* **2a** to move or pass abruptly from one state, topic, etc to another, *esp* to rise quickly: *She leapt to her feet; The idea leapt into his mind.* **b** (+ at) to seize an opportunity, offer, etc eagerly. ➤ *verb trans* to pass over (something) by leaping. ➤➤ **leaper** *noun*. [Old English *hlēapan*]

leap² *noun* **1a** a jump, or the distance covered by it. **b** a place leaped over or from. **2** a sudden transition, *esp* a rise or increase. ✲ **a leap in the dark** an action undertaken in uncertainty of the outcome.

by/in leaps and bounds very rapidly: *His maths has come on in leaps and bounds this year.*

leapfrog¹ *noun* a game in which one player bends down and another leaps over them with legs apart.

leapfrog² *verb trans and intrans* (**leapfrogged, leapfrogging**) **1** to leap over (somebody or something) in or as if in leapfrog. **2** to progress rapidly by passing over (rivals, obstacles, intermediate stages, etc).

leap second *noun* a second added or removed to synchronize one time scale with another, *esp* to make atomic time coincide with solar time.

leapt /lept/ *verb* past tense and past part. of LEAP¹.

leap year *noun* a year with an extra day added to make it coincide with the solar year, *esp* a year in the Gregorian calendar with 29 February as the 366th day. [prob from the 'leap' made by any date after February in a leap year over the weekday on which it would normally fall]

learn /luhn/ *verb* (*past tense and past part.* **learned** /luhnd, luhnt/ *or* **learnt** /luhnt/) ➤ *verb trans* **1a** to gain knowledge of or skill in (something): *learn a trade.* **b** to memorize (something): *We have to learn our lines for the play.* **c** to come to be able (to do something): *They are learning to cope on their own.* **d** to come to realize or know (something): *She learned that he was ill.* **2** *non-standard* to teach (somebody). ➤ *verb intrans* to acquire knowledge or skill. ➤➤ **learnable** *adj*, **learner** *noun*. [Old English *leornian*]

Usage note

Learn is not used in standard English to mean 'teach'. It never takes a personal pronoun or a person's name as a direct object: *I learned my acting skills from her; she taught me to act.*

learned /'luhnid/ *adj* **1** characterized by or associated with learning; erudite. **2** /luhnd/ acquired by learning: *learned versus innate behaviour patterns.* ➤➤ **learnedly** *adv*, **learnedness** *noun*.

learning *noun* acquired knowledge or skill, *esp* knowledge acquired by study or education: *with just enough of learning to misquote* — Byron.

learning curve *noun* **1** the rate at which somebody learns something, e.g. a new job or procedure, or the rate at which new knowledge has to be assimilated. **2** a graphical representation of this, typically in the form of a curve.

learning difficulties *pl noun* difficulties in learning basic skills at the same rate as people of the same age, often caused by mental handicap.

learnt /luhnt/ *verb* past tense and past part. of LEARN.

lease¹ /lees/ *noun* **1** a contract putting the land or property of one party at the disposal of another, usu for a stated period and rent. **2** the period of such a contract. ✲ **new lease of life** a renewed period of healthy activity, strength, or usefulness.

lease² *verb trans* **1** to grant (property) by lease. **2** to hold (property) under a lease. ➤➤ **leasable** *adj*. [Anglo-French *lesser* from Old French *laissier* to let, from Latin *laxare* to loosen, from *laxus* slack]

leaseback *noun* an arrangement by which one party sells or gives something to another but continues to have the use of it in return for rent or hire.

leasehold *noun* **1** tenure by lease. **2** property held by lease. ➤➤ **leaseholder** *noun*.

leash¹ /leesh/ *noun* **1** a line or strap for leading or restraining a dog or other animal. **2** a restraint or check. [Middle English *lees, leshe*, from Old French *laisse*, from *laissier* (see LEASE²) in the sense 'to let run on a long lead']

leash² *verb trans* to put (e.g. a dog) on a leash.

least¹ /leest/ *adj* **1a** smallest in quantity or extent. **b** used in the names of plants and animals: of a kind distinguished by small size: *the least bittern.* **c** smallest possible; slightest: *I haven't the least idea.* **2** lowest in rank, degree, or importance. [Old English *lǣst*, superl of *lǣssa* LESS¹]

least² *noun* **1** the smallest number or amount: *It's the least I can do; to say the least.* **2** somebody or something that is lowest in importance: *That's the least of my worries.* ✲ **at least 1** as a minimum; if not more: *It costs at least £50.* **2** if nothing else; at any rate: *At least it is legal.* **not in the least** not at all.

least³ *adv* to the smallest degree or extent: *least-known; when we least expected it.* ✲ **least of all** especially not: *Nobody, least of all the children, paid attention.* **not least** especially: *This is worrying news, not least for the shareholders.*

least common denominator *noun* = LOWEST COMMON DENOMINATOR.

least common multiple *noun* = LOWEST COMMON MULTIPLE.

least squares *pl noun* (*treated as sing.*) a method of fitting a curve to a set of points representing statistical data in such a way that the sum of the squares of the distances of the points from the curve is a minimum.

leastways *adv chiefly dialect* at least; at any rate: *He isn't married, leastways that's what he told me.*

leastwise *adv* = LEASTWAYS.

leather[1] /'ledhə/ *noun* **1a** animal skin dressed for use. **b** (*used before a noun*) made of leather: *leather shoes*. **2** something wholly or partly made of leather, e.g.: **a** a piece of chamois or similar material used for polishing metal or glass. **b** (*in pl*) leather clothing, *esp* a motorcyclist's jacket and trousers. [Old English *lether*]

leather[2] *verb trans* (**leathered, leathering**) **1** to cover (something) with leather. **2** *informal* to beat (a person or animal) with a strap; to thrash (them).

leatherback /'ledhəbak/ *noun* the largest existing sea turtle, which has a flexible CARAPACE (back covering) composed of a mosaic of small bones embedded in a thick leathery skin: *Dermochelys coriacea.*

leatherette /ledhə'ret/ *noun* an imitation leather.

leatherjacket *noun* **1** *Brit* the tough-skinned larva of the crane fly, which lives in the soil and feeds on the roots of plants. **2** any of various tropical fishes with rough or leathery skin.

leathern /'ledhən/ *adj archaic* made of or resembling leather: *I saw her hand; she has a leathern hand … I verily did think her old gloves were on, but 'twas her hands* — Shakespeare.

leatherneck *noun NAmer, informal* used *esp* by sailors: a member of the marines. [from the leather neckband formerly part of a marine's uniform]

leathery *adj* resembling leather in appearance or consistency, *esp* tough.

leave[1] /leev/ *verb* (*past tense and past part.* **left** /left/) ➤ *verb trans* **1a** to go away from (a place). **b** to desert or abandon (somebody). **c** to withdraw from (an organization, institution, etc): *He left school at 15*. **2** to put, station, deposit, or deliver (something), *esp* before departing. **3a** to cause or allow (something or somebody) to be or remain in a specified or unaltered condition: *His manner left me cold*. **b** (*also* + off/out) to fail to include, use, or take (something): *She left her notes at home; They left his name off the list*. **c** to permit (something) to be or remain subject to the action or control of a specified person or thing: *Just leave everything to me; We left nothing to chance*. **d** to allow (somebody) to do or continue something without interference: *I'll leave you to take care of things*. **4** to bequeath (property). **5** to have (members of one's family) remaining after one's death. **6** to have (a quantity) remaining or as a remainder: *Ten from twelve leaves two*. **7** to cause (something) to remain as an aftereffect. ➤ *verb intrans* to depart; to set out. ✳ **leave alone/be** *informal* to stop or refrain from interfering with, annoying, disturbing, or interrupting (somebody or something): *They won't leave me be.* **leave a lot to be desired** to be less than satisfactory. **leave go** *informal* to stop holding (something). **leave off** to stop or cease (doing something): *Leave off teasing your sister.* **leave somebody standing** to surpass somebody spectacularly. **leave well alone** to avoid meddling. ➤➤ **leaver** *noun*. [Old English *læfan*]

Usage note —————————

leave *or* let? There are one or two phrases in which *leave* is often used as a substitute for *let*, especially *leave alone, leave be*, and *leave go*. These are acceptable in conversational English, but the latter two should not be used in formal writing. *Leave somebody alone* needs special care since it can mean both *let somebody alone* (not interfere with them) and, literally, to leave somebody on their own.

leave[2] *noun* **1** authorized absence, e.g. from employment. **2** *formal* permission to do something: *by your leave*. ✳ **take one's leave** (*often* + of) to say farewell; to leave. [Old English *léaf*]

leave[3] *verb intrans* to produce leaves; to leaf. [Middle English *leven*, from *leef* leaf]

leaved *adj* (*used in combinations*) having leaves of the kind or number specified: *palmate-leaved; a four-leaved clover.*

leaven[1] /'lev(ə)n/ *noun* **1a** a substance, e.g. yeast, used to produce fermentation or a gas in dough, batter, etc to lighten it and make it rise. **b** a mass of fermenting dough reserved for this purpose. **2**

something that modifies or lightens something. [Middle English *levain* via French from Latin *levare* to raise]

leaven[2] *verb trans* (**leavened, leavening**) **1** to produce fermentation in (dough, batter, etc) and make it rise by adding leaven. **2** to mingle or permeate (something) with a modifying, tempering, or enlivening element.

leaves /leevz/ *noun* pl of LEAF[1].

leave-taking *noun* a departure or farewell.

leavings *pl noun* remains or residue.

Lebanese /lebə'neez/ *noun* (*pl* **Lebanese**) a native or inhabitant of the Lebanon, country in SW Asia. ➤➤ **Lebanese** *adj.*

Lebensraum /'layb(ə)nzrowm/ *noun* territory believed to be necessary for national existence or self-sufficiency; *specif* land Nazi Germany attempted to take in central and eastern Europe. [German *Lebensraum*, from *Leben* living, life + *Raum* space]

leccy /'leki/ *noun Brit, informal* electricity: *The leccy's been cut off.*

lech[1] /lech/ *noun informal, derog* **1** a lecherous man. **2** a lascivious act or urge.

lech[2] *verb intrans informal, derog* (*usu* + after) to behave lasciviously towards somebody; to lust after them: *leching after schoolgirls.*

lecher *noun* a lecherous man. [Middle English *lechour* from Old French *lecheor*, from *lechier* to lick, live in debauchery, of Germanic origin]

lechery *noun* inordinate sexual desire or indulgence in sexual activity; debauchery or lasciviousness. ➤➤ **lecherous** /-rəs/ *adj*, **lecherously** *adv.*

lecithin /'lesithin/ *noun* a PHOSPHOLIPID (fatty chemical compound) found in animals and plants, e.g. in nerve tissue and egg yolk, that is used in the manufacture of margarine, chocolate, etc to stabilize oil and water mixtures and retard the deterioration of fats and oils. [Greek *lekithos* yolk of an egg + -IN[1]]

lectern /'lektuhn/ *noun* a reading desk, *esp* one from which the Bible is read in church. [Middle English *lettorne* via French from medieval Latin *lectrum*, from Latin *legere* to read]

lection /'leksh(ə)n/ *noun archaic* a variant reading in a particular copy or edition of a text. [Latin *lection-, lectio* act of reading, from *legere* to read]

lectionary *noun* (*pl* **lectionaries**) a book or list of scriptural texts proper to each day of the church year. [medieval Latin *lectionarium* from *lection-, lectio* liturgical lesson for a particular day, from Latin: see LECTION]

lector /'lektaw/ *noun* **1** the reader of a lesson in a church service. **2** a lecturer in some universities. [late Latin *lector* reader, from Latin *legere* to read]

lecture[1] /'lekchə/ *noun* **1** a discourse given to an audience, *esp* for instruction. **2** a reproof delivered at length; a reprimand. [Middle English in the senses 'reading, text', via French and late Latin from Latin *lectus*, past part. of *legere* to read]

lecture[2] *verb intrans* to deliver a lecture or series of lectures. ➤ *verb trans* **1** to deliver a lecture to (an audience, a class of students, etc). **2** to reprove (somebody) at length or severely.

lecturer /'lekchərə/ *noun* **1** somebody who lectures. **2** a British university or college teacher below professorial rank.

lectureship *noun* the office or position of an academic lecturer.

LED *abbr* light-emitting diode, a small semiconductor diode that emits light when an electric current is passed through it and that is used on display screens, instrument panels, etc.

led /led/ *verb* past tense and past part. of LEAD[1].

lederhosen /'laydəhohz(ə)n/ *pl noun* traditional leather shorts that often have H-shaped braces and are worn by men in Austria, Bavaria, etc. [German *Lederhosen* from early High German *Lederhose*, from *Leder* leather + *Hose* trousers]

ledge /lej/ *noun* **1** a narrow horizontal surface that projects from a vertical or steep surface, e.g. a wall or rock face. **2** an underwater ridge or reef. **3** a mineral-bearing lode or vein. ➤➤ **ledged** *adj*, **ledgy** *adj*. [Middle English *legge* bar of a gate, prob from *leggen*: see LAY[1]]

ledger[1] /'lejə/ *noun* **1** a book containing the complete record of a company's accounts. **2** a horizontal piece of timber secured to the uprights of scaffolding. **3** = LEDGER TACKLE. [Middle English *legger*, prob from *leyen, leggen*: see LAY[1]]

ledger[2] *verb intrans* (**ledgered, ledgering**) to fish with ledger tackle.

ledger line or **leger line** noun in music, a short line added above or below a stave to extend its range.

ledger tackle noun fishing tackle arranged so that the weight and bait rest on the bottom.

lee[1] /lee/ noun 1 protecting shelter. 2 the side, e.g. of a ship, that is sheltered from the wind or that faces the direction towards which the wind is blowing. [Old English *hlēo*]

lee[2] adj of or on the lee side: *The rocky point … was in sight, broad on the lee bow* — Captain Marryat.

leeboard noun either of two movable flat surfaces attached to the outside of the hull of a sailing vessel that can be lowered to reduce leeway.

leech[1] /leech/ noun 1 any of numerous species of flesh eating or bloodsucking freshwater worms having a flattened segmented body with a sucker at each end: class Hirudinea. 2 a person who leeches on another. 3 archaic a physician or surgeon: *Make each prescribe to other, as each other's leech* — Shakespeare. [Old English *lǣce*; sense 3 may be a different word, the two coming together because the worm was long used by physicians to bleed patients]

leech[2] verb trans in medicine, esp in former times, to use leeches to draw blood from (a patient) as a method of treatment. ➤ verb intrans (often + on/off) to gain or seek to gain profit or advantage from another person, esp by clinging persistently.

leech[3] noun 1 either vertical edge of a square sail. 2 the rear edge of a fore-and-aft sail. [Middle English *leche* from early Low German *līk* boltrope]

leek /leek/ noun 1 a plant of the lily family that is related to the onion and garlic and is widely cultivated for its mildly pungent leaves and thick white edible stalk and bulb: *Allium porrum*. 2 the stalk and bulb of this plant, used as a vegetable. [Old English *lēac*]

leer[1] /lia/ verb intrans to give a lascivious, knowing, or sly look. ➤➤ **leering** adj, **leeringly** adv. [orig in the sense 'to look sideways'; prob from obsolete *leer* cheek, via Middle English from Old English *hlēor*]

leer[2] noun a lascivious, knowing, or sly look.

leery adj (**leerier, leeriest**) (often + of) suspicious or wary: *He was leery of strangers*. ➤➤ **leeriness** noun.

lees /leez/ pl noun the sediment of a liquor, e.g. wine, during fermentation and ageing. [Middle English *lie* via French from medieval Latin *lia*, of Gaulish origin]

lee shore noun a shore lying off a ship's lee side.

leet /leet/ noun Scot a list of candidates for a job or position. [prob from Old French *litte, lite*, variant of *liste* LIST[1]]

leeward[1] /'leewǝd; nautical 'looh·ǝd/ adj and adv in or facing the direction towards which the wind is blowing: compare WINDWARD[1].

leeward[2] noun the side or direction towards which the wind is blowing: compare WINDWARD[2].

lee wave noun a stationary wave formed by an air current on the sheltered side of a mountain.

leeway noun 1a an allowable margin of freedom or variation; tolerance. b Brit a margin of shortcoming in performance, esp due to lost or wasted time: *She has a lot of leeway to make up after her absence*. 2 off-course sideways movement of a ship in the direction of the wind.

left[1] /left/ adj 1a of, on, or being the side of somebody or something that is nearer the west when the front faces north. b of, on, or being the side of something that is closer to the left hand of an observer positioned directly in front: *the top left corner of the screen*. c located on the left side when facing downstream: *the left bank of a river*. 2 (often **Left**) of the left or left wing in politics.

Word history
Old English *lyst, left* weak; the left hand usually being weaker. The use of *left* and *right* to indicate political groups derives from the seating arrangements in the French National Assembly in 1789. The conservatives and royalists sat on the President's right (originally the place of honour due to the nobles); the republicans sat on his left, with the most radical of them at the far end; and moderates sat in the centre. This seating arrangement is now traditional in many legislatures; in the House of Commons, however, the government sits on the Speaker's right regardless of its persuasion.

left[2] adv on or towards the left.

left[3] noun 1a the part on the left side. b the location or direction of the left side. c the left hand, or a blow struck with it. 2 (often **the**

Left) (treated as sing. or pl). a those professing socialist or radical political views. b = LEFT WING (1A), (1B).

left[4] verb past tense and past part. of LEAVE[1].

left-back noun in football, hockey, etc, a defensive player on the left wing.

Left Bank noun the bohemian district of Paris situated on the left bank of the Seine. [translation of French *Rive Gauche*]

left-hand adj 1 situated on the left: *the left-hand side*. 2 of, designed for, or done with the left hand.

left-handed[1] adj 1 using the left hand habitually or more easily than the right. 2 of, designed for, or done with the left hand: *left-handed scissors*. 3 said of a rotary motion or spiral curve: anticlockwise. 4 ambiguous or double edged: *a left handed compliment*. 5 clumsy or awkward. ➤➤ **left-handedly** adv, **left-handedness** noun.

left-handed[2] adv using the left hand: *I had to sign left-handed because my right arm was in plaster*.

left-hander noun 1 a left-handed person. 2 a blow struck with the left hand.

leftism noun (often **Leftism**) left-wing principles and policy, or advocacy of these. ➤➤ **leftist** noun and adj.

left-luggage noun 1 Brit a room, e.g. at a railway station, where passengers' luggage may be left temporarily for a small fee. 2 (used before a noun) of or for the temporary storage of luggage: *a left-luggage locker*.

left-luggage office noun = LEFT-LUGGAGE (1).

leftover noun (also in pl) an unused or unconsumed residue, esp of food. ➤➤ **leftover** adj.

leftward /'leftwǝd/ adj towards or on the left.

leftwards (NAmer **leftward**) adv towards the left.

left wing noun 1 (often **Left Wing**). a the more socialist division of a group or party. b the members of a European legislative body holding more radical political views and occupying the left side of a legislative chamber: compare RIGHT WING, WING[1]. 2 in sport, the left side of the field when facing towards the opposing team, or the players positioned on this side. ➤➤ **left-winger** noun.

left-wing adj 1 belonging to or characteristic of the left wing in politics. 2 professing socialist or radical political views.

lefty noun (pl **lefties**) 1 informal a left-wing person. 2 a left-handed person.

leg /leg/ noun 1a a limb or analogous appendage of a person or animal used for supporting the body and for walking: *Good Launcelot Gobbo, use your legs … run away* — Shakespeare. b an artificial replacement for a human leg. c a joint of meat from the hind leg of an animal, esp above the hock. 2 the part of a garment that covers the leg. 3 something resembling a leg in form or function, e.g.: a a pole or bar serving as a support or prop, e.g. for a tripod or a table. b a branch of a forked or jointed object, e.g. a compass. 4a a portion of a trip; a stage. b the part of a relay race run by one competitor. c a round of a competition, or one of two or more events or games constituting a round. d the course and distance sailed on a single tack. 5a = LEG SIDE. b in cricket, a fielding position on the leg side of the pitch: *short leg*. c (used before a noun) said of a ball bowled in cricket: moving or tending to move in the direction of the off side: *a leg spin*. d (used before a noun) in, on, or towards the leg side of a cricket field: *the leg stump*. 6 either side of a triangle as distinguished from the base or hypotenuse. * **have legs 1** informal said of an idea, etc: to be of interest, be worth exploring or developing. 2 informal said of a film or play: to have long-term popularity. **not have a leg to stand on** not to have the least support or basis for one's position, esp in a controversy. [Middle English from Old Norse *leggr*]

leg. abbr legato.

legacy /'legǝsi/ noun (pl **legacies**) 1 a gift of money or property by will; a bequest. 2 something passed on by an ancestor or predecessor or remaining from the past: *the bitter legacy of two world wars*. [Middle English *legacie* office of a legate, bequest, via French or medieval Latin from Latin *legatus*: see LEGATE]

legal /'leegl/ adj 1 of law: *the legal profession*. 2 permitted by law. 3 established by or deriving authority from law. 4 recognized in common law as distinguished from equity. ➤➤ **legally** adv. [Middle English via French from Latin *legalis*, from *leg-, lex* law]

legal aid noun money from public funds to pay for legal advice or representation for those who cannot afford it.

legalese /leegl'eez/ *noun* the specialized language or jargon of the legal profession.

legalise /'leegl·iez/ *verb trans* see LEGALIZE.

legalism *noun* strict or excessive conformity to the law or to a moral code. >>> **legalist** *noun and adj*, **legalistic** /-'listik/ *adj*, **legalistically** /-'listikli/ *adv*.

legality /li'galiti/ *noun* (*pl* **legalities**) **1** the state of being legal; lawfulness. **2** (*in pl*) the requirements and procedures of the law.

legalize *or* **legalise** /'leegl·iez/ *verb trans* to make (something) legal; to give legal validity or sanction to (it). >>> **legalization** /-'zaysh(ə)n/ *noun*.

legal tender *noun* currency that a creditor is bound by law to accept as payment of a debt.

legate /'legət/ *noun* **1** an official delegate or messenger. **2** a representative of the pope. >>> **legateship** *noun*, **legatine** /-'tin/ *adj*. [Middle English via Old French from Latin *legatus* deputy, emissary, past part. of *legare* to depute, send as emissary, bequeath, from *leg-*, *lex* law]

legatee /legə'tee/ *noun* a person to whom a legacy is bequeathed.

legation /li'gaysh(ə)n/ *noun* **1a** a diplomatic mission, *esp* one in a foreign country headed by a minister. **b** the official residence of a diplomat on such a mission. **2** the rank or office of a legate. [Middle English *legacioun* via French from Latin *legation-*, *legatio*, from *legare*: see LEGATE]

legato /li'gahtoh/ *adj and adv* said of a piece of music: to be performed in a smooth and connected manner. >>> **legato** *noun*. [Italian *legato*, literally 'tied']

leg before wicket *adj* said of a batsman or batswoman in cricket: out because of having obstructed with a part of the body, *esp* the legs, a ball that would otherwise have hit the wicket.

leg break *noun* in cricket, a slow bowled ball that turns from the leg side towards the off side when it bounces.

leg bye *noun* in cricket, a run scored after the ball has touched a part of the batsman's or batswoman's body but not the bat or hands: compare BYE[1] (2), EXTRA[2] (4).

legend /'lej(ə)nd/ *noun* **1a** a story coming down from the past, *esp* one popularly regarded as historical although not verifiable. **b** a body of such stories: *a character in Celtic legend*. **c** a similar story of recent origin. **2** a person, act, or thing that inspires legends: *a legend in her own lifetime*. **3a** an inscription or title on an object, e.g. a coin. **b** a caption. **c** the key to a map, chart, etc. [Middle English *legende* via French from medieval Latin *legenda* things to be read, from Latin *legere* to gather, select, read]

legendary *adj* **1** of, described in, or characteristic of legend. **2** celebrated as if in legend; very famous: *a legendary figure in the world of jazz*.

legerdemain /ˌlejədə'mayn/ *noun* **1** manual skill or dexterity in conjuring; sleight of hand. **2** a display of artful skill, trickery, or adroitness: *political legerdemain*. [Middle English from early French *leger de main* light of hand]

leger line /'lejə/ *noun* see LEDGER LINE.

legged *adj* (*used in combinations*) having legs of the kind or number specified: *a four-legged animal*.

leggings /'legingz/ *pl noun* **1** very close-fitting stretchy trousers worn *esp* by women or children. **2** a close-fitting usu protective covering, e.g. of leather, that reaches from the ankles to the knees or thighs.

leggy *adj* (**leggier, leggiest**) **1** having disproportionately long legs: *a leggy colt*. **2** said *esp* of a woman: having attractively long legs. **3** said of a plant: having unnaturally long thin stems; spindly. >>> **legginess** *noun*.

leghorn *noun* **1a** fine plaited straw made from an Italian wheat. **b** a hat made from this straw. **2** (**Leghorn**) /le'gawn/ a domestic fowl of a hardy breed originating in the Mediterranean. [*Leghorn*, former name of Livorno, port in Italy from where the straw and fowls were exported]

legible /'lejəbl/ *adj* capable of being read or deciphered: *legible handwriting*. >>> **legibility** /-'biliti/ *noun*, **legibly** *adv*. [Middle English from late Latin *legibilis*, from Latin *legere* to read]

legion[1] /'leej(ə)n/ *noun* **1** the principal unit of the ancient Roman army comprising 3000–6000 foot soldiers and cavalry. **2a** a large military force: *the Foreign Legion*. **b** a national association of ex-servicemen: *the Royal British Legion*. **3** (*also in pl*) a very large

number; a multitude: *legions of football fans*. [Middle English via French from Latin *legion-*, *legio*, from *legere* to gather]

legion[2] *adj* many or numerous: *The problems are legion*.

legionary[1] *adj* of or being a legion. [Latin *legionarius*, from *legion-*, *legio*: see LEGION[1]]

legionary[2] *noun* (*pl* **legionaries**) a member of a legion, *esp* a Roman legion.

legionnaire /leejə'neə/ *noun* a member of a legion, *esp* a foreign legion or an ex-servicemen's association. [French *légionnaire* from Latin *legionarius*: see LEGIONARY[1]]

legionnaire's disease *noun* a serious infectious disease resembling pneumonia that is caused by a bacterium and often affects groups of people associated in one place, e.g. a hotel or hospital. [from its outbreak at a convention of the American Legion (an ex-servicemen's association) in 1976]

legislate /'lejislayt/ *verb intrans* to make or enact laws. >>> *verb trans* to bring (something) about by legislation. [back-formation from LEGISLATOR]

legislation /leji'slaysh(ə)n/ *noun* laws or the making of laws.

legislative /'lejislətiv/ *adj* **1** having the power or performing the function of a legislature. **2a** of legislating. **b** created by a legislature, *esp* as distinguished from an executive or judicial body. **3** of or created by legislation. >>> **legislatively** *adv*.

legislator *noun* a maker of laws, *esp* a member of a legislative body. [Latin *legis lator* proposer of a law, from *legis*, genitive of *lex* law + *lator* proposer, from *latus*, past part. of *ferre* to carry, propose]

legislature /'lejisləchə/ *noun* a body of people having the power to legislate.

legit /li'jit/ *adj informal* legitimate.

leg it *verb intrans* (**legged it, legging it**) *informal* **1** to walk or run fast; to hurry: *We legged it to the station*. **2** to run away: *He broke the window and then legged it*.

legitimate[1] /li'jitimət/ *adj* **1a** in accordance with law: *a legitimate government*. **b** ruling by or based on the strict principle of hereditary right: *a legitimate claim to the throne*. **2** neither spurious nor false; genuine: *a legitimate grievance*. **3** recognized as lawful offspring; born in wedlock. **4** conforming to recognized principles or accepted rules and standards. **5** relating to serious dramatic works acted on stage by professional actors, as opposed to music hall, some forms of musical comedy, etc: *legitimate theatre*. **6** in accordance with reason or logic: *a legitimate deduction*. >>> **legitimacy** /-si/ *noun*, **legitimately** *adv*. [medieval Latin *legitimatus*, past part. of *legitimare* to legitimate, from Latin *legitimus* legitimate, from *leg-*, *lex* law]

legitimate[2] /li'jitimayt/ *verb trans* **1a** to give legal status to (something). **b** to justify (something). **2** to give (an illegitimate child) the legal status of one legitimately born. >>> **legitimation** /-'maysh(ə)n/ *noun*, **legitimatization** /-mətie'zaysh(ə)n/ *noun*, **legitimization** /-mie'zaysh(ə)n/ *noun*.

legitimatize *or* **legitimatise** /li'jitimətiez/ *verb trans* = LEGITIMATE[2].

legitimise /li'jitimiez/ *verb trans* see LEGITIMIZE.

legitimism /li'jitimiz(ə)m/ *noun* support for a legitimate monarch or government. >>> **legitimist** *noun and adj*.

legitimize *or* **legitimise** /li'jitimiez/ *verb trans* = LEGITIMATE[2].

legless *adj* **1** *chiefly Brit, informal* very drunk. **2** having no legs.

Lego /'legoh/ *noun trademark* a toy construction kit. [contraction of Danish *leg godt* play well]

leg-of-mutton *or* **leg-o'-mutton** *adj* said of a sleeve or sail: having an approximately triangular shape.

leg-pull *noun* a playful trick or deception. [from the phrase *pull somebody's leg*]

legroom *noun* space in which to extend the legs while seated.

leg rope *noun Aus, NZ* a rope used to secure an animal by one of its hind legs.

leg side *noun* the side of a cricket field away from which the receiving batsman's or batswoman's feet are turned: compare OFF SIDE.

legume /'legyoohm/ *noun* **1** any of a large family of plants, shrubs, and trees having pods containing seeds and root nodules containing nitrogen-fixing bacteria and including important food and forage plants, e.g. peas, beans, or clovers: family Leguminosae. **2** the usu edible pod or seed of such a plant. >>> **leguminous**

/li'gyoohminǝs/ *adj.* [French *légume* from Latin *legumin-, legumen* leguminous plant, from *legere* to gather]

leg-up *noun informal* **1** assistance in mounting a horse, climbing a wall, etc. **2** a helping hand; a boost.

leg-warmers *pl noun* knitted leg coverings resembling long footless socks, often worn by dancers during practice.

legwork *noun* work involving physical activity and usu forming the basis of more creative or mentally exacting work.

lei[1] /lay/ *noun* a wreath or necklace of flowers or leaves that is a symbol of affection in Polynesia. [Hawaiian *lei*]

lei[2] *noun* pl of LEU.

Leibnizian[1] /lieb'nitsi-ǝn/ *adj* of the German philosopher and mathematician Gottfried von Leibniz (1616–1716) or his work.

Leibnizian[2] *noun* a follower of Leibniz.

Leicester /'lestǝ/ *noun* **1** an orange-red cheese with a mild flavour and a firm texture. **2** an animal of a breed of white-faced sheep with long exceptionally fine white fleece originating in England and bred for meat. [named after *Leicester*, county town of Leicestershire in central England, where both originated]

Leics *abbr* Leicestershire.

leishmaniasis /leeshmǝ'nie-ǝsis/ *noun* a disease caused by any of a genus of parasitic protozoans (single-celled organisms; see PROTOZOAN). [scientific Latin from *Leishmania*, genus name of the causative organisms, named after Sir William *Leishman* d.1926, Scottish pathologist]

leister[1] /'leestǝ/ *noun* a spear with three or more barbed prongs for catching fish, *esp* salmon. [Old Norse *ljóstr*, from *ljósta* to strike]

leister[2] *verb trans* (**leistered, leistering**) to spear (a fish) with a leister.

leisure /'lezhǝ/ *noun* **1** freedom provided by the cessation of activities, *esp* time free from work or duties: *To be able to fill leisure intelligently is the last product of civilization* — Bertrand Russell. **2** unhurried ease: *How many inner resources one needs to tolerate a life of leisure without fatigue* — Natalie Clifford Barney. ✳ **at leisure/at one's leisure 1** at an unhurried pace. **2** at one's convenience. ➤➤ **leisured** *adj*. [Middle English *leiser* via Old French from Latin *licēre* to be allowed]

leisure centre *noun* a public building offering facilities for a variety of leisure activities, such as a swimming pool, gym, and function rooms.

leisurely[1] *adj* characterized by leisure; unhurried. ➤➤ **leisureliness** *noun*.

leisurely[2] *adv* without haste; deliberately.

leisurewear *noun* casual clothes suitable for sport or relaxation.

leitmotiv *or* **leitmotif** /'lietmohteef/ *noun* **1** a musical phrase that signals an idea, person, or situation, *esp* in the operas of Wagner. **2** a recurring theme, *esp* in a literary work. [German *Leitmotiv*, from *leiten* to lead + *Motiv* motive, from French *motif*]

lek[1] /lek/ *noun* the basic monetary unit of Albania, divided into 100 qindarka. [Albanian *lek*]

lek[2] *noun* an area where black grouse or other social birds congregate to carry on display and courtship behaviour. [prob from Swedish *lek* sport or play]

lekker /'lekǝ/ *adj SAfr, informal* pleasant or nice. [Afrikaans *lekker*, from Dutch]

LEM /lem/ *abbr* lunar excursion module.

lemma /'lemǝ/ *noun* (*pl* **lemmas** *or* **lemmata** /'lemǝtǝ/) **1** a proposition accepted as true for the sake of demonstrating another proposition. **2a** the argument or theme of a composition prefixed as a title or introduction. **b** a heading or introduction, or a subsidiary part of one. [via Latin from Greek *lēmma* thing taken, assumption, from *lambanein* to take]

lemming /'leming/ *noun* **1** any of several species of small furry volelike rodents with a short tail, *esp* one of a species living in northern mountains that periodically undergoes mass migrations resulting in the death of many through drowning in the sea: genus *Lemmus*. **2** a member of a group mindlessly pursuing a course of action that will lead to mass destruction. [Norwegian *lemming*]

lemon /'lemǝn/ *noun* **1a** an oval yellow citrus fruit with a thick rind and acid flesh. **b** the stout thorny tree, related to the orange and grapefruit, that bears this fruit: *Citrus limon*. **2** a pale yellow colour. **3** *informal* somebody or something that is unsatisfactory or worthless; a dud. ➤➤ **lemony** *adj*. [Middle English *lymon* via French from medieval Latin *limon-, limo*, from Arabic *laymūn* citrus fruit]

lemonade /lemǝ'nayd/ *noun* a soft drink, often carbonated, made or flavoured with lemon.

lemon balm *noun* a bushy plant of the mint family that has white or pinkish flowers and is often cultivated for its fragrant lemon-scented leaves: *Melissa officinalis*.

lemon cheese *noun* = LEMON CURD.

lemon curd *noun* a conserve made from lemons, sugar, eggs, and butter.

lemongrass *noun* a robust grass that grows in tropical regions and is the source of an essential oil with an odour of lemon or verbena: *Cymbopogon citratus*.

lemon sole *noun* a brown flatfish of N Atlantic and European waters that is highly valued for food: *Microstomus kitt*. [*lemon* from French *limande*, a flatfish]

lempira /'lempirǝ/ *noun* the basic monetary unit of Honduras, divided into 100 centavos. [American Spanish *lempira*, named after *Lempira* d.1539, Mayan chief who resisted the Spanish conquerors of Honduras]

lemur /'leemǝ/ *noun* any of numerous tree-dwelling mammals of Madagascar that are related to the monkeys and typically have a pointed muzzle, large eyes, and a long furry tail: family Lemuridae. [scientific Latin *lemur* from Latin *lemures* (pl) ghosts]

lend /lend/ *verb* (*past tense and past part.* **lent** /lent/) ➤ *verb trans* **1a** to give (something) to somebody for temporary use on condition that it be returned: *She lent me her umbrella*. **b** to give (money) to somebody for temporary use on condition of repayment, usu with interest. **2a** to give the assistance or support of (something); to add or contribute (it): *a dispassionate and scholarly manner which lends great force to his criticisms* — Times Literary Supplement. **b** (*usu* + to) to adapt or apply (oneself or itself) to something: *a topic that lends itself admirably to class discussion*. ➤ *verb intrans* to make loans, *esp* on a professional basis. ✳ **lend an ear** to listen. ➤➤ **lender** *noun*. [Middle English *lenen, lenden*, from Old English *lænan*, from *læn* loan]

Usage note

lend, loan, *and* **borrow**. These words are sometimes confused. To *lend* means 'to allow somebody to take and use something that is yours': *they lent me their lawn mower*. To *borrow* means the opposite 'to take and use something that belongs to somebody else': *I borrowed their lawn mower*. To show who lent the thing borrowed use *from*: *I borrowed ten pounds from Bob*. To *loan* means the same as to *lend* and is mainly used with reference to money: *The bank loaned them £100,000*. *Loan* is also a noun: *a loan of £10,000; the loan of our lawn mower*.

lending library *noun chiefly Brit* the lending department of a public library.

lend-lease *noun* the transfer of goods and services to an ally in a common cause; *specif* the system by which the USA gave material aid to the Allies in World War II.

length /length/ *noun* **1** the quality or state of being long. **2a** the longer or longest dimension of an object. **b** the extent from end to end: *the length of a piece of string*. **c** the vertical extent of something, e.g. hair or clothing: *the length of her skirt; shoulder-length hair*. **d** the full extent of something: *We walked the length of the street*. **3a** duration or extent in time: *the length of a broadcast*. **b** relative duration or stress of a sound. **c** extent from beginning to end: *the length of the book*. **4** the length of something taken as a unit of measure: *an arm's length apart; His horse led by a length; She swam two lengths of the pool*. **5** (*also in pl, but treated as sing.*) the degree to which something, e.g. a course of action, is carried; a limit or extreme: *He went to great lengths to learn the truth*. **6a** a long expanse or stretch: *lengths of hair*. **b** a piece of something long and narrow: *a length of pipe; a 2m length of fabric*. **7** in cricket, the distance down the pitch that a bowled ball travels before bouncing. ✳ **at length 1** fully; comprehensively. **2** for a long time. **3** finally; at last. [Old English *lengthu* from *lang* long]

lengthen *verb* (**lengthened, lengthening**) ➤ *verb intrans* to become longer. ➤ *verb trans* to make (something) longer.

lengthways *adv and adj* in the direction of the length: *Bricks are generally laid lengthways*.

lengthwise *adv and adj* = LENGTHWAYS.

lengthy *adj* (**lengthier, lengthiest**) **1** of great or unusual length; long. **2** excessively or tediously protracted. ➤➤ **lengthily** *adv*, **lengthiness** *noun*.

lenient /'leeni·ənt/ *adj* **1** having or showing a mild, merciful, or tolerant nature; not severe: *lenient treatment of offenders.* **2** *archaic* exerting a soothing or easing influence. ➤➤ **lenience** *noun,* **leniency** /-si/ *noun,* **leniently** *adv.* [Latin *lenient-, leniens,* present part. of *lenire* to soften, soothe, from *lenis* soft, mild]

Leninism /'leniniz(ə)m/ *noun* the communist principles and policies advocated by Vladimir Ilyich Lenin. ➤➤ **Leninist** *noun and adj,* **Leninite** /-niet/ *noun and adj.* [named after V I *Lenin* (Ulyanov) d.1924, Russian political leader]

lenitive[1] /'lenitiv/ *adj archaic* said of a drug: relieving pain or stress. [early French *lenitif* from medieval Latin *lenitivus,* from Latin *lenire:* see LENIENT]

lenitive[2] *noun archaic* a lenitive drug.

lenity /'leniti/ *noun formal* gentleness or mercy. [French *lénité* from Latin *lenitat-, lenitas,* from *lenis* soft, mild]

leno /'leenoh/ *noun* (*pl* **lenos**) **1** an open weave in which pairs of warp yarns cross one another and lock the weft yarns in position. **2** a fabric, e.g. gauze, made with such a weave. [French *linon* linen fabric, from *lin* flax, from Latin *linum*]

lens /lenz/ *noun* **1a** a piece of glass or other transparent material with two opposite regular surfaces, at least one of which is curved, that is used to form an image by focusing rays of light. **b** a combination of two or more lenses, e.g. in a camera or microscope. **2** a device for directing or focusing radiation other than light, e.g. sound waves or electrons. **3** something shaped like an optical lens with both sides convex. **4** a transparent lens-shaped or nearly spherical body in the eye that focuses light rays on the retina. ➤➤ **lensed** *adj,* **lensless** *adj.* [Latin *lent-, lens* LENTIL; from its shape]

Lent /lent/ *noun* the 40 weekdays from Ash Wednesday to Easter Saturday observed by Christians as a time of penitence and fasting in commemoration of Christ's period of fasting in the wilderness. ➤➤ **Lenten** *adj.* [Middle English *lente* springtime, Lent, from Old English *lencten*]

lent *verb* past tense and past part. of LEND.

lenticel /'lentisel/ *noun* any of numerous pores in the stems of woody plants through which gases are exchanged between the atmosphere and the stem tissues. [Latin *lenticella,* dimin. of *lent-, lens* LENTIL]

lenticular /len'tikyoolə/ *adj* **1** having the shape of a lens with both sides convex. **2** of a lens. [Latin *lenticularis* lentil-shaped, from *lenticula:* see LENTIL]

lentil /'lentl/ *noun* **1** a Eurasian plant of the pea family, cultivated for its small flattish round edible seeds, typically yellow or orange in colour, that are rich in protein: *Lens culinaris.* **2** a seed of this plant, used as a vegetable *esp* in soups. [Middle English via Old French from Latin *lenticula,* dimin. of *lent-, lens* lentil]

lentivirus /'lentivie·ərəs/ *noun* any of a subfamily of viruses, including the human immunodeficiency virus, that begins producing symptoms a long time after infection. [scientific Latin *lentivirus,* from Latin *lentus* slow + VIRUS]

lent lily *noun Brit* the European wild daffodil: *Narcissus pseudonarcissus.*

lento /'lentoh/ *adj and adv* said of a piece of music: to be performed in a slow manner. [Italian *lento* slow, from Latin *lentus* pliant, sluggish, slow]

Leo /'leeoh/ *noun* **1** in astronomy, a constellation (the Lion) depicted as a lion. **2a** in astrology, the fifth sign of the zodiac. **b** a person born under this sign. [Latin *leo* lion]

leone /li'ohni/ *noun* the basic monetary unit of Sierra Leone, divided into 100 cents. [named after Sierra *Leone*]

Leonine /'lee·ənien/ *adj* **1** of or relating to any of the popes named Leo: *the Leonine Wall.* **2a** said of medieval Latin verse: in hexameter or elegiac metre with internal rhyme. **b** said of English verse: having internal rhyme. [Middle English, from the name *Leo,* from Latin *leo* LION]

leonine /'lee·ənien/ *adj* of or resembling a lion; having the characteristics, e.g. courage, popularly ascribed to lions. [Middle English via Old French from Latin *leoninus,* from *leon-, leo:* see LION]

leopard /'lepəd/ *noun* or **leopardess** /-des/ *noun* **1** a big cat of S Asia and Africa that has a tawny or buff coat with black spots arranged in broken rings or rosettes: *Panthera pardus.* **2** a heraldic representation of a lion walking with its head turned towards the observer.

[Middle English via Old French and late Latin from Greek *leopardos,* from *leōn* LION + *pardos* leopard]

leopard seal *noun* a large predatory Antarctic seal having a grey coat spotted with black: *Hydrurga leptonyx.* Also called SEA LEOPARD.

leotard /'lee·ətahd/ *noun* a close-fitting stretchy one-piece garment worn by dancers, gymnasts, and others performing physical exercises. [named after Jules *Léotard* d.1870, French trapeze performer, who invented it]

leper /'lepə/ *noun* **1** a person suffering from leprosy. **2** a person shunned for moral or social reasons; an outcast. [Middle English *lepyre* from *lepre* leprosy, via Old French and late Latin from Greek *lepra,* from *lepein* to peel]

lepid- or **lepido-** *comb. form* forming words, denoting: flake or scale: *lepidopteran.* [via Latin from Greek *lepid-, lepis* scale, from *lepein* to peel]

lepidolite /le'pidəliet/ *noun* a violet-coloured mineral that consists of a mica containing lithium.

lepidopteran /lepi'doptərən/ *noun* any of a large order of insects comprising the butterflies and moths that are caterpillars in the larval stage and have four wings covered with minute overlapping scales when adult: order Lepidoptera. ➤➤ **lepidopteran** *adj,* **lepidopterous** /-rəs/ *adj.* [from the Latin order name, from LEPID- + Greek *pteron* wing]

lepidopterist /lepi'doptərist/ *noun* a person who collects or studies butterflies and moths.

leporine /'lepərien/ *adj* of or resembling a hare. [Latin *leporinus,* from *lepor-, lepus* hare]

leprechaun /'leprikawn/ *noun* a mischievous elf of Irish folklore. [Irish Gaelic *leipreachán* from early Irish *lúchorpán,* from *lú* small + *corpán,* dimin. of *corp* body, from Latin *corpus*]

leprosy /'leprəsi/ *noun* a bacterial disease characterized by the formation of lumps or patches on the skin that enlarge and spread, loss of sensation with eventual paralysis, wasting of muscle, and production of deformities and mutilations.

Word history
LEPROUS + -Y[2]. The word replaced Middle English *lepre* (see LEPER) in the 16th cent.

leprous /'leprəs/ *adj* of, resembling, or suffering from leprosy. [Middle English from late Latin *leprosus* leprous, from *lepra* leprosy, from Greek: see LEPER]

-lepsy *comb. form* forming nouns, denoting: attack or seizure: *catalepsy.* [early French *-lepsie* via late Latin from Greek *-lēpsia,* from *lēpsis,* from *lambanein* to take or seize]

lepta /'leptə/ *noun* pl of LEPTON[1].

lepto- *comb. form* forming words, with the meaning: narrow or slender: *leptospirosis.* [Greek *leptos* thin, fine]

lepton[1] /'lepton/ *noun* (*pl* **lepta** /'leptə/) a former unit of currency in Greece, worth 100th of a drachma (up to the introduction of the euro in 2002). [Greek *lepton,* neuter of *leptos* small]

lepton[2] *noun* any of a group of elementary particles, e.g. an electron or muon, that take part in weak interactions with other elementary particles. ➤➤ **leptonic** /lep'tonik/ *adj.* [Greek *leptos* small + -ON[2]]

lepton number *noun* a quantum number equal to the number of leptons minus the number of antileptons.

leptospirosis /,leptohspie'rohsis/ *noun* any of several diseases of human beings and domestic animals, e.g. Weil's disease, caused by infection with spirochaetes (spiral-shaped bacteria; see SPIROCHAETE) and characterized by fever, muscle pains, and sometimes jaundice. [scientific Latin *leptospirosis* from *Leptospira,* genus name of the spirochaetes, from Greek LEPTO- + *speira* coil]

lesbian /'lezbi·ən/ *noun* a female homosexual. ➤➤ **lesbian** *adj,* **lesbianism** *noun.* [via Latin from Greek *Lesbios* of *Lesbos,* island in the Aegean Sea, home of Sappho *fl.* c.600 BC, Greek poetess whose work expressed love and affection for women]

lese majesty /leez/ *noun* **1a** a crime, e.g. treason, committed against a sovereign power. **b** an offence violating the dignity of a ruler. **2** any attack on or affront to dignity, importance, or authority. [early French *lese majesté* from Latin *laesa majestas,* literally 'injured majesty']

lesion /'leezh(ə)n/ *noun* **1** an abnormal change in the structure of an organ or tissue due to injury or disease, *esp* a well-defined area or patch of structural change. **2** an injury or wound. [Middle English via French from Latin *laesion-*, *laesio*, from *laedere* to injure]

less¹ /les/ *adj* **1a** smaller in quantity or extent: *of less importance*; *It weighs three pounds less.* **b** *informal* fewer: *less than three*; *I've had less problems with this car.* **2** lower in rank, degree, or importance: *James the Less*; *no less a person than the president.* [Old English *læs* (adv and noun) and *læssa* (adj)]

Usage note
less *or* fewer? See note at FEWER.

less² *adv* to a smaller degree or extent: *He sleeps less in summer*; *much less angrily.* ✷ **less and less** to a progressively smaller degree or extent. **less than** by no means; not at all: *She was being less than honest in her replies.*

less³ *prep* diminished by (something); minus (it): *£100 less tax.*

less⁴ *noun* a smaller portion or quantity. ✷ **less of 1** not so truly or greatly: *He's less of a fool than I thought.* **2** *informal* stop doing or saying something: *Less of your cheek!*

-less *suffix* **1** forming adjectives from nouns, with the meanings: **a** destitute of, not having: *childless*; *hopeless.* **b** free from: *painless*; *careless.* **2** forming adjectives from verbs, with the meaning: unable to so act or be acted on: *tireless*; *stainless.* [Middle English *-les*, *-lesse* from Old English *-lēas*, from *lēas* devoid, false]

lessee /le'see/ *noun* somebody who holds property under a lease. [Middle English from Anglo-French *lessé*, from *lesser*: see LEASE²]

lessen *verb* (**lessened, lessening**) ➤ *verb trans* to reduce (something) in size, extent, etc. ➤ *verb intrans* to diminish or decrease.

lesser *adj and adv* less in size, quality, or significance: *lesser-known*; *the lesser of two evils.*

lesser celandine *noun* = CELANDINE (1).

lesson /'les(ə)n/ *noun* **1a** a period of instruction. **b** a reading or exercise to be studied. **2a** an instructive or warning example: *the lessons history holds for us.* **b** something, *esp* a piece of wisdom, learned by study or experience: *He has not learned the lessons of life who does not every day surmount a fear* — Ralph Waldo Emerson. **3** a passage from sacred writings read in a service of worship. [Middle English via Old French and late Latin from Latin *lection-*, *lectio* act of reading, from *legere* to read]

lessor /'lesaw, le'saw/ *noun* somebody who grants property by lease. [Middle English *lessour* from Anglo-French, from *lesser*: see LEASE²]

lest /lest/ *conj* **1** so that not; in case: *I obeyed her lest she should be angry.* **2** used after an expression of fear, anxiety, etc: that: *I was afraid lest she be angry.* [Middle English *les the*, *leste*, from Old English *thȳ lǣs the*, literally 'by which less that']

Usage note
Lest should be followed by a verb in the subjunctive or by a verb formed with should: *lest it rain before we are finished*; *lest there should be any doubt about the seriousness of the situation.*

let¹ /let/ *verb trans* (**letting**, *past tense and past part.* **let**) **1a** to give opportunity to (somebody or something), whether by positive action or by failure to prevent them; to allow (somebody) to do something: *She lets the children play in the yard*; *He let his beard grow.* **b** to allow (something or somebody) to move or pass in a specified way: *Don't let the dogs loose*; *Please let us through.* **2** to cause (something) to happen: *to let it be known.* **3** compare LET'S. **4** used in the imperative to introduce a request or proposal: *Let us go now*; *Just let him try.* **5** in mathematics, used to express a proposition or assumption: *Let AB be equal to BC.* **6a** to allow somebody the use of (accommodation) for rent or lease. **b** to assign (a contract) after receiving bids. ✷ **let alone/be** to stop or refrain from disturbing or interrupting (somebody or something). **let fall/drop** to mention (something) casually as if by accident. **let fly** to aim a blow or lose one's temper. **let go** see GO¹. **let into** to insert (something) into a surface: *a tablet let into the wall.* **let loose on** to give (somebody) freedom of access to something: *You can't let him loose on the files just yet.* **let oneself go 1** to behave with relaxed ease or abandonment. **2** to allow one's appearance to deteriorate. [Old English *lǣtan*]

Usage note
let *or* leave? See note at LEAVE¹.

let² *noun Brit* an act or period of letting premises, e.g. a flat.

let³ *noun* **1** a serve, shot, or rally in tennis, squash, etc that does not count, e.g. because of obstruction or dispute, and must be replayed. **2** *formal* something that impedes; an obstruction: *without* let or hindrance. [Middle English *lette* obstruction, from Old English *lettan* to hinder]

let⁴ *verb trans* (**letting**, *past tense and past part.* **letted** *or* **let**) to hinder or impede (somebody or something).

-let *suffix* forming nouns, with the meanings: **1** a smaller or lesser person or thing: *booklet*; *starlet.* **2** an article worn on a specified part of the body: *anklet.* [Middle English from early French *-elet*, from *-el*, dimin. suffix (from Latin *-ellus*) + -ET]

letdown *noun informal* a disappointment or disillusionment.

let down *verb trans* **1** to fail or disappoint (somebody) in loyalty or support. **2** to make (a garment) longer. **3** to deflate (a tyre).

lethal /'leeth(ə)l/ *adj* **1** relating to or capable of causing death. **2** gravely damaging or destructive; devastating: *a lethal combination.* ➤➤ **lethality** /lee'thaliti/ *noun*, **lethally** *adv.* [Latin *letalis*, *lethalis*, from *letum* death]

lethargy /'lethəji/ *noun* **1** lack of energy or interest. **2** abnormal drowsiness. ➤➤ **lethargic** /li'thahjik/ *adj*, **lethargically** /li'thahjikli/ *adv.* [Middle English *litargie* via late Latin from Greek *lēthargia*, from *lēthargos* forgetful, lethargic, from *lēthe* forgetfulness + *argos* lazy]

Lethe /'leethi/ *noun* **1** in Greek mythology, the river in Hades the waters of which when drunk caused the souls of the dead to forget their life on earth. **2** (*often* **lethe**) *literary* forgetfulness; oblivion. ➤➤ **Lethean** /'leethi-ən/ *adj.* [via Latin from Greek *Lēthē*, from *lēthē* forgetfulness]

let in *verb trans* allow (a person or animal) to enter a building or room. ✷ **let in for** to involve (somebody, *esp* oneself) in something undesirable: *I didn't know what I was letting myself in for.* **let in on** to allow (somebody) to share confidential information.

let off *verb trans* **1** to excuse (somebody) from duty, punishment, etc. **2** to cause (a gun, bomb, or firework) to explode.

let on *verb trans and intrans informal* **1** to reveal or admit (something, *esp* secret information). **2** to pretend (something): *She let on that she was a stranger.*

let out *verb trans* **1** to utter or emit (a sound). **2** to allow (a person or animal) to leave or escape. **3a** to utter or emit (a sound). **b** to reveal (confidential information). **4** to excuse (somebody) from an obligation or responsibility. **5** *chiefly Brit* to rent out (property, etc). **6** to make (a garment) wider or looser.

let-out *noun Brit, informal* something, e.g. an exclusion clause in a contract, that provides an opportunity to escape or be released from an obligation.

let's /lets/ *contraction* used *esp* to introduce a suggestion: let us: *Let's face it, they'll probably refuse*; *Let's go.*

Lett /let/ *noun dated* = LATVIAN (1). ➤➤ **Lettish** *adj.* [German *Lette* from Latvian *Latvi*]

letter¹ /'letə/ *noun* **1** a symbol, usu written or printed, representing a speech sound and constituting a unit of an alphabet. **2** a written or printed message addressed to a person or organization and usu sent through the post: *Nobody knows how to write letters, and yet one has 'em, one does not know why. They serve one to pin up one's hair —* Congreve. **3** (*in pl, but treated as sing. or pl*). **a** literature. **b** learning, *esp* scholarly knowledge of or achievement in literature: *a man of letters.* **4** (**the letter**) the precise wording; the strict or literal meaning: *the letter of the law.* **5** in printing, a style of type. ✷ **to the letter** precisely or literally: *We obeyed their instructions to the letter.* [Middle English via Old French from Latin *littera* letter of the alphabet, *litterae* (pl) epistle, literature]

letter² *verb trans* (**lettered, lettering**) **1** to set (something) down in letters. **2** to mark (something) with letters.

letter bomb *noun* an explosive device concealed in an envelope or package and intended to detonate when the envelope or package is opened.

letter box *noun* **1** *Brit* a hole in a door or a box outside a house to receive material delivered by post. **2** = POSTBOX.

lettered *adj dated* learned or educated.

letterhead *noun* **1** a printed heading on a sheet of writing paper showing the name, address, etc of a person or organization. **2** stationery printed with such a heading, or a sheet of this.

lettering *noun* the letters used in an inscription, *esp* as regards their style or quality.

letter of credence *noun* a formal document authorizing the power of a diplomatic agent to act for a government.

letter of credit *noun* a letter issued by a bank authorizing the bearer to draw on the issuing bank or on its agent in another country up to a certain sum.

letter of marque *noun* in former times, a licence granted by a government to a private person to fit out an armed ship to plunder enemy shipping as a privateer. [Middle English *marque* reprisals, via French from Old Provençal *marca*, from *marcar* to mark, seize as a pledge, of Germanic origin]

letterpress *noun* **1** a method of printing from an inked raised surface, or matter produced by this method. **2** *Brit* printed text, e.g. of a book, as distinct from pictorial illustrations.

letters patent *pl noun* a formal open document, e.g. from a sovereign, conferring on somebody a right or privilege, *esp* the sole right to exploit their invention.

Lettish *noun* = LATVIAN (2).

lettuce /'letis/ *noun* **1** a common garden plant with succulent edible leaves that are eaten raw in salads: *Lactuca sativa*. **2** any of various similar or related plants, e.g. a lamb's lettuce. [Middle English *letuse* via Old French from Latin *lactuca*, from *lact-*, *lac* milk; from its milky juice]

letup *noun* *informal* a cessation or lessening of effort, activity, or intensity: *There has been no letup in the hostilities.*

let up *verb intrans* **1** to diminish or become less intense. **2** to relax one's efforts or activities. ✳ **let up on** to become less severe towards (somebody).

leu /'layooh/ *noun* (*pl* **lei** /lay/) **1** the basic monetary unit of Romania, divided into 100 bani. **2** the basic monetary unit of Moldova. [Romanian *leu* lion, from Latin *leo*: see LION]

leuc- or **leuco-** or **leuk-** or **leuko-** *comb. form* forming words, with the meanings: **1** white; colourless: *leucocyte*; *leucorrhoea*. **2** white matter of the brain: *leucotomy*. [Latin *leuc-*, *leuco-* from Greek *leuk-*, *leuko-*, from *leukos* white]

leucine /'loohseen/ *noun* an amino acid found in most proteins and an essential constituent of the human diet. [LEUC- + -INE²]

leuco- *comb. form* see LEUC-.

leucoblast (*NAmer* **leukoblast**) /'loohkohblast/ *noun* a bone-marrow cell that gives rise to a white blood cell. ⪢ **leucoblastic** /-'blastik/ *adj*.

leucocyte (*NAmer* **leukocyte**) /'lyoohkəsiet/ *noun* = WHITE BLOOD CELL. ⪢ **leucocytic** /-'sitik/ *adj*.

leucoma /looh'kohmə/ *noun* a dense white opaque part in the cornea of the eye. [via late Latin from Greek *leukōma*, from *leukos* white]

leucorrhoea (*NAmer* **leukorrhea**) /loohkə'ree-ə/ *noun* a thick whitish discharge from the vagina resulting *esp* from inflammation of its lining.

leucotomy /looh'kotəmi/ *noun* (*pl* **leucotomies**) = LOBOTOMY.

leuk- *comb. form* see LEUC-.

leukaemia (*NAmer* **leukemia**) /looh'keemi·ə/ *noun* a type of cancer that is characterized by an abnormal increase in the number of white blood cells in the body tissues, *esp* the blood. [Latin *leukaemia*, from Greek *leukos* white + *haima* blood]

leuko- *comb. form* see LEUC-.

leukoblast /'loohkohblast/ *noun* *NAmer* see LEUCOBLAST.

leukocyte /'loohkəsiet/ *noun* *NAmer* see LEUCOCYTE.

leukorrhea /loohkə'reeə/ *noun* *NAmer* see LEUCORRHOEA.

Lev. or **Levit.** *abbr* Leviticus (book of the Bible).

lev /lef/ *noun* (*pl* **leva** /'levə/) the basic monetary unit of Bulgaria, divided into 100 stotinki. [Bulgarian *lev* lion]

lev- or **levo-** *comb. form* *NAmer* see LAEV-. [French *lévo-* from Latin *laevus* left]

Levant /li'vant/ *noun* (**the Levant**) *archaic* the countries of the eastern Mediterranean. [French *levant* rising, sunrise, from present part. of *lever* to rise: see LEVEE¹]

levant /li'vant/ *verb intrans* *Brit, archaic* to abscond, *esp* to run away from a unpaid debt. [perhaps from Spanish *levantar* to break camp, derivative of Latin *levare* to raise]

levanter *noun* a strong easterly Mediterranean wind.

levator /li'vaytə/ *noun* a muscle that raises a part of the body: compare DEPRESSOR. [Latin *levator* from *levare* to raise]

levee¹ /'levi/ *noun* **1** a reception of visitors formerly held by a person of rank on rising from bed. **2** a reception, usu in honour of a particular person. [French *levé*, from *lever* to rise or raise, from Latin *levare* to raise]

levee² *noun* *chiefly NAmer* **1a** an embankment constructed to prevent flooding. **b** the natural embankment of silt deposited by a river. **2** a river landing place. **3** a continuous dyke or ridge for confining areas of land to be irrigated. [French *levée*, fem past part. of *lever*: see LEVEE¹]

level¹ /'levəl/ *noun* **1a** a horizontal line, plane, or surface. **b** a horizontal state or condition. **c** the equilibrium of a fluid marked by a horizontal surface of even altitude: *Water seeks its own level*. **2a** a position of height, *esp* in relation to the ground: *eye level*. **b** a layer or tier in a vertical structure, e.g. a floor in a building. **3a** a position or place in a scale or rank, e.g. of value or importance: *a high level of academic excellence*. **b** a stage of progress. **4** the size or amount of something specified: *the noise level*. **5a** a device, e.g. a spirit level, for establishing a horizontal line or plane. **b** in surveying, an instrument used to measure relative heights. **6** (*also in pl*) a practically horizontal or flat area, *esp* of land. ✳ **on the level** *informal* honest; genuine. [Middle English via early French *livel* from Latin *libella*, dimin. of *libra* weight, balance]

level² *adj* **1a** having no part higher than another: *a level surface*. **b** parallel with the plane of the horizon: *on level ground*. **c** said of a spoon, cup, etc used as a measure: filled just to the edge or rim with a flat surface: *a level tablespoonful of sugar*. **d** (*often +* with) of or at the same height: *The pictures are not level*. **2a** even or unvarying in magnitude: *a level temperature*. **b** equal in advantage, progression, or standing: *He drew level with the leader*. **c** steady or unwavering: *She spoke in level tones*. **3** distributed evenly; uniform: *level stress*. ✳ **a level playing field** a situation in which nobody has an unfair advantage. **do one's level best** to do one's very best; to make every effort. ⪢ **levelly** *adv*, **levelness** *noun*.

level³ *verb* (**levelled, levelling**, *NAmer* **leveled, leveling**) ➤ *verb trans* **1** (*also +* off) to make (a line or surface) horizontal; to make (it) level, even, or uniform. **2a** (*often +* at) to bring (e.g. a weapon) to a horizontal aiming position. **b** (+ at/against) to aim or direct (criticism, an accusation, etc) at somebody. **3** to bring (people or things) to a common level, plane, or standard; to equalize (them): *Love levels all ranks* — W S Gilbert. **4** to lay (a building, village, etc) level with the ground; to raze (it). **5** to find the heights of different points in (a land area). ➤ *verb intrans* **1** (+ out/off) to attain or come to a level; to become level: *The plane levelled off at 10,000m*. **2** (*often* + at) to aim a gun or other weapon horizontally. **3** *informal* (+ with) to deal frankly and openly with somebody: *I'll level with you, I have no direct experience in this field.*

level crossing *noun* *Brit* the crossing of a railway and a road on the same level.

leveler *noun* *NAmer* see LEVELLER.

levelheaded *adj* having sound judgment; sensible. ⪢ **levelheadedly** *adv*, **levelheadedness** *noun*.

leveller (*NAmer* **leveler**) *noun* **1** something that tends to reduce differences between people. **2** (**Leveller**) a member of a radical group during the English Civil War who advocated legal equality and religious tolerance.

level of attainment *noun* in British education, any of ten positions on a scale used to assess the ability of school pupils.

level pegging *adj* *Brit* (*used after a noun*) said of two contestants: equal. [from the practice of keeping score by putting pegs into parallel rows of holes]

lever¹ /'leevə/ *noun* **1a** a bar used for prising up or dislodging something. **b** an inducing or compelling force; a tool: *attempts to use food as a political lever* — Time. **2a** a rigid bar used to exert a pressure or sustain a weight at one end by applying force at the other and pivoting it on a support. **b** a projecting part by which a mechanism is operated or adjusted. [Middle English via Old French from Latin *levare* to raise]

lever² *verb trans* (**levered, levering**) to prise, raise, or move (something) with or as if with a lever.

leverage¹ /'leevərij/ *noun* **1** the action of a lever or the mechanical advantage gained by it. **2** power or influence. **3** = GEARING (2).

leverage² *verb trans* to finance (a buyout or other speculative business deal) largely by borrowing, in the expectation that interest repayments on the loan can be paid out of the profits of the deal:

the leveraged buyout, so-called because over 90% of the purchase money is usually borrowed — The Economist.

leveret /'lev(ə)rit/ *noun* a hare in its first year. [Middle English via French from Latin *lepor-, lepus* hare]

leviathan /lə'vie-əthən/ *noun* **1** (*often* **Leviathan**) a biblical sea monster. **2** something very large or powerful. [Middle English via late Latin from Hebrew *liwyāthān*]

levigate /'levigayt/ *verb trans* **1** to grind (something) to a fine smooth powder, *esp* while in a moist condition. **2** to make (something) into a mixture of uniform texture, e.g. a gel. ➤➤ **levigation** /-'gaysh(ə)n/ *noun*. [Latin *levigatus*, past part. of *levigare*, from *levis* smooth]

Levit. *abbr* see LEV.

levitate /'levitayt/ *verb intrans* to rise or float in the air, *esp* in apparent defiance of gravity. ➤ *verb trans* to cause (something or somebody) to levitate. ➤➤ **levitation** /-'taysh(ə)n/ *noun*, **levitator** *noun*. [Latin *levis* light in weight + -ATE⁴]

Levite /'leeviet/ *noun* a member of the priestly Hebrew tribe of Levi; *specif* one assigned to lesser ceremonial offices. [Middle English via late Latin from Greek *Leuitēs*, from *Leui* Levi, third son of Jacob, from Hebrew]

Levitical /lə'vitikl/ *adj* of the Levites or Leviticus. [via late Latin from Greek *Leuitikos*, from *Leui*: see LEVITE]

levity /'leviti/ *noun* lack of seriousness, *esp* excessive or unseemly frivolity. [Latin *levitat-, levitas* lightness, frivolity, from *levis* light in weight]

levo- *comb. form* NAmer see LAEV-.

levodopa /leevoh'dohpə/ *noun* Brit = L-DOPA.

levorotatory *adj* NAmer see LAEVOROTATORY.

levulose *noun* NAmer see LAEVULOSE.

levy¹ /'levi/ *noun* (*pl* **levies**) **1a** the imposing or collection of a tax, fine, etc. **b** an amount levied. **2** *archaic*. **a** the enlistment or conscription of men for military service. **b** (*treated as sing. or pl*) troops raised by levy. [Middle English via early French *levee*, from *lever*: see LEVEE¹]

levy² *verb trans* (**levies, levied, levying**) **1a** to impose, collect, or demand (something, e.g. a tax) by legal authority. **b** to seize (property) in accordance with a legal judgment. **2** *archaic* to enlist or conscript (somebody) for military service. **3** *archaic* (*often* + on/upon) to prepare for and make (war). ➤➤ **leviable** *adj*.

lewd /loohd/ *adj* sexually coarse or suggestive; obscene or salacious: *lewd songs*. ➤➤ **lewdly** *adv*, **lewdness** *noun*. [Old English *lǣwede* not in holy orders, lay, hence 'uneducated, ignorant' (13th cent.), later 'vulgar, vile, obscene']

lewis /'looh·is/ *noun* a device consisting of wedges or curved metal bars used to grip and hoist large stones or blocks. [prob from Old French *lous*, pl of *lou* a kind of siege engine, literally 'wolf', from Latin *lupus*]

Lewis acid *noun* in chemistry, a substance that can accept an electron pair from a donor compound to form a covalent bond. [named after Gilbert N *Lewis* d.1946, US chemist]

Lewis base *noun* in chemistry, a substance that can donate an electron pair to an acceptor compound to form a covalent bond. [named after Gilbert N *Lewis* d.1946, US chemist]

Lewis gun *noun* a light air-cooled machine gun operated by gas, used *esp* in World War I. [named after Isaac *Lewis* d.1931, US army officer and inventor]

lewisite /'looh·isiet/ *noun* a liquid that causes blisters, developed as a poison gas for war use. [named after Winford *Lewis* d.1943, US chemist, who developed it]

lexeme /'lekseem/ *noun* a unit of language that has independent meaning without being added to another word or word part and that cannot be understood from the meanings of its constituent elements, e.g. the word *garden* or the phrase *kick the bucket*; compare MORPHEME. [LEXICON + -EME]

lexical /'leksikl/ *adj* **1** of words or the vocabulary of a language as distinguished from its grammar and construction. **2** of a lexicon. ➤➤ **lexically** *adv*.

lexicography /leksi'kogrəfi/ *noun* the compiling or editing of dictionaries. ➤➤ **lexicographer** *noun*, **lexicographic** /-'grafik/ *adj*, **lexicographical** /-'grafikl/ *adj*. [LEXICON + -GRAPHY]

lexicology /leksi'koləji/ *noun* a branch of linguistics concerned with the meaning and use of words. ➤➤ **lexicological** /-'lojikl/ *adj*.

[French *lexicologie*, from late Greek *lexikon* (see LEXICON) + *-logie* -LOGY]

lexicon /'leksikən/ *noun* **1** the vocabulary of a language, individual, or subject. **2** a dictionary, *esp* of Greek, Latin, or Hebrew. [late Greek *lexikon*, neuter of *lexikos* of words, from Greek *lexis* word, speech, from *legein* to say]

lexigraphy /lek'sigrafi/ *noun* a system of writing in which each character stands for a word. [Greek *lexis* (see LEXICON) + -GRAPHY]

lexis /'leksis/ *noun* the complete vocabulary of a language. [Greek *lexis*: see LEXICON]

ley¹ /lay/ *noun* arable land used temporarily for hay or grazing. [variant of LEA]

ley² *noun* an alignment of landmarks held to mark the course of a prehistoric trackway and associated by some people with paranormal phenomena. [variant of LEA in the sense 'tract of open ground']

Leyden jar /'liedən/ *noun* an early form of CAPACITOR (device for storing electrical energy) consisting of a glass jar coated inside and outside with metal foil and having the inner coating connected to a conducting rod passed through the insulating stopper. [named after *Leiden, Leyden*, city in the Netherlands, where it was invented]

Leyland cypress /'laylənd/ *noun* = LEYLANDII.

leylandii /lay'landi·ie/ *noun* (*pl* **leylandii**) a fast-growing hybrid conifer that is widely cultivated for screening: *× Cupressocyparis leylandii*. [from the Latin taxonomic name, named after Christopher J *Leyland* d.1926, British horticulturalist, who first grew it]

ley line *noun* = LEY².

LF *abbr* low frequency.

lf *abbr* in printing, light face.

LGBT *abbr* lesbian, gay, bisexual, transgender.

LGV *abbr* large goods vehicle.

LH *abbr* luteinizing hormone.

lh *abbr* left hand.

Lhasa apso /'lahsə 'apsoh/ *noun* (*pl* **Lhasa apsos**) a small dog of a breed originating in Tibet, having a dense coat of long straight hair and a tail that curls over the back. [*Lhasa*, capital of Tibet + Tibetan *apso*]

LI *abbr* **1** Light Infantry. **2** Long Island.

Li *abbr* the chemical symbol for lithium.

liability /lie-ə'biliti/ *noun* (*pl* **liabilities**) **1** being liable. **2** something for which one is liable, *esp* a debt. **3** a hindrance or drawback.

liable /'lie-əbl/ *adj* **1** legally responsible. **2** (+ to) exposed or subject to something: *liable to a fine; You're liable to get hurt*. **3** habitually likely to do something: *She's liable to get annoyed*. [(assumed) Anglo-French *liable* from early French *lier* to bind or tie, from Latin *ligare*]
Usage note
See note at APT.

liaise /li'ayz/ *verb intrans* **1** (*often* + with) to establish a connection and cooperate. **2** to maintain communication, e.g. between departments of an organization. [back-formation from LIAISON]

liaison /li'ayzon/ *noun* **1** communication, e.g. between departments of an organization. **2a** a close bond or connection. **b** an illicit sexual relationship. **3** in cookery, a substance or mixture used to thicken or bind liquids, e.g. soups or sauces. **4** the pronunciation, e.g. in French *est-il*, of an otherwise silent consonant before a word beginning with a vowel sound. [French *liaison* from early French *lier*: see LIABLE]
Usage note
Liaison is often misspelt. It has two *i*s and one *a*.

liana /li'ahnə/ *or* **liane** /li'ahn/ *noun* a climbing plant, *esp* of tropical rain forests, that roots in the ground. [French *liane*]

liar /'lie-ə/ *noun* a person who tells lies, *esp* habitually: *The best liar is he who makes the smallest amount of lying go the longest way* — Samuel Butler. [Old English *lēogere*, from *lēogan* LIE⁴]

Lias /'lie-əs/ *noun* a geological epoch, the first epoch of the Jurassic period, lasting from about 208 million to 178 million years ago. ➤➤ **Liassic** /lie'asik/ *adj*. [French *Lias* from Middle English *lyas*, a kind of limestone, from Old French *liais* hard limestone]

Lib. *abbr* Liberal.

lib /lib/ *noun* (*often* **Lib**) *informal* liberation: *women's lib*. ➤➤ **libber** *noun*.

libation /lie'baysh(ə)n/ *noun* **1** a liquid used in a sacrifice to a god, or an act of pouring such a liquid. **2** *humorous* an alcoholic drink. [Middle English from Latin *libation-, libatio,* from *libare* to pour as an offering]

Lib Dem /,lib 'dem/ *noun informal* a Liberal Democrat.

libel[1] /'liebl/ *noun* **1** defamation of somebody by published writing or pictorial representation as distinguished from spoken words or gestures: compare SLANDER[1]. **2** a false defamatory written statement. ⇒ **libellous** *adj.* [Middle English *libell* written declaration, via French from Latin *libellus,* dimin. of *liber book*]

libel[2] *verb trans* (**libelled, libelling,** *NAmer* **libeled, libeling**) to make or publish a libel about (somebody). ⇒ **libeller** *noun,* **libellist** *noun.*

liberal[1] /'lib(ə)rəl/ *adj* **1a** broad-minded or tolerant, *esp* not bound by authoritarianism, orthodoxy, or tradition. **b** advocating or favouring individual rights and freedom. **2a** (*often* **Liberal**) based on or advocating political liberalism. **b** (**Liberal**) in Britain, of, belonging to, or supporting the Liberal Democrats. **3** said of education, studies, etc: intended to provide general knowledge and develop intellectual capacities rather than professional or vocational skills. **4a** generous or openhanded: *a liberal giver.* **b** abundant or ample: *a liberal helping.* **5** not literal; loose: *a liberal interpretation of the rules.* ⇒ **liberality** /libə'raliti/ *noun,* **liberally** *adv,* **liberalness** *noun.* [Middle English via French from Latin *liberalis* suitable for a freeman, generous, from *liber free*]

liberal[2] *noun* **1** a person who is not strict in the observance of orthodox ways, e.g. in religion; somebody with liberal views: *No true liberal should feel any resentment at the growth of black consciousness* — Steve Biko. **2a** (*often* **Liberal**) a supporter of political liberalism or a member of a Liberal party. **b** (**Liberal**) in Britain, a Liberal Democrat.

liberal arts *pl noun* **1** *chiefly NAmer* the cultural branches of learning, e.g. language, literature, history, etc, as opposed to science and technology; the arts or humanities. **2** the medieval studies comprising the TRIVIUM (grammar, rhetoric, and logic) and QUADRIVIUM (music, geometry, arithmetic, and astronomy).

Liberal Democrat *noun* a member or supporter of a British political party created in 1988 from the former Liberal and Social Democratic parties.

liberalise /'librəliez/ *verb trans and intrans* see LIBERALIZE.

liberalism *noun* **1** broad-mindedness or tolerance. **2** (*often* **Liberalism**) a political philosophy based on belief in progress, moderate social and economic reform, and the protection of political and civil liberties.

Editorial note
Liberalism has pervaded many modern ideologies in its respect for individual development and human rights. It has sustained both libertarians, who argue for minimal state intervention and maximal personal choice, and welfare-liberals, who have come to see liberty and human well-being as mutually dependent and the enablement of these values as a prime responsibility of the state towards its citizens — Professor Michael Freeden.

⇒ **liberalist** *noun,* **liberalistic** /-'listik/ *adj.*

liberalize *or* **liberalise** *verb trans and intrans* to become or cause (something) to become liberal. ⇒ **liberalization** /-'zaysh(ə)n/ *noun,* **liberalizer** *noun.*

liberal studies *pl noun* studies of the arts or humanities, *esp* as a supplementary course for students of science and technology or those pursuing a professional or vocational qualification.

liberate /'libərayt/ *verb trans* **1** to set (somebody or something) free; *specif* to free (a country) from foreign domination. **2** to free (somebody) from social conventions, injustices, or discrimination. **3** to release (a gas, atom, etc) from chemical combination. **4** *euphem or humorous* to steal (something). ⇒ **liberated** *adj,* **liberator** *noun.* [Latin *liberatus,* past part. of *liberare,* from *liber free*]

liberation /libə'raysh(ə)n/ *noun* **1** liberating or being liberated. **2** the seeking of equal rights and status: *gay liberation.* ⇒ **liberationist** *noun.*

liberation theology *noun* a theory or movement holding that theology involves a political commitment to change society by liberating humankind from social and political injustice.

Liberian /lie'biəri·ən/ *noun* a native or inhabitant of Liberia, country in W Africa. ⇒ **Liberian** *adj.*

libertarian /libə'teəri·ən/ *noun* **1** an advocate of liberty. **2** a believer in free will. ⇒ **libertarian** *adj,* **libertarianism** *noun.*

libertine /'libəteen/ *noun* **1** a person who is unrestrained by convention or morality; *specif* a person who leads a dissolute life: *It is easier to make a saint out of a libertine than out of a prig* — George Santayana. **2** a freethinker, *esp* in religious matters. ⇒ **libertinage** /-nij/ *noun,* **libertine** *adj,* **libertinism** /-tiniz(ə)m/ *noun.* [Middle English *libertyn* freedman, from Latin *libertinus* of a freedman, from *libertus* freedman, from *liber free*]

liberty /'libəti/ *noun* (*pl* **liberties**) **1a** the power to do as one pleases. **b** freedom from physical restraint or dictatorial control: *Liberty is, to the lowest rank of every nation, little more than the choice of working or starving* — Dr Johnson. **c** the enjoyment of various rights and privileges: *civil liberty.* **d** the power of choice.

Editorial note
Liberty is individual freedom of which there are two forms: firstly, a sense of freedom and release from the chains of external control (negative liberty), and secondly an internal freedom of choice (positive liberty). This also entails the notion of self-determination, which leads to inequality with others. It can also involve the taking of risks, which may not result in the desired outcome — Helena Kennedy.

2 a right or immunity awarded or granted; a privilege. **3** *informal* (*also in pl*): **a** a breach of etiquette or propriety: *He was reprimanded for taking liberties with female colleagues.* **b** a risk or chance: *She took foolish liberties with her health.* **c** an action going beyond normal or authorized limits: *I took a few liberties with the original text.* **4a** a short authorized absence from naval duty, usu for less than 48 hours. **b** (*used before a noun*) having or used for such a period of shore leave: *a liberty man; a liberty boat.* ✳ **at liberty 1** free. **2** at leisure; unoccupied. [Middle English via French from Latin *libertat-, libertas,* from *liber free*]

Liberty bodice *noun Brit, trademark* a sleeveless undergarment made from thick cotton, formerly worn by girls and women.

liberty cap *noun* a close-fitting conical cap used as a symbol of liberty, e.g. during the French Revolution.

Liberty Hall *noun informal* a place where one can do as one likes.

liberty horse *noun* a circus horse that performs without a rider.

libidinous /li'bidinəs/ *adj* having or marked by strong sexual desire; lascivious. ⇒ **libidinously** *adv,* **libidinousness** *noun.* [Middle English via French from Latin *libidinosus,* from *libidin-, libido:* see LIBIDO]

libido /li'beedoh/ *noun* (*pl* **libidos**) **1** sexual drive. **2** in psychoanalysis, emotional or mental energy derived from primitive biological urges. ⇒ **libidinal** /li'bid(ə)nəl/ *adj,* **libidinally** /li'bid(ə)nəli/ *adv.* [Latin *libidin-, libido* desire, lust, from *libēre* to please]

Libra /'leebrə/ *noun* **1** in astronomy, a constellation (the Scales) depicted as a pair of scales. **2a** in astrology, the seventh sign of the zodiac. **b** a person born under this sign. ⇒ **Libran** *noun and adj.* [Latin *libra* scales, pound]

libra /'leebrə/ *noun* (*pl* **librae** /'leebree/) an ancient Roman unit of weight equal to about 12oz (0.34kg). [Latin *libra* scales, pound]

librarian /lie'breəri·ən/ *noun* a person who manages or assists in a library. ⇒ **librarianship** *noun.*

library /'liebri/ *noun* (*pl* **libraries**) **1a** a room, building, or other place in which books, periodicals, CDs, videos, etc are kept for reference or for borrowing by the public. **b** a collection of such books, CDs, etc. **2** a collection resembling or suggesting a library: *a library of computer programs.* **3** a series of related books issued by a publisher. [Middle English via medieval Latin *librarium,* neuter of Latin *librarius* of books, from *libr-, liber book*]

libration /lie'braysh(ə)n/ *noun* an apparent or real oscillation of the moon or other celestial body that causes parts at the edge of the disc to become alternately visible and invisible. [Latin *libration-, libratio,* from *librare* to balance, from *libra* scales]

libretto /li'bretoh/ *noun* (*pl* **libretti** /-tee/ *or* **librettos**) the text of a work that is both theatrical and musical, e.g. an opera. ⇒ **librettist** *noun.* [Italian *libretto,* dimin. of *libro* book, from Latin *libr-, liber book*]

Librium /'libri·əm/ *noun trademark* the tranquillizing drug chlordiazepoxide. [invented name, perhaps based on *equilibrium*]

Libyan /'libi·ən/ *noun* a native or inhabitant of Libya, country in N Africa. ⇒ **Libyan** *adj.*

lice /lies/ *noun* pl of LOUSE.

licence (*NAmer* **license**) /'lies(ə)ns/ *noun* **1a** permission granted by authority to engage in a particular business, e.g. selling alcoholic drink, or activity, e.g. driving a vehicle, that would otherwise be unlawful. **b** a document giving evidence of such permission. **2a**

freedom of action. **b** permission to act. **3** freedom claimed by an artist or writer to alter facts or deviate from rules, *esp* for the sake of the effect gained: *poetic licence.* **4a** freedom that allows or is used with irresponsibility. **b** disregard for rules of propriety or personal conduct. [Middle English via French from Latin *licentia*, from *licent-*, *licens*, present part. of *licēre* to be permitted]

Usage note ───────────────
licence *or* license? In British English *licence* is the only spelling for the noun meaning 'freedom of action' or 'a document authorizing the holder to do something': *a licence to kill; May I see your licence, please?* The spelling for the equivalent verb in British and American English is *license*: *You are only licensed to drive vehicles in categories C, D, and E.* Thus also *licensed premises* and a *licensed restaurant* – ones that have been granted a licence to serve alcoholic drink. In American English, the spelling *license* is used for both the verb and the noun.

license /'lies(ə)ns/ *verb trans* **1** to give official permission to (somebody) to do something, e.g. to drive a vehicle. **2** to give official permission for (something, e.g. the sale of alcoholic drink). ➤➤ **licensable** *adj,* **licensor** *noun.*

Usage note ───────────────
license *or* licence? See note at LICENCE.

licensed *adj* **1** being premises on which alcoholic drink may be lawfully sold and consumed: *a licensed restaurant.* **2** said of a vehicle, gun, etc: owned or used by somebody who has a licence to do so.

licensee /lies(ə)n'see/ *noun* the holder of a licence, *esp* a licence to sell alcoholic drink.

license plate *noun NAmer* a renewable numberplate showing that the vehicle to which it is attached is licensed.

licentiate /lie'senshi·ət/ *noun* **1** a person licensed to practise a profession. **2** an academic degree awarded by some European universities. ➤➤ **licentiateship** *noun.* [medieval Latin *licentiatus,* past part. of *licentiare* to allow, from Latin *licentia:* see LICENCE]

licentious /lie'senshəs/ *adj* **1** behaving in a sexually unrestrained manner. **2** *archaic* showing or marked by disregard for strict rules of correctness. ➤➤ **licentiously** *adv,* **licentiousness** *noun.* [Latin *licentiosus* from *licentia:* see LICENCE]

lichee /'liechee/ *noun* see LYCHEE.

lichen /'liek(ə)n, 'lich(ə)n/ *noun* **1** a complex plant made up of an alga and a fungus growing in symbiotic association on a solid surface, e.g. a rock or tree trunk. **2** a skin disease characterized by raised spots. ➤➤ **lichened** *adj,* **lichenous** /-nəs/ *adj.* [via Latin from Greek *leichēn, lichēn*]

lich-gate /lich/ *noun* see LYCH-GATE.

licit /'lisit/ *adj* not forbidden by law; permissible. ➤➤ **licitly** *adv.* [early French *licite* from Latin *licitus,* past part. of *licēre* to be permitted]

lick¹ /lik/ *verb trans* **1a** to pass the tongue over (something), *esp* in order to taste, moisten, or clean it. **b** (*usu* + up) to take (food or drink) into the mouth with the tongue; to lap (it). **2** to flicker or play over (something) like a tongue: *flames licking the walls.* **3** *informal.* **a** to strike (somebody) repeatedly; to thrash (them). **b** to get the better of (something); to overcome (it): *She has licked every problem.* **c** to defeat (somebody), *esp* decisively or thoroughly: *We licked the opposition.* ➤ *verb intrans* **1** to lap with or as if with the tongue. **2** to dart like a tongue: *flames licking at the windows.* ✳ **lick into shape** to put (something or somebody) into proper form or condition: *Mr Turner reckoned that it took him a term to lick boys into shape* — Somerset Maugham. **lick one's wounds** to recover after defeat or humiliation. **lick somebody's boots** *informal* to behave sycophantically towards somebody, *esp* with a view to getting a favour from them. ➤➤ **licker** *noun.* [Old English *liccian*]

lick² *noun* **1a** an act of licking. **b** *informal* a small amount; a touch: *a lick of paint.* **2** = SALT LICK. **3** *informal* an improvised piece of jazz or pop music usu added into a written composition. **4** *informal* a blow. **5** *informal* speed or pace: *The car was travelling at quite a lick.* ✳ **a lick and a promise** *informal* something hastily and not thoroughly done, *esp* a quick wash.

lickerish or **liquorish** /'likərish/ *adj* **1** lecherous. **2** *archaic.* **a** fond of good food. **b** greedy or desirous. ➤➤ **lickerishly** *adv.* [alteration of Middle English *lickerous,* ultimately from Old French *lecheor:* see LECHER]

lickety-split /,likiti 'split/ *adv NAmer, informal* at great speed. [prob from LICK¹ + SPLIT¹]

licking *noun informal* **1** a sound thrashing; a beating. **2** a severe setback; a defeat.

lickspittle *noun* an obsequious subordinate; a toady.

licorice /'likəris/ *noun NAmer* see LIQUORICE.

lictor /'liktə/ *noun* an officer of ancient Rome who carried the FASCES (symbol of authority) and accompanied the chief magistrates in public appearances. [Latin *lictor,* perhaps related to *ligare* to bind]

lid /lid/ *noun* **1** a hinged or detachable cover for a receptacle. **2** an eyelid. **3** the OPERCULUM (flap covering seeds or spores) in mosses. ✳ **put the lid on something** *chiefly Brit* to ruin or put paid to something. ➤➤ **lidded** *adj,* **lidless** *adj.* [Old English *hlid*]

lido /'leedoh, 'liedoh/ *noun* (*pl* **lidos**) **1** a public open-air swimming pool. **2** a fashionable beach resort. [named after *Lido,* a beach resort near Venice in Italy]

lie¹ /lie/ *verb intrans* (**lying,** past tense **lay** /lay/, past part. **lain** /layn/) **1a** to be or to stay at rest in a horizontal position; to rest or recline. **b** (*often* + down) to assume a horizontal position. **c** to be or remain in a specified state or condition: *They were lying in wait, The machinery lay idle for days.* **2a** said of something inanimate: to be or remain in a flat or horizontal position on a surface: *Books were lying on the table.* **b** said of snow: to remain on the ground without melting. **3** to have as a direction; to lead: *The route lay to the west.* **4a** to occupy a specified place or position: *Hills lie behind us; The responsibility lies with us.* **b** (+ on) to have an adverse or disheartening effect on (somebody); to weigh on (them): *Remorse lay heavily on her.* **c** said of an action, claim, etc in a court of law: to be sustainable or admissible. ✳ **lie low** to strive to avoid notice: *Old hippies don't die, they just lie low until the laughter stops and their time comes round again* — Joseph Gallivan. [Old English *licgan*]

Usage note ───────────────
lie *or* lay? See note at LAY¹.

lie² *noun* **1** the way, position, or situation in which something lies: *the lie of the land.* **2** a place frequented by an animal, bird, or fish.

lie³ *noun* **1** an untrue or false statement, *esp* when made with intent to deceive: *Good lies need a leavening of truth to make them palatable* — William McIlvanney. **2** something that misleads or deceives: *living a lie.* ✳ **give the lie to** to show (something) to be false or untrue.

lie⁴ *verb intrans* (**lies, lied, lying**) **1** to make an untrue statement with intent to deceive; to speak falsely. **2** to create a false or misleading impression: *The camera never lies.* [Old English *lēogan*]

Liebfraumilch /'leebfrowmilsh/ *noun* a white wine made in the Rhine valley, or a similar wine made elsewhere. [German *Liebfraumilch,* alteration of *Liebfrauenmilch,* from *Liebfrauenstift,* literally 'dear lady's monastery', religious foundation in Worms, Germany dedicated to the Virgin Mary, where it was first produced + *Milch* milk]

lied /leed, leet/ *noun* (*pl* **lieder** /'leedə/) a German song, *esp* a 19th-cent. setting of a lyrical poem with piano accompaniment. [German *Lied* song, from Old High German *liod*]

lie detector *noun* an instrument for detecting physical evidence, e.g. a change in pulse or breathing rate, of the mental tension that accompanies telling lies.

lie down *verb intrans* to submit meekly or abjectly to defeat, disappointment, or insult: *He won't take that criticism lying down.*

lie-down *noun chiefly Brit* a brief rest, *esp* on a bed.

lief /leef/ *adv archaic* soon; gladly: *I'd as lief go as not.* [Old English *lēof* (adj)]

liege¹ /leej/ *adj* **1a** said of a lord: entitled to feudal allegiance. **b** said of a vassal: owing feudal allegiance. **2** faithful; loyal. [Middle English via Old French from late Latin *laeticus,* from *laetus* serf, of Germanic origin]

liege² *noun* **1** a feudal superior. **2a** a feudal vassal. **b** a loyal subject.

liege lord *noun* = LIEGE² (1).

liege man *noun* (*pl* **liege men**) **1** = LIEGE² (2A). **2** a devoted follower.

lie in *verb intrans* **1** *chiefly Brit* to stay in bed later than usual in the morning. **2** *archaic* to be in bed to give birth to a child.

lie-in *noun chiefly Brit* an instance of staying in bed later than usual.

lien /leen, 'lee·ən/ *noun* the legal right to hold another's property until a debt is paid. [early French *lien* tie, band, from Latin *ligamen,* from *ligare* to bind]

lie off *verb intrans* said of a ship: to be or keep a small distance away from the shore or another ship.

lierne /li'uhn/ *noun* a nonstructural rib in a vaulted ceiling that passes from one main rib to another. [French *lierne* from early French *lier* to bind, tie, from Latin *ligare*]

lie to *verb intrans* said of a ship: to be stationary with the bows pointing into the wind.

lieu /l(y)ooh/ ✱ **in lieu** in substitution; instead. [early French *lieu* place, from Latin *locus*]

lie up *verb intrans* said of a ship: to remain in dock or out of commission.

Lieut. *abbr* Lieutenant.

lieutenant /lef'tenənt, *NAmer* looh'tenənt/ *noun* **1** an official empowered to act for a higher official; a deputy or representative. **2a** an officer in the Royal Navy and US navy ranking below a lieutenant commander. **b** an officer in the British army and Royal Marines ranking below a captain. **c** *NAmer* a fire or police officer ranking below a captain. ⟫ **lieutenancy** /-si/ *noun*. [Middle English from early French *lieutenant*, from *lieu* (see LIEU) + *tenant* holding, from *tenir* to hold, from Latin *tenēre*]

lieutenant colonel *noun* an officer ranking below a colonel in the British and US armies, US air force, Royal Marines, and US Marines.

lieutenant commander *noun* an officer in the Royal Navy and US navy ranking below a commander.

lieutenant general *noun* an officer ranking below a general in the British army, the Royal Marines, and the US army, air force, and marines.

lieutenant governor *noun* **1** a deputy or subordinate governor. **2a** in the USA, an elected official serving as deputy to the governor of a state. **b** in Canada, the formal head of government of a province, appointed by the federal government as a representative of the Crown.

life /lief/ *noun* (*pl* **lives** /lievz/) **1a** the quality that distinguishes a living and functional being from a dead body or inanimate object. **b** a state of matter, e.g. a cell or an organism, characterized by capacity for metabolism, growth, reaction to stimuli, and reproduction.

Editorial note
The characteristics of living organisms include the capacity to maintain a constant internal environment, to respond to and transform their external environment, to grow and develop, and to self-replicate, producing more or less identical copies of themselves. Living beings are thermodynamically open, deriving energy from their environments in order to sustain and transform themselves, a process known as autopoiesis, or self-creation — Professor Steven Rose.

2a the sequence of physical and mental experiences that make up the existence of an individual. **b** an aspect of the process of living: *the sex life of the frog*. **c** a state or condition of existence: *life after death*. **3a** the period from birth to death or to the present time: *I have lived here all my life*. **b** a specific phase of earthly existence: *his adult life*. **c** the period from an event or the present time until death: *a member for life*. **d** *informal* a sentence of life imprisonment: *He got life for the murder*. **4** a biography. **5** a way or manner of living: *a holy life*. **6a** a person: *Many lives were lost in the disaster*. **b** living beings, e.g. of a specified kind or environment: *forest life*. **7a** the living form considered as a model: *painted from life*. **b** (*used before a noun*) using a living model: *a life class*. **8a** the period of usefulness, effectiveness, or functioning of something inanimate: *the expected life of torch batteries*. **b** a period of existence, e.g. of a subatomic particle: compare HALF-LIFE. **9a** the active part of human existence, *esp* in a wide range of circumstances or experiences: *She left home to see life*. **b** activity from living things; movement: *stirrings of life*. **c** the activities of a specified sphere, area, or time: *the political life of the country*. **10** any of several chances to participate given to a contestant in some games, one of which is forfeited each time they lose. **11** (*used before a noun*) of, being, or provided by life insurance: *a life policy*. ✱ **be the life and soul of the party** to be in a lively mood and keep everyone around one entertained. **for the life of me** *informal* no matter how hard I try: *I can't for the life of me remember her name*. **get a life** *informal* (*usu in imperative*) to have a bit of sense, relax, and get more out of life: *I've just one more thing to say – Simon, get a life and some new clichés* — Hot Press. **not on your life** *informal* certainly not. [Old English *līf*]

life-and-death *adj* involving death or risk to life; vitally important: *a life-and-death decision*.

life assurance *noun chiefly Brit* = LIFE INSURANCE.

lifebelt *noun chiefly Brit* a buoyant ring for keeping a person afloat.

lifeblood *noun* **1** *literary* the blood necessary to life. **2** a vital or life-giving force.

lifeboat *noun* **1a** a shore-based boat for use in saving lives at sea. **b** a boat carried by a ship for use in an emergency. **2** something designed to rescue, e.g. a fund set up to help small investors or employees when a large company fails.

lifebuoy *noun chiefly Brit* a buoyant float to which a person may cling in the water.

life coach *noun* somebody who advises clients on how to better organize and improve the quality of their personal and professional lives.

life cycle *noun* the series of stages in form and functional activity through which an organism passes during its lifetime.

life expectancy *noun* the expected length of somebody's or something's life, based on statistical evidence.

lifeguard *noun* an expert swimmer employed to safeguard others at a swimming pool or beach.

life imprisonment *noun* a sentence of imprisonment for a long time, given in Britain for murder and other very serious crimes.

life insurance *noun* insurance providing for payment of a stipulated sum to a beneficiary on the death of the insured person or to the insured person at the end of a fixed period.

life jacket *noun* an inflatable or buoyant device that is designed to keep a person afloat and is either worn continuously or put on in an emergency by the passengers and crew of a boat, ship, or aircraft.

lifeless *adj* **1a** dead. **b** inanimate. **2** having no living beings: *a lifeless planet*. **3** lacking qualities expressive of life and vigour; dull: *a lifeless voice*. ⟫ **lifelessly** *adv*, **lifelessness** *noun*.

lifelike *adj* accurately representing or imitating real life: *a lifelike sculpture of a horse*.

lifeline *noun* **1** a rope or line for saving or safeguarding life, e.g.: **a** one stretched along the deck of a ship for use in rough weather. **b** one fired to a ship in distress by means of a rocket. **c** one by which a diver is lowered and raised. **d** one for lowering or raising a person to safety. **2** something, *esp* a sole means of communication, regarded as indispensable for the maintenance or protection of life.

lifelong *adj* lasting or continuing throughout life.

life peer *or* **life peeress** *noun* a British peer whose title is not hereditary. ⟫ **life peerage** *noun*.

life preserver *noun* **1** a life jacket, lifebuoy, etc. **2** *Brit* a small club with a weighted head.

lifer *noun informal* a person sentenced to life imprisonment.

life raft *noun* a usu inflatable raft carried on ships, aircraft, etc for use in an emergency at sea.

lifesaver *noun* **1** somebody or something that saves life. **2** somebody or something timely and effective in the prevention or relief of distress or difficulty. **3** *Aus* a lifeguard, *esp* on a surfing beach. ⟫ **lifesaving** *adj and noun*.

life science *noun* a branch of science, e.g. biology, medicine, anthropology, or sociology, that deals with living organisms and life processes: compare PHYSICAL SCIENCE. ⟫ **life scientist** *noun*.

life-size *adj* of natural size; of the size of the original: *a life-size statue*.

life-sized *adj* = LIFE-SIZE.

life span *noun* **1** the duration of existence of an individual. **2** the average length of life of a kind of organism or of a material object, *esp* in a particular environment or in specified circumstances.

lifestyle *noun* an individual's way of life, or the activities, possessions, etc associated with this.

life-support system *noun* a system that provides all or some of the items necessary for maintaining the life of a person.

life table *noun* a table showing life expectancy and death rate for people of a given age, job, etc, used *esp* for insurance purposes.

lifetime *noun* **1** the length of time for which a living being exists: *during my grandfather's lifetime*. **2** the length of time for which a thing remains useful, valid, etc.

LIFO /'liefoh/ *abbr* last in first out.

lift¹ /lift/ *verb trans* **1a** to raise (something or somebody) from a lower to a higher position; to elevate (them). **b** to raise (somebody or something) in rank, condition, intensity, etc: *The news lifted their spirits.* **c** to pick (something or somebody) up in order to move them: *She lifted the jar off the shelf.* **2** to put an end to (a blockade or siege) by withdrawing the surrounding forces. **3** to revoke or rescind (something): *The embargo has been lifted.* **4** to take up (e.g. a root crop) from the ground. **5** to hit (a ball, shuttlecock, etc) into the air. **6** *informal* to plagiarize (something). **7** *informal* to steal (something): *She had her purse lifted.* **8** *informal* to arrest (somebody). ➤ *verb intrans* **1** to ascend or rise. **2** to disperse upwards: *until the fog lifts.* ➤➤ **liftable** *adj*, **lifter** *noun*. [Middle English *liften* from Old Norse *lypta*]

lift² *noun* **1** *Brit* a device for conveying people or objects from one level to another, esp in a building. **2a** the act or an instance of lifting. **b** the power or force required or used for lifting. **3** a free ride as a passenger in a motor vehicle. **4** a slight rise or elevation of ground. **5** the distance or extent to which something rises or is lifted. **6** a feeling of cheerfulness, pleasure, or encouragement, usu a temporary one: *Her new haircut gave her a real lift.* **7** the component of the aerodynamic force acting on an aircraft or wing that is perpendicular to the relative wind and usu constitutes the upward force opposing the pull of gravity. **8** an organized transport of people, equipment, or supplies, *esp* an airlift. **9** any of the layers forming the heel of a shoe.

lift off *verb intrans* said of an aircraft, spacecraft, or missile: to take off vertically.

lift-off *noun* a vertical takeoff by an aircraft, spacecraft, or missile.

lig¹ /lig/ *verb intrans* (**ligged, ligging**) *Brit, informal* to obtain refreshment or entertainment at another's expense; to freeload. ➤➤ **ligger** *noun*. [prob from English dialect *lig* to lie, variant of LIE⁴]

lig² *noun Brit, informal* a party, show, or other function at which free refreshment or entertainment is provided.

ligament /'ligəmənt/ *noun* a tough band of tissue connecting two or more bones or cartilages or supporting an organ and keeping it in place. ➤➤ **ligamentary** /-'ment(ə)ri/ *adj*, **ligamentous** /-'mentəs/ *adj*. [Middle English via medieval Latin from Latin *ligamentum* band, tie, from *ligare* to bind or tie]

ligand /'lig(ə)nd/ *noun* an ion, molecule, etc joined by many bonds to a central atom in a complex chemical compound. [Latin *ligandus*, from *ligare* to bind or tie]

ligate /li'gayt/ *verb trans* to tie (something, e.g. an artery) with a ligature. ➤➤ **ligation** /li'gaysh(ə)n/ *noun*. [Latin *ligatus*, past part. of *ligare* to bind or tie]

ligature /'ligəchə/ *noun* **1a** something that is used to bind; *specif* a thread used in surgery. **b** something that unites or connects. **2** the act of binding or tying. **3** in music, a slur or tie. **4** in printing, a character consisting of two or more letters or characters joined together, e.g. ﬂ. [Middle English via French from late Latin *ligatura*, from Latin *ligare* to bind or tie]

liger /'liegə/ *noun* the hybrid offspring of a male lion and a female tiger.

-light *comb. form* having a relatively low content, *esp* of something considered undesirable or harmful: *caffeine-light.*

light¹ /liet/ *noun* **1a** something that makes vision possible by stimulating the sense of sight. **b** electromagnetic radiation in the wavelength range that is visible to the human eye. **2** a source of light, e.g. a lamp or a candle. **3** illumination provided by a celestial body; *specif* daylight. **4** a flame or spark for lighting something, e.g. a cigarette. **5** (*also in pl*) a traffic light: *The lights were red.* **6** a particular illumination in a place: *a studio with a north light.* **7a** spiritual illumination. **b** understanding or knowledge. **8** enlightening information or explanation: *He shed some light on the problem.* **9** a particular aspect or appearance in which something is viewed: *They now saw the matter in a different light.* **10** a medium, e.g. a window, through which light is admitted. **11** a specified expression perceived as being in somebody's eyes: *the light of love in his eyes.* **12** (*in pl*) a set of principles, standards, or opinions: *true by your lights.* **13** = LEADING LIGHT. ✳ **bring to light** to disclose or reveal (something): *What your wisdoms could not discover, these shallow fools have brought to light* — Shakespeare. **come to light** to be revealed or disclosed. **in the light of** with the insight provided by: *in the light of his confession.* **see the light 1** to understand suddenly; to gain insight. **2** to undergo conversion. **see the light of day 1** to be born

or come into existence. **2** to be published or come to public attention. ➤➤ **lightless** *adj*, **lightproof** *adj*. [Old English *lēoht, liht*]

light² *adj* **1** having plenty of light; bright: *a light airy room.* **2a** pale in colour or colouring. **b** said of colour: medium in saturation and high in lightness. ➤➤ **lightish** *adj*, **lightness** *noun.*

light³ *verb* (*past tense* **lit**, *past part.* **lit** /lit/ *or* **lighted**) ➤ *verb intrans* **1** to become illuminated. **2** to catch fire. ➤ *verb trans* **1** to set fire to (something). **2a** to conduct or guide (somebody) with a light. **b** to provide light in (a place).

light⁴ *adj* **1a** having little weight; not heavy. **b** designed to carry a comparatively small load: *a light van.* **c** of the smaller variety: *a light gun.* **d** having relatively little weight in proportion to bulk: *Aluminium is a light metal.* **e** containing less than the legal, standard, or usual weight: *a light coin.* **f** carrying little or no cargo: *The ship returned light.* **2** not abundant or intense. **3a** said of sleep or a sleeper: easily disturbed. **b** exerting a minimum of force or pressure; gentle or soft: *a light touch.* **c** resulting from very slight pressure; faint: *light print.* **4a** easily endurable: *light taxation.* **b** requiring little effort: *light work.* **5** graceful, deft, or nimble: *light on his feet.* **6a** lacking seriousness; frivolous. **b** of little importance; trivial. **7** free from care; cheerful: *a light heart.* **8** intended chiefly to entertain: *light reading.* **9a** said of a drink: having a comparatively low alcoholic content or a mild flavour: *a light white wine.* **b** said of food: having a low calorie or fat content. **10a** easily digested: *a light dessert.* **b** well risen: *a light cake.* **11** lightly armoured, armed, or equipped: *light cavalry.* **12** easily pulverized; crumbly: *light soil.* **13** dizzy or giddy: *I felt light in the head.* **14** said of industry: requiring relatively small investment and usu producing small consumer goods. ➤➤ **lightish** *adj*, **lightly** *adv*, **lightness** *noun*. [Old English *lēocht, liht*]

light⁵ *adv* **1** lightly. **2** with the minimum of luggage: *travelling light.*

light⁶ *verb intrans* (*past tense and past part.* **lit** /lit/ *or* **lighted**) **1** (+ on/upon) to settle or alight: *A bird lit on the lawn.* **2** (+ on/upon) to arrive by chance; to happen: *I lit upon a solution.* **3** *NAmer, informal* (+ into) to attack (somebody). [Old English *līhtan*, from *lēocht*, from *līht* LIGHT⁴]

light air *noun* a wind having a speed of 1 to 5km/h (1 to 3mph).

light box *noun* a box containing an electric light and having a translucent lid, used for viewing photographic transparencies, etc.

light breeze *noun* a wind having a speed of 6 to 11km/h (4 to 7mph).

light bulb *noun* a glass bulb containing a filament or gas that gives off light when heated by electricity.

light-emitting diode *noun* see LED.

lighten¹ *verb* (**lightened, lightening**) ➤ *verb trans* **1** to reduce the weight of (something). **2** to relieve (somebody's mind) of a burden. **3** to make (something) less wearisome; to alleviate (it): *More company increases happiness, but does not lighten or diminish misery* — Thomas Traherne. **4** to make (something) less serious or more cheerful. ➤ *verb intrans* **1** to become lighter or less burdensome. **2** to become less serious or more cheerful: *His mood lightened.* [Middle English *lihten*, from LIGHT⁴]

lighten² *verb* (**lightened, lightening**) ➤ *verb trans* **1** to make (a place) light or bright; to illuminate (it). **2** to make (a colour, hair, etc) lighter or paler. ➤ *verb intrans* **1** to grow lighter; to brighten. **2** to discharge flashes of lightning. [Middle English *lightenen*, from LIGHT²]

lightening /'liet(ə)ning/ *noun* a sensation, experienced in late pregnancy, of a lessening of pressure on the diaphragm when the head of the foetus engages in the pelvis.

Usage note

lightening *or* lightning? See note at LIGHTNING.

lighten up *verb intrans informal* (*usu in imperative*) to stop being quite so humourless; to unbend: *What a spoilsport ... objecting to the Spitting Image royal puppets being displayed ... Lighten up, Ma'am. It's only a joke* — Today.

lighter¹ *noun* a device for lighting a cigarette, cigar, etc.

lighter² *noun* a large flat-bottomed barge used in unloading or loading ships. [Middle English from early Dutch *lichten* to unload]

lighterage /'lietərij/ *noun* the loading, unloading, or transport of goods by means of a lighter.

light-fingered *adj* **1** expert at or given to stealing, *esp* by picking pockets. **2** having a light and dexterous touch: *a light-fingered pianist.*

light-flyweight *noun* a weight in amateur boxing or wrestling of not more than 48kg (106lb).

light-footed *adj* moving gracefully and nimbly. ➤➤ **light-footedly** *adv*.

light-headed *adj* **1** faint or dizzy. **2** frivolous. ➤➤ **light-headedly** *adv*, **light-headedness** *noun*.

light-hearted *adj* **1** free from care or worry; cheerful. **2** not serious; playful or amusing. ➤➤ **light-heartedly** *adv*, **light-heartedness** *noun*.

light-heavyweight *noun* **1** a weight in boxing of 72.5–79.5kg (160–175lb) if professional or 75–81kg (165–179lb) if amateur. **2** a weight in professional or amateur wrestling of not more than 90kg (198lb).

lighthouse /'liet·hows/ *noun* a tower, mast, etc equipped with a powerful light to warn or guide shipping at sea.

lighting *noun* **1** an artificial supply of light, or the apparatus providing it. **2** the arrangement of lights, *esp* to produce a particular effect. **3** the effect produced by light, e.g. in painting or photography.

lighting-up time *noun* *Brit* the time when motorists are required by law to have the lights of their vehicles on.

light into *verb trans* *NAmer, informal* to attack (somebody).

light meter *noun* a small and often portable device for measuring the degree of illumination, *esp* an exposure meter.

light-middleweight *noun* a weight in amateur boxing of 67–71kg (148–157lb).

lightness *noun* the attribute of objects or colours by which more or less of the incident light is reflected or transmitted.

lightning /'lietning/ *noun* **1** the flashing of light produced by a discharge of atmospheric electricity between two clouds or between a cloud and the earth. **2** (*used before a noun*) very quick, short, or sudden: *a lightning strike*. [Middle English, from *lightenen*: see LIGHTEN²]

Usage note
lightning *or* lightening? The flash in a thunderstorm is *lightning* without an *e*. *Lightening* comes from the verb *lighten*: if you see a *lightening* in the sky, dawn is about to break or the clouds are about to part.

lightning conductor (*NAmer* **lightning rod**) *noun* a metal rod fixed to the highest point of a building or mast and connected to the earth or water below as a protection against damage by lightning.

light opera *noun* = OPERETTA.

light out *verb intrans* *NAmer, informal* to leave in a hurry: *He lit out for home as soon as he could.* [LIGHT⁶]

light pen *noun* **1** a pen-shaped photoelectric device that is pointed at or moved over a VDU screen to communicate with a computer. **2** a hand-held pen-shaped device used to read bar codes.

light pollution *noun* excessive artificial light, e.g. from street lamps, causing the night sky to be unnaturally bright and obscuring faint stars.

light railway *noun* a transport system using small trains, usu in a city.

light reaction *noun* in biochemistry, the phase of PHOTO-SYNTHESIS (use of sunlight by green plants to obtain nutrients) for which light is necessary. It involves the conversion of light energy to chemical energy for storage in the form of the chemical compound ATP, and the splitting of water molecules into hydrogen and oxygen: compare DARK REACTION.

lights *pl noun* the lungs of a slaughtered sheep, pig, etc, used *esp* as food for pets. [Middle English *lightes*, from LIGHT⁴]

lightship *noun* a moored vessel equipped with a powerful light to warn or guide shipping at sea.

light show *noun* an entertainment of ever-changing coloured light, *esp* as part of a pop concert.

lightsome /'liets(ə)m/ *adj literary* **1** airy or nimble: *He walked with a lightsome step.* **2** free from care; light-hearted: *Then was Christian glad and lightsome* — Bunyan. **3** full of light; bright: *Her room was warm and lightsome* — James Joyce. ➤➤ **lightsomely** *adv*, **lightsomeness** *noun*.

lights-out *noun* **1** a prescribed bedtime for people living in an institution, e.g. a boarding school or prison. **2** a command or signal for putting out lights.

light up *verb trans* **1a** to illuminate (something), *esp* in a sudden or conspicuous manner: *Fireworks lit up the night sky.* **b** to make (something) more animated or cheerful. **2** to ignite (a cigarette, pipe, etc). ➤ *verb intrans* **1a** to become illuminated or lit: *The sky lit up.* **b** to become more cheerful. **2** to start smoking a cigarette, pipe, etc.

lightweight¹ *noun* **1a** a weight in boxing of 59–61kg (130–135lb) if professional or 57–60kg (126–132lb) if amateur. **b** a weight in wrestling of not more than 70kg (154lb) if professional or not more than 68kg (150lb) if amateur. **2** somebody of little ability or importance.

lightweight² *adj* **1** having less than average weight: *a lightweight fabric.* **2** lacking in seriousness or profundity; inconsequential. **3** in boxing or wrestling, of or involving lightweights: *the lightweight championship.*

light-welterweight *noun* a weight in amateur boxing of 60–63.5kg (132–140lb).

light-year *noun* in astronomy, a unit of length equal to the distance that light travels in one year in a vacuum, approximately 9460 thousand million km (about 5878 thousand million mi).

lign- *or* **ligni-** *or* **ligno-** *comb. form* forming words, denoting: **1** wood: *lignin; ligneous.* **2** lignin and: *lignocellulose.* [Latin *lign-, ligni-*, from *lignum* wood, from *legere* to gather]

ligneous /'ligni-əs/ *adj* of or resembling wood; woody. [Latin *ligneus*, from *lignum*: see LIGN-]

ligni- *comb. form* see LIGN-.

lignify /'lignifie/ *verb trans* (**lignifies, lignified, lignifying**) to convert (a plant cell) into wood or woody tissue. ➤➤ **lignification** /-fi'kaysh(ə)n/ *noun*. [French *lignifier* from Latin *lignum*: see LIGN-]

lignin /'lignin/ *noun* a substance that together with cellulose forms the woody cell walls of plants and the cementing material between them.

lignite /'ligniet/ *noun* a brownish black coal that is harder than peat but usu retains the texture of the original wood. Also called BROWN COAL. ➤➤ **lignitic** /lig'nitik/ *adj*. [French *lignite* from Latin *lignum*: see LIGN-]

ligno- *comb. form* see LIGN-.

lignocaine /'lignəkayn/ *noun* a synthetic local anaesthetic.

lignocellulose /lignoh'selyoolohs/ *noun* any of several substances constituting the essential part of woody cell walls and consisting of cellulose closely associated with lignin.

lignum vitae /,lignəm 'vietee/ *noun* (*pl* **lignum vitae**s) **1** any of several tropical American trees with blue or purple flowers: genus *Guaiacum.* **2** the very hard dark wood of any of these trees. [Latin *lignum vitae* wood of life, because its resin was used medicinally]

ligroin /'ligroh·in/ *noun* a petroleum extract that boils usu in the range 20–135°C and is used *esp* as a solvent. [origin unknown]

ligulate /'ligyoolət/ *adj* **1** shaped like a strap: *the ligulate corolla of a flower.* **2** having ligules.

ligule /'ligyoohl/ *noun* a strap-shaped membranous outgrowth of a leaf, *esp* of the sheath of a blade of grass. [Latin *ligula* small tongue, strap, dimin. of *lingua* tongue]

Ligurian /li'gyoori·ən/ *noun* a native or inhabitant of Liguria in NW Italy. ➤➤ **Ligurian** *adj*.

likable *or* **likeable** /'liekəbl/ *adj* pleasant or agreeable. ➤➤ **likability** /-'biliti/ *noun*, **likableness** *noun*, **likably** *adv*.

like¹ /liek/ *prep* **1a** having the characteristics of (something or somebody); similar to (them): *His house is like a palace.* **b** typical of (somebody or something): *It was just like her to do that.* **2a** in the manner of (somebody or something); similarly to (them): *Don't act like a fool.* **b** to the same degree as (something): *This dress fits like a glove.* **3** appearing to be, threaten, or promise (something): *It looks like rain.* **4a** of the class of (something): *a subject like physics.* **b** used to introduce an example: such as: *foods that are high in fibre, like wholemeal bread.* ✳ **like anything/crazy** *informal* used to emphasize a verb: *They ran like anything.* **like that 1** in that way: *Don't eat like that.* **2** without demur or hesitation: *You can't change jobs just like that.* [Middle English from Old Norse *likr, glikr*]

Usage note
like *and* such as. Sometimes the use of *like* can be ambiguous: *a boy like you* could mean either 'a boy, for example, you' or 'a boy who resembles you'. The ambiguity can be avoided if *like* is used to introduce a comparison and *such as* is used to introduce an example. However in the latter case, the use of *such as* is normally restricted to more formal contexts.

like² *conj informal* **1** in the same way as: *if she can sing like she can dance.* **2** as if: *He acts like he knows what he's doing.*

like³ *noun* somebody or something that is similar or equal to another, *esp* in excellence, magnitude, etc; a counterpart: *You never saw the like of it; Her like will never be seen again.* ✻ **the like** similar things: *football, tennis, and the like.* **the likes of** *informal* people similar to and usu including (the specified person): *I wouldn't lend money to the likes of her.*

like⁴ *adj* similar in appearance, character, or quantity: *suits of like design.*

like⁵ *adv* **1** likely or probably: *'It would have much amazed you.' 'Very like, very like.'* — Shakespeare; *He'll come as like as not.* **2** *informal* so to speak: *He went up to her casually, like.*

like⁶ *verb trans* **1a** to find (something or somebody) agreeable, acceptable, or pleasant: *She likes playing games.* **b** to feel about (something); to regard (it): *How would you like a change?* **2** to wish or choose (to have, be, or do something); to want (it): *He likes us to come early.* ➤ *verb intrans* to feel inclined; to choose: *You can leave any time you like.* [Old English *līcian*]

like⁷ *noun* a liking or preference: *my likes and dislikes.*

-like *comb. form* forming adjectives from nouns, with the meaning: resembling or characteristic of: *bell-like; ladylike.*

Usage note
Adjectives ending in *-like* may be written with or without a hyphen (*catlike, hair-like*) although common compound adjectives ending in *-like* are usually written without a hyphen (*childlike, lifelike*). When *-like* is attached to a word ending in *-ll* a hyphen is added (*bell-like*). When the root word ends in a single *l*, the spelling with or without a hyphen is permissible: *owllike* or *owl-like*.

likeable *adj* see LIKABLE.

likelihood /'lieklihood/ *noun* probability: *In all likelihood it will rain.*

likely¹ /'liekli/ *adj* (**likelier, likeliest**) **1** having a high probability of being or occurring: *likely to succeed; the likely result.* **2a** reliable or credible: *a likely enough story.* **b** used ironically: incredible: *A likely story!* **3** promising: *a likely candidate.* **4** seeming appropriate; suitable: *a likely spot for a picnic.* [Middle English from Old Norse *glíkligr*, from *glíkr* LIKE¹]

Usage note
See note at APT.

likely² *adv* probably: *He will most likely give up.* ✻ **as likely as not** very probably.

Usage note
Likely is not used on its own as an adverb meaning 'probably' in British English. A sentence such as *They will likely try again* is acceptable in American English, but not in British English. However phrases such as *quite likely, more than likely*, and *very likely* present no problems: *They have very likely been delayed; She will more than likely call again.*

like-minded *adj* having a similar outlook or disposition. ➤➤ **like-mindedly** *adv*, **like-mindedness** *noun*.

liken *verb trans* (**likened, likening**) (+ to) to discover or point out the resemblance of (somebody or something) to another; to compare (them): *The building has been likened to a giant mushroom.*

likeness *noun* **1** resemblance. **2** a copy or portrait: *a good likeness of her.* **3** an appearance or semblance.

likewise *adv* **1** moreover; in addition. **2** in like manner; similarly: *Go and do likewise.*

liking *noun* **1** favourable regard: *I looked upon her with a soldier's eye, that liked, but had a rougher task in hand than to drive liking to the name of love* — Shakespeare. **2** taste or fondness: *She developed a liking for exotic foods.* ✻ **take a liking to** to develop a fondness for (a person or thing): *She took a liking to the newcomer.* **to one's liking** satisfactory: *Things were not to his liking.*

likuta /li'koohtə/ *noun* (*pl* **makuta** /mah-/) a former unit of currency in Zaïre (now the Democratic Republic of Congo), worth 100th of a zaïre. [from Kikongo, a Bantu language spoken in the Congo and adjacent areas]

lilac /'lielək, 'lielak/ *noun* **1** any of several species of European shrubs of the olive family with heart-shaped leaves and large clusters of fragrant white or pale pinkish purple flowers: genus *Syringa.* **2** a pale pinkish purple colour. [early French *lilac* (modern *lilas*) via Arabic and Persian from Sanskrit *nīla* dark blue]

lilangeni /leelang'gayni/ *noun* (*pl* **emalangeni** /i,malang'gayni/) the basic monetary unit of Swaziland, divided into 100 cents. [Bantu *li-langeni*, literally 'member of the royal family']

liliaceous /lili'ayshəs/ *adj* of lilies or the lily family.

Lilliputian /lili'pyoohsh(ə)n/ *noun* somebody or something that is remarkably small. ➤➤ **Lilliputian** *adj.* [named after *Lilliput*, imaginary country of tiny people in *Gulliver's Travels* by Jonathan Swift d.1745, Irish satirist]

Li-Lo /'lie loh/ *noun* (*pl* **Li-Los**) *trademark* an airbed. [alteration of *lie low*]

lilt¹ /lilt/ *verb intrans* to sing or speak rhythmically and with varying pitch. ➤➤ **lilting** *adj*, **liltingly** *adv.* [Middle English *lulten*; earlier history unknown]

lilt² *noun* **1** a rhythmic swing, flow, or rising and falling inflection in music or speech. **2** a light springy motion: *a lilt in her step.*

lily /'lili/ *noun* (*pl* **lilies**) **1a** any of various plants that grow from bulbs and have variously coloured showy flowers: genus *Lilium.* **b** any of various similar or related plants, e.g. a water lily. **c** a flower of any of these plants. **2** in heraldry, a fleur de lis. [Old English *lilie* from Latin *lilium*, from Greek *leirion*]

lily-livered /'livəd/ *adj* lacking courage; cowardly.

lily of the valley *noun* (*pl* **lilies of the valley**) a low perennial plant of the lily family that has large leaves and fragrant bell-shaped white flowers: genus *Convallaria.*

lily pad *noun* a large flat floating leaf of a water lily.

lily-white *adj* **1** pure white. **2** irreproachable or pure.

lima bean /'leemə, 'liemə/ *noun* **1** a bean plant of tropical American origin widely cultivated for its flat edible seeds: *Phaseolus lunatus.* **2** a seed of this plant, used as a vegetable. [named after *Lima*, capital city of Peru]

limb¹ /lim/ *noun* **1** any of the projecting paired appendages of an animal body used *esp* for movement and grasping, *esp* a leg or arm of a human being. **2** a large primary branch of a tree. **3** an extension or branch; *specif* any of the four branches or arms of a cross. **4** an active member or agent: *limbs of the law.* ✻ **out on a limb** in an exposed and unsupported position. ➤➤ **limbless** *adj.* [Old English *lim*]

limb² *noun* **1** the outer edge of the apparent disc of a celestial body. **2** the broad flat part of a petal or sepal furthest from its base. **3** the graduated margin of a curve or circle in an instrument for measuring angles. [Latin *limbus* border]

limbed *adj* (*usu used in combinations*) having limbs of the kind or number specified: *strong-limbed.*

limber¹ /'limbə/ *adj* supple in body or mind; flexible. ➤➤ **limberness** *noun.* [origin unknown]

limber² *noun* the detachable front part of a gun carriage consisting of a frame supporting two wheels and an ammunition box used as a seat. [Middle English *lymour*; earlier history unknown]

limber up *verb intrans* to prepare for physical action by gentle exercise: *He limbered up before the match.*

limbic /'limbik/ *adj* of or being a group of structures in the brain, including the hypothalamus and hippocampus, that are concerned with emotion and motivation: *the limbic system.* [Latin *limbicus* of a border or margin, from *limbus* border]

limbo¹ /'limboh/ *noun* **1** in Roman Catholic theology, an abode of the souls of those who died before receiving Christian baptism and are barred from heaven. **2a** a place or state of restraint or confinement, or of neglect or oblivion. **b** an intermediate or transitional place or state. [Middle English from medieval Latin *limbo*, ablative of *limbus* border]

limbo² *noun* (*pl* **limbos**) a W Indian acrobatic dance that involves bending over backwards and passing under a low horizontal pole. [from LIMBER¹]

limbo³ *verb intrans* (**limbos, limboed, limboing**) to dance the limbo.

Limburger /'limbuhgə/ *noun* a creamy soft white to yellow cheese with a strong smell and flavour. [Flemish *Limburger* of *Limburg*, a province in NE Belgium where it was orig made]

lime¹ /liem/ *noun* **1a** a caustic solid consisting of calcium oxide and some magnesium oxide, obtained by heating calcium carbonate, e.g. in the form of shells or limestone, to a high temperature, and used in building and in agriculture. Also called QUICKLIME. **b** calcium hydroxide, occurring as a dry white powder, made by treating caustic lime with water. **c** = CALCIUM: *carbonate of lime.* **2** *archaic* birdlime. >>> **limy** *adj.* [Old English *līm*]

lime² *verb trans* **1** to treat or cover (e.g. soil) with lime. **2** *archaic.* **a** to trap (a bird) with birdlime. **b** to smear (e.g. a twig) with birdlime.

lime³ *noun* **1** any of a genus of trees with heart-shaped leaves and clusters of yellow flowers, often planted along streets and avenues: genus *Tilia.* **2** the light fine-grained wood of this tree. [alteration of Middle English *line*, from Old English *lind* linden tree]

lime⁴ *noun* **1a** a small green citrus fruit with acid juicy pulp used as a flavouring and as a source of vitamin C. **b** the spiny tropical citrus tree that bears this fruit: *Citrus aurantifolia.* **2** a soft drink made from sweetened lime juice: *lager and lime.* **3** a bright greenish yellow colour. [French *lime* via Provençal from Arabic *līma*]

limeade /liem'ayd/ *noun* a soft drink consisting of sweetened lime juice mixed with plain or carbonated water.

limekiln *noun* a kiln or furnace for reducing calcium-containing material, e.g. limestone or shells, to lime for burning.

limelight *noun* **1** (**the limelight**) the centre of public attention. **2** an intense white light formerly used for stage lighting, produced by directing a flame on a cylinder of lime.

limerick /'limərik/ *noun* a humorous verse form of five lines with a rhyme scheme of aabba.

Word history
named after *Limerick*, a city and county in Eire. It is thought that a refrain, 'Will you come up to Limerick?', was once added between the verses of a limerick at a party.

limestone *noun* a widely-occurring rock consisting mainly of calcium carbonate.

limewash *noun* a mixture of lime and water used as a coating, e.g. for walls.

limewater *noun* **1** an alkaline solution of calcium hydroxide in water used as an antacid. **2** natural water containing calcium carbonate or calcium sulphate in solution.

limey *noun* (*pl* **limeys**) (*often* **Limey**) *NAmer, Aus, informal, derog* a British person, formerly *esp* a sailor. [shortening of *lime-juicer*, from the British practice of drinking lime juice to prevent scurvy on ships]

limit¹ /'limit/ *noun* **1a** a line or point that cannot or should not be passed. **b** a boundary, edge, or terminus. **c** (*in pl*) the place enclosed within a boundary: *You must not go off limits.* **2a** something that bounds, restrains, or confines: *He worked within the limits of his knowledge; She set a limit on his spending.* **b** the furthest point or extreme degree of something: *They tax my patience to the limit.* **c** a prescribed maximum or minimum amount, quantity, or number: *a speed limit.* **3a** a number whose difference from the value of a function approaches zero as the value of the independent variable approaches some given number. **b** a number that for an infinite sequence of numbers is such that ultimately each of the remaining terms of the sequence differs from this number by less than any given amount. **✳ to be the limit** *informal* to be exasperating or intolerable. >>> **limitless** *adj,* **limitlessly** *adv,* **limitlessness** *noun.* [Middle English via French from Latin *limit-, limes* boundary]

limit² *verb trans* (**limited, limiting**) **1** to restrict (somebody or something) to specific bounds or limits: *The specialist can no longer limit himself to his speciality.* **2** to curtail or reduce (something) in quantity or extent; to curb (it): *We must limit the power of aggressors.* >>> **limitable** *adj,* **limitative** *adj,* **limiter** *noun.*

limitation /limi'taysh(ə)n/ *noun* **1** something that is limiting, e.g.: **a** a restriction or curb. **b** a defect, undesirable quality, or weak point. **2** the act or an instance of limiting. **3** in law, a period defined by statute after which a claimant is barred from bringing a legal action. >>> **limitational** *adj.*

limited *adj* **1** confined within limits; restricted: *limited success.* **2** said of a monarchy or government: restricted as to the scope of powers. **3** lacking the ability to grow or do better: *a bit limited; a bit thick in the head* — Virginia Woolf. **4** *Brit* being a limited company. >>> **limitedly** *adv,* **limitedness** *noun.*

limited company *noun* a company in which the responsibility of an individual shareholder for the company's debts is limited according to the amount of the company's capital that he or she contributed.

limited liability *noun Brit* liability, e.g. of a shareholder or shipowner, limited by law or contract.

limn /lim/ *verb trans archaic or literary* to represent (something) by drawing or painting it, or to describe (it) in words. >>> **limner** *noun.* [Middle English *luminen, limnen* to illuminate a manuscript, via French from Latin *illuminare*: see ILLUMINATE]

limnology /lim'noləji/ *noun* the scientific study of physical, chemical, biological, and meteorological conditions in lakes and bodies of fresh water. >>> **limnological** /-'lojikl/ *adj,* **limnologist** *noun.* [Greek *limnē* pool, marshy lake + -LOGY]

limo /'limoh/ *noun* (*pl* **limos**) *informal* = LIMOUSINE.

limousine /limə'zeen, 'liməzeen/ *noun* a large luxurious motor car, *esp* one with a glass partition separating the driver from the passengers: *All we want is a limousine and a ticket for the peepshow* — Louis MacNeice.

Word history
French *limousine* 'cloak from *Limousin*', a former province of France where they were worn. The car was so named because the original model, unlike similar vehicles of the period, had a roof or canopy that protected the driver.

limp¹ /limp/ *verb intrans* **1** to walk with an uneven step to avoid putting the full weight of the body on an injured leg. **2** to proceed slowly or with difficulty: *The plane limped home.* [prob from Middle English *lympen* to fall short, of Germanic origin]

limp² *noun* a limping movement or gait.

limp³ *adj* **1a** lacking firmness and stiffness; drooping or shapeless. **b** said of a book cover: not stiff or rigid. **2** lacking energy. >>> **limply** *adv,* **limpness** *noun.* [prob related to LIMP¹]

limpet /'limpit/ *noun* a marine mollusc that has a low conical shell with a broad opening beneath for its large suction foot, that enables it to cling very tightly to rock when disturbed: families Acmaeidae and Patellidae. [Old English *lempedu* from late Latin *lampreda*]

limpet mine *noun* an adhesive or magnetic explosive device; *esp* one designed to cling to the hull of a ship.

limpid /'limpid/ *adj* **1** transparent or clear: *limpid streams.* **2** clear and simple in style: *limpid prose.* >>> **limpidity** /lim'piditi/ *noun,* **limpidly** *adv,* **limpidness** *noun.* [French *limpide* from Latin *limpidus,* prob from *lympha, limpa*: see LYMPH]

limp-wristed *adj informal, offensive* said of a man, *esp* a homosexual: = EFFEMINATE.

linage /'lienij/ *noun* the number of lines in a piece of printed or written matter.

linchpin or **lynchpin** /'linchpin/ *noun* **1** a locking pin inserted crosswise, e.g. through the end of an axle or shaft. **2** somebody or something regarded as a vital or coordinating factor: *She was the linchpin of the organization.* [Middle English, from Old English *lynis* linchpin + *pinn* PIN¹]

Lincoln green /'lingk(ə)n/ *noun* **1** a bright green colour. **2** cloth of Lincoln green. [named after *Lincoln*, a city in E England where the cloth was orig made]

Lincs /lingks/ *abbr* Lincolnshire.

linctus /'lingktəs/ *noun* any of various syrupy usu medicated liquids used to relieve throat irritation and coughing. [Latin *linctus* past part. of *lingere* to lick]

lindane /'lindayn/ *noun* a type of benzene hexachloride used as an insecticide and weedkiller, now often restricted in use because it persists in the environment. [named after T van der *Linden* fl.1940, Dutch chemist]

linden /'lind(ə)n/ *noun* = LIME³.

line¹ /lien/ *noun* **1a** a long narrow mark across a surface, e.g. one made by a pencil. **b** in mathematics, a straight or curved path that is traced by a moving point and has length but no breadth. **2a** something, e.g. a ridge or seam, that is distinct, elongated, and narrow. **b** a narrow crease, e.g. on the face; a wrinkle. **3** a real or imaginary straight line oriented in terms of stable points of reference: *It lies on a line between London and Glasgow.* **4a** a circle of latitude or longitude on a sphere. **b** (**the Line**) the equator. **5a** a boundary demarcating an area, or separating it from another one; a border: *the state line.* **b** a mark, e.g. on a map, indicating the position of a boundary or the outline of an area, or connecting points of e.g. equal height or depth. **6a** a marked or imaginary line across or at the limit of a playing area such as a football field, that regulates the playing of a game. **b** a line marking the starting or *esp* finishing point for a race. **7** a railway track. **8a** a defining outline; an edge or contour: *the line of a building.* **b** the marks that collectively shape the formal design of a picture as distinguished from the shading or colour. **9** a rank of objects of one kind; a row. **10a** a horizontal row of written or printed characters. **b** a single row of words in a poem. **c** (*in pl*) a piece of poetry: *The work was entitled 'Lines on the Death of a Favourite Goldfish'.* **d** a short letter; a note. **11a** a short sequence of words spoken by an actor playing a particular role. **b** (*in pl*) all of the text making up a particular role. **12** *Brit* (*in pl*) a specified number of lines of writing to be copied as a school punishment. **13** *NAmer* a queue. **14** a related series of people or things coming one after the other in time; a family. **15** an arrangement of operations in industry permitting various stages of manufacture to take place in sequence. **16a** in music, any of the horizontal parallel strokes on a stave. **b** a succession of musical notes, *esp* in a melodic phrase. **17** a thin horizontal section of the image on a television screen. **18** in physics, a narrow part of a spectrum distinguished by being noticeably more or less bright than neighbouring areas. **19** a thread, string, cord, or rope, *esp*: a clothesline. **b** a rope used on a ship. **c** a device for catching fish that consists of a cord with hooks and is attached to a rod or other fishing gear. **d** a length of material, e.g. cord, used in measuring and levelling: *a plumb line.* **20a** a conducting wire or cable conveying electrical power through a circuit or system or carrying a telecommunications signal. **b** a telephone connection. **21** a continuous length of piping for conveying a liquid or gas. **22** a particular type of merchandise, product, or service: *We don't carry that line.* **23a** a course of conduct, action, or thought; a policy: *What's their line on education for the under-fives?* **b** a field of activity, interest, or business: *He's in the clothing line.* **24a** a specified manner or theme when talking or writing: *a hefty line in home psychoanalysis* — Derek Jewell. **b** *informal* insincere talk used to deceive or persuade somebody: *She believed his line about having lost all his money.* **25** (*in pl*) a general plan; a model: *I'm writing something on the lines of a guidebook.* **26** a group of vehicles, ships, aeroplanes, etc carrying passengers or goods regularly over a route, or the company owning or operating these vehicles: *a shipping line.* **27a** a linked series of trenches and fortifications, *esp* facing the enemy. **b** a military formation in which the different elements, e.g. soldiers or companies, are abreast of each other. **c** (**the line**) regular and numbered infantry regiments of the army as opposed to auxiliary forces or troops guarding the sovereign: *a regiment of the line.* **28** a state of agreement or conformity: *We must bring her into line; He had strayed out of line.* **29** *slang* a quantity of cocaine arranged in a long narrow strip for snorting. **above the line** in accounting, denoting money used for current expenditure. **all along the line** at every point, or in every aspect of something. **below the line** in accounting, denoting money used for capital expenditure. **draw the line** to set a limit, *esp* as regards what is or is not acceptable: *I don't mind if you put pressure on them, but I draw the line at violence.* **fall in/into line** to conform. **get a line on** *informal* to find out something about. **hold the line 1** to remain connected and wait while making a telephone call. **2** to resist an attack without retreating or making concessions. **in line for** in the right position for; likely to get. **in line with** conforming to. **lay it on the line** to speak bluntly or make the situation absolutely clear. **on the line** at risk: *Several jobs were on the line.* **out of line** *chiefly NAmer* behaving in an unacceptable fashion, *esp* rudely and disrespectfully. **the end of the line** the point at which something stops, or beyond which no further progress is possible. [Middle English, partly from Old French *ligne* and partly from Old English *līne*, both ultimately from Latin *linea* (*fibra*) flax (fibre), from *linum* flax]

line[2] *verb trans* **1** to form a line along (something): *Pedestrians lined the streets.* **2** to form (something) into a line or lines; to line (it) up. **3** to mark (something) with a line or cover (it) with lines.

line[3] *verb trans* **1a** to cover the inner surface of (something): *He lined the cloak with silk.* **b** to serve as the lining of (something): *Tapestries lined the walls.* **2** to put something inside (something); to fill (it). [Middle English *linen*, from Old English *līnen*: see LINEN; because linen was often used for linings]

lineage /'liniij/ *noun* **1** a line of descent from a common ancestor or source. **2** in biology, a group of organisms belonging to the same line of descent. [Middle English *linage* via Old French *lignage* from Latin *linea*: see LINE[1]]

lineal /'lini-əl/ *adj* **1** consisting of, or being in, a direct line of ancestry or descent: compare COLLATERAL[1]. **2** composed of or arranged in lines; linear. ➤➤ **lineally** *adv.*

lineament /'lini-əmənt/ *noun* **1** (*also in pl*) a distinctive outline, feature, or contour of a body or figure, *esp* a face. **2** in geology, a linear feature, e.g. of the earth or a planet, revealing a characteristic in the underlying structure. [Middle English from Latin *lineamentum*, from *linea*: see LINE[1]]

linear /'lini-ə/ *adj* **1a** arranged in or resembling a line. **b** consisting of or relating to lines. **2a** characterized by an emphasis on line; *esp* having clearly defined outlines. **b** said of script: composed of simply drawn lines with little attempt at pictorial representation. **3a** involving a single dimension. **b** said of an equation, function, etc: containing any number of variables, all of the first degree, and, in the case of two variables, represented graphically by a straight line. **4** consisting of a straight chain of atoms. **5** elongated with nearly parallel sides: *a linear leaf.* **6** having or being a response or output that is directly proportional to the input: *A good amplifier is linear.* ➤➤ **linearity** /-'ariti/ *noun*, **linearly** *adv.*

linear accelerator *noun* a device in which charged particles are accelerated in a straight line by successive impulses from a series of electric fields.

Linear B *noun* a linear form of writing used in Crete and on the Greek mainland from the 15th cent. to the 12th cent. BC.

linear motor *noun* an electric motor having linear rather than cylindrical main components. It has been used to propel a vehicle over a track.

linear programming *noun* a mathematical method of solving practical problems, e.g. the allocation of resources, by considering the interaction of many separate linear functions.

lineation /lini'aysh(ə)n/ *noun* **1** the action of marking with lines. **2** an arrangement of lines. [Middle English *lineacion* outline, from Latin *lineation-, lineatio*, from *lineare* to make straight, from *linea*: see LINE[1]]

linebacker *noun* in American football, a defensive player positioned close behind the linemen.

line dancing *noun* a type of dancing to country and western music, performed by people in rows executing a sequence of steps simultaneously. ➤➤ **line dancer** *noun.*

line drawing *noun* a drawing composed only of lines, e.g. drawn with a pen or pencil.

line feed *noun* in computing, a control character that moves a printer or a screen onto the next line.

lineman *noun* (*pl* **linemen**) **1** *Brit* somebody who lays railway tracks. **2** *NAmer* somebody who repairs and installs telephone or power lines. **3** in American football, any of the offensive or defensive players positioned at the line of scrimmage.

line manager *noun* a person in an organization who has immediate authority over employees on the next level down in the hierarchy. ➤➤ **line management** *noun.*

linen /'linin/ *noun* **1** a hard-wearing cloth or yarn made from flax. **2a** household articles, e.g. sheets and tablecloths, made typically, *esp* formerly, of linen. **b** *archaic* washable underclothing: *When my ablutions were completed, I was put into clean linen of the stiffest character … and trussed up in my tightest … suit* — Dickens. [Old English *līnen*, from *līn* flax, from Latin *linum*]

linenfold *noun* a carved or moulded ornament representing vertical folds of linen, characteristic of Tudor panelling.

line of battle *noun* the arrangement of troops in a line for fighting.

line of credit *noun* the amount of credit made available, e.g. by a bank, to a particular individual or organization.

line of fire *noun* the path or expected path of a missile, bullet etc.

line of force *noun* a line in a magnetic, electric, or gravitational field whose tangent at any point gives the direction of the field at that point.

line of scrimmage *noun* in American football, an imaginary line parallel to the goal lines that marks the point to which the ball was carried on the last play and from which the next play begins.

line of sight *noun* a straight line from an observer's eye to a distant point towards which he or she is looking.

line-out *noun* **1** in Rugby Union, a method of returning the ball to play after it has crossed a touchline which involves throwing it in between two lines of forwards from each team. **2** the opposing lines of forwards drawn up for a line-out.

line printer *noun* a high-speed printing device that prints each line as a unit rather than character by character.

liner¹ *noun* **1** a passenger ship belonging to a shipping company and usu sailing scheduled routes. **2** somebody or something that makes, draws, or uses lines. **3** = EYELINER.

liner² *noun* **1** something used to line an item of clothing or a container: *a bin liner; a nappy liner.* **2** a replaceable metal lining for reducing the wear of a mechanism.

liner note *noun chiefly NAmer* a sleeve note for a compact disc or gramophone record.

linesman *noun* (*pl* **linesmen**) **1** an official who assists the referee or umpire in various games, *esp* in determining if a ball or player is out of the prescribed playing area. **2** *chiefly Brit* somebody who sets up or repairs telephone lines, electric power cables, etc.

line up *verb intrans* to assume an orderly arrangement in a line: *Line up for inspection.* ➤ *verb trans* **1** to put (people or things) into alignment. **2** to assemble or organize (people or things).

line-up *noun* **1** a line of people arranged for inspection or as a means of identifying a suspect. **2a** a group of people or items assembled for a particular purpose: *the line-up for tonight's show.* **b** a list of players playing for a team: *England's line-up includes Owen and Beckham.*

ling¹ /ling/ *noun* any of several species of large long-bodied food fishes of the cod family, found in shallow seas off Greenland and Europe: genus *Molva*. [Middle English *lenge*, prob from early Dutch]

ling² *noun* = HEATHER (1). [Middle English, from Old Norse *lyng*]

ling. *abbr* linguistics.

-ling *suffix* forming nouns, denoting: **1** somebody connected with: *hireling; sibling.* **2** a young, small, or lesser kind of: *duckling; princeling.* **3** somebody having (a specified quality or attribute): *underling; darling.* [Old English]

linga /'linggə/ *or* **lingam** /'linggəm/ *noun* a phallus symbolic of the divine generative power and of the Hindu god Siva: compare YONI. [Sanskrit *linga* (nominative *lingam*) mark, phallus]

Lingala /ling'gahlə/ *noun* a Bantu language of the Congo. ➤➤ **Lingala** *adj.* [the name in a local language]

lingam /'linggəm/ *noun* see LINGA.

linger /'linggə/ *verb intrans* (**lingered, lingering**) **1a** to delay going, *esp* because of reluctance to leave; to tarry. **b** to be protracted or slow in disappearing: *The smell of burning lingered for several days.* **2a** (+ over/on/upon) to spend a long time doing, dealing with, or looking at something, usu because it gives pleasure. **b** to be slow to act; to procrastinate. **3** (*often* + on) to continue in a failing or moribund state. ➤➤ **lingerer** *noun,* **lingering** *adj,* **lingeringly** *adv.* [Middle English (northern) *lengeren* to dwell, frequentative of *lengen* to prolong, from Old English *lengan*]

lingerie /'lonh·zhəri, 'lan(h)-* (*French* lɛ̃ʒri)/ *noun* women's underwear and nightclothes. [French *lingerie,* from *linge* linen, ultimately from Latin *linum*]

lingo /'linggoh/ *noun* (*pl* **lingoes** *or* **lingos**) *informal* **1** a foreign language. **2** the special vocabulary of a particular subject; jargon. [prob via Provençal *lingo* or Portuguese *lingoa,* from Latin *lingua* tongue]

lingua franca /,linggwə 'frangkə/ *noun* (*pl* **lingua francas** *or* **linguae francae** /,linggwie 'frangkie/) **1** a language used as a common or commercial tongue among people not speaking the same native language. **2** a mode of communication representing or resembling a common language: *This explains why 'camp', the secret argot of homosexuality, is also the lingua franca of theatreland —* The Economist; *the lingua franca of popular music —* Punch. **3** a language formerly spoken in Mediterranean ports that consisted of a mixture of Italian with French, Spanish, Greek, and Arabic elements. [Italian *lingua franca,* literally 'Frankish language']

lingual /'linggwəl/ *adj* **1a** to do with or in the region of the tongue. **b** articulated with the tongue. **2** = LINGUISTIC. ➤➤ **lingually** *adv.* [Latin *lingualis,* from *lingua* tongue]

linguini *or* **linguine** /ling'gweeni/ *pl noun* (*treated as sing. or pl*) pasta in the form of flat strands. [Italian *linguine,* literally 'little tongue', from *lingua* tongue, from Latin]

linguist /'linggwist/ *noun* **1** somebody accomplished in languages. **2** somebody who studies linguistics. [Latin *lingua* tongue, language]

linguistic /ling'gwistik/ *adj* relating to language or linguistics. ➤➤ **linguistically** *adv.*

linguistics *pl noun* (*treated as sing.*) the scientific study of human language with regard to its nature, structure, and use.

Editorial note
Linguistics developed in the early 20th cent., its focus on contemporary languages distinguishing it from the earlier study of language history, known as philology. It has since emerged as a major academic discipline, with many branches (e.g. phonetics, grammar, semantics), inter-disciplinary connections (for example sociolinguistics, psycholinguistics, computational linguistics), and applications (for example in translation, language teaching, and speech pathology) — Professor David Crystal.

➤➤ **linguistician** /-'stish(ə)n/ *noun.*

liniment /'linimənt/ *noun* a liquid preparation that is applied to the skin, *esp* to allay pain or irritation. [Middle English from late Latin *linimentum,* from Latin *linire* to smear]

lining /'liening/ *noun* **1** a protective or decorative layer of a different material used to cover the inside of something, e.g. a garment. **2** fabric used specifically to make linings.

link¹ /lingk/ *noun* **1** a connecting element, e.g. a single ring or division of a chain. **2** a connection, relationship, or correspondence between people or things: *They sought a link between smoking and cancer.* **3a** a system or connection that enables people, machines, etc to communicate with each other. **b** a means of transportation between one place and another. **4** a unit of length equal to 7.92in (20.12cm), formerly used in surveying. ➤➤ **linker** *noun.* [Middle English *linke* loop, from Old Norse *hlekkr*]

link² *verb trans* **1** to join or connect (two or more things or people): *a road that links two towns.* **2** to suggest that (people or things) are significantly associated or have a relationship with each other: *His name has been romantically linked with hers.* ➤ *verb intrans* (*often* + up) to become connected by a link.

link³ *noun* a torch of flaming pitch, formerly used to light the way through the streets. [perhaps from late Latin *linchinus* candle, from Greek *lyknos* light]

linkage /'lingkij/ *noun* **1** the act or an instance of linking or being linked. **2** a system of links. **3** in genetics, the relationship between genes on the same chromosome that causes them to be inherited together. **4** in electronics, the degree of electromagnetic interaction expressed as the product of the number of turns of a coil and the magnetic flux linked by the coil.

linkman *noun* (*pl* **linkmen**) a broadcaster whose function is to link and introduce separate items, *esp* in a news programme.

links *pl noun* **1** (*treated as sing. or pl*) a golf course. **2** *Scot* sand hills, *esp* along the seashore. [Old English *hlincas* rising ground, pl of *hlinc* ridge]

linkup *or* **link-up** *noun* **1** the establishment of a physical or non-physical connection or contact: *the linkup of two spacecraft.* **2a** something that serves as a linking device or factor. **b** a means of communication between people, machines, or places.

linn /lin/ *noun chiefly Scot* **1a** a pool at the base of a waterfall. **b** = WATERFALL. **2** a steep precipice. [Scottish Gaelic *linne* pool]

Linnaean *or* **Linnean** /li'nee-ən/ *adj* following or relating to the systematic methods of the Swedish botanist Linnaeus who established the system of binomial nomenclature for all living things. [from Carolus *Linnaeus* (Latinized name of Carl von Linné) d.1778, Swedish botanist]

linnet /'linit/ *noun* any of three species of common small African and Eurasian finches with brown plumage, the male having a red breast and forehead: genus *Acanthis.* [early French *linette,* from *lin* flax, from Latin *linum*; because it feeds on linseed]

lino /'lienoh/ *noun* (*pl* **linos**) *chiefly Brit, informal* = LINOLEUM.

linocut *noun* a design cut in relief on a piece of linoleum, or a print made from this.

linoleate /li'nohliayt/ *noun* a salt or ester of linoleic acid.

linoleic acid /linə'layik, -'leeik/ *noun* a liquid polyunsaturated fatty acid found in oils obtained from plants, e.g. linseed or peanut oil, and essential for mammalian nutrition: formula $C_{18}H_{32}O_2$. [Latin *linum* flax + OLEIC ACID]

linolenate /linə'laynayt, -'leenayt/ *noun* a salt or ester of linolenic acid.

linolenic acid /linə'laynik, -'leenik/ *noun* a liquid polyunsaturated fatty acid found in drying oils, e.g. linseed oil, and essential for mammalian nutrition: formula $C_{18}H_{30}O_2$. [irreg from LINOLEIC ACID]

linoleum /li'nohli-əm/ *noun* a floor covering with a canvas back and a coloured or patterned surface of hardened linseed oil and a filler, e.g. cork dust. [Latin *linum* flax + *oleum* oil]

Linotype /'lienətiep, 'lienohtiep/ *noun trademark* a keyboard-operated typesetting machine that produces each line of type in the form of a solid metal slug. [alteration of *line of type*]

linsang /'linsang/ *noun* **1** any of several species of carnivorous mammals with thick spotted or banded fur, related to the civets and genets and found in SE Asia: genus *Prionodon*. **2** a similar mammal found in W Africa: genus *Poiana*. [Malay *linsang*]

linseed /'linseed/ *noun* the seed of flax used as a source of linseed oil, as a medicine, or as animal feed. [Old English *līnsæd*, from *līn* flax + *sæd* seed]

linseed oil *noun* a yellowish oil obtained from flaxseed and used in paint, varnish, printing ink, and linoleum and for conditioning cricket bats.

linsey-woolsey /,linzi 'woolzi/ *noun* **1** a coarse sturdy fabric of wool and linen or cotton: *Some had linsey-woolsey frocks, some gingham ones, and a few of the young ones had on calico* — Mark Twain. **2** *archaic* nonsense; flannel: *But what linsey-woolsey hast thou to speak to us again?* — Shakespeare. [Middle English *lynsy wolsye*, prob from *Lindsey*, a village in Suffolk, England where linen was produced + *wolle* wool + *-sey* rhyming suffix]

linstock /'linstok/ *noun* a staff formerly used to hold a lighted match for firing cannon. [Dutch *lontstok*, from *lont* match + *stok* stick]

lint /lint/ *noun* **1** a soft absorbent material with a fleecy surface that is made from linen and is used chiefly for surgical dressings. **2** the fibrous coat of thick hairs that covers cotton seeds. **3** fluff or shreds of fibre from cloth. ➤➤ **linty** *adj*. [Middle English *lynnet* flax prepared for spinning, ultimately from Latin *linum* flax]

lintel /'lintl/ *noun* a horizontal architectural member spanning and usu carrying the load above an opening. [Middle English via French from late Latin *limitaris* threshold, from *limit-, limes* boundary]

linter *noun* **1** (*in pl*) the fuzz of short fibres that sticks to cottonseed after the ginning process. **2** a machine for removing linters.

lion /'lie-ən/ *or* **lioness** /-nes/ *noun* **1** a flesh-eating big cat of open or rocky areas of Africa and formerly southern Asia that has a tawny body with a tufted tail and in the male a shaggy blackish or dark brown mane: *Panthera leo*. **2** a courageous or ferocious person. **3** *dated* a person of interest or importance: *literary lions*. **4** (**the Lion**) the constellation and sign of the zodiac Leo. [Middle English via Old French from Latin *leon-, leo*, from Greek *leōn*]

lionhearted *adj* courageous and brave.

lionize *or* **lionise** *verb trans* to treat (somebody) as an object of great interest or importance. ➤➤ **lionization** /-'zaysh(ə)n/ *noun*, **lionizer** *noun*. [LION + -IZE; from the idea of a lion being something unusual or spectacular]

lion's share *noun* the largest or best portion.

lip[1] /lip/ *noun* **1** either of the two fleshy folds that surround the mouth. **2a** a fleshy edge or margin, e.g. of a wound. **b** = LABIUM. **3** the edge of a hollow vessel or cavity; *esp* one shaped to make pouring easy. **4** *informal* impudent or insolent talk, *esp* in reply. ✳ **lick one's lips** to show that one is looking forward to eating or doing something with great pleasure. **pass one's lips** to be eaten, drunk, or spoken. ➤➤ **lipless** *adj*, **lip-like** *adj*. [Old English *lippa*]

lip[2] *verb trans* (**lipped, lipping**) **1** to touch (something) with the lips; *esp* to kiss (it). **2** *said of water*: to lap against (something). **3** *said of a golf ball*: to reach the edge of (the hole) without dropping in.

lip- *comb. form* see LIPO-.

lipa /'leepə/ *noun* (*pl* **lipa** *or* **lipas**) a unit of currency in Croatia, worth 100th of a kuna. [Serbo-Croatian *lipa*, literally 'lime tree']

lipase /'lipayz, 'lipays, 'liepayz/ *noun* an enzyme that accelerates the HYDROLYSIS (chemical breakdown) or synthesis of fats or the breakdown of lipoproteins. [Greek *lipos* fat + -ASE]

lip gloss *noun* a cosmetic for giving a gloss to the lips.

lipid /'lipid, 'liepid/ *noun* any of various substances that with proteins and carbohydrates form the principal structural components of living cells, and that include fats, waxes, and related and derived compounds. [French *lipide* from Greek *lipos* fat]

Lipizzaner *or* **Lippizaner** /lipit'sahnə/ *noun* a breed of horses developed in Austria and used in dressage displays. [German *Lipizzaner*, named after *Lipizza, Lippiza*, stud near Trieste, formerly the Austrian Imperial Stud]

lipo- *or* **lip-** *comb. form* forming words, with the meaning: fat or fatty: *lipoprotein; lipoma*. [Greek *lipos* fat]

lipogenesis /liepə'jenəsis/ *noun* the formation of fatty acids in the living body. ➤➤ **lipogenic** /-ik/ *adj*.

lipoid[1] /'lipoyd, 'liepoyd/ *adj* resembling fat.

lipoid[2] *noun* **1** a fat-like substance. **2** = LIPID.

lipoidal /li'poydl, lie-/ *adj* = LIPOID[1].

lipoma /li'pohmə/ *noun* (*pl* **lipomas** *or* **lipomata** /-tə/) a tumour of fatty tissue.

lipoprotein /lipoh'prohteen, lie-/ *noun* a protein that has a lipid molecule attached to it and carries lipids in the bloodstream.

liposome /'lipəsohm, 'lie-/ *noun* a microscopic sphere composed of layers of fatty tissue, which occurs naturally in cells or is manufactured artificially for medical research.

liposuction /'lipohsuksh(ə)n, 'lie-/ *noun* a technique in plastic surgery for the removal of excess body fat, e.g. on the thighs and buttocks, in which the fat is drawn out through a metal tube by vacuum suction.

lipped *adj* (*usu used in combinations*) having a lip or lips, *esp* of a specified kind or number: *tight-lipped*.

Lippizaner /lipit'sahnə/ *noun* see LIPIZZANER.

lippy *adj* (**lippier, lippiest**) *informal* cheeky or impudent.

lip-read *verb* (*past tense and past part.* **lip-read** /'lipred/) ➤ *verb trans* to understand (speech) by lip-reading. ➤ *verb intrans* to use lip-reading. ➤➤ **lip-reader** *noun*.

lip-reading *noun* the act of watching the movements of a person's lips and deducing from them what he or she is saying.

lipsalve *noun* an ointment for sore or chapped lips.

lip service *noun* support expressed in words but not in actions: *They paid lip service to hygiene by washing down the building once a year.*

lipstick *noun* **1** a waxy solid cosmetic for colouring the lips. **2** a stick of this, with its case.

lip-synch[1] *or* **lip-sync** /'lipsingk/ *noun* the exact synchronization of lip movement with recorded speech or song.

lip-synch[2] *verb intrans* to move the lips in lip-synch with a recording.

liquate /'liekwayt/ *verb trans* to separate (*esp* a metal) from an ore, alloy, etc by selective melting. ➤➤ **liquation** /lie'kwaysh(ə)n/ *noun*. [Latin *liquatus*, past part. of *liquare* to make liquid]

liquefacient /likwi'faysh(ə)nt/ *noun* something that liquefies a substance or promotes liquefaction.

liquefaction /likwi'faksh(ə)n/ *noun* **1** the process of making or becoming liquid. **2** the state of being liquid. [Middle English via late Latin from Latin *liquefactus*, past part. of *liquefacere*, from *liquēre* to be fluid + *facere* to make]

liquefy *or* **liquify** /'likwifie/ *verb* (**liquefies** *or* **liquifies, liquefied** *or* **liquified, liquefying** *or* **liquifying**) ➤ *verb trans* to reduce (something) to a liquid state. ➤ *verb intrans* to become liquid. ➤➤ **liquefiable** *adj*, **liquefier** *noun*. [early French *liquefier* from Latin *liquefacere*: see LIQUEFACTION]

liquescent /li'kwes(ə)nt/ *adj* being or tending to become liquid. [Latin *liquescent-, liquescens*, present part. of *liquescere* to become fluid, from *liquēre* to be fluid]

liqueur /li'kyooə/ *noun* a strong usu sweet alcoholic drink flavoured, e.g. with fruit or aromatics, usu drunk after a meal. [French *liqueur*, from Old French *licour* liquor: see LIQUOR[1]]

liquid[1] /'likwid/ *adj* **1** flowing freely like water. **2** neither solid nor gaseous; in a state where the constituent molecules can move freely among themselves but do not tend to separate like those of gases: *liquid mercury*. **3a** shining and clear: *large liquid eyes*. **b** smooth and unconstrained in movement. **4a** *said of sounds*: flowing, pure, and free of harshness. **b** *said of a consonant*: articulated without friction and capable of being prolonged like a vowel: *The consonants /r/ and /l/ are liquid consonants in British English.* **5** *said of assets*: consisting of or capable of ready conversion into cash. ➤➤ **liquidly** *adv*, **liquidness** *noun*. [Middle English via French from Latin *liquidus*, from *liquēre* to be fluid]

liquid[2] *noun* **1** a substance that is liquid, *esp* one that is liquid at normal temperatures. **2** a liquid consonant.

liquid air *noun* air in the liquid state that is intensely cold and used chiefly as a refrigerant.

liquidambar /likwi'dambə/ *noun* **1** any of several North American or Asian trees of the witch hazel family that bear a round fruit and have star-shaped leaves: genus *Liquidambar*. **2** the resin from such a tree, used in medicine. [Latin genus name, from *liquidus* (see LIQUID[1]) + late Latin *ambar, ambra*: see AMBER]

liquidate /'likwidayt/ *verb trans* **1a** to settle (a debt), *esp* by payment. **b** to bring the commercial activities of (e.g. a business) to an end and use the assets towards paying off the debts. **2** to convert (assets) into cash. **3** *informal* to get rid of (somebody); to kill (them). ➤ *verb intrans* **1** to liquidate debts, damages, or accounts. **2** to be or become liquidated. ➤➤ **liquidation** /-'daysh(ə)n/ *noun*. [late Latin *liquidatus*, past part. of *liquidare* to melt, from Latin *liquidus*: see LIQUID[1]]

liquidator *noun* a person appointed by law to liquidate a company.

liquid crystal *noun* a liquid having certain physical, *esp* optical, properties shown by crystalline solids but not by ordinary liquids.

liquid crystal display *noun* a display of numbers or symbols, e.g. in a digital watch or calculator, produced by applying an electric field to liquid crystal cells in order to change the amount of light they reflect.

liquidise /'likwidiez/ *verb trans* see LIQUIDIZE.

liquidiser *noun* see LIQUIDIZER.

liquidity /li'kwiditi/ *noun* **1** the state of being liquid. **2** the liquid assets of a company.

liquidize *or* **liquidise** *verb trans* to cause (something solid) to be liquid; *esp* to mash or process (e.g. fruit or vegetables) into a liquid.

liquidizer *or* **liquidiser** *noun chiefly Brit* a domestic electric appliance for grinding, pureeing, liquidizing, or blending foods.

liquid measure *noun* a unit or series of units for measuring liquid capacity.

liquid paraffin *noun* a colourless oily mixture of chemical compounds obtained from petroleum, used as a laxative.

liquify /'likwifie/ *verb trans and intrans* see LIQUEFY.

liquor[1] /'likə/ *noun* **1** alcoholic drink, *esp* spirits. **2** any liquid substance, *esp* water in which food has been cooked. **3** a solution of a drug in water. [Middle English via Old French *licour* from Latin *liquor*, from *liquēre* to be fluid]

liquor[2] *verb trans* (**liquored, liquoring**) **1** to dress (e.g. leather) with oil or grease. **2** to steep (e.g. malt) in water.

liquorice (*NAmer* **licorice**) /'likərish, -ris/ *noun* **1** a European plant of the pea family that has spikes of blue flowers and is cultivated for its roots: *Glycyrrhiza glabra*. **2a** a sweet flavoured with liquorice: *liquorice allsorts*. **b** the pungent black dried root of liquorice, extracts of which are used in brewing, confectionery, and as a laxative. [Middle English *licorice* via Old French and late Latin from Greek *glykyrrhiza*, from *glykys* sweet + *rhiza* root]

liquorish /'likərish/ *adj* see LICKERISH.

lira /'liərə/ *noun* (*pl* **lire** /'liərə, 'liəray/ *or* **liras**) **1** the former basic monetary unit of Italy and San Marino (in Italy replaced by the euro in 2002). **2** the basic monetary unit of Malta, divided into 100 cents. **3** the basic monetary unit of Turkey, divided into 100 kurus. [Italian *lira* from Latin *libra* scales, pound]

lisente /li'sente/ *noun* pl of SENTE.

lisle /liel/ *noun* a smooth tightly twisted thread usu made of long-staple cotton: *schoolgirls of the 50s in brown lisle stockings and lace-ups*. [from *Lisle*, former name of Lille, a city in N France where it was first made]

lisp[1] /lisp/ *verb intrans* **1** to pronounce /s/ and /z/ imperfectly, *esp* by giving them the sounds of /th/ and /dh/. **2** to speak with a lisp. **3** to speak in childish tones: *As yet a child, nor yet a fool to fame, I lisped in numbers, for the numbers came* — Pope. ➤ *verb trans* to utter (something) in a lisping voice. ➤➤ **lisper** *noun*, **lisping** *adj*, **lispingly** *adv*. [Old English *-wlyspian*]

lisp[2] *noun* a speech defect or affectation characterized by lisping.

lissom *or* **lissome** /'lis(ə)m/ *adj* flexible, lithe, or supple: *A robe of samite ... that more expressed than hid her, clung about her lissome limbs* — Tennyson. ➤➤ **lissomness** *noun*. [alteration of *lithesome*, from LITHE + -SOME[1]]

list[1] /list/ *noun* a series or catalogue of words or numbers, e.g. representing people or objects of a particular kind, usu arranged in order so as to be easily found: *a guest list; a shopping list*. [French *liste* from Italian *lista*, of Germanic origin]

list[2] *verb trans* **1** to make a list of (things or people). **2** to include (something or somebody) on a list. **3** *Brit* to include (a building) in an official list as being of architectural or historical importance and hence protected from demolition. **4** *archaic* to recruit (somebody).

list[3] *verb intrans* to lean to one side: *The ship was listing badly*. [origin unknown]

list[4] *noun* a sideways tilt, *esp* of a ship's hull.

list[5] *noun* **1** (*in pl*). **a** the enclosed area for a tournament, or the fence surrounding this. **b** a scene of competition. **2** a band or strip of material; *esp* a selvage. [Old English *līste*]

list[6] *verb trans archaic* to please (somebody); to suit (them). ➤ *verb intrans archaic or literary* to wish or choose: *The wind bloweth where it listeth* — Bible. [Old English *lystan*]

list[7] *noun archaic* a desire.

list[8] *verb intrans archaic* = LISTEN[1]. [Old English *hlystan*, from *hlyst* hearing, from *hlysnan* to listen]

listed *adj* **1** *Brit* said of a building: protected by being included in an official list as being historically or architecturally important. **2** said of a company: having shares that are quoted on the main market of the London Stock Exchange.

listen[1] /'lis(ə)n/ *verb intrans* (**listened, listening**) **1** to pay attention to sound: *listening to music*. **2** to hear or consider with thoughtful attention; to heed: *I warned her, but she wouldn't listen*. **3** to be alert to catch an expected sound: *We listened for his step*. ➤➤ **listener** /'lisnə/ *noun*. [Old English *hlysnan*]

listen[2] *noun informal* an act of listening: *Have a listen to this*.

listen in *verb intrans* **1** to tune in to or monitor a broadcast. **2** to listen to a conversation, *esp* surreptitiously.

listening post *noun* **1** an advanced position used by troops to gather information about the enemy's movements. **2** a place where information, e.g. about another country or area, is received and monitored.

lister /'listə/ *noun NAmer* a plough that has a double mouldboard and turns up soil on each side of the furrow.

listeria /li'stiəri-ə/ *noun* any of a genus of rod-shaped bacteria that cause listeriosis in humans and many species of wild and domesticated animals: genus *Listeria*, *esp Listeria monocytogenes*. [Latin genus name, named after Joseph *Lister* d.1912, English bacteriologist]

listeriosis /li,stiəri'ohsis/ *noun* an often fatal food poisoning, caused by infection with listeria, usu characterized by flu-like symptoms, septicaemia, and meningitis and, in pregnant women, miscarriages.

listing *noun* **1** the act or an instance of making a list or including something in a list. **2a** an entry in a list. **b** a list or catalogue.

listless *adj* characterized by indifference, lack of energy, and disinclination for exertion; languid. ➤➤ **listlessly** *adv*, **listlessness** *noun*. [Middle English *listles*, from LIST[7] + -les -LESS]

list price *noun* the basic price of an item as published in a catalogue, price list, or advertisement but subject to discounts, e.g. trade or quantity discounts.

lit /lit/ *verb* past tense and past part. of LIGHT[3], LIGHT[6].

lit. *abbr* **1** literally. **2** literature. **3** litre.

litany /'lit(ə)ni/ *noun* (*pl* **litanies**) **1a** a prayer consisting of a series of petitions by the leader, each of which is followed by a response, usu the same response, from the congregation. **b** (**the Litany**) a prayer in the Anglican Book of Common Prayer consisting of set petitions and responses. **2** any repetitive recital: *Haley relieved himself by repeating over a not very select litany of imprecations on himself* — Harriet Beecher Stowe. [Middle English *letanie* via Old French and late Latin from late Greek *litaneia* prayer, from Greek *litē* entreaty, from *litanos* entreating]

litas /'leetas/ *noun* (*pl* **litas**) the basic monetary unit of Lithuania, divided into 100 centas. [Lithuanian *litas*]

litchi /'liechee/ *noun* see LYCHEE.

lite /liet/ *adj* **1** said of food or drink: low in calories, alcohol, fat or sugar. **2** *NAmer, informal* having little substance: *lite music*. [alteration of LIGHT[4]]

-lite *comb. form* forming nouns, denoting: minerals, rocks, and fossils: *graptolite*. [French *-lite*, alteration of *-lithe*, from Greek *lithos* stone]

liter /'leetə/ *noun NAmer* see LITRE.

literacy /'lit(ə)rəsi/ *noun* **1** the ability to read and write: compare ORACY. **2** skill in or knowledge of a particular subject.

literal[1] /'lit(ə)rəl/ *adj* **1** having or denoting the factual, ordinary, or primary meaning of a word or expression, as opposed to a figurative one. **2a** keeping strictly to the basic and straightforward meaning of a written text, e.g. that of the Bible. **b** reproduced word for word; exact or verbatim: *a literal translation*. **3** relating to or expressed in letters. **4** characterized by a lack of imagination; prosaic: *He took a very literal approach to the subject.* ⟫ **literality** /litə'raliti/ *noun*, **literalness** *noun*. [Middle English via French and late Latin from Latin *litteralis* of a letter, from *littera*: see LETTER[1]]

literal[2] *noun Brit* in printing, a misprint involving a single letter.

literalism *noun* **1** adherence to the literal meanings of words or texts, *esp* the rejection of allegorical or metaphorical interpretations of biblical texts. **2** realistic portrayal in literature or art. ⟫ **literalist** *noun*, **literalistic** /-'listik/ *adj*.

literally *adv* **1** in the literal sense; without metaphor or exaggeration. **2** with exact equivalence; verbatim: *Follow the instructions literally.* **3** *informal* used to intensify a metaphorical or hyperbolic expression: *She was literally tearing her hair out.*

Usage note
Literally is commonly used to show that a familiar phrase or idiom is especially relevant or should be understood in a real or physical sense: *He was literally red with anger.* It is also used informally as a kind of intensifier in metaphor, in which the literal meaning is apparently absurd: *He was literally beside himself with anger.* This last use is justifiable in linguistic terms, but is controversial.

literary /'lit(ə)rəri/ *adj* **1** relating to, constituting, or concerning literature: *literary criticism*. **2a** = WELL-READ. **b** producing or connected with literature as a profession: *Disraeli was a literary as well as a political figure*. **3** characteristic of the style or vocabulary of works of literature; more formal or picturesque than ordinary writing or speech. ⟫ **literarily** *adv*, **literariness** *noun*.

literate[1] /'lit(ə)rət/ *adj* **1** able to read and write. **2** educated or cultured, *esp* versed in literature or creative writing. **3** possessing knowledge or skill in a particular field of activity: *computer literate*. ⟫ **literately** *adv*. [Middle English *literat* from Latin *litteratus* marked with letters, literate, from *litterae* letters, literature, pl of *littera* LETTER[1]]

literate[2] *noun* a literate person.

literati /litə'rahtee/ *pl noun* the educated class; the intelligentsia. [obsolete Italian *literati* from Latin, pl of *litteratus*: see LITERATE[1]]

literature /'lit(ə)rəchə/ *noun* **1** writings in prose or verse, *esp* writings having artistic value or expression and expressing ideas of permanent or universal interest: *What makes literature interesting is that it does not survive its translation. The characters in a novel are made out of the sentences. That's what their substance is* — Jonathan Miller.

Editorial note
Literature comprises works where style or form offers pleasure in excess of the content, which is often, but not necessarily, fictional. The term thus represents a classification that depends on a value judgment. The category, not widely identified before the 19th cent., is now in question, as it has become increasingly evident that it represents the taste of a particular race, class, or gender at a specific historical moment — Professor Catherine Belsey.

2 the body of writings on a particular subject: *scientific literature*. **3** printed matter, e.g. leaflets or circulars. [Middle English via French from Latin *litteratura*, from *litteratus*: see LITERATE[1]]

lith- *comb. form* see LITHO-.

-lith *comb. form* forming nouns, denoting: stone or rock: *megalith*; *granolith*. [Latin *-lithus* and French *-lithe* from Greek *lithos* stone]

litharge /'lithahj/ *noun* a fused lead monoxide, *esp* a red form used in making ceramics and glass. [Middle English via French and Latin from Greek *lithargyros*, from *lithos* stone + *argyros* silver]

lithe /liedh/ *adj* flexible or supple: *a lithe plant stem; a lithe dancer*. ⟫ **lithely** *adv*, **litheness** *noun*. [Old English *līthe* gentle, soft]

lithia /'lithi-ə/ *noun* a white oxide of lithium, used for absorbing carbon dioxide and water vapour: formula Li_2O. [scientific Latin *lithia* from Greek *lithos* stone]

lithic /'lithik/ *adj* **1** of or relating to stone. **2** *dated* relating to stones in the internal organs of the body. **3** relating to lithium. [Greek *lithikos*, from *lithos* stone]

-lithic *comb. form* forming adjectives, with the meaning: relating to or characteristic of a specified stage in human beings' use of stone implements: *Neolithic*. [LITHIC]

lithium /'lithi-əm/ *noun* **1** a silver-white soft metallic chemical element of the alkali metal group that is the lightest metal known, and is used in alloys: symbol Li, atomic number 3. **2** the lithium ion when used in the treatment of manic-depressive conditions. [scientific Latin *lithium*, from LITHIA]

lithium carbonate *noun* a lithium salt used in the glass and ceramic industries and to treat manic-depressive psychosis: formula Li_2CO_3.

litho /'liethoh/ *noun* (*pl* **lithos**) **1** = LITHOGRAPH[1]. **2** = LITHOGRAPHY.

litho- or **lith-** *comb. form* forming words, with the meaning: stone: *lithograph*; *lithotomy*. [Latin *litho-* from Greek, from *lithos* stone]

lithograph[1] /'lithəgrahf, -graf/ *noun* a print made by lithography. ⟫ **lithographic** /-'grafik/ *adj*, **lithographically** /-'grafikli/ *adv*.

lithograph[2] *verb trans* to produce, copy, or portray (something) by lithography.

lithography /li'thogrəfi/ *noun* the process of printing from a surface, e.g. a stone or a metal plate, on which the image to be printed is ink receptive and the blank area ink-repellent. ⟫ **lithographer** *noun*. [German *Lithographie*, from LITHO- + *-graphie* -graphy]

lithology /li'tholəji/ *noun* the study of the composition, shape, etc of rocks and rock formations. ⟫ **lithological** /-'lojikl/ *adj*.

lithophyte /'lithəfiet/ *noun* a plant that grows on rock. [French *lithophyte*, from LITHO- + -PHYTE]

lithopone /'lithəpohn/ *noun* a white pigment consisting essentially of zinc sulphide and barium sulphate. [LITHO- + Greek *ponos* work]

lithosphere /'lithəsfiə/ *noun* the solid rocky crust of the earth or another celestial body.

lithotomy /li'thotəmi/ *noun* (*pl* **lithotomies**) the surgical removal of a stone, *esp* from the urinary bladder. [via late Latin from Greek *lithotomia* urinary bladder, from *lithotomein* to perform a lithotomy, from LITHO- + *temnein* to cut]

lithotripsy /'lithohtripsi/ *noun* a non-surgical method for the treatment of kidney stones that uses a lithotripter to reduce the stones to very small particles which can be passed out with the urine. [LITHO- + Greek *tripsis* rubbing, from *tribein* to rub]

lithotripter /'lithohtriptə/ *noun* an instrument that fragments kidney stones with ultrasound waves. [Greek *lithos* stone + *tribein* to rub, pound]

Lithuanian /lithyoo'ayni-ən/ *noun* **1** a native or inhabitant of Lithuania, country on the SE shore of the Baltic Sea. **2** the Baltic language of the people of Lithuania. ⟫ **Lithuanian** *adj*.

litigable *adj* able to be the subject of a lawsuit.

litigant /'litig(ə)nt/ *noun* a person engaged in a lawsuit. ⟫ **litigant** *adj*.

litigate /'litigayt/ *verb intrans* to carry on a lawsuit. ⟫ *verb trans* to contest (an issue) at law. ⟫ **litigation** /-'gaysh(ə)n/ *noun*, **litigator** *noun*. [Latin *litigatus*, past part. of *litigare*, from *lit-, lis* lawsuit + *agere* to drive]

litigious /li'tijəs/ *adj* **1** inclined to engage in lawsuits. **2** subject to litigation. **3** tending to argue; disputatious. ⟫ **litigiously** *adv*, **litigiousness** *noun*. [Middle English via French from Latin *litigiosus*, from *litigium* dispute, from *litigare*: see LITIGATE]

litmus /'litməs/ *noun* a colouring matter from lichens that turns red in acid solutions and blue in alkaline solutions and is used as an acid-alkali indicator. [Middle English from Old Norse *lit-mosi*, from *litr* dye + *mosi* moss]

litmus paper *noun* absorbent paper coloured with litmus and used as an indicator of acidity or alkalinity.

litotes /lie'tohteez/ *noun* (*pl* **litotes**) understatement in which an affirmative is expressed by the negative of its opposite (e.g. in *not a bad singer*). [Greek *litotēs*, from *litos* simple]

litre (*NAmer* **liter**) /'leetə/ *noun* a metric unit of capacity equal to one cubic decimetre (about 1.75 pints). [French *litre* via late Latin from Greek *litra* a weight]

LittD /,lit 'dee/ *abbr* Doctor of Letters. [Latin *Litterarum Doctor*]

litter[1] /'litə/ *noun* **1a** rubbish or waste products, *esp* in a public place. **b** an untidy accumulation of objects, e.g. papers. **2** a group of offspring of an animal, born at one birth. **3a** = CAT LITTER. **b** straw or similar material used as bedding for animals. **c** the uppermost slightly decayed layer of organic matter on the forest floor.

4a a covered and curtained couch carried by people or animals. **b** a stretcher or other device for carrying a sick or injured person. [Middle English via Old French from medieval Latin *lectaria*, Latin *lectus* bed]

litter[2] *verb* (**littered, littering**) ➤ *verb trans* **1a** to strew (an area) with litter, *esp* scattered articles: *Don't litter the desk-top with papers.* **b** to scatter (things) about in disorder. **2** *archaic* to provide (e.g. a horse) with litter as a bed. ➤ *verb intrans* to strew litter.

littérateur /ˌlitərə'tuh (*French* literatœːr)/ *noun* a literary person; *esp* a professional writer. [French *littérateur* from Latin *litterator* critic, from *litteratus*: see LITERATE[1]]

litterbug *noun informal* a litter lout.

litter lout *noun Brit, informal* a person who carelessly drops rubbish in public places.

little[1] /'litl/ *adj* **1** small in size or extent; tiny: *his little feet.* **2** said of a person: young or younger: *She has two little sisters.* **3** said of a plant or animal: small in comparison with related forms: *little owl.* **4** narrow or mean: *the pettiness of little minds.* **5** small in importance or interest; trivial. **6** pleasingly small: *He's a cute little thing.* **7** amounting to only a small quantity; not much: *We had little or no time.* **8** short in duration; brief: *Wait a little while.* **9** (**a little**) at least some though not much: *Fortunately he had a little money in the bank.* ➤➤ **littleness** *noun.* [Old English *lytel*]

little[2] *adv* (**less, least**) **1** (**a little**) to a small extent or degree. **2** (*usu in combination*) to no great degree or extent; not much: *little-known.* **3** hardly or not at all: *He cared little for his neighbours.*

little[3] *noun* **1a** only a small portion or quantity; not much: *We understood little of his speech; I'll do what little I can.* **b** (**a little**) a small amount or portion: *Have a little of this cake.* **2** (**a little**) a short time or distance: *Let's walk for a little.*

Little Bear *noun* = URSA MINOR.

little by little *adv* by small degrees or amounts; gradually.

Little Dipper *noun NAmer* = URSA MINOR.

little englander *noun* (*often* **Little Englander**) an opponent of British involvement in international affairs, *esp* in the 19th cent.

little finger *noun* the fourth and smallest finger of the hand counting the index finger as the first.

little grebe *noun* a brown diving bird that is similar in shape to a duck, the smallest European grebe: *Tachybaptus ruficollis.*

Little League *noun NAmer* (*often used before a noun*) a commercially sponsored baseball league for children aged from 8 to 12.

little owl *noun* an insect-eating owl found in Africa and Eurasia, which is distinguished by its small size and squat flat-headed appearance: *Athene noctua.*

little people *pl noun* the imaginary beings, e.g. fairies, elves, etc, of folklore.

little toe *noun* the outermost and smallest digit of the foot.

littoral[1] /'litərəl/ *adj* relating to or occurring on or near the shore of a sea or lake. [Latin *litoralis*, from *litor-, litus* seashore]

littoral[2] *noun* a coastal region; *esp* the intertidal zone.

liturgical /li'tuhjikl/ *adj* **1** relating to or having the characteristics of liturgy. **2** using or favouring the use of liturgy: *liturgical churches.* ➤➤ **liturgically** *adv.*

liturgist /'litəjist/ *noun* **1** a person who follows, compiles, or leads a liturgy. **2** a specialist in the study of formal public worship.

liturgy /'litəji/ *noun* (*pl* **liturgies**) **1** (*often* **Liturgy**) the form of service used in the celebration of Communion, *esp* in the Orthodox Church. **2** a prescribed form of public worship. [via late Latin from Greek *leitourgia*, from *leitourgos* minister]

livable *or* **liveable** /'livəbl/ *adj* **1a** suitable for living in. **b** (+ with) pleasant to live with. **2** possible to continue or cope with; endurable. ➤➤ **livability** /-'biliti/ *noun*, **livableness** *noun.*

live[1] /liv/ *verb intrans* **1** to be alive; to have the life of an animal or plant. **2** to continue alive: *His illness was so serious, he was lucky to live.* **3** to maintain oneself; to subsist: *She lived by writing; He lived by his wits.* **4** to conduct or pass one's life: *Yet we have gone on living, living and partly living* — T S Eliot. **5** to occupy a home; to dwell: *They had always lived in the country.* **6a** to attain eternal life. **b** to remain in human memory or record. **7** to have a life rich in experience: *the right to live, not merely to exist.* **8** (+ together/with) to cohabit. **9** *chiefly Brit, informal* said of a thing: to be found in a specified place, *esp* normally or usually: *Where does this jug live?* ➤ *verb trans* **1** to pass, spend, or experience (one's life): *She lived*

three years as a nun. **2** to enact or practise (something): *living a lie.* ✳ **live it up** *informal* to enjoy an exciting or extravagant social life or social occasion: *lived it up with wine and song.* **live through** to survive (an unpleasant or dangerous experience): *I hope we won't have to live through another war.* **live up to** to act or be in accordance with (*esp* a standard expected by somebody). [Old English *libban*]

live[2] /liev/ *adj* **1** having life. **2** containing living organisms: *live yogurt.* **3** exerting force or containing energy, e.g.: **a** glowing: *live coals.* **b** connected to a source of electric power. **c** said of ammunition, bombs, etc: unexploded, unfired. **d** driven by or imparting motion or power. **e** said of a nuclear reactor or nuclear bomb: charged with material capable of undergoing fission. **4** of continuing or current interest: *live issues.* **5** said *esp* of a rock: not quarried or cut; native. **6** in play in a game: *a live ball.* **7a** performed, performing, or recorded in the presence of an audience: *live music.* **b** said of an audience: actually present at the event or performance. **8** broadcast as it happens: *a live television programme.* [short for ALIVE]

live[3] /liev/ *adv* **1** in person and in front of an audience: *They rarely perform live nowadays.* **2** simultaneously as it happens: *This concert is being broadcast live from the Wigmore Hall.*

liveable /'livəbl/ *adj* see LIVABLE.

lived-in *adj* **1** showing agreeable signs of having been used and occupied; comfortable and homely. **2** said of a person's face: lined or wrinkled apparently as a result of a person's life experiences.

live down /liv/ *verb trans* to cause (e.g. a crime or mistake) to be forgotten, *esp* by future good behaviour: *I had made a mistake and couldn't live it down.*

live in /liv/ *verb intrans* to live at one's place of work: *The housekeeper is required to live in.*

live-in /liv/ *adj* **1** living at one's place of employment: *a live-in maid.* **2** living with somebody else in his or her home: *her live-in lover.*

livelihood /'lievlihood/ *noun* something, *esp* a job, that provides a person with the means to support themselves. [alteration of Middle English *livelode* course of life, from Old English *liflad*, from *lif* LIFE + *lad* course]

live load /liev/ *noun* in engineering, a variable load or force on a structure, e.g. moving traffic on a bridge: compare DEAD LOAD.

livelong /'livlong/ *adj chiefly literary* whole or entire: *the livelong day.* [Middle English *lef long*, from *lef* LIEF + LONG[1]; the spelling changed in the 16th cent. by association with LIVE[1]]

lively /'lievli/ *adj* (**livelier, liveliest**) **1a** briskly alert, active, and energetic: *lively children.* **b** done or conducted with energy, vigour, or emotional intensity: *a lively debate.* **2** full of life, movement, or incident: *The crowded streets made a lively scene.* **3** intellectually active, perceptive, and questioning: *lively minds.* **4** having a striking, stimulating, or exciting effect on the mind or senses: *a lively description.* **5a** moving with speed and force, often in unpredictable ways: *a lively sea.* **b** said of a pitch or playing surface: causing sharp unpredictable movements of the ball. **6** said of a boat or car: responsive to the helm or controls and exciting to sail or drive in. **7** *Brit, humorous* full of possibly disagreeable or dangerous consequences: *We were given a lively time by enemy artillery.* ➤➤ **livelily** *adv*, **liveliness** *noun.* [Old English *liflic*, from *lif* LIFE]

liven /'liev(ə)n/ *verb* (**livened, livening**) ➤ *verb trans* (*often* + up) to make (something) more lively. ➤ *verb intrans* (*often* + up) to become more lively: *The party was quiet at first, but soon livened up.*

live oak /liev/ *noun* any of several N American evergreen oaks; *esp* one that is cultivated for its tough wood used in shipbuilding: *Quercus virginiana.*

live out /liv/ *verb intrans* to live outside one's place of work: *Owing to the shortage of college rooms, some students must live out.* ➤ *verb trans* **1** to live till the end of (a period of time): *Will the sick man live out the month?* **2** to enact or carry out in real life (something previously only imagined).

liver[1] /'livə/ *noun* **1a** a large vascular glandular organ of vertebrates that secretes bile and causes changes in the blood, e.g. by converting blood sugar into glycogen. **b** any of various large digestive glands of invertebrates. **2** the liver of an animal, e.g. a calf or pig, eaten as food. **3** a dark reddish brown. [Old English *lifer*]

liver[2] *noun* a person who lives, *esp* in a specified way: *a clean liver.*

liver fluke *noun* any of various worms that invade and damage the liver of mammals, *esp* sheep: *Fasciola hepatica* and other species.

liveried /'livərid/ *adj* wearing a livery: *a liveried chauffeur.*

liverish *adj* **1** suffering from liver disorder; bilious. **2** peevish or irascible. >> **liverishness** *noun*.

Liverpudlian /livə'pudli·ən/ *noun* **1** a native or inhabitant of Liverpool. **2** the dialect or accent of the people of Liverpool. >> **Liverpudlian** *adj*. [alteration, influenced by PUDDLE[1], of *Liverpool*, a city in England + -IAN]

liver salts *pl noun* mineral salts taken in water as a cure for indigestion.

liver sausage *noun* a sausage consisting chiefly of cooked minced liver, often with pork trimmings.

liver spot *noun* a brown mark on the skin caused by an accumulation of pigment cells, frequently occurring in older people.

liverwort *noun* a plant of a class related to and resembling the mosses but differing in reproduction and development: class Hepaticae. [so called because of its shape, thought to resemble the liver]

livery[1] *noun* (*pl* **liveries**) **1a** the distinctive clothing worn by a member of a livery company or guild. **b** the distinctive uniform of servants employed by an individual or a single household. **c** a distinctive colour scheme, e.g. on aircraft, distinguishing an organization or group. **2** the legal delivering of property. **3** = LIVERY STABLE. ✱ **at livery** said of a horse: kept and fed for the owner in a livery stable.

Word history
Middle English via Old French *livrer* to dispense, deliver, from Latin *liberare* to free. The word originally denoted the provision of food and clothing to one's retainers, or the food or clothing supplied, hence distinctive clothing or uniform.

livery[2] *adj* **1** resembling liver, e.g. in colour or texture. **2** = LIVERISH.

livery company *noun* any of various London craft or trade associations that are descended from medieval guilds. [so called because of the distinctive clothing formerly worn by members]

liveryman *noun* (*pl* **liverymen**) a freeman of the City of London who is a member of a livery company.

livery stable *noun* **1** an establishment where horses are stabled and fed for their owners. **2** an establishment that hires out horses.

lives /lievz/ *noun* pl of LIFE.

livestock /'lievstok/ *noun* animals kept or raised for use or pleasure; *esp* farm animals kept for use and profit.

live wire /liev/ *noun informal* an alert, active, or aggressive person.

livid /'livid/ *adj* **1** *informal* very angry; enraged: *He was livid at his son's disobedience*. **2** discoloured by bruising. **3** unnaturally white or pale; ashen or pallid. >> **lividity** /li'viditi/ *noun*, **lividly** *adv*, **lividness** *noun*. [French *livide* from Latin *lividus*, from *livēre* to be blue]

living[1] /'living/ *adj* **1a** having the characteristics of life; alive; not dead. **b** still in use, *esp* still spoken: *a living language*. **2** true to life; exact: *He's the living image of his grandfather*. **3** used as an intensifier: *She scared the living daylights out of him*. **4** *literary* in its natural place or condition: *hewn from the living rock*. ✱ **in living memory** in a time that people who are alive now can remember.

living[2] *noun* **1a** means of subsistence; a livelihood: *earning a living*. **b** *Brit* = BENEFICE. **2** the condition of being alive. **3** a way of life.

living death *noun* a life so full of misery that death would be preferable.

living fossil *noun* an organism (e.g. a horseshoe crab or coelacanth) that has remained essentially unchanged from much earlier geological times and whose close relatives are usu extinct.

living room *noun* a room in a home used for everyday activities.

living wage *noun* a wage sufficient to provide an acceptable standard of living.

living will *noun* a document detailing a person's wishes with regard to medical treatment, in case they are ever in a situation where they are unable to give informed consent, e.g. to being kept alive on a life support system.

Livonian /li'vohni·ən/ *noun* a native or inhabitant of Livonia on the Baltic Sea. >> **Livonian** *adj*.

lizard /'lizəd/ *noun* any member of a suborder of reptiles distinguished from snakes by two pairs of functional limbs (sometimes lacking in burrowing lizards), external ears, and eyes with movable lids: suborder Lacertilia. [Middle English *liserd* via French from Latin *lacerta*]

LJ *abbr* Lord Justice.

Lk. *abbr* Luke (book of the Bible).

ll. *abbr* lines.

'll *contraction* will or shall: *You'll be late*.

llama /'lahmə/ *noun* **1** any of several wild and domesticated S American ruminant mammals with a woolly fleece related to the camels but smaller and without a hump; *esp* the domesticated guanaco: *Lama glama*. **2** cloth made from the hair of the llama. [Spanish *llama* from Quechua]

llano /'l(y)ahnoh/ *noun* (*pl* **llanos**) an open grassy plain, *esp* in Spanish America. [Spanish *llano* plain, from Latin *planum* from *planus* PLAIN[1]]

LLB *abbr* Bachelor of Laws. [Latin *Legum Baccalaureus*]

LLD *abbr* Doctor of Laws. [Latin *Legum Doctor*]

LLM *abbr* Master of Laws. [Latin *Legum Magister*]

Lloyd's /loydz/ *noun* an association of London underwriters specializing in marine insurance and shipping news and insuring against losses of almost every kind: *We shall all go together when we go … Lloyd's of London will be loaded when we go* — Tom Lehrer. [named after Edward *Lloyd* d.1726, English coffee-house keeper whose premises in London became the centre of shipbroking and marine insurance business]

lm *abbr* lumen.

LMS *abbr* local management of schools.

LNG *abbr* liquefied natural gas.

lo /loh/ *interj archaic* used to call attention or to express wonder or surprise. ✱ **lo and behold** *usu humorous* used to greet the surprise appearance of somebody or something or to introduce a surprising event in a story. [Old English *lā*]

loach /lohch/ *noun* any of a family of small freshwater fishes related to the carps, which have a long slender body and spines round the mouth: family Cobitidae. [Middle English *loche*, from Old French]

load[1] /lohd/ *noun* **1a** an amount, *esp* a large or heavy one, that is carried, supported, or borne; a burden. **b** (*often in combinations*) the quantity that can be carried at one time by a specified means: *a boatload of tourists*. **2** the forces to which a structure is subjected: *the load on the arch*. **3** a burden of responsibility, anxiety, etc: *Hearing you say that took a load off her mind*. **4** external resistance overcome by a machine or other source of power. **5a** power output, e.g. of a power plant. **b** a device to which power is delivered. **6** the amount of work to be performed by a person, machine, etc. **7** *informal* (*also in pl*) a large quantity or amount; a lot: *She's talking a load of rubbish*; *There's loads of room on the back seat*. ✱ **get a load of** *informal* to pay attention to (something surprising). **get/have a load on** *NAmer, informal* to be intoxicated or drunk. [Old English *lād* support, carrying]

load[2] *verb trans* **1a** to put a load in or on (e.g. a vehicle): *load a van with furniture*. **b** to place (something) in or on a vehicle or ship: *load the furniture into the van*. **2** to encumber or oppress (somebody) with something heavy, laborious, or disheartening; to burden (them): *The company is loaded down with debts*. **3a** to weight or shape (dice) so that they fall unfairly. **b** to make (something) subject to one-sided or prejudicial influences; to bias (it). **c** to charge (something) with emotional associations or hidden implications: *a loaded statement*. **4a** to insert something into (a device) so that it is ready to operate, *esp* to put bullets, ammunition, etc into (a gun): *Fortunately, the pistol wasn't loaded*. **b** to place or insert (e.g. a film or tape) in a device or piece of equipment. **5** to affect, often adversely, (the output of a preceding stage of an electrical circuit). > *verb intrans* **1** to receive a load. **2** to put a load on or in a carrier, device, or container; *esp* to insert the charge in a firearm. ✱ **load the dice** (*often + against/in favour of*) to prearrange all the elements of a situation, *esp* to somebody's advantage or disadvantage: *The dice of God are always loaded* — Ralph Waldo Emerson. >> **loader** *noun*.

loaded *adj* **1** carrying a load. **2** said of a question, argument, etc: misleading or biased. **3** said of e.g. a dice: weighted so that it falls unfairly. **4** *informal* drunk or intoxicated. **5** *informal* having a large amount of money.

loading *noun* **1** a cargo, weight, or stress placed on something. **2** an amount added, e.g. to the net premium in insurance, to represent business expenses, extra risks, or profit. **3** *Aus* a weighting added to a wage or salary.

loading gauge *noun Brit* a bar suspended over railway tracks to show how high a train may be loaded.

load line *noun* = PLIMSOLL LINE.

loadstar *noun* see LODESTAR.

loadstone *noun* see LODESTONE.

loaf[1] /lohf/ *noun* (*pl* **loaves** /lohvz/) **1** a mass of baked bread usu having a regular shape and standard weight. **2** a shaped or moulded and often symmetrical mass of food, e.g. sugar or chopped cooked meat. **3** *Brit, informal* the head or brains: *Use your loaf!* [Old English *hlāf*; (sense 3) rhyming slang *loaf (of bread)* head]

loaf[2] *verb intrans* to spend time in idleness. [prob back-formation from LOAFER]

loafer *noun* **1** a person who loafs; an idler or slacker. **2** *trademark* a low leather shoe similar to a moccasin but with a broad flat heel. [perhaps short for landloafer, from German *Landläufer* tramp; (sense 2) from *Loafer*, a trademark]

loam /lohm/ *noun* **1** rich crumbly soil consisting of a mixture of clay, silt, and sand. **2** a mixture of clay, sand, and other materials used e.g. for plastering. ➤➤ **loaminess** *noun*, **loamy** *adj*. [Old English *lām*]

loan[1] /lohn/ *noun* **1a** money lent at interest. **b** something lent, usu for the borrower's temporary use. **2** permission to use something temporarily. **3** a loanword. ✴ **on loan** being kept or used by a borrower. [Middle English *lon* from Old Norse *lān*]

loan[2] *verb trans* to lend (something): *The portrait has been loaned to the gallery by its unnamed owner.* ➤➤ **loanable** *adj*, **loaner** *noun*.
Usage note
See note at LEND.

loan shark *noun informal* a person who lends money to individuals at exorbitant rates of interest.

loan translation *noun* a word or phrase introduced into a language through translation of the elements of a term in another language, e.g. *superman* from German *Übermensch*. Also called CALQUE.

loanword *noun* a word taken from another language and at least partly naturalized.

loath *or* **loth** /lohth/ *adj* (*usu* + to) unwilling to do something; reluctant: *I was loath to leave the warmth of the fire.* ✴ **nothing loath** perfectly willing to fall in with a proposal, etc: *Neither of us seemed disposed to continue digging, and when he suggested a meal, I was nothing loath* — H G Wells. [Old English *lāth* hostile, repulsive]
Usage note
loath, loth, *or* loathe? *Loath* and *loth* are alternative spellings of the same word, an adjective meaning 'reluctant': *She was very loath to part with the money. Loath* is the preferred spelling in modern English. *Loathe* is a verb meaning 'to dislike intensely': *I absolutely loathe greasy food.*

loathe /lohdh/ *verb trans* to dislike (somebody or something) intensely, often with a feeling of disgust. ➤➤ **loather** *noun*. [Old English *lāthian*, from *lāth* hostile, repulsive]
Usage note
loathe, loath, *or* loth? See note at LOATH.

loathing /'lohdhing/ *noun* extreme dislike; disgust; detestation.

loathsome /'lohdhs(ə)m, 'lohths(ə)m/ *adj* giving rise to loathing; hateful; disgusting. ➤➤ **loathsomely** *adv*, **loathsomeness** *noun*. [Middle English *lothsum*, from *loth* evil, from Old English *lāth*, from *lāth* (adj) hostile, repulsive]

loaves /lohvz/ *noun* pl of LOAF[1].

lob[1] /lob/ *verb* (**lobbed**, **lobbing**) ➤ *verb trans* **1** to throw, hit, or propel (e.g. a ball) gently or in a high arc. **2** in sports, to hit or kick the ball over (an opponent) in a high arc: *She lobbed him as he came in to the net.* ➤ *verb intrans* to hit a ball easily in a high arc, *esp* in tennis, squash, etc.
Word history
obsolete *lob* pollock, later 'lout, loosely hanging object' prob of Low German or Flemish origin. The verb originally meant 'to behave like a lout', hence 'to move or to throw something clumsily or carelessly'.

lob[2] *noun* **1** a ball that is lobbed. **2** in cricket, a ball bowled in a high arc.

lobar /'lohbə/ *adj* relating to or affecting a lobe, e.g. the lobe of a lung.

lobate /'lohbayt/ *adj* **1** having or resembling a lobe or lobes. **2** said of a bird: having separate fringed toes. ➤➤ **lobation** /loh'baysh(ə)n/ *noun*. [Latin *lobatus*, from late Latin *lobus*: see LOBE]

lobby[1] /'lobi/ *noun* (*pl* **lobbies**) **1a** a porch or small entrance hall. **b** a large entrance hall serving as a foyer, e.g. in a hotel or theatre.

2 an anteroom of a legislative chamber, *esp* either of two anterooms to which members of either of the Houses of Parliament go to vote during a division. **3** (*treated as sing. or pl*) a group of people engaged in lobbying as representatives of a particular interest group. [late Latin *lobium* gallery, of Germanic origin]

lobby[2] *verb* (**lobbies**, **lobbied**, **lobbying**) ➤ *verb intrans* to try to influence members of a legislative body in favour of or against a policy or course of action. ➤ *verb trans* **1** to try to influence (e.g. a member of a legislative body) with respect to a particular issue. **2** to secure the passage of (legislation) by influencing public officials. ➤➤ **lobbyer** *noun*, **lobbyist** *noun*.

lobby correspondent *noun Brit* a parliamentary correspondent, e.g. of a newspaper, given information unofficially by Ministers, which may be used without naming the source.

lobe /lohb/ *noun* a curved or rounded projection or division; *esp* such a projection or division of a bodily organ or part. ➤➤ **lobed** *adj*. [early French *lobe* via late Latin *lobus* from Greek *lobos*]

lobectomy /loh'bektəmi/ *noun* (*pl* **lobectomies**) surgical removal of a lobe of an organ, e.g. a lung, or gland.

lobelia /loh'beelyə, lə-/ *noun* any of a genus of widely distributed and cultivated herbaceous plants with clusters of small showy blue or red flowers: genus *Lobelia*. [Latin genus name, named after Matthias de *Lobel* d.1616, Flemish botanist]

loblolly pine /'lobloli/ *noun* a pine of the southern USA with flaky reddish bark, long needles in groups of three, and spiny-tipped cones: *Pinus taeda*. [*loblolly* a thick gruel, in the US; because the tree grows in swampy ground]

lobola /lə'bohlə/ *or* **lobolo** /-loh/ *noun* an African custom whereby the groom's family gives the bride's family a payment in cattle or cash shortly before a wedding. [Bantu *ukulobola* to pay a bride price]

lobotomize *or* **lobotomise** /lə'botəmiez/ *verb trans* to perform a lobotomy on (somebody).

lobotomy /lə'botəmi/ *noun* (*pl* **lobotomies**) a brain operation used, *esp* formerly, in the treatment of some mental disorders, e.g. violent psychoses, in which nerve fibres in the cerebral cortex are cut in order to change behaviour. [LOBE + -TOMY]

lobscouse /'lobskows/ *noun* a dish formerly eaten by sailors, made by stewing or baking meat with vegetables and ship's biscuit. [origin unknown]

lobster /'lobstə/ *noun* (*pl* **lobsters** *or collectively* **lobster**) **1** any of a family of large edible ten-legged marine crustaceans that have stalked eyes, a pair of large claws, and a long abdomen: family Homaridae. **2** the flesh of a lobster used as food. [Old English *loppestre*, modification of Latin *locusta* crustacean, lobster, prob influenced by Old English *loppe* spider]

lobster pot *noun* a basket used as a trap for catching lobsters.

lobster thermidor /'thuhmidaw/ *noun* a dish of lobster cooked in a cream sauce and served in its shell with a grilled cheese topping. [French *Thermidor*, the eleventh month of the French Revolutionary calendar, from Greek *thermē* heat + *dōron* gift]

lobule /'lobyoohl/ *noun* a small lobe. ➤➤ **lobular** *adj*, **lobulate** *adj*.

lobworm /'lobwuhm/ *noun* a large earthworm used as bait by anglers; a lugworm. [obsolete *lob* (see LOB[1]) in the sense 'a loosely hanging object' + WORM[1]]

local[1] /'lohk(ə)l/ *adj* **1** characteristic of or belonging to a particular place; not general or widespread: *local news.* **2** primarily serving the needs of a particular limited district: *local government.* **3** involving or affecting only a restricted part of a living organism: *local anaesthetic.* **4** characterized by or relating to position in space. ➤➤ **locally** *adv*. [Middle English via French from late Latin *localis*, from Latin *locus* place]

local[2] *noun* **1** a local person or thing: *I spoke to some friendly locals.* **2a** *Brit, informal* the neighbourhood pub. **b** *NAmer* a local branch of an organization; *esp* a union branch.

local anaesthetic *noun* an anaesthetic that causes loss of sensation in a specific area of the body only and does not cause the patient to lose consciousness.

local area network *noun* a communications system linking together computer terminals in an office building, manufacturing plant, etc.

local authority *noun Brit* the body of people who have political and administrative power in a British city, district, etc.

local colour *noun* the description in a literary work of the features and peculiarities of a particular locality and its inhabitants.

locale /loh'kahl/ *noun* a place or locality, *esp* when viewed in relation to a particular event or characteristic; a scene. [modification of French *local*: see LOCAL[1]]

local government *noun* the government of a specific local subdivision of a major political unit.

localise *verb trans* see LOCALIZE.

localism *noun* 1 affection or partiality for a particular place, *esp* to the exclusion of others. 2 a local idiom or custom.

locality /loh'kaliti/ *noun* (*pl* **localities**) 1 a particular place, situation, or location: *His head was as bald as the palm of my hand, but his hair in falling seemed to have stuck to his chin, and had prospered in the new locality* — Joseph Conrad. 2 the fact or condition of having a location in space or time.

localize *or* **localise** *verb trans* 1 to restrict (something) to a particular place. 2 to assign (something) to or keep (it) within a definite locality. 3 to give local characteristics to (something). >>> **localizable** *adj*, **localization** /-ie'zaysh(ə)n/ *noun*.

local option *noun* the right of an area's local government to regulate an activity, e.g. the sale of alcohol, in that area.

local time *noun* time based on the meridian through a particular place, as contrasted with that of an area in which the time is standardized.

locate /loh'kayt/ *verb trans* 1 to determine, discover, or indicate the position, site, or limits of (something). 2 to set or establish (something) in a particular spot. >>> *verb intrans* NAmer to establish oneself or one's business in a particular place; to settle. >>> **locatable** *adj*, **locater** *noun*. [Latin *locatus*, past part. of *locare* to place, from *locus* place]

location /loh'kaysh(ə)n/ *noun* 1 a particular place or position. 2 a place outside a studio where a broadcast or film is made: *The outdoor scenes were filmed on location in Yorkshire.* 3 SAfr under the apartheid system, a segregated residential area for blacks on the outskirts of a town or city. >>> **locational** *adj*.

locative[1] /'lokətiv/ *adj* denoting a grammatical case expressing the idea of location in or movement towards a particular place. [Latin *locus* place + -ATIVE]

locative[2] *noun* the locative case or a word in this case.

loc. cit. /,lok 'sit/ *abbr* in the place cited. [Latin *loco citato* in the place cited]

loch /lokh/ *noun* a lake or nearly landlocked arm of the sea in Scotland. [Middle English from Scottish Gaelic]

lochia /'loki·ə/ *noun* a discharge of blood and mucus from the womb following childbirth. >>> **lochial** *adj*. [via Latin from Greek *lochia*, neuter pl of *lochios* of childbirth, from *lochos* childbirth]

loci /'lohsie, 'lohkie/ *noun* pl of LOCUS.

lock[1] /lok/ *noun* 1 a fastening that can be opened and often closed only by means of a particular key or combination. 2 an enclosed section of waterway, e.g. a canal, which has gates at each end and in which the water level can be raised or lowered to move boats from one level to another. 3 in wrestling, a hold secured on a usu specified body part. 4 *chiefly Brit* the extent to which the front wheels of a vehicle are turned to change the direction of travel. 5 = LOCK FORWARD. 6 *archaic* a gunlock. [Old English *loc*]

lock[2] *verb trans* 1a to fasten the lock of (something). b to make (something) fast with or as if with a lock. 2 to shut (somebody) in or out, or to make (something) secure or inaccessible, by or as if by means of locks: *He had locked himself away from the curious world.* 3a to fix (something) immovably by means of a securing mechanism or through parts becoming jammed. b to fix (somebody or something) in a particular situation or method of operation: *Administration and students were locked in conflict.* 4a to hold (somebody) in a close embrace. b to grapple (somebody) in combat. 5 to move or permit (e.g. a ship) to pass by raising or lowering it in a lock. >>> *verb intrans* 1a to be fitted and fastenable with a lock. b to become locked, e.g. when closed. 2 to become fixed or jammed immovably. * **lock horns** to engage in an argument or dispute. >>> **lockable** *adj*.

lock[3] *noun* 1a a curl, tuft, etc of hair. b *literary* (*in pl*) the hair of the head. 2 a tuft or bunch of wool, cotton, etc. [Old English *locc*]

locker *noun* 1 a cupboard or compartment that may be closed with a lock; *esp* one for individual storage use. 2 a chest or compartment on board ship.

locket /'lokit/ *noun* a small case usu of precious metal that has space for a memento, e.g. a small picture, and is usu worn on a chain round the neck. [early French *loquet* dimin. of *loc* latch, lock, of Germanic origin; related to Old English *loc* LOCK[1]]

lock forward *noun* in rugby, either of two players positioned inside the second row of the scrum.

lockjaw *noun* 1 an early symptom of tetanus characterized by spasm of the jaw muscles and inability to open the jaws. 2 = TETANUS.

locknut *noun* 1 a nut screwed hard up against another to prevent either of them from moving. 2 a nut so constructed that it locks itself when screwed up tight.

lock on *verb trans* (often + to) to sight and follow (a target) automatically by means of a radar beam or sensor.

lockout *noun* a whole or partial closing of a business by an employer in order to gain concessions from or resist demands of employees.

lock out *verb trans* 1 to prevent (somebody) from entering a place by locking the door, gate, etc. 2 to subject (a body of employees) to a lockout.

locksmith *noun* somebody who makes or mends locks as an occupation.

lockstep *noun* a mode of marching in step as closely as possible.

lockstitch *noun* a sewing machine stitch formed by looping together two threads, one on each side of the material being sewn.

lock, stock, and barrel *adv* wholly or completely. [from the principal parts of a flintlock]

lockup *noun* 1 a prison, *esp* a small or temporary one. 2 *Brit* a shop or garage that can be locked up. 3 an investment that is meant to be held over a long term.

lock up *verb trans* 1 to lock (a building): *Have you locked up the house?* 2 to put (somebody) in prison or a place of confinement. 3 to invest (capital) in such a way that it cannot easily be converted into ready money.

loco[1] /'lohkoh/ *noun* (*pl* **locos**) *informal* a locomotive.

loco[2] *adj informal* out of one's mind. [Spanish *loco* insane]

locomotion /lohkə'mohsh(ə)n/ *noun* the act or power of moving from place to place. [Latin *locus* place + MOTION[1]]

locomotive[1] /lohkə'mohtiv/ *noun* an engine that moves under its own power, *esp* one that moves railway carriages and wagons.

locomotive[2] *adj* 1 relating to or assisting movement from place to place. 2 moving, or able to move, by self-propulsion.

locomotor *adj* 1 = LOCOMOTIVE[2]. 2 affecting or involving the locomotive organs of the body.

locoweed *noun* any of several leguminous plants of N America that cause madness in livestock: genera *Astragalus* and *Oxytropis*. [Spanish *loco* crazy + WEED[1]]

loculus /'lokyoolas/ *noun* (*pl* **loculi** /-lee/) a small chamber or cavity, *esp* in a plant or animal body. >>> **locular** *adj*. [Latin *loculus* compartment, dimin. of *locus* place]

locum /'lohkəm/ *noun informal* somebody, *esp* a doctor or cleric, filling an office for a time or temporarily taking the place of another. [short for LOCUM TENENS]

locum tenens /'tenenz/ *noun* (*pl* **locum tenentes** /te'nenteez, -tiz/) *formal* = LOCUM. [late Latin *locum tenens* one holding a place]

locus /'lohkəs, 'lokəs/ *noun* (*pl* **loci** /'lohsie, 'lohkie/) 1 a place or locality. 2 in mathematics, the set of all points whose location is determined by a stated condition or conditions. 3 in genetics, the position on a chromosome of a particular gene or allele. [Latin *locus* place]

locust /'lohkəst/ *noun* 1 any of numerous migratory short-horned grasshoppers that often travel in vast swarms in warm and tropical parts of Asia and Africa, stripping the areas they pass through of all vegetation: genera *Locusta* and *Melanophus*: compare GRASSHOPPER. 2 any of various hard-wooded trees of the pea family, e.g.: a the carob tree: *Ceratonia siliqua*. b a tall N American tree with thorns and hanging clusters of fragrant white flowers: *Robinia pseudoacacia*. [Middle English from Latin *locusta* locust, crustacean; (sense 2) from the pods allegedly resembling locusts]

locust tree *noun* = LOCUST (2).

locution /lə'kyoohsh(ə)n/ *noun* 1 a word or expression characteristic of a region, group, or cultural level. 2 a style or manner of speaking. [Middle English *locucioun* from Latin *locution-, locutio*, from *loqui* to speak]

lode /lohd/ *noun* an ore deposit. [Old English *lād* course, support]

loden *noun* **1** a thick woollen waterproof cloth used for making coats *esp* in Germany and Austria. **2** a dull greyish green colour typical of this cloth. [German *Loden* from Old High German *lodo* coarse cloth]

lodestar *or* **loadstar** *noun* **1** a star that guides, *esp* the pole star. **2** something that serves as a guiding star. [Middle English *lode sterre*, from LODE in an obsolete sense 'course, way']

lodestone *or* **loadstone** *noun* **1** a piece of magnetized mineral iron oxide. **2** something that strongly attracts; a magnet. [LODE in an obsolete sense 'course, way' + STONE[1]; from the magnet's use in navigation]

lodge[1] /loj/ *noun* **1** a house lived in only during a particular season, e.g. the hunting season. **2a** a small house orig for the use of a game-keeper, caretaker, porter, etc. **b** a porter's room, e.g. at the entrance to a college, block of flats, etc. **c** the house where the head of a university college lives, *esp* in Cambridge. **d** (*often* **Lodge**) a large house or hotel. **3a** the meeting place of a branch of a fraternal organization: *a Masonic lodge*. **b** a particular branch of such an organization, or its members collectively. **4** a den or lair of an animal or a group of animals, e.g. beavers or otters. **5** a Native American tent or dwelling. [Middle English from Old French *loge* hut, of Germanic origin]

lodge[2] *verb trans* **1** to provide temporary, *esp* rented, accommodation for (somebody). **2** to fix (something) firmly in place. **3** to lay (e.g. a complaint) before an authority. **4** to deposit (e.g. money) for safekeeping. **5** to place or vest (e.g. power) in somebody or something. **6** to beat (e.g. a crop) flat to the ground. ➤ *verb intrans* **1a** to occupy a place, *esp* temporarily. **b** to be a lodger. **2** to come to rest, *esp* to become firmly fixed, in a particular place: *The bullet lodged in his chest.* **3** said of hay or grain crops: to fall or lie down.

lodger *noun* somebody who occupies a rented room in somebody else's house.

lodging *noun* **1** a place to live; a dwelling. **2a** a temporary place to stay: *a lodging for the night.* **b** (*in pl*) a rented room or rooms for residing in, usu in a private house rather than a hotel.

lodging house *noun* a house where lodgings are provided and let.

loess /'loh·is, les/ *noun* a usu yellowish brown loamy deposit found in Europe, Asia, and N America and believed to be chiefly deposited by the wind. ➤➤ **loessial** *adj*. [German *Löss*]

loft[1] /loft/ *noun* **1a** = ATTIC. **b** *NAmer* an upper room or floor. **2a** a gallery in a church or hall. **b** (*often in combination*) an upper floor in a barn or warehouse used for storage: *a hayloft.* **c** a shed or coop for pigeons. **3a** in golf, the backward slant of the face of a club head. **b** a stroke or shot using this. [Old English from Old Norse *lopt* air]

loft[2] *verb trans* to propel (e.g. a ball) high up into the air: *I lofted the ball over midwicket.*

lofty *adj* (**loftier, loftiest**) **1** rising to a great height; impressively high: *lofty mountains.* **2a** elevated in character and spirit; noble: *Who would not sing for Lycidas? He knew himself to sing, and build the lofty rhyme* — Milton. **b** elevated in position; superior. **3** having a haughty overbearing manner; supercilious. ➤➤ **loftily** *adv*, **lofti-ness** *noun*.

log[1] /log/ *noun* **1** a usu bulky piece or length of unshaped timber ready for sawing or for use as firewood. **2a** the record of the rate of a ship's speed or daily progress. **b** the full nautical record of a ship's voyage. **c** the full record of a flight by an aircraft. **3** an apparatus for measuring the rate of a ship's motion through the water; formerly consisting of a wooden float tied to a line. **4** any of various records of performance: *a computer log.* [Middle English *logge*, prob of Scandinavian origin]

log[2] *verb* (**logged, logging**) ➤ *verb trans* **1** to enter details of or about (something) in a log. **2a** to move or attain (e.g. an indicated distance, speed, or time) as noted in a log. **b** to sail a ship or fly an aircraft for (an indicated distance or period of time). **c** (*often* + up) to have (something) to one's credit: *He usually logged about 30,000 miles a year in his car.* **3** to cut (trees) for timber. ➤ *verb intrans* to cut logs for timber.

log[3] *noun* = LOGARITHM.

-log *comb. form NAmer* see -LOGUE.

loganberry /'lohgənb(ə)ri, -beri/ *noun* (*pl* **loganberries**) **1** a sweet red edible berry, a hybrid of a raspberry and a dewberry. **2** the prickly plant that bears this fruit: *Rubus loganobaccus.* [named after James H *Logan* d.1928, US lawyer and horticulturalist, who first grew it]

logarithm /'logəridh(ə)m/ *noun* the exponent that indicates the power to which a number is raised to produce a given number: *The logarithm of 100 to the base 10 is 2.* ➤➤ **logarithmic** /-'ridhmik/ *adj*, **logarithmically** /-'ridhmikli/ *adv*. [Latin *logarithmus*, from Greek *logos* ratio + *arithmos* number]

logbook *noun* **1** a book used to record the details of a ship's voyage or an aircraft's flight. **2** *Brit* = REGISTRATION DOCUMENT.

loge /lohzh/ *noun* a private box in a theatre. [French *loge*: see LODGE[1]]

logger *noun NAmer* a lumberjack.

loggerhead *noun* **1** any of various very large marine turtles; *esp* a flesh-eating turtle of the W Atlantic: *Caretta caretta.* **2** an iron tool consisting of a long handle ending in a ball or bulb used to melt tar or to heat liquids. **3** *archaic* a fool or dunce: *'Where hast thou been, Hal?' 'With three or four loggerheads amongst three or fourscore hogsheads'* — Shakespeare. ✱ **at loggerheads** in quarrelsome disagreement: *For nearly two years, England played with a manager and captain at loggerheads* — Today. [prob from English dialect *logger* block of wood + HEAD[1]]

loggia /'loj(i)ə/ *noun* (*pl* **loggias** *or* **loggie** /'lojie/) a roofed open gallery behind a colonnade or arcade. [Italian *loggia* from French *loge*: see LODGE[1]]

logic /'lojik/ *noun* **1a** a science that deals with the formal principles and structure of thought and reasoning and assesses reasoned arguments on the basis of their validity or invalidity. **b** a specified branch or system of logic. **c** a particular mode of reasoning viewed as valid or faulty: *I couldn't follow his logic.* **2** rationality or a rationally discernible sequence in thought or argument, as opposed to irrationality or emotionalism. **3** an inevitable progression of cause and effect following a particular event, set of circumstances, etc. **4a** the fundamental principles and the connection of circuit elements for performing Boolean operations, e.g. those needed for arithmetical computation, in a computer. **b** the circuits themselves. ➤➤ **logician** /lo'jish(ə)n, lə-/ *noun*. [Middle English *logik* via French and Latin from Greek *logikē*, fem of *logikos* of reason, from *logos* word, reason]

logical *adj* **1** of or conforming with logic: *a logical argument.* **2** capable of reasoning or of using reason in an orderly fashion: *a logical thinker.* ➤➤ **logicality** /-'kaliti/ *noun*, **logically** *adv*.

logical positivism *noun* a philosophical movement of the 20th cent. stressing linguistic analysis and rejecting metaphysical theories. ➤➤ **logical positivist** *noun*.

logic bomb *noun* a computer virus designed to become active in specific circumstances.

log in *verb intrans* = LOG ON.

logistics /lo'jistiks, lə-/ *pl noun* (*treated as sing. or pl*) **1** the work of planning and organizing the details of a large and complex operation. **2** the management of the flow of materials through an organization or manufacturing process. **3** the aspect of military science dealing with the transportation, quartering, and supplying of troops in military operations. ➤➤ **logistic** *adj*, **logistically** *adv*. [French *logistique* art of calculating, logistics, from Greek *logistikē* art of calculating, from *logizein* to calculate, from *logos* reason]

logjam /'logjam/ *noun* **1** a deadlock or impasse. **2** a mass of logs jammed together in a river, causing a blockage.

logo /'logoh, 'lohgoh/ *noun* (*pl* **logos**) an identifying symbol used by a company, e.g. in its advertising. [LOGOGRAM *or* LOGOTYPE]

logo- *comb. form* forming words, denoting: thought or speech: *logogram; logorrhoea.* [Greek *logo-* from *logos* word]

log off *verb intrans* to end a session at a computer terminal by performing a fixed set of operations, *esp* by entering a command.

logogram /'logəgram/ *noun* a character or sign used, e.g. in shorthand, to represent an entire word: compare IDEOGRAM, PICTOGRAPH.

Logoi /'logoy/ *noun* pl of LOGOS.

log on *verb intrans* to begin a session at a computer terminal by performing a fixed set of operations, *esp* by entering a command and a password.

logorrhoea (NAmer **logorrhea**) /logə'riə/ noun excessive and often incoherent talkativeness or wordiness. [Latin logorrhoea, from Greek logos word + rhoia flow]

Logos /'logos/ noun (pl **Logoi** /'logoy/) **1** in philosophy, cosmic reason that gives order and form to the world. **2** (**the Logos**) the divine wisdom manifest in the creation and redemption of the world, identified in Christian thought with the second person of the Trinity. [Greek logos speech, word, reason]

logotype /'logətiep/ noun **1** a single block or piece of type that prints a whole word, e.g. the name of a newspaper. **2** an identifying symbol, e.g. for advertising; a logo.

log out verb intrans = LOG OFF.

logrolling noun NAmer **1** the trading of votes by members of a legislature to secure favourable action on projects of mutual interest. **2** a sport in which people treading logs try to dislodge one another. [(sense 1) from a former US custom of neighbours assisting one another in rolling logs]

-logue (NAmer **-log**) comb. form forming nouns, denoting: conversation; talk: duologue; epilogue. [Middle English -logue via Old French and Latin from Greek -logos, from legein to speak]

logwood noun **1** a Central American and W Indian tree of the pea family with hard heavy wood: Haematoxylon campechianum. **2** the brown or reddish brown heartwood of this tree, which yields a dye.

-logy or **-ology** comb. form forming nouns, denoting: **1** doctrine, theory, or science: ethnology. **2** oral or written expression: phraseology. **3** writings of a specified kind or on a specified subject: trilogy; hagiology. [Middle English -logie via Old French and Latin from Greek, from logos word]

loin /loyn/ noun **1a** the part of a human being or quadruped on each side of the spinal column between the hipbone and the lower ribs. **b** a cut of meat comprising this part of one or both sides of a carcass with the adjoining half of the vertebrae included. **2** (in pl). **a** the upper and lower abdominal regions and the region about the hips. **b** the pubic region; the crotch. **c** the genitals. ✳ **gird (up) one's loins** see GIRD[1]. [Middle English loyne via French from Latin lumbus]

loincloth noun a cloth worn about the hips and covering the genitals.

loiter /'loytə/ verb intrans (**loitered, loitering**) **1** to remain in an area for no obvious reason; to hang about. **2** to make frequent pauses while travelling; to dawdle. ➤➤ **loiterer** noun. [Middle English loiteren, prob from early Dutch loteren to waggle, be loose]

loll /lol/ verb intrans **1** to recline, lean, or move in a lazy or excessively relaxed manner; to lounge: I won't lie neither, but loll and lean upon one elbow: with one foot a little dangling off, jogging in a thoughtful way — Congreve. **2** to hang down loosely: His tongue lolled out. [Middle English lollen, prob of imitative origin]

Lollard /'loləd/ noun any of the followers of the English religious reformer John Wycliffe who travelled in the 14th and 15th cents as lay preachers throughout England and Scotland. ➤➤ **Lollardism** noun, **Lollardry** noun. [Middle English, from Middle Dutch lollaert, literally 'mumbler' (orig applied to a charitable brotherhood, and later to various religious groups), from lollen to mumble]

lollipop /'lolipop/ noun **1** a large often round flat sweet of boiled sugar on the end of a stick. **2** Brit an ice lolly. [prob from English dialect lolly tongue + POP[1]]

lollipop man or **lollipop lady** noun (pl **lollipop men** or **lollipop ladies**) Brit, informal somebody controlling traffic to allow children to cross busy roads, esp near a school. [from the warning sign he or she carries, shaped like a lollipop]

lollop /'loləp/ verb intrans (**lolloped, lolloping**) to move or proceed with an ungainly loping motion. [LOLL + -op as in GALLOP[1]]

lollo rosso /,loloh 'rosoh/ noun a variety of lettuce with curly reddish leaves and a slightly bitter taste. [Italian lollo rosso]

lolly /'loli/ noun (pl **lollies**) **1** a lollipop or ice lolly. **2** Brit, informal = MONEY. [short for LOLLIPOP]

Lombard /'lombahd, 'lombəd/ noun **1** a member of a Teutonic people who invaded Italy and settled in the Po valley in the sixth cent. **2** a native or inhabitant of Lombardy in N Italy. ➤➤ **Lombardic** /lom'bahdik/ adj. [Middle English Lumbarde via French and Old Italian from Latin Langobardus, of Germanic origin]

Lombardy poplar /'lombədi/ noun a much planted tall narrow European poplar with upward-sloping branches: Populus nigra italica. [Lombardy, a district of Italy where it originated]

Londoner /'lund(ə)nə/ noun a native or inhabitant of London.

London pride /'lundn/ noun a plant of the saxifrage family with small pinkish white flowers growing out of a rosette of leaves: Saxifraga urbium.

lone /lohn/ adj **1** only or sole. **2** situated alone or separately; isolated. **3** formal having no company; solitary. [Middle English, short for ALONE]

lonely adj (**lonelier, loneliest**) **1** sad from being alone or without friends. **2** cut off from others; solitary. **3** not frequented by people; desolate. ➤➤ **loneliness** noun.

lonely hearts pl noun lonely people seeking companions or spouses: a lonely hearts club.

loner noun a person or animal that prefers solitude.

lonesome[1] /'lohns(ə)m/ adj **1** chiefly NAmer = LONELY. **2** remote or desolate: like one, that on a lonesome road doth walk in fear and dread, and having once turned round walks on, and turns no more his head; because he knows, a frightful fiend doth close behind him tread — Coleridge. ➤➤ **lonesomely** adv, **lonesomeness** noun.

lonesome[2] ✳ **on/by one's lonesome** informal by oneself; alone.

lone wolf noun a person who prefers to work, act, or live alone.

long[1] /long/ adj **1a** extending for a considerable distance. **b** having greater length or height than usual. **2a** having a specified length: 2 metres long. **b** forming the chief linear dimension: the long side of the room. **3** extending over a considerable or specified time: a long friendship; two hours long. **4** containing a large or specified number of items or units: a long list; 300 pages long. **5a** said of a speech sound or syllable: of relatively long duration. **b** being one of a pair of similarly spelt vowel sounds that is longer in duration: There is a long 'a' in fate. **c** bearing a stress or accent. **6a** having the capacity to reach or extend a considerable distance: a long left jab. **b** hit for a considerable distance: a long drive from the tee. **7a** said of betting odds: greatly differing in the amounts wagered on each side. **b** subject to great odds; unlikely: a long chance. **8** owning or accumulating securities or goods, esp in anticipation of an advance in prices: They are now long on wheat. ✳ **before long** in a short time; soon. **be long** informal to take a long time: Will you be long in there? **in the long run** in the course of sufficiently prolonged time, trial, or experience. **long in the tooth** past one's best days; old [from the fact that the gums recede in old age, making the teeth appear longer]. **long on** informal having a large amount of, or being well endowed with: He's long on good looks, but rather short on brains. **not by a long chalk** see CHALK[1]. ➤➤ **longish** adj. [Old English long, lang]

long[2] adv (**longer, longest**) **1** for a long time: I was excited long before the big day. **2** throughout a specified period: all night long. **3** said of somebody striking a ball: over a long distance or past the target. ✳ **no longer 1** not now, though usu previously: They're no longer at that address. **2** not for a greater length of time: I could wait no longer and left. **so/as long as 1** during and up to the end of the time that; while. **2** = PROVIDING. **so long** informal goodbye.

long[3] noun **1** a long period of time: We couldn't stay for long. **2** a long syllable. ✳ **the long and (the) short** the gist; the outline: The long and the short of it was that we had to walk home.

long[4] verb intrans (often + for) to feel a strong desire or craving, esp for something not likely to be attained: They longed for peace. [Old English langian to prolong, dwell on, yearn]

long. abbr longitude.

long ago noun the distant past. ➤➤ **long-ago** adj.

longboat noun the largest boat carried by a sailing vessel.

longbow noun **1** the medieval English yew or ash bow of about 2m (6ft) in length. **2** a similar bow used in archery.

long-dated adj **1** said of gilt-edged stocks or bonds: redeemable after a long period, usu 15 years or more. **2** said of a bill of exchange: payable after three or more months.

long-day adj said of a plant: producing flowers only on exposure to long periods of daylight.

long-distance[1] adj **1** covering or effective over a long distance: a long-distance race. **2** said of telephone communications: between points a long distance apart: a long-distance call.

long-distance[2] adv by long-distance telephone: I called her long-distance.

long division *noun* arithmetical division in which the calculations corresponding to the division of parts of the dividend by the divisor are written out.

long-drawn *adj* = LONG-DRAWN-OUT.

long-drawn-out *adj* extended to a great length; protracted.

long drink *noun* a cool refreshing drink containing a comparatively large quantity of liquid but little or no alcohol.

longeron /'lonjərən/ *noun* a fore-and-aft framing member of an aircraft fuselage. [French *longeron*, from *allonger* to make long, ultimately from Latin *longus* long]

longevity /lon'jeviti, long-/ *noun* great length of life: *a study of longevity.* [late Latin *longaevitas* from Latin *longaevus* long-lived, from *longus* long + *aevum* age]

longhair *noun* a person with, or usu thought of as having, long hair, e.g. a hippie or somebody of an artistic, *esp* avant-garde, temperament.

longhand *noun* ordinary writing; handwriting.

long haul *noun* **1** a lengthy usu difficult period of time: *the long haul back to health.* **2** the transport of goods or passengers over long distances.

long-headed *adj* *dated* having unusual foresight or wisdom. ⟫⟫ **long-headedness** *noun*.

long hop *noun* in cricket, an easily hit short-pitched delivery of a ball.

longhorn *noun* a breed of long-horned cattle of Spanish derivation.

longhorn beetle *noun* any of various beetles usu distinguished by their very long antennae: family Cerambycidae.

longing *noun* a strong desire, *esp* for something difficult to attain. ⟫⟫ **longing** *adj*, **longingly** *adv*.

longitude /'lonjityoohd, 'longgityoohd/ *noun* the angular distance of a point on the surface of a celestial body, *esp* the earth, measured E or W from a prime meridian, e.g. that of Greenwich: compare LATITUDE. [Middle English from Latin *longitudin-, longitudo* length, from *longus* long]

longitudinal /lonji'tyoohdinl, longgi-/ *adj* **1** relating to length or the lengthways dimension. **2** placed or running lengthways. **3** dealing with the growth and change of an individual or group over a period of years: *longitudinal studies.* ⟫⟫ **longitudinally** *adv*.

longitudinal wave *noun* a wave, e.g. a sound wave, in which the particles of the medium vibrate in the direction of the line of advance of the wave: compare TRANSVERSE WAVE.

long johns /jonz/ *pl noun informal* underpants with legs extending usu down to the ankles. [from the name *John*]

long jump *noun* an athletic field event consisting of a jump for distance from a running start. ⟫⟫ **long jumper** *noun*.

long leg *noun* in cricket, a fielding position near the boundary behind the batsman on the leg side of the pitch.

long-life *adj* said of a commercial product: processed so as to be long-lasting: *long-life milk.*

long-lived /'livd/ *adj* **1** characterized by long life: *a long-lived family.* **2** long-lasting or enduring. ⟫⟫ **long-livedness** /'liv(i)dnis/ *noun*.

long off *noun* in cricket, a fielding position near the boundary behind the bowler on the off side of the pitch.

long on *noun* in cricket, a fielding position near the boundary behind the bowler on the leg side of the pitch.

long-range *adj* **1** relating to or fit for long distances: *long-range rockets.* **2** involving or taking into account a long period of time: *long-range planning.*

longship *noun* a long open ship propelled by oars and a sail and used by the Vikings principally to carry warriors.

longshore *adj* on, along, or relating to the shore. [from *along shore*]

longshore drift *noun* a process by which material is moved along a shore by a current flowing parallel to the shore-line.

longshoreman *noun* (*pl* **longshoremen**) *NAmer* = DOCKER.

long shot *noun* **1** a venture that involves considerable risk and has little chance of success. **2a** a competitor, e.g. in a horse race, given little chance of winning. **b** a bet on such a competitor made at long odds. ✱ **by a long shot** by a great deal.

longsighted *or* **long-sighted** *adj* unable to see things that are close to the eyes clearly. ⟫⟫ **longsightedly** *adv*, **longsightedness** *noun*.

long-standing *adj* of long duration.

long stop *noun* **1** in cricket, a now largely disused fielding position directly, and some distance, behind the wicketkeeper to stop balls missed by the latter, or a fielder occupying this position. **2** *Brit* somebody or something that provides a final line of defence should normal procedures fail.

long-suffering *adj* patiently enduring pain, difficulty, or provocation. ⟫⟫ **long-sufferingly** *adv*.

long suit *noun* **1** in card games, the suit of which one has the greatest number of cards in one's hand. **2** the activity or quality in which a person excels: *Diplomacy wasn't exactly her long suit.*

long-tailed tit *noun* a very small Eurasian tit with a long tail and largely black, pink, and white plumage: *Aegithalos caudatus.*

long-term *adj* occurring over or involving a relatively long period of time.

long ton *noun* a unit of weight equal to 2240lb (about 1016kg).

longueur /long'guh (*French* lɔ̃gœːr)/ *noun* (*pl* **longueurs** /long'guh(z) (*French* lɔ̃gœːr)/) a dull and tedious part or period. [French *longueur* length, from *long* long, from Latin *longus*]

long vacation *noun* the long summer holiday of British law courts and universities.

long wave *noun* a band of radio waves typically used for sound broadcasting and covering wavelengths of 1000m or more.

longways *adv* = LENGTHWAYS.

long weekend *noun* a short holiday including a weekend.

long-winded /'windid/ *adj* tediously long in speaking or writing. ⟫⟫ **long-windedly** *adv*, **long-windedness** *noun*.

longwise *adv chiefly NAmer* = LENGTHWAYS.

lonicera /lo'nisərə/ *noun* a shrub of the genus *Lonicera*; a honeysuckle. [named after Adam *Lonitzer* d.1586, German botanist]

loo¹ /looh/ *noun Brit, informal* = TOILET. [perhaps modification of French *l'eau* the water, or perhaps from *Waterloo*, an early 20th-cent. trade name for lavatory cisterns]

loo² *noun* an old card game in which the winner of each trick takes a portion of the pool while losing players have to contribute to the next pool. [short for obsolete *lanterloo*, from French *lanturelu* piffle]

loofah /'loohfə/ *noun* a dried seed pod of any of several plants of the cucumber family that is used as a bath sponge. [Latin genus name *Luffa*, from Arabic *lūfa*]

look¹ /look/ *verb trans* **1** to find out or learn (something) by the use of one's eyes: *Look what time it starts; Look what you've done!* **2** to regard (something) intensely; to examine (it): *I couldn't look him in the eye; Don't look a gift horse in the mouth.* **3** to express (something) by the eyes or facial expression: *She looked daggers at him.* **4** to have an appearance that befits or accords with (something): *He really looked the part.* ➤ *verb intrans* **1a** to use the power of sight; *esp* to make a visual search. **b** to direct one's attention: *I'll look into the matter.* **c** to direct the eyes: *Look at him!* **2** to have the appearance of being; to appear or seem: *She looks very ill.* **3** to have a specified outlook: *The house looked east.* ✱ **look after** to take care of (somebody or something). **look here** used to attract attention or for emphasis. **look into** to investigate (something). **look sharp** to be quick; to hurry. [Old English *lōcian*]

look² *noun* **1** an act of looking; a glance: *Stolen looks are nice in chapels* — Leigh Hunt. **2a** a facial expression: *She had a funny look on her face.* **b** (*in pl*) physical appearance, *esp* when pleasing: *He's always worrying about his looks; She has kept her looks.* **c** the general appearance of or impression created by somebody or something: *He has the look of a loser about him.* **3** a style or fashion: *This year's look is aggressive and spiky.*

look³ *interj* used to attract attention or to show annoyance: *Look, what are we going to do about it?*

lookalike *noun* somebody or something that looks like another; a double.

look back *verb intrans* (*often* + to/on) to consider past events; to remember. ✱ **not look back** to continue to make successful progress: *After his initial success, he never looked back.*

look down *verb intrans* (+ on/upon) to have an attitude of superiority or contempt: *He snobbishly looks down on the poor.*

looker *noun* **1** (*often in combination*) a person having an appearance of a specified kind: *a good-looker.* **2** *informal* an attractive person, *esp* a woman.

look for *verb trans* **1** to try to find (something). **2** to expect or hope to get (something): *We were looking for rather more than they eventually offered; They came here looking for a fight.*

look in *verb intrans* to pay a short visit: *I'll look in on her on my way home.*

look-in *noun informal* **1** a chance to take part. **2** a chance of success.

looking glass *noun* = MIRROR[1].

look on *verb intrans* to be a spectator, *esp* to witness an event without getting involved in it. ➤ *verb trans* (*usu* + as) to consider (somebody or something) in the specified way: *I prefer to look on it as a challenge.*

lookout *noun* **1** a place or structure affording a wide view for observation. **2a** somebody engaged in keeping watch. **b** a careful watch: *Keep a lookout for traffic wardens.* **3** *Brit, informal* a matter of care or concern: *It's your lookout if you do such a silly thing.* **4** *chiefly Brit* a future possibility; a prospect.

look out *verb intrans* **1** (*usu in imperative*) to take care. **2** to keep watching: *Look out for your parents.* ➤ *verb trans chiefly Brit* to choose (something) by inspection; to select (it): *I'll look out a suit for your interview.*

look over *verb trans* to examine (something).

look-see *noun informal* a relatively quick assessment or investigation.

look to *verb trans* **1** (*often* + for) to rely on (somebody or something) to do or provide something: *You're the person they usually look to for financial advice.* **2** to pay careful attention to (something), *esp* to make sure that (it) is in good order: *They should look to their own moral standards before they start criticizing other people's.*

look up *verb intrans* to improve in prospects or conditions: *Business is looking up.* ➤ *verb trans* **1** to search (information) for in or as if in a reference work: *Look up a phone number in the directory.* **2** to pay a usu short visit to (somebody): *I looked up my friend while I was there.* **3** (+ to) to have an attitude of respect: *They always looked up to their parents.*

loom[1] /loohm/ *noun* a frame or machine for weaving together yarns or threads into cloth. [Middle English *lome* tool, loom, from Old English *gelōma* tool]

loom[2] *verb intrans* **1** to come into sight indistinctly, in enlarged or distorted and menacing form, often as a result of atmospheric conditions. **2a** to appear in an impressively great or exaggerated form. **b** to take shape as an impending occurrence: *Our exams loomed large.* [prob from Low German or Dutch]

loom[3] *noun* the indistinct and exaggerated appearance of something seen on the horizon or through fog or darkness.

loon[1] /loohn/ *noun informal* a mad or silly person. [Middle English *loun* rogue, idler, influenced by LOONY[2]]

loon[2] *noun NAmer* = DIVER (3A). [of Scandinavian origin]

loon[3] *verb intrans Brit, informal* to behave in a crazy or excited manner, usu as a result of intoxication.

loony[1] *adj* (**loonier, looniest**) *informal* crazy or foolish. ➤➤ **looniness** *noun.*

loony[2] *noun* (*pl* **loonies**) a crazy or foolish person. [by shortening and alteration from LUNATIC[1]]

loony bin *noun informal, derog* a hospital or home for people who are mentally ill.

loop[1] /loohp/ *noun* **1** a partially closed figure that has a curved outline surrounding a central opening. **2a** something shaped like a loop, *esp* a ring or curved piece used to form a fastening or handle. **b** a manoeuvre in which an aircraft passes successively through a climb, inverted flight, and a dive, and then returns to normal flight. **3** a zigzag-shaped intrauterine contraceptive device. **4** a piece of film or magnetic tape whose ends are spliced together so as to reproduce the same material continuously. **5** a series of instructions, e.g. for a computer, that is repeated until a terminating condition is reached. **6** a closed electric circuit. **7** = LOOP LINE. ✳ **knock somebody for a loop** to surprise or disconcert somebody greatly. [Middle English *loupe*, of unknown origin]

loop[2] *verb intrans* **1** to make, form, or move in a loop or loops. **2** to execute a loop in an aircraft. ➤ *verb trans* **1a** to make a loop in, on, or about (something). **b** to fasten (something) with a loop. **2** to join (two courses of loops) in knitting. **3** to form a loop with (something): *I looped the wool round the knitting needle.* ✳ **loop the loop** to perform a loop in an aircraft.

looper *noun* **1** a small hairless caterpillar that moves in a series of loops by arching its body: families Geometridae and Noctuidae. Also called INCHWORM, MEASURING WORM. **2** a device on a sewing machine for making loops.

loophole[1] *noun* **1** a means of escape; *esp* an ambiguity or omission in a text through which its intent may be evaded. **2** a small opening through which missiles, firearms, etc may be discharged or light and air admitted: *The nice Morn on th'Indian steep from her cabined loop-hole peep* — Milton. [Middle English *loupe* embrasure, loophole + HOLE[1]]

loophole[2] *verb trans* to make loopholes in (e.g. a wall).

loop line *noun* a railway line that leaves and later rejoins a main line.

loop of Henle /'henli/ *noun* a part of each NEPHRON (tubular unit) in a kidney through which water resorption takes place. [named after Friedrich J *Henle* d.1885, German pathologist]

loop stitch *noun* a needlework stitch consisting of a series of interlocking loops.

loopy *adj* (**loopier, loopiest**) *informal* slightly crazy or foolish.

loose[1] /loohs/ *adj* **1a** not rigidly fastened or securely attached. **b** having worked partly free from attachments: *The masonry is loose at the base of the wall.* **c** not tight-fitting: *a loose cardigan.* **2a** free from a state of confinement or restraint and able to move about at will: *a lion loose in the streets.* **b** not kept together in a bundle, container, or binding: *loose hair.* **3** not dense, close, or compact in structure or arrangement. **4** not tightly drawn or stretched; slack. **5a** lacking in precision, exactness, or care: *a loose translation.* **b** permitting freedom of interpretation: *The wording of the document is very loose.* **6** *dated.* **a** lacking restraint or self-control; careless; irresponsible: *a loose tongue.* **b** dissolute or promiscuous: *loose living.* **7a** said of a cough: produced freely and accompanied by rising of mucus. **b** said of the bowels: producing frequent, very fluid stools. ➤➤ **loosely** *adv*, **looseness** *noun.* [Middle English *lous* from Old Norse *lauss*]

Usage note

loose or **lose**? The spelling of these two words can cause problems. *Loose,* spelt with *-oo-* and pronounced with a soft *s* to rhyme with *goose* is mainly used as an adjective meaning 'not tight': *a loose-fitting dress; the knot has worked loose. Lose* with one *o* and pronounced to rhyme with *whose* is a verb meaning 'to be unable to find': *I'm always losing my spectacles.*

loose[2] *verb trans* **1** to free (somebody or something) from restraint; to release (them). **2** to untie, unfasten, or detach (something). **3** to make (something) less tight; to relax or loosen (it). **4** (*often* + off) to fire or discharge (e.g. a bullet or a volley).

loose[3] *adv* in a loose manner; loosely: *The rope hung loose.*

loose[4] *noun* (*usu* **the loose**) in rugby, open play that is characterized by free passing of the ball. ✳ **on the loose** free from restraint; *specif* having escaped from prison.

loose box *noun Brit* an individual enclosure within a barn or stable in which an animal may move about freely.

loose cannon *noun* somebody who acts independently and disruptively, rather than following the norms of an organization or group.

loose cover *noun Brit* a removable protective usu cloth cover for an article of furniture, e.g. an upholstered chair.

loose end *noun* an incomplete or unexplained detail. ✳ **at a loose end** bored or unoccupied.

loose head *noun* in rugby, the front-row forward on the hooker's left when the ball is put into the scrum.

loose-leaf *adj* said of an album or book: bound so that individual leaves can be detached or inserted: *a loose-leaf photograph album.*

loosen *verb* (**loosened, loosening**) ➤ *verb trans* **1** to make (something) loose or looser: *She loosened her belt.* **2** to cause or permit (something) to become less strict. ➤ *verb intrans* to become loose or looser. ➤➤ **loosener** *noun.*

loosen up *verb intrans* **1** to become more relaxed. **2** to warm up one's muscles before exercising.

loosestrife *noun* **1** any of a genus of plants of the primrose family with leafy stems and yellow or white flowers: genus *Lysimachia.* **2** any of a genus of plants of the henna family including some with showy spikes of purple flowers: genus *Lythrum.* [intended as translation of Greek *lysimacheios* loosestrife (from *Lysimachos*, the name of its discoverer), as if it was from *lysis* act of loosing + *machesthai* to fight]

loot[1] /looht/ *noun* **1** goods, usu of considerable value, taken in war; spoils. **2** something taken illegally, e.g. by force or deception: *the robbers' loot*. **3** *informal* money. [Hindi *lūṭ* to loot]

loot[2] *verb trans and intrans* **1** to plunder or sack (a place) in war. **2** to seize and carry away (something) by force or illegally, *esp* in war or public disturbance. ➤➤ **looter** *noun*.

lop[1] /lop/ *verb trans* (**lopped, lopping**) **1a** to cut off branches or twigs from (a tree). **b** to cut (a limb) from a person. **2** (+ off/away) to remove or do away with (something) as unnecessary or undesirable: *We lopped several thousand off the annual budget.* ➤➤ **lopper** *noun*. [Middle English *loppe* small branches, twigs]

lop[2] *noun* small branches and twigs cut from a tree.

lop[3] *verb intrans* (**lopped, lopping**) **1** said of animal ears: to hang downwards; to droop. **2** to slouch or lope. [perhaps imitative]

lope[1] /lohp/ *noun* an easy bounding gait capable of being sustained for a long time: *The wolf started off at an easy lope in a manner that plainly showed he was going somewhere* — Jack London. [Middle English *loup, lope* leap, from Old Norse *hlaup*]

lope[2] *verb intrans* to go, move, or ride at a lope.

lop-eared *adj* said of an animal: having ears that droop. [LOP[3]]

lopsided *adj* **1** having one side heavier or lower than the other. **2** lacking in balance, symmetry, or proportion. ➤➤ **lopsidedly** *adv*, **lopsidedness** *noun*. [LOP[3]]

loquacious /lə'kwayshəs/ *adj formal* = TALKATIVE. ➤➤ **loquaciously** *adv*, **loquaciousness** *noun*, **loquacity** /lə'kwasiti/ *noun*. [Latin *loquac-, loquax*, from *loqui* to speak]

loquat /'lohkwət, 'lohkwot/ *noun* **1** a small yellow edible plumlike fruit. **2** the ornamental Asiatic evergreen tree of the rose family, with reddish branches, that bears this fruit: *Eriobotrya japonica*. [Chinese (Cantonese) *lauh gwat*, from *lauh* rush + *gwat* orange]

lor /law/ *interj Brit, informal* used to express surprise, amazement, or dismay. [from the interjection LORD[2]]

loran /'lawrən/ *noun* a system of navigation in which the intervals between reception of pulsed signals sent out by widely spaced radio stations is used to determine position. [contraction of *long-range navigation*]

Lord[1] /lawd/ *noun* **1a** (**the Lord**) God, *esp*, for Christians, God the Father. **b** (**the Lord** or **Our Lord**) Jesus Christ. **2** (**the Lords**) the House of Lords. **3** used as the title of a lord or as a prefix to some official titles: *Lord Advocate*. ✳ **My Lord** used as a form of address to judges, bishops, and noblemen.

Lord[2] *interj* used to express surprise, amazement, or dismay: *Oh Lord!; Good Lord!*

lord[1] *noun* **1** a man of rank or high position, e.g.: **a** a British nobleman, e.g. a baron, marquess, earl, or viscount. **b** the son of a duke or marquess or the eldest son of an earl. **c** a feudal tenant holding land directly from the king. **d** a bishop of the Church of England. **2a** a ruler by hereditary right, to whom service and obedience are due. **b** somebody from whom a feudal fee or estate is held. **3** somebody who has achieved domination or who exercises leadership or great power in some area: *press lords*. ➤➤ **lordless** *adj*, **lord-like** *adj*. [Old English *hlāford*, from *hlāf* loaf + *weard* keeper; compare with LADY]

lord[2] ✳ **lord it over** to act like a lord; *esp* to put on airs: *He likes to lord it over his friends.*

Lord Advocate *noun* the chief law officer of the Crown in Scotland.

Lord Chamberlain *noun* the chief officer of the British royal household.

Lord Chancellor *noun* an officer of state who presides over the House of Lords, serves as head of the judiciary, and is usu a member of the cabinet.

Lord Chief Justice *noun* the president of the Queen's Bench Division of the High Court.

Lord Justice *noun* (*pl* **Lords Justices**) = LORD JUSTICE OF APPEAL.

Lord Justice of Appeal *noun* (*pl* **Lords Justices of Appeal**) a judge of the Court of Appeal.

Lord Lieutenant *noun* (*pl* **Lords Lieutenant** or **Lord Lieutenants**) an official representative of a sovereign in a British county.

lordly *adj* (**lordlier, lordliest**) **1a** of or having the characteristics of a lord; dignified. **b** grand or noble. **2** disdainful and arrogant. ➤➤ **lordliness** *noun*.

Lord Mayor *noun* the mayor of the City of London and other large British cities.

lordosis /law'dohsis/ *noun* an abnormal forward curvature of the spine: compare KYPHOSIS, SCOLIOSIS. ➤➤ **lordotic** /law'dotik/ *adj*. [via Latin from Greek *lordōsis*, from *lordos* curving forwards]

Lord President of the Council *noun* (*pl* **Lord Presidents of the Council**) the president of the Privy Council.

Lord Privy Seal *noun* a member of the British Cabinet with no departmental duties.

Lord Provost *noun* the provost of a Scottish district council.

lords and ladies *noun* = CUCKOOPINT.

Lord's Day *noun* (*usu* **the Lord's Day**) = SUNDAY[1]. [from the Christian belief that Christ rose from the dead on Sunday]

lordship *noun* **1** the authority or power of a lord; dominion. **2** (**Lordship**) used as a title to address or refer to a bishop, a High Court Judge, or a peer: *His Lordship is not at home.*

Lord's Prayer *noun* (**the Lord's Prayer**) the prayer taught by Jesus beginning 'Our Father'. [Matthew 6:9–13, Luke 11:2–4]

Lords Spiritual *pl noun* the archbishops and senior bishops in the House of Lords.

Lord's Supper *noun* (*usu* **the Lord's Supper**) = HOLY COMMUNION.

Lords Temporal *pl noun* the peers in the House of Lords who are not bishops.

lore /law/ *noun* a specified body of knowledge or tradition: *bird lore; ghost lore*. [Old English *lār*]

lorgnette /law'nyet/ *noun* (*also in pl*) a pair of glasses or opera glasses with a handle: *There was a Miss Mayblunt, no longer in her teens, who looked at the world through lorgnettes, and with the keenest interest* — Kate Chopin. [French *lorgnette*, from *lorgner* to take a sidelong look at]

lorica /lo'rieka/ *noun* (*pl* **loricae** /-kee/) a hard protective case or shell of an aquatic invertebrate animal. ➤➤ **loricate** /'lorikayt/ *adj*. [Latin *lorica* breastplate, from *lorum* strap]

lorikeet /'lorikeet, lori'keet/ *noun* any of numerous small treedwelling parrots mostly of Australasia, with bright-coloured plumage: subfamily Lorunae. [LORY + -*keet* as in PARAKEET]

loris /'lawris/ *noun* any of several small nocturnal slow-moving treedwelling primates of S and SE Asia: family Lorisidae. [French *loris*, perhaps from obsolete Dutch *loeris* simpleton]

lorry /'lori/ *noun* (*pl* **lorries**) *Brit* a large motor vehicle for carrying loads by road. ✳ **fall off the back of a lorry** see FALL[1]. [perhaps from English dialect *lurry* to pull, drag]

lory /'lawri/ *noun* (*pl* **lories**) any of several species of small Australasian or Indonesian parrots with long slender protuberances on the upper surface of the tongue, which form a brushlike organ used for extracting nectar from flowers: family Loridae. [Malay *luri*]

lose /loohz/ *verb* (*past tense and past part.* **lost** /lost/) ➤ *verb trans* **1** to miss (something) from one's possession or from its customary or expected place; to fail to find (something). **2** to suffer deprivation of (something); to cease to have (something), *esp* in an unforeseen or accidental manner: *He lost his leg in an accident.* **3a** to suffer loss through the death of or final separation from (somebody): *They had lost a son in the war.* **b** said of a pregnant woman: to have a miscarriage of (a baby). **4a** to be defeated in (a conflict or contest). **b** to fail to gain (something competed for). **5** to fail to use (e.g. an opportunity); to let (a chance) slip by. **6a** to have less of (something): *The aircraft began to lose height.* **b** to free oneself from or be rid of (something): *He's dieting to lose some weight.* **7** to fail to perceive (something) with the senses or the mind: *I lost part of what was said.* **8** to cause the loss of (something): *One careless statement lost her the election.* **9** to fail to keep or maintain (e.g. one's balance). **10a** to fail to keep (somebody or something) in sight or in mind: *I lost him in the crowd.* **b** *informal* to escape from or shake off (a pursuer). **11** to withdraw (oneself) from immediate reality: *He lost himself in a book.* **12** (*usu in passive*) to cause the destruction of (something) or the death of (somebody). **13** said of a watch or clock: to run slow by (a specified amount). ➤ *verb intrans* **1** to suffer a defeat. **2a** to be deprived of something of value; to fail to benefit. **b** (*often* + on) to make a financial loss. **3** said of a watch or clock: to run slow. ✳ **lose face** to lose one's dignity or reputation [from the Chinese custom of hiding the face with a fan as a sign of shame or humiliation]. **lose heart** to become dispirited. **lose it** *informal* to lose control of oneself. **lose one's way 1** to be unable to find the correct direction to go in; to get lost. **2** to go astray intellectually or morally. **lose sight of** to fail to take into account. **lose the plot** *informal* to lose one's sense or good judgment; to lose sight of one's aims or intentions: *The project seemed to be going well, but eventually I realized I had just lost the plot.* **lose track of** to fail to be aware of or to follow (something). [Middle English *losen* from Old English *losian* to perish, lose, from *los* destruction]

Usage note

lose or loose? See note at LOOSE[1].

lose out *verb intrans* **1** (*often* + on) to make a loss. **2** to be the loser, *esp* unluckily.

loser *noun* **1** somebody who loses, *esp* consistently. **2** somebody or something that does poorly; a failure.

loss /los/ *noun* **1a** the act or an instance of losing possession. **b** the harm or privation resulting from loss or separation. **2** a person, thing, or amount lost: *The woman who retired is a great loss to her firm.* **3** failure to gain, win, obtain, or use something. *The team went home downhearted after their loss.* **4** an amount by which cost exceeds revenue: *We made a loss on the sale of the house.* ✱ **at a loss 1** uncertain or puzzled. **2** not making enough money to cover costs. [Middle English *los*, prob back-formation from *lost*, past part. of *losen*: see LOSE]

loss adjuster *noun* somebody who investigates insurance claims and decides how much compensation to award.

loss leader *noun* an article sold at a loss in order to draw customers.

lost[1] /lost/ *adj* **1a** unable to find the way. **b** no longer visible. **c** bewildered or helpless. **2a** ruined or destroyed physically or morally. **b** damned. **3a** no longer possessed: *one's lost youth.* **b** no longer known: *the lost art of letter-writing.* **4** (*usu* + in) rapt or absorbed: *lost in reverie.* ✱ **be lost for words** to be unable to think what to say, e.g. because of shock. **be lost on somebody** to be unnoticed or unappreciated by somebody. **get lost** *informal* (*usu in imperative*) to go away.

lost[2] *verb* past tense and past part. of LOSE.

lost cause *noun* a cause that has lost all prospect of success.

lost generation *noun* **1** the generation considered socially and emotionally disadvantaged as a result of reaching adulthood during and immediately following World War I. **2** the potentially talented young men killed in World War I.

lot[1] /lot/ *noun* **1** *informal* (*also in pl*) a considerable amount or number: *a lot of illness; He has lots of friends.* **2** (**the lot**) *chiefly Brit* the whole amount or number: *He ate up the whole lot.* **3** *informal* (*treated as sing. or pl*) a number of associated people; a set: *Hello, you lot.* **4** an article or a number of articles offered as one item, e.g. in an auction sale: *What am I bid for lot 16?* **5a** an object used as a counter when deciding a question by chance: *They drew lots for who was to go.* **b** the use of lots as a means of making a choice, or the choice made in this way. **6a** something that falls to somebody by lot; a share. **b** one's way of life or worldly fate; fortune: *A policeman's lot is not a happy one* — W S Gilbert. **7a** a portion of land; *esp* one with fixed boundaries designated on a plot or survey: *a parking lot.* **b** a film studio and its adjoining property. ✱ **a lot 1** *informal* much, considerably, or to a great extent: *I drove a lot faster; The place has changed a lot since we were last here.* **2** *informal* often or frequently: *She goes there a lot.* **draw/cast lots** to decide an issue by random selection, using objects of unequal length, with different markings, etc. **throw in one's lot with** to join forces or ally oneself with. [Old English *hlot*]

lot[2] *verb trans* (**lotted, lotting**) **1** to form or divide (e.g. land) into lots. **2** to allot or apportion (something).

loth /lohth/ *adj* see LOATH.

Usage note

loth, loath, or loathe? See note at LOATH.

lothario /lə'thahrioh/ *noun* (*pl* **lotharios**) (*often* **Lothario**) a man whose chief interest is seducing women. [named after *Lothario*, seducer in the play *The Fair Penitent* by Nicholas Rowe d.1718, English dramatist]

loti /'lohti/ *noun* (*pl* **maloti** /ma'lohti/) the basic monetary unit of Lesotho, divided into 100 lisente. [of Bantu origin; named after the *Maloti* mountains of Lesotho]

lotion /'lohsh(ə)n/ *noun* a medicinal or cosmetic liquid for external use. [Latin *lotion-*, *lotio* act of washing, from *lavere* to wash]

lots *adv informal* much or considerably: *She is lots older than me.* [pl of LOT[1]]

lottery /'lot(ə)ri/ *noun* (*pl* **lotteries**) **1** a way of raising money by the sale or the distribution of numbered tickets some of which are later randomly selected to entitle the holder to a prize. **2** an event or affair whose outcome is decided or apparently decided by chance: *Buying a secondhand car is a lottery.* [early French *loterie* from early Dutch *loterij*, from *lot* lot]

lotto /'lotoh/ *noun* **1** a children's game similar to bingo. **2** *NAmer, Aus* = LOTTERY. [Italian *lotto* lottery, lotto, from French *lot* lot, of Germanic origin]

lotus /'lohtəs/ *noun* **1** any of various water lilies including several represented in ancient Egyptian and Hindu art and religious symbolism: *Nymphaea lotus* and other species. **2** any of a genus of widely distributed upright herbaceous plants, e.g. bird's-foot trefoil: genus *Lotus*. **3** a fruit considered in Greek legend to cause indolence and dreamy contentment. [via Latin from Greek *lōtos* from Hebrew *lōt* myrrh, (sense 2) Latin genus name]

lotus-eater *noun* somebody who lives in dreamy indolence. [named after the *lotus-eaters*, a mythical people living in indolence caused by lotus fruit, translation of Greek *Lōtophagoi*]

lotus position *noun* a yoga position in which one sits with legs folded, the feet resting on the thighs, and the arms resting on the knees. [translation of Sanskrit *padmāsana*, from *padma* lotus (symbolizing transcendence of external impulse and sensation) + *āsana* seat, posture]

louche /loohsh/ *adj* morally dubious; disreputable or seedy. [French *louche*, literally 'cross-eyed', from Latin *luscus* one-eyed]

loud[1] /lowd/ *adj* **1** marked by or producing a high volume of sound. **2** clamorous or noisy. **3** obtrusive or offensive in appearance; flashy: *a loud checked suit.* ➤➤ **loudly** *adv,* **loudness** *noun.* [Old English *hlūd*]

loud[2] *adv* in a loud manner. ✱ **out loud** aloud.

louden *verb trans and intrans* (**loudened, loudening**) to become, or to make (something), loud or louder.

loud-hailer *noun chiefly Brit* = MEGAPHONE.

loudmouth *noun informal* a person who frequently talks in a loud offensive way. ➤➤ **loudmouthed** *adj.*

loudspeaker *noun* an electromechanical device that converts electrical energy into acoustic energy and that is used to reproduce sounds.

Lou Gehrig's disease /,loo 'gerigz/ *noun* = AMYOTROPHIC LATERAL SCLEROSIS. [named after Henry Louis *Gehrig* d.1941, US baseball player, who died from it]

lough /lokh/ *noun* a loch in Ireland. [Middle English, of Celtic origin]

louis /'looh·i/ *noun* = LOUIS D'OR.

louis d'or /,looh·i 'daw (*French* lwi dɔr)/ *noun* (*pl* **louis d'or** /,looh·i (*French* lwi)/) **1** a French gold coin first struck in 1640 and issued until the Revolution. **2** the French 20-franc gold piece issued after the Revolution; a napoleon. [French *louis d'or*, from *Louis* XIII d.1643, King of France + *d'or* of gold]

lounge[1] /lownj/ *verb intrans* to act or move idly or lazily; to loll. [origin unknown]

lounge[2] *noun* **1** a room in a private house for sitting in; a sitting room. **2** a room in a public building providing comfortable seating. **3** a waiting room, e.g. at an airport.

lounge bar *noun Brit* = SALOON (1A).

lounge lizard *noun dated* a man who passes his time idly in fashionable society, *esp* in the company of women.

lounger *noun* **1** a comfortable chair, *esp* an extended one: *a sun lounger.* **2** somebody who lounges.

lounge suit *noun Brit* a man's suit for wear during the day and on informal occasions.

loupe /loohp/ *noun* a small optical magnifying instrument used by jewellers and watchmakers. [French *loupe* gem of imperfect brilliancy; lump]

lour[1] *or* **lower** /'lowə/ *verb intrans* **1** to scowl or look sullen. **2** said of the weather: to become dark, gloomy, and threatening. ➤➤ **louring** *adj,* **louringly** *adv.* [Middle English *louren*; earlier history unknown]

lour² _or_ **lower** /'lowə/ _noun_ a sullen expression.

louse /lows/ _noun_ (_pl_ **lice** /lies/) **1a** any of various small wingless usu flattened insects parasitic on warm-blooded animals: orders Anoplura and Mallophaga. **b** (_usu in combination_) any of various small insects or related animals that live on other animals, e.g. fish, or on plants. **c** (_usu in combination_) any of several small arthropods that are not parasitic: _book louse; wood louse_. **2** (_pl_ **louses**) _informal_ a contemptible person. [Old English _lūs_]

louse up /lows/ _verb trans informal_ to make a mess of (something); to spoil (it).

lousewort _noun_ any of a genus of plants of the foxglove family with spikes of two-lipped flowers: genus _Pedicularis_. [from the belief that sheep feeding on it became infested with vermin]

lousy /'lowzi/ _adj_ (**lousier, lousiest**) **1** _informal_ very bad, unpleasant, useless, etc: _'House Beautiful' is play lousy_ — Dorothy Parker. **2** _informal_ very mean; despicable: _a lousy trick to play_. **3** _informal_ (+ with) containing or covered with large numbers of; teeming with: _The place was lousy with police_. **4** infested with lice. ⫸ **lousily** _adv_, **lousiness** _noun_.

lout /lowt/ _noun_ a rough ill-mannered person, usu a man or youth. ⫸ **loutish** _adj_. [perhaps from Old Norse _lūtr_ bent down, from _lūta_ to bow down]

louvre (_NAmer_ **louver**) /'loohvə/ _noun_ **1** any one of a set of slanted fixed or movable strips of metal, wood, glass, etc fitted across an opening to allow the flow of air or sound but to exclude rain or sun and to provide privacy. **2** a roof lantern or turret with slatted apertures for the escape of smoke or admission of light. ⫸ **louvred** _adj_. [Middle English _lover_ from early French _lovier_]

lovable _or_ **loveable** /'luvəbl/ _adj_ having qualities that inspire love or affection; sweet, charming, or amiable. ⫸ **lovability** /-'biliti/ _noun_, **lovableness** _noun_, **lovably** _adv_.

lovage /'luvij/ _noun_ any of several aromatic perennial plants of the carrot family; _esp_ a European plant sometimes cultivated as a herb or flavouring agent: _Levisticum officinale_. [Middle English _lovache_ via Anglo-French from late Latin _levisticum_, alteration of Latin _ligusticum_, neuter of _ligusticus_ of _Liguria_, coastal region of NW Italy]

love¹ /luv/ _noun_ **1** a strong feeling of attachment, tenderness, and protectiveness for another person: _maternal love for a child_. **2** attraction or devotion based on sexual desire: _Love is only one of many passions_ — Dr Johnson. **3** warm interest in and enjoyment of something: _love of music_. **4a** the object of interest and enjoyment: _Music was his first love_. **b** a person who is loved; a darling: _my one and only love_. **c** an assurance of love: _Give her my love_. **5** (**Love**) a god or personification of love. **6** a score of zero in tennis, squash, etc. **7** _Brit, informal_ used as a friendly or affectionate form of address: _Would you like a seat, love?_ ✳ **for love** for charity or pleasure, not for payment. **for love or money** (_usu in negative contexts_) in any possible way: _You couldn't get a ticket for love or money_. **for the love of** for the sake of. **make love** to have sexual intercourse. **make love to** _dated_ to woo or court (somebody). [Old English _lufu_; (sense 6) from the phrase _to play for love_ to play for nothing, i.e. without stakes]

love² _verb trans_ **1** to feel passionate devotion or tenderness for (somebody). **2** to feel a great liking, attachment, or enthusiasm for (somebody or something). ⪢ _verb intrans_ to feel love or affection, or to experience desire.

loveable _adj_ see LOVABLE.

love affair _noun_ **1** an often temporary sexual liaison or romantic attachment between people. **2** a lively enthusiasm: _He's got a love affair with hang-gliding_.

love apple _noun archaic_ = TOMATO. [prob translation of French _pomme d'amour_; the tomato was formerly believed to have aphrodisiac qualities]

lovebird _noun_ any of various small usu grey or green parrots that show great affection for their mates: genus _Agapornis_.

lovebite _noun_ a temporary red mark produced by biting or sucking an area of one's partner's skin, _esp_ the neck, in sexual play.

love child _noun euphem_ an illegitimate child.

love feast _noun_ a meal eaten together by a Christian congregation in token of brotherly love.

love-in-a-mist _noun_ a European garden plant of the buttercup family with pale blue or white flowers enveloped in numerous very fine leaves: _Nigella damascena_.

loveless _adj_ **1** without love: _a loveless marriage_. **2** unloving or unloved. ⫸ **lovelessly** _adv_, **lovelessness** _noun_.

love-lies-bleeding _noun_ any of various plants of the amaranth family widely cultivated for their drooping clusters of small usu scarlet or purple flowers: genus _Amaranthus_.

lovelorn /'luvlawn/ _adj_ sad because of unrequited love. [_lorn_ forsaken, from Middle English _loren_, past part. of _lesen_ to lose, from Old English _lēosan_]

lovely¹ _adj_ (**lovelier, loveliest**) **1** delicately or delightfully beautiful. **2** very pleasing; fine: _a lovely view_. ⪢ **lovelily** _adv_, **loveliness** _noun_. [Old English _luflic_ loving, lovable, from _lufu_ love + -_līc_ -LY¹]

lovely² _noun_ (_pl_ **lovelies**) _informal_ a beautiful woman.

lovemaking _noun_ **1** sexual activity; _esp_ sexual intercourse. **2** _archaic_ courtship.

love match _noun_ a marriage or engagement undertaken for love rather than financial or other advantages.

love nest _noun informal_ a small secret flat, room, or house used for conducting a usu illicit sexual relationship.

lover _noun_ **1** a person with whom somebody has a sexual relationship, _esp_ outside marriage. **2** somebody who is keen on something: _a lover of the theatre; a dog lover_.

love seat _noun_ an S-shaped double chair or settee that allows two people to sit side by side though facing in opposite directions.

lovesick _adj_ languishing with love. ⪢ **lovesickness** _noun_.

lovey _noun_ (_pl_ **loveys**) _Brit, informal_ used as a friendly or affectionate form of address: _What's the matter, lovey?_

lovey-dovey /ˌluvi 'duvi/ _adj informal_ excessively loving or romantic. [LOVEY + _dovey_, from DOVE¹ + -Y⁴]

loving _adj_ feeling or showing love; affectionate: _loving care; a loving glance_. ⪢ **lovingly** _adv_.

loving cup _noun_ a large ornamental drinking vessel with two or more handles that is passed among a group of people for all to drink from.

low¹ /loh/ _adj_ **1a** not measuring much from the base to the top; not high: _a low wall_. **b** situated or rising only a little above the ground or some other reference point: _a low bridge_. **c** near the horizon: _It was evening, and the sun was low_. **2a** situated below the normal level or the base of measurement: _low ground_. **b** situated near the bottom: _low down on the list_. **c** marking a nadir or bottom: _the low point of her career_. **3** of less than the usual degree, size, amount, or value: _low pressure; Prices are low at the moment_. **4** considered comparatively unimportant: _a low priority_. **5a** said of sound: not shrill or loud; soft. **b** said of a note: depressed in pitch. **6a** lacking strength, health, or vitality; weak: _He's been very low with pneumonia_. **b** lacking spirit or vivacity; depressed: _low spirits_. **7a** lacking dignity or formality: _a low style of writing_. **b** morally reprehensible: _He played a low trick on her_. **c** coarse or vulgar: _low language_. **8** unfavourable or disparaging: _She had a low opinion of him_. **9** humble in character or status: _people of low birth_. **10** said of a gear: designed for slow speed. **11** said of women's clothing: cut deep at the neck to reveal the upper part of the chest and breasts. **12** said of a vowel: = OPEN¹ (12). ⪢ **lowness** _noun_. [Middle English _lah, low_, from Old Norse _lāgr_]

low² _noun_ **1** a relatively or unusually small amount or depressed level: _Sales have reached a new low_. **2** a region of low atmospheric pressure.

low³ _adv_ at or to a low place, altitude, or degree: _She fired low and hit him in the leg_.

low⁴ _verb intrans_ to make the deep sustained throat sound characteristic of a cow. [Old English _hlōwan_]

low⁵ _noun_ a lowing sound.

lowborn _adj_ born to parents of low social rank.

lowboy _noun NAmer_ a low chest or side table that is supported on short legs.

lowbred _adj_ **1** rude or vulgar. **2** = LOWBORN.

lowbrow _adj informal, derog_ catering for or having unsophisticated or unintellectual tastes, _esp_ in the arts. ⪢ **lowbrow** _noun_.

Low Church _adj_ tending, _esp_ in the Anglican Church, to minimize emphasis on the priesthood, sacraments, and ceremonial and often to emphasize evangelical principles. ⪢ **Low Churchman** _noun_.

low comedy _noun_ comedy bordering on farce and depending on physical action and situation rather than wit and characterization: compare HIGH COMEDY.

low-density lipoprotein *noun* any of a group of lipoproteins that are found in plasma and are the major carriers of cholesterol in the blood.

lowdown *noun* (**the lowdown**) *informal* useful information: *Get the lowdown on each city with these guides written by the locals!*

low-down *adj informal* underhand or despicable.

lower[1] /ˈloh-ə/ *adj* **1** relatively low in position, rank, or order. **2** less advanced in the scale of evolutionary development: *lower organisms*. **3** constituting the popular, more representative, and often, e.g. in Britain, more powerful branch of a legislative body consisting of two houses: *the lower chamber*. **4a** beneath the earth's surface. **b** (*often* **Lower**) being an earlier division of the named geological period or series: *Lower Carboniferous*. **5** being the southern part of a specified area: *lower New York State*.

lower[2] /ˈloh-ə/ *verb* (**lowered, lowering**) ➤ *verb trans* **1a** to cause (something) to descend; to move, direct, or let (it) down: *lowered the boat over the side of the ship*; *lower your aim*. **b** to reduce the height of (something): *lowered the ceiling*. **2a** to reduce (something) in value, amount, degree, strength, or pitch: *They have lowered the price*; *Lower your voice*. **b** to bring (somebody) down; to degrade (them): *I wouldn't lower myself to speak to them*. ➤ *verb intrans* **1** to move down; to drop. **2** = DIMINISH (1).

lower[3] /ˈlohə/ *verb intrans* see LOUR[1].

lower[4] /ˈlohə/ *noun* see LOUR[2].

lower case /ˈloh-ə/ *noun* lower-case letters. [from the compositor's practice of keeping such letters in the lower of a pair of type cases]

lower-case /ˈloh-ə/ *adj* said of a letter: belonging to the series typically used elsewhere than at the beginning of sentences or proper names, e.g. a, b, c rather than A, B, C.

lower chamber /ˈloh-ə/ *noun* = LOWER HOUSE.

lower class /ˈloh-ə/ *noun* (*treated as sing. or pl*) a social class occupying a position below the middle class. ➤➤ **lower-class** *adj.*

lowerclassman /ˌloh-əˈklahsmən/ *noun* (*pl* **lowerclassmen**) *NAmer* a member of the freshman or sophomore class in a college or secondary school.

lower criticism /ˈloh-ə/ *noun dated* textual criticism, *esp* of biblical texts: compare HIGHER CRITICISM.

lower deck /ˈloh-ə/ *noun* **1** a deck below the main deck of a ship. **2** (*treated as sing. or pl*) the petty officers and crew of a ship or navy as distinguished from the officers: compare QUARTERDECK.

lower house /ˈloh-ə/ *noun* the larger legislative house in a parliament that has two chambers, usu made up of elected members.

lowermost /ˈloh-əmohst/ *adj* lowest.

lower regions /ˈloh-ə/ *pl noun archaic* = HELL.

lowest common denominator *noun* **1** the lowest common multiple of two or more denominators. **2** *derog* something, e.g. a level of taste, that typifies or is common, acceptable, or comprehensible to all or the greatest possible number of people.

lowest common multiple *noun* the smallest number that is a multiple of each of two or more numbers.

low frequency *noun* a radio frequency in the range between 30 and 300kHz.

Low German *noun* the German dialects of N Germany; = PLATTDEUTSCH.

low-impact *adj* **1** said of physical exercise: making no stressful demands on the body. **2** causing little environmental harm.

low-key *adj* of low intensity; restrained.

low-keyed *adj* = LOW-KEY.

lowland *noun* **1** (*also in pl*) low or level country. **2** (**the Lowlands**) the central and E part of Scotland lying between the Highlands and the Southern Uplands. ➤➤ **lowlander** *noun*.

Low Latin *noun* the Latin language in its later stages and nonclassical forms, e.g. Medieval Latin.

low-level *adj* **1** occurring, done, or placed at a low level. **2** being of low importance or rank: *low-level talks*. **3** said of a computer language: in which each word, symbol, etc is equivalent to one machine code instruction and which deals directly with memory addresses and processor registers.

lowlife *noun* (*pl* **lowlifes**) **1** the life of immoral people and criminals as treated in the arts, *esp* in its more picturesquely sordid aspects. **2** *informal* a criminal or immoral person.

low-loader *noun* a truck or railway carriage with a low load-carrying platform.

lowly[1] *adj* (**lowlier, lowliest**) **1** humble and modest in manner or spirit. **2** low in the scale of biological or cultural evolution. **3** ranking low in a social or economic hierarchy. ➤➤ **lowliness** *noun*.

lowly[2] *adv* **1** in a humble or meek manner. **2** in a low position, manner, or degree.

low-lying *adj* lying below the normal level or surface or below the base of measurement or mean elevation: *low-lying clouds*.

low mass *noun* (*often* **Low Mass**) a mass recited by a single celebrant: compare HIGH MASS.

low-pitched *adj* **1** said of sound: not shrill; deep. **2** said of a roof: sloping gently.

low profile *noun* a mode of operation or behaviour intended to attract little attention: *The Government has been keeping a low profile over the disturbances* — The Guardian.

low-profile *adj* **1** not projecting far above the surface or base; low. **2** intended to attract little attention; unobtrusive.

low relief *noun* sculpture with forms barely projecting from the background; bas-relief.

low-rent *adj informal* **1** said of accommodation: cheap and shabby. **2** said of a person: of low character and having poor tastes.

low-rise *adj* said of a building: usu constructed with up to four storeys: *a low-rise classroom building*.

low season *noun* a usu periodic time of low or reduced profitability, e.g. from sales, or business opportunity; *esp* a period when the number of visitors to a holiday resort is low.

low-spirited *adj* dejected or depressed. ➤➤ **low-spiritedly** *adv*, **low-spiritedness** *noun*.

Low Sunday *noun* the Sunday following Easter. [prob from the contrast of ordinary services on this day after the Easter celebrations]

low-tech /tek/ *adj* using low technology.

low technology *noun* technology that is simple and unsophisticated, used *esp* to perform basic tasks.

low-tension *adj* **1** having a low voltage. **2** relating to apparatus for use at low voltages.

low tide *noun* **1** the tide when the water reaches its lowest level. **2** the time when this occurs.

low water *noun* = LOW TIDE: compare HIGH WATER, WATER[1] (8).

low-water mark *noun* the level of the sea at low tide.

lox[1] /loks/ *noun* liquid oxygen. [contraction of *liquid oxygen*]

lox[2] *noun* smoked salmon. [Yiddish *laks*]

loyal /ˈloyəl/ *adj* **1** unswerving in support for or allegiance to a person, country, or cause; faithful. **2** showing such allegiance: *her loyal determination to help the party*. ➤➤ **loyally** *adv*. [early French *loial* from Latin *legalis* legal]

loyalist *noun* somebody loyal to a government or sovereign, *esp* in time of revolt. ➤➤ **loyalism** *noun*.

loyalty *noun* (*pl* **loyalties**) **1** being loyal. **2** a feeling of allegiance or duty.

loyalty card *noun Brit* a card issued by a retailer, e.g. a supermarket, to reward regular customers by giving them points towards discounts on future purchases.

lozenge /ˈlozinj/ *noun* **1** a small often medicated sweet: *Miss Wepley rarely had recourse to her lozenges, but in case she should be taken with a fit of coughing she wished to have the emergency duly provided for —* Saki. **2** a figure with four equal sides and two acute and two obtuse angles; a diamond or rhombus: *marble walks arranged in black and white lozenges* — Henry James. **3** in heraldry, a diamond-shaped charge on a coat of arms. [Middle English from Old French *losenge* small cake, window pane]

LP[1] *noun* a gramophone record designed to be played at 33⅓ revolutions per minute and typically having a diameter of 30.5cm (12in.) and a playing time of 20–25 minutes per side. [short for *long-playing record*]

LP[2] *or* **l.p.** *abbr* low pressure.

LPG *abbr* liquefied petroleum gas.

L-plate *noun Brit* a sign bearing a letter L fixed to the front and back of a motor vehicle to show that the driver is not yet qualified. [L short for *learner*]

LPO *abbr* London Philharmonic Orchestra.

Lr *abbr* the chemical symbol for lawrencium.

LRP *abbr* lead replacement petrol.

LS *abbr* Lesotho (international vehicle registration).

LSB *abbr* in computing, least significant bit.

LSD *noun* a drug taken illegally for its potent action in producing hallucinations and altered perceptions. [short for LYSERGIC ACID DIETHYLAMIDE]

L.S.D. *abbr Brit* pounds, shillings, and pence. [Latin *librae, solidi, denarii* pounds, shillings, and pence]

LSE *abbr* **1** London School of Economics. **2** London Stock Exchange.

LSO *abbr* London Symphony Orchestra.

LT *abbr* Lithuania (international vehicle registration).

Lt. *abbr* Lieutenant.

LTA *abbr* Lawn Tennis Association.

Ltd *abbr Brit* Limited.

LtG *abbr* Lieutenant General.

Lu *abbr* the chemical symbol for lutetium.

luau /'looh·ow/ *noun* a Hawaiian feast. [Hawaiian *lu'au*]

lubber /'lubə/ *noun* **1** a big clumsy person. **2** a clumsy seaman; a landlubber. ➤➤ **lubberly** *adj and adv.* [Middle English *lobre, lobur*, perhaps related to *lob* lout: see LOB[1]]

lubber line *noun* a fixed line on the compass of a ship or aircraft that is aligned with the fore-and-aft line of the craft.

lubra /'loohbrah, 'loohbrə/ *noun Aus* an Australian aboriginal woman. [Tasmanian *lubara*]

lubricant /'loohbrikənt/ *noun* **1** a substance, e.g. grease or oil, capable of reducing friction, heat, and wear when introduced as a film between solid surfaces. **2** something that lessens or prevents difficulty: *Alcohol can be a great lubricant.* ➤➤ **lubricant** *adj.*

lubricate /'loohbrikayt/ *verb trans* **1** to make (something) smooth or slippery. **2** to apply a lubricant to (something). ➤➤ *verb intrans* to act as a lubricant. ➤➤ **lubrication** /-'kaysh(ə)n/ *noun*, **lubricator** *noun.* [Latin *lubricatus*, past part. of *lubricare*, from *lubricus* slippery]

lubricious /looh'brishəs/ *adj formal* **1** lecherous or salacious. **2** slippery or smooth: *a lubricious skin.* ➤➤ **lubriciously** *adv*, **lubricity** /looh'brisiti/ *noun.* [Latin *lubricus* slippery, easily led astray]

lubricous /'loohbrikəs/ *adj* = LUBRICIOUS.

Lucan *or* **Lukan** /'loohkən/ *adj* relating to St Luke or the Gospel of Luke. [late Latin *lucanus*, from *Lucas* Luke, from Greek *Loukas*]

lucent /'loohs(ə)nt/ *adj literary* **1** glowing with light; luminous. **2** clear or translucent. ➤➤ **lucency** /-si/ *noun*, **lucently** *adv.* [Latin *lucent-, lucens*, present part. of *lucēre* to shine, from *luc-, lux* light]

lucerne /looh'suhn/ *noun* = ALFALFA. [French *luzerne* from Provençal *luserno* glow-worm, ultimately from Latin *lucēre* to shine (see LUCENT); from the plant's shiny seeds]

lucid /'loohsid/ *adj* **1** clear to the understanding; plain: *The morbid logician seeks to make everything lucid, and succeeds in making everything mysterious* — G K Chesterton. **2** having full use of one's faculties; sane. ➤➤ **lucidity** /looh'siditi/ *noun*, **lucidly** *adv*, **lucidness** *noun.* [Latin *lucidus* from Latin *lucēre*: see LUCENT]

Lucifer /'loohsifə/ *noun* **1** used as a name of the devil. **2** the planet Venus when appearing as the morning star.

Word history

Old English from Latin *lucifer* light-bearing, from *luc-, lux* light + *-fer* -FER. Originally a name given to the morning star; used in the Bible (Isaiah 14:12) as an epithet for a king of Babylon who tried to rival God and was cast into hell, said by early Church fathers to represent an archangel who was driven out of heaven because of his pride, later identified with Satan.

luck /luk/ *noun* **1** whatever good or bad events happen to a person by chance. **2** the tendency for a person to be consistently fortunate or unfortunate. ✳ **down on one's luck** going through a time of hardship, poverty, or unsuccess. **hard/tough/worse luck!** *informal* used to express commiseration. **no such luck** *informal* unfortunately not. **try one's luck** attempt to do something that may or may not succeed. [Middle English *lucke* from early Dutch *luc*]

luckless *adj* unlucky or unfortunate. ➤➤ **lucklessly** *adv*, **lucklessness** *noun.*

luck out *verb intrans NAmer* to prosper or succeed, *esp* through chance or good fortune.

lucky *adj* (**luckier, luckiest**) having, resulting from, or bringing good luck. ➤➤ **luckily** *adv*, **luckiness** *noun.*

lucky dip *noun Brit* an attraction, e.g. at a fair, in which small prizes can be drawn unseen from a receptacle.

lucrative /'loohkrətiv/ *adj* producing wealth; profitable. ➤➤ **lucratively** *adv*, **lucrativeness** *noun.* [Middle English *lucratif* via French from Latin *lucrativus*, from *lucrari* to gain, from *lucrum* gain]

lucre /'loohkə/ *noun* money, wealth, or profit. [Middle English from Latin *lucrum* gain]

lucubrate /'loohkyoobrayt/ *verb intrans formal* to study or write, *esp* at night.

lucubration /loohkyoo'braysh(ə)n/ *noun formal* **1** laborious study or meditation, *esp* when done at night. **2** studied or pretentious expression in speech or writing. [Latin *lucubration-, lucubratio* study by night, work produced at night, from *lucubrare* to work by lamplight]

lud /lud/ *noun* (*usu* **m'lud**) *Brit* used to address a judge in court. [alteration of LORD[1]]

Luddite /'ludiet/ *noun* **1** a member of a group of early 19th-cent. English workmen who destroyed labour-saving machinery as a protest against unemployment. **2** somebody opposed to technological progress or innovations. ➤➤ **Luddism** *noun.* [named after Ned *Ludd* fl.1779, half-witted Leicestershire villager who destroyed stocking frames]

ludicrous /'loohdikrəs/ *adj* amusing because of obvious absurdity or incongruity. ➤➤ **ludicrously** *adv*, **ludicrousness** *noun.* [Latin *ludicrus*, from *ludus* play, sport]

ludo /'loohdoh/ *noun* a simple board game played on a square board with counters and dice in which the first to reach the home square wins. [Latin *ludo* I play, from *ludere* to play, from *ludus* play, sport]

luff[1] /luf/ *noun* the forward edge of a fore-and-aft sail. [Middle English, denoting a device for changing the course of a ship, from early French *lof* weather side of ship, luff]

luff[2] *verb intrans* (*often* + up) to sail nearer the wind. ➤ *verb trans* to raise or lower (a jib on a crane).

Luftwaffe /'looftvahfə, 'looftwahfə/ *noun* the German Air Force, *esp* during World War II. [German *Luftwaffe*, from *Luft* air + *Waffe* weapon]

lug[1] /lug/ *verb trans* (**lugged, lugging**) to drag, pull, or carry (something) with great effort. [Middle English *luggen* to pull by the hair or ear, drag, prob of Scandinavian origin]

lug[2] *noun* = LUGSAIL.

lug[3] *noun* **1** something, e.g. a handle, that projects like an ear. **2** *Brit, dialect or humorous* an ear. **3** a clumsy man. [Middle English (Scot) *lugge* ear, perhaps from Middle English *luggen*: see LUG[1]]

luge[1] /loohzh/ *noun* a small toboggan that is ridden in a supine position and used in racing. [Swiss French *luge*]

luge[2] *verb intrans* to ride on a luge.

Luger /'loohgə/ *noun trademark* a German automatic pistol. [named after George *Luger* d.1923, German firearms expert]

luggage /'lugij/ *noun* cases, bags, etc containing the belongings that accompany a traveller. [LUG[1] + -AGE]

lugger *noun* a small fishing or coasting boat that carries one or more lugsails. [LUGSAIL]

lughole *noun Brit, dialect or humorous* an ear.

lugsail /'lugsayl, 'lugsəl/ *noun* a four-sided fore-and-aft sail attached to an obliquely hanging yard. [perhaps from LUG[3]]

lugubrious /lə'goohbri·əs/ *adj* mournful, *esp* exaggeratedly or affectedly so. ➤➤ **lugubriously** *adv*, **lugubriousness** *noun.* [Latin *lugubris*, from *lugēre* to mourn]

lugworm *noun* any of a genus of marine worms that burrow in sand and are used for bait: genus *Arenicola*. [origin unknown]

Lukan *adj* see LUCAN.

lukewarm /loohk'wawm/ *adj* **1** moderately warm; tepid. **2** lacking conviction; indifferent. ➤➤ **lukewarmly** *adv*, **lukewarmness** *noun.* [Middle English, from *luke* tepid + WARM[1]]

lull[1] /lul/ *verb trans* **1** to cause (somebody) to sleep or rest; to soothe (them). **2** to cause (somebody) to relax vigilance, *esp* by deception.

➤ *verb intrans* to become less in intensity or strength. [Middle English *lullen*, prob of imitative origin]

lull² *noun* a temporary pause or decline in activity.

lullaby /'luləbie/ *noun* (*pl* **lullabies**) a song to quieten children or lull them to sleep. [LULL¹ + BYE-BYE]

lulu /'loohlooh/ *noun informal* somebody or something that is remarkable or wonderful. [prob from *Lulu*, nickname for *Louise*]

lum /lum/ *noun chiefly Scot* a chimney. [orig in the sense 'sky light': perhaps via Old French from Latin *lumen* light, airshaft, opening]

luma /'loohmə/ *noun* (*pl* **luma** *or* **lumas**) a unit of currency in Armenia, worth 100th of a dram. [Armenian *luma*]

lumbago /lum'baygoh/ *noun* muscular pain of the lumbar region of the back. [Latin *lumbago*, from *lumbus* loin]

lumbar /'lumbə/ *adj* to do with or in the region of the loins or the vertebrae between the thoracic vertebrae and sacrum: *the lumbar region*. [Latin *lumbaris*, from Latin *lumbus* loin]

lumbar puncture *noun* a medical procedure in which a hollow needle is inserted into the spinal cord, e.g. to give a drug or to withdraw cerebrospinal fluid for diagnosis.

lumber¹ /'lumbə/ *verb intrans* (**lumbered**, **lumbering**) to move heavily or clumsily. [Middle English *lomeren*; earlier history unknown]

lumber² *noun* **1** surplus or disused articles, e.g. furniture, that are stored away: *Knowledge, which we often see to be no better than lumber in men of dull understanding, was, in him, true, evident, and actual wisdom* — James Boswell. **2** *NAmer* timber or logs, *esp* when dressed for use.

Word history ⎯⎯⎯⎯⎯⎯⎯⎯⎯⎯⎯⎯
perhaps from *Lombard* in the obsolete sense 'pawnshop', from the use of pawnshops as storehouses of disused property. In the medieval period many pawnbrokers and moneylenders were Lombards.

lumber³ *verb trans Brit, informal* to encumber or saddle (somebody) with something: *I was lumbered with the bill as usual.* ➤ *verb intrans NAmer* to cut down and saw timber. ➤➤ **lumberer** *noun*.

lumberjack *noun* a person engaged in logging.

lumberjacket *noun* a heavy hip-length usu brightly checked woollen jacket that is fastened up to the neck.

lumberyard *noun NAmer* = TIMBERYARD.

lumen /'loohmin/ *noun* (*pl* **lumina** /-nə/ *or* **lumens**) **1** the cavity of a tubular organ: *the lumen of a blood vessel.* **2** the SI unit of luminous flux equal to the amount of light emitted in a solid angle of one steradian by a point source of light with an intensity of one candela. ➤➤ **luminal** *adj*. [Latin *lumin-*, *lumen* light, air shaft, opening]

luminance /'loohminəns/ *noun* the luminous intensity of a surface in a given direction per unit of projected area.

luminary /'loohmin(ə)ri/ *noun* (*pl* **luminaries**) **1** a person brilliantly outstanding in some respect: *Another darling weakness of the Academy is that none of its luminaries must 'arrive' in a hurry … By the time they have painted a thousand or so square yards of canvas, their work begins to be recognized* — Saki. **2** a natural body that gives light, e.g. the sun or moon. [Middle English *luminarye* via French from late Latin *luminaria*, pl of *luminare* lamp, heavenly body, from *lumin-*, *lumen* light]

luminesce /loohmi'nes/ *verb intrans* to exhibit luminescence. [back-formation from *luminescent*: see LUMINESCENCE]

luminescence *noun* an emission of light that occurs at low temperatures and that is produced by physiological processes, as in the firefly, by chemical action, by friction, or by electrical action. ➤➤ **luminescent** *adj*. [Latin *lumin-*, *lumen* light + -ESCENCE]

luminiferous /loohmi'nifərəs/ *adj archaic* transmitting, producing, or yielding light. [Latin *lumin-*, *lumen* light + -IFEROUS]

luminosity /loohmi'nositi/ *noun* (*pl* **luminosities**) **1a** being luminous. **b** something luminous. **2a** the relative quantity of light. **b** the relative brightness of something.

luminous /'loohminəs/ *adj* **1** emitting or full of light; bright. **2** relating to light or luminous flux. ➤➤ **luminously** *adv*, **luminousness** *noun*. [Middle English from Latin *luminosus*, from *lumin-*, *lumen* light]

luminous flux *noun* radiant flux in the visible-wavelength range.

lumme /'lumi/ *interj Brit, informal* used to express surprise. [contraction of *love me* (in the expression *Lord love me!*)]

lummox /'luməks/ *noun informal* a clumsy or stupid person. [origin unknown]

lump¹ /lump/ *noun* **1** a usu compact piece or mass of indefinite size and shape: *a lump of coal.* **2** an abnormal swelling. **3** *informal* a heavy thickset person; *specif* one who is stupid or dull. **4** (**the lump**) *Brit, informal* the whole group of casual non-union building workers. ✳ **a lump in one's throat** a dry feeling in the throat caused by emotion. [Middle English, prob of Germanic origin]

lump² *verb trans* **1** (*usu* + together) to group (things) without discrimination. **2** to make lumps on, in, or of (something). ➤ *verb intrans* **1** to become formed into lumps. **2** (*usu* + along) to move in a heavy way.

lump³ *verb trans informal* to put up with (something): *If you don't like it, you're just going to have to lump it.* [lump to be sulky, dislike, of imitative origin]

lumpectomy /lum'pektəmi/ *noun* (*pl* **lumpectomies**) the surgical removal of a tumour, *esp* in breast cancer, together with a minimal amount of surrounding tissue.

lumpen *adj informal* stupid or unenlightened. [back-formation from LUMPENPROLETARIAT; influenced by LUMP¹]

lumpenproletariat /,lumpənprohli'teəri-ət/ *noun* (*treated as sing. or pl*) in Marxist theory, the poorest people in society, e.g. homeless people, who are seen as being unenlightened and not interested in revolution. [German *Lumpenproletariat* lowest section of the proletariat, from *Lumpen* rags + *Proletariat* proletariat]

lumpfish *noun* (*pl* **lumpfishes** *or collectively* **lumpfish**) = LUMPSUCKER.

lumpish *adj* **1** dull or sluggish. **2** heavy or awkward. ➤➤ **lumpishly** *adv*, **lumpishness** *noun*.

lumpsucker *noun* a sea fish of the N Atlantic with a large rounded body and pelvic fins that are modified into a sucker so that the fish can attach itself to rocks, stones, etc: *Cyclopterus lumpus.* [early Dutch *lumpe* cod + SUCKER¹]

lump sum *noun* a large sum of money given in a single payment.

lumpy *adj* (**lumpier**, **lumpiest**) **1** filled or covered with lumps. **2** said of water: characterized by choppy waves. **3** said of a person: having a thickset clumsy appearance. ➤➤ **lumpily** *adv*, **lumpiness** *noun*.

lunacy /'loohnəsi/ *noun* (*pl* **lunacies**) **1** wild foolishness; extravagant folly. **2** *no longer in technical use.* **a** insanity interrupted by lucid intervals. **b** insanity amounting to lack of capability or responsibility in law. [LUNATIC¹]

luna moth /'loohnə/ *noun* a large N American moth with crescent-shaped markings and long tails on the hind wings: *Actias luna.* [Latin *luna* moon]

lunar /'loohnə/ *adj* **1a** found on or relating to the moon. **b** designed for use on the moon: *lunar vehicles.* **2** measured by the time taken for the moon to orbit the earth: *a lunar month.* [Latin *lunaris*, from *luna* moon]

lunar eclipse *noun* an eclipse in which the moon passes partly or wholly through the earth's shadow.

lunar month *noun* the period of time, averaging 29½ days, between two successive new moons.

lunar year *noun* a period of twelve lunar months.

lunate¹ /'loohnayt/ *adj* shaped like a crescent. [Latin *lunatus*, past part. of *lunare* to bend in a crescent, from *luna* moon]

lunate² *noun* (*also* **lunate bone**) a crescent-shaped bone of the CARPUS (wrist), which articulates with the bones of the lower arm.

lunatic¹ /'loohnətik/ *noun* **1** *no longer in technical use* a mentally ill person: *All are lunatics, but he who can analyse his delusion is a philosopher* — Ambrose Bierce. **2** a foolish or foolhardy person. [Middle English *lunatik* from Old French *lunatique* or late Latin *lunaticus*, both from Latin *luna* moon; from the former belief that lunacy fluctuates with the phases of the moon]

lunatic² *adj* **1** *archaic* insane. **2** wildly foolish.

lunatic asylum *noun dated* a hospital or home for people who are mentally ill.

lunatic fringe *noun* the extremist or fanatical members of a political or social movement.

lunation /looh'naysh(ə)n/ *noun* in astronomy, = LUNAR MONTH. [Middle English *lunacioun* from late Latin *lunation-*, *lunatio*, from Latin *luna* moon]

lunch[1] /lunch/ *noun* a midday meal. ✳ **out to lunch** *informal* crazy or out of touch with reality. [short for LUNCHEON]

lunch[2] *verb intrans* to eat lunch. ➢ *verb trans* to provide (somebody) with lunch or take (them) out to lunch. ➢➢ **luncher** *noun*.

lunch box *noun* **1** a box to carry food for e.g. a worker's or schoolchild's lunch. **2** *coarse slang* a man's genitals, *esp* as detectable under tight-fitting clothes.

luncheon /'lunch(ə)n/ *noun formal* = LUNCH[1]. [English dialect *luncheon* large lump, alteration of *lunch* lump, piece of food, perhaps alteration of LUMP[1]]

luncheon meat *noun* a precooked mixture of meat, e.g. pork, and cereal shaped in a loaf.

luncheon voucher *noun Brit* a voucher given to an employee as a benefit and exchangeable for food in some restaurants or shops.

lunette /looh'net/ *noun* **1** a semicircular window opening in a wall, vault, or dome. **2** a semicircular section of wall that is partly surrounded by a vault, often filled by windows or by a mural or sculpture. **3** a temporary fortification consisting of two walls forming a projecting angle. **4** a case used to hold the consecrated host in the Roman Catholic Church. [French *lunette*, dimin. of *lune* moon, from Latin *luna*]

lung /lung/ *noun* either of the usu paired compound saclike organs in the chest that constitute the basic respiratory organ of air-breathing vertebrates. [Old English *lungen*]

lunge[1] /lunj/ *verb intrans* to make a sudden forward movement or thrust. ➢ *verb trans* to thrust (e.g. a weapon) forward. [by shortening and alteration from obsolete *allonge* to make a thrust with a sword, from French *allonger* to lengthen]

lunge[2] *noun* **1** a sudden thrust or forceful forward movement. **2** the act of plunging forward.

lunge[3] *noun* a long rein used to hold and guide a horse in breaking and training. [French *longe* from Latin *longus* long]

lunge[4] *verb trans* to guide (a horse) on a lunge in a circular course round the trainer.

lungfish *noun* (*pl* **lungfishes** *or collectively* **lungfish**) any of various fishes that breathe by a modified air bladder as well as gills: order Dipneusti or Cladistia.

lungi /'loonggi/ *noun* (*pl* **lungis**) a usu cotton cloth worn variously as a loincloth, turban, or sash, *esp* by Indians. [Hindi *luṅgī*, from Persian]

lungwort *noun* any of several species of European plants of the borage family with usu white-spotted leaves covered in rough hairs, and blue or pink flowers: genus *Mertensia*. [because it was formerly used to treat lung diseases, and its leaves are supposed to resemble a diseased lung]

lunisolar /loohni'sohlə/ *adj* of or attributed to the moon and the sun. [Latin *luna* moon + SOLAR[1]]

lunula /'loohnyoohlə/ *noun* (*pl* **lunulae** /-lee/) the crescent-shaped whitish mark at the base of a fingernail. [Latin *lunula* crescent-shaped ornament, dimin. of *luna* moon]

lunule /'loohnyoohl/ *noun* = LUNULA.

lupin *or* **lupine** /'loohpin/ *noun* any of a genus of leguminous plants, some of which are cultivated for fertilizer, fodder, their edible seeds, or their long spikes of flowers: genus *Lupinus*. [Middle English *lupine* from Latin *lupinus*: see LUPINE]

lupine /'loohpien/ *adj* relating to or resembling a wolf. [Latin *lupinus*, from *lupus* wolf]

lupus /'loohpəs/ *noun* any of several diseases characterized by ulcers or scaly patches on the skin, *esp* tuberculosis of the skin. [Latin *lupus* wolf; orig denoting an ulcerous or cancerous condition, said to eat the skin like a wolf]

lupus erythematosus /ˌerətheemə'tohsəs/ *noun* a slowly progressive systemic disease marked by degenerative changes to connective tissue, reddish skin lesions, arthritic changes, lesions of internal organs, and wasting. [Latin *lupus erythematosus*, from LUPUS + Greek *eruthēma* reddening]

lupus vulgaris /vool'gahris, vul-/ *noun* a tuberculous disease of the skin marked by ulceration and scarring. [Latin *lupus vulgaris* common lupus]

lurch[1] /luhch/ *noun* an abrupt, uncontrolled, and jerky movement. [origin unknown]

lurch[2] *verb intrans* **1** to move in an abrupt, uncontrolled, and jerky manner. **2** to stagger and sway.

lurch[3] *noun* in cribbage, a decisive defeat in which an opponent wins a game by more than double the defeated player's score. ✳ **in the lurch** in a vulnerable and unsupported position; deserted. [early French *lourche* defeated by a lurch, deceived]

lurcher *noun* any of several types of swift-running dogs that are crosses between greyhound or whippet and another breed, e.g. the collie or terrier. [English dialect *lurch* to prowl, from Middle English *lorchen*, prob alteration of *lurken* LURK[1]]

lure[1] /lyooə, looə/ *noun* **1a** somebody or something used to entice or decoy. **b** a decoy for attracting animals so that they can be captured, e.g. an artificial bait used for catching fish. **2** a bunch of feathers and often meat attached to a long cord and used by a falconer to recall a bird. **3** the power to appeal or attract: *the lure of success*. [Middle English from early French *loire*, of Germanic origin]

lure[2] *verb trans* **1** to attract (a person or an animal) with something that promises pleasure, food, or gain. **2** to recall (a hawk) by means of a lure.

Lurex /'lyooəreks/ *noun trademark* a type of thread which is partly coated so as to give a metallic appearance.

lurgy /'luhgi/ *noun* (*pl* **lurgies**) *Brit, humorous* an illness, *esp* a widespread minor infection: *Half the staff are down with the dreaded lurgy*. [prob from ALLERGY]

lurid /'l(y)ooərid/ *adj* **1** unnaturally or unattractively bright in colour; gaudy. **2** sensational or shocking: *lurid newspaper reports of the crime*. **3** wan and ghastly pale in appearance. ➢➢ **luridly** *adv*, **luridness** *noun*. [Latin *luridus* pale yellow, sallow]

lurk[1] /luhk/ *verb intrans* **1a** to lie hidden in wait, *esp* with evil intent. **b** to move furtively or inconspicuously. **2** to be present but undetected; *esp* to be a hidden threat. ➢➢ **lurker** *noun*. [Middle English *lurken*; earlier history unknown]

lurk[2] *noun Aus, informal* a ruse or stratagem; a racket.

luscious /'lushəs/ *adj* **1** having a delicious taste or smell: *quite overcanopied with luscious woodbine* — Shakespeare. **2** said *esp* of a woman: extremely attractive. **3** richly luxurious or appealing to the senses. ➢➢ **lusciously** *adv*, **lusciousness** *noun*. [Middle English *lucius*, perhaps alteration of *licius*, short for DELICIOUS]

lush[1] /lush/ *adj* **1** producing or covered by luxuriant growth: *lush grass*. **2** opulent or sumptuous. **3** *informal* sexually attractive or voluptuous. **4** *informal* luscious, delicious, or generally very enjoyable. ➢➢ **lushly** *adv*. [Middle English *lusch* soft, tender; perhaps ultimately from Latin *laxus* loose]

lush[2] *noun chiefly NAmer, informal* a heavy drinker; an alcoholic. [origin unknown]

lush[3] *verb intrans NAmer* to drink heavily.

lust[1] /lust/ *noun* **1** strong sexual desire, *esp* as opposed to love. **2** an intense longing; a craving. ➢➢ **lustful** *adj*, **lustfully** *adv*, **lustfulness** *noun*. [Old English *lust* pleasure, desire]

lust[2] *verb intrans* (*usu* + for/after) to have an intense desire or craving, *esp* a sexual desire.

luster /'lustə/ *noun and verb NAmer* see LUSTRE[1], LUSTRE[2], LUSTRE[3].

lusterware *noun* see LUSTREWARE.

lustra /'lustrə/ *noun* pl of LUSTRUM.

lustral *adj* relating to a ceremony of religious purification. [Latin *lustralis*, from *lustrum*: see LUSTRUM]

lustrate /'lustrayt/ *verb trans* to purify (somebody or something) ceremonially. ➢➢ **lustration** /lu'straysh(ə)n/ *noun*. [Latin *lustratus*, past part. of *lustrare* to brighten, purify, from *lustrum*: see LUSTRUM]

lustre[1] (*NAmer* **luster**) /'lustə/ *noun* **1a** a glow of reflected light; a sheen. **b** the property of a mineral that is determined by the amount and quality of light reflected from its surface. **2** glory or distinction. **3a** a glass pendant used *esp* to ornament a chandelier. **b** a decorative object, e.g. a chandelier, hung with glass pendants. **4** a lustrous fabric with cotton warp and a wool, mohair, or alpaca weft. **5** an iridescent glaze used to decorate pottery or porcelain. ➢➢ **lustreless** *adj*. [early French *lustre* from Old Italian *lustro*, from *lustrare* to shine, from Latin *lustrare*: see LUSTRATE]

lustre[2] (*NAmer* **luster**) *noun* = LUSTRUM.

lustre[3] (*NAmer* **luster**) *verb trans* to give lustre or distinction to (something).

lustreware (*NAmer* **lusterware**) *noun* ceramic ware decorated with an iridescent glaze.

lustrous /'lustrəs/ *adj* softly and evenly shining: *a lustrous satin; the lustrous glow of an opal.* ➤➤ **lustrously** *adv*, **lustrousness** *noun*.

lustrum /'lustrəm/ *noun* (*pl* **lustrums** or **lustra** /'lustrə/) a period of five years. [Latin *lustrum*, purification of the Roman people made every five years after the census]

lusty *adj* (**lustier**, **lustiest**) full of vitality; healthy and vigorous. ➤➤ **lustily** *adv*, **lustiness** *noun*. [LUST[1] in a Middle English sense 'life, vigour']

lutanist /'loohtinist/ *noun* see LUTENIST.

lute[1] /looht/ *noun* a stringed musical instrument with a large pear-shaped body, a neck with a fretted fingerboard, and pairs of strings tuned in unison. [Middle English from French *lut*, via Old Provençal from Arabic *al 'ūd*, literally 'the wood']

lute[2] *noun* a substance, e.g. cement or clay, used for sealing or packing joints or for coating a porous surface to make it impervious to a liquid or gas. [Middle English, from Latin *lutum* clay]

lute[3] *verb trans* to seal or coat (something) with lute.

luteal /'loohti·əl/ *adj* relating to or involving the CORPUS LUTEUM (hormone-producing body present in the ovary during pregnancy).

lutecium /looh'teeshi·əm/ *noun* see LUTETIUM.

lutein /'loohti·in, 'loohteen/ *noun* an orange pigment occurring in plants, animal fat, egg yolk, and the CORPUS LUTEUM (hormone-producing body present in the ovary during pregnancy). [Latin *luteum* egg yolk, neuter of *luteus* (see LUTEOUS) + -IN[1]]

luteinizing hormone or **luteinising hormone** /'loohteeniez-ing/ *noun* a hormone from the front lobe of the pituitary gland that in the female stimulates ovulation and in the male the synthesis of androgen.

lutenist /'loohtinist/ or **lutanist** *noun* a lute player. [late Latin *lutanista*, from *lutana* lute, prob from early French *lut*: see LUTE[1]]

luteotrophic hormone /ˌloohtioh'trohfik, -'trofik/ *noun* = PRO-LACTIN. [Latin *luteum* as in CORPUS LUTEUM + -TROPHIC]

luteous /'loohti·əs/ *adj* of a yellow colour tinged with green or brown. [Latin *luteus* yellowish, from *lutum*, a plant used for dyeing yellow]

lutetium or **lutecium** /looh'teeshi·əm/ *noun* a silver-white metallic chemical element of the rare-earth group found in ytterbium alloys: symbol Lu, atomic number 71. [scientific Latin, from *Lutetia*, ancient name of Paris, home of French chemist G *Urbains* d.1938, who discovered it]

Lutheran[1] /'loohthərən/ *noun* a member of a Lutheran church.

Lutheran[2] *adj* relating to religious doctrines, e.g. justification by faith alone, or Protestant churches derived from Martin Luther or his followers. ➤➤ **Lutheranism** *noun*. [Martin *Luther* d.1546, German religious reformer]

luting /'loohting/ *noun* = LUTE[2].

lutz /loots, luts/ *noun* in ice-skating, a jump from one skate with a complete turn in the air and a return to the other skate. [prob named after Gustave *Lussi* b.1898, Swiss figure skater, its inventor]

luvvie or **luvvy** /'luvi/ *noun* (*pl* **luvvies**) *Brit, informal or humorous* an actor, *esp* seen as affected: *He is director of the Royal National Theatre, and thus head boy of that dramatic sub-species known to brutish non-Thespians as the 'luvvies'* — The Economist. [variant of LOVEY, supposed to be much used by the acting profession]

lux /luks/ *noun* (*pl* **lux**) the SI unit of illumination, equal to one lumen per square metre. [Latin *lux* light]

luxate /'luksayt/ *verb trans* to dislocate (a part of the body). ➤➤ **luxation** /luk'saysh(ə)n/ *noun*. [Latin *luxatus*, past part. of *luxare*, from *luxus* dislocated]

luxe /luks, looks/ *noun* = LUXURY. [French *luxe* luxury, from Latin *luxus*: see LUXURY]

Luxembourgish /'luksəmbawrish/ or **Luxemburgish** /'luksəmbuhgish/ *noun* a dialect of German which is one of the official languages of Luxembourg. ➤➤ **Luxembourgish** *adj*, **Luxemburgish** *adj*.

luxuriant /lug'zhooəri·ənt/ *adj* **1** characterized by abundant growth. **2a** exuberantly rich and varied; prolific. **b** richly or excessively ornamented: *luxuriant prose.* ➤➤ **luxuriance** *noun*, **luxuriantly** *adv*. [Latin *luxurians*, present part. of *luxuriare* to grow abundantly or excessively, from *luxuria*: see LUXURY]

Usage note

luxuriant or **luxurious**? These two words are sometimes confused. *Luxuriant* means 'growing thickly and abundantly': *luxuriant vegetation*. *Luxurious* is the adjective connected with the ordinary sense of *luxury*: *the sort of luxurious accommodation you would expect from a five-star hotel.*

luxuriate /lug'zhooəriayt/ *verb intrans* (*often* + in) to enjoy oneself consciously; to revel. [Latin *luxuriatus*, past part. of *luxuriare*: see LUXURIANT]

luxurious /lug'zhooəri·əs/ *adj* **1** extremely comfortable and usu furnished with articles of high quality and sumptuous appearance. **2** *literary* fond of luxury or self-indulgence. ➤➤ **luxuriously** *adv*, **luxuriousness** *noun*.

Usage note

luxurious or **luxuriant**? See note at LUXURIANT.

luxury /'lukshəri/ *noun* (*pl* **luxuries**) **1** great ease or comfort based on habitual or liberal use of expensive items without regard to cost: *lived in luxury.* **2a** something desirable but costly or difficult to obtain: *Love is like any other luxury. You have no right to it unless you can afford it* — Trollope. **b** something relatively expensive adding to pleasure or comfort but not indispensable. [Middle English *luxurie* via French from Latin *luxuria* rankness, luxury, excess, from *luxus* abundance, pleasure]

LV *abbr* **1** Latvia (international vehicle registration). **2** *Brit* luncheon voucher.

LW *abbr* **1** long wave. **2** low water.

lwei /lə'way/ *noun* (*pl* **lwei** or **lweis**) a unit of currency in Angola, worth 100th of a kwanza. [of Bantu origin]

LWM *abbr* low-water mark.

lx *abbr* lux.

LXX *abbr* Septuagint.

-ly[1] *suffix* forming adjectives, with the meanings: **1** like in appearance, manner, or nature; having the characteristics of: *queenly*; *fatherly*. **2** recurring regularly at intervals of; every: *hourly*; *daily*. [Old English *-līc*, *-lic*]

-ly[2] *suffix* forming adverbs, with the meaning: in (such) a manner: *slowly*; *frankly*. [Old English *-līce*, *-lice*, from *-līc* -LY[1]]

lycanthrope /'liekənthrohp, lie'kanthrohp/ *noun* **1** *literary* = WERE-WOLF. **2** a person with the symptoms of lycanthropy. [via Latin from Greek *lykanthrōpos* werewolf, from *lykos* wolf + *anthrōpos* man]

lycanthropy /lie'kanthrəpi/ *noun* **1** the transformation of a human being into a wolf, held to be possible by witchcraft or magic. **2** a psychological delusion that one has become a wolf. ➤➤ **lycanthropic** /-'thropik/ *adj*.

lycée /'leesay (*French* lise)/ *noun* a French public secondary school. [French *lycée* from Latin *Lyceum*: see LYCEUM]

lyceum /lie'see·əm/ *noun* **1** = LYCÉE. **2** (*often* **Lyceum**) a public building, cinema, theatre, etc. **3** *NAmer, archaic* a hall for public lectures or discussions, or an organization responsible for presenting such a programme. [Latin *Lyceum* gymnasium near Athens where Aristotle taught, from Greek *Lykeion*, neuter of *Lykeios*, epithet of Apollo, god of poetry; the gymnasium took its name from a temple of Apollo nearby]

lychee or **lichee** or **litchi** /'liechee/ *noun* **1** a small oval fruit with a hard scaly outer covering and a small hard seed surrounded by edible soft white fragrant pulp. **2** the Chinese tree that bears this fruit: *Litchi chinensis*. [Chinese (Pekinese) *lizhi*]

lych-gate or **lychgate** or **lich-gate** /lich/ *noun* a roofed gate at the entrance to a churchyard traditionally used as a resting place for a coffin during part of a burial service. [Middle English *lycheyate*, from Old English *līc* body, corpse + *geate* GATE[1]]

lychnis /'liknis/ *noun* any of a genus of plants of the pink family with heads of showy red, pink, or white flowers: genus *Lychnis*. [Latin genus name, ultimately from Greek *lukhnos* a red flower, from *lychnos* lamp]

lycopodium /ˌliekə'pohdi·əm/ *noun* **1** any of a large genus of erect or creeping club mosses with evergreen one-nerved leaves: genus *Lycopodium*. **2** a fine yellowish powder of lycopodium spores used in pharmacy and as a component of fireworks and flashlight powders. [Latin genus name, from Greek *lykos* wolf + *podion*, dimin. of *pod-*, *pous* foot; from the shape of the plant's root]

Lycra /'liekrə/ *noun trademark* a synthetic stretchy yarn made from polyurethane and used chiefly in tight-fitting sportswear and swimwear.

lyddite /'lidiet/ *noun* a high explosive composed chiefly of picric acid. [named after *Lydd*, a town in Kent, SE England where it was orig tested]

lye /lie/ *noun* **1** a strong alkaline liquid rich in potassium carbonate, leached from wood ashes, and used in making soap. **2** a strong alkaline solution, e.g. of sodium hydroxide or potassium hydroxide. [Old English *lēag*]

lying[1] /'lieing/ *verb* present part. of LIE[1].

lying[2] *verb* present part. of LIE[4].

lying-in *noun* (*pl* **lyings-in** *or* **lying-ins**) *archaic* confinement for childbirth: *The Lord … took away my most dear, precious, meek, and loving wife, in childbed, after three weeks' lying-in* — Thomas Shepard.

lykewake /'liekwayk/ *noun Brit* a watch held over a dead body. [Middle English *lych wake*, from Old English *līc* body, corpse + WAKE[2]]

Lyme disease /liem/ *noun* an infectious disease characterized by recurring attacks of fever, joint pain, chronic lethargy, and a rash, sometimes involving serious complications of the heart and nervous system, caused by a tick-borne bacterium. [named after Old *Lyme*, a town in Connecticut, USA, where the disease was identified in 1975]

lymph /limf/ *noun* a pale fluid resembling blood plasma that contains white blood cells but normally no red blood cells, which circulates in the lymphatic vessels, and bathes the cells of the body. [Latin *lympha* water goddess, water, from Greek *nymphē* NYMPH]

lymph- *or* **lympho-** *comb. form* forming words, denoting: lymph or lymphatic tissue: *lymphocyte*. [Latin *lympha*: see LYMPH]

lymphatic[1] /lim'fatik/ *adj* **1** of, involving, or produced by lymph, lymphoid tissue, or lymphocytes. **2** conveying lymph: *lymphatic vessels*. **3** lacking physical or mental energy; sluggish.

lymphatic[2] *noun* a vessel that contains or conveys lymph.

lymphatic system *noun* the network of vessels that transport lymph to the bloodstream.

lymph gland *noun* = LYMPH NODE.

lymph node *noun* any of the rounded masses of lymphoid tissue that occur along the course of the lymphatic vessels and in which lymphocytes are formed.

lympho- *comb. form* see LYMPH-.

lymphocyte /'limfəsiet/ *noun* a white blood cell that is present in large numbers in lymph and blood and defends the body by immunological responses to invading or foreign matter, e.g. by producing antibodies. ➤➤ **lymphocytic** /-'sitik/ *adj.*

lymphoid /'limfoyd/ *adj* **1** relating to or resembling lymph. **2** relating to or constituting the tissue characteristic of the lymph nodes.

lymphoma /lim'fohmə/ *noun* (*pl* **lymphomas** *or* **lymphomata** /-tə, -'mahtə/) cancer of the lymph nodes.

lynch /linch/ *verb trans* to put (somebody) to death illegally by mob action. ➤➤ **lyncher** *noun*. [LYNCH LAW]

lynchet /'linchit/ *noun Brit* a terrace formed on a hillside by prehistoric cultivation. [English dialect *lynch*, from Old English *hlinc* ridge of land + -ET]

lynch law *noun* the punishment of presumed crimes or offences usu by death without due process of law. [prob named after William *Lynch* d.1820, US citizen who organized extralegal tribunals in Virginia]

lynchpin *noun* see LINCHPIN.

lynx /lingks/ *noun* (*pl* **lynxes** *or collectively* **lynx**) any of various wildcats with relatively long legs, a short stubby tail, a mottled coat, and often tufted ears, e.g. the common lynx of N Europe and Asia,

and the bobcat: *Lynx lynx* and other species. [via Latin from Greek *lynx*]

lynx-eyed *adj* having keen eyesight.

lyonnaise /lee·ə'nayz/ *adj* cooked in the way traditional in Lyons, often with onions. [French *lyonnaise* in the manner of Lyons, from fem of *lyonnais* of Lyons, from *Lyon* Lyons, a city in southwestern France]

lyrate /'lie·ərət/ *adj* shaped like a lyre.

lyre /'lie·ə/ *noun* a stringed musical instrument of the harp family with a U-shaped frame and a crossbar from which the strings were stretched to the sound box at the base, used by the ancient Greeks, *esp* to accompany song and recitation. [Middle English *lire* via Old French and Latin from Greek *lyra*]

lyrebird *noun* either of two Australian songbirds the male of which displays tail feathers in the shape of a lyre during courtship: genus *Menura*.

lyric[1] /'lirik/ *noun* **1** (*in pl*) the words of a popular song. **2** a lyric poem.

lyric[2] *adj* **1a** suitable for being set to music and sung. **b** having a beautifully melodious or songlike quality. **2** expressing direct personal emotion: *lyric poetry*. **3** said of a singer: having a light voice and a melodic style. [early French *lyrique* or Latin *lyricus* from Greek *lyrikos*, from *lyra* LYRE]

lyrical *adj* **1** = LYRIC[2]. **2** full of admiration or enthusiasm: *She waxed lyrical about their new kitten.* ➤➤ **lyrically** *adv.*

lyricism /'lirisiz(ə)m/ *noun* **1a** a pleasantly melodious, flowing, and songlike quality, *esp* in music. **b** a directly personal and intense style or quality in an art. **2** great enthusiasm or exuberance.

lyricist /'lirisist/ *noun* a writer of lyrics.

lyrist /'lie·ərist/ *noun* **1** somebody who plays the lyre. **2** /'lirist/ = LYRICIST.

lyse /lies, liez/ *verb trans and intrans* to undergo or cause (a cell) to undergo lysis. [back-formation from Latin *lysis*: see LYSIS]

lysergic acid /lie'suhjik/ *noun* an acid obtained from alkaloids that occur in the fungus ergot, and from which the drug LSD is obtained: formula $C_{16}H_{16}N_2O_2$. [blend of HYDROLYSIS + ERGOT]

lysergic acid diethylamide /die,ethil'aymied, die·ə'thieləmied/ *noun* = LSD.

lyses /'lieseez/ *noun* pl of LYSIS.

lysin /'liesin/ *noun* a substance capable of causing lysis; *esp* an antibody capable of causing disintegration of red blood cells or micro-organisms.

lysine /'lieseen, 'liesin/ *noun* a basic amino acid found in most proteins and an essential constituent of the human diet.

lysis /'liesis/ *noun* (*pl* **lyses** /'lieseez/) **1** a process of disintegration or dissolution of cells. **2** the gradual decline of a disease process, e.g. fever. ➤➤ **lytic** /'litik/ *adj*, **lytically** /'litikli/ *adv*. [via Latin from Greek *lysis* act of loosening, dissolution, remission of fever, from *lyein* to loosen]

-lysis *comb. form* forming nouns, denoting: decomposition, disintegration, or breaking down: *electrolysis*; *autolysis*. [Latin *-lysis* via Latin and Greek from Greek *lysis*: see LYSIS]

Lysol /'liesol/ *noun trademark* a mildly corrosive solution of cresol and soap, formerly used as a disinfectant. [-LYSIS + -OL[1]]

-lyte *comb. form* forming nouns, denoting: a substance capable of undergoing the process or change specified: *electrolyte*. [Greek *lytos* that may be untied, soluble, from *lyein* to loosen]

-lytic *suffix* forming adjectives, with the meaning: of or effecting decomposition: *hydrolytic enzymes*. [Greek *lytikos* able to loosen, from *lyein* to loosen]

M¹ *or* **m** *noun* (*pl* **M's** *or* **Ms** *or* **m's**) **1a** the 13th letter of the English alphabet. **b** a written character or design denoting this letter. **c** the sound represented by this letter, one of the English consonants. **2** an item designated as M, *esp* the 13th in a series. **3** the Roman numeral for 1000.

M² *abbr* **1** Mach. **2** Malta (international vehicle registration). **3** mark. **4** Master. **5** mega-. **6** Member. **7** Monsieur. **8** motorway.

m *abbr* **1** in cricket, maiden over. **2** male. **3** mare. **4** married. **5** masculine. **6** mass. **7** metre. **8** mile. **9** milli-. **10** million. **11** minute. **12** month.

'm *contraction* am: *I'm going.*

MA *abbr* **1** Massachusetts (US postal abbreviation). **2** Master of Arts. **3** Military Academy. **4** Morocco (international vehicle registration).

ma /mah/ *noun informal* an affectionate name for one's mother.

ma'am /mam, mahm; *unstressed* məm/ *noun* used in the USA as a respectful form of address for any woman, and in Britain *esp* when addressing the Queen or a royal princess: madam.

Maasai /'masie/ *noun* see MASAI.

Mac /mak/ *noun informal* **1** *NAmer* a form of address for a man whose name is not known to the speaker. **2** *dated* a form of address for a Scotsman. [*Mac-, Mc-*, common Scottish and Irish patronymic prefix]

mac *or* **mack** *noun Brit, informal* a raincoat. [short for MACKINTOSH]

macabre /mə'kahb(r)ə/ *adj* **1** ghastly; gruesome: *Spare us the macabre details; a macabre sense of humour.* **2** relating to or depicting the grimmer or uglier aspects of death. [French *macabre* from *danse macabre* dance of death, from early French *danse Macabé* dance of the Maccabees, prob from a mystery play]

macadam /mə'kadəm/ *noun* small broken stones compacted into a solid mass, *esp* bound together with tar or asphalt, used in making a road surface: compare TARMACADAM. [named after John *McAdam* d.1836, Scottish engineer]

macadamia /makə'daymi-ə/ *noun* **1** an edible waxy round nut. **2** any of a genus of Australian evergreen trees, with clusters of white flowers, that bear this nut: genus *Macadamia*. [from the Latin genus name, named after John *Macadam* d.1865, Australian chemist]

macadamize /mə'kadəmiez/ *or* **macadamise** *verb trans* to construct or finish (a road) with macadam.

macaque /mə'kahk/ *noun* any of several species of short-tailed monkeys of S Asia and the E Indies, with cheek pouches in which food is stored: genus *Macaca*. [French *macaque* from Portuguese *macaco*]

macaroni /makə'rohni/ *noun* (*pl* **macaronis** *or* **macaronies**) **1** (*used as sing. or pl*) pasta made from durum wheat and shaped in hollow tubes that are wider in diameter than spaghetti. **2** an English dandy of the 18th cent. who affected continental ways. [Italian *maccheroni*, pl of *maccherone*, from Italian dialect *maccarone* dumpling, macaroni]

macaronic /makə'ronik/ *adj* denoting a type of burlesque verse characterized by a mixture of Latin and vernacular words, the latter sometimes given Latin inflections. [Latin *macaronicus* from Italian dialect *maccarone* macaroni]

macaroon /makə'roohn/ *noun* a small cake or biscuit composed chiefly of egg whites, sugar, and ground almonds or occasionally coconut. [French *macaron* from Italian dialect *maccarone* macaroni]

Macassar oil /mə'kasə/ *noun* a preparation containing oil formerly used for dressing the hair. [named after *Macassar*, former name for Ujung Pandang, a city in Indonesia from where the oil's ingredients reputedly originated]

macaw /mə'kaw/ *noun* any of several species of long-tailed large and showy parrots of S and Central America: genus *Ara* and other genera. [Portuguese *macau*]

Macc. *abbr* Maccabees (books of the Apocrypha).

Maccabees /'makəbeez/ *pl noun* **1** a priestly family who led a Jewish revolt against Seleucid rule and reigned over Palestine from 142 to 63 BC. **2** (*treated as sing.*) either of two narrative and historical books included in the Roman Catholic canon of the Old Testament and in the Protestant Apocrypha. ⟫⟫ **Maccabean** /-'bee-ən/ *adj.* [Greek *Makkabaioi*, pl of *Makkabaios*, surname of Judas Maccabaeus, Jewish patriot of the second cent. BC]

McCarthyism /mə'kahthiiz(ə)m/ *noun* a fanatical campaign against alleged Communists in the US senate and in public life, carried on by Senator McCarthy in the early 1950s mainly by means of unsubstantiated charges and damaging innuendo. ⟫⟫ **McCarthyist** *noun and adj*, **McCarthyite** /-iet/ *noun and adj.* [named after Joseph R McCarthy d.1957, US politician]

McCoy /mə'koy/ ✳ **the real McCoy** *informal* something that is neither imitation nor substitute; the genuine article: *We thought the Gucci watch was fake but it turned out to be the real McCoy.* [alteration of *Mackay* in the phrase *the real Mackay* the true chief of the Mackay clan, a position often disputed]

Mace /mays/ *noun trademark* a riot control agent in aerosol form, containing tear gas. [prob from MACE¹]

mace¹ *noun* **1** a heavy medieval spiked staff or club. **2** an ornamental staff used as a symbol of authority. [Middle English from early French *masse, mace* large hammer]

mace² *noun* an aromatic spice consisting of the dried external fibrous covering of a nutmeg. [Middle English via French from Latin *macir*, an East Indian spice, from Greek *makir*]

macédoine /masə'dwahn, 'masədoyn/ *noun* a mixture of fruits or vegetables served sometimes in jelly as a salad, cocktail, or garnish. [French *macédoine*, earlier meaning 'mixture, medley', from

Macédoine Macedonia, a region of SE Europe; perhaps from the mixture of races in Macedonia, or in Alexander the Great's empire]

Macedonian /masi'dohni-ən/ *noun* **1** a native or inhabitant of the ancient kingdom of Macedonia in SE Europe, the modern republic of Macedonia in the Balkans, or the region of Macedonia in Greece. **2** the Slavonic language of modern Macedonia. **3** the language of ancient Macedonia, of uncertain affinity but probably Indo-European. ➤➤ **Macedonian** *adj.*

macerate /'masərayt/ *verb trans* **1** to cause (food) to become soft or separated into constituent elements by steeping in fluid. **2** *archaic* to cause (somebody) to waste away. ➤ *verb intrans* to soften and wear away, *esp* as a result of being wetted. ➤➤ **maceration** /-'raysh(ə)n/ *noun*, **macerator** *noun*. [Latin *maceratus*, past part. of *macerare* to soften, steep]

McGuffin /mə'gufin/ *noun* an incident or device in a book or film that precipitates the action, important to the main characters but overlooked by the reader or audience. [coined by Alfred Hitchcock d.1980, English film director; from a story containing such a plot feature]

Mach /mak, mahk/ *noun* = MACH NUMBER: *an aeroplane flying at Mach two.*

machair /'makhə/ *noun* on the west coast of Scotland and the Western Isles, a flat strip of sandy grass-grown land close to the shore, used for grazing: *The weed is carted from the shore to the machairs … and laid out to dry* — Chambers Journal. [Gaelic *machair*]

machete /mə'sheti/ *noun* a large heavy knife used for cutting vegetation and as a weapon. [Spanish *machete* from *macho* sledge-hammer]

Machiavelli /,makiə'veli/ *noun* = MACHIAVELLIAN[2].

Machiavellian[1] /,maki-ə'veli-ən/ *adj* cunning, opportunist, and deceitful. [named after Niccolò *Machiavelli* d.1527, Italian statesman and political theorist, who advocated unethical means to gain or maintain power]

Machiavellian[2] *noun* a Machiavellian person, *esp* a politician.

Machiavellianism *noun* the political theory of Machiavelli; *esp* the view that politics is amoral and that any means, however unscrupulous, can justifiably be used in securing or retaining political power.

machicolate /mə'chikəlayt/ *verb trans* (*usu as past part.*) to provide (a fortification) with machicolations: *a machicolated and battlemented tower.* [late Latin *machicolare* from Old French *machicoller* from *machicoleis* machicolation, from *macher* to crush + *col* neck]

machicolation /ma,chikə'laysh(ə)n/ *noun* an opening between the corbels of a projecting parapet or in the floor of a gallery or roof of a portal for discharging missiles upon assailants below.

machinate /'makinayt, 'mash-/ *verb intrans* (*often* + against) to scheme or plot, *esp* to do harm. ➤➤ **machinator** *noun*. [Latin *machinatus*, past part. of *machinari*, from *machina* machine, contrivance]

machination /maki'naysh(ə)n, mash-/ *noun* a scheming move intended to accomplish some usu discreditable end.

machine[1] /mə'sheen/ *noun* **1a** a combination of parts that transmit forces, motion, and energy one to another in a predetermined manner: *a sewing machine.* **b** an instrument, e.g. a lever or pulley, designed to transmit or modify the application of power, force, or motion. **c** a combination of mechanically, electrically, or electronically operated parts for performing a task. **d** a coin-operated device: *a cigarette machine.* **2a** a person or organization that operates with mechanical efficiency. **b** the controlling or inner organization, e.g. of a group or activity: *the war machine.* [early French *machine* structure, fabric, via Latin from Greek *mēchanē* (Doric dialect *machana*), from *mēchos* means, expedient]

machine[2] *verb trans* **1** to shape, finish, or operate on (something) with a machine. **2** to sew (something) using a sewing machine: *Machine the zip in place.* ➤➤ **machinability** /-'biliti/ *noun*, **machinable** *adj*, **machineable** *adj*.

machine code *noun* a system of symbols and rules for coding information in a form usable by a machine, e.g. a computer.

machine gun *noun* an automatic gun for rapid continuous fire.

machine-gun *verb trans* (**machine-gunned, machine-gunning**) to fire at (somebody or something) with a machine gun. ➤➤ **machine-gunner** *noun*.

machine language *noun* = MACHINE CODE.

machine-readable *adj* directly usable by a computer: *machine-readable text.*

machinery *noun* **1a** machines in general or as a functioning unit. **b** the working parts of a machine. **2** the system or organization by which an activity or process is controlled: *the machinery of government.*

machine tool *noun* a usu power-driven machine designed for cutting or shaping wood, metal, etc. ➤➤ **machine-tooled** *adj*.

machinist *noun* **1** a person who operates a machine, *esp* a sewing machine. **2** a person who makes, assembles, or repairs machinery.

machismo /mə'kizmoh, mə'chizmoh/ *noun* an exaggerated awareness and assertion of masculinity. [Mexican Spanish *machismo* from Spanish *macho* male]

Mach number /mak, mahk/ *noun* a number representing the ratio of the speed of a body to the speed of sound in the surrounding atmosphere: *A Mach number of two indicates a speed that is twice that of sound.* [named after Ernst *Mach* d.1916, Austrian physicist]

macho[1] /'machoh/ *adj* toughly or aggressively virile: *They think it's macho to be violent.* [Spanish *macho* male, from Latin *masculus* masculine]

macho[2] *noun* (*pl* **machos**) **1** machismo. **2** a man who is aggressively virile.

macintosh /'makintosh/ *noun* see MACKINTOSH.

mack /mak/ *noun Brit, informal* see MAC.

mackerel /'mak(ə)rəl/ *noun* (*pl* **mackerels** or collectively **mackerel**) **1** a fish of the N Atlantic that has a green back with dark blue bars and a silvery belly and is one of the most important food fishes: *Scomber scombrus.* **2** any of various usu small or medium-sized related fishes. [Middle English *makerel* from Old French *maquerel*, of uncertain origin]

mackerel shark *noun* = PORBEAGLE.

mackerel sky *noun* a sky covered with rows of altocumulus or cirrocumulus clouds, resembling the patterns on a mackerel's back.

mackintosh or **macintosh** /'makintosh/ *noun chiefly Brit* a raincoat. [named after Charles *Macintosh* d.1843, Scottish chemist and inventor, who patented the rubberized cloth orig used to make such coats]

mackle /'makl/ *noun* a blur or double impression on a printed sheet. [French *macule* spot, mackle, from Latin *macula* spot, stain]

macle /'makl/ *noun* **1** a compound crystal consisting of two or more similar individual crystals in contact; = TWIN[1] (3). **2** a dark or discoloured spot, e.g. in a mineral. [French *macle* wide-meshed net, lozenge, macle, of Germanic origin]

McNaghten rules or **M'Naghten** or **McNaughten** /mək'nawt(ə)n/ *pl noun* in English law, a set of four rules that establish how far an insane person is responsible for criminal acts. [named after Daniel *McNaghten*, the murderer whose case in 1843 led to the establishment of the rules]

macr- *comb. form* see MACRO-.

macramé /mə'krahmi/ *noun* **1** the art of tying threads or cords in patterns. **2** a coarse lace so produced, or decorative articles made from it. [French *macramé* from Italian *macramè*, via Turkish from Arabic *migramah* embroidered veil]

macro /'makroh/ *noun* (*pl* **macros**) **1** a single computer instruction that stands for a complete sequence of operations. **2** = MACRO LENS.

macro- or **macr-** *comb. form* forming words, with the meanings: **1** long in duration or size: *macrobiotic.* **2** large or abnormally large: *macrophyte.* [via French and Latin from Greek *makr-*, *makro-* long, from *makros* long, large]

macrobiotic /,makrohbie'otik/ *adj* relating to or denoting a restricted diet, *esp* one consisting chiefly of whole grains or whole grains and vegetables, that is usu undertaken with the intention of promoting health and prolonging life.

macrobiotics *noun* (*treated as sing.*) a macrobiotic system or diet.

macrocarpa /makroh'kahpə/ *noun* a Californian cypress grown in New Zealand and elsewhere to provide hedging or windbreaks: *Cupressus macrocarpa.* [scientific Latin *macrocarpa*, from MACRO- + *-carpa*, fem of *-carpus* -CARPOUS]

macrocephalic /,makrohsi'falik/ *adj* = MACROCEPHALOUS.

macrocephalous /makroh'sefələs/ *adj* having an exceptionally large head or cranium. ➤➤ **macrocephaly** /-li/ *noun*.

macroclimate /'makrohkliemət/ *noun* the predominant or normal climate of a large region.

macrocosm /'makrəkoz(ə)m/ *noun* **1** the universe. **2** a complex that is a large-scale reproduction of one of its constituents. ➤➤ **macrocosmic** /-'kozmik/ *adj*, **macrocosmically** /-'kozmikli/ *adv*. [MACRO- + Greek *kosmos* order, universe]

macroeconomics /ˌmakroh·ekə'nomiks, -eekə'nomiks/ *pl noun* (*treated as sing.*) a study of large-scale economics, e.g. of a nation: compare MICROECONOMICS. ➤➤ **macroeconomic** *adj*.

macroevolution /ˌmakroh-eevə'loohsh(ə)n/ *noun* evolutionary change affecting broad groups of organisms, e.g. families and genera, and involving relatively large and complex steps or changes. ➤➤ **macroevolutionary** *adj*.

macroinstruction *noun* **1** = MACRO. **2** = MACRO (1).

macro lens *noun* a lens with which subjects can be photographed at very close range.

macromolecule /makroh'molikyoohl/ *noun* a large molecule, e.g. of a protein or rubber, built up from smaller chemical structures. ➤➤ **macromolecular** /-'lekyoolə/ *adj*.

macron /'makron/ *noun* a mark (¯) placed over a vowel or syllable to show a long or stressed sound. [Greek *makron*, neuter of *makros* long]

macronutrient /makroh'nyoohtri-ənt/ *noun* a nutrient element of which relatively large quantities are essential to the growth and welfare of a plant.

macrophage /'makrohfayj, -fahzh/ *noun* any of various large cells that are distributed throughout the body tissues, ingest foreign matter and debris, and may be attached to the fibres of a tissue or take the form of a mobile white blood cell. [MACRO- + -PHAGE]

macrophyte /'makrohfiet/ *noun* a plant that is part of the macroscopic plant life of a body of water.

macropod /'makrəpod, 'makroh-/ *noun* any of a family of Australasian herbivorous marsupials that comprises the kangaroos and wallabies: family Macropodidae.

macroscopic /makrə'skopik/ *adj* **1** large enough to be observed by the naked eye. **2** considered in terms of large units or elements. ➤➤ **macroscopically** *adv*. [MACRO- + -SCOPIC (as in MICROSCOPIC)]

macrostructure /'makrohstrukchə/ *noun* the structure of a metal, body part, the soil, etc revealed by visual examination with little or no magnification. ➤➤ **macrostructural** *adj*.

macula /'makyoolə/ *noun* (*pl* **maculae** /-lee/ *or* **maculas**) **1** a blotch or spot; *esp* a macule. **2** an anatomical structure, e.g. the MACULA LUTEA, having the form of a spot differentiated from surrounding tissues. ➤➤ **macular** *adj*. [Latin *macula* spot]

macula lutea /'loohti-ə/ *noun* (*pl* **maculae luteae** /'loohti-ee/) a small yellowish area lying slightly to the side of the centre of the retina that constitutes the region of best vision. [Latin *macula lutea* yellow spot]

maculation /makyoo'laysh(ə)n/ *noun* the arrangement of spots and markings on an animal or plant.

macule /'makyoohl/ *noun* a discoloured spot on the skin that is not raised above the surface. [French *macule* from Latin *macula* spot]

macumba /mə'koombə/ *noun* a Brazilian religious cult combining features of voodoo and of Christianity. [Portuguese *Macumba*]

macushla /mə'kooshlə/ *noun Irish* used as an affectionate form of address: my darling. [Irish *mo* my + *cuisle* pulse]

mad[1] /mad/ *adj* (**madder, maddest**) **1** mentally disordered; insane. **2** utterly foolish; senseless. **3** carried away by intense anger. **4** carried away by enthusiasm or desire: *mad for thy love?* — Shakespeare. **5** said of a dog: affected with rabies. **6** intensely excited or distraught; frantic. **7** characterized by intense and often chaotic activity: *make a mad dash for cover; in a mad rush.* ✳ **like mad** *informal* very hard, fast, loud, etc: *shout like mad.* **mad keen** *informal* very enthusiastic. [Old English *gemǽd*, past part. related to *gemād* silly, mad]

mad[2] *verb* (**madded, madding**) *archaic or literary* to drive (a person) mad: *This music mads me* — Shakespeare.

Madagascan /madə'gaskən/ *noun* a native or inhabitant of the island of Madagascar. ➤➤ **Madagascan** *adj*.

madam /'madəm/ *noun* **1** used without a name as a form of respectful address to a woman, sometimes used obliquely: *Will madam have the fish?* **2** (**Madam**) used with *Dear* as a conventional

form of address at the beginning of a letter. **3** (**Madam**) used in direct address as a conventional title of respect before a woman's title of office: *Madam Chairman.* **4** the female head of a brothel. **5** *Brit, informal* a conceited or petulant young lady or girl: *She's a real little madam.* [Middle English from Old French *ma dame* my lady]

madame /'madəm (*French* madam)/ *noun* (*pl* **mesdames** /'maydam, may'dam/) used as a title equivalent to *Mrs* before the name of a married French-speaking woman or used without a name as a generalized term of direct address. [French *madame* from Old French *ma dame* my lady]

madcap[1] /'madkap/ *adj* characterized by impulsiveness or recklessness: *another of her madcap exploits.*

madcap[2] *noun* a person who is impulsive or reckless.

mad cow disease *noun informal* BSE (bovine spongiform encephalopathy).

madden *verb trans* (**maddened, maddening**) **1** to drive (somebody) mad. **2** to exasperate or enrage (somebody). ➤➤ **maddeningly** *adv*.

madder *noun* **1** a Eurasian plant with whorled leaves and small yellowish flowers: *Rubia tinctorum.* **2** a red dye prepared from the root of this plant. [Old English *mædere*]

madding *adj archaic or literary* **1** acting as if mad; frenzied: *far from the madding crowd's ignoble strife* — Gray. **2** tending to infuriate or drive one mad; maddening: *How have mines eyes out of their spheres been fitted in the distraction of this madding fever!* — Shakespeare.

made /mayd/ *verb* past tense and past part. of MAKE[1]. ✳ **get/have it made** *informal* to be certain of success; to be in a fortunate situation.

Madeira /mə'diərə/ *noun* a fortified wine from Madeira.

Madeira cake *noun Brit* a very rich sponge cake.

madeleine /'madəlin, -layn/ *noun* a small rich cake made from a sponge mixture and baked in a small mould and often decorated with jam and coconut. [French *madeleine*, prob named after *Madeleine* Paulmier, 19th-cent. French pastry cook]

mademoiselle /ˌmadmwə'zel (*French* madmwazεl)/ *noun* (*pl* **mademoiselles** *or* **mesdemoiselles** /ˌmaydmwə'zel (*French* medmwazεl)/) **1** (**Mademoiselle**) used as a title equivalent to *Miss* for an unmarried French-speaking girl or woman. **2** a young Frenchwoman. **3** *dated* a French governess or female language teacher. [French *mademoiselle* from Old French *ma damoisele* my young lady]

made-to-measure *adj* said of a garment: made according to an individual's measurements in order to achieve a good fit.

made-up *adj* **1** wearing make-up. **2** fancifully conceived or falsely devised; fictional. **3** of a road: covered in tarmac.

madhouse /'mad-hows/ *noun* **1** *dated* a lunatic asylum. **2** *informal* a place of uproar or confusion.

madly *adv informal* **1a** with great energy; frantically: *The children were charging madly around.* **b** without restraint; passionately. **2** extremely: *It was madly expensive.*

madman *noun* (*pl* **madmen**) **1** a man who is insane. **2** a crazy or reckless man: *He was hit by one of those madmen driving at well over the speed limit.*

madness *noun* **1a** insanity. **b** extreme folly or recklessness. **2** any of several ailments of animals characterized by frenzied behaviour, *esp* rabies.

Madonna /mə'donə/ *noun* (**the Madonna**) the Virgin Mary. [Italian *Madonna* from Old Italian *ma donna* my lady]

Madonna lily *noun* a white Mediterranean lily with trumpet-shaped flowers: *Lilium candidum.*

madras /mə'dras, mə'drahs/ *noun* **1** a fine usu cotton plain-woven shirting and dress fabric, usu in brightly coloured checked or striped designs. **2** a spicy curry, typically made with meat: *duck madras.* [named after *Madras*, a city in India, where the fabric was orig produced]

madrasa /mə'drasə/ *or* **madrasah** *or* **medrese** /me'dresay/ *noun* (*pl* **madrasas**) a college of Islamic instruction. [Arabic *madrasa*, from *darasa* to study]

madrepore /madri'paw/ *noun* any of an order of reef-building corals of tropical seas: order Madreporaria. ➤➤ **madreporian** *adj and noun*. [French *madrépore* from Italian *madrepora*, from *madre* mother + *poro* pore]

madrigal /'madrig(ə)l/ *noun* **1a** an unaccompanied and often complex secular song for several voices. **b** any part song; a glee. **2** a short medieval love poem. ▶▶ **madrigalian** /-'gali·ən, -'gayli·ən/ *adj*, **madrigalist** *noun*. [Italian *madrigale* via medieval Latin *carmen matricale* simple song, from Latin *matricalis* of the womb, from *matric-, matrix* womb]

madrilene /madri'leen, -'len/ *noun* a CONSOMMÉ (clear soup) flavoured with tomato juice and served cold. [French (*consommé à la*) *madrilène*, Madrid-style (consommé), from Spanish *madrileño* of Madrid]

madwoman *noun* (*pl* **madwomen**) **1** a woman who is insane. **2** a crazy or reckless woman.

Maecenas /mie'seenəs/ *noun* a generous patron, *esp* of literature or art. [named after Gaius *Maecenas* d.8 BC, Roman statesman and patron of literature]

maelstrom /'maylstrohm, 'maylstrəm/ *noun* **1** a powerful whirlpool. **2** something resembling a maelstrom in turbulence and violence. [early Dutch (modern *maalstroom*), from *malen* to grind + *strom* stream]

maenad /'meenad/ *noun* **1** a female participant in ancient Greek ritual orgies in honour of Dionysus. **2** a frenzied woman: *Blanche Stroeve was in the cruel grip of appetite … she was a Maenad* — Somerset Maugham. ▶▶ **maenadic** /mee'nadik/ *adj*. [via Latin from Greek *mainad-, mainas* a madwoman, a Bacchante, from *mainesthai* to be mad]

maestoso /mie'stohshoh/ *adj and adv* said of a piece of music: to be performed in a majestic stately manner. [Italian *maestoso* from Latin *majestosus*, from *majestas* majesty]

maestro /'miestroh/ *noun* (*pl* **maestros** or **maestri** /'miestree/) a master in an art; *esp* an eminent composer, conductor, or teacher of music. [Italian *maestro* master, from Latin *magister* master]

Mae West /may/ *noun informal, dated* an inflatable life jacket. [named after *Mae West* d.1980, US actress noted for her full figure]

MAFF /maf/ *abbr Brit* Ministry of Agriculture, Fisheries, and Food.

Mafia /'mafi·ə/ *noun* **1** (**the Mafia**) (*treated as sing. or pl*) a secret society of Sicilian political terrorists. **2** a secret criminal organization originating in Sicily and prevalent *esp* in the USA, chiefly concerned with the financial control of illicit activities, e.g. vice and narcotics. **3** (*often* **mafia**) an excessively influential coterie of a usu specified kind: *the presumptions of the mental health mafia* — R J Neuhaus. [Italian *mafia* from Sicilian dialect, in the senses 'boldness', 'bragging']

mafioso /mafi'ohsoh/ *noun* (*pl* **mafiosi** /-see/) a member of the Mafia. [Italian *mafioso* from *mafia* Mafia]

mag /mag/ *noun informal* a magazine.

mag. *abbr* **1** magnesium. **2** magnetic. **3** magnetism. **4** magnitude.

magainin /mə'gaynin/ *noun* any of a group of antibiotic substances derived from the skin of a frog. [Hebrew *magain* a shield]

magazine /magə'zeen, 'mag-/ *noun* **1a** a usu illustrated periodical, bound in paper covers, containing miscellaneous pieces by different authors. **b** a television or radio programme containing a number of usu topical items, often without a common theme. **2a** a holder from which cartridges can be fed into a gun chamber automatically. **b** a lightproof chamber for films or plates in a camera or for film in a film projector. **3a** a storeroom for arms, ammunition, or explosives, e.g. gunpowder. **b** a stock of arms and ammunition.

Word history
early French *magazine* via Old Provençal from Arabic *makhāzin*, pl of *makhzan* storehouse. From its original meaning 'storehouse' the word was used in book titles in the 17th cent. to suggest a store of information, giving rise in the 18th cent. to its chief current meaning of a periodical.

magdalen or **magdalene** /'magdələn/ *noun* **1** (*often* **Magdalen**) *archaic* a reformed prostitute: *Magdalens … worn out and penitent courtesans at Rome* — Nathan Bailey. **2** an institution or refuge for reformed prostitutes: *Asylums and Magdalenes are not the proper remedies for these abuses* — Mary Wollstonecraft. [named after Mary *Magdalen* or *Magdalene*, a woman healed by Jesus of evil spirits (Luke 8:2), identified with a reformed prostitute (Luke 7:36–50): compare MAUDLIN]

Magdalenian /magdə'leeni·ən/ *adj* of the latest Palaeolithic culture in Europe characterized by implements of flint, bone, and ivory and by cave paintings. [French *magdalénien* from *La Madeleine*, rock shelter in SW France where objects from this culture were found]

mage /mayj/ *noun* a wise man; a sage; a magician; = MAGUS: *And there I saw mage Merlin* — Tennyson. [Middle English from Latin *magus* wise man]

Magen David /,mawgən 'dayvid/ *noun* a star of David, used as a Jewish symbol. [Hebrew *māghēn Dāwidh*, literally 'shield of David', from David d.c.962 BC, King of Judah and Israel]

magenta[1] /mə'jentə/ *adj* **1** of a deep purplish red colour. **2** in photography and colour printing, of a pinkish red colour. ▶▶ **magenta** *noun*. [named after *Magenta*, a town in N Italy, site of a battle in 1859 just before magenta dye was discovered]

magenta[2] *noun* the dye FUCHSIN.

maggot /'magət/ *noun* a soft-bodied legless grub that is the larva of a two-winged fly, e.g. the housefly or blowfly. ▶▶ **maggoty** *adj*. [Middle English *mathek, maddok, magotte*, of Scandinavian origin]

magi /'mayjie/ *noun* pl of MAGUS.

Magian[1] /'mayji·ən/ *noun* a magus.

Magian[2] *adj* relating to the Magi. ▶▶ **Magianism** *noun*.

magic[1] /'majik/ *noun* **1** the use of means, e.g. charms, rites, incantations, or spells, believed to have supernatural power over natural forces. **2** the art of producing illusions by sleight of hand. **3a** an extraordinary power or influence producing surprising results and defying explanation. **b** something that seems to cast a spell: *the magic of the voice*. [Middle English *magik* via French and Latin from Greek *magikē*, fem of *magikos* Magian, magical, from *magos* magus, sorcerer]

magic[2] *adj* **1** relating to magic. **2** having seemingly supernatural qualities. **3** *informal* very good; marvellous: *Their new record is really magic*. ▶▶ **magical** *adj*, **magically** *adv*.

magic[3] *verb trans* (**magicked, magicking**) *informal* used *esp* to and by children: to create, transform, transport, or remove (something) by or as if by magic: *In the morning the spots had all been magicked away*.

magical realism *noun* = MAGIC REALISM.

magic bullet *noun informal* a drug or other medical remedy that can target specific cells, tissue, etc in the body without causing harmful side effects.

magic eye *noun* **1** *informal* a photoelectric cell. **2** a miniature cathode-ray tube that emits a variable light and can be used as a visual indicator for tuning a device, e.g. a radio worked by valves.

magician /mə'jish(ə)n/ *noun* **1** somebody skilled in magic. **2** a conjurer. **3** a person extraordinarily skilled at something; a wonder-worker: *She's a magician with pastry*.

magic lantern *noun* an early device for the projection of still pictures from slides.

magic mushroom *noun informal* a fungus that has hallucinogenic properties.

magic realism *noun* the depiction in art and literature of fantastic, surrealistic, and mythical elements in a style of scrupulous realism.

Editorial note
Associated with modern South American writers like Jorge Luis Borges and Gabriel García Márquez, magic realism has also been identified in a number of European (Italo Calvino, Milan Kundera) and Asian novelists (Salman Rushdie). It involves the displacement of history and a universal sense of the fantastic, presented as a commonplace. Márquez speaks of the crushing effects of linear time, and of fantasy not as an invention but a condition. It also represents the modern novel in a state of imaginative play — Professor Malcolm Bradbury.

▶▶ **magic realist** *noun and adj*.

magic square *noun* a square array of numbers in which the sum of each vertical, horizontal, or diagonal row is the same: compare SQUARE[1].

magilp /mə'gilp/ *noun* see MEGILP.

Maginot Line /'mazhinoh (*French* maʒino)/ *noun* a line of defensive fortifications built in NE France before World War II. [named after André *Maginot* d.1932, French minister of war]

magister /'majistə, məj'istə/ *noun* (*pl* **magistri** /-trie/) *archaic* used as a title or form of address to a scholar, *esp* a university teacher: master. [Latin *magister* master, teacher, tutor]

magisterial /maji'stiəri·əl/ *adj* **1a** assuming authority, *esp* inappropriately; high-handed; dictatorial: *adopt a magisterial tone*. **b** said of a performance, literary or artistic work, etc: authoritative; definitive; masterly. **2** relating to the office of a magistrate.

>> **magisterially** *adv.* [late Latin *magisterialis* of authority, from *magisterium* office of a master, from *magister* master]

magistracy /'majistrəsi/ *noun* (*pl* **magistracies**) **1** the office or power of a magistrate. **2** magistrates considered as a group.

magistral /'majistrəl/ *adj chiefly archaic* **1** relating to a master's authority; dictatorial; = MAGISTERIAL. **2** said of a medical prescription: specially made up to treat a particular case. >> **magistrally** *adv.* [late Latin *magistralis* relating to a master or teacher from *magistr-*, *magister* master]

magistrate /'majistrayt, -strət/ *noun* a civil legislative or executive official, e.g.: **a** a principal official exercising governmental powers. **b** a paid or unpaid local judicial officer who presides in a magistrates' court. >> **magistrature** *noun.* [Middle English *magistrat* from Latin *magistratus* magistracy, magistrate, from *magistr-*, *magister* master, political superior]

magistrates' court *noun* a court of summary jurisdiction for minor criminal cases and preliminary hearings.

magistri /'majistrie, mə'jistrie/ *noun* pl of MAGISTER.

Maglemosian /magli'mohsi·ən, -sh(ə)n/ *adj* relating to or belonging to the first Mesolithic culture of N Europe, between about 8000 and 5000 BC, which was characterized by its forest and lakeside settlements and its woodworking tools, fishing tackle, and dugout canoes. [named after *Maglemose*, a site on the island of Sjaelland (Zealand) in Denmark where objects from this culture were found]

maglev /'maglev/ *noun* a railway system in which an electrically driven train is raised and held above the track by powerful magnets. [short for *magnetic levitation*]

magma /'magmə/ *noun* **1** molten rock material within the earth from which an igneous rock results by cooling. **2** *dated* a thin medieval paste or suspension, e.g. of a precipitate in water. >> **magmatic** /mag'matik/ *adj.* [Latin *magmat-*, *magma* dregs, from Greek *magma* thick unguent, from *massein* to knead]

Magna Carta *or* **Magna Charta** /,magnə 'kahtə/ *noun* **1** a charter of liberties to which the English barons forced King John to assent in 1215. **2** any document similarly constituting a fundamental guarantee of rights and privileges. [medieval Latin *Magna Carta* great charter]

magna cum laude /,magnə kum 'lawdi/ *adv chiefly NAmer* used in reference to the gaining of degrees, etc: with distinction. [Latin *magna cum laude* with great praise]

magnanimity /magnə'nimiti/ *noun* the quality of being magnanimous; generosity. [Latin *magnanimitas*, from *magnus* great + *animus* spirit]

magnanimous /mag'naniməs/ *adj* showing nobility of feeling and generosity of mind; not subject to petty feelings: *a magnanimous gesture.* >> **magnanimously** *adv.*

magna opera /,magnə 'ohpərə, 'opərə/ *noun* pl of MAGNUM OPUS.

magnate /'magnayt/ *noun* **1** a prominent and wealthy industrialist or businessman; a tycoon. **2** *archaic* a person of wealth or influence; a great man in some sphere: *the associate of Johnson, Burke … and other magnates* — Washington Irving. [Middle English *magnates* (pl) via late Latin *magnat-*, *magnas* great man, used in pl, from Latin *magnus* great]

magnesia /mag'neezh(y)ə, -zyə/ *noun* **1** a white oxide of magnesium used *esp* in making cements, insulation, fertilizers, and rubber. **2** magnesium oxide or hydrated magnesium carbonate used in medicine as an antacid and mild laxative. >> **magnesian** *adj.* [scientific Latin *magnesia* from *magnes carneus* a white earth, literally 'flesh magnet', from its propensity for sticking to the lips; compare MAGNET]

magnesite /'magnəsiet/ *noun* magnesium carbonate occurring as a mineral and used *esp* in making heat-resistant materials, e.g. bricks for lining furnaces.

magnesium /mag'neezi·əm/ *noun* a silver-white metallic chemical element of the alkaline-earth group, which burns with an intense white light, is lighter than aluminium, and is used in making light alloys: symbol Mg, atomic number 12. [scientific Latin *magnesium* from MAGNESIA in its obsolete sense 'manganese']

magnet /'magnit/ *noun* **1** a body that has the property of attracting iron and producing a magnetic field outside itself, *esp* a mass of iron, steel, etc that has this property artificially imparted. **2** something that attracts: *The island is a magnet for tax evaders.*

Word history

Middle English *magnete* via French from Latin *magnet-*, *magnes*, from Greek *magnēs lithos* stone of Magnesia. Magnesia, an ancient city in Asia Minor, was said to have large deposits of magnetic iron ore.

magnet- *or* **magneto-** *comb. form* forming words, with the meaning: magnetic force, magnetism, or magnetic: *magnetometer*; *magneton*; *magnetoelectric.* [Latin *magnet-*, *magnes* magnet]

magnetic /mag'netik/ *adj* **1a** relating to magnetism or a magnet. **b** capable of being magnetized. **c** working by magnetic attraction. **d** relating to or produced by the earth's magnetism. **2** possessing an extraordinary power or ability to attract or charm: *a magnetic personality.* >> **magnetically** *adv.*

magnetic dip *noun* the angle formed with the horizon by a magnetic needle free to rotate in the vertical plane.

magnetic equator *noun* an imaginary line on the earth's surface, roughly parallel to the geographical equator and connecting all points at which the magnetic dip is zero. Also called ACLINIC LINE.

magnetic field *noun* a region of space near a body possessing magnetism or carrying an electric current in which magnetic forces can be detected.

magnetic flux *noun* **1** the strength or effect of the magnetic forces acting in a particular area of a magnetic field. **2** lines of force used to represent this.

magnetic inclination *noun* = MAGNETIC DIP.

magnetic mine *noun* a mine that is detonated by the proximity of the magnetic field of a metal body such as a ship's hull or a tank.

magnetic moment *noun* a measure of the TORQUE[1] (force producing rotation) exerted on a magnetic needle, a particle or group of particles having electric charge, or a similar magnetic system when placed in a magnetic field; the quantity obtained by multiplying the distance between the poles of a magnet by the strength of either pole.

magnetic needle *noun* a slender bar of magnetized iron, steel, etc that when freely suspended indicates the direction of a magnetic field in which it is placed, and that is the essential part of a magnetic compass.

magnetic north *noun* the northerly direction in the earth's magnetic field as indicated by a horizontal magnetic needle.

magnetic pole *noun* **1** either of two small nonstationary regions in the N and S geographical polar areas of the earth or another celestial body towards which a magnetic needle points from any direction. **2** either of the regions of a magnet at which the magnetic forces set up by the magnet are strongest.

magnetic resonance *noun* the resonant vibration of electrons, atoms, molecules, or nuclei when in a magnetic field in response to radio waves at particular frequencies.

magnetic resonance imaging *noun* in medicine, the use of magnetic resonance to create a scanned image of a part of the body, e.g. the brain or spinal cord.

magnetic storm *noun* a marked local disturbance of the earth's magnetic field, prob related to sunspot activity.

magnetic tape *noun* a ribbon of thin paper or plastic with a magnetizable coating for use in recording sound or video signals and in computing.

magnetise *verb trans* see MAGNETIZE.

magnetism *noun* **1a** a physical phenomenon existing in various forms, which is associated with moving particles having electric charge and involves the setting up of a field of force, is shown by magnets and electric currents, and includes the attraction for iron observed in magnets. **b** a branch of physics dealing with magnetic phenomena. **2** an ability to attract or charm: *personal magnetism.*

magnetite /'magnitiet/ *noun* iron oxide occurring as a black mineral strongly attracted by a magnet.

magnetize *or* **magnetise** *verb trans* **1** to cause (something) to become magnetic. **2** to attract (people) or be a focus for their attention, as though through magnetism: *She … set off along Piccadilly, the flick of her skirt, the lift of her mane, the jangling of her beads and bangles magnetizing male attention* — Melvyn Bragg. >> **magnetizable** *adj,* **magnetization** /-'zaysh(ə)n/ *noun,* **magnetizer** *noun.*

magneto /mag'neetoh/ *noun* (*pl* **magnetos**) an alternator with permanent magnets formerly used to generate a high voltage for the ignition in an internal-combustion engine. [short for *magneto-electric machine*]

magneto- *comb. form* see MAGNET-.

magnetoelectric /mag‚neetoh·i'lektrik/ *adj* relating to or characterized by an electric current or a voltage produced by magnetic means: *magnetoelectric induction*. ➤➤ **magnetoelectrically** *adv*, **magnetoelectricity** /-'trisiti/ *noun*.

magnetohydrodynamic /mag‚neetoh·hiedrohdie'namik/ *adj* relating to or denoting phenomena arising from the motion of electrically conducting fluids in the presence of electric and magnetic fields. ➤➤ **magnetohydrodynamics** *pl noun*.

magnetometer /magni'tomitə/ *noun* an instrument for measuring magnetic intensity, *esp* of the earth's magnetic field. ➤➤ **magnetometry** /-tri/ *noun*.

magnetomotive force /mag‚neetoh'mohtiv/ *noun* a factor that is the cause of a MAGNETIC FLUX.

magneton /'magniton, mag'nieton/ *noun* a unit in which the MAGNETIC MOMENT of a particle, e.g. an atom, is measured.

magnetopause /mag'neetohpawz/ *noun* the outer boundary of a magnetosphere. [MAGNETOSPHERE + Latin *pausa* stop]

magnetoresistance /mag'neetoh·rizist(ə)ns/ *noun* influence on the electrical resistance of a metal exerted by an external magnetic field.

magnetosphere /mag'neetosfiə/ *noun* a region surrounding a celestial body, *specif* the earth, in which charged particles are trapped by its magnetic field. ➤➤ **magnetospheric** /-'sferik/ *adj*.

magnetron /'magnitron/ *noun* an electronic valve that in the presence of an externally applied magnetic field is used as a high-power microwave source, e.g. for a radar transmitter. [MAGNET + -TRON]

Magnificat /mag'nifikat/ *noun* **1** the canticle of the Virgin Mary in Luke 1:46–55. **2** a musical setting of this. [Middle English from Latin *magnificat* (it) magnifies, from *magnificare* (see MAGNIFY); from the first word of the canticle]

magnification /‚magnifi'kaysh(ə)n/ *noun* **1** the process of magnifying or of being magnified. **2** the apparent enlargement of an object by a microscope, telescope, etc. **3a** the degree to which something is magnified. **b** a measure of the magnifying power of an optical instrument or lens.

magnificent /mag'nifis(ə)nt/ *adj* **1a** sumptuous in structure and adornment. **b** strikingly beautiful or impressive. **2** sublime: *her magnificent prose*. **3** exceptionally fine or excellent: *a magnificent day*. ➤➤ **magnificence** *noun*, **magnificently** *adv*. [Latin *magnificent-*, stem of *magnificentior*, comparative form of *magnificus* accomplishing great things, from *magnus* great + *facere* to do]

magnifico[1] /mag'nifikoh/ *noun* (*pl* **magnificoes**) *informal* a person of high position or distinguished appearance and manner.

Ɯord history

Italian *magnifico* magnificent, from Latin *magnificus* noble, splendid. The word orig meant a Venetian nobleman.

magnifico[2] *adj informal* (*exclamatory or predicative*) magnificent; splendid; wonderful. [Italian *magnifico* magnificent]

magnify /'magnifie/ *verb trans* (**magnifies, magnified, magnifying**) **1** said of a lens or optical instrument, etc: to enlarge (something) in appearance. **2** to increase or exaggerate the significance of (something): *We magnify our own troubles*. **3** *archaic* to glorify (God): *My soul doth magnify the Lord* — Bible. ➤➤ **magnifier** *noun*. [Middle English *magnifien* via French from Latin *magnificare*, from *magnificus* noble, splendid]

magnifying glass *noun* a single optical lens for magnifying.

magniloquent /mag'nilǝkwǝnt/ *adj* speaking in or characterized by a high-flown, often bombastic, style or manner; grandiloquent: *a large basket containing his 'fiambreras' – that magniloquent Castilian word for cold collation* — Longfellow. ➤➤ **magniloquence** *noun*, **magniloquently** *adv*. [Latin *magniloquus*, from *magnus* great + *loqui* to speak]

magnitude /'magnityoohd/ *noun* **1a** size or extent: *List the planets in order of magnitude; the magnitude of the swing towards Labour*. **b** a numerical quantity or value. **2** importance or significance: *the magnitude of the proposed task; a disaster of unprecedented magnitude*. **3** the brightness of a celestial body, *esp* a star, measured on a logarithmic scale in which a difference of five units corresponds to the multiplication or division of the brightness of light by 100. [Middle English from Latin *magnitudo* from *magnus* great]

magnolia[1] /mag'nohli·ǝ/ *noun* any of a genus of shrubs or trees with evergreen or deciduous leaves and usu large white, yellow, rose, or purple flowers: genus *Magnolia*. [from the Latin genus name, named after Pierre *Magnol* d.1715, French botanist]

magnolia[2] *adj* of a very pale pinkish white colour. ➤➤ **magnolia** *noun*.

magnox /'magnoks/ *noun* an alloy of magnesium with small quantities of the metals aluminium and beryllium that is used to enclose rods of uranium fuel in some nuclear reactors. [short for *magnesium no oxidation*]

magnum /'magnǝm/ *noun* (*pl* **magnums**) **1** a wine bottle holding twice the usual amount (about 1.5l). **2a** a cartridge of standard size with an extra-powerful charge. **b** a firearm using such cartridges. [Latin *magnum*, neuter of *magnus* great]

magnum opus /'ohpǝs/ *noun* (*pl* **magnum opuses** or **magna opera** /‚magnǝ 'ohpǝrǝ, 'opǝrǝ/) the greatest achievement of an artist, writer, etc. [Latin *magnum opus* great work]

magpie /'magpie/ *noun* **1** any of several species of birds of the crow family with very long tails and black-and-white plumage: genus *Pica*. **2** any of several species of birds resembling or related to the magpie; *esp* an Australian bird with black-and-white plumage: genus *Gymnorhina*. **3** a person who chatters noisily. **4** a person who collects objects in a random fashion. **5a** the outermost ring but one on a target. **b** a shot that hits this ring.

Ɯord history

Mag (a nickname for *Margaret*) + PIE[2]. The bird was formerly known as a *maggotpie*, *maggot* representing Margaret (compare the use of first names in Robin redbreast and Tomtit), and *pie* being *pied*, an allusion to its black and white plumage.

maguey /'magway/ *noun* **1a** any of several species of Mexican fleshy-leaved agaves used to make the alcoholic drink pulque: *Agave atrovirens* and other species. **b** a plant related to the agaves: genus *Furcraea*. **2** a hard fibre derived from magueys and used for twine. [Spanish *maguey* from Taino]

magus /'maygǝs/ *noun* (*pl* **magi** /'mayjie/) **1a** a member of a Zoroastrian hereditary priestly class in ancient Persia. **b** (*often* **Magus**) any of the three wise men from the East who traditionally paid homage to the infant Jesus. **2** a magician or sorcerer. [Middle English via Latin from Greek *magos* magus, sorcerer]

Magyar /'magyah/ *noun* **1** a member of the Finno-Ugric people of Hungary. **2** a Uralic language spoken in Hungary, Romania, and other countries; = HUNGARIAN (2). ➤➤ **Magyar** *adj*. [Hungarian *Magyar*]

Mahabharata /‚mah·hǝ'bahrǝtǝ/ *noun* one of two great Hindu epics, written in Sanskrit and dating in part from about 300 BC, relating the story of the war in N India between the Pandava and Kaurava brothers, descendants of Bharata, and containing the poem *Bhagavad-Gita*. [Sanskrit *mahā* great + *Bhārata*, that is, 'great epic of the Bharata dynasty']

maharajah or **maharaja** /mahhǝ'rahjǝ/ *noun* a Hindu Indian prince ranking above a rajah. [Sanskrit *mahārāja*, from *mahat* great + *rājan* raja]

maharani or **maharanee** /mah'rahnee/ *noun* **1** the wife of a maharaja. **2** a Hindu Indian princess ranking above a rani. [Hindi *mahārānī*, from *mahā* great + *rānī* rani]

maharishi /mahhǝ'rishi/ *noun* a Hindu teacher of mystical knowledge. [Sanskrit *mahārṣi*, from *mahat* great + *ṛṣi* sage and poet]

mahatma /mǝ'hatmǝ/ *noun* used as a title of honour, *esp* by Hindus: a person revered for outstanding moral and spiritual qualities. [Sanskrit *mahātman* great-souled, from *mahat* great + *ātman* soul]

Mahayana /mah·hǝ'yahnǝ/ *noun* a branch of Buddhism prevalent in Tibet, China, and Japan that includes ritual and devotional practices: compare THERAVADA. [Sanskrit *mahāyāna*, literally 'great vehicle']

Mahdi /'mahdi/ *noun* **1** the expected messiah of Muslim tradition. **2** a leader claiming to be this messiah. ➤➤ **Mahdism** *noun*, **Mahdist** *noun and adj*. [Arabic *mahdīy* one rightly guided]

Mahican /mǝ'heek(ǝ)n/ *noun* (*pl* **Mahicans** or *collectively* **Mahican**) **1** a member of a Native American people formerly living in the environs of the Hudson river. **2** the Algonquian language spoken by these people. ➤➤ **Mahican** *adj*. [the Mahican name]

mahi-mahi /'mahhi mahhi/ *noun* a tropical food fish with an iridescent blue body: *Coryphaena hippurus*. [Hawaiian *mahi-mahi*]

mah-jong or **mah-jongg** /ˌmah ˈjong/ noun a game of Chinese origin usu played by four people, with 144 tiles that are drawn and discarded until one player secures a winning hand. [Chinese dialect ma tsiang literally 'sparrows']

mahlstick /'mawlstik/ noun a maulstick.

mahogany[1] /məˈhog(ə)ni/ noun (pl **mahoganies** or collectively **mahogany**) 1 any of several species of tropical trees: genus Swietenia. 2 the usu dark-coloured moderately hard and heavy wood of these trees, widely used for fine cabinetwork. [origin unknown]

mahogany[2] adj of a reddish brown colour. ⇒ **mahogany** noun.

mahonia /məˈhohni·ə/ noun a N American and Eurasian evergreen shrub of the barberry family, with spiny leaves and clusters of small yellow flowers: genus Mahonia. [from the Latin genus name, named after Bernard McMahon d.1816, US botanist]

mahout /məˈhowt/ noun a keeper and driver of an elephant. [Hindi mahāwat, mahāut]

Mahratta /məˈrahtə/ noun see MARATHA.

Mahratti /məˈrahti/ noun see MARATHI.

mahseer /'mahsi·ə/ noun any of several species of large edible carps of N India: genus Barbus. [Sanskrit mahā great + śaphara carp]

maid /mayd/ noun 1 a female servant. 2 archaic or literary. a an unmarried girl or woman: It is not the fashion for the maids in France to kiss before they are married — Shakespeare. b a virgin: Then up he rose and donned his clo'es and dupped [undid] the chamber door, let in the maid that out a maid never departed more — Shakespeare. [Middle English maide, short for MAIDEN[1]]

maidan /mieˈdahn/ noun a parade ground or esplanade in Asia. [Hindi maidān from Arabic]

maiden[1] /'mayd(ə)n/ noun 1 archaic or literary. a an unmarried girl or woman. b a virgin. 2 in cricket, an over in which no runs are credited to the batsman. 3 a horse that has never won a race. ⇒ **maidenhood** noun, **maidenish** adj, **maidenliness** noun, **maidenly** adj. [Old English mægden, mæden, dimin. of mægeth]

maiden[2] adj 1 not married: a maiden aunt. 2 said of a female animal: never having been mated or borne young. 3 denoting the first venture of somebody or something untried: a ship's maiden voyage; a new MP's maiden speech in Parliament. 4a said of a horse: that has never won a race. b said of a horse race: for horses that have never won a race. 5 archaic not previously touched, used, etc; fresh; virgin: Refresh the beds with a few barrowfuls of maiden earth.

maidenhair noun any of several species of ferns with fronds that have delicate spreading branches: genus Adiantum.

maidenhair fern noun = MAIDENHAIR.

maidenhair tree noun = GINKGO.

maidenhead noun 1 archaic a woman's virginity: a merry song which bore some relation to matrimony and the loss of a maidenhead — Henry Fielding. 2 the HYMEN. [Middle English maidenhed, from MAIDEN[1] + -hed -HOOD]

maiden name noun the surname of a woman prior to taking her husband's name on marriage.

maiden over noun = MAIDEN[1] (2).

maid of honour noun (pl **maids of honour**) 1 NAmer a bride's principal unmarried wedding attendant. 2 an unmarried noblewoman whose duty it is to attend a queen or princess. 3 a puff pastry tartlet filled with custard.

maidservant noun dated a female servant: He has no children, keeps one maidservant, and is comfortably off — Conan Doyle.

maigre /'maygə/ adj 1 said of days in the calendar of the Roman Catholic Church: prescribed for fasting or for not eating meat. 2 said of food: suitable for eating on maigre days; specif not containing meat or meat juices. [French maigre, literally 'meagre']

mail[1] /mayl/ noun 1a posted items, e.g. letters and parcels, that are conveyed from one post office to another. b a delivery of letters, etc to an address, or the batch delivered: Has the mail arrived? 2 the postal system. 3 email. [Middle English male pack, bag, from Old French, of Germanic origin]

mail[2] verb trans 1 to send (e.g. a letter) by post. 2a to send (somebody) mail. b to send (something) by email. ⇒ **mailable** adj.

mail[3] noun 1 armour made of interlocking metal rings, chains, or sometimes plates. 2 the hard protective covering, e.g. a shell, carapace, or scales, of certain animals. ⇒ **mailed** adj. [Middle English maille via French from Latin macula spot, mesh]

mail[4] verb trans to cover or clothe (somebody or something) with or as if with mail.

mailbag noun 1 a bag used to carry mail. 2 = POSTBAG (2).

mailbox noun 1 NAmer a letter box. 2 in computing, a file where email messages are stored.

mailer noun 1 chiefly NAmer a person who sends mail; the sender. 2 a container, e.g. a tube, used for sending items by post. 3 in computing, a program for sending email.

mailing list noun an organization's list of the names and addresses to which it regularly sends information.

maillot /'mieyoh (French majo)/ noun 1 tights for dancers, acrobats, or gymnasts: the gymnast whose maillot is loose — Henry James. 2 a tight-fitting top or jersey, e.g. one worn for cycling. 3 NAmer a woman's one-piece usu strapless swimsuit. [French maillot swaddling cloth]

mailman noun (pl **mailmen**) NAmer a postman.

mail merge noun in computing, the merging of names and addresses held on a database with a letter template to create personalized letters.

mail order noun an order for goods that is received and fulfilled by post. ⇒ **mail-order** adj.

mailshot noun an advertising or information leaflet posted to a great many people at one time.

maim /maym/ verb trans to mutilate, disfigure, or wound (a person or animal) seriously; to cripple (them). [Middle English maynhen, maymen from Old French maynier]

main[1] /mayn/ adj chief or principal: a main road; our main objective. ✱ **by main force** using sheer strength. [Middle English, from attributive use of Old English mægen strength, reinforced by Old Norse megn strong]

main[2] noun 1 a principal pipe, duct, or cable carrying gas, electricity, or water: the water main. 2 (**the mains**) the central source of water, gas, or electricity supplied to an area for use by a large number of consumers: turn off the gas at the mains. 3a a mainmast. b a mainsail. 4 (**the main**) archaic a mainland: They ... tried to make a landing on the main — Byron; the Spanish main. 5 literary or archaic the open sea: to traverse climes beyond the Western Main — Goldsmith. 6 archaic physical strength. ✱ **in/for the main** on the whole. **with all one's might and main** with all one's strength: tugging with all my might and main.

main[3] noun in the game of HAZARD[1] (3), a number exceeding four and not exceeding nine called by a player before throwing the dice. [prob from MAIN[2]]

mainbrace noun the brace attached to the main yard of a sailing ship.

main clause noun a clause functioning as the chief element in a complex sentence and able to stand alone as a sentence, e.g. he laughed in he laughed when he heard.

mainframe noun a large computer that can run several independent programs simultaneously or is connected to other smaller computers.

mainland noun the largest land area of a continent, country, etc, considered in relation to smaller offshore islands. ⇒ **mainlander** noun.

mainline verb trans slang to inject (a narcotic or other drug of abuse) into a vein: mainlining heroin. ⇒ verb intrans slang (+ on) to inject a narcotic, etc into a vein: mainline on barbiturates. ⇒ **mainliner** noun.

main line noun 1 a principal railway line. 2 NAmer a main road. 3 slang a major vein into which drugs can be injected.

mainly adv in most cases or for the most part; chiefly.

main man noun 1 a leading figure on whom others rely, in a team or organization. 2 informal a close and trusted companion: Bob's my main man ... I hope you're not offended by that — Esquire.

mainmast /'maynmahst, -məst/ noun a sailing vessel's principal mast.

mainsail /'maynsayl, -s(ə)l/ noun 1 the lowest square sail on the mainmast of a square-rigged ship. 2 the principal fore-and-aft sail on the mainmast of a fore-and-aft-rigged ship.

main sequence noun a series of classifications to which most stars except giants, supergiants, and white dwarfs belong.

mainsheet noun a rope by which the mainsail of a sailing boat is controlled and secured.

mainspring *noun* 1 the chief spring, *esp* of a watch or clock. 2 the chief motive, agent, or cause of something: *We have no modern English plays in which the natural attraction of the sexes for one another is made the mainspring of the action* — George Bernard Shaw.

mainstay *noun* 1 a chief support or main part of something: *Bananas are the mainstay of their economy.* 2 a rope or wire stretching forward from the head of the mainmast of a sailing ship and providing its chief support.

mainstream[1] *noun* (**the mainstream**) the prevailing influences, values, and activities of a group or society: *His work is outside the mainstream of modern science fiction.*

mainstream[2] *adj* belonging to or constituting the mainstream: *a video aimed at a mainstream audience; children with special needs in mainstream schools.*

maintain /mayn'tayn/ *verb trans* 1 to keep (something) in its required state of operation, repair, efficiency, or validity: *maintain a motor bike; maintain a mortgage.* 2 to sustain (something) against opposition or danger; to defend (it): *a position she will find difficult to maintain.* 3 to continue or keep up (something): *He couldn't maintain his composure.* 4 to support, sustain, or provide for (e.g. dependants): *She has a family to maintain.* 5 to affirm (something) in argument; to assert (it): *She maintained that she had never seen him before.* ➤➤ **maintainable** *adj*, **maintainer** *noun*. [Middle English *mainteinen* via Old French and late Latin from Latin *manu tenēre* to hold in the hand]

maintained school *noun* a school provided, controlled, or aided by a British local education authority.

maintenance /'mayntinəns/ *noun* 1 the work of maintaining or the state of being maintained. 2 the upkeep of property or equipment. 3 *chiefly Brit* payments for the support of one spouse by another, *esp* of a woman by a man, pending or following legal separation or divorce. 4 in law, the former offence of interference in a case by an uninvolved party, e.g. by the providing of funds.

maintop *noun* a platform at the top of the mainmast of a square-rigged ship.

main-topmast *noun* the mast section above the mainmast in a square-rigged sailing ship, rising from the maintop.

maiolica /mə'yolikə/ *noun* see MAJOLICA.

maisonette /mays(ə)n'et/ *noun* a part of a house, usu on two floors, let or sold separately. [French *maisonnette*, dimin. of *maison* house, via Old French from Latin *mansion-, mansio* dwelling place]

mai tai /'mei tei/ *noun chiefly NAmer* a cocktail consisting of rum, curaçao, grenadine, and fruit juice. [of Polynesian origin]

maître d' /metrə 'dee/ *noun* (*pl* **maître d's** /dees/) *informal* = MAÎTRE D'HÔTEL.

maître d'hôtel /ˌmetrə doh'tel/ *noun* (*pl* **maîtres d'hôtel** /ˌmetrə/) 1 the manager or owner of a hotel or restaurant. 2 a head waiter. 3 a head steward; a major-domo. [French *maître d'hôtel*, literally 'master of house']

maize /mayz/ *noun* 1 a tall widely cultivated cereal grass bearing seeds on elongated ears: *Zea mays.* 2 the ears or edible seeds of this plant. [Spanish *maíz* from Taino *mahiz*]

Maj. *abbr* Major.

majestic /mə'jestik/ *adj* 1 having or showing great grandeur or dignity; noble: *The president gave a majestic wave.* 2 having an impressive bearing or aspect; magnificent. ➤➤ **majestically** *adv*.

majesty /'majəsti/ *noun* (*pl* **majesties**) 1a impressive bearing or aspect. b greatness or splendour of quality or character. 2 sovereign power. 3 (**Majesty**) used in addressing or referring to a king or queen: *Your Majesty.* [Middle English *maieste* via Old French from Latin *majestat-, majestas* greatness, grandeur, dignity, sovereign power]

majolica /mə'jolikə, mə'yol-/ *or* **maiolica** /mə'yol-/ *noun* a type of early Italian tin-glazed earthenware. [Italian *maiolica* from late Latin *Majolica* Majorca]

major[1] /'mayjə/ *adj* 1 notable or conspicuous in effect or scope; considerable: *a major improvement.* 2 involving serious risk to life; serious: *a major illness.* 3 greater in importance, size, rank, or degree: *one of our major poets.* 4a said *esp* of a musical scale or mode: having semitones between the third and fourth and the seventh and eighth steps, giving the pattern: tone, tone, semitone, tone, tone, tone, semitone. b denoting or based on a major scale: *in a major key; a sonata in C major.* c denoting a musical interval equivalent to the distance between the first and the second, third, sixth, or seventh notes of a major scale: *a major third.* d said of a chord: having a musical interval of four semitones between the lowest note and the next note above it. 5 *dated* used after a surname: the elder of two brothers in a British public school: *Jennings major.* [Middle English *maiour* from Latin *major*, compar of *magnus* great, large]

major[2] *noun* 1 an officer in the British army, the Royal Marines, and the US army, air force, and marines, ranking below a lieutenant colonel. 2 a major musical interval, scale, key, or mode. 3 an important company or organization. 4 *chiefly NAmer.* a a main subject of academic study. b a student specializing in a specified subject: *He is a history major.* 5 in law, a person who has attained the age of majority. 6 in logic: a a major term. b a major premise.

major[3] *verb intrans* (**majored, majoring**) *chiefly NAmer* (+ in) to take courses in one's major subject: *She majored in chemistry.*

major axis *noun* in geometry, the chord of an ellipse passing through its focuses.

Majorcan /mə'yawkən/ *noun* a native or inhabitant of the Balearic island of Majorca. ➤➤ **Majorcan** *adj*.

major-domo /ˌmayjə 'dohmoh/ *noun* (*pl* **major-domos**) a man, e.g. a head steward, who has charge of a large household. [via Spanish and Italian from medieval Latin *major domus* chief of the house]

majorette /mayjə'ret/ *noun* a baton-twirling girl or woman in a decorative approximation to a military outfit who marches ahead of, or as a member of, a procession usu accompanying a band. [short for DRUM MAJORETTE]

major general *noun* an officer in the British army, the Royal Marines, and the US army, air force, and marines, ranking below a lieutenant general.

majority /mə'joriti/ *noun* (*pl* **majorities**) 1a a number greater than half of a total. b the amount by which such a greater number exceeds the remaining smaller number. 2 the greatest in number of two or more groups constituting a whole: *in the majority of cases; The majority of students live in.* 3 in voting: a *Brit* the number by which the votes cast for the winning party exceed those for its nearest rival. b *NAmer* the number by which the votes cast for the winning party exceed those for the remaining parties. 4 the age, usu 18 or 21, at which full legal rights and responsibilities are acquired: *attain one's majority.* 5 the military office, rank, or commission of a major: *I am surprised that the Prince should have offered you a majority, when he knows very well that nothing short of lieutenant colonel will satisfy others* — Scott. ✳ **be in the majority** to constitute the larger group: *Conference business was conducted in English since English speakers were in the majority.*

Usage note

the majority of Properly, *the majority of* should be followed by a plural noun or pronoun (*The majority of homes now boast a computer, The majority of us know how to use a computer*), and its use with singular mass nouns (*the majority of literature*) avoided.

major league *noun* a league of highest classification in US professional sport, *esp* baseball.

majorly *adv informal* extremely: *I was majorly unpleased* — Julian Barnes.

major premise *noun* in logic, the statement that contains the description of the subject of the conclusion drawn in a logical syllogism: *If Venus is a goddess, and we accept the major premise that all goddesses are immortal, we conclude that Venus must be immortal.*

major suit *noun* in bridge, either of the suits of hearts or spades, which are of superior scoring value: compare MINOR SUIT.

major term *noun* in logic, the term that states what is asserted of the subject of a major premise, e.g. *are immortal* in *All goddesses are immortal.*

majuscule /'majiskyoohl/ *noun* a letter in a style of handwriting employing only capital or UNCIAL[1] (rounded or curved capital) letters. ➤➤ **majuscular** /mə'juskyoolə/ *adj*, **majuscule** *adj*. [French *majuscule* from Latin *majusculus* rather large, dimin. of *major* greater, larger]

make[1] /mayk/ *verb* (*past tense and past part.* **made**) ➤ *verb trans* 1a to form (something) or put it together from ingredients or components: *a factory that makes cars.* b to create or produce (something) by work or action: *She made herself a cup of coffee.* c (+ into) to change or transform (something) into something else: *We can make the material into a curtain.* 2a to bring (something) about by effort: *The two sides made peace.* b to cause (somebody or something) to be or become: *The journey made us tired.* **c** to cause (something) to appear or seem to; to represent (something) in a certain way: *In the film they make the battle take place in winter.* **d** to produce (something) as an end product: *The navy will make a man of you; They made a mess of the job.* **3a** to perform or carry out (something): *He made a speech; Let's make an early start.* **b** to draft or produce a version of (a document, etc): *You should make a will.* **c** to enact or establish (e.g. a law). **d** to formulate (e.g. a plan) in the mind. **e** to put (something) forward for acceptance: *She made me a promise; Did you make an offer?* **4a** to cause (somebody or something) to act in a specified way: *Rain makes the flowers grow.* **b** to compel (somebody) to do something: *She was made to return.* **5a** to appoint (somebody) to a job: *They made him bishop.* **b** *chiefly NAmer, informal* to achieve (a rank or position): *They said she could make team captain.* **c** to be capable of becoming or of serving as (something): *Rags make the best paper; He will make a good husband.* **6a** to combine to form (something); to constitute (something): *We need 14 people to make a quorum; Hydrogen and oxygen make water.* **b** to amount to (a total): *Four and four make eight.* **7a** to gain (e.g. money) by working, trading, dealing, etc. **b** to score (e.g. points) in a game or sport: *The visiting side made 120 runs.* **8** to compute or estimate (something) in terms of a stated time or an amount: *I make that six biscuits you've had so far; What time do you make it?* **9** to be integral or essential to the existence or success of (something): *That bright paint really makes the room; It made my day.* **10** to reach or attain (something): *The plane never made the airfield; The story even made the national papers.* **11** to be in time for (e.g. a train). **12a** to assemble and set alight the materials for (a fire). **b** to renew or straighten the bedclothes on (a bed). **13a** in bridge or another card game, to fulfil (a contract). **b** to win a trick with (a card). **c** to shuffle (a pack of cards) in preparation for dealing. **14** *informal* to persuade (somebody) to consent to sexual intercourse. ➤ *verb intrans* **1** to set out or go in a specified direction: *He made towards the door; They were making for the coast.* **2** to behave as if beginning a specified action: *He made as if to hand it over.* **3** to act or behave in a specified way: *to make merry.* **4** said of the tide: to start to ebb or flow. ✳ **make away/off with** to take or steal (something). **make believe** to pretend or feign. **make do** to manage with the limited means at hand. **make it 1** *informal* to be successful. **2** *informal* to have sexual intercourse. **make like** *NAmer, informal* to imitate (something); to pretend to be (it). **make something of 1** to attribute a specified degree of significance to (something): *She tends to make too much of her problems.* **2** to understand (something): *I could make nothing of the play.* **make way** to give room. **make with** *NAmer, informal* to produce or do (something): *She's always making with the funny remarks.* ➤➤ **makable** *adj*, **makeable** *adj*, **maker** *noun*. [Old English *macian*]

make² *noun* **1a** the manner or style in which something is constructed. **b** a place or origin of manufacture; a brand. **2** the type or process of making or manufacturing. ✳ **on the make 1** *informal* rising or attempting to rise to a higher social or financial status. **2** *informal* in search of a sexual partner or sexual adventure.

make-believe *noun* **1** the activity of pretending or imagining. **2** something imaginary or pretended. ➤➤ **make-believe** *adj*.

make off *verb intrans* to leave in haste. ✳ **make off with** to steal (something).

make out *verb trans* **1** to manage to see, hear, or understand (something or somebody), often with some difficulty: *We could just make out the lighthouse.* **2** to write out or draft (a document): *Make out the cheque to me.* **3** to claim or pretend (that something is so): *He made out that he had never heard of me.* ➤ *verb intrans informal* **1** to fare or manage: *How is he making out in his new job?* **2** *NAmer* to engage in sexual activity.

makeover *noun* **1** the refurbishing of a garment, piece of furniture, room, etc. **2** the remodelling of somebody's appearance with a different hairstyle, clothes, and make-up.

make over *verb trans* **1** to give (somebody) a new look with a different hairstyle, clothes, and make-up. **2** to remake or redesign (e.g. a room). **3** to transfer the title of (property): *He made over the estate to his eldest son.*

Maker *noun* **(the/our/one's Maker)** God.

makeshift¹ *adj* being a crude and temporary expedient. ➤➤ **makeshift** *noun: using a box as a makeshift table.*

makeshift² *noun* a crude and temporary expedient.

make up *verb trans* **1** to invent (a story or excuse), sometimes in order to deceive. **2** said of parts: to constitute (a whole). **3** to

prepare; to put together. **4a** to prepare (something); to put (something) together: *I'll make up a bed for you; They are making up the prescription.* **b** to produce (e.g. clothes) by cutting and sewing. **c** to arrange typeset matter into (columns or pages) for printing. **5** to apply cosmetics to (the face). **6** to compensate for (a deficiency); *esp* to make (e.g. a required amount or number) complete. **7** to settle (differences). ➤ *verb intrans* **1** to become reconciled. **2** (+ for) to compensate for a disappointment or something lost or missing: *We will have to make up for lost time.* **3** to apply cosmetics. **4** to assemble a finished article; *esp* to complete a garment by sewing together. ✳ **make it up** to become reconciled after a quarrel. **make it up to** to compensate (somebody) for a disappointment or unfairness.

make-up *noun* **1** cosmetics, e.g. lipstick and mascara, applied, *esp* to the face, to give colour or emphasis. **2a** the way in which the parts of something are put together. **b** physical, mental, and moral constitution.

makeweight *noun* **1** something added to bring a weight to a desired value. **2** something of little intrinsic value thrown in to fill a gap.

making *noun* **1** the process of producing or developing something: *What goes into the making of an actor.* **2a** (*in pl*) the ingredients or parts needed to make something: *We've got the makings of a fruit salad.* **b** *informal* profits or earnings. **c** *NAmer, Aus, informal* (*in pl*) paper and tobacco used for rolling one's own cigarettes. ✳ **have the makings of** to have the right qualities for becoming a certain thing: *You have the makings of a pianist.* **in the making** in the process of becoming, forming, or developing. **of one's own making** brought on by oneself: *a crisis of their own making.*

mako¹ /'mahkoh/ *noun* (*pl* **makos**) either of two Australian species of shark that are notable sport fish and considered dangerous: *Isurus glaucus* and *Isurus oxyrhynchus.* Also called BLUE POINTER. [Maori *mako*]

mako² /'mahkoh, 'makoh/ *noun* (*pl* **makos**) a small evergreen New Zealand tree with red berries: *Aristotelia racemosa.*

makuta /mah'koohtə/ *noun* pl of LIKUTA.

MAL *abbr* Malaysia (international vehicle registration).

Mal. *abbr* Malachi (book of the Bible).

mal- *comb. form* forming words, with the meanings: **1a** bad or badly: *malpractice.* **b** faulty or faultily: *malfunction.* **c** deficiently: *malnourished.* **2** abnormal or abnormally: *malformation; malformed.* **3** not: *malcontent; maladroit.* [Middle English via French *mal* from Latin *male* badly, from *malus* bad]

malabsorption /maləb'zawpsh(ə)n/ *noun* the deficient absorption of food substances, vitamins, etc, e.g. vitamin B_{12}, from the stomach and intestines.

malac- or **malaco-** *comb. form* forming words, with the meaning: soft: *malacostracan.* [Greek *malakos* soft]

malacca /mə'lakə/ *noun* **1** a type of cane, often of mottled appearance, from an Asiatic rattan palm: *Calamus rotang: There were also two long sharp-ribbed settees of malacca cane* — Herman Melville. **2** a walking stick made from this. [named after *Malacca*, a city and state in Malaysia]

malachite /'maləkiet/ *noun* hydrated copper carbonate occurring as a green mineral and used for ornaments. [Middle English *melochites* via Latin from Greek *molochitēs* from *molochē* mallow]

malaco- *comb. form* see MALAC-.

malacology /malə'koləji/ *noun* a branch of zoology dealing with molluscs. ➤➤ **malacological** /-'lojikl/ *adj*, **malacologist** *noun*.

malacostracan /malə'kostrəkən/ *noun* any of a major subclass of crustaceans including the crabs, woodlice, lobsters, and shrimps: subclass Malacostraca. ➤➤ **malacostracan** *adj*. [from the Latin subclass name, from MALACO- + Greek *ostrakon* shell]

maladjusted /malə'justid/ *adj* manifesting behavioural difficulties through failure to cope with one's social environment and conditions of life. ➤➤ **maladjustment** *noun*.

maladminister /maləd'ministə/ *verb trans* (**maladministered**, **maladministering**) *formal* to administer (something) incompetently or corruptly. ➤➤ **maladministration** /-'straysh(ə)n/ *noun*.

maladroit /malə'droyt/ *adj* clumsy or inept: *a maladroit remark.* ➤➤ **maladroitly** *adv*, **maladroitness** *noun*. [French *maladroit* from early French, from MAL- + ADROIT]

malady /'malədi/ *noun* (*pl* **maladies**) a disease or disorder: *My sister is in her own room, nursing that essentially feminine malady, a slight* *headache* — Wilkie Collins. [Middle English *maladie* via Old French from Latin *male habitus* in bad condition]

Malaga /ˈmaləgə/ *noun* a usu sweet fortified wine from the Málaga region of Spain.

Malagasy /maləˈgasi/ *noun* (*pl* **Malagasies** *or collectively* **Malagasy**) **1** a native or inhabitant of the Malagasy Republic (Madagascar). **2** the Austronesian language of Madagascar. ⋙ **Malagasy** *adj*.

malaise /maˈlez, məˈlayz/ *noun* **1** an indeterminate feeling of debility or lack of health, often accompanying the start of an illness. **2** a vague sense of mental or moral unease. **3** social or economic disquiet: *the general malaise which affects the entire retail sector* — The Guardian. [French *malaise*, from Old French *mal* bad + *aise* comfort]

malamute *or* **malemute** /ˈmaləmyooht/ *noun* a breed of powerful heavy-coated Alaskan dog with erect ears and a plumy tail. [Inuit *Malimuit*, an Alaskan people who developed the breed]

malapropism /ˈmaləpropiz(ə)m/ *noun* an incongruous misapplication of a word, as in 'polo bears' or 'neon stockings'.

Word history
named after Mrs *Malaprop*, a character often misusing words in *The Rivals*, a comedy by R B Sheridan d.1816, Irish dramatist. The many gaffes made by Mrs Malaprop (named from MALAPROPOS[1]) include the observation: 'As headstrong as an allegory [alligator] on the banks of the Nile'.

malapropos[1] /ˌmaləprəˈpoh/ *adv formal or literary* in an inappropriate or inopportune way: *She had spoken malapropos, as she realized too late.* [French *mal à propos* not to the purpose]

malapropos[2] *adj formal or literary* inappropriate or inopportune: *It will give him a hearty laugh at present, and put him on his guard against laughing when it might be very mal-a-propos* — Scott.

malaria /məˈleəri·ə/ *noun* a disease caused by protozoan parasites in the red blood cells, transmitted by the bite of mosquitoes, and characterized by periodic attacks of chills and fever. ⋙ **malarial** *adj*, **malarian** *adj*, **malarious** /-ri·əs/ *adj*. [Italian *malaria* from *mala aria* bad air; from the former belief that it was caused by gases from marshy places]

malarkey /məˈlahki/ *noun informal* nonsense: *Half that stuff about matching bullets to guns is scientific malarkey* — Gavin Lyall. [origin unknown]

malathion /maləˈthieon, -ən/ *noun* an insecticide used against household flies and greenfly. [*maleate*, a salt of maleic acid + THI- + -ON[1]]

Malawian /məˈlahwi·ən/ *noun* a native or inhabitant of Malawi in S central Africa. ⋙ **Malawian** *adj*.

Malay /məˈlay/ *noun* **1** a member of a people of the Malay peninsula and adjacent islands. **2** the Austronesian language spoken in the Malay peninsula. ⋙ **Malay** *adj*.

Word history
early Dutch *Malayo* (now *Maleier*) from Malay *Mĕlayu*. Malay words that have passed into English include *amok, bamboo, caddy, cockatoo, gingham, gong, gutta-percha, kapok, ketchup, rattan, sago*, and *sarong*.

Malayalam /məˈlayəlam, maliˈahləm/ *noun* a Dravidian language of SW India. ⋙ **Malayalam** *adj*.

Malayan /məˈlayən/ *noun* = MALAY.

Malayo- *comb. form* forming words, with the meaning: Malayan and: *Malayo-Indonesian*.

Malayo-Polynesian /məˈlayoh/ *adj* Austronesian.

Malaysian /məˈlayzi·ən, -zh(ə)n/ *noun* a native or inhabitant of Malaysia. ⋙ **Malaysian** *noun*.

malcontent[1] /ˈmalkənˈtent/ *noun* a discontented person; *esp* somebody violently opposed to a government or regime.

malcontent[2] *adj* dissatisfied with the existing state of affairs: *awed by the greatness of the universe and malcontent with what the philosophers told me* — Somerset Maugham. [early French *malcontent*, from Old French *mal* badly + *content* pleased]

malcontented *adj* = MALCONTENT[2].

mal de mer /ˌmal də ˈmeə/ *noun* seasickness. [French *mal de mer*]

Maldivian /ˈmoldivi·ən, molˈdie-/ *noun* **1** a native or inhabitant of the Maldives, islands in the Indian Ocean. **2** the Indic language spoken in the Maldives. ⋙ **Maldivian** *adj*.

male[1] /mayl/ *adj* **1** relating to or denoting the sex that fertilizes or inseminates the female to produce offspring. **2** said of a plant or flower: having stamens but no ovaries. **3** relating to or character-

istic of the male sex. **4** made up of male individuals: *a male voice choir*. **5** designed for fitting into a corresponding hollow part: *a male electric plug*. ⋙ **maleness** *noun*. [Middle English via French from Latin *masculus*, dimin. of *mar-, mas* male]

Usage note
male *or* masculine? *Male* is used to describe the sex that does not bear offspring, and plants or flowers that do not produce fruit or seeds: *a male deer is called a stag. Masculine* is used only of human beings, not plants or animals, and describes qualities and behaviour that are characteristic of or traditionally ascribed to men rather than women: *He doesn't think pink sheets are very masculine. Masculine* is also used to classify nouns, adjectives, and pronouns in some languages, in contrast to those that are feminine or neuter.

male[2] *noun* a male person, animal, or plant.

male bonding *noun* a process in which men spend time together and form close friendships.

male chauvinist *noun* a man who believes in the inherent superiority of men over women and is excessively loyal to his own sex. ⋙ **male chauvinism** *noun*.

malediction /maləˈdiksh(ə)n/ *noun literary* a curse: *He whispered to himself a malediction … upon the ship, upon the men* — Joseph Conrad. ⋙ **maledictory** /-ˈdikt(ə)ri/ *adj*. [Middle English *malediccioun* via late Latin from Latin *maledicere* to speak evil of, from *male* badly + *dicere* to speak, say]

malefaction /maliˈfaksh(ə)n/ *noun formal or literary* an evil deed; a crime: *hanged for their malefactions*.

malefactor /ˈmalifaktə/ *noun* **1** *formal or literary* a person who commits a crime: *Overcoats and waterproofs hung like gibbeted malefactors* — James Joyce. **2** a wrongdoer. [Middle English from Latin *malefactor* from *malefactus*, past part. of *malefacere* to do evil, from *male* badly + *facere* to do]

male fern *noun* a fern from which an extract is obtained that is used to treat tapeworm infestation: *Dryopteris filix-mas*.

malefic /məˈlefik/ *adj literary* **1** said of stars or planets: having malign influence. **2** said of magic, etc: harmful or malicious: *the malefic arts*. ⋙ **maleficence** *noun*, **maleficent** *adj*. [Latin *maleficus* wicked, mischievous, from *male* badly + -*ficus* doing, from *facere* to do]

maleic acid /məˈlee·ik/ *noun* a crystalline acid used in making plastics: formula $C_4H_4O_4$. [French *maléique*, alteration of *malique* malic; from its formation by dehydration of malic acid]

male menopause *noun* a mid-life crisis that causes emotional upheaval in a man, thought to resemble the effects of the menopause on women.

malemute /ˈmaləmyooht/ *noun* see MALAMUTE.

malevolent /məˈlevələnt/ *adj* intending or wishing harm; full of hate: *She treated me to a malevolent glare.* ⋙ **malevolence** *noun*, **malevolently** *adv*. [Latin *malevolent-, malevolens*, from *male* badly + *volent-, volens*, present part. of *velle* to wish]

malfeasance /malˈfeez(ə)ns/ *noun* in law, misconduct or wrongdoing, *esp* by a public official. [MAL- + early French *faisance* doing, execution]

malformation /malfəˈmaysh(ə)n/ *noun* anomalous, abnormal, or faulty formation or structure. ⋙ **malformed** *adj*.

malfunction[1] /malˈfungksh(ə)n/ *verb intrans* to fail to operate in the normal manner.

malfunction[2] *noun* a failure to operate in the normal manner.

Malian /ˈmahli·ən/ *noun* a native or inhabitant of Mali in W Africa. ⋙ **Malian** *adj*.

malic acid /ˈmalik/ *noun* an acid found in the juices of certain fruits, e.g. apples, and other plants: formula $C_4H_6O_5$. [French *malique* from Latin *malum* apple]

malice /ˈmalis/ *noun* **1** a conscious desire to do harm; spite. **2** a premeditated desire to commit a crime. [Middle English via Old French from Latin *malitia* ill will, from *malus* bad]

malice aforethought *noun* in law, predetermination to commit a violent crime, which must be proved in order to make a killing constitute an act of murder.

malicious /məˈlishəs/ *adj* **1** motivated by malice: *malicious gossip*. **2** intended to cause harm: *malicious damage to property*. ⋙ **maliciously** *adv*, **maliciousness** *noun*.

malign[1] /məˈlien/ *adj* **1** evil in nature or effect: *malign influences*. **2** malevolent: *Iago's … malign genius* — Independent. **3** *archaic* said of a disease: malignant or virulent. ⋙ **malignity** /məˈligniti/ *noun*,

malignly *adv.* [Middle English *maligne* via French from Latin *malignus*, from *male* badly + *gignere* to beget]

malign² *verb trans* to speak ill of (somebody), *esp* spitefully or unfairly.

malignancy /mə'lignənsi/ *noun* (*pl* **malignancies**) **1a** a malignant tumour. **b** the presence of a malignant tumour or disease. **c** the degree to which a growth, etc is malignant. **2** malevolence; malignity.

malignant /mə'lignənt/ *adj* **1a** harmful; malevolent: *a malignant spirit; with a malignant expression in her eyes.* **b** passionately and relentlessly malevolent. **2** said of a tumour or disease: tending to infiltrate and spread. ➤➤ **malignantly** *adv.* [late Latin *malignant-, malignans, present part. of malignari, from malignus* malign]

malinger /mə'linggə/ *verb intrans* (**malingered, malingering**) to pretend illness or incapacity so as to avoid duty or work. ➤➤ **malingerer** *noun.* [French *malingre* sickly]

Malinke /mə'lingki/ *noun* (*pl* **Malinkes** *or collectively* **Malinke**) **1** a member of a W African people living in Mali, Senegal, and the Ivory Coast, noted for using cowrie shells as currency. **2** the Mande language of this people. [name of the people in Malinke]

mall /mawl, mal/ *noun* **1** a large covered shopping precinct, usu with associated parking space. **2** a public promenade, often bordered by trees. [named after The *Mall*, a promenade in London, orig an alley used for playing pall-mall (an old game played with balls and mallets)]

mallard /'malahd, 'maləd/ *noun* (*pl* **mallards** *or collectively* **mallard**) a common large wild duck that is the ancestor of the domestic ducks: *Anas platyrhynchos.* [Middle English from early French *mallart*]

malleable /'mali·əbl/ *adj* **1** said *esp* of metals or other materials: capable of being beaten or rolled into a desired shape. **2** easily shaped by outside forces or influences: *when one is young and malleable.* ➤➤ **malleability** /-'biliti/ *noun*, **malleableness** *noun*, **malleably** *adv.* [Middle English *malliable* via French from Latin *malleus* hammer]

mallee /'mali/ *noun* any of several low-growing shrubby Australian eucalyptuses: *Eucalyptus dumosa* and *Eucalyptus oleosa.* [from an Aboriginal language]

malleolus /mə'lee·ələs/ *noun* (*pl* **malleoli** /-lie/) in anatomy, a bony protuberance, *esp* those at each side of the ankle, forming the lower ends of the tibia and fibula. [scientific Latin from Latin *malleolus*, dimin. of *malleus* hammer, in reference to the hammerhead-like shape of such protuberances]

mallet /'malit/ *noun* **1** a hammer with a large, usu wooden or soft metal head, used e.g. for hitting a chisel. **2** a long-handled implement with a large usu cylindrical wooden head for striking the ball in croquet or polo. [Middle English *maillet* from Old French *maillet*, dimin. of *mail* hammer, from Latin *malleus* hammer]

malleus /'mali·əs/ *noun* (*pl* **mallei** /'maliie/) the outermost of the chain of three small bones that transmit sound to the inner ear of mammals; = HAMMER¹ (2C): compare INCUS, STAPES. [Latin *malleus* hammer]

mallow /'maloh/ *noun* any of numerous species of plants with usu deeply cut lobed leaves and showy pink, purple, or white flowers: genus *Malva.* [Old English *mealwe* from Latin *malva*]

malm /mahm/ *noun* **1** a soft crumbly limestone rock or soil. **2** a brick made from clay and chalk. [Old English *mealm-*]

malmsey /'mahmzi/ *noun* **1** the sweetest variety of Madeira wine. **2** formerly, a sweet white wine imported from Greece. [Middle English *malmesey* from late Latin *Malmasia* Monemvasia, a village in Greece where it was orig produced]

malnourished /mal'nurisht/ *adj* suffering from malnutrition; undernourished.

malnutrition /malnyooh'trish(ə)n/ *noun* faulty or inadequate nutrition.

malocclusion /malə'kloohzh(ə)n/ *noun* a defect in the meeting and alignment of the upper and lower teeth when the jaws are brought together.

malodorous /mal'ohd(ə)rəs/ *adj formal* smelling bad.

maloti /mə'lohti/ *noun* pl of LOTI.

malpractice /mal'praktis/ *noun* **1** failure to exercise due professional skill or care. **2** an instance of improper conduct; malfeasance.

malt¹ /mawlt/ *noun* **1** grain softened in water, allowed to germinate, then roasted and used in brewing and distilling. **2** unblended malt whisky produced in a particular area: *the finest Highland malts.* **3** *NAmer* = MALTED MILK. ➤➤ **maltiness** *noun*, **malty** *adj.* [Old English *mealt*]

malt² *verb trans* **1** to convert (grain) into malt. **2** to make (e.g. liquor) with malt or malt extract. ➤ *verb intrans* to become malt.

maltase /'mawltayz, 'maltayz/ *noun* an enzyme that accelerates the breakdown of the sugar maltose to glucose, is found in plants, bacteria, and yeasts, and is secreted by the intestines during digestion.

malted milk /'mawltid/ *noun* **1** a soluble powder prepared from dried milk and malted cereals. **2** a drink made by dissolving this powder with milk.

Maltese /mawl'teez/ *noun* (*pl* **Maltese**) **1** a native or inhabitant of Malta, an island in the Mediterranean. **2** the Semitic language spoken in Malta. ➤➤ **Maltese** *adj.*

Maltese cross *noun* a cross consisting of four equal arms that broaden from the centre and have their ends indented by a shallow V.

malt extract *noun* a sweet light-brown syrup prepared from an infusion of malt and water.

malt house *noun* a building where malt is prepared and stored.

Malthusian /mal'thyoohzi·ən/ *adj* relating to Malthus or his theory that population tends to increase faster than its means of subsistence and that widespread poverty inevitably results unless population growth is checked. ➤➤ **Malthusian** *noun*, **Malthusianism** *noun.* [named after Thomas *Malthus* d.1834, English economist and clergyman]

maltings *noun* (*pl* **maltings**) (*treated as sing.*) a building where malt is prepared and stored.

malt liquor *noun* a fermented alcoholic drink, e.g. beer or ale, made with malt.

maltose /'mawltohz, 'mawltohs/ *noun* a sugar formed by the breakdown of starch. [French *maltose* from MALT¹]

maltreat /mal'treet/ *verb trans* to treat (a person or animal) cruelly or roughly. ➤➤ **maltreatment** *noun.* [French *maltraiter* from early French, from MAL- + *traiter* to treat]

maltster /'mawltstə/ *noun* a person who makes or deals in malt.

malt whisky *noun* whisky distilled from malted barley.

malvaceous /mal'vayshəs/ *adj* relating to or denoting plants of the mallow family (Malvaceae), including e.g. cotton and okra. [scientific Latin *malvaceus* from Latin *malva* mallow]

Malvasia /malvə'see·ə, -zee·ə/ *noun* **1** a variety of grape used in the production of red and white wine, *esp* in Italy, and to make MALMSEY (sweet Madeira wine). **2** a wine produced from this grape. [Italian *Malvasia* Monemvasia: see MALMSEY]

malversation /malvuh'saysh(ə)n/ *noun formal* corruption in office. [early French *malversation* from *malverser* to be corrupt, from *mal* bad + *verser* to turn, handle, from Latin *versare* from *versus*, past part. of *vertere* to turn]

mam /mam/ *noun informal* **1** *chiefly Brit* an affectionate name for one's mother. **2** *chiefly NAmer* used as a form of address for a woman. [(sense 1) short for *mama*; (sense 2) a variant of *ma'am*]

mama *or* **mamma** /mə'mah, 'mumə/ *noun* **1** *informal* an affectionate name for one's mother. **2** /*usu* 'mumə/*NAmer, informal* a mature woman. [baby talk]

mamba /'mambə/ *noun* any of several species of tropical African venomous snakes related to the cobras but with no hood: genus *Dendroaspis.* [Zulu *im-amba*]

mambo¹ /'mamboh/ *noun* (*pl* **mambos**) **1** a ballroom dance of Haitian origin that resembles the rumba. **2** the music for this. [American Spanish *mambo*]

mambo² *verb intrans* (**mamboes, mamboed, mamboing**) to dance the mambo.

Mameluke /'mamilook/ *noun* a member of a politically powerful Egyptian military class, descended from Turkish slaves, who occupied the sultanate from 1250 to 1517 and remained as a ruling class until 1811. [French *mameluk* from Arabic *mamlūk* slave]

mamilla *or* **mammilla** /mə'milə/ *noun* (*pl* **mamillae** *or* **mammillae** /-lie/) **1** a nipple. **2** a nipple-shaped part, structure, or protuberance. [Latin *mammilla, mamilla* breast, nipple, dimin. of *mamma* breast]

mamillary *or* **mammillary** /'mamiləri/ *adj* **1** relating to or resembling the breasts, e.g. in being smoothly rounded. **2** said of a mineral: having smooth convex surfaces.

mamma¹ /mə'mah, 'mumə/ *noun* see MAMA. [Latin *mamma* mother, breast, of baby-talk origin]

mamma² /'mamə/ *noun* (*pl* **mammae** /'mamee/) a mammary gland with its accessory parts; a breast or udder.

mammal /'maməl/ *noun* any of a class of higher vertebrates comprising humans and all other animals that have mammary glands and nourish their young with milk: class Mammalia. ➤➤ **mammalian** /mə'mayli-ən/ *adj.* [late Latin *mammalis* of the breast, from Latin *mamma* breast]

mammalogy /mə'maləji/ *noun* a branch of zoology dealing with mammals. ➤➤ **mammalogist** *noun*.

mammary /'maməri/ *adj* relating to or in the region of the mammary glands or breasts.

mammary gland *noun* the milk-producing gland in female mammals, e.g. the breast in women.

mammilla /ma'milə/ *noun* see MAMILLA.

mammillary /'mamiləri/ *adj* see MAMILLARY.

mammogram /'maməgram/ *noun* an X-ray photograph of the breasts.

mammography /mə'mogrəfi/ *noun* the examination of the breasts by taking X-ray photographs, e.g. for early detection of cancer.

Mammon /'mamən/ *noun* (*also* **mammon**) material wealth or possessions, *esp* considered as an evil: *the shuffling worldly wisdom of men, who, forgetting that they cannot serve God and mammon, endeavour to blend contradictory things* — Mary Wollstonecraft. [late Latin *mammona* via Greek from Aramaic *māmōnā* riches]

mammoth¹ /'maməth/ *noun* any of several extinct species of large hairy long-tailed Pleistocene elephants: genus *Mammuthus*. [Russian *mamont, mamot*]

mammoth² *adj* of very great size: *a mammoth task; mammoth business conglomerates.*

mammy /'mami/ *noun* (*pl* **-ies**, *pl* **mammies**) **1** *Brit, informal* an affectionate name for one's mother. **2** *NAmer, offensive* a black nanny of white children, *esp* formerly in the southern USA. [alteration of MAMMA¹]

Man. *abbr* Manitoba.

man¹ /man/ *noun* (*pl* **men** /men/) **1** an adult human male. **2** an individual or person: *A man could get killed doing that.* **3** the human race. **4a** a two-legged primate mammal that is the sole representative of a distinct family and is anatomically related to the great apes but is distinguished from them, *esp* by greater brain development and a capacity for articulate speech and abstract reasoning: *Homo sapiens.* **b** any extinct member of this species. **5** (*usu used in combinations*) a man belonging to a usu specified category, e.g. by birth, residence, membership, or occupation: *a townsman; a businessman; a dustbin man.* **6a** a husband. **b** a male sexual partner: *find a new man.* **7** (*in pl*). **a** a member of the ranks of a military force: *officers and men.* **b** the working force, as distinguished from the employer and usu the management. **c** the members of a team. **8** (**the/your/our man**) the most suitable person: *If you want a good worker, he's your man.* **9** a person possessing the qualities traditionally associated with manhood, e.g. courage and fortitude: *He was a man, take him for all in all* — Shakespeare; *Come on, be a man!* **10** any of the pieces moved by each player in various board games, e.g. chess or draughts. **11** (*often* **the Man**) *NAmer, slang* the police. **12** (*often* **the Man**) *NAmer, slang* the white establishment. ✳ **be one's own man** to be independent-minded, not answerable to others. **man and boy** from childhood: *He had worked with cattle man and boy.* **man to man 1** frankly, as one man to another. **2** in football, etc, with each player marking an opponent. **to a man** without exception. ➤➤ **manless** *adj,* **manlike** *adj.* [Old English *man, mann*]

Usage note

Man can be used without an indefinite or definite article to mean the human species or the whole human race: *Man is a political animal.* This usage is, however, felt by many people to be inappropriate in the modern age since it suggests that the male defines or embodies the species, ignoring the female. *Man* should not be used unthinkingly in any context to mean 'men and women' or 'the human race'. Substitutes are *humanity, human beings, the human race, humans, humankind, people,* or, occasionally, *individual* or *person: one person, one vote.* Many compounds with 'man' (and 'woman') can be altered to gender-inclusive forms: *man-hours* to

working hours; man-made to *artificial* or *synthetic; cameraman* and *camerawoman* to *camera operator; fireman* and *firewoman* to *firefighter; policeman* and *policewoman* to *police officer.*

man² *verb trans* (**manned, manning**) to provide (e.g. a machine or a place) with the necessary people: *workers who man the production lines; Man the pumps!*

man³ *interj informal* used to express intensity of feeling: *Man, what a game!*

mana /'mahnə/ *noun* in Polynesia and Melanesia, the power of elemental forces embodied in an object or person. [Maori *mana*]

man about town *noun* a worldly and socially active man.

manacle¹ /'manəkl/ *noun* **1** (*usu in pl*) a shackle or handcuff. **2** (*usu in pl*) a restraint: *the manacles of etiquette.* [Middle English *manicle* via French from Latin *manicula,* dimin. of *manus* hand]

manacle² *verb* **1** to confine (the hands) with manacles. **2** to subject (somebody) to a restraint: *Writers of all kinds are manacled servants of the public. We write frankly and fearlessly but then we 'modify' before we print* — Mark Twain.

manage /'manij/ *verb trans* **1** to conduct the running of (a business). **2** to control or supervise (a person or an animal). **3** to guide or have charge of (a sports team, athlete, entertainer, etc). **4** to use (e.g. money) economically: *He managed his resources carefully.* **5** to succeed in handling (e.g. something cumbersome): *I can't manage the crate by myself.* **6a** to contrive (to do something): *We managed to warn them in time.* **b** to succeed in accomplishing (something): *She managed a smile.* **7** to be able to fit in (something): *I'm full – I don't think I can manage a dessert; Can you manage dinner one evening next week?* ➤ *verb intrans* to be able to cope with a difficult situation; *esp* to use one's finances to the best advantage. ➤➤ **manageability** /-'biliti/ *noun,* **manageable** *adj,* **manageableness** *noun,* **manageably** *adv.* [Italian *maneggiare* from *mano* hand, from Latin *manus* hand]

managed currency *noun* a currency that is subject to government control, *esp* with regard to the exchange rate.

managed fund *noun* an investment fund that is run by an institutional investor, e.g. an insurance company on behalf of a small investor.

management *noun* **1** the activity, work, or art of managing. **2** (*usu* **the management**) (*treated as sing. or pl*) the collective body of those who manage or direct an enterprise: *The management take no responsibility for articles left on the premises.*

management buyout *noun* the purchase of a business company by its managers, usu with financial backing from a bank or other outside source of finance.

manager *or* **manageress** /-jə'res/ *noun* **1** a person who manages a business, etc, or controls a group of personnel. **2** a person who directs a sports team, player, entertainer, etc. **3** a member of the House of Commons or House of Lords who is chosen to organize something that concerns both Houses. **4** in computing, a program that organizes a resource or process: *Click on 'File Manager'.* **5** anybody who has to manage anything: *He's a poor manager of his time.* ➤➤ **managerial** /-'jiəri-əl/ *adj,* **managerially** /-'jiəri-əli/ *adv,* **managership** *noun.*

managing *adj* denoting a post bearing executive responsibility: *managing director; managing editor.*

mañana /man'yahnə/ *adv* at an indefinite time in the future. [Spanish *mañana* tomorrow, from earlier *cras mañana,* literally 'tomorrow early']

manat /'manat/ *noun* (*pl* **manat**) **1** the basic monetary unit of Azerbaijan, divided into 100 gopik. **2** the basic monetary unit of Turkmenistan, divided into 100 tenge.

man-at-arms *noun* (*pl* **men-at-arms**) a soldier, *esp* formerly a heavily armed and usu mounted soldier.

manatee /'manətee/ *noun* any of several species of tropical aquatic plant-eating mammals with broad tails: genus *Trichechus.* [Spanish *manatí* from Carib *manáti*]

manchester /'manchestə/ *noun Aus, NZ* **1** (*also* **Manchester**) linen goods, e.g. sheets: *manchester and soft furnishings.* **2** (*also* **Manchester**) a household linen department in a shop: *downstairs in the manchester department.* [short for *Manchester wares,* named after *Manchester,* a city in England where such goods were orig made]

manchineel /manchi'niəl/ *noun* a tropical American tree of the spurge family, which has poisonous yellow to reddish apple-like fruit and a milky sap that causes blisters: *Hippomane mancinella*. [French *mancenille* from Spanish *manzanilla*, dimin. of *manzana* apple]

Manchu /man'chooh/ *noun* (*pl* **Manchus** *or collectively* **Manchu**) **1** a member of the orig nomadic native people of Manchuria, of Tartar stock, who established a dynasty in China in 1644. **2** the Tungusic language spoken by these people. ➤ **Manchu** *adj*.

manciple /'mansipl/ *noun archaic* a steward or caterer, *esp* in a college or monastery. [Middle English via Anglo-Norman French from Latin *mancipium* act of purchase, from *mancip-*, *manceps* purchaser]

Mancunian /mang'kyoohni-ən, man-/ *noun* a native or inhabitant of Manchester, a city in England. ➤ **Mancunian** *adj*. [medieval Latin *Mancunium* Manchester]

-mancy *comb. form* forming nouns, denoting: divination: *necromancy*. [Middle English *-mancie* via Old French and Latin from Greek *-manteia*, from *mantis* diviner, prophet]

mandala /'mahndələ/ *noun* a Hindu or Buddhist symbol in the form of a circle enclosing a square with a deity on each of its four sides used to represent the universe. [Sanskrit *maṇḍala* circle]

mandamus /man'dayməs/ *noun* (*pl* **mandamuses**) a judicial writ requiring something to be carried out. [Latin *mandamus* we command, from *mandare* to entrust, command]

mandarin /'mandərin, -'rin/ *noun* **1** (**Mandarin**). **a** the primarily northern dialect of Chinese used by the court and officials under the Empire. **b** the chief dialect of Chinese that has a standard variety spoken in the Beijing area. **2** a public official in the Chinese Empire ranked according to any of nine grades. **3a** a person of position and influence, *esp* in literary or bureaucratic circles: *the mandarins of the Foreign Office; the fashion mandarins*. **b** an elder and often reactionary member of such a circle. **4a** a yellow to orange loose-skinned citrus fruit. **b** the small spiny Chinese orange tree that bears this fruit: *Citrus reticulata*. [Portuguese *mandarin* via Malay from Sanskrit *mantrin* counsellor, from *mantra* counsel; (sense 4) French *mandarine*, ultimately from Portuguese *mandarin* (prob referring to the yellow colour of the official's robes)]

mandarin collar *noun* a narrow stand-up collar.

mandarin duck *noun* a brightly marked crested Asian duck, often found domesticated: *Aix galericulata*.

mandarin orange *noun* = MANDARIN (4A).

mandatary /'mandət(ə)ri/ *noun* see MANDATORY².

mandate¹ /'mandayt/ *noun* **1** an authoritative command from a superior. **2** an authorization to act on behalf of another, e.g.: **a** in law, a commission to a person to carry out a particular task gratuitously. **b** written permission to somebody to use another person's bank account for transactions. **3** the authority to act on behalf of the electorate perceived as given to the winner of an election. **4a** formerly, an order granted by the League of Nations to a member nation for the establishment of a responsible government over a conquered territory. **b** a mandated territory. [early French *mandat* from Latin *mandatum*, neuter past part. of *mandare* to entrust, command, from *manus* hand + *dare* to give]

mandate² /'mandayt/ *verb trans* **1** to give (somebody) a mandate: *A representative, as distinct from a delegate, is not mandated to vote in any particular way*. **2** to make (something) mandatory: *He mandated reform of the curriculum*. **3** to administer or assign (e.g. a territory) under a mandate.

mandatory¹ /'mandət(ə)ri/ *adj* **1** containing or constituting a command: *The measures are advisable although not mandatory*. **2** compulsory or obligatory: *a mandatory sentence of life imprisonment*. ➤ **mandatorily** *adv*.

mandatory² *or* **mandatary** *noun* (*pl* **mandatories**) a nation or person holding a mandate.

Mandelbrot set /'mandlbrot/ *noun* a complex FRACTAL (geometric shape divisible into parts that match the original) image generated by a computer drawing the coordinates produced by the repeated application of a mathematical equation. [named after Benoit *Mandelbrot* b.1924, US mathematician]

mandible /'mandibl/ *noun* **1a** the jaw. **b** the lower jaw together with its surrounding soft parts. **c** the upper or lower part of a bird's bill. **2** any of various mouth parts in insects or other invertebrates for holding or biting food. ➤ **mandibular** /man'dibyoolə/ *adj*, **mandibulate** /man'dibyoolayt/ *adj*. [early French via late Latin from Latin *mandere* to chew]

Mandinka /mən'dingkə/ *noun* (*pl* **Mandinkas** *or collectively* **Mandinka**) **1** a member of a W African people inhabiting Senegal, Gambia, and Sierra Leone. **2** the Mande language spoken by this people.

mandolin *or* **mandoline** /mandə'lin/ *noun* **1** a stringed musical instrument of the lute family with four pairs of strings and a fretted neck. **2** a utensil with adjustable blades set in a frame, for slicing vegetables. [Italian *mandolino*, dimin. of *mandola* lute]

mandragora /man'dragərə/ *noun* = MANDRAKE: *Give me to drink mandragora … that I might sleep out this great gap of time my Antony is away* — Shakespeare. [Old English: compare MANDRAKE]

mandrake /'mandrayk/ *noun* **1** a Mediterranean plant of the potato family with whitish or purple flowers and a large forked root traditionally thought to resemble the human form: *Mandragora officinarum*. **2** the root of a mandrake, formerly used to promote conception, as a laxative, or to induce sleep or hypnosis: *Go, and catch a falling star, get with child a mandrake root* — John Donne.

Word history

Middle English from Old English MANDRAGORA from Latin and Greek *mandragoras*. The form *mandrake* is thought to come from MAN¹, because of the shape of the root + DRAKE² dragon, because of its special properties.

mandrel *or* **mandril** /'mandrəl/ *noun* **1** an axle or spindle inserted into a hole in a workpiece to support it during machining. **2** a metal bar round which material, e.g. metal, may be cast, shaped, etc. [prob modification of French *mandrin* lathe]

mandrill /'mandril/ *noun* a large gregarious baboon found in W Africa, the male of which has red and blue striped cheeks and hindquarters: *Mandrillus sphinx*. [prob from MAN¹ + DRILL⁶]

mane /mayn/ *noun* **1** long thick hair growing on the neck of a horse, male lion, etc. **2** long thick hair on a person's head. ➤ **maned** *adj*. [Old English *manu*]

man-eater *noun* **1** an animal that will kill and eat humans: *You needn't be afraid of the lion … There hasn't been a man-eater around here for two years* — Edgar Rice Burroughs. **2** *informal* a woman of sexually predatory habits. ➤ **man-eating** *adj*.

manège /ma'nezh/ *noun* **1** a school for training horses and teaching horsemanship, or an enclosed area in which this is done. **2** the movements or paces of a trained horse. **3** horsemanship. [French *manège* from Italian *maneggio* training of a horse, from *maneggiare* to MANAGE]

manes /'mahnayz/ *pl noun* (*also* **Manes**) the spirits of the ancient Roman dead to which graveside sacrifices were made. [Latin *manes*]

maneuver /mə'noohvə/ *noun and verb NAmer* see MANOEUVRE¹ and MANOEUVRE².

man Friday *noun* a trustworthy male assistant. [named after *Friday*, a character in the novel *Robinson Crusoe* by Daniel Defoe d.1731, English writer]

manful /'manf(ə)l/ *adj* showing courage and resolution: *with a manful effort to grin*. ➤ **manfully** *adv*, **manfulness** *noun*.

manga /'manggə/ *noun* a Japanese cartoon genre found in comic books and animated films, characteristically on science-fiction or fantasy themes. [Japanese *manga*]

mangabey /'manggəbi/ *noun* any of several species of long-tailed African monkeys: genus *Cercocebus*. [named after *Mangabey*, a region of Madagascar]

manganese /'manggə'neez/ *noun* a greyish white brittle metallic chemical element, used mainly in alloys: symbol Mn, atomic number 25. ➤ **manganic** /mang'ganik/ *adj*, **manganous** /'manggənəs/ *adj*. [French *manganèse* via Italian from late Latin *magnesia* magnesia]

mange /maynj/ *noun* any of various contagious skin diseases affecting domestic animals or sometimes human beings, characterized by inflammation and loss of hair and caused by a minute parasitic mite. [Middle English *manjewe* from early French *mangeue* itching, from *mangier* to eat]

mangel-wurzel /'manggl wuhzl/ *noun* a large yellow to orange type of beet grown as food for livestock. [German *Mangoldwurzel*, *Mangelwurzel*, from *Mangold* beet + *Wurzel* root]

manger /'maynjə/ *noun* a trough or open box in a stable for holding feed. [Middle English *mangeour*, *manger* via French from Latin *manducare* to chew, devour, from *manducus* glutton, from *mandere* to chew]

mangetout /'monjtooh, 'monzhtooh/ *noun* (*pl* **mangetouts** *or collectively* **mangetout** /'monjtooh, 'monzhtooh/) a variety of garden pea with thin flat edible pods. [French *mangetout*, from *manger* to eat + *tout* all]

mangey /'maynji/ *adj* see MANGY.

mangle[1] /'manggl/ *verb trans* **1** to hack or crush (something): *bodies mangled in the car accident.* **2** to spoil (something) by inept rendering: *One of the children was mangling Handel's 'Harmonious Blacksmith' on the piano.* ⏩ **mangler** *noun.* [Middle English *manglen* via Anglo-French from Old French *maynier* to maim]

mangle[2] *noun* **1** a machine with rollers for squeezing water from laundry. **2** *NAmer* a machine with heated rollers for pressing laundry. [Dutch *mangel* via German and Middle High German from Latin *manganum* philtre, mangonel]

mangle[3] *verb trans* to squeeze or press (laundry) with a mangle.

mango /'manggoh/ *noun* (*pl* **mangoes** *or* **mangos**) **1** a yellowish red fruit with a firm skin, large stone, and juicy edible pulp. **2** the tropical evergreen tree that bears this fruit: *Mangifera indica.* [Portuguese *manga* from Tamil *mān-kāy*]

mangold /'manggohld, 'manggəld/ *noun* = MANGEL-WURZEL.

mangonel /'manggənel/ *noun* a military engine formerly used to throw rocks, stones, etc. [Middle English from early French *mangonel*, prob from medieval Latin *manganellus*, from Greek *manganon* charm, philtre, ballista, pulley block]

mangosteen /'manggohsteen/ *noun* **1** a dark reddish brown fruit with thick rind and edible flesh. **2** the E Indian tree that bears this fruit: *Garcinia mangostana.* [Malay *mangustan*]

mangrove /'manggrohv/ *noun* any of various tropical maritime trees or shrubs with roots that grow above ground and form dense masses: genera *Rhizophora, Avicennia* and other genera. [prob from Portuguese *mangue* mangrove + GROVE]

mangy *or* **mangey** /'maynji/ *adj* (**mangier, mangiest**) **1** suffering or resulting from mange. **2** having many worn or bare spots; shabby. ⏩ **manginess** *noun.*

manhandle /man'handl, 'man-/ *verb trans* **1** to move or manoeuvre (a large, heavy, or cumbersome object) by human force. **2** to handle (somebody or something) roughly.

manhattan /man'hatn/ *noun* (*also* **Manhattan**) a cocktail consisting of vermouth, whisky, and sometimes a dash of bitters. [named after *Manhattan*, a borough of New York City, USA]

manhole *noun* a covered opening in a floor, pavement, etc, giving access to an underground system, *esp* a sewer.

manhood *noun* **1** the condition of being an adult male as distinguished from a child or female. **2** *literary* (*treated as sing. or pl*) the adult males of a country, etc collectively: *calling again on her young manhood to defend her shores.* **3** manly qualities, such as physical strength and sexual prowess. **4** *euphem or humorous* a man's masculinity, as represented by his penis: *I thought I was about to be deprived of my manhood.*

man-hour *noun* a unit of one hour's work by one person, used *esp* as a basis for cost accounting and wage calculation.

manhunt *noun* an organized hunt for somebody, *esp* a criminal.

mania /'mayni-ə/ *noun* **1** abnormal excitement and euphoria marked by mental and physical hyperactivity and disorganization of behaviour. **2** an excessive or unreasonable enthusiasm or obsession. [Middle English via late Latin from Greek *mania* from *mainesthai* to be mad]

-mania *comb. form* forming nouns, denoting: **1** abnormal obsession or desire: *megalomania.* **2** excessive enthusiasm: *Beatlemania.*

maniac[1] /'mayniak/ *noun* **1** a person who behaves in a wild, violent, or uncontrolled way. **2** a person characterized by an inordinate or uncontrollable enthusiasm for something. **3** *archaic* an insane person; a lunatic. [late Latin *maniacus* maniacal, from Greek *maniakos* from *mania* mania]

maniac[2] *adj* = MANIACAL.

maniacal /mə'nie-əkl/ *adj* **1** affected with or suggestive of madness: *If great reasoners are often maniacal, it is equally true that maniacs are commonly great reasoners* — G K Chesterton. **2** characterized by ungovernable frenzy: *an expression of maniacal rage.* ⏩ **maniacally** *adv.*

manic[1] /'manik/ *adj* affected by, relating to, or resembling mania: *manic tendencies; bouts of manic activity.* ⏩ **manically** *adv.*

manic[2] *noun* a person suffering from mania.

manic-depressive[1] *adj* affected by or denoting a mental disorder characterized by alternating mania and extreme depression.

manic-depressive[2] *noun* a person suffering from a manic-depressive disorder.

Manichaean *or* **Manichean** /mani'kee-ən/ *noun* **1** a believer in a religious dualism originating in Persia in the third cent. AD and teaching the release of the spirit from matter through austere living. **2** a believer in religious or philosophical dualism, regarded as heretical, *esp* by the Roman Catholic Church. ⏩ **Manichaean** *adj*, **Manichaeanism** *noun*, **Manichaeism** /'manikeeiz(ə)m/ *noun.* [late Latin *manichaeus* from Greek *Manichaios* Manes d.c.276 AD, founder of the sect]

manicure[1] /'manikyooə/ *noun* a treatment for the care of the hands and fingernails. [French *manicure*, from Latin *manus* hand + French *-icure* (as in *pédicure* pedicure)]

manicure[2] *verb trans* **1** to give a manicure to (somebody). **2** to trim (e.g. a lawn) closely and evenly: *Even if it [the pampered town cat] does go outside, there is little to hunt on the manicured lawns* — Desmond Morris. ⏩ **manicurist** *noun.*

manifest[1] /'manifest/ *adj* readily perceived by the senses, e.g. sight or mind; obvious: *He concurred, with manifest relief.* ⏩ **manifestly** *adv.* [Middle English, ultimately from Latin *manifestus*, literally 'that is grasped by the hand']

manifest[2] *verb trans* to make (e.g. a quality) evident or certain by showing or displaying it: *He chose his companions for some individuality of character which they manifested* — Charles Lamb. ➤ *verb intrans* said of a spirit, ghost, etc: to appear in visible form.

manifest[3] *noun* a list of passengers or an invoice of cargo, *esp* for a ship.

manifestation /manife'staysh(ə)n/ *noun* **1** the process of manifesting or of being manifested, or an instance of this: *It was yet another manifestation of her eagerness to please.* **2** something that manifests; evidence; proof: *conclusive manifestation of his guilt.* **3** a sign, e.g. materialization, of the presence of a spirit.

manifesto /mani'festoh/ *noun* (*pl* **manifestos** *or* **manifestoes**) a public declaration of intentions, *esp* by a political party before an election. [Italian *manifesto* denunciation, indication, from *manifestare* to manifest, from Latin *manifestus* manifest]

manifold[1] /'manifohld/ *adj* many and varied: *Darwin was undiscouraged by the manifold difficulties of the fossil record* — Philip E Johnson. ⏩ **manifoldly** *adv*, **manifoldness** *noun.* [Old English *manigfeald*, from *manig* MANY[1] + *-feald* -FOLD]

manifold[2] *noun* a hollow fitting, e.g. connecting the cylinders of an internal combustion engine with the exhaust pipe, with several outlets or inlets for connecting one pipe with several other pipes.

manikin *or* **mannikin** /'manikin/ *noun* **1** a little man. **2** an anatomical model of the body for use in medical or art instruction. **3** = MANNEQUIN. [Dutch *mannekijn*, dimin. of *man* man]

Manila *or* **Manilla** /mə'nilə/ *noun* **1** a fibre obtained from the leaf-stalk of a banana plant. Also called ABACA. **2** a strong and durable paper of a brownish or buff colour with a smooth finish, made orig from this fibre. **3** a cigar made in the city of Manila. [named after *Manila*, the capital of the Philippine Islands]

Manila hemp *noun* = MANILA (1).

Manila paper *noun* = MANILA (2).

Manilla /mə'nilə/ *noun* see MANILA.

manilla *noun* a horseshoe-shaped metal bracelet used as money by some peoples of W Africa. [Portuguese *manilha* or Spanish *manilla*]

man in the street *noun* an average or typical person, *esp* for statistical purposes: *But the man in the street will say: how can it get worse? And: why should it get better?* — Independent.

manioc /'maniok/ *noun* = CASSAVA. [French *manioc* and Spanish and Portuguese *mandioca* from Tupi *manioca*]

maniple /'manipl/ *noun* **1** a subdivision of the ancient Roman legion consisting of either 120 or 60 men. **2** a long narrow strip of silk worn over the left arm by clerics of or above the order of sub-deacon. [Latin *manipulus* handful; (sense 1) from the custom of using a handful of hay on a pole as a military standard; (sense 2) from its having been orig held in the hand]

manipulate /mə'nipyoolayt/ *verb trans* **1** to handle or operate (something), *esp* skilfully: *Children have difficulty manipulating scissors.* **2a** to manage or use (something) skilfully: *manipulate the situation.* **b** to control or influence (somebody) by artful, unfair, or insidious means, *esp* to one's own advantage: *She saw her colleagues only in terms of how they could be manipulated.* **3** to examine and treat (a fracture, sprain, etc) by moving bones into the proper position manually. ➤➤ **manipulability** /-lə'biliti/ *noun*, **manipulable** *adj*, **manipulatable** *adj*, **manipulation** /-'laysh(ə)n/ *noun*, **manipulative** /-lətiv/ *adj*, **manipulator** *noun*, **manipulatory** /-lət(ə)ri/ *adj*. [back-formation from *manipulation*, via French from Latin *manipulus* handful]

Manitoban /mani'tohbən/ *noun* a native or inhabitant of the province of Manitoba in Canada. ➤➤ **Manitoban** *adj*.

manitou /'manitooh/ *noun* a supernatural force held by the Algonquians of N America to pervade the natural world. [of Algonquian origin]

mankind *noun* (*treated as sing. or pl*) **1** the human race: *Know then thyself, presume not God to scan; the proper study of mankind is man* — Pope. **2** men as distinguished from women.

Usage note

The same objection is often raised to the use of *mankind* to mean 'human beings as a race or species' as to the use of *man* in the same sense: it seems sexist. The expressions *humanity, humankind, human beings*, and *the human race* will generally fit neatly into any context where *mankind* might be employed and should be preferred. See also note at MAN[1].

manky /'manki/ *adj* (**mankier, mankiest**) *Brit, informal* nasty or dirty. [prob from English dialect *mank* mutilated, defective, via Old French from Latin *mancus* maimed]

manlike *adj* **1** resembling or characteristic of a man, e.g. as distinct from an animal. **2** resembling or characteristic of a man rather than a woman or child: *She had quickly understood the admiration which shone, manlike, in the eyes of the men* — Jack London.

manly *adj* (**manlier, manliest**) **1** having or showing the qualities traditionally thought to befit a man; *esp* in being courageous or strong. **2** marked by such qualities; appropriate or suitable for a man: *manly sports*. ➤➤ **manliness** *noun*.

man-made *adj* **1** made or produced by human beings rather than nature. **2** synthetic or artificial.

manna /'manə/ *noun* **1a** in the Bible, food miraculously supplied to the Israelites in their journey through the wilderness. **b** divinely supplied spiritual nourishment. **2** a usu sudden and unexpected source of benefit: *the Hill Inn, a renowned hostelry dispensing manna from heaven to weary Three Peaks walkers* — A Wainright. **3** a sweet substance exuded from plants that yields mannitol and acts as a mild laxative, *esp* obtained from the European flowering ash: *Fraxinus ornus*. [Old English via late Latin and Greek from Hebrew *mān*]

manned *adj* **1** equipped with people. **2** said of a spacecraft: carrying a human crew.

mannequin /'manikin/ *noun* **1a** an artist's, tailor's, or dressmaker's model of the human figure. **b** such a model used for displaying clothes in a shop. **2** a person who models clothing, *esp*, formerly, a woman. [French *mannequin* from Dutch *mannekijn*: see MANIKIN]

manner /'manə/ *noun* **1** the mode or method in which something is done or happens: *They worked in a brisk manner*. **2** a method of artistic execution or mode of presentation; a style. **3** *chiefly literary* a kind or sort: *Of that there is no manner of doubt* — W S Gilbert. **4** a characteristic or distinctive bearing, air, or deportment: *his poised gracious manner; a cool offhand manner*. **5** (*in pl*). **a** social conduct or rules of conduct as shown in the prevalent customs. **b** social behaviour evaluated as to politeness; *esp* conduct indicating good background: *a child with no manners*. ✳ **in a manner of speaking** in one sense; in a way. **to the manner born** accustomed from birth or as if from birth: *though I am native here and to the manner born* — Shakespeare. ➤➤ **mannerless** *adj*. [Middle English *manere* via Old French from Latin *manuaria*, fem of *manuarius* of the hand, from *manus* hand]

mannered *adj* **1** (*used in combinations*) having manners of the kind specified: *well-mannered*. **2** having an artificial or stilted character.

mannerism *noun* **1** a characteristic gesture or trait; an idiosyncrasy. **2a** exaggerated or affected adherence to a particular style in art or literature. **b** (**Mannerism**) a style of art in Italy and elsewhere in Europe between about 1520 and 1610, characterized by elongation of the human figure, CONTRAPPOSTO (exaggerated twisting), jewel-like colour, and eroticism, leading exponents being Bronzino, Pontormo, and Parmigianino. ➤➤ **mannerist** *noun and adj*, **manneristic** /-'ristik/ *adj*. [Italian *maniera* style]

mannerly *adj* showing or having good manners; polite. ➤➤ **mannerliness** *noun*.

mannikin /'manikin/ *noun* see MANIKIN.

mannish *adj* said of a woman, her appearance, or manner: resembling, befitting, or typical of a man rather than a woman: *She had square mannish shoulders*. ➤➤ **mannishly** *adv*, **mannishness** *noun*.

manoeuvre[1] (*NAmer* **maneuver**) /mə'n(y)oohvə/ *noun* **1** a movement requiring skill and dexterity: *breathtaking skateboarding manoeuvres*. **2** a strategic move adopted in a social or political situation: *A series of adroit manoeuvres on her part had resulted in rapid promotion*. **3** (*in pl*). **a** a military or naval movement. **b** a large-scale training exercise for the armed forces. [French *manœuvre* via Old French and late Latin from Latin *manu operare* to work by hand]

manoeuvre[2] (*NAmer* **maneuver**) *verb* (**manoeuvres, manoeuvred, manoeuvring**) ➤ *verb intrans* **1** to perform a manoeuvre. **2** to use stratagems. ➤ *verb trans* **1** to move or deploy (troops). **2** to shift (something) into the desired position: *manoeuvre a vehicle into a parking space*. **3** to edge (a person) into a certain position as part of a plan or scheme: *Before you realize it you'll find yourself manoeuvred into a corner and be unable to refuse*. ➤➤ **manoeuvrability** /mə,n(y)oohv(ə)rə'biliti/ *noun*, **manoeuvrable** *adj*, **manoeuvrer** *noun*.

man of God *noun* **1** a clergyman. **2** a godly man, e.g. a saint or prophet.

man of letters *noun* **1** a scholar. **2** a reputable author: *nineteenth-century men of letters*.

man of straw *noun* **1** a person of no moral stamina. **2** a financially unreliable person. **3** *dated* a sham argument or adversary, set up only to be easily countered.

man of the cloth *noun* a clergyman: *The number of times their new minister was seen slipping into Jake's and Nell's brewery ... worried some of his congregation. For a man of the cloth to spend so much time there suggested all manner of things* — New Scientist.

man of the house *noun* the chief male in a household.

man-of-war *or* **man-o'-war** *noun* (*pl* **men-of-war** *or* **men-o'-war**) **1** a warship of the days of sail; *broadly* a warship. **2** = FRIGATE BIRD. **3** = PORTUGUESE MAN-OF-WAR.

manometer /mə'nomitə/ *noun* an instrument, typically consisting of a U-shaped tube filled with liquid, e.g. mercury, used for measuring the pressure of gases and vapours. ➤➤ **manometric** /manoh'metrik/ *adj*. [French *manomètre*, from Greek *manos* sparse, thin, rare + French *-mètre* -METER[2]]

manor /'manə/ *noun* **1** a landed estate. **2** a former unit of English rural territorial organization; *esp* such a unit in the Middle Ages consisting of an estate under a lord who held a variety of rights over land and tenants including the right to hold court. **3** a house owned or formerly owned by the lord of a manor. **4** *Brit, informal* one's territory or home ground. **5** *Brit, informal* a district or area of police administration. ➤➤ **manorial** /mə'nawri-əl/ *adj*. [Middle English *maner* from Old French *manoir* to sojourn, dwell, from Latin *manēre* to remain]

man-o'-war /manə'waw/ *noun* (*pl* **men-o'-war**) see MAN-OF-WAR.

manpower *noun* the total supply of people available for work or service.

manqué /'mongkay (*French* mãke)/ *adj* (*used after a noun*) that could have been but failed to be what is specified: *His prose suggests that he is a poet manqué*. [French *manqué*, past part. of *manquer* to lack, fail]

mansard /'mansahd, 'mansəd/ *noun* a roof with a lower steeper slope and a higher shallower one on all four sides.

Word history

French *mansarde*, named after François *Mansart* d.1666, French architect. He rebuilt part of the château of Blois using this type of roof.

mansard roof *noun* = MANSARD.

manse /mans/ *noun* the residence of a Presbyterian or Baptist clergyman: *Some of the things she said reminded one that she was a daughter of the manse*. [Middle English *manss* mansion house, via late Latin from Latin *mansus*: see MANSION]

manservant *noun* (*pl* **menservants**) a male servant, *esp* a valet.

-manship *suffix* forming nouns, denoting: the art or skill of somebody who practises an activity: *horsemanship; gamesmanship*.

mansion /'mansh(ə)n/ *noun* **1a** the house of the lord of a manor. **b** a large imposing residence. **2** a separate apartment in a large structure. **3** (*in pl*) used in residence names: a large building divided into flats. [Middle English via French from Latin *mansion-, mansio*, from *mansus*, past part. of *manēre* to remain, dwell]

manslaughter *noun* the unlawful killing of somebody without malicious intent, e.g. by avoidable negligence or in the course of an unlawful act: compare MURDER[1].

manta /'mantə/ *noun* = MANTA RAY.

manta ray /'mantə/ *noun* an extremely large flat ray of warm seas: *Manta birostris*. [American Spanish *manta* from Spanish *manta* blanket; from its being caught in traps resembling large blankets]

manteau /'mantoh/ *noun* (*pl* **manteaus** /-tohz/) formerly, a woman's loose gown or cape; = MANTUA. [French *manteau* outer garment, from Latin *mantellum* cloak]

mantel *or* **mantle** /'mantl/ *noun* **1** a mantelpiece. **2** a mantelshelf.

mantelet /'mantlit/ *noun* see MANTLET.

mantelpiece *or* **mantlepiece** *noun* **1** an ornamental structure round a fireplace. **2** a mantelshelf. [early French *mantel* mantle]

mantelshelf *or* **mantleshelf** *noun* a shelf forming part of or above a mantelpiece.

mantes /'manteez/ *noun* pl of MANTIS.

mantic /'mantik/ *adj* relating to divination; prophetic. [Greek *mantikos* from *mantis* prophet]

manticore /'mantikaw/ *noun archaic or literary* a mythical beast having a lion's body and a man's face, along variously with porcupine's quills or a scorpion's tail. [Middle English, via Old French and Latin from Greek *martichoras* (misread as *mantichoras*) man-eater, tiger, of Persian origin]

mantilla /man'tilə/ *noun* a light scarf worn over the head and shoulders, *esp* by Spanish and Latin-American women. [Spanish *mantilla*, dimin. of *manta* mantle]

mantis /'mantis/ *noun* (*pl* **mantises** *or* **mantes** /'manteez/) any of a genus of insects that feed on other insects and clasp their prey in forelimbs that are held as if in prayer: genus *Mantis*: compare PRAYING MANTIS. [via Latin from Greek *mantis*, literally 'diviner, prophet']

mantissa /man'tisə/ *noun* in mathematics, the part of a common logarithm following the decimal point. [Latin *mantisa, mantissa* makeweight]

mantle[1] /'mantl/ *noun* **1** a loose sleeveless garment worn over other clothes; a cloak. **2** something that covers, envelops, or conceals. **3** a role or persona that one adopts or takes over from somebody else: *William Hague has assumed the unlikely mantle of Dirty Harry.* **4a** a fold or lobe in the body wall of snails, mussels, etc that lines the shell and contains shell-secreting glands. **b** the soft external body wall that lines the hard outer covering of barnacles, sea squirts, and related animals. **5** the feathers covering the back and wings of a bird, *esp* when different in colour from the rest of the plumage. **6** a lacy hood or sheath treated with a solution of the chemical elements cerium and thorium that when placed over the flame of a gas or oil lamp increases the amount of light given off. **7** the part of the earth that lies between the crust and the central core. [Middle English *mantel* via Old French from Latin *mantellum* cloak]

mantle[2] *verb trans* to cover (something) with or as if with a mantle. ➤ *verb intrans* to blush: *her rich face mantling with emotion* — Disraeli.

mantle[3] *noun* see MANTEL.

mantlepiece *noun* see MANTELPIECE.

mantleshelf *noun* see MANTELSHELF.

mantlet *or* **mantelet** /'mantlit/ *noun* **1** a very short cape or cloak formerly worn by women. **2** the movable frontal plate of the turret of an armoured fighting vehicle. **3** a movable shelter formerly used by besiegers when attacking. [Middle English from early French *mantelet*, dimin. of *mantel, manteau* mantle]

man-to-man *adj* **1** characterized by frankness and honesty. **2** denoting a defensive system in football, basketball, etc in which each player marks one specific opponent.

mantra /'mantrə/ *noun* **1** orig in Hinduism or Buddhism, a word or sound used to focus the mind and help concentration, e.g. as a preliminary to meditation. **2** a VEDIC[1] hymn. [Sanskrit *mantra* sacred counsel, formula, from *manyate* he thinks]

mantrap *noun* a trap for catching trespassers or poachers.

mantua /'mantyooə/ *noun* a usu loosely fitting gown worn in the 17th and 18th cents. [alteration of French *manteau, mantel* cloak, influenced by *Mantua*, a town in N Italy]

manual[1] /'manyooəl/ *adj* **1** relating to or involving the hands: *manual dexterity.* **2** requiring or using physical skill and energy: *manual labour.* **3** worked or done by hand as distinct from by machine or automatically: *a manual gear change.* ➤➤ **manually** *adv.* [Middle English *manuel* via French from Latin *manualis* from *manus* hand]

manual[2] *noun* **1** a book of instructions; a handbook. **2** a keyboard for the hands; *specif* any of the several keyboards of an organ that control separate divisions of the instrument. **3** a vehicle that has manual transmission. **4** the set movements in the handling of a weapon during a military drill or ceremony.

manubrium /mə'nyoohbri-əm/ *noun* (*pl* **manubria** /-bri-ə/ *or* **manubriums**) the uppermost segment of the sternum in human beings and many other mammals, articulating with the collarbone. [Latin *manubrium* handle, from *manus* hand]

manufactory /manyoo'fakt(ə)ri/ *noun* (*pl* **manufactories**) *archaic* a factory.

manufacture[1] /manyoo'fakchə/ *noun* **1** the large-scale making of wares by hand or by machinery. **2** an industry using mechanical power and machinery. **3** the act or process of producing something. [early French *manufacture* from Latin *manu factus* made by hand]

manufacture[2] *verb trans* **1** to make (materials) into a product suitable for use. **2** to make (wares) from raw materials by hand or by machinery, *esp* on a large scale. **3** to invent or fabricate (something): *manufacture a plausible excuse.* **4** to produce (something) as if by manufacturing: *writers who manufacture stories for television.* ➤➤ **manufacturing** *noun.*

manufacturer *noun* an employer in a manufacturing industry.

manuka /'mahnookə/ *noun* an evergreen New Zealand shrub that forms large areas of scrub: *Leptospermum scoparium.* [Maori *manuka*]

manumit /manyoo'mit/ *verb trans* (**manumitted, manumitting**) to give (slaves) their freedom. ➤➤ **manumission** /-'mish(ə)n/ *noun.* [Middle English *manumitten* via French from Latin *manumittere*, literally 'to send forth from the hand' from *manus* hand + *mittere* to let go, send]

manure[1] /mə'nyooə/ *noun* material that fertilizes land; *esp* the faeces of domestic animals.

manure[2] *verb trans* to enrich (land) by the application of manure.

Word history
Middle English *manouren* to till, cultivate, via French from Latin *manu operare* to work by hand. The original sense of working by hand (see also MANOEUVRE[1]) came in time to be narrowed to the act of cultivating and then to the dressing that was added to the soil.

manus /'maynəs/ *noun* (*pl* **manus**) the farthest section of the forelimb of a vertebrate animal, consisting of the wrist and hand in a human being or the equivalent part in other vertebrates. [Latin *manus* hand]

manuscript /'manyooskript/ *noun* a composition or document written by hand or typed as distinguished from a printed copy. [late Latin *manuscriptum* from neuter of Latin *manu scriptus* written by hand]

Manx /mangks/ *noun* the Celtic language of the people of the Isle of Man, closely related to Irish and Gaelic but having an anglicized spelling, now spoken only by students of the language. ➤➤ **Manx** *adj.* [alteration of earlier *Maniske* from Old Norse *Mana* Isle of Man]

Manx cat *noun* a breed of short-haired domestic cats associated with the Isle of Man, that have no tail, or a mere stump.

Manxman *noun* (*pl* **Manxmen**) a male native or inhabitant of the Isle of Man.

Manx shearwater /'shiəwawtə/ *noun* a small black-and-white N Atlantic shearwater: *Puffinus puffinus.*

Manxwoman *noun* (*pl* **Manxwomen**) a female native or inhabitant of the Isle of Man.

many[1] /'meni/ *adj* (**more, most**) (*also used in combinations*) amounting to a large but unspecified number: *I have spent many years in teaching; many-coloured hand-woven fabrics.* ✳ **a good/ great many** numerous: *She's said to have had a great many offers in her time.* **as many** the same in number: *see three plays in as many days.* **many a** more than one: *Many a good candidate has failed that test.* **many's the** on more than one (occasion, etc): *Many's the time I've vowed never to have him back.* [Old English *manig*]

many[2] *pronoun* (*treated as pl*) a large number of people or things: *Many prefer to stay at home; Many of them are homeless; I haven't got as many as you.*

many[3] *noun* (**the many**) *literary* the great majority: *rank, material possessions, and other things esteemed by the many.*

many-sided *adj* having many sides or aspects: *her many-sided personality.* >> **many-sidedness** *noun.*

manzanilla /manzə'nilə/ *noun* a pale very dry sherry. [Spanish *manzanilla*, literally 'camomile' (which the sherry's flavour is said to resemble), dimin. of *manzana* apple]

Maoism /'mowiz(ə)m/ *noun* Marxism-Leninism as developed in China chiefly by Mao Zedong. >> **Maoist** *noun and adj.* [named after *Mao Zedong* d.1976, Chinese political leader]

Maori /'mowri/ *noun* (*pl* **Maoris** *or collectively* **Maori**) **1** a member of the Polynesian aboriginal people of New Zealand. **2** the Austronesian language of the Maori people.

Word history

the Maori name. Maori words that have passed into worldwide English all refer to the flora and fauna of New Zealand: *kiwi, kowhai, mako, moa, rata*, and so on. A few Maori words of more general reference have entered the English spoken within New Zealand, such as *puku, tapu, utu*, and *whare*.

map[1] /map/ *noun* **1a** a representation on a reduced scale and usu a flat surface of part of the earth's surface, showing geographical features, political divisions, population distribution, etc. **b** a similar representation of the surface of another planet, the moon, etc. **2** a representation of something in a maplike form. **3** a theoretical arrangement of genes along a chromosome; a genetic map. * **put something on the map** to make something well known. **wipe something off the map** to consign something to oblivion. [Latin *mappa* napkin, towel]

map[2] *verb trans* (**mapped, mapping**) **1a** to make a map of (something). **b** to delineate (something) as if on a map. **c** to survey (an area) in order to make a map. **2** in mathematics, to assign to every element of (a set) an element of the same or another set. **3** (*often* + *out*) to plan in detail: *We mapped out a programme.* >> **mappable** *adj*, **mapper** *noun*, **mapping** *noun.*

maple /'maypl/ *noun* **1** any of several species of trees of the sycamore family that have broad leaves with three to seven pointed lobes and clusters of paired broad flat winged seeds: genus *Acer*. **2** the hard light-coloured close-grained wood of this tree, which is used for flooring and furniture. [Old English *mapul-*]

maple sugar *noun NAmer* sugar made by boiling maple syrup.

maple syrup *noun* syrup made by concentrating the sap of sugar maple trees.

map reference *noun* a pair of coordinates for finding a point on a map, such as its longitude and latitude, or a letter and number leading vertically and horizontally to a square of reference.

maquette /ma'ket/ *noun* a small preliminary model of a sculpture, e.g. in wax or clay. [French *maquette* from Italian *macchietta*, dimin. of *macchia* sketch]

maquillage /maki'yahzh (*French* makijaʒ)/ *noun* cosmetics; makeup. [French *maquillage* from *maquiller* to make up]

maquis /ma'kee/ *noun* (*pl* **maquis** /ma'kee/) **1** scrubland vegetation of Mediterranean coastal areas, consisting mainly of broadleaved evergreen shrubs, e.g. laurels and myrtles, or small trees, e.g. olives and figs. **2** (**Maquis**). **a** (**the Maquis**) the French Resistance movement during World War II. **b** a member of this movement. [French *maquis* from Italian *macchie*, pl of *macchia* thicket, spot]

Mar. *abbr* March.

mar /mah/ *verb trans* (**marred, marring**) to detract from the perfection or wholeness of (something); to spoil (it): *Striving to better, oft we mar what's well* — Shakespeare. [Old English *mierran* to obstruct, waste]

marabou /'marabooh/ *noun* **1** a large grey and white African stork that has an inflatable pouch of pink skin at its throat and feeds on carrion: *Leptoptilos crumeniferus*. **2** a soft fluffy material prepared from marabou or turkey feathers and used for trimming hats or clothes. [French *marabout* marabout]

marabout /'marabooh/ *noun* **1** a Muslim holy man of N Africa. **2** a shrine marking the grave of such a Muslim holy man. [French *marabout* via Portuguese from Arabic *murābiṭ* hermit, monk]

maraca /mə'rakə/ *noun* a dried gourd or a rattle like a gourd that is used as a rhythm instrument, usu one of a pair. [Portuguese *maracá* from Tupi *maráka*]

marae /mah'rie/ *noun* **1** the courtyard of a Maori meeting house as the central meeting ground of a village. **2** formerly, in Polynesia, a sacred enclosure or open-air place of worship. [of Polynesian origin]

maranta /mə'rantə/ *noun* any of a genus of ornamental tropical plants that are cultivated for their variegated leaves: genus *Maranta*. [from the Latin genus name, named after Bartolommeo *Maranta*, 16th-cent. Italian herbalist]

maraschino /marə'sheenoh, -'skeenoh/ *noun* (*pl* **maraschinos**) **1** a sweet liqueur distilled from the fermented juice of a bitter wild cherry. **2** a usu large cherry preserved in true or imitation maraschino. [Italian *maraschino* from *marasca* bitter wild cherry]

maraschino cherry *noun* = MARASCHINO (2).

marasmus /mə'razməs/ *noun* severe malnutrition, *esp* in the very young, sometimes due to malabsorption of nutrients, resulting in emaciation and growth retardation. >> **marasmic** *adj.* [late Latin *marasmus* from Greek *marasmos* from *marainein* to waste away]

Maratha *or* **Mahratta** /mə'rahtə/ *noun* (*pl* **Marathas** *or collectively* **Maratha**) **1** a member of the Marathi-speaking people of the state of Maharashtra in W central India. **2** a member of the princely warrior caste of the former Hindu kingdom of this region. [Marathi *Marāṭhā* and Hindi *Marhaṭṭā* from Sanskrit *Mahārāṣṭra* great kingdom]

Marathi *or* **Mahratti** /mə'rahti/ *noun* the chief Indic language of the state of Maharashtra in W central India. [Marathi *marāṭhī*]

marathon /'marəth(ə)n/ *noun* **1** a long-distance race; *specif* a foot race of 42.2km (about 26mi 385yd) that is contested on an open course in major athletics championships. **2** (*also used before a noun*) an event or activity characterized by great length or concentrated effort: *With a marathon effort the book was completed on time; a 24-hour pot-throwing marathon.*

Word history

named after *Marathon* in Greece, site of a victory of Greeks over invading Persians in 490 BC, the news of which was carried to Athens by a long-distance runner. In the original account by the Greek historian Herodotus, the messenger Pheidippides ran from Athens to Sparta before the battle to ask for help.

maraud /mə'rawd/ *verb intrans* to roam about in search of plunder. > *verb trans* to raid or pillage (a place). >> **marauder** *noun.* [French *marauder* from *maraud* rogue, vagabond]

marble[1] /'mahbl/ *noun* **1** crystalline limestone in which the original crystals have dissolved slowly, usu under the influence of heat and pressure, and recrystallized to form a hard rock that can be polished to a very smooth finish. **2** a little ball made of a hard substance, e.g. glass, and used in various children's games. **3** (*in pl, but treated as sing.*) any of several games played with marbles, the object of which is to hit a mark or hole, to hit another player's marble, or to knock as many marbles as possible out of a ring. **4** *informal* (*in pl*) elements of common sense, *esp* sanity: *persons who are born without all their marbles* — Arthur Miller. >> **marbly** *adj.* [Middle English via Old French and Latin from Greek *marmaros* shining stone]

marble[2] *verb trans* to give a veined or mottled appearance to (e.g. the edges of a book).

marbled *adj* **1a** made of or veneered with marble. **b** characterized by an extensive use of marble as an architectural or decorative feature: *ancient marbled cities.* **2** said of meat: marked by a mixture of fat and lean. **3** denoting a type of sponge cake in which a layer of e.g. chocolate mixture has been folded into plain mixture, giving a variegated effect.

marbling *noun* coloration or markings resembling or suggestive of marble.

Marburg disease /'mah'buhg/ *noun* a severe viral infection, transmitted to humans from African green monkeys, which causes high fever and sometimes death. [named after *Marburg*, a city in Germany, where the first human outbreak occurred]

marc /mahk/ *noun* **1** the organic residue remaining after an extraction process, e.g. the pressing of grapes. **2** brandy made from the residue of grapes after pressing. [French *marc* from early French *marchier* to trample]

marcasite /'mahkə'seet, 'mahkəsiet/ *noun* **1** a white or pale yellow form of the mineral iron pyrites, used in jewellery. **2** polished steel or a similar white metal used for making jewellery. [Middle English *marchasite* via late Latin from Arabic *marqashīthā*]

marcato /mah'kahtoh/ *adj and adv* said of a piece of music: to be performed with emphasis. [Italian *marcato* marked, accented]

March /mahch/ *noun* the third month of the year. [Middle English via Old French from Latin *Martius* of Mars, the Roman god of war]

march[1] /mahch/ *verb intrans* **1** to move along steadily, usu in step with others. **2a** to move in a direct purposeful manner. **b** to make steady progress: *Time marches on.* **3** to participate in an organized march. ➤ *verb trans* to cause (e.g. an army) to march: *They marched him off to the police station.* [Old French *marchier* to trample, march]

march[2] *noun* **1a** the action of marching. **b** a regular measured stride or rhythmic step used in marching. **c** steady forward movement: *the march of progress.* **2** a musical composition, usu in duple or quadruple time, that has a strongly accentuated beat and is designed or suitable to accompany marching. **3** a procession of people organized as a demonstration of support or protest. ✳ **on the march 1** marching: *an army on the march.* **2** moving steadily; advancing: *Tottenham's fine victory … was full of reassuring evidence that the Terry Venables vision is on the march again* — Today.

march[3] *noun* (*often* **the Marches**) (*usu in pl*) a border region; *esp* a tract of land between two countries whose ownership is disputed: *the Welsh marches.* [Middle English *marche* from Old French *marche*, of Germanic origin]

march[4] *verb intrans* (+ with) to have common borders or frontiers with another territory: *a region that marches with Canada in the north.*

marcher[1] *noun* a person who marches, *esp* for a specified cause: *a peace marcher.*

marcher[2] *noun* a person who inhabits a border region.

March hare *noun* a brown hare in its breeding season, noted for eccentric behaviour such as boxing, leaping, and running round in circles: *The March Hare will be much the most interesting, and perhaps, as this is May, it won't be raving mad – at least not as mad as it was in March* — Lewis Carroll.

marching orders *pl noun* **1** official notice for troops to move. **2** notice of dismissal: *Any more fouls like that and you'll be given your marching orders.*

marchioness /mahshə'nes, 'mahshənis/ *noun* **1** the wife or widow of a marquess. **2** a woman having in her own right the rank of a marquess. [medieval Latin *marchionissa* from *marchion-*, *marchio* marquess, from *marca* border region]

marchpane /'mahchpayn/ *noun archaic* marzipan: *Good thou, save me a piece of marchpane* — Shakespeare. [Italian *marzapane* marzipan]

Mardi Gras /,mahdi 'grah/ *noun* a carnival period culminating on Shrove Tuesday often observed, e.g. in New Orleans, with parades and festivities. [French *Mardi Gras*, literally 'fat Tuesday'; from its being the last day of feasting before the fasting of Lent]

mardy /'mahdi/ *adj* (**mardier**, **mardiest**) *Brit, dialect* sulky: *a mardy child.* [dialect *mard* spoilt (of a child), alteration of *marred*, past part. of MAR]

mare[1] /meə/ *noun* the female of a horse or other equine animal, *esp* when fully mature or of breeding age. [Old English *mere*]

mare[2] /'mahray/ *noun* (*pl* **maria** /'mahri·ə/) a large dark area on the surface of the moon or Mars. [Latin *mare* sea]

mare's nest /meəz/ *noun* a false discovery, illusion, or deliberate hoax. [earlier *discover a mare's nest*, that is, make an unprecedented or astonishing find]

mare's tail /meəz/ *noun* **1** a common aquatic plant with long shoots covered with narrow leaves: *Hippuris vulgaris.* **2** a long streak of cirrus cloud.

margarine /mahjə'reen, 'mahj-/ *noun* a substitute for butter made usu from vegetable oils churned with ripened skimmed milk to a smooth emulsion.

Word history
French *margarine* from Greek *margaron* pearl, from the lustre of the organic compounds first used to make it. Originally applied to a fatty substance found in animal fats, *margarine* became established as a name for a butter substitute in the 1870s.

margarita /mahgə'reetə/ *noun* a cocktail consisting chiefly of tequila and lemon or lime juice, traditionally served in a salt-rimmed glass. [Mexican Spanish *margarita*, prob from the forename *Margarita*]

margay /'mahgay/ *noun* a small American spotted cat resembling the ocelot: *Felis wiedi.* [French *margay* from Tupi *maracaja*]

marge[1] /mahj/ *noun Brit, informal* margarine.

marge[2] *noun literary* a margin or rim: *by the flowrie marge of a fresh stream* — Spenser. [early French *marge* from Latin *margo*]

margin[1] /'mahjin/ *noun* **1a** the part of a page or sheet outside the main body of printed or written matter. **b** a vertical line, usu on the left-hand side of a page, e.g. of an exercise book, marking a margin. **2a** the outside limit of an area, etc; the edge. **b** a part adjoining an edge; a rim or border. **c** (*usu in pl*) the periphery of a community, movement, organization, etc, where those not wholly committed or not wholly accepted find themselves: *Those on the margins of a culture know more about its centre than the centre can ever know about the margins* — Screen. **3a** a spare amount or measure or degree allowed: *She left no margin for error in her calculations.* **b** a bare minimum below which or an extreme limit beyond which something becomes impossible or is no longer desirable: *a joke that was on the margin of good taste.* **4** the difference between one amount and another: *The bill was passed by a one-vote margin.* **5a** in business, the limit below which the level of return is insufficient to warrant continued economic activity. **b** the difference between net sales and the cost of merchandise sold, from which expenses are met or profit derived. **6** cash or collateral that is deposited by a client with a broker, e.g. a stockbroker, to protect the broker from loss on a contract. **7** *Aus* a supplement to a basic wage, given to an employee who has extra skills. ➤➤ **margined** *adj.* [Middle English from Latin *margin-*, *margo* border]

margin[2] *verb trans* **1** to provide (something) with a border. **2** to place (something) with a broker as a deposit.

marginal[1] *adj* **1** written or printed in the margin. **2** relating to or situated at a margin or border. **3** close to the lower limit of qualification, acceptability, or function. **4** relating to or providing a nominal profit margin. **5** denoting a constituency where the Member of Parliament was elected with only a small majority. **6** representing a slight difference: *a marginal improvement.* ➤➤ **marginality** /-'naliti/ *noun*, **marginally** *adv.* [late Latin *marginalis* from Latin *margin-*, *margo* edge]

marginal[2] *noun* **1** a marginal constituency. **2** an aquatic plant that grows in shallow water close to the land.

marginalia /mahji'nayli·ə/ *pl noun* marginal notes, e.g. in a book. [medieval Latin *marginalia*, neuter pl of *marginalis*: see MARGINAL[1]]

marginalize *or* **marginalise** *verb trans* to treat (a person or thing) as peripheral or unimportant, or banish them from the focal area of concern: *His wing of the party was in effect marginalized and reduced to splenetic outrage on the fringes of the conference* — The Observer. ➤➤ **marginalization** /-'zaysh(ə)n/ *noun.*

marginate /'mahjinayt/ *adj* having a margin that is distinct in colour, shape, etc: *marginate leaves.* ➤➤ **margination** /-'naysh(ə)n/ *noun.*

margravate /'mahgrəvət/ *noun* the territory of a margrave.

margrave /'mahgrayv/ *noun* **1** the hereditary title of some princes of the Holy Roman Empire. **2** a member of the German nobility corresponding in rank to a British marquess. [Dutch *markgraaf* from early Dutch *marcgrave* count of a border territory]

margravine /'mahgrəveen/ *noun* the wife of a margrave.

marguerite /mahgə'reet/ *noun* = OXEYE DAISY. [early French *margarite* pearl, daisy, via Latin from Greek *margaritēs* from *margaron* pearl]

Mari /'mahri/ *noun* (*pl* **Maris** *or collectively* **Mari**) **1** a member of a people living in the Volga valley in Russia. **2** the Uralic language of this people. ➤➤ **Mari** *adj.*

maria /'mahri·ə/ *noun* pl of MARE[2].

mariachi /mari'ahchi/ *noun* (*pl* **mariachis**) **1** a group of Mexican street musicians. **2** a member of such a group. **3** the folk music traditionally played by such a group. [Mexican Spanish *mariachi*]

marigold /'marigohld/ *noun* any of several species of composite plants of the daisy family with showy yellow or red flower heads: genera *Tagetes* and *Calendula.* [Middle English, from *Mary*, mother of Jesus + Middle English *gold* marigold, corn marigold]

marijuana *or* **marihuana** /mari'(h)wahnə/ *noun* a usu mild form of cannabis that is smoked for its intoxicating effect. [Mexican Spanish *mariguana, marihuana*]

marimba /mə'rimbə/ *noun* a percussion instrument of Southern Africa and Central America which resembles a large xylophone, has a dried gourd shell or similar object beneath each bar to give resonance, and is played with soft-headed hammers. [of African origin]

marina /mə'reenə/ *noun* a dock or basin providing secure moorings for motorboats, yachts, etc. [Italian and Spanish *marina* seashore, fem of *marino* (adj) marine, from Latin *marinus*: see MARINE¹]

marinade¹ /mari'nayd/ *noun* **1** a blend of oil, wine or vinegar, herbs, and spices in which meat, fish, etc is soaked to enrich its flavour or make it tender. **2** the food so treated, or a dish of such food. [French *marinade* from Spanish *marinada* from *marinar* to pickle in brine, from *marino* marine]

marinade² *verb trans* to soak (e.g. meat) in a marinade.

marinara /mari'nahrə/ *adj* (*used after a noun*) said of food: cooked with a spicy tomato sauce containing onions and garlic: *spaghetti marinara*. [Italian (*alla*) *marinara* in the style of a sailor]

marinate /'marinayt/ *verb trans* to marinade (food). [prob from Italian *marinato*, past part. of *marinare* to marinade, from *marino* marine]

marine¹ /mə'reen/ *adj* **1** relating to or belonging to the sea: *marine life; marine biology*. **2** relating to the navigation or commerce of the sea: *marine law*. [Middle English from Latin *marinus* of the sea, from *mare* sea]

marine² *noun* **1** any of a class of soldiers serving on shipboard or in close association with a naval force. **2** seagoing ships of a specified nationality or class: *the mercantile marine*. **3** a seascape.

mariner /'marinə/ *noun formal or literary* a seaman or sailor. [Middle English via Old French from late Latin *marinarius* from Latin *marinus*: see MARINE¹]

Mariolatry /meəri'olətri/ *noun* excessive veneration of the Virgin Mary. [Latin *Maria* Mary + -*latry* as in IDOLATRY]

marionette /,mari-ə'net/ *noun* a small-scale usu wooden figure with jointed limbs that is moved from above by attached strings or wires. [French *marionnette* from early French *maryonete* from *Marion*, dimin. of *Marie* Mary]

marital /'maritl/ *adj* **1** relating to marriage or to the relationship between husband and wife: *marital tensions*. **2** relating to a husband: *assert one's marital rights*. >> **maritally** *adv*. [Latin *maritalis* from *maritus* husband]

maritime /'maritiem/ *adj* **1** relating to navigation or commerce on the sea: *a maritime museum*. **2** associated with or found near the sea: *maritime vegetation*. **3** said of a climate: having small variations in seasonal temperatures because of the influence of the sea. [Latin *maritimus* from *mare* sea]

marjoram /'mahjəram, -rəm/ *noun* **1** a usu fragrant and aromatic plant of the mint family with small pale purple or pink flowers, and leaves that are used as a herb: *Origanum marjorana*. **2** = OREGANO. [alteration of Middle English *majorane* via French from late Latin *majorana*]

mark¹ /mahk/ *noun* **1** an impression on the surface of something; *esp* a scratch, stain, etc that spoils the appearance of a surface. **2** something, e.g. a line, notch, or fixed object, designed to record position. **3a** a symbol used for identification or indication of ownership. **b** a distinguishing characteristic. **c** a symbol, *esp* a cross, made in place of a signature by a person who cannot write. **d** a written or printed symbol: *punctuation marks*. **4** a sign or token: *The directors presented him with a gold watch as a mark of their esteem*. **5** a figure that registers a point or level reached or achieved: *the halfway mark in the first period of play*. **6** a symbol used as a judgment of merit, *esp* one used by a teacher to express an estimate of a student's work or conduct. **7** an assessment of merits; a rating: *get high marks for honesty if nothing else*. **8** a trademark. **9** (**Mark**) used with a number to specify a particular model of a vehicle, weapon, machine, etc. **10** a goal or target, e.g. the jack in a game of bowls. **11** the starting line or position in a track event. **12a** in rugby, the action of a player making a mark in the ground with the heel and shouting 'Mark' after catching a ball that has been kicked, knocked, or thrown forward by a member of the opposing team, after which a free kick is awarded. **b** the mark so made. **c** in Australian Rules football, a catch of a ball that has been kicked at least ten yards by an opponent, after which a free kick is awarded. **13** any of the points on a sounding line for measuring depths that corresponds to a depth in whole fathoms and is distinctively marked, e.g. by a piece of leather or coloured cloth. ✱ **a soft/easy mark** a potential dupe or victim: *Tourists are seen as a soft mark*. **be quick/slow off the mark** to react or respond smartly or sluggishly. **close to/near the mark** not far off the truth. **leave its mark** to leave a trace or trauma: *The financial strains have left their mark*. **make one's mark** to make one's name or leave behind a record of one's achievement: *young actors all eager to make their mark*. **off/wide of the mark** not

accurate, apt, or appropriate: *a judgment that was obviously wide of the mark*. **of mark** *literary* of distinction: *writers of mark*. **on your marks** used as a command to competitors in a race to take their starting positions. **somebody's mark** somebody's level of taste or appreciation. **up to the mark** (*usu with a negative*) reaching the desired standard: *Rhadames wasn't quite up to the mark in this production*. [Old English *mearc* boundary, frontier, sign]

mark² *verb trans* **1** to make or leave a mark on (something). **2a** to evaluate or give a mark to (a piece of written work). **b** to add appropriate symbols, characters, or other marks to (e.g. a text). **c** to indicate (something) by a mark or symbol. **3** to register or record (something): *Mark the date in your diary*. **4** to put something inside a book so as to identify (a page). **5a** to characterize or distinguish (something): *the flamboyance that marks her stage appearance*. **b** to be a sign of (something): *This treaty will mark the friendship between our countries*. **c** to be the occasion of (something notable): *This year marks the 50th anniversary of the organization*. **6** (*usu* + off) to set (something) apart by or as if by a line or boundary. **7a** to label (merchandise) so as to indicate price or quality. **b** to designate (something or somebody) with or as if with a mark: *She had been marked for greatness from an early age*. **8** to observe or take notice of (something): *You mark my words!* **9a** in a team sport, to stay close to (an opponent), *esp* to prevent the opponent from getting or passing the ball. **b** in rugby or Australian Rules football, to make a mark on catching (the ball). >> *verb intrans* to become or make something stained, scratched, etc. ✱ **mark time 1** to keep the time of a marching step by moving the feet alternately without advancing. **2** to pass the time unproductively while waiting for an opportunity to progress or advance. **mark you** used to draw attention to a point: *He meets his death five miles from the school, not by a bullet, mark you ... but by a savage blow* — Conan Doyle. [Old English *mearcian*]

mark³ *noun* (*often* **Mark**) the former basic monetary unit of Germany, divided into 100 pfennigs (replaced by the euro in 2002). [Old English *marc*, prob of Scandinavian origin]

markdown *noun* **1** a reduction in price. **2** the amount of this.

mark down *verb trans* **1** to put a lower price on (an item for sale). **2** to reduce the number of marks awarded to (a candidate). **3** (+ as) to characterize somebody in a certain way, *esp* unfavourably: *He evidently had me marked down as an ignoramus*.

marked *adj* **1a** having natural marks: *wings marked with white*. **b** made identifiable by marking: *a marked card*. **2** having a distinctive or emphasized character: *a marked American accent*. **3** being an object of attack, suspicion, or vengeance: *a marked man*. **4a** said of a word or form: distinguished from a basic form, e.g. the singular, by the presence of a particular linguistic feature, e.g. *s* indicating the plural form. **b** said of a sense of a word: giving a judgment as to quality, size, etc as in *a large house*, as distinct from a use such as *a house not quite as large as its neighbours*. >> **markedly** /'mahkidli/ *adv*.

marker *noun* **1** something used to mark a position, place, direction, etc. **2** a felt-tip pen with a broad tip, *esp* in a fluorescent colour. **3** a person who marks something. **4** in a team game, a player who marks an opponent.

market¹ /'mahkit/ *noun* **1a** a meeting together of people for the purpose of trade, by private purchase and sale. **b** an open space, building, etc where provisions, livestock, etc are sold. **2a** a geographical area offering opportunities for the sale of products: *the foreign market*. **b** a section of the community where there is a taste or demand for certain wares: *Thank heaven ... for a good man's love; for I must tell you friendly in your ear: sell when you can; you are not for all markets* — Shakespeare. **c** an opportunity for selling: *trying to create new markets for their product*. **d** commercial activity; extent of trading: *a flagging market*. **e** the area of economic activity in which the forces of supply and demand affect prices: *market value*.

Editorial note ――――――――――――

The term market is typically used as an abstract description of any decentralized environment in which transactions can occur, especially in which outcomes tend to be determined by a multiplicity of traders. It can refer to legal markets, illegal (black) markets, and non-monetary markets (such as that of individuals searching for husbands or wives). Although 'market forces' are usually associated with low levels of outside formal regulation, it is increasingly recognized that any market exists within a set of rules and norms — Evan Davis.

――――――――――――――――――――――

✱ **be in the market for** to be interested in buying (something): *We are in the market for a house*. **on the market** available for purchase. [Middle English via French from Latin *mercatus* trade, marketplace, from past part. of *mercari* to trade, from *merc-, merx* merchandise]

market² *verb* (**marketed, marketing**) ➤ *verb trans* to sell (something) or offer it for sale. ➤ *verb intrans dated* to deal in a market. ➤➤ **marketability** /-'biliti/ *noun*, **marketable** *adj*.

marketeer /mahki'tia/ *noun* **1** a person who trades in a market. **2** a person who supports a particular type of market: *a free marketeer*.

market forces *pl noun* the mechanism of supply and demand operating within a system of free enterprise.

market garden *noun* a plot in which vegetables are grown for market. ➤➤ **market gardening** *noun*, **market gardener** *noun*.

marketing *noun* the skills and functions, including packaging, promotion, and distribution, involved in selling goods.

market-maker *noun* a wholesale dealer in securities who is prepared to buy and sell specified securities at all times.

marketplace *noun* **1** an open place in a town where markets are held. **2** an opportunity for selling: *The marketplace is the interpreter of supply and demand*.

market research *noun* research, e.g. the collection and analysis of information about consumer preferences, dealing with the patterns or state of demand for a particular product in a market. ➤➤ **market researcher** *noun*.

market-test *verb trans* to put (some operation of a public-sector concern) out to tender, *esp* with a view ultimately to total privatization.

market value *noun* the value of an asset if sold in a free market; a price at which both buyers and sellers are willing to do business: compare BOOK VALUE.

markhor /'mahkaw/ *noun* a large Himalayan wild goat with long spiralled horns and a coat that is reddish brown in summer and grey and silky in winter: *Capra falconeri*. [Persian *mārkhōr*, literally 'snake eater', from *mār* snake + *-khōr* eating]

marking *noun* **1** a mark or marks. **2** an arrangement, pattern, or disposition of marks.

markka /'mahka/ *noun* (*pl* **markkaa** /'mahkah/ *or* **markkas**) the former basic monetary unit of Finland, divided into 100 penni (replaced by the euro in 2002). [Finnish *markka* from Swedish *mark* a unit of value]

Markov chain /'mahkof/ *noun* in statistics, a random sequence of states in which the probability of occurrence of a future state depends only on the present state and not on the path by which it was reached. [named after A A *Markov* d.1922, Russian mathematician]

Markov model *noun* = MARKOV CHAIN.

marksman *or* **markswoman** *noun* (*pl* **marksmen** *or* **markswomen**) a person skilled in hitting a mark or target. ➤➤ **marksmanship** *noun*.

markup *noun* **1** an increase in price. **2** the amount of this. **3** an amount added to the price of something to guarantee the seller a profit.

mark up *verb trans* **1** to set a higher price on (something). **2** to edit (a text) by adding appropriate symbols, characters, or other marks to it.

markup language *noun* in desktop publishing and typesetting, a set of codes in a text that determines type styles, format, etc.

marl¹ /mahl/ *noun* a crumbly earthy deposit, e.g. of silt or clay, which contains calcium carbonate and is used as a fertilizer for lime-deficient soils. ➤➤ **marly** *adj*. [Middle English via French from late Latin *margila*, dimin. of Latin *marga* marl]

marl² *verb trans* to fertilize (land) with marl.

marlin¹ /'mahlin/ *noun* any of several species of large oceanic game fishes that have a spear-shaped projection extending from the snout: genera *Makaira* and *Tetrapterus*. [short for MARLINSPIKE; from the appearance of its snout]

marlin² *noun* = MARLINE.

marline /'mahlin/ *noun* a thin two-stranded usu tarred rope used on board ship. [Dutch *marlijn*, alteration of *marling*, from *meren, marren* to tie, moor]

marlinspike *or* **marlinespike** *noun* a pointed steel tool used to separate strands of rope or wire.

marmalade /'mahmolayd/ *noun* a clear sweetened preserve made from citrus fruit, *esp* oranges, and usu containing pieces of fruit peel. [Portuguese *marmelada* quince conserve, from *marmelo*

quince, via Latin from Greek *melimēlon* a sweet apple, from *meli* honey + *mēlon* apple]

Marmite /'mahmiet/ *noun trademark* a concentrated yeast extract used as a savoury spread. [French *marmite* stock pot, earthenware cooking pot]

marmite *noun* a large earthenware or cast-iron cooking pot with a lid. [French *marmite* pot, kettle, earlier 'hypocrite' (the development having reference to the concealed contents), from *marmotter* to mutter + *mite* cat]

marmoreal /mah'mawri-əl/ *adj literary* made of or resembling marble or a marble statue: *her marmoreal neck and shoulders*. [Latin *marmoreus* from *marmor* marble, from Greek *marmaros*]

marmoset /'mahməzet/ *noun* any of several species of small S and Central American monkeys with long tails and silky fur: genera *Callithrix* and *Cebuella*. [Middle English *marmusette* from early French *marmoset* grotesque figure, from *marmouser* to mumble, of imitative origin]

marmot /'mahmət/ *noun* any of a genus of burrowing rodents with short legs and coarse fur: genus *Marmota*. [French *marmotte*, perhaps from *marmotter* to chatter, in reference to their cry]

marocain /'marəkayn/ *noun* a kind of ribbed crepe, used as a dress fabric. [French *marocain* Moroccan]

Maronite /'marəniet/ *noun* a member of a Syrian Christian Church now existing chiefly in the Lebanon. [late Latin *maronita* from *Maron-, Maro*, name of fifth-cent. AD Syrian monk, said to have founded the sect]

Maroon /mə'roohn/ *noun* a descendant of a fugitive black slave of the W Indies and Guiana. [modification of American Spanish *cimarrón* wild, savage]

maroon¹ *verb trans* **1** (*usu as past part.*) to abandon (somebody) on a desolate island or coast. **2** (*usu as past part.*) to isolate (somebody) in a helpless state. [MAROON]

maroon² *adj* of a dark brownish red colour. ➤➤ **maroon** *noun*. [French *marron* Spanish chestnut]

maroon³ *noun* an explosive rocket used as a distress signal. [French *marron* Spanish chestnut; from the noise of a chestnut exploding in a fire]

marque¹ /mahk/ *noun* a make of vehicle, as distinct from a particular model. [French *marque* mark, brand, from *marquer* to mark, of Germanic origin]

marque² *noun* = LETTER OF MARQUE. [Middle English via French from Old Provençal *marca* from *marcar* to mark, seize as pledge, of Germanic origin]

marquee /mah'kee/ *noun* **1** a large tent, e.g. for an outdoor party or exhibition. **2** *NAmer* a permanent canopy projecting over an entrance, e.g. of a hotel or theatre. [a false singular formed from French *marquise* MARQUISE, assumed to be a plural]

Marquesan /mah'kayz(ə)n/ *noun* a native or inhabitant of the Marquesas Islands in the South Pacific. ➤➤ **Marquesan** *adj*.

marquess /'mahkwis/ *noun* a member of the British peerage ranking below a duke and above an earl. ➤➤ **marquessate** *noun*. [MARQUIS]

marquetry *or* **marqueterie** /'mahkitri/ *noun* decorative work consisting of pieces of wood, ivory, etc inlaid in a wood veneer that is then applied to a surface, e.g. of a piece of furniture. [early French *marqueterie* from *marqueter* to chequer, inlay, from *marque* mark]

marquis /'mahkwis/ *noun* **1** a nobleman in Europe ranking above a count and below a duke. **2** a marquess. ➤➤ **marquisate** *noun*. [Middle English *marquis, markis* from early French *marquis*, alteration of *marchis* from *marche* MARCH³]

marquise /mah'keez/ *noun* **1** a marchioness. **2** a gem or ring setting shaped like an oval with pointed ends. **3** *archaic* a marquee. [French *marquise*, fem of *marquis*: see MARQUIS]

marram grass /'marəm/ *noun* a strong wiry grass that grows on sandy shores and prevents erosion: *Ammophila arenaria*. [of Scandinavian origin; related to Old Norse *marálmr* a beach grass]

marriage /'marij/ *noun* **1a** the state of being husband and wife or the mutual relation it represents: *Marriage is so unlike anything else. There is something awful in the nearness it brings* — George Eliot. **b** the institution whereby a man and a woman are joined in a special kind of social and legal dependence. **2** an act or the rite of marrying; *esp* the wedding ceremony. **3** an intimate or close union: *a marriage of minds; the marriage of lyrics and melody*.

➤ **marriageable** *adj.* [Middle English *mariage* from early French *mariage* from *marier* to marry]

marriage of convenience *noun* a marriage contracted for advantage rather than for love.

married[1] /'marid/ *adj* **1** joined in marriage. **2** relating to married people: *married bliss*.

married[2] *noun* (*pl* **marrieds**) a married person: *young marrieds*.

marrons glacés /ˌmaronh 'glasay/ *pl noun* chestnuts candied or preserved in syrup. [French *marrons glacés* iced chestnuts]

marrow /'maroh/ *noun* **1a** a plant of the gourd family cultivated for its smooth-skinned elongated fruit: *Cucurbita pepo*. **b** a fruit of this plant, used as a vegetable; a vegetable marrow. **2a** a soft tissue that fills the cavities and porous part of most bones and in which red blood cells and certain white blood cells are produced. **b** the substance of the spinal cord. **3** the inmost, best, or essential part; the core: *you, the injured pith and marrow of this land* — Dickens. ✱ **to the marrow** through and through: *chilled to the marrow; a sportsman to his marrow*. [Old English *mearg*]

marrowbone /'marəbohn/ *noun* a bone rich in marrow.

marrowfat /'marohfat/ *noun* any of several types of large pea.

marry[1] /'mari/ *verb* (**marries, married, marrying**) ➤ *verb trans* **1a** to take (somebody) as a spouse. **b** to give (somebody) in marriage. **c** to perform the ceremony of marriage for (a couple). **2** to bring (two or more things) together closely, harmoniously, and usu permanently: *successfully marrying apparently disparate elements*. **3** to splice (rope ends) so as not to increase their width. ➤ *verb intrans* **1a** to take a spouse: *I had often wondered why young women should marry, as they have so much more freedom, and so much more attention paid to them while unmarried, than when married* — Dr Johnson. **b** to become husband and wife. **2** to join in a close or harmonious relationship: *These wines marry well*. ✱ **marry into** to become a member of (a family) or obtain (something) by marriage: *She married into a prominent family; marry into money*. [Middle English *marien* via Old French from Latin *maritare* from *maritus* (adj) married, (noun) husband]

marry[2] *interj archaic* used for emphasis, *esp* in assertion or concurrence: *Marry, well remembered* — Shakespeare. [Middle English *marie* from *Marie*, the Virgin Mary]

Marsala /mah'sahlə/ *noun* a sweet fortified wine from Sicily. [named after *Marsala*, a town in Sicily, where it was orig made]

marsh /mahsh/ *noun* an area of soft wet land usu covered with sedges, rushes, etc. ➤➤ **marshiness** *noun*, **marshy** *adj*. [Old English *merisc, mersc*]

marshal[1] /'mahsh(ə)l/ *noun* **1** an officer of the highest military rank. **2a** a chief officer in the USA responsible for court processes in a district. **b** the head of a US police or fire department. **3a** a person who arranges and directs a ceremony. **b** a person who arranges the procedure at races. **4** an official in Britain who assists a circuit judge. ➤➤ **marshalship** *noun*. [Middle English from Old French *mareschal*, of Germanic origin]

marshal[2] *verb* (**marshalled, marshalling,** *NAmer* **marshaled, marshaling**) ➤ *verb trans* **1** to place (e.g. soldiers) in proper rank or position. **2** to bring together and order (e.g. facts) in an effective way. **3** to lead (a group of people) ceremoniously or solicitously; to usher (them). **4** in heraldry, to combine (coats of arms) so as to indicate marriage, descent, etc.

marshalling yard *noun* a place where railway vehicles are shunted and assembled into trains.

marshal of the Royal Air Force *noun* an officer of the highest rank in the Royal Air Force.

marsh fever *noun* malaria.

marsh gas *noun* methane.

marsh harrier *noun* a small brown bird of prey that nests in large dense reed beds and is seen over open fields and marshes in Europe, N Africa, and Asia: *Circus aeruginosus*.

marshmallow *noun* **1** a pink-flowered Eurasian marsh plant of the mallow family: *Althaea officinalis*. **2** a light spongy confection formerly made from the root of the marshmallow, and now made from sugar, albumen, and gelatin.

marsh marigold /'marigohld/ *noun* a European and N American marsh plant of the buttercup family with large bright yellow flowers: *Caltha palustris*. Also called KINGCUP.

marsupia /mah's(y)oohpi·ə/ *noun* pl of MARSUPIUM.

marsupial[1] /mah's(y)oohpi·əl/ *noun* any of an order of lower mammals including the kangaroos, wombats, and opossums, the females of which have a pouch on the abdomen for carrying young, and do not develop a placenta: order Marsupialia. [scientific Latin *marsupialis* from Latin *marsupium*: see MARSUPIUM]

marsupial[2] *adj* **1** relating to or denoting a marsupial. **2** relating to or forming a marsupium or pouch.

marsupium /'mahs(y)oohpi·əm/ *noun* (*pl* **marsupia** /-pi·ə/) the abdominal pouch of a marsupial, formed by a fold of the skin and enclosing the mammary glands. [via Latin from Greek *marsypion*, dimin. of *marsypos* pouch]

mart /maht/ *noun* a place of trade, e.g. an auction room or market: *a cattle mart*. [Middle English from Middle Dutch *marct, mart*]

martagon lily /'mahtagən/ *noun* a Eurasian lily with mottled reddish purple flowers that resemble turbans: *Lilium martagon*. [Middle English *mortagon* from late Latin *martagon*, ultimately from Turkish *martağan* type of turban]

Martello /mah'teloh/ *noun* a circular masonry fort or blockhouse formerly used, e.g. in Britain, for coastal defence. [alteration of Cape *Mortella*, Corsica, where such a tower was captured by a British fleet in 1794]

Martello tower *noun* = MARTELLO.

marten /'mahtin/ *noun* (*pl* **martens** or collectively **marten**) any of several species of tree-dwelling mammals with slender bodies that are related to weasels: genus *Martes*. [Middle English *martryn* from Old French *martrine*, fem of *martrin* of a marten, from *martre* marten, of Germanic origin]

martensite /'mahtinziet/ *noun* the chief constituent of steel hardened by rapid cooling. ➤➤ **martensitic** /-'zitik/ *adj*. [named after Adolf *Martens* d.1914, German metallurgist]

martial /'mahsh(ə)l/ *adj* **1** relating to, denoting, or suited to a warrior: *I know not how, but martial men are given to love* — Bacon. **2** relating to war; warlike. ➤➤ **martially** *adv*. [Middle English from Latin *martialis* of the god Mars, from *Mart-, Mars* Mars]

martial art *noun* an Oriental art of combat, e.g. judo or karate, practised as a sport.

martial law *noun* the law administered by military forces in occupied territory or in an emergency.

Martian[1] /'mahsh(ə)n/ *adj* relating to or coming from the planet Mars. [Middle English from Latin *Mart-, Mars* the planet Mars]

Martian[2] *noun* a supposed inhabitant of Mars.

martin /'mahtin/ *noun* any of various small swallows with short tails, *esp* the house martin or sand martin. [early French *martin* from St *Martin*; prob from the migration of martins around Martinmas: compare MARTLET]

martinet /mahti'net/ *noun* a strict disciplinarian.

Word history
named after Jean *Martinet* d.1672, French army officer. The Marquis de Martinet served in Louis XIV's own regiment of infantry and introduced a system of drill to train and discipline new recruits. He died at the siege of Duisburg.

martingale /'mahtingayl/ *noun* **1** one or more straps fastened to the girth of a horse's harness, passed between the forelegs, and attached to the reins, noseband, or bit, for checking the upward movement of the horse's head. **2** in betting, any of several systems in which the stake is doubled every time a bet is lost. **3** a cable securing the boom of a jib to the stem or stern of a ship. [early French *martingale*]

martini /mah'teeni/ *noun* **1** a cocktail made of gin and dry vermouth. **2** (**Martini**) *trademark* a type of sweet or dry vermouth. **3** a glass or measure of martini. [prob named after *Martini* and Rossi, Italian firm selling vermouth]

Martiniquan or **Martinican** /mahti'neek(ə)n/ *noun* a native or inhabitant of Martinique in the Windward Islands. ➤➤ **Martiniquan** *adj*.

Martinmas /'mahtinməs, -mas/ *noun* 11 November celebrated as the feast of St Martin. [Middle English *martinmasse*, from St *Martin* d.397, patron saint of France, + *masse* mass]

martlet /'mahtlit/ *noun* **1** in heraldry, a representation of a swallow without feet, used e.g. in indicating descent, to denote a fourth son. **2** *archaic or literary* a martin: *this guest of summer, the temple-haunting martlet* — Shakespeare. [Middle English, in the sense 'a swift', from Old French *merlet* martin, influenced by *martinet*: compare MARTIN]

martyr¹ /'mahtə/ *noun* **1** a person who is put to death because of their religious beliefs. **2** any person who suffers for any cause or set of beliefs: *the Tolpuddle martyrs.* **3** a victim of constant suffering: *a martyr to migraine.* **4** a person who behaves unnecessarily, even pointedly, in a self-sacrificing manner: *OK, be a martyr if you must.* ⨠ **martyrdom** *noun.* [Old English *martir* via late Latin from Greek *martyr-, martys,* literally 'witness']

martyr² *verb trans* **1** to put (somebody) to death as a martyr. **2** to inflict agonizing pain on (somebody): *racked with sciatics, martyred with the stone* — Pope.

martyrize *or* **martyrise** *verb trans* to make (somebody) a martyr. ⨠ **martyrization** /-'zaysh(ə)n/ *noun.*

martyrology /mahtə'roləji/ *noun* that part of ecclesiastical history concerned with the lives and sufferings of martyrs. ⨠ **martyrological** /-'lojikl/ *adj,* **martyrologist** *noun.*

marvel¹ /'mahv(ə)l/ *noun* something or somebody amazing: *the marvels of modern technology; How did you manage it? You're a marvel!* [Middle English *mervel* via Old French from late Latin *mirabilia,* neuter pl of Latin *mirabilis* wonderful, from *mirari* to wonder]

marvel² *verb intrans* (**marvelled, marvelling,** *NAmer* **marveled, marveling**) (+ at) to be filled with surprise, wonder, or amazed curiosity: *I never cease to marvel at your memory.*

marvellous (*NAmer* **marvelous**) /'mahvələs/ *adj* **1** causing wonder. **2** of the highest kind or quality. ⨠ **marvellously** *adv,* **marvellousness** *noun.*

marvel of Peru /pə'roo/ *noun* = FOUR-O'CLOCK.

Marxism /'mahksiz(ə)m/ *noun* the political and economic principles and policies advocated by Karl Marx, which stress the importance of human labour in determining economic value, the struggle between classes as an instrument of social change, and dictatorship of the proletariat.

Editorial note
Marx claimed to replace utopian ideas of socialism with a scientific theory that would demonstrate the inevitable breakdown of capitalism. His insights about class inequalities have proved more durable than his suggestion for building a Communist society. The irony is that Communism actually came to exhibit structural flaws and injustices of a kind that Marx supposed unique to a market economy — Professor Peter Clarke.

⨠ **Marxist** *noun and adj.* [named after Karl *Marx* d.1883, German political philosopher and economist]

Marxism-Leninism /'leniniz(ə)m/ *noun* a theory and practice of communism developed by Lenin from the doctrines of Marx. ⨠ **Marxist-Leninist** *noun and adj.*

marzipan /'mahzipan/ *noun* a paste made from ground almonds, sugar, and egg whites, used for coating cakes or shaped into small sweets. [German *Marzipan* from Italian *marzapane* a medieval coin, marzipan, from Arabic *mawthabān,* a medieval coin]

Masai *or* **Maasai** /'masie/ *noun* (*pl* **Masais** *or collectively* **Masai**) **1** a member of a pastoral and hunting people of Kenya and Tanzania. **2** the Nilotic language of Kenya and Tanzania. [the Masai name for this people]

masala /mə'sahlə/ *noun* a mixture of spices ground into a powder or paste, used in Indian cooking. [Urdu *maṣālaḥ*]

masc. *abbr* masculine.

mascara /ma'skahrə/ *noun* a cosmetic for colouring, *esp* darkening, the eyelashes. [Italian *maschera* mask]

mascarpone /maskə'pohni/ *noun* a soft rich Italian cream cheese. [Italian *mascarpone*]

mascon /'maskon/ *noun* in astronomy, any of the concentrations of mass that are situated just under the surface of the moon and have strong gravitational pull. [short for *mass concentration*]

mascot /'maskot, 'maskət/ *noun* a person, animal, or object adopted as a good luck symbol. [French *mascotte* from Provençal *mascoto* from *masco* witch]

masculine¹ /'maskyoolin/ *adj* **1a** male. **b** having qualities appropriate to a man: *her deep masculine voice.* **2** in grammar, of, belonging to, or being the gender that normally includes most words or grammatical forms referring to males. **3** denoting a rhyme that occurs between stressed final syllables, e.g. *sigh, cry, deny.* ⨠ **masculinely** *adv,* **masculinity** /-'liniti/ *noun.* [Middle English *masculin* via French from Latin *masculinus* from *masculus* (noun) male, dimin. of *mas* male]

Usage note
masculine *or* male? See note at MALE¹.

masculine² *noun* a word or morpheme of the masculine gender.

masculinize *or* **masculinise** *verb trans* to give a predominantly masculine character to (somebody); *esp* to cause (a female) to take on male characteristics. ⨠ **masculinization** /-'zaysh(ə)n/ *noun.*

maser /'mayzə/ *noun* a device that works like a laser for amplifying or generating microwave radiation. [acronym from *microwave amplification by stimulated emission of radiation*]

mash¹ /mash/ *noun* **1** crushed malt or grain meal steeped and stirred in hot water to ferment. **2** a mixture of bran or similar feeds and usu hot water for livestock. **3** a soft pulpy mass. **4** *Brit, informal* mashed potatoes. [Old English *māsc*]

mash² *verb trans* **1** to crush or pound (something) to a soft pulpy state. **2** to heat and stir (e.g. crushed malt) in water as part of the process of brewing beer. **3** *Brit, dialect* to brew (tea). ⨠ **masher** *noun.*

mashie /'mashi/ *noun dated* a metal golf club used for shots of medium distance and for height. [perhaps from French *massue* club]

mask¹ /mahsk/ *noun* **1a** a covering or partial covering for the face used for disguise or protection. **b** a figure of a head worn on the stage in ancient times to identify the character and project the voice. **c** a grotesque false face worn at carnivals or in rituals. **d** a copy of a face made by sculpting or by means of a mould: *a death mask.* **2** something that disguises or conceals; *esp* a pretence or facade: *Her mask of gentility occasionally slipped.* **3** in photography, a translucent or opaque screen to cover part of the sensitive surface in taking or printing a photograph, so that only part of the image or scene appears in the final picture. **4** a device covering the mouth and nose, used: **a** to promote breathing, e.g. by connection to an oxygen supply. **b** to remove noxious gases from the air. **c** to prevent the spread of infective material breathed out, e.g. by a surgeon. **5** a face pack. [early French *masque* from Old Italian *maschera*]

mask² *verb trans* **1** to provide, cover, or conceal (something) with a mask. **2** to conceal (something) from view. **3** to make (e.g. a flavour) indistinct or imperceptible: *Peppermint had been added to mask the bitter taste.* **4** to cover (something) up: *He posed as a door-to-door salesman in order to mask his real purpose.* **5** to cover (something) for protection: *Mask the edges of the glass before painting the frames.* **6** to modify the size or shape of (e.g. a photograph) by means of a mask. ⨠ **masked** *adj.*

masked ball *noun* a ball at which the participants wear masks.

masking tape *noun* an adhesive tape used to cover a surface and keep it free from paint when painting an adjacent area.

masochism /'masəkiz(ə)m/ *noun* **1** the act or an instance of obtaining pleasure or gratification, *esp* sexual pleasure, by being physically or mentally abused: compare SADISM. **2** apparent enjoyment of something tiresome or painful. ⨠ **masochist** *noun,* **masochistic** /-'kistik/ *adj,* **masochistically** /-'kistikli/ *adv.* [named after Leopold von Sacher-*Masoch* d.1895, Austrian novelist, who described the condition]

mason /'mays(ə)n/ *noun* **1** a skilled worker with stone. **2** (**Mason**) a freemason. [Middle English from Old French *maçon,* prob of Germanic origin]

Masonic /mə'sonik/ *adj* relating to Freemasons or Freemasonry.

masonry /'mays(ə)nri/ *noun* **1** something built of stone or brick. **2** (**Masonry**) Freemasonry.

masque /mahsk/ *noun* **1** a short allegorical dramatic entertainment of the 16th and 17th cents performed by masked actors. **2** = MASQUERADE¹ (1). [early French *masque:* see MASK¹]

masquerade¹ /maskə'rayd/ *noun* **1** a social gathering of people wearing masks and often fantastic costumes. **2** disguise: *Everyone is to go in masquerade* — Horace Walpole. **3** something that is merely show; pretence: *In public they kept up a masquerade; though the marriage was increasingly loveless.* [early French *masquerade* from Old Italian dialect *mascarada* from Old Italian *maschera* mask]

masquerade² *verb intrans* **1** to disguise oneself or to wear a disguise. **2** (+ as) to assume the appearance of something that one is not: *It's easy enough to put on a white coat and masquerade as a hospital doctor.* ⨠ **masquerader** *noun.*

Mass. *abbr* Massachusetts.

mass¹ /mas/ *noun* **1** (**Mass**) the liturgy or a celebration of the Eucharist, *esp* in Roman Catholic and Anglo-Catholic churches. **2** a musical setting for the ORDINARY² (invariable parts) of the Mass.

✳ hear mass to attend mass without taking Communion. [Old English *mæsse*, ultimately from Latin *missa*, fem of *missus*, past part. of *mittere* to send; perhaps from the words of dismissal (*Ite, missa est*) at the end of the service]

mass² *noun* **1** a quantity of matter or the form of matter that holds or clings together in one body. **2** in physics, the property of a body that is a measure of its resistance to having its speed or position changed when a force is applied to it, causes it to have weight in a gravitational field, and is commonly taken as a measure of the amount of material it contains. **3** an unbroken expanse; a bulk: *a mountain mass; a mass of colour.* **4** the principal part or main body: *a section that had broken away from the mass.* **5** *informal* (in *pl*) a large quantity, amount, or number: *There was masses of food left over.* **6** a large body of people in a compact group. **7** (the masses) (in *pl*) the body of ordinary people as contrasted with the elite: *All the world over, I will back the masses against the classes* — W E Gladstone. **✳ in the mass** in total. [Middle English *masse* via French from Latin *massa* from Greek *maza* barley cake; perhaps related to Greek *massein* to knead]

mass³ *verb trans* to assemble (usu homogeneous elements) into a mass: *the massed pipe bands.* **➤** *verb intrans* to assemble into a mass.

mass⁴ *adj* **1** relating to or intended for the mass of the people: *a mass market.* **2** participated in by or affecting a large number of individuals: *mass suicide; mass murder.* **3** large-scale: *mass production.*

massacre¹ *noun* **1** the ruthless and indiscriminate killing of large numbers of people. **2** *informal* a complete defeat.

massacre² /'masəkə/ *verb trans* **1** to kill (people) deliberately and violently; to slaughter (them). **2** *informal* to defeat (an opponent or opposing team) severely. [early French *massacre*]

massage¹ /'masahj, 'masahzh, mə'sahzh, mə'sahj/ *noun* the kneading, rubbing, etc of the body in order to relieve aches, tone muscles, give relaxation, etc. [French *massage* from *masser* to massage, from Arabic *massa* to stroke]

massage² *verb trans* **1** to perform massage on (somebody). **2** (+ in/into) to rub a substance, e.g. oil, into (the skin or the scalp). **3** to adjust (data) so as to present a particular appearance: *The government has been accused of massaging hospital waiting list figures.* **✳ massage somebody's ego** to flatter somebody and make them feel good about themselves. **➤➤** **massager** *noun*.

massasauga /masə'sawgə/ *noun* a small N American rattlesnake: *Sistrurus catenatus.* [alteration of *Mississauga*, a town in SE Ontario, Canada]

mass defect /'deefekt/ *noun* in physics, the difference between the mass of an isotope and its mass number.

massé /'masi/ *noun* a shot in billiards, snooker, etc made with a nearly vertical cue so as to drive the cue ball in a curved path. [French *massé*, past part. of *masser* to make a massé shot, from *masse* sledgehammer, from early French *mace* mace]

masseter /ma'seetə/ *noun* a large muscle that raises the lower jaw and assists in chewing. [via Latin from Greek *masētēr* from *masasthai* to chew]

masseur /ma'suh/ *or* **masseuse** /ma'suhz/ *noun* a man or woman who practises massage and physiotherapy. [French *masseur, masseuse* from *masser* to massage]

massicot /'masikot/ *noun* yellow lead monoxide used as a pigment. [Middle English *masticot* via French from Old Italian *massicotto* pottery glaze]

massif /'maseef, ma'seef/ *noun* a principal mountain mass that gives rise to a number of peaks towards its summit. [French *massif* (adj) massive]

massive /'masiv/ *adj* **1a** large, solid, or heavy: *a massive oak door.* **b** impressively large: *shifting his massive bulk; Massive crowds are expected.* **2a** large or impressive in scope or degree: *There has been a massive response.* **b** large in comparison to what is typical: *a massive dose of penicillin.* **c** extensive and severe: *a massive haemorrhage.* **3a** said of a mineral: not obviously crystalline. **b** said of a rock: fairly uniform in appearance; homogeneous. **➤➤** **massively** *adv*, **massiveness** *noun*. [Middle English *massiffe* from early French *massif* from *masse* mass]

mass-market *adj* said of a product: designed for or aimed at a wide range of people.

mass media *pl noun* broadcasting, newspapers, and other means of communication designed to reach large numbers of people.

mass noun *noun* a noun, e.g. *sand* or *justice*, that characteristically denotes a substance or concept and not an individual item, that does not form a plural, and that cannot be used with the indefinite article; = UNCOUNTABLE NOUN: compare COUNT NOUN.

mass number *noun* in physics, the number of protons and neutrons in the nucleus that expresses the mass of an isotope.

mass-produce *verb trans* to produce (goods) in large quantities by standardized mechanical processes. **➤➤** **mass-produced** *adj*, **mass production** *noun*.

mass spectrograph *noun* an apparatus that separates a stream of charged particles, e.g. electrons or fragments of a molecule, according to mass, usu with photographic recording of the data.

mass spectrometer *noun* an apparatus similar to a mass spectrograph but usu adapted for the electrical measurement of data.

mass spectrum *noun* the spectrum of a stream of charged particles produced by a mass spectrograph or mass spectrometer.

mast¹ /mahst/ *noun* **1** a tall pole or structure rising from the keel or deck of a ship, esp for carrying sails. **2** a vertical pole or lattice supporting a radio or television aerial. **✳ before the mast** as an ordinary sailor, not an officer: *I told the second mate, with whom I had been pretty thick when he was before the mast* — R H Dana. [Old English *mæst*]

mast² *verb trans* to equip (a ship) with a mast.

mast³ *noun* beechnuts, acorns, etc accumulated on the forest floor and often serving as food for animals, e.g. pigs. [Old English *mæst*; prob related to MEAT]

mastaba /'mastəbə/ *noun* an Egyptian tomb that is oblong in shape with sloping sides and a flat roof. [Arabic *maṣṭabah* stone bench]

mast cell *noun* a large cell that occurs in connective tissue and contains histamine, serotonin, and heparin which may be released on disruption of the cell, e.g. as a result of an antigen-antibody reaction at the cell surface, and may cause responses such as inflammation or an allergic reaction. [translation of German *Mastzelle*, from *Mast* food, mast + *Zelle* cell]

mastectomy /ma'stektəmi/ *noun* (*pl* **mastectomies**) the excision or amputation of a breast. [Greek *mastos* breast + -ECTOMY]

masted *adj* (*used in combinations*) having masts of the number or kind specified: *a two-masted vessel.*

master¹ /'mahstə/ *noun* **1a** a person having control or authority over another; a ruler or governor. **b** an owner, *esp* of a slave or animal. **c** a male teacher. **d** an employer. **e** the male head of a household. **f** a person qualified to command a merchant ship. **g** the head of a college. **h** a presiding officer in an institution or society, e.g. a Masonic lodge, or at a function. **2** (*often* **Master**) somebody who directs a hunt and has overall control of the pack of hounds used in it. **3a** (**Master**) used as a title for a youth or boy too young to be called *Mr.* **b** (**Master**) *archaic* Mr: *I am glad to see you, Master Page.* **c** (*often* **Master**) a revered religious leader. **4** (*often* **Master**) an officer of the Supreme Court of England and Wales with responsibility for preliminary or procedural matters in High Court cases. **5** a person holding an academic degree higher than a bachelor's but lower than a doctor's. **6** an artist, performer, player, exponent of something, etc who is extremely skilled or accomplished: *He was a master of disguise.* **7** in chess or bridge, somebody who has won a specified number of games in tournaments. **8** a workman qualified to teach apprentices: *He had his master's certificate.* **9** a person or thing that conquers or masters; a victor or superior: *if you can dream and not make dreams your master* — Kipling; *In this young obscure challenger the champion had found his master.* **10** a mechanism or device that controls the operation of another: compare SLAVE¹ (3). **11** an original film, recording, etc from which copies can be made. [Old English *magister* via Old French *maistre* from Latin *magister*; related to Latin *magnus* great]

master² *verb trans* (**mastered, mastering**) **1a** to become skilled or proficient in the use of (a device, etc): *manage to master the controls.* **b** to gain a thorough understanding of (a subject): *mastering Spanish irregular verbs.* **2** to become master of (somebody or something); to overcome (them).

master³ *adj* **1** controlling: *a master switch.* **2** principal or main: *the master bedroom.* **3** qualified to teach apprentices: *a master carpenter.*

master aircrew *noun* a member of the Royal Air Force having a rank equal to that of warrant officer.

master-at-arms *noun* (*pl* **masters-at-arms**) a petty officer responsible for maintaining discipline aboard ship.

master builder *noun* **1** *chiefly archaic* a builder skilled in the planning and construction of buildings, before the growth of architecture as a profession. **2** an independent builder who employs workmen.

master class *noun* a class in which an eminent musician, actor, etc advises and corrects advanced pupils.

masterful /'mahstəf(ə)l/ *adj* **1** inclined to take control and dominate: *his masterful personality*. **2** having or showing the technical, artistic, or intellectual skill of a master: *a masterful exhibition of eloquent fact and subtlety* — Joseph Heller. ⟫⟫ **masterfully** *adv*, **masterfulness** *noun*.

Usage note
masterful or masterly? Both these words can be used to mean 'having or showing the skill of a master', but *masterly* should be preferred in this sense: *a masterly performance*. The main sense of *masterful* is 'showing strength or dominance': *a masterful type who took charge in any situation*. In modern usage *masterly* cannot be used in this sense.

master gunnery sergeant *noun* a non-commissioned officer in the US marines ranking below a warrant officer and equal to a sergeant major.

master key *noun* a key designed to open several different locks.

masterly *adj* demonstrating exceptional expertise: *a masterly translation*. ⟫⟫ **masterliness** *noun*.

Usage note
masterly or masterful? See note at MASTERFUL.

master mason *noun* **1** a fully trained and skilled mason, *esp* one that employs and trains others. **2** a Freemason who has attained the rank of third degree.

mastermind[1] *noun* **1** a person who masterminds a project. **2** a person of outstanding intellect.

mastermind[2] *verb trans* to be the intellectual force behind (a project).

master of arts *or* **Master of Arts** *noun* the recipient of a master's degree, usu in an arts subject.

master of ceremonies *noun* **1** a person who determines the procedure to be observed on a state or public occasion. **2** a person who acts as host, *esp* by introducing speakers, performers, etc, at an event.

master of science *or* **Master of Science** *noun* the recipient of a master's degree in a scientific subject.

Master of the Rolls *noun* the presiding judge of the Court of Appeal in England and Wales.

masterpiece *noun* **1** a work done with extraordinary skill; *esp* the supreme creation of a type, period, or person. **2** a piece of work that qualifies a craftsman as a member of a guild; a test piece. [prob translation of Dutch *meesterstuk* or German *Meisterstück* in the original sense 'work done to qualify as a master craftsman']

masterstroke *noun* a masterly or inspired move.

mastery *noun* **1a** the authority of a master. **b** the upper hand in a contest or competition. **2a** possession or display of great skill or technique. **b** skill or knowledge that makes one master of a subject: *the arduous steps by which he reached such mastery over his art as he ever acquired* — Somerset Maugham. [Middle English *maistrie* from Old French *maistrie* from *maistre* master]

masthead[1] *noun* **1** the top of a mast. **2** the name of a newspaper displayed on the top of the first page.

masthead[2] *verb* **1** to send (a sailor) up to the masthead *esp* as a form of punishment: *If you masthead a sailor for not doing his duty, why should you not weathercock a parishioner for refusing to pay tithes?* — Sydney Smith. **2** to fly (a sail or flag) from the masthead: *Our yards were mast-headed* — R H Dana.

mastic /'mastik/ *noun* **1** an aromatic resin that exudes from mastic trees and is used in varnishes. **2** = MASTIC TREE. **3** a substance like putty used as a protective coating or cement. [Middle English *mastik* via Latin from Greek *mastichē*]

masticate /'mastikayt/ *verb trans* **1** to grind or crush (food) before swallowing; to chew (it). **2** to soften or reduce (something) to pulp, e.g. by crushing. ⟫ *verb intrans* to chew. ⟫⟫ **mastication** /-'kaysh(ə)n/ *noun*, **masticator** *noun*, **masticatory** *adj*. [late Latin *masticatus*, past part. of *masticare*, from Greek *mastichan* to gnash the teeth]

mastic tree *noun* a small S European evergreen tree of the sumach family that yields mastic: *Pistacia lentiscus*.

mastiff /'mastif/ *noun* a breed of very large powerful deep-chested smooth-coated dogs used chiefly as guard dogs. [Middle English *mastif*, ultimately from Latin *mansuetus* tame, past part. of *mansuescere* to tame, from *manus* hand + *suescere* to accustom]

mastitis /ma'stietis/ *noun* inflammation of the breast or udder, usu caused by infection. [late Latin *mastitis*]

mastodon /'mastədon/ *noun* any of numerous extinct mammals similar to the related mammoths and elephants but with a different form of molar teeth: *when Aunt is calling to Aunt like mastodons bellowing across primeval swamps* — P G Wodehouse. [Latin *mastodont-*, *mastodon*, from Greek *mastos* breast, nipple + *odont-*, *odōn*, *odous* tooth; from the nipple-shaped projections on the molar teeth]

mastoid[1] /'mastoyd/ *adj* relating to the mastoid process. [via Latin from Greek *mastoeidēs* from *mastos* breast]

mastoid[2] *noun* **1** the mastoid process. **2** = MASTOIDITIS.

mastoiditis /mastoy'dietis/ *noun* inflammation of the mastoid process.

mastoid process *noun* a somewhat conical prominent or projecting part of the temporal bone behind the ear.

masturbate /'mastəbayt/ *verb intrans* to practise masturbation on oneself. ⟫ *verb trans* to practise masturbation on (another person). ⟫⟫ **masturbator** *noun*, **masturbatory** *adj*. [Latin *masturbatus*, past part. of *masturbari*]

masturbation /mastə'baysh(ə)n/ *noun* stimulation of the genitals accomplished by any means except sexual intercourse.

mat[1] /mat/ *noun* **1** a piece of thick fabric used as a covering for an area of floor, e.g. a doormat or a bathmat. **2a** a relatively thin usu decorative piece of material, e.g. cork or plastic, used under an object, *esp* to protect a surface, e.g. from heat, moisture, or scratches. **b** a mouse mat. **3** a large thick pad or cushion used as a surface for wrestling, tumbling, and gymnastics. **4** a mass of intertwined or tangled strands. ✱ **on the mat** *informal* in trouble; due to be punished. [Old English *meatte* from late Latin *matta*]

mat[2] *verb* (**matted**, **matting**) ⟫ *verb intrans* said of fibres, hair, etc: to become tangled or intertwined. ⟫ *verb trans* to form (fibres, hairs, etc) into a tangled mass.

mat[3] *verb trans* see MATT[3].

mat[4] *adj* see MATT[1].

mat[5] *noun* see MATT[2].

mat[6] *noun* = MATRIX (2).

matador /'matədaw/ *noun* **1** a bullfighter who has the principal role and who kills the bull in a bullfight. **2** a game played with dominoes. **3** in some card games, a high card. [Spanish *matador*, literally 'killer', from *matar* to kill]

matai /'mahtie/ *noun* a New Zealand evergreen tree with wood that is used to make floors: *Podocarpus spicatus*. [Maori *matai*]

match[1] /mach/ *noun* **1a** a contest between two or more teams or individuals. **b** in tennis, a contest completed when one player or side wins a specified number of sets. **2** a person or thing that is the equal of another: *Volkswagen's new hatchback is a match for its main rivals* — Daily Telegraph. **3** a person or thing able to cope with another: *When it came to arguments, his brother was no match for him.* **4a** one thing that corresponds exactly to another: *The wall colour is an exact match for the carpet.* **b** a pair of things that correspond exactly: *They're an excellent match.* **5a** a prospective partner in marriage: *Her parents regarded him as a suitable match for her.* **b** a marriage union: *It was a marriage of convenience rather than a love match; rumours about a royal match.* ✱ **meet one's match** to encounter somebody capable of holding their own against one; to meet one's equal. [Old English *mæcca*; related to MAKE[1]]

match[2] *verb trans* **1a** to cause (two things) to correspond; to make (them) harmonious: *matching lifestyle to income.* **b** to be the exact counterpart or equal of (something): *Does this scarf match my dress OK?* **2a** to be equal to (something or somebody): *Nobody can match her in speedy mental calculation.* **b** to pit (a person or thing) in competition or opposition: *matching his strength against his enemy's.* **c** to provide (somebody) with worthy competition: *The contestants were well matched.* **3** to fit (two things) together or make them suitable for fitting together. **4** *archaic* to join (a couple, or one person to another) in marriage: *an idle king … matched with an aged wife* — Tennyson. **5** to equalize (electrical impedances) in order to maximize the power transfer from one to another. ➤ *verb intrans* **1** to be exactly or nearly alike. **2** to go well together; to correspond. ➤➤ **matchable** *adj*, **matching** *adj*.

match³ *noun* **1** a short slender piece of wood, cardboard, etc tipped with a mixture that ignites when subjected to friction. **2** formerly, a chemically prepared wick or cord used in firing firearms or powder. [Middle English *macche* wick, from early French *meiche*]

matchboard *noun* a board with a groove cut along one edge and a tongue along the other so as to fit snugly with the edges of similarly cut boards.

match-fit *adj* in a good enough state of physical fitness to perform creditably in a match.

matchless *adj* having no equal; peerless: *But observe the matchless judgment of our Shakespeare* — Coleridge. ➤➤ **matchlessly** *adv*.

matchlock *noun* **1** a mechanism by which a slow-burning cord is lowered over a hole in the breech of a musket to ignite the charge. **2** a musket equipped with a matchlock.

matchmaker *noun* a person who arranges marriages or speculatively introduces one party to another. ➤➤ **matchmaking** *noun*.

match play *noun* a golf competition scored by number of holes won rather than strokes played: compare STROKE PLAY. ➤➤ **match player** *noun*.

match point *noun* a situation in tennis, badminton, etc in which a player will win the match by winning the next point.

matchstick *noun* **1** the wooden stem of a match. **2** (*used before a noun*) **a** made of matchsticks: *a matchstick model*. **b** denoting a figure drawn with single straight lines: *suggestions for exercises, illustrated with matchstick figures*.

matchwood *noun* **1** wood suitable for matches. **2** wood splinters: *The door had been reduced to matchwood.*

mate¹ /mayt/ *noun* **1a** *Brit, Aus* used as a familiar form of address between men: a friend. **b** (*often in combination*) an associate or companion: *a flatmate; a playmate*. **c** an assistant to a more skilled workman: *a builder's mate*. **2** an officer on a merchant ship ranking below the captain. **3a** a marriage partner. **b** either member of a breeding pair of animals. [Middle English, prob from early Low German *mât* comrade]

mate² *verb intrans* **1** said of animals: to come together to breed: *They mate for life*. **2** to join together; to connect: *gears that mate well*. ➤ *verb trans* **1** to join (two animals) together, or (one animal) to another, as mates. **2** to join or fit (two parts) together.

mate³ *verb trans* in chess, to checkmate (an opponent). [Middle English *maten* via Old French from Arabic *mât* (in *shāh māt*): see CHECKMATE¹]

mate⁴ *noun* in chess, checkmate.

maté /'matay, 'mahtay/ *noun* **1** a tealike aromatic beverage made from leaves, which is drunk chiefly in S America. **2** the S American holly that bears these leaves: *Ilex paraguayensis*. [via French from American Spanish *mate* from Quechua *mati*]

matelot /'mat(ə)loh/ *noun Brit, informal* a sailor. [early French *matelot* from early Dutch *mattenoot*, from *matte* mat, bed + *noot* companion; from when sailors had to share hammocks in pairs]

mater /'maytə/ *noun Brit, dated, informal* an affectionate name for one's mother. [Latin *mater* mother]

materfamilias /,maytəfə'mili·əs, ,mah-/ *noun* (*pl* **matresfamilias** /,maytrayz-, ,mahtrayz-/) a female head of a household. [Latin *materfamilias*, from *mater* mother + *familias*, archaic genitive of *familia* household]

material¹ /mə'tiəri·əl/ *noun* **1** the elements, constituents, or substances of which something is composed or can be made. **2** matter that has usu specified qualities which give it individuality: *sticky material*. **3** data that may be worked into a more finished form: *collecting material for her autobiography*. **4** a person considered with a view to being suitable or successful: *I don't think he's officer material*. **5** cloth; fabric. **6** (*in pl*) apparatus necessary for doing or making something: *assemble the requisite materials*.

material² *adj* **1** relating to, derived from, or consisting of matter; *esp* physical: *the material world*. **2a** bodily: *appear in material form*. **b** relating to matter rather than form: *a material cause*. **3a** important or significant: *constitute a material advantage*. **b** (+ to) relevant: *facts material to the investigation*. **4** of or concerned with physical rather than spiritual things: *material comforts; material possessions*. **5** in philosophy, relating to the substance of reasoning rather than the form. ➤➤ **materiality** /-'aliti/ *noun*. [Middle English *materiel*

via French from late Latin *materialis* from Latin *materia*: see MATTER¹]

materialise *verb intrans* see MATERIALIZE.

materialism *noun* **1** a preoccupation with or stress on material rather than spiritual things. **2a** a theory that only physical matter is real and that all processes and phenomena can be explained by reference to matter. **b** a doctrine that the highest values lie in material well-being and material progress.

Editorial note
Traditionally, materialism was a doctrine stating that whatever occurs is reducible to movements of expanded material objects, the latter being defined by spatial properties. Thus conceived, materialism is the belief that all events are really physical, and the question whether mental processes (feelings, thoughts, impressions) can be thus interpreted and whether some realities (e.g. mathematical objects, musical creations) have a separate kind of existence, has been discussed for centuries. Often a person who cares only for material goods is called a 'materialist' — Professor Leszek Kołakowski.

➤➤ **materialist** *noun and adj*, **materialistic** /-'listik/ *adj*, **materialistically** /-'listikli/ *adv*.

materialize *or* **materialise** *verb intrans* **1** said of a ghost or spirit: to assume bodily form. **2** to become reality; to become tangible: *promises of money which never materialized*. **3** to put in an appearance. ➤ *verb trans* to cause (a ghost or spirit) to appear in bodily form. ➤➤ **materialization** /-'zaysh(ə)n/ *noun*.

materially *adv* **1** to a considerable degree; substantially. **2** in terms of material things.

materia medica /mətiəriə 'medikə/ *noun* **1** substances used in the composition of medical remedies; drugs; medicine. **2a** the branch of medical science that deals with the sources, nature, properties, and preparation of drugs. **b** a written account of materia medica. [scientific Latin *materia medica* medical matter]

materiel /mə,tieri'el/ *noun* equipment, apparatus, and supplies used by the armed forces. [French *matériel* (adj used as a noun)]

maternal /mə'tuhnl/ *adj* **1** relating to or characteristic of a mother. **2** related through one's mother: *my maternal grandfather*. ➤➤ **maternally** *adv*. [Middle English via French from Latin *maternus* from *mater* mother]

maternity /mə'tuhniti/ *noun* **1** motherhood. **2** (*used before a noun*) relating to pregnancy or pregnant women: *the maternity department; a maternity dress*.

mateship *noun Aus* good fellowship between friends and working companions; camaraderie.

matey¹ *or* **maty** /'mayti/ *noun* used as a form of address: mate.

matey² *or* **maty** *adj* (**matier, matiest**) *informal* friendly. ➤➤ **mateyness** *noun*, **matily** *adv*, **matiness** *noun*.

math /math/ *noun NAmer* mathematics: *Take the sales, subtract the loss, you get this big positive number. The math is quite straightforward* — Bill Gates.

mathematical /mathə'matikl/ *adj* **1** relating to mathematics. **2** rigorously exact. ➤➤ **mathematically** *adv*. [via Latin from Greek *mathēmatikos* from *mathēmat-, mathēma* mathematics, from *manthanein* to learn]

mathematics /mathə'matiks/ *pl noun* (*treated as sing. or pl*) **1** the science of numbers and their operations, interrelations, and combinations and of space configurations and their structure, measurement, etc. **2** the calculations or mathematical operations involved in a particular problem, field of study, etc. ➤➤ **mathematician** /-'tish(ə)n/ *noun*.

maths *pl noun Brit* (*treated as sing. or pl*) mathematics.

matin¹ /'matin/ *adj archaic or literary* relating to matins or to the early morning.

matin² *noun* = MATINS (3).

matinal /'matinl/ *adj* = MATIN¹.

matinée /'matinay/ *noun* a musical or dramatic performance during the day, *esp* the afternoon. [French *matinée*, literally 'morning', via Old French from Latin *matutinum*, neuter of *matutinus* of the morning, from *Matuta*, goddess of morning; from the fact that performances were formerly also given in the morning]

matinée coat *noun* = MATINÉE JACKET.

matinée jacket *noun Brit* a cardigan worn by babies.

matins /'matinz/ *pl noun* (*treated as sing. or pl*) **1** (*often* **Matins**) the night office forming with lauds the first of the canonical hours. **2** a daily morning office of the Anglican Church. **3** *literary* the morning song of birds: *Ere the first cock his matin sings* — Milton. [Middle English *matines* via Old French from Latin *matutinae*, fem pl of *matutinus*: see MATINÉE]

matresfamilias /ˌmaytrayzfəˈmili·əs, ˌmahtrayz-/ *noun* pl of MATERFAMILIAS.

matri- *comb. form* forming words, denoting: mother: *matriarch*. [Latin *matr-, matri-* from *matr-, mater* mother]

matriarch /ˈmaytriahk/ *noun* a woman who rules a family, group, or state; *specif* a mother who is the head of her family. ➤➤ **matriarchal** *adj*.

matriarchy *noun* (*pl* **matriarchies**) a system of social organization in which the female is the head of the family, and descent and inheritance are traced through the female line.

matrices /ˈmaytriseez/ *noun* pl of MATRIX.

matricide /ˈmaytrisied, ˈmat-/ *noun* **1** the act of murdering one's mother. **2** a person who commits matricide. ➤➤ **matricidal** /ˌmaytriˈsiedl, ˌmat-/ *adj*. [Latin *matricida* and *matricidium*, from MATRI- + *-cida* and *-cidium* -CIDE]

matriculate /məˈtrikyoolayt/ *verb intrans* **1** to be admitted as a member of a college or university. **2** *SAfr* to pass an examination at the end of one's time at school. ➤ *verb trans* to admit (somebody) as a member of a college or university. ➤➤ **matriculation** /-ˈlaysh(ə)n/ *noun*. [late Latin *matriculatus*, past part. of *matriculare*, from *matricula* public roll, dimin. of *matric-, matrix* list, from Latin *matrix*: see MATRIX]

matrilineal /matriˈlini·əl, may-/ *adj* relating to or tracing descent through the maternal line. ➤➤ **matrilineally** *adv*.

matrilocal /ˈmatrilohkl, ˈmaytri-/ *adj* relating to or having a marriage system in which the married couple live with the wife's family.

matrimony /ˈmatriməni/ *noun* marriage. ➤➤ **matrimonial** /-ˈmohni·əl/ *adj*, **matrimonially** *adv*. [Middle English via French from Latin *matrimonium* from *matr-, mater* mother, matron]

matrix /ˈmaytriks/ *noun* (*pl* **matrices** /-seez/ *or* **matrixes**) **1** a substance, environment, etc within which something else originates or develops. **2** a mould in which something is cast or from which a surface in relief, e.g. a piece of type, is made by pouring or pressing. **3** the natural material in which something, e.g. a fossil, gem, or specimen for study, is embedded. **4** the substance between the cells of a tissue that holds them together. **5** a rectangular array of mathematical elements treated as a unit and subject to special algebraic laws. **6** something resembling a mathematical matrix, *esp* in rectangular arrangement of elements into rows and columns. [Latin *matrix* womb, from *matr-, mater* mother]

matron /ˈmaytrən/ *noun* **1** a woman in charge of living arrangements in a school, residential home, etc. **2** *Brit* a woman in charge of the nursing in a hospital; a senior nursing officer. **3** a married woman, *esp* one who is dignified and mature. **4** *NAmer* a female prison warden. [Middle English *matrone* via French from Latin *matrona* from *matr-, mater* mother]

matronly *adj* **1** suitable to a mature married woman: *matronly dignity*. **2** said of a female figure: inclined to stoutness. ➤➤ **matronliness** *noun*.

matron of honour *noun* a bride's principal married wedding attendant.

matronymic /matrəˈnimik/ *or* **metronymic** /met-/ *noun* a name derived from that of the bearer's mother or maternal ancestor: compare PATRONYMIC. [Latin *matr-, mater* mother, following the pattern of PATRONYMIC]

Matt. *abbr* Matthew (book of the Bible).

matt¹ *or* **mat** *or* **matte** /mat/ *adj* lacking lustre or gloss; *esp* having an even surface free from shine or highlights. [French *mat* via Old French from Latin *mattus* drunk]

matt² *or* **mat** *or* **matte** *noun* **1** a roughened or dull finish, e.g. on gilt or paint. **2** a border round a picture acting as a frame or as a contrast between picture and frame. [French *mat* dull colour, unpolished surface]

matt³ *or* **mat** *or* **matte** *verb trans* (**matted, matting**) to make (e.g. metal or colour) matt.

matte /mat/ *noun* a crude mixture of sulphides formed in smelting copper, lead, etc sulphide ores. [French *matte*]

matter¹ /ˈmatə/ *noun* **1a** the substance of which a physical object is composed. **b** a physical substance occupying space and having mass. **c** something of a particular kind or for a particular purpose:

vegetable matter; reading matter. **d** material, e.g. faeces, urine, or pus, discharged from the living body.

Editorial note ——————————————————
The most fundamental definition of matter is that it consists of fermions (half-integral spin particles, such as electrons and quarks) held together by the exchange of bosons (integral spin particles, such as photons and gluons). The elucidation of the structure of matter is the domain of physics; its transformation from one substance to another is the domain of chemistry. Biology is the science of living matter — Professor Peter Atkins.

2 (**the matter**) a source of disquiet: *What's the matter?* **3a** a subject of interest or concern: *the matter in hand*. **b** a subject of disagreement or proceedings at law. **c** something to be dealt with; an affair or concern: *I have a few personal matters to take care of; It's no laughing matter*. **4a** material for treatment in thought, fields of knowledge, discourse, or writing: *Her style is elegant, but the matter is so dull*. **b** the content of or ideas contained in verbal or written material as distinguished from the form in which this content is expressed. **c** *archaic* meaningful content in what is said; substance: *More matter, with less art* — Shakespeare; *I was born to speak all mirth and no matter* — Shakespeare. **5** in Aristotelian philosophy, the formless substance that can take form to become any existing thing. **6a** that part of a legal case which deals with facts rather than principles of law. **b** something to be proved in a court of law. **7a** something written or printed. **b** type set up for printing. ✳ **a matter of** a period of time reckoned merely in (minutes, hours, days, etc): *They would know the result in a matter of hours*. **as a matter of fact** in truth; actually. **for that matter** so far as that is concerned. **in the matter of** concerning (something or somebody). **no matter 1** that is of no importance. **2** regardless or irrespective of a certain thing: *He would be calm no matter what the provocation*. [Middle English *matere* via Old French from Latin *materia* matter, physical substance, from *mater* mother]

matter² *verb intrans* (**mattered, mattering**) **1** to be of importance. **2** *technical* to form or discharge pus.

matter of course *noun* something routine or to be expected as a natural consequence: *assume that the witnesses summoned in force … have perjured themselves as a matter of course* — W S Gilbert.

matter-of-fact *adj* keeping to or concerned with fact; *esp* not fanciful or imaginative. ➤➤ **matter-of-factly** *adv*, **matter-of-factness** *noun*.

matting *noun* material, e.g. hemp, for mats.

mattins /ˈmatinz/ *noun* = MATINS.

mattock /ˈmatək/ *noun* a digging tool with a head like that of a pick and often a blade like that of an axe or adze. [Old English *mattuc*]

mattress /ˈmatris/ *noun* **1** a fabric case filled with resilient material, e.g. feathers, foam rubber, or an arrangement of coiled springs, used as, or on, a bed. **2a** a mass of interwoven brush and poles to protect a bank from erosion, or a similar mass serving as a foundation in soft ground. **b** a concrete slab or raft used as a foundation or footing. [Middle English *materas* via Old French from Arabic *maṭraḥ* place where something is thrown]

maturate /ˈmatyoorayt/ *verb intrans* said of a boil or abscess: to form pus; to suppurate. ➤➤ **maturative** /-tiv/ *adj*.

maturation /matyooˈraysh(ə)n/ *noun* **1** the process of becoming mature: *sexual maturation; changes in the wine during the maturation process*. **2** the formation of pus; suppuration. ➤➤ **maturational** *adj*.

mature¹ /məˈtyooə/ *adj* **1** characteristic of or being in a condition of full or adult development; full-grown. **2** physically, emotionally, or mentally advanced. **3a** having completed natural growth and development; ripe. **b** having attained a final or desired state: *mature wine*. **4** based on slow careful consideration: *a mature judgment*. **5** due for payment: *a mature loan*. ➤➤ **maturely** *adv*. [Middle English from Latin *maturus* ripe]

mature² *verb intrans* **1** to become mature. **2** to become due for payment: *The policy matures next year*. ➤ *verb trans* to bring (e.g. food or drink) to full development or completion.

mature student *noun* an entrant to British higher education who is older than usual, *esp* one who is over 25.

maturity /məˈtyooəriti/ *noun* **1** the quality or state of being mature; *esp* full development. **2** the date when a bond, note, insurance policy, etc becomes due.

matutinal /matyooˈtienl/ *adj literary* of or occurring in the morning: *Is all this precious time to be lavished on the matutinal repair and* *beautifying of an elderly person, who never goes abroad?* — Nathaniel Hawthorne. [late Latin *matutinalis* from Latin *matutinus*: see MATINÉE]

maty¹ /'mayti/ *noun* see MATEY¹.

maty² *adj* see MATEY².

matzo *or* **matzoh** /'matsoh/ *or* **matzah** /'matsa/ *noun* (*pl* **matzoth** /'matsoht, 'matsohth/ *or* **matzos** *or* **matzohs**) a wafer of unleavened bread eaten during Passover. [Yiddish *matse* from Hebrew *maṣṣāh*]

maudlin /'mawdlin/ *adj* weakly and effusively sentimental; tearful. [alteration of Mary *Magdalen*, the spelling reflecting the earlier pronunciation of the name; from the practice of depicting her as a weeping, penitent sinner: compare MAGDALEN]

maul¹ /mawl/ *verb trans* **1** said of an animal: to attack and tear the flesh of (an animal or person). **2** to handle (somebody or something) roughly. ➤➤ **mauler** *noun*. [Middle English *mallen* via Old French from Latin *malleus* hammer]

maul² *noun* **1** in Rugby Union, a situation in which one or more players from each team close round the player carrying the ball who tries to get the ball out to his or her own team: compare RUCK¹. **2** a heavy two-handed hammer. [see MAUL¹]

maulstick *noun* a stick used by painters to support and steady the hand while working. [Dutch *maalstok*, from early Dutch *malen* to paint + Dutch *stok* stick]

maunder /'mawndə/ *verb intrans* (**maundered, maundering**) **1** to act or wander idly. **2** to speak in a rambling or indistinct manner. [prob imitative]

Maundy /'mawndi/ *noun* the distribution of Maundy money.

Maundy money *noun* specially minted coins given to selected poor people by the British Sovereign in a ceremony on Maundy Thursday.

Maundy Thursday *noun* the Thursday before Easter observed in commemoration of the Last Supper. [Middle English *maunde* ceremony of washing the feet of the poor on Maundy Thursday, via Old French from Latin *mandatum* command; from Jesus' words in John 13:34]

Mauritanian /mori'tayni·ən/ *noun* a native or inhabitant of Mauritania in W Africa. ➤➤ **Mauritanian** *adj*.

Mauritian /mə'rishən/ *noun* a native or inhabitant of Mauritius, an island in the Indian Ocean. ➤➤ **Mauritian** *adj*.

mausoleum /mawsə'lee·əm/ *noun* (*pl* **mausoleums** *or* **mausolea** /-'lee·ə/) a large and elaborate tomb; *esp* a stone building with places for entombment of the dead above ground.

Word history
via Latin from Greek *mausōleion* from *Mausōlos* Mausolus d.c.353 BC, ruler of Caria in Asia Minor, for whom a magnificent tomb was erected. Mausolus' tomb was one of the Seven Wonders of the World.

mauve¹ /mohv/ *adj* of a pinkish purple to bluish purple colour. ➤➤ **mauve** *noun*. [French *mauve* mallow, from Latin *malva* mallow]

mauve² *noun* a dyestuff that produces a mauve colour.

maven /'mayv(ə)n/ *noun chiefly NAmer* an expert or enthusiast: *Picasso mavens and all sorts of experts* — The Guardian. [Yiddish *meyvn* from Hebrew *mēḇīn* understanding]

maverick /'mav(ə)rik/ *noun* **1** an independent and nonconformist individual. **2** *NAmer* an unbranded range animal; *esp* a motherless calf.

Word history
named after Samuel A *Maverick* d.1870, US pioneer who did not brand his calves. The practice soon arose of calling unbranded cattle *mavericks* and the term was then extended to independent-minded or masterless people.

mavis /'mayvis/ *noun literary* a song thrush. [Middle English from early French *mauvis*]

maw /maw/ *noun* **1** an animal's stomach or crop. **2** the throat, gullet, or jaws, *esp* of a voracious flesh-eating animal. [Old English *maga*]

mawkish /'mawkish/ *adj* **1** sickly or feebly sentimental. **2** *archaic or dialect* having an insipid often unpleasant taste. ➤➤ **mawkishly** *adv*, **mawkishness** *noun*. [Middle English *mawke* maggot, from Old Norse *mathkr*]

max. *abbr* maximum.

maxi /'maksi/ *noun* (*pl* **maxis**) a floor-length coat, skirt, etc. [MAXI-]

maxi- *comb. form* forming words, with the meanings: **1** extra long: *a maxi-skirt*. **2** extra large: *a maxi-yacht*. [shortened from MAXIMUM¹]

maxilla /mak'silə/ *noun* (*pl* **maxillae** /-lee/ *or* **maxillas**) **1a** the jaw. **b** either of two bones of the upper jaw of a human or other higher vertebrate. **2** any of the one or two pairs of mouthparts behind the mandibles in insects and other arthropods. ➤➤ **maxillary** *adj*. [Latin *maxilla*, dimin. of *mala* jaw]

maxim /'maksim/ *noun* a succinct expression of a general truth, fundamental principle, or rule of conduct. [Middle English *maxime* via French and late Latin from Latin *maxima*, fem of *maximus*: see MAXIMUM¹]

maxima /'maksimə/ *noun* pl of MAXIMUM¹.

maximal *adj* **1** the greatest or most comprehensive: *make maximal use of the therapists' time*. **2** being an upper limit: *on a maximal dose*. ➤➤ **maximally** *adv*.

maximin /'maksimin/ *noun* the maximum of a mathematical set of minimum values, *esp* the largest of a set of minimum possible gains each of which occurs in the least advantageous outcome of a strategy followed by a participant in a situation governed by game theory: compare MINIMAX. ➤➤ **maximin** *adj*. [blend of MAXIMUM¹ and MINIMUM¹]

maximize *or* **maximise** *verb trans* to increase (something) to a maximum or to the highest possible degree: *maximize profits*. ➤➤ **maximization** /-'zaysh(ə)n/ *noun*.

maximum¹ /'maksiməm/ *noun* (*pl* **maxima** /-mə/ *or* **maximums**) the greatest amount, number, intensity, level, or extent possible or recorded: *when speed of growth is at a maximum*. [Latin *maximum*, neuter of *maximus* greatest, superl of *magnus* great]

maximum² *adj* of or being a maximum.

maxwell /'makswəl, 'makswel/ *noun* the unit of magnetic flux in the centimetre-gram-second system. [named after James Clerk *Maxwell* d.1879, Scottish physicist]

May *noun* the fifth month of the year. [Middle English via Old French *mai* (adj) from *Maia*, Roman goddess]

may¹ /may/ *verb aux* (*third person sing. present tense* **may**, *past tense* **might** /miet/) **1** used to express permission or opportunity: *You may go now*; *What is this, may I ask?* **2** used to express possibility: *They may be right*; *The road may well be closed*. **3** used to express a wish or hope: *Long may the good weather last*. ✴ **be that as it may** whether that is true or not; in spite of that. [Old English *mæg*]

Usage note
may *or* can? See note at CAN¹.

may² *noun* hawthorn or hawthorn blossom. [MAY, the month when it comes into flower]

Maya /'mie·ə/ *noun* (*pl* **Mayas** *or collectively* **Maya**) **1** a member of a group of Native American peoples inhabiting the Yucatán peninsula. **2** the Mayan language spoken in Yucatán. [Spanish *Maya*, from Mayan]

maya *noun* **1** the diverse world as perceived by the senses, held in Hinduism to conceal the unity of absolute being. **2** deceptive appearance or illusion. [Sanskrit *māyā*]

Mayan *noun* **1** a member of the Maya people. **2** a family of Native American languages of Central America, including Maya and Tzeltal. ➤➤ **Mayan** *adj*.

mayapple *noun* **1** an edible egg-shaped yellow fruit. **2** the N American plant that bears this fruit: *Podophyllum peltatum*. [MAY, the month in which the fruit appears]

maybe /'maybee, 'maybi/ *adv* perhaps. [Middle English from (*it*) *may be*]

maybug *noun* a cockchafer.

Mayday *noun* used as an international radio distress signal. [French *m'aider* help me]

May Day *noun* 1 May, celebrated as a springtime festival and in many countries as a public holiday in honour of working people.

mayest /'mayist/ *or* **mayst** /mayst/ *verb* archaic second person sing. present of MAY¹.

mayflower *noun* any of various plants that bloom in the spring.

mayfly *noun* (*pl* **mayflies**) any of an order of insects with an aquatic nymph and a short-lived fragile adult with membranous wings: order Ephemeroptera.

mayhap /'mayhap/ *adv archaic, esp dialect* perhaps: *'I'll tie her to the leg of the loom ... with a good long strip of something.' 'Well, mayhap that'll do'.* — George Eliot. [from the phrase *(it) may hap*]

mayhem /'mayhem/ *noun* **1** a state of great confusion or disorder. **2** needless or wilful damage. **3** formerly, in law, the crime of wilfully injuring somebody in order to render them defenceless. [Middle English *mayme* the crime of maiming a person, from Old French *mahaim* loss of a limb, from *maynier* to maim]

maying *or* **Maying** *noun archaic* the celebrating of May Day.

mayn't /'maynt/ *contraction* may not.

mayonnaise /maya'nayz/ *noun* a thick dressing, e.g. for salad, made with egg yolks, vegetable oil, and vinegar or lemon juice. [French *mayonnaise*, prob from *mahonnais* of Mahon, port and capital of Minorca]

mayor /mea/ *noun* the chief executive or nominal head of a city or borough. ➤➤ **mayoral** *adj*. [Middle English *maire* via Old French from Latin *major* greater]

mayoralty /'mearalti/ *noun* (*pl* **mayoralties**) the office or term of office of a mayor. [Middle English *mairaltee* from Old French *mairalté* from *maire* mayor]

mayoress /'mearis, mea'res/ *noun* **1** the wife of a mayor. **2** a woman who is a mayor.

maypole *noun* a tall ribbon-wreathed pole forming a centre for dances, *esp* on May Day.

May queen *noun* a girl chosen to preside over a May Day festival.

mayst /mayst/ *verb archaic* second person sing. present of MAY[1].

mayweed *noun* **1** a foul-smelling Eurasian plant with white flowers like daisies: *Anthemis cotula*. **2** a similar related plant that is scentless: *Tripleurospermum inodurum*. [Old English *mægtha* mayweed + WEED[1]]

maze[1] /mayz/ *noun* **1a** a network of paths designed to confuse and puzzle those who attempt to walk through it. **b** a drawn representation of such a network, designed as a puzzle. **c** something intricately or confusingly complicated: *a maze of regulations*. **2** *archaic* a state of bewilderment: *I'm in a maze yet, like a dog in a dancing-school* — Congreve. ➤➤ **mazy** *adj*. [Middle English, prob from AMAZE]

maze[2] *verb trans archaic or dialect* to bewilder or perplex (somebody): *The spring, the summer, the ... autumn, angry winter, change their wonted liveries; and the mazed world ... now knows not which is which* — Shakespeare. [Middle English *mazen*; prob related to Old English *āmasian* to confuse: see AMAZE]

mazel tov /'maz(ə)l tof, tov/ *interj* used by Jews: well done; congratulations. [Hebrew *mazzāl ṭōḇ*, literally 'good star']

mazer /'mayzə/ *noun* a large drinking bowl orig of a hard wood. [Middle English from Old French *mazere*, of Germanic origin]

mazuma /mə'zoohmə/ *noun NAmer, informal* money. [Yiddish *mezumen* from Hebrew *mĕzummān* fixed, appointed]

mazurka /mə'zuhkə/ *noun* **1** a Polish folk dance in moderate triple time. **2** music for such a dance. [via French from Polish *mazurka* woman of the province Mazovia]

mazzard /'mazəd/ *noun* a sweet cherry, *esp* a wild sweet cherry used as a rootstock for grafting. [origin unknown]

MB *abbr* Bachelor of Medicine. [Latin *Medicinae Baccalaureus*]

Mb *abbr* megabyte(s).

MBA *abbr* Master of Business Administration.

mbaqanga /(ə)mbah'kanggə/ *noun* a style of popular music in S Africa. [Zulu *umbaqanga* mixture]

MBE *abbr* Member of the Order of the British Empire.

mbira /(ə)m'biərə/ *noun* an African musical instrument that consists of tuned metal or wooden strips mounted on a gourd resonator or wooden box, which vibrate when plucked with the thumb or fingers. [of Bantu origin]

MBO *abbr* management buyout.

MC *abbr* **1** Master of Ceremonies. **2** *NAmer* Member of Congress. **3** *Brit* Military Cross. **4** Monaco (international vehicle registration).

Mc *abbr* megacycle(s).

MCC *abbr* Marylebone Cricket Club.

mcg *abbr* microgram.

MCh *abbr* Master of Surgery. [Latin *Magister Chirurgiae*]

MCom *abbr* Master of Commerce.

MD *abbr* **1** Doctor of Medicine. **2** *Brit* Managing Director. **3** mentally deficient. **4** Maryland (US postal abbreviation). **5** Moldova (international vehicle registration). [(sense 1) Latin *Medicinae Doctor*]

Md[1] *abbr* the chemical symbol for mendelevium.

Md[2] *abbr* Maryland.

MDF *abbr* medium density fibreboard.

MDMA *abbr* methylenedioxymethamphetamine (the drug Ecstasy).

MDT *abbr* Mountain Daylight Time.

ME *abbr* **1** Middle English. **2** myalgic encephalomyelitis. **3** Maine (US postal abbreviation).

Me *abbr* **1** Maine. **2** Maître.

me[1] /mee/ *pronoun* used as the objective case: I: *He looked at me; You're fatter than me; It's me*. [Old English *mē*]

me[2] *noun* something suitable for me: *That dress isn't really me*.

me[3] *or* **mi** /mee/ *noun* in music, the third note of a major scale in the tonic sol-fa system, or the note E in the fixed-doh system. [Middle English *mi*: see GAMUT]

mea culpa /,mayah 'koolpah, 'kulpə/ *noun* a formal or humorous acknowledgment of personal fault. [Latin *mea culpa* through my fault]

mead[1] /meed/ *noun* a fermented alcoholic drink made of water, honey, malt, and yeast: *All that can be said against mead is that 'tis rather heady* — Hardy. [Old English *medu*]

mead[2] *noun archaic or literary* a meadow: *the myriad cricket of the mead* — Tennyson. [Old English *mæd*]

meadow /'medoh/ *noun* an area of moist low-lying usu level grassland. [Old English *mædwe*]

meadowlark *noun* any of several species of N American songbirds that are largely brown and buff and typically have a yellow breast marked with a black crescent: genus *Sturnella*.

meadow saffron *noun* a lilac-flowered European crocus: *Colchicum autumnale*. Also called NAKED LADIES.

meadowsweet *noun* a tall Eurasian plant of the rose family with creamy-white fragrant flowers: *Filipendula ulmaria*.

meagre (*NAmer* **meager**) /'meegə/ *adj* **1** deficient in quality or quantity: *meagre helpings*. **2** having little flesh: *his meagre frame*. ➤➤ **meagrely** *adv*, **meagreness** *noun*. [Middle English *megre* via French from Latin *macr-, macer* lean]

meal[1] /meel, miəl/ *noun* **1** the portion of food taken or provided at one time to satisfy appetite. **2** the time of eating a meal. ✳ **make a meal of something** *informal* to carry something out in an unduly laborious way. [Old English *mæl*]

meal[2] *noun* **1** the usu coarsely ground seeds of a cereal grass or pulse. **2** a product resembling this, *esp* in texture. [Old English *melu*]

mealie /'meeli/ *noun SAfr* an ear of maize. [Afrikaans *mielie* via Portuguese from Latin *milium* millet]

meals on wheels *pl noun* (*treated as sing. or pl*) a service whereby meals are brought to the housebound.

meal ticket *noun informal* somebody or something that can be milked as a source of income: *Some lawyers were deliberately spinning out cases and were on to a meal ticket* — The Scotsman. [from US sense of a voucher entitling the holder to a meal]

mealworm *noun* the larva of the meal beetle that infests grain products and is often raised as food for insect-eating animals, bait for fishing, etc: *Tenebrio molitor*.

mealy *adj* (**mealier, mealiest**) **1** soft, dry, and crumbly. **2** containing meal. **3** covered with meal or fine granules. **4** said *esp* of a horse: flecked with another colour. **5** pallid or blanched: *a mealy complexion*. ➤➤ **mealiness** *noun*.

mealybug *noun* any of numerous scale insects with a white powdery covering that are pests, *esp* of fruit trees: family Pseudococcidae.

mealy-mouthed *adj* hypocritically unwilling to speak plainly or directly, e.g. for fear of incurring odium.

mean[1] /meen/ *adj* **1** not generous; stingy. **2** characterized by petty malice; spiteful or nasty: *a mean trick*. **3** particularly bad-tempered, unpleasant, or disagreeable: *the meanest horse I ever saw; That was a mean storm last night*. **4** of poor shabby inferior quality or status: *the meaner quarters of the city*. **5** lacking distinction or eminence;

merely ordinary: *the meanest flower that blows* — Wordsworth; *no mean feat.* **6** *dated* of low social position; humble: *of mean birth.* **7** *informal* excellent or impressive: *He blows a mean trumpet!* ➤➤ **meanly** *adj,* **meanness** *noun.* [Old English *gemæne*]

mean² *verb trans (past tense and past part.* **meant** /ment/) **1** to have (something) in mind as a purpose; to intend (it): *I mean to go; She meant no offence.* **2** to serve or intend to convey, produce, or indicate (something); to signify (it): *'Nisi' means 'unless'; Red means danger; This means war.* **3** to intend (something) for a particular use or purpose: *It isn't meant to relieve pain.* **4** (*usu* + to) to have significance or importance: *Her family means a lot to her; The remark meant nothing to me.* ✳ **I mean** used to correct, explain, or expatiate: *Are you bringing Samantha, I mean Sacha?; Have you got change? For the meter, I mean; Shall we leave now? I mean, there's nothing to stay for.* **mean well** to have good intentions. [Old English *mænan*]

mean³ *noun* **1** a middle point between extremes. **2** a value that lies within a range of values and is estimated according to a prescribed law; *esp* an arithmetic mean. [MEAN⁴]

mean⁴ *adj* **1** occupying a position about midway between extremes; average: *the mean temperature.* **2** occupying a middle position; intermediate in space, order, time, kind, or degree. [Middle English *mene* from early French *meien* from Latin *medianus* median]

meander¹ /mɪˈandə/ *verb intrans* (**meandered, meandering**) **1** said of a river or road: to follow a winding or intricate course. **2** to wander aimlessly or casually without definite direction. ➤➤ **meandering** *adj,* **meanderingly** *adv.*

meander² *noun* **1** a turn or winding of a stream. **2** a winding path, course, or pattern.

Word history
Latin *maeander* from Greek *Maiandros* (now *Menderes*), a river in Asia Minor. The Menderes is supposed to have given the legendary figure Daedalus the idea of building a labyrinth in which to imprison the Minotaur.

mean deviation *noun* in statistics, the mean of the values of the numerical differences between the numbers of a set, e.g. statistical data, and their mean or MEDIAN² (value in the middle of the range).

meanie or **meany** /ˈmeeni/ *noun* (*pl* **meanies**) *informal* a narrow-minded or ungenerous person.

meaning¹ *noun* **1** that which is conveyed or which one intends to convey, *esp* by language: *some word that teems with hidden meaning – like Basingstoke* — W S Gilbert. **2** significant quality; value: *It gives a new meaning to life; This has no meaning in law.* **3** implication of a hidden or special significance: *a glance full of meaning.* **4** sense or significance: *What was the meaning of his dream?*

meaning² *adj* significant or expressive: *She shot him a meaning glance.* ➤➤ **meaningly** *adv.*

meaningful /ˈmeeningf(ə)l/ *adj* **1** having meaning; significant. **2** having a hidden or special significance; expressive: *a meaningful glance.* **3** having a purpose; worthwhile: *She was looking for a deep and meaningful relationship.* ➤➤ **meaningfully** *adv,* **meaningfulness** *noun.*

meaningless *adj* **1** devoid of meaning. **2** having no purpose; futile. ➤➤ **meaninglessly** *adv,* **meaninglessness** *noun.*

mean life *noun* the average time during which an atom, nucleus, or other, usu unstable, system exists in a particular form.

means *pl noun* **1** (*treated as sing. or pl*). **a** that which enables a desired purpose to be achieved: *the increasing use of email as a means of communication; the means of production.* **b** the method used to attain an end: *They used any means at their disposal.* **2** (*treated as pl*) resources available for disposal; *esp* wealth: *a man of means.* ✳ **by all means** of course; certainly: *go ahead by all means.* **by any means** (*in negative contexts*) at all: *He won't be persuaded by any means.* **by means of** with the help or use of: *She escaped by means of a ladder.* **by no means** not at all; in no way: *He is by no means rich.*

mean solar time *noun* = MEAN TIME.

means test *noun* an examination into somebody's financial state to determine their eligibility for public assistance, for a student grant, etc.

means-test *verb trans* to subject (somebody) to, or make (something) conditional on, a means test.

mean sun *noun* a fictitious sun used for timekeeping that moves at a constant rate along the celestial equator.

meant /ment/ *verb* past tense and past part. of MEAN².

meantime¹ *noun* the intervening time: *You pack, and in the meantime I'll phone the station.*

meantime² *adv* meanwhile.

mean time *noun* time that is based on the motion of the MEAN SUN (fictitious sun used for timekeeping): compare APPARENT TIME.

meanwhile¹ *adv* **1** during the intervening time: *I'll see you later, but meanwhile, get some sleep.* **2** during the same period: *Meanwhile, down on the farm, things were happening.*

meanwhile² *noun* the meantime: *In the meanwhile, please don't do anything silly.*

meany *noun* (*pl* **meanies**) see MEANIE.

measles /ˈmeezlz/ *pl noun* (*treated as sing.*) **1** an infectious viral disease, usu affecting children, marked by a rash of distinct red circular spots and high fever. **2** infestation with larval tapeworms, *esp* in pigs or pork. [(sense 1) Middle English *meseles,* pl of *mesel* spot characteristic of measles, an alteration (influenced by *mesel* leper) of *masel*; (sense 2) Middle English *mesel* infested with tapeworms or leprous, via Old French from Latin *misellus* leper, wretch, dimin. of *miser* miserable]

measly /ˈmeezli/ *adj* (**measlier, measliest**) **1** *informal* contemptibly small or few, worthless or insignificant: *They offered us a measly £50 for the lot.* **2** infected with measles. **3** containing larval tapeworms: *measly pork.*

measurable /ˈmezh(ə)rəbl/ *adj* capable of being measured; *specif* large or small enough to be measured. ➤➤ **measurability** /mezh(ə)rəˈbiliti/ *noun,* **measurably** *adv.*

measure¹ *verb trans* **1a** to ascertain the size, amount, or degree of (something) in terms of a standard unit or in comparison with something else: *We measured the rainfall over one month.* **b** to have (a specified measurement): *The carpet measured 3m by 2m.* **c** (+ out) to take or allot (something) in measured amounts: *Measure out 60g of flour.* **2a** to estimate or appraise the quality, value, etc of (something): *Some improvements in the school were easy to measure.* **b** (+ against) to judge (somebody or something) by a criterion. **3** to choose or control (something) with cautious restraint; to regulate (it): *He measured his words to suit the occasion.* **4** *archaic* to travel over (a certain distance); to traverse (it). ➤ *verb intrans* to take or make a measurement. [Middle English *mesure* via Old French from Latin *mensura* from *mensus,* past part. of *metiri* to measure]

measure² *noun* **1a** a step planned or taken to achieve an end: *We must take measures to improve sales.* **b** a proposed legislative act or bill. **2a** a standard or unit of measurement: *The metre is a measure of length.* **b** a system of standard units of measure: *metric measure.* **3** an instrument or utensil for measuring. **4** a measured quantity: *a measure of whisky.* **5a** an appropriate or due portion: *We must give them their just measure.* **b** a moderate extent, amount, or degree: *With the new job came a measure of respectability.* **6a** poetic rhythm measured by quantity or accent; metre. **b** musical time. **c** a metrical unit; a foot. **7** *NAmer* the notes and rests that form a bar of music. **8** *archaic* a slow and stately dance. **9** the width of a full line of type or print. **10** (*in pl*) rock strata: *coal measures.* ✳ **beyond measure** to a great extent: *Her singing annoyed him beyond measure.* **for good measure** in addition to the main item or to what is strictly necessary. **get the measure of** to get to know the character or abilities of (somebody) or the nature or requirements of (something).

measured *adj* **1** rhythmical; *esp* slow and regular: *a measured tread.* **2** carefully controlled or thought out: *a measured remark.* ➤➤ **measuredly** *adv.*

measureless *adj* having no observable limit; immeasurable.

measurement *noun* **1** the act or an instance of measuring. **2** a figure, extent, or amount obtained by measuring. **3** a system of standard measuring units.

measure up *verb intrans* to have the necessary ability, skill, or qualities; to be adequate. ➤ *verb trans* to measure (something): *We measured up the room to plan the new kitchen.*

measuring worm *noun* = LOOPER (1).

meat /meet/ *noun* **1** animal flesh used as food. **2** *chiefly NAmer* the edible part of something as distinguished from a husk, shell, or other covering. **3** *archaic* food; *esp* solid food as distinguished from drink. **4** the core or essence of something. ✳ **be meat and drink to 1** *Brit* to be a source of real enjoyment to (somebody). **2** *Brit* to be a routine task for (somebody). **easy meat** *informal* an easy prey. **meat and potatoes** *chiefly NAmer* basic or everyday aspects or matters. ➤➤ **meatless** *adj.* [Old English *mete*]

meatball *noun* **1** a small ball-shaped mass of minced meat, usu beef, for cooking. **2** *NAmer, informal* a stupid person.

meatloaf *noun* a dish consisting of minced meat, usu with flavourings, made into the shape of a loaf and baked.

meatus /mi'aytəs/ *noun* (*pl* **meatuses** *or* **meatus**) the opening to the outside of a natural body passage. [Latin *meatus* passage, course, from *meare* to go, pass: see PERMEATE]

meaty /'meeti/ *adj* (**meatier**, **meatiest**) **1** consisting of, tasting like, or with a similar texture to meat. **2** strong-looking, fleshy, or heavily built. **3** rich in ideas or points to think about or discuss. ⟫⟫ **meatily** *adv*, **meatiness** *noun*.

Mecca /'mekə/ *noun* a place regarded as a goal by a specified group of people: *Liverpool is a Mecca for Beatles fans*. [named after *Mecca*, city in Saudi Arabia, birthplace of the prophet Muhammad and holy city of Islam]

Meccano /mi'kahnoh/ *noun trademark* a toy construction set, largely made up of perforated strips of metal or plastic. [invented word based on MECHANICAL[1]]

mech. *abbr* **1** mechanic. **2** mechanical. **3** mechanics.

mechanic /mi'kanik/ *noun* **1** a skilled worker who repairs or maintains machinery. **2** *archaic* a manual worker; an artisan. [prob from early French *mechanique*, *mecanique* (adj and noun) via Latin from Greek *mēchanikos* from *mēchanē* machine: see MACHINE[1]]

mechanical[1] *adj* **1a** operated by a machine or machinery. **b** relating to machinery or machines. **2** done as if by machine; lacking in spontaneity. **3** of, dealing with, or in accordance with the principles of mechanics: *mechanical energy*; *mechanical engineering*. **4** in philosophy, said of a theory: explaining phenomena by the laws of physics and chemistry. ⟫⟫ **mechanically** *adv*, **mechanicalness** *noun*. [Middle English *mechanicall*, ultimately from Greek *mēchanikos*: see MECHANIC]

mechanical[2] *noun* **1** (*in pl*) the working parts of something, e.g. a car. **2** *archaic* a manual worker.

mechanical advantage *noun* the ratio of the force that performs the useful work of a machine to the force that is applied to the machine.

mechanical drawing *noun* a drawing, e.g. of a machine or architectural plan, done with the aid of instruments.

mechanical engineering *noun* the branch of engineering concerned with the design, construction, and operation of machines. ⟫⟫ **mechanical engineer** *noun*.

mechanician /mekə'nish(ə)n/ *noun* a person who designs or makes machinery.

mechanics *pl noun* **1** (*treated as sing. or pl*) the branch of science that deals with energy and forces, and their effect on moving and stationary bodies. **2** (*treated as sing. or pl*) the practical application of mechanics to the design, construction, or operation of machines or tools. **3** (*treated as pl*) the working parts of something. **4** (*treated as pl*) the functional details of something.

mechanise /'mekəniez/ *verb trans* see MECHANIZE.

mechanism /'mekəniz(ə)m/ *noun* **1** a set of moving parts designed to perform a particular function, *esp* inside a piece of machinery. **2** a process or technique for achieving a result. **3** in philosophy, a theory that all natural phenomena are mechanically determined and capable of explanation by the laws of physics and chemistry. ⟫⟫ **mechanist** *noun*. [Latin *mechanismus* from Greek *mēchanē* machine: see MACHINE[1]]

mechanistic /mekə'nistik/ *adj* relating to the doctrine of mechanism. ⟫⟫ **mechanistically** *adv*.

mechanize *or* **mechanise** /'mekəniez/ *verb trans* **1a** to equip (e.g. a factory) with machinery, *esp* in order to replace human or animal labour. **b** to equip (a force) with armed and armoured motor vehicles. **2** to make (something) mechanical, automatic, or monotonous. ⟫⟫ **mechanization** /-'zaysh(ə)n/ *noun*, **mechanizer** *noun*.

mechano- *comb. form* forming words, with the meaning: involving mechanical processes; mechanical: *mechanotherapy*.

mechanoreceptor /'mekənoh·riseptə/ *noun* a sensory end organ of a nerve, e.g. a touch receptor, that responds to a mechanical stimulus, e.g. a change in pressure or tension. ⟫⟫ **mechanoreceptive** /-tiv/ *adj*.

mechanotherapy /,mekənoh'therəpi/ *noun* the treatment of clinical disorders or injuries by manual or mechanical means, *esp* by providing specific exercises.

Mechlin /'meklin/ *noun* = MECHLIN LACE.

Mechlin lace *noun* a variety of PILLOW LACE (lace made using bobbins on a padded surface), used in dressmaking and millinery. It is generally characterized by delicate floral patterns outlined with a heavier thread. [named after *Mechlin* (now *Mechelen*), a town in N Belgium, where the lace was orig produced]

MEcon /,em i'kon/ *abbr* Master of Economics.

meconium /mi'kohni·əm/ *noun* a dark greenish mass that accumulates in the bowels during foetal life and is discharged shortly after birth. [via Latin from Greek *mēkōnion* poppy juice, from *mēkōn* poppy]

meconopsis /meekə'nopsis/ *noun* (*pl* **meconopses** *or collectively* **meconopsis** /-'nopseez/) any of a genus of ornamental Eurasian poppies, including the blue poppy: genus *Meconopsis*. [Latin genus name, from Greek *mēkōn* poppy]

MEd /,em 'ed/ *abbr* Master of Education.

Med /med/ *noun* (**the Med**) *informal* the Mediterranean Sea. [short for *Mediterranean*]

med. *abbr* **1** medical. **2** medicine. **3** medieval. **4** medium.

médaillon /may'dieyonh/ *noun* (*pl* **médaillons** /may'dieyonh/) a small round cut of meat or fish: *médaillons of lamb*. [French *médaillon*, literally 'medallion']

medal /'medl/ *noun* a piece of metal with a stamped design, emblem, inscription, etc that commemorates a person or event or is awarded for excellence or achievement. ⟫⟫ **medalled** *adj*, **medallic** /mi'dalik/ *adj*. [early French *medaille* from Old Italian *medaglia* coin worth half a denarius, medal, from late Latin *medialis* middle, from Latin *medius*]

medalist *noun NAmer* see MEDALLIST.

medallion /mi'dalyən/ *noun* **1** a pendant in the shape of a medal. **2** a decorative tablet, panel, etc, often bearing a figure or portrait in relief. [French *médaillon* from Italian *medaglione*, augmentative of *medaglia*: see MEDAL]

medallist (*NAmer* **medalist**) *noun* **1** a person who has received a medal as an award, *esp* for sporting achievement. **2** a designer, engraver, or maker of medals.

medal play *noun* golf scored by the number of strokes played; stroke play.

meddle /'medl/ *verb intrans* (*usu* + in/with) to interest oneself in what is not one's concern; to interfere in something unduly. ⟫⟫ **meddler** *noun*. [Middle English *medlen* from Old French *mesler*, *medler*, ultimately from Latin *miscēre* to mix: see MIX[1]]

meddlesome /'medls(ə)m/ *adj* given to interfering in other people's business, or characterized by a desire to interfere or invade people's privacy: *It seemed to her that her aunt was meddlesome; and from this came a vague apprehension that she would spoil something —* Henry James. ⟫⟫ **meddlesomely** *adv*, **meddlesomeness** *noun*.

Mede /meed/ *noun* a native or inhabitant of ancient Media in Persia. ⟫⟫ **Median** *noun and adj*. [Middle English via Latin *Medus* from Greek *Mēdos*]

medevac[1] *or* **medivac** /'medivak/ *noun NAmer* the transport by air of people who need medical attention. [blend of MEDICAL[1] + *evacuation* (see EVACUATE)]

medevac[2] *or* **medivac** *verb trans* (**medevacked** *or* **medevaced**, **medevacking** *or* **medevacing**) to transport (a patient) by air to a place providing medical attention.

media[1] /'meedi·ə/ *noun* **1** pl of MEDIUM[1]. **2** the means of communication, such as the press and television, supplying news and information to the general public. **3** (*used before a noun*) relating to, involved in, or staged by the communications media: *a media event*.

Usage note

Media is a plural form, the plural of *medium*: *Television is a medium*; *Television and radio are media*. The form *a media* is grammatically incorrect. The form *the media* meaning 'all the various institutions that spread news and information' should be followed by a plural verb: *The media have shown little interest in this event. He looks forward to an age where the media is redundant – The Guardian*. This last use is incorrect.

media[2] *noun* (*pl* **mediae** /'meedi·ee/) the middle muscular part of the wall of a blood or lymph vessel. [late Latin *media*, fem of *medius* middle]

mediaeval /medi'eevl/ *adj* see MEDIEVAL.

media event *noun* an event staged by the media or specifically in order to attract coverage by the media.

medial /'meedi·əl/ *adj* **1** being, occurring in, or extending towards the middle; median. **2** said of a speech sound: pronounced in the middle of the mouth; central. ➤➤ **medially** *adv.* [late Latin *medialis* from Latin *medius* middle]

median[1] /'meedi·ən/ *adj* **1** *technical* lying in the plane that divides an animal into right and left halves: *a median vein*. **2** of or constituting a statistical median. [via French from Latin *medianus* from *medius* middle]

median[2] *noun* **1a** a statistical value in an ordered set of values below and above which there is an equal number of values, or which is the arithmetic mean of the two middle values if there is no one middle value. **b** a vertical line that divides the HISTOGRAM (type of graph) of a FREQUENCY DISTRIBUTION (frequency with which values of a variable occur) into two parts of equal area. **2a** a line from a point of intersection of two sides of a triangle to the midpoint of the opposite side. **b** a line joining the midpoints of the nonparallel sides of a trapezium. **3** = MEDIAN STRIP. ➤➤ **medianly** *adv.*

median strip *noun NAmer* a central reservation, e.g. between the two halves of a dual carriageway.

mediant /'meedi·ənt/ *noun* in music, the third note of a diatonic scale. [Italian *mediante* from late Latin *mediant-*, *medians*, present part. of *mediare* to be in the middle]

mediastinum /ˌmeedi·ə'stienəm/ *noun* (*pl* **mediastina** /-nə/) **1** the space in the chest between the membranes enclosing the lungs, containing the heart, trachea, etc. **2** a membrane dividing the two parts of an organ or cavity. ➤➤ **mediastinal** *adj.* [Latin *mediastinum*, neuter of *mediastinus* medial, from *medius* middle]

media studies *pl noun* (*treated as sing.*) an academic subject in which the workings, methods, and effects of the mass media are studied.

mediate[1] /'meediayt/ *verb intrans* to intervene between parties in order to reconcile them. ➤ *verb trans* **1** to bring about (a settlement) by mediation. **2** to act as a mediator in (a dispute). **3** to act as intermediary agent in bringing, effecting, or communicating (something). **4** *technical* to transmit or effect (something) by acting as an intermediate mechanism or agency. ➤➤ **mediation** /-'aysh(ə)n/ *noun*, **mediator** *noun*, **mediatory** /--ət(ə)ri/ *adj.* [late Latin *mediatus*, past part. of *mediare* to be in the middle, from Latin *medius* middle]

mediate[2] /'meedi·ət/ *adj* acting through an intervening agent or agency; indirect. ➤➤ **mediately** *adv.*

medic[1] /'medik/ *noun informal* a medical doctor or student. [Latin *medicus* physician]

medic[2] *noun* see MEDICK.

medicable /'medikəbl/ *adj* curable or remediable. [Latin *medicabilis* from *medicare* to heal]

Medicaid /'medikayd/ *noun* in the USA, a system of hospital care and medical insurance for people on low incomes, funded by the government. [MEDICAL[1] + AID[2]]

medical[1] /'medikl/ *adj* relating to physicians or the science or practice of medicine. ➤➤ **medically** *adv.* [via French from late Latin *medicalis* from Latin *medicus* physician, from *mederi* to heal]

medical[2] *noun* an examination to determine a person's physical fitness.

medical certificate *noun* a certificate signed by a doctor giving an assessment of a person's state of health, *esp* of a person's fitness or unfitness for work.

medicalize or **medicalise** /'medikəliez/ *verb trans* to view (something) as a medical problem, *esp* unnecessarily: *The system medicalizes childbirth*. ➤➤ **medicalization** /-'zaysh(ə)n/ *noun*.

medical officer *noun* a doctor who is responsible for health services in an organization, local authority, etc.

medical practitioner *noun* a physician or surgeon.

medical tourism *noun* travel abroad partly or wholly for medical treatment.

medicament /mi'dikəmənt/ *noun* a medicine.

Medicare /'medikeə/ *noun* **1** in the USA, a system of medical insurance for people over 65 years of age, sponsored by the government. **2** in Canada and Australia, a system of universal health care partly financed by taxes. [blend of MEDICAL[1] and CARE[1]]

medicate /'medikayt/ *verb trans* **1** to treat (a patient, wound, etc) medicinally. **2** to impregnate (something) with a medicinal substance: *medicated soap*. ➤➤ **medicative** *adj.* [Latin *medicatus*, past part. of *medicare* to heal]

medication /medi'kaysh(ə)n/ *noun* **1** a medicine, drug, or remedy. **2** treatment with drugs.

Medicean /medi'seeən, -'cheeən/ *adj* of or relating to the Medici family, rulers of Florence from the 15th cent. until 1737, when the line ended. Having acquired great wealth in the 13th cent. through banking and commerce, members of the family presided over a great period of cultural achievement, amassing great libraries and encouraging artists and writers.

medicinal[1] /mə'dis(ə)nl/ *adj* **1** used to cure disease or relieve pain. **2** relating to or involving medicines or drugs. ➤➤ **medicinally** *adv.*

medicinal[2] *noun* a medicinal substance.

medicine /'med(ə)sin/ *noun* **1** the science and art of the maintenance of health and the prevention and treatment of disease, *esp* using nonsurgical methods. **2** a substance or preparation used in treating or preventing disease. **3** among some peoples, an object held to have remedial or magical properties, or the magical power of such an object; a charm or fetish. ✳ **give somebody a taste/dose of their own medicine** to treat somebody in the same unpleasant way that they have treated somebody else. **take one's medicine** to accept one's punishment; to submit to something unpleasant. [Middle English via Old French from Latin *medicina*, fem of *medicinus* of a physician, from *medicus* physician]

medicine ball *noun* a heavy ball used for throwing and catching as a form of exercise.

medicine man *noun* among Native Americans and some other peoples, a healer or sorcerer believed to have supernatural powers; a shaman.

medick or **medic** /'medik/ *noun* any of several species of small plants of the pea family with purple or yellow flowers: genus *Medicago*. [Middle English *medike* via Latin from Greek *mēdikē*, fem of *mēdikos* Median, from *Mēdia* Media, an ancient country of the Persian empire]

medico /'medikoh/ *noun* (*pl* **medicos**) *informal* a medical doctor or student. [via Italian from Latin *medicus* physician]

medieval or **mediaeval** /medi'eevl/ *adj* **1** dating from or typical of the Middle Ages. **2** *informal* extremely old-fashioned or out of date. ➤➤ **medievally** *adv.* [Latin *medius* middle + *aevum* age]

medievalism *noun* **1** medieval qualities, character, or beliefs. **2** devotion to or copying of the institutions, arts, and practices of the Middle Ages.

medievalist *noun* a specialist in or devotee of medieval history, culture, or languages.

medieval Latin *noun* liturgical and literary Latin of the 7th–15th cents.

mediocre /meedi'ohkə/ *adj* of ordinary or average quality. [French *médiocre* from Latin *mediocris*, literally 'halfway up a mountain', from *medius* middle + *ocris* stony mountain]

mediocrity /meedi'okriti, medi-/ *noun* (*pl* **mediocrities**) **1a** the quality or state of being mediocre: *Only mediocrity can be trusted to be always at its best* — Max Beerbohm. **b** mediocre ability or value. **2** a mediocre person.

meditate /'meditayt/ *verb intrans* **1** to empty the mind of thoughts and fix the attention on one matter, *esp* as a religious or spiritual exercise. **2** to engage in deep or serious reflection. ➤ *verb trans* (*often* + on/upon) to focus one's attention on (something); to consider or plan (something) in the mind. ➤➤ **meditative** /-tiv/ *adj*, **meditatively** /-tivli/ *adv*, **meditativeness** *noun*, **meditator** *noun*. [Latin *meditatus*, past part. of *meditari*]

meditation /medi'taysh(ə)n/ *noun* **1** the act or an instance of meditating. **2** a written or spoken communication of the results of extended study of a topic.

Mediterranean /ˌmeditə'rayni·ən/ *adj* **1** of or characteristic of the Mediterranean Sea or the region around it. **2** said of a climate: characterized by hot dry summers and relatively warm but wet winters. **3** said of a white-skinned person: characterized by medium or short stature, slender build, and a dark complexion. ➤➤ **Mediterranean** *noun*. [Latin *mediterraneus* inland, from *medius* middle + *terra* land]

medium[1] /'meedi·əm/ *noun* (*pl* **media** /'meediə/ or **mediums**) **1a** a means of doing something; a vehicle. **b** a channel or means of communication, *esp* one, e.g. television, designed to reach large numbers of people. **2** a material or technical means of artistic expression: *She found watercolour a satisfying medium*. **b** a mode of artistic expression: *He discovered his true medium as a writer*. **3** a substance regarded as the means of transmission of a force or effect: *Air is the medium that conveys sound.* **4** a liquid, e.g. oil or water, with which dry colouring material can be mixed. **5** (*pl* **mediums**) a person through whom others seek to communicate with the spirits of the dead. **6** a middle position or state. **7a** a surrounding or enveloping substance; *esp* a MATRIX (natural material in which a fossil, gem, etc is embedded). **b** a nutrient system for the artificial cultivation of cells or organisms, *esp* bacteria. **c** a liquid or solid in which animal or plant structures are placed, e.g. for preservation. [Latin *medium*, neuter of *medius* middle]

medium² *adj* intermediate or average in amount, quality, position, or degree.

medium frequency *noun* a radio frequency in the range between 300 and 3000 kilohertz.

medium wave *noun chiefly Brit* a band of radio waves, typically used for sound broadcasting, covering wavelengths between about 180m and 600m.

medivac¹ /'medivak/ *noun* see MEDEVAC¹.

medivac² *verb trans* see MEDEVAC².

medlar /'medlə/ *noun* **1** a small brown fruit like a crab apple that is not eaten until it has begun to decay and that is used in preserves. **2** the small Eurasian tree of the rose family that bears this fruit: *Mespilus germanica.* [Middle English *medeler* from early French *meslier, medlier* from *mesle, medle* medlar fruit, via Latin from Greek *mespilon*]

medley /'medli/ *noun* (*pl* **medleys**) **1** a mixture, *esp* a confused mixture. **2** a musical composition made up of a series of songs or short musical pieces. **3** a swimming race in which different strokes are used for different sections of the race. [Middle English *medle* from early French *medlee*, fem of *medlé*, past part. of *medler* to mix]

Médoc /'medok, may'dok/ *noun* (*pl* **Médoc**) a red wine produced in the Médoc district of SW France.

medrese /me'dresay/ *noun* see MADRASA.

medulla /mi'dulə/ *noun* (*pl* **medullae** /-lee/ *or* **medullas**) **1** the inner region of an organ or tissue in the body, e.g. the kidney. **2** the internal tissue of a plant; the pith. ⋙ **medullary** /-ri/ *adj*. [Latin *medulla* pith, marrow]

medulla oblongata /oblong'gahtə/ *noun* (*pl* **medulla oblongatas** *or* **medullae oblongatae** /-tee/) the pyramid-shaped part of the brainstem of vertebrates that merges into the spinal cord. [scientific Latin *medulla oblongata*, literally 'oblong medulla']

medusa /mi'dyoohzə/ *noun* (*pl* **medusae** /-zee/ *or* **medusas**) **1** a jellyfish. **2** the umbrella-shaped free-swimming form of a class of animals related to the jellyfish that produces sperm and eggs for sexual reproduction. ⋙ **medusoid** /-zoyd/ *adj and noun*. [Latin *Medusa*, one of the three Gorgons with snakes for hair; from the resemblance of some species to a head with snake-like curls]

meed /meed/ *noun archaic* just reward, recompense, or compensation: *He must not float upon his watery bier unwept, and welter to the parching wind, without the meed of some melodious tear* — Milton. [Old English *mēd*]

meek /meek/ *adj* **1** patient and without resentment; long-suffering. **2** lacking spirit and courage; timid or submissive. ⋙⋙ **meekly** *adv*, **meekness** *noun*. [Middle English from Old Norse *mjúkr* soft, pliant]

meerkat /'miəkat/ *noun* any of several small flesh-eating S African mammals related to the mongooses, which live in colonies and stand up by their burrows to look out for danger, or as a way of threatening other animals: several species, *esp Suricata suricatta* and *Cynictis penicillata.* [via Afrikaans from Dutch *meerkat* a kind of monkey, from Middle Dutch *meercatte* monkey, from *meer* sea + *catte* cat]

meerschaum /'miəshəm/ *noun* **1** a fine light white clayey mineral that is a form of magnesium silicate, found chiefly in Turkey and used *esp* for tobacco pipes. **2** a tobacco pipe with a bowl made of meerschaum. [German *Meerschaum*, from *Meer* sea + *Schaum* foam]

meet¹ /meet/ *verb* (*past tense and past part.* **met** /met/) ⋙ *verb trans* **1a** to come into the presence of (somebody) by accident or design: *We met in the street; I'll meet you tomorrow for lunch.* **b** to receive or greet (somebody) in an official capacity: *The mayor met the visiting dignitaries.* **c** to become acquainted with (somebody): *Have you met my sister?* **d** to encounter (somebody) as antagonist or foe; to oppose (them): *The teams will meet in the final.* **2** (*often* + with) to encounter or experience (something): *He met his death during the war; Her efforts met with much criticism.* **3** to answer or respond to

(something): *His speech was met with loud catcalls.* **4** to come into contact or conjunction with (something); to join (it): *This is where the river meets the sea.* **5** to conform to (something), *esp* exactly and precisely; to satisfy (it): *The nursery school didn't meet their needs.* **6** to pay (a cost) fully; to settle (it). ⋙ *verb intrans* **1** to become acquainted: *We met at the party.* **2** to come together: *The cars met in a head-on collision; The athletes meet on Wednesdays.* **3** to join at a fastening: *The waistcoat won't meet.* ✳ **meet somebody halfway** to make concessions to somebody. [Old English *mētan*]

meet² *noun* **1** the assembling of participants for a hunt or for competitive sports. **2** an athletics meeting.

meet³ *adj archaic* suitable or proper: *O Caledonia! stern and wild, meet nurse for a poetic child!* — Scott. ⋙ **meetly** *adv*, **meetness** *noun*. [Old English *gemǣte*; related to *mētan*: see METE¹]

meeting *noun* **1** an assembly of people for a common purpose, *esp* for a formal discussion. **2** a coming together, *esp* of two or more people. **3** an organized sporting event, e.g. for horse racing or athletics.

meeting house /'meetinghows/ *noun* a building used for worship by Quakers and some other religious groups.

mefloquine /'meflǝkween/ *noun* a drug used for the prevention or treatment of malaria. [METHYL + FLUORO- + QUINOLINE]

meg- *comb. form* see MEGA-.

mega¹ /'megǝ/ *adj informal* very big, famous, prestigious, or important. [MEGA-]

mega² *adv* extremely or extraordinarily.

mega- *or* **meg-** *comb. form* forming words, with the meanings: **1** great or large: *megalith.* **2** one million (10⁶): *megawatt; megohm.* **3** in computing, 2²⁰: *megabyte.* [Greek *megas* large]

megabit /'megǝbit/ *noun* a unit of computer information equal to one million bits or, strictly, 2²⁰ bits.

megabuck /'megǝbuk/ *noun informal* **1** one million dollars. **2** (*in pl*) a large amount of money.

megabyte /'megǝbiet/ *noun* a unit of computer storage equal to one million bytes or, strictly, 2²⁰ bytes.

megacycle /'megǝsiekl/ *noun no longer in technical use* a megahertz.

megadeath /'megǝdeth/ *noun* used as a unit in predicting the effects of atomic warfare: one million deaths.

megafauna /'megǝfawnǝ/ *noun* the larger land animals inhabiting a particular region or living during a particular geological period.

megaflop /'megǝflop/ *noun* a unit of processing speed for computers, equal to one million, or, strictly, 2²⁰ floating-point operations per second.

megahertz /'megǝhuhts/ *noun* (*pl* **megahertz**) a unit of frequency equal to one million hertz.

megal- *or* **megalo-** *comb. form* forming words, with the meanings: **1** large or of giant size: *megaloblast.* **2** grandiose: *megalomania.* [via Latin from Greek *megal-, megas* large]

megalith /'megǝlith/ *noun* a huge undecorated block of stone; *esp* one used in prehistoric monuments: *I saw the horses: huge in the dense grey – ten together – megalith-still* — Ted Hughes. ⋙ **megalithic** /-'lithik/ *adj*.

megalo- *comb. form* see MEGAL-.

megaloblast /'megǝlohblahst/ *noun* a large abnormal red blood cell that sometimes appears in the blood, *esp* in cases of pernicious anaemia. ⋙ **megaloblastic** /-'blastik/ *adj*.

megalomania /,megǝlǝ'mayni·ǝ/ *noun* **1** an obsessive craving for power or unhealthy delight in wielding it over other people. **2** a mental disorder characterized by delusory feelings of personal omnipotence and grandeur: compare SUPERIORITY COMPLEX. ⋙ **megalomaniac** /-ak/ *adj and noun*, **megalomaniacal** /-mǝ'nie·ǝkl/ *adj*.

megalopolis /megǝ'lopǝlis/ *noun* **1** a very large city. **2** a densely populated urban region embracing one or several metropolises. ⋙ **megalopolitan** /-'polit(ǝ)n/ *noun and adj*.

megalosaur /'megǝlǝsaw, -lohsaw/ *or* **megalosaurus** /,megǝlǝ'sawrǝs, -loh'sawrǝs/ *noun* a very large carnivorous dinosaur of the Jurassic and early Cretaceous periods that walked on two legs. [scientific Latin *megalosaurus*, from MEGALO- + Greek *sauros* lizard]

megaphone /'megǝfohn/ *noun* a hand-held funnel-shaped device used to amplify or direct the voice. ⋙ **megaphonic** /-'fonik/ *adj*.

megapode /'megəpohd/ *noun* any of several species of large birds found in Australia, New Guinea, and nearby islands, that live on the ground and lay their eggs in a large mound of earth and decaying vegetable matter so that they incubate by natural heat: family Megapodiidae. Also called MOUND-BUILDER.

megastar /'megəstah/ *noun informal* a superstar. ⟫⟫ **megastardom** *noun*.

megastore /'megəstaw/ *noun* a superstore, *esp* one that sells a particular type of product.

megathere /'megəthiə/ *noun* an extinct giant ground-living mammal resembling a sloth that lived in America during the Miocene and Pleistocene epochs: genus *Megatherium*. [Latin genus name, from MEGA- + Greek *thērion* wild animal]

megatherium /megə'thiəriəm/ *noun* (*pl* **megatheriums** *or* **megatheria** /megə'thiəri·ə/) = MEGATHERE.

megaton /'megətun/ *noun* an explosive force produced by an atom or hydrogen bomb equivalent to that of one million tons of TNT.

megavolt /'megəvohlt, -volt/ *noun* a unit of electromotive force equal to one million volts.

megawatt /'megəwot/ *noun* a unit of power equal to one million watts.

me generation *noun* a generation of young people in the 1970s and 1980s considered as being intensely concerned with their own well-being and comfortable lifestyle.

Megger /'megə/ *noun trademark* an instrument that generates a high voltage and is used to test and measure the resistance of electrical insulation. [perhaps from MEGOHM]

megilp *or* **magilp** /mə'gilp/ *noun* a mixture of linseed oil and varnish or turpentine used, *esp* formerly, as a thinner for oil paints. [origin unknown]

megohm /'megohm/ *noun* a unit of electrical resistance equal to one million ohms.

megrim[1] /'meegrəm/ *noun archaic* **1** (*in pl*) low spirits. **2** a fancy or whim. **3** migraine. [Middle English *migreime* from early French *migraine*]

megrim[2] *noun* **1** any of several small flatfishes found off the N Atlantic coast, *esp* a European flatfish: *Lepidorhombus whiffiagonis*. **2** = SCALDFISH. [origin unknown]

meibomian gland /mie'bohmi·ən/ *noun* any of the small sebaceous glands in the human eyelid. [named after Heinrich Meibom d.1700, German anatomist]

meiosis /mie'ohsis/ *noun* (*pl* **meioses** /-seez/) **1** a specialized process of nuclear division in gamete-producing cells by which one of each pair of chromosomes passes to each resulting gametic cell which thus has half the number of chromosomes of the original cell and is usually genetically unique: compare MITOSIS, CELL DIVISION. **2** = LITOTES. ⟫⟫ **meiotic** /mie'otik/ *adj*, **meiotically** /mie'otikli/ *adv*. [via Latin from Greek *meiōsis* diminution, from *meioun* to diminish, from *meiōn* less]

Meissen /'mies(ə)n/ *noun* a type of porcelain developed in the 18th cent. at Meissen in Germany.

-meister *comb. form* forming nouns, denoting: a person who is good at a particular thing: *a web-meister; a spin-meister.* [German *Meister* master]

Meistersinger /'miestəzingə (*German* maɪstərziyər)/ *noun* (*pl* **Meistersinger** *or* **Meistersingers**) a member of any of various German guilds formed chiefly in the 15th and 16th cents for the cultivation of poetry and music. [German *Meistersinger*, from *Meister* master + *Singer* singer]

meitnerium /mietniəriəm/ *noun* an unstable radioactive chemical element made artificially by high-energy ion bombardment: symbol Mt, atomic number 109. [named after Lise *Meitner* d.1968, Austrian physicist]

melamine /'meləmin, -meen/ *noun* **1** a chemical compound with a high melting point used *esp* in the making of melamine resins: formula $C_3H_6N_6$. **2** a plastic made from melamine or melamine resin. [German *Melamin*]

melamine resin *noun* a resin that becomes permanently rigid after heating, made from melamine and used in moulded products, adhesives, and coatings.

melan- *or* **melano-** *comb. form* forming words, with the meanings: **1** black or dark: *melanin*. **2** melanin: *melanocyte; melanophore.*

[Middle English via French and Latin from Greek *melan-*, *melas* black]

melancholia /melən'kohli·ə/ *noun* **1** melancholy. **2** *dated* an abnormal mental condition characterized by feelings of extreme depression and worthlessness. ⟫⟫ **melancholiac** /-ak/ *noun*. [late Latin *melancholia* melancholy]

melancholy[1] /'melənkəli, -koli/ *noun* **1** a feeling or state of deep sadness or depression. **2** = MELANCHOLIA (2). **3** = BLACK BILE. ⟫⟫ **melancholic** /-'kolik/ *adj and noun*, **melancholically** /-'kolikli/ *adv*.

Word history

Middle English *malencolie* via French and late Latin from Greek *melancholia*, from *melan-* black + *cholē* bile. An excess of black bile was formerly believed to cause depression.

melancholy[2] *adj* **1** depressed in spirits; dejected: *If there is a hell upon earth, it is to be found in a melancholy man's heart* — Robert Burton. **2** causing sadness; depressing.

Melanesian /melə'neezyən, -zh(y)ən/ *noun* **1** a native or inhabitant of Melanesia, region in the W Pacific. **2** a language group consisting of the Austronesian languages of Melanesia. ⟫⟫ **Melanesian** *adj*.

melange /'maylonhzh, may'lonhzh (*French* melɑ̃:ʒ)/ *noun* a mixture of incongruous elements: *The team were forced to wear a multi-coloured melange of club strips and borrowed jerseys* — Stuart Cosgrove. [French *mélange* from early French *mesler*, *meler* to mix]

melanin /'melənin/ *noun* a dark brown or black pigment in the hair, skin, and eyes of people and animals. It is responsible for tanning when the skin is exposed to sunlight.

melanism /'meləniz(ə)m/ *noun* an increased amount of black or dark-coloured pigmentation of skin, feathers, hair, etc. ⟫⟫ **melanic** /mi'lanik/ *adj*.

melano- *comb. form* see MELAN-.

melanocyte /mi'lanəsiet, 'melənoh-/ *noun* a cell in the EPIDERMIS (outer skin layer) that produces melanin.

melanocyte-stimulating hormone *noun* a hormone from the pituitary gland in vertebrates that produces darkening of the skin: compare MELATONIN.

melanoma /melə'nohmə/ *noun* (*pl* **melanomas** *or* **melanomata** /-tə/) a tumour of the cells in the skin and retina that produce melanin, which may be malignant and can be caused by exposure to sunlight.

melanophore /mi'lanohfaw, 'melənohfaw/ *noun* a melanin-containing pigment-bearing cell, found *esp* in fishes, amphibians, and reptiles.

melanosis /melə'nohsis/ *noun* the abnormal deposition of pigments, *esp* melanin, in the tissues of the body. ⟫⟫ **melanotic** /-'notik/ *adj*.

melatonin /melə'tohnin/ *noun* a hormone from the pineal gland in vertebrates that produces lightening of the skin: compare MELANOCYTE-STIMULATING HORMONE. [prob from *melanocyte* + *serotonin*]

Melba toast /'melbə/ *noun* very thin crisp toast. [named after Dame Nellie *Melba* d.1931, Australian operatic soprano]

meld[1] /meld/ *verb trans* to combine or blend (two or more different substances or things) together to form a single substance or thing. ⟫ *verb intrans* to combine. [blend of *melt* and *weld*]

meld[2] *noun* a combination or blend.

meld[3] *verb trans* to declare (a card or combination of cards) for a score in a card game such as rummy or canasta. [German *melden* to announce]

meld[4] *noun* a run or set of cards that is or can be melded in a card game.

melee /'melay/ *noun* a confused or riotous struggle; *esp* a general hand-to-hand fight. [French *mêlée* from Old French *meslee* from *mesler* to mix]

melic /'melik/ *adj* said of poetry: intended to be sung. [Latin *melicus* from Greek *melikos* from *melos* song: see MELODY]

melilot /'melilot/ *noun* a yellow-flowered plant of the pea family, widely cultivated to enrich the soil and for hay, and that is a common weed of cultivated land: genus *Melilotus*. [Middle English *mellilot* via French and Latin from Greek *melilōtos*, from *meli* honey + *lōtos* clover, lotus]

meliorate /'meeli·ərayt/ *verb* *trans* = AMELIORATE. ➤➤ **melioration** /-'raysh(ə)n/ *noun*, **meliorative** /-rətiv/ *adj.* [late Latin *melioratus*, past part. of *meliorare*, from Latin *melior* better]

meliorism /'meeliəriz(ə)m/ *noun* the belief that the world can be improved by human effort. ➤➤ **meliorist** *adj and noun*, **melioristic** /-'ristik/ *adj.*

melisma /mə'lizmə/ *noun* (*pl* **melismas** *or* **melismata** /-tə/) a group of notes or tones sung on one syllable, *esp* in PLAINSONG (medieval Christian chant). ➤➤ **melismatic** /meliz'matik/ *adj.* [via Latin from Greek *melisma* melody, from *melizein* to sing]

melliferous /mə'lifərəs/ *adj* producing or yielding honey. [Latin *mellifer*, from *mell-, mel* honey + *-fer* -FEROUS]

mellifluent /mə'lifloo-ənt/ *adj* = MELLIFLUOUS.

mellifluous /mə'lifloo-əs/ *adj* said of a sound or voice: sounding sweet and flowing smoothly. ➤➤ **mellifluously** *adv*, **mellifluousness** *noun.* [late Latin *mellifluus*, from Latin *mell-, mel* honey + *fluere* to flow]

mellophone /'meləfohn/ *noun* a circular valved brass instrument with a range similar to that of the French horn. [MELLOW[1] + -PHONE]

Mellotron /'melətron/ *noun* trademark an electronic keyboard instrument in which the sound source is a prerecorded tape.

mellow[1] /'meloh/ *adj* **1** rich and soft: *mellow lighting.* **2a** made gentle by age or experience. **b** relaxed or genial, *esp* because of intoxication. **3** *archaic* said of a fruit: tender and sweet because ripe. **4** said of earth: soft and like loam. ➤➤ **mellowly** *adv*, **mellowness** *noun.* [Middle English *melowe*]

mellow[2] *verb intrans* to become mellow, *esp* to become more genial. ➤ *verb trans* to make (somebody or something) mellow.

melodeon *or* **melodion** /mə'lohdi·ən/ *noun* **1** a type of small accordion used in folk music. **2** a small organ similar to the harmonium, in which the air is drawn through reeds by suction bellows. [German *Melodion* from *Melodie* melody]

melodic /mə'lodik/ *adj* **1** relating to or having melody. **2** said of a part in a musical composition: playing the melody. **3** melodious. ➤➤ **melodically** *adv.*

melodic minor scale *noun* a musical scale that has semitones between the second and third and seventh and eighth steps ascending, and between the second and third and fifth and sixth steps descending: compare HARMONIC MINOR SCALE.

melodion /mə'lohdi·ən/ *noun* see MELODEON.

melodious /mə'lohdi·əs/ *adj* **1** having a pleasant sound or tune. **2** relating to melody. ➤➤ **melodiously** *adv*, **melodiousness** *noun.*

melodist /'melədist/ *noun* **1** a composer of melodies. **2** *archaic* a singer.

melodrama /'melədrahmə/ *noun* **1a** a work, e.g. a film or play, characterized by crude emotional appeal and by the predominance of plot and action over characterization. **b** the dramatic genre comprising such works. **2** sensational or sensationalized events, language, or behaviour. **3** formerly, a sensational drama interspersed with songs. ➤➤ **melodramatic** /-drə'matik/ *adj*, **melodramatically** /-drə'matikli/ *adv*, **melodramatist** /-'dramətist/ *noun.* [modification of French *mélodrame*, from Greek *melos* music + French *drame* drama]

melodramatics /,melədrə'matiks/ *pl noun* overemotional or exaggerated behaviour.

melody /'melədi/ *noun* (*pl* **melodies**) **1** a rhythmic succession of single notes organized as an aesthetic whole; a tune. **2** the principal part in a harmonic composition. **3** an agreeable succession or arrangement of sounds. [Middle English *melodie* via Old French and late Latin from Greek *melōidia* chanting, music, from *melos* musical phrase, song + *aeidein* to sing]

melon /'melən/ *noun* **1** a large, usu round or oval fruit with a hard rind, sweet juicy edible flesh and a central cavity packed with many seeds. **2** the plant of the cucumber family that bears this fruit: *Cucumis melo.* **3** a waxy mass in the head of some whales and dolphins that is believed to focus sound signals. [Middle English via French from late Latin *melon-, melo*, short for Latin *melopepon-, melopepo*, from Greek *mēlopepōn*, from *mēlon* apple + *pepōn* an edible gourd]

melt[1] /melt/ *verb intrans* **1** to become altered from a solid to a liquid state by heating. **2** to dissolve or disintegrate: *These chocolates melt in the mouth.* **3** to be or become mild, tender, or gentle. **4** to disappear as if by dissolving: *His anger melted.* **5** to lose distinct outline;

to blend: *I tried to melt into the background.* ➤ *verb trans* **1** to reduce (a substance) from a solid to a liquid state by heating. **2** (+ down) to melt (e.g. scrap metal) for reuse. **3** to cause (something) to dissolve or disappear. **4** to make (somebody) tender or gentle. ➤➤ **meltable** *adj*, **melter** *noun*, **meltingly** *adv.* [Old English *meltan*; related to Latin *mollis* soft]

melt[2] *noun* **1a** molten material. **b** the mass melted at a single operation. **2** the act or process of melting. **3** *chiefly NAmer* an open sandwich, burger, or other dish topped with melted cheese.

melt[3] *noun* the spleen, *esp* when used as food. [Old English *milte*]

meltdown *noun* **1** the overheating to melting point of the uranium fuel in the core of a nuclear reactor, so that it burns through its container and allows dangerous radioactivity to escape. **2** a catastrophic collapse, e.g. of an economy or market. **3** *informal* a state of furious rage or of mental breakdown.

meltemi /mel'temi/ *noun* a dry northwesterly wind that blows during the summer months in the northeastern Mediterranean. [via modern Greek *meltémi* from Turkish *meltem*]

melting point *noun* the temperature at which a solid melts.

melting pot *noun* **1** a vessel in which metals or other materials are melted down. **2** a place or situation in which diverse ideas, peoples, traditions, etc come together and mix. **3** an uncertain situation; a state of flux: *Her fate was still in the melting pot.*

melton /'meltən/ *noun* a heavy smooth woollen or wool and cotton fabric used for making overcoats and jackets. [named after *Melton* Mowbray, town in Leicestershire where such cloth was made]

meltwater *or* **meltwaters** *noun* water from the melting of ice or snow, *esp* from a glacier.

member /'membə/ *noun* an individual or unit belonging to or forming part of a group or organization, e.g. a team or a church. ➤➤ **membership** *noun.* **1** (**Member**) a person entitled to sit in a legislative body; *esp* a Member of Parliament. **2** a person of a low rank of certain orders of knighthood. **3** a constituent part of a whole, e.g.: **a** in mathematics, an element of a set. **b** in logic, a component of a class. **c** either of the expressions on either side of a mathematical equation or inequality. **d** a part of a sentence, *esp* a clause. **4a** *archaic* a part of the human body, *esp* a limb. **b** the penis. **5** a unit of structure in a plant body. **6** a beam or similar load-bearing structure in a building. [Middle English *membre* via Old French from Latin *membrum* limb]

membership *noun* **1** the state or status of being a member. **2** (*treated as sing. or pl*) the members of an organization, or the number of its members.

membrane /'membrayn/ *noun* **1** a thin pliable sheet or layer covering, lining, or connecting organs or cells in animals and plants. **2** a thin pliable sheet of material. ➤➤ **membraneous** /mem'braynəs/ *adj*, **membranous** /'membrənəs/ *adj.* [Latin *membrana* skin, parchment, from *membrum* limb]

meme /meem/ *noun* a behavioural or cultural trait that is passed on by other than genetic means, e.g. by imitation.

Editorial note
The term 'meme' was coined in 1976 by Richard Dawkins as an example of a replicator, that is, information copied in an evolutionary process. Examples are habits, skills, stories, or games that are passed on by imitation. Memes range from valuable inventions, scientific theories, or artistic creations to 'viruses of the mind' such as chain letters or false beliefs — Dr Susan Blackmore.

➤➤ **memetic** *adj.* [Greek *mimēma*, literally 'that which is imitated', by analogy with *gene*]

memento /mə'mentoh/ *noun* (*pl* **mementos** *or* **mementoes**) something, e.g. a souvenir, that serves as a reminder of past events. [Middle English from Latin *memento* remember, imperative of *meminisse* to remember]

memento mori /'mawri/ *noun* (*pl* **memento mori**) a reminder of mortality, *esp* a human skull. [Latin *memento mori*, literally 'remember that you must die']

memo /'memoh/ *noun* (*pl* **memos**) *informal* a memorandum.

memoir /'memwah/ *noun* **1** a narrative or biography written from personal experience. **2** (*in pl*) an autobiography, *esp* one written by a public figure. **3** a learned essay on a particular topic. **4** (*in pl*) the records of a learned society. ➤➤ **memoirist** *noun.* [French *mémoire* memory, from Latin *memoria*]

memorabilia /ˌmem(ə)rəˈbiliˌə/ *pl noun* objects valued because of their connection with memorable people or events. [Latin *memorabilia*, neuter pl of *memorabilis*: see MEMORABLE]

memorable /ˈmem(ə)rəbl/ *adj* 1 worth remembering; notable. 2 easy to remember. ➤➤ **memorability** /-ˈbiliti/ *noun*, **memorably** *adv*. [Middle English from Latin *memorabilis* from *memorare* to remind, mention, from *memor* mindful]

memorandum /meməˈrandəm/ *noun* (*pl* **memorandums** *or* **memoranda** /-də/) 1 a usu brief communication for internal circulation, e.g. within an office. 2 an often unsigned informal record or communication; a written reminder. 3 a document recording the terms of a legal agreement, the formation of a company, etc. [Middle English from Latin *memorandum*, neuter of *memorandus* to be remembered, gerundive of *memorare*]

memorial[1] /məˈmawriˌəl/ *noun* 1 something, *esp* a monument, that commemorates a person or event. 2 a historical record. 3 a statement of facts addressed to a government or parliament, often accompanied by a petition. 4 a memorandum or note; *specif* an informal diplomatic communication.

memorial[2] *adj* serving to commemorate a person or event. ➤➤ **memorially** *adv*.

memorialize *or* **memorialise** /meˈmawriəliez/ *verb trans* to remember or commemorate (something).

memorize *or* **memorise** /ˈmeməriez/ *verb trans* to commit (facts or information) to memory; to learn (something) by heart. ➤➤ **memorizable** *adj*, **memorization** /-ˈzaysh(ə)n/ *noun*.

memory /ˈmem(ə)ri/ *noun* (*pl* **memories**) 1 the brain's or an individual's ability to remember experience in general or to recall particular experiences: *She was endowed with extraordinary powers of memory.* 2 the store of things learned and retained from an individual's experience: *I searched my memory for his name.* 3 an image or impression of somebody or something stored in the brain: *She had no memory of the incident; It brought back many happy memories of our last visit.* 4 the time within which past events can be or are remembered: *The event was within living memory.* 5 commemorative remembrance: *The townspeople had erected a statue in memory of their previous MP.* 6a a device, *esp* in a computer, into which data can be inserted for storage, and from which it may be extracted when wanted. b the capacity of a device for storing information. 7 the capacity of a material, e.g. metal or plastic, to show effects resulting from past treatment, or to return to a former condition. ✲ **a trip/walk down memory lane** a nostalgic review of events or objects from the past. [Middle English *memorie* via French from Latin *memoria*, from *memor* mindful]

memsahib /ˈmemsahhib, ˈmemsahb/ *noun Indian, dated* used as a term of address: a married European woman. [Hindi *memṣāḥib*, from English *ma'am* + Hindi *ṣāḥib* sahib, from Arabic *ṣāḥib* friend, lord]

men /men/ *noun* pl of MAN[1].

men- *or* **meno-** *comb. form* forming words, denoting: menstruation: *menorrhagia*. [via scientific Latin from Greek *mēn* month]

menace[1] /ˈmenis/ *noun* 1 a person or thing that is threatening or dangerous. 2 a threatening atmosphere or tone. 3 an annoying person. [Middle English via French from Latin *minacia* from *minac-, minax* threatening, from *minari* to threaten]

menace[2] *verb trans* to threaten or show intent to harm (somebody or something). ➤➤ **menacer** *noun*, **menacing** *adj*, **menacingly** *adv*.

ménage /meˈnahzh, mayˈnahzh/ *noun* a household. [French *ménage* from Old French *mesnage* dwelling, ultimately from Latin *mansion-, mansio* mansion]

ménage à trois /ah ˈtrwah/ *noun* (*pl* **ménages à trois** /ah ˈtrwah/) a sexual relationship involving three people, *esp* a situation in which a third person lives with a married couple. [French *ménage à trois* household for three]

menagerie /məˈnajəri/ *noun* 1 a place where animals are kept and trained, *esp* for exhibition. 2 a zoo. [French *ménagerie* from early French *menagerie* management of a household or farm, from *ménage*: see MÉNAGE]

ménages à trois *noun* pl of MÉNAGE À TROIS.

menaquinone /menəkwiˈnohn/ *noun* a vitamin found in putrefying organic matter and synthesized by bacteria in the intestines; vitamin K$_2$. [*methyl* + *naphthoquinone*]

menarche /ˈmenahki/ *noun* the first menstrual period; the onset of menstruation. [scientific Latin *menarche*, from Greek *mēn* month + *archē* beginning]

mend[1] /mend/ *verb trans* 1 to restore (something) to a sound condition or working order; to repair (it). 2 to improve or rectify (something): *She tried to mend her ways; He made an unsuccessful attempt to mend matters.* 3 to add fuel to (a fire). ➤ *verb intrans* 1 to undergo improvement. 2 to improve in health; to heal. ➤➤ **mendable** *adj*, **mender** *noun*. [Middle English *menden*, short for *amenden*: see AMEND]

mend[2] *noun* a mended place or part; a repair. ✲ **on the mend** improving, *esp* in health.

mendacious /menˈdayshəs/ *adj* given to or characterized by deception or falsehood; lying. ➤➤ **mendaciously** *adv*. [Latin *mendac-, mendax* lying, false]

mendacity /menˈdasiti/ *noun* (*pl* **mendacities**) 1 *formal* a tendency to untruthfulness: *Lying! Lying hardly comes into it. I overdo it. I get carried away in an ecstasy of mendacity* — George Bernard Shaw. 2 a lie. [late Latin *mendacitas* from Latin *mendac-, mendax* lying, false]

mendelevium /mendəˈleeviˌəm/ *noun* a radioactive metallic chemical element that is artificially produced: symbol Md, atomic number 101. [scientific Latin *mendelevium*, named after Dmitri *Mendeleev* d.1907, Russian chemist]

Mendelian /menˈdeeliˌən/ *adj* relating to or according with Mendel's laws, the principles of heredity put forward by Gregor Mendel, *esp* the genetic principle that genes occur in pairs, each GAMETE (sex cell) receiving one member of each pair, so that an organism has one gene of each pair randomly passed on from each of its parents. ➤➤ **Mendelian** *noun*, **Mendelism** /ˈmendəliz(ə)m/ *noun*. [named after Gregor *Mendel* d.1884, Austrian botanist]

mendicant[1] /ˈmendikənt/ *noun* 1 a beggar. 2 (*often* **Mendicant**) a friar living off alms. ➤➤ **mendicancy** /-si/ *noun*, **mendicity** /menˈdisiti/ *noun*. [Latin *mendicant-, mendicans*, present part. of *mendicare* to beg, from *mendicus* beggar]

mendicant[2] *adj* 1 given to begging. 2 said of a member of a religious order: dependent on begging.

mending *noun* clothes or other items that need to be mended by sewing or darning.

menfolk *pl noun* men in general, *esp* the men of a family or community.

MEng /ˌem ˈeng/ *abbr* Master of Engineering.

menhaden /menˈhayd(ə)n/ *noun* (*pl* **menhadens** *or collectively* **menhaden**) any of several species of large fishes of the herring family abundant along the Atlantic coast of the USA where they are used for bait or converted into oil or fertilizer: *Brevoortia tyrannus* and other species. [of Algonquian origin]

menhir /ˈmenhiə/ *noun* a single upright roughly shaped monolith, usu of prehistoric origin. [French *menhir*, from Breton *men* stone + *hir* long]

menial[1] /ˈmeeniˌəl/ *adj* 1 said of work: lacking in interest or status and involving little skill. 2 *dated* relating to servants or to their status; lowly: *the situation of governesses, the only one in which even a well-educated woman … can struggle for a subsistence; and even this is a dependence next to menial* — Mary Wollstonecraft. ➤➤ **menially** *adv*. [Middle English *meynial* from *meynie* household, retinue, from Old French *mesnie*, ultimately from Latin *mansion-, mansio* dwelling]

menial[2] *noun* a domestic servant.

Ménière's disease /məˈnyeaz/ *noun* a disorder of the inner ear causing recurrent attacks of dizziness, ringing in the ears, and deafness. [named after Prosper *Ménière* d.1862, French physician]

meningeal /məˈninjiˌəl/ *adj* relating to or in the region of the meninges.

meninges /məˈninjeez/ *noun* pl of MENINX.

meningitis /meninˈjietis/ *noun* inflammation of the meninges (membranes enveloping the brain and spinal cord; see MENINX), usu caused by bacterial, fungal, or viral infection. ➤➤ **meningitic** /-ˈjitik/ *adj*.

meningococcus /məˌningˈgohˈkokəs/ *noun* (*pl* **meningococci** /-ˈkok(s)ee, -ˈkok(s)ie/) a bacterium that causes meningitis of the brain and spinal cord: *Neisseria meningitidis*. ➤➤ **meningococcal** *adj*.

meninx /'meningks, 'meeningks/ *noun* (*pl* **meninges** /məˈninjeez/) any of the three membranes, the dura mater, pia mater, and arachnoid, that envelop the brain and spinal cord. [scientific Latin *meninx* from Greek *mēning-, mēninx* membrane]

meniscus /məˈniskəs/ *noun* (*pl* **menisci** /məˈnisie/ *or* **meniscuses**) **1** the curved concave or convex upper surface of a column of liquid. **2** a lens that is concave on one side and convex on the other. **3** a crescent-shaped body or figure. **4** a fibrous cartilage within a joint, *esp* of the knee. [scientific Latin *meniscus* from Greek *mēniskos*, dimin. of *mēnē* moon, crescent]

Mennonite /'menəniet/ *noun* a member of a Protestant group derived from the 16th-cent. Anabaptist movement in Friesland and characterized by congregational autonomy and rejection of military service. [German *Mennonit*, named after *Menno* Simons d.1561, Frisian religious reformer who founded the group]

meno /'menoh/ *adv* in music, used as an instruction meaning less, e.g. less fast, less loudly. [Italian *meno* less]

meno- *comb. form* see MEN-.

menopause /'menəpawz/ *noun* the natural cessation of menstruation occurring usu between the ages of 45 and 50, or the time in a woman's life at which this occurs. ➤➤ **menopausal** /-'pawzl/ *adj*. [MENO- + Greek *pausis* PAUSE¹]

menorah /miˈnawrə/ *noun* a candelabrum, usu with seven branches, that is a symbol of Judaism. A menorah was used to light the temple in Jerusalem, and they are now used at Hanukkah, when the candles are lit on successive nights. [Hebrew *měnōrāh* candlestick]

menorrhagia /menəˈrayji·ə/ *noun* abnormally heavy bleeding in menstruation.

menorrhoea /menəˈriə/ *noun* normal menstrual bleeding.

mensch /mench/ *noun NAmer, informal* somebody who is honourable, decent, and trustworthy. [Yiddish *mensh* from German *Mensch*, literally 'person']

menses /'menseez/ *pl noun* **1** (*also treated as sing.*) the menstrual flow. **2** (*treated as sing.*) the time of menstruation. [Latin *menses*, pl of *mensis* month]

Menshevik /'menshəvik/ *noun* a member of the less radical wing of the Russian Social Democratic Party before and during the Russian Revolution. They believed in the gradual achievement of socialism by parliamentary methods. ➤➤ **Menshevism** *noun*, **Menshevist** *noun*. [Russian *men'shevik* from *men'she* less; so-called because they formed the minority group of the party]

mens rea /ˌmenz ˈree·ə/ *noun* criminal intent. [Latin *mens rea*, literally 'guilty mind']

men's room *noun chiefly NAmer* a men's toilet.

menstrua /'menstrooə/ *noun* pl of MENSTRUUM.

menstrual /'menstrooəl/ *adj* of or relating to menstruation. [Latin *menstrualis*, from *menstruum* menses, from *mensis* month]

menstrual cycle *noun* the cycle of ovulation and menstruation experienced by women after they reach puberty, and also by some other female primates.

menstruate /'menstrooayt/ *verb intrans* said of a woman or other female primate: to discharge blood, secretions, and tissue debris from the uterus at intervals of approximately 28 days as part of the natural reproductive cycle, if a pregnancy has not occurred. [late Latin *menstruatus*, past part. of *menstruari* to menstruate, from Latin *menstrua* menses]

menstruation /menstrooˈaysh(ə)n/ *noun* the discharging of blood, secretions, and tissue debris from the uterus that recurs in nonpregnant primate females of breeding age at approximately monthly intervals; a single occurrence of this.

menstruous /'menstrooəs/ *adj* = MENSTRUAL.

menstruum /'menstrooəm/ *noun* (*pl* **menstruums** *or* **menstrua** /'menstrooə/) **1** menses. **2** *archaic* in alchemy, a solvent. [Latin *menstruus* monthly; (sense 2) from the comparison made by alchemists between a base metal in a solvent undergoing transmutation into gold and an ovum in the womb being supposedly transformed by menstrual blood]

mensurable /'menshərəbl/ *adj* capable of being measured; measurable. [late Latin *mensurabilis*, from *mensurare* to measure, from *mensura* measure]

mensural /'menshərəl/ *adj* **1** of or involving measurement. **2** of or being POLYPHONIC (several-part vocal) music originating in the

13th cent. with each note having a definite and exact time value. [late Latin *mensuralis* measurable, from Latin *mensura* measure]

mensuration /menshəˈraysh(ə)n/ *noun* **1** measurement. **2** geometry applied to the computation of lengths, areas, or volumes from given dimensions or angles. [late Latin *mensuration-, mensuratio*, from *mensurare* to measure]

-ment *suffix* forming nouns from verbs, denoting: **1** the concrete result, object, or agent of the action specified: *embankment*; *entanglement*. **2** an action or process: *encirclement*; *development*. **3** the place of a specified action: *encampment*. [Middle English via Old French from Latin *-mentum*]

mental /'mentl/ *adj* **1a** relating to the mind or its activity: *mental health*; *mental processes*. **b** relating to intellectual as contrasted with emotional or physical activity: *mental ability*; *a mental age of three*. **2** performed or experienced in the mind: *mental arithmetic*. **3a** of or relating to a psychiatric disorder: *mental illness*. **b** intended for the care of people suffering from a psychiatric disorder: *a mental hospital*. **4** *informal* mad. ➤➤ **mentally** *adv*. [Middle English via French from late Latin *mentalis*, from Latin *ment-, mens* mind: see MIND¹]

mental age *noun* a measure used in psychological testing that expresses an individual's mental attainment in terms of the number of years it takes an average child to reach the same level: compare INTELLIGENCE QUOTIENT.

mental block *noun* a temporary inability to remember something or to carry out a mental task.

mental defective *noun dated* a person who suffers from severe learning difficulties.

mental deficiency *noun dated* the condition of being of below average intelligence and suffering from severe learning difficulties.

mental handicap *noun dated, sometimes offensive* an impairment of a person's intellectual abilities, through brain damage or underdevelopment, that renders him or her unable to live a fully independent life. ➤➤ **mentally handicapped** *adj*.

mentalism *noun* a doctrine that only individual minds are real and that the external world exists or has properties only to the extent that it is represented in a conscious mind. ➤➤ **mentalist** *noun and adj*, **mentalistic** *adj*.

mentality /menˈtaliti/ *noun* (*pl* **mentalities**) **1** a mode of thought; mental disposition or outlook. **2** mental power or capacity; intelligence.

mentation /menˈtaysh(ə)n/ *noun technical* mental activity. [Latin *ment-, mens* mind + -ATION]

menthol /'menthol/ *noun* an alcohol that occurs *esp* in mint oils and has the smell and cooling properties of peppermint. ➤➤ **mentholated** /'menthəlaytid/ *adj*. [German *Menthol* from Latin *mentha* mint]

mention¹ /'mensh(ə)n/ *noun* **1** a brief reference to somebody or something; a passing remark. **2** a formal citation for outstanding achievement. [Middle English *mencioun* via Old French from Latin *mention-, mentio*, from *ment-, mens* mind]

mention² *verb trans* **1** to refer to (somebody or something) briefly in speech or writing. **2** to cite (somebody or something) for outstanding achievement. ➤➤ **mentionable** *adj*.

mentor¹ /'mentaw/ *noun* **1** a wise and trusted adviser. **2** an experienced member of an organization or institution entrusted with training and advising younger or less experienced members. [named after *Mentor*, tutor of Odysseus's son Telemachus in Homer's *Odyssey*]

mentor² *verb trans* (**mentored, mentoring**) to act as a mentor to (somebody). ➤➤ **mentoring** *noun*.

menu /'menyooh/ *noun* (*pl* **menus**) **1a** a list of the dishes that may be ordered, e.g. in a restaurant, or that are to be served, e.g. at a banquet. **b** the dishes themselves. **2** a list of available programs, functions, commands, etc, displayed on a computer screen, from which the user can select a particular option. [French *menu* small, detailed, from Latin *minutus* very small]

meow¹ /mee'ow/ *verb intrans* see MIAOW¹.

meow² *noun* see MIAOW².

MEP *abbr* Member of the European Parliament.

meperidine /məˈperədeen/ *noun* = PETHIDINE. [blend of *methyl* + *piperidine*]

Mephistopheles /mefi'stofəleez/ *noun* a devil in medieval mythology, the one to whom Faust, in the German legend, sold his soul. **≫ Mephistophelean** /mi,fistə'feeli·ən/ *adj*, **Mephistophelian** *adj.*

mephitic /mi'fitik/ *adj* said of a gas or vapour: foul-smelling, noxious, or poisonous. [Latin *mephiticus* from *mephitis* poisonous gas emitted from the earth]

-mer *comb. form* forming nouns, denoting: something that is a specified type of polymer or isomer: *tautomer*. [Greek *meros* part]

mercantile /'muhkəntiel/ *adj* **1** relating to merchants or trading: *mercantile law*. **2** relating to mercantilism. [via French from Italian *mercante* merchant, from Latin *mercant-*, *mercans*, present part. of *mercari* to trade]

mercantilism /'muhkəntəliz(ə)m, -tieliz(ə)m/ *noun* an economic system first prominent in the 17th cent. that was intended to increase the power and wealth of a nation by strict governmental regulation of the national economy. **≫ mercantilist** *noun and adj.*

mercaptan /muh'kaptan/ *noun no longer in technical use* another name for THIOL. [German *Mercaptan* via Danish from medieval Latin *mercurium captans*, literally 'seizing mercury']

Mercator's projection or **Mercator projection** /muh'kaytəz/ *noun* a map projection showing the lines of longitude as parallel evenly spaced straight lines and the lines of latitude as parallel straight lines whose distance from each other increases with their distance from the equator. This projection causes the shapes of large areas to become greatly distorted with increasing distance from the equator: compare PETERS' PROJECTION. [named after Gerardus *Mercator* (Gerhard Kremer) d.1594, Flemish geographer who invented the system of map projection]

mercenary¹ /'muhs(ə)nri/ *noun* (*pl* **mercenaries**) a soldier who is hired to fight for a foreign country. [Middle English in the sense 'hireling', from Latin *mercenarius* from *merced-*, *merces* wages]

mercenary² *adj* acting primarily for financial reward. **≫ mercenariness** *noun.*

mercer /'muhsə/ *noun Brit esp* formerly, a dealer in fine textile fabrics, e.g. silk. **≫ mercery** *noun.* [Middle English from Old French *mercier* merchant, from *mers* merchandise, from Latin *merc-*, *merx*: see MARKET¹]

mercerize or **mercerise** *verb trans* to give (e.g. cotton thread or fabrics) lustre and strength by chemical treatment under tension with an alkali, e.g. caustic soda. [named after John *Mercer* d.1866, English calico printer]

merchandise¹ /'muhchəndies/ *noun* **1** goods for sale, e.g. in a shop. **2** products developed and sold to promote a film, band, etc. [Middle English *marchaundise* from Old French *marcheandise*, from *marcheant* merchant]

merchandise² or **merchandize** /'muhchəndiez/ *verb trans* **1a** to promote the sale of (goods) through skilful packaging and presentation. **b** to publicize (an idea, product, etc). **2** *archaic* to buy and sell (goods) in business. **≫ merchandiser** *noun.*

merchandising /'muhchəndiezing/ *noun* **1** sales promotion, including market research, development of new products, coordination of manufacture and marketing, and effective advertising, presentation, and packaging. **2** commercial products developed to exploit the popularity of something or somebody, e.g. a film, band, or football team.

merchandize /'muhchəndiez/ *verb trans* see MERCHANDISE².

merchant /'muhchənt/ *noun* **1a** a wholesaler. **b** *chiefly NAmer* a shopkeeper. **2** *informal, derog* a person who indulges in a specified activity: *a doom merchant; a squeegee merchant*. **3** (*used before a noun*) of or used in commerce: *merchant ships*. [Middle English *marchant* from Old French *marcheant*, ultimately from Latin *mercatus*, past part. of *mercari* to trade]

merchantable *adj* of commercially acceptable quality; marketable.

merchant bank *noun chiefly Brit* a firm of private bankers that handles bills of exchange and guarantees new issues of securities. **≫ merchant banker** *noun.*

merchantman *noun* (*pl* **merchantmen**) a ship used in commerce.

merchant marine *noun chiefly NAmer* = MERCHANT NAVY.

merchant navy *noun chiefly Brit* the privately or publicly owned commercial ships of a nation, or the crews of these ships.

Mercian /'muhsi·ən/ *noun* **1** a native or inhabitant of the ancient Anglo-Saxon kingdom of Mercia in central England. **2** the dialect of Old English spoken in Mercia. **≫ Mercian** *adj.*

merciful /'muhsif(ə)l/ *adj* **1** having, showing, or inclined to mercy. **2** constituting a benefit or blessing, *esp* a relief from suffering: *Her death was a merciful release.* **≫ mercifully** *adv*, **mercifulness** *noun.*

merciless /'muhsilis/ *adj* having no mercy; pitiless. **≫ mercilessly** *adv*, **mercilessness** *noun.*

mercurial¹ /muh'kyooəri·əl/ *adj* **1a** characterized by rapid and unpredictable changes of mood. **b** lively, quick-witted, fast-talking, and unpredictable. **2** of, containing, or caused by mercury. **3** (**Mercurial**) associated with the planet Mercury. **≫ mercuriality** /-'aliti/ *noun*, **mercurially** *adv.*

mercurial² *noun* a drug or chemical containing mercury.

mercury¹ /'muhkyoori/ *noun* a silver-white heavy poisonous metallic chemical element that is liquid at ordinary temperatures, and is used in thermometers, barometers, etc: symbol Hg, atomic number 80. **≫ mercuric** /muh'khyoorik/ *adj*, **mercurous** /-rəs/ *adj.* [Middle English *mercurie* from Latin *Mercurius* Mercury, god of commerce, skill, etc, and the planet Mercury]

mercury² *noun* any of a genus of poisonous European woodland plants that includes DOG'S MERCURY: genus *Mercurialis*. [Latin genus name, from *mercurialis* of the god Mercury]

mercury lamp *noun* = MERCURY-VAPOUR LAMP.

mercury-vapour lamp *noun* a lamp in which an electric discharge takes place through mercury vapour causing a characteristic greenish blue light that is used for street lighting and as a source of ultraviolet radiation.

mercy¹ /'muhsi/ *noun* (*pl* **mercies**) **1** compassion or forbearance shown *esp* to an offender or an enemy. **2** a fortunate circumstance: *It was a mercy they found her before she froze.* **3** (*used before a noun*) giving or bringing help and relief to people in distress: *a mercy flight; a mercy mission.* **✳ at the mercy of** wholly in the power of (somebody or something); with no way to protect oneself against (them). [Middle English via Old French *merci* from Latin *merced-*, *merces* price paid, wages, from *merc-*, *merx* merchandise]

mercy² *interj archaic* used to express surprise.

mercy killing *noun* the killing of somebody who is suffering from a terminal disease; euthanasia.

mere¹ /miə/ *adj* **1a** being what is specified and nothing else: *a mere child.* **b** *archaic* downright; utter; nothing less than what is specified: *I have … engaged my friend to his mere enemy* — Shakespeare; *people, all swol'n and ulcerous … the mere despair of surgery* — Shakespeare. **2** (**the merest**) the slightest: *I only caught the merest glimpse of the castle.* [Middle English from Latin *merus* pure, unmixed]

mere² *noun literary* a lake, *esp* a small one. [Old English]

mere³ /'meri/ *noun* a ceremonial Maori hand weapon made of bone or greenstone. [Maori *mere*]

-mere *comb. form* forming nouns, denoting: part or segment: *blastomere*. [French *-mère* from Greek *meros* part]

merely *adv* only; simply; no more than.

merengue or **meringue** /mə'renggay/ *noun* a ballroom dance, orig from Dominica and Haiti, in which the dancers take alternate long and short sliding steps, keeping the legs stiff, or a piece of music for this, usu in duple time. [American Spanish *merengue*, ultimately from French *méringue* MERINGUE¹]

meretricious /merə'trishəs/ *adj* **1** attractive in a showy or tawdry way. **2** based on pretence or insincerity; specious. **3** *archaic* of or like a prostitute. **≫ meretriciously** *adv*, **meretriciousness** *noun.* [Latin *meretricius* from *meretric-*, *meretrix* prostitute, from *merēre* to earn]

merganser /muh'gansə/ *noun* any of various usu crested fish-eating and diving sawbill ducks, *esp* the red-breasted merganser: *Mergus serrator.* [scientific Latin *merganser*, from Latin *mergus* a waterfowl (from *mergere*: see MERGE) + *anser* goose]

merge /muhj/ *verb intrans* **1** to combine or unite. **2** to blend or come together gradually without abrupt change. **≻ verb trans** to cause (two or more things) to combine or blend. [Latin *mergere* to dip, plunge]

merger *noun* **1** a combining or combination, *esp* of two organizations, e.g. business concerns. **2** in law, the absorption of one estate, contract, or interest in another.

meridian /mə'ridi·ən/ *noun* **1** a circle on the surface of the earth or other celestial body passing through both poles, or the representation of this on a map or globe. **2** in astronomy, a circle passing through the poles of the CELESTIAL SPHERE (imaginary circle against which stars and planets appear to be placed) and the zenith of a given place. **3** *literary* a high point, *esp* of success or greatness. **4** in acupuncture, one of the pathways in the body along which vital energy is said to flow. [Middle English via French from Latin *meridianus* from *meridies* noon, south, irreg from *medius* mid + *dies* day]

meridional[1] /mə'ridi·ənəl/ *adj* **1** relating to or situated in the south, *esp* of France; southern. **2** relating to a meridian. [Middle English via French from late Latin *meridionalis*, irreg from Latin *meridies*: see MERIDIAN]

meridional[2] *noun* an inhabitant of the south, *esp* of France.

meringue[1] /mə'rang/ *noun* **1** a mixture of stiffly beaten egg whites and sugar baked until crisp. **2** a small cake, cream-filled shell, or other confection made with meringue or having a meringue topping. [French *méringue*]

meringue[2] /mə'renggay/ *noun* see MERENGUE.

merino /mə'reenoh/ *noun* (*pl* **merinos**) **1** a sheep of a fine-woolled white breed originating in Spain. **2** a soft wool or wool and cotton clothing fabric resembling cashmere. [Spanish *merino*]

meristem /'meristem/ *noun* a plant tissue that is the major area of growth and is made up of small cells capable of dividing indefinitely. ⟩⟩ **meristematic** /-'matik/ *adj*. [Greek *meristos* divided (from *merizein* to divide) + English *-em* as in *system*]

merit[1] /'merit/ *noun* **1** worth or excellence. **2** a good level in passing an exam, higher than a pass but lower than a distinction. **3** (*usu in pl*) a good or praiseworthy quality; a virtue. **4** (*in pl*) spiritual credits believed to be earned by performance of righteous acts and to ensure future benefits. **5** (*in pl*) the intrinsic rights and wrongs of a case, *esp* a legal case. ✳ **on its merits** in accordance with its intrinsic good or bad qualities. [Middle English via Old French from Latin *meritum*, from neuter of *meritus*, past part. of *merēre* to deserve, earn]

merit[2] *verb trans* (**merited, meriting**) to be worthy of (something); to deserve (it).

meritocracy /meri'tokrasi/ *noun* (*pl* **meritocracies**) **1** government by people chosen on the basis of their ability. **2** a society in which talented people hold power. **3** a ruling class of talented and educated people. ⟩⟩ **meritocratic** /-'kratik/ *adj*. [MERIT[1] + -O- + -CRACY]

meritorious /meri'tawri·əs/ *adj* **1** deserving of reward or honour. **2** *chiefly NAmer* said of a legal action or claim: likely to succeed on merit. ⟩⟩ **meritoriously** *adv*, **meritoriousness** *noun*. [Middle English from Latin *meritorius* that brings in money, from *merēre*: see MERIT[1]]

merle *or* **merl** /muhl/ *noun Scot or archaic* the European blackbird. [Middle English via French from Latin *merula*]

merlin /'muhlin/ *noun* a small N American and European falcon with pointed wings: *Falco columbarius*. [Middle English *meriloun* from Old French *esmerillon*, of Germanic origin]

merlon /'muhlən/ *noun* any of the solid sections between the indentations of a battlemented parapet. [via French from Italian *merlone*, augmentative of *merlo* battlement]

Merlot /'meəloh, meə'loh/ *noun* **1** a variety of grape used in the production of wine, often blended with Cabernet Sauvignon grapes. **2** a red wine produced from this grape. [French *Merlot*]

mermaid /'muhmayd/ *noun* a mythical sea creature usu represented with a woman's head and trunk and a fish's tail: *Teach me to hear mermaids singing* — John Donne; *I have heard the mermaids singing, each to each. I do not think that they will sing to me* — T S Eliot. [Middle English *mermaide*, from *mere* sea, lake + *maide* maid]

mermaid's purse *noun* the leathery egg case of a skate, ray, or related fish.

merman /'muhman/ *noun* (*pl* **mermen**) a mythical sea creature usu represented with a man's head and trunk and a fish's tail.

-merous *comb. form* forming adjectives, with the meaning: possessing the number of parts specified: *pentamerous*. [via Latin from Greek *meros* part]

Merovingian[1] /meroh'vinji·ən/ *adj* relating to or associated with the Frankish dynasty that ruled in Gaul and part of Germany from about AD 500 to AD 751. [French *mérovingien* from medieval Latin

Merovingi Merovingians, named after *Merovaeus* Merowig d.458, Frankish founder of the dynasty]

Merovingian[2] *noun* a member of the Merovingian dynasty.

merriment /'merimənt/ *noun* light-hearted gaiety or fun.

merry /'meri/ *adj* (**merrier, merriest**) **1** cheerful and lively; jolly. **2** marked by fun, laughter, and enjoyment. **3** *Brit, informal* slightly drunk; tipsy. ✳ **make merry** *literary* to celebrate or indulge in jollity. ⟩⟩ **merrily** *adv*, **merriness** *noun*. [Old English *myrge, merge* pleasant, delightful]

merry andrew /'androoh/ *noun archaic* a clown, jester, or joker.

merry-go-round *noun* **1** a revolving fairground machine with model horses or vehicles that people ride on. **2** a busy round of activity.

merrymaking *noun* happy, festive activity; fun. ⟩⟩ **merrymaker** *noun*.

merrythought *noun chiefly Brit, dated* the wishbone of a bird.

mes- *or* **meso-** *comb. form* forming words, with the meanings: **1** mid or in the middle: *Mesolithic*. **2** intermediate, e.g. in size or type: *mesomorph; meson*. [via Latin from Greek *mesos*: see MID[1]]

mesa /'maysə/ *noun* a usu isolated hill, *esp* in the SW USA, with steeply sloping sides and a level top. [Spanish *mesa* table, from Latin *mensa*]

mésalliance /me'zali·əns/ *noun* a marriage to somebody of inferior social position. [French *mésalliance*, from *més-* MIS[1] + *alliance*]

mescal /me'skal/ *noun* **1** = MAGUEY (IA). **2** a colourless Mexican spirit distilled from the sap of an agave. **3** = PEYOTE (I). [Spanish *mezcal, mescal*, from Nahuatl *mexcalli* mescal liquor]

mescal button *noun* a dried button-like protuberance of a peyote cactus, chewed for its hallucinogenic effect.

mescaline *or* **mescalin** /'meskəlin, -leen/ *noun* a hallucinogenic drug obtained from peyote cacti.

Mesdames /may'dahm/ *noun* pl of MRS.

mesdames /may'dam/ *noun* pl of MADAME.

mesdemoiselles /ˌmaydəmwah'zel/ *noun* pl of MADEMOISELLE.

mesembryanthemum /meˌzembri'anthiməm, mi-/ *noun* (*pl* **mesembryanthemums**) any of a genus of chiefly S African fleshy leaved herbaceous plants with bright flowers: genus *Mesembryanthemum*. [Latin genus name, from Greek *mesēmbria* midday (from *mes-* + *hēmera* day) + *anthemon* flower]

mesencephalon /mesen'sef(ə)lon/ *noun* the midbrain. ⟩⟩ **mesencephalic** /-'falik/ *adj*.

mesenchyme /'mesengkiem/ *noun* a loosely organized fibrous tissue of the MESODERM (embryonic tissue layer) of an embryo, giving rise to such structures as connective tissues, blood, bone, and cartilage. ⟩⟩ **mesenchymal** *adj*. [from Greek *mesos* middle + *enkhuma* infusion]

mesentery /'mez(ə)nteri, 'mes-/ *noun* (*pl* **mesenteries**) any of several folds of the peritoneum of vertebrates, which surround the intestines and connected organs and join them with the rear wall of the abdominal cavity. ⟩⟩ **mesenteric** /mez(ə)n'terik, mes-/ *adj*. [scientific Latin *mesenterium* via early French *mesentere* from Greek *mesenterion*, from *mes-* + *enteron* intestine]

mesh[1] /mesh/ *noun* **1a** the cords, wires, etc that make up a net; a network: *wire mesh*. **b** a woven, knitted, or knotted fabric with evenly spaced small holes. **2** an open space in a net, network, etc. **3a** an interlocking or intertwining arrangement or construction. **b** (*usu in pl*) a web or snare. **4** the contact of teeth in a set of gears: *in mesh*. **5** in computing, a network of connections having two or more connections between each pair of items. **6** in computing, a set of finite elements that represent a geometric object to be modelled or analysed. [prob from early Dutch *maesche*]

mesh[2] *verb intrans* **1** said of the teeth of a gearwheel: to be in or come into mesh. **2** to become entangled. **3** to fit together properly; to coordinate or harmonize. ⟩ *verb trans* **1** to catch or entangle (something). **2** to cause (something) to coordinate or harmonize. **3** to represent (a geometric object) as a set of finite elements. ⟩⟩ **meshed** *adj*.

meshuga *or* **meshugga** *or* **meshugah** /mə'shoohgə, mə'shoogə/ *adj chiefly NAmer, informal* crazy or mad. [Yiddish *meshuge*]

mesial /'meezi·əl/ *adj* relating to or in the region of the plane that divides an animal into right and left halves. ⟩⟩ **mesially** *adv*.

mesic[1] /'meezik/ *adj* containing or requiring a moderate amount of moisture: compare HYDRIC, XERIC: *a mesic habitat; a mesic plant*.

mesic² /'meezik, 'mezik/ *adj* of a meson.

mesmeric /mez'merik/ *adj* **1** exerting a hypnotic influence or having a hypnotic effect; completely absorbing. **2** *archaic* relating to mesmerism. ⋙ **mesmerically** *adv*.

mesmerise /'mezməriez/ *verb* see MESMERIZE.

mesmerism /'mezməriz(ə)m/ *noun* hypnotism, *esp* as formerly practised and expounded by Franz Mesmer and his disciples. [named after F A *Mesmer* d.1815, Austrian physician and hypnotist]

mesmerize *or* **mesmerise** /'mezməriez/ *verb trans* **1** to fascinate (somebody); to rivet (them). **2** *archaic* to hypnotize (somebody). ⋙ **mesmerization** /-'zaysh(ə)n/ *noun*, **mesmerizer** *noun*.

mesne /meen/ *adj* in law, occurring or placed between two other things; intermediate. [Middle English from early French *meien* in the middle: see MEAN⁴]

mesne profits *pl noun* payments that a landlord can claim from a tenant occupying property after the end of a tenancy.

meso- *comb. form* see MES-.

mesoblast /'meezəblast/ *noun* the embryonic cells that give rise to mesoderm. ⋙ **mesoblastic** / 'blastik/ *adj*.

mesocarp /'mezohkahp/ *noun* the middle layer of the PERICARP (ripened ovary wall enclosing the seeds) of a fruit.

mesocephalic /,mesohse'falik/ *adj* having a medium-sized head.

mesoderm /'mesohduhm/ *noun* **1** the middle of the three primary germ layers of an embryo that is the source of bone, muscle, connective tissue, and the inner layer of the skin in the adult: compare ECTODERM, ENDODERM. **2** the tissue that derives from this germ layer. ⋙ **mesodermal** /-'duhml/ *adj*.

Mesolithic /mesoh'lithik/ *adj* relating to or dating from a transitional period of the Stone Age between the Palaeolithic and the Neolithic, extending from about 12,000 to 3000 BC, following the withdrawal of ice sheets and marked by a rising temperature that allowed new types of vegetation to grow. The people were hunter-gatherers who used flint tools, and had not progressed to an agricultural way of life.

mesomorph /'mesohmawf/ *noun* a person with a compact body shape and muscular build: compare ECTOMORPH, ENDOMORPH. ⋙ **mesomorphic** *adj*, **mesomorphy** *noun*. [short for MESODERM + -MORPH]

meson /'meezon/ *noun* any of a group of unstable elementary particles including the pions and kaons that are bosons and have a mass between that of an electron and a proton. ⋙ **mesonic** /mee'zonik/ *adj*. [MES- + -ON²]

mesophyll /'mesohfil/ *noun* the soft tissue forming the internal structures of a leaf between layers of epidermis. [scientific Latin *mesophyllum*, from MESO- + Greek *phyllon* leaf]

mesophyte /'mesohfiet/ *noun* a plant that grows under medium conditions of moisture. ⋙ **mesophytic** /-'fitik/ *adj*.

Mesopotamian /,mesəpə'taymi-ən/ *noun* a native or inhabitant of Mesopotamia. ⋙ **Mesopotamian** *adj*.

mesosphere /'mesohsfia/ *noun* a layer of the upper atmosphere which extends from the top of the stratosphere (50km; 30mi) to an altitude of about 85km (about 50mi) and in which photochemical reactions take place. ⋙ **mesospheric** /-'sferik/ *adj*.

mesothelia /mesoh'theeli-ə/ *noun* pl of MESOTHELIUM.

mesothelioma /,mesohtheeli'ohmə/ *noun* (*pl* **mesotheliomas** *or* **mesotheliomata** /-'tə/) a tumour of the lining of the peritoneum, lungs, heart, etc, often occurring after prolonged contact with blue asbestos dust. [scientific Latin *mesothelioma* from MESOTHELIUM]

mesothelium /mesoh'theeli-əm/ *noun* (*pl* **mesothelia** /-li-ə/) surface tissue derived from mesoderm, which lines the body cavity of an embryo of a vertebrate animal and develops into the linings of the abdomen, heart, and lungs, and into muscle. ⋙ **mesothelial** *adj*. [scientific Latin *mesothelium*, from MESO- + EPITHELIUM]

mesotrophic /mesoh'trohfik/ *adj* said of a body of water: having a moderate amount of dissolved nutrients, e.g. chemical compounds or food: compare EUTROPHIC, OLIGOTROPHIC.

Mesozoic /mesoh'zoh-ik/ *adj* relating to or dating from a geological era (between the Palaeozoic and Cenozoic eras, and including the Triassic, Jurassic, and Cretaceous periods), lasting from about 245 million to about 65 million years ago, and marked *esp* by the appearance of dinosaurs, marine and flying reptiles, and evergreen trees. ⋙ **Mesozoic** *noun*.

mesquite /me'skeet/ *noun* any of several species of spiny trees or shrubs of the pea family that form extensive thickets in the SW USA and Mexico and bear sugar-rich pods, known as mesquite beans, used as a livestock feed: genus *Prosopis*. [Spanish *mesquite* from Nahuatl *mizquitl*]

mess¹ /mes/ *noun* **1** an untidy, disordered, dirty, or generally unpleasant state or condition. **2** *euphem* the excrement of a domestic animal. **3a** a prepared dish of soft or liquid food. **b** a usu unappetizing mixture of ingredients eaten together. **4** a disorganized situation resulting from misunderstanding, blundering, or misconduct. **5** a person whose appearance is untidy or whose life and affairs are in disorder. **6** a place where servicemen or women eat their meals: *the officers' mess*. ✳ **make a mess of** *informal* to perform (a task, etc) incompetently: *I made a mess of my German oral*.

Word history
Middle English *mes* via Old French from late Latin *missus* course at a meal, from *missus*, past part. of *mittere* to put, send. The word originally signified a portion of food, then mixed food, especially for an animal and so, ultimately, an untidy state. Another early meaning was a small group of people sitting together at a banquet and being served from the same dishes. This gave rise to the 'mess' in which soldiers eat.

mess² *verb intrans* **1a** to make a mess. **b** *euphem* said of a domestic animal: to defecate. **2a** (*usu* + with) to handle or play with something, *esp* carelessly. **b** *informal* (*usu* + with) to interfere or meddle with something or somebody. **3** to take meals in a mess: *They messed together during the war.* ⋙ *verb trans* **1** to make (something or somebody) look untidy. **2** to defecate on (something): *He had messed his trousers.*

mess about *verb intrans* **1** to waste time, *esp* by behaving in a silly way. **2** to dabble, potter, or simply work according to one's whim or mood. **3** (*usu* + with) to conduct an affair with somebody: *She was messing about with someone else's husband.* ⋙ *verb trans Brit, informal* to treat (somebody) without due consideration: *Why don't you stop messing him about and give him a definite date?*

message¹ /'mesij/ *noun* **1** a communication in writing, in speech, or by signals. **2** a central theme or idea intended to inspire, urge, warn, enlighten, advise, etc. **3** a communication from a prophet or religious leader. **4** *Scot, Irish* an errand. **5** (*in pl*) shopping. ✳ **be on/off message** *informal* chiefly in politics, to make statements that accord or do not accord with officially approved policy. **get the message** *informal* to understand what somebody is saying. [Middle English via Old French from late Latin *missaticum*, from Latin *missus*, past part. of *mittere* to send]

message² *verb trans* to send (somebody) a message, *esp* an email.

message stick *noun* a stick with symbolic patterns carved on it, traditionally used by Australian aborigines to carry messages from one community to another.

mess around *verb trans and intrans* = MESS ABOUT.

messeigneurs /mese'nyuh/ *noun* pl of MONSEIGNEUR.

messenger¹ /'mesinjə/ *noun* a person who carries a message or does an errand. [Middle English *messangere* from Old French *messagier*, from *message*]

messenger² *verb trans chiefly NAmer* to send (something) by a messenger.

messenger RNA *noun* an RNA that carries the code for a particular protein from the cell's DNA to the RIBOSOME (the specialized structure in a cell) and there acts as a template for the formation of the protein: compare TRANSFER RNA.

mess hall *noun chiefly NAmer* a communal dining room where members of the armed forces have their meals together, or a building containing such a room.

messiah /mə'sie-ə/ *noun* **1** (**the Messiah**). **a** the expected king and deliverer of the Jews. **b** Jesus, regarded by Christians as fulfilling this role. **2** a professed leader of a cause. ⋙ **messiahship** *noun*. [Hebrew *māshīaḥ* and Aramaic *měshīḥā* anointed]

messianic /mesi'anik/ *adj* **1** associated with a messiah or the Messiah. **2** marked by idealistic enthusiasm for a cherished cause. ⋙ **messianism** /mə'sie-əniz(ə)m, 'mesi-ə-/ *noun*. [late Latin *Messias* + Latin *-anicus* as in *romanicus* Romanic]

messieurs /me'syuh, mə'syuhz/ *noun* pl of MONSIEUR.

mess jacket *noun* a short fitted man's jacket reaching to the waist and worn by a military officer as part of a uniform on formal occasions in the mess.

mess kit *noun* **1** a compact kit of cooking and eating utensils for soldiers, campers, etc. **2** formal evening wear worn by military officers in the mess.

messmate *noun* a fellow member of a ship's mess.

Messrs /'mesəz/ *noun* pl of MR. [shortening of French MESSIEURS]

messuage /'meswij/ *noun* in law, a house with its outbuildings and land. [Middle English from Anglo-French, prob alteration of Old French *mesnage*: see MÉNAGE]

mess up *verb trans informal* **1** to make a mess of (something); to spoil (it). **2** to cause (somebody) to be psychologically upset.

messy *adj* (**messier, messiest**) **1** marked by confusion, disorder, or dirt. **2** lacking neatness or precision; slovenly. **3** unpleasantly or tryingly difficult to deal with. ➤➤ **messily** *adv*, **messiness** *noun*.

mestiza /me'steezə/ *noun* (*pl* **mestizas**) a woman of mixed European and Native American ancestry. [Spanish *mestiza*, fem of *mestizo* mixed, via late Latin *mixticius* from Latin *mixtus*, past part. of *miscēre* to mix]

mestizo /me'steezoh/ *noun* (*pl* **mestizos**) a man of mixed European and Native American ancestry. [Spanish *mestizo*: see MESTIZA]

met /met/ *verb* past tense and past part. of MEET[1].

met. *abbr* **1** meteorological. **2** meteorology. **3** metropolitan.

meta- *or* **met-** *prefix* forming words, denoting: **1a** a position behind or beyond: *metacarpus*. **b** a later or more highly organized or specialized form: *metazoan*. **2** a change or transformation: *metamorphosis; metabolism*. **3** something more comprehensive or of a higher or second order: *metapsychology; metalanguage*. **4** a substitution at two positions in the benzene ring that are separated by one carbon atom: compare ORTH-, PARA-[1]. [via Latin from Greek *meta* among, with, after]

metabolise /mi'tabəliz/ *verb trans and intrans* see METABOLIZE.

metabolism /mə'tabəliz(ə)m/ *noun* all the processes involved in the building up and destruction of living tissue; *specif* the chemical changes in living cells by which energy is provided and new material is assimilated. ➤➤ **metabolic** /metə'bolik/ *adj*, **metabolically** *adv*. [Greek *metabolē* change, from *metaballein* to change]

metabolite /mə'tabəliet/ *noun* **1** a product of metabolism. **2** a substance essential to the metabolism of a particular organism or to a particular metabolic process.

metabolize *or* **metabolise** /mi'tabəliez/ *verb trans and intrans* to process (a substance) by, or to undergo the processes of, metabolism. ➤➤ **metabolizable** *adj*, **metabolizer** *noun*.

metacarpus /metə'kahpəs/ *noun* (*pl* **metacarpi** /-pie/) **1** the group of five long bones in the hand between the wrist and fingers. **2** the equivalent set of bones between the ankle and toes in the forefoot of an animal. ➤➤ **metacarpal** *adj and noun*. [scientific Latin *metacarpus*]

metacentre (*NAmer* **metacenter**) /'metəsentə/ *noun* the point of intersection of the vertical line through the centre of buoyancy of a floating body, e.g. a ship, with the vertical line through the new centre of buoyancy when the body is displaced, e.g. by being heeled over. ➤➤ **metacentric** /-'sentrik/ *adj*.

metafiction /'metəfiksh(ə)n/ *noun* literary fiction in which conventional realistic narrative is subordinate to, and often undercut by, a self-conscious exposure of the storytelling process itself. ➤➤ **metafictional** /-'fiksh(ə)nl/ *adj*.

metage /'meetij/ *noun* the official measuring of the weight of something, e.g. coal. [METE[1] + -AGE]

metagenesis /metə'jenəsis/ *noun* = ALTERNATION OF GENERATIONS. [scientific Latin *metagenesis*]

metal[1] /'metl/ *noun* **1** any of various usu hard and shiny substances that are ductile and capable of being melted and fused, e.g. iron, copper, or mercury, *esp* chemical elements, that are good conductors of electricity and heat, form positive ions by loss of electrons, and yield basic oxides and hydroxides. **2** glass in its molten state. **3** either of the heraldic tinctures gold or silver. **4** = ROAD METAL. **5** (*in pl*) the rails of a railway line. [Middle English via Old French from Latin *metallum* mine, metal, from Greek *metallon*]

metal[2] *verb trans* (**metalled, metalling**, *NAmer* **metaled, metaling**) **1** to cover or provide (something) with metal. **2** *Brit* to surface (a road) with broken stones.

metalanguage /'metəlanggwij/ *noun* the language and terminology used to talk analytically about language itself.

metal detector *noun* an electronic device that gives an audible or visual signal when it detects the presence of metal objects, e.g. buried coins or concealed wiring.

metaled *adj NAmer* see METALLED.

metalize *verb trans NAmer* see METALLIZE.

metalled (*NAmer* **metaled**) *adj* said of a road: covered with a surface of broken stones.

metallic /mi'talik/ *adj* **1** of, containing, like, or being metal. **2** having a particularly lustrous reflective quality: *metallic paint*. **3** said of a sound: sharp and ringing, like metal striking metal. **4** bitter or acrid in taste. **5** yielding metal. ➤➤ **metallically** *adv*.

metalliferous /metə'lifərəs/ *adj* yielding or containing metal. [Latin *metallifer*, from *metallum* metal + *-fer* -FEROUS]

metallize *or* **metallise** (*NAmer* **metalize**) *verb trans* **1** to treat, combine, or coat (something) with a metal. **2** to make (something) metallic. ➤➤ **metallization** /-'zaysh(ə)n/ *noun*.

metallography /metə'logrəfi/ *noun* the study of the microscopic structure of metals. ➤➤ **metallographer** *noun*, **metallographic** /mi,talə'grafik/ *adj*, **metallographical** /mi,talə'grafikl/ *adj*, **metallographically** /mi,talə'grafikli/ *adv*. [French *métallographie*, from Latin *metallum* metal + French *-graphie* -GRAPHY]

metalloid[1] /'metəloyd/ *noun* an element, e.g. arsenic, having some properties of typical metals and some properties of typical nonmetals; a semimetal.

metalloid[2] *adj* **1** resembling a metal. **2** of or being a metalloid.

metalloidal *adj* = METALLOID[2].

metallurgy /mə'taləji, 'metəluhji/ *noun* the branch of science concerned with the properties of metals and their extraction, production and refining. ➤➤ **metallurgic** /metə'luhjik/ *adj*, **metallurgical** /metə'luhjikl/ *adj*, **metallurgically** /metə'luhjikli/ *adv*, **metallurgist** *noun*. [Latin *metallurgia*, from Greek *metallon* + Latin *-urgia* -URGY]

metalwork *noun* **1** the craft of shaping things out of metal. **2** products made from metal. ➤➤ **metalworker** *noun*, **metalworking** *noun*.

metamere /'metəmiə/ *noun* = SOMITE. ➤➤ **metameric** /-'merik/ *adj*, **metamerism** /mə'taməriz(ə)m/ *noun*.

metamorphic /metə'mawfik/ *adj* **1** said of rock: having undergone metamorphism. **2** of or involving metamorphosis. ➤➤ **metamorphically** *adv*.

metamorphism /metə'mawfiz(ə)m/ *noun* a change in rock effected *esp* by heat and pressure and resulting in a more compact and crystalline structure.

metamorphose /metə'mawfohz, -'fohz/ *verb intrans* **1** said of an insect or amphibian: to undergo metamorphosis. **2** to be transformed. ➤ *verb trans* **1** to change (something) completely; to transform (it). **2** to cause (rock) to undergo metamorphism. [early French *metamorphoser* from *metamorphose* metamorphosis, from Latin *metamorphosis*]

metamorphosis /metə'mawfəsis/ *noun* (*pl* **metamorphoses** /-seez/) **1** a marked abrupt change in the form or structure of an insect or amphibian occurring in the course of development, e.g. the change from a tadpole to a frog. **2a** change of form, structure, or substance, *esp* by supernatural means. **b** a striking alteration, e.g. in appearance or character. [via Latin from Greek *metamorphōsis* from *metamorphoun* to transform, from META- + *morphē* form]

metaphase /'metəfayz/ *noun* the second stage of cell division in which the chromosomes become arranged in line horizontally to the spindle in preparation for division to take place: compare ANAPHASE, PROPHASE.

metaphor /'metəfə, -faw/ *noun* **1** a figure of speech in which a word or phrase literally denoting one kind of object or idea is applied to another to suggest a likeness or analogy between them, e.g. in *the ship ploughs the sea*: compare SIMILE: *Science is all metaphor* — Timothy Leary; *All slang is metaphor, and all metaphor is poetry* — G K Chesterton. **2** an object, activity, or idea treated as a metaphor. ➤➤ **metaphoric** /-'forik/ *adj*, **metaphorical** /-'forikl/ *adj*, **metaphorically** /-'forikli/ *adv*. [via French from Latin *metaphora* from Greek *metapherein* to transfer, from META- + *pherein* to bear]

metaphrase[1] /'metəfrayz/ *noun* a close or word-for-word translation. ➤➤ **metaphrastic** /-'frastik/ *adj*. [via Latin *metaphrasis* from Greek *metaphrazein* to translate, from META- + *phrazein* to tell]

metaphrase[2] *verb trans* **1** to translate (a text) word for word. **2** to alter the wording of (a text).

metaphysic /metəˈfizik/ noun a particular system of metaphysics. [Middle English metaphesyk from medieval Latin Metaphysica: see METAPHYSICS]

Metaphysical /metəˈfizikl/ noun a metaphysical poet.

metaphysical adj **1** of or relating to metaphysics. **2** highly abstract or abstruse: metaphysical reasoning. **3** beyond nature or what is physical; supernatural. **4** (often **Metaphysical**) of or being English poetry, esp of the early 17th cent., that is marked by ingenious witty imagery expressing subtleties of thought and emotion. ➤➤ **metaphysically** adv.

metaphysics pl noun (treated as sing. or pl) **1** a division of philosophy concerned with ultimate causes and the underlying nature of things; esp ontology.

Editorial note ────────────────────
Metaphysics is the enquiry into the ultimate nature of reality. It seeks to determine what genuinely and fundamentally exists, and what existence itself is. It asks whether, in addition to physical reality, such things as deity, abstract objects like numbers, and values such as goodness and beauty, exist in the universe, and if so, in what way — Dr Anthony Grayling.

2 pure or speculative philosophy. **3** informal abstract and impractical theorizing. ➤➤ **metaphysician** /-ˈzish(ə)n/ noun. [medieval Latin Metaphysica, title of Aristotle's treatise on the subject, from Greek (ta) meta (ta) physika, literally 'the (works) after the physical (works)'; from its position in his collected works]

metaplasia /metəˈplayzi-ə/ noun abnormal replacement of cells of one type by cells of another. ➤➤ **metaplastic** /-ˈplastik/ adj.

metapsychology /ˌmetəsieˈkoləji/ noun the branch of psychology involved with a philosophical study of mental processes that cannot be examined by experimentation. ➤➤ **metapsychological** /-ˈlojikl/ adj.

metastable /metəˈstaybl/ adj **1** said of a state of equilibrium: stable as long as it is subject only to a small degree of disturbance. **2** said of a substance or particle: unstable in theory but lasting long enough for practical purposes. ➤➤ **metastability** /-stəˈbiliti/ noun.

metastasis /miˈtastəsis/ noun (pl **metastases** /-seez/) a secondary growth of a malignant tumour at a site distant from the primary growth. ➤➤ **metastatic** /metəˈstatik/ adj. [via late Latin from Greek metastasis, from methistanai to change, from META- + histanai to set]

metastasize or **metastasise** /miˈtastəsiez/ verb intrans said of cancer cells: to spread to other parts of the body by metastasis.

metatarsus /metəˈtahsəs/ noun (pl **metatarsi** /-sie/) **1** the bones in the foot between the ankle and toes. **2** the equivalent bones in the hind foot of a four-legged animal. ➤➤ **metatarsal** adj and noun.

metatherian /metəˈthiəri-ən/ noun any of a group of mammals comprising the marsupials: subclass Metatheria. ➤➤ **metatherian** adj. [from the Latin name, from META- + Greek thēria, pl of thērion wild animal]

metathesis /məˈtathəsis/ noun (pl **metatheses** /-seez/) **1** the transposition of two phonemes in a word, e.g. in Old English bridd, Modern English bird. **2** = DOUBLE DECOMPOSITION. ➤➤ **metathetic** /metəˈthetik/ adj, **metathetical** /metəˈthetikl/ adj. [Greek metathesis from metatithenai to transpose, from META- + tithenai to place]

metathorax /metəˈthawraks/ noun the rear segment of the thorax of an insect. ➤➤ **metathoracic** /-ˈrasik/ adj.

metazoan /metəˈzoh-ən/ noun any member of a kingdom or sub-kingdom of animals comprising all those with multicellular bodies differentiated into tissues, except sponges and protozoans. ➤➤ **metazoan** adj. [scientific Latin Metazoa, group name, from META- + -ZOA]

mete[1] /meet/ verb trans **1** (+ out) to distribute, allot, or inflict (something): Swift punishment was meted out to all offenders. **2** archaic to measure (something). [Old English metan]

mete[2] noun a boundary or boundary stone. [Middle English via Old French from Latin meta boundary]

metempsychosis /meˌtempsieˈkohsis/ noun (pl **metempsychoses**) the passing of the soul at death into another body; reincarnation. [via late Latin from Greek metempsychōsis, from META- + en in + psychē soul]

meteor /ˈmeeti-ə, ˈmeetiaw/ noun **1** a small particle of matter from space, observable directly only when it falls into the earth's atmosphere and is heated by friction so that it glows. **2** the streak of light produced by the fall of a meteor. [Middle English via French and Latin from Greek meteōron phenomenon in the sky, from neuter of meteōros high in the air]

meteoric /meetiˈorik/ adj **1** associated with a meteor or meteorite. **2** resembling a meteor in speed or in sudden and temporary brilliance: She enjoyed a meteoric rise to fame. **3** said of water: derived from condensation or precipitation. ➤➤ **meteorically** adv.

meteorite /ˈmeeti-əriet/ noun a rock from interplanetary space that reaches the surface of the earth. ➤➤ **meteoritic** /-ˈritik/ adj.

meteoroid /ˈmeeti-əroyd/ noun an object in orbit round the sun that becomes a meteor or meteorite when it meets the earth's atmosphere. ➤➤ **meteoroidal** /-ˈroydl/ adj.

meteorology /ˌmeeti-əˈrolaji/ noun **1** the science of the atmosphere and its phenomena, esp weather and weather forecasting. **2** the weather or atmospheric phenomena of a region. ➤➤ **meteorological** /-ˈlojikl/ adj, **meteorologically** /-ˈlojikli/ adv, **meteorologist** noun. [via French from Greek meteōrologia, from meteōron phenomenon in the sky + -logia -LOGY]

meteor shower noun the phenomenon observed when members of a group of meteors encounter the earth's atmosphere and their luminous paths appear to spray out from a single point.

meter[1] /ˈmeetə/ noun an instrument for measuring and recording the amount of something, e.g. gas, electricity, or parking time used. [-METER[2]]

Usage note ────────────────────
meter or metre? In British English a metre is a measurement of length equal to 100cm, while a meter is a measuring instrument: to read the meter. Likewise, in British English, the rhythmic pattern of a line of poetry is its metre, though the words for specific types of metre end in -er: hexameter; iambic pentameter. In American English the spelling meter is used for all these senses.

meter[2] verb trans (**metered, metering**) to measure (something) by means of a meter.

meter[3] noun NAmer see METRE[1], METRE[2].

-meter[1] comb. form forming nouns, denoting: a measure or unit of metrical verse: pentameter.

-meter[2] comb. form forming nouns, denoting: an instrument or means for measuring: barometer. [French -mètre from Greek metron measure]

meth /meth/ noun informal methamphetamine. [by contraction]

meth- or **metho-** comb. form forming words, denoting: methyl: methacrylic.

methacrylic acid /methəˈkrilik/ noun an acid used esp in making acrylic resins or plastics: formula $C_4H_6O_2$.

methadone /ˈmethədohn/ or **methadon** /-don/ noun a synthetic narcotic drug used esp as a substitute narcotic in the treatment of heroin addiction and as a painkiller. [from its chemical name, 6-di-methylamino-4,4-diphenyl-3-heptanone]

methamphetamine /methamˈfetəmin/ noun an amphetamine drug, used illegally as a stimulant. [METH- + AMPHETAMINE]

methanal /ˈmethənal/ noun = FORMALDEHYDE.

methane /ˈmeethayn/ noun a colourless, odourless flammable gas that is a member of the alkane series of organic chemical compounds, is a product of decomposition of plant or animal matter in marshes and mines, and is used as a fuel and as a raw material in synthesis of chemical compounds: formula CH_4.

methanoic acid /methəˈnoh-ik/ noun = FORMIC ACID.

methanol /ˈmethənol/ noun a volatile flammable poisonous liquid alcohol that is added to ethyl alcohol to make it unfit to drink and is used as a solvent and as a raw material in synthesis of chemical compounds: formula CH_3OH.

Methedrine /ˈmethədrin/ noun trademark methamphetamine. [METH- + BENZEDRINE]

metheglin /məˈtheglin/ noun a Welsh form of mead, with added spices. [Welsh meddyglyn, from meddyg physician + llyn liquor]

methinks /miˈthingks/ verb intrans (past tense **methought** /miˈthawt/) archaic it seems to me. [Old English mē thincth, from mē (dative of ic I) + thincth (it) seems, from thyncan to seem]

methionine /miˈthie-əneen, -nien/ noun a sulphur-containing amino acid that is found in most proteins and is an essential constituent of human diet: formula $CH_3S(CH_2)_2CH(NH_2)COOH$. [METHYL + Greek theion sulphur + -INE[2]]

metho- comb. form see METH-.

method /'methəd/ *noun* **1** a systematic procedure for doing something, or the regular way in which something is done: *You know my methods* — Conan Doyle. **2a** an orderly arrangement or system: *Though this be madness, yet there is method in't* — Shakespeare. **b** the habitual practice of orderliness and regularity. **3** (**the Method**) a dramatic technique by which an actor seeks to identify closely with the inner personality of the character being portrayed. [via French and Latin from Greek *methodos*, from META- + *hodos* way]

methodical /mə'thodikl/ *adj* arranged, characterized by, or performed with method or order; systematic. ➤➤ **methodic** *adj*, **methodically** *adv*.

methodise *verb trans* see METHODIZE.

Methodism *noun* the doctrines and practice of the Methodist Church.

Methodist *noun* a member of any of the denominations deriving from the Wesleyan revival in the Church of England, having an evangelical character and stressing personal and social morality. ➤➤ **Methodist** *adj*, **Methodistic** /-'distik/ *adj*. [METHOD + -IST[1]; in the orig sense 'a person devoted to a particular method']

methodize *or* **methodise** *verb trans* to organize (something) in accordance with a method; to systematize (it). ➤➤ **methodizer** *noun*.

methodology /methə'doləji/ *noun* (*pl* **methodologies**) the body of methods and rules employed by a science or discipline. ➤➤ **methodological** /-'lojikl/ *adj*, **methodologically** /-'lojikli/ *adv*, **methodologist** *noun*. [Latin *methodologia*, from *methodus* method + -OLOGY]

methotrexate /methə'treksayt/ *noun* a synthetic anticancer drug used to treat lymphomas and some forms of leukaemia: formula $C_{20}H_{22}N_8O_5$. [METH- + -*trexate*, of unknown origin]

methought /mi'thawt/ *verb* past tense of METHINKS: *Methought I was enamoured of an ass* — Shakespeare.

meths /meths/ *noun Brit, informal* methylated spirits. [by contraction]

Methuselah /mi'thyoohzələ/ *noun* **1** a person who has lived to a great age. **2** a champagne bottle holding eight times the usual amount. [named after *Methuselah*, a biblical patriarch said to have lived 969 years (Genesis 5:27)]

methyl /'methil, 'meethil, 'meethiel/ *noun* a chemical group, CH_3, derived from the gas methane by removing one hydrogen atom. ➤➤ **methylic** /mə'thilik/ *adj*. [back-formation from METHYLENE]

methyl alcohol *noun* = METHANOL.

methylate /'methilayt/ *verb trans* **1** to impregnate or mix (something) with methanol or methylated spirits. **2** to introduce the methyl group into (something, e.g. a compound). ➤➤ **methylated** *adj*, **methylation** /-'laysh(ə)n/ *noun*.

methylated spirits *or* **methylated spirit** *noun* alcohol mixed with an adulterant, *esp* methanol, to make it undrinkable and therefore exempt from duty.

methylene /'methəleen/ *noun* a chemical group, CH_2, with a valency of two, that is derived from the gas methane by removing two hydrogen atoms. [French *méthylène*, from Greek *methy* wine + *hylē* wood]

methylene blue *noun* an oxidizing dye used *esp* to stain biological specimens, and as an antidote in cyanide poisoning.

methylphenidate /methil'fenidayt, meethil-, meethiel-/ *noun* a drug used in the treatment of attention deficit disorder and narcolepsy, acting as a stimulant on the central nervous system: formula $C_{14}H_{19}NO_2$.

metical /meti'kal/ *noun* (*pl* **meticais** /meti'kiesh/) the basic monetary unit of Mozambique, divided into 100 centavos. [via Portuguese from Arabic *mithqāl* a unit of weight]

meticulous /mə'tikyooləs/ *adj* marked by extreme or excessive care over detail: *Every detail, from the pearl pin in the black satin cravat to the lavender spats over the varnished shoes, spoke of the meticulous care in dress for which he was famous* — Conan Doyle. ➤➤ **meticulously** *adv*, **meticulousness** *noun*.

Word history
Latin *meticulosus* timid, from *metus* fear. Although the earlier uses of *meticulous* were derogatory, it now usually indicates approval. Its original sense (from the 17th cent.) was 'fearful, timid', but this sense has long been obsolete. In the 19th cent. it came to mean 'overconcerned with details, fussy'. Now it usually signifies 'commendably precise'.

métier /'maytyay/ *noun* **1** one's trade. **2** something, e.g. an activity, in which one is expert or successful; one's forte. [French *métier* from alteration of Latin *ministerium* work, ministry]

métis /me'tees/ *noun* (*pl* **métis** /me'tees/) a person of mixed race, *esp* somebody who is half French Canadian and half Native American. [French *métis* from late Latin *mixticius* mixed]

metoestrus /me'teestrəs/ *noun* the period of regression and recuperation that follows OESTRUS (a period of sexual excitement) in a mammal's sexual cycle.

metol /'meetol/ *noun* a soluble white chemical compound used in photographic developers: formula $C_{14}H_{20}N_2O_6S$. [German *Metol*, a name arbitrarily chosen by the inventor]

Metonic cycle /mi'tonik/ *noun* a period of 19 years, after which the new and full moons occur again on the same cycle of dates. [named after *Meton*, fifth-cent. BC Greek astronomer]

metonym /'metənim/ *noun* a word used in metonymy. ➤➤ **metonymic** /-'nimik/ *adj*, **metonymical** /-'nimikl/ *adj*, **metonymically** /-'nimikli/ *adv*. [back-formation from METONYMY]

metonymy /mi'tonəmi/ *noun* (*pl* **metonymies**) a figure of speech in which the word for a part, aspect, or attribute of a thing is used to mean the thing itself, e.g. *the White House* used to mean the US president and executive or *wheels* used to mean a car. [via Latin from Greek *metōnymia*, literally 'change of name']

metope /'metohp, 'metəpi/ *noun* the space between two triglyphs (square projections; see TRIGLYPH) of a Doric frieze, often adorned with carvings. [Greek *metopē*, from META- + *opē* opening]

metre[1] (*NAmer* **meter**) /'meetə/ *noun* the basic metric SI unit of length equal to 100 centimetres (about 39.37in.). [French *mètre* from Greek *metron* measure]

Usage note
metre *or* meter? See note at METER[1].

metre[2] (*NAmer* **meter**) *noun* **1** the rhythm of verse, determined by the number and type of feet in a line. **2** the basic recurrent rhythmical pattern of accents and beats per bar in a piece of music. [Old English *mēter* via Latin *metrum* from Greek *metron* measure, metre]

Usage note
metre *or* meter? See note at METER[1].

metre-kilogram-second *adj* relating to a system of units based on the metre, the kilogram, and the second.

metric[1] /'metrik/ *adj* using decimal units of measure based on the metre, litre, and kilogram as standards.

metric[2] *noun informal* the metric system.

metric[3] *adj* relating to or using a poetic metre.

-metric *or* **-metrical** *comb. form* forming adjectives corresponding to nouns in -*meter* or -*metry*: *chronometric*; *geometric*.

metrical[1] *adj* relating to or composed in poetic metre. ➤➤ **metrically** *adv*.

metrical[2] *adj* to do with measurement. ➤➤ **metrically** *adv*.

-metrical *comb. form* see -METRIC.

metricate /'metrikayt/ *verb trans* to change (measurements) into the metric system. ➤➤ **metrication** /-'kaysh(ə)n/ *noun*.

metrics *pl noun* (*treated as sing. or pl*) the aspect of prosody that deals with metrical structure.

metric system *noun* a decimal system of weights and measures based on the metre, the litre, and the kilogram.

metric ton *or* **metric tonne** *noun* a tonne.

Metro /'metroh/ *noun* (*pl* **Metros**) *Can* the inner urban area of a Canadian city, *esp* of Toronto, or its administration. [short for *Metropolitan*]

metro *noun* (*pl* **metros**) an underground railway system in a city, *esp* Paris. [French *métro*, short for *chemin de fer métropolitain* metropolitan railway]

metrology /mi'troləji/ *noun* the science of weights and measures or of measurement. ➤➤ **metrological** /metrə'lojikl/ *adj*. [French *métrologie* from Greek *metrologia* theory of ratios, from *metron* measure]

metronidazole /metrə'niedəzohl/ *noun* a synthetic drug used to treat infections by protozoa (single-celled organisms; see PROTOZOAN), *esp* vaginal trichomoniasis: formula $C_6H_9N_3O_3$. [METHYL + -*tron*- (prob from *nitro*) + IMIDAZOLE]

metronome /'metrənohm/ *noun* a device designed to help musicians by marking the speed of a beat with a regularly repeated tick. >>> **metronomic** /metrə'nomik/ *adj.* [Greek *metron* + *-nomos* controlling, from *nomos* law]

metronymic /metrə'nimik/ *noun* see MATRONYMIC. [Greek *mētr-*, *mētēr* mother + *onyma*, *onoma* name]

metropolis /mi'tropəlis/ *noun* **1a** the chief or capital city of a country, state, or region. **b** a large or important city. **2** a place, *esp* a city, regarded as a centre of a specified activity. [via Latin from Greek *mētropolis*, from *mētr-*, *mētēr* mother + *polis* city]

metropolitan[1] /metrə'polit(ə)n/ *adj* **1** relating to, situated in, or characteristic of a metropolis. **2** of or constituting a parent state, as opposed to an overseas colony or dependency: *metropolitan France*. **3** relating to a metropolitan or the see of a metropolitan. [late Latin *metropolitanus* relating to the see of a metropolitan, ultimately from Greek *mētropolis* chief city]

metropolitan[2] *noun* **1a** in the Eastern Churches, the head of an ecclesiastical province, ranking above an archbishop and below a patriarch. **b** in the Church of England or Roman Catholic Church, an archbishop or chief bishop of a province. **2** a person who lives in a metropolis.

metropolitan county *noun* any of the six areas in England, each centred on a large city, that formed an administrative unit for purposes of local government between 1974 and 1986.

metropolitan district *noun* any of the six areas in England that formerly made up the metropolitan counties. Since 1986 they have functioned as unitary local authorities, each with its own elected council.

metrorrhagia /meetrə'rayji-ə, met-/ *noun* profuse bleeding from the uterus, *esp* between menstrual periods. [scientific Latin *metrorrhagia*]

-metry *comb. form* forming nouns, denoting: the art, process, or science of measuring the thing specified: *chronometry*. [Middle English *-metrie* via French from Latin *-metria*, from Greek *metrein* to measure]

mettle /'metl/ *noun* **1** strength of spirit or temperament. **2** staying quality; stamina. ✳ **on one's mettle** ready to do one's best. [alteration of METAL[1]]

mettlesome /'metls(ə)m/ *adj* spirited.

meunière /muh'nyeə (*French* mønjɛːr)/ *adj* with a sauce of melted butter, parsley, and lemon juice: *sole meunière*. [French (*à la*) *meunière*, in the manner of a miller's wife]

MeV *abbr* million electron volts.

mew[1] /myooh/ *verb intrans* to utter the high-pitched, plaintive sound characteristic of a cat or a gull. [Middle English *mewen*, of imitative origin]

mew[2] *noun* a mewing sound.

mew[3] *noun* a cage or building used to keep trained falcons in, *esp* when they are moulting. [Middle English *mewe* from early French *mue* from *muer* to moult, from Latin *mutare* to change]

mew[4] *verb trans* **1** (*often* + up) to shut (somebody) up in something; to confine (them). **2** to keep (a moulting hawk) in a mew. > *verb intrans* said of a trained falcon: to moult. [Middle English *mewen* from *mewe*: see MEW[3]]

mewl /myoohl/ *verb intrans* **1** to cry weakly; to whimper: *at first the infant, mewling and puking in the nurse's arms* — Shakespeare. **2** to mew. [imitative]

mews /myoohz/ *noun* (*pl* **mews**) *Brit* **1** a street or row of houses converted from former stables, or built in this style. **2** a set of stables built round an open courtyard.

Word history —————————
pl of MEW[3], originally referring to the royal stables built on the site of the king's hawk mews at Charing Cross in London in the 16th cent. The modern meaning of converted dwellings was acquired in the early 19th cent.

MEX *abbr* Mexico (international vehicle registration).

Mexican /'meksik(ə)n/ *noun* a native or inhabitant of Mexico. >>> **Mexican** *adj.*

Mexican wave *noun* a wavelike movement made by a large number of seated people, *esp* spectators in a sports stadium, in which several adjacent files of people in unison stand up, raise their arms, and then sit down again. This procedure is repeated rapidly by successive files until it has passed through the whole crowd.

[from its first appearance during the football World Cup finals in Mexico in 1986]

meze /'mayzay/ *noun* (*pl* **meze** *or* **mezes**) an assortment of simple snacks served as appetizers, e.g. in Middle Eastern countries. [Turkish *meze*]

mezereon /mə'ziəri-ən/ *noun* a small European shrub with fragrant purple flowers and poisonous red berries: *Daphne mezereum*. [Middle English *mizerion* via late Latin from Arabic *māzariyūn*]

mezuzah /mə'zoohzə/ *noun* (*pl* **mezuzahs** *or* **mezuzoth** /-zoht/) a small oblong case containing a parchment inscribed with religious texts, fixed to the doorpost by some Jewish families as a sign of their faith. [Hebrew *mĕzūzāh* doorpost]

mezzanine[1] /'mezəneen/ *noun* **1** a low-ceilinged storey between two main storeys, e.g. the ground and first floors, of a building; *esp* an intermediate storey that projects in the form of a balcony. **2a** *NAmer* the lowest balcony in a theatre. **b** *Brit* the area beneath the stage in a theatre. [via French from Italian *mezzanino*, dimin. of *mezzano* middle, from Latin *medianus* middle, median]

mezzanine[2] *adj* of or relating to a form of financing, *esp* for the takeover of a large company, made up of high-yield unsecured loans repayable only after other commitments have been met in case of bankruptcy.

mezza voce /ˌmetsə 'vohchi/ *adj and adv* said of a piece of music: to be performed at medium volume. [Italian *mezza voce* half voice]

mezzo /'metsoh/ *noun* (*pl* **mezzos**) = MEZZO-SOPRANO. [Italian *mezzo* half]

mezzo forte *adj and adv* said of a piece of music: to be performed in a moderately loud manner. [Italian *mezzo forte* half loud]

mezzo piano /pi'ahnoh/ *adj and adv* said of a piece of music: to be performed in a moderately soft manner. [Italian *mezzo piano* half soft]

mezzo-rilievo /ri'leevoh, ree'lyayvoh/ *noun* (*pl* **mezzo-rilievos**) sculptural relief which is halfway between bas-relief and high relief and in which about half of the circumference of the design stands out from the surrounding area. [Italian *mezzorilievo*, from *mezzo* half + *rilievo* relief]

mezzo-soprano *noun* (*pl* **mezzo-sopranos**) a female singing voice between soprano and contralto, or a singer with this voice. [Italian *mezzosoprano*]

mezzotint[1] *noun* **1** a method of engraving on copper or steel by scraping or burnishing a roughened surface to produce light and shade. **2** a print produced by this method. [modification of Italian *mezzatinta*, from *mezza* (fem of *mezzo*) half + *tinta* tint]

mezzotint[2] *verb trans* to engrave (a plate) in mezzotint. >>> **mezzotinter** *noun.*

MF *abbr* medium frequency.

mf *abbr* mezzo forte.

MFH *abbr* Master of Foxhounds.

Mg *abbr* the chemical symbol for magnesium.

mg *abbr* milligram(s).

Mgr *abbr* **1** Monseigneur. **2** Monsignor.

mgr *abbr* manager.

mho /moh/ *noun* (*pl* **mhos**) = SIEMENS. [backward spelling of OHM]

MHR *abbr Aus, NAmer* Member of the House of Representatives.

MHz *abbr* megahertz.

MI *abbr* **1** Michigan (US postal abbreviation). **2** *Brit* military intelligence.

mi[1] /mee/ *noun* in music, the third note of a major scale in the tonic sol-fa system, or the note E in the fixed-doh system. [late Latin: see GAMUT]

mi[2] *abbr* **1** mile(s). **2** mileage.

MI5 *noun no longer in official use* the British government agency responsible for internal security and counterintelligence. [short for *Military Intelligence, section 5*]

MI6 *noun no longer in official use* the British government agency responsible for counterintelligence and security overseas. [short for *Military Intelligence, section 6*]

MIA *abbr chiefly NAmer* missing in action.

miaow[1] *or* **meow** /mi'ow, myow/ *verb intrans* to make the characteristic cry of a cat. [imitative]

miaow[2] *or* **meow** *noun* a miaowing sound.

miasma /mi'azmə/ *noun* (*pl* **miasmas** *or* **miasmata** /-tə/) *literary* **1** a heavy or foul-smelling vapour, e.g. one from a swamp formerly believed to cause disease. **2** a pervasive influence or atmosphere that tends to weaken or corrupt: *the miasma of poverty.* ➤➤ **miasmal** *adj,* **miasmatic** /mee-əz'matik/ *adj,* **miasmic** /-'mik/ *adj.* [via Latin from Greek *miasma* defilement, from *miainein* to pollute]

Mic. *abbr* Micah (book of the Bible).

mica /'miekə/ *noun* any of various coloured or transparent silicate materials occurring as crystals that readily separate into very thin flexible leaves. ➤➤ **micaceous** /mie'kayshəs/ *adj.* [Latin *mica* grain, crumb]

mice /mies/ *noun* pl of MOUSE¹.

micelle /mi'sel/ *noun* a molecular aggregate that forms a particle in a COLLOID (solution containing suspended particles). ➤➤ **micellar** *adj.* [scientific Latin *micella* from Latin *mica* crumb]

Mich. *abbr* Michigan.

Michaelmas /'mik(ə)lməs/ *noun* the Christian feast of St Michael the Archangel, celebrated on 29 September. [Old English *Michaeles mæsse* Michael's mass]

Michaelmas daisy *noun* any of several asters widely grown as garden plants, with daisy-like flowers that bloom in the autumn: *Aster novi-belgii.*

Michaelmas term *noun Brit* the university term beginning in October.

Michigander /mishi'gandə/ *noun* a native or inhabitant of the state of Michigan.

mick¹ *or* **Mick** /mik/ *noun offensive* **1** an Irishman. **2** a Roman Catholic. [*Mick*, nickname for *Michael*, common Irish forename]

mick² *noun Aus* the reverse side of a coin. [origin unknown]

mickey¹ /'miki/ *noun informal* = MICKEY FINN. [shortening]

mickey² ✷ **take the mickey** *chiefly Brit, informal* to make fun of, tease, or ridicule (somebody). ➤➤ **mickey-taking** *noun.* [prob from *Mickey Bliss*, rhyming slang for *piss*]

Mickey Finn /fin/ *noun informal* an alcoholic drink doctored with a drug, e.g. to make the drinker unconscious.

Word history

perhaps from the name *Mickey Finnish*. The term is said to come from a notorious figure in 19th-cent. Chicago.

Mickey Mouse *adj informal* trivial or petty. [*Mickey Mouse*, cartoon character created by Walt Disney d.1966, US film producer]

mickle¹ /'mikl/ *adj Scot, N Eng, or archaic* great or much. ➤➤ **mickle** *adv.* [Old English *micel*]

mickle² *noun Scot, N Eng, or archaic* a great amount.

Micmac *or* **Mi'kmaq** /'mikmak/ *noun* (*pl* **Micmacs** *or* **Mi'kmaqs** *or* collectively **Micmac** *or* **Mi'kmaq**) **1** a member of a Native American people of E Canada. **2** the Algonquian language spoken by this people. [Micmac *Migmag*, literally 'allies']

micr- *comb. form* see MICRO-.

micra /'miekrə/ *noun* pl of MICRON.

micro¹ /'miekroh/ *adj* very small or microscopic.

micro² *noun* (*pl* **micros**) **1** a microcomputer. **2** a microprocessor.

micro- *or* **micr-** *comb. form* forming words, denoting: **1** smallness or a reduced size: *microdot.* **2** a reduced concept or scope: *microclimate.* **3** a factor of one millionth (10^{-6}): *microsecond.* [Middle English via Latin from Greek *mikr-, mikro-,* from *mikros, smikros* small, short]

microbe /'miekrohb/ *noun* a micro-organism, *esp* a bacterium that causes disease. ➤➤ **microbial** /mie'krohbi-əl/ *adj,* **microbic** /mie'krohbik/ *adj.* [MICRO- + Greek *bios* life]

microbiology /,miekrohbie'oləji/ *noun* the biology of viruses, bacteria and other microscopic biological organisms. ➤➤ **microbiological** /-'lojikl/ *adj,* **microbiologically** /-'lojikli/ *adv,* **microbiologist** *noun.*

microburst /'miekrohbuhst/ *noun* an incidence of extreme local turbulence, usu consisting of a downward rush of cold air that is very dangerous to aircraft taking off or landing.

microcephaly /miekroh'sefəli/ *noun* abnormal smallness of the head, associated with incomplete development of the brain. ➤➤ **microcephalic** /-si'falik/ *adj,* **microcephalous** *adj.* [scientific Latin *microcephalus* (adj), from MICRO- + Greek *kephalē* head]

microchip /'miekrohchip/ *noun* = CHIP¹ (5).

microcircuit /'miekrohsuhkit/ *noun* a compact electronic circuit, *esp* an integrated circuit. ➤➤ **microcircuitry** *noun.*

microclimate /'miekrohkliemət/ *noun* a climate restricted to a small area or habitat and different from that of the surrounding region. ➤➤ **microclimatic** /-'matik/ *adj,* **microclimatically** *adv,* **microclimatology** /-'toləji/ *noun.*

microcomputer /'miekrohkəmpyoohtə/ *noun* a small self-contained computer that is based on one or more microprocessors.

microcopy¹ /'miekrohkopi/ *noun* (*pl* **microcopies**) a photographic copy in which graphic matter is greatly reduced in size.

microcopy² *verb trans* (**microcopies, microcopied, microcopying**) to make a microcopy of (something).

microcosm /'miekrəkoz(ə)m/ *noun* **1** something, e.g. a community or situation, regarded as having the characteristics of a larger whole: *Therapy is supposed to be a microcosm of your relationships, with the therapist taking on multiple roles* — Esquire. **2** human life or human nature regarded as an epitome of the universe. ➤➤ **microcosmic** /-'kozmik/ *adj.* [Middle English via medieval Latin *microcosmus* from Greek *mikros kosmos* small world]

microcrystal /'miekrohkristl/ *noun* a crystal visible only under the microscope. ➤➤ **microcrystalline** /-'krist(ə)lien/ *adj,* **microcrystallinity** /-'liniti/ *noun.*

microdot /'miekrohdot/ *noun* **1** a photographic reproduction of printed matter reduced to the size of a single dot for security or ease of transmission. **2** a small tablet containing a hallucinogenic drug.

microeconomics /,miekroheekə'nomiks, -ekə'nomiks/ *pl noun* (*treated as sing. or pl*) a study of economics in terms of individual areas of activity, e.g. a firm, household, or prices: compare MACROECONOMICS. ➤➤ **microeconomic** *adj.*

microelectronics /,miekrohilek'troniks, -elik'troniks/ *pl noun* (*treated as sing. or pl*) a branch of electronics that deals with or produces miniaturized electronic circuits and components. ➤➤ **microelectronic** *adj.*

microevolution /,miekroheevə'loohsh(ə)n, -evə'loohsh(ə)n/ *noun* in biology, evolutionary change resulting from selective accumulation of minute variations. ➤➤ **microevolutionary** *adj.*

microfiche /'miekrohfeesh/ *noun* a sheet of microfilm containing rows of very small images of pages of printed matter. [French *microfiche,* from MICRO- + *fiche* peg, tag, slide]

microfilm¹ /'miekrəfilm/ *noun* a photographic film on which graphic matter, e.g. printing, can be recorded in miniaturized form.

microfilm² *verb trans* to make a microfilm of (e.g. a document or text).

microgram /'miekrəgram/ *noun* a metric unit of mass equal to one millionth of a gram.

micrograph /'miekrəgrahf/ *noun* a photograph or graphic reproduction of an object as seen through a microscope.

microgravity /'miekrohgraviti/ *noun* an environment in which conditions of near weightlessness are experienced, e.g. by an astronaut in an orbiting spacecraft.

microgroove /'miekrohgroohv/ *noun* the fine spiral groove on a long-playing or extended-play record.

microhabitat /miekroh'habitat/ *noun* a small usu specialized and isolated habitat, e.g. a decaying tree stump.

microinstruction /,miekrohin'struksh(ə)n/ *noun* a very low-level instruction, sequences of which are stored within a computer processor and correspond to a single machine operation.

microlight /'miekrəliet/ *noun chiefly Brit* a very small light aircraft for one or two people.

microlith /'miekrohlith/ *noun* a tiny flint blade tool, *esp* of the Mesolithic period, often set in a bone or wooden haft. ➤➤ **microlithic** /-'lithik/ *adj.*

micromanage /'miekrohmanij/ *verb trans NAmer* to oversee and control the minor details of (something). ➤➤ **micromanagement** *noun,* **micromanager** *noun.*

micromanipulation /,miekrohmənipyoo'laysh(ə)n/ *noun* dissection and injection of tissue or cells under the microscope using fine needles controlled by a series of levers.

micrometer /mie'kromitə/ *noun* **1** an instrument for measuring distances between objects seen through a microscope or telescope. **2** a gauge for making precise measurements of length by means of a spindle moved by a finely threaded screw. [French *micromètre,* from MICRO- + *-mètre* -METER²]

micrometre (*NAmer* **micrometer**) /'miekrohmeetə/ *noun* a metric unit of length equal to one millionth of a metre.

micrometry /mie'kromətri/ *noun* measurement with a micrometer.

microminiaturization or **microminiaturisation** /,miekroh-minichərie'zaysh(ə)n/ *noun* the process of producing things, *esp* electronic components, in an extremely small size.

micron /'miekron/ *noun* (*pl* **microns** or **micra** /'miekrə/) *no longer in technical use* one millionth part of a metre. [via Latin from Greek *mikron*, neuter of *mikros* small]

Micronesian /miekrə'neezhən, -zi·ən/ *noun* **1** a native or inhabitant of Micronesia, a group of islands in the W Pacific. **2** a group of Austronesian languages spoken in Micronesia. ▶▶ **Micronesian** *adj*.

micronutrient /miekroh'nyoohtri·ənt/ *noun* a nutrient, e.g. a trace element, required in small quantities.

micro-organism /miekroh'awgəniz(ə)m/ *noun* an organism of microscopic size or smaller, e.g. a bacterium.

microphage /'miekrohfayj, -fahzh/ *noun* a small PHAGOCYTE (cell that engulfs and destroys foreign matter).

microphone /'miekrəfohn/ *noun* a device that converts sounds into electrical signals, *esp* for transmission or recording. ▶▶ **microphonic** /-'fonik/ *adj*.

microphotograph /miekroh'fohtəgrahf/ *noun* a reduced photograph that must be magnified for viewing; a microcopy. ▶▶ **microphotography** /-'togrəfi/ *noun*.

microprint /'miekrəprint/ *noun* a photographic copy of graphic matter in reduced size.

microprocessor /miekroh'prohsesə/ *noun* an integrated circuit forming the central processing unit of a small computer.

micropyle /'miekrohpiel/ *noun* **1** in biology, an opening in the surface of an ovule of a flowering plant through which the pollen tube penetrates. **2** in zoology, a differentiated area of the surface of an egg through which the sperm enters. [MICRO- + Greek *pylē* gate]

microscope /'miekrəskohp/ *noun* **1** an optical instrument consisting of a lens or combination of lenses mounted above a base plate and used to magnify minute objects. **2** an instrument, e.g. an electron microscope, using radiations other than light to produce enlarged images of minute objects. [Latin *microscopium*, from MICRO- + -*scopium* -SCOPE]

microscopic /miekrə'skopik/ *adj* **1** invisible or indistinguishable without the use of a microscope. **2** *informal* very small. **3** of or conducted with the microscope or microscopy. **4** characterized by great attention to detail. ▶▶ **microscopical** *adj*, **microscopically** *adv*.

microscopy /mie'kroskəpi/ *noun* the use of a microscope. ▶▶ **microscopist** *noun*.

microsecond /'miekrohsekənd/ *noun* one millionth of a second.

microsome /'miekrohsohm/ *noun* a minute particle seen in a fraction obtained by heavy centrifugation (spinning under gravity; see CENTRIFUGE[2]) of broken cells viewed through an electron microscope, usually fragments of ENDOPLASMIC RETICULUM (system of interconnected double membranes in cell cytoplasm). ▶▶ **microsomal** /-'sohml/ *adj*. [German *Mikrosom*, from MICRO- + Greek *sōma* body]

microstructure /'miekrohstrukchə/ *noun* the structure of a mineral, alloy, living cell, etc, which can be seen through a microscope. ▶▶ **microstructural** *adj*.

microsurgery /miekroh'suhjəri/ *noun* minute surgical dissection or manipulation of living tissue, usu under a microscope, e.g. in eye surgery. ▶▶ **microsurgical** /-'suhjikl/ *adj*.

microswitch /'miekrohswich/ *noun* an electrical switch that can be operated by a small usu delicate movement.

microteaching /'miekrohteeching/ *noun* the teaching of a small group for a short time, *esp* as practice for a trainee teacher.

microtome /'miekrohtohm/ *noun* an instrument for cutting sections, e.g. of plant or animal tissues, for microscopic examination.

microtone /'miekrohtohn/ *noun* a musical interval smaller than a semitone. ▶▶ **microtonal** /-'tohnl/ *adj*, **microtonality** /-'naliti/ *noun*, **microtonally** /-'tohnəli/ *adv*.

microtubule /miekroh'tyoohbyoohl/ *noun* any of the minute cylindrical structures in cells that are widely distributed in cytoplasm and are made up of protein subunits.

microwave[1] /'miekrəwayv/ *noun* **1** a band of very short electromagnetic waves of between 0.001m and 0.3m in wavelength. **2** a microwave oven.

microwave[2] *verb trans* to cook or heat (food) in a microwave oven. ▶▶ **microwavable** *adj*, **microwaveable** *adj*.

microwave background *noun* microwave radiation detected by astronomers that appears to pervade all space and is thought to be a relic of the big bang that formed the universe.

microwave oven *noun* an oven in which food is cooked by the heat produced as a result of the interaction between penetrating microwaves and the substance of the food.

micturate /'miktyoorayt/ *verb intrans formal* to urinate. ▶▶ **micturition** /-'rish(ə)n/ *noun*. [Latin *micturire* from *mictus*, past part. of *mingere*]

mid[1] /mid/ *adj* **1** being the part in the middle or midst: *She lived in the mid 19th century.* **2** occupying a middle position. **3** said of a vowel: articulated with the tongue midway between the upper and lower areas of the mouth. [Old English *midde*; related to Latin *medius*, Greek *mesos*]

mid[2] *prep literary* amid.

mid- *comb. form* forming words, denoting: **1** the middle part or point of something: *mid-August*; *in mid-sentence*. **2** something of medium size or between the two extremes of a range of things: *midiron*.

midair /mid'eə/ *noun* a point or region in the air above ground level.

Midas touch /'miedəs/ *noun* the talent for making wealth out of any activity one turns one's hand to. [named after *Midas*, a king of Phrygia in Greek mythology, to whom the god Dionysus gave the power to turn anything into gold by touching it]

mid-Atlantic *adj* said of language: halfway between American and British English.

midbrain /'midbrayn/ *noun* the middle of the three primary divisions of the vertebrate brain in both its fully developed and embryonic forms.

midday /-'day/ *noun* the middle part of the day; noon.

midden /'mid(ə)n/ *noun* **1** a dunghill. **2** = KITCHEN MIDDEN. [Middle English *midding*, of Scandinavian origin]

middle[1] /'midl/ *adj* **1** equally distant from the extremes of something; central. **2** intermediate, e.g. in rank or quality. **3** (**Middle**) denoting a form intermediate in time or development: *Middle English*. **4** said of a verb form or voice: typically asserting that one both performs and is affected by the action represented; expressing reflexive or reciprocal action. [Old English *middel*; related to Latin *medius*]

middle[2] *noun* **1** a middle part, point, or position. **2** *informal* the waist and abdomen. **3** a middle verb form or voice.

middle[3] *verb trans* in cricket, tennis, etc, to hit (a shot) correctly with the middle of the bat or racket.

middle age *noun* the period of life from about 40 to about 60: *middle age … between youth and old age, variously reckoned to suit the reckoner* — Chambers Dictionary. ▶▶ **middle-aged** *adj*.

middle-aged spread *noun* an increase in girth, *esp* round the waist, associated with middle age.

Middle Ages *pl noun* (*usu* **the Middle Ages**) the period of European history from about AD 1000 to about 1500, or more technically, from the deposition of the last Roman emperor in the West in AD 476 to the fall of Constantinople in 1453.

middle-age spread *noun* = MIDDLE-AGED SPREAD.

Middle America *noun* **1** the middle classes of the USA. **2** the midwestern states of the USA. **3** Central America and Mexico. ▶▶ **Middle American** *adj and noun*.

middlebrow *adj informal, derog* having a quite easily accessible intellectual content and conventional form: *Somerset Maugham's Cakes and Ale mocks a vain middlebrow bestseller called Alroy Kear, modelled on Hugh Walpole* — New Statesman.

middle C *noun* in music, the note designated by the first ledger line below the treble staff and the first above the bass staff.

middle class *noun* (*also in pl, but treated as sing. or pl*) a class occupying a position between upper and lower, consisting *esp* of business and professional people. ▶▶ **middle-class** *adj*.

middle distance *noun* the part of a picture or view between the foreground and the background.

middle-distance *adj* in athletics, denoting a race over a distance between 400m and 1500m (or between 440yd and 1mi).

middle ear *noun* a cavity through which sound waves are transmitted by a chain of tiny bones from the eardrum to the inner ear.

Middle East *noun* the countries of SW Asia and N Africa, usu taken to include Turkey, Libya, Egypt, Lebanon, Syria, Israel, Jordan, the states of the Arabian Peninsula, Iran, and Iraq. ➤➤ **Middle Eastern** *adj*.

middle eight *noun* the short middle section of a conventionally organized popular song, often eight bars in length and differing in tune and character from the rest of the song.

Middle England *noun* a collective term for middle-class, middle-income people living in small towns or suburban or rural areas, who have conventional political, social, and moral views.

Middle English *noun* English from about 1150 to 1500.

middle game *noun* the part of a chess game following the opening moves when players attempt to gain and exploit positional and material advantage: compare END GAME, OPENING¹ (2A).

middle ground *noun* **1** a standpoint midway between extremes. **2** = MIDDLE DISTANCE.

Middle High German *noun* the form of HIGH GERMAN (German as orig spoken in S Germany) used from around 1200 to around 1500.

Middle Low German *noun* the form of LOW GERMAN (German as orig spoken in N Germany) used from around 1200 to around 1500.

middleman *noun* (*pl* **middlemen**) an intermediary between two parties; *esp* a dealer intermediate between the producer of goods and the retailer or consumer.

middle management *noun* the group of people who manage and direct the departments or groups within an organization, but are not responsible for its overall management. ➤➤ **middle manager** *noun*.

middle name *noun* **1** a person's name between the first name and the surname. **2** a quality of character for which somebody is well known: *Generosity is her middle name.*

middle-of-the-road *adj* **1** conforming to the majority in taste, attitude, or conduct. **2** moderate in political conviction.

middle passage *noun* (*usu* **the middle passage**) the Atlantic crossing from W Africa to the Caribbean made by ships involved in the slave trade. This was the central section of a round trip for European slave ships, which took them from Europe to Africa, from Africa to America, and from America back to Europe.

middle school *noun* **1** in Britain, a school, or part of a school, for pupils aged 8–12 or 9–13. **2** in the USA and Canada, a junior high school.

middle-sized *adj* neither large nor small; of medium size.

middle term *noun* in logic, the term of a SYLLOGISM (a formal deductive argument) that occurs in both premises.

middleware *noun* computer software that has an intermediate function between the operating system and the various applications that are run on the machine.

middle watch *noun* the part of a ship's watch between midnight and 4 a.m.

middleweight *noun* **1** a weight in boxing of 70–72.5kg (154–160lb) if professional or 71–75kg (157–165lb) if amateur. **2** a weight in wrestling of 76–80kg (166–176lb) if professional or 75–82kg (165–180lb) if amateur.

middling *adj* **1** of middle or moderate size, degree, or quality. **2** mediocre or second-rate. ➤➤ **middling** *adv*, **middlingly** *adv*. [Middle English (Scot) *mydlyn*, prob from *mid, middle* mid]

middlings *pl noun* (*treated as sing. or pl*) a granular product or by-product of grain milling used in animal feeds.

Middx *abbr* Middlesex.

middy /'midi/ *noun* (*pl* **middies**) **1** *informal* a midshipman. **2** a loosely fitting blouse with a sailor collar, formerly worn by women and children. [by shortening and alteration]

midfield /'midfeeld, mid'feeld/ *noun* **1** the part of a pitch or playing field midway between the goals. **2** the group of players in a football team who act as a link between the defenders and strikers. ➤➤ **midfielder** *noun*.

midge /mij/ *noun* **1** a small two-winged fly often found near water. Some of them feed on blood: families Ceratopogonidae and Chironomidae. **2** used in the names of other small flies whose larvae produce galls or damage the leaves of plants. **3** *informal* a small person. [Old English *mycg*; related to Latin *musca*, Greek *myia* fly]

midget /'mijit/ *noun* **1** a very small person; a dwarf. **2** (*used before a noun*) of a much smaller size than usual: *a midget submarine.* [MIDGE + -ET]

midgut /'midgut/ *noun* the middle part of the digestive tract, that in vertebrates includes the small intestine.

MIDI /'midi/ *noun* (*often used before a noun*) a standard specification for linking up electronic musical instruments to a computer: *a MIDI synthesizer.* [acronym from *Musical Instrument Digital Interface*]

midi /'midi/ *noun* (*pl* **midis**) a woman's skirt, dress, or coat that extends to the mid-calf. [MID¹ + -*i* as in MINI¹, MAXI]

midi- *comb. form* forming words, denoting: medium size or length.

midinette /,midi'net/ *noun* a young seamstress working for a fashion house in Paris, or a saleswoman in a clothes shop. [French *midinette*, from *midi* midday + *dinette* quick meal; prob because seamstresses were only allowed time for a quick snack at lunch]

midiron /'midie·ən/ *noun* in golf, a club used for drives over a medium distance, such as a 4, 5, or 6 iron.

midi system *noun Brit* a compact unit consisting of parts making up a hi-fi system.

midland /'midlənd/ *noun* the central region of a country. ➤➤ **midland** *adj*.

Midlands *noun* (**the Midlands**) part of the central area of England, usually taken as comprising Leicestershire, Nottinghamshire, Derbyshire, Staffordshire, the West Midlands metropolitan district, and the E parts of Herefordshire and Worcestershire. ➤➤ **Midlander** *noun*.

mid-life crisis *noun* a loss of confidence and purpose that may affect a person in early middle age, with the realization that the pattern of his or her life is now established.

midline /'midlien, 'midlien/ *noun* the middle line or plane, *esp* of the body or a part of the body.

midmost *adj literary* positioned in or near the middle of something. ➤➤ **midmost** *adv*.

midnight /'midniet/ *noun* the middle of the night; *specif* twelve o'clock at night.

midnight sun *noun* the sun visible at midnight in the arctic or antarctic summer.

mid-off *noun* in cricket, a fielding position near the bowler on the off side of the pitch, or a fielder in this position.

mid-on *noun* in cricket, a fielding position near the bowler on the leg side of the pitch, or a fielder in this position.

midpoint *noun* a point midway between the beginning and end of something.

Midrash /'midrash/ *noun* (*pl* **Midrashim** /mid'rashim/) a commentary on a Hebrew biblical text. [Hebrew *midhrāsh* exposition, explanation]

midrib *noun* the large central vein of a leaf.

midriff /'midrif/ *noun* **1** the middle part of the human torso. **2** = DIAPHRAGM (I). [Old English *midhrif*, from *midde* mid + *hrif* belly]

midship /'midship/ *noun* the middle section of a ship or boat.

midshipman /'midshipmən/ *noun* (*pl* **midshipmen**) **1a** a young person training to become a naval officer in the Royal Navy. **b** a cadet in the US navy. **2** an American toadfish with organs that produce light along the underside of its body: genus *Porichthys*.

midships *adv* amidships.

midst¹ /midst/ *noun archaic or literary* the inner or central part or point of something. ✳ **in somebody's midst** among a group of people, or within a group or organization: *It was clear that we had an informer in our midst.* **in the midst of 1** in the middle of (something); surrounded or beset by (something). **2** during or around the midpoint of (something): *I arrived in the midst of the celebrations.* [Middle English *middest*, alteration of *middes*, back-formation from *amiddes* amid]

midst² *prep archaic or literary* amid.

midstream *noun* the part of a stream towards the middle. ✳ **in midstream 1** in the middle of a stream or river. **2** in the middle of a process or activity.

midsummer *noun* **1** the period around the middle of summer. **2** the summer solstice.

Midsummer Day *or* **Midsummer's Day** *noun* the feast of the nativity of John the Baptist, celebrated on 24 June.

midterm /'midtuhm/ *noun* **1** the period around the midpoint of an academic term, a term of office, or a pregnancy. **2** *NAmer* an examination held in the middle of an academic term.

midway[1] *adv and adj* halfway.

midway[2] *noun NAmer* a central section of a fair, carnival, or exhibition, containing sideshows and other attractions.

midweek *noun* the middle of the week. ➤➤ **midweek** *adj and adv.*

Midwest *noun* the N central part of the USA, including the states of Ohio, Illinois, Michigan, Indiana, Minnesota, Iowa, Missouri, Nebraska, and Kansas. ➤➤ **Midwestern** *adj.*

mid-wicket *noun* in cricket, a fielding position on the leg side equidistant from each wicket, or a fielder in this position.

midwife /'midwief/ *noun* (*pl* **midwives**) a nurse trained to assist women in childbirth. [Middle English *midwif*, from *mid* with + *wif* woman]

midwifery /'midwifəri, mid'wif-/ *noun* the job, study, or techniques of assisting at childbirth; obstetrics.

midwife toad *noun* either of two rather small toads of central and SW Europe, the male of which carries the strings of eggs laid by the female until they hatch: *Alytes obstetricans* and *Alytes cisternasi.*

midwinter *noun* **1** the period around the middle of winter. **2** the winter solstice.

mien /meen/ *noun* a person's air or bearing, *esp* as expressive of mood or personality: *One praised her ankles, one her eyes, one her dark hair and lovesome mien* — Tennyson. [by shortening and alteration from DEMEAN[2]]

mifepristone /mife'pristohn/ *noun* a synthetic steroid given to induce abortion early in a pregnancy, which it does by blocking the action of the hormone progesterone. [Dutch *mifepriston*, from *mife-* (aminophenol) + *-pr-* (propyl) + *-ist-* (oestradiol) + -ONE]

miff[1] /mif/ *verb trans informal* to make (somebody) cross or peeved. [origin unknown]

miff[2] *noun informal* **1** an irritable or sulky mood. **2** a trivial quarrel.

might[1] /miet/ *verb* the past tense of MAY[1] used to express: **1** permission or possibility: *He asked whether he might come; The king might do nothing without parliament's consent.* **2** a past or present possibility that is unfulfilled: *I might well have been killed; If he were older he might understand.* **3** a purpose or intention in the past: *I wrote it down so that I might not forget it.* **4** expectation or obligation: *You might at least apologize; They might have offered to help.* **5** a polite or ironic question: *Who might you be?* [Old English *meahte, mihte*]

might[2] *noun* great power or strength. ✳ **with might and main** with all the strength or power that one has. [Old English *miht*]

mightily /'miet(ə)l·i/ *adv* very much: *It amused us mightily* — Charles Dickens.

mightn't /'mietnt/ *contraction* might not.

mighty[1] /'mieti/ *adj* (**mightier, mightiest**) **1** powerful or strong. **2** imposingly great: *the mighty mountains.* **3** *informal* very large or loud: *a mighty crash.* ➤➤ **mightiness** *noun.*

mighty[2] *adv chiefly NAmer, informal* to a great degree; extremely: *a mighty big man.*

mignonette /minyə'net/ *noun* any of several species of annual garden plants with fragrant greenish yellow flowers: genus *Reseda.* [French *mignonnette*, dimin. of *mignon* darling]

migraine /'meegrayn/ *noun* a recurrent severe headache usu associated with disturbances of vision, sensation, and movement often on only one side of the body. ➤➤ **migrainous** *adj.* [French *migraine* via late Latin from Greek *hēmikrania* pain in one side of the head, from HEMI- + *kranion* cranium]

migrant /'miegrənt/ *noun* **1** an animal that moves from one habitat to another for feeding or breeding. **2** a person who moves regularly in order to find seasonal work. ➤➤ **migrant** *adj.* [Latin *migrant-, migrans*, present part. of *migrare*]

migrate /mie'grayt/ *verb intrans* **1** said of an animal: to pass seasonally from one region or climate to another for feeding or breeding. **2** said of a person: to move from one country or locality to another. **3** to move or change position: *Filarial worms migrate within the human body.* **4** in computing, to change from one hardware or software system to another. ➤➤ **migration** *noun*, **migrational** *adj*, **migrator** *noun.* [Latin *migratus*, past part. of *migrare*]

migratory /'miegrət(ə)ri/ *adj* wandering or roving.

mihrab /'meerab, 'meerəb/ *noun* a niche in the wall of a mosque that indicates the direction towards Mecca. [Arabic *miḥrāb*]

mikado /mi'kahdoh/ *noun* (*pl* **mikados**) a title formerly used for the emperor of Japan. [Japanese *mikado*, from *mi* magnificent + *kado* door]

mike[1] /miek/ *noun informal* a microphone. [by shortening and alteration]

mike[2] *verb trans informal* to place a microphone in or near (something).

Mi'kmaq /'mikmak/ *noun* see MICMAC.

mil[1] /mil/ *noun* a unit of length equal to 1000th of an inch (about 0.0254mm) used *esp* for the diameter of wire and formerly in precision engineering. [Latin *mille* thousand]

mil[2] *abbr* **1** millilitres. **2** millimetres. **3** *informal* millions.

milady /mi'laydi/ *noun* (*pl* **miladies**) formerly used as a term of address to an Englishwoman of noble or gentle birth. [via French from English *my lady*]

milage /'mielij/ *noun* see MILEAGE.

Milanese /milə'neez/ *noun* (*pl* **Milanese**) a native or inhabitant of the city of Milan in N Italy. ➤➤ **Milanese** *adj.*

milch /milch/ *adj* said of a domestic animal: bred or used primarily for milk production. [Old English *-milce*]

milch cow *noun* **1** a cow kept for its milk. **2** a source of easily acquired gain: *Industry is being made the milch cow of the economy.*

mild[1] /mield/ *adj* **1** gentle in nature or manner. **2** not severe: *a mild case of chickenpox.* **3** not strong in flavour or effect: *a mild curry; mild painkillers.* **4** not extreme, *esp* not acutely felt or strongly expressed: *She looked up in mild surprise.* **5** said of the weather: quite warm. ➤➤ **mildly** *adv*, **mildness** *noun.* [Old English *milde*]

mild[2] *noun Brit* a dark-coloured beer not flavoured with hops.

mildew[1] /'mildyooh/ *noun* a usu whitish growth on the surface of organic matter, e.g. paper or leather, or living plants, caused by fungi. ➤➤ **mildewy** *adj.* [Old English *meledēaw* honeydew]

mildew[2] *verb trans* to affect (something) with mildew. ➤ *verb intrans* to be affected with mildew.

mild steel *noun* a type of strong steel that is easily worked, containing a low proportion of carbon.

mile /miel/ *noun* **1a** (*also* **statute mile**) a unit of distance equal to 1760yd (about 1.61km). **b** = NAUTICAL MILE. **c** an old Roman unit equal to 1000 paces (about 1.48km). **2** (*often in pl*) a large distance or amount: *We travelled miles that day.* ✳ **miles from nowhere** in an extremely remote place. [Old English *mīl*, ultimately from Latin *milia* miles, from *milia passuum* thousands of paces]

mileage *or* **milage** /'mielij/ *noun* **1a** a total length, distance, or distance covered, in miles. **b** the number of miles travelled over a period of time. **2** an allowance for travelling expenses at a certain rate per mile. **3** the average distance in miles a vehicle will travel for an amount of fuel. **4** *informal* the benefit derived from something or the amount of service it has given: *She has had quite a bit of mileage out of that particular story.*

Mile High Club *noun* a notional set of people who have had sexual intercourse in a high-flying aircraft.

mileometer *or* **milometer** /mie'lomitə/ *noun Brit* an instrument fitted in a car or other vehicle to record the number of miles it travels.

milepost *noun* **1** *chiefly NAmer, Aus* a post indicating the distance in miles from or to a given point. **2** a post indicating one mile from the end of a race. **3** a significant new stage or development.

miler *noun* a person or horse that competes in mile races.

miles *adv informal* very much: *He's miles happier in that new job.*

milestone *noun* **1** a stone serving as a milepost. **2** a crucial stage in something's development.

milfoil /'milfoyl/ *noun* **1** yarrow. **2** a water plant with submerged leaves divided into very narrow segments: genus *Myriophyllum.*

Also called WATER MILFOIL. [Middle English via Old French from Latin *millefolium*, from *mille* thousand + *folium* leaf]

miliaria /mili'eəri·ə/ *noun* = PRICKLY HEAT. [Latin *milaria*, fem of *miliarius* of millet]

miliary /'milyəri/ *adj* said of a disease: characterized by many small projections, blisters, or nodules resembling millet seed. [Latin *miliarius* of millet, from *milium* millet]

milieu /'meelyuh, meel'yuh (*French* miljø)/ *noun* (*pl* **milieus** *or* **milieux** /'meelyuh(z), meel'yuh(z) (*French* miljø)/) a person's environment or setting. [French *milieu* midst, from *mi* middle + *lieu* place]

militant /'milit(ə)nt/ *adj* **1** aggressively active, e.g. in a cause; combative. **2** engaged in warfare or combat. ➤➤ **militancy** /-si/ *noun*, **militant** *noun*, **militantly** *adv*. [Middle English via French from Latin *militant-*, *militans*, present part. of *militare* to engage in warfare]

militarise /'militəriez/ *verb trans* see MILITARIZE.

militarism /'militəriz(ə)m/ *noun* **1** a policy of aggressive military preparedness. **2** the glorification of military virtues and ideals. ➤➤ **militarist** *noun*, **militaristic** /-'ristik/ *adj*.

militarize *or* **militarise** /'militəriez/ *verb trans* **1** to equip (somebody or something) with military forces and defences. **2** to give a military character to (something). ➤➤ **militarization** /-'zaysh(ə)n/ *noun*, **militarized** *adj*.

military[1] /'milit(ə)ri/ *adj* **1** relating to or characteristic of soldiers, arms, or war. **2** carried on or supported by armed force: *a military dictatorship*. ➤➤ **militarily** *adv*. [early French *militaire* from Latin *militaris*, from *milit-*, *miles* soldier]

military[2] *noun* (**the military**) a country's armed forces.

military police *noun* (*treated as pl*) a branch of an army that carries out police functions within it. ➤➤ **military policeman** *noun*, **military policewoman** *noun*.

militate /'militayt/ *verb intrans* (*usu* + against) to have significant weight or effect against something. [Latin *militatus*, past part. of *militare* to engage in warfare, from *milit-*, *miles* soldier]

Usage note

militate *or* **mitigate**? These two words are sometimes confused. *Militate* is related in form and meaning to *militant* and *military*, and its earliest meaning is 'to serve as a soldier' or 'to fight'. It is usually followed by *against* and in modern English means 'to exert a powerful influence against' or 'make very difficult or unlikely': *Present circumstances militate against an early resumption of peace talks*. *Mitigate* is followed by a direct object and means 'to make less severe': *measures intended to mitigate the harshness of prison life*.

militia /mi'lishə/ *noun* **1** (*treated as sing. or pl*) a body of citizens with some military training who are called on to fight only in an emergency. **2** (*treated as sing. or pl*) in the USA, the whole body of citizens declared by law as being subject to call to military service. ➤➤ **militiaman** *noun*. [Latin *militia* military service, from *milit-*, *miles* soldier]

milk[1] /milk/ *noun* **1a** a white or creamy liquid secreted by the mammary glands of female mammals for the nourishment of their young. **b** the milk of cows, goats and similar animals used as food for humans. **2** a liquid similar to milk, e.g.: **a** the latex of a plant. **b** the juice of a coconut. **c** a cosmetic lotion, *esp* a cleanser. [Old English *meolc, milc*]

milk[2] *verb trans* **1** to draw milk from (a cow, goat, etc). **2** to extract sap or venom from (something). **3a** to draw all possible advantage from (a situation or person): *He milked the audience for applause*. **b** to extract money from (somebody) over a period of time.

milk-and-water *adj* weak or insipid: *milk-and-water liberalism*.

milk bar *noun Brit* a snack bar that sells milk drinks, particularly milk shakes, and other light refreshments.

milk chocolate *noun* solid chocolate made with the addition of milk, which is mild and sweet in taste.

milker *noun* **1** a person who milks cows or other animals. **2** an animal kept to supply milk, or considered from the point of view of the amount and quality of milk it supplies.

milk fever *noun* **1** a disease of cows, sheep, goats, etc that have recently given birth, caused by a drain on the body's mineral reserves during the establishment of the milk flow. **2** a feverish disorder caused by infection after childbirth.

milk float *noun Brit* a light *usu* electrically propelled vehicle for carrying milk for domestic delivery.

milk leg *noun* a painful swelling of the leg after childbirth caused by thrombosis in the veins.

milkmaid *noun archaic* a girl or woman who works in a dairy.

milkman *noun* (*pl* **milkmen**) a man who sells or delivers milk.

Milk of Magnesia *noun Brit, trademark* a white suspension of magnesium hydroxide in water, used as an antacid and mild laxative.

milk pudding *noun Brit* a pudding consisting of rice, tapioca, sago, etc boiled or baked in sweetened milk.

milk round *noun* **1** *Brit* a regular route for delivering milk. **2** a series of visits to universities made by representatives of large firms in the hope of recruiting people who are about to graduate.

milk run *noun* a regular journey, e.g. by an aircraft.

milk shake *noun* a beverage made of milk and a flavouring syrup, thoroughly shaken or blended.

milksop *noun* a weak and timid person.

milk sugar *noun* = LACTOSE.

milk tooth *noun* a tooth of a mammal, *esp* a child, that is replaced later in life.

milkweed *noun* a plant that secretes milky latex: genus *Asclepias*.

milkwort *noun* any of several species of herbaceous plants and shrubs with small white, pink, or blue flowers, formerly believed to increase the milk in nursing mothers: genus *Polygala*.

milky *adj* (**milkier, milkiest**) **1** containing milk. **2** resembling milk in colour or consistency. **3** cloudy or semi-opaque: *The old man had milky blue eyes*. ➤➤ **milkily** *adv*, **milkiness** *noun*.

Milky Way *noun* **1** a broad irregular band of faint light that stretches completely round the celestial sphere and is caused by the light of the many stars forming the galaxy of which the sun and the solar system are a part. **2** the galaxy to which the solar system belongs. [Middle English, translation of Latin *via lactea*]

mill[1] /mil/ *noun* **1** a building provided with machinery for grinding grain into flour. **2** a machine or apparatus for grinding grain. **3** a machine or hand-operated device for crushing or grinding a solid substance, e.g. coffee beans or peppercorns. **4** a building or collection of buildings with machinery for manufacturing. **5** = MILLING MACHINE. ✳ **go/be put through the mill** to undergo an unpleasant or trying experience. [Old English *mylen*, ultimately from Latin *mola* mill, millstone, from *molere* to grind]

mill[2] *verb trans* **1** to grind (grain or a similar substance) into flour, meal, or powder. **2** to shape or dress (metal) by means of a rotary cutter. **3** to give a raised rim or a ridged edge to (a coin). **4** to thicken (wool) by fulling it. ➤ *verb intrans* (+ about/around) to move in a confused swirling mass. ➤➤ **millable** *adj*, **milled** *adj*.

millboard *noun* strong cardboard suitable for book covers and for panelling in furniture. [alteration of *milled board*]

milldam *noun* a dam to make a millpond.

millefeuille /'meelfœi/ *noun* a small cake made of layers of puff pastry with jam and cream in between. [French *millefeuilles*, literally 'one thousand leaves']

millefiori /milifi'awri/ *noun* ornamental glass produced by cutting cross-sections of variously sized and coloured fused bundles of glass rods. [Italian *millefiori*, from *mille* thousand (from Latin) + *fiori*, pl of *fiore* flower, from Latin *flor-*, *flos*]

millefleurs /'meelfluh/ *noun* a design consisting of many small flowers and leaves, used *esp* on tapestry and porcelain. [French *millefleurs*, literally 'a thousand flowers']

millenarian /mili'neəri·ən/ *adj* **1** relating to or believing in the imminent Second Coming of Christ. **2** relating to a thousand years. ➤➤ **millenarian** *noun*.

millenarianism *noun* **1** the belief that a 1000-year period of blessedness will immediately follow or precede the Second Coming of Christ. **2** the belief that there will be a future golden age. ➤➤ **millenarianist** *adj and noun*.

millenary[1] /mi'lenəri/ *noun* (*pl* **millenaries**) **1** a group of a thousand units or things. **2** a period of a thousand years. **3** a thousandth anniversary. [late Latin *millenarium*, neuter of *millenarius* of a thousand, from Latin *milleni* one thousand each, from *mille* thousand]

millenary[2] *adj* **1** relating to or consisting of a thousand. **2** suggesting a millennium.

millennia /mi'leni·ə/ *noun* pl of MILLENNIUM.

millennialism /mil'eni·əlizm/ *noun* = MILLENARIANISM. ➤➤ **millennialist** *adj and noun.*

millennium /mi'leni·əm/ *noun* (*pl* **millennia** /-ni·ə/ *or* **millenniums**) **1a** a period of a thousand years, *esp* measured from the traditional date of the birth of Christ. **b** a thousandth anniversary. **2** the date on which one period of a thousand years ends and another begins. **3a** the thousand years mentioned in the Bible (Rev. 20) during which holiness is to prevail and Christ is to reign on earth. **b** a future golden age. ➤➤ **millennial** *adj*. [Latin *mille* thousand + late Latin *-ennium* as in *biennium* period of two years]
Usage note —————————————————
Millennium is spelt with two *l*'s and two *n*'s, separated by an *e*.

millennium bug *noun* an inherent weakness in the dating software used in the operating systems and programs of many computers, caused by storing the year as two digits only. Some computers were unable to recognize the fact that the year 2000 (represented by the digits 00) followed the year 1999 (represented by the digits 99).

millepede /'milipeed/ *noun* see MILLIPEDE.

millepore /'milipaw/ *noun* a stony reef-building coral: genus *Millepora*. [Latin *mille* thousand + *porus* pore]

miller /'milə/ *noun* a person who owns or works a mill, *esp* for corn.

miller's-thumb *noun* a small freshwater fish of Europe and N America, with a flattened head and body: *Cottus gobio*.

millesimal /mi'lesim(ə)l/ *adj* relating to division into thousandths; a thousandth. ➤➤ **millesimal** *noun*, **millesimally** *adv*. [Latin *millesimus* thousandth, from *mille* thousand]

millet /'milit/ *noun* **1** any of various small-seeded annual cereal and forage grasses cultivated for their grain and used as food, *esp* one cultivated in Europe and Asia: *Panicum miliaceum*. **2** the seed of any of these grasses. [Middle English *milet* via French from Latin *milium*]

milli- *comb. form* forming words, denoting: 1000th part of a specified unit: *milligram*. [via French from Latin *milli-* thousand, from *mille*]

milliard /'miliahd, 'milyahd/ *noun Brit, dated* a thousand millions (10^9). [French *milliard* from *mille* thousand]

millibar /'milibah/ *noun* a unit of pressure equal to 1000th of a bar.

milligram *or* **milligramme** /'miligram/ *noun* one thousandth of a gram. [French *milligramme*, from MILLI- + *gramme* gram]

millilitre (*NAmer* **milliliter**) /'mililleetə/ *noun* one thousandth of a litre (0.002 pints).

millimetre (*NAmer* **millimeter**) /'milimeetə/ *noun* one thousandth of a metre (about 0.039in.). [French *millimètre*, from MILLI- + *mètre* metre]

milliner /'milinə/ *noun* a person who designs, makes, or sells women's hats: *Young ladies of rank and position do occasionally have private debts which they dare not acknowledge … Sometimes the milliner and the jeweller are at the bottom of it* — Wilkie Collins. ➤➤ **millinery** *noun*. [irreg from *Milan*, city in N Italy; from the importation of women's finery from Italy in the 16th cent.]

milling machine *noun* a machine tool for shaping metal against rotating milling cutters.

million /'milyən/ *noun* (*pl* **millions** *or* **million**) **1** the number 1,000,000 (10^6), or the quantity represented by it. **2** *informal* (*also in pl*) an indefinitely large number: *There are millions of things to think about*. ➤➤ **million** *adj*, **millionth** *adj and noun*. [Middle English *milioun* via early French *milion* from Old Italian *milione*, augmentative of *mille* thousand, from Latin *mille*]

millionaire /milyə'neə/ *or* **millionairess** /-'neəres/ *noun* a man or woman whose wealth is estimated at a million or more money units. [French *millionnaire*, from *million* million]

millipede *or* **millepede** /'milipeed/ *noun* any of numerous species of invertebrate animals related to the centipedes, usu with a cylindrical segmented body and two pairs of legs on each segment: class Diplopoda. [Latin *millepeda* a small crawling animal, from *mille* thousand + *ped-, pes* foot]

millisecond /'milisekənd/ *noun* one thousandth of a second.

millpond *noun* a pond produced by damming a stream to produce a head of water for operating a mill.

millrace *noun* a channel in which water flows to and from a mill wheel, or the usu swift-flowing current in such a channel. [Middle English *milnras*, from *miln, mille* mill + *ras* race, current]

Mills bomb /milz/ *noun* an oval hand grenade with a serrated exterior, used *esp* by British forces during World War I. [named after Sir William *Mills* d.1932, English inventor]

millstone *noun* **1** either of a pair of circular stones that rotate against each other and are used for grinding grain. **2** a heavy or crushing burden.

millstream *noun* a stream flowing past a mill and used to turn a mill wheel.

mill wheel *noun* a waterwheel that drives a mill.

millwright /'milriet/ *noun* a person who plans, builds, or maintains mills.

milometer /mie'lomitə/ *noun* see MILEOMETER.

milord /mi'lawd/ *noun* formerly used as a term of address to an Englishman of noble or gentle birth. [via French from English *my lord*]

milt /milt/ *noun* the male reproductive glands of fishes when filled with secretion, or the secretion of these glands. [Old English *milte* spleen]

Miltonian /mil'tohni·ən/ *adj* of or characteristic of the poet John Milton or his work. ➤➤ **Miltonian** *noun*. [John *Milton* d.1674, English poet]

Miltonic /mil'tonik/ *adj* = MILTONIAN.

mime[1] /miem/ *noun* **1a** the art of portraying a character or telling a story by gesture and body movement. **b** a performance of mime. **c** a performer of mime. **2** an ancient dramatic entertainment representing scenes from life, usu in a ridiculous manner. [Latin *mimus* from Greek *mimos* imitator, actor]

mime[2] *verb intrans* **1** to act a part with gesture and body movement rather than words. **2** to pretend to sing or play a musical instrument, *esp* during a prerecorded performance. ➤ *verb trans* to act or express (something) using mime. ➤➤ **mimer** *noun*.

Mimeograph /'mimi·əgrahf/ *noun trademark* a duplicating machine for making copies from a stencil through which ink is pressed. [Greek *mimeomai* I imitate + -GRAPH]

mimeograph *verb trans* to make copies of (something) using a Mimeograph.

mimesis /mi'meesis/ *noun* **1** in art or literature, the imitative representation of reality. **2** in biology or sociology, imitation or mimicry. [via Latin from Greek *mimēsis* from *mimeisthai* to imitate]

mimetic /mi'metik/ *adj* **1** imitative. **2** relating to, characterized by, or exhibiting mimicry. ➤➤ **mimetically** *adv*. [via Latin from Greek *mimētikos* from *mimeisthai* to imitate]

mimic[1] /'mimik/ *verb trans* (**mimicked, mimicking**) **1** to imitate (somebody or something, e.g. their voice or mannerisms), *esp* slavishly; to ape (them). **2** to ridicule (somebody or something) by imitation. **3** to simulate (something). **4** in biology, to resemble (something) by mimicry. [via Latin from Greek *mimikos* from *mimos* mime]

mimic[2] *noun* somebody or something that mimics another or others.

mimic[3] *adj* **1a** imitative. **b** imitation; mock: *a mimic battle*. **2** of mime or mimicry. ➤➤ **mimical** *adj*.

mimicry /'mimikri/ *noun* **1** the act or an instance of mimicking. **2** in biology, resemblance of one organism to another that secures it an advantage, e.g. protection from predators.

mimosa /mi'mohzə, -sə/ *noun* **1** any of a genus of tropical and subtropical trees, shrubs, and non-woody plants of the pea family that have globular heads of small yellow flowers and leaves that droop or close in response to light, touch, etc: genus *Mimosa*. **2** an acacia tree with sweetly scented yellow flowers in compact globular clusters: *Acacia dealbata*. [from the Latin genus name, from *mimus* mime; from its apparent imitation of animal sensitivity when touched]

mimulus /'mimyooləs/ *noun* any of a genus of plants that includes the monkey flower: genus *Mimulus*. [from the Latin genus name, from Latin *mimus* mime; prob from the masklike shape of the flowers]

Min. *abbr* **1** Minister. **2** Ministry.

min. *abbr* **1** minimum. **2** minor. **3** minute (unit of time).

mina /'mienə/ *noun* see MYNAH.

minaret /minə'ret/ *noun* a slender tower attached to a mosque and surrounded by one or more projecting balconies from which the summons to prayer is made. ⟫ **minareted** *adj.* [via French from Turkish *minare* from Arabic *manārah* lighthouse]

minatory /ˈminət(ə)ri/ *adj formal* menacing; threatening. [late Latin *minatorius* from Latin *minatus*, past part. of *minari* to threaten]

mince[1] /mins/ *verb trans* to cut or chop (meat, etc) into very small pieces. ⟩ *verb intrans* to walk with short steps in an affected manner. ✳ **not mince matters/one's words** to speak honestly and frankly. ⟫ **mincer** *noun*. [Middle English *mincen* from early French *mincer*, ultimately from Latin *minutia* smallness]

mince[2] *noun chiefly Brit* minced meat.

mincemeat *noun* a mixture of raisins, finely chopped apples, suet, spices, etc, sometimes flavoured with brandy, used *esp* to fill pies. ✳ **make mincemeat of** to defeat (somebody) soundly and conclusively.

mince pie *noun* a small round pie filled with mincemeat, eaten *esp* at Christmas.

mincing *adj* affectedly dainty or delicate: *trying to speak in a small mincing treble* — George Eliot. ⟫ **mincingly** *adv*.

mind[1] /miend/ *noun* **1** the organized conscious and unconscious mental processes of an organism that result in reasoning, thinking, perceiving, etc: *It is wonderful … how little the mind is actually employed in the discharge of any profession* — Dr Johnson. **2a** recollection; memory: *time out of mind*. **b** attention; concentration. **3** the normal condition of the mental faculties: *He lost his mind*. **4a** an intention or desire: *I've a good mind to withdraw my offer*. **b** an opinion or view: *of the same mind*. **5** a disposition or mood: *her state of mind*. **6** the mental attributes of a specified group: *the scientific mind*. **7** a person considered as an intellectual being: *She is one of the finest minds of the academic world*. **8a** the intellect and rational faculties as contrasted with the emotions. **b** the human spirit and intellect as opposed to the body and the material world: *mind over matter*. ✳ **a piece of one's mind** a severe scolding. **bear/keep in mind** to think of (something), *esp* at the appropriate time; not to forget (it). **bring to mind** to cause (something) to be recalled. **change one's mind** to alter a decision or adopt a different plan. **cross one's mind** said of a thought: to occur to one. **on one's mind** occupying or troubling one's thoughts: *She can't work with the problem of the mortgage on her mind*. **out of one's mind** insane. **put somebody in mind of something** to remind somebody of something; to make them think of it. [Old English *gemynd*; related to Latin *ment-, mens* mind]

mind[2] *verb trans* **1** to be concerned or care about (something): *I don't mind what we do*. **b** to object to (something): *I don't mind the noise*. **2** to attend to (something) closely: *Mind how you behave*. **3** to pay attention to or follow (advice, instructions, or orders). **4a** to be careful or sure to do (something): *Mind you finish your homework!* **b** to be cautious about (something): *Mind the step*. **5** to give protective care to (somebody or something); to look after (them): *I'm minding my neighbours' children*. ⟩ *verb intrans* **1** (*often* + out) to be attentive or wary. **2** to be or become concerned; to care: *Never mind!* ✳ **mind you** take this fact into account; notice this: *mind you, I don't blame him*.

mind-bending *adj informal* **1** at the limits of understanding or credibility. **2** = MIND-BLOWING. ⟫ **mind-bender** *noun*, **mind-bendingly** *adv*.

mind-blowing *adj informal* **1** of or causing a psychic state similar to that produced by a psychedelic drug. **2** mentally or emotionally exhilarating. ⟫ **mind-blower** *noun*, **mind-blowingly** *adv*.

mind-boggling *adj informal* causing great surprise or wonder. ⟫ **mind-bogglingly** *adv*.

minded *adj* **1** (*used in combinations*) having a specified kind of mind: *narrow-minded*. **2** inclined; disposed: *He was not minded to report his losses*.

minder *noun* **1a** a person who looks after somebody or something. **b** = CHILDMINDER. **2** *chiefly Brit, informal* a person who provides physical protection to another or others, e.g.: a person who acts as a bodyguard and assistant to a person operating outside or on the edge of the law. **b** a person who accompanies a famous or important person, e.g. a politician, to monitor and control their contact with the media or the public.

mindful /ˈmiendf(ə)l/ *adj* (*often* + of) keeping something in mind; aware of something: *mindful of her responsibilities*. ⟫ **mindfully** *adv*, **mindfulness** *noun*.

mindless *adj* **1** devoid of thought or intelligence; senseless: *mindless violence*. **2** involving or requiring little thought or concentration: *mindless work*. **3** (+ of) inattentive to or heedless of something: *mindless of the danger*. ⟫ **mindlessly** *adv*, **mindlessness** *noun*.

mind-numbing *adj* extremely dull or boring. ⟫ **mind-numbingly** *adv*.

mind reader *noun* a person who can or is thought to be able to perceive what another person is thinking. ⟫ **mind reading** *noun*.

mindset *noun* a habitual attitude of mind; a set of basic assumptions that influences judgment and action: *small-minded imperial freebooters, comically limited by the mindset of their time* — The Listener.

mind's eye *noun* the faculty of visual memory or imagination: *'My father – I think I see my father.' 'O, where, my lord?' 'In my mind's eye, Horatio.'* — Shakespeare.

mine[1] /mien/ *pronoun* the one or ones that belong to me or are associated with me: *The book is mine; Mine are on the table; children younger than mine*. ✳ **of mine** belonging to or associated with me: *friends of mine*. [Old English *mīn*: see MY[1]]

mine[2] *adj archaic* used before a vowel or *h* or after a noun: my: *mine host; mistress mine*.

mine[3] *noun* **1a** an excavation from which mineral substances are taken, *esp* a system of tunnels and pits along with associated buildings etc. **b** an ore deposit. **2** (*often* + of) a rich source of something: *a mine of information*. **3** an encased explosive designed to destroy enemy personnel, vehicles, or ships. **4** an underground passage beneath an enemy position. [Middle English, from early French *mine*, prob of Celtic origin; related to Welsh *mwyn* ore]

mine[4] *verb trans* **1a** to obtain (ore, coal, etc) from a mine. **b** to dig into (the earth) for ore, coal, etc. **2** to seek valuable material in (something). **3** to place military mines in, on, or under (something): *They mined the harbour*. **4a** to dig an underground passage to gain access to or cause the collapse of (an enemy position). **b** = UNDERMINE. ⟩ *verb intrans* **1** to dig a mine. **2** to extract ore, coal, etc from a mine or mines, *esp* as an industry. ⟫ **mining** *noun*.

minefield *noun* **1** an area of land or water where explosive mines have been laid as a defence. **2** something that is full of hidden dangers or difficulties.

minelayer *noun* a vessel or aircraft for laying explosive mines.

miner *noun* **1** a person who works in a mine. **2** (*used in combinations*) any of various insects that burrow or tunnel into plant tissue: *a leaf miner*.

mineral[1] /ˈmin(ə)rəl/ *noun* **1a** a solid homogeneous crystalline inorganic substance. **b** any of various naturally occurring substances, e.g. stone, coal, or petroleum, obtained by drilling, mining, etc. **2** something that is neither animal nor plant. **3** *Brit* (*usu in pl*) an effervescent non-alcoholic drink. [Middle English from late Latin *minerale*, from neuter of *mineralis* (adj), from *minera* mine, ore, from Old French *miniere* mine]

mineral[2] *adj* of, being, or containing a mineral or minerals.

mineralize *or* **mineralise** *verb trans* **1a** to convert (organic matter) into a mineral or inorganic compound. **b** to impregnate (water, etc) with a mineral. **2** to transform (a metal or rock) into an ore. ⟫ **mineralization** /-ˈzaysh(ə)n/ *noun*.

mineral kingdom *noun* the one of the three basic groups of natural objects that includes inorganic objects: compare ANIMAL KINGDOM, PLANT KINGDOM.

mineralogy /minəˈraləji/ *noun* a branch of geology dealing with the structure, properties, and classification of minerals. ⟫ **mineralogical** /-ˈlojikl/ *adj*, **mineralogist** *noun*.

mineral oil *noun* an oil of mineral origin, e.g. petroleum, as opposed to one derived from plants.

mineral water *noun* water naturally or artificially impregnated with mineral salts or gases, e.g. carbon dioxide.

mineral wool *noun* any of various lightweight synthetic fibrous materials used *esp* in heat and sound insulation.

minestrone /miniˈstrohni/ *noun* a rich thick vegetable soup usu containing pasta. [Italian *minestrone*, augmentative of *minestra* from *minestrare* to serve, dish up, from Latin *ministrare* from *minister* servant]

minesweeper *noun* a ship designed for removing or neutralizing explosive mines. ⟫ **minesweeping** *noun*.

Ming /ming/ *noun* **1** a Chinese dynasty dating from 1368 to 1644. **2** (*used before a noun*) of or being Chinese porcelain produced during this dynasty: *a Ming vase*. [Chinese (Pekingese) *ming* luminous]

mingle /'ming-gl/ *verb trans* **1** to bring or mix (things) together. **2** to mix (something) with something else. ➤ *verb intrans* **1** to become mingled. **2** to mix with or go among a group of people: *mingling with the crowd*. [Middle English *menglen*, frequentative of *mengen* to mix, from Old English *mengan*]

mingy /'minji/ *adj* (**mingier, mingiest**) *informal* mean or miserly. [perhaps blend of MEAN¹ and STINGY]

mini¹ /'mini/ *noun* (*pl* **minis**) **1** something small of its kind, e.g. a motor car. **2** = MINISKIRT. [MINI-]

mini² *adj* small of its kind; miniature.

mini- *comb. form* forming nouns, with the meanings: **1** miniature; small of its kind: *minicomputer*. **2** having a hemline several inches above the knee: *miniskirt*. [short for MINIATURE]

miniature¹ /'minicha/ *noun* **1a** a copy or representation on a much reduced scale. **b** something that is small of its kind. **2** a very small painting, e.g. a portrait on ivory or metal. **3** a painting in an illuminated manuscript. **4** the art of painting miniatures. ➤ **miniaturist** *noun*. [Italian *miniatura* art of illuminating a manuscript, via medieval Latin from Latin *miniatus*, past part. of *miniare* to colour with minium: see MINIUM]

miniature² *adj* **1** on a small or reduced scale: *a miniature railway*. **2** much smaller than the standard size: *a miniature poodle*.

miniaturize *or* **miniaturise** *verb trans* **1** to design or construct (something) as a small copy. **2** to reduce (something) in scale. ➤ **miniaturization** /-'zaysh(ə)n/ *noun*.

minibar /'minibah/ *noun* a selection of drinks etc, often in a small refrigerator, for the use of guests in a hotel room and usu paid for at the end of the stay.

minibus /'minibus/ *noun* a small bus for carrying about ten passengers.

minicab /'minikab/ *noun* a taxi that can be hired by telephone but that cannot cruise in search of passengers.

minicomputer /'minikəmpyoohtə/ *noun* a type of small and relatively inexpensive computer, which replaced the mainframe for many purposes in the 1970s and was itself rendered obsolete by the microcomputer in the 1990s.

MiniDisc /'minidisk/ *noun trademark* a small CD on which it is possible to record sound or data.

minim /'minim/ *noun* **1** in music, a note with the time value of two crotchets or half a semibreve. **2** a unit of capacity equal to one sixtieth of a fluid drachm, approximately one drop of liquid. **3** in calligraphy, a short vertical stroke. **4** a small ancient Roman coin. [Latin *minimus* least]

minima /'minimə/ *noun* pl of MINIMUM¹.

minimal /'miniml/ *adj* of or being a minimum; constituting the least possible. ➤ **minimally** *adv*.

minimal art *noun* abstract art, *esp* sculpture, consisting of simple geometric forms and plain colours.

minimalism *noun* **1a** a type of design characterized by simplicity of form and arrangement. **b** a type of music characterized by the repetition of simple elements. **c** = MINIMAL ART.

Editorial note ——————
A style of music that originated in the USA in the 1960s and was pioneered by LaMonte Young and Terry Riley, but which achieved its greatest refinement in the works of Steve Reich and Philip Glass. Minimalism relies upon the repetition of usually simple, rhythmically stable musical figures and static harmony to achieve its effect. Though the era of pure minimalism was relatively short, its influence on both sides of the Atlantic was far-reaching, for it offered composers an alternative to the complex methods of organization that had been dominant since the end of World War II — Andrew Clements.

2 advocacy of moderating or restricting the powers of a political organization. ➤ **minimalist** *noun and adj*.

minimax /'minimaks/ *noun* the minimum of a mathematical set of maximum values, *esp* the smallest of a set of maximum possible losses each of which occurs in the most unfavourable outcome of a strategy followed by a participant in a situation governed by game theory; compare MAXIMIN. [MINIMUM¹ + MAXIMUM¹]

minimize *or* **minimise** /'minimiez/ *verb trans* **1** to reduce (something) to a minimum: *The effect of increasing affluence is to minimize the importance of economic goals* — J K Galbraith. **2** to represent (something) at less than true value; to play (it) down. ➤ **minimization** /-'zaysh(ə)n/ *noun*, **minimizer** *noun*.

minimum¹ /'miniməm/ *noun* (*pl* **minima** /-mə/ *or* **minimums**) **1** the least quantity or value assignable, admissible, or possible. **2** the lowest degree or amount reached or recorded. [Latin *minimum*, neuter of *minimus* smallest]

minimum² *adj* of or being a minimum.

minimum wage *noun* a wage fixed by law or contract as the least that may be paid to employees.

minion /'minyən/ *noun* **1** a servile attendant. **2** *derog* a minor official. [early French *mignon* darling, from *mignot* dainty]

minipill /'minipil/ *noun* an oral contraceptive in the form of a pill taken daily by a woman and containing only progesterone.

miniseries /'minisiəriz/ *noun* (*pl* **miniseries**) a television drama screened in a small number of episodes.

miniskirt /'miniskuht/ *noun* a woman's skirt with the hemline several inches above the knee.

minister¹ /'ministə/ *noun* **1a** a member of the clergy, *esp* in a Protestant or nonconformist Church. **b** a person who assists the officiant in Christian worship. **c** the superior of any of several religious orders. **2** a high officer of state managing a division of government. **3** a diplomatic representative accredited to a foreign state. **4** a person who acts for or in place of another; an agent. **5** *archaic* somebody or something that produces an effect; a cause or instrument. ➤ **ministerial** /-'stiəri-əl/ *adj*, **ministerially** /-'stiəri-əli/ *adv*. [Middle English *ministre* via Old French from Latin *minister* servant; related to Latin *minor* smaller]

minister² *verb* (**ministered, ministering**) ➤ *verb intrans* **1** to perform the functions of a minister of religion. **2** (+ to) to give assistance, care, or service to people who are sick or in need. ➤ *verb trans archaic* to provide or supply (something).

minister-general *noun* = MINISTER¹ (1C).

Minister of State *noun* a government minister ranking below a Secretary of State.

Minister of the Crown *noun* in Britain and Canada, a member of the cabinet.

minister without portfolio *noun* a government minister with no specific departmental responsibilities.

ministration /mini'straysh(ə)n/ *noun* **1** *formal or humorous* (*also in pl*) an act of assistance, care, or service: *The angel of his life had been snatched away and given to a rude man of earth and iron, who could neither need nor appreciate her ministrations* — Nathaniel Hawthorne. **2** ministering, *esp* in religious matters. ➤ **ministrant** /-strənt/ *noun and adj*.

ministry /'ministri/ *noun* (*pl* **ministries**) **1a** a government department presided over by a minister. **b** the building in which the business of a ministry is transacted. **c** the group of ministers constituting a cabinet. **2** the body of ministers of religion; the clergy. **3** the period of service or office of a minister of religion or government. **4** the office, duties, or functions of a minister of religion or government. **5** = MINISTRATION.

minium /'mini-əm/ *noun archaic* = RED LEAD. [Middle English from Latin *minium* cinnabar, red lead, of Iberian origin]

minivan *noun* a small van with removable seats.

miniver /'minivə/ *noun* a white fur used chiefly for lining or trimming robes of state. [Middle English *meniver* from Old French *menu vair* small vair]

mink /mingk/ *noun* (*pl* **minks** *or collectively* **mink**) **1** any of several species of semiaquatic flesh-eating mammals that resemble weasels and have partially webbed feet and a soft thick coat: genus *Mustela*. **2a** the soft fur or pelt of the mink, which varies in colour from white to dark reddish brown. **b** (*used before a noun*) made from this fur: *a mink coat*. [Middle English *mynk*]

minke whale /'mingkə, 'mingki/ *noun* a small RORQUAL (whalebone whale) of northern seas: *Balaenoptera acutorostrata*. [prob from *Meincke*, reputedly the name of a Norwegian whaling gunner]

Minn. *abbr* Minnesota.

minneola /mini'ohlə/ *noun* a citrus fruit with a thin reddish orange skin that is a cross between a tangerine and a grapefruit. [perhaps named after *Mineola*, town in Texas, USA]

minnesinger /'minising-ə/ *noun* a member of a class of German lyric poets and musicians of the 12th to the 14th cent. [German *Minnesinger*, from Middle High German *Minne* love + *Singer* singer]

minnow /'minoh/ *noun* (*pl* **minnows** *or collectively* **minnow**) **1a** a small dark-coloured freshwater fish, related to the carp, that is found in the upper parts of rivers: *Phoxinus phoxinus*. **b** any of various small fish resembling or related to the minnow. **2** something small or insignificant of its kind. [Middle English *menawe*; related to Old English *myne* minnow]

Minoan[1] /mi'noh-ən/ *adj* of or being a highly developed Bronze Age culture of Crete from around 3000 to 1100 BC. [via Latin from Greek *minōios* from *Minōs* Minos, legendary king of Crete]

Minoan[2] *noun* a native or inhabitant of ancient Crete.

minor[1] /'mienə/ *adj* **1a** inferior in importance, size, rank, or degree: *a minor poet*. **b** comparatively unimportant: *a minor alteration*. **c** not serious or involving risk to life: *a minor illness*. **2** said of a person: not having attained majority. **3a** said *esp* of a musical scale: having semitones between the second and third, fifth and sixth, and sometimes seventh and eighth steps. **b** being or based on a minor scale: *in a minor key*. **c** being a musical interval less by a semitone than a corresponding major interval. **d** said of a chord: having an interval of a minor third between the root and the next note above it. **4a** said of a premise in logic: containing the subject of a conclusion drawn in a syllogism, e.g. *Venus is a goddess* in *If all goddesses are immortal, and Venus is a goddess, then Venus must be immortal*. **b** said of a term in logic: being the subject of a minor premise, e.g. *Venus* in *Venus is a goddess*. **5** *Brit, dated* used after a surname: being the younger of two brothers, *esp* at a public school: *Jones minor*. [Middle English from Latin *minor* smaller, inferior; related to Latin *minuere* to lessen]

minor[2] *noun* **1** a person who has not attained majority. **2** a minor musical interval, scale, key, etc. **3** in logic, a minor premise or term. **4** *NAmer* a student's subsidiary subject.

minor[3] *verb intrans* (**minored, minoring**) *NAmer* (+ in) to study something as a subsidiary subject.

minor axis *noun* the chord of an ellipse that passes through the centre and is perpendicular to the major axis.

Minorcan /mi'nawkən/ *noun* a native or inhabitant of the Balearic island of Minorca. >> **Minorcan** *adj*.

minor canon *noun* a canon in the Church of England who assists in services but has no vote in the CHAPTER (2).

minority /mie'noriti, mi-/ *noun* (*pl* **minorities**) **1a** the period before attainment of the age of majority. **b** the state of being a legal minor. **2** (*treated as sing. or pl*) the smaller of two groups constituting a whole; *specif* a group with less than the number of votes necessary for control. **3** (*treated as sing. or pl*) a group of people who share common characteristics or interests differing from those of the majority of a population.

minor league *noun NAmer* a league of lower classification than the major league in US professional sport, *esp* baseball.

minor order *noun* (*usu in pl*) any of the Roman Catholic or Eastern Orthodox clerical orders that are lower in rank than major orders.

minor planet *noun* an asteroid.

minor suit *noun* in bridge, either of the suits of clubs or diamonds, which are of inferior scoring value: compare MAJOR SUIT.

Minotaur /'mienətaw, 'min-/ *noun* in Greek mythology, a monster with the body of a man and the head of a bull, kept by Minos in a labyrinth on Crete and ultimately killed by Theseus. [Middle English via French from Latin *Minotaurus* from Greek *Minōtauros*, from *Minōs* Minos, legendary king of Crete + *tauros* bull]

minster /'minstə/ *noun* a large or important church often having cathedral status. [Old English *mynster*, from late Latin *monasterium* monastery]

minstrel /'minstrəl/ *noun* **1** a medieval singer, poet, or musical entertainer. **2** any of a group of entertainers with blackened faces giving a performance of supposedly Negro singing, dancing, etc. [Middle English *menestrel* via Old French from late Latin *ministerialis* imperial household officer, from Latin *ministerium* service, from *minister* servant]

minstrelsy /'minstrəlsi/ *noun* **1** the singing and playing of a minstrel. **2** (*treated as sing. or pl*) a group of minstrels. **3** songs or poems composed or performed by minstrels. [Middle English *minstralcie*, from early French *menestralsie* from *menestrel* minstrel]

mint[1] /mint/ *noun* **1a** any of several species of plants that have whorled leaves with a characteristic strong taste and smell, used *esp* as a flavouring: genus *Mentha*. **b** the flavour of mint. **2** a sweet, chocolate, etc flavoured with peppermint. >> **minty** *adj*.

Word history
Old English *minte*; related to Old High German *minza*, ultimately from Latin *mentha* mint. The plant is said to be so called from Minthe, a nymph who was loved by Pluto and who was then turned by Pluto's jealous wife Proserpina into the plant named after her.

mint[2] *noun* **1** a place where coins, medals, etc are made. **2** *informal* a vast sum or amount of money.

Word history
Old English *mynet* coin, money, related to Old High German *munizza* coin, ultimately from Latin *moneta* mint, coin, from *Moneta*, epithet of Juno. The connection with the Roman goddess Juno arises from the fact that the Romans coined money in the temple of Juno Moneta.

mint[3] *verb trans* **1** to make (coins, etc) by stamping metal. **2** to fabricate or invent (a new word, etc). >> **minter** *noun*.

mint[4] *adj* unspoilt, as if fresh from a mint; pristine or perfect: *in mint condition*.

mintage /'mintij/ *noun* **1** the action, process, or cost of minting coins. **2** coins produced in a single period of minting.

mint julep *noun* = JULEP.

minuend /'minyooend/ *noun* in mathematics, a number from which another is to be subtracted. [Latin *minuendum*, neuter of *minuendus*, gerundive of *minuere* to lessen]

minuet /minyoo'et/ *noun* **1** a slow graceful dance in triple time. **2** music for or in the rhythm of this dance, typically as a movement in a symphony, suite, etc. [early French *menuet* tiny, delicate, dimin. of *menu* small]

minus[1] /'mienəs/ *prep* **1** diminished by: *Seven minus four is three*. **2** *informal* without: *minus his hat*. [Middle English from Latin *minus* less, from neuter of *minor* smaller]

minus[2] *noun* (*pl* **minuses**) **1** = MINUS SIGN. **2** a negative quantity. **3** a deficiency or defect.

minus[3] *adj* **1** less than zero; negative: *a minus quantity*. **2** having negative qualities, *esp* involving a disadvantage: *a minus factor*. **3** used after a grade: falling lower than the specified grade: *a mark of B minus*. **4** of or having a negative electric charge.

minuscule[1] /'minəskyoohl/ *adj* **1** very small: *Perry, with his minuscule armada of two frigates and two sailing vessels, arrived at ... the very mouth of Tokyo Bay on 8 July 1853* — Simon Winchester. **2a** of, in, or being a lower-case letter or letters. **b** written in minuscules. [French *minuscule* from Latin *minusculus* rather small, dimin. of *minor* smaller]

Usage note
Minuscule meaning 'tiny' or 'a small letter' (see MINUSCULE[2]) is spelt with one *i* and two *u*'s. It can never be spelt *miniscule*.

minuscule[2] *noun* **1** a lower-case letter. **2** a style of small cursive handwriting used in ancient and medieval manuscripts. >> **minuscular** /mi'nuskyoolə/ *adj*.

minus sign *noun* the symbol (–), denoting subtraction or a negative quantity, e.g. in $8 - 6 = 2$ or $-10°$.

minute[1] /'minit/ *noun* **1a** a unit of time equal to one sixtieth of an hour. **b** a unit of angular measurement equal to one sixtieth of a degree. **2** a distance that can be covered in approximately one minute: *We lived five minutes from the station*. **3** *informal* a short space of time; a moment. **4a** a short note or memorandum. **b** (*in pl*) the official record of the proceedings of a meeting. [Middle English via French from late Latin *minuta*, from Latin *minutus* small, past part. of *minuere* to lessen]

minute[2] *verb* **1** to make notes or a brief summary of (a meeting); to take the minutes of (it). **2** to record (something) in the minutes of a meeting etc.

minute[3] /mie'nyooht/ *adj* **1** extremely small. **2** of minor importance; petty. **3** marked by painstaking attention to detail. >> **minutely** *adv*, **minuteness** *noun*. [Latin *minutus* small: see MINUTE[1]]

minute gun /'minit/ *noun* a gun fired at one-minute intervals at funerals, commemoration ceremonies, etc, or as a distress signal.

minute hand /'minit/ *noun* the long hand that marks the minutes on the face of a watch or clock.

minuteman /'minitman/ *noun* (*pl* **minutemen**) in the American Revolution, a member of a group of armed men pledged to be ready for action at a minute's notice.

minute steak /'minit/ *noun* a small thin steak that can be quickly cooked.

minutia /mi'nyoohshi·ə, mie-/ *noun* (*pl* **minutiae** /-shi·ee/) (*usu in pl*) a small, precise, or minor detail. [Latin *minutiae* trifles, details, pl of *minutia* smallness, from *minutus* small: see MINUTE¹]

minx /mingks/ *noun* a flirtatious or cunning girl or young woman. [origin unknown]

Miocene /'mie·əseen/ *adj* relating to or dating from a geological epoch, the fourth epoch of the Tertiary period, lasting from about 23.5 million to 5.2 million years ago, and marked *esp* by the first appearance of apes. >> **Miocene** *noun.* [Greek *meiōn* less + -CENE]

miosis *or* **myosis** /mie'ohsis/ *noun* (*pl* **mioses** *or* **myoses** /-seez/) excessive smallness or contraction of the pupil of the eye >> **miotic** /mie'otik/ *adj and noun.* [Latin *miosis* from Greek *myein* to be closed (of the eyes) + -OSIS]

mips /mips/ *abbr* million instructions per second (measure of computing speed).

miracle /'mirəkl/ *noun* **1** an extraordinary and welcome event that manifests or is attributed to divine intervention in human affairs. **2** an astonishing and wonderful event, thing, or accomplishment. **3** somebody or something that is a remarkable example or instance of the specified thing: *This watch is a miracle of precision.* **4** (*used before a noun*) being a miracle: *miracle drugs.* [Middle English via Old French from Latin *miraculum* from *mirari* to wonder at]

miracle play *noun* a medieval drama based on episodes from the Bible or the life of a saint: compare MORALITY PLAY, MYSTERY PLAY.

miraculous /mi'rakyooləs/ *adj* **1** of the nature of a miracle; supernatural. **2** evoking wonder like a miracle; marvellous: *For murther, though it have no tongue, will speak with most miraculous organ —* Shakespeare. **3** capable of working miracles. >> **miraculously** *adv,* **miraculousness** *noun.* [early French *miraculeux* from medieval Latin *miraculosus* from Latin *miraculum* miracle]

mirage /'mirahzh, mi'rahzh/ *noun* **1** an optical illusion appearing *esp* as a pool of water or as the reflection of distant objects and caused by the reflection of rays of light by a layer of heated air. **2** something illusory and unattainable. [French *mirage* from *mirer* to look at, from Latin *mirari* to wonder at]

MIRAS /'mierəs/ *abbr Brit* formerly, Mortgage Interest Relief at Source.

mire¹ /'mie·ə/ *noun* **1** a tract of soft waterlogged ground; a marsh or bog. **2** soft mud or slush. **3** a situation of great difficulty, complexity, or involvement: *sinking into the mire of debt.* >> **miry** *adj.* [Middle English, from Old Norse *mȳrr*; related to Old English *mōs* bog: see MOSS]

mire² *verb trans* **1** to cause (somebody or something) to sink or stick fast in or as if in a mire: *mired in detail and confusion.* **2** to cover or soil (somebody or something) with mire.

mirepoix /miə'pwah/ *noun* (*pl* **mirepoix**) a mixture of diced vegetables sautéed and used in sauces or as a bed on which to braise meat. [French *mirepoix*, prob named after Charles de Lévis, duc de Mirepoix d.1757, French diplomat and general]

mirid /'mie·ərid, 'mirid/ *noun* = CAPSID¹.

mirk¹ /muhk/ *noun* see MURK¹.

mirk² *adj* see MURK².

mirky *adj* = MURKY (1).

mirror¹ /'mirə/ *noun* **1** a smooth or polished surface, e.g. of metal or silvered glass, that forms images by reflection. **2** something that gives a true representation: *Art is the mirror of life.* >> **mirrorlike** *adj.* [Middle English *mirour* from Old French *mirer* to look at, from Latin *mirari* to wonder at]

mirror² *verb trans* (**mirrored, mirroring**) **1** to reflect (somebody or something) in a mirror, or as if in a mirror. **2** to copy, represent, or correspond to (something) exactly.

mirror ball *noun* a large sphere covered with squares of reflective glass that is hung from the ceiling in a dance hall or nightclub and revolves to create a decorative lighting effect.

mirror carp *noun* a domesticated variety of the carp with large shiny scales.

mirror image *noun* something that has its parts reversely arranged in comparison with an otherwise identical thing.

mirror writing *noun* words written backward with reversed characters, resembling normal writing when reflected in a mirror.

mirth /muhth/ *noun* happiness or amusement accompanied with laughter. >> **mirthful** *adj,* **mirthfully** *adv,* **mirthfulness** *noun,* **mirthless** *adj.* [Old English *myrgth* from *myrge*: see MERRY]

MIRV /muhv/ *noun* an intercontinental missile having multiple warheads that may be directed to separate targets. [acronym from *multiple independently-targeted re-entry vehicle*]

mis-¹ *prefix* **1** forming verbs and their derivatives, with the meanings: **a** badly; wrongly; unfavourably: *misjudge*; *misbehave.* **b** not: *misunderstand.* **2** forming nouns and their derivatives, with the meanings: **a** bad; wrong: *misdeed*; *misfit.* **b** opposite or lack of: *mistrust*; *misfortune.* **c** suspicious; apprehensive: *misgiving.* [Old English, of Germanic origin; related to Old English *missan* to miss]

mis-² *or* **miso-** *comb. form* forming nouns and their derivatives, denoting: hatred: *misogamy.* [Greek, from *misein* to hate]

misadventure /misəd'venchə/ *noun* **1** a misfortune or mishap. **2** (*also* **death by misadventure**) in law, death due to an action not intended to cause harm. [Middle English *mesaventure* from Old French *mesavenir* to chance badly, from *mes-* MIS-¹ + *avenir* to chance, happen]

misaligned /misə'liend/ *adj* not correctly aligned. >> **misalignment** *noun.*

misalliance /misə'lie·əns/ *noun* an improper or unsuitable alliance, *esp* a mésalliance. [modification of French *mésalliance*]

misanthrope /'miz(ə)nthrohp/ *noun* a person who hates or distrusts other people or humankind in general. >> **misanthropic** /-'thropik/ *adj,* **misanthropical** /-'thropikl/ *adj,* **misanthropy** /mi'zanthrəpi/ *noun.* [Greek *misanthrōpos* hating mankind, from MIS-² + *anthrōpos* man]

misanthropist /mi'zanthrəpist/ *noun* = MISANTHROPE.

misapply /misə'plie/ *verb trans* (**misapplies, misapplied, misapplying**) to apply or use (something) wrongly. >> **misapplication** /,misapli'kaysh(ə)n/ *noun.*

misapprehend /,misapri'hend/ *verb trans* to misunderstand (something). >> **misapprehension** /-'hensh(ə)n/ *noun,* **misapprehensive** /-'hensiv/ *adj.*

misappropriate /misə'prohpriayt/ *verb trans* to appropriate or take (something) wrongly, e.g. by theft or embezzlement. >> **misappropriation** /-'aysh(ə)n/ *noun.*

misbecome /misbi'kum/ *verb trans* (*past tense* **misbecame,** *past part.* **misbecome**) *formal* to be inappropriate or unbecoming to: *It misbecomes you to speak ill of your parents.*

misbegotten /misbi'gotn/ *adj* **1** having a disreputable or improper origin; ill-conceived: *misbegotten notions.* **2** wretched; contemptible: *a misbegotten scoundrel.* **3** *archaic* illegitimate; bastard.

misbehave /misbi'hayv/ *verb intrans* to behave badly. >> **misbehaviour** /-'hayvyə/ *noun.*

misbelief /misbi'leef/ *noun* a false belief.

misc. *abbr* **1** miscellaneous. **2** miscellany.

miscalculate /mis'kalkyoolayt/ *verb trans* to calculate or assess (something) wrongly. > *verb intrans* to make an incorrect calculation or assessment. >> **miscalculation** /-'laysh(ə)n/ *noun.*

miscall /mis'kawl/ *verb trans* **1** to call (somebody or something) by the wrong name; to misname (them). **2** *archaic, dialect* to speak ill of (somebody); to abuse (them).

miscarriage /mis'karij/ *noun* **1** the expulsion of a human foetus before it is capable of survival outside the womb, *esp* between the 12th and 20th weeks of pregnancy. **2** a failure in administration: *a miscarriage of justice.*

miscarry /mis'kari/ *verb intrans* (**miscarries, miscarried, miscarrying**) **1** to suffer miscarriage of a foetus. **2** to fail to achieve an intended purpose; to go wrong: *The plan miscarried.* **3** said of mail etc: to fail to reach an intended destination. **4** *archaic* said of ships: to come to harm; to be wrecked: *In the narrow seas that part the French and English, there miscarried a vessel of our country —* Shakespeare.

miscast /mis'kahst/ *verb trans* (*past tense and past part.* **miscast**) **1** to cast (an actor) in an unsuitable role. **2** to cast an unsuitable actor in (a role).

miscegenation /,misiji'naysh(ə)n/ *noun* interbreeding of races, *esp* between people of different skin colour. [Latin *miscēre* to mix + *genus* race]

miscellanea /misə'layni·ə/ *pl noun* a miscellaneous collection, *esp* of literary works. [Latin *miscellanea*, neuter pl of *miscellaneus*]

miscellaneous /misə'layni·əs/ *adj* **1** consisting of diverse items or members. **2** having various characteristics or capabilities: *As a writer I was too miscellaneous* — George Santayana. ≫ **miscellaneously** *adv*, **miscellaneousness** *noun*. [Latin *miscellaneus* from *miscellus* mixed, from *miscēre* to mix]

miscellany /mi'seləni/ *noun* (*pl* **miscellanies**) **1** a mixture of various things. **2** a book containing miscellaneous literary pieces. ≫ **miscellanist** *noun*. [modification of French *miscellanées* (pl) from Latin MISCELLANEA]

mischance /mis'chahns/ *noun* **1** bad luck. **2** a piece of bad luck. [Middle English *mischaunce* from Old French *meschance*, from *mes-* MIS-[1] + *chance* chance, luck]

mischief /'mischif/ *noun* **1** often playful action that annoys or irritates, usu without causing or intending serious harm. **2** somebody or something that causes harm or annoyance. **3** a specific injury or damage from a particular agent: *He did himself a mischief on the barbed wire.* **4** the quality or state of being mischievous. [Middle English *meschief* from Old French *meschief* calamity, from *mes-* MIS-[1] + *chief* head, end]

mischievous /'mischivəs/ *adj* **1a** disruptively playful: *a mischievous puppy.* **b** playfully provocative; arch: *a mischievous glance.* **2** able or tending to cause annoyance, unrest, or minor injury: *mischievous behaviour.* **3** harmful; malicious: *mischievous gossip.* ≫ **mischievously** *adv*, **mischievousness** *noun*.

misch metal /mish/ *noun* an alloy of rare-earth metals used *esp* in tracer bullets and as a flint in lighters. [German *Mischmetall*, from *mischen* to mix + *Metall* metal]

miscible /'misibl/ *adj* said *esp* of a liquid: capable of being mixed; *specif* capable of being mixed with another liquid in any proportion without separating. ≫ **miscibility** /-'biliti/ *noun*. [medieval Latin *miscibilis* from Latin *miscēre* to mix]

misconceive /miskən'seev/ *verb trans* to interpret (something) wrongly; to misunderstand (it). ≫ **misconceiver** *noun*.

misconceived *adj* badly judged, planned, or conceived: *a misconceived notion.*

misconception /miskən'sepsh(ə)n/ *noun* a false or mistaken idea, opinion, or attitude, *esp* one based on misunderstanding or ignorance.

misconduct[1] /mis'kondukt/ *noun* **1** intentional wrongdoing; *specif* deliberate violation of a law or standard: *professional misconduct.* **2** bad or improper behaviour; *specif* adultery. **3** mismanagement of responsibilities: *misconduct of the company's affairs.*

misconduct[2] /miskən'dukt/ *verb trans formal* **1** to conduct (oneself) badly or improperly. **2** to mismanage (something).

misconstrue /miskən'strooh/ *verb trans* (**misconstrues, misconstrued, misconstruing**) to construe (something) wrongly; to misinterpret (it). ≫ **misconstruction** /-'struksh(ə)n/ *noun*.

miscount /mis'kownt/ *verb trans* to count (things or people) wrongly. ≻ *verb intrans* to make an incorrect count. [Middle English *misconten* from early French *mesconter* from *mes-* MIS-[1] + *conter* to count]

miscreant[1] /'miskri·ənt/ *noun* **1** a person who behaves criminally or maliciously. **2** *archaic* a heretic or unbeliever. [Middle English *miscreaunt* disbelieving, from early French *mescreant*, present part. of *mescroire* to disbelieve, from *mes-* MIS-[1] + *croire* to believe, from Latin *credere*]

miscreant[2] *adj* **1** behaving criminally or maliciously. **2** *archaic* heretical or unbelieving.

miscue[1] /mis'kyooh/ *noun* **1a** in billiards or snooker, a faulty stroke in which the cue slips. **b** in other sports, e.g. cricket, a faulty hit etc. **2** a mistake or blunder; *specif* an error made in reading.

miscue[2] *verb* (**miscues, miscued, miscueing** *or* **miscuing**) ≻ *verb intrans* **1** to make a miscue. **2** said of an actor: to answer the wrong cue or to fail to answer the right one. ≻ *verb trans* to hit (a shot, etc) in a faulty manner.

misdate /mis'dayt/ *verb trans* to date (a letter, occurrence, etc) wrongly.

misdeal[1] /mis'deel/ *verb trans and intrans* (*past tense and past part.* **misdealt** /mis'delt/) to deal (cards) incorrectly.

misdeal[2] *noun* the act or an instance of misdealing.

misdeed /mis'deed/ *noun* a wrong deed; an offence.

misdemeanour (*NAmer* **misdemeanor**) /misdi'meenə/ *noun* **1** a minor crime, *esp* one formerly technically distinguished from a felony. **2** a minor offence or wrongdoing.

misdirect /misdi'rekt, misdie'rekt/ *verb trans* **1** to give a wrong direction or instruction to (somebody). **2** to direct (effort, etc) wrongly or inappropriately. **3** to address (mail) incorrectly. ≫ **misdirection** /-sh(ə)n/ *noun*.

misdoubt /mis'dowt/ *verb trans archaic* **1** to doubt the reality or truth of (something). **2** to suspect (somebody or something).

mise-en-scène /,meez onh 'sen (*French* miz ã sɛn)/ *noun* **1** the arrangement of actors, props, and scenery on a stage in a theatrical production. **2** the environment or setting in which something takes place: *Be ready to describe to me the locality, the accessories – how shall I put it – the mise en scène* — Henry James. [French *mise en scène*, literally '(action of) putting on stage']

miser /'miezə/ *noun* a mean grasping person, *esp* one who lives miserably in order to hoard wealth. [Latin *miser* miserable, wretched]

miserable /'miz(ə)rəbl/ *adj* **1a** in a pitiable state of distress or unhappiness. **b** habitually gloomy or morose. **2a** wretchedly inadequate or meagre: *a miserable hovel.* **b** causing or characterized by extreme discomfort or unhappiness: *a miserable childhood.* **3** shameful; contemptible: *a miserable failure.* ≫ **miserableness** *noun*, **miserably** *adv*. [Middle English via French from Latin *miserabilis* wretched, pitiable, from *miserari* to pity, from *miser* wretched]

misère /mi'zeə/ *noun* in solo whist, etc, a declaration made by a player undertaking to win no tricks in the next game. [French *misère*, literally 'poverty, misery']

miserere /mizə'reəri/ *noun* **1a** (**Miserere**) the 51st Psalm. **b** a plea or lament, *esp* a cry for mercy. **2** = MISERICORD (I). [Latin *miserere* be merciful, from *misereri* to be merciful, from *miser* wretched; from the first word of the 51st Psalm]

misericord *or* **misericorde** /mi'zerikawd/ *noun* **1** a ledge on the underside of the hinged seat of a choir stall to support the occupant in a standing position when the seat is turned up. **2** in former times, a relaxation of certain rules for monks and nuns, or a place where such rules were relaxed. [medieval Latin *misericordia* seat in church, from Latin *misericord-*, *misericors* merciful, from *misereri* + *cord-*, *cor* heart]

miserly *adj* **1** of or characteristic of a miser; mean. **2** said of an amount: small and inadequate. ≫ **miserliness** *noun*.

misery /'mizəri/ *noun* (*pl* **miseries**) **1** physical or mental suffering or discomfort; great unhappiness or distress. **2** a cause of great suffering or distress. **3** *chiefly Brit, informal* a grumpy, morose, or querulous person. [Middle English *miserie*, *misere*, via French from Latin *miseria*, from *miser* wretched]

misfeasance /mis'feez(ə)ns/ *noun* the improper performance of a lawful action. ≫ **misfeasor** *noun*. [early French *mesfaisance* from *mesfaire* to do wrong, from *mes-* MIS-[1] + *faire* to make, do, from Latin *facere*]

misfire[1] /mis'fie·ə/ *verb intrans* **1** said of a motor vehicle, engine, etc: to have the explosive or propulsive charge fail to ignite at the proper time. **2** said *esp* of a firearm: to fail to fire. **3** to fail to have an intended effect: *As criticism, this essay misfires* — Stephen Spender.

misfire[2] /'misfie·ə/ *noun* the act or an instance of misfiring.

misfit /'misfit/ *noun* **1** a person who is poorly adjusted to their environment. **2** something that fits badly.

misfortune /mis'fawchən/ *noun* **1** bad luck. **2** a distressing or unfortunate incident or event.

misgive /mis'giv/ *verb* (*past tense* **misgave** /mis'gayv/, *past part.* **misgiven** /mis'giv(ə)n/) ≻ *verb trans literary* to make (somebody) fearful or apprehensive. ≻ *verb intrans literary* to be fearful or apprehensive.

misgiving *noun* a feeling of doubt, suspicion, or apprehension, *esp* concerning a future event.

misgovern /mis'guvən/ *verb trans* to govern (a nation, etc) badly. ≫ **misgovernment** *noun*.

misguide /mis'gied/ *verb trans* to lead (somebody) astray; to mislead (them). ≫ **misguidance** *noun*.

misguided *adj* directed by mistaken ideas, principles, or motives. ≫ **misguidedly** *adv*, **misguidedness** *noun*.

mishandle /mis'handl/ *verb trans* **1** to treat (somebody or something) roughly; to maltreat (them). **2** to mismanage (a situation, crisis, etc).

mishap /'mis·hap/ *noun* an unfortunate accident: *He asked the waves, he asked the felon winds what hard mishap hath doomed this gentle swain* — Milton. [Middle English, from MIS-[1] + HAP[1] happening, chance, from Old Norse *happ* good luck]

mishear /mis'hiə/ *verb* (*past tense and past part.* **misheard** /mis'huhd/) ➤ *verb trans* to hear (something) wrongly. ➤ *verb intrans* to misinterpret what is heard.

mishit[1] /mis'hit/ *verb trans* (**mishitting**, *past tense and past part.* **mishit**) to hit (a ball or stroke) in a faulty manner.

mishit[2] /'mis hit/ *noun* a faulty hit, shot, or stroke

mishmash /'mishmash/ *noun informal* a hotchpotch or jumble. [partly reduplication of MASH[1], partly from Middle High German *misch-masch*, reduplication of *mischen* to mix]

Mishnah *or* **Mishna** /'mishnə/ *noun* the collection of Jewish traditions chiefly concerned with the law that was compiled about AD 200 and forms the basis of the Talmud. ➤➤ **Mishnaic** /mish'nayik/ *adj*. [Hebrew *mishnāh* instruction, oral law, from *shānāh* to repeat, learn]

misinform /misin'fawm/ *verb trans* to give untrue or misleading information to (somebody). ➤➤ **misinformation** /-'maysh(ə)n/ *noun*.

misinterpret /misin'tuhprit/ *verb trans* (**misinterpreted, misinterpreting**) to understand or explain (something) wrongly. ➤➤ **misinterpretation** /-'taysh(ə)n/ *noun*, **misinterpreter** *noun*.

misjudge /mis'juj/ *verb trans* **1** to estimate (something) wrongly. **2** to judge (somebody) wrongly, *esp* to have an unjustly bad opinion of (them). ➤ *verb intrans* to make a mistaken judgment. ➤➤ **misjudgment** *noun*.

miskey /mis'kee/ *verb trans* to make an error in keying (words, numbers, etc) on a keyboard or keypad.

Miskito /mi'skeetoh/ *noun* (*pl* **Miskitos** *or collectively* **Miskito**) **1** a member of a Native American people of Nicaragua and Honduras. **2** the Amerind language of this people. **3** an English creole language spoken on the Atlantic coast of Nicaragua and Honduras. [the Miskito name]

mislay /mis'lay/ *verb trans* (*past tense and past part.* **mislaid** /mis'layd/) to put or leave (something) in a place that is subsequently forgotten; to lose (it) temporarily.

mislead /mis'leed/ *verb trans* (*past tense and past part.* **misled** /mis'led/) **1** to lead (somebody) into a mistaken action or belief. **2** to lead (somebody) in a wrong direction. ➤➤ **misleader** *noun*, **misleading** *adj*, **misleadingly** *adv*.

mismanage /mis'manij/ *verb trans* to manage (a situation, finances, etc) wrongly or incompetently. ➤➤ **mismanagement** *noun*.

mismatch[1] /mis'mach/ *verb trans* to match (people or things) incorrectly or unsuitably, e.g. in marriage.

mismatch[2] /'mismach/ *noun* a poor, wrong, or unsuitable match.

misname /mis'naym/ *verb trans* to call (somebody or something) by the wrong or an inappropriate name.

misnomer /mis'nohmə/ *noun* **1** an incorrect or inappropriate name or designation. **2** the use of such a name or designation. [Middle English *misnoumer* from early French *mesnommer* to misname, from *mes-* MIS-[1] + *nommer* to name, from Latin *nominare*]

miso /'meesoh/ *noun* a thick brown salty paste made from fermented soya beans, used to flavour savoury dishes. [Japanese *miso*]

miso- *comb. form* see MIS-[2].

misogamist /mi'sogəmist, mie-/ *noun* a person who hates marriage. ➤➤ **misogamy** /-mi/ *noun*. [MIS-[2] + Greek *gamos* marriage]

misogynist /mi'soj(ə)n·ist, mie-/ *noun* a person who hates women. ➤➤ **misogynistic** /-'nistik/ *adj*, **misogynous** /-nəs/ *adj*, **misogyny** /-ni/ *noun*. [Greek *misogynēs*, from MIS-[2] + *gynē* woman]

misplace /mis'plays/ *verb trans* **1** to put (something) in the wrong place. **2** = MISLAY. ➤➤ **misplacement** *noun*.

misplaced *adj* **1** directed towards the wrong or an unsuitable object or outcome: *misplaced enthusiasm*. **2** used at the wrong or an inappropriate time or place: *misplaced humour*.

misplay[1] /mis'play/ *noun* a wrong or unskilful action, *esp* in a game; an error.

misplay[2] *verb trans* to play (a ball, card, etc) wrongly or unskilfully.

misprint[1] /'misprint/ *noun* a printing error.

misprint[2] /mis'print/ *verb trans* to print (something) incorrectly.

misprision[1] /mis'prizh(ə)n/ *noun* in law, formerly, concealment of treason or other serious crime by somebody who is not actually a participant: *Amyas was guilty of something like misprision of treason in not handing him over to the nearest justice* — Charles Kingsley. [Middle English from early French *mesprison* error, wrongdoing, from Old French *mespris*, past part. of *mesprendre* to make a mistake, from *mes-* MIS-[1] + *prendre* to take, from Latin *prehendere* to seize]

misprision[2] *noun archaic or literary* **1** the scorning or undervaluing of something: *it seemed an insult to Ruth Hailey and a misprision of her kindly wishes* — Israel Zangwill. **2** a misunderstanding: *There is some strange misprision in the princes* — Shakespeare.

misprize /mis'priez/ *verb trans* to scorn or undervalue (something): *clinging with silent love and faith to one who, misprized by others, was worthy in her thoughts* — George Eliot. [early French *mesprisier* from MIS-[1] + *prisier* to appraise]

mispronounce /misprə'nowns/ *verb trans* to pronounce (a word or name) wrongly. ➤➤ **mispronunciation** /-nunsi'aysh(ə)n/ *noun*.

misquote /mis'kwoht/ *verb trans* **1** to quote (something) incorrectly. **2** to repeat or report incorrectly what was said by (somebody). ➤➤ **misquotation** /-'taysh(ə)n/ *noun*.

misread /mis'reed/ *verb trans* (*past tense and past part.* **misread** /mis'red/) to read or interpret (something) incorrectly.

misreport /misri'pawt/ *verb trans* to report (something) falsely or inaccurately.

misrepresent /ˌmisrepri'zent/ *verb trans* to represent (something) falsely; to give an untrue or misleading account of (it). ➤➤ **misrepresentation** /-'taysh(ə)n/ *noun*.

misrule[1] /mis'roohl/ *verb trans* to rule (a nation, etc) incompetently; to misgovern (it).

misrule[2] *noun* **1** misruling or being misruled. **2** disorder; anarchy.

Miss. *abbr* Mississippi.

miss[1] /mis/ *verb trans* **1** to fail to hit, reach, meet, catch, or attain (something): *We missed the train; She missed her step and fell heavily.* **2** to discover or feel the absence of (something), *esp* with regret: *I didn't miss my cheque book for several days; He missed his wife desperately.* **3** to escape or avoid (something): *I narrowly missed being run over.* **4** (*often* + out) to leave (something) out; to omit (it). **5** to fail to understand, sense, or experience (something): *You're missing the point.* **6** to fail to attend (work, school, an appointment, etc). **7** to fail to watch, listen to, or take part in (a show, party, etc). **8** to fail to take advantage of (an opportunity, etc). ➤ *verb intrans* **1** to fail to hit something. **2** to misfire: *The engine missed.* **✳ miss out on** to fail to have or experience (something desirable): *people who missed out on further education.* **miss the boat** *informal* to fail to take advantage of an opportunity. [Old English *missan*; related to German *missen* to miss]

miss[2] *noun* **1** a failure to hit something. **2** a failure to attain a desired result. **✳ give (something) a miss** *chiefly Brit, informal* to avoid, bypass, or omit (something) deliberately: *language learners give Russian a miss* — Times Educational Supplement.

miss[3] *noun* **1** (**Miss**). **a** used as a title preceding the name of an unmarried woman or a girl. **b** used e.g. before the name of a place or a line of activity to form a title awarded to a usu young unmarried woman: *Miss World.* **2a** (*often* **Miss**) used as a term of address to a young woman. **b** used as a term of address to a female schoolteacher. **3** *derog or humorous* a young unmarried woman or a girl. [short for MISTRESS]

Usage note

Miss, Mrs, *or* Ms? See note at Ms.

missal /'misl/ *noun* a book containing all that is said or sung at mass for the whole year. [Middle English *messel* via French from medieval Latin *missale*, neuter of *missalis* of the mass, from late Latin *missa* mass]

missel thrush /'misl/ *noun* see MISTLE THRUSH.

misshape[1] /mis'shayp/ *verb trans* (*past tense* **misshaped**, *past part.* **misshaped** *or* **misshapen**) *archaic* to shape (something or somebody) badly; to deform (them). ➤➤ **misshapen** *adj*, **misshapenly** *adv*, **misshapenness** *noun*.

misshape[2] /'misshayp/ *noun* something badly shaped or deformed; *specif* a misshapen chocolate, biscuit, etc, sold at a reduced price.

missile /'misiel/ *noun* **1** an object thrown or projected, usu so as to strike something at a distance. **2** a self-propelled weapon that travels through the air; a ballistic missile or guided missile. [Latin *missile*, from neuter of *missilis* capable of being thrown, from *missus*, past part. of *mittere* to throw, send]

missilery /'misielri/ *noun* **1** the science dealing with the design, manufacture, and use of missiles. **2** missiles collectively.

missing *adj* **1** absent or lost. **2** not confirmed as either alive or dead: *missing in action.*

missing link *noun* **1** an item needed to complete a continuous series. **2** a hypothetical intermediate form between human beings and their anthropoid ancestors.

mission[1] /'mish(ə)n/ *noun* **1a** a ministry commissioned by a religious organization to propagate its faith or carry on humanitarian work, usu abroad. **b** assignment to or work in a field of missionary enterprise. **c** a mission establishment. **d** (*in pl*) organized missionary work. **e** a campaign to increase church membership or strengthen Christian faith. **2** (*treated as sing. or pl*) a body of people sent to perform a service or carry on an activity, e.g.: **a** a group sent to a foreign country to negotiate, advise, etc. **b** a permanent embassy or legation. **3** a specific task with which a person or group is charged. **4a** a definite military, naval, or aerospace task. **b** a flight operation of an aircraft or spacecraft in the performance of a mission. **5** a calling or vocation. [late Latin *mission-, missio* religious mission, from Latin *missus*, past part. of *mittere* to send]

mission[2] *verb trans* to carry on a religious mission among or in (a people).

missionary[1] *noun* (*pl* **missionaries**) a person undertaking a mission, *esp* somebody in charge of a religious mission in a remote part of the world.

missionary[2] *adj* **1** relating to, engaged in, or devoted to missions. **2** characteristic of a missionary: *missionary zeal.*

missionary position *noun* a position for sexual intercourse in which the woman lies underneath and face to face with the man, regarded as the conventional position. [from its being reputedly advocated as the proper position by missionaries to primitive peoples]

mission creep *noun* **1** the gradual escalation of the role and actions of a military force in an area of conflict, e.g. from peacekeeping to active combat. **2** a similar widening of the aims, role, or activities of any body.

mission statement *noun* a formal statement of the policies, aims, values, etc of a company or other organization.

missis /'misiz/ *noun* see MISSUS.

Mississippian /misi'sipi-ən/ *adj* **1** of the US state of Mississippi, its people, or the Mississippi River. **2** relating to or dating from a geological period of the Palaeozoic era in N America that precedes the Pennsylvanian and that corresponds to the earlier subdivision of the Carboniferous period. ➤➤ **Mississippian** *noun.*

missive /'misiv/ *noun formal or humorous* a written communication; a letter. [early French *lettre missive*, literally 'letter intended to be sent']

misspell /mis'spel/ *verb trans* (*past tense* **misspelt** /mis'spelt/, *past part.* **misspelt** *or* **misspelled**) to spell (something) incorrectly. ➤➤ **misspelling** *noun.*

misspend /mis'spend/ *verb trans* (*past tense and past part.* **misspent** /mis'spent/) to spend (money, time, etc) wrongly or foolishly; to squander (it): *his misspent youth.*

misstate /mis'stayt/ *verb trans* to state (something) incorrectly; to give a false account of (it). ➤➤ **misstatement** *noun.*

misstep /mis'step/ *noun* **1** a wrong step. **2** a blunder.

missus *or* **missis** /'misiz/ *noun* (*pl* **missuses** *or* **missies**) **1** *informal or humorous* somebody's wife: *Have you met the missus?* **2** *informal* used as a term of address to a married woman. [alteration of MISTRESS]

missy /'misi/ *noun* (*pl* **missies**) *informal* used as a term of address to a young girl.

mist[1] /mist/ *noun* **1a** water in the form of diffuse particles in the atmosphere, *esp* near the earth's surface. **b** condensed water vapour on a surface, *esp* on glass. **2** (*also in pl*) something that dims or obscures: *the mists of time.* **3** a film, *esp* of tears, before the eyes. **4a**

a cloud of small particles suggestive of a mist. **b** a suspension of a finely divided liquid in a gas. [Old English; related to Middle Dutch *mist* mist, Greek *omichlē*]

mist[2] *verb intrans* (*often* + up/over) to be or become covered with or obscured by mist. ➤ *verb trans* to cover (something) with mist, or as if with mist.

mistake[1] /mi'stayk/ *verb trans* (*past tense* **mistook** /mi'stook/, *past part.* **mistaken** /mi'stayk(ə)n/) **1a** to misunderstand the meaning, intention, or significance of (something or somebody). **b** to estimate (something) wrongly. **2a** to identify (somebody or something) wrongly: *I mistook him for his brother.* **b** to confuse (somebody or something) with another. **3** to choose (something) wrongly: *She mistook her way in the dark.* ➤➤ **mistakable** *adj.* [Middle English *mistaken* from Old Norse *mistaka* to take by mistake, from MIS-[1] + *taka* to take]

mistake[2] *noun* **1** a wrong action or statement arising from faulty judgment, inadequate knowledge, or carelessness. **2** a misunderstanding of the meaning or significance of something.

mistaken *adj* **1** said of an action, idea, etc: based on wrong thinking; incorrect: *in the mistaken belief that he was honest.* **2** said of a person: wrong in opinion: *If you think he's honest, you're mistaken.* ➤➤ **mistakenly** *adv,* **mistakenness** *noun.*

mister /'mistə/ *noun* **1** (**Mister**) = MR. **2** (*often* **Mister**) used as a generalized informal term of address to a man who is a stranger; sir. [alteration of MASTER[1]]

mistime /mis'tiem/ *verb trans* to time (something) badly; to do or say (it) at the wrong or inappropriate time.

mistle thrush *or* **missel thrush** /'misl/ *noun* a large Eurasian thrush with greyish brown upper parts and larger spots on its underparts than the song thrush: *Turdus viscivorus.* [Old English *mistel* mistletoe + THRUSH[1]; from its feeding on mistletoe berries]

mistletoe /'misltoh/ *noun* **1** a European shrub that grows as a parasite on the branches of trees and has thick leaves, small yellowish flowers, and waxy white glutinous berries: *Viscum album.* **2** any of various similar or related plants. [Old English *misteltān*, from *mistel* mistletoe, basil + *tān* twig]

mistook /mi'stook/ *verb* past tense of MISTAKE[1].

mistral /'mistrəl, mi'strahl/ (*French* mistral)/ *noun* a strong cold dry northerly wind of S France. [via French from Provençal *mistral* masterful, from Latin *magistralis*]

mistreat /mis'treet/ *verb trans* to treat (somebody or something) badly. ➤➤ **mistreatment** *noun.*

mistress /'mistris/ *noun* **1a** a woman in a position of power, authority, possession, or control. **b** *archaic* the female head of a household. **2** a woman who has achieved mastery of a subject or skill. **3** a woman with whom a man has a continuing sexual relationship outside marriage. **4** *chiefly Brit* a female schoolteacher: *the maths mistress.* **5** *archaic* a sweetheart. **6** (**Mistress**) *archaic* used as a title preceding the name of a woman and now superseded by *Mrs, Miss,* and *Ms.* [Middle English *maistresse,* from Old French *maistresse,* fem of *maistre* master]

Mistress of the Robes *noun* in Britain, a high-ranking female member of the royal household who is in charge of the Queen's wardrobe.

mistrial /'mistrie-əl/ *noun* **1** a trial declared void because of some error in the proceedings. **2** *NAmer* a trial that is inconclusive, e.g. because the jury cannot reach agreement.

mistrust[1] /mis'trust/ *verb trans* **1** to have little trust in (somebody or something); to be suspicious of (them). **2** to doubt the reliability or effectiveness of (something): *She mistrusted her own judgment.*

mistrust[2] *noun* a lack of trust; distrust. ➤➤ **mistrustful** *adj,* **mistrustfully** *adv,* **mistrustfulness** *noun.*

misty *adj* (**mistier, mistiest**) **1a** covered with or obscured by mist: *a misty windscreen.* **b** consisting of or marked by mist: *a misty morning.* **2** not clear; indistinct, blurred or vague. ➤➤ **mistily** *adv,* **mistiness** *noun.*

misunderstand /,misundə'stand/ *verb trans* (*past tense and past part.* **misunderstood** /-'stood/) **1** to fail to understand (something or somebody). **2** to interpret (something) incorrectly.

misunderstanding *noun* **1** a failure to understand; a misinterpretation: *Is an intelligent human being likely to be much more than a large-scale manufacturer of misunderstanding?* — Philip Roth. **2** *euphem* a disagreement; a dispute.

misunderstood *verb* past tense and past part. of MIS-UNDERSTAND.

misusage /mis'yoohsij/ *noun* **1** bad treatment; abuse. **2** wrong or improper use, *esp* of words. [early French *mesusage*, from *mes-* MIS-[1] + USAGE]

misuse[1] /mis'yoohz/ *verb trans* **1** to put (something) to wrong or improper use. **2** to abuse or maltreat (somebody or something). ⟩⟩ **misuser** *noun*.

Usage note ⎯⎯⎯⎯⎯⎯⎯⎯
misuse *or* abuse? See note at ABUSE[1].

misuse[2] /mis'yoohs/ *noun* **1** incorrect or improper use. **2** maltreatment; abuse.

MIT *abbr* Massachusetts Institute of Technology.

mite /miet/ *noun* **1** any of a large order of small to minute invertebrate animals related to the spiders and ticks that often infest animals, plants, and stored foods: order Acari. **2a** a very small child or animal. **b** a very small amount or particle. **3** formerly, a small coin or sum of money; *specif* a Flemish coin of low value. ✱ **a mite** *informal* to a small extent; somewhat: *I'm a mite hungry* [Old English *mite*; related to Middle Dutch *mite* mite, small copper coin]

miter[1] /'mietə/ *noun NAmer* see MITRE[1].

miter[2] *verb trans NAmer* see MITRE[2].

mither /'miedhə/ *verb intrans chiefly N Eng dialect* to make a fuss or pester somebody. [of unknown origin]

Mithraism /'mithrayiz(ə)m/ *noun* the cult of Mithras, an ancient Persian god of light, which flourished in the late Roman Empire and had as its central ceremony the sacrifice of a bull. ⟩⟩ **Mithraic** /mi'thrayik/ *adj*, **Mithraist** *noun*. [via Latin from Greek *Mithras* from Old Persian *Mithra*]

mithridatism /'mithridaytiz(ə)m/ *noun* tolerance to a poison acquired by taking gradually increased doses of it. [from Greek *Mithridatēs* Mithridates VI d.63 BC, king of Pontus, who reputedly inured himself to poisons in this way]

mitigate /'mitigayt/ *verb trans* **1** to make (something) less harsh or hostile. **2a** to make (something) less severe or painful; to alleviate (it). **b** to lessen the seriousness of (something): *mitigating circumstances*. ⟩⟩ **mitigable** *adj*, **mitigation** /-'gaysh(ə)n/ *noun*, **mitigator** *noun*, **mitigatory** /-gaytəri, -gat(ə)ri/ *adj*. [Middle English *mitigaten* from Latin *mitigatus*, past part. of *mitigare* to soften, from *mitis* soft]

Usage note ⎯⎯⎯⎯⎯⎯⎯⎯
mitigate *or* militate? See note at MILITATE.

mitochondrion /mietoh'kondri-ən/ *noun* (*pl* **mitochondria** /-dri-ə/) in biology, any of several round or long specialized parts of a cell that are found outside the nucleus, are rich in fats, proteins, and enzymes, and produce energy through cellular respiration. ⟩⟩ **mitochondrial** *adj*, **mitochondrially** *adv*. [scientific Latin *mitochondrion*, from Greek *mitos* thread + *chondrion*, dimin. of *chondros* grain]

mitosis /mie'tohsis/ *noun* (*pl* **mitoses** /-seez/) the formation during cell division of two new nuclei from a dividing nucleus, each having the same number of chromosomes as the original nucleus, or the type of cell division in which this occurs: compare MEIOSIS (1), CELL DIVISION. ⟩⟩ **mitotic** /mie'totik/ *adj*. [scientific Latin *mitosis*, from Greek *mitos* thread]

mitral /'mietrəl/ *adj* **1** resembling a mitre. **2** of or being the heart valve situated between the upper and lower chambers on the left-hand side.

mitre[1] (*NAmer* **miter**) /'mietə/ *noun* **1** a tall pointed divided ceremonial hat with two bands hanging down at the back, worn by bishops and abbots. **2a** a joint made by cutting the ends of two pieces of wood or other material obliquely so that they form a right angle when fitted together. **b** a diagonal join in sewing that resembles this, e.g. at the corner of a hem. [Middle English via French and Latin from Greek *mitra* headband, turban]

mitre[2] (*NAmer* **miter**) *verb trans* **1a** to cut (something, e.g. the ends of pieces of wood) obliquely to make a mitre. **b** to join (pieces) in a mitre. **c** to form (a corner, etc) by means of a mitre. **2** to confer a mitre on (somebody) and thus raise (them) to the rank of abbot or bishop.

mitre box *noun* a device for guiding a handsaw at the proper angle in making a mitre joint in wood.

mitre joint (*NAmer* **miter joint**) *noun* = MITRE[1] (2A).

mitt /mit/ *noun* **1a** a glove that leaves the fingers or the ends of the fingers uncovered. **b** = MITTEN (1). **c** a baseball catcher's protective glove. **2** *informal* a hand: *Keep your mitts off it!* [short for MITTEN]

mitten /'mit(ə)n/ *noun* **1** a covering for the hand and wrist that has one section for all four fingers and another for the thumb. **2** = MITT (1A). **3** *informal* (*in pl*) boxing gloves. [Middle English *mitain* from Old French *mitaine*, prob from *mite* mitten]

mittimus /'mitiməs/ *noun* **1** a warrant formerly sent to the keeper of a prison to receive and detain a specified person. **2** formerly, a writ used to send records from one court to another. [Latin *mittimus* we send, from *mittere* to send]

mitzvah /'mitsvə/ *noun* (*pl* **mitzvoth** /'mitsvoht/) **1** a commandment of the Jewish law. **2** an act considered in the Jewish religion as being praiseworthy or charitable. [Hebrew *miṣwah*]

mix[1] /miks/ *verb trans* **1a** to combine or blend (ingredients) into one mass. **b** to combine (one ingredient) with another or others. **c** to prepare (something) by mixing ingredients: *to mix a drink*. **2** to bring (different things or elements) into close association: *to mix business with pleasure*. **3** to drink (different types of alcoholic drink) in succession. **4** to control the balance of (various sounds), *esp* during the recording of a film, broadcast, record, etc: compare DUB[2]. **5** to crossbreed (animals, plants, etc). ⟩ *verb intrans* **1a** to become mixed. **b** to be capable of mixing. **2** to seek or enjoy the fellowship or company of others. **3** (+ in) to become actively involved: *He decided not to mix in politics*. **4** to interbreed. ✱ **mix and match** to select complementary items from different sources to form a whole. **mix it** *informal* to start an argument or fight. [Middle English *mixen*, back-formation from *mixte* mixed, via French from Latin *mixtus*, past part. of *miscere* to mix]

mix[2] *noun* **1** the act or an instance of mixing. **2** a product of mixing; *specif* a commercially prepared mixture of food ingredients: *a cake mix*. **3** a combination: *the right mix of jobs, people, and amenities* — The Times. **4** the proportion in which elements are mixed or combined. **5a** a combination of recordings, *esp* one having the individual sounds adjusted to provide a pleasing blend. **b** a version of a musical recording that has been mixed to produce a different type of sound from the original: *a dance mix*.

mixed *adj* **1** combining diverse elements. **2** made up of or involving people of different sexes, races, religions, etc: *in mixed company*. **3** including or accompanied by conflicting or dissimilar elements: *mixed feelings*. **4** deriving from two or more races or breeds: *a person of mixed blood*. [Middle English *mixte*: see MIX[1]]

mixed bag *noun* a miscellaneous collection; an assortment.

mixed blessing *noun* something with both advantages and disadvantages, e.g. a desirable situation or occurrence that also has undesirable elements.

mixed doubles *pl noun* (*treated as sing.*) in tennis, badminton, etc, a game or match with one male player and one female player on each side.

mixed economy *noun* an economic system in which private enterprise and nationalized industries coexist.

mixed farming *noun* the growing of crops and rearing of livestock on the same farm.

mixed grill *noun Brit* a dish of several meats and vegetables grilled and served together.

mixed marriage *noun* a marriage between people of different races or religions.

mixed martial arts *noun* = ULTIMATE FIGHTING.

mixed metaphor *noun* a combination of incongruous metaphors, e.g. in *iron out bottlenecks*.

mixed number *noun* a number, e.g. $5\frac{2}{3}$, composed of an integer and a fraction.

mixed-up *adj informal* being in a state of perplexity, uncertainty, or disorder; confused.

mixer *noun* **1** a container, device, or machine for mixing something, e.g. food or concrete. **2** a person considered with respect to their sociability: *She was shy and a poor mixer*. **3** a non-alcoholic drink intended to be mixed with an alcoholic drink, *esp* spirits. **4a** an electronic device used to combine *esp* sound signals from a number of sources in variable proportions for recording, broadcasting, etc. **b** a person who operates such a device.

mixer tap *noun* a tap that supplies hot water, cold water, or a mixture of the two in variable proportions through a single outlet.

mixture /'mikschə/ *noun* **1** the act or an instance of mixing. **2a** a product of mixing; a combination or blend. **b** a combination of two or more components or ingredients in varying proportions that retain their own properties. **3** the relative proportions of the constituents of a mixture; *specif* the proportion of fuel to air produced in a carburettor. [Old French *misture* from Latin *mixtura* from *mixtus*: see MIX[1]]

mix up *verb trans* **1** to mistake or confuse (somebody or something) for another: *You're mixing her up with her sister.* **2** to make (something) untidy or disordered. **✳ be/get mixed up in** to be or become involved in an illegal or suspect activity or with an undesirable group: *He was mixed up in drug trafficking.*

mix-up *noun informal* a state or instance of confusion.

mizzen *or* **mizen** /'miz(ə)n/ *noun* **1** the mast behind the mainmast in a sailing vessel. **2** the principal fore-and-aft sail on a mizzenmast. [Middle English *meson* from early French *misaine*, perhaps from Italian *mezzana* mizzensail]

mizzenmast *noun* = MIZZEN (1).

mizzle[1] /'mizl/ *verb intrans chiefly dialect* = DRIZZLE[1]. [Middle English *miseln*]

mizzle[2] *noun* = DRIZZLE[2]. **➤➤ mizzly** *adj*.

mizzle[3] *verb intrans chiefly Brit, informal* to depart suddenly. [origin unknown]

MK *abbr* Macedonia (international vehicle registration).

Mk *abbr* **1** Mark (book of the Bible). **2** mark (unit of currency or numbered model).

mks *abbr* metre-kilogram-second (system of units).

mkt *abbr* market.

ml *abbr* **1** mile. **2** millilitre.

MLA *abbr* **1** Member of the Legislative Assembly. **2** *NAmer* Modern Language Association.

MLC *abbr* Member of the Legislative Council.

MLD *abbr* minimum lethal dose.

MLitt /,em 'lit/ *abbr* Master of Letters. [Latin *Magister Litterarum*]

Mlle *abbr* Mademoiselle.

Mlles *abbr* Mesdemoiselles.

MLR *abbr* minimum lending rate.

MM *abbr* **1** Maelzel's metronome. **2** Messieurs. **3** *Brit* Military Medal.

mm *abbr* millimetre.

MMC *abbr Brit* Monopolies and Mergers Commission.

Mme *abbr* Madame.

Mmes *abbr* Mesdames.

mmf *abbr* magnetomotive force.

MMR *abbr* measles, mumps, and rubella (vaccination).

MMS *abbr* **1** multimedia messaging (service). **2** multimedia message.

MMus /,em 'mus/ *abbr* Master of Music.

MN *abbr* **1** *Brit* Merchant Navy. **2** Minnesota (US postal abbreviation).

Mn *abbr* the chemical symbol for manganese.

MNA *abbr* Member of the National Assembly (of Quebec).

mnemonic[1] /ni'monik/ *adj* **1** assisting or intended to assist the memory. **2** of memory or mnemonics. **➤➤ mnemonically** *adv*. [Greek *mnēmonikos* from *mnēmōn* mindful, from *mimnēskesthai* to remember]

mnemonic[2] *noun* a mnemonic device or code.

mnemonics *pl noun* (*treated as sing. or pl*) the art of or a system for improving the memory.

MO *abbr* **1** Medical Officer. **2** Missouri (US postal abbreviation). **3** modus operandi. **4** money order.

Mo[1] *abbr* the chemical symbol for molybdenum.

Mo[2] *abbr* Montana.

mo *or* **mo'** /moh/ *noun chiefly Brit, informal* a very short space of time; a moment. [short for MOMENT]

mo. *abbr* month.

-mo *suffix* forming nouns, denoting: the number of leaves for a book made by folding a sheet of paper: *sixteenmo*. [from DUODECIMO]

moa /'moh·ə/ *noun* any of several species of very large extinct flightless birds of New Zealand: *Dinornis maximus* and other species. [Maori *moa*]

Moabite /'moh·əbiet/ *noun* a member of an ancient Semitic people related to the Hebrews. **➤➤ Moabite** *adj*. [Middle English, from late Latin *Moabita, Moabites* from Greek *Mōabitēs* from *Mōab* Moab, ancient kingdom in Syria]

moan[1] /mohn/ *noun* **1a** a low prolonged sound usu of pain or grief. **b** a sound resembling this, *esp* a mournful sound made by the wind. **2** *informal* a complaint. [Middle English *mone*]

moan[2] *verb intrans* **1** to produce a moan. **2** *informal* to complain or grumble: *always moaning about something.* **➤ verb trans** **1** to utter (something) with moans or in a low mournful voice. **2** *literary* to lament or bewail (something); to bemoan (it). **➤➤ moaner** *noun*, **moanful** *adj*.

moat[1] /moht/ *noun* a deep wide trench, usu filled with water, constructed round a castle or other fortified place. [Middle English *mot, mote* from Old French *mote* bank, mound]

moat[2] *verb trans* to surround (a building or place) with or as if with a moat: *a moated grange*.

mob[1] /mob/ *noun* **1** (*also before a noun*) a large, disorderly, or riotous crowd: *lynched by an angry mob; mob rule.* **2a** a large group: *a mob of schoolchildren.* **b** *chiefly Brit, informal* a particular group or class of people: *He's joined the plainclothes mob.* **3** (**the mob**) the masses; the populace: *endeavour to stand out from the mob.* **4** (*usu* **the Mob**) *chiefly NAmer* the Mafia or a similarly organized criminal gang. **5a** *chiefly Aus* a flock, drove, or herd of animals. **b** *now Aus* a vast number or amount: *The broadening waters flowed through a mob of wooded islands* — Joseph Conrad.

Word history
short for earlier *mobile*, from Latin *mobile vulgus* fickle crowd. The term was first applied to people by members of the Green Ribbon Club, a late 17th-cent. political club.

mob[2] *verb trans* (**mobbed, mobbing**) **1** to attack (somebody) in a large crowd or group. **2** to crowd round (somebody), *esp* out of curiosity or admiration. **3** to crowd into (a building or place).

mob cap *noun* a woman's full soft cap with a frill round the edge, worn indoors *esp* in the 18th cent. [prob from obsolete *mab, mob*, slattern, careless dress, from *Mab* short for *Mabel*]

mobile[1] /'mohbiel/ *adj* **1** capable of moving or being moved. **2** changing readily in expression or mood. **3** capable of or undergoing movement into a different social class: *upwardly mobile.* **4** marked by or having the use of a vehicle or vehicles for transport: *a mobile library.* **➤➤ mobility** /moh'biliti, mə-/ *noun*. [via French from Latin *mobilis* from *movēre* to move]

mobile[2] *noun* **1** a decorative structure with suspended parts that are moved by air currents. **2** = MOBILE PHONE: *People who wear hearing aids will neither be able to use digital mobiles, nor work with colleagues who use them* — The Economist.

mobile home *noun* a caravan, *esp* one used as permanent accommodation.

mobile phone *noun* a portable telephone for use in a cellular radio system.

mobilize *or* **mobilise** /'mohbiliez/ *verb trans* **1a** to assemble and make ready (troops) for active service. **b** to marshal (resources) for action. **2a** to put (something) into movement or circulation. **b** to release (something stored in the body) for use in an organism. **➤ verb intrans** to be mobilized. **➤➤ mobilizable** *adj*, **mobilization** /-'zaysh(ə)n/ *noun*.

Möbius strip /'muhbi·əs/ *noun* a one-sided surface that is constructed from a rectangle by holding one end, rotating the opposite end through 180°, and joining it to the first end. [named after August *Möbius* d.1868, German mathematician]

mobocracy /mo'bokrəsi/ *noun* (*pl* **mobocracies**) **1** rule by the masses. **2** (*treated as sing. or pl*) the masses as a ruling class.

mobster /'mobstə/ *noun informal* a member of a criminal gang.

MOC *abbr* Mozambique (international vehicle registration).

moccasin /'mokəsin/ *noun* **1** a soft leather heelless shoe with the sole brought up the sides of the foot and joined with a puckered seam to a U-shaped piece lying on top of the foot. **2** any shoe with such a puckered seam on the upper. **3** = WATER MOCCASIN. [of Algonquian origin]

mocha /'mokə, 'mohkə/ *noun* **1** a coffee of superior quality; *specif* a coffee with small green or yellow beans grown on the Arabian peninsula. **2** a flavouring obtained from a strong coffee infusion or from a mixture of cocoa or chocolate with coffee. **3** a pliable suede-finished glove leather made from African sheepskin. [named after *Mocha*, seaport in Yemen, from where the coffee was first shipped]

mock[1] /mok/ *verb trans* **1** to treat (somebody or something) with contempt or ridicule; to deride (them). **2** to disappoint, frustrate, or delude (somebody or something). **3** to copy or mimic (somebody or something) in fun or derision. ➤ *verb intrans* to jeer or scoff. ➤➤ **mocker** *noun*, **mocking** *adj*, **mockingly** *adv*. [Middle English *mocken* from early French *mocquer* from Old French *moquier*]

mock[2] *noun* **1** (*also in pl*) a school examination used as practice for an official one. **2** an object of derision or ridicule.

mock[3] *adj* being or having the character of an imitation; simulated: *mock cream; a mock battle*.

mockers ✳ **put the mockers on 1** *Brit, informal* to ruin or put an end to (something): *The rain put the mockers on our plans*. **2** *Brit, informal* to bring misfortune to (somebody). [perhaps modification (influenced by MOCK[1]) of Yiddish *makeh* boil, sore, plague, from Hebrew *makāh* blow, wound, plague]

mockery *noun* (*pl* **mockeries**) **1** jeering or contemptuous behaviour or words. **2** an object of derision or ridicule. **3** a deceitful or contemptible imitation; a travesty. **4** something insultingly or ridiculously inappropriate. ✳ **make a mockery of something** to undermine it or render it pointless: *If these major mining proposals within our most prized countryside are given the go-ahead now, they will make a mockery of the government's future conservation proposals —* Climber and Hill Walker.

mock-heroic[1] *adj* using heroic style, character, or action for satirical effect in the treatment of an unheroic subject: *a mock-heroic poem*.

mock-heroic[2] *noun* a mock-heroic composition or the mock-heroic technique.

mockingbird *noun* a songbird of the USA that imitates the calls of other birds: *Mimus polyglottos*.

mockney or **Mockney** /'mokni/ *noun* a fake cockney accent. ➤➤ **mockney** *adj*. [MOCK[3] + COCKNEY]

mock orange *noun* any of several species of ornamental shrubs of the saxifrage family with showy fragrant white flowers: *Philadelphus coronarius* and other species.

mock turtle soup *noun* a soup made from a calf's head in imitation of turtle soup.

mock-up *noun* a full-sized model or representation, e.g. for study, testing, or display.

MOD *abbr Brit* Ministry of Defence.

mod[1] /mod/ *noun* (*usu* **Mod**) a Gaelic competitive festival of the arts, *esp* singing and recitation, held in Scotland. [Scottish Gaelic *mòd* from Old Norse *mōt* meeting; related to Old English *mōt* MOOT[1]]

mod[2] *noun* (*often* **Mod**) a member of a group of young people in Britain, *esp* in the 1960s, noted for their neat appearance and stylish clothing: compare ROCKER (2). [short for MODERN[1]]

mod. *abbr* **1** moderate. **2** moderato. **3** modern.

modal /'mohdl/ *adj* **1** of general form or structure, as opposed to particular substance or content. **2** of or being a grammatical form or category indicating mood; *specif* of or being an auxiliary verb expressing necessity, possibility, etc, e.g. *can, must*, or *may*. **3** of modality in logic. **4** of or being in a musical mode; *specif* being in one of the church modes rather than a major or minor key. **5** of or having a statistical mode. ➤➤ **modally** *adv*. [Latin *modalis* from Latin *modus* late: see MODE]

modal auxiliary verb *noun* in grammar, a verb such as *will, shall, should, would, may, might*, that helps another verb to form tenses, voices, and moods that cannot be indicated by INFLECTION (verb ending).

modality /moh'daliti/ *noun* (*pl* **modalities**) **1** a modal quality or attribute; a form. **2** the classification of logical propositions according to the possibility, impossibility, contingency, or necessity of their content.

mod cons /,mod 'konz/ *pl noun Brit, informal* modern conveniences, *esp* household fittings or devices designed to increase comfort or save time: *a house with all mod cons*.

mode /mohd/ *noun* **1** a way of doing something: *a mode of transport*. **2** a particular functional arrangement or condition: *a space-*

craft in orbiting mode. **3a** a particular form or variety of something. **b** a form or manner of expression; a style. **4** a prevailing fashion or style, e.g. of dress or behaviour. **5** = MOOD[2] (1). **6** = MOOD[2] (2). **7** an arrangement of the eight notes of a musical scale within an octave in any of several fixed schemes that use different patterns of tones and semitones between successive notes. **8** in statistics, the most frequently occurring value in a set of data. **9** in physics, any of various stable patterns of which a vibrating or oscillating body or system is capable. [Middle English *moede* from Latin *modus* measure, manner, musical mode; (sense 4) French *mode* from Latin *modus*]

model[1] /'modl/ *noun* **1a** a replica of something in three dimensions. **b** a representation of something to be constructed. **c** (*used before a noun*) of or being such a replica or representation: *a model aeroplane*. **2** structural design: *He built his home on the model of an old farmhouse*. **3a** an example used for reproducing or copying or worthy of imitation or emulation: *This essay is a model of clarity*. **b** (*used before a noun*) being or providing such an example: *a model student*. **4a** somebody or something that serves as a pattern for an artist. **b** a person who poses for an artist or photographer. **c** a person who is employed to wear or use merchandise, *esp* clothing, in order to display it: *a fashion model*. **5** a type or design of an article or product, e.g. a garment or car. **6** a description or analogy used to help visualize something, e.g. an atom, that cannot be directly observed. **7** a system of postulates, data, and inferences presented as a mathematical description of an entity or state of affairs, which may be stored in a computer. [early French *modelle* from Old Italian *modello* from Latin *modulus* small measure, from *modus*: see MODE]

model[2] *verb* (**modelled, modelling**, *NAmer* **modeled, modeling**) ➤ *verb trans* **1a** to shape (something) in a mouldable material. **b** to produce a model of (something): *using a computer to model the problem*. **2** to plan, construct, or fashion (something) in imitation of a particular model: *modelled on the US constitution*. **3** to display (something), *esp* by wearing it. ➤ *verb intrans* **1** to work as a model, *esp* a fashion model. **2** to design, produce, or imitate forms: *modelling in clay*. ➤➤ **modeller** *noun*.

modem /'mohdəm/ *noun* an electronic device that converts digital data from a computer into an audio signal that can be transmitted via a telephone line. [blend of *modulator* + *demodulator*]

moderate[1] /'mod(ə)rət/ *adj* **1a** avoiding extremes of behaviour or expression; practising reasonable restraint: *a moderate drinker*. **b** calm, mild, or temperate: *a moderate climate*. **c** within reasonable limits: *moderate wage demands*. **d** avoiding extreme political or social measures; not radical. **2** being average or somewhat less than average in quality, amount, degree, or extent: *only moderate success*. ➤➤ **moderately** *adv*. [Middle English from Latin *moderatus* past part. of *moderare* to moderate]

moderate[2] /'modərayt/ *verb trans* **1** to lessen the intensity or extremeness of (something). **2** to preside over (a meeting or debate). **3** to ensure consistency of grading in (examination papers or results). **4** in physics, to slow down (neutrons) with a moderator. ➤ *verb intrans* **1** to act as a moderator. **2** to decrease in violence, severity, intensity, or extremeness.

moderate[3] /'mod(ə)rət/ *noun* a person who holds moderate views or favours a moderate course. [MODERATE[1]]

moderate breeze *noun* a wind having a speed of 20 to 28km/h (13 to 18mph).

moderate gale *noun* a wind having a speed of 50 to 61km/h (about 32 to 38mph).

moderation /modə'raysh(ə)n/ *noun* **1** the process of moderating or of being moderated. **2** the avoidance of extremes, *esp* in personal behaviour; restraint; self-control: *Moderation is a virtue only in those who are thought to have an alternative —* Henry Kissinger. ✳ **in moderation** within reasonable limits.

Moderations *pl noun* the first honours examination at Oxford University in some subjects.

moderato /modə'rahtoh/ *adj and adv* said of a piece of music: to be performed at a moderate tempo. [Italian *moderato* from Latin *moderatus*: see MODERATE[1]]

moderator /'modəraytə/ *noun* **1** a person who arbitrates; a mediator. **2** a person who presides over an assembly, meeting, debate, etc, e.g.: **a** the presiding officer of a Presbyterian governing body. **b** the officer presiding over certain Oxbridge examinations. **3** a person who moderates examination papers or results. **4** in physics, a substance used for slowing down neutrons in a nuclear reactor. ➤➤ **moderatorship** *noun*.

modern[1] /'modən/ *adj* **1a** of or characteristic of a period extending from a particular point in the past to the present time. **b** of or characteristic of the present or the immediate past; contemporary. **2** involving recent techniques, styles, or ideas: *modern art*. **3** (**Modern**) constituting the present or most recent period of a language. **4** *archaic* ordinary; everyday; commonplace: *They say miracles are past; and we have our philosophical persons to make modern and familiar things supernatural and causeless* — Shakespeare. ➤➤ **modernity** /mo'duhniti, mə-/ *noun,* **modernness** *noun.* [late Latin *modernus* from Latin *modo* just now, from *modus* measure]

modern[2] *noun* a person of modern times or having modern views.

modern English *noun* English since the late 15th cent.

modern history *noun* the period of history from the end of the Middle Ages to the present day.

modernise *verb* see MODERNIZE.

modernism *noun* **1** a practice, usage, or expression characteristic of modern times. **2** (*often* **Modernism**) a tendency in theology to adapt traditional doctrine to contemporary thought, *esp* by minimizing supernatural elements. **3** the theory and practices of modern art, literature, music, etc, *esp* a search for new forms of expression involving a deliberate break with the past.

Editorial note ───────────────
The dominant 20th-cent. experimental movement in literature and the arts, modernism displaced tradition and the classical. Its weapons were a radical new aesthetic (free verse, stream-of-consciousness prose, etc), an avant-garde posture, a revolt against existing cultural institutions, and a celebration of artistic independence (bohemia). Modernism peaked internationally around World War I, declined with World War II, leaving a major new tradition for successors to face — Professor Malcolm Bradbury.

➤➤ **modernist** *noun and adj,* **modernistic** /-'nistik/ *adj.*

modernize *or* **modernise** *verb trans* to adapt (something) to modern needs, style, or standards. ➤ *verb intrans* to adopt modern views, habits, or techniques. ➤➤ **modernization** /-'zaysh(ə)n/ *noun,* **modernizer** *noun.*

modern pentathlon *noun* a contest in which all participants compete in a 300m freestyle swimming race, a 4000m cross-country run, a 5000m 30-jump equestrian steeplechase, épée fencing, and target shooting at 25m.

modest /'modist/ *adj* **1** having or showing a moderate estimate of one's abilities or worth; not boastful or self-assertive. **2** arising from or characteristic of a modest nature. **3** small or limited in size, amount, or aim: *a modest salary.* **4** carefully observant of proprieties of dress and behaviour; decent. ➤➤ **modestly** *adv,* **modesty** *noun.* [Latin *modestus* moderate; related to Latin *modus* measure]

modicum /'modikəm/ *noun* a small or limited amount: *without a modicum of truth.* [Middle English from Latin *modicum,* neuter of *modicus* moderate, from *modus* measure]

modification /ˌmodifi'kaysh(ə)n/ *noun* **1a** a small or limited change made to something. **b** the making of such a change. **2** the limiting of a statement; a qualification. ➤➤ **modificatory** *adj.*

modifier /'modifie·ə/ *noun* **1** a word or word group that qualifies or limits the meaning of another, e.g. *horror* in *horror film.* **2** somebody or something that modifies another.

modify /'modifie/ *verb* (**modifies, modified, modifying**) ➤ *verb trans* **1a** to make minor changes in (something). **b** to make basic changes in (something), often for a specific purpose: *Wings are arms modified for flying.* **2** to make (something) less extreme. **3** in grammar, to limit (a word or phrase) in meaning; to qualify (it). ➤ *verb intrans* to undergo change. ➤➤ **modifiable** *adj.* [Middle English *modifien* from early French *modifier* from Latin *modificare* to measure, moderate, from *modus*: see MODE]

modi operandi /'mohdee, -die/ *noun* pl of MODUS OPERANDI.

modish /'mohdish/ *adj* fashionable; stylish. ➤➤ **modishly** *adv,* **modishness** *noun.*

modiste /moh'deest/ *noun dated* a person who makes and sells fashionable women's clothing, *esp* dresses and hats. [French *modiste* from *mode* style, mode]

modi vivendi /'mohdee, -die/ *noun* pl of MODUS VIVENDI.

Mods /modz/ *pl noun informal* = MODERATIONS.

modular /'modyoolə/ *adj* **1** of or based on a module or modulus. **2** consisting of or constructed from modules. ➤➤ **modularity** /-'lariti/ *noun.*

modulate /'modyoolayt/ *verb trans* **1** to vary (one's voice, etc) in tone, pitch, etc. **2** to keep (something) in proper measure or

proportion; to temper or regulate (it). **3** to vary the amplitude, frequency, or phase of (one of two combined waves) to match the variations of the other, *esp* in combining a radio wave with the sound or vision signal it carries. ➤ *verb intrans* in music, to pass by regular chord or melodic progression from one key or tonality into another. ➤➤ **modulation** /-'laysh(ə)n/ *noun,* **modulator** *noun.* [Latin *modulatus,* past part. of *modulari* to play, sing, from *modulus:* see MODULUS]

module /'modyoohl/ *noun* **1** any of a set of standardized units for use together in construction, e.g. of buildings, computers, or furniture: *factory-built modules, assembled on site.* **2** a unit or section of an educational course, treating a specific subject or topic. **3** an independent unit that is part of the total structure of a space vehicle. **4** a standard or unit of measurement. [Latin *modulus:* see MODULUS]

modulus /'modyooləs/ *noun* (*pl* **moduli** /-lie/) **1** a number or quantity that expresses the degree in which a physical property is possessed by a substance or body. **2a** the positive square root of the sum of the squares of the real and imaginary parts of a complex number. **b** a number that is used to divide another number in order to find out the remainder. **c** the factor by which a logarithm of a number to one base is multiplied to obtain the logarithm of the number to a new base. [Latin *modulus* small measure, dimin. of *modus* measure]

modus operandi /ˌmohdəs opə'randi, -'randie/ *noun* (*pl* **modi operandi** /ˌmohdee, ˌmohdie/) a method or procedure. [late Latin *modus operandi* way of operating]

modus vivendi /vi'vendee, -die/ *noun* (*pl* **modi vivendi** /ˌmohdee, ˌmohdie/) **1** a practical compromise, *esp* between opposed or quarrelling parties. **2** a manner of living; a way of life. [late Latin *modus vivendi* manner of living]

Mogadon /'mogədon/ *noun trademark* = NITRAZEPAM. [invented name, perhaps based on Greek *mogos* toil, trouble + *donax* arrow]

moggie *or* **moggy** /'mogi/ *noun* (*pl* **moggies**) *Brit, informal* a cat. [prob alteration of *Maggie,* nickname for *Margaret*]

mogul[1] /'mohg(ə)l/ *noun* **1** (**Mogul, Moghul**) a member of a Muslim dynasty of Turkish and Mongolian origin that ruled India from the 16th to the 18th cent. **2** *informal* a great, wealthy, or powerful person; a magnate. [Persian *Mughul* from Mongolian *Mongol*]

mogul[2] *noun* a built-up mound of snow causing a bump on a ski slope. [prob of Scandinavian origin; related to Norwegian dialect *muge* heap]

MOH *abbr* Medical Officer of Health.

mohair /'mohheə/ *noun* **1** the long silky hair of the Angora goat. **2** a fabric or yarn made wholly or partly from this hair: compare ANGORA (2A). [modification (by association with *hair*) of early Italian *mocaiarro* from Arabic *mukhayyar,* literally 'choice']

Mohammedan /mə'hamid(ə)n/ *adj* see MUHAMMADAN.

Mohawk /'mohhawk/ *noun* (*pl* **Mohawks** *or collectively* **Mohawk**) **a** a member of a Native N American people of the Mohawk river valley in New York State. **b** the Iroquoian language of this people. ➤➤ **Mohawk** *adj.* (*often* **mohawk**) a turn in ice-skating from an edge of one foot to the same edge of the other foot in the opposite direction: compare CHOCTAW. [of Algonquian origin; related to Narraganset *Mohowaùuck,* literally 'they eat living things']

Mohican /moh'heekən/ *noun* **1** see MAHICAN. **2** (*often* **mohican**) a punk hairstyle in which the head is shaved except for a strip of erect hair running from front to back.

Moho /'moh·hoh/ *noun* (**the Moho**) the zone beneath the earth's surface at which studies of seismic waves indicate a transition in the materials making up the earth, and that represents a distinct boundary separating the earth's crust from the underlying mantle. [short for *Mohorovičic discontinuity,* named after Andrija Mohorovicić d.1936, Yugoslav seismologist]

Mohorovicic discontinuity /ˌmohhə'rohvichich/ *noun* = MOHO.

Mohs' scale /mohz/ *noun* a scale of hardness for minerals. [named after Friedrich *Mohs* d.1839, German mineralogist]

moidore /'moydaw/ *noun* a former Portuguese gold coin. [modification of Portuguese *moeda de ouro* coin of gold]

moiety /'moyiti/ *noun* (*pl* **moieties**) **1** either of two equal or approximately equal parts; a half. **2** any of the portions into which something is divided. [Middle English *moite* from early French *moité* from late Latin *medietat-*, *medietas* from Latin *medius* middle]

moil[1] /moyl/ *verb intrans archaic, dialect* **1** to work hard; to drudge: *toiling and moiling.* **2** to be in a state of continuous agitation; to churn or swirl. ➤ *verb trans archaic, dialect* to make (something) wet or dirty. ➤➤ **moiler** *noun.* [Middle English *moillen* to moisten, make dirty, from early French *moillier*, ultimately from Latin *mollis* soft]

moil[2] *noun* **1** laborious work; drudgery. **2** confusion or turmoil.

moiré[1] /'mwahray (*French* mware)/ *or* **moire** /mwah/ *adj* said of a fabric: having an irregular wavy finish or a wavy watered appearance. [French *moiré* like watered mohair, from *moire* MOHAIR]

moiré[2] *or* **moire** *noun* **1** an irregular wavy finish on a fabric. **2** a fabric having a wavy watered appearance. **3** a wavy shimmering pattern seen when two geometrically regular patterns, e.g. two sets of parallel lines or two grids, are superimposed, *esp* at an acute angle.

moist /moyst/ *adj* **1** slightly wet; damp. **2** of or having high humidity. ➤➤ **moistly** *adv,* **moistness** *noun.* [Middle English *moiste* from early French *moiste*, ultimately from Latin *mucidus* slimy, from *mucus* mucus]

moisten /'moysn/ *verb trans* to make (something) moist. ➤ *verb intrans* to become moist.

moisture /'moyschə/ *noun* liquid diffused as vapour or condensed as tiny droplets. [Middle English, modification of early French *moistour*, from *moiste*: see MOIST]

moisturize *or* **moisturise** *verb trans* to add or restore moisture to (the skin, etc). ➤➤ **moisturizer** *noun.*

mojo /'mohjoh/ *noun* (*pl* **mojos**) *chiefly NAmer* **1** a magic spell or charm. **2** magic. [prob of W African origin]

moke /mohk/ *noun informal* **1** *Brit* a donkey. **2** *Aus* a horse, *esp* one of poor quality. [origin unknown]

mol /mohl/ *noun* see MOLE[5].

mol. *abbr* **1** molecular. **2** molecule.

molal /'mohlal/ *adj* of or being a solution containing one mole of solute per kilogram of solvent. [MOLE[5]]

molality /moh'laliti/ *noun* (*pl* **molalities**) the concentration of a solution measured in terms of the number of moles of solute per kilogram of solvent.

molar[1] /'mohlə/ *noun* a grinding tooth with a rounded or flattened surface; *specif* any of the teeth towards the back of the jaw in mammals. [Latin *molaris*, from *mola* millstone]

molar[2] *adj* of or located near the molars.

molar[3] *adj* **1** of or containing one mole of a substance: *molar volume.* **2** of or being a solution containing one mole of solute per litre of solution. [Latin *moles* mass]

molarity /moh'lariti/ *noun* (*pl* **molarities**) the concentration of a solution measured in terms of the number of moles of solute per litre of the solution.

molar tooth *noun* = MOLAR[1].

molasses /mə'lasiz/ *noun* **1** the darkest most viscous syrup remaining after all sugar that can be separated by crystallization has been removed during the refining of raw sugar. **2** *NAmer* treacle or golden syrup. [Portuguese *melaço* from late Latin *mellaceum* grape juice, from Latin *mell-*, *mel* honey]

mold[1] /mohld/ *noun NAmer* see MOULD[1].

mold[2] *verb trans NAmer* see MOULD[2].

mold[3] *noun NAmer* see MOULD[3].

mold[4] *noun NAmer* see MOULD[4].

Moldavian /mol'dayvi·ən/ *noun* **1** a native or inhabitant of Moldavia. **2** = MOLDOVAN. ➤➤ **Moldavian** *adj.*

molder *verb intrans NAmer* see MOULDER.

molding *noun NAmer* see MOULDING.

Moldovan /mol'dohv(ə)n/ *noun* a native or inhabitant of Moldova. ➤➤ **Moldovan** *adj.*

moldy *adj NAmer* see MOULDY.

mole[1] /mohl/ *noun* **1** any of several species of small burrowing insect-eating mammals with tiny eyes, concealed ears, and soft fur: *Talpa europaea* and other species. **2a** a person who spends a long period of time establishing a position of trust within an institution in order secretly to further the interests of a rival organization or government, e.g. by spying. **b** a person who leaks secret informa-

tion about an organization in which they are involved. [Middle English; related to Middle Low German *mol*]

mole[2] *noun* a dark-coloured permanent spot, mark, or small lump on the human body. [Old English *māl*; related to Old High German *meil* spot]

mole[3] *noun* **1** a massive structure formed of masonry, large stones, etc laid in the sea as a pier or breakwater. **2** a harbour formed by a mole. [via French from Old Italian *molo* from late Greek *mōlos*, from Latin *moles* mass, exertion]

mole[4] *noun* an abnormal mass in the womb, *esp* one containing foetal tissues. [French *môle* from Latin *mola*, literally 'mill, millstone']

mole[5] *or* **mol** /mohl/ *noun* the basic SI unit of amount of substance equal to the amount of a substance that contains the same number of atoms, molecules, ions, etc as there are atoms in 0.012kg of carbon-12. [German *Mol*, short for *Molekula* molecule]

mole[6] /'mohlay/ *noun* a spicy Mexican sauce made with chillis and chocolate. [Mexican Spanish *mole* from Nahuatl *molli* a sauce or stew]

mole cricket *noun* any of several genera of large crickets with enormously developed front legs for use in digging: family Gryllotalpidae.

molecular /mə'lekyoolə/ *adj* of, produced by, or consisting of molecules: *molecular oxygen.* ➤➤ **molecularity** /-'lariti/ *noun,* **molecularly** *adv.*

molecular biology *noun* a branch of biology dealing with the structure, organization, and functioning of the molecules of living matter.

molecular formula *noun* a chemical formula that gives the total number of atoms of each chemical element in a molecule: compare STRUCTURAL FORMULA.

molecular weight *noun* = RELATIVE MOLECULAR MASS.

molecule /'molikyoohl/ *noun* the smallest unit of a substance that retains its characteristic properties, usu consisting of two or more atoms of the same or different chemical elements bonded together. [French *molécule* from late Latin *molecula*, dimin. of Latin *moles* mass]

molehill *noun* a mound of earth thrown up by a burrowing mole. ✳ **make a mountain out of a molehill** to overdramatize a minor problem.

mole rat *noun* any of several genera of small Eurasian and African rodents resembling true moles in behaviour or appearance: families Bathyergidae and Muridae.

moleskin *noun* **1** the skin of the mole used as fur. **2** a heavy durable cotton fabric with a short thick velvety nap on one side used *esp* for casual wear and work clothes. **3** (*in pl*) clothes, *esp* trousers or overalls, made of moleskin.

molest /mə'lest/ *verb trans* to annoy, disturb, or attack (somebody); *specif* to abuse or attack (them) sexually. ➤➤ **molestation** /mohle'staysh(ə)n/ *noun,* **molester** *noun.* [Middle English *molesten* via early French *molester* from Latin *molestare*, from *molestus* burdensome, annoying, from *moles* mass]

moll /mol/ *noun informal* **1** a gangster's female friend or companion. **2** a prostitute. [*Moll*, nickname for *Mary*]

mollie *or* **molly** /'moli/ *noun* (*pl* **mollies**) any of several species of small black or brightly coloured tropical or subtropical fishes, often kept as an aquarium fish: genus *Poecilia* (formerly *Mollienisia*). [short for Latin genus name *Mollienisia*, named after François Mollien d.1850, French statesman]

mollify /'molifie/ *verb trans* (**mollifies, mollified, mollifying**) **1** to lessen the anger or hostility of (somebody). **2** to reduce (something) in intensity or severity. ➤➤ **mollification** /-fi'kaysh(ə)n/ *noun,* **mollifier** *noun.* [Middle English *mollifien* via early French *mollifier* from late Latin *mollificare* from Latin *mollis* soft]

mollusc (*NAmer* **mollusk**) /'moləsk/ *noun* any of a large phylum of invertebrate animals including the snails, shellfish, and squids, that have a soft unsegmented body often enclosed in a shell: phylum Mollusca. ➤➤ **molluscan** /mo'luskən/ *adj.* [French *mollusque* from Latin *Mollusca*, phylum name, neuter pl of *molluscus* soft, from *mollis*]

molly /'moli/ *noun* (*pl* **mollies**) see MOLLIE.

mollycoddle[1] /'molikodl/ *verb trans* to treat (somebody) with excessive indulgence, attention, or protection. [*Molly* (nickname for *Mary*) + CODDLE]

mollycoddle² *noun* a spoilt or effeminate man or boy.

Molotov cocktail /'molətof/ *noun* a crude hand grenade made from a bottle filled with petrol or other inflammable liquid with a wick, usu a saturated rag, that is ignited just before it is thrown. [named after Vyacheslav M *Molotov* d.1986, Soviet statesman]

molt¹ /mohlt/ *verb trans and intrans NAmer* see MOULT¹.

molt² *noun NAmer* see MOULT².

molten /'mohlt(ə)n/ *adj* liquefied by heat; melted. [Middle English, past part. of *melten* to melt]

molto /'moltoh/ *adv* used in music: much; very: *molto sostenuto*. [Italian *molto* from Latin *multum*, neuter of *multus* much]

mol. wt *abbr* molecular weight.

moly /'mohli/ *noun* (*pl* **molies**) **1** a S European plant with small yellow flowers that is related to the onions and garlics: *Allium moly*. **2** in Greek mythology, a magic herb with white flowers and black roots, given to Odysseus to counteract Circe's spells. [via Latin from Greek *mōlu*]

molybdenite /mə'libdəniet/ *noun* a greyish blue mineral that consists of molybdenum disulphide and is the chief ore of molybdenum: formula MoS₂. [scientific Latin *molybdena*]

molybdenum /mə'libdənəm/ *noun* a silver-white metallic chemical element that is hard and is used *esp* in strengthening and hardening steel: symbol Mo, atomic number 42. [scientific Latin *molybdenum* from *molybdena* lead ore, molybdenite, via Latin from Greek *molybdaina* from *molybdos* lead]

mom /mom/ *noun NAmer, informal* = MUM¹. [variant of MAMA]

moment /'mohmənt/ *noun* **1a** a very brief interval of time. **b** a specific point in time. **2a** present time: *at the moment*. **b** a time of excellence or prominence: *She has her moments*. **3** *formal* importance in influence or effect: *a matter of great moment*. **4** a stage in historical or logical development: *one moment in the history of thought* — T S Eliot. **5a** a tendency to produce motion, *esp* rotational motion about a point or axis. **b** a measure of the tendency to produce rotational motion, equal to the product of a force and its perpendicular distance from a particular axis or point. [Middle English via French from Latin *momentum* movement, moment, from *movēre* to move]

momenta /mə'mentə/ *noun* pl of MOMENTUM.

momentarily /'mohmənt(ə)rili, mohmən'tarili/ *adv* **1** for a very short time. **2** *chiefly NAmer* very soon or immediately. **3** at any moment: *I momentarily expected his coming* — Charlotte Brontë.

momentary *adj* lasting a very short time; transitory. ⋙ **momentariness** *noun*.

momently *adv archaic or literary* **1** from moment to moment; continually: *The danger is momently increasing*. **2** for a very short time; momentarily.

moment of inertia *noun* a measure of the amount of resistance a body offers to having its rotational speed changed; the ratio of the TORQUE¹ (force causing rotation) applied to a body to the acceleration thus produced.

moment of truth *noun* **1** a moment of testing or crisis on the outcome of which everything depends. **2** the moment of the final sword thrust in a bullfight.

momentous /mə'mentəs/ *adj* of great consequence or significance. ⋙ **momentously** *adv*, **momentousness** *noun*.

momentum /mə'mentəm/ *noun* (*pl* **momenta** /-tə/) **1** the ability or tendency to continue onwards possessed by an object in motion or an operation in progress. **2** in physics, a property of a moving body that determines the length of time required to bring it to rest when under the action of a constant force; the result of multiplying the mass of a body by its velocity. **3** impetus or driving force: *The debate gathered momentum*. [Latin *momentum* movement]

momma /'momə, 'mumə/ *noun* **1** *NAmer, informal* = MOM. **2** a buxom mature woman. [variant of MAMA]

mommy /'momi/ *noun* (*pl* **mommies**) = MOM.

Mon /mohn/ *noun* (*pl* **Mons** *or collectively* **Mon**) **1** a member of a major ethnic group of Myanmar (formerly Burma) and Thailand. **2** the language of this group. [the Mon name]

Mon. *abbr* Monday.

mon. *abbr* monetary.

mon- *or* **mono-** *comb. form* forming words, with the meanings: **1** one; single; alone: *monaural; monoplane*. **2** containing one specified atom, radical, or group: *monohydric; monoxide*. [Middle English via French and Latin from Greek *monos* alone, single]

monad /'mohnad, 'monad/ *noun* **1** a fundamental unit or entity; one. **2** in the philosophy of Leibniz, an elementary indivisible spiritual entity or substance forming with others a harmonious system that is the basis of the material world. **3** *dated* a minute single-celled organism. ⋙ **monadic** /moh'nadik, mo-/ *adj*, **monadism** *noun*. [late Latin *monad-*, *monas*, from Greek *monos* alone]

monadelphous /monə'delfəs/ *adj* said of stamens: united by the filaments into one group, usu forming a tube around the carpels. [MON- + Greek *adelphos* brother + -OUS]

monadnock /mə'nadnok/ *noun* a hill or ridge of hard rock that rises above surrounding eroded land. [named after Mount *Monadnock* in New Hampshire, USA]

monandry /mo'nandri/ *noun* **1** the state, practice, or custom of having only one husband at a time. **2** the condition of a flower with a single stamen or a plant with such flowers. ⋙ **monandrous** /-drəs/ *adj*.

monarch /'monək/ *noun* **1** a person who reigns over a kingdom or empire. **2** somebody or something occupying a commanding or preeminent position. **3** a large migratory N American butterfly that has orange-brown wings with black veins and borders and larvae that feed on milkweed: *Danaus plexippus*. ⋙ **monarchal** /mə'nahkl/ *adj*, **monarchial** /mə'nahki·əl/ *adj*, **monarchic** /mə'nahkik/ *adj*, **monarchical** /mə'nahkikl/ *adj*. [late Latin *monarcha* from Greek *monarchos*, from MON- + *-archos*: see -ARCH]

monarchism /'monəkiz(ə)m/ *noun* the principle of government by monarchy, or support for this principle. ⋙ **monarchist** *noun and adj*, **monarchistic** /-'kistik/ *adj*.

monarchy /'monəki/ *noun* (*pl* **monarchies**) **1** absolute sovereignty or undivided rule by a single person. **2** a government or state in which sovereignty is actually or nominally held by a monarch. **3** the institution represented by the sovereign and the royal family: *The monarchy is a labour-intensive industry* — Harold Wilson.

monastery /'monəst(ə)ri/ *noun* (*pl* **monasteries**) a residence occupied by a religious community, *esp* of monks, or the community itself. [Middle English *monasterie* via late Latin from late Greek *monastērion* from Greek *monazein* to live alone, from *monos* single]

monastic¹ /mə'nastik/ *adj* **1** of monasteries, monks, or nuns. **2** resembling, e.g. in seclusion or austerity, life in a monastery. ⋙ **monastically** *adv*, **monasticism** /-siz(ə)m/ *noun*.

monastic² *noun* a monk, nun, or other person with a monastic way of life.

monatomic /monə'tomik/ *adj* **1** consisting of one atom or of molecules containing one atom. **2** said of a chemical compound: having one atom or chemical group that can be replaced by another in a chemical reaction. ⋙ **monatomically** *adv*.

monaural /mon'awrəl/ *adj* **1** of or involving only one ear. **2** using only one channel to record or reproduce sound; monophonic. ⋙ **monaurally** *adv*.

monazite /'monəziet/ *noun* a yellowish to reddish brown mineral that is a phosphate of cerium and lanthanum and often contains thorium. [German *Monazit*, from Greek *monazein* to live alone; from its rarity]

Monday /'munday, 'mundi/ *noun* the second day of the week, following Sunday. [Old English *monendæg* day of the moon, a translation of Latin *lunae dies*]

monecious /mə'neeshəs, mo-/ *adj NAmer* see MONOECIOUS.

Monégasque /monay'gask/ *noun* a native or inhabitant of the Mediterranean principality of Monaco. ⋙ **Monégasque** *adj*. [French *Monégasque*]

Monel metal /mo'nel/ *noun trademark* a corrosion-resistant nickel and copper alloy. [from the name of Andrew *Monell* d.1921, President of the company that produced it]

monetarism /'munitariz(ə)m/ *noun* an economic theory that the most effective way of controlling the economy is by controlling only the supply of money.

Editorial note

Monetarism cannot be seen as one uniform creed; but common to most dedicated believers is the fatalistic view that governments are unable to generate long-term economic growth by attempting to raise public or private spending. This is because only by increasing the money supply can spending overall be increased; and increases in the money supply simply lead to higher prices. Naturally, monetarism has been associated with a minimalist view of the government's role in economic management — Evan Davis.

>>> **monetarist** *noun and adj.*

monetary /'munit(ə)ri/ *adj* of money or its circulation in the economy. >>> **monetarily** *adv.* [late Latin *monetarius* of a mint, of money, from Latin *moneta* mint, money]

monetize *or* **monetise** /'munitiez/ *verb trans* 1 to convert (something) into money. 2 to establish (something) as legal tender. >>> **monetization** /-'zaysh(ə)n/ *noun.* [Latin *moneta* mint, money + -IZE]

money /'muni/ *noun* (*pl* **moneys** *or* **monies**) 1 something generally accepted as a medium of exchange, a measure of value, or means of payment, *esp* officially printed, coined, or stamped currency. 2 a form or denomination of coin or paper money. 3 wealth reckoned in terms of money: *Money couldn't buy friends, but you got a better class of enemy* — Spike Milligan. 4 (*in pl*) a sum or sums of money. * **for one's money** in one's opinion. **in old money** *informal* in formerly used units of measurement: *20 degrees celsius, that's 68 degrees Fahrenheit in old money.* **in the money** *informal* having a lot of money, *esp* money gained suddenly as winnings, profits, etc. [Middle English *moneye* from early French *moneie* from Latin *moneta* mint, money: see MINT²]

moneybags *noun* (*pl* **moneybags**) *informal* a wealthy person.

money changer *noun* 1 a person whose occupation is the exchanging of kinds or denominations of currency. 2 *chiefly NAmer* a device for dispensing small change.

moneyed *or* **monied** *adj* 1 having much money; wealthy. 2 consisting of or derived from money: *moneyed power.*

moneyer *noun archaic* an authorized coiner of money; a minter. [Middle English from Old French *monier* from late Latin *monetarius* master of a mint, coiner, from *monetarius* (adj) of a mint]

money-grubber *noun informal* a person who is greedily bent on accumulating money, *esp* by sordid or unscrupulous means. >>> **money-grubbing** *adj and noun.*

moneylender *noun* a person whose business is lending money and charging interest on it. >>> **moneylending** *adj and noun.*

money-maker *noun* 1 a profitable product or enterprise, *esp* one that produces much profit. 2 a person who succeeds in accumulating wealth. >>> **money-making** *adj and noun.*

money spider *noun* a small spider supposed to bring luck to the person on whom it crawls: family Linyphiidae.

money-spinner *noun chiefly Brit, informal* a highly successful money-making product or enterprise. >>> **money-spinning** *adj and noun.*

moneywort *noun* = CREEPING JENNY.

-monger *comb. form* forming nouns, denoting: 1 a trader or dealer: *fishmonger.* 2 a person who attempts to stir up or spread something that is usu petty or discreditable: *gossipmonger; warmonger.* [Old English *mangere*, from Latin *mangon-, mango* dealer]

mongo /'monggoh/ *noun* (*pl* **mongo** *or* **mongos**) a unit of currency in Mongolia, worth 100th of a tugrik. [Mongolian *möngö* silver]

Mongol /'monggol, 'monggl/ *noun* 1 a member of any of the Mongoloid peoples of Mongolia, north China, and central Asia. 2 = MONGOLIAN. 3 a person of Mongoloid racial stock. 4 (**mongol**) *offensive* a person who is affected with Down's syndrome. >>> **Mongol** *adj.* [Mongolian *Mongol*]

Mongolian /mong'gohli-ən/ *noun* 1 a native or inhabitant of Mongolia. 2 any of a group of Altaic languages of central Asia, Mongolia, and northern China. >>> **Mongolian** *adj.*

Mongolic /mong'golik/ *adj* = MONGOLOID¹ (1).

mongolism *noun offensive* = DOWN'S SYNDROME.

Mongoloid¹ /'mongg(ə)loyd/ *adj* 1 of, constituting, or characteristic of a major racial stock including peoples of N and E Asia, Malaysians, Inuit, and some Native Americans. 2 (**mongoloid**) *offensive* of or affected with Down's syndrome.

Mongoloid² *noun* a member of a Mongoloid people.

mongoose /'monggoohs/ *noun* (*pl* **mongooses**) any of numerous species of ferret-sized agile mammals of Asia, Africa, and S Europe that have grey-brown fur, short legs, and a long furry tail, and feed on eggs and small animals: family Herpestidae. [Hindi *māgūs* from Prakrit *maṅguso*]

mongrel /'monggrəl, 'munggrəl/ *noun* 1 a dog, *esp* one of unknown ancestry, resulting from the interbreeding of diverse breeds. 2 a cross between different types of person, animal, plant, or thing. >>> **mongrelism** *noun,* **mongrelly** *adj.* [prob from Middle English *mong* mixture, short for *ymong*, from Old English *gemong* crowd]

mongrelize *or* **mongrelise** *verb trans* to make a mongrel of (something or somebody). >>> **mongrelization** /-'zaysh(ə)n/ *noun.*

monicker /'monikə/ *noun* see MONIKER.

monied /'munid/ *adj* see MONEYED.

monies /'muniz/ *noun* pl of MONEY.

moniker *or* **monicker** /'monikə/ *noun informal* a name or nickname. [origin unknown]

moniliform /mo'nilifawm/ *adj* in biology, jointed or constricted at regular intervals so as to resemble a string of beads: *moniliform insect antennae.* [Latin *monile* necklace + -IFORM]

monism /'mohniz(ə)m, 'mon-/ *noun* 1 a doctrine that a complex entity, e.g. the universe, is basically simple and undifferentiated. 2 a doctrine asserting that mind and matter are not separate entities. >>> **monist** *noun,* **monistic** /moh'nistik, mo-/ *adj.* [German *Monismus*, from Greek *monos* single + -ISM]

monition /moh'nish(ə)n/ *noun* 1 an admonition or warning. 2 a formal notice from an ecclesiastical authority, *esp* a bishop, requiring that somebody refrain from something. [Middle English *monicioun* via French from Latin *monition-, monitio*, from *monitus*, past part. of *monēre* to warn]

monitor¹ /'monitə/ *noun* 1 a pupil appointed to help a teacher, e.g. by keeping order or performing a specific task. 2 somebody or something that monitors or is used in monitoring, e.g. a device for observing a biological condition or function: *a heart monitor.* 3a a receiver used to view the picture being picked up by a television camera. b a screen displaying information from a computer. 4 any of several species of large lizards of tropical Asia, Africa, and Australia that are closely related to the iguanas: genus *Varanus.* 5 in former times, a small warship with heavy firepower for its size. >>> **monitorial** /-'tawri-əl/ *adj,* **monitorship** *noun.* [Latin *monitor* one who warns, overseer, from *monitus*, past part. of *monēre* to warn; (sense 4) from its supposedly giving warning of the presence of crocodiles; (sense 5) named after *Monitor*, first ship of this type]

monitor² *verb trans* (**monitored, monitoring**) 1 to observe, inspect, listen to, or record (something), *esp* for a special purpose over a period of time. 2 to regulate or control the operation of (a machine or process). 3 to check (a broadcast, etc) for quality or content.

monitor lizard *noun* = MONITOR¹ (4).

monitory¹ /'monit(ə)ri/ *adj formal* warning or admonitory. [Latin *monitorius* from *monitus*: see MONITOR¹]

monitory² *noun* (*pl* **monitories**) *formal* a letter containing an admonition or warning.

monitress /'monitris/ *noun* a female monitor.

monk /mungk/ *noun* a male member of a religious order who lives usu in a monastery under vows of poverty, chastity, etc. >>> **monkhood** *noun.* [Old English *munuc* via late Latin from Greek *monachos* single, from *monos* alone]

monkey¹ /'mungki/ *noun* 1 any of the primate mammals, with the exception of human beings and usu the lemurs and tarsiers, *esp* any of the smaller longer-tailed primates as contrasted with the apes: families Cebidae, Callitrichidae, and Cercopithecidae. 2 *informal* a mischievous child; a scamp. 3 any of various machines, implements, or vessels, *esp* the falling weight of a pile driver. 4 *Brit, informal* the sum of £500. 5 *slang* a desperate desire for or addiction to drugs. * **have a monkey on one's back** *slang* to be addicted to or dependent on drugs. **make a monkey of (somebody)** to make (somebody) appear ridiculous. [prob of low German origin; related to Old Spanish *mona* monkey]

monkey² *verb intrans informal* 1 (*often* + about/around) to act in an absurd or mischievous manner. 2 (+ with) to meddle or tamper with something.

monkey business *noun informal* mischievous or underhand activity.

monkey flower *noun* any of several species of plants with yellow or red flowers resembling those of the snapdragon: genus *Mimulus.*

monkey jacket *noun* a short fitted uniform jacket reaching to the waist.

monkey nut *noun Brit* a peanut.

monkey-puzzle *noun* a widely planted S American evergreen conifer tree that has a network of intertwined branches covered with spirals of stiff sharp needlelike leaves: *Araucaria araucana*. Also called CHILE PINE. [from the notion that even a monkey would have difficulty climbing it]

monkey shines *pl noun NAmer* = MONKEY TRICKS.

monkey suit *noun informal* a dinner suit.

monkey's wedding *noun SAfr, informal* a mixture of sunshine and rain.

monkey tricks *pl noun informal* mischievous or underhand acts.

monkey wrench *noun* a large spanner with one fixed and one adjustable jaw.

monkfish *noun (pl* **monkfishes** *or collectively* **monkfish) 1** an edible fish that lives on the bottom of the sea, has a flattened body with large winglike pectoral fins, and is closely related to the sharks and rays: *Squatina squatina*. **2** = ANGLERFISH.

monkish *adj* **1** of a monk or monks. **2** *often derog* practising strict self-denial; ascetic.

monkshood *noun* a very poisonous Eurasian plant often cultivated for its showy spikes of white or purplish flowers: *Aconitum napellus*.

mono[1] /'monoh/ *adj* **1** = MONOPHONIC. **2** = MONOCHROME[2].

mono[2] *noun* **1** monophonic sound reproduction. **2** reproduction in monochrome.

mono- *comb. form* see MON-.

monoacid *noun* an acid having one acid hydrogen atom.

monoamine /monoh'ameen/ *noun* an AMINE (chemical compound) that has one carbon-containing chemical group attached to the nitrogen atom; *specif* one that functions as a NEUROTRANSMITTER (substance that transmits nerve impulses), e.g. noradrenalin.

monobasic /monoh'baysik/ *adj* said of an acid: having only one replaceable hydrogen atom in each molecule.

monocarpic /monoh'kahpik/ *adj* said of a plant: bearing fruit only once and then dying.

monochord /'monǝkawd/ *noun* an instrument that is used for measuring and demonstrating the mathematical relations of musical notes and consists of a single string stretched over a sounding board with a movable bridge set on a graduated scale. [Middle English *monocorde* via French and late Latin from Greek *monochordon*, from MONO- + *chordē* string]

monochromatic /,monohkrǝ'matik/ *adj* **1** having or consisting of one colour or hue. **2** said of light or other radiation: of a single wavelength. ⏩ **monochromatically** *adv.* [via Latin from Greek *monochrōmatos*, from MONO- + *chrōmat-, chrōma* colour]

monochromator /'monohkrǝmaytǝ/ *noun* a device used in physics to isolate radiation of a single wavelength.

monochrome[1] /'monǝkrohm/ *noun* **1** reproduction or execution in shades of one colour, black and white, or shades of grey. **2** a painting, drawing, or photograph in monochrome. ⏩ **monochromic** /-'krohmik/ *adj,* **monochromist** *noun.* [Latin *monochroma* fem of *monochromos* of one colour, from Greek *monochrōmos*]

monochrome[2] *adj* **1** of or executed in shades of a single colour. **2** reproducing or transmitting visual images in black, white, and tones of grey; black-and-white: *monochrome television; a monochrome photograph.* **3** lacking in variety or interest; dull: *Universities these days are desperately monochrome* — N Smart.

monocle /'monǝkl/ *noun* a device to improve vision consisting of a single lens for one eye, held in position by the facial muscles. ⏩ **monocled** *adj.* [via French from late Latin *monoculus* having one eye, from MON- + Latin *oculus* eye]

monocline /'monǝklien/ *noun* a fold or bend in rock in which all the rock layers slope in one direction at a constant angle. ⏩ **monoclinal** /-'klienl/ *adj and noun.*

monoclinic /monoh'klinik/ *adj* of or being a system of crystal structure characterized by three unequal axes, two of which are not at right angles to each other.

monoclinous /monoh'klienǝs/ *adj* said of a plant: having both stamens and ovaries in the same flower: compare DICLINOUS.

[scientific Latin *monoclinus*, literally 'having one bed', from MONO- + Greek *klinē* bed]

monoclonal antibody /monǝ'klohnl/ *noun* an antibody produced by a single clone of cells that is pure and specific for a single antigenic determinant and is used in research, diagnosis, therapy, and biotechnology.

monocoque /'monǝkok/ *noun* **1** a type of construction, e.g. of a fuselage, in which the outer skin carries all or nearly all the stresses. **2** a type of vehicle construction in which the body is integral with the chassis. [French *monocoque* from MONO- + *coque* shell, from Latin *coccum* excrescence on a tree, from Greek *kokkos* berry]

monocot /'monǝkot/ *noun* = MONOCOTYLEDON.

monocotyledon /,monohkoti'leedn/ *noun* any of a class of flowering plants including all those that have a single COTYLEDON (leaf produced by a germinating seed) and typically long narrow leaves with parallel veins, e.g. the grasses, orchids, and lilies: class Monocotyledoneae: compare DICOTYLEDON. ⏩ **monocotyledonous** /-nǝs/ *adj.* [MONO- + COTYLEDON]

monocracy /mo'nokrǝsi/ *noun (pl* **monocracies)** government by a single person; autocracy. ⏩ **monocrat** /'monǝkrat/ *noun,* **monocratic** /-'kratik/ *adj.*

monocular /mo'nokyoolǝ/ *adj* of, involving, or suitable for use with only one eye. ⏩ **monocularly** *adv.* [late Latin *monoculus* having one eye: see MONOCLE]

monoculture /'monohkulchǝ/ *noun* the cultivation of a single agricultural product to the exclusion of other uses of the land.

monocycle /'monohsiekl/ *noun* = UNICYCLE.

monocyte /'monǝsiet/ *noun* a large white blood cell that is present in small numbers in the blood and defends the body by engulfing and digesting harmful or unwanted matter.

monody /'monǝdi/ *noun (pl* **monodies) 1** an ode sung by one voice, *esp* in a Greek tragedy. **2** a poem lamenting somebody's death. **3** a style of music that has one melody with little or no accompaniment. ⏩ **monodic** /mǝ'nodik/ *adj,* **monodist** *noun.* [via late Latin from Greek *monōidia* from *monōidos* singing alone, from MON- + *aidein* to sing]

monoecious (*NAmer* **monecious**) /mǝ'neeshǝs, mo-/ *adj* **1** having separate female and male flowers on the same plant: compare DIOECIOUS. **2** having male and female reproductive organs in the same organism; hermaphrodite. [MONO- + Greek *oikos* house]

monofil /'monohfil/ *noun* = MONOFILAMENT.

monofilament /monǝ'filǝmǝnt/ *noun* a single untwisted strand of synthetic fibre, e.g. of nylon.

monogamy /mǝ'nogǝmi/ *noun* **1** the state, practice, or custom of being married to one person at a time: *Bigamy is having one husband too many. Monogamy is the same* — anonymous, quoted by Erica Jong. **2** in zoology, the habit of having only one mate. ⏩ **monogamist** *noun,* **monogamous** /-mǝs/ *adj,* **monogamously** /-mǝsli/ *adv.* [French *monogamie* via late Latin from Greek *monogamia* from *monogamos* monogamous, from MONO- + *gamos* marriage]

monogenesis /monoh'jenǝsis/ *noun* **1** unity of origin; development from a single source or common ancestor. **2** the theory or belief that all organisms are descended from a single cell or all human beings from a single pair of ancestors. ⏩ **monogenetic** /-'netik/ *adj.* [late Latin *monogenesis*]

monogenic /monǝ'jenik/ *adj* of or being an inheritable characteristic controlled by a single gene, *esp* by either of a pair of genes coding for contrasting forms of that characteristic. ⏩ **monogenically** *adv.*

monogeny /mǝ'nojǝni/ *noun* = MONOGENESIS.

monogram[1] /'monǝgram/ *noun* a design usu formed of the interwoven initials of a name. ⏩ **monogrammatic** /-'matik/ *adj.* [late Latin *monogramma* from MONO- + Greek *gramma* letter]

monogram[2] *verb trans* (**monogrammed, monogramming**) to mark (something) with a monogram.

monograph[1] /'monǝgrahf, -graf/ *noun* **1** a treatise on a small area of learning. **2** a written account of a single thing. ⏩ **monographic** /-'grafik/ *adj.*

monograph[2] *verb trans* to write a monograph on (something). ⏩ **monographer** /mo'nogrǝfǝ/ *noun,* **monographist** /mo'nogrǝfist/ *noun.*

monogyny /mə'nojəni/ *noun* the state, practice, or custom of having only one wife at a time. ⫸ **monogynous** /-nəs/ *adj.* [MONO- + Greek *gynē* woman, wife]

monohull /'monohhul/ *noun* a boat with a single hull, e.g. as opposed to a catamaran.

monohybrid /monoh'hiebrid/ *noun* an organism or strain of organisms that has two different versions of one particular gene.

monohydric /monoh'hiedrik/ *adj* 1 containing one atom of hydrogen that is capable of reacting as an acid. 2 containing one hydroxyl group in the molecule.

monokini /monoh'keeni/ *noun* a one-piece swimming costume, *esp* a topless bikini. [MONO- + -*kini* as in BIKINI]

monolayer /'monohlayə/ *noun* a single continuous layer of film that is one cell or one molecule in thickness.

monolingual /monoh'ling·gwəl/ *adj* knowing or using only one language.

monolith /'monəlith/ *noun* 1 a single large block of stone, often in the form of an obelisk or column. 2 a massive structure. 3 a complex structure or organization in which individual parts function together as a single powerful whole. [French *monolithe* consisting of a single stone, via Latin from Greek *monolithos*, from MONO- + *lithos* stone]

monolithic /monə'lithik/ *adj* 1 formed of a single large block of stone. 2 said e.g. of an electronic current: formed from or produced in or on a single crystal: *a monolithic silicon chip.* 3 constituting a single unit. 4 constituting a massive uniform whole: *the monolithic totalitarian state.*

monologize *or* **monologise** /mo'nolojiez/ *verb intrans* to utter or perform a monologue.

monologue /'monəlog/ *noun* 1a a long speech by an actor alone or as if alone on stage. b a dramatic sketch performed by one actor. 2 a long usu tedious speech that monopolizes a conversation. ⫸ **monologic** /-'lojik/ *adj*, **monological** /-'lojikl/ *adj*, **monologist** /-gist, -jist/ *noun*, **monologuist** /-gist/ *noun*. [French *monologue*, from MONO- + -LOGUE (as in DIALOGUE)]

monomania /monoh'mayni·ə/ *noun* obsessional preoccupation with or concentration on a single object or idea. ⫸ **monomaniac** /-ak/ *noun and adj*, **monomaniacal** /-mə'nie·əkl/ *adj*. [late Latin *monomania*]

monomer /'monəmə/ *noun* any of the identical units that combine to form a polymer. ⫸ **monomeric** /-'merik/ *adj*. [MONO- + -MER (as in POLYMER)]

monometallic /,monohmi'talik/ *adj* 1 consisting of or using one metal. 2 of monometallism.

monometallism /monoh'metl·iz(ə)m/ *noun* the adoption of one metal only as a monetary standard. ⫸ **monometallist** *noun*.

monomial[1] /mo'nohmi·əl/ *noun* a mathematical expression consisting of a single term, e.g. $3xy^2$. [blend of MONO- and -*nomial* as in BINOMIAL[1]]

monomial[2] *adj* said of a mathematical expression: consisting of a single term.

monomolecular /,monohmə'lekyoolə/ *adj* only one molecule thick: *a monomolecular film.*

monomorphic /monoh'mawfik/ *adj* 1 said of a species: showing little variation, e.g. in appearance, between members or sexes. 2 said of an organism: showing little structural change during the life cycle. 3 said of a chemical compound: having a single crystalline form.

monomorphous /monoh'mawfəs/ *adj* = MONOMORPHIC.

mononucleosis /,monohnyoohkli'ohsis/ *noun* 1 the presence of an abnormally large number of monocytes in the blood. 2 = INFECTIOUS MONONUCLEOSIS.

monophonic /monoh'fonik/ *adj* 1 of or being a system for sound recording or reproduction that uses only one channel between the source of the signal and its final point of use: compare STEREOPHONIC. 2 having a single melodic line with little or no accompaniment. ⫸ **monophonically** *adv*.

monophthong /'monəfthong/ *noun* a simple vowel sound, e.g. /i/ in *bid*. ⫸ **monophthongal** /-'thonggl/ *adj*. [late Greek *monophthongos* single vowel, from MONO- + Greek *phthongos* sound]

Monophysite /mo'nofisiet/ *noun* a person who holds the doctrine that there is only one nature in the person of Christ and that this nature is divine. ⫸ **Monophysitic** /,monohfi'sitik/ *adj*, **Monophysitism** *noun*. [via late Latin from early Greek *Monophysitēs* from MONO- + Greek *physis* nature]

monoplane /'monəplayn/ *noun* an aeroplane with only one main pair of wings.

monopole /'monəpohl/ *noun* 1 a hypothetical single concentrated electric charge or magnetic pole, or a hypothetical particle having such a pole. 2 a radio aerial consisting of a single straight radiating element.

monopolise /mə'nopəliez/ *verb trans* see MONOPOLIZE.

monopolist /mo'nopəlist/ *noun* a person who has or favours a monopoly. ⫸ **monopolistic** /-'listik/ *adj*.

monopolize *or* **monopolise** /mə'nopəliez/ *verb trans* 1 to assume exclusive possession, control, or use of (something): *monopolizing the conversation.* 2 to obtain or exploit a monopoly of (a market, etc). ⫸ **monopolization** /-'zaysh(ə)n/ *noun*, **monopolizer** *noun*.

monopoly /mə'nopəli/ *noun* (*pl* **monopolies**) 1a exclusive ownership or control, e.g. of a commodity or market, through legal privilege, command of supply, concerted action, etc: *Like many businessmen of genius he learned that free competition was wasteful, monopoly efficient* — Mario Puzo. b a person or group having a monopoly. c something, *esp* a commodity, controlled by a monopoly. 2 exclusive possession, control, or use of something. 3 (**Monopoly**) *trademark* a board game in which players buy, sell, rent and mortgage properties with the aim of bankrupting their opponents. [via Latin from Greek *monopōlion* from MONO- + *pōlein* to sell]

monorail /'monərayl/ *noun* a single rail serving as a track for a wheeled vehicle.

monosaccharide /monoh'sakəried/ *noun* a sugar, e.g. glucose, that cannot be broken down to simpler sugars.

monoski /'monohskee/ *noun* a wide ski attached to both feet of the skier. ⫸ **monoskier** *noun*, **monoskiing** *noun*.

monosodium glutamate /,monəsohdi·əm 'gloohtəmayt/ *noun* a white chemical compound added to foods to intensify their natural flavour.

monostable /'monohstaybl/ *adj* said e.g. of an electrical circuit: having only one stable state.

monosyllabic /,monəsi'labik/ *adj* 1 consisting of one syllable or of monosyllables. 2 using or speaking only monosyllables. 3 pointedly brief in answering or commenting; terse. ⫸ **monosyllabically** *adv*. [French *monosyllabique*, from *monosyllabe*: see MONOSYLLABLE]

monosyllable /'monəsiləbl/ *noun* a word of one syllable, *esp* one used as a complete utterance: *answering in monosyllables.* [modification of French or late Latin from Greek *monosyllabon* neuter of *monosyllabos* having one syllable, from MONO- + *syllabē* syllable]

monotheism /'monohtheeiz(ə)m/ *noun* the doctrine or belief that there is only one God. ⫸ **monotheist** *noun*, **monotheistic** /-'istik/ *adj*, **monotheistically** /-'istikli/ *adv*.

monotint /'monətint/ *noun* = MONOCHROME[1].

monotone[1] /'monətohn/ *noun* 1 a succession of speech sounds in one unvarying pitch. 2 a single unvaried musical note. 3 a tedious sameness or repetition. [Greek *monotonos*: see MONOTONOUS]

monotone[2] *adj* 1 having a uniform colour. 2 unvarying or unvaried.

monotonic /monə'tonik/ *adj* 1 uttered in a monotone. 2 said e.g. of a mathematical function: increasing continuously or decreasing continuously. ⫸ **monotonically** *adv*.

monotonous /mə'not(ə)nəs/ *adj* 1 tediously uniform or repetitive. 2 uttered or sounded in one unvarying tone. ⫸ **monotonously** *adv*, **monotonousness** *noun*, **monotony** /-ni/ *noun*. [Greek *monotonos*, from MONO- + *tonos* tone]

monotreme /'monohtreem/ *noun* any of an order of egg-laying mammals including the platypus and echidna: order Monotremata. ⫸ **monotrematous** /-'treemətəs, -'tremətəs/ *adj*. [Latin *Monotremata*, order name, from MONO- + Greek *trēmat-*, *trēma* hole]

Monotype /'monətiep/ *noun trademark* a keyboard-operated typesetting machine that casts and sets metal type in separate characters.

monotype *noun* a single impression on paper taken from a painting on glass or metal.

monotypic /monoh'tipik/ *adj* **1** having only a single type or representative. **2** said of a genus: comprising only one species.

monounsaturated /,monoh·un'sachooraytid/ *adj* said of a fat or oil: having only one double or triple chemical bond.

monovalent /monoh'vaylənt/ *adj* in chemistry, having a valency of one; univalent.

monoxide /mə'noksied/ *noun* an oxide containing one atom of oxygen.

monozygotic /,monohzie'gotik/ *adj* said of twins: derived from a single egg; identical.

monozygous /mono'ziegəs/ *adj* = MONOZYGOTIC.

monseigneur /monse'nyuh/ *noun* (*pl* **messeigneurs** /mayse'n-yuh/) (*often* **Monseigneur**) used as a title for a French dignitary, e.g. a prince or bishop. [French *monseigneur*, literally 'my lord']

monsieur /mə'syuh/ *noun* (*pl* **messieurs** /mə'syuh, mə'syuhz/) (*often* **Monsieur**) used by or to a French-speaking man as a title equivalent to *Mr* or as a term of direct address equivalent to *sir*. [early French *monsieur*, literally 'my lord']

monsignor /mon'seenyə, monsee'nyaw/ *noun* (*pl* **monsignori** /-'nyawree/) (*often* **Monsignor**) used as a title for certain high-ranking Roman Catholic priests, e.g. prelates and officers of the papal court. [Italian *monsignore* from French *monseigneur*]

monsoon /mon'soohn/ *noun* **1** a seasonal wind of S Asia blowing from the SW in summer and the NE in winter. **2** the season of the SW monsoon, marked by very heavy rains. ⏩ **monsoonal** *adj*. [early Dutch *monssoen* from Portuguese *monção* from Arabic *mawsim* time, season]

mons pubis /,monz 'pyoohbis/ *noun* (*pl* **montes pubis** /,monteez/) a rounded raised mass of fatty tissue over the pubic bone. [scientific Latin *mons pubis*, literally 'pubic hill']

monster /'monstə/ *noun* **1** an imaginary animal of incredible shape or form that is usu dangerous or horrifying: *She is a monster without being a myth* — Oscar Wilde. **2** an animal or plant of *esp* grotesquely abnormal form or structure. **3a** something exceptionally large for its kind. **b** *informal* (*used before a noun*) exceptionally large: *monster tomatoes*. **4** a person of appalling ugliness, wickedness, or cruelty. [Middle English *monstre* via French from Latin *monstrum* omen, monster, prob from *monēre* to warn, remind]

monstera /mon'stiərə/ *noun* any of a genus of tropical American evergreen climbing plants that includes the Swiss cheese plant: genus *Monstera*. [from the Latin genus name, perhaps from Latin *monstrum* monster]

monstrance /'monstrəns/ *noun* in the Roman Catholic Church, a vessel in which the consecrated HOST⁴ (holy bread) is exposed for veneration. [via French from late Latin *monstrantia*, from Latin *monstrant-, monstrans*, present part. of *monstrare* to show]

monstrosity /mon'strositi/ *noun* (*pl* **monstrosities**) **1** the quality or state of being monstrous: *the utter monstrosity of the crime*. **2** something deviating wildly from the normal; a monster or freak. **3** an excessively bad or shocking example; a hideous thing: *The old town hall was a red-brick monstrosity*. **4** something of terrifying size, force, or complexity.

monstrous /'monstrəs/ *adj* **1a** having the qualities or appearance of a monster. **b** extraordinarily large. **c** extraordinarily ugly or vicious. **2a** outrageously wrong or ridiculous. **b** shocking; appalling. ⏩ **monstrously** *adv*, **monstrousness** *noun*.

mons veneris /,monz 'venəris/ *noun* (*pl* **montes veneris** /,monteez/) the mons pubis of a woman or girl. [scientific Latin *mons veneris*, literally 'hill of Venus']

Mont. *abbr* Montana.

montage /monh'tahzh/ *noun* **1a** a picture made by combining or overlapping several separate pictures. **b** a literary, musical, or artistic composition made up of different elements. **2a** a method of film editing in which the chronological sequence of events is interrupted by juxtaposed or rapidly succeeding shots. **b** a film sequence using montage. [French *montage* from *monter* to mount]

montane /'montayn/ *adj* of or found in mountainous areas, *esp* the relatively moist cool slopes just below the tree line. [Latin *montanus* of a mountain: see MOUNTAIN]

Montanist /'montənist/ *noun* an adherent of a heretical Christian sect of the late second cent. stressing the continuing prophetic gifts of the Holy Spirit. ⏩ **Montanism** *noun*. [named after *Montanus*, second-cent. schismatic in Asia Minor]

montbretia /mon(t)'breeshə/ *noun* a widely grown hybrid plant of the iris family with bright yellow or orange flowers: *Crocosmia × crocosmiflora*. [scientific Latin *montbretia*, named after A F E Coquebert de *Montbret* d.1801, French naturalist]

monte /'monti/ *noun* **1** a card game in which players select any two of four exposed cards and bet that one of them will be matched before the other as cards are dealt one at a time from the pack. **2** a card game in which players bet on which of three face-down cards is which. [Spanish *monte*, literally 'bank', via Italian from Latin *mont-, mons* mountain]

Montenegrin /monti'neegrin/ *noun* **1** a native or inhabitant of Montenegro in the Balkans. **2** the Serbo-Croatian language as spoken in Montenegro, traditionally written in the Cyrillic alphabet but now written in either Cyrillic or the Latin letters. ⏩ **Montenegrin** *adj*.

montes pubis /,monteez 'pyoohbis/ *noun* pl of MONS PUBIS.

Montessori /monti'sawri/ *adj* of or being a system of teaching young children through play. [named after Maria *Montessori* d.1952, Italian physician and educationist]

montes veneris /,monteez 'venəris/ *noun* pl of MONS VENERIS.

Montezuma's revenge /monti'zoohmaz/ *noun informal* sickness and diarrhoea contracted on a visit to Mexico. [named after *Montezuma* II, the last Aztec emperor]

month /munth/ *noun* **1a** any of the twelve divisions of the year corresponding approximately with the period of the moon's rotation around the earth and being between 28 and 31 days in duration. Also called CALENDAR MONTH. **b** a period of four weeks. **c** the interval between the same date in adjacent months. **2** (*in pl*) an indefinite, usu protracted, period of time: *He's been gone for months*. **3** one ninth of the typical duration of human pregnancy: *in her eighth month*. ✳ **a month of Sundays** *informal* a very long period of time. [Old English *mōnath*; related to Old High German *mānōd* month, Old English *mōna* moon]

monthly¹ /'munthli/ *adj* **1** payable or reckoned by the month. **2** done, occurring, or published every month.

monthly² *adv* every month, once a month, or by the month.

monthly³ *noun* (*pl* **monthlies**) **1** a monthly periodical. **2** *dated, informal* (*in pl*) a menstrual period.

monument /'monyoomənt/ *noun* **1** a memorial stone, sculpture, or structure erected to commemorate a person or event. **2** a structure or site of historical or archaeological importance. **3** a lasting evidence or reminder of somebody or something notable or influential. **4** an exceptional example of something: *a monument to bad taste*. [Middle English in the senses 'burial place, legal record', from Latin *monumentum* memorial, from *monēre* to remind]

monumental /monyoo'mentl/ *adj* **1a** of, serving as, or resembling a monument: *a monumental inscription*. **2a** very great in degree: *their monumental arrogance*. **b** imposing or outstanding: *a monumental work*. ⏩ **monumentally** *adv*.

moo¹ /mooh/ *verb intrans* to make the deep characteristic noise of a cow. [imitative]

moo² *noun* a mooing sound.

mooch /moohch/ *verb intrans informal* **1** (+ around/about/along) to wander aimlessly or disconsolately. **2** *NAmer* to sponge or cadge. ▸ *verb trans informal* **1** to steal (something). **2** to cadge, beg, or scrounge (something). ⏩ **moocher** *noun*. [prob from French dialect *muchier* to hide, lurk]

mood¹ /moohd/ *noun* **1a** a predominant emotion, feeling, or frame of mind. **b** the right frame of mind: *You must be in the mood, or you'll fall asleep* — The Listener. **c** the evocation of mood in art, literature, music, etc. **2** a fit of often silent anger or bad temper. **3** a prevailing attitude: *They misjudged the mood of the public*. [Old English *mōd*]

mood² *noun* **1a** a distinct form or set of forms of a verb used to express whether the action or state it denotes is considered a fact, a possibility, or a wish: *the subjunctive mood*. **b** a similar distinct form or set of verb forms used to express whether a sentence is a statement, a command, or a question: *the interrogative mood*. **2** in logic, any of several traditional subclasses of the forms of the SYLLOGISM (statement consisting of two premises and a conclusion). [alteration of MODE]

moody *adj* (**moodier, moodiest**) **1** sullen or gloomy. **2** subject to sharply fluctuating moods; temperamental. ⏩ **moodily** *adv*, **moodiness** *noun*.

Moog /moohg, mohg/ *noun trademark* a musical synthesizer. [named after its inventor, R A *Moog* b.1934, US engineer]

moola *or* **moolah** /'moohlə/ *noun informal* money. [origin unknown]

mooli /'moohli/ *noun* a type of radish with a large white root. Also called DAIKON. [Hindi *mūlī* from Sanskrit *mūla* root]

moon¹ /moohn/ *noun* **1a** (**the Moon**) the earth's natural satellite that shines by reflecting the sun's light. **b** the appearance or visibility of the moon from the earth: *a full moon.* **c** a satellite of a planet. **2** *literary* a month: *many moons ago.* *** over the moon** *informal* absolutely delighted. **≫ moonless** *adj,* **moonlike** *adj.* [Old English *mōna*; related to Old High German *māno* moon, Latin *mensis* month, Greek *mēn* month, *mēnē* moon]

moon² *verb intrans* **1** *informal* (*often* + around/about) to move about listlessly. **2** *informal* (*often* + around/about) to spend time in idle gazing or daydreaming. **3** *informal* to expose one's buttocks to somebody as a joke or insult.

moonbeam *noun* a ray of light from the moon.

mooncalf *noun* (*pl* **mooncalves**) a fool or simpleton: *He explained with a mooncalf simplicity to everyone in the carriage* — G K Chesterton.

moon-faced *adj* having a very round face.

moonfish *noun* (*pl* **moonfishes** *or collectively* **moonfish**) **1** any of various silvery or yellowish sea fishes with thin deep bodies: *Selene setapinnis* and other species. **2** = OPAH.

Moonie /'moohni/ *noun informal* a member of the Unification Church, a religious sect founded in 1954 by Sun Myung Moon, whose adherents live in communes, donate all their possessions to the movement, and believe that the founder has been given a divine mission to complete the task of uniting the whole world in a perfect sinless family. [named after Sun Myung *Moon* b.1920, Korean industrialist and religious leader]

moonlight¹ *noun* the light of the moon.

moonlight² *verb intrans* (*past tense and past part.* **moonlighted**) *informal* to hold a second job, *esp* a secret or illegal one done at night, in addition to one's regular work. **≫ moonlighter** *noun.*

moonlight flit *noun Brit, informal* an act of leaving a place in secret, *esp* at night, to avoid paying rent or other money that is owed.

moonlit *adj* illuminated by or as if by the moon.

moonquake *noun* a ground tremor on the moon.

moonrat *noun* any of several species of insect-eating mammals of SE Asia with a long snout, long naked tail, and whitish grey fur: *Echinosorex gymnurus* and other species.

moonscape /'moohnskayp/ *noun* **1** the surface of the moon as seen or as depicted. **2** a similarly barren or devastated landscape.

moonshine *noun* **1** the light of the moon. **2** empty talk; nonsense. **3** *chiefly NAmer, informal* illegally distilled or smuggled spirits, *esp* whisky.

moonshiner *noun chiefly NAmer, informal* a maker, smuggler, or seller of illicit spirits.

moon shot *noun informal* the launching of a spacecraft to the moon or its vicinity.

moonstone *noun* a transparent or milky-white translucent variety of feldspar with a pearly lustre, that is used as a gem.

moonstruck *adj* affected by or as if by the moon; *specif* mentally unbalanced or romantically sentimental.

moony *adj* (**moonier, mooniest**) *informal* inanely dreamy.

Moor /maw, mooə/ *noun* a member of the mixed Arab and Berber people that conquered Spain in the eighth cent. AD. **≫ Moorish** *adj.* [Middle English *More* via French from Latin *Maurus* inhabitant of Mauretania, ancient country of N Africa]

moor¹ *noun chiefly Brit* an expanse of open uncultivated peaty upland that is typically overgrown by heathers, grasses, etc. [Old English *mōr*; related to Old High German *meri* sea]

moor² *verb trans* to fasten (a vessel or buoy) with cables, lines, etc. **≫ verb intrans** to secure a vessel, etc by mooring it. [Middle English *moren*; related to early Dutch *meren, maren* to tie, moor]

moorage /'mawrij, 'mooərij/ *noun* **1** a place to moor. **2** a charge made for mooring.

moorcock *noun Brit* a male red grouse.

moorhen *noun* any of several species of common blackish birds of the rail family that nest in reeds and bushes near fresh water: *Gallinula chloropus* and other species.

mooring *noun* **1** (*also in pl*) a place where or an object to which a ship, boat, etc can be made fast. **2** (*usu in pl*) a line, chain, etc used to moor a vessel: *She may have dragged her moorings.* **3** (*usu in pl*) a moral principle used as a guide to behaviour: *He's lost his moorings.*

Moorish idol *noun* a tropical marine fish with a compressed body and yellow and black stripes, found around coral reefs: *Zanclus cornutus.*

moorland *noun Brit* an area consisting of moors.

moose /moohs/ *noun* (*pl* **moose**) **1** a large N American deer that belongs to the same species as the European elk and has very large flattened antlers: *Alces alces.* **2** *NAmer* the European elk. [of Algonquian origin; related to Natick *moos* moose]

moot¹ /mooht/ *noun* **1** an early English local assembly held for debate, administration, and legal matters. **2** a mock court in which law students argue hypothetical cases. [Old English *mōt*; related to MEET¹]

moot² *verb trans* to put (an idea) forward for discussion.

moot³ *adj* open to question; debatable: *It's a moot point.*

mop¹ /mop/ *noun* **1** an implement consisting of a head made of absorbent material fastened to a long handle and used *esp* for cleaning floors. **2** something that resembles a mop, *esp* a shock of untidy hair. [Middle English *mappe*; perhaps related to Latin *mappa* napkin, towel]

mop² *verb trans* (**mopped, mopping**) **1** to clean or wipe (a floor or other surface) with or as if with a mop. **2** (*often* + up) to clean or soak up (water or other liquid) with or as if with a mop. **≫ mopper** *noun.*

mope¹ /mohp/ *verb intrans* to give oneself up to brooding; to become listless or dejected. **≫ moper** *noun,* **mopy** *adj.* [prob from obsolete *mop, mope* fool]

mope² *noun informal* **1** a person who mopes. **2** (**the mopes**) (*treated as sing. or pl*) low spirits. **3** a fit of sulking or low spirits: *She's having a mope in her bedroom.*

moped /'mohped/ *noun* a low-powered motorcycle; *specif* one with an engine capacity of 50cc or under. [Swedish *moped*, blend of *motor* MOTOR¹ + *pedal* PEDAL¹]

mopoke /'mohpohk/ *noun* = BOOBOOK.

moppet /'mopit/ *noun informal* an endearing young child, *esp* a sweet little girl. [obsolete *mop* fool, child + -ET]

mop up *verb trans* **1a** to absorb, take up, or deal with (*esp* a remnant or remainder). **b** to complete (a project, transaction, etc). **2** to eliminate (remaining resistance, enemy forces, etc) after a battle by killing or taking prisoners.

moquette /mo'ket/ *noun* a carpet or upholstery fabric with a velvety pile. [French *moquette*]

MOR *abbr* middle-of-the-road (said of music).

mor /maw/ *noun* a humus usu found in forests that forms a distinct layer above the underlying soil. [Danish *mor*]

moraine /mo'rayn/ *noun* an accumulation of earth and stones carried and deposited by a glacier. **≫ morainal** *adj,* **morainic** /-nik/ *adj.* [French *moraine*]

moral¹ /'morəl/ *adj* **1a** of or being the principles of right and wrong in human behaviour; ethical. **b** expressing or teaching a conception of right behaviour: *a moral poem.* **c** conforming to a standard of right behaviour or to the dictates of one's conscience: *a moral person; one's moral obligations.* **d** sanctioned by or resulting from one's ethical judgment: *Moral indignation is jealousy with a halo —* H G Wells. **2** providing encouragement and approval: *moral support.* **3** said of a victory: having the appearance of a defeat but being morally right. **4** very probable though not proved: *a moral certainty.* **≫ morally** *adv.* [Middle English via French from Latin *moralis* from *mor-, mos* custom]

Usage note

moral *or* **morale**? These two words are sometimes confused. *Moral*, the adjective, pronounced /'moral/, means 'relating to principles of right and wrong' (*moral judgments*) or 'showing a proper sense of right and wrong' (*a moral person*). As a noun, *moral* usually means 'the moral lesson to be drawn from a story' (see MORAL²). *Morale*, pronounced /mə'rahl/, means 'the general mood of a group of people': *The general decided to lay on a concert party to boost the troops' morale.*

moral[2] *noun* **1** the moral significance of or practical lesson to be learned from a story, event, experience, etc. **2** (*in pl*) moral practices or teachings; standards of behaviour.

morale /məˈrahl/ *noun* the mental and emotional condition, e.g. of enthusiasm or loyalty, of an individual or group, *esp* at a particular time or with regard to the task at hand. [modification of French *moral*]

Usage note

morale *or* moral? See note at MORAL[1].

moralise *verb* see MORALIZE.

moralism *noun* **1** a conventional moral attitude or saying. **2** an often exaggerated emphasis on moral rectitude.

moralist *noun* **1** a person who is concerned with moral principles and problems. **2** *often derog* a person who is concerned with regulating the morals of others: *The infliction of cruelty with a good conscience is a delight to moralists* — Bertrand Russell. **3** a person who leads a moral life. ➤ **moralistic** /-ˈlistik/ *adj*, **moralistically** /-ˈlistikli/ *adv*.

morality /məˈraliti/ *noun* (*pl* **moralities**) **1a** right behaviour or moral correctness. **b** degree of conformity to moral standards: *She questioned the morality of his act.* **2** a system or sphere of moral conduct: *Christian morality.*

Editorial note

Morality is sometimes identified with ethics, and sometimes contrasted with it. If contrasted, the moral is thought of more narrowly, as the right, the obligatory, that which is our duty; the ethical is taken to concern proper or correct behaviour more generally. Virtues of character such as steadfastness, modesty, and self-respect are more properly thought of as ethical than as moral. Charity, kindness, and considerateness would be moral virtues. Morality is also sometimes thought of as a system or set of rules or principles that can be applied to particular cases to tell us what to do. But to be appropriately sensitive to the needs and concerns of others seems to be different from approaching them with a set of rules in hand — Professor Jonathan Dancy.

morality play *noun* a form of allegorical drama popular *esp* in the 15th and 16th cents, in which the characters personify moral or abstract qualities such as pride or youth: compare MIRACLE PLAY, MYSTERY PLAY.

moralize *or* **moralise** *verb intrans* to talk about matters of morality, and in particular about the moral lapses of other people, *esp* to do so tediously or sanctimoniously. ➤ *verb trans* **1** to interpret (something) from a moral perspective, or draw a moral from (it): *Critics have made mistaken attempts to moralize the film.* **2** to make (somebody or something) moral or morally better. ➤➤ **moralization** /-ˈzaysh(ə)n/ *noun*, **moralizer** *noun*.

moral majority *noun* **1** the reputedly major part of a society who uphold traditional moral values. **2** (**the Moral Majority**) a political and social movement in the USA which favours conservative and authoritarian policies based on Protestant fundamentalist beliefs.

moral philosophy *noun* the branch of philosophy dealing with ethics.

moral support *noun* assistance or backing that involves some form of psychological effect rather than a physical or tangible effect: *If you're going to complain, I'll go with you for moral support.*

moral theology *noun* the branch of theology that deals with ethics.

moral victory *noun* a situation involving apparent defeat, but from which some form of ethical consolation can be taken.

morass /məˈras/ *noun* **1** a marsh or swamp. **2** a confused and disorganized situation; circumstances that overwhelm or trap a person or impede progress: *a morass of lies and deception.* [Dutch *moeras*, modification of Old French *maresc* marsh, of Germanic origin]

moratorium /morəˈtawri-əm/ *noun* (*pl* **moratoriums** *or* **moratoria** /-ri-ə/) **1** (*often* + on) a suspension of activity, *esp* a temporary one agreed between all involved. **2** a legally authorized delay in the performance of an obligation or the payment of a debt. [late Latin *moratorium*, neuter of *moratorius* dilatory, from Latin *moratus*, past part. of *morari* to delay]

Moravian /məˈrayvi-ən/ *noun* **1a** a native or inhabitant of Moravia, the region forming the eastern part of the Czech Republic. **b** the dialect of the Czech language of the people of Moravia. **2** a member of the Moravian Church, a Protestant denomination derived from the Hussite movement for religious reform during the 15th cent. in Bohemia and Moravia. ➤➤ **Moravian** *adj*.

moray /ˈmoray, ˈmawray/ *noun* any of numerous species of large often brightly coloured eels that live in warm seas and have sharp teeth capable of inflicting a savage bite. One species found in the Mediterranean Sea is valued for food, but the flesh of some species is toxic and may cause illness or death: family Muraenidae. [Portuguese *moréia* via Latin from Greek *myraina*]

moray eel *noun* = MORAY.

morbid /ˈmawbid/ *adj* **1** abnormally susceptible to or characterized by gloomy feelings, *esp* having an unnatural preoccupation with death. **2** showing an interest in grisly and gruesome things, *esp* those involving death and disease: *morbid interest in other people and their doings* — D H Lawrence. **3** indicative of or relating to disease or things that are diseased. ➤➤ **morbidly** *adv*, **morbidness** *noun*. [Latin *morbidus* diseased, from *morbus* disease]

morbid anatomy *noun* the scientific study of diseased organs and tissues.

morbidity /mawˈbiditi/ *noun* (*pl* **morbidities**) **1** the quality of being morbid; morbidness. **2** the relative incidence of a disease.

morbific /mawˈbifik/ *adj dated* causing disease. [Latin *morbus* disease + -FIC]

mordacious /mawˈdayshəs/ *adj formal* **1** sarcastic. **2** given to biting. ➤➤ **mordacity** /mawˈdasiti/ *noun*. [Latin *mordac-, mordax* biting, from *mordēre* to bite]

mordant[1] /ˈmawd(ə)nt/ *adj* **1** caustic or sharply critical in thought, manner, or style: *mordant wit.* **2** acting as a mordant. **3** burning; pungent. ➤➤ **mordancy** /-si/ *noun*, **mordantly** *adv*. [early French *mordant*, present part. of *mordre* to bite, from Latin *mordēre*]

mordant[2] *noun* **1** a chemical that fixes a dye by combining with it to form an insoluble compound. **2** a corroding substance used in etching.

mordent /ˈmawd(ə)nt/ *noun* a musical ornament made by a quick alternation of a principal note with either of the immediately adjacent notes. [via German from Italian *mordente* from Latin *mordent-, mordens*, present part. of *mordēre* to bite]

more[1] /maw/ *adj* **1** greater in quality, quantity, or number: *This was something more than she expected; Seven is two more than five.* **2** additional; further: *Three more guests arrived; Have some more tea; What more do you want?* **✳ nothing more than/neither more nor less than** simply; plainly. [Old English *māra*]

more[2] *adv* **1a** as an additional amount: *There's not much more to do.* **b** moreover; again: *Summer is here once more.* **2** to a greater degree, extent, or amount: *You should practise more; I'm more sad than angry; It costs more than making your own beer.* **3** used with an adjective or adverb to form the comparative: *They're much more evenly matched now.* **✳ more and more** to a progressively increasing degree; with increasing frequency. **more often than not** at most times; usually. **more or less 1** to some extent or degree; somewhat: *We were more or less pleased with the results.* **2** almost: *It's more or less over.* **3** approximately: *It's more or less 6 foot long.* **more than** very: *We were more than happy to help.*

more[3] *noun* **1** a greater or additional quantity, amount, or part: *We hope to see more of her; Tell me more; There's more to this than meets the eye.* **2** additional ones: *More were found as the search continued.* **✳ more of** nearer to being (something specified) than something else: *It's more of a sofa than a bed.*

moreish *or* **morish** *or* **more-ish** *adj Brit, informal* so tasty as to cause a desire for more: *These biscuits are very moreish.*

morel /moˈrel/ *noun* **1** a large edible fungus with a light yellowish brown cap: *Morchella esculenta.* **2** any of several species of related fungi: genus *Morchella.* [French *morille*, of Germanic origin]

morello /məˈreloh/ *noun* (*pl* **morellos**) a cultivated sour cherry with a dark-red skin, used *esp* in jams: *Prunus cerasus.* [prob modification of Flemish *amarelle, marelle*, from late Latin *amarellum* a cultivated cherry, from Latin *amarus* sour]

moreover *adv* in addition to what has been said.

mores /ˈmawreez, ˈmawrayz/ *pl noun* the customs or conventions of a particular group. [Latin *mores*, pl of *mor-, mos* custom]

Moresco /məˈreskoh/ *noun and adj* (*pl* **Morescos**) see MORISCO.

moresque *or* **Moresque** /mawˈresk/ *adj* said of art or architecture: having a Moorish style, design, or influence. [via French from Spanish *morisco* from *moro* Moor, from Latin *Maurus*]

morganatic /mawgə'natik/ *adj* relating to or denoting a marriage between people of different rank in which the rank of the inferior partner remains unchanged and the children do not succeed to the titles or property of the parent of higher rank. ➤➤ **morganatically** *adv.*

Word history
late Latin *matrimonium ad morganaticam* marriage with morning gift. The husband's gift to his wife on the first morning of their marriage was all that the wife was entitled to from the marriage.

morgen /'mawgən/ *noun* (*pl* **morgen**) **1** a Southern African and former Dutch unit of land area equal to about 0.85 hectares (about 2.1 acres). **2** formerly in Scandinavia and Prussia, a unit of land area equal to about 0.3 hectares (about 0.66 acres). [Dutch *morgen*, literally 'morning'; from the idea that it is the amount of land that can be ploughed in one morning]

morgue /mawg/ *noun* **1a** a mortuary. **b** *informal* a gloomy, dispiriting, or deserted place. **2** a collection of reference works and files in a newspaper office, used *esp* in compiling information for obituaries. [French *Morgue*, the name of a Paris mortuary]

moribund /'moribund/ *adj* **1** dying. **2** having almost completely lost former vigour, vitality, or drive; nearing the end of existence: *an attitude of disgust and resentment towards the Life Force that could only arise in a diseased and moribund community in which Ibsen's Hedda Gabler would be the typical woman* — George Bernard Shaw. ➤➤ **moribundity** /-'bunditi/ *noun.* [Latin *moribundus* from *mori* to die]

morion /'mawri·ən/ *noun* a high-crested 16th-cent. helmet with no visor. [early French *morion*]

Morisco /mə'riskoh/ *or* **Moresco** /mə'reskoh/ *noun* (*pl* **Moriscos** *or* **Moriscoes**) a Spanish Moor, *esp* one who had become a baptized Christian. ➤➤ **Morisco** *adj.* [Spanish *morisco*: see MORESQUE]

morish /'mawrish/ *adj* see MOREISH.

Mormon /'mawmən/ *noun* a member of the Church of Jesus Christ of Latter-Day Saints, founded in 1830 in the USA by Joseph Smith, and following precepts contained in the Book of Mormon, a sacred text that he discovered. ➤➤ **Mormon** *adj,* **Mormonism** *noun.*

morn /mawn/ *noun literary* morning. [Old English *morgen*]

mornay *or* **Mornay** /'mawnay/ *adj* **1** denoting a rich creamy cheese sauce: *mornay sauce.* **2** (*used after a noun*) denoting food served in this sauce: *cod mornay.* [named after *Mornay*, 19th-cent. French chef who invented the sauce]

morning /'mawning/ *noun* **1a** the time from midnight to noon or sunrise to noon. **b** the dawn. **2** the beginning or an early period, e.g. of time or life: *The morning and spring of your life are past* — Henry David Thoreau. ✳ **in the morning 1** during the morning. **2** tomorrow morning. **the morning after** the unpleasant aftereffects, *esp* a hangover, felt on the morning after a night of excessive drinking, etc, or the time when these unpleasant aftereffects are felt. [Middle English, from MORN + *-ing* (as in EVENING)]

morning-after pill *noun* an oral contraceptive that blocks implantation of a fertilized egg in the human womb and so prevents conception. [from its being taken after rather than before sexual intercourse]

morning coat *noun* a man's TAILCOAT (jacket with long split back) that is worn on formal occasions during the day.

morning dress *noun* men's dress for formal occasions during the day, such as weddings, usu consisting of a black morning coat and striped trousers.

morning glory *noun* any of several species of usu twining plants of the bindweed family with showy trumpet-shaped flowers: genus *Ipomoea.*

mornings *adv* chiefly NAmer, informal in the morning; on any morning.

morning sickness *noun* nausea and vomiting occurring, *esp* in the morning, during the earlier months of a woman's pregnancy.

morning star *noun* a bright planet, *esp* Venus, seen in the eastern sky before or at sunrise.

Moro /'mawroh/ *noun* (*pl* **Moros** *or collectively* **Moro**) **1** a member of any of several Muslim peoples of the S Philippines. **2** the Austronesian language of the Moro peoples. [Spanish *Moro* Moor, from Latin *Maurus*: see MOOR]

Moroccan /mə'rokən/ *noun* a native or inhabitant of Morocco. ➤➤ **Moroccan** *adj.*

morocco /mə'rokoh/ *noun* (*pl* **moroccos**) a fine leather made from goatskin tanned with sumach. [named after *Morocco*, country in N Africa where it was orig made]

moron /'mawron/ *noun* **1** *informal* a very stupid person. **2** a term used formerly to classify a person with a learning disability who has an IQ of between 50 and 70. ➤➤ **moronic** /mə'ronik/ *adj,* **moronically** /mə'ronikli/ *adv,* **moronism** *noun,* **moronity** /mə'roniti/ *noun.* [Greek *mōros* foolish, stupid]

morose /mə'rohs/ *adj* **1** marked by or expressive of gloom. **2** having a gloomy disposition. ➤➤ **morosely** *adv,* **moroseness** *noun.* [Latin *morosus* capricious, from *mor-, mos* will]

morph[1] /mawf/ *noun* any of two or more variant forms of an animal or plant. [Greek *morphē* form]

morph[2] *noun* the realization in speech or writing of a MORPHEME. [back-formation from MORPHEME]

morph[3] *noun* in cinematography, an image altered by MORPHING. [Greek *morphē* form]

morph[4] *verb intrans* in cinematography, to undergo MORPHING (alteration of image by computer program). ➤ *verb trans* to alter (an image) in this way.

morph. *abbr* **1** morphological. **2** morphology.

morph- *or* **morpho-** *comb. form* forming words, denoting: form: *morphogenesis.* [via German from Greek *morphē* form]

-morph *comb. form* forming nouns, denoting: a person or thing having a specified form: *endomorph; isomorph.* ➤➤ **-morphic** *comb. form,* **-morphous** *comb. form,* **-morphy** *comb. form.* [Greek *-morphos* from *morphē* form]

morpheme /'mawfeem/ *noun* the smallest indivisible unit of language that has a meaning, e.g. 'cat' or the various elements of a word such as 'lovingly', which is composed of three morphemes, 'love', '-ing', and '-ly', realized in speech and writing by a MORPH[2]: compare LEXEME. ➤➤ **morphemic** /maw'feemik/ *adj,* **morphemically** /maw'feemikli/ *adv.* [French *morphème* from Greek *morphē* form (as in *phonème* phoneme)]

morphemics /maw'feemiks/ *pl noun* (*treated as sing.*) **1** the study of morphemes and word structure. **2** the structure of a language in terms of morphemes.

morphia /'morfi·ə/ *noun dated* morphine.

-morphic *comb. form* see -MORPH.

morphine /'mawfeen/ *noun* the principal alkaloid of opium that is an addictive narcotic drug and is medicinally used as a powerful painkiller. ➤➤ **morphinic** /maw'feenik, maw'finik/ *adj,* **morphinism** *noun.* [French *morphine*, from *Morpheus* Roman god of dreams and sleep]

morphing *noun* in cinematography, the changing of one image into another by means of a computer program.

-morphism *comb. form* forming nouns, denoting: **1** a quality or state of having a particular form: *heteromorphism.* **2** conceptualization in a particular form: *anthropomorphism.* [via late Latin from Greek *-morphos* from *morphē* form]

morpho- *comb. form* see MORPH-.

morphogenesis /mawfoh'jenəsis/ *noun* **1** the formation and differentiation of tissues and organs during embryonic development or evolution. **2** the formation and development of land forms. ➤➤ **morphogenetic** /-'netik/ *adj.* [scientific Latin *morphogenesis*, from MORPHO- + GENESIS]

morphology /maw'foləji/ *noun* **1** the form and structure of animals and plants, or the scientific study concerned with this. **2a** the study and description of word formation in a language including inflection, derivation, and compounding. **b** the system of word-forming elements and processes in a language. **3** the structure or form of something, or the study of it. ➤➤ **morphologic** /-'lojik/ *adj,* **morphological** /-'lojikl/ *adj,* **morphologically** /-'lojikli/ *adv,* **morphologist** *noun.* [German *Morphologie*, from MORPHO- + -LOGY]

-morphous *comb. form* see -MORPH.

-morphy *comb. form* see -MORPH.

Morris chair /'moris/ *noun* an armchair with an adjustable back and loose cushions. [named after William *Morris* d.1896, English writer, artist, and designer]

morris dance *noun* any of several traditional English dances that are performed by groups of people, usu men, wearing costumes to which small bells are attached and carrying handkerchiefs or small sticks. ⋙ **morris dancer** *noun*, **morris dancing** *noun*, **morris man** *noun*. [Middle English *moreys daunce*, from *moreys* Moorish (from *More* Moor) + *daunce* dance]

morrow /'moroh/ *noun* **1** (*usu* **the morrow**) *archaic or literary* the next day. **2** the period of time following something. **3** the morning. [Middle English *morn, morwen* morning]

Morse /maws/ *noun* a signalling code in which letters of the alphabet are represented by combinations of dots and dashes, which are transmitted as short and long sounds, e.g. bleeps, or flashes of light. [named after Samuel *Morse* d.1872, US artist and inventor]

Morse code *noun* = MORSE.

morsel /'mawsl/ *noun* **1** a small piece of food. **2** a small quantity; a scrap. [Middle English from Old French *morsel*, dimin. of *mors* bite, from Latin *morsus*, past part. of *mordēre* to bite]

mortadella /ˌmawtə'delə/ *noun* a large smooth-textured steamed Italian sausage made from spiced pork or beef and usu served sliced as a cold meat. [Italian, an irregular diminutive of Latin *murtatum* seasoned with myrtle berries, applied to a sausage with myrtle berry flavouring]

mortal[1] /'mawtl/ *adj* **1a** not living for ever; subject to death. **b** of human existence. **2a** causing or about to cause death; fatal. **b** continuing until death: *mortal combat*. **3** marked by relentless hostility: *a mortal enemy*. **4** very great, intense, or severe: *They cowered away in mortal terror*. **5** of or connected with death: *He was in his last mortal agony*. **6** *informal*. **a** humanly conceivable: *every mortal thing*. **b** very tedious and prolonged: *We waited three mortal hours for him to show up*. [Middle English via French from Latin *mortalis*, from *mort-, mors* death]

mortal[2] *noun* **1** a human being. **2** *informal* a person of a specified kind: *He's an odd sort of mortal.*

mortality /maw'taliti/ *noun* (*pl* **mortalities**) **1** the state of being mortal. **2** the death of large numbers of people, animals, etc. **3** the human race: *Take these tears, mortality's relief* — Pope. **4a** the number of deaths in a given time or place. **b** the ratio of deaths in a given time to population. **c** the number of things lost, or the rate of loss or failure, *esp* of businesses.

mortality table *noun* = LIFE TABLE.

mortally *adv* **1** in a deadly or fatal manner: *mortally wounded*. **2** to an extreme degree; intensely: *She was mortally offended.*

mortal sin *noun* in Christian theology, a sin, e.g. murder, of such gravity that it totally debars the soul from divine grace: compare VENIAL SIN. ⋙ **mortal sinner** *noun*.

mortar[1] /'mawtə/ *noun* **1** a strong usu bowl-shaped vessel, e.g. of stone, in which substances are pounded or ground with a pestle, used *esp* in cooking and pharmacy. **2** a light usu muzzle-loading artillery gun having a tube that is short in relation to its calibre, a smooth bore, and a low muzzle velocity. Mortars are used by infantry for firing shells at high angles over short distances. [Old English *mortere* from Old French *mortier* from Latin *mortarium*]

mortar[2] *verb* (**mortared, mortaring**) to fire shells at (somebody or something) with a mortar or mortars.

mortar[3] *noun* a mixture of cement, lime, gypsum plaster, etc with sand and water, that hardens and is used to join bricks, stones, etc or for plastering. [Middle English *morter* from Old French *mortier* from Latin *mortarium*; in this sense, orig something mixed in a MORTAR[1] (1)]

mortar[4] *verb trans* (**mortared, mortaring**) to plaster, fix, or join (something) with mortar.

mortarboard *noun* **1** a square board with a handle underneath, used by bricklayers for holding mortar; = HAWK[1] (3). **2** an academic cap consisting of a close-fitting crown with a stiff flat square attached on top.

mortgage[1] /'mawgij/ *noun* **1** an agreement by which a person borrows money, e.g. from a bank or building society, usu to buy a house, and the lending organization is given the right to take possession of the borrower's property, e.g. the house, if the loan is not repaid in accordance with the terms stipulated in the agreement. **2** the loan received through such an agreement. **3** the deed containing the loan agreement. **4** the sum paid, usu monthly, towards repayment of the loan and any interest accruing. [Middle English *morgage* from Old French *mortgage*, from *mort* dead (from Latin *mortuus*) + *gage* security, pledge]

mortgage[2] *verb trans* **1** to transfer the ownership of (property) by a mortgage. **2** to make (*esp* oneself) subject to a claim or obli-

gation: *The middle-aged are mortgaged to life* — Oscar Wilde. ⋙ **mortgageable** *adj*.

mortgagee /mawgi'jee/ *noun* the lender in a mortgage, usu a bank or building society.

mortgagor /'mawgijə, mawgi'jaw/ *or* **mortgager** /'mawgijə/ *noun* the borrower in a mortgage, usu a person buying a house who uses the property as security.

mortice[1] /'mawtis/ *noun* see MORTISE[1].

mortice[2] *verb trans* see MORTISE[2].

mortician /maw'tish(ə)n/ *noun chiefly NAmer* an undertaker. [Latin *mort-, mors* death + -ICIAN]

mortify /'mawtifie/ *verb* (**mortifies, mortified, mortifying**) ⋙ *verb trans* **1** to subject (somebody) to feelings of shame or acute embarrassment. **2** to subdue (e.g. bodily needs and desires), *esp* by abstinence or self-inflicted suffering. ⋙ *verb intrans* said of flesh: to become necrotic or gangrenous. ⋙ **mortification** /-fi'kaysh(ə)n/ *noun*, **mortifying** *adj*, **mortifyingly** *adv*. [Middle English *mortifien* to kill, subdue, from early French *mortifier* from late Latin *mortificare*, from Latin *mort-, mors* death]

mortise[1] *or* **mortice** /'mawtis/ *noun* a usu rectangular cavity cut into a piece of material, e.g. wood, to receive a protrusion, *esp* a tenon, of another piece. [Middle English *mortays* from early French *mortaise*]

mortise[2] *or* **mortice** *verb trans* **1** to join or fasten (something) securely, *specif* by a mortise and tenon joint. **2** to cut or make a mortise in (e.g. a piece of wood).

mortise lock *noun* a lock that is designed to be fitted into a mortise in the edge of a door, as distinct from a lock fitted to the door's surface.

mortmain /'mawtmayn/ *noun* **1** a non-transferable possession of lands or buildings by an ecclesiastical or other corporation. **2a** property or other gifts nontransferably bequeathed to a church or corporation. **b** (*usu* **in mortmain**) the status of such property or gifts. [Middle English *morte-mayne* from early French *mortemain*, from *morte* (fem of *mort* dead, from Latin *mortuus*) + *main* hand (from Latin *manus*)]

mortuary[1] /'mawtyooəri, 'mawchəri/ *noun* (*pl* **mortuaries**) a room or building in which dead bodies are kept before burial or cremation. [Middle English *mortuarie* gift claimed by the church from a dead person's estate, from Latin *mortuarium*, neuter of *mortuarius* of the dead, from *mortuus* dead]

mortuary[2] *adj* of death or the burial of the dead: *a mortuary urn*.

morula /'mooroolə/ *noun* (*pl* **morulae** /-lee/) the embryo of a metazoan animal at a very early stage in its development, preceding the blastula stage, consisting of a solid globular mass of cells: compare BLASTULA, GASTRULA. [scientific Latin *morula*, dimin. of Latin *morum* mulberry]

morwong /'maw-wong/ *noun* (*pl* **morwongs** *or collectively* **morwong**) any of several genera of large brightly coloured edible fishes that are found around the coasts of Australasia and have a tapering body, thick lips, and a long dorsal fin: family Cheilodactylidae. [from the name in an Aboriginal language]

Mosaic /mə'zayik, moh-/ *adj* of Moses, the biblical prophet and lawgiver, or the institutions or writings attributed to him. [late Latin *Mosaicus* from *Moses*]

mosaic[1] *noun* **1a** decorative work made from small pieces of different coloured material, e.g. glass or stone, inlaid to form pictures or patterns: compare TESSERA. **b** a picture or pattern produced from this. **c** (*used before a noun*) in the form of a mosaic or composed of mosaic: *a mosaic floor*. **2** something like a mosaic. **3a** an organism, or part of one, composed of cells with different genetic make-up; = CHIMERA (3). **b** a virus disease of plants, e.g. tobacco, characterized *esp* by diffuse yellow and green mottling of the foliage. **4** an arrangement of photosensitive cells in the tube of a television camera. [Middle English *musycke* via French from Latin *musaicum*, alteration of *musivum*, neuter of *musivus* of a muse, artistic, from Latin *Musa* muse]

mosaic[2] *verb trans* (**mosaicked, mosaicking**) **1** to form (something) into a mosaic. **2** to decorate (something) with a mosaic. ⋙ **mosaicist** /-sist/ *noun*.

mosaic disease *noun* = MOSAIC[1] (3B).

mosaicism /moh'zayisizəm/ *noun* in biology, the condition of an organism or body part being composed of cells with different genetic make-up.

moschatel /ˈmoskəˌtel/ *noun* a small perennial plant that is found in woods and other shady places and that has heads of five greenish yellow flowers that smell of musk and are arranged at right angles like the faces of a cube: *Adoxa moschatellina*.

Moselle *or* **Mosel** /mohˈzel/ *noun* a typically light-bodied white table wine made in the valley of the Moselle. [German *Moselwein*, from *Mosel* Moselle, river in Germany + *Wein* wine]

Moses basket /ˈmohzəz/ *noun* a baby's wicker cot, usu with handles for portability. [with allusion to the basket containing the baby Moses that was hidden in the bulrushes (Exodus 2:3)]

mosey¹ /ˈmohzi/ *verb intrans* (**moseys, moseyed, moseying**) *informal* (*usu* + along/around/off) to go in a leisurely, unhurried, or aimless way; to wander or saunter. [origin unknown]

mosey² *noun informal* a casual and unhurried walk: *I'll have a mosey along later and see what's happening.*

mosh /mosh/ *verb intrans Brit, informal* to dance in an energetic bouncing way, often deliberately colliding with other dancers, usu to heavy metal, thrash, or punk music. **⋙ mosher** *noun*. [prob an alteration of MASH² or MUSH²]

mosh pit *noun Brit, informal* an area just in front of a stage at a gig where people mosh.

Moslem /ˈmozlim/ *noun* see MUSLIM.

mosque /mosk/ *noun* a building used for public worship by Muslims. [early French *mosquee* via Italian and Spanish from Arabic *masjid* temple, from *sajada* to prostrate oneself]

mosquito /moˈskeetoh/ *noun* (*pl* **mosquitoes** *or* **mosquitos**) any of various species of two-winged flies, the females of which suck the blood of animals and humans, often transmitting diseases such as malaria and yellow fever to them: family Culicidae. [Spanish *mosquito* dimin. of *mosca* fly, from Latin *musca*]

mosquito net *noun* a net or screen hung across a door or window or round a bed to keep out mosquitoes.

moss /mos/ *noun* **1a** any of a phylum of primitive plants with small leafy stems bearing sex organs at the tip: phylum Bryophyta. **b** many of these plants growing together and covering a surface. **c** any of various similar plants, such as lichens. **2** *chiefly Scot* a peat bog. **⋙ mossiness** *noun*, **mosslike** *adj*, **mossy** *adj*. [Old English *mōs* bog]

moss agate *noun* an agate containing brown, black, or green mosslike markings.

moss animal *noun* = BRYOZOAN.

mossie *or* **mozzie** /ˈmozi/ *noun chiefly Aus, informal* = MOSQUITO.

moss rose *noun* a variety of garden rose with glandular mossy growths on the calyxes (leaflike parts surrounding the flowers; see CALYX) and flower stalks, and fragrant white, pink, or red flowers: *Rosa centifolia muscosa*.

moss stitch *noun* a knitting stitch made up of alternate plain and purl stitches, with each plain stitch knitted as a purl and each purl one knitted as a plain on the following row.

mosstrooper *noun* a person who lived by raiding and plundering in the Scottish–English border area during the 17th cent.

most¹ /mohst/ *adj* **1** the majority of: *Most people think so.* **2** greatest in quantity or extent: *the most ability.* **✳ for the most part** in most cases or respects; mainly. [Old English *mǣst*]

most² *adv* **1** (*often* **the most**) to the greatest degree or extent: *What I like most about him is his smile.* **2** used with an adjective or adverb to form the superlative: *That was the most challenging job he ever had.* **3** very: *Her argument was most persuasive.*

most³ *noun* the greatest quantity, number, or amount: *It's the most I can do; She spends most of her time in bed; Most became discouraged and left.* **✳ at most/at the most** as a maximum limit: *It'll take him an hour at most to finish the job.* **be the most** *informal* to be the best, greatest, etc of all. **make the most of** to use (something) or present (oneself) to the best advantage or with the best effect.

most⁴ *adv archaic, dialect, or NAmer* almost.

-most *suffix* forming adjectives, with the meanings: **1** most; to the highest possible degree: *innermost; utmost.* **2** nearest to (a specified place or part): *topmost; hindmost.* [Middle English, alteration of *-mest* (as in *formest* foremost)]

Most Honourable *adj* a title given to marquesses, marchionesses, members of the Privy Council, and holders of the Order of the Bath.

mostly *adv* **1** for the greatest part; mainly. **2** in most cases; usually.

Most Reverend *adj* a title given to Anglican archbishops and Irish Roman Catholic bishops.

most significant bit *noun* in computing, the bit in a binary number that is of the highest numerical value.

MOT¹ *or* **MoT** *noun* **1** in the UK, a compulsory annual roadworthiness test for motor vehicles older than a certain age. In general, MOT tests are compulsory for motor vehicles three years old and over; for taxis, ambulances, large goods vehicles, and large passenger-carrying vehicles, they are compulsory from one year onwards. **2** a certificate to show that a vehicle has passed such a test. [short for *Ministry of Transport*, the government department that introduced the test, now called Department of Transport]

MOT² *or* **MoT** *verb trans* (**MOTs, MOTing, MOTed** *or* **MOT'd**) **1** (*usu in passive*) to put (a vehicle) through an MOT test. **2** to carry out an MOT test on (a vehicle).

mot /moh/ *noun* (*pl* **mots** /moh(z)/) a pithy or witty saying; a shortened form of BON MOT. [French *mot* word, saying, from Latin *muttum* grunt]

MOT certificate *noun* = MOT¹ (2).

mote /moht/ *noun* a small particle, *esp* a particle of dust suspended in the air. [Old English *mot*]

motel /mohˈtel/ *noun* a roadside hotel, usu with the rooms arranged around a parking area, catering *esp* for passing motorists. [blend of MOTOR¹ and HOTEL]

motet /mohˈtet/ *noun* a choral composition on a sacred text. [Middle English from early French *motet*, dimin. of *mot* word]

moth /moth/ *noun* **1** any of numerous species of flying insects similar to butterflies: order Lepidoptera.

Editorial note ————————————————

Moths can be distinguished from butterflies by the form of their antennae, which vary in shape and are often feathery but never end in knobs as butterflies' antennae do. Moths generally have stouter bodies and proportionately smaller wings than butterflies, are mostly duller in colour, and most species fly at night rather than during the day. Their larvae are usu plant-eating caterpillars.

2 = CLOTHES MOTH. [Old English *moththe*]

mothball¹ *noun* a ball of naphthalene or, formerly, camphor, used to keep moths from clothing, linen, etc. **✳ in/into mothballs 1** in or into a state of temporary rejection or suspension, *esp* because of a lack of interest or relevance; on ice or on hold: *We'll put that idea in mothballs for the moment.* **2** in or into a state of indefinitely long protective storage: *Many ships were put into mothballs after the war.*

mothball² *verb trans* **1a** to postpone (work, etc) indefinitely. **b** to reject or set aside (a plan, project, etc that is of no further or current use or interest). **2a** to withdraw (a ship or aeroplane) from service: *Several airliners were mothballed during the fuel shortage.* **b** to take (a factory) out of operation temporarily.

moth-eaten *adj* **1** damaged by moths or moth larvae: *moth-eaten clothes.* **2a** very worn-out or shabby in appearance. **b** antiquated; outmoded: *Religion … that vast moth-eaten musical brocade created to pretend we never die* — Philip Larkin.

mother¹ /ˈmudhə/ *noun* **1a** a female parent of a child or offspring: *All women become like their mothers. That is their tragedy* — Oscar Wilde. **b** a female acting as the parent of a child or offspring she did not give birth to. **c** the characteristics or feelings of or associated with a mother: *His tears brought out the mother in her.* **d** (*used before a noun*) of a female parent; bearing the relationship of female parent: *a mother hen.* **2** (*used before a noun*) derived from, or as if from, one's mother: *English is her mother tongue.* **3a** a woman considered as the originator, inventor, or founder of something. **b** a source, origin, or producer of something: *Necessity is the mother of invention.* **c** (*used before a noun*) denoting or relating to the source or origin of something: *This is the mother church of several churches in the district.* **4** something that provides protection or nourishment: *The forest is our mother, our shelter, and the source of our food.* **5** *informal, sometimes considered offensive* a very big, good, bad, or otherwise notable or extreme example of something: *I've got the mother of a hangover this morning.* **6a** a woman in authority. **b** (*often used as a term of address*) a mother superior: *What is your opinion, Reverend Mother?* **7** *archaic* used *esp* as a term of address: an old or elderly woman. **8** *taboo* = MOTHERFUCKER. **⋙ motherhood** *noun*, **motherless** *adj*, **motherlessness** *noun*. [Old English *mōdor*; related to Latin *mater*, Greek *mētēr*]

mother² *verb trans* (**mothered, mothering**) **1** *often derog* to care for or protect (a person, animal, etc) like a mother, sometimes to an excessive or unnecessary degree. **2a** *dated* to give birth to (a baby). **b** to give rise to (something); to initiate or produce (it). ➤ **mothering** *noun*.

mother³ *noun* a slimy membrane of yeast and bacterial cells that develops on the surface of alcoholic liquids undergoing vinegar-producing fermentation and is added to wine or cider to produce vinegar. [related to early Dutch *modder* mud, lees, dregs; possibly also connected with MOTHER¹ in the sense of 'source' or 'provider']

motherboard *noun* a printed circuit board that contains the main electronic components of a computer and into which other boards can be slotted so that the computer can operate various peripherals such as a disk drive.

Mother Carey's chicken /'keəriz/ *noun* = STORM PETREL. [said to be from Latin *mater cara* or Spanish *madre cara* dear mother, referring to the Virgin Mary]

mother country *noun* **1** one's native country; the country in which one was born and grew up. **2** a country from which settlers or colonists emigrate.

motherfucker *noun taboo* **1** a contemptible or offensive person or thing. **2** an exceptional, formidable, or impressive person or thing. ➤ **motherfucking** *adj*.

Mother Goose rhyme *noun chiefly NAmer* = NURSERY RHYME. [named after *Mother Goose*, fictional author of *Mother Goose's Melodies*, collection of nursery rhymes published in London about 1760]

Mothering Sunday *noun Brit, dated* = MOTHER'S DAY. [said to be orig connected with the former custom in parts of England of *mothering*, i.e. visiting the mother church of a district, during Lent, but generally understood as a day on which mothers are honoured, visited, and given gifts]

mother-in-law *noun* (*pl* **mothers-in-law**) the mother of one's husband or wife.

motherland *noun* one's native country.

mother lode *noun* **1** the major vein of ore, e.g. in an area. **2** a good source or supply of something.

motherly *adj* **1** characteristic of a mother. **2** showing the characteristics associated with a mother, e.g. care and kindness. ➤ **motherliness** *noun*.

mother-of-pearl *noun* the hard pearly iridescent substance forming the inner layer of the shells of certain molluscs, *esp* abalones and oysters. Also called NACRE.

mother of the chapel *noun* (*pl* **mothers of the chapel**) a woman who is the shop steward in charge of a union branch in the publishing or printing industry.

mother of vinegar *noun* = MOTHER³.

mother's boy *noun* a boy or man regarded as depending too much on his mother or as being excessively influenced by her.

Mother's Day *noun* a day set aside for the honouring of mothers, the second Sunday in May in the USA, Canada, and Australia, and the fourth Sunday of Lent in Britain. Also called MOTHERING SUNDAY.

mother ship *noun* **1** a spaceship which acts as a service and supply base and usu a launch base for one or more smaller craft. **2** a ship that provides supplies and facilities for a number of smaller craft.

mother superior *or* **Mother Superior** *noun* the head of a religious community of women.

mother tongue *noun* **1** one's native language. **2** a language from which another language derives.

mother wit *noun* a person's natural intelligence and common sense: *As long as wit is mother wit it can be as wild as it pleases* — G K Chesterton.

mothproof¹ *adj* resistant to attack by moths or the larvae of moths, *esp* clothes moths.

mothproof² *verb trans* to make (e.g. clothing) mothproof.

mothy *adj* (**mothier, mothiest**) **1** containing or infested with moths. **2** moth-eaten. **3** mothlike.

motif /moh'teef/ *noun* **1a** a recurring element forming a theme in a work of art or literature, *esp* a dominant idea or central theme. **b** in music, a short, but prominent, sequence of notes, often one that undergoes development when repeated during the piece. **2a** a

repeated design or colour. **b** a single decoration, such as a logo, e.g. on an item of clothing. **3** a leitmotiv. [French *motif* motive, motif]

motile /'mohtiel/ *adj* said of a cell, sperm, protozoan, etc: exhibiting or capable of movement. ➤ **motility** /moh'tiliti/ *noun*. [Latin *motus*, past part. of *movēre* to move]

motion¹ /'mohsh(ə)n/ *noun* **1a** the act, process, or an instance of changing position; a movement. **b** the way in which somebody or something moves. **c** the ability to move. **2** the act or an instance of moving part of the body; a gesture: *He made a beckoning motion with his hand.* **3** a moving part or mechanism. **4a** a proposal for action, *esp* a formal proposal made in a deliberative assembly. **b** an application made to a court or judge to obtain an order, ruling, or direction. **5a** (*also in pl*) an evacuation of the bowels. **b** the matter evacuated from the bowels at one time; a stool. **6** an impulse or inclination of the mind or will: *the motions of humanity to good or evil* — T S Eliot. **7** a melodic change of pitch. ✱ **go through the motions** to carry out an activity half-heartedly or mechanically; to do the minimum necessary without enthusiasm or serious intent: *You'd better at least go through the motions of apologizing.* **in motion** moving or functioning. **set in motion** to get (something) started or to initiate (something): *set an enquiry in motion.* ➤ **motional** *adj*, **motionless** *adj*, **motionlessly** *adv*, **motionlessness** *noun*. [Middle English *mocioun* via French from Latin *motion-, motio* movement, from *motus*, past part. of *movēre* to move]

motion² *verb trans* to direct (somebody or something) by a gesture: *She motioned me to sit down.*

motion picture *noun* **1** *chiefly NAmer* a cinema film. **2** (*used before a noun*) relating to a cinema film or films: *the motion-picture industry.*

motivate /'mohtivayt/ *verb trans* to provide (somebody) with a motive or incentive to do something: *I was asked how I would motivate the boys to learn French.* ➤ **motivator** *noun*.

motivation /mohti'vaysh(ə)n/ *noun* **1** the act or an instance of motivating or being motivated. **2** a motivating force, influence, or incentive that directs one's action towards achieving a desired goal; a motive. **3** enthusiasm or drive. ➤ **motivational** *adj*, **motivationally** *adv*.

motive¹ /'mohtiv/ *noun* **1** a need, desire, etc that causes somebody to act. **2** a recurrent phrase or figure that is developed through the course of a musical composition; = MOTIF. ➤ **motiveless** *adj*, **motivelessly** *adv*, **motivelessness** *noun*. [Middle English from early French *motif*: see MOTIVE²]

motive² *adj* **1** moving or tending to move to action; motivating. **2** of or causing motion: *motive energy.* [early French *motif* from late Latin *motivus* from Latin *motus*, past part. of *movēre* to move]

motive power *noun* **1a** something such as water or steam whose energy is used to impart motion to machinery. **b** the energy itself. **2** the locomotives, *esp* steam ones, of a railway thought of collectively.

motivity /moh'tiviti/ *noun* the power of moving or producing movement.

mot juste /,moh 'zhoohst (*French* mo ʒyst)/ *noun* (*pl* **mots justes** /,moh 'zhoost (*French* mo ʒyst)/) the exactly right or most appropriate word or phrasing. [French *mot juste*]

motley¹ /'motli/ *adj* (**motlier, motliest**) **1** composed of varied, often disreputable or unsightly, elements: *The Natural Law Party ... is not a motley collection of ageing hippies, but an arm of a wealthy and complex organisation* — Daily Telegraph. **2** multicoloured. [Middle English, perhaps from *mot* mote, speck]

motley² *noun* **1a** a woollen fabric of mixed colours made in England between the 14th and 17th cents. **b** the characteristic clothing of a jester, made of motley. **2** a haphazard mixture of often incompatible elements: *The lanes are a motley of blank walls and doorways* — Colin Thubron.

motocross /'mohtohkros/ *noun* the sport of racing motorcycles across country on a rugged usu hilly course: compare AUTOCROSS, RALLYCROSS. [blend of MOTOR¹ + CROSS-COUNTRY²]

motor¹ /'mohtə/ *noun* **1** any of various machines or devices that transform energy into motion, e.g. **a** a small compact engine. **b** an internal-combustion engine, *esp* a petrol engine. **c** a machine that transforms electrical energy into mechanical energy in the form of rotational movement. **d** (*used before a noun*) equipped with or driven by a motor: *a motor vehicle.* **2** *chiefly Brit.* **a** *informal* a motor vehicle, *esp* a car. **b** (*used before a noun*) of or for motor vehicles: *the motor trade.* **3a** somebody or something that imparts motion. **b**

(*used before a noun*) causing or imparting motion. **c** (*used before a noun*) said of a nerve or nerve fibre: conveying nerve impulses from the brain, spinal cord, or a nerve centre to a muscle, gland, etc in order to cause contraction, secretion, etc. **d** (*used before a noun*) of or involving muscles or muscular movement. ➤➤ **motorless** *adj*. [Latin *motor* from *motus*, past part. of *movēre* to move]

motor[2] *verb intrans* (**motored, motoring**) **1** to travel by car. **2** *informal* to make rapid progress. ➤➤ **motorable** *adj*.

motor bike *noun informal* a motorcycle.

motorboat or **motor boat** *noun* a usu small boat propelled by a motor.

motorcade /'mohtəkayd/ *noun* a procession of motor vehicles. [MOTOR + CAVALCADE]

motor car *noun* **1** *Brit* = CAR (1). **2** *chiefly NAmer* a self-propelled railway carriage.

motorcycle[1] *noun* a two-wheeled motor vehicle that can carry one or two people astride the engine.

motorcycle[2] *verb intrans* to travel by motorcycle. ➤➤ **motorcyclist** *noun*.

motorise *verb trans* see MOTORIZE.

motorist *noun* somebody who drives a car.

motorize or **motorise** *verb trans* **1** to equip (e.g. a vehicle) with a motor. **2** to provide (e.g. troops) with motor-driven equipment, e.g. for transport. ➤➤ **motorization** /-'zaysh(ə)n/ *noun*.

motorman *noun* (*pl* **motormen**) a driver of a motor-driven vehicle, e.g. a bus or underground train.

motormouth *noun informal* a brashly talkative person.

motor racing *noun* the sport of racing in cars that are specially designed for speed.

motor scooter *noun* a type of light motorcycle having a seat so placed that the driver sits in front of rather than astride the enclosed engine.

motor vehicle *noun* a road vehicle powered by a motor, *esp* an internal-combustion engine.

motorway *noun Brit* a major road, designed for high-speed traffic, that has separate carriageways for different directions and certain restrictions on the types of vehicle and driver allowed on it.

motte /mot/ *noun* a specially constructed mound of earth on which a fortified wooden tower was built, *esp* as part of the type of Norman castle called a motte and bailey. [French *motte* from Old French *mote, motte* mound]

MOT test *noun* = MOT[1] (1).

mottle[1] /'motl/ *noun* **1** an irregular pattern of spots or blotches on a surface. **2** a coloured spot or blotch. [prob back-formation from *motley*]

mottle[2] *verb trans* to mark (something) with mottles. ➤➤ **mottled** *adj*.

motto /'motoh/ *noun* (*pl* **mottoes** or **mottos**) **1** a short expression of a guiding principle; a maxim: *'Honesty is the best policy' has always been my motto.* **2** a usu humorous or sentimental saying, or a piece of paper with such a saying printed on it, *esp* found in party crackers. **3a** a sentence, phrase, or word inscribed on something as appropriate to or indicative of its character or use: *She asked if I could translate the Latin motto on the sundial.* **b** a quotation at the front of a book, start of a chapter, etc, appropriate to its theme; = EPIGRAPH. [Italian *motto* saying, word, from Latin *muttum* grunt, from *muttire* to mutter]

moue /mooh/ *noun* a little grimace; a pout. [French *moue*, of Germanic origin]

mouflon or **moufflon** /'moohflonh/ *noun* (*pl* **mouflons** /'moohflonh/ *or collectively* **mouflon**) any member of a race of small wild reddish brown sheep of the mountains of Corsica and Sardinia: *Ovis musimon.* The female has no horns, but the males have large curling horns. The mouflon is thought to be one of the ancestors of the domestic sheep. [French *mouflon* from Italian dialect *movrone* from late Latin *mufron-, mufro*]

mouillé /'mweeay, 'moohay (*French* muje)/ *adj* said of a consonant: pronounced with the front of the tongue near or touching the hard palate; palatalized. [French *mouillé*, literally 'moistened']

moujik /'moohzhik/ *noun* see MUZHIK. [French *moujik* from Russian]

mould[1] (*NAmer* **mold**) /mohld/ *noun* **1** a cavity, dish, or form in which a substance, e.g. a jelly or a metal casting, is shaped. **2** the frame on or round which an object is constructed. **3** something formed in or on a mould; a moulding. **4** a fixed pattern or form. **5** distinctive character or type: *We need to recruit more men of his mould.* ✱ **break the mould 1** to bring about fundamental changes in an established system: *They set out to break the mould of British politics.* **2** to produce somebody or something unique: *They broke the mould when they made her.* [Middle English *mold, molde*, from Old French *modle* from Latin *modulus*, dimin. of *modus* measure]

mould[2] (*NAmer* **mold**) *verb trans* **1** to give shape to (something). **2** to form (something) in a mould. **3** to exert a steady formative influence on (a person, opinions, etc). **4** to fit closely to the contours of (a person's body, etc). **5** to ornament (something) with moulding or carving: *moulded picture frames.* ➤➤ **mouldable** *adj*, **moulder** *noun*.

mould[3] (*NAmer* **mold**) *noun* **1** an often woolly growth on the surface of damp or decaying organic matter. **2** the fungus that produces this. [Middle English *mowlde*, prob of Scandinavian origin]

mould[4] (*NAmer* **mold**) *noun* crumbling soft soil suited to plant growth, *esp* soil rich in humus. [Old English *molde*]

mouldboard *noun* a curved plate on a ploughshare for lifting and turning the soil.

moulder (*NAmer* **molder**) *verb intrans* (**mouldered, mouldering**, *NAmer* **moldered, moldering**) (*often* + away) to crumble into dust or decayed fragments, *esp* gradually. [perhaps from MOULD[1]]

moulding (*NAmer* **molding**) *noun* **1** an article produced by moulding. **2** a decorative recessed or embossed surface. **3** a decorative band or strip used for ornamentation or finishing, e.g. on a cornice.

mouldy (*NAmer* **moldy**) *adj* (**mouldier, mouldiest**) **1** of, resembling, or covered with a mould-producing fungus. **2** old and mouldering; fusty, crumbling. **3** *informal*. **a** miserable or nasty. **b** stingy. **c** bad.

moules marinière /,mool marin'yiə/ *pl noun* (*also* **moules à la marinière**) mussels that are cooked in a white wine sauce and served in their shells, usu as a starter. [French *moules à la marinière*, literally 'mussels in the marine style']

moulin /'moohlanh (*French* mulɛ̃)/ *noun* a nearly cylindrical vertical shaft worn in a glacier by water from melting snow and ice. [French *moulin*, literally 'mill', from late Latin *molinum*]

moult[1] (*NAmer* **molt**) /mohlt/ *verb trans and intrans* said of birds, animals, etc: to shed or cast off (hair, feathers, shell, horns, or an outer layer) periodically. [alteration of Middle English *mouten* from Old English *-mūtian* to change, from Latin *mutare*]

moult[2] (*NAmer* **molt**) *noun* an instance or the process or time of moulting.

mound[1] /mownd/ *noun* **1a** a heap or pile. **b** a large quantity: *I've got a mound of unanswered letters to deal with.* **2** a small hill. **3** an artificial bank or hill of earth or stone, e.g. for defence or as a place of burial. **4** in baseball, the slightly elevated ground on which a pitcher stands to deliver the ball. [origin unknown]

mound[2] *verb trans* **1** to form (something) into a mound. **2** *archaic* to enclose or fortify (a place) with a fence or a ridge of earth.

Mound Builder *noun* a member of an indigenous people inhabiting a region around the Mississippi River in the USA during prehistoric times, who built huge burial and effigy mounds.

mound-builder *noun* = MEGAPODE.

mount[1] /mownt/ *verb intrans* **1** (*often* + up) to increase in amount, extent, or degree. **2** (*often* + up) to get up on or into something above ground level, *esp* to seat oneself on a horse, etc for riding. **3** to rise or ascend. ➤ *verb trans* **1a** to go up or climb (a hill, stairs, etc). **b** to seat or place oneself on (something raised): *The speaker mounted the platform.* **2a** to lift up, raise or erect (e.g. a barrier). **b** to place (e.g. artillery or other weapons) in position for use. **c** to initiate and carry out (e.g. an assault or strike); to organize (e.g. a campaign). **3a** to set (somebody) on an animal or other means of conveyance: *He mounted his little daughter on a donkey.* **b** to provide (e.g. troops) with animals for riding. **4** to station somebody as or act as (a defence, escort, observer, etc): *They were ordered to mount guard over the palace.* **5a** to attach (something) to a support. **b** to arrange or assemble (e.g. a photograph) for use or display. **c** to prepare (e.g. a specimen) for examination or display. **6** to organize and present (e.g. a show) for public viewing or performance: *The local operatic society mounted a sumptuous opera.* **7** said of a male animal: to climb onto (a female animal) for copulation. ➤➤ **mountable**

adj, **mounter** *noun*. [Middle English *mounten* from early French *monter*; ultimately from Latin *mont-*, *mons* mountain]

mount² *noun* **1** something on which somebody or something is mounted, e.g.: **a** the material, e.g. cardboard, on which a picture is mounted. **b** a jewellery setting. **c** an attachment for an accessory. **d** a hinge, card, etc for mounting a stamp in a stamp collection. **e** a slide for a specimen in microscopy. **2a** a horse for riding. **b** the act or an instance of mounting, e.g. of a horse or bicycle. **c** an opportunity to ride a horse, *esp* in a race.

mount³ *noun* **1** *literary* a hill: *from foggy mount and marshy plain* — Byron. **2** used in hill or mountain names: *Mount Olympus*; *Mount Everest*. [Old English *munt* and Old French *mont* from Latin *mont-*, *mons* mountain]

mountain /'mownt(ə)n/ *noun* **1** a landmass that projects conspicuously above its surroundings and is higher than a hill. **2a** (*also in pl*) a vast amount or quantity. **b** a supply, *esp* of a specified usu agricultural commodity, in excess of demand: *a butter mountain*. [Middle English from Old French *montaigne*, ultimately from Latin *montanus* of a mountain, from *mont-*, *mons* mountain]

mountain ash *noun* **1** any of several species of trees of the rose family usu with small red fruits; ROWAN: genus *Sorbus*. **2** in Australia, any of several species of eucalyptus trees: genus *Eucalyptus*.

mountain avens *noun* a low-growing perennial plant of the rose family, with flowers having eight white petals and yellow stamens: *Dryas octopetala*.

mountain bike *noun* a wide-tyred heavy-duty bicycle with a large number of gears, orig designed to cope with rugged terrain. ➤➤ **mountain biker** *noun*, **mountain biking** *noun*.

mountaineer¹ /mowntə'niə/ *noun* **1** a person who climbs mountains. **2** *dated* a person who lives in a mountainous region. [MOUNTAIN + -EER]

mountaineer² *verb intrans* to climb mountains, *esp* as a pastime.

mountaineering /mowntə'niəring/ *noun* the pastime or technique of climbing mountains and rock faces.

mountain goat *noun* **1** any goat or goatlike animal that inhabits mountainous regions, noted proverbially for its agility and surefootedness. **2** a goatlike animal related to the antelopes that inhabits the Rocky Mountains of N America, having a shaggy white coat and short curved horns: *Oreamnos americanus*.

mountain laurel *noun* an evergreen shrub of eastern N America that has poisonous leathery leaves and clusters of pink or white spring-blooming flowers: *Kalmia latifolia*. Also called CALICO BUSH.

mountain lion *noun* = PUMA.

mountainous /'mowntənəs/ *adj* **1** said of a region: containing many mountains. **2** resembling a mountain; huge. ➤➤ **mountainously** *adv*.

mountain sickness *noun* = ALTITUDE SICKNESS.

mountebank /'mowntibangk/ *noun* **1** a swindler or charlatan. **2** formerly, somebody who sold quack medicines to the public, e.g. from a bench or stall. ➤➤ **mountebankery** *noun*. [Italian *montambanco*, from *monta in banco!* climb on the bench! (referring to the raised platform used to attract an audience)]

mounted *adj* **1a** riding on a horse, etc. **b** operating on horseback: *mounted police*. **2** said of a photograph, stamp, etc: on a mounting.

Mountie *or* **Mounty** /'mownti/ *noun* (*pl* **Mounties**) *informal* a member of the Royal Canadian Mounted Police.

mounting *noun* = MOUNT² (backing or support).

mounting block *noun* a block, platform with steps, or convenient stone from which a rider may mount a horse.

Mounty *noun* see MOUNTIE.

mourn /mawn/ *verb intrans* to feel or express, e.g. in a conventional manner, grief or sorrow, *esp* for a death: *a time to mourn and a time to dance* — Bible. ➤ *verb trans* to feel or express grief or sorrow for (a death, serious loss, etc). ➤➤ **mourner** *noun*. [Old English *murnan*]

mournful /'mawnf(ə)l/ *adj* **1** gloomy or sad. **2** expressing, causing, or filled with sorrow. ➤➤ **mournfully** *adv*, **mournfulness** *noun*.

mourning *noun* **1** the act or state of somebody who is mourning. **2a** an outward sign, e.g. black clothes or a black armband, of grief for a person's death: *After her husband died, she wore mourning for the rest of her life*. **b** a period of time during which signs of grief are shown.

mourning dove *noun* a wild dove of the USA, with a long pointed tail, bluish grey upper parts, and a plaintive call: *Zenaida macroura*.

mousaka /mooh'sahkə/ *noun* see MOUSSAKA.

mouse¹ /mows/ *noun* (*pl* **mice** /mies/) **1a** any of numerous species of small rodents with a pointed snout, grey to brown fur, and a long slender almost hairless tail: family Muridae. **b** the common house mouse: *Mus musculus*. **2** (*pl also* **mouses**) in computing, a small box, with a movable ball under it, that is connected to a computer and that, when moved across a desk or mat, causes a cursor to move across a VDU screen, so enabling the operator to point to and execute commands, e.g. by means of icons, or change data. **3** a timid person; *esp* a shy or very quiet girl or woman. **4** *informal* = BLACK EYE. [Old English *mūs*; related to Latin *mus*, Greek *mys*]

mouse² /mows, mowz/ *verb intrans* **1** to hunt for mice. **2** (*often* + about) to move stealthily. **3** in computing, to use a mouse to execute a command, etc. ➤ *verb trans* **1** *chiefly NAmer* (+ out) to search for (something) carefully. **2** in computing, to use a mouse to make (one's way) to an icon, menu, specified part of a VDU screen, etc.

mouse deer *noun* = CHEVROTAIN.

mouse mat *or* **mouse pad** *noun* a non-slip mat with a surface that gives better contact for the manipulation of a computer mouse than the surface of a desk does.

mouse potato *noun informal* a person who spends a large part of their leisure time using a computer, *esp* surfing the Internet or playing computer games. [modelled on COUCH POTATO]

mouser /'mowsə/ *noun* an animal, *esp* a cat, used to catch mice.

mousetrap *noun* **1** a trap for mice. **2** *Brit, informal* low-quality cheese.

mousetrapping *noun* the process of trapping an Internet user in a particular website by means of software codes that cause more of the website's pages to be displayed when the user attempts to leave the site.

mousey *adj* see MOUSY.

moussaka *or* **mousaka** /mooh'sahkə/ *noun* a Greek dish consisting of layers of minced lamb or other meat, aubergine, tomato, and cheese with a cheese or savoury custard topping. [Modern Greek *mousakas* from Turkish *musakka*]

mousse¹ /moohs/ *noun* **1** a light sweet or savoury cold dish usu containing cream, gelatin, and whipped egg whites. **2** a frothy cosmetic preparation applied to the hair to hold it in a desired style. [French *mousse* moss, froth, from late Latin *mulsa* mixture of honey and water]

mousse² *verb trans* to put mousse on (hair) in order to style.

mousseline /'moohsleen/ *noun* **1** a fine sheer fabric (e.g. of rayon) that resembles muslin. **2** a frothy sauce, e.g. a hollandaise sauce that has whipped cream or beaten eggs added to it. **3** a delicate type of blown glass. [French *mousseline* muslin: see MUSLIN]

moustache (*NAmer* **mustache**) /mə'stahsh, mə'stash/ *noun* **1** the hair growing or allowed to grow on somebody's upper lip. **2** hair or bristles round the mouth of a mammal. **3** any mark round the mouth that resembles a moustache: *a milky moustache*. ➤➤ **moustached** *adj*. [via French from Old Italian *mustaccio* from Greek *moustaki*, dimin. of *mystak-*, *mystax* upper lip, moustache]

Mousterian /mooh'stiəri·ən/ *adj* relating to or associated with a Lower Palaeolithic culture characterized by well-made flint tools. ➤➤ **Mousterian** *noun*. [French *moustérien*, named after Le Moustier, cave in Dordogne, France, where remains from this culture were found]

mousy *or* **mousey** /'mowsi/ *adj* (**mousier, mousiest**) **1** of or resembling a mouse, e.g.: **a** quiet or stealthy. **b** timid; lacking personality. **2** said of hair: light greyish brown. **3** infested with mice. ➤➤ **mousily** *adv*, **mousiness** *noun*.

mouth¹ /mowth/ *noun* (*pl* **mouths** /mowdhz/) **1a** the opening through which food passes into a person's or animal's body and through which speech, etc flows. **b** the cavity in the head bounded externally by the lips and enclosing the tongue, gums, and teeth. **c** the front part of this cavity: *He punched him in the mouth*. **2** something like a mouth, *esp* in affording entrance or exit, e.g.: **a** the place where a river enters a sea, lake, etc. **b** the opening of a cave, volcano, harbour, etc. **c** the opening of a container. **3** an individual requiring food: *There are just too many mouths to feed*. **4a** utterance: *He finally gave mouth to his feelings*. **b** a way of speaking: *He really* *does have a foul mouth.* **c** a person who speaks on behalf of another person, an organization, etc; = MOUTHPIECE (3). **5** *informal.* **a** a tendency to talk too much, *esp* boastfully; boastful talk, *esp* if not followed by action: *He's all mouth.* **b** impertinent language. **6** a grimace made with the lips. **7** a horse's response to pressure on the bit. ✳ **down in the mouth/at mouth 1** sad or dejected. **2** sulky. **keep one's mouth shut** to remain silent. **watch one's mouth** *informal* to be careful about what one says, *esp* to avoid saying something impertinent or obscene. ➤➤ **mouthed** /mowdhd/ *adj,* **mouthless** *adj,* **mouthlike** *adj.* [Old English *mūth*]

mouth² /mowdh/ *verb trans* **1** to say (something), *esp* insincerely or pompously. **2** to repeat (something) without comprehension. **3** to form (words) soundlessly with the lips. **4** to take (something) into the mouth, or move (it) around in the mouth. ➤ *verb intrans* **1** to talk insincerely or pompously. **2** (*usu* + at) to grimace.

mouthful /'mowthf(ə)l/ *noun* (*pl* **mouthfuls**) **1a** as much as the mouth will hold. **b** the amount, e.g. of food, put into the mouth at one time. **2** a small quantity. **3a** a word or phrase that is very long or difficult to pronounce. **b** *Brit, informal* a rude or angry answer or remark: *I really gave him a mouthful.* **c** *chiefly NAmer, informal* a very apt or significant comment or statement: *You sure said a mouthful there.*

mouth off /mowdh/ *verb intrans informal* **1** to express opinions or complaints loudly and forcefully. **2** to talk impertinently or abusively.

mouth organ /mowth/ *noun* a harmonica.

mouthpart /'mowthpaht/ *noun* a structure or appendage near or forming part of the mouth of an insect or other arthropod.

mouthpiece /'mowthpees/ *noun* **1** something placed at or forming a mouth. **2** a part of e.g. a musical instrument or a telephone that goes in the mouth or is put next to the mouth. **3** somebody or something that expresses or interprets another's views.

mouth-to-mouth /,mowth tə 'mowth/ *adj* denoting a method of artificial respiration in which the rescuer places his or her mouth over the victim's mouth and blows air into the lungs forcefully every few seconds to inflate them.

mouthwash /'mowthwosh/ *noun* a liquid medical preparation for cleansing and freshening the mouth and freshening the breath.

mouth-watering /mowth/ *adj* **1** stimulating or appealing to the appetite; appetizing. **2** extremely attractive. ➤➤ **mouth-wateringly** *adv.*

mouthy /'mowdhi/ *adj* (**mouthier, mouthiest**) excessively talkative or inclined to talk too much, *esp* impudently or boastfully.

movable¹ *or* **moveable** /'moohvəbl/ *adj* **1** capable of being moved. **2** said of a church festival, etc: changing date from year to year: *movable holidays.* **3** *esp* in law, denoting personal property that can be moved, e.g. the furniture in a house that has been sold. ➤➤ **movability** /-'biliti/ *noun,* **movableness** *noun,* **movably** *adv.*

movable² *or* **moveable** *noun* (*usu in pl*) *esp* in law, an item of movable personal property, as distinguished from buildings, land, etc.

movable-doh *adj* in tonic sol-fah, denoting the system of treating doh as the keynote of every major scale, ray as the second note, etc: compare FIXED-DOH.

movable feast *noun* an annual religious festival, e.g. Easter, not celebrated on the same date each year.

move¹ /moohv/ *verb intrans* **1** (*also* + along/on) to go or progress in a particular direction or to a particular place or position. **2** to change position, shape, or arrangement: *He can talk without his lips moving.* **3a** to change to a new activity, topic, etc: *We'd better move on to the next item.* **b** to change one's opinion or stance: *They seem to be moving to a more radical position.* **4a** to change one's residence, office location, school, etc. **b** to change one's job. **5** to pass one's life in a specified environment, or belong to a specified group: *She moves in the most fashionable circles.* **6a** to take action: *They waited several days before moving.* **b** to make progress: *After a slow start, things really began to move.* **7** to operate or function, *esp* mechanically. **8** (*usu* + for) to make a formal request, application, or appeal: *We move for an adjournment.* **9a** in board games, to transfer a piece from one position to another: *It's your turn to move.* **b** said of a piece: to change position in a particular way according to the rules: *Bishops move diagonally.* **10** said of goods: to change hands by being sold. **11** said of the bowels: to discharge faeces; to empty. ➤ *verb trans* **1** (*also* + along/on) to change the place or position of (somebody or something); to cause or force (somebody or something) to go or progress in a particular direction or to a particular place or

level: *The police moved the onlookers back.* **2** to change the position, shape, or arrangement of (something): *You can see him moving his lips.* **3a** to take (furniture and possessions) from one residence or location to another: *We're moving house tomorrow.* **b** to perform this service for (somebody): *We're being moved by a local removal firm.* **c** to transfer (somebody) to another place, organization, etc. **4** to put (somebody) into activity or rouse (them) up from inactivity; to prompt (somebody) to action: *The report finally moved the Government to take action.* **5** (*often* + to) to affect (somebody) in such a way as to lead to a specified show of emotion: *The story moved her to tears.* **6** to propose (something) formally: *He moved that the meeting be adjourned.* **7** to transfer (a piece in a board game) from one position to another. **8** to cause (goods) to change hands through sale or rent. **9** to cause (the bowels) to empty. [Middle English *moven* from early French *movoir* from Latin *movēre*]

move² *noun* **1a** a movement; a change of position, posture, etc: *Don't make a move! There's a snake at your feet.* **b** a way of moving, e.g. in dance, martial arts, etc. **2** a step taken so as to gain an objective; a manoeuvre: *We'll let them make the first move.* **3** a change of residence or location. **4a** the act or an instance of moving a piece, e.g. in chess. **b** the turn of a player to move. ✳ **get a move on** to hurry up. **make a move on** to make advances towards (somebody), *esp* of a sexual nature. **on the move 1** in a state of moving about from place to place: *They're constantly on the move.* **2** in a state of moving ahead or making progress: *Civilization is always on the move.* **3** very busy.

moveable¹ *adj* see MOVABLE¹.

moveable² *noun* see MOVABLE².

move in *verb intrans* **1** to take up occupation of a residence or place of work. **2a** (*often* + on) to approach and surround a place from various directions: *Police were moving in on the scene.* **b** (*often* + on) to try to take over or gain control.

movement *noun* **1a** the act or process of moving, *esp* a change of place, position, or posture. **b** a particular instance or manner of moving. **c** (*usu in pl*) an action or activity: *troop movements.* **d** (*in pl*) the activities of a person, *esp* during a specified time: *He couldn't account for his movements on the night of the robbery.* **2** an organized effort to promote an end or the body of people involved in it: *We are the true peace movement* — Margaret Thatcher. **3** a trend, *esp* in prices. **4** the moving parts of a mechanism that transmit motion. **5** in music, a unit or division having its own key, rhythmic structure, and themes and forming a separate part of an extended musical composition. **6a** the development of the action in a work of literature. **b** the quality of a book, play, etc of having a quickly moving plot. **7** the act of emptying the bowels or the faeces evacuated.

move on *verb intrans* to change one's residence or location for another.

move out *verb intrans* to leave a residence or place of work.

move over *verb intrans* **1** to move along a seat, etc in order to make room. **2** (*often* + to) to change allegiance.

mover *noun* **1** somebody or something that moves, removes, or sets something in motion. **2** the instigator or driving force behind something: *She is one of the prime movers in the anti-hunting lobby.* **3** somebody who proposes a motion formally, e.g. at a meeting. **4** *chiefly NAmer* a person or company that carries out removals.

movers and shakers *pl noun* people of power and influence, who can introduce or back new developments. [from lines in the poem 'Ode' by Arthur O'Shaughnessy d.1881, 'We are the movers and shakers of the world for ever, it seems']

move up *verb intrans* **1** to move along a seat, etc in order to make room for others. **2** to be promoted or move to a higher level.

movie /'moohvi/ *noun* **1** a cinema film. **2** (**the movies**) **a** cinema films collectively. **b** the cinema industry. [*moving picture*]

moving *adj* **1** marked by or capable of movement. **2** evoking a deep emotional response. **3** producing or transferring motion or action: *This was the moving spirit behind the scheme.* **4** relating to a change of residence or location. ➤➤ **movingly** *adv.*

moving picture *noun chiefly NAmer* a film; a movie.

moving staircase *noun* an escalator.

mow /moh/ *verb* (*past tense* **mowed**, *past part.* **mowed** *or* **mown** /mohn/) ➤ *verb trans* **1** to cut down (a crop, *esp* hay or corn); to cut (grass). **2** to cut down the grass, etc of (e.g. a field), to cut the grass of (a lawn, etc). ➤ *verb intrans* to cut down grass, etc. ➤➤ **mower** *noun,* **mowings** *pl noun.* [Old English *māwan*]

mow down *verb trans* **1** to kill, destroy, or knock down (somebody or something), *esp* in great numbers or mercilessly. **2** to overcome (an enemy, opponent, etc) swiftly and decisively.

mown /mohn/ *verb* past part. of MOW.

Mozambican /mohzəm'beek(ə)n/ *noun* a native or inhabitant of Mozambique in SE Africa. ➤➤ **Mozambican** *adj*.

Mozartian[1] *or* **Mozartean** /moh'tsahti-ən/ *adj* relating to Wolfgang Amadeus Mozart d.1791, Austrian composer, or characteristic of his music.

Mozartian[2] *or* **Mozartean** *noun* an admirer or follower of Mozart and his music.

mozzarella /motsə'relə/ *noun* a moist white unsalted unripened curd cheese. [Italian *mozzarella*, a dimin. of *mozza* a type of cheese, from *mozzare* to cut off]

mozzie /'mozi/ *noun* see MOSSIE.

MP *abbr* **1** Member of Parliament. **2** Metropolitan Police. **3** Military Police. **4** Military Policeman or -woman. **5** Mounted Police.

mp *abbr* **1** mezzo piano. **2** (*also* **m.p.**) melting point.

MP3 *noun* a standard format for compressing a sequence of sound, e.g. music, into a small file without losing the original quality of the sound, or the technology connected with this. [from .mp3, indicating files of this type; abbr of Motion Picture Experts Group-1, Audio Layer-3]

mpg *abbr* miles per gallon.

mph *abbr* miles per hour.

MPhil /,em 'fil/ *abbr* Master of Philosophy.

mpm *abbr* metres per minute.

mps *abbr* metres per second.

MPV *abbr* multipurpose vehicle.

MR *abbr* Master of the Rolls.

Mr /'mistə/ *noun* (*pl* **Messrs** /'mesəz/) **1** used as a conventional title of courtesy before a man's surname. **2** used in direct address before a man's title of office: *May I ask one more question, Mr Chairman?* **3** used before the name of a place or of a profession or activity or before some epithet to form a title applied to a male viewed or recognized as a representative of the thing indicated: *Here comes Mr Football.* [Middle English, abbr of *maister* master; *Messrs* abbr of French *Messieurs*, pl of *Monsieur*]

MRC *abbr* Brit Medical Research Council.

MRCGP *abbr* Member of the Royal College of General Practitioners.

MRCP *abbr* Member of the Royal College of Physicians.

MRCS *abbr* Member of the Royal College of Surgeons.

MRCVS *abbr* Member of the Royal College of Veterinary Surgeons.

MRI *abbr* magnetic resonance imaging.

MRM *abbr* mechanically recovered meat.

mRNA *abbr* messenger RNA.

MRP *abbr* manufacturer's recommended price.

MRPhS *abbr* Member of the Royal Pharmaceutical Society.

Mrs /'misiz/ *noun* (*pl* **Mesdames** /may'dahm/) **1a** used as a conventional title of courtesy before a married woman's surname: *I spoke to Mrs Smith.* **b** used before the name of a place or of a profession or activity or before some epithet to form a title applied to a married woman viewed or recognized as a representative of the thing indicated: *And here she is, Mrs Tennis 1999.* **2** (*often* **the/my Mrs**) *informal* a person's wife: *I took the Mrs along to the pub.* [abbr of MISTRESS; *Mesdames* from French, pl of *Madame*]

Usage note
Mrs, Ms, or Miss? See note at Ms.

MRSA *abbr* methicillin-resistant (or multiple-resistant) *Staphylococcus aureus* (a bacterium that is highly resistant to antibiotics).

MS *abbr* **1** (*also* **M.S.**) in music, left hand. **2** manuscript. **3** Master of Surgery. **4** Mauritius (international vehicle registration). **5** Mississippi (US postal abbreviation). **6** multiple sclerosis. [(sense 1) Italian *mano sinistra* left hand]

Ms /məz, miz/ *noun* used instead of Mrs or Miss, *esp* when the woman's marital status is unknown or irrelevant.

Usage note
Ms, Mrs, or Miss? Traditionally, the title *Miss* was used by a woman before marriage together with her maiden name, while *Mrs* was used after marriage together with her husband's surname: *Miss Jones became Mrs Smith*

when she married. From the 1950s onwards, the title *Ms* began to be used by women who did not wish to disclose their marital status, thought it irrelevant, or felt an all-purpose title for women equivalent to *Mr* was needed. This title was also used by some people when writing to or addressing women whose marital status was unknown: it is very useful for this purpose. *Ms* is gradually acquiring wider acceptance, especially among younger people. Some people, however, dislike its associations with feminism and insist on using or being addressed by the traditional titles.

ms *abbr* **1** millisecond. **2** manuscript.

MSB *abbr* in computing, = MOST SIGNIFICANT BIT.

MSC *abbr* Brit Manpower Services Commission.

MSc *abbr* Master of Science.

MS-DOS /,em es 'dos/ *abbr* trademark Microsoft disk operating system.

msec *abbr* millisecond.

MSF *abbr* Brit Manufacturing, Science, and Finance (trade union).

MSG *abbr* monosodium glutamate.

Msgr *abbr* **1** Monseigneur. **2** Monsignor.

MSP *abbr* **1** Member of the Scottish Parliament. **2** music service provider, a commercial company providing music via the Internet in the form of MP3 files.

MSS *or* **mss** *abbr* manuscripts.

MT *abbr* Montana (US postal abbreviation).

Mt[1] *abbr* **1** Mount. **2** Matthew (book of the Bible).

Mt[2] *abbr* the chemical symbol for meitnerium.

MTB *abbr* **1** motor torpedo boat. **2** mountain bike.

MTech /,em 'tek/ *abbr* Master of Technology.

mth *abbr* month.

mu /myooh/ *noun* the twelfth letter of the Greek alphabet (M, μ), equivalent to and transliterated as roman m. [Greek *my*]

much[1] /much/ *adj* (**more** /maw/, **most** /mohst/) **1** *chiefly formal* great in quantity or extent: *I have much pleasure in proposing this motion.* **2** used with a negative word to suggest or emphasize smallness of quantity or extent: *We don't have much money.* **3** used in questions about quantity or extent: *How much milk is there?* [Middle English *muche* large, much, from *michel, muchel* from Old English *micel, mycel*]

much[2] *adv* **1a** to a great degree or extent; considerably: *She's much happier now; Much to my surprise, John did come to the party.* **b** *formal* very: *The Queen said she was much amused by the story.* **c** by far: *He is much the fatter of the two.* **d** nearly, approximately: *He looks much the way his father did.* **e** frequently, often: *He was a much married man, having had no fewer than seven wives.* **2** used with a negative word to suggest or emphasize smallness of degree or extent: *She's not much better off than she was before.* **3** used in questions about degree or extent: *How much happier are they, though?* ✱ **much as 1** (*also* **as much as**) however much; even though: *Much as I would like to stay, it's time I was on my way.* **2** to a similar extent or degree, or in a similar way: *I would treat her much as I treat all my other students.* **much less** and certainly not: *She can't even walk, much less run.*

much[3] *noun* **1** a great quantity, amount, or part: *So little done, so much to do* — Cecil Rhodes; *The wailing went on for much of the night.* **2a** used with a negative word to suggest or emphasize smallness of amount or extent: *There's not much to do around here; He's not much of a help, is he?* **b** used with a negative word to suggest or emphasize poor quality, unimpressiveness, etc: *I don't think much of that idea; The house was not much to look at, but it had potential.* **3** used to ask questions about amount or extent: *How much did it cost?* **4** a certain amount: *I'll say this much for him, he tries.* ✱ **a bit much** *informal* rather excessive or unreasonable. **as much 1** the same quantity: *Give him as much again.* **2** that; so: *I thought as much! You've been at the biscuits again.* **make much of 1** to understand: *I can't make much of all these scribbles.* **2** to treat something as of great importance or significance: *He made much of the fact that the dog hadn't barked.* **3** to treat (somebody) as being important; to flatter or fawn on (them). **not up to much** not very good. **too much 1** *informal, dated* wonderful; exciting. **2** terrible; awful. **too much for 1** more than a match for: *They were too much for the other team and won 10-nil.* **2** beyond the endurance of: *His remarks were just too much for me and I walked out.*

muchness *noun* *informal or dated* amount or magnitude. ✱ **much of a muchness** *Brit* said of two or more things, etc: very similar;

having little to differentiate them in quality, etc: *This way is longer, but the other way is busier, so the journey times are much of a muchness.*

mucilage /'myoohsilij/ *noun* **1** a thick gelatinous substance produced by plants and obtained *esp* from seaweeds, hard when dry but swelling in water to form a slimy mass. **2** a thick sticky solution, e.g. of a gum, used *esp* as an adhesive. [Middle English *muscilage* from late Latin *mucilago* mucus, musty juice, from Latin *mucus* mucus]

mucilaginous /myoohsi'lajinəs/ *adj* **1** sticky, like glue. **2** of mucilage; full of or secreting mucilage. [late Latin *mucilaginosus* from *mucilagin-, mucilago* mucus]

muck /muk/ *noun* **1a** soft moist farmyard manure. **b** dark highly organic soil. **2** dirt or filth, *esp* if moist or slimy. **3** mire or mud. **4** *informal* coarse or disgusting speech or writing. ⟫⟫ **muckily** *adv*, **muckiness** *noun*, **mucky** *adj*. [Middle English *muk*, prob of Scandinavian origin]

muck about *verb intrans* chiefly *Brit, informal* **1** to engage in aimless or silly activity; to waste time. **2** (+ with) to interfere with or spoil (something): *The garden looked fine before they started mucking about with it.* ⟫ *verb trans* chiefly *Brit, informal* to treat (somebody) discourteously or inconsiderately, causing them inconvenience: *The hotel kept mucking us about and changing our rooms.*

muck around *verb intrans* = MUCK ABOUT.

mucker[1] *noun* *Brit, informal* a friend or pal. [MUCK IN + -ER[2]]

mucker[2] *noun* *informal* a disagreeable person. [prob alteration (influenced by *muck*) of *fucker* or from German *Mucker* hypocrite, bigot]

muck in *verb intrans* *Brit, informal* **1** to share or join in a task: *If we all mucked in together, we'd get the job done in no time.* **2** to share sleeping accommodation.

muckle *adj and noun* = MICKLE[1], MICKLE[2].

muck out *verb intrans* to remove manure or filth, *esp* from an animal's quarters. ⟫ *verb trans* to clear (e.g. a stable) of manure.

muckrake *verb intrans* to search out and publicly expose real or apparent misconduct of prominent individuals. ⟫⟫ **muckraker** *noun*, **muckraking** *noun*.

Word history

obsolete *muckrake* a rake for dung. The term was coined by President Theodore Roosevelt in 1906 to describe journalists who exposed corruption. He compared them to the 'man with the muckrake' in Part II of John Bunyan's *Pilgrim's Progress* (1684) who 'could look no way but downwards'.

mucksweat *noun* *Brit* **1** a heavy sweat. **2** a state of great anxiety or impatience.

muck up *verb trans* *informal* **1** to bungle or spoil (something). **2** chiefly *Brit* to make (something) dirty or messy.

mucoprotein /'myoohkohprohteen/ *noun* a protein found in body fluids and tissues that contains complex nitrogenous polysaccharides and a higher proportion of carbohydrate than glycoproteins.

mucosa /myooh'kohzə/ *noun* (*pl* **mucosae** /-zee/ *or* **mucosas**) = MUCOUS MEMBRANE. ⟫⟫ **mucosal** *adj*. [scientific Latin *mucosa*, fem of Latin *mucosus* mucous]

mucous /'myoohkəs/ *adj* **1** of mucus. **2** secreting or covered with mucus. [Latin *mucosus* from *mucus* nasal mucus]

mucous membrane *noun* a membrane, rich in glands secreting mucus, that lines body passages and cavities, e.g. the mouth, with openings to the exterior.

mucus /'myoohkəs/ *noun* a thick slippery secretion produced by mucous membranes, e.g. in the nose, which it moistens and protects. [Latin *mucus* nasal mucus]

mud /mud/ *noun* **1** soft wet earth or any sticky mixture of a solid and a liquid resembling this. **2** abusive or malicious remarks or charges. ✳ **here's mud in your eye** an informal and humorous drinking toast. **sling/throw mud at** to make abusive or malicious remarks about (somebody) or subject (them) to malicious charges. **somebody's name is mud** *informal* the person concerned is held in contempt or is very unpopular. [Middle English *mudde*, prob from Middle Low German *mudde*]

mudbank *noun* a bank of mud in a river or the sea.

mudbath *noun* **1** a bath in heated mud, e.g. at a spa, for the relief of rheumatism, arthritis, etc. **2** something in a muddy state or with a lot of mud: *By the second half, the goalmouth was just a mudbath.*

muddle[1] /'mudl/ *verb trans* **1a** to confuse (somebody): *Explain it more slowly! You're muddling me.* **b** to make (somebody) stupefied or thick-headed, *esp* with alcohol. **2** (*often* + up) to confuse (two or more people or things) in one's mind; to mix (them) up: *I always get 'partly' and 'partially' muddled up.* **3** (*often* + up) to get (things) out of the required arrangement and into a confused mess, etc: *I've got all these papers sorted into their appropriate piles, so don't muddle them up again.* **4** to make a mess of (something); to bungle (it). **5** chiefly *NAmer* to mix or stir (a drink) gently. ⟫ *verb intrans* (+ along/on) to proceed or get along in a confused aimless way. ⟫⟫ **muddled** *adj*, **muddler** *noun*, **muddling** *noun and adj*, **muddlingly** *adv*, **muddly** *adj*. [prob from early Dutch *moddelen* to make muddy, from *modde* mud]

muddle[2] *noun* **1** a state of confusion: *Muddle is the extra unknown personality in any committee* — Anthony Sampson. **2** a confused mess. **3** a mix-up or mistake: *There's been a muddle over the tickets.*

muddleheaded *adj* **1** mentally confused. **2** inept or bungling. ⟫⟫ **muddleheadedly** *adv*, **muddleheadedness** *noun*.

muddle through *verb intrans* to succeed in spite of incompetence or lack of understanding, method, or planning.

muddy[1] *adj* (**muddier, muddiest**) **1a** full of or covered with mud. **b** like mud: *a muddy colour.* **c** not clear; cloudy: *a muddy liquid.* **2a** lacking in clarity or brightness: *He had only a rather muddy recollection of what had happened.* **b** obscure in meaning; muddled, confused. ⟫⟫ **muddily** *adv*, **muddiness** *noun*. [MUD + -Y[1]]

muddy[2] *verb trans* (**muddies, muddied, muddying**) to make (something) dirty, stained, cloudy, dull, or confused: *Don't muddy the clean floor; He always brings up irrelevant points that muddy the issues.*

mudfish *noun* (*pl* **mudfishes** *or collectively* **mudfish**) **1** any of various species of fishes that burrow into mud in order to survive drought: *Protopterus annectens* and members of the genus *Neochanna.* **2** = BOWFIN.

mudflap *noun* a flap suspended behind the wheel of a vehicle to prevent mud, splashes, etc being thrown up.

mudflat *noun* (*also in pl*) a muddy area of ground exposed at low tide but covered at high tide.

mudguard *noun* a metal or plastic guard over the wheel of a bicycle, motorcycle, etc to deflect or catch mud.

mudlark *noun* **1** *orig* a destitute child in Victorian London, *esp* one who tried to find useful or saleable objects in the tidal mud of the Thames. **2** anyone who tries to find useful or saleable objects in river mud.

mudpack *noun* a face-pack containing fuller's earth.

mud puppy *noun* a large American salamander that has bright red external gills and a grey to brown body usu marked with bluish black spots: *Necturus maculosus.*

mudskipper *noun* any of several species of small fishes of the goby family of Asia and Polynesia that have fleshy modified front fins enabling them to leave the water and move about actively on mud: genus *Periopthalmodon* and other genera.

mudslinging *noun* directing offensive epithets, invective, and scandalous allusions or charges against a political opponent, competitor, etc. ⟫⟫ **mudslinger** *noun*.

mudstone *noun* a hardened shale produced by the consolidation of mud.

muesli /'m(y)oohzli/ *noun* (*pl* **mueslis**) a dish of Swiss origin, usu eaten at breakfast, consisting of rolled oats, dried fruit, nuts, grated apple, etc. [Swiss German *Müsli* from German *Mus* soft food, pulp + *-li* (German *-lein*) dimin. suffix]

muezzin /mooh'ezin/ *noun* in Islam, a mosque official who calls the faithful to prayer at fixed daily times, usu from a minaret: compare IMAM. [Arabic *mu'adhdhin* one who calls people to prayer]

muff[1] /muf/ *noun* **1** a warm cylindrical wrap in which both hands are placed. **2** *coarse slang* a woman's genitalia. [Dutch *mof* from early French *moufle* mitten, from late Latin *muffula*]

muff[2] *verb trans* **1** to handle (something) awkwardly; to bungle (an attempt, etc). **2a** to fail to hold (a ball) when attempting a catch. **b** to bungle (a catch). [perhaps from MUFF[1]]

muff[3] *noun* **1** a failure to hold a ball in attempting a catch. **2** any bungled or failed attempt. **3** *informal* a timid, awkward or incompetent person, *esp* in sports: *I was a hopeless muff at tennis.*

muffin /'mufin/ *noun* **1** in Britain, a light round yeast-leavened bun usu split into two, toasted and buttered. **2** in the USA and Canada, a round sweet individual-sized cake. [origin unknown]

muffle[1] /'mufl/ *verb trans* **1** (*often* + up) to wrap (somebody, oneself, or something) up so as to conceal or protect (them, oneself, or it): *muffled themselves in the cocoon of middle-aged habit and convention* — Aldous Huxley. **2a** to wrap or pad (something) to dull the sound it makes. **b** to deaden the sound of (a gun, drum, hammer, etc). **3a** to keep down or suppress (something): *muffled laughter*. **b** to prevent (somebody) from expressing something. ➤ *verb intrans* (+ up) to wrap up for warmth or protection. [Middle English *muflen*, perhaps from early French *moufle* mitten]

muffle[2] *noun* a chamber in a furnace or kiln where articles can be heated without direct contact with flames or combustion products. [French *moufle*, literally 'mitten']

muffler *noun* **1** a warm scarf worn round the neck. **2** a device for deadening sound, e.g. on a drum, piano, bell, etc. **3** *NAmer* a silencer for a motor vehicle.

mufti[1] /'mufti/ *noun* (*pl* **muftis**) a professional Muslim jurist. [Arabic *muftī*]

mufti[2] *noun* civilian or ordinary clothes worn by somebody who is usually in uniform, *esp* a member of the armed forces or the police force. [prob from MUFTI[1]]

mug[1] /mug/ *noun* **1a** a large usu cylindrical drinking cup. **b** = MUG-FUL. **2** *informal* the face or mouth of somebody. **3** *Brit, informal* somebody who is easily deceived; a sucker. [prob of Scandinavian origin]

mug[2] *verb trans* (**mugged, mugging**) to assault and rob (somebody), *esp* in the street or some other public place. ➤ **mugger** *noun*, **mugging** *noun*. [prob from obsolete *mug* to punch in the face, from MUG[1]]

mugful /'mugf(ə)l/ *noun* (*pl* **mugfuls**) the amount a mug holds or could hold.

muggins /'muginz/ *noun* (*pl* **mugginses** or **muggins**) *informal* a stupid or gullible person, *esp* used when referring to oneself: *Muggins here lost her passport*. [prob from the surname *Muggins*, influenced by MUG[1]: compare JUGGINS]

muggy /'mugi/ *adj* (**muggier, muggiest**) said of the weather: warm, damp, and close. ➤➤ **muggily** *adv*, **mugginess** *noun*. [English dialect *mug* drizzle, prob of Scandinavian origin]

mug's game *noun chiefly Brit, informal* an activity that is liable to involve loss, failure, or danger: *Gambling is a mug's game*. [MUG[1] (3)]

mug shot *noun informal* a photograph of a person's face, *esp* one used by police for identification purposes. [MUG[1] (2)]

mug up *verb trans Brit, informal* to study (something) hard, e.g. before an exam. ➤ *verb intrans* (*often* + on) to study something hard; to swot. [origin unknown]

mugwort *noun* a tall Eurasian composite plant with small brownish flower heads that is common on waste ground and in hedgerows: *Artemisia vulgaris*. [Old English *mucgwyrt*, from *mucg-* (prob related to Old English *mycg* midge) + *wyrt* wort]

mugwump /'mugwump/ *noun chiefly NAmer* a person who remains aloof or apart, *esp* an independent in politics. [obsolete slang *mugwump* important person, from Algonquian *mugguomp* or *mugquomp* a great chief or war leader]

Muhammadan or **Mohammedan** /mə'hamid(ə)n/ *adj dated, now usu considered offensive* of Muhammad or Islam; = MUSLIM. ➤➤ **Muhammadan** *noun*, **Muhammadanism** *noun*. [named after *Muhammad* d.632, Arab prophet and founder of Islam + -AN[1] (1)]

mujahedin or **mujaheddin** or **mujahedeen** or **mujahideen** or **mujahidin** /,moohjahə'deen, -he'deen/ *pl noun* Islamic resistance fighters opposing the Soviet-backed government and Soviet troops in Afghanistan in the 1980s. ➤➤ **mujahedin** *adj*. [Arabic *mujāhidīn* from *mujāhadah* striving, struggling, from *jahada* to strive, struggle]

mukluk /'mukluk/ *noun* a boot, usu made of sealskin or reindeer skin, traditionally worn by North American Inuits. [Yupik *maklak* large seal]

mulatto /myooh'latoh/ *noun* (*pl* **mulattoes** or **mulattos**) a person who has one parent who is black and one who is white: *Grape is my mulatto mother in this frozen whited country* — Ted Hughes. ➤➤ **mulatto** *adj*. [Spanish *mulato* from *mulo* mule, from Latin *mulus*]

mulberry /'mulb(ə)ri/ *noun* (*pl* **mulberries**) **1a** an edible red, purple, or white fruit resembling a raspberry. **b** any of several species of trees of the fig family that bear this fruit: genus *Morus*. **2** a dark purple or purplish black colour. ➤➤ **mulberry** *adj*. [Middle English *murberie, mulberie*, from Old French *moure* (from Latin *morum*) + Middle English *berie* berry]

mulch[1] /mulch/ *noun* a protective covering, e.g. of compost, spread on the ground to control weeds, enrich the soil, etc. [perhaps from English dialect *melch* soft, mild; prob from Old English *melsc* mellow]

mulch[2] *verb trans* **1** to put mulch on or round (e.g. a plant). **2** to treat (ground or soil) with mulch.

mulct[1] /mulkt/ *noun formal* a fine or penalty. [Latin *multa, mulcta*]

mulct[2] *verb trans formal* **1** to punish (somebody) by a fine. **2a** to swindle (somebody). **b** to obtain (something) by swindling.

mule[1] /myoohl/ *noun* **1a** the sterile offspring of a mating between a female horse and an ass: compare HINNY[1]. **b** a sterile hybrid animal or plant, *esp* a cross between a canary and another bird. **2** a very stubborn person. **3** a machine for simultaneously drawing and twisting fibre into yarn or thread and winding it onto spindles. [Old English *mūl*, reinforced in Middle English by Old French *mul*, from Latin *mulus*]

mule[2] *noun* a backless shoe or slipper. [early French *mule* a kind of slipper, from Latin *mulleus* shoe worn by magistrates]

muleta /m(y)ooh'laytə/ *noun* a small cape attached to a stick and used by a matador during the final stage of a bullfight. [Spanish *muleta* crutch, muleta, dimin. of *mula* she-mule, from Latin *mula*, fem of *mulus*]

muleteer /myoohlə'tiə/ *noun* somebody who drives mules. [French *muletier* from *mulet*, dimin. of Old French *mul* mule]

mulga /'mulgə/ *noun* (*pl* **mulgas** or *collectively* **mulga**) **1** a shrubby plant that is widespread in the drier parts of Australia and is often used as fodder: *Acacia aneura*. **2** the wood of this tree. **3** land covered with this plant. **4** (**the mulga**) *Aus, informal* the outback. [native name in Australia]

muliebrity /myoohli'ebriti/ *noun chiefly literary* **1** the quality or status of being a woman; femininity. **2** womanhood. [late Latin *muliebritat-, muliebritas*, from Latin *muliebris* of a woman, from *mulier* woman]

mulish /'myoohlish/ *adj* unreasonably and inflexibly obstinate. ➤➤ **mulishly** *adv*, **mulishness** *noun*. [MULE[1] + -ISH]

mull[1] /mul/ *verb trans* to heat, sweeten, and flavour (e.g. wine or beer) with spices. [origin unknown]

mull[2] *noun* used *esp* in place names: a headland or peninsula in Scotland: *Mull of Galloway*. [Middle English (Scots) *mole*, prob from Old Norse *mūli* projecting crag, snout, muzzle]

mull[3] *noun* crumbly soil humus forming a layer of mixed organic matter and mineral soil and merging into the underlying mineral soil. [German *Mull* from Danish *muld* from Old Norse *mold* dust, soil]

mull[4] *noun* a soft fine sheer fabric of cotton, silk, or rayon. [by shortening and alteration from earlier *mulmul* muslin, from Hindi *malmal*]

mullah /'mulə, 'moolə/ *noun* a Muslim of a quasi-clerical class trained in traditional Islamic law and doctrine. ➤➤ **mullahism** *noun*. [Turkish *molla* and Persian and Hindi *mulla*, from Arabic *mawlā*]

mullein or **mullen** /'mulən/ *noun* any of several species of plants of the figwort family, most of which have woolly leaves and spikes of usu yellow flowers: genus *Verbascum*. [Middle English *moleyne* from Old French *moleine*; of Celtic origin]

muller /'mulə/ *noun* a pestle usu for grinding substances, e.g. artists' pigments, on a slab. [Middle English *molour*, prob from *mullen* to grind]

Müllerian mimicry /moo'liəri·ən, myooh-/ *noun* mimicry between two or more inedible or dangerous species, considered to reduce the difficulties of recognition by potential predators: compare BATESIAN MIMICRY. [named after Fritz *Müller* d.1897, German zoologist]

mullet /'mulit/ *noun* (*pl* **mullets** or *collectively* **mullet**) any of several species of red, golden, or grey food fishes, many of which have two barbels (thin sensory projections; see BARBEL[2]) on the chin: families Mullidae and Mugilidae. [Middle English *molet* from early French *mulet* via Latin from Greek *myllos*]

mulligatawny /ˌmuligəˈtawni/ *noun* a rich meat soup of Indian origin seasoned with curry. [Tamil *mi akutaṇṇi* a strongly seasoned soup, from *mi aku* pepper + *taṇṇi* water]

mullion[1] /ˈmulyən/ *noun* a slender vertical bar placed *esp* between panes or panels, e.g. of a window or door: compare TRANSOM (ID). [prob alteration of earlier *monial* mullion, from Middle English *moynel, moniel* from early French *moinel* middle]

mullion[2] *verb trans* (**mullioned, mullioning**) to fit a mullion or mullions in (a window, etc).

mullock /ˈmulək/ *noun* **1** *Aus, NZ* mining refuse. **2** *Brit dialect, Aus, NZ* rubbish; nonsense. *** poke mullock at** to make fun of or ridicule (somebody or something). [Middle English *mullok* rubbish, refuse, from *mul, mol* dust]

mull over *verb trans* to consider (something) at length. [Middle English *mullen* to grind, from *mul, mol* dust]

mulloway /ˈmuləway/ *noun* (*pl* **mulloways** or collectively **mulloway**) a large predatory edible marine fish that lives in Australian coastal waters: *Johnius antarctica*.

multi- *comb. form* forming words, with the meanings: **1a** many; multiple; much: *multistorey*. **b** more than two: *multilateral; multivalent*. **c** more than one: *multiparous*. **2** many times over: *multimillionaire*. [Middle English, via French from Latin *multus* much, many]

multiaccess /multiˈakses/ *adj* said of a computer system: allowing two or more users simultaneous access and use.

multicolour /ˈmultikulə/ (*NAmer* **multicolor**) *adj* = MULTI-COLOURED.

multicoloured /ˈmultikuləd/ (*NAmer* **multicolored**) *adj* having or composed of various colours.

multicultural /multiˈkulchərəl/ *adj* relating to, composed of, designed for, promoting, or denoting a combination of several distinct cultures: *a multicultural urban environment*. >>> **multiculturalism** *noun*, **multiculturalist** *noun*, **multiculturally** *adv*.

multifaceted /multiˈfasitid/ *adj* having several distinct facets or aspects: *He has a brain that is well able to cope with the multifaceted problems of foreign policy*.

multifactorial /ˌmultifakˈtawri-əl/ *adj* having or involving a variety of elements: *a multifactorial study*. >>> **multifactorially** *adv*.

multifarious /multiˈfeəri-əs/ *adj* having or occurring in great variety; diverse. >>> **multifariously** *adv*, **multifariousness** *noun*. [Latin *multifarius*, from MULTI- + -*farius* (related to *facere* to make, do)]

multiflora /multiˈflawrə/ *noun* an orig Chinese and Japanese variety of rose growing as a shrub, with clusters of small white or pink flowers: *Rosa multiflora*. It is the ancestor of many garden varieties such as the floribunda roses.

multiform /ˈmultifawm/ *adj* having many forms or appearances. >>> **multiformity** /-ˈfawmiti/ *noun*. [French *multiforme* from Latin *multiformis*, from MULTI- + -*formis* -FORM]

multigym /ˈmultijim/ *noun* an exercise apparatus with a variety of weights and levers, used for toning the muscles of the body.

multilateral /multiˈlat(ə)rəl/ *adj* **1** participated in by more than two parties. **2** having many sides. >>> **multilaterally** *adv*.

multilayer /multiˈlayə/ *adj* = MULTILAYERED.

multilayered /multiˈlayəd/ *adj* having or involving several distinct layers, strata, or levels: *the multilayered tropical rain forest*.

multilingual /multiˈlinggwəl/ *adj* **1** written or spoken in several languages. **2** using or able to use several languages: *a multilingual translator*. >>> **multilingualism** *noun*, **multilingually** *adv*.

multimedia /multiˈmeedi-ə/ *noun* (*often used before a noun*) the use of several means of expression or communication, e.g.: **a** the use of different media, such as television, video, etc, in education, marketing, etc: *multimedia resource materials*. **b** the use of different materials and media as a means of artistic expression. **c** the handling of various media, such as text, graphics, and sound, by a computer.

multimedia messaging or **multimedia messaging service** *noun* the transmission of text, sound, and images by mobile phone: compare PHOTO MESSAGING, PICTURE MESSAGING. >>> **multimedia message** *noun*.

multimillionaire /ˌmultimilyəˈneə/ *noun* somebody whose wealth is estimated at many millions of money units.

multinational[1] /multiˈnash(ə)nəl/ *adj* **1** of more than two nations: *a multinational alliance; a multinational society*. **2** operating or having branches, etc in more than two countries: *a multinational company*.

multinational[2] *noun* a multinational company.

multipack /ˈmultipak/ *noun* a pack containing several items of the same type, e.g. bottles, cans, batteries, etc, sold as a single unit at a lower price than the items would cost if sold separately.

multiparous /mulˈtipərəs/ *adj* **1** producing many or more than one offspring at a birth. **2** having given birth one or more times previously. [late Latin *multiparus*, from MULTI- + -*parus* -PAROUS]

multipartite /multiˈpahtiet/ *adj* **1** having many parts or sections. **2** = MULTILATERAL, MULTIPARTY. [Latin *multipartitus*, from MULTI- + *partitus*, past part. of *partire* to divide, from *part-, pars* part]

multiparty /multiˈpahti/ *adj* of or involving more than two political parties: *Our two-party system cloaks a multiparty reality* — Dean Acheson.

multiphase /ˈmultifayz/ *adj* = MULTIPHASIC.

multiphasic /multiˈfayzik/ *adj* having various phases or elements.

multiple[1] /ˈmultipl/ *adj* **1** consisting of, including, or involving more than one part, element, etc. **2** many; manifold: *multiple achievements*. **3** shared by many: *multiple ownership*. **4** having several functions or uses. **5** said of a fruit: formed by coalescence of the ripening ovaries of several flowers: *A pineapple is a multiple fruit*. [via French from Latin *multiplex*, from MULTI- + -*plex* fold]

multiple[2] *noun* **1** the product of a quantity by an integer: *35 is a multiple of seven*. **2** *chiefly Brit* = MULTIPLE STORE.

multiple-choice *adj* having several answers from which one is to be chosen: *a multiple-choice exam question*.

multiple sclerosis *noun* a chronic condition characterized by progressively developing partial or complete paralysis and jerking muscle tremor resulting from the formation of patches of hardened tissue in nerves of the brain and spinal cord that have lost their myelin.

multiple store *noun chiefly Brit* a chain store.

multiple unit *noun* a train that has one or more carriages containing motors for propulsion and is used mainly for local services.

multiplex[1] /ˈmultipleks/ *adj* **1** manifold; multiple. **2** said of a cinema building: having several auditoriums. **3** involving, relating to, or denoting a communications system allowing several messages to be transmitted simultaneously by the same circuit or channel. [Latin *multiplex*: see MULTIPLE[1]]

multiplex[2] *noun* **1** a cinema building with several auditoriums screening various films. **2** a multiplex communications system.

multiplex[3] *verb* to send (messages or signals) by a multiplex system. >>> **multiplexer** or **multiplexor** *noun*.

multiplicable /multiˈplikəbl/ *adj* capable of being multiplied.

multiplicand /ˌmultipliˈkand/ *noun* a number that is to be multiplied by another (the multiplier). [Latin *multiplicandus*, gerundive of *multiplicare*]

multiplication /ˌmultipliˈkaysh(ə)n/ *noun* **1** the act or process or an instance of multiplying or being multiplied. **2** a mathematical operation that at its simplest is an abbreviated process of adding an integer to itself a specified number of times (e.g. $2 \times 3 = 2 + 2 + 2$) and that is extended to other numbers in accordance with laws that are valid for integers. >>> **multiplicative** /-ˈplikətiv/ *adj*, **multiplicatively** /-ˈplikətivli/ *adv*. [Middle English *multiplicacioun* via French from Latin *multiplication-, multiplicatio*, from *multiplicatus*, past part. of *multiplicare* to multiply]

multiplication sign *noun* the symbol (×) denoting that the quantities on either side of it are to be multiplied together.

multiplication table *noun* any of a number of tables that show the results of multiplying two numbers together.

multiplicity /multiˈplisiti/ *noun* (*pl* **multiplicities**) **1** the quality or state of being multiple or various. **2** a great number: *a multiplicity of errors*. [early French *multiplicité* from late Latin *multiplicitat-, multiplicitas* from Latin *multiplic-, multiplex* multiple]

multiplier /ˈmultiplie-ə/ *noun* **1** a number by which another number (the multiplicand) is multiplied. **2** an instrument or device for multiplying or intensifying some effect. **3** a person or thing that multiplies, e.g. a key-operated machine or mechanism or circuit on a machine that multiplies figures and records the products. **4** the ratio between the total increase in national income arising from the change in one of the components of aggregate demand, e.g. investment, government expenditure, or exports, and the change in that component. [MULTIPLY[1] + -ER[2]]

multiply[1] /'multiplie/ *verb* (**multiplies, multiplied, multiplying**) ➤ *verb trans* **1** to increase (people, things, etc) in number, *esp* greatly. **2a** to combine (numbers) by multiplication: *Multiply seven and eight.* **b** (*usu in passive*) to combine a number with (another number) by multiplication: *7 multiplied by 8 is 56.* ➤ *verb intrans* **1a** to become greater in number; spread. **b** to breed or propagate. **2** to perform multiplication. ➤➤ **multipliable** *adj.* [Middle English *multiplien* from Old French *multiplier* from Latin *multiplicare*, from *multiplic-, multiplex* multiple]

multiply[2] /'multipli/ *adv* in a multiple manner; in several ways.

multiprocessing /multi'prohsesing/ *noun* the processing of several computer programs at the same time, *esp* such processing done by a computer system with several processors sharing a single memory.

multiprocessor /multi'prohsesə/ *noun* a computer system consisting of several processors sharing a single memory, so allowing MULTIPROCESSING.

multiprogramming /multi'prohgraming/ *noun* a technique for executing several independent computer programs simultaneously, e.g. by sequentially taking one instruction from each program.

multipronged /multi'prongd/ *adj* having several distinct aspects or elements.

multipurpose /multi'puhpəs/ *adj* serving several purposes.

multiracial /multi'raysh(ə)l/ *adj* composed of, involving, or representing various races. ➤➤ **multiracialism** *noun.*

multistage /'multistayj/ *adj* **1** having successive operating stages, *esp* having propulsion units that operate in turn: *multistage rockets.* **2** conducted in stages: *a multistage investigation.* **3** said of a pump, turbine, etc: having more than one rotor.

multistorey[1] /multi'stawri/ *adj* said of a building: having several storeys.

multistorey[2] *noun* (*pl* **multistoreys**) a multistorey car park.

multitasking /multi'tahsking/ *noun* the execution of a number of tasks simultaneously by a computer.

multitrack /multi'trak/ *adj* of or involving several separately recorded sound tracks.

multitude /'multityoohd/ *noun* **1** a great number; a host. **2** a crowd. **3** (**the multitude**) ordinary people; the masses. **4** the state of being many. [Middle English via French from Latin *multitudin-, multitudo,* from *multus* much]

multitudinous /multi'tyoohdinəs/ *adj formal* **1** composed of a multitude of individuals. **2** existing in a great multitude; numerous. **3** existing in or consisting of innumerable elements or aspects. ➤➤ **multitudinously** *adv,* **multitudinousness** *noun.*

multivalent /multi'vaylənt/ *adj* **1** = POLYVALENT. **2** having many values, meanings, or appeals. ➤➤ **multivalence** *noun,* **multivalency** /-si/ *noun.*

multiverse /'multivuhs/ *noun* a multiple universe, comprising a possibly infinite multiplicity of universes existing beside our own universe.

mum[1] /mum/ *noun chiefly Brit, informal* = MOTHER[1]. [short for MUMMY[1]]

mum[2] *adj* silent; not divulging information: *We'll need to keep mum about this.* ✴ **mum's the word** do not tell anyone about this. [prob imitative of a sound made with closed lips]

mum[3] *verb intrans* (**mummed, mumming**) to take part in mumming. [see MUMMING]

mumble[1] /'mumbl/ *verb trans and intrans* to speak or say (words) in a low and indistinct voice. ➤➤ **mumbler** *noun,* **mumbling** *adj and noun,* **mumblingly** *adv.* [Middle English *momelen,* of imitative origin]

mumble[2] *noun* something that is difficult to understand because it is said in a low and indistinct voice.

mumbo jumbo /,mumboh 'jumboh/ *noun* **1** elaborate but meaningless ritual. **2** meaningless or complicated activity or language that obscures and confuses. [*Mumbo Jumbo,* an idol or deity once held to have been worshipped in Africa]

mu-meson /myooh 'meezon/ *noun* = MUON.

mummer /'mumə/ *noun* **1** a person who takes part in mumming. **2** *chiefly archaic, derog or humorous* an actor in the theatre.

mummery /'muməri/ *noun* (*pl* **mummeries**) **1** a performance of mumming. **2** an absurd or pretentious ceremony or performance.

mummify /'mumifie/ *verb* (**mummifies, mummified, mummifying**) ➤ *verb trans* **1** to embalm and dry (the body of a dead animal or human being). **2** to cause (something) to dry up and shrivel. **3** to preserve (something) outdated or in an outdated form: *mummified customs that have long outlasted their usefulness* — Dean Inge. ➤ *verb intrans* to dry up and shrivel like a mummy. ➤➤ **mummification** /-fi'kaysh(ə)n/ *noun.*

mumming *noun* **1** the practice of performing in a traditional pantomime. **2** the custom of going about merrymaking in disguise during festivals. [Middle English *mommyng* from *mommen* to perform in a pantomime, from early French *momer* to go masked]

mummy[1] /'mumi/ *noun* (*pl* **mummies**) *chiefly Brit, informal* an affectionate name for one's mother. [baby talk, variant of MAMA, MAMMA[1]]

mummy[2] *noun* (*pl* **mummies**) **1** a body embalmed for burial in the manner of the ancient Egyptians. **2** an unusually well-preserved dead body. [Middle English *mummie* powdered parts of a mummified body used as a drug, from early French *momie* from late Latin *mumia* mummy, powdered mummy, from Arabic *mūmiyah* bitumen, mummy, from Persian *mūm* wax]

mumps /mumps/ *pl noun* (*treated as sing. or pl*) an infectious viral disease marked by swelling of the parotid glands and mainly affecting children. [pl of obsolete *mump* grimace]

mumsy /'mumzi/ *adj* (**mumsier, mumsiest**) *Brit, informal* **1** warm and sympathetic; motherly. **2** homely; comfortable. **3** dowdy and old-fashioned. [MUM[1] + -*sy* (as in *flimsy*)]

mun. *abbr* municipal.

munch /munch/ *verb* to chew (food) with a crunching sound and visible movement of the jaws. ➤➤ **muncher** *noun.* [Middle English *monchen,* prob of imitative origin]

Munchausen's syndrome /'moonsh,howzənz, 'munsh-/ *noun* a psychiatric disorder in which sufferers pretend to have various serious illnesses in order to get medical treatment, often in hospital. To this end, they sometimes inflict severe injuries on their bodies or describe their symptoms so accurately that surgery is required. ✴ **Munchausen's syndrome by proxy** a similar psychiatric disorder in which sufferers harm other people, usu children, to attract medical attention. [named after Baron *Munchausen,* the eponymous hero of a book (1785) of fantastic stories about his daring but implausible exploits]

munchies /'munchiz/ *pl noun* **1** (*usu* **the munchies**) *informal* a craving for food. **2** snacks of various kinds.

mundane /mun'dayn/ *adj* **1** practical and ordinary, *esp* to the point of dull familiarity. **2** of this world, e.g. in contrast to heaven. ➤➤ **mundanely** *adv,* **mundaneness** *noun,* **mundanity** *noun.* [Middle English *mondeyne* from early French *mondain* from late Latin *mundanus* from Latin *mundus* world]

mung bean /mung/ *noun* **1** a small edible green or yellow bean grown in tropical climates. **2** the erect bushy plant that bears this bean, grown *esp* as the chief source of bean sprouts: *Vigna radiata.* [Hindi *mūng* from Sanskrit *mudga*]

municipal /myooh'nisipl/ *adj* **1a** of a municipality. **b** relating to, denoting, or having local self-government. **2** restricted to one locality. ➤➤ **municipally** *adv.* [Latin *municipalis* from *municip-, municeps* inhabitant of a municipality, literally 'undertaker of duties', from *munus* duty, service + *capere* to take]

municipal building *noun* (*also in pl*) a building where the council and administrative staff of a town, etc work.

municipalise *verb trans* see MUNICIPALIZE.

municipality /,myoohnisi'paliti/ *noun* (*pl* **municipalities**) **1** a political unit, such as a town, city, or district, having corporate status and some self-government. **2** the governing body of such a unit.

municipalize or **municipalise** *verb trans* **1** to invest control of (some function, etc) in a municipality. **2** to make (a town, district, etc) a municipality. ➤➤ **municipalization** /-'zaysh(ə)n/ *noun.*

munificent /myooh'nifis(ə)nt/ *adj formal* **1** giving or bestowing with great generosity. **2** characterized by great liberality. ➤➤ **munificence** *noun,* **munificently** *adv.* [Latin *munificent-,* from *munificus* generous, from *munus* service, gift]

muniments /'myoohnimənts/ *pl noun* in law, documents kept as evidence of title or privilege. [Middle English via Old French from Latin *munimentum* defence, from *munire* to fortify]

munition /myooh'nish(ə)n/ *verb trans* to supply (e.g. troops) with munitions. [via French from Latin *munition-, munitio* from *munitus*, past part. of *munire* to fortify]

munitions *pl noun* armaments, ammunition, military equipment, stores, etc.

Munro /mun'roh/ *noun* (*pl* **Munros**) a British mountain over 3000 feet (914.4 metres) in height. [named after Sir Hugh *Munro* d.1919, who compiled a list of such mountains in Scotland; the term orig applied only to Scottish mountains]

muntjac or **muntjak** /'muntjak/ *noun* any of several species of small deer of SE Asia, India, and China, with brown coats, short horns, and a cry like a dog's bark: genus *Muntiacus*. [prob modification of Javanese *mindjangan* deer]

muon /'myooh·on/ *noun* an unstable elementary particle similar to but heavier than the electron, that occurs *esp* in cosmic rays. Also called MU-MESON. ➤➤ **muonic** /myooh'onik/ *adj*. [contraction of *mu-meson*, from *mu* (taken as a symbol for *meson*, and used to distinguish it from the short-lived pi-meson, i.e. pion)]

mural¹ /'myooərəl/ *noun* a work of art, e.g. a painting, applied directly onto a wall. ➤➤ **muralist** *noun*. [Latin *muralis* from *murus* wall]

mural² *adj* of, resembling, or applied to a wall.

murder¹ /'muhdə/ *noun* **1** the crime of unlawfully and intentionally killing somebody: compare MANSLAUGHTER. **2** *informal* something that is very difficult, dangerous, or disagreeable: *It was murder trying to find a parking space.* ✴ **get away with murder** *informal* to do whatever one likes without being punished or having to face the consequences. **scream/yell/cry blue/bloody murder** *informal* to make a huge fuss or a loud protest: *The fans will scream blue murder if the price of tickets goes up again.* [Old English *morthor*, reinforced in Middle English by Old French *murdre*]

murder² *verb* (**murdered, murdering**) ➤ *verb trans* **1** to kill (somebody) unlawfully and intentionally. **2** to slaughter (somebody or something) brutally. **3a** to destroy (something). **b** *informal* to mutilate, mangle, or ruin (something): *She absolutely murdered the Chopin piece.* **c** *informal* to beat (a person, team, etc) comprehensively: *They murdered the opposition.* **d** *informal* to eat or drink (something) with enthusiasm: *I could murder a pizza.* ➤ *verb intrans* to commit murder. ➤➤ **murderer** *noun*, **murderess** /-ris/ *noun*.

murderous /'muhd(ə)rəs/ *adj* **1a** having the purpose or capability of murder. **b** characterized by or causing murder or bloodshed. **2** *informal*. **a** fiercely unpleasant; strong: *I don't know how people survive in that murderous heat.* **b** dangerous: *They followed a narrow murderous track over the mountains.* ➤➤ **murderously** *adv*, **murderousness** *noun*.

murex /'myooəreks/ *noun* (*pl* **murices** /'myooəriseez/ or **murexes**) a spiny-shelled tropical marine gastropod mollusc that yields a purple dye: genus *Murex*. [from the genus name, from Latin *murex* purple fish]

muriatic acid /myooəri'atik/ *noun archaic* = HYDROCHLORIC ACID. ➤➤ **muriate** /'myooəri·ət, -ayt/ *noun*. [French *acide muriatique* from Latin *muriaticus* pickled in brine, from *muria* brine]

murices /'myooəriseez/ *noun* pl of MUREX.

murine /'myooərien, -rin/ *adj* of mice, rats, and similar rodents. [Latin *murinus* from *mur-, mus* mouse]

murk¹ or **mirk** /muhk/ *noun* **1** gloom; darkness. **2** fog. [Middle English *mirke*, prob from Old Norse *myrkr*]

murk² or **mirk** *adj Scot or archaic* dark and gloomy.

murky *adj* (**murkier, murkiest**) **1a** dark and gloomy: *a murky night.* **b** said of air: foggy; misty. **c** said of water: cloudy, muddy, or dirty. **2** obscure or unknown but probably deliberately so in order to conceal something dishonest, immoral, unfavourable, etc: *The newspapers started to investigate his murky past.* **3** deliberately vague or impenetrable: *murky official rhetoric.* ➤➤ **murkily** *adv*, **murkiness** *noun*.

murmur¹ /'muhmə/ *noun* **1a** a low indistinct continuous sound. **b** a subdued or gentle utterance. **c** a half-suppressed or muttered complaint. **2** an atypical sound of the heart indicating an abnormality. ✴ **without a murmur** without complaining. [Middle English *murmure* via French from Latin *murmur* murmur, roar, of imitative origin]

murmur² *verb intrans* **1** to make a murmur. **2** to complain or grumble. ➤ *verb trans* to say (something) in a murmur: *He murmured an apology for being late.* ➤➤ **murmurer** *noun*, **murmuring** *adj and noun*, **murmuringly** *adv*.

murmurous /'muhmərəs/ *adj* **1** filled with or making murmurs. **2** low and indistinct. ➤➤ **murmurously** *adv*.

murphy /'muhfi/ *noun* (*pl* **murphies**) *informal* a potato. [*Murphy*, a common Irish surname; from the potato having formerly been the staple food of Ireland]

Murphy's law *noun informal* a facetious principle that states that, if it is possible for something to go wrong or turn out badly, then it will do just that. Also called SOD'S LAW. [from the surname *Murphy*]

murrain /'murin/ *noun* **1** any of various highly infectious diseases, e.g. red water and anthrax, that affect cattle and other domestic animals. **2** *archaic* a plague, *esp* one affecting domestic animals or plants. [Middle English *moreyne* from early French *morine* from *morir* to die, from Latin *mori*]

murther¹ /'muhdhə/ *noun archaic or dialect* = MURDER¹: *I'll have these players play something like the murther of my father before mine uncle* — Shakespeare.

murther² *verb trans and intrans* (**murthered, murthering**) *archaic* = MURDER².

mus. *abbr* **1** museum. **2** music. **3** musical. **4** musician.

MusB /,mus 'bee/ *abbr* Bachelor of Music. [Latin *Musicae Baccalaureus*]

Mus Bac /,mus 'bak/ *abbr* = MusB.

Muscadet /'muskəday (*French* myskadɛ)/ *noun* **1** a variety of grape used in the production of very dry white wine, *esp* near Nantes in NE France. **2** a wine produced from this grape. [via French from Provençal *muscadet*, a variety of grape, from *muscat* musky: see MUSCAT]

muscadine /'muskədien, -din/ *noun* **1** a grapevine of the southern USA with musky fruits borne in small clusters: *Vitis rotundifolia*. **2** a grape from this variety of vine. [prob alteration of MUSCATEL]

muscat /'muskət, 'muskat/ *noun* **1** any of several varieties of cultivated grape used in the production of sweet white wine and raisins. **2** = MUSCATEL (1). [via French from Provençal *muscat* musky, from *musc* musk, from late Latin *muscus*]

muscatel /muskə'tel/ or **muscadel** /-'del/ *noun* **1** a sweet white wine produced from muscat grapes. **2** a raisin made from muscat grapes. [Middle English *muskadelle* via French from Old Provençal *muscadel* resembling musk, from *muscat* musky: see MUSCAT]

muscle /'musl/ *noun* **1a** a tissue made of modified elongated cells that contract and relax when stimulated to produce motion. **b** an organ consisting of this tissue that moves a part of the body. **2a** muscular strength; brawn. **b** power or force: *They called on the government to use its economic muscle to promote peace.* ➤➤ **muscled** *adj*, **muscly** *adj*. [via French from Latin *musculus*, dimin. of *mus* mouse; from the supposed mouselike form of some muscles]

muscle-bound *adj* **1** having enlarged muscles with impaired elasticity, often as a result of excessive exercise. **2** lacking flexibility; rigid.

muscle in *verb intrans informal* (*often* + on) to interfere or take a share in something forcibly.

muscleman *noun* (*pl* **musclemen**) **1** a strong muscular man; a body-builder. **2** a man who is hired to give people physical protection or to intimidate opponents.

muscovado /muskə'vahdoh/ *noun* unrefined sugar obtained as crystals after sugarcane juice has been evaporated and the molasses drained off. [via Spanish from Portuguese (*açúcar*) *mascavado*, from *açúcar* sugar + *mascavado*, past part. of *mascavar* to adulterate, separate raw sugar (from molasses)]

Muscovite /'muskəviet/ *noun* **1** a native or inhabitant of Moscow. **2** *archaic* a Russian. **3** (**muscovite**) a form of mica. ➤➤ **Muscovite** *adj*. [see MUSCOVY]

Muscovy /'muskəvi/ *noun* **1** *archaic* Russia. **2** a former Russian principality that had Moscow as its capital. [late Latin *Muscovia*, *Moscovia* Moscow]

Muscovy duck *noun* a widely domesticated large S American crested duck: *Cairina moschata*. In the wild, the ducks are green, while domesticated forms may be green, grey, white, or a mixture of these colours. [prob alteration of *musk duck*]

muscul- *or* **musculo-** *comb. form* forming words, with the meanings: **1** muscle: *muscular.* **2** muscular and: *musculoskeletal.* [Latin *musculus* muscle]

muscular /'muskyoolə/ *adj* **1a** of or affecting muscle or the muscles. **b** having well-developed musculature. **2** having strength of expression or character; vigorous. ▶▶ **muscularity** /-'lariti/ *noun*, **muscularly** *adv*.

muscular dystrophy *noun* progressive wasting of muscles occurring as a hereditary disease: compare DYSTROPHY.

musculature /'muskyooləchə/ *noun* the system of muscles of the body or part of the body. [French *musculature* from Latin *musculus* muscle]

musculo- *comb. form* see MUSCUL-.

musculoskeletal /,muskyooloh'skelitəl/ *adj* denoting, relating to, or affecting both the muscular and skeletal systems of the body.

MusD /,mus 'dee/ *abbr* Doctor of Music.

Mus Doc /,mus 'dok/ *abbr* = MusD.

muse¹ /myoohz/ *verb intrans* to become absorbed in thought; to engage in daydreaming. ▶▶ *verb trans* to think or say (something) reflectively. ▶▶ **muser** *noun*. [Middle English *musen* from early French *muser* to gape, idle, muse, from *muse* mouth of an animal, from late Latin *musus*]

muse² *noun* the act or an instance of reflective thinking.

muse³ *noun* **1** (**Muse**) any of the nine sister goddesses in Greek mythology who were the patrons of the arts and sciences.

Editorial note ———
In Greek mythology the Muses were the daughters of Zeus and Mnemosyne. Their names were Calliope (epic poetry), Clio (history), Euterpe (flute-playing), Thalia (comedy), Melpomene (tragedy), Terpsichore (choral lyric and dancing), Erato (lyric poetry), Polyhymnia (hymns and pantomime), and Urania (astronomy).

2a (*sometimes* **the muse**) a source of inspiration, *esp* for a creative artist: *To a historian libraries are food, shelter, and even muse* — Barbara Tuchman. **b** a woman who is a source of inspiration to a creative artist, *esp* a poet. [Middle English via French and Latin from Greek *Mousa*]

musette /myooh'zet/ *noun* **1** a small bagpipe having a soft sweet tone. **2a** a quiet pastoral air that often has a drone bass and is adapted for the musette. **b** a dance performed to the tune of a musette. **3** a small knapsack or a similar bag with one shoulder strap. [early French *musette*, dimin. of *muse* bagpipe, from *muser* to muse, play the bagpipe]

museum /myooh'zee-əm/ *noun* an institution devoted to the acquiring, care, study, and display of objects of historical, artistic, cultural, or scientific interest or value, or a place exhibiting such objects. [Latin *Museum* library, study, from Greek *Mouseion*, neuter of *Mouseios* of the Muses, from *Mousa* Muse]

museum piece *noun* **1** an object interesting enough for a museum to display. **2** *Brit, informal* somebody or something regarded as being absurdly old-fashioned.

mush¹ /mush/ *noun* **1a** a soft mass of semiliquid material. **b** *NAmer* a thick maize porridge. **2** mawkish sentimentality. **3** /moosh/ *Brit, informal*. **a** a person's face or mouth. **b** used *esp* to address somebody: a person: *Oi, mush, how's it going?* [prob alteration of MASH¹]

mush² *verb trans* to reduce (something) to a mush.

mush³ *verb intrans* to travel, *esp* over snow, with a sledge drawn by dogs. [prob from French *marcher* to go, advance]

mush⁴ *interj* a command to sledge dogs to start pulling or to travel more quickly. [see MUSH³]

mush⁵ *noun* a journey, *esp* over snow, with a sledge drawn by dogs.

mushroom¹ /'mushroohm, -room/ *noun* **1a** the enlarged, *esp* edible, fleshy fruiting body of a class of fungus, consisting typically of a stem bearing a flattened or domed cap: compare TOADSTOOL. **b** *informal* any fungus. **2a** something like a mushroom, e.g. in shape or rapidity of growth. **b** (*used before a noun*) said of growth, development, expansion, etc: happening rapidly and often suddenly. **3** a pale brownish pink colour. [Middle English *musseroun* from early French *mousseron* from late Latin *mussirion-, mussirio*]

mushroom² *verb intrans* **1** to spring up suddenly or multiply or grow rapidly. **2** to form a mushroom shape. **3** to pick wild mushrooms: *go mushrooming.*

mushroom cloud *noun* the mushroom-shaped cloud of dust, etc that forms above a nuclear explosion.

mushy /'mushi/ *adj* (**mushier, mushiest**) **1** having the consistency of mush. **2** mawkishly sentimental. ▶▶ **mushily** *adv*, **mushiness** *noun*.

music /'myoohzik/ *noun* **1a** vocal, instrumental, or mechanical sounds that have rhythm, melody, or harmony: *Music is spiritual. The music business is not* — Van Morrison. **b** the science or art of writing music. **c** a musical accompaniment: *The play was set to music by this hitherto unknown young composer.* **d** the score of a musical composition set down on paper. **2** an agreeable sound; euphony: *the music of the nightingale.* ✴ **music to one's ears** something (e.g. news or information) that one is very pleased to hear or learn: *To hear that she'd had her comeuppance at last was music to my ears.* [Middle English *musik* via Old French and Latin from Greek *mousikē* any art presided over by the Muses, *esp* music, from fem of *mousikos* of the Muses, from *Mousa* Muse]

musical¹ *adj* **1** having the pleasing harmonious qualities of music. **2** having an interest in or talent for music. **3** set to or accompanied by music. **4** of music, musicians, or music lovers. ▶▶ **musicality** /-'kaliti/ *noun*, **musically** *adv*.

musical² *noun* a film or theatrical production that consists of songs, dances, and dialogue based on a unifying plot.

musical box *noun* a container enclosing an apparatus that reproduces music mechanically when activated.

musical chairs *pl noun* **1** (*treated as sing.*) a children's game in which players march to music round a row of chairs numbering one less than the players and scramble for seats when the music stops. At each turn, the player not finding a seat is eliminated and a seat removed in order to eliminate a further player at the next turn. **2** any situation involving people making frequent changes of position.

musical comedy *noun* a musical, *esp* one of a sentimental or humorous nature.

music box *noun NAmer* = MUSICAL BOX.

music centre *noun Brit, dated* a usu stereophonic system that houses a record player, a radio, and a cassette tape recorder in a single unit.

music drama *noun* **1** a form of opera in which the action is not interrupted by formal song divisions, e.g. recitatives or arias, and the music is determined solely by dramatic appropriateness. **2** an opera of this form. [German *Musikdrama*, term coined by Richard Wagner d.1883, German composer]

music hall *noun* **1** entertainments consisting of a variety of unrelated acts, e.g. acrobats, comedians, singers, and dancers. **2** *esp* formerly, a theatre where such entertainments are performed.

musician /myooh'zish(ə)n/ *noun* a composer, conductor, or performer of music, *esp* an instrumentalist. ▶▶ **musicianly** *adj*, **musicianship** *noun*.

musicology /myoohzi'kolə ji/ *noun* the study of music as a branch of knowledge or field of research. ▶▶ **musicological** /-'lojikl/ *adj*, **musicologist** *noun*. [Italian *musicologia*, from Latin *musica* music + *-logia* -LOGY]

music stool *noun* a stool usu having an adjustable height and used by a pianist.

musing /'myoohzing/ *noun* meditation or reflection. ▶▶ **musingly** *adv*.

musique concrète /mooh,zeek kong'kret (*French* myzik kɔ̃krɛt)/ *noun* a montage of recorded natural sounds, e.g. voices, traffic noise, and bird calls, arbitrarily modified and arranged. Also called CONCRETE MUSIC. [French *musique concrète*, literally 'concrete music']

musk /musk/ *noun* **1a** a substance with a penetrating persistent smell that is obtained from a gland of the male musk deer and used as a perfume fixative. **b** a similar substance from another animal or a synthetic substitute. **c** the odour of musk. **2** any of various plants with musky smells: *esp Mimulus moschatus, Malva moschatus,* and related species. ▶▶ **muskiness** *noun*, **musky** *adj*. [Middle English *muske* via French and late Latin from Persian *mushk*, ultimately from Sanskrit *muṣka* scrotum; from the shape of the musk deer's musk bag]

musk deer *noun* a small heavy-limbed hornless deer of central Asia, the male of which produces musk: *Moschus moschiferus.*

muskeg /'muskeg/ *noun* **1** a sphagnum bog of northern N America, often with tussocks. **2** a usu thick deposit of partially decayed vegetable matter of wet northern regions. [Cree *maskēk* swamp]

muskellunge /'muskilunj/ *noun* (*pl* **muskellunges** *or collectively* **muskellunge**) the largest species of pike, found in the lakes and rivers of the Great Lakes region of N America and valued as a game and food fish: *Esox masquinongy*. [Canadian French *maskinongé* Ojibwa *māskinōshē*]

musket /'muskit/ *noun* a heavy large-calibre firearm with a smooth bore, fired from the shoulder. [early French *mousquet* from Old Italian *moschetto* arrow for a crossbow, musket, from dimin. of *mosca* fly, from Latin *musca*]

musketeer /muskə'tiə/ *noun* **1** a soldier armed with a musket. **2** a soldier of the household guard of the French monarch in the 17th and 18th cents. [modification of early French *mousquetaire*, from *mousquet* musket]

musketry /'muskitri/ *noun* **1** muskets collectively or troops armed with muskets. **2** musket fire. **3** the art or technique of using a musket or other small firearms.

muskmelon *noun* **1** any of various melons that have orange coloured flesh with a musky flavour and a rind with raised netlike markings. **2** a plant that bears this type of melon: *Cucumis melo*.

musk ox *noun* a thickset shaggy-coated wild ox of Greenland and northern N America that gives off a strong musky odour: *Ovibos moschatus*.

muskrat *noun* (*pl* **muskrats** *or collectively* **muskrat**) **1** an aquatic rodent of N America with thick brown fur, a long scaly tail, webbed hind feet, and musk glands at the base of the tail: *Ondatra zibethica*. **2** the fur of this animal. [prob by folk etymology from a word of Algonquian origin; related to Natick *musquash* muskrat]

musk rose *noun* a rose of the Mediterranean region with white musky flowers: *Rosa moschata*.

Muslim /'moozlim, 'muzlim/ *or* **Moslem** /'mozləm/ *noun* an adherent of Islam. ⮞ **Muslim** *adj*. [Arabic *muslim*, literally 'one who surrenders (to God)']

muslin /'muzlin/ *noun* a delicate plain-woven cotton fabric. [French *mousseline* from Italian *mussolina* from Arabic *mawṣiliy* of Mosul, city in Iraq where it was orig made]

muso /'myoohsoh/ *noun* (*pl* **musos**) **1** *Brit, informal*. **a** *chiefly derog* a musician, *esp* one who plays pop music and is more concerned with technique than with content or expression. **b** a person who has a strong interest in or vast knowledge of music, *esp* pop music. **c** (*used before a noun*) denoting or relating to music, musicians, music enthusiasts, etc *esp* in the pop music world: *Fiona will know who sang that – she's a real muso head*. **2** *chiefly Aus, NZ, informal* a musician, *esp* one who plays professionally. [a contraction of MUSIC *or* MUSICIAN + -O[1]]

musquash /'muskwosh/ *noun archaic* = MUSKRAT. [of Algonquian origin]

muss[1] /mus/ *noun NAmer, informal* a state of disorder; mess. ⮞ **mussy** *adj*. [origin unknown]

muss[2] *verb trans NAmer, informal* (*often* + up) to make (something) untidy; to disarrange or dishevel (it).

mussel /'musl/ *noun* **1** a marine bivalve mollusc with a dark elongated shell: family Mytilidae. **2** a freshwater bivalve mollusc whose shell has a lustrous mother-of-pearl lining and which sometimes produces pearls: family Unionidae. [Old English *muscelle*, ultimately from Latin *musculus* muscle, mussel]

Mussulman /'muslmən, 'moos-/ *noun* (*pl* **Mussulmen** *or* **Mussulmans**) *archaic* a Muslim. [Persian *musulmān*, modification of Arabic *muslim*]

must[1] /məs(t), *strong* must/ *verb aux* (*third person sing. present tense* **must**, *past tense in reported speech* **must**) **1** to have to; to be obliged to: *You must stop at the lights; She said we must not park outside the house*. **2** to be required or necessary: *Propaganda, to be effective, must be believed. To be believed, it must be credible. To be credible, it must be true* — Hubert Humphrey. **3** to be supposed or likely: *It must be lunch time*. **4** used to express insistence: *You must stay for dinner*. **5** used to express certainty, usu in ironic contexts: *You must be joking*. [Old English *moste*, past indicative and subjunctive of *motan* to be allowed to, have to]

must[2] /must/ *noun* an essential or prerequisite.

must[3] *noun* grape juice before and during fermentation. [Old English from Latin *mustum*, from neuter of *mustus* young, fresh, new]

must[4] *noun* mould or mustiness. [back-formation from MUSTY]

must[5] *noun* see MUSTH.

mustache /mə'stahsh, mə'stash/ *noun* see MOUSTACHE.

mustachio /mə'stahshioh, mə'stash-/ *noun* (*pl* **mustachios**) (*also in pl*) a moustache, *esp* a large or elaborate one. ⮞ **mustachioed** *adj*. [Spanish *mostacho* from Italian *mustaccio*: see MOUSTACHE]

mustang /'mustang/ *noun* the small hardy feral or semi-wild horse of the western plains of the USA. [Mexican Spanish *mestengo* from Spanish *mesteño* strayed, from *mesta* annual roundup of cattle that disposed of strays, from late Latin (*animalia*) *mixta* mixed (animals)]

mustard /'mustəd/ *noun* **1** a pungent yellow or brownish paste or powder used as a condiment or in medicine, *esp* as an emetic or counterirritant, and ground from the seeds of any of several related plants belonging to the cabbage family. **2** any of several species of these plants, with lobed leaves, yellow flowers, and straight seed pods: genera *Brassica* and *Sinapis*. **3** a brownish yellow colour. ⮞ **mustard** *adj*, **mustardy** *adj*. [Middle English from Old French *mostarde* from *moust* must, from Latin *mustum*: see MUST[3]]

mustard gas *noun* an irritant and blister-inducing oily liquid used as a poison gas, *esp* in chemical warfare.

mustard plaster *noun* a plaster containing powdered mustard, used in medicine, e.g. to ease inflammation.

mustelid /'mustilid, mu'stelid/ *noun technical* any of a family of predatory mammals such as a weasel, ferret, badger, skunk, marten, or otter: family Mustelidae. ⮞ **musteline** *adj*.

muster[1] /'mustə/ *verb* (**mustered, mustering**) ⮞ *verb trans* **1a** to assemble or convene (e.g. troops). **b** to call the roll of (e.g. a body of troops). **2** (*often* + up) to summon (*esp* courage, nerve) in response to a need: *He'd need all the courage he could muster*. ⮞ *verb intrans* said *esp* of troops: to come together; to congregate. [Middle English *mustren* to show, muster, from Old French *monstrer* from Latin *monstrare* to show]

muster[2] *noun* **1a** the act or an instance of assembling, e.g. for military inspection, duty, etc. **b** an assembled group; a collection. **2** *Aus, NZ* the act or process of rounding up livestock. ✳ **pass muster** to be acceptable; to be of a satisfactory standard: *This slipshod work would never pass muster*.

muster in *verb trans NAmer* to enrol (somebody) formally into the armed forces.

muster out *verb trans NAmer* to discharge (somebody) from the armed forces.

muster roll *noun* a register of the officers and men in a military unit or ship's company.

musth *or* **must** /must/ *noun* a periodic state of frenzy in certain large male mammals, e.g. elephants and camels, usu connected with the rutting season. [Hindi *mast* intoxicated, from Persian]

mustn't /'musnt/ *contraction* must not.

musty *adj* (**mustier, mustiest**) **1a** affected by mould, damp, or mildew. **b** tasting or smelling of damp and decay. **2a** trite or stale: *a musty proverb. The musty elegance of the old hotel*. **c** out of date: *That's a rather musty concept nowadays*. ⮞ **mustily** *adv*, **mustiness** *noun*. [perhaps alteration (influenced by MUST[3]) of earlier *moisty* moist]

mutable /'myoohtəbl/ *adj* **1** capable of or liable to change or alteration. **2** capable of or subject to mutation. ⮞ **mutability** /-'biliti/ *noun*, **mutableness** *noun*, **mutably** *adv*. [Latin *mutabilis*, from *mutare* to change]

mutagen /'myoohtəjən/ *noun* something that causes genetic mutation or increases its frequency. ⮞ **mutagenesis** /-'jenəsis/ *noun*, **mutagenic** /-'jenik/ *adj*, **mutagenically** /-'jenikli/ *adv*, **mutagenicity** /-'nisiti/ *noun*. [MUTATION + -GEN]

mutant[1] /'myoohtənt/ *noun* an animal, organism, cell, etc that has undergone mutation. [Latin *mutant-, mutare* to change]

mutant[2] *adj* relating to, affected by, showing, etc mutation.

mutate /myooh'tayt/ *verb trans* to cause (something) to undergo mutation. ⮞ *verb intrans* to undergo mutation. ⮞ **mutator** *noun*. [back-formation from MUTATION]

mutation /myooh'taysh(ə)n/ *noun* **1a** the act or an instance of changing; alteration: *There is nothing exempt from the peril of mutation* — Sir Walter Raleigh. **b** an alteration, *esp* a significant and fundamental one. **2a** a relatively permanent change in an organism's hereditary material. **b** an individual or strain differing from others of its type and resulting from such a change. **3** in linguistics, a sound-change resulting from the phonetic or linguistic environment, e.g. UMLAUT in Germanic languages or the change of the initial consonant of a Celtic word under the influence of a preceding sound. ➤➤ **mutational** *adj*, **mutationally** *adv*. [Middle English *mutacioun* via French from Latin *mutation-*, *mutatio*, from *mutatus*, past part. of *mutare* to change]

mutatis mutandis /m(y)ooh,tahtis m(y)ooh'tandis/ *adv* with the necessary changes having been made. [Latin *mutatis mutandis*, literally 'things being changed that have to be changed']

mutch /much/ *noun* a close-fitting linen cap formerly worn by women and children, *esp* in Scotland. [Middle English from Dutch *mutse*, from Latin *almucia* AMICE]

mute[1] /myooht/ *adj* **1a** not speaking. **b** unable to speak; dumb. **2a** felt but not expressed: *mute sympathy*. **b** in law, refusing to plead: *a mute defendant*. **3** said of a letter: appearing in the spelling of a word but not pronounced: *The 'b' of 'lamb' is mute*. ➤➤ **mutely** *adv*, **muteness** *noun*. [Middle English *muet* via Old French from Latin *mutus*]

mute[2] *noun* **1** a person who cannot or does not speak. **2** a device attached to a musical instrument to reduce, soften, or muffle its tone. **3** in law, a person who refuses to plead. **4** formerly, a hired mourner. **5** *esp* formerly, a mime actor. **6** = STOP[2] (5).

mute[3] *verb trans* **1** to muffle or reduce the sound of (e.g. a musical instrument). **2** to tone down (a colour, etc).

muted *adj* **1** subdued: *a muted response*; *muted lighting*. **2** said of a musical instrument or the sound it produces: provided with or produced or modified by the use of a mute. ➤➤ **mutedly** *adv*.

mute swan *noun* the common white swan of Europe and W Asia, so called because it produces no loud notes: *Cygnus olor*.

muti /'moohti/ *noun informal* in South Africa, medicine, *esp* of the herbal or traditional type. [Zulu *umuthi* medicinal plant]

mutilate /'myoohtilayt/ *verb trans* **1a** to injure or damage (somebody, something, or a body part) severely. **b** to deprive (somebody) of a limb or other essential body part. **2** to damage or deface (e.g. a text): *The censors had mutilated the script*. ➤➤ **mutilation** /-'laysh(ə)n/ *noun*, **mutilator** *noun*. [Latin *mutilatus*, past part. of *mutilare*, from *mutilus* mutilated, maimed]

mutineer /myoohti'niə/ *noun* somebody who mutinies.

mutinous /'myoohtinəs/ *adj* **1** tending to mutiny; rebellious. **2** of or constituting mutiny. ➤➤ **mutinously** *adv*, **mutinousness** *noun*.

mutiny[1] /'myoohtini/ *noun* (*pl* **mutinies**) open resistance to authority, *esp* concerted revolt of e.g. soldiers or a naval crew against discipline or a superior officer. [obsolete *mutine* to rebel, from early French *se mutiner* from *mutin* mutinous, from *meute* revolt, ultimately from Latin *movēre* to move]

mutiny[2] *verb intrans* (**mutinies, mutinied, mutinying**) to take part in a mutiny; to rebel against authority, a command, etc.

mutism *noun* the state of being mute, *esp* speechlessness caused by psychological reasons rather than by physiological damage.

mutt /mut/ *noun informal* **1** *often humorous or derog* a dog, *esp* a mongrel. **2** a dull or stupid person. [short for MUTTONHEAD]

mutter[1] /'mutə/ *verb* (**muttered, muttering**) ➤ *verb intrans* **1** to utter sounds or words in a low or indistinct voice. **2** to utter muffled threats or complaints. ➤ *verb trans* to utter (something) in a low or indistinct voice. ➤➤ **mutterer** *noun*. [Middle English *muteren*]

mutter[2] *noun* muttered sounds or words.

mutton /'mutn/ *noun* the flesh of a mature sheep used as food. ✱ **mutton dressed as lamb** *Brit, informal, derog* a middle-aged or elderly woman dressed in clothing more suited to a younger person. ➤➤ **muttony** *adj*. [Middle English *motoun* from Old French *moton* ram, wether, of Celtic origin]

mutton bird *noun* any of several species of Australasian shearwaters (seabirds of the petrel family; see SHEARWATER), the young of which are caught for their feathers, oil, and edible flesh: family Procellariidae. [so called because its cooked flesh tastes like mutton]

muttonchops *pl noun* side-whiskers that are narrow at the temple and broad by the lower jaws.

muttonchop whiskers *pl noun* = MUTTONCHOPS.

muttonhead *noun informal, dated* a slow-witted or stupid person; a blockhead. ➤➤ **muttonheaded** *adj*.

mutual /'myoohtyooəl, 'myoohchəl/ *adj* **1a** directed by each towards the other: *Human life consists in mutual service* — Charlotte Gilman. **b** said of two or more people, groups, etc: having the same specified feeling for each other: *They had long been mutual enemies*.

2 shared by two or more people, groups, etc; in common: *I believe we have a mutual friend*. **3** relating to or denoting a type of insurance, or insurance company providing it, in which the policy holders constitute the members of the insuring company, sharing profits and expenses, there being no other shareholders. ➤➤ **mutuality** /-'aliti/ *noun*, **mutually** *adv*. [Middle English from French *mutuel* from Latin *mutuus* lent, borrowed, mutual; related to Latin *mutare* to change]

Usage note
mutual, reciprocal, or **common**? These three words are sometimes confused. *Mutual* and *reciprocal* can both mean 'directed towards each other'. Two people can be said to share *a mutual* or *reciprocal hatred*, if they hate each other. They can also, however, be said to share *a common hatred* if they both independently hate the same other thing or other person. Because *common* has several other meanings apart from 'shared', *mutual* is sometimes used where the strictly correct word would be *common*. The best-known example is *our mutual friend*, meaning 'your friend as well as mine', a phrase that is now generally acceptable and reinforced by the title of Dickens' novel, whereas *our common friend* might be thought to mean 'our vulgar friend'.

mutual induction *noun* the production of an electromotive force in a circuit by a change of current in another circuit linked to it by a magnetic field.

mutualism *noun* **1** the doctrine or practice that mutual dependence is essential for social welfare. **2** a situation or condition in which two dissimilar organisms live together for the benefit of both of them; = SYMBIOSIS. ➤➤ **mutualist** *noun*, **mutualistic** /-'listik/ *adj*.

mutuel /'myoohtyooəl, 'myoohchəl/ *noun NAmer* = PARI-MUTUEL (system for betting).

muumuu /'moohmooh/ *noun* a brightly coloured loose, often long, dress of a type traditionally worn by women in Hawaii. [Hawaiian *mu'umu'u*, literally 'cut off']

Muzak /'myoohzak/ *noun trademark* recorded background music played in public places.

muzhik *or* **moujik** /'moohzhik/ *noun* a Russian peasant, *esp* in tsarist times. [Russian *muzhik*]

muzzle[1] /'muzl/ *noun* **1a** the projecting jaws and nose of a dog or other animal. **b** a covering for the mouth of an animal used to prevent biting, barking, etc. **2** the discharging end of a pistol, rifle, etc. [Middle English *musell* from early French *musel*, dimin. of *muse* mouth of an animal, from late Latin *musus*]

muzzle[2] *verb trans* **1** to fit (e.g. a dog) with a muzzle. **2** to restrain (a person) from free expression; to gag (them). ➤➤ **muzzler** *noun*.

muzzle-loader *noun* a firearm that is loaded through the muzzle. ➤➤ **muzzle-loading** *adj*.

muzzy /'muzi/ *adj* (**muzzier, muzziest**) **1** said of a person, recollection, etc: mentally confused; befuddled. **2a** said of an image: blurred; unclear. **b** said of a sound: indistinct. ➤➤ **muzzily** *adv*, **muzziness** *noun*. [perhaps blend of *muddled* and FUZZY]

MV *abbr* **1** megavolt. **2** motor vessel.

mv *abbr* millivolt.

MVO *abbr* Member of the Royal Victorian Order.

MW *abbr* **1** Malawi (international vehicle registration). **2** medium wave. **3** megawatt.

mW *abbr* milliwatt.

Mx *abbr* maxwell.

MY *abbr* motor yacht.

my[1] /mie/ *adj* **1** belonging to or associated with me: *my house*; *my children*; *my being chosen*; *my acquittal*. **2** used in expressions of surprise, horror, disbelief, etc: *My God!*; *A millionaire my foot! He's got no more money than I have*. [Middle English *mi* from Old English *mīn* my, mine, genitive of *ic* I: see MINE[1]]

my[2] *interj* (*also reduplicated*) used to express surprise, distress, pleasure, etc: *Oh my! What a mess!*; *My, oh my, that was some party!*

my- *or* **myo-** *comb. form* forming words, denoting: muscle: *myocardium*. [via late Latin from Greek *mys* mouse, muscle]

myalgia /mie'aljə/ *noun* pain in one or more muscles. ➤➤ **myalgic** /-jik/ *adj*. [MY- + -ALGIA]

myalgic encephalomyelitis *noun dated* = CHRONIC FATIGUE SYNDROME.

myalism /'mie-əliz(ə)m/ *noun* a form of popular religion in the West Indies, involving spirit possession and ritual sacrifice. [prob from a West African language, possibly related to Hausa *myal* sorcerer + -ISM]

myall /'mie·awl/ *noun* **1** any of various species of Australian acacia trees with hard fragrant wood: genus *Acacia*. **2** a member of an indigenous Australian people who lives in a traditional way. [Aboriginal name]

myasthenia /mie·əs'theeni·ə/ *noun* muscular weakness. ⟫⟫ **myasthenic** *adj*. [MY- + ASTHENIA]

myasthenia gravis /'grahvis/ *noun* a disease characterized by progressive weakness and exhaustibility of voluntary muscles without wasting. [scientific Latin *myasthenia gravis*, literally 'grave myasthenia']

myc- *or* **myco-** *comb. form* forming words, denoting: fungus: *mycology*; *mycosis*. [via late Latin from Greek *mykēt-, mykēs* fungus, mushroom]

mycelium /mie'seeli·əm/ *noun* (*pl* **mycelia** /-li·ə/) the mass of interwoven hyphae (threadlike filaments; see HYPHA) that forms the body of a fungus and is usu submerged in another body, e.g. soil or the tissues of a host. ⟫⟫ **mycelial** *adj*. [scientific Latin *mycelium*, from MYC- + Greek *hēlos* nail, wart, callus]

Mycenaean *or* **Mycenian** /miesi'nee·ən/ *adj* relating or belonging to or denoting a late Bronze Age culture that flourished at Mycenae, a city of ancient Greece, and whose influence spread to other Peloponnesian cities. ⟫⟫ **Mycenaean** *noun*.

mycetozoan /mie,setə'zoh·ən/ *noun* = SLIME MOULD. ⟫⟫ **mycetozoan** *adj*. [Latin *Mycetozoa*, order of protozoans, from Greek *mykēt-, mykēs* fungus + Latin *-zoa* animals]

myco- *comb. form* see MYC-.

mycoflora /'miekoflawrə/ *noun* the fungi characteristic of a region or special environment. [MYCO- + FLORA]

mycology /mie'koləji/ *noun* the scientific study of fungal life or fungi. ⟫⟫ **mycologic** /-'lojik/ *adj*, **mycological** /-'lojikl/ *adj*, **mycologically** /-'lojikli/ *adv*, **mycologist** *noun*. [scientific Latin *mycologia*, from MYCO- + -LOGY]

mycoplasma /miekoh'plazmə/ *noun* (*pl* **mycoplasmas** *or* **mycoplasmata** /-tə/) any of various minute micro-organisms without cell walls that are intermediate in some respects between viruses and bacteria and are mostly parasitic, usu in mammals: order Mycoplasmatales. ⟫⟫ **mycoplasmal** *adj*. [from the Latin genus name, from MYCO- + PLASMA]

mycorrhiza /mieko'riezə/ *noun* (*pl* **mycorrhizae** /-zee/ *or* **mycorrhizas**) the symbiotic (mutually beneficial; see SYMBIOSIS) association of the MYCELIUM (body) of a fungus with the roots of a flowering plant such as an orchid. ⟫⟫ **mycorrhizal** *adj*. [scientific Latin *mycorrhiza*, from MYCO- + Greek *rhiza* root]

mycosis /mie'kohsis/ *noun* (*pl* **mycoses** /-seez/) infection with or disease caused by a fungus. ⟫⟫ **mycotic** /mie'kotik/ *adj*. [MYC- + -OSIS]

mycotoxin /miekoh'toksin/ *noun* a toxic substance produced by a fungus, *esp* a mould.

myel- *or* **myelo-** *comb. form* forming words, denoting: marrow; spinal cord: *myelitis*. [via late Latin from Greek *myelos* marrow, from *mys* mouse, muscle]

myelin /'mie·əlin/ *noun* a soft white fatty material that forms a thick sheath about the cytoplasmic core of nerve cells adapted for fast conduction of nervous impulses. ⟫⟫ **myelinic** /-'linik/ *adj*.

myelinated /'mie·əlinaytid/ *adj* said of a nerve fibre: having a sheath of myelin. ⟫⟫ **myelination** /-'naysh(ə)n/ *noun*.

myelitis /mie·ə'lietəs/ *noun* inflammation of the spinal cord or the bone marrow.

myelo- *comb. form* see MYEL-.

myelogenic /,mie·əloh'jenik/ *adj* = MYELOGENOUS.

myelogenous /mie·ə'lojinəs/ *adj* relating to or produced by the bone marrow.

myeloid /'mie·əloyd/ *adj* **1** relating to or in the region of the spinal cord. **2** relating to or resembling bone marrow.

myeloma /mie·ə'lohmə/ *noun* (*pl* **myelomas** *or* **myelomata** /-mətə/) a tumour of the bone marrow, usu one that is malignant. ⟫⟫ **myelomatous** /-təs/ *adj*.

mynah *or* **myna** *or* **mina** /'mienə/ *noun* any of various Asian starlings, *esp* a largely black one that can easily be taught to pronounce words: *Gracula religiosa* and other species. [Hindi *mainā*]

myo- *comb. form* see MY-.

myocardium /mieoh'kahdi·əm/ *noun* (*pl* **myocardia** /-di·ə/) the middle muscular layer of the heart wall. ⟫⟫ **myocardial** *adj*, **myocarditis** /-'dietəs/ *noun*. [scientific Latin *myocardium*, from MYO- + Greek *kardia* heart]

myofibril /mieoh'fiebril, -'fibril/ *noun* any of the long thin parallel contractile filaments of a striated muscle cell. ⟫⟫ **myofibrillar** *adj*. [MYO- + Latin *fibrilla* fibril]

myoglobin /mie·ə'glohbin, 'mie-/ *noun* a red protein that brings oxygen to the muscles and allows it to be stored there, similar to haemoglobin in the blood.

myology /mie'oləji/ *noun* the scientific study of muscles. ⟫⟫ **myologic** /-'lojik/ *ad*, **myological** /-'lojikl/ *adj*, **myologist** *noun*. [via French from Latin *myologia*, from MY- + -OLOGY]

myope /'mieohp/ *noun* a person who is affected by myopia. [French *myope* via late Latin from Greek *myōps*, from *myein* to be closed + *ōps* eye, face]

myopia /mie'ohpi·ə/ *noun* **1** defective vision of distant objects resulting from the visual images being focused in front of the retina; shortsightedness: compare HYPERMETROPIA. **2** a lack of ability or a deliberate unwillingness to be intellectually objective or to see the validity of other people's opinions; narrow-mindedness. ⟫⟫ **myopic** /mie'opik, mie'ohpik/ *adj*, **myopically** /mie'opikli, mie'ohpikli/ *adv*. [via late Latin from Greek *myōpia* from *myōps*: see MYOPE]

myosin /'mie·əsin/ *noun* a fibrous protein that reacts with actin to form the principal contractile element of muscles.

myosis /mie'ohsis/ *noun* see MIOSIS.

myosotis /mie·ə'sohtis/ *noun* any of a genus of plants of the borage family including the forget-me-not: genus *Myosotis*. [from the Latin genus name, from Greek *myosōtis*, from *my-, mys* mouse + *ōt-, ous* ear]

myriad[1] /'miri·əd/ *noun* **1** (*also in pl*) an indefinitely large number: *There were myriads of people at the fair.* **2** *archaic* ten thousand. [Greek *myriad-, myrias*, from *myrioi* countless, ten thousand]

myriad[2] *adj* innumerable; countless: *Men ... exploit and injure in a myriad subtle ways* — Ann Oakley.

myriapod *or* **myriopod** /'miri·əpod/ *noun* a millipede, centipede, or related arthropod with a body made up of numerous similar segments bearing jointed legs. [Greek *myrioi* countless, ten thousand + *pod-, pous* foot]

myrmidon /'muhmid(ə)n/ *noun* a subordinate who carries out orders unquestioningly. [Latin *Myrmidon-, Myrmido*, from Greek *Myrmidōn*, one of the legendary Thessalian people accompanying Achilles to the Trojan War]

myrobalan /mie'robələn, mi-/ *noun* **1** an Asian plum tree used extensively as a rootstock; = CHERRY PLUM. **2a** the dried bitter fruit of certain E Indian trees, used chiefly in leather tanning and in inks. **b** any of several species of the trees that bear this fruit: genus *Terminalia*. [via French and Latin from Greek *myrobalanos*, from *myron* perfume + *balanos* acorn]

myrrh /muh/ *noun* an aromatic gum resin obtained from various African and Asian trees, used e.g. in perfumes, medicines, and incense. [Old English *myrre* via Latin from Greek *myrra*, of Semitic origin]

myrtle /'muhtl/ *noun* an evergreen S European bushy shrub with shiny leaves, fragrant white or rosy flowers, and black berries, or any of numerous related shrubs or trees found in S America and Australasia: genus *Myrtus*. [Middle English *mirtille* via French and Latin from Greek *myrtos*, prob of Semitic origin]

myself /mie'self/ *pronoun* **1** used reflexively to refer to the person speaking or writing: *I have hurt myself.* **2** used for emphasis: *I myself said it.* ✳ **be myself** to be fit or healthy as normal: *I'm not quite myself today.* [Middle English, alteration of earlier *meself*]

Mysian /'miesi·ən/ *noun* a native or inhabitant of Mysia, an ancient region of northwestern Asia Minor. ⟫⟫ **Mysian** *adj*.

mysterious /mi'stiəri·əs/ *adj* **1** difficult to comprehend. **2** containing, suggesting, or implying mystery. ⟫⟫ **mysteriously** *adv*, **mysteriousness** *noun*.

mystery[1] /'mist(ə)ri/ *noun* (*pl* **mysteries**) **1a** something or somebody not understood or beyond understanding; an enigma: *One may say that the eternal mystery of the world is its comprehensibility* — Albert Einstein. **b** something that cannot be explained: *His disappearance remains a mystery.* **c** a profound, enigmatic, or secretive quality or character: *Nobody has explained the mystery of the Mona*

Lisa's smile. **d** the secret or specialized practices peculiar to an occupation or group of people: *The mysteries of cooking were quite beyond her.* **e** (*used before a noun*) mysterious; unexplained: *She is suffering from some mystery illness.* **2** a fictional work dealing usu with the solution of a mysterious crime. **3a** a religious truth that is disclosed by revelation alone and even so is not fully understandable. **b** any of the 15 events, e.g. the Nativity, the Crucifixion, or the Assumption, serving as a subject for meditation during the saying of the rosary. **c** (**Mystery**) a Christian sacrament; *specif* Communion. **d** (*also in pl*) a secret religious rite believed, e.g. in certain ancient religions, to impart enduring bliss. **e** a cult devoted to such rites. **4** = MYSTERY PLAY. [Middle English *mysterie* via Latin from Greek *mystērion*, from *myein* to be closed (of the eyes or lips)]

mystery² *noun* (*pl* **mysteries**) *archaic* **1** a trade or craft. **2** a body of people engaged in a particular trade, business, or profession; a guild. [Late Latin *misterium, mysterium*, alteration of *ministerium* service, occupation, from *minister* servant]

mystery play *noun* a medieval religious drama based on episodes from the Scriptures or the lives of the saints: compare MIRACLE PLAY, MORALITY PLAY. [French *mystère* from Latin *mysterium*]

mystery tour *noun Brit* a pleasure trip, *esp* by coach, to a destination that is not made known to those taking part when they set out.

mystic¹ /'mistik/ *noun* a person who believes that God or ultimate reality can be, or can only be, apprehended by direct personal experience, *esp* somebody who orders his or her life towards this goal. [see MYSTICAL]

mystic² *adj* = MYSTICAL.

mystical *adj* **1** having a sacred or spiritual meaning not given by normal modes of thought or feeling. **2** of or resulting from a person's direct experience of communion with God or ultimate reality. **3** of mysteries or esoteric rites. **4** of mysticism or mystics. **5a** mysterious or incomprehensible. **b** obscure or esoteric. **c** arousing awe and wonder. ➤➤ **mystically** *adv*. [Middle English *mistik* from Latin *mysticus* of mysteries, from Greek *mystikos*, from *myein* to be closed (of the eyes or lips)]

mysticism /'mistisiz(ə)m/ *noun* **1** the experience of mystical union or direct communion with ultimate reality reported by mystics. **2** the belief that direct knowledge of God, spiritual truth, or ultimate reality can be attained through subjective experience, e.g. intuition or insight. **3** vague speculation; a belief without sound basis.

mystification /,mistifi'kaysh(ə)n/ *noun* the act or an instance of mystifying or being mystified.

mystify /'mistifie/ *verb trans* (**mystifies, mystified, mystifying**) **1** to perplex or bewilder (somebody). **2** to make (something) appear mysterious or obscure. ➤➤ **mystifier** *noun*, **mystifyingly** *adv*. [French *mistifier* from *mystère* mystery, from Latin *mysterium* mystery]

mystique /mi'steek/ *noun* **1** a mystical reverential atmosphere or quality associated with a person or thing. **2** an esoteric skill or aura of secrecy peculiar to an occupation or activity, *esp* when regarded by outsiders as intriguing or puzzling. [French *mystique* from Latin *mysticus*; see MYSTICAL]

myth /mith/ *noun* **1a** a traditional story that embodies popular beliefs or explains a practice, belief, or natural phenomenon. **b** a body of myths; = MYTHOLOGY. **2** a parable or allegory. **3a** a person or thing having a fictitious existence. **b** a belief subscribed to

uncritically by some groups: *To explode a myth is accordingly not to deny the facts but to re-allocate them* — Gilbert Ryle. [Greek *mythos* tale, speech, myth]

mythic /'mithik/ *adj* = MYTHICAL.

mythical /'mithikl/ *adj* **1** based on or described in a myth. **2** invented or imagined. ➤➤ **mythically** *adv*.

mythicize *or* **mythicise** /'mithisiez/ *verb trans* to treat (somebody or something) as the basis of a myth, or to make (them or it) the basis of a myth. ➤➤ **mythicist** /-sist/ *noun*, **mythicizer** *noun*.

mytho- *comb. form* forming words, denoting: myth: *mythology*.

mythoi /'miethoy, 'mothoy/ *noun* pl of MYTHOS.

mythological /mithə'lojikl/ *adj* **1** relating to or dealt with in mythology or myths. **2** lacking factual or historical basis. ➤➤ **mythologically** *adv*.

mythologize *or* **mythologise** /mi'tholəjiez/ *verb trans* to build a myth round (a person, thing, event, etc). ➤➤ *verb intrans* to relate, classify, and explain myths. ➤➤ **mythologizer** *noun*.

mythology /mi'tholəji/ *noun* (*pl* **mythologies**) **1** a body of myths, *esp* those dealing with the gods and heroes of a particular people. **2** a study of myths. **3** a body of beliefs, usu with little factual foundation, lending glamour or mystique to somebody or something. ➤➤ **mythologist** *noun*. [French *mythologie* via late Latin from Greek *mythologia* legend, myth, from *mythologein* to relate myths, from *mythos* + *logos* speech]

mythomania /mithoh'mayni-ə/ *noun* an excessive tendency to tell lies or exaggerate. ➤➤ **mythomaniac** /-ak/ *noun and adj*.

mythopoeia /,mithoh'peeə/ *noun* the composition or making of a myth or myths. ➤➤ **mythopoeic** *adj*. [Greek *mythopoiia*, from *mythos* myth + *poien* to make]

mythos /'miethos, 'mithos/ *noun* (*pl* **mythoi** /'miethoy, 'mothoy/) **1** a pattern of beliefs expressing, often symbolically, the characteristic or common attitudes in a group or culture. **2** a theme or plot. [Greek *mythos* myth]

my word *interj* used to express surprise or astonishment.

myx- *or* **myxo-** *comb. form* forming words, denoting: **1** mucus: *myxoedema*. **2** slime: *myxomycete*. [Greek *myxa* mucus]

myxedema /miksə'deemə/ *noun NAmer* = MYXOEDEMA.

myxoedema (*NAmer* **myxedema**) /miksə'deemə/ *noun* thickening and dryness of the skin and loss of vigour resulting from severe HYPOTHYROIDISM (deficient activity of the thyroid gland).

myxoma /mik'sohmə/ *noun* (*pl* **myxomas** *or* **myxomata** /-tə/) a soft tumour made up of mucous or gelatinous connective tissue. ➤➤ **myxomatous** /-təs/ *adj*.

myxomatosis /,miksəmə'tohsis/ *noun* a severe and usu fatal viral disease of rabbits characterized by swelling of the mucous membranes and the formation of tumour-like tissue below the skin. It has been deliberately introduced in order to control the population in some areas.

myxomycete /miksoh'mieseet, -mie'seet/ *noun* any of a class of slime moulds that live on decaying vegetation and in moist soil: class Myxomycetes. ➤➤ **myxomycetous** /-mie'seetəs/ *adj*. [MYX- + Greek *mykēt-, mykēs* fungus]

myxovirus /'miksohvie(ə)rəs/ *noun* any of a group of viruses that includes the influenza and mumps viruses.

N¹ *or* **n** *noun* (*pl* **N's** *or* **Ns** *or* **n's**) **1a** the 14th letter of the English alphabet. **b** a written character or design denoting this letter. **c** the sound represented by this letter, one of the English consonants. **2** an item designated as N, *esp* the 14th in a series.

N² *abbr* **1** (*also* **Kt**) in chess, knight. **2** used on electric plugs: neutral. **3** in place names, New. **4** in physics, newton or newtons. **5** in chemistry, referring to solutions: normal. **6** North. **7** Northern. **8** Norway (international vehicle registration). **9** (*used in combinations*) nuclear: *N power; the N bomb.*

N³ *abbr* the chemical symbol for nitrogen.

n¹ *abbr* **1** name. **2** (*usu used in combinations*) in physics, etc, nano-. **3** in grammar, neuter. **4** in grammar, nominative. **5** in grammar, noun. **6** noon. **7** in index reference to footnote, note. **8** in printing, en.

n² *adj* **1** in mathematics, etc, a symbol for an indefinite number. **2** *informal* a vast number: *n things to do.*

n- *abbr* used in chemistry, with reference to straight-chain hydrocarbons, normal.

'n' *or* **'n** *conj informal* and: *fish 'n' chips.*

-n *suffix* see -EN¹, -EN², -EN³.

NA *abbr* **1** Netherlands Antilles (international vehicle registration). **2** North America.

Na *abbr* the chemical symbol for sodium. [scientific Latin *natrium* sodium, from NATRON]

n/a *abbr* **1** in banking, no account. **2** not applicable. **3** not available.

NAACP *abbr NAmer* National Association for the Advancement of Colored People.

NAAFI *or* **Naafi** /'nafi/ *noun* **1** the organization which runs shops and canteens in British military establishments. **2** any of these shops or canteens. [acronym from *Navy, Army, and Air Force Institutes*]

naan /nahn/ *noun* see NAN².

naartje /'nahchi/ *noun SAfr* a tangerine. [Afrikaans *naartje* from Tamil *nārattai* citrus]

nab /nab/ *verb trans* (**nabbed, nabbing**) *informal* **1** to arrest or apprehend (somebody). **2** to catch hold of or grab (something): *Nab a couple of chairs.* [perhaps alteration of English dialect *nap* (compare KIDNAP), prob of Scandinavian origin]

Nabataean *or* **Nabatean** /nabə'tee-ən/ *noun* **1** a member of an ancient Arab trading people, allies of the Romans from AD 63, whose capital was Petra (now in Jordan). **2** the now extinct form of Aramaic spoken by this people. ➤➤ **Nabataean** *adj.* [Latin *Nabat(h)aeus*, related to Arabic *Nabaṭ* concerning the Nabataeans]

nabe /nayb/ *noun NAmer, informal* **1** a neighbourhood. **2** a local cinema. **3** a neighbour.

nabob /'naybob/ *noun* **1** (*also* **nawab**) a provincial governor of the Mogul empire in India. **2** said orig of an Englishman grown rich in India: a man of great wealth. ➤➤ **nabobess** /-'bes/ *noun.* [Spanish *nabab* or Portuguese *nababo*, both from Urdu *nawwāb*, from Arabic *nuwwāb*, pl of *nāʾib* governor]

NACAB *abbr* National Association of Citizens' Advice Bureau.

nacelle /na'sel/ *noun* a housing for an aircraft engine. [French *nacelle*, literally 'small boat', from late Latin *navicella*, dimin. of Latin *navis* ship]

nacho /'nachoh/ *noun* (*pl* **nachos**) a Mexican savoury consisting of a piece of tortilla covered with melted cheese, chopped peppers, etc. [Mexican Spanish *nacho*, of uncertain origin; said to represent a pet form of *Ignazio*, name of chef who invented the dish]

NACODS /'naykodz/ *abbr* Brit National Association of Colliery Overmen, Deputies, and Shotfirers.

nacre /'naykə/ *noun* mother-of-pearl. ➤➤ **nacred** *adj*, **nacreous** /'naykri-əs/ *adj.* [French *nacre* via early Italian *naccara* drum, mother-of-pearl, from Arabic *naqqārah* drum; compare NAKER]

NAD *abbr* nicotinamide-adenine dinucleotide, a widely occurring compound that is a cofactor of numerous enzymes that catalyse oxidation or reduction reactions.

Na-dené /nah 'deni/ *or* **Na-dene** /nə 'deen/ *noun* a family of Native American languages spoken in Alaska, E Canada, and NW USA. [Tlingit *naa* tribe + N Athabaskan *dene* people, tribe]

nadir /'naydiə, 'nadiə/ *noun* **1** in astronomy, the point of the celestial sphere that is directly opposite the ZENITH and vertically downward from the observer. **2** a person's or thing's lowest or worst point: *The relationship between the Soviet Union's two dominant politicians here reached its nadir* — The Economist. [Middle English via French from Arabic *naẓīr* opposite]

naevus (*NAmer* **nevus**) /'neevəs/ *noun* (*pl* **naevi** /'neevie/) a congenital pigmented area on the skin; a birthmark. [Latin *naevus* blemish, birthmark]

naff /naf/ *adj* Brit, informal lacking sophistication, coolness, or style; crassly stupid: *naff musicals; a naff thing to say.* ➤➤ **naffness** *noun.* [possibly alteration of EFF, or backwards spelling of *fan* for FANNY]

naffing *adj and adv* Brit, informal an intensive used to express irritation or contempt: *a naffing bore; naffing awful.*

naff off *verb intrans* Brit, informal (*usu in imperative*) used in contemptuous dismissal of somebody, their opinions, etc.

nafka /'nafkə/ *noun* the basic monetary unit of Eritrea, divided into 100 cents.

NAFTA or **Nafta** /'naftə/ abbr North American Free Trade Agreement.

nag¹ /nag/ noun a horse, esp one that is old or in poor condition. [Middle English nagge; related to Dutch negge small horse]

nag² verb (**nagged, nagging**) ⟩ verb intrans **1** (often + at) to find fault incessantly. **2** said of a pain or worry: to be a persistent source of annoyance or discomfort. ⟩ verb trans to subject (a person) to constant scolding or urging. ⟩⟩ **nagger** noun, **nagging** adj, **naggingly** adv. [orig dialect in the sense 'to gnaw', prob of Scandinavian origin]

nag³ noun **1** a person, esp a woman, who nags habitually. **2** a nagging feeling.

Naga /'nahgə/ noun (pl **Nagas** or collectively **Naga**) **1** a member of a group of peoples living in the Naga hills of India and Myanmar. **2** any of the Tibeto-Burman languages spoken by these peoples. ⟩⟩ **Naga** adj. [perhaps from Sanskrit naga mountain]

naga /'nahgə/ noun in Hindu mythology, one of a race of semi-divine beings, partly human and partly cobra, associated with water and with initiation. [Sanskrit nāga serpent]

nagana /nə'gahnə/ noun a fatal disease of hoofed cattle in tropical Africa caused by a TRYPANOSOME (type of parasite) and transmitted by tsetse flies. [Zulu u-nakane, ulu-nakane]

Nah. abbr Nahum (book of the Bible).

NAHT abbr Brit National Association of Head Teachers.

Nahuatl /na'wahtl/ noun (pl **Nahuatls** or collectively **Nahuatl**) **1** a group of Native American peoples of S Mexico and Central America. **2** a Uto-Aztecan language of central Mexico (see also AZTEC).

Word history
via Spanish from Nahuatl Nahuatl, sing. of Nahua the Nahuatl people. Words from the Nahuatl language that were picked up by the Spanish conquistadores and settlers, and then passed into English, include avocado, cacao, chilli, chocolate, coyote, and tomato.

Nahuatlan /na'wahtlən/ noun the subgroup of the Uto-Aztecan languages of which Nahuatl is the last-known member. ⟩⟩ **Nahuatlan** adj.

naiad /'nied/ noun (pl **naiads** or **naiades** /'nie-ədeez/) **1** (often **Naiad**) a water nymph in classical mythology living in springs, rivers, etc. **2** the aquatic larva of a mayfly, dragonfly, damselfly, etc. **3** an underwater plant with narrow leaves and tiny flowers: genus Najas. [French naïade via Latin from Greek naiad-, naias, from naein to flow]

naiant /'nayənt/ adj in heraldry, said of a fish or other sea creature: swimming horizontally. [Anglo-Norman naiant, variant of Old French noiant, present part. of noier to swim, from Latin natare]

naif¹ or **naïf** /nah'eef/ adj = NAIVE. [French naïf: see NAIVE]

naif² or **naïf** noun a naive person.

nail¹ /nayl/ noun **1** a slender pointed and headed spike designed to be hammered or driven into a surface, to join materials, serve as a support, etc. **2a** a horny sheath protecting the upper end of each finger and toe of human beings and other primates. **b** a claw or other structure corresponding to this. **c** in some soft-billed birds, a horny growth on the upper MANDIBLE (segment of beak). **3a** formerly, a unit of cloth measurement, equivalent to 2¼ inches. **b** formerly, a unit of weight for beef, wool, or other commodity, equivalent to seven or eight pounds. ✱ **a nail in the coffin of** a step towards the destruction, extinction, or disappearance of (something or somebody). **hit the nail on the head** to speak appositely. **on the nail** said of payment: immediate. ⟩⟩ **-nailed** comb. form, **nailless** adj. [Old English nægel]

nail² verb trans **1** (often + down/together) to fasten (something) with or as if with a nail or nails. **2** informal to trap, catch, or arrest (a criminal, etc). **3** informal to detect or expose (a lie or liar). **4** chiefly NAmer, informal. **a** in sport, to strike (a ball) successfully. **b** in sport, said of a player: to outwit (an opponent). **c** in baseball, said of a fielder: to put out (a runner) by throwing to a base.

nail-biting adj informal characterized by or causing emotional tension or anxiety: another nail-biting contest.

nail bomb noun an explosive device containing nails, used typically by terrorists in crowded areas, with the intention of causing mutilation.

nailbrush noun a small firm-bristled brush for cleaning the fingernails.

nail down verb trans **1** to define, identify, or establish (something) clearly. **2** to secure a definite promise or decision from (somebody).

nail enamel noun NAmer = NAIL POLISH.

nailer noun **1** formerly, a person who makes nails. **2** a power tool for driving in nails. ⟩⟩ **nailery** noun.

nail file noun a small metal file or emery board for shaping the fingernails.

nail head noun an architectural ornament resembling the enlarged head of a nail, also used on leather clothing, upholstery, etc.

nail polish noun coloured or clear varnish applied to the fingernails or toenails for adornment.

nail punch noun a tool used to COUNTERSINK a nail head (bring it flush with or sink it below the surrounding surface).

nail set noun = NAIL PUNCH.

nail sickness noun structural deterioration resulting from the corrosion of the nails holding the structure together.

nail varnish noun chiefly Brit = NAIL POLISH.

nainsook /'naynsook/ noun a soft lightweight cotton cloth. [Hindi nainsukh, from nain eye + sukh delight]

naira /'nierə/ noun (pl **naira**) the basic monetary unit of Nigeria, divided into 100 kobo. [contraction of Nigeria]

naissant /'nays(ə)nt/ adj in heraldry, said e.g. of an animal: arising from the middle of a FESS (broad horizontal stripe) or other device, with only the forepart shown. [French naissant, literally 'being born', from naître to be born, from Latin nasci]

naive or **naïve** /nah'eev, nie'eev/ adj **1** ingenuous or unsophisticated. **2** lacking in worldly wisdom or informed judgment; credulous. **3** said of art or artists: either self-taught or untutored, or, as with Gauguin or Picasso, rejecting Western sophistication in favour of a stronger, simpler African or Pacific style; = PRIMITIVE¹. ⟩⟩ **naively** adv, **naiveness** noun. [French naïve, fem of naïf innocent, guileless, from Old French naif inborn, natural, from Latin nativus: see NATIVE¹]

naivety or **naïvety** or **naiveté** or **naïveté** /nah'eeviti, nah'eevti, nie-/ noun (pl **naiveties** or **naïveties** or **naivetés** or **naïvetés**) **1** naive behaviour; lack of sophistication or worldliness. **2** a naive remark or action.

naked /'naykid/ adj **1** having no clothes on. **2a** said of a tree, plant, animal, or bird: without foliage, or without fur, hair, or feathers. **b** said of a light: not shaded: a naked bulb. **c** said of a sword, dagger, etc: without its scabbard or sheath. **3** open and undisguised: naked greed. **4** literary unarmed or defenceless; vulnerable to attack. ✱ **the naked eye** one's eyesight unaided by a magnifying glass, microscope, or telescope: impossible to see with the naked eye. **the naked truth** the harsh facts, unconcealed or undisguised. ⟩⟩ **nakedly** adv, **nakedness** noun. [Old English nacod]

naked boys pl noun = NAKED LADIES.

naked ladies pl noun (treated as pl or sing.) = MEADOW SAFFRON: Colchicum autumnale.

naked lady noun a leafless pink orchid of Australia and New Zealand.

naker /'naykə/ noun archaic the kettledrum: a flourish of the Norman trumpets mingled with the deep and hollow clang of the nakers — Scott. [Middle English via early French nacaire from Arabic naqqārah drum: compare NACRE]

NALGO /'nalgoh/ abbr Brit National and Local Government Officers Association.

naloxone /'naləksohn/ noun a drug obtained from morphine and used in the treatment of drug overdoses. [contraction of N-allylnoroxymorphone, from N³ + ALLYL + NOR- + OXY-² + MORPHINE + -ONE]

naltrexone /nal'treksohn/ noun a drug, $C_{20}H_{23}NO_4$, that opposes the action of narcotics, esp heroin, and is used in the treatment of drug addiction to lessen withdrawal symptoms. [contraction of N-allylnoroxymorphone (see NALOXONE), with the arbitrary insertion of trex as in METHOTREXATE]

NAM abbr Namibia (international vehicle registration).

Nam /nam/ or **'Nam** /nahm/ noun NAmer, informal Vietnam, esp with reference to the Vietnam War.

Nama /'nahmə/ noun (pl **Namas** or collectively **Nama**) **1** a member of one of the Khoikhoi peoples of Namibia. **2** the Khoisan language spoken by these peoples. Also called KHOIKHOI. ⨠ **Nama** adj. [the Nama name]

namaskar /nəməs'kah/ noun a traditional Indian gesture of greeting, performed by joining the palms in front of the face or chest and bowing. Also called NAMASTE². [Hindi namaskar from Sanskrit namaskāra, from namas bowing + kāra action]

namaste¹ /nəməs'tay/ interj a traditional Indian word of greeting. [Hindi namaste, from Sanskrit nāmas bowing + te to you]

namaste² noun = NAMASKAR.

namby-pamby¹ /ˌnambi 'pambi/ adj 1 insipidly sentimental. 2 lacking resolution or firmness; soft. ⨠ **namby-pambyism** noun.

Word history

Namby-Pamby, satirical nickname given to Ambrose Philips d.1749, English writer of pastoral verse. Ambrose Philips was a versatile minor poet whose works include a few adulatory odes addressed to the young children of wealthy people. The jingling style of these odes, and their transparent intention of ingratiating Philips with the parents, aroused the scorn of the hack writer Henry Carey. His parody 'Namby-Pamby, or a panegyric upon the new versification' (1726) is written in an exaggerated form of baby talk which turns Philips' name into Namby-Pamby: 'Namby-Pamby, pilly-piss,/ Rhimy-pim'd on Missy Miss'. The parody became well known, and within a short time namby-pamby had become established in the language.

namby-pamby² noun (pl **namby-pambies**) a namby-pamby person.

name¹ /naym/ noun 1 a word or phrase identifying a person, place or thing, by which they are known, referred to, or addressed. 2 a famous or important person, company, etc: She's quite a name in the pop world. 3 one's reputation: She's trying to clear her name. 4 Brit in insurance, an underwriter with Lloyd's. ✳ **by/of the name of** called: a dog by the name of Montmorency. **call somebody names** to apply abusive epithets to somebody or insult them verbally. **get/have a name for** to acquire or have a reputation for (something): I don't want to get a name for unpunctuality. **in all but name** effectively though not officially: She is leader in all but name. **in name only** officially, or in outward form, but not in reality: He is head of the firm in name only. **in/under the name of** 1 reserved, etc, for (so-and-so): booked in the name of Chesney. 2 for the sake of (a cause, etc): crimes perpetrated in the name of religion. **make a name for oneself** to become well-known. **the name of the game** informal the main point to note or recognize in relation to some activity. **to one's name** (usu in negative contexts) in one's possession: He hadn't a penny to his name. [Old English nama, noma]

name² verb trans 1 to give a name to (a person, animal, place, or thing). 2 to identify or mention (a person, etc) by name. 3 to appoint or nominate (a person): Her successor has been named. 4 Brit said of the Speaker of the House of Commons: to mention (an MP) by name as having disobeyed the chair, and so ban them from the House. 5 to specify (a sum, date, etc). ✳ **name after** (NAmer **name for**) to give (somebody or something) the same name as somebody or something else. **name for** NAmer to give (somebody or something) the same name as somebody or something else. **name names** to mention specific people, esp in distributing blame. **name the day** to decide on a date for one's wedding. ⨠ **nameable** adj, **namer** noun.

name-calling noun the use of abusive language, esp when resorted to in place of reasoned argument.

namecheck¹ noun the public mention of somebody or something specifically by name, e.g. in a broadcast programme.

namecheck² verb trans chiefly NAmer, informal to refer to (somebody) specifically by name.

name day noun the feast day of the saint after whom one is named.

name-drop verb intrans (**name-dropped, name-dropping**) to indulge in name-dropping.

name-dropping noun the practice of trying to impress others by the apparently casual mention of prominent people as acquaintances or contacts.

nameless adj 1a having no name; without a name. b not named; anonymous: the nameless reviewer. 2 obscure, undistinguished, or forgotten: nameless generations of students. 3 archaic said of a child: illegitimate. 4a hard to define: nameless fears. b too terrible to describe: nameless atrocities. ⨠ **namelessly** adv, **namelessness** noun.

namely adv that is to say: and he wore exactly the same face as yesterday – namely, a very unhappy one — Henry James.

nameplate noun a plate or plaque bearing a name.

namesake noun somebody or something with the same name as the person or thing in question: My acquaintance Jane Eyre was nothing like her literary namesake. [prob from for the name's sake]

nametape noun a piece of tape attached to a garment or other piece of property that bears the owner's name.

Namibian /nə'mibi-ən/ noun a native or inhabitant of Namibia. ⨠ **Namibian** adj.

nan¹ /nan/ noun Brit, informal used by children: one's grandmother. [perhaps a child's pronunciation of GRAN]

nan² /nahn/ or **naan** noun a traditional Indian type of leavened bread, usu formed into large flat leaf-shaped pieces. [Urdu and Persian nan]

nana¹ or **nanna** /'nanə/ noun Brit, informal used by children: one's grandmother. [perhaps a child's pronunciation of NANNY¹ or GRANNY]

nana² /'nahnə/ noun Brit, informal a silly idiot; a fool. [probably from BANANA]

nan bread noun = NAN².

nancy /'nansi/ or **nance** /nans/ noun (pl **nancies**) offensive an effeminate or homosexual man. [from the female name Nancy]

nancy boy noun = NANCY.

NAND /nand/ noun 1 an operation in electronics and computer logic that produces an output which is the inverse of that of an AND² circuit. 2 (used before a noun) denoting a GATE¹ or circuit that generates an output signal unless there are signals on all its inputs. [blend of NOT¹ + AND]

nandrolone /'nandrəlohn/ noun an anabolic steroid, similar to testosterone, which is an illegal substance for athletes.

nankeen /nang'keen/ noun 1 (often used before a noun) esp formerly, a durable brownish yellow cotton fabric orig made in China: to find myself in the heat … with a pair of silk stockings and nankeen pantaloons — Coleridge. 2 (in pl) esp formerly, a pair of trousers made of nankeen. [named after Nanjing, also written Nanking, city in China, where the fabric was first manufactured]

nanna /'nanə/ noun see NANA¹.

nanny¹ or **nannie** /'nani/ noun (pl **nannies**) chiefly Brit a child's nurse; a nursemaid. [orig a child's name for a nurse; nickname for Ann]

nanny² verb (**nannies, nannied, nannying**) ⨠ verb trans 1 to look after (children) as a nanny. 2 to treat (people) with an interfering overprotectiveness. ⨠ verb intrans to work as a children's nanny.

nanny goat noun informal a female domestic goat. [from Nanny, nickname for Ann]

nanny state noun a state the government of which takes upon itself to decide what is best for people and so to interfere to an unwarrantable extent in the way they live their lives.

nano- comb. form forming words, denoting: a one-thousand-millionth (10^{-9}) part of a unit, etc: nanosecond. [Greek nanos dwarf]

nanometre (NAmer **nanometer**) /'nahnəmeetə/ noun one thousand-millionth of a metre.

nanosecond /'nahnohsekənd/ noun one thousand-millionth of a second.

nanotechnology /ˌnanohtek'noləji/ noun the technology of manufacturing and measuring objects of microscopically small size, esp between 0.1 and 100 nanometres: nanotechnology, a revolutionary new engineering concept — Irish Times.

Nansen bottle /'nans(ə)n/ noun a waterproof container for collecting samples of sea water, usu one of several lowered on a line to take in water at a range of depths, closing automatically as they fill. [named after F Nansen d.1930, Norwegian explorer and scientist, who invented it]

naos /'nayos/ noun 1 in an ancient Greek temple, the innermost chamber, containing the shrine with an image of the deity: compare CELLA. 2 in a Byzantine church, the nave or main body. [Greek naos temple, inner shrine]

nap¹ /nap/ verb intrans (**napped, napping**) to take a short sleep, esp during the day. ✳ **catch somebody napping** to catch somebody when they are unprepared or inattentive. [Old English hnappian]

nap² *noun* a short sleep, *esp* during the day: *I never take a nap after dinner but when I have had a bad night, and then the nap takes me* — Dr Johnson.

nap³ *noun* **1** a hairy or downy surface, e.g. on a woven fabric; a pile. **2** *Aus.* **a** bedding or blankets. **b** a bedroll. ➤➤ **napless** *adj*, **napped** *adj*. [Middle English *noppe* from early Dutch or early Low German *noppe* flock of wool, nap]

nap⁴ *verb trans* (**napped, napping**) to raise a nap on (fabric or leather).

nap⁵ *noun* **1** = NAPOLEON (2). **2** *Brit.* **a** in horse-racing, the act or instance of betting all one's money on a single potential winner. **b** a tipster's selection for such a bet. ✳ **go nap 1** to try to take all five tricks in the game of napoleon. **2** to risk all in a single venture.

nap⁶ *verb trans* (**napped, napping**) *Brit* in horse racing, to recommend (a horse) as a possible winner: *the three-year-old napped to win the 3.30 at Sandown.*

napa /'napə/ *noun* see NAPPA.

napalm¹ /'naypahm/ *noun* **1** a thickener consisting of a mixture of aluminium soaps. **2** petrol jellied with napalm and used *esp* in incendiary bombs and flamethrowers. [blend of *naphthenate* (a salt of naphthene) + PALMITATE]

napalm² *verb trans* to attack (troops) with napalm.

nape /nayp/ *noun* the back of the neck. [Middle English; earlier history unknown]

napery /'naypəri/ *noun* household linen; *esp* table linen. [Middle English from Old French *naperie*, from *nappe*: see NAPPE]

nap hand *noun* **1** in the game of napoleon, a hand of cards on which a player would be justified in going nap. **2** a favourable chance that invites the taking of risks. **3** *informal* a series of five successes, victories, or winning points, in a sport, game, etc.

naphth- *or* **naphtho-** *comb. form* forming words, denoting: naphthalene: *naphthol.* [NAPHTHA and NAPHTHALENE]

naphtha /'nafthə/ *noun* **1** petroleum. **2** any of various liquid hydrocarbon mixtures used chiefly as solvents. [via Latin from Greek *naphtha*, of Iranian origin]

naphthalene /'nafthəleen/ *noun* a hydrocarbon usu obtained by distillation of coal tar and used *esp* in mothballs, and the synthesis of organic chemicals. ➤➤ **naphthalenic** /-'lenik/ *adj*. [alteration of earlier *naphthaline*, from NAPHTHA]

naphthene /'naftheen/ *noun* any of a group of chemical compounds (cycloalkanes; see CYCLOALKANE), many of which occur in petroleum. ➤➤ **naphthenic** /naf'theenik/ *adj*. [NAPHTHA + -ENE]

naphtho- *comb. form* see NAPHTH-.

naphthol /'nafthol/ *noun* either of two chemical compounds, $C_{10}H_7OH$, that are derivatives of naphthalene, found in COAL TAR or made synthetically, and used in the manufacture of dyes.

Napierian logarithm /nə'piəri·ən, nay-/ *noun* = NATURAL LOGARITHM. [named after John *Napier*: see NEPER]

Napier's bones /'naypi·əz/ *pl noun* formerly, a set of rods of ivory or other material, marked with figures for facilitating multiplication and division. [named after John *Napier*: see NEPER]

napkin /'napkin/ *noun* **1** a square piece of material, e.g. linen or paper, used at table to wipe the lips or fingers and protect the clothes. **2** *chiefly Brit, formal* a baby's nappy. **3** *chiefly NAmer* = SANITARY TOWEL. [Middle English *nappekin*, dimin. of *nappe* tablecloth, from Old French: see NAPPE]

napoleon /nə'pohli·ən/ *noun* **1** a former French 20-franc gold coin. **2** a card game resembling whist played with hands of five cards in which players bid to name the numbers of tricks they will take. [French *napoléon*, named after *Napoleon* I d.1821, Emperor of France]

Napoleonic /nə,pohli'onik/ *adj* relating to or resembling Napoleon I: *the Napoleonic Wars.*

nappa *or* **napa** /'napə/ *noun* a soft leather prepared from sheep or goat skin by tawing (treating with mineral salts; see TAW¹), used for gloves, handbags, etc. [named after *Nappa*, town in California, USA, where it is produced]

nappe /nap/ *noun* **1** a mountain-forming structure resulting from a large mass thrust over other rocks. **2** a smooth sheet of water flowing over a dam or weir. **3** in geometry, a SHEET¹ (surface of a figure), *esp* either of two sheets of a cone on either side of the vertex. [French *nappe* tablecloth, sheet, from Latin *mappa* cloth]

napped *adj* said of a fabric: having a raised surface, or NAP³ (1).

napper /'napə/ *noun Brit, informal* a person's head. [prob from NAP¹, with the idea of nodding off]

nappy¹ /'napi/ *noun* (*pl* **nappies**) *chiefly Brit* a shaped pad or a square piece of towelling worn by babies to absorb and retain urine and faeces and usu drawn up between the legs and fastened at the waist. [shortening of NAPKIN]

nappy² *adj* (**nappier, nappiest**) **1** *NAmer, informal* said of a black person's hair: tightly curly; fuzzy. **2** said of beer: having a frothy head. [orig 'shaggy'; from early Dutch *noppigh* or early Low German *noppich*, from *noppe* NAP³]

nappy rash *noun* a skin rash concentrated round a baby's genital and anal area, caused by irritation from the ammonia in a urine-soaked nappy.

narc *or* **nark** /nahk/ *noun NAmer, informal* a government agent or other official who investigates violations of the narcotics regulations. [shortening of *narcotics agent*]

narcissi /nah'sisie/ *noun pl* of NARCISSUS.

narcissism /'nahsisiz(ə)m/ *noun* **1** abnormal interest in or admiration for oneself or one's appearance: *At their worst, contemporary heroes and heroines are stomach-churning models of narcissism* — Daily Telegraph. **2** sensual pleasure derived from contemplating one's own body. ➤➤ **narcissist** *noun and adj*, **narcissistic** /-'sistik/ *adj*. [named after *Narcissus*, a youth in Greek mythology who fell in love with his own reflection in a pool, pined away, and was turned into a narcissus]

narcissus /nah'sisəs/ *noun* (*pl* **narcissi** /-sie/ *or* **narcissuses**) any of several species of daffodils with pale outer petals and a shallow orange or bright yellow CORONA¹ (central crown): *Narcissus poeticus* and other species. [via Latin from Greek *narkissos*, perhaps from *narkē* numbness, with reference to the plant's narcotic properties]

narco /'nahkoh/ *noun* (*pl* **narcos**) *NAmer, informal* **1** a dealer in drugs. **2** a narcotics investigation agent; = NARC.

narco- *comb. form* forming words, with the meanings: **1** relating to insensibility, torpor, or numbness: *narcolepsy.* **2** relating to the use of or trade in narcotic drugs: *narcoterrorism.* [Greek *narkē* numbness]

narcoanalysis /,nahkohə'nalisis/ *noun* psychoanalysis of a patient who has been put into a trance with the aid of barbiturate drugs.

narcolepsy /'nahkəlepsi/ *noun* an abnormal tendency to brief spells of deep sleep. ➤➤ **narcoleptic** /-'leptik/ *noun and adj*.

narcosis /nah'kohsis/ *noun* drowsiness, stupor, or unconsciousness produced by narcotics or other chemicals. [Greek *narkōsis* action of benumbing, from *narkoun*: see NARCOTIC¹]

narcosynthesis /nahkoh'sinthisis/ *noun* psychotherapy of a patient with the use of barbiturates to release suppressed or repressed thoughts and emotions.

narcoterrorism /nahkoh'terəriz(ə)m/ *noun* terrorism engaged in by powerful drug dealers to deter their opponents. ➤➤ **narco-terrorist** *noun and adj*.

narcotic¹ /nah'kotik/ *noun* **1** a drug that induces drowsiness, stupor, or unconsciousness, and relieves pain. **2** any drug, *esp* an illegal or addictive one, that affects mood and behaviour and is taken for recreational rather than medical purposes. [Middle English *narkotik* via Old French and late Latin from Greek *narkō-tikos* benumbing, from *narkoun* to benumb, from *narkē* numbness]

narcotic² *adj* **1** like, being, or yielding a narcotic: *narcotic plants.* **2** inducing mental lethargy; soporific: *narcotic drugs.* **3** relating to narcotics or to addiction to narcotics. ➤➤ **narcotically** *adv*.

narcotize *or* **narcotise** /'nahkətiez/ *verb trans* **1** to treat (somebody) with or subject (them) to a narcotic. **2** to put (somebody) into a state of narcosis. ➤ *verb intrans* to act as a narcotizing agent. ➤➤ **narcotism** *noun*.

nard /nahd/ *noun* the Himalayan SPIKENARD plant. [Middle English *narde* via French and Latin from Greek *nardos*, prob ultimately from Sanskrit *nalada* spikenard]

nardoo /'nahdooh/ *noun* **1** an Australian fern with cloverlike fronds: *Marsilea drummondii.* **2** the spore-producing body of this fern, ground into flour by Aboriginals. [from Aboriginal Diyari *nardu* or Kalimaroi *naahdu*]

nares /'neəreez/ *pl noun* (*sing.* **naris** /'neəris/) the nostrils. ➤➤ **narial** *adj*. [Latin *nares* the nostrils, pl of *naris* nostril, nose]

narghile *or* **nargileh** /'nahgili/ *noun* a WATER PIPE (oriental smoking apparatus), *esp* with several flexible tubes: compare

HOOKAH. [Persian *nārgīla*, from *nārgīl* coconut (of which the bowls were orig made), from Sanskrit *nārikela*]

naris /'neəris/ *noun* sing. of NARES.

nariyal /'nahri·əl/ *noun Indian English* a coconut. [Hindi *nāriyal*]

nark[1] /nahk/ *noun informal* **1** *Brit, Aus, NZ* a police informer: *a copper's nark.* **2** *Aus, NZ* an annoying person or thing. **3** a whingeing or complaining person. [Romany *nāk* nose]

nark[2] *verb intrans* **1** *Brit, Aus, NZ, informal (often + on)* to spy or inform on people, *esp* for the police. **2** to complain or whinge. ➤ *verb trans informal (usu in passive)* to offend or affront (somebody): *I was narked by her remark.*

nark[3] *noun* see NARC.

narky *adj* (**narkier, narkiest**) *Brit, informal* easily annoyed; irritable.

Narraganset /narə'gansit/ *noun* (*pl* **Narragansets** or collectively **Narraganset**) **1** a member of a Native American people of Rhode Island. **2** the extinct Algonquian language of this people. ➤➤ **Narraganset** *adj.* [Narraganset *narraganset*, literally 'people of the promontory']

narrate /nə'rayt/ *verb trans* **1** to relate or tell (a story). **2** to give a spoken commentary in accompaniment to (a film, etc). ➤➤ **narrator** /nə'raytə, 'narətə/ *noun.* [Latin *narratus*, past part. of *narrare* to relate, from *gnarus* knowing]

narration /nə'raysh(ə)n/ *noun* **1** the act of narrating a story, etc. **2** a story or narrative. ➤➤ **narrational** *adj.*

narrative[1] /'narətiv/ *noun* **1** something that is related or narrated; a story. **2** the narrated parts of a novel or other literary work, as distinct from the dialogue. **3** the art or practice of narration.

narrative[2] *adj* of or relating to narration. ➤➤ **narratively** *adv,* **narrativity** /-'tiviti/ *noun.*

narratology /narə'toləji/ *noun* a branch of literary analysis or criticism that deals with narrative.

Editorial note _____
Narratology is the study of the poetics of fiction, exploring the nature of narrative systems and devices, and has been of increasing importance in modern culture. It is now a key part of critical theory and of writing and artistic production, exploring the mechanics of all types of storytelling, for example film scripting and direction, for the purpose of refining artistic and media techniques — Professor Malcolm Bradbury.

➤➤ **narratological** /-tə'lojikl/ *adj,* **narratologist** *noun.*

narrow[1] /'naroh/ *adj* **1** of little width, *esp* in comparison with height or length. **2** of less than standard width: *a narrow-gauge railway.* **3** limited in size or scope; restricted: *a narrow field of study.* **4** inflexible in attitudes or beliefs. **5** only just sufficient or successful: *won by a narrow majority; a narrow escape.* **6** in speech, denoting a vowel sound made with the tongue drawn back so as to narrow the pharynx, e.g.: **a** the vowels *e* and *i*, as distinct from the BROAD[1] vowels *a, o,* and *u.* **b** the vowel sound *ee* in contrast to *i;* = TENSE[1] (3). **✳ in narrow circumstances** in poverty. ➤➤ **narrowness** *noun.* [Old English *nearu*]

narrow[2] *noun* (*in pl*) a narrow sea passage; = STRAIT[2].

narrow[3] *verb trans* **1** to make (something) narrow or narrower: *arteries narrowed by a thick deposit.* **2** (*often + down*) to restrict the scope or sphere of (research, an enquiry, etc). **3** to close (one's eyes) slightly in focusing one's attention on something. ➤ *verb intrans* to become narrow or narrower: *His eyes narrowed.*

narrowband *adj* said of radio or television transmission: involving signals over a narrow range of frequencies.

narrowboat *noun* a canal barge with a BEAM[1] (width) of 2.1m (7ft) or less.

narrowcast[1] *verb trans* (*past tense and past part.* **narrowcast**) to transmit (a programme) to a restricted region or audience, e.g. by cable television. [blend of NARROW[1] and BROADCAST[1]]

narrowcast[2] *noun* a narrowcast transmission.

narrow gauge *noun* a railway gauge narrower than the standard gauge of 1.435m (4ft 8¹/₂ inches).

narrowly *adv* **1** by a narrow margin; only just: *He narrowly escaped a parking fine.* **2** with close concentration: *He looked at her narrowly.*

narrow-minded *adj* lacking tolerance or breadth of vision; bigoted. ➤➤ **narrow-mindedly** *adv,* **narrow-mindedness** *noun.*

narrow money *noun* in economics, ready money in the form of notes or cash, for use in direct exchange.

narthex /'nahtheks/ *noun* **1** the western portico or inner porch of an early church. **2** in modern churches, a vestibule at the west end. [Greek *narthēx* giant fennel, cane, casket (because boxes were made from it), which in late Greek came to mean 'church portico']

narwhal or **narwal** /'nahwəl/ *noun* a small arctic whale, the male of which has a long twisted ivory tusk: *Monodon monoceros.* [Norwegian or Danish *narhval*, Swedish *narval*, or Dutch *narwal*, all ultimately from Old Norse *nāhvalr*, from *nār* corpse + *hvalr* whale; from its colour]

nas- or **naso-** or **nasi-** *comb. form* forming words, with the meanings: **1** nose: *nasal.* **2** nasal; nasal and: *nasogastric.* [Latin *nasus* nose]

NASA /'nahsə/ *abbr NAmer* National Aeronautics and Space Administration.

nasal[1] /'nayzl/ *adj* **1** relating to the nose. **2** said of speech sounds: **a** uttered through the nose with the mouth passage closed, e.g. *m, n, ng.* **b** uttered with resonance through the nose but with both the mouth and nose passage open, e.g. French *en, un.* **3** said of somebody's speech, of a language, etc: characterized by resonance produced through the nose: *speaking in a nasal whine.* ➤➤ **nasality** /nay'zaliti/ *noun,* **nasally** *adv.* [Middle English via late Latin *nasalis* from Latin *nasus* nose]

nasal[2] *noun* a nasal speech sound.

nasalize or **nasalise** *verb trans* to utter (speech sounds) with resonance through the nose: *The nasalized vowel in Gaelic 'cnoc' (hill) is reflected in the Manx spelling 'cronk'.* ➤➤ **nasalization** /-'zaysh(ə)n/ *noun.*

nascent /'nas(ə)nt, 'nays(ə)nt/ *adj* **1** *formal* in the process of being born; just beginning to develop: *a nascent spirit of rebellion.* **2** said of hydrogen: freshly produced in a reactive form. ➤➤ **nascence** *noun,* **nascency** /-si/ *noun.* [Latin *nascent-, nascens,* present part. of *nasci* to be born]

naseberry /'nayzb(ə)ri/ *noun* (*pl* **naseberries**) = SAPODILLA. [alteration by folk etymology of Portuguese or Spanish *néspera* medlar]

nasi- or **naso-** *comb. form* see NAS-.

nasogastric /nayzoh'gastrik/ *adj* said e.g. of a feeding tube: reaching the stomach via the nose.

nasopharynx /nayzoh'faringks/ *noun* the upper part of the pharynx, connecting with the nasal passages. ➤➤ **nasopharyngeal** /-rin'jee·əl/ *adj.*

nastic /'nastik/ *adj* said of the movement of a plant part: caused by an external stimulus but not influenced by its direction. [Greek *nastos* close-pressed, from *nassein* to press]

nasturtium /nə'stuhsh(ə)m/ *noun* a widely cultivated plant with circular leaves and bright orange, red, or yellow flowers, and pungent seeds: *Tropaeolum majus.* [Old English from Latin *nasturtium, nasturcium,* a kind of cress, prob from *naris* or *nasus* nose + *torquēre* to twist; from its strong smell]

nasty[1] /'nahsti/ *adj* (**nastier, nastiest**) **1** unpleasant, repugnant, or disgusting: *a nasty smell; nasty weather.* **2** said of people or their behaviour: spiteful. **3** uncharitable: *a nasty suspicion.* **4** harmful or dangerous: *a nasty situation; a nasty wound.* **✳ turn nasty** to become violent or vicious if provoked, etc. ➤➤ **nastily** *adv,* **nastiness** *noun.* [Middle English; earlier history unknown]

nasty[2] *noun* (*pl* **nasties**) *informal* a nasty or offensive person or thing: *video nasties.*

NAS/UWT *abbr Brit* National Association of Schoolmasters and Union of Women Teachers.

nat. *abbr* **1** national. **2** nationalist. **3** natural.

natal[1] /'naytl/ *adj* related to or associated with one's birth: *a natal star.* [Middle English from Latin *natalis,* from *nasci* to be born]

natal[2] *adj* see NATES.

natality /nə'taliti/ *noun* the birthrate.

natant /'naytənt/ *adj formal* floating or swimming in water: *natant decapods.* [Latin *natant-, natans,* present part. of *natare* to swim]

natation /nə'taysh(ə)n/ *noun formal* the activity or art of swimming. [Latin *natation-, natatio,* from *natare* to swim, float]

natatorial /nayta'tawri·əl/ *adj* relating to or adapted to swimming.

natatory /'naytət(ə)ri/ *adj* = NATATORIAL.

natch /nach/ *adv informal* often used as an interjection: naturally.

nates /'nayteez/ *pl noun* the buttocks. ➤➤ **natal** *adj.* [Latin *nates,* pl of *natis* buttock]

NATFHE /'natfee/ *abbr Brit* National Association of Teachers in Further and Higher Education.

natheless *or* **nathless** /'naythlis/ *adv archaic* nevertheless; nonetheless: *He had tortured the lady with exceeding tortures, natheless she would not confess to him aught* — Richard Burton. [Old English, from *nā* never + THE[1] + *lǣs* LESS[1]]

nation /'naysh(ə)n/ *noun* (*treated as sing. or pl*) **1** (*treated as sing. or pl*). **a** a people with a common origin, tradition, and language. **b** a community of people possessing a more or less defined territory and government.

Editorial note ────────
Belonging to a nation is nothing if not emotional commitment. Like being a member of a family, it does not essentially depend on a rational calculation of advantage or merit – though it may engender pseudo-rational claims to superiority, whether in war or sport. National heroes exemplify this sort of self-image, often idealized rather than truly representative — Professor Peter Clarke.

2 a tribe or federation of tribes, e.g. of Native Americans. **3** (**the nations**) *archaic* the gentiles or heathen: *Why do the nations so furiously rage together?* — Bible. [Middle English *nacioun* via French from Latin *nation-, natio* birth, race, nation, from *nasci* to be born]

national[1] /'nash(ə)nəl/ *adj* **1** relating to or belonging to a nation. **2** said of an industry, etc: belonging to or maintained by the central government. **3** denoting a coalition government formed by most or all major political parties. **4** denoting a newspaper produced for sale throughout the country, as distinct from a local one. ⟫ **nationally** *adv.*

national[2] *noun* **1** a citizen of a specified nation: *an Egyptian national*. **2** a national newspaper in contrast to a local one: *It made the headlines in all the nationals*. **3** (*usu in pl*) a competition that is national in scope.

national anthem *noun* a patriotic hymn or song officially adopted by a nation for use on public or ceremonial occasions.

National Assembly *noun* **1** an elected legislative body in many countries. **2** in revolutionary France, the elected legislative body of 1789–91.

national assistance *or* **National Assistance** *noun* formerly, in Britain, a weekly welfare allowance designed to supplement low incomes, replaced in 1965 by SUPPLEMENTARY BENEFIT, and in 1988 by INCOME SUPPORT.

national bank *noun* **1** a bank that officially provides banking services for the government, implements its monetary decisions, e.g. on credit regulation, and issues bank notes; = CENTRAL BANK. **2** in the USA, a commercial bank that is chartered under the federal government and is required to be a member of the Federal Reserve System.

national call *noun* a telephone call made to a number beyond the local area but within the caller's country.

National Certificate *noun Brit* a technician's qualification obtained at either of two levels by part-time study.

national curriculum *noun* in England and Wales since 1989, a curriculum designed to operate throughout the state-maintained school system, with set attainment targets and assessment of pupils taking place at four stages, the core subjects being English, mathematics, and science, and the other required subjects art, design, technology, geography, history, music, physical education, and a foreign language.

national debt *noun* the amount of money owed by the government of a country.

National Diploma *noun Brit* an advanced qualification, usu in a technical or applied subject, obtained at either of two levels typically by part-time or sandwich-course study.

National Football *noun Aus* = AUSTRALIAN RULES FOOTBALL.

National Front *noun Brit* an extreme right-wing political party asserting the racial superiority of the indigenous British population over immigrants, e.g. blacks.

national grid *noun* **1** in Britain, a country-wide network of high-voltage cables between major power stations. **2** in Britain, the system of coordinates used for map reference by the Ordnance Survey.

National Guard *noun* a militia force recruited by each state of the USA and equipped by the federal government, available for service to either.

National Health *noun* = NATIONAL HEALTH SERVICE.

National Health Service *noun* the British system of medical care, started in 1948, by which every person is entitled to medical treatment paid for mainly by taxation.

national hunt *or* **National Hunt** *noun* **1** in Britain, the sport of horse-racing over jumps; steeplechasing. **2** the body controlling this sport.

national income *noun* the total sum of earnings of residents of a nation, including wages and salaries of employees, interest, income from rent, and gross trading profits of companies and public utilities, and income from abroad measured over some specified time period, usu one year.

national insurance *or* **National Insurance** *noun Brit* a compulsory social-security scheme funded by contributions from employers, employees, and the government, which insures the individual against sickness, retirement, and unemployment.

nationalise *verb trans* see NATIONALIZE.

nationalism *noun* **1** loyalty and devotion to one's nation; *esp* the exalting of one's nation above all others.

Editorial note ────────
Nationalism has often been regarded as a benign force, expressing the essential identity of immemorially distinct peoples. Yet destructive passions can be unleashed in its name. Moreover, the concept itself is now challenged by a recognition that it appeals to a sense of community that is 'imagined', whether its appeal is to historical or territorial settlement, shared ethnicity or common religion — Professor Peter Clarke.

2 the pursuit of political independence for one's country or nation.

nationalist *noun* **1** a loyal and enthusiastic supporter of one's own country. **2** (**Nationalist**) a member of a political group advocating national independence or strong national government. ⟫ **nationalist** *adj*, **nationalistic** /-'listik/ *adj*, **nationalistically** /-'listikli/ *adv.*

nationality /nash(ə)'naliti/ *noun* (*pl* **nationalities**) **1** the fact or status of belonging to a particular nation. **2** national character. **3** an ethnic group within a larger unit.

nationalize *or* **nationalise** *verb trans* **1** to transfer control or ownership of (an industry or other major concern) to the state government. **2** to give a national character to (architecture, etc). **3** = NATURALIZE. ⟫ **nationalization** /-'zaysh(ə)n/ *noun*, **nationalizer** *noun.*

National Lottery *noun* in Britain, a state-controlled lottery inaugurated in 1994.

national park *noun* an area of special scenic, historical, or environmental importance, preserved and maintained by the government for public enjoyment or the preservation of wildlife, etc.

national product *noun* the value of the goods and services produced in a nation during a year.

National Savings *pl noun* (*treated as sing. or pl*) in Britain, a savings scheme run by the government through the Post Office, funds being deposited in the National Savings Bank and made available for government use.

national service *noun* a statutory period of compulsory service in one's country's armed forces. ⟫ **national serviceman** *noun*, **national servicewoman** *noun.*

National Socialism *noun* the policies of the Nazis, including anti-Semitism, territorial expansion, state control of the economy, and the placing of supreme power in the hands of Hitler as Führer. ⟫ **National Socialist** *noun and adj.*

National Trust *noun* a charitable trust for the preservation of places of historic interest and natural beauty in Britain.

nation-state *noun* a sovereign state inhabited by a relatively homogeneous people as opposed to several nationalities.

nationwide *adj and adv* throughout the whole country: *a new nationwide road-safety initiative; available from good stores nationwide.*

native[1] /'naytiv/ *adj* **1** belonging to or being the place of one's birth: *one's native land.* **2** belonging to a particular place by birth: *a native Yorkshireman.* **3** said of a plant, etc: living or growing naturally in a particular region; indigenous. **4** produced or originating in a particular place or in the vicinity; local: *native industries.* **5** inborn; innate: *native wit.* **6** simple; unaffected: *native charm.* **7** found in nature, *esp* in a pure form: *mining native silver.* ✳ **go native** *derog* said of a person living abroad: to adopt the way of life of the local population. ⟫ **natively** *adv*, **nativeness** *noun.*

[Middle English *natif* via French from Latin *nativus*, from *nasci* to be born]

native² *noun* **1** a person born or reared in a particular place: *a native of Devon.* **2** *dated, offensive* an original or indigenous inhabitant, *esp* of a country colonized by Europeans. **3** a plant, animal, etc living or growing in a particular locality. **4** *chiefly humorous* a local resident; *esp* a person who lives in a place permanently, as distinguished from a visitor or a temporary resident: *day-trippers who disturb the peace of the natives.*

Usage note
There are few problems with *native* used as an adjective: *native land, native language*, and *native Yorkshireman* are all unexceptionable. It is with the noun that the trouble starts. The noun *native* is extremely offensive if used to mean simply 'a non-white person', and scarcely less so if used to mean 'an original (and by implication usually uncivilized) inhabitant of a country'. The only currently safe use of the noun *native* is in the meaning 'a person who was born in a particular place': *I am a native of Hertfordshire.* See also note at NATIVE AMERICAN.

Native American *noun* **1** a member of any of the indigenous races of N America. **2** more generally, a member of any of the indigenous races of N, S, or Central America; = AMERICAN INDIAN.

Usage note
This is now generally accepted as the correct term to use for a person whose ancestors lived in America before the arrival of Europeans. The term *Red Indian* for a Native (North) American should be avoided. See also note at AMERICAN INDIAN.

native bear *noun* *Aus* = KOALA.

native-born *adj* born in the place indicated: *Nowak is a native-born Scot despite his Polish name.*

native cat *noun* *Aus* = DASYURE.

native companion *noun* *Aus* = BROLGA.

native dog *noun* *Aus* = DINGO.

native hen *noun* a moorhen native to Australia, with a greenish beak: *Gallinula ventralis* of Australia and *Gallinula mortierii* of Tasmania.

native rock *noun* local rock in its original site, not quarried or imported.

native speaker *noun* a person who speaks the language in question as their native language: *native speakers of English.*

nativism *noun* **1** a policy of favouring native inhabitants as opposed to immigrants. **2** the revival or perpetuation of an indigenous culture. **3** in psychology, a theory emphasizing that behaviour and personality are innately determined. ➤➤ **nativist** *noun and adj,* **nativistic** /-'vistik/ *adj.*

nativity /nə'tiviti/ *noun* (*pl* **nativities**) **1** one's birth. **2a** (**the Nativity**) the birth of Jesus Christ. **b** the festival celebrating this; Christmas. **c** a painting or other artistic representation of this. **3** *dated* a horoscope or birth chart. [Middle English *nativite* via French from Latin *nativitat-, nativitas* birth, from *nativus* relating to birth, innate, from *nasci* to be born]

nativity play *noun* a play about the birth of Christ, usu including the adoration of the shepherds and the visit of the three wise men, performed at Christmas.

NATO *or* **Nato** /naytoh/ *abbr* North Atlantic Treaty Organization.

natriuresis /,naytriyooə'reesis/ *noun* the excretion of an excessive quantity of sodium in the urine. ➤➤ **natriuretic** /-'retik/ *adj.* [scientific Latin *natrium* sodium, from NATRON + Latin *uresis* from Greek *ourēsis* urination]

natron /'naytron, 'naytrən/ *noun* hydrated sodium carbonate occurring as a mineral and used in ancient times in embalming. [French *natron* via Spanish and Arabic from Greek *nitron*: see NITRE]

NATSOPA /nat'sohpə/ *abbr* National Society of Operative Printers, Graphical, and Media Personnel.

natter¹ /'natə/ *verb intrans* (**nattered, nattering**) *chiefly Brit, informal* to chatter or gossip. [prob imitative]

natter² *noun* the act or an instance of nattering.

natterjack /'natəjak/ *noun* a common brownish yellow W European toad with short hind legs, which runs rather than hops: *Bufo calamita.* [origin unknown]

natty /'nati/ *adj* (**nattier, nattiest**) *informal* **1** said of clothes or their wearer: neat and trim; spruce. **2** said of a gadget, contrivance, etc: clever, neat, or apt. ➤➤ **nattily** *adv,* **nattiness** *noun.* [perhaps alteration of *netty*, from obsolete *net* neat, clean, from French: see NEAT¹]

Natufian /na'toohfi·ən/ *adj* in archaeology, denoting a late Mesolithic Middle-Eastern culture of about 10,000–8000 BC, significant for showing the beginnings of agriculture and permanent settlement. [from *Wādi en-Natūf*, Palestinian site yielding finds]

natural¹ /'nach(ə)rəl/ *adj* **1** existing in or produced by nature without human intervention: *natural scenery; natural resources.* **2** relating to nature as an object of study and research: *the natural environment.* **3** relating to the physical world: *Natural laws describe phenomena of the physical universe.* **4** in accordance with or determined by nature: *a more natural lifestyle.* **5** true to nature: *painted in natural colours.* **6** in a state of nature unenlightened by culture or morality: *natural man.* **7** based on an inherent moral sense: *natural justice.* **8a** related by blood rather than by adoption: *his natural parents.* **b** *archaic* illegitimate: *Monmouth was the natural son of Charles II.* **9a** innate; inherent: *a natural talent for languages.* **b** having a specified character or attribute by nature: *a natural athlete.* **c** not disguised or altered in appearance or form: *leave one's hair its natural shade.* **10a** said of fabric: unbleached or undyed. **b** off-white or creamy beige in colour. **11a** happening in accordance with the ordinary course of nature: *death from natural causes.* **b** normal, expected. *Events followed their natural course.* **c** following from the nature of the case; warranted by the facts: *a perfectly natural assumption to make in the circumstances.* **12** free from affectation or constraint: *natural, spontaneous behaviour.* **13** said of musical notes: **a** neither sharp nor flat. **b** having the pitch modified by the natural sign. **14** denoting a brass instrument such as a trumpet or horn, without valves or keys. **15** in bridge, denoting a bid that reflects one's cards. ➤➤ **naturalness** *noun.* [Middle English, in the sense 'of a certain status by birth', via Old French from Latin *naturalis* of nature, from *natura*: see NATURE]

natural² *noun* **1** *informal* a person having natural skills, talents, or abilities: *As an actor, he was a natural.* **2** *informal* a person or thing likely to be particularly suitable or successful. **3a** a sign (♮) placed on the musical stave to indicate that the following note or notes are not sharp or flat. **b** a note to which the natural sign applies. **4** in cards, etc, a result or combination that immediately wins. **5** *Brit, informal* one's life: *... never worked so hard in all my natural* — Compton Mackenzie. **6** *archaic* a person born mentally defective.

natural-born *adj* **1** equipped by nature to be the specified thing: *He was a natural-born salesman.* **2** *archaic* = NATIVE-BORN: *No person except a natural-born citizen ... shall be eligible to the office of President* — US Constitution.

natural childbirth *noun* the management of labour by the mother, through special breathing and relaxation techniques, so that the use of drugs is kept to a minimum.

natural classification *noun* scientific classification of plants and animals according to characteristics signifying relationship, as opposed to the artificial system used by Linnaeus in plant taxonomy.

natural gas *noun* **1** a combustible mixture of methane and other hydrocarbons, occurring naturally underground and used chiefly as a fuel and as raw material in industry. **2** any gas that flows out from the earth's crust through natural openings or bored wells.

natural history *noun* **1** the usu amateur study, *esp* in the field, of natural objects, e.g. plants and animals, often in a particular area. **2** the natural development of an organism, disease, etc over a period of time. **3** a treatise on some aspect of nature.

natural immunity *noun* immunity with which one is born, resulting from genetic inheritance, as distinct from immunity acquired through the production of antibodies in response to antigens.

naturalise *verb trans* see NATURALIZE.

naturalism *noun* **1** realism in art or literature, *esp* when emphasizing scientific observation of life without idealization of the ugly. **2** a philosophical theory discounting supernatural explanations of the origin of the universe and attributing it to natural properties and causes. **3** action or thought based on natural desires and instincts. **4** in moral philosophy, the view that it is possible to derive ethical statements from non-ethical ones. ➤➤ **naturalistic** /-'listik/ *adj,* **naturalistically** /-'listikli/ *adv.*

naturalist *noun* **1** a follower or advocate of naturalism. **2** a student of natural history. ➤➤ **naturalist** *adj.*

naturalize *or* **naturalise** *verb trans* **1** to admit (a foreigner) to the citizenship of a country. **2** (*in passive*). **a** said of a plant or animal: to become established in the wild in an area where it is not indigenous: *naturalized species.* **b** said of an originally foreign word, e.g.

shampoo: to develop the phonology and grammatical features of a native word: *naturalized English*.

natural language *noun* a language that has developed naturally as a means of human communication, as distinct from an invented or artificial language, a code, or computer language.

natural law *noun* **1a** the set of moral principles that are understood to govern human conduct. **b** any one of these principles. **2** a law of nature that is an observed pattern operating in relation to natural phenomena.

natural life *noun* the span of life that in normal circumstances is likely for a person or animal.

natural logarithm *noun* a logarithm with *e* as base. Also called NAPIERIAN LOGARITHM.

naturally *adv* **1** by nature: *naturally timid*. **2** as might be expected; of course: *Naturally, we shall be there*. **3** in a natural manner: *Behave naturally*.

natural magic *noun* in medieval tradition, magic that is worked on people, for good or ill, by manipulating nature, e.g. by making images under certain astrological conditions and administering herbal concoctions, as distinct from invoking evil spirits: *Thou mixture rank, of midnight weeds collected … thy natural magic and dire property on wholesome life usurp immediately* — Shakespeare.

natural number *noun* the number 1 or any positive whole number, e.g. 3, 12, 432.

natural philosophy *noun archaic* natural or physical science, *esp* physics.

natural religion *noun* religion that proceeds from reasoned argument rather than divine revelation: *Theology … is a science in the strictest sense of the word. I will tell you … what it is not – not 'physical evidences' for God, not 'natural religion'* — Cardinal Newman.

natural resources *pl noun* industrial materials and capacities, e.g. mineral deposits and waterpower, supplied by nature.

natural science *noun* any of the sciences dealing with the physical world and its phenomena, including physics, chemistry, biology, and geology. **>>> natural scientist** *noun*.

natural selection *noun* a natural process that tends to result in the survival of organisms best adapted to their environment and the elimination of organisms carrying undesirable traits that have resulted from genetic mutation: compare SELECTION, STRUGGLE FOR EXISTENCE.

Editorial note
Natural selection is the theory of the driving force of evolution, proposed by Charles Darwin (1809–82) and, independently, by Alfred Wallace (1823–1913). It uniquely accounts for adaptation: the illusion that living organisms are well designed. Genetic variation in a population is randomly generated by mutation and sexual recombination, and nonrandomly sampled by natural selection. The fittest survive, and future generations inherit what qualified them to do so — Professor Richard Dawkins.

natural theology *noun* knowledge of God's existence and his works that is arrived at through observation and reasoning, rather than through divine revelation; = DEISM.

natural virtue *noun* any of the virtues, specifically justice, prudence, temperance, and fortitude, of which humans are capable: compare THEOLOGICAL VIRTUE.

natural wastage *noun* reduction of staff numbers by non-replacement of employees who leave as they retire, etc.

natural year *noun* = SOLAR YEAR.

nature /'naychə/ *noun* **1** the physical world in terms of landscape, plants, and animals, as distinct from human creations. **2** a creative force apprehended as controlling these phenomena. **3** a way of life taken as representing mankind's original or natural condition: *back to nature*. **4** the physical constitution or motivating forces of an organism. **5** the inherent character or constitution of a person or thing; essence. **6** disposition or temperament. **7** an individual's inborn or inherited characteristics, as distinct from those attributable to NURTURE[1]: *an inquisitive person by nature*. **8** a kind or class of thing: *documents of a confidential nature*.

Editorial note
Nature can refer either to the external world or to individuals, and contrasts the biological with the cultural or the artificial. Human nature now usually refers to basic biological drives, to which cultural attributes are added; but in Aristotelian thought, human nature was the fullest development of an individual's being. Acts are sometimes justified as being natural; but the justification is rarely convincing and is referred to in ethics as the naturalistic fallacy — Dr Mark Ridley.

* **against nature** unnatural. **in a state of nature 1** quite naked. **2a** in a morally unregenerate state. **b** in an uncivilized state. **c** in an uncultivated condition. **in the nature of things** inevitable or inevitably. **in the nature of** by way of or describable as (a certain thing). **somebody's better nature** somebody's capacity for kindness, tolerance, etc. **the nature of the beast** the unalterable character of something. [Middle English *nature* via Old French from Latin *natura*, from *natus*, past part. of *nasci* to be born]

nature cure *noun* = NATUROPATHY.

nature reserve *noun* an area of great botanical or zoological interest protected from exploitation by human beings.

nature study *noun* the study of plants, animals, and the natural world in general, *esp* as a school subject at elementary level.

nature trail *noun* a walk, e.g. in a nature reserve, planned to indicate points of interest to the observer of nature.

naturism *noun* **1** = NUDISM, *esp* communal nudism as a means of being in harmony with nature and other people. **2** the worship of nature and natural objects. **>>> naturist** *adj and noun*.

naturopathy /naychə'ropəthi/ *noun* treatment of disease emphasizing stimulation of the natural healing processes, including the use of herbal medicines, diet control, exercise, and massage. **>>> naturopath** /'naychərəpath/ *noun*, **naturopathic** /-'pathik/ *adj*.

NAU *abbr* Nauru (international vehicle registration).

naught[1] /nawt/ *noun* **1** *archaic or literary* nothing. **2** *NAmer* the arithmetical symbol 0; ZERO[1] or NOUGHT (1). *** come to naught** said of a plan, etc: to fail; to be foiled. **set at naught** to belittle or express scorn for (something). [Old English *nāwiht, nawht*, from *nā* (see NO[1]) + *wiht* creature, thing]

Usage note
naught *or* nought? In British English *nought* is the usual spelling for the word meaning '0' or 'zero': *a one followed by six noughts*. This word is usually spelt *naught* in American English. In both British English and American English *naught* is a rather literary term meaning 'nothing': *come to naught*.

naught[2] *adj archaic* wicked; immoral: *And can I think, after all this, that my daughter can be naught? What, a whore?* — Congreve. [orig in sense 'inferior, worthless']

naughty /'nawti/ *adj* (**naughtier, naughtiest**) **1** said of a child: badly behaved; mischievous; disobedient. **2** *archaic* criminally wicked: *A sort of naughty persons, lewdly bent … have practised dangerously against your state* — Shakespeare. **3** *euphem or humorous* slightly improper: *naughty pictures*. **4** *archaic* bad; unpleasant: *'Tis a naughty night to swim in* — Shakespeare. **>>> naughtily** *adv*, **naughtiness** *noun*. [NAUGHT[2] + -Y[1]]

nauplius /'nawpli-əs/ *noun* (*pl* **nauplii** /'nawpliie/) the larva of many crustaceans (lobsters, crabs, shrimps, etc; see CRUSTACEAN) in the first stage after leaving the egg, with an unsegmented body, a single eye, and three pairs of limbs. [via Latin from Greek *nauplios*, a kind of shellfish, named after *Nauplios*, son of Poseidon, Greek god of the sea]

nausea /'nawzi-ə/ *noun* **1** a feeling of discomfort in the stomach accompanied by a distaste for food and an urge to vomit. **2** extreme disgust. **>>> nauseant** *noun and adj*. [via Latin from Greek *nausia, nautia* seasickness, from *naus* ship]

nauseate /'nawziayt/ *verb trans* to affect (somebody) with nausea or disgust: *I was nauseated by her hypocrisy*. **>>> nauseating** *adj*, **nauseatingly** *adv*.

nauseous /'nawzi-əs, 'nawshəs/ *adj* **1** affected with nausea or disgust: *feeling nauseous*. **2** disgusting: *nauseous sentiment*. **>>> nauseously** *adv*, **nauseousness** *noun*.

nautch /nawch/ *noun* an entertainment in India performed by professional dancing girls. [Hindi *nāc* from Sanskrit *nrtya* dancing]

nautical /'nawtikl/ *adj* relating to or associated with seamen, navigation, or ships. **>>> nautically** *adv*. [via Latin from Greek *nautikos*, from *nautēs* sailor, from *naus* ship]

nautical mile *noun* any of various units of distance used for sea and air navigation based on the length of a minute of arc of a great circle of the earth, *esp* a former British unit equal to 6080ft (about 1853.18m), replaced in 1970 by an international unit equal to 1852m (about 6076.17ft): compare SEA MILE.

nautilus /'nawtiləs/ *noun* (*pl* **nautiluses** or **nautili** /-lie/) **1** any of several species of cephalopod molluscs (class including octopuses and squids; see CEPHALOPOD), with a light spiral shell, upright during swimming, that inhabit the Pacific and Indian Oceans:

genus *Nautilus*. **2** = PAPER NAUTILUS. [via Latin from Greek *nautilos* nautilus, sailor, in reference to its sail-like appearance when swimming]

NAV *abbr* net asset value.

Navaho /'navəhoh/ *noun* see NAVAJO.

navaid /'navayd/ *noun* an electronic device or system that assists a navigator. [contraction of *navigation aid*]

Navajo or **Navaho** /'navəhoh/ *noun* (pl **Navajos** or **Navahos** or collectively **Navajo** or **Navaho**) **1** a member of a Native American people of New Mexico, Utah, and Arizona. **2** the Athabaskan language of this people. [shortened from Spanish *Apaches de Navajó* Apaches of Navajo, from Tewa *Navahu*, name of a pueblo]

naval /'nayvl/ *adj* **1** relating to a navy. **In naval uniform. 2** consisting of or involving warships: *a naval expedition*. [Latin *navalis* relating to ships, naval, from *navis* ship]

naval architect *noun* a person who designs ships. ⏵⏵ **naval architecture** *noun*.

naval stores *pl noun* **1** materials and articles used in shipping. **2** products such as turpentine and pitch, obtained from resinous conifers, *esp* pines, which were formerly used in the construction and maintenance of wooden ships.

Navaratri /navə'rahtri/ or **Navaratra** /-trə/ *noun* a nine-day Hindu festival held during the September-to-October period to celebrate the slaying of demons by Rama and the goddess Durga. [Sanskrit *navaratri* nine nights]

navarin /'navərin, -ranh/ *noun* a mutton or lamb casserole cooked with turnip and other root vegetables. [French *navarin* from *navet* turnip]

nave[1] /nayv/ *noun* the main long central space of a church lying to the west of the chancel and usu flanked by aisles. [late Latin sense of Latin *navis* ship, prob from the similarity of the roof to an upturned hull]

nave[2] *noun* the hub of a wheel. [Old English *nafu*; related to Old English *nafela* NAVEL]

navel /'nayvl/ *noun* **1** the depression in the middle of the abdomen marking the point of former attachment of the umbilical cord. **2** the central point of a place: *the navel of the state* — Shakespeare. [Old English *nafela*]

navel-gazing *noun humorous* **1** unproductive self-analysis, *esp* at a time when urgent or positive action is required. **2** obsession with a single narrow issue, *esp* when matters of more general importance must be considered.

navel orange *noun* a seedless orange with a pit at the top enclosing a small secondary fruit.

navelwort *noun* = PENNYWORT (1).

navicular /nə'vikyoolə/ *noun* a bone shaped like a boat, *esp* one in the ankle. ⏵⏵ **navicular** *adj*. [Latin *navicularis* relating to boats, from *navicula* boat, dimin. of *navis* ship]

navigable /'navigəbl/ *adj* **1** said of a river, channel, etc: suitable for ships to pass through or along. **2** said of a vessel or craft: capable of being steered. ⏵⏵ **navigability** /-'biliti/ *noun*, **navigableness** *noun*, **navigably** *adv*.

navigate /'navigayt/ *verb trans* **1** to plan or direct the course of (a ship or aircraft, *esp* with the aid of maps and instruments. **2** to sail through (seas) or travel across (terrain). **3** in computing, to explore (the Internet) using hypertext links. ⏵ *verb intrans* **1** to direct the route of a ship or aircraft. **2** said of a car passenger: to read the map and advise the driver about the route. [Latin *navigatus*, past part. of *navigare* to sail, from *navis* ship + *agere* to drive]

navigation /navi'gaysh(ə)n/ *noun* **1** the activity of navigating. **2** the science of determining position, course, distance travelled, and the best course to be steered in a ship or aircraft. **3** traffic on any stretch of water; the passage of vessels. **4** *now chiefly dialect* a canal or other navigable inland waterway. ⏵⏵ **navigational** *adj*, **navigationally** *adv*.

navigation lights *pl noun* the set of lights displayed at night by a ship or aircraft to indicate position and direction.

navigator *noun* **1** the person in charge of navigating a ship or aircraft. **2** formerly, an explorer by sea: *those who ... believed ... in contradiction to the discoveries of the philosophers and the experience of the navigators ... that the earth was flat* — Thomas Paine. **3** a car passenger who directs the driver en route, with the help of a map, etc. **4** (**Navigator**) *trademark* a computer program for browsing on

the Internet and finding sites or information. **5** *archaic* a construction worker on a NAVIGATION (4).

navvy /'navi/ *noun* (pl **navvies**) *Brit* an unskilled labourer. [shortening of NAVIGATOR (5)]

navy /'nayvi/ *noun* (pl **navies**) **1** a nation's ships of war and support vessels together with the organization needed for maintenance. **2** (often **Navy**) (treated as sing. or pl) the branch of a country's armed services supplying the crews and the supporting personnel for these ships. **3** = NAVY BLUE. **4** *archaic or literary* a fleet of ships. [Middle English *navie* via Old French from late Latin *navia*, from Latin *navis* ship]

navy blue *adj* (often used before a noun) of a deep dark blue colour: *a navy-blue suit*. ⏵⏵ **navy blue** *noun*. [from the colour of the British naval uniform]

navy yard *noun NAmer* a naval dockyard.

nawab /nə'wahb/ *noun* **1** = NABOB (1). **2** a Muslim of high or noble status. [Urdu *nawwāb*: see NABOB]

nay[1] /nay/ *adv* **1** *literary* not merely this but even: *She was happy, nay, ecstatic*. **2** *N Eng or archaic* no. * **not dare say somebody nay** to be afraid to refuse somebody what they want. [Middle English *nay* no, from Old Norse *nei*, from *ne* not + *ei* ever]

nay[2] *noun* **1** a denial or refusal. **2** a vote or voter against something.

naysay /'naysay/ *verb trans* (**naysays** /'naysez/, **naysaid** /'naysed/, **naysaying**) *chiefly NAmer* to deny, reject, oppose, or say no to (something). ⏵⏵ **naysaying** *noun*.

naysayer *noun chiefly NAmer* a person who has a negative, gloomy, or pessimistic attitude to something.

Nazarene /'nazəreen/ *noun* **1** a native or inhabitant of Nazareth in Galilee (now N Israel), childhood home of Jesus Christ. **2** (**the Nazarene**) Jesus Christ. **3a** used by Jews or Muslims: a Christian. **b** a member of a Jewish sect of early Christians. **4** a member of an early 19th-cent. group of German painters that tried to restore the Renaissance by imitating e.g. Dürer, il Perugino, and the youthful Raphael. [Greek *Nazarēnos*, from *Nazaret* Nazareth]

Nazarite /'nazəriet/ *noun* see NAZIRITE.

Nazi[1] /'nahtsi/ *noun* (pl **Nazis**) **1** a member of the National Socialist German Workers' Party, which controlled Germany from 1933 to 1945. **2** *derog* a person with fascist, authoritarian, or racist attitudes. ⏵⏵ **Naziism** *noun*, **Nazism** /'nahtsiz(ə)m/ *noun*. [German *Nazi*, shortened from *Nationalsozialist* national socialist]

Nazi[2] *adj* of or relating to Nazis or Naziism.

Nazify /'nahtsifie/ *verb trans* (**Nazifies, Nazified, Nazifying**) to convert (a person or a nation) to Naziism. ⏵⏵ **Nazification** /-fi'kaysh(ə)n/ *noun*.

Nazirite or **Nazarite** /'nazəriet/ *noun* a Jew of biblical times consecrated to God by a vow to avoid drinking wine, cutting the hair, and being defiled by the presence of a corpse. ⏵⏵ **Naziritism** *noun*. [via late Latin from Greek *naziraios, nazaraios*, from Hebrew *nāzīr*, literally 'consecrated']

NB *abbr* **1** Nebraska. **2** New Brunswick (US postal abbreviation). **3** note well. [(sense 3) Latin *nota bene*]

Nb *abbr* the chemical symbol for niobium.

nb *abbr* in cricket, no ball.

NBA *abbr* **1** *NAmer* National Basketball Association. **2** *NAmer* National Boxing Association. **3** formerly, in Britain, Net Book Agreement.

NBC *abbr* **1** *NAmer* National Broadcasting Company. **2** in relation to weapons or warfare: nuclear, biological, and chemical.

nbg *abbr Brit, informal* no bloody good.

NC *abbr* **1** *Brit* national curriculum. **2** network computer. **3** North Carolina (US postal abbreviation). **4** numerical control.

NC-17 *abbr NAmer* classification of cinema films: no children under 17.

NCB *abbr Brit* formerly, National Coal Board (renamed British Coal).

NCC *abbr* **1** *Brit* National Curriculum Council. **2** Nature Conservancy Council.

NCO *abbr* non-commissioned officer.

NCP *abbr Brit* National Car Parks.

NCT *abbr Brit* National Childbirth Trust.

NCU *abbr Brit* National Communications Union.

ND *abbr* North Dakota (US postal abbreviation).

Nd *abbr* the chemical symbol for neodymium.

nd *abbr* no date.

-nd *suffix chiefly Brit* used after the figure 2 to indicate the ordinal number second: *2nd; 72nd.*

N Dak *abbr* North Dakota.

Ndebele /əndə'beeli, -'bayli/ *noun (pl* **Ndebeles** *or collectively* **Ndebele)** **1** a member of a people of Zimbabwe and NE South Africa. **2** a major language of Zimbabwe. **3** one of the official languages of South Africa. ⋙ **Ndebele** *adj.* [from Ndebele *Ndebele* from Sotho *Matebele*]

NDP *abbr* **1** net domestic product. **2** *Can* New Democratic Party.

NDT *abbr Can* Newfoundland Daylight Time.

NE *abbr* **1** Nebraska (US postal abbreviation). **2** New England. **3** Northeast. **4** Northeastern. **5** Northeast (London postcode).

Ne *abbr* the chemical symbol for neon.

né /nay/ *adj* the masculine of NÉE: originally called (such and such): *David Swinton, né Schwitzer.* [French *né* born, masc past part. of *naître* to be born, from Latin *nasci*]

ne- *comb. form* see NEO-.

Neanderthal¹ /ni'andətawl/ *noun* **1** an extinct Palaeolithic species of human that inhabited Europe widely between 120,000 and 35,000 years ago, characterized by a receding forehead and prominent brow ridges, and producing flints worked on one side only.

Editorial note _____

Neandert(h)al(er) is an early form of human being, named after a site in the Neander Valley (or Tal) near Düsseldorf, Germany, where its robust fossil bones were uncovered in 1856. It is an archaic form of *Homo sapiens*, known as *Homo sapiens neanderthalensis*, characterized by a large brain, massive brow-ridges, a receding chin, and a heavy muscular build. Neanderthals occupied parts of the Old World from about 200,000 to 28,000 years ago. Debate still rages as to whether they are at least part ancestral to modern humans or represent an evolutionary dead-end — Dr Paul Bahn.

2 *informal* a man who is primitive in appearance, behaviour, or attitudes. ⋙ **Neanderthaloid** /-təloyd/ *adj.* [named after *Neandertal*, a valley near Düsseldorf, Germany, where skeletal remains were found]

Neanderthal² *adj* **1** of, like, or being Neanderthal man. **2** *informal* resembling a caveman or primitive person in appearance, behaviour, or attitudes; *esp* reactionary.

Neanderthal man *noun* = NEANDERTHAL¹.

neap /neep/ *noun* a tide just after the first and third quarters of the moon, when the difference between high and low tide is at its smallest. [Old English *nēp* as in *nēpflōd* neap tide]

Neapolitan /nee-ə'politn/ *adj* **1** of or relating to the city of Naples. **2** said of ice cream: having different-coloured layers. ⋙ **Neapolitan** *noun.* [Latin *Neapolitanus* from *Neapolis* Naples, from Greek *neos* new + *polis* city]

neap tide *noun* = NEAP.

near¹ /niə/ *adv* **1** (*often* + to) at or to only a short distance away: *living near to one's parents; The exams were drawing near.* **2** (*used before an adjective*) almost: *with near-disastrous results.* ✳ **near on** almost; close on: *near on 40 deaths.* [Middle English from Old Norse *naer* nearer, from *nā* near]

near² *prep* near to: *near the edge; Call me nearer the time.*

near³ *adj* **1** close in place, time, or connection: *the nearest shop; in the near future; a near relation.* **2** almost but not quite a certain thing: *a near disaster.* **3** denoting the side of a vehicle nearest the kerb, that is the left when traffic keeps to the left; nearside: compare OFF³. ✳ **a near go/thing** an unpleasant or disastrous experience narrowly avoided. ⋙ **nearness** *noun.*

near⁴ *verb trans* to approach (a place or point): *as we neared the house; My researches were nearing their conclusion.* ➤ *verb intrans* to get near; to approach: *as the millennium neared.*

nearby /niə'bie/ *adv and adj* close at hand: *live nearby; a nearby café.*

Nearctic /ni'ahktik/ *adj* of or being the biogeographic subregion that includes Greenland and arctic and temperate N America. [NEO- + ARCTIC¹]

near-death experience *noun* a distinctive experience, typically an OUT-OF-BODY EXPERIENCE, recounted upon recovery by somebody who has been on the point of dying.

Near East *noun* **1** the countries of SW Asia between the Mediterranean coast and India. **2** *dated* the Balkan states and the region formerly dominated by Ottoman Empire.

near gale *noun* = MODERATE GALE.

nearly *adv* **1** almost but not quite: *nearly a year later; I nearly fell over.* **2** closely: *nearly related.* ✳ **not nearly** by no means: *not nearly enough.*

near-market *adj* said of scientific research or projects: close to development for commercial use.

near miss *noun* **1** something one does not quite achieve: *She didn't get a first in her finals, but was told it was a near miss.* **2** a near-collision between vehicles, *esp* aircraft.

near money *noun* financial assets, such as BILL OF EXCHANGE, that can be converted easily into cash.

nearside *noun Brit* the left-hand side of a vehicle or the road: compare OFF SIDE: *He hit a car parked on his nearside.*

nearsighted *adj* able to see near things more clearly than distant ones; myopic. ⋙ **nearsightedly** *adv,* **nearsightedness** *noun.*

neat¹ /neet/ *adj* **1** tidy or orderly: *a neat pile; neat handwriting.* **2** elegantly simple: *a neat description.* **3** entirely satisfactory; well-defined or precise: *a neat solution.* **4** adroit: *neat footwork.* **5** *NAmer, informal* excellent. **6** said of spirits: without addition or dilution; straight: *neat brandy; I drink my whisky neat.* ⋙ **neatly** *adv,* **neatness** *noun.* [French *net* clean, from Latin *nitidus* bright, neat, from *nitēre* to shine]

neat² *noun (pl* **neats** *or collectively* **neat)** *archaic* the common domestic ox or cow: *Silence is only commendable in a neat's tongue dried* — Shakespeare. [Old English *nēat*]

neaten *verb trans* (**neatened, neatening**) to make (something) neat or neater.

neath *or* **'neath** /neeth/ *prep literary* beneath: *The milestones into headstones change, 'neath every one a friend* — J R Lowell.

neat's-foot oil *noun* a pale yellow oil made by boiling the feet and shinbones of cattle, used chiefly as a leather dressing.

NEB *abbr* **1** *Brit* National Enterprise Board. **2** New English Bible.

Neb *abbr* Nebraska.

neb /neb/ *noun archaic or dialect* **1** the nose: *For the neb o'them's never out o' mischief* — Scott. **2** an animal's snout or bird's beak. **3** a small pointed end; a tip: *I have so worn out the neb of my pen* — Thomas Fuller. [Old English *nebb*]

nebbish /'nebish/ *noun NAmer, informal* a timid or inadequate man. ⋙ **nebbishy** *adj.* [Yiddish *nebekh* poor, luckless, prob of Slavic origin]

Nebr *abbr* Nebraska.

nebula /'nebyoolə/ *noun (pl* **nebulas** *or* **nebulae** /-lee/) **1** a cloudy patch on the cornea. **2a** any of many immense bodies of highly rarefied gas or dust in interstellar space. **b** *dated* = GALAXY. ⋙ **nebular** *adj.* [Latin *nebula* mist, cloud]

nebular hypothesis *noun* the astronomical theory that the solar system has evolved from a hot gaseous nebula.

nebulise /'nebyooliez/ *verb trans* see NEBULIZE.

nebuliser *noun* see NEBULIZER.

nebulize *or* **nebulise** /'nebyooliez/ *verb trans* to reduce (a liquid) to a fine spray or atomize (it). ⋙ **nebulization** /-'zaysh(ə)n/ *noun.* [Latin *nebula* mist, cloud + -IZE]

nebulizer *or* **nebuliser** *noun* a device for discharging a liquid, *esp* a medicine for inhaling, in the form of a fine spray; = ATOMIZER.

nebulosity /nebyoo'lositi/ *noun (pl* **nebulosities**) **1** the quality of being nebulous. **2** a mass of nebulous matter; = NEBULA (2A).

nebulous /'nebyooləs/ *adj* **1** said of ideas, etc: indistinct or vague: *nebulous notions of natural justice.* **2** relating to or resembling a nebula; nebular. **3** hazy; misty. ⋙ **nebulously** *adv,* **nebulousness** *noun.*

nebuly /'nebyooli/ *adj* said of a dividing line or border in heraldry: in the form of deeply interlocking curves; wavy. [French *nébulé* from medieval Latin *nebulatus*, from Latin *nebula* cloud, in reference to the wavy edge of a cloud]

NEC *abbr* National Executive Committee.

nécessaire /nese'seə/ *noun* a small decorative case for scissors, tweezers, cosmetics, pencils, etc: *Gwendolen ... thrust necklace, cambric, scrap of paper, and all into her nécessaire* — George Eliot. [French *nécessaire* necessary]

necessarian /nesi'seəri·ən/ *noun and adj* = NECESSITARIAN.

necessarily /'nesəs(ə)rəli, nesə'serəli/ *adv* as a necessary consequence; inevitably.

necessary[1] /'nesəs(ə)ri, 'nesəseri/ *adj* **1** essential; indispensable. **2** inevitable; inescapable: *seeing that death, a necessary end, will come when it will come* — Shakespeare. **3** logically unavoidable: *a necessary conclusion*. **4** in philosophy, denoting something that cannot be denied without contradiction of some other statement: *'All spinsters are unmarried' is a necessary truth*. **5** acting under compulsion; not free: *a necessary agent*. [Middle English from Latin *necessarius*, from *necesse* needful, unavoidable]

necessary[2] *noun* (*pl* **necessaries**) **1** an indispensable item; an essential: *My necessaries are embark'd* — Shakespeare. **2** (**the necessary**). **a** *informal* the action required; the needful: *Do the necessary*. **b** *Brit, informal* money.

necessitarian /nə,sesi'teəri·ən/ *noun* a person who subscribes to the philosophy of NECESSITARIANISM. ⋙ **necessitarian** *adj*.

necessitarianism *noun* the philosophical doctrine of DETERMINISM.

necessitate /nə'sesitayt/ *verb trans* to make (something) necessary or unavoidable: *changes in his lifestyle necessitated by his drop in salary*.

necessitous /nə'sesitəs/ *adj formal* lacking life's necessities; needy, impoverished: *They were, in fact, a necessitous family; numerous, too* — Jane Austen. ⋙ **necessitously** *adv*, **necessitousness** *noun*.

necessity /nə'sesiti/ *noun* (*pl* **necessities**) **1** the quality of being necessary, indispensable, or unavoidable: *no necessity to decide immediately*. **2** impossibility of a contrary order or condition, *esp* in a specified sphere: *physical necessity*. **3** pressing need or desire: *Necessity is the mother of invention*. **4** *literary or archaic* poverty; want: *You shall not seal to such a bond for me; I'll rather dwell in my necessity* — Shakespeare. **5** something necessary or indispensable: *the daily necessities of life*. ✲ **of necessity** necessarily: *the conclusion that must of necessity follow*. [Middle English via Old French *necessite* from Latin *necessitat-, necessitas*, from *necesse* needful, unavoidable]

neck[1] /nek/ *noun* **1** the part of a person or animal that connects the head with the body. **2** a cut of beef, mutton, etc taken from this part: *neck of lamb*. **3** the part of a garment that covers the neck. **4** a relatively narrow part shaped like a neck, e.g.: **a** the constricted end of a bottle. **b** the slender part of a fruit near its attachment to the plant. **c** (*usu* **neck of the womb**) = CERVIX. **d** the part of a stringed musical instrument extending from the body and supporting the fingerboard and strings. **e** a narrow stretch of land, *esp* an isthmus. **f** a column of solidified MAGMA (molten rock) from a volcanic vent. **5** *Brit, informal* insolent boldness; cheek. ✲ **breathe down somebody's neck** see BREATHE. **by a neck** by a narrow margin: *He won by a neck*. **catch/get it in the neck** *informal* to be severely rebuked or punished. **neck and neck** keeping abreast in a race. **neck of the woods** *usu humorous* a district or locality, *esp* if undistinguished. **neck or nothing** risking everything. **save one's neck** to make good one's escape from a compromising situation, etc. **up to one's neck** deeply involved in (some business). ⋙ **neckless** *adj*. [Old English *hnecca* back of the neck]

neck[2] *verb intrans informal* to kiss and caress in sexual play.

neckband *noun* a doubled or reinforced band of fabric forming the neck piece of a garment or providing the base for the attachment of a collar.

neckcloth *noun* a large cravat of various styles, typically white, worn by men from the mid- 17th to mid- 19th cent: *a merry-eyed, small-featured, grey-haired man, with his chin propped up by an ample, many-creased white neckcloth* — George Eliot.

necked *adj* (*usu used in combinations*) having a neck, or a neck of the specified kind: *long-necked*.

neckerchief /'nekəcheef, -chif/ *noun esp* formerly, a square of fabric folded and worn round the neck, *esp* by men: *He was usually muffled in an enormous silk neckerchief* — D H Lawrence. [Middle English, from NECK[1] + KERCHIEF]

necking *noun* in classical architecture, a plain concave band between the capital and shaft of a Tuscan column.

necklace[1] /'neklis/ *noun* **1** a string of jewels, beads, etc worn round the neck as an ornament. **2** a petrol-soaked tyre placed round the neck of a victim and set alight, used in black townships in South

Africa in the 1980s as a means of lynching suspected government collaborators.

necklace[2] *verb trans* to kill (somebody) by means of a tyre necklace.

necklet /'neklit/ *noun* an ornament for wearing round the neck, typically rigid and close-fitting.

neckline *noun* the upper edge of a garment that forms the opening for the neck and head.

necktie *noun chiefly NAmer* = TIE[2] (2): *My necktie rich and modest, but asserted by a simple pin* — T S Eliot.

necktie party *noun NAmer, informal* a lynching or hanging.

neckwear *noun* clothing that is worn round the neck, such as a tie or scarf.

necr- *or* **necro-** *comb. form* forming words, denoting: **1** corpse; corpses: *necrophilia*. **2** conversion to dead tissue: *necrosis*. [Greek *nekros* dead body]

necrobiosis /,nekrohbie'ohsis/ *noun* the normal degeneration and death of cells that compose bodily tissues. ⋙ **necrobiotic** /-'otik/ *adj*.

necrology /ni'kroləji/ *noun* (*pl* **necrologies**) **1** a list of the recently dead. **2** an obituary. ⋙ **necrological** /nekrə'lojikl/ *adj*, **necrologist** *noun*.

necromancy /'nekrəmansi/ *noun* **1** the conjuring up of the spirits of the dead in order to predict or influence the future. **2** magic or sorcery generally. ⋙ **necromancer** *noun*, **necromantic** /-'mantik/ *adj*, **necromantically** /-'mantikli/ *adv*. [Middle English *nigromancie*, via Old French from medieval Latin *nigromantia*, an alteration, by folk assocation with Latin *nigr-, niger* black (hence sense 2) of late Latin *necromantia*, from Greek *nekros* corpse + Latin *-mantia* -MANCY]

necrophagous /ni'krofəgəs/ *adj* said of a bird, animal, or insect: feeding on corpses or carrion.

necrophilia /nekrə'fili·ə/ *noun* obsession with, erotic interest in, or sexual intercourse with corpses. ⋙ **necrophile** /'nekrəfiel/ *noun*, **necrophiliac** /-ak/ *adj and noun*, **necrophilic** /-ik/ *adj*, **necrophilism** /ni'krofiliz(ə)m/ *noun*.

necrophobia /nekrə'fohbi·ə/ *noun* an irrational fear of death or corpses.

necropolis /ni'kropəlis/ *noun* (*pl* **necropolises** *or* **necropoleis** /-lays/) a cemetery, *esp* a large elaborate cemetery of an ancient city. [Greek *nekropolis* city of the dead, from *nekros* corpse + *polis* city]

necropsy /'nekropsi/ *noun* (*pl* **necropsies**) examination of a body after death; AUTOPSY, POSTMORTEM[1] (1).

necroscopy /ni'kroskəpi/ *noun* (*pl* **necroscopies**) = NECROPSY.

necrosis /ni'krohsis/ *noun* (*pl* **necroses** /-seez/) the death of living tissue through disease, injury, or interruption of the blood supply. ⋙ **necrotic** /ni'krotik/ *adj*. [Greek *nekrōsis*, from *nekroun* to make dead, from *nekros* corpse]

necrotize *or* **necrotise** /'nekrətiez/ *verb intrans* to undergo necrosis. ➤ *verb trans* to cause necrosis in (cells or tissues). [Greek *nekrōtikos* necrotic, from *nekroun*]

necrotizing fasciitis /fashi'ietis/ *noun* inflammation of the fascia of a muscle or organ, rapidly causing destruction of the tissue overlying it.

nectar /'nektə/ *noun* **1** a sweet liquid secreted by the flowers of many plants that is collected and made into honey by bees. **2** in classical mythology, the drink of the gods. **3** any delicious drink. ⋙ **nectarous** *adj*. [via Latin from Greek *nektar* drink of the gods]

nectarine /'nektərin, -reen/ *noun* **1** a type of peach with a smooth thin downless skin and firm flesh. **2** the tree that bears this fruit: *Prunus persica*. [from *nectarine* like nectar, from NECTAR + -INE[1]]

nectary *noun* (*pl* **nectaries**) a plant gland, found in flowers, leaves, or stipules, that secretes nectar. [scientific Latin *nectarium*, from *nectar* (see NECTAR) + *-arium* -ARY[1]]

NEDC *abbr* National Economic Development Committee.

neddy /'nedi/ *noun* (*pl* **neddies**) **1** a child's word for a donkey. **2** *Aus, informal* a horse, *esp* a racehorse. [from *Ned*, nickname for *Edward*]

née *or* **nee** /nay/ *adj* used to identify a married woman by her maiden name: born as: *Mary Thomson, née Wilkinson*. [French *née*, fem of *né*: see NÉ]

need[1] /need/ *verb trans* **1** to be in need of or require (something). **2** to be constrained or required to do something: *We need to discuss* this urgently. ➤ **verb aux** (*third person sing. present tense* **need**) (*chiefly in questions or with negatives*) to be under necessity or obligation to do something: *She need not decide straight away*; *Need you shout?* [Old English *nēdian*]

need² *noun* **1** obligation: *No need to apologize*. **2** sufficient reason; grounds: *There's no need to worry*. **3** (*also in pl*) something one requires: *The corner shop supplies nearly all our needs*. **4** a physiological or psychological requirement relating to one's well-being: *emotional needs*. **5** a condition requiring supply or relief: *His friends deserted him in his hour of need*. **6** poverty; want. ✱ **if need be** if necessary. **in need of** requiring (a certain treatment, etc): *furniture in need of a good polish*. [Old English *nēd, nēod*]

need-blind *adj NAmer* denoting a system of university admissions by which applicants are assessed according to their academic ability regardless of their capacity to pay for tuition.

needful /'needf(ə)l/ *adj* **1** necessary or requisite: *Do whatever is needful*. **2** *archaic* needy. ✱ **the needful** *informal* what is needed, *esp* money. ➤➤ **needfulness** *noun*.

needle¹ /'needl/ *noun* **1** a small slender usu steel instrument with an eye for thread at one end and a sharp point at the other, used for sewing. **2** any of various similar larger instruments without an eye that are used for carrying thread or yarn and making stitches, e.g. in crocheting or knitting. **3** a type of needle designed to carry sutures when sewing tissues in surgery. **4** a slender hollow pointed end of a hypodermic syringe. **5** a slender pointed indicator on a dial, e.g. the MAGNETIC NEEDLE of a compass. **6** a stylus for playing records. **7** a pointed crystal. **8** a sharp pinnacle of rock. **9** = OBELISK (1). **10** a needle-shaped leaf, *esp* of a conifer. **11** a slender pointed rod controlling a fine inlet or outlet, e.g. in a valve. **12** a beam used to take the load of a wall while supported at each end. **13** *Brit, informal* (*often before a noun*) ill feeling; hostility: *a needle match*. ✱ **give somebody the needle** *informal* to nag, rebuke, or criticize somebody. ➤➤ **needlelike** *adj*. [Old English *nǣdl*]

needle² *verb trans* **1** *literary* to sew or pierce (something) with a needle, or as if with a needle: *the fairy-cupped elf-needled mat of moss* — Robert Browning. **2** *informal* to provoke (somebody) by persistent teasing or gibes. ➤➤ **needler** *noun*, **needling** *noun*.

needlecord *noun* a fine corduroy with close ribs and a flattish pile.

needlecraft *noun* the art of needlework.

needlefish *noun* (*pl* **needlefishes** *or collectively* **needlefish**) = GARFISH.

needlepoint *noun* **1** (*also* **needlelace**) lace worked with a needle over a paper or parchment pattern: compare PILLOW LACE. **2** embroidery worked on canvas usu in a simple even stitch, e.g. cross-stitch or tent stitch: compare GROS POINT, PETIT POINT.

needless *adj* not needed; unnecessary: *needless fears*. ✱ **needless to say** naturally; of course: *Needless to say, I jumped at the chance*. ➤➤ **needlessly** *adv*, **needlessness** *noun*.

needletime *noun* *chiefly Brit* the programme time allocated, by agreement with the Musicians' Union, for the broadcasting of music from records.

needle valve *noun* a valve with a long narrow tapering closure.

needlewoman *noun* (*pl* **needlewomen**) a woman who does needlework, *esp* skilfully.

needlework *noun* **1** the activity of sewing or embroidery. **2** sewn work or embroidery. ➤➤ **needleworker** *noun*.

needn't /'neednt/ *contraction* need not. ✱ **needn't have** was under no necessity to (do something) but did: *I needn't have got up so early*.

needs *adv archaic* necessarily. ✱ **needs must/must needs** must inevitably: *He still drags a chain along that needs must clog his flight* — Dryden; *This strict court of Venice must needs give sentence 'gainst the merchant there* — Shakespeare. **needs must when the devil drives** one must occasionally do things one would rather not do. [Old English *nēdes*, genitive of *nēd* NEED²]

needy *adj* (**needier, neediest**) in want; impoverished. ➤➤ **neediness** *noun*.

neem *or* **nim** /neem/ *noun* a SE Asian tree the wood of which is similar to mahogany, with fruit and seeds that yield an aromatic medicinal oil, leaves that have insecticidal properties, bark from which a tonic is prepared, and a trunk that produces a gum: *Azadirachta indica*. [Hindi *nīm* from Sanskrit *nimba*]

neep /neep/ *noun Scot and N Eng* a turnip. [Old English *nǣp* turnip, from Latin *napus*]

ne'er /neə/ *adv literary* never.

ne'er-do-well *noun* **1** an idle worthless person. **2** (*used before a noun*) idle and worthless: *ne'er-do-well loafers*.

nefarious /ni'feəri-əs/ *adj* iniquitous; criminal; evil. ➤➤ **nefariously** *adv*, **nefariousness** *noun*. [Latin *nefarius* abominable, from *nefas* crime, from *ne-* not + *fas* right, divine law]

neg /neg/ *noun informal* a photographic negative.

neg. *abbr* negative.

nega- *comb. form* forming words, denoting: a negative or minus unit of measurement, e.g. one saved as a result of energy conservation: *nega-watt*.

negate /ni'gayt/ *verb trans* **1** to nullify (something) or make (it) ineffective or invalid: *A slip at this stage could negate the whole experiment*. **2** to deny the existence or truth of (something): *Marx negated the … claim of capitalism to be the only possible natural system* — Maurice Bloch. **3** in grammar or logic, to make (a statement, clause, etc) negative. ➤➤ **negater** *noun*, **negator** *noun*, **negatory** /'neg-, ni'gaytəri/ *adj*. [Latin *negatus*, past part. of *negare* to say no, deny]

negation /ni'gaysh(ə)n/ *noun* **1a** a denial or contradiction of something. **b** in logic or grammar, a negative statement, *esp* an assertion of the falsity of a given proposition. **2** something that represents the absence or opposite of something actual or positive: *Anarchy is the negation of government*. ➤➤ **negational** *adj*.

negative¹ /'negətiv/ *adj* **1** indicating or expressing denial, prohibition, or refusal: *a negative reply*. **2** denoting the absence or the contradiction of something: *'Non-human' is a negative term*. **3** expressing negation: *negative words such as 'no' and 'not'*. **4** lacking positive qualities: *a negative personality*. **5** said of a number: less than zero: *-2 is a negative number*. **6** said of an angle: extending or generated in a direction opposite to an arbitrarily chosen positive direction, *esp* clockwise. **7** being, relating to, or charged with electricity of which the electron is the elementary unit. **8** gaining electrons. **9** having lower electric potential and constituting the part towards which the current flows from the external circuit. **10** said of a test result: not affirming the presence of the organism or condition in question. **11** said of plant tropism: turning away from a source of stimulation. **12** denoting pressure that is less than the pressure of the atmosphere. **13** said of a photographic image: having the light and dark parts of the subject reversed. ➤➤ **negatively** *adv*, **negativity** /-'tiviti/ *noun*. [Middle English from late Latin *negativus*, from *negare* to deny]

negative² *noun* **1** in grammar, etc, a word such as *no, not,* or *never* that expresses negation, denial, or refusal, or a statement employing such an expression. **2** in logic, etc, something that is the opposite or negation of the thing in question: *a proposition and its negative*. **3** a minus number. **4** an undesirable aspect or feature of something; a minus factor. **5** a photographic image, usu on transparent film, used for printing positive pictures, with the light and dark of the original reversed. **6** the plate of a battery that has the lower electric potential. ✱ **in the negative** said of a response, etc: indicating negation, denial, or refusal.

negative³ *verb trans* **1** to reject, veto, or refuse to accept or approve (a proposal, etc). **2** to contradict, disprove, or demonstrate the falsity of (a statement, claim, argument, etc). **3** to nullify (something) or render (it) ineffective: *new methods of cover-up that negative the work of the enquiry*.

negative equity *noun* a situation placing the owner of a mortgaged property potentially in debt when the market value of the property falls below the amount of mortgage left to be repaid.

negative feedback *noun* the return of part of the output of a system, e.g. an electronic or mechanical one, in inverted form to the input, in order to produce changes, usu of a corrective nature, e.g. to reduce distortion in an amplifier; compare POSITIVE FEEDBACK.

negative geotropism *noun* the response to gravity of a plant stem that grows upwards regardless of the position in which it is placed.

negative income tax *noun* a system of subsidy payments to families with incomes below a stipulated level, proposed as a substitute for or supplement to social-security payments.

negative pole *noun* that pole of a magnet which turns southwards when the magnet swings freely.

negative resistance *noun* in electronics, a property exhibited by certain devices, e.g. the MAGNETRON (valve used e.g. in a radar transmitter), in which the current decreases as the applied voltage increases.

negative sign *noun* = MINUS SIGN.

negativism *noun* **1** an attitude or system of thought marked by strong mistrust or disbelief of accepted opinions or ideas. **2** a tendency to refuse to do, to do the opposite of, or to do something at variance with what is asked. ➤➤ **negativist** *noun*, **negativistic** /-ˈvistik/ *adj*.

neglect¹ /niˈglekt/ *verb trans* **1** to fail to give (a person, animal, or thing) proper care and attention: *The garden had been neglected.* **2** to fail (to do something required of one): *He neglected to report the accident to the police.* **3** to disregard, or fail to act in accordance with (one's duties, somebody's advice, etc). ➤➤ **neglecter** *noun*. [Latin *neglectus*, past part. of *neglegere* to disregard, from *neg-* not + *legere* to choose]

neglect² *noun* **1** failure to give, or the resulting lack of, proper care and attention: *houses suffering from neglect.* **2** the act of neglecting something: *neglect of duty.*

neglectful /niˈglektf(ə)l/ *adj* (*often* + of) careless, heedless, or forgetful: *neglectful of his own health.* ➤➤ **neglectfully** *adv*, **neglectfulness** *noun*.

negligee *or* **négligé** /ˈneglizhay/ *noun* a woman's light decorative dressing gown, often designed to be worn with a matching nightdress. [French *négligé*, past part. of *négliger* to neglect, from Latin *neglegere* (see NEGLECT¹); in reference to its use as casual wear]

negligence /ˈneglijəns/ *noun* **1** carelessness or forgetfulness. **2** in law, the offence of failing to take due care, when this is judged to have contributed to or caused the damage in question. [Latin *negligentia*, variant of *neglegentia*, from *neglegere*: see NEGLECT¹]

negligent /ˈneglijənt/ *adj* **1** inclined to neglect one's duties, etc; neglectful: *negligent parenting.* **2** casual: *Holmes strolled round the house with his hands in his pockets and a negligent air which was unusual with him* — Conan Doyle.

negligible /ˈneglijəbl/ *adj* so slight or insignificant as to be not worth considering; trifling. ➤➤ **negligibility** /-ˈbiliti/ *noun*, **negligibly** *adv*.

negotiable /niˈgohshəbl/ *adj* **1** transferable to another person: *negotiable securities.* **2** said of a road, route, passage, etc: capable of being passed along or through. **3** capable of being dealt with or settled through discussion: *The salary is negotiable.* ➤➤ **negotiability** /-ˈbiliti/ *noun*.

negotiable instrument *noun* a cheque, BILL OF EXCHANGE, or other legal document that is freely negotiable.

negotiate /niˈgohshiayt/ *verb intrans* to confer with others affected by a disputed issue, with the aim of reaching agreement over it. ➤ *verb trans* **1** to achieve (a settlement, etc) by discussion with others. **2** to pass or deal with (an obstacle en route): *while negotiating a bend at speed.* **3** to transfer (a cheque or BILL OF EXCHANGE) to somebody else's legal possession. **4** to convert (a cheque) into cash. ➤➤ **negotiant** *noun*, **negotiator** *noun*, **negotiatory** /-shətri/ *adj*. [Latin *negotiatus*, past part. of *negotiari* to do business, from *neg-* not + *otium* leisure]

negotiation /ni,gohshiˈaysh(ə)n/ *noun* (*also in pl*) the act or an instance of conferring in order to reach agreement over a disputed issue.

Negress /ˈneegris/ *noun now offensive* a woman or girl of black African race.

Negrillo /niˈgriloh/ *noun* (*pl* **Negrillos** *or* **Negrilloes**) a member of any of a group of black peoples of short stature that inhabit Central Africa. [Spanish *negrillo*, dimin. of *negro*: see NEGRO]

Negrito /niˈgreetoh/ *noun* (*pl* **Negritos** *or* **Negritoes**) a member of any of a group of black peoples of short stature that inhabit SE Asia and Melanesia. [Spanish *negrito* dimin. of *negro*: see NEGRO]

negritude /ˈnegrityoohd, ˈnee-/ *noun* **1** the fact or quality of being of black African race. **2** conscious pride in the African heritage. [French *négritude*, from *nègre* Negro, from Latin *nigr-*, *niger* black]

Negro /ˈneegroh/ *noun* (*pl* **Negroes**) *now offensive* a member or descendant of any of a group of black peoples native to Africa south of the Sahara Desert. ➤➤ **Negro** *adj*. [Spanish or Portuguese *negro* black, from Latin *nigr-*, *niger*]

Usage note
Negro, black, *and* coloured. See note at BLACK².

Negroid /ˈneegroyd/ *adj sometimes offensive* belonging to one of the divisions of humankind represented by the indigenous races of central and S Africa, characterized by dark brown skin, tightly curled black hair, full lips, and a short wide nose.

negroni /niˈgrohni/ *noun* (*pl* **negronis**) a cocktail composed of gin, Campari, and vermouth. [Italian *negroni*, said to be named after a nobleman called Negroni who invented it]

Negrophobia /neegrohˈfohbi-ə/ *noun* an irrational fear or dislike of black people. ➤➤ **Negrophobe** /ˈnee-/ *noun*.

Negus /ˈneegəs/ *noun* formerly, the title of the supreme sovereign of Ethiopia. [Amharic *n'gus* king]

negus *noun* a drink of wine, hot water, sugar, lemon juice, and nutmeg. [named after Francis Negus d.1732, English colonel who invented it]

Neh. *abbr* Nehemiah (book of the Bible).

neigh¹ /nay/ *verb intrans* to make the characteristic cry of a horse. [Middle English *neyen* from Old English *hnægan*]

neigh² *noun* a neighing sound.

neighbor /ˈnaybə/ *noun NAmer* = NEIGHBOUR¹.

neighbour¹ (*NAmer* **neighbor**) /ˈnaybə/ *noun* **1** a person who lives next door, or very close, to one: *Let's invite the neighbours round.* **2** a person next to one, or a country, etc next to one's own: *chatting to one's dinner-party neighbour; our EU neighbours.* **3** *archaic* one's fellow human being: *Love thy neighbour.* [Old English *nēahgebūr*, from *nēah* NIGH + *gebūr* dweller]

neighbour² (*NAmer* **neighbor**) *verb trans literary or archaic* to adjoin or lie near to (a place): *the Jewish quarter that neighbours Old Town Square.* ➤ *verb intrans* **1** dated to be neighbours: *We neighboured in our youth.* **2** *literary* (+ on/upon) to adjoin somewhere.

neighbourhood (*NAmer* **neighborhood**) *noun* **1** the area surrounding one's own home. **2** the area around the thing specified. **3** a particular place or location: *a leafy neighbourhood.* ✳ **in the neighbourhood of** approximately (a certain amount): *in the neighbourhood of £20,000.*

neighbourhood watch *noun* a scheme organized within a local community, by which members take joint responsibility for keeping a watch on each other's property, as a way of discouraging burglaries.

neighbouring (*NAmer* **neighboring**) *adj* nearby; adjacent: *the neighbouring village.*

neighbourly (*NAmer* **neighborly**) *adj* like or typical of a neighbour, *esp* in being helpful or friendly: *a neighbourly gesture.*

neither¹ /ˈniedhə, ˈneedhə/ *adj* not the one or the other of two; not either: *neither hand.* [Middle English, alteration of Old English *nauther*, from *nā* not, NO¹ + *hwæther* which of two, whether]

neither² *pron* not the one or the other of two: *neither of us.*
Usage note
Neither, like *either*, should be followed by a verb in the singular when it is the subject of a sentence: *Neither of them was caught.* If two or more particular things or people are being mentioned, *neither* is followed by *nor*, not by *or*: *Neither Janet nor her sister is coming* (see NEITHER³). Both pronunciations (ˈniedhə or ˈneedhə) are acceptable: British English tends to prefer the former and American English the latter.

neither³ *conj* used with NOR¹: not either: *neither here nor there.*

neither⁴ *adv* **1** similarly not; also not; = NOR²: '*I can't understand it.*' '*Neither can I.*' **2** *archaic or dialect* either: *I saw Mark Antony offer him a crown — yet 'twas not a crown neither — 'twas one of these coronets* — Shakespeare.

nekton /ˈnekton/ *noun* a collective term for aquatic animals, such as whales or squid, that swim freely independent of water currents, as distinct from PLANKTON. ➤➤ **nektonic** /nekˈtonik/ *adj*. [German *Nekton* from Greek *nēkton*, neuter of *nēktos* swimming, from *nēchein* to swim]

nelly /ˈneli/ ✳ **not on your nelly** *informal* certainly not; not on your life. [from rhyming slang *Nelly Duff* for PUFF² in the sense 'life']

nelson /ˈnels(ə)n/ *noun* a wrestling hold in which leverage is applied against one's opponent's head, neck, and arm. [prob from the name *Nelson*, but the reason is unknown]

nemat- *or* **nemato-** *comb. form* forming words, denoting: **1** thread: *nematocyst.* **2** nematode: *nematology.* [Greek *nēmat-*, *nēma* thread]

nematic /ni'matik/ *adj* denoting, in chemistry or physics, the phase of a LIQUID CRYSTAL (liquid with molecular structure like that of crystalline solids) characterized by having the molecules oriented in parallel lines rather than in layers: compare CHOLESTERIC, SMECTIC.

nemato- *comb. form* see NEMAT-.

nematocyst /'nemətəsist/ *noun* any of the minute stinging organs of jellyfish or other coelenterates.

nematode /'nemətohd/ *noun* any of a phylum of elongated cylindrical worms parasitic in animals or plants or living freely in soil or water, including the threadworms, roundworms, and eelworms: phylum Nematoda. [scientific Latin, from NEMAT- + -ōda from Greek *oidēs* -OID]

nematology /nemə'toləji/ *noun* a branch of zoology that deals with nematodes. ➤➤ **nematological** /-'lojikl/ *adj,* **nematologist** *noun.*

Nembutal /'nembyootahl/ *noun trademark* the drug PENTOBARBITONE. [*Na* (symbol for sodium) + the initial letters of ETHYL, METHYL, and BUTYL]

nemertean /ni'muhti-ən/ *noun* any of a phylum of ribbon-like often vividly coloured marine worms: phylum Nemertea. Also called RIBBON WORM. ➤➤ **nemertean** *adj,* **nemertine** /-tien/ *adj and noun,* **nemertinean** /nemə'tini-ən/ *adj and noun.* [scientific Latin from Greek *Nēmertēs* Nemertes, one of the Nereids (sea nymphs)]

nemeses /'neməseez/ *noun* pl of NEMESIS.

nemesia /ni'meezh(y)ə/ *noun* any of a genus of S African plants of the foxglove family cultivated for their colourful flowers: genus *Nemesia.* [scientific Latin from Greek *nemesion* catchfly]

nemesis /'neməsis/ *noun* (pl **nemeses** /-seez/) **1** retribution or vengeance. **2** a person or thing that is the agent of this. **3** one's downfall or ruin, *esp* if deserved: *A Nemesis attends the woman who plays the game of elusiveness too often, in the utter contempt for her that, sooner or later, her old admirers feel* — Hardy. [Latin *Nemesis* goddess of divine retribution, from Greek *nemesis* retribution, from *nemein* to give what is due]

nemophila /ni'mofilə/ *noun* any of several species of a N American annual trailing plant grown for its blue flowers: *Nemophila menziesii* and other species. [scientific Latin *nemophila,* fem of *nemophilus* glade-loving, from Greek *nemos* glade, grove + *philein* to love]

nene *or* **ne-ne** /'naynay/ *noun* a goose of the Hawaiian Islands, at one time almost extinct, now re-established in the wild after breeding in captivity: *Branta sandvicensis.* [Hawaiian *nēnē*]

Nenets /'nenets/ *noun* (pl **Nenets** *or* **Nentsy** *or* **Nentsi** /'nentsi/) **1** a member of a nomadic reindeer-herding people of Arctic Russia and Siberia. **2** the Samoyedic language of this people. [Russian *Nenets,* the name of this people, from Nenets, a real person]

neo- *or* **ne-** *comb. form* forming words, with the meanings: **1** new; recent: *neonate.* **2** of a later period or phase: *Neolithic.* **3** in a revived form: *neoclassicism.* **4** of the New World: *Neotropical.* [Greek *neos* new]

neoclassic /neeoh'klasik/ *adj* = NEOCLASSICAL.

neoclassical /neeoh'klasikl/ *adj* relating to or constituting a revival or adaptation of the classical, *esp* in literature, music, art, or architecture: *the neoclassical façade.*

Editorial note
Neoclassical is a term used across the arts to describe works that hark back to the proportions and gestures of an earlier 'classic' period, but in music defining a style that achieved enormous influence between the two world wars and persists in some composers' language today – though 'neobaroque' might be a more accurate description. Composers like Stravinsky and Hindemith felt compelled to recycle the forms and key schemes of the 17th and 18th cents, sensing that modernism had pushed the boundaries of harmony and tonality as far as they could go — Andrew Clements.

➤➤ **neoclassicism** /-siz(ə)m/ *noun,* **neoclassicist** /-sist/ *noun and adj.*

neocolonialism /neeohkə'lohni-əliz(ə)m/ *noun* the economic and political policies by which a great power indirectly extends its influence over other territories, *esp* former dependencies. ➤➤ **neocolonial** *adj,* **neocolonialist** *noun and adj.*

neocortex /neeoh'kawteks/ *noun* (pl **neocortices**) the back part of the CORTEX (area of brain controlling higher-thought ability) that is unique to mammals, considered the most recently evolved part of the cortex and responsible for sight and hearing. ➤➤ **neocortical** *adj.*

neo-Darwinism *or* **Neo-Darwinism** /neeoh'dahwiniz(ə)m/ *noun* a theory that explains evolution in terms of natural selection and population genetics and specifically denies the possibility of inheriting acquired characteristics. ➤➤ **neo-Darwinian** /-'wini-ən/ *adj and noun,* **neo-Darwinist** *noun.*

neodymium /neeoh'dimi-əm/ *noun* a silver-grey metallic chemical element of the rare-earth group that occurs in monazite and bastnasite, and is used in colouring glass: symbol Nd, atomic number 60. [NEO- + DIDYMIUM]

Neogene /'nee-əjeen/ *adj* in geological chronology, of or relating to the later subdivision of the Tertiary period, covering the Miocene and Pliocene epochs, lasting from about 25 million to about 2 million years ago. ➤➤ **Neogene** *noun.* [Greek *neogenēs* newborn, of new type, from *neos* new + *-genēs* born, produced, of the type specified]

neo-Gothic[1] /neeoh'gothik/ *adj* denoting a 19th-cent. architectural style imitating Gothic and other medieval styles and characterized by vaulting, pointed arches, castellation and mock fortification generally.

neo-Gothic[2] *noun* the neo-Gothic style of architecture.

neo-Impressionism /neeoh-im'presh(ə)niz(ə)m/ *noun* a late 19th-cent. development of Impressionism in France, whose chief exponents were Seurat, Signac, and Camille Pissarro, their work being characterized by formal composition and the use of DIVISIONISM (pointillism).

neoliberalism /neeoh'lib(ə)rəliz(ə)m/ *noun* a modern economic doctrine which favours a market-driven society with minimal government intervention in business and reduced public expenditure on social services, along with privatization, free trade, restrictions on trade-unionism, etc. ➤➤ **neoliberal** *adj and noun.*

Neolithic /nee-ə'lithik/ *adj* relating to or dating from the last period of the Stone Age, a geological period characterized by polished stone implements.

Editorial note
Neolithic literally means the 'New Stone Age', i.e. the final part of the Stone Age, the period generally associated with a basic change from hunting and gathering to farming: people now began settling down in villages, cultivating crops, keeping domestic livestock, and making and using pottery and stone tools, but with as yet no usage of metal. The dating of the Neolithic is quite variable, beginning in the Near East around 8000 BC and lasting into the 2nd millennium BC in northern Europe — Dr Paul Bahn.

➤➤ **Neolithic** *noun.*

neologise *verb intrans* see NEOLOGIZE.

neologism /ni'oləjiz(ə)m/ *noun* **1** a new word, usage, or expression. **2** the practice of introducing or using new words or expressions. ➤➤ **neological** /-'lojikl/ *adj,* **neologistic** /-'jistik/ *adj,* **neology** *noun.* [French *néologisme,* from *néo-* NEO- + Greek *logos* word]

neologize *or* **neologise** *verb intrans* to introduce new words or expressions.

Neo-Melanesian /neeohmelə'neezyən, -zh(y)ən/ *noun* an English-based PIDGIN (tongue evolved for communication between speakers of different languages) spoken in Papua New Guinea, Melanesia, and NE Australia. Also called TOK PISIN.

neomycin /nee-ə'miesin/ *noun* an antibiotic or mixture of antibiotics effective against a wide range of micro-organisms and obtained from a soil bacterium, *Streptomyces fradiae,* that is used for surface treatment of local infections or to sterilize the intestine before surgery. [NEO- + MYC- + -IN[1]]

neon /'neeon/ *noun* **1** a gaseous chemical element of the noble gas group, used in fluorescent signs and lighting: symbol Ne, atomic number 10. **2** fluorescent signs and lighting using neon. **3** a lamp in which the gas contains a large proportion of neon. **4** (*used before a noun*) of or relating to neon: *a neon sign.* ➤➤ **neoned** *adj.* [Greek *neon,* neuter of *neos* new]

neonate /'nee-ənayt/ *noun technical* a newborn child less than a month old. ➤➤ **neonatal** /-'naytl/ *adj,* **neonatologist** /-'toləjist/ *noun,* **neonatology** /-'toləji/ *noun.* [scientific Latin *neonatus,* from NEO- + *natus,* past part. of *nasci* to be born]

neon lamp *noun* = NEON LIGHT.

neon light *noun* **1** a glass tube or bulb that contains neon at low pressure, emitting a red glow, used for advertising signs. **2** generally, any fluorescent tubular lamp.

neon tetra /'tetrə/ *noun* a small tropical fish of the CHARACIN family with a glowing blue-green band along each side and a red band on the tail, sought after for aquariums: *Paracheirodon innesi*.

neophobia /neeoh'fohbi·ə/ *noun* irrational dislike or fear of anything new and unfamiliar. ➤➤ **neophobe** /'nee-/ *noun*, **neophobic** /-bik/ *adj*.

neophyte /'nee·əfiet/ *noun* **1** a new convert to a religious faith. **2** a recently ordained priest or a novice in a religious order. **3** a beginner in a subject, skill, etc. [via ecclesiastical Latin from Greek *neophytos* newly planted, newly converted, from *neos* new + *phyein* to bring forth]

neoplasm /'nee·əplaz(ə)m/ *noun* an abnormal growth of tissue; a tumour. ➤➤ **neoplastic** /-'plastik/ *adj*.

neoplasticism /nee·ə'plastisiz(ə)m/ *noun* a severely abstract style of painting of 1912 onwards in which only rectangles strictly parallel to the vertical and horizontal axes figured, and only primary colours, along with white, black, and grey, were allowed, its chief exponents being the Dutch artist Piet Mondrian (d.1944) and members of the group De Stijl. [French *néoplasticisme*, translating Dutch *nieuwe beelding* new forming]

Neoplatonism /neeoh'playtəniz(ə)m/ *noun* a modified form of PLATONISM (philosophy of Plato) developed in the third cent. AD, incorporating Pythagorean and Aristotelian features, along with elements of oriental mysticism. ➤➤ **Neoplatonic** /-plə'tonik/ *adj*, **Neoplatonist** *noun*.

neoprene /'nee·əpreen/ *noun* a synthetic rubber resistant to oils. [NEO- + -*prene* as in ISOPRENE]

neorealism /neeoh'ree·əliz(ə)m/ *noun* a movement in filmmaking, originating in Italy in the 1940s, intended to give an authentic depiction of the social problems of ordinary people. ➤➤ **neorealist** *adj and noun*, **neorealistic** /-'listik/ *adj*.

neostigmine /neeoh'stigmien/ *noun* a synthetic drug that is used in the treatment of MYASTHENIA GRAVIS (disease causing muscular weakness and exhaustion), ILEUS (obstruction of the intestine), and GLAUCOMA (eye disease). [NEO- + -*stigmine* as in *physostigmine*, a drug obtained from *Physostigma venenosum* the Calabar bean]

neoteny /nee'ot(ə)ni/ *noun* **1** in zoology, the retention of some larval or immature characters in adulthood. **2** in zoology, the attainment of sexual maturity during the larval stage, e.g. in the axolotl. ➤➤ **neotenic** /nee·ə'tenik/ *adj*, **neotenous** *adj*. [scientific Latin *neotenia*, from NEO- + Greek *teinein* to stretch]

neoteric /nee·ə'terik/ *adj* of recent origin; modern. [via late Latin from Greek *neōterikos* youthful, modern, from *neōteros*, compar of *neos* new, young]

Neotropic /neeoh'tropik/ *adj* = NEOTROPICAL.

Neotropical /neeoh'tropikl/ *adj* relating to or denoting the region comprising tropical America and the W Indies.

Neozoic /nee·ə'zoh·ik/ *adj and noun* = CAINOZOIC.

NEP *abbr* Nepal (international vehicle registration).

Nepalese /nepə'leez/ *noun and adj* (*pl* **Nepalese**) see NEPALI.

Nepali /ni'pawli/ *noun* (*pl* **Nepalis** or collectively **Nepali**) **1** a native or inhabitant of Nepal. **2** the official Indic language of Nepal. Also called NEPALESE. ➤➤ **Nepali** *adj*. [Hindi *naipālī* of Nepal]

nepenthes /ni'pentheez/ *noun* **1** (also **nepenthe** /-'penthi/) a potion used by the ancients to induce forgetfulness of pain or sorrow, described by Homer in the *Odyssey*. **2** any of a genus of plants that includes the pitcher plants: genus *Nepenthes*. ➤➤ **nepenthean** /-thi·ən/ *adj*. [Greek *nēpenthēs* banishing pain or sorrow, from *nē-* not + *penthos* grief, sorrow]

neper /'neepə/ *noun* in physics, a logarithmic unit used for expressing the ratio between two currents, voltages, or power levels. [*Neperus*, Latinized form of *Napier*, in reference to John *Napier* d.1617, Scottish mathematician and inventor of logarithms]

nepeta /ni'peetə/ *noun* any of a genus of plants that includes catmint and other plants with spikes of blue or violet flowers: genus *Nepeta*. [Latin *nepeta* calamint, formerly classified within this genus]

nepheline /'nefəlin/ *noun* a mineral occurring in igneous rocks, variously brown, green, or colourless, a silicate of sodium, potassium, and aluminium. ➤➤ **nephelinic** /-'linik/ *adj*. [French *néphéline* from Greek *nephelē* cloud; because the mineral fragments turn cloudy when immersed in nitric acid]

nephelite /'nefəliet/ *noun* = NEPHELINE.

nephelometer /nefe'lomitə/ *noun* an instrument for measuring light absorption as a means of determining the concentration or size of suspended particles in a liquid. [Greek *nephelē* cloud + -METER[2]]

nephew /'nefyooh/ *noun* the son of one's brother or sister or of one's brother-in-law or sister-in-law. [Middle English *nevew* via Old French *neveu* from Latin *nepot-, nepos* grandson, nephew]

nephology /ni'foləji/ *noun* the study of clouds. [Greek *nephos* cloud + -LOGY]

nephr- *or* **nephro-** *comb. form* forming words, denoting: kidney; kidneys: *nephrectomy; nephrology*. [Greek *nephros* kidney]

nephrectomy /ni'frektəmi/ *noun* (*pl* **nephrectomies**) the surgical removal of a kidney.

nephridia /ni'fridi·ə/ *noun* pl of NEPHRIDIUM.

nephridiopore /ni'fridi·əpaw/ *noun* the external orifice of a NEPHRIDIUM.

nephridium /ni'fridi·əm/ *noun* (*pl* **nephridia** /-di·ə/) **1** a tubular glandular organ for excreting waste matter, characteristic of various invertebrate animals, e.g. earthworms. **2** an excretory structure, *esp* a NEPHRON. ➤➤ **nephridial** *adj*. [scientific Latin *nephridium*, dimin. of Greek *nephros* kidney]

nephrite /'nefriet/ *noun* a green, white, or black variety of jade, of comparatively little value, that is a silicate of calcium and magnesium. [German *Nephrit* from Greek *nephros* kidney; because it was worn as a remedy for kidney diseases]

nephritic /ni'fritik/ *adj* **1** relating to the kidneys; = RENAL. **2** relating to or affected with nephritis.

nephritis /ni'frietəs/ *noun* inflammation of the kidneys.

nephro- *comb. form* see NEPHR-.

nephrology /ni'froləji/ *noun* the branch of medicine specializing in the study of the kidney, its function and diseases. ➤➤ **nephrological** /-'lojikl/ *adj*, **nephrologist** *noun*.

nephron /'nefron/ *noun* any of the million or so tubular units in the kidney of a vertebrate that secrete urine into the ureter. [German *Nephron* from Greek *nephros* kidney]

nephroscope /'nefrəskohp/ *noun* an instrument that can be inserted through the skin to facilitate examination of the kidneys.

nephrosis /ni'frohsis/ *noun* degenerative, as distinct from inflammatory, kidney disease.

nepit /'nepit/ *noun* see NIT[4].

ne plus ultra /ˌnay ploos 'ooltrə/ *noun* the highest point, most advanced stage, or greatest degree, of something: *I could subscribe cordially to every one of the thirty-nine articles, which do indeed appear to me to be the ne plus ultra of human wisdom* — Samuel Butler. [Latin *ne plus ultra*, literally 'not further beyond', a warning to sailors supposedly inscribed on the Pillars of Hercules at Gibraltar]

nepotism /'nepətiz(ə)m/ *noun* favouritism shown to a relative, e.g. by appointment to office. ➤➤ **nepotist** *noun*.

Word history

French *népotisme* from Italian *nepotismo*, from *nepote* nephew, from Latin *nepot-, nepos* grandson, nephew. The reference is to the 'nephews' of some popes (in many cases their illegitimate sons) who were given privileges and career advancement.

neptunium /nep'tyoohni·əm/ *noun* a silvery radioactive metallic chemical element artificially produced by bombarding uranium with neutrons: symbol Np, atomic number 93. [named after the planet *Neptune*, because Neptune is next to Uranus in terms of distance from the sun, and the element was discovered shortly after URANIUM]

NERC *abbr Brit* Natural Environment Research Council.

nerd *or* **nurd** /nuhd/ *noun informal* **1** a boring or socially inept person. **2** a person obsessed with computing; a computer freak. ➤➤ **nerdish** *adj*, **nerdishness** *noun*, **nerdy** *adj*. [origin unknown]

nereid /'niəri·id/ *noun* a POLYCHAETE (using bristles for propulsion) marine worm: family Nereidae. [scientific Latin *Nereidae* from Greek *Nēreidai*, sea nymphs, daughters of the sea god Nereus]

nerine /ni'rieni, nə'reenə/ *noun* a S African plant grown from a bulb, with white, pink, red, or orange flowers that have twisted strap-like petals: genus *Nerine*. [scientific Latin *nerine*, from Greek *Nērēis*, name of a sea nymph]

nerite /'niəriet/ *noun* any of several species of gastropod molluscs with globular, brightly streaked shells, found mainly in warm shallow coastal waters: *Theodoxus fluviatilis* and other species. [Latin *nerita* sea mussel, formerly used as genus name, from Greek *nērītēs*, *nēreitēs* sea snail, sea mussel, named after the sea god Nereus]

neritic /ne'ritik/ *adj* denoting, or belonging to the region of shallow water adjoining the seacoast: *neritic organisms*. [from NERITE]

neroli /'niərəli/ *noun* a fragrant pale yellow essential oil obtained from the flowers of the orange tree and used *esp* in cologne and as a flavouring. [via French from Italian *neroli*, said to be named in honour of Anna Maria de La Trémoille d.1722, princess of *Nerole*, its reputed discoverer]

nervate /'nuhvayt/ *adj* said of leaves: having nerves or ribs.

nervation /nuh'vaysh(ə)n/ *noun* the arrangement of nerves or ribs in a leaf.

nervature /'nuhvəchə/ *noun* = NERVATION.

nerve[1] /nuhv/ *noun* **1** any of the threadlike bands of nervous tissue that connect parts of the nervous system with the other organs, conduct nervous impulses, and are made up of axons (conducting away from the nerve cell; see AXON) and dendrites (conducting to the nerve cell; see DENDRITE), together with protective and supportive structures. **2** a combination of courage, self-discipline, adventurous spirit, and tenacity: *Most stunts take a bit of nerve*. **3** *informal* cheek; audacity: *You've got a nerve, asking for another loan.* **4** (*in pl*) feelings of acute nervousness or anxiety. **5** the sensitive pulp of a tooth. **6** *archaic* a sinew or tendon: *He sweats, strains his young nerves* — Shakespeare. **7** an unbranched rib in a leaf, *esp* of a moss. ✳ **hit/touch a nerve** to mention a subject that causes one's hearer particular distress. [Latin *nervus* sinew, nerve]

nerve[2] *verb trans* **1** to brace (somebody) or lend (them) courage or strength: *The drink had nerved her*. **2** (*also* + up/for) to prepare (oneself) psychologically for a challenge: *all nerved up for the battle*.

nerve block *noun* anaesthesia induced in a particular part of the body by injecting a local anaesthetic close to the nerves that supply it.

nerve cell *noun* = NEURON.

nerve centre *noun* **1** a group of connected nerve cells associated with a particular bodily function. **2** the control centre or headquarters of an operation; a source of leadership or energy: *A small ... man sat tilted back in a swivel chair, in a corner which seemed the nerve centre of the establishment* — Christopher Morley.

nerved *adj* (*usu used in combinations*) **1** said of a leaf: having ribs or nerves: *a five-nerved leaf*. **2** said of a person: having nerves of the type specified: *not a job for a weak-nerved individual*.

nerve fibre *noun* the AXON (thread of nerve tissue) leading from a NEURON (nerve cell).

nerve gas *noun* a deadly gas, *esp* an organophosphate, that interferes with nerve transmission and disrupts the vital functions, e.g. respiration.

nerve impulse *noun* a surge of electric current that travels along a nerve fibre following stimulation and serves to transmit either a record of sensation from the affected nerve ending, or an instruction to act to a nerve ending connected with a muscle or gland.

nerveless *adj* **1** lacking strength or vigour; inert: *The pen dropped from his nerveless fingers*. **2** not agitated or afraid; cool. **3** said of a leaf or an anatomical part: without nerves: *nerveless hind wings*. ⋙ **nervelessly** *adv*, **nervelessness** *noun*.

nerve-racking *or* **nerve-wracking** *adj* placing a great strain on the nerves; hair-raising.

nervine[1] /'nuhvien, 'nuhveen/ *noun* a medicine used for calming the nerves. [late Latin *nervinus* relating to sinews or nerves, from Latin *nervus* sinew, NERVE[1], possibly via French *nervin*]

nervine[2] *adj* said of a medicine: used to calm the nerves.

nervous /'nuhvəs/ *adj* **1** relating to the nerves: *nervous tissue*. **2** anxious or apprehensive: *I was so nervous before my driving test*. **3** constitutionally anxious or easily upset: *persons of a nervous disposition*. **4** said of an ailment such as a headache: caused by anxious anticipation. ⋙ **nervously** *adv*, **nervousness** *noun*. [Latin *nervosus*, from *nervus* sinew, NERVE[1]]

nervous breakdown *noun* a mental and emotional disorder in which worrying, depression, severe tiredness, etc prevent one from coping with one's responsibilities.

nervous system *noun* the brain, spinal cord, or other nerves and nervous tissue together forming a system for interpreting stimuli from the sense organs and transmitting impulses to muscles, glands, etc.

nervous wreck *noun informal* a description of somebody in a severely stressed condition: *This wedding business is turning me into a nervous wreck*.

nervure /'nuhvyooə/ *noun* **1** in an insect, any of the chitinous (horny; see CHITIN) ribs supporting the wings. **2** any of the veins, *esp* the principal vein, of a leaf. [French *nervure*, from *nerf* sinew, from Latin *nervus* sinew, NERVE[1]]

nervy *adj* (**nervier, nerviest**) **1** *chiefly Brit* suffering from nervousness or anxiety. **2** *NAmer, informal* brash or imprudent. **3** *archaic or literary* sinewy; strong: *Death, that dark spirit, in's nervy arm doth lie* — Shakespeare. ⋙ **nerviness** *noun*.

nescience /'nesi·əns, 'nesh(ə)ns/ *noun literary* ignorance; lack of knowledge: *There was in Adam a nescience of many things* — Henry Manning. ⋙ **nescient** *adj*. [late Latin *nescientia*, from Latin *nescient-, nesciens*, present part. of *nescire*: see NICE]

nesh /nesh/ *adj* **1** *dialect* weak or delicate. **2** *dialect* timid or cowardly. **3** *archaic* said of meat or vegetation: soft, tender, pliant, or succulent. [Old English *hnesce* delicate, soft, tender]

ness /nes/ *noun archaic* found in place names: a cape or headland: *Fife Ness*. [Old English *næss*; related to *nosu* NOSE[1]]

-ness *suffix* forming nouns from adjectives, denoting: **1** a state or quality, or an instance of it: *goodness; a kindness*. **2** degree or amount: *thickness*. **3** a region of a certain character: *a wilderness*. [Old English *-nes*]

nest[1] /nest/ *noun* **1** a structure built by a bird for laying eggs in, and for sheltering its young. **2** a place or structure where other creatures, e.g. insects, breed or shelter: *an ants' nest*. **3** a cosy retreat, corner, or hollow: *The child made a nest among the cushions*. **4** a den or haunt: *a nest of forgers*. **5** a set of things in a range of sizes, that fit one inside the other: *a nest of tables*. ⋙ **nestful** (*pl* **nestfuls**) *noun*. [Old English *nest* nest, brood]

nest[2] *verb intrans* **1** said of birds: to construct or occupy a nest ready for rearing young. **2** said of tables, etc: to fit one inside the other. ⋗ *verb trans* **1** to fit (a set of tables, etc) one inside the other. **2** to insert (lexical, linguistic, or computer data) within a hierarchically arranged framework, typically in a subordinate position. ⋙ **nester** *noun*.

nest box *noun* a specially constructed box provided for a bird to nest in.

nest egg *noun* **1** a real or artificial egg left in a nest to induce a fowl to continue to lay there. **2** an amount of money saved up as a reserve.

nesting box *noun* = NEST BOX.

nestle /'nesl/ *verb intrans* **1** (*often* + against/round/into/up to) to settle snugly or comfortably: *nestling round their mother*. **2** said e.g. of a place: to lie in a sheltered position: *a village nestling in the hollow*. ⋗ *verb trans* to press (oneself, one's head, etc) closely and affectionately, e.g. against someone. [Old English *nestlian* to make a nest, from NEST[1]]

nestling /'nes(t)ling/ *noun* a young bird that has not abandoned the nest.

Nestor *or* **nestor** /'nestaw/ *noun* a patriarch or mentor: *I would in due time be a Nestor, an elder of the people* — James Boswell. [named after *Nestor*, wise old king of Pylos in Greek mythology]

Nestorian /ne'stawri·ən/ *adj* relating to or denoting a church following the doctrine that divine and human persons remained separate in the incarnate Christ. ⋙ **Nestorian** *noun*, **Nestorianism** *noun*. [*Nestorius* d.451, patriarch of Constantinople]

net[1] /net/ *noun* **1** an open meshed fabric of any of various degrees of coarseness or fineness, twisted, knotted, or woven together at regular intervals. **2** a device made of net for catching fish, birds, or insects. **3** a net barricade which divides a tennis, badminton, etc court in half and over which a ball or shuttlecock must be hit. **4** a football, hockey, etc goal, enclosed by net at back and sides: *He slammed the ball into the back of the net*. **5** (*usu in pl*) a practice cricket pitch surrounded by nets: *In the nets he could maintain an accuracy which seemed beyond him under the tension of actual play* — John Arlott. **6** *Brit, informal* (*in pl*) net curtains. **7** arrangements made for trapping or ensnaring somebody: *caught in the net*. **8** = NETWORK[1], *esp* **a** a group of communications or broadcasting stations under unified control. **b** an interlinked series of computers. **c** (**the Net**) the INTERNET. ✳ **fall/slip through the net** to escape the elaborate system set up to entrap one. **spread one's net wide** to set up a widespread system of contacts, etc, so as to be sure of finding what one wants. ⟫ **netful** noun, **netless** adj, **netlike** adj, **netty** adj. [Old English net, nett]

net² verb trans (**netted, netting**) **1** to cover or enclose (something) with a net, or as if with a net: They netted the fruit trees to keep the birds off. **2** to catch (a fish, etc) in a net, or as if in a net. **3a** to hit (a ball) into the net for the loss of a point in a game in tennis, badminton, etc. **b** to hit or kick (a ball or puck) into the goal for a score in hockey, football, etc. **4** to make a net out of (rope, string, etc). ⟫ **netter** noun.

net³ or Brit **nett** adj **1** free from all charges or deductions, e.g.: **a** remaining after all deductions, e.g. for taxes, outlay, or loss: compare GROSS¹ (2A): net earnings. **b** excluding all TARE² (deduction for weight of container): net weight. **2** final; ultimate: the net result. [Middle English in the sense 'clean, pure' from French net: see NEAT¹]

net⁴ or Brit **nett** verb trans (**netted, netting**) **1** to make (a sum) by way of profit; to clear (it). **2** to get possession of (something) for oneself: ... succeeded in netting more of the goods of this world — John Wain.

net⁵ noun a net amount, profit, weight, price, or score.

net asset value noun the total value of the assets of an organization, minus its capital charges and liabilities.

netball noun a game, usu played by women, between teams of seven players who try to score goals by tossing an inflated ball through a high horizontal ring on a post at each end of a hard court.

Net Book Agreement noun formerly, in Britain, a voluntary agreement by which booksellers sold books only at the prices decided by the publishers.

net domestic product noun a country's gross domestic product with a certain amount deducted to allow for the depreciation of CAPITAL GOODS (goods used in production).

nether /'nedhə/ adj **1** beneath the earth's surface: the nether regions. **2** formal lower or under. ⟫ **nethermost** adj. [Old English nithera, from nither down]

Netherlander /'nedhəlandə/ noun a native or inhabitant of the Netherlands. ⟫ **Netherlandish** adj.

nether regions pl noun **1** the world of the dead; the underworld; Hades. **2** Hell. **3** euphem a person's bottom and genital area.

netherworld noun the world of the dead; the underworld.

netiquette /'netiket/ noun the code of behaviour commonly observed by users of the Internet. [blend of NET¹ + ETIQUETTE]

Netizen noun an Internet user, esp one who actively contributes to the development of the Net. [NET¹ (8C) + CITIZEN]

net national product noun = NET DOMESTIC PRODUCT.

net present value noun the total income expected from a project over its whole life, discounted at an interest rate to equal its capital value now, and set against its total costs.

net profit noun the gross profit of an operation or transaction minus expenses such as operating costs, employees' wages, overheads, and depreciation.

net realizable value noun the net value of an asset regarded as a selling prospect.

net statutory income noun a person's total taxable income assessed for a particular tax year, after personal allowances have been deducted.

netsuke /'netsooki, 'nets(ə)ki/ noun (pl **netsuke** or **netsukes**) a small and often intricately carved toggle, e.g. of ivory, used to fasten a pouch to a kimono sash. [Japanese netsuke, from ne root, bottom + tsukeru to attach]

nett /net/ adj and verb trans see NET³, NET⁴.

netting noun a fabric or other material consisting of a network of interlocked threads, wires, etc: wire netting.

nettle¹ /'netl/ noun **1** any of several species of a widely distributed plant with greenish flowers and jagged leaves covered with stinging hairs: Urtica dioica and other species. **2** (used in combinations) any of various plants like the nettle: dead nettle. ✻ **grasp the nettle** to tackle a problem with bold determination. [Old English netel]

nettle² verb trans **1** said of a remark, etc: to goad or sting (somebody): Nettled by the criticism, she retaliated fiercely. **2** to strike or sting (somebody) with or as if with nettles.

nettle rash noun a raised itchy skin rash caused by allergy; = URTICARIA.

nettlesome /'netls(ə)m/ adj chiefly NAmer **1** causing irritation or annoyance. **2** easily annoyed; testy; irritable.

net ton noun a unit of total internal capacity, e.g., in the case of a ship, with tonnage deducted to allow for crew accommodation, operating machinery, etc.

net-top box noun a device that makes it possible to access the Internet via a television set.

network¹ noun **1** a structure of crisscrossing cords, wires, etc, secured at the intersections, e.g. by knots. **2** any system of intersecting horizontal and vertical lines. **3** a system of interconnected railways, roads, etc. **4** a group of broadcasting stations linked together for a simultaneous broadcast. **5** an arrangement of connected electrical conductors. **6** a set of interconnected computers or terminals.

network² verb trans **1** Brit to broadcast (a programme) on a network. **2** to link up (computers or terminals) so as to interact with each other. ➤ verb intrans to create useful contacts for oneself by talking and interacting with others.

networker noun **1** a person working from home or a remote office through a link to a central network. **2** a person who networks with others with similar interests in order to establish useful contacts.

Neufchâtel /'nuhshatel (French nœʃatɛl)/ noun a soft white cheese similar to cream cheese but containing less fat. [named after Neufchâtel, town in France where it is made]

neume or **neum** /nyoohm/ noun **1** in medieval plainsong, a note or group of notes assigned to one syllable. **2** any of a set of written symbols used to show this. [late Latin neuma from Greek pneuma breath]

neur- or **neuro-** comb. form forming words, with the meanings: **1** nerve; nervous system: neural; neurosurgeon. **2** neural; neural and: neuromuscular. [Greek neuron nerve, sinew]

neural /'nyooərəl/ adj **1** relating to a nerve or the nervous system. **2** dated denoting an anatomical part lying towards the spine as distinct from the front of the body; = DORSAL: compare HAEMAL, VENTRAL. ⟫ **neurally** adv.

neural chip noun = NEUROCHIP.

neural computer noun = NEUROCOMPUTER.

neuralgia /nyoo(ə)'raljə/ noun intense paroxysms of pain radiating along the course of a nerve, esp in the head or face. ⟫ **neuralgic** /-jik/ adj.

neural net noun = NEURAL NETWORK.

neural network noun a computer system modelled on the human brain, which is designed to learn by trial and error, as distinct from being programmed.

neural tube noun a hollow structure in the embryo of a mammal, from which the brain and spinal cord form.

neurasthenia /nyooərəs'theeni·ə/ noun dated an emotional disorder causing severe fatigue, depression, etc. ⟫ **neurasthenic** /-nik/ adj, **neurasthenically** /-nikli/ adv.

neurilemma /nyooəri'lemə/ noun see NEUROLEMMA.

neuritis /nyooə'rietəs/ noun inflammation of a nerve or nerves, causing pain, sensory disturbances due to impaired function, etc. ⟫ **neuritic** /nyooə'ritik/ adj.

neuro- comb. form see NEUR-.

neuroanatomy /,nyooəroh-ə'natəmi/ noun the study of the structure of the nervous system. ⟫ **neuroanatomical** /-anə'tomikl/ adj, **neuroanatomist** noun.

neurobiology /,nyooərohbie'oləji/ noun the anatomy, physiology, and biochemistry of the nervous system. ⟫ **neurobiological** /-'lojikl/ adj, **neurobiologist** noun.

neurochemistry /nyooəroh'kemistri/ noun the biochemistry of nerves or of the transmission of impulses along them. ⟫ **neurochemical** /-ikl/ adj, **neurochemist** /'nyoo-/ noun.

neurochip /'nyooərohchip/ noun a semiconductor chip for use in a NEURAL NETWORK (computer system modelled on the brain).

neurocomputer /,nyooərohkəm'pyoohtə/ noun a computer using a NEURAL NETWORK (system modelled on the brain) to imitate the working of the brain.

neuroendocrine /nyooəroh'endəkrien/ adj relating to the interaction of the nervous system and the ENDOCRINE¹ (hormonal) system in controlling certain functions.

neurofibril /nyooəroh'fiebril/ *noun* any of the fine protein fibres made up of bundles of neurofilaments, that are found in a nerve cell and are associated with the transport of substances along the length of the cell. ➤➤ **neurofibrillary** /-'briləri/ *adj*.

neurofibroma /,nyooərohfie'brohmə/ *noun* (*pl* **neurofibromas** *or* **neurofibromata** /-mətə/) a tumour formed on the sheath of a nerve cell, malignant in some cases.

neurofibromatosis /,nyooərohfie,brohmə'tohsis/ *noun* the morbid formation of fibromata throughout the body.

neurofilament /'nyooərohfiləmənt/ *noun* any of the microscopic threadlike filaments that make up a neurofibril.

neurogenesis /nyooəroh'jenəsis/ *noun* the growth and development of the nerves and nervous tissue.

neurogenic /nyooəroh'jenik/ *adj* arising in or controlled by the nervous system: *neurogenic shock*.

neuroglia /nyoo(ə)'rogli-ə/ *noun* supporting tissue that is intermingled with the impulse-conducting cells of nervous tissue in the brain, spinal cord, and ganglia. Also called GLIA. ➤➤ **neuroglial** *adj*. [NEURO- + Greek *glia* glue]

neurohormone /'nyooərohhawmohn/ *noun* a hormone, such as noradrenaline, that is produced in the nervous system rather than by endocrine glands.

neurolemma /nyooərə'lemə/ *or* **neurilemma** /nyooəri-/ *noun* the thin delicate outer sheath surrounding a nerve fibre. ➤➤ **neurolemmal** *adj*. [scientific Latin *neurolemma*, from NEURO- + Greek *eilēma* covering, coil, from *eilein* to wind]

neuroleptic[1] /nyooərə'leptik/ *noun* a drug that reduces nervous tension by depressing nerve activity; = TRANQUILLIZER. [NEURO- + Greek *lēpsis* seizing, from *lambanein* to seize]

neuroleptic[2] *adj* said of a drug: having a tranquillizing effect.

neurolinguistic programming /,nyooərohling'gwistik/ *noun* a form of therapy designed to alter set patterns of thought and behaviour and increase self-awareness.

neurolinguistics *pl noun* (*treated as sing. or pl*) the branch of linguistics concerned with language-processing in the brain.

neurology /nyoo(ə)'roləji/ *noun* the study of the nervous system, its structure, and its function. ➤➤ **neurologic** /-'lojik/ *adj*, **neurological** /-'lojikl/ *adj*, **neurologically** /-'lojikli/ *adv*, **neurologist** *noun*.

neuroma /nyooə'rohmə/ *noun* (*pl* **neuromas** *or* **neuromata** /-tə/) = NEUROFIBROMA.

neuromuscular /nyooəroh'muskyoolə/ *adj* involving nervous and muscular cells, tissues, etc: *a neuromuscular junction*.

neuron /'nyooəron/ *or* **neurone** /'nyooərohn/ *noun* any of the many specialized cells each with an AXON and dendrites (fibres respectively transmitting impulses from and to the cell body; see DENDRITE) that form the functional units of the nervous system. ➤➤ **neuronal** /'nyooərənəl, nyoo'rohnl/ *adj*, **neuronic** /nyoo(ə)'ronik/ *adj*. [Greek *neuron* nerve, sinew]

neuropathology /,nyooərohpə'tholəji/ *noun* the study of the diseases of the nervous system. ➤➤ **neuropathological** /-pathə'lojikl/ *adj*, **neuropathologist** *noun*.

neuropathy /nyoo(ə)'ropəthi/ *noun* any dysfunctional state of the nerves or nervous system. ➤➤ **neuropathic** /-'pathik/ *adj*, **neuropathically** /-'pathikli/ *adv*.

neuropeptide /nyooəroh'peptied/ *noun* a POLYPEPTIDE (amino-acid chain) that serves as a NEUROTRANSMITTER (medium transmitting nerve impulse).

neurophysiology /,nyooərohfizi'oləji/ *noun* the physiology of the nervous system. ➤➤ **neurophysiological** /-'lojikl/ *adj*, **neurophysiologist** *noun*.

neuropsychiatry /,nyooərohsie'kie-ətri/ *noun* a branch of medicine concerned with both the psychological and physiological aspects of mental disorder. ➤➤ **neuropsychiatric** /-ki'atrik/ *adj*, **neuropsychiatrically** /-ki'atrikli/ *adv*, **neuropsychiatrist** *noun*.

neuropsychology /,nyooərohsie'koləji/ *noun* the study of the way brain function, the nervous system, and behaviour interrelate. ➤➤ **neuropsychological** /-'lojikl/ *adj*, **neuropsychologist** *noun*.

neuropteran /nyoo(ə)'roptərən/ *noun* any of an order of insects including the lacewings, usu having a fine network of veins in their wings: order Neuroptera. ➤➤ **neuropteran** *adj*, **neuropterous** /-rəs/ *adj*. [NEURO-, in the sense 'veined' + Greek *pteron* wing]

neuroscience /nyooəroh'sie-əns/ *noun* **1** any of the sciences dealing with the nervous system and the brain. **2** the body of such sciences.

neurosis /nyoo(ə)'rohsis/ *noun* (*pl* **neuroses** /-seez/) a nervous disorder, unaccompanied by disease of the nervous system, in which phobias, compulsions, anxiety, and obsessions make normal life difficult.

neurosurgery /nyooəroh'suhjəri/ *noun* surgery to a part of the nervous system. ➤➤ **neurosurgeon** /'nyooərohsuhj(ə)n/ *noun*, **neurosurgical** /-jikl/ *adj*.

neurotic[1] /nyoo(ə)'rotik/ *adj* **1** relating to or caused by a neurosis: *neurotic behaviour*. **2** affected by a neurosis; hypersensitive or obsessive about something. **3** *informal* unduly anxious: *neurotic about punctuality*. ➤➤ **neurotically** *adv*, **neuroticism** /-siz(ə)m/ *noun*.

neurotic[2] *noun* a person who is emotionally unstable or is affected with a neurosis: *A neurotic can perfectly well be a literary genius, but his greatest danger is always that he will not recognize when he is dull* — Louis S Auchincloss.

neurotomy /nyooə'rotəmi/ *noun* (*pl* **neurotomies**) the severing of a nerve by surgery in order to produce sensory loss, give relief from pain, or suppress involuntary movements.

neurotoxin /nyooəroh'toksin/ *noun* any poison that acts on the nervous system, *esp* a poisonous protein such as that in snake venom. ➤➤ **neurotoxic** /-'toksik/ *adj*, **neurotoxicity** /-tok'sisiti/ *noun*.

neurotransmitter /,nyooərohtrans'mitə, -tranz'mitə/ *noun* a substance, e.g. acetylcholine, that is released at a nerve ending and transmits nerve impulses across the SYNAPSE (gap between nerve cells).

Editorial note
There are at least 50 different types of neurotransmitter. Nerve endings (synapses) are packed with small vesicles containing neurotransmitters; when an impulse arrives down the nerve it triggers the release of these chemicals, which diffuse across the synaptic junction to the post-synaptic neuron or muscle, where they interact with protein receptors in the membrane, either exciting or inhibiting its activity — Professor Steven Rose.

➤➤ **neurotransmission** /-'mish(ə)n/ *noun*.

neurotrophic /nyooəroh'trofik/ *adj* relating to the growth of nervous tissue.

neurotropic /nyooəroh'tropik/ *adj* attracted to or growing in nerve tissue: *neurotropic drugs; a neurotropic virus*. ➤➤ **neurotropism** /-'trohpiz(ə)m/ *noun*.

neuston /'nyoohston/ *noun* minute organisms that float or swim in the surface film of water. ➤➤ **neustonic** /nyooh'stonik/ *adj*. [German *Neuston* from Greek *neuston*, neuter of *neustos* swimming, from *nein* to swim; modelled on PLANKTON]

neut. *abbr* neuter.

neuter[1] /'nyoohtə/ *adj* **1** in grammar, denoting or belonging to the gender of nouns that is neither masculine nor feminine. **2** said of an animal: **a** lacking generative organs, or having non-functioning ones. **b** castrated or spayed. **3** said of a flower or plant: without pistils or stamens. [Latin *neuter* neither, from *ne* not + *uter* either]

neuter[2] *noun* **1** in grammar, a neuter noun or other neuter form. **2** an infertile insect in a group of social insects, *esp* a worker bee or ant. **3** a spayed or castrated animal.

neuter[3] *verb trans* (**neutered**, **neutering**) **1** to spay or castrate (a domestic animal). **2** to render (something) feeble or ineffective, or emasculate (it).

neutral[1] /'nyoohtrəl/ *adj* **1** said of a country or a person: not engaged on either side of a war, dispute, etc. **2** impartial or unbiased. **3** of indefinite character; having no strongly distinctive characteristics. **4** denoting a colour that is any shade of beige or grey. **5** denoting chemical substances having a pH value of about 7, so neither acid nor alkaline. **6** not electrically charged, or neither positive nor negative; not live, as the blue-covered wire in an electric plug. **7** in speech, denoting the vowel schwa (/ə/) or the vowel sound (/ah/) made with the lips neither spread nor rounded. ➤➤ **neutralism** *noun*, **neutralist** *noun*, **neutralistic** /-'listik/ *adj*, **neutrality** /nyooh'traliti/ *noun*, **neutrally** *adv*. [Latin *neutralis* grammatically neuter, from *neuter*: see NEUTER[1]]

neutral[2] *noun* **1** a neutral person or state. **2** a neutral colour or shade, *esp* beige. **3** the gear position in which no gear is engaged. **4** an electrically neutral or non-live terminal, etc.

neutralize *or* **neutralise** *verb trans* **1** to nullify or render (something) ineffective by having the opposite effect. **2** to make (a substance) chemically neutral. **3** to disarm (a bomb) or render (it) safe. **4** *euphem* to kill (somebody). ➤➤ **neutralization** /-'zaysh(ə)n/ *noun*.

neutretto /nyooh'tretoh/ *noun* (*pl* **neutrettos**) in particle physics, the neutrino associated with the muon. [NEUTRINO + dimin. suffix -*etto*]

neutrino /nyooh'treenoh/ *noun* (*pl* **neutrinos**) either of two forms of an uncharged elementary particle that is created in the process of particle decay, e.g. inside a star, is believed to be massless, and interacts only slightly with other matter. [Italian *neutrino*, dimin. of *neutro* neutral]

neutron /'nyoohtron/ *noun* an uncharged elementary particle with a mass about that of the proton, present in the nuclei of all atoms except those of normal hydrogen. [NEUTRAL¹ + -ON³]

neutron bomb *noun* a nuclear bomb that produces relatively large amounts of radiation in the form of neutrons and a relatively small blast, being designed to destroy life while leaving buildings, etc intact.

neutron gun *noun* a device for discharging a beam of fast neutrons.

neutron number *noun* the number of neutrons in the nucleus of an atom: symbol *N*.

neutron star *noun* any of various very dense celestial bodies that consist mainly of closely packed neutrons thought to be the remainder of a much larger star the core of which collapsed under its own gravity.

neutropenia /nyoohtrə'peeni·ə/ *noun* a dearth of neutrophils (see NEUTROPHIL¹) in the blood, exposing the system to infection. [NEUTRAL¹ + Greek *penia* lack, need]

neutrophil¹ /'nyoohtrafil/ or **neutrophile** /-fiel/ *noun* a white blood cell that has neutrophilic granules in its cytoplasm and is present in large numbers in the blood.

neutrophil² *adj* = NEUTROPHILIC.

neutrophilic /nyoohtrə'filik/ *adj* said of a cell or cell tissue: staining to the same degree with both acidic and alkaline dyes. [NEUTRAL¹ + -PHILIC]

Nev. *abbr* Nevada.

névé /'nevay (French neve)/ *noun* partly compacted granular snow, *esp* forming the surface part of the upper end of a glacier. [Swiss French *névé* glacier, from Latin *niv-, nix* snow]

never /'nevə/ *adv* **1** not ever; at no time: *I've never skied.* **2** used emphatically for *not*: *This will never do.* **3** surely not: *'I've resigned.' 'Never!'* ✳ **never fear** don't worry. **Well, I never!** used to express incredulity. [Old English *næfre*, from *ne* not + *æfre* EVER]

nevermore *adv literary* never again: *They parted, nevermore to meet.*

never-never or **the never-never** *noun informal* **1** *Brit* = HIRE PURCHASE. **2** *Aus* the outback, or remote desert country.

never-never land *noun* an ideal or imaginary place. [from *Never Land* (or *Never Never Land*) in *Peter Pan* by J M Barrie d.1937, Scottish writer]

nevertheless /,nevədhə'les/ *adv* in spite of that; yet; however: *true but nevertheless unkind.*

nevus /'neevəs/ *noun* (*pl* **nevi** /'neevie/) *NAmer* see NAEVUS.

new¹ /nyooh/ *adj* **1** recently bought, made, built, etc: *new shoes; the new sports complex.* **2** just invented or discovered: *a new technique; the new planet.* **3** fresh; unused: *Start a new sheet of paper.* **4** doing something for the first time: *new parents; I'm new to the Internet.* **5** replacing the previous one: *the new prime minister.* **6** fresh; unfamiliar; different: *a new hairstyle; visiting new places.* **7** refreshed; regenerated: *She woke a new woman.* **8** said of potatoes, etc: harvested early in the season. **9** denoting the post-medieval or Renaissance form of an ancient or classical language such as Greek, Latin, or Hebrew; = MODERN¹ (3). ➤➤ **newness** *noun*. [Old English *nīwe*]

new² *adv* (*used in combinations*) newly or recently: *new-mown grass.*

New Age or **new age** *noun* **1** (*often used before a noun*) a cultural movement of the late 1980s, characterized by popular enthusiasm for alternative beliefs and disciplines, including astrology, mysticism, meditation, and holistic medicine: *So off to the therapist, the new-age aquarian bubble bath and Christianity* — Marxism Today, 1990. **2** a gentle dreamy melodic style of popular music typical of the late 1980s, using synthesizers and acoustic instruments and incorporating sounds from nature. ➤➤ **New-Ager** *noun*, **New-Agey** *adj*.

New-Age music *noun* = NEW AGE (2).

New-Age traveller *noun* a member of an itinerant group of enthusiasts for New-Age culture, adopting an unconventional lifestyle, associated mainly with the 1980s and early 1990s.

newbie /'nyoohbi/ *noun* (*pl* **newbies**) *informal* a person who is new and inexperienced at something; a novice.

newborn¹ *noun* (*pl* **newborn** or **newborns**) a recently born child or animal: *a study of jaundice in the newborn.*

newborn² *adj* **1** just born: *newborn babies.* **2** said of hope, zeal, etc: reborn; regenerated: *with newborn vigour.*

new brutalism *noun* in architecture, = BRUTALISM.

Newcastle disease /'nyoohkahsl, 'nyoohkasl/ *noun* = FOWL PEST. [named after *Newcastle*-upon-Tyne, city in NE England, where it was first recorded in 1927]

new chum *noun* **1** *Aus* a person new to something; a novice. **2** *Aus, NZ formerly*, a recent immigrant from Britain.

newcomer *noun* **1** (*often* + to) a recent arrival. **2** (*often* + to) a beginner or novice: *newcomers to the Internet.*

newel /'nyooh·əl/ *noun* **1** an upright post about which the steps of a spiral staircase wind. **2** a principal post supporting either end of a staircase handrail. [Middle English *nowell* via Old French *nouel* knob, stone of a fruit, from late Latin *nucalis* like a nut, from Latin *nuc-, nux* nut]

newel post *noun* = NEWEL (2).

New Englander *noun* a native or inhabitant of the New-England region of the USA, comprising the states of Maine, New Hampshire, Vermont, Massachusetts, Rhode Island, and Connecticut.

newfangled /nyooh'fanggld, 'nyooh-/ *adj derog* or *humorous* modern and unnecessarily complicated or gimmicky. ➤➤ **newfangledness** *noun*. [Middle English *newefangel* fond of novelty, from NEW¹ + Old English *fangen*, past part. of *fōn* to take, seize]

newfound *adj* newly discovered: *my newfound friend; newfound confidence.*

Newfoundland /nyooh'fowndlənd/ *noun* a large intelligent dog of a breed with coarse dense, usu black, hair. [named after *Newfoundland*, island off Canada's east coast, where the breed originated]

newie /'nyooh·i/ *noun* (*pl* **newies**) *Brit, informal* a new person or thing, e.g. a newly released music album.

newish *adj* fairly new.

new issue *noun* an issue of shares being offered for the first time to the public.

new-laid *adj* said of an egg: just laid.

New Left *noun* a radical left-wing movement originating in Britain in the late 1950s.

New Look or **the New Look** *noun* a style of women's clothing introduced in 1947, featuring full calf-length skirts, partly in celebration of the availability of fabric after wartime austerity.

newly *adv* **1** lately; recently: *a newly married couple.* **2** anew: *newly painted.*

newlywed¹ *adj* recently married.

newlywed² *noun* a recently married person.

new man *noun* a man who rather than adopting an aggressively male social role participates in activities traditionally regarded as more appropriate to women, e.g. childcare, cooking, and housework.

Newmarket /'nyoohmahkit/ *noun* a card game in which players bet on matching cards in their hand against four court cards taken from a second pack of cards. [named after *Newmarket*, town in E England]

new maths (*NAmer* **new math**) *pl noun* (*treated as sing. or pl*) mathematics that is based on set theory, *esp* as taught in primary and secondary schools.

new moon *noun* **1** the phase of the moon when its dark side is towards the earth. **2** the thin crescent moon seen a few days after this.

news *pl noun* (*treated as sing.*) **1** information about something that has recently happened: *wonderful news about the baby.* **2** information about recent events in the world, reported in the newspapers, or on radio and television. **3** (**the news**) a broadcast report of such events. ✳ **that's news to me** that's the first I've heard of it. **the good news is... the bad news is...** used to prepare one's listener for welcome and unwelcome facts. ⏵⏵ **newsless** adj. [Middle English, plural of NEW¹, orig with a plural verb, translating late Latin *nova* or Old French *noveles* new things]

news agency noun (pl **news agencies**) an organization that collects news items for distribution to newspapers.

newsagent noun chiefly Brit a retailer of newspapers and magazines.

newsboy noun a boy who delivers newspapers. Also called PAPERBOY.

newscast noun a broadcast news report. ⏵⏵ **newscaster** noun, **newscasting** noun. [blend of NEWS + BROADCAST²]

news conference noun = PRESS CONFERENCE.

newsdealer noun NAmer = NEWSAGENT.

newsflash noun a brief broadcast reporting an important item of news, *esp* one that interrupts a programme.

newsgirl noun a girl who delivers newspapers. Also called PAPERGIRL.

newsgroup noun a forum of Internet users or email correspondents who exchange news and views about topics of mutual interest.

newshound noun informal a newspaper reporter or journalist, *esp* one of the persistent investigative type.

newsie /'nyoohzi/ noun (pl **newsies**) see NEWSY².

newsletter noun a publication in the form of a printed sheet, pamphlet, or small-format newspaper, containing news and articles relevant to a particular group, association, etc, for circulation to its members.

newsman noun (pl **newsmen**) a man who gathers, reports, or comments on the news; a reporter or correspondent.

newsmonger /'nyoohzmunggə/ noun archaic a person who makes it their business to circulate news; a gossip: *Protestations of impartiality I shall make none. They … are perfect nonsense, when used by a news-monger* — William Cobbett.

newspaper noun a printed daily or weekly publication consisting of folded sheets and containing news reports, articles, photographs, and advertising.

newspaperman or **newspaperwoman** noun (pl **newspapermen** or **newspaperwomen**) a journalist employed by a newspaper.

newspeak or **Newspeak** noun propagandistic language marked by euphemism, circumlocution, and the inversion of customary meanings. [*Newspeak*, a language 'designed to diminish the range of thought', in the novel *Nineteen Eighty-Four* by George Orwell d.1950, English writer]

newsprint noun cheap paper made chiefly from wood pulp and used mostly for newspapers.

newsreader noun a broadcaster who reads the news.

newsreel noun a short film dealing with current events.

newsroom noun a place, e.g. an office, where news is prepared for publication or broadcast.

news sheet noun = NEWSLETTER.

newsstand noun a stall where newspapers and periodicals are sold.

New Stone Age noun (**the New Stone Age**) the NEOLITHIC period.

New Style adj the method of dating based on the Gregorian calendar, which superseded the Julian calendar and was introduced in Scotland in 1600 and in England and Wales in 1752.

newsvendor noun a person who sells newspapers, *esp* in the street at a regular place.

news wire noun **1** a teleprinter transmitting latest news stories and stock-market results. **2** a similarly up-to-the-minute news service accessible via the Internet.

newswoman noun (pl **newswomen**) a woman who gathers, reports, or comments on the news; a reporter or correspondent.

newsworthy adj (**newsworthier, newsworthiest**) sufficiently interesting to warrant reporting.

newsy¹ adj (**newsier, newsiest**) said of a letter, etc: full of news, *esp* personal news. ⏵⏵ **newsiness** noun.

newsy² or **newsie** noun (pl **newsies**) **1** NAmer, Aus a NEWSBOY or NEWSGIRL. **2** NAmer a reporter or journalist.

newt /nyooht/ noun any of various small amphibians of the salamander type, with a long slender body and tail and short legs.

Word history
Middle English, alteration of *ewte*, from Old English *efeta*, whence the doublet EFT. This word has gained its initial *n* sound through a process that has also affected *nickname* and is opposite to that undergone by *adder*, *apron*, and *umpire* (see note at ADDER). When *ewt* was preceded by the indefinite article, the two words were confused: *an ewt* was taken as *a newt*. The latter form was established by the 15th cent.

New Testament noun the second part of the Christian Bible, comprising the canonical Gospels and Epistles, the books of Acts, and the book of Revelation.

newton /'nyooht(ə)n/ noun the SI unit of force equal to the force that would impart an acceleration of one metre per second per second to a free mass of one kilogram. [named after Sir Isaac *Newton* d.1727, English mathematician and scientist]

Newtonian /nyooh'tohni·ən/ adj relating to, following, or agreeing with Sir Isaac Newton or his discoveries: *Newtonian mechanics*.

Newtonian telescope noun a reflecting telescope for astronomical observation constructed so that light collected by a concave mirror is brought to a focus outside the top of the tube by means of a small plane mirror set at 45° to it.

Newton's law of gravitation noun the law that the force of attraction between any two massive particles is directly proportional to the product of their masses, divided by the square of the distance between them.

Newton's laws of motion pl noun three laws of motion that underlie Newtonian mechanics: (1) that a body continues at rest or in motion in a straight line unless acted on by an external force; (2) that the change in momentum of a moving body is proportional to, and in the same direction as, the force causing it; (3) that the force exerted by one body on another is equal and opposite to the force exerted by the latter on the former.

Newton's rings pl noun an optical phenomenon whereby, when a convex lens is placed on a flat glass plate, a dark spot surrounded by bright and dark rings is visible to the observer at the point of contact.

new town noun in Britain, any of several towns planned and built as a unit since 1946.

new wave noun **1** (often **New Wave**) a cinematic movement characterized by improvisation, abstraction, a subjective treatment of chronology and symbolism, and the frequent use of experimental photographic techniques. **2** a style of rock music that developed from PUNK ROCK and is usu more complex musically while retaining an emphasis on social comment. [translation of French *nouvelle vague*]

New World noun (**the New World**) the W hemisphere, *esp* the continental landmass of N and S America.

New Year noun **1** the first day or days of a calendar year. **2** the festive period around 31 December and 1 January.

New Year's Day noun 1 January, observed as a public holiday in many countries.

New Year's Eve noun 31 December, *esp* the evening.

New Yorker noun a native or inhabitant of the US city or state of New York.

New Zealander /'zeeləndə/ noun a native or inhabitant of New Zealand.

New Zealand flax noun = FLAX-LILY or PHORMIUM.

next¹ /nekst/ adj **1** immediately adjacent or following, e.g. in place or order: *the next house*. **2** immediately after the present or a specified time: *next week*. [Old English *nīehst*, superl of *nēah* NIGH]

next² adv **1** in the time, place, or order nearest or immediately succeeding: *Next we drove home; the next-closest school*. **2** on the following occasion or the first occasion to come: *when next we meet*. ✳ **as good/well, etc as the next man** as good, well, etc, as anybody: *I think I'm as generous as the next man*. **next but one** not the next one but the one after: *the next house but one*.

next³ prep archaic or dialect nearest or adjacent to (something): *Wear wool next the skin*.

next⁴ noun **1** a person or thing that is next: *laughing one minute and crying the next*. **2** something forthcoming: *to be contained in our next*.

next door adv in or to the next building, room, etc: *living next door to us*.

next-door *adj* situated or living in the next building, room, etc: *my next-door neighbours.*

next of kin *noun* (*pl* **next of kin**) the person most closely related to oneself.

next to¹ *prep* immediately following or adjacent to: *Sit next to Mary; Next to gin I like sherry best.*

next to² *adv* very nearly; almost: *The article told me next to nothing.*

nexus /'neksəs/ *noun* (*pl* **nexuses** *or* **nexus** /'neksəs/) **1** a connection or link: *It makes money seem the only social nexus — Nation Review.* **2** a connected group or series: *a nexus of causes.* **3** the focus or nub of something: *those dinner parties which had now become the nexus of her social life — Sara Maitland.* [Latin *nexus* a joining together, band, past part of *nectere* to bind]

Nez Percé /ˌnez 'puhs (*French* ne pɛrse)/ *noun* (*pl* **Nez Percé** *or* **Percés** /'puhsiz (*French* pɛrse)/) a member of a Native American people of Idaho, Washington, and Oregon. [French *nez percé*, literally 'pierced nose'; from the nose pendants which some of them wore]

NF *abbr* **1** National Front. **2** Newfoundland (US postal abbreviation).

NFL *abbr NAmer* National Football League, the chief professional league for American football.

Nfld *abbr* Newfoundland.

NFU *abbr Brit* National Farmers' Union.

NG *abbr* **1** *NAmer* National Guard. **2** New Guinea.

ng *abbr* no good.

NGA *abbr Brit* formerly, National Graphical Association.

ngaio /'nieoh/ *noun* (*pl* **ngaios**) a small tree of New Zealand with white wood and edible fruit: *Myoporum laetum.* [Maori *ngaio*]

ngati /'nahti/ *noun* (*pl* **ngati**) *NZ* a clan or tribe. [Maori *ngati*]

NGO *abbr* non-governmental organization.

NGR *abbr* Nigeria (international vehicle registration).

ngultrum /en'gooltrəm, eng-/ *noun* the basic monetary unit of Bhutan.

Nguni /n'goohni/ *noun* (*pl* **Ngunis** *or collectively* **Nguni**) **1** a member of a group of Bantu-speaking peoples of southern Africa. **2** the Bantu languages of the Nguni, including Swazi, Xhosa, and Zulu. ⟩⟩ **Nguni** *adj.* [the Zulu name]

ngwee /(ə)ng'gwee/ *noun* (*pl* **ngwee**) a unit of currency in Zambia, worth 100th of a kwacha. [native name in Zambia, literally 'bright']

NH *abbr* New Hampshire (US postal abbreviation).

NHI *abbr Brit* National Health Insurance.

NHS *abbr Brit* National Health Service.

NI *abbr* **1** *Brit* National Insurance. **2** Northern Ireland. **3** *NZ* North Island.

Ni *abbr* the chemical symbol for nickel.

niacin /'nie-əsin/ *noun* = NICOTINIC ACID. [*nicotinic acid* + -IN¹]

nib /nib/ *noun* **1a** the writing point of a pen, from which the ink is distributed, or either of its divisions. **b** the sharpened point of a quill pen. **2** any small pointed or projecting part. **3** (*in pl*) shelled and crushed coffee or cocoa beans, nuts, etc. **4** *archaic* a beak, bill, or nose. ⟩⟩ **nibbed** *adj.* [early Dutch *nib* beak]

nibble¹ /'nibl/ *verb trans* **1a** to bite (something) cautiously, gently, or playfully: *They have reached the ear-nibbling stage.* **b** to eat or chew (something) in small bites. **2** to produce (a hole, etc) by repeated small bites. ⟩ *verb intrans* **1** (*usu* + at) to take gentle, small, or cautious bites: *nibbling at the bait.* **2** to show cautious or qualified interest: *one firm offer and a couple of others nibbling.* ⟩⟩ **nibbler** *noun.* [Middle English, of Germanic origin]

nibble² *noun* **1** an act of nibbling. **2** a very small amount, e.g. of food. **3** *informal* (*in pl*) savoury morsels served at a reception, etc: *wine and nibbles.*

niblick /'niblik/ *noun* formerly, a number nine iron golf club with a lofted metal head, designed for short high shots, *esp* out of long grass or a bunker. [perhaps NIBBLE¹ + -*ick* -OCK]

nibs ✳ **his nibs** *informal* an important or self-important man or one who demands a lot of attention. [alteration of *nabs*, of unknown origin]

NIC /'nik/ *abbr* **1** newly-industrializing country. **2** Nicaragua (international vehicle registration).

NiCad (*NAmer* **Nicad**) /'niekad/ *noun trademark* a storage battery or cell for recharging portable equipment, with an alkaline electrolyte, and nickel and cadmium electrodes. [shortening of *nickel cadmium battery*]

Nicam *or* **NICAM** /'niekam/ *noun* in British television transmission, a digital system by means of which standard video signals are provided with high-quality stereo sound. [acronym from *near instantaneously companded* (compressed and expanded) *audio multiplex*]

Nicaraguan /nikə'ragyooən, -'ragwən/ *noun* a native or inhabitant of Nicaragua in central America. ⟩⟩ **Nicaraguan** *adj.*

NICE /nies/ *abbr* National Institute for Clinical Excellence.

nice /nies/ *adj* **1** pleasant or agreeable: *This is a very nice day, and we are taking a very nice walk, and you are two very nice young ladies in* Every commendation on every subject is comprised in that one word — Jane Austen. **2** said of a person: kind, considerate, or accommodating. **3** socially respectable: *She comes from a nice home.* **4** satisfactorily performed, competent, or skilful: *Nice shot!* **5** ironic fine: *She's a nice one to complain.* **6** subtle: *a nice distinction.* **7** tricky: *a nice dilemma.* **8** *archaic* fastidious, precise, discriminating, or scrupulous: *not over-nice in their methods.* **9** *archaic* delicate: *But these are nice plants and are kept mostly under glass — Celia Fiennes.* **10** *archaic* coy or shy: *They are … bashful, very shy, and nice of being touched —* Aphra Behn. **11** *archaic* loose-living: *He put out of his court all nyce and wanton people — John Rastell.* **12** *archaic* foolish or ignorant: *So it is bot a nyce sinne of gold to ben to covoitous — John Gower.* ✳ **nice and** pleasantly; agreeably: *nice and warm.* **nice one** *informal* used to express admiration for an adroit move. **nice try** *informal* used to express ironic sympathy over a failed ploy. ⟩⟩ **nicely** *adv,* **niceness** *noun.*

Word history
Middle English, in the sense 'foolish', via Old French *nice* simple, silly, from Latin *nescius* ignorant, from *nescire* not to know, from *ne-* not + *scire* to know. *Nice* has undergone numerous shifts of meaning. Before the 16th cent. most of its meanings were highly derogatory: 'foolish', 'strange', 'lazy', and 'effeminate' among them. Even the senses 'fastidious', 'precise', and 'delicate', which probably gave rise to the sense 'pleasant', were originally derogatory. The use of *nice* as a general term of approval became fashionable in the late 18th cent.

nice-looking *adj* good-looking; attractive: *Some hostesses … will forgive anything … as long as one is nice-looking — Saki.*

Nicene Creed /'nieseen/ *noun* a Christian creed expanded from a creed issued by the first Council of Nicaea in AD 325, beginning 'I believe in one God'. [late Latin *Nicenus, Nicaenus* of Nicaea, city of Asia Minor]

nicety /'niesiti/ *noun* (*pl* **niceties**) **1** a fine point or distinction: *the niceties of grammar.* **2** subtlety or precision: *She put the point with great nicety.* **3** a point of etiquette or protocol: *no time for niceties.* **4** an elegant or refined feature. ✳ **to a nicety** to the point at which the thing in question is at its best: *roasted to a nicety.* [Middle English *nicete* folly, from Old French from *nice*: see NICE]

niche¹ /neesh, nich/ *noun* **1** a recess in a wall, *esp* for a statue. **2** a place or activity for which a person is best suited: *He has found his niche in life.* **3** the ecological role of an organism in a community, *esp* in regard to food consumption. **4** (*often used before a noun*) a specialized but rewarding retailing opportunity: *niche marketing.* [French *niche* from *nicher* to nest, ultimately from Latin *nidus* nest]

niche² *verb trans* to place (a person, etc) in or as if in a niche: *When the boom in improvisational comedy came along later, however, Merton niched himself rather better — The Face.*

Nichiren /'nishərən/ *noun* a Japanese Buddhist sect founded by the reformer Nichiren d.1282, using the Lotus SUTRA (Buddhist scripture) as its basic text.

Nichrome /'niekrohm/ *noun trademark* a nickel and chromium alloy with a high electrical resistance.

nick¹ /nik/ *noun* **1** a small cut, notch, or groove. **2** the point at which the back or side wall of a squash court meets the floor. **3** a line where two planes meet: = EDGE¹ (2). **4** (**the nick**) *Brit, informal* a prison or police station. ✳ **in good/bad nick** *Brit, informal* in good or bad condition. **in the nick of time** at the final critical moment; just before it would be too late. [Middle English *nyke*, prob alteration of *nocke* NOCK¹]

nick² *verb trans* **1** to make a nick in (something). **2** to cut (a part of the body, etc) slightly: *I nicked myself shaving.* **3** *Brit, informal* to steal (something). **4** *Brit, informal* to arrest (somebody): *He was nicked for shoplifting.* **5** *NAmer* (+ for) to cheat or overcharge (somebody) to the extent of a certain sum, etc. **6** *informal* to hit, guess, or catch (something) exactly. ➤ *verb intrans chiefly Aus, informal* (+ off/away, etc) to depart hastily or surreptitiously.

nickel[1] /'nik(ə)l/ *noun* **1** a silver-white metallic chemical element that is hard and malleable, with similar magnetic properties to iron, capable of a high polish and resistant to corrosion, occurs naturally in various ores, and is used in coins and in alloys: symbol Ni, atomic number 28. **2a** a US coin containing one part of nickel to three of copper, and worth five cents. **b** the sum of five US cents. [German *Kupfernickel* niccolite (a mineral largely composed of a nickel arsenide), prob from *Kupfer* copper + *Nickel* goblin; from the deceptive copper colour of niccolite]

nickel[2] *verb trans* (**nickelled, nickelling**, *NAmer* **nickeled, nickeling**) to coat (a metal) with nickel.

nickel-and-dime[1] *adj NAmer, informal* unimportant; small-time: *a nickel-and-dime business venture.* [orig denoting a store selling goods at five or ten cents]

nickel-and-dime[2] *verb trans NAmer, informal* (*usu in passive*) **1** said of small expenses or other harassments: to undermine or ruin (somebody) little by little. **2** to amass (a considerable sum) little by little. ➤ *verb intrans NAmer, informal* to spend money sparingly; to penny-pinch.

nickel brass *noun* an alloy of copper and zinc with a small amount of nickel.

nickelodeon /nikə'lohdi·ən/ *noun dated* a jukebox. [NICKEL[1] + -*odeon* as in MELODEON]

nickel silver *noun* a silver-white alloy of copper, zinc, and nickel. Also called GERMAN SILVER.

nickel steel *noun* stainless steel strengthened by the addition of chromium and nickel.

nicker[1] /'nikə/ *noun* (*pl* **nicker**) *Brit, informal* the sum of £1: *fifty nicker.* [origin unknown]

nicker[2] *verb intrans* (**nickered, nickering**) said of a horse: to whinny. [perhaps alteration of *neigh*, or imitative]

nicknack /'niknak/ *noun* see KNICK-KNACK.

nickname[1] *noun* **1** a familiar or humorous name used in place of or in addition to a proper name. **2** a familiar form of a personal name, e.g. *Bob* for *Robert.*

Word history
Middle English *nekename* additional name, alteration (by incorrect division of *an ekename*) of *ekename*, from *eke* also (from Old English *eac*) + NAME[1]. See NEWT for another example of a word that, through misunderstanding, gained an initial *n*.

nickname[2] *verb trans* to give (a person or thing) a nickname: *an ornate building we had nicknamed 'the Wedding Cake'.*

Niçois[1] /nee'swah/ *or* **Niçoise** /nee'swahz/ *adj* **1** relating to or belonging to the French city of Nice. **2** (*usu after a noun*) denoting dishes garnished with tomatoes, anchovies, and capers: *salade Niçoise.* [French *Niçois* (masc), *Niçoise* (fem)]

Niçois[2] *or* **Niçoise** *noun* (*pl* **Niçois** *or* **Niçoises** /nee'swahz/) a native or inhabitant of the French city of Nice.

Nicol prism /'nikl/ *or* **nicol prism** *noun* a prism consisting of two pieces of the transparent variety of the mineral calcite cemented together, used *esp* to obtain a ray of polarized light. [named after William *Nicol* d.1851, Scottish physicist, who invented it]

nicotiana /ˌnikəti'ahnə/ *noun* any of several species of a plant related to the tobacco plant, with fragrant tubular flowers: *esp Nicotiana alata.* [scientific Latin *nicotiana herba* tobacco plant, named after Jacques *Nicot* d.1600, French diplomat and scholar, who introduced tobacco into France]

nicotinamide /nikə'tinəmied/ *noun* a vitamin of the vitamin B complex that is used by the body in a similar way to nicotinic acid. [NICOTINE + AMIDE]

nicotinamide-adenine dinucleotide *noun* = NAD.

nicotine /'nikəteen/ *noun* a poisonous chemical compound, the alkaloid that occurs in tobacco, used as an agricultural insecticide, causing disorders of the respiratory system, dizziness, increased blood pressure, and disturbances of hearing and vision: formula $C_{10}H_{14}N_2$. ➤ **nicotinic** /-'tinik/ *adj.* [French *nicotine* from scientific Latin *nicotiana*: see NICOTIANA]

nicotine patch *noun* a skin patch impregnated with nicotine, worn by somebody attempting to give up smoking cigarettes, to control their craving for tobacco.

nicotinic acid /nikə'tinik/ *noun* a vitamin of the vitamin B complex that is found widely in animals and plants, deficiency in which results in PELLAGRA (skin disease). ➤➤ **nicotinate** /'nikətinayt/ *noun.* [*nicotinic* from NICOTINE + -IC[1]]

nictate /'niktayt/ *verb intrans technical* to blink. ➤➤ **nictation** /nik'taysh(ə)n/ *noun.* [Latin *nictatus*, past part. of *nictare* to blink, and late Latin *nictitatus*, past part. of *nictitare*, frequentative of *nictare*]

nictitate /'niktitayt/ *verb intrans* = NICTATE.

nictitating membrane *noun* in birds, reptiles, and some mammals, e.g. cats, a thin membrane capable of extending across the eyeball under the eyelids.

nidation /nie'daysh(ə)n/ *noun* in mammals, the process by which a fertilized egg attaches itself to the wall of the uterus. [Latin *nidus* nest + -ATION]

nide /nied/ *noun* the nest or brood of a pheasant. [Latin *nidus* nest, perhaps via French *nid*]

nidi /'niedie, 'niedee/ *noun* pl of NIDUS.

nidicolous /ni'dikələs/ *adj* said of young birds: remaining in the nest for a comparatively long time after hatching; = ALTRICIAL: compare NIDIFUGOUS. [Latin *nidus* nest + -*colous* inhabiting]

nidification /ˌnidifi'kaysh(ə)n/ *noun* the act, process, or technique of building a nest. [late Latin *nidification-, nidificatio*, from Latin *nidificare* to build a nest, from *nidus* nest]

nidifugous /ni'difyoogəs/ *adj* said of young birds: leaving the nest comparatively soon after hatching; = PRECOCIAL: compare NIDICOLOUS. [Latin *nidus* nest + *fugere* to flee, escape]

nidify /'nidifie/ *verb intrans* (**nidifies, nidified, nidifying**) said of birds: to build a nest. [from Latin *nidificare* to build a nest, from *nidus* nest]

nidus /'niedəs/ *noun* (*pl* **nidi** /'niedie, 'niedee/ *or* **niduses**) **1** a nest or breeding place, *esp* a place in an animal or plant where bacteria or other organisms lodge and multiply. **2** a place where something originates, develops, or is found or fostered: *the Sorbonne, formerly the nidus of pedantry* — Maurice Keatinge. [Latin *nidus* nest]

niece /nees/ *noun* a daughter of one's brother or sister or of one's brother-in-law or sister-in-law. [Middle English *nece* granddaughter, niece, via Old French from Latin *neptis* granddaughter, niece, fem of *nepot-, nepos* grandson, nephew]

niello /ni'eloh/ *noun* (*pl* **nielli** /-lie, -lee/ *or* **niellos**) **1** a black enamel-like compound of sulphur with silver, copper, and lead, used for filling in incised designs on silver or other metals. **2** decorated work of this kind, or an example of it. ➤➤ **nielloed** *adj.* [Italian *niello* from Latin *nigellus*: see NIGELLA]

niente /ni'entay/ *adj and adv* said of a piece of music: with the sound or tone fading away to nothing. [Italian *niente* nothing]

Niersteiner /'niəshtienə/ *noun* a white Rhine wine produced in the region of the German town of Nierstein.

Nietzschean /'neetshi·ən/ *adj* relating to the philosophical teachings of Friedrich Nietzsche, *esp* his doctrine of the superman. ➤➤ **Nietzschean** *noun.* [Friedrich *Nietzsche* d.1900, German philosopher]

niff[1] /nif/ *noun Brit, informal* an unpleasant smell. ➤➤ **niffy** *adj.* [orig dialect, perhaps from SNIFF[1]]

niff[2] *verb intrans Brit, informal* to smell unpleasant; to stink.

nifty /'nifti/ *adj* (**niftier, niftiest**) *informal* **1** very good or effective: *a nifty gadget.* **2** cleverly conceived or executed: *nifty fingering.* ➤➤ **niftily** *adv*, **niftiness** *noun.* [origin unknown]

nigella /nie'jelə/ *noun* any of various species of a plant with finely segmented leaves and white, blue, or yellow flowers, *esp* LOVE-IN-A-MIST. [scientific Latin *nigella*, fem of Latin *nigellus* blackish, dimin. of *niger* black; in reference to the plant's black seeds]

Niger-Congo /'niejəˌkonggoh/ *noun* a large language family of sub-Saharan Africa which includes the Bantu, Kwa, and Mande languages. ➤➤ **Niger-Congo** *adj.* [named after the *Niger* and *Congo* rivers]

Nigerian /nie'jiəri·ən/ *noun* a native or inhabitant of Nigeria in W Africa. ➤➤ **Nigerian** *adj.*

niggard /'nigəd/ *noun* a mean or stingy person. ➤➤ **niggard** *adj.* [Middle English, ultimately of Scandinavian origin]

niggardly *adj* **1** grudgingly mean; miserly. **2** provided in meagre amounts: *niggardly praise.* ➤➤ **niggardliness** *noun*, **niggardly** *adv.*

nigger /'nigə/ *noun offensive or derog* a black person, *esp* one of African race. [alteration of *neger* adj, via French *nègre* from Spanish or Portuguese *negro*: see NEGRO]

niggle /'nig'l/ *verb intrans* **1** said of a pain or worry: to cause minor but persistent discomfort or anxiety. **2** to find fault constantly in a petty way. ⟫ **niggle** *noun,* **niggler** *noun,* **niggly** *adj.* [prob of Scandinavian origin]

niggling *adj* **1** petty: *niggling criticisms.* **2** persistently annoying: *niggling doubts.* ⟫ **nigglingly** *adv.*

nigh /nie/ *adv, adj, and prep archaic* near in place, time, or relation: *nigh on 50 years; Evening drew nigh; She was nigh her time.* [Old English *nēah*]

night /niet/ *noun* **1** the period of darkness from dusk to dawn caused by the earth's daily rotation. **2** an evening characterized by a specified event or activity: *Thursday is bingo night; opening night.* **3** darkness; nightfall: *Night was approaching.* **4** *literary* a state of affliction, ignorance, or obscurity: *Discharge my followers; let them hence away, from Richard's night to Bolingbroke's fair day —* Shakespeare. [Old English *niht*]

nightbird *noun* = NIGHT OWL.

night blindness *noun* reduced vision in dim light, *esp* at night. ⟫ **night-blind** *adj.*

nightcap *noun* **1** formerly, a cloth cap worn in bed: *He ... put on his dressing-gown and slippers, and his nightcap —* Dickens. **2** a drink taken at bedtime.

nightclothes *or* **night clothes** *pl noun* clothes worn for sleeping in: *He was clad only in a pink dressing gown, which covered his night clothes —* Conan Doyle.

nightclub *noun* a place of entertainment open at night that has a floor show, provides music and space for dancing, and usu serves drinks and food. ⟫ **nightclubber** *noun,* **nightclubbing** *noun.*

night crawler *noun chiefly NAmer* an earthworm that emerges at night, often collected for use as fishing bait.

nightdress *noun* a woman's or girl's nightgown.

nightfall *noun* dusk.

nightgown *noun* a loose garment for sleeping in.

nighthawk *noun* **1** a nightjar, owl, or similar bird that flies at night. **2** *NAmer* = NIGHT OWL.

night heron *noun* any of several species of small, nocturnally active herons with a short neck: genus *Nycticorax.*

nightie *or* **nighty** /'nieti/ *noun* (*pl* **nighties**) *informal* a nightdress.

nightingale /'nietinggayl/ *noun* a small migratory thrush with brown plumage and a red-brown tail, noted for the sweet song of the male, typically heard at night: *Luscinia megarhynchos.* [Old English *nihtegale,* from *niht* NIGHT + *galan* to sing]

nightjar *noun* any of several species of Eurasian insect-eating birds with large eyes and greyish brown plumage that are active at night and have a characteristic discordant call: *Caprimulgus europaeus* and other species. Also called GOATSUCKER. [NIGHT + JAR[2]]

night latch *noun* a door lock whose bolt is operated from the outside by a key and from the inside by a knob.

nightlife *noun* late evening entertainment or social life.

night light *noun* **1** a dim light kept burning all night long, *esp* in the bedroom. **2** a small squat slow-burning candle designed for this purpose.

nightlong *or* **night-long** *adj and adv literary* throughout the night: *Night-long within mine arms in love and sleep she lay —* Ernest Dowson.

nightly[1] *adj* **1** happening at night: *one's nightly slumbers.* **2** happening every night: *nightly air raids.*

nightly[2] *adv* every night: *performing nightly at eight.*

nightmare *noun* **1** a frightening or distressing dream. **2** an experience or situation that causes anxiety or terror or seems beyond one's control: *Their filing system was a nightmare.* ⟫ **nightmarish** *adj,* **nightmarishly** *adv.*

Word history
Middle English, from NIGHT + Old English *mære,* an evil spirit believed to suffocate people in their sleep. This evil spirit was sometimes also known as the *nighthag* or the *riding of the witch.*

night owl *noun informal* somebody who tends to be most active at night.

nights *adv informal* regularly every night: *people who work nights.*

night safe *noun* a safe accessible from the exterior wall of a bank, used for depositing money when the bank is closed.

night school *noun* classes, often in subjects leading to a qualification, held in the evening.

nightshade *noun* any of several plants related to the potato, typically with poisonous red or black berries, *esp Solanum dulcamara* (WOODY NIGHTSHADE), *Atropa belladonna* (DEADLY NIGHTSHADE), and *Solanum nigrum* (BLACK NIGHTSHADE). [Old English *nihtscada,* prob from *niht* NIGHT + *sceadu* SHADE[1], in reference to the colour of the berries]

nightshirt *noun* a long loose shirt for sleeping in.

nightside *noun* the side of a planet or moon that is not in daylight.

night soil *noun* human excrement collected for fertilizing the soil.

nightstand *noun* = NIGHT TABLE.

nightstick *noun NAmer* a club carried by a policeman: compare TRUNCHEON.

night table *noun NAmer* a small bedside table.

night time *noun* the time from dusk to dawn. ⟫ **night-time** *adj.*

night watchman *noun* (*pl* **night watchmen**) **1** a person who keeps watch, e.g. over a building, by night. **2** in cricket, a relatively inexpert batsman who is sent in to bat towards the end of a day's play so that a more expert batsman need not face the bowling until the following day.

nightwear *noun* clothing for wearing in bed; nightclothes.

nighty *noun* (*pl* **nighties**) see NIGHTIE.

nigrescent /ni'gres(ə)nt/ *adj literary* verging on black; blackish; dusky: *the glossy ermine ... or scarcer sable with nigrescent locks —* Hans Busk. ⟫ **nigrescence** *noun.* [Latin *nigrescent-, nigrescens,* present part. of *nigrescere* to become black, grow dark, from *nigr-, niger* black]

nigritude /'nigrityoohd/ *noun formal* blackness. [Latin *nigritudo,* from *nigr-, niger* black]

nihilism /'nie-əliz(ə)m, 'nihi-/ *noun* **1** a view that rejects all values and beliefs as meaningless or unfounded. **2** the philosophical view that nothing has real existence; extreme scepticism. **3** (*often* **Nihilism**) the doctrine of a 19th-cent. Russian revolutionary party that social conditions are so bad as to make destruction desirable for its own sake. **4** terrorism or anarchy. ⟫ **nihilist** *noun and adj,* **nihilistic** /-'listik/ *adj.* [German *Nihilismus,* from Latin *nihil* nothing]

nihility /ni'hiliti/ *noun* **1** nothingness: *what God originally created ... that matter which ... he first made from his spirit or from nihility —* Poe. **2** a non-existent thing. **3** a trifle. [late Latin *nihilitas* nothingness, from Latin *nihil* nothing]

nihil obstat /,nie-əl 'obstat, ,nihil/ *noun* **1** authoritative or official approval. **2** in the Roman Catholic Church, a certificate confirming that a publication is doctrinally and morally unexceptionable. [Latin *nihil obstat* nothing hinders]

-nik *suffix* forming nouns, denoting: a person who is associated with a particular activity or cause: *beatnik; refusenik; computernik.* [Yiddish *-nik* agent suffix, the word form suggested also by Russian *sputnik*]

Nikkei average /'nikay/ *noun* = NIKKEI INDEX.

Nikkei index *noun* a figure indicating the average closing price of 225 representative stocks on the Tokyo Stock Exchange. [*Nihon Keizai Shimbun,* Japanese Economic Journal, the group calculating and issuing the index]

nil /nil/ *noun* nothing, zero: *a score of two points to nil.* ⟫ **nil** *adj.* [Latin *nil,* contraction of *nihil* nothing]

nil desperandum /,nil despə'randəm/ *interj* never lose hope. [Latin *nil* nothing (see NIL) + *desperandum* to be despaired of, verbal noun from *desperare:* see DESPAIR[1], from Horace's *nil desperandum Teucro duce* no cause to despair with Teucer as your leader, Odes 1.vii.27]

Nile green /niel/ *noun* a pale bluish green. ⟫ **Nile-green** *adj.* [developed from EAU-DE-NIL]

Nile perch *noun* a large predatory freshwater fish of NE and central Africa, caught as food: *Lates niloticus.* [named after the river *Nile* in E Africa]

nilgai /'nilgie/ *noun* (*pl* **nilgais** *or collectively* **nilgai**) a large Indian antelope, the male having short horns: *Boselaphus tragocamelus.*

[Hindi *nīlgaī*, fem of *nīlgāw* blue bull, from Sanskrit *nīla* dark blue + *go* bull, cow]

Nilo-Saharan /nielohsə'hahrən/ *noun* a group of languages comprising the Nilotic family and other languages of N and E Africa. ➤➤ **Nilo-Saharan** *adj*.

Nilotic /nie'lotik/ *adj* 1 denoting or belonging to the Nile or Nile region, or its people or languages. 2 denoting a group of Nilo-Saharan languages spoken in Sudan and E Africa. [via Latin from Greek *Neilōtikos*, from *Neilos* the river Nile in E Africa]

nilpotent /nil'pohtənt/ *adj* denoting a mathematical entity that is equal to zero when raised to some power: *nilpotent matrices*. [Latin *nil* (see NIL) + *potent-, potens* having power: see POTENT[1]]

nim[1] /nim/ *noun* any of various games in which each player in turn draws objects from one or more piles and attempts to take the last object or force their opponent to take it. [prob from Middle English *nim* to take, from Old English *niman*, or from German *nimm!* take!]

nim[2] /neem/ *noun* see NEEM.

nimbi /'nimbie, 'nimbee/ *noun* pl of NIMBUS.

nimble /'nimbl/ *adj* 1 quick, light, and easy in movement. 2 quick and clever in thought and understanding. ➤➤ **nimbleness** *noun*, **nimbly** *adv*. [Old English *nǽmel, numol* quick to comprehend, from *niman* to take; *-b-* introduced in the 16th cent. to aid pronunciation]

nimbostratus /nimboh'strahtəs, -'straytəs/ *noun* a cloud formation consisting of a dark rainy cloud layer, occurring at medium altitude, between about 450 and 3000m (about 1500 and 10,000ft). [scientific Latin, from NIMBUS + STRATUS]

nimbus /'nimbəs/ *noun* (*pl* **nimbi** /'nimbie, 'nimbee/ *or* **nimbuses**) 1 a heavy grey rain-bearing cloud. 2 a luminous vapour, cloud, or atmosphere surrounding a god or goddess. 3 a luminous circle about the head of a representation of a god, saint, or sovereign: compare AUREOLE. [Latin *nimbus* rainstorm, cloud, bright mist surrounding a god, hence, in ecclesiastical Latin, a saint's aureole]

Nimby /'nimbi/ *noun* (*pl* **Nimbys** *or* **Nimbies**) a person who, while not objecting in principle to a specified kind of development, etc, is averse to its occurring in their immediate neighbourhood. [acronym from *Not In My Back Yard*]

nimiety /ni'mieiti/ *noun literary* an excess or superfluity: *A more serious blemish... with most modern poetry, is nimiety, the tendency to dilute the general effect by repetition* — Illustrated London News. [late Latin *nimietas*, from Latin *nimius* too much, adj, from *nimis* adv]

niminy-piminy /,nimeni 'pimeni/ *adj* affectedly dainty or delicate. [prob fanciful coinage perhaps influenced by NAMBY-PAMBY[1]]

Nimrod *or* **nimrod** /'nimrod/ *noun literary* a huntsman. [named after *Nimrod*, great-grandson of Noah, described in Genesis 10:9 as 'a mighty hunter']

nincompoop /'ningkəmpoohp/ *noun* a silly or foolish person. [perhaps from French *nicodème* simpleton, named after the Pharisee *Nicodemus* (John 3: 1–10), but the form is not satisfactorily explained]

nine /nien/ *noun* 1 the number 9, or the quantity represented by it. 2 something having nine parts or members. 3a the age of 9 years. b the hour three hours before midday or midnight. ✳ **dressed to/up to the nines** *informal* dressed very smartly or elaborately. ➤➤ **nine** *adj*, **ninefold** *adj and adv*. [Old English *nigon*]

nine days' wonder *noun* something that creates a short-lived sensation.

nine-eleven *or* **9/11** *noun chiefly NAmer* 11 September 2001, the date of the destruction of the World Trade Centre in New York in a terrorist attack.

ninepins *pl noun* 1 (*treated as sing.*) the games of skittles (see SKITTLE). 2 (*in sing.*) a skittle. ✳ **go down/drop/fall like ninepins** to fall over, fall ill, or die, in large numbers.

nineteen /nien'teen/ *adj and noun* the number 19, or the quantity represented by it. ✳ **talk nineteen to the dozen** *informal* to talk or converse volubly. ➤➤ **nineteenth** *adj and noun*. [Old English *nigontīne*, from *nigon* NINE + *tien* TEN]

Nineteen Eighty-Four *noun* an era, *esp* a future era, envisaged as having all aspects of life controlled by an all-seeing totalitarian government. [*Nineteen Eighty-Four*, futuristic novel by George Orwell d.1950, English writer]

nineteenth hole *noun humorous* the bar of a golf club or other gathering place. [from its being resorted to after the 18 holes on a standard golf course]

nine-to-five *adj* said of a job: a requiring one to work normal office hours only. b providing regular employment and paying a regular wage.

ninety /'nienti/ *adj and noun* (*pl* **nineties**) 1 the number 90, or the quantity represented by it. 2 (*in pl*) the numbers 90 to 99; *specif* a range of temperatures, ages, or dates within a century characterized by these numbers. ➤➤ **ninetieth** /'nienti·əth/ *adj and noun*. [Old English *nigontig*, short for *hundnigontig* group of ninety, from *hund* HUNDRED + *nigon* NINE + *-tig* group of ten]

ning-nong /'ningnong/ *noun Aus, NZ, informal* a fool. [of uncertain origin]

ninhydrin /nin'hiedrin/ *noun* an oxidizing agent used *esp* for the detection of amino acids and polypeptides. [formerly a trademark, from *nin* of unknown origin + HYDR- + -IN[1]]

ninja /'ninjə/ *noun* (*pl* **ninja** *or* **ninjas**) a person skilled in ninjutsu. [Japanese *ninja* spy]

ninjutsu /nin'jootsooh/ *noun* the Japanese martial art of espionage and camouflage. [Japanese *nin* stealth + *jutsu* art, skill, science]

ninny /'nini/ *noun* (*pl* **ninnies**) *humorous, informal* a silly or foolish person. [perhaps by shortening and alteration from *an innocent*]

ninon /'neenon, 'nienon (French ninɔ̃)/ *noun* a fine smooth sheer fabric, orig silk. [prob from French *Ninon*, nickname for *Anne*]

ninth /nienth/ *adj and noun* 1 denoting a person or thing having the position in a sequence corresponding to the number nine. 2 one of nine equal parts of something. 3 in music, an interval of nine degrees of a diatonic scale, or the combination of two notes at such an interval. ➤➤ **ninthly** *adv*. [Old English *nigotha*]

niobium /nie'ohbi·əm/ *noun* a silver-grey metallic chemical element that is ductile, occurs naturally in columbite and tantalite, and is used in superconductive alloys: symbol Nb, atomic number 41. [scientific Latin from Greek *Niobē*, daughter of Tantalus in Greek mythology, from its occurrence in tantalite]

Nip /nip/ *noun derog* a Japanese. [short for *Nipponese*, from Japanese *Nippon* Japan]

nip[1] *verb* (**nipped, nipping**) ➤ *verb trans* 1 to catch hold of (something) and squeeze or pinch it sharply. 2 (*often* + off) to sever (something) by or as if by pinching sharply: *nip off the dead heads*. 3 to give a small, sharp bite to (somebody or something). 4 said of cold or frost: to injure (e.g. a plant) or numb (a part of the body). ➤ *verb intrans chiefly Brit, informal* to go quickly or briefly; to hurry: *nip out to the shops*. ✳ **nip something in the bud** to prevent the growth, development, or success of something at an early stage: *They nipped the rebellion in the bud*. [Middle English *nippen*, of Germanic origin]

nip[2] *noun* 1 a sharp stinging cold: *a nip in the air*. 2 a sharp squeeze, *esp* between finger and thumb; a pinch. 3 a small, sharp bite. 4 *chiefly NAmer* a pungent flavour; a tang. ✳ **nip and tuck 1** *chiefly NAmer* neck and neck. 2 a piece of cosmetic surgery. **put the nips in** *Aus, NZ* to put pressure on somebody in order to extort money from them.

nip[3] *noun* a small measure or drink of spirits. [prob short for *nipperkin*, a small liquor container, of Low German or Dutch origin]

nip[4] *verb* (**nipped, nipping**) to take nips of (a drink).

nipa /'neepə, 'niepə/ *noun* 1 a palm tree with creeping roots found in the mangrove swamps of India and the islands of the Pacific: *Nypa fruticans*. 2 an alcoholic drink made from the juice of this tree. [Spanish or Portuguese *nipa* from Malay *nipah* nipa palm]

nipper *noun* 1 (*in pl*) any of various devices, e.g. pincers or pliers, for gripping or cutting. 2 *chiefly Brit, informal* a child; *esp* a small boy.

nipple /'nipl/ *noun* 1 the protuberance of a mammary gland, e.g. a breast, from which milk is drawn in the female. 2 an artificial teat through which a bottle-fed infant feeds. 3 a device with a hole through which the discharge of a liquid can be regulated. 4 a small projection through which oil or grease is injected into machinery. [earlier *neble, nible*, prob dimin. of NEB or NIB]

nipplewort *noun* a plant of the daisy family with small yellow flower heads, growing in woodland and wasteland: *Lapsana communis*.

nippy *adj* (**nippier, nippiest**) 1 nimble and lively: *nippy little cars*. 2 said of the weather: chilly. ➤➤ **nippily** *adv*, **nippiness** *noun*.

NIREX /'niereks/ *abbr Brit* Nuclear Industry Radioactive Waste Executive.

nirvana /nuh'vahnə/ *noun* **1** (*often* **Nirvana**) a Hindu and Buddhist state of final bliss and freedom from the cycle of rebirth, attainable through the extinction of desire and individual consciousness.

Editorial note

(Sanskrit) Nirvana ('blowing out') is a term found in ancient Indian religions for the state of liberation from suffering. Best-known from Buddhism, it is the cessation of suffering that enlightened beings enter upon death. The question of what remains of consciousness in nirvana has been persistent in Buddhist philosophy. In common English parlance, nirvana has come to mean any ultimate state of satisfaction — Professor Donald Lopez.

2 a place or state of peaceful relief from pain or anxiety. [Sanskrit *nirvāṇa* act of extinguishing, from *nis-* out + *vāti* it blows]

nisei /'neesay, nee'say/ *noun* (*pl* **nisei** or **niseis**) a child of immigrant Japanese parents who is born and educated in the USA. [Japanese *nisei* second generation, from *ni* second + *sei* generation]

nisi /'niesie, 'neezee/ *adj* (*used after a noun*) taking effect at a specified time unless previously modified or avoided: *a decree nisi.* [Latin *nisi* unless]

Nissen hut /'nis(ə)n/ *noun* a prefabricated shelter with a semi-circular arching roof of corrugated iron and a concrete floor. [named after Peter *Nissen* d.1930, Brit mining engineer, who invented it]

nit[1] /nit/ *noun* the egg or larva of a louse or other parasitic insect. [Old English *hnitu*]

nit[2] *noun chiefly Brit, informal* a nitwit.

nit[3] *noun* a unit of luminance equal to one candela per square metre. [Latin *nitor* brightness]

nit[4] or **nepit** /'nepit/ *noun* a unit of information equal to 1.44 bits. [blend of *Napierian* or *Neperian* (see NEPER) + DIGIT]

nit[5] *interj Aus, informal* used to warn of somebody's approach. ✳ **keep nit** to keep a look-out. [prob variant of NIX[2]]

niter /'nietə/ *noun NAmer* see NITRE.

niterie /'nietəri/ *noun* (*pl* **niteries**) *informal* a nightclub: *Hottest gossip-point round the Hollywood niteries is Amber Lush's latest escort* — David Lodge. [facetious misspelling of NIGHT + -ERY]

nitinol /'nitinol/ *noun* an alloy of nickel and titanium. [the chemical symbols NI and TI + the initials of *Naval Ordnance Laboratory*]

nitpick *verb intrans* to criticize in a petty and often unjustified way.

nit-picking *noun* petty and often unjustified criticism. ➤➤ **nitpicking** *adj.* [NIT[1]]

nitr- or **nitro-** *comb. form* forming words, denoting: **1** a chemical compound that contains the nitro group -NO₂: *nitrobenzene.* **2** a chemical compound that contains nitric acid, nitrogen, or nitrates: *nitrocellulose.* [Greek *nitron*: see NITRE]

nitrate[1] /'nietrayt/ *noun* **1** a salt or ester of nitric acid. **2** sodium or potassium nitrate used as a fertilizer.

nitrate[2] *verb trans* to treat or combine (a substance) with nitric acid or a nitrate. ➤➤ **nitration** /nie'traysh(ə)n/ *noun,* **nitrator** *noun.*

nitrazepam /nie'trazipam/ *noun* a synthetic drug with actions similar to those of diazepam, widely used as a hypnotic in sleeping pills. Also called MOGADON. [NITR- + -*azepam* as in DIAZEPAM]

nitre (*NAmer* **niter**) /'nietə/ *noun* = POTASSIUM NITRATE. [Middle English via Old French *nitre* and Latin *nitrum* from Greek *nitron, natron* from Egyptian *ntry*]

nitric /'nietrik/ *adj* relating to or containing nitrogen, *esp* with a relatively high valency: *nitric oxide.*

nitric acid *noun* a corrosive inorganic liquid acid, used *esp* as an oxidizing agent and in making fertilizers, dyes, etc: formula HNO₃.

nitric oxide *noun* a colourless poisonous gas that is obtained from nitrogen or ammonia and reacts in air to produce brown fumes of nitrogen dioxide gas: formula NO.

nitride /'nietried/ *noun* a compound of nitrogen with one other element: *boron nitride.*

nitrification /,nietrifi'kaysh(ə)n/ *noun* the process of nitrifying; *specif* the oxidation, e.g. by bacteria, of ammonium salts first to nitrites and then to nitrates.

nitrify /'nietrifie/ *verb trans* (**nitrifies, nitrified, nitrifying**) to combine or impregnate (a substance) with nitrogen or one of its compounds. [French *nitrifier,* from *nitr-* NITR-]

nitrile /'nietriel, -tril/ *noun* an organic compound containing the cyanide group.

nitrite /'nietriet/ *noun* a salt or ESTER (alcohol compound) of nitrous acid.

nitro[1] /'nietroh/ *adj* (*often as comb. form*) denoting the univalent group NO₂ or containing it in the molecular structure: *nitrobenzene.* [NITRO-]

nitro[2] *noun* (*pl* **nitros**) any of various nitrated chemical compounds; *esp* NITROGLYCERINE.

nitro- *comb. form* see NITR-.

nitrobacterium /,nietrohbak'tiəri·əm/ *noun* (*pl* **nitrobacteria** /-ri·ə/) any soil bacterium that is involved in the process of nitrification by which ammonium compounds are converted into compounds that can be used by plants; a nitrate bacterium or a nitrite bacterium.

nitrobenzene /nietroh'benzeen/ *noun* an oily liquid with an almond smell, used *esp* as a solvent and in making aniline.

nitrocellulose /nietroh'selyoolohs, -lohz/ *noun* = CELLULOSE NITRATE.

nitrogen /'nietrəj(ə)n/ *noun* a trivalent gaseous chemical element that constitutes about 78% by volume of the atmosphere and is found in combined form as a constituent of all living things: symbol N, atomic number 7. [French *nitrogène,* from *nitro-* NITRO- + -*gène* -GEN]

nitrogen cycle *noun* the continuous circulation of nitrogen and nitrogen-containing compounds from air to soil to living organisms and back to air, involving nitrogen fixation, nitrification, decay, and denitrification.

nitrogen dioxide *noun* a red-brown highly poisonous gas that is formed by the combination of nitric oxide with oxygen and is used in the manufacture of nitric acid and in rocket fuel to provide oxygen needed for combustion: formula NO₂.

nitrogen fixation *noun* assimilation of atmospheric nitrogen into chemical compounds, whether as a biological or industrial process; *specif* this process performed by soil micro-organisms, *esp* in the root nodules of leguminous plants, e.g. clover. ➤➤ **nitrogen-fixer** *noun,* **nitrogen-fixing** *noun.*

nitrogen monoxide *noun* = NITRIC OXIDE.

nitrogen mustard *noun* any of various poisonous compounds that cause blistering of the skin, are related to mustard gas but contain nitrogen instead of sulphur, and are used in the treatment of some cancers.

nitrogen narcosis *noun* a state of euphoria and exhilaration that occurs, *esp* in deep-water diving, when nitrogen in normal air is breathed at a higher than normal pressure, blunting the subject's awareness of danger and ability to think clearly.

nitrogenous /nie'trojinəs/ *adj* containing nitrogen or a nitrogen compound.

nitroglycerine /nietroh'glisəreen, -rin/ or **nitroglycerin** /nietroh'-glisərin/ *noun* an oily explosive liquid used chiefly in making dynamite and, as a weak solution in water, in medicine to dilate the blood vessels: formula C₃H₅(ONO₂)₃.

nitromethane /nietroh'meethayn/ *noun* an oily liquid obtained from methane and used as a solvent and rocket fuel: formula CH₃NO₂.

nitros- or **nitroso-** *comb. form* forming words, with the meaning: containing the univalent group NO in the molecular structure: *nitrosamine.* [scientific Latin *nitrosus*: see NITROUS]

nitrosamine /nie'trohsəmeen, -min/ *noun* any of various compounds, in some cases cancer-producing, containing the group NNO in their molecular structure.

nitroso- *comb. form* see NITROS-.

nitrous /'nietrəs/ *adj* relating to or containing nitrogen, *esp* with a relatively low valency. [Latin *nitrosus,* from *nitrum*: see NITRE]

nitrous acid *noun* an unstable acid containing less oxygen than nitric acid and occurring only in solution or in the form of its salts: formula HNO₂.

nitrous oxide *noun* a gas used as a general anaesthetic, *esp* in obstetrics and dentistry: formula N₂O.

nitty-gritty /,niti 'griti/ *noun informal* the important basic realities. ➤➤ **nitty-gritty** *adj.* [prob reduplication based on GRIT[1]]

nitwit /'nitwit/ *noun informal* a scatterbrained or stupid person. ➤➤ **nit-witted** *adj.* [prob from NIT[2] + WIT[1]]

NIV *abbr* New International Version (of the Bible).

nival /'niev(ə)l/ *adj* describing or relating to a permanently snow-covered region. [Latin *nivalis* snowy, from *niv-, nix* snow]

nivation /nie'vaysh(ə)n/ *noun* ground erosion that takes place beside or under a snow bank as a result of the alternation of freeze and thaw. [Latin *niv-, nix* snow + -ATION]

niveous /'nivi·əs/ *adj literary* snowy or snow-like: *a pure and niveous white* — Sir Thomas Browne; *the niveous stole of winter* — James Hurdis. [Latin *niveus* snowy, from *niv-, nix* snow]

nix[1] /niks/ *noun informal* nothing. [German *nichts* nothing]

nix[2] *interj* **1** *NAmer, informal* no. **2** *Brit, dated* used to warn of the approach of somebody in authority.

nix[3] *verb trans NAmer, informal* to veto, forbid, or cancel (a suggestion, deal, etc.).

nix[4] *or* **nixie** /'niksi·/ *noun* a water sprite of Germanic folklore. [German *Nixe* from Old High German *nihhus*]

nizam /ni'zahm/ *noun* the title of any of a line of sovereigns of Hyderabad in India, reigning from 1713 to 1950. ⟫ **nizamate** /-mayt/ *noun.* [Hindi *niẓām* order, governor, from Arabic]

Nizari /ni'zahri/ *noun* (*pl* **Nizaris**) a member of an Ismaili Muslim sect founded in 1094, now living mainly in India under the leadership of the Aga Khan. [named after *Nizar*, an Egyptian Ismaili imam whom the Nizaris supported]

NJ *abbr* New Jersey (US postal abbreviation).

NL *abbr* Netherlands (international vehicle registration).

NLP *abbr* **1** natural language processing. **2** neurolinguistic programming.

NM *abbr* New Mexico (US postal abbreviation).

nm *abbr* **1** nanometre. **2** nautical mile.

N Mex *abbr* New Mexico.

NMR *abbr* nuclear magnetic resonance.

NNE *abbr* north-northeast.

NNP *abbr* net national product.

NNW *abbr* north-northwest.

No[1] *abbr* the chemical symbol for nobelium.

No[2] *or* **Noh** /noh/ *noun* (*pl* **No** *or* **Noh**) a classic Japanese dance-drama, or such dance-drama as a form. [Japanese *nō* talent]

No. *abbr NAmer* north.

no[1] /noh/ *interj* **1** used in answers expressing negation, dissent, denial, or refusal; contrasted with yes: *No, I'm not going.* **2** used like a question tag, demanding assent to the preceding statement: *You approve, no?* **3** or rather; nay: *happy, no, ecstatic.* **4** used as an interjection to express incredulity: *'She's 17.' 'No!'* ✳ **not take no for an answer** to be persistent in trying to persuade somebody. [Old English *nā*, from *ne* not + *ā* always]

no[2] *adv* **1** used to mean 'not' in negating an alternative choice: *whether his mother would let him or no.* **2** (*in comparisons*) not in any respect or degree: *no better than before.* **3** *chiefly Scot* not: *It's no right.* ✳ **no can do** *informal* I can't manage what you ask. **no longer/more** not any more; not as formerly.

no[3] *adj* **1** not any: *no money; there's no denying; no parking.* **2** hardly any; very little: *I'll be finished in no time.* **3** not a; quite other than a: *He's no expert.* **4** used before a noun phrase to give force to an opposite meaning: compare NOT[1]: *in no uncertain terms.* ✳ **no fear** *informal* certainly not. **no place** *NAmer* nowhere. **no problem** *informal* used in assent: OK; all right. **no through road** used in signs: passage blocked or not allowed. **no two ways about it** there's no doubt about it; it's quite clear. **no way** *informal* used in emphatic refusal or denial: certainly not! **no worries** *informal* fine; OK; there's no difficulty.

no[4] *noun* (*pl* **noes** *or* **nos**) a negative reply or vote. ✳ **the noes have it** the votes against are in the majority.

no. *abbr* **1** in cricket, not out. **2** number. [(sense 2) Latin *numero*, ablative of *numerus* NUMBER[1]]

no-account *adj chiefly NAmer, informal* said usu of a person: insignificant: *Her boyfriend was a no-account sponger called Mike.* ⟫ **no-account** *noun.*

Noachian /noh'ayki·ən/ *adj* relating to the Biblical patriarch Noah.

noah /'noh·ə/ *noun Aus, informal* a shark. [shortened from *Noah's ark*, rhyming slang]

nob[1] /nob/ *noun* **1** *informal* a person's head. **2** in the game of cribbage, in the expression *his nob* or *his nobs*, a jack of the same suit

as the card turned by the dealer, that scores one point for the holder: *one for his nob.* [prob alteration of KNOB]

nob[2] *noun chiefly Brit, informal* a wealthy or influential person. ⟫ **nobby** *adj.* [orig Scots, in the spelling *knab*; earlier history unknown]

no-ball[1] *noun and interj* often as a call from the umpire: an illegal delivery of the ball in cricket which cannot take a wicket and counts one run to the batsman's side if the batsman does not score a run off it.

no-ball[2] *verb trans* said of an umpire in cricket: to declare (a bowler) to have delivered, or (a delivery) to be, a no-ball. ➤ *verb intrans* to bowl a no-ball.

nobble /'nobl/ *verb trans informal* **1** to incapacitate (*esp* a racehorse), *esp* by drugging. **2** to win (somebody) over to one's side, *esp* by dishonest means. **3** to get hold of (something), *esp* dishonestly. **4** to swindle or cheat (somebody). [origin unknown]

nobbler *noun* **1** a person who nobbles a horse, person, or thing. **2** *Aus, NZ* a drink of spirits.

nobby *adj* see NOB[2].

Nobelist /noh'belist/ *noun chiefly NAmer* a winner of a Nobel prize.

nobelium /noh'beeli·əm/ *noun* a radioactive metallic chemical element that is artificially produced: symbol No, atomic number 102. [scientific Latin, named after the *Nobel* Institute of Physics in Stockholm (from Alfred *Nobel*; see NOBEL PRIZE), who first claimed to have produced it; it was later produced at the University of California]

Nobel prize /noh'bel/ *noun* any of various annual prizes established by the will of Alfred Nobel for the encouragement of people who work for the interests of humanity, e.g. in the fields of peace, literature, medicine, and physics. [named after Alfred *Nobel* d.1896, Swedish manufacturer, inventor, and philanthropist]

nobiliary /noh'bilyəri/ *adj* relating to the nobility: *nobiliary particles such as de or von.* [French *nobiliaire* from Latin *nobilis*; see NOBLE[1]]

nobility /noh'biliti/ *noun* (*pl* **nobilities**) **1** the quality of being noble. **2** aristocratic or high-born rank. **3** (*treated as sing. or pl*) the people making up a noble class: *a scion of the nobility.* [Old French *nobilité* from Latin *nobilitat-, nobilitas* from *nobilis*: see NOBLE[1]]

nobilmente /nohbil'mentay/ *adv* said of a piece of music: to be performed in a noble manner. [Italian *nobilmente* nobly]

noble[1] /'nohbl/ *adj* **1** gracious and dignified in character or bearing: *of noble mien.* **2** famous; notable: *a noble victory.* **3** of or relating to high birth or exalted rank: *noble lords; of noble rank.* **4** of fine quality; excellent: *a noble vintage.* **5** imposing; stately: *a noble sight.* **6** having or showing a magnanimous character or high ideals: *noble deeds; It was noble of you to sacrifice your Sunday afternoons to help us.* **7** chemically inert or unreactive: compare BASE[4]: *noble metals.* ✳ **the noble art/science** *archaic or literary* boxing. ⟫ **nobleness** *noun*, **nobly** *adv.* [Old French *noble* from Latin *nobilis* knowable, well known, noble, from *noscere* to come to know]

noble[2] *noun* **1** a person of noble rank or birth. **2** a former English gold coin worth 6s 8d: *Pray thee, Sir John, let it be but twenty nobles; i'faith I am loath to pawn my plate* — Shakespeare.

noble gas *noun* any of a group of gaseous elements that react only slightly with other elements and include helium, neon, argon, krypton, xenon, and radon. Also called INERT GAS.

nobleman *noun* (*pl* **noblemen**) a man of noble rank.

noble metal *noun* a metal, *esp* gold, silver, or platinum, that is unreactive, is unaffected by acids, and does not corrode.

noble rot *noun* a mould that grows on over-ripe grapes and is deliberately cultivated to give certain wines, e.g. the Sauternes, their distinctive flavour: *Botrytis cinerea.* [translation of French *pourriture noble*]

noble savage *noun* the idealized concept of primitive man presented in the philosophy of Jean-Jacques Rousseau and popularized by Romantic literature: *The liberal must understand that the days of the Noble Savage are gone* — Steve Biko.

noblesse /noh'bles, no'bles/ *noun* (*treated as sing. or pl*) the members of a country's nobility. [French *noblesse* from Old French *noblesce* nobility, from *noble*: see NOBLE[1]]

noblesse oblige /o'bleezh/ *phrase* rank brings its responsibilities. [French *noblesse oblige*, literally 'nobility obliges']

noblewoman *noun* (*pl* **noblewomen**) a woman of noble rank.

nobody[1] /'nohbədi, 'nohbodi/ *pronoun* no person; not anybody: *Nobody likes me.*

nobody[2] *noun* (*pl* **nobodies**) a person of no influence or consequence.

no-brainer *noun NAmer, informal* (*often used before a noun*) a procedure that demands minimal intellectual effort: *one of those no-brainer decisions.*

nociceptive /nohsi'septiv/ *adj* in physiology: **a** said of a stimulus: painful. **b** said of a reflex or a stimulus-receiving structure: responding to a nociceptive stimulus, so as to protect the body from injury. [Latin *nocēre* to harm + RECEPTIVE]

nociceptor /'nohsiseptə/ *noun* a sensory RECEPTOR (stimulus-receiving structure) that responds to painful stimuli. [Latin *nocēre* to harm + RECEPTOR]

nock[1] /nok/ *noun* **1** a notch cut at the end of an archer's bow to hold the string. **2** a notch in the arrow into which the bowstring fits. [Middle English *nocke* notched tip on the end of a bow, prob from early Dutch *nocke* summit, tip]

nock[2] *verb trans* **1** to fit (an arrow) to a bowstring. **2** to make a nock in (e.g. a bow or arrow).

no-claim bonus *or* **no-claims bonus** *noun Brit* a discount allowed in an insurance premium, e.g. for motor insurance, when no claim has been made under the policy in previous years.

noct- *or* **nocti-** *comb. form* forming words, denoting: night: *noctambulation; noctilucent; nocturnal.* [Latin *noct-, nox* night]

noctambulist /nok'tambyoolist/ *noun* a sleepwalker; = SOMNAMBULIST. ⋙ **noctambulism** *noun.* [NOCT- + Latin *ambulare* to walk]

nocti- *comb. form* see NOCT-.

noctiluca /nokti'loohkə/ *noun* (*pl* **noctilucae** /-'loohkee, -'loohsee/) a marine single-celled animal that propels itself through the water by flagella (whiplike structures; see FLAGELLUM) and emits light, often causing phosphorescence of the sea: genus *Noctiluca.* [scientific Latin *noctiluca* something that shines by night, from *noct-, nox* night + *lucēre* to shine]

noctilucent cloud /nokti'loohs(ə)nt/ *noun* a thin luminous usu coloured cloud seen in the night sky at a height of about 80 kilometres (50 miles), *esp* in summer in high latitudes. [NOCTI- + Latin *lucent-, lucens,* present part. of *lucēre* to shine]

noctuid /'noktyooid/ *noun* any of a large family of nocturnal moths, typically with pale or coloured hindwings, whose larvae, including the cutworms, are in many cases destructive agricultural pests: family Noctuidae. ⋙ **noctuid** *adj.* [scientific Latin Noctuidae, from *Noctua,* literally 'night owl', name of moth genus, from *noct-, nox* night]

noctule /'noktyoohl/ *noun* a large reddish brown insect-eating bat with rounded ears: *Nyctalus noctula.* [French *noctule* from late Latin *noctula* small owl, dimin. of Latin *noctua* owl]

nocturn /'noktuhn/ *noun* a principal division of MATINS (first of the daily services in the Catholic Church), orig said at night. [Middle English via Old French *nocturne* from late Latin *nocturnum,* neuter of Latin *nocturnus* of the night, from *noct-, nox* night]

nocturnal /nok'tuhnl/ *adj* **1** relating to or occurring in the night. **2** said of an animal: active at night: *a nocturnal predator.* ⋙ **nocturnally** *adv.* [late Latin *nocturnalis,* from Latin *nocturnus:* see NOCTURN]

nocturnal emission *noun* an ejaculation of semen that takes place during sleep, *esp* in conjunction with an erotic dream.

nocturne /'noktuhn/ *noun* a work of art dealing with evening or night; *esp* a dreamy pensive composition for the piano. [French *nocturne:* see NOCTURN]

nocuous /'nokyoo-əs/ *adj literary* harmful; noxious: *a nocuous kind of grass, namely the dreaded spear-grass* — Carl Lumholtz. ⋙ **nocuously** *adv.* [Latin *nocuus* harmful, from *nocēre* to harm]

nod[1] /nod/ *verb* (**nodded, nodding**) ➤ *verb intrans* **1** to make a short downward movement of the head, e.g. in assent, understanding, or greeting. **2** to make repeated down-and-up movements with the head: *nod violently.* **3** said of flowers or trees: to bend or sway gently downwards or forwards. **4** to become drowsy or sleepy: *nod in front of the fire.* **5** to make a slip or error in a moment of inattention: *Even Homer sometimes nods.* ➤ *verb trans* **1** to incline (one's head) in a quick downward movement. **2** to express (assent, etc) by a nod: *They nodded their approval.* ✳ **a nodding acquaintance** a slight acquaintance: *one acquires a nodding acquaintance with most specialisms.* **be on nodding terms with** to know (somebody) well

enough to nod to them by way of greeting. **nod something through** to approve it with a nod, as distinct from a formal vote, etc. ⋙ **nodder** *noun.* [Middle English *nodden,* of Germanic origin]

nod[2] *noun* an act of nodding. ✳ **give somebody/something the nod** to choose them or approve the choice of them. **go through on the nod** said of a proposal, etc: to be accepted by informal general consent. **Land of Nod** the world of slumbers; sleep.

noddle[1] /'nodl/ *noun informal* a person's head. [Middle English *nodle* back of the head or neck; earlier history unknown]

noddle[2] *verb informal* to nod (one's head). [from NOD[1]]

noddy[1] /'nodi/ *noun* (*pl* **noddies**) any of several species of stout-bodied terns of tropical seas: genera *Anous* and *Procelsterna.* [perhaps a reference to the bird's nodding action during courtship]

noddy[2] *noun* (*pl* **noddies**) (*in pl*) footage of a television interviewer's reactions to an interviewee's words, for strategic insertion into the edited version of the interview. [NOD[1]]

node /nohd/ *noun* **1** in anatomy or pathology, any normal or abnormal knot, thickness, or swelling: *a lymph node.* **2** in a plant, the point on a stem at which one or more leaves are attached. **3** in astronomy, either of the points where the orbit of a celestial body or artificial satellite intersects a defined plane, e.g. ecliptic plane or the equator. **4** in mathematics, the point where a curve intersects itself. **5** in physics: **a** a point, line, etc of a vibrating body at which the vibration is at a minimum. **b** a point where current or voltage is zero. **6** in computing: **a** a point in a network where lines cross or branch. **b** a computer terminal or peripheral attached to a network. [Latin *nodus* knot, node]

node of Ranvier /'ranvi-ə, 'ronhviay/ *noun* a constriction in the MYELIN sheath (protective fatty sheath) of a myelinated nerve fibre. [named after Louis *Ranvier* d.1922, French histologist who first described them]

nod off *verb intrans* to fall asleep, *esp* unintentionally while in a sitting position.

nodose /'nohdohs, noh'dohs/ *adj technical* having protuberances, *esp* if conspicuous. ⋙ **nodosity** /noh'dositi/ *noun.* [Latin *nodosus* knotty, from *nodus* knot]

nodule /'nodyoohl/ *noun* **1** any small hardish rounded mass, e.g. an abnormal aggregation of cells in the body. **2** a small rounded lump of a mineral or mineral aggregate. **3** a swelling on the root of a leguminous plant, e.g. clover, containing symbiotic bacteria that convert atmospheric nitrogen into a form in which it can be used by the plant. ⋙ **nodular** *adj,* **nodulated** *adj,* **nodulation** /-'laysh(ə)n/ *noun.* [Latin *nodulus,* dimin. of *nodus* knot, NODE]

Noel *or* **Noël** /noh'el/ *noun* Christmas, used e.g. on Christmas cards, and in the refrains of Christmas carols. [French *noël* Christmas, carol, ultimately from Latin *natalis* birthday, from *natalis* relating to birth, from *nasci* to be born]

noes /nohz/ *noun* pl of NO[4].

noetic /noh'etik/ *adj* relating to or based on the intellect. [Greek *noētikos* intellectual, from *noein* to think, from *nous* mind]

nog *or* **nogg** /nog/ *noun* **1** a drink, usu alcoholic, containing beaten egg. **2** in E Anglia, a strong local beer. [origin unknown]

noggin /'nogin/ *noun* **1** a small mug or cup. **2** a small measure of spirits, usu 0.142 litres (¼pt). **3** *informal* a person's head. [origin unknown]

no-go *adj* denoting an area of prohibited or restricted access, *esp* one within a city that has been closed off by paramilitaries, with access denied to the police and army.

Noh /noh/ *noun* see NO[2].

no-hit game *noun* = NO-HITTER.

no-hitter *noun* in baseball, a game in which no hits are scored off the pitcher's throws.

no-hoper *noun informal* a person who has no chance of success.

nohow /'nohhow/ *adv* **1** *NAmer, informal* used emphatically with a negative: *Salad ain't fit for a dog to eat, no-how* — David Graham Phillips. **2** *archaic* in poor shape: *'You don't look very well, my lad.' 'I dunno … I feel anyhow or nohow'* — D H Lawrence.

noil /noyl/ *noun* (*usu in pl*) a short fibre or knot combed out of a textile fibre, e.g. silk, before spinning. [perhaps via Old French *noel* from late Latin *nodellus,* dimin. of Latin *nodus* knot, NODE]

noir /nwah/ *adj* said of a film or cinematic technique: typical, or reminiscent, of the FILM NOIR style of film-making. [French *noir* black]

noise[1] /noyz/ *noun* **1** loud confused discordant sound, e.g. of shouting; din. **2** a sound, *esp* if sudden or harsh. **3** unwanted signals or fluctuations in an electrical circuit. **4** irrelevant or meaningless information occurring with desired information in the output of a computer. **5** (*usu in pl*) remarks intended to convey an attitude or response: *make encouraging noises.* * **make a noise** to make a fuss as a way of getting due attention. **noises off 1** sounds made offstage for the benefit of the audience. **2** unwanted background noise. ➤ **noiseless** *adj*, **noiselessly** *adv*. [Middle English via Old French *noise* strife, quarrel, noise, evidently from Latin *nausea* (see NAUSEA)]

noise[2] *verb trans dated* (+ about/abroad) to spread (news) by gossip or hearsay.

noisette /nwah'zet (*French* nwazɛt)/ *noun* **1** a small round thick boneless slice of lamb or other meat. **2** a chocolate containing hazelnuts. [French *noisette* hazel nut, dimin. of *nois*, *noix* nut, from Latin *nuc-*, *nux*]

noisome /'noys(ə)m/ *adj literary* repellent; offensive: *the noisome weeds which without profit suck the soil's fertility from wholesome flowers* — Shakespeare. ➤ **noisomely** *adv*, **noisomeness** *noun*. [Middle English *noysome*, from *noy*, variant of ANNOY + -SOME[1]]

noisy /'noyzi/ *adj* (**noisier**, **noisiest**) **1** making a lot of noise: *noisy neighbours.* **2** full of noise: *a noisy office.* **3** said of a radio transmission, etc: characterized by interference that obscures the main signal. ➤ **noisily** *adv*, **noisiness** *noun*.

nolens volens /ˌnohlenz 'vohlenz/ *adv* whether or not one wants; perforce: *Three or four years would make me a sailor in every respect, mind and habit, as well as body – nolens volens* — R H Dana. [Latin *nolens* unwilling, *volens* willing, pres parts. respectively of *nolle* not to want and *volle* to want]

noli me tangere /ˌnohli may 'tanggəray/ *noun* a warning against touching or interference. [Latin *noli me tangere* do not touch me]

nolle prosequi /ˌnoli 'prosikwie/ *noun* an entry on the record of a legal action stating that the prosecutor or plaintiff will not proceed with part or all of their suit or prosecution. [Latin *nolle prosequi* to be unwilling to pursue]

no-load *adj NAmer* said of shares in a mutual fund: sold directly to the buyer without sales commission.

nolo contendere /ˌnohloh kon'tendəri/ *noun* in the USA, a legal plea by which the defendant accepts conviction without admitting guilt, in expectation of being able to deny the charges in a separate case. [Latin *nolo contendere* I do not want to contend]

nom. *abbr* nominative.

noma /'nohmə/ *noun* (*pl* **nomas**) gangrene of the lining of the cheek and lips, often spreading from a gum ulcer, occurring usu in people suffering from severe malnutrition or weakness. [scientific Latin *noma*, from Greek *nomē* spreading ulcer, from *nemein* (used of an ulcer) to spread, literally 'to graze']

nomad /'nohmad/ *noun* **1** a member of a people that wanders from place to place, usu seasonally and within a well-defined territory. **2** a person who wanders aimlessly from place to place. ➤ **nomad** *adj*, **nomadic** /noh'madik/ *adj*, **nomadically** /noh'madikli/ *adv*, **nomadism** *noun*. [via Latin from Greek *nomad-*, *nomas* roaming, member of a pastoral tribe, from *nemein* to graze]

no-man's-land *noun* **1a** an area of waste or unclaimed land. **b** an unoccupied area between opposing armies. **2** an area of anomalous, ambiguous, or indefinite character: *That whole question of private judgment versus authority is No-Man's-Land for us* — Harold Frederic.

nombril /'nombril/ *noun* in heraldry, the point halfway between the FESS (horizontal bar across the middle) and the base of a shield. [French *nombril* navel]

nom de guerre /ˌnom də 'geə/ *noun* (*pl* **noms de guerre** /ˌnom/) an assumed name; a pseudonym: *Wicked impostors go round lecturing under my nom de guerre* — Mark Twain. [French *nom de guerre*, literally 'name of warfare']

nom de plume /ˌnom de 'ploohm/ *noun* (*pl* **noms de plume** /ˌnom/) a pseudonym under which an author writes. [alteration of French *nom de guerre* pseudonym, with substitution of French *plume* pen]

nome /nohm/ *noun* **1** a province of ancient Egypt. **2** an administrative region of modern Greece. [Greek *nomos* division, from *nemein* to divide]

nomen /'nohmən, 'nohmen/ *noun* (*pl* **nomina** /'nominə/) an ancient Roman's family name, usu the second of three names, e.g. *Julius* in *Caius Julius Caesar*. [Latin *nomin-*, *nomen* name]

nomenclature /no'menkləchə/ *noun* **1** a name or designation. **2** the activity or an instance of selecting names for things, *esp* within a particular system. **3** a system of terms used in a particular science, discipline, or art: *botanical nomenclature.* ➤ **nomenclator** /'nohmenklaytə/ *noun*, **nomenclatural** /-'klaychərəl, -klə'chooərəl/ *adj*. [Latin *nomenclatura* calling by name, list of names, from *nomen* name + *calatus*, past part. of *calare* to call]

nomina /'nominə/ *noun* pl of NOMEN.

nominal[1] /'nominl/ *adj* **1** said of the status of somebody or something: being so in name only: *He remained the country's nominal leader.* **2** said of a sum of money: very small: *a nominal fee.* **3** said of a quantity or measurement: not necessarily corresponding to that specified. **4** *informal* in space travel etc, functioning satisfactorily. **5** in grammar, having the function of a noun: *a nominal group such as 'a large white house'.* ➤ **nominally** *adv*. [Latin *nominalis* relating to names, from *nomin-*, *nomen* name]

nominal[2] *noun* in grammar, a word or word group functioning as a noun.

nominal definition *noun* in logic, a definition of a particular thing that distinguishes it from other things by describing it in terms of its properties or characteristics, without saying what it essentially is.

nominalise *verb trans* see NOMINALIZE.

nominalism *noun* a theory that abstract things and general ideas are mere names and have no independent reality inside or outside the mind. ➤ **nominalist** *adj*, **nominalist** *noun*, **nominalistic** /-'listik/ *adj*.

nominalize *or* **nominalise** *verb trans* to form a noun from (a verb or adjective), as, for example *upkeep* from *keep up*, or *warmth* from *warm*. ➤ **nominalization** /-'zaysh(ə)n/ *noun*. [NOMINAL[2]]

nominal value *noun* **1** the value stated on a cheque, share certificate, etc. **2** the value stated on a coin or note; = FACE VALUE.

nominate[1] /'nominayt/ *verb trans* **1** to appoint or recommend (somebody) for appointment. **2** to propose (somebody) for an honour, award, or candidature. **3** *literary* to designate or specify (somebody or something) by name: *Sight may distinguish of colours; but suddenly to nominate them all, it is impossible* — Shakespeare. ➤ **nomination** /-'naysh(ə)n/ *noun*, **nominator** *noun*. [Latin *nominatus*, past part. of *nominare*, from *nomin-*, *nomen* name]

nominate[2] /'nominayt, -nət/ *adj* said of a subspecies: having the same name as its species, as with *Homo sapiens sapiens*.

nominative[1] /'nominətiv/ *adj* **1** denoting a grammatical case expressing the subject of a verb. **2** /-'naytiv/ said of an office-bearer, etc: appointed by nomination as distinct from election.

nominative[2] *noun* the nominative case or a word in this case.

nominee /nomi'nee/ *noun* **1** a person who is nominated as a candidate or nominated to an office. **2** (*often used before a noun*) a person or company nominated to act on behalf of somebody else, or to hold stock on their behalf: *a nominee shareholder.*

nomogram /'nomgram, 'noh-/ *noun* a graphic representation that consists of several lines marked off to scale and arranged in such a way that by using a straight edge to connect known values on two lines an unknown value can be read at the point of intersection with another line. ➤ **nomographic** /-'grafik/ *adj*, **nomography** /no'mogrəfi, noh-/ *noun*. [Greek *nomos* law + -GRAM]

nomograph /'noməgrahf, -graf, 'nohməgrahf, -graf/ *noun* = NOMOGRAM.

nomological /nomə'lojikl/ *adj* in philosophy, etc, denoting basic non-logical physical laws or rules of reasoning: *a nomological deductive argument*. [Greek *nomos* law + -*logical*]

no more *adv informal or dialect* neither: *She's not satisfied and no more am I.*

nomothetic /nomə'thetik/ *adj* in philosophy, etc, denoting general or universal laws. [Greek *nomothetikos* of law-making, from *nomothetein* to make laws, from *nomos* law + *tithenai* to place, put]

nomothetical /nom'əthetikl/ *adj* = NOMOTHETIC.

-nomy *comb. form* forming nouns, denoting: **1** a system of laws or principles governing a specified field; the science of something: *agronomy*; *astronomy*. **2** management: *economy*. **3** government or rule: *autonomy*. [Greek *-nomia*, related to *nemein* to distribute, *nomos* law]

non- *prefix* forming nouns and adjectives, with the meanings: **1** not of the class or category specified: *non-alcoholic; nonviolent; non-fiction.* **2** the reverse or absence of the thing specified: *nonconformity; nonpayment; nonexistence.* **3** designed not to have a typical tendency: *non-stick; non-iron; non-flammable.* **4** failure to be or refraining from being the thing specified: *non-smoker; nonbeliever; non-combatant.* **5** hardly definable as the thing specified: *non-event.* [Middle English via French from Latin *non* not]

Usage note

non- or **non?** *Non* as a prefix is generally used with a hyphen in British English to preserve the identity of the word elements, especially in forms such as *non-event* and *non-native,* and in longer words such as *non-productive* and *non-professional.* In American English, and increasingly in British English, you will find *non-* words spelt as single words: *nonstandard; nonviolence.* Some words have become familiar as single words, for example *nonconformist* and *nonentity.*

non-A, non-B hepatitis *noun* a viral type of hepatitis resulting usu from a transfusion containing infected blood, so not caused by the agents responsible for HEPATITIS A or HEPATITIS B. Also called HEPATITIS C.

nona- *or* **non-** *comb. form* forming words, with the meanings: **1** nine: *nonagon.* **2** containing nine atoms, groups, or chemical equivalents in the molecular structure. [Latin *nonus* ninth]

non-addictive *adj* said of a drug or other substance taken into the body: not causing addiction.

nonage /'nohnij, 'nonij/ *noun* a period or state of youth or immaturity. [Middle English from Old French *nonage,* literally 'not the age', from NON- + AGE[1]]

nonagenarian /ˌnohnəjiˈneəri·ən, ˌnon-/ *noun* a person between 90 and 99 years old. >>> **nonagenarian** *adj.* [Latin *nonagenarius* containing ninety, ultimately from *nonaginta* ninety]

non-aggression *adj* said of an agreement, pact, treaty, etc between states: containing an undertaking on both or all sides to refrain from aggressive acts towards each other.

nonagon /'nonəgən/ *noun* a polygon with nine angles and nine sides.

non-alcoholic *adj* said of a drink: containing no alcohol: *non-alcoholic or low-alcohol beers.*

non-aligned *adj* said of a state or country, *esp* during the cold war: not allied with any of the superpowers. >>> **non-alignment** *noun.*

non-allergenic *adj* said of skin preparations, etc: specially formulated so as not to cause an allergic reaction: compare HYPOALLERGENIC.

non-allergic *adj* = NON-ALLERGENIC.

nonane /'nohnayn, 'nonayn/ *noun* a colourless saturated liquid that is a member of the alkane series of organic chemical compounds and is found in petroleum spirit: formula C_9H_{20}. [NONA- (indicating nine carbon atoms) + -ANE]

nonce[1] /nons/ *adj* said of words, expressions etc: occurring only once; devised for one specific occasion: *nonce usages; a nonce meaning.* [from *for the nonce*; see NONCE[2]]

nonce[2] ✱ **for the nonce 1** *literary* for the present; for the time being: *This idea satisfied me, and I dismissed my curiosity for the nonce* — Poe. **2** *archaic* for the purpose: *I'll have prepared him a chalice for the nonce* — Shakespeare. [Middle English *the nanes,* alteration, by misdivision, of *then anes* in such phrases as *to then anes* for the one purpose, from *then* dative sing. of THE[1] + *anes:* see ONCE[1]]

nonce[3] *noun* Brit, *slang* a sexual deviant, *esp* one convicted of an offence such as child molestation. [orig prison slang, of unknown derivation]

nonchalant /'nonshələnt/ *adj* giving an impression of easy unconcern or indifference: *He presently smiled an easy, nonchalant smile* — Mark Twain. >>> **nonchalance** *noun,* **nonchalantly** *adv.* [French *nonchalant,* present part. of Old French *nonchaloir* to disregard, from NON- + *chaloir* to concern, from Latin *calēre* to be warm or roused]

non-classified *adj* said of information: not officially classified as secret.

non-collegiate *adj* **1** said of a university: established as a single institution rather than consisting of a number of separate colleges. **2** said of a student, e.g. at Oxford or Cambridge: independent; not enrolled as a member of any college.

non-com /'nonkom/ *noun informal* = NON-COMMISSIONED OFFICER.

non-combatant /non'kombət(ə)nt, -'bat(ə)nt/ *noun* in wartime, a civilian, army chaplain, etc who does not engage in combat. >>> **non-combatant** *adj.*

non-commissioned officer *noun* a subordinate officer, e.g. a sergeant, in the armed forces appointed from among the personnel who do not hold a commission.

non-committal /nonkə'mitl/ *adj* giving no clear indication of attitude or feeling: *in a non-committal voice.* >>> **non-committally** *adv.*

non compos mentis /ˌnon kompos 'mentis/ *adj* not of sound mind. [Latin *non compos mentis* not in control of one's mind]

non-conductor *noun* a substance that conducts heat, electricity, etc only very slightly under normal conditions.

nonconformist *noun* **1** a person who does not conform to a generally accepted pattern of thought or behaviour. **2** (*often* **Nonconformist**) a person who does not conform to an established Church; *specif* a member of a Protestant body separated from the Church of England. >>> **Nonconformism** *noun,* **nonconformism** *noun,* **Nonconformist** *adj,* **nonconformist** *adj.*

nonconformity *noun* **1** refusal to conform to an established creed, rule, or practice. **2** absence of correspondence or agreement.

non-content *noun* a member of the House of Lords who votes against a particular motion.

non-contributory *adj* said of a pension: paid for by regular contributions from the employer only, and not requiring contributions from the employee.

non-controversial *adj* said of a topic, issue, etc: not of a kind to cause heated debate; not divisive: *non-controversial general-interest material.*

non-cooperation *noun* **1** refusal to cooperate. **2** this as a form of protest. >>> **non-cooperationist** *noun,* **non-cooperative** /-'op(ə)rətiv/ *adj,* **non-cooperator** /-'opəraytə/ *noun.*

nonda /'nondə/ *noun* **1** a yellow plum-like fruit of the Australian tropics with an astringent taste. **2** the tree bearing this fruit, growing in groves on sand ridges: *Parinari nonda.* [prob from an Aboriginal language of Queensland]

non-delivery *noun esp* in legal contexts, the failure to provide or deliver goods.

non-denominational *adj* said of a religious foundation, system of religious instruction, etc: not attached or specific to any particular Christian denomination, therefore open or acceptable to Christians of all denominations.

nondescript[1] /'nondiskript/ *adj* **1** lacking distinctive or interesting qualities; dull: *of nondescript appearance and personality.* **2** *orig,* belonging to no particular class or kind; hard to classify; neither one thing nor another: *a nondescript animal.* [orig in the scientific sense 'not previously described'; from NON- + Latin *descriptus,* past part. of *describere:* see DESCRIBE]

nondescript[2] *noun* **1** a person or thing of unknown type: *What it was, whether bear or man or monkey, I could in no wise tell … Behind me the murderers, before me this lurking nondescript* — Stevenson. **2** a person or thing not worth classifying: *ranging from the landlord to the lowest stable nondescript* — Dickens; *It was the old-fashioned wheeled nondescript belonging to the captain, and Thomasin sat in it alone* — Hardy.

non-destructive *adj* said of scientific testing procedures: not involving harm to or destruction of the specimen.

non-disjunction *noun* in genetics, the failure of two chromosomes to separate during cell division, with the result that one daughter cell has both and the other neither of the chromosomes.

non-domiciled *adj* said of an individual, e.g. a party in a legal agreement: not living in his or her country of origin: *non-domiciled nationals.*

non-drinker *noun* a person who abstains from alcohol.

non-drip *adj* **1** said of paint: maintaining a coherent consistency when wet, and so not inclined to drip. **2** said of liquid-containers: designed so as not to ooze the contents: *a non-drip lid.*

non-drying oil *noun* a highly saturated oil, e.g. olive oil, that is unable to solidify when exposed in a thin film to air.

none[1] /nun/ *pronoun* (*treated as sing. or pl when referring to a pl noun or pronoun*) **1** not any: *None of the money is missing; None of the* *telephones is/are working; lots of applicants, but none is/are suitable.* **2** literary nobody: *None lament/laments his departure.* **3** not any such thing or person: *Stale bread is better than none.* ✱ **none but** only: *none but her closest friends.* **none other than** used in identifying somebody or something surprising: *The culprit was none other than the common cold virus.* **want none of something** to refuse to be connected with it. [Old English *nān*, from *ne* not + *ān* ONE¹]

Usage note

None can be used with a singular or a plural verb, depending on the meaning. If you want to emphasize the individuals in a group, you use the singular, and *none* is equivalent to 'not one': *None of them is a professional actor.* When you want to emphasize a group or collection of people or things, the plural is more usual and *none* is equivalent to the plural meaning of 'not any': *None of them are professional actors.* A singular construction can often sound formal or pedantic: *None of them is over eighteen.* When *none* is used of non-countable things, it is treated as singular and is equivalent to the singular meaning of 'not any': *None of the cheese is left.*

none² *adv* (*used with a compar*) not in the least; not at all: *none the worse for her adventure; an explanation that left me none the wiser.* ✱ **none too** not very: *none too clever.* **none too soon 1** only just in time. **2** and high time too.

none³ /nohn/ *or* **nones** *or* **None** *or* **Nones** *noun* in the Roman Catholic Church, the fifth of the canonical hours (times set for divine service; see CANONICAL HOUR) that was orig fixed for 3 p.m. [late Latin *nona*: see NOON]

nonentity /no'nentiti/ *noun* (*pl* **nonentities**) **1** somebody or something of little importance or interest. **2** something that does not exist or exists only in the imagination. **3** non-existence.

nones /nohnz/ *pl noun* (*treated as sing. or pl*) **1** in the ancient Roman calendar, the ninth day before the ides, that is the fifth of the month, but the seventh of March, May, July, and October: compare CALENDS, IDES. **2** see NONE³. [Middle English *nonys* via Old French from Latin *nonas*, fem accusative pl of *nonus* ninth]

non-essential *adj* not indispensable; not absolutely required: *non-essential purchases; exclude non-essential traffic from city centres.* ⟫ **non-essential** *noun*.

non est factum /ˌnon est 'faktəm/ *noun* in law, the plea on the part of a defendant that a written agreement is invalid because he or she misunderstood it at the time of signing. [Latin *non est factum* it was not done]

nonesuch *or* **nonsuch** *noun* **1** literary, chiefly archaic a person or thing without an equal; a paragon: *His equal … I never met with … before … he is a none-such* — Thomas Hull; *The Scripture … presenteth Solomon's [temple] as a Nonesuch, or peerless structure* — Thomas Fuller. **2** a small species of MEDICK (plant): *Medicago lupulina.* ⟫ **nonesuch** *adj*.

nonet /noh'net, no'net/ *noun* **1** a piece of music for nine voices or instruments. **2** a group of nine singers or instrumentalists. [Italian *nonetto*, from *nono* ninth, from Latin *nonus*]

nonetheless /ˌnundhə'les/ *or* **none the less** *adv* nevertheless.

non-euclidean *or* **non-Euclidean** *adj* not assuming or in accordance with all of Euclid's postulates: *non-euclidean geometry.*

non-event /ˌnoni'vent/ *noun* **1** an event that hardly deserves the name, having turned out to be dull or inconsequential. **2** an event that does not take place.

non-executive director *noun* a director of a commercial company who is not one of its full-time employees.

non-existent *adj* **1** not real; existing only in the imagination: *fears over non-existent dangers.* **2** totally absent: *Toilet arrangements were non-existent.*

non-factive *adj* in linguistics, said of a verb such as *believe* or *think*: taking as its object a clause that may or may not convey a fact: compare CONTRAFACTIVE, FACTIVE.

nonfeasance /non'feez(ə)ns/ *noun* failure to act according to a legal requirement. [NON- + obsolete *feasance* doing, execution, from Old French *faisance* act, from *faire* to make, do, from Latin *facere*]

non-ferrous *adj* relating to or denoting a metal other than iron, or not containing iron.

non-fiction *noun* prose writing based directly on fact; literature other than novels and stories. ⟫ **non-fictional** *adj*.

non-figurative *adj* said of art: not depicting objects, scenes, etc from the natural world; abstract; = NON-OBJECTIVE, NON-REPRESENTATIONAL.

non-finite *adj* **1** not subject to limits of size or extent: *a non-finite quantity.* **2** in grammar, said of a verb form or clause: not restricted as to tense, person, or number.

non-flam /ˌnon 'flam/ *adj informal* non-flammable.

non-flammable *adj* difficult or impossible to set alight. ⟫ **non-flammability** /-'biliti/ *noun*.

non-fulfilment *noun* **1** failure to fulfil something such as a contract, requirement, or condition. **2** failure to achieve something such as a desire.

non-functional *adj* **1** having no function, or not having its standard function: *a non-functional organ; non-functional wings.* **2** not in working order; not operational.

nong /nong/ *noun Aus, NZ, informal* a fool or simpleton. [prob shortened from NING-NONG]

non-governmental *adj* **1** denoting an organization, typically a large one, such as a cultural body, a charity, or a professional body, having recognized official status but independent of the government. **2** not relating to the affairs of government: *non-governmental business.*

non-Hodgkin's lymphoma *noun* any of a variety of malignant lymphomas, having in common the absence of the giant cells characteristic of HODGKIN'S DISEASE.

non-human *adj* **1** not belonging to the human class: *non-human primates.* **2** not of human origin: *some non-human agency.*

nonillion /noh'nilyən/ *noun* **1** *Brit* the number one followed by 54 zeros (10^{54}). **2** *NAmer* the number one followed by 30 zeros (10^{30}). [French *nonillion*, from Latin *nonus* ninth + *-illion* as in MILLION]

non-inductive *adj* not inductive; *esp* having negligible electrical INDUCTANCE (capacity to induce an electric current).

non-inflammable *adj* = NON-FLAMMABLE.

non-interference *noun* abstention from interfering, *esp* the policy or practice of not interfering in the internal affairs of another state.

non-intervention *noun* the policy of not intervening, *esp* in the affairs of another state. ⟫ **non-interventionist** *noun and adj*.

non-invasive *adj* **1** said of medical or surgical procedures: not involving a large incision or the introduction of instruments into the body. **2** said of a tumour, etc: not spreading dangerously or transferring to other parts of the body. **3** said of a plant: not inclined to upset ecological balance by taking over the habitat of established plants.

non-ionic *adj* **1** not ionic. **2** said of a detergent: not producing ions in solution in water.

nonjoinder /non'joyndə/ *noun* failure to include a necessary party in a legal action.

non-judgmental *adj* open-minded; not judging others according to one's personal criteria, *esp* of morality: *a sympathetic, non-judgmental attitude towards Aids sufferers.*

nonjuring /non'jooəring/ *adj* being a nonjuror: *the nonjuring bishops.* [NON- + Latin *jurare* to swear]

nonjuror *noun* **1** a person refusing to take an oath. **2** (*usu* **Nonjuror**) a member of the clergy in Britain who refused to take an oath of allegiance to William and Mary after 1688.

non-linear *adj* **1** not arranged in, or involving, a straight line. **2** not following a linear progression or sequence; random: *non-linear narrative.* **3** said of a mathematical equation: including terms not of the first degree, that is, terms representing squares or cubes. ⟫ **non-linearity** /-'ariti/ *noun*, **non-linearly** *adv*.

non-logical *adj* said of thought processes: intuitive, or based on experience; not involving a chain of reasoning.

non-member *noun* a person, state, etc, that is not a member of the body in question. ⟫ **non-membership** *noun*.

non-metal *noun* a chemical element, e.g. boron or carbon, that is not a metal. ⟫ **non-metallic** /-'talik/ *adj*.

non-moral *adj* not relating to moral principles: *non-moral considerations.*

non-native *adj* **1** said of the speaker of a language: having acquired the language in question in later life, as distinct from having spoken it from early childhood. **2** said of a plant or animal: introduced into the country in question; not indigenous.

non-natural *adj* **1** denoting a sense of a word that is not its natural one. **2** in philosophy, denoting ethical properties such as good or evil. **3** said of land use: not in accordance with nature.

non-negative *adj* said of a number: either positive, or equal to zero.

non-negotiable *adj* **1** said of a decision, etc: final; not open to discussion or alteration. **2** said of a document such as a cheque, voucher, etc: not transferable to the ownership of another person.

non-nuclear *adj* not having or using nuclear power or weapons: *a non-nuclear country*.

no-no /'noh noh/ *noun* (*pl* **no-nos**) *informal* something to be avoided; something quite unacceptable: *Having your ears pierced was an absolute no-no in those days*.

non-objective *adj* **1** said of a judgment, etc: influenced by personal considerations; not objective. **2** said of paintings, etc: abstract; = NON-REPRESENTATIONAL, NON-FIGURATIVE.

non-observance *noun* **1** (+ of) failure to obey (a rule or law), or to keep (a tradition or ritual): *non-observance of Sunday*. **2** failure to notice or observe something.

no-nonsense *adj* **1** serious; businesslike. **2** without trifles or frills.

non-operational *adj* **1** not working; not in use: *non-operational locomotives*. **2** not actively functioning as such: *a non-operational director*.

nonpareil /'nonpərel, nonpə'rayl/ *noun literary, chiefly archaic* somebody or something having no equal: *though you were crowned the nonpareil of beauty* — Shakespeare. ➤➤ **nonpareil** *adj*. [French *nonpareil* adj, from NON- + *pareil* equal, ultimately from Latin *par* equal]

non-persistent /nonpə'sist(ə)nt/ *adj* not persistent, e.g.: **a** decomposed rapidly in the environment, e.g. by micro-organisms: *non-persistent insecticides*. **b** relating to a micro-organism or virus capable of existing in a VECTOR[1] (2A).

non-person *noun* (*pl* **non-persons**) **1** a person who usu for political or ideological reasons is removed from official recognition or consideration. **2** a person regarded as of no interest or significance: *Economically she is a non-person* — Observer Magazine.

non placet /,non 'playset, ,nohn 'plaket/ *noun* in an ecclesiastical or academic assembly, a negative vote. [Latin *non placet* it does not please]

nonplus[1] /non'plus/ *verb trans* (**nonplussed, nonplussing,** *NAmer* **nonplused, nonplusing**) (*often as past part.*) **1** to perplex or disconcert (somebody) or put them at a loss: *The guide was bewildered, nonplussed* — Mark Twain. **2** *chiefly NAmer* used in the opposite sense through misapprehension of *non-* as NON-: to fail to perturb or upset (somebody): *Branson was nonplussed by Elliot's refusal – in fact it constituted the perfect challenge* — M Brown. [orig in the sense 'to bring to a nonplus'; from NONPLUS[2]]

nonplus[2] *noun archaic* the state of being perplexed, disconcerted, or at a loss: *Dubious words … puzzle men's reason, and bring them to a nonplus* — John Locke. [Latin *non plus* no further]

non-polar *adj* not polar; *esp* not having or requiring the presence of electrical poles: *a non-polar solvent*.

non-prescription *adj* said of medicines, etc: available for purchase without a prescription.

non-productive *adj* **1** failing to produce or yield: *a non-productive oil well*. **2** said of a cough: dry. ➤➤ **non-productiveness** *noun*.

non-professional *adj* **1** not professionally trained or earning one's living as such: *filmed on location using non-professional actors*. **2** not belonging to one of the recognized professions.

non-profit *adj NAmer* = NON-PROFITMAKING.

non-profitmaking *adj* said of an organization: not constituted or run with the intention of making a profit.

non-proliferation *noun* stoppage of the proliferation of something, *esp* nuclear weapons.

non-proprietary *adj* **1** said of a product or preparation: not registered as a brand or protected by a trademark. **2** said of computer hardware or software: of a pattern that is in the public domain, so not restricted to a single manufacturer.

non prosequitur /,non pro'sekwitə, ,nohn/ *noun* formerly, a judgment given in favour of the defendant, where the plaintiff fails to launch the action within the time limit. [Latin *non prosequitur* he does not prosecute]

non-racial *adj* not involving racial distinctions: *a fully-integrated, non-racial democracy*.

non-representational *adj* said of art: not representing natural or actual objects, figures, etc; abstract; = NON-FIGURATIVE, NON-OBJECTIVE. ➤➤ **non-representationalism** *noun*.

non-resident *adj* **1** not living in the place, country, etc in question: *a non-resident property-owner*. **2** said of a job or academic course: not requiring residence in the place of work or study. **3** said of computer software: not kept permanently in the memory. ➤➤ **non-residence** *noun*, **non-residency** /-si/ *noun*, **non-resident** *noun*.

non-residential *adj* **1** said of a job: not requiring residence in the workplace. **2** said of an institution, etc: not providing accommodation for residents. **3** said of property: suitable as commercial premises rather than private housing.

non-resistance *noun* **1** passive submission to authority. **2** the principle of not resisting violence by force.

non-restrictive *adj* **1** not tending to limit or restrict. **2** in grammar, denoting or adding to rather than identifying a modified word or phrase: *a non-restrictive clause*: compare RESTRICTIVE.

non-return *adj* said of a valve: allowing the flow of air or liquid in one direction only.

non-returnable *adj* said of containers, *esp* bottles: not returnable to a dealer in exchange for a deposit.

non-rigid *adj* **1** said of materials: not rigid; flexible or pliable. **2** said of an airship: maintaining form by pressure of contained gas. ➤➤ **non-rigidity** /-'jiditi/ *noun*.

non-scientific *adj* **1** not relating to science. **2** not using scientific methods. ➤➤ **non-scientist** *noun*.

nonsecretor *noun* a person of blood group A, B, or AB who does not secrete the corresponding antigen in bodily fluids, e.g. saliva.

non-sectarian *adj* not affiliated with or restricted to a particular religious sect or denomination: *non-sectarian schools; a non-sectarian political party*.

nonsense /'nonsəns/ *noun* **1** meaningless words or language: *write nonsense*. **2** foolish or absurd language, conduct, or thought. **3** frivolous or insolent behaviour: *stand no nonsense*. **4** used interjectionally to express forceful disagreement. ✳ **make a nonsense of** to compromise (e.g. a principle or ruling) to such an extent as to make it untenable: *building concessions that make a nonsense of our stated conservation policy*. ➤➤ **nonsensical** /non'sensikl/ *adj*, **nonsensically** /non'sensikli/ *adv*, **nonsensicalness** /non'sensiklnis/ *noun*.

nonsense verse *noun* humorous or whimsically absurd verse.

non sequitur /,non 'sekwitə/ *noun* **1** a conclusion that does not follow from the premises. **2** a statement that does not follow logically from anything previously said. [Latin *non sequitur* it does not follow]

non-skid *adj* said of e.g. a tyre or road surface: designed or equipped to prevent skidding.

non-slip *adj* designed to reduce or prevent slipping: *non-slip soles*.

non-smoker *noun* **1** a person who does not smoke. **2** a train compartment in which smoking is not permitted. ➤➤ **non-smoking** *adj*.

non-social *adj* not socially oriented; lacking a social component.
Usage note —————
non-social, antisocial, asocial, unsociable, *or* unsocial? See note at ANTI-SOCIAL.

non-specific urethritis *noun* infection of the URETHRA (canal carrying urine from the bladder) that is sexually transmitted but caused by bacteria other than gonococci (those causing gonorrhoea; see GONOCOCCUS).

non-standard *adj* **1** not conforming to a required norm or standard: *non-standard envelopes*. **2** said of language: not conforming in pronunciation, grammatical construction, idiom, or word choice to accepted usage.

non-starter *noun* **1** somebody or something that is sure to fail. **2** a plan, etc that is bound to prove impracticable. **3** a competitor, racehorse, etc that fails to take part in a race.

non-stick *adj* **1** said of a pan surface: treated so that food does not stick to it during cooking. **2** said of a pan: having such a surface.

non-stop *adj* **1** continuous: *non-stop rain*. **2** said of a journey: with no intermediate stops: *non-stop flights*. ➤➤ **non-stop** *adv*.

nonsuch /'nunsuch/ *noun* see NONESUCH.

nonsuit[1] *noun* a judgment against a plaintiff for failure to prosecute, or inability to establish, a case. [Middle English, from Anglo-French *nounsuyte*, from *noun-* NON- + Old French *siute* following, pursuit]

nonsuit[2] *verb trans* to dismiss the suit of (a plaintiff) for failure to prosecute, or inability to establish, a case.

non-swimmer *noun* a person who cannot swim, or who is not among those swimming: *No non-swimmers beyond this point.*

non-technical *adj* **1** not involving science or technology: *non-technical work.* **2** denoting a popular or non-scientific term for something: *a cerebral infarction, or stroke, to use its non-technical name.*

non-transferable *adj* said of a cheque, voucher, ticket, etc: not able to be transferred to the possession of another person.

non-trivial *adj* **1** not trivial; significant. **2** in mathematics, denoting a solution to an equation in which at least one unknown value is not equal to zero.

non troppo /non 'tropoh/ *adv* used to qualify a musical direction: not to excess. [Italian *non troppo* not too much]

non-U /,non 'yooh/ *adj* said of words, social conduct, etc: not characteristic of the upper classes. [NON- + U[5]]

non-uniform *adj* **1** subject to variation; not uniform: *non-uniform in length.* **2** not involving the wearing of uniform: *a non-uniform job.* ➤➤ **non-uniformity** /-'fawmiti/ *noun*, **non-uniformly** *adv.*

non-union *adj* not belonging to or connected with a trade union: *non-union plumbers; a non-union job.*

non-use /non'yoohs/ *noun* failure to use, or abstention from using, something: *non-use of contraceptives.* ➤➤ **non-usage** /-sij/ *noun*, **non-user** /non'yoohzə/ *noun.*

non-verbal *adj* said e.g. of communication: not involving words or speech: *voluntary or involuntary non-verbal signals, such as smiling or blushing.* ➤➤ **non-verbally** *adv.*

non-violence *noun* **1** abstention from violence on moral grounds. **2** passive resistance or peaceful demonstration for political ends. ➤➤ **non-violent** *adj*, **non-violently** *adv.*

non-white *noun* a person not of mainly Caucasian or European descent, *esp* one of black African descent. ➤➤ **non-white** *adj.*

non-word *noun* a string of letters or speech sounds that has the appearance or sound of a word but is not accepted as one.

nonyl /'noniel, 'nohniel, 'nohnil/ *noun* (*used before a noun*) denoting an alkyl radical, -C₉H₁₉, derived from NONANE. [NONA- (indicating nine carbon atoms) + -YL]

non-zero *adj* not equal to zero; either positive or negative.

noodle[1] /'noohdl/ *noun humorous* **1** a silly or foolish person. **2** *NAmer* the head. [perhaps alteration of NODDLE[1]]

noodle[2] *noun* (*usu in pl*) a narrow flat ribbon of pasta made with egg. [German *Nudel*]

nook /nook/ *noun* a small secluded or sheltered place; a corner or recess: *a cosy nook.* ✳ **every nook and cranny** everywhere possible, *esp* as representing the coverage or penetration of an exhaustive search, etc. [Middle English *noke, nok*; earlier history unknown]

nooky *or* **nookie** /'nooki/ *noun informal* lovemaking; sexual intercourse. [perhaps from NOOK]

noon /noohn/ *noun* **1** twelve o'clock in the day; midday. **2** the highest or culminating point. [Old English *nōn* ninth hour from sunrise, orig about 3pm, from late Latin *nona*, from *nona hora* ninth hour, from *nonus* ninth; associated with the service of NONE[3] or NONES, therefore becoming earlier as the service was held earlier]

noonday *noun literary* (*often used before a noun*) the middle of the day; noon: *in the noonday heat.*

no one *or* **no-one** *pronoun* nobody.

noontide *noun literary* the middle of the day; noon: *It being about noontide the air was clear and motionless* — Hardy.

noontime *noun NAmer* = NOONTIDE.

noose[1] /noohs/ *noun* a loop with a running knot that tightens as the rope is pulled. ✳ **put one's head in a noose** to put oneself into a vulnerable position or bring about one's own downfall. [prob from Provençal *nous* knot, from Latin *nodus*]

noose[2] *verb trans* **1** to secure (a quarry) by a noose. **2** to make a noose in (a rope).

Nootka /'nootkə, 'noohtkə/ *noun* (*pl* **Nootkas** *or collectively* **Nootka**) **1** a member of a Native American people of Vancouver Island and NW Washington. **2** the language of this people. ➤➤ **Nootka** *adj*. [named after *Nootka* Sound, an inlet on Vancouver Island]

nootropic /noh-ə'tropik/ *noun* a drug used to enhance memory or sharpen other mental functions. ➤➤ **nootropic** *adj*. [Greek *noos* mind + -TROPIC]

nopal /'nohpl/ *noun* **1** any of several species of a Mexican cactus similar to the prickly pear, cultivated as food for the cochineal insect: *esp Nopalea cochinellifera.* **2** (*usu* **nopales** /noh'pahles/) the edible flesh of this cactus, used in Mexican cuisine. [Spanish *nopal* from Nahuatl *nopalli* cactus]

no-par *adj* said of securities: not having a PAR[1] (stated or face) value.

nope /nohp/ *adv chiefly NAmer, informal* no.

NOR /naw/ *noun* (*usu before another noun*) **1** in computing, denoting a logic circuit that has two or more inputs and one output, the output signal being 1 if all the inputs are 0, and 0 if any of the inputs is 1. **2** in electronics, denoting a gate or circuit that has an output only if there is no signal on any of the input connections. [from the conjunction NOR[1], because of the similarity of its function in logic]

nor[1] /naw/ *conj* **1** used with NEITHER[3]: and not; and not either: *neither she nor I; She neither knew nor cared.* **2** *archaic or literary* neither: *Nor heaven nor earth have been at peace tonight* — Shakespeare. **3** *dialect, chiefly archaic* than: *I know better nor you* — George Eliot. ✳ **nor yet** *literary* but also not; and also not: *neither unseemly short, nor yet exceeding long* — Spenser. [contraction of Old English *nother* neither]

nor[2] *adv and conj* and not; neither: *'I don't approve.' 'Nor do I'; It didn't seem hard, nor was it.*

nor' /naw/ *noun* (*used in combinations*) north: *nor'easter.*

nor- *comb. form* forming nouns, denoting: an organic compound derived from the one specified through the replacement of one or more methyl groups with hydrogen atoms: *noradrenaline; norepinephrine.* [shortening of NORMAL[1], orig denoting a compound without methyl substituents]

noradrenalin *or* **noradrenaline** /norə'drenəlin/ *noun* a compound from which adrenalin is formed in the body and which is the major NEUROTRANSMITTER (medium transmitting nerve impulses) released from the nerve endings of the sympathetic nervous system.

Norbertine /'nawbətien, -tin/ *noun* a member of the religious order founded by St Norbert in the 12th cent; = PREMONSTRATENSIAN. ➤➤ **Norbertine** *adj.*

Nordic[1] /'nawdik/ *adj* **1** relating to or belonging to a tall, fair, long-headed, blue-eyed physical type characteristic of the Germanic peoples of N Europe, *esp* Scandinavia. **2** said of competitive ski events: consisting of ski jumping and cross-country racing: compare ALPINE[2] (3). [French *nordique*, from *nord* north]

Nordic[2] *noun* a person of Nordic physical type or of a supposed Nordic division of the Caucasian race; *esp* one from N Europe.

nor'easter /naw'reestə/ *noun* = NORTHEASTER.

norepinephrine /,norepi'nefrin, nori'pinəfrin/ *noun chiefly NAmer* = NORADRENALIN.

Norfolk jacket /'nawfək/ *noun esp* formerly, a man's semifitted belted single-breasted jacket with box pleats: *He was dressed like a gentleman, in Norfolk jacket and knickerbockers, with a cloth cap on his head* — Conan Doyle. [named after *Norfolk*, county of England]

nori /'nawri/ *noun* in Japanese cuisine, edible seaweed, used e.g. to wrap sushi portions. [Japanese *nori*]

noria /'nawri-ə/ *noun* a device for raising water from a stream into irrigation channels, consisting of a chain of buckets that revolves round a wheel driven by the current. [Spanish *noria* from Arabic *nā'ūra*]

norite /'nawriet/ *noun* a granular igneous rock similar in composition to GABBRO. [*Norway*, Scandinavian country + -ITE[1]]

nork /nawk/ *noun Aus, slang* (*usu in pl*) a female breast. [said to be from *Norco* a brand of butter whose wrapping showed a cow's udder]

norm /nawm/ *noun* **1** an authoritative standard; a model. **2** a principle of correctness that is binding upon the members of a group, and serves to regulate action and judgment. **3** a set standard of development or achievement, usu derived from the average achievement of a large group. **4** a pattern typical of a social group. **5** in mathematics, the square root of the sum of the squares of the absolute values of the elements of a MATRIX or of the components of a VECTOR[1]. [Latin *norma* rule, pattern, literally 'carpenter's square']

normal[1] /'nawml/ *adj* **1** conforming to or constituting a norm, rule, or principle: *normal behaviour*. **2** occurring naturally: *normal immunity*. **3** having average intelligence or development. **4** free from mental disorder. **5** *dated* said of a chemical solution: having a concentration of one gram equivalent weight of a solute in one litre. **6** in geometry, said of a line or plane: intersecting another at right angles; perpendicular. **7** in statistics, relating to, involving, or being a normal curve or normal distribution. ➤➤ **normalcy** /- si/ *noun*, **normality** /naw maliti/ *noun*, **normally** *adv*. [Latin *normalis*, from *norma*: see NORM]

normal[2] *noun* **1** somebody or something that is normal. **2** in geometry, a line or plane intersecting another at right angles.

normal curve *noun* in statistics, the symmetrical bell-shaped curve of a normal distribution.

normal distribution *noun* in statistics, a frequency distribution whose graph is a standard symmetrical bell-shaped curve.

normalize *or* **normalise** *verb trans* **1** to make (something abnormal or irregular) normal: *try to normalize relations*. **2** to multiply (e.g. a VECTOR[1] or mathematical function) by a factor which makes an associated value, e.g. a norm or integral, equal to one. ➤➤ **normalizable** *adj*, **normalization** /-'zaysh(ə)n/ *noun*, **normalizer** *noun*.

normal school *noun* in N America, *esp* formerly, a teacher-training college. [translation of French *école normale*; because the first such college was intended as a model or norm]

Norman /'nawmən/ *noun* **1** a member of a people of mixed Frankish and Scandinavian stock who settled in Normandy in the tenth cent. **2** any of the Norman-French conquerors of England in 1066, or their descendants. **3** the northern form of Old French spoken by the medieval Normans. **4** a style of architecture characterized, *esp* in its English form, by semicircular arches and heavy pillars: compare ROMANESQUE[1]. ➤➤ **Norman** *adj*. [Middle English via Old French *Normant* from Old Norse *Northmann-*, *Northmathr* Norseman, from *northr* north + *mann-*, *mathr* man]

Norman French *noun* = NORMAN (3).

normative /'nawmətiv/ *adj* **1** serving as or prescribing a norm: *a normative code of procedure*. **2** said of a statement: conveying a value judgment as distinct from a fact. ➤➤ **normatively** *adv*, **normativeness** *noun*. [French *normatif*, from *norme* norm, from Latin: see NORM]

Norn[1] /nawn/ *noun* in Norse mythology, any of the three Norse goddesses of fate. [Old Norse]

Norn[2] *noun* a medieval form of Norse formerly spoken in Orkney and Shetland. [Old Norse *Norræn*, from *northr* north]

Norplant /'nawplahnt/ *noun trademark* a contraceptive implant for women from which there is a controlled release of the synthetic hormone LAEVONORGESTREL. [blend of *Laevonorgestrel* + *implant*]

Norse[1] /naws/ *noun* **1** (**the Norse**) (*treated as pl*) the Norwegians, or generally, the Scandinavians of the medieval period. **2** = OLD NORSE. [obsolete Dutch *noorsch*, adj, Norwegian, Scandinavian, alteration of *noordsch* northern, from *noord* north]

Norse[2] *adj* Scandinavian; *esp* of ancient or medieval Scandinavia or Norway.

Norseman *noun* (*pl* **Norsemen**) a native or inhabitant of ancient or medieval Scandinavia.

north[1] /nawth/ *noun* **1** the direction in which a compass needle normally points, 90° anticlockwise from east. **2** (*often* **North**) regions or countries lying to the north of a specified or implied point of orientation. [Old English]

north[2] *adj and adv* **1** at, towards, or coming from the north. **2** said of the wind: blowing from the north. **✳ north by east** in a position or direction between north and north-northeast. **north by west** in a position or direction between north and north-northwest.

North American *noun* a native or inhabitant of North America, *esp* of the USA or Canada. ➤➤ **North American** *adj*.

Northants /naw'thants/ *abbr* Northamptonshire.

northbound *adj and adv* going or moving north: *the northbound carriageway*.

northeast[1] *noun* **1** the direction midway between north and east. **2** (*often* **Northeast**) regions or countries lying to the northeast of a specified or implied point of orientation. ➤➤ **northeastward** /-wəd/ *adj and adv*, **northeastwards** /-wədz/ *adv*.

northeast[2] *adj and adv* **1** at, towards, or coming from the northeast. **2** said of the wind: blowing from the northeast.

northeaster *noun* a wind blowing from the northeast.

northeasterly[1] *adj and adv* **1** in a northeastern position or direction. **2** said of the wind: blowing from the northeast.

northeasterly[2] *noun* (*pl* **northeasterlies**) a wind blowing from the northeast.

northeastern *adj* in or towards the northeast; inhabiting the northeast.

norther *noun NAmer* a strong cold wind blowing from the north over Florida, Texas, and the Gulf of Mexico.

northerly[1] /'nawdhəli/ *adj and adv* **1** in a northern position or direction. **2** said of the wind: blowing from the north.

northerly[2] *noun* (*pl* **northerlies**) a wind blowing from the north.

northern /'nawdhən/ *adj* in or towards the north; inhabiting the north. ➤➤ **northernmost** *adj*.

Northerner *noun* a native or inhabitant of the North.

northern hemisphere *noun* the half of the globe north of the equator.

northern lights *pl noun* = AURORA BOREALIS.

northernmost *adj* found or situated furthest north: *The island's northernmost extremity*.

North Germanic *noun* a group of Germanic languages comprising Swedish, Norwegian, Danish, Icelandic, and Faeroese. Also called SCANDINAVIAN.

northing *noun* **1** distance due north in latitude from the preceding point of measurement. **2** northerly progress.

North Korean *noun* a native or inhabitant of North Korea. ➤➤ **North Korean** *adj*.

northland *or* **northlands** *or* **Northland** *or* **Northlands** *noun literary* land in the north; the north of a country.

north light *noun* strong natural light without direct sunlight, traditionally preferred by artists as the dominant illumination for a studio.

Northman *noun* (*pl* **Northmen**) *archaic* a Norseman.

north-northeast[1] *noun* the direction midway between north and northeast.

north-northeast[2] *adj and adv* at, towards, or coming from the north-northeast.

north-northwest[1] *noun* the direction midway between north and northwest: *I am but mad north-north-west* — Shakespeare.

north-northwest[2] *adj and adv* at, towards, or coming from the north-northwest.

north pole *noun* **1a** (*often* **North Pole**) the northernmost point of the rotational axis of the earth or another celestial body. **b** the northernmost point on the CELESTIAL SPHERE (imaginary sphere surrounding the earth on whose surface the stars appear to be placed) about which the stars seem to revolve. **2** the northward-pointing pole of a magnet.

North Star *noun* = POLE STAR.

Northumb. *abbr* Northumberland.

Northumbrian /naw'thumbri·ən/ *noun* **1** a native or inhabitant of the region of Northumbria or the county of Northumberland in N England. **2** the English dialect of ancient or modern Northumbria. ➤➤ **Northumbrian** *adj*. [obsolete *Northumber* inhabitant of England north of the river Humber, from Old English *Northhymbre*, pl]

northward /'nawthwəd/ *adj and adv* towards the north; in a direction going north.

northwards *adv* towards the north; northward.

northwest[1] *noun* **1** the direction midway between north and west. **2** (*often* **Northwest**) regions or countries lying to the northwest of a specified or implied point of orientation. ➤➤ **northwestward** /-wəd/ *adj and adv*, **northwestwards** /-wədz/ *adv*.

northwest² *adj and adv* **1** at, towards, or coming from the north-west. **2** said of the wind: blowing from the northwest.

northwester *noun* a wind blowing from the northwest.

northwesterly¹ *adj and adv* **1** in a northwestern position or direction. **2** said of the wind: blowing from the northwest.

northwesterly² *noun* (*pl* **northwesterlies**) a wind blowing from the northwest.

northwestern *adj* in or towards the northwest; inhabiting the northwest.

Norway lobster /'nawway/ *noun* a smallish European lobster, widely fished for the table: *Nephrops norvegicus*. [named after *Norway*, country in Scandinavia]

Norway maple *noun* a Eurasian maple with yellow flowers which appear before the leaves, widely cultivated as an ornamental tree: *Acer platanoides*.

Norway rat *noun* = BROWN RAT.

Norway spruce *noun* a European spruce with long cones, grown for its timber and traditionally used as a Christmas tree: *Picea abies*.

Norwegian /naw'weejən/ *noun* **1** a native or inhabitant of Norway. **2** the North Germanic language of Norway. ⟫ **Norwegian** *adj*.

Word history
late Latin *Norvegia, Norwegia* Norway, from Old Norse *Norvegr* north way. Words from modern Norwegian that have passed into English reflect the physical features, fauna, legends, and activities of the country. They include *auk, fjord, floe, kraken, krill, lemming, ski, slalom,* and *troll.* (For the contribution of the older Norwegian vocabulary, see note at OLD NORSE).

nor'wester /naw'westə/ *noun* **1** = NORTHWESTER. **2a** an oilskin jacket. **b** an oilskin hat; SOU'WESTER.

nos. *abbr* numbers.

nos- or **noso-** *comb. form* forming words, denoting: disease: *nosology*. [Greek *nosos* illness, disease]

nose¹ /nohz/ *noun* **1** the projecting part above the mouth on the face of a person or animal, containing the nostrils and used for breathing and smelling. **2** the snout or muzzle of an animal. **3** the sense of smell: *use one's nose.* **4** the aroma or bouquet of something, *esp* wine. **5** an instinct for detecting a certain thing: *have a nose for a good story.* **6** *informal* an act of investigating: *have a nose round the premises.* **7** the front end of a vehicle. **8** a projecting part of something. ✳ **by a nose** used in reference to a win: by a narrow margin. **cut off one's nose to spite one's face** to damage one's own interests in one's eagerness to take revenge on another. **follow one's nose** see FOLLOW. **get one's nose in front** to manoeuvre oneself into a leading position. **get up somebody's nose** *informal* to annoy somebody. **give somebody a bloody nose** *informal* to defeat or thrash somebody soundly. **keep one's nose clean** *informal* to stay out of trouble. **keep one's nose out of** *informal* to refrain from interfering in (e.g. somebody else's business). **look down one's nose at** *informal* to show or express disdain for (a person or thing). **nose to tail** said of vehicles: in a long slowly-moving queue. **not see further than one's nose/the end of one's nose** *informal* to be circumscribed in one's judgment. **on the nose 1** *informal* said of betting on a horse: to win, as distinct from being placed. **2** *NAmer* precisely. **3** *Aus, NZ* bad-smelling; offensive. **pay through the nose** *informal* to pay exorbitantly. **put somebody's nose out of joint** *informal* to offend or affront somebody. **rub somebody's nose in it** *informal* to remind somebody mischievously of a painful failure or mistake. **turn one's nose up at** *informal* to show or express disdain for (a person or thing). **with one's nose in the air** haughtily. ⟫ **noseless** *adj*, **noselike** *adj*. [Old English *nosu*]

nose² *verb trans* **1** said of an animal: to push its nose into or against (a person or thing) or nuzzle them. **2** to sniff (something) investigatively. **3** *literary* to scent (something) or detect it using one's sense of smell: *But indeed, if you find him [the dead Polonius] not within this month, you shall nose him as you go up the stair, into the lobby —* Shakespeare. ➤ *verb intrans* **1** (*often* + about/around) to pry: *You wouldn't want the police nosing round.* **2** said of a vehicle or driver: to pull slowly forward: *just nosing out of the garage.*

nose bag *noun* a bag for feeding a horse or other animal, that covers the muzzle and is fastened on top of the head.

noseband *noun* the part of a bridle that passes over a horse's nose.

nosebleed *noun* an attack of bleeding from the nose.

nose candy *noun NAmer, informal* cocaine.

nose cone *noun* the protective cone forming the front section of a spacecraft, missile, or aircraft.

nosed *adj* (*used in combinations*) having a nose of the kind specified: *snub-nosed.*

nose dive *noun* **1** a downward nose-first plunge of an aircraft or other flying object. **2** a sudden dramatic drop: *Profits took a nose dive.*

nose-dive *verb intrans* to make a nose dive.

no-see-um /noh'see-əm/ *noun NAmer* any tiny biting insect, *esp* a midge.

nose flute *noun* a flute played by blowing into it through one nostril while the other is plugged.

nosegay *noun* a small bunch of flowers; a posy. [NOSE¹ + GAY² in the obsolete sense 'ornament']

nose guard *noun* = NOSE TACKLE.

nose job *noun informal* a surgical operation to improve the shape of the nose.

nose leaf *noun* a leaf-like structure on a bat's nose, having an important function in echolocation.

nosema /noh'seemə/ *noun* any of a genus of parasites that cause disease in insects: genus *Nosema*. [Latin genus name, from Greek *nosēma* disease]

nosepiece *noun* **1** a piece of armour for protecting the nose. **2** the end piece of a microscope to which the lens nearest the specimen is attached. **3** *NAmer* = NOSEBAND.

nose rag *noun informal* a handkerchief.

nose ring *noun* a ring fixed through the nose *esp* of a bull, for leading it.

nose tackle *noun* in American football, a defensive LINEMAN (player on line of scrimmage) positioned so as to face the offensive centre.

nose wheel *noun* the landing wheel under the nose of an aircraft.

nosey *adj* see NOSY.

nosh¹ /nosh/ *verb trans informal* to chew or munch (food). ➤ *verb intrans informal* to eat. ⟫ **nosher** *noun*. [Yiddish *nashn* to nibble, from German *naschen* to eat on the sly]

nosh² *noun informal* food; a meal.

noshery *noun* (*pl* **nosheries**) *informal* an eating place; a snack bar or restaurant.

no-show *noun informal* a person who has made a reservation or appointment but fails to attend or cancel.

nosh-up *noun Brit, informal* a large meal.

no-side *noun* in rugby, the end of a game; full time.

nosing /'nohzing/ *noun* **1** the usu rounded edge of a stair tread that projects over the riser, or metal edging for protecting this. **2** any similar round-edged moulding. [NOSE¹ + -ING²]

noso- *comb. form* see NOS-.

nosocomial /nosoh'kohmi-əl/ *adj* said of a disease: having originated in hospital. [Greek *nosokomos* an attendant on the sick, from *nosos* disease + *komein* to tend]

nosode /'nosohd/ *noun* a homoeopathic medicine prepared from the secretions collected in the course of a disease.

nosology /no'soləji/ *noun* a branch of medical science that deals with the classification of diseases. ⟫ **nosologic** /-'lojik/ *adj*, **nosological** /-'lojikl/ *adj*, **nosologically** /-'lojikli/ *adv*, **nosologist** *noun*.

nostalgia /no'staljə/ *noun* **1** a wistful or excessively sentimental yearning for something past or irrecoverable. **2** the evocation of or indulgence in such sentiment: *an evening of reminiscence and nostalgia.* **3** homesickness. ⟫ **nostalgic** /-jik/ *adj and noun*, **nostalgically** /-jikli/ *adv*. [scientific Latin *nostalgia*, from Greek *nostos* homecoming + -ALGIA]

nostalgie de la boue /nostal,zhee də la 'booh/ *noun* a craving for a degraded or depraved state or way of life. [French *nostalgie de la boue* longing for mud]

nostoc /'nostok/ *noun* a single-celled blue-green alga which forms a gelatinous mass: genus *Nostoc*. [name invented by Paracelsus d.1541, Swiss alchemist]

Nostratic /no'stratik/ *noun* **1** a hypothetical language family including Indo-European, Afro-Asiatic, Dravidian, Altaic, and other languages. **2** the postulated ancestral language of this family.

➤➤ Nostratic *adj.* [German *nostratisch*, from Latin *nostrat-*, *nostras* of our country, from *noster* our]

nostril /'nostrəl/ *noun* either of the two external openings of the nose. **➤➤ -nostrilled** *comb. form*. [Old English *nosthyrl*, from *nosu* NOSE[1] + *thyrel* hole]

nostro account /'nostroh/ *noun* a bank account held by a British bank at a foreign bank, usu in the foreign currency: compare VOSTRO ACCOUNT. [Italian *nostro* our, from Latin *noster*]

nostrum /'nostrəm/ *noun* (*pl* **nostrums**) **1** a medicine of secret composition recommended by its preparer usu without proof of its effectiveness: *He was ... imploring information as to the composition and action of innumerable quack nostrums* — Conan Doyle. **2** a facile or questionable remedy. [Latin *nostrum*, in the sense 'something of our own devising', neuter of *noster* our, ours]

nosy *or* **nosey** /'nohzi/ *adj* (**nosier, nosiest**) *informal* inquisitive; prying. **➤➤ nosily** *adv*, **nosiness** *noun*. [NOSE[1]]

nosy parker /'pahkə/ *noun Brit, informal* a busybody. [said to be named after Matthew *Parker* d.1575, Archbishop of Canterbury, known for his detailed investigations into church affairs]

NOT /not/ *noun* (*usu used before a noun*) **1** in computing, denoting a logic circuit that has one input and one output, the output signal being 1 if the input is 0, and 0 if the input is 1. **2** in electronics, denoting a gate or circuit that has an output signal only if there is no input signal. [NOT[1], because of the similarity of its function in logic]

not[1] /not/ *adv* **1a** (*also, as suffix* **-n't**) used usu with an auxiliary verb or *be* to form negatives: *He will not budge*; *It isn't ready*; *Didn't they know?* **b** used with verbal nouns and infinitives: *Not passing the test would be a disappointment*; *He told us not to complain*. **2** used as substitute for a whole negative clause: *'Was it a mistake?' 'I hope not'*; *whether we agree or not*; *Have you finished? If not, why not?* **3** used to negate other words: *'How is she?' 'Not well'*; *George III, not George II*. **4** less than (a surprisingly small amount): *not five minutes later*. **5** used to give force to an opposite meaning: compare NO[3]: *not a million miles away*; *not without reason*; *not a few of us*. **6** *informal, humorous* used after a statement to deny it emphatically: *That's a great suggestion – not!* ✱ **not a** used before words representing a minimum unit to indicate a complete absence of something: *not a word*; *not a crumb*. **not at all 1** definitely not: *'Is that silly?' 'Not at all'.* **2** used as a deprecatory response to thanks. **not but what** *dated or dialect* nevertheless: *Not but what he was wrong to do it.* **not least** in particular: *It was a shock to everyone, not least her parents.* **not nearly** far from: *not nearly complete.* **not that** though it should not be inferred that: *not that I approve.* **not very** (*also* **not so**) not; not at all: *not very nice*; *not so great.* [Middle English, contraction of NOUGHT]

not[2] *or* **Not** *adj* said of art paper: not hot-pressed, and having a slightly textured surface. [NOT[1]]

not- *or* **noto-** *comb. form* forming words, with the meaning: back or back part: *notochord*. [Greek *nōton*, *nōtos* back]

nota bene /ˌnohtə 'benay/ *interj* used to call attention to something important. [Latin *nota bene* mark well]

notability /nohtə'biliti/ *noun* (*pl* **notabilities**) **1** a prominent person. **2** being notable.

notable[1] /'nohtəbl/ *adj* **1** worthy of note; remarkable: *one notable error*. **2** distinguished; prominent: *some notable writers*. **➤➤ notableness** *noun*.

Usage note

notable *or* **noticeable?** These two words are close in meaning but there is nevertheless a clear distinction between them. *Notable* means 'worthy of notice' and thus, often, 'important' or 'remarkable': *a notable achievement*. *Noticeable*, on the other hand, means 'visible' or 'perceptible': *a noticeable improvement in quality*. A *notable difference* between two things would generally be a large as well as significant one, whereas a *noticeable* difference might only be very small.

notable[2] *noun* **1** a prominent person. **2** (*often* **Notable**) (*in pl*) a group of people summoned, *esp* in France when it was a monarchy, to act as a deliberative body.

notably *adv* **1** remarkably: *They were a notably longlived family*. **2** in particular: *in several of her novels, most notably The Bell*.

notaphily /noh'tafəli/ *noun* the collecting of banknotes as a hobby. **➤➤ notaphilic** /-'filik/ *adj*, **notaphilist** *noun*. [Latin *nota* NOTE[1] + -PHILY]

notarial /noh'teəri·əl/ *adj* relating to or executed by a notary: *a notarial style of expression*; *notarial records*. **➤➤ notarially** *adv*.

notarize *or* **notarise** /'nohtəriez/ *verb trans chiefly NAmer* (*often as past part.*) to validate (a document, etc) as a notary public: *a notarized statement*.

notary /'nohtəri/ *noun* (*pl* **notaries**) a public officer appointed to administer oaths and draw up and authenticate documents. [Middle English *notary* clerk, notary public, from Latin *notarius* clerk, secretary, from *notarius* relating to shorthand, from *nota* shorthand character, NOTE[1]]

notary public *noun* (*pl* **notaries public** *or* **notary publics**) = NOTARY.

notate /noh'tayt/ *verb trans* to put (e.g. music in aural form) into notation. [back-formation from NOTATION]

notation /noh'taysh(ə)n/ *noun* **1** a system or set of marks, signs, symbols, figures, characters, or abbreviated expressions used to present e.g. mathematical, musical, or choreographical elements. **2** *chiefly NAmer* an annotation or note. **➤➤ notational** *adj*. [Latin *notation-*, *notatio*, from *notare*: see NOTE[2]]

notch[1] /noch/ *noun* **1** a V-shaped indentation. **2** a slit or cut used as a record. **3** any of the holes in a belt for receiving the tongue of the buckle. *tighten one's belt a notch.* **4** a degree or point on a scale **5** a step or level: *go up a notch.* **6** *NAmer* a deep narrow pass; a gap. **➤➤ notched** *adj*. [Anglo-Norman *noche*, prob misdivision of *an oche*, from Old French *oche* notch]

notch[2] *verb trans* **1** to make a notch in (something). **2** (*often* + up) to mark or record (e.g. an addition to a score) with or as if with a notch. **3** (+ up) to score or achieve (e.g. a success).

notchy *adj* (**notchier, notchiest**) said of a manual gear change: operating jerkily, suggestive of slotting the lever into narrow notches.

note[1] /noht/ *noun* **1** (*also in pl*) a memorandum; a condensed or informal record: *take lecture notes*; *make a note of her surname and address*. **2** a brief comment or explanation: *programme notes for a concert*. **3** a printed comment or reference set apart from the text of a book: *in the notes for chapter 12*. **4** a short informal letter. **5** = PROMISSORY NOTE. **6** a piece of paper money. **7** a letter or form certifying something: *a sick note*. **8** a formal diplomatic communication. **9** a scholarly or technical essay shorter than an article and restricted in scope: *submit a note on the bronze buckle found in the excavation*. **10** a sound having a definite pitch, *esp* made by a musical instrument or the human voice: *She can't reach the high notes any longer*. **11** a call or sound; *esp* the musical call of a bird: *Then nightly sings the staring owl: 'Tu-who; to-whit, tu-who' – a merry note* — Shakespeare. **12** a written symbol used to indicate the duration and pitch of a tone by its shape and position on the musical stave. **13** a key of a piano, organ, etc: *the black notes*. **14** a characteristic feature: *the essential notes of his satire* — F R Leavis. **15** an element in a flavour, taste, smell, etc: *the distinctive note of basil*. **16** a feeling or element of something: *a note of sadness in her voice*; *The talks ended on an optimistic note.* ✱ **hit/strike the right/wrong/a false note** to act appropriately or inappropriately. **of note 1** distinguished: *scholars of note.* **2** significant: *Nothing of note occurred.* **strike/sound a note of** to introduce an element of something: *sound a note of caution.* **take note** (*often* + of) to pay attention: *While waiting she took note of her surroundings*; *Prospective parents, take note!* **➤➤ noteless** *adj*. [Old French *note* from Latin *nota* mark, character, written note]

note[2] *verb trans* **1** to pay due attention to (information being presented to one): *Please note the change of address*; *Please note that the office is closed on 2 January.* **2** to notice or observe (something): *She noted his lack of enthusiasm*; *I note that you're a fan of Raymond Chandler.* **3** (*often* + down) to record (information) in writing; to make a note of (something): *note down her phone number.* **4** to make special mention of (a fact): *He was a keen walker, a fact noted by his biographers.* **➤➤ noter** *noun*. [Middle English *noten* via Old French from Latin *notare* to mark, note, from *nota* mark, character, NOTE[1]]

notebook *noun* a book for notes or memoranda.

notecase *noun Brit, dated* a wallet for carrying bank notes.

note cluster *noun* a musical chord consisting of several adjacent notes.

noted *adj* well-known; famous: *one noted critic*. **➤➤ notedly** *adv*, **notedness** *noun*.

notelet /'nohtlit/ *noun* a folded sheet of paper bearing a printed design on the front, for a brief informal letter.

notepad *noun* **1** a pad of paper for writing notes on. **2** a small hand-held computer with which a stylus is used for inputting data.

notepaper *noun* paper for letter-writing.

note row /roh/ *noun* = TONE-ROW.

noteworthy *adj* worthy of or attracting attention; notable: *a noteworthy remark.* ➤➤ **noteworthily** *adv,* **noteworthiness** *noun.*

nothing /'nuthing/ *pronoun and noun* **1** not anything; no thing: *nothing in the letter box; nothing greasy.* **2** a thing of no consequence or significance: *It's nothing – don't worry; He would be nothing without his title.* **3** *informal* (used before a noun) denoting something worthless: *a nothing person; a nothing job.* **4** an unremarkable thing: *It was nothing for trains from the provinces to be five or six hours late* — Muriel Spark. **5** what is non-existent: *Nothing can be made out of nothing* — Shakespeare. **6** in calculating, nought: *Three from three is nothing.* **7** no truth or significance: *There was nothing in the rumour.* **8** (+ of) no hint or trace of (something): *There was nothing of the shrinking violet about Helen.* **9** *NAmer, informal* used in emphatic contradiction: *'It's an improvement.' 'Improvement nothing!'* ✱ **for nothing 1** without pay or without paying: *work for nothing; travel for nothing.* **2** to no purpose: *all that work for nothing.* **leave nothing to the imagination** to be over-explicit or too revealing. **like nothing on earth 1** severely indisposed or embarrassed. **2** grotesque; outlandish. **next to nothing** almost nothing; very little. **nothing daunted** not depressed or unnerved; undaunted. **nothing but** only: *He's nothing but trouble.* **nothing doing 1** *informal* used to refuse cooperation. **2** *informal* no progress. **nothing if not** very definitely (a certain thing): *nothing if not a tryer.* **nothing less than/short of** sheer; downright: *That's nothing short of blackmail.* **nothing like 1** not resembling (a person or thing) in the least. **2** not nearly; by no means: *nothing like complete; nothing like as easy.* **nothing much** very little. **nothing/nothing else for it** no alternative; no other solution: *nothing for it but to swim the river.* **nothing to** insignificant in comparison with (something else): *Your astonishment is nothing to mine.* **nothing to do with 1** no connection with (the person or thing mentioned). **2** not the business of (the person mentioned). **stop at nothing** to be quite ruthless. **sweet nothings** *humorous* affectionate exchanges between lovers. **there's nothing to it** it's perfectly simple. **think nothing of 1** to despise (somebody or something). **2** to be unperturbed at (something): *think nothing of cycling 50 miles.* **think nothing of it** used as a deprecatory response to thanks, etc. [Old English *nān thing, nāthing,* from *nā, nān* (see NO[1]) + THING]

nothingness *noun* **1** nonexistence. **2** utter insignificance. **3** a void; emptiness. **4** a metaphysical entity opposed to and devoid of being.

notice[1] /'nohtis/ *noun* **1** attention or observation: *It had escaped my notice.* **2** advance warning: *The timetable is subject to change without notice.* **3** formal notification of one's intention to terminate an agreement, typically relating to employment or tenancy: *hand in one's notice; give the landlord three weeks' notice.* **4** polite or favourable attention; favour: *She had very little notice from any but him* — Jane Austen. **5** a placard or poster displaying information. **6** a brief announcement in a newspaper, etc: *put a notice in the local paper.* **7** a short critical account or review of a production, etc: *receive some flattering notices.* ✱ **at a moment's/at short notice** with little or no warning. **put somebody on notice/serve notice on somebody** to warn somebody of an imminent occurrence. **take no notice of** to disregard or pay no heed to (somebody or something). **take notice of** to observe or treat (somebody or something) with special attention: *He was used to being taken notice of.* [Middle English *notise* knowledge, information, via Old French from Latin *notitia* fame, knowledge, from *notus* known, past part. of *noscere* to come to know]

notice[2] *verb trans* **1** to take notice of or become aware of (something): *He noticed that she wore no ring; No one noticed the substitution.* **2** to attract comment; to become well-known: *beginning to be noticed.* **3** *archaic* to comment upon or refer to (something): *Mr Garrick's judicious alteration of this play has been already noticed in a former number* — London Chronicle 1766. **4** *archaic* to acknowledge acquaintance with (a person): *By Mrs. Hurst and Miss Bingley they were noticed only by a curtsey* — Jane Austen. **5** *chiefly NAmer* to give (somebody) formal notice of something. ➤ *verb intrans* to become aware of something: *I'm sorry, I didn't notice.*

noticeable *adj* **1** deserving notice; significant: *a noticeable improvement.* **2** capable of being noticed; perceptible: *walking with a noticeable limp.* ➤➤ **noticeably** *adv.*

Usage note

noticeable *or* notable? See note at NOTABLE[1].

notice board *noun chiefly Brit* a board on which notices may be displayed.

notifiable /'nohtifie·əbl/ *adj* said of a disease: required by law to be reported to official health authorities.

notification /,nohtifi'kaysh(ə)n/ *noun* **1** the act or an instance of notifying. **2** something written that gives notice: *receive notification of the intended repair work.*

notify /'nohtifie/ *verb trans* (**notifies, notified, notifying**) **1** (*also* + of) to give, *esp* formal or official, notice to (somebody): *All the parties concerned were notified of his intentions.* **2** to make (something) known: *We shall notify the date to you in due course.* ➤➤ **notifier** *noun.* [Middle English via Old French *notifier* from late Latin *notificare* to make known, from Latin *notus:* see NOTICE[1]]

notion /'nohsh(ə)n/ *noun* **1** a broad general concept: *Our notions of right and wrong.* **2** (*usu in negative contexts*) a conception or impression: *With all her knowledge of history, Alice had no very clear notion how long ago anything had happened* — Lewis Carroll. **3** a whim or fancy: *odd notions.* **4** an intention: *She had given up her notion of going to university.* **5** *chiefly NAmer* (*in pl*) small articles of merchandise, e.g. haberdashery. [Latin *notion-, notio,* from *noscere* to come to know]

notional /'nohsh(ə)nl/ *adj* **1** theoretical; speculative; adduced for the purpose of forward planning: *figures calculated on the lines of a notional profit for the coming year.* **2** existing only in the mind; imaginary: *for yourself and a notional partner.* **3** relating to or denoting a notion or idea; conceptual: *the notional boundaries between academic disciplines.* **4** said of a word: having an actual meaning in a sentence rather than a mere grammatical function: *'Has' is notional in 'he has luck', relational in 'he has gone'.* **5** in language-teaching, denoting a syllabus aimed at developing effective communication. **6** *chiefly NAmer* given to fanciful moods or ideas. ➤➤ **notionality** /-'naliti/ *noun,* **notionally** *adv.*

noto- *comb. form* see NOT-.

notochord /'nohtəkawd/ *noun* a cartilaginous rod that forms the longitudinal support of the body in the lancelet, lamprey, etc and in the embryos of higher vertebrates. ➤➤ **notochordal** /-'kawdl/ *adj.* [NOTO- + Latin *chorda* cord]

notoriety /nohtə'rieiti/ *noun* (*pl* **notorieties**) **1** the state of being notorious: *a womanizer of some notoriety.* **2** a notorious person.

notorious /noh'tawri·əs/ *adj* well-known for something bad or unfavourable; infamous: *a notorious gambler; a district notorious for crime; Swimming pools were a notorious source of eye and ear infections.* ➤➤ **notoriously** *adv.*

Word history

late Latin *notorius* well-known, earlier 'making known', from *notus,* past part. of *noscere* to come to know. The sense was possibly influenced by late Latin *notorium* notorious offence, earlier 'information', 'indictment', neuter of *notorius.*

notornis /noh'tawnis/ *noun* (*pl* **notornis** /-nis/) a flightless bird of New Zealand, also called the takahe: genus *Notornis.* [scientific Latin *notornis,* from Greek *notos* south + *ornis* bird]

not proven /'prohv(ə)n/ *adj* in a Scottish court of law, used as a verdict on a charge where evidence is insufficient to convict the accused.

no-trump *adj* denoting a bid, contract, or hand in bridge suitable to play without any suit being trumps. ➤➤ **no-trump** *noun,* **no-trumper** *noun.*

Nottingham lace /'notingəm/ *noun* a kind of flat machine-made lace, orig produced in Nottingham.

Notts /nots/ *abbr* Nottinghamshire.

notwithstanding[1] /notwidh'standing, notwith-/ *prep* (*also after the noun*) in spite of (something): *notwithstanding my reluctance; her objections notwithstanding.* [Middle English, from NOT[1] + *withstanding,* present part. of WITHSTAND, modelled on Old French *non obstant* not obstructing]

notwithstanding[2] *adv* nevertheless: *Notwithstanding, they will have to pay costs.*

notwithstanding[3] *conj* (*usu* + that) although: *notwithstanding that he had taken the proper precautions.*

nougat /'nugat, 'noohgah/ *noun* a sweet consisting of nuts or fruit pieces in a semisolid sugar paste. [French *nougat* from Old Provençal *nogat,* from *noga* nut, from Latin *nuc-, nux*]

nougatine /'noohgəteen/ *noun* chocolate-covered nougat.

nought /nawt/ *noun and pronoun* **1** the arithmetical symbol 0; zero. **2** = NAUGHT[1] (1). [variant spelling of NAUGHT[1]]

Usage note

nought *or* naught? See note at NAUGHT[1].

noughties /'nawtiz/ *pl noun* (**the noughties**) *informal* the years of the decade 2000 to 2009. [from NOUGHT, by analogy with *the twenties, the thirties,* etc]

noughts and crosses *pl noun* (*usu treated as sing.*) a game in which two players alternately put noughts and crosses in nine square spaces arranged in a grid in an attempt to get a row of three noughts or three crosses.

noumenon /'noohminon, 'now-/ *noun* (*pl* **noumena** /-nə/) **1** in Kantian philosophy, a thing in itself, as distinct from a thing as apprehended by the senses. **2** an object or experience perceived by the senses rather than by thought or intuition. ➤➤ **noumenal** *adj.* [German *Noumenon* from Greek *nooumenon* that which is apprehended by thought, from *noein* to think, conceive, from *nous* mind]

noun /nown/ *noun* a word that is: **a** a term for a person, thing, animal, place, quality, or state. **b** a name identifying a person, thing, animal, or place. [Middle English from Anglo-French *noun* name, noun, via Old French from Latin *nomen* name]

noun phrase *noun* in grammar, a group of words such as, e.g. *a general practitioner,* that can function like a noun as the subject of a sentence, or as an object after a verb or preposition.

nourish /'nurish/ *verb trans* **1** to nurture or rear (e.g. a child or animal). **2** to encourage the growth of or foster (something): *teachers that can nourish talent in their pupils; bitter memories that nourished his hatred.* **3** to provide (e.g. soil or a plant) with nutriment; to feed (it). **4** to cherish or entertain (an idea, feeling, etc): *She had long nourished a desire to write.* ➤➤ **nourisher** *noun,* **nourishing** *adj.* [Middle English via Old French from Latin *nutrire* to suckle, nourish]

nourishment *noun* **1** food or nutriment. **2** the process of nourishing or of being nourished.

nous /nows/ *noun* **1** the mind, reason, or intellect. **2** *chiefly Brit* practical common sense; gumption. [Greek *noos, nous* mind]

nouveau /'noohvoh (*French* nuvo)/ *adj informal* **1** = NOUVEAU RICHE: *nouveau landowners.* **2** used facetiously to denote the latest trend or wave of a type: *a nouveau hippy; the nouveau soul scene.* [French *nouveau* new]

nouveau riche /'reesh (*French* riʃ)/ *noun* (*pl* **nouveaux riches** /,noohvoh 'reesh/) a person who has recently become rich, *esp* one who displays their wealth unsubtly. ➤➤ **nouveau riche** *adj.* [French *nouveau riche* new rich]

nouveau roman /roh'mahn (*French* romã)/ *noun* a type of novel originating in France in the 1950s that rejects such traditional novelistic features as coherent plot, simple chronology, and rounded characterization, presenting instead something closer to real experience in all its randomness. [French *nouveau roman* new novel]

nouveaux riches /,noohvoh 'reesh/ *noun* pl of NOUVEAU RICHE.

nouvelle /nooh'vel/ *adj informal* relating to or reflecting the practices of NOUVELLE CUISINE: *The food's a bit nouvelle.* [French *nouvelle,* fem of *nouveau* new]

nouvelle cuisine /kwi'zeen/ *noun* a style of cooking originating in France that uses high quality ingredients and emphasizes the natural flavours and textures of the food rather than allowing them to be smothered, e.g. by heavy rich sauces. [French *nouvelle cuisine* new cooking]

nouvelle vague /'vahg (*French* nuvɛl vag)/ *or* **Nouvelle Vague** *noun* = NEW WAVE (1). [French *nouvelle vague* new wave]

Nov. *abbr* November.

nova /'nohvə/ *noun* (*pl* **novas** *or* **novae** /'nohvee, 'nohvie/) a double star system that becomes suddenly much brighter as a result of a thermonuclear explosion and then fades away to its former obscurity over months or years. ➤➤ **novalike** *adj.* [scientific Latin, fem of Latin *novus* new, such stars being at first thought to be newly formed]

novaculite /'nohvakyooliet/ *noun* a very hard fine-grained rock containing silica, used for making whetstones. [Latin *novacula* razor + -ITE[1]]

novae /'nohvee, 'nohvie/ *noun* pl of NOVA.

novation /noh'vaysh(ə)n/ *noun* in law, the substitution of a new obligation for an old one, e.g. by substituting a new contract, creditor, or debtor for a previous one, carried out with the consent of all parties concerned. [late Latin *novation-, novatio* renewal, legal novation, from Latin *novare* to make new, from *novus* new]

novel[1] /'novl/ *noun* **1** an invented prose narrative that is usu long and complex and deals *esp* with human experience and social behaviour.

Editorial note

'Novel' describes an extended prose narrative, usually realistic, structured, multiply storied, strong in characters. The modern novel is commonly dated from Cervantes' Don Quixote (1605), though prose narratives existed before. It became a popular form across Europe in the 18th cent. and, with Balzac, Dickens, Tolstoy, and Dostoevsky, a great social and moral record of the 19th cent. In the 20th cent. it acquired greater experimental complexity and psychological depth. As a popular commercial product and a form of art, it is now the dominant genre — Professor Malcolm Bradbury.

2 (**the novel**) the literary class or genre represented by novels. [Italian *novella,* short for *novella storia* new story, from Latin *novellus,* dimin. of *novus* new]

novel[2] *adj* **1** new and unlike anything previously known: *a novel feeling.* **2** original and striking, *esp* in conception or style: *a novel approach.* ➤➤ **novelly** *adj.* [Middle English, in the sense 'young, fresh', via Old French from Latin *novellus,* dimin. of *novus* new]

novelette /novə'let/ *noun* a short novel or long short story, often of a sentimental nature. ➤➤ **novelettish** *adj.*

novelise *verb trans* see NOVELIZE.

novelist *noun* a writer of novels.

novelistic /novə'listik/ *adj* relating to or typical of novels.

novelize *or* **novelise** *verb trans* (*often as past part*) to convert (a story) from another form, e.g. a play or cinema film, into a novel. ➤➤ **novelization** *noun.*

novella /no'velə/ *noun* (*pl* **novellas** *or* **novelle** /-lay/) **1** a short novel, usu more complex than a short story. **2** a substantial short story or narrative tale, *esp* of a satirical nature.

Editorial note

As a short prose narrative or long tale, the novella goes back to Boccaccio's Decameron (1471) and earlier. For the Romantics it became a form of long short story, poetic and fantastic, more precise than the novel, focused around a single event. Striking modern examples of novellas are Conrad's Heart of Darkness (1902), Kafka's Metamorphosis (1912) and Mann's Death in Venice (1913) — Professor Malcolm Bradbury.

[Italian *novella;* see NOVEL[1]]

novelty /'nov(ə)lti/ *noun* (*pl* **novelties**) **1** something new and unusual: *a novelty to have breakfast in bed.* **2** the quality or state of being novel: *The novelty had worn off.* **3** a small manufactured often cheap article for personal or household adornment: *a shop selling gifts and novelties.* **4** (*used before a noun*) denoting an article designed to amuse by virtue of its unusualness: *novelty socks.* [Old French *novelte,* from *novel:* see NOVEL[2]]

November /noh'vembə/ *noun* the eleventh month of the year. [Middle English via Old French from Latin *November* ninth month, from *novem* nine: see SEPTEMBER]

novena /noh'veenə/ *noun* (*pl* **novenas** *or* **novenae** /-nee/) in the Roman Catholic Church, nine days' devotion of prayers for the intercession of a particular saint for a special purpose. [late Latin *novena,* fem of Latin *novenus* nine each, from *novem* nine]

novice /'novis/ *noun* **1** a person admitted to probationary membership of a religious community. **2** a new or inexperienced person in a job, etc; a beginner. **3** a racehorse that has yet to win a certain number of races. [Middle English via Old French from late Latin *novicius* newly captured slave, inexperienced person, from *novus* new]

novitiate *or* **noviciate** /noh'vishi·ət, -ayt/ *noun* **1** the state of being a novice, or the duration of this. **2** a house where novices are trained. **3** a novice, *esp* in a religious order. [French *noviciat,* from medieval Latin *noviciatus,* from *novicius:* see NOVICE]

novocaine /'nohvəkayn/ *noun* = PROCAINE. [from Latin *novus* new + COCAINE]

now[1] /now/ *adv* **1a** at the present time: *It's now 5.30; Not now; can you wait?* **b** often added for clarity when reporting the situation as it stands: *I've been living here 20 years now; They now have three children.* **c** immediately: *See to it now.* **d** as things have turned out; in the light of recent developments: *It doesn't matter now; A spring election is now certain.* **e** used to express irritation at the latest in a series of similar occurrences: *What's the trouble now?* **f** used in narrative to refer to the time in question: *It was now snowing heavily.* **2** used in conversation or discourse: **a** to mark a transition, emphasize a point, etc: *Now then, let's deal with this other matter; Let me see now, how old is she?* **b** to comfort, exhort, admonish, or respond quizzically: *Now, now, don't cry; There now, it's OK; 'Mum, I need some money.' 'Do you now?'* ✳ **by now** as things are or were: *She must be eighty by now; By now the hints and rumours were fairly thick* — The Economist. **for now** for the present: *all for now.* **just now** in the immediate past: *He was here just now.* **now and/every now and again/then** occasionally: *see them every now and then.* **now for** let's turn our attention to (something): *Now for breakfast.* **now... now** at one moment... at the next: *saying now one thing and now the opposite.* **now or never** used to indicate urgency: *Make the move – it's now or never.* **now you're talking** *informal* used in enthusiastic response. **up to now** so far. ➤➤ **nowness** *noun*. [Old English *nū*]

now² *conj* (*often* + that) as a result of the circumstance that; since: *He had time to rationalize the family finances now that he had retired; Now we're all here, how about starting on the food?*

nowadays /'nowədayz/ *adv* in these modern times, in contrast to the past; today. [Middle English, from NOW¹ + Old English *a daeges* during the day]

noway /'nohway/ *or* **noways** /'nohwayz/ *adv NAmer or archaic* in no way whatever; not at all.

nowhere /'nohweə/ *adv and pronoun* not anywhere: *The plant is found nowhere else; The path led nowhere; I've got nowhere to put my CDs.* ✳ **be/come nowhere** to be unplaced in a race, or perform without distinction in a competition. **get/go nowhere/nowhere fast** to make no progress. **get somebody nowhere** to be of no benefit to them: *Quarrelling will get us nowhere.* **nowhere near** not nearly: *nowhere near enough.* **the middle of nowhere** somewhere remote from a town or civilization.

nowise /'nohwiez/ *adv* = NOWAY.

nowt /nowt/ *noun N Eng* nothing. [variant of NAUGHT¹]

NOx *noun* oxides of nitrogen, *esp* as a pollutant in the atmosphere.

noxious /'nokshəs/ *adj* **1** harmful to living things: *noxious fumes.* **2** *literary* morally harmful; unwholesome: *noxious influences.* ➤➤ **noxiously** *adv*, **noxiousness** *noun*. [Latin *noxius*, from *noxa* harm]

noyau /'nwayoh/ *noun* (*pl* **noyaux** /'nwayohz/) a brandy liqueur flavoured with the kernels of fruit stones. [French *noyau* kernel, ultimately from Latin *nuc-*, *nux* nut]

nozzle /'nozl/ *noun* a projecting part with an opening that usu serves as an outlet; *esp* a short tube with a taper or constriction used on a hose, pipe, etc to speed up or direct a flow of fluid. [dimin. of NOSE¹]

NP *abbr* Notary Public.

Np *abbr* the chemical symbol for neptunium.

np *abbr* **1** new paragraph. **2** no place (of publication).

NPA *abbr* Newspaper Publishers' Association.

NPD *abbr* new product development.

NPL *abbr* National Physical Laboratory.

NPV *abbr* net present value.

nr *abbr* near.

NRA *abbr* **1** *NAmer* National Rifle Association. **2** *Brit* National Rivers Authority.

NRSV *abbr* New Revised Standard Version (of the Bible).

NRV *abbr* net realizable value.

NS *abbr* **1** in dates, New Style. **2** Nova Scotia (US postal abbreviation).

NSA *abbr NAmer* National Security Agency.

NSB *abbr Brit* National Savings Bank.

NSC *abbr NAmer* National Security Council.

NSF *abbr NAmer* National Science Foundation.

NSPCC *abbr Brit* National Society for the Prevention of Cruelty to Children.

NST *abbr Can* Newfoundland Standard Time.

NSTC *abbr* the broadcasting system for television used in Japan and N America. [National Television Standard Committee]

NSU *abbr* non-specific urethritis.

NSW *abbr* New South Wales.

NT *abbr* **1** National Trust. **2** New Testament. **3** Northern Territory. **4** Northwest Territories. **5** in bridge, no trumps.

-n't *contraction and suffix* used with auxiliary verbs, modal auxiliary verbs, and 'be' and 'have' as ordinary verbs: not: *isn't; won't; couldn't.*

nth /enth/ *adj* **1** denoting an unspecified member of an ordinally numbered series: *Suppose every nth bag is opened and checked.* **2** *informal* denoting the last in a long series of instances: *warning you for the nth time.* ✳ **to the nth degree** to the utmost: *exaggerated to the nth degree.* [N² + -TH¹]

NTP *abbr* normal temperature and pressure.

nt wt *abbr* net weight.

n-type *adj* said of a semiconductor: having an excess of electrons: compare P-TYPE. [contraction of *negative-type*]

nu /nyooh/ *noun* the 13th letter of the Greek alphabet (N, ν), equivalent to and transliterated as roman n. [Greek *ny*, of Semitic origin; related to Hebrew *nūn*, 14th letter of the alphabet]

nuance /'nyoohonhs (*French* nyɑ̃:s)/ *noun* a subtly distinct gradation in colour, meaning, or tone; a shade: *nuances of expression.* ➤➤ **nuanced** *adj*. [French *nuance* shade of colour, subtle distinction, from *nuer* to shade, from *nue* cloud, from Latin *nubes*]

nub /nub/ *noun* **1a** a knob, lump, or protuberance: *a nub of coal.* **b** a small nugget of metal or chunk of rock. **2** (**the nub**) the gist or crux of a matter: *the nub of his discourse.* [alteration of English dialect *knub*, from early Low German *knubbe, knobbe* knob]

Nuba /'noohbə/ *noun* (*pl* **Nubas** *or collectively* **Nuba**) a member of a people inhabiting the Sudan. ➤➤ **Nuba** *adj*. [Latin *Nubae* the Nubians]

nubbin /'nubin/ *noun* **1** a small lump or protuberance. **2** *NAmer* something diminutive or undeveloped of its kind: *a nubbin of a nose.* [dimin of NUB]

nubble /'nubl/ *noun* a small knob or lump. [dimin. of NUB]

nubbly /'nubli/ *adj* (**nubblier, nubbliest**) = NUBBY.

nubby /'nubi/ *adj* (**nubbier, nubbiest**) *chiefly NAmer* **1** said of fabric: having a rough knobbly texture. **2** blunt or stubby; lumpy. [prob from NUBBLE]

Nubian /'nyoohbi·ən/ *adj* **1** a native or inhabitant of the region of N Sudan and S Egypt corresponding to ancient Nubia. **2** a group of Nilo-Saharan languages of Sudan and S Egypt. **3** a goat of a short-haired breed with long legs and drooping ears, orig from Africa. ➤➤ **Nubian** *adj*.

nubile /'n(y)oohbiel/ *adj* said of a girl: **a** of marriageable age. **b** young and sexually attractive. ➤➤ **nubility** /n(y)ooh'biliti/ *noun*. [French *nubile* marriageable from Latin *nubilis*, from *nubere* to marry, literally 'to veil oneself', from *nubes* cloud]

nubuck /'nyoohbuk/ *noun* cowhide rubbed on the flesh side to give a soft suede-like finish.

nucellus /nyooh'seləs/ *noun* (*pl* **nucelli** /-lie, -lee/) in botany, the central part of an ovule, containing the embryo sac. [scientific Latin; prob from *nucleus*: see NUCLEUS]

nucha /'nyoohkə/ *noun* (*pl* **nuchae** /'nyoohkee/) the nape of the neck. ➤➤ **nuchal** *adj*. [late Latin *nucha* MEDULLA OBLONGATA (the part of the spinal cord within the skull), from Arabic *nukhā* spinal marrow]

nuci- *comb. form* forming words, with the meaning: relating to nuts: *nuciferous.* [Latin *nuc-*, *nux* nut]

nuciferous /nyooh'sifərəs/ *adj* said of a tree: producing nuts.

nucle- *or* **nucleo-** *comb. form* forming words, with the meanings: **1** nucleus or nuclear: *nucleon.* **2** related to nucleic acid: *nucleoprotein.* [French *nuclé-, nucléo-*, from Latin *nucleus*: see NUCLEUS]

nuclear /'nyoohkliə/ *adj* **1** relating to or constituting a nucleus: *the nuclear family.* **2** relating to the atomic nucleus, atomic energy, the atom bomb, or atomic power: *nuclear force.*

nuclear bomb *noun* a bomb whose explosive force is the result either of NUCLEAR FUSION or NUCLEAR FISSION.

nuclear chemistry *noun* the branch of chemistry dealing with nuclear reaction.

nuclear disarmament *noun dated* the reduction or giving up of nuclear weapons on the part of the countries possessing them.

nuclear energy *noun* energy that can be liberated by changes in the nucleus of an atom, *esp* by fission of a heavy nucleus or fusion of light nuclei.

nuclear family *noun* a family unit that consists of husband, wife, and children: compare EXTENDED FAMILY.

nuclear fission *noun* the splitting into two halves of the nucleus of an atom, whether spontaneously or as a result of the impact of a particle, *esp* with a release of energy.

nuclear force *noun* the attractive force that binds nucleons together in an atomic nucleus.

nuclear fuel *noun* a fuel that consists of a substance that can sustain a fission chain reaction and is therefore usable as a source of nuclear energy.

nuclear fusion *noun* a reaction in which two nuclei combine or fuse together, with a release of energy.

nuclear isomer *noun* any of two or more atomic nuclei that have the same atomic number and the same mass number but different energy states.

nuclear magnetic resonance *noun* a technique for finding the MAGNETIC RESONANCE (absorption of electromagnetic radiation) of an atomic nucleus, used e.g. in body-scanning to determine structure.

nuclear medicine *noun* the branch of medicine specializing in the use of radioactive nuclides in the diagnosis and treatment of disease.

nuclear physics *noun* (*treated as sing.*) the branch of physics concerned with atomic nuclei, their behaviour and interactions, *esp* as a source of energy.

nuclear power *noun* 1 power produced by a nuclear reactor, *esp* if electric or motive. 2 a country possessing nuclear weapons. ➤➤ **nuclear-powered** *adj*.

nuclear reaction *noun* the change that takes place in the structure and energy content of an atomic nucleus as a result of interaction with a particle or another nucleus.

nuclear reactor *noun* an apparatus in which a self-sustaining reaction occurs, involving the breakdown of the nuclei of atoms of uranium, plutonium, etc with the release of large amounts of energy.

nuclear threshold *noun* in a war, etc, the stage at which the use of nuclear weapons becomes a likelihood or reality.

nuclear umbrella *noun* the protection supposedly afforded by alliance with a country that possesses nuclear weapons.

nuclear waste *noun* radioactive waste, *esp* from the use or reprocessing of nuclear fuel.

nuclear winter *noun* a state of darkness and extreme cold on earth, caused by clouds of dust and smoke blocking sunlight, which some scientists consider a likely consequence of a nuclear war.

nuclease /'nyoohkliayz, -ays/ *noun* any of various enzymes that promote the breakdown of nucleic acids.

nucleate[1] /'nyoohkliayt/ *verb intrans* 1 to form a nucleus. 2 said of villages or settlements: to cluster round a centre. ➤➤ **nucleation** /-'aysh(ə)n/ *noun*, **nucleator** *noun*.

nucleate[2] /'nyoohkli-ət, -ayt/ *adj* having a nucleus or nuclei: *nucleated cells*.

nucleated /'nyoohkliaytid/ *adj* = NUCLEATE[2].

nuclei /'nyoohkliie/ *noun* pl of NUCLEUS.

nucleic acid /nyooh'klayik, nyooh'kleeik/ *noun* RNA, DNA, or another complex organic substance present in living cells, composed of a chain of nucleotide molecules linked to each other.

nuclein /'nyoohkliin/ *noun* = NUCLEOPROTEIN.

nucleo- *comb. form* see NUCLE-.

nucleolus /nyooh'klee-ələs, -'ohləs/ *noun* (*pl* **nucleoli** /-lie, -lee/) a spherical body in the nucleus of a cell that is prob the site of the synthesis of ribosomes (specialized cell parts; see RIBOSOME). ➤➤ **nucleolar** *adj*. [Latin *nucleolus*, dimin. of *nucleus*: see NUCLEUS]

nucleon /'nyoohklion/ *noun* either of two elementary particles, that is, a proton or a neutron, that are found *esp* in an atomic nucleus. ➤➤ **nucleonic** /-'onik/ *adj*. [NUCLE- + -ON[2]]

nucleonics /nyoohkli'oniks/ *pl noun* (*treated as sing.*) the physics and technical applications of nucleons, the atomic nucleus, or nuclear energy.

nucleophile /'nyoohkli-əfiel/ *noun* a substance, e.g. a negative ion, with an affinity for atomic nuclei. ➤➤ **nucleophilic** /-'filik/ *adj*, **nucleophilicity** /-fi'lisiti/ *noun*.

nucleoprotein /,nyoohklioh'prohteen/ *noun* a compound of a protein, e.g. a histone, with a nucleic acid, e.g. DNA, forming the major constituent of chromosomes.

nucleoside /'nyoohkli-əsied/ *noun* any of several compounds, e.g. adenosine, consisting of a purine or pyrimidine base combined with deoxyribose or ribose and occurring *esp* as a constituent of nucleotides. [NUCLEO- + GLYCOSIDE]

nucleosynthesis /,nyoohklioh'sinthəsis/ *noun* the production, e.g. in the sun, of chemical elements from simple components, e.g. hydrogen nuclei or protons.

nucleotide /'nyoohkli-ətied/ *noun* any of several compounds that form the structural units of RNA and DNA and consist of a nucleoside combined with a phosphate group. [formed irregularly from NUCLEO- + -IDE]

nucleus /'nyoohkli-əs/ *noun* (*pl* **nuclei** /'nyoohkliie, 'nyoohkli-ee/ *or* **nucleuses**) 1 a small bright and dense part of a galaxy or head of a comet. 2 a central point, mass, etc about which gathering, concentration, etc takes place: e.g. **a** a usu round ORGANELLE (specialized structure within a cell) containing the chromosomes and surrounded by a membrane. **b** a discrete mass of nerve cells in the brain or spinal cord. **c** the positively charged central part of an atom that accounts for nearly all of the atomic mass and consists of protons and usu neutrons. [Latin *nucleus* kernel, dimin. of *nuc-*, *nux* nut]

nuclide /'nyoohklied/ *noun* an atom with a particular number of protons and neutrons in its nucleus. ➤➤ **nuclidic** /nyooh'klidik/ *adj*. [NUCLEUS + Greek *eidos* form]

nude[1] /n(y)oohd/ *adj* 1 without clothing; naked. 2 relating to or involving nudity: *nude scenes*; *nude bathing*. 3 *literary* without natural covering or adornment; bare: *nude trees*. 4 lacking something essential to legal validity, e.g., in the case of a contract, not supported by CONSIDERATION (something that makes a promise legally binding). ➤➤ **nudely** *adv*, **nudeness** *noun*. [Latin *nudus* naked]

nude[2] *noun* 1 a representation, e.g. in painting or sculpture, of a nude human figure: *Renoir's nudes*. 2 a nude person. ✳ **in the nude** in a state of nakedness: *walking about in the nude*.

nudge[1] /nuj/ *verb trans* 1 to poke (somebody) gently with one's elbow, *esp* to draw their attention to something. 2 to push (something) gently: *She felt the dog's nose nudging her hand*. 3 to move (something) slightly in a certain direction: *Yearly profits had been nudged over the million mark*. 4 to encourage (somebody) gently to do something by hints and reminders: *nudge them towards giving us a loan*. ✳ **nudge nudge** *informal* interjected to add salacious suggestiveness to one's words: *Yer average gig-goer is still stuck in the 'wink wink, nudge nudge' mentality of the '70s* — New Musical Express. ➤➤ **nudger** *noun*. [prob of Scandinavian origin]

nudge[2] *noun* 1 the act of nudging or pushing gently. 2 a gentle hint or reminder: *Perhaps he needs a nudge*.

nudibranch /'n(y)oohdibrangk/ *noun* any of an order of shell-less marine molluscs, having external gills and strikingly coloured bodies; the sea-slugs: order Nudibranchia. ➤➤ **nudibranch** *adj*, **nudibranchiate** /-'brangki-ət, -ayt/ *adj and noun*. [Latin *nudus* naked, exposed + *branchia* gill]

nudie /'nyoohdi/ *adj informal* said of photos, magazines, etc: showing naked people and mildly pornographic images.

nudism *noun* the cult or practice of going nude as much as possible. ➤➤ **nudist** *adj and noun*.

nudity *noun* the state of being nude or naked; nakedness: *Nudity is a form of dress* — John Berger.

nudnik /'noodnik/ *noun NAmer, informal* a silly tedious pest of a person. [Yiddish *nudnik* from Russian *nudnyĭ* tedious + -NIK]

nuée ardente /,nyooay ah'donht/ *noun* a glowing cloud of gas, volcanic ash, and fragments of lava flowing out of a volcano. [French *nuée ardente* burning cloud]

Nuer /'nooh-ə/ *noun* (*pl* **Nuers** *or collectively* **Nuer**) 1 a member of an African people of Ethiopia and SE Sudan. 2 the Nilotic language of this people. [Dinka *Nuer*, local name of this people]

nugatory /'nyoohgət(ə)ri/ *adj formal* 1 trifling; inconsequential: *nugatory remarks*. 2 said of a law, etc: invalid or inoperative. [Latin *nugatorius*, from *nugari* to trifle, from *nugae* jests, trifles]

nugget /'nugət/ *noun* 1 a solid lump, *esp* of a precious metal in its natural state. 2 a useful fact: *a nugget of information*. ➤➤ **nuggety** *adj*. [prob dimin. of English dialect *nug* lump, block]

nuisance /'nyoohs(ə)ns/ *noun* **1** a circumstance, person or thing that is a source of trouble, annoyance, or inconvenience. **2** in law, the actionable offence of behaving in an offensive or harmful way in public or towards an individual: *commit a nuisance*. ✳ **nuisance value** the significance that a person or thing has solely by virtue of being a source of annoyance. [Middle English *nusaunce* injury, from Old French *nuisir* to harm, from Latin *nocēre*]

nuisance ground *noun Can* a rubbish dump.

NUJ *abbr Brit* National Union of Journalists.

nuke[1] /'nyoohk/ *noun informal* a nuclear weapon.

nuke[2] *verb trans informal* **1** to attack (a population) with nuclear weapons. **2** *NAmer* to cook (food) in a microwave oven.

null[1] /nul/ *adj* **1** having no force in law; invalid: *declare a marriage null and void*. **2** amounting to nothing; nil: *the null effect of arms embargoes*. **3** without character or distinction: *intellectually null*. **4** in mathematics: **a** = EMPTY[1] (4). **b** having zero as a limit: *null sequence*. **c** said of a matrix: having all the elements equal to zero. **5a** said of an electrical instrument: indicating, e.g. by a zero reading on a scale, when current or voltage is zero. **b** relating to or denoting a method of measurement in which an unknown quantity, e.g. of electric current, is compared with a known quantity of the same kind and found equal by a null instrument. [French *nul* not any, from Latin *nullus*, from *ne-* not + *ullus* any]

null[2] *noun* **1** zero on a scale. **2** a minimum or zero value of an electric current or of a radio signal. **3** a meaningless group of letters or characters included in a coded message to hinder interpretation by unauthorized people.

nulla[1] /'nulə/ *noun* (*pl* **nullas**) in printing, a zero or nought. [alteration of NULL[2]]

nulla[2] *noun* = NULLA-NULLA.

nullah /'nulə/ *noun* in India, a gully or ravine. [Hindi *nālā* brook, ravine]

nulla-nulla /,nulə 'nulə/ *noun* a hardwood club used by Australian aboriginals. [Dharuk (Aboriginal language) *ngalla-ngalla*]

null hypothesis *noun* a statistical hypothesis to be tested and accepted or rejected in favour of an alternative; *specif* the hypothesis that an observed difference, e.g. between the means of two samples, is due to chance alone.

nullify /'nulifie/ *verb trans* (**nullifies, nullified, nullifying**) **1** to make (something) legally null and void. **2** to render (something) ineffective or cancel it out. ⟫ **nullification** /-fi'kaysh(ə)n/ *noun*.

nullipara /nu'lipərə/ *noun* (*pl* **nulliparae** /-ree/) a female that has not borne offspring. ⟫ **nulliparous** /-rəs/ *adj*. [scientific Latin *nullipara*, from Latin *nullus* none + *-para*, from *parere* to give birth to]

nullity /'nuliti/ *noun* (*pl* **nullities**) **1** in law, something that is legally null and void. **2** the state of being legally null and void; invalidity. **3** something of no worth or importance. **4** nothingness.

NUM *abbr Brit* National Union of Mineworkers.

Num. *abbr* Numbers (book of the Bible).

num. *abbr* numeral.

numb[1] /num/ *adj* **1** devoid of sensation, *esp* as a result of cold or anaesthesia. **2** devoid of emotion e.g. as a result of shock. ⟫ **numbly** *adv*, **numbness** *noun*. [Middle English *nomen*, literally 'taken (with paralysis)', past part. of *nimen* to take, from Old English *niman*]

numb[2] *verb trans* **1** to make (a person or a bodily part) numb: *numb the fingers; numb the senses; numbed by the shock*. **2** to reduce the sharpness of (a pain). ⟫ **numbed** *adj*.

numbat /'numbat/ *noun* a small Australian marsupial with a long snout, bushy tail, and black-and-white-striped back, that feeds on termites: *Myrmecobius fasciatus*. [Nyungar (Aboriginal language) *numbat*]

number[1] /'numbə/ *noun* **1** any of the words, or the numerals, digits or other symbols representing them, that are used in counting or calculating quantities, and in referring to things by their position in a series. **2** arithmetic; calculation: *no feeling for number*. **3** several: *A number of questions arise*. **4** numerical superiority: *have the advantage of numbers*. **5** in grammar, singular and plural, or the inflections and word forms that distinguish them. **6** *literary* (*in pl*) metrical lines; verses: *These numbers will I tear, and write in prose* — Shakespeare. **7** a numeral or set of digits used to identify or designate somebody or something: *a car number; a telephone number*. **8** a member of a group or sequence designated by *esp* consecutive

numbers. **9** an individual or item, e.g. a single act in a variety show or a single issue of a periodical, singled out from a group: *A big production number closed the show*. **10** a piece of pop or jazz music. **11** *informal*. **a** something viewed in terms of the advantage or enjoyment obtained from it: *He has a cushy number in his father's firm; drives round in a fast little number*. **b** an article of *esp* women's clothing: *wearing a chic little black number*. **12** *informal* a person or individual, *esp* an attractive girl: *a red-headed number with bedroom eyes* — Raymond Chandler. **13** a certain identified group of individuals: *Some students hunted, but he was not of their number*. ✳ **any number** *informal* a large number: *She's had any number of proposals*. **by numbers** following instructions of the simplest kind, *esp* where each step is indicated by a number. **do a number on somebody** *NAmer, informal* to disparage or humiliate somebody comprehensively. **have somebody's number** to understand somebody's real motives or game. **somebody's number is up** *informal* somebody is doomed. **without number** innumerable: *times without number*. [Middle English from Old French *nombre*, from Latin *numerus*]

Usage note

number of. The phrase *a number of* meaning 'some' or 'several' should be used with a verb in the plural: *There are a number of things to discuss; A number of you, I know, disagree*. When *number* means 'the overall quantity' in *the number of* it is used with a singular verb: *The number of meningitis cases is increasing*.

number[2] *verb* (**numbered, numbering**) ➤ *verb trans* **1** to amount to (a certain total): *In those days the choir numbered barely 25*. **2** to enumerate and assign numbers to (things in a series): *Don't forget to number the programmes*. **3** (*usu* + among) to regard (a person or thing) as being included in a certain group: *proud to number her among my friends*. ➤ *verb intrans* (*usu* + among) to be regarded as included in a certain group: *He numbers among the people I can really trust*. ✳ **somebody's days are numbered** somebody is likely to die, fall from power, etc, very soon. ⟫ **numberable** *adj*.

Number 10 *noun* Number 10 Downing Street, official residence in London of the British Prime Minister.

number-cruncher *noun* **1** a powerful computer or program that processes large amounts of numerical data very quickly: compare CRUNCHER. **2** *derog* a statistician. ⟫⟫ **number-crunching** *noun and adj*.

numbered account *noun* a bank account identified by a number as distinct from a personal name, *esp* in a Swiss bank.

number eight *noun* the player positioned in the back row of the scrum in rugby union.

numberless *adj* innumerable; countless.

number one *noun* **1** something that is first in rank, order, or importance: *It was number one in her list of priorities*. **2** *informal* oneself and one's interests, as deserving prior consideration: *always thinking of number one*. **3** *euphem* used by or to children: an act of urinating.

numberplate *noun chiefly Brit* a rectangular identifying plate fastened to a vehicle and bearing the vehicle's registration number.

Numbers *pl noun* (*treated as sing.*) the mainly narrative fourth book of the Old Testament. [so called because of the account of a census of the tribes of Israel in chapters 1–4]

numbers game *noun* **1** *derog* the manipulation of statistics for one's own purposes. **2** *NAmer* an illegal lottery based on unpredictable combinations of numbers in published figures, e.g. stock-market prices, sports results, the official lottery, etc.

numbers racket *noun NAmer* = NUMBERS GAME (2).

number theory *noun* a branch of mathematics dealing with integers and their properties.

number two *noun* **1** a second-in-command. **2** *euphem* used by or to children: an act of defecating.

numbfish *noun* (*pl* **numbfishes** or collectively **numbfish**) any of several electric rays that numb their prey with a severe electric shock, *esp Hypnos monopterygium*.

numbles /'numblz/ *noun archaic* = UMBLES.

numbskull *noun* see NUMSKULL.

numdah /'numdə/ *noun* an embroidered felt or woollen rug made in the Middle East or the Indian subcontinent. [Urdu *namdā* from Persain *namad* carpet]

numen /'nyoohmin/ *noun* (*pl* **numina** /-nə/) a divine force associated with a place or natural object. [Latin *numen* deity, divinity, divine will, literally 'a nod']

numerable /'nyoohm(ə)rəbl/ *adj* capable of being counted.

numeracy /'nyoohmərəsi/ *noun Brit* the quality or state of being numerate.

numeraire /'nyoohmə'reə/ *noun* in economics, a commodity that acts as standard for measuring value or for currency exchange: *using gold as the numeraire*. [French *numéraire* coin, specie, from late Latin *numerarius* relating to numbers, from Latin *numerus* NUMBER¹]

numeral¹ /'nyoohm(ə)rəl/ *noun* a conventional symbol that represents a natural number or zero. [via French from late Latin *numeralis* relating to numbers, from Latin *numerus* NUMBER¹]

numeral² *adj* relating to or expressing numbers. ➤➤ **numerally** *adv.*

numerate /'nyoohm(ə)rət/ *adj* understanding basic mathematics; able to use numbers in calculation. [coined from Latin *numerus* NUMBER¹ on the model of LITERATE¹]

numeration /nyoohmə'raysh(ə)n/ *noun* 1 counting. 2 designating by a number. 3 expressing in words numbers written as numerals. 4 a system of numbering or counting. ➤➤ **numerate** /'nyoohmərayt/ *verb trans.* [Middle English from Latin *numeration-, numeratio*, from *numerare* to count, from *numerus* NUMBER¹]

numerator /'nyoohməraytə/ *noun* the part of a fraction that is above the line and signifies the number of parts of the denominator that is shown by the fraction.

numeric /nyooh'merik/ *adj* = NUMERICAL.

numerical /nyooh'merikl/ *adj* relating to, expressed in, or involving numbers or a number system: *the numerical superiority of the enemy; a numerical code.* ➤➤ **numerically** *adv.* [late Latin *numericus*, from Latin *numerus* NUMBER¹]

numerology /nyoohmə'roləji/ *noun* the study of the occult significance of numbers. ➤➤ **numerological** /-'lojikl/ *adj,* **numerologist** *noun.* [Latin *numerus* NUMBER¹ + -OLOGY]

numero uno /,noohməroh 'oohnoh/ *noun informal* the foremost person or thing. [Italian *numero uno* number one]

numerous /'nyoohm(ə)rəs/ *adj* consisting of many units or individuals. ➤➤ **numerously** *adv,* **numerousness** *noun.* [Middle English from Latin *numerosus*, from *numerus* NUMBER¹]

numerus clausus /,nyoohmərəs 'klowzəs/ *noun* a restriction limiting the intake of applicants, e.g. for a university course, to a fixed maximum number. [Latin *numerus clausus* closed number]

numina /'nyoohminə/ *noun* pl of NUMEN.

numinous /'nyoohminəs/ *adj* 1 awe-inspiring or mysterious. 2 filled with a sense of the presence of divinity. [Latin *numin-, numen* divinity, deity]

numismatics /nyoohmiz'matiks/ *pl noun* (*treated as sing.*) the study or collection of coinage, coins, paper money, medals, tokens, etc. ➤➤ **numismatic** *adj,* **numismatically** *adv,* **numismatist** /nyooh'miz-/ *noun,* **numismatology** /-'toləji/ *noun.* [French *numismatique,* via Latin from Greek *nomismat-, nomisma* current coin, from *nomizein* to have in use, from *nomos* custom, law]

nummulite /'numyooliet/ *noun* in palaeontology, the disc-shaped porous shell of a fossil PROTOZOAN (single-celled animal) of the Tertiary period. [Latin *nummulus,* dimin. of *nummus* coin + -ITE¹]

numnah /'numnə/ *noun* a piece of leather, sheepskin, etc placed under a horse's saddle to prevent chafing. [Urdu *namdā*: see NUMDAH]

numpty /'numpti/ *noun* (*pl* **numpties**) *Scot, informal* an idiot. [origin unknown]

numskull *or* **numbskull** /'numskul/ *noun* a dull or stupid person. [NUMB¹ + SKULL]

nun /nun/ *noun* 1 a female member of a religious order living in a convent under vows of chastity, poverty, etc and often engaged in educational or nursing work. 2 a pigeon with a crest on its head reminiscent of a nun's hood. ➤➤ **nunlike** *adj,* **nunnish** *adj.* [Old English *nunne* from ecclesiastical Latin *nonna,* fem of *nonnus* monk]

nunatak /'nunətak/ *noun* an isolated pointed rock mass projecting above the surface of an inland snow or ice field. [Eskimo *nunataq*]

nun buoy *noun* a circular buoy with tapering top and bottom, used to mark the right-hand side of a channel leading into a harbour, painted green in British waters and red in US waters. [obsolete *nun* child's spinning top, of unknown origin]

Nunc Dimittis /,noongk di'mitis, ,nungk/ *noun* a canticle based on the prayer of Simeon in the Bible, Luke 2, 29–32. [Latin *nunc dimittis* now allow to go, the first words of the canticle]

nunchaku /nun'chakooh/ *noun* (*pl* **nunchaku** *or* **nunchakus**) a weapon used in oriental martial arts as a defence against frontal attack, consisting of two hardwood sticks each 30cm (a foot) long, joined together by a body-width cord, thong, or chain. [Okinawan Japanese *nunchaku* from a Taiwanese word for a farm implement, prob meaning 'two diggers']

nunciature /'nunsi·əchə, 'nunshi-/ *noun* the office of a papal nuncio or the duration of this. [Italian *nunziatura,* from *nunzio*: see NUNCIO]

nuncio /'nunsioh, 'nunshioh/ *noun* (*pl* **nuncios**) a papal ambassador to a civil government. [Italian *nunzio* from Latin *nuntius* messenger]

nuncle /'nungkl/ *noun archaic* used as a familiar form of address for one's uncle, or for his superiors by a court fool: *Prithee, nuncle, be contented!* — Shakespeare. [prob by misdivision of *mine uncle*]

nuncupative /'nungkyoopətiv/ *adj* in law, said of a will or testament: declared orally, e.g. by a mortally wounded soldier or sailor or other fatally injured person. [late Latin *nuncupativus* from Latin *nuncupare* to declare, from *nomen* name + *capere* to take]

nunnery /'nunəri/ *noun* (*pl* **nunneries**) a convent of nuns.

nuoc mam /nwok 'mahm/ *noun* a spicy sauce used in Vietnamese cuisine, made from the liquor of decomposing fish. [Vietnamese *nuoc mam*]

NUPE /'nyoohpi/ *abbr Brit* National Union of Public Employees.

Nupe /'noohpay/ *noun* (*pl* **Nupes** *or collectively* **Nupe**) 1 a member of a people of W central Nigeria. 2 the Niger-Congo language of this people. ➤➤ **Nupe** *adj.* [named after *Nupe,* a former kingdom in W Africa]

nuptial¹ /'nupsh(ə)l/ *adj* 1 relating to marriage. 2 in zoology, characteristic of or occurring in the breeding season: *a nuptial flight.* ➤➤ **nuptiality** /nupshi'aliti/ *noun.* [Latin *nuptialis,* from *nuptiae,* pl, wedding, from *nubere*: see NUBILE]

nuptial² *noun* (*usu in pl*) a wedding: *Isabel at first had thought of celebrating her nuptials in her native land* — Henry James.

nuptial plumage *noun* the brilliantly coloured plumage developed in the males of many birds prior to the start of the breeding season: compare ECLIPSE PLUMAGE.

NUR *abbr Brit* National Union of Railwaymen.

nuraghe /noo'rahgay/ *or* **nuragh** /noo'rahg/ *noun* (*pl* **nuraghi** /noo'rahgi/) any of many round stone towers in Sardinia, built in the Bronze Age and Iron Age. ➤➤ **nuraghic** /-gik/ *adj.* [Sardinian *nuraghe*]

nurd /nuhd/ *noun* see NERD.

Nurofen /'nyooərəfen/ *noun trademark* the painkilling drug IBUPROFEN.

nurse¹ /nuhs/ *noun* 1 a person skilled or trained in caring for the sick or infirm, *esp* under the supervision of a physician. 2 *dated* a woman employed to take care of a young child. 3 *archaic* = WET NURSE. 4 a member of the worker caste in an ant, bee, etc society, that cares for the young. 5 in forestry, a tree planted to provide shelter for others. [Middle English via Old French *nurice* from late Latin *nutricia* nurse, fem of Latin *nutricius*: see NUTRITIOUS]

nurse² *verb trans* 1 to tend (e.g. a sick person): *nurse her back to health.* 2 to suckle (a baby). 3 to rear or nurture (a child). 4 to attempt to cure (e.g. an illness or injury) by appropriate treatment: *nurse a cold.* 5 to hold (e.g. a baby) lovingly or caressingly. 6 to hold or handle (something) carefully: *nursing his laptop on his knee.* 7 to hold (a drink), drinking it slowly. 8 to nourish and promote the growth of (a plant, etc): *nursed one's tomatoes.* 9 to harbour (a feeling) in one's mind: *nurse a grievance.* 10 to attend to the needs or whims of (a person) to keep their goodwill: *You have to nurse your best customers.* 11 in billiards, to play shots that keep (the balls) together. ➤ *verb intrans* 1 to act or serve as a nurse: *How long have you been nursing?* 2 said of a mother: to suckle an offspring. 3 said of a baby: to suck at the breast. [alteration of NOURISH by association with NURSE¹]

nurse³ *noun* a grey shark of Australia, found in shallow coastal waters: *Odontaspis arenarius.* [orig *nusse,* alteration of HUSS by misdivision of *an huss*]

nursehound *noun* a large spotted European dogfish of NE Atlantic waters: *Scyliorhinus stellaris.* [NURSE³ + HOUND¹]

nurseling /'nuhsling/ *noun* see NURSLING.

nursemaid *noun* a girl or woman employed to look after children.

nursery /'nuhs(ə)ri/ *noun* (*pl* **nurseries**) **1** a child's bedroom or playroom. **2a** a place where small children are looked after in their parents' absence. **b** = NURSERY SCHOOL. **3** a place where young animals, e.g. fish, grow or are cared for. **4** an area where plants, trees, etc are grown for propagation, sale, or transplanting.

nursery cannon *noun* in billiards, a strike that keeps the three balls close together.

nursery class *noun* a class attached to a primary school for the education of children aged between three and five.

nurseryman *noun* (*pl* **nurserymen**) a person whose occupation is the cultivation of plants, usu for sale.

nursery nurse *noun* a person trained to look after babies and young children in nurseries and crèches.

nursery rhyme *noun* a short traditional story in rhyme for children.

nursery school *noun* a school for children aged usu from three to five.

nursery slope *noun* a usu gentle ski slope for beginners.

nursery stakes *noun* a race for two-year-old horses.

nurse shark *noun* any of several sharks with barbels (thin sensory projections; see BARBEL²) round the nose: *esp Ginglymostoma cirratum*. [NURSE³]

nursing home *noun* a usu private hospital or home, where care is provided for the aged, chronically ill, etc.

nursing officer *noun* a nurse of the next rank below a senior nursing officer.

nursling *or* **nurseling** /'nuhsling/ *noun* formerly, a child under the care of a nurse, *esp* a wetnurse.

nurture¹ /'nuhchə/ *noun* **1** training; upbringing. **2** the provision of food and nourishment. **3** the environmental, educational, etc factors that influence the inherent genetic make-up or NATURE of an individual. [Middle English via Old French *norriture* from late Latin *nutritura* act of nursing, from Latin *nutrire* to suckle, NOURISH]

nurture² *verb trans* **1** to give care and nourishment to (a child). **2** to rear or bring up (a child). **3** to encourage and develop (an interest, talent, etc). **4** to cherish (a hope, ambition, etc). ➤ **nurturance** *noun*, **nurturant** *adj*, **nurturer** *noun*.

NUS *abbr Brit* **1** National Union of Seamen. **2** National Union of Students.

NUT *abbr Brit* National Union of Teachers.

nut¹ /nut/ *noun* **1** a dry fruit or seed consisting of a hard separable rind or shell and often edible kernel; the kernel itself. **2** a typically hexagonal usu metal block that has a central hole with an internal screw thread cut on it, and can be screwed onto a piece, *esp* a bolt, with an external thread to tighten or secure something. **3a** a small fitting at the end of a violin bow with a screw adjusting the tension of the hair. **b** the ridge in a stringed instrument, e.g. a violin, over which the strings pass on the upper end of the fingerboard. **4** a small piece or lump: *a nut of butter*. **5** *informal* a person's head. **6** *informal*. **a** an insane or wildly eccentric person. **b** an ardent enthusiast: *a tennis nut*. **7** *informal*. **a** (*as an interjection, in pl*) nonsense! **b** *coarse slang* (*in pl*) a man's testicles. ✳ **a tough/hard nut (to crack)** a person or problem that is difficult to deal with. **do one's nut** *informal* to get very angry. **nuts and bolts 1** the basic practical issues. **2** the working parts. **use a sledgehammer to crack a nut** to be unduly forceful in tackling something comparatively small and simple. ➤ **nutlike** *adj*. [Old English *hnutu*]

nut² *verb* (**nutted, nutting**) ➤ *verb intrans* to gather or seek nuts: *The children were allowed to go nutting*. ➤ *verb trans informal* to butt (somebody) with one's head.

nutant /'nyooht(ə)nt/ *adj* said of a flower head: nodding; drooping. [Latin *nutant-, nutans*, present part. of *nutare*: see NUTATION]

nutation /nyooh'taysh(ə)n/ *noun* **1** a slight nodding of the earth's axis superimposed on its normal PRECESSION (motion like that of a spinning top). **2** a spontaneous usu irregular spiral movement of a growing stem, tendril, root, etc. **3** *literary or technical* the act of nodding the head. ➤ **nutate** *verb intrans*, **nutational** *adj*. [Latin *nutation-, nutatio* from *nutare* to nod, rock, frequentative of *nuere* to nod]

nut-brown *adj* of the colour of a ripe hazelnut.

nutcase *noun informal* a nut; a mad person.

nutcracker *noun* (*also in pl*) an implement for cracking nuts, usu consisting of two hinged metal arms between which the nut is held and compressed.

nutgall *noun* **1** a nut-shaped GALL⁴ (insect-caused growth) that forms on oaks and other trees. **2** a gall that forms inside hazel buds.

nuthatch /'nut·hach/ *noun* a Eurasian tree-climbing bird with bluish grey upper parts and a black stripe through the eye region: *esp Sitta europaea*. [Middle English, from NUT¹ + obsolete *hatch*, related to HACK¹, from its habit of hacking at nuts with its beak]

nuthouse /'nut·hows/ *noun informal, derog* a mental hospital.

nutlet /'nutlit/ *noun* **1** a small nut. **2** a small fruit similar to a nut. **3** the stone in each of the fleshy segments that collectively form the fruit of a raspberry, blackberry, etc.

nut loaf *noun* a vegetarian dish consisting of chopped or ground nuts, vegetables, and herbs, mixed with a binding ingredient such as egg, and shaped into a loaf for baking and slicing.

nutmeg /'nutmeg/ *noun* **1** a round hard aromatic seed used as a spice. **2** the Indonesian tree that bears this seed: *Myristica fragrans*. [Middle English *notemuge* via Old French from Old Provençal *noz muscada*, from *noz* nut (from Latin *nuc-, nux*) + *muscada*, fem of *muscat*: see MUSCAT]

nutria /'nyoohtri·ə/ *noun* **1** a coypu. **2** the fur of the coypu. [Spanish *nutria*, alteration of Latin *lutra* otter]

nutrient /'nyoohtri·ənt/ *noun* something that provides nourishment. ➤➤ **nutrient** *adj*. [Latin *nutrient-, nutriens*, present part. of *nutrire* to NOURISH]

nutriment /'nyoohtrimənt/ *noun* something that nourishes or promotes growth; nourishment. [Latin *nutrimentum* nourishment, from *nutrire* to NOURISH]

nutrition /nyooh'trish(ə)n/ *noun* **1** nourishing or being nourished; *specif* all the processes by which an organism takes in and uses food. **2** the branch of science concerned with nutrients and their assimilation. ➤➤ **nutritional** *adj*, **nutritionally** *adv*, **nutritionist** *noun*. [late Latin *nutrition-, nutritio*, from Latin *nutrire* to NOURISH]

nutritious /nyooh'trishəs/ *adj* nourishing. ➤➤ **nutritiously** *adv*, **nutritiousness** *noun*. [Latin *nutricius* giving nourishment, from *nutric-, nutrix* nurse]

nutritive /'nyoohtritiv/ *adj* **1** relating to nutrition. **2** nourishing. ➤➤ **nutritively** *adv*. [late Latin *nutritivus* from *nutrire* to NOURISH]

nuts /nuts/ *adj informal* **1** (+ on) passionately keen or enthusiastic: *He's nuts on ice-hockey*. **2** crazy; mad: *Bull terriers are my first real love. My home is a shrine to them and a talking point for my friends, who think I'm completely nuts* — Dogs Today; *The way he turns on the television as soon as he walks into the room drives me nuts* — Best. [NUT¹]

nutshell /'nut·shel/ *noun* the hard outside covering enclosing the kernel of a nut. ✳ **in a nutshell** in brief; in essence: *the whole story in a nutshell*.

nutso /'nutsoh/ *noun* (*pl* **nutsos**) *NAmer, informal* a crazy person; an eccentric. [from NUTS]

nutter /'nutə/ *noun chiefly Brit, informal* a crazy fool; an idiot; a lunatic.

nutty *adj* (**nuttier, nuttiest**) **1** containing nuts; full of nuts. **2** having a flavour like that of nuts. **3** *informal* eccentric or silly; crazy. ➤➤ **nuttiness** *noun*.

nux vomica /ˌnuks 'vomikə/ *noun* (*pl* **nux vomica**) **1** a poisonous seed containing strychnine and other alkaloids. **2** the S Asian tree that bears these seeds: *Strychnos nux-vomica*. [Latin *nux* nut + *vomica* emetic]

nuzzle /'nuzl/ *verb intrans* to lie close or snug; to nestle: *nuzzling up against their mother in the basket*. ➤ *verb trans* **1** to rub (something or somebody) affectionately with the nose or face. **2** to root or dig (something) out with the snout. [Middle English *noselen* to bring the nose towards the ground, from NOSE¹]

NV *abbr* Nevada (US postal abbreviation).

NVQ *abbr Brit* National Vocational Qualification.

NW *abbr* **1** Northwest. **2** Northwestern. **3** Northwest (London postcode).

NWT *abbr* Northwest Territories (of Canada).

NY *abbr* New York (US postal abbreviation).

nyaff /nyaf/ *noun Scot, informal* a stupid annoying person. [orig as a verb, meaning 'to yap like a dog']

nyala /nˈyahlə/ *noun* (*pl* **nyalas** or *collectively* **nyala**) a S African antelope with a crest of white hair along its length: *Tragelaphus angasi*. [Venda (Bantu language) *dzi-nyálà* nyala buck]

Nyanja /ˈnyanjə/ *noun* (*pl* **Nyanjas** or *collectively* **Nyanja**) **1** a member of a people of Malawi and E and central Zambia. **2** a Niger-Congo language of Malawi and Zambia. [local name, literally 'lake']

NYC *abbr* New York City.

nyct- or **nycto-** *comb. form* forming words, denoting: night; darkness. [Greek *nykt, nyx* night]

nyctalopia /niktəˈlohpi-ə/ *noun* = NIGHT BLINDNESS. [scientific Latin from Greek *nykt-, nyx* night + *alaos* blind + *ōps* eye]

nyctitropic /niktiˈtropik, -ˈtrohpik/ *noun* relating to or denoting a movement of a plant part at nightfall, e.g. the closing of a flower. ⫸ **nyctitropism** /nikˈtitrəpiz(ə)m, niktiˈtroh-/ *noun*.

nycto- *comb. form* see NYCT-.

nyctophobia /niktəˈfohbi-ə/ *noun* intense, *esp* irrational, fear of the night or of darkness. [NYCTO- + -PHOBIA]

nylon /ˈnielon, ˈnielən/ *noun* **1** any of numerous strong tough elastic synthetic polyamide materials fashioned into fibres, sheets, etc and used *esp* in textiles and plastics. **2** nylon fabric or yarn. **3** (*in pl*) stockings made of nylon. [coined word modelled on COTTON, RAYON, etc]

nymph /nimf/ *noun* **1** any of the minor female spirits of nature in classical mythology. **2** *literary* a girl, *esp* a beautiful one. **3** any of various immature insects; *esp* a larva of a dragonfly or other insect with incomplete metamorphosis. ⫸ **nymphal** *adj*, **nymphean** /ˈnimfi-ən/ *adj*. [Middle English *nimphe* via Old French from Latin *nympha* bride, nymph, from Greek *nymphē*]

nympha /ˈnimfə/ *noun* (*pl* **nymphae** /ˈnimfie/) either of the LABIA MINORA (inner lips of the vulva). [Latin *nympha*: see NYMPH]

nymphet /ˈnimfit/ or **nymphette** /nimˈfet/ *noun* a sexually desirable girl in early adolescence: *Between ... nine and fourteen there occur maidens who ... reveal their true nature which is not human but nymphic*

... and these chosen creatures I propose to designate as 'nymphets' — Vladimir Nabokov.

Word history

French *nymphette*, dimin. of *nymphe*: see NYMPH. Orig a poetic word for a young nymph; the current sense was introduced by V Nabokov d.1977, Russian-born American writer, in his novel *Lolita*.

nympho /ˈnimfoh/ *noun* (*pl* **nymphos**) *informal* a nymphomaniac.

nympholepsy /ˈnimfəlepsi/ *noun literary* a frenzy of emotion, usu inspired by something unattainable. ⫸ **nympholept** /-lept/ *noun*, **nympholeptic** /-ˈleptik/ *adj*. [Greek *nympholēptos* frenzied, literally 'caught by nymphs', from *nymphē* NYMPH + -O- + *lambanein* to seize, on the model of EPILEPSY]

nymphomania /nimfəˈmayni-yə/ *noun* excessive sexual desire in a female: compare SATYRIASIS. ⫸ **nymphomaniac** /-ak/ *noun and adj*, **nymphomaniacal** /ˌnimfohməˈnie-əkl/ *adj*. [scientific Latin, from *nymphae* inner lips of the vulva (pl of *nympha*: see NYMPH) + -O- + MANIA]

Nynorsk /n(y)oohˈnawsk/ *noun* a literary form of Norwegian based on the spoken dialects of Norway: compare BOKMÅL. [Norwegian *Nynorsk*, literally 'new Norwegian' from *ny* new + *Norsk* Norwegian]

NYO *abbr* National Youth Orchestra.

NYSE *abbr* New York Stock Exchange.

nystagmus /niˈstagməs/ *noun* a rapid involuntary oscillation of the eyeballs, e.g. from dizziness. ⫸ **nystagmic** /-mik/ *adj*. [scientific Latin, from Greek *nystagmos* drowsiness, from *nystazein* to doze]

nystatin /ˈniestatin, ni-/ *noun* an antibiotic used chiefly for treating fungal infections. [acronym from *New York State*, where it was first manufactured, + -IN[1]]

Nyungar /ˈnyoongə/ *noun* an Aboriginal language of SW Australia, now no longer spoken. [Nyungar *Nyungar*, literally 'man']

NZ *abbr* New Zealand (international vehicle registration).

NZBC *abbr* New Zealand Broadcasting Commission.

O¹ *or* **o** *noun* (*pl* **O's** *or* **Os** *or* **o's**) **1a** the 15th letter of the English alphabet. **b** a written character or design denoting this letter. **c** the sound represented by this letter, one of the English vowels. **2** an item designated as O, *esp* the 15th in a series. **3** a representation in speech of 'zero' or 'nought', *esp* in a series of numbers.

O² /oh/ *interj* = OH¹, used *esp* in addressing somebody or expressing a wish: *O Mary, at thy window be, it is the wish'd, the trysted hour!* — Burns. [Middle English]

O³ *noun* see OH².

O⁴ *abbr* **1** Ohio. **2** a blood type of the ABO system, lacking both the A and B antigens. **3** Ocean. **4** Old.

O⁵ *abbr* the chemical symbol for oxygen.

o *abbr* **1** octavo. **2** old. **3** in cricket, over.

o' *or* **o** /ə/ *prep* **1** of: *one o'clock*. **2** *chiefly dialect* on. [Middle English *o*, *o-*, contraction of ON¹ and OF]

o-¹ *or* **oo-** *comb. form* forming nouns, denoting: **1** egg: *oology*. **2** ovum: *oocyte*. [Greek *ōi-*, *ōio-*, from *ōion* egg]

o-² *comb. form* = ORTH-: *o-xylene*.

-o- *suffix* used as a connective vowel to join word elements of Greek and other origin: *milometer*; *elastomer*. [Middle English via Old French and Latin from Greek *-o-*, thematic vowel of many nouns and adjectives in combination]

-o¹ *suffix informal* forming nouns and adjectives, denoting: somebody or something that is, has the qualities of, or is associated with: *cheapo*; *wino*; *beano*. [perhaps from OH¹]

-o² *suffix informal* forming interjections from other parts of speech: *righto*. [prob from OH¹]

oaf /ohf/ *noun* a clumsy slow-witted person. ⟫ **oafish** *adj*, **oafishly** *adv*, **oafishness** *noun*. [variant of obsolete *auf* changeling, from Old Norse *alfr* elf]

oak /ohk/ *noun* (*pl* **oaks** *or collectively* **oak**) **1** any of numerous species of trees or shrubs of the beech family, usu having lobed leaves and producing acorns: genus *Quercus*. **2** the tough hard wood of this tree. ⟫ **oaken** *adj*. [Old English *āc*]

oak apple *noun* a large round gall produced on oak stems or leaves by a gall wasp.

oak leaf *adj* denoting a type of lettuce with leaves similar in shape to the leaves of an oak tree.

oak-leaf cluster *noun* a bronze or silver cluster of oak leaves and acorns added to various US military decorations to signify a second or subsequent award of the basic decoration.

oakum /'ohkəm/ *noun* hemp or jute fibre obtained by untwisting old rope impregnated with tar or a tar derivative and used in packing joints and stopping up gaps between the planks of a ship. [Middle English *okum* from Old English *ācumba* tow]

O & M *abbr* organization and methods.

OAP *abbr Brit* old age pensioner.

oar¹ /aw/ *noun* **1** a long usu wooden shaft with a broad blade at one end used for propelling or steering a boat. **2** an oarsman or oarswoman. ✳ **put/stick one's oar in** to interfere. ⟫ **oared** *adj*, **oarless** *adj*. [Old English *ār*]

oar² *verb trans and intrans chiefly literary* to row (a boat).

oarfish *noun* (*pl* **oarfishes** *or collectively* **oarfish**) a very long, thin soft-bodied sea fish that is found in deep waters: *Regalecus glesne*.

oarlock *noun chiefly NAmer* = ROWLOCK.

oarsman *or* **oarswoman** *noun* (*pl* **oarsmen** *or* **oarswomen**) somebody who rows a boat, *esp* in a racing crew. ⟫ **oarsmanship** *noun*.

OAS *abbr* **1** Organisation de l'Armée Secrète, a former organization dedicated to retaining French rule in Algeria. **2** Organization of American States.

oases /oh'ayseez/ *noun* pl of OASIS.

Oasis /oh'aysis/ *noun trademark* a highly water-absorbent foam-based material into which cut flowers and other plants may be stuck for display.

oasis *noun* (*pl* **oases** /-seez/) **1** a fertile area in a desert or other dry region. **2** a place or time affording relaxation or relief. [via late Latin from Greek *oasis*]

oast /ohst/ *noun* a kiln for drying hops or malt. [Old English *āst*]

oast house *noun* a usu circular building housing an oast.

oat /oht/ *noun* **1a** (*usu in pl*) a widely cultivated cereal grass with a loosely branched flower head, producing grain that is used mainly as a livestock feed: *Avena sativa*: *Oats: a grain, which in England is generally given to horses but in Scotland supports the people* — Dr Johnson. **b** (*usu in pl*) any of several related grasses: genus *Avena*. **c** (*in pl*) a crop or field of oats. **2** an oat seed. ✳ **feel one's oats 1** *NAmer, informal* to feel full of energy. **2** *NAmer, informal* to be full of one's own importance. **get one's oats** *Brit, informal* to have sex. **sow one's wild oats** see SOW². ⟫ **oaten** *adj*, **oaty** *adj*. [Old English *āte*]

oatcake *noun* a usu crisp savoury biscuit made of oatmeal.

oat grass *noun* = WILD OAT.

oath /ohth/ *noun* (*pl* **oaths** /ohdhz/) **1a** a solemn calling upon God or a revered person or thing to witness to the true or binding nature of a declaration. **b** something, e.g. a promise, formally confirmed by an oath: *an oath of allegiance*. **c** a form of expression used in taking an oath. **b** any swearword. ✳ **my oath** *Aus* an expression of agreement. **on/under oath** bound by a solemn promise to tell the truth. [Old English *āth*]

oatmeal *noun* **1** meal made from oats, used *esp* in porridge and oatcakes. **2** a greyish beige colour. ➤➤ **oatmeal** *adj*.

OAU *abbr* Organization of African Unity.

OB *abbr* outside broadcast.

ob. *abbr* he or she died. [Latin *obiit*, from *obire* to die]

ob- *or* **oc-** *or* **of-** *or* **op-** *or* **os-** *prefix* forming words, with the meanings: **1** out or forth: *obtrude; offer*. **2** exposed: *obverse*. **3** so as to involve compliance: *obey; observe*. **4** against or in opposition to: *obloquy; opponent*. **5** resisting: *obstinate*. **6** in the way of; hindering: *obstacle; obstruct*. **7** hidden or concealed: *obfuscatory; occult*. **8** inversely: *obovate*. [Middle English via Old French from Latin *ob* in the way of, on account of]

Obad. *abbr* Obadiah (book of the Bible).

obbligato[1] *or* **obligato** /obli'gahtoh/ *adj* said of a musical part or accompaniment: not to be omitted. [Italian *obbligato* obligatory, past part. of *obbligare* to oblige, from Latin *obligare*: see OBLIGE]

obbligato[2] *or* **obligato** *noun* (*pl* **obbligatos** *or* **obligatos** *or* **obbligati** *or* **obliqati** /-tee/) an elaborate, *esp* melodic, accompaniment usu played by a single instrument and not to be omitted from the piece.

obconic /ob'konik/ *adj* shaped like an inverted cone.

obconical /ob'konikl/ *adj* = OBCONIC.

obcordate /ob'kawdayt/ *adj* said of leaves: heart-shaped with the notch at the end furthest from the stalk.

obdurate /'obdyoorət, 'objoorət/ *adj* **1** stubbornly refusing to change opinions, decisions, or courses of action. **2** not inclined to feel sympathy or be swayed by feelings of sympathy; hardhearted: *If you remain callous and obdurate, I shall perish as he did, and you will know why* — W S Gilbert. ➤➤ **obduracy** /-si/ *noun*, **obdurately** *adv*, **obdurateness** *noun*. [Middle English from Latin *obduratus*, past part. of *obdurare* to harden, from OB- + *durare* to harden, from *durus* hard]

OBE *abbr* Officer of the Order of the British Empire.

obeah /'ohbi·ə/ *noun* **1** (*often* **Obeah**) sorcery and magic ritual of a kind practised by some people in the West Indies. **2** a charm used in this form of sorcery and magic. [Twi *ōbayifo*, a creeper used in making charms]

obeahman *noun* (*pl* **obeahmen**) a man who is expert in the practice of obeah.

obedience /ə'beedi·əns, oh-/ *noun* **1a** the act or an instance of obeying. **b** the quality or state of being obedient. **2** a sphere of jurisdiction, *esp* in the Church.

obedient /ə'beedi·ənt, oh-/ *adj* submissive to the will or authority of a superior. ➤➤ **obediently** *adv*. [Middle English via Old French from Latin *oboedient-, oboediens*, present part. of *oboedire*: see OBEY]

obeisance /oh'bay(i)səns/ *noun* **1** a movement or gesture made as a sign of respect or submission. **2** deference or homage. ➤➤ **obeisant** *adj*, **obeisantly** *adv*. [Middle English *obeisaunce* from early French *obeissance*, from *obeissant*, present part. of *obeir*: see OBEY]

obeli /'obilee/ *noun* pl of OBELUS.

obelisk /'obəlisk/ *noun* **1** an upright four-sided usu monolithic pillar that gradually tapers towards the top and ends in a pyramid. **2** = DAGGER (2). [early French *obelisque* via Latin from Greek *obeliskos*, dimin. of *obelos* spit, pointed pillar]

obelus /'obiləs/ *noun* (*pl* **obeli** /-lee/) **1** a symbol (– or ÷) chiefly used in ancient manuscripts to mark a passage of doubtful authenticity. **2** = DAGGER (2). [via late Latin from Greek *obelos* spit, pointed pillar, obelus]

obese /oh'bees/ *adj* very overweight, *esp* unhealthily overweight according to medical criteria concerning the risk to health of excessive weight. ➤➤ **obesity** *noun*. [Latin *obesus*, past part. of *obedere* to eat up, from OB- + *edere* to eat]

obey /ə'bay, oh'bay/ *verb trans* **1** to submit to the commands or authority of (somebody or something): *We were taught to obey our teachers; He had simply obeyed a whim*. **2** to comply with (instructions); to execute (them). ➤ *verb intrans* to act obediently. [Middle English *obeien* via Old French *obeir* from Latin *oboedire*, from OB- + *audire* to hear]

obfuscate /'obfəskayt/ *verb trans* **1** to make (something) obscure or difficult to understand. **2** to confuse or bewilder (somebody). ➤➤ **obfuscation** /-'skaysh(ə)n/ *noun*, **obfuscatory** /-'skayt(ə)ri/ *adj*.

[late Latin *obfuscatus*, past part. of *obfuscare*, from OB- + Latin *fuscus* dark brown]

obi[1] /'ohbi/ *noun* = OBEAH.

obi[2] *noun* a broad sash worn with a Japanese kimono. [Japanese *obi* belt]

obit /'obit, 'ohbit/ *noun informal* an obituary.

obiter dictum /,obitə 'diktəm/ *noun* (*pl* **obiter dicta** /'diktə/) **1** an incidental observation made by a judge which is not material to his or her judgment and therefore not binding. **2** an incidental remark or observation. [late Latin *obiter dictum* something said in passing]

obituary[1] /ə'bityoo(ə)ri/ *noun* (*pl* **obituaries**) a notice of a person's death printed in a newspaper, etc, usu with a short biography: *There's no such thing as bad publicity except your own obituary* — Brendan Behan. ➤➤ **obituarist** *noun*. [medieval Latin *obituarium*, from Latin *obitus* death]

obituary[2] *adj* announcing a death.

obj. *abbr* **1** object. **2** objective.

object[1] /'objikt/ *noun* **1a** something that is capable of being seen and touched. **b** something that is considered or examined: *an object of study*. **c** in philosophy, something external to the thinking or perceiving mind. **2** something or somebody that arouses an emotion or provokes a reaction or response: *an object of derision*. **3** an end towards which effort, action, etc is directed; a goal: *What's the object of the exercise?* **4** a noun or noun equivalent appearing in a prepositional phrase or representing the goal or the result of the action of its verb, e.g. *house* in *we built a house*. **5** in computing, a component of a software system. **6** *dated* somebody or something that is ridiculous, outlandish, or pathetic in appearance: *He looked a real object*. *** no object** not a problem or obstacle; not something that will restrict one's actions: *If money's no object, then buy the house*. ➤➤ **objectless** *adj*. [Middle English, ultimately from Latin *objectum*, neuter of *obicere* to throw in the way, present, hinder, from OB- + *jacere* to throw]

object[2] /əb'jekt/ *verb* ➤ *verb intrans* **1** (*often* + to) to oppose something with words or arguments. **2** (*often* + to) to feel dislike or disapproval: *I object to his condescending manner*. ➤ *verb trans* to state (something) as an objection: *They objected that the statement was misleading*. ➤➤ **objector** *noun*. [Middle English *objecten* from Latin *objectus*, past part. of *obicere*: see OBJECT[1]]

object ball *noun* the ball first struck by the cue ball in snooker, billiards, etc.

object glass *noun* = OBJECTIVE[2] (4).

objectify /əb'jektifie/ *verb trans* (**objectifies**, **objectified**, **objectifying**) **1** to represent (something abstract) as a concrete thing. **2** to reduce (something or somebody) to the status of a mere object. ➤➤ **objectification** /-fi'kaysh(ə)n/ *noun*.

objection /əb'jeksh(ə)n/ *noun* **1** (*often* + to) a reason or argument presented in opposition. **2** (*often* + to) a feeling or statement of dislike, disapproval, or opposition.

objectionable *adj* unpleasant or offensive. ➤➤ **objectionableness** *noun*, **objectionably** *adv*.

objective[1] /əb'jektiv/ *adj* **1a** concerned with or expressing the nature of external reality rather than personal feelings or beliefs. **b** dealing with facts without distortion by personal feelings or prejudices. **2** constituting an object: e.g.: **a** existing independently of the mind. **b** belonging to the external world and observable or verifiable. **3** said of a symptom of disease: perceptible to other people as well as the affected individual. **4** denoting a grammatical case that follows a preposition or a transitive verb. ➤➤ **objectively** *adv*, **objectiveness** *noun*, **objectivity** /objik'tiviti/ *noun*.

objective[2] *noun* **1** something towards which efforts are directed; a goal. **2** something to be attained or achieved by a military operation. **3** in grammar, the objective case or a word in this case. **4** the lens or system of lenses nearest to the object being viewed in a telescope, microscope, etc.

objectivism *noun* **1** emphasis on what is real or objective, rather than on thoughts or feelings, e.g. in art and literature. **2** in philosophy, the theory that objective reality exists and is not simply created by our apparent perception of it. ➤➤ **objectivist** *noun*, **objectivistic** /-'vistik/ *adj*.

object language *noun* in semantics and logic, a language described by means of another language; everyday language as opposed to metalanguage.

object lesson *noun* something that serves as a concrete illustration of a principle.

objet d'art /ˌobzhay 'dah (*French* ɔbʒɛ dar)/ *noun* (*pl* **objets d'art** /ˌobzhay (*French* ɔbʒɛ)/) a usu small article of some artistic value. [French *objet d'art* art object]

objet trouvé /ˈtroohvay (*French* truve)/ *noun* (*pl* **objets trouvé** /ˈtroohvay/) a natural or manufactured object displayed as having artistic value. [French *objet trouvé* found object]

objurgate /ˈobjuhgayt/ *verb trans formal* to denounce or reproach (somebody) harshly; to castigate (them). ➤➤ **objurgation** /-ˈgaysh(ə)n/ *noun*. [Latin *objurgatus*, past part. of *objurgare*, from OB- + *jurgare* to quarrel]

oblast /ˈoblahst/ *noun* (*pl* **oblasts** or **oblasti** /-tee/) an administrative subdivision of a constituent republic of the former Soviet Union. [Russian *oblast*]

oblate[1] /ˈoblayt/ *adj* said of a spheroid: flattened or depressed at the poles: compare PROLATE. ➤➤ **oblateness** *noun*. [OB- + *-latus* as in Latin *prolatus*: see PROLATE]

oblate[2] *noun* a member of any of several Roman Catholic communities whose life is devoted to religious service but who has not taken monastic vows. [medieval Latin *oblatus*, literally 'one offered up', past part. of *offerre*: see OFFER[1]]

oblation /ə'blaysh(ə)n/ *noun* 1 (**Oblation**) the act of offering to God the bread and wine used at Communion. 2 an offering made for religious purposes. ➤➤ **oblational** *adj*, **oblatory** /-təri/ *adj*. [Middle English *oblacioun* via French from late Latin *oblation-*, *oblatio* from Latin *oblatus*, past part. of *offerre*: see OFFER[1]]

obligate[1] /ˈobligayt/ *verb trans* to compel (somebody) legally or morally. ➤➤ **obligator** *noun*. [Latin *obligatus*: see OBLIGATE[2]]

obligate[2] /ˈobligayt, -gət/ *adj* in biology: **a** restricted to one characteristic mode of life: *an obligate parasite*. **b** always happening irrespective of environmental conditions: *obligate parasitism*. ➤➤ **obligately** *adv*. [Middle English in the sense 'bound by law or duty, obliged', from Latin *obligatus*, past part. of *obligare*: see OBLIGE]

obligati /obli'gahtee/ *noun* pl of OBLIGATO.

obligation /obli'gaysh(ə)n/ *noun* 1 something one is bound to do; a duty. 2 indebtedness for a service or favour: *Her kindness has put me under an obligation to her*. 3 something, e.g. a contract or promise, that binds somebody to a course of action. 4 a financial commitment: *The company was unable to meet its financial obligations*.

obligato /obli'gahtoh/ *adj and noun* see OBBLIGATO[1], OBBLIGATO[2].

obligatory /ə'bligət(ə)ri/ *adj* 1 needing to be done; compulsory. 2 binding in law or conscience. 3 relating to or enforcing an obligation: *a writ obligatory*. ➤➤ **obligatorily** *adv*.

oblige /ə'bliej/ *verb trans* 1 to compel (somebody) by force or circumstance. 2a (*usu in passive*) to put (somebody) in one's debt by a favour or service: *We're much obliged to you for all your help*. **b** to do a favour for (somebody): *She obliged the assembled company with a song*. ➤ *verb intrans* to do something as a favour; to be of service: *He's always ready to oblige*. [Middle English *obligen* via Old French from Latin *obligare* to bind to, from OB- + *ligare* to tie]

obligee /obli'jee/ *noun* in law, somebody to whom another person is obligated.

obliging /ə'bliejing/ *adj* eager to help; accommodating. ➤➤ **obligingly** *adv*, **obligingness** *noun*.

obligor /obli'gaw/ *noun* somebody who places himself or herself under a legal obligation.

oblique[1] /ə'bleek/ *adj* **1a** neither perpendicular nor parallel; sloping. **b** said of a cone, cylinder, etc: having the axis not perpendicular to the base. **c** said of a triangle: having no right angle. **d** said of an angle: greater than but not a multiple of 90°. **2** not straightforward or explicit; indirect: *oblique references to financial difficulties*. **3** said of a muscle: lying at an angle to the main axis of the body or of the limb of which it is a part and with one end not attached to bone. ➤➤ **obliquely** *adv*, **obliqueness** *noun*. [Middle English *oblike* from Latin *obliquus*]

oblique[2] *noun* 1 something, e.g. a line, that is oblique. 2 any of several muscles that are oblique, *esp* any of the thin flat muscles forming the middle and outer layers of the side walls of the abdomen. 3 = SOLIDUS (1).

oblique[3] *verb intrans* to move in an oblique direction.

oblique case *noun* any grammatical case other than the nominative or vocative.

obliquity /ə'blikwiti/ *noun* (*pl* **obliquities**) deviation from being parallel or perpendicular, or the amount of such deviation.

obliterate /ə'blitərayt/ *verb trans* **1** to destroy all trace or indication of (something). **2** to make (something) illegible or imperceptible, e.g. by drawing a line through it. **3** to cause (e.g. a blood vessel or other body part) to collapse or disappear. **4** to cancel (a postage stamp). ➤➤ **obliteration** /-'raysh(ə)n/ *noun*, **obliterative** /-tiv/ *adj*, **obliterator** *noun*. [Latin *oblitteratus*, past part. of *oblitterare*, from OB- + *littera* LETTER[1]]

oblivion /ə'blivi·ən/ *noun* **1** the state of forgetting or being oblivious. **2a** the state of being forgotten. **b** the state of no longer existing; extinction. **3** an official disregarding of offences. [Middle English via French from Latin *oblivion-*, *oblivio*, from *oblivisci* to forget]

oblivious /ə'blivi·əs/ *adj* (+ of/to) lacking conscious knowledge; completely unaware. ➤➤ **obliviously** *adv*, **obliviousness** *noun*.

Word history

The original sense of *oblivious*, dating from the 15th cent., was 'forgetful' or 'no longer aware'. Since the mid-19th cent. it has been increasingly used to mean 'unaware' or 'unconscious', without any suggestion of forgetting.

oblong[1] /ˈoblong/ *adj* deviating from a square by being longer, *esp* rectangular with adjacent sides of unequal length. [Middle English from Latin *oblongus*, from OB- + *longus* long]

oblong[2] *noun* something that is oblong in shape; a rectangle.

obloquy /ˈoblokwi/ *noun* (*pl* **obloquies**) **1** strongly worded condemnation. **2** discredit or disgrace. [late Latin *obloquium*, from *obloqui* to speak against, from OB- + *loqui* to speak]

obnoxious /əb'nokshəs/ *adj* highly offensive or repugnant. ➤➤ **obnoxiously** *adv*, **obnoxiousness** *noun*. [Latin *obnoxius*, from OB- + *noxa* harm]

oboe /ˈohboh/ *noun* a woodwind musical instrument with a DOUBLE REED (two flat pieces of cane that vibrate to make the sound when blown across) and a conical tube and a usual range from B flat below middle C upwards for about 2½ octaves. ➤➤ **oboist** *noun*. [Italian *oboe* from French *hautbois*: see HAUTBOY]

oboe d'amore /dah'mawray/ *noun* an oboe with a pear-shaped free end and sombre tone that has a lower range than the true oboe and is used *esp* in baroque music. [Italian *oboe d'amore*, literally 'oboe of love']

obol /ˈobol/ *noun* an ancient Greek coin worth one sixth of a drachma. [via Latin from Greek *obolos*, variant of *obelos* spit, pointed pillar]

obovate /o'bohvayt/ *adj* said of a leaf: ovate with the narrower end nearest the stalk.

obs. *abbr* **1** obsolete. **2** obstetrical. **3** obstetrics.

obscene /əb'seen/ *adj* **1** offending standards of *esp* sexual propriety or decency; *specif* inciting sexual depravity: *The police confiscated various obscene publications*. **2** repugnant, *esp* morally. ➤➤ **obscenely** *adv*. [early French *obscène* from Latin *obscenus*, *obscaenus*]

obscenity /əb'seniti/ *noun* (*pl* **obscenities**) **1** the quality or state of being obscene. **2** an obscene act or utterance.

obscurantism /obskyoo'rantiz(ə)m/ *noun* opposition to the advancement of knowledge or the revealing of facts. ➤➤ **obscurant** /ob'skyooərənt/ *noun*, **obscurantist** *noun and adj*. [French *obscurantisme*, from Latin *obscurant-*, *obscurans*, present part. of *obscurare*: see OBSCURE[1]]

obscure[1] /əb'skyooə/ *adj* **1** hard to understand, *esp* because not clearly expressed; abstruse. **2** not well-known or widely acclaimed: *He's writing a thesis on some obscure poet*. **3** difficult to see or identify; indistinct. **4** dark; dim. **5** denoting the unstressed vowel /ə/. ➤➤ **obscurely** *adv*, **obscureness** *noun*. [Middle English via French from Latin *obscurus* dark, from OB- + *-scurus* covered]

obscure[2] *verb trans* **1** to prevent (something) from being seen, identified, or discovered; to conceal (it). **2** to make (something) indistinct or unintelligible. **3** to make (something) dark or dim. ➤➤ **obscuration** /obskyoo'raysh(ə)n/ *noun*.

obscurity /əb'skyooəriti/ *noun* (*pl* **obscurities**) **1** the quality or state of being obscure. **2** an obscure person or thing.

obsequies /ˈobsikwiz/ *pl noun formal* a funeral ceremony; funeral rites. [Middle English *obsequie* via French from medieval Latin *obsequiae*, alteration of Latin *exsequiae*, *exequiae* funeral rites, by association with *obsequium* dutiful service]

obsequious /əb'seekwi·əs/ *adj* **1** showing a servile willingness to oblige or admire; fawning. **2** *archaic* paying due respect; dutiful. >>> **obsequiously** *adv*, **obsequiousness** *noun*.

Word history

Middle English from Latin *obsequiosus* compliant, ultimately from *obsequi* to comply, from OB- + *sequi* to follow. In its original use (from the 15th cent.) this word was approbatory, meaning 'obedient', 'dutiful': *I see you are obsequious in your love* – Shakespeare. Perhaps reflecting a loss of the ideal of service and obedience, it is now always used in a derogatory sense.

observable¹ /əb'zuhvəbl/ *adj* capable of being observed; discernible. >>> **observably** *adv*.

observable² *noun* something that can be observed.

observance /əb'zuhv(ə)ns/ *noun* **1a** (*usu in pl*) a customary practice, rite, or ceremony. **b** a rule governing members of a religious order. **2** an act of complying with a custom, rule, or law: *It is a custom more honoured in the breach than the observance* — Shakespeare. **3** *archaic* respect; attention.

observant /əb'zuhv(ə)nt/ *adj* **1** quick to notice; alert. **2** paying close attention; watchful. **3** (+ of) careful to observe rules, etc; mindful. >>> **observantly** *adv*.

observation /obzə'vaysh(ə)n/ *noun* **1a** the act or an instance of observing. **b** the faculty of observing. **2** the gathering of information by noting facts or occurrences: *weather observations*. **3** a remark or comment. **4** the condition of somebody or something that is observed: *He was kept under observation at the hospital*. >>> **observational** *adj*, **observationally** *adv*. [early French from Latin *observation-*, *observatio*, from *observare*: see OBSERVE]

observation car *noun NAmer* a railway carriage with large windows and often a partly transparent roof that affords passengers a broad view.

observatory /əb'zuhvət(ə)ri/ *noun* (*pl* **observatories**) a building or institution for the observation and interpretation of astronomical or other natural phenomena. [Latin *observatorium*, from *observare*: see OBSERVE]

observe /əb'zuhv/ *verb trans* **1** to perceive or take note of (something), *esp* by concentrated attention. **2a** to act in due conformity with (e.g. a law): *They were careful to observe local customs*. **b** to celebrate or perform (e.g. a ceremony or festival) according to a prescribed or traditional form. **3** to utter (something) as a comment: *They observed that things weren't what they used to be*. **4** to make a medical or scientific observation on or of (somebody or something). [Middle English *observen* via French from Latin *observare* to guard, watch, observe, from OB- + *servare* to keep]

observer *noun* **1** somebody sent to observe but not participate officially in something, e.g. a conference or congress. **2** somebody who accompanies the pilot of an aircraft to make observations.

obsess /əb'ses/ *verb trans* (*usu in passive*) to preoccupy (somebody) intensely or abnormally. >>> *verb intrans* (*usu* + on/over) to be obsessed by something; to brood over it obsessively. >>> **obsessed** *adj*. [Latin *obsessus*, past part. of *obsidēre* to besiege, beset, from OB- + *sedēre* to sit]

obsession /əb'sesh(ə)n/ *noun* **1** the state of being obsessed; *specif* a persistent disturbing preoccupation with an often unreasonable idea, associated with a psychiatric disorder. **2** loosely, something that preoccupies somebody. >>> **obsessional** *adj*, **obsessionally** *adv*.

obsessive¹ /əb'sesiv/ *adj* **1** relating to or tending to suffer from obsession. **2** excessive to the point of abnormality: *our obsessive need for quick solutions* — Adlai Stevenson. >>> **obsessiveness** *noun*.

obsessive² *noun* somebody who is obsessive.

obsessive-compulsive *adj* denoting a disorder in which a particular type of behaviour is frequently repeated as a means of keeping fears or other unwelcome thoughts at bay.

obsidian /əb'sidi·ən/ *noun* a usu black volcanic glass-like rock that splits to give a convex surface. [Latin *obsidianus*, false manuscript reading for *obsianus lapis* stone of *Obsius*, a Roman traveller named by Pliny as its supposed discoverer]

obsolesce /obsə'les/ *verb intrans* to become obsolete.

obsolescent /obsə'les(ə)nt/ *adj* going out of use; becoming obsolete. >>> **obsolescence** *noun*. [Latin *obsolescent-*, *obsolescens*, present part. of *obsolescere*: see OBSOLETE]

obsolete /'obsəleet, -'leet/ *adj* **1** no longer in use; defunct. **2** no longer in vogue; outmoded. **3** in biology, said e.g. of an organ or

body part: rudimentary compared to that of an earlier or related species; vestigial. >>> **obsoletely** *adv*, **obsoleteness** *noun*. [Latin *obsoletus*, past part. of *obsolescere* to grow old, become disused, from OB- + *solere* to be accustomed]

obstacle /'obstəkl/ *noun* something that hinders or obstructs. [Middle English via French from Latin *obstaculum*, from *obstare* to stand in the way, to stand by, from OB- + *stare* to stand]

obstacle course *noun* **1** an area of land containing obstacles, e.g. walls and ditches, to be surmounted, *esp* by soldiers undergoing training. **2** an activity containing a series of obstacles or difficulties.

obstacle race *noun* a race in which the runners must negotiate contrived obstacles.

obstetric /əb'stetrik, ob-/ *adj* relating to childbirth or obstetrics. >>> **obstetrically** *adv*. [Latin *obstetric-*, *obstetrix* midwife, from *obstare*: see OBSTACLE]

obstetrical /əb'stetrikl, ob-/ *adj* = OBSTETRIC.

obstetrics *pl noun* (*treated as sing. or pl*) a branch of medicine dealing with the care and treatment of women before, during, and after childbirth. >>> **obstetrician** /obstə'trish(ə)n/ *noun*.

obstinate /'obstinət/ *adj* **1** clinging stubbornly to an opinion, decision, or course of action; unyielding. **2** not easily subdued, remedied, or removed: *an obstinate fever*. >>> **obstinacy** /-si/ *noun*, **obstinately** *adv*. [Middle English from Latin *obstinatus*, past part. of *obstinare* to be resolved]

obstreperous /əb'strep(ə)rəs/ *adj* **1** aggressively resistant to control or authority; unruly. **2** noisy and boisterous; clamorous. >>> **obstreperously** *adv*, **obstreperousness** *noun*. [Latin *obstreperus*, from *obstrepere* to clamour against, from OB- + *strepere* to make a noise]

obstruct /əb'strukt/ *verb trans* **1** to block or close (something) up with an obstacle: *The road has been obstructed by a landslide*; *The fence obstructs the view*. **2** to impede the progress of (something or somebody); to hinder (it or them). >>> **obstructive** /-tiv/ *adj*, **obstructively** /-tivli/ *adv*, **obstructiveness** /-tivnis/ *noun*, **obstructor** *noun*. [Latin *obstructus*, past part. of *obstruere*, from OB- + *struere* to build]

obstruction /əb'struksh(ə)n/ *noun* **1** something that obstructs. **2** a condition of being clogged or blocked. **3** an attempted delay of business in a deliberative body, e.g. Parliament. **4** a foul, e.g. in football or hockey, in which a player gets between an opponent and the ball so as to restrict the opponent's playing of the ball.

obstructionism *noun* the deliberate hindering or delaying of business, e.g. the business of a legislative body. >>> **obstructionist** *noun and adj*, **obstructionistic** /-'nistik/ *adj*.

obtain /əb'tayn/ *verb trans* to gain (something) by effort or request; to acquire (it). >>> *verb intrans formal* to be generally accepted or practised; to be in existence: *Fortunately we have a record of many of the customs that obtained at the time*. >>> **obtainability** /-'biliti/ *noun*, **obtainable** *adj*, **obtainer** *noun*, **obtainment** *noun*. [Middle English *obteinen* via French from Latin *obtinēre* to hold on to, possess, from OB- + *tenere* to hold]

obtest /ob'test, əb'test/ *verb trans and intrans archaic* to make an earnest plea to (somebody); to beseech (them). >>> **obtestation** /obte'staysh(ə)n/ *noun*. [early French *obtester* from Latin *obtestari* to call to witness, beseech, from OB- + *testari*: see TESTAMENT]

obtrude /əb'troohd/ *verb intrans* to thrust oneself or itself forward with unwarranted or unwelcome assertiveness. >>> *verb trans* **1** to thrust (something) out. **2** to assert (something) without the right to or without being asked. **3** to push (oneself) forward obtrusively. >>> **obtruder** *noun*, **obtrusion** /-zh(ə)n/ *noun*. [Latin *obtrudere* to thrust at, from OB- + *trudere* to thrust]

obtrusive /əb'troohsiv, -ziv/ *adj* **1** unduly, irritatingly, or disturbingly noticeable. **2** forward in manner; pushy. >>> **obtrusively** *adv*, **obtrusiveness** *noun*. [Latin *obtrusus*, past part. of *obtrudere*: see OBTRUDE]

obtund /ob'tund/ *verb trans* to reduce the sharpness of (feelings, etc); to deaden (them): *obtunded reflexes*. [Middle English *obtunden* from Latin *obtundere*: see OBTUSE]

obtuse /əb'tyoohs/ *adj* **1** lacking sensitivity or mental alertness. **2a** said of an angle: greater than 90° but less than 180°. **b** said of a triangle: having an obtuse angle. **c** not pointed or acute. **3** said of a leaf: rounded at the end furthest from the stalk. >>> **obtusely** *adv*, **obtuseness** *noun*. [Latin *obtusus* blunt, dull, past part. of *obtundere* to beat against, blunt, from OB- + *tundere* to beat]

obverse[1] /'obvuhs/ *adj* **1** facing the observer or opponent. **2** said of a leaf: with the base narrower than the top. **3** constituting a counterpart or complement. ➤➤ **obversely** *adv*. [Latin *obversus*, past part. of *obvertere* to turn towards, from OB- + *vertere* to turn]

obverse[2] *noun* **1a** the side of a coin, medal, or currency note that bears the principal design and lettering and is regarded as the front: compare REVERSE[3]. **b** the more conspicuous of two possible sides or aspects. **2a** a counterpart to a fact or truth. **b** in logic, a proposition that can be directly inferred from another by denying the opposite of it: *'All dogs are animals' and 'No dogs are not animals' are obverses.*

obvert /ob'vuht/ *verb trans* **1** to turn (something) so that it faces the other way and the other side is seen. **2** in logic, to produce the obverse of (a proposition). [Latin *obvertere* to turn towards: see OBVERSE[1]]

obviate /'obviayt/ *verb trans* **1** to anticipate and dispose of (a difficulty, etc) in advance: *Their objections are thus obviated.* **2** to make (something) unnecessary. ➤➤ **obviation** /-'aysh(ə)n/ *noun*. [late Latin *obviatus*, past part. of *obviare* to meet, withstand, from OB- + *via* way]

obvious /'obvi·əs/ *adj* **1** evident to the senses or understanding; clear. **2** lacking subtlety; unsubtle: *The symbolism of the novel was rather obvious.* ➤➤ **obviously** *adv*, **obviousness** *noun*. [Latin *obvius*, from *obviam* in the way, from OB- + *via* way]

OC *abbr* Brit Officer Commanding.

o/c *abbr* overcharge.

oc- *prefix* see OB-.

ocarina /okə'reenə/ *noun* a simple wind instrument with an elongated egg-shaped body, a projecting mouthpiece, and usu eight finger holes and two thumb holes. [Italian *ocarina* from *oca* goose; from its shape]

Occam's razor *or* **Ockham's razor** /'okəmz/ *noun* a scientific principle that explanations should include as little reference as possible to things that are not known for certain. [named after William of *Occam* (or *Ockham*) d.1349, English scholastic philosopher]

occas. *abbr* occasionally.

occasion[1] /ə'kayzh(ə)n/ *noun* **1** a time at which something occurs: *I've caught her out in a lie on several occasions.* **2** a suitable opportunity or circumstance: *This is hardly the occasion for laughter.* **3** *formal* a state of affairs that provides a reason or grounds: *You have no occasion to be annoyed.* **4** *formal* the immediate or incidental cause: *His insulting remark was the occasion of a bitter quarrel.* **5** a special event or ceremony: *The wedding was quite an occasion.* ✳ **on occasion** from time to time. **rise to the occasion** to perform well when a situation demands it. **take occasion** to make use of an opportunity when it arises. [Middle English via French from Latin *occasion-*, *occasio*, from *occidere* to fall, fall down, happen, from OC- + *cadere* to fall]

occasion[2] *verb trans* (**occasioned, occasioning**) *formal* to bring (something) about; to cause (it).

occasional *adj* **1** occurring at irregular or infrequent intervals. **2** acting in a specified capacity from time to time: *an occasional golfer.* **3** designed for use as the occasion demands: *an occasional table.* **4** composed for a particular occasion: *occasional verse.*

occasionally *adv* at irregular or infrequent intervals; now and again.

Occident /'oksid(ə)nt/ *noun* (**the Occident**) *formal or literary* the countries of the West, as distinct from the Orient. [Middle English via French from Latin *occident-*, *occidens*, present part. of *occidere* (see OCCASION[1]) in the sense 'to set' (of the sun)]

Occidental /oksi'dentl/ *noun* a member of any of the indigenous peoples of the Occident.

occidental *or* **Occidental** *adj* of or situated in the Occident; western. ➤➤ **occidentalism** *noun*, **occidentally** *adv*.

occidentalize *or* **occidentalise** /oksi'dentl·iez/ *verb intrans* to become occidental, e.g. in culture. ➤ *verb trans* to make (somebody or something) occidental.

occipita /ok'sipitə/ *noun* pl of OCCIPUT.

occipital /ok'sipitl/ *adj* relating to or located in the back part of the head or skull. ➤➤ **occipitally** *adv*. [medieval Latin *occipitalis*, from Latin *occipit-*, *occiput*: see OCCIPUT]

occipital lobe *noun* the back lobe of each CEREBRAL HEMISPHERE (front portion of the brain) that contains the areas that interpret visual impulses.

occiput /'oksipət/ *noun* (*pl* **occiputs** *or* **occipita** /ok'sipitə/) the back part of the head. [Latin *occipit-*, *occiput*, from OC- + *capit-*, *caput* head]

Occitan /'ositən/ *noun* the Romance language of the people of Languedoc in southern France, including medieval literary Provençal: compare PROVENÇAL. ➤➤ **Occitan** *adj*.

occlude /ə'kloohd/ *verb trans* **1** to stop up (a passage or opening); to block (it). **2** to obstruct or hinder (something). **3** to take up and hold (e.g. a gas) by absorption or adsorption. ➤ *verb intrans* **1** said of teeth: to fit together with the cusps of the opposing teeth when the mouth is closed. **2** to become occluded. ➤➤ **occludent** *adj*, **occlusive** /-siv/ *adj*. [Latin *occludere*, from OC- + *claudere* to shut, close]

occluded front *noun* = OCCLUSION (3).

occlusion /ə'kloohzh(ə)n/ *noun* **1** the act or an instance of occluding or being occluded. **2** the complete obstruction of the breath passage in the articulation of a speech sound. **3** a weather front formed by a cold front overtaking a warm front and lifting the warm air above the earth's surface. [from Latin *occlusus*, past part. of *occludere*: see OCCLUDE]

occult[1] /o'kult/ *noun* (**the occult**) matters regarded as involving the action or influence of supernatural agencies or some secret knowledge of them.

occult[2] /o'kult, 'okult/ *adj* **1** involving supernatural powers. **2** known only to the initiated few; esoteric. **3** not easily understood; abstruse. **4** in medicine, not present, manifest, or detectable by the unaided eye: *occult blood loss.* ➤➤ **occultly** *adv*. [Latin *occultus*, past part. of *occulere* to cover up, from OC- + *celare* to hide]

occult[3] /o'kult/ *verb trans* **1** to hide (something) from view, *esp* by putting something else in front of it. **2** to conceal (a celestial body) by occultation. ➤ *verb intrans* to become concealed by occultation. [Latin *occultare*, from *occultus*: see OCCULT[2]]

occultation /okul'taysh(ə)n/ *noun* the eclipsing of one celestial body by another, usu much larger, one: compare ECLIPSE[1], TRANSIT[1].

occultism /'okultiz(ə)m/ *noun* belief in or study of the action or influence of supernatural powers. ➤➤ **occultist** *noun*.

occupancy /'okyoopənsi/ *noun* (*pl* **occupancies**) **1** the act or an instance of taking and holding possession of land, a property, etc. **2** the act or an instance of becoming an occupant, or the state of being an occupant. **3** the state of being occupied. **4** a period of occupation. **5** the proportion of a building, e.g. a hotel, that is occupied.

occupant /'okyoopənt/ *noun* **1** somebody who occupies a particular building, *esp* a resident. **2** somebody who takes possession of vacant land in order to become its owner. **3** somebody who occupies a particular position.

occupation /okyoo'paysh(ə)n/ *noun* **1a** an activity by which one earns a living. **b** an activity in which one engages: *'I must admit I smoke.' 'I am glad to hear it. A man should always have an occupation of some kind.'* — Oscar Wilde. **2a** the occupancy of land. **b** tenure. **3a** the act of taking possession or the holding and control of a place or area, *esp* by a foreign military force. **b** the period of time for which a place or area is occupied. [Middle English *occupacioun* via French from Latin *occupation-*, *occupatio*, from *occupare*: see OCCUPY]

occupational *adj* of or resulting from a particular occupation: *occupational hazards.* ➤➤ **occupationally** *adv*.

occupational psychology *noun* the branch of psychology that deals with behaviour in the workplace.

occupational therapy *noun* creative activity used as therapy for promoting recovery or rehabilitation. ➤➤ **occupational therapist** *noun*.

occupy /'okyoopie/ *verb trans* (**occupies, occupied, occupying**) **1** to engage the attention or energies of (somebody). **2** to fill up (a portion of space or time). **3** to take or maintain possession of (e.g. land or a building). **4** to reside in or use (a building) as an owner or tenant. **5** to hold (a particular job or position). ➤➤ **occupier** *noun*. [Middle English *occupien* to take possession of, occupy, via French from Latin *occupare* to seize, take over, from OC- + *capere* to take]

occur /ə'kuh/ *verb intrans* (**occurred, occurring**) **1** to become the case; to happen. **2** to be found; to exist. **3** (+ to) to come to mind: *It occurs to me that I haven't posted the letter.* [Latin *occurrere* to run into, to present itself, from OC- + *currere* to run]

occurrence /ə'kurəns/ *noun* **1** something that takes place; an event. **2** the act or an instance of occurring.

ocean /'ohsh(ə)n/ *noun* **1a** any or all of the large expanses of salt water that together cover nearly ¾ of the earth's surface: *How inappropriate to call this planet Earth when it is clearly Ocean* — Arthur C Clarke. **b** *literary* the sea. **2** *informal* (*in pl*) a huge amount: *No need to hurry, we've got oceans of time.* [Middle English *occean* via Latin from Greek *Ōkeanos* a river once believed to encircle the earth, at that time thought to consist of a single land mass]

oceanarium /ohshə'neəri·əm/ *noun* (*pl* **oceanariums** *or* **oceanaria** /-ri·ə/) a large marine aquarium.

oceangoing *adj* said of a ship: designed for travel on the ocean.

Oceanian /ohsi'ahni·ən, ohshi-/ *noun* a native or inhabitant of Oceania, islands in the central and southern Pacific Ocean including Melanesia, Micronesia, and Polynesia, and often also taken to include New Zealand and sometimes Australia and New Guinea. ➤➤ **Oceanian** *adj*.

oceanic /ohshi'anik/ *adj* of, produced by, or occurring in the ocean, *esp* the open sea.

oceanography /ohshə'nogrəfi/ *noun* the science dealing with oceans and their form, biology, and resources. ➤➤ **oceanographer** *noun*, **oceanographic** /-'grafik/ *adj*, **oceanographical** /-'grafikl/ *adj*, **oceanographically** /-'grafikli/ *adv*.

oceanology /ohshə'noləji/ *noun* oceanography, *esp* the applied technological aspects of oceanography. ➤➤ **oceanological** /-'lojikl/ *adj*, **oceanologist** *noun*.

ocellate /'osilayt, oh'selayt, -lət/ *adj* = OCELLATED.

ocellated /'osilaytid, oh'selaytid/ *adj* **1** having ocelli. **2** resembling an ocellus. ➤➤ **ocellation** /-'laysh(ə)n/ *noun*.

ocellus /oh'seləs, o-/ *noun* (*pl* **ocelli** /-lie/) **1** a minute simple eye or eyespot of an invertebrate animal, e.g. an insect. **2** a spot of colour encircled by a band of another colour, e.g. on a peacock's tail feather or a butterfly's wing. ➤➤ **ocellar** *adj*. [Latin *ocellus*, dimin. of *oculus* eye]

ocelot /'osəlot/ *noun* a medium-sized wildcat with a yellow or greyish coat dotted and striped with black, native to C and S America: *Felis pardalis.* [French *ocelot* from Nahuatl *ocelotl* jaguar]

och /okh/ *interj* Scot, Irish an expression of surprise, impatience, or regret. [Scottish and Irish Gaelic]

oche /'oki/ *noun* the line behind which a player must stand when throwing darts at a dartboard. [Middle English *oche* groove, notch, from early French *oche*]

ocher /'ohkə/ *noun* NAmer see OCHRE.

ochone /ə'khohn/ *interj* Scot, Irish an expression of sorrow or regret used chiefly by Gaelic speakers. [Scottish Gaelic *ochòin*, Irish Gaelic *ochón*]

ochre (*NAmer* **ocher**) /'ohkə/ *noun* **1** a brownish yellow colour. **2** an earthy usu red or yellow pigment made from impure iron ore. ➤➤ **ochreous** /'ohkri·əs/ *adj*. [Middle English *oker* via French and Latin from Greek *ōchra*, fem of *ōchros* yellow]

-ock *suffix* forming nouns, denoting: a small or young kind of: *hillock; bullock.* [Old English *-oc*]

ocker /'okə/ *or* **Ocker** *noun* Aus, NZ, informal an Australian, *esp* one regarded as uncultivated or loutish. [nickname for *Oscar*, used for a character in an Australian television series (1965–68)]

Ockham's razor /'okəmz/ *noun* see OCCAM'S RAZOR.

o'clock /ə'klok/ *adv* **1** used in specifying the exact hour when telling the time. **2** used for indicating position or direction as if on a clock dial: *Aircraft approaching at six o'clock.* [contraction of *of the clock*]

OCR *abbr* **1** optical character reader. **2** optical character recognition.

Oct. *abbr* October.

oct. *abbr* octavo.

octa- *or* **octo-** *or* **oct-** *comb. form* forming words, with the meanings: **1** eight: *octoroon.* **2** containing eight atoms, groups, or chemical equivalents in the molecular structure: *octane.* [Greek *okta-, oktō-, okt-*, from *okto* eight]

octad /'oktad/ *noun* a group or series of eight. [Greek *oktad-, oktas* number 8, body of 8 men, from *oktō* eight]

octagon /'oktəgon, -gən/ *noun* a polygon with eight angles and eight sides. ➤➤ **octagonal** /ok'tagənl/ *adj*, **octagonally** /ok'tagənəli/ *adv*. [via Latin from Greek *oktagōnon*, from *okta-* OCTA- + *-gōnon* -GON]

octahedra /oktə'heedrə/ *noun* pl of OCTAHEDRON.

octahedral /oktə'heedrəl/ *adj* **1** having eight plane faces. **2** of or formed in octahedrons. ➤➤ **octahedrally** *adv*.

octahedron /oktə'heedrən/ *noun* (*pl* **octahedrons** *or* **octahedra** /-drə/) a polyhedron with eight faces.

octal /'okt(ə)l/ *adj* relating to a number system having eight as its base.

octameter /ok'tamitə/ *noun* a line of verse consisting of eight metrical feet.

octane /'oktayn/ *noun* a colourless liquid that is a member of the alkane series of organic chemical compounds that occurs *esp* in petroleum: formula C_8H_{18}.

octane number *noun* a number that is used to measure or indicate the antiknock properties of a liquid motor fuel and that increases as the probability of knocking decreases: compare CETANE NUMBER.

octane rating *noun* = OCTANE NUMBER.

octant /'oktənt/ *noun* **1** any of the eight parts into which a space is divided by three coordinate planes. **2** an eighth part of a circle. **3a** the position or aspect of a celestial body that lies at an angle of 45° to another celestial body. **b** an instrument used formerly for measuring altitudes of a celestial body from a ship or aircraft. [Latin *octant-, octans* eighth of a circle, from *octo* eight]

octavalent /oktə'vaylənt/ *adj* in chemistry, having a valency of eight.

octave /'oktiv, 'oktayv/ *noun* **1a** a musical interval of eight notes on the diatonic scale. **b** the whole series of notes or piano, organ, etc keys within this interval that form the unit of the modern diatonic scale. **c** a note separated from a lower note by this interval. **2** a group of eight lines of verse, *esp* the first eight of a sonnet. **3** an eight-day period of religious observances beginning with a festival day, or the final day of this period. **4** in fencing, the last of eight parrying positions. **5** any group of eight. [Middle English from Latin *octava*, fem of *octavus* eighth, from *octo* eight]

octavo /ok'tayvoh/ *noun* (*pl* **octavos**) **1** a size of book page that is created when a standard sheet is folded into 8 leaves or 16 pages, approximately 16 × 23cm or 6 × 9in. **2** a book with this size of page. [Latin *octavo*, ablative of *octavus*: see OCTAVE]

octennial /ok'teni·əl/ *adj* **1** taking place every eight years. **2** lasting for a period of eight years. [Latin *octennium* period of eight years, from OCTA- + *annus* year]

octet /ok'tet/ *noun* **1** a group of eight instruments, voices, or performers. **2** a musical composition for an octet. **3** = OCTAVE (2). **4** in chemistry, the stable arrangement of eight electrons in the outer shell of an atom of a noble gas.

octillion /ok'tilyən/ *noun* **1** Brit the number one followed by 48 zeros (10^{48}). **2** NAmer the number one followed by 27 zeros (10^{27}). [Latin *octo* eight + *-illion* as in MILLION]

octo- *comb. form* see OCTA-.

October /ok'tohbə/ *noun* the tenth month of the year. [Middle English *Octobre* via French from Latin *October* eighth month of the Roman calendar, from *octo* eight: see SEPTEMBER]

octocentenary /,oktohsen'teenəri, -'tenəri/ *noun* (*pl* **octocentenaries**) an 800th anniversary.

octodecimo /oktoh'desimoh/ *noun* **1** a size of book page that is created when a standard sheet is folded into 16 leaves or 32 pages, approximately 10 x 16cm or 4 x 4¼in. **2** a book with this size of page. [Latin *octodecimo*, ablative of *octodecimus* eighteenth, from *octodecim* eighteen, from OCTO- + *decem* ten]

octogenarian¹ /,oktojə'neəri·ən/ *noun* a person between 80 and 89 years old. [Latin *octogenarius* containing eighty, ultimately from *octoginta* eighty]

octogenarian² *adj* aged between 80 and 89 years.

octopi /'oktəpie/ *noun* pl of OCTOPUS.

octopod¹ /'oktəpod/ *noun* any of an order of cephalopod molluscs with eight arms that includes the octopuses: order Octopoda. ➤➤ **octopodan** /ok'topədən, -'pohdən/ *adj*, **octopodous** /ok'topədəs/ *adj*. [Greek *oktōpod-, oktōpous* scorpion, from *oktō* OCTO- + *pod-, pous* foot]

octopod² *adj* of or belonging to the octopods.

octopus /'oktəpəs/ *noun* (*pl* **octopuses** *or* **octopi** /-pie/) **1** any of several genera of molluscs that are related to the squids and cuttle-fishes and have eight muscular arms equipped with two rows of suckers: genus *Octopus* and other genera. **2** something that has many radiating branches or a far-reaching controlling influence: *the family – that dear octopus from whose tentacles we never quite escape* — Dodie Smith. [Greek *oktōpous*: see OCTOPOD¹]

octoroon /oktə'roohn/ *noun archaic* a person of one eighth black ancestry. [OCTO- + *-roon* as in QUADROON]

octosyllable /'oktohsiləbl/ *noun* a word or line of eight syllables. **➤➤ octosyllabic** /-'labik/ *adj*.

octroi /'oktrwah/ *noun* in France and some other European countries, a tax levied on goods brought into some towns. [French *octroi*, literally 'concession', from *octroyer* to grant, from medieval Latin *auctorizare* to authorize, from *auctor*: see AUTHOR¹]

octuple¹ /'oktoohp(ə)l, ok'toohp(ə)l/ *adj* eight times as many or as much. [French *octuple* from Latin *octuplus*, from *octo* eight]

octuple² /ok'toohp(ə)l/ *verb trans* to increase or multiply (something) by eight times. **➤** *verb intrans* to increase by eight times.

octuple³ *noun* a quantity eight times larger than another.

ocul- *or* **oculo-** *comb. form* forming nouns, denoting: eye, or eye and something: *oculist*. [Latin *ocul-*, from *oculus* eye]

ocular¹ /'okyoolə/ *adj* **1** performed or perceived with the eyes. **2** of the eye: *ocular muscles*. [late Latin *ocularis* of eyes, from Latin *oculus* eye]

ocular² *noun* an eyepiece.

ocularist *noun* somebody who makes artificial eyes.

oculist /'okyoolist/ *noun* an ophthalmologist or optician. [French *oculiste* from Latin *oculus* eye]

oculo- *comb. form* see OCUL-.

OD¹ *noun* an overdose of a drug. [short for OVERDOSE¹]

OD² *verb intrans* (**OD's, OD'd, OD'ing**) to take an overdose of a drug.

OD³ *abbr* **1** officer of the day. **2** on demand. **3** ordnance datum. **4** outer diameter. **5** overdraft. **6** overdrawn.

od /od, ohd/ *noun* a mysterious force formerly believed to pervade the universe. [German *Od*, coined by Baron Karl von Reichenbach d.1869, German natural philosopher]

odalisque /'ohdəlisk/ *noun* a female slave or concubine in a harem. [French *odalisque* from Turkish *odal k*, from *oda* chamber + *lik* function]

odd /od/ *adj* **1** different from the usual or conventional; strange. **2a** left over when others are paired or grouped. **b** not matching: *odd socks*. **3a** said of a number: not divisible by two without leaving a remainder. **b** marked by an odd number: *The tables are all on odd pages*. **4a** not regular or planned; casual or occasional; spare: *at odd moments*. **b** scattered or remote: *You can still find them in odd corners of the world*. **5** (*in combination*) somewhat more than the specified number: *300-odd pages*. **➤➤ oddly** *adv*, **oddness** *noun*. [Middle English *odde* from Old Norse *oddi* point of land, triangle, odd number]

oddball¹ *noun informal* an eccentric or peculiar person.

oddball² *adj* eccentric; peculiar; odd.

Oddfellow *noun* a member of the Independent Order of Oddfellows, an English charitable society with secret traditions reminiscent of the Freemasons.

oddity /'oditi/ *noun* (*pl* **oddities**) **1** an odd person, thing, event, or trait. **2** oddness or strangeness.

odd jobs *pl noun* various nonspecialized household jobs, *esp* miscellaneous repairs or manual work. **➤➤ odd-jobber** *noun*, **odd-job man** *noun*.

odd man out *noun* somebody or something that differs in some respect from all the others in a set or group.

oddment *noun* **1** something left over; a remnant. **2** (*in pl*) miscellaneous things; odds and ends.

odds *pl noun* **1** the probability, expressed as a ratio, that one thing will rather happen than another: *The odds are that he will be dismissed*; *The odds are 50 to one against the newcomer*. **2** the ratio between the amount to be paid off for a winning bet and the amount of the bet: *odds of three to one*. **3a** an amount by which one thing exceeds or falls short of another in terms of strength, support, etc: *They won the election against considerable odds*. **b** a difference in

terms of advantage or disadvantage: *It makes no odds*. **✳ at odds** in disagreement or at variance. **give/lay odds** to offer a bet in which the odds are favourable to the other person. **over the odds** *Brit* more than is right, fair, or acceptable. **take odds 1** to offer a bet in which the odds are favourable to oneself. **2** to accept a bet with odds favourable to the other person.

odds and ends *pl noun* miscellaneous items or remnants.

odds-on *adj* **1** viewed as having a better than even chance to win: *the odds-on favourite*. **2** not involving much risk and therefore likely to succeed: *It was odds-on that the game would be called off*.

odd trick *noun* each trick in excess of six won by the declarer's side at bridge.

ode /ohd/ *noun* a LYRIC² poem (expressing intense personal emotion), often addressed to a particular person or thing, marked by a usu exalted tone and varying metre and length of line. [early French *ode* via late Latin from Greek *ōidē* song]

-ode¹ *comb. form* forming nouns, denoting: **1** way or path: *electrode*. **2** electrode: *diode*. [Greek *-odos*, from *hodos* road, way]

-ode² *comb. form* forming nouns and adjectives, denoting: resembling, or something resembling: *geode*.

odeum /'oh·dee·əm, 'ohdi·əm/ *or* **odeon** /-ən/ *noun* (*pl* **odea** /'oh·dee·ə, 'ohdi·ə/) a small roofed theatre in ancient Greece and Rome. [via Latin from Greek *ōideion*, from *ōidē* song]

odious /'ohdi·əs/ *adj* arousing hatred or revulsion: *an odious crime*. **➤➤ odiously** *adv*, **odiousness** *noun*. [Middle English via French from Latin *odiosus*, from *odium*: see ODIUM]

odium /'ohdi·əm/ *noun formal* general condemnation or disgrace associated with a despicable act: *Few [slave-owners] are willing to incur the odium attaching to the reputation of being a cruel master* — Frederick Douglass. [Latin *odium* hatred, from *odisse* to hate]

odometer /oh'domitə/ *noun* an instrument for measuring the distance travelled, e.g. by a vehicle. [French *odomètre* from Greek *hodometron*, from *hodos* way, road + *metron* measure]

odont- *or* **odonto-** *comb. form* forming words, denoting: tooth: *odontology*. [French *odont-* from Greek *odont-, odous* tooth]

-odont *comb. form* forming adjectives and nouns, with the meaning: having teeth, or something that has teeth, of the nature specified: *glyptodont*. [Greek *odont-, odous* tooth]

odonto- *comb. form* see ODONT-.

odontoglossum /oh,dontə'glosəm/ *noun* (*pl* **odontoglossums**) an epiphytic (growing on other plants; see EPIPHYTE) tropical American orchid with showy flowers: genus *Odontoglossum*. [Latin ODONTO- + Greek *glōssa* tongue]

odontoid process /oh'dontoyd/ *noun* a toothlike projection from the front end of the second vertebra in the neck on which the first vertebra and the head rotate.

odontology /ohdon'toləji, od-/ *noun* the science dealing with the structure, development, and diseases of the teeth. **➤➤ odontological** /-'lojikl/ *adj*, **odontologist** *noun*.

odor /'ohdə/ *noun NAmer* see ODOUR.

odoriferous /ohdə'rif(ə)rəs/ *adj* giving off an odour, *esp* a pleasant odour. **➤➤ odoriferously** *adv*.

odorous /'ohdərəs/ *adj* having a characteristic scent or odour. **➤➤ odorously** *adv*.

odour (*NAmer* **odor**) /'ohdə/ *noun* **1** the quality of something that stimulates the sense of smell; a scent. **2** *chiefly derog* a characteristic quality; a savour: *an odour of sanctity*. **3** *formal* repute or favour: *They were in bad odour for a while after the scandal*. **➤➤ odourless** *adj*. [Middle English *odour* via French from Latin *odor* smell, scent]

odyssey /'odəsi/ *noun* (*pl* **odysseys**) a long and wandering journey or quest. [named after the *Odyssey*, epic poem by Homer recounting the long wanderings of Odysseus, king of Ithaca in Greek mythology]

OE *abbr* **1** Old English. **2** Old Etonian.

Oe *abbr* oersted.

OECD *abbr* Organization for Economic Cooperation and Development.

oecumenical /ekyoo'menikl, ee-/ *adj* see ECUMENICAL.

OED *abbr* Oxford English Dictionary.

oedema (*NAmer* **edema**) /i'deemə/ *noun* abnormal swelling caused by an accumulation of serum-derived liquid in the spaces between tissue cells. [Greek *oidēma* swelling, from *oidein* to swell]

Oedipus complex /'eedipəs, 'ed-/ *noun* in Freudian psychology, an adult personality disorder resulting from the sexual attraction developed by a child towards the parent of the opposite sex with accompanying jealousy of the parent of the same sex: compare ELECTRA COMPLEX. ⏵⏵ **Oedipal** *adj.* [named after *Oedipus*, figure in Greek mythology who unknowingly killed his father and married his mother]

oeillade /uh'yahd (*French* œjad)/ *noun literary* a glance, *esp* an amorous or provocative one: *Page's wife … examined my parts with most judicious oeillades* — Shakespeare. [French *oeillade*, from *oeil* eye, from Latin *oculus*]

OEM *abbr* own or original equipment manufacturer, a company that builds computers to individual customers' specifications using components manufactured by others.

oenology (*NAmer* **enology**) /ee'nolaji/ *noun* the science of wine and winemaking. ⏵⏵ **oenologist** *noun*. [Greek *oinos* wine + -LOGY]

oenophile (*NAmer* **enophile**) /'eenəfiel/ *noun* a wine connoisseur. [Greek *oinos* wine + -PHILE]

o'er /aw, 'oh·ə/ *adv and prep literary* over.

oersted /'uhstəd/ *noun* a unit of magnetic field strength in the centimetre-gram-second system, equal to 79.58 amperes per metre. [named after Hans Christian *Oersted* d.1851, Danish physicist who discovered the magnetic effect of an electric current]

oesophago- or **oesophago-** (*NAmer* **esophag-** or **esophago-**) *comb. form* forming words, with the meaning: oesophagus, or oesophagus and: *oesophageal*.

oesophagi /ee'sofəgie/ *noun* pl of OESOPHAGUS.

oesophago- *comb. form* see OESOPHAG-.

oesophagus /ee'sofəgəs/ *noun* (*pl* **oesophagi** /-gie/) the muscular tube leading from the back of the mouth to the stomach; the gullet. ⏵⏵ **oesophageal** /-'jee·əl/ *adj*. [Middle English *ysophagus* from Greek *oisophagos*, from *oisein* to be going to carry + *phagein* to eat]

oestr- or **oestro-** (*NAmer* **estr-** or **estro-**) *comb. form* forming words, denoting: oestrus: *oestrogen*.

oestradiol (*NAmer* **estradiol**) /eestrə'dieol, es-/ *noun* the major oestrogenic steroid sex hormone in human females, used in treating abnormal absence of menstruation and menopausal symptoms. [*oestrin*, an oestrogenic hormone + DI-[1] + -OL[1]]

oestriol (*NAmer* **estriol**) /'eestriol, 'es-/ *noun* an oestrogenic steroid hormone used *esp* in the treatment of menopausal symptoms. [*oestrin*, an oestrogenic hormone + TRI- + -OL[1]]

oestro- *comb. form* see OESTR-.

oestrogen (*NAmer* **estrogen**) /'eestrəj(ə)n, 'es-/ *noun* any of several steroid hormones that stimulate the development of secondary sex characteristics in female vertebrates and promote oestrus in lower mammals. ⏵⏵ **oestrogenic** /-'jenik/ *adj*, **oestrogenically** /-'jenikli/ *adv*. [OESTRUS + -GEN]

oestrone (*NAmer* **estrone**) /'eestrohn, 'estrohn/ *noun* an oestrogen that is a derivative of oestradiol and has similar actions and uses. [*oestrin*, an oestrogenic hormone + -ONE]

oestrus (*NAmer* **estrus**) /'eestrəs, 'estrəs/ *noun* a regularly recurrent state of sexual excitability in the female of most lower mammals when she will copulate with the male; heat. ⏵⏵ **oestral** *adj*, **oestrous** /'eestrəs, 'estrəs/ *adj*. [Latin *oestrus* gadfly, frenzy, from Greek *oistros*]

oestrus cycle *noun* the series of changes in a female mammal occurring from one period of oestrus to the next.

oeuvre /'uhvrə (*French* œ:vr)/ *noun* (*pl* **oeuvres** /'uhvrə (*French* œ:vr)/) the total work produced by a writer, artist, or composer. [French *œuvre* work, from Latin *opera*]

of /əv; *strong* ov/ *prep* **1** used to indicate origin or derivation: *a man of noble birth*; *She died of pneumonia*; *the plays of Shaw*. **2a** composed or made from: *a crown of gold*; *an inch of rain*. **b** containing: *a cup of water*. **3** from among: *most of the army*; *one of his last poems*. **4a** belonging or related to: *the leg of the chair*; *a friend of John's*. **b** possessing or characterized by: *a man of courage*; *an area of hills*. **c** connected with: *the king of England*; *the time of arrival*. **5a** in respect to: *slow of speech*; *We have high hopes of him*. **b** directed towards: *love of nature*. **6** used to show separation or removal: *She gave of her time*; *They cheated him of his rights*. **7** used to indicate apposition: *the city of Rome*; *the art of painting*. **8** *NAmer* to a specified hour; to: *a quarter of four*. **9** *informal* in or during: *We go there of an evening*. ＊ **of a** used to suggest or describe a resemblance; -like: *that palace of a house*; *a big brute of a dog*. [Old English *of*, adv and prep]

of- *prefix* see OB-.

ofay /'ohfay, oh'fay/ *noun slang, derog* used by African-Americans: a white person. [origin unknown]

of course *adv* **1** as might be expected; naturally: *Of course I shall come*. **2** used in reply to express agreement or permission. **3** used to introduce a well-known fact or to invite agreement: *Words are, of course, the most powerful drug used by mankind* — Kipling.

off[1] /of/ *adv* **1a** from a place or position: *She marched off*; *Try to frighten them off*. **b** away from land: *The ship stood off to sea*. **2a** away in space or ahead in time: *She stood ten paces off*; *Christmas is a week off*. **b** from a course; aside: *They turned off into a lay-by*. **c** into sleep or unconsciousness: *I must have dozed off*. **3a** so as not to be in contact: *He took his coat off*. **b** so as not to be attached: *The handle came off*. **c** so as to be divided: *a surface marked off into squares*; *a corner screened off*. **4a** to or in a state of discontinuance or suspension: *Shut off the engine*; *The game was rained off*; *The radio is off*. **b** so as to be completely finished or no longer existent: *One by one they killed them off*; *I'm going upstairs to sleep it off*. **c** in or into a decayed state: *The cream's gone off*. **5** away from an activity or function: *I never take time off for lunch*. **6** offstage: *Noises off*. **7** *slang* to a point of orgasm or ejaculation: *She brought him off*. ＊ **off with** take off; cut off: *Off with his head!* [Old English *of*: see OF]

off[2] *prep* **1a** used to indicate physical separation or distance from: *Take it off the table*; *He jumped off his bike*. **b** lying or turning aside from: *I got it in a shop just off the high street*. **c** away from: *I'm taking a week off work*; *off-centre*. **2** used to indicate the source from which something derives or is obtained: *We dined off oysters*; *She bought it off a friend*. **3a** not occupied in: *When are you off duty?* **b** no longer interested in or using: *He's off drugs*; *I've gone off science fiction*. **c** below the usual standard or level of: *He was definitely off his game*.

off[3] *adj* **1a** started on the way: *They went off on a spree*. **b** not taking place or staying in effect; cancelled: *The match is off*. **c** said of a dish on a menu: no longer being served. **2a** not up to standard: *I'm having an off day*. **b** not busy; slack: *off season*. **3** no longer fresh and beginning to decay: *This fish is off*. **4** provided: *She's pretty well off*; *How are you off for socks?* **5a** in, on, or towards the side of a cricket field that the batsman's or batswoman's body faces when they are receiving. **b** said of a ball bowled in cricket: moving or tending to move in the direction of the leg side: *an off break*. **6a** being the right-hand one of a pair: *the off wheel of a cart*. **b** situated to one side; adjoining: *We had a bedroom with a dressing room off*. **7** *informal* said of behaviour: not what one has a right to expect, *esp* rather unkind or dishonest: *It was a bit off to leave without a word of thanks!*

off[4] *verb intrans* to go away; to leave. ⏵ *verb trans NAmer, slang* to kill (somebody).

off[5] *noun* **1** the start or outset: *ready for the off*. **2** a signal to start. **3** in cricket, = OFF SIDE (1).

off. *abbr* **1** office. **2** officer. **3** official.

offal /'ofl/ *noun* **1** the liver, heart, kidney, etc of a butchered animal used as food. **2** the by-products of milling used *esp* for animal feeds. **3** refuse. [Middle English, from *of* OFF[1] + FALL[1]]

off and on *adv* at irregular intervals; from time to time.

offbeat[1] *noun* an unaccented beat of a musical bar.

offbeat[2] *adj informal* unusual or unconventional.

off-break *noun* a slow bowled ball in cricket that turns from the off side towards the leg side when it bounces.

off chance *noun* a remote possibility. ＊ **on the off chance** just in case: *I came on the off chance of seeing you*.

off-colour *adj* **1** unwell: *She's feeling a bit off-colour*. **2** *chiefly NAmer* somewhat indecent; risqué.

offcut *noun* a piece, e.g. of paper or wood, that is left after the original piece required has been cut.

offence (*NAmer* **offense**) /ə'fens/ *noun* **1** something that provokes a sense of outrage. **2** a feeling of displeasure or resentment, or a cause of it. **3a** a sin or misdeed. **b** an illegal act; a crime. **4** a military attack; an assault. **5** /'ofens/ *chiefly NAmer* the attacking team, players, or positions in a team sport. ＊ **give offence** to offend somebody. **take offence** to be offended. ⏵⏵ **offenceless** *adj*. [Middle English via French from Latin *offensa*, from *offendere* to strike against, OFFEND]

offend /ə'fend/ *verb trans* **1** to cause (somebody) to feel indignation or disgust. **2** to cause (somebody or something) pain or displeasure; to hurt (them): *colours that offend the eye.* ➤ *verb intrans* **1** to cause displeasure, difficulty, or discomfort. **2** to commit a crime or wrongdoing. **3** (*often* + against) to break a moral or divine law. ➤➤ **offender** *noun.* [Middle English *offenden* via French from Latin *offendere* to strike against, offend]

offense /ə'fens/ *noun NAmer* see OFFENCE.

offensive[1] /ə'fensiv/ *adj* **1** causing indignation or outrage. **2** arousing physical disgust; repellent. **3a** aggressive or attacking. **b** of or designed for attack: *offensive weapons.* ➤➤ **offensively** *adv,* **offensiveness** *noun.*

offensive[2] *noun* **1** the position or attitude of an attacking party: *They took the offensive.* **2** an *esp* military attack on a large scale.

offer[1] /'ofə/ *verb* (**offered, offering**) ➤ *verb trans* **1a** to present (something) for acceptance, rejection, or consideration. **b** to present (something) in order to satisfy a requirement: *Candidates may offer Welsh as one of their foreign languages.* **2a** to make (something) available; to provide (it): *The hotel offers a full range of facilities.* **b** to present (goods) for sale. **3** to declare one's willingness (to do something): *They offered to help me.* **4** to display (a quality): *She offered stubborn resistance.* **5** to present (something) in performance or exhibition. **6** to tender (something) as payment. **7** (*often* + up) to present (e.g. a prayer or sacrifice) in an act of worship or devotion. ➤ *verb intrans* **1** to make an offer for consideration, acceptance, etc. **2** *archaic* to present itself; to occur. ➤➤ **offerer** *noun.* [Latin *offerre* to present, tender, from OF- + *ferre* to carry]

offer[2] *noun* **1** an undertaking to do or give something. **2** a price named by a prospective buyer. **3** *archaic* a proposal, *specif* a proposal of marriage: *It is always incomprehensible to a man that a woman should ever refuse an offer of marriage* — Jane Austen. ✳ **on offer 1** for sale at a reduced price. **2** available to use or buy. **under offer** said of property: provisionally sold subject to the signing of contracts.

offer document *noun* a document giving details of a proposed takeover, sent by the predator company to the shareholders of the target company.

offering *noun* **1** the act or an instance of offering. **2** something offered, *esp* a sacrifice ceremonially offered as a part of worship. **3** a contribution to the support of a church or other religious organization.

offertory /'ofət(ə)ri/ *noun* (*pl* **offertories**) **1** (*often* **Offertory**) the offering of the Communion bread and wine to God before consecration, or a text recited or sung while this is happening. **2** the collection and presentation of the offerings of the congregation at public worship. [medieval Latin *offertorium,* from Latin *offerre:* see OFFER[1]]

offhand[1] *adj* **1** without proper respect, courtesy, or warmth; curt. **2** informal or casual. ➤➤ **offhandedly** *adv,* **offhandedness** *noun.*

offhand[2] *adv* without forethought or preparation: *I couldn't give you the figures offhand.*

offhanded *adj* = OFFHAND[1].

office /'ofis/ *noun* **1a** a room in which the administrative, clerical, or professional work of an organization is performed. **b** a group of people sharing such a room. **c** a building where the business of a particular organization is carried out. **d** a place, *esp* a small room, where a particular service is provided: *the lost property office.* **e** *chiefly Brit* (*in pl*) the rooms, buildings, or outhouses in which the activities attached to the service of a house are carried on. **f** *chiefly Brit, euphem* (*usu in pl*) a lavatory. **2a** (**Office**) a major administrative unit in some governments: *the Foreign Office.* **b** a subdivision of some government departments. **3a** a position giving authority to exercise a public function: *the office of Prime Minister.* **b** a position with special duties or responsibilities: *the insolence of office* — Shakespeare. **c** a position of authority or power: *He's been in office for three years now.* **4a** *formal* an *esp* beneficial service or action carried out for another: *I obtained the post through her good offices.* **b** (*usu in pl*) a minor duty or task. **5** a prescribed form or service of worship. [Middle English via Old French from Latin *officium* service, duty, office, from *opus* work + *facere* to make, do]

officebearer *noun* somebody who holds an official position, such as president, secretary or treasurer, in a club, church, or other organization.

office block *noun* a large building containing offices.

office boy *noun* a young man employed to run errands in an office.

office girl *noun* a young woman employed to run errands in an office.

officer[1] /'ofisə/ *noun* **1a** somebody who holds a position of authority or command in the armed forces; *specif* a commissioned officer. **b** a master or any of the mates of a merchant or passenger ship. **c** a member of a police force. **2** somebody who holds a position with special duties or responsibilities, e.g. in a government or business. **3** a rank in the Order of the British Empire. [Middle English via French and medieval Latin from Latin *officium:* see OFFICE]

officer[2] *verb trans* (**officered, officering**) **1** to supply (an organization, etc) with officers. **2** to command or direct (e.g. a military unit) as an officer.

officer of arms *noun* any of the officials of a monarch or government responsible for creating and granting heraldic arms.

official[1] /ə'fish(ə)l/ *adj* **1** prescribed or sanctioned by an authority; authorized. **2** relating to a position of authority or to the duties of somebody who holds such a position. **3** holding a position of authority. **4** suitable for or characteristic of people in positions of authority; formal. ➤➤ **officially** *adv.*

Usage note

official *or* officious? A letter, a document, or an announcement can be *official* ('written or made by someone in authority'). Only a person or their words or behaviour can be *officious* in its ordinary meaning. It is an uncomplimentary word meaning 'bossy and interfering'.

official[2] *noun* somebody who holds a position of authority, *esp* in a public organization or institution: *government officials.* ➤➤ **officialdom** *noun.*

officialese /ə,fishə'leez/ *noun* the characteristic language of official statements, typically wordy, pompous, or obscure.

officialism *noun* the lack of flexibility and excessive adherence to routine regarded as typical of the behaviour of officials, *esp* government officials.

Official Receiver *noun* a public official appointed to administer a bankrupt's property.

officiant /ə'fishi-ənt, -si-ənt/ *noun* a priest who officiates at a religious ceremony.

officiate /ə'fishiayt/ *verb intrans* **1** to perform an *esp* religious ceremony, function, or duty: *The bride's brother officiated at the wedding.* **2** to act as an official or in an official capacity. ➤➤ **officiation** /-'aysh(ə)n/ *noun,* **officiator** *noun.*

officinal /ofi'sienl/ *adj* **1** medicinal: *officinal herbs.* **2** *archaic* said of medicine: kept ready-prepared at a pharmacy. ➤➤ **officinally** *adv.* [medieval Latin *officinalis* of a storeroom, from *officina* storeroom, workshop, from Latin *officium:* see OFFICE]

officious /ə'fishəs/ *adj* **1** given to or marked by overzealousness in exercising authority or carrying out duties. **2** said *esp* of a diplomatic agreement: informal or unofficial. ➤➤ **officiously** *adv,* **officiousness** *noun.* [Latin *officiosus,* from *officium:* see OFFICE]

Usage note

officious *or* official? See note at OFFICIAL[1].

offie /'ofi/ *noun Brit, informal* an off-licence.

offing *noun* the part of the deep sea visible from the shore. ✳ **in the offing** likely to happen in the near future.

offish *adj informal* inclined to be aloof or distant. ➤➤ **offishly** *adv,* **offishness** *noun.*

off-key *adj and adv* varying in pitch from the proper tone of a melody.

off-label *adj* denoting the use of a medicinal drug for a purpose other than that for which it has been tested and approved: *This paper outlines the risks in off-label prescribing.* ➤➤ **off-labelling** *noun.*

off-licence *noun Brit* a shop, part of a pub, etc licensed to sell alcoholic drinks to be consumed off the premises.

off limits *adv and adj* not to be entered; out-of-bounds: *No topic is off limits for discussion.*

off-line[1] *adj* **1** not controlled directly by a computer: compare ON-LINE[1]. **2** not currently connected to a computer or network: compare ON-LINE[1].

off-line[2] *adv* while not controlled by or connected to a computer.

off-load *verb trans* **1** to unload (cargo). **2** to get rid of (something unwanted).

off-message *adj* said of a politician: deviating from official party policy.

off-peak *adj* taking place or used at a time of less than the maximum demand or activity: *off-peak electricity; off-peak travel.*

off-piste *adj and adv* away from regular skiing runs, on unprepared slopes.

offprint *noun* a separately printed excerpt, e.g. an article from a magazine.

off-putting *adj chiefly Brit, informal* disagreeable or disconcerting.

off-road *adj and adv* for or on rough terrain rather than prepared road surfaces.

off-roader *noun* an off-road vehicle.

off sales *pl noun Brit* drinks and food sold, *esp* by a pub, for consumption off the premises.

offscreen *adv and adj* out of sight of the film or television viewer.

off season *noun* a time of suspended or reduced activity in business or trade. ➤➤ **off-season** *adv and adj.*

offset[1] *verb* (**offsetting,** *past tense and past part.* **offset**) ➤ *verb trans* **1a** to balance (something): *Credits offset debits.* **b** to compensate or make up for (something). **2** to print (e.g. a book) using the offset process. **3** to place (something) to one side. ➤ *verb intrans* to form an offset.

offset[2] *noun* **1** something that serves to compensate for something else. **2a** a printing process in which an inked impression from a plate is first made on a rubber surface and then transferred to paper. **b** in printing, = SET-OFF (4). **3** a short shoot or bulb growing out to the side from the base of a plant. **4a** an offshoot, *esp* of a family or race. **b** a spur in a range of hills. **5** an abrupt bend in an object by which one part is turned aside out of line. **6** in surveying, a distance measured at a right angle to the main line of survey. **7** in architecture, a horizontal or sloping ledge on a wall formed by the wall becoming thinner above it.

offset litho *noun* offset printing from photolithographic plates.

offshoot *noun* **1** a branch of a plant's main stem. **2** something that develops out of something else.

offshore *adj and adv* **1** away from the shore. **2** at a distance from the shore. **3** located or operating abroad, usu taking advantage of tax benefits: *an offshore fund.*

offside *adv and adj* illegally in advance of the ball or puck in a team game.

off side *noun* **1** the side of a cricket field that the batsman's or batswoman's body faces when they are receiving: compare LEG SIDE. **2** *chiefly Brit* the right side of a vehicle, furthest from the kerb: compare NEARSIDE.

offspin *noun* spin that causes a cricket ball bowled at slow speed to turn from the off side towards the leg side when it bounces. ➤➤ **off-spinner** *noun.*

offspring *noun* (*pl* **offspring**) the progeny of a person, animal, or plant; young. [Old English *ofspring,* from *of* OFF[1] + *springan* SPRING[1]]

offstage *adv and adj* **1** on a part of the stage not visible to the audience. **2** behind the scenes, away from the public gaze.

off-the-cuff *adj informal* not prepared in advance; impromptu.

off-the-peg *adj chiefly Brit* said of clothes: made beforehand to fit standard sizes, as distinct from being made to measure.

off-the-record *adj* unofficial or in confidence, or given or made unofficially or in confidence.

off-the-shelf *adj* available as a stock item, not specially designed or custom-made.

off-the-wall *adj informal* strikingly eccentric; crazy.

off-white *adj* of a yellowish or greyish white colour. ➤➤ **off-white** *noun.*

OFM *abbr* Order of Friars Minor, i.e. the Franciscans.

OFS *abbr* Orange Free State.

OFT *abbr Brit* Office of Fair Trading.

oft /oft/ *adv literary* often. [Old English]

often /'of(t)ən/ *adv* **1** at many times. **2** in many cases: *They often die young.* ✳ **as often as not** for much of the time.

Word history
Middle English alteration of OFT. The *t* in *often* appears to have been pronounced until late in the 17th cent., but then to have become silent and remained so throughout the 18th and 19th cents. The increasingly common modern spelling pronunciation with the *t* sound reinserted was stigmatized in the 1930s as 'vulgar' but it is now established as a standard alternative to the traditional pronunciation.

o.g. *abbr* own goal.

ogam /'ogəm, 'oh-əm/ *noun* see OGHAM.

ogee /'ohjee/ *noun* **1** a moulding in the form of a shallow S-shaped curve. **2** a pointed arch with shallow S-shaped sides. [from OGIVE, the orig sense; from the use of such mouldings in ogives]

ogham *or* **ogam** /'ogəm, 'oh-əm/ *noun* a 20-character alphabet used in ancient Celtic and Pictish inscriptions, with notches for vowels and lines that met at or cut across a straight line (e.g. the edge of a stone) for consonants. ➤➤ **oghamic** /o'gamik, 'oh-əmik/ *adj.* [Irish Gaelic *ogham* from early Irish *ogom, ogum*]

ogival /oh'jievl/ *adj* having the form of an ogive or an ogee.

ogive /'ohjiev/ *noun* a diagonal arch or rib across a Gothic vault. [French *ogive*]

ogle[1] /'ohgl/ *verb trans and intrans* to glance or stare at (somebody) with sexual interest, *esp* obviously and distastefully: *Léonie did not want to watch Therese clamber on his knee, twist her blonde curls with one finger, ogle him* — Michèle Roberts. ➤➤ **ogler** *noun.* [prob from Low German *oegeln,* from *oog* eye]

ogle[2] *noun* an openly and distastefully lecherous glance or stare.

O grade *noun* **1** a former secondary school examination in Scotland, replaced by the Standard Grade. **2** a pass at O grade.

ogre /'ohgə/ *or* **ogress** /'ohgris/ *noun* **1** a hideous giant of folklore believed to feed on human beings. **2** a dreaded person or thing. ➤➤ **ogreish** /'ohgərish/ *adj.* [French *ogre*]

OH *abbr* Ohio (US postal abbreviation).

oh[1] /oh/ *interj* an expression of surprise, pain, disappointment, etc, or used to introduce a remark when addressing somebody. [variant spelling of O[2]]

oh[2] *or* **O** *noun* zero. [from the similarity of the symbol for zero to the letter O]

ohc *abbr* overhead camshaft.

ohm /ohm/ *noun* the SI unit of electrical resistance equal to the resistance between two points of a conductor when a constant potential difference of one volt applied to these points produces a current of one ampere. ➤➤ **ohmic** /'ohmik/ *adj,* **ohmically** /'ohmikli/ *adv.* [named after Georg Simon *Ohm* d.1854, German physicist who studied the measurement of electrical resistance]

ohmmeter /'ohmeetə/ *noun* an instrument for measuring electrical resistance.

OHMS *abbr* On His/Her Majesty's Service.

Ohm's law /ohmz/ *noun* the principle that the flow of electric current through a conductor is directly proportional to the potential difference, provided that the temperature remains constant, and is inversely proportional to the resistance. [named after G S *Ohm* (see OHM) who formulated it]

oho /oh'hoh/ *interj* an expression of amused surprise, exultation, etc. [Middle English, from O[2] + HO[1]]

-oholic *comb. form* see -HOLIC.

OHP *abbr* overhead projector.

OHT *abbr* overhead transparency.

ohv *abbr* overhead valve.

oi[1] /oy/ *noun* an aggressive type of punk music popular in the early 1980s, with lyrics that often advocated racism and violence. [prob from *oi, oy,* interj used to attract attention, express warning, etc]

oi[2] *interj informal* used to attract somebody's attention.

-oic *suffix* forming adjectives, with the meaning: containing a carboxyl group or a derivative of one: *benzoic acid.* [-O- + -IC[1]]

-oid *suffix* **1** forming nouns, denoting: something resembling a specified object or having a specified quality: *humanoid.* **2** forming adjectives, with the meaning: having the form or appearance of: *anthropoid.* [early French *-oïde* via Latin *-oïdes* from Greek *-oeidēs,* from *eidos* appearance, form]

oidium /oh'idi-əm/ *noun* (*pl* **oidia** /-di-ə/) **1a** any of various fungi many of which are the spore-bearing stages of powdery mildews. **b** any of the asexual spores borne by such a fungus. **2** a powdery mildew, *esp* on grapes, caused by an oidium. [O-[1] + -IDIUM]

oik /oyk/ *noun slang* a vulgar, loud, or otherwise obnoxious man; a yob. [origin unknown]

oil¹ /oyl/ *noun* **1** any of numerous smooth greasy substances that burn readily, are liquid or at least easily liquefiable on warming, and are soluble in ether and similar chemical compounds but not in water. **2a** = PETROLEUM. **b** any of various substances derived from petroleum, used for fuel, lubrication, etc. **c** *Brit* = PARAFFIN. **d** (*used before a noun*) relating to petroleum, a petroleum derivative, or paraffin: *an oil rig; an oil stove*. **3** a substance of oily consistency, used cosmetically, in cooking, in medicine, etc: *bath oil; olive oil*. **4a** = OIL PAINT: *a portrait painted in oils*. **b** = OIL PAINTING. **5** *Aus* information or gen. [Middle English *oile* via Old French from Latin *oleum* oil, olive oil, from Greek *elaion*, from *elaia* OLIVE]

oil² *verb trans* to apply oil to (something), *esp* in order to lubricate it. ▶ *verb intrans* to change from a solid fat into an oil by melting. ✳ **oil the wheels** to help things run smoothly. ▶▶ **oiler** *noun*.

oilbird *noun* a nocturnal bird of S America and Trinidad valued because oil can be extracted from the fat of its young and used as a substitute for butter: *Steatornis caripensis*.

oil cake *noun* the solid residue of an oil-bearing crop such as linseed left after the oil has been extracted and used mainly as an animal feed.

oilcan *noun* a container with a long nozzle designed to release oil in a controlled flow, e.g. for lubricating machinery.

oilcloth *noun* cotton cloth treated with oil and used for table and shelf coverings.

oilfield *noun* a region rich in petroleum deposits, *esp* one producing petroleum in commercial quantities.

oil-fired *adj* said of a heating system, etc: fuelled by oil.

oil gland *noun* a gland that secretes oil, e.g. the uropygial gland.

oilman *noun* (*pl* **oilmen**) a man who owns or works for an oil company.

oil of turpentine *noun* = TURPENTINE¹ (1B).

oil of vitriol *noun* *no longer in technical use* concentrated sulphuric acid.

oil paint *noun* paint consisting of ground pigment mixed with oil.

oil painting *noun* **1** the art of painting with oil paints. **2** a painting done with oil paints. ✳ **be no oil painting** *informal* to be rather unattractive physically.

oil palm *noun* an African palm tree with fruit that yields palm oil: *Elaeis guineensis*.

oil rig *noun* the equipment for drilling an oil well, with or without the platform that supports it.

oil sand *noun* sandstone deposits impregnated with bitumen or other petroleum derivatives.

oilseed *noun* a seed or crop, e.g. rape, grown largely for oil.

oil shale *noun* shale from which oil can be distilled.

oilskin *noun* **1** an oiled waterproof cloth used for coverings and garments. **2** an oilskin or plastic raincoat. **3** (*in pl*) an oilskin or plastic suit of coat and trousers, worn by fishermen, etc.

oil slick *noun* a film of oil floating on an expanse of water.

oilstone *noun* a sharpening stone used with a surface coating of oil.

oil well *noun* a well drilled in the earth from which petroleum is obtained.

oily *adj* (**oilier, oiliest**) **1** of, resembling, containing, or covered with oil. **2** too eager to please, flatter, or admire; ingratiating. ▶▶ **oilily** *adv*, **oiliness** *noun*.

oink¹ /oyngk/ *verb intrans* said of a pig: to make a characteristic grunting noise. [imitative]

oink² *noun* the grunting noise of a pig.

ointment /'oyntmənt/ *noun* a soothing or healing oily cream applied to the skin. [Middle English from Old French *oignement*, modification of Latin *unguentum*: see UNGUENT]

OIRO *abbr* offers in the region of.

Ojibwa /oh'jibway, -wə/ *or* **Ojibway** /oh'jibway/ *noun* (*pl* **Ojibwas** *or* **Ojibways** *or collectively* **Ojibwa** *or* **Ojibway**) **1** a member of a Native American people orig from north of Lake Huron. **2** an Algonquin language spoken in north central USA and Ontario. [Ojibwa *ojib-ubway* a kind of moccasin worn by the Ojibwa]

OK¹ *or* **okay** *interj* an expression of agreement or permission.
Word history
perhaps abbr of *oll korrect*, humorous alteration of *all correct*. It is almost certain that *OK* arose as part of a vogue for facetious abbreviations in newspapers in Boston and New York in the late 1830s. *OK* stood for 'oll korrect', just as *OW* stood for 'oll wright' or 'all right' and *KG* for 'know go' or 'no go'. It was taken up and used as a slogan during the presidential campaign of 1840 by supporters of the Democratic candidate Martin Van Buren, whose nickname 'Old Kinderhook' (from his birthplace, Kinderhook) coincidentally had the initials of OK. By the end of 1840 the term was widely popularized in the USA, although it was not common in Britain before the 20th cent. Other origins have been proposed: Choctaw *oke* 'it is', Scottish *och aye*, the Haitian port *Aux Cayes*, a railway freight agent named *Obadiah Kelly*, and so on. None of these has any basis in fact.

OK² *or* **okay** *adv and adj* quite good or well, but not outstandingly so.

OK³ *or* **okay** *verb trans* (**OK's, OK'd, OK'ing** *or* **okays, okayed, okaying**) to give approval or authorization to (something); to sanction (it).

OK⁴ *or* **okay** *noun* (*pl* **OK's** *or* **okays**) an approval or endorsement.

OK⁵ *abbr* Oklahoma (US postal abbreviation).

okapi /oh'kahpi/ *noun* (*pl* **okapis** *or collectively* **okapi**) an African mammal closely related to the giraffe but with a shorter neck and black and cream rings on the upper parts of the legs: *Okapia johnstoni*. [local name in Africa]

okay /oh'kay/ *interj, adv and adj, verb trans, and noun* see OK¹, OK², OK³, OK⁴.

okeydoke /ohki'dohk/ *or* **okeydokey** /-ki/ *interj informal* an expression of agreement or permission. [reduplication of OK¹]

Okla *abbr* Oklahoma.

okra /'ohkrə, 'okrə/ *noun* **1** a tall annual plant of the mallow family cultivated for its mucilaginous green pods: *Abelmoschus esculentus*. **2** the pods of this plant, used as a vegetable, *esp* in soups and stews. [of W African origin]

-ol¹ *suffix* forming nouns, denoting: a chemical compound containing a hydroxyl group; alcohol: *glycerol; phenol; ethanol*. [from ALCOHOL]

-ol² *comb. form* see -OLE.

old¹ /ohld/ *adj* **1** advanced in years or age; senior. **2** having existed for a specified period of time: *three years old*. **3a** dating from the past, *esp* the remote past: *old traditions*. **b** persisting from an earlier time: *an old ailment*. **c** of long standing: *an old friend*. **4** experienced: *an old hand*. **5** former: *one of her old students*. **6a** worn with time or use. **b** no longer in use; discarded. **7** (**Old**) constituting an early period in the development of a language: *Old English*. **8a** long familiar: *the same old story*. **b** used as an intensifier: *a high old time; any old time*. **9** used to express affection or in various informal forms of address: *You can always rely on old George; I say, old boy, can you lend me a fiver?* ▶▶ **older** *adj*, **oldish** *adj*, **oldness** *noun*. [Old English *eald*]
Usage note
older *or* **elder**? See note at ELDER¹

old² *noun* **1** used in combinations to denote a person or animal of a specified age: *a three-year-old*. **2** an old or earlier time: *men of old*.

old Adam *noun* the sinful nature inherent in man. [named after *Adam*, the first man and first sinner according to the Bible (Genesis 2:7–3:24)]

old age *noun* the final stage of the normal life span.

old age pension *noun* a retirement pension. ▶▶ **old age pensioner** *noun*.

Old Bill *noun* = BILL.

old boy *noun chiefly Brit* **1** a former pupil of a particular school, *esp* a public school. **2** used as an informal term of address for a man. **3** *informal* an old man, *esp* one who is sprightly or resilient.

old boy network *noun chiefly Brit* the system of favouritism operating among people of a similar privileged background, *esp* among former pupils of public schools.

Old Church Slavonic *noun* a Slavonic language surviving as the liturgical language of the Orthodox Church.

old country *noun* (**the old country**) an immigrant's country of origin.

olden *adj literary* of a bygone era.

Old English *noun* the earliest form of the English language, dating from around the seventh to the eleventh cents; Anglo-Saxon.

Old English sheepdog *noun* a dog of an English breed of medium-sized sheepdogs with a very long shaggy coat.

olde-worlde /ˌohld 'wuhld, ˌohldi 'wuhldi/ *adj* belonging to a past age, or quaintly or tastelessly imitating earlier styles. [pseudo-archaic spelling of OLD-WORLD]

old-fashioned *adj* 1 belonging to or characteristic of a past era; outdated. 2 clinging to the customs, tastes, or fashions of a past era. ⟩⟩ **old-fashionedly** *adv*.

old-fashioned look *noun dated* a knowing or disapproving look.

old firm *noun* (**the old firm**) *informal* a group of old friends, colleagues, or associates.

Old French *noun* the earliest form of the French language, dating from the 9th to approximately the late 14th cents.

old girl *noun chiefly Brit* 1 a former pupil of a particular school. *esp* a public school. 2 used as an informal term of address to a woman. 3 *informal* an old woman, *esp* one who is sprightly or resilient.

Old Glory *noun* the flag of the USA.

old gold *adj* of a dull brownish yellow colour. ⟩⟩ **old gold** *noun*.

old guard *noun* (*treated as sing. or pl*) the conservative members of a group or party, often the founding members.

old hand *noun* somebody with a great deal of experience; a veteran.

old hat *adj* 1 tediously familiar or overused; hackneyed. 2 laughably old-fashioned.

Old High German *noun* High German before the twelfth cent.

oldie /'ohldi/ *noun* somebody or something old, *esp* a popular song from the past.

old lady *noun* 1 an elderly woman. 2 *informal* somebody's wife or mother.

old maid *noun* 1 *derog* a single woman of advanced age; a spinster: *I would always trust the old wives' fables against the old maids' facts* — G K Chesterton. 2 *informal* a prim fussy person. 3 a simple card game in which each player tries to avoid holding a designated unpaired card at the end. ⟩⟩ **old-maidish** *adj*.

old man *noun informal* 1 an elderly man. 2a somebody's husband or father. b (**the old man**) a man in authority, e.g. one's employer, manager, or commander.

old-man's beard *noun* 1 any of several species of clematis that have long grey feathery flower parts: genus *Clematis*. 2 any of several species of greenish grey lichens that grow in long hair-like strands on the trunks and branches of trees: genus *Usnea*.

old master *noun* 1 a distinguished European painter of the 16th to early 18th cents. 2 a painting produced by an old master.

old moon *noun* the moon in its last phase, before the new moon.

Old Nick *noun informal* the devil.

Old Norse *noun* the early forms of the North Germanic language as used in Scandinavia and Iceland.

Word history
The substantial Old Norse element in the English vocabulary comes from the Scandinavians, mostly from Denmark and Norway, who raided England from the late eighth cent., settled in the country from the mid-ninth cent., and became rulers of the region north and east of a line from London to Chester. Thousands of Old Norse words entered English by the 13th cent., including *awkward, both, dirt, fellow, hit, husband, ill, leg, outlaw, rag, root, scale, sky, take, want, window,* and the pronouns *they, them, their.* Since Old Norse was quite closely related to English, some words (e.g. *bleak, kettle*) result from a mixture of Old English and Old Norse; some (e.g. *dane* and *drag*) could have originally come from either language; and in a few cases, Old Norse words have survived alongside their Old English equivalents, sometimes with a different meaning or only in dialect (*skirt/shirt, kirk/church, scale/shell*).

Old North French *noun* the northern dialects of Old French, *esp* of Normandy and Picardy.

Old Prussian *noun* a Baltic language of NE Poland that survived until the 17th cent.

Old Saxon *noun* the West Germanic language spoken by the ancient Saxons.

old school *noun* (**the old school**) adherents of traditional ideas and practices.

old school tie *noun* 1 a tie displaying the colours of an English public school, worn by former pupils. 2 (**the old school tie**) the conservatism and upper-class solidarity traditionally attributed to former members of British public schools.

old stager *noun* somebody with years of experience and service; an old hand.

oldster /'ohldstə/ *noun chiefly NAmer, informal* an elderly person.

Old Stone Age *noun* (**the Old Stone Age**) the PALAEOLITHIC period.

Old Style *noun* the former method of reckoning dates, according to the Julian calendar.

Old Testament *noun* a collection of writings forming the Jewish canon of Scripture and the first part of the Christian Bible.

old-time *adj* belonging to or characteristic of a period in the recent past.

old-timer *noun* 1 somebody with years of experience and service; a veteran. 2 *chiefly NAmer* an old man.

old wives' tale *noun* a traditional superstitious notion.

old woman *noun informal* 1 an elderly woman. 2 somebody's wife or mother. 3 *informal, derog* a timid, prim, or fussy person, *esp* a man. ⟩⟩ **old-womanish** *adj*.

Old World *noun* (**the Old World**) Europe, Asia, and Africa, the parts of the world known to Europeans before the discovery of America.

old-world *adj* 1 belonging or relating to Europe, Asia, or Africa. 2 reminiscent of a past age, *esp* quaintly charming.

olé /oh'lay/ *interj* a cry of approval or success, *esp* at bullfights. [Spanish *ole, olé* from Arabic *wa-llāh*, from *wa-* and + *allāh* God]

ole- *or* **oleo-** *comb. form* forming words, denoting: oil: *oleic*. [French *olé-, oléo-* from Latin *ole-*, from *oleum*: see OIL[1]]

-ole *or* **-ol** *comb. form* forming nouns, denoting: 1 a chemical compound containing a five-membered ring of atoms, usu not all of which are carbon atoms: *pyrrole*. 2 a chemical compound containing an ether group: *anisole*. [Latin *oleum*: see OIL[1]]

oleaceous /ohli'ayshəs/ *adj* said of plants: belonging to the olive family. [Latin genus name *Oleaceae*, from *olea* olive tree, from Greek *elaia* OLIVE]

oleaginous /ohli'ajinəs/ *adj* 1 resembling, containing, or producing oil; oily. 2 obsequious or unctuous in manner: *Then we went in to face this perfectly oleaginous and crepuscular little registrar* — Julian Barnes. ⟩⟩ **oleaginously** *adv*, **oleaginousness** *noun*. [early French *oleagineux* from Latin *oleagineus* of an olive tree, from *olea*: see OLEACEOUS]

oleander /ohli'andə/ *noun* a poisonous evergreen shrub of the periwinkle family with fragrant white, pink, or red flowers: *Nerium oleander*. [medieval Latin *oleander*]

oleaster /oli'astə/ *noun* any of several species of large shrubs or small trees with yellow flowers and fruits that resemble olives, planted *esp* to provide shelter in dry windy regions: genus *Elaeagnus*. [Latin *oleaster*, from *olea*: see OLEACEOUS]

olefin *or* **olefine** /'ohlifin, -feen/ *noun* an ALKENE (one of a series of chemical compounds composed of carbon and hydrogen). ⟩⟩ **olefinic** /-'finik/ *adj*. [French (*gaz*) *oléfiant* ethylene, from Latin *oleum*: see OIL[1]]

oleic /oh'leeik/ *adj* 1 relating to, derived from, or contained in oil. 2 of oleic acid. ⟩⟩ **oleate** /'ohliayt/ *noun*.

oleic acid *noun* an unsaturated fatty acid found as glycerides in natural fats and oils: formula $C_{18}H_{34}O_2$.

oleo- *comb. form* see OLE-.

oleograph /'ohli-əgrahf, -graf/ *noun* a CHROMOLITHOGRAPH (colour picture) printed on cloth to resemble an oil painting. ⟩⟩ **oleographic** /-'grafik/ *adj*, **oleography** /-'ogrəfi/ *noun*. [OLEO- + -GRAPH]

oleomargarine /ˌohliohmahjə'reen/ *noun* 1 an oily extract from beef fat used in margarine. 2 *NAmer, dated* margarine.

oleoresin /ˌohlioh'rezin/ *noun* a solution of resin in oil occurring naturally as a plant product, e.g. turpentine, or made synthetically. ⟩⟩ **oleoresinous** /-nəs/ *adj*.

oleum /'ohli-əm/ *noun* a heavy oily strongly corrosive solution of sulphur trioxide in sulphuric acid. [Latin *oleum*: see OIL[1]]

O level *noun* 1 a former secondary school examination in England and Wales, replaced by the GCSE. 2 a pass at O level.

olfaction /ol'faksh(ə)n/ *noun formal or technical* 1 the act or an instance of smelling. 2 the sense of smell. ⟩⟩ **olfactive** /-tiv/ *adj*, **olfactory** /-t(ə)ri/ *adj*. [Latin *olfactus*, past part. of *olfacere* to smell, from *olēre* to smell + *facere* to make, do]

olig- *or* **oligo-** *comb. form* forming words, with the meaning: few: *oligarchy.* [medieval Latin from Greek *oligos,* olig-, *oligo-* small, *oligoi* few]

oligarch /'oligahk/ *noun* a member of an oligarchy. [Greek *oligarchēs,* from OLIG- + *-archēs* -ARCH]

oligarchy *noun* (*pl* **oligarchies**) **1** government by a small group. **2** a state or organization in which a small group exercises control, *esp* for its own interests. **3** a small group exercising such control. ➤➤ **oligarchic** /-'gahkik/ *adj,* **oligarchical** /-'gahkikl/ *adj.*

oligo- *comb. form* see OLIG-.

Oligocene /o'ligohseen, 'ol-/ *adj* relating to or dating from a geological epoch, the third epoch of the Tertiary period, lasting from about 35.5 million to about 23.5 million years ago, and marked by extensive movements of the earth's crust that produced new mountain ranges, diminished forests, rising grasses, and the appearance of the first primates. ➤➤ **Oligocene** *noun.* [Greek OLIGO- + *kainos* new or recent; from the scarcity of new life forms during this period]

oligochaete /'oligohkeet/ *noun* any of a class of freshwater and terrestrial annelid worms, including the earthworm, with relatively few bristles along the body: class Oligochaeta: compare POLYCHAETE. [OLIGO- + Greek *chaitē* long hair]

oligoclase /'oligohklays, o'lig-/ *noun* a common feldspar mineral of the plagioclase series found in many rocks, e.g. granite. [German *Oligoklas,* from Greek OLIGO- + *klasis* breaking]

oligomer /ə'ligəmə/ *noun* a POLYMER (large molecule consisting of repeated molecular units) containing relatively few structural units. ➤➤ **oligomeric** /,oligoh'merik/ *adj,* **oligomerization** /oli,gohmərie'zaysh(ə)n/ *noun.* [OLIGO- + -MER]

oligopoly /oli'gopəli/ *noun* a market situation in which each of a few producers affects the market without any one of them having decisive control over it. ➤➤ **oligopolist** *noun,* **oligopolistic** /-'listik/ *adj.* [OLIGO- + MONOPOLY]

oligospermia /,oligoh'spuhmi·ə/ *noun* the condition of there being abnormally few sperm in one's semen.

oligotrophic /,oligoh'trofhik/ *adj* **1** deficient in plant nutrients: *oligotrophic boggy acid soils.* **2** said of a body of water: having abundant dissolved oxygen: compare EUTROPHIC, MESOTROPHIC.

olingo /o'linggoh/ *noun* (*pl* **olingos**) any of several species of small mammals of the raccoon family that live in trees in tropical American rainforests: genus *Bassaricyon.* [American Spanish *olingo,* from a Mayan word]

olio /'ohlioh/ *noun* (*pl* **olios**) **1** a highly spiced stew of Spanish origin. **2** a miscellaneous collection of items. [modification of Spanish *olla* stew, pot, from Latin *aulla* cooking pot]

olivaceous /oli'vayshəs/ *adj* of an olive-green colour.

olive /'oliv/ *noun* **1** a small green or purplish black stone fruit used as a food and a source of oil. **2** the small evergreen tree that bears this fruit, grown *esp* in the Mediterranean: *Olea europaea.* **3** a dull yellowish green colour resembling that of an unripe olive. ➤➤ **olive** *adj.* [Middle English via Old French from Latin *oliva* from Greek *elaia*]

olive branch *noun* an offer or gesture of conciliation or goodwill.

Word history
with reference to the biblical story of Noah, in which a dove released from the Ark returned carrying an olive twig, showing that the flood had receded and that God and man were reconciled (Genesis 8:11).

olive drab *noun* **1** a wool or cotton fabric of a greyish olive colour. **2** a uniform made of this fabric. **3** a greyish green colour.

olive-green *adj* olive, or of a green colour that is lighter and stronger than olive. ➤➤ **olive green** *noun.*

olive oil *noun* a pale yellow to golden oil obtained from ripe olives and used extensively in cooking and as a salad oil.

olivine /'oliveen, -vien/ *noun* a usu greenish mineral that is a silicate of magnesium and iron. Also called CHRYSOLITE. ➤➤ **olivinic** /-'vinik/ *adj,* **olivinitic** /-vi'nitik/ *adj.* [German *Olivin* from Latin *oliva:* see OLIVE]

olla podrida /,olə po'dreedə/ *noun* (*pl* **olla podridas** *or* **ollas podridas**) a rich seasoned stew of many different meats and vegetables that is a traditional Spanish and Latin American dish. [Spanish *olla podrida,* literally 'rotten pot']

olm /ohlm, olm/ *noun* a European cave-dwelling aquatic salamander with non-functional eyes: *Proteus anguinus.* [German *Olm*]

Olmec /'olmek/ *noun* (*pl* **Olmecs** *or collectively* **Olmec**) a member of an ancient indigenous people of Central and South America. ➤➤ **Olmec** *adj.* [Nahuatl *Olmecatl,* literally 'people who live in the rubber country']

ology /'oləji/ *noun* (*pl* **ologies**) *informal* a science or any other field of study. [from *geology, psychology,* etc]

-ology *comb. form* = -LOGY.

oloroso /ohlə'rohsoh, ol-/ *noun* (*pl* **olorosos**) a golden-coloured, full-bodied, sweet sherry. [Spanish *oloroso* fragrant, ultimately from Latin *olēre* to smell]

olympiad /ə'limpiad/ *noun* **1** (*often* **Olympiad**) any of the four-year intervals between Olympian games by which time was reckoned in ancient Greece. **2** a holding of the modern Olympic Games. [early French *Olympiade* via Latin *Olympiad-, Olympias* from Greek *Olympia,* site in Greece of ancient games]

Olympian[1] /ə'limpi·ən/ *adj* **1** of the ancient Greek region of Olympia. **2** outstandingly great: *Olympian achievements.* **3a** characteristic of or befitting a god. **b** supremely aloof or detached.

Olympian[2] *noun* **1** an inhabitant of the ancient Greek region of Olympia. **2** any of the ancient Greek deities dwelling on Olympus. **3** a loftily detached or superior person. **4** *chiefly NAmer* a participant in the modern Olympic Games.

Olympian Games *pl noun* (**the Olympian Games**) the ancient Olympic Games.

Olympic /ə'limpik/ *adj* **1** relating to ancient Olympia; Olympian. **2** of or executed in the Olympic Games.

Olympic Games *pl noun* (*treated as sing. or pl*) **1** (**the Olympic Games**) an international sports meeting held once every four years in a different host country. **2** an ancient Greek festival held every four years at Olympia, with athletic, literary, and musical contests.

Olympics *pl noun* (**the Olympics**) (*treated as sing. or pl*) the modern Olympic Games.

OM *abbr* Brit Order of Merit.

-oma *suffix* (*pl* **-omas** *or* **-omata**) forming nouns, denoting: tumour: *adenoma; fibroma.* [Latin *-omat-, -oma* from Greek *-ōmat-, -ōma*]

Omani /oh'mahni/ *noun* (*pl* **Omanis**) a native or inhabitant of Oman. ➤➤ **Omani** *adj.*

omasum /oh'mays(ə)m/ *noun* (*pl* **omasa** /-sə/) the third stomach of a ruminant mammal, lying between the reticulum and the abomasum. [Latin *omasum* tripe of a bullock]

ombre (*NAmer* **omber**) /'ombə/ *noun* a card game for three players using a pack of 40 cards, popular in Europe in the 17th and 18th cents. [Spanish *hombre* man, from Latin *homo*]

ombré /'ombray/ *adj* said *esp* of fabrics: graduated in colour from light to dark. [French *ombré,* past part. of *ombrer* to shade, ultimately from Latin *umbra* shade]

ombudsman /'omboodzmən/ *noun* (*pl* **ombudsmen**) a government official appointed to investigate complaints made by individuals against government or public bodies. [Swedish *ombudsman* representative, from Old Norse *umbothsmathr,* from *umboth* commission + *mathr* man]

-ome *suffix* forming nouns, denoting: part: *rhizome.* [see -OMA]

omega /'ohmigə, 'om-/ *noun* **1** the 24th and last letter of the Greek alphabet (Ω, ω), equivalent to and transliterated as roman ō. **2** the last one in a series, order, etc. [Greek *ō mega,* literally 'large O']

omelette (*NAmer* **omelet**) /'omlit/ *noun* a mixture of beaten eggs cooked until set in a shallow pan and often served folded in half over a filling: compare SPANISH OMELETTE. [French *omelette,* alteration of early French *alumelle,* literally 'knife blade', ultimately from Latin *lamina* thin plate]

omen[1] /'ohmən/ *noun* an event or phenomenon believed to be a sign of some future occurrence. [Latin *omin-, omen*]

omen[2] *verb trans and intrans* (**omened, omening**) to be an omen of (something).

omentum /oh'mentəm/ *noun* (*pl* **omenta** /-tə/ *or* **omentums**) a fold of peritoneum connecting or supporting the stomach and other abdominal parts. ➤➤ **omental** *adj.* [Latin *omentum*]

omertà /ohmə'tah/ *noun* the code of silence about the Mafia's activities observed by its members and associates. [Italian dialect *omertà* from Italian *umiltà* humility]

omicron /oh'miekrən/ *noun* the 15th letter of the Greek alphabet (O, o), equivalent to and transliterated as roman o. [Greek *o mikron*, literally 'small o']

ominous /'ominəs/ *adj* suggesting or signalling future disaster or evil. ⟫⟫ **ominously** *adv*, **ominousness** *noun*. [Latin *ominosus*, from *omin-*, *omen* OMEN[1]]

omission /ə'mish(ə)n/ *noun* **1** the act or an instance of omitting or being omitted: *sins of omission*. **2** something neglected or left undone. [Middle English *omissioun* via late Latin *omission-*, *omissio*, from Latin *omittere*: see OMIT]

omit /ə'mit/ *verb trans* (**omitted, omitting**) **1** to leave (something or somebody) out or unmentioned. **2** to fail to do (something). ⟫⟫ **omissible** /ə'misibl/ *adj*. [Middle English *omitten* from Latin *omittere* to let fall, from OB- + *mittere* to let go, send]

ommatidium /omə'tidi·əm/ *noun* (*pl* **ommatidia** /-di·ə/) any of the many parts that form the compound eye of an insect, crab, or other arthropod, each corresponding to a simple eye. ⟫⟫ **ommatidial** *adj*. [Greek *ommatidion*, dimin. of *ommat-*, *omma* eye]

omni- *comb. form* forming words, with the meaning: all or universally: *omnidirectional*. [Latin *omni-* from *omnis* all]

omnibus /'omnibəs/ *noun* **1a** a book containing reprints of a number of works, usu by one author. **b** a television or radio programme consisting of two or more programmes, usu episodes of a series, orig broadcast separately. **c** (*used before a noun*) being an omnibus: *an omnibus edition of the works of Jane Austen*. **2** *formal*, *dated* a bus: *The handbag … seems to be mine. Yes, here is the injury it received through the upsetting of a Gower Street omnibus in younger and happier days* — Oscar Wilde. [French *omnibus* bus, from Latin *omnibus* for all, dative pl of *omnis* all]

omnicompetent /omni'kompit(ə)nt/ *adj* **1** competent in all matters. **2** competent to legislate or make judgments on all matters. ⟫⟫ **omnicompetence** *noun*.

omnidirectional /,omnidi'reksh(ə)nl, -die'reksh(ə)nl/ *adj* moving or capable of moving in all directions, *esp* receiving or transmitting radio waves equally well in all directions.

omnifarious /omni'feəri·əs/ *adj* of all varieties, forms, or kinds. [late Latin *omnifarius*, from OMNI- + Latin *-farius* as in MULTIFARIOUS]

Omnipotent /om'nipət(ə)nt/ *noun* (**the Omnipotent**) God.

omnipotent *adj* having unlimited or very great power or influence. ⟫⟫ **omnipotence** *noun*, **omnipotently** *adv*. [Middle English via French from Latin *omnipotent-*, *omnipotens*, from OMNI- + *potent-*, *potens*: see POTENT[1]]

omnipresent /omni'prez(ə)nt/ *adj* present in all places at all times. ⟫⟫ **omnipresence** *noun*.

omniscience /om'nisi·əns/ *noun* **1** the quality of being all-knowing. **2** all-embracing knowledge: *All other men are specialists, but his specialism is omniscience* — Conan Doyle.

omniscient /om'nisi·ənt, om'nish(ə)nt/ *adj* **1** having infinite awareness or understanding. **2** possessed of complete knowledge; all-knowing. ⟫⟫ **omnisciently** *adv*. [medieval Latin *omniscientia* omniscience, from OMNI- + Latin *scientia*: see SCIENCE]

omnium-gatherum /,omni·əm 'gadhərəm/ *noun* (*pl* **omnium-gatherums**) a miscellaneous collection of things or people. [Latin *omnium*, genitive pl of *omnis* all + GATHER[1] + Latin *-um* noun ending]

omnivorous /om'nivərəs/ *adj* **1** feeding on both animal and vegetable substances. **2** avidly taking in, and *esp* reading, everything. ⟫⟫ **omnivore** /'omnivaw/ *noun*, **omnivorously** *adv*, **omnivorousness** *noun*. [Latin *omnivorus*, from OMNI- + -VOROUS]

ON *abbr* **1** Old Norse. **2** Ontario.

on[1] /on/ *prep* **1** in contact with or supported from below by: *There's a fly on the ceiling; Can you stand on one foot?* **2** attached or fastened to: *She had a dog on a lead*. **3** carried on the person of: *Have you got a match on you?* **4** very near to, *esp* along an edge or border: *He visited a number of towns on the frontier; Walton-on-Thames*. **5a** within the limits of an area: *There are deer on the hills; There's a picture on page 17*. **b** at the usual standard or level of: *He was on form tonight*. **c** positioned at or towards: *On his right was the then president*. **d** in the direction of; against: *The protesters marched on Westminster*. **e** with regard to; concerning: *She's very keen on sports*. **f** staked on the success of: *I had £5 on his horse*. **g** doing or carrying out a specified action or activity: *I'm here on business*. **h** working for, supporting,

or belonging to: *He's on their side*. **i** working at or in charge of: *I'll ask the man on the gate*. **6a** having as a basis or source, e.g. of knowledge or comparison: *I have it on good authority; Prices are down on last year*. **b** at the expense of; paid for by: *Drinks are on the house*. **7a** in the state or process of: *The house is on fire; Why don't we buy it while it's on offer?* **b** in the specified manner: *I got it on the cheap*. **c** using as a medium: *She played it on the clarinet*. **d** using by way of transport: *He left on the early train*. **e** sustained or powered by: *We live on vegetables; He's on a low income*. **f** regularly taking: *Hundreds of teachers are on Valium*. **8a** at the time of: *You can get the books cash on delivery*. **b** on the occasion of or immediately after and usu in consequence of: *He fainted on hearing the news*. **c** in the course of: *I saw Van Morrison when he was on tour*. [Old English *an, on*]

on[2] *adv* **1** so as to be supported from below: *Put the top on*. **2** so as to be worn: *She has new shoes on*. **3** so as to be attached: *Sew the buttons on*. **4a** ahead or forwards in space or time: *40 years on, nothing has changed; It's getting on for five*. **b** with the specified part forward: *The cars crashed head on*. **c** without interruption: *She chattered on and on*. **d** in continuance or succession: *and so on*. **5a** in or into operation: *Let's switch the light on; Will you get the potatoes on?* **b** in or into an activity or function: *The night shift came on*.

on[3] *adj* **1a** taking place: *The game is on*. **b** performing or broadcasting: *We're on in ten minutes*. **c** intended or planned: *He has nothing on for tonight*. **d** worn as clothing: *She went out with just a cardigan on*. **2a** committed to a bet. **b** in favour of a win: *The odds are two to one on*. **3** *chiefly Brit* (*usu in negative contexts*) possible or practicable: *You can't refuse, it's just not on*. **4a** *chiefly Brit, informal* nagging: *She's always on at him about his hair*. **b** *informal* talking dully, excessively, or incomprehensibly: *What are you on about?* **5** in cricket, on or towards the side of the field that is opposite to the side that the batsman's or batswoman's body faces when they are receiving: *an on drive*.

-on[1] *suffix* forming nouns, denoting: a chemical compound: *parathion; interferon*. [alteration of -ONE]

-on[2] *suffix* forming nouns, denoting: **1** elementary particle: *electron; baryon*. **2** unit or quantum: *photon*. **3** basic operational unit of genetic material: *operon*. [from -*on* in ION]

-on[3] *suffix* forming nouns, denoting: inert gas: *neon*. [from -*on* in ARGON]

onager /'onəjə/ *noun* **1** a small Asian wild ass with a broad stripe on its back: *Equus hemionus onager*. **2** a heavy catapult-like machine used in ancient and medieval times for hurling rocks in battle. [Middle English via Latin from Greek *onagros*, from *onos* ass + *agros* field]

on and off *adv* at irregular and usu infrequent intervals; from time to time.

onanism /'ohnəniz(ə)m/ *noun* **1** = COITUS INTERRUPTUS. **2** masturbation. ⟫⟫ **onanistic** /-'nistik/ *adj*. [named after *Onan*, who 'spilled his seed on the ground' to avoid impregnating his brother's wife (Genesis 38:9)]

ONC *abbr Brit* formerly, Ordinary National Certificate.

once[1] /wuns/ *adv* **1** one time and no more: *They met only once; He shaves once a week*. **2** at some indefinite time in the past; formerly: *There once lived a king*. **3** by one degree of relationship: *second cousin once removed*. **4** even one time; ever: *They've never once lost a match at home*. ✳ **once again/more 1** now again as before: *They were back home once again*. **2** for one more time. **once and for all/once for all** for the final or only time; conclusively. **once in a while** occasionally. **once or twice** a few times. **once upon a time** used as a traditional formula to begin a children's story: at some time in the past. [Middle English *anes, ones*, genitive of *an, on* ONE[1]]

once[2] *noun* one single time: *Once is enough; Do it just this once*. ✳ **all at once 1** all at the same time. **2** without warning; suddenly. **at once 1** at the same time; simultaneously: *They both spoke at once*. **2** without delay; immediately. **for once** on this occasion only, or at least.

once[3] *conj* from the moment when; as soon as: *Once he arrives we can start; Once over the wall we're safe*.

once-over *noun informal* a swift appraising glance: *I gave him the once-over*.

oncer /'wunsə/ *noun Brit, dated, informal* a £1 note.

onchocerciasis /,ongkohsuh'kie·əsis/ *noun* (*pl* **onchocerciases** /-seez/) infection with or a disease caused by parasitic worms of the genus *Onchocerca*, *esp* river blindness, a disease that causes blindness in humans and that is caused by a worm, native to Africa but now also present in parts of tropical America, which is transmitted by biting flies. [scientific Latin, from Latin genus name *Onchocerca* (from Greek *onkos* barbed hook + *kerkos* tail) + -IASIS]

oncogene /'ongkohjeen/ *noun* a gene, e.g. in some viruses, that causes cancer. [Greek *onkos* mass + GENE]

oncogenic /ongkoh'jenik/ *adj* relating to or causing the formation of tumours. ▶▶ **oncogenesis** /-'jenəsis/ *noun*, **oncogenically** /-'jenikli/ *adv*, **oncogenicity** /-'nisiti/ *noun*. [Greek *onkos* mass + -GENIC or -GENOUS]

oncogenous /ong'kojinəs/ *adj* = ONCOGENIC.

oncology /ong'koləji/ *noun* the study and treatment of cancer and malignant tumours. ▶▶ **oncological** /ongkə'lojikl/ *adj*, **oncologist** *noun*. [Greek *onkos* mass + -LOGY]

oncoming¹ *adj* **1** approaching from the front. **2** coming nearer in time or space; advancing.

oncoming² *noun* approach; onset.

oncost *noun* = OVERHEAD³.

OND *abbr* Brit formerly, Ordinary National Diploma.

on dit /,on 'dee (*French* 5 di)/ *noun* (*pl* **on dits** /'dee, 'deez (*French* di)/) a piece of gossip; a rumour. [French *on dit*, literally 'they say, it is said']

one¹ /wun/ *adj* **1a** being a single unit or thing: *I can only find one sock.* **b** being the first of the stated kind: *on page one.* **2** being a particular but unspecified instance: *I saw her early one morning.* **3** the same; identical: *We were both of one mind.* **4a** constituting a unified entity: *The combined elements form one substance.* **b** being in a state of agreement; united: *I am one with the rest of you in this matter.* **5** being some unspecified future time: *We might try it one weekend; One day I'll get you out of this place.* **6a** being a particular object or person: *Close first one eye then the other.* **b** being the only individual of an indicated or implied kind: *She's the one and only person who can help us.* ✳ **one and the same** the very same. [Old English *ān*]

one² *pronoun* (*pl* **ones**) **1** an indefinitely indicated person; anybody at all: *One has a duty to one's public.* **2** used to refer to a noun or noun phrase previously mentioned or understood: *two grey shirts and three red ones; The question is one of great importance.*

Usage note
One is a useful word for making statements that apply to everyone in general and no one in particular: *One seldom makes that particular mistake twice. You* can serve the same purpose (*You can't make an omelette without breaking eggs*) and sounds less formal and impersonal. It must be clear, however, that *you* is intended to have a general meaning and does not refer to a particular person or particular people. *One* does sound rather formal, but it does not sound too affected unless it is being used in place of *I*.

one³ *noun* **1** the number 1, or the quantity represented by it. **2a** the age of 1 year. **b** the hour one hour after midday or midnight. **3** the first in a set or series: *He takes a one in shoes.* **4a** a single person or thing. **b** a unified entity: *They all rose up as one and clamoured for more pay.* **c** a particular example or instance: *Last night was one of the coldest nights this year.* **d** a certain specified person: *The police are looking for one George Hopkins.* **5a** a blow or stroke: *She socked him one on the jaw.* **b** a drink: *We've just time for a quick one.* **c** a joke or story: *Have you heard this one?* **6** something having a denomination of one: *I'll take the money in ones.* **7a** a person with a liking for or interest in a specified thing; an enthusiast: *He's rather a one for baroque music.* **b** a bold, amusing, or remarkable character: *Oh, you are a one!* ✳ **at one** in a state of agreement or harmony. **for one** not to mention others. **one after another/the other** in succession. **one and all** everybody. **one and only** the only person one loves: *But darling, you're my one and only!* **one by one** singly or successively. **one or other** either; any: *One or other of us should go to the funeral.* **one or two** a few.

-one *suffix* forming nouns, denoting: ketone, or a compound related or analogous to a ketone: *acetone.* [alteration of -ENE]

one another *pronoun* (*not used as the subject of a verb*) each of two or more in reciprocal action or relationship.

Usage note
one another or each other? See note at EACH OTHER.

one-armed bandit *noun* a type of gambling machine that is operated by a lever on one side of the machine. [from the lever, and the machine's tendency to divest you of your money]

one-dimensional *adj* lacking depth; superficial. ▶▶ **one-dimensionality** *noun*.

one-horse *adj* **1** pulled by one horse: *a one-horse open sleigh.* **2** *informal* of little importance or interest: *a one-horse town.* **3** with only one contender: *a one-horse race.*

oneiric /oh'nierik/ *adj* of or relating to dreams; dreamy. [Greek *oneiros* dream]

one-liner *noun* a short funny remark.

one-man *adj* **1** consisting of only one man or one person. **2** done or produced by only one man or one person.

one-man band *noun* **1** a street entertainer who has a number of musical instruments attached to his or her body in such a way that they can be played at the same time. **2** somebody who operates on their own, e.g. running a business single-handedly, or the business, etc run by such a person.

oneness *noun* **1** the state or fact of being only one in number; singleness: *Put in something about the Supernal Oneness* — Poe. **2** the state or fact of being whole, identical, or in agreement.

one-night stand *noun* **1** a sexual relationship lasting only one night, or a person with whom one has such a relationship. **2** a performance given only once in any particular place.

one-off¹ *adj chiefly Brit* made or intended as a single and unrepeated item or occurrence: *a one-off job.*

one-off² *noun* somebody or something that is unique.

one-on-one *adj* = ONE-TO-ONE (2).

one-piece *adj* consisting of or made in a single undivided piece: *a one-piece swimming costume.*

oner /'wunə/ *noun informal* a single attempt: *We did it in a oner.*

onerous /'ohnərəs, 'on-/ *adj* representing or involving a burden; troublesome. ▶▶ **onerously** *adv*, **onerousness** *noun*. [Middle English via French from Latin *onerosus*, from *oner-*, *onus* burden]

oneself *pronoun* **1** used reflexively to refer to an indefinitely indicated person or to people in general: *Innocence ends when one is stripped of the delusion that one likes oneself* — Joan Didion. **2** used for emphasis: *It is hard to believe unless one has seen it oneself.* ✳ **be oneself** to be fit or healthy as normal: *One is never quite oneself immediately after an operation.*

one-sided *adj* **1** giving favour unfairly to one party in a dispute, contest, etc; biased. **2a** having or occurring on one side only. **b** having one side prominent or more developed. ▶▶ **one-sidedly** *adv*, **one-sidedness** *noun*.

one-step *noun* a ballroom dance marked by quick walking steps, or a piece of music for this dance.

one-time *adj* former.

one-to-one *adj* **1** pairing each element of a set uniquely with an element of another set. **2** involving contact between somebody, e.g. a teacher, and one other person only: *one-to-one tuition.*

one-track *adj* interested or absorbed in one thing only: *a one-track mind.*

one-two *noun* **1** a combination of two quick blows in boxing, usu with different hands and in rapid succession. **2** a pass in football whereby one player kicks the ball to another and runs forward immediately to receive the return.

one up *adj* in a position of advantage.

one-upmanship /'upmənship/ *noun* the art of gaining a psychological advantage over others by professing social or professional superiority.

one-way *adj* **1** moving in or allowing movement in only one direction: *one-way traffic.* **2** involving no collaboration or reciprocation; unilateral.

one-woman *adj* **1** consisting of only one woman. **2** done or produced by only one woman.

one-world *adj* illustrating or promoting the belief that the various communities of the world depend on each other socially, economically, and ecologically.

ongoing *adj* **1** actually in progress. **2** growing or developing.

onion /'unyən/ *noun* **1** an Asian plant of the lily family widely cultivated for its pungent smelling, strong tasting edible bulb that has a brown papery skin: *Allium cepa.* **2** the bulb of this plant, used as a vegetable. ✳ **know one's onions** *Brit, informal* to be very knowledgeable about something. [Middle English via French from Latin *union-*, *unio*, perhaps from *unus* one]

onionskin *noun* a thin, strong, very lightweight paper.

on-line[1] *adj* **1** controlled directly by, or directly linked to, a computer: compare OFF-LINE[1]. **2** currently connected to a computer or network: compare OFF-LINE[1]. **3** in operation or production.

on-line[2] *adv* **1** while controlled by or linked to a computer or network. **2** into operation or production.

onlooker /'onlookə/ *noun* a passive spectator. ➤➤ **onlooking** *adj.*

only[1] /'ohnli/ *adj* **1** alone in its class or kind; sole: *This is the only detergent that contains fabric softener.* **2** unquestionably the best: *It's the only way to travel.* **3** without a brother or sister: *an only child.* [Old English *ānlīc*, from *ān* ONE[3] + *lic* -LY[1]]

only[2] *adv* **1a** nothing more than; merely: *only a little one; If it would only rain!* **b** solely or exclusively: *That is something known only to him.* **2** by a very small amount or margin: *We only just caught the bus.* **3a** in the final outcome: *It will only make you sick.* **b** with nevertheless the final result: *They won the battle, only to lose the war.* **4** no earlier than: *I saw her only last week; She has only just left.* ✳ **only too** very much, sometimes regrettably so: *It's only too true that love is blind.*

Usage note

The notion that the adverb *only* should always be placed next to the word in the sentence that it refers to is a superstition that runs counter to the natural position of such modifying words in English (compare *often* and *usually*). The typical position is between the subject and the verb in sentences such as *I only drink wine at weekends* and after an auxiliary verb in sentences such as *I can only lend you a pound.* (Compare *I often drink wine at weekends* and *I can usually lend you a pound.*) In ordinary conversation, the tone of voice makes it clear that *only* refers forward to the phrase *at weekends* and not more immediately to the words *drink* or *wine*, and that you do not mean (for example) *I drink wine at weekends but I don't cook with it* or *I drink wine at weekends but not beer.* In more formal written English, especially in legal documents, the position of *only* becomes more important, because in these contexts the language needs to be precise. So a contract, for example, might include the wording *This penalty will be applied only if the contractor has been warned in writing at least three weeks in advance of the due date.* But in ordinary English *only* would go after the verb *will.*

only[3] *conj informal* **1** but or however: *They look very nice, only we can't use them.* **2** were it not for the fact that: *I'd tell you, only you'll just spread it around.*

on-message *adj* said of a politician: following official party policy.

o.n.o. *abbr* used with prices of goods for sale: or nearest offer.

on-off *adj* occurring or existing from time to time; intermittent: *an on-off relationship.*

onomastic /onə'mastik/ *adj* relating to or consisting of a name. [Greek *onomastikos*, from *onomazein* to name, from *onoma* name]

onomastics *pl noun* (*treated as sing. or pl*) the science or study of proper names.

onomatopoeia /ˌonəmatə'pee·ə/ *noun* the formation or use of words intended to be a vocal imitation of the sound associated with the thing or action designated, e.g. *buzz, cuckoo.* ➤➤ **onomatopoeic** /-'peeik/ *adj,* **onomatopoeically** /-'peeikli/ *adv.* [via late Latin from Greek *onomatopoiia,* from *onomat-, onoma* name + *poiein* to make]

onrush /'onrush/ *noun* a forceful rushing forwards.

onset /'onset/ *noun* **1** a time or point at which something begins; a commencement. **2** an attack or assault.

onshore *adj and adv* **1** towards or moving towards the shore. **2** on or near the shore.

onside *adv and adj* **1** in a position permitted by the rules of the game; not offside. **2** in agreement or support, or into a position of agreement or support.

onslaught /'onslawt/ *noun* a fierce attack. [modification of Dutch *aanslag* act of striking, by association with obsolete *slaught* slaughter]

on stream *adj and adv* in or into production: *More oil fields are soon due to come on stream.*

Ont. *abbr* Ontario.

ont- *or* **onto-** *comb. form* forming nouns, denoting: **1** being or existence: *ontology.* **2** organism: *ontogeny.* [Greek *ont-, ōn,* present part. of *einai* to be]

-ont *comb. form* forming nouns, denoting: cell or organism: *symbiont.* [from ONT-]

on-the-job *adj* denoting something learned, gained, or done while working in a job.

onto *or* **on to** /'ontə; *strong* 'ontooh/ *prep* **1** to a position on. **2** in or into a state of awareness about: *They put the police onto him.* **3** indicating a mathematical set, each element of which is the image of at least one element of another set: *a function mapping the set S onto the set T.* **4** *chiefly Brit* in or into contact with: *We've been onto the council about the drains.*

Usage note

There is no objection to spelling *onto* as a single word when it means 'to a position on': *The book fell onto the floor.* Some people have reservations about using *onto* after a verb that is often followed by the preposition *on.* In a sentence such as *We walked on to the end of the lane* ('until we reached'), *onto* would be incorrect. Compare *We walked onto the end of the red carpet* ('we walked forward and stood on'), in which *onto* is correct. Sentences such as *She latched on to the idea at once* and *I want to move on to another topic* are, however, a grey area. *Onto* is increasingly being used in them, but the safer option is to use *on to.* The form *onto* has been used throughout this dictionary.

onto- *comb. form* see ONT-.

ontogenesis /ontə'jenəsis/ *noun* (*pl* **ontogeneses** /-seez/) the entire set of processes involved in the development of an individual organism: compare PHYLOGENESIS. ➤➤ **ontogenetic** /-'netik/ *adj,* **ontogenetically** /-'netikli/ *adv.*

ontogeny /on'tojəni/ *noun* = ONTOGENESIS.

ontological /ontə'lojikl/ *adj* **1** of ontology. **2** relating to or based on being or existence. ➤➤ **ontologically** *adv.*

ontology /on'toləji/ *noun* a branch of philosophy concerned with the nature of being.

Editorial note

By 'the nature of being' (which is the subject of 'ontology') we mean first the nature of 'beings'. What sorts of things are there? Material objects, for one, as occupiers of space-time. Beyond them (or instead of them) there may be such further things as events, states of affairs, persons, numbers, ideas, qualities, waves. As well as asking about beings, we may ask what 'being' itself is. Plato and Heidegger take this question to be very important; Aristotle and many others think it is senseless and so needs no answer — Professor Jonathan Dancy.

➤➤ **ontologist** *noun.*

onus /'ohnəs/ *noun* **1a** a duty or responsibility. **b** blame. **2** the burden of proof in a legal case. [Latin *onus*]

onward[1] /'onwəd/ *adj* directed or moving onwards; forward.

onward[2] *adv* = ONWARDS.

onwards *adv* towards or at a point lying ahead in space or time; forwards: *From his childhood onwards, he had wanted to act.*

onychophoran /oni'kofərən/ *noun* any of a small phylum of small tropical slug-like animals that have segmented bodies and short stumpy legs: phylum Onychophora. [scientific Latin from Greek *onych-, onyx* claw + -O- + *-phoros* -PHORE]

-onym *comb. form* forming nouns, denoting: **1** name: *pseudonym.* **2** word: *antonym.* [Middle English via Latin *-onymum* from Greek *-ōnymon,* from *onyma* name]

onyx /'oniks/ *noun* **1** a translucent variety of quartz with layers of different colours, typically green and white or black, or brown and white. **2** a translucent or semitranslucent calcium carbonate mineral, usu calcite, with marble-like bands of colour. [Middle English *onix* via Old French and Latin from Greek *onyx,* literally 'claw, nail']

oo- *comb. form* see O-[1].

oocyte /'oh·əsiet/ *noun* a cell that becomes an ovum after it has divided.

oodles /'oohdlz/ *pl noun informal* a great quantity; a lot. [perhaps alteration of HUDDLE[2]]

oogamete /oh·ə'gameet/ *noun* a relatively large immobile female GAMETE (sex cell).

oogamous /oh'ogəməs/ *adj* having or involving a small mobile male GAMETE (sex cell) and a large immobile female gamete. ➤➤ **oogamy** /-mi/ *noun.*

oogenesis /oh·ə'jenəsis/ *noun* the formation and maturation of eggs or ova. ➤➤ **oogenetic** /-'netik/ *adj.*

ooh /ooh/ *interj* an expression of amazement or pleased surprise.

oolite /'oh·əliet/ *noun* a rock, *esp* limestone, consisting of small round grains, *esp* of calcium carbonate. ➤➤ **oolitic** /-'litik/ *adj.* [prob from French *oolithe,* from O-[1] + *-lithe* -LITE]

oolith /'oh·əlith/ *noun* any of the small round grains that make up oolite.

oology /oh'oləji/ *noun* the study or collecting of birds' eggs. ⟫ **oological** /-'lojikl/ *adj,* **oologically** /-'lojikli/ *adv,* **oologist** *noun.*

oolong /'oohlong/ *noun* a dark China tea that is partially fermented before drying. [Chinese (Pekingese) *wulong,* literally 'black dragon']

oompah /'oompah/ *noun* the deep, often rhythmical sound of a tuba, euphonium, or similar brass band instrument. [imitative]

oomph /oom(p)f/ *noun informal* **1** vitality or enthusiasm. **2** sexual attractiveness. [imitative]

oops /oops, oohps/ *interj* an expression of apology or surprise, *esp* when causing an accident or making a mistake.

oospore /'oh-əspaw/ *noun* a fertilized plant spore that grows into the phase of a plant producing sexual spores: compare ZYGOSPORE.

ooze[1] /oohz/ *verb intrans* **1a** to pass or flow slowly through small openings. **b** to diminish gradually. **2** to exude moisture. ⟩ *verb trans* **1** to emit (something) slowly. **2** to display (a quality) in abundance: *She positively oozed vitality.* [Middle English *wosen* from Old English *wōs* sap, juice]

ooze[2] *noun* **1** an infusion of vegetable material, e.g. bark, used for tanning leather. **2** something that oozes. ⟫ **oozy** *adj.*

ooze[3] *noun* **1** a soft deposit of mud, slime, debris, etc on the bottom of a body of water. **2** a marsh or bog, or its muddy ground. ⟫ **oozy** *adj.* [Old English *wāse* mire]

OP *abbr* **1** observation post. **2** opposite prompt, used to designate the part of a theatre stage offstage to the right of the actors. **3** Order of Preachers, i.e. the Dominicans. **4** organophosphate. **5** out of print. [(sense 3) Latin *Ordo Praedicatorum*]

op /op/ *noun informal* a military or surgical operation.

op. *abbr* opus.

op- *prefix* see OB-.

opacity /oh'pasiti/ *noun* (*pl* **opacities**) **1** the quality of being opaque. **2** obscurity of meaning; unintelligibility. **3** an opaque spot on a normally transparent structure, e.g. the lens of the eye. [French *opacité* shadiness, from Latin *opacitat-, opacitas,* from *opacus* shaded, dark]

opah /'ohpə/ *noun* a large brilliantly coloured marine fish with rich oily red flesh: *Lampris guttatus.* Also called KINGFISH. [Ibo *úbá*]

opal /'ohp(ə)l/ *noun* a transparent to translucent mineral consisting of a hydrated silica and used in its opalescent forms as a gem. [Latin *opalus* from Sanskrit *upala* stone, jewel]

opalescent /ohpə'les(ə)nt/ *adj* reflecting a milky iridescent light. ⟫ **opalescence** *noun.*

opal glass *noun* glass to which fluorides have been added to give it a milky translucent quality.

opaline[1] /'ohpəlien/ *adj* resembling opal; opalescent.

opaline[2] *noun* = OPAL GLASS.

opaque[1] /oh'payk/ *adj* **1** not able to be seen through; not transparent or translucent: *People were so ridiculous with their illusions … thinking their own lies opaque while everyone else's were transparent —* George Eliot. **2** hard to understand; unintelligible. ⟫ **opaquely** *adv,* **opaqueness** *noun.* [Latin *opacus* shaded, dark]

opaque[2] *noun* something opaque, *esp* an opaque paint for blocking out portions of a photographic negative or print.

op art /op/ *noun* a style of art characterized by the repeated use of geometric shapes and patterns designed to create optical illusions and visual uncertainty. ⟫ **op artist** *noun.*

op. cit. /,op 'sit/ *abbr* in the work cited. [Latin *opere citato*]

ope /ohp/ *verb trans and intrans archaic* to open. [variant of OPEN[2]]

OPEC /'ohpek/ *abbr* Organization of Petroleum Exporting Countries.

open[1] /'ohp(ə)n/ *adj* **1a** allowing access or passage; not shut or locked: *an open door.* **b** having no enclosing or confining barrier: *the open hillside.* **c** presenting no obstacle to passage or view. **d** having the parts or surfaces spread out or unfolded. **2a** not fastened or sealed: *The bottle was open.* **b** not covered or protected: *an open boat; an open wound.* **3** in operation, *esp* ready for business or use: *The shop won't be open yet.* **4a** exposed to general view or knowledge; public: *They regarded him with open hatred.* **b** vulnerable to attack or question; liable: *Whether they'll succeed is open to doubt.* **5a** available: *That's the only course open to us.* **b** not taken up with duties or engagements: *Keep an hour open on Friday.* **c** not finally decided or settled: *It's an open question whether GM foods are safe.* **d** available

for a qualified applicant; vacant. **e** remaining available for use or filling until cancelled: *We can place an open order for more items.* **f** not restricted to a particular category of participants; *specif* contested by both amateurs and professionals. **6a** willing to receive and consider: *I'm always open to suggestions.* **b** candid or frank. **c** willing to consider new ideas; unprejudiced: *an open mind.* **d** having a relatively liberal structure, with freedom of belief, information, etc: *the open society.* **7** generous; openhanded. **8** free from checks or restraints: *an open economy.* **9** containing many small openings or spaces; *specif* porous. **10a** having relatively wide spacing between words or lines: *open type.* **b** said of a compound word: with elements separated by a space in writing or printing, e.g. in *ski lift.* **11a** said of a string on a musical instrument: not stopped by the finger. **b** said of a note: produced on a musical instrument without fingering the strings, valves, slides, or keys. **12** said of a vowel: articulated with the tongue low in the mouth. **13** said of a mathematical set: containing a neighbourhood of every element. **14** *Brit* said of a cheque: payable in cash to the person, organization, etc named on it; not crossed. ✳ **with open arms** in a welcoming or enthusiastic manner. ⟫ **openness** *noun.* [Old English]

open[2] *verb* (**opened, opening**) ⟩ *verb trans* **1** to change or move (something) from a closed position: *to open a window.* **2** to gain access to the contents of (a container, package, etc). **3a** to make (a business, shop, etc) available for business: *The Bank opened a new branch in the High Street.* **b** to declare (something) available for use, *esp* ceremonially. **c** to make the necessary arrangements for (e.g. a bank account), *esp* by depositing money. **4** to unfold or spread out (something). **5** to do the first part of (an activity): *They opened the meeting with a prayer.* **6** to begin (e.g. the bidding, betting, or play) in a card game. **7** in cricket, to begin (a side's round of batting or bowling). ⟩ *verb intrans* **1** to become open. **2** to begin an activity: *He opened with a prayer.* **3** (+ into/onto) to give access: *The door opens onto a terrace.* **4** (*often* + out) to extend or unfold: *The view opened out in front of us.* ⟫ **openable** *adj.*

open[3] *noun* **1** (**the open**) a large outdoor space, *esp* in the countryside. **2** (*often* **Open**) a contest, competition, or tournament in which anybody can compete. ✳ **bring into/be in the open** to be, or cause (something) to be, generally known.

open[4] *adv* openly.

open air *noun* (**the open air**) a large outdoor space; outdoors.

open-air *adj* outdoor.

open-and-shut *adj* easily settled: *an open-and-shut case.*

opencast *adj* said of a mine or mining: worked from or carried out on the earth's surface by removing material covering the mineral mined for.

open chain *noun* in chemistry, an arrangement of atoms in a chain whose ends are not joined to form a ring.

open circuit *noun* an incomplete circuit of electrical components through which current cannot flow.

open-circuit television *noun* a television system or installation in which programmes are broadcast so that they are available to any receivers within range.

open court *noun* a court or trial to which the public are admitted.

open day *noun* a day on which an institution is open to the public.

open door *noun* **1** a policy of equal commercial relations with all nations. **2** a policy of unrestricted access. ⟫ **open-door** *adj.*

open-ended *adj* without any definite limits or restrictions, e.g. of time or purpose, set in advance. ⟫ **open-endedness** *noun.*

opener *noun* **1a** a device that opens something: *a bottle opener.* **b** somebody who begins something; *specif* an opening batsman or batswoman. **2** (*in pl*) cards of sufficient value for a player to open the betting in a poker game. **3** the first item or event in a series. ✳ **for openers** *informal* to start with.

open-faced *adj* **1** with a facial expression that suggests frankness and lack of duplicity. **2** said of a watch: with no glass cover over the face.

openhanded *adj* generous in giving. ⟫ **openhandedly** *adv,* **openhandedness** *noun.*

openhearted *adj* **1** kind, generous, or affectionate. **2** candidly straightforward. ⟫ **openheartedly** *adv,* **openheartedness** *noun.*

open-hearth *adj* of, produced by, or used in the open-hearth steelmaking process.

open-hearth process *noun* a process of making steel from pig iron in a reverberatory furnace.

open-heart surgery *noun* surgery in which the heart is actually exposed and blood circulation performed by machine.

open house /hows/ ✳ **keep open house** to be ready to receive visitors at all times.

opening[1] *noun* **1** a space through which something can pass; a gap. **2a** an often standard series of moves made at the beginning of a game of chess or draughts: compare END GAME, MIDDLE GAME. **b** a first performance. **3a** a favourable opportunity; a chance. **b** an opportunity for employment; a vacancy. **4** the act or an instance of becoming open or making something open.

opening[2] *adj* **1** coming at or marking the beginning of something. **2** relating to an opening: *opening night.*

opening time *noun* the time at which a business, shop, etc opens; *specif* the statutory time at which a pub may open for the sale of alcohol.

open learning *noun* flexible further education for part-time students, such as that involving study at home with broadcast, recorded or printed lesson material.

open letter *noun* a letter, *esp* of protest, appeal, or explanation, usu addressed to an individual but intended for the general public, and published in a newspaper, periodical, etc.

openly *adv* in an open and frank manner.

open market *noun* a market based on free competition and an unrestricted flow of goods, e.g. between countries.

open marriage *noun* a marriage in which both partners agree to retain a considerable degree of the social and sexual independence they enjoyed when they were single.

open-minded *adj* receptive to new arguments or ideas. ⫸ **open-mindedly** *adv*, **open-mindedness** *noun*.

openmouthed /ohp(ə)n'mowdhd/ *adj* having the mouth open, *esp* in surprise.

open out *verb intrans* to speak freely.

open-plan *adj* having no or few internal dividing walls: *an open-plan house.*

open prison *noun* a prison that has less restrictive security than a conventional one, to which criminals considered unlikely to attempt escape may be sent.

open question *noun* **1** a question to which the answer needs to be more complex than a simple *yes* or *no*. **2** a matter that has yet to be decided or resolved.

open-reel *adj* = REEL-TO-REEL.

open sandwich *noun* a sandwich without a top slice of bread.

open season *noun* a period during which it is legal to kill or catch game or fish protected at other times by law.

open secret *noun* a supposed secret that is in fact widely known.

open sesame /'sesəmi/ *noun* a means of gaining access to something otherwise inaccessible. [*open sesame* the magical command used by Ali Baba to open the door of the robbers' den in the Arabic folk tale *Ali Baba and the Forty Thieves*]

open shop *noun* a place of work in which employment is not dependent on membership of a trade union: compare CLOSED SHOP.

Open University *noun* (**the Open University**) the non-residential British university that caters mainly for adults studying part-time and operates mainly through correspondence courses and broadcast programmes.

open up *verb intrans* **1** to allow access to a building. **2** said of a game, competition, etc: to become more interesting, *esp* because more closely contested. **3** to start to speak more freely. **4** to start shooting weapons. ➤ *verb trans* to make (something) available or accessible: *The deal opened up important new possibilities for trade.*

open verdict *noun* a verdict at an inquest that records a death but does not state its cause.

openwork *noun* ornamental work (e.g. in fabric or metal) that is perforated or pierced. ⫸ **open-worked** *adj*.

opera[1] /'oprə/ *noun* **1a** a drama set to music and made up of vocal pieces with orchestral accompaniment and usu other orchestral music (e.g. an overture): *I do not mind what language an opera is sung in so long as it is a language I don't understand* — Edward Appleton. **b** the performance of such a drama, or the score for it.

Editorial note
Opera is one of the most familiar musical terms, yet the most complex and multi-faceted of all musical genres if not of all art forms. First designated favola in musica, opera originated in 1590s Florence as an attempt to merge drama and music in the manner of Greek tragedy. The ground-breaking characteristic of this form was its declamatory monodic style, or recitative, but it also included arias, choruses, and instrumental music. These components (plus vocal ensembles) are still the basis of today's Grand Opera which encompasses a dazzling array of masterpieces by living and dead composers, served in performance by a vast panoply of highly skilled artists and technicians — Amanda Holden.

2 the branch of the arts concerned with such works. **3** a company performing operas. **4** a theatre where operas are performed; an opera house. [Italian *opera* work, opera, from Latin *opera* work, pains, from *opus, opus* work]

opera[2] /'op(ə)rə/ *noun* pl of OPUS.

operable /'op(ə)rəbl/ *adj* **1** suitable for surgical treatment: *an operable cancer*. **2** fit, possible, or desirable to use; practicable. ⫸ **operability** /-'biliti/ *noun*, **operably** *adv*.

opéra bouffe /,op(ə)rə 'boohf (*French* ɔpera buf)/ *noun* (*pl* **opéras bouffes** /,op(ə)rə 'boohf/) = OPERA BUFFA. [French *opéra bouffe* from Italian *opera buffa*]

opera buffa /'boohfə/ *noun* (*pl* **opera buffas**) a farcical or satirical opera, *esp* of a form popular in the 18th cent. [Italian *opera buffa* comic opera]

opéra comique /ko'meek (*French* kɔmik)/ *noun* (*pl* **opéras comiques** /,op(ə)rə ko'meek/) = COMIC OPERA. [French *opéra comique*]

opera glasses *pl noun* small binoculars suitable for use at the opera or theatre.

opera hat *noun* a man's collapsible top hat.

opera house *noun* a theatre designed for the performance of opera.

operand /'opə'rand/ *noun* something, *esp* a quantity, on which an operation is performed, e.g. in mathematics. [Latin *operandum*, from *operari*: see OPERATE]

operant[1] /'op(ə)rənt/ *adj* effective or functioning.

operant[2] *noun* **1** an OPERATOR (1A). **2** a type of behaviour, e.g. bar pressing by a rat to obtain food, that operates on the environment to produce rewarding effects.

opera seria /'siəri-ə/ *noun* (*pl* **opera serias**) an 18th-cent. opera with a heroic or legendary subject. [Italian *opera seria* serious opera]

operate /'opərayt/ *verb intrans* **1** to exert power or influence; to act: *There were several factors operating against our success.* **2** to produce a desired effect. **3** to be in effect; to function. **4** to be in action; *specif* to carry out trade or business. **5** (*often* + on) to perform surgery. **6** to carry on a military or naval action or mission. ➤ *verb trans* **1a** to cause (e.g. a machine) to function; to work (it). **b** to put or keep (e.g. a business) in operation; to manage (it). **2** to cause (something) to happen; to bring (it) about. [Latin *operatus*, past part. of *operari* to work, from *oper-, opus* work]

operatic /opə'ratik/ *adj* **1** relating to opera. **2** overtly theatrical in behaviour; flamboyant. ⫸ **operatically** *adv*.

operatics /opə'ratiks/ *pl noun* (*treated as sing. or pl*) the performance of operas.

operating system *noun* the computer software that supports and controls the running of a computer and its associated equipment, e.g. by keeping track of the different programs running simultaneously.

operating table *noun* a high table on which a patient lies while undergoing surgery.

operating theatre *noun* *Brit* a room in a hospital where surgical operations are carried out.

operation /opə'raysh(ə)n/ *noun* **1a** the act or an instance of operating or being operated, or the method of operating. **b** something done or to be done; an activity. **2** the state of being functional or operative: *The plant is now in operation.* **3** a procedure carried out on a living body with special instruments, usu for the repair of damage or the restoration of health. **4** any of various mathematical or logical processes, e.g. addition, carried out to derive one expression from others according to a rule. **5** a usu military action, mission, or manoeuvre and its planning. **6** a business or financial transaction. **7** a single step performed by a computer in the execution of a program.

operational *adj* **1** of or based on operations. **2a** of, involved in, or used for the execution of commercial, military, or naval operations. **b** currently functioning or in a state in which functioning is now possible. ➤➤ **operationally** *adv*.

operationalism *noun* the theory in the philosophy of science that a concept can only properly be defined in terms of repeatable operations of observation, measurement, etc, e.g. the concept of weight should be defined in terms of repeatable acts of weighing. ➤➤ **operationalist** *noun*, **operationalistic** /-'listik/ *adj*.

operational research *noun* the application of scientific, *esp* mathematical, methods to the study and analysis of problems involving complex systems, e.g. business management, economic planning, and the waging of war.

operations research *noun* = OPERATIONAL RESEARCH.

operations room *noun* a room from which military or other operations are controlled.

operative[1] /'op(ə)rətiv/ *adj* **1** in force or operation. **2a** significant or relevant: *I might come, but 'might' is the operative word.* **b** producing an appropriate effect; efficacious. **3** based on, consisting of, or using a surgical operation. ➤➤ **operatively** *adv*, **operativeness** *noun*.

operative[2] *noun* **1** a worker. **2** a secret agent. **3** *NAmer* a private detective.

operator *noun* **1a** somebody who operates a machine or device. **b** somebody who owns or runs a business, organization, etc: *a tour operator.* **c** somebody who works on a telephone switchboard. **2** a mathematical or logical symbol denoting an operation to be performed. **3** *informal* a shrewd and skilful manipulator.

operculum /o'puhkyooləm/ *noun* (*pl* **opercula** /-lə/ *or* **operculums**) **1** a lid or covering flap, e.g. of a moss capsule or the gills of a fish. **2** a hard plate at the end of the foot in many gastropod molluscs that closes the shell when the animal is retracted. ➤➤ **opercular** *adj*, **operculate** /-lət, -layt/ *adj*, **operculated** /-laytid/ *adj*. [Latin *operculum* cover, from *operire* to shut, cover]

operetta /opə'retə/ *noun* a less formal or serious, and usu romantic or humorous, form of opera that includes dancing and spoken dialogue. ➤➤ **operettist** *noun*. [Italian *operetta*, dimin. of *opera*: see OPERA[1]]

operon /'opəron/ *noun* a set of genes on a chromosome encoding proteins that function together as a unit and are expressed together. [OPERATOR + -ON[2]]

ophicleide /'ofiklied/ *noun* a brass musical instrument of low range with finger-operated keys for varying the pitch, superseded in the 19th cent. by the tuba. [French *ophicléide*, from Greek *ophis* snake + *kleid-, kleis* key]

ophidian[1] /o'fidi-ən/ *adj* of or resembling snakes. [via Latin from Greek *ophid-, ophis* snake]

ophidian[2] *noun technical* a snake.

ophite /'ofiet/ *noun* any of various usu green and often mottled rocks, e.g. serpentine. [Latin *ophite* from Greek *ophitēs* (*lithos*) serpentine (stone), from *ophis* snake]

ophthalm- *or* **ophthalmo-** *comb. form* forming words, denoting: eye or eyeball: *ophthalmology.* [Greek *ophthalmos* eye]

ophthalmia /of'thalmi-ə, op-/ *noun* inflammation of the conjunctiva or the eyeball. [Middle English *obtalmia* via late Latin *ophthalmia* from Greek *ophthalmos* eye]

ophthalmic /of'thalmik, op-/ *adj* of or situated near the eye.

ophthalmic optician *noun* an optician qualified to test eyesight and prescribe correctional lenses.

ophthalmo- *comb. form* see OPHTHALM-.

ophthalmologist /ofthal'moləjist, op-/ *noun* a physician who specializes in ophthalmology: compare OPTICIAN.

ophthalmology /ofthal'moləji, op-/ *noun* the branch of medical science dealing with the structure, functions, and diseases of the eye. ➤➤ **ophthalmological** /-'lojikl/ *adj*, **ophthalmologically** /-'lojikli/ *adv*.

ophthalmoscope /of'thalməskohp, op-/ *noun* an instrument used to view the retina and other structures inside the eye. ➤➤ **ophthalmoscopic** /-'skopik/ *adj*, **ophthalmoscopy** /-'moskəpi/ *noun*.

-opia *comb. form* forming nouns, denoting: the condition of having a specified visual defect: *myopia.* [Greek *-ōpia*, from *ōps* eye]

opiate[1] /'ohpi-ət, -ayt/ *adj* **1** containing or mixed with opium. **2** inducing sleep; narcotic.

opiate[2] *noun* **1** a preparation or derivative of opium; a narcotic. **2** something that induces inaction or calm.

opine /oh'pien/ *verb trans formal* to state (something) as an opinion. [early French *opiner* from Latin *opinari* to have an opinion]

opinion /ə'pinyən/ *noun* **1** a view or judgment formed about a particular matter: *I'm of the opinion that he's lying.* **2a** a belief that is not supported by positive knowledge. **b** a generally held view. **3a** a formal expression by an expert of his or her professional judgment or advice, *esp* a barrister's written advice to a client. **b** *chiefly NAmer* a formal expression of the principles on which a legal decision is based. ✱ **matter of opinion** something about which people differ and which cannot be decided objectively or proved conclusively one way or the other. [Middle English via French from Latin *opinion-, opinio*, from *opinari* to have an opinion]

opinionated /ə'pinyənaytid/ *adj* always ready to express one's own opinions and dismissive of other people's. ➤➤ **opinionatedly** *adv*, **opinionatedness** *noun*.

opinion poll *noun* a survey conducted by questioning people selected at random or by quota in order to establish public opinion on some matter.

opium /'ohpi-əm/ *noun* **1** an addictive drug consisting of the dried juice of the unripe seed capsules of the opium poppy, containing morphine and other narcotic alkaloids: *Thou hast the keys of Paradise, oh just, subtle, and mighty opium* — De Quincey. **2** something that has an addictive effect, *esp* something that inhibits thought or action: *Has anything replaced religion as the opium of the people?* [Middle English via Latin from Greek *opion* poppy juice, dimin. of *opos* sap]

opium den *noun* a place where opium can be bought and smoked.

opium poppy *noun* an annual Eurasian poppy cultivated as the source of opium or for its edible seeds or showy flowers: *Papaver somniferum.*

opossum /ə'posəm/ *noun* (*pl* **opossums** *or collectively* **opossum**) **1** any of numerous species of American tree-dwelling marsupials with a prehensile tail: family Didelphidae. **2** = POSSUM (2). [Virginia Algonquian *âpäsûm* white animal]

opp. *abbr* opposite.

opponent[1] /ə'pohnənt/ *noun* **1** somebody who takes the opposite side in a contest, conflict, etc. **2** in anatomy, an opponent muscle. [Latin *opponent-, opponens*, present part. of *opponere*: see OPPOSE]

opponent[2] *adj* **1** *formal* opposing. **2** said of a muscle: opposing or counteracting and limiting the action of another.

opportune /'opətyoohn, -'tyoohn/ *adj* **1** suitable or convenient for a particular occurrence or action: *It seemed an opportune moment to discuss money.* **2** occurring at an appropriate time: *an opportune offer.* ➤➤ **opportunely** *adv*, **opportuneness** *noun*. [Middle English via French from Latin *opportunus*, literally 'blowing towards the harbour', hence 'seasonable, favourable' from OP- + *portus* harbour, PORT[1]]

opportunism /opə'tyoohniz(ə)m/ *noun* the taking advantage of opportunities or circumstances, *esp* with little regard for principles or consequences.

opportunist /opə'tyoohnist/ *noun* somebody who seizes opportunities with little regard for principles or consequences.

opportunistic /ˌopətyooh'nistik/ *adj* **1** tending to seize opportunities with little regard for principles or consequences. **2** said of a disease: caused by a micro-organism that has little or no effect on healthy people but attacks those whose immune systems have been weakened in some way.

opportunity /opə'tyoohniti/ *noun* (*pl* **opportunities**) **1** a favourable set of circumstances. **2** a chance for advancement or progress.

opposable /ə'pohzəbl/ *adj* **1** capable of being opposed or resisted. **2** said of a thumb or other digit: capable of being placed opposite and against the remaining digits.

oppose /ə'pohz/ *verb trans* **1** to be hostile to or against (somebody or something); to offer resistance to (them or it). **2** to place (something) opposite or against something else so as to provide a counterbalance, contrast, etc to it. ➤➤ **opposer** *noun*, **opposing** *adj*. [French *opposer* from Latin *opponere*, from OP- + *ponere* to place]

opposed *adj* set in opposition; contrary.

opposite[1] /'opəzit/ *adj* **1a** in a position with regard to somebody or something else that is at the other end or side of an intervening line or space: *We were on opposite sides of the road.* **b** said of angles: on opposite sides of a point where two lines intersect. **2a** occupying an opposing position: *We need to consider the opposite sides of the question.* **b** diametrically different; contrary. **3** being the other of a matching or contrasting pair: *the opposite sex.* **4** said of plant parts: situated in pairs at the same level on opposite sides of an axis: compare ALTERNATE[1]: *opposite leaves.* **>> oppositely** *adv,* **oppositeness** *noun.* [Middle English via French from Latin *oppositus,* past part. of *opponere:* see OPPOSE]

opposite[2] *prep* **1** across from and usu facing: *We sat opposite each other.* **2** in a role complementary to: *He played opposite the leading lady.*

opposite[3] *adv* on or to an opposite side.

opposite[4] *noun* **1** something or somebody opposed or contrary. **2** an antonym.

opposite number *noun* a counterpart.

opposition /opə'zish(ə)n/ *noun* **1** the act or an instance of placing something opposite or of being so placed. **2a** hostility. **b** hostile or contrary action. **3** (*treated as sing. or pl*). **a** the body of people opposing something. **b** (*often* **Opposition**) the main political party opposing the party in power. **4** in astronomy, an opposite position of the sun and another celestial body in which their longitude differs by 180°. **5** in logic, the relation between two propositions having the same subject and predicate but differing in quantity or quality or both. **>> oppositional** *adj.*

oppress /ə'pres/ *verb trans* **1** to crush (e.g. a people) by harsh or authoritarian rule: *The most potent weapon in the hands of the oppressor is the mind of the oppressed* — Steve Biko. **2** to weigh heavily on the mind or spirit of (somebody). **>> oppressor** *noun.* [Middle English *oppressen* via French from medieval Latin *oppressare,* from Latin *oppressus,* past part. of *opprimere* to press against, from OP- + *premere* PRESS[1]]

oppression /ə'presh(ə)n/ *noun* **1** the act or an instance of oppressing or being oppressed. **2** unjust or harsh exercise of authority or power. **3** a sense of being mentally weighed down.

oppressive /ə'presiv/ *adj* **1** unreasonably harsh or severe; authoritarian. **2** causing a sense of being mentally weighed down. **3** said of the weather: stiflingly warm and lacking in breeze; close. **>> oppressively** *adv,* **oppressiveness** *noun.*

opprobrious /ə'prohbri·əs/ *adj formal* **1** sharply critical, scornful, or abusive: *opprobrious language.* **2** bringing the disrespect of others; shameful. **>> opprobriously** *adv.*

opprobrium /ə'prohbri·əm/ *noun formal* **1** the public disgrace or contempt that results from shameful behaviour. **2** something that brings disgrace. [Latin *opprobrium* from *opprobrare* to reproach, from OP- + *probrum* disgrace]

oppugn /ə'pyoohn/ *verb trans formal* to cast doubt on (something). **>> oppugner** *noun.* [Middle English *oppugnen* from Latin *oppugnare* to attack, from OP- + *pugnare* to fight]

ops /ops/ *pl noun* operations, *esp* military operations. [by shortening]

-opsis *comb. form* forming nouns, denoting: a thing, e.g. a plant part, resembling something: *caryopsis.* [Greek *-opsis,* from *opsis* appearance, vision]

opsonin /'opsənin/ *noun* an antibody in blood serum that makes foreign cells more susceptible to the action of phagocytes. **>> opsonic** /op'sonik/ *adj.* [Latin *opsonium* relish (ultimately from Greek *opson* food) + -IN[1]]

-opsy *comb. form* forming nouns, denoting: examination: *autopsy.* [Greek *-opsia,* from *opsis* appearance, vision]

opt /opt/ *verb intrans* (*often* + for) to make a choice in favour of or against something. [French *opter* from Latin *optare*]

opt. *abbr* **1** in grammar, optative. **2** optical. **3** optician. **4** optics. **5** optional.

optative[1] /'optətiv/ *adj* of or belonging to a grammatical mood, e.g. in Greek, expressing wish or desire.

optative[2] *noun* the optative mood or a verb form expressing this.

optic[1] /'optik/ *adj* of vision or the eye. [early French *optique* via medieval Latin from Greek *optikos,* from *opsesthai* to be going to see]

optic[2] *noun* **1** any of the lenses, prisms, or mirrors of an optical instrument. **2** *Brit* a device that delivers a measure of alcoholic

spirit when fitted to the neck of an inverted bottle. **3** *archaic or humorous* the eye.

optical *adj* **1** of optics. **2a** visual: *an optical illusion.* **b** visible: *an optical galaxy.* **c** designed to aid vision: *an optical instrument.* **3** of or using light: *optical microscopy.* **>> optically** *adv.*

optical activity *noun* the ability of some substances to rotate the plane of vibration of polarized light.

optical art *noun formal* = OP ART.

optical character reader *noun* an electronic device that can read documents, books, tables, or other data by measuring the variation in the light reflected from the paper.

optical character recognition *noun* a process whereby handwritten or printed material is scanned electronically for inputting to a computer system.

optical fibre *noun* a very thin glass or plastic fibre used in fibre optics to transmit light.

optical glass *noun* a high-quality glass used *esp* for making lenses.

optical illusion *noun* something that deceives the observer into believing that they are seeing something they are not.

optical isomer *noun* in chemistry, each of two or more isomers that are mirror images of each other and rotate plane-polarized light in opposite directions.

optic axis *noun* a line in a doubly refracting medium along which double refraction does not occur.

optician /op'tish(ə)n/ *noun* somebody who prescribes correctional lenses for eye defects or supplies spectacles on prescription; an ophthalmic optician.

optics *pl noun* **1** (*treated as sing. or pl*) the science of the nature, properties, and uses of light, or radiation, or particles that behave like light. **2** optical properties or components.

optima /'optimə/ *noun* pl of OPTIMUM[2].

optimal /'optiml/ *adj* most satisfactory; optimum. **>> optimally** *adv.*

optimise *verb trans* see OPTIMIZE.

optimism /'optimiz(ə)m/ *noun* **1** a tendency to emphasize favourable aspects of situations or events or to expect the best possible outcome; hopefulness. **2a** the doctrine that this world is the best possible world. **b** the belief that good will in the end triumph over evil.

Editorial note _____

As William James saw, optimism involves confidence that we can act well, that our projects can succeed, and that they can make the world a better place or adapt it to one's needs or ends. Leibniz held that a perfect and benevolent God would inevitably create the best of all possible worlds. His response to the problem that the world contains natural evils was that a world without such evils would inevitably display other imperfections; for example, it might lack the elegant law-governed structure or the great natural variety of this one — Professor Christopher Hookway.

>> optimist *noun,* **optimistic** /-'mistik/ *adj,* **optimistically** /-'mistikli/ *adv.* [French *optimisme* from Latin *optimum:* see OPTIMUM[2]]

optimize *or* **optimise** /'optimiez/ *verb trans* to make (something) as effective or advantageous as possible. **>> optimization** /-'zaysh(ə)n/ *noun.*

optimum[1] /'optiməm/ *adj* most favourable or desirable.

optimum[2] *noun* (*pl* **optima** /-mə/ *or* **optimums**) something that is most favourable to a particular end. [Latin *optimum,* neuter of *optimus* best]

option[1] /'opsh(ə)n/ *noun* **1a** an alternative course of action; a choice. **b** an item offered in addition to or in place of standard equipment. **2** the act or an instance of choosing, or the right to choose. **3** a right to buy or sell something, e.g. designated securities or commodities, at a specified price during a stipulated period, or a contract giving this right. *** keep/leave one's options open** to not commit oneself by opting for something. [French *option* from Latin *option-, optio* free choice, from *optare* to choose]

option[2] *verb trans* (**optioned, optioning**) to grant or take an option on (something).

optional *adj* available as a choice; not compulsory. **>> optionally** *adv.*

optometry /op'tomətri/ *noun* the art or profession of examining the eye for defects and prescribing correctional lenses or exercises but not drugs or surgery. **>>> optometric** /-'metrik/ *adj*, **optometrist** *noun*. [Greek *optos* seen + -METRY]

opt out *verb intrans* **1** to choose not to participate in something. **2** *Brit* said e.g. of a school: to choose to withdraw from local authority control and manage financial and administrative affairs independently.

opulent /'opyoolant/ *adj* **1** showing evidence of great wealth; luxurious. **2** having great wealth; rich. **3** in plentiful supply; abundant. **>>> opulence** *noun*, **opulently** *adv*. [Latin *opulentus*, from *ops* power, wealth, help]

opuntia /o'punshi·ə/ *noun* any of a genus of cacti that includes the prickly pears: genus *Opuntia*. [Latin *opuntia* a plant growing around *Opus*, ancient city in Greece]

opus /'ohpəs/ *noun* (*pl* **opera** /'op(ə)rə/ *or* **opuses**) **1** a musical composition or set of compositions, usu numbered in the order of issue. **2** an artistic work of any kind. [Latin *oper-*, *opus* work]

opuscule /o'puskyoohl/ *noun* a small or minor work, e.g. of literature. [French *opuscule* from Latin *opusculum*, dimin. of *opus* work]

opus Dei /'day·ee/ *noun* **1** in the Christian Church, worship that follows the forms prescribed in the liturgy, regarded as the Christian duty to God. **2** (**Opus Dei**) a Roman Catholic organization whose members are dedicated to living according to Christian principles and promoting such principles in all spheres of life. [medieval Latin *opus Dei* work of God]

OR *abbr* **1** operating room. **2** operational research. **3** Oregon (US postal abbreviation). **4** other ranks. **5** owner's risk.

or[1] /ə; *strong* aw/ *conj* **1a** used to join two sentence elements of the same class or function and often introduced by *either* to indicate that what immediately follows is another or a final alternative: *either sink or swim; whether you like it or not*. **b** used before the second and later of several suggestions to indicate approximation or uncertainty: *five or six days*. **2** used after a negative and not: *She never drinks or smokes*. **3** used to introduce an alternative word mentioned by way of definition or explanation of another word: *a heifer or young cow*. **4** used to indicate the result of rejecting a preceding choice: *Hurry or you'll be late*. **5** used to introduce an afterthought: *Shall I tell you more – or am I boring you?* [Middle English *other* from Old English *othθe*]

Usage note
When *or* connects two nouns that are both singular the verb following them must be singular: *…if your money or your luggage is stolen*. If it connects two plural nouns, the verb is plural: *…when your relatives or your friends come to visit*. If *or* separates a singular and a plural noun or two different personal pronouns, the rule is that the verb should agree with whichever comes second: *What if my money or my valuables go missing?; Either you or he has made a mistake*.

or[2] /aw/ *noun* in heraldry, a yellow or gold tincture. [early French *or* gold, from Latin *aurum*]

-or[1] *suffix* forming nouns, denoting: somebody or something that performs a specified action: *vendor*. [Middle English from Old French *-eur*, *-eor* and Latin *-or*]

-or[2] *suffix* forming nouns, denoting: **1** a quality, condition, or state of: *horror; tremor*. **2** an instance of a specified quality or state: *error*. [Middle English via Old French *-eur* from Latin *-or*]

orache *or* **orach** /'orich/ *noun* any of several species of plants of the goosefoot family with green, white, or red leaves, one variety of which is cultivated and eaten like spinach: genus *Atriplex*. [Middle English *orage*, via Anglo-French *arasche* and Latin *atriplex* from Greek *atraphaxys*]

Oracle /'orəkl/ *noun* trademark a service provided by ITV which transmits information, e.g. the weather or sports results, on usu special channels: compare TELETEXT.

oracle *noun* **1a** an often cryptic answer to some question, usu regarding the future, purporting to come from a deity. **b** a priest or priestess who delivers oracles, or a shrine housing them. **2** a person giving wise or authoritative decisions, or a statement by them. [Middle English via French from Latin *oraculum*, from *orare* to speak]

oracular /o'rakyoolə/ *adj* **1** of or being an oracle. **2** resembling an oracle in authority or obscurity of expression. **>>> oracularly** *adv*. [Latin *oraculum*: see ORACLE]

oracy /'orəsi/ *noun* the ability to understand speech and to express oneself intelligibly in words: compare LITERACY. [Latin *or-*, *os* mouth, modelled on LITERACY]

oral[1] /'awrəl, 'orəl/ *adj* **1a** uttered in words; spoken. **b** using speech. **c** involving spoken questions and answers rather than written ones: *an oral examination*. **2a** of, given through, or affecting the mouth: *A fast word about oral contraception. I asked a girl to go to bed with me and she said 'no'* — Woody Allen. **b** in psychoanalysis, of or relating to the first stage of sexual development in which gratification is derived from eating, sucking, and later by biting: compare ANAL, GENITAL. **>>> orality** /aw'raliti, o-/ *noun*, **orally** *adv*. [Latin *or-*, *os* mouth]

Usage note
oral or aural? See note at AURAL.

oral[2] *noun* an oral examination.

oral history *noun* history based on traditions handed down in a community or the memories of those who have taken part in important events which are recorded orally, e.g. on a tape recorder, rather than in written documents.

oral sex *noun* sexual activity in which the genitals of one person are stimulated by the lips and/or tongue of another.

Orange /'orənj/ *adj* of Orangemen: *an Orange lodge*. **>>> Orangeism** *noun*.

orange *noun* **1a** a spherical fruit with a reddish yellow leathery aromatic rind and sweet juicy edible pulp. **b** any of several species of small evergreens of the rue family that bear this fruit: genus *Citrus*. **2** any of several trees or fruits resembling the orange. **3** the colour of oranges, between red and yellow in the spectrum. **4** a drink made from oranges. **>>> orange** *adj*. [Middle English, via Old French, Arabic and Persian from Sanskrit *nāranṅga* orange tree, of Dravidian origin]

orangeade /orən'jayd/ *noun* a beverage of sweetened orange juice mixed with still or carbonated water.

orange flower water *noun* a solution of NEROLI (extract of orange flowers) in water, used as a food flavouring and formerly as a toilet water.

Orangeman *noun* (*pl* **Orangemen**) a member of a Protestant loyalist society in Northern Ireland and elsewhere. [named after William III of England d.1702, Prince of *Orange*, city in France, Protestant ruler who deposed the Roman Catholic James II]

orange peel *noun* a pitted surface, e.g. on porcelain, like that of an orange.

orange pekoe /'peekoh/ *noun* **1** a black tea made from the tiny leaf and bud at the end of the stalk. **2** broadly, Indian or Sri Lankan tea of good quality.

orangery /'orənj(ə)ri/ *noun* (*pl* **orangeries**) a protected place, e.g. a greenhouse, for growing oranges in cool climates.

orangestick *noun* a thin usu orangewood stick with a pointed end used in manicuring.

orangewood *noun* the wood of the orange tree used *esp* for turning and carving.

orangey /'orinji/ *adj* see ORANGY.

orangish *adj* rather orange.

orang-utan *or* **orang-utang** /,awrang-oo'tan, -'tang/ *noun* a largely plant-eating tree-dwelling anthropoid ape of Borneo and Sumatra with orange-brown skin and hair and very long arms: *Pongo pygmaeus*. [Malay *orang hutan*, from *orang* man + *hutan* forest]

orangy *or* **orangey** /'orənji/ *adj* resembling an orange, *esp* in taste or colour.

orate /o'rayt/ *verb intrans* to speak in an elevated and often pompous manner. [back-formation from ORATION]

oration /o'raysh(ə)n/ *noun* a speech delivered in a formal and dignified manner. [Latin *oration-*, *oratio* speech, oration, from *orare* to plead, speak, pray]

orator /'orətə/ *noun* **1** somebody who delivers an oration. **2** a skilled public speaker. [Middle English *oratour* via French from Latin *orator*, from *orare* to plead, speak, pray]

oratorio /orə'tawrioh/ *noun* (*pl* **oratorios**) a choral work based usu on a religious subject and composed chiefly of recitatives, arias, and choruses without action or scenery. [Italian *oratorio*, named after the *Oratorio* di San Filippo Neri (Oratory of St Philip Neri) in Rome, where musical religious services were held in the 16th cent.]

oratory[1] /'orət(ə)ri/ *noun* (*pl* **oratories**) **1** a place of prayer, *esp* a private or institutional chapel. **2** (**Oratory**) a congregation, house, or church of the Oratorians, a branch of the Roman Catholic

Church that has secular priests. [Middle English *oratorie* from late Latin *oratorium*, from Latin *orare* to plead, speak, pray]

oratory[2] *noun* **1** the art of public speaking. **2** public speaking characterized by impressive or excessive eloquence. [Latin *oratoria*, from *orator*: see ORATOR]

orb /awb/ *noun* **1** a golden globe surmounted by a cross, symbolizing royal power and justice. **2** a spherical object. **3** *literary* any planet or celestial body. **4** *literary* an eye. [early French *orbe* from Latin *orbis* circle, disc, orb]

orbicular /aw'bikyoolə/ *adj* **1** spherical. **2** said of e.g. a leaf: circular. ⨠ **orbicularity** /-'lariti/ *noun*, **orbicularly** *adv*, **orbiculate** /-lət/ *adj*. [Middle English *orbiculer* via French from late Latin *orbicularis*, from Latin *orbiculus*, dimin. of *orbis* circle, disc, ORB]

orbit[1] /'awbit/ *noun* **1a** a path followed by one celestial body or object in its revolution round another, e.g. that of the earth round the sun. **b** the path of an electron around the nucleus of an atom. **c** one complete revolution by a celestial body or object round another. **2** a sphere of activity or influence. **3** *literary* the eye. **4** in anatomy, the bony socket of the eye. **5** the skin around a bird's eye. ⨠ **orbital** *adj*. [Latin *orbita*, from *orbis* circle, disc, ORB]

orbit[2] *verb* (**orbited, orbiting**) ⨠ *verb trans* **1** to revolve in an orbit round (e.g. a celestial body). **2** to send (a spacecraft or satellite) into space and make it revolve in an orbit. ⨠ *verb intrans* to travel in circles.

orbital[1] *adj* **1** relating to the orbit of a celestial body or an object in space. **2** said of a road: bypassing and *esp* almost circling a major city.

orbital[2] *noun* **1** an area round an atom or molecule inside which there is a high probability of finding one or two of the electrons that orbit round the atomic nuclei. **2** a road that passes around a town; a bypass.

orbiter *noun* a spacecraft designed to orbit a celestial body without landing on its surface.

orc /awk/ *noun* a fairytale monster of varying description, most commonly a human-like creature. [perhaps from Latin *orcus* hell, or Italian *orco* demon, monster; used by J R R Tolkien d.1973, British writer, for one of a race of small, warlike, ogreish people]

orca /'awkə/ *noun* = KILLER WHALE.

Orcadian /aw'kaydi·ən/ *noun* a native or inhabitant of the Orkney Islands off northern Scotland. ⨠ **Orcadian** *adj*. [Latin *Orcades* Orkney Islands]

orch. *abbr* **1** orchestra. **2** orchestral. **3** orchestrated by.

orchard /'awchəd/ *noun* a usu enclosed area in which fruit trees are planted. [Old English *ortgeard*, prob from Latin *hortus* garden + Old English *geard* YARD[2]]

orchestra /'awkistrə/ *noun* **1** a large group of musicians organized to perform ensemble music, *esp* a group comprising string, woodwind, brass, and percussion sections. **2** = ORCHESTRA PIT. **3** *NAmer* the stalls in a theatre. **4** the circular space used by the chorus in front of the stage in an ancient Greek theatre. [via Latin from Greek *orchēstra*, from *orcheisthai* to dance]

orchestral /aw'kestrəl/ *adj* of or composed for an orchestra. ⨠ **orchestrally** *adv*.

orchestra pit *noun* in a theatre, the space in front of the stage where the members of the orchestra sit.

orchestra stalls *pl noun* in a theatre, the rows of seats that form the section of the stalls nearest the stage.

orchestrate /'awkistrayt/ *verb trans* **1** to compose or arrange (music) for an orchestra. **2** to provide (e.g. a performance) with orchestration: *She was asked to orchestrate the ballet.* **3** to arrange or control (something) cleverly to achieve the desired outcome. ⨠ **orchestrator** *noun*.

orchestration /awki'straysh(ə)n/ *noun* **1** the act or an instance of orchestrating something. **2** the arrangement of music for performance by an orchestra, or the style of such an arrangement.

orchid /'awkid/ *noun* any of a large family of plants related to the grasses and lilies and usu having striking three-petalled flowers with an enlarged liplike middle petal: family Orchidaceae. ⨠ **orchidaceous** /-'dayshəs/ *adj*. [Latin genus name, from *orchis*: see ORCHIS]

orchidectomy /awki'dektəmi/ *noun* (*pl* **orchidectomies**) the surgical removal of one or both testicles. [irreg from Greek *orchis* testicle + -ECTOMY]

orchil /'awchil, 'awkil/ *noun* **1** a violet dye obtained from certain lichens. **2** any of several species of lichens from which this dye is obtained: genus *Roccella* and other genera. [Middle English *orchell* from Old French *orcheil*]

orchis /'awkis/ *noun* an orchid having fleshy roots and a spurred lip, native to northern regions: genus *Orchis*. [Latin genus name, from Greek *orchis* testicle, orchid, from the shape of the tubers]

orchitis /aw'kietəs/ *noun* inflammation of the testicles. [Greek *orchis* testicle + -ITIS]

ord. *abbr* **1** order. **2** ordinary. **3** ordnance.

ordain /aw'dayn/ *verb trans* **1** to invest (somebody) officially with priestly or presbyterial authority, e.g. by the laying on of hands. **2a** to order (something) by appointment, decree, or law; to command (it). **b** to make (something) destined to happen; to foreordain (it). ⨠ **ordainment** *noun*. [Middle English *ordeinen* via Old French and late Latin from Latin *ordinare* to put in order, appoint, from *ordin-, ordo* arrangement, group, ORDER[1]]

ordeal /aw'deel/ *noun* **1** any severe or testing experience. **2** a method formerly used to determine guilt or innocence by submitting the accused to dangerous or painful tests whose outcome was believed to depend on divine or supernatural intervention: *ordeal by fire*. [Old English *ordāl*]

order[1] /'awdə/ *noun* **1a** a specific rule, regulation, or authoritative direction. **b** the rule of law or proper authority: *the white moderate who is more devoted to order than to justice* — Martin Luther King. **2a** a direction to purchase, sell, or supply goods or to carry out work. **b** goods bought or sold. **c** a written direction to pay money to somebody. **3** a proper, orderly, or functioning condition: *out of order*. **4a** a sociopolitical system, or a division of it: *the present economic order*. **b** regular, correct, suitable, or harmonious arrangement. **5a** customary procedure, *esp* in debate: *Mr chairman, I'd like to raise a point of order*. **b** a prescribed form of a religious service. **6a** a religious body or community living under a specific rule and often required to take vows of renunciation of earthly things. **b** any of the several grades of the Christian ministry. **c** (*in pl*) the office of a person in the Christian ministry: *holy orders*. **7a** a rank or group in a community. **b** a category in the classification of living things ranking above the family and below the class. **8** any rank or level. **9a** a category or kind. **b** arrangement of objects or events according to sequence in space, time, value, importance, etc: *list the names in alphabetical order*. **c** the number of times mathematical differentiation is applied successively: *derivatives of higher order*. **d** the number of columns or rows in a square matrix. **e** the number of elements in a finite mathematical group. **10a** a style of building, *esp* any of the classical styles of building: *the Doric order*. **b** a column and entablature proportioned and decorated according to one of the classical styles. **11** the style of dress and equipment for a specified purpose: *troops in full marching order*. **12** a military decoration. * **in/of the order of** about as much or as many as; approximately. **in order that** so that. **in order to** for the purpose of. **on order** having been ordered. **out of order 1** not in correct order. **2** not in working condition. **3** not following correct procedure; not allowed by the rules. **4** *informal* not acceptable or appropriate. **to order** according to the specifications of an order: *furniture made to order*. [early French *ordre* via medieval Latin from Latin *ordin-, ordo* arrangement, group, class]

order[2] *verb* (**ordered, ordering**) ⨠ *verb trans* **1** to put (things) in order; to arrange (them). **2a** to give (somebody) an order; to command (them). **b** to command (somebody) to go or come to a specified place. **c** to place an order for (something): *This is not what we ordered*. **d** to command or prescribe (an action, etc). ⨠ *verb intrans* to give or place an order.

order arms *noun* a drill position in which the rifle is held vertically beside the right leg with the butt resting on the ground. [from the command *order arms!*]

ordered *adj* **1** marked by regularity or self-discipline. **2a** with elements arranged in a regular or harmonious order. **b** in mathematics, having a specified first element: *a set of ordered pairs*.

order in council or **Order in Council** *noun* an order made by the British sovereign on the advice of the privy council, giving the force of law to administrative regulations.

orderly[1] *adj* **1a** arranged in order; neat. **b** liking or exhibiting order; methodical. **2** well behaved or peaceful. ⨠ **orderliness** *noun*.

orderly[2] *noun* (*pl* **orderlies**) **1** a soldier assigned to carry messages, relay orders, etc for a superior officer. **2** a hospital attendant who does routine or heavy work, e.g. carrying supplies or moving patients.

orderly room *noun* the administration office of a military unit.

order of magnitude *noun* a range of magnitude extending from a particular value to ten times that value.

order of the day *noun* **1a** an agenda, e.g. of business to be attended to. **b** a proclamation or instructions issued by a commanding officer. **2** the characteristic or dominant feature or activity. **3** *informal* the only option available.

order paper *noun* a programme of the day's business in a legislative assembly.

ordinal[1] /'awdinl/ *noun* **1** = ORDINAL NUMBER. **2a** (**Ordinal**) the forms of religious service for ordination, or a book containing them. **b** a book containing the Roman Catholic services to be used on every day of the year.

ordinal[2] *adj* **1** of a specified order or rank in a series. **2** in biology, relating to an order in taxonomy. [late Latin *ordinalis* from Latin *ordin-, ordo* arrangement, group, ORDER[1]]

ordinal number *noun* a number designating the place, e.g. first, second, or third, occupied by an item in an ordered set: compare CARDINAL NUMBER.

ordinance /'awdinəns/ *noun* **1** an authoritative order or regulation. **2** a prescribed usage, practice, or ceremony. [Middle English from French *ordenance*, ultimately from Latin *ordinant-, ordinans*, present part. of *ordinare*: see ORDAIN]

ordinand /'awdinand/ *noun* a candidate for ordination; a trainee priest. [late Latin *ordinandus*, verbal noun from *ordinare*: see ORDAIN]

ordinary[1] /'awdn(ə)ri, 'awd(ə)nri/ *adj* **1** routine or usual; customary. **2** not exceptional; commonplace. **3** said of a differential equation: involving only two variables and their first derivatives. >> **ordinarily** /'awd(ə)nərili, ,awdə'neərili/ *adv*, **ordinariness** *noun*. [Middle English *ordinarie* from Latin *ordinarius*, from *ordin-, ordo* ORDER[1]]

ordinary[2] *noun* (*pl* **ordinaries**) **1** (*often* **Ordinary**) the invariable parts of the Roman Catholic mass: compare PROPER[2]. **2** any of the simplest heraldic charges used in coats of arms, e.g. a chevron. **3** a bishop or judge having jurisdiction over a constituted territory or group in his own right, not by delegation. **4** *NAmer* = PENNY-FARTHING. **5** *Brit, archaic*. **a** a tavern or eating house serving regular meals at a fixed price. **b** a meal served at such a place. * **out of the ordinary** not usual or customary. [Middle English *ordinarie* via Anglo-French and medieval Latin from Latin *ordinarius*: see ORDINARY[1]]

Ordinary grade *noun* = O GRADE.

Ordinary level *noun* = O LEVEL.

ordinary seaman *noun* the lowest rank in the Royal Navy, below able seaman.

ordinary share *noun* a share entitling the holder to dividends or assets only after the claims of debenture holders and preference shares have been met: compare PREFERENCE SHARE.

ordinate /'awdinət/ *noun* the coordinate of a point in a plane Cartesian coordinate system obtained by measuring parallel to the y-axis: compare ABSCISSA. [Latin *linea ordinate applicata* line applied in an orderly manner]

ordination /awdi'naysh(ə)n/ *noun* the act or an instance of ordaining somebody as a priest, minister, or elder, or their being ordained.

ordnance /'awdnəns/ *noun* **1a** military supplies. **b** a government department dealing with military supplies. **2** heavy artillery: *Let all the battlements their ordnance fire* — Shakespeare. [Middle English variant of ORDINANCE]

ordnance datum *noun* a standard mean sea level used by the Ordnance Survey.

Ordnance Survey *noun* a British or Irish government organization that produces a survey of Great Britain or Ireland published as a series of detailed maps.

ordonnance /'awdənəns (*French* ɔrdɔnɑ̃ːs)/ *noun* arrangement of parts in art, architecture, and literature. [French *ordonnance*, alteration of early French *ordenance*: see ORDINANCE]

Ordovician /awdə'vishi-ən/ *adj* relating to or dating from a geological period, the second period of the Palaeozoic era, lasting from about 510 million to about 439 million years ago, and marked by

the first appearance of vertebrates in the sea. >> **Ordovician** *noun*. [Latin *Ordovices*, ancient people in N Wales]

ordure /'awdyooə/ *noun formal* excrement. [Middle English from Old French *ord* foul, from Latin *horridus*: see HORRID]

ore /aw/ *noun* a mineral containing a metal or other valuable constituent for which it is mined. [Old English *ār*]

öre /'uhrə/ *noun* (*pl* **öre**) a unit of currency in Sweden, worth 100th of a krona. [Swedish *öre* from Latin *aureus* a gold coin, literally 'golden', from *aurum* gold]

øre /'uhrə/ *noun* (*pl* **øre**) a unit of currency in Denmark and Norway, worth 100th of a krone. [Danish and Norwegian *øre*, prob from Latin *aureus* a gold coin: see ÖRE]

Oreg *abbr* Oregon.

oregano /ori'gahnoh, ə'regənoh/ *noun* a bushy plant of the mint family whose leaves are used as a herb in cooking: *Origanum vulgare*. [American Spanish *orégano* via Spanish and Latin from Greek *origanon*]

orfe /awf/ *noun* (*pl* **orfes**) a golden-yellow European freshwater fish that is a popular pond and aquarium fish: *Idus idus*. [German *Orfe* via Old High German *orvo* and Latin *orphus* from Greek *orphos*]

org. *abbr* **1** organic. **2** organization. **3** organized.

organ /'awgən/ *noun* **1a** a musical instrument consisting of sets of pipes activated by compressed air and controlled by keyboards. **b** an electronic keyboard instrument producing a sound approximating to that of an organ. **c** = REED ORGAN. **d** any of various similar cruder instruments. **2** a specialized biological structure, e.g. the heart or a leaf, consisting of tissues and performing some specific function in an organism: *My brain? It's my second-favourite organ* — Woody Allen. **3** a subordinate organization that performs specialized functions: *He's written a book on the various organs of government*. **4** *formal* a newspaper or periodical. **5** *informal* a penis. [partly from Old English *organa* via Latin *organum* from Greek *organon* tool, instrument, partly via Old French *organe* from Latin *organum*]

organ- *or* **organo-** *comb. form* forming words, with the meanings: **1** organ or organs: *organoleptic*. **2** organic: *organophosphate*. [Middle English via medieval Latin from Latin *organum*: see ORGAN]

organa /'awgənə/ *noun pl* of ORGANON.

organdie *or* **organdy** /'awgəndi/ *noun* a very fine transparent muslin with a stiff finish. [French *organdi*]

organelle /awgə'nel/ *noun* a part of a cell, e.g. a mitochondrion, that has a specialized structure and usu a specific function. [Latin *organum*: see ORGAN]

organ-grinder *noun* **1** an itinerant street musician who operates a barrel organ, traditionally accompanied by a monkey who dances to the tunes played. **2** *informal* the partner who has authority; the boss.

organic /aw'ganik/ *adj* **1a** of or derived from living organisms. **b** denoting the production of food, etc carried out using fertilizer solely of plant or animal origin without the aid of chemical fertilizers, pesticides, etc, or the food, etc so produced: *organic farming*. **2a** of or arising in a bodily organ. **b** affecting the structure of the organism: *an organic disease*. **3a** forming an integral element of a whole. **b** having systematic coordination of parts. **c** resembling or developing in the manner of an organism. **4** containing carbon compounds, *esp* those occurring in living organisms, or denoting the branch of chemistry dealing with these. **5** of or constituting the law by which a government exists. >> **organically** *adv*.

organisation /,awgənie'zaysh(ə)n/ *noun* see ORGANIZATION.

organise /'awgəniez/ *verb trans* see ORGANIZE.

organism *noun* **1** an individual member of a biological species; a being. **2** a complex structure of interdependent and subordinate elements. >> **organismal** /-'nizml/ *adj*, **organismic** /-'nizmik/ *adj*.

organist /'awgənist/ *noun* somebody who plays the organ.

organization *or* **organisation** /,awgənie'zaysh(ə)n/ *noun* **1a** the act or an instance of organizing or being organized. **b** the condition or manner of being organized. **2a** an association or society: *charitable organizations*. **b** an administrative and functional body, e.g. a business or a political party. >> **organizational** *adj*.

organize *or* **organise** *verb trans* **1** to arrange or form (elements) into a complete or functioning whole. **2** to arrange (something) by systematic planning and effort. **3** to persuade (people) to associate in an organization, *esp* to unionize (workers): *organized labour*. **4** *archaic* to cause (something) to develop an organic structure. > *verb intrans* **1** to arrange elements into a whole. **2** to form an organization, *esp* a trade union. ➤ **organizer** *noun*. [Middle English from medieval Latin *organizare*, from Latin *organum*: see ORGAN]

organo- *comb. form* see ORGAN-.

organoleptic /ˌawgənoh'leptik, aw,ganə-/ *adj* **1** involving or using one or more of the sense organs: *organoleptic evaluation of foods*. **2** being, affecting, or relating to qualities, e.g. taste and smell, that stimulate the sense organs. [French *organoleptique*, from Greek *organon* organ + *-leptikos* receptive, from *lambanein* to take]

organon /'awgənon/ *noun* (*pl* **organons** or **organa** /-ə/) a set of principles for scientific or philosophical investigation. [Greek *organon* tool, ORGAN]

organophosphate /aw,ganə'fosfayt/ *noun* an organic compound, *esp* a pesticide, containing phosphorus.

organum /'awgənəm/ *noun* an early style of Western music based on plainsong and combining various melodies. [Latin *organum*: see ORGAN]

organza /aw'ganzə/ *noun* a sheer dress fabric resembling organdie, usu made of silk, rayon, or nylon. [prob alteration of *Lorganza*, a trademark]

organzine /'awgənzeen/ *noun* a raw silk yarn used for warp threads in fine fabrics. [French *organsin* from Italian *organzino*, prob from *Organzi*, former Italian name of *Urgench*, town in Uzbekistan where it was first manufactured]

orgasm /'awgaz(ə)m/ *noun* **1** the climax of sexual excitement, occurring typically as the culmination of sexual intercourse. **2** any intensely pleasurable sensation. ➤ **orgasmic** /aw'gazmik/ *adj*, **orgastic** /aw'gastik/ *adj*. [Greek *orgasmos*, from *organ* to grow ripe, be lustful]

orgeat /'awzhah (*French* ɔrʒa)/ *noun* a sweet syrup or drink made with almonds and usu orange flower water and used *esp* as a cocktail ingredient. [French *orgeat* from early French *orge* barley, from Latin *hordeum*]

orgy /'awji/ *noun* (*pl* **orgies**) **1a** a wild party characterized by, or organized to provide the opportunity for, sexual promiscuity. **b** drunken revelry. **2** an excessive or frantic indulgence in a specified activity: *an orgy of destruction*. **3** the secret rites of an ancient Greek or Roman deity, often accompanied by ecstatic singing and dancing. ➤ **orgiastic** /awji'astik/ *adj*. [early French *orgie* via Latin from Greek *orgia* secret rites or revels]

-orial *suffix* forming adjectives, with the meaning: of, belonging to, or connected with: *sensorial*. [Middle English from Latin *-orius* -ORY² + Middle English -AL¹]

oribi /'orəbi, 'aw-/ *noun* (*pl* **oribis** or collectively **oribi**) a small graceful tan-coloured antelope of S and E Africa with short horns: *Ourebia ourebi*. [Afrikaans *oribi* from Khoikhoi]

oriel window /'awri·əl/ *noun* a bay window projecting from an upper storey and supported by a corbel or bracket. [Middle English *oriel* porch, oriel window, from early French *oriol* porch]

orient¹ /'awri·ənt, 'o-/ *noun* **1** (**the Orient**) *dated* the countries of eastern Asia, *esp* China, Japan, and their neighbours. **2** a pearl of great lustre. [Middle English via French from Latin *orient-, oriens* rising, east, present part. of *oriri* to rise]

orient² /'awri·ent, 'o-/ *verb trans* to orientate (oneself or something). [French *orienter*, from Latin *orient-, oriens*: see ORIENT¹]
Usage note
orient *or* orientate? Both forms of the word are correct. *Orient* is more often used in American English, *orientate* in British English.

orient³ /'awri·ənt, 'o-/ *adj* **1** *literary* lustrous or sparkling: *orient gems*. **2** *archaic* oriental.

Oriental *noun offensive* a member of any of the indigenous peoples of the Orient.

oriental /awri'entl, o-/ *adj* **1** (*often* **Oriental**). **a** relating to or characteristic of the Orient. **b** relating or belonging to any of the indigenous peoples of the Orient. **2** (**Oriental**) of or being the biogeographic region that includes Asia S and SE of the Himalayas and part of the Malay archipelago. **3** said of a pearl or other precious stone: of superior grade, lustre, or value.

orientalism *or* **Orientalism** *noun* **1** a characteristic feature of the peoples or culture of the Orient. **2** scholarship or learning in oriental subjects.

orientalist *noun* (*often* **Orientalist**) a specialist in oriental subjects.

orientate /'awri·əntayt, 'o-/ *verb trans chiefly Brit* **1** to ascertain (one's own) bearings in unfamiliar surroundings. **2** to cause (somebody or oneself) to adjust to an unfamiliar environment or situation. **3a** to cause (something) to face or point towards the east; *specif* to build (a church or temple) with the longitudinal axis pointing eastwards. **b** to set (something) in a definite position, *esp* in relation to the points of the compass.
Usage note
orientate *or* orient? See note at ORIENT².

orientation /ˌawri·ən'taysh(ə)n, ˌo-/ *noun* **1a** the act or an instance of orientating or being orientated. **b** an arrangement, alignment, or relative position. **2** a lasting tendency of thought, inclination, or interest: *a person's sexual orientation*. **3** change of position by an organism, or part of one, in response to an external stimulus. ➤ **orientational** *adj*.

orientation course *noun chiefly NAmer* a course that is designed to introduce people to a new situation or organization.

orienteer¹ /ˌawri·ən'tiə/ *verb intrans* to take part in orienteering.

orienteer² *noun* a person who takes part in orienteering.

orienteering *noun* a sport in which contestants have to cross usu difficult unfamiliar country on foot using a map and compass to navigate their way between checkpoints. [modification (influenced by -EER) of Swedish *orientering*, from *orientera* to orient]

orifice /'orifis/ *noun* an opening through which something may pass, *esp* one in the body. ➤ **orificial** /-'fish(ə)l/ *adj*. [via French from Latin *orificium*, from *or-, os* mouth + *-ficium* from *-ficus*: see -FIC]

oriflamme /'oriflam/ *noun* a banner, symbol, or ideal inspiring devotion or courage. [Middle English *oriflamble* the sacred red banner of St Denis (used as the banner of the kings of France in battle), via French from medieval Latin *aurea flamma* golden flame]

orig. *abbr* **1** origin. **2** original. **3** originally.

origami /ori'gahmi/ *noun* the Japanese art or process of folding paper into complex shapes. [Japanese *origami*, from *oru* to fold + *kami* paper]

origanum /ə'rigənəm, ori'gahnəm/ *noun* oregano or marjoram. [Middle English from Latin *origanum* wild marjoram, from Greek *origanon*]

origin /'orijin/ *noun* **1** a source or starting-point. **2** ancestry or parentage. **3** in anatomy, the more fixed or central attachment or end of a muscle. **4** in mathematics, the point of intersection of axes, e.g. on a graph, where the value of the variables is zero. [Middle English *origine* via French from Latin *origin-, origo*, from *oriri* to rise]

original¹ /ə'rijənl/ *adj* **1** initial or earliest. **2a** not secondary, derivative, or imitative. **b** being the first instance or source of a copy, reproduction, or translation. **3** inventive or creative. ➤ **originally** *adv*.

original² *noun* **1** something from which a copy, reproduction, or translation is made. **2** an eccentric person.

originality /ə,rijə'naliti/ *noun* (*pl* **originalities**) **1** freshness or novelty, e.g. in design or style. **2** the power of imaginative and independent thought or creation. **3** the quality or state of being original.

original sin *noun* in Christianity, the innate sinfulness of all human beings that is supposed to have resulted from Adam's disobedience of God.

originate /ə'rijənayt/ *verb intrans* to begin or come into existence. ➤ *verb trans* to bring (something) into existence; to initiate (it). ➤ **origination** /-'naysh(ə)n/ *noun*, **originator** *noun*.

O-ring /'oh/ *noun* a circular rubber ring used in machinery as a seal.

oriole /'awriohl, 'awri·əl/ *noun* **1** any of a family of usu brightly coloured songbirds of Africa, Europe, and Asia: family Oriolidae. **2** any of a family of American songbirds with black and either orange or yellow plumage: family Icteridae. [French *oriol* from Latin *aureolus*, dimin. of *aureus* golden, from *aurum* gold]

orison /'oriz(ə)n/ *noun archaic* a prayer: *Nymph, in thy orisons be all my sins remembered* — Shakespeare. [Middle English via Old French from Latin *oration-, oratio*: see ORATION]

-orium *suffix* (*pl* **-oriums** or **-oria**) forming nouns, denoting: a place for a particular function: *crematorium*. [Latin *-orium*, from neuter of *-orius* -ORY²]

Oriya /o'ree(y)ə/ *noun* (*pl* **Oriyas** *or collectively* **Oriya**) **1** a native or inhabitant of the state of Orissa in E India, or a member of a people originating in this region. **2** the Indic language of the Oriya. ➤➤ **Oriya** *adj*. [Hindi *Uriya*]

Orlon /'awlon/ *noun trademark* an acrylic fibre or fabric. [invented name, modelled on *nylon*]

orlop deck /'awlop/ *noun* the lowest deck in a ship that has four or more decks. [Middle English *overlop* deck of a single-decker, from early Low German *overlōp*, literally 'something that overleaps']

ormer /'awmə/ *noun* an ABALONE (type of shellfish), *esp* one common in the Channel Islands. [French dialect *ormer*, ultimately from Latin *auris maris* ear of the sea; because of its shape]

ormolu /'awməlooh/ *noun* gilded brass or bronze used to decorate furniture, ornaments, etc. [French *or moulu*, literally 'ground gold']

ornament[1] /'awnəmənt/ *noun* **1a** something that adds beauty to a person or thing, e.g. a piece of jewellery or a decorative carving. **b** a small decorative object. **c** decoration or embellishment: *a building without ornament*. **2** a person who adds honour or importance to something. **3** in music, an embellishing note or notes not belonging to the essential harmony or melody. [Middle English via French from Latin *ornamentum* equipment, decoration, from *ornare* to furnish, embellish]

ornament[2] /'awnəmənt/ *verb trans* to decorate or embellish (something).

ornamental[1] /awnə'mentl/ *adj* **1** used or intended as an ornament; decorative. **2** said of a plant: cultivated for its beauty. ➤➤ **ornamentally** *adv*.

ornamental[2] *noun* a plant cultivated for its beauty.

ornamentation /,awnəmen'taysh(ə)n/ *noun* **1** ornamenting or being ornamented. **2** something that ornaments; a decoration or embellishment.

ornate /aw'nayt/ *adj* **1** elaborately or excessively decorated. **2** affectedly elaborate or florid in style: *ornate prose*. ➤➤ **ornately** *adv*, **ornateness** *noun*. [Middle English *ornat* from Latin *ornatus*, past part. of *ornare* to furnish, embellish]

ornery /'awnəri/ *adj NAmer, informal* bad-tempered or cantankerous. ➤➤ **orneriness** *noun*. [alteration of ORDINARY[1]]

ornith- *or* **ornitho-** *comb. form* forming words, denoting: bird: *ornithology*. [via Latin from Greek *ornith-, ornis*]

ornithischian /awni'thiski·ən/ *noun* a dinosaur with a pelvic structure similar to that of a bird: compare SAURISCHIAN. ➤➤ **ornithischian** *adj*. [ORNITH- + Greek *ischion* hip joint]

ornitho- *comb. form* see ORNITH-.

ornithology /awnə'tholəji/ *noun* a branch of zoology dealing with birds. ➤➤ **ornithological** /-'lojikl/ *adj*, **ornithologically** /-'lojikli/ *adv*, **ornithologist** *noun*. [scientific Latin *ornithologia*, from ORNITHO- + *-logia* -LOGY]

oro-[1] *comb. form* forming words, denoting: mountain: *orogeny*. [Greek *oros*]

oro-[2] *comb. form* forming words, denoting: mouth: *oropharynx*. [Latin *or-, os*]

orogenesis /awroh'jenəsis/ *noun* = OROGENY.

orogeny /o'rojəni/ *noun* the process of mountain formation, *esp* by folding of the earth's crust. ➤➤ **orogenetic** /-'netik/ *adj*, **orogenic** /-'jenik/ *adj*.

orography /o'rogrəfi/ *noun* a branch of physical geography that deals with mountains. ➤➤ **orographic** /-'grafik/ *adj*, **orographical** /-'grafikl/ *adj*. [ORO-[1] + GEOGRAPHY]

oropharynx /awroh'faringks/ *noun* the part of the pharynx at the back of the mouth. ➤➤ **oropharyngeal** /-farin'jeeəl/ *adj*.

orotund /'orətund, 'oroh-/ *adj* **1** said of the voice: marked by fullness of sound; sonorous or resonant. **2** said of writing or speech: pompous or bombastic. ➤➤ **orotundity** /-'tunditi/ *noun*. [modification of Latin *ore rotundo*, literally 'with round mouth']

orphan[1] /'awf(ə)n/ *noun* **1** a child whose parents are dead. **2** a child whose father or mother is dead. ➤➤ **orphanhood** *noun*. [late Latin *orphanus* from Greek *orphanos* bereaved]

orphan[2] *verb trans* (**orphaned, orphaning**) to make (somebody) an orphan.

orphanage /'awf(ə)nij/ *noun* an institution for the care of orphans.

orphic /'awfik/ *adj* **1** (**Orphic**) relating to Orpheus or Orphism. **2** mystic or oracular. [Latin *Orphicus* from Greek *Orphikos*, from *Orpheus*, poet and musician in Greek mythology]

Orphism /'awfiz(ə)m/ *noun* an ancient Greek mystery religion. [named after *Orpheus* (see ORPHIC), its reputed founder]

orphrey /'awfri/ *noun* (*pl* **orphreys**) an ornamental border or band, *esp* on an ecclesiastical vestment. [Middle English *orfrey* via French from medieval Latin *aurifrigium*, from Latin *aurum* gold + *Phrygius* Phrygian]

orpiment /'awpimənt/ *noun* an orange to yellow mineral consisting of arsenic trisulphide and formerly used as a pigment: formula As_2S_3. [Middle English via French from Latin *auripigmentum*, from *aurum* gold + *pigmentum*: see PIGMENT[1]]

orpine /'awpin/ *noun* a plant with fleshy leaves and pink or purple flowers: *Sedum telephium*. [Middle English *orpin* from early French, from *orpiment*: see ORPIMENT; orig applied to a sedum with yellow flowers]

orrery /'orəri/ *noun* (*pl* **orreries**) a clockwork apparatus showing the relative positions and motions of celestial bodies in the solar system. [named after Charles Boyle d.1731, fourth Earl of *Orrery*, for whom one was made]

orris /'oris/ *noun* **1** a European iris with a fragrant RHIZOME (thick underground stem) that is used in perfumery: *Iris florentina*. **2** the fragrant rhizome of this or a related plant, prepared for use in perfumery. [prob alteration of IRIS]

orrisroot *noun* = ORRIS (2).

orth- *or* **ortho-** *comb. form* forming words, with the meanings: **1** straight, upright, vertical, or perpendicular: *orthorhombic*. **2** correct or corrective: *orthodontics*. **3** in chemistry, containing the highest possible number of hydroxyl groups or molecules of water. **4** in chemistry, involving substitution at two neighbouring positions in the benzene ring: compare META-, PARA-[1]. [Middle English via French and Latin from Greek, from *orthos* straight, right]

orthochromatic /,awthəkrə'matik, ,awthoh-/ *adj* said of photographic film or emulsion: sensitive to light of all colours except red.

orthoclase /'awthəklayz, -klays/ *noun* a common feldspar mineral, usu white or pink in colour, consisting of potassium aluminium silicate: formula $KAlSi_3O_8$. [German *Orthoklas*, from ORTH- + Greek *klasis* breaking, from *klan* to break]

orthodontia /awthə'donshi·ə/ *noun* = ORTHODONTICS. [scientific Latin *orthodontia*, from ORTH- + Greek *odont-, odous* tooth]

orthodontics /awthə'dontiks/ *pl noun* (*treated as sing. or pl*) a branch of dentistry dealing with the correction of irregularities of the teeth. ➤➤ **orthodontic** *adj*, **orthodontist** *noun*.

orthodox /'awthədoks/ *adj* **1a** conforming to established, dominant, or official doctrine, e.g. in religion: *'Do you know where the wicked go after death?' 'They go to hell,' was my ready and orthodox answer* — Charlotte Brontë. **b** in accordance with proper practice; conventional: *It points also to an orthodox burial with proper accompaniment of medical certificate and official sanction* — Conan Doyle. **2a** (**Orthodox**) relating or belonging to any of the Eastern Churches headed by the patriarch of Constantinople that separated from the Western Church in the eleventh cent. and have characteristic doctrines, liturgy, and forms of organization: *the Greek Orthodox Church*. **b** (*usu* **Orthodox**) of or being Judaism that keeps to strict and traditional interpretation of the TORAH (Jewish scripture) and authoritative rabbinic tradition: *an Orthodox Jew*. ➤➤ **orthodoxly** *adv*. [via French and Latin from late Greek *orthodoxos*, from ORTH- + *doxa* opinion]

orthodoxy *noun* (*pl* **orthodoxies**) **1** being orthodox. **2** an orthodox belief or practice.

orthodromic /,awthə'dromik/ *adj* said *esp* of a nerve impulse or fibre: proceeding or conducting in the usual direction: compare ANTIDROMIC. [ORTH- + *drom-*, from Greek *dromos* racecourse, running + -IC]

orthoepy /'awthoh·əpi/ *noun* the study of correct pronunciation. ➤➤ **orthoepic** /-'epik/ *adj*, **orthoepist** *noun*. [scientific Latin *orthoepia* from Greek *orthoepeia*, from ORTH- + *epos* word]

orthogenesis /awthə'jenəsis/ *noun* **1** evolution of species held to occur in a particular usu predetermined direction independent of external factors. **2** the theory that the development of society passes through the same stages in every culture. ➤➤ **orthogenetic** /-'netik/ *adj*, **orthogenetically** /-'netikli/ *adv*.

orthogonal /aw'thogənl/ *adj* said of lines, planes, axes, etc: perpendicular to one another. ➤ **orthogonally** *adv*. [via French and Latin from Greek *orthogōnios*, from ORTH- + *gōnia* angle]

orthographic /awthə'grafik/ *adj* relating to orthography. ➤ **orthographically** *adv*.

orthographical /awthə'grafikl/ *adj* = ORTHOGRAPHIC.

orthography /aw'thogrəfi/ *noun* (*pl* **orthographies**) **1** correct spelling. **2** the spelling system of a language. **3** the part of language study that deals with letters and spelling and their relationship with the sounds they represent. ➤ **orthographer** *noun*. [Middle English *ortografie* via French and Latin from Greek *orthographia*, from ORTH- + *graphein* to write]

orthopaedics (*NAmer* **orthopedics**) /awthə'peediks/ *pl noun* (*treated as sing. or pl*) a branch of medicine dealing with the correction or prevention of skeletal and muscular deformities, *esp* by surgery. ➤ **orthopaedic** *adj*, **orthopaedist** *noun*. [French *orthopédique* (adj), from *orthopédie* orthopedics, from ORTH- + Greek *paid-, pais* child]

orthopteran *or* **orthopteron** /aw'thoptərən/ *noun* (*pl* **orthopterans** *or* **orthopterons** *or* **orthoptera** /-rə/) any of an order of large insects including the crickets and grasshoppers, with biting mouthparts and either two pairs of wings or none: order Orthoptera. ➤ **orthopteran** *adj*, **orthopterous** /-rəs/ *adj*. [from the Latin order name, from ORTH- + Greek *pteron* wing]

orthoptics /aw'thoptiks/ *pl noun* (*treated as sing. or pl*) the study of disorders of vision, *esp* those caused by weak eye muscles, and the use of exercises and other non-surgical methods to correct them. ➤ **orthoptic** *adj*, **orthoptist** *noun*.

orthorexia nervosa /awthə'reksi-ə/ *or* **orthorexia nervosa** /nuh'vohzə/ *noun* an obsessive concern with eating only health-giving food. ➤ **orthorexic** *noun and adj*. [scientific Latin, from ORTH- + Greek *orexia* appetite + Latin *nervosa* nervous]

orthorhombic /awthə'rombik/ *adj* relating to or being a system of crystal structure characterized by three unequal axes at right angles to each other.

orthoscopic /awthə'skopik/ *adj* **1** giving an image in correct and normal proportions. **2** giving a flat field of view. [ORTH- + -SCOPIC]

ortolan /'awtələn/ *noun* a small brown and greyish green European bunting that is eaten as a delicacy, *esp* in France: *Emberiza hortulana*. [French *ortolan* from Italian *ortolano*, literally 'gardener', from Latin *hortulanus*, from *hortulus*, dimin. of *hortus* garden]

Orwellian /aw'weli-ən/ *adj* characteristic of the British novelist George Orwell (d.1950) or his writings, *esp* in depicting the way in which people are manipulated by an authoritarian state.

-ory¹ *suffix* forming nouns, denoting: **1** a place for a particular function: *observatory*; *refectory*. **2** something that serves a particular function: *directory*. [Middle English *-orie* from Latin *-orium*, neuter of *-orius*]

-ory² *suffix* forming adjectives, with the meanings: **1** of or involving: *gustatory*; *compulsory*. **2** serving for or producing: *justificatory*. [Middle English *-orie* via French from Latin *-orius*]

oryx /'oriks/ *noun* (*pl* **oryxes** *or collectively* **oryx**) any of a genus of large African antelopes with long straight horns: genus *Oryx*. [Latin *oryx* a gazelle, from Greek *orux* pickaxe, antelope (from its pointed horns), from *oryssein* to dig]

OS *abbr* **1** Old Style. **2** operating system. **3** ordinary seaman. **4** Ordnance Survey. **5** out of stock. **6** outsize.

O/S *abbr* outstanding.

Os *abbr* the chemical symbol for osmium.

os- *prefix* see OB-.

Osage orange /'ohsayj/ *noun* **1** an ornamental N American tree of the fig family with shiny oval leaves and hard bright orange wood: *Maclura pomifera*. **2** the small inedible orangelike fruit of this tree. [named after the *Osage*, a Native North American people who used to use the wood of this tree for making bows]

Oscan /'oskən/ *noun* an Italic language formerly spoken in S Italy, extinct by the first cent. AD. ➤ **Oscan** *adj*. [Latin *Oscus* + -AN¹]

Oscar /'oskə/ *noun* any of a number of gold statuettes awarded annually by the American Academy of Motion Picture Arts and Sciences for outstanding achievement in the cinema. Also called ACADEMY AWARD. [named after *Oscar* Pierce, 20th-cent. US wheat and fruit grower whom the statuette allegedly resembled]

oscillate /'osilayt/ *verb intrans* **1a** to swing backward and forward like a pendulum. **b** to move or travel back and forth between two points. **2** to vary between opposing beliefs, feelings, courses of action, etc. **3** in physics, to undergo oscillation. ➤ *verb trans* in physics, to cause (something) to undergo oscillation. ➤ **oscillatory** /-lət(ə)ri/ *adj*. [Latin *oscillatus*, past part. of *oscillare* to swing, from *oscillum* swing]

oscillation /osi'laysh(ə)n/ *noun* **1** the act of oscillating. **2** a variation or fluctuation. **3** in physics, a regular change from a maximum to a minimum, *esp* a flow of electricity periodically changing direction. **4** a single swing from one extreme limit to the other.

oscillator *noun* **1** a device for producing electrical oscillations in the form of alternating current, *esp* a radio-frequency or audio-frequency signal generator. **2** somebody or something that oscillates.

oscillogram /ə'siləgram/ *noun* a permanent record made by an oscillograph or oscilloscope. [Latin *oscillare* (see OSCILLATE) + -GRAM]

oscillograph /ə'siləgrahf, -graf/ *noun* an instrument for recording oscillations, *esp* electrical ones. ➤ **oscillographic** /-'grafik/ *adj*, **oscillography** /osi'logrəfi/ *noun*. [French *oscillographe*, from Latin *oscillare* (see OSCILLATE) + French *-graphe* -GRAPH]

oscilloscope /ə'siləskohp/ *noun* an instrument in which electrical oscillations register as a temporary visible wave form on the fluorescent screen of a cathode-ray tube. ➤ **oscilloscopic** /-'skopik/ *adj*. [Latin *oscillare* (see OSCILLATE) + -SCOPE]

oscine /'osien/ *adj* belonging or relating to a suborder of birds with vocal cords specialized for singing. [Latin *oscin-, oscen* bird used in divination, from OS- + *canere* to sing]

oscula /'oskyoolə/ *noun* pl of OSCULUM.

oscular /'oskyoolə/ *adj* **1** relating to the mouth or to kissing. **2** relating to an osculum.

osculate /'oskyoolayt/ *verb trans and intrans* **1** *humorous or formal* to kiss (somebody). **2** said of curves or surfaces: to touch and have a common tangent with (another curve or surface). ➤ **osculation** /-'laysh(ə)n/ *noun*, **osculatory** /'oskyoolət(ə)ri/ *adj*. [Latin *osculatus*, past part. of *osculari*, from *osculum* kiss, dimin. of *os* mouth]

osculum /'oskyooləm/ *noun* (*pl* **oscula** /-lə/) in zoology, an opening in a living sponge from which a current of water flows out. [Latin *osculum*, dimin. of *os* mouth]

-ose¹ *suffix* forming adjectives, with the meanings: **1** full of or possessing the quality of: *verbose*; *bellicose*. **2** having, consisting of, or resembling: *ramose*. ➤ **-osity** *suffix*. [Middle English from Latin *-osus*]

-ose² *suffix* forming nouns, denoting: a carbohydrate, *esp* a sugar: *amylose*; *fructose*. [from GLUCOSE]

osier /'ohzhə/ *noun* **1** a willow with pliable twigs that are used for furniture and basketry: *Salix viminalis*. **2** a willow twig used in basketry. [Middle English via French from medieval Latin *auseria* osier bed]

-osis *suffix* (*pl* **-oses** *or* **-osises**) forming nouns, denoting: **1a** an action, process, or state: *hypnosis*; *metamorphosis*. **b** an abnormal or pathological condition: *thrombosis*. **2** the increase or formation of something: *fibrosis*. [Middle English via Latin from Greek *-ōsis*, from *-ō-* (stem of causative verbs ending in *-oun*) + *-sis* (suffix of action)]

-osity *suffix* see -OSE¹.

Osmanli /oz'manli/ *noun dated* an Ottoman. [Turkish *osmanl*, named after *Osman* d.1326, founder of the Ottoman Empire]

osmiridium /ozmi'ridi-əm, os-/ *noun* a hard naturally occurring alloy of iridium and osmium that is used *esp* for pen nibs. [OSMIUM + IRIDIUM]

osmium /'ozmi-əm/ *noun* a blue-grey metallic chemical element of the platinum group that is hard and brittle, is the heaviest metal known, occurs naturally in platinum ores, and is used in alloys: symbol Os, atomic number 76. ➤ **osmic** /'ozmik/ *adj*. [scientific Latin *osmium*, from Greek *osmē* smell]

osmoregulation /ˌozmohregyoo'laysh(ə)n, ˌos-/ *noun* the usu automatic regulation of osmotic pressure or water content, *esp* in the body of an organism. [OSMOSIS + REGULATION]

osmose /'ozmohs, 'osmohs/ *verb intrans* to pass by osmosis. [back-formation from OSMOSIS]

osmosis /oz'mohsis, os-/ *noun* **1** movement of a solvent through a selectively permeable membrane (i.e. one that allows only certain small particles, molecules, etc to pass through) into a solution of higher concentration, which tends to equalize the concentrations on the two sides of the membrane. **2** a process of absorption or diffusion suggestive of osmosis, e.g. the assimilation of knowledge. ➤➤ **osmotic** /oz'motik, os-/ *adj*, **osmotically** /-'motikli/ *adv.* [short for *endosmosis*, from END- + Greek *ōsmos* act of pushing, from *ōthein* to push]

osmotic pressure /oz'motik, os-/ *noun* pressure associated with osmosis and dependent on concentration and temperature, *esp* the pressure that must be applied to a solution to prevent osmosis.

osmunda /oz'mundə/ *noun* any of a genus of large ferns: genus *Osmunda*. [from the Latin genus name, via medieval Latin from Old French *osmonde*]

osprey /'ospray, 'ospri/ *noun* (*pl* **ospreys**) **1** a large fish-eating hawk with dark brown and white plumage: *Pandion haliaetus.* **2** a feather used to decorate hats. [Middle English *ospray* via French from Latin *ossifraga*, literally 'bone-breaking', a bird mentioned by Pliny; probably the lammergeier, which drops its prey from a height to break the bones and get at the marrow]

ossein /'osiin/ *noun* the COLLAGEN (fibrous protein) of bones. [OSSEOUS + -IN[1]]

osseous /'osi-əs/ *adj technical* consisting of bone; bony. [Latin *osseus*, from *oss-, os* bone]

Ossetian /o'seesh(ə)n/ *noun* **1** (*also* **Ossete**) a native or inhabitant of Ossetia in the central Caucasus. **2** (*also* **Ossetic**) the Iranian language of the Ossetians. ➤➤ **Ossetian** *adj.*

ossicle /'osikl/ *noun* a small bone or bony structure, *esp* one in the middle ear. [Latin *ossiculum*, dimin. of *oss-, os* bone]

ossify /'osifie/ *verb* (**ossifies, ossified, ossifying**) ➤ *verb intrans* **1** to become bone. **2** to become inflexible in habit or attitude. ➤ *verb trans* to change (e.g. cartilage) into bone. ➤➤ **ossification** /-fi'kaysh(ə)n/ *noun.* [French *ossifier*, from Latin *oss-, os* bone]

osso bucco /,osoh 'boohkoh/ *noun* an Italian dish made from sliced shin of veal including marrowbone braised with tomatoes and white wine. [Italian *ossobucco* marrowbone]

ossuary /'osyooəri/ *noun* (*pl* **ossuaries**) a place or container for the bones of the dead. [late Latin *ossuarium* from Latin, neuter of *ossuarius* of bones, from *oss-, os* bone]

oste- *or* **osteo-** *comb. form* forming words, denoting: bone: *osteitis; osteopathy.* [via scientific Latin from Greek *osteon*]

osteitis /osti'ietəs/ *noun* inflammation of bone.

ostensible /o'stensəbl/ *adj* seeming to be so, but not necessarily true or real. ➤➤ **ostensibly** *adv.* [French *ostensible* from Latin *ostensus*, past part. of *ostendere* to show, from OS- + *tendere* to stretch]

ostensive /o'stensiv/ *adj* defining something by demonstration, e.g. by displaying or pointing to the thing or quality being defined. ➤➤ **ostensively** *adv.* [late Latin *ostensivus* from Latin *ostendere*: see OSTENSIBLE]

ostentation /ostən'taysh(ə)n/ *noun* unnecessary display of wealth, knowledge, etc designed to impress or attract attention. ➤➤ **ostentatious** /-shəs/ *adj*, **ostentatiously** /-shəsli/ *adv*, **ostentatiousness** /-shəsnis/ *noun.* [Middle English *ostentacioun* via French from Latin *ostentation-, ostentatio*, from *ostentare* to display ostentatiously, from *ostendere*: see OSTENSIBLE]

osteo- *comb. form* see OSTE-.

osteoarthritis /,ostioh·ah'thrietəs/ *noun* a degenerative form of arthritis usu associated with increasing age. ➤➤ **osteoarthritic** /-'thritik/ *adj.*

osteology /osti'oləji/ *noun* a branch of anatomy dealing with the bones. ➤➤ **osteological** /-'lojikl/ *adj*, **osteologically** /-'lojikli/ *adv*, **osteologist** *noun and adj.*

osteoma /osti'ohmə/ *noun* (*pl* **osteomas** *or* **osteomata** /-tə/) a benign tumour composed of bone tissue.

osteomalacia /,ostiohmə'layshi-ə/ *noun* softening of the bones, *esp* in adults and elderly people, usu caused by a deficiency of vitamin D or calcium and equivalent to rickets in children and young people. [scientific Latin *osteomalacia*, from OSTE- + Greek *malakia* softness, from *malakos* soft]

osteomata /osti'ohmətə/ *noun* pl of OSTEOMA.

osteomyelitis /,ostiohmie·ə'lietəs/ *noun* an infectious inflammatory disease of bone or bone marrow.

osteopathy /osti'opəthi/ *noun* a system of treatment of disease based on the manipulation of bones or other parts of the body. ➤➤ **osteopath** /'osti-əpath/ *noun*, **osteopathic** /-'pathik/ *adj*, **osteopathically** /-'pathikli/ *adv.*

osteophyte /'osti-əfiet/ *noun* an abnormal outgrowth from a bone. ➤➤ **osteophytic** /-'fitik/ *adj.*

osteoporosis /,ostiohpə'rohsis/ *noun* a disease that causes enlargement of the internal cavities in the bones and makes them thin, brittle, and porous. Also called BRITTLE BONE DISEASE. [scientific Latin *osteoporosis*, from OSTE- + *porosis* porosity, from Latin *porus* PORE[1]]

ostinato /osti'nahtoh/ *noun* (*pl* **ostinatos**) a musical figure repeated persistently at the same pitch throughout a composition: compare IMITATION (3), SEQUENCE[1] (6). [Italian *ostinato* obstinate, from Latin *obstinatus*: see OBSTINATE]

ostler (*NAmer* **hostler**) /'oslə/ *noun* in former times, a groom or stableman at an inn: *Richardson used to say, that had he not known who Fielding was, he should have believed he was an ostler —* Dr Johnson. [Middle English *osteler, hosteler* innkeeper, ostler, from HOSTEL]

Ostmark /'ostmahk/ *noun* the basic monetary unit of the former German Democratic Republic. [German *Ostmark*, literally 'East mark']

ostracize *or* **ostracise** /'ostrəsiez/ *verb trans* **1** to exclude (somebody) by general consent from a group or society: *The wives and families of the traitors were ostracized, while the corner groceryman who sold provisions to them was boycotted —* Jack London. **2** in ancient Greece, to send (somebody) into temporary exile by popular vote. ➤➤ **ostracism** /'ostrəsiz(ə)m/ *noun.* [Greek *ostrakizein* to banish by voting with potsherds, from *ostrakon* shell, potsherd; a vote to banish somebody was registered by writing his name on a potsherd]

ostrich /'ostrich, *also* 'ostrij/ *noun* **1** a swift-running flightless bird of N Africa, the largest of existing birds, that has dark plumage, a naked head, long legs, and two toes on each foot: *Struthio camelus.* **2** a person who refuses to face up to unpleasant realities. [Middle English via French from vulgar Latin *avis struthio*, from Latin *avis* bird + *struthio* ostrich, ultimately from Greek *strouthos*; (sense 2) from the belief that the ostrich when pursued hides its head in the sand and believes itself to be unseen]

Ostrogoth /'ostrəgoth/ *noun* a member of the E division of the Goths (N German invaders of the Roman Empire in the fourth and fifth cents; see GOTH). ➤➤ **Ostrogothic** /-'gothik/ *adj.* [late Latin *Ostrogothi* eastern Goths, of Germanic origin]

OT *abbr* **1** occupational therapy. **2** occupational therapist. **3** Old Testament. **4** overtime.

ot- *or* **oto-** *comb. form* forming words, denoting: **1** ear: *otitis.* **2** ear and: *otolaryngology.* [Greek *ōt-, ōto-*, from *ōt-, ous* ear]

otalgia /oh'taljə/ *noun* in medicine, earache.

OTC *abbr* **1** Officers' Training Corps. **2** over-the-counter.

OTE *abbr* on target earnings, the projected remuneration of a sales representative or other person on commission.

other[1] /'udhə/ *adj* **1a** being the remaining one or ones of two or more: *She held on with one hand and waved with the other one.* **b** being the one or ones distinct from that or those previously mentioned: *He is taller than the other boys.* **c** second; alternate: *I phone my mother every other day.* **2a** not the same; different: *opinions other than her own.* **b** far or opposite: *He lives the other side of town.* **3** additional or further: *John and two other boys.* **4** recently past: *I saw her the other evening.* ✽ **the other thing** an alternative that is not explicitly stated: *If you don't like it, you can do the other thing!* [Old English *ōther*]

other[2] *pronoun* **1** the remaining or opposite one: *We slid from one side to the other; The others came later.* **2** a different or additional one: *some film or other; There are many others on the market.* ✽ **no other** *archaic* nothing else: *We can do no other.*

other-directed *adj* directed in thought and action primarily by external influences rather than by one's own values.

otherness *noun* the state of being other or different.

other ranks *pl noun chiefly Brit* military persons not holding commissioned rank.

otherwise[1] *adv* **1** in different circumstances: *She might otherwise have left.* **2** in other respects: *an otherwise excellent dinner.* **3** in a different way: *They were otherwise engaged.* **4** if not; or else: *Do what I say, otherwise you'll be sorry.* **5** used to express the opposite: *mothers,* *whether married or otherwise; guilty unless proved otherwise.* [Old English *on ōthre wīsan* in another manner]

otherwise² *adj* of a different kind: *How can I be otherwise than grateful?*

other woman *noun* the female lover of a married man.

other world *noun* the spirit world or the afterlife.

otherworldly *adj* concerned with spiritual or intellectual matters rather than the material world. ➤➤ **otherworldliness** *noun*.

otic /'ohtik/ *adj* relating to or in the region of the ear. [Greek *ōtikos*, from *ōt-, ous* ear]

-otic¹ *suffix* forming adjectives corresponding to nouns ending in -osis, with the meanings: **1** of or characterized by a specified action, process, or condition: *hypnotic, symblock.* **2** having an abnormal or pathological condition: *thrombotic; neurotic.* ➤➤ **-otically** *suffix*. [Greek *-ōtikos,* adjectival ending]

-otic² *comb. form* forming adjectives, with the meaning: having a specified relationship to the ear: *periotic.* [Greek *ōtikos*: see OTIC]

otiose /'ohshiohs, 'ohtiohs/ *adj* **1** *formal* futile or pointless; lacking use or effect. *otiose rhetoric.* **2** *archaic* at leisure; idle. ➤➤ **otiosely** *adv,* **otioseness** *noun.* [Latin *otiosus,* from *otium* leisure]

otitis /oh'tietəs/ *noun* inflammation of the ear.

oto- *comb. form* see OT-.

otolaryngology /,ohtohlaring'goləji/ *noun* = OTORHINOLARYNGOLOGY. ➤➤ **otolaryngological** /-lə,ringgə'lojikl/ *adj,* **otolaryngologist** *noun.* [OTO- + LARYNG- + -OLOGY]

otolith /'ohtohlith/ *noun* any of many minute lumps of calcite and protein in the internal ear that are receptors for the sense of balance. ➤➤ **otolithic** /-'lithik/ *adj.* [French *otolithe,* from OTO- + -*lithe* -LITH]

otology /oh'toləji/ *noun* a branch of medicine dealing with the ear. ➤➤ **otological** /-'lojikl/ *adj,* **otologist** *noun.*

otorhinolaryngology /,ohtoh,rienoh,laring'goləji/ *noun* a branch of medicine dealing with the ear, nose, and throat. [OTO- + RHINO- + LARYNG- + -OLOGY]

otoscope /'ohtəskohp/ *noun* a medical instrument for examining the eardrum and outer ear.

OTT *abbr* over-the-top.

ottar /'otə/ *noun* see ATTAR.

ottava rima /oh,tahvə 'reemə/ *noun* in poetry, a form of stanza having eight lines of ten syllables each in English or eleven syllables each in Italian with a rhyme scheme of *abababcc.* [Italian *ottava rima* eighth rhyme]

otter /'otə/ *noun* (*pl* **otters** *or collectively* **otter**) **1a** any of several species of aquatic fish-eating mammals related to the weasels that have webbed and clawed feet, a long streamlined body, and dark brown fur: genus *Lutra* and other genera. **b** the fur of an otter. **2** a piece of fishing tackle consisting of a submerged board to which baited lines are attached. [Old English *otor*]

otter board *noun* either of two boards that keep the mouth of a trawl net open.

otter hound *noun* a hound of a breed originating in Britain, having a wiry shaggy coat, long drooping ears, and a keen sense of smell. [from its use in hunting otters]

otto /'otoh/ *noun* see ATTAR. [by alteration]

Ottoman /'otəmən/ *adj* **1** of the Turks or Turkey; Turkish. **2** of the Ottoman Empire, a former Turkish sultanate in SE Europe, W Asia, and N Africa, founded around 1300 and dissolved after World War I. [French *ottoman,* prob via Italian from Arabic *'othmānī,* from *'Othmān* Osman d.1326, founder of the Ottoman Empire]

ottoman *noun* (*pl* **ottomans**) **1** (**Ottoman**) a Turk, *esp* of the Ottoman Empire. **2a** a usu heavily upholstered box or seat without a back or arms. **b** a cushioned stool for the feet. **3** a heavy corded fabric. [(senses 2, 3) French *ottomane,* fem of *ottoman*: see OTTOMAN]

OU *abbr* Open University.

ou /oh/ *noun* *SAfr, informal* a fellow. [Afrikaans *ou,* prob from *ou* old, from Dutch *ouwe* old man]

ouabain /wah'bah·in, 'wahbah·een/ *noun* a poisonous chemical compound obtained from several African shrubs or trees of the periwinkle family and used in medicine as a heart stimulant. [French *ouabaïo,* an African tree that yields ouabain, from Somali *waba yo*]

ouananiche /wahnə'neesh/ *noun* NAmer a landlocked Atlantic salmon that lives in the lakes of SE Canada. [Canadian French *ouananiche* from Algonquian]

oubliette /,oohbli'et/ *noun* a dungeon with an opening only at the top. [French *oubliette* from *oublier* to forget, from Latin *oblivisci*]

ouch /owch/ *interj* used to express sudden sharp pain.

ought¹ /awt/ *verb aux* (*third person sing. present tense* **ought,** *past tense in reported speech* **ought**) **1** used to express moral obligation: *We ought to pay our debts; He said we ought not to say such things.* **2** used to express what is advisable or recommended: *The paint ought to be left to dry overnight; You ought to see her dance.* **3** used to express probability or expectation: *They ought to have arrived by now.* [Old English *ahte,* past tense of *agan* to OWE]

usage note

The negative form of *ought* is *ought not,* which can be shortened to *oughtn't. Oughtn't we to let them know in advance?* The form *didn't ought* is not standard English. The form *ought to have* is used to express an unfulfilled obligation in the past: *You ought to have told us* (but you did not).

ought² *pronoun* = AUGHT.

ought³ *noun* = NOUGHT. [perhaps from incorrect division of *a nought*]

oughtn't /'awtnt/ *contraction* ought not.

ouguiya /ooh'gee·ə/ *noun* the basic monetary unit of Mauritania, divided into five khoums. [French *ouguiya* from Arabic *'ukiyya,* ultimately from Latin *uncia*: see OUNCE¹]

Ouija board /'weejə, 'weeji/ *noun trademark* a board with letters, numbers, and other signs around the edge and a moving pointer that is used to produce messages, answers to questions, etc in spiritualistic seances. [French *oui* yes + German *ja* yes]

ounce¹ /owns/ *noun* **1a** a unit of weight equal to one sixteenth of a pound (about 28.35g). **b** a unit of troy weight or apothecaries' weight equal to one twelfth of a pound or 480 grains (about 31g). **c** = FLUID OUNCE. **2** (*usu with a negative*) the least amount: *The Queen is the prescriptive sovereign of one realm only, the United Kingdom: elsewhere neither she nor her so-called representatives the governors-general possess an ounce of prescriptive sovereignty* — Enoch Powell. [Middle English via French from Latin *uncia* twelfth part, ounce, from *unus* one]

ounce² *noun* = SNOW LEOPARD. [Middle English *unce, once* from Old French *once,* alteration of *lonce* (the *l* being taken for the definite article *l*'), ultimately from Latin *lync-, lynx* LYNX]

our /'owə, ah/ *adj* **1** belonging to or associated with us: *our house; our children; our being chosen; our rescue.* **2** belonging to or associated with people in general: *Our nearest relative is the chimpanzee.* **3** used by writers and monarchs as a formal word for *my.* [Old English *ūre*]

-our *suffix* = -OR².

Our Father *noun* the Lord's Prayer. [from its opening words]

Our Lady *noun* = VIRGIN MARY.

ours /'owəz, ahz/ *pronoun* the one or ones that belong to us or are associated with us: *Ours has a sunroof; children younger than ours; Are these books ours?* *** of ours** belonging to or associated with us: *friends of ours.*

ourself /owə'self, ah'self/ *pronoun* used instead of *myself* when *we* is used instead of *I,* e.g. by a monarch: *We will ourself in person to this war* — Shakespeare; *We have shaken hands with the world's business; we have done with it; we have discharged ourself of it* — Charles Lamb.

ourselves /owə'selvz, ah'selvz/ *pronoun* **1** used reflexively to refer to the people speaking or to a person speaking and associated people: *We washed ourselves in the stream.* **2** used for emphasis: *We designed the kitchen ourselves.* *** be ourselves** to be fit or healthy as normal: *We weren't quite ourselves that day.*

-ous *suffix* forming adjectives, with the meanings: **1** full of, characterized by, or possessing the quality of something: *clamorous; envious.* **2** in chemistry, having a valency relatively lower than in compounds or ions named with an adjective ending in *-ic: ferrous; mercurous.* ➤➤ **-ously** *suffix.* [Middle English; partly from Old French *-ous, -eus, -eux,* partly from Latin *-us*]

ousel /'oohzl/ *noun* see OUZEL.

-ously *suffix* see -OUS.

oust /owst/ *verb trans* **1** to take the place of (somebody); to supplant (them). **2** to deprive (somebody) of possession, *esp* of land. [Anglo-French *ouster* via Old French *oster* from Latin *obstare* to stand against, from OB- + *stare* to stand]

ouster *noun* illegal dispossession. [Anglo-French *ouster*: see OUST]

out[1] */owt/ adv* **1a** away from the inside or centre: *They went out into the garden.* **b** from among other things: *Separate out the bad apples.* **c** away from the shore, the city, or one's homeland: *out at sea; out in the country.* **d** away from a particular place, *esp* one's home or business: *out for lunch; out on strike.* **e** clearly in or into view: *if the sun stays out.* **f** said of a flower: in or into full bloom. **2a** not in the proper place: *You left a word out.* **b** inaccurate in reckoning: *more than £10 out.* **3** no longer in vogue or fashion. **4a** to or in a state of extinction or completion: *The candle had burned out; before the year is out.* **b** to the fullest extent or degree; completely: *Hear me out; We must clean out the attic.* **c** in or into a state of determined effort: *out to fight pollution.* **5a** aloud: *She cried out.* **b** in or into public knowledge or circulation: *The truth leaked out.* **c** *informal* used with a superlative: in existence; ever: *the funniest thing out.* **6** so as to be eliminated, *esp* from a game: *bowled out.* **7** in or into a state of unconsciousness. **8** used on a two-way radio to indicate that a message is complete and no reply is expected. ✳ **have it out** *informal* to settle a matter of contention by discussion or a fight. **out of 1a** from within to the outside of (something): *She walked out of the room.* **b** beyond the range or limits of (something): *out of sight.* **c** away from (something): *while I was out of town.* **2a** used to indicate a change in quality, state, or form: *I woke out of a deep sleep.* **b** used to indicate a position or state away from what is correct or desirable: *out of alignment.* **3a** used to indicate origin or cause: *He came out of fear.* **b** using (something) as a material: *The hut was built out of old timber.* **c** said *esp* of horses: having (the specified animal) as a mother: *a colt out of an ordinary mare.* **4** used to indicate exclusion from or deprivation of (something): *out of breath.* **5** from among (a number or group): *One out of four survived.* **out of it** not part of a group, activity, or fashion. [Old English *ūt*]

Usage note
The use of *out* to mean *out of* is standard in American English but seems rather casual in British English and is better avoided in formal writing or speech: *She simply turned and walked out of* (American also *walked out*) *the door.*

out[2] *verb intrans* to become publicly known: *The truth will out.* ➤ *verb trans* **1** to expel, eject, or dismiss (somebody or something); to put or throw (them) out. **2** *informal* to reveal that (somebody) is homosexual.

out[3] *adj* **1** directed or serving to direct outwards: *the out tray.* **2** not permissible, possible, or worth considering: *Your suggestion's definitely out.* **3a** in cricket, baseball, etc, not allowed to continue batting. **b** said of a ball, shot, etc: landing outside the prescribed area. **4** *informal* open about one's homosexuality.

out[4] *prep non-standard or NAmer* out of.

Usage note
See note at OUT[1].

out[5] *noun* a way of escaping from an embarrassing or difficult situation: *She's now looking for an out.*

out- *prefix* forming words, with the meanings: **1** forth: *outcry; outburst; outrush.* **2** result or product: *output; outcome.* **3** in a manner that goes beyond, surpasses, or excels: *outmanoeuvre; outstrip.* **4** located outside; external: *outbuilding.* [OUT[1]]

outage */'owtij/ noun* a period of nonoperation, e.g. of a power supply.

out-and-out *adj* being completely as specified at all times or from every point of view: *an out-and-out liar.*

outback */'owtbak/ noun* remote rural country, *esp* in Australia.

outbalance */owt'baləns/ verb trans* to exceed (something) in value or importance.

outbid */owt'bid/ verb trans* (**outbidding**, *past tense and past part.* **outbid**) to make a higher bid than (somebody).

outboard[1] */'owtbawd/ adv* in a lateral direction from the hull of a ship or the fuselage of an aircraft. [OUT- + BOARD[1] in the sense 'ship's side']

outboard[2] *adj* **1** situated outboard. **2** having, using, or limited to the use of an outboard motor.

outboard[3] *noun* **1** a motor, propeller, and rudder attached as a unit to the stern of a small boat. **2** a boat with an outboard motor.

outboard motor *noun* = OUTBOARD[3] (1).

outbound */'owtbownd/ adj* outward-bound: *outbound traffic.*

outbrave */owt'brayv/ verb trans* **1** to face or resist (somebody) defiantly. **2** to be braver than (somebody).

outbreak */'owtbrayk/ noun* **1** a sudden or violent breaking out of activity: *the outbreak of war.* **2** a sudden rise in the incidence of something, *esp* a disease: *an outbreak of measles.*

outbreed */owt'breed/ verb trans (past tense and past part.* **outbred**) to cause (animals or plants that are not closely related) to interbreed. ➤➤ **outbreeding** */'owtbreeding/ noun.*

outbuilding */'owtbilding/ noun* a smaller building separate from but belonging to a main building.

outburst */'owtbuhst/ noun* **1** a violent expression of feeling. **2** a surge of activity or growth.

outcast */'owtkahst/ noun* a person who is cast out by society. ➤➤ **outcast** *adj.*

outcaste[1] */'owtkahst/ noun* **1** a Hindu who has been ejected from his or her CASTE (hereditary social class). **2** a person who has no caste.

outcaste[2] *verb trans* to make (somebody) an outcaste.

outclass */owt'klahs/ verb trans* to excel or surpass (somebody or something) in quality, skill, etc.

outcome */'owtkum/ noun* a result or consequence.

outcrop[1] */'owtkrop/ noun* the part of a rock formation that appears at the surface of the ground.

outcrop[2] *verb intrans* (**outcropped, outcropping**) to project as an outcrop.

outcry */'owtkrie/ noun (pl* **outcries**) **1** a public expression of anger or disapproval. **2** a loud cry; a clamour.

outdated */owt'daytid/ adj* old-fashioned or obsolete; outmoded.

outdid */owt'did/ verb* past tense of OUTDO.

outdistance */owt'dist(ə)ns/ verb trans* to go far ahead of (somebody), e.g. in a race.

outdo */owt'dooh/ verb trans* (**outdoes** */owt'duz/, past tense* **outdid** */owt'did/, past part.* **outdone** */owt'dun/*) to surpass (somebody) in action or performance.

outdoor */'owtdaw/ adj* **1** of or performed outdoors: *outdoor pursuits.* **2** not enclosed; without a roof: *an outdoor restaurant.*

outdoors[1] */'owtdawz/ adv* outside a building; in or into the open air.

outdoors[2] *noun* **1** the open air. **2** the world remote from human habitation: *the great outdoors.*

outer[1] */'owtə/ adj* **1** situated or belonging on the outside; external: *the outer covering.* **2** away from a centre; situated farther out: *the outer planets.* ➤➤ **outermost** *adj.*

outer[2] *noun* **1** the ring on a shooting target that is outermost and worth the least score, or a shot that hits this ring. **2** *Aus, NZ* the part of the spectator area at a racecourse or sports ground that is outside the enclosure.

outer bar *noun* (**the outer bar**) in Britain, junior barristers who are not Queen's Counsels or King's Counsels.

outer ear *noun* the visible part of the ear together with the canal through which sound waves reach the eardrum.

outer space *noun* space outside the earth's atmosphere.

outerwear */'owtəweə/ noun* clothing to be worn over other clothes or outdoors.

outface */owt'fays/ verb trans* **1** to confront (somebody) unflinchingly; to defy (them). **2** to cause (somebody) to waver or submit by staring at them.

outfall */'owtfawl/ noun* the outlet for a river, lake, drain, sewer, etc.

outfield */'owtfeeld/ noun* **1a** the part of a cricket field beyond the prepared section on which the wickets are laid out. **b** the part of a baseball field outside a line connecting the bases. **c** the defensive fielding positions that lie in the outfield, or the players in these positions. **2** farmland that is farthest from the main buildings of a farm. ➤➤ **outfielder** *noun.*

outfit[1] */'owtfit/ noun* **1a** a set of garments worn together, often for a specified occasion or activity. **b** a complete set of equipment needed for a particular purpose. **2** *informal* (*treated as sing. or pl*) a group that works as a team.

outfit[2] *verb trans* (**outfitted, outfitting**) to provide (somebody) with an outfit or equipment.

outfitter *noun* somebody who supplies outfits or equipment, *esp* a retailer in men's clothing.

outflank /owt'flangk/ *verb trans* **1** to go round the flank of (an opposing force); to outmanoeuvre (them). **2** to gain an advantage over (somebody) by doing something unexpected.

outflow /'owtfloh/ *noun* **1** the act or process of flowing out. **2** something that flows out.

outfox /owt'foks/ *verb trans* to get the better of (somebody) by cunning.

outgeneral /owt'jen(ə)rəl/ *verb trans* (**outgeneralled, outgeneralling,** *NAmer* **outgeneraled, outgeneraling**) to get the better of (somebody), *esp* by using superior military tactics.

outgo[1] /owt'goh/ *verb trans* (**outgoes,** *past tense* **outwent** /owt'went/, *past part.* **outgone** /owt'gon/) **1** to go beyond or exceed (something). **2** to outdo or outstrip (somebody).

outgo[2] /'owtgoh/ *noun* outlay; expenditure.

outgoing[1] *adj* **1a** retiring or withdrawing from a position: *the outgoing president.* **b** going away; departing: *outgoing ships.* **2** friendly or sociable.

outgoing[2] *noun* **1** the act or an instance of going out. **2** (*in pl*) expenditure, *esp* overheads.

outgone /owt'gon/ *verb* past part. of OUTGO[1].

outgrow /owt'groh/ *verb trans* (*past tense* **outgrew** /owt'grooh/, *past part.* **outgrown** /owt'grohn/) **1** to grow or increase faster than (somebody or something). **2** to grow too large for (e.g. clothes). **3** to lose or leave behind (e.g. a habit) as one grows older.

outgrowth /'owtgrohth/ *noun* **1** something that grows out of something else. **2** the process of growing out. **3** a consequence or by-product.

outgun /owt'gun/ *verb trans* (**outgunned, outgunning**) to surpass (somebody) in firepower, weaponry, or shooting; *broadly* to defeat (them).

outhouse /'owt·hows/ *noun* **1** an outbuilding. **2** *chiefly NAmer* an outside toilet.

outing /'owting/ *noun* **1** a short pleasure trip. **2** *informal* the act of revealing the homosexuality of somebody, *esp* a public figure, against their will.

outjockey /owt'joki/ *verb trans* *dated* to outwit (somebody) by deception.

outlandish /owt'landish/ *adj* **1** strikingly unusual; bizarre. **2** *archaic* foreign. ⟫⟫ **outlandishly** *adv.* [Old English *ūtlendisc* foreign, from *ūtland* outlying land, foreign country, from *ūt* OUT[1] + *land* LAND[1]]

outlast /owt'lahst/ *verb trans* to last longer than (something or somebody).

outlaw[1] /'owtlaw/ *noun* **1** a fugitive from the law. **2** somebody excluded from the protection of the law. [Old English *ūtlaga* from Old Norse *ūtlagi,* from *ūt* out + *lag-, lög* law]

outlaw[2] *verb trans* **1** to make (something) illegal; to ban (it). **2** to deprive (somebody) of the protection of the law. ⟫⟫ **outlawry** /-ri/ *noun.*

outlay /'owtlay/ *noun* expenditure or payment.

outlet /'owtlit/ *noun* **1a** a place or opening through which something is let out; an exit or vent. **b** a means of release or satisfaction for an emotion or drive. **2** an agency, e.g. a shop or dealer, through which a product is marketed: *retail outlets.* **3** *chiefly NAmer* an electric socket. [OUT[1] + LET[1]]

outlier /'owtlie·ə/ *noun* **1** something separated or lying away from a main or related body. **2** a formation of younger rocks surrounded by older ones. [OUT[1] + LIE[1] + -ER[2]]

outline[1] /'owtlien/ *noun* **1** a line bounding the outer limits of something or indicating its shape. **2** a drawing with no shading or detail. **3a** a condensed or general treatment of a subject. **b** a summary of a written work. **4** a preliminary plan or draft showing the main features only.

outline[2] *verb trans* **1** to draw the outline of (something). **2** to indicate the principal features of (something).

outlive /owt'liv/ *verb trans* **1** to live longer than (somebody). **2** to survive the effects of (something).

outlook /'owtlook/ *noun* **1** a view from a particular place: *a house with a pleasant outlook.* **2** an attitude or point of view. **3** a prospect for the future.

outlying /'owtlie·ing/ *adj* remote from a centre or main point.

outmanoeuvre (*NAmer* **outmaneuver**) /owtmə'n(y)oohvə/ *verb trans* to defeat (somebody) by more skilful manoeuvring.

outmatch /owt'mach/ *verb trans* to prove superior to (somebody).

outmoded /owt'mohdid/ *adj* **1** no longer in fashion. **2** no longer acceptable; obsolete. ⟫⟫ **outmodedness** *noun.*

outnumber /owt'numbə/ *verb trans* (**outnumbered, outnumbering**) to exceed (people or things) in number.

out-of-body experience *noun* a feeling of being separate from one's body and so able to observe oneself as if from a distance.

out-of-bounds *adv and adj* outside the prescribed boundaries or limits.

out-of-court *adj* said of a settlement: agreed between disputing parties without the intervention of a court of law.

out-of-date *adj* **1** old-fashioned or obsolete; outmoded. **2** no longer valid or usable: *an out-of-date season ticket.*

out-of-doors *adv* = OUTDOORS[1].

out-of-pocket *adj* **1** requiring an outlay of cash: *out-of-pocket expenses.* **2** having spent or lost more money than one can afford.

out-of-the-way *adj* **1** off the beaten track; remote. **2** unusual.

outpace /owt'pays/ *verb trans* to surpass (somebody or something) in speed, growth, development, etc.

outpatient /'owtpaysh(ə)nt/ *noun* a patient who visits a hospital for diagnosis or treatment but does not stay there overnight: compare INPATIENT.

outperform /owtpə'fawm/ *verb trans* to do better than (something or somebody) in performance or achievement: *a sports car that outperforms them all.*

outplacement /'owtplaysmənt/ *noun* advice and assistance in finding new jobs for redundant employees, usu provided or paid for by the company making them redundant.

outplay /owt'play/ *verb trans* to play better than and defeat (somebody) in a game.

outpoint /owt'poynt/ *verb trans* to defeat (somebody) by scoring more points, *esp* in boxing.

outport /'owtpawt/ *noun* **1** a port that is auxiliary to a major port and generally more able to handle larger vessels. **2** *Can* a small fishing village, *esp* in Newfoundland.

outpost /'owtpohst/ *noun* **1** a post or detachment established at a distance from a main body of troops, *esp* to protect it from surprise attack. **2a** an outlying or frontier settlement. **b** an outlying branch of a main organization or body.

outpouring /'owtpawring/ *noun* **1** (*usu in pl*) an outburst of powerful emotion. **2a** the act of pouring out. **b** something that pours out.

output[1] /'owtpoot/ *noun* **1a** the amount produced by somebody in a given time. **b** the act or process of producing. **2a** agricultural or industrial production. **b** mental or artistic production. **3a** something, e.g. power or energy, produced by a machine or system. **b** the terminal for the output on an electrical device. **c** the information produced by a computer.

output[2] *verb trans* (**outputting,** *past tense and past part.* **output**) to produce (something) as output.

outrage[1] /'owtrayj/ *noun* **1** the anger and resentment aroused by injury or insult. **2** an act that violates accepted standards of behaviour or taste: *an outrage alike against decency and dignity* — John Buchan. **3** an act of violence or brutality. [Middle English from Old French *outrage* excess, outrage, from *outrer* to carry to excess, ultimately from Latin *ultra* beyond]

outrage[2] *verb trans* **1** to arouse intense anger or resentment in (somebody). **2** to violate the standards or principles of (something). **3** *euphem* to rape (somebody).

outrageous /owt'rayjəs/ *adj* **1** going beyond all standards of propriety, decency, or taste; shocking or offensive. **2** not conventional or moderate; extravagant: *When I was young, the old regarded me as an outrageous young fellow, and now that I'm old the young regard me as an outrageous old fellow* — Fred Hoyle. ⟫⟫ **outrageously** *adv,* **outrageousness** *noun.*

outran /owt'ran/ *verb* past tense of OUTRUN.

outrank /owt'rangk/ *verb trans* **1** to rank higher than (somebody). **2** to exceed (something) in importance.

outré /'oohtray (*French* utre)/ *adj* violating convention or propriety; bizarre. [French *outré,* past part. of *outrer:* see OUTRAGE[1]]

outreach¹ /owt'reech/ *verb trans* to reach further than (somebody or something).

outreach² /'owtreech/ *noun* **1** involvement with and education of people in the community: *the theatre's outreach programme.* **2** the act or extent of reaching out.

outride /owt'ried/ *verb trans* (*past tense* **outrode** /owt'rohd/, *past part.* **outridden** /owt'rid(ə)n/) **1** to ride better, faster, or farther than (somebody). **2** said of a ship: to ride out (a storm).

outrider /'owtriedə/ *noun* **1** a mounted attendant or motorcyclist who rides ahead of or beside a carriage or car as an escort or guard. **2** *NAmer* a person on horseback who herds cattle.

outrigger /'owtrigə/ *noun* **1a** a spar, beam, or framework projecting from a ship's side, e.g. to secure a mast. **b** a projecting framework by which a float is attached beside a canoe to give it greater stability, or a canoe so equipped. **2** a member projecting from a main structure to provide additional stability or support something. [perhaps an alteration, by association with RIG², of obsolete *outligger* a spar for extending a sail, from Dutch *uitligger* outlier]

outright¹ /owt'riet/ *adv* **1** completely; altogether. **2** instantaneously; on the spot. **3** without reservation; directly: *She asked him outright.* **4** without restrictions: *I purchased the property outright.*

outright² /'owtriet/ *adj* **1** being completely or exactly what is stated: *an outright lie.* **2** without reservation; direct. **3** without restrictions: *an outright purchase.*

outrode /owt'rohd/ *verb* past tense of OUTRIDE.

outrun /owt'run/ *verb trans* (**outrunning**, *past tense* **outran** /owt'ran/, *past part.* **outrun**) **1** to run faster than (somebody). **2** to exceed or surpass (something).

outsell /owt'sel/ *verb trans* (*past tense and past part.* **outsold** /owt'sohld/) **1** to exceed (something) in numbers sold. **2** to surpass (somebody) in selling or salesmanship.

outset /'owtset/ *noun* (**the outset**) the beginning or start.

outshine /owt'shien/ *verb trans* (*past tense and past part.* **outshone** /owt'shon/) **1** to shine brighter than (something). **2** to outdo or surpass (something or somebody).

outside¹ /owt'sied, 'owtsied/ *noun* **1** the outer side or surface of something. **2** an outer manifestation; an appearance. **3** the part surrounding or beyond the boundaries of something. **4a** the side of a pavement that is nearer the traffic. **b** the side of a curve or bend that has the longer edge. **c** the side of a carriageway that is nearer the middle of the road. **d** in sport, the section of a playing area towards the sidelines. **e** (*in pl*) the outer sheets of a ream of paper. **✳ at the outside** at the most: *The crowd numbered 10,000 at the outside.*

outside² *adj* **1** of or being on, near, or towards the outside: *an outside lavatory; an outside telephone line; driving in the outside lane.* **2a** originating elsewhere: *an outside broadcast; outside agitators.* **b** not belonging to one's regular occupation or duties: *outside interests.* **3** maximum: *outside odds.* **4** barely possible; remote: *an outside chance.*

outside³ /owt'sied/ *adv* **1** on or to the outside: *Wait outside in the passage.* **2** outdoors. **3** *chiefly Brit, informal* not in prison. **✳ outside of 1** *chiefly NAmer* beyond the limits of (something). **2** *chiefly NAmer* except for or apart from (something).

outside⁴ /'owtsied, owt'sied/ *prep* **1** on or to the outside of (e.g. a place): *We live a mile outside Cambridge.* **2** beyond the limits of (something): *outside my experience.* **3** except or besides (something or somebody): *She has few interests outside her children.*

outside broadcast *noun* a television or radio broadcast recorded or filmed on location, not in a studio.

outsider /owt'siedə/ *noun* **1** somebody who does not belong to a particular group. **2** a competitor who has only a remote chance of winning.

outsize¹ /'owtsiez/ *adj* of an exceptionally large or larger than standard size.

outsize² *noun* an outsize person or thing, e.g. a garment.

outskirts /'owtskuhts/ *pl noun* the parts of a town or city that are farthest from the centre.

outsmart /owt'smaht/ *verb trans* to get the better of (somebody); to outwit (them).

outsold /owt'sohld/ *verb* past tense and past part. of OUTSELL.

outsource /'owtsaws/ *verb trans and intrans* to obtain (components, services, etc) from outside suppliers.

outspan¹ /owt'span/ *verb* (**outspanned, outspanning**) *SAfr* to unharness (e.g. oxen) from a wagon. [from Dutch *uitspannen* to unyoke, from *uit* out + *spannen* to yoke, harness]

outspan² /'owtspan/ *noun SAfr* a place to camp or graze animals when travelling by wagon.

outspoken /owt'spohk(ə)n/ *adj* direct and open in speech or expression; frank. ➤➤ **outspokenly** *adv*, **outspokenness** *noun*.

outspread¹ /owt'spred/ *verb trans* (*past tense and past part.* **outspread**) to spread (something) out; to extend (it).

outspread² *adj* spread or stretched out; fully extended.

outstanding /owt'standing/ *adj* **1a** marked by excellence or distinction. **b** standing out from a group; conspicuous. **2a** unpaid: *There are several bills outstanding.* **b** continuing or unresolved. ➤➤ **outstandingly** *adv*.

outstare /owt'steə/ *verb trans* to stare at (somebody) for longer than they can stare back.

outstation /'owtstaysh(ə)n/ *noun* a remote or outlying station.

outstay /owt'stay/ *verb trans* **1** to stay beyond the time or limits of (something): *He outstayed his welcome.* **2** to stay or last longer than (other people): *She outstayed her rivals.*

outstretch /owt'strech/ *verb trans* **1** to stretch (something) out; to extend (it): *with outstretched arms.* **2** to go beyond the limits of (something).

outstrip /owt'strip/ *verb trans* (**outstripped, outstripping**) **1** to go faster or farther than (somebody or something); to leave (them) behind. **2** to do better than or get ahead of (somebody). **3** to be greater than or grow faster than (something): *Demand has outstripped supply.* [OUT- + obsolete *strip* to move fast]

outswing /'owtswing/ *noun* the swing of a bowled cricket ball from the leg to the off side: compare INSWING. ➤➤ **outswinger** *noun.*

out-take *noun* a section of film, recording, etc that is cut out during editing.

out tray *noun* a tray on a desk for papers, letters, etc that have been dealt with.

outturn /'owttuhn/ *noun* **1** a quantity produced; output. **2** a result or outcome.

outvote /owt'voht/ *verb trans* to defeat (somebody) by a majority of votes.

outward¹ /'owtwəd/ *adj* **1a** situated on or directed towards the outside. **b** being or going away from home: *the outward voyage.* **2** relating to external appearances; superficial: *outward calm.* ➤➤ **outwardness** *noun.*

outward² *noun* the external part or appearance.

outward³ *adv NAmer* see OUTWARDS.

Outward Bound *noun trademark* an organization that provides adventure training for young people.

outward-bound *adj* going in an outward direction, e.g. away from a home port.

outwardly *adv* in outward appearance; superficially.

outwards (*NAmer* **outward**) *adv* towards the outside; away from the centre.

outwear /owt'weə/ *verb trans* (*past tense* **outwore** /owt'waw/, *past part.* **outworn** /owt'wawn/) to last longer than (something).

outweigh /owt'way/ *verb trans* to exceed (something) in weight, value, or importance.

outwent /owt'went/ *verb* past tense of OUTGO¹.

outwit /owt'wit/ *verb trans* (**outwitted, outwitting**) to get the better of (somebody) by superior cleverness.

outwith /'owtwidh/ *prep Scot* outside.

outwore /owt'waw/ *verb* past tense of OUTWEAR.

outwork /'owtwuhk/ *noun* **1** a minor defensive position constructed outside a fortified area. **2** work done for a business or organization off its premises usu by employees based at home. ➤➤ **outworker** *noun*, **outworking** *noun.*

outworn¹ /owt'wawn/ *adj* no longer useful or acceptable; outmoded.

outworn² /owt'wawn/ *verb* past part. of OUTWEAR.

ouzel *or* **ousel** /'oohzl/ *noun* **1** = RING OUZEL. **2** = DIPPER (2). **3** *archaic* the European blackbird. [Old English *ōsle* blackbird]

ouzo /'oohzoh/ *noun* an unsweetened Greek spirit flavoured with aniseed that is usu drunk with water. [modern Greek *ouzon, ouzo*]

ov- or **ovi-** or **ovo-** *comb. form* forming words, denoting: **1** egg: *oviform.* **2** ovum: *oviduct.* [Latin *ov-, ovi-,* from *ovum*]

ova /'ohvə/ *noun* pl of OVUM.

oval[1] /'ohvl/ *adj* having the shape of an egg or ellipse. ⨠ **ovality** /oh'valiti/ *noun,* **ovally** *adv,* **ovalness** *noun.* [late Latin *ovalis* of an egg, from Latin *ovum* egg]

oval[2] *noun* **1** an oval figure or object. **2a** an oval sports field or track. **b** *Aus* a ground for Australian Rules football.

ovariectomy /oh,veəri'ektəmi, ,ohvəri-/ *noun* (*pl* **ovariectomies**) the surgical removal of an ovary. [scientific Latin *ovariectomia,* from *ovarium* (see OVARY) + *-ectomia* -ECTOMY]

ovary /'ohvəri/ *noun* (*pl* **ovaries**) **1** either of the pair of female reproductive organs that produce eggs and female sex hormones in human beings and other animals. **2** the hollow rounded part at the base of a CARPEL (female reproductive organ of a flowering plant) that contains one or more ovules (structures that develop into seeds; see OVULE). ⨠ **ovarian** /oh'veəri-ən, oh'va-/ *adj.* [scientific Latin *ovarium* from Latin *ovum* egg]

ovate /'ohvayt/ *adj* shaped like an egg: *an ovate leaf.*

ovation /oh'vaysh(ə)n/ *noun* **1** an expression of popular acclaim, *esp* sustained and enthusiastic applause. **2** a ceremony, of less importance than a triumph, attending the entrance into ancient Rome of a victorious general. [Latin *ovation-, ovatio,* from *ovare* to exult]

oven /'uv(ə)n/ *noun* an enclosed compartment or chamber used for baking, heating, or drying, *esp* one used in a kitchen for cooking food. [Old English *ofen*]

ovenbird *noun* any of numerous species of small S American songbirds that build dome-shaped nests of mud: family *Furnariidae.* [from the shape of its nest]

oven glove *noun Brit* a cloth pad or mitten used for handling hot cooking pots and dishes.

oven-ready *adj* said of food: sold ready to be cooked without further preparation.

ovenware *noun* heat-resistant dishes in which food can be cooked in an oven.

over[1] /'ohvə/ *adv* **1a** across a barrier: *Can you climb over?* **b** across an intervening space: *The whole family went over to the States.* **c** to a particular place: *Let's ask them over for drinks.* **d** downwards from an upright position: *I fell over.* **e** so as to bring the underside up: *He turned his cards over.* **f** so as to be reversed: *We need to change the two pictures over.* **g** from one person or side to another: *Hand it over.* **2** beyond some quantity or limit: *£10 or over; The show ran a minute over.* **3a** in excess; remaining: *There wasn't much over; Three into seven goes twice and one over.* **b** till a later time: *Can you stay over till Monday?* **4a** so as to cover the whole surface: *windows boarded over.* **b** from beginning to end; through: *I read the article over.* **5a** at an end: *The day is over.* **b** used on a two-way radio to indicate that a message is complete and a reply is expected. **6a** used to show repetition: *ten times over; She had to start all over again.* **b** *chiefly NAmer* once more: *Do your sums over.* ✳ **over and over** repeatedly. **over with** finished or completed. [Old English *ofer*]

over[2] *prep* **1a** higher than (something or somebody): *He towered over his mother.* **b** vertically above but not touching (something or somebody): *A lamp hung over the table.* **c** used to indicate downward movement: *She hit him over the head; He must have fallen over the cliff.* **d** from one side of (a barrier or intervening space) to the other; across (it): *We climbed over the gate; The geese flew over the lake.* **e** so as to cover (something or somebody): *She laid a blanket over the child.* **f** all through or throughout (something): *She showed me all over the house.* **2a** used to indicate authority, power, or jurisdiction: *He never respected those over him.* **b** used to indicate superiority, advantage, or preference: *a big lead over the others.* **3** more than (the specified number or amount): *It shouldn't cost over £5.* **4** by means of (a medium or channel of communication): *over the radio; over the phone.* **5a** during (a period of time): *over the past 25 years; I wrote it over the weekend.* **b** past or beyond (something): *We're over the worst.* **6** used to indicate an object of care or reference: *watching over the children; We all laughed over the incident.* **7** used to indicate an object of occupation or activity: *sitting over their wine.* ✳ **over against** as opposed to; in contrast with. **over and above** besides; in addition to.

over[3] *noun* in cricket, any of the divisions of an innings during which one bowler bowls six balls from the same end of the pitch. [from the umpire's cry of *over* (i.e. change to the other end) after the sixth ball]

over- *comb. form* forming words, with the meanings: **1** upper or higher: *overlord.* **2** outer or covering: *overcoat.* **3a** excessive: *overcompensation.* **b** excessively: *overwork.* **4** above: *overarch.* **5** downwards: *overthrow.*

overabundance /,ohvərə'bund(ə)ns/ *noun* an excess or surfeit. ⨠ **overabundant** *adj.*

overact /ohvə'(r)akt/ *verb trans and intrans* to perform (a part) with undue exaggeration.

overage[1] /ohvə'rayj/ *adj* beyond a specified age limit. [OVER[2] + -AGE[1]]

overage[2] /'ohvərij/ *noun* a surplus or excess. [OVER- + -AGE]

overall[1] /ohvə'rawl/ *adv* **1** as a whole. **2** from end to end.

overall[2] /'ohvərawl/ *noun* **1** (*in pl*) a protective garment resembling a boiler suit or dungarees. **2** *chiefly Brit* a usu loose-fitting protective coat worn over other clothing.

overall[3] *adj* including everything.

overarch /ohvə'rahch/ *verb trans* to form an arch over (something).

overarching /ohvə'rahching/ *adj* **1** forming an arch overhead. **2** dominating or embracing everything else.

overarm /'ohvərahm/ *adj and adv* with the hand and arm brought forward and down from above shoulder level.

overate /ohvə'ret, -'rayt/ *verb* past tense of OVEREAT.

overawe /ohvə'(r)aw/ *verb trans* to fill (somebody) with respect or fear.

overbalance[1] /ohvə'baləns/ *verb trans* **1** to cause (somebody or something) to lose balance. **2** to outweigh (something). ⨠ *verb intrans* to lose balance and fall.

overbalance[2] /ohvə'baləns/ *noun* an excess of weight, value, etc.

overbear /ohvə'beə/ *verb trans* (*past tense* **overbore** /-'baw/, *past part.* **overborne** /-'bawn/) **1a** to domineer over (somebody). **b** to surpass (something) in importance or relevance; to outweigh (it). **2** to bring (something or somebody) down by superior weight or force.

overbearing *adj* harshly masterful or domineering. ⨠ **overbearingly** *adv.*

overbid /ohvə'bid/ *verb* (**overbidding**, *past tense and past part.* **overbid**) ⨠ *verb intrans* **1** in an auction, to bid in excess of value. **2** in bridge, to bid more than the scoring capacity of one's hand. ⨠ *verb trans* **1** in an auction, to bid in excess of (another person's bid). **2** in bridge, to bid more than the value of (one's hand). ⨠ **overbid** /'oh-/ *noun.*

overbite /'ohvəbiet/ *noun* in dentistry, the projection of the upper front teeth over the lower when the jaws are in contact.

overblown[1] /ohvə'blohn/ *adj* inflated or pretentious. [BLOW[1]]

overblown[2] *adj* past the prime of bloom: *overblown roses.* [BLOW[4]]

overboard /'ohvəbawd/ *adv* over the side of a ship or boat into the water. ✳ **go overboard 1** to be very enthusiastic. **2** to go to extremes. **throw overboard** to abandon (something).

overbook /ohvə'book/ *verb trans and intrans* to take bookings for (e.g. a hotel or flight) in excess of the space available.

overbore /ohvə'baw/ *verb* past tense of OVERBEAR.

overborne /ohvə'bawn/ *verb* past part. of OVERBEAR.

overbuild /ohvə'bild/ *verb trans* (*past tense and past part.* **overbuilt** /-'bilt/) **1a** to build (houses) in excess of demand. **b** to put up too many buildings in (an area). **2** to build on top of (something). **3** to build (something) too elaborately.

overburden[1] /ohvə'buhd(ə)n/ *verb trans* (**overburdened, overburdening**) to place an excessive burden on (somebody). ⨠ **overburdensome** *adj.*

overburden[2] /'ohvəbuhd(ə)n/ *noun* **1** soil, rock, etc overlying a useful geological deposit, e.g. of coal. **2** an excessive burden.

overcall /ohvə'kawl/ *verb trans and intrans* to make a higher bid than (the previous bid or player) in a card game. ⨠ **overcall** /'oh-/ *noun.*

overcame /ohvə'kaym/ *verb* past tense of OVERCOME.

overcapitalize *or* **overcapitalise** /ohvə'kapitəliez/ *verb trans* **1** to put a nominal value on the capital of (a company) higher than the actual cost or fair market value. **2** to supply capital for (e.g. a business venture) beyond what is warranted or legally permitted. ⟫ **overcapitalization** /-'zaysh(ə)n/ *noun*.

overcast[1] /'ohvəkahst, ohvə'kahst/ *adj* **1** said of the sky or weather: cloudy. **2** sewn with long stitches passing over a raw edge to prevent fraying.

overcast[2] /'ohvəkahst/ *noun* a covering of clouds over the sky.

overcast[3] /ohvə'kahst/ *verb trans* (*past tense and past part.* **overcast**) **1** to darken or overshadow (something). **2** to sew over (a raw edge, *esp* with long slanting widely spaced stitches, to prevent fraying.

overcharge /ohvə'chahj/ *verb trans* **1** to charge (somebody) too much. **2** to charge (a battery) too much. **3** to fill (something) too full. ➤ *verb intrans* to make an excessive charge. ⟫ **overcharge** /'oh-/ *noun*.

overcloud /ohvə'klowd/ *verb trans* **1** to cover (something) with clouds. **2** to make (something) dim or dark.

overcoat /'ohvəkoht/ *noun* **1** a warm usu thick coat for wearing outdoors over other clothing. **2** a protective coat of paint or varnish.

overcome /ohvə'kum/ *verb* (*past tense* **overcame** /-'kaym/, *past part.* **overcome**) ➤ *verb trans* **1** to deal with (a problem, handicap, etc) successfully; to surmount (it). **2** to overpower or overwhelm (somebody): *They were overcome with emotion.* **3** to defeat (somebody or something). ➤ *verb intrans* to gain superiority; to win. [Old English *ofercuman*, from *ofer* OVER[1] + *cuman* COME[1]]

overcompensate /ohvə'kompensayt/ *verb intrans* to try to make up for a weakness or failing by exaggerating some other trait. ⟫ **overcompensation** /-'saysh(ə)n/ *noun*.

overcook /ohvə'kook/ *verb trans* to cook (something) too much or for too long.

overcrop /ohvə'krop/ *verb trans* (**overcropped, overcropping**) to exhaust (land) by continuous cultivation.

overcrowd /ohvə'krowd/ *verb trans* to cause (a place) to be too crowded.

overdo /ohvə'dooh/ *verb trans* (**overdoes** /-'duz/, *past tense* **overdid** /-'did/, *past part.* **overdone** /-'dun/) **1a** to do or use (something) to excess. **b** to exaggerate (something). **2** to cook (food) too much. ✳ **overdo it/things** to exhaust oneself, *esp* through overwork.

overdose[1] /'ohvədohs/ *noun* a dangerously excessive dose of drugs, medicine, etc.

overdose[2] *verb intrans* to take an overdose. ➤ *verb trans* to give (somebody) an overdose. ➤ **overdosage** /-sij/ *noun*.

overdraft /'ohvədrahft/ *noun* **1** an act of overdrawing at a bank or the state of being overdrawn. **2** the sum overdrawn. **3** a loan facility whereby an account-holder is permitted to overdraw up to a prescribed limit.

overdraw /ohvə'draw/ *verb* (*past tense* **overdrew** /-'drooh/, *past part.* **overdrawn** /-'drawn/) ➤ *verb trans* **1** to withdraw more money from (a bank account) than the balance, with or without authorization. **2** to exaggerate or overstate (something). ➤ *verb intrans* to overdraw a bank account.

overdrawn /ohvə'drawn/ *adj* **1** said of a bank account: in deficit. **2** said of a person: having an overdrawn account.

overdress[1] /ohvə'dres/ *verb* to dress (oneself) too elaborately or formally: *She was overdressed, but not badly dressed* — Somerset Maugham.

overdress[2] /'ohvədres/ *noun* a dress worn over another dress or over a jumper, blouse, etc.

overdrew /ohvə'drooh/ *verb* past tense of OVERDRAW.

overdrive[1] /'ohvədriev/ *noun* a transmission gear in a motor vehicle that provides a ratio higher than the normal top gear and is used at high speeds to lower fuel consumption and reduce wear. ✳ **go into overdrive** to be extremely active: *My imagination went into overdrive.*

overdrive[2] /ohvə'driev/ *verb trans* (*past tense* **overdrove** /-'drohv/, *past part.* **overdriven** /-'driv(ə)n/) to overwork or overuse (somebody or something).

overdub[1] /ohvə'dub/ *verb trans* (**overdubbed, overdubbing**) to record (new sounds) on top of an existing recording.

overdub[2] /'ohvədub/ *noun* an instance of overdubbing.

overdue /ohvə'dyooh/ *adj* **1a** unpaid when due. **b** delayed beyond the proper or appointed time. **2** more than ready or ripe.

overeat /ohvə'reet/ *verb intrans* (*past tense* **overate** /-'ret, -'rayt/, *past part.* **overeaten** /-'reet(ə)n/) to eat to excess.

over-egg ✳ **over-egg the pudding** to make something more elaborate than is necessary.

overestimate /ohvə'restimayt/ *verb trans* **1** to estimate (something) as being more than the actual amount or size. **2** to place too high a value on (something); to overrate (it). ⟫ **overestimate** /-mət/ *noun*, **overestimation** /-'maysh(ə)n/ *noun*.

overexpose /,ohvərik'spohz/ *verb trans* **1** to expose (something or somebody) excessively. **2** to expose (e.g. photographic film) to too much light. ⟫ **overexposure** /-zhə/ *noun*.

overextend /,ohvərik'stend/ *verb trans* **1** to extend (something) beyond a safe or reasonable point. **2** to impose an excessive burden of work, financial commitment, etc on (somebody, *esp* oneself).

overfeed /ohvə'feed/ *verb trans and intrans* (*past tense and past part.* **overfed** /-'fed/) to feed (a person or animal) to excess.

overfish /ohvə'fish/ *verb trans* to deplete (a fishing ground or stock of fish) by fishing excessively.

overflew /ohvə'flooh/ *verb* past tense of OVERFLY.

overflight /'ohvəfliet/ *noun* a passage over an area in an aircraft.

overflow[1] /ohvə'floh/ *verb intrans* **1** to flow over or beyond a brim, edge, or limit. **2** to be filled with something: *I am overflowing with gratitude.* ➤ *verb trans* **1** to cover (something) with or as if with water. **2** to flow over the brim, edge, or limit of (something).

overflow[2] /'ohvəfloh/ *noun* **1** a flowing over, *esp* of liquid. **2** something that flows over. **3** an excess of people, things, etc that cannot be accommodated. **4** an outlet or receptacle for surplus liquid.

overfly /ohvə'flie/ *verb trans* (**overflies**, *past tense* **overflew** /-'flooh/, *past part.* **overflown** /-'flohn/) to fly over (a place), *esp* in an aircraft.

overfold /'ohvəfohld/ *noun* a geological formation in which layers of rock fold upwards into an ANTICLINE (arch) with one side more steeply sloping than the other.

overgrew /ohvə'grooh/ *verb* past tense of OVERGROW.

overground /'ohvəgrownd/ *adj and adv* on the surface; not underground: *overground railway.*

overgrow /ohvə'groh/ *verb* (*past tense* **overgrew** /-'grooh/, *past part.* **overgrown** /-'grohn/) ➤ *verb trans* **1** to grow over (something) so as to cover it with vegetation. **2** to grow beyond (something); to outgrow (it). ➤ *verb intrans* to grow excessively. ⟫ **overgrowth** /'ohvəgrohth/ *noun*.

overgrown /ohvə'grohn/ *adj* **1** grown over or choked with vegetation. **2** grown too large.

overhand /'ohvəhand/ *adj and adv* with the hand brought forward and down from above shoulder level.

overhand knot *noun* a simple knot used *esp* to prevent the end of a rope or cord from fraying or from passing through a hole.

overhang[1] /ohvə'hang/ *verb* (*past tense and past part.* **overhung** /-'hung/) ➤ *verb trans* **1** to project over or beyond (something). **2** to threaten (somebody or something). ➤ *verb intrans* to project so as to be over or beyond something.

overhang[2] /'ohvəhang/ *noun* **1** something that overhangs, or the extent by which something overhangs. **2** a projection of the roof or upper storey of a building beyond the wall of the lower part.

overhaul /ohvə'hawl/ *verb trans* **1** to examine (e.g. a machine) thoroughly and carry out any necessary repairs. **2** to overtake (somebody or something). ⟫ **overhaul** /'oh-/ *noun*. [orig in the senses 'to slacken (a rope), release (a tackle)'; OVER[1] + HAUL[1]]

overhead[1] /ohvə'hed/ *adv* above one's head.

overhead[2] /'ohvəhed/ *adj* operating, situated, or coming from above.

overhead[3] /'ohvəhed/ *noun* **1a** (*also in pl*) a business expense, e.g. rent, insurance, or heating, that is not chargeable to a particular part of the work or product: compare FIXED COSTS, VARIABLE COST. **b** (*used before a noun*) of or being such an expense: *overhead costs.* **2** a stroke in squash, tennis, etc made above head height.

overhead projector *noun* a device that projects a magnified image of a horizontal transparency onto a screen via a mirror.

overhear /ohvə'hiə/ *verb trans and intrans* (*past tense and past part.* **overheard** /-'huhd/) to hear (somebody speaking or something said) without the speaker's knowledge or intention.

overheat /ohvə'heet/ *verb trans* **1** to heat (something) to excess. **2** to stimulate or excite (something or somebody) unduly. **3** to cause (an economy) to overheat. ➤ *verb intrans* **1** to become overheated. **2** said of an economy: to undergo rapid inflation caused by excessive demand.

overhung /ohvə'hung/ *verb* past tense of OVERHANG[1].

overindulge /,ohvərin'dulj/ *verb trans* **1** to indulge in (something) to an excessive degree. **2** to indulge (somebody) to an excessive degree. ➤ *verb intrans* to indulge in something to an excessive degree. ➤➤ **overindulgence** *noun*, **overindulgent** *adj*.

overissue /ohvə'rish(y)ooh, -'risyooh/ *verb trans* (**overissues, overissued, overissuing**) to issue (shares, banknotes, etc) in excess of the limit of capital, credit, or authority. ➤➤ **overissue** *noun*.

overjoyed /ohvə'joyd/ *adj* extremely pleased; elated.

overkill /'ohvəkil/ *noun* **1** the capability of destroying an enemy or target with a force, *esp* of nuclear weapons, that is larger than required. **2** an excess of something beyond what is required or suitable for a particular purpose: *the satirical overkill in Dickens* — John Fowles.

overlaid /ohvə'layd/ *verb* past tense and past part. of OVERLAY[1].

overlain /ohvə'layn/ *verb* past part. of OVERLIE.

overland[1] /'ohvəland/ *adv and adj* by, on, or across land rather than sea or air.

overland[2] *verb trans and intrans Aus* in former times, to drive (livestock) overland for long distances. ➤➤ **overlander** *noun*.

overlap /ohvə'lap/ *verb* (**overlapped, overlapping**) ➤ *verb trans* to extend over and cover a part of (something). ➤ *verb intrans* **1** said of two or more things: to overlap each other. **2** to coincide partly; to have something in common. ➤➤ **overlap** /'oh-/ *noun*.

overlay[1] /ohvə'lay/ *verb trans* (*past tense and past part.* **overlaid** /-'layd/) **1** to lay or spread (something) over a surface; to superimpose (it). **2** (+ with) to cover or decorate (a surface) with something laid or spread over it: *The primer is overlaid with a thin layer of oil paint.*

overlay[2] /'ohvəlay/ *noun* **1** something laid or spread over something else; a covering. **2a** a transparent sheet of drawings, designs, etc to be superimposed on another sheet, e.g. to add detail. **b** a decorative veneer.

overlay[3] /'ohvəlay/ *verb* past tense of OVERLIE.

overleaf /ohvə'leef/ *adv* on the other side of the page.

overlie /ohvə'lie/ *verb trans* (*past tense* **overlay** /-'lay/, *past part.* **overlain** /-'layn/) to lie or be situated on top of (something).

overload /ohvə'lohd/ *verb trans* to load (something) to excess. ➤➤ **overload** /'oh-/ *noun*.

overlocking /'ohvəloking/ *noun* the act or process of oversewing a raw edge of fabric using a small machine stitch to prevent unravelling. ➤➤ **overlocker** *noun*.

overlong /ohvə'long/ *adj and adv* too long.

overlook[1] /ohvə'look/ *verb trans* **1a** to fail to notice (something); to miss (it): *It's better to be looked over than overlooked* — Mae West. **b** to ignore (something). **c** to excuse (something). **2** to have or provide a view of (something) from above: *a room overlooking the garden.* **3** *archaic* to supervise (something). **4** *archaic* to look on (somebody) with the evil eye.

overlook[2] /'ohvəlook/ *noun NAmer* a high place commanding a good view.

overlord /'ohvəlawd/ *noun* **1** a lord who is superior to other lords. **2** an absolute or supreme ruler. ➤➤ **overlordship** *noun*.

overly *adv* to an excessive degree. [Middle English, from OVER[1] + -LY[1]]

overman[1] /ohvə'man/ *verb trans* (**overmanned, overmanning**) to provide (something) with too many workers: *The ship is overmanned.*

overman[2] /'ohvəmən, -man/ *noun* (*pl* **overmen**) **1** a foreman or overseer. **2** = SUPERMAN.

overmantel /'ohvəmantl/ *noun* an ornamental often shelved structure above a mantelpiece.

overmaster /ohvə'mahstə/ *verb trans* (**overmastered, overmastering**) to overpower (somebody), to subdue (them).

overmatch /ohvə'mach/ *verb trans chiefly NAmer* **1** to be stronger, more skilful, etc than (an opponent); to defeat (them). **2** to match (somebody) with a superior opponent: *a badly overmatched boxer.*

overmighty /ohvə'mieti/ *adj* exercising or claiming undue power.

overmuch /ohvə'much/ *adj and adv and noun* too much.

overnice /ohvə'nies/ *adj* too fastidious or fussy: *As a young cannibal, he was not overnice in the matter of diet* — Edgar Rice Burroughs.

overnight[1] /ohvə'niet/ *adv* **1** during or throughout the night: *travel overnight.* **2** for a single night: *stay overnight.* **3** suddenly.

overnight[2] /'ohvəniet/ *adj* **1** done, occurring, operating, or used during the night. **2** lasting throughout the night or for a single night. **3** sudden: *an overnight success.*

overpaid /ohvə'payd/ *verb* past tense and past part. of OVERPAY.

overpass[1] /'ohvəpahs/ *noun* = FLYOVER (1).

overpass[2] /ohvə'pahs/ *verb trans* **1** to pass over or through (something). **2** to exceed or surpass (something).

overpay /ohvə'pay/ *verb trans* (*past tense and past part.* **overpaid** /-'payd/) to pay (somebody) too much.

overpitch /ohvə'pich/ *verb* to bowl (a ball) in cricket so that it bounces nearer the batsman's or batswoman's wicket than intended and can be easily hit.

overplay /ohvə'play/ *verb trans* **1** to exaggerate (e.g. a dramatic role). **2** to give too much emphasis to (something). ✳ **overplay one's hand** to overestimate one's capacities.

overplus /'ohvəplus/ *noun* a surplus. [Middle English, partial translation of early French *surplus:* see SURPLUS]

overpopulation /,ohvəpopyoo'laysh(ə)n/ *noun* the condition of having a population so dense as to cause environmental deterioration or impaired quality of life. ➤➤ **overpopulated** /ohvə'pop-/ *adj*.

overpower /ohvə'powə/ *verb trans* (**overpowered, overpowering**) **1** to defeat or overcome (somebody or something) by superior force. **2** to be so strong or intense as to overwhelm (somebody or something): *The flavour of the cheese overpowers the other ingredients.* ➤➤ **overpowering** *adj*, **overpoweringly** *adv*.

overprice /ohvə'pries/ *verb trans* to price (something) too high.

overprint[1] /ohvə'print/ *verb trans* to print over (something) with something additional.

overprint[2] /'ohvəprint/ *noun* **1** something added by or as if by overprinting. **2** a printed marking added to a postage stamp to alter the original or to commemorate a special event.

overproduce /,ohvəprə'dyoohs/ *verb trans and intrans* to produce an excess of (something). ➤➤ **overproduction** /-'duksh(ə)n/ *noun*.

overproof /ohvə'proohf/ *adj* containing more alcohol than proof spirit does.

overprotect /,ohvəprə'tekt/ *verb trans* to protect (e.g. a child) excessively or unduly. ➤➤ **overprotection** /-sh(ə)n/ *noun*, **overprotective** *adj*.

overqualified /ohvə'kwolified/ *adj* having more education, training, or experience than a job calls for.

overran /ohvə'ran/ *verb* past tense of OVERRUN.

overrate /ohvə'rayt/ *verb trans* to rate (something or somebody) too highly.

overreach /ohvə'reech/ *verb trans* **1** to defeat (oneself) by trying to do or gain too much. **2** to reach above or beyond (something). **3** to get the better of (somebody), typically by unscrupulous or crafty methods. ➤ *verb intrans* said of a horse: to strike the hind foot against the forefoot.

overreact /,ohvəri'akt/ *verb intrans* to show an excessive or exaggerated reaction. ➤➤ **overreaction** /-sh(ə)n/ *noun*.

override[1] /ohvə'ried/ *verb trans* (*past tense* **overrode** /-'rohd/, *past part.* **overridden** /-'rid(ə)n/) **1** to prevail over (something); to dominate (it): *Fear overrode all other emotions.* **2a** to set (e.g. a decision) aside by superior authority; to annul (it). **b** to take manual control of (e.g. an automatic control). **3** to overlap (something).

override[2] /'ohvəried/ *noun* a device or system used to override a control.

overrider /'ohvəriedə/ *noun Brit* a vertical attachment to a motor vehicle bumper to prevent it from interlocking with another in a collision.

overriding /'ohvərieding/ *adj* more important than any other: *overriding considerations.*

overripe /ohvə'riep/ *adj* having passed beyond maturity or ripeness towards decay.

overrode /ohvə'rohd/ *verb* past tense of OVERRIDE[1].

overrule /ohvə'roohl/ *verb trans* **1** to reject or disallow (a decision, judgment, objection, etc) by superior authority. **2** to overrule the decision, argument, objection, etc of (somebody).

overrun /ohvə'run/ *verb* (**overrunning**, *past tense* **overran** /-'ran/, *past part.* **overrun**) ➤ *verb trans* **1a** to swarm or spread over (a place); to infest (it). **b** to invade and occupy (a place) in large numbers. **2a** to run or go beyond or past (something): *The plane overran the runway.* **b** to exceed (something, e.g. an allowed cost or time). ➤ *verb intrans* to exceed a desired or expected limit in time or space: *The lecture overran by five minutes.* ➤➤ **overrun** /'oh-/ *noun*.

oversaw /ohvə'saw/ *verb* past tense of OVERSEE.

oversea /ohvə'see/ *adj* = OVERSEAS[2] (2).

overseas[1] /ohvə'seez/ *adv* beyond or across the sea; abroad: *travel overseas.*

overseas[2] *adj* **1** of, from, to, or in places across the sea; foreign: *overseas markets*; *overseas students here in London.* **2** relating to transport across the sea.

overseas[3] *noun* a place or places across the sea; a foreign country or foreign countries.

oversee /ohvə'see/ *verb trans* (*past tense* **oversaw** /-'saw/, *past part.* **overseen** /-'seen/) to watch and direct (a task, operation, etc). ➤➤ **overseer** /'ohvəsiə/ *noun*.

oversell /ohvə'sel/ *verb trans* (*past tense and past part.* **oversold** /-'sohld/) **1** to sell more of (something) than is available. **2** to make excessive claims for (something or somebody); to praise (them) too highly.

oversensitive /ohvə'sensətiv/ *adj* unduly or extremely sensitive. ➤➤ **oversensitiveness** *noun*.

overset /ohvə'set/ *verb trans* (**oversetting**, *past tense and past part.* **overset**) **1** to tip (something) over; to overturn (it). **2** to disturb or upset somebody).

oversew /'ohvəsoh/ *verb trans* (*past part.* **oversewn** /-sohn/, *or* **oversewed**) to sew over (an edge or two edges placed together), *esp* with small closely worked stitches, to make a neat or firm seam.

oversexed /ohvə'sekst/ *adj* having an abnormally strong sexual drive: *overpaid, overfed, oversexed, and over here* — Tommy Trinder.

overshadow /ohvə'shadoh/ *verb trans* **1** to cast a shadow over (something). **2** to exceed (something) in importance; to outweigh (it).

overshoe /'ohvəshooh/ *noun* a shoe worn over another as protection, e.g. from rain or snow.

overshoot /ohvə'shooht/ *verb trans* (*past tense and past part.* **overshot** /-'shot/) **1** to shoot or pass over or beyond (e.g. a target) and miss it. **2** said of an aircraft: to fly or taxi beyond the end of a runway. ➤➤ **overshoot** /'oh-/ *noun*.

overshot /'ohvəshot/ *adj* **1** having or being an upper jaw that projects beyond the lower jaw. **2** said of a waterwheel: operated by the weight of water passing over and flowing from above.

oversight /'ohvəsiet/ *noun* **1** an inadvertent omission or error. **2** supervision.

oversimplify /ohvə'simplifie/ *verb trans* (**oversimplifies, oversimplified, oversimplifying**) to simplify (something) to such an extent as to cause distortion, misunderstanding, or error. ➤➤ **oversimplification** /-fi'kaysh(ə)n/ *noun*.

oversize /ohvə'siez, 'ohvəsiez/ *adj* of above average or normal size.

oversized /ohvə'siezd, 'ohvəsiezd/ *adj* = OVERSIZE.

overskirt /'ohvəskuht/ *noun* a skirt worn over another skirt or over a dress.

oversleep /ohvə'sleep/ *verb intrans* (*past tense and past part.* **overslept** /-'slept/) to sleep beyond the intended time for waking.

oversold /ohvə'sohld/ *verb* past tense and past part. of OVERSELL.

overspend[1] /ohvə'spend/ *verb* (*past tense and past part.* **overspent** /-'spent/) ➤ *verb trans* **1** to spend more than (an allotted amount). **2** to spend or use (something) to excess. ➤ *verb intrans* to spend beyond one's means.

overspend[2] /'ohvəspend/ *noun* an amount spent that exceeds the available budget.

overspent /ohvə'spent/ *verb* past tense and past part. of OVERSPEND[1].

overspill /'ohvəspil/ *noun* **1** something that spills over; an excess. **2** *chiefly Brit* the movement of excess urban population into less crowded areas, e.g. new towns, or the excess population itself.

overspread /ohvə'spred/ *verb trans* (*past tense and past part.* **overspread**) to spread over or above (something).

overstate /ohvə'stayt/ *verb trans* to state (something) in too strong terms; to exaggerate (it). ➤➤ **overstatement** *noun*.

overstay /ohvə'stay/ *verb trans* to stay beyond the time or limits of (something): *She overstayed her welcome.*

oversteer /ohvə'stiə/ *verb intrans* said of a motor vehicle: to steer into a sharper turn than the driver intends. ➤➤ **oversteer** /'ohvəstiə/ *noun*.

overstep /ohvə'step/ *verb trans* (**overstepped, overstepping**) to exceed or transgress (something): *overstepping the bounds of good taste.* ✳ **overstep the mark** to go beyond what is acceptable.

overstrung /ohvə'strung/ *adj* **1** too highly strung; too sensitive. **2** said of a piano: having strings in sets that cross each other at an oblique angle.

overstuff /ohvə'stuf/ *verb trans* to cover (e.g. a chair) completely and thickly with upholstery.

oversubscribe /,ohvəsəb'skrieb/ *verb trans* to subscribe or apply for more of (something) than is available or offered for sale. ➤➤ **oversubscription** /-'skripsh(ə)n/ *noun*.

overt /'ohvuht, oh'vuht/ *adj* open to view; not concealed. ➤➤ **overtly** *adv*. [Middle English from early French *ouvert*, *overt*, past part. of *ouvrir* to open, ultimately from Latin *aperire*]

overtake /ohvə'tayk/ *verb* (*past tense* **overtook** /-'took/, *past part.* **overtaken** /-'tayk(ə)n/) ➤ *verb trans* **1** to catch up with and move past (somebody or something). **2** to catch up with and do better than (somebody). **3** to come upon (somebody) suddenly: *Misfortune overtook them.* ➤ *verb intrans* *chiefly Brit* to catch up with and pass another vehicle going in the same direction. [Middle English *overtaken*, from OVER[1] + *taken* to take]

overtax /ohvə'taks/ *verb trans* **1** to tax (somebody) too heavily. **2** to put too great a burden or strain on (somebody).

over-the-counter *adj* **1** said of a drug or medicine: able to be sold lawfully without prescription. **2** not traded on an organized securities exchange, e.g. the stock market: *over-the-counter transactions.*

overthrow[1] /ohvə'throh/ *verb trans* (*past tense* **overthrew** /-'throoh/, *past part.* **overthrown** /-'throhn/) **1** to cause the downfall of (somebody or something); to remove (them) from power. **2** to overturn or upset (something). **3** to throw (a ball) further than intended.

overthrow[2] /'ohvəthroh/ *noun* **1** the act or an instance of overthrowing. **2a** in cricket, a return of the ball from a fielder that passes beyond the fielders near the wickets. **b** a further run scored from this.

overthrust /'ohvəthrust/ *noun* in geology, a fault in which one mass of rock is forced over another.

overtime /'ohvətiem/ *noun* **1** time in excess of a set limit, *esp* working time in excess of a standard working day or week. **2** the wage paid for overtime. **3** *NAmer* = EXTRA TIME. ➤➤ **overtime** *adv*.

overtone /'ohvətohn/ *noun* **1a** in music, any of the higher tones produced simultaneously with the FUNDAMENTAL[2] (principal or lowest note). **b** = HARMONIC[2] (1). **2** (*also in pl*) a secondary effect, quality, or meaning; a suggestion.

overtook /ohvə'took/ *verb* past tense of OVERTAKE.

overtop /ohvə'top/ *verb trans* (**overtopped, overtopping**) **1** to rise above the top of (something). **2** to surpass (somebody or something).

overtrain /ohvə'trayn/ *verb trans* to train (e.g. an athlete) more than is desirable for maximum efficiency. ➤ *verb intrans* to engage in excessive training.

overtrick /'ohvətrik/ *noun* in contract bridge, a card trick won in excess of the number bid: compare UNDERTRICK.

overtrousers /'ohvətrowzəz/ *pl noun* waterproof or protective trousers worn over other trousers.

overtrump /ohvə'trump/ *verb trans and intrans* to trump (a player or card) with a higher trump card than the highest previously played on the same trick.

overture /'ohvətyooə, -chə/ *noun* **1a** the orchestral introduction to a musical dramatic work. **b** an orchestral concert piece written *esp* as a single movement. **2** (*also in pl*). **a** an initiative towards an agreement, negotiation, or relationship. **b** something introductory; a prelude. [Middle English *overture* opening, from early French, ultimately from Latin *apertura*: see APERTURE]

overturn /ohvə'tuhn/ *verb trans* **1** to cause (something) to turn over; to upset or invert (it). **2** to overthrow or destroy (something). **3** to cancel or reverse (e.g. a decision). ➤ *verb intrans* to turn over. ➤➤ overturn /'oh-/ *noun*.

overuse[1] /ohvə'joohs/ *noun* excessive use.

overuse[2] /ohvə'jooz/ *verb trans* to use (something) excessively.

overview /'ohvəvyooh/ *noun* a usu brief general survey.

overweening /ohvə'weening/ *adj* **1** arrogant or presumptuous. **2** immoderate or exaggerated. [Middle English *overwening*, present part. of *overwenen* to be arrogant, from OVER[1] + *wenen* to imagine, from Old English *wēnan*]

overweight[1] /ohvə'wayt/ *adj* exceeding the expected, normal, or proper weight.

overweight[2] /'ohvəwayt/ *noun* weight above what is normal, average, or required.

overweight[3] /ohvə'wayt/ *verb trans* **1** to give too much weight or consideration to (something). **2** to weight (something) excessively; to overload (it).

overwhelm /ohvə'welm/ *verb trans* **1** to defeat or overcome (e.g. an army) by superior force or numbers. **2** to affect (somebody) with intense emotion: *I was overwhelmed by their generosity.* **3** to cover (something) over completely; to submerge (it). ➤➤ **overwhelming** *adj*, **overwhelmingly** *adv*. [Middle English *overwhelmen*, from OVER[1] + *whelmen* to turn over, cover up]

overwind /ohvə'wiend/ *verb trans* (*past tense and past part.* **overwound** /-'wownd/) to wind (e.g. a watch) too much.

overwinter /ohvə'wintə/ *verb intrans* (**overwintered, overwintering**) to survive or spend the winter.

overwork /ohvə'wuhk/ *verb trans* **1** to cause (somebody) to work too hard or too long. **2** to make excessive use of (something). ➤ *verb intrans* to work too hard or too long. ➤➤ **overwork** *noun*.

overwound /ohvə'wownd/ *verb* past tense and past part. of OVERWIND.

overwrite /ohvə'riet/ *verb* (*past tense* **overwrote** /-'roht/, *past part.* **overwritten** /-'ritn/) ➤ *verb trans* **1** to write (something) in an inflated or pretentious style. **2a** to write on top of (existing writing). **b** to destroy (existing data) in a computer file by replacing it with new data. ➤ *verb intrans* to write too much or pretentiously.

overwrought /ohvə'rawt/ *adj* **1** extremely excited or agitated. **2** too elaborate in construction or design. [archaic past part. of OVERWORK]

ovi- *comb. form* see OV-.

oviduct /'ohvidukt/ *noun* the tube through which eggs pass from an ovary. ➤➤ **oviductal** /-'duktl/ *adj*. [scientific Latin *oviductus*, from OVI- + *ductus*: see DUCT[1]]

oviform /'ohvifawm/ *adj* egg-shaped.

ovine /'ohvien/ *adj* of or resembling sheep. [late Latin *ovinus*, from Latin *ovis* sheep]

oviparous /oh'vipərəs/ *adj* involving or producing eggs that hatch outside the mother's body: compare VIVIPAROUS. ➤➤ **oviparity** /-'pariti/ *noun*, **oviparously** *adv*. [Latin *oviparus*, from OVI- + *-parus* -PAROUS]

oviposit /ohvi'pozit/ *verb intrans* (**oviposited, ovipositing**) said *esp* of an insect: to lay eggs. ➤➤ **oviposition** /-'zish(ə)n/ *noun*. [prob back-formation from OVIPOSITOR]

ovipositor *noun* a specialized organ, *esp* of an insect, for laying eggs. [scientific Latin *ovipositor*, from OVI- + Latin *positor* somebody or something that places, from *ponere* to place]

ovo- *comb. form* see OV-.

ovoid /'ohvoyd/ *adj* shaped like an egg. ➤➤ **ovoid** *noun*. [French *ovoïde* from Latin *ovum* egg]

ovoidal /oh'voydl/ *adj* = OVOID.

ovolo /'ohvəloh/ *noun* (*pl* **ovolos**) in architecture, a rounded convex moulding. [Italian *ovolo*, dimin. of *uovo, ovo* egg, from Latin *ovum*]

ovotestis /ohvoh'testis/ *noun* (*pl* **ovotestes** /-teez/) a GONAD (organ producing sex cells), e.g. in some snails, that produces both eggs and sperm.

ovoviviparous /,ohvohvi'vipərəs/ *adj* producing eggs that develop and hatch within the mother's body. ➤➤ **ovoviviparity** /-'pariti/ *noun*. [OVO- + Latin *viviparus*: see VIVIPAROUS]

ovulate /'ovyoolayt/ *verb intrans* to produce eggs or discharge them from an ovary. ➤➤ **ovulation** /-'laysh(ə)n/ *noun*, **ovulatory** /-lət(ə)ri/ *adj*.

ovule /'ovyoohl, 'oh-/ *noun* **1** a reproductive structure within the ovary of a seed plant that develops into a seed after fertilization of the egg cell it contains. **2** a small egg, *esp* one in an early stage of growth. ➤➤ **ovular** /'ovyoolə/ *adj*. [scientific Latin *ovulum*, dimin. of Latin *ovum* egg]

ovum /'ohvəm/ *noun* (*pl* **ova** /'ohvə/) a female GAMETE (reproductive cell) in animals that when fertilized can develop into a new individual. [Latin *ovum* egg]

ow /ow/ *interj* used to express sudden mild pain. [Middle English]

owe /oh/ *verb trans* **1a** to be under obligation to pay (money) to somebody. **b** to be under obligation to give or show (something) to somebody: *I owe you an explanation.* **c** to be indebted to (somebody): *She still owes me for the tickets.* **2** (*usu* + to) to have or enjoy (something) as a result of the action or existence of something or somebody else: *He owes his success to luck.* ➤ *verb intrans* to be in debt. [Old English *āgan*]

owing /'oh·ing/ *adj* unpaid; due. ✳ **owing to** because of: *The train was delayed owing to a signal failure.*

Usage note

owing to or due to? See note at DUE[1].

owl /owl/ *noun* any of an order of chiefly nocturnal birds of prey with a large head, a short neck, large eyes, and a short hooked bill: order Strigiformes. [Old English *ūle*]

owlet /'owlit/ *noun* a small or young owl.

owlish *adj* **1** having a round face or a wide-eyed stare. **2** solemn or wise. ➤➤ **owlishly** *adv*.

own[1] /ohn/ *adj* used after a possessive: belonging to, relating to, or done by oneself or itself: *He cooked his own dinner.* [Old English *āgen*]

own[2] *verb trans* **1** to have or hold (something) as property; to possess (it). **2** to acknowledge or admit (something). ➤ *verb intrans* (+ to) to acknowledge something to be true or valid. ➤➤ **owner** *noun*, **ownership** *noun*.

own[3] *pronoun* used after a possessive: one or ones belonging to oneself or itself: *a country with oil of its own.* ✳ **on one's own 1** in solitude; alone: *She lives on her own.* **2** without assistance or control.

own-brand *adj* of or being goods offered for sale under the label or trade name of the retail distributor, e.g. a chain store.

owner-occupier *noun* somebody who owns the house they live in.

own goal *noun* **1** a goal, *esp* in football, accidentally scored by a player against his or her own team. **2** an action that brings unfortunate results to the person who took it: *To burgle the police car was a classic own goal* — Daily Telegraph.

own up *verb intrans* to confess a fault or wrongdoing frankly.

owt /owt/ *pronoun* N Eng anything. [variant of AUGHT]

ox /oks/ *noun* (*pl* **oxen** /'oks(ə)n/ *or collectively* **ox**) **1** a domestic species of bovine mammal: *Bos taurus*. **2** an adult castrated male ox. [Old English *oxa*]

ox- *or* **oxo-** *comb. form* forming words, with the meaning: containing a carbonyl group in the molecular structure; ketone: *oxoacetic acid*. [French, from *oxygène*: see OXYGEN]

oxalate /'oksəlayt/ *noun* a salt or ester of oxalic acid.

oxalic acid /ok'salik/ *noun* a poisonous strong acid that occurs in various plants and is used *esp* as a bleach: formula $C_2H_2O_4$. [translation of French (*acide*) *oxalique*, from Latin *oxalis* OXALIS]

oxalis *noun* any of a genus of plants, e.g. the wood sorrel, with leaves that contain oxalic acid and usu white, pink, or yellow flowers: genus *Oxalis*. [from the Latin genus name, from Greek *oxys* acid, sharp]

oxbow /'oksboh/ *noun* **1** a U-shaped collar round a draught ox's neck for supporting the yoke. **2a** a U-shaped river bend. **b** a curved lake formed from such a bend in a meandering river.

oxbow lake *noun* = OXBOW (2B).

Oxbridge /'oksbrij/ *noun* the universities of Oxford and Cambridge: *Rough and ready, your chum seems … Somewhat different* *from your dandy friends at Oxbridge* — Thackeray. [blend of *Oxford* + *Cambridge*]

oxen /'oks(ə)n/ *noun* pl of OX.

oxer /'oksə/ *noun* an obstacle for horses to jump consisting of a hedge, rails, and sometimes a ditch. [orig in the sense 'hedge or fence to restrain cattle'; from OX + -ER²]

oxeye daisy *noun* a leafy-stemmed European plant with long white ray flowers: *Chrysanthemum leucanthemum.*

Oxford /'oksfəd/ *noun* a low shoe laced or tied over the instep. [named after *Oxford*, city in England]

Oxford bags *pl noun* wide-legged trousers.

Oxford blue *noun* a dark blue colour. [adopted as the colour of Oxford University]

Oxford movement *noun* a High Church movement within the Church of England that began at Oxford in 1833.

oxidant /'oksid(ə)nt/ *noun* = OXIDIZING AGENT.

oxidation /oksi'daysh(ə)n/ *noun* **1** the act or process of oxidizing. **2** the state or result of being oxidized. ⟫⟫ **oxidational** *adj,* **oxidative** /-tiv/ *adj.* [French *oxidation*, from *oxider, oxyder* to oxidize]

oxidation number *noun* the degree of or potential for oxidation of a chemical element or an atom, which is usu expressed as a positive or negative number representing the ionic or effective electric charge; valency.

oxidation state *noun* = OXIDATION NUMBER.

oxide /'oksied/ *noun* a compound of oxygen with a chemical element or group. ⟫⟫ **oxidic** /ok'sidik/ *adj.* [French *oxide, oxyde*, from OX- + *-ide* from *acide*: see ACID¹]

oxidize *or* **oxidise** /'oksidiez/ *verb trans* **1** to combine (a substance) with oxygen. **2** to remove hydrogen atoms from (something). **3** to cause (e.g. an atom, ion, or molecule) to lose one or more electrons. ▸ *verb intrans* **1** to combine with oxygen. **2** to undergo a loss of hydrogen atoms or electrons. ⟫⟫ **oxidizable** *adj,* **oxidizer** *noun.* [OXIDE + -IZE]

oxidizing agent *noun* a substance that oxidizes something, *esp* chemically, e.g. by gaining electrons: compare REDUCING AGENT.

oxlip *noun* a Eurasian primula similar to the cowslip but unscented and having larger flowers: *Primula elatior.* [Old English *oxanslyppe,* literally 'ox dung', from *oxa* OX + *slypa, slyppe* paste]

oxo- *comb. form* see OX-.

Oxon. *abbr* **1** Oxfordshire. **2** used chiefly with academic awards: of Oxford: *MA (Oxon.).* [(sense 1) medieval Latin *Oxonia*; (sense 2) medieval Latin *Oxoniensis*]

Oxonian /ok'sohni-ən/ *noun* **1** a native or inhabitant of Oxford. **2** a student or graduate of Oxford University. ⟫⟫ **Oxonian** *adj.* [medieval Latin *Oxonia* Oxford]

oxpecker *noun* either of two species of African birds that perch on large animals and feed on ticks; = TICKBIRD: genus *Buphagus.*

oxtail *noun* the tail of an ox, used *esp* in making soup.

oxter /'okstə/ *noun chiefly Scot, Irish, N Eng* the armpit or the crook of the arm: *a babie in her oxter* — Allan Ramsay. [Old English *ōxta*]

oxtongue *noun* **1** a plant with rough tongue-shaped leaves: genus *Picris.* **2** the tongue of an ox used as meat.

oxy-¹ *comb. form* forming words, denoting: sharpness: *oxytocin.* [Greek *oxys* sharp]

oxy-² *comb. form* forming words, with the meaning: containing or using oxygen: *oxyacetylene; oxyhaemoglobin.* [French *oxy-*, from *oxygène*: see OXYGEN]

oxyacetylene /,oksi-ə'set(ə)lin, -leen/ *adj* of or using a mixture of oxygen and acetylene, *esp* for producing a hot flame: *an oxyacetylene torch.*

oxyacid /'oksiasid/ *noun* an acid that contains oxygen.

oxygen /'oksij(ə)n/ *noun* a colourless odourless gaseous chemical element that forms about 21% by volume of the atmosphere, is found combined in water, most minerals, and many organic compounds, and is essential for the life of most organisms: symbol O, atomic number 8. ⟫⟫ **oxygenic** /-'jenik/ *adj.* [French *oxygène*, from Greek *oxys* acid, sharp + French *-gène* -GEN]

oxygenate /'oksijənayt/ *verb trans* to impregnate, combine, or supply (e.g. blood) with oxygen. ⟫⟫ **oxygenation** /-'naysh(ə)n/ *noun,* **oxygenator** *noun.*

oxygen mask *noun* a device worn over the nose and mouth through which oxygen is supplied from a storage tank.

oxygen tent *noun* a canopy placed over somebody in bed within which a flow of oxygen-enriched air can be maintained.

oxyhaemoglobin /,oksiheemə'glohbin/ *noun* HAEMOGLOBIN (red blood pigment) loosely combined with oxygen that it releases to the tissues.

oxymoron /oksi'mawron/ *noun* (*pl* **oxymora** /-rə/) a combination of contradictory or incongruous words, e.g. *cruel kindness.* [late Greek *oxymōron*, neuter of *oxymōros* pointedly foolish, from Greek *oxys* sharp, keen + *mōros* foolish]

oxytetracycline /,oksitetrə'sieklien/ *noun* an antibiotic obtained from a bacterium (*Streptomyces rimosus*) and used in the treatment of a large number of infections including whooping cough and pneumonia.

oxytocin /oksi'tohsin/ *noun* a hormone secreted by the back lobe of the pituitary gland that stimulates contractions of the muscular wall of the womb, *esp* during childbirth, and assists the release of milk. ⟫⟫ **oxytocic** /-sik/ *adj.* [Greek *oxytokia* sudden delivery, from OXY-¹ + *tokos* childbirth, from *tiktein* to bear, beget]

oyer and terminer /,oyər and 'tuhminə/ *noun* in former times, a commission authorizing a British judge to hear and decide a criminal case before a court of assize. [Anglo-French *oyer et terminer*, literally 'to hear and determine']

oyez /oh'yay, oh'yes/ *interj* uttered by a court official or public crier to gain attention. [Middle English from Anglo-French *oyez* hear ye, imperative pl of *oir* to hear, from Latin *audire*]

oyster /'oystə/ *noun* **1** any of several species of edible marine invertebrate animals that have a rough irregular hinged shell and are found in coastal waters or estuaries: family Ostreidae. **2** a pinkish white colour, sometimes with a greyish tone. **3** a small mass of meat contained in a hollow of the pelvic bone on each side of the back of a fowl. [Middle English *oistre* via French and Latin from Greek *ostreon*]

oyster bed *noun* a place where oysters grow or are cultivated.

oystercatcher *noun* any of several species of wading birds that have stout legs, black or black and white plumage, and a heavy wedge-shaped orange beak adapted for opening shellfish: genus *Haematopus.*

oyster mushroom *noun* an edible mushroom with a soft grey cap that is shaped like an oyster: *Pleurotus ostreatus.*

oyster plant *noun* **1** = SALSIFY (1). **2** a N European creeping plant of the forget-me-not family that has blue flowers and grows in coastal areas: *Mertensia maritima.*

Oz /oz/ *noun informal* Australia. [by shortening and alteration]

oz. *abbr* ounce. [Italian *onza*]

Ozalid /'ozəlid/ *noun trademark* **1** a machine or process for producing positive prints of typeset material. **2** a print produced by this machine or process.

ozocerite /ohzoh'siəriet/ *or* **ozokerite** /-'kiəriet/ *noun* a waxy substance often found with petroleum that is white when pure, often smells unpleasant, and is used in making candles, electrical insulation, etc. [German *Ozokerit*, from Greek *ozein* to smell + *kēros* wax]

ozone /'ohzohn/ *noun* **1** a form of oxygen with three atoms in each molecule that is a bluish gas with a pungent smell and is formed naturally in the upper atmosphere by the action of ultraviolet solar radiation on oxygen, and can be generated commercially for use as a sterilizing, purifying, bleaching, or oxidizing agent: formula O_3. **2** *informal* pure and refreshing air. ⟫⟫ **ozonic** /oh'zohnik, oh'zonik/ *adj,* **ozonous** /-nəs/ *adj.* [German *Ozon* from Greek *ozōn,* present part. of *ozein* to smell]

ozone-friendly *adj* not harmful to or damaging the ozone layer; *specif* not using or containing chlorofluorocarbons.

ozone layer *noun* an atmospheric layer at heights of approximately 30–50km (20–30mi) that has a high ozone content and protects the earth by absorbing ultraviolet radiation from the sun.

ozonize *or* **ozonise** *verb trans* **1** to convert (oxygen) into ozone. **2** to treat, impregnate, or combine (a substance) with ozone. ⟫⟫ **ozonization** /-'zaysh(ə)n/ *noun,* **ozonizer** *noun.*

ozonosphere /oh'zohnəsfiə, oh'zon-/ *noun* = OZONE LAYER.

P¹ *or* **p** *noun* (*pl* **P's** *or* **Ps** *or* **p's**) **1a** the 16th letter of the English alphabet. **b** a written character or design denoting this letter. **c** the sound represented by this letter, one of the English consonants. **2** an item designated as P, *esp* the 16th in a series.

P² *abbr* **1** parking. **2** in chess, pawn. **3** in physics, poise. **4** Portugal (international vehicle registration). **5** proprietary.

P³ *abbr* the chemical symbol for phosphorus.

p *abbr* **1** page. **2** participle. **3** past. **4** pence. **5** penny. **6** per. **7** in music, piano. **8** pico-. **9** pint. **10** power. **11** pressure.

PA *abbr* **1** Panama (international vehicle registration). **2** Pennsylvania (US postal abbreviation). **3** personal assistant. **4** Press Association. **5** public address. **6** purchasing agent.

Pa¹ *abbr* pascal.

Pa² *abbr* the chemical symbol for protactinium.

pa /pah/ *noun informal* an affectionate name for one's father. [short for PAPA]

p.a. *abbr* per annum.

paan *or* **pan** /pahn/ *noun* a betel leaf filled with spices and chewed as a stimulant, *esp* by Indians. [Hindi *pān* from Sanskrit *parṇa* wing, leaf]

pa'anga /pah'ang(g)ə/ *noun* (*pl* **pa'anga**) the basic monetary unit of Tonga, divided into 100 seniti. [Tongan *pa'anga* seed]

pabulum /'pabyooləm/ *noun* bland or unsatisfying intellectual matter or entertainment. [Latin *pabulum* food, fodder, from *pascere* to feed]

PABX *abbr Brit* private automatic branch exchange.

paca /'pakə, 'pahkə/ *noun* either of two species of large S and Central American burrowing rodents; *esp* a common edible rodent of S America that has a brown coat spotted with white and a hide used for leather: genus *Agouti*. [Portuguese and Spanish *paca* from Tupi *páca*]

PACE /pays/ *abbr Brit* Police and Criminal Evidence Act.

pace¹ /pays/ *noun* **1a** a step in walking. **b** the distance covered by a single step, usu taken to be about 0.75m (about 30in.). **c** a manner of walking; a tread. **2a** a gait of a horse, *esp* a gait in which a horse has been trained to move. **b** a fast two-beat gait in which the horse moves its two left legs and its two right legs in unison alternately. **3** rate of movement: *She started off up the hill at a tremendous pace*. **4** rate or speed of doing something: *The pace of change quickened as the century neared its end*. ✳ **keep pace with** to move, change, or progress at the same speed as somebody or something. **off the pace** behind the leader or leaders in a race or contest. **put somebody through their paces** to test somebody by making them demonstrate their abilities. **set the pace** to control the speed at which a race is run or an activity progresses. **stand/stay the pace** to be able to maintain the same speed as others. [Middle English

pas via Old French from Latin *passus*, literally 'stretch of the leg', from *pandere* to stretch, spread]

pace² *verb intrans* **1** to walk with a slow or measured tread. **2** said *esp* of a horse: to go at a pace. ➤ *verb trans* **1a** (*often* + out/off) to measure (a distance) by pacing. **b** to traverse (e.g. a room) at a walk. **2** said of a horse: to cover (a course) by pacing. **3** to set or regulate the pace of (e.g. a race); *specif* to go ahead of (e.g. a runner) as a pacemaker. **4** to keep pace with (somebody).

pace³ /'paysi/ *prep* used when contradicting or disagreeing with somebody: with due respect to: *This, pace the bishop, is not a religious issue*. [Latin *pace*, ablative of *pac-, pax* peace, permission]

pace bowler /pays/ *noun* in cricket, somebody who bowls the ball fast and without spin.

pace car /pays/ *noun* in motor racing, a car that leads the field of competitors through a warm-up lap but does not participate in the race.

pacemaker /'paysmaykə/ *noun* **1a** somebody or something that sets the pace, e.g. in a race. **b** somebody who takes the lead or sets an example. **2a** an electronic device implanted in the body that applies regular electric shocks to stimulate or steady the heartbeat. **b** the area of tissue in the heart or other body part that serves to establish and maintain a rhythmic activity. ➤➤ **pacemaking** *noun*.

pacer /'paysə/ *noun* **1** somebody who or something which paces; *specif* a horse whose gait is the pace. **2** = PACEMAKER (1).

pacesetter /'pays·setə/ *noun* = PACEMAKER (1). ➤➤ **pacesetting** *noun and adj*.

pacey /'paysi/ *adj* see PACY.

pacha /'pahshə, 'pashə/ *noun* see PASHA.

pachycephalosaur /paki'sef(ə)ləsaw/ *noun* a plant-eating dinosaur of the late Cretaceous period that had a thick dome-shaped skull and walked on two feet. [Greek *pachys* thick + CEPHAL- + *sauros* lizard]

pachyderm /'pakiduhm/ *noun* an elephant, rhinoceros, pig, or other usu thick-skinned hoofed nonruminant mammal. ➤➤ **pachydermal** /-'duhml/ *adj*, **pachydermatous** /-'duhmətəs/ *adj*. [French *pachyderme* from Greek *pachydermos* thick-skinned, from *pachys* thick + *derma* skin]

pachytene /'pakiteen/ *noun* in genetics, the stage of meiosis in which the paired chromosomes shorten and thicken and split longitudinally into two chromatids. [Greek *pachys* thick + *-tene*, from Latin *taenia*, ribbon, band]

Pacific /pə'sifik/ *noun* (**the Pacific**) the Pacific Ocean: *like stout Cortez when with eagle eyes he stared at the Pacific* — Keats. [*Pacific Ocean*, translation of Latin *Mar Pacifico* peaceful sea, named by the

Portuguese explorer Ferdinand Magellan d.1521, because he encountered no storms there]

pacific *adj* **1** having a mild peaceable nature. **2** tending to bring about peace; conciliatory. **3** (**Pacific**) belonging to, relating to, or being in the region of the Pacific Ocean. ➤➤ **pacifically** *adv.* [Middle English via early French *pacifique* from Latin *pacificus*, from *pac-*, *pax* PEACE + *facere* to make]

pacifier /'pasifie-ə/ *noun* **1** somebody or something that pacifies. **2** *NAmer* a baby's dummy.

pacifism /'pasifiz(ə)m/ *noun* opposition to war as a means of settling disputes; *specif* refusal to bear arms on moral or religious grounds. ➤➤ **pacifist** *noun and adj.* [French *pacifisme*, from *pacifique*: see PACIFIC]

pacify /'pasifie/ *verb trans* (**pacifies, pacified, pacifying**) **1** to allay the anger or agitation of (somebody). **2** to restore (e.g. a country) to a peaceful state; to subdue (it). ➤➤ **pacification** /-fi'kaysh(ə)n/ *noun*, **pacificatory** /pə'sifikət(ə)ri/ *adj.* [Middle English *pacifien* from Latin *pacificare*, from *pac-*, *pax* PEACE]

pack[1] /pak/ *noun* **1a** a light, non-rigid paper, cardboard, or plastic container for goods, often together with its contents. **b** the amount contained in a pack. **c** *chiefly NAmer* = PACKET[1] (1A). **2** a bundle or bag for goods or equipment carried on the shoulders or back; *specif* a knapsack or rucksack. **3** a full set of playing cards. **4a** a group, set, or collection of things, *esp* a large one: *a pack of lies.* **b** a set of related documents usu in a folder or similar container: *an information pack.* **5** (*treated as sing. or pl*). **a** a number of wild or domesticated animals, kept together or naturally grouping together, *esp* for hunting. **b** an organized group of submarines or other naval craft. **c** an organized group of people, *esp* of Cub Scouts or Brownie Guides. **d** the forwards in a rugby team, *esp* when acting together, e.g. in a scrum. **e** the main group of runners, riders, etc in a race when bunched together behind the leaders. **6** a compact manufactured article designed to perform a specific function. **7** a concentrated mass of e.g. snow; *specif* = PACK ICE. **8** a pad of wet absorbent material such as gauze for application to the body for therapeutic purposes, *esp* to fill a bleeding cavity temporarily. **9** = FACE-PACK. **10** the quantity of food packaged or preserved in a particular season. [Middle English, of Low German or Dutch origin]

pack[2] *verb trans* **1** to place (an item or items, goods, etc) in a container, *esp* for transportation or storage or for carrying on a journey. **2** to cover, fill, or surround (something) with packing material, *esp* for protection. **3a** to fill (a room or space) completely. **b** (+ with) to include a large amount or quantity in (something): *a guidebook packed with information.* **4a** (+ in/into) to fit (a large number of things or people) into a relatively small space or (a large number of activities) into a short period of time. **b** *informal* (+ in) to attract a large number of (people). **5** *informal* (+ in/up) to bring (something) to an end; to finish with (something). **6** *chiefly NAmer, informal* to carry or wear (e.g. a gun). **7** to increase the density of (something); to compress (something). ➤ *verb intrans* **1** (*often* + away/up) to put belongings, goods, etc into containers ready for transportation or storage. **2** (*often* + away) to be suitable for packing, *esp* to be foldable or collapsible for easy storage or transport. **3** (+ into) to enter in large numbers and fill a place. **4** to become built up or compacted in a layer or mass. **5** (+ down) said of rugby forwards: to gather into a tight formation ready for a scrum. **✳ pack a punch 1** to be capable of hitting hard. **2** to be very strong or effective, or capable of making an impact. ➤➤ **packable** *adj*, **packer** *noun.*

pack[3] *verb trans* to influence the composition of (e.g. a jury) so as to influence the verdict. [orig in the sense 'to make a secret agreement'; perhaps alteration of PACT]

package[1] /'pakij/ *noun* **1a** an object or number of objects wrapped or packed up together; a parcel. **b** a wrapper or container in which something is packed. **2** a number of related items, proposals, etc presented for sale, acceptance, etc as a whole, e.g.: **a** a group of contract benefits gained through collective bargaining usu between management and union. **b** a ready-made computer program or set of programs for carrying out a relatively generalized operation, e.g. accounting or stock control, sold as a self-contained product. **c** = PACKAGE DEAL. **d** = PACKAGE HOLIDAY.

package[2] *verb trans* **1a** to make (something) into a package. **b** to enclose (something) in a package or covering. **2** to group (various items) together for sale or presentation as a whole. **3** to present (a person or product) in a way that will appeal to an audience. **4** said of a small publishing company: to compile or organize the writing

and illustration of (a book) on behalf of a publisher. ➤➤ **packaged** *adj*, **packager** *noun.*

package deal *noun* **1** an offer or agreement involving a number of related items and making acceptance of one item dependent on the acceptance of all. **2** the items offered in a deal of this type.

package holiday *noun* a holiday organized by a travel agent or tour operator who arranges all the transport and accommodation and charges an inclusive price.

package tour *noun* = PACKAGE HOLIDAY.

packaging *noun* **1** material used for packing. **2** the design and manufacture of materials used for packing goods. **3** the promotion of the image of a product or person via the media.

pack animal *noun* an animal, e.g. a donkey, used for carrying packs.

pack drill *noun* a military punishment consisting of marching up and down in full kit. **✳ no names, no pack drill** *informal* mentioning no names, so nobody gets blamed: *There's a certain party – no names no pack-drill – who's fairly doggin' me to get information* — Edgar Wallace.

packed *adj* **1** very full or crowded, or filled to capacity: *The show has been playing to packed houses.* **2** (*usu used in combinations*). **a** containing a large quantity or number of something: *an action-packed story.* **b** compressed or compacted: *hard-packed snow.*

packet[1] /'pakit/ *noun* **1a** a small container usu of paper or cardboard, usu together with its contents: *a packet of biscuits.* **b** = PARCEL[1] (1). **2** in computing, a unit of data sent as part of a message from one user to another through a packet-switching network. **3** (**a packet**) *Brit, informal* a large sum of money: *It must have cost a packet.* **4** *dated* a passenger boat carrying mail and cargo on a regular schedule. [Anglo-French *pacquet*, dimin. of PACK[1]; (sense 4) short for *packet boat*]

packet[2] *verb* (**packeted, packeting**) to wrap (something) in a packet.

packet boat *noun* = PACKET[1] (4).

packet-switching network *noun* a digital communications system in which messages are transmitted as many separate packets of data which are reassembled in the correct order by the receiving equipment.

packhorse *noun* a horse used for carrying packs.

pack ice *noun* sea ice crushed together into a large floating mass.

packing *noun* **1** the action, process, or method of packing something. **2** material used to pack goods.

pack off *verb trans informal* to send (somebody) away, *esp* abruptly or unceremoniously.

pack rat *noun* any of numerous species of N American rodents, similar to the rat, that live in woodland and collect forest debris near their nests. The best-known species has cheek pouches and a bushy tail: genus *Neotoma* and other genera.

packsaddle *noun* a saddle designed to support a pack on an animal's back.

pack up *verb intrans* **1a** to put things, *esp* tools and equipment, away in containers or in their usual storage places. **b** *informal* to finish work or some other activity. **2** *informal* to cease to function.

pact /pakt/ *noun* an agreement or treaty; *esp* an international treaty. [Middle English via French from Latin *pactum*, neuter past part. of *pacisci* to agree, contract]

pacy or **pacey** /'paysi/ *adj* (**pacier, paciest**) *Brit* having pace; fast or speedy.

pad[1] /pad/ *noun* **1** a thin flat mat or cushion, e.g.: **a** padding used to shape an article of clothing. **b** a padded guard worn to shield body parts, *esp* the legs of a batsman, against impact. **c** a piece of absorbent material used as a surgical dressing or protective covering. **d** a piece of material saturated with ink for inking the surface of a rubber stamp. **2a** the foot of an animal. **b** the cushioned thickening of the underside of the toes of cats, dogs, etc. **3** a number of sheets of paper, e.g. for writing or drawing on, fastened together at one edge. **4a** a flat surface for a vertical takeoff or landing. **b** = LAUNCH PAD. **5** *informal* living quarters. **6** a large floating leaf of a water lily. [origin unknown]

pad[2] *verb* (**padded, padding**) ➤ *verb trans* **1** to provide (something) with a pad or padding. **2** (*often* + out) to expand or fill out (speech or writing) with superfluous matter. ➤ *verb intrans* **1** (+ up) said of a cricketer: to put on pads ready to go out and bat. **2** (+ up) said of a batsman: to defend one's wicket by deliberately blocking or deflecting the ball with one's pads.

pad³ verb (**padded, padding**) ➤ verb intrans to walk with a muffled step. ➤ verb trans to traverse (an area) on foot: *padding the quiet streets*. [perhaps from early Dutch *paden* to follow a path, from *pad* path]

pad⁴ noun a padding sound.

padding noun material with which something is padded.

paddle¹ /'padl/ noun **1a** a usu wooden implement similar to but smaller than an oar, used to propel and steer a small craft, e.g. a canoe. **b** an implement with a short handle and broad flat blade used for stirring, mixing, hitting, etc. **2** any of the broad boards at the circumference of a paddle wheel or waterwheel. **3** a flattened limb or flipper of a bird or mammal that swims. [Middle English *padell*; earlier history unknown]

paddle² verb intrans **1** to move over water by paddling a craft. **2** to swim with short strokes as an animal does. ➤ verb trans to propel (a craft) by a paddle. * **paddle one's own canoe** to be independent and self-reliant. ➤➤ **paddler** noun.

paddle³ verb intrans to walk, play, or wade in shallow water. ➤➤ **paddler** noun. [prob frequentative of PAD³]

paddle⁴ noun an act of paddling: *We went for a paddle in the sea*.

paddle steamer noun a vessel propelled by a pair of paddle wheels mounted amidships or by a single paddle wheel at the stern.

paddle wheel noun a power-driven wheel with paddles round its circumference used to propel a boat.

paddock /'padək/ noun **1** a small usu enclosed field, *esp* for pasturing or exercising animals. **2** a field where racehorses are saddled and paraded before a race. **3** an area at a motor-racing track where cars, motorcycles, etc are parked and worked on before a race. [Old English *pearroc*]

Paddy /'padi/ noun (pl **Paddies**) derog, offensive an Irish person. [*Paddy*, a common Irish nickname for *Patrick*]

paddy¹ noun (pl **paddies**) **1** = PADDYFIELD. **2** threshed unmilled rice. [Malay *padi*]

paddy² noun (pl **paddies**) *Brit, informal* a temper tantrum: *She always goes off in a paddy when she doesn't get her own way.* [from PADDY]

paddyfield noun a field of wet land in which rice is grown.

paddymelon noun see PADEMELON.

paddy wagon noun NAmer, informal a police vehicle in which prisoners are carried.

Word history
prob from PADDY. Many policemen in New York were Irish.

pademelon or **paddymelon** /'padimelən/ noun any of several species of small wallaby found in the Australian coastal scrub: genus *Thylogale*. [alteration of earlier *paddymalla*, from Dharuk, an Aboriginal language]

padlock¹ /'padlok/ noun a portable lock with a shackle that can be passed through a staple or link and then secured. [Middle English *padlok*, from *pad-* (of unknown origin) + *lok* LOCK¹]

padlock² verb trans to secure (something) using a padlock.

padre /'pahdri/ noun informal **1** a Christian priest. **2** a military chaplain. [Spanish or Italian or Portuguese *padre*, literally 'father', from Latin *pater*]

pad saw noun a narrow pointed fine-toothed saw used for cutting tight curves; a keyhole saw. [PAD¹ in the sense 'tool handle']

paean /'pee-ən/ noun a joyously exultant song or hymn of praise, tribute, thanksgiving, or triumph: *Under his breath, with a furtive exultation, he began once again the paean of victory and devastation* — Saki. [Latin *paean* hymn of thanksgiving to Apollo, from Greek *paian, paiōn*, from *Paian, Paiōn*, epithet of Apollo in the hymn]

paederast noun see PEDERAST.

paederasty noun see PEDERASTY.

paediatrician /ˌpeedi-ə'trish(ə)n/ noun a specialist in paediatrics.

paediatrics (NAmer **pediatrics**) /peedi'atriks/ pl noun (treated as sing. or pl) medicine dealing with the development, care, and diseases of children. ➤➤ **paediatric** adj.

paedo- (NAmer **pedo-**) comb. form forming words, denoting: child: *paedophile*. [Greek *paid-, paido-* from *paid-, pais* child, boy]

paedomorphosis /ˌpeedoh·maw'fohsis/ noun evolutionary development of an organism that involves retention of juvenile characteristics by the adult.

paedophile (NAmer **pedophile**) /'peedəfiel/ noun a person affected with paedophilia.

paedophilia (NAmer **pedophilia**) /peedə'fili-ə/ noun sexual desire directed towards children.

paella /pie'elə/ noun a saffron-flavoured Spanish dish containing rice, meat, seafood, and vegetables. [Catalan *paella* pot, pan, via French from Latin *patella*: see PATELLA]

paeon /'pee-ən/ noun a metrical foot of four syllables with one long or stressed and three short or unstressed syllables. [via Latin from Greek *paian, paiōn*: see PAEAN; paeans used this metre]

paeony /'pee-əni/ noun (pl **paeonies**) see PEONY.

pagan /'paygən/ noun **1** a follower of a polytheistic religion. **2** an irreligious person. ➤➤ **pagan** adj, **paganish** adj, **paganism** noun.

Word history
Middle English via late Latin from Latin *paganus* country dweller, civilian, from *pagus* country district. In Christian Latin the sense 'civilian' was applied to somebody who did not belong to the 'army' of Christ.

page¹ /payj/ noun **1** a leaf of a book, magazine, etc, or a single side of a leaf. **2** something, e.g. an event, worth being recorded in writing: *an exciting page in Germany's history*. **3** a sizable subdivision of computer memory used chiefly for convenience of reference in programming. **4** an electronic document published on the World Wide Web. [early French *page* from Latin *pagina*, from *pangere* to fasten]

page² verb trans to paginate (e.g. a book). ➤ verb intrans (often + through) to turn pages, *esp* in a haphazard manner.

page³ noun **1** a boy serving as an honorary attendant at a formal function, e.g. a wedding. **2** somebody employed to deliver messages or run errands. **3** a boy being trained for the medieval rank of knight and in the personal service of a knight. **4** a young man or boy attending on a person of rank. [Middle English via Old French from Italian *paggio*, prob ultimately from Greek *pais* child, boy]

page⁴ verb trans **1** to summon (somebody) by repeatedly calling out their name over a public-address system. **2** to summon (somebody) by a coded signal emitted by a short-range radio transmitter.

pageant /'paj(ə)nt/ noun **1** a show or exhibition; *esp* a colourful spectacle with a series of tableaux, dramatic presentations, or a procession, expressing a common theme. **2** an ostentatious display. [Middle English *pagyn, padgeant* scene of a play, via late Latin from Latin *pagina*: see PAGE¹]

pageantry /'paj(ə)ntri/ noun colourful or splendid display; spectacle.

page boy noun **1** a boy serving as a page. **2** a usu shoulder-length woman's hairstyle in which the ends of the hair are turned under in a smooth roll.

page-jacking noun the process of diverting Internet users from a website they are searching for to some other site that somebody wants them to visit. [PAGE¹ + HIJACK¹]

pager noun a small portable electronic device that can be used to communicate with somebody, e.g. by emitting an audible tone or sending a text message.

page-three adj Brit pictured, or attractive enough to be pictured, on page three of a tabloid newspaper where photographs of topless young women are regularly featured.

page-turner noun **1** a person or device that turns pages, *esp* an assistant who turns the pages of a score for a musician. **2** informal a compulsively readable book.

paginate /'pajinayt/ verb trans to number the sides of the leaves of (e.g. a book) in a sequence: compare FOLIATE². ➤➤ **pagination** /-'naysh(ə)n/ noun. [Latin *pagina*: see PAGE¹]

pagoda /pə'gohdə/ noun a tower with many storeys, with upturned projecting roofs at the division of each storey and erected *esp* as a Buddhist temple or memorial in the Far East. [Portuguese *pagode* oriental idol, temple]

pagoda tree noun a leguminous tree of SE Asia with ornamental creamy-white flowers that hang in clusters: *Sophora japonica*.

pah /pah/ interj used to express contempt or disgust.

Pahlavi /'pahlavi/ or **Pehlevi** /'pay-/ noun **1** the Iranian language of Sassanian Persia, used in classical literature. **2** a Semitic script used for writing Pahlavi. [Persian *pahlawī*, from *Pahlav* Parthia, from Old Persian *Parthava*]

paid /payd/ *verb* past tense and past part. of PAY¹. ✳ **put paid to** to bring to an abrupt end; to destroy.

paid-up *adj* **1** having paid the necessary fees to be a full member of a group or organization. **2** showing the characteristic attitudes and behaviour of a specified group to a marked degree: *a fully paid-up member of the awkward squad.*

pail /payl/ *noun* a bucket, *esp* a wooden or metal one. ➤➤ **pailful** *noun*. [Middle English *payle, paille*, prob from Old English *pægel*, a small measure of liquid]

paillasse /'palias/ *noun* see PALLIASSE.

paillette /pal'yet/ *noun* a small shiny object, e.g. a spangle, used to decorate clothing. [French *paillette*, dimin. of *paille* straw, from Latin *palea*]

pain¹ /payn/ *noun* **1** a basic bodily sensation induced by a harmful stimulus or physical disorder and characterized by physical discomfort, e.g. pricking, throbbing, or aching. **2** mental or emotional distress: *'I believe I gave you some pain.' 'Does that please you?' 'Infinitely; I love to give pain.'* — Congreve. **3** *informal* somebody or something that annoys or is a nuisance: *She's a real pain.* **4** (*in pl*) the trouble involved or care taken in doing something: *I got no thanks for my pains.* **5** (*in pl*) the painful muscular contractions involved in childbirth; labour. ✳ **be at pains to do something** to take special care to do something. **on/under pain of** subject to penalty or punishment of: *They were ordered to leave the country on pain of death.* **pain in the neck** *informal* a source of annoyance; a nuisance. [Middle English via Old French from Latin *poena* punishment, pain, from Greek *poinē* payment, penalty]

pain² *verb trans* to make (somebody) suffer or cause distress to (them); to hurt (them).

pained *adj* showing pain or distress; troubled or annoyed.

painful /'paynf(ə)l/ *adj* **1a** causing or feeling pain. **b** distressing or annoying. **2** proceeding slowly and usu involving great effort or exertion: *their painful progress up the hill.* **3** *informal* very bad; awful. ➤➤ **painfully** *adv,* **painfulness** *noun.*

painkiller *noun* a drug, e.g. morphine or aspirin, that relieves pain. ➤➤ **painkilling** *adj.*

painless *adj* **1** not causing any pain: *a painless injection.* **2** easy or effortless: *Changing banks was relatively painless.* ➤➤ **painlessly** *adv,* **painlessness** *noun.*

painstaking *adj* showing diligent care and effort. ➤➤ **painstakingly** *adv,* **painstakingness** *noun.*

paint¹ /paynt/ *verb trans* **1a** to apply colour, pigment, paint, or cosmetics to (something). **b** to apply (something) with a movement resembling that used in painting. **2a** to represent (something or somebody) in colours on a surface by applying pigments. **b** to decorate (something) by painting. **c** (+ out/over) to conceal (something) by covering it with paint. **3a** to describe or evoke (something) as if by painting: *Her novel paints glowing pictures of rural life.* **b** to depict (somebody or something) as having specified or implied characteristics: *He's not as black as he's painted.* ➤ *verb intrans* to practise the art of painting. ✳ **paint the town red** *informal* to go out and celebrate exuberantly. [Middle English *painten* via Old French from Latin *pingere* to tattoo, embroider, paint]

paint² *noun* **1** a mixture of a pigment and a suitable liquid which forms a closely adherent coating when spread on a surface. **2a** pigment, *esp* in compressed form. **b** an applied coat of paint: *wet paint; Don't scratch the paint.* **3** *informal* make-up, *esp* rouge. ➤➤ **painty** *adj.*

paintball *noun* **1** a war game involving contestants equipped with special guns that fire dye-filled pellets. **2** a pellet used in this game. ➤➤ **paintballer** *noun,* **paintballing** *noun.*

paintbox *noun* a metal box containing small blocks of water-colour pigment.

paintbrush *noun* a brush for applying paint.

painted lady *noun* any of several species of migratory butterflies with wings mottled in brown, orange, red, and white: *Cynthia cardui* and other species.

painter¹ *noun* **1** an artist who paints. **2** somebody who applies paint, e.g. to a building, *esp* as an occupation.

painter² *noun* a line used for securing or towing a boat. [Middle English *paynter*, prob from early French *pendoir, pentoir* clothesline, from *pendre* to hang]

painterly *adj* **1** relating to or typical of a painter; artistic. **2** denoting a style of painting that emphasizes colour, tone, and texture rather than line. ➤➤ **painterliness** *noun.*

painting *noun* **1** a product of painting; *esp* a painted work of art. **2** the art or occupation of painting.

paintwork *noun* a painted surface: *He had damaged the paintwork of the car.*

pair¹ /peə/ *noun* **1** two corresponding things usu used together: *a pair of shoes.* **2a** two corresponding bodily parts: *a beautiful pair of eyes.* **b** a single thing made up of two connected corresponding pieces: *a pair of trousers.* **3** a couple in love, engaged, or married: *They were a devoted pair.* **4** two playing cards of the same value in a hand. **5** two horses harnessed side by side. **6** two mated animals. **7** a partnership between two people, *esp* in a contest against another partnership. **8** two members from opposite sides of a deliberative body who agree that neither will vote if either is absent so that the balance between the two sides is maintained. [Middle English *paire* via Old French from Latin *paria* equal things, neuter pl of *par* equal]

pair² *verb trans* **1** (*often* + up) to arrange (things) in pairs: *She succeeded in pairing the socks.* **2** to arrange a voting pair between (Members of Parliament).

pair off *verb trans* to cause (two people) to form a pair, *esp* male and female: *Anxious mothers are trying to pair off their children.* ➤ *verb intrans* to form a couple or a group of two: *They paired off for the next dance.*

pair production *noun* the transformation of a quantum of radiant energy into an electron and a positron.

pair up *verb trans* to organize (people or things) in pairs. ➤ *verb intrans* = PAIR OFF.

paisa /'piesə/ *noun* (*pl* **paise** /'piesay, 'piesə/) **1** a unit of currency in India, Nepal, and Pakistan, worth 100th of a rupee. **2** a unit of currency in Bangladesh worth 100th of a taka. [Hindi *paisā*]

paisley /'payzli/ *noun* **1** a pattern of colourful abstract teardrop-shaped figures. **2** (*used before a noun*) woven or printed with this pattern: *paisley pyjamas.* ➤➤ **paisley** *adj.* [named after *Paisley*, a town in Scotland where a woollen cloth was made with this pattern]

Paiute /'pieyooht/ *noun* (*pl* **Paiutes** or collectively **Paiute**) **1** a member of a Native American people orig of Utah, Arizona, Nevada, and California. **2** the language spoken by these people. [Spanish *payute*]

pajamas /pə'jahməz/ *pl noun NAmer* see PYJAMAS.

pak choi /ˌpak 'choy/ (*NAmer* **bok choy** /ˌbok/) *noun* a Chinese cabbage with long dark green leaves and succulent white stems. [Chinese (Cantonese) *baahk choi* white vegetable]

pakeha /'pahkəhah, pah'kee·ə/ *noun* (*pl* **pakehas** or collectively **pakeha**) *NZ* somebody who is not a Maori; a white New Zealander. [Maori *pakeha*]

Paki /'paki/ *noun Brit, informal, offensive* = PAKISTANI.

Pakistani /paki'stahni, pah-/ *noun* a native or inhabitant of Pakistan, or a person whose family came from Pakistan. ➤➤ **Pakistani** *adj.*

pakora /pə'kawrə/ *noun* an Indian savoury snack consisting of diced vegetables or meat dipped in batter made from chickpea flour and fried. [Hindi *pakoṛā*]

PAL /pal/ *abbr* phase alternation line (a system of transmitting colour television programmes).

pal /pal/ *noun informal* **1** a close friend. **2** used as a familiar form of address, *esp* to a stranger: *Put that back, pal.* [Romany *phral, phal* brother, friend, from Sanskrit *bhrātr*]

palace /'palis/ *noun* **1a** a large stately house. **b** a large public building. **2** the official residence of a ruler, e.g. a sovereign or bishop. [Middle English *palais* via Old French from Latin *palatium*, from *Palatium*, the Palatine Hill in Rome where the emperors' residences were built]

paladin /'palədin/ *noun* **1** a champion of a medieval prince. **2** a knight renowned for chivalry and valour. **3** one of the twelve legendary companions and peers of Charlemagne. [French *paladin* via Italian and late Latin from Latin *palatinus* palace official, from *palatium*: see PALACE]

palae- *or* **palaeo-** (*NAmer* **pale-, paleo-**) *comb. form* forming words, with the meanings: **1** involving or dealing with ancient forms or conditions: *palaeobotany.* **2** early, primitive, or archaic:

Palaeolithic. [Greek *palai-, palaio-,* from *palaios* ancient, from *palai* long ago]

Palaearctic (*NAmer* **Palearctic**) /pali'ahktik/ *adj* denoting, relating to, or coming from a biogeographic region that includes Europe and N Asia, Arabia, and Africa.

palaeo- *comb. form* see PALAE-.

palaeobotany (*NAmer* **paleobotany**) /,palioh'botəni/ *noun* a branch of botany dealing with fossil plants. ⟫⟫ **palaeobotanical** /-'tanikl/ *adj,* **palaeobotanist** *noun.*

Palaeocene (*NAmer* **Paleocene**) /'paliohseen/ *adj* relating to or dating from a geological epoch, the first epoch of the Tertiary period, lasting from about 65 million to about 56.5 million years ago and marked by the emergence of mammals. ⟫⟫ **Palaeocene** *noun.*

palaeoclimate (*NAmer* **paleoclimate**) /'paliohkliemit/ *noun* the climate of an age in the geological past. ⟫⟫ **palaeoclimatic** /-'matik/ *adj.*

palaeoclimatology (*NAmer* **paleoclimatology**) /,paliohkliemə'tolǝji/ *noun* a science dealing with the climate of prehistoric ages. ⟫⟫ **palaeoclimatologist** *noun.*

palaeoecology (*NAmer* **paleoecology**) /,palioh-i'kolǝji/ *noun* a branch of ecology that is concerned with the characteristics of environments in the geological past and with their relationships to the plants and animals of prehistoric times. ⟫⟫ **palaeoecological** /-eekə'lojikl/ *adj,* **palaeoecologist** *noun.*

palaeography (*NAmer* **paleography**) /pali'ogrǝfi/ *noun* the study of ancient writings and inscriptions. ⟫⟫ **palaeographer** *noun,* **palaeographical** /-'grafikl/ *adj,* **palaeographically** /-'grafikli/ *adv.*

Palaeolithic (*NAmer* **Paleolithic**) /,pali-ǝ'lithik/ *adj* relating to or dating from the earliest period of the Stone Age, lasting from about 750,000 to about 15,000 years ago, and marked *esp* by the development and use of crude, chipped stone implements.

Editorial note
Palaeolithic literally means the 'Old Stone Age', i.e. the first and longest part of the Stone Age, spanning the period from the very first recognizable stone tools (c.2.5 million years ago) to the retreat of the glacial ice in the northern hemisphere around 10,000 years ago. Throughout this long period, people lived as hunter-gatherers. The Palaeolithic in some parts of the Old World is subdivided into three phases — the Lower Palaeolithic (the period of early human forms), the Middle (generally associated with Neanderthals in some areas) and Upper (the period of fully modern humans). The equivalent term in the New World is Palaeoindian — Dr Paul Bahn.

⟫⟫ **Palaeolithic** *noun.*

palaeomagnetism (*NAmer* **paleomagnetism**) /,palioh'-magnǝtiz(ǝ)m/ *noun* the study of the intensity and direction of residual magnetization in ancient rocks. ⟫⟫ **palaeomagnetic** /-'netik/ *adj.*

palaeontology (*NAmer* **paleontology**) /,palion'tolǝji/ *noun* a science dealing with the life of past geological periods as discovered from fossil remains. ⟫⟫ **palaeontological** /-'lojikl/ *adj,* **palaeontologist** *noun.* [French *paléontologie* from *palé-* PALAEO- + Greek *onta* living things + French *-logie* -LOGY]

Palaeozoic (*NAmer* **Paleozoic**) /,pali-ǝ'zoh-ik/ *adj* relating to or dating from a geological era (before the Mesozoic era and including the Cambrian, Ordovician, Silurian, Devonian, Carboniferous, and Permian periods), lasting from about 570 million to about 245 million years ago, and marked *esp* by the appearance of fish, land plants, amphibians, and reptiles. ⟫⟫ **Palaeozoic** *noun.*

palais /'palay, 'pali/ *noun Brit* a public dance hall. [French *palais de danse* dance palace]

palais de danse /də donhs/ *noun* = PALAIS.

palanquin *or* **palankeen** /'palǝnkeen/ *noun* a litter formerly used in eastern Asia to carry one person, and usu hung from poles borne on the bearers' shoulders. [Portuguese *palanquim* from Javanese *pĕlanɱki,* from Sanskrit *palyanka* bed, couch]

palatable /'palǝtǝbl/ *adj* 1 pleasant to the taste. 2 = ACCEPTABLE: *She did not find the suggestion at all palatable.* ⟫⟫ **palatability** /-'biliti/ *noun,* **palatably** *adv.*

palatal[1] /'palǝtl/ *adj* 1 to do with or in the region of the palate. 2 said of a speech sound: formed with the front of the tongue near or touching the hard palate. ⟫⟫ **palatally** *adv.*

palatal[2] *noun* a palatal speech sound, such as *j, y,* or *sh.*

palatalize *or* **palatalise** *verb trans* to pronounce (a sound) as a palatal sound; to make (it) palatal. ⟫⟫ **palatalization** /-'zaysh(ǝ)n/ *noun.*

palate /'palǝt/ *noun* 1 the roof of the mouth, separating it from the nasal cavity. **2a** the sense of taste. **2b** a usu intellectual taste or liking: *The novel was too pessimistic for my palate.* **3** flavour, *esp* the flavour of wine. [Middle English from Latin *palatum*]

palatial /pǝ'laysh(ǝ)l/ *adj* 1 suitable for a palace; magnificent and luxurious. 2 relating to a palace. ⟫⟫ **palatially** *adv.* [Latin *palatium:* see PALACE]

palatinate /pǝ'latinǝt/ *noun* the territory of a palatine.

palatine[1] /'palǝtien/ *noun* a feudal lord, e.g. a count or bishop, with sovereign power. [Latin *palatinus,* from *palatinus* of the palace, from *palatium:* see PALACE]

palatine[2] *adj* said of a feudal lord in the Middle Ages: possessing sovereign authority within a particular territory.

palatine[3] *adj* to do with or in the region of the palate.

palatine[4] *noun* either of a pair of bones that are situated behind and between the two bones of the upper jawbone and form the hard palate.

palatine bone *noun* = PALATINE[4].

palaver[1] /pǝ'lahvǝ/ *noun* **1a** a tediously involved procedure; fuss or bother: *All the palaver of getting passports made our holiday a real nightmare.* **b** unnecessary or time-consuming talk: *We understand one another without any palaver, don't we, old fellow?* — Louisa M Alcott. **c** a particular business or area of interest, or the jargon associated with it: *I have been a quartz miner ... I know all the palaver of that business* — Mark Twain. **2** *dated* a long discussion; a parley: *Next morning a solemn palaver (as the natives of Madagascar call their national convention) was held* — Scott.

palaver[2] *verb intrans* (**palavered, palavering**) 1 to talk in an idle or tedious way. 2 *dated* to hold talks or a parley: *They were coming to palaver with the Sheik* — Edgar Rice Burroughs. [Portugese *palavra* word, speech, via late Latin from Greek *parabolē:* see PARABLE]

palazzo /pǝ'latsoh/ *noun* (*pl* **palazzi** /-see/) a large imposing residential or civic building in Italy, or a building that imitates the appearance of an Italian palazzo. [Italian *palazzo* from Latin *palatium:* see PALACE]

palazzo pants *pl noun* loose wide-legged trousers for women.

pale[1] /payl/ *adj* 1 deficient in colour or intensity of colour; pallid: *a pale face.* 2 not bright or brilliant; dim: *a pale sun shining through the fog.* 3 feeble or faint: *a pale imitation.* 4 said of a colour: not deep or dark; light and whitish: *a pale pink.* ⟫⟫ **palely** *adv,* **paleness** *noun,* **palish** *adj.* [Middle English via French from Latin *pallidus:* see PALLID]

pale[2] *verb intrans* 1 to become pale. 2 to seem inferior or less important: *He was so worried about the children that everything else seemed to pale into insignificance.*

pale[3] *noun* 1 an upright post forming part of a fence. 2 formerly, a territory or district within certain bounds or under a particular jurisdiction. 3 a broad vertical band down the centre of a heraldic shield. **✳ beyond the pale** in violation of good manners or social convention. [Middle English via French from Latin *palus* stake]

pale- *comb. form NAmer* see PALAE-.

Palearctic /pali'ahktik/ *adj NAmer* see PALAEARCTIC.

paleface /'paylfays/ *noun derog* a white person, *esp* as distinguished from a Native American.

paleo- *comb. form NAmer* see PALAE-.

paleobotany /,palioh'botəni/ *noun NAmer* see PALAEOBOTANY.

Paleocene /'paliohseen/ *adj NAmer* see PALAEOCENE.

paleoclimate /'paliohkliemit/ *noun NAmer* see PALAEOCLIMATE.

paleoclimatology /,paliohkliemə'tolǝji/ *noun NAmer* see PALAEO-CLIMATOLOGY.

paleography /pali'ogrǝfi/ *noun NAmer* see PALAEOGRAPHY.

Paleolithic /,pali-ǝ'lithik/ *adj NAmer* see PALAEOLITHIC.

paleomagnetism /,palioh'magnǝtiz(ǝ)m/ *noun NAmer* see PALAEOMAGNETISM.

paleontology /,palion'tolǝji/ *noun NAmer* see PALAEONTOLOGY.

Paleozoic /,pali-ǝ'zoh-ik/ *adj NAmer* see PALAEOZOIC.

Palestinian /palǝ'stini-ǝn/ *noun* a native or inhabitant of Palestine. ⟫⟫ **Palestinian** *adj.*

palette /'palit/ *noun* **1** a thin board held by a painter for mixing pigments. **2a** the set of colours put on the palette. **b** a particular range, quality, or use of colour. **c** a comparable range, quality, or use of available elements, *esp* in another art, e.g. music. **d** the range of colours a computer is able to display on a VDU. [French *palette*, dimin. of *pale* spade, shovel, from Latin *pala* spade]

palette knife *noun* a knife with a flexible steel blade and no cutting edge, used by artists for mixing and applying paints or in cooking.

palfrey /'pawlfri/ *noun* (*pl* **palfreys**) *archaic* a saddle horse other than a war-horse, *esp* for a woman. [Middle English via Old French from late Latin *paraveredus*, from Greek *para-* beside + Latin *veredus* light-horse]

Pali /'pahli/ *noun* the language of the canonical scriptures of Theravada Buddhism, closely related to Sanskrit. [Sanskrit *pāli* row, series of Buddhist sacred texts]

palimony /'paliməni/ *noun informal* an allowance ordered by a court to be paid by one member of an unmarried couple formerly living together to the other. [blend of PAL and ALIMONY]

palimpsest /'palimpsest/ *noun* writing material, e.g. a parchment or tablet, reused after earlier writing has been erased. [via Latin from Greek *palimpsēstos* scraped again, from *palin* again + *psēn* to rub, scrape]

palindrome /'palindrohm/ *noun* a word, sentence, etc that reads the same backwards or forwards. ➤➤ **palindromic** /-'dromik/ *adj*. [Greek *palindromos* running back again, from *palin* back, again + *dramein* to run]

paling /'payling/ *noun* **1** a fence made of stakes or pickets. **2** a stake used in such a fence.

palingenesis /palin'jenəsis/ *noun* the recurrence of biological characteristics, e.g. the gill slits in a human embryo, that are derivations from distant ancestral forms rather than adaptations of recent origin. ➤➤ **palingenetic** /-'netik/ *adj*. [Latin *palingenesis*, from Greek *palin* again + Latin *genesis* birth]

palisade¹ /pali'sayd/ *noun* **1** a fence of stakes, *esp* for defence. **2** a long strong stake pointed at the top and set close together with others as a defence. **3** *NAmer* (*in pl*) a line of steep cliffs. [French *palissade*, ultimately from Latin *palus* stake]

palisade² *verb trans* to surround or fortify (something) with palisades.

palisade layer *noun* a layer of cells containing many chloroplasts (cell part containing chlorophyll; see CHLOROPLAST) lying beneath the upper skin of green leaves.

pall¹ /pawl/ *noun* **1** something heavy or dark that covers or conceals: *a pall of thick black smoke*. **2a** a square of linen used to cover the chalice containing the wine used at Communion. **b** a heavy cloth draped over a coffin or tomb. **3** = PALLIUM (1B). **4** in heraldry, a Y-shaped device. [Old English *pæll* from Latin *pallium* cloak]

pall² *verb intrans* to cease to be interesting or attractive: *The notion of Freddy succeeding at anything was a joke that never palled* — George Bernard Shaw. [Middle English *pallen* to become weak or stale, short for *appallen*: see APPAL]

palladia /pə'laydi-ə/ *noun* pl of PALLADIUM².

Palladian /pə'laydi-ən/ *adj* denoting a classical style of architecture based on the examples and principles of Andrea Palladio. ➤➤ **Palladianism** *noun*. [Andrea *Palladio* d.1580, Italian architect]

palladium¹ /pə'laydi-əm/ *noun* a silver-white metallic chemical element of the platinum group that occurs naturally in various ores, and is used *esp* in electrical contacts and as a catalyst: symbol Pd, atomic number 46. [Latin *palladium*, named after *Pallas*, an asteroid which was discovered just before the element]

palladium² *noun* (*pl* **palladia** /-di-ə/) something that gives protection; a safeguard.

Word history
via Latin from Greek *palladion*, from *Pallad-, Pallas*, epithet of Athene, Greek goddess of wisdom. The safety of Troy was believed to depend on a statue of Athene.

pallbearer /'pawlbeərə/ *noun* a person who helps to carry the coffin at a funeral or is part of its immediate escort.

pallet¹ /'palit/ *noun* **1** a portable platform intended for handling, storing, or moving materials and packages. **2** a flat-bladed wooden tool used by potters for shaping clay. **3** a lever or surface in a timepiece that receives an impulse from the escapement wheel and imparts motion to a balance or pendulum. [early French *palette*: see PALETTE]

pallet² *noun* **1** a straw-filled mattress. **2** a small hard often makeshift bed. [Middle English *pailet* from French *paillette*: see PAILLETTE]

palletize *or* **palletise** *verb trans* to place, transport, or store (something) on pallets. ➤➤ **palletization** /-'zaysh(ə)n/ *noun*.

pallia /'pali-ə/ *noun* pl of PALLIUM.

palliasse *or* **pailliasse** /'palias/ *noun* a thin straw mattress. [modification of French *paillasse*, from *paille*: see PAILLETTE]

palliate /'paliayt/ *verb trans* **1** to lessen the unpleasantness of (e.g. a disease) without removing the cause. **2** to disguise the gravity of (a fault or offence) by excuses or apologies; to extenuate (it). **3** to moderate the intensity of (something). ➤➤ **palliation** /-'aysh(ə)n/ *noun*, **palliator** *noun*. [late Latin *palliatus*, past part. of *palliare* to cloak, conceal, from *pallium* cloak]

palliative /'pali-ətiv/ *noun* something, e.g. a drug, that palliates. ➤➤ **palliative** *adj*, **palliatively** *adv*.

pallid /'palid/ *adj* **1** lacking colour; wan. **2** lacking sparkle or liveliness; dull. ➤➤ **pallidly** *adv*, **pallidness** *noun*. [Latin *pallidus*, from *pallēre* to be pale]

pallium /'pali-əm/ *noun* (*pl* **pallia** /'pali-ə/ *or* **palliums**) **1a** a white woollen band in the shape of two Y's that meet on the shoulders, worn *esp* by a pope or archbishop. **b** a draped rectangular cloth worn as a cloak, *esp* by men of ancient Rome. **2** the mantle of a mollusc, bird, etc. **3** the cerebral cortex. ➤➤ **pallial** *adj*. [Latin *pallium* coverlet, cloak]

pallor /'palə/ *noun* deficiency of facial colour; paleness: *The pallor of girls' brows shall be their pall* — Wilfred Owen. [Latin *pallor*, from *pallēre* to be pale]

pally *adj* (**pallier, palliest**) *informal* = FRIENDLY¹ (1): *He was very pally with the local vicar.*

palm¹ /pahm; *NAmer* pah(l)m/ *noun* **1** any of a family of tropical or subtropical trees, shrubs, or climbing plants related to the lilies, grasses, and orchids and usu having a simple stem and a crown of large leaves: family Palmae. **2** a leaf of the palm as a symbol of victory, distinction, or rejoicing. [Old English *palma*, ultimately from Latin *palma* PALM², the leaf being thought to resemble an open hand]

palm² *noun* **1** the concave part of the human hand between the bases of the fingers and the wrist. **2** a unit of measurement based on the length, e.g. about 200mm or 8in., or breadth, e.g. about 100mm or 4in., of the human hand. **✳ in the palm of one's hand** entirely under one's control. ➤➤ **palmar** /'palmə/ *adj*. [Middle English *paume* via French from Latin *palma*]

palm³ *verb trans* **1** to conceal (e.g. a playing card) in or with the hand. **2** to pick up (something) stealthily.

palmate /'palmayt/ *adj* **1** resembling a hand with the fingers spread: *a palmate antler*. **2** having lobes radiating from a common point: *a palmate leaf*. **3** said of an aquatic bird: having the front toes webbed.

palmated /'palmaytid/ *adj* = PALMATE.

palmcorder /'pahmkawdə/ *noun* a video camera and recorder that is small enough to be held in the palm of the hand. [blend of PALM² + CAMCORDER]

palmer /'pahmə/ *noun* a pilgrim, *esp* one wearing two crossed palm leaves as a sign of a visit to the Holy Land.

palmetto /pal'metoh/ *noun* (*pl* **palmettos** *or* **palmettoes**) any of several usu low-growing fan-leaved palms, *esp* the cabbage palmetto of the USA: *Sabal palmetto*. [modification of Spanish *palmito* little palm, from Latin *palma*: see PALM¹]

palmistry /'pahmistri/ *noun* the art or practice of reading a person's character or future from markings on the palms. ➤➤ **palmist** *noun*. [Middle English *pawmestry*, prob from *paume* palm + *maistrie* mastery]

palmitate /'palmitayt/ *noun* a salt or ester of palmitic acid.

palmitic acid /pal'mitik/ *noun* a waxy fatty acid occurring as glycerides in most fats and fatty oils: formula $C_{16}H_{32}O_2$. [from *palmitin* (an ester of glycerol and palmitic acid), from French *palmitine*, prob from *palmite* pith of the palm tree, from Spanish *palmito*: see PALMETTO]

palm off *verb trans* **1** (*often* + on) to get rid of (something unwanted or inferior) by deceiving somebody into taking it: *He* *palmed his old car off on his cousin.* **2** *informal* (+ with) to trick (somebody) into believing something untrue or accepting something worthless: *She tried to palm me off with some story about a sick aunt.*

palm oil *noun* an edible fat obtained from the fruit of several palms and used in soap and candles.

Palm Sunday *noun* the Sunday before Easter celebrated as a festival in the Christian Church commemorating Christ's triumphal entry into Jerusalem. [from the palm branches strewn in Christ's path]

palmtop /'pahmtop/ *noun* a small computer that can be held in the palm of the hand.

palmy /'pahmi/ *adj* (**palmier, palmiest**) **1** marked by prosperity; flourishing: *palmy days.* **2** bearing palms or having many palms: *a palmy shoreline.*

palmyra /pal'mie·ərə/ *noun* a tall fan-leaved palm cultivated in Asia for its hard wood, fibre, and sugar-rich sap: *Borassus flabellifer.* [Portuguese *palmeira* palm tree, from Latin *palma*: see PALM¹]

palomino /palə'meenoh/ *noun* (*pl* **palominos**) **1** a light tan or cream-coloured, usu slender-legged horse. **2** (**Palomino**) a variety of grape used in the production of fortified wine, *esp* sherry. [American Spanish *palomino* from Spanish, literally 'like a dove', from Latin *palumbinus*, from *palumbes* ringdove]

palp /palp/ *noun* a segmented touch- or taste-sensitive feeler on the mouthparts of an insect or other arthropod. ⫸ **palpal** *adj.* [Latin *palpus* caress, soft palm of the hand, from *palpare* to stroke, caress]

palpable /'palpəbl/ *adj* **1** capable of being touched or felt; tangible. **2** easily perceptible by the mind; obvious: *a palpable falsehood.* ⫸ **palpability** /-'biliti/ *noun,* **palpably** *adv.* [Middle English from late Latin *palpabilis,* from Latin *palpare* to stroke, caress]

palpate /'palpayt/ *verb trans* to examine (a part of the body), *esp* medically, by touch. ⫸ **palpation** /pal'paysh(ə)n/ *noun.* [earliest as *palpation,* from Latin *palpation-, palpatio,* from *palpare* to stroke, caress]

palpebral /'palpibrəl/ *adj* to do with or in the region of the eyelids. [late Latin *palpebralis,* from Latin *palpebra* eyelid]

palpi /'palpie, 'palpee/ *noun* pl of PALPUS.

palpitant /'palpit(ə)nt/ *adj* marked by trembling or throbbing.

palpitate /'palpitayt/ *verb intrans* **1** to beat rapidly and strongly; to throb: *a palpitating heart.* **2** to tremble, shake, or flutter. ⫸ **palpitation** /-'taysh(ə)n/ *noun.* [Latin *palpitatus,* past part. of *palpitare,* frequentative of *palpare* to stroke]

palpus /'palpəs/ *noun* (*pl* **palpi** /'palpie, 'palpee/) = PALP. [Latin *palpus*: see PALP]

palstave /'pawlstayv/ *noun* a type of Bronze age axe designed to fit into a split wooden handle. [Danish *pålstav* from Old Norse *pālstafr,* a heavy missile, prob from *pāll* spade, hoe + *stafr* staff]

palsy¹ /'pawlzi, 'polzi/ *noun* (*pl* **palsies**) *dated* paralysis or uncontrollable tremor of the body or a part of the body. [Middle English *parlesie* via French from Latin *paralysis*: see PARALYSIS]

palsy² *verb trans* (**palsies, palsied, palsying**) to affect (a part of the body) with palsy; to paralyse (it).

palter /'pawltə, 'poltə/ *verb intrans* (**paltered, paltering**) *archaic* **1** to act insincerely or deceitfully; to equivocate. **2** (+ with) = HAGGLE. ⫸ **palterer** *noun.* [origin unknown]

paltry /'pawltri/ *adj* (**paltrier, paltriest**) **1** extremely or insultingly small; meagre: *a paltry sum.* **2** mean and petty: *a paltry trick.* ⫸ **paltriness** *noun.* [English dialect *palt, pelt* rubbish, rags]

paludal /pəl'yoohdl, 'palyoodl/ *adj* relating to marshes or fens. [Latin *palud-, palus* marsh + -AL¹]

palynology /pali'noləji/ *noun* a branch of botany dealing with pollen and spores. ⫸ **palynological** /-'lojikl/ *adj,* **palynologist** *noun.* [Greek *palynein* to sprinkle, from *palē* fine meal, + -LOGY]

pampas /'pampəs/ *noun* (*treated as sing. or pl*) an extensive generally grass-covered plain of temperate S America. [American Spanish *pampas* from Quechua *pampa* plain]

pampas grass *noun* a tall S American grass with large silky flower heads frequently cultivated as an ornamental plant: *Cortaderia selloana.*

pamper /'pampə/ *verb trans* (**pampered, pampering**) to treat (a person or an animal) with extreme or excessive care and attention: *They always pampered their guests.* [Middle English *pamperen,* prob of Dutch origin]

pampero /pam'peəroh/ *noun* (*pl* **pamperos**) a strong cold wind from the W or SW that blows over the pampas. [American Spanish *pampero* from *pampas*: see PAMPAS]

pamphlet /'pamflit/ *noun* a usu small unbound printed publication with a paper cover, often dealing with topical matters: *a pamphlet on genetically modified crops.*

Word history ─────────────
Middle English *pamflet* unbound booklet, from *Pamphilet,* popular name of 'Pamphilus, seu De Amore'. This work (which translates as 'Pamphilus' or 'On Love') was a popular 12th-cent. Latin love poem.

pamphleteer¹ /pamfli'tiə/ *noun* a writer of pamphlets, *esp* political ones attacking something or urging a cause.

pamphleteer² *verb intrans* to write and publish pamphlets.

pan¹ /pan/ *noun* **1** a round metal container or vessel, usu with a long handle, used on the hob of a cooker or over an open fire to heat or cook food. **2** any of various usu broad, shallow, and open receptacles for domestic use, e.g. a dustpan or a bedpan. **3** either of the receptacles in a pair of scales. **4** a round shallow metal container for separating a heavy mineral, e.g. gold, from lighter waste by washing. **5** *Brit* the bowl of a toilet. **6** the part of the gunlock in old guns or pistols that holds a small charge of powder directly ignited, e.g. by the spark from the flint, to set off the main charge. **7** a natural or artificial hollow or depression in land, e.g. a saltpan. **8** a drifting fragment of the flat thin ice that forms in bays or along the shore. **9** a compacted often clayey layer in soil that is impenetrable to plant roots; hardpan. **10** a drum in a steel band. [Old English *panne*]

pan² *verb* (**panned, panning**) ⫸ *verb intrans* **1** to wash earth, gravel, etc in a pan in search of metal, e.g. gold. **2** to yield precious metal in panning. ⫸ *verb trans* **1** *informal* to subject (a person, their work, a product, etc) to damning criticism: *Some new American cars have been panned as dumpy and boring* — The Economist. **2a** to wash (earth, gravel, etc) in a pan. **b** to separate (e.g. gold) by panning.

pan³ *verb* (**panned, panning**) ⫸ *verb intrans* **1** to rotate a film or television camera horizontally so as to keep a moving object in view or obtain a panoramic effect. **2** said of a camera: to undergo panning. ⫸ *verb trans* to cause (a camera) to pan. [PANORAMA]

pan⁴ *noun* **1** the act or process of panning a camera. **2** the movement of the camera in a panning shot.

pan⁵ /pahn/ *noun* see PAAN.

pan- *comb. form* forming words, with the meanings: **1** all or completely: *panchromatic.* **2a** relating to all of a specified group: *Pan-American.* **b** advocating or involving the union of the group specified: *Pan-Asian.* [Greek *pan-,* from *pan,* neuter of *pant-, pas* all, every]

panacea /panə'see·ə/ *noun* a remedy for all maladies; a cure-all. ⫸ **panacean** *adj.* [via Latin from Greek *panakeia,* from PAN- + *akeisthai* to heal, from *akos* remedy]

panache /pə'nash/ *noun* **1** dash or flamboyance in style and action; verve. **2** an ornamental tuft, e.g. of feathers, *esp* on a helmet. [early French *pennache* via Old Italian from late Latin *pinnaculum* small wing, dimin. of Latin *pinna* wing, feather]

panada /pə'nahdə/ *noun* a thick paste of flour or breadcrumbs used as a base for a sauce or as a binder for forcemeat. [Spanish *panada* from *pan* bread, from Latin *panis*]

Pan-African /,pan 'afrik(ə)n/ *adj* relating to all the people of Africa, *esp* in terms of their political cooperation or their independence. ⫸ **Pan-Africanism** *noun.*

panama /panə'mah, 'panə-/ *or* **Panama** *noun* a lightweight hat of plaited straw. [American Spanish *panamá,* named after *Panama,* a country in Central America]

Panamanian /panə'mayni·ən/ *noun* a native or inhabitant of Panama in central America. ⫸ **Panamanian** *adj.*

Pan-American /,pan ə'merik(ə)n/ *adj* relating to all the people of North, South, and Central America, *esp* in terms of their political or economic cooperation. ⫸ **Pan-Americanism** *noun.*

Pan-Arab /,pan 'arəb/ *adj* relating to all the people of the Arab states, *esp* in terms of their political cooperation. ⫸ **Pan-Arabism** *noun.*

panatella /panə'telə/ *noun* a long slender straight-sided cigar. [American Spanish *panatella* a long thin biscuit, ultimately from Latin *panis* bread]

pancake[1] *noun* **1** a flat cake made from thin batter and cooked on both sides usu in a frying pan. **2** make-up compressed into a flat cake or stick form.

pancake[2] *verb intrans* **1** said of an aircraft: to make a pancake landing. **2** *informal* to become flattened. ➤ *verb trans* **1** said of a pilot: to make a pancake landing in (an aircraft). **2** *informal* to flatten (something).

Pancake Day *noun* Shrove Tuesday, marked by the eating of pancakes.

Word history
pancakes were traditionally made to use up eggs and fat before the fast of Lent.

pancake landing *noun* a landing in which an aircraft descends in an approximately horizontal position with little forward motion.

pancetta /pan'chetə/ *noun* belly of pork that has been cured and spiced, used *esp* in Italian cooking. [Italian *pancetta*, dimin. of *pancio* belly, from Latin *pantex* intestine]

panchromatic /pankrə'matik/ *adj* said of photographic film: sensitive to light of all colours in the visible spectrum.

pancreas /'pangkri-əs/ *noun* a large compound gland in vertebrates that secretes digestive enzymes into the intestines and the hormones insulin and glucagon into the blood. ➤➤ **pancreatic** /-'atik/ *adj*. [via Latin from Greek *pankreas*, from PAN- + *kreas* flesh, meat]

pancreatic juice /pangkri'atik/ *noun* an alkaline liquid containing digestive enzymes secreted by the pancreas into the duodenum.

pancreatin /pan'kree-ətin, 'pangkri-ətin/ *noun* a digestive medicine containing a mixture of pancreatic enzymes obtained from animals.

pancreatitis /,pangkri-ə'tietəs/ *noun* inflammation of the pancreas.

panda /'pandə/ *noun* **1** a large black-and-white plant-eating mammal of western China resembling a bear but related to the raccoons: *Ailuropoda melanoleuca*. Also called GIANT PANDA. **2** a long-tailed Himalayan flesh-eating mammal resembling the American raccoon and having long chestnut fur spotted with black: *Ailurus fulgens*. Also called RED PANDA. [French *panda*, from the Nepalese name of the red panda]

panda car *noun* *Brit* a small car used by police patrols, *esp* in urban areas. [from its orig having black and white bodywork]

pandanus /pan'daynəs/ *noun* (*pl* **pandanuses**) a tropical tree or shrub with slender stems and swordlike leaves that yield fibre; the screw pine: genus *Pandanus*. [Latin genus name, from Malay *pandan*]

pandect /'pandekt/ *noun* **1** a complete code of the laws of a country or system of law. **2** a treatise covering an entire subject. [late Latin *Pandectes*, sixth-cent. digest of Roman civil law, ultimately from Greek *pandektēs* all-receiving, all-containing, from PAN- + *dekhesthai* to receive]

pandemic[1] /pan'demik/ *adj* said of a disease: occurring over a wide area and affecting an exceptionally high proportion of the population. [via late Latin from Greek *pandēmos* of all the people, from PAN- + *dēmos* the people]

pandemic[2] *noun* an outbreak of a pandemic disease.

pandemonium /pandi'mohni-əm/ *noun* a scene of wild and noisy confusion; a tumult; uproar. [Latin *pandemonium* abode of all demons, hell, from PAN- + Greek *daimōn* evil spirit]

pander[1] /'pandə/ *verb intrans* (**pandered, pandering**) (+ to) to encourage or exploit the weaknesses or vices of others; *esp* to provide gratification for others' desires: *The audience is vulgar and stupid, you've got to pander to them* — Herman Wouk.

pander[2] *noun* **1** *dated* a pimp. **2** *archaic* somebody who panders to another's desires.

Word history
Middle English, named after *Pandarus*, Lycian ally of the Trojans in the Trojan War. He appears in Boccaccio's *Filostrato*, and subsequently in Chaucer's *Troilus and Criseyde* and Shakespeare's *Troilus and Cressida*, as the go-between who seduces Cressida on Troilus' behalf.

pandit /'pundit/ *noun* often used as an honorary title: a wise or learned man in India, *esp* a scholarly expert in Hindu religion and philosophy. [Hindi *paṇḍit* from Sanskrit *paṇḍita*]

P & L *abbr* profit and loss.

P & O *abbr* Peninsular and Oriental (Steamship Company).

Pandora's box /pan'dawrəz/ *noun* a prolific source of troubles.

Word history
from Greek mythology, in which a box or, in an earlier version, a jar containing all the evils of life, and Hope, was given by the gods to Pandora, the first woman. When it was opened the evils escaped into the world and only Hope remained. There is a later version in which the jar contained blessings rather than evils; but the occasional use of *Pandora's box* to mean a storehouse of unfamiliar contents is more probably due to the idea of a cornucopia or the influence of various legends about the opening of mysterious boxes.

p & p *abbr* *Brit* postage and packing.

pane /payn/ *noun* **1** a piece, section, or side of something; *esp* a framed sheet of glass in a window or door. **2** any of the sections into which a sheet of postage stamps is cut for distribution. [Middle English *pan, pane* strip of cloth, pane, via French from Latin *pannus* cloth, rag]

panegyric /pani'jirik/ *noun* a speech or piece of writing in praise of somebody or something: *He concluded with a panegyric upon modern chemistry* — Mary Shelley. ➤➤ **panegyrical** *adj*, **panegyrist** /pani'jirist, -'jie-ərist/ *noun*. [via Latin from Greek *panēgyrikos*, literally 'of or for a festival assembly', from *panēgyris* festival assembly]

panegyrize or **panegyrise** /'panijiriez/ *verb trans archaic* to eulogize (somebody or something).

panel[1] /'panl/ *noun* **1** a separate or distinct part of a surface, e.g.: **a** a thin usu rectangular board set in a frame, e.g. in a door. **b** a usu sunken or raised section of a surface set off by a margin. **c** a flat usu rectangular piece of construction material, e.g. plywood or precast concrete, usu attached to a frame. **d** a thin flat piece of wood on which a picture is painted. **e** a piece of fabric forming a vertical section of or insert in a garment: *a skirt made with eight panels*. **2** a usu vertical mounting for controls or dials, e.g. on the dashboard of a car or aircraft. **3** a flat often insulated support, e.g. for computer machinery or parts of an electrical device, usu with controls on one face. **4a** a group of people selected to render some service, e.g. as a committee of investigation or arbitration. **b** a group of people who discuss topics before an audience, e.g. on television or radio. **c** a group of entertainers or guests who appear as contestants in a quiz or guessing game on radio or television. **5** a list of people summoned for service as jurors. **6** in Scottish law, somebody accused of a crime. **7** *Brit* a list of doctors in a particular area available for consultation by National Health Service patients. [Middle English, in the senses 'piece of cloth', 'slip of parchment', 'list of jurors', via French from Latin *pannus* cloth]

panel[2] *verb trans* (**panelled, panelling**, *NAmer* **paneled, paneling**) to furnish or decorate (e.g. a wall) with panels usu of timber: *a panelled living room*.

panel beater *noun* a person whose job is to repair the metal bodywork of motor vehicles, *esp* by beating out dents.

panelling (*NAmer* **paneling**) *noun* panels joined in a continuous surface; *esp* decorative wood panels joined to line a room.

panellist (*NAmer* **panelist**) *noun* a member of a panel, *esp* a discussion or advisory panel or a radio or television panel.

panel pin *noun* a short slender nail used for woodwork.

panel saw *noun* a fine saw for cutting thin wood.

panettone /pani'tohnay, -ni/ *noun* (*pl* **panettoni** /-ni/) a rich Italian fruitcake, traditionally eaten at Christmas. [Italian *panettone* from *panetto* cake, dimin. of *pane* bread, from Latin *panis*]

pan-fry *verb trans* (**pan-fries, pan-fried, pan-frying**) to fry (food) in a pan in a small amount of oil or fat.

pang /pang/ *noun* **1** a brief piercing spasm of pain. **2** a sharp attack of mental anguish: *pangs of remorse*. [origin unknown]

panga /'panggə/ *noun* a large broad-bladed African knife; a machete. [from Swahili]

pangolin /pang'gohlin/ *noun* any of several species of nocturnal insect-eating Asiatic and African mammals that have a body covered with large overlapping horny scales: genera *Manis* and *Phataginus*. [Malay *peng-guling* from *guling* rolling over; from its habit of rolling itself into a ball]

panhandle[1] *noun* *NAmer* a narrow strip of land projecting from one territory or state into another or between others.

panhandle² *verb intrans NAmer, informal* to beg in the street. ➤ **panhandler** *noun.* [earliest as *panhandler*, prob from the resemblance of the beggar's extended forearm to the handle of a pan]

Panhellenic /panhe'lenik/ *adj* relating to all Greece or all the people of Greece, *esp* in terms of their political cooperation. ➤ **Panhellenism** *noun.*

panic¹ /'panik/ *noun* **1** a sudden overpowering feeling of fear, *esp* a sudden unreasoning terror that spreads rapidly through a group. **2** (*used before a noun*) of or arising from a panic: *a wave of panic buying.* ➤ **panicky** *adj.* [French *panique* panic-stricken, from Greek *panikos*, from *Pan*, the Greek god of the woods, whose sudden appearance was said to cause irrational fear]

panic² *verb* (**panicked, panicking**) ➤ *verb intrans* to be affected with panic: *I panicked when I realized that the door was locked.* ➤ *verb trans* to cause (somebody) to feel panic.

panic attack *noun* a sudden disabling feeling of extreme anxiety or terror.

panic button *noun* an emergency control or signalling device; *esp* one used to activate an alarm or summon help. ✳ **press the panic button** *informal* to panic or to cause other people to react with alarm or an extreme sense of urgency.

panic grass *noun* any of various forage or cereal grasses, e.g. millet: genus *Panicum* and other genera. [Middle English *panik* via French or Latin from Latin *panicum*, from *panus* swelling, ear of millet]

panicle /'panikl/ *noun* **1** a flower head in which the main stem branches and the flowers are borne on short stalks. **2** a loosely branched flower cluster in the shape of a pyramid. ➤ **panicled** *adj.* [Latin *panicula*, dimin. of *panus* swelling]

panic room *noun esp* in the US, a secure room in a house or flat, typically with a steel door and concrete walls, floor, and ceiling, affording special protection against intruders or other dangers.

panic stations *noun Brit, informal* a state of confused anxiety caused by a sudden emergency.

panic-stricken *adj* overcome with panic.

Panjabi /poon'jahbi/ *noun and adj* see PUNJABI.

panjandrum /pan'jandrəm/ *noun humorous* a powerful personage or self-important official. [*Grand Panjandrum*, the burlesque title of an imaginary personage in some nonsense lines by Samuel Foote d.1777, English actor and dramatist]

pannacotta /panə'kotə/ *noun* an orig. Italian dessert of sweetened flavoured cream heated and solidified with gelatin and chilled before serving. [Italian, from *panna* cream + *cotta* cooked]

pannage /'panij/ *noun* the mainly historical right to feed animals, e.g. pigs, in a wood. [Middle English via Old French from late Latin *pastionaticum*, from *pastion-, pastio* feeding, from *pascere* to feed]

panne /pan/ *noun* a silk or rayon velvet with lustrous pile flattened in one direction. [French *panne*, ultimately from Latin *pinna* feather, wing]

pannier /'pani·ə/ *noun* **1** a large basket; *esp* either of a pair carried on the back of an animal. **2** either of a pair of bags or boxes fixed on either side of the rear wheel of a bicycle or motorcycle. **3** a hoop petticoat or looped-up overskirt, formerly worn to give extra width to the sides of a skirt at hip level. [Middle English *panier* via French from Latin *panarium* bread basket, from *panis* bread]

pannikin /'panikin/ *noun Brit* a small metal pan or cup. [PAN¹ + *-nikin* as in *cannikin* a small metal cup, from Dutch *kanneken*, dimin. of *kan* can]

panoply /'panəpli/ *noun* **1** a magnificent or impressive array: *the full panoply of a military funeral.* **2a** a full suit of armour. **b** ceremonial dress. ➤ **panoplied** *adj.* [Greek *panoplia*, from PAN- + *hopla* arms, armour, pl of *hoplon* tool, weapon]

panoptic /pan'optik/ *adj* showing a whole view at a time. [Greek *panoptēs* seeing everything, from PAN- + *optos* visible]

panorama /panə'rahmə/ *noun* **1a** an unobstructed or complete view of a landscape or area. **b** a comprehensive presentation or survey of a series of events. **2a** a large pictorial representation encircling the spectator. **b** a picture exhibited by being unrolled before the spectator. ➤ **panoramic** /-'ramik/ *adj,* **panoramically** /-'ramikli/ *adv.* [PAN- + Greek *horama* sight, from *horan* to see]

pan out *verb intrans* to turn out as specified; *esp* to succeed. [PAN²]

panpipes *pl noun* a wind instrument consisting of a graduated series of short vertical pipes bound together with the mouthpieces

in an even row. [named after *Pan*, Greek god of woods, its legendary inventor]

pansy /'panzi/ *noun* (*pl* **pansies**) **1** a hybrid garden plant derived from wild pansies and violets, with flowers that have rounded velvety petals: *Viola x wittrockiana* or *Viola tricolorhortensis*. **2** *informal, derog* an effeminate man or male homosexual. [early French *pensée*, literally 'thought', fem past part. of *penser* to think, from Latin *pensare* to ponder]

pant¹ /pant/ *verb intrans* **1a** to breathe quickly, spasmodically, or in a laboured manner. **b** to run panting: *I panted along beside the bicycle.* **c** to make a puffing sound. **2** to long eagerly; to yearn: *as pants the hart for cooling streams* —Nahum Tate and Nicholas Brady. **3** to throb or pulsate. ➤ *verb trans* to utter (something) with panting; to gasp (it): *He panted his apologies for arriving so late.* [Middle English *panten* prob from French *pantaisier* to be agitated, ultimately from Greek *phantasioun* to cause to imagine, from *phantasia*: see FANTASY¹]

pant² *noun* **1** a panting breath: *as if this earth in fast thick pants were breathing* — Coleridge. **2** a puffing sound.

pant- or **panto-** *comb. form* forming words, with the meaning: all: *pantisocracy; pantomime.* [early French *pant-* via Latin from Greek, from *pant-, pas* all, every]

pantalettes (*NAmer* **pantalets**) /pantə'lets/ *pl noun* a trouser-like undergarment with a ruffle at the bottom of each leg, worn *esp* by women and children in the early 19th cent. [dimin. of PANTALOONS]

Pantaloon /pantə'loohn/ *noun* a stock character in the commedia dell'arte who is usu a skinny old dotard wearing spectacles, slippers, and a tight-fitting combination of trousers and stockings. [Italian *Pantalone*, prob named after the patron saint of Venice, *San Pantaleone*]

pantaloons *pl noun* **1** loose-fitting trousers worn by women, usu gathered at or above the ankle. **2** tight-fitting trousers formerly worn by men, usu fastened under the instep with straps.

pantechnicon /pan'teknikən/ *noun Brit* a large van, *esp* for transporting household possessions, furniture, etc. [short for *pantechnicon van*, named after the *Pantechnicon*, a building in London established for the sale of works of art but later used as a furniture warehouse, from PAN- + Greek *technikon*, neuter of *technikos* technical, artistic]

pantheism /'panthee·iz(ə)m/ *noun* **1** a doctrine that equates God with the forces and laws of nature. **2a** the worship of all the gods of different religions and cults. **b** toleration of such worship, e.g. at certain periods of the Roman empire. ➤ **pantheist** *noun,* **pantheistic** /-'istik/ *adj,* **pantheistical** /-'istikl/ *adj,* **pantheistically** /-'istikli/ *adv.* [French *panthéisme*, from *panthéiste* pantheist, from English *pantheist*, from PAN- + *-theist* from Greek *theos* god]

pantheon /'panthi·ən/ *noun* **1** the gods of a people collectively, *esp* the officially recognized gods. **2** a building serving as the burial place of or containing memorials to famous dead. **3** a group of illustrious persons. [Middle English *Panteon*, a temple at Rome, via Latin from Greek *pantheion* temple of all the gods, from PAN- + *theos* god]

panther /'panthə/ *noun* (*pl* **panthers** or collectively **panther**) **1** a leopard, *esp* of the black colour phase. **2** *NAmer* = PUMA. [Middle English *pantere* via Old French and Latin from Greek *panthēr*]

pantie girdle *noun* see PANTY GIRDLE.

panties /'pantiz/ *pl noun* pants for women or children; knickers.

pantihose /'pantihohz/ *pl noun* see PANTYHOSE.

pantile /'pantiel/ *noun* a roofing tile whose transverse section is a flattened S-shape. ➤ **pantiled** *adj.* [PAN¹ + TILE¹]

pantisocracy /panti'sokrəsi/ *noun* (*pl* **pantisocracies**) a system of social organization in which all people are equal in rank and rule equally. ➤ **pantisocratic** /-'kratik/ *adj.* [Greek PANT- + *isokratia* equal rule, from *isos* equal + *kratos* power]

panto /'pantoh/ *noun* (*pl* **pantos**) *Brit, informal* = PANTOMIME.

panto- *comb. form* see PANT-.

pantograph /'pantəgrahf, -graf/ *noun* **1** an instrument for copying something, e.g. a map, on a predetermined scale consisting of four light rigid bars jointed in parallelogram form. **2** a collapsible and adjustable framework mounted on an electric vehicle, e.g. a railway locomotive, for collecting current from an overhead wire: compare TROLLEY. ➤ **pantographic** /-'grafik/ *adj.* [French *pantographe*, from PANTO- + *-graphe* -GRAPH]

pantomime /'pantəmiem/ *noun* **1** a British theatrical and musical entertainment of the Christmas season based on a nursery tale with stock roles and topical jokes. **2a** communication of a story by bodily or facial movements, *esp* in drama or dance. **b** a work or performance in which the story is communicated in this way. **3** something absurd or meaningless; a farce. ⟫⟫ **pantomimic** /-'mimik/ *adj*. [Latin *pantomimus*, from PANTO- + *mimus*: see MIME[1]]

pantothenic acid /pantə'thenik/ *noun* a thick oily acid that is a vitamin of the vitamin B complex, is found in all living tissues, and is essential for cell growth: formula $C_9H_{17}NO_5$. [Greek *pantothen* from all sides, from *pant-*, *pas* all; because it is widespread]

pantry /'pantri/ *noun* (*pl* **pantries**) a room or cupboard used for storing provisions or tableware. [Middle English *panetrie* from Old French *panetier* servant in charge of the pantry, from *pan* bread, from Latin *panis*]

pants[1] /pants/ *pl noun* **1** *Brit* an undergarment that covers the crotch and hips and that may extend to the waist and partly down each leg; underpants. **2** *NAmer* trousers. * **bore/scare the pants off somebody** *informal* to bore/scare somebody very much. **by the seat of one's pants** *informal* by instinct and experience rather than by logic or using mechanical aids. **catch somebody with their pants down** *informal* to take somebody by surprise and at a disadvantage. [short for PANTALOONS]

pants[2] *adj Brit*, *informal* of very poor quality or not at all enjoyable; awful; terrible: *The film was pants, but we had a fab meal afterwards.*

pantsuit *or* **pants suit** *noun NAmer* = TROUSER SUIT.

panty girdle *or* **pantie girdle** /'panti/ *noun* a woman's girdle shaped like pants.

pantyhose *or* **pantihose** /'pantihohz/ *pl noun NAmer* = TIGHTS.

panzer /'panzə/ *noun* a tank, *esp* a German tank of World War II. [German *Panzer* coat of mail, armour, from Old French *pancière*, from *pance*, *panche* belly, from Latin *pantex* intestine]

pap[1] /pap/ *noun* **1** soft food for infants or invalids. **2** something, e.g. a novel, lacking solid value or substance. [Middle English, prob via early Low German or early Dutch *pappe* from Latin *pappare* to eat]

pap[2] *noun chiefly dialect* a nipple or teat. [Middle English *pappe*, prob of Scandinavian origin]

papa /pə'pah, 'papə/ *noun informal* an affectionate name for one's father. [French *papa* via late Latin from Greek *pappas* father]

papacy /'paypəsi/ *noun* (*pl* **papacies**) **1** the office of pope. **2** the period of a pope's reign. **3** (**Papacy**) the system of government of the Roman Catholic Church of which the pope is the supreme head. [Middle English *papacie* from late Latin *papa*: see POPE]

papain /pə'pay·in, pə'pie·in/ *noun* an enzyme in the juice of unripe papaya, used to tenderize meat. [PAPAYA + -IN[1]]

papal /'paypl/ *adj* relating to a pope or the Papacy. ⟫⟫ **papally** *adv*. [Middle English via French from late Latin *papa*: see POPE]

paparazzo /papə'ratsoh/ *noun* (*pl* **paparazzi** /-si/) a freelance photographer who specializes in taking sensational or newsworthy photographs of famous people. [Italian *paparazzo*, named after a character in the film *La Dolce Vita* by Federico Fellini]

papaveraceous /pə,payvə'rayshəs, pə,pav-/ *adj* relating to plants of the poppy family. [Latin family name *Papaveraceae*, from *papaver* POPPY]

papaverine /pə'payvəreen, pə'pav-, -rin/ *noun* a drug obtained from opium that causes the relaxation of smooth muscle, e.g. of the gut and blood vessels, and is thus used to treat certain types of colic and to relieve spasm in blood vessels, e.g. in the brain. [Latin *papaver* POPPY + -INE[2]]

papaw /pə'paw/ *noun* see PAWPAW.

papaya /pə'pie·ə/ *noun* **1** a large edible tropical fruit that is roughly oval in shape and has a yellow skin, orange flesh, and a central cavity filled with round black seeds. **2** the tropical American tree that bears this fruit: *Carica papaya*. [Spanish *papaya* from Carib or Arawak]

paper[1] /'paypə/ *noun* **1** a material for writing, drawing, printing on, etc made from compacted vegetable fibres, e.g. wood or cloth, in the form of thin sheets. **2a** (*also in pl*) a piece of paper containing a written or printed statement; a document: *naturalization papers.* **b** (*in pl*) documents carried as proof of identity or status. **c** (*in pl*) official documents relating to the cargo, ownership, etc of a ship. **d** (*in pl*) an individual's personal documents and records, miscellaneous writings, diaries, etc: *The manuscript was found among his papers after his death.* **3** = NEWSPAPER. **4a** a formal written composition, e.g. one designed for publication or intended to be read aloud. **b** a government report or discussion document. **5a** a set of questions to be answered during a single examination. **b** a set of answers to examination questions written by a candidate. **6** a paper container or wrapper. **7** = WALLPAPER[1]. **8** *informal* a ticket; *esp* a free pass to a theatrical performance. **9** (*used before a noun*) existing only in theory; nominal. * **on paper 1** in writing. **2** in theory; hypothetically: *They are the better team on paper.* [Middle English *papir* via French and Latin from Greek *papyros* PAPYRUS]

paper[2] *verb trans* (**papered**, **papering**) **1** to cover or line (something) with paper; *esp* to apply wallpaper to (a wall). **2** *informal* to give out free tickets for (a performance): *They had to paper the theatre for the opening night.* ⟫⟫ **paperer** *noun*.

paperback *noun* a book with a flexible paper binding: compare HARDBACK.

paperbark *noun* an Australian tree with papery bark: genus *Melaleuca*.

paperboy *noun* a boy who delivers newspapers.

paper chase *noun* a type of cross-country race in which some of the runners scatter bits of paper as a trail which others follow to find and catch them.

paper clip *noun* a small clip made from two loops of wire, used for holding sheets of paper together.

papergirl *noun* a girl who delivers newspapers.

paperhanger *noun* somebody who wallpapers walls, *esp* professionally.

paperknife *noun* (*pl* **paperknives**) a blunt ornamental knife for slitting envelopes or uncut pages.

paperless *adj* using computers rather than paper to communicate and store information: *the paperless office of the future.*

paper money *noun* bank notes.

paper mulberry *noun* an Asian variety of mulberry, the bark of which was formerly used in papermaking, *esp* in Japan: *Broussonetia papyrifera.*

paper nautilus *noun* a mollusc related to the octopuses and squids, the female of which lays its eggs in a delicate papery shell: genus *Argonauta.*

paper over *verb trans* **1** to gloss over, explain away, or patch up (e.g. major differences), *esp* in order to maintain a semblance of unity. **2** to hide or conceal (e.g. a crack) with wallpaper.

paper tape *noun* a ribbon of paper with a pattern of holes punched in it to represent information or instructions, formerly used in a computer, telex machine, etc.

paper-thin *adj* extremely thin or insubstantial.

paper tiger *noun* a person, power, etc, represented as strong or threatening, but actually ineffectual: *That was only the first occasion that Chairman Khrushchev reminded Chairman Mao that the paper tiger had nuclear teeth* — Peter Lewis. [translation of a Chinese phrase used by Mao Zedong d.1976, Chinese political leader]

paperweight *noun* a usu small heavy object used to hold down loose papers on a desk.

paperwork *noun* routine clerical or record-keeping work, often incidental to a more important task.

papery *adj* resembling paper in thinness or consistency: *papery leaves.*

papier-mâché /,papyay 'mashay, ,paypə/ *noun* a light strong moulding material made of paper pulped with glue, used for making boxes, trays, etc. [French *papier mâché*, literally 'chewed paper']

papilla /pə'pilə/ *noun* (*pl* **papillae** /-lee/) **1** a small projecting nipple-shaped body part. **2** a piece of connective tissue extending into and nourishing the root of a hair, feather, etc. ⟫⟫ **papillary** *adj*, **papillate** /'papilayt/ *adj*, **papillose** /'papilohs/ *adj*. [Latin *papilla* nipple]

papilloma /papi'lohmə/ *noun* (*pl* **papillomas** *or* **papillomata** /-tə/) a benign tumour, e.g. a wart, produced by an overgrowth of epithelial tissue. [PAPILLA + -OMA]

papillon /'papilon/ *noun* a dog of a breed of small slender toy spaniels with large butterfly-shaped ears. [French *papillon* butterfly, from Latin *papilion-*, *papilio*]

papist or **Papist** /'paypist/ noun (often **Papist**) derog = ROMAN CATHOLIC[1]. ▶▶ **papism** noun, **papist** adj, **papistry** /-stri/ noun. [early French papiste from late Latin papa: see POPE]

papoose /pə'poohs/ noun **1** a young Native American child. **2** a bag worn on the back, used for carrying a baby. [Algonquian papoòs]

pappus /'papəs/ noun (pl **pappi** /'papie/) a tuft of usu hairy appendages crowning the ovary or fruit in various plants, e.g. the dandelion. ▶▶ **pappose** /'papohs/ adj. [via Latin from Greek pappos old man, old man's beard]

paprika /'paprikə, pə'preekə/ noun a mild to hot red condiment consisting of the finely ground dried pods of any of various cultivated sweet peppers: compare CAYENNE PEPPER, CHILLI. [Hungarian paprika via Serbian from Greek peperi]

Pap smear /pap/ noun a method for the early detection of cancer in which cells, e.g. from mucous membrane in the cervix, are scraped off and examined under the microscope. [named after George N Papanicolaou d.1962, US medical scientist]

Pap test noun = PAP SMEAR.

Papuan /'papyooən/ noun **1** a native or inhabitant of Papua or Papua New Guinea in the W Pacific. **2** any of a mixed group of languages of New Guinea and nearby islands. ▶▶ **Papuan** adj.

papule /'papyoohl/ or **papula** /-lə/ noun (pl **papules** or **papulae** /-lee/) a small solid usu conical projection from the skin. ▶▶ **papular** adj. [Latin papula pustule]

papyri /pə'pie·ərie/ noun pl of PAPYRUS.

papyrology /papi'roləji/ noun the study of ancient papyrus manuscripts. ▶▶ **papyrologist** noun. [PAPYRUS + -LOGY]

papyrus /pə'pie·ərəs/ noun (pl **papyruses** or **papyri** /-rie/) **1** a tall sedge of the Nile valley: Cyperus papyrus. **2** the pith of the papyrus plant, esp when made into a material for writing on. **3** a usu ancient manuscript written on papyrus. [Middle English via Latin from Greek papyros]

par[1] /pah/ noun **1** in golf, the standard score of a good player for each hole of a golf course, or a score equal to this. **2a** an amount taken as an average or norm. **b** an accepted standard; specif a usual standard of physical condition or health. **3a** the established value of the monetary unit of one country expressed in terms of the monetary unit of another country. **b** the money value assigned to each share of stock in the charter of a company. ✳ **on a par with** equal to. **par for the course** what is to be expected in a particular situation. [Latin par one that is equal, from par equal]

par[2] verb trans (**parred, parring**) to score par on (a hole in golf).

par. abbr paragraph.

par- prefix see PARA-[1].

para[1] /'parə/ noun (pl **paras**) informal **1** a paratrooper. **2** = PARAGRAPH[1].

para[2] /'pahrə/ noun (pl **paras** or **para**) a unit of currency in parts of Yugoslavia, worth 100th of a dinar. [Turkish para from Persian pārah piece]

para-[1] or **par-** prefix forming words, with the meanings: **1a** beside or alongside: parathyroid; parallel. **b** beyond: paranormal; paradox. **2** in chemistry, involving substitution at two opposite positions in the benzene ring that are separated by two carbon atoms: compare META-, ORTH-: paradichlorobenzene. **3a** associated in a subsidiary or auxiliary capacity: paramedical. **b** closely resembling or related to: paratyphoid. [Middle English via French and Latin from Greek, from para beside, beyond]

para-[2] comb. form forming words, denoting: an object that protects: parasol.

parabasis /pə'rabəsis/ noun (pl **parabases** /-seez/) an address to the audience by the chorus in a classical Greek comedy. [Greek parabasis from parabainein to go aside, step forward]

parabiosis /,parəbie'ohsis/ noun the anatomical and physiological union of two organisms, e.g. Siamese twins, or an artificial union produced as an experiment. ▶▶ **parabiotic** /-'otik/ adj. [Latin parabiosis, from PARA-[1] + -BIOSIS]

parable /'parəbl/ noun a usu short story illustrating a moral or religious principle. [Middle English via French and late Latin parabola comparison, speech, parabola, from Greek parabolē setting alongside, from paraballein to compare, from PARA-[1] + ballein to throw]

parabola /pə'rabələ/ noun a symmetrical curve of the kind generated when a cone is intersected by a plane parallel to its side:

compare ELLIPSE, HYPERBOLA. [via late Latin from Greek parabolē: see PARABLE]

parabolic /parə'bolik/ adj **1** of or having the form of a parabola: motion in a parabolic curve. **2** expressed by or being a parable. ▶▶ **parabolical** adj, **parabolically** adv.

paraboloid /pə'rabəloyd/ noun a surface some plane sections of which are parabolas: compare ELLIPSOID, HYPERBOLOID. ▶▶ **paraboloidal** /-'loydl/ adj.

paracetamol /parə'seetəmol, -'setəmol/ noun a chemical compound that is widely used as a painkiller and in the synthesis of other chemical compounds. [contraction of para-acetamidophenol]

parachronism /pə'rakrəniz(ə)m/ noun an error in dating something, esp assigning something to a date later than the correct one.

parachute[1] /'parəshooht/ noun a folding expanse of light fabric attached by lines to a harness, that opens out into an umbrella shape to ensure a safe descent of a person or object through the air from a great height, e.g. from an aeroplane. ▶▶ **parachutist** noun. [French parachute, from PARA-[2] + chute fall]

parachute[2] verb intrans to descend by means of a parachute. ▶ verb trans to drop (e.g. supplies) by parachute.

Paraclete /'parəkleet/ noun = HOLY SPIRIT. [Middle English Paraclit via French and late Latin from Greek Paraklētos, literally 'advocate', from parakalein to call to one's side, from PARA-[1] + kalein to call]

parade[1] /pə'rayd/ noun **1** a public procession. **2** a formal assembly or march past by a body of troops before a superior officer. **3** a succession of things or people on display. **4** an ostentatious display or demonstration of something: He made a parade of his superior knowledge. **5** chiefly Brit a row of shops. **6** a place for strolling; a promenade. [French parade from Spanish parada display, ultimately from Latin parare to prepare]

parade[2] verb intrans **1** to march in a procession. **2** to walk up and down, esp in a vain, grand, or eye-catching manner. **3** (+ as) = MASQUERADE[2] (2): myths which parade as modern science. ▶ verb trans **1** to cause (people or vehicles) to manoeuvre or march. **2** to exhibit (something) ostentatiously: Wrestling … superstars of the European Rampage Again Tour paraded their machismo before a frenzied audience at Wembley Arena — Daily Telegraph. ▶▶ **parader** noun.

paradiddle /'parədid(ə)l/ noun a pattern in drumming, consisting of four beats played with alternate sticks, either left, right, left, left, or right, left, right, right. [imitative]

paradigm /'parədiem/ noun **1** an example or pattern, esp an outstandingly clear or typical example. **2** in grammar, an example of a conjugation or declension showing a word in all its inflectional forms. **3** a model used in science as a framework for ideas. ▶▶ **paradigmatic** /-dig'matik/ adj. [via late Latin from Greek paradeigma, from paradeiknynai to show side by side, from PARA-[1] + deiknynai to show]

paradise /'parədies/ noun **1a** (often **Paradise**) = HEAVEN. **b** (often **Paradise**) the place or state of perfect happiness enjoyed by Adam and Eve before the first sin; the Garden of Eden. **2** an intermediate place or state where the righteous dead await resurrection and judgment; limbo. **3** an idyllic place or state. ▶▶ **paradisaical** /-di'sayəkl/ adj, **paradisal** adj, **paradisiacal** /-di'sie·əkl/ adj, **paradisical** /-'dizikl/ adj. [Middle English paradis via Old French paradis and late Latin paradisus from Greek paradeisos enclosed park, of Iranian origin]

parados /'parədos/ noun a bank of earth behind a fortified place or trench. [French parados, from PARA-[2] + dos back, from Latin dorsum]

paradox /'parədoks/ noun **1a** a statement that is apparently contradictory or absurd and yet might be true. **b** a self-contradictory statement that at first seems true. **2** something, e.g. a person, condition, or act, with seemingly contradictory qualities or phases. **3** a tenet contrary to received opinion. ▶▶ **paradoxical** /-'doksikl/ adj, **paradoxically** /-'doksikli/ adv. [via Latin from Greek paradoxon, neuter of paradoxos contrary to expectation, from PARA-[1] + doxa opinion]

paradoxical sleep noun a state of sleep in which the pattern of brain waves is similar to that of a waking state, and which is characterized by dreaming, rapid eye movements, and vascular congestion of the sex organs. Also called REM SLEEP.

paraesthesia (*NAmer* **paresthesia**) /paris'theezyə, -zh(y)ə/ *noun* a sensation of prickling or tingling on the skin with no physical cause. [Latin *paraesthesia*, from PARA-¹ + AESTHESIA]

paraffin /'parəfin/ *noun* **1** a usu waxy inflammable mixture of hydrocarbons obtained from distillates of wood, coal, petroleum, etc and used chiefly in candles, chemical synthesis, and cosmetics. **2** *Brit* an inflammable liquid hydrocarbon obtained by distillation of petroleum and used *esp* as a fuel. **3** *no longer in technical use* = ALKANE. [German *Paraffin* from Latin *parum* too little + *affinis* related; because it does not easily form compounds with other substances]

paragliding /'parəglieding/ *noun* the sport of travelling through the air by means of a specially-designed rectangular parachute after being released at a height, e.g. from a aeroplane. ⨠ **paraglider** *noun*.

paragon /'parəgən/ *noun* a model of excellence, or a perfect pattern of a particular quality: *He had within himself a fund of common sense to draw upon, so that to espouse a paragon of wisdom would be but to carry water to the fountain* — Henry James. [early French *paragon* from Old Italian *paragone* touchstone, from *paragonare* to test on a touchstone, from Greek *parakonan*, literally 'to sharpen against', hence 'to compare']

paragraph¹ /'parəgrahf, -graf/ *noun* **1a** a usu indented division of a written composition that develops a single point or idea. **b** a composition or news item that is complete in one paragraph. **2** a sign, e.g. (¶), used as a reference mark or to indicate the beginning of a paragraph. ⨠ **paragraphic** /-'grafik/ *adj*. [via French and late Latin from Greek *paragraphos* line used to mark change of persons in a dialogue, from *paragraphein* to write alongside, from PARA-¹ + *graphein* to write]

paragraph² *verb trans* to divide (a piece of writing) into paragraphs.

Paraguayan /'parəgwie-ən/ *noun* a native or inhabitant of Paraguay in S America. ⨠ **Paraguayan** *adj*.

parakeet *or* **parrakeet** /'parəkeet/ *noun* a small slender long-tailed parrot: subfamily Psittacinae. [Spanish *periquito*, Italian *parrochetto* or early French *perroquet* PARROT¹]

paraldehyde /pə'raldihied/ *noun* a synthetic drug used as a sedative and hypnotic to control convulsions.

paralipsis /parə'lipsis/ *noun* a rhetorical device in which the speaker uses a formula, e.g. 'not to mention . . .' or 'to say nothing of . . .', that, taken literally, suggests that something is not going to be spoken of, but in fact gives it greater emphasis. [via late Latin from Greek *paraleipsis* omission, from *paraleipein* to leave out, from PARA-¹ + *leipein* to leave]

parallax /'parəlaks/ *noun* **1** the apparent displacement or the difference in apparent direction of an object as seen from two different points not on the same straight line. **2** in astronomy, the difference in direction of a planet, star, or other celestial body as measured from two points on the earth or on the earth's orbit round the sun. ⨠ **parallactic** /-'laktik/ *adj*. [early French *parallaxe* from Greek *parallaxis*, from *parallassein* to change, alternate, ultimately from PARA-¹ + *allos* other]

parallel¹ /'parəlel/ *adj* **1a** extending in the same direction and always being the same distance apart: *parallel rows of trees*. **b** everywhere equally distant: *Concentric spheres are parallel*. **2** in computing, processing a number of items of data simultaneously. **3** of or being an electrical circuit having a number of conductors in parallel. **4a** analogous or comparable. **b** said of phrases, sentences, etc: having identical types of word in corresponding positions. **c** said of musical keys: having the same first note. **d** said of two or more melodies or musical parts: keeping the same distance apart in musical pitch. [via Latin from Greek *parallēlos* beside another, from PARA-¹ + *allēlōs* one another]

parallel² *noun* **1** somebody or something equal or similar in all essential particulars; a counterpart. **2** a comparison to show resemblance: *She drew a parallel between the two states*. **3a** a parallel line, curve, or surface. **b** a line on a map or globe representing any of the imaginary circles on the surface of the earth that are parallel to the equator. **c** in printing, a sign ‖ used as a reference mark. **4** a method of connecting two or more electric components or circuits to a power source in which each is separately connected to both terminals of the source and receives the same voltage.

parallel³ *verb trans* (**paralleled, paralleling**) **1** to run parallel to (something else). **2a** to equal or match (something): *No one has paralleled my success in business*. **b** to follow a similar course to (something); to correspond to (it): *Her career paralleled mine*.

parallel bars *pl noun* a pair of bars supported horizontally 1.7m (5ft 7in.) above the floor usu by a common base, used in a gymnastic event.

parallelepiped /,parəleli'pieped, ,parəle'lepiped/ *noun* a polyhedron with faces that are parallelograms. [Greek *parallēlepipedon*, from *parallēlos* (see PARALLEL¹) + *epipedon* plane surface]

parallel import *noun* an imported item, often a pharmaceutical product brought in by an unlicensed dealer, that undercuts the price of a locally manufactured article.

parallelism *noun* **1** the quality or state of being parallel. **2** a resemblance or correspondence.

parallelogram /parə'leləgram/ *noun* a quadrilateral with opposite sides parallel and equal. [via late Latin from Greek *parallēlogrammon*, neuter of *parallēlogrammos* bounded by parallel lines, from *parallēlos* (see PARALLEL¹) + *grammē* line]

parallel processing *noun* the processing by a computer of a number of items of data simultaneously.

parallel ruler *noun* an instrument for drawing parallel lines, consisting of two connected movable straight edges.

paralogism /pə'raləjiz(ə)m/ *noun* in logic, an unintentionally false argument. ⨠ **paralogist** *noun*. [early French *paralogisme* via late Latin from Greek *paralogismos*, from *paralogos* unreasonable, from PARA-¹ + *logos* reason]

Paralympics /parə'limpiks/ *pl noun* (*treated as sing. or pl*) an international sports contest for disabled athletes, organized like the Olympic Games. ⨠ **Paralympic** *adj*. [blend of *paraplegic* (see PARAPLEGIA) and OLYMPICS]

paralyse (*NAmer* **paralyze**) /'parəliez/ *verb trans* **1** to affect (somebody or a body part) with paralysis. **2** to make (somebody or something) powerless or ineffective. **3** to make (somebody or something) immobile; to transfix (them). [French *paralyser*, back-formation from *paralysie* paralysis, from Latin: see PARALYSIS]

paralysis /pə'raləsis/ *noun* (*pl* **paralyses** /-seez/) **1** loss or partial loss of function, *esp* when involving motion or sensation in a part of the body. **2** loss of the ability to move. **3** a state of powerlessness or incapacity to act. [via Latin from Greek *paralysis*, from *paralyein* to disable, from PARA-¹ + *lyein* to loosen]

paralytic¹ /parə'litik/ *adj* **1** of, resembling, or affected with paralysis. **2** *chiefly Brit, informal* very drunk. ⨠ **paralytically** *adv*.

paralytic² *noun* a person suffering from paralysis.

paralyze /'parəliez/ *verb trans NAmer* see PARALYSE.

paramagnetic /,parəmag'netik/ *adj* denoting or relating to a substance that in a magnetic field is slightly attracted towards points of higher field intensity. ⨠ **paramagnetism** /-'magnətiz(ə)m/ *noun*.

paramatta /parə'matə/ *noun* see PARRAMATTA.

paramecium /parə'meesi-əm/ *noun* (*pl* **paramecia** /-si-ə/ *or* **parameciums**) a single-celled animal that has an elongated body covered with CILIA (hairlike projections) and an oblique funnel-shaped groove bearing the mouth at the tip: genus *Paramecium*. [Latin genus name, from Greek *paramēkēs* oval]

paramedic /parə'medik/ *noun* **1** a person, e.g. a member of an ambulance crew, who is trained to carry out emergency medical procedures. **2** a person whose job supports the job of doctors in a hospital, e.g. a laboratory technician. ⨠ **paramedical** *adj*.

parameter /pə'ramitə/ *noun* **1** an arbitrary constant whose value characterizes a member of a system, e.g. a family of curves. **2** a quantity, e.g. a mean or variance, that describes a statistical population. **3** any of a set of physical properties whose values determine the characteristics or behaviour of something. **4** *informal* a factor or characteristic, *esp* a limiting one: *We must work within the parameters of time and budget*. ⨠ **parametric** /parə'metrik/ *adj*, **parametrically** /parə'metrikli/ *adv*. [Latin *parameter*, from PARA-¹ + Greek *metron* measure]

paramilitary¹ /parə'milit(ə)ri/ *adj* formed on a military pattern, *esp* as a potential auxiliary military force: *a paramilitary border patrol*.

paramilitary² *noun* (*pl* **paramilitaries**) a member of a paramilitary force.

paramnesia /parəm'neezi·ə/ *noun* a disorder of the memory involving the recall of events that did not in fact take place, e.g. déjà vu. [Latin *paramnesia*, from PARA-¹ + *-mnesia* as in AMNESIA]

paramount /'parəmownt/ *adj* superior to all others; supreme. ⏩ **paramountcy** /-si/ *noun*. [Anglo-French *paramont*, from Old French *par* by + *amont* above]

paramour /'parəmooə/ *noun archaic* an illicit lover; *esp* a mistress. [Middle English, from *par amour* by way of love, from Old French]

parang /'parang/ *noun* a heavy Malaysian or Indonesian knife. [Malay *parang*]

paranoia /parə'noyə/ *noun* **1** a mental disorder characterized by delusions of persecution or grandeur. **2** a tendency towards excessive or irrational suspiciousness and distrustfulness of others. ⏩ **paranoiac** /-ak/ *adj and noun*, **paranoid** /'parənoyd/ *adj and noun*. [via Latin from Greek *paranoia* madness, from *paranous* demented, from PARA-¹ + *nous* mind]

paranormal /parə'nawml/ *adj* not scientifically explainable; supernatural.

Editorial note

Paranormal phenomena consist of psychokinesis or PK (effects of mind on matter), and three types of extrasensory perception or ESP — telepathy (mind-to-mind communication), clairvoyance (acquisition of information from a distant object or event), and precognition (seeing into the future). They are inexplicable on any generally accepted scientific theory, and their existence, if proven, would overthrow fundamental principles of physics — Dr Susan Blackmore.

⏩ **paranormally** *adv*.

parapenting /'parəpenting/ *noun* the sport of paragliding down the side of a mountain from a high point. ⏩ **parapenter** *noun*. [French *parapente*, from PARACHUTE¹ + *pente* slope]

parapet /'parəpit, -pet/ *noun* **1** a wall, rampart, or mound of earth or stone to protect soldiers. **2** a low wall or balustrade to protect the edge of a platform, roof, or bridge. ⏩ **parapeted** *adj*. [Italian *parapetto*, from *parare* to shield + *petto* chest]

paraph /'paraf/ *noun* a flourish at the end of a signature, orig executed as an anti-forgery device. [early French *paraph* from Latin *paragraphus*: see PARAGRAPH¹]

paraphernalia /,parəfə'nayli·ə/ *noun* (*treated as sing. or pl*) all the trappings and impedimenta associated with any particular pursuit or production. [late Latin *paraphernalia* personal belongings of a married woman, from Greek *parapherna*, from PARA-¹ + *phernē* dowry]

paraphrase¹ /'parəfrayz/ *noun* a restatement of a text, passage, or work giving the meaning in another form. [early French *paraphrase* via Latin from Greek *paraphrasis*, from *paraphrazein* to paraphrase, from PARA-¹ + *phrazein* to tell]

paraphrase² *verb trans* to make a paraphrase of (e.g. a text). ⏩ **paraphrasable** *adj*.

paraphrastic /parə'frastik/ *adj* explaining or translating more clearly and amply; having the nature of a paraphrase. ⏩ **paraphrastically** *adv*.

paraplegia /parə'pleejə/ *noun* paralysis of the lower half of the body including the legs, usually resulting from injury or disease: compare HEMIPLEGIA, QUADRIPLEGIA. ⏩ **paraplegic** /-jik/ *adj and noun*. [via Latin from Greek *paraplēgiē* hemiplegia, from PARA-¹ + *plēgiē* -PLEGIA]

parapsychology /,parəsie'kolaji/ *noun* the investigation of evidence for the occurrence of psychic phenomena, e.g. telepathy and clairvoyance.

Editorial note

Parapsychology was established as an academic discipline in the 1930s by J B and Louisa Rhine, who also coined the term 'extrasensory perception' (ESP) and devised laboratory techniques for investigating paranormal phenomena. Parapsychologists use scientific methods and statistical techniques, but their claims to have demonstrated ESP and PK (effects of mind on matter) remain controversial and are not accepted by most scientists — Dr Susan Blackmore.

⏩ **parapsychological** /-'lojikl/ *adj*, **parapsychologist** *noun*.

paraquat /'parəkwot, -kwat/ *noun* a very poisonous herbicide used as a weedkiller. [PARA-¹ + QUATERNARY¹]

parasail¹ /'parəsayl/ *verb intrans* to take part in the sport of parasailing.

parasail² *noun* a parachute used in the sport of parasailing.

parasailing *noun* the sport of rising into the air and parachuting down while wearing a specially modified parachute and being towed by a motor boat.

parascend /'parəsend/ *verb intrans* to take part in the sport of parascending. [back-formation from PARASCENDING]

parascending *noun* the sport of rising into the air and parachuting down while wearing a specially modified parachute and being towed by a motor vehicle or a boat. ⏩ **parascender** *noun*. [PARA-² + *ascending*, present part. of ASCEND]

paraselene /,parəse'leeni/ *noun* (*pl* **paraselenae** /-nee, -nie/) a bright spot seen on circles of light surrounding the moon. ⏩ **paraselenic** /-'lenik/ *adj*. [Latin *paraselene*, from PARA-¹ + Greek *selēnē* moon]

parasite /'parəsiet/ *noun* **1** an organism living in or on another organism and drawing its nourishment directly from it, often harming it in the process. **2** a person who depends on somebody else for existence or support without making a useful or adequate return. ⏩ **parasitic** /-'sitik/ *adj*, **parasitical** /-'sitikl/ *adj*, **parasitically** /-'sitikli/ *adv*. [early French *parasite* via Latin from Greek *parasitos*, from PARA-¹ + *sitos* grain, food]

parasitise /'parəsitiez, -sietiez/ *verb trans* see PARASITIZE.

parasitism /'parəsitiz(ə)m/ *noun* an intimate association between organisms of two or more kinds in which a parasite benefits at the expense of a host.

parasitize *or* **parasitise** /'parəsitiez, -sietiez/ *verb trans* to infest or live on or with (an organism) as a parasite. ⏩ **parasitization** /-'zaysh(ə)n/ *noun*.

parasitoid /'parəsitoyd, -sietoyd/ *noun* an insect, *esp* a wasp, that develops within the body of e.g. another insect and eventually kills it.

parasitology /,parəsi'tolaji, -sie'tolaji/ *noun* a branch of biology dealing with parasites and parasitism, *esp* among animals. ⏩ **parasitologist** *noun*.

parasol /'parəsol/ *noun* a lightweight umbrella used as a protection from the sun. [French *parasol* from Old Italian *parasole*, from *parare* to shield + *sole* sun, from Latin *sol*]

parasuicide /parə'sooh·isied/ *noun* an attempt to cause harm to oneself, e.g. by taking an overdose, but not actually to kill oneself.

parasympathetic /,parəsimpə'thetik/ *adj* denoting or relating to the part of the autonomic nervous system that contains nerves that induce secretion, increase the tone and contractility of smooth muscle, and cause the dilation of blood vessels.

parasynthesis /parə'sinthəsis/ *noun* in linguistics, the formation of words by adding a prefix, suffix, etc to a compound, e.g. *brown-haired* from *brown hair* + *-ed*. ⏩ **parasynthetic** /-'thetik/ *adj*.

paratha /pə'rahtə/ *noun* a flat type of Indian unleavened bread. [Hindi *parāthā*]

parathion /parə'thieon/ *noun* a very poisonous insecticide used in farming. [PARA-¹ + THIO- + PHOSPHATE + -ON¹]

parathyroid /parə'thieroyd/ *noun* any of four small endocrine glands near the thyroid gland that produce a hormone.

paratroops /'parətroohps/ *pl noun* troops trained and equipped to parachute into combat areas from an aeroplane. ⏩ **paratrooper** *noun*.

paratyphoid /parə'tiefoyd/ *noun* a disease caused by salmonella, which resembles typhoid fever and is commonly contracted by eating contaminated food.

paravane /'parəvayn/ *noun* a torpedo-shaped device towed underwater by a ship to sever the moorings of mines. [PARA-² + VANE]

par avion /pah(r) a'vyon (*French* par avyɔ̃)/ *adv* used on mail: by airmail. [French *par avion* by aeroplane]

parboil /'pahboyl/ *verb trans* to boil (e.g. vegetables) briefly as a preliminary or incomplete cooking procedure. [Middle English *parboilen* to parboil, also 'to boil thoroughly', via French and late Latin from Latin PER- + *bullire* to boil]

parbuckle¹ /'pahbukl/ *noun* a sling of rope fastened overhead that is used for hoisting or lowering a cylindrical object, e.g. a cask. [origin unknown]

parbuckle² *verb trans* to raise or lower (something) by means of a parbuckle.

parcel¹ /'pahsl/ *noun* **1** an object or objects wrapped in brown paper or other material, *esp* for sending by post. **2** a plot of land. **3** a collection or group of people, animals, or things; a lot: *The whole* *story was a parcel of lies.* [Middle English via French from Latin *particula*: see PARTICLE]

parcel[2] *verb trans* (**parcelled, parcelling**, *NAmer* **parceled, parceling**) **1** (*often* + up) to make (something) up into a parcel; to wrap (it). **2** (+ out) to divide (something) into parts; to distribute (it). **3** to cover (e.g. a rope) with strips of canvas.

parch /pahch/ *verb trans* **1** to make (e.g. land) dry or scorched. **2** to roast (e.g. peas) slightly in a dry heat. ➤ *verb intrans* to become dry or scorched. [Middle English *parchen*; earlier history unknown]

parched *adj* **1** *informal* said of a person: extremely thirsty. **2** said of land: dry because of lack of rainfall.

parchment *noun* **1** the skin of an animal, *esp* of a sheep or goat, prepared as material for writing on. **2** strong paper made to resemble parchment. **3** a parchment manuscript. [Middle English *parchemin* via Old French and Latin from Greek *pergamēnē*, fem of *Pergamēnos, Pergamum*, an ancient city in Asia Minor]

pard /pahd/ *noun archaic or literary* a leopard: *not charioted by Bacchus and his pards, but on the viewless wings of poesy* — Keats. [Middle English *parde* via Old French and Latin from Greek *pardos*]

pardon[1] /'pahdn/ *noun* **1** excuse or forgiveness for a fault, offence, or discourtesy. **2** a release from legal penalties. **3** in the Christian Church, formerly, an indulgence.

pardon[2] *verb trans* (**pardoned, pardoning**) **1** to absolve (somebody) from the consequences of a fault or crime. **2** to allow (an offence) to pass without punishment. ✳ **pardon/excuse my French** see FRENCH[2]. **pardon me** used in courteous denial or apology: *Pardon me, I didn't quite catch what you said.* ➤ **pardonable** *adj*, **pardonably** *adv*. [Middle English *pardonen* via French from late Latin *perdonare* to grant freely, from PER- + Latin *donare* to give]

pardoner *noun* a medieval preacher delegated to raise money by granting indulgences.

pare /peə/ *verb trans* **1a** to cut or shave off the outer surface of (something); to peel (it). **b** to trim off the outer edges of (*esp* the nails): *Let not him that plays the lion pare his nails, for they shall hang out for the lion's claws* — Shakespeare. **2** (*often* + down/away) to diminish (something) gradually as if by paring: *We managed to pare the costs right down.* ➤➤ **parer** *noun*. [Middle English *paren* via French from Latin *parare* to prepare, acquire]

paregoric /pari'gorik/ *noun* a camphorated tincture of opium, formerly used to relieve pain and coughing. [French *parégorique* relieving pain, via late Latin from Greek *parēgorikos*, from *parēgorein* to talk over, soothe, from PARA-[1] + *agoreuein* to speak]

parenchyma /pə'rengkimə/ *noun* **1** a fleshy tissue of the leaves, fruits, stems, etc of higher plants that consists of thin-walled living cells: compare COLLENCHYMA, SCLERENCHYMA. **2** the essential and distinctive tissue of an organ or an abnormal growth, as distinguished from its supportive framework. ➤➤ **parenchymatous** /parən'kiemətəs, -'kimətəs/ *adj*. [via Latin from Greek *parenchyma* visceral flesh, from *parenchein* to pour in beside, from PARA-[1] + *chein* to pour]

parent[1] /'peərənt/ *noun* **1** a father or mother. **2** an animal or plant regarded in relation to its offspring. **3** the material or source from which something is derived. **4** *archaic* an ancestor. ➤➤ **parental** /pə'rentl/ *adj*, **parentally** /pə'ren-/ *adv*, **parenthood** *noun*. [Middle English via French from Latin *parent-, parens*, present part. of *parere* to give birth to]

parent[2] *verb trans* to be or act as the parent of (a child).

parentage /'peərəntij/ *noun* descent from parents or ancestors; lineage: *a woman of noble parentage.*

parent company *noun* a company that owns other subsidiary companies.

parenteral /pa'rentərəl/ *adj* **1** situated or occurring outside the intestine. **2** said of a drug: introduced into the body other than through the intestines, e.g. by injection. ➤➤ **parenterally** *adv*. [PARA-[1] + Greek *enteron* intestine]

parenthesis /pə'renthəsis/ *noun* (*pl* **parentheses** /-seez/) **1a** an amplifying or explanatory word or phrase inserted in a passage and set off, in writing, by punctuation. **b** either or both of the curved marks (or) used in writing and printing to enclose a parenthesis or to group a symbolic unit in a logical or mathematical expression. Also called BRACKET[1] (1A). **2** an interlude or interval. ➤➤ **parenthetic** /parən'thetik/ *adj*, **parenthetical** /parən'thetikl/ *adj*, **parenthetically** /parən'thetikli/ *adv*. [via late Latin from Greek *parenthesis*, from *parentithenai* to insert, from PARA-[1] + *tithenai* to place]

parenthesize *or* **parenthesise** /pə'renthəsiez/ *verb trans* to make a parenthesis of (e.g. a clause). ➤ *verb intrans* to digress.

parenting *noun* the caring for and raising of a child.

parent-teacher association *noun* (*treated as sing. or pl*) an organization of teachers at a school and the parents of their pupils, which works for the improvement of the school.

parergon /pa'ruhgon/ *noun* (*pl* **parerga** /-gə/) supplementary or subsidiary work; work undertaken apart from one's regular employment. [via Latin from Greek *parergon*, from PARA-[1] + *ergon* work]

paresis /pə'reesis, 'parəsis/ *noun* (*pl* **pareses** /-seez/) **1** slight or partial paralysis. **2** insanity and paralysis resulting from syphilis. ➤➤ **paretic** /pə'retik/ *adj*. [via Latin from Greek *paresis*, from *parienai* to let fall, from PARA-[1] + *hienai* to let go]

paresthesia /paris'theezyə, -zh(y)ə/ *noun NAmer* see PARAESTHESIA.

par excellence /pahr 'eks(ə)ləns (*French* par ɛksɛlɑ̃:s)/ *adj* (*used after a noun*) being the best example of a kind; without equal: *the dictionary par excellence.* [French *par excellence*, literally 'by excellence']

parfait /pah'fay/ *noun* a frozen flavoured dessert that resembles custard and contains whipped cream and eggs. [French *parfait*, literally 'something perfect', from *parfait*: see PERFECT[1]]

parget[1] /'pahjit/ *verb trans* (**pargeted, pargeting**) to coat (a wall) with plaster, *esp* ornamentally. [Middle English *pargetten* from early French *parjeter* to throw on top of, from *par-* thoroughly (from PER-) + *jeter*: see JET[1]]

parget[2] *noun* plasterwork, *esp* in raised ornamental figures on walls.

pargeting /'pahjiting/ *noun* = PARGET[2].

parhelia /pah'heeli-ə/ *noun* pl of PARHELION.

parhelic circle /pah'heelik/ *noun* a luminous circle or halo parallel to the horizon at the altitude of the sun, caused by the sun's rays reflecting off ice crystals in the atmosphere.

parhelion /pah'heeli-ən/ *noun* (*pl* **parhelia** /-li-ə/) any one of several bright spots that often appear on the parhelic circle: compare ANTHELION. ➤➤ **parhelic** /-lik/ *adj*. [via Latin from Greek *parēlion*, from PARA-[1] + *hēlios* sun]

pariah /pə'rie-ə/ *noun* **1** = OUTCAST. **2** formerly, a member of a low caste of S India and Burma (now Myanmar).

Word history
Tamil *paṟaiyan* drummer, from *paṟai* drum. Pariahs were traditionally the drummers for religious processions.

pariah dog *noun* = PYE-DOG.

parietal[1] /pə'rie-ətl/ *adj* **1a** relating to or in the region of the walls of an anatomical part or cavity. **b** forming or relating to the upper rear wall of the skull. **2** said of a developing seed or its support: attached to the main wall of the ovary. **3** *NAmer* concerning life or regulations within a college. [early French *parietal*, from Latin *pariet-, paries* wall of a cavity or hollow organ]

parietal[2] *noun* a parietal part, e.g. a bone or scale.

parietal bone *noun* either of a pair of bones of the top and side of the skull.

parietal lobe *noun* the middle lobe of each cerebral hemisphere; the lobe that contains an area concerned with the interpretation of the body sensations of touch, temperature, etc.

pari-mutuel /,pari 'myoohtyooəl/ *noun* **1** a betting pool in which those who bet on the winners of the first three places share the total amount bet, minus a percentage for the management. **2** *NAmer* = TOTALIZATOR (I). [French *pari mutuel*, literally 'mutual stake']

paring /'peəring/ *noun* **1** the act of cutting away an edge or surface. **2** something pared off: *apple parings.*

Paris green /'paris/ *noun* a very poisonous bright green powder that is used as an insecticide and pigment. [named after Paris, capital of France]

parish /'parish/ *noun* **1** a subdivision of a diocese served by a single church or clergyman. **2** a unit of local government in rural England, often coinciding with an original ecclesiastical parish. [Middle English *parisshe* via French from late Latin *parochia*, from late Greek *paroikia*, from *paroikos* neighbour, Christian, from Greek PARA-[1] + *oikos* dwelling]

parishioner /pə'rish(ə)nə/ *noun* a member or inhabitant of a parish.

parish-pump *adj Brit* having a restricted outlook or limited interest; parochial: *smacked less of a serious schism than of a parish-pump quarrel* — Times Literary Supplement.

parish register *noun* a book containing records of baptisms, marriages, and burials in a parish.

Parisian /pə'rizi·ən/ *noun* a native or inhabitant of Paris. ➤➤ **Parisian** *adj*.

parity[1] /'pariti/ *noun* **1** the quality or state of being equal or equivalent. **2** equivalence of a commodity price expressed in one currency to its price expressed in another. **3a** the property of an integer with respect to being odd or even: *Three and seven have the same parity*. **b** the state of being odd or even that is the basis of a method of detecting errors in binary-coded data. **4** the property whereby a quantity, e.g. the charge of an elementary particle, changes from positive to negative or vice versa or remains unaltered during a particular interaction or reaction. [Latin *paritas*, from *par* equal]

parity[2] *noun* **1** the state or fact of having borne offspring. **2** the number of children previously borne. [-PAROUS + -ITY]

parity check *noun* a check made on computer data by which errors are detected.

park[1] /pahk/ *noun* **1a** an area of land for recreation in or near a city or town. **b** an area maintained in its natural state as a public property. **2** an enclosed area of lawns, woodland, pasture, etc attached to a country house and used as a game reserve or for recreation. **3** an often landscaped site for a number of buildings housing establishments of a similar type: *a science park*. **4a** (*usu in combination*) an area set aside for vehicles to be parked in. **b** a space to park one's vehicle. **5** an assigned space for military animals, vehicles, or materials. **6a** (**the park**) *Brit, informal* the playing area for a ball game played on grass, *esp* a football pitch. **b** *NAmer* an arena or stadium used for ball games. [Middle English via Old French *pare* from medieval Latin *parricus*, of Germanic origin]

park[2] *verb trans* **1** to leave or place (a vehicle) for a time, *esp* at the roadside or in a car park or garage. **2** to assemble (e.g. equipment or stores) in a military dump or park. **3** *informal* to set and leave (somebody or something) temporarily: *She parked her boyfriend at the bar; Park yourself over there while I make us a cup of tea.* ➤ *verb intrans* to park a vehicle.

parka /'pahkə/ *noun* **1** a warm, weatherproof thigh-length jacket with a hood. **2** a similar hooded garment made of fur or animal hide worn by Arctic peoples. [Aleut *parka* skin, outer garment, from Russian *parka* pelt]

park-and-ride *noun* an urban transport system in which public transport takes passengers into the centre of a town from large car parks situated on the outskirts.

parkin /'pahkin/ *noun* a thick heavy ginger cake made with oatmeal and treacle. [origin unknown]

parking lot *noun NAmer* an outdoor car park.

parking meter *noun* a coin-operated device which registers the payment and displays the time allowed for parking a motor vehicle.

Parkinsonism /'pahkins(ə)niz(ə)m/ *noun* = PARKINSON'S DISEASE.

Parkinson's disease /'pahkins(ə)nz/ *noun* a long-lasting progressive nervous disease, marked by tremor, weakness of resting muscles, and a peculiar gait. ➤➤ **parkinsonian** /-'sohni·ən/ *adj*. [named after James *Parkinson* d.1824, English physician, who first described it]

Parkinson's Law *noun* an observation in office organization that work expands so as to fill the time available for its completion. [named after C Northcote *Parkinson* d.1993, English historian, who formulated it]

parkland *noun* land with clumps of trees and shrubs in cultivated condition suitable for use as a park.

parkway *noun NAmer* a broad landscaped road or highway.

parky *adj* (**parkier, parkiest**) *Brit, informal* = CHILLY (1). [origin unknown]

Parl. *abbr* **1** Parliament. **2** Parliamentary.

parlance /'pahləns/ *noun* a manner of speaking and choice of words: *in legal parlance*. [early French *parlance* from Old French *parler*: see PARLEY[1]]

parlando /pah'landoh/ *adj and adv* said of a piece of music: to be delivered or performed in an unsustained style suggestive of speech. [Italian *parlando* speaking, from *parlare* to speak, ultimately from late Latin *parabola*: see PARABLE]

parlay[1] /'pahli/ *verb trans NAmer* to bet (a sum of money) in a parlay. [French *paroli* parlay, from Italian dialect *parolo*, from *paro* equal, from Latin *par*]

parlay[2] *noun NAmer* an accumulator bet.

parley[1] /'pahli/ *verb intrans* to speak with another; to confer; *specif* to discuss terms with an enemy. [early French *parler* to speak, ultimately from late Latin *parabola*: see PARABLE]

parley[2] *noun* (*pl* **parleys**) a conference for discussion of points in dispute; *specif* a conference under truce to discuss terms with an enemy.

parliament /'pahləmənt, 'pahlyəmənt/ *noun* **1** (*often* **Parliament**). **a** the supreme legislative body of the UK that consists of the House of Commons and the House of Lords and is called together and dissolved by the sovereign. **b** a similar body in another nation or state. **2** a formal conference for the discussion of public affairs. [Middle English from Old French *parlement*, from *parler*: see PARLEY[1]]

parliamentarian /,pahləmən'teəri·ən/ *noun* **1** *Brit* a Member of Parliament. **2** an expert in parliamentary rules and practice. **3** (*often* **Parliamentarian**) an adherent of the parliament during the English Civil War. ➤➤ **parliamentarian** *adj*.

parliamentary /pahlə'ment(ə)ri/ *adj* **1** of, appropriate to, or enacted by a parliament. **2** supporting the parliament during the English Civil War.

Parliamentary Commissioner for Administration *noun* the official title of the government ombudsman in the UK.

parliamentary private secretary *noun* a Member of Parliament in the UK who assists a government minister.

parlour (*NAmer* **parlor**) /'pahlə/ *noun* **1a** *dated* a room in a private house for the entertainment of guests. **b** a room in an inn, hotel, or club for conversation or semiprivate uses. **2** a shop or business: *a funeral parlour; a beauty parlour*. **3** a place for milking cows. [Middle English from Old French *parlour*, from *parler*: see PARLEY[1]]

parlour game *noun* an indoor word game, board game, etc.

parlous /'pahləs/ *adj often humorous* giving cause for concern or alarm; precarious; bad or serious: *Given the parlous state of our finances, there'll be no holiday for us this year.* ➤➤ **parlously** *adv*. [Middle English, alteration of *perilous*: see PERIL]

Parmesan /pahmi'zan, 'pah-/ *noun* a very hard dry strongly flavoured cheese that is often used grated. [French *parmesan* of *Parma*, a city in Italy where it originated]

parochial /pə'rohki·əl/ *adj* **1** belonging to or relating to a church parish. **2** limited or provincial in outlook; concerned only with local affairs; lacking a wider or imaginative view: *The average English critic is a don manqué, hopelessly parochial when not exaggeratedly teutonophile* — Constant Lambert. ➤➤ **parochially** *adv*. [Middle English *parochiall* via French from late Latin *parochialis*, from *parochia*: see PARISH]

parochialism *noun* selfish pettiness or narrowness, e.g. of interests, opinions, or views.

parody[1] /'parədi/ *noun* (*pl* **parodies**) **1** a literary or musical work in which the style of an author is imitated for comic or satirical effect.

Editorial note ━━━━━━━━━━━━━━━━━━━━
Parody is common in literature as a form of mocking imitation, and was employed by many major writers – Sterne, Fielding, Dickens, etc – often to develop a new genre based on upturning something previous. In 'postmodern' culture it has a more serious role as a mocking or self-doubting style, expressing the ironic, over-quoted, unreal nature of artistic forms and institutions — Professor Malcolm Bradbury.

2 a feeble or ridiculous imitation. ➤➤ **parodic** /pə'rodik/ *adj*, **parodist** *noun*. [via Latin from Greek *parōidia*, from PARA-[1] + *aidein* to sing]

parody[2] *verb trans* (**parodies, parodied, parodying**) to imitate (somebody) for comic or satirical effect.

parol /'parəl/ *adj* legal, given by word of mouth: *parol evidence*. [early French *parole*: see PAROLE[1]]

parole[1] /pə'rohl/ *noun* **1** a conditional release of a prisoner. **2** a pledge of one's honour; *esp*, formerly, the promise of a prisoner of war to fulfil stated conditions in consideration of release or the granting of privileges. **3** the linguistic behaviour of an individual speaker of a language: compare LANGUE. [early French *parole* speech, parole, from late Latin *parabola*: see PARABLE]

parole² *verb trans* to put (a prisoner) on parole. ⟫⟫ **parolee** /-'lee/ *noun.*

paronomasia /ˌparənoh'maysi-ə/ *noun* a play on words; a pun. [via Latin from Greek *paronomasia*, from *paronomazein* to call with a slight change of name, from PARA-¹ + *onomazein* to name, from *onoma* name]

parotid gland /pə'rotid/ *noun* either of a pair of large salivary glands below and in front of the ear. ⟫⟫ **parotid** *adj.* [via Latin from Greek *parōtid-, parōtis*, from PARA-¹ + *ōt-, ous* ear]

parotitis /parə'tietəs/ *noun* inflammation of the parotid glands; *esp* mumps.

-parous *comb. form* forming adjectives, with the meaning: giving birth to or producing (the specified number or type of) offspring: *biparous; viviparous.* [Latin *-parus*, from *parere* to give birth to, produce]

paroxysm /'parəksiz(ə)m/ *noun* **1** a fit, attack, or sudden increase or recurrence of disease symptoms; a convulsion: *a paroxysm of coughing.* **2** a sudden violent emotion or action: *a paroxysm of rage.* ⟫⟫ **paroxysmal** /-'sizməl/ *adj.* [via French and late Latin from Greek *paroxysmos*, from *paroxynein* to stimulate, exasperate, from PARA-¹ + *oxynein* to sharpen]

parp /pahp/ *verb trans* to make a sound like that of a car horn. ⟫⟫ **parp** *noun and interj.* [imitative]

parquet /'pahkay, 'pahki/ *noun* **1** a floor or flooring made of blocks of wood laid in geometrical patterns. **2** *NAmer* the stalls in a theatre. [early French *parquet*, literally 'small enclosure', dimin. of *parc*: see PARK¹]

parquetry /'pahkitri/ *noun* work in the form of usu geometrically patterned wood laid or inlaid, *esp* for floors.

parr /pah/ *noun* (*pl* **parrs** or collectively **parr**) a young salmon actively feeding in fresh water. [origin unknown]

parrakeet /'parəkeet/ *noun* see PARAKEET.

parramatta *or* **paramatta** /parə'matə/ *noun* a fine lightweight dress fabric of silk and wool or cotton and wool. [named after *Parramatta*, a city in SE Australia, site of a prison where it was first made for convicts' clothing]

parricide /'parisied/ *noun* **1** the act of murdering one's father or mother. **2** a person who commits parricide. ⟫⟫ **parricidal** /-'siedl/ *adj.* [Latin *parricida* and *parricidium*, from *parri-* relative, of unknown origin + *-cida* and *-cidium* from *caedere* to cut, to kill]

parrot¹ /'parət/ *noun* any of numerous species of large tropical birds, typically with brightly coloured plumage, a curved hooked beak, and in some cases the ability to mimic speech: order Psittaciformes. [prob irreg from early French *perroquet*]

parrot² *verb trans* (**parroted, parroting**) to repeat or imitate (e.g. another's words) without understanding or thought.

parrot-fashion *adv* without regard for meaning: *He learned it parrot-fashion.*

parrot fish *noun* a spiny-finned sea fish with teeth that are fused into a cutting plate like a beak: families Scaridae and Labridae.

parry¹ /'pari/ *verb trans* (**parries, parried, parrying**) **1** to ward off (e.g. a blow). **2** to evade (e.g. an accusation) *esp* by an adroit answer. [prob from French *parez*, imperative of *parer* to parry, via Old Provençal from Latin *parare* to prepare]

parry² *noun* (*pl* **parries**) **1** an act of parrying a blow. **2** a defensive or evasive reply.

parse /pahz/ *verb trans* to resolve (e.g. a sentence) into component parts of speech and describe them grammatically. [Latin *pars orationis* part of speech]

parsec /'pahsek/ *noun* a unit of distance used in astronomy equal to about 3.25 light years; the distance at which the radius of the earth's orbit subtends an angle of one second of arc. [PARALLAX + SECOND⁴]

Parsi *or* **Parsee** /'pahsee, pah'see/ *noun* a Zoroastrian descended from Persian refugees settled principally in Bombay. [Persian *pārsī*, from *Pārs* Persia]

parsimonious /pahsi'mohni-əs/ *adj* spending as little money or using as few resources as possible; frugal; stingy: *He was, I had discovered, parsimonious about small expenditures* — Willa Cather. ⟫⟫ **parsimoniously** *adv*, **parsimoniousness** *noun.*

parsimony /'pahsiməni/ *noun* the quality of being careful with money or resources; thrift or stinginess. [Middle English *parcimony* from Latin *parsimonia*, from *parcere* to spare]

parsley /'pahsli/ *noun* an orig S European plant of the carrot family widely cultivated for its leaves, which are used as a herb or garnish in cooking: *Petroselinum crispum.* [Old English *petersilie* via late Latin from Greek *petroselinon*, from *petra* rock + *selinon* parsley]

parsnip /'pahsnip/ *noun* **1** a European plant of the carrot family with large leaves and yellow flowers cultivated for its long edible tapering root: *Pastinaca sativa.* **2** the root of this plant, used as a vegetable. [Middle English *pasnepe* via French from Latin *pastinaca*, from *pastinum* two-pronged dibble]

parson /'pahs(ə)n/ *noun* **1** the clergyman in charge of an Anglican parish. **2** any clergyman. [Middle English *persone* via Old French and late Latin from Latin *persona*: see PERSON]

parsonage /'pahsənij/ *noun* the house provided by a church for its parson.

parson's nose *noun* the fatty extension of the rump of a cooked fowl.

part¹ /paht/ *noun* **1** any of the often indefinite or unequal subdivisions into which something is divided and which together constitute the whole. **2a** an essential portion or integral element: *I never felt I was part of what was going on there.* **b** an amount equal to another amount: *Mix one part of the powder with three parts of water.* **c** an exact fraction of a quantity. **3** a certain amount or a contributing factor but not the whole: *That's part of the reason why I phoned you.* **4** a separable and replaceable piece in a machine; a component. **5** an organ, member, or other constituent element of a plant or animal body. **6** any of the opposing sides in a conflict or dispute: *He took his son's part in the argument.* **7** a division of a literary work. **8a** a vocal or instrumental line or melody in music arranged for more than one voice or instrument. **b** a particular voice or instrument in a piece of music. **c** the written music for a particular voice or instrument. **9a** an actor's role in a play. **b** a written copy of the lines of such a role. **10** somebody's contribution to or role in an action or event: *The government denied it had any part in the strike.* **11** (*in pl*) an unspecified territorial area: *She took off for parts unknown; Are you from these parts?* **12** *dated* (*in pl*) personal abilities; talents: *a man of parts.* **13** *NAmer* a parting in the hair. ✳ **for one's part** as far as one is concerned. **for the most part** see MOST¹. **in part** in some degree; partially. **look the part** to have a physical appearance appropriate to one's role or function. **on the part of somebody/on somebody's part** by, from, or on behalf of somebody. **play a part** **1** to pretend to be something one is not. **2** to have something to do with (something); to be instrumental in (it): *I played a part in her promotion.* **take part** (*often* + in) to join in; to share or participate. **take something in good part** to accept (e.g. a joke or critical remark) without offence. [Old French and Old English *part*, both from Latin *part-, pars*]

part² *verb intrans* **1a** to separate from or take leave of somebody. **b** to take leave of one another. **2** to become separated into parts: *The clouds parted and the sun appeared.* **3** to become separated, detached, or broken: *The strands of the rope parted.* **4** (+ with) to relinquish possession or control, *esp* reluctantly: *When one parts with one's cruelty, one parts with one's power; and when one has parted with that, I fancy one's old and ugly* — Congreve. ⟫ *verb trans* **1a** to divide (something) into parts. **b** to separate (the hair) by combing on each side of a line. **2a** to remove (somebody) from contact or association with somebody else; to separate (two people): *till death us do part.* **b** to hold (e.g. combatants) apart. [Middle English *parten* via Old French *partir* from Latin *partire* to divide, from *part-, pars* PART¹]

part³ *adv* = PARTLY: *A centaur is part man part horse.*

partake /pah'tayk/ *verb intrans* (*past tense* **partook** /pah'took/, *past part.* **partaken** /-k(ə)n/) *formal* (+ in/of) to take a part or share; to participate: *She partook of some wine; He doesn't often partake in sports.* ⟫⟫ **partaker** *noun.* [earliest as *partaker*, alteration of *part taker*]

part and parcel *noun* an essential part or element.

parterre /pah'teə/ *noun* **1** an ornamental garden with paths between the beds. **2** *NAmer* a theatre pit. [French *parterre*, from *par terre* on the ground]

part-exchange¹ *noun Brit* a method of paying for something whereby part of the payment takes the form of goods, the balance being made up in money: *He bought a new car and gave his old one in part-exchange.*

part-exchange[2] *verb trans* to give or take (something) in part-exchange.

parthenogenesis /ˌpahthinohˈjenəsis/ *noun* reproduction by development of an unfertilized gamete that occurs *esp* among lower plants and invertebrate animals. ⟫ **parthenogenetic** /-ˈnetik/ *adj.* [scientific Latin *parthogenesis*, from Greek *parthenos* virgin + Latin *genesis* birth]

Parthian /ˈpahthi-ən/ *noun* a native or inhabitant of ancient Parthia in SW Asia. ⟫ **Parthian** *adj.*

Parthian shot *noun* = PARTING SHOT. [from the Parthian horsemen's practice of shooting arrows backwards while in real or feigned flight]

partial[1] /ˈpahsh(ə)l/ *adj* **1** of a part rather than the whole; not general or total: *a partial solution.* **2** inclined to favour one party more than the other; biased. **3** (+ to) markedly fond of somebody or something: *partial to beans.* ⟫ **partially** *adv.* [Middle English *parcial* via French from late Latin *partialis*, from Latin *part-, pars* PART[1]]

Usage note

partially *or* **partly**? These two words are often interchangeable, but there is a subtle distinction between them that is worth noting. *Partly* is the preferable choice with the meaning 'as regards one part': *The building is constructed partly of brick and partly of stone. Partially* is the preferable choice with the meaning 'to a limited extent; incompletely': *partially sighted. Partly* is used more commonly than *partially* to introduce an explanatory clause or phrase, sometimes in the expression *partly … partly: Partly because of the weather and partly because of the weak economy, profits were down last year.*

partial[2] *noun* an overtone in music.

partial derivative *noun* in mathematics, the derivative of a function of several variables with respect to any one of them, the remaining variables being treated as constants.

partial differential equation *noun* in mathematics, a differential equation containing at least one partial derivative.

partial differentiation *noun* the process of finding a partial derivative.

partiality /pahshiˈaliti/ *noun* (*pl* **partialities**) **1** unfair preference for somebody or something; bias. **2** a special taste or liking.

partial pressure *noun* in chemistry, the pressure exerted by a specified gas in a mixture of gases.

partible /ˈpahtəbl/ *adj* said of a property or estate: capable of being divided up.

participate /pahˈtisipayt, pə-/ *verb intrans* to join with others in doing something; to be involved or have a part or share in something: *He never participates in class discussions.* ⟫ **participant** *noun,* **participation** /-ˈpaysh(ə)n/ *noun,* **participator** *noun,* **participatory** /-pət(ə)ri/ *adj.* [Latin *participatus,* past part. of *participare,* ultimately from *part-, pars* PART[1] + *capere* to take]

participle /ˈpahtisipl, pahˈtis-/ *noun* a verbal form, e.g. *singing* or *sung,* that has the function of an adjective and at the same time can be used in compound verb forms. ⟫ **participial** /-ˈsipi-əl/ *adj,* **participially** /-ˈsipi-əli/ *adv.* [Middle English via French from Latin *participium,* from *participare:* see PARTICIPATE]

particle /ˈpahtikl/ *noun* **1** a minute quantity or fragment, *esp* of a physical substance. **2** a minute subdivision of matter, *esp* at sub-atomic level, e.g. an electron or proton. **3a** a minor unit of speech including all uninflected words or all words except nouns and verbs. **b** an affix, e.g. *un-.* [Middle English from Latin *particula,* dimin. of *part-, pars* PART[1]]

particle-beam weapon *noun* an electronic weapon that uses a high-velocity beam of electrons, protons, or hydrogen atoms to destroy enemy targets.

particle board *noun* a board made of very small pieces of wood bonded together, e.g. with a synthetic resin.

particle physics *noun* a branch of physics dealing with the constitution, properties, and interactions of elementary particles.

parti-coloured *or* **particoloured** (*NAmer* **parti-colored** *or* **particolored**) /ˈpahti kuləd/ *adj* showing different colours or tints: *parti-coloured threads.* [*parti-* alteration of PARTY[3]]

particular[1] /pəˈtikyoolə/ *adj* **1** denoting or relating to a single person or thing; specific: *She wasn't the particular person I had in mind.* **2** worthy of notice; special, unusual: *There was nothing in the letter of particular importance.* **3** detailed or exact. **4a** concerned over or attentive to details; meticulous. **b** hard to please; exacting: *The cat is very particular about her food.* **5** said of a proposition in logic:

predicating a term of some but not all members of a specified class: compare UNIVERSAL[1] (4). [Middle English *particuler* via French from late Latin *particularis* of a small part, from Latin *particula:* see PARTICLE]

particular[2] *noun* an individual fact, point, circumstance, or detail: *Particulars are not to be examined till the whole has been surveyed* — Dr Johnson. ✳ **in particular** specifically or especially: *The House of Peers, throughout the war, did nothing in particular, and did it very well* — W S Gilbert.

particular average *noun* accidental partial damage to or loss of an insured ship or cargo affecting only the shipowner or the owner of the cargo: compare GENERAL AVERAGE.

particularise *verb trans* see PARTICULARIZE.

particularism *noun* **1** exclusive or special devotion to a particular interest. **2** a political theory that each political group has a right to promote its own interests without regard to those of larger groups. ⟫ **particularist** *noun,* **particularistic** /-ˈristik/ *adj.*

particularity /pəˌtikyooˈlariti/ *noun* (*pl* **particularities**) **1a** (*usu in pl*) a minute detail; a particular. **b** an individual characteristic; a peculiarity. **2** the quality or state of being particular as opposed to universal. **3** the quality or state of being fastidious in behaviour or expression.

particularize *or* **particularise** *verb trans formal* to state (something) in detail; to specify (it). ⟫ *verb intrans formal* to go into details. ⟫ **particularization** /-ˈzaysh(ə)n/ *noun.*

particularly *adv* **1** to an unusual degree: *She particularly wanted to meet you.* **2** in detail; specifically: *But I particularly asked you to get milk.*

particulate /pahˈtikyoolət, -layt/ *noun* a substance consisting of minute separate particles. ⟫ **particulate** *adj.* [Latin *particula* (see PARTICLE) + -ATE[1]]

parting *noun* **1a** the act or an instance of parting from somebody: *Parting is such sweet sorrow* — Shakespeare. **b** (*used before a noun*) given, taken, or performed at parting: *a parting kiss.* **2** *Brit* the line where the hair is parted. **3** a place or point where a division or separation occurs.

parting shot *noun* a pointed remark or hostile gesture made when leaving.

parti pris /ˌpahti ˈpree/ *noun* (*pl* **partis pris** /ˌpahti ˈpree/) a preconceived opinion; a prejudice or bias. [French *parti pris,* literally 'side taken']

partisan /ˈpahtizan, -ˈzan/ *noun* **1** a firm adherent to a party, faction, cause, or person; *esp* one exhibiting blind, prejudiced, and unreasoning allegiance. **2** a member of a guerrilla band operating behind enemy lines. ⟫ **partisan** *adj,* **partisanship** *noun.* [early French *partisan* from Old Italian *partigiano,* from *parte* part, party]

partis pris /ˌpahti ˈpree/ *noun pl* of PARTI PRIS.

partita /pahˈteetə/ *noun* (*pl* **partitas** *or* **partite** /-tay, -tee/) a musical suite. [Italian *partita* from *partire* to divide, from Latin *partire:* see PART[2]]

partite[1] /ˈpahtiet/ *adj* **1** (*usu in combination*) divided into a usu specified number of parts: *tripartite.* **2** cleft nearly to the base: *a partite leaf.* [Latin *partitus,* past part. of *partire:* see PART[2]]

partite[2] /pahˈteetay, -tee/ *noun pl* of PARTITA.

partition[1] /pahˈtish(ə)n, pə-/ *noun* **1a** division into parts. **b** a part or section of a whole. **2** something that divides; *esp* a light interior dividing wall. ⟫ **partitioner** *noun,* **partitionist** *noun.* [Middle English from Latin *partition-, partitio,* from *partire:* see PART[2]]

partition[2] *verb trans* **1** to divide (e.g. a country) into parts or shares. **2a** to divide (e.g. a room) by a partition. **b** (*usu* + off) to enclose (an area) or separate (it) off from a larger one with a partition: *Can we partition off part of the room to use as an office?*

partitive[1] /ˈpahtətiv/ *adj* in grammar, of or denoting a part of a whole. ⟫ **partitively** *adv.*

partitive[2] *noun* in grammar, a noun or pronoun indicating a partitive construction.

partly *adv* not completely; to some extent or degree; as one constituent among two or more.

Usage note

partly *or* **partially**? See note at PARTIAL[1].

partner[1] /ˈpahtnə/ *noun* **1a** a member of a partnership. **b** an associate or colleague in a joint venture. **2a** either of a couple who dance together. **b** somebody who plays with one or more others in a game against an opposing side. **c** a person with whom one is having a sexual relationship; a spouse, lover, etc. [Middle English *partener*, alteration of *parcener*, from Anglo-French, from Latin *partition-, partitio*: see PARTITION[1]]

partner[2] *verb trans* (**partnered, partnering**) to act as a partner to (somebody).

partnership *noun* **1** the state of being a partner; association. **2a** two or more joint principals in a business. **b** a legal relation between two such people. **3** an association involving close cooperation.

part of speech *noun* a class of words, e.g. nouns and adverbs, distinguished according to the kind of idea denoted and the function performed in a sentence.

partook /pah'took/ *verb* past tense of PARTAKE.

partridge /'pahtrij/ *noun* (*pl* **partridges** or collectively **partridge**) any of numerous species of medium-sized stout-bodied African and Eurasian game birds with variegated plumage: genera *Perdix, Alectoris*, and other genera. [Middle English *partrich* via Old French and Latin from Greek *perdik, perdix*]

part song *noun* a usu unaccompanied song consisting of two or more voice parts with one part carrying the melody.

part-time[1] *adj* involving or working less than the customary or standard hours: *a part-time job; part-time students.* >>> **part-timer** *noun*.

part-time[2] *adv* for part of the time: *worked part-time in a bookshop.*

parturient /pah'tyooəri·ənt/ *adj formal* about to bring forth young. [Latin *parturient-, parturiens*, present part. of *parturire* to be in labour, from *parere* to produce]

parturition /pahtyoo'rish(ə)n/ *noun formal* = CHILDBIRTH. [late Latin *parturition-, parturitio*, from Latin *parturire*: see PARTURIENT]

partway *adv* to some extent; partially or partly.

part work *noun Brit* a regularly published series of magazines devoted to one subject that is designed to be bound together in e.g. book form.

party[1] /'pahti/ *noun* (*pl* **parties**) **1** a social gathering: *a birthday party.* **2** a group of people holding broadly similar views, organized to take part in politics. **3** a group of people organized to carry out an activity or fulfil a function together: *a search party.* **4** a person or group taking one side of a question, dispute, or contest. **5** a person or group participating in a legal action or proceeding; a participant; *the guilty party.* **6** *informal* a particular individual. [Middle English *partie* part, party, from Old French *partie*, from *partir*: see PART[2]]

party[2] *verb intrans* (**parties, partied, partying**) *informal* to attend a social gathering; to celebrate: *They were out partying till dawn.*

party[3] *adj* said of a heraldic shield: divided into parts of different tinctures. [Old French *parti*, ultimately from Latin *partire*: see PART[2]]

party line *noun* **1** the official principles of a political party. **2** a single telephone line shared by two or more subscribers.

party-pooper /'poohpə/ *noun informal* somebody who spoils a party by refusing to join in the fun. [*pooper* from POOP[3]]

party wall *noun* a wall that divides two adjoining properties and in which each owner has a joint interest.

parvenu /'pahvənyooh/ *noun* a person of low social position who has recently or suddenly acquired wealth or power; an upstart. >>> **parvenu** *adj.* [French *parvenu*, past part. of *parvenir* to arrive, from Latin *pervenire*, from *per* through + *venire* to come]

parvis or **parvise** /'pahvis/ *noun* an enclosed space in front of a church. [Middle English *parvis* via French from late Latin *paradisus*: see PARADISE]

parvovirus /'pahvohvie·ərəs/ *noun* any of a family of very small viruses that contain DNA, found *esp* in rodents and dogs: family Parvoviridae. [Latin *parvus* small + VIRUS]

pas /pah/ *noun* (*pl* **pas** /pah, pahz/) a dance step or combination of steps. [French *pas* from Latin *passus* step]

Pascal /pa'skal/ *noun* a high-level computer language based on Algol that is used as a teaching language in computer studies and for business and commercial applications. [named after Blaise *Pascal* d.1662, French mathematician and philosopher]

pascal /pa'skal/ *noun* the SI unit of pressure equal to the pressure produced by a force of one newton applied uniformly over an area of one square metre. [named after Blaise *Pascal*: see PASCAL]

Pascal's triangle *noun* a set of numbers arranged in a triangle, each of which is obtained by adding together the numbers above it, and which is used to determine the coefficients of the terms in an expansion made using the binomial theorem. [named after Blaise *Pascal*: see PASCAL]

paschal /'paskl/ *adj* **1** relating to the Jewish Passover. **2** relating or appropriate to Easter. [Middle English via Old French from late Latin *paschalis*, from Greek *pascha* Passover, from Hebrew *pesaḥ*]

pas de deux /,pah də 'duh/ *noun* (*pl* **pas de deux** /'duh, 'duhz/) a dance or set of dance steps for two performers. [French *pas de deux*, literally 'step for two']

pash /pash/ *noun Brit, informal, dated* a hero-worshipping adolescent infatuation; a crush. [from PASSION]

pasha or **pacha** /'pahshə, 'pashə/ *noun* a man of high rank or office, e.g. in Turkey or N Africa: *Glubb Pasha.* [Turkish *paşa*]

pashmina /push'meenə/ *noun* **1** a fine woollen fabric made from the hair of goats. **2** a shawl made of this fabric. [Persian *pashmina* from *pašm* wool]

Pashto /'pooshtoh/ *noun* the Indo-Iranian language of the Pathan people of E Afghanistan and parts of Pakistan. [Persian *pashtu*, from Pashto]

paso doble /,pasoh 'dohblay/ *noun* a ballroom dance with two beats to the bar, based on a Latin American march step, or the music for this dance. [Spanish *paso doble* double step]

pasqueflower /'paskflowə/ *noun* a low-growing plant of the buttercup family with large, usu white or purple, early spring flowers: *Pulsatilla vulgaris.*

Word history
modification of early French *passefleur*, from *passer* (see PASS[1]) + *fleur* flower, from Latin *flor-, flos*. The modification came about by association with archaic *Pasque* Easter, because it blooms in early Spring.

pasquinade /paskwi'nayd/ *noun* a lampoon or satire, *esp* one posted in a public place: *The white walls of the barracks were covered with epigrams and pasquinades levelled at Cortes* — William Hickling Prescott. [early French *pasquinade* from Italian *pasquinata*, from *Pasquino*, the name given to a statue in Rome on which lampoons were posted]

pass[1] /pahs/ *verb intrans* **1a** to move or proceed in a specified direction: *The column of soldiers passed down the road.* **b** to go by or move past: *She waved from the train window as it passed.* **c** to go across, over, or through: *Allow no one to pass.* **2** said of time: to elapse: *An hour had passed before we realized it.* **3** to go from one quality or state to another: *Their mood passed from disbelief to anger.* **4** to complete its course and cease: *The trouble passed very quickly.* **5** to go uncensured or unchallenged: *I will let that remark pass.* **6** (*often* + to) to go from the control or possession of one person or group to that of another: *The throne passed to the king's daughter.* **7** to take place as a mutual exchange or transaction: *Angry words passed between them.* **8a** to be successful in an examination or test. **b** to become approved by a legislative or executive body. **c** to be accepted or regarded as adequate or fitting: *Will she pass in a crowd?* — Jonathan Swift. **9** (*often* + for) to resemble somebody or something closely enough to be mistaken for them: *She would certainly pass for 18.* **10** to happen or occur: *What passed at the interview?* **11** in a team game, to send the ball to another player. **12** to decline an offer or opportunity. **13** to decline to bid, bet, or play in a card game. **14** *euphem* (*often* + on/away/over) to die. >>> *verb trans* **1** to go across, over, or through (something). **2** to go past or by (something). **3** to go past (another vehicle) in the same direction. **4** to surpass or exceed (something). **5** to advance or develop beyond (e.g. a particular stage). **6** to spend (time). **7** to transfer (something) from one person to another: *Please pass the salt.* **8** to move or place (something): *Pass the rope around the tree.* **9** in a team game, to send (the ball) to another player. **10** in tennis, to hit a ball past (an opponent). **11** to emit or discharge (a fluid) from the body: *The patient was passing blood.* **12a** to be successful in (an examination or test). **b** to judge (a candidate) to be successful in an examination. **c** to accept or approve (somebody or something) after examination. **13** to secure the approval of (e.g. a legislative body). **14** to cause or permit (a law or proposal) to win approval or legal or official sanction. **15a** to pronounce (e.g. a judgment or sentence). **b** to utter (e.g. a comment or a remark). **16** to omit a regularly scheduled declaration and payment of (a dividend). **✳ in passing** as a relevant digression; parenthetically. **pass the time of day** to give or exchange friendly greetings. >>> **passer** *noun*. [Middle English *passen* from Old French *passer*, ultimately from Latin *passus* step] passed or past? These two words, which are pronounced the same, are sometimes confused. *Passed* is the only standard form of the past tense and past participle of *to pass*: *We passed the house on our way to the bus stop; That danger has now passed. Past* is used for all other forms: noun, adjective, preposition and adverb: *That's all in the past; Past mistakes should be forgotten; half past three; The car drove past.* As a rule of thumb, *passed* rarely follows *is* and *past* rarely follows *has*.

pass[2] *noun* **1** the act or an instance of passing. **2a** a written permission to move about freely in a place or to leave or enter it. **b** a written leave of absence from a military post or station for a brief period. **c** a permit or ticket allowing free travel or admission. **3a** the passing of an examination: *I got two A-level passes.* **b** Brit the passing of a university examination without honours. **4** *informal* a sexually inviting gesture or approach. *Did he make a pass at you?* **5** a single complete mechanical operation, e.g. in manufacturing or data processing. **6a** a transference of objects by deceptive means, *esp* sleight of hand. **b** a moving of the hands over or along something. **7a** an act of passing a ball or puck to a teammate, e.g. in football, or a ball or puck so passed. **b** in tennis, a ball hit to the side and out of reach of an opponent. **8** in card games, an announcement of a decision not to bid, bet, play, or draw an additional card. **9** a single passage or movement of a man-made object, e.g. an aircraft, over a place or towards a target. **10** a usu distressing or bad state of affairs: *Things have come to a pretty pass when you can't buy English butter.* **11** a thrust or lunge in fencing. [partly from Middle English *passe* from early French, from *passer*: see PASS[1]; partly from PASS[1]]

pass[3] *noun* a narrow passage over a comparatively low point in a mountain range. [Middle English from Old French *pas*, from Latin *passus* step]

passable *adj* **1a** barely good enough; tolerable: *The food was passable.* **b** pretty good: *She … became, in less than a year, a very passable imitation of an English lady in dress and carriage* — Kipling. **2** capable of being passed, crossed, or travelled on: *passable roads.* ⟫ **passably** *adv*.

passacaglia /pasə'kahlyə/ *noun* an instrumental musical composition in moderately slow triple time consisting of variations usu on a ground bass. [modification of Spanish *pasacalle*, from *pasar* to pass + *calle* street; because it used to be played for dancing in the street]

passage[1] /'pasij/ *noun* **1a** the action or process of passing from one place or condition to another. **b** the act or an instance of moving through or past something. **2a** a way through or along which one can move. **b** a corridor or lobby giving access to the different rooms or parts of a building or apartment. **3a** a specified act of travelling or passing, *esp* by sea or air: *a rough passage.* **b** a right to be conveyed as a passenger: *The fugitives secured a passage to France.* **c** a right, liberty, or permission to pass. **4** the passing of a legislative measure. **5a** a brief usu noteworthy portion of a written work or speech. **b** a phrase or short section of a musical composition. **6** /pa'sahzh/ incubation of a pathogen, e.g. a virus, in culture, a living organism, or a developing egg. [Middle English from early French, from *passer*: see PASS[1]]

passage[2] /pa'sahzh/ *verb trans* to subject (e.g. a virus) to passage.

passageway /'pasijway/ *noun* = CORRIDOR (1).

passant /'pas(ə)nt/ *adj* (*used after a noun*) said of a heraldic animal: walking with the farther forepaw raised: *leopard passant.* [early French *passant*, present part. of *passer*: see PASS[1]]

passata /pə'sahtə/ *noun* a thick purée of tomatoes, used in Italian cooking. [Italian *passata*]

passband *noun* a band of frequencies, e.g. in an electronic circuit or a light filter, that is transmitted with maximum efficiency.

passbook *noun* **1** a building society account-holder's book in which deposits and withdrawals are recorded. **2** an identity document that formerly had to be carried by nonwhites in S Africa.

pass by *verb trans* to escape the notice of (somebody). ⟫ *verb intrans* to go past.

passé /'pahsay, 'pasay/ *adj* **1** no longer fashionable or current; out-of-date; outmoded: *They … pronounce Fielding to be low, and Mozart to be passé* — Frederic Harrison. **2** past one's prime. [French *passé*, past part. of *passer*: see PASS[1]]

passed pawn *noun* in chess, a pawn that has no enemy pawn in front of it on its own or an adjacent file.

passenger /'pasinjə/ *noun* **1** somebody who travels in, but does not operate, a public or private conveyance. **2** a member of a group who contributes little or nothing to the functioning or productivity of the group. [Middle English from early French *passager* passing, from *passage* act of passing, from *passer*: see PASS[1]]

passenger pigeon *noun* an extinct but formerly abundant N American migratory pigeon: *Ectopistes migratorius.*

passe-partout /,pahs pah'tooh/ *noun* **1** a strong paper gummed on one side and used *esp* for mounting pictures. **2** archaic a master key: *Why, this wench is the passe-partout, a very master-key to everybody's strong-box* — Congreve. [French *passe-partout*, from *passe partout* pass everywhere]

passer-by *noun* (*pl* **passers-by**) a person who happens by chance to pass by a particular place.

passerine[1] /'pasərien/ *adj* belonging to the largest order of birds that consists chiefly of perching songbirds, e.g. finches, warblers, and thrushes. [Latin *passerinus* of sparrows, from *passer* sparrow]

passerine[2] *noun* a passerine bird.

passim /'pasim/ *adv* used to refer to the occurrence of an item in a piece of text: at various points or frequently throughout the text. [Latin *passim* from *passus* scattered, past part. of *pandere* to spread]

passing[1] *adj* **1** going by or past: *a passing pedestrian.* **2a** having a brief duration: *a passing whim.* **b** carried out quickly or casually. **3** used in or for passing: *a passing place in a road.*

passing[2] *noun* *euphem* an instance of dying; death: *They mourned her passing.*

passing note *noun* a melodic but discordant note interposed between essential notes of adjacent chords.

passion /'pash(ə)n/ *noun* **1a** intense, driving, or uncontrollable feeling. **b** an outbreak of anger. **2a** ardent affection; love. **b** a strong liking, devotion, or interest. **c** strong sexual desire. **d** the object of somebody's devotion or enthusiastic interest. **3a** (*usu* **Passion**) the sufferings of Christ between the night of the Last Supper and his death. **b** a musical setting of a gospel account of the Passion story. ⟫ **passional** *adj*, **passionless** *adj*. [Middle English via Old French from late Latin *passion-, passio-* from Latin *pati* to suffer]

passionate /'pash(ə)nət/ *adj* **1** capable of, affected by, or expressing intense feeling, *esp* love, hatred, or anger. **2** extremely enthusiastic; keen: *a passionate interest in sport.* ⟫ **passionately** *adv*, **passionateness** *noun*.

passionflower *noun* a chiefly tropical plant with usu showy flowers and pulpy often edible berries: genus *Passiflora*. [from the fancied resemblance of parts of the flower to the instruments of Christ's crucifixion]

passionfruit *noun* an edible fruit from any of various passion-flowers; *esp* a granadilla.

passion play *noun* a dramatic representation of the passion and crucifixion of Christ.

Passion Sunday *noun* the fifth Sunday in Lent.

Passiontide *noun* the last two weeks of Lent.

Passion Week *noun* the second week before Easter.

passive[1] /'pasiv/ *adj* **1** said of a person: lacking in energy, will, or initiative; meekly accepting. **2** offering no resistance; submissive. **3** acted on, receptive to, or influenced by external forces or impressions. **4a** in grammar, said of a verb form or voice: expressing an action that is done to the grammatical subject of a sentence, e.g. *was hit* in *the ball was hit.* **b** said of a sentence: containing a passive verb form. **5** said of an electronic device: using no electrical power for amplifying or controlling an electrical signal: *Capacitors and resistors are passive devices.* **6** operating solely by means of the power of an input signal: *A passive communication satellite simply reflects television signals.* **7** operating by intercepting signals emitted from a target: *a passive homing missile.* **8** in or characterized by a state of chemical inactivity, *esp* resistant to corrosion. **9** not involving expenditure of chemical energy: *passive transport across a cell membrane.* ⟫ **passively** *adv*, **passiveness** *noun*, **passivity** /pa'siviti/ *noun*. [Middle English from Latin *passivus* from *pati* to suffer]

passive[2] *noun* **1** a passive verb form. **2** the passive voice of a verb.

passive immunity *noun* immunity acquired by transfer of antibodies, e.g. by injection of blood serum from an individual with active antibodies.

passive resistance *noun* resistance characterized by nonviolent non-cooperation.

passive smoking *noun* the involuntary inhalation of tobacco smoke from cigarettes, pipes, or cigars which other people are smoking.

passkey *noun* = MASTER KEY.

pass law *noun* a former S African law, abolished in 1986, restricting the movements of nonwhites, forcing them to live in certain areas, and requiring them to carry identification at all times.

pass off *verb trans* **1** to misrepresent (somebody or something) with the intention of deceiving people: *She passed herself off as a millionairess.* **2** to disregard (an awkward remark). ➤ *verb intrans* **1** to take place and be completed: *His stay in France passed off smoothly.* **2** to complete its course and cease: *His headache had passed off by lunchtime.*

pass out *verb intrans* **1** to lose consciousness. **2** *chiefly Brit* to finish a period of military training.

Passover *noun* the Jewish festival celebrating the liberation of the Israelites from slavery in Egypt. [from the exemption of the Israelites from the slaughter of the first-born in Egyptian (Exodus 12:23–7)]

pass over *verb trans* **1** to ignore (something) and continue. **2** to ignore or disregard the claims of (somebody) to advancement.

passport *noun* an official document issued by a government as proof of identity and nationality to one of its citizens for use when leaving or reentering the country and affording some protection when abroad. [early French *passeport*, from *passer* (see PASS¹) + *port* PORT¹]

pass up *verb trans* to decline or reject (e.g. an opportunity).

password *noun* **1** a word or phrase that must be spoken by a person before being allowed into a place, *esp* past a guard. **2** a word or combination of letters and numbers used to gain access to part of a computer system.

past¹ /pahst/ *adj* **1a** just gone or elapsed: *for the past few months.* **b** having gone by; earlier: *past generations; in years past.* **2** finished or ended: *Winter is past.* **3** of or constituting the verb tense that expresses action or state in time gone by. **4** preceding or former: *a past president.* [Middle English, past part. of *passen*: see PASS¹]

Usage note

past *or* passed? See note at PASS¹.

past² *prep* **1a** beyond the age of or for (something): *He's past 80; She's past playing with dolls.* **b** subsequent to (a time): *half past two.* **2a** at the farther side of (something); beyond (it). **b** up to and then beyond (something): *I drove past the house.* **3** beyond the capacity, range, or sphere of (something): *past belief.* ✳ **not put it past somebody** *informal* to believe somebody to be perfectly capable of doing something: *I wouldn't put it past her to cheat.* **past it** *informal* no longer effective or in one's prime.

past³ *noun* **1a** time gone by. **b** something that happened or was done in the past: *He didn't regret the past.* **2** in language, a verb form expressing past events. **3** a past life, history, or course of action; *esp* one that is kept secret: *She has a past, you know.*

past⁴ *adv* so as to pass by the speaker: *Children ran past.*

pasta /'pastə/ *noun* dough formed into various shapes and used fresh or dried, e.g. as spaghetti. [via Italian from late Latin *pasta*: see PASTE¹]

paste¹ /payst/ *noun* **1** a soft, thick, mouldable mixture or composition, e.g.: **a** a preparation of flour or starch and water used as an adhesive. **b** clay or a clay mixture used in making pottery or porcelain. **2a** a smooth preparation of meat, fish, etc used as a spread. **b** a usu sweet doughy confection: *almond paste.* **c** a fat-enriched dough used *esp* for pastry. **3** a brilliant glass used in making imitation gems. [Middle English via French from late Latin *pasta* dough, paste, ultimately from Greek *passein* to sprinkle]

paste² *verb trans* **1** to stick (something) with paste. **2** in computing, to insert (e.g. an image or piece of text) into a document. **3** *informal* to thrash or defeat (somebody).

pasteboard *noun* board made by pasting together sheets of paper.

pastel¹ /'pastl, *NAmer* pas'tel/ *noun* **1** a paste of powdered pigment mixed with gum, or a crayon made of this. **2** a drawing in pastel. **3** any of various pale or light colours. ➤➤ **pastelist** *noun*, **pastellist** *noun*. [French *pastel* via Italian from late Latin *pastellus* woad, dimin. of *pasta*: see PASTE¹]

pastel² *adj* pale and light in colour.

pastern /'pastən/ *noun* **1** a part of a horse's foot extending from the fetlock to the hoof. **2** a part of another animal's leg corresponding to this. [early French *pasturon*, from *pasture* pasture, hobble for a pastured animal (tied around the pasterns), from late Latin *pastura*: see PASTURE¹]

paste-up *noun* a piece of copy for photographic reproduction consisting of text and artwork in the proper positions.

pasteurisation /ˌpahstyoorie'zaysh(ə)n, pas-/ *noun* see PASTEURIZATION.

pasteurise /'pahstyooriez, pas-/ *verb trans* see PASTEURIZE.

pasteurization *or* **pasteurisation** /ˌpahstyoorie'zaysh(ə)n, pas-/ *noun* partial sterilization of a substance, *esp* a liquid, e.g. milk, by heating for a short period. [named after Louis *Pasteur* d.1895, French chemist, who devised the process]

pasteurize *or* **pasteurise** /'pahstyooriez, 'pas-/ *verb trans* to subject (e.g. milk) to pasteurization. ➤➤ **pasteurizer** *noun*.

pasticcio /pa'stichoh/ *noun* (*pl* **pasticcios**) = PASTICHE. [Italian *pasticcio*, literally 'pasty', from late Latin *pasta*: see PASTE¹]

pastiche /pa'steesh/ *noun* a literary, artistic, or musical work that imitates the style of a previous work. [French *pastiche* from Italian *pasticcio*: see PASTICCIO]

pastie /'pasti/ *noun* see PASTY¹.

pastille *or* **pastil** /'past(ə)l/ *noun* **1** an aromatic or medicated lozenge. **2** a small cone of aromatic paste, burned to fumigate or scent a room. [French *pastille* from Latin *pastillus* small loaf, lozenge. dimin. of *panis* bread]

pastime /'pahstiem/ *noun* something, e.g. a hobby, game, etc, that amuses and serves to make time pass agreeably.

pastis /pa'stees/ *noun* (*pl* **pastis** /pa'stees/) an alcoholic drink flavoured with aniseed. [French *pastis*, literally 'mixture', ultimately from late Latin *pasta*: see PASTE¹]

past master *noun* somebody who is expert or experienced in a particular activity. [alteration of *passed master*; somebody who has passed as a master in a guild or society]

pastor /'pahstə/ *noun* somebody who has responsibility for the spiritual welfare of a group; *esp* the minister in charge of a congregation: *The shades of night were falling fast; the rain was falling faster, when through an alpine village passed, an alpine village pastor* — A E Housman, parodying Longfellow. ➤➤ **pastorate** /-rət/ *noun*, **pastorship** *noun*. [Middle English *pastour* via Old French from Latin *pastor* shepherd, herdsman, from *pascere* to feed, graze]

pastoral¹ *adj* **1a** used for or based on livestock rearing. **b** of the countryside; not urban. **c** portraying rural life, *esp* in an idealized and conventionalized manner: *pastoral poetry.* **d** pleasingly peaceful and innocent; idyllic. **2a** providing spiritual care or guidance for a church congregation. **b** providing personal guidance and care for school pupils or students. ➤➤ **pastoralism** *noun*, **pastorally** *adv*. [Middle English from Latin *pastoralis*, from *pastor*: see PASTOR]

pastoral² *noun* **1** a letter addressed by a bishop to a diocese. **2a** a pastoral literary work. **b** a depiction of country life, *esp* one that is idealized. **c** = PASTORALE.

pastorale /pastə'rahl/ *noun* (*pl* **pastorales** *or* **pastorali** /-lee/) an instrumental composition or opera with a pastoral theme. [Italian *pastorale* pastoral, ultimately from late Latin *pastor*: see PASTOR]

pastoralist *noun* *Aus* a farmer who keeps grazing animals, e.g. cattle or sheep.

past participle *noun* a participle, e.g. finished, expressing a past event.

past perfect¹ *adj* of or constituting a verb tense, e.g. *had finished*, that expresses completion of an action at or before a past time.

past perfect² *noun* in language, a verb form expressing the completion of an action before a time in the past.

pastrami /pa'strahmi/ *noun* a highly seasoned smoked beef. [Yiddish *pastrami* from Romanian *pastramă*]

pastry /'paystri/ *noun* (*pl* **pastries**) **1** a fat-enriched dough that is used to make baked dishes, e.g. pies, flans, and tarts. **2** an article of food made with pastry, *esp* a sweet tart or small cake. [Middle English, from PASTE¹]

pasturage /'pahstyoorij, 'pahschərij/ *noun* = PASTURE¹.

pasture¹ /'pahschə/ *noun* **1** land used for grazing. **2** plants, e.g. grass, grown for feeding grazing animals. **3** the feeding of livestock; grazing. [Middle English via French from late Latin *pastura* grazing, from Latin *pascere* to feed]

pasture[2] *verb intrans* to graze on pasture. ➤ *verb trans* to feed (e.g. cattle) on pasture.

pasty[1] *or* **pastie** /'pasti/ *noun* (*pl* **pasties**) a small usu savoury pie or pastry case with a filling, baked without a container. [Middle English *pastee* from early French *pasté*, from *paste*: see PASTE[1]]

pasty[2] /'paysti/ *adj* (**pastier, pastiest**) resembling paste; *esp* pallid and unhealthy in appearance. ➤➤ **pastiness** *noun*.

pat[1] /pat/ *noun* **1** a light tap, *esp* with the hand or a flat instrument. **2** a light tapping sound. **3** a small mass of something, e.g. butter. ✳ **a pat on the back** an expression of congratulation or praise. [Middle English *patte*, prob of imitative origin]

pat[2] *verb trans* (**patted, patting**) **1** to strike (something) lightly with the open hand or some other flat surface. **2** to flatten, smooth, or put (something) into place or shape with light blows: *He patted his hair into place*. **3** to tap or stroke (a person or an animal) gently with the hand to soothe, caress, or show approval.

pat[3] *adj* **1** prompt or immediate. **2** suspiciously appropriate; contrived: *a pat answer*. **3** learned, mastered, or memorized exactly.

pat[4] *adv* in a pat manner; aptly or promptly. ✳ **have something off pat** to have memorized something so that one can say it without hesitation.

pat. *abbr* **1** patent. **2** patented.

pataca /pə'tahkə/ *noun* the basic monetary unit of Macao, divided into 100 avos. [Portuguese *pataca*]

patagium /pə'tayji-əm/ *noun* (*pl* **patagia** /-ji-ə/) a wing membrane; *esp* the fold of skin connecting the forelimbs and hind limbs of a gliding animal, e.g. a flying squirrel. [Latin *patagium* gold edging on a tunic]

Patagonian /patə'gohni-ən/ *noun* a native or inhabitant of Patagonia in S America. ➤➤ **Patagonian** *adj*.

patch[1] /pach/ *noun* **1** a piece of material used to mend or cover a hole or reinforce a weak spot. **2a** a cover, e.g. a piece of adhesive plaster, applied to a wound. **b** a shield worn over the socket of an injured or missing eye. **3a** a small piece; a scrap. **b** a small area distinct from its surroundings: *damp patches on the wall*. **c** a small piece of land usu used for growing vegetables: *a cabbage patch*. **4** a piece of cloth sewn on a garment as an ornament or insignia. **5** a piece of adhesive plaster impregnated with a drug, which is worn on the skin to allow the drug to be absorbed. **6** a temporary connection in a communications system. **7** a small file supplied to correct a fault in a computer program. **8** *chiefly Brit, informal* a usu specified period: *Their marriage was going through a bad patch*. **9** *chiefly Brit* an area for which a particular individual or unit, e.g. of police, has responsibility. **10** a tiny piece of black silk formerly worn on the face, *esp* by women in the 17th cent. and 18th cents, to set off the complexion. ✳ **not a patch on** *Brit, informal* not nearly as good as. [Middle English *pacche*, perhaps from early French *pieche*, variant of *piece*: see PIECE[1]]

patch[2] *verb trans* **1** to mend or cover (e.g. a hole or weak spot) with a patch: *He patched the elbow of his jacket; We treated the squint by patching the good eye for ten minutes every day*. **2** to provide (something) with a patch. **3** *informal* (*often* + up/together) to mend or put together (something), *esp* in a hasty or shabby fashion: *They were attempting to patch up their marriage*. **4** *informal* (+ up) to bring (a quarrel, dispute, etc) to an end. **5a** to make a patch in (a computer program). **b** to make a change in (data stored on a computer) without following the standard routine for this procedure. **6** to connect (e.g. circuits) by a patch cord. ➤➤ **patcher** *noun*.

patchboard *noun* a board which has sets of linked sockets for making temporary circuit connections by means of patch cords.

patch cord *noun* a wire with a plug at each end that is used to link sockets on a patchboard.

patchouli *or* **patchouly** /pə'choohli/ *noun* **1** an E Indian shrubby plant of the mint family that yields a fragrant essential oil: *Pogostemon cablin*. **2** a heavy perfume made from patchouli oil. [Tamil *paccui*]

patch panel *noun* = PATCHBOARD.

patch pocket *noun* a flat pocket attached to the outside of a garment.

patch test *noun* a test for allergies in which small amounts of various substances are applied to the skin.

patchwork *noun* **1** work consisting of pieces of cloth of various colours and shapes sewn together. **2** something composed of miscellaneous or incongruous parts.

patchy *adj* (**patchier, patchiest**) **1** uneven in quality; incomplete: *My knowledge of French is patchy*. **2** said of certain types of weather: appearing in patches: *patchy fog*. ➤➤ **patchily** *adv*, **patchiness** *noun*.

pate /payt/ *noun archaic or humorous* the head: *his bald pate*. [Middle English; earlier history unknown]

pâté /'patay/ *noun* a rich savoury paste of seasoned and spiced meat, fish, etc. [French *pâté* from early French *pasté*: see PASTY[1]]

pâté de foie gras /,patay də ,fwah 'grah (*French* fwa gra)/ *noun* pâté made from the liver of a specially fattened goose. [French *pâté de foie gras* pâté of fat liver]

patella /pə'telə/ *noun* (*pl* **patellae** /-lee/) = KNEECAP[1]. ➤➤ **patellar** *adj*. [Latin *patella*, dimin. of *patina* shallow dish]

paten /'pat(ə)n/ *noun* **1** a plate holding the bread used at Communion. **2** a thin circular metal plate. [Middle English via Old French from Greek *patanē* plate]

patent[1] /'payt(ə)nt, 'pat(ə)nt/ *noun* **1** an official document conferring a right or privilege. **2a** a document giving an inventor the exclusive right to make, use, or sell an invention for a specified period. **b** the monopoly or right so granted. **c** a patented invention. **3** a privilege or licence. [Middle English, orig in *letters patent* an open letter or document conferring a right; via French from Latin *patent-, patens*, present part. of *patēre* to be open]

patent[2] /'payt(ə)nt, 'pat(ə)nt/ *adj* **1** /'paytənt/ readily visible or intelligible; not hidden or obscure; perfectly obvious: *It was so patent a truth that if he were not a doctor there was nothing else he could be, that a doctor he persisted in being* — Henry James. **2** protected by or made under a patent. **3** protected by a trademark or a trade name so as to establish proprietary rights like those conveyed by a patent; proprietary: *patent drugs*. **4** said of a passage or duct in the body: affording free passage; unobstructed: *a patent opening*. ➤➤ **patency** /'payt(ə)nsi/ *noun*, **patently** /'pay-/ *adv*.

patent[3] /'payt(ə)nt, 'pat(ə)nt/ *verb trans* to obtain a patent for (an invention). ➤➤ **patentable** *adj*.

patentee /payt(ə)n'tee, pat-/ *noun* somebody to whom a grant is made or a privilege secured by patent.

patent leather /'payt(ə)nt/ *noun* a leather with a hard smooth glossy surface, used for shoes.

patent medicine /'payt(ə)nt/ *noun* a medicine that is made and marketed under a patent, trademark, etc.

patent office /'payt(ə)nt, 'pat(ə)nt/ *noun* a government office for granting patents.

pater /'paytə/ *noun Brit, dated, informal* an affectionate name for one's father. [Latin *pater*]

paterfamilias /,paytəfə'milias, ,pa-/ *noun* (*pl* **patresfamilias** /,pahtrayz-/) the male head of a household. [Latin *paterfamilias*, from *pater* father + *familias*, archaic genitive of *familia*: see FAMILY]

paternal /pə'tuhnl/ *adj* **1** relating to fatherhood; typical of or appropriate to a father: *paternal benevolence*. **2** related through one's father: *a paternal grandfather*. ➤➤ **paternally** *adv*. [Latin *paternus* from *pater* father]

paternalism *noun* a system under which a government or organization deals with its subjects or employees in an authoritarian but benevolent way, *esp* by supplying all their needs and regulating their conduct. ➤➤ **paternalist** *noun and adj*, **paternalistic** /-'listik/ *adj*, **paternalistically** /-'listikli/ *adv*.

paternity /pə'tuhniti/ *noun* **1** being a father. **2** origin or descent from a father.

paternity test *noun* the comparison of the genetic attributes, e.g. blood groups, of a mother, a child, and a man to determine whether the man could be the child's father.

paternoster /patə'nostə, 'patə-/ *noun* **1a** (*often* **Paternoster**) the Lord's Prayer, *esp* in Latin. **b** (*often* **Paternoster**) the recital of this in the Roman Catholic Church. **c** a large rosary bead that indicates when the Lord's Prayer should be recited. **2** a type of lift without doors that moves continuously, allowing people to step on and off as it moves. **3** a weighted fishing line with a row of hooks. [Middle English via late Latin from Latin *pater noster* our father (the first words of the prayer)]

path /pahth/ *noun* (*pl* **paths** /pahdhz/) **1** a track formed by the frequent passage of people or animals. **2** a track specially constructed for a particular use: *a garden path*. **3a** a course or route: *the path of a planet*. **b** a way of life, conduct, or thought: *His path through life was difficult*. **4** in computing, the route taken by an operating system when searching through directories to locate a file, or a series of characters indicating this route. ➤➤ **pathless** *adj.* [Old English *pæth*]

path- *or* **patho-** *comb. form* forming words, denoting: pathological state or disease: *pathogen*. [Latin from Greek *pathos* suffering]

-path *comb. form* forming nouns, denoting: **1** a practitioner of the system of medicine specified: *naturopath*. **2** a sufferer from a disorder affecting a particular part: *psychopath*. [back-formation from -PATHY]

Pathan /pə'tahn/ *noun* a member of a Pashto-speaking people of NW Pakistan and SE Afghanistan, the principal ethnic group of Afghanistan. [Hindi *Paṭhān*]

pathetic /pə'thetik/ *adj* **1a** deserving or arousing pity; pitiful. **b** *informal* contemptible or inadequate: *a pathetic performance*. **2** *archaic* of or affecting the emotions. ➤➤ **pathetically** *adv.* [via late Latin from Greek *pathētikos* capable of feeling, pathetic, from *paschein* to experience, suffer]

pathetic fallacy *noun* the attribution of human characteristics or feelings to animals or inanimate objects, or natural phenomena, e.g. in *the cruel sea*.

pathfinder *noun* **1** somebody who travels through unexplored regions to mark out a new route. **2** somebody who makes an important discovery, e.g. in a field of knowledge.

pathname *noun* in computing, the full description of the location of a file in a hierarchical filing system.

patho- *comb. form* see PATH-.

pathogen /'pathə(ə)n/ *noun* a bacterium, virus, or other disease-causing agent. ➤➤ **pathogenic** /-'jenik/ *adj*, **pathogenicity** /-'nisiti/ *noun.*

pathogenesis /pathə'jenəsis/ *noun* the origination and development of a disease. ➤➤ **pathogenetic** /-'netik/ *adj.* [scientific Latin *pathogenesis*, from PATHO- + *genesis*: see GENESIS]

pathological /pathə'lojikl/ (*NAmer* **pathologic**) *adj* **1** involving or caused by disease. **2** *informal.* **a** having no reasonable foundation; irrational: *She had a pathological fear of publicity.* **b** habitual or compulsive: *a pathological liar.* **3** of pathology. ➤➤ **pathologically** *adv.*

pathology /pə'tholəji/ *noun* **1** the study of the essential nature of diseases, *esp* their causes and the structural and functional changes that they produce. **2** the anatomical and physiological abnormalities that constitute or characterize a particular disease. ➤➤ **pathologist** *noun.* [via Latin from Greek *pathologia* study of the emotions, from PATHO- + -LOGY]

pathos /'paythos/ *noun* **1** a quality evoking pity or compassion: *the pathos of the scene.* **2** an emotion of sympathetic pity. [Greek *pathos* suffering, experience, emotion, from *paschein* to experience or suffer]

pathway *noun* **1** a path, course, or progression. **2** a sequence of biochemical reactions occurring in a living cell, e.g. those reactions by which a substance is broken down to yield energy: *metabolic pathways*.

-pathy *comb. form* forming nouns, denoting: **1** a feeling: *empathy*; *telepathy*. **2** a disorder of a particular part or system: *neuropathy*. **3** a system of medicine based on a particular factor: *osteopathy*. [Latin *-pathia* from Greek *-patheia*, from *pathos*: see PATHOS]

patience /'paysh(ə)ns/ *noun* **1a** the capacity to bear pain, trouble, delay, etc calmly or without complaint. **b** forbearance under provocation or strain. **2** *chiefly Brit* any of various card games that can be played by one person and usu involve the arranging of cards in a prescribed pattern or sequence.

patient[1] /'paysh(ə)nt/ *adj* showing or having patience; calm and forbearing. ➤➤ **patiently** *adv.* [Middle English *pacient* via French from Latin *patient-, patiens*, present part. of *pati* to suffer]

patient[2] *noun* a person awaiting or receiving medical care.

patina /'patinə/ *noun* **1** a green or brown film formed on copper and bronze by weathering or simulated weathering and valued as aesthetically pleasing. **2** a surface appearance of something, e.g. polished wood, that has grown more beautiful with age or use. [Latin *patina* shallow dish]

patio /'patioh/ *noun* (*pl* **patios**) **1** a paved area adjoining a house, often used for sitting or eating outdoors. **2** an open inner court characteristic of houses in Spain or Latin America. [Spanish *patio* courtyard]

patio door *noun* a glass door leading to a patio or balcony.

patisserie /pə'teesəri, pə'tis-/ *noun* **1** an establishment where pastries and cakes are made and sold. **2** pastries and cakes. [French *pâtisserie* from early French *pastiserie* pastry, from late Latin *pasta*: see PASTE[1]]

Patna rice /'patnə/ *noun* a long-grained rice suitable for use in savoury dishes. [named after *Patna*, city in India, near where it was orig produced]

patois /'patwah/ *noun* (*pl* **patois** /'patwahz/) **1** a provincial dialect other than the standard or literary dialect. **2** the terminology or jargon of a particular group. [French *patois*]

patr- *or* **patri-** *or* **patro-** *comb. form* forming words, denoting: father: *patronymic*. [*patr-, patri-* from Latin, from *patr-, pater* father; *patr-, patro-* from Greek, from *patr-, patēr* father]

patresfamilias /,pahtrayzfə'milias/ *noun* pl of PATERFAMILIAS.

patri- *comb. form* see PATR-.

patrial /'paytri-əl/ *noun* formerly, a person with a legal right to reside in Britain because a parent or grandparent was born there. ➤➤ **patriality** /-'aliti/ *noun.* [medieval Latin *patrialis* of one's fatherland, from Latin *patria* fatherland, from *pater* father]

patriarch /'paytriahk/ *noun* **1a** a man who is head of a patriarchy. **b** any of the biblical fathers of the human race or of the Hebrew people. **c** a man who is the father or founder, e.g. of a race, science, religion, or class of people. **d** the oldest member or representative of a group. **e** a venerable old man. **2a** any of the bishops of the sees of Constantinople, Alexandria, Antioch, and Jerusalem or of the ancient see of Rome. **b** the head of any of various Eastern churches. **c** a Roman Catholic bishop next in rank to the pope. ➤➤ **patriarchal** /-'ahkl/ *adj.* [Middle English *patriarche* via French and Latin from Greek *patriarchēs*, from *patria* lineage (from *patr-, patēr* father) + *-archēs*: see -ARCH]

patriarchate /'paytriahkit/ *noun* the office or jurisdiction of a patriarch.

patriarchy *noun* (*pl* **patriarchies**) **1** a system or an instance of social organization marked by the supremacy of the father in the family, the legal dependence of wives and children, and the reckoning of descent and inheritance through the male line. **2** a society governed by men.

patrician /pə'trish(ə)n/ *noun* **1** a person of high birth; an aristocrat. **2** a member of any of the original citizen families of ancient Rome: compare PLEBEIAN[1] (1A), PROLETARIAT (3). **3** *NAmer* a person of breeding and cultivation. ➤➤ **patrician** *adj.* [Middle English *patricion* via French from Latin *patricius* of a noble father, from *patr-, pater* father]

patriciate /pə'trishi-ət/ *noun* **1** (*treated as sing. or pl*) a patrician class. **2** the position or rank of a patrician in ancient Rome.

patricide /'patrisied/ *noun* **1** the act of killing one's father. **2** somebody who commits patricide. ➤➤ **patricidal** /-'siedl/ *adj.* [Latin *patricida* and *patricidium*, from PATRI- + *-cida* and *-cidium*, from *caedere* to cut, to kill]

patrilineal /patri'lini-əl/ *adj* relating to or tracing descent through the paternal line.

patrimony /'patriməni/ *noun* (*pl* **patrimonies**) **1a** property inherited from one's father or male ancestor. **b** something derived from one's ancestors; heritage. **2** formerly, an estate or endowment belonging by ancient right to a church. ➤➤ **patrimonial** /-'mohni-əl/ *adj.* [Middle English *patrimonie* via French from Latin *patrimonium*, from *patr-, pater* father]

patriot /'patri-ət, 'paytri-ət/ *noun* a person who loves and zealously supports their country: *No matter that patriotism is too often the refuge of scoundrels. Dissent, rebellion, and all-round hell-raising remain the true duty of patriots* — Barbara Ehrenreich. ➤➤ **patriotic** /-'otik/ *adj*, **patriotically** /-'otikli/ *adv*, **patriotism** *noun.* [French *patriote* via Latin from Greek *patriōtēs*, from *patrios* of one's father, from *patr-, patēr* father]

patristic /pə'tristik/ *adj* of the fathers of the early Christian Church, or their writings.

patristical /pə'tristikl/ *adj* = PATRISTIC.

patristics /pə'tristiks/ *pl noun* (*treated as sing. or pl*) the study of the writings and theology of the fathers of the early Christian Church.

patro- *comb. form* see PATR-.

patrol[1] /pə'trohl/ *noun* **1** a person or group sent to travel round or along a district, site, road, etc for observation or the maintenance of security. **2** the action of carrying out a patrol. **3** a reconnaissance or combat mission, or the people employed on such a mission. **4**

an aircraft or ship with patrolling duties. **5** a subdivision of a Scout troop or Guide company that has six to eight members.

patrol² *verb trans and intrans* (**patrolled, patrolling**) to carry out a patrol of (an area). ➤➤ **patroller** *noun*. [French *patrouiller* to tramp round in the mud, from *patte* paw + dialect *gadrouille* dirty water]

patrol car *noun* a car used by police to patrol motorways, etc.

patrolman *noun* (*pl* **patrolmen**) *NAmer* a police officer assigned to a beat.

patrology /pəˈtroləji/ *noun* (*pl* **patrologies**) **1** = PATRISTICS. **2** a collection of patristic works. [Latin *patrologia*, from Greek PATRO- + *-logia* -LOGY]

patrol wagon *noun NAmer, Aus, NZ* an enclosed van used by police to carry prisoners; a Black Maria.

patron /ˈpaytrən/ *noun* **1** a person who uses wealth or influence to help an individual, institution, or cause: *Is not a patron, my Lord, one who looks with unconcern on a man struggling for life in the water, and, when he has reached ground, encumbers him with help? —* Dr Johnson. **2** a person who is chosen, named, or honoured as a special guardian, protector, or supporter. **3** a regular customer of a pub, restaurant, etc. **4a** a patrician in ancient Rome who granted protection to a client. **b** the former owner of a freed slave in ancient Rome. **5** *Brit* formerly, a holder of the right to grant a benefice in the Church of England. [Middle English from medieval Latin *patronus* patron, defender, pattern, from Latin *patr- pater* father]

patronage /ˈpatrənij, ˈpay-/ *noun* **1** the support or influence of a patron. **2** the power to control appointments to government jobs or the right to privileges. **3** the granting of favours in a condescending way. **4** the custom provided by the patrons of an establishment or service. **5** the position of a patron in ancient Rome.

patroness /ˈpaytrənis, -ˈnes/ *noun* **1** a woman who uses wealth or influence to help an individual, institution, or cause. **2** a woman who is chosen, named, or honoured as a special guardian, protector, or supporter.

patronize *or* **patronise** /ˈpatrəniez/ *verb trans* **1** to adopt an air of condescension towards (somebody). **2** to be a regular customer of (a pub, hotel, etc). **3** to act as a patron of (an individual, institution, or cause). ➤➤ **patronizer** *noun*, **patronizing** *adj*, **patronizingly** *adv*.

patron saint *noun* a saint regarded as protecting a particular person, group, church, etc.

patronymic /patrəˈnimik/ *noun* a name derived from that of the bearer's father or paternal ancestor, usu by the addition of an affix: compare MATRONYMIC. [via late Latin from Greek *patronymikos* (adj), from *patronymia* patronymic, from PATRO- + *onyma* name]

patsy /ˈpatsi/ *noun* (*pl* **patsies**) *chiefly NAmer, informal* a person who is duped or victimized; a sucker. [perhaps from Italian *pazzo* fool]

patten /ˈpatn/ *noun* a sandal or overshoe set on a wooden sole or metal device, worn formerly to keep one's feet out of the mud. [Middle English from early French *patin*, from *patte* paw, hoof]

patter¹ /ˈpatə/ *verb intrans* (**pattered, pattering**) **1** to strike lightly, rapidly, and repeatedly: *Rain pattered against the window pane*. **2** to run with quick light steps. [frequentative of PAT²]

patter² *noun* a quick succession of taps or pats.

patter³ *noun* **1a** the rapid talk of a comedian. **b** the talk with which some entertainers accompany their routine. **c** the glib talk of a salesperson. **2** the jargon of a profession or group.

patter⁴ *verb intrans* (**pattered, pattering**) to talk glibly and volubly. [Middle English *patren* to gabble a prayer, from PATERNOSTER]

pattern¹ /ˈpat(ə)n/ *noun* **1** a repeated decorative design, e.g. on fabric. **2** a natural or chance arrangement or sequence: *the pattern of events*. **3** a design, model, or set of instructions for making something: *a dress pattern*. **4** a model for making a mould into which molten metal is poured to form a casting. **5** a form or model proposed for imitation; an example. **6** a specimen or sample, e.g. of wallpaper. [Middle English *patron* via French from medieval Latin *patronus*: see PATRON]

pattern² *verb trans* **1** to decorate (something) with a pattern. **2** (+ on/after) to make or model (something) according to a pattern. **3** to arrange (something) as a pattern.

patty /ˈpati/ *noun* (*pl* **patties**) **1** a small flat cake of chopped food, *esp* minced meat. **2** a little pie or pasty. **3** *NAmer* a round peppermint covered with chocolate. [French *pâté*: see PÂTÉ]

patulous /ˈpatyooləs/ *adj* spreading widely from a centre: *a tree with patulous branches*. [Latin *patulus* from *patēre* to be open]

paua /ˈpowə/ *noun* **1** an edible shellfish of New Zealand with a rainbow-coloured shell that is often used as an ornament: *Haliotis iris*. **2** a fishhook made from a paua shell. [Maori *paua*]

paucity /ˈpawsiti/ *noun* smallness of number or quantity; insufficiency or scarcity. [Middle English *paucite* via French from Latin *paucitat-, paucitas*, from *paucus* little]

Pauli exclusion principle /ˈpawli/ *noun* = EXCLUSION PRINCIPLE. [named after Wolfgang *Pauli* d.1958, Austrian-born US physicist who formulated it]

Pauline /ˈpawlien/ *adj* relating to or characteristic of the apostle Paul (1st cent. AD).

Paul Jones /ˌpawl ˈjohnz/ *noun* a ballroom dance during which the couples change partners. [prob named after John *Paul Jones* d.1792, US naval officer]

paulownia /pawˈlohni-ə/ *noun* a small Chinese tree of the figwort family with fragrant violet flowers: genus *Paulownia*. [Latin genus name, named after Anna *Paulovna* d.1865, Russian princess]

paunch /pawnch/ *noun* **1** a large or protruding belly or stomach. **2** = RUMEN. ➤➤ **paunchiness** *noun*, **paunchy** *adj*. [Middle English via French from Latin *pantic-, pantex* intestine]

pauper /ˈpawpə/ *noun* **1** a very poor person. **2** formerly, somebody supported by charity or from public funds. ➤➤ **pauperism** *noun*. [Latin *pauper*: see POOR]

pauperize *or* **pauperise** *verb trans* to reduce (somebody) to poverty or destitution. ➤➤ **pauperization** /-ˈzaysh(ə)n/ *noun*.

paupiette /pohˈpyet/ *noun* a thin slice of meat or fish rolled round a stuffing. [French *paupiette*, derivative of early French *poulpe* pulp, from Latin *pulpa*]

pause¹ /pawz/ *noun* **1** a temporary stop, e.g. for rest or thought: *The notes I handle no better than many pianists. But the pauses between the notes – ah, that is where the genius resides! —* Artur Schnabel. **2** the sign denoting a FERMATA (the lengthening of a musical note or rest). **3** a break in a line of poetry. **4** a mechanism on a video or tape recorder that enables the tape to be stopped temporarily during playing or recording. ✱ **give somebody pause** to make somebody hesitate: *For in that sleep of death what dreams may come … must give us pause —* Shakespeare. [Middle English via Latin *pausa* from Greek *pausis*, from *pauein* to stop]

pause² *verb intrans* **1** to stop temporarily. **2** to linger for a time. ➤ *verb trans* to cause (something, e.g. a recording) to stop temporarily: *She paused the video when the phone rang*.

pavane *or* **pavan** /pəˈvan, pəˈvahn/ *noun* a stately court dance introduced into England in the 16th cent., or a piece of music for this dance. [early French *pavane* via Old Spanish *pavana* from Old Italian *Pavana*, from *Pavo*, dialect name of the city of Padua]

pave /payv/ *verb trans* to cover (a piece of ground) with material, e.g. stone or concrete, to form a firm flat surface for walking or travelling on. ✱ **pave the way for** to prepare a smooth easy way for (something); to facilitate development of (something). ➤➤ **paved** *adj*, **paver** *noun*, **paving** *noun*. [Middle English *paven* via French *paver* from Latin *pavire* to strike or stamp]

pavé /ˈpavay/ *noun* **1** a setting in which jewels are set closely together to conceal a metal base. **2** a pavement. [French *pavé*, past part. of *paver*: see PAVE]

pavement *noun* **1** *Brit* a surfaced raised walk for pedestrians at the side of a road. **2** *NAmer* the artificially covered surface of a road. **3** in geology, a level area of bare rock. [Middle English via French from Latin *pavimentum* beaten floor, from *pavire* to strike or stamp]

pavement artist *noun Brit* a person who draws coloured pictures on the pavement in the hope of getting money from passers-by.

pavilion¹ /pəˈvilyən/ *noun* **1** *Brit* a permanent building on a sports ground, *esp* a cricket ground, containing changing rooms, etc. **2a** a light ornamental structure in a garden, park, etc. **b** a temporary structure erected at an exhibition by an individual exhibitor. **c** a large often sumptuous tent. **3** a projecting or visually distinct part of a building forming part of a symmetrical composition. **4** any of several detached or semidetached units into which a building, e.g. a hospital, is divided. [Middle English *pavilon* via French from Latin *papilion-, papilio* butterfly; because the flaps of a tent were thought to resemble a butterfly's wings]

pavilion[2] *verb trans* (**pavilioned, pavilioning**) *literary* **1** to provide (a place) with a pavilion. **2** to put (something) in or as if in a pavilion.

pavior or **paviour** /'payvyə/ *noun* **1** a paving stone. **2** *archaic* a person who paves. [Middle English *pavier* from *paven*: see PAVE]

pavlova /pav'lohvə/ *noun* a dessert made of meringue topped with cream and fruit. [named after Anna *Pavlova* d.1931, Russian ballet dancer]

Pavlovian /pav'lohvi-ən/ *adj* **1** of Ivan Pavlov (d.1936), Russian physiologist, or his work and theories on conditioning, *esp* his demonstration of the conditioned reflex. **2** said of a reaction: produced automatically in response to a stimulus; predictable.

paw[1] /paw/ *noun* **1** the clawed, padded foot of a lion, dog, or other animal. **2** *informal* a human hand. [Middle English from early French *poue*, prob of Germanic origin]

paw[2] *verb trans and intrans* **1** *informal* to feel or touch (somebody) clumsily or indecently. **2** to touch, scrape, or strike (something) with a paw or hoof.

pawky /'pawki/ *adj* (**pawkier, pawkiest**) *chiefly Scot, N Eng* having a dry wit; sardonic. ➤➤ **pawkily** *adv*, **pawkiness** *noun*. [Scottish and N English dialect *pawk* trick]

pawl /pawl/ *noun* a pivoted tongue or sliding bolt on one part of a machine that is adapted to fall into notches on another part, e.g. a ratchet wheel, so as to permit motion in only one direction. [perhaps modification of Dutch *pal*]

pawn[1] /pawn/ *noun* **1** in chess, any of eight pieces of each colour of least value. Pawns have the power to move forward, usu one square at a time, and diagonally when capturing another piece. **2** somebody who can be used to further the purposes of somebody else. [Middle English *pown* via French from Latin *pedon-, pedo* foot soldier, from *ped-, pes* foot]

pawn[2] *verb trans* to deposit (something) with a pawnbroker as a pledge or security.

pawn[3] *noun* **1** the state of being deposited with somebody as a pledge or security, e.g. for a loan: *My ring was in pawn.* **2** something deposited or pledged in this way. [Middle English *paun* from early French *pan* pledge, security, of Germanic origin]

pawnbroker *noun* a person who lends money on the security of personal property pledged, which can be sold if the money is not repaid. ➤➤ **pawnbroking** *noun*.

pawnshop *noun* a pawnbroker's shop.

pawpaw or **papaw** /'pawpaw/ *noun* **1** = PAPAYA. **2a** a N American tree of the custard-apple family with purple flowers and a yellow edible fruit: *Asimina triloba*. **b** the edible fruit of this tree.

PAX *abbr Brit* private automatic (telephone) exchange.

pax[1] /paks/ *noun* **1** a tablet decorated with a sacred figure, e.g. of Christ, ceremonially kissed by participants at mass. **2** = KISS OF PEACE. [Middle English from Latin *pax* PEACE]

pax[2] *interj Brit, informal, dated* used by children as an indication that they wish to stop fighting or participating in a game.

pay[1] /pay/ *verb* (*past tense and past part.* **paid** /payd/) ➤ *verb trans* **1** to give money to (somebody) in return for goods or services. **2a** to give (money) in return for goods, property, or services. **b** to discharge a debt or obligation for (a bill or account). **3** to transfer or dispose of (money): *I have paid a large sum into the bank.* **4** to give or forfeit (something) in reparation or retribution: *to pay a penalty.* **5** to give or offer (attention, one's respects, etc). **6** to make (a call or visit). **7a** to earn (an amount) as a return: *an investment paying 5%.* **b** to be profitable or advantageous to (somebody): *It would pay us to wait a little longer.* ➤ *verb intrans* **1a** (*often* + for) to give money in return for something: *Who paid for the meal?* **b** to discharge a debt or obligation. **2** to make amends or be punished: *You will pay for this.* **3** to be worth the expense or effort: *It pays to be patient.* ✳ **pay court to** to flatter (somebody). **pay through the nose** see NOSE[1]. ➤➤ **payee** /pay'ee/ *noun*, **payer** *noun*. [Middle English *payen* via French from Latin *pacare* to pacify, from *pac-, pax* PEACE]

pay[2] *noun* **1** money paid as a salary or wage. **2** (*used before a noun*) requiring payment for its use: *pay TV.* ✳ **in the pay of** employed by (somebody).

pay[3] *verb trans* (*past tense and past part.* **payed**) to coat (the seams of a wooden ship) with a waterproof substance. [obsolete French *peier* from Latin *picare*, from *pic-, pix* PITCH[3]]

payable *adj* that may, can, or must be paid.

payback *noun* **1** financial return, e.g. from an investment. **2** *informal* an act of retaliation or revenge.

pay back *verb trans* **1** to repay (money owed). **2** to get revenge on (somebody).

paybed *noun* in Britain, a hospital bed in a National Health Service hospital which is paid for by the occupant.

pay channel *noun* a television channel paid for separately by the viewer.

payday *noun* the day of the week or month on which wages, etc are regularly paid.

pay dirt *noun* **1** *NAmer* earth or ore that yields a profit to a miner. **2** *chiefly NAmer, informal* a useful or remunerative discovery or object: *They had hit pay dirt with their latest scheme.*

PAYE *abbr Brit* pay as you earn, a system of deducting income tax from pay before an employee receives it.

payee /pay'ee/ *noun* a person receiving payment, e.g. somebody to whom a cheque is made out.

paying guest *noun* a lodger.

payload *noun* **1** the revenue-producing load that a vehicle can carry. **2** the explosive charge carried in the warhead of a missile. **3** the load carried in a spacecraft that relates directly to the purpose of the flight, as opposed to the load necessary for operation.

paymaster *noun* **1** an officer or agent whose duty it is to pay salaries or wages. **2** a person or organization employing and controlling somebody.

paymaster general *noun* (*pl* **paymasters general** or **paymaster generals**) (*often* **Paymaster General**) a British government minister, orig in charge of payments, who is often made a member of the cabinet and entrusted with special functions.

payment *noun* **1** the act of paying: *Alas! how deeply painful is all payment!* — Byron. **2** a sum of money paid. **3** a recompense, e.g. a reward or punishment.

paynim /'paynim/ *noun archaic* a non-Christian, *esp* a Muslim. [Middle English *painim* via Old French from late Latin *paganismus* from *paganus* pagan]

payoff *noun informal* **1a** a payment received, e.g. on being discharged from employment or as a bribe. **b** a profit or reward. **2** a decisive fact or factor resolving a situation or bringing about a definitive conclusion. **3** the climax of an incident or chain of events; *specif* the denouement of a narrative.

pay off *verb trans* **1** to give all that is due to (somebody), *esp* when discharging an employee. **2** to pay (a debt or a creditor) in full. **3** to bribe (somebody). ➤ *verb intrans informal* to yield returns; to be successful or profitable.

payola /pay'ohlə/ *noun chiefly NAmer* an undercover or indirect payment for unofficial promotion of a commercial product. [prob alteration of PAYOFF]

pay out *verb trans* **1** to give out or disburse (money). **2** to slacken (a rope) and allow it to run out gradually.

pay-out *noun* a large payment of money.

pay-per-view *noun* a service offered by cable or satellite television companies by which subscribers pay an additional fee to watch a particular programme.

payphone *noun* a public telephone that is operated by coins or a phonecard.

payroll *noun* **1** a list of those entitled to be paid by a company and of the amounts due to each. **2** the sum necessary to pay all those on a payroll.

pay TV *noun* a television broadcasting system in which viewers pay a subscription to watch a particular channel.

pay up *verb trans* to pay (money owed) in full or on demand.

PB *abbr* in athletics, personal best.

Pb *abbr* the chemical symbol for lead. [Latin *plumbum*]

pb *abbr* paperback.

PBS *abbr NAmer* Public Broadcasting Service.

PBX *abbr* private branch (telephone) exchange.

PC *abbr* **1** personal computer. **2** police constable. **3** political correctness. **4** politically correct. **5** Privy Councillor.

pc *abbr* **1** per cent. **2** postcard.

PCB *abbr* **1** polychlorinated biphenyl. **2** printed circuit board.

P-Celtic *noun* = BRYTHONIC. [from the development in these languages of the phoneme *p* from Indo-European *qu*]

PCI *abbr* peripheral component interconnect.

pcm *abbr* pulse code modulation.

PCP *abbr* **1** phencyclidine. **2** pneumocystis carinii pneumonia.

pct *abbr* NAmer per cent.

PCV *abbr* Brit passenger-carrying vehicle.

PD *abbr* **1** per diem. **2** NAmer police department. **3** potential difference. **4** public domain.

Pd *abbr* the chemical symbol for palladium.

pd *abbr* paid.

Pde *abbr* in street names, Parade.

PDQ *adv informal* immediately. [short for *pretty damn quick*]

PDSA *abbr Brit* People's Dispensary for Sick Animals.

PDT *abbr* Pacific daylight time (time zone).

PE *abbr* **1** Peru (international vehicle registration). **2** physical education.

pea /pee/ *noun* **1a** a widely cultivated leguminous climbing plant with pods containing round protein-rich green seeds: *Pisum sativum.* **b** a seed of this plant, used as a vegetable. **2** used in the names of various leguminous plants related to or resembling the pea, e.g. the chick-pea. [back-formation from *pease* (taken as a pl), from Old English *pise* via Latin *pisum* from Greek *pison*]

pea-brain *noun informal* a stupid person. ⟫⟫ **pea-brained** *adj.*

peace /pees/ *noun* **1a** a state of tranquillity or quiet. **b** public order and security maintained by law or custom: *a breach of the peace.* **2a** mutual concord, *esp* between countries: *I would rather have peace in the world than be President* — Harry S Truman. **b** an agreement to end hostilities. **3** freedom from disquieting or oppressive thoughts or emotions: *peace of mind.* **4** harmony in personal relations. **5 (the peace)** in the Christian Church, an action such as a handshake or kiss, exchanged as a symbol of love or harmony. ✳ **at peace 1** in a state of concord or tranquillity. **2** *euphem* dead. **hold one's peace** to remain silent in spite of having something to say. **keep the peace** to avoid or prevent discord or civil disturbance. [Middle English *pees* via French from Latin *pac-, pax*]

peaceable *adj* **1** disposed to peace; not inclined to dispute or quarrel. **2** free from strife or disorder. ⟫⟫ **peaceableness** *noun*, **peaceably** *adv.*

peace corps *noun* a body of trained volunteer personnel sent by the US government to assist developing nations.

peace dividend *noun* the money saved on armaments that is available for other purposes when a nation reduces its military capacity.

peaceful /'peesf(ə)l/ *adj* **1** untroubled by conflict, agitation, or commotion; quiet or tranquil. **2** devoid of violence or force: *a peaceful demonstration.* **3** not inclined to dispute or quarrel; peaceable. ⟫⟫ **peacefully** *adv*, **peacefulness** *noun.*

peacekeeping *noun* the preserving of peace; *esp* international enforcement and supervision of a truce between hostile states or communities. ⟫⟫ **peacekeeper** *noun.*

peacemaker *noun* somebody who makes peace, *esp* by reconciling opposing sides. ⟫⟫ **peacemaking** *noun and adj.*

peace offering *noun* **1** something given or done to produce peace or reconciliation. **2** in the Bible, an offering to God.

peace pipe *noun* = CALUMET.

peace sign *noun* a sign made by holding the palm outwards and forming a V with the index and middle fingers, used to indicate the desire for peace.

peacetime *noun* **1** a time when a nation is not at war. **2** (*used before a noun*) relating to a time of peace: *a peacetime government.*

peach¹ /peech/ *noun* **1a** an edible fruit with a large stone, thin downy skin, and sweet yellow flesh. **b** the low spreading tree, belonging to the rose family, that bears this fruit: *Prunus persica.* **2** a light yellowish pink colour. **3** *informal* a particularly excellent or attractive person or thing. ✳ **peaches and cream** said of a complexion: clear and pale, with pink cheeks. ⟫⟫ **peach** *adj.* [Middle English *peche* via French from Latin *persicum*, neuter of *persicus* Persian]

peach² *verb intrans informal* to turn informer: *He peached on his accomplices.* [Middle English *pechen*, short for *apechen* to accuse, from early French *empechier*: see IMPEACH]

peach melba /'melbə/ *noun* a dish of peaches topped with ice cream and raspberry purée. [named after Dame Nellie *Melba* d.1931, Australian operatic soprano]

peachy *adj* (**peachier, peachiest**) **1** resembling a peach in taste, smell, colour, or texture. **2** *chiefly NAmer, informal* very pleasing; excellent. ⟫⟫ **peachiness** *noun.*

peacock /'peekok/ *noun* **1** a male peafowl with very large brightly coloured tail feathers that are tipped with eyelike spots and can be erected and spread in a fan: *'You know her curiously shrill voice?' 'Yes, she is a peacock in everything but beauty.'* — Oscar Wilde. **2** a peafowl. [Middle English *pecok*, from Old English *pēa* peafowl (from a prehistoric Germanic word borrowed from Latin *pavon-, pavo* peacock) + *cok* COCK¹]

peacock blue *adj* of a lustrous greenish blue colour. ⟫⟫ **peacock blue** *noun.*

peacock butterfly *noun* a butterfly with large eyespots on the wings: *Inachis io.*

peacock ore *noun* = BORNITE.

peafowl *noun* any of several species of very large ground-living pheasants of SE Asia and the Indian subcontinent: *Pavo cristatus* and other species. [*pea-* as in PEACOCK + FOWL¹]

pea green *adj* of a light yellowish green colour. ⟫⟫ **pea green** *noun.*

peahen *noun* a female peafowl. [Middle English *pehenne*, from Old English *pēa* (see PEACOCK) + *henn* HEN]

pea jacket *noun* a heavy woollen double-breasted jacket formerly worn by sailors. [by folk etymology from Dutch *pijjekker*, from *pij*, a kind of cloth + *jekker* jacket]

peak¹ /peek/ *noun* **1a** the top of a hill or mountain ending in a point, or a hill or mountain with a pointed top. **b** something resembling a mountain peak. **2** a projecting part on the front of a cap or hood. **3a** a high point in a course of development, *esp* as represented on a graph. **b** the highest level or greatest degree. **4** a sharp or pointed end. **5a** the upper rearmost corner of a four-cornered fore-and-aft sail. **b** the narrow part of a ship's bow or stern. **6** (*used before a noun*) at or reaching the maximum of capacity, value, or activity: *peak productivity; peak traffic hours.* [perhaps alteration of PIKE⁷]

peak² *verb intrans* to reach a maximum or high point.

peak³ *verb intrans archaic* to grow thin or sickly. [origin unknown]

peaked¹ *adj* said of a cap: having a peak.

peaked² *adj* = PEAKY.

peak flow meter *noun* a device used to measure a person's lung capacity, e.g. to monitor asthma.

peak load *noun* maximum demand or density, e.g. of electricity or traffic.

peak time *noun* the time of greatest demand for a service, e.g. television programmes or public transport.

peaky *adj* (**peakier, peakiest**) looking pale and wan; sickly.

peal¹ /peel/ *noun* **1** the loud ringing of bells. **2a** in bell-ringing, a complete set of changes rung on a set of bells. **b** a set of bells tuned to the notes of the major scale for change ringing. **3** a loud prolonged sound: *peals of laughter.* [Middle English, in the sense 'bell rung as a summons to church', short for *appel* appeal, from *appelen*: see APPEAL²]

peal² *verb intrans* **1** said of bells: to ring loudly or in a peal. **2** said of laughter or thunder: to make a loud prolonged sound.

peanut *noun* **1a** a widely cultivated leguminous plant with pods containing one to three seeds that ripen in the earth: *Arachis hypogaea.* **b** the pod or oily edible seed of this plant. **2** *informal* (*in pl*) a trifling amount of money.

peanut butter *noun* a spread made from ground peanuts.

pear /peə/ *noun* **1** a yellowish brown edible fruit, which widens at the end furthest from the stalk. **2** the tree, belonging to the rose family, that bears this fruit: genus *Pyrus.* [Old English *peru* from Latin *pirum*]

pearl¹ /puhl/ *noun* **1a** a hard round lustrous mass, usu milky-white in colour, formed in the shell of some molluscs, *esp* oysters, and used as a gem. **b** an artificial imitation of this. **c** = MOTHER-OF-PEARL. **2** somebody or something very rare or precious. **3** a slightly bluish grey or white colour. ⟫⟫ **pearl** *adj.* [Middle English via French *perle* from Latin *pernula*, dimin. of *perna* haunch, sea mussel]

pearl² *verb trans* to set or adorn (something) with or as if with pearls. ➤ *verb intrans* **1** *literary* to form drops or beads like pearls. **2** to fish or search for pearls.

pearl³ *noun Brit* = PICOT. [alteration of PURL¹]

pearl ash *noun archaic* potassium carbonate in its commercial form.

pearl barley *noun* barley that has been ground into medium-sized grains.

pearler *noun* a person who dives for pearls, or a boat involved in the pearl business.

pearlized *or* **pearlised** *adj* given a lustrous or iridescent surface or finish: *pearlized nail polish.*

pearl millet *noun* a tall cereal grass grown in Africa, Asia, and S USA for its edible seeds and for forage: *Pennisetum glaucum.*

pearlwort *noun* a very small plant of the pink family with minute white or green flowers: genus *Sagina.*

pearly¹ *adj* (**pearlier, pearliest**) resembling, containing, or decorated with pearls or mother-of-pearl. ➤➤ **pearliness** *noun.*

pearly² *noun* (*pl* **pearlies**) *Brit* **1** (*in pl*) the clothes worn by a pearly king or queen, or the buttons used to decorate these clothes. **2** *informal* (*in pl*) teeth.

Pearly Gates *pl noun informal* the gates of heaven. [from the reference in Revelation 21:21]

pearly king *or* **pearly queen** *noun* a man or woman who is a member of a family of London costermongers traditionally entitled to dress in clothes covered with pearl buttons on ceremonial occasions.

pearmain /'peəmayn/ *noun* any of various pear-shaped eating apples. [Middle English *permayn*, a type of pear, via French from Latin *Parmensis* of Parma, city in Italy]

pear-shaped *adj* having a figure with wide hips and a narrow upper body. ✳ **go pear-shaped** *Brit, informal* to go wrong.

peart /piət, pyuht/ *adj NAmer, dialect* lively. [variant of PERT]

peasant /'pez(ə)nt/ *noun* **1** a member of a class of usu poor people, e.g. small landowners or farm labourers, of low social status. **2** *informal* an uneducated or rude person. ➤➤ **peasantry** *noun.* [Middle English *paissaunt* from French *paisent*, ultimately from Latin *pagus* country district]

peascod *noun* see PEASECOD.

pease /peez/ *noun archaic* a pea or peas. [see PEA]

peasecod *or* **peascod** *noun archaic* a pea pod. [Middle English *pesecod*, from *pese* PEASE + *cod* bag, husk, from Old English]

pease pudding *noun chiefly Brit* a puree of boiled split peas, usu served with ham, gammon, or bacon.

peashooter /'peeshoohtə/ *noun* a toy blowpipe for shooting peas.

pea-souper /'soohpə/ *noun* **1** *Brit, informal* a heavy yellowish fog. **2** *Can, derog* a French Canadian.

peat /peet/ *noun* partially carbonized vegetable tissue formed by partial decomposition in water of various plants, e.g. mosses, found in large bogs. It is used as a fuel for domestic heating and as a fertilizer. ➤➤ **peaty** *adj.* [Middle English *pete* from medieval Latin *peta*]

peat moss *noun* **1** = SPHAGNUM. **2** a peat bog.

pebble¹ /'pebl/ *noun* **1** a small rounded stone, worn smooth by the action of water or sand. **2** = ROCK CRYSTAL. **3** *informal* (*used before a noun*) very thick: *pebble lenses.* ➤➤ **pebbly** *adj.* [Middle English *pobble* from Old English *papolstān*, from *papol-* (prob imitative) + *stān* STONE¹]

pebble² *verb trans* to pave or cover (something) with pebbles or something resembling pebbles.

pebbledash *noun chiefly Brit* a finish for exterior walls consisting of small pebbles embedded in a stucco base. ➤➤ **pebbledashed** *adj.*

pec /pek/ *noun informal* (*usu in pl*) a pectoral muscle.

pecan /'peekən, pi'kan/ *noun* **1** a smooth oblong edible nut. **2** a large hickory tree of the USA and Mexico that bears this nut: *Carya illinoensis.* [French *pacane,* of Algonquian origin]

peccable /'pekəbl/ *adj formal* prone to sin. [early French *peccable,* ultimately from Latin *peccare* to stumble or sin]

peccadillo /pekə'diloh/ *noun* (*pl* **peccadilloes** *or* **peccadillos**) a slight or trifling offence. [Spanish *pecadillo,* dimin. of *pecado* sin, from Latin *peccatum,* neuter past part. of *peccare* to stumble or sin]

peccant /'pekənt/ *adj archaic* **1** guilty or sinning. **2** producing disease. ➤➤ **peccancy** *noun.* [Latin *peccant-, peccans,* present part. of *peccare* to stumble or sin]

peccary /'pekəri/ *noun* (*pl* **peccaries**) any of several species of largely nocturnal American mammals related to and resembling the pigs: family Tayassuidae. [Carib *pikari*]

peck¹ /pek/ *verb trans* **1** to strike or pierce (something) with the beak or a pointed tool. **2** to make (a hole) by pecking. **3** to kiss (somebody) perfunctorily. **4** said of a bird: to pick up (e.g. a worm) with the beak. ➤ *verb intrans* **1** to strike, pierce, or pick up something with or as if with the beak. **2** *informal* to eat reluctantly and in small bites: *She just pecked at her food.* [Middle English *pecken,* alteration of *piken* to pierce]

peck² *noun* **1** an impression or hole made by pecking. **2** a quick sharp stroke. **3** a light kiss.

peck³ *noun* **1** a unit of volume or capacity equal to 2gall (9.092l). **2** *archaic* a large quantity or number: *a peck of troubles.* [Middle English *pek* from Old French]

peck⁴ *verb intrans* said of a horse: to stumble on landing from a jump. [alteration of PICK⁴ in the sense 'to pitch']

pecker *noun NAmer, coarse slang* a penis. ✳ **keep one's pecker up** *Brit, informal* to stay cheerful in the face of adversity [from an earlier meaning of the word].

pecking order *noun* **1** the natural hierarchy within a flock of birds, *esp* poultry, in which each bird pecks another lower in the scale without fear of retaliation. **2** a social hierarchy.

peckish *adj chiefly Brit, informal* slightly hungry.

peck order *noun* = PECKING ORDER.

pecorino /pekə'reenoh/ *noun* a hard pungent Italian cheese made from sheep's milk. [Italian *pecorino* of ewes, from *pecora* ewe, from Latin *pecora* ewe, sheep]

pecs /peks/ *pl noun informal* pectoral muscles.

pecten /'pekten/ *noun* (*pl* **pectines** /'pektineez/ *or* **pectens**) **1** a body part that resembles a comb; *esp* a folded membrane projecting inwards from the retina of a bird or reptile. **2** = SCALLOP¹ (IA). [Latin *pectin-, pecten* comb, scallop]

pectin /'pektin/ *noun* a water-soluble substance that binds adjacent cell walls in plant tissues and yields a gel that acts as a setting agent in jams and fruit jellies. ➤➤ **pectic** /'pektik/ *adj.* [French *pectine,* ultimately from Greek *pēgnynai* to fix or coagulate]

pectines /'pektineez/ *noun* pl of PECTEN.

pectoral¹ /'pekt(ə)rəl/ *adj* relating to or in the region of the chest. [French *pectoral* from Latin *pectoralis,* from *pector-, pectus* breast]

pectoral² *noun* **1** a pectoral muscle. **2** something worn on the chest, e.g. a breastplate.

pectoral fin *noun* either of the fins of a fish that correspond to the forelimbs of a quadruped.

pectoral muscle *noun* any of the muscles connecting the front walls of the chest with the bones of the upper arm and shoulder, of which there are two on each side in human beings.

peculate /'pekyoolayt/ *verb trans formal* to embezzle (public funds). ➤➤ **peculation** /-'laysh(ə)n/ *noun,* **peculator** *noun.* [Latin *peculatus,* past part. of *peculari,* from *peculium:* see PECULIAR¹]

peculiar¹ /pi'kyoohlyə/ *adj* **1** different from the usual or normal; strange or curious. **2** (+ to) belonging exclusively to somebody or something: *a style of architecture peculiar to this area.* **3** *formal* special or distinctive; particular: *He had received peculiar favours.* ➤➤ **peculiarly** *adv.* [Middle English *peculier* from Latin *peculiaris* of private property, special, from *peculium* private property, from *pecu* cattle]

peculiar² *noun chiefly Brit* something exempt from ordinary jurisdiction; *esp* a church or parish independent of the diocese in which it is situated.

peculiarity /pi,kyoohli'ariti/ *noun* (*pl* **peculiarities**) **1** a distinguishing characteristic. **2** the state of being peculiar.

pecuniary /pi'kyoohni·əri/ *adj formal* of or measured in money. ➤➤ **pecuniarily** *adv.* [Latin *pecuniarius,* from *pecunia* money, from *pecu* cattle]

-ped *or* **-pede** *comb. form* forming nouns, denoting: a foot or feet: *quadruped; centipede.* [Latin *ped-, pes* foot]

pedagogics /pedə'gojiks/ *pl noun dated* (*treated as sing. or pl*) pedagogy. ➤➤ **pedagogic** *adj*, **pedagogical** *adj*, **pedagogically** *adv*.

pedagogue /'pedəgog/ *noun formal or humorous* a teacher. [Middle English *pedagoge* via French and Latin from Greek *paidagōgos* slave who escorted children to school, from *paid-*, *pais* child + *agōgos* leader, from *agein* to lead]

pedagogy /'pedəgogy, -ji/ *noun* (*pl* **pedagogies**) the science, profession, or theory of teaching.

pedal[1] /'pedl/ *noun* **1** a lever operated by the foot, *esp* one of the two that drive the chainwheel of a bicycle, one used to control a motor vehicle, or one pressed in playing a musical instrument. **2** = PEDAL-NOTE (2). [early French *pedale* via Italian from Latin *pedalis*: see PEDAL[3]]

pedal[2] *verb* (**pedalled, pedalling**, *NAmer* **pedaled, pedaling**) ➤ *verb intrans* **1** to use or work a pedal or pedals. **2** to ride a bicycle. ➤ *verb trans* to work the pedals of (a bicycle, piano, etc). ➤➤ **pedaller** *noun*.

pedal[3] /'pedl, 'peedl/ *adj* relating to or in the region of the foot or feet. [Latin *pedalis*, from *ped-*, *pes* foot]

pedal-note *noun* **1** any of the lowest notes that can be sounded on a brass instrument, being eight notes below the normal range. **2** a single sustained note, usu in the bass, that sounds against changing harmonies in the other parts. [from the playing of the lowest notes on the organ by means of pedals]

pedalo /'pedəloh/ *noun* (*pl* **pedalos** *or* **pedaloes**) *Brit* a small pleasure boat that is propelled by paddles turned by pedals.

pedal point *noun* = PEDAL-NOTE (2).

pedal pushers *pl noun* calf-length trousers worn by women and girls.

pedal steel guitar *noun* an electronically amplified guitar that is mounted on a stand with pedals, the pitch of which can be varied by use of the pedals or by sliding a steel bar across the frets.

pedant /'ped(ə)nt/ *noun* a person who is unnecessarily concerned with detail, *esp* in the presentation or use of knowledge: *this dried-up pedant, this elaborator of small explanations about as important as the surplus stock of false antiquities kept in a vendor's back chamber* — George Eliot. ➤➤ **pedantic** /pi'dantik/ *adj*, **pedantically** /pi'dantikli/ *adv*, **pedantry** *noun*. [early French *pedant* from Italian *pedante*]

peddle /'pedl/ *verb trans* **1a** to sell (goods) as a pedlar. **b** to sell (illegal drugs). **2** *derog* to seek to disseminate (ideas or opinions): *He was accused of peddling racist views.* ➤ *verb intrans* to sell goods as a pedlar. [back-formation from PEDDLER, PEDLAR]

peddler *noun* **1** a person who peddles something: *a drug peddler*. **2** *NAmer* see PEDLAR.

-pede *comb. form* see -PED.

pederast *or* **paederast** /'pedərast/ *noun* a man who has sexual intercourse with a boy. ➤➤ **pederastic** /-'rastik/ *adj*. [Greek *paiderastēs*, literally 'lover of boys', from *paid-*, *pais* child, boy + *erastēs* lover, from *erasthai* to love]

pederasty *or* **paederasty** /'pedərasti/ *noun* sexual intercourse between a man and a boy.

pedestal /'pedistl/ *noun* **1a** a base supporting a column. **b** the base of an upright structure, e.g. a statue. **2** a supporting column of a washbasin or a toilet. **3** a base or foundation. **4** a position of uncritical esteem or idealized respect: *He put his wife on a pedestal.* [early French *piedestal* from Old Italian *piedestallo*, from *pie di stallo* foot of a stall]

pedestrian[1] /pi'destri·ən/ *noun* **1** a person going on foot; a walker. **2** (*used before a noun*) of or for pedestrians: *a pedestrian precinct.*

pedestrian[2] *adj* dull or commonplace; unrelieved by flights of fancy: *'Sedate' is a better word for these essays. And two of them might be called even pedestrian. No harm in that: pedestrian documentation is what there is a call for* — Donald Davie. ➤➤ **pedestrianly** *adv*. [Latin *pedestr-*, *pedester*, literally 'going on foot', from *ped-*, *pes* foot]

pedestrian crossing *noun Brit* a marked stretch of road on which pedestrians crossing the road have priority over the traffic in certain circumstances.

pedestrianize *or* **pedestrianise** *verb trans* to convert (e.g. a street) to a paved area for pedestrians only. ➤➤ **pedestrianization** /-'zaysh(ə)n/ *noun*.

pediatrics /peedi'atriks/ *pl noun NAmer* see PAEDIATRICS.

pedicab /'pedikab/ *noun* a covered tricycle used as a taxi in some Asian countries. [PEDAL[1] + -I- + CAB]

pedicel /'pedis(ə)l/ *noun* **1** a plant stalk that supports a fruiting or spore-bearing organ. **2** a narrow basal attachment of an animal organ or part, e.g. the narrow stalk joining a spider's abdomen to the rest of its body. ➤➤ **pedicellate** /pe'dis(ə)layt/ *adj*. [scientific Latin *pedicellus*, dimin. of Latin *pediculus* louse]

pedicle /'pedikl/ *noun* **1** = PEDICEL. **2** part of a skin graft that is still attached to its original site. [Latin *pediculus*, dimin. of *ped-*, *pes* foot]

pediculosis /pi,dikyoo'lohsis/ *noun* infestation with lice. ➤➤ **pediculous** /pi'dikyooləs/ *adj*. [Latin *pediculus* louse + -OSIS]

pedicure[1] /'pedikyooə/ *noun* a treatment for the care of the feet and toenails. [French *pédicure*, from Latin *ped-*, *pes* foot + *curare* to take care, from *cura* care]

pedicure[2] *verb trans* to give a pedicure to (somebody).

pedigree /'pedigree/ *noun* **1** the recorded purity of breed of an individual or strain. **2a** an ancestral line, *esp* a distinguished one; a lineage. **b** a genealogical table. **3** the origin and history of something. **4** (*used before a noun*) of, being, or producing animals with a pedigree: *a pedigree dog.* ➤➤ **pedigreed** *adj*. [Middle English *pedegru* from early French *pie de grue* crane's foot, from the branching shape of a family tree]

pediment /'pedimənt/ *noun* **1** the triangular piece of wall in the angle formed by the two slopes of a roof in classical architecture. **2** a broad, gently sloping surface of bedrock that is situated at the base of a steeper slope, often thinly covered with deposited gravel and sand. It occurs as a result of the erosion of rock layers in arid regions. ➤➤ **pedimental** /-'mentl/ *adj*, **pedimented** *adj*. [alteration of obsolete *periment*, prob alteration of PYRAMID[1]]

pedipalp /'pedipalp/ *noun* either of the second pair of appendages of an arachnid, e.g. a spider, that are near the mouth and are often modified for a special function. [scientific Latin *pedipalpus*, from *ped-*, *pes* foot + *palpus* see PALP]

pedlar (*NAmer* **peddler**) /'pedlə/ *noun* a person who travels about offering small wares for sale. [Middle English *pedlere*, alteration of *peddere*, from *ped* wicker basket]

pedo- *comb. form NAmer* see PAEDO-.

pedology /pi'doləji/ *noun* the scientific study of soils. ➤➤ **pedological** /peedə'lojikl/ *adj*, **pedologist** *noun*. [Greek *pedon* earth + -LOGY]

pedometer /pi'domitə/ *noun* an instrument that records the distance a walker covers by responding to body motion at each step. [French *pédomètre*, from Latin *ped-*, *pes* foot + French -*mètre* -METER[2]]

pedophile /'peedəfiel/ *noun NAmer* see PAEDOPHILE.

peduncle /pi'dungkl/ *noun* **1** a stalk bearing a flower, flower cluster, or fruit. **2** a narrow stalklike part by which some larger part or the whole body of an organism is attached. ➤➤ **peduncular** /-kyoolə/ *adj*, **pedunculate** /-kyoolit/ *adj*. [scientific Latin *pedunculus*, dimin. of Latin *ped-*, *pes* foot]

pee[1] /pee/ *verb intrans informal* to urinate. [initial letter of PISS[1]]

pee[2] *noun informal* **1** an act of urinating. **2** urine.

peek[1] /peek/ *verb intrans* **1** to take a brief look; to glance. **2** (*often* + in/out) to peer through a crack or hole or from a place of concealment. **3** to stick up or out, so as to be just visible: *Snowdrops peeked through the newly fallen snow.* [Middle English *piken*; earlier history unknown]

peek[2] *noun* a brief or furtive look; a glance.

peekaboo[1] *or* **peek-a-boo** /'peekəbooh/ *noun* a game for amusing a baby in which one repeatedly hides and reappears, typically exclaiming 'Peekaboo!'.

peekaboo[2] *adj* **1** said of a garment: trimmed with eyelet embroidery or made from sheer fabric: *a peekaboo blouse.* **2** said of a hairstyle: having a fringe that covers one eye.

peel[1] /peel/ *verb trans* **1** to strip off an outer layer of (e.g. a fruit or vegetable). **2** to remove (something) by stripping it: *He peeled the label off the can.* ➤ *verb intrans* **1** to come off in sheets or scales. **2** to lose an outer layer, e.g. of skin. [Middle English *pelen* via French from Latin *pilare* to remove the hair from, from *pilus* hair]

peel[2] *noun* **1** the skin or rind of a fruit or vegetable. **2** (*also* **skin peel**) the cosmetic removal of one or more layers of skin, *esp* from the face: compare ACID PEEL.

peel[3] *noun archaic* a long-handled shovel for getting bread, pies, etc into or out of an oven. [Middle English *pele* via French from Latin *pala*, from *pangere* to fix]

peel[4] *or* **pele** *noun* a small fortified tower built in the 16th cent. along the Scottish–English border. [Middle English *pel* stockade, stake, via French from Latin *palus* stake, PALE[3]]

peeler[1] *noun* a knife or other utensil for peeling fruit or vegetables.

peeler[2] *noun Brit, informal, archaic* a policeman. [named after Sir Robert *Peel* d.1850, English statesman who founded the Irish constabulary]

peelie-wally /'peeliwali/ *adj Scot* sickly, pale, or ill-looking. [prob reduplication of *peelie*, prob alteration of PALE[1]]

peeling *noun* (*usu in pl*) a strip of skin, rind, etc that has been stripped off a vegetable or fruit.

peel off *verb trans* to remove (something) by peeling. ➤ *verb intrans* **1** to come off by peeling. **2** *Brit* to take off one's clothes. **3** to break away from a group or formation, e.g. of marchers or aircraft.

peel tower *noun* = PEEL[4].

peen[1] *or* **pein** /peen/ *noun* the hemispherical or wedge-shaped end of the head of a hammer that is opposite the face and is used for bending, shaping, or cutting the material struck. [prob of Scandinavian origin]

peen[2] *or* **pein** *verb trans* to draw, bend, or flatten (something) by hammering with a peen.

peep[1] /peep/ *verb intrans* **1** to look cautiously or slyly, *esp* through an aperture; to peek. **2** (*often* + out) to begin to emerge from concealment; to show slightly. [Middle English *pepen*, perhaps alteration of *piken* PEEK[1]]

peep[2] *noun* **1** a brief or furtive look; a glance. **2** the first faint appearance of something: *at the peep of dawn*.

peep[3] *verb intrans* **1** to make a feeble shrill sound as of a bird newly hatched; to cheep. **2** to make a high-pitched electronic sound; to bleep. **3** to utter the slightest sound: *Every time he peeps, she jumps to see what's the matter* — Benjamin Spock. [Middle English *pepen*, of imitative origin]

peep[4] *noun* a peeping sound.

peeper[1] *noun* **1** somebody who peeps; *esp* a voyeur. **2** *informal* (*usu in pl*) an eye.

peeper[2] *noun* a small brown N American tree frog that peeps shrilly in the spring: *Hyla crucifer*. Also called SPRING PEEPER.

peephole *noun* a hole or crevice to peep through, *esp* a hole in a door through which callers can be observed.

Peeping Tom *noun* (*often* **peeping Tom**) a voyeur.

Word history
named after *Peeping Tom*, legendary 11th-cent. figure who peeped at Lady Godiva as she rode naked through Coventry. According to legend, Earl Leofric imposed heavy taxes on his tenants, which his wife begged him to remove. He said he would do so only if she rode naked through the town. She did so, and Leofric kept his promise. The figure of Peeping Tom is a much later addition to the story. According to some, he was struck blind for trying to look at her.

peep show *noun* **1** an entertainment or object, e.g. an erotic film, or painting, viewed through a small opening or a magnifying glass. **2** a show featuring erotic entertainment, e.g. striptease.

peep sight *noun* a rear sight for a gun having an adjustable metal piece pierced with a small hole to peep through in aiming.

peepul /'peepul/ *noun* see PIPAL.

peer[1] /piə/ *verb intrans* **1** to look curiously or searchingly, *esp* at something difficult to discern. **2** to be partially visible; to peep. [perhaps by shortening and alteration from APPEAR]

peer[2] *noun* **1** a duke, marquess, earl, viscount, or baron of the British nobility: *The House of Peers made no pretence to intellectual eminence or scholarship sublime* — W S Gilbert. **2** a person who belongs to the same group in society as another, *esp* determined by age, grade, or status. ✳ **without peer** unequalled. [Middle English from Old French *per* equal, one's equal, from Latin *par*]

peerage /'piərij/ *noun* **1** the rank or title of a peer. **2** (**the peerage**) (*treated as sing. or pl*) the body of peers. **3** a book containing a list of peers with their family histories, trees, and titles.

peeress /'piəris/ *noun* **1** a woman having the rank of a peer. **2** the wife or widow of a peer.

peer group *noun* a group of people of approximately the same age or status.

peerless *adj* matchless or incomparable. ➤➤ **peerlessly** *adv*.

peer review *noun* the evaluation of a person's work, *esp* academic research work, by qualified people working in the same field. ➤➤ **peer-review** *verb trans*.

peeve[1] /peev/ *verb trans informal* to make (somebody) peevish or resentful; to annoy (somebody): *He was peeved at not being invited to the party*. [back-formation from PEEVISH]

peeve[2] *noun informal* a particular grievance; a grudge.

peevish *adj* querulous in temperament or mood; fretful. ➤➤ **peevishly** *adv*, **peevishness** *noun*. [Middle English *pevish* spiteful; earlier history unknown]

peewee /'peewee/ *noun* **1** *Scot* the lapwing. **2** see PEWEE. [imitative]

peewit *or* **pewit** /'peewit/ *noun Brit* the lapwing. [imitative]

peg[1] /peg/ *noun* **1** a small pointed or tapered piece of wood, metal, or plastic used to pin down or fasten things or to fit into or close holes; a pin: *a tent peg*. **2** *Brit* = CLOTHES PEG. **3** a projecting piece used to hold or support something: *He hung his hat on the peg in the hall*. **4** any of the pins turned to regulate the pitch of the strings of a musical instrument. **5** a predetermined level at which something, e.g. a price, is fixed. **6** in baseball, a fast throw to a base to get a runner out. **7** *informal* a person's leg. **8** *Brit* a drink, *esp* of spirits. ✳ **off the peg** *chiefly Brit* said of clothes: mass-produced; ready-made. **square peg in a round hole** see SQUARE[2]. **take somebody down a peg or two** to reduce somebody's sense of self-importance. [Middle English *pegge*, prob from early Dutch]

peg[2] *verb trans* (**pegged, pegging**) **1** to fix or mark (something) with pegs. **2** to fix or hold (prices, etc) at a predetermined level. **3** *NAmer, informal* to label (somebody) as something: *They had her pegged as a high-flier*. **4** in baseball, to throw (a ball) fast to a base to get a runner out.

peg away *verb intrans informal* (*often* + at) to work hard and steadily at something: *She's pegging away at her essay*.

pegboard *noun* a board pierced at regular intervals with holes into which hooks or pegs may be inserted for the storage or display of articles.

peg leg *noun informal* an artificial leg, or a person with an artificial leg.

pegmatite /'pegmətiet/ *noun* a coarse variety of granite occurring as dykes or veins, or a formation resembling this. [French *pegmatite* from Greek *pēgmat-*, *pēgma* something fastened together, from *pēgnynai* to fasten together]

peg out *verb intrans* **1** *chiefly Brit, informal* to die. **2** in croquet, to finish a game by hitting the peg with the ball. **3** in cribbage, to score the winning point in a game. ➤ *verb trans* to mark or secure (something) by pegs: *They pegged out the boundaries of the estate; I pegged out the washing*.

peg top *noun* a spinning top with a metal pin through the centre.

peg-top *adj dated* said of a garment: wide at the hips and narrow at the bottom.

Pehlevi /'payləvi/ *noun* see PAHLAVI.

PEI *abbr* Prince Edward Island.

peignoir /'paynwah/ *noun* a woman's loose negligee or dressing gown. [French *peignoir*, literally 'garment worn while combing the hair', from *peigner* to comb, ultimately from Latin *pecten* comb]

pein[1] /peen/ *noun* see PEEN[1].

pein[2] *verb trans* see PEEN[2].

pejorative /pi'jorətiv/ *adj* expressing criticism; disparaging. ➤➤ **pejoratively** *adv*. [late Latin *pejoratus*, past part. of *pejorare* to make or become worse, from Latin *pejor* worse]

pekan /'pek(ə)n/ *noun NAmer* = FISHER (1). [Canadian French *pekan* from Algonquian]

peke /peek/ *noun* (*often* **Peke**) *informal* = PEKINGESE (1). [by shortening and alteration]

Pekinese /peeki'neez/ *noun* see PEKINGESE.

Peking duck /pee'king/ *noun* a Chinese dish of crispy roast duck usu served with thin pancakes, spring onions, and plum sauce.

Pekingese *or* **Pekinese** /peeki'neez/ *noun* (*pl* **Pekingese** *or* **Pekinese**) **1** a small short-legged dog of a breed with a broad flat face and a long thick soft coat. **2a** a native or inhabitant of Beijing (formerly Peking). **b** the dialect of Mandarin Chinese spoken in Beijing. ⨠ **Pekingese** *adj.* [named after *Peking, Pekin,* now usu written Beijing, city in NE China]

Peking man *noun* an extinct Pleistocene man known from skeletal and cultural remains at Choukoutien in China.

pekoe /'peekoh/ *noun* a black tea of superior quality. [Chinese (Amoy) *pek ho,* literally 'white down'; because the leaves are picked when they are young and downy]

pelage /'pelij/ *noun* the hairy covering of a mammal. [French *pelage* from Latin *pilus* hair]

Pelagian /pi'layji·ən/ *noun* a person who follows the British monk and theologian Pelagius (4th cent. AD) in denying original sin and holding that people's salvation depends on their own efforts rather than divine grace. ⨠ **Pelagian** *adj,* **Pelagianism** *noun.*

pelagic /pe'lajik/ *adj* **1** of the open sea. **2** said of fish: living at or above moderate depths in the sea: compare DEMERSAL. [via Latin from Greek *pelagikos,* from *pelagos* sea]

pelargonium /pelə'gohni·əm/ *noun* any of a genus of southern African plants of the geranium family with showy red, pink, or white flowers: genus *Pelargonium.* [Latin genus name, irreg from Greek *pelargos* stork; apparently because its capsules resemble a stork's bill: compare CRANESBILL, GERANIUM]

Pelasgian /pi'lazgi·ən/ *noun* a member of an ancient people inhabiting Greece and the E islands of the Mediterranean. ⨠ **Pelasgian** *adj.* [Greek *pelasgios* (adj) Pelasgian, from *Pelasgoi* Pelasgians]

pele /peel/ *noun* see PEEL⁴.

pelf /pelf/ *noun archaic* money or riches. [Middle English from early French *pelfre* booty]

pelham /'peləm/ *noun* a bit for a horse having a bar mouthpiece and used with a restraining chain and one or two reins. [prob from the name *Pelham*]

pelican /'pelikən/ *noun* any of several species of large web-footed birds with a very large bill containing a pouch that can be distended for catching and keeping fish: genus *Pelecanus.* [Old English *pellican* via Latin from Greek *pelekan*]

pelican crossing *noun* in Britain, a crossing at which the movement of vehicles and pedestrians is controlled by pedestrian-operated traffic lights. [irreg from *pedestrian light controlled crossing*]

pelisse /pi'lees/ *noun* **1** a full-length frock-coat, with a wide collar, worn by women in the early 19th cent.: *If I thought it would not tempt her to go out in sharp winds and grow coarse, I would send her a new hat and pelisse* — Jane Austen. **2** a long cloak or coat made, lined, or trimmed with fur; *esp* one formerly part of a hussar's uniform. [French *pelisse* from late Latin *pellicia* of fur, from Latin *pellis* skin]

pellagra /pe'lagrə, pe'laygrə/ *noun* a disease associated with a deficiency of nicotinic acid in the diet, marked by inflammation and flaking of the skin, loss of appetite, diarrhoea, and disorders of the central nervous system. ⨠⨠ **pellagrous** *adj.* [Italian *pellagra* from *pelle* skin (from Latin *pellis*) + *-agra* as in PODAGRA]

pellet¹ /'pelit/ *noun* **1** a small rounded or spherical body, e.g. of food or medicine. **2** a piece of small shot. **3** a mass of undigested food regurgitated by a bird of prey. [Middle English *pelote* via French from Latin *pilota,* dimin. of *pila* ball]

pellet² *verb trans* (**pelleting, pelleted**) **1** to form or compact (something) into pellets. **2** to strike (something) with or as if with pellets.

pellicle /'pelikl/ *noun technical* a thin skin or film, e.g. the outer layer of a single-celled organism, or a growth of bacteria on the surface of a liquid culture. [early French *pellicule* from Latin *pellicula,* dimin. of *pellis* skin]

pellitory¹ /'pelit(ə)ri/ *noun* (*pl* **pellitories**) (*also* **pellitory-of-Spain**) a S European composite plant, the root of which was formerly used for medicinal purposes: *Anacyclus pyrethrum.* [Middle English *peletre* via French *piretre* from Latin *pyrethrum*: see PYRETHRUM]

pellitory² *noun* (*pl* **pellitories**) (*also* **pellitory-of-the-wall**) a plant of the nettle family with inconspicuous flowers, growing in crevices in walls and rocks: genus *Parietaria.* [Middle English *paritorie* via French from Latin *pariet-, paries* wall]

pell-mell¹ /,pel'mel/ *adv and adj* **1** in confusion or disorder. **2** in confused haste. [early French *pelemele* from Old French *pesle mesle,* reduplication of *mesle-,* stem of *mesler* to mix or mingle]

pell-mell² *noun* confusion or disorder.

pellucid /pi'l(y)oohsid/ *adj* **1** clear or transparent. **2** easy to understand. ⨠ **pellucidly** *adv.* [Latin *pellucidus,* from *per* through + *lucidus* lucid]

Pelmanism /'pelmaniz(ə)m/ *noun* **1** a system of memory training. **2** (*often* **pelmanism**) a card game in which players try to turn up pairs of playing cards spread at random face down on a table by remembering the failed attempts of previous turns. [named after the *Pelman* Institute, founded in London in 1898 for training the mind]

pelmet /'pelmit/ *noun* a length of board or fabric placed above a window to conceal curtain fixtures. [prob modification of French *palmette* palm leaf design, from *palme* palm from Latin *palma*]

pelorus /pi'lawrəs/ *noun* a navigational instrument having two sight vanes mounted on a rotatable ring by which bearings are taken. [perhaps named after *Pelorus,* said to have been Hannibal's pilot]

pelota /pi'lotə/ *noun* **1a** = JAI ALAI. **b** any of various other Spanish or Latin-American court games. **2** the ball used in pelota. [Spanish *pelota* from Old French *pelote* little ball, ultimately from Latin *pilla* ball]

peloton /'pelətonh/ *noun* the main group of riders in a cycle race. [French *peloton* platoon, ball, from Old French *pelote* little ball (see PELOTA); from the tightly-packed bunch of riders]

pelt¹ /pelt/ *verb trans* **1** to strike (somebody) with a succession of blows or missiles: *They pelted him with stones.* **2** to hurl or throw (missiles). ⨠ *verb intrans* **1** said of rain, etc: to fall heavily and continuously. **2** to run fast: *The children pelted down the road.* [Middle English *pelten*; earlier history unknown]

pelt² *noun archaic* speed or force. ✻ **(at) full pelt** with great speed or force.

pelt³ *noun* **1** an undressed animal skin with its hair, wool, or fur. **2** an animal skin stripped of hair or wool before tanning. [Middle English, ultimately from Latin *pellis* skin]

peltate /'peltayt/ *adj* said of a leaf: shaped like a shield; *specif* having the stem or support attached to the lower surface. [prob from scientific Latin *peltatus,* from Latin *pelta* small shield, from Greek *peltē*]

peltry /'peltri/ *noun* animal pelts. [Middle English from Anglo-French *pelterie,* from Latin *pellis* skin]

pelves /'pelveez/ *noun* pl of PELVIS.

pelvic /'pelvik/ *adj* relating to or in the region of the pelvis.

pelvic fin *noun* either of the fins of a fish, situated one on each side of the lower surface of the body, that correspond to the hind limbs of a four-legged animal.

pelvic girdle *noun* the bony or cartilaginous arch that supports the hind limbs of a vertebrate.

pelvic inflammatory disease *noun* inflammation of the female reproductive organs, caused by bacterial infection and characterized by lower abdominal pain and high fever.

pelvis /'pelvis/ *noun* (*pl* **pelvises** *or* **pelves** /'pelveez/) **1** a basin-shaped structure in the skeleton of many vertebrates that is formed by the pelvic girdle and adjoining bones of the spine. **2** the funnel-shaped cavity of the kidney into which urine is discharged. [Latin *pelvis* basin]

Pembroke table /'pembrək/ *noun* a small four-legged table with a drawer and drop leaves. [named after *Pembrokeshire,* county of Wales]

pemmican *or* **pemican** /'pemikən/ *noun* a concentrated food consisting of dried pounded meat mixed with melted fat traditionally made by Native Americans, or a similar preparation of beef and dried fruits used for emergency rations. [Cree *pimikân*]

pemphigus /'pemfigəs/ *noun* a disease characterized by large blisters on the skin, often accompanied by itching. [scientific Latin *pemphigus* from Greek *pemphig-, pemphix* breath, pustule]

PEN /pen/ *abbr* International Association of Poets, Playwrights, Editors, Essayists, and Novelists.

Pen. *abbr* peninsula.

pen¹ /pen/ *noun* **1** an implement for writing or drawing with ink, e.g. a ballpoint or fountain pen. **2** (**the pen**) writing as an occupation. **3** an electronic device used with a computer, e.g. to choose an item from a menu or to enter data. **4** the horny feather-shaped internal shell of a squid. [Middle English *penne* quill pen, via French from Latin *penna, pinna* feather]

pen² *verb trans* (**penned, penning**) to write (a letter, poem, article, etc.).

pen³ *noun* **1** a small enclosure for farm animals, *esp* pigs. **2** a small place of confinement or storage. **3** a heavily fortified dock for a submarine. [Old English *penn*]

pen⁴ *verb trans* (**penned, penning**) to shut (an animal or a person) in a pen.

pen⁵ *noun* a female swan. [origin unknown]

pen⁶ *noun NAmer, informal* a prison. [short for PENITENTIARY¹]

penal /'peenl/ *adj* **1** of, relating to, or prescribing punishment. **2** said of an offence: liable to punishment. **3** harsh: *penal taxation*. **>>> penally** *adv.* [Middle English via French from Latin *poenalis*, from *poena*: see PAIN¹]

penal code *noun* a code of laws concerning crimes and their punishment.

penalize *or* **penalise** /'peenəliez/ *verb trans* **1** to inflict a penalty on (somebody): *Growing old's like being increasingly penalized for a crime you haven't committed* — Anthony Powell. **2** to put (somebody) at a serious or unfair disadvantage. **3** to declare (an act) punishable by law. **>>> penalization** /-'zaysh(ə)n/ *noun.*

penal servitude *noun* a sentence of imprisonment with hard labour.

penalty /'pen(ə)lti/ *noun* (*pl* **penalties**) **1** a punishment legally imposed or incurred for committing a crime. **2a** a disadvantage imposed for violation of the rules of a sport. **b** (*in pl*) in bridge, points scored by the side that defeats the opposing contract. **3** a forfeiture to which a person agrees to be subject if conditions are not fulfilled: *a penalty clause in the contract*. **4** = PENALTY KICK. **5** disadvantage, loss, or suffering due to some action: *He paid the penalty for his heavy drinking*. [medieval Latin *poenalitas* from Latin *poenalis*, from *poena*: see PAIN¹]

penalty area *noun* a rectangular area 40m (44yd) wide and 16m (18yd) deep in front of each goal on a football pitch.

penalty box *noun* **1** = PENALTY AREA. **2** in ice hockey, an area alongside the rink to which penalized players are confined.

penalty kick *noun* **1** a free kick at the goal in football. **2** a free kick in rugby.

penalty point *noun* a punishment for a driving offence, e.g. speeding, which is marked on a person's licence. An accumulation of penalty points can lead to disqualification.

penalty rates *pl noun Aus, NZ* formerly, increased rates of pay for working outside normal hours.

penalty shoot-out *noun* in football, a method of deciding the winner of a drawn match, in which players from each team alternately try to score a goal with a penalty kick.

penalty spot *noun* a spot 11m (12yd) in front of the goal on a football pitch, from which penalty kicks are taken.

penance¹ /'penəns/ *noun* **1** an act of self-abasement or devotion performed to show repentance for sin. **2** a sacramental rite of the Roman Catholic, Orthodox, and some Anglican Churches involving confession and a penance directed by the confessor. [Middle English via French from Latin *paenitentia* penitence, from *paenitēre* to be sorry]

penance² *verb trans archaic* to impose a penance on (somebody).

penannular /pen'anyoolə/ *adj* in archaeology, having the form of a ring with a small break in the circumference: *a penannular ornament*. [Latin *paene, pene* almost + ANNULAR]

penates /pi'nahteez, pi'nayteez/ *pl noun* the ancient Roman gods charged, in conjunction with Vesta, with watching over domestic property: compare LARES. [Latin *Penates*, from *penus* provision of food]

pence /pens/ *noun* pl of PENNY.

penchant /'ponhshonh/ *noun* (*often* + for) a strong leaning; a liking: *With a turn for literary expression myself, and a penchant for forcible figures and phrases, I appreciated ... the peculiar vividness ... of his metaphors* — Jack London. [French *penchant*, present part. of *pencher* to incline, from Latin *pendicare*, from *pendere* to weigh]

pencil¹ /'pensl/ *noun* **1** an implement for writing, drawing, etc, consisting of or containing a slender cylinder of a solid marking substance, e.g. graphite. **2** a small medicated or cosmetic roll or stick for local applications: *a styptic pencil*. **3** a set of light rays, *esp*

when diverging from or converging to a point. **4** something long and thin like a pencil: *a pencil of light*. [Middle English *pensel* paintbrush, via French from Latin *penicillus* brush, literally 'little tail', dimin. of *penis* tail, PENIS]

pencil² *verb trans* (**pencilled, pencilling,** *NAmer* **penciled, penciling**) to draw, write, or mark (something) with a pencil. **※ pencil something in** to make a provisional appointment, etc. **>>> penciller** *noun.*

pendant¹ /'pendənt/ *noun* **1** an ornament hanging from a chain worn round the neck. **2** an electric light fitting suspended from the ceiling. **3** the bar or ring of metal on a pocket watch to which the chain is attached. **4** a pennant. **5** a short rope to which tackles are attached, e.g. on the mast of a ship. **6** /'pendənt, 'pādā/ a companion piece or supplement to a work of art, literature, or music. [Middle English *pendaunt* from French *pendant*, present part. of *pendre* to hang down, from Latin *pendēre*]

pendant² *adj* = PENDENT.

pendent /'pendənt/ *adj* **1** supported from above; suspended: *pendent icicles*. **2** jutting or leaning over; overhanging: *a pendent cliff*. **3** remaining undetermined; pending. **4** in grammar, said of a sentence: incomplete. **>>> pendency** *noun.* [Middle English *pendaunt*: see PENDANT¹]

pendentive /pen'dentiv/ *noun* a triangular concave corner part that supports a circular dome over a square or polygonal space. [French *pendentif* from Latin *pendent-, pendens*, present part. of *pendēre* to hang down]

pending¹ /'pending/ *prep* while awaiting; until: *She was excluded pending the next meeting of the governors*. [French *pendant*: see PENDANT¹]

pending² *adj* **1** not yet decided or dealt with: *There was a libel action pending*. **2** imminent or impending: *a pending general election*.

pendragon /pen'dragən/ *noun* the leader among the ancient British chiefs. [Middle English from Welsh *pendragon*, from *pen* chief + *dragon* military standard, literally 'dragon', ultimately from Greek *drako* DRAGON]

pendulous /'pendyooləs/ *adj* hanging downwards: *pendulous jowls*. **>>> pendulously** *adv.* [Latin *pendulus*, from *pendēre* to hang down]

pendulum /'pendyooləm/ *noun* **1** a body suspended from a fixed point so as to swing freely under the action of gravity and commonly used to regulate the mechanism of a clock. **2** something that changes regularly, *esp* going from one extreme to another: *the pendulum of public opinion*. [Latin *pendulum*, neuter of *pendulus*: see PENDULOUS]

peneplain *or* **peneplane** /'peeniplayn/ *noun* an almost flat land surface produced by erosion. [Latin *paene, pene* almost + PLAIN² or PLANE¹]

penes /'peeneez/ *noun* pl of PENIS.

penetralia /peni'trayli·ə/ *pl noun* the innermost or most secret and hidden parts of a place or thing. [Latin *penetralia*, neuter pl of *penetralis* inner, from *penetrare* to PENETRATE]

penetrance /'penitrəns/ *noun* the proportion of individuals possessing a particular gene that show the characteristic associated with that gene; a measure of the frequency with which a gene shows its effect.

penetrant /'penitrənt/ *noun* a substance that increases the penetration of a liquid, e.g. into porous material.

penetrate /'penitrayt/ *verb trans* **1a** to pass into or through (something). **b** to enter (an organization or a market), *esp* by overcoming resistance. **c** to insert the penis into the vagina or anus of (a sexual partner). **2a** to see into or through (something): *trying to penetrate the darkness*. **b** to discover the inner contents or meaning of (something). **3** to diffuse through or into (something). **> verb intrans** to be absorbed by the mind; to be understood: *I heard what he said, but it didn't penetrate*. **>>> penetrability** /-trə'biliti/ *noun,* **penetrable** *adj,* **penetrator** *noun.* [Latin *penetratus*, past part. of *penetrare*]

penetrating *adj* **1** having the power of entering, piercing, or pervading: *a penetrating shriek; a penetrating wind*. **2** acute or discerning: *He had some penetrating insights into life*. **>>> penetratingly** *adv.*

penetration /peni'traysh(ə)n/ *noun* **1** the act or an instance of penetrating. **2** the depth to which something penetrates. **3** the ability to discern deeply and acutely: *a critic gifted with great powers of penetration*.

penetrative /'penitrətiv/ *adj* **1** able to pass into or through something. **2** having discernment or insight. **3** said of sexual activity: involving insertion of the penis into the vagina or anus of a partner.

penetrometer /peni'tromitə/ *noun* an instrument for measuring firmness or consistency, e.g. of soil. [Latin *penetrare* to penetrate + -METER²]

pen-friend *noun chiefly Brit* a person, *esp* one in another country, with whom a friendship is made through correspondence.

penguin /'penggwin/ *noun* any of several species of flightless aquatic birds of the southern hemisphere, with a dark back and white or pale belly, wings resembling flippers, and webbed feet: family Spheniscidae. [perhaps from Welsh *pen gwyn* white head]

penicillate /peni'silət/ *adj* having a tuft of fine filaments: *a penicillate stigma*. [scientific Latin *penicillatus* from Latin *penicillus*: see PENCIL¹]

penicillin /peni'silin/ *noun* any of several antibiotics or antibacterial drugs, orig obtained from moulds, that act by interfering with the growth of bacterial cell walls. [scientific Latin *Penicillium*, genus name of fungi, from Latin *penicillus*: see PENCIL¹]

penile /'peeniel/ *adj* relating to or in the region of the penis.

peninsula /pi'ninsyoolə/ *noun* a usu narrow strip of land jutting out into or almost surrounded by water. ➤➤ **peninsular** *adj*. [Latin *paeninsula*, from *paene* almost + *insula* island]

penis /'peenis/ *noun* (*pl* **penises** or **penes** /'peeneez/) the male organ of copulation by which semen is introduced into the female, also used by mammals for urination. [Latin *penis* penis, tail]

penitent¹ /'penit(ə)nt/ *adj* feeling or expressing sorrow for sins or offences. ➤➤ **penitence** *noun*, **penitently** *adv*. [Middle English via French from Latin *paenitent-, paenitens*, present part. of *paenitēre* to be sorry]

penitent² *noun* **1** somebody who repents of sin. **2** in the Roman Catholic Church, somebody under church censure but admitted to penance, *esp* under the direction of a confessor.

penitential /peni'tensh(ə)l/ *adj* of penitence or penance: *O, how I fear thee, living God … and worship thee with trembling hope, and penitential tears* — F W Faber. ➤➤ **penitentially** *adv*.

penitentiary¹ /peni'tensh(ə)ri/ *noun* (*pl* **penitentiaries**) **1** *NAmer* a prison for the confinement of people convicted of serious crimes. **2a** an officer in some Roman Catholic dioceses vested with power from the bishop to absolve in certain special cases. **b** a tribunal of the papal court concerned with granting pardons for sin and excusing penitents wholly or partly from penance in this world or the next. [Middle English *penitenciary* officer dealing with penitents, from medieval Latin *paenitentiarius*, from *paenitentia*: see PENANCE¹]

penitentiary² *adj NAmer* of or incurring confinement in a penitentiary.

penknife /'pennief/ *noun* (*pl* **penknives** /'pennievz/) a small pocketknife. [from its original use for mending quill pens]

penlight *noun* a small electric torch resembling a fountain pen in size or shape.

penman *noun* (*pl* **penmen**) **1** somebody skilled in writing with a pen; *esp* a professional copyist or scribe. **2** *dated* somebody with a specified quality or style of handwriting: *a poor penman*. **3** an author. ➤➤ **penmanship** *noun*.

Penn. *abbr* Pennsylvania.

pen name *noun* an author's pseudonym.

pennant /'penənt/ *noun* **1** any of various nautical flags used for identification or signalling. **2** a flag that tapers to a point or has a swallowtail. **3** *NAmer* a flag denoting the holding of a championship, e.g. in a professional baseball league. **4** = PENDANT¹ (5). [blend of PENDANT¹ + PENNON]

pennate /'penayt/ *adj* = PINNATE. [Latin *pennatus* feathered or trimmed, from *penna, pinna* feather]

penne /'peni/ *pl noun* (*treated as sing. or pl*) pasta in the form of short tubes with diagonally cut ends. [Italian *penne*, literally 'quills']

penni /'peni/ *noun* (*pl* **penniä** /'peni-ə/ or **pennis**) a former unit of currency in Finland, worth 100th of a markka (up to the introduction of the euro in 2002). [Finnish *penni*]

penniless /'penilis/ *adj* lacking money; poor. ➤➤ **pennilessness** *noun*.

pennon /'penən/ *noun* a pennant; *esp* a long triangular or swallow-tailed streamer attached to the head of a lance as a knight's personal flag. [Middle English from early French *penon*, literally 'large feather', ultimately from Latin *penna* feather]

penn'orth /'penəth/ *noun* = PENNYWORTH.

Pennsylvania Dutch /pens(ə)l'vayni-ə/ *noun* **1** (*treated as pl*) a people descended from 18th-cent. German immigrants to E Pennsylvania. **2** a dialect of High German spoken in E Pennsylvania.

Pennsylvania German *noun* = PENNSYLVANIA DUTCH (2).

Pennsylvanian *adj* **1** of or relating to the US state of Pennsylvania. **2** relating to or dating from a geological period of the Palaeozoic era in N America that follows the Mississippian and that corresponds to the later subdivision of the Carboniferous period ➤➤ **Pennsylvanian** *noun*.

penny /'peni/ *noun* (*pl* **pennies** or **pence** /pens/) **1a** a unit of currency in Britain and many other countries, worth 100th of a pound. **b** a bronze coin representing a former British monetary unit worth 240th of a pound. **2** *NAmer, informal* a cent. **3** a denarius. **4** (*in negative contexts*) the least amount of money: *He didn't have a penny*. ✱ **a penny for your thoughts** used to ask somebody what they are thinking about. **be ten/two a penny** *chiefly Brit* to be very common or plentiful and therefore worth little. **the penny drops** *chiefly Brit, informal* the true meaning finally dawns [refers to slot machines activated by the dropping of an inserted penny]. [Old English *penning, penig*]

-penny *comb. form Brit* forming adjectives, with the meaning: costing the number of pence specified: *ninepenny*.

penny black *noun* the first adhesive postage stamp, issued in Britain in 1840.

penny dreadful *noun* formerly, a novel of violent adventure or crime orig costing a penny.

penny-farthing *noun Brit* an early type of bicycle having a small rear wheel and a large front wheel. [from the relative sizes of the old penny and farthing coins]

penny-pinching *adj* mean, niggardly, or stingy. ➤➤ **penny-pincher** *noun*, **penny-pinching** *noun*.

pennyroyal *noun* **1** a European mint with pink or lilac flowers and small aromatic leaves: *Mentha pulegium*. **2** an aromatic American plant of the mint family: *Hedeoma pulegioides*. [alteration of early French *poullieul real*, literally 'royal thyme'; from its value as a medicinal plant]

penny shares *pl noun* shares with a market price of less than 20p.

pennyweight *noun* a unit of troy weight equal to one twentieth of an ounce troy (about 1.56g).

penny whistle *noun* a small simple musical pipe with a whistle mouthpiece and finger holes.

penny-wise *adj* careful with small amounts. ✱ **penny-wise and pound-foolish** prudent in dealing with small sums or matters but extravagant or wasteful with large ones.

pennywort *noun* **1** a European plant that grows on rocks and walls and has long spikes of whitish green to pink flowers: *Umbilicus rupestris*. **2** a marsh plant with small pinkish green flowers and shiny round leaves: *Hydrocotyle vulgaris*.

pennyworth *noun* **1** an amount that can be bought for a penny. **2** a small quantity; a modicum: *He had not a pennyworth of common sense*. **3** *archaic* value for the money spent; a bargain: *I got a good pennyworth*. **4**✱ **put in one's pennyworth** *Brit* to contribute to a discussion.

penology /pee'nolǝji/ *noun* a branch of criminology dealing with prison management and the treatment of offenders. ➤➤ **penological** /-'lojikl/ *adj*, **penologist** *noun*. [Greek *poinē* penalty + -LOGY]

pen pal *noun* a pen-friend.

pen pusher *noun informal* a person whose work involves boring or repetitive writing at a desk; *specif* a clerk.

pensile /'pensiel/ *adj* pendent or hanging: *the pensile nest of a bird*. [Latin *pensilis*, from *pendēre* to hang]

pension¹ /'pensh(ə)n/ *noun* **1** a fixed sum paid regularly to a person, e.g. following retirement or as compensation for a wage-earner's death: *a widow's pension; a private pension plan*. **2** a regular payment made, *esp* formerly, to somebody as patronage or as a reward for service. ➤➤ **pensionless** *adj*. [Middle English via French from Latin *pension-, pensio*, from *pendere* to pay]

pension² *verb trans* to grant or pay a pension to (somebody).

pension³ /ˈponhsyonh/ *noun* a hotel or boarding house, *esp* in continental Europe. [French *pension*]

pensionable *adj* relating to entitlement to receive a pension: *of pensionable age; a pensionable employee.*

pensioner *noun* a person who receives or lives on a pension, *esp* an old-age pension.

pension off *verb trans* to dismiss or retire (somebody) from service with a pension.

pensive /ˈpensiv/ *adj* sadly or deeply thoughtful. >> **pensively** *adv*, **pensiveness** *noun*. [Middle English *pensif* via French from Latin *pensare* to ponder, from *pensus*, past part. of *pendēre* to weigh]

penstemon /ˈpenˈsteemən/ *noun* see PENTSTEMON.

penstock /ˈpenstok/ *noun* **1** a valve, sluice, or gate for regulating a flow, e.g. of water. **2** a conduit or pipe for conducting water to a hydroelectric station. [PEN³ in the sense 'dam' + STOCK¹]

pent /pent/ *adj literary* pent-up. [past part. of obsolete *pend* to confine, from Middle English *penden*, alteration of *pennen* PEN⁴]

penta- *or* **pent-** *comb. form* forming words, with the meanings: **1** five: *pentahedron; pentode.* **2** containing five atoms, groups, or chemical equivalents in the molecular structure. [Middle English from Greek, from *pente*]

pentacle /ˈpentəkl/ *noun* a pentagram. [medieval Latin *pentaculum*, from Greek *pente* five]

pentad /ˈpentad/ *noun* a group or series of five. [Greek *pentad-*, *pentas*, from *pente* five]

pentadactyl /pentəˈdaktil/ *adj* having five digits on the hand or foot. [via Latin from Greek *pentadaktylos*, from PENTA- + *daktylos* finger, toe]

Pentagon /ˈpentəgon/ *noun* (**the Pentagon**) the US military establishment. [the *Pentagon* building, a five-sided building housing the headquarters of the US Department of Defense in Arlington, Virginia]

pentagon *noun* a polygon with five angles and five sides. >> **pentagonal** /penˈtagənl/ *adj*. [Greek *pentagōnon*, neuter of *pentagōnos* pentagonal, from PENTA- + *gōnia* angle]

pentagram /ˈpentəgram/ *noun* a five-pointed star used as a magical symbol. [Greek *pentagrammon*, from PENTA- + *-grammon* (related to *gramma* -GRAM)]

pentahedron /pentəˈheedrən, -ˈhedrən/ *noun* (*pl* **pentahedrons** *or* **pentahedra** /-drə/) a polyhedron with five faces. >> **pentahedral** *adj*. [PENTA- + -HEDRON]

pentamerous /penˈtamərəs/ *adj* **1** divided into or consisting of five parts. **2** said of a flower: having each whorl of petals, sepals, stamens, etc consisting of five or a multiple of five members. [Latin *pentamerus* from Greek PENTA- + Latin *-merus* -MEROUS]

pentameter /penˈtamitə/ *noun* a line of verse consisting of five metrical feet. [via Latin from Greek *pentametros* having five metrical feet, from PENTA- + *metron* METRE¹]

pentamidine /penˈtamideen/ *noun* an antibiotic drug used *esp* to treat PCP in patients with Aids. [PENTANE + AMIDE + -INE²]

pentane /ˈpentayn/ *noun* a volatile liquid that is a member of the alkane series of organic chemical compounds and is obtained from petroleum: formula C_5H_{12}.

pentangle /ˈpentanggl/ *noun* a pentagram.

pentanoic acid /pentəˈnohˈik/ *noun* a liquid acid obtained from valerian or manufactured synthetically, used in perfumes and pharmaceuticals: formula $C_5H_{10}O_2$.

pentaprism /ˈpentəpriz(ə)m/ *noun* a five-sided prism, *esp* in a camera, which gives a constant deviation of 90° to light from any direction.

Pentateuch /ˈpentətyoohk/ *noun* the first five books of the Old Testament: Genesis, Exodus, Leviticus, Numbers, and Deuteronomy. >> **Pentateuchal** /-ˈtyoohkl/ *adj*. [via late Latin from Greek *Pentateuchos*, from PENTA- + *teuchos* tool, vessel, book]

pentathlete /penˈtathleet/ *noun* an athlete who competes in the pentathlon.

pentathlon /penˈtathlən/ *noun* **1** = MODERN PENTATHLON. **2** a women's athletic contest in which all contestants compete in the 100m hurdles, shot put, high jump, long jump, and 200m sprint. [Greek *pentathlon* athletic contest involving five events, from PENTA- + *athlon* contest]

pentatonic /pentəˈtonik/ *adj* of, in, or being a musical scale consisting of five notes: *a pentatonic tune.*

pentavalent /pentəˈvaylənt/ *adj* in chemistry, having a valency of five.

Pentecost /ˈpentikost/ *noun* **1** a festival of the Christian Church observed on the seventh Sunday after Easter, commemorating the descent of the Holy Spirit on the apostles. **2** the Jewish festival of Shabuoth, observed on the 50th day after the second day of Passover. [Old English *pentecosten* via Latin from Greek *pentēkostē*, literally '50th day']

Pentecostal /pentiˈkostl/ *adj* **1** of or belonging to any of various evangelical Christian bodies laying particular emphasis on the gifts of the Holy Spirit, e.g. speaking in tongues and healing. **2** of or relating to Pentecost. >> **Pentecostalism** *noun*, **Pentecostalist** *adj and noun*.

penthouse /ˈpentˈhows/ *noun* **1** a dwelling on the roof or in the uppermost part of a building, usu structurally distinct: *a penthouse flat.* **2** *archaic* a structure, e.g. a shed or roof, attached to and sloping from a wall or building. [by folk etymology from Middle English *pentis* via French from medieval Latin *appenticium* appendage, from Latin *appendic-, appendix* appendage, from *appendere*: see APPEND]

pentimento /pentiˈmentoh/ *noun* (*pl* **pentimenti** /-tee/) a reappearance in a painting of underlying work that has been painted over. [Italian *pentimento* repentance, correction, from *pentire* to repent, from Latin *paenitere*]

pentobarbital /pentəˈbahbitl/ *noun NAmer* = PENTOBARBITONE.

pentobarbitone /pentəˈbahbitohn/ *noun* a barbiturate used, *esp* formerly, in sleeping pills and to prevent convulsions: formula $C_{11}H_{18}N_2O_3$. Also called NEMBUTAL.

pentode /ˈpentohd/ *noun* a THERMIONIC VALVE (device for regulating a flow of electricity) that has an anode and a cathode to and from which electrons flow and three grids that control the flow of electricity and improve the performance of the valve.

pentose /ˈpentohz, ˈpentohs/ *noun* any of various monosaccharides (simple sugars; see MONOSACCHARIDE), e.g. ribose, that contain five carbon atoms in the molecule.

Pentothal /ˈpentəthal/ *noun trademark* thiopentone.

pentstemon *or* **pentemon** /penˈ(t)steemən/ *noun* a N American plant with bright showy flowers and five stamens: genus *Penstemon*. [alteration of the Latin genus name *Penstemon*, from PENTA- + Greek *stēmōn* thread]

pent-up *adj* confined or held in check: *pent-up feelings.*

pentyl /ˈpentiel, ˈpentil/ *noun* a chemical group derived from pentane by the removal of a hydrogen atom: formula C_5H_{11}. [PENTANE + -YL]

penult /piˈnult, peˈnult/ *noun* in linguistics, the next to last syllable of a word. [Latin *paenultima*, fem of *paenultimus* almost last, from *paene* almost + *ultimus* last]

penultimate¹ /piˈnultimit, pe-/ *adj* last but one: *the penultimate chapter of a book.*

penultimate² *noun* a penult.

penumbra /piˈnumbrə/ *noun* (*pl* **penumbrae** /-bree/ *or* **penumbras**) **1** a region of partial darkness, e.g. in an eclipse, in a shadow surrounding the UMBRA (region of total darkness). **2** a less dark region surrounding the dark centre of a sunspot. >> **penumbral** *adj*. [scientific Latin *penumbra*, from Latin *paene* almost + *umbra* shadow]

penurious /piˈnyooəriˌəs/ *adj formal* **1** marked by or suffering from penury; very poor. **2** frugal. >> **penuriously** *adv*, **penuriousness** *noun*.

penury /ˈpenyoori/ *noun* severe poverty. [Middle English from Latin *penuria* want]

peon /ˈpeeˈən/ *noun* **1** (*pl* **peones** /payˈohneez/) an agricultural labourer in Spanish America. **2** an Indian or Sri Lankan infantryman, orderly, or other worker. **3** *chiefly NAmer* a drudge or menial. **4** (*pl* **peones** /payˈohneez/) = BANDERILLERO. >> **peonage** /-nij/ *noun*. [Portuguese *peão* and French *pion* from medieval Latin *pedon-, pedo*: see PAWN¹]

peony *or* **paeony** /ˈpeeˈəni/ *noun* (*pl* **peonies** *or* **paeonies**) a plant with very large showy red, pink, or white flowers: genus *Paeonia*. [Middle English *piony* via French and Latin from Greek *paiōnia*, from *Paiōn* Paeon, mythical physician of the gods]

people[1] /'peepl/ *pl noun* **1** human beings in general. **2** a group of persons considered collectively: *business people.* **3** (*used with a possessive adjective*) the members of a family or kinship: *His people have been farmers for generations.* **4** (**the people**) the mass of a community. **5** (**the people**) the citizens of a state who are qualified to vote. **6** (*treated as sing. or pl*) a body of persons that are united by a common culture and that often constitute a politically organized group: *the Jewish people.* ✱ **of all people** used to show surprise: *Fancy having an affair with Richard of all people.* [Middle English *peple* via Anglo-French *poeple* from Latin *populus*]

Usage note
people or persons? *People* is generally used as the plural of *person: one person; two people.* The form *persons* is reserved for formal or legal contexts: *committed by a person or persons unknown.*

people[2] *verb trans* **1** to supply or fill (a place) with people: *The purpose of population is not ultimately peopling earth. It is to fill heaven* — Graham D Leonard. **2** (*usu in passive*) to dwell in or inhabit (a place).

people carrier *noun* a large car with three rows of seats.

people mover *noun* **1** a means of transporting people over short distances, e.g. a moving pavement in an airport. **2** = PEOPLE CARRIER.

PEP /pep/ *abbr* **1** *Brit* personal equity plan. **2** Political and Economic Planning.

pep[1] /pep/ *noun informal* energy or high spirits. [short for PEPPER[1]]

pep[2] *verb trans* (**pepped, pepping**) (*usu* + up) to fill (somebody or something) with energy or enthusiasm.

peperoni /pepə'rohni/ *noun* see PEPPERONI.

peplum /'peplǝm/ *noun* a short skirt or flounce attached to the waistline of a blouse, jacket, or dress. [Latin *peplum* from Greek *peplos* robe or shawl]

pepo /'peepoh/ *noun* (*pl* **pepos**) a fleshy fruit with many seeds and a hard rind, e.g. a pumpkin, melon, or cucumber. [via Latin *pepo* large melon, from Greek *pepōn* ripe]

pepper[1] /'pepə/ *noun* **1** any of various tropical and mostly climbing shrubs with aromatic leaves; *esp* one with berries from which black pepper and white pepper are prepared: genus *Piper*. **2** the ground black or white powder obtained from the peppercorns of these shrubs. **3** (*used with a qualifying term*) any of various products similar to pepper; *esp* a pungent condiment obtained from capsicums: *cayenne pepper*. **4a** = SWEET PEPPER. **b** = HOT PEPPER. **c** a capsicum whose fruits are hot peppers or sweet peppers. [Old English *pipor* via a prehistoric Germanic word from Latin *piper*, ultimately from Sanskrit *pippalī* peppercorn, berry]

pepper[2] *verb trans* (**peppered, peppering**) **1** to sprinkle or season (food) with pepper. **2** to cover or fill (something) extensively with many instances of a thing: *The manager peppered his report with statistics.* **3** to shower (somebody or something) with shot or other missiles.

pepper-and-salt *adj* **1** said of a fabric or garment: having black and white or dark and light colour intermingled in small flecks. **2** said of hair: having streaks of grey.

peppercorn *noun* a dried berry of the pepper plant, used as a spice or ground as powder.

peppercorn rent *noun Brit* a very small amount of money paid as a nominal rent.

pepper mill *noun* a small pot used for grinding peppercorns by hand.

peppermint *noun* **1a** a mint plant with dark green tapering leaves and whorls of small pink flowers: *Mentha piperita*. **b** an aromatic essential oil obtained from this. **2** a sweet flavoured with peppermint oil. ⟫⟫ **pepperminty** *adj*.

pepperoni *or* **peperoni** /pepə'rohni/ *noun* a spicy Italian beef and pork sausage. [Italian *peperone* chilli, from Latin *piper*: see PEPPER[1]]

pepper pot *noun* **1** *Brit* a small container with a perforated top used for sprinkling ground pepper on food. **2** a W Indian stew of vegetables and meat or fish, highly seasoned usu with the juice of a bitter cassava.

peppery *adj* **1** hot or pungent: *a peppery meal.* **2** hot-tempered or touchy: *a peppery old man.* **3** strong or fierce: *a peppery speech.* ⟫⟫ **pepperiness** *noun*.

pep pill *noun informal* a tablet of a stimulant drug.

peppy *adj* (**peppier, peppiest**) *chiefly NAmer, informal* energetic and high-spirited. ⟫⟫ **peppily** *adv*, **peppiness** *noun*.

pepsin /'pepsin/ *noun* an enzyme of the stomach that breaks down most proteins in an acid environment. [German *Pepsin* from Greek *pepsis* digestion, from *pessein* to cook or digest]

pep talk *noun informal* a talk designed to encourage somebody.

peptic /'peptik/ *adj* of or promoting digestion. [via Latin from Greek *peptikos*, from *peptos* cooked, from *peptein, pessein* to cook or digest]

peptic ulcer *noun* an ulcer caused by the action of pepsin and stomach acid on the mucous membranes of the digestive tract.

peptide /'peptied/ *noun* a short chain of two or more amino acids joined by bonds linking the amino group of one to the CARBOXYL (acid) group of another. [PEPTONE + -IDE]

peptone /'peptohn/ *noun* any of various water-soluble products of protein breakdown. [German *Pepton* from Greek, neuter of *peptos*: see PEPTIC]

per /pə/ *strong* puh/ *prep* **1** with respect to every; for each: *£30 per head per week.* **2** by the means or agency of (something); through. ✱ **as per** according to (something): *as per list price.* **as per usual** *informal* as usual. [Latin *per* through, by means of, by]

per- *prefix* forming words, with the meanings: **1a** through or throughout: *perambulate; pervade.* **b** thoroughly or very: *perfervid; perfect.* **2** to the bad; to destruction: *perjure; perdition.* **3a** containing a large proportion of a specified chemical element or group: *peroxide.* **b** containing an atom in a high oxidation state in its molecular structure: *perchloric acid.* [French or Latin, through, throughout, thoroughly, to destruction, from PER]

peradventure[1] /pərəd'venchə, puh-/ *adv archaic* perhaps or possibly. [Middle English from Old French *per aventure* by chance]

peradventure[2] *noun archaic* doubt or chance.

perambulate /pə'rambyoolayt/ *verb intrans formal* to stroll. ⟫ *verb trans* **1** *formal* to travel over or through (a place) on foot. **2** *Brit* formerly, to walk round (e.g. a parish) to establish the boundaries. ⟫⟫ **perambulation** /-'laysh(ə)n/ *noun*, **perambulatory** /-lət(ə)ri/ *adj*. [Latin *perambulatus*, past part. of *perambulare*, from PER- through + *ambulare* to walk]

perambulator *noun formal* a pram.

per annum /'anəm/ *adv* in or for each year. [medieval Latin *per annum*]

percale /pə'kayl/ *noun* a closely woven cotton cloth used for clothing, sheeting, and industrial uses. [French *percale* from Persian *pargālah*]

per capita /'kapitə/ *adv and adj* by or for each person. [medieval Latin *per capita* by heads]

per caput /'kapoot/ *adv and adj* = PER CAPITA.

perceive /pə'seev/ *verb trans* **1** to become aware of (something) through the senses; *esp* to see or observe (something). **2** to regard (somebody or something) in the specified way: *She is perceived as being tough.* ⟫⟫ **perceivable** *adj*, **perceivably** *adv*, **perceiver** *noun*. [Middle English *perceiven* via Old French *perceivre* from Latin *percipere*, from PER- + *capere* to take]

per cent[1] /'sent/ *adv* in or for each hundred: *47 per cent of the electorate.* [PER + Latin *centum* hundred]

per cent[2] *noun* (*pl* **per cent**) **1** one part in a hundred: *She gave half a per cent of her income to charity.* **2** a percentage: *a large per cent of the total.*

percentage /pə'sentij/ *noun* **1** a proportion expressed as per cent of a whole: *What percentage of the population own their own houses?* **2** a share of winnings or profits: *They did him out of his percentage.* **3** any proportion of a whole: *Only a small percentage of the children have their own bedroom.* **4** *informal* an advantage or profit: *There wasn't any percentage in nagging him further.*

percentile /pə'sentiel/ *noun* **1** in statistics, any of 99 values in a FREQUENCY DISTRIBUTION (arrangement showing frequency with which values of a variable occur) that divide it into 100 parts, each containing 1% of the individuals, items, etc under consideration. **2** any of the 100 groups of individuals, items, etc comprising such a part or interval. [prob from PER CENT[2] + -ILE]

percept /'puhsept/ *noun* a mental impression of a perceived object. [back-formation from PERCEPTION]

perceptible /pə'septibl/ *adj* capable of being perceived: *There was a perceptible change in her tone.* **>>> perceptibility** /-'biliti/ *noun*, **perceptibly** *adv*.

perception /pə'sepsh(ə)n/ *noun* **1** an awareness of one's surroundings that is produced by the operation of the senses.

Editorial note

Perception is generally held to be our primary source of knowledge. The way in which this works, however, is disputed. Some hold that perception is the occurrence of sensory ideas in the mind, which in some way reveal the nature of their external causes. Others hold that perception is a direct awareness of the external, unmediated by prior knowledge of anything internal. There is a related debate about whether sensory experience is itself conceptual. If it is not, the world is not presented to us in conceptual form; rather, we impose such a form on what we receive, by categorization or conceptualization — Professor Jonathan Dancy.

2a a result of perceiving; an observation. **b** a mental image; a concept. **3** intuitive discernment; insight or understanding: *He has little perception of what is required.* **>>> perceptional** *adj*. [Latin *perception-, perceptio* act of perceiving, from *percipere*: see PERCEIVE]

perceptive /pə'septiv/ *adj* **1** capable of or exhibiting keen perception; observant or discerning: *a perceptive scholar.* **2** characterized by sympathetic understanding or insight. **3** relating to perception: *I had had such extraordinary evidence of the quickness of his perceptive faculties* — Conan Doyle. **>>> perceptively** *adv*, **perceptiveness** *noun*, **perceptivity** /-'tiviti/ *noun*.

perceptual /pə'septyooəl/ *adj* of or involving perception, *esp* in relation to immediate sensory experience. **>>> perceptually** *adv*.

perch¹ /puhch/ *noun* **1** a roost for a bird. **2** a resting place or vantage point; a seat. [Middle English via French *perche* from Latin *pertica* pole]

perch² *verb intrans* to alight, settle, or rest, *esp* briefly or precariously. **>** *verb trans* to place (somebody or something) on a perch, height, or precarious spot: *She perched the hat on her head.*

perch³ *noun* (*pl* **perches** or collectively **perch**) **1** a small European freshwater fish with vertical stripes and spiny fins: *Perca fluviatilis.* **2** any of numerous fishes with a bony skeleton that are related to or resemble the European perch. [Middle English *perche* via French and Latin from Greek *perkē*]

perch⁴ *noun chiefly Brit* **1** a former unit of length equal to one quarter of a chain (about 5.029m). **2** a former unit of area equal to one hundred and sixtieth of an acre (about 25.29 square m). [Middle English in the sense 'measuring pole' from French *perche*: see PERCH¹]

perchance /pə'chahns/ *adv archaic or literary* perhaps or possibly. [Middle English from early French *per chance* by chance]

Percheron /'puhshəron/ *noun* a powerful draught horse of a breed that originated in the Perche region of France. [French *percheron* from *le Perche*, region of N France]

perchloric acid /pə'klawrik/ *noun* a strong corrosive acid that has the highest proportion of oxygen of any acid of chlorine and is a powerful oxidizing agent when heated: formula $HClO_4$.

percipient¹ /pə'sipi·ənt/ *adj* perceptive or discerning. **>>> percipience** *noun*, **percipiently** *adv*. [Latin *percipient-, percipiens*, present part. of *percipere*: see PERCEIVE]

percipient² *noun* somebody who is able to perceive things, *esp* somebody who is telepathic.

percoid /'puhkoyd/ *adj* of or belonging to a very large suborder of spiny-finned fishes with a bony skeleton, including the perches, sunfishes, sea basses, and sea breams: suborder Percoidea. **>>> percoid** *noun*. [derivative of Latin *perca* perch]

percolate /'puhkəlayt/ *verb intrans* **1** said of a liquid or gas: to pass through a porous substance; *esp* so that a soluble constituent is extracted. **2** said of coffee: to be prepared in a percolator. **3** to spread gradually through a group or area; to diffuse: *Sunlight percolated into our rooms; The news finally percolated down to us.* **>** *verb trans* to prepare (coffee) in a percolator. **>>> percolation** /-'laysh(ə)n/ *noun*. [Latin *percolatus*, past part. of *percolare*, from PER- + *colare* to sieve]

percolator *noun* a coffee pot in which boiling water passes repeatedly through a perforated basket containing ground coffee beans.

per contra /'kontrə/ *adv* on the contrary. [Italian *per contra* by the opposite side (of the ledger)]

percuss /pə'kus/ *verb trans* in medicine, to perform percussion on (a body part). [Latin *percussus*, past part. of *percutere*: see PERCUSSION]

percussion /pə'kush(ə)n/ *noun* **1a** the beating or striking of a musical instrument. **b** (*used before a noun*) denoting a musical instrument played by beating or striking. **c** percussion instruments that form a section of a band or orchestra. **2** the striking of sound on the ear. **3** in medicine, the tapping of the surface of the body to determine, from the sound produced, the condition of the parts beneath. **>>> percussive** /pə'kusiv/ *adj*, **percussively** *adv*, **percussiveness** *noun*. [Latin *percussion-, percussio*, from *percutere* to beat, from PER- + *quatere* to shake]

percussion cap *noun* a small container containing an explosive charge, e.g. for a toy gun.

percussionist *noun* a person who plays percussion instruments.

percutaneous /puhkyoo'tayni·əs/ *adj* in medicine, done or effected through the skin: *the percutaneous absorption of an ointment.* **>>> percutaneously** *adv*.

per diem¹ /'dee·em/ *adj and adv* by the day or for each day. [medieval Latin *per diem*]

per diem² *noun* a daily allowance or fee.

perdition /pə'dish(ə)n/ *noun* in Christianity, eternal damnation; hell. [Middle English *perdicion* from Latin *perdition-, perditio*, from *perdere* to destroy, from PER- + *dare* to give]

perdurable /puh'dyooərəbl/ *adj formal* very durable; eternal. [Middle English via French from Latin *perdurare* to endure, from PER- + *durare* to last]

père /peə/ *noun* used after the surname of a father to distinguish him from a son of the same name: *Clark père was an idler with a taste for expensive yachts* — Geoffrey Hulton. [French *père* father, from Latin *patr-, pater*]

Père David's deer /'dayvidz/ *noun* a large grey deer with long slender antlers, now found only in captivity: *Elaphurus davidianus.* [named after *Père* Armand *David* d.1900, French missionary and naturalist, who discovered it in China where it originated]

peregrinate /'perigrinayt/ *verb intrans archaic or humorous* to walk; to make a peregrination.

peregrination /,perigri'naysh(ə)n/ *noun archaic or humorous* a long and wandering journey, *esp* in a foreign country. **>>> peregrinator** /'perigrinaytə/ *noun*. [early French *peregrination* from Latin *peregrination-, peregrinatio*, from *peregrinari* to travel abroad, from *peregrinus* foreign, foreigner, from *peregre* abroad, from PER- + *ager* field]

peregrine¹ /'perigrin/ *noun* a smallish fast-flying falcon with dark grey wings and back, formerly much used in falconry: *Falco peregrinus.* [Middle English *peregrine* wandering, widely distributed, from Latin *peregrinus*: see PEREGRINATION]

peregrine² *adj archaic* strange or foreign.

peregrine falcon *noun* = PEREGRINE¹.

peremptory /pə'rempt(ə)ri/ *adj* **1** characterized by imperious or arrogant self-assurance: *a peremptory tone.* **2** expressive of urgency or command: *a peremptory call.* **3** in law, admitting no contradiction or refusal: *a peremptory court order.* **>>> peremptorily** *adv*, **peremptoriness** *noun*. [late Latin *peremptorius* deadly, decisive, from Latin *peremptus*, past part. of *perimere* to take entirely, destroy, from PER- + *emere* to take]

perennial¹ /pə'reni·əl/ *adj* **1** lasting throughout the year or for several years. **2** said of a plant: living for several years, usu with new herbaceous growth each year: compare ANNUAL¹, BIENNIAL¹. **3** lasting for a long time or forever; constant: *Politics provide a perennial topic of argument.* **>>> perennially** *adv*. [Latin *perennis*, from PER- + *annus* year]

perennial² *noun* a plant living for more than two years.

perestroika /perə'stroykə/ *noun* the restructuring of a system or organization; *esp* the political and social reform of the communist system of the former Soviet Union. [Russian *perestroika* from *perestroit* to reconstruct or reorganize, from *pere-* RE- + *stroit* to construct]

perfect¹ /'puhfikt/ *adj* **1a** entirely without fault or defect; flawless. **b** satisfactory in every respect: *The holiday was perfect.* **c** corresponding to an ideal standard or abstract concept: *a perfect gentleman.* **2a** accurate or exact: *a perfect circle.* **b** lacking in no essential detail; complete. **3** absolute or utter: *I felt a perfect fool.* **4** in grammar, of or constituting a verb tense or form that expresses an action or state completed at the time of speaking or at a time spoken of. **5a** of a flower: having both stamens and carpels. **b** said of a fungus: having sexual or asexual reproductive stages; producing both sexual and asexual spores. **6** in mathematics, said of an integer: equal to the sum of all the integers by which it can be divided without leaving a remainder, including 1 but excluding itself, e.g. 6 or 28. **7a** denoting the musical intervals fourth, fifth, and octave, which are the same in major and minor keys. **b** said of a cadence: passing from a dominant or subdominant to a tonic chord. ⟫ **perfectly** *adv*, **perfectness** *noun*. [Middle English *parfit* via French *parfait* from Latin *perfectus*, past part. of *perficere* to carry out, perfect, from PER- + *facere* to make or do]

perfect[2] *noun* the verb tense that expresses a completed action or state, or a verb form expressing this, e.g. *I have finished*.

perfect[3] /'pə'fekt/ *verb trans* **1** to make (something) perfect; to improve or refine. **2** to bring (something) to final form. ⟫ **perfecter** *noun*, **perfectibility** /-'biliti/ *noun*, **perfectible** *adj*.

perfecta *noun chiefly NAmer* a bet, e.g. on a horse or dog race, that involves forecasting the first two finishers in correct order. [American Spanish (*quiniela*) *perfecta* perfect (quinella)]

perfect binding /'puhfikt/ *noun* bookbinding in which single leaves are held together with adhesive at the spine.

perfect gas /'puhfikt/ *noun* = IDEAL GAS.

perfection /pə'feksh(ə)n/ *noun* **1a** making or being perfect. **b** freedom from fault or defect. **c** full development; maturity: *Greek civilization slowly flowered to perfection.* **2** unsurpassable accuracy or excellence, or an example of this: *The cruellest thing a man can do to a woman is to portray her as perfection* — D H Lawrence.

perfectionism *noun* **1** a disposition to regard as unacceptable anything short of perfection, *esp* in one's own work. **2** the doctrine that a state of perfection is attainable. ⟫ **perfectionist** *adj and noun*.

perfective /pə'fektiv/ *adj* said of a form of a verb: expressing action as complete: compare IMPERFECTIVE[1]. ⟫ **perfective** *noun*.

perfecto /pə'fektoh/ *noun* (*pl* **perfectos**) a thick cigar that tapers almost to a point at each end. [Spanish *perfecto* perfect, from Latin *perfectus*: see PERFECT[1]]

perfect participle /'puhfikt/ *noun* a participle expressing a completed event.

perfect pitch /'puhfikt/ *noun* = ABSOLUTE PITCH (2).

perfervid /puh'fuhvid/ *adj literary* particularly fervid; ardent: *I had framed a humble and beseeching and perfervid petition to Congress begging the government to build the monument* — Mark Twain. [Latin *perfervidus*, from PER- + *fervidus*: see FERVID]

perfidious /pə'fidi·əs/ *adj* faithless or disloyal; treacherous. ⟫ **perfidiously** *adv*, **perfidiousness** *noun*.

perfidy /'puhfidi/ *noun literary* faithlessness or disloyalty; treachery. [Latin *perfidia* from *perfidus* faithless, from *per fidem decipere* to betray, literally 'to deceive by trust']

perfoliate /pə'fohli·ət, -ayt/ *adj* **1** said of a leaf: having a base that curves completely round the stem so that the stem appears to pass through the leaf. **2** said of a plant: having perfoliate leaves. [Latin *perfoliata* perfoliate plant, from PER- + *foliata*, fem of *foliatus*: see FOLIATE[1]]

perforate[1] /'puhfərayt/ *verb trans* **1** to make a hole through or in (something). **2** to make a line of holes in or between (e.g. postage stamps in a sheet) to make separation easier. ⟫ **perforated** *adj*, **perforation** /-'raysh(ə)n/ *noun*, **perforator** *noun*. [Latin *perforatus*, past part. of *perforare* to bore through, from PER- + *forare* to bore]

perforate[2] /'puhfərit/ *adj* perforated: *a perforate shell.*

perforce /pə'faws/ *adv formal* by force of circumstances; unavoidably. [Middle English from early French *par force* by force]

perform /pə'fawm/ *verb trans* **1** to do (something); to carry (something) out: *The computer can perform several tasks at once.* **2** to do (something) in a formal manner or according to prescribed ritual: *The priest performed the marriage ceremony.* **3** to give a rendering of (a dramatic or musical piece). ⟫ *verb intrans* **1** to carry out an action or pattern of behaviour; to act or function: *He performs well under pressure.* **2** to give a dramatic or musical performance. **3** said of an investment: to yield profits. ⟫ **performable** *adj*, **performer** *noun*. [Middle English *performen* from Anglo-French *performer*, alteration of Old French *perfournir*, from PER- + *fournir* to complete]

performance /pə'fawməns/ *noun* **1** the act or an instance of performing: *in the performance of her duties.* **2** a presentation to an audience of a play, a piece of music, a dance, etc. **3** the ability to perform or work: *Good engine performance requires good tuning.* **4** *informal.* **a** a lengthy or troublesome process or activity: *Going through customs*

was such a performance! **b** a display of bad behaviour. **5** in linguistics, the manifestation of language capacity in actual speech and writing: compare COMPETENCE.

performance art *noun* art that combines an element of theatre with visual or auditory elements, e.g. a sculpture or tableau of which the artist forms a part. ⟫ **performance artist** *noun*.

performative /pə'fawmətiv/ *noun* an expression that constitutes the performance of the specified act by virtue of its utterance, e.g. *I bet* or *I declare war.* ⟫ **performative** *adj*.

performing arts *pl noun* arts, e.g. music and drama, that are performed to an audience.

perfume[1] /'puhfyoohm/ *noun* **1** a pleasant-smelling liquid preparation, e.g. of floral essences, applied to the skin: *Here's the smell of the blood still. All the perfumes of Arabia will not sweeten this little hand* — Shakespeare. **2** a sweet or pleasant smell; a fragrance. [early French *perfum* prob from Old Provençal *perfumar* to perfume, from PER- + *fumar* to smoke, from Latin *fumare*]

perfume[2] /'puhfyoohm, pə'fyoohm/ *verb trans* **1** to fill or imbue (something) with a sweet smell. **2** to apply perfume to (something). ⟫ **perfumed** *adj*.

perfumery /pə'fyoohm(ə)ri/ *noun* (*pl* **perfumeries**) **1** the manufacture of perfumes. **2** a place where perfumes are made or sold. ⟫ **perfumer** *noun*.

perfunctory /pə'fungkt(ə)ri/ *adj* characterized by routine or superficiality; mechanical or cursory: *Jude sat watching her ... easy, curiously nonchalant risings and sittings, and her perfunctory genuflections* — Hardy. ⟫ **perfunctorily** *adv*, **perfunctoriness** *noun*. [late Latin *perfunctorius* from Latin *perfunctus*, past part. of *perfungi* to accomplish or get through with, from PER- + *fungi* to perform]

perfuse /pə'fyoohz/ *verb trans* **1** to suffuse (something) with a colour, liquid, etc. **2** in medicine, to force a fluid through (an organ or tissue), *esp* by way of the blood vessels. ⟫ **perfusion** /-zh(ə)n/ *noun*, **perfusionist** /-zh(ə)nist/ *noun*. [Latin *perfusus*, past part. of *perfundere* to pour over, from PER- + *fundere* to pour]

pergola /'puhgələ/ *noun* an arbour made by training plants over a trellis, or the trellis itself. [Italian *pergola* from Latin *pergula* projecting roof, from *pergere* to come or go forwards]

perhaps /pə'haps, praps/ *adv* **1** possibly but not certainly; maybe: *Perhaps I'm mistaken.* **2** used in polite requests: *Perhaps you would open the window.*

peri /'piəri/ *noun* (*pl* **peris**) a supernatural being in Persian folklore descended from fallen angels and excluded from paradise until penance is accomplished. [Persian *perī* fairy, genius, modification of Avestan *pairikā* witch]

peri- *prefix* forming words, with the meanings: **1** round or about: *periscope; peripatetic.* **2** near: *perihelion; perigee.* **3** enclosing or surrounding: *perimeter; peritoneum.* [Latin from Greek, from *peri* round, in excess]

perianth /'perianth/ *noun* the outer part of a flower, surrounding the reproductive parts, *esp* when not differentiated into petals and sepals. [scientific Latin *perianthium*, from PERI- + Greek *anthos* flower + -IUM]

periapt /'periapt/ *noun archaic* an amulet or charm. [early French *periapte* from Greek *periapton*, from *periaptein* to fasten round (oneself), from PERI- + *haptein* to fasten]

pericardia /peri'kahdi·ə/ *noun* pl of PERICARDIUM.

pericarditis /,perikah'dietis/ *noun* inflammation of the pericardium.

pericardium /peri'kahdi·əm/ *noun* (*pl* **pericardia** /-di·ə/) **1** the membranous sac that surrounds the heart of vertebrates. **2** the space surrounding the heart in arthropods and molluscs. ⟫ **pericardial** *adj*. [scientific Latin from Greek *perikardion*, neuter of *perikardios* round the heart, from PERI- + *kardia* heart]

pericarp /'perikahp/ *noun* the structure that surrounds the seed or seeds of a fruit and consists of the ripened and modified wall of a plant ovary. [scientific Latin from Greek *perikarpion* pod, from PERI- + -*karpion* -CARP]

perichondrium /peri'kondri·əm/ *noun* the membrane of fibrous connective tissue that surrounds cartilage except at joints. [scientific Latin, from PERI- + Greek *chondros* grain, cartilage]

periclase /'periklays/ *noun* a mineral consisting of magnesium oxide, found in marble and limestone. [German *Periklas* via Italian from Greek *periklasis* act of twisting or breaking round, from *periklan* to twist or break round, from PERI- + *klan* to break; because it cleaves perfectly]

periclinal /peri'klienl/ *adj* **1** said of a fold in sedimentary rock: dome-shaped. **2** said of a cell wall: parallel to the outer surface of a plant. [Greek *periklinēs* sloping on all sides, from PERI- + *klinein* to lean]

pericranium /peri'krayni·əm/ *noun* (*pl* **pericrania** /-ni·ə/) the strong external membrane of the skull. [scientific Latin from Greek *perikranion*, neuter of *perikranios* round the skull, from PERI- + *kranion* skull]

pericycle /'perisiekl/ *noun* a thin layer of cells that surrounds the central vascular part of many stems and roots. ➤➤ **pericyclic** /-'sieklik/ *adj*. [French *péricycle* from Greek *perikyklos* spherical, from PERI- + *kyklos* circle]

periderm /'periduhm/ *noun* the outer protective layer of woody roots and stems that consists of cork and adjacent tissues. ➤➤ **peridermal** /-'duhml/ *adj*. [scientific Latin *peridermis*, from PERI- + DERMIS]

peridot /'peridot/ *noun* a deep yellowish green transparent gem consisting of silicates of iron and magnesium. [French *péridot* from Old French *peritot*]

perigee /'perijee/ *noun* the point nearest the earth reached by the moon or a satellite in its orbit: compare APOGEE (1). [early French *perigee* via Latin from Greek *perigeion*, neuter of *perigeios* near the earth, from PERI- + *gē* earth]

periglacial /peri'glayshl/ *adj* relating to an area that borders on a glacier or ice sheet.

perigynous /pə'rijinəs/ *adj* **1** said of a floral organ, e.g. a petal or sepal: borne on a ring or cup of the receptacle surrounding an ovule: compare EPIGYNOUS, HYPOGYNOUS. **2** said of a flower: having perigynous petals, sepals, etc. ➤➤ **perigyny** *noun*. [scientific Latin *perigynus*, from PERI- + *-gynus* -GYNOUS]

perihelion /peri'heeli·ən/ *noun* (*pl* **perihelia** /-li·ə/) the point in the path of a planet, comet, etc that is nearest to the sun: compare APHELION. [scientific Latin *perihelion*, from PERI- + Greek *hēlios* sun]

peril /'peril/ *noun* exposure to the risk of being injured, destroyed, or lost; danger. ➤➤ **perilous** *adj*, **perilously** *adv*, **perilousness** *noun*. [Middle English via French from Latin *periculum* danger]

perilune /'periloohn/ *noun* the point in the path of a body orbiting the moon that is nearest the centre of the moon: compare APOLUNE. [PERI- + Latin *luna* moon]

perilymph /'perilimf/ *noun* the liquid inside the labyrinth of the inner ear that acts as a shock absorber and in the transmission of sound vibrations.

perimeter /pə'rimitə/ *noun* **1** the boundary of a closed plane figure, or the length of this. **2** the outer edge or limits of something. **3** (*used before a noun*) denoting a line, strip, fence, etc bounding an area: *a perimeter fence*. **4** an instrument used to measure field of vision. ➤➤ **perimetric** /peri'metrik/ *adj*. [French *périmètre* via Latin from Greek *perimetros*, from PERI- + *metron* measure]

perinatal /peri'naytl/ *adj* relating to the time immediately before and after childbirth. ➤➤ **perinatally** *adv*.

perineum /peri'nee·əm/ *noun* (*pl* **perinea** /-'nee·ə/) the area between the anus and the genitals. ➤➤ **perineal** *adj*. [via Latin from Greek *perinaion*, from PERI- + *inein* to empty out]

period /'piəri·əd/ *noun* **1** a portion of time. **2** a chronological division; a stage of history. **3** (*used before a noun*) of a particular historical period: *period costume*. **4** a division of geological time that is part of an era and is subdivided into epochs. **5** any of the divisions of the school day. **6** a single occurrence of menstruation. **7** *chiefly NAmer* a full stop. **8** in physics, the interval of time that elapses before a cyclic motion or phenomenon begins to repeat itself. **9** in mathematics, a number that does not change the value of a periodic function when added to the independent variable; *esp* the smallest such number. **10** in chemistry, a horizontal row of elements in the periodic table. **11** in astronomy, the time taken by a body, e.g. a planet, to make one complete rotation on its axis. **12** in rhetoric, a well-proportioned sentence of several clauses. [early French *periode* via Latin from Greek *periodus* circuit, period of time, rhetorical period, from PERI- + *hodos* way]

periodic /piəri'odik/ *adj* **1** recurring at regular intervals. **2** consisting of or containing a series of repeated stages: *periodic decimals; a periodic vibration*. **3** expressed in or characterized by rhetorical periods. **4** relating to the periodic table. ➤➤ **periodicity** /-'disiti/ *noun*.

periodical¹ *adj* **1** recurring at regular intervals. **2** said of a magazine or journal: published at fixed intervals, e.g. weekly or quarterly: *the tenth Muse, who now governs the periodical press* — Trollope. ➤➤ **periodically** *adv*.

periodical² *noun* a periodical publication.

periodic function *noun* a mathematical function, e.g. a sine or cosine, the possible values of which all recur at regular intervals.

periodic table *noun* an arrangement of chemical elements in the order of their atomic numbers that shows a periodic variation in their properties.

Editorial note ────────────
The periodic table is divided into vertical groups and horizontal periods. The elements in a given group show close family similarities, as do diagonally related neighbours. Metallic elements lie to the left of the table and non-metallic elements lie to the right; they are separated by a diagonal band of metalloids. The table is used as a basis for the systematic discussion of the elements — Professor Peter Atkins.

periodontal /,peri·ə'dontl/ *adj* relating to or in the region of the tissues surrounding a tooth.

periodontics /,peri·ə'dontiks/ *pl noun* (*treated as sing. or pl*) the branch of dentistry that deals with diseases of the supporting structures of the teeth. ➤➤ **periodontist** *noun*. [scientific Latin *periodontium*, from PERI- + Greek *odont-, odous, odōn* tooth]

periodontology /,peri·ədon'toləji/ *noun* = PERIODONTICS.

period piece *noun* a piece of fiction, art, furniture, or music, the special value of which lies in its evocation of a historical period.

perioperative /peri'opərətiv/ *adj* at the time of a surgical operation: *perioperative deaths*.

periosteum /peri'osti·əm/ *noun* (*pl* **periostea** /-ti·ə/) the covering of connective tissue that closely surrounds all bones except at the joints. ➤➤ **periosteal** *adj*. [scientific Latin from Greek *periosteon*, neuter of *periosteos* round the bone, from PERI- + *osteon* bone]

periostitis /,perio'stietis/ *noun* inflammation of the periosteum.

peripatetic¹ /,peripə'tetik/ *adj* **1** travelling or itinerant. **2** said of a teacher, e.g. a music teacher: unattached to a particular school; teaching in various schools. **3** (**Peripatetic**) Aristotelian. ➤➤ **peripatetically** *adv*, **Peripateticism** /-siz(ə)m/ *noun*. [early French *peripatetique* from Greek *peripatētikos*, from *peripatein* to walk up and down, discourse while pacing (as did Aristotle), from PERI- + *patein* to tread]

peripatetic² *noun* **1** a peripatetic teacher. **2** (**Peripatetic**) a follower of Aristotle or an adherent of Aristotelianism.

peripeteia /,peripi'tie·ə, -'tee·ə/ *noun formal* a sudden or unexpected reversal of circumstances or situation, e.g. in a tragedy. [Greek *peripeteia* from *peripiptein* to fall round, change suddenly, from PERI- + *piptein* to fall]

peripheral¹ /pə'rif(ə)rəl/ *adj* **1** of, involving, or forming a periphery: *a peripheral wall*. **2** of minor significance: *a peripheral issue*. **3a** relating to or situated at or near the surface of the body. **b** of, being, or supplying the part of the nervous system other than the brain and the spinal cord. **4** auxiliary or supplementary: *a peripheral device*. ➤➤ **peripherally** *adv*.

peripheral² *noun* a device, e.g. a printer or scanner, connected to a computer and able to exchange signals with it.

periphery /pə'rif(ə)ri/ *noun* (*pl* **peripheries**) **1** the outer limits or edge of something. **2** a less important or central position. [early French *peripherie* via Latin from Greek *periphereia*, from *peripherein* to carry round, from PERI- + *pherein* to carry]

periphrasis /pə'rifrəsis/ *noun* (*pl* **periphrases** /-seez/) the use of circumlocution or roundabout phrasing, e.g. *I was of the opinion that* instead of *I thought that*. [via Latin from Greek *periphrasis*, from *periphrazein* to express periphrastically, from PERI- + *phrazein* to point out]

periphrastic /peri'frastik/ *adj* **1** of or characterized by periphrasis. **2** formed by the use of function words or auxiliaries instead of by inflection, e.g. *more fair* as contrasted with *fairer*. ➤➤ **periphrastically** *adv*.

perique /pə'reek/ *noun* a rich-flavoured aromatic Louisiana tobacco. [Louisiana French *périque*, said to be the nickname of Pierre Chenet, who first grew it]

periscope /'periskohp/ *noun* a tubular optical instrument containing lenses, mirrors, or prisms for seeing objects not in the direct line of sight. ➤➤ **periscopic** /-'skopik/ *adj*.

perish /'perish/ *verb intrans* **1** to die, *esp* in a terrible or sudden way. **2** to be ruined or destroyed: *recollection of a past already long since perished* — Philip Sherrard. **3** to deteriorate or rot: *The rubber had begun to perish.* ➤ *verb trans* said of cold or exposure: to weaken or numb (somebody): *We were perished with cold.* ✱ **perish the thought** *informal* used to express horror at or firm rejection of an idea. [Middle English *perisshen* via French from Latin *perire*, from PER- + *ire* to go]

perishable[1] *adj* liable to rot or decay: *It is a well-known fact that love is an emotion that is almost as perishable as eggs* — H L Mencken. ➤ **perishability** /-'biliti/ *noun*.

perishable[2] *noun* (*in pl*) things, *esp* items of food, that are liable to rot or decay.

perisher *noun Brit, informal* an annoying or troublesome person or thing; *esp* a mischievous child.

perishing *adj* **1** *Brit, informal* extremely cold. **2** *dated* damnable or confounded: *I wish this perishing bus strike would end.* ➤ **perishingly** *adv.*

perisperm /'perispuhm/ *noun* nutritive tissue derived from the nucleus and surrounding the embryo of a seed. [PERI- + Greek *sperma* seed]

perissodactyl /pə,risoh'daktil/ *noun* any of an order of hoofed mammals, e.g. the horse, tapir, or rhinoceros, that do not chew the cud and that usu have an odd number of toes on each foot: order Perissodactyla. ➤ **perissodactyl** *adj.* [from the Latin order name, from Greek *perissos* odd in number + *daktylos* finger, toe]

peristalsis /peri'stalsis/ *noun* successive waves of involuntary contraction passing along the walls of a hollow muscular structure, *esp* the intestine, and forcing the contents onward. ➤ **peristaltic** *adj,* **peristaltically** *adv.* [scientific Latin from Greek *peristaltikos* peristaltic, from *peristellein* to wrap round, from PERI- + *stellein* to place]

peristome /'peristohm/ *noun* **1** the region round the mouth in various invertebrate animals, e.g. starfish, earthworms, and some single-celled organisms. **2** the fringe of projections surrounding the opening of the spore-bearing capsule of a moss. [scientific Latin *peristoma*, from PERI- + Greek *stoma* mouth]

peristyle /'peristiel/ *noun* a colonnade surrounding a building or court. [French *péristyle* via Latin from Greek *peristylon*, neuter of *peristylos* surrounded by a colonnade, from PERI- + *stylos* pillar]

peritoneum /,peritə'nee·əm/ *noun* (*pl* **peritoneums** *or* **peritonea** /-'nee·ə/) the smooth transparent membrane that lines the cavity of the abdomen of a mammal and covers the organs of the abdomen and pelvis. ➤ **peritoneal** *adj.* [late Latin from Greek *peritonaion*, neuter of *peritonaios* stretched round, from PERI- + *teinein* to stretch]

peritonitis /,peritə'nietəs/ *noun* inflammation of the peritoneum, causing severe abdominal pain.

periwig /'periwig/ *noun* = PERUKE. ➤ **periwigged** *adj.* [modification of early French *perruque*: see PERUKE]

periwinkle[1] /'periwingkl/ *noun* any of various trailing evergreen plants with blue or white flowers: genera *Vinca* and *Catharanthus.* [Old English *perwince* from Latin *pervinca*]

periwinkle[2] *noun* any of numerous species of small edible marine snails with a spiral shell: family *Littorinidae.* [Middle English alteration of Old English *pinewincle*, from Latin *pina*, a kind of mussel (from Greek) + Old English *-wincle* shell]

perjure /'puhjə/ *verb trans* to make (oneself) guilty of perjury. ➤ **perjurer** *noun.* [early French *perjurer* from Latin *perjurare*, from PER- + *jurare*: see JURY[1]]

perjured *adj* **1** said of evidence: containing deliberate untruths. **2** guilty of committing perjury.

perjury /'puhj(ə)ri/ *noun* (*pl* **perjuries**) the voluntary violation of an oath, *esp* the telling of an untruth in a court of law. ➤ **perjurious** /-'jwariəs/ *adj.*

perk[1] /puhk/ *noun informal* a privilege or benefit incidental to regular salary or wages: *A company car is a perk of the job.* [by shortening and alteration from PERQUISITE]

perk[2] *verb intrans informal* said of coffee: to percolate. [by shortening and alteration]

perk up *verb intrans and trans* to recover one's vigour or cheerfulness, *esp* after a period of weakness or depression, or cause (somebody) to recover in this way: *She perked up when the letter arrived.* [Middle English *perken* to perch, be jaunty, perhaps from early French *perche*: see PERCH[1]]

perky *adj* (**perkier, perkiest**) **1** lively; jaunty: *a perky tune.* **2** briskly self-assured; cocky: *a perky salesman.* ➤ **perkily** *adv,* **perkiness** *noun.*

perlite /'puhliet/ *noun* a greyish volcanic glass that appears to be composed of small globular bodies. When expanded by heat it forms a lightweight aggregate used in concrete and plaster, or as a soil conditioner to assist drainage. [French *perlite* from *perle*: see PEARL[1]]

perm[1] /puhm/ *noun* a long-lasting wave set in the hair by chemicals. [short for PERMANENT WAVE]

perm[2] *verb trans* to give a perm to (the hair).

perm[3] *noun Brit, informal* a permutation; *specif* any of the possible combinations of teams that can be chosen in the football pools.

perm[4] *verb trans Brit, informal* to permute (something); *specif* to pick out and combine (a specified number of teams in the football pools) in all the possible permutations: *Perm any eight from eleven.*

permafrost /'puhməfrost/ *noun* a layer of permanently frozen ground in very cold regions, e.g. the Arctic and Antarctic. [blend of PERMANENT[1] + FROST[1]]

Permalloy /'puhməloy/ *noun trademark* an easily magnetized and demagnetized alloy of about 80% nickel and 20% iron. [contraction of *permeable alloy*]

permanent[1] /'puhmənənt/ *adj* **1** continuing or enduring without fundamental or marked change; lasting or stable: *The word permanent had its own kind of revenge on those who misused it, for the Bible said that nothing was permanent and everything came and went* — Janet Frame. **2** not subject to replacement according to political circumstances: *She is a Permanent Undersecretary at the Home Office.* ➤ **permanence** *noun,* **permanency** *noun,* **permanently** *adv.* [Middle English via French from Latin *permanent-, permanens*, present part. of *permanēre* to endure, from PER- + *manēre* to remain]

permanent[2] *noun NAmer* = PERM[1].

permanent magnet *noun* a magnet that retains its magnetism after removal of the magnetizing force.

permanent tooth *noun* any of the second set of teeth of a mammal that replace the milk teeth and typically last into old age.

permanent wave *noun* = PERM[1].

permanent way *noun Brit* the rails, sleepers, and ballast that make up the track of a railway system.

permanganate /pə'manggənit, -nayt/ *noun* a dark purple salt containing manganese.

permeability /,puhmi·ə'biliti/ *noun* **1** the state or quality of being permeable. **2** the property of a magnetizable substance that determines the ease with which it becomes a magnet and thus the effect it has on the MAGNETIC FLUX (strength of magnetic forces) operating in the region around it.

permeable /'puhmi·əbl/ *adj* capable of being permeated; *esp* having pores or openings that permit liquids or gases to pass through: *a permeable membrane.*

permeance /'puhmi·əns/ *noun* **1** permeation. **2** the permeability of a piece of a magnetizable substance equal to the reciprocal of the magnetic RELUCTANCE (resistance to the passage of a magnetic force).

permeate /'puhmiayt/ *verb trans* **1** to spread or diffuse throughout (something): *He was fundamentally and outwardly abject ... it was the element of his nature which permeated all his acts and passions and emotions* — Joseph Conrad. **2** to pass through the pores, gaps, cracks, etc of (something). ➤ **permeation** /-'aysh(ə)n/ *noun.* [Latin *permeatus*, past part. of *permeare*, from PER- + *meare* to go, pass]

Permian /'puhmi·ən/ *adj* relating to or dating from a geological period, the last period of the Palaeozoic era, lasting from about 290 million to about 245 million years ago, and marked by the expansion of reptiles. ➤ **Permian** *noun.* [named after *Perm*, region in Russia where strata of this period are easily seen]

permissible /pə'misibl/ *adj* allowable. ➤ **permissibility** /-'biliti/ *noun,* **permissibly** *adv.* [Middle English from medieval Latin *permissibilis*, from Latin *permittere*: see PERMIT[1]]

permission /pə'mish(ə)n/ *noun* formal consent; authorization. [Middle English via French from Latin *permission-, permissio*, from *permittere*: see PERMIT[1]]

permissive /pə'misiv/ *adj* **1** tolerant; *esp* accepting a relaxed social or sexual morality: *the permissive age.* **2** allowing but not enforcing;

optional: *permissive legislation.* ➤➤ **permissively** *adv,* **permissiveness** *noun.* [French *permissif* from Latin *permittere*: see PERMIT¹]

permit¹ /pə'mit/ *verb* (**permitted, permitting**) ➤ *verb trans* **1** to give (somebody) authorization to do something: *You are not permitted to leave the building.* **2** to consent to (something), usu expressly or formally: *The hospital won't permit access to the records.* **3** to make (something) possible: *technology that permits high-quality reproduction of sound and images.* ➤ *verb intrans* **1** to give an opportunity; to allow: *weather permitting.* **2** *formal* (+ of) to allow for something: *The wording permits of the following interpretations.* ➤➤ **permitter** *noun.* [Latin *permittere* to let through, permit, from PER- + *mittere* to let go, send]

permit² /'puhmit/ *noun* a written warrant allowing the holder to do or keep something: *a gun permit.*

permittivity /puhmi'tiviti/ *noun* the ability of a DIELECTRIC² (substance that does not contain an electric current) to store electrical potential energy when placed in an electric field.

permutate /'puhmyootayt/ *verb trans* to change the order or arrangement of (something).

permutation /puhmyoo'taysh(ə)n/ *noun* **1** any of the various possible ordered arrangements of a set of objects, numbers, letters, etc, or the changing from one to another of these: compare COMBINATION. **2** a variation or change, e.g. in character or condition, brought about by rearrangement of existing elements. **3** *Brit* a combination of teams that can be chosen in the football pools. ➤➤ **permutational** *adj.* [Middle English *permutacioun* exchange, transformation, via French from Latin *permutation-, permutatio,* from *permutare*: see PERMUTE]

permute /pə'myooht/ *verb trans* to change the order or arrangement of (objects, numbers, etc), *esp* to arrange them successively in all possible ways. [Middle English *permuten* via French from Latin *permutare,* from PER- + *mutare* to change]

pernicious /pə'nishəs/ *adj* highly injurious or destructive; deadly: *I am inclined to believe irreligion equally pernicious with gin and tea —* Dr Johnson. ➤➤ **perniciously** *adv,* **perniciousness** *noun.* [early French *pernicieux* from Latin *perniciosus,* from *pernicies* destruction, from PER- + *nec-, nex* violent death]

pernicious anaemia *noun* anaemia marked by a decrease in the number of red blood cells, which is caused by a reduced ability to absorb vitamin B_{12}.

pernickety /pə'nikiti/ *adj chiefly Brit, informal* **1** fussy about small details; fastidious: *a pernickety teacher.* **2** requiring precision and care: *a pernickety job.* [perhaps alteration of PARTICULAR¹]

Pernod /'puhnoh, 'peənoh/ *noun trademark* a French aperitif with a strong aniseed flavour.

peroneal /perə'nee·əl/ *adj* relating to or in the region of the fibula. [scientific Latin *peroneus,* from *perone* fibula, from Greek *peronē,* literally 'pin, buckle': compare FIBULA]

Peronist /'perənist/ *noun* a supporter of Juan Péron (d.1974), Argentinian soldier and statesman. ➤➤ **Peronist** *adj.*

perorate /'perərayt/ *verb intrans formal* **1** to deliver a long, pompous, or highly rhetorical oration. **2** to conclude a speech. [Latin *peroratus,* past part. of *perorare* to declaim at length, wind up an oration, from PER- + *orare* to speak]

peroration /perə'raysh(ə)n/ *noun* the concluding part of a discourse, in which the main points are summed up. [Middle English *peroracyon* from Latin *peroration-, peroratio,* from *perorare*: see PERORATE]

perovskite /pə'rofskiet/ *noun* a yellow, brown, or black mineral consisting mainly of calcium titanate. [named after L A *Perovsky* d.1856, Russian mineralogist]

peroxide¹ /pə'roksied/ *noun* **1** an OXIDE (compound of oxygen with one other element or group) containing a high proportion of oxygen; *esp* a compound containing the peroxy chemical group –O–O–. **2** *not in technical use* hydrogen peroxide.

peroxide² *verb trans* to bleach (hair) with hydrogen peroxide.

peroxy /pə'roksi/ *noun* (*used in combinations*) the bivalent chemical radical –O–O–.

perp /puhp/ *noun NAmer, informal* the perpetrator of a crime. [by shortening]

perpendicular¹ /puhpən'dikyoolə/ *adj* **1** being or standing at right angles to the plane of the horizon or a given line or plane. **2** extremely steep; precipitous. **3** (**Perpendicular**) of, being, or built in a style of Gothic architecture prevalent in England from the late

14th to the 16th cent. characterized by large windows, an emphasis on vertical lines, and sometimes fan vaults. ➤➤ **perpendicularity** /-'lariti/ *noun,* **perpendicularly** *adv.* [Middle English *perpendiculer* via French from Latin *perpendicularis,* from *perpendiculum* plumb line, from PER- + *pendēre* to hang]

perpendicular² *noun* a line, plane, or surface at right angles to the plane of the horizon or to another line or surface.

perpetrate /'puhpitrayt/ *verb trans* to be guilty of performing or doing (something wrong); to commit. ➤➤ **perpetration** /-'traysh(ə)n/ *noun,* **perpetrator** *noun.* [Latin *perpetratus,* past part. of *perpetrare,* from PER- + *patrare* to accomplish]

perpetual /pə'pechoo(ə)l, -tyoo(ə)l/ *adj* **1** continuing or valid forever; everlasting. **2** holding something, e.g. an office, for life or for an unlimited time. **3** said of an investment: having no fixed maturity date; irredeemable: *a perpetual bond.* **4** occurring repeatedly; constant: *a perpetual complaint.* **5** said of a plant: blooming continuously throughout the season. ➤➤ **perpetually** *adv.* [Middle English *perpetuel* via French from Latin *perpetuus,* from PER- + *petere* to go to]

perpetual calendar *noun* **1** a table for finding the day of the week for a wide range of dates. **2** a display, e.g. on a frame or stand, that can be adjusted by means of movable words and figures to show the date of any day in any year.

perpetual check *noun* in chess, an endless succession of checks which results in a draw.

perpetual motion *noun* the hypothetical continuous operation of an isolated machine without the introduction of energy from an external force.

perpetuate /pə'pechooayt, -tyooayt/ *verb trans* to cause (something) to last indefinitely: *The storyteller perpetuates the oral tradition of the village.* ➤➤ **perpetuation** /-'aysh(ə)n/ *noun,* **perpetuator** *noun.* [Latin *perpetuatus,* past part. of *perpetuare,* from *perpetuus*: see PERPETUAL]

perpetuity /puhpi'tyooh-iti/ *noun* (*pl* **perpetuities**) **1** the quality or state of being perpetual; eternity. **2** an estate limited so that it cannot be disposed of for a period longer than that allowed by law. **3a** an ANNUITY (regular payment of money) payable for life. **b** an investment, e.g. a bond, with no fixed maturity date. [Middle English *perpetuite* via French from Latin *perpetuitat-, perpetuitas,* from *perpetuus*: see PERPETUAL]

perplex /pə'pleks/ *verb trans* **1** to puzzle or confuse (somebody): *Her attitude completely perplexes me.* **2** to complicate (an issue or topic). ➤➤ **perplexed** *adj,* **perplexedly** /-sidli/ *adv,* **perplexing** *adj,* **perplexingly** *adv.* [obsolete *perplex* involved, perplexed, from Latin *perplexus,* from PER- + *plexus* involved, from *plectere* to braid, twine]

perplexity /pə'pleksiti/ *noun* (*pl* **perplexities**) the state of being perplexed or bewildered, or something that causes such a state. [Middle English *perplexite* via Old French from late Latin *perplexitat-, perplexitas,* from Latin *perplexus*: see PERPLEX]

per pro /'proh/ *prep* used to indicate that a person is signing a letter or document on behalf of somebody else: *In the sequence 'Smith per pro Jones', Smith is the writer of the document and Jones is signing on behalf of Smith.* [abbr of Latin *per procurationem* through the agency (of)]

perquisite /'puhkwizit/ *noun* **1** *formal* a perk. **2** formerly, something held or claimed as a special or exclusive right or possession. [Middle English, denoting property acquired by other means than inheritance, from late Latin *perquisitum* acquisition, literally 'something sought', from Latin *perquirere* to search for thoroughly, from PER- + *quaerere* to seek]

Usage note

perquisite or prerequisite? *Perquisite* is the full and formal form of the common word *perk*: the *perquisites of an office* are the additional or fringe benefits somebody acquires by being in office over and above the position and the salary. *Prerequisite* is usually followed by the preposition *for* and means 'a necessary condition or attribute': *The presentation of a passport or a birth certificate is a prerequisite for the issuing of a marriage licence.*

perron /'perən/ *noun* an outdoor stairway leading up to a building entrance, or a platform at its top. [French *perron* from Old French *perre, pierre* rock, stone, via Latin from Greek *petra*]

perry /'peri/ *noun* (*pl* **perries**) **1** an alcoholic drink made from fermented pear juice. **2** a glass or measure of perry. [Middle English *peirrie* via French from Latin *pirum* PEAR]

pers. *abbr* **1** person. **2** personal.

per se /'say/ *adv* by, of, or in itself; intrinsically. [Latin *per se*]

persecute /'puhsikyooht/ *verb trans* **1** to harass (somebody) in a manner designed to injure or afflict them, *esp* because of their race, religion, political beliefs, etc. **2** to annoy (somebody) with persistent or urgent approaches, attacks, pleas, etc; to pester (them). >>> **persecution** /-'kyoohsh(ə)n/ *noun*, **persecutive** /-tiv/ *adj*, **persecutor** *noun*, **persecutory** /-'kyooht(ə)ri/ *adj*. [early French *persecuter*, back-formation from *persecuteur* persecutor, from late Latin *persecutor*, from Latin *persequi* to pursue, persecute, from PER- + *sequi* to follow]

persecution complex /puhsi'kyoohsh(ə)n/ *noun* a strong and irrational belief that one is hated and being persecuted by other people.

perseverance /puhsi'viərəns/ *noun* **1** persevering; steadfastness. **2** in Christianity, the Calvinistic doctrine that the elect, once saved, continue in a state of grace.

perseverate /puh'sevərayt/ *verb intrans* in psychology, to manifest perseveration.

perseveration /puh,sevə'raysh(ə)n/ *noun* in psychology, continuation or repetition of something, usu to an excessive or exceptional degree. [Latin *perseveration-, perseveratio*, from *perseverare*: see PERSEVERE]

persevere /puhsi'viə/ *verb intrans* (*often* + in/with) to persist in a state, enterprise, or undertaking in spite of adverse influences, opposition, or discouragement. [Middle English *perseveren* via French from Latin *perseverare* to follow strictly, from PER- + *severus* SEVERE]

Persian /'puhsh(ə)n, 'puhzh(ə)n/ *noun* **1** a native or inhabitant of ancient Persia or modern Iran. **2** the Indo-Iranian language of ancient Persia and modern Iran, varieties of which are spoken also in Afghanistan and Tajikistan. **3** = PERSIAN CAT. >>> **Persian** *adj*.

Word history
Words of Persian origin that have passed into English include *baksheesh, bazaar, caravan, shawl, spinach, taffeta,* and *turban*. There are also several English words that have been borrowed from Persian but are ultimately of Arabic origin, such as *attar, ayatollah,* and *sherbet. Kiosk* derives from the Turkish adaptation of a Persian word.

Persian carpet *noun* a carpet or rug made, *esp* in medieval Persia or modern Iran, to a traditional pattern by knotting wool, or rarely silk, yarn by hand onto a woven backing.

Persian cat *noun* a short-nosed, rather flat-faced, domestic cat with long silky fur.

Persian lamb *noun* **1** the young of the karakul sheep. **2** the pelt of the karakul lamb, characterized by very silky, tightly curled fur.

Persian rug *noun* = PERSIAN CARPET.

persiflage /'puhsiflahzh/ *noun formal* frivolous bantering talk. [French *persiflage*, from *persifler* to banter, from PER- + *siffler* to whistle, hiss, boo, from Latin *sibilare*, of imitative origin]

persimmon /puh'simən/ *noun* **1** a round yellow, orange, or red fruit with flesh that is extremely astringent when unripe but edible when fully ripened. **2** either of two species of trees of the ebony family that have hard fine wood and that bear this fruit: genus *Diospyros*. [alteration of Algonquian *pessimmins*]

persist /pə'sist/ *verb intrans* **1** (*often* + in/with) to go on resolutely or stubbornly in spite of opposition or warning. **2** (*often* + with) to be insistent in the repetition or pressing of a question, opinion, etc. **3** to continue to exist, *esp* past a usual, expected, or normal time. **4** to continue: *Rain is likely to persist throughout the night.* >>> **persister** *noun*. [early French *persister* from Latin *persistere*, from PER- + *sistere* to take a stand, stand firm]

persistent *adj* **1a** persisting or inclined to persist in a course of action, etc. **b** continuing or recurring: *The most persistent sound which reverberates through man's history is the beating of war drums —* Arthur Koestler. **c** continuing to exist in spite of interference or treatment: *a persistent cough.* **2** said of a chemical substance: broken down only slowly in the environment: *persistent pesticides.* **3** remaining beyond the usual period: *a persistent leaf.* **4a** remaining without change in function or structure. **b** said of a structure characteristic of a young or larval stage: remaining in the adult: *persistent gills.* >>> **persistence** *noun*, **persistency** /-si/ *noun*, **persistently** *adv*. [Latin *persistent-, persistens*, present part. of *persistere*: see PERSIST]

persistent vegetative state *noun* a medical condition resulting from brain damage, e.g. from a traffic accident, or brain degeneration, e.g. from Alzheimer's disease, in which a patient is unconscious and shows no signs of thought, feeling, or responsiveness to stimuli. Although reflex activities such as breathing continue, the patient is kept alive only by medical intervention, e.g. intravenous feeding.

persnickety /pə'snikiti/ *adj* **1** *NAmer* = PERNICKETY. **2** snobbish. [alteration of PERNICKETY]

person /'puhs(ə)n/ *noun* (*pl* **people** /'peepl/ *or formal* **persons**) **1a** a human being considered as having a character of their own, or as being different from all others: *You're just the person I wanted to see.* **b** a human being considered with regard to a particular characteristic, preference, etc: *I'm very much a hands-on person.* **2** a living human body or its outward appearance: *She was small and neat of person; We're insured against damage to person and property.* **3** any of three forms of verb or pronoun that indicate reference to the speaker, to somebody or something spoken to, or to somebody or something spoken of: compare FIRST PERSON, SECOND PERSON, THIRD PERSON. **4** (*usu* **Person**) any of the three modes of being in the Trinity as understood by Christians. **5** in law, an individual, corporation, etc with recognized legal rights and duties. *** in person** in one's own bodily presence: *He appeared in person last time.* [Middle English via Old French from Latin *persona* actor's mask, character in a play, person, prob from Etruscan *phersu* mask]

Usage note
persons or **people**? See note at PEOPLE[1].

-person *comb. form* forming nouns, denoting: a person who performs a role or function: *chairperson*.

persona /pə'sohnə/ *noun* **1** (*pl* **personas** *or* **personae** /-nee, -nie/) a role or character adopted by a person. **2** (*pl* **personae**) (*in pl*) the characters in a fictional work: compare DRAMATIS PERSONAE. **3** (*pl* **personas**) an individual's social facade, which, *esp* in Jungian psychology, reflects the role that the individual is playing in life: compare ANIMA. [Latin *persona*: see PERSON]

personable *adj* pleasing in person; attractive. >>> **personableness** *noun*, **personably** *adv*.

personae /puh'sohnee, -nie/ *noun* pl of PERSONA.

personage /'puhs(ə)nij/ *noun* **1** a person of rank, note, or distinction, *esp* somebody distinguished in presence and personal power. **2** a dramatic, fictional, or historical character. **3** *formal* a human individual; a person.

persona grata /puh,sohnə 'grahtə/ *noun* (*pl* **personae gratae** /puh,sohnee 'grahtee/) a person who is personally acceptable or welcome to another person, etc: *You'll be persona grata on the committee with all your fund-raising experience!* [Latin *persona grata*, literally 'acceptable person']

personal *adj* **1** of or affecting a person; private: *It was not done purely for personal financial gain.* **2a** done in person without the intervention of another; proceeding from a single person: *It will receive my personal attention; The Prime Minister made a personal appearance at the conference.* **b** carried on between individuals directly: *She had a personal interview with the Managing Director.* **c** said of argumentation, etc; relating issues to oneself; subjective rather than objective: *You're blessed with a woman's brain: vague, slippery, inexact, interested only in the personal aspect of a thing —* Henry Handel Richardson. **3** of the person or body: *personal hygiene.* **4a** of the private affairs of an individual: *Keep your nose out of my personal business!* **b** referring to the character, conduct, motives, or private affairs of an individual, often in an offensive manner: *Don't make personal remarks.* **5** existing as a person: *I don't believe in a personal God.* **6** in law, said of personal property: *a personal estate.* **7** denoting grammatical person. [Middle English via French from late Latin *personalis*, from Latin *persona*: see PERSON]

personal ad *noun informal* an advertisement, notice, or other message printed in the personal column of a newspaper.

personal assistant *noun* a person performing administrative and secretarial duties as assistant to a business executive, etc.

personal column *noun* a section of a newspaper containing personal messages, requests, notices, and advertisements that private individuals and organizations pay to have published.

personal computer *noun* a microcomputer for personal or business use, *esp* for such applications as word processing, financial analysis, and computer games.

personal equity plan *noun* in Britain, an investment scheme whereby individuals are permitted to invest a limited annual sum in British shares without paying tax on capital gains or dividend income; now replaced by the ISA.

personal estate *noun* = PERSONAL PROPERTY.

personal identification number *noun* = PIN NUMBER.

personalise *verb trans* see PERSONALIZE.

personality /puhs(ə)'naliti/ *noun* (*pl* **personalities**) **1** (*in pl*) reference, *esp* critical, to a particular person: *Let's keep personalities out of this debate.* **2** the totality of an individual's behavioural and emotional tendencies; a distinguishing complex of individual or group characteristics. **3a** distinction or excellence of personal and social traits. **b** a person who has distinction or excellence of personal or social traits: *He's quite a personality.* **c** a person of importance, prominence, renown, or notoriety: *He's a well-known TV personality.* [Middle English *personalite* from late Latin *personalitat-*, *personalitas*, from *personalis* personal, from Latin *persona*: see PERSON]

personality cult *noun* the officially encouraged slavish admiration of a leader.

personalize *or* **personalise** *verb trans* **1** to make (something) personal or individual, e.g.: **a** to mark (something) as the property of a particular person. **b** to design or make (something) so as to fit in with a particular person's wishes or needs. **2** to focus (an argument, etc) on personalities rather than issues. **3** to personify (a quality, etc). ⟫⟫ **personalization** /-'zaysh(ə)n/ *noun.*

personally *adv* **1** in person: *Proverbs are always platitudes until you have personally experienced the truth of them* — Aldous Huxley. **2** as a person; in personality: *She's personally attractive but not very trustworthy.* **3** for oneself; as far as oneself is concerned: *Personally, I don't think much of it.* **4** as directed against oneself in a personal way: *Don't take my remarks about your plan personally.*

personal organizer *noun* **1** a loose-leaf file holding a diary, address book, notebook, and printed sheets of information. **2** a small computerized device offering similar facilities.

personal pronoun *noun* a pronoun, e.g. *I*, *you*, or *they*, that expresses a distinction of person.

personal property *noun* in law, all property other than freehold estates and interests in land.

personal stereo *noun* a very small cassette player or CD player which may be carried on a belt or in a pocket and listened to through earphones: compare WALKMAN.

personalty /'puhs(ə)nəlti/ *noun* personal property: compare REALTY. [Anglo-French *personalté* from late Latin *personalitat-*, *personalitas*: see PERSONALITY]

persona non grata /puh,sohnə non 'grahtə/ *noun* a person who is personally unacceptable or unwelcome to another person, etc. [Latin *persona non grata*, literally 'person not acceptable']

personate /'puhs(ə)nayt/ *verb trans formal* **1** to impersonate or represent (somebody). **2** to assume (some character or capacity) with fraudulent intent. ⟫⟫ **personation** /-'naysh(ə)n/ *noun,* **personative** /-nətiv/ *adj,* **personator** *noun.*

personification /pə,sonifi'kaysh(ə)n/ *noun* **1** the act or an instance of personifying an inanimate object, abstract quality, idea, etc. **2** an embodiment or incarnation: *She's the personification of good sense.*

personify /pə'sonifie/ *verb trans* (**personifies, personified, personifying**) **1** to conceive of or represent (an inanimate object, abstract quality, etc) as having human qualities or human form. **2** to be the embodiment of (some quality) in human form: *He was kindness personified.* ⟫⟫ **personifier** *noun.*

personnel /puhsə'nel/ *noun* **1** (*treated as sing. or pl*) a body of people employed, e.g. in a factory, office, or organization, or engaged on a project. **2** a division of an organization concerned with the employees and their welfare at work. [French *personnel* via German from late Latin *personale*, neuter of *personalis* personal, from Latin *persona*: see PERSON]

perspective /pə'spektiv/ *noun* **1a** the aspect of an object of thought from a particular standpoint: *Try to get a different perspective on your problem.* **b** the true relationship or relative importance of things, or the capacity to discern this: *We need to see these events in their historical perspective; Do get things in perspective. It's not that important that she didn't come to your party.* **2a** the way in which the relationship of solid objects to each other in space appears to the eye, or the technique of accurately representing this on a flat or curved surface. **b** linear perspective; the representation of space in art by converging parallel lines. **c** (*used before a noun*) of, using, or seen in perspective: *a perspective drawing.* **d** a picture or view giving a distinctive impression of distance; a vista. ⟫⟫ **perspectively** *adv.* [Middle English from late Latin *perspectiva*, from *perspectivus*

of sight, optical, from Latin *perspicere* to look through, see clearly, from PER- + *specere* to look]

Perspex /'puhspeks/ *noun trademark* a transparent acrylic plastic. [from Latin *perspicere*: see PERSPECTIVE]

perspicacious /puhspi'kayshəs/ *adj* of acute mental vision or discernment. ⟫⟫ **perspicaciously** *adv,* **perspicaciousness** *noun,* **perspicacity** /-'kasiti/ *noun.* [Latin *perspicac-*, *perspicax*, from *perspicere*: see PERSPECTIVE]

perspicuous /pə'spikyooəs/ *adj* plain to the understanding, *esp* because of clarity and precision of presentation: *a perspicuous argument.* ⟫⟫ **perspicuity** /puhspi'kyooh-iti/ *noun,* **perspicuously** *adv,* **perspicuousness** *noun.* [Latin *perspicuus* transparent, perspicuous, from *perspicere*: see PERSPECTIVE]

perspiration /puhspi'raysh(ə)n/ *noun* **1** sweating. **2** sweat. ⟫⟫ **perspiratory** /pə'spie-ərət(ə)ri/ *adj.*

perspire /pə'spie-ə/ *verb intrans* to sweat. [French *perspirer*, from Latin PER- + *spirare* to blow, breathe]

persuade /pə'swayd/ *verb trans* **1** to move (somebody) by argument, reasoning, evidence, or entreaty to a belief, position, or course of action. **2** (*often* + of) to cause (somebody) to think or feel certain about something; to convince (them): *The icy roads persuaded him of the need to drive carefully.* **3** (+ from/out of) to get (something) with difficulty from somebody: *They finally persuaded an answer out of her.* ⟫⟫ **persuadability** /-'biliti/ *noun,* **persuadable** *adj,* **persuader** *noun.* [Latin *persuadēre*, from PER- + *suadēre* to advise, urge]

persuasible /pə'swaysəbl, -zəbl/ *adj* persuadable. ⟫⟫ **persuasibility** /-'biliti/ *noun.* [via French from Latin *persuasibilis* persuasive, from *persuadēre*: see PERSUADE]

persuasion /pə'swayzh(ə)n/ *noun* **1a** persuading or being persuaded. **b** persuasiveness: *She has great powers of persuasion.* **2a** an opinion held with complete assurance. **b** a particular system of religious beliefs, or a group adhering to it. **3** a kind or sort: *He always hangs about with people of the same persuasion as himself.* [Middle English *persuasioun* via French from Latin *persuasion-*, *persuasio*, from *persuadēre*: see PERSUADE]

persuasive /pə'swaysiv, -ziv/ *adj* tending or able to persuade. ⟫⟫ **persuasively** *adv,* **persuasiveness** *noun.*

pert /puht/ *adj* **1** impudent and forward; saucy. **2** trim and chic; jaunty: *a pert little hat.* ⟫⟫ **pertly** *adv,* **pertness** *noun.* [Middle English in the sense 'open, bold, forward', modification of Old French *apert* from Latin *apertus* open, from *aperire* to open]

pertain /pə'tayn/ *verb intrans* **1a** (*usu* + to) to belong to somebody or something or exist as a part, attribute, feature, function, or right: *He deplores the destruction and havoc pertaining to war.* **b** (*also* + to) to be appropriate: *The criteria that pertain elsewhere do not apply here.* **2** *formal* (+ to) to have reference to something: *She has shelves of books pertaining to birds.* [Middle English *perteinen* via French from Latin *pertinēre* to reach to, belong, from PER- + *tenēre* to hold]

pertinacious /puhti'nayshəs/ *adj formal* clinging resolutely to an opinion, purpose, or design, often to the point of stubbornness. ⟫⟫ **pertinaciously** *adv,* **pertinaciousness** *noun,* **pertinacity** /-'nasiti/ *noun.* [Latin *pertinac-*, *pertinax* from PER- + *tenac-*, *tenax* tenacious, from *tenēre* to hold]

pertinent /'puhtinənt/ *adj* clearly relevant to the matter in hand: *all the pertinent details.* ⟫⟫ **pertinence** *noun,* **pertinency** /-si/ *noun,* **pertinently** *adv.* [Middle English via French from Latin *pertinent-*, *pertinens*, present part. of *pertinēre*: see PERTAIN]

perturb /pə'tuhb, puh'tuhb/ *verb trans* **1** (*usu in passive*) to disturb (somebody) greatly in mind; to trouble (them). **2** to throw (something) into confusion or disorder. **3** to cause (a moving object, celestial body, etc) to deviate from a theoretically regular motion such as a regular path of orbit. ⟫⟫ **perturbable** *adj,* **perturbation** /puhtə'baysh(ə)n/ *noun,* **perturbational** /puhtə'baysh(ə)nl/ *adj,* **perturbed** *adj,* **perturbing** *adj,* **perturbingly** *adv.* [Middle English *perturben* via French from Latin *perturbare* to throw into confusion, from PER- + *turbare* to disturb]

pertussis /pə'tusis/ *noun* = WHOOPING COUGH. [Latin *pertussis*, from PER- + *tussis* cough]

peruke /pə'roohk/ *noun* a long curly wig worn by men in the 17th and 18th cent.; = PERIWIG. [early French *perruque* from Old Italian *parrucca*, *perrucca* hair, wig]

peruse /pə'roohz/ *verb trans formal* **1** to examine or consider (a document, etc) with attention and in detail; to study (it). **2** to look over the contents of (a book, etc). ⟫⟫ **perusal** *noun,* **peruser** *noun.*

[Middle English *perusen*, prob from PER- + Middle English *usen* to use]

Peruvian /pə'roohvi-ən/ *noun* a native or inhabitant of Peru in S America. ▶▶ **Peruvian** *adj*. [Latin *Peruvia* Peru]

perv[1] *or* **perve** /puhv/ *noun informal* **1** a sexual pervert. **2** *Aus, NZ* a lustful or lecherous look. ▶▶ **pervy** *adj*.

perv[2] *or* **perve** *verb intrans Aus, NZ, informal* (*often* + at/on) to look lustfully or lecherously at somebody.

pervade /pə'vayd/ *verb trans* to be or become diffused throughout every part of (something). ▶▶ **pervasion** /-zh(ə)n/ *noun*, **pervasive** /-siv, -ziv/ *adj*, **pervasively** /-sivli, -zivli/ *adv*, **pervasiveness** /-sivnis, -zivnis/ *noun*. [Latin *pervadere* to go through, pervade, from PER- + *vadere* to go]

perve[1] /puhv/ *noun* see PERV[1].

perve[2] *verb intrans* see PERV[2].

perverse /pə'vuhs/ *adj* **1a** obstinate in opposing what is right, reasonable, or accepted; wrongheaded. **b** arising from or indicative of stubbornness or obstinacy. **2** unreasonably opposed to the wishes of others; uncooperative, contrary. **3** in law, being contrary to the evidence or to the direction of the judge on a point of law: *a perverse verdict.* ▶▶ **perversely** *adv*, **perverseness** *noun*, **perversity** *noun*. [Middle English from Latin *perversus*, past part. of *pervertere*: see PERVERT[1]]

perversion /pə'vuhsh(ə)n/ *noun* **1** the act or an instance of perverting. **2** something perverted, *esp* abnormal sexual behaviour. ▶▶ **perversive** /-siv/ *adj*.

pervert[1] /pə'vuht/ *verb trans* **1** to cause (somebody) to turn aside or away from what is good, true, or morally right; to corrupt (them). **2a** to divert (something) to a wrong use or purpose; to misuse (it). **b** to twist the meaning or sense of (something); to misinterpret (it). ▶▶ **perverter** *noun*. [Middle English *perverten* via French from Latin *pervertere* to overturn, corrupt, pervert, from PER- + *vertere* to turn]

pervert[2] /'puhvuht/ *noun* a perverted person; *specif* a person given to some form of sexual perversion.

perverted /pə'vuhtid/ *adj* **1** marked by perversion, *esp* sexual perversion. **2** corrupt. ▶▶ **pervertedly** *adv*, **pervertedness** *noun*.

pervious /'puhvi-əs/ *adj* **1** permeable: *pervious soil.* **2** *formal* (+ to) willing to consider arguments, new ideas, etc: *pervious to reason.* ▶▶ **perviousness** *noun*. [Latin *pervius*, from PER- + *via* way]

Pesach /'paysahkh/ *noun* = PASSOVER. [Hebrew *Pesah*]

peseta /pə'saytə/ *noun* the former basic monetary unit of Spain, divided into 100 centimos, also used in Andorra (in Spain replaced by the euro in 2002). [Spanish *peseta*, dimin. of *peso*: see PESO]

pesewa /pi'saywah/ *noun* a unit of currency in Ghana, worth 100th of a cedi. [Fanti *pesewa* penny]

pesky /'peski/ *adj* (**peskier, peskiest**) *informal* troublesome or annoying. ▶▶ **peskily** *adv*, **peskiness** *noun*. [prob from PEST + -Y[1]]

peso /'paysoh/ *noun* (*pl* **pesos**) **1** the basic monetary unit of certain Spanish-speaking Latin American countries, e.g. Argentina, Chile, Mexico, Uruguay, and the Philippines. **2** a former silver coin of Spain and Spanish America worth eight reals. [Spanish *peso*, literally 'weight', from Latin *pensum*, from *pendēre* to weigh]

pessary /'pesəri/ *noun* (*pl* **pessaries**) **1** a vaginal suppository. **2** a device worn in the vagina to support the uterus or prevent conception. [Middle English *pessarie* from late Latin *pessarium*, from Greek *pessos* oval stone for playing draughts, pessary]

pessimism /'pesimiz(ə)m/ *noun* **1** a tendency to stress the adverse aspects of a situation or event or to expect the worst possible outcome: *Pessimism, when you get used to it, is just as agreeable as optimism* — Arnold Bennett. **2** in philosophy, the doctrine that this is the worst of all possible worlds.

Editorial note

The modern scientific view appears to encourage pessimism. It eliminates human freedom, the bases of religious belief, and objective values: people become the puppets of their bodily states and upbringing. William James embraced religious belief and human freedom as satisfactory beliefs since they offered an escape from this pessimistic outcome — Professor Christopher Hookway.

▶▶ **pessimist** *noun*, **pessimistic** /-'mistik/ *adj*, **pessimistically** /-'mistikli/ *adv*. [French *pessimisme* from Latin *pessimus* worst]

pest /pest/ *noun* **1** somebody or something that pesters or annoys; a nuisance. **2** a plant or animal capable of causing damage or

carrying disease. **3** (*usu* **the pest**) *archaic* a pestilence, *esp* bubonic plague. [early French *peste* from Latin *pestis* plague, pestilence]

pester /'pestə/ *verb trans* (**pestered, pestering**) to harass or annoy (somebody) with petty irritations and demands. [modification of early French *empestrer* to hobble, embarrass, ultimately from IN-[2] + Latin *pastor* herdsman]

pester power *noun* the commercial influence exercised by children who pester their parents into buying them things they want, e.g. because they have seen them advertised on television.

pesticide /'pestisied/ *noun* a chemical used to destroy insects and other pests of crops, domestic animals, etc. ▶▶ **pesticidal** /-'siedl/ *adj*.

pestiferous /pe'stif(ə)rəs/ *adj* **1** *humorous* annoying. **2** *formal* dangerous to society; pernicious. **3** *literary* carrying or propagating infection. ▶▶ **pestiferously** *adv*. [Middle English from Latin *pestifer* pestilential, noxious, from *pestis* plague, pestilence + -*fer* -FEROUS]

pestilence /'pestiləns/ *noun* a virulent and devastating epidemic disease; *specif* BUBONIC PLAGUE. [Middle English via Old French from Latin *pestilent-, pestilens*: see PESTILENTIAL]

pestilent /'pestilənt/ *adj* = PESTILENTIAL.

pestilential /pesti'lensh(ə)l/ *adj* **1** *archaic* causing displeasure or annoyance; irritating. **2** morally harmful; pernicious. **3** destructive of life; deadly. ▶▶ **pestilentially** /-'lensh(ə)li/ *adv*, **pestilently** *adv*. [Middle English from Latin *pestilent-, pestilens* pestilential, from *pestis* plague]

pestle[1] /'pesl/ *noun* **1** a club-shaped implement for pounding substances in a mortar. **2** any of various devices for pounding, stamping, or pressing. [Middle English *pestel* via French from Latin *pistillum*]

pestle[2] *verb trans and intrans* to pound or pulverize (something) with or as if with a pestle.

pesto /'pestoh/ *noun* a paste made from crushed basil leaves, garlic, pine nuts, olive oil, and Parmesan cheese, often eaten with pasta. [Italian *pesto* from *pestare* to pound, crush]

PET /pet/ *abbr* **1** polyethylene terephthalate. **2** positron emission tomography. **3** pre-eclamptic toxaemia.

Pet. *abbr* Peter (books of the Bible).

pet[1] /pet/ *noun* **1** an animal, bird, etc kept for companionship, amusement, etc rather than work or food. **2** somebody who is treated with unusual kindness or consideration; a favourite. **3** *chiefly Brit* used chiefly as an affectionate form of address: darling. [perhaps back-formation from Middle English *pety* small, alteration of PETIT]

pet[2] *adj* **1a** kept or treated as a pet. **b** for pet animals: *a pet shop.* **2** expressing fondness or endearment: *He always refers to his wife by some silly pet name.* **3** favourite: *Art was my pet subject at school.* **4** strongest; particular: *My pet hate is washing up.*

pet[3] *verb* (**petted, petting**) ▷ *verb trans* **1** to stroke (an animal, etc) in a gentle or loving manner. **2** to treat (somebody) with unusual or excessive kindness and consideration; to pamper (them). ▷ *verb intrans* to engage in amorous embracing, caressing, etc. ▶▶ **petter** *noun*.

pet[4] *noun* a fit of peevishness, sulkiness, or anger. [origin unknown]

PETA *abbr* People for the Ethical Treatment of Animals.

peta- *comb. form* forming words, denoting: thousand billion (10^{15}). [from PENTA-, 10^{15} being equal to 1000^5]

petal /'petl/ *noun* any of the modified, often brightly coloured, leaves of the COROLLA (flower) of a flowering plant. ▶▶ **petalled** *adj*, **petal-like** *adj*. [via Latin from Greek *petalon* leaf]

-petal *comb. form* forming adjectives, with the meaning: moving or tending towards: *centripetal*. [from Latin *petere* to seek]

petaline /'petəlien/ *adj* of or like a petal.

petaloid /'petəloyd/ *adj* **1** resembling a petal, *esp* in shape or bright colour. **2** consisting of petal-like parts.

petalous /'petələs/ *adj* (*used in combinations*) having a given number or type of petals: *polypetalous*.

pétanque /pay'tongk (*French* petãk)/ *noun* = BOULE[1]. [French *pétanque* from Provençal *pèd tanco* foot fixed]

petard /pi'tahd/ *noun* **1** formerly, a case containing an explosive for military demolitions. **2** formerly, a firework that explodes with a loud report. ✳ **be hoist with one's own petard** to be the victim of one's own scheming or trickery. [early French *petard* from *peter* to break wind, ultimately from Latin *pedere*]

petechia /pə'teeki·ə/ *noun* (*pl* **petechiae** /-ki·ee/) a minute bleeding or blood-filled spot that appears in the skin or MUCOUS MEMBRANE, *esp* in some infectious diseases, e.g. TYPHOID, as a result of the leaking of blood from an underlying blood vessel. >> **petechial** *adj.* [scientific Latin *petechia* from Italian *petecchia*, derivative of Latin *impetigo*]

peter /'peetə/ *noun informal* **1** a safe. **2** *Aus, NZ* a cell. [from the name *Peter*]

peter away *verb intrans* = PETER OUT.

peterman *noun* (*pl* **petermen**) *archaic* a safebreaker.

peter out *verb intrans* to diminish gradually and come to an end; to give out. [origin unknown]

Peter Pan /pan/ *noun* **1** a man who seems never to age. **2** an immature man. [*Peter Pan*, hero of the play *Peter Pan, or the boy who wouldn't grow up* by Sir James Barrie d.1937, Scottish novelist and dramatist]

Peter principle *noun* (**the Peter principle**) the proposition that members of a hierarchical organization, such as a business, tend to be promoted until they reach a position that is beyond their capabilities. [named after Laurence *Peter* d.1990, Canadian-born US educator, who formulated the theory]

petersham /'peetəshəm/ *noun* **1** a heavy corded ribbon used for belts and put round hats. **2** a rough nubbly woollen cloth, or a coat made of this cloth. [named after Charles Stanhope, Lord *Petersham* d.1851, English colonel who wore a petersham coat]

Peter's pence *pl noun* (*treated as sing.*) an annual tribute of a penny, formerly paid by each householder in England to the papal see. [from the tradition that St Peter founded the papal see]

Peters' projection *noun* a PROJECTION (representation of latitude and longitude on flat surface) in which regions and countries of the world are shown in their correct relative sizes but therefore with distorted shapes: compare MERCATOR'S PROJECTION.

pethidine /'pethideen, -din/ *noun* a synthetic narcotic drug with actions and uses similar to those of morphine but with less sedative effect, often used to relieve labour pains. [blend of PIPERIDINE and ETHYL]

pétillant /'payteeyonh (*French* petijã)/ *adj* said of a wine: mildly effervescent. [French *pétillant*, present part. of *pétiller* to effervesce with a crackling sound, from early French *peter*: see PETARD]

petiole /'petiohl/ *noun* **1** the stalk by which a leaf is attached to a stem. **2** in insects, etc, a slender stalk joining two larger parts or structures, such as the narrow waist-like part of the bodies of bees, ants, wasps, etc; = PEDICEL. >> **petiolar** /-'ohlə/ *adj*, **petiolate** /-layt, -lət/ *adj*, **petiolated** /-laytid/ *adj*, **petioled** *adj*. [French *pétiole* from Latin *petiolus* small foot, fruit stalk, from *ped-*, *pes* foot]

petit /'peti/ *adj* in law, said of a crime: petty; minor. [Middle English from Old French *petit* small: compare PETTY]

petit bourgeois *or* **petty bourgeois** /'booəzh-wah (*French* pəti burʒwa)/ *noun* (*pl* **petits bourgeois** /,peti 'booəzh-wah/) a member of the petite bourgeoisie, *esp* a conventional and conservative person: *This section of Brooklyn has a tone and atmosphere peculiarly French … one can quite imagine oneself in some smaller Parisian boulevard frequented by the petit bourgeois* — Christopher Morley. >> **petit bourgeois** *adj*.

petite /pə'teet/ *adj* said of a woman: having a small trim figure. [French *petite*, fem of *petit* small]

petite bourgeoisie /booəzh·wah'zee (*French* pətit burʒwazi)/ *or* **petty bourgeoisie** *noun* (*treated as sing. or pl*) the lower middle class, *esp* as considered conventional and conservative in attitudes and behaviour. [French *petite bourgeoisie*, literally 'small bourgeoisie']

petit four /'faw (*French* pəti fur)/ *noun* (*pl* **petits fours** *or* **petit fours** /,peti 'fawz (*French* fur)/) a small fancy cake or biscuit, usu iced. [French *petit four*, literally 'small oven']

petition[1] /pi'tish(ə)n/ *noun* **1a** a formal written request made to somebody in authority, e.g. a government, *esp* one made by a large number of people. **b** a document embodying such a request, usu signed by a large number of people: *They handed in a petition with thousands of signatures.* **2** an earnest request; an entreaty. **3** a formal request for legal action addressed to a court. **4** something asked or requested. **5** the act of requesting something. >> **petitionary** *adj*.

[Middle English via French from Latin *petition-*, *petitio*, from *petere* to seek, request, demand]

petition[2] *verb trans* to present a petition to (somebody). >> **verb intrans** (*usu* + for) to make a request by petition for something to be done: *They petitioned for his immediate release.* >>> **petitioner** *noun*.

petitio principii /pi,tishioh prin'kipi·ee/ *noun* a logical fallacy in which what is to be proved is assumed without justification to be true as a premise. [Latin *petitio principii*, literally 'postulation of the beginning', i.e. begging the question]

petit mal /'mal/ *noun* mild epilepsy, or a mild epileptic attack lasting only a short time: compare GRAND MAL. [French *petit mal* small illness]

petit point /'poynt (*French* pəti pwɛ̃)/ *noun* **1** = TENT STITCH. **2** needlepoint embroidery worked on canvas across single threads in tent stitch: compare GROS POINT, NEEDLEPOINT. [French *petit point* small point]

petit pois /'pwah, pətee (*French* pəti pwa)/ *noun* (*pl* **petits pois** /,peti 'pwah(z) (*French* pəti pwa)/) (*usu in pl*) a small young, slightly sweet, green pea. [French *petit pois* small pea]

petits bourgeois /,peti 'booəzh·wah/ *noun* pl of PETIT BOURGEOIS.

petits fours /,peti 'fawz/ *noun* pl of PETIT FOUR.

petits pois /,peti 'pwah(z)/ *noun* pl of PETIT POIS.

petr- *or* **petri-** *or* **petro-** *comb. form* forming words, denoting: stone; rock: *petrology.* [Greek *petr-*, *petro-*, from *petros* stone and *petra* rock]

Petrarchan sonnet /pi'trahkən/ *noun* a sonnet consisting of an OCTAVE (eight-line section) rhyming *abba abba* and a SESTET (six-line section) rhyming in any of various patterns, e.g. *cde cde* or *cdc cdc*. [named after *Petrarch* (Francesco *Petrarca*) d.1374, Italian poet, who used this form]

petrel /'petrəl/ *noun* any of numerous species of seabirds, such as albatrosses, shearwaters, fulmars, and storm petrels, with thick plumage, webbed feet, hooked bills, and distinctive tubular nostrils. They characteristically fly far from land, and come ashore only to breed: order Procellariiformes.

Word history

alteration of earlier *pitteral*, perhaps a nickname for *Peter*. The link with *Peter* may have come about because of the supposed similarity between the storm petrel flying low with its legs dangling, appearing to walk on the surface of the ocean while feeding, and Saint Peter's walking on the Sea of Galilee (Matthew 14:29).

petri- *comb. form* see PETR-.

petri dish *or* **Petri dish** /'peetri/ *noun* a small shallow glass or plastic dish with a loose cover, used *esp* for cultures of micro-organisms. [named after Julius *Petri* d.1921, German bacteriologist, who invented it]

petrifaction /petri'faksh(ə)n/ *noun* **1** the act or an instance of petrifying. **2** something petrified.

petrification /,petrifi'kaysh(ə)n/ *noun* = PETRIFACTION.

petrify /'petrifie/ *verb* (**petrifies, petrified, petrifying**) >> *verb trans* **1** (*usu in passive*) to paralyse (somebody) with fear, amazement, or awe; to make (them) very afraid: *I was petrified at the thought of speaking in public.* **2a** to convert (something) into stone or a hard or stony substance. **b** to make (something) hard or fixed as if by turning it to stone: *while he munches a petrified sandwich and waits for the train* — Mark Twain. **3** to make (somebody or something) lifeless or inactive; to deaden (them). >> *verb intrans* to become stone or of stony hardness or rigidity. [early French *petrifier* from medieval Latin *petrificare*, from Latin *petra* rock, from Greek]

petro- *comb. form* **1** see PETR-. **2** forming words, denoting: petroleum: *petrodollar.*

petrochemical[1] /petroh'kemikl, petrə-/ *noun* a chemical obtained from petroleum or natural gas. >> **petrochemistry** /-mistri/ *noun*.

petrochemical[2] *adj* **1** relating to petrochemistry, petrochemicals, or the properties and processing of petroleum and natural gas. **2** obtained from petrochemicals.

petrodollar /'petrohdolə/ *noun* a unit of foreign exchange obtained by a petroleum-exporting country by sales abroad.

petroglyph /'petrəglif/ *noun* an ancient or prehistoric carving, painting, or inscription on a rock. [French *pétroglyphe*, from PETRO- + -*glyph* from Greek *glyphē*: see GLYPH]

petrography /pe'trografi/ *noun* the description and systematic classification of rocks. ➤ **petrographer** *noun,* **petrographic** /-'grafik/ *adj,* **petrographical** /-'grafikl/ *adj,* **petrographically** /-'grafikli/ *adv.*

petrol /'petrəl/ *noun chiefly Brit* a volatile inflammable liquid hydrocarbon mixture refined from petroleum and used as a fuel for internal-combustion engines. [French (*essence de*) *pétrole* (essence of) petroleum]

petrolatum /petrə'laytəm/ *noun* = PETROLEUM JELLY. [scientific Latin, from PETRO- + Latin *-atum*]

petrol bomb *noun* a simple hand-thrown bomb consisting of a bottle filled with petrol and having a piece of rag in the neck to act as a fuse when ignited.

petroleum /pə'trohli·əm/ *noun* a dark oily inflammable liquid composed of a mixture of hydrocarbons, widely occurring in the upper strata of the earth, and refined for use as petrol, naphtha, etc. [PETRO- + Latin *oleum*: see OIL¹]

petroleum jelly *noun* a semisolid mixture of hydrocarbons obtained from petroleum, used as an ointment.

petrology /pe'trolǝji/ *noun* a science that deals with the origin, structure, composition, etc of rocks. ➤ **petrologic** /-'lojik/ *adj,* **petrological** /-'lojikl/ *adj,* **petrologically** /-'lojikli/ *adv,* **petrologist** *noun.*

petrol station *noun Brit* a place where petrol is sold to vehicle drivers, usu also having a shop where newspapers, confectionery, etc may be bought; = FILLING STATION.

petrosal /pi'trohs(ə)l/ *adj* = PETROUS (2).

petrous /'petrəs, 'peetrəs/ *adj* **1** resembling stone, *esp* in hardness. **2** of the hard dense part of the human temporal bone that contains the internal hearing organs. [early French *petreux* from Latin *petrosus,* from *petra* rock, from Greek]

petticoat /'petikoht/ *noun* **1a** a woman's light undergarment hanging from the waist or shoulders; an underskirt or slip. **b** an outer skirt formerly worn by women and small children. **2** *humorous or derog* (*used before a noun*) characteristic of or exercised by women: *a petticoat government.* ➤ **petticoated** *adj.* [Middle English *petycote* short tunic, petticoat, from *pety* small (from Old French *petit*) + *cote*: see COAT¹]

pettifog /'petifog/ *verb intrans* (**pettifogged, pettifogging**) *archaic* **1** to quibble over insignificant details. **2** to engage in legal chicanery. ➤ **pettifoggery** *noun.* [back-formation from PETTIFOGGER]

pettifogger *noun archaic* **1** a quibbler. **2** a lawyer of inferior quality, *esp* one who resorts to trickery. [prob from PETTY + obsolete *fogger,* perhaps from *Fugger,* 15th- and 16th-cent. German family of financiers and merchants]

pettifogging *adj archaic* **1** quibbling. **2** petty or trivial.

pettish /'petish/ *adj* peevish or petulant. ➤ **pettishly** *adv,* **pettishness** *noun.* [prob from PET⁴]

petty /'peti/ *adj* (**pettier, pettiest**) **1** trivial. **2** having secondary rank or importance. **3** small-minded. **4** in law, said of a crime, etc: minor; = PETIT. ➤ **pettily** *adv,* **pettiness** *noun.* [Middle English *pety* small, minor, alteration of PETIT]

petty bourgeois *noun* see PETIT BOURGEOIS. ➤ **petty bourgeoisie** *noun.*

petty cash *noun* cash kept on hand, e.g. in an office, for payment of minor items.

petty larceny *noun NAmer, no longer used technically in Britain* theft of property below a value specified by law: compare GRAND LARCENY.

petty officer *noun* a rank of NON-COMMISSIONED OFFICER in the navy, or a person of that rank.

petty sessions *pl noun* (*treated as sing. or pl*) = MAGISTRATES' COURT.

petulant /'petyoolənt/ *adj* characterized by expressions or bouts of childish bad temper, often for no real reason; peevish. ➤ **petulance** *noun,* **petulantly** *adv.* [early French *petulant,* from Latin *petulant-, petulans* impudent, from *petere*: see PETITION¹]

petunia /pi'tyoohnyə, -ni·ə/ *noun* a plant of the nightshade family with large brightly coloured funnel-shaped flowers: genus *Petunia.* [Latin genus name, from obsolete French *petun* tobacco, from Tupi *petyn*; tobacco belongs to another genus of the nightshade family]

pew /pyooh/ *noun* **1a** a bench fixed in a row for the use of the congregation in a church. **b** a high compartment with such benches for the accommodation of a group, e.g. a family. **2** *Brit, informal* a seat: *Do take a pew.* [Middle English *pewe* from early French *puie* balustrade, from Latin *podium* parapet, podium, from Greek *podion* base]

pewee *or* **peewee** /'peewee/ *noun* any of several species of small olive grey N American flycatchers: genus *Contopus.* [imitative]

pewit /'peewit/ *noun* see PEEWIT.

pewter /'pyoohtə/ *noun* **1** any of various alloys containing tin, *esp* one of tin and lead used formerly, or a modern alloy containing copper and antimony. **2** plates, tankards, etc made of pewter. [Middle English from early French *peutre*]

pewterer *noun* a person who works with pewter and makes plates, tankards, etc.

peyote /pay'ohti, pi-/ *noun* **1** a small cactus with rounded stems covered with small jointed protuberances that contain mescaline and are chewed by some Native Americans for their hallucinogenic effect: *Lophophora williamsii.* **2a** = MESCAL BUTTON. **b** = MESCALINE. [Mexican Spanish *peyote,* from Nahuatl *peyotl*]

pF *abbr* picofarad.

pf *abbr* pfennig.

pfennig *or* **Pfennig** /'(p)fenig, '(p)fenikh (German 'pfɛniç)/ *noun* (*pl* **pfennigs** *or* **pfennige** /-gə/) a former unit of currency in Germany, worth 100th of a mark (up to the introduction of the euro in 2002). [German *Pfennig,* from Old High German *pfenning*]

pfg *abbr* pfennig.

PFI *abbr* Private Finance Initiative.

PG¹ *adj* in Britain, a classification of cinema films suitable for all ages but for which parental guidance is recommended for children under 12 because some scenes may be considered unsuitable for such children. ➤ **PG** *noun.* [Parental Guidance]

PG² *abbr* **1** paying guest. **2** postgraduate.

pg *abbr* page.

PGA *abbr* Professional Golfers' Association.

pH *noun* a figure used to express the acidity or alkalinity of a solution on a scale of 0 to 14 with 7 representing neutrality. pH is the negative logarithm of the hydrogen-ion concentration of a solution in moles per litre; thus, a solution with a concentration of 10^{-7} has a pH value of 7. [German, from *Potenz* power + *H,* symbol for hydrogen]

phaeton /'fayt(ə)n/ *noun* a light open four-wheeled carriage. [named after *Phaëthon,* character in Greek legend who attempted to drive the chariot of the sun]

phag- *or* **phago-** *comb. form* forming words, with the meaning: eating; devouring: *phagocyte.* [Greek, from *phagein* to eat]

phage /fayj/ *noun* = BACTERIOPHAGE. [by shortening]

-phage *comb. form* see -PHAGY.

-phagia *comb. form* see -PHAGY.

phago- *comb.form* see PHAG-.

phagocyte /'fagəsiet/ *noun* a macrophage, white blood cell, etc that characteristically engulfs foreign material, e.g. bacteria, and consumes debris, e.g. from tissue injury. ➤ **phagocytic** /-'sitik/ *adj,* **phagocytically** /-'sitikli/ *adv.*

phagocytize *or* **phagocytise** /'fagəsietiez/ *verb trans* = PHAGOCYTOSE.

phagocytose /'fagəsietohs, -tohz/ *verb trans* to take (solid matter) into the cell or consume (it) by phagocytosis.

phagocytosis /,fagəsie'tohsis/ *noun* (*pl* **phagocytoses** /-seez/) the uptake and usu destruction of extracellular solid matter by phagocytes: compare PINOCYTOSIS. ➤ **phagocytotic** /-'totik/ *adj,* **phagocytotically** /-'totikli/ *adv.*

-phagy *or* **-phagia** *comb. form* forming nouns, denoting: **1** eating: *anthropophagy.* **2** destroying: *bacteriophagy.* ➤ **-phage** *comb. form,* **-phagous** *comb. form.* [Greek *phagein* to eat]

phalange /'falanj/ *noun* = PHALANX (3). [French *phalange* from Greek *phalang-,* PHALANX]

phalangeal /falan'jee·əl/ *adj* see PHALANX.

phalanger /fə'lanjə/ *noun* any of various small marsupials of the Australian region that live in trees and have thick fur and a long tail. Some species have flaps of skin between their front and hind limbs by means of which they can glide between trees: family Phalangeridae. [Greek *phalang-, phalanx* finger or toe bone]

phalanges /fə'lanjeez/ *noun* pl of PHALANX (3).

phalanx /'falangks/ *noun* **1** (*pl* **phalanxes**). **a** (*treated as sing. or pl*) a closely massed arrangement of people, animals, or things. **b** a body of people organized for a common purpose: *the whole phalanx of professional conservatism* — Lytton Strachey. **2** (*pl* **phalanxes**) (*treated as sing. or pl*) a body of troops, *esp* those of ancient Greece, in close array behind a wall of shields. **3** (*pl* **phalanges** /fə'lanjeez/) any of the digital bones of the hand or foot of a vertebrate. ⟩⟩ **phalangeal** /-'jee-əl/ *adj.* [via Latin from Greek *phalang-, phalanx* battle line, digital bone]

phalarope /'falərohp/ *noun* (*pl* **phalaropes** *or collectively* **phalarope**) any of a genus of small wading birds that have lobed toes and are good swimmers: genus *Phalaropus*. [French *phalarope* from Latin *phalaropus*, from Greek *phalaris* coot + *pous* foot]

phalli /'falie/ *noun* pl of PHALLUS.

phallic /'falik/ *adj* of or resembling a phallus. ⟩⟩ **phallically** *adv.*

phallicism /'falisiz(ə)m/ *noun* the worship of generative power as symbolized by the phallus.

phallism /'falis(ə)m/ *noun* = PHALLICISM.

phallocentric /faloh'sentrik/ *adj* **1** centred on the phallus. **2** of or holding a belief in maleness as the norm and in the supremacy of men over women.

phallus /'faləs/ *noun* (*pl* **phalli** /'falie/ *or* **phalluses**) the penis, or a symbol or representation of the penis, *esp* an erect penis, as a symbol of generative power or male dominance. [via Latin from Greek *phallos* penis, representation of the penis]

phanerogam /'fanərohgam/ *noun* formerly, a spermatophyte. ⟩⟩ **phanerogamic** /-'gamik/ *adj*, **phanerogamous** /-'rogəməs/ *adj*. [French *phanérogame*, from Greek *phaneros* visible + *gamos* marriage]

Phanerozoic /,fanərə'zoh-ik, fə,nerə-/ *adj* relating to or dating from a geological aeon that comprises the Palaeozoic, Mesozoic, and Cainozoic eras, i.e. the last 570 million years, before which fossils are extremely rare. ⟩⟩ **Phanerozoic** *noun*. [Greek *phaneros* visible + -ZOIC²]

phantasm /'fantaz(ə)m/ *noun literary* **1** an illusion. **2a** a ghost or spectre. **b** a figment of the imagination; a fantasy. ⟩⟩ **phantasmal** /fan'tazm(ə)l/ *adj*, **phantasmic** /fan'tazmik/ *adj*.

Word history
Middle English *fantasme* from Old French *fantasme* from Latin *phantasma*, from Greek, from *phantazein* to present to the mind, from *phantos* visible. The spelling of this and many other words now beginning with *ph*- changed from the 16th cent. onwards under the influence of Latin and Greek.

phantasmagoria /fan,tazmə'gawri-ə/ *noun* **1** an optical effect by which figures on a screen appear to dwindle into the distance or to rush towards the observer with enormous increase of size. **2** a constantly shifting, confused succession of things seen or imagined, e.g. in a dreaming or feverish state. ⟩⟩ **phantasmagoric** /-'gorik/ *adj*, **phantasmagorical** /-'gorikl/ *adj*. [French *fantasmagorie*, from *fantasme* (see PHANTASM) + *-agorie*, prob from Greek *ageirein* to assemble, collect]

phantasy¹ /'fantəsi/ *noun* (*pl* **phantasies**) *archaic* = FANTASY¹.

phantasy² *verb trans and intrans* (**phantasies, phantasied, phantasying**) *archaic* = FANTASY².

phantom¹ /'fantəm/ *noun* **1a** something, e.g. a ghost, apparent to the senses but with no substantial existence. **b** something elusive or unreal; a will-o'-the-wisp: *that treacherous phantom which men call Liberty* — John Ruskin. **c** something existing only in the imagination: *His dreams were troubled by phantoms of the past.* **2** something existing in appearance only; a form without substance. ⟩⟩ **phantomlike** *adv and adj.* [Middle English *fantosme, fantome* from early French *fantosme*, modification of Latin *phantasma*: see PHANTASM]

phantom² *adj* **1** of the nature of, suggesting, or being a phantom. **2** fictitious, dummy, or non-existent: *phantom voters*.

phantom limb *noun* the feeling that a person may have after losing an arm or a leg that the amputated limb is still present and attached to the body, sometimes experienced as feelings of pain in the supposed limb.

phantom pregnancy *noun* a physiological state resembling pregnancy.

pharaoh /'fearoh/ *noun* (*often* **Pharaoh**) a ruler of ancient Egypt. ⟩⟩ **pharaonic** /fea'ronik/ *adj.* [via late Latin from Greek *pharaō* from Hebrew *par'ōh*, from Egyptian *pr-'o*, literally 'great house']

pharaoh ant *noun* a small red ant that is a household and greenhouse pest throughout the world: *Monomorium pharaonis*. [so called because the ants were wrongly believed to be one of the plagues of ancient Egypt]

pharisaic /fari'say·ik/ *adj* **1** (**Pharisaic**) of the Pharisees. **2** marked by hypocritical self-righteousness. ⟩⟩ **Pharisaism** *noun*, **pharisaism** /'farisayiz(ə)m/ *noun*. [via late Latin from late Greek *pharisaikos*, from Greek *pharisaios*: see PHARISEE]

pharisaical /fari'say·ikl/ *adj* = PHARISAIC.

pharisee /'farisee/ *noun* **1** (**Pharisee**) a member of a Jewish party noted for strict adherence to the Torah. **2** a pharisaic person. ⟩⟩ **phariseeism** *or* **Phariseeism** *noun*. [Old English *farise* via Latin from Greek *pharisaios*, from Aramaic *pĕrīshayyā*, pl of *pĕrīshā*, literally 'separated']

pharmaceutic /fahmə'syoohtik/ *adj* = PHARMACEUTICAL¹.

pharmaceutical¹ /fahmə'syoohtikl/ *adj* of or engaged in pharmacy or in the manufacture of medicinal substances. ⟩⟩ **pharmaceutically** *adv.* [via late Latin from Greek *pharmakeutikos*, from *pharmakeuein*: see PHARMACY]

pharmaceutical² *noun* a medicinal drug.

pharmaceutics *pl noun* **1** (*treated as sing.*) the preparation and dispensing of medicinal drugs. **2** medicinal drugs.

pharmaco- *comb. form* forming words, denoting: medicine; drug: *pharmacology.* [Greek *pharmako-*, from *pharmakon* magic charm, poison, drug]

pharmacognosy /fahmə'kognəsi/ *noun* the study of drugs from natural sources, *esp* plants. ⟩⟩ **pharmacognostic** /-'nostik/ *adj*, **pharmacognostical** /-'nostikl/ *adj*. [Greek *pharmakon* magic charm, poison, drug + *-gnōsia* knowledge, from *gnōsis*]

pharmacology /fahmə'koləji/ *noun* **1** the science of drugs and their effect on living things. **2** the properties and effects of a particular drug: *the pharmacology of morphine.* ⟩⟩ **pharmacologic** /-'lojik/ *adj*, **pharmacological** /-'lojikl/ *adj*, **pharmacologically** /-'lojikli/ *adv*, **pharmacologist** *noun*.

pharmacopoeia (*NAmer* **pharmacopeia**) /,fahmǝkə'pee-ə/ *noun* **1** a book describing drugs, chemicals, and medicinal preparations: compare DISPENSATORY. **2** a stock of drugs. ⟩⟩ **pharmacopoeial** *adj*. [via Latin from late Greek *pharmakopoiia* preparation of drugs, from PHARMACO- + Greek *poiein* to make]

pharmacy /'fahməsi/ *noun* (*pl* **pharmacies**) **1** the preparation and dispensing of medicinal drugs. **2a** a place where medicines are compounded or dispensed. **b** a chemist's shop. ⟩⟩ **pharmacist** *noun*. [via late Latin from Greek *pharmakeia* administration of drugs, from *pharmakeuein* to administer drugs, from *pharmakon* magic charm, poison, drug]

pharos /'fearos/ *noun* a lighthouse or beacon to guide ships.

Word history
from the tall lighthouse build about 280 BC on the island of *Pharos* at Alexandria on the Mediterranean coast of Egypt. The lighthouse was one of the Seven Wonders of the World.

pharyng- *or* **pharyngo-** *comb. form* forming words, denoting: pharynx: *pharyngitis.* [Greek, from *pharyng-, pharynx*]

pharyngal /fə'ringgl/ *adj* = PHARYNGEAL.

pharyngeal /farin'jee·əl, fə'rinji·əl/ *adj* **1** to do with or in the region of the pharynx. **2** said of a consonant: produced in the pharynx. [Latin *pharyngeus*, from *pharyng-, pharynx*, from Greek]

pharynges /fə'rinjeez/ *noun* pl of PHARYNX.

pharyngitis /farin'jietəs/ *noun* inflammation of the pharynx.

pharyngo- *comb. form* see PHARYNG-.

pharynx /'faringks/ *noun* (*pl* **pharynges** /fə'rinjeez/ *or* **pharynxes**) in vertebrates, the part of the alimentary canal between the mouth cavity and the oesophagus. [via Latin from Greek *pharyng-, pharynx* throat, pharynx]

phase¹ /fayz/ *noun* **1** a discernible part or stage in a course, development, or cycle: *Her style changed in the later phases of her career.* **2** an aspect or part, e.g. of a problem, under consideration. **3** a particular appearance or state in a regularly recurring cycle of changes: *the phases of the moon.* **4** in physics, a particular stage of progress reached in a regularly recurring motion or cyclic process with respect to a standard or reference position or assumed starting point; the point to which a rotation, oscillation, or periodic variation has advanced, considered in its relation to a standard or starting position. **5** a homogeneous, physically distinct, and mechanically separable portion of matter present in a complex mixture the constituents of which have different physical states: *Ice in an ice-and-water mixture constitutes the solid phase.* **6** a cyclically recurring or geographical variation in the appearance, e.g. coat or plumage colours, of an animal or bird. ✳ **in phase 1** synchronized or correlated. **2** said of two or more waves: having the same phase; reaching a maximum value simultaneously. **out of phase 1** not synchronized or correlated. **2** said of two or more waves: not having the same phase; not reaching a maximum value simultaneously. [Greek *phasis* appearance of a star, phase of the moon, from *phainein* to show, appear]

phase² *verb trans* **1** (*usu in passive*) to conduct or carry out (a project, etc) by planned phases. **2** (*also* + with) to schedule (operations, etc) or contract for (goods or services) to be performed or supplied as required. **3** to adjust (something) so as to be in phase with something else.

phase-contrast microscope *noun* a microscope that changes differences in the phase of the light transmitted through or reflected by the object into differences of intensity in the image and is used *esp* for examining biological specimens that have not been stained.

phase in *verb trans* to introduce the practice, production, or use of (something) in gradual stages. ▸ **phase-in** *noun.*

phase modulation *noun* a modulation of the phase of a wave, *esp* a radio carrier wave by the characteristics of the signal carried, or a method of transmitting using this: compare AMPLITUDE MODULATION, FREQUENCY MODULATION.

phase out *verb trans* to discontinue the practice, production, or use of (something) in gradual stages. ▸ **phase-out** *noun.*

-phasia *comb. form* forming nouns, denoting: speech or language disorder: *aphasia.* ▸ **-phasic** *comb. form.* [Greek *phasis* utterance, from *phanai* to speak, say]

phasic /ˈfayzik/ *adj* of a phase or phases, occurring in phases.

-phasic *comb. form* see -PHASIA.

phasor /ˈfayzə/ *noun* a regularly alternating quantity, e.g. current or voltage, that is represented graphically by a directed line segment the length of which represents the magnitude and the direction of the phase: compare VECTOR¹, SCALAR² (2). [blend of PHASE¹ + VECTOR¹]

phatic /ˈfatik/ *adj* said of speech: expressing feelings or establishing an atmosphere of sociability rather than communicating ideas. ▸ **phatically** *adv.* [Greek *phatos* spoken, from *phanai* to speak, say]

PhD *abbr* Doctor of Philosophy. [Latin *philosophiae doctor*]

pheasant /ˈfez(ə)nt/ *noun* (*pl* **pheasants** *or collectively* **pheasant**) **1** any of numerous species of large long-tailed and brightly coloured birds, orig from Asia, many of which are reared as ornamental or game birds: genus *Phasianus* and other genera. **2** the flesh of a pheasant used as food. [Middle English *fesaunt* via French and Latin from Greek *phasianos*, literally 'of the Phasis', river in Colchis, ancient country in Asia]

phen- *or* **pheno-** *comb. form* forming words, with the meanings: **1a** of or derived from benzene: *phenol.* **b** containing phenyl: *phenobarbitone.* **2** showing; visible: *phenotype.* [obsolete *phene* benzene, from French *phène*, from Greek *phainein* to show, from its occurrence in illuminating gas]

phenacetin /fiˈnasətin/ *noun* a white crystalline compound used as a painkiller and to relieve fever. [PHEN- + ACETYL + -IN¹]

phencyclidine /fenˈsieklideen/ *noun* **1** a synthetic drug used in veterinary medicine as an anaesthetic. **2** this drug used illegally as a hallucinogenic. Also called ANGEL DUST.

phenix /ˈfeeniks/ *noun NAmer* see PHOENIX.

pheno- *comb. form* see PHEN-.

phenobarbital /feenohˈbahbit(ə)l/ *noun NAmer* = PHENOBARBITONE.

phenobarbitone /feenohˈbahbitohn/ *noun* a barbiturate used *esp* as a sedative and anticonvulsant in the treatment of epilepsy.

phenocryst /ˈfenəkrist, ˈfee-/ *noun* any of the prominent embedded crystals of a porphyry rock. ▸ **phenocrystic** /fenəˈkristik, fee-/ *adj.* [French *phénocryste*, from PHENO- + Greek *krystallos* CRYSTAL¹]

phenol /ˈfeenol/ *noun* **1** a caustic poisonous acidic chemical compound present in coal tar, a derivative of benzene containing a HYDROXYL (OH) group in place of a hydrogen atom. It is used in dilute solution as a disinfectant. Also called CARBOLIC ACID. **2** any of various acidic chemical compounds analogous to phenol in that they contain one or more hydroxyl groups attached to a ring of atoms similar to a BENZENE RING (ring of six carbon atoms). ▸ **phenolic** /fiˈnolik/ *adj.* [PHEN- + -OL¹]

phenology /fiˈnoləji/ *noun* the relations between climate and periodic biological phenomena, e.g. bird migration or plant flowering, or the study of these relations. ▸ **phenological** /feenəˈlojikl/ *adj,* **phenologically** /feenəˈlojikli/ *adv.* [*phenomena*, pl of PHENOMENON + -LOGY]

phenolphthalein /feenol fthaliin, -ˈleen/ *noun* a synthetic compound used in medicine as a purgative and in chemical analysis as an indicator of alkalinity. It is brilliant red in alkaline solutions. [PHENOL + PHTHALIC ACID + -IN¹]

phenomena /fiˈnominə/ *noun* pl of PHENOMENON.

phenomenal *adj* **1** extraordinary or remarkable: *The show was a phenomenal success.* **2** relating to or being a phenomenon, e.g.. **a** known through the senses rather than through thought or intuition. **b** concerned with phenomena rather than with hypotheses. ▸ **phenomenally** *adv.*

phenomenalism *noun* a theory which holds that knowledge of the external world is limited to or reducible to descriptions of phenomena as perceived by the senses. ▸ **phenomenalist** *noun,* **phenomenalistic** /-ˈlistik/ *adj,* **phenomenalistically** /-ˈlistikli/ *adv.*

phenomenological /fi,nominəˈlojikl/ *adj* **1** of phenomenology or phenomenalism. **2** = PHENOMENAL (2). ▸ **phenomenologically** *adv.*

phenomenology /fi,nomiˈnoləji/ *noun* **1** the description of the formal structure of what is directly experienced and of consciousness, in abstraction from any consideration of causal connections between what is experienced and the external world. **2a** the description of a related group of phenomena: *the phenomenology of religion.* **b** an analysis produced by phenomenological investigation. ▸ **phenomenologist** *noun.* [German *Phänomenologie*, from *Phänomenon* phenomenon + -OLOGY]

phenomenon /fiˈnominən/ *noun* (*pl* **phenomena** /-nə/) **1** an observable fact or event. **2a** an object of sense perception rather than of thought or intuition. **b** a fact or event that can be scientifically described and explained. **3a** a notable or remarkable circumstance or occurrence: *The precision with which those accustomed to watchfulness ... sleep, is not the least of the phenomena of our mysterious being. The head is no sooner on the pillow than consciousness is lost* — J Fenimore Cooper. **b** (*pl usu* **phenomenons**) an exceptional, unusual, or abnormal person, thing, or event; a prodigy. [via late Latin from Greek *phainomenon*, from *phainomenos*, present part. of *phainesthai* to appear]

Usage note

phenomenon *and* phenomena. *Phenomenon* is a singular noun. *Phenomena* is its plural and should never be used as if it were singular: *a strange phenomenon that occurs during an eclipse; the strange phenomena that occur during eclipses.*

phenothiazine /feenohˈthie-əzeen/ *noun* **1** a synthetic compound used in chemical synthesis and in veterinary medicine against parasitic worms. **2** any of various phenothiazine derivatives, e.g. chlorpromazine, used as tranquillizing agents, *esp* in the treatment of schizophrenia. [PHENO- + THI- + AZINE]

phenotype /ˈfeenətiep/ *noun* the visible characteristics of an organism that are produced by the interaction of the organism's genes and the environment: compare GENOTYPE. ▸ **phenotypic** /-ˈtipik/ *adj,* **phenotypical** /-ˈtipikl/ *adj,* **phenotypically** /-ˈtipikli/ *adv.* [German *Phänotypus* from Greek *phainein* to show + *typos*: see TYPE¹]

phenyl /ˈfenil, ˈfeenil, ˈfeeniel/ *noun* (*often used in combinations*) a univalent radical $-C_6H_5$ that is derived from benzene by removal of one hydrogen atom. ▸ **phenylic** /feˈnilik, fə-/ *adj.* [French *phényle*, from PHEN- + -YL]

phenylalanine /fenilˈaləneen, feeˈ-/ *noun* an amino acid found in most proteins that is essential for human development and health.

phenylketonuria /fenilkeetəˈnyooəri.ə, feeˈ-/ *noun* an inherited metabolic disease in human beings that results in severe mental deficiency if untreated from birth. ▸ **phenylketonuric** /-rik/ *adj and noun.* [PHENYL + KETONE + -URIA]

pheromone /'ferəmohn/ *noun* a chemical substance that is produced by an animal and stimulates one or more behavioural responses in other individuals of the same species. ⟫⟫ **pheromonal** /-'mohnl/ *adj.* [Greek *pherein* to carry + *-mone* as in HORMONE]

phew /fyooh/ *interj* used to express shock, relief, or exhaustion.

phi /fie/ *noun* the 21st letter of the Greek alphabet (Φ, φ), equivalent to and transliterated as roman ph. [later Greek *phi* from Greek *phei*]

phial /'fie·əl/ *noun* a small closed or closable vessel, *esp* for holding liquid medicine. [Middle English via Latin from Greek *phialē*]

Phi Beta Kappa /,fie beetə 'kapə/ *noun* an American college fraternity, membership of which is based on academic distinction, or a member of this fraternity. [*Phi Beta Kappa Society*, from *phi* + *beta* + *kappa*, initials of the society's Greek motto *philosophia biou kybernētēs* philosophy the guide of life]

Phil. *abbr* **1** Philadelphia. **2** Philharmonic. **3** Philippians (book of the Bible).

phil. *abbr* philosophy.

phil- *or* **philo-** *comb. form* forming words, with the meanings: **1** loving: *philanthropy*. **2** having an affinity for: *philoprogenitive*. [Middle English via French and Latin from Greek *philos* dear, friendly]

-phil *comb. form* see -PHILE.

philadelphus /filə'delfəs/ *noun* (*pl* **philadelphuses**) any of a genus of ornamental shrubs of the hydrangea family with white cup-shaped flowers with a scent like orange blossom, *esp* MOCK ORANGE: genus *Philadelphus*. [Latin genus name, from Greek *philadelphos* brotherly, from PHIL- + *adelphos* brother]

philander /fi'landə/ *verb intrans* (**philandered, philandering**) **1** said of a man: to flirt. **2** said of a man: to have many casual love affairs. ⟫⟫ **philanderer** *noun.* [obsolete *philander* lover, philanderer, prob named after *Philander*, stock name for a lover in early romances, from Greek PHIL- + *andr-, anēr* man]

philanthropic /filən'thropik/ *adj* **1** of or characterized by philanthropy; humanitarian. **2** dispensing or receiving aid from funds set aside for humanitarian purposes: *a philanthropic institution*. ⟫⟫ **philanthropically** *adv.*

philanthropical /filən'thropikl/ *adj* = PHILANTHROPIC.

philanthropy /fi'lanthrəpi/ *noun* (*pl* **philanthropies**) **1** goodwill to one's fellow human beings, *esp* active effort to promote the welfare of others. **2** a philanthropic act or gift. ⟫⟫ **philanthrope** /'filənthrohp/ *noun,* **philanthropist** *noun.* [via late Latin from Greek *philanthrōpia*, from *philanthrōpos* loving mankind, from PHIL- + *anthrōpos* man]

philately /fi'latəli/ *noun* the study and collection of postage stamps. ⟫⟫ **philatelic** /-'telik/ *adj,* **philatelically** /-'telikli/ *adv,* **philatelist** *noun.* [French *philatélie*, from PHIL- + Greek *ateleia* exemption from payment, from A-² + *telos* toll, tax; because the stamp exempts the recipient from paying]

-phile *or* **-phil** *comb. form* forming nouns, with the meanings: **1** a person having a fondness or liking for: *Francophile*. **2** something having an affinity for: *thermophile*. ⟫⟫ **-phile** *comb. form.* [French *-phile* from Greek *-philos*, from *philos* loving]

Philem. *abbr* Philemon (book of the Bible).

philharmonic /filə'monik, fil(h)ah-/ *adj* used *esp* in the names of choirs, orchestras, etc: fond of or devoted to music. [French *philharmonique* from Italian *filarmonico* music-loving, from *fil-* PHIL- + *armonia* harmony, from Latin *harmonia*: see HARMONY]

philhellene /'filheleen/ *noun* an admirer or supporter of Greece or the Greeks. ⟫⟫ **philhellenic** /filhe'leenik, -'lenik/ *adj.* [Greek *philellēen*, from PHIL- + *Hellēen* Hellene]

-philia *or* **-phily** *comb. form* forming nouns, denoting: **1** a liking for or interest in: *Francophilia*. **2** an abnormal appetite or liking for: *necrophilia*. ⟫⟫ **-philiac** *comb. form.* [Greek *philia* friendship, from *philos* dear]

philibeg /'filibeg/ *noun* see FILIBEG.

-philic *comb. form* forming adjectives, with the meaning: having an affinity or liking for: *necrophilic*. [Greek *-philos*, from *philos* dear]

philippic /fi'lipik/ *noun literary* a speech or declamation full of bitter invective. [early French *philippique* from Latin *philippica*; the *orationes philippicae* were speeches of Cicero against Mark Antony, the name being a translation of Greek *philippikoi logoi*, literally 'speeches relating to Philip', speeches of Demosthenes against Philip II of Macedon]

Philippine /'filipeen/ *adj* **1** of or relating to the Republic of the Philippines, archipelago in the S China Sea. **2** = FILIPINO.

philistine /'filistien/ *noun* **1** (**Philistine**) a native or inhabitant of ancient Philistia. **2** (*often* **Philistine**) a person who professes indifference or opposition to intellectual or aesthetic values. ⟫⟫ **philistinism** /-stiniz(ə)m/ *noun.* [from *Philistia*, ancient country in SW Palestine]

Phillips screw /'filips/ *noun trademark* a screw with a cross-shaped slot in the head. [named after Henry F *Phillips* d.1958, American businessman, the original manufacturer]

Phillips screwdriver *noun trademark* a screwdriver with a cross-shaped tip for turning Phillips screws.

phillumenist /fi'loohmənist/ *noun* a person who collects books of matches or matchbox labels. [PHIL- + Latin *lumen* light + -IST¹]

philo- *comb. form* see PHIL-.

philodendron /filə'dendrən/ *noun* (*pl* **philodendrons** *or* **philodendra** /-drə/) a plant of the arum family cultivated for its showy foliage: genus *Philodendron*. [Latin genus name, from Greek *Philodendron*, neuter of *philodendros* loving trees, from PHILO- + *dendron* tree; because many species are climbers which, in the wild, use trees for support]

philogyny /fi'lojini/ *noun formal* fondness for or admiration of women. ⟫⟫ **philogynist** *noun.* [Greek *philogynia*, from PHILO- + *gynē* woman]

philology /fi'loləji/ *noun* **1** the study of the historical development of a language or the comparison of different languages, *esp* based on the analysis of texts; historical linguistics and/or comparative linguistics. **2** the study of ancient texts. **3** the study of texts as a field of study that sheds light on cultural history. **4** *dated* the study of literature. ⟫⟫ **philologian** /-'lohji·ən/ *noun,* **philological** /-'lojikl/ *adj,* **philologically** /-'lojikli/ *adv,* **philologist** *noun.* [French *philologie* via Latin from Greek *philologia* love of learning and literature, ultimately from PHILO- + *logos* word, speech]

philoprogenitive /,filohproh'jenətiv/ *adj formal* **1** producing many offspring; prolific. **2** of love of one's offspring. [PHILO- + Latin *progenitus*, past part. of *progignere*: see PROGENITOR]

philosopher /fi'losəfə/ *noun* **1a** a specialist in philosophy: *Organic life … has developed gradually from the protozoan to the philosopher* — Bertrand Russell. **b** a scholar or thinker. **2** a person whose philosophical viewpoint enables them to meet trouble with equanimity. [Middle English via French and Latin from Greek *philosophos* lover of wisdom, from PHILO- + *sophos* wise]

philosopher's stone *noun* a substance believed by alchemists to have the power of transmuting base metals into gold.

philosophic /filə'sofik/ *adj* = PHILOSOPHICAL.

philosophical /filə'sofikl/ *adj* **1** of philosophers or philosophy. **2** calm in the face of trouble. ⟫⟫ **philosophically** *adv.*

philosophize *or* **philosophise** /fi'losəfiez/ *verb intrans* **1** to engage in philosophical reasoning. **2** to expound a trite or superficial philosophy.

philosophy /fi'losəfi/ *noun* (*pl* **philosophies**) **1a** the study of the nature of knowledge and existence and the principles of moral and aesthetic value: *Philosophy is at once the most sublime and the most trivial of human pursuits* — William James. **b** the philosophical principles or teachings of a specified individual, group, period, or field of study: *Kantian philosophy; the philosophy of science*. **2** the sum of beliefs and attitudes of a specified individual, group, or period: *the vegetarian philosophy*. **3** equanimity in the face of trouble or stress. [Middle English *philosophie* via French and Latin from Greek *philosophia*, from *philosophos*: see PHILOSOPHER]

-philous *comb. form* forming adjectives, with the meaning: having a liking or affinity for: *coprophilous*. [Greek *-philos*, from *philos* dear, loving, friendly]

philtre (*NAmer* **philter**) /'filtə/ *noun* a potion or drug reputed to have the power to arouse sexual passion or desire. [early French *philtre* via Latin from Greek *philtron*, from *philein* to love, from *philos* dear, loving]

-phily *comb. form* see -PHILIA.

phimosis /fie'mohsis/ *noun* (*pl* **phimoses** /-seez/) tightness of the foreskin preventing its retraction. [Greek *phimōsis*, literally 'muzzling', from *phimos* muzzle]

phiz /fiz/ *noun* = PHIZOG.

phizog /fi'zog/ *noun Brit, informal* a person's face, or the expression on their face. [by shortening and alteration from PHYSIOGNOMY]

phleb- *or* **phlebo-** *comb. form* forming words, denoting: vein: *phlebitis*. [Middle English *fleb-* via French and Latin from Greek *phleb-, phlebo-*, from *phleb-, phleps* vein]

phlebitis /fli'bietəs/ *noun* inflammation of a vein.

phlebo- *comb. form* see PHLEB-.

phlebotomize *or* **phlebotomise** *verb trans* to draw blood from (somebody) by phlebotomy; to bleed (them).

phlebotomy /fli'botəmi/ *noun* (*pl* **phlebotomies**) the letting or taking of blood in the treatment or diagnosis of disease. ➤➤ **phlebotomist** *noun.* [Middle English *fleobotomie* via French and late Latin from Greek *phlebotomia*, from PHLEBO- + -TOMY]

phlegm /flem/ *noun* 1 thick mucus secreted in abnormal quantities in the respiratory passages. **2a** intrepid coolness; composure. **b** dull or apathetic coldness or indifference. **3** one of the four humours in medieval physiology, considered to be cold and moist and to cause sluggishness. ➤➤ **phlegmy** /'flemi/ *adj.* [Middle English *fleume* via French and late Latin from Greek *phlegma* flame, inflammation, phlegm, from *phlegein* to burn]

phlegmatic /fleg'matik/ *adj* 1 having or showing a slow and stolid temperament. **2** resembling, consisting of, or producing phlegm. ➤➤ **phlegmatically** *adv.*

phloem /'floh·em/ *noun* a complex vascular tissue of higher plants that functions chiefly in the conduction of soluble food substances, e.g. sugars: compare XYLEM. [German *Phloem* from Greek *phloios, phloos* bark]

phlogiston /flo'jist(ə)n/ *noun* the supposed essence of fire formerly regarded as a material substance which was given off when a substance burned or was oxidized. [via Latin from Greek *phlogiston*, neuter of *phlogistos* inflammable, from *phlogizein* to set on fire]

phlox /floks/ *noun* (*pl* **phloxes** *or collectively* **phlox**) an American plant with red, purple, white, or variegated flowers: genus *Phlox*. [Latin genus name, from Latin *phlox* a flame-coloured flower, from Greek, flame, wallflower]

-phobe *comb. form* forming nouns, denoting: a person afraid of or averse to: *Francophobe*. [Greek *-phobos*: see PHOBIA]

phobia /'fohbi-ə/ *noun* an exaggerated and illogical fear of something. [late Latin *-phobia* from Greek, from *-phobos* fearing, from *phobos* fear, flight]

-phobia *comb. form* forming nouns, denoting: abnormal fear or dislike of: *claustrophobia*.

phobic /'fohbik/ *adj* 1 of or being a phobia. **2** motivated by or based on withdrawal from an unpleasant stimulus: *a phobic response to light.*

-phobic *comb. form* forming adjectives, with the meanings: 1 having an aversion for: *Anglophobic*. **2** lacking affinity for or chemical attraction to: *hydrophobic*. [-*phobic* via French *-phobique* and Late Latin *-phobicus* from Greek *-phobikos* from *-phobia; -phobous* via late Latin *-phobus* from Greek *-phobos*: see PHOBIA]

-phobous *comb. form* = -PHOBIC.

phoebe /'feebi/ *noun* any of three species of FLYCATCHER (insect-catching bird) found in the USA and northern S America: genus *Sayornis*. [of imitative origin, influenced by the name *Phoebe*]

Phoenician /fə'neesh(ə)n/ *noun* 1 a native or inhabitant of ancient Phoenicia in SW Asia. **2** an ancient Semitic language of Phoenicia. ➤➤ **Phoenician** *adj.*

phoenix (NAmer **phenix**) /'feeniks/ *noun* 1 a mythical bird believed to live for 500 years, burn itself on a pyre, and rise alive from the ashes to live another cycle. **2** something that appears to arise from its own ashes, or be reborn after its own destruction. **3** somebody or something that is unique and of notable beauty, quality, etc. ➤➤ **phoenix-like** *adj.* [Old English *fenix* via Latin *phoenix* from Greek *phoinix* purple, crimson, Phoenician, phoenix, date palm]

pholidot /'folidot/ *noun* a member of an order of mammals that consists solely of the pangolins: order Pholidota. [via Latin from Greek *pholidōtos* scaly, from *pholis, pholid-* scale]

phon /fon/ *noun* the unit of measurement of perceived loudness of sound. It is measured on a scale beginning at zero for the faintest audible sound, with the number of phons of a given sound being equal to the intensity in decibels of a pure tone of a frequency of 1000 hertz judged by the average listener to be equal in loudness to the given sound. [Greek *phōnē* voice, sound]

phon. *abbr* phonetics.

phon- *or* **phono-** *comb. form* forming words, denoting: sound; voice; speech: *phonograph*. [Greek *phōn-, phōno-*, from *phōnē* voice, sound]

phonate /foh'nayt/ *verb intrans* to produce vocal sounds, *esp* speech sounds. ➤➤ **phonation** /-sh(ə)n/ *noun,* **phonatory** /'fohnət(ə)ri/ *adj.*

phone[1] /fohn/ *noun* 1 = TELEPHONE[1]. **2** (*also in pl*) = EARPHONE. [by shortening]

phone[2] *verb trans and intrans* (*also* + back/in/up) = TELEPHONE[2].

phone[3] *noun* in phonetics, a simple speech sound. [Greek *phōnē* voice, sound]

-phone *comb. form* 1 forming nouns, denoting: sound: *homophone; telephone; xylophone*. **2** forming nouns, with the meaning: speaker of: *Anglophone*. [Greek *-phōnos* sounding, from *phōnē* voice, sound]

phone book *noun* = TELEPHONE DIRECTORY.

phonecard *noun* a small plastic card that can be used to make prepaid telephone calls from some public telephones.

phone-in *noun* a broadcast programme in which viewers or listeners can participate by telephone.

phoneme /'fohneem/ *noun* the smallest unit of speech that can be used to differentiate words, e.g. /b/, /p/, and /f/, which differentiate the words *bin, pin,* and *fin*: compare ALLOPHONE. [French *phonème* from Greek *phōnēma* speech sound, utterance, from *phōnein*: see PHONETIC]

phonemic /fə'neemik/ *adj* 1 of phonemes. **2** phonetically distinctive. ➤➤ **phonemically** *adv.*

phonemics *pl noun* 1 (*treated as sing. or pl*) the study of phonemes. **2** the phonemic system of a language. ➤➤ **phonemicist** /-sist/ *noun.*

phonetic /fə'netik/ *adj* **1a** of spoken language or speech sounds. **b** of the study of phonetics. **2** representing speech sounds by symbols that each have one value only. ➤➤ **phonetically** *adv.* [Greek *phōnētikos*, from *phōnein* to sound with the voice, from *phōnē* voice, sound]

phonetics *pl noun* 1 (*treated as sing. or pl*) the study and classification of speech sounds. **2** the system of speech sounds of a language. ➤➤ **phonetician** /fohnə'tish(ə)n, fon-/ *noun,* **phonetist** /'fohnətist/ *noun.*

phoney[1] *or* **phony** /'fohni/ *adj* (**phonier, phoniest**) *informal* 1 not genuine or real, e.g.: **a** intended to deceive, mislead, or defraud; counterfeit. **b** sham: *The phoney tinsel of Hollywood* — Oscar Levant. **c** false: *He was using a phoney name.* **2** said of a person: pretentious. ➤➤ **phoneyness** *noun,* **phonily** *adv,* **phoniness** *noun.* [origin unknown]

phoney[2] *or* **phony** *noun* (*pl* **phoneys** *or* **phonies**) somebody or something that is phoney.

-phonia *comb. form* 1 = -PHONY (1): *dysphonia*. **2** forming nouns, denoting: a speech or voice disorder: *aphonia*. [-PHONY + -IA[1]]

phonic /'fonik/ *adj* 1 of or producing sound; acoustic. **2a** of speech sounds. **b** of phonics. ➤➤ **phonically** *adv.* [Greek *phōnē* voice, sound + -IC[1]]

-phonic *comb. form* forming adjectives, with the meanings: 1 of sound: *quadraphonic*. **2** of a speech or voice disorder: *aphonic*.

phonics *pl noun* (*treated as sing. or pl*) a method of teaching reading and pronunciation through the phonetic value of letters, syllables, etc.

phono /'fohnoh/ *adj* 1 said of a plug used in audio and video equipment: in which the central prong of the plug is one conductor and the outer cylinder is the other conductor. **2** said of a socket: accepting a phono plug. [shortening of PHONOGRAPH]

phono- *comb. form* see PHON-.

phonocardiogram /fohnoh'kahdi·əgram/ *noun* in medicine, a printed record of the sounds made by the heart.

phonocardiograph /fohnoh'kahdi·əgrahf, -graf/ *noun* a device for making phonocardiograms. ➤➤ **phonocardiographic** /-'grafik/ *adj,* **phonocardiography** /-'ogrəfi/ *noun.*

phonogram /'fohnəgram/ *noun* a character used, e.g. in shorthand, to represent a spoken sound. ➤➤ **phonogramic** /-'gramik/ *adj,* **phonogramically** /-'gramikli/ *adv,* **phonogrammic** *adj,* **phonogrammically** *adv.*

phonograph /'fohnəgrahf, -graf/ *noun* **1** an early device for recording or reproducing sound in which a stylus cuts or follows a groove on a cylinder. **2** *NAmer* = GRAMOPHONE or RECORD PLAYER. ➤➤ **phonographic** *adj*.

phonology /fə'noləji/ *noun* (*pl* **phonologies**) **1** the study of the sound system (PHONEMICS) of a language or languages. **2** the phonemic system of a language. ➤➤ **phonological** /fohnə'lojikl/ *adj*, **phonologically** /fohnə'lojikli/ *adv*, **phonologist** *noun*.

phonon /'fohnon/ *noun* a quantum of energy in the form of vibrations, e.g. sound. [PHON- + -ON²]

phony¹ /'fohni/ *adj* (**phonier, phoniest**) see PHONEY¹.

phony² *noun* (*pl* **phonies**) see PHONY².

-phony *comb. form* forming nouns, denoting: **1** sound: *telephony*; *euphony*. **2** a speech or voice disorder; = -PHONIA (2). [Middle English *-phonie* via French and Latin from Greek *-phōnia*, from *-phōnos* sounding, from *phōnē* voice, sound]

phooey /'fooh-i/ *interj informal* used to express scorn or incredulity.

-phore *comb. form* forming nouns, denoting: bearer; carrier: *gametophore*; *semaphore*. ➤➤ **-phorous** *comb. form*. [Greek *-phoros* from *pherein* to carry]

-phoresis *comb. form* (*pl* **-phoreses**) forming nouns, denoting: transmission: *electrophoresis*. [Greek *phorēsis* act of carrying, from *phorein* to carry, wear, frequentative of *pherein* to carry]

phormium /'fawmi-əm/ *noun* (*pl* **phormiums**) **1** any of various plants of the agave family having long dark green lance-shaped leaves that are a source of a fibre used in ropes, mats, etc; = FLAX-LILY; NEW ZEALAND FLAX: genus *Phormium*. **2** the fibre obtained from the leaves of these plants. [Greek *phormion* mat, basket]

-phorous *comb. form* see -PHORE.

phosgene /'fozjeen/ *noun* a very poisonous colourless gas that is a severe respiratory irritant and was formerly used in warfare. [Greek *phōs* light + -GEN, -*gene*; because it was obtained orig by the action of sunlight on a mixture of chlorine and carbon monoxide]

phosph- *or* **phospho-** *comb. form* forming words, denoting: **1** phosphorus: *phosphide*. **2** phosphate: *phospholipid*.

phosphate /'fosfayt/ *noun* **1** a salt or ester of a phosphoric acid. **2** any of several phosphates used as fertilizers. ➤➤ **phosphatic** /fos'fatik/ *adj*. [French *phosphate*, from *acide phosphorique* phosphoric acid]

phosphatide /'fosfətied/ *noun* = PHOSPHOLIPID.

phosphene /'fosfeen/ *noun* an impression of light due to excitation of the retina caused by pressure on the eyeball. ➤➤ **phosphenic** /fos'feenik/ *adj*. [Greek *phōs* light + *phainein* to show]

phosphide /'fosfied/ *noun* a binary compound of phosphorus with an element or radical.

phosphine /'fosfeen/ *noun* **1** a colourless, extremely poisonous, inflammable gas, a compound of phosphorus and hydrogen that has a smell of decaying fish. **2** any of various organic chemical compounds derived from this gas.

phospho- *comb. form* see PHOSPH-.

phospholipid /fosfoh'lipid/ *noun* any LIPID (fatty compound) containing a PHOSPHATE (compound of phosphoric acid), found in all living cells, *esp* in membranes; = PHOSPHATIDE.

phosphor /'fosfə/ *noun* a substance showing phosphorescence. [via Latin from Greek *phōsphoros*, literally 'light bringer', from *phōs-* light + *pherein* to carry, bring]

phosphor- *or* **phosphoro-** *comb. form* forming words, denoting: phosphorus: *phosphoric*; *phosphorous*.

phosphor bronze *noun* any of a number of varieties of bronze containing a small amount of phosphorus, resistant to corrosion and used in bearings, gears, etc.

phosphoresce /fosfə'res/ *verb intrans* to exhibit phosphorescence.

phosphorescence /fosfə'res(ə)ns/ *noun* **1** light emission that is caused by the absorption of radiation and continues for a noticeable time after the radiation has stopped. **2** lasting emission of light without noticeable heat. **3** emitted light. ➤➤ **phosphorescent** *adj*.

phosphoric /fos'forik/ *adj* of or containing phosphorus, *esp* in its higher valency.

phosphoric acid *noun* any of several forms of acid used *esp* in preparing phosphates, e.g. for fertilizers, in rustproofing metals, and as a flavouring in soft drinks.

phosphorite /'fosfəriet/ *noun* calcium phosphate occurring as a mineral. ➤➤ **phosphoritic** /-'ritik/ *adj*.

phosphoro- *comb. form* see PHOSPHOR-.

phosphorous /'fosf(ə)rəs/ *adj* of or containing phosphorus, *esp* in its lower valency.

phosphorus /'fosf(ə)rəs/ *noun* **1** a non-metallic chemical element of the nitrogen family that occurs widely, *esp* as phosphates: symbol P, atomic number 15.

Editorial note
The two main forms are white phosphorus, which is a soft waxy solid that is poisonous, phosphorescent, and highly inflammable, and red phosphorus, which is less reactive, does not phosphoresce, and is used in safety matches, There is also an even less reactive black variety, somewhat resembling graphite.

2 a phosphorescent substance or body, *esp* one that shines or glows in the dark; = PHOSPHOR. [via Latin from Greek *phōsphoros*: see PHOSPHOR]

phosphorylate /fos'forilayt/ *verb trans* to combine (an organic compound) with an inorganic phosphate group.

phosphorylation /fos,fori'laysh(ə)n/ *noun* the combining of an organic compound with an inorganic phosphate group, *esp* the conversion of carbohydrates into their phosphates in metabolic processes. ➤➤ **phosphorylative** /fos'forilativ/ *adj*.

phossy jaw /'fosi/ *noun informal* formerly, gangrene of the lower jaw caused by prolonged exposure to phosphorus, a condition once commonly suffered by those employed in the making of safety matches when white phosphorus was used.

phot /foht/ *noun* a unit of illumination in the centimetre-gram-second system, equal to one lumen per square centimetre. [Greek *phōt-, phōs* light]

phot. *abbr* **1** photograph. **2** photographic. **3** photography.

phot- *or* **photo-** *comb. form* forming words, with the meanings: **1** light; radiant energy: *photic*; *photography*. **2** photograph or photographic: *photoengraving*. **3** photoelectric: *photocell*. [Greek *phōt-, phōto-*, from *phōt-, phōs* light]

photic /'fohtik/ *adj* **1** of or involving light, *esp* in its effect on living organisms. **2** said of a layer or level of the sea, etc: penetrated by the sun's light sufficiently to allow photosynthesis and plant growth. ➤➤ **photically** *adv*.

photo¹ /'fohtoh/ *noun* (*pl* **photos**) **1** = PHOTOGRAPH¹. **2** (*used before a noun*) involving photography: *a photo finish*; *a photo session*.

photo² *verb trans and intrans* (**photoes, photoed, photoing**) = PHOTOGRAPH².

photo- *comb. form* see PHOT-.

photoautotrophic /fohtoh,awtə'trohfik/ *adj* said of an organism: capable of synthesizing food from inorganic substances, e.g. carbon dioxide, using energy from light: compare CHEMOAUTOTROPHIC. ➤➤ **photoautotrophically** *adv*.

photocall /'fohtohkawl/ *noun* a session at which a person is photographed, typically for the purpose of publicity, e.g. in the press.

photo CD *noun* a compact disc that can be used to store images which can be displayed from it onto a video or television screen.

photocell /'fohtohsel/ *noun* = PHOTOELECTRIC CELL.

photochemistry /fohtoh'kemistri/ *noun* the effect of radiant energy in producing chemical changes, or the branch of chemistry that deals with this. ➤➤ **photochemical** *adj*, **photochemically** *adv*, **photochemist** *noun*.

photochromic /fohtə'krohmik/ *adj* of a substance that is capable of changing colour on exposure to radiant energy, e.g. light, or using such a substance: *photochromic glass*. ➤➤ **photochromism** *noun*. [PHOTO- + CHROM- + -IC¹]

photocomposition /,fohtoh,kompə'zish(ə)n/ *noun* a typesetting process involving the composition of text directly on film or photosensitive paper for reproduction.

photoconductivity /,fohtoh,konduk'tiviti/ *noun* electrical conductivity that is affected by exposure to radiation, *esp* light. ➤➤ **photoconductive** /-'duktiv/ *adj*, **photoconductor** /-'duktə/ *noun*.

photocopy¹ /'fohtəkopi, 'fohtoh-/ *noun* (*pl* **photocopies**) a reproduction of printed text, photographs, etc by a process involving photography.

photocopy² *verb* (**photocopies, photocopied, photocopying**) ➤ *verb trans* to make a photocopy of (something). ➤ *verb intrans*

1 to make photocopies. **2** to be reproduced as photocopies: *Photographs don't photocopy very well.* ➤➤ **photocopiable** *adj,* **photocopier** *noun.*

photodegradable /ˌfohtohdiˈgraydəbl/ *adj* capable of being broken down, *esp* into simpler harmless products, by the action of light, *esp* sunlight: compare BIODEGRADABLE. ➤➤ **photodegradability** /-ˈbiliti/ *noun.*

photodynamic therapy /ˌfohtohdieˈnamik/ *noun* a therapeutic treatment, e.g. for cancers and eye disorders, in which a light-sensitive drug is introduced into the affected area, e.g. by intravenous injection, and is then activated by light, usu from a laser, and destroys a tumour or unwanted tissue.

photoelectric /ˌfohtohˈiˈlektrik/ *adj* involving, relating to, or using any of various electrical effects caused by the interaction of radiation, e.g. light, with matter, *esp* involving or using the release of electrons due to such interaction. ➤➤ **photoelectrically** *adv,* **photoelectricity** /-ˈtrisiti, -elikˈtrisiti/ *noun.*

photoelectric cell *noun* a CELL¹ (device producing electricity) whose electrical properties are modified by the action of light, used in burglar alarms, exposure meters, etc; = PHOTOCELL.

photoelectron /ˌfohtohˈiˈlektron/ *noun* an electron released in photoemission. ➤➤ **photoelectronic** /-ˈtronik, -elikˈtronik/ *adj.*

photoemission /ˌfohtohˈiˈmish(ə)n/ *noun* the release of electrons from a metal by radiation, *esp* light. ➤➤ **photoemissive** /-siv/ *adj,* **photoemitter** /-ˈmitə/ *noun.*

photoengraving /ˌfohtohˈinˈgrayving/ *noun* a process for making line and halftone blocks by photographing an image on a metal plate and then etching, or a plate made by this process.

photo finish *noun* **1** a race finish so close that the winner is only revealed by a photograph of the contestants as they cross the finishing line, or any similar close finish. **2** any close contest.

photofit /ˈfohtohfit/ *noun* (*often* **Photofit**) a means of constructing a likeness of a person's face from photographs, *esp* for identification, or a likeness produced in this way.

photog. *abbr* **1** photograph. **2** photographer. **3** photographic. **4** photography.

photogenic /fohtəˈjenik/ *adj* **1** looking attractive in photographs. **2** producing or generating light; luminescent: *photogenic bacteria.* ➤➤ **photogenically** *adv.*

photogram /ˈfohtəgram/ *noun* **1** a shadow-like image made without a camera by placing objects between light-sensitive paper and a light source. **2** *archaic* a photograph.

photogrammetry /fohtohˈgramitri/ *noun* the use of *esp* aerial photographs to obtain reliable measurements. ➤➤ **photogrammetric** /-ˈmetrik/ *adj,* **photogrammetrist** *noun.* [PHOTOGRAM + -METRY]

photograph¹ /ˈfohtəgrahf, -graf/ *noun* a picture or likeness obtained by photography.

photograph² *verb trans* to take a photograph of (somebody or something). ➤ *verb intrans* **1** to take a photograph or photographs. **2** to undergo being photographed. ➤➤ **photographable** *adj,* **photographer** /fəˈtografə/ *noun.*

photographic /fohtəˈgrafik/ *adj* **1** relating to, obtained by, or used in photography. **2** capable of retaining vivid impressions; = EIDETIC: *He's got a photographic memory.* ➤➤ **photographically** *adv.*

photography /fəˈtografi/ *noun* the art or process of producing images on a sensitized surface, e.g. a film, by the action of radiant energy, *esp* light: *Photography, because it stops the flow of life, is always flirting with death* — John Berger.

photogravure /ˌfohtohgrəˈvyooə/ *noun* a process for making prints from an intaglio plate prepared by photographic methods, or a picture produced in this way.

photojournalism /fohtohˈjuhnəliz(ə)m/ *noun* journalism which places more emphasis on photographs than on written material. ➤➤ **photojournalist** *noun,* **photojournalistic** /-ˈlistik/ *adj.*

photolyse (*NAmer* **photolyze**) /ˈfohtəliez/ *verb trans* to cause (something) to undergo photolysis.

photolysis /fohˈtoləsis/ *noun* chemical decomposition by the action of radiant energy, *esp* light. ➤➤ **photolytic** /-ˈlitik/ *adj,* **photolytically** /-ˈlitikli/ *adv.*

photolyze /ˈfohtəliez/ *verb trans NAmer* see PHOTOLYSE.

photo messaging *noun* the transmission and reception by mobile phone of photographs taken by means of a built-in camera or camera attachment: compare MULTIMEDIA MESSAGING. ➤➤ **photo message** *noun.*

photometer /fohˈtomitə/ *noun* an instrument for measuring light intensity, illumination, or brightness. ➤➤ **photometric** /-ˈmetrik/ *adj,* **photometrically** /-ˈmetrikli/ *adv,* **photometry** /-tri/ *noun.*

photomicrograph¹ /fohtəˈmiekrəgrahf, -graf/ *noun* a photograph of an object magnified under a microscope. ➤➤ **photomicrographic** /-ˈgrafik/ *adj,* **photomicrographical** /-ˈgrafikl/ *adj,* **photomicrography** /-ˈkrogrəfi/ *noun.*

photomicrograph² *verb trans* to make a photomicrograph of (a specimen, etc).

photomontage /ˌfohtohmonˈtahzh/ *noun* the technique of producing a picture made up of several juxtaposed, overlapping, or superimposed photographs, or a picture produced in this way.

photomosaic /ˌfohtohmohˈzayik/ *noun* a picture consisting of an arrangement of consecutive aerial photographs covering a wide area of ground.

photomultiplier /fohtohˈmultiplie-ə/ *noun* a device that increases the brightness of an electronic image, e.g. a television picture, by multiplying the number of electrons released by photoelectric emission.

photon /ˈfohton/ *noun* a QUANTUM (very small quantity) of electromagnetic radiation. ➤➤ **photonic** /fohˈtonik/ *adj.* [PHOT- + -ON²]

photo-offset *noun* offset printing from photolithographic plates.

photo opportunity *noun* an event staged primarily to give newspaper and magazine photographers a chance to get good pictures of a famous or important person; = PHOTOCALL.

photoperiod /ˈfohtohˈpiəri-əd/ *noun* the relative lengths of alternating periods of lightness and darkness as they affect the growth and maturity of an organism. ➤➤ **photoperiodic** /-ˈodik/ *adj,* **photoperiodically** /-ˈodikli/ *adv,* **photoperiodism** *noun.*

photophobia /fohtohˈfohbi-ə/ *noun* **1** painful sensitiveness to strong light. **2** fear of sunlight or well-lit places. ➤➤ **photophobic** /-bik/ *adj.*

photophore /ˈfohtohfaw/ *noun* a light-emitting organ, *esp* any of the luminous spots on various marine fishes.

photopositive /fohtohˈpozətiv/ *adj* moving or turning towards light.

photorealism /fohtohˈreeliz(ə)m, -ˈriəl-/ *noun* extremely realistic representation of detail as an artistic style, *esp* in painting or sculpture. ➤➤ **photorealist** *noun and adj.*

photoreceptor /ˌfohtohriˈseptə/ *noun* a receptor for light stimuli; a light-sensitive organ or cell. ➤➤ **photoreception** /-sh(ə)n/ *noun,* **photoreceptive** /-tiv/ *adj.*

photosensitise /fohtohˈsensitiez/ *verb trans* see PHOTOSENSITIZE.

photosensitive /fohtohˈsensətiv/ *adj* sensitive or sensitized to radiant energy, *esp* light. ➤➤ **photosensitivity** /-ˈtiviti/ *noun.*

photosensitize *or* **photosensitise** /fohtohˈsensitiez/ *verb trans* to make (something) sensitive, or abnormally sensitive, to the influence of radiant energy, *esp* light. ➤➤ **photosensitization** /-ˈzaysh(ə)n/ *noun.*

photosetting /ˈfohtohseting/ *noun* = PHOTOCOMPOSITION.

photosphere /ˈfohtəsfiə/ *noun* the luminous surface layer of the sun or another star. ➤➤ **photospheric** /-ˈsferik/ *adj.*

Photostat /ˈfohtəstat/ *noun* **1** *trademark* a device for making a photographic copy of written, printed, or graphic material. **2** (*also* **photostat**) a copy made in this way.

photostat *verb trans* (**photostatted, photostatting**) to copy (something) on a Photostat or similar device. ➤➤ **photostatic** /-ˈstatik/ *adj.*

photosynthesis /fohtohˈsinthəsis/ *noun* the synthesis of organic chemical compounds from carbon dioxide using radiant energy, *esp* light; *specif* the formation of carbohydrates in the chlorophyll-containing tissues of plants exposed to light: compare CHEMOSYNTHESIS. ➤➤ **photosynthetic** /-ˈthetik/ *adj,* **photosynthetically** /-ˈthetikli/ *adv.*

photosynthesize *or* **photosynthesise** /fohtohˈsinthəsiez/ *verb trans and intrans* to produce (something) by means of photosynthesis.

phototaxis /fohtoh'taksis/ *noun* the movement of an organism towards or away from light. ➤➤ **phototactic** /-tik/ *adj*, **phototactically** /-tikli/ *adv*.

phototropism /foh'totrəpiz(ə)m, fohtoh'trohpiz(ə)m/ *noun* the turning or curving of an organism, *esp* a plant, or of one of its parts, towards or away from light. ➤➤ **phototropic** /-'tropik, -'trohpik/ *adj*, **phototropically** /-'tropikli, -'trohpikli/ *adv*.

phototypesetting /fohtoh'tiepseting/ *noun* = PHOTOCOMPOSITION. ➤➤ **phototypesetter** *noun*.

phototypography /ˌfohtohtie'pogrəfi/ *noun* = PHOTOCOMPOSITION. ➤➤ **phototypographic** /-'grafik/ *adj*.

photovoltaic /ˌfohtohvol'tayik/ *adj* of or using the generation of an electromotive force when radiant energy such as light falls on the boundary between dissimilar substances in close contact: *a photovoltaic cell; the photovoltaic effect*.

phrasal /'frayzl/ *adj* **1** of a phrase. **2** consisting of a phrase. ➤➤ **phrasally** *adv*.

phrasal verb *noun* a compound verb consisting of a simple verb plus an adverb, a preposition, or both, *esp* one in which the meaning cannot be deduced from the meanings of the words from which it is formed, e.g. *put up with* or *fall out*.

phrase¹ /frayz/ *noun* **1** a group of two or more grammatically related words that do not form a clause, e.g. a preposition with the words it governs. **2** a brief idiomatic or pithy expression; a catchphrase: *She's good at turning a phrase*. **3** a mode or form of speech; diction. **4** a group of musical notes forming a natural unit of melody that is usu three or four bars in length. [via Latin from Greek *phrasis*, from *phrazein* to point out, explain, tell]

phrase² *verb trans* **1** to express (something) in words or in appropriate or telling terms: *a politely phrased rejection*. **2** to divide (music, a part, etc) into melodic phrases.

phrase book *noun* a book containing words and idiomatic expressions of a foreign language and their translation.

phraseology /frayzi'oləji/ *noun* (*pl* **phraseologies**) **1** the phrases used by a particular group, or the way in which they are used: *To be candid, in Middlemarch phraseology, meant, to use an early opportunity of letting your friends know that you did not take a cheerful view of their capacity, their conduct, or their position* — George Eliot. **2** a manner of putting words and phrases together; a style. **3** choice of words. ➤➤ **phraseological** /-'lojikl/ *adj*, **phraseologically** /-'lojikli/ *adv*. [Latin *phraseologia*, from Greek *phrase-*, *phrasis* speech, diction + *-logia* -LOGY]

phrasing *noun* **1** a style of expression; phraseology. **2** the art, act, method, or result of grouping notes into musical phrases.

phratry /'fraytri/ *noun* (*pl* **phratries**) a tribal subdivision. [Greek *phratria*, from *phratēr* member of the same clan, member of a phratry]

phren- *or* **phreno-** *comb. form* forming words, denoting: **1** mind: *phrenology*. **2** diaphragm: *phrenic*. [Greek, from *phren-*, *phrēn* diaphragm, mind]

phrenetic /fri'netik/ *adj archaic* = FRENETIC.

phrenic /'frenik/ *adj* of the diaphragm. [scientific Latin *phrenicus*, from Greek *phren-*, *phrēn* diaphragm, mind]

phreno- *comb. form* see PHREN-.

phrenology /fri'noləji/ *noun* the formerly popular study of the shape of the skull as a supposed indicator of mental faculties and character. ➤➤ **phrenological** /frenə'lojikl, free-/ *adj*, **phrenologically** /frenə'lojikli, free-/ *adv*, **phrenologist** *noun*.

Phrygian /'friji-ən/ *noun* **1** a native or inhabitant of ancient Phrygia in Asia Minor. **2** the ancient language of Phrygia, probably belonging to the Indo-European family. ➤➤ **Phrygian** *adj*.

Phrygian bonnet *noun* = PHRYGIAN CAP.

Phrygian cap *noun* a close-fitting conical cap; = LIBERTY CAP. [because such a cap was worn by the ancient Phrygians]

Phrygian mode *noun* a MODE (fixed arrangement of eight notes) which may be represented on the white keys of the piano on a scale from E to E.

phthalic acid /'(f)thalik/ *noun* an acid obtained by oxidation of various benzene derivatives: formula $C_8H_6O_4$. [short for obsolete *naphthalic acid*, from NAPHTHALENE]

phthisis /'(f)thiesis, 'tiesis/ *noun* (*pl* **phthises** /'(f)thieseez, 'tieseez/) a progressive wasting condition, *esp* lung tuberculosis. [via Latin from Greek *phthisis*, from *phthinein* to waste away]

phut¹ /fut/ *noun* a dull sound as of something bursting. [imitative]

phut² ✳ **go phut** *chiefly Brit, informal* to break or break down: *The bulb's just gone phut*.

pH value *noun* = PH.

phyco- *comb. form* forming words, denoting: seaweed or algae. [Greek *phykos* seaweed]

phycology /fie'koləji/ *noun* the study of algae. ➤➤ **phycological** /-'lojikl/ *adj*, **phycologist** *noun*.

phyl- *or* **phylo-** *comb. form* forming words, denoting: tribe; race; phylum: *phylogenesis*. [Latin from Greek, from *phylē*, *phylon* tribe, race]

-phyl *comb. form* see -PHYLL.

phyla /'fielə/ *noun* pl of PHYLUM.

phylactery /fi'lakt(ə)ri/ *noun* (*pl* **phylacteries**) **1** either of two small square leather boxes containing passages from scripture, traditionally worn on the left arm and forehead by Jewish men during morning weekday prayers. **2** = AMULET. [Middle English *philaterie* via Latin from Greek *phylaktērion* amulet, phylactery, from *phylak-*, *phylax* guard]

phyll- *or* **phyllo-** *comb. form* forming words, denoting: leaf: *phyllotaxy*. [Greek *phyllon* leaf]

-phyll *or* **-phyl** *comb. form* forming nouns, denoting: leaf: *chlorophyll*. [Greek *phyllon* leaf]

phyllo /'feeloh/ *noun* see FILO.

phyllo- *comb. form* see PHYLL-.

phyllode /'filohd/ *noun* a flat expanded leaf stalk that resembles the blade of a foliage leaf and fulfils the same functions. [scientific Latin *phyllodium* from Greek *phyllōdēs* like a leaf, from *phyllon* leaf]

phylloquinone /fieloh'kwinohn, filə-/ *noun* a naturally occurring vitamin found *esp* in green plants; vitamin K_1. [PHYLLO- + *quinone*]

phyllotaxis /filoh'taksis/ *noun* (*pl* **phyllotaxes** /-seez/) = PHYLLOTAXY.

phyllotaxy /filoh'taksi/ *noun* (*pl* **phyllotaxies**) the arrangement of leaves on a stem, or the study of such arrangements. ➤➤ **phyllotactic** /-'taktik/ *adj*. [PHYLLO- + -TAXIS]

-phyllous *comb. form* forming adjectives, with the meaning: having the specified number or type of leaves, leaflets, or leaflike parts: *diphyllous*. [scientific Latin *-phyllus* from Greek *-phyllos*, from *phyllon* leaf]

phylloxera /filok'siərə/ *noun* a plant louse that is destructive to many plants such as grapevines: *Phylloxera vitifoliae*. ➤➤ **phylloxeran** *adj and noun*. [PHYLLO- + Greek *xēros* dry]

phylo- *comb. form* see PHYL-.

phylogenesis /fieloh'jenəsis/ *noun* (*pl* **phylogeneses** /-seez/) **1** the evolutionary history of a type of organism or a genetically related group of organisms, e.g. a species: compare ONTOGENESIS. **2** the history or course of the development of something such as a word or custom. ➤➤ **phylogenetic** /-'netik/ *adj*, **phylogenetically** /-'netikli/ *adv*, **phylogenically** /-nikli/ *adv*.

phylogeny /fi'lojəni/ *noun* (*pl* **phylogenies** /fi'lojəniz/) the evolution of a genetically related group of organisms, e.g. a race or species, or the history of this. ➤➤ **phylogenic** /fieloh'jenik/ *adj*.

phylum /'fieləm/ *noun* (*pl* **phyla** /'fielə/) **1** a major group of related species in the classification of plants and animals. **2** a group of language families or a group of languages more remotely related than those of a family. [scientific Latin, from Greek *phylon* tribe, race]

phys. *abbr* **1** physical. **2** physician. **3** physics. **4** physiological. **5** physiology.

physalis /'fisəlis, 'fie-/ *noun* any of a genus of plants with bell-shaped flowers and balloon-like calyxes (outer part of flower head; see CALYX): genus Physalis. [via Latin from Greek *physallis* bladder; from the shape of the calyx]

physi- *or* **physio-** *comb. form* forming words, with the meanings: **1** nature: *physiography*. **2** physical: *physiotherapy*. [French from Latin, from Greek, from *physis* growth, nature]

physic¹ /'fizik/ *noun archaic* **1** a medicinal preparation, e.g. a drug, *esp* a purgative. **2** medical treatment. [Middle English *physik, phisic* natural science, art of medicine, via Old French *fisique* and Latin *physica*, from Greek *physikē* natural science, from *physikos* of nature, from *physis* growth, nature]

physic[2] *verb trans* (**physicked, physicking**) *archaic* to administer medicine to (somebody), *esp* to purge (them). [Middle English *phisiken*, from *phisik*: see PHYSIC[1]]

physical[1] /'fizikl/ *adj* **1a** having material existence; perceptible, *esp* through the senses, and subject to the laws of nature. **b** of material things: *the physical world.* **2a** of the body: *a physical examination.* **b** concerned or preoccupied with the body and its needs, as opposed to spiritual matters. **c** involving forceful bodily contact: *a physical sport like American football.* **d** involving or enjoying affectionate touching, often of a sexual nature: *He's a very physical person.* **e** *informal* using or involving force and aggression: *If you don't tell us, we're going to have to get physical.* **3a** of sciences such as physics, chemistry, and astronomy. **b** of or involving physics: *physical chemistry.* >> **physically** *adv.* [Middle English, from late Latin *physicalis*, from Latin *physica*: see PHYSIC[1]]

physical[2] *noun* **1** a medical examination of a person's body to determine their health and fitness. **2** (*in pl*) existing stocks or commodities that can be bought and sold and used at the present time, as opposed to futures.

physical anthropology *noun* a branch of anthropology concerned with the comparative study of the physical evolution of human beings and their variation and classification, *esp* through measurement and observation: compare CULTURAL ANTHROPOLOGY. >> **physical anthropologist** *noun.*

physical chemistry *noun* the branch of chemistry concerned with the relationship between the chemical structure of substances and their physical properties.

physical education *noun* instruction in sports, athletic games, and gymnastics for the development and health of the body.

physical geography *noun* geography that deals with the exterior physical features and changes of the earth rather than political boundaries, etc.

physicality /fizi'kaliti/ *noun* intensely physical orientation; predominance of the physical, usu at the expense of the mental, spiritual, or social.

physical jerks *pl noun Brit, informal* strenuous bodily exercises carried out for the sake of health and fitness.

physical science *noun* the natural sciences, such as physics, astronomy, or chemistry, that deal primarily with nonliving materials, or any one of these: compare LIFE SCIENCE. >> **physical scientist** *noun.*

physical therapy *noun NAmer* = PHYSIOTHERAPY.

physical training *noun dated* = PHYSICAL EDUCATION.

physician /fi'zish(ə)n/ *noun* a person skilled in the art of healing; *specif* a doctor of medicine, as opposed to a surgeon. [Middle English *fisicien*, from Old French, from *fisique*: see PHYSIC[1]]

physicist /'fizisist/ *noun* an expert or specialist in physics.

physico- *comb. form* forming words, with the meanings: **1** physical: *physicogeographical.* **2** physical and: *physicochemical.* [via Latin from Greek *physikos* of nature: see PHYSIC[1]]

physics /'fiziks/ *pl noun* **1** (*treated as sing. or pl*) a science that deals with matter and energy and their properties and interactions in such fields as mechanics, heat, electricity, magnetism, atomic structure, etc. **2** (*treated as pl*) the physical properties and phenomena of a particular system. [Latin *physica*: see PHYSIC[1]]

physio /'fizioh/ *noun* (*pl physios*) *Brit, informal* **1** a physiotherapist. **2** = PHYSIOTHERAPY.

physio- *comb. form* see PHYSI-.

physiocrat /'fiziohkrat/ *noun* (*also* **Physiocrat**) a member of a school of political economists founded in 18th-cent. France, characterized chiefly by a belief that government policy should not interfere with the operation of natural economic laws and free trade and that land and its produce is the source of all wealth. >> **physiocracy** /-'okrəsi/ *noun*, **physiocratic** /-'kratik/ *adj.* [French *physiocrate*, from PHYSIO- + -CRAT]

physiognomy /fizi'onəmi/ *noun* (*pl physiognomies*) **1** the facial features, *esp* when revealing qualities of mind or character: *the freshness and candor of their physiognomy* — Walt Whitman. **2** an external aspect; *also* inner character or quality revealed outwardly: *the physiognomy of a political party.* **3** the art of judging character from outward appearance. >> **physiognomic** /,fizi·ə(g)'nomik/ *adj*, **physiognomical** /,fizi·ə(g)'nomikl/ *adj*, **physiognomically** /,fizi·ə(g)'nomikli/ *adv*, **physiognomist** *noun.* [Middle English *phisonomie* via French and Latin from Greek *physiognōmonia*, from

physiognōmōn judging character by the features, from *physis* nature, physique, appearance + *gnōmōn* interpreter]

physiography /fizi'ogrəfi/ *noun* (*pl physiographies*) **1** a description of nature or natural phenomena. **2** physical geography. >> **physiographer** *noun*, **physiographic** /-'grafik/ *adj*, **physiographical** /-'grafikl/ *adj.*

physiol. *abbr* physiology.

physiologic /,fizi·ə'lojik/ *adj* = PHYSIOLOGICAL.

physiological /,fizi·ə'lojikl/ *adj* **1** of physiology. **2** characteristic of or appropriate to an organism's healthy or normal functioning: *This test allows us to determine the physiological level of various substances in the blood.* >> **physiologically** *adv.*

physiology /fizi'oləji/ *noun* **1** the branch of biology that deals with the functions and activities of life or of living matter, e.g. organs, tissues, or cells, and the physical and chemical phenomena involved. **2** the physiological activities of an organism, or part of one, or a particular bodily function: *the physiology of sex.* >> **physiologist** *noun.* [Latin *physiologia* natural science, from Greek PHYSIO- + -LOGY]

physiotherapy /,fizioh'therəpi/ *noun* the treatment of disease, injury, etc by physical and mechanical means, e.g. massage and regulated exercise. >> **physiotherapist** *noun.* [scientific Latin *physiotherapia*, from PHYSIO- + *therapia*: see THERAPY]

physique /fi'zeek/ *noun* the form or structure of a person's body. [French *physique*, literally 'physical, bodily', from Latin *physicus* of nature, from Greek *physikos*: see PHYSIC[1]]

phyt- *or* **phyto-** *comb. form* forming words, denoting: plant: *phytotoxin.* [Greek *phyton* plant, from *phyein* to bring forth]

-phyte *comb. form* forming nouns, denoting: **1** a plant having the characteristic or habitat specified: *saprophyte.* **2** pathological growth: *osteophyte.* >> **-phytic** *comb. form.* [Greek *phyton*: see PHYT-]

phyto- *comb. form* see PHYT-.

phytochemistry /fietoh'kemistri/ *noun* the chemistry of plants, plant processes, and plant products. >> **phytochemical** *adj*, **phytochemist** /'fie-/ *noun.*

phytochrome /'fietəkrohm/ *noun* a compound of a protein with a light-sensitive biological pigment, that exists in two forms, is present in traces in many plants, and plays a role in many developmental processes and in initiating flowering when activated by infrared light.

phytoplankton /fietoh'plangktən/ *noun* planktonic plant life: compare ZOOPLANKTON. >> **phytoplanktonic** /-'tonik/ *adj.*

phytotoxic /fietoh'toksik/ *adj* poisonous to plants. >> **phytotoxicity** /-'sisiti/ *noun.*

phytotoxin /fietoh'toksin/ *noun* **1** a poisonous substance produced by a plant. **2** a substance poisonous to plants.

PI *abbr* **1** Philippine Islands (international vehicle registration). **2** private investigator.

pi[1] /pie/ *noun* (*pl pis* /piez/) **1** the 16th letter of the Greek alphabet (Π, π), equivalent to and transliterated as roman p. **2a** the ratio of the circumference of a circle to its diameter with a value, to eight decimal places, of 3.14159265. **b** the symbol (π) denoting this ratio. [later Greek *pi*, from Greek *pei*, of Semitic origin]

pi[2] *adj Brit, derog, informal* pious. [by shortening]

pi[3] *noun NAmer* see PIE[3].

pi[4] *verb trans NAmer* see PIE[4].

piacular /pie'akyoolə/ *adj formal* **1** making atonement; expiatory. **2** requiring atonement; sinful. [Latin *piacularis*, from *piaculum* sacrificial offering, from *piare* to appease]

piaffe[1] /pi'af/ *verb intrans* said of a horse: *esp* in dressage, to perform a slow trot on the spot with legs raised high. [French *piaffer* to strut]

piaffe[2] *or* **piaffer** /pi'afə/ *noun* the action or an instance of piaffing.

pia mater /,pie·ə 'mahtə, ,pee·ə, 'maytə/ *noun* the thin innermost membrane that envelops the brain and spinal cord. [Latin *pia mater*, literally 'tender mother']

pianism /'pee·əniz(ə)m/ *noun* the art or technique of piano playing, or skill in playing the piano.

pianissimo /pee·ə'nisimoh/ *adj and adv* said of a piece of music: to be performed very softly. [Italian *pianissimo*, superl of *piano*: see PIANO[2]]

pianist /'pee-ənist/ *noun* a person who plays the piano, *esp* a skilled or professional performer.

pianistic /pee-ə'nistik/ *adj* **1** of or characteristic of the piano. **2** skilled in or well adapted to piano playing. ➤➤ **pianistically** *adv.*

piano[1] /pi'anoh/ *noun* (*pl* **pianos**) a large keyboard musical instrument consisting of a large wooden case enclosing steel wire strings that sound when struck by felt-covered hammers operated from a keyboard of black and white keys. [Italian *piano*, short for *pianoforte*: see PIANOFORTE]

piano[2] /pi'ahnoh, 'pyahnoh/ *adj and adv* said of a piece of music: to be performed in a soft or quiet manner. [Italian *piano* soft, from late Latin *planus* smooth, level]

piano accordion *noun* an accordion with a small piano-like keyboard for the right hand. ➤➤ **piano accordionist** *noun.*

pianoforte /pi,anoh'fawti/ *noun formal* a piano.

Word history
Italian *pianoforte* from *piano e forte* soft and loud: see PIANO[2], FORTE[2]. The prototype of the modern pianoforte, originating in Italy in the early 18th cent., was called 'soft-loud' because its mechanism of hammers striking strings allowed its tone to be easily varied. This set it apart from the two keyboard instruments popular at the time: the harpsichord, in which quills pluck the strings, had a loud tone that could scarcely be varied; the clavichord, using a striking or pressing mechanism, had a tone that could be modified to some extent but was always soft.

Pianola /pee-ə'nohlə/ *noun trademark* a mechanical piano operated by the pressure of air through perforations in a paper roll; = PLAYER PIANO. [prob a dimin. of PIANO[1]]

piano roll *noun* the perforated paper roll that operates a player piano.

piassava /pi-ə'sahvə/ *noun* **1** any of several stiff coarse fibres obtained from S American and African palms and used *esp* in making ropes or brushes. **2** any of the trees from which this fibre is obtained: *Attalea funifera*, *Leopoldinia piassaba*, or *Raphia vinifera*. [Portuguese *piassaba* from Tupi *piaçaba*]

piastre (*NAmer* **piaster**) /pi'astə/ *noun* a unit of currency in certain Middle Eastern countries, e.g. Egypt and Syria, worth 100th of the basic monetary unit. [French *piastre* from Italian *piastra* thin metal plate, coin]

piazza /pi'atsə/ *noun* (*pl* **piazzas**) **1** (*pl also* **piazze** /-si/) an open square, *esp* in an Italian town. **2** *chiefly Brit* a covered passageway with one or both sides in the form of open arches. **3** *NAmer, archaic* a veranda. [Italian *piazza* from Latin *platea* broad street]

pibroch /'peebrokh, 'peebrok/ *noun* music for the Scottish Highland bagpipes in the form of a set of martial or mournful variations. [Scottish Gaelic *piobaireachd* pipe-music, from *piobair* piper]

pic /pik/ *noun* (*pl* **pics** or **pix** /piks/) *informal* a photograph. [short for PICTURE[1]]

pica[1] /'piekə/ *noun* **1** a unit of one sixth of an inch (4.23mm) or 12 points used in measuring typographical material. Also called EM. **2** a size of typewriter type providing 10 characters to the linear inch. **3** a former size of printing type equal to 12 point. [prob from medieval Latin *pica*, literally 'magpie', a name given to a 15th-cent. collection of church rules]

pica[2] *noun* the pathological craving for and eating of inappropriate substances, e.g. chalk or ashes. [Latin *pica* magpie]

picador /'pikədaw/ *noun* (*pl* **picadors** or **picadores** /-'dawrayz/) a horseman who in a bullfight prods the bull with a lance to weaken its neck and shoulder muscles. [Spanish *picador*, from *picar* to prick]

picaninny /'pikənini, -'nini/ *noun* (*pl* **picaninnies**) *NAmer* see PICCANINNY.

picaresque /pikə'resk/ *adj* of a type of fiction narrating in loosely linked episodes the adventures of a rogue. [Spanish *picaresco*, from *pícaro* rogue]

picaroon /pikə'roohn/ *noun archaic* a rogue; a roguish unscrupulous adventurer. [Spanish *picarón*, augmentative of *pícaro* rogue]

picayune[1] /pikə'yoohn/ *noun* **1a** a five-cent piece. **b** a small coin of Spanish origin, formerly current in the southern USA. **2** *NAmer, informal* something trivial or somebody unimportant. [French *picaillon* halfpenny, from Provençal *picaioun*, from *picaio* money, from *pica* to jingle]

picayune[2] *adj NAmer, informal* **1** of little value; paltry. **2** petty; small-minded. ➤➤ **picayunish** *adj.*

piccalilli /pikə'lili/ *noun* a hot relish of chopped vegetables, mustard, and spices. [perhaps from PICKLE[1] + CHILLI]

piccaninny (*NAmer* **picaninny** or **pickaninny**) /'pikəni, -'nini/ *noun* (*pl* **piccaninnies** or *NAmer* **picaninnies** or *NAmer* **pickaninnies**) *offensive* a small black child or, in Australia, a small Aboriginal child. [prob modification of Portuguese *pequenino* very little, from *pequeno* small]

piccolo /'pikəloh/ *noun* (*pl* **piccolos**) a small flute whose range is an octave higher than that of an ordinary flute. ➤➤ **piccoloist** *noun.* [Italian *piccolo*, short for *piccolo flauto* small flute]

piccy /'piki/ *noun* (*pl* **piccies**) *informal* a picture or photograph.

pick[1] /pik/ *verb trans* **1** to choose or select (somebody or something): *When choosing between two evils, I always like to pick the one I never tried before* — Mae West. **2a** to remove (a flower or fruit) by plucking it from the plant or tree. **b** to remove the flowers or fruit from (a plant or tree). **3a** to remove (something) bit by bit or one at a time: *A dog was picking the meat from a bone; She stopped to pick hairs off his jacket.* **b** to remove unwanted matter from (the nose or teeth) with a finger or pointed instrument. **4** to eat (food) in small amounts fussily or with little appetite. **5** to pierce or penetrate (something) with a pointed instrument. **6** to loosen (something) or pull it apart with a sharp point. **7** to make (a hole) by digging at a surface. **8** to steal from (somebody's) pocket. **9** to provoke (a quarrel or fight). **10** to pluck the strings of (a guitar or banjo string) with a plectrum or the fingers. **11** to unlock (a lock) with a device other than the key, e.g. a piece of wire. **12** to make (one's) way carefully on foot. ➤ *verb intrans* **1** (+ at) to pull at something repeatedly with the fingers. **2** (+ at) to eat food sparingly and with little appetite. **3** (+ at) to find fault with somebody or something, *esp* in a petty way. ✱ **pick through/over** to sort (a number of items). **pick and choose** to choose the best of something. **pick holes in** to find faults or inadequacies in (something). **pick on** to single (somebody) out for unpleasant or unfair treatment. **pick somebody's brains** to obtain ideas or information from somebody who is well informed. **pick to pieces** to subject (somebody or something) to harsh criticism. ➤➤ **pickable** *adj.* [Middle English *piken*; earlier history unknown]

pick[2] *noun* **1** the act or privilege of choosing or selecting; a choice: *Take your pick.* **2** (*treated as sing. or pl*) the best or choicest: *the pick of the herd.* **3** the portion of a crop gathered at one time: *the first pick of grapes.*

pick[3] *noun* **1** a heavy iron or steel tool with a long wooden handle and a head that is pointed at one or both ends. **2** a toothpick. **3** *informal* a plectrum. [Middle English *pik*, variant of PIKE[6]]

pick[4] *verb trans* to throw (a shuttle) across the loom. [Middle English *pykken*, alteration of *picchen* PITCH[2]]

pick[5] *noun* **1** the act or an instance of throwing the shuttle across a loom. **2** one weft thread taken as a unit of fineness of fabric.

pickaback[1] /'pikəbak/ *adv* = PIGGYBACK[1].

pickaback[2] *noun* = PIGGYBACK[2].

pickaback[3] *adj* = PIGGYBACK[3].

pickaninny /'pikənini, -'nini/ *noun* (*pl* **pickaninnies**) *NAmer* see PICCANINNY.

pickaxe[1] (*NAmer* **pickax**) *noun* = PICK[3] (1). [alteration of Middle English *pikois*, *pikeis* from Old French *picois*, from *pic* pick, from Latin *picus* woodpecker]

pickaxe[2] (*NAmer* **pickax**) *verb trans* to hit or break (something) with a pickaxe.

picked *adj* choice; prime.

picker *noun* **1** a person or machine that picks something, *esp* crops. **2** a person or the part of a loom that threads the shuttle. **3** *informal* a person who plays the guitar or banjo: *He's a great guitar-picker.*

pickerel /'pik(ə)rəl/ *noun* (*pl* **pickerels** or *collectively* **pickerel**) *chiefly Brit, dialect* a young or small pike. [Middle English *pikerel*, dimin. of PIKE[1]]

picket[1] /'pikit/ *noun* **1a** a person or group of people posted by a trade union at a place of work affected by a strike to try to persuade workers not to go in or to prevent them doing so. **b** a person or group of people posted for a demonstration or protest. **2** (*treated as sing. or pl*). **a** a small body of troops detached to guard an army from surprise attack. **b** a detachment kept ready in camp for such duty. **3a** a pointed or sharpened stake or post. **b** (*used before a noun*) consisting of pickets: *a picket fence.* [French *piquet*, from early French *piquer* to prick]

picket[2] *verb* (**picketed, picketing**) ➤ *verb trans* **1a** to post pickets at (a place of work, etc). **b** to walk or stand in front of (a place of work, etc) as a picket. **2a** to guard (an army) with a picket. **b** to post (a detachment of troops) as a picket. **3** to enclose, fence, or fortify (a place) with pickets. **4** to tether (something). ➤ *verb intrans* to serve as a picket. ➤ **picketer** *noun*.

picket line *noun* a line of people picketing a business, organization, etc.

pickings *pl noun* **1** gleanable or eatable fragments; scraps. **2** yield or return for effort expended; *esp* rewards obtained by dishonest or dubious means.

pickle[1] /'pikl/ *noun* **1a** a brine or vinegar solution in which foods, e.g. meat, fish, or vegetables, are preserved. **b** food, e.g. a mixture of chopped vegetables, preserved in a brine or vinegar solution: compare CHUTNEY. **c** (*also in pl*) a vegetable that has been preserved in a brine or vinegar solution, e.g. an onion or *esp* in the USA and Canada, a cucumber. **2** *informal* a difficult or confused situation; a mess: *I could see no way out of the pickle I was in* — Stevenson. **3** any of various solutions, e.g. of acid, used in industrial cleaning or processing. **4** *Brit, informal* a mischievous or troublesome child. [Middle English *pekille*, prob from early Dutch *pekel, peekel*]

pickle[2] *verb trans* to treat, preserve, or clean (something) in or with a pickle.

pickled *adj* **1** preserved in brine or vinegar. **2** *informal* drunk.

picklock *noun* **1** a tool for picking locks. **2** a burglar.

pick-me-up *noun informal* something that stimulates or restores; a tonic.

pick off *verb trans* to aim at and shoot (members of a group one by one).

pick out *verb trans* **1** to select or distinguish (one person or thing) in a group. **2** to make (something) clearly visible, *esp* as distinguished from a background: *The fences were picked out in red.* **3** to play the notes of (a tune) by ear or one by one.

pickpocket *noun* a person who steals from pockets or bags.

pickup *noun* **1a** the act or an instance of picking up. **b** a stop to pick up passengers, goods, etc. **2** somebody or something picked up, e.g.: **a** a hitchhiker or passenger who is given a lift. **b** a temporary casual acquaintance, *esp* one made with the intention of having sex. **3** a light motor truck having an open body with low sides and tailboard. **4a** a device on a record player that converts mechanical movements into electrical signals, or this device and the slender arm to which it is attached. **b** a device on a guitar that converts the vibrations of the strings into electrical signals. **5** a device, e.g. a microphone or a television camera, for converting sound or an image into electrical signals. **6** interference, e.g. to reception, from an adjacent electrical circuit or system.

pick up *verb trans* **1** to take hold of (somebody or something) from the ground or a lower level and lift them up. **2** to take (passengers or goods) into a vehicle. **3** to collect or buy (somebody or something) on one's way. **4a** to acquire (something) casually or by chance: *She picked up an antique vase at a jumble sale.* **b** to acquire (information or knowledge): *I picked up a bit of French while I was abroad.* **c** to be infected with (a germ or disease). **5** to begin a casual relationship with (somebody), often with sexual intentions. **6a** to arrest or apprehend (somebody). **b** to find and follow (a trail). **c** to receive (a radio signal, etc). **d** to hear or understand (something): *I didn't pick up what he said.* **7** to increase (speed). **8a** to resume or continue (a conversation, discussion, etc). **b** (+ on) to question or criticize (somebody): *I'd like to pick you up on something you just said.* **9** *chiefly NAmer* to clean up or tidy (a room). ➤ *verb intrans* **1** to recover or improve: *Business is beginning to pick up again.* **2** to resume after a break; to continue. **3** (+ on) to resume discussion of a point. ✻ **pick oneself up 1** to stand up again after falling. **2** to recover after a setback. **pick up the bill** to accept the cost of or responsibility for something.

pickup truck *noun* = PICKUP (3).

Pickwickian /pik'wiki·ən/ *adj* **1** characteristic of Samuel Pickwick, a character in the novel *Pickwick Papers* by Charles Dickens (d.1870), *esp* in being simple and generous. **2** said of a word or expression: intended or taken in a sense other than the obvious or literal one: *He had used the word in its Pickwickian sense* — Dickens.

picky *adj* (**pickier, pickiest**) fussy or choosy: *She's such a picky eater.* ➤ **pickily** *adv*, **pickiness** *noun*.

picnic[1] /'piknik/ *noun* **1** an informal meal eaten in the open, the food eaten at such a meal, or an outing including such a meal. **2** *informal* a pleasant or amusingly carefree experience: *Don't expect marriage to be a picnic.* **3** *informal* an easily accomplished task or

feat. ➤➤ **picnicky** *adj*. [German *Picknick* from French *pique-nique*, from *piquer* to pick, peck + Old French *nique* something of little value]

picnic[2] *verb intrans* (**picnicked, picnicking**) to have or go on a picnic. ➤➤ **picnicker** *noun*.

pico- *comb. form* forming nouns, denoting: one million millionth (10^{-12}) part of a specified unit: *picogram.* [Spanish *pico* beak, small amount]

picot /'peekoh/ *noun* any of a series of small ornamental loops on ribbon or lace. [French *picot* small point, from *pic* prick, from *piquer* to prick]

picotee /pikə'tee/ *noun* a flower having petals of one basic colour with a margin of another colour, *esp* a carnation having light petals with dark edges. [French *picoté* pointed, from *picoter* to mark with points, from *picot*: see PICOT]

picr- *or* **picro-** *comb. form* forming words, with the meaning: bitter: *picric acid.* [French, from Greek *pikr-, pikro-*, from *pikros* sharp, bitter]

picric acid /'pikrik/ *noun* a strong toxic yellow acid used *esp* in powerful explosives, as a dye, and as an antiseptic: formula $C_6H_3N_3O_7$.

picro- *comb. form* see PICR-.

Pict /pikt/ *noun* a member of the Celtic people who once occupied northern Britain and later became amalgamated with the Scots in AD 843 under Kenneth MacAlpin. [Middle English *Pictes* Picts, from late Latin *Picti*, perhaps from Latin *picti* painted people, from *pictus*: see PICTURE[1]]

Pictish *noun* the language of the Picts. ➤➤ **Pictish** *adj*.

pictogram /'piktəgram/ *noun* = PICTOGRAPH.

pictograph /'piktəgrahf, -graf/ *noun* **1** an ancient or prehistoric drawing or painting, often on a rock wall. **2** any of the symbols used in a system of picture writing such as Chinese or Egyptian hieroglyphics: compare IDEOGRAM, LOGOGRAM. **3** a diagram representing statistical data by pictorial forms. ➤➤ **pictographic** /-'grafik/ *adj*, **pictography** /pik'tografi/ *noun*. [Latin *pictus* (see PICTURE[1]) + -GRAPH]

pictorial[1] /pik'tawri·əl/ *adj* **1** of painting or drawing, or of a painting or drawing: *pictorial perspective.* **2** consisting of or illustrated by pictures: *These paintings are pictorial records of a battle between the Egyptians and the Hittites.* **3** said of language, writing, etc: suggesting or conveying visual images; graphic. ➤➤ **pictorially** *adv*, **pictorialness** *noun*. [late Latin *pictorius*, from Latin *pictor* painter, from *pingere* to paint]

pictorial[2] *noun* a newspaper or magazine with many pictures in it and in which information is conveyed more by the pictures than by text.

picture[1] /'pikchə/ *noun* **1** a design or representation made by painting, drawing, photography, etc. **2a** a mental image: *I have a picture of the house in my mind.* **b** a description so vivid or graphic as to suggest a mental image or give an accurate idea of something: *She painted a vivid picture of life in Victorian England.* **c** a presentation of the relevant or characteristic facts concerning a problem or situation: *The report draws an alarming picture of the economic future.* **3a** an image or copy: *He was the picture of his father.* **b** the perfect example: *She looked the picture of health.* **c** a striking or picturesque sight: *His face was a picture when he heard the news.* **4a** a transitory visible image or reproduction, e.g. on a television screen: *He adjusted the television for a brighter picture.* **b** a cinema film. **c** *chiefly Brit, informal* (*in pl*) the cinema: *What's on at the pictures?* **5** a situation: *Let's just look at the overall political picture.* ✻ **in the picture** *informal* fully informed and up to date. [Middle English from Latin *pictura*, from *pictus*, past part. of *pingere* to paint]

picture[2] *verb trans* **1** to paint, draw, or photograph a representation, image, or visual conception of (somebody or something); to depict (them). **2** to describe (something) graphically in words. **3** to form a mental image of (something); to imagine (it).

picture book *noun* a book, *esp* for young children, that consists wholly or chiefly of pictures.

picture card *noun* a playing card with a picture on it, i.e. a jack, queen, or king: = COURT CARD.

picture hat *noun* a woman's decorated hat with a broad brim.

picture house /hows/ *noun Brit, dated* a cinema.

picture messaging *noun* the transmission and reception of pictures as well as text by mobile phone: compare MULTIMEDIA MESSAGING. ➤➤ **picture message** *noun*.

picture postcard *noun* a postcard with a picture or photograph, typically of a holiday resort or place of interest, on one side.

picture-postcard *adj* picturesque: *picture-postcard villages*.

picture rail *noun* a rail of wood or plaster fixed to the walls of a room for pictures to be hung from.

picturesque /pikchə'resk/ *adj* **1** quaintly or charmingly attractive. **2** evoking striking mental images; vivid: *picturesque language*. ➤➤ **picturesquely** *adv*, **picturesqueness** *noun*. [French *pittoresque* from Italian *pittoresco*, from *pittore* painter, from Latin *pictor*: see PICTORIAL[1]]

picture tube *noun* a cathode-ray tube in a television set, having at one end a screen of luminescent material onto which a beam of electrons is projected, so producing visible images.

picture window *noun* a large single-paned window usu facing an attractive view.

PID *abbr* pelvic inflammatory disease.

piddle[1] /'pidl/ *verb intrans informal* **1** (*usu* + about/around) to act or work in an idle or trifling manner. **2** to urinate. ➤ *verb trans informal* (*usu* + away) to waste (time): *He's just piddling his life away*. ➤➤ **piddler** *noun*. [origin unknown]

piddle[2] *noun informal* **1** urine. **2** the act or an instance of urinating.

piddling *adj informal* trivial or paltry.

piddock /'pidək/ *noun* a bivalve mollusc that bores holes in wood, clay, and rocks: family Pholadidae. [origin unknown]

pidgin /'pijin/ *noun* **1** a language based on two or more languages and used for purposes of communication, *esp* for trade, between people with different native languages: compare CREOLE. **2** (*used before a noun*) being a pidgin that is a form of or is derived from a given language: *pidgin English*. [*Pidgin English*, oriental modification of *business English*]

pi-dog /'piedog/ *noun* see PYE-DOG.

pie[1] /pie/ *noun* a dish consisting of a sweet or savoury filling covered or encased by pastry and baked in a container. ✳ **pie in the sky** *informal* an illusory hope or prospect of future happiness; misplaced optimism. [Middle English, perhaps the same word as PIE[2], the contents of a pie being likened to a collection of objects collected by a magpie]

pie[2] *noun archaic or dialect* **1** a magpie. **2** a variegated animal. [Middle English via French from Latin *pica* magpie]

pie[3] (*NAmer* **pi**) *noun* **1** printers' type that is spilt or mixed. **2** a muddle. [origin unknown]

pie[4] (*NAmer* **pi**) *verb trans* (**pies, pied, pieing** *or* **piing**) **1** to spill or throw (type or typeset matter) into disorder. **2** to mix (things) up; to muddle (them).

piebald[1] /'piebawld/ *adj* **1** said *esp* of a horse: of different colours; *specif* spotted or blotched with different colours, *esp* black and white. **2** composed of incongruous parts; heterogeneous. [PIE[2] + BALD in the sense 'streaked with white']

piebald[2] *noun* a piebald horse or other animal.

piece[1] /pees/ *noun* **1a** a part of a whole, *esp* a part detached, cut, or broken from a whole, or one of the elements from which something is made: *We've lost one of the pieces of this jigsaw; Would you like a piece of cake?* **b** a distinct separate bit or item of something: *There were pieces of paper all over the floor.* **c** an instance or occurrence: *That was a piece of luck!* **d** a portion marked off: *We bought a piece of land to build a house on.* **e** a standard quantity, *esp* of length, weight, or size, in which something is made or sold. **2** an object or individual regarded as a unit of a kind or class; an example: *There were fine teak tables for sale, copied from antique pieces.* **3a** a literary, artistic, dramatic, or musical work. **b** a passage to be recited. **4** a statement of one's opinion, etc; something one wants to say: *I've said my piece and I'll say no more.* **5** a coin, *esp* of a specified value: *a ten-pence piece.* **6a** a small object of some shape used in playing a board game. **b** a chess piece other than a pawn. **7a** a gun: *an artillery piece.* **b** *informal* a firearm. **8** *informal* a person, *esp* a woman: *He said his new neighbour was a tasty piece.* **9a** *Brit, dialect* a snack meal, *esp* one prepared at home and taken to eat at one's place of work. **b** *Scot* a sandwich: *a cheese piece.* **10** *NAmer, informal* a short distance. **11** *Aus, NZ* (*usu in pl*) a fragment of fleece or wool. ✳ **go to pieces** to suffer a mental breakdown; to lose control of oneself, e.g. because of stress, shock, or anger. **in one piece** unharmed; without being damaged: *It was a horrific journey, but we arrived in one piece.* **of a piece** alike; consistent; of the same kind. **piece by piece** by one piece after another; by degrees; in small stages: *They built up the case against him piece by piece.* **take something to pieces** to dismantle something; to reduce (it) to its component parts. **take to pieces** to be able to be dismantled or reduced to component parts. **tear/pull something to pieces** to criticize something severely; to show the faults or flaws in it. **tear somebody to pieces** to criticize somebody harshly. **to pieces** into fragments: *The vase fell to pieces in her hands.* [Middle English from Old French, ultimately of Gaulish origin]

piece[2] *verb trans* **1** (*often* + together) to join (parts of something) into a whole: *He pieced the story together from the accounts of witnesses.* **2** (*often* + up) to repair, renew, or complete (something) by adding pieces; to patch (it). ➤➤ **piecer** *noun*.

pièce de résistance /,pyes də rə'zistanhs (*French* pjɛs də rezistɑ̃s)/ *noun* (*pl* **pièces de résistance** /,pyes/) **1** an outstanding item; a showpiece. **2** the chief dish of a meal. [French *pièce de résistance*, literally 'piece of resistance']

piece goods *pl noun* **1** fabrics made and sold in standard lengths. **2** *chiefly NAmer* fabrics sold from the bolt by the retailer in lengths specified by the customer.

piecemeal[1] *adv* **1** one piece at a time; gradually. **2** in pieces or fragments; apart. [PIECE[1] + *-meal*, from Old English *mǣlum* at a time, from *mael*: see MEAL[1]]

piecemeal[2] *adj* done, made, or accomplished piece by piece or in a fragmentary or unsystematic way.

piece of cake *noun informal* something easily accomplished.

piece of eight *noun* (*pl* **pieces of eight**) a former Spanish coin worth eight reals.

piece of work *noun informal* a person: *The manager's a nasty piece of work.*

piece rate *noun* a system whereby wages are calculated according to a set rate per unit produced.

pièces de résistance /,pyes də 'rɛzistanhs/ *noun pl of* PIÈCE DE RÉSISTANCE.

piecework *noun* work that is paid for at a set rate per unit. ➤➤ **pieceworker** *noun*.

pie chart *noun* a graphical means of showing the composition of a whole, each component being represented by a sector of a circle, the size of which is proportional to the magnitude of the component. [PIE[1]]

piecrust *noun* the baked pastry covering of a pie.

piecrust table *noun* a round table with a decorative edge resembling the edge of a pie crust.

pied /pied/ *adj* having patches of two or more colours.

pied-à-terre /,pyay dah 'teə (*French* pje ta tɛr/ *noun* (*pl* **pieds-à-terre** /,pyay/) a temporary or second lodging, e.g. a flat in a city kept by somebody who lives in the country. [French *pied-à-terre*, literally 'foot on the ground']

piedmont[1] /'peedmont/ *adj* lying or formed at the base of mountains: *piedmont glaciers*. [*Piedmont*, region of Italy at the foot of the Alps]

piedmont[2] *noun* an area of land or a sloping land form at the foot of a mountain or mountains.

pie-dog *noun* see PYE-DOG.

pied piper *noun* (*often* **Pied Piper**) a person who offers strong but delusive enticement.

Word history
named after *The Pied Piper of Hamelin*, title and hero of a poem by Robert Browning d.1889, English poet. The poem recounts a German folk tale about a piper who first rids the town of Hamelin (Hameln, near Hanover) of rats, and then, when payment for this service is refused, leads away the children of the town to a nearby hill, where they disappear through a door never to be seen again.

pieds-à-terre /,pyay dah 'teə/ *noun pl of* PIED-À-TERRE.

pie-eyed *adj informal* drunk. [prob from PIE[4]]

pier /piə/ *noun* **1** a structure extending into navigable water for use as a landing place, promenade, etc. **2** an intermediate support for the adjacent ends of two bridge spans. **3a** a vertical structural support, e.g. for a wall. **b** a short section of wall between two openings. [Middle English *per* from medieval Latin *pera*]

pierce /piəs/ *verb trans* **1** to enter (something) or thrust into (it) sharply or painfully: *The thorn pierced his finger.* **2** to make a hole in or through (something); to perforate (it). **3** to force or make a way into or through (something): *A light pierced the darkness.* **4** to penetrate (something) with the eye or mind; to discern (it). **5** to move or affect the emotions of (somebody), *esp* sharply or painfully: *Grief pierced his heart when he heard of his son's death.* **6** to sound sharply through (quietness, etc): *A shriek pierced the stillness of the evening.* **7** said of cold: to penetrate the clothing, body, etc of (a person): *The cold pierced them to the bone.* ➤ *verb intrans* **1** to force a way into or through something. **2** to penetrate. [Middle English *percen* from Old French *percer*, ultimately from Latin *pertusus*, past part. of *pertundere* to pierce, from *per* through + *tundere* to beat, pound]

pierced *adj* **1** having holes. **2** decorated with perforations.

piercing *adj* **1** penetratingly loud or shrill: *piercing cries.* **2** bright and seeming to be able to see through or into things clearly: *piercing eyes.* **3** penetratingly cold: *a piercing winter wind.* **4** strongly unkind and hurtful: *piercing sarcasm.* **5** perceptive: *a piercing mind.* ➤➤ **piercingly** *adv.*

pier glass *noun* a tall mirror, *esp* one designed to occupy the wall space between two windows.

pieris /ˈpiəris/ *noun* a N American and Asian shrub of the heath family, having panicles (flower heads with flowers on rows of stalks; see PANICLE) of small white urn-shaped flowers: genus *Pieris*. [Latin genus name, literally 'Muse', from *Pieria*, a district in N Greece said to be the home of the Muses]

Pierrot /ˈpiəroh/ *noun* **1** a stock comic character of old French pantomime usu having a whitened face, baggy white clothing, and a pointed hat. **2** (**pierrot**) a member of a group of performers dressed like Pierrot, or of any similar group of entertainers, e.g. at seaside resorts or in public parks. [French *Pierrot*, dimin. of *Pierre* Peter]

pier table *noun* a table designed to be placed against the wall between two windows, often under a PIER GLASS.

pietà /peeayˈtah, pyayˈtah/ *noun* (*often* **Pietà**) a representation of the Virgin Mary mourning over the dead body of Christ. [Italian *pietà* pity, from Latin *pietat-, pietas*: see PIETY]

pietism /ˈpie-ətiz(ə)m/ *noun* **1a** emphasis on personal devotional experience rather than theology. **b** exaggerated religious sentiment. **2** (**Pietism**) a religious movement originating in 17th-cent. Germany stressing Bible study and personal religious experience. ➤➤ **Pietist** *noun,* **pietist** *noun,* **pietistic** /-ˈtistik/ *adj,* **pietistical** /-ˈtistikl/ *adj,* **pietistically** /-ˈtistikli/ *adv.*

piety /ˈpieiti/ *noun* (*pl* **pieties**) **1** the quality or state of being pious; religious devotion. **2** a conventional belief adhered to unthinkingly: *the depressing pieties of the Culture Religion of Modernism —* Leslie Fiedler. **3** an act inspired by piety: *His soul took up again her burden of pieties, masses and prayers and sacraments and mortifications —* James Joyce. **4** dutifulness, *esp* to parents: *filial piety.* [Old French *piete* piety, pity, from Latin *pietat-, pietas*, from *pius* dutiful]

piezo- *comb. form* forming words, denoting: pressure: *piezometer; piezoelectric.* [Greek *piezein* to press]

piezoelectric /pie,eezoh-iˈlektrik, ,peezoh-/ *adj* of or by means of piezoelectricity: *the piezoelectric effect; a cigarette lighter with piezoelectric ignition.* ➤➤ **piezoelectrically** *adv.*

piezoelectricity /pie,eezoh-elikˈtrisiti, ,peezoh-, -ilekˈtrisiti/ *noun* **1** electricity or electric polarity due to pressure, *esp* in a crystalline substance such as quartz. **2** the creation of pressure in such a crystalline substance due to electricity.

piezometer /pie-əˈzomitə/ *noun* an instrument for measuring pressure or compressibility. ➤➤ **piezometric** /pie,eezəˈmetrik/ *adj,* **piezometry** /-tri/ *noun.*

piffle¹ /ˈpifl/ *noun informal* trivial nonsense. [prob imitative]

piffle² *verb intrans informal* to talk or act in a trivial or ineffective way.

piffling *adj informal* trivial or derisory.

pig¹ /pig/ *noun* **1a** *chiefly Brit* any of several species of stout-bodied short-legged omnivorous mammals with a thick bristly skin and a long mobile snout, *esp* the domesticated varieties: family Suidae. **b** *NAmer* a young pig. **c** used in the names of some other animals: *guinea pig.* **d** pork. **2** *informal* a person who is like or suggestive of a pig in habits or behaviour, e.g. in dirtiness, greed, or selfishness: *a male chauvinist pig; He made a pig of himself at the buffet.* **3** *slang, derog* a police officer. **4** *Brit, informal* something difficult or

unpleasant: *Writing dictionaries can be a pig of a job.* **5** a shaped mass of cast crude metal, *esp* iron. ✱ **a pig in a poke** something offered in such a way as to obscure its value, lack of value, or real nature [from the practice of putting a cat in a poke (bag) to fool a customer into thinking they were buying a sucking pig]. **make a pig's ear of something** *informal* to make a mess of something; to do or handle it badly. [Middle English *pigge* from (assumed) Old English *picga*]

pig² *verb* (**pigged, pigging**) ➤ *verb intrans* said of a sow: to give birth to piglets; to farrow. ➤ *verb trans* **1** said of a sow: to give birth to (piglets). **2** *informal* **a** to eat (food) greedily: *She pigged all the cream cakes.* **b** to overindulge (oneself): *He pigged himself on cream cakes.* ✱ **pig it** *informal* to live like a pig, in filth and squalor.

pigeon¹ /ˈpij(ə)n/ *noun* **1** any of numerous birds with a stout body and smooth and compact plumage, many of which are domesticated or live in urban areas: family Columbidae. **2** *NAmer, informal* a person who is easily tricked or swindled; the victim of a trick or swindle. [Middle English from early French *pijon* from late Latin *pipion-, pipio* young bird, from Latin *pipire* to chirp]

pigeon² *noun Brit, informal* a matter of special concern; business: *That's not my pigeon — someone else can deal with it.* [alteration of PIDGIN]

pigeon breast *noun* a deformity of the chest marked by a sharply projecting breastbone. ➤➤ **pigeon-breasted** *adj.*

pigeon chest *noun* = PIGEON BREAST.

pigeonhole¹ *noun* **1** a small open compartment, e.g. in a desk or cabinet, for letters or documents. **2** a neat category which usu fails to reflect actual complexities: *He's got a psychological pigeonhole for every misfit.* **3** a hole for a pigeon to nest in.

pigeonhole² *verb trans* **1** to assign (somebody or something) to a category, *esp* in an overly restrictive way. **2a** to place (mail, etc) in the pigeonhole of a desk or any similar place. **b** to lay (a proposal, etc) aside for the time being.

pigeon-toed *adj* having the toes turned in.

piggery *noun* (*pl* **piggeries**) **1** a place where pigs are kept. **2** dirty, greedy, or nasty behaviour: *male chauvinist piggery.*

piggish *adj* **1** of or resembling a pig, *esp* in being dirty, greedy, bad-mannered etc. **2** *Brit, informal* obstinate. ➤➤ **piggishly** *adv,* **piggishness** *noun.*

piggy¹ *noun* (*pl* **piggies**) **1** used by or to children: a pig, *esp* a little pig. **2** used by or to children: a toe. ✱ **piggy in the middle 1** a children's game in which two people throw something, e.g. a ball, to one another while a person standing between them tries to intercept it. **2** *informal* a person who is caught in an awkward or harmful situation between two others who are in disagreement or conflict: *The union and the managers are in dispute, and we're piggy in the middle.*

piggy² *adj* (**piggier, piggiest**) **1** of or resembling a pig: *The man had little piggy eyes.* **2** like a pig in being dirty, greedy, bad-mannered, etc; = PIGGISH. ➤➤ **piggily** *adv,* **pigginess** *noun.*

piggyback¹ *adv* up on the back and shoulders: *She carried the child piggyback up the stairs.* [alteration of earlier *a pick back, a pick pack,* of unknown origin]

piggyback² *noun* a ride on somebody's back and shoulders: *He gave his injured friend a piggyback.*

piggyback³ *adj* **1** being up on the shoulders and back: *Children love piggyback rides.* **2** being or relating to something carried as an extra load on the back of a vehicle, e.g. an aircraft. **3** in medicine, denoting a type of heart transplant which leaves the patient's own heart functioning along with the transplanted heart.

piggy bank *noun* a box for a child to collect and keep money in, often in the shape of a pig.

pigheaded *adj* obstinate; stubborn. ➤➤ **pigheadedly** *adv,* **pigheadedness** *noun.*

pig-ignorant *adj informal* **1** extremely ignorant. **2** very stupid: *That was a pig-ignorant thing to do.*

pig iron *noun* crude iron from the blast furnace, before refining.

pig lead *noun* lead cast in pigs.

piglet /ˈpiglit/ *noun* a young pig.

pigmeat *noun* the meat of a pig, i.e. pork, ham, or bacon.

pigment¹ /ˈpigmənt/ *noun* **1** a substance that colours other materials, *esp* a powdered substance that is mixed with a liquid in which it is relatively insoluble and is used to colour paints, inks, plastics, etc. **2** any of various colouring matters in animals and plants. ➤➤ **pigmentary** /-t(ə)ri/ *adj.* [Latin *pigmentum*, from *pingere* to paint]

pigment² /pig'ment/ *verb trans* to colour (something) with pigment, or as if with pigment.

pigmentation /pigmən'taysh(ə)n/ *noun* **1** coloration with or deposition of pigment in an animal or plant. **2** discoloration of body tissue caused by excessive deposition of pigment.

pigmy /'pigmi/ *noun* (*pl* **pigmies**) see PYGMY.

pignut *noun* **1a** a common Eurasian plant of the carrot family, with edible tubers; = EARTHNUT: *Conopodium majus*. **b** one of these tubers. **2** *chiefly NAmer*. **a** any of several hickory trees with bitter-flavoured nuts: genus *Carya*. **b** the nut of the pignut.

pig out *verb intrans informal* (*often* + on) to eat a large amount of food: *We pigged out on doughnuts and cream cakes*.

pigpen *noun NAmer* a pigsty.

pigskin *noun* **1** the skin of a pig, or leather made from the skin of a pig. **2** *NAmer, informal* a football.

pigsticking *noun* the hunting of wild boar on horseback with a spear. ➤➤ **pigsticker** *noun*.

pigsty *noun* (*pl* **pigsties**) **1** an enclosure with a covered shed for pigs. **2** a dirty, untidy, or neglected place.

pigswill /'pigswil/ *noun* waste food fed to pigs.

pigtail *noun* **1a** a tight plait of hair, *esp* when worn singly at the back of the head. **b** either of two bunches of hair worn loose or plaited at either side of the head, *esp* by young girls. **2** a thin twist of tobacco. ➤➤ **pigtailed** *adj.*

pika /'piekə, 'peekə/ *noun* any of various species of small tailless mammals related to the rabbits, that are found, mostly in mountainous regions, in Asia, E Europe, and western N America: genus *Ochotona*. [Tungusic *piika*]

pike¹ /piek/ *noun* (*pl* **pikes** *or collectively* **pike**) **1** a large long-snouted bony fish widely distributed in cooler parts of the N hemisphere and valued for food and as a game fish: *Esox lucius*. **2** any of various fish related to or resembling the pike. [Middle English, from *pike* pikestaff, spike; from the shape of its head]

pike² *noun* a weapon consisting of a long wooden shaft with a pointed steel head that was used by foot soldiers until superseded by the bayonet. [early French *pique*, from *piquer* to prick, ultimately from Latin *picus* woodpecker]

pike³ *verb trans* formerly, to attack, pierce, or kill (somebody) with a pike.

pike⁴ *noun* a body position, e.g. in diving, in which the hands touch the toes or clasp the legs at the knees, the hips are bent forward, and the knees are straight. ➤➤ **piked** *adj.* [prob from PIKE¹]

pike⁵ *noun NAmer* = TURNPIKE.

pike⁶ *noun* a point or spike. [Old English *pīc*]

pike⁷ *noun Brit* a mountain or hill, *esp* in the Lake District, with a peaked summit. [Middle English, perhaps of Scandinavian origin]

pike⁸ *verb intrans NAmer, Aus, NZ, informal* (*usu* + on/out) to let somebody down by avoiding doing something or failing to do it: *He was supposed to be giving us a hand but he's piked on us.* [orig in the sense 'to go away', perhaps from *pikestaff*, a pilgrim's staff, with the idea of taking up the staff when setting out]

pikelet /'pieklit/ *noun Brit, dialect* a crumpet. [by shortening and alteration from earlier *bara-picklet*, from Welsh *bara pyglyd* pitchy bread]

pikeman *noun* (*pl* **pikemen**) an infantry soldier armed with a pike.

pikeperch *noun* (*pl* **pikeperches** *or collectively* **pikeperch**) any of several species of carnivorous freshwater fishes of the perch family that resemble pikes: genus *Stizostedion*.

piker *noun NAmer, Aus, NZ, informal* **1** a cautious gambler who makes only small bets. **2** a mean or miserly person. **3** a person who does things in a small or trivial way. **4** a shirker; a person who lets others down. [PIKE⁸]

pikestaff *noun* **1** formerly, a spiked staff for use on slippery ground. **2** formerly, the staff of a foot soldier's pike.

pil- *or* **pili-** *or* **pilo-** *comb. form* forming words, denoting: hair: *piliferous*. [Latin *pilus* hair]

pilaf *or* **pilaff** /'peelaf, 'pilaf/ *or* **pilau** /'peelow, pi'low/ *or* **pilaw** /pi'law/ *noun* a dish of seasoned rice or wheat, with meat, vegetables, etc. [Persian and Turkish *pilāv*]

pilaster /pi'lastə/ *noun* a shallow pier or a flat representation of a usu classical column in shallow relief projecting slightly from a wall. [early French *pilastre* from Italian *pilastro* from Latin *pila* pillar]

pilau /'peelow, pi'low/ *or* **pilaw** /pi'law/ *noun* see PILAF.

pilchard /'pilchəd/ *noun* **1** a food fish of the herring family that occurs in large schools along the coasts of Europe: *Sardina pilchardus*. **2** any of a number of sardines related to the pilchard: genus *Sardinops* and other genera. [origin unknown]

pile¹ /piel/ *noun* **1a** a quantity of things heaped together. **b** (*also in pl*) a large quantity, number, or amount: *There's a pile of stuff still to be read; She's got piles of friends.* **c** a heap of wood for burning a corpse or a sacrifice; = PYRE. **2** a great amount of money; a fortune: *Now that he has made his pile, he can live in luxury.* **3** a large building or group of buildings: *They live in a large Elizabethan pile in the country.* **4** a nuclear reactor. **5** a vertical series of alternate discs of two dissimilar metals, e.g. copper and zinc, separated by discs of cloth or paper moistened with an electrolyte for producing an electric current. [Middle English via French from Latin *pila* pillar]

pile² *verb trans* **1** (*often* + up) to lay or place (things) in a pile. **2** to put or heap (things) in large quantities: *She piled potatoes on his plate.* ➤ *verb intrans* (+ into/out of) to get into or out of a vehicle in a confused rush: *The children piled into the car.* ✳ **pile into** said of a vehicle: to crash into (something). **pile it on** *informal* to exaggerate.

pile³ *noun* **1** a soft raised surface on a fabric or carpet, consisting of cut threads or loops. **2** soft hair, down, fur, or wool. ➤➤ **piled** *adj.* [Middle English via French from Latin *pilus* hair]

pile⁴ *noun* a beam of timber, steel, reinforced concrete, etc driven into the ground to carry a vertical load. [Old English *pīl* pointed stake, arrow, ultimately from Latin *pilum* javelin]

pile⁵ *verb trans* to drive piles into (the ground). ➤➤ **piling** *noun.*

pilea /'pieli·ə, 'pil-/ *noun* pl of PILEUM.

pileate /'pieli·ət, -ayt, 'pil-/ *adj* **1** said of birds: crested. **2** said of fungi: having a cap. [Latin *pileatus* wearing a cap, from *pileus* felt cap]

pileated /'pieliaytid, 'pil-/ *adj* = PILEATE.

pile-driver *noun* a machine for driving piles into the ground.

pilei /'pieliie/ *noun* pl of PILEUS.

piles /'pielz/ *pl noun* haemorrhoids. [Middle English from Latin *pila* ball, from the spherical shape of an external haemorrhoid]

pileum /'pieli·əm, 'pil-/ *noun* (*pl* **pilea** /'pieli·ə, 'pil-/) the top of a bird's head from the bill to the base of the skull. [scientific Latin from Latin *pilleum, pileum* felt cap, variant of *pilleus, pileus*]

pile up *verb intrans* **1** to accumulate: *The work had piled up over the holidays.* **2** *informal* said of vehicles: to crash into one another.

pile-up *noun informal* a collision involving usu several motor vehicles and causing damage or injury.

pileus /'pieli·əs/ *noun* (*pl* **pilei** /'pieliie/) the cap of many fungi, e.g. mushrooms. [Latin *pileus, pilleus* felt cap]

pilewort *noun* any of a number of plants, such as the lesser celandine, once thought to be a remedy for piles.

pilfer /'pilfə/ *verb trans and intrans* (**pilfered, pilfering**) to steal (items of little value) stealthily in small amounts. ➤➤ **pilferage** /-rij/ *noun,* **pilferer** *noun.* [early French *pelfrer,* from *pelfre* booty]

pilgrim /'pilgrim/ *noun* **1** a person making a pilgrimage. **2** *archaic or literary* a traveller. [Middle English via Old French from late Latin *pelegrinus,* alteration of Latin *peregrinus* foreigner: see PEREGRINATION]

pilgrimage¹ /'pilgrimij/ *noun* **1** a journey to a shrine or sacred place as an act of devotion, in order to acquire spiritual merit, or as a penance. **2** a long journey or search undertaken for sentimental reasons, out of duty, as a process of self-discovery, etc: *Real love is a pilgrimage* — Anita Brookner. **3** the course of life on earth.

pilgrimage² *verb intrans* to go on a pilgrimage.

Pilgrim Fathers *pl noun* (**the Pilgrim Fathers**) the English colonists who settled at Plymouth, Massachusetts, USA, in 1620.

pili- *comb. form* see PIL-.

piliferous /pieˈlifərəs/ *adj* said of a leaf, etc: covered in hair or having a hairy or hairlike tip.

Pilipino /piləˈpeenoh/ *noun* the Tagalog-based official language of the Philippines, archipelago in the S China Sea. [Pilipino, from Spanish *Filipino* Philippine]

pill[1] /pil/ *noun* **1a** a small solid mass of medicine to be swallowed whole. **b** (**the Pill**) an oral contraceptive in the form of a pill, taken daily by a woman over a monthly cycle or 21 days of a monthly cycle. **2** something repugnant or unpleasant that must be accepted or endured: *The loss of salary was a bitter pill to swallow.* **3** something resembling a pill in size or shape. **4** *NAmer, informal* a disagreeable or tiresome person. [Latin *pilula*, dimin. of *pila* ball]

pill[2] *verb trans* to dose (a person or animal) with pills. ➤ *verb intrans* said of a fabric: to become rough with or mat into little balls of fibre: *Brushed woollens often pill.*

pillage[1] /ˈpilij/ *noun* **1** the act or an instance of looting or plundering, *esp* in war. **2** something taken as booty. [Middle English from early French, from *piller* to plunder, from *peille* rag, from Latin *pilleum, pilleus* felt cap]

pillage[2] *verb trans and intrans* **1** to plunder (a place) ruthlessly; to loot (it). **2** to take (something) as plunder. ➤➤ **pillager** *noun*.

pillar[1] /ˈpilə/ *noun* **1a** a firm upright support for a superstructure. **b** an ornamental column or shaft. **c** anything like a pillar in shape: *a pillar of cloud.* **2** a person perceived as a prop or mainstay of their class, group, etc: *We are peers of highest station, paragons of legislation, pillars of the British nation* — W S Gilbert. **3** a solid mass of coal, ore, etc left standing to support a mine roof. ✳ **from pillar to post** from one place or one situation to another. [Middle English via Old French from medieval Latin *pilare*, from Latin *pila*]

pillar[2] *verb trans* (**pillared, pillaring**) to support or decorate (a building) with or as if with pillars.

pillar box *noun* a red pillar-shaped public postbox.

pillar-box red *adj* of a vivid scarlet colour. ➤➤ **pillar-box red** *noun.*

pillbox *noun* **1** a box for pills, *esp* a shallow round box made of pasteboard. **2** a small low concrete weapon emplacement. **3** a small round brimless hat with a flat crown and straight sides, worn *esp* by women.

pillion[1] /ˈpilyən/ *noun* a saddle or seat for a passenger on a motorcycle or motor scooter. [orig in the sense 'light saddle'; Scottish Gaelic *pillean* or Irish Gaelic *pillín*, dimin. of *peall* covering, couch]

pillion[2] *adv* on a pillion, or as if on a pillion: *riding pillion.*

pilliwinks /ˈpiliwingks/ *pl noun* an old instrument of torture that crushed the victim's fingers. [Middle English *pyrwykes, pyrewinkes*; earlier history unknown]

pillock /ˈpilək/ *noun Brit, informal* a stupid or objectionable person. [English dialect *pill, pilluck, pillick* penis, of Scandinavian origin]

pillory[1] /ˈpiləri/ *noun* (*pl* **pillories**) **1** a device for publicly punishing offenders, consisting of a wooden frame with holes to hold the head and hands. **2** any means for exposing a person to public scorn or ridicule. [Middle English from Old French *pilori, pellori*, prob from Latin *pila* pillar]

pillory[2] *verb trans* (**pillories, pilloried, pillorying**) **1** to put (somebody) in a pillory. **2** to expose (somebody) to public contempt, ridicule, or scorn.

pillow[1] /ˈpiloh/ *noun* **1** a usu rectangular cloth container filled with soft material such as feathers or synthetic fibre and used to support the head of a reclining or sleeping person. **2** something resembling a pillow, *esp* in form, such as a padded support used in lace-making. [Old English *pyle, pylu*, ultimately from Latin *pulvinus* cushion, pillow]

pillow[2] *verb trans* **1** to rest or lay (something) on a pillow, or as if on a pillow. **2** to serve as a pillow for (something).

pillowcase *noun* a removable washable cover, *esp* of cotton or nylon, for a pillow.

pillow lace *noun* lace worked with bobbins over a padded support: compare NEEDLEPOINT.

pillow lava *noun* lava solidified in rounded masses.

pillow slip *noun* = PILLOWCASE.

pillow talk *noun* intimate conversation in bed between lovers, often as exploited by secret agents masquerading as escorts.

pilo- *comb. form* see PIL-.

pilocarpine /pielohˈkahpeen/ *noun* a chemical compound that is obtained from the leaves of the jaborandi shrub and is used *esp* in eyedrops to contract the pupil of the eye. [Latin *Pilocarpus*, genus name of jaborandi shrub]

pilose /ˈpielohs/ *adj* said of leaves, etc: covered with soft hair. ➤➤ **pilosity** /pieˈlositi/ *noun.* [Latin *pilosus*, from *pilus* hair]

pilot[1] /ˈpielət/ *noun* **1** a person who handles or is qualified to handle the controls of an aircraft or spacecraft. **2** a person who is qualified and usu licensed to conduct a ship into and out of a port or in specified waters. **3** a trial run of a project or a trial programme on radio or television, e.g. to test public opinion or reaction. **4** a piece that guides a tool or machine part. **5** (*used before a noun*) serving as a guide, activator, or trial: *pilot holes; pilot lamps; a pilot scheme.* **6** *archaic* a guide or leader. ➤➤ **pilotless** *adj.* [early French *pilote* from medieval Latin *pilota*, alteration of *pedota*, ultimately from Greek *pēdon* oar]

pilot[2] *verb trans* (**piloted, piloting**) **1a** to act as pilot of (an aircraft, spacecraft, etc). **b** to direct the course of (a ship). **2** to test (a product, programme idea, etc) by means of a pilot. **3** to guide, lead, or conduct (a project, person, etc) over a difficult course.

pilotage /ˈpielətij/ *noun* **1** the piloting of a ship, aircraft, spacecraft, etc. **2** the fee paid to a ship's pilot. **3** the navigation of an aircraft by direct observation of landmarks and use of charts.

pilot balloon *noun* a small unmanned balloon sent up to show the direction and speed of the wind.

pilot-cloth *noun* a thick blue woollen cloth used *esp* for seamen's coats.

pilot fish *noun* a small oceanic fish of warm and tropical seas that is marked with distinctive dark-coloured vertical bands and often swims in the company of a large fish, *esp* a shark: *Naucrates ductor.*

pilothouse /ˈpielətˌhows/ *noun* a WHEELHOUSE (place for steering and navigational equipment) on a ship.

pilot lamp *noun* = PILOT LIGHT (1).

pilot light *noun* **1** an indicator light showing whether power is on or where a switch or circuit breaker is located. **2** a small permanent flame used to ignite gas at a burner, e.g. on a gas cooker or a central-heating boiler.

pilot officer *noun* an officer of the lowest rank in the Royal Air Force.

Pils /pilz, pils/ *noun* (*pl* **Pils**) a Pilsner, or any lager beer of a similar type.

Pilsner *or* **Pilsener** /ˈpilznə, ˈpilsnə/ *noun* a light beer with a strong flavour of hops. [German *Pilsner* of *Pilsen* (now Plzen), city in the Czech Republic, where it was first brewed]

pilule /ˈpilyoohl/ *noun* a little pill. ➤➤ **pilular** *adj.* [early French from Latin *pilula*: see PILL[1]]

pimento /piˈmentoh/ *noun* (*pl* **pimentos**) **1** see PIMIENTO. **2** = ALLSPICE. [Spanish *pimiento* allspice, pepper, from late Latin *pigmenta*, pl of *pigmentum* plant juice, from Latin: see PIGMENT[1]]

pi-meson /ˈpie meez(ə)n/ *noun* = PION. [*pi*, representing the initial letter of *primary radiation*]

pimiento /piˈmyentoh/ *or* **pimento** /piˈmentoh/ *noun* (*pl* **pimientos** *or* **pimentos**) any of various sweet peppers with a mild sweet flavour that are used *esp* as a garnish and as a stuffing for olives. [Spanish *pimiento*: see PIMENTO]

pimp[1] /pimp/ *noun* **1a** a man who solicits clients for a prostitute or brothel and takes some of their earnings. **b** a person who supplies or procures whatever is needed to satisfy another person's lusts or vices. **2** *Aus, informal* an informer. [origin unknown]

pimp[2] *verb intrans* to act as a pimp.

pimpernel /ˈpimpənel/ *noun* any of several species of plants of the primrose family, such as the scarlet pimpernel: genera *Anagallis* and *Lysimachia*. [Middle English *pimpernele* via French from late Latin *pimpinella*, a medicinal herb, perhaps from Latin *piper*: see PEPPER[1]]

pimple /ˈpimpl/ *noun* **1** a small solid inflamed elevation of the skin, usu containing pus. **2** any swelling or protuberance like a pimple. ➤➤ **pimpled** *adj*, **pimply** *adj.* [Middle English *pinple*, of Germanic origin]

PIN /pin/ *abbr* = PIN NUMBER.

pin[1] /pin/ *noun* **1a** a small thin pointed piece of metal with a head used *esp* for fastening cloth, paper, etc. **b** = SAFETY PIN. **c** an ornament or badge fastened to clothing with a pin. **d** a type of small nail: *a panel pin.* **2a** a relatively long and slender piece of solid material, e.g. wood or metal, used for fastening separate articles together, as a safety catch, or as a support. **b** something resembling a pin, *esp* in slender elongated form: *a rolling pin.* **3a** any of the bottle-shaped wooden pieces constituting the target in various games, e.g. skittles and tenpin bowling. **b** the staff of the flag marking a hole on a golf course. **c** the peg at which a quoit is pitched. **4** a projecting metal bar on a plug that is inserted into a socket. **5** a wooden peg set in the head of a stringed instrument, by means of which the tension of a string can be adjusted. **6** *informal* (*usu in pl*) a leg: *He's still a bit wobbly on his pins.* **7** something of small value; a trifle. **8** in chess, a move that prevents a piece from moving away from the king or another more valuable piece, or the position of the piece that is prevented from moving. [Old English *pinn*]

pin² *verb trans* (**pinned, pinning**) **1** to fasten or attach (something) with a pin or pins. **2** to hold (somebody or something) firmly so they cannot move. **3** in chess, to make (an opposing piece) unable to move without exposing the king to check or a valuable piece to capture. ✳ **pin one's hopes on** to rely on completely. **pin something on** to assign the blame or responsibility for something on (somebody or something).

pina colada /ˌpeenə kəˈlahdə/ *or* **piña colada** /ˌpeenyə, ˌpeenə/ *noun* a drink made from rum, coconut milk, and pineapple juice. [Spanish *piña colada*, literally 'strained pineapple']

pinafore /ˈpinəfaw/ *noun Brit* **1** an apron, usu with a bib. **2** a sleeveless dress designed to be worn over a blouse or sweater. [PIN² + AFORE, because originally the apron bib was pinned to the front of the wearer's dress]

pinafore dress *noun* = PINAFORE (2).

pinball *noun* a game in which a ball is propelled across a sloping surface at pins and targets that score points if hit.

pinball machine *noun* an amusement device for playing pinball and automatically recording the score.

pinboard *noun* a flat board made of, or having a covering layer of, cork, on which messages, memos, and photographs can be pinned.

pince-nez /ˈpans nay, ˈpins (*French* pɛ̃s ne)/ *noun* (*pl* **pince-nez**) glasses clipped to the nose by a spring. [French *pince-nez*, from *pincer* to pinch + *nez* nose]

pincer /ˈpinsə/ *noun* **1a** (*in pl*) an instrument having two short handles and two grasping jaws working on a pivot and used for gripping things. **b** the front claw of a lobster, crab, etc, resembling a pair of pincers. **2** either part of a two-pronged attack aiming to surround an enemy position. ⟫⟫ **pincerlike** *adj.* [Middle English *pinceour*, from early French *pincier* to PINCH¹]

pinch¹ /pinch/ *verb trans* **1a** to squeeze (something) tightly and usu painfully between the finger and thumb or between the jaws of an instrument. **b** to squeeze or compress (something) painfully: *These shoes pinch my toes.* **2** *informal* to steal (something). **3** *slang* said of the police: to arrest (somebody). **4a** to cause physical or mental pain to (somebody or something). **b** (*usu in passive*) to cause (somebody, *esp* their face) to appear thin or shrunken. **c** to cause (a plant, etc) to shrivel or wither. **5** (*usu* + back/off/out) to prune the tip of (a plant or shoot), usu to correct growth or induce branching. **6** to subject (somebody) to strict economy or deprivation. **7** to sail (a ship) too close to the wind. ⟫ *verb intrans* **1** to be too tight, *esp* painfully so: *My new shoes pinch.* **2** to be frugal: *They have to pinch and save to live.* **3** said of a ship: to sail too close to the wind. [Middle English *pinchen*, from Old French *pinchier, pincier*]

pinch² *noun* **1a** an act of pinching; a squeeze. **b** as much as may be taken between the finger and thumb: *a pinch of snuff.* **c** a very small amount. **2** (**the pinch**). **a** a critical juncture; an emergency: *When it comes to the pinch, human beings are heroic* — George Orwell. **b** pressure or stress: *when the pinch of foreign competition came at last* — G M Trevelyan. **c** hardship; privation: *After a year of sanctions, they began to feel the pinch.* **3** *slang* a robbery. **4** *slang* a raid or arrest made by the police. ✳ **at a pinch** in an emergency.

pinchbeck¹ /ˈpinchbek/ *noun* **1** an alloy of copper and zinc used *esp* to imitate gold in jewellery. **2** something sham or counterfeit. [named after Christopher *Pinchbeck* d.1732, English watchmaker, who invented the alloy]

pinchbeck² *adj* **1** made of pinchbeck. **2** sham, counterfeit, or imitative.

pincushion *noun* a small cushion in which pins are stuck ready for use, *esp* in sewing.

pin down *verb trans* **1** to force (somebody) to be decisive or explicit about their intentions. **2** to define or categorize (something) clearly: *She had a feeling of unease that was difficult to pin down.* **3** to restrict the movement of (an enemy or fugitive) by surrounding them or firing on them etc.

pine¹ /pien/ *noun* **1a** any of numerous species of coniferous evergreen trees which have long slender needles: genus *Pinus*: compare FIR. **b** any of a number of related or similar but unrelated trees. **2** the straight-grained white or yellow wood of a pine. ⟫⟫ **piney** *adj,* **piny** *adj.* [Old English *pīn* from Latin *pinus*]

pine² *verb intrans* **1** (*often* + away) to lose vigour or health, e.g. through grief; to languish. **2** (+ for) to yearn intensely and persistently, *esp* for something unattainable; to long for it: *pining for her lost youth.* [Old English *pīnian* to suffer, cause suffering to, ultimately from Latin *poena*: see PAIN¹]

pineal body /ˈpiniˈal/ *noun* a small appendage of the brain of most vertebrates that has the structure of an eye in a few reptiles and that secretes melatonin and other hormones. [French *pinéal* from Latin *pinea* pinecone, from the shape of the gland]

pineal gland *noun* = PINEAL BODY.

pineapple *noun* **1a** a large oval prickly fruit with succulent yellow flesh. **b** the tropical plant with rigid spiny leaves and a dense head of small flowers, related to the grasses, lilies, and orchids, that bears this fruit: *Ananas comosus.* **2** *informal* a hand grenade. [Middle English *pinappel* pinecone, from *pin, pine* PINE¹ + *appel* APPLE, fruit]

pineapple weed *noun* a European or North American plant of the daisy family with small rounded heads of yellow florets (tiny flowers; see FLORET) without rays (petal-like parts; see RAY¹) that smell of pineapple when crushed: the European *Matricaria matricarioides* and the North American *Matricaria discoidea.*

pinecone *noun* a cone of a pine tree.

pine kernel *noun* = PINE NUT.

pine marten *noun* a slender Eurasian marten with a yellowish patch on the chest and throat: *Martes martes.*

pine nut *noun* the edible seed of any of various chiefly western N American pine trees.

pineta /pieˈneetə/ *noun* pl of PINETUM.

pinetum /pieˈneetəm/ *noun* (*pl* **pineta** /-tə/) a plantation of pine trees or other conifers, *esp* an ornamental one or one used for botanical research. [Latin *pinetum*, from *pinus* PINE¹]

pin feather *noun* an immature feather still encased or partially encased in a white horny sheath and before its veins have expanded.

pinfold¹ *noun* a pound for stray animals, *esp* cattle. [Old English *pundfald*, from *pund-* POUND⁴ + *fald* FOLD³]

pinfold² *verb trans* to collect or confine (a stray animal or animals) in a pinfold or similar enclosure.

ping¹ /ping/ *noun* a sharp ringing sound. [imitative]

ping² *verb intrans* to make a sharp ringing sound. ⟫ *verb trans* **1** to cause (something) to make a sharp ringing sound. **2** *NAmer* = PINK⁵. ⟫⟫ **pinger** *noun.* [imitative]

pingin /ˈpingˈgin/ *noun* (*pl* **pingin**) a unit of currency in Ireland, worth 100th of a punt.

Ping-Pong /ˈping pong/ *noun trademark* = TABLE TENNIS. [imitative]

pinhead *noun* **1** the head of a pin. **2** something very small or insignificant. **3** *informal* a stupid person. ⟫⟫ **pinheaded** *adj,* **pinheadedness** *noun.*

pinhole *noun* a very small hole made with, or as if with, the point of a pin.

pinhole camera *noun* a photographic camera with a minute aperture and no lens.

pinion¹ /ˈpinyən/ *noun* **1** the section of a bird's wing where the flight feathers grow. **2** *literary* a bird's feather; a quill. ⟫⟫ **pinioned** *adj.* [Middle English via early French *pignon* from Latin *pinna* feather]

pinion² *verb trans* (**pinioned, pinioning**) **1a** to disable or restrain (somebody) by holding or binding their arms. **b** to hold or bind (a person's arms) in order to disable or restrain them. **c** to shackle (somebody or something). **2** to restrain (a bird) from flight, *esp* by cutting off the pinion of a wing.

pinion³ *noun* a gear with a small number of teeth designed to mesh with a larger gear wheel or rack. [French *pignon* from *peigne* comb, from Latin *pecten*]

pink¹ /pingk/ *adj* **1** of a colour midway between red and white: *a pink rosy complexion*. **2** said of a person or their political views: slightly left of centre. **3** relating to homosexuals or homosexuality. **4** said of a fox-hunter's coat: scarlet. ✴ **turn/go pink** to blush. ➤➤ **pinkish** *adj*, **pinkly** *adv*, **pinkness** *noun*. [from PINK³, and orig used in describing the flower. The noun is earlier, and may be from 'pink eye': see PINK³]

pink² *noun* **1a** any of various shades of colour midway between red and white. **b** pale red fabric, clothes, paint, etc. **2a** a fox-hunter's scarlet coat, or the colour of it. **b** a fox-hunter wearing this type of coat. ✴ **in the pink** in good health: *He looks in the pink, despite his recent operation*. **2** said of a business, economy, etc: flourishing or prospering. **3** in the very best of condition, health, etc: *The racehorses look in the pink of condition*. [perhaps from *pink eye*: see PINK³. Recorded earlier than PINK¹]

pink³ *noun* **1** any of various species of plants related to the carnation and widely grown for their attractive and sometimes scented flowers: genus *Dianthus*. **2** a pink, red, white, or variegated flower of one of these plants. [from Middle English *pink* small, of unknown origin, in *pink eye* a small or half-shut eye, which the flowers resemble]

pink⁴ *verb trans* **1** to cut a zigzag pattern on the edge of (fabric) to prevent fraying. **2** to decorate (leather or something made of leather) with a perforated pattern. **3** *dated* to stab, pierce, or nick (something or somebody) slightly. [Middle English *pinken* to stab or nick, prob from early Dutch]

pink⁵ *verb intrans* said of an internal-combustion engine: to make a series of popping or rattling noises as an indication that the combustion of the fuel-air mixture in the cylinders is faulty; to KNOCK¹. [imitative]

pink⁶ *noun archaic* a small square-rigged sailing vessel with a narrow overhanging stern. [early Dutch *pin(c)ke*]

pink elephants *pl noun informal* any of various hallucinations supposedly arising from heavy drinking or the use of drugs.

pinkeye *noun* a highly contagious conjunctivitis that affects human beings and various domestic animals.

pink gin *noun* **1** a drink consisting of gin flavoured with angostura bitters which give the drink a pale pink colour. **2** a glass or measure of pink gin.

pinkie *or* **pinky** /pingki/ *noun* (*pl* **pinkies**) *informal* the little finger. [prob from Dutch *pinkje*, dimin. of *pink* little finger]

pinking shears *pl noun* shears or scissors with a saw-toothed inner edge on the blades, used to give a zigzag edge on cloth to prevent fraying. [PINK⁴]

pinko /pingkoh/ *noun* (*pl* **pinkos** *or* **pinkoes**) *chiefly derog* somebody who holds political views that are left of centre. [PINK¹ + -O¹]

pinky¹ /pingki/ *noun* (*pl* **pinkies**) see PINKIE.

pinky² *adj* (**pinkier**, **pinkiest**) pinkish.

pin money *noun* **1** extra money earned or given for casual spending. **2** *archaic* an allowance given by a husband to his wife for personal expenditure, e.g. on clothing.

pinna /pinə/ *noun* (*pl* **pinnae** /pinee/ *or* **pinnas**) **1** a leaflet or primary division of a pinnate leaf or frond. **2** the largely cartilaginous projecting portion of the outer ear in humans and other mammals. **3** any winglike or finlike appendage. ➤➤ **pinnal** *adj*. [Latin *pinna* feather]

pinnace /pinəs/ *noun dated* any of various ship's boats. [early French *pinace*, prob via Spanish *pinaza* from Latin *pinus* PINE¹]

pinnacle¹ /pinəkl/ *noun* **1** the highest or most successful point of development or achievement: *Being made professor was the pinnacle of her career*. **2** a mountain peak or similar towering structure. **3** an architectural ornament resembling a small spire and used *esp* to crown a buttress. [Middle English *pinacle* via French from late Latin *pinnaculum* gable, from Latin *pinna* feather, point]

pinnacle² *verb trans* **1** to put a pinnacle on (a building, buttress, or roof). **2** to raise (something) on or as if on a pinnacle. **3** to crown (something) with a pinnacle.

pinnae /pinee/ *noun* pl of PINNA.

pinnate /pinayt, pinət/ *adj* said of a leaf: resembling a feather, *esp* in having similar parts arranged on opposite sides of an axis like

the barbs on the shaft of a feather. ➤➤ **pinnately** *adv*, **pinnation** /pinaysh(ə)n/ *noun*. [Latin *pinnatus* feathered, from *pinna* feather]

pinniped /piniped/ *noun* any of an order of carnivorous aquatic mammals including the seals, walruses, and sea lions, that have a streamlined body and flippers that enable them to move gracefully through water, but whose land movements are comparatively ungainly: order Pinnipedia. ➤➤ **pinniped** *adj*. [Latin *pinna* wing, fin + *ped* foot]

pinnule /pinyoohl/ *noun* **1** any of the secondary branches of a pinnate leaf. **2** an animal's small winglike or finlike part or organ. ➤➤ **pinnulate** /-lat, -layt/ *adj*, **pinnulated** /-laytid/ *adj*. [Latin *pinnula*, dimin. of *pinna* feather]

PIN number *noun* a four-digit number usu linked to a plastic card, such as a cheque card, and known only to the holder of that card, that is used as a security check when the card is used, e.g. to withdraw money from a cash dispenser. [abbr of *personal identification number*]

pinny /pini/ *noun* (*pl* **pinnies**) *informal* = PINAFORE (1).

pinochle *or* **pinocle** /peenukl/ *noun* **1** a card game similar to bezique played with a 48-card pack containing two each of the ace, king, queen, jack, ten, and nine in each suit, for two or more players who try to score points and win tricks. **2** the combination of queen of spades and jack of diamonds that scores 40 points in this game. [origin unknown]

pinocytosis /ˌpienohsie'tohsis, pin-/ *noun* (*pl* **pinocytoses** /-seez/) the intake of small droplets of fluid by a cell through the formation of small fluid-filled sacs in the cell's cytoplasmic membrane: compare PHAGOCYTOSIS. [scientific Latin, from Greek *pinein* to drink + CYT- + -OSIS]

pinole /pinohli/ *noun* a finely ground flour made from parched corn blended with a mixture of ground mesquite beans, sugar, and spices. [American Spanish *pinole* from Nahuatl *pinolli*]

piñon *or* **pinyon** /pinyohn, pinyohn/ *noun* **1** a low-growing pine tree with edible seeds: *Pinus cembroides*. **2** an edible seed from this tree. [American Spanish *piñón* from Spanish *piña* pinecone, from Latin *pinea*]

Pinot /peenoh/ *noun* **1** any of several varieties of grape, including Pinot noir and Pinot blanc, related to Chardonnay and used in the production of red and white wine. **2** a wine produced from this grape. [French *Pinot*, alteration of *Pineau*, dimin. of *pin* PINE¹, so called because a cluster of these grapes resembles a pinecone]

pinotage /peenohtahzh/ *noun* **1** a variety of grape that is a hybrid of Pinot noir, used in the production of red wine, *esp* in S Africa. **2** a wine produced from this grape.

pinpoint¹ *verb trans* to fix, determine, or identify (the site of something) with precision: *Rescue teams in helicopters were able to pinpoint the scene of the crash*.

pinpoint² *adj* **1** extremely precise: *He works with pinpoint accuracy*. **2** extremely small, fine, or precise: *a pinpoint target*.

pinpoint³ *noun* **1** a very small point or area: *You can see a pinpoint of light at the end of the tube*. **2** the sharp end of a pin.

pinprick *noun* **1** a small puncture made by a pin or a similar sharp point. **2** a petty irritation or annoyance.

pins and needles *pl noun* (*treated as sing. or pl*) a pricking tingling sensation in a limb or the fingers or toes when they are recovering from numbness.

pinstripe *noun* **1** a very thin stripe, *esp* on a fabric. **2** (*usu in pl*) a suit or trousers with pinstripes. ➤➤ **pinstriped** *adj*.

pint /pient/ *noun* **1** a unit of capacity equal to one eighth of a gallon (0.568l in Britain or 0.473l in the USA for liquid measure; 0.551l in Britain and the USA for dry measure). **2** *Brit, informal* a pint of beer. [Middle English *pinte* from French]

pintable *noun* = PINBALL MACHINE.

pintail *noun* (*pl* **pintails** *or collectively* **pintail**) any of several species of slender grey and white dabbling ducks with an upwardly pointing tail: genus *Anas*.

pintle /pintl/ *noun* a usu upright pivot on which another part, *esp* a rudder, turns. [Old English *pintel* penis]

pinto¹ /pintoh/ *noun* (*pl* **pintos** *or* **pintoes**) *NAmer* a piebald or blotched horse or pony. [American Spanish *pinto* painted, ultimately from Latin *pingere* to paint]

pinto² *adj NAmer* pied; mottled; piebald.

pinto bean *noun* a mottled bean that resembles the kidney bean in size and shape and is grown for food and fodder, *esp* in SW United States.

pint-size *adj* very small, *esp* smaller than normal.

pint-sized *adj* = PINT-SIZE.

pin tuck *noun* a very narrow usu ornamental tuck in a garment, *esp* a shirt front or dress bodice.

pin-up *noun* **1** a picture or poster of a sexually attractive person, usu either a famous celebrity or somebody seductively or scantily clothed. **2** a person appearing in such a picture or photo.

pinwheel *noun* **1** = CATHERINE WHEEL. **2** *NAmer* = WINDMILL¹ (2).

pinworm *noun* a small nematode worm that lives parasitically in the colon, rectum, and anus regions of humans and other vertebrates; = THREADWORM.

Pinyin /'pin'yin/ *noun* the standard modern spelling system for transliterating Chinese characters into the roman alphabet. [Chinese (Pekingese) *pinyin*, from *pin* spell + *yin* sound]

pinyon /'pinyohn, pin'yohn/ *noun* see PIÑON.

piolet /pi·ə'lay (*French* pjɔlɛ)/ *noun* an ice axe used in mountaineering. [French *piolet*, literally 'little pick']

pion /'pieon/ *noun* in physics, any of several positive, negative, or neutral unstable elementary particles of the meson family responsible for the force between nucleons. ⟫⟫ **pionic** /pie'onik/ *adj*. [from PI¹ + -ON²]

pioneer¹ /pie·ə'niə/ *noun* **1a** a person or group that originates or helps open up a new line of thought or activity or a new method or technical development. **b** any of the first people to settle in a territory. **c** (*used before a noun*) relating to or used by a pioneer or pioneers: *pioneer technology; a pioneer trail*. **2** a member of a military unit engaging in light construction and defensive works. [early French *peonier* foot soldier, ultimately from Latin *pedon-, pedo*: see PAWN¹]

pioneer² *verb intrans* to act as a pioneer. ⟩ *verb trans* **1** to originate or take part in the development of (something): *The institute pioneered the cloning of sheep*. **2** to open or prepare (land, a trail, etc) for others to follow and settle.

pious /'pie·əs/ *adj* **1** devout; deeply religious. **2** sacred or devotional, *esp* as distinct from being profane or secular. **3** dutiful; reverential. **4** marked by sham or hypocritical virtue; sanctimonious. ⟫⟫ **piously** *adv*, **piousness** *noun*. [Latin *pius* dutiful, pious]

pip¹ /pip/ *noun* **1** a small fruit seed of an apple, orange, etc. **2** any of the divisions marked on the skin of a pineapple. ⟫⟫ **pipless** *adj*. [shortened form of PIPPIN]

pip² *verb trans* (**pipped, pipping**) to remove the pips from (a fruit).

pip³ *noun* (*usu in pl*) a short high-pitched tone, *esp* one of a series given as a time signal in a radio broadcast or as an indication on a payphone that the caller should insert more money. **2** a blip on a radar screen or instrument. [imitative]

pip⁴ *verb* (**pipped, pipping**) ⟩ *verb trans* said of a hatching bird: to crack open (its eggshell). ⟩ *verb intrans* **1** said of a bird: to make a shrill noise. **2** said of a radar screen, etc: to blip.

pip⁵ *noun* **1a** any of the dots on dice and dominoes that indicate numerical value. **b** any of the symbols on a set of playing cards that indicate suit and rank. **2** a star worn, *esp* on the shoulder, to indicate an army officer's rank. [origin unknown]

pip⁶ *noun* a disease of poultry marked by the formation of a scale or crust on the bird's tongue and the presence of thick mucus in its throat. ✳ **give somebody the pip** *informal, dated* to cause somebody to feel disgust or irritation or to be depressed. [Middle English *pippe* from early Dutch, prob ultimately from Latin *pituita* phlegm]

pip⁷ *verb trans* (**pipped, pipping**) **1** *informal* to beat (somebody or something) by a narrow margin: *Katy just pipped Jo for first place*. **2** *dated* to wound (somebody or something) with a gun. ✳ **pip at the post** to beat (somebody) at the very last minute, *esp* in a race or competition. [origin unknown]

pipal *or* **peepul** /'peepl/ *noun* a large long-lived Indian fig tree: *Ficus religiosa*. [Hindi *pīpal*]

pipe¹ /piep/ *noun* **1a** a long tube or hollow body for conducting a liquid, gas, etc. **b** a tubular or cylindrical object, part, or passage, *esp* one in the body. **c** a roughly cylindrical vein of ore. **2a** a wood, clay, etc tube with a mouthpiece at one end, and at the other a small bowl in which plant material, *esp* tobacco, is burned for

smoking: *He lit his pipe*. **b** an amount of tobacco held in the bowl of a pipe. **3a** any of various simple musical instruments consisting of a tube with holes in it, the holes being covered by the fingers in varying configurations to produce different notes when air is blown into the tube. **b** (*in pl*) a set of different lengths of musical pipes joined together; = PANPIPES. **c** (**the pipes**) bagpipes. **d** any cylindrical tube that produces music, e.g. on an organ. **e** a boatswain's whistle. **4** a large cask used *esp* for wine and oil and often used as a measure of capacity equivalent to two hogsheads or 105 imperial gallons (477.3l). **5** a high-pitched noise, *esp* a shrill birdsong. ✳ **put that in one's pipe and smoke it** *informal* to be forced to accept a situation or fact despite one's objections or its disadvantages. ⟫⟫ **pipeful** (*pl* **pipefuls**) *noun*. [Old English *pīpa* musical pipe, from Latin *pipare* to cheep, of imitative origin: compare FIFE]

pipe² *verb trans* **1** to convey (a fluid substance, *esp* water, gas, or oil) along a pipe, pipeline, or a series of pipes. **2** to transmit (a radio or television broadcast, music, or an electrical signal) along wires or cables. **3a** to put (a decoration or message) on a cake, etc in icing or cream using a bag with a nozzle: *He piped 'Happy Birthday Jane' on the cake*. **b** to decorate (a cake, etc) in this way. **c** to decorate or cover something with (icing or cream). **4a** to trim (clothing, soft furnishings, etc) with decorative cord, etc. **b** to attach (decorative cord, etc) to clothes or soft furnishings. **5** to install a system of pipes in (a building, etc). **6** to connect (something) by means of a pipe or pipes. **7** to say in a shrill voice: *She was quick to pipe her objection*. **8a** to play (a tune) on a pipe, pipes, or bagpipes. **b** to use a pipe, pipes, or bagpipes to welcome or escort (somebody or something) ceremonially: *The crew piped the admiral aboard; Morag piped the haggis to the table*. **c** to use a boatswain's pipe to tell (sailors) to assemble for work, mealtimes, inspection, etc: *Harry piped the crew to swabbing duty*. ⟩ *verb intrans* **1** to play a pipe, pipes, or bagpipes. **2** said of a bird: to sing in a shrill, high-pitched way. **3** said of somebody, *esp* a child: to speak in a high-pitched voice: *'Honest, Mum,' piped Molly, 'I never touched him'*.

pipe bomb *noun* a homemade bomb formed from a length of pipe capped at both ends and packed with explosives and nails or other missiles.

pipe clay *noun* a fine white clay used *esp* for making tobacco pipes and for whitening leather and other materials.

pipe-clay *verb trans* to whiten or clean (leather, etc) with pipe clay.

pipe cleaner *noun* a piece of flexible wire covered with tufted fabric which is used to clean the stem of a tobacco pipe.

piped music *noun* recorded background music played through loudspeakers in public places.

pipe down *verb intrans informal* to stop talking or making noise.

pipe dream *noun* an unattainable or fantastic plan or hope. [from the fantasies brought about by smoking an opium pipe]

pipefish *noun* (*pl* **pipefishes** *or collectively* **pipefish**) any of numerous species of long slender marine fishes related to the sea horses that have tube-shaped snouts and bodies covered with bony plates: family Syngnathidae.

pipeline¹ *noun* **1** a line of pipe with pumps, valves, and control devices for conveying liquids, gases, etc. **2a** the processes that supplies pass through from source to user. **b** something considered as a continuous set of processes which somebody must go through or be subjected to: *Children have to pass along the educational pipeline*. **3** a direct channel for information. ✳ **in the pipeline** in the process of being done, completed, developed, or delivered: *An upgraded version of the software is in the pipeline*.

pipeline² *verb trans* to convey (a fluid substance) along a pipeline.

pipe major *noun* the principal player in a pipe band or a non-commissioned officer who trains the members of an army pipe band.

pipe of peace *noun* = CALUMET.

pipe organ *noun* = ORGAN (1A).

piper /'piepə/ *noun* **1** somebody who plays a pipe, pipes, or bagpipes. **2** somebody who makes, lays, or repairs pipes.

piperidine /pi'perədeen, -din/ *noun* a liquid HETEROCYCLIC (having a ring of atoms of more than one kind) organic compound with a peppery smell like that of ammonia. [Latin *piper* (see PEPPER¹) + -IDE + -INE²]

pipette (*NAmer* **pipet**) /pi'pet/ *noun* a narrow usu calibrated tube that has a small-bore aperture at the lower end and usu widens into a bulb in the middle, into which a liquid is drawn by suction and retained by closing the upper end, and that is used e.g. for measuring liquids or for transferring or dispensing measured quantities of liquid. [French *pipette*, dimin of *pipe* pipe, cask, ultimately from Latin *pipare*: see PIPE[1]]

pipe up *verb intrans* to begin to play, sing, or speak, *esp* unexpectedly.

piping /ˈpieping/ *noun* **1** a quantity or system of pipes. **2a** a narrow cord trimming used to decorate upholstery, garments, etc. **b** a thin cordlike line of icing or cream used to decorate cakes, etc. **3a** the act or an instance of producing music on a pipe, pipes, or bagpipes. **b** the act or an instance of producing a high-pitched sound, note, or call: *the piping of a blackbird*.

piping hot *adj* so hot as to sizzle or hiss; very hot.

pipistrelle /pipiˈstrel/ *noun* any of a genus of small insect-eating bats: genus *Pipistrellus*. [French *pipistrelle* via Italian *pipistrello* from Latin *vespertilio* bat, from *vesper* evening]

pipit /ˈpipit/ *noun* any of numerous species of small songbirds resembling larks, most of which have brown plumage streaked with darker brown or black: genus *Anthus*. [imitative]

pipkin /ˈpipkin/ *noun dated* a small earthenware or metal cooking pot. [origin unknown]

pippin /ˈpipin/ *noun* any of several varieties of eating apple with usu yellow skins strongly flushed with red. [Middle English *pepin* from French]

pipsqueak *noun informal* a small or insignificant person.

piquant /ˈpeekənt/ *adj* **1** having an agreeably stimulating taste; savoury: *She ordered pasta in a piquant sauce.* **2** pleasantly stimulating to the mind. ➤➤ **piquancy** /-si/ *noun*, **piquantly** *adv.* [early French *piquant*, present part. of *piquer* to sting, prick]

pique[1] /peek/ *noun* resentment resulting from wounded pride, or the bad temper that results from this: *In a fit of pique, he handed in his resignation.*

pique[2] *verb trans* (**piques, piqued, piquing**) **1** to arouse anger or resentment in (somebody), *esp* by offending or insulting them. **2** (*usu* + on/upon) to pride or congratulate (oneself), *esp* in respect of a particular accomplishment: *He piques himself on his skill as a cook.* [early French *piquer* to prick, sting]

piqué *or* **pique** /ˈpeekay/ *noun* a durable ribbed fabric made from cotton, rayon, or silk. [French *piqué* from early French *piquer* to prick, quilt]

piquet /piˈket/ *noun* **1** a card game for two players played with a 32-card pack with no cards below the seven, the ace being high. **2** = PICKET[1] (2). [French *piquet*, of unknown origin]

piracy /ˈpie-ərəsi/ *noun* (*pl* **piracies**) **1** the act or an instance of committing robbery or illegal violence on the high seas, or a similar act, e.g. hijacking, on board an aircraft in flight. **2** the infringement of a copyright, patent, etc. [via medieval Latin from late Greek *peirateia*, from Greek *peiratēs*: see PIRATE[1]]

piranha /piˈrahn(y)ə/ *noun* any of several species of small S American freshwater fishes with strong jaws and sharp teeth which they use for ripping flesh from their prey: genus *Serrosalmus* and other genera. [Portuguese *piranha*, from Tupi *pirá* fish + *sainha* tooth]

pirate[1] /ˈpie-ərət/ *noun* **1a** somebody who commits piracy. **b** a ship used in piracy. **2a** somebody who appropriates another person's work, ideas, etc without permission: *a video pirate.* **b** (*used before a noun*) relating to something that has been obtained without the owner's permission: *That stall sells pirate videos.* **3** (*used before a noun*) denoting or relating to an unauthorized radio station. ➤➤ **piratic** /pieˈratik/ *adj*, **piratical** /pieˈratikl/ *adj*, **piratically** /pieˈratikli/ *adv.* [Middle English via French and Latin from Greek *peiratēs*, from *peiran* to attempt, attack]

pirate[2] *verb trans* **1** to reproduce (somebody else's work, ideas, etc) without authorization. **2** to take or appropriate (goods) by piracy. **3** to commit piracy on (a ship, aircraft, etc). ➤ *verb intrans* to commit or practise piracy.

pirogue /piˈrohg/ *noun* a long narrow canoe made from a hollowed-out tree trunk and used mainly in the Caribbean and the waters round Central America. [French *pirogue* from Galibi *piragua*]

pirouette[1] /piroo'et/ *noun* in ballet and skating, a fast spin of the body, *esp* one performed on the toes or ball of one foot while the other foot is raised. [French *pirouette*, literally 'teetotum']

pirouette[2] *verb intrans* to perform a pirouette.

pis /piez/ *noun* pl of PI[1].

pis aller /ˌpeez aˈlay/ *noun* (*pl* **pis allers** /aˈlay(z)/) a last resource or device; an expedient. [French *pis* worse + *aller* to go]

pisc- *or* **pisci-** *comb. form* forming words, denoting: fish: *pisciculture; piscivorous.* [Latin *piscis* fish]

piscary /ˈpisk(ə)ri/ *noun* (*pl* **piscaries**) **1** *chiefly Brit, dated* the right of fishing in waters belonging to another. **2** = FISHERY (2). [Latin *piscaria* fishing rights, from *piscis* fish]

piscatorial /piskəˈtawri-əl/ *adj* = PISCATORY.

piscatory /ˈpiskət(ə)ri/ *adj* relating to fish, fishing, or anglers: *a most unfortunate place for the execution of those piscatory tactics which had been invented along the velvet margins of quiet English rivulets —* Washington Irving. [Latin *piscatorius*, from *piscatus*, past part. of *piscari* to fish, from *piscis* fish]

Pisces /ˈpieseez/ *noun* **1** in astronomy, a constellation (the Fish or Fishes) depicted as two fishes joined at the tails. **2a** in astrology, the twelfth sign of the zodiac. **b** a person born under this sign. ➤➤ **Piscean** /ˈpiesi-ən/ *adj and noun.* [Latin *pisces*, pl of *piscis* fish]

pisci- *comb. form* see PISC-.

pisciculture /ˈpisikulchə/ *noun* the breeding and rearing of fish under artificial or controlled conditions, *esp* for scientific research or for farming purposes. ➤➤ **piscicultural** *adj*, **pisciculturist** *noun.*

piscina /piˈseenə/ *noun* (*pl* **piscinas** *or* **piscinae** /-nee/) in the Roman Catholic Church, a stone basin with a drain where water used in the Mass can be poured away. [Latin *piscina*, literally 'fish-pond', from *piscis* fish]

piscine /ˈpisien/ *adj* relating to or characteristic of fish. [Latin *piscis* fish + -INE[1]]

piscivorous /piˈsivərəs/ *adj* said of an animal: feeding only or mainly on fish. ➤➤ **piscivore** /ˈpisivaw/ *noun.*

pish /pish/ *interj dated* used to express disdain or contempt. [origin unknown]

pisiform[1] /ˈpisifawm/ *adj* pea-shaped. [Latin *pisiformis*, from *pisum* (see PEA) + *forma* FORM[1]]

pisiform[2] *noun* a small rounded bone of the wrist or carpus on the side of the little finger or ulna in most mammals.

pismire /ˈpismie-ə/ *noun archaic or dialect* an ant. [Middle English *pissemire*, from *pisse* urine + *mire* ant]

piss[1] /pis/ *verb intrans coarse slang* **1** to urinate. **2** (*often* + down) to rain heavily. ➤ *verb trans coarse slang* **1** to urinate in or on (something): *piss the bed.* **2** to discharge (something) in one's urine: *to piss blood.* ✻ **piss on** *chiefly Brit, coarse slang* to treat (somebody or something) with contempt. [Middle English *pissen* from early French *pisser*, prob imitative]

piss[2] *noun coarse slang* **1** urine. **2** an instance of urinating. ✻ **take the piss** *Brit, coarse slang* to make fun of, tease, or mock somebody or something.

piss about *verb intrans chiefly Brit, coarse slang* to waste time doing something that has no value.

piss around *verb intrans* = PISS ABOUT.

pissed *adj* **1** *Brit, coarse slang* drunk. **2** *NAmer, slang* very angry or upset.

piss off *verb intrans Brit, coarse slang* to go away. ➤ *verb trans coarse slang* to cause (somebody) to be annoyed or fed up: *His sloppy work really pisses me off.*

pissoir /piˈswah/ *noun* a public urinal, *esp* in the street in some European countries. [French *pissoir* from *pisser*: see PISS[1]]

piss up *verb trans chiefly Brit, coarse slang* to ruin (something) or make a complete mess of (it).

piss-up *noun chiefly Brit, coarse slang* a heavy drinking session.

pistachio /piˈstahshioh/ *noun* (*pl* **pistachios**) **1a** a pale green or yellowish edible nut, often roasted and salted or used to flavour confectionery, *esp* ice cream. **b** a small deciduous tree with greenish or brownish flowers, from which pistachio nuts are obtained: *Pistacia vera.* **2** the green colour of pistachios. [Italian *pistacchio* via Latin from Greek *pistakion* a pistachio nut, of Persian origin]

piste /peest/ *noun* a prepared slope for skiing. [French *piste*, literally 'racetrack']

pistil /ˈpistil/ *noun* in botany, the female parts of a flowering plant, comprising the OVARY (the part where the seeds develop), the STYLE[1] (an extension of the ovary), and the STIGMA (the top of the style where pollen is deposited). [Latin *pistillum* PESTLE[1]; from its shape]

pistillate /'pistilət, -layt/ *adj* said of a plant: having pistils but no stamens: compare STAMINATE.

pistol /'pistl/ *noun* a short firearm intended to be aimed and fired with one hand. [early French *pistole* via German from Czech *píšt'ala* pipe, whistle]

pistole /pi'stohl/ *noun* any of various former European coins, usu of gold, in circulation during the 17th and 18th cents. [Middle English from early French *pistolet*: see PISTOL]

pistoleer /pistə'liə/ *noun archaic* a person, *esp* a soldier, armed with a pistol.

pistol grip *noun* **1** a grip or handle on a shotgun, rifle, tool, etc shaped like a pistol stock. **2** (*used before a noun*) denoting a piece of equipment that has this type of grip or handle: *a pistol-grip saw.*

pistol-whip *verb trans* (**pistol-whipped, pistol-whipping**) to beat (somebody or something) with the butt or barrel of a pistol.

piston /'pist(ə)n/ *noun* **1** a sliding disc or short cylinder fitting within a cylinder in which it moves back and forth or up and down by or against fluid pressure. In an internal-combustion engine, it turns a crankshaft to produce motion. **2** a sliding valve in a cylinder in a brass instrument, which, when depressed, alters a note's pitch. **3** a button on an organ that controls a group of stops. [French *piston* from Italian *pistone*, ultimately from Latin *pinsere* to crush]

piston ring *noun* a springy split metal ring for sealing the gap between a piston and a cylinder wall.

piston rod *noun* a rod attached to a piston for driving a wheel or producing motion.

pit¹ /pit/ *noun* **1a** a hole, shaft, or cavity in the ground. **b** a mine where coal or minerals are excavated. **c** a mine shaft. **d** (*used before a noun*) relating to or used in mining: *a pit pony.* **2** (*often* **the pits**) an area at the side of a motor-racing track for servicing, refuelling, and tyre changing. **3a** a natural hollow in the surface of the body. **b** an indented scar left in the skin by a disease such as chickenpox. **c** the bottom of an anatomical part: *the pit of the stomach.* **4** a sunken area in a garage, workshop, etc where a mechanic can work on the underside of vehicles. **5** the area on the floor of a stock exchange where specified commodities are traded. **6** *archaic* an enclosed area where animals, *esp* bears, are made to fight each other. **7a** (**the Pit**) *literary* = HELL. **b** (**the pits**) *informal* the worst imaginable: *That job was just the pits.* **8** *Brit, informal* a person's bed: *He often lies in his pit until lunchtime.* **9a** (**the pit**) *chiefly Brit* the floor of a theatre auditorium. **b** = ORCHESTRA PIT. **10** = PITFALL (1). [Old English *pytt*, ultimately from Latin *puteus* a well]

pit² *verb* (**pitted, pitting**) ➤ *verb trans* **1** to make small holes or indentations in the surface of (something): *Acne had pitted her skin.* **2a** (+ against) to set (a person or oneself) in competition with another person. **b** (+ against) to use (one's mental resources) to try to solve a problem, etc: *Pit your wits against this conundrum.* **c** *dated* (+ against) to cause (cocks, dogs, etc) to fight against each other as a form of sport that is now illegal, usu in a pit or enclosure and with bets being taken on the outcome. ➤ *verb intrans* **1** to become marked by small holes or indentations. **2** said of a racing-car driver: to go into the pits for refuelling, a change of tyres, or servicing.

pit³ *noun chiefly NAmer* a stone in a fruit such as a plum or cherry. [Dutch *pit* kernel]

pit⁴ *verb trans* (**pitted, pitting**) *chiefly NAmer* to remove the pit from (a fruit).

pita /'pitə/ *noun NAmer* see PITTA.

pita bread *noun NAmer* see PITTA BREAD.

pit-a-pat¹ *or* **pitapat** /'pitəpat/ *noun* a series of light tapping sounds. [imitative]

pit-a-pat² *or* **pitapat** *adv and adj* with light tapping sounds.

pit bull *noun* = PIT BULL TERRIER.

pit bull terrier *noun* a US breed of short-haired terrier with a powerful stocky muscular body, orig bred for fighting and still having a reputation for fierceness. [so called because of the PIT¹ where they were put to fight]

pitch¹ /pich/ *noun* **1a** *chiefly Brit* a piece of ground with boundaries and other areas marked on it, used for playing a team sport. **b** in cricket, = WICKET (1B). **2a** in baseball and cricket, the act or an instance of a pitcher or bowler delivering a ball to a batter or batsman, or the ball or quality of ball so delivered. **b** in golf, a shot made with a lofted club causing the ball to travel in a high arc. **3** a slope, *esp* of a roof, or the degree of this. **4** a level or degree, *esp* an

advanced or extreme one: *a high pitch of effectiveness.* **5** *informal* a special and usu persuasive way of speaking or arguing: *an aggressive sales pitch.* **6** *chiefly Brit* a place regularly used or claimed by a person, *esp* a street vendor or performer. **7a** the distinctive quality that a sound has according to the frequency of the vibrations produced at the sound's source, with fast vibrations producing a higher pitch than slow ones. **b** in music, height or depth of tone. **c** any of various standardized levels for achieving the height or depth of tone of specific musical instruments. **8** an erratic heaving motion, *esp* an up-and-down movement of a ship, aircraft, or vehicle. **9** *technical.* **a** the distance between one point and another, *esp* the distance between one point on the tooth of a cog or gear and the corresponding point on the next tooth. **b** the degree to which the blade of a propeller slants in relation to its axis of rotation. ✳ **make a pitch for** to put forward a bid or claim for (something). [from PITCH²]

pitch² *verb trans* **1a** to throw (something) in a careless, rough, or casual way; to toss. **b** to cause (a ship, aircraft, or vehicle) to travel with a specified motion. **2a** said of a pitcher in baseball: to throw (a ball) from the mound towards the batter. **b** said of a bowler in cricket: to throw (a ball) towards the batsman so that it bounces at a specified point or in a particular way. **c** in golf, to use a lofted club to hit (a ball), causing it to travel in a high arc and land with backspin. **3a** in music, to set (a piece of music, one's voice, or an instrument) at a particular pitch. **b** to express (a speech, piece of writing, etc) at a specified level or to adapt (it) for a particular audience. **c** to set (something, e.g. hopes or aspirations) at a specified level. **4a** to develop or direct (a product, etc) towards a particular type of customer or section of the market. **b** to set (a price) at a specified level. **5** to erect (a tent, etc) temporarily. **6** to give (a roof) a specified downward incline from the ridge. **7** to pave (a road) with stones. ➤ *verb intrans* **1a** to move to or fall heavily, *esp* forwards or downwards. **b** said of a ship, aircraft, or vehicle: to move with or be affected by a heaving or rocking motion. **2a** in golf, to strike the ball with a lofted club. **b** said of a ball in golf and cricket: to land or bounce in a specified place or way. **c** in baseball, to act as a pitcher. ✳ **pitch into** *informal* to attack (somebody or something) physically or verbally. [Middle English, perhaps from Old English *picung* stigmata]

pitch³ *noun* **1** a black or dark viscous substance obtained as a residue in the distillation of organic materials, *esp* tars, or any of various similar substances. **2** resin obtained from various conifers. [Old English *pic*, ultimately from Latin *pix*]

pitch⁴ *verb trans dated* to cover, smear, or treat (something) with pitch.

pitch and putt *noun* a game similar to golf but played on a much shorter course using only two clubs, a lofted one and a putter.

pitch-black *adj* completely black or dark.

pitchblende /'pichblend/ *noun* a radium-containing uranium oxide occurring as a brown to black lustrous mineral. [German *Pechblende*, from *Pech* pitch + *Blende* blende]

pitch-dark *adj* **1** too dark for a person to see. **2** too dark to be seen.

pitched battle *noun* **1** a battle between armies fought on previously chosen ground, rather than a chance encounter. **2** a fierce conflict.

pitcher¹ *noun* a large jug, *esp* an earthenware or china one with a handle formerly used for holding water for washing the face and hands. [Middle English *picher* from early French *pichier* from Latin *picarius* goblet]

pitcher² *noun* somebody who pitches; *specif* the player who pitches in a baseball game.

pitcher plant *noun* any of various insectivorous plants whose specially modified leaves form fluid-filled basins in which insects become trapped: families *Sarraceniaceae, Nepenthaceae,* and others.

pitchfork¹ *noun* a long-handled fork with two or three long curved prongs used *esp* for lifting and tossing hay. [Middle English *pikfork* from *pik* (see PICK³) + FORK¹]

pitchfork² *verb trans* **1** to lift and toss (hay, straw, etc) with a pitchfork. **2** to thrust (somebody) into a position, office, etc, *esp* suddenly or without preparation.

pitch in *verb intrans informal* to contribute energetically to an activity.

pitch pine *noun* any of various N American pine trees grown commercially for their timber, which is used in the construction of buildings and in the manufacture of furniture, and as a source of turpentine: genus *Pinus*.

pitch pipe *noun* a small musical pipe used to establish the required pitch in singing or in tuning an instrument.

pitch up *verb intrans* **1** *informal* to arrive; to turn up. **2** in cricket: to deliver a ball so that it bounces near the person batting, making it awkward to hit.

pitchy *adj* (**pitchier, pitchiest**) **1** relating to, resembling, or covered with PITCH³. **2** very dark in colour. ⋙ **pitchiness** *noun*.

piteous /'piti-əs/ *adj* causing or deserving pity or compassion. ⋙ **piteously** *adv*, **piteousness** *noun*.

pitfall *noun* **1** a hidden or not easily recognized danger or difficulty. *She was neither clear-sighted nor accurate, and in her attempts to describe morals, manners, and even facts, was unable to avoid the pitfalls of exaggeration* — Trollope. **2** a trap or snare, *esp* a camouflaged pit used to capture animals.

pith¹ /pith/ *noun* **1a** the white tissue surrounding the flesh and directly below the skin of a citrus fruit. **b** the spongy cellular tissue in the stems of most vascular plants. **2a** the essential part of something: *individuality, which was the very pith of liberty* — Harold Laski. **b** meaning or substance: *He made a speech that lacked pith.* **3** *archaic* the marrow of an animal's spinal cord. [Old English *pitha*]

pith² *verb trans* **1** to remove the pith from (a plant part). **2** to kill or immobilize (an animal) by severing the spinal cord.

pithead *noun* the top of a mining pit and the ground and buildings around it.

pithecanthropus /ˌpithikan'throhpəs, pithi'kan-/ *noun* (*pl* **pithecanthropi** /-pie/) any of the primitive extinct humans known from skeletal remains from Javanese Pliocene gravels: compare JAVA MAN. ⋙ **pithecanthropoid** /-'kanthrəpoyd/ *adj*. [scientific Latin, from Greek *pithēkos* ape + *anthrōpos* human being]

pith helmet *noun* a hat made from the pith of any of various Indian swamp plants and worn in tropical regions to protect the head and the back of the neck from the sun.

pithos /'pithos/ *noun* (*pl* **pithoi** /'pithoy/) a large earthenware or ceramic jar used in classical times for storing oil or grain. [Greek *pithos*]

pithy *adj* (**pithier, pithiest**) **1** said of language, a speech, etc: full of meaning or substance and concisely expressed. **2** said of a plant or plant part: resembling pith or having a great deal of pith. ⋙ **pithily** *adv*, **pithiness** *noun*.

pitiable /'piti-əbl/ *adj* **1** deserving or arousing pity. **2** contemptibly inadequate: *a pitiable excuse.* ⋙ **pitiableness** *noun*, **pitiably** *adv*.

pitiful /'pitif(ə)l/ *adj* **1** deserving or arousing pity or commiseration. **2** woefully small or inadequate. **3** *archaic* full of pity; compassionate. ⋙ **pitifully** *adv*, **pitifulness** *noun*.

pitiless /'pitilis/ *adj* showing little or no pity; merciless. ⋙ **pitilessly** *adv*, **pitilessness** *noun*.

pitman *noun* **1** (*pl* **pitmen**) a male mine worker. **2** (*pl* **pitmans**) *NAmer* = CONNECTING ROD.

piton /'peeton/ *noun* a spike or peg that is driven into a rock or ice surface as a support, *esp* for a rope, in mountaineering. [French *piton*, literally 'ringbolt']

pitot /'peetoh/ *noun* a tube with a short right-angled bend that is used with a manometer to measure the velocity of fluid flow. [named after Henri *Pitot* d.1771, French physicist who invented it]

pitot tube *noun* = PITOT.

pit pony *noun* *Brit*, *dated* a small horse formerly used in mines to pull trucks loaded with coal.

pitprop *noun* a support, usu of wood, used in a mine.

pit saw *noun* a handsaw worked by two men, one of whom stands on or above the log being sawn and the other below it, usu in a pit.

pit stop *noun* **1** in motor racing, a stop at the pits (see PIT¹ (2)) for refuelling, changing tyres, or servicing. **2** *informal* a break from work or during a journey for a rest or refreshments.

pitta (*NAmer* **pita**) /'pitə/ *noun* slightly leavened bread, typically flat and oval in shape, that is often split open to hold a savoury filling. [Greek *pitta*, literally 'cake, pie']

pitta bread (*NAmer* **pita bread**) *noun* = PITTA.

pittance /'pit(ə)ns/ *noun* a small amount or allowance, *esp* a meagre wage or inadequate remuneration. [Middle English via early French *pitance* from Latin *pietantia*, from *pietas* PITY¹]

pitter-patter¹ /'pitə ˌpatə/ *noun* a rapid succession of light tapping sounds. [imitative]

pitter-patter² *verb intrans* (**pitter-pattered, pitter-pattering**) to make or move with a series of light tapping sounds: *Rain was pitter-pattering against the window.*

pitter-patter³ *adj and adv* with a succession of light tapping sounds.

pituitary¹ /pi'tyooh-it(ə)ri/ *adj* of the pituitary gland. [Latin *pituita* phlegm, from the former belief that the pituitary gland secreted phlegm]

pituitary² *noun* a small two-lobed endocrine organ attached to the brain which secretes many important hormones controlling growth, metabolism, the function of other endocrine glands, etc.

pituitary body *noun* = PITUITARY².

pituitary gland *noun* = PITUITARY².

pit viper *noun* any of various venomous snakes, including the rattlesnakes, that have a heat-sensitive pit on each side of the head and hollow perforated fangs: subfamily *Crotalinae*.

pity¹ /'piti/ *noun* (*pl* **pities**) **1** sympathetic sorrow or compassion for the suffering, distress, or unhappiness of another. **2** something to be regretted; a source of disappointment: *It's a pity you can't go.* ✳ **for pity's sake** used to express exasperation or as an urgent appeal. **have/take pity on** to have sympathy for or show mercy towards (somebody or something). **more's the pity** used to express regret or disappointment. [Middle English *pite* via French from Latin *pietas* piety, pity]

pity² *verb trans* (**pities, pitied, pitying**) to feel pity for (somebody or something). ⋙ **pitying** *adj*, **pityingly** *adv*.

pityriasis /pitə'rie-əsis/ *noun* any of various skin diseases that are characterized by the shedding of fine scurfy scales. [scientific Latin from Greek *pityriasis* scurf, from *pityron* bran]

più mosso /ˌpyooh 'mosoh/ *adj and adv* said of a piece of music: to be performed more quickly. [Italian *più mosso* more animated]

pivot¹ /'pivət/ *noun* **1** a shaft or pin on which something, *esp* a mechanized part, turns. **2** a person, thing, or factor that has a major or central role, function, or effect: *It was as if the pivot and pole of his life, from which he could not escape, was his mother* — D H Lawrence. **3** the person or position that a body of troops uses as a reference point when manoeuvring. [French *pivot*, of unknown origin]

pivot² *verb* (**pivoted, pivoting**) ⋙ *verb intrans* to turn on a pivot, or as if on a pivot. ⋙ *verb trans* **1** to cause (something) to pivot. **2** to provide (something) with a pivot or pivots. **3** to mount (something) on a pivot. **4** (*usu* + on) to depend on (something or somebody). ⋙ **pivotable** *adj*.

pivotal *adj* **1** vitally important; crucial: *The prime minister played a pivotal role in the peace talks.* **2** relating to or constituting a pivot. ⋙ **pivotally** *adv*.

pix¹ /piks/ *noun* pl of PIC.

pix² *noun* see PYX.

pixel /'piksəl/ *noun* **1** one of thousands of tiny spots on a computer display screen that together can be manipulated to form an image or character. **2** one of thousands of tiny spots produced by a printer on paper that together form a printed image or character. [blend of PIX¹ + the first syllable of ELEMENT]

pixie *or* **pixy** /'piksi/ *noun* (*pl* **pixies**) a fairy or elf, *esp* one typically depicted in folklore as a small human with large pointed ears and wearing a pointed hat. ⋙ **pixieish** *adj*. [origin unknown]

pixilated *or* **pixillated** /'piksilaytid/ *adj* **1** bemused, confused, or crazy. **2** *informal*, *dated* drunk. ⋙ **pixilation** /-'laysh(ə)n/ *noun*. [from PIXIE, based on similar forms such as *elated* and *stimulated*]

pixy /'piksi/ *noun* (*pl* **pixies**) see PIXIE.

pizazz /pə'zaz/ *noun* see PIZZAZZ.

pizz. *abbr* pizzicato.

pizza /'peetsə/ *noun* (*pl* **pizzas**) a round base of baked bread dough spread with a mixture of tomatoes, cheese, herbs, etc. [Italian *pizza*, literally 'pie']

pizzazz *or* **pizazz** *or* **pzazz** /pə'zaz/ *noun* an attractive and often flamboyant combination of spirited vitality and glamorous style: *He always dresses with such pizzazz.* [origin uncertain, but said to have been coined by Diana Vreeland d.1989, US fashion expert and magazine editor]

pizzeria /peetsə'riə/ *noun* (*pl* **pizzerias**) a place where pizzas are made or sold. [Italian *pizzaria*, from *pizza* PIZZA]

pizzicato /pitsi'kahtoh/ *adj and adv* said of a piece of music for stringed instruments: to be performed by plucking instead of bowing. >> **pizzicato** *noun*. [Italian *pizzicato*, from *pizzicare* to pinch, pluck]

pizzle /'pizəl/ *noun archaic* **1** an animal's penis, *esp* a bull's: *'Sblood, you starveling, you elf-skin, you dried neat's tongue, you bull's pizzle, you stockfish* — Shakespeare. **2** a bull's penis used as a whip for flogging offenders. [Low German *pesel* or Flemish *pezel*]

PK *abbr* Pakistan (international vehicle registration).

Pk *abbr* used in street names: Park.

pk *abbr* **1** peck. **2** peak.

pkg *abbr* package.

pkt *abbr* packet.

PKU *abbr* phenylketonuria.

PL *abbr* Poland (international vehicle registration).

Pl *abbr* used in street names: Place.

pl. *abbr* **1** platoon. **2** plural.

PLA *abbr* **1** People's Liberation Army. **2** *Brit* Port of London Authority.

placable /'plakəb(ə)l/ *adj archaic* easily calmed or appeased. >> **placability** /-'biliti/ *noun,* **placably** *adv.*

placard[1] /'plakahd/ *noun* a sign or notice for display, placed on a wall or carried as part of a demonstration. [Middle English *placquart* formal document, from early French *plaquier*: see PLAQUE]

placard[2] *verb trans* **1** to cover (something) with or as if with placards. **2** to give public notice of (a meeting, demonstration, concert, etc) by means of placards.

placate /plə'kayt/ *verb trans* to soothe or mollify (somebody), *esp* by concessions; to appease (them). >> **placation** /-sh(ə)n/ *noun,* **placative** /-tiv, 'plakətiv/ *adj,* **placatory** /-t(ə)ri, 'plakə-/ *adj.* [Latin *placatus,* past part. of *placare* to please]

place[1] /plays/ *noun* **1a** a position or point in space. **b** an identifiable spot, *esp* on the surface of something. **c** the point one has reached in reading a book, etc. **2** a city, town, or other geographical location. **3a** an area or a building or other structure that has a specified function or that is referred to with familiarity: *a parking place; a place to eat.* **b** a building, house, room, etc that is occupied by a specified person. **4a** a space occupied by or assigned to somebody or something. **b** a position that a person takes or is assigned to at a table, *esp* for a meal or during a meeting, etc. **c** a position that is assigned to somebody for work, study, etc, or in a team or competition. **5a** a role, right, or duty: *It's not my place to tell you what to do.* **b** a prestigious position in society: *the endless quest for preferment and place* — Time. **c** a suitable setting or an appropriate occasion: *There's no place for that kind of language here.* **6a** a position held or won by something or somebody in sequence with another or others, *esp* in a competition or race. **b** *Brit* in a race, any of the first three or sometimes first four positions, *esp* other than first. **c** *NAmer* in a race, *esp* a horse race, second position. **d** in mathematics, a position that a figure has in a series of others, *esp* a figure that follows the point in decimal notation. **7a** (*often* **Place**) a short, usu residential street or a town square with houses or offices. **b** a country estate or house with substantial grounds. * **all over the place** in a state of complete confusion or disarray. **another place** *Brit* used in the House of Commons to refer to the House of Lords, and vice versa. **be going places** to be achieving success. **give place to** to be superseded by (somebody or something). **go places 1** to travel widely. **2** to succeed. **in place of** as an alternative to or substitute for (somebody or something). **know one's place** to be aware of and accept one's position or status, *esp* when it is an inferior or humble one. **out of place 1** in the wrong place or position. **2** said of a person, activity, etc: uncomfortable or incongruous in particular surroundings. **put somebody in their place** to humiliate (somebody) or prove (them) wrong, *esp* when they have shown arrogance or presumptuousness. **take one's place** to go into one's assigned or usual position. **take place** to happen. **take the place of** to be or act as a substitute for (somebody or something). [Middle English via Old French from Latin *platea* open space, from Greek *plateia hodos* broad way]

place[2] *verb trans* **1a** to put (something or somebody) in a specified position or condition. **b** to cause (somebody, oneself, or something) to be in a specified position, condition, or situation: *The* army *placed her under house arrest.* **2a** to assert or assign a role to (a quality, attribute, etc): *He places great emphasis on accuracy.* **b** to estimate (a figure, value, etc) at a specified level. **3** to remember or identify (somebody or something): *I couldn't place his face.* **4** to find employment or a home for (somebody). **5a** to put (an advertisement or notice) in a newspaper, etc. **b** to submit or confirm (a bet, order, etc).

placebo /plə'seeboh/ *noun* (*pl* **placebos**) **1a** a medication or treatment regime that has no physiological effect and is prescribed for the patient's psychological benefit. **b** a substance that has no effects and which is used as a control against another substance, *esp* a drug, which is known to have or is being tested for a specific effect. **2** something that has a soothing or calming effect, *esp* something said or done only to please another person. **3** the Roman Catholic vespers for the dead. [Latin *placebo* I shall please, from *placēre* to please]

placebo effect *noun* an improvement in the health of a person who has been given a substance that contains no active ingredients. The positive response is attributable only to the person's belief that the substance will produce a beneficial result.

place card *noun* a card with a guest's name on it indicating the guest's place at table during a formal dinner.

placed *adj* said of a competitor at the end of a race, etc: in a leading place, *esp* second or third.

placekick *noun* in American football, rugby, and Association Football, a kick at a ball placed or held in a stationary position on the ground.

place-kick *verb intrans* said of a player: to take a placekick. >> **place-kicker** *noun.*

placeman *noun* (*pl* **placemen**) a political appointee to a public office, *esp* one who is given the post in recognition of previous political support and who is expected to continue giving allegiance.

place mat *noun* a tablemat for one person's place at a table.

placement *noun* **1** the act or an instance of putting somebody or something in a specified place, or the result or effect of doing this. **2a** the act or an instance of finding work or a school for somebody or of finding a home for a person or animal. **b** a workplace, school, or home found for a person or animal. **3** a temporary spell of work, *esp* one that allows a student to gain practical experience: *The college is sending us two trainee nursery nurses on placement for a month.*

place name *noun* the name of a geographical locality, such as a town, or a geographical feature, such as a mountain, lake, etc.

placenta /plə'sentə/ *noun* (*pl* **placentas** *or* **placentae** /-tee/) **1** a large rounded vascular organ that develops in the uterus during pregnancy in most higher mammals. It is linked to the foetus by the umbilical cord and provides the foetus with oxygen and nourishment. **2** the part of the ovary in a flowering plant to which the ovules are attached. [Latin *placenta* flat cake, from Greek *plakous*]

placental[1] *adj* **1** relating to a placenta. **2** relating to or typical of a mammal that can develop a placenta. Also called EUTHERIAN.

placental[2] *noun* a placental mammal.

placentation /plasen'taysh(ə)n/ *noun* **1** the development of the placenta and attachment of the foetus to the uterus during pregnancy. **2** the particular type of form and structure of a mammalian or plant placenta.

placer /'plasə/ *noun* (*often used before a noun*) an alluvial or glacial deposit containing particles of valuable minerals, *esp* gold: *placer deposits.* [American Spanish *placer* deposit, shoal, from *plaza* place, from Latin *platea*: see PLACE[1]]

place setting *noun* a set of cutlery, dishes, and glasses arranged on a table for the use of one person.

placet /'playset/ *noun Brit* an assenting vote given at a church or university assembly signalled by saying *placet.* [Latin *placet* it pleases, from *placēre* to please]

placid /'plasid/ *adj* not easily upset or excited; calm: *He has an unusually placid disposition.* >> **placidity** /plə'siditi/ *noun,* **placidly** *adv,* **placidness** *noun.* [Latin *placidus,* from *placēre* to please]

placing *noun* **1** the act or an instance of putting something in position. **2** (*in pl*) the positions or rankings given to competitors during or following a race or other competition. **3** a position taken up by somebody looking for work. **4** a sale or new issue of a large block of shares not offered to the general public.

placket /'plakit/ *noun* **1** a slit in a garment, *esp* a skirt, for a fastening or pocket. **2** a flap of fabric covering this. [alteration of PLACARD¹ in an obsolete sense 'garment worn under an open coat']

placoid /'plakoyd/ *adj* said of the scales of fish: toothlike in structure, with an enamel surface and an interior composed of dentine: compare CTENOID, GANOID. [Greek *plak-*, *plax* flat surface + -OID]

plafond /pla'fon/ *noun* an ornately decorated ceiling or a painting or other decoration on such a ceiling. [French *plafond* ceiling, from *plat* flat + *fond* bottom]

plagal /'playgl/ *adj* **1** said of a mode in church music: having the KEYNOTE¹ (the note on which the mode is based) on the fourth scale step: compare AUTHENTIC. **2** said of a cadence: passing from a subdominant to a tonic chord. [Latin *plagalis*, ultimately from Greek *plagios* oblique, sideways, from *plagos* side]

plage /plahzh/ *noun* a bright region on the sun caused by light from gas clouds and often associated with a sunspot. [French *plage* beach, region, ultimately from Greek *plagos* side]

plagiarise *verb trans* see PLAGIARIZE.

plagiarism /'playjəriz(ə)m/ *noun* **1** the act or an instance of plagiarizing. **2** something plagiarized. >> **plagiarist** *noun*, **plagiaristic** /-'ristik/ *adj*.

plagiarize *or* **plagiarise** /'playjəriez/ *verb trans and intrans* to appropriate and pass off (the ideas or words of another) as one's own. >> **plagiarizer** *noun*. [Latin *plagiarius* kidnapper, from *plagium* kidnapping, from Greek *plagion*]

plagioclase /'playji-əklays, -klayz/ *noun* a TRICLINIC (having three unequal axes) feldspar, *esp* one containing calcium or sodium. [Greek *plagios* (see PLAGAL) + *klasis* breaking]

plague¹ /playg/ *noun* **1** any of several epidemic virulent diseases that cause many deaths, *esp* a fever caused by a bacterium carried by rat fleas and transmitted to humans via their bite: compare BUBONIC PLAGUE. **2** a large destructive influx of insects or animals that cause widespread damage: *a plague of locusts*. **3** an outbreak or constant occurrence of something harmful or unwelcome. [Middle English *plage* via French from Latin *plaga* blow, strike]

plague² *verb trans* (**plagues, plagued, plaguing**) **1** to annoy or harass (somebody) continually. **2** to infest or afflict (a people, area, etc) with disease, calamity, etc. >> **plaguer** *noun*.

plaguey *or* **plaguy** *adj* archaic, *informal* causing irritation or annoyance; troublesome.

plaice /plays/ *noun* (*pl* **plaice**) **1** a large edible N Atlantic European flatfish with a brown skin flecked with orange that is valued commercially: *Pleuronectes platessa*. **2** a related N American fish: *Hippoglossoides platessoides*. [Middle English via Old French *plaïs* from late Latin *platessa* from Greek *platys* broad, flat]

plaid /plad/ *noun* **1** a rectangular length of tartan worn over the left shoulder as part of Highland dress. **2** a usu twilled woollen fabric with a tartan pattern. **3** *chiefly NAmer* tartan. >> **plaided** *adj*. [Scottish Gaelic *plaide* blanket]

Plaid Cymru /,plied 'kumri/ *noun* the Welsh Nationalist Party. [Welsh *Plaid Cymru* Party of Wales]

plain¹ /playn/ *adj* **1a** not fancy or decorated: *a plain dress*. **b** said of a fabric: without a pattern. **c** consisting of a single colour: *a plain white shirt*. **d** flat or smooth. **2** free of added substances; pure: *Just a glass of plain water, please*. **3** unobstructed: *She shoplifted in plain view of the store detective*. **4** obvious; easy to understand; unambiguous: *He made it perfectly plain that he didn't want to go*. **5** free from deceitfulness or subtlety; candid: *She's known for her plain speaking*. **6** lacking special distinction or affectation; ordinary: *I'm just a plain country girl*. **7a** characterized by simplicity; not complicated: *plain home cooking*. **b** not rich or elaborately prepared or decorated. **8** said of a person: not particularly attractive: *I have known several Jacks, and they all, without exception, were more than usually plain* — Oscar Wilde. **9** said of knitting: done in rows of knit stitches. **10** said of an envelope: unmarked with nothing to identify its source or contents. **11** used for emphasis: utter; absolute: *That was just plain stupidity!* >> **plainly** *adv*, **plainness** *noun*. [Middle English via French from Latin *planus* flat, plain]

plain² *noun* **1a** an extensive area of level or rolling treeless country. **b** a broad unbroken expanse of land. **2** = KNIT² (1).

plain³ *adv* **1** in a plain manner; clearly or simply. **2** totally; utterly: *It's just plain daft*.

plain⁴ *verb intrans* archaic **1** to mourn or lament. **2** to complain. **3** to make a mournful or wailing noise. [Middle English via early French *plaindre* from Latin *plangere* to lament]

plainchant *noun* = PLAINSONG. [French *plain-chant*, literally 'plain song']

plain chocolate *noun* Brit chocolate that has no milk added to it, making it darker in colour and more bitter in taste than milk chocolate.

plain clothes *pl noun* **1** ordinary civilian dress as opposed to uniform, *esp* a police uniform. **2** (*used before a noun*) not wearing a uniform: *a plain-clothes detective*.

plain dealing *noun* straightforward honesty: *He's a businessman noted for his plain dealing*.

plain flour *noun* Brit flour that has no raising agent added to it, used in making biscuits, pastry, etc: compare SELF-RAISING FLOUR.

plain sailing *noun* easy or uninterrupted progress.

Word history

this expression derives from *plane sailing*, a simple former method of navigation based on the working hypothesis that the earth's surface is a plane rather than a sphere. Although it is first recorded in English (in the late 17th cent.) in the form *plain sailing*, this stems from the lack of clear distinction between the spellings *plane* and *plain* at the time. The spelling *plane sailing* became usual in the 19th cent., but has now been replaced by *plain sailing*, which arose by association with *plain* meaning 'simple, straightforward'.

Plains Indian *noun* any member of the Native American tribes, such as the Cheyenne, Crow, Dakota, and Pawnee, formerly living on the Great Plains of N America.

plainsman *noun* (*pl* **plainsmen**) a man who lives on a plain, *esp* one of the early settlers in the US prairie regions.

plainsong *noun* **1** unaccompanied vocal music of the medieval church, *esp* GREGORIAN CHANT. **2** a liturgical chant of any of various Christian rites.

plain-spoken *adj* candid or blunt in what one says. >> **plain-spokenness** *noun*.

plain stitch *noun* = KNIT² (1).

plainswoman /'playnzwoomən/ *noun* (*pl* **plainswomen**) a woman who lives on a plain, *esp* one of the early settlers in the US prairie regions.

plaint /playnt/ *noun* **1** Brit a legal document in which the grounds of a complaint are recorded for submission to a court of law. **2** *archaic* a protest. [Middle English from early French *plainte*, ultimately from Latin *plangere* to lament, beat one's breast in grief]

plaintext *noun* computer-generated text in its non-encrypted or decrypted form.

plaintiff /'playntif/ *noun* somebody who brings a civil legal action against another in a court of law: compare DEFENDANT. [Middle English *plaintif* from early French *plaintif* plaintive, grieving, from *plainte*: see PLAINT]

plaintive /'playntiv/ *adj* expressing sorrow or sounding very sad; mournful. >> **plaintively** *adv*, **plaintiveness** *noun*. [Middle English from early French *plaintif* grieving, from *plainte*: see PLAINT]

plain weave *noun* a simple weave in which the weft yarns pass alternatively over and under the warp yarns. >> **plain-weave** *adj*, **plain-woven** *adj*.

plait¹ *or* **plat** /plat/ *noun* **1** a length of plaited material, *esp* hair or rope, made up of three or more interwoven strands. **2** *archaic* = PLEAT¹. [Middle English from early French *pleit* from Latin *plicare* to fold]

plait² *or* **plat** *verb trans* **1a** to interweave the strands of (hair, rope, etc) to form a plait or plaits. **b** to make (something) by plaiting. **2** *archaic* = PLEAT². >> **plaiter** *noun*.

plan¹ /plan/ *noun* **1** a detailed account or proposal of how something can be done or achieved: *Accountants presented a plan for expanding the business*. **2** a proposed or intended course of action: *If you have no plans for this evening, we could go to the cinema*. **3** a financial arrangement, *esp* one that is designed to give security in the future: *a personal savings plan*. **4a** a detailed map of an area, usu on a large scale: *a plan of the city centre*. **b** a diagram or outline of something: *This plan shows where the drainage will go; Here is the seating plan for the conference*. **c** a technical drawing in the horizontal plane of the structure of something, *esp* a building or a single floor of a building. * **go (according) to plan** said of an event, etc: to turn out as intended or arranged: *If everything goes to* *plan, the baby will be born in April.* **plan of action/attack** a scheme for doing or achieving something in which all the elements have been decided in advance. **the/one's best plan** the/one's most appropriate or sensible way of proceeding. [early French *plan* ground plan, plane surface, from *planter*: see PLANT²]

plan² *verb trans* (**planned, planning**) **1** to arrange (something) in advance: *We're planning a school reunion next year; It's always best to plan ahead.* **2** (+ to/on) to intend (to do something): *We don't plan to get married just yet; I'm not planning on going.* **3** to design (something): *I planned the layout of the new kitchen myself.*

plan- *or* **plano-** *comb. form* forming words, with the meaning: level or flat: *planoconcave.*

planar /'playnə/ *adj* of, being, or lying in a mathematical plane. ➤ **planarity** /play'nariti/ *noun.*

planarian /plə'neəri·ən/ *noun* any of various nonparasitic and mostly aquatic flatworms: order Tricladida. [Latin name *Planaria* of one genus of the order, from *planus* flat]

planchet /'plahnchit/ *noun* a plain metal disc for stamping to make a coin, medal, etc. [French *planchet*, dimin. of *planche*: see PLANK¹]

planchette /plan'shet/ *noun* a small often heart-shaped board on castors with a pencil attached to it, used at séances and spiritualist meetings in the belief that it will spell out telepathic messages when touched lightly with the fingers. [French *planchette*, fem of *planchet*: see PLANCHET]

Planck's constant /plangks/ *or* **Planck constant** *noun* in physics, a fundamental constant that is equal to the energy of a quantum of electromagnetic radiation divided by its frequency and which has a value of 6.626×10^{-34} joule-seconds. [named after Max *Planck* d.1947, German physicist]

plane¹ /playn/ *noun* **1a** in mathematics, a surface on which any two included points can be joined by a straight line lying wholly within the surface. **b** a flat or level physical surface. **2** a level of existence, consciousness, or development: *on the intellectual plane.* **3a** *informal* an aeroplane. **b** any of the main supporting surfaces of an aeroplane. [Latin *planum* a level surface, from *planus* flat, level]

plane² *adj* **1** having no elevations or depressions; flat. **2a** of or dealing with geometric planes. **b** lying in a plane: *a plane curve.* [Latin *planus* flat, level]

plane³ *verb intrans* **1a** said of a bird: to fly with the wings motionless. **b** said of something airborne: to glide. **2** said of a speedboat, surfboard, etc: to skim across the surface of the water. [French *planer*, from *plan* PLANE¹; from the plane formed by the wings of a soaring bird]

plane⁴ *noun* a tool with a sharp blade protruding from the base of a flat metal or wooden stock for smoothing or shaping a wooden surface by removing thin shavings. [Middle English via French from Latin *planare* to make level, from *planus* level]

plane⁵ *verb trans* **1** to make (a surface, *esp* a wooden one) flat or even with a plane: *She planed the sides of the door.* **2** (*often* + away/down) to remove (something) by planing. ➤ **planer** *noun.*

plane⁶ *noun* a large deciduous tree with deeply cut lobed leaves and thin bark that is shed in flakes: genus *Platanus.* [Middle English via French from Latin *platanus*; from Greek *platanos*, from *platys* broad; because of its broad leaves]

plane polarization *noun* a process in which the vibrations of electromagnetic radiation, *esp* those of light, are confined to a single direction.

planet /'planit/ *noun* **1a** any of the nine celestial bodies, Mercury, Venus, earth, Mars, Jupiter, Saturn, Uranus, Neptune, or Pluto, that move round our sun in various elliptical orbits: *like some watcher of the skies when a new planet swims into his ken* — Keats. **b** (**the planet**) the earth. **c** any celestial body which orbits a star and which is of substantial size but is not massive enough to become a star itself. **2** in astrology, any of the nine celestial bodies that orbit our sun, together with the sun and moon, thought of in terms of their influence on a person's life, etc. ✳ **on another planet** *informal* out of touch with reality. [Middle English *planete* via Old French from late Latin *planeta*, modification of Greek *planēt-*, *planēs*, literally 'wanderer', from *planasthai* to wander]

plane table *noun dated* a field surveying instrument that consists of a drawing board on a tripod and an alidade.

planetarium /plani'teəri·əm/ *noun* (*pl* **planetariums** *or* **planetaria** /-ri·ə/) **1a** an optical projector for showing images of celestial bodies and effects as seen in the night sky. **b** a domed building or

room where these images are shown. **2** a model of the solar system; an ORRERY.

planetary /'planit(ə)ri/ *adj* **1a** of a planet. **b** having a motion like that of a planet: *planetary electrons.* **2** of or belonging to the earth; terrestrial. **3** *literary* erratic or wandering. **4** in astrology, influenced by a planet. **5** said of a gear: being one of a set that travels around another central gear.

planetary nebula *noun* a bright ring-shaped expanding nebula of fluorescent gas around a star.

planetesimal /plani'tesim(ə)l/ *noun* any of numerous small solid celestial bodies that may aggregate to form larger planets. [from PLANET + *-esimal* as in INFINITESIMAL²]

planetoid /'planitoyd/ *noun* = ASTEROID¹. ➤ **planetoidal** /-'toydl/ *adj.*

planform *noun* a view in the horizontal plane of an object, *esp* an aircraft wing, from above.

plangent /'planj(ə)nt/ *adj literary* **1** said of a sound: loudly reverberating. **2** said of a sound: having an expressive, *esp* plaintive, quality. ➤ **plangency** *noun*, **plangently** *adv.* [Latin *plangent-*, *plangens*, present part. of *plangere* to lament, beat one's breast in grief]

planimeter /plə'nimitə/ *noun* an instrument for measuring the area of a plane figure by tracing its boundary line. ➤ **planimetric** /-'metrik/ *adj*, **planimetry** /-tri/ *noun.* [Latin *planum* plane + -METER²]

planish /'planish/ *verb trans* to toughen and finish (metal) by hammering. ➤ **planisher** *noun.* [from early French *planiss-*, stem of *planir* to make smooth]

planisphere /'planisfiə/ *noun* a polar projection of the celestial sphere and the stars on a plane to show the relative positions of the constellations at any given time. ➤ **planispheric** /-'sferik/ *adj.* [from Latin *planisphaerium* from *planum* (see PLANE¹) + *sphaera* (see SPHERE¹)]

plank¹ /plangk/ *noun* **1** a long thick piece of wood, *esp* a piece of sawn timber used in constructing floors, roofs, and walls. **2** a major article in an official programme, *esp* a policy that is fundamental to the declared aims of a political party. ✳ **walk the plank** to be made to walk off the end of a plank jutting out from a ship, *esp* by pirates. [Middle English from early French *planche*, dialect form of *planche*, from Latin *planca* board, fem of *plancus* flat]

plank² *verb trans* **1** to cover or floor (an area) with planks. **2** *NAmer, Irish* to put (something or oneself) down heavily, forcefully, or clumsily.

planking *noun* a number of planks thought of collectively, *esp* when used, or to be used, together to construct a floor, boat, etc.

plankton /'plangktən/ *noun* the minute animals and plants, mainly microscopic diatoms and protozoans, but also tiny crustaceans, fish eggs, and larvae, that float near the surface of seas and lakes: compare NEKTON. ➤ **planktonic** /plangk'tonik/ *adj.* [German *Plankton* from Greek *planktos* drifting, from *plazesthai* to wander]

planned economy *noun* an economy in which a nation's central government sets and controls the levels of investment, production, prices, and incomes rather than allowing market forces to determine them.

planned obsolescence *noun* a way of increasing consumer demand for manufactured goods by making them less durable than they could be, *esp* by using materials that soon wear out, stopping the production of spare parts, and frequently updating or modifying the design or function.

planner *noun* **1** somebody who plans something, *esp* a person who draws plans or who is involved in town planning. **2** a chart on which one can mark appointments, holidays, tasks, etc.

planning permission *noun Brit* formal permission given by a local authority for the erection or alteration of buildings or other structures.

plano- *comb. form* see PLAN-.

planoconcave /ˌplaynohkon'kayv/ *adj* said *esp* of a lens: flat on one side and concave on the other.

planoconvex /ˌplaynohkon'veks/ *adj* said *esp* of a lens: flat on one side and convex on the other.

plant¹ /plahnt/ *noun* **1a** any of various living but immobile multicellular organisms such as trees and flowers that typically have cellulose cell walls, root systems for absorbing water and inorganic substances, and leaves that manufacture nutrients. **b** a tree, shrub, vine, etc that is, or can be, planted, *esp* a soft-stemmed or fleshy-stemmed nonwoody plant smaller than a shrub or tree. **2a** a building or collection of buildings where large-scale manufacturing or processing takes place. **b** machinery and equipment necessary for a large-scale manufacturing or processing operation to function: *The company is investing in new plant.* **3a** a person who secretly infiltrates an organization in order to spy, gain information, or cause trouble. **b** something that has surreptitiously been put in a person's belongings, home, etc with the intention of incriminating them: *He claimed the stash of drugs was a police plant.* **c** somebody placed in an audience to assist a performer. **4** in snooker, a shot in which the cue ball strikes one of two balls that are touching or lying close together, so that the other is potted.

plant[2] *verb trans* **1a** to put (a seed, plant, bulb, etc) in a place with the right conditions to encourage germination or growth: *One guy plants bananas; another plants cocoa; I'm a writer, I plant lines* — Derek Walcott. **b** to give (a place) over to the germination or growth of a specified plant or crop: *Monty planted the field with potatoes.* **2** to put or settle (something, somebody, or oneself) firmly in a specified place: *She planted herself in the most comfortable arm-chair.* **3** to send (somebody) to infiltrate an organization to spy, gain information, or cause trouble: *The company planted a mole in their rival's laboratories.* **4** to place or hide (an explosive device). **5** to establish (an idea, etc) in somebody's mind. **6** to put (something incriminating) surreptitiously in somebody's belongings, home, etc: *He said somebody must have planted the gun on him.* **7** to establish or found (a new colony, community, etc). **8a** to put (young fish, spawn, oysters, etc) in water, *esp* in a lake or river to improve the fishing or in a fish farm for cultivation. **b** to stock (a stretch of water) with young fish, spawn, oysters, etc. **9** *informal* to land (a punch or blow). [Old English *plantian* and early French *planter*, both from Latin *plantare* to plant, fix in place]

Plantagenet[1] /plan'taj(ə)nit/ *adj* belonging to or denoting the English royal house that ruled from 1154 to 1485. [early French *Plantagenet*, literally 'sprig of broom', from Latin *planta* sprig + *genista* broom, a representation of which appeared on the family's crest, later becoming the nickname of Geoffrey of Anjou, father of Henry III]

Plantagenet[2] *noun* a member of the Plantagenet dynasty.

plantain[1] /'plantayn, 'plantin/ *noun* any of numerous species of short-stemmed plants with dense spikes of minute greenish or brownish flowers and usu a rosette of oval or sword-shaped leaves, typically found growing on wasteland or road verges: genus *Plantago.* [Middle English via French from Latin *plantagin-, plantago*, from *planta* sole of the foot, because of its broad leaves]

plantain[2] *noun* **1** a green-skinned fruit, resembling a banana but more angular in form, that is a staple food in many tropical regions. **2** the large treelike plant that bears this fruit: *Musa paradisiaca.* [Spanish *plantano* plane tree, from Latin *platanus*: see PLANE[6]]

plantain lily *noun* = HOSTA.

plantar /'plantə/ *adj* relating to the sole of the foot. [Latin *plantaris* from *planta* sole]

plantation /plahn'taysh(ə)n, plan-/ *noun* **1** a large estate where commercial crops, such as coffee, tea, tobacco, and rubber, are grown, *esp* in tropical areas. **2** an area where trees are grown for commercial purposes. **3** *dated* a settlement in a new country or region; a colony.

planter *noun* **1** somebody who owns or manages a plantation: *a tea planter.* **2** a container in which ornamental plants are grown. **3** a machine for planting seeds, bulbs, etc, *esp* one designed to cover a large area quickly. **4** *archaic* somebody who settles or founds a new colony.

planter's punch *noun* any of various rum-based cocktails made with lime, lemon, orange, or pineapple juice, sugar, grenadine, soda water, and sometimes angostura bitters. [so called because it was a favourite drink of 19th-cent. sugar-plantation owners and managers]

plantigrade[1] /'plantigrayd/ *adj* said of humans and certain mammals, such as bears: walking on the sole with the heel touching the ground: compare DIGITIGRADE[1]. [French *plantigrade*, from Latin *planta* sole + -*gradus* walking]

plantigrade[2] *noun* a plantigrade animal.

plant kingdom *noun* the one of the three basic groups of natural objects that includes all living and extinct plants: compare ANIMAL KINGDOM, MINERAL KINGDOM.

plantlet /'plantlit/ *noun* a small plant, *esp* a young plant.

plant louse *noun* an aphid or other small insect that lives as a parasite on plants.

plant out *verb trans* to transplant (e.g. seedlings or a house plant) from a pot, seed tray, etc to open ground.

plaque /plak, plahk/ *noun* **1a** a commemorative or decorative inscribed tablet, *esp* one fixed to a wall. **b** an ornamental brooch, *esp* the badge of an honorary order. **2a** a film of mucus on teeth where bacteria multiply: compare TARTAR (2). **b** a localized abnormal patch in a body part or on the surface of a body part, often the result of injury or a build-up of mineral deposits. [French *plaque* from *plaquier* to lay flat, from early Dutch *placken* to piece, patch]

plash[1] /plash/ *noun* **1** *literary* a shallow or muddy pool. **2** a splashing noise. >>> **plashy** *adj.* [Middle English *plasche*, of imitative origin]

plash[2] *verb trans* *literary* to break the surface of (water) with a splash. > *verb intrans* *literary* to cause a splashing or spattering effect.

-plasia *or* **-plasy** *comb. form* forming nouns, denoting: development, formation, or growth: *hyperplasia.* [scientific Latin from Greek *plasis* moulding, from *plassein* to mould]

plasm /'plaz(ə)m/ *noun* **1** = GERM PLASM. **2** = PLASMA. [late Latin *plasma*: see PLASMA]

plasm- *or* **plasmo-** *comb. form* forming words, denoting: plasma or cytoplasm: *plasmin; plasmolysis.* [late Latin *plasma*: see PLASMA]

-plasm *comb. form* forming nouns, denoting: structural material of a living organism, *esp* of a cell: *endoplasm.* [from PROTOPLASM]

plasma /'plazmə/ *noun* **1a** the fluid part of blood, lymph, or milk in which material such as corpuscles, fat globules, and other cells are suspended. **b** a sterilized preparation made from the plasma of donated blood and used in transfusions. Also called BLOOD PLASMA. **2** a former name for PROTOPLASM or CYTOPLASM. **3** a highly ionized gas containing approximately equal numbers of positive ions and electrons. **4** a green variety of chalcedony used as a semiprecious gemstone. >>> **plasmatic** /plaz'matik/ *adj.* [late Latin *plasma* mould, image, from Greek *plassein* to mould]

plasma torch *noun* a device that heats a gas by electrical means to form a plasma for high-temperature operations, *esp* in melting metal.

plasmid /'plazmid/ *noun* a piece of DNA in *esp* bacteria that exists and reproduces independently of the cell's chromosomes, used for carrying introduced genes of commercial value.

plasmin /'plazmin/ *noun* an enzyme that breaks down the fibrin of blood clots.

plasminogen /plaz'minəjən/ *noun* the substance found in blood plasma and serum from which plasmin is formed.

plasmo- *comb. form* see PLASM-.

plasmodium /plaz'mohdi·əm/ *noun* (*pl* **plasmodia** /-di·ə/) **1** a stage in the cycle of certain simple organisms, such as the slime moulds, in which a mass of protoplasm with many nuclei is formed. **2** any of a genus of parasitic protozoans, including the species that causes malaria: genus *Plasmodium.* >>> **plasmodial** *adj.* [scientific Latin, from PLASM- + -*odium* thing resembling]

plasmolysis /plaz'moləsis/ *noun* shrinking of the cytoplasm away from the wall of a living cell due to water loss by osmosis, *esp* in a plant that has been deprived of water. >>> **plasmolytic** /-'litik/ *adj.*

-plast *comb. form* forming nouns, denoting: a living cell or a small body of living material: *protoplast.* [Greek *plastos* moulded, from *plassein* to mould]

plaster[1] /'plahstə/ *noun* **1** a paste-like mixture, e.g. of lime, water, and sand, that hardens on drying and is used *esp* for coating walls, ceilings, and partitions. **2** an adhesive strip, often with a small pad in the middle, used for covering and protecting small cuts, blisters, etc. **3** a rigid dressing made from plaster of Paris and used for immobilizing a broken bone, *esp* in a limb, to allow it to heal in the correct position. >>> **plastery** *adj.* [Old English *plaster* and Old French *plastre*, both from Latin *plastrum*, from Greek *emplassein* to plaster on, from EN-[1] + *plassein* to mould]

plaster[2] *verb trans* (**plastered, plastering**) **1** to coat (a wall, ceiling, etc) with plaster. **2** to apply plaster to (a wall, ceiling, etc). **3a** to cover over or conceal (something) with a coat of plaster. **b** to coat or cover (something) thickly with a specified substance: *She plastered her face with make-up.* **c** to cause (something) to lie flat or stick to another surface: *He plastered his hair down; The heavy rain* *plastered his shirt to his body.* **4** *informal.* **a** to put (a large number of things) on a specified surface: *Sophie plastered posters all over her bedroom walls.* **b** to publish or display (something) conspicuously: *The scandal was plastered across the front page of every tabloid newspaper.* **5** to apply a plaster cast to (a broken limb, etc). **6** *informal, dated* to inflict heavy damage, injury, or casualties on (a person or target), *esp* by a concentrated or unremitting attack. ⋙ **plasterer** *noun.*

plasterboard *noun* a board with a plaster core used *esp* as a substitute for plaster on interior walls.

plaster cast *noun* = PLASTER¹ (3).

plaster down *verb trans* = PLASTER² (3C).

plastered *adj informal* drunk.

plastering *noun* **1** a coating with, or as if with, plaster. **2** *informal* a decisive defeat.

plaster of Paris /'paris/ *noun* a white powder made from gypsum that forms a quick-setting paste when mixed with water, and which is chiefly used for making casts for broken limbs, etc and moulds, *esp* in sculpture. [named after *Paris*, capital city of France, where it was first produced]

plasterwork *noun* plaster on interior walls, *esp* when it has a decorative effect.

plastic¹ /'plastik/ *noun* **1** any of numerous synthetic organic polymers that, while soft, can be moulded, cast, etc into shapes and then set to have a rigid or slightly elastic form. Plastic is used in the manufacture of a wide variety of things, as an artificial fibre, and as a coating material. **2** *informal* = PLASTIC MONEY.

plastic² *adj* **1** made of plastic or a material resembling plastic. **2a** capable of being moulded; soft and pliable. **b** said of a person: easily influenced; impressionable. **3** said of an art form: involving moulding or modelling to create three-dimensional objects. **4** said of a scientific technique: showing or involving permanent distortion of a solid form through the application of a temporary force which does not lead to fracturing. **5** involving or relating to a formative or creative power: *the plastic forces of nature.* **6** said of a medium such as poetry or film: involving or allowing creativity or freedom of interpretation. **7** *derog* artificial: *Sinister influences are at work to turn Fiji into another Hawaii, that plastic paradise further along the route — Observer.* ⋙ **plastically** *adv.* [via Latin from Greek *plastikos* relating to moulding, from *plassein* to mould]

-plastic *comb. form* forming adjectives, with the meanings: developing, forming, or growing: *thromboplastic.* [Greek *-plastikos:* see PLASTIC²]

plastic art *noun* (*usu in pl*) any form of visual art, such as sculpture, ceramics, or architecture, that involves the use of modelling or moulding to produce a three-dimensional object or effect.

plastic bomb *noun* a bomb made with a plastic explosive.

plastic bullet *noun* a bullet made from PVC or other plastic material for use in riot control and crowd dispersal, causing less damage than a conventional bullet: compare RUBBER BULLET.

plastic explosive *noun* a pliable doughlike explosive substance that can be moulded by hand to fit and adhere to a surface.

Plasticine /'plastiseen/ *noun trademark* a soft pliable coloured substance used, *esp* by children, for play and modelling. [PLASTIC² + -INE²]

plasticise *verb trans* see PLASTICIZE.

plasticiser *noun* see PLASTICIZER.

plasticity /plas'tisiti/ *noun* **1** the capacity a material has for being moulded or altered. **2** the ability to retain a shape produced by pressure deformation.

plasticize *or* **plasticise** /'plastisiez/ *verb trans* to add (something) to a substance, material, etc in order to give or increase flexibility. ⋙ **plasticization** /-'zaysh(ə)n/ *noun.*

plasticizer *or* **plasticiser** *noun* a chemical added *esp* to rubbers and plastics to give or increase flexibility.

plasticky *adj* made of or resembling plastic, *esp* in being artificial or of poor quality.

plastic money *noun informal* a credit card, or credit cards collectively.

plastic surgery *noun* surgery concerned with the repair, restoration, or cosmetic improvement of parts of the body chiefly by the grafting of tissue. ⋙ **plastic surgeon** *noun.*

plastid /'plastid/ *noun* any of various organelles (specialized structures; see ORGANELLE) of plant cells that function as centres

of photosynthesis, store starch, oil, etc, or contain pigment. ⋙ **plastidial** /pla'stidi-əl/ *adj.* [German *Plastid* from Greek *plastos* moulded, from *plassein* to mould]

plastination /plasti'naysh(ə)n/ *noun* the preservation of biological specimens by a process in which body fluids and fat are replaced by substances such as silicone rubber, epoxy resins, or polyester. ⋙ **plastinated** /'plastinaytid/ *adj.*

plastron /'plastrən/ *noun* **1** a quilted pad worn in fencing to protect the chest, waist, and sides. **2** the underside of the shell of a tortoise or turtle. Also called BREASTPLATE. **3a** a shirt front, *esp* the starched and sometimes embroidered or frilled front of a man's evening or dress shirt. **b** the front part of a type of dress bodice popular during the 19th cent. ⋙ **plastral** *adj.* [early French *plastron* from Italian *piastrone,* augmentative of *piastra* thin metal plate, from Latin *emplastrum:* see PLASTER¹]

-plasty *comb. form* forming nouns, denoting: the surgical alteration, replacement, or formation of a specified part of the body: *rhinoplasty.* [Greek *plassein* to mould]

-plasy *comb. form* see -PLASIA.

plat¹ /plat/ *noun* = PLAIT¹.

plat² *verb trans* (**platted, platting**) = PLAIT².

plat³ *noun chiefly NAmer* **1** a small plot of land. **2** a map that shows features such as the position of streets, buildings, areas of waste ground, etc and often proposed developments. [Middle English, variant of PLOT¹]

plat⁴ *verb trans* (**platted, platting**) *chiefly NAmer* to make a map of (an area), *esp* one that shows existing features and proposed developments.

platan /'plat(ə)n/ *noun* = PLANE⁶. [Middle English via Latin from Greek *platanus:* see PLANE⁶]

plat du jour /,plah doo 'zhooə (*French* pla dy ʒu:r)/ *noun* (*pl* **plats du jour** /,plah/) a dish featured by a restaurant on a particular day in addition to those offered on the regular menu. [French *plat du jour,* literally 'plate of the day']

plate¹ /playt/ *noun* **1a** a flat and usu circular dish from which food is eaten or served. **b** an amount of food held by or served on this type of dish: *a plate of ravioli.* **c** *NAmer* a complete course of a meal served on this type of dish; a platter: *I'll have the seafood plate, thank you.* **d** *Aus, NZ* a dish filled with food and brought by a guest as a contribution to a party: *Sheila was asked to bring a savoury plate.* **e** a flat dish, often of silver or wood, that is passed round a church congregation for donations of money. **f** *esp* in the Roman Catholic Church, a small flat dish held under a person's chin at communion to catch any crumbs of consecrated bread. **2a** a flat sheet or strip of metal, *esp* one that is rolled or hammered to become very thin and used to coat another metal. **b** metal or metal objects coated in this: *a collection of silver plate.* **c** tableware and other household articles made of gold or silver. **d** a flat piece of metal that overlaps and articulates with many other similar pieces to form armour. **e** armour that is constructed from these. **3a** a thin piece of metal or plastic with an inscription on it. **b** a strip used for identifying something: *a personalized numberplate; Thieves had changed the van's registration plates.* **4a** a piece of metal or other material used for strengthening or joining purposes. **b** a moulded piece of plastic with an artificial tooth or teeth attached to it. **c** *informal* a set of dentures. **5a** a flat piece of a naturally occurring material, often one of several fused together to form an organic structure such as the outer covering of an animal's body or the shell of a turtle, tortoise, etc. **b** any of the rigid but mobile blocks that together form the earth's crust: see also PLATE TECTONICS. **6a** a sheet of metal or other material with text or an image on it, used for printing multiple copies of the text or image. **b** an impression taken from this type of sheet or from a woodcut. **c** a full-page book illustration, *esp* one produced on high-quality paper. **d** a sheet coated with a light-sensitive film used in early cameras to capture an image. **7a** a sporting competition in which the prize is a large flat dish, usu a silver or gold one with engraving. **b** a sporting competition, *esp* in horseracing, in which the prize is a silver or gold cup, bowl, etc. **c** a large dish, cup, or bowl awarded in a sporting competition. **8** a small light-weight horseshoe used *esp* for racehorses. **9** in baseball, = HOME PLATE. **10** in architecture, a horizontal supporting member, *esp* in a wood-frame construction, e.g. a WALL PLATE. **11** *chiefly NAmer.* **a** a thin piece of metal used in a battery, capacitor, cell, etc as an electrode. **b** the anode in an electron valve or tube. ✱ **on a plate** without having to make any great effort: *She was handed the opportunity on a plate.* **on one's plate** to be dealt with or worked on: *I've got too much on my plate to take on any new contracts.* [Middle English via French *plat* from Latin *plata* plate armour, ultimately from Greek *platys* flat]

plate² *verb trans* **1** to coat (a surface, *esp* a metallic one, or a metal object) with a thin layer of rolled or hammered metal, usu gold, silver, or steel. **2** to add or attach a decorative, protective, or strengthening plate or plates to (something). **3** to form (metal) into plate by rolling or hammering. **4** to serve (food) on a plate: *Meals in this restaurant are always plated in imaginative ways.* **5** in printing, to produce (an image, copy, etc) from a plate.

plate armour *noun* = PLATE¹ (2E).

plateau¹ /'platoh/ *noun* (*pl* **plateaus** *or* **plateaux** /'platohz/) **1** a wide, fairly flat area of ground that is much higher than the land around it. **2** a state of stability or a lack of change, *esp* after a period of activity: *House prices appear to have reached a plateau.* [French *plateau* from early French *plat* flat, ultimately from Greek *platys*]

plateau² *verb intrans* (**plateaus, plateaued, plateauing**) to become stable or reach a stage where there is little or no change, *esp* after a period of activity: *Stock market prices have plateaued recently.*

plateful /'playtf(ə)l/ *noun* (*pl* **platefuls**) as much as a plate will hold.

plate glass *noun* (*often used before a noun*) rolled, ground, and polished sheet glass, used *esp* in shop and office windows: *Across the meadows he could see the flats of the council estate, the sun striking their plate-glass windows and making them blaze as if the whole place was on fire* — Ruth Rendell.

platelayer *noun Brit* a person who lays and maintains railway track.

platelet /'playtlit/ *noun* = BLOOD PLATELET.

platen /'plat(ə)n/ *noun* **1** a flat plate that exerts pressure, *esp* in a printing press where it holds the paper against the type. **2** the roller of a typewriter against which the paper is held. [early French *plateine* metal plate, from *plat*: see PLATEAU¹]

plateresque /platə'resk/ *adj* (*also* **Plateresque**) said *esp* of Spanish architecture: ornate in style with decorative parts that resemble motifs used in silverware. [Spanish *plateresco* from *platero* silversmith, from *plata* silver, ultimately from Greek *platys* flat]

plate tectonics *pl noun* (*treated as sing.*) the study of the formation of the major structures of the earth's surface, *esp* in the context of the theory that the LITHOSPHERE (earth's crust) is composed of rigid plates (see PLATE¹ (5B)) that can interact with each other at their boundaries because of the molten nature of the mantle below them. ➤➤ **platetectonic** *adj*, **platetectonically** *adv*.

platform /'platfawm/ *noun* **1a** a raised area, *esp* in a hall, where a speaker or performer can be seen by the audience. **b** (*used before a noun*) present on a platform, e.g. because of being important: *The platform party included the mayor and her husband.* **c** a level horizontal surface that is raised above the area around it: *The artefacts were displayed on individual platforms.* **d** a raised area by the track at a railway station where passengers can wait for and board or leave trains. **e** an area on a bus where passengers pay fares and wait to alight. **2** a raised structure housing the equipment used for drilling for oil and gas. **3** in computing, the combination of a particular type of CPU and operating system, which determines what programs can be run. **4** in space technology, an orbiting structure used for launching missiles, rockets, satellites, etc. **5** an official policy, *esp* a declared political one that distinguishes one party or group from the others and is used as a means of attracting support. **6** an opportunity, means, or place where opinions can be expressed; a forum: *An Internet newsgroup offers a good platform for interactive discussions.* **7** (*usu in pl*) a shoe with a built-up sole: *Julian wore five-inch black platforms.* [French *platforme* a ground plan, from *plat* (see PLATEAU¹) + *forme* FORM¹]

platform game *noun* a type of computer game in which a player's object is to manipulate a character through various obstacles and so progress from one level or platform to the next, the levels usually becoming progressively more testing of the player's skills.

plating /'playting/ *noun* **1** a thin coating of metal. **2** a coating of metal plates.

platinize *or* **platinise** /'platiniez/ *verb trans* to coat (something, *esp* another metal) with platinum. ➤➤ **platinization** /-'zayshən/ *noun*.

platinum /'platinəm/ *noun* **1** a greyish white precious metallic chemical element that is heavy and does not corrode, occurs

naturally in copper and nickel ores, and is used *esp* as a catalyst and in making jewellery: symbol Pt, atomic number 78. **2** (*used before a noun*) silvery in colour. [Spanish *platina*, dimin. of *plata*: see PLATERESQUE]

platinum black *noun* a soft dull black powder of platinum used as a catalyst.

platinum blonde¹ *or* **platinum blond** *adj* said *esp* of hair: having a pale silvery-blonde colour.

platinum blonde² *or* **platinum blond** *noun* somebody, *esp* a woman, with silvery-blonde hair.

platinum disc *noun* a music award in the form of a framed platinum record given to an artist, group, etc in Britain for selling 300,000 copies of an album.

platinum metals *pl noun* a group of six metals, ruthenium, osmium, rhodium, iridium, palladium, and platinum, with similar physical and chemical properties and a tendency to occur naturally together.

platitude /'platityoohd/ *noun* **1** a trite remark stating the self-evident, typically made for the sake of something to say: *Where in this small talking world can I find a longitude with no platitude?* — Christopher Fry. **2** triteness. ➤➤ **platitudinous** /-'tyoohdinəs/ *adj*. [French *platitude*, from *plat*: see PLATEAU¹]

platitudinize *or* **platitudinise** /plati'tyoohdiniez/ *verb intrans* to utter platitudes.

platonic /plə'tonik/ *adj* **1** (**Platonic**) characteristic of or relating to Plato or Platonism. **2** said of a friendship or love: close but not sexual. ➤➤ **platonically** *adv*. [via Latin from Greek *Platōnikos*, from *Platōn* Plato d.349 BC, Greek philosopher]

Platonic body *noun* = PLATONIC SOLID.

Platonic solid *noun* any one of the five regular convex solids described by Plato, i.e. the tetrahedron (four triangular faces), the hexahedron (six square faces), the octahedron (eight triangular faces), the dodecahedron (twelve pentagonal faces), and the icosahedron (twenty triangular faces).

Platonism /'playtəniz(ə)m/ *noun* the philosophy of Plato, according to which actual things, such as cats and beds, and ideas, such as truth or beauty, are copies of transcendent ideas which are the objects of true knowledge. ➤➤ **Platonist** *noun*, **Platonistic** /-'nistik/ *adj*.

platoon /plə'toohn/ *noun* (*treated as sing. or pl*) **1** a subdivision of a military company normally consisting of two or more sections or squads, each composed of ten to twelve soldiers. **2** a group of people sharing a common characteristic or activity: *a platoon of waiters.* [from French *peloton* small detachment, literally 'a small ball': see PELOTON]

plats du jour /ˌplah doo 'zhooə/ *noun pl* of PLAT DU JOUR.

Plattdeutsch /'platdoych/ *noun* = LOW GERMAN. [German *Plattdeutsch* from Dutch *Platduitsch*, literally 'Low German', from *plat* flat, low + *duitsch* German]

platteland /'plutəlunt/ *noun SAfr* remote rural areas. [Afrikaans *platteland* from Dutch, literally 'flatland']

platter /'platə/ *noun* **1** a large often oval plate used *esp* for serving meat. **2** a meal that consists of a variety of foods served on one plate: *a cold meat platter.* **3** *NAmer, dated* a gramophone record. ✻ **on a (silver) platter** *informal* used to indicate something that is given or achieved easily or effortlessly: *He handed her the job on a silver platter.* ➤➤ **platterful** (*pl* **platterfuls**) *noun*. [Middle English *plater* via Anglo-French from early French *plat*: see PLATE¹]

platy- *comb. form* forming words, with the meaning: flat, *esp* broad and flat: *platypus.* [Greek *platys* broad, flat]

platyhelminth /plati'helminth/ *noun* any of a phylum of various soft-bodied flattened worms, including the planarians, flukes, and tapeworms: phylum Platyhelminthes. ➤➤ **platyhelminthic** /-'minthik/ *adj*. [Greek *platys* broad, flat + *helminth-*, *helmis* worm]

platypus /'platipəs/ *noun* (*pl* **platypuses**) a small aquatic Australian and Tasmanian primitive egg-laying mammal that has a fleshy bill resembling that of a duck, webbed feet, and a broad flattened tail: *Ornithorhynchus anatinus.* Also called DUCK-BILLED PLATYPUS. [via Latin from Greek *platypous* flat-footed, from *platys* broad, flat + *pous* foot]

platyrrhine /'platirien/ *noun* **1a** any of a group of American monkeys, e.g. the marmosets, tamarins, and capuchins, which have flattened noses with widely spaced nostrils, and prehensile tails: compare CATARRHINE. **b** (*used before a noun*) relating to or denoting this group of monkeys or a monkey that belongs to this group. **2a** a person with a broad flattened nose. **b** (*used before a noun*) relating to or denoting this type of person. [PLATY- + Greek *rhin-, rhis* nose + -INE¹]

plaudit /'plawdit/ *noun* (*usu in pl*) an expression of enthusiastic approval. [Latin *plaudite* applaud, pl imperative of *plaudere* to applaud, a command given to the audience by Roman actors at the end of a play]

plausible /'plawzǝbl/ *adj* **1** apparently fair, reasonable, or valid but often specious: *a highly plausible pretext*. **2** said of a person: persuasive or believable, but deceptive. ⟫⟫ **plausibility** /-'biliti/ *noun*, **plausibly** *adv*. [Latin *plausibilis* worthy of applause, from *plaudere* to applaud]

play¹ /play/ *verb trans* **1a** to take part in (a sport, game, etc). **b** to compete with (another person or team) in a sport or game: *Fred was playing his brother at draughts*. **2** to choose or use (a player, side, etc) in a certain way or for a certain role. **3a** to strike (a ball) or carry out (a shot) in a sport. **b** to move (a piece) or lay (a card, etc) at one's turn in a game. **4a** to make music on (a specified instrument). **b** to produce (a piece of music, notes, etc) on a musical instrument: *The band played a waltz*. **5** to cause (a radio, record player, compact disc, etc) to produce sounds. **6a** to perform (a role) in a drama, film, etc. **b** to take on (a role) in play: *The children were playing Star Wars*. **c** to have the attributes or role of (somebody or something): *He tried to play the peacemaker without success*. **7** to apply (a joke, trick, etc) for fun or deception. **8** to deal with (something) in a specified way: *The boss tried to play the issue discreetly*. **9** to bet on (horses, etc). **10** to buy and sell shares on (the stock market). ⟩ *verb intrans* **1a** to engage in activities for enjoyment or recreation. **b** (+ with) to use something for amusement or fun: *The child was playing with an old box*. **2a** to behave or speak in a light-hearted way. **b** (+ with) to treat somebody or something frivolously: *He should stop playing with the poor girl's feelings*. **3a** to act or behave in a specified way: *I always try to play fair*. **b** (+ at) to engage in an activity in a desultory or half-hearted way: *You can't play at being a parent*. **4** to take part in a sport or game: *He usually plays for a local team*. **5** to produce music: *The band started playing*. **6** to take part in a play, film, etc: *She played opposite Olivier in Hamlet*. **7** to exist or feature briefly, intermittently, or freely: *The lights played on the water*. ✽ **play ball** *informal* to cooperate. **play fast and loose** to act irresponsibly. **play for time** to concoct delays in order to gain an advantage. **play hard to get** *informal* to assume an attitude of indifference to personal advances. **play into the hands of somebody** to act in a way that gives an opponent or rival an advantage. **play it by ear** to use one's instincts and adapt to circumstances in a course of action. **play it cool** to give an impression of nonchalance. **play one's cards right** to act correctly or successfully. **play somebody for** to treat somebody in a specified way: *Don't play me for a complete idiot*. **play the field** to engage in sexual encounters with several partners. **play the game** to behave fairly. **play with oneself** to masturbate. **play with fire** see FIRE¹. **to play with** at one's disposal: *a lot of money to play with*. ⟫⟫ **playability** /-ǝ'biliti/ *noun*, **playable** *adj*. [Old English *plag(i)en* to exercise]

play² *noun* **1a** activity that is done for fun, recreation, or amusement: *I love watching children at play*. **b** fun that is derived from a joke, trick, etc: *They didn't mean any harm, it was only done in play*. **2** a piece of dramatic literature meant to be acted out on stage or broadcast on television or radio: *The play's the thing wherein I'll catch the conscience of the King* — Shakespeare. **3a** conduct of a specified nature, *esp* in sports or games, or in dealing with other people: *I'm here to ensure fair play*. **b** an action that is designed to have a specified effect or outcome: *It's just a play for sympathy*. **4** in a sport, game, etc: **a** a move or the action: *It's your play*; *The referee stopped play after the illegal tackle*. **b** the period during which the action takes place: *Rain stopped play*. **c** the set boundaries within which the action takes place: *The ball went out of play*. **d** the quality or type of action; the level of skill: *The competition featured some outstanding play*. **e** *NAmer* a manoeuvre or move. **5a** ease or freedom of movement, *esp* of a machine part. **b** freedom or scope: *Try to give full play to the child's imagination*. **c** brief, intermittent, or free motion: *The play of the snowflakes against the car windscreen is mesmerizing*. ✽ **call into play** to bring (somebody or something) into operation. **in/into play 1** in/into condition or position to be legitimately played. **2** in/into operation or consideration. **make a play for** to take deliberate action to try to obtain (somebody or something). **out of play** not in play.

playa /'plah·yǝ/ *noun* the flat bottom of an undrained desert basin that occasionally becomes a shallow lake. [Spanish *playa* beach, from Latin *plagia*]

play about *verb intrans* **1** to behave irresponsibly. **2** (+ with) to tinker with something. **3** *informal* to have a sexual affair.

play-act *verb intrans* **1** to pretend or make believe. **2** to behave in a misleading, insincere, or histrionic manner. ⟩ *verb trans* to act (a part or role), on stage or in reality. ⟫⟫ **play-acting** *noun*, **play-actor** *noun*. [earliest as *play-acting*]

play along *verb intrans* **1** (*often* + with) to pretend to cooperate with somebody or something. **2** to give a musical accompaniment to somebody or something or join in with music being played.

play around *verb intrans* = PLAY ABOUT.

playback *noun* **1** the act or an instance of reproducing previously recorded images or sound. **2** a button or device that activates this process.

play back *verb trans* to reproduce (sound or pictures) from (a recorded medium).

playbill *noun* an advertising poster giving details of a theatrical production, e.g. the dates and times, venue, ticket prices, and cast list.

playboy *noun* a wealthy man who devotes himself to luxury and personal, *esp* sexual, enjoyment.

play down *verb trans* to minimize the importance of (an incident, *esp* an embarrassing or compromising one).

played out *adj* worn or tired out.

player *noun* **1** a person who takes part in a sport, game, etc. **2** a person who plays a musical instrument: *a trumpet player; an accomplished player of the harp*. **3** a device for playing back music, videos, etc from a cassette, compact disc or other disc, record, etc: *a cassette player*. **4** a person or group taking part in some activity or working in a specified way or at a specified level: *The appointee must be an excellent team player*. **5** *literary, dated* an actor in the theatre.

player-manager *noun* somebody who manages a sports team, *esp* a professional football team, and who also plays for it.

player piano *noun* a piano containing a mechanical device that operates the keys automatically; a PIANOLA.

playfellow *noun dated* = PLAYMATE.

playful /'playf(ǝ)l/ *adj* **1** full of fun; high-spirited: *a playful kitten*. **2** humorously light-hearted or good-natured: *the playful tone of her voice*. ⟫⟫ **playfully** *adv*, **playfulness** *noun*.

playground *noun* **1** a piece of land for children to play on, *esp* one attached to a school or in a park, etc with swings, slides, etc. **2** an area favoured for recreation or amusement: *The town was a gambler's playground*.

playgroup *noun chiefly Brit* a supervised group of children below school age who play together regularly.

playhouse /'playhows/ *noun* **1** a theatre, used *esp* in names of theatres. **2** a toy house for children to play in.

playing card *noun* any of a set of usu 52 thin rectangular pieces of cardboard etc, used in playing numerous card games. Each has an identical design on one side and distinguishing marks or pictures on the other, indicating one of the four suits (see SUIT¹ (2A)) and one of the 13 ranks (ace to ten and jack, queen, king). There may also be two jokers (see JOKER).

playing field *noun* (*also in pl*) a field used for playing organized games and often divided into several separate pitches.

playlet /'playlit/ *noun* a short play.

playlist¹ *noun* a list of the songs or musical pieces chosen to be broadcast on a radio programme or played by a disc jockey during a session at a club or by a band at a concert.

playlist² *verb trans* to include (a song or piece of music) on a playlist.

playmaker *noun* a player in a team sport who creates attacking moves and scoring opportunities.

playmate *noun* a friend with whom somebody, *esp* a child, regularly plays.

play off *verb intrans* said of two teams or players: to take part in a play-off. ⟩ *verb trans* to bring (other people) into conflict for one's own advantage.

play-off *noun* a final contest or an extra match played to determine a winner.

play on words *noun* a pun.

play out *verb trans* **1** to finish or use up (a person's energy, strength, etc). **2** to unreel (a fishing line, etc).

playpen *noun* a portable usu collapsible enclosure in which a baby or young child may play safely.

playroom *noun* a room set aside for children to play in.

playschool *noun* a place where preschool children meet for sessions of supervised play, storytelling, singing, etc.

playsuit *noun dated* a garment, *esp* dungarees, for children to play in.

plaything *noun* **1** a toy. **2** a person regarded or treated dismissively.

play up *verb trans* **1** to give special emphasis or prominence to (something): *The press played up the political scandal.* **2** *Brit* to cause pain or distress to (somebody): *My feet have been playing me up.* ➤ *verb intrans* **1** *Brit* to be troublesome or mischievous. **2** *Brit* to fail to function properly: *The television is playing up again.*

playwright /'playriet/ *noun* somebody who writes plays.

plaza /'plahzə/ *noun* (*pl* **plazas**) **1** a public square in a city or town. **2** *chiefly NAmer* a shopping complex with extensive facilities. [Spanish *plaza*, from Latin *platea* broad street]

plc *abbr* (*also* **PLC**) public limited company.

plea /plee/ *noun* **1** an earnest request or appeal, *esp* one made in an urgent or emotional way. **2** an accused person's answer to an indictment: *a plea of guilty.* **3** something offered by way of excuse or justification. **4** an allegation made by a party in support of his or her case. [Middle English via early French *plaid* from Latin *placitum* decision, decree, from *placēre* PLEASE¹]

plea bargaining *noun* the act or process of pleading guilty to a lesser charge in order to avoid standing trial for a more serious one.

pleach /pleech/ *verb trans* to interlace (twigs or branches) to form a hedge or canopy. [Middle English *plechen* via French from Latin *plectere* to braid]

plead /pleed/ *verb* (*past tense and past part.* **pleaded** *or* **plead** /pled/ *or NAmer, Scot* **pled** /pled/) ➤ *verb intrans* **1** (*usu* + for) to make an impassioned or earnest request or appeal for something: *He pleaded for mercy.* **2** (*usu* + with) to make an impassioned or earnest request or appeal to somebody: *I'm pleading with you not to go.* **3a** said of a lawyer, etc: to appear in a court of law on behalf of an accused party. **b** said of an accused person in a court of law: to answer an accusation in a specified way: *I've decided to plead not guilty.* ➤ *verb trans* **1** to give or offer (a specified condition) as an excuse or reason: *Plead ignorance and you might get off with a warning.* **2** said of a lawyer: to argue (a case) on behalf of an accused party. **3** said of an accused person: to put forward (a reason) or invoke (a point of law), *esp* as a form of defence: *She pleaded it was done in self-defence.* ➤➤ **pleadable** *adj*, **pleader** *noun.* [early French *plaidier* to go to law, from *plaid*: see PLEA]

pleading¹ *noun* **1** the advocacy of a case in a court. **2** any of the formal usu written allegations made alternately by the parties in a legal action. **3** the act or an instance of making an impassioned or earnest request or appeal.

pleading² *adj* said of a look, etc: imploring. ➤➤ **pleadingly** *adv.*

pleasance /'plez(ə)ns/ *noun* a secluded garden or landscaped area laid out with trees and walks, *esp* one attached to a large house. [Middle English from early French *plaisance*, from *plaisant*: see PLEASANT]

pleasant /'plez(ə)nt/ *adj* **1** having qualities that tend to give pleasure; agreeable: *We spent a pleasant day sightseeing.* **2** said of a person: likable; friendly and helpful or thoughtful. **3** *archaic* facetious; determined to have one's little joke: *Well, sweet queen, you are pleasant with me* — Shakespeare. ➤➤ **pleasantly** *adv*, **pleasantness** *noun.* [Middle English *plesaunt* from early French *plaisant*, present part. of *plaisir*: see PLEASE¹]

pleasantry /'plez(ə)ntri/ *noun* (*pl* **pleasantries**) **1** a polite but trivial remark: *We exchanged pleasantries.* **2** *dated* a humorous act or remark; a joke.

please¹ /pleez/ *verb trans* **1** to give a feeling of satisfaction, pleasure, or contentment to (somebody). **2** *formal* to be the wish or will of (somebody or something): *If it please the court, I'll call my next witness.* ✳ **if you please 1** used to indicate surprise or indignation: *And then, if you please, he had the cheek to ask for his money back.* **2** if you want to. **please oneself** to do as one likes.

➤➤ **pleasing** *adj*, **pleasingly** *adv.* [Middle English *plesen* via French *plaisir* from Latin *placēre*]

please² *adv* **1** used in a polite request or an urgent appeal: *Could you please open the window; Oh, please let me go to the party, mum.* **2** (*also* **yes, please**) used as a polite or enthusiastic affirmative reply. **3** used to indicate surprise or indignation: *Oh, please – you can't be serious!*

pleased *adj* **1** satisfied or contented: *She had a pleased expression on her face; I'm so pleased you could come.* **2** glad or willing (to do something): *I'm always pleased to help.* **3** (+ with) happy about or contented with something: *She was very pleased with the price she got for the car.* ✳ **as pleased as Punch** extremely happy or satisfied. **pleased to meet you** used when somebody is introduced to a person for the first time. **pleased with oneself** smugly satisfied.

pleasurable /'plezh(ə)rəbl/ *adj* pleasant; enjoyable. ➤➤ **pleasurability** /-'biliti/ *noun*, **pleasurableness** *noun*, **pleasurably** *adv.*

pleasure¹ *noun* **1a** a feeling of satisfaction or contentment: *His face glowed with pleasure.* **b** a source of enjoyment and delight: *It's always a pleasure to talk to her; Good wine is one of life's pleasures.* **c** enjoyment or recreation, *esp* in contrast to necessity: *Are you here on business or pleasure?* **2** sensual gratification or indulgence: *They lead a life of idle pleasure.* **3** a wish or desire, *esp* when there are various options available: *'What's your pleasure?' 'I'll have a brandy, please'.* ✳ **a/my pleasure** used as a polite reply to an expression of gratitude. **at His/Her Majesty's pleasure** *Brit* detained in prison. **have the pleasure** *formal* used in formulating a polite request: *May I have the pleasure of the next dance?* **take pleasure in** to derive pride and satisfaction from (something): *She takes great pleasure in finding faults in people.* **with pleasure** willingly or gladly, used *esp* as a way of politely accepting an offer or invitation. [Middle English *plesure* from early French *plaisir* (see PLEASE¹), used as a noun]

pleasure² *verb trans archaic* to give sexual pleasure to (somebody).

pleat¹ /pleet/ *noun* a fold in cloth made by doubling material over on itself and stitching or pressing it in place. ➤➤ **pleated** *adj*, **pleatless** *adj.* [Middle English *plete*, variant of PLAIT¹]

pleat² *verb trans* to make a pleat or pleats in (something). ➤➤ **pleater** *noun.*

pleb /pleb/ *noun chiefly Brit, informal, derog* = PLEBEIAN¹.

plebby *adj* (**plebbier, plebbiest**) *chiefly Brit, derog* = PLEBEIAN².

plebeian¹ /pli'bee-ən/ *noun* **1a** a member of the common people in ancient Rome: compare PATRICIAN. **b** a member of a lower class in any society. **2** *derog* a coarse or uneducated person. ➤➤ **plebeianism** *noun.* [Latin *plebeius* of the common people, from *plebs* common people]

plebeian² *adj* **1** of plebeians. **2** crude or coarse in manner or style; common. ➤➤ **plebeianly** *adv.*

plebiscite /'plebisiet/ *noun* **1** a vote by the people of an entire country or district for or against a proposal, *esp* on an important issue such as choosing a new government or ruler: compare REFERENDUM. **2** any similar expression of public opinion. ➤➤ **plebiscitary** /plə'bisit(ə)ri/ *adj.* [Latin *plebis scitum*, literally 'decree of the common people']

plectrum /'plektrəm/ *noun* (*pl* **plectra** /'plektrə/ *or* **plectrums**) **1** a small thin piece of plastic, metal, etc used to pluck the strings of a stringed instrument, *esp* a guitar. **2** a similar mechanical part in a harpsichord or other instrument whose strings are plucked. [via Latin from Greek *plēktron*, from *plēssein* to strike]

pled /pled/ *verb* past tense and past part. of PLEAD.

pledge¹ /plej/ *noun* **1** a solemn and binding promise or undertaking. **2** an undertaking, *esp* to donate money to charity. **3** something given as a token of love, remembrance, loyalty, etc. **4** something handed over to an authority as security, redeemable only on the fulfilment of a promise, discharge of a debt, etc. **5** (**the pledge**) an undertaking to abstain from drinking alcohol. **6** *archaic* a toast or drink to a person's health. ✳ **in pledge** held as security for a loan: *His watch is in pledge.* [Middle English from French *plege* from Latin *plebere* to pledge, of Germanic origin]

pledge² *verb trans* **1** to promise (something or to do something): *They pledged their allegiance to the flag.* **2** to deposit (something) as security. **3** to bind (somebody) by or as if by a solemn promise. **4** *archaic* to drink the health of (somebody). ➤➤ **pledger** *noun*, **pledgor** /ple'jaw/ *noun.*

pledgee /ple'jee/ *noun* somebody to whom a pledge is given.

pledget /'plejit/ *noun* a compress or pad used to apply medication or absorb discharges, *esp* from a wound. [origin unknown]

-plegia *comb. form* forming nouns, denoting: a type of paralysis: *hemiplegia*. [via Latin from Greek *-plēgiē*, from *plēssein* to strike]

-plegic *comb. form* forming adjectives, denoting: suffering from a type of paralysis: *paraplegic*.

plein air /,playn 'eə/ *adj* denoting or relating to painting that is done outdoors, *esp* when applied to French Impressionist painting of the 19th cent. ➤➤ **pleinairist** *noun.* [French *plein air* open air]

pleio- *or* **pleo-** *or* **plio-** *comb. form* forming words, with the meaning: more: *pleonasm*. [from Greek *pleiōn* more]

Pleistocene /'pliestəseen/ *adj* relating to or dating from a geological epoch, the first epoch of the Quaternary period, lasting from about 1.64 million to about 10,000 years ago, and marked *esp* by glaciation and the first appearance of human beings. ➤➤ **Pleistocene** *noun.* [Greek *pleistos* most + *kainos* new or recent]

plenary[1] /'pleenəri/ *adj* **1** absolute; unqualified: *plenary power.* **2** said of a meeting, lecture, etc: attended by all entitled to be present: *There was a plenary session, after which the conference split into discussion groups.* [Latin *plenarius*, from *plenus* full]

plenary[2] *noun* (*pl* **plenaries**) a plenary meeting or session.

plenipotentiary[1] /,plenipə'tensh(ə)ri/ *noun* (*pl* **plenipotentiaries**) somebody, *esp* a diplomat, invested with full power to transact business. [Latin *plenipotentiarius*, from *plenus* full + *potentia*: see POTENTIAL[1]]

plenipotentiary[2] *adj* **1** said *esp* of a diplomat: having or invested with full power: *She was appointed minister plenipotentiary.* **2** giving a person full power.

plenitude /'plenityoohd/ *noun formal* **1** an abundance: *Your stomachs are round with the plenitude of eating* — Jack London. **2** the condition of being ample, full, or complete. [Middle English *plenitude* via French from Latin *plenitudo*, from *plenus* full]

plenteous /'plenti-əs/ *adj literary* plentiful. ➤➤ **plenteously** *adv,* **plenteousness** *noun.* [Middle English from early French *plentiveus*, from *plentif* abundant, from *plenté*: see PLENTY[1]]

plentiful /'plentif(ə)l/ *adj* **1** characterized by, constituting, or existing in plenty. **2** containing or yielding plenty: *a plentiful land.* ➤➤ **plentifully** *adv,* **plentifulness** *noun.*

plenty[1] /'plenti/ *noun* (*pl* **plenties**) **1a** (*treated as sing. or pl*) a full or more than adequate amount or supply: *You've had plenty of time to finish the job; There's plenty more.* **b** a large number or amount: *He's in plenty of trouble.* **2** ample supplies: *years of plenty.* ✴ **in plenty** being more than adequate amount or supply: *We've got books in plenty in the library.* [Middle English from early French *plenté*, ultimately from Latin *plenus* full]

plenty[2] *adj Scot, NAmer* ample: *There's still plenty work to be done.*

plenty[3] *adv informal* **1** quite or abundantly: *I think it's plenty warm enough.* **2** chiefly NAmer to a considerable or extreme degree; very: *We were plenty hungry.*

plenum /'pleenəm/ *noun* (*pl* **plenums** *or* **plena** /'pleenə/) **1** an assembly or meeting at which all the people eligible to attend are present; = PLENARY[2]. **2** in physics, a space that is completely filled with matter: compare VACUUM[1] (1A). [Latin *plenum*, neuter of *plenus* full]

pleo- *comb. form* see PLEIO-.

pleochroism /plee'okroh·iz(ə)m/ *noun* the property of a crystal of showing different colours when viewed by light from different angles. ➤➤ **pleochroic** /plee-ə'krohik/ *adj.* [PLEO- + Greek *khrōs* skin, colour + -ISM]

pleomorphism /pleeoh'mawfiz(ə)m/ *noun* the occurrence in the life cycle of an animal or plant of more than one form. ➤➤ **pleomorphic** /-fik/ *adj.* [PLEO- + -MORPHISM]

pleonasm /'plee-ənaz(ə)m/ *noun* **1** the use of more words than are necessary to convey an intended sense. **2** a superfluous word or phrase. ➤➤ **pleonastic** /-'nastik/ *adj,* **pleonastically** /-'nastikli/ *adv.* [via Latin from Greek *pleonasmos*, from *pleonazein* to be excessive or superfluous, from *pleiōn* more]

plesiosaur /'pleesi·əsaw/ *noun* a Mesozoic marine reptile with a flattened body, a long neck, and limbs flattened into paddles. [scientific Latin *Plesiosaurus*, name of the type genus, from Greek *plēsios* close (meaning 'closely related') + *sauros* lizard]

plessor /'plesə/ *noun* see PLEXOR.

plethora /'plethərə/ *noun* **1** (*usu* + of) a large, and *esp* excessive, quantity: *We have to keep abreast of a plethora of regulations.* **2** *not now used technically* an abnormal excess of a fluid, *esp* blood, in the body. ➤➤ **plethoric** /ple'thorik/ *adj.* [via medieval Latin from Greek *plēthōra*, literally 'fullness', from *plēthein* to be full]

pleur- *or* **pleuro-** *comb. form* forming words, with the meaning: relating to, affecting, or positioned in or near the pleura or pleurae: *pleuropneumonia.* [from Greek *pleura*: see PLEURA[1]]

pleura[1] /'plooərə/ *noun* (*pl* **pleurae** /'plooəree/ *or* **pleuras**) the delicate membrane that lines each half of the thorax of mammals and surrounds the lung of the same side. ➤➤ **pleural** *adj.* [scientific Latin from Greek *pleura*, literally 'side (of the body)', rib]

pleura[2] /'plooərə/ *noun* pl of PLEURON.

pleurisy /'plooərisi/ *noun* inflammation of the pleura, usu with fever and painful breathing. ➤➤ **pleuritic** /-'ritik/ *adj.* [Middle English *pluresie* via French from Latin *pleuritis*, from Greek *pleura*: see PLEURA[1]]

pleuro- *comb. form* see PLEUR-.

pleuron /'plooəron/ *noun* (*pl* **pleura** /-rə/) a side part of each segment of the body of an insect. [Greek *pleuron* side of the body]

pleuropneumonia /,plooərohnyooh'mohni·ə/ *noun* inflammation of the pleura and lungs.

Plexiglas /'pleksiglahs/ *noun NAmer, trademark* a type of transparent plastic made from acrylic resin and used mainly as a substitute for glass. [Greek *plēxis* (see PLEXOR) + GLASS[1]]

plexor /'pleksə/ *or* **plessor** /'plesə/ *noun* a small rubber-headed hammer used for testing body reflexes and in PERCUSSION (tapping the body as a means of medical diagnosis). [Greek *plēxis* percussion (from *plēssein* to strike) + -OR[1]]

plexus /'pleksəs/ *noun* (*pl* **plexus** *or* **plexuses**) **1** a network of interconnected blood vessels or nerves. **2** a network of parts or elements in a structure or system. ➤➤ **plexiform** /'pleksifawm/ *adj.* [Latin *plexus* braid, network, from past part. of *plectere* to braid]

pliable /'plie·əbl/ *adj* **1** easily bent without breaking; flexible. **2** yielding readily to others; compliant. ➤➤ **pliability** /-'biliti/ *noun,* **pliableness** *noun,* **pliably** *adv.* [Middle English from early French *pliable*, from *plier*: see PLY[1]]

pliant /'plie·ənt/ *adj* = PLIABLE. ➤➤ **pliancy** /-si/ *noun,* **pliantly** *adv,* **pliantness** *noun.* [Middle English from early French *pliant*, present part. of *plier*: see PLY[1]]

plicate /'pliekayt/ *adj* in biology and geology, folded lengthways like a fan; pleated or ridged: *a plicate leaf.* ➤➤ **plicately** *adv,* **plicateness** *noun,* **plication** /pli'kaysh(ə)n/ *noun.* [Latin *plicatus*, past part. of *plicare* to fold]

plicated /'plie·kaytid/ *adj* = PLICATE.

plié /'pleeay/ *noun* (*pl* **pliés**) the action in ballet of bending the knees outwards while holding the back straight. [French *plié*, past part. of *plier*: see PLY[1]]

pliers /'plie·əz/ *pl noun* a tool with a pair of pincers with jaws for holding small objects or for bending and cutting wire. [from PLY[1]]

plight[1] /pliet/ *noun* a condition of extreme hardship, difficulty, or danger: *the plight of the homeless.* [Middle English *plit* from Anglo-French *pleit* fold, ultimately from Latin *plicare* to fold; the spelling was influenced by PLIGHT[2]]

plight[2] *verb trans archaic* to promise (something) solemnly: *plight one's troth.* [Old English *plihtan* to endanger]

plimsoll /'plims(ə)l/ *noun Brit, dated* a shoe with a rubber sole and canvas top worn *esp* for sports. [prob from the supposed resemblance of the upper edge of the rubber to the Plimsoll line on a ship]

Plimsoll line *noun* one of a set of markings indicating the different levels to which a vessel may legally be loaded in various seasons and waters. [named after Samuel *Plimsoll* d.1898, English leader of shipping reform, who advocated its use]

Plimsoll mark *noun* = PLIMSOLL LINE.

plink[1] /plingk/ *verb intrans* to make a quick sharp tinkling noise: *I can hear someone plinking on the piano.* ➤ *verb trans* to make (a musical instrument) produce this noise.

plink[2] *noun* a quick sharp tinkling noise. ➤➤ **plinky** *adj.*

plinth /plinth/ *noun* **1** a usu square block serving as a base for a pedestal, column, statue, etc. **2** a part of a structure forming a continuous foundation or base. [via Latin from Greek *plinthos* brick]

plio- *comb. form* see PLEIO-.

Pliocene /'plieohseen, 'plie-əseen/ *adj* relating to or dating from a geological epoch, the last epoch of the Tertiary period, lasting from about 5.2 million to about 1.64 million years ago, and marked by the appearance of many modern mammals. >> **Pliocene** *noun.* [PLIO- + Greek *kainos* new or recent]

pliosaur /'plie-əsaw/ *noun* any of various marine reptiles of the Mesozoic era, plesiosaurs with short necks, large heads, and powerful jaws. [scientific Latin *Pliosaurus*, name of the type genus, from Greek *pleiōn* more + *sauros* lizard]

plissé[1] *or* **plisse** /'pleesay/ *adj* said of a fabric: having a permanently puckered finish. [French *plissé* pleated, past part. of *plisser* to pleat, from *plier*: see PLY[1]]

plissé[2] *or* **plisse** *noun* (*pl* **plisses** *or* **plisses**) fabric with a permanently puckered finish.

PLO *abbr* Palestine Liberation Organization.

plod[1] /plod/ *verb* (**plodded, plodding**) >> *verb intrans* **1a** (*often* + along/on) to walk heavily or slowly; to trudge. **b** (*often* + along) to proceed slowly or tediously: *The story just plods endlessly.* **2** to work laboriously and monotonously: *He was plodding through stacks of unanswered letters.* >> *verb trans* to tread slowly or heavily along or over (something): *I remember the days when people plodded the streets all day, looking for work.* >> **plodder** *noun,* **ploddingly** *adv.* [imitative]

plod[2] *noun* **1** a slow trudging walk. **2a** (*also* **PC Plod/Mr Plod**) *Brit, informal* a policeman. **b** (**the plod/PC Plod/Mr Plod**) (*treated as pl*) the police. [(sense 2) from Mr Plod the Policeman, a character in the Noddy stories by Enid Blyton d.1968]

-ploid *comb. form* forming words, denoting: a specified number of sets of chromosomes in a cell: *polyploid.* [from DIPLOID[1] and HAPLOID[1]]

ploidy /'ploydi/ *noun* the degree of repetition of the haploid number of chromosomes in a cell. [from -PLOID]

plonk[1] /plongk/ *verb trans* to put (something or oneself) down heavily, clumsily, or carelessly. [imitative]

plonk[2] *noun* the act or sound of plonking.

plonk[3] *noun chiefly Brit, informal* cheap or inferior wine. [short for earlier *plink-plonk,* perhaps modification of French *vin blanc* white wine]

plonker *noun* **1** *informal* a stupid or useless person. **2** *coarse slang* a man's penis. [orig as a dialect word meaning 'something large'; from PLONK[1]]

plook *or* **pluke** /ploohk/ *noun Scot* a spot or pimple. >> **plooky** *adj,* **plukey** *adj.* [origin unknown]

plop[1] /plop/ *verb* (**plopped, plopping**) >> *verb intrans* **1** to drop or move suddenly with a sound suggestive of something dropping into water. **2** to allow the body to drop heavily: *She plopped into a chair.* >> *verb trans* to drop or throw (something) into liquid without making much of a splash: *He plopped some ice into his drink.* [imitative]

plop[2] *noun* the act or a sound of plopping.

plosion /'plohzh(ə)n/ *noun* the release of obstructed breath that occurs in the articulation of plosive consonants. [from EXPLOSION]

plosive[1] /'plohsiv, 'plohziv/ *noun* a consonant such as *b, p,* or *d* that is articulated by blocking the outward flow of air through the mouth, e.g. with the lips or tongue, and then allowing air to escape in a sharp burst. [from EXPLOSIVE[1]]

plosive[2] *adj* relating to a plosive.

plot[1] /plot/ *noun* **1** a secret plan, *esp* one made by two or more people to do something illegal, harmful, or dishonest. **2** the sequence of events or main story of a literary work, film, etc. **3** a small piece of land, *esp* one used or designated for a specific purpose: *a vegetable plot.* **4** a chart or other graphic representation. **5** *NAmer* = GROUND PLAN (1). >> **plotless** *adj,* **plotlessness** *noun.* [Old English]

plot[2] *verb* (**plotted, plotting**) >> *verb trans* **1a** to make a plot, map, or plan of (something). **b** to mark or note (something) on or as if on a map or chart: *The navigator plotted the ship's position.* **2** to plan or contrive (something), *esp* secretly: *They plotted the overthrow of the government.* **3a** to assign a position to (a point) by means of coordinates. **b** to draw (a curve) by means of plotted points. **c** to represent (an equation) by means of a curve so constructed. **4** to invent or devise the plot of (a literary work, film, etc). **5** to lay (a garden, etc) out in plots. >> *verb intrans* to form a plot; to scheme.

plotter *noun* **1** somebody who secretly plans something, *esp* something evil, underhand, or treacherous. **2** a computer output device that prints hard copies of line-based graphics, such as charts, diagrams, or technical drawings, using pens or electrostatic charges and toner.

plough[1] (*NAmer* **plow**) /plow/ *noun* **1** any of various devices used to cut, lift, and turn over soil, *esp* in preparing ground for sowing. **2** ploughed land. **3** (**the Plough**) a formation of seven stars in the northern sky. [Old English *plōh,* ultimately from a prehistoric Germanic word]

plough[2] (*NAmer* **plow**) *verb intrans* **1** to use a plough. **2** (*often* + into) to force a way, *esp* violently: *The car ploughed into a group of spectators.* **3** (*often* + through) to proceed steadily and laboriously; to plod: *We had to plough through hundreds of applications.* >> *verb trans* **1a** to turn, break up, or work (earth or land) with a plough. **b** to make (a furrow) with a plough. **2** (*often* + in/into) to invest (money or resources): *The government is ploughing more money into education.* **3** to remove snow from (a road) with a snowplough. **4** *Brit, dated* to fail (an examination), or to fail an examination in (a subject): *I usually ploughed French.* >> **ploughable** *adj,* **plougher** *noun.*

plough back *verb trans* to reinvest (profits) in an industry.

ploughman (*NAmer* **plowman**) *noun* (*pl* **ploughmen** *or NAmer* **plowmen**) somebody who guides a plough; *broadly* a farm labourer.

ploughman's lunch *noun Brit* a cold lunch of bread, cheese, and usu pickles, often served in a pub.

ploughshare (*NAmer* **plowshare**) /'plowsheə/ *noun* the part of a plough that cuts the furrow. [Middle English, from PLOUGH[1] + *schare* ploughshare, from Old English *scaer*]

plover /'pluvə/ *noun* (*pl* **plovers** *or collectively* **plover**) **1** any of numerous species of wading birds with a short beak and usu a stout compact build: family Charadriidae. **2** any of various related or similar birds. [Middle English via French from Latin *pluvia* rain]

plow[1] /plow/ *noun NAmer* see PLOUGH[1].

plow[2] *verb NAmer* see PLOUGH[2].

plowman *noun* (*pl* **plowmen**) *NAmer* see PLOUGHMAN.

plowshare *noun NAmer* see PLOUGHSHARE.

ploy /ploy/ *noun* a cunningly devised or contrived plan or act, *esp* one intended to embarrass or frustrate an opponent or to secure a personal advantage. [prob from EMPLOY[1]]

PLP *abbr Brit* Parliamentary Labour Party.

PLR *abbr Brit* Public Lending Right.

pluck[1] /pluk/ *verb trans* **1a** to take a firm hold of (something) and remove it: *I would … have plucked my nipple from his boneless gums and dashed the brains out* — Shakespeare. **b** to pick (a flower, fruit, etc): *She plucked a particularly fine bloom for his buttonhole.* **2a** to pull out (feathers) from a chicken, etc. **b** to remove the feathers from (a bird's carcass). **3a** to pull out (hairs), *esp* from the eyebrows. **b** to neaten (the eyebrows) by pulling some of the hairs out. **4a** to produce sounds from (a stringed musical instrument) using the fingers or a plectrum. **b** to use the fingers or a plectrum on (the strings of a musical instrument). **5** *slang* to swindle (somebody). >> *verb intrans* (+ at) to tug: *She plucked at the folds of her skirt.* >> **plucker** *noun.* [Old English *pluccian*]

pluck[2] *noun* **1** courage and determination. **2** the heart, liver, and lungs of a slaughtered animal, *esp* as food. **3** an act or instance of plucking or pulling.

pluck up *verb trans* **1** to summon up or muster (the necessary courage, etc) to do something difficult or frightening: *He plucked up the nerve to ask her out.* **2** to pull out or uproot (something).

plucky *adj* (**pluckier, pluckiest**) showing spirited courage and determination, *esp* when faced with a difficulty or danger. >> **pluckily** *adv,* **pluckiness** *noun.*

plug[1] /plug/ *noun* **1** something used to seal a hole, often tightly enough to prevent anything escaping; a stopper. **2a** an insulated device with metal prongs that connects an electrical appliance to an electricity supply at a socket. **b** *not in technical use* an electric socket. **3** *informal* a publicity boost, *esp* given on a television or radio programme: *He went on the chat show to give his new book a plug.* **4a** tobacco in a large compressed cake. **b** a small piece taken from such a cake, used for chewing rather than smoking. **5** a mass of solidified magma that blocks the top of an extinct volcano. **6** *informal* = SPARK PLUG. **7** (*also* **plug plant**) a young plant with its roots encased in a small mass of soil or compost, ready for planting out. [early Dutch *plugge*]

plug² *verb* (**plugged, plugging**) ➤ *verb trans* **1** to block, close, or secure (a hole or gap) with a plug. **2** *informal* to publicize (a book, film, etc), *esp* by media promotion: *She plugged her autobiography on daytime TV.* **3** *informal* to shoot (somebody or something): *The cop plugged him in the leg.* ➤ *verb intrans* (*usu* + away) to work doggedly and persistently: *He plugged away at his homework.* ➤➤ **plugger** *noun.*

plug and play *noun* in computing, a system which automatically detects and configures new peripherals such as printers, modems, monitors, etc without any instruction from a user.

plughole *noun Brit* a hole in a sink, basin, bath, or shower tray where the water drains away and which can often be temporarily sealed with a rubber plug. ✳ **go down the plughole** *informal* to be wasted or beyond use, or to fail dismally, often with no hope of recovery: *Her business went down the plughole.*

plug in *verb trans* to attach or connect (an electrical appliance) to a power point.

plug-in¹ *noun* a computer module or software program designed to be added to a system to enhance or upgrade an existing feature or function or to supply an extra one.

plug-in² *adj* of or being a plug-in: *a plug-in sound card.*

plug plant *noun* = PLUG¹ (7).

plug-ugly¹ *noun* (*pl* **plug-uglies**) *chiefly NAmer, informal* a gangster, villain, or rowdy person. [from the name of a criminal gang, the Plug Uglies, that operated in several US cities during the 1850s, from PLUG² + UGLY]

plug-ugly² *adj chiefly NAmer, informal* said of a person: very ugly indeed.

pluke *noun* = PLOOK.

plum /plum/ *noun* **1a** an edible globular to oval smooth-skinned fruit with yellow, purple, red, or green skin and an oblong seed. **b** any of several species of trees and shrubs of the rose family that bear this fruit: genus *Prunus.* **2** *informal.* **a** something excellent or superior, *esp* an opportunity or position offering exceptional advantages. **b** (*used before a noun*) denoting this kind of opportunity, etc: *a plum job.* **3** a dark reddish purple colour. [Old English *plūme* from Latin *prunum*: see PRUNE¹]

plumage /'ploohmij/ *noun* all of a bird's feathers. ➤➤ **plumaged** *adj.* [Middle English from early French *plume*: see PLUME¹]

plumb¹ /plum/ *noun* **1** a lead weight attached to a cord and used to determine the depth of water or to gauge the verticality of a surface, line, or edge. **2** any of various weights, such as a sinker for a fishing line. [Middle English via early French *plomb* from Latin *plumbum* lead]

plumb² *adv* **1** *informal* exactly; precisely: *His house is plumb in the middle of the island.* **2** *chiefly NAmer, informal* completely; absolutely: *Have you gone plumb crazy?* **3** *archaic* straight down or up; vertically.

plumb³ *verb trans* **1** to measure (the depth of water) with a plumb. **2** to examine (something) minutely and critically, *esp* in order to understand it: *He was plumbing the book's complexities.* **3** to adjust or test (the trueness or verticality of a surface, line, or edge) by a plumb line. **4a** to supply (a house, etc) with plumbing. **b** to connect or join (a pipe, tap, etc) to a system of pipes or to a drain. **5** to experience or endure, or explore and describe (the most extreme form of something unpleasant or unwelcome): *He had plumbed the depths of human misery.*

plumb⁴ *adj* **1** exactly vertical or true. **2** said of a cricket wicket: flat and allowing little or no horizontal or vertical deviation of the bowled ball.

plumb- *or* **plumbo-** *comb. form* forming words, denoting: lead: *plumbism.* [from Latin *plumbum* lead]

plumbago /plum'baygoh/ *noun* (*pl* **plumbagos**) **1** a plant of the thrift family with spikes of attractive blue, grey, or red flowers: genus *Plumbago.* **2** *archaic* = GRAPHITE. [Latin *plumbago* lead ore, from *plumbum* lead]

plumb bob *noun* a metal bob or weight of a plumb line.

plumbeous /'plumbi·əs/ *adj* said *esp* of the colour of some birds' plumage: dull grey. [Latin *plumbeus* leaden, from *plumbum* lead]

plumber /'plumə/ *noun* somebody who installs, repairs, and maintains water piping and fittings, central heating systems, etc.

[Middle English, meaning 'a dealer or worker in lead', from early French *plombier*, ultimately from Latin *plumbum* lead]

plumbic /'plumbik/ *adj* of or containing tetravalent lead: compare PLUMBOUS.

plumb in *verb trans* to connect (a bath, shower, toilet, etc, or an appliance, *esp* a washing machine) to a water supply.

plumbing /'pluming/ *noun* **1** a plumber's occupation or trade. **2** the system of pipes, tanks, and fixtures installed or required in supplying the water, sanitation, and heating in a house or building. **3** *Brit, euphem* the organs, etc involved in excretion, *esp* those of the urinary tract: *She was off work because of trouble with her plumbing.*

plumbism /'plumbiz(ə)m/ *noun* chronic or acute lead poisoning.

plumb line *noun* a line that has a weight at one end and is used *esp* to determine verticality.

plumbo- *comb. form* see PLUMB-.

plumbous /'plumbəs/ *adj* of or containing bivalent lead: compare PLUMBIC.

plumb rule *noun* a plumb line and bob attached to a strip of wood and used by surveyors and builders to test if a wall, etc is vertical.

plume¹ /ploohm/ *noun* **1a** a bird's feather, *esp* a long attractive and brightly coloured one used for display. **b** a cluster of distinctive feathers. **2** a feather or cluster of feathers worn e.g. in a hat, as a decoration. **3** something resembling a feather in shape, appearance, or lightness: *a plume of smoke.* **4** a feathery or feather-like part of an animal or plant. **5** a column of molten material rising from the earth's mantle. ➤➤ **plumed** *adj.* [Middle English via French from Latin *pluma* soft feather, down]

plume² *verb trans* **1** to provide or decorate (something) with plumes. **2** *archaic* (*usu* + on/upon) to pride or congratulate (oneself). **3** *archaic* said of a bird: to preen and arrange (its feathers or itself).

plummet¹ /'plumit/ *verb intrans* (**plummeted, plummeting**) to fall sharply and abruptly: *Share prices plummeted today.*

plummet² *noun* **1** a fall or drop, *esp* one that is rapid or unexpected. **2** a plumb or plumb line. [Middle English from early French *plombet* ball of lead, dimin. of *plomb*: see PLUMB¹]

plummy *adj* (**plummier, plummiest**) **1** said of somebody's voice or accent: characteristic of or resembling that of the English upper classes, often in an affected or exaggerated way. **2** sought after or desirable: *Ewan landed a plummy role in the film.* **3** resembling or tasting of plums.

plumose /'ploohmohs/ *adj technical* **1** having feathers or plumes. **2** feathery. **3** having a main shaft bearing small filaments: *the plumose antennae of an insect.* ➤➤ **plumosely** *adv.*

plump¹ /plump/ *adj* having a full rounded form; slightly fat: *His voice was as smooth and suave as his countenance, as he advanced with a plump little hand extended* — Conan Doyle. ➤➤ **plumpish** *adj,* **plumply** *adv,* **plumpness** *noun.* [Middle English, meaning 'dull, blunt', of Germanic origin]

plump² *verb trans* **1** (*also* + up) to make (something) become rounder or fuller: *She plumped the cushions.* **2** (*also* + out/up) to cause (somebody or something) to become fat or fatter. ➤ *verb intrans* (*also* + out) to become fat or fatter.

plump³ *verb intrans* **1** (*usu* + down/into) to drop or sink suddenly or heavily: *Exhausted, she plumped down in the chair.* **2** (+ for) to decide on something out of several choices or courses of action: *I'll plump for beer rather than wine.* ➤ *verb trans* to drop, throw, or place (something or oneself) suddenly or heavily. [Middle English *plumpen*, prob. of imitative origin]

plump⁴ *noun* a sudden plunge, fall, or blow, or the sound of this.

plump⁵ *adv* **1** *informal* with a sudden or heavy drop: *The toddler sat down plump on his bottom.* **2** *dated* without qualification; directly.

plum pudding *noun* a rich boiled or steamed pudding containing dried fruit, *esp* raisins, and spices.

plum tomato *noun* a type of oval tomato, orig an Italian variety, that is often tinned and used in making sauces, etc.

plumule /'ploohmyoohl/ *noun* **1** a rudimentary bud in an embryonic plant which will develop into a shoot during germination. **2** a down feather, either in a young bird or in the insulating layer below the contour feathers of some adult birds, *esp* aquatic ones. ➤➤ **plumulose** /-lohs/ *adj.* [Latin *plumula*, dimin. of *pluma* soft feather, down]

plumy /'ploohmi/ *adj* (**plumier, plumiest**) **1** of or resembling a feather or feathers. **2** consisting of or decorated with feathers.

plunder[1] /'plundə/ *verb* (**plundered, plundering**) ➤ *verb trans* **1** to pillage or sack (a town, etc). **2a** to take (goods) by force, *esp* in a war, riot, or disturbance. **b** to take goods forcibly from (somewhere): *Looters plundered the shop.* ➤ *verb intrans* to commit robbery or looting. ➤➤ **plunderer** *noun.* [German *plundern* from early German *plunder*, literally 'household goods']

plunder[2] *noun* **1** something taken by force, theft, or fraud; loot. **2** the act or an instance of plundering or pillaging.

plunge /'plunj/ *verb trans* **1a** to move (something) with a sharp, usu downward motion. **b** to cover (a distance) in a downward direction: *The car plunged 100m down the cliff.* **2** to immerse (something, *esp* a food) in a liquid: *Plunge the tomatoes in boiling water and then remove the skins.* **3** to cause (a place) to be in a usu dangerous or unwelcome condition: *A power cut plunged the building into darkness.* **4** to sink (a plant or a plant in a pot) into the ground. ➤ *verb intrans* **1** (*usu* + into) to jump or dive, *esp* in water: *We all plunged into the swimming pool.* **2** to move with a sharp, usu downward motion: *The car careered off the road and plunged down the cliff.* **3** to fall rapidly, suddenly, or unexpectedly: *Profits have plunged to an alltime low.* [Middle English *plungen* from early French *plongier*, ultimately from Latin *plumbum* lead, plummet]

plunge[2] *noun* **1** a dive or swim. **2** a sudden downward movement; a sharp fall, *esp* in value: *a plunge in share prices.* ✳ **take the plunge** *informal* to decide to do something, *esp* after considering the potential risks: *He took the plunge and became self-employed.*

plunge pool *noun* a small but relatively deep pool, usu of cold water, that people jump into between or after sauna sessions.

plunger *noun* **1a** a device, such as a piston in a pump, that acts with a plunging or thrusting motion. **b** a rubber suction cup on a handle used for clearing blocked pipes, drains, etc. **2** *informal* a reckless gambler or speculator.

plunk[1] /plungk/ *verb trans* **1** to play (a keyboard instrument) so as to produce a hollow, metallic, or harsh sound. **2** *informal* (*also* + down) to set (something or oneself) down suddenly; to plump. ➤➤ **plunker** *noun.* [imitative]

plunk[2] *noun* a hollow, metallic, or harsh sound.

plup. *abbr* pluperfect.

pluperfect[1] /plooh'puhfikt/ *adj* = PAST PERFECT[1]. [contraction of Latin *plus quam perfectus*, literally 'more than perfect']

pluperfect[2] *noun* the pluperfect tense, or a verb in this tense.

plural[1] /'plooərəl/ *adj* **1** in grammar, said of a word or word form: denoting more than one, or in some languages more than two or three, persons, things, or instances: compare DUAL[1], SINGULAR[1]. **2** consisting of or containing more than one kind, thing, or class: *a plural society.* ➤➤ **plurally** *adv.* [Middle English via French from Latin *pluralis*, from *plus* more]

plural[2] *noun* in grammar, the plural number, the inflectional form denoting it, or a word in that form.

pluralise *verb trans and intrans* see PLURALIZE.

pluralism *noun* **1** a state of society in which members of diverse social groups develop their traditional cultures or special interests within a common civilization. **2** the holding of two or more offices or positions, *esp* benefices, at the same time. ➤➤ **pluralist** *adj and noun*, **pluralistic** /-'listik/ *adj*, **pluralistically** /-'listikli/ *adv.*

plurality /plooə'raliti/ *noun* (*pl* **pluralities**) **1a** the state of being plural or numerous. **b** a large number or quantity. **2** a benefice or other position or office held by pluralism.

pluralize *or* **pluralise** *verb trans* **1** to make (something) become more numerous. **2** to put (a word) into its plural form. **3** to cause (something) to consist of more than one part. ➤ *verb intrans* **1** said of a member of the clergy: to hold more than one official position or benefice at the same time. **2** to become plural in form.

pluri- *comb. form* forming words, with the meaning: more than one; several; multi-: *pluriaxial*. [from Latin *plur-*, from *plus* more]

plus[1] /plus/ *prep* **1** increased by; with the addition of: *Four plus five equals nine; We have to repay the debt plus interest.* **2** and also: *The job needs experience plus patience.* [Latin *plus* more]

plus[2] *noun* (*pl* **pluses** *or* **plusses**) **1** an added quantity. **2** a positive factor, quantity, or quality. **3** a surplus. **4** = PLUS SIGN.

plus[3] *adj* **1** arithmetically or electrically positive. **2** additional and welcome: *A plus factor is its nearness to the shops.* **3** said *esp* of an

academic grade: slightly higher than that specified: *He got a B plus for his essay.*

plus[4] *conj* and moreover: *plus he has to watch what he says* — Punch.

plus ça change /plooh sa 'shonzh/ *phrase* used to express the opinion or acknowledge the fact that things never really change. [from French *plus ça change, plus c'est la même chose* the more it changes, the more it is the same thing]

plus fours *pl noun* loose wide trousers gathered on a band and finishing just below the knee. [from the extra four inches of length allowed for the loose overhang at the knee]

plush[1] /plush/ *noun* a fabric with an even pile that is longer and less dense than the pile of velvet. [from early French *peluche* from *peluchier* to pluck, ultimately from Latin *pilus* hair]

plush[2] *adj* **1** made of or resembling plush. **2** luxurious, expensive, or lavish: *We spent the night in a plush hotel.* ➤➤ **plushly** *adv*, **plushness** *noun.*

plushy *adj* = PLUSH[2] (2).

plus sign *noun* a sign (+) denoting addition or a positive quantity.

plutocracy /plooh'tokrəsi/ *noun* (*pl* **plutocracies**) **1** government by a controlling class of wealthy people. **2** a state that is governed by wealthy people. **3** a class of wealthy people who govern a state. ➤➤ **plutocratic** /-'kratik/ *adj*, **plutocratically** /-'kratikli/ *adv.* [Greek *ploutokratia*, from *ploutos* wealth + *-kratia* -CRACY]

plutocrat /'plootohkrat/ *noun* **1** *often derog* a person whose status or power is based on or dependent on their wealth. **2** a member of a plutocracy.

pluton /'ploohton/ *noun* a large body of igneous rock. [back-formation from PLUTONIC]

Plutonian /plooh'tohni-ən/ *adj* **1** relating to the underworld or the Greek god Pluto. **2** relating to the planet Pluto.

plutonic /plooh'tonik/ *adj* **1** said of igneous rock: formed by solidification of a molten magma deep within the earth. **2** (**Plutonic**) = PLUTONIAN (1).

plutonium /plooh'tohni-əm/ *noun* a silvery radioactive metallic chemical element similar to uranium that is formed in atomic reactors, and is used in weapons and as a fuel for atomic reactors: symbol Pu, atomic number 94. [named after the planet Pluto, because Pluto is next to Neptune in terms of distance from the sun and the element was discovered shortly after NEPTUNIUM]

pluvial[1] /'ploohvi-əl/ *adj* **1** of or caused by rain. **2** characterized by abundant rainfall. [Latin *pluvialis* from *pluvia* rain]

pluvial[2] *noun* a prolonged geological period of wetter than average weather.

ply[1] /plie/ *verb trans* (**plies, plied, plying**) to twist (strands of rope or yarn) together. [Middle English *plien* to fold, via early French *plier* from Latin *plicare*]

ply[2] *noun* (*pl* **plies**) **1a** a strand in a yarn, wool, etc. **b** any of several layers of cloth usu sewn together or sheets of wood laminated together. **c** (*used before a noun*) specifying the number of strands or layers something has: *two-ply wood; four-ply wool*. **2** *informal* = PLYWOOD.

ply[3] *verb* (**plies, plied, plying**) ➤ *verb trans* **1a** to use (a tool, etc) steadily and diligently: *He was busily plying his axe.* **b** to practise or perform (an occupation) steadily and diligently: *He's been plying his trade for over thirty years.* **2a** to keep furnishing or supplying something to (somebody): *She plied them with drinks.* **b** to keep asking (somebody) questions: *Once he'd been rescued, he was plied with questions by the press.* **3** said of a ship, taxi, etc: to go or travel over or on (a specified route) regularly. ➤ *verb intrans* **1** said of a boatman, taxi driver, etc: to wait regularly in a particular place for custom: *The streets were packed with taxis plying for hire.* **2** (+ between) to travel regularly: *There's a ferry that plies between the islands.* [Middle English *plien*, short for *applien*: see APPLY]

Plymouth Brethren /'pliməth/ *pl noun* a Christian religious body whose first congregation was founded about 1830 at Plymouth in Devon, most branches of which practise believers' baptism and which has no ordained clergy.

Plymouth Rock *noun* a breed of medium-sized domestic chicken. [named after *Plymouth Rock* in Massachusetts, USA, where the Pilgrim Fathers are supposed to have landed in 1620]

plywood *noun* a light structural material consisting of thin sheets of wood glued or cemented together with the grains of adjacent layers arranged crosswise, usu at right angles.

PM *abbr* **1** postmortem. **2** Prime Minister. **3** Provost Marshal.

Pm *abbr* the chemical symbol for promethium.

p.m. *abbr* post meridiem, used to indicate the time after midday.

PMG *abbr* **1** Paymaster General. **2** Postmaster General.

PMS *abbr* premenstrual syndrome.

PMT *abbr* premenstrual tension.

pn *abbr* promissory note.

PNdB *abbr* perceived noise decibel or decibels.

pneum- *or* **pneumo-** *or* **pneumon-** *or* **pneumono-** *comb. form* forming words, with the meanings: **1** air; gas: *pneumothorax*. **2** a lung or the lungs: *pneumonectomy*; *pneumogastric*. **3** pneumonia: *pneumococcus*. [from Greek *pneumōn* lung]

pneumat- *or* **pneumato-** *comb. form* forming words, denoting: **1** air; vapour; gas: *pneumatics*. **2** respiration: *pneumatometer*. **3** spirit: *pneumatology*. [from Greek *pneumat-*, *pneuma* air]

pneumatic[1] /nyooh'matik/ *adj* **1** relating to air, gas, or wind. **2a** said of a machine or tool: operated by gas or air under pressure or by a vacuum. **b** containing air under pressure: *a pneumatic tyre*. **3** said of the bones of birds: having air-filled cavities, an adaptation which makes them lighter in flight. ⟫ **pneumatically** *adv*, **pneumaticity** /-'tisiti/ *noun*. [via Latin from Greek *pneumatikos*, from *pneuma* air, breath, spirit]

pneumatic[2] *noun* a tyre that is filled with air under pressure.

pneumatic drill *noun* a large mechanical drill, operated by compressed air, and used *esp* for breaking up a road surface by repeatedly striking it.

pneumatics *pl noun* (*treated as sing. or pl*) the branch of science that deals with the study of the mechanical properties of gases.

pneumato- *comb. form* see PNEUMAT-.

pneumatology /nyoohmə'toləji/ *noun* the branch of theology that is concerned with spiritual matters and spirits, *esp* the Holy Spirit. ⟫ **pneumatological** /-'lojikl/ *adj*.

pneumatometer /nyoohmə'tomitə/ *noun* **1** an instrument for measuring the force exerted by the lungs in breathing. **2** an instrument for measuring air entering and leaving the lungs; = SPIROMETER.

pneumatophore /'nyoohmətəhfaw/ *noun* a muscular gas-containing sac that serves as a float on a hydrozoan colony, e.g. the Portuguese man-of-war. ⟫ **pneumatophoric** /nyooh,matə'forik/ *adj*.

pneumo- *comb. form* see PNEUM-.

pneumococcus /nyoohmoh'kokəs/ *noun* (*pl* **pneumococci** /-'kok(s)ie/) a bacterium that causes acute pneumonia. ⟫ **pneumococcal** /-kl/ *adj*, **pneumococcic** /-'kok(s)ik/ *adj*.

pneumoconiosis /ˌnyoomohkoni'ohsis/ *noun* a crippling disease of the lungs, *esp* of miners, caused by the habitual inhalation of irritant mineral or metallic particles: compare SILICOSIS. [PNEUMO- + Greek *konis* dust + -OSIS]

pneumogastric /nyoohmoh'gastrik/ *adj* **1** relating to or affecting the lungs and stomach. **2** *dated* = VAGAL.

pneumon- *comb. form* see PNEUM-.

pneumonectomy /nyoomoh'nektəmi/ *noun* the surgical removal of a lung or part of a lung.

pneumonia /nyooh'mohni·ə/ *noun* a lung infection that causes the air sacs to fill with pus, as a result of which the lungs change from a soft spongy consistency to become quite solid. ⟫ **pneumonic** /nyoo'monik/ *adj*. [via Latin from Greek *pneumōn* lung]

pneumono- *comb. form* see PNEUM-.

pneumothorax /nyoohmoh'thawraks/ *noun* the presence of gas or air in the pleural cavity, occurring *esp* as a result of disease or injury, and resulting in the collapse of the lung.

PNG *abbr* Papua New Guinea (international vehicle registration).

p-n junction *or* **pn junction** *noun* a boundary between a p-type semiconductor and an n-type semiconductor that functions as a rectifier in a diode, photocell, transistor, etc.

PNP *abbr* positive-negative-positive, denoting a device consisting of an n-type semiconductor between two p-type semiconductors.

PO *abbr* **1** Petty Officer. **2** Pilot Officer. **3** postal order. **4** Post Office.

Po *abbr* the chemical symbol for polonium.

po /poh/ *noun* (*pl* **pos**) *Brit, informal* = CHAMBER POT. [from POT[1]]

poach[1] /pohch/ *verb trans* to cook (e.g. fish or an egg) in a simmering liquid, *esp* milk, water, or stock. [Middle English *pochen* from early French *pochier*, literally 'to put into a bag', from *poche* bag, pocket]

poach[2] *verb trans* **1** to take (game or fish) illegally by hunting on land or fishing in a river without the owner's permission. **2** to take (ideas, work, etc belonging to somebody else) and use them or it to one's own advantage. **3** to entice (an employee working for another company) to come and work for one's own company. **4** to trespass on (land). **5** said of a horse or its rider: to cause (land) to break up into muddy patches. **6** said of somebody playing doubles in tennis or badminton: to take or try to take (a shot or shots that belong to their partner). ⟫ *verb intrans* **1** (+ on) to encroach on somebody else's territory: *what happens to a poet when he poaches on a novelist's preserves* — Virginia Woolf. **2** said *esp* of a striker in football: to wait around the opposing team's goal area for a scoring opportunity. ⟫⟫ **poacher** *noun*. [French *pocher* to trample, trespass, prob of Germanic origin]

POB *abbr* Post Office box.

pochard /'pohchəd/ *noun* (*pl* **pochards** *or collectively* **pochard**) **1** a diving duck, the males of which have reddish brown heads: *Aythya ferina*. **2** any of several species of related ducks: genera *Netta* and *Aythya*. [origin unknown]

pock /pok/ *noun* **1** a pustule in an eruptive disease, *esp* smallpox. **2** = POCKMARK. ⟫⟫ **pocky** *adj*. [Old English *pocc* pustule]

pocket[1] /'pokit/ *noun* **1** a small bag that is sewn or inserted in a garment and open at the top or side. **2** a supply of money; financial resources: *We sell a range of second-hand cars to suit all pockets*. **3** a pouchlike compartment for storage: *Stick the book in the pocket beside the driver's seat*. **4** any of several openings at the corners or sides of a billiard or snooker table into which balls are propelled. **5** a small isolated area or group: *pockets of unemployment*. **6a** a cavity, *esp* one in the earth that contains a deposit of gold, water, etc. **b** = AIR POCKET. ✳ **in pocket** in the position of having made a profit. **in somebody's pocket** under that person's control or influence. **line one's pocket** to make money, *esp* by dishonest means. **out of pocket** having suffered a financial loss. **put one's hand in one's pocket** to spend one's own money. ⟫⟫ **pocketful** (*pl* **pocketfuls**) *noun*. [Middle English *poket* from early French *pokete*, dimin. of *poke*, dialect variant of *poche* pouch, bag]

pocket[2] *verb trans* (**pocketed, pocketing**) **1a** to put or enclose (something) in or as if in one's pocket: *He pocketed his change*. **b** to appropriate (something) for one's own use; to steal (it): *She pocketed the money she had collected for charity*. **2** to accept (something unpleasant): *You'll just have to pocket their insults*. **3** to set aside or suppress (something): *He pocketed his pride and apologized*. **4** to drive (a ball) into a pocket of a billiard or snooker table.

pocket[3] *adj* **1** small enough to be carried in the pocket: *a pocket camera*. **2** small; miniature: *a pocket submarine*.

pocket battleship *noun* a small powerful battleship, *esp* one built by Germany in the 1930s so as to come within treaty limitations of tonnage and armament.

pocketbook *noun* **1** *Brit* a small notebook: *The policeman noted the details in his pocketbook*. **2** *NAmer* a wallet or small money bag.

pocket borough *noun* an English parliamentary constituency which, before reform in 1832, was under the control of one person or family, usu the dominant landowner.

pocketknife *noun* a knife that has one or more blades that fold into the handle, making it safe and small enough to be carried in the pocket.

pocket money *noun* money for small personal expenses, *esp* a weekly sum given to a child.

pocket-size *or* **pocket-sized** *adj* = POCKET[3] (I).

pocket watch *noun* a watch designed to be carried in a person's pocket, e.g. on the end of a chain, as opposed to on a person's wrist.

pockmark *noun* a mark or pit in the skin left by smallpox, chickenpox, etc. ⟫⟫ **pockmarked** *adj*.

poco /'pohkoh/ *adv* used in music: somewhat: *poco allegro*. [Italian *poco* little, from Latin *paucus* a few]

poco a poco /ˌpohkoh ah 'pohkoh/ *adv* used in music: gradually. [Italian *poco a poco* little by little]

POD *abbr* pay on delivery.

pod[1] /pod/ *noun* **1a** a long seed capsule or fruit, *esp* of the pea, bean, or other leguminous plant, and the seeds contained inside it. **b** the empty capsule once the seeds have been removed or dispersed. **2** an egg case of a locust or similar insect. **3** a streamlined compartment under the wings or fuselage of an aircraft, used as a container for fuel, etc. **4** a detachable compartment on a spacecraft or aircraft. [prob a back-formation from Middle English *podware, podder* field crops, of unknown origin]

pod² *verb* (**podded, podding**) ➤ *verb intrans* said of a leguminous plant: to produce pods. ➤ *verb trans* to remove (peas, beans, etc) from a pod.

pod³ *noun* a small group of animals, *esp* whales, seals, or other marine animals, swimming or living close together. [origin unknown]

-pod *or* **-pode** *comb. form* forming words, denoting: a specified type of foot or a specified number of feet: *arthropod; megapode.* [Greek *-podos* from *pod-, pous* foot]

podagra /pə'dagrə/ *noun* gout of the foot, *esp* the big toe. ➤➤ **podagral** *adj.* [Middle English from Latin *podagra*, from Greek *pod-, pous* foot+ *agra* trap]

-pode *comb. form* see -POD.

podge /poj/ *noun* **1** *chiefly Brit. informal* a fat person. **2** excess fat or an area on a person's body where there is excess fat. [prob alteration of *pudge*, of unknown origin]

podgy *adj* (**podgier, podgiest**) short and plump; chubby.

podia /'pohdi·ə/ *noun* pl of PODIUM.

podiatry /po'die·ətri/ *noun chiefly NAmer* = CHIROPODY. ➤➤ **podiatric** /podi'atrik/ *adj,* **podiatrist** *noun.* [Greek *pod-, pous* foot + -IATRY]

podium /'pohdi·əm/ *noun* (*pl* **podiums** *or* **podia** /'pohdi·ə/) **1a** a small raised platform for an orchestral conductor, lecturer, public speaker, nightclub dancer, etc. **b** *NAmer* a lectern. **2a** a continuous base or platform supporting a wall of columns of a building. **b** a low block providing contrast to a multistorey block or smaller area. [via Latin from Greek *podion*, dimin. of *pod-, pous* foot]

-podium *comb. form* forming nouns, denoting: a specified type of foot: *pseudopodium.* [via Latin from Greek *podion*: see PODIUM]

podzol /'podzol/ *or* **podsol** /'podsol/ *noun* any of a group of soils that have a grey upper layer from which humus and compounds of iron and aluminium have leached to enrich the layer below. ➤➤ **podzolic** /pod'zolik/ *adj,* **podzolization** /-lie'zaysh(ə)n/ *noun.* [Russian *podzol*, from *pod* under + *zola* ashes]

poem /'poh·əm/ *noun* **1** a literary composition in verse, often with rhyme and following a set rhythm and using words for their sound as well as meaning. **2** a creation, experience, or object suggesting a poem: *The interior was a poem of chinoiserie.* [early French *poeme* via Latin from Greek *poiēma* something created, from *poiein* to create]

poesy /'poh·əzi, -si/ *noun* (*pl* **poesies**) *archaic or literary* **1** a poem or group of poems; poetry. **2** the art or composition of poetry. [Middle English *poesie* via French and Latin from Greek *poiēsis*, from *poiein* to create]

poet /'poh·it/ *noun* **1** somebody who writes poetry. **2** a creative artist with special sensitivity for a specified medium: *a poet of the piano.* [Middle English via French from Latin *poeta* from Greek *poiētēs* maker, from *poiein* to create]

poetaster /poh·i'tastə/ *noun* an inferior poet. [from Latin *poeta* (see POET) + -ASTER]

poetess /'poh·ites/ *noun dated* a woman who writes poetry.

poetic /poh'etik/ *adj* **1a** relating to or characteristic of poets or poetry. **b** having qualities associated with poetry, such as grace, beauty, or nobility. **2** written in verse. ➤➤ **poetically** *adv,* **poeticism** /-siz(ə)m/ *noun.*

poetical /poh'etikl/ *adj* = POETIC.

poeticize *or* **poeticise** /poh'etisiez/ *verb trans* to give (something) a poetic quality or form.

poetic justice *noun* an outcome in which vice is punished and virtue rewarded in a manner that is particularly or ironically appropriate.

poetic licence *noun* **1** allowable departure from the normal rules of grammar, factual accuracy, etc for the purpose of achieving a particular literary effect. **2** *informal* liberties taken with rules or conventions of any kind.

poetics *pl noun* **1** (*treated as sing. or pl*) the study of poetry and the techniques used by poets. **2** (*treated as sing.*) a treatise on poetry or aesthetics.

poetize *or* **poetise** *verb intrans* to write poetry. ➤ *verb trans* = POETICIZE. ➤➤ **poetizer** *noun.*

poet laureate *noun* (*pl* **poets laureate** *or* **poet laureates**) (*often* **Poet Laureate**) in Britain, a poet appointed for life by the sovereign as a member of the royal household and expected to compose poems for state occasions.

poetry /'poh·itri/ *noun* **1a** literary writing in the form of a poem or poems. **b** the art of writing poetry. **2** a quality of beauty, grace, and great feeling: *poetry in motion.*

po faced /pəh/ *adj Brit, informal* having a foolishly solemn humourless, or disapproving expression. [from PO]

pogo /'pohgoh/ *verb intrans* (**pogoes, pogoed, pogoing**) to jump or dance up and down in a jerky uncontrolled way, *esp* to punk music. [from POGO STICK]

pogo stick *noun* a pole with a spring at the bottom and two footrests on which somebody can jump up and down or move along. [formerly a trademark; of unknown origin]

pogrom /'pogrəm/ *noun* an organized massacre of people from a particular ethnic group, *esp* of Jews in eastern Europe and Russia. [via Yiddish from Russian *pogrom*, literally 'devastation']

poi¹ /poy/ *noun* a Hawaiian food made from the root of the taro plant, which is cooked, pounded, and kneaded to a paste and often allowed to ferment. [Hawaiian and Samoan *poi*]

poi² *noun* (*pl* **poi** *or* **pois**) **1** a ball of flax suspended on a string and swung by Maori women in certain dances. **2** a dance performed with a poi. [Maori *poi*]

-poiesis *comb. form* forming nouns, denoting: production or formation: *erythropoiesis.* [via scientific Latin from Greek *poiēsis* creation]

poignant /'poynyənt/ *adj* **1a** said of reflections, memories, experiences, etc: causing or renewing distress or pity; painfully sad: *Her whole attitude and bearing brought to Sépincourt the poignant, the bewildering conviction that he held no place in her thoughts* — Kate Chopin. **b** said of regret or distress: acute; bitter: *If the distress be not poignant enough to keep the eyes unclosed, they will be sure to open to sensations of softened pain and brighter hope* — Jane Austen. **2** *archaic* to the point; apt: *Her illustrations were apposite and poignant* — Charles Lamb. ➤➤ **poignance** *noun,* **poignancy** /-si/ *noun,* **poignantly** *adv.* [Middle English *poinant* from early French *poignant*, present part. of *poindre* to prick, from Latin *pungere* to prick, sting]

poikilotherm /poy'kiləthuhm/ *noun* a living organism, e.g. a frog, with a variable body temperature that is usu slightly higher than the temperature of its environment. ➤➤ **poikilothermal** /-'thuhml/ *adj,* **poikilothermic** /-'thuhmik/ *adj,* **poikilothermy** /-'thuhmi/ *noun.* [Greek *poikilos* variegated + -THERM]

poilu /'pwahlooh/ *noun* a soldier in the French infantry, *esp* one who fought in World War I. [French *poilu* hairy, suggesting ruggedness and bravery]

poinciana /poynsi'ahnə/ *noun* any of several species of ornamental tropical trees or shrubs with bright orange or red flowers: genera *Caesalpinia* and *Delonix*. [Latin *Poinciana*, former genus name, named after M De Poinci, 17th-cent. governor of the Antilles]

poind /pind/ *verb trans* in Scots law, to take forceful legal possession of (e.g. a debtor's property); to impound or distrain (it). [Scots *punden, pynden* from Old English *pyndan* to dam up, from *pund-* enclosure]

poinsettia /poyn'seti·ə/ *noun* a small shrub of the spurge family bearing delicate yellow flower clusters surrounded by bright red, showy bracts (leaflike structures; see BRACT): *Euphorbia pulcherrima.* [Latin *Poinsettia*, former genus name, named after Joel R Poinsett d.1851, US diplomat, who introduced it to the USA from Mexico]

point¹ /poynt/ *noun* **1a** an individual detail; an item. **b** a distinguishing detail: *Tact is one of her strong points.* **c** the most important element of a discussion or matter: *You've missed the whole point of the joke.* **2** an end or object to be achieved; a purpose: *There is no point in continuing this discussion.* **3a** the sharp, tapering, or narrowly rounded end of something; a tip. **b** any of the sharp projections on a garden fork or similar implement; a tine. **c** a projecting and usu tapering piece of land. **d** the tip of a projecting body part. **e** (*in pl*) the extremities of an animal, *esp* when of a different colour from the rest of the body. **f** (*in pl*) in ballet, the tips of the toes. **g** the contact or discharge extremity of an electrical device, e.g. a sparking plug or contact breaker. **4a** a very small mark; a dot. **b** a full stop. **c** a decimal point. **d** a dot, stroke, or other diacritic used to indicate or modify sounds, e.g. in Hebrew, Arabic, or phonetic script. **5a** a geometric element that has a position but no extent or magnitude. **b** a geometric element determined by an ordered set of coordinates. **6a** a precisely indicated position: *He walked to a point 50 yards north of the building.* **b** an exact moment: *At this point he was interrupted.* **c** (**the point**) the time interval immediately before something indicated; the verge: *at the point of death.* **d** a particular step, stage, or degree in development: *She had reached the point where nothing seemed to matter anymore.* **e** a definite position on a scale: *boiling point.* **7a** any of the 32 evenly spaced compass directions. **b** the 11° 15′ interval between two successive compass points. **8a** a unit of counting in the scoring of a game or contest. **b** a unit used in evaluating something. **c** a unit used in quoting prices (e.g. of shares, bonds, and commodities). **d** in printing, a unit of measurement of type size and spacing equal to 0.351mm (about $^1/_{72}$in). **e** a unit of weight of precious stones, *esp* diamonds, equal to 2mg (0.01 carat). **9** *Brit* (*in pl*) a device made of usu two movable rails and necessary connections and designed to turn a train from one track to another. **10** *Brit* an electric socket. **11** (*usu in pl*) in former times, a piece of cord or ribbon with metal tags at the ends, used to fasten or lace garments. **12a** in cricket, a fielding position close to the batsman and more or less in line with the stumps on the off side. **b** a player in this position. **13** in lacrosse, a defensive player or the position of such a player. **14** the rigidly intent attitude of a gundog when marking game for a hunter. ✳ **beside the point** irrelevant. **make a point of** to take particular care to (do something). **to the point** relevant or pertinent: *a suggestion that was to the point.* **up to a point** to a certain extent; not completely. [Middle English, partly from Old French *point* puncture, small spot, point in time or space, partly from Old French *pointe* sharp end, both ultimately from Latin *pungere* to prick]

point² *verb intrans* **1** (*often* + at/to) to indicate the position or direction of something, *esp* by extending a finger: *She pointed at the house across the road.* **2** to be extended or turned in a particular direction: *The ship was pointing north.* **3** (+ to) to indicate the fact or probability of something: *The evidence all pointed to an accidental death.* **4** to indicate the presence of game: *a dog that points well.* ➤ *verb trans* **1** to cause (something) to be turned or aimed in a particular direction. **2** to scratch out the old mortar from the joints of (brickwork, etc) and fill in with new material. **3** to provide (something) with a point: *He was pointing a pencil with a knife.* **4** said of a gundog: to indicate the presence and place of (game) for a hunter by a point. **5** to mark signs or points in (e.g. psalms or Hebrew writing).

point-blank¹ *adv* **1** at such close range that a missile travels in a straight line and cannot miss the target: *He fired point-blank at the intruder.* **2** directly and without explanation: *She refused point-blank.* [POINT² + BLANK² in the sense 'centre of a target']

point-blank² *adj* **1** at or being a very close range of firing: *I fired at point-blank range.* **2** direct or blunt: *a point-blank refusal.*

point duty *noun* traffic regulation carried out by a police officer or other official stationed at a particular point, *esp* a road junction.

pointe /pwant (*French* pwɛ̃t)/ *noun* a ballet position in which the body is balanced on the extreme tip of the toe. [French *pointe*: see POINT¹]

pointed /'poyntid/ *adj* **1** having a point. **2** said *esp* of a critical remark: clearly aimed at a particular person or group. **3** conspicuous: *pointed indifference.* ➤➤ **pointedly** *adv*, **pointedness** *noun.*

pointer *noun* **1a** a rod used to point at things on maps, charts, etc. **b** a needle that indicates a reading on a dial or other scale. **2** a useful suggestion or hint; a tip. **3** a large strong gundog of a smooth-haired breed that hunts by scent and indicates the presence of game by pointing.

pointillism /'pwantiliz(ə)m, 'poyn-/ *noun* in art, the technique of applying small strokes or dots of pure colour to a surface so that from a distance they blend together. ➤➤ **pointillist** *noun and adj.* [French *pointillisme*, from *pointiller* to stipple, from *point*: see POINT¹]

point lace *noun* = NEEDLEPOINT (1).

pointless *adj* devoid of meaning, relevance, or purpose; senseless: *a pointless remark.* ➤➤ **pointlessly** *adv*, **pointlessness** *noun.*

point of honour *noun* a matter that somebody considers to have a serious effect on their honour or reputation.

point of no return *noun* **1** the point in a long-distance journey at which return to the starting point becomes impossible, e.g. because of insufficient fuel or supplies. **2** a critical point, e.g. in a course of action, at which turning back or reversal becomes impossible.

point of order *noun* a question relating to procedure in an official meeting.

point of sale *noun* in retail distribution, the place at which a product is sold.

point-of-sale *adj* denoting advertising or promotional material accompanying a product at its point of sale.

point of view *noun* **1** a position from which something or somebody is observed, considered, or evaluated. **2** an opinion or attitude.

point out *verb trans* to direct somebody's attention to (something).

point source *noun* a source of light or other energy that is concentrated at a point and considered to have no dimensions.

point-to-point *noun* a cross-country steeplechase for amateur riders on hunting horses. ➤➤ **point-to-pointer** *noun.*

point up *verb trans* to emphasize or show the importance of (something).

poise¹ /poyz/ *noun* **1a** easy self-possessed assurance of manner; composure or dignity. **b** a particular way of carrying oneself, *esp* with grace or elegance. **2** a stable balanced state; equilibrium: *a poise between widely divergent impulses* — F R Leavis. [Middle English *poyse* weight, heaviness, via early French *pois*, *peis* from Latin *pensum*, from *pendere* to weigh]

poise² *verb trans* **1** to hold or carry (something) in equilibrium; to balance (it): *She walked along with a water jar poised on her head.* **2** to hold (something) supported or suspended without motion in a steady position: *He waited with his hand poised over the alarm button.* ➤ *verb intrans* to be poised. [Middle English *poisen* to weigh, ponder, via French from Latin *pensare*: see PENSIVE]

poise³ /pwahz/ *noun* a cgs unit of dynamic viscosity; the viscosity of a liquid or gas that would require a force of one dyne per square centimetre to move either of two parallel layers one centimetre apart with a velocity of one centimetre per second relative to the other layer. [French *poise*, named after Jean Louis Marie *Poiseuille* d.1869, French physician and anatomist]

poised /poyzd/ *adj* **1a** marked by composure or dignity; self-possessed. **b** marked by balance or equilibrium. **2** in a state or position of readiness: *poised for action; poised to jump.*

poison¹ /'poyz(ə)n/ *noun* **1a** a substance that through its chemical action kills or harms a living organism. **b** something that destroys or corrupts. **2** in chemistry or nuclear physics, a substance that inhibits the activity of another substance or the course of a reaction or process: *a catalyst poison.* [Middle English via Old French *poison* drink, poisonous drink, poison, from Latin *potion-*, *potio*: see POTION]

poison² *verb trans* (**poisoned, poisoning**) **1a** to harm or kill (a person, animal, or plant) with poison. **b** to taint or contaminate (something) with poison. **2** to exert a harmful influence on (something or somebody); to corrupt (them): *Their minds had been poisoned.* **3** to inhibit the activity, course, or occurrence of (something). ➤➤ **poisoner** *noun*, **poisoning** *noun.*

poison³ *adj* poisoned or poisonous: *poison gas.*

poisoned chalice *noun* something given or awarded, e.g. a task or responsibility, that is likely to bring misfortune or unpopularity to the receiver.

poison ivy *noun* **1** a N American climbing plant of the sumach family that has greenish flowers and white berries and produces an oil that causes an intensely itching skin rash: *Rhus radicans.* **2** any of several related plants.

poisonous /'poyz(ə)nəs/ *adj* **1** having the properties or effects of poison. **2** malicious. ➤➤ **poisonously** *adv.*

poison-pen letter *noun* a letter written, usu anonymously, with malicious intent to frighten or offend.

poison pill *noun* in business, any of various strategies employed by a company to make a takeover bid unattractive or impracticable to an unwelcome prospective purchaser.

Poisson distribution /'pwahsonh/ *noun* in statistics, a probability distribution that is often used to model the number of outcomes of discrete events, e.g. traffic accidents, that occur in a fixed time. [named after Siméon *Poisson* d.1840, French mathematical physicist, who first described it]

poke¹ /pohk/ *verb trans* **1a** to hit (something or somebody) with a fingertip or something sharp; to prod (them): *She poked him in the ribs.* **b** to produce (something) by piercing, stabbing, or jabbing: *I poked a hole in the lid.* **2** to cause (something) to project: *She poked her head out of the window.* **3** to stir the coals or logs of (a fire) so as to promote burning. **4** *informal* to hit (somebody) with the fist; to punch (them): *I poked him in the nose.* **5** *coarse slang* said of a man: to have sexual intercourse with (a woman). ➤ *verb intrans* **1** to make a prodding, jabbing, or thrusting movement, *esp* repeatedly. **2** (+ about/around) to look about or through something in a random manner; to rummage: *We found it while poking around in the attic.* **3** to be stuck out; to protrude: *The dog's nose poked through the bars of the gate.* **4** *coarse slang* said of a man: to have sexual intercourse. ✳ **poke one's nose into** to meddle in or interfere with (*esp* something that does not concern one). [Middle English *poken*, prob of Germanic origin]

poke² *noun* **1** a prod or jab. **2** *informal* a punch. **3** *coarse slang* an act of sexual intercourse. **4** a women's bonnet with a projecting brim at the front, worn *esp* in the 18th and 19th cents.

poke³ *noun NAmer, Scot* a bag or sack. [Middle English from Old French *poke*: see POCKET¹]

poke bonnet *noun* = POKE² (4).

poker¹ *noun* a metal rod for poking a fire.

poker² *noun* any of several card games in which a player bets that the value of his or her hand is greater than that of the hands held by others, who must equal or raise the bet or drop out. [prob modification of French *poque*, a card game similar to poker]

poker face *noun* an inscrutable face that reveals no hint of a person's thoughts or feelings. ➤➤ **poker-faced** *adj.* [from the need of poker players to conceal the true quality of their hands]

pokerwork *noun* **1** decorative designs burned into wood or other material using a heated metal rod. **2** the art of doing pokerwork.

pokeweed *noun* a coarse N American plant with white flowers, dark purple juicy berries, and a poisonous root: *Phytolacca americana.* [modification of *puccoon* a plant used in dyeing, of Algonquian origin]

pokey *noun NAmer, informal* a jail. [origin unknown]

poky or **pokey** /'pohki/ *adj* (**pokier, pokiest**) **1** *informal* small and cramped. **2** *NAmer* annoyingly slow. ➤➤ **pokily** *adv*, **pokiness** *noun*. [POKE¹]

Polack /'pohlak/ *noun NAmer, offensive* a Polish person. [Polish *Polak*]

polar /'pohlə/ *adj* **1** of or in the region around a geographical pole. **2** of the poles of a magnet. **3** in chemistry, exhibiting polarity, *esp* having groups with opposing properties at opposite ends: *a polar molecule*; *a polar solvent.* **4** completely opposite in nature, tendency, or action. **5a** resembling a pole or axis round which all else revolves; pivotal. **b** serving as a guide in the manner of the Pole Star. [Latin *polaris* from *polus*: see POLE³]

polar bear *noun* a large white bear native to arctic regions: *Thalarctos maritimus.*

polar circle *noun* either the Arctic Circle or the Antarctic Circle.

polar coordinate *noun* in geometry, either of two numbers that locate a point in a plane by its distance along a line from a fixed point and the angle this line makes with a fixed line.

polar distance *noun* **1** in geometry, the angular distance of a point on the surface of a sphere from the nearest pole. **2** in astronomy, the angular distance of a star from the celestial pole.

polarimeter /pohlə'rimitə/ *noun* **1** an instrument for determining the amount of polarization of light. **2** an instrument for measuring the amount of optical rotation produced by an optically active substance, e.g. a sugar solution. ➤➤ **polarimetric** /-'metrik/ *adj*, **polarimetry** /-tri/ *noun*. [*polarization* (see POLARIZE) + -METER²]

polariscope /poh'lariskohp/ *noun* **1** an instrument for studying the properties of or examining substances in polarized light. **2** = POLARIMETER (2). ➤➤ **polariscopic** /-'skopik/ *adj*. [*polarization* (see POLARIZE) + -SCOPE]

polarise /'pohləriez/ *verb* see POLARIZE.

polarity /pə'larəti, poh-/ *noun* (*pl* **polarities**) **1** the quality or condition of a body that has opposite properties or powers in opposite directions. **2** magnetic attraction towards a particular object or in a specific direction. **3** the particular state of having either a positive

or negative electrical charge. **4** the state or an instance of being diametrically opposed.

polarize or **polarise** /'pohləriez/ *verb trans* **1a** to cause (e.g. light waves) to vibrate in a definite or restricted pattern or direction. **b** to give (something) electrical or magnetic polarity. **2** to divide (e.g. people or their opinions) into two opposing factions or categories. ➤ *verb intrans* to become polarized. ➤➤ **polarizable** *adj*, **polarization** /-'zaysh(ə)n/ *noun*, **polarizer** *noun*. [French *polariser* from Latin *polaris* polar, from *polus*: see POLE³]

polarography /pohlə'rogrəfi/ *noun* a method of analysing chemical substances or solutions that uses electrolysis.

Polaroid /'pohləroyd/ *noun* **1** *trademark.* **a** a light-polarizing material used in sunglasses to prevent glare and in various optical devices. **b** (*in pl*) sunglasses with lenses made from this material. **2a** a camera that produces a finished print soon after the photograph has been taken. **b** a photographic print from such a camera. [POLARIZE + -OID]

polder /'pohldə, 'pohldə/ *noun* an area of low land reclaimed from a body of water, *esp* in the Netherlands. [Dutch *polder*]

Pole /pohl/ *noun* a native or inhabitant of Poland in E Europe. ➤➤➤ **Polish** *adj*. [German *Pole*, of Slavonic origin]

pole¹ *noun* **1a** a long thin usu cylindrical piece of wood, metal, etc. **b** a shaft that extends from the front axle of a wagon between the horses or other animals pulling it. **2** = ROD (4). **3** = POLE POSITION. ✳ **up the pole 1** *chiefly Brit, informal* slightly mad; crazy. **2** *chiefly Brit, informal* misguided or mistaken. [Old English *pāl* stake, pole, from Latin *palus* stake]

pole² *verb trans* **1** to push or propel (e.g. a boat) with a pole. **2** to support (e.g. a crop) on poles.

pole³ *noun* **1** either extremity of an axis of a sphere or of a body, *esp* the earth, resembling a sphere. **2a** either of the two terminals of an electric cell, battery, or dynamo. **b** any of two or more regions in a magnetized body at which the magnetism is concentrated. **3** in biology, either of the anatomically or physiologically differentiated areas at opposite ends of an axis in an organism or cell. **4** in geometry, the fixed point in a system of polar coordinates that serves as the ORIGIN (position where values are zero). **5a** either of two related opposites. **b** something serving as a guiding influence or centre of attraction: *The business of education in this case, is only to conduct the shooting tendrils to a proper pole* — Mary Wollstonecraft. ✳ **poles apart** having nothing in common; totally unrelated. [Middle English *pool* via Latin *polus* from Greek *polos* pivot, pole]

poleaxe¹ (*NAmer* **poleax**) *noun* **1** a battle-axe with a short handle and often a hook or spike opposite the blade. **2** an axe used, *esp* formerly, in slaughtering cattle. [Middle English *polax, pollax*, from *pol* POLL¹ in the sense 'striking end of a tool' + *ax* AXE¹]

poleaxe² (*NAmer* **poleax**) *verb trans* **1** to attack, strike, or fell (somebody) with a poleaxe. **2** *informal* to give (somebody) a great shock; to stupefy (them).

polecat *noun* (*pl* **polecats** or *collectively* **polecat**) **1** a carnivorous mammal with dark brown fur that is native to Europe, Asia, and N Africa, is related to the weasel, and is noted for its unpleasant smell: *Mustela putorius.* **2** *NAmer* = SKUNK (1). [Middle English *polcat*, prob from early French *poul, pol* cock + CAT¹, because it preys on poultry]

pole dancer *noun* an erotic dancer in a nightclub, who performs around a vertical pole. ➤➤➤ **pole dancing** *noun*.

polemic /pə'lemik/ *noun* **1** an aggressive attack on or refutation of somebody's opinions or principles. **2** an argument or controversy. **b** (*in pl, but treated as sing. or pl*) the art or practice of disputation or controversy. ➤➤➤ **polemic** *adj*, **polemical** *adj*, **polemically** *adv*, **polemicist** /-sist/ *noun*. [French *polémique* via medieval Latin from Greek *polemikos* warlike, hostile, from *polemos* war]

polemicize or **polemicise** /pə'lemisiez/ *verb intrans* to engage in aggressive verbal attacks, argument, or controversy.

polenta /pə'lentə/ *noun* **1** fine maize flour used in Italian cooking. **2** cooked polenta served as a thick paste with fish, meat, etc or sliced and fried.

Word history

via Italian from Latin *polenta*, literally 'pearl barley'. In Old and Middle English *polenta*, borrowed directly from Latin, denoted pearl barley or a kind of porridge made from it or, later, from chestnut or corn meal. In the 17th and 18th cents the word appeared mainly in travel writing, referring to porridge made usually of maize, a staple food of Mediterranean peasants.

In modern use the word has been reborrowed from Italian and refers exclusively to fine maize meal as used in Italy.

pole position *noun* in motor racing, a position on the inside of the front row of the starting grid, awarded to the driver who was fastest in the practice or qualifying session.

Pole Star *noun* a star in the constellation Ursa Minor that lies very close to the N celestial pole.

polestar *noun* **1** a directing principle; a guide. **2** a centre of attraction.

pole vault *noun* an athletic field event consisting of a jump over a high crossbar with the aid of a long flexible pole.

pole-vault *verb intrans* to compete in the pole vault. ➤➤ **pole-vaulter** *noun*.

police[1] /pə'lees/ *noun* **1** (*treated as sing. or pl*) a body of trained people entrusted by a government with maintenance of public order and enforcement of laws. **2** (*treated as pl*) members of this body; police officers: *We called the police*. **3** (*treated as sing. or pl*) an organized body having similar functions within a more restricted sphere: *railway police*. [early French *police* government, via late Latin *politia* from Greek *politeia*, ultimately from *polis* city, state]

police[2] *verb trans* **1** to control (an area, event, etc) by use of police. **2** to supervise the operation or administration of (e.g. an industry or election), *esp* to prevent violation of rules.

police dog *noun* a dog trained to assist the police, e.g. in catching criminals or detecting drugs.

police force *noun* = POLICE[1] (1).

policeman *noun* (*pl* **policemen**) a man who is a member of the police.

police officer *noun* a member of the police.

police state *noun* a country or state characterized by repressive governmental control of political, economic, and social life, usu enforced by secret police.

police station *noun* the headquarters of a local police force.

policewoman *noun* (*pl* **policewomen**) a woman who is a member of the police.

policy[1] /'polisi/ *noun* (*pl* **policies**) **1a** a definite course of action selected from among alternatives, *esp* in the light of given conditions. **b** an overall plan embracing general goals and procedures and intended to guide and determine decisions. **2** wise or sensible procedure: *It's bad policy to smoke*. [Middle English *policie* government, policy, via French from late Latin *politia*: see POLICE[1]]

policy[2] *noun* (*pl* **policies**) a contract of insurance. [alteration of earlier *police*, via French, Old Italian, and medieval Latin, ultimately from Greek *apodeixis* proof, from *apodeikenai* to show, prove]

policyholder *noun* a person or company holding an insurance policy.

polio /'pohlioh/ *noun* = POLIOMYELITIS.

poliomyelitis /,pohliohmie-ə'lietis/ *noun* an infectious viral disease, *esp* of children, characterized by inflammation of the nerve cells of the spinal cord, paralysis, and wasting of skeletal muscles, often resulting in permanent disability and deformity. [scientific Latin *poliomyelitis*, from Greek *polios* grey + *myelos* marrow]

-polis *comb. form* forming nouns, denoting: city: *megalopolis*. [late Latin *-polis*, ultimately from Greek *polis* city state]

Polish /'pohlish/ *noun* the Slavonic language of Poland in E Europe. ➤➤ **Polish** *adj*.

polish[1] /'polish/ *verb trans* **1** to make (something) smooth and glossy, usu by rubbing it. **2** to make (somebody or something) more refined. **3** (*often + up*) to bring (e.g. a skill) to a highly developed or finished state; to improve or perfect (it): *a polished performance*; *I must polish up my French before the holiday*. **4** to remove the outer husk of (rice) by milling. ➤ *verb intrans* to become smooth or glossy by or as if by friction. ➤➤ **polisher** *noun*. [Middle English *polisshen* via Old French from Latin *polire*]

polish[2] /'polish/ *noun* **1** a preparation used to produce a gloss and sometimes a colour for the protection and decoration of a surface: *furniture polish*; *nail polish*. **2** the act or an instance of polishing: *give the table a polish*. **3** a smooth glossy surface. **4** refinement, elegance, or social grace.

polish off /'polish/ *verb trans* to consume or dispose of (something) rapidly or completely.

politburo /'politbyooəroh/ *noun* (*pl* **politburos**) the principal policy-making and executive committee of a communist party. [Russian *politbyuro*, contraction of *politicheskoye byuro* political bureau]

polite /pə'liet/ *adj* (**politer**, **politest**) **1** showing or characterized by consideration and deference towards others; courteous. **2** showing or characterized by correct social usage; refined. ➤➤ **politely** *adv*, **politeness** *noun*. [Middle English in the sense 'polished, burnished', from Latin *politus*, past part. of *polire* to POLISH[1]]

politesse /poli'tes/ *noun* formal politeness; decorousness. [French *politesse* from Old Italian *pulito* polite, polished, ultimately from Latin *polire* to POLISH[1]]

politic /'politik/ *adj* **1** wise or expedient: *a politic decision*. **2** shrewd in managing or dealing with people and situations. [Middle English *politik* via French from Latin *politicus*, from Greek *politikos* political, from *politēs* citizen, from *polis* city]

Usage note ⎯⎯⎯⎯⎯⎯⎯⎯⎯⎯
politic or **political**? See note at POLITICAL.

political /pə'litikl/ *adj* **1** relating to government or public affairs. **2a** relating to politics, *esp* party politics. **b** active in or sensitive to politics: *highly political students*. **3** involving or charged with acts against a government: *political criminals*. **4** concerned with relationships of power within an organization rather than matters of practicality or principle. ➤➤ **politically** *adv*. [Latin *politicus*: see POLITIC]

Usage note ⎯⎯⎯⎯⎯⎯⎯⎯⎯⎯
political or **politic**? These two words are not interchangeable. *Political* is much the commoner word and means, broadly, 'having to do with politics'. *Politic* means 'sensible or advantageous under the circumstances' and can be used in contexts that have nothing at all to do with politics: *It might be politic to postpone your trip*.

political correctness *noun* the quality of being politically correct, or adherence to politically correct forms and conventions: *Political correctness is the natural continuum from the party line ... a self-appointed group of vigilantes imposing their views on others* — Doris Lessing.

political economy *noun* **1** a social science dealing with the interrelationship of political and economic processes. **2** *dated* = ECONOMICS (1). ➤➤ **political economist** *noun*.

politically correct *adj* having or showing sensitivity to the risk of offending particular groups of people and therefore careful to avoid judgmental or discriminatory words or actions.

political prisoner *noun* somebody who has been imprisoned for their political beliefs, affiliations, or activities.

political science *noun* a social science concerned chiefly with political institutions and processes. ➤➤ **political scientist** *noun*.

politician /poli'tish(ə)n/ *noun* **1** a person experienced or engaged in politics, *esp* a political representative voted into office. **2** *NAmer*, *derog* somebody who uses underhand methods for personal advancement.

politicize *or* **politicise** /pə'litisiez/ *verb trans* **1** to give (something) a political tone or character. **2** to make (somebody) aware of political issues or politically active. ➤ *verb intrans* to discuss or engage in politics. ➤➤ **politicization** /-'zaysh(ə)n/ *noun*.

politicking /'politiking/ *noun* *chiefly derog* political activity, *esp* insincere or opportunistic attempts to win votes or support.

politico /pə'litikoh/ *noun* (*pl* **politicos**) *informal*, *chiefly derog* a politician or political person. [Italian *politico* or Spanish *político*, both from Latin *politicus*: see POLITIC]

politico- *comb. form* forming adjectives, with the meaning: political and: *politico-diplomatic*. [Latin *politicus*: see POLITIC]

politics /'politiks/ *pl noun* **1** (*treated as sing. or pl*). **a** the art or science of government. **b** = POLITICAL SCIENCE. **2** (*treated as sing. or pl*). **a** the activities associated with government; political affairs. **b** political life as a profession. **3** a person's political sympathies. **4** (*treated as sing. or pl*) the complex of relations between human beings in society or within an organization.

Editorial note ⎯⎯⎯⎯⎯⎯⎯⎯⎯⎯
Politics is often colloquially associated with an unscrupulous drive for power, but it is an inevitable feature of human organization, of the containment – or pursuit – of conflict, and the realization of collective ends and values. It occurs in all human interaction involving the exercise of influence and the distribution of scarce resources, but is particularly salient at the level of states, aspiring to endow politics with authority — Professor Michael Freeden.

[Greek *politika*, neuter pl of *politikos*: see POLITIC]

polity /'politi/ *noun* (*pl* **polities**) **1** a country or state regarded as a politically organized unit. **2** a form of government or social organization. [late Latin *politia*: see POLICE[1]]

polka[1] /'polka, 'pohlkə/ *noun* **1** a lively dance of Bohemian origin with two beats to the bar. **2** a piece of music for or in the rhythm of this dance. [via French and German from Czech *půlka* half-step, from *půl* half]

polka[2] *verb intrans* (**polkas, polkaed, polkaing**) to dance the polka.

polka dot /'pohlkə/ *noun* any of many regularly distributed dots in a textile design. ➤➤ **polka-dot** *adj,* **polka-dotted** *adj.*

poll[1] /pohl/ *noun* **1a** the casting or recording of votes. **b** (*in pl*) the place where votes are cast: *at the polls.* **c** the number of votes recorded: *a heavy poll.* **2** a survey conducted by the questioning of people selected at random or by quota, or the results of such a survey: *an opinion poll.* **3** the head or scalp. **4** a hornless animal. **5** the broad or flat end of the head of a striking tool, e.g. a hammer. [Middle English *pol, polle* head, from early Low German; (senses 1 and 2) from the idea of counting heads and hence votes]

poll[2] *verb trans* **1** to receive (a usu specified number of votes). **2** to receive and record the votes of (e.g. a constituency or an electorate). **3** to question (people) in a poll. **4a** to cut off or cut short (e.g. the hair or horns of domestic livestock). **b** to cut off or cut short the hair or horns of (e.g. domestic livestock). **5** to remove the top of (e.g. a tree); *specif* to pollard (it). ➤➤ *verb intrans* to cast one's vote. ➤➤ **pollee** /poh'lee/ *noun,* **poller** *noun.*

pollack *or* **pollock** /'polək/ *noun* (*pl* **pollacks** *or* **pollocks** *or collectively* **pollack** *or* **pollock**) a N Atlantic food fish related to and resembling the cod but darker and with a more obviously protruding lower jaw: *Pollachius pollachius.* [Scots *podlok,* of unknown origin]

pollan /'polən/ *noun* (*pl* **pollans** *or collectively* **pollan**) a freshwater food fish related to the salmons and trouts that is found in some Irish lakes: *Coregonus pollan.* [Irish *pollán,* perhaps from *pol* pool]

pollard[1] /'polǝd/ *noun* **1** a tree cut back to the main stem to promote the growth of a dense head of foliage. **2** a hornless animal of a usu horned kind. [POLL[2] + -ARD]

pollard[2] *verb trans* to make a pollard of (a tree).

pollen /'polən/ *noun* the minute granules that are discharged as a fine dust from the ANTHER (part of male reproductive organ) of a flower and serve to fertilize the ovules. ➤➤ **pollinic** /pǝ'linik/ *adj.* [Latin *pollen* fine flour, dust]

pollen basket *noun* a smooth area on each hind leg of a bee that serves to collect and transport pollen.

pollen count *noun* a figure representing the amount of pollen in the air, available as a warning to people affected by hay fever or other allergic conditions.

pollex /'poleks/ *noun* (*pl* **pollices** /'poliseez/) *technical* the first digit of the forelimb; the thumb. ➤➤ **pollical** /'polikl/ *adj.* [Latin *pollic-, pollex* thumb, big toe]

pollin- *or* **pollini-** *comb. form* forming words, denoting: pollen: *pollinate; pollinium.* [scientific Latin *pollin-, pollen*: see POLLEN]

pollinate /'polǝnayt/ *verb trans* to place pollen on the STIGMA (female reproductive organ) and so fertilize (a flower or plant). ➤➤ **pollination** /-'naysh(ǝ)n/ *noun,* **pollinator** *noun.*

pollini- *comb. form* see POLLIN-.

pollinium /pǝ'lini-ǝm/ *noun* (*pl* **pollinia** /-ni-ǝ/) a coherent mass of pollen grains, often with a stalk bearing an adhesive disc that clings to insects.

polliwog *or* **pollywog** /'poliwog/ *noun dialect, NAmer* a tadpole. [alteration of Middle English *polwygle,* prob from *pol* POLL[1] + *wiglen* WIGGLE[1]]

pollock /'polǝk/ *noun* see POLLACK.

pollster /'pohlstǝ/ *noun* somebody who conducts a poll or compiles data obtained by a poll.

poll tax *noun* any tax of a fixed amount per person levied on adults.

pollute /pǝ'looht/ *verb trans* **1** to contaminate (something), *esp* with toxic substances: *pollute the environment.* **2** to make (somebody) morally impure; to corrupt or defile (them). ➤➤ **pollutant** *noun,* **polluter** *noun.* [Middle English *polluten* from Latin *pollutus,* past part. of *polluere* to pollute, defile, ultimately from Latin *lutum* mud]

pollution /pǝ'loohsh(ǝ)n/ *noun* **1** the act of polluting or the state of being polluted: *Even the most ardent environmentalist doesn't really want to stop pollution … He wants to have the right amount of pollution* — Milton Friedman. **2** material that pollutes.

Pollyanna /poli'anǝ/ *noun* an irrepressible optimist. ➤➤ **Pollyannaish** *adj.* [named after *Pollyanna,* heroine of the novel *Pollyanna* by Eleanor Porter d.1920, US fiction writer]

pollywog /'poliwog/ *noun* see POLLIWOG.

polo /'pohloh/ *noun* a game of Eastern origin played by teams of usu four players on horseback using mallets with long flexible handles to drive a wooden ball into the opponents' goal. [Balti *polo* ball]

polonaise /polǝ'nayz/ *noun* **1a** a stately Polish processional dance in moderate time with three beats to the bar. **b** a piece of music for or in the rhythm of this dance. **2** a short-sleeved elaborate dress with a fitted waist and loops of material drawn up at the sides and back to reveal a decorative underskirt. [French *polonaise,* fem of *polonais* Polish]

polo neck *noun chiefly Brit* a very high closely fitting collar worn folded over, or a jumper with such a collar.

polonium /pǝ'lohni·ǝm/ *noun* a radioactive metallic chemical element that occurs naturally in uranium ores, and is used in nuclear research and to remove static electricity: symbol Po, atomic number 84. [scientific Latin *polonium* from medieval Latin *Polonia* Poland]

polony /pǝ'lohni/ *noun* = BOLOGNA. [alteration of *Bologna*]

polo shirt *noun* a casual knitted cotton shirt with a soft collar and buttons at the neck.

poltergeist /'poltǝgiest/ *noun* a mischievous ghost said to be responsible for unexplained noises and throwing objects about. [German *Poltergeist,* from *poltern* to knock + *Geist* spirit]

poltroon /pol'troohn/ *noun archaic* a spiritless coward. [early French *poultron* from Old Italian *poltrone,* perhaps from Latin *pullus* young of an animal]

poly /'poli/ *noun* (*pl* **polys**) *Brit, informal* a polytechnic.

poly- *comb. form* forming words, with the meanings: **1** many or much: *polyphonic; polygyny.* **2** excessive or abnormally great: *polyphagia.* **3** containing two or more specified ions or chemical groups in the molecular structure: *polyamide.* **4** polymer of: *polytetra-fluoroethylene.* [Middle English via Latin from Greek *polys* much]

polyamide /poli'amied, -mid/ *noun* a chemical compound characterized by more than one amide group or a synthetic fibre made from this, e.g. nylon.

polyandry /'poliandri/ *noun* **1** the fact of having more than one husband or male mate at a time: compare POLYGAMY, POLYGYNY. **2** a flower's possession of a large number of stamens. ➤➤ **polyandrous** /-'andrǝs/ *adj.* [Greek *polyandria* having many men, from POLY- + *andr-, anēr* man]

polyanthus /poli'anthǝs/ *noun* (*pl* **polyanthuses** *or* **polyanthi** /-thie/) a flowering plant that is a hybrid between the wild primrose and primula: *Primula × polyantha.* [scientific Latin *polyanthus* from Greek *polyanthos* blooming, from POLY- + *anthos* flower]

polyatomic /,poli·ǝ'tomik/ *adj* said of a molecule: containing more than two atoms.

poly bag *noun Brit, informal* a small bag made of thin usu transparent polythene; a plastic bag.

polycarbonate /poli'kahbǝnayt, -nǝt/ *noun* any of various tough transparent plastics characterized by high impact strength and high softening temperature.

polychaete /'polikeet/ *noun* any of a class of chiefly marine annelid worms with many bristles, usu arranged in pairs, along the body: class Polychaeta: compare OLIGOCHAETE. ➤➤ **polychaetous** /-'keetǝs/ *adj.* [Greek *polychaitēs* having much hair, from POLY- + *chaitē* mane]

polychlorinated biphenyl /poli'klawrinaytid/ *noun* any of several chemical compounds that are produced by replacing the hydrogen atoms in biphenyl with chlorine, have various industrial applications, and are poisonous environmental pollutants.

polychromatic /,polikrǝ'matik/ *adj* **1** showing a variety or a change of colours; multicoloured. **2** containing or denoting radiation with more than one wavelength. ➤➤ **polychromatism** /-'krohmǝtiz(ǝ)m/ *noun.* [Greek *polychrōmatos,* from POLY- + *chrōmat-, chrōma* colour]

polychrome /'polikrohm/ *adj* relating to, made with, or decorated in several colours: *polychrome pottery*. ➤➤ **polychromy** /-mi/ *noun*. [Greek *polychrōmos*, from POLY- + *chrōma* colour]

polyclinic /'poliklinik/ *noun* a clinic offering a wide range of medical services.

polycotton /'polikotən/ *noun* a fabric that is blend of polyester and cotton. ➤➤ **polycotton** *adj*.

polycrystalline /poli'kristəlien/ *adj* composed of many crystals, *esp* of varying orientation.

polycyclic /poli'sieklik, -'siklik/ *adj* 1 said e.g. of a plant or shell: having more than one ring or whorl. 2 said of a chemical compound: having two or more fused rings of atoms in the molecule.

polycystic /poli'sistik/ *adj* in medicine, having or characterized by the presence of many cysts.

polycythaemia (*NAmer* **polycythemia**) /polisie'theemi-ə/ *noun* in medicine, a condition marked by an abnormal increase in the number of circulating red blood cells. [scientific Latin *polycythaemia*, from POLY- + CYT- + -HAEMIA]

polydactyl /poli'daktil/ *adj* having more fingers or toes than normal. ➤➤ **polydactyly** /-li/ *noun*. [Greek *polydaktylos*, from POLY- + *daktylos* finger]

polydactylous /poli'daktiləs/ *adj* = POLYDACTYL.

polyester /poli'estə/ *noun* 1 a polymer containing ester groups used *esp* in making fibres or plastics. 2 a synthetic fibre made from polyester.

polyethylene /poli'ethileen/ *noun* = POLYTHENE.

polygamy /pə'ligəmi/ *noun* 1 the practice or condition of being married to more than one person at a time, *esp* marriage in which a husband has more than one wife: compare POLYANDRY, POLYGYNY: *in pious times … before polygamy was made a sin* — Dryden. 2 in zoology, the practice of having more than one mate during a single breeding season. 3 in botany, the condition of bearing both hermaphrodite and unisexual flowers on the same plant. ➤➤ **polygamist** *noun*, **polygamous** *adj*, **polygamously** *adv*. [early French *polygamie* via late Latin from Greek *polygamia*, from POLY- + -*gamia* -GAMY]

polygene /'polijeen/ *noun* any of a group of genes that collectively control the inheritance of or modify the expression of a characteristic. ➤➤ **polygenic** /poli'jenik/ *adj*.

polygenesis /poli'jenəsis/ *noun* origin from more than one ancestral line or stock. ➤➤ **polygenetic** /-'netik/ *adj*, **polygenetically** /-'netikli/ *adv*.

polyglot[1] /'poliglot/ *adj* 1 speaking several languages; multilingual. 2 containing text in several languages. [Greek *polyglōttos*, from POLY- + *glōtta* language]

polyglot[2] *noun* 1 somebody who speaks several languages. 2 (**Polyglot**) a book, *esp* a Bible, containing versions of the same text in several languages. ➤➤ **polyglottal** /-'glotəl/ *adj*.

polygon /'poligən, -gon/ *noun* a two-dimensional geometric figure, usu closed, with three or more straight sides. ➤➤ **polygonal** /pə'lig(ə)nl/ *adj*. [via late Latin from Greek *polygōnon*, from POLY- + *gōnia* angle]

polygonum /pə'ligənəm/ *noun* any of a genus of plants of the dock family with thickened stem joints and small usu white, red, or green flowers: genus *Polygonum*. [from the Latin genus name, from Greek *polygonon* knotgrass, from POLY- + *gony* knee, joint]

polygraph /'poligrahf, -graf/ *noun* an instrument for recording variations of the pulse rate, blood pressure, etc simultaneously, *esp* one used as a lie detector. ➤➤ **polygraphic** /-'grafik/ *adj*.

polygyny /pə'lijini/ *noun* 1 the fact of having more than one wife or female mate at a time: compare POLYANDRY, POLYGAMY. 2 a flower's possession of a large number of ovaries. ➤➤ **polygynous** *adj*. [POLY- + Greek *gyne* woman]

polyhedron /poli'heedrən/ *noun* (*pl* **polyhedrons** *or* **polyhedra** /-drə/) a solid geometric figure with four or more plane faces. ➤➤ **polyhedral** *adj*. [Greek *polyedron*, from POLY- + *hedron* side]

polymath /'polimath/ *noun* somebody who has a wide range of learning or accomplishments. ➤➤ **polymathic** /-'mathik/ *adj*, **polymathy** /pə'limathi/ *noun*. [Greek *polymathēs* very learned, from POLY- + *manthanein* to learn]

polymer /'polimə/ *noun* a chemical compound or mixture of compounds consisting essentially of repeating structural units and formed by chemical combination of many small molecules.

polymeric /-'merik/ *adj*. [earliest as *polymeric*, from Greek *polymerēs* having many parts, from POLY- + *meros* part]

polymerase /'polimərayz, -rays/ *noun* an enzyme that speeds up the formation of polymers; *specif* any of several enzymes that take part in the formation of DNA or RNA.

polymerize *or* **polymerise** /'polimeriez, pə'limeriez/ *verb intrans* to undergo a chemical reaction in which two or more small molecules combine to form larger molecules that contain repeating structural units of the original molecules. ➤➤ *verb trans* to cause (something) to polymerize. ➤➤ **polymerization** /-'zaysh(ə)n/ *noun*.

polymerous /pə'limərəs/ *adj* in biology, having or consisting of many parts.

polymorph /'polimawf/ *noun* 1 a polymorphic organism or substance, or any of its forms. 2 = GRANULOCYTE.

polymorphic /poli'mawfik/ *adj* having, assuming, or occurring in various forms, characters, or styles. ➤➤ **polymorphism** *noun*. [Greek *polymorphos*, from POLY- + -*morphē* form]

polymorphonuclear leucocyte /polimawfoh'nyoohkli-ə/ *noun* = GRANULOCYTE.

polymorphous /poli'mawfəs/ *adj* = POLYMORPHIC.

Polynesian /poli'neezyən, -'neezh(y)ən/ *noun* 1 a native or inhabitant of Polynesia, islands in the central and southern Pacific. 2 a group of Austronesian languages, including Maori and Samoan. ➤➤ **Polynesian** *adj*.

polynomial[1] /poli'nohmi-əl/ *noun* 1 in mathematics, a sum of two or more algebraic terms each of which consists of a constant multiplied by one or more variables raised to a power. 2 a Latin name for an animal or plant that consists of three or more terms, e.g. one denoting a subspecies. [POLY- + -*nomial* as in BINOMIAL[1]]

polynomial[2] *adj* 1 consisting of several terms. 2 involving or expressed as polynomials.

polynucleotide /poli'nyoohkli-ətied/ *noun* a polymer composed of a chain of linked repeating nucleotides, as in DNA or RNA.

polynya /polə'nyah/ *noun* an area of open water in sea ice. [Russian *polyn'ya*]

polyp /'polip/ *noun* 1 a sea anemone, coral, or related organism with a hollow cylindrical body that is attached at one end and has a central mouth surrounded by tentacles at the other. 2 a small abnormal tissue growth, usu with a stalk, projecting from the surface of a mucous membrane. ➤➤ **polypoid** /-poyd/ *adj*, **polypous** /-pəs/ *adj*. [early French *polype* octopus, nasal tumour, via Latin *polypus* from Greek *polypous*, from POLY- + *pous* foot]

polypary /'polip(ə)ri/ *noun* (*pl* **polyparies**) the common structure or tissue in which the polyps of certain compound organisms, e.g. corals, are embedded.

polypeptide /poli'peptied/ *noun* a long chain of amino acids joined by peptide bonds.

polyphagia /poli'fayji-ə/ *noun* 1 abnormally excessive appetite or eating. 2 the habit of feeding on many kinds of food. ➤➤ **polyphagous** /pə'lifəgəs/ *adj*.

polyphase /'polifayz/ *adj* said of an electrical device: having, using, or producing two or more phases of alternating current.

polyphonic /poli'fonik/ *adj* 1 said of music: consisting of several different parts played or sung simultaneously. 2 said of a musical instrument: producing more than one note at a time. 3 having several different sounds or voices. ➤➤ **polyphonically** *adv*.

polyphonous /pə'lifənəs/ *adj* = POLYPHONIC. ➤➤ **polyphonously** *adv*.

polyphony /pə'lifəni/ *noun* a polyphonic style of musical composition. [Greek *polyphōnia* variety of tones, from POLY- + *phōnē* voice, sound]

polyphyletic /polifi'letik/ *adj* derived from more than one ancestral line or stock. ➤➤ **polyphyletically** *adv*, **polyphyleticism** /-siz(ə)m/ *noun*. [Greek *polyphylos* of many tribes, from POLY- + *phylē* tribe]

polypi /'polipie/ *noun* pl of POLYPUS.

polyploid[1] /'poliployd/ *adj* having three or more homologous sets of chromosomes: compare DIPLOID[1], HAPLOID[1]. ➤➤ **polyploidy** /-di/ *noun*.

polyploid[2] *noun* a polyploid cell or organism.

polypod /'polipod/ *adj* said of insect larvae: having many legs or leglike structures. ➤➤ **polypod** *noun*. [Greek *polypod-, polypous* having many feet: see POLYP]

polypody /pə'lipədi/ *noun* (*pl* **polypodies**) any of a genus of widely distributed ferns that have creeping underground stems: genus *Polypodium*. [Middle English *polypodie* via Latin from Greek *polypodion*, from POLY- + *pod-*, *pous* foot]

polypropylene /poli'prohpileen, -'propileen/ *noun* any of various plastics or fibres that are polymers of propylene.

polypus /'polipəs/ *noun* (*pl* **polypi** /-pie/) = POLYP (2). [Latin *polypus*: see POLYP]

polyrhythm /'poliridh(ə)m/ *noun* in music, the simultaneous combination of contrasting rhythms. >>> **polyrhythmic** /-'ridh-mik/ *adj*.

polysaccharide /poli'sakəried/ *noun* a carbohydrate, e.g. cellulose or starch, consisting of chains of monosaccharide molecules.

polysemous /poli'seeməs, pə'lisiməs/ *adj* said of a word or phrase: having many meanings. >>> **polysemy** /-mi/ *noun*. [via late Latin from Greek *polysēmos*, from POLY- + *sēma* sign]

polystyrene /poli'stie-əreen/ *noun* a rigid transparent polymer of styrene with good insulating properties used *esp* in moulded products, foams, and sheet materials.

polysyllabic /,polisi'labik/ *adj* **1a** having two or more syllables. **b** having many syllables. **2** characterized by polysyllabic words. >>> **polysyllabically** *adv*. [medieval Latin *polysyllabus* from Greek *polysyllabos*, from POLY- + *syllabē* syllable]

polysyllabical /,polisi'labikl/ *adj* = POLYSYLLABIC.

polysyllable /'polisiləbl/ *noun* a polysyllabic word: *My father was losing his remarkably moderated tone, and threatening polysyllables* — George Meredith. [medieval Latin *polysyllaba*, fem of *polysyllabus*: see POLYSYLLABIC]

polytechnic¹ /poli'teknik/ *noun* in Britain a higher-education institution offering full-time, sandwich, and part-time courses for qualifications up to degree level with a bias towards the vocational. Not widely used after 1992 when polytechnics were permitted to call themselves universities. [French *polytechnique* from Greek *polytechnos* skilled in many arts, from POLY- + *technē* art]

polytechnic² *adj* relating or devoted to instruction in many technical arts or applied sciences.

polytetrafluoroethylene /,politetrəflooəroh'ethileen/ *noun* a tough translucent plastic used *esp* for non-stick coatings, e.g. in cooking utensils, for insulation, and for artificial body parts, e.g. hip joints.

polytheism /'polithiiz(ə)m/ *noun* belief in or worship of two or more gods. >>> **polytheist** *noun*, **polytheistic** /-'istik/ *adj*. [French *polythéisme*, ultimately from Greek *polytheos* of many gods, from POLY- + *theos* god]

polythene /'politheen/ *noun* any of various lightweight plastics that are polymers of ethylene and are used *esp* for packaging, insulation, and making moulded articles, e.g. bowls, buckets, etc. [contraction of POLYETHYLENE]

polytonality /,politoh'naliti/ *noun* in music, the simultaneous use of two or more keys. >>> **polytonal** /-'tohnl/ *adj*, **polytonally** /-'tohnəli/ *adv*.

polyunsaturated /,poliun'sachooraytid/ *adj* said of a fat or oil: rich in double and triple chemical bonds.

polyurethane /poli'yooərithayn/ *noun* any of various polymers used *esp* in foams, paints, and resins.

polyvalent /poli'vaylənt/ *adj* **1a** in chemistry, having a valency greater than two. **b** in chemistry, having more than one valency. **2** said of a vaccine, antibody, etc: effective against or counteracting more than one toxic substance, antigen, etc. >>> **polyvalence** *noun*.

polyvinyl /poli'vienl/ *adj* of or being a polymerized vinyl chemical compound, resin, or plastic.

polyvinyl acetate /poli'vienl/ *noun* a colourless synthetic resin made from vinyl acetate and used *esp* in paints, adhesives, and sealants.

polyvinyl chloride *noun* = PVC.

polyzoan /poli'zoh-ən/ *noun* = BRYOZOAN. >>> **polyzoan** *adj*. [Latin phylum name *Polyzoa*, from POLY- + -ZOA]

pom /pom/ *noun informal* **1** (*often* **Pom**) = POMERANIAN. **2** (*often* **Pom**) = POMMY.

pomace /'pumis/ *noun* a pulpy residue, *esp* of apples crushed to extract juice for cider-making. [prob from medieval Latin *pomacium* cider, from Latin *pomum* apple, fruit]

pomade¹ /pə'mayd, pə'mahd/ *noun* a perfumed ointment for the hair or scalp. [early French *pommade* ointment formerly made from apples, from Latin *pomum* apple, fruit]

pomade² *verb trans* to apply pomade to (the hair or scalp).

pomander /pə'mandə, po-/ *noun* **1** a mixture of aromatic substances enclosed in a perforated bag or other container and used to scent clothes, to perfume a room, or, in former times, to guard against infection. **2** a container for such a mixture. [Middle English from early French *pome d'ambre*, literally 'apple or ball of amber']

pomatum /pə'maytəm/ *noun* = POMADE¹. [Latin *pomatum* from *pomum*: see POMADE¹]

pome /pohm/ *noun* in botany, a fruit consisting of an outer thickened fleshy layer and a central core with the seeds enclosed in a capsule, e.g. an apple. [Middle English via French from late Latin *pomum* apple, fruit]

pomegranate /'pomigranət/ *noun* **1** a thick-skinned reddish fruit about the size of an orange that contains many seeds surrounded by edible crimson pulp. **2** the tree that bears this fruit, native to W Asia and N Africa: *Punica granatum*. [Middle English *poumgarnet* from early French *pomme grenate*, literally 'seedy apple']

pomelo /'pomiloh/ *noun* (*pl* **pomelos**) **1** = SHADDOCK (1). **2** *chiefly NAmer* = GRAPEFRUIT (1). [alteration of earlier *pompelmous*, from Dutch *pompelmoes*]

Pomeranian /pomə'rayni-ən/ *noun* a small dog of a breed with long straight hair, pointed ears and muzzle, and a curling tail. [named after *Pomerania*, region of N Europe]

pomfret cake /'pumfrit, 'pomfrit/ *noun* = PONTEFRACT CAKE. [from *Pomfret*, earlier form of *Pontefract*]

pomiculture /'pomikulchə/ *noun* the growing of fruit. [Latin *pomum* fruit + CULTURE¹]

pommel¹ /'puməl, 'poməl/ *noun* **1** the raised part at the front and top of a saddle. **2** a knob on the hilt of a sword. **3** either of the pair of removable handles on the top of a pommel horse. [Middle English from early French *pomel* little fruit, from late Latin *pomum* apple, fruit]

pommel² /'puməl/ *verb trans* (**pommelled, pommelling, *NAmer* pommeled, pommeling**) = PUMMEL. [POMMEL¹]

pommel horse /'puməl, 'poməl/ *noun* **1** a leather-covered vaulting horse with two handles on the top, used for swinging and balancing exercises. **2** a men's gymnastic event using the pommel horse.

Pommy or **Pommie** /'pomi/ *noun* (*pl* **Pommies**) *Aus, NZ, informal, chiefly derog* a British person. [short for POMEGRANATE, prob alteration (from the redness of the fruit and British complexions) of rhyming slang *Jimmy Grant* immigrant]

pomology /po'moləji, poh-/ *noun* the branch of horticulture concerned with the growing of fruit. >>> **pomological** /pomə'lojikl/ *adj*, **pomologist** *noun*. [scientific Latin *pomologia*, from Latin *pomum* fruit + -*logia* -LOGY]

pomp /pomp/ *noun* **1** a stately or ceremonial display of magnificence; splendour. **2** ostentatious display of self-importance or boastfulness. [Middle English via French and Latin from Greek *pompē* act of sending, escort, procession, pomp, from *pempein* to send]

pompadour /'pompədooə, -daw/ *noun* **1** a woman's hairstyle in which the hair is turned back into a loose full roll round the face. **2** *NAmer* a man's hairstyle in which the hair is combed back into a mound curving over the forehead. [named after the Marquise de *Pompadour* d.1764, mistress of Louis XV of France]

pompano /'pompənoh/ *noun* (*pl* **pompanos** or *collectively* **pompano**) **1** any of a family of marine fish: family Carangidae. **2** a N American food fish of the butterfish family found in coastal Pacific waters: *Peprilus simillimus*. [Spanish *pámpano*]

pom-pom¹ or **pompom** /'pom pom/ *noun* **1** an ornamental ball or tuft used *esp* on clothing, hats, etc. **2** = POMPON (1). [alteration of POMPON]

pom-pom² or **pompom** *noun* an automatic gun mounted on ships and used against aircraft in World War II. [imitative]

pompon /'pompon(h)/ *noun* **1** a chrysanthemum or dahlia with small rounded flower heads. **2** = POM-POM¹ (1). [French *pompon* from early French *pompe* tuft of ribbons]

pomposity /pom'positi/ *noun* (*pl* **pomposities**) **1** pompous demeanour, speech, or behaviour. **2** a pompous gesture, habit, or act.

pompous /'pompəs/ *adj* **1** self-important or pretentious: *a pompous politician.* **2** excessively elevated or ornate: *pompous rhetoric.* **3** *archaic* characterized by pomp; magnificent or splendid. >>> **pompously** *adv,* **pompousness** *noun.*

ponce¹ /pons/ *noun Brit, informal* **1** = PIMP¹ (1A). **2** *derog* a man who behaves in an effeminate manner. [perhaps from obsolete *pounce* talon of bird of prey, act of pouncing: see POUNCE¹]

ponce² *verb intrans Brit, informal* **1** = PIMP². **2** (+ around/about) to act in a frivolous, showy, or effeminate manner.

poncey /'ponsi/ *adj* see PONCY.

poncho /'ponchoh/ *noun* (*pl* **ponchos**) a cloak resembling a blanket with a slit in the middle for the head, orig worn in S America. [American Spanish *poncho* from Araucanian *pontho* woollen fabric]

poncy or **poncey** /'ponsi/ *adj Brit, informal* frivolous, showy, or effeminate.

pond /pond/ *noun* **1** a relatively small body of fresh water. **2** (**the Pond**) *informal* the Atlantic Ocean. [Middle English *ponde* artificially confined body of water, alteration of *pounde:* see POUND⁴]

ponder /'pondə/ *verb* (**pondered, pondering**) >>> *verb trans* to give careful and often lengthy thought or consideration to (something): *I pondered my next move.* >>> *verb intrans* (*often* + over) to think or consider, *esp* quietly, soberly, and deeply. >>> **ponderer** *noun.* [Middle English *ponderen* via French from Latin *ponderare* to weigh, ponder, from *ponder-, pondus* weight]

ponderable /'pond(ə)rəbl/ *adj* capable of being weighed or appraised; appreciable. [late Latin *ponderabilis,* from Latin *ponderare:* see PONDER]

ponderosa pine /pondə'rohsə/ *noun* **1** a tall N American pine tree with long needles: *Pinus ponderosa.* **2** the strong reddish wood of this tree. [Latin *ponderosa,* fem of *ponderosus:* see PONDEROUS, from the tree's drooping shape]

ponderous /'pond(ə)rəs/ *adj* **1** unwieldy or clumsy because of weight and size: *These two young creatures were the Honourable Mary and the Honourable Kate – scarcely appearing large enough as yet to bear the weight of such ponderous prefixes* — Hardy. **2** oppressively dull: *ponderous prose.* >>> **ponderosity** /pondə'rositi/ *noun,* **ponderously** *adv,* **ponderousness** *noun.* [Middle English via French from Latin *ponderosus,* from *ponder-, pondus* weight]

pond skater *noun* any of numerous species of long-legged insects that move about on the surface of water: genus *Gerris* and other genera.

pondweed *noun* an aquatic plant with a jointed stem, floating or submerged leaves, and spikes of greenish flowers: genus *Potamogeton.*

pone /pohn/ *noun* = CORN PONE. [Algonquian *pone* bread]

pong¹ /pong/ *verb intrans Brit, informal* to emit an unpleasant smell; to stink. [origin unknown]

pong² *noun* an unpleasant smell; a stink.

ponga /'pongə/ or **punga** /'pungə/ *noun* a tall tree fern native to New Zealand: *Cyathea dealbata.* [Maori *ponga*]

pongee /pon'jee/ *noun* **1** a thin soft fabric of Chinese origin woven from raw silk and usu left unbleached and undyed. **2** an imitation of this fabric in cotton or rayon. [Chinese (Pekingese) *benji,* also written *pen-chi,* woven at home, from *ben* own + *ji* loom]

pongid /'ponjid/ *noun* any of a family of anthropoid apes: family Pongidae. >>> **pongid** *adj.* [from the Latin family name, from Congolese *mpungu* ape]

poniard /'ponyəd/ *noun* a small slender dagger: *She speaks poniards, and every word stabs* — Shakespeare. [early French *poignard,* from *poing* fist, from Latin *pugnus*]

pons /ponz/ *noun* (*pl* **pontes** /'ponteez/) a broad mass of nerve fibres on the lower front surface of the brain. [see PONS VAROLII]

pons asinorum /asi'nawrəm/ *noun* a critical test of ability imposed on the inexperienced or ignorant. [Latin *pons asinorum,* literally 'asses' bridge', a name orig applied to the proposition that the base angles of an isosceles triangle are equal, considered to be a stumbling-block for students of geometry]

pons Varolii /və'rohli·ee, -liie/ *noun* = PONS. [scientific Latin *pons Varolii,* literally 'bridge of Varoli', named after Costanzo *Varoli* d.1575, Italian surgeon and anatomist]

pont /pont/ *noun SAfr* a ferry in the form of a flat-bottomed boat pulled across a river by means of a rope or cable. [Dutch *pont* from early Dutch *ponte* ferry boat]

Pontefract cake /'pontifrakt/ *noun* a small flat circular liquorice sweet. [named after *Pontefract,* town in Yorkshire, England, place of its manufacture]

pontes /'ponteez/ *noun* pl of PONS.

pontifex /'pontifeks/ *noun* (*pl* **pontifices** /pon'tifiseez/) a member of the council of priests in ancient Rome. [Latin *pontific-, pontifex,* from *pont-, pons* bridge + *facere* to make]

pontifex maximus /'maksiməs/ *noun* **1** the pope. **2** the head of the council of priests in ancient Rome. [Latin *pontifex maximus* greatest pontiff]

pontiff /'pontif/ *noun* **1** the pope. **2** *esp* in former times, a bishop. [French *pontife* from Latin *pontific-, pontifex:* see PONTIFEX]

pontifical¹ /pon'tifikl/ *adj* **1a** of the pope; papal. **b** of a bishop or pontifex. **2** pretentiously dogmatic. >>> **pontifically** *adv.* [Latin *pontificalis,* from *pontific-, pontifex:* see PONTIFEX]

pontifical² *noun* **1** a book containing the forms for sacraments and rites performed by a bishop. **2** (*in pl*) the ceremonial robes of a bishop; *specif* the vestments worn by a bishop or cardinal celebrating a pontifical mass.

pontifical mass *noun* the solemn celebration of the Roman Catholic Mass by a bishop or cardinal.

pontificate¹ /pon'tifikayt/ *verb intrans* **1** to speak or express opinions in a pompous or dogmatic way. **2** to officiate at a pontifical mass. >>> **pontification** /-'kaysh(ə)n/ *noun,* **pontificator** *noun.* [medieval Latin *pontificatus,* from Latin *pontific-, pontifex:* see PONTIFEX]

pontificate² /pon'tifikət/ *noun* the office or term of office of the pope.

pontifices /pon'tifiseez/ *noun* pl of PONTIFEX.

pontine /'pontien/ *adj* of the pons.

pontoon¹ /pon'toohn/ *noun* **1** a flat-bottomed boat or portable float used in building a floating temporary bridge or in salvage work. **2** a floating landing stage, e.g. in a marina. [French *ponton* floating bridge, punt, from Latin *ponton-, ponto,* from *pons* bridge]

pontoon² *noun* a gambling card game in which the object is to be dealt cards scoring more than those of the dealer up to but not exceeding 21. [prob alteration of VINGT-ET-UN]

pony /'pohni/ *noun* (*pl* **ponies**) **1** a small horse, *esp* a member of any of several breeds of stocky horses under 14.2 hands in height. **2** (**the ponies**) *slang* racehorses or horse racing. **3** *Brit, informal* a sum of £25. **4a** a small liqueur glass. **b** a small measure of spirits. [prob from obsolete French *poulenet,* dimin. of French *poulain* colt, ultimately from Latin *pullus* young of an animal, foal]

ponytail *noun* a hairstyle in which the hair is drawn back tightly and tied at the back of the head.

pony trekking *noun* the pastime of riding ponies long distances cross-country in a group, usu at a leisurely pace.

poo¹ /pooh/ *noun informal* faeces. [POOH¹]

poo² *verb intrans* (**poos, pooed, pooing**) *informal* to defecate.

pooch /poohch/ *noun informal* a dog. [origin unknown]

poodle /'poohdl/ *noun* **1** a dog of an active intelligent breed having a thick curly coat that is often clipped and shaved in a distinctive way. **2** a servile person. [German *Pudel,* short for *Pudelhund* splashing dog, the poodle being orig trained as a water dog]

poof or **pouf** /poohf, poof/ or **poofter** /'pooftə/ *noun Brit, informal, derog* **1** an effeminate man. **2** a homosexual man. [perhaps an alteration of PUFF²]

pooh¹ /pooh/ *interj* used to express contempt, disapproval, or distaste at an unpleasant smell. [imitative]

pooh² *noun* = POO¹.

pooh³ *verb intrans* = POO².

pooh-bah /bah/ or **Pooh-Bah** *noun* a person holding many public or private offices. [named after *Pooh-Bah,* character bearing the title Lord-High-Everything-Else in the comic opera *The Mikado* by W S Gilbert d.1911, English librettist and poet, and A S Sullivan d.1900, English composer]

pooh-pooh *verb trans* to express contempt for (something or somebody); to disparage or dismiss (them): *Congress ... pooh-poohed Mr Bush's first proposals as inadequate* — The Economist. [from POOH¹]

pool¹ /poohl/ *noun* **1** a small body of standing water or other liquid; a puddle: *a rock pool; a pool of blood.* **2** a small and relatively deep body of still or slow-moving water in a stream or river. **3** = SWIM-MING POOL. **4** something resembling a pool, e.g. in depth or shape: *pools of light*. [Old English *pōl*]

pool² *noun* **1** the combined stakes of the players of a gambling game. **2** any of various games played on a billiard table with six pockets and usu 15 numbered balls: compare BILLIARDS, SNOOKER¹. **3a** a collective supply of things for common use. **b** a facility or service to which a number of people, e.g. the members of a business organization, have access: *a typing pool*. **4** a combination of investments managed for a common purpose. **5** an association or agreement between business organizations for the purpose of gaining control of a market by driving out competition. **6** (*in pl*) = FOOTBALL POOLS. [French *poule* hen, perhaps from a hen being used as the target and prize in a game]

pool³ *verb trans* to combine (e.g. resources or effort) in a common stock or for a common purpose.

poontang /ˈpoohntang/ *noun chiefly NAmer, coarse slang* **1** sexual intercourse with a woman. **2** a woman regarded as a sexual object. [prob from French *putain* whore]

poop¹ /poohp/ *noun* a raised structure or deck at the stern of a ship above the main deck. [early French *poupe* from Latin *puppis* stern]

poop² *verb trans* said of a wave or sea: to break over the stern of (a ship). ➤ *verb intrans* said of a ship: to receive a wave or sea over the stern.

poop³ *verb trans chiefly NAmer, informal* (*usu in passive, often* + out) to exhaust (somebody); to tire (them) out. ➤ *verb intrans NAmer, informal* (+ out) to withdraw or fail through exhaustion, loss of courage, etc. [origin unknown]

poop⁴ *noun informal* faeces. [slang *poop* excrement (from Middle English *poupen* to blow a horn, later to break wind, defecate, of imitative origin)]

poop⁵ *verb intrans informal* to defecate.

pooper-scooper /ˈpoohpə skoohpə/ *noun* a dog owner's portable device for picking up and removing faeces left by the dog in public places. [POOP⁴ + SCOOP²]

poop-scoop /ˈpoohp skoohp/ *noun* = POOPER-SCOOPER.

poor /pooə, paw/ *adj* **1a** lacking sufficient money or material possessions. **b** of or characterized by poverty. **2a** less than adequate; meagre: *a poor harvest*. **b** (+ in) lacking in something specified: *a diet poor in calcium*. **3** inferior in quality, value, skill, etc: *in poor health; a poor essay*. **4** inspiring pity: *Poor old soul!* **5** humble or unpretentious: *in my poor opinion*. ➤➤ **poorness** *noun*. [Middle English *poure* via Old French from Latin *pauper*, from *paucus* little + *parare* to acquire]

poor box *noun* a box, e.g. in a church, into which money for the poor can be put.

poorhouse /ˈpooəhows, ˈpawˌhows/ *noun* = WORKHOUSE (1).

poor law *noun* a law that in former times provided for the relief of the poor.

poorly¹ *adv* in a poor, inadequate, or inferior manner.

poorly² *adj* somewhat ill; unwell.

poort /pooət/ *noun SAfr* a narrow pass between mountains. [Afrikaans *poort* from Dutch *poort* gate]

poor white *noun chiefly derog* a member of an inferior or under-privileged white social group, *esp* in the southern USA.

poove /poohv/ *noun Brit, informal, derog* = POOF. [by alteration]

POP *abbr* **1** point of presence, a point of entry to a computer network. **2** *Brit* Post Office preferred (size of envelope).

pop¹ /pop/ *verb* (**popped, popping**) ➤ *verb intrans* **1** to make or burst with a sharp explosive sound. **2** *informal* to go or come suddenly or quickly: *I just popped out to do some shopping.* **3** said of eyes: to appear to protrude from the sockets, e.g. in amazement. ➤ *verb trans* **1** to cause (something) to explode or burst open: *She popped the balloon.* **2** *informal* to put (something) suddenly or quickly: *He popped a sweet into his mouth.* **3** *informal* to take (drugs) orally or by injection: *popping pills.* **4** *informal* to shoot at (somebody or something). **5** *Brit, informal* to pawn (something). ✴ **pop one's clogs** *Brit, informal* to die. **pop the question** *informal* to propose marriage. [Middle English *poppen*, of imitative origin]

pop² *noun* **1** a popping sound. **2** a flavoured carbonated soft drink. [(sense 2) from the sound of pulling a cork from a bottle]

pop³ *adv informal* with or as if with a popping sound; suddenly.

pop⁴ *noun chiefly NAmer, informal* an affectionate name for one's father. [short for POPPA]

pop⁵ *adj* **1** of pop music: *pop singer*. **2** denoting a mass culture widely disseminated through the media. [short for POPULAR]

pop⁶ *noun* = POP MUSIC.

pop. *abbr* population.

pop art *noun* art that incorporates items from popular culture and the mass media, e.g. comic strips. ➤➤ **pop artist** *noun*.

popcorn *noun* **1** a variety of maize with kernels that swell up and burst open when heated to form a white starchy mass. **2** the swollen and burst kernels eaten as a snack.

pope /pohp/ *noun* **1** (*often* **Pope**) the bishop of Rome as head of the Roman Catholic Church. **2** a priest of an Eastern Orthodox Church. **3** = RUFF⁴. [Old English *pāpa* via late Latin from Greek *pappas, papas,* title of bishops, literally 'father'; (sense 2) from Russian *pop* via Old Slavonic *popŭ* from Greek *pappas, papas*]

popery /ˈpohp(ə)ri/ *noun derog* Roman Catholicism.

pop-eyed *adj* having staring or bulging eyes, e.g. as a result of surprise or excitement.

popgun *noun* **1** a toy gun that shoots a cork or pellet and produces a popping sound. **2** *informal* an inadequate or inefficient firearm.

popinjay /ˈpopinjay/ *noun* **1** a conceited or supercilious person: *It's a song of a popinjay, bravely born, who turned up his noble nose in scorn* — W S Gilbert. **2** *archaic* a parrot. [Middle English *papejay* parrot, via French from Arabic *babghā'*]

popish /ˈpohpish/ *adj derog* Roman Catholic. ➤➤ **popishly** *adv*.

poplar /ˈpoplə/ *noun* **1** any of a genus of slender quick-growing trees of the willow family: genus *Populus*. **2** = TULIP TREE (1). [Middle English *poplere* via French from Latin *populus*]

poplin /ˈpoplin/ *noun* a strong usu cotton fabric in plain weave with fine crosswise ribs. [obsolete French *papeline*, prob ultimately from medieval Latin *papalis* papal, because poplin was first made in the French city of Avignon, residence of the popes in exile during the 14th cent.]

popliteal /pop'liti-əl, -'tee-əl/ *adj* in anatomy, of the back part of the leg behind the knee joint. [Latin *poplit-, poples* ham, back of the knee]

pop music *noun* modern commercially promoted popular music that is usu simple in form and has a strong beat.

pop off *verb intrans informal* **1** to leave suddenly. **2** to die unexpectedly.

poppa /ˈpopə/ *noun NAmer, informal* an affectionate name for one's father. [alteration of PAPA]

poppadom *or* **poppadum** /ˈpopədom, -dum/ *noun* a crisp wafer-thin pancake of deep-fried dough eaten chiefly with Indian food. [Tamil *pappaṭam*]

popper *noun* **1** *Brit, informal* = PRESS-STUD. **2** *informal* a capsule of amyl nitrite that is crushed and inhaled. **3** *NAmer* a device for making popcorn.

poppet /ˈpopit/ *noun* **1** *chiefly Brit, informal* a lovable or enchanting person or animal. **2** a mushroom-shaped valve that moves up and down from its seating when a force is applied in the direction of the stem. [Middle English *popet*: see PUPPET]

poppet valve *noun* = POPPET (2).

popping crease *noun* either of the lines drawn perpendicularly across a cricket pitch 4ft (about 1.22m) in front of each wicket and behind which the batsman must have a foot or the bat on the ground to avoid being run out or stumped: compare BOWLING CREASE.

popple /ˈpop(ə)l/ *verb intrans* said of water: to flow gently with a bubbling sound. [early Dutch *poppelen* to murmur, of imitative origin]

poppy /ˈpopi/ *noun* (*pl* **poppies**) **1** any of numerous species of plants with showy red, orange, or yellow flowers, including a plant that grows wild in cornfields, the opium poppy, and several plants cultivated for ornament: genus *Papaver* and other genera. **2** an artificial red poppy worn in the period leading up to Remembrance Sunday. [Old English *popæg, popig,* modification of Latin *papaver*]

poppycock *noun informal* empty talk; nonsense. [Dutch dialect *pappekak*, literally 'soft dung']

Poppy Day *noun Brit, informal* = REMEMBRANCE SUNDAY.

the red poppy, the seeds of which germinate in disturbed ground, grew prolifically on the battlefields of N France in World War I. For this reason, and because of its blood-red colour, the flower came to symbolize those killed in the two World Wars; artificial poppies are sold in aid of disabled ex-servicemen and -women and are laid on war memorials on Remembrance Sunday.

poppyhead *noun* a carved decoration on the end of a church pew.

pop socks *pl noun* calf-length nylon stockings worn under long skirts or trousers.

popsy /'popsi/ *noun* (*pl* **popsies**) *Brit, informal, dated* a girlfriend, or any attractive young woman. [from POPPET]

populace /'popyoolǝs/ *noun* (*treated as sing. or pl*) the general public; the masses. [early French *populace* via Italian *popolaccio* rabble, ultimately from Latin *populus* the people, a people]

popular /'popyoolǝ/ *adj* **1a** generally liked or admired: *a very popular girl*. **b** liked or favoured by a particular person or group: *These drinks are popular with children*. **2** suited to the needs, means, tastes, or understanding of the general public: *a popular history of the war*. **3** of or used by the general public. **4** widespread or prevalent: *a popular misconception*. ⨾⨾⨾ **popularity** /-'lariti/ *noun*, **popularly** *adv*. [Latin *popularis* of the people, from *populus* the people, a people]

popular front *noun* a coalition of left-wing political parties organized against a common opponent, *esp* those opposing fascism since 1935.

popularize *or* **popularise** *verb trans* **1** to cause (something or somebody) to be generally liked, accepted, or well-known. **2** to present (something) in a generally understandable or interesting form: *popularizing science*. ⨾⨾⨾ **popularization** /-'zaysh(ǝ)n/ *noun*, **popularizer** *noun*.

populate /'popyoolayt/ *verb trans* **1** to occupy or inhabit (a place). **2** to provide (a place) with inhabitants; to people (it). [Latin *populatus*, past part. of *populare* to people, from *populus* people]

population /popyoo'laysh(ǝ)n/ *noun* **1** (*treated as sing. or pl*) the whole number of people living in a place. **2** (*treated as sing. or pl*) a body of people with something in common: *a floating population of drifters*. **3** a set of individuals or items from which samples are taken for statistical measurement. **4** a group of organisms of a particular species inhabiting a particular area. **5** the act of populating a place. [Latin *population-*, *populatio*, from *populare*: see POPULATE]

population explosion *noun* a vast usu rapid increase in the size of a population.

populist /'popyoolist/ *noun* **1** a member of a political party claiming to represent ordinary people. **2** somebody who has or cultivates an appeal to ordinary people. ⨾⨾⨾ **populism** *noun*, **populist** *adj*, **populistic** /-'listik/ *adj*. [Latin *populus* the people]

populous /'popyoolǝs/ *adj* having many inhabitants; densely populated. ⨾⨾⨾ **populously** *adv*, **populousness** *noun*. [Latin *populosus*, from *populus* people]

pop-up *adj* **1** denoting or having a device that causes its contents to spring up or stand out in relief: *a pop-up toaster*; *a pop-up book*. **2** of or being a computer facility, e.g. a menu, that can be brought up onto the screen during the running of a program to provide the user with a set of options, instructions, etc.

porbeagle /'pawbeegl/ *noun* a shark of the N Atlantic and Pacific oceans with a pointed nose and crescent-shaped tail: *Lamna nasus*. [Cornish *porgh-bugel*, literally 'harbour shepherd']

porcelain /'paws(ǝ)lin/ *noun* **1a** a hard nonporous translucent ceramic ware made from a mixture of kaolin, quartz, and feldspar fired at a high temperature. Also called HARD-PASTE PORCELAIN. **b** a translucent ceramic ware made from a mixture of refined clay and ground glass fired at a low temperature. Also called SOFT-PASTE PORCELAIN. **2** objects made of porcelain. ⨾⨾⨾ **porcellaneous** /pawsǝ'layni-ǝs/ *adj*, **porcellanous** /paw'selǝnǝs/ *adj*. [early French *porcelaine* cowrie shell, porcelain (because the finish of porcelain resembles the surface of the shell), via Italian *porcello* vulva, literally 'little pig', from Latin *porcus* pig, vulva, from the shape of the shell]

porch /pawch/ *noun* **1** a covered entrance to a building, *esp* one that projects from the doorway. **2** *NAmer* = VERANDA. [Middle English *porche* via French from Latin *porticus*: see PORTICO]

porcine /'pawsien/ *adj* of or resembling a pig or pigs. [Latin *porcinus*, from *porcus* pig]

porcupine /'pawkyoopien/ *noun* any of various relatively large ground-living or tree-dwelling rodents having stiff sharp bristles

mingled with the hair: families Hystricidae and Erethizontidae. [Middle English *porkepin* via early French *porc espin* from Old Italian *porcospino*, from Latin *porcus* pig + *spina* prickle, SPINE]

porcupine fish *noun* a spiny fish of tropical seas that can inflate its body to ward off predators: *Diodon hystrix*.

pore[1] /paw/ *noun* a minute opening, *esp* one in the skin, through which liquids or gases pass. [Middle English via French from Latin *porus*, from Greek *poros* passage, pore]

pore[2] *verb intrans* **1** (*usu* + over) to study something closely or attentively. **2** (+ on/over/upon) to reflect or meditate on something. [Middle English *pouren*; earlier history unknown]

porgy /'pawgi/ *noun* (*pl* **porgies** *or collectively* **porgy**) **1** a spiny-finned food fish native to the coasts of Europe and America: *Pagrus pagrus*. **2** any of numerous species of related fishes: family Sparidae. [Spanish and Portuguese *pargo*, ultimately from Greek *phagros* sea bream]

poriferan /paw'rif(ǝ)rǝn/ *noun* any of a phylum of aquatic invertebrates of the sponge family: phylum Porifera. ⨾⨾⨾ **poriferal** *adj*, **poriferan** *adj*. [Latin *porus* (see PORE[1]) + *-fer* -FEROUS]

pork /pawk/ *noun* the flesh of a pig used as food. [Middle English via French from Latin *porcus* pig]

pork barrel *noun chiefly NAmer, informal* a government project yielding rich benefits for a particular constituency, usu introduced to gain political support. ⨾⨾⨾ **pork-barrelling** *noun*. [from the practice of preserving meat in a barrel for future use]

porker *noun* **1** a young pig fattened for food. **2** *informal, offensive* a person who is overweight.

pork pie *noun* a pie filled with minced pork that has a raised crust and is usu served cold.

porkpie hat *noun* a man's hat with a low crown, a flat top, and usu a turned-up brim. [from its shape]

porky[1] *adj* (**porkier**, **porkiest**) **1** of or resembling pork. **2** *informal* rather overweight.

porky[2] *noun* (*pl* **porkies**) *Brit, slang* (*usu in pl*) a lie, *esp* a trivial one: *You've bin telling porkies, PC – and in my manor we're strictly kosher —* Independent. [rhyming slang *pork pie*]

porn[1] /pawn/ *noun informal* pornography.

porn[2] *or* **porno** /'pawnoh/ *adj informal* pornographic.

pornography /paw'nografi/ *noun* **1** books, photographs, films, etc containing erotic material intended to cause sexual excitement. **2** the production of pornography. ⨾⨾⨾ **pornographer** *noun*, **pornographic** /-'grafik/ *adj*, **pornographically** /-'grafikli/ *adv*. [Greek *pornographos* (adj) writing about prostitutes, from *pornē* prostitute + *graphein* to write]

porous /'pawrǝs/ *adj* **1** permeable to liquids and gases. **2** having pores or spaces. ⨾⨾⨾ **porosity** /paw'rositi/ *noun*, **porously** *adv*, **porousness** *noun*. [Middle English from early French *poreaux*, from Latin *porus*: see PORE[1]]

porphyria /paw'firi-ǝ/ *noun* any of various hereditary metabolic disorders characterized *esp* by discoloured urine, extreme sensitivity to light, and phases of mental derangement. [from PORPHYRIN, which is excreted in the urine]

porphyrin /'pawfirin/ *noun* any of various pigments obtained *esp* from chlorophyll or haemoglobin. [Greek *porphyra* purple]

porphyry /'pawfiri/ *noun* **1** a rock consisting of crystals of the mineral feldspar embedded in a compact dark red or purple mass of surrounding rock. **2** any igneous rock having distinct crystals in a relatively fine-grained base. ⨾⨾⨾ **porphyritic** /-'ritik/ *adj*. [Middle English *porfurie* via Latin *porphyrites* from Greek *porphyritēs* (*lithos*) (stone) like Tyrian purple, from *porphyra* purple]

porpoise /'pawpǝs/ *noun* (*pl* **porpoises** *or collectively* **porpoise**) **1** a small gregarious whale with a blunt snout that resembles a dolphin and is about 2m (6ft) long: *Phocoena phocoena*. **2** any of several species of related whales: family Phocoenidae. [Middle English *porpoys* via French from medieval Latin *porcopiscis*, from Latin *porcus* pig + *piscis* fish]

porridge /'porij/ *noun* **1** a soft food made by boiling oatmeal or another cereal in milk or water until thick. **2** *Brit, informal* time spent in prison. [alteration of POTTAGE]

porringer /'porinjǝ/ *noun* a small bowl from which soft or liquid foods, e.g. soup or porridge, are eaten. [alteration of Middle English *poteger*, *potinger*, from early French *potager* of pottage, from *potage*: see POTTAGE]

port[1] /pawt/ *noun* **1** a town or city with a harbour where ships may take on and discharge cargo and passengers. **2** = PORT OF ENTRY. [Old English via Old French from Latin *portus* harbour]

port[2] *noun* the left side of a ship or aircraft looking forward: compare STARBOARD[1]. ≫ **port** *adj.* [orig the side turned towards the harbour wall when moored]

port[3] *verb trans* to turn (the helm of a ship or boat) to the left.

port[4] *noun* a fortified sweet wine of rich taste and aroma made in Portugal. [named after *Oporto*, seaport in Portugal from where the wine was orig shipped]

port[5] *noun* **1** an opening, e.g. in machinery, allowing liquid or gas to enter or escape. **2** a socket or circuit by which a computer communicates with a printer, disk drive, etc. **3a** an opening in a ship's side for loading and unloading cargo. **b** = PORTHOLE (1). **4** a hole in an armoured vehicle or fortification through which guns may be fired. **5** *chiefly Scot* a gate or gateway, e.g. of a walled town or fortress. [Middle English *porte* via French from Latin *porta* passage, gate]

port[6] *verb trans* **1** to carry (a military weapon) diagonally in front of the body with a muzzle pointing upwards to the left. *port arms*. **2** in computing, to transfer (software) from one type of system to another. [Middle English via French from Latin *portare* to carry]

port[7] *noun Aus, informal* a bag or case, *esp* one used by travellers. [short for PORTMANTEAU]

portable[1] /'pawtəbl/ *adj* **1** capable of being carried or moved about, *esp* because small or light: *a portable typewriter*. **2** said of computer software: able to be ported without modification. ≫ **portability** /-'biliti/ *noun*, **portably** *adv.* [Middle English via French from late Latin *portabilis*, from Latin *portare* to carry]

portable[2] *noun* something, e.g. a television or typewriter, that is portable.

portage[1] /'pawtij/ *noun* **1** the carrying of boats or their cargo overland from one body of navigable water to another. **2** the route followed in portage, or a place where such a transfer is necessary. **3** *archaic* the act or cost of carrying or transporting. [Middle English from early French *portage*, from *porter* to carry, from Latin *portare*]

portage[2] *verb trans* to carry (a boat or its cargo) from one body of water to another.

Portakabin /'pawtəkabin/ *noun trademark* a portable prefabricated hut, e.g. for use on building sites. [contraction and alteration of *portable cabin*]

portal[1] /'pawtl/ *noun* **1** a door, gateway, or entrance, *esp* one that is grand or imposing. **2** in computing, an Internet site providing numerous links to other sites and other information. [Middle English via French and medieval Latin from Latin *porta* gate]

portal[2] *adj* in anatomy, of the transverse opening on the underside of the liver where most of the major blood vessels enter. [scientific Latin *portalis* from Latin *porta* gate]

portal vein *noun* a vein that begins and ends in capillaries and that transfers blood from one part of the body to another without passing through the heart, *esp* the vein carrying blood from the digestive organs and spleen to the liver.

portamento /pawtə'mentoh/ *noun* (*pl* **portamenti** /-tee/) in music, a continuous gliding movement from one note to another by the voice, a trombone, or a bowed stringed instrument. [Italian *portamento*, literally 'act of carrying', from *portare* to carry, from Latin]

portative /'pawtətiv/ *adj* **1** *formal* relating to carrying or used for carrying things. **2** *archaic* = PORTABLE[1] (1). [Middle English *portatif* via French from medieval Latin *portatil* portable, from Latin *portare* to carry]

portcullis /pawt'kulis/ *noun* a usu iron or wood grating that can be lowered between grooves to prevent passage through the gateway of a fortified place. [Middle English *port colice*, from early French *porte coleïce* sliding door]

port de bras /ˌpaw də 'brah/ *noun* the technique and practice of arm movement in ballet. [French *port de bras* carriage of the arm]

Porte /pawt/ *noun* the government of the Ottoman empire. [French *Porte*, short for *Sublime Porte* sublime gate, from the gate of the sultan's palace where justice was administered]

porte cochere /ˌpawt ko'sheə (*French* pɔrt kɔʃɛr)/ *noun* **1** a passageway through a building designed to let vehicles pass from the street to an inner courtyard. **2** a roofed structure extending from the entrance of a building over an adjacent driveway and sheltering those getting into or out of vehicles. [French *porte cochère* coach door]

portend /paw'tend/ *verb trans* to be an omen, warning, or sign of (something unpleasant or momentous to come); to foreshadow (it). [Middle English *portenden* from Latin *portendere*, from por- PRO-[2] + *tendere* to stretch]

portent /'pawt(ə)nt, 'pawtent/ *noun* **1** something foreshadowing a coming event; an omen. **2** prophetic indication or significance. **3** *archaic* a marvel or prodigy. [Latin *portentum* from *portendere*: see PORTEND]

portentous /paw'tentəs/ *adj* **1** of or being a portent. **2** eliciting amazement or wonder; prodigious. **3** self-consciously important or solemn; pompous. ≫ **portentously** *adv*, **portentousness** *noun*.

porter[1] /'pawtə/ *noun chiefly Brit* a gatekeeper or doorkeeper, *esp* of a large building, who usu regulates entry and answers enquiries. [Middle English via Old French from late Latin *portarius*, from Latin *porta* gate]

porter[2] *noun* **1** somebody employed to carry luggage, e.g. in a hotel or railway station. **2** somebody employed to move patients or equipment in a hospital. **3** *NAmer* a sleeping-car attendant. **4** a heavy dark brown beer brewed from partly browned malt. [Middle English *portour* via French from late Latin *portator*, from Latin *portare* to carry; (sense 4) short for *porter's beer*]

porterage /'pawt(ə)rij/ *noun* the work performed by a porter, or a charge made for it.

porterhouse /'pawtəhows/ *noun* **1** a large steak cut from the back end of the sirloin above the ribs and containing part of the fillet. **2** in former times, an establishment where porter and other drinks were sold and sometimes steaks were served.

portfire *noun* a portable slow-burning fuse used in former times for firing cannons and igniting explosives in mining.

portfolio /pawt'fohlioh/ *noun* (*pl* **portfolios**) **1** a hinged cover or flexible case for carrying loose papers, pictures, etc. **2** a set of drawings, photographs, etc assembled and presented as evidence of creative talent. **3** the office or responsibilities of a government minister or member of a cabinet: *the defence portfolio*. **4** the securities held by an investor. [Italian *portafoglio*, from *portare* to carry (from Latin) + *foglio* leaf, sheet]

porthole *noun* **1** a small window in the side of a ship or aircraft. **2** = PORT[5] (4). [PORT[5]]

portico /'pawtikoh/ *noun* (*pl* **porticoes** or **porticos**) a roof supported by columns and attached to a building, usu as a porch at the entrance, *esp* in classical architecture. [Italian *portico* from Latin *porticus* porch, from *porta* gate]

portiere /pawti'eə/ *noun* a curtain hanging across a doorway. [French *portière* from *porte* door, from Latin *porta* gate]

portion[1] /'pawsh(ə)n/ *noun* **1** a part or share of something, e.g.: **a** a helping of food. **b** a share of an estate received by gift or inheritance. **c** *archaic* a dowry. **2** *archaic* an individual's lot or fate. [Middle English via Old French from Latin *portion-, portio*]

portion[2] *verb trans* **1** (*usu* + out) to divide (something) into portions and distribute it. **2** to give (somebody) a portion.

portionless *adj archaic* having no dowry or inheritance.

Portland cement /'pawtlənd/ *noun* a cement capable of setting underwater made by roasting a mixture of finely ground lime and clay in a kiln. [from its resemblance to PORTLAND STONE]

Portland stone *noun* a type of limestone widely used in building. [named after the Isle of *Portland*, peninsula in Dorset, England, where the limestone is found]

portly /'pawtli/ *adj* (**portlier, portliest**) **1** rather overweight; stout. **2** *archaic* stately or dignified. ≫ **portliness** *noun*. [Middle English *port* deportment, bearing, via French from Latin *portare* to carry + -LY[1]]

portmanteau /pawt'mantoh/ *noun* (*pl* **portmanteaus** or **portmanteaux** /-tohz/) **1** a large bag or case for a traveller's belongings that opens into two equal parts. **2** (*used before a noun*) denoting something that combines two or more uses or qualities. [early French *portemanteau*, from *porter* to carry (from Latin *portare*) + *manteau* mantle, from Latin *mantellum*]

portmanteau word *noun* = BLEND[2] (2).

portmanteaux /pawt'mantohz/ *noun pl* of PORTMANTEAU.

port of call *noun* **1** a port where ships customarily stop during a voyage. **2** a stop included in an itinerary.

port of entry *noun* a place, e.g. a harbour or airport, where goods and people may be permitted to pass into or out of a country subject to clearing through customs.

portrait /'pawtrit, 'pawtrayt/ *noun* **1** a pictorial likeness of a person. **2** any portrayal or representation, e.g. in a novel, film, etc. **3** (*used before a noun*) of or being a printed format in which the body of text, illustration, etc is higher than it is wide: compare LANDSCAPE¹. ►►► **portraitist** *noun*, **portraiture** /'pawtrichə/ *noun*. [early French *portrait*, past part. of *portraire*: see PORTRAY]

portray /paw'tray/ *verb trans* **1** to make a picture of (something or somebody). **2a** to describe or depict (something or somebody), *esp* in words: *a novel portraying life in the armed forces*. **b** to represent (somebody or something) in a particular way: *The documentary portrayed him as a tyrant*. **3** to play the role of (somebody) in a film, play, etc. ►►► **portrayal** *noun*, **portrayer** *noun*. [Middle English *portraien* via early French *portraire* from Latin *protrahere* to draw forth, reveal, expose, from PRO-² + *trahere* to draw]

Port Salut /ˌpaw sa'looh (*French* pɔr saly)/ *noun* a pale yellow mild-flavoured cheese. [named after *Port du Salut*, Trappist abbey in NW France, where it was orig made]

Portuguese /pawchoo'geez, pawtyoo'geez/ *noun* (*pl* **Portuguese**) **1** a native or inhabitant of Portugal. **2** the Romance language of the people of Portugal, Brazil, and some other countries. ►►► **Portuguese** *adj*. [Portuguese *português*]

Portuguese man-of-war *noun* a coelenterate that resembles the jellyfish, has very long stinging tentacles, and floats on the surface of the sea: *Physalia physalis*.

POS *abbr* point of sale.

pose¹ /pohz/ *verb trans* **1** to place (e.g. a model) in a particular position or attitude, *esp* for artistic purposes. **2** to constitute (e.g. a problem or threat). **3** to present (e.g. a question) for attention or consideration. ► *verb intrans* **1** to assume or sustain a posture for artistic purposes: *posing for the photographers*. **2** (+ as) to pretend to be somebody other than oneself: *The attackers posed as insurance salesmen*. **3** *Brit, informal* to behave or dress in a self-consciously stylish way calculated to attract attention and impress others. [Middle English *posen* via early French *poser* from late Latin *posit-*, *ponere* to stop, rest, pause, ultimately from Latin *pausa*: see PAUSE¹]

pose² *noun* **1** a sustained posture assumed for artistic purposes, e.g. in acting or modelling. **2** an assumed attitude or mode of behaviour intended to impress or deceive others.

pose³ *verb trans* to puzzle or baffle (somebody). [shortening of *appose* to question, variant of OPPOSE]

poser¹ *noun* a puzzling or baffling question. [POSE³]

poser² *noun* **1** *Brit, informal* somebody who dresses or behaves in a self-consciously stylish way designed to attract attention and impress others. **2** = POSEUR (1). [POSE¹]

poseur /poh'zuh/ *noun* **1** an affected or insincere person. **2** = POSEUR² (1). [French *poseur* from *poser*: see POSE¹]

posey or **posy** /'pohzi/ *adj* (**posier, posiest**) *informal* pretentious: *an effective but slightly posey awakening-of-lesbian-desires item with an appealing cast and silly fantasy touches* — New Musical Express.

posh¹ /posh/ *adj informal* **1** very fine; splendid: *a posh new car*. **2** socially exclusive or fashionable, *esp* upper-class: *a posh Knightsbridge address*.

Word history ————————
perhaps from obsolete *posh* money, dandy. Often said to stand for 'port out, starboard home', indicating the shadier, and therefore more desirable and expensive, side of a ship travelling to the Indian subcontinent from Britain, but there is no evidence to support this theory.

posh² *adv informal* in a posh way, *esp* in an educated or upper-class accent: *talk posh*.

posit /'pozit/ *verb trans* (**posited, positing**) **1** to assume or put forward (something) as fact, *esp* for the purposes of an argument; to postulate (it). **2** to place (something) in position. [Latin *positus*, past part. of *ponere* to place]

position¹ /pə'zish(ə)n/ *noun* **1a** the place occupied by somebody or something: *a house in an attractive position overlooking the sea*. **b** the proper place for something: *The cars are now in position*. **c** a place occupied by troops for strategic reasons. **d** the part of a field or playing area in which a member of a sports team generally operates: *Which position do you play?* **2** the way in which somebody or something is disposed or arranged: *in a vertical position*. **3a** a condition or situation: *I am not in a position to make such a decision*. **b** social or official rank or status. **c** a situation that confers advantage or

preference: *jockeying for position*. **4** *formal* a post or job. **5** an opinion: *She made her position on the issue clear*. **6** in logic, the statement of a proposition or thesis. **7** a market commitment in securities or commodities. **8** in music, the disposition of the notes of a chord. [via early French *position* from Latin *position-, positio*, from *ponere* to place]

position² *verb trans* to put (something or somebody) in a proper or specified position.

positional *adj* of, fixed by, or dependent on position: *positional astronomy*.

positive¹ /'pozitiv/ *adj* **1a** concentrating on what is good or beneficial; optimistic: *He has a positive attitude towards his illness*. **b** capable of being constructively applied; helpful: *positive criticism*. **2a** marked by or indicating acceptance, approval, or affirmation. **b** showing the presence of something sought or suspected to be present: *a positive test for blood*. **3a** expressed clearly or peremptorily: *Her answer was a positive no*. **b** fully assured; confident or certain: *I'm positive that he is right*. **c** incontestable: *positive proof*. **d** utter: *a positive disgrace*. **4a** real or active: *a positive influence for good in the community*. **b** having or expressing actual existence or quality as distinguished from deprivation or deficiency. **c** not speculative; empirical. **5** numerically greater than zero: *+2 is a positive integer*. **6a** extending or generated in a direction arbitrarily or customarily taken as that of increase or progression: *positive angles*. **b** directed or moving towards a source of stimulation: *a positive response to light*. **7** said of a photographic image: having the light and dark parts corresponding to those of the original subject. **8a** of, being, or charged with electricity of which the proton is the elementary unit. **b** losing electrons. **c** having higher electric potential and constituting the part from which the current flows to the external circuit. **9** in grammar, of or constituting the simple form of an adjective or adverb that expresses no degree of comparison. ►►► **positively** *adv*, **positiveness** *noun*, **positivity** /-'tiviti/ *noun*. [Middle English, in the sense 'formally laid down', via Old French *positif* from Latin *positivus*, from *posit-, ponere* to place]

positive² *noun* **1** something positive, e.g. something about which an affirmation can be made. **2** a positive photograph or a print from a negative. **3** the positive degree or form of an adjective or adverb. **4** a positive number.

positive discrimination *noun* a bias in favour of members of a group that is discriminated against or inadequately represented in a particular situation.

positive feedback *noun* the return of part of the output of a system, e.g. an electronic or mechanical one, to the input, reinforcing the input energy by an increase in output energy: compare NEGATIVE FEEDBACK.

positive vetting *noun* investigation into the character of a candidate for the civil service that makes use of any secret information gathered by the security services.

positivism *noun* **1** a theory rejecting theology and metaphysics in favour of knowledge based on the scientific observation of natural phenomena. **2** = LOGICAL POSITIVISM. ►►► **positivist** *adj and noun*, **positivistic** /-'vistik/ *adj*. [French *positivisme*, from *positif* (see POSITIVE¹) + *-isme* -ISM]

positron /'pozitron/ *noun* a positively charged elementary particle that has the same mass and magnitude of electrical charge as the electron and is its ANTIPARTICLE (counterpart capable of producing mutual annihilation). Also called ANTI-ELECTRON. [POSITIVE¹ + *-tron* as in ELECTRON]

posology /pə'soləji/ *noun* a branch of medicine dealing with the quantities in which drugs should be administered. ►►► **posological** /-ə'lojikl/ *adj*. [French *posologie*, from Greek *posos* how much + French *-logie* -LOGY]

poss. *abbr* **1** in grammar, possessive. **2** possible.

posse /'posi/ *noun* **1** (*treated as sing. or pl*) in former times, a body of people summoned by a sheriff to assist in enforcing the law or preserving the public peace, usu in an emergency. **2** a large group, often with a common interest. [medieval Latin *posse comitatus*, literally 'power or authority of the county']

possess /pə'zes/ *verb trans* **1a** to have and hold (something) as property; to own (it). **b** to have (something) as an attribute, knowledge, or skill. **2a** to influence (somebody) so strongly as to direct their actions: *Whatever possessed her to act like that?* **b** said of a demon, evil spirit, etc: to enter into and control (somebody). **3** (+ of/with) to make (somebody) the owner or holder of something. **4** to have sexual intercourse with (a woman). ►►► **possessor** *noun*.

[Middle English *possessen* via French from Latin *possessus*, past part. of *possidēre* to occupy, to sit in power, from *posis* power + *sidere* to sit]

possessed *adj* influenced or controlled by something, e.g. an evil spirit or a passion.

possession /pə'zesh(ə)n/ *noun* **1a** the state of having or owning something. **b** in law, control or occupancy, e.g. of property, without regard to ownership. **c** in sport, control of the ball by a player or team. **2a** something owned or controlled: *personal possessions; colonial possessions.* **b** (*in pl*) wealth or property. **3** domination by something, e.g. an evil spirit or a passion.

possessive[1] /pə'zesiv/ *adj* **1** insisting on undivided love or attention: *a possessive mother.* **2** reluctant to share or give up possessions **3** denoting a grammatical case expressing ownership or a relation corresponding to ownership: *the possessive pronouns 'mine' and 'ours'.* ⟫ **possessively** *adv,* **possessiveness** *noun.*

possessive[2] *noun* the possessive case or a word in this case.

possessory /pə'zes(ə)ri/ *adj formal* of or having possession: *a possessory interest.*

posset /'posit/ *noun* a comforting hot beverage of sweetened and spiced milk curdled with ale or wine, formerly used as a remedy for colds. [Middle English *poshet, possot*; earlier history unknown]

possibility /posə'biliti/ *noun* (*pl* **possibilities**) **1** the condition or fact of being possible. **2a** something possible. **b** a candidate, competitor, etc who is reasonably likely to be selected, win, etc. **3** (*usu in pl*) potential or prospective value: *The house had great possibilities.*

possible[1] /'posəbl/ *adj* **1** within the limits of ability, capacity, or realization. **2** capable of occurring or being done according to nature, custom, manners, etc. **3** that may or may not occur: *It is possible but not probable that he will win.* **4** having a specified potential use, quality, etc: *a possible housing site.* [Middle English via French from Latin *possibilis*, from *posse*: see POTENT[1]]

possible[2] *noun* **1** something possible: *Politics is the art of the possible.* **2** somebody or something that may be selected for a specified role, task, etc.

possibly *adv* **1** it is possible that; maybe: *He possibly missed the train.* **2** used as an intensifier with *can* or *could*: *You can't possibly eat all that cake; I did all I possibly could to help her.*

possum /'pos(ə)m/ *noun* **1** = OPOSSUM (1). **2** *Aus, NZ* = PHALANGER. ✳ **play possum** *informal* to pretend to be ignorant, asleep, or dead in order to deceive somebody. [shortening of OPOSSUM]

post[1] /pohst/ *noun* **1** a piece of timber, metal, etc fixed firmly in an upright position, *esp* as a stay or support. **2** a pole marking the starting or finishing point of a race, *esp* a horse race. ✳ **first past the post** see FIRST[3]. [Old English, ultimately from Latin *postis* doorpost, beam]

post[2] *verb trans* **1** (*often* + up) to fasten (e.g. a notice) to a wall, board, etc in a public place. **2** to publish, announce, or advertise (something) by or as if by use of a placard, poster, etc.

post[3] *noun* **1** *chiefly Brit.* **a** the letters, parcels, etc handled by a postal system; mail. **b** a single collection or delivery of post: *The last post goes at 5.30; Today's post is on your desk.* **c** a postal system. **d** information or a message posted on an Internet site. **2** in former times, any of a series of stopping-places along a fixed route where messengers on horseback passed letters, parcels, etc to a fresh rider, or any of the messengers involved in such relays. [early French *poste* relay station, courier, via Old Italian *posta* from Latin *posita*, fem past part. of *ponere* to place]

post[4] *verb trans* **1** to send (something) by post. **2** to provide (somebody) with the latest news; to inform (them): *I kept her posted on the latest gossip.* **3a** to enter (an item) in a ledger. **b** to make entries in (e.g. a ledger). **4** to make (a message or piece of information) public on the Internet. ⟩ *verb intrans* **1** in former times, to travel with post-horses. **2** *archaic* to ride or travel with haste; to hurry.

post[5] *adv* with great speed; express.

post[6] *noun* **1a** the place at which somebody, e.g. a sentry, is stationed. **b** the place at which a body of troops is stationed; a camp. **2a** an office or position to which a person is appointed; a job. **b** a duty or task to which a person is assigned. **3** a trading post or settlement. **4** *Brit* either of two military bugle calls giving notice of the time for retiring at night. [early French *poste* via Old Italian *posto* from Latin *positum*, neuter past part. of *ponere* to place]

post[7] *verb trans* **1** to station (e.g. a sentry or body of troops) somewhere: *Guards were posted at the doors.* **2** *chiefly Brit* to send

(somebody) to work in a different unit or location: *She was posted to the Tokyo office.*

post- *prefix* forming words, with the meaning: after, subsequent, or later: *postdate; postscript; post-operative.* [Middle English from Latin *post* (adv and prep)]

postage /'pohstij/ *noun* the fee for sending something by post.

postage stamp *noun* an adhesive or printed stamp used as evidence of prepayment of postage.

postal *adj* **1** relating to or denoting a system for the conveyance of letters, parcels, etc between a large number of users. **2** conducted by post: *a postal vote.* ⟫ **postally** *adv.*

postal card *noun NAmer* = POSTCARD.

postal code *noun* = POSTCODE.

postal order *noun Brit* an order issued by a post office for payment of a specified sum of money usu at another post office.

postbag *noun* **1** *Brit* = MAILBAG. **2** a single batch of mail delivered to one address, *esp* letters from the general public to a person or organization.

postbox *noun* **1** a secure receptacle for the posting of outgoing mail, *esp* a public box erected in the street. **2** = LETTER BOX (1).

postcard *noun* a card, often bearing a picture of a place, on which a message can be written and sent by post without an enclosing envelope.

post chaise *noun* a four-wheeled horse-drawn carriage seating two to four people, used in former times for the rapid transporting of mail and passengers.

postclassical *adj* of or being a period, e.g. in art, literature, or civilization, following a classical period.

postcode *noun* a combination of letters and numbers that is used in the postal address of a place in Britain to assist sorting: compare ZIP CODE.

postcode lottery *noun Brit* disparities in the medical treatment provided by different health authorities or in the social care provided by different local authorities, so making the level of care a person receives dependent on where they live.

post-coital *adj* occurring in or done during the period immediately following sexual intercourse.

postdate *verb trans* **1a** to mark (a document, e.g. a cheque) with a future date, usu in order to stall action, e.g. payment. **b** to assign to (an event) a later date than that of actual occurrence. **2** to follow (something) in time.

postdoctoral /pohst'doktərəl/ *adj* of or engaged in advanced academic or professional work beyond a doctor's degree: *a postdoctoral fellowship.*

poster *noun* **1** a large advertisement displayed in a public place. **2** a large printed picture hung on a wall for decoration.

poste restante /ˌpohst 'restont/ *noun chiefly Brit* a postal service in which mail is kept for a limited period of time at a post office for collection by the person to whom it is addressed, or the department holding such mail. [French *poste restante*, literally 'mail remaining']

posterior[1] /po'stiəri-ə/ *adj* **1** later in time or order. **2** situated behind or towards the back, *esp* towards the back of the body: compare ANTERIOR. **3** said of a plant part: on the same side as or facing the main stem. ⟫ **posteriority** /-'oriti/ *noun,* **posteriorly** *adv.* [Latin *posterior*, compar of *posterus* coming after, from *post* after]

posterior[2] *noun informal* the buttocks.

posterity /po'steriti/ *noun* **1** all future generations. **2** (*treated as sing. or pl*) all the descendants of one ancestor. [Middle English *posterite* via French from Latin *posteritat-, posteritas*, from *posterus*: see POSTERIOR[1]]

postern /'postən, 'pohstuhn/ *noun* a lesser door or gate of a castle or other large building. [Middle English *posterne* via Old French from late Latin *posterula*, dimin. ultimately of Latin *posterus*: see POSTERIOR[1]]

poster paint *noun* an opaque watercolour paint containing gum.

post-feminist *adj* denoting feminist ideas that are a development or moderation of those of the original feminist movement. ⟫ **post-feminism** *noun,* **post-feminist** *noun.*

post-free *adv chiefly Brit* = POSTPAID.

post-glacial *adj* occurring after an age of glaciation.

postgraduate /pohst'gradyooət/ *noun* **1** a student continuing higher education after completing a first degree. **2** (*used before a noun*) of or being such a student or their studies: *a postgraduate course.*

posthaste *adv* with all possible speed. [POST³ + HASTE¹]

post horn *noun* a simple brass or copper wind instrument without valves or keys but with a cupped mouthpiece, used *esp* by guards of mail coaches in the 18th and 19th cents.

post-horse *noun* a horse formerly kept at an inn for use by travellers or mail carriers.

posthumous /'postyooməs/ *adj* **1** following or occurring after death: *posthumous fame.* **2** published after the death of the author or composer. **3** born after the death of the father. ⟫⟫ **posthumously** *adv.* [Latin *posthumus*, alteration (influenced by *humus* ground) of *postumus* late-born, posthumous, superl of *posterus*: see POSTERIOR¹]

postie /'pohsti/ *noun informal* a postman or postwoman.

postilion *or* **postillion** /po'stilyən/ *noun* a person who rides on the nearside leading horse of a team drawing a coach to guide them in the absence of a coachman. [early French *postillon* mail carrier using post-horses, from Italian *postiglione*, from *posta*: see POST³]

postimpressionism *noun* a theory or practice in art originating in France in the late 19th cent. that reacted against the naturalist tendency of impressionism by stressing the formal or subjective elements in a painting. ⟫⟫ **postimpressionist** *adj and noun*, **postimpressionistic** /-'nistik/ *adj.* [French *postimpressionnisme*]

post-industrial *adj* of or being a period characterized by the decline of heavy industry and the emergence of other forms of economic activity, e.g. those based on information technology in the late 20th cent.

posting *noun* an appointment to a post or command.

Post-it *noun trademark* a coloured label with an adhesive strip along one edge, which can be temporarily attached to and easily removed from any surface and may be used for messages, reminders, etc.

postman *noun* (*pl* **postmen**) a man who delivers the post.

postman's knock *noun* a children's game in which a kiss is the reward for the pretended delivery of a letter.

postmark¹ *noun* a cancellation mark showing the date and place of posting of a piece of mail.

postmark² *verb trans* to mark (an envelope or package) with a postmark.

postmaster *noun* a man in charge of a post office.

postmaster general *noun* (*pl* **postmasters general**) an official in charge of a national post office.

post meridiem /məˈridi·əm/ *adj* after noon, the full form of P.M. [Latin *post meridiem* after midday]

postmillennial *adj* **1** of the period following a millennium. **2** of postmillennialism.

postmillennialism *noun* the belief that Christ will return only after the MILLENNIUM (thousand-year period mentioned in the Bible). ⟫⟫ **postmillennialist** *noun.*

postmistress *noun* a woman in charge of a post office.

postmodernism *noun* in the arts, any movement that rejects or moderates the ideas of a previous movement considered modernist, often encompassing a reinterpretation of classical ideas, forms, and practices.

Editorial note ⎯⎯⎯⎯⎯⎯⎯⎯⎯⎯⎯⎯⎯⎯⎯⎯
The term 'postmodernism' has broadly come to define experimental tendencies in the western arts and architecture after the decline of Modernism in 1945. Particularly associated with post-industrial society and 'the cultural logic of late capitalism', it suggests multiple quotation, cultural crossover, multicultural borrowing. Formerly characterizing the postwar avant-garde, it is now a generalized term for the knowing, hi-tech, pluralist character of contemporary society — Professor Malcolm Bradbury.

⟫⟫ **postmodern** *adj*, **postmodernist** *noun and adj.*

postmortem¹ /pohst'mawtəm/ *noun* **1** an examination of a body after death to determine the cause of death or the character and extent of changes produced by disease. **2** an analysis or discussion of an event after it is over, *esp* after it has failed.

postmortem² *adj* **1** occurring after death. **2** following the event: *a postmortem appraisal of the game.* [Latin *post mortem* after death]

postmortem examination *noun* = POSTMORTEM¹ (1).

postnatal *adj* relating to the period following childbirth. ⟫⟫ **postnatally** *adv.*

postnuptial *adj* **1** occurring after marriage. **2** relating to the period after animals have mated. ⟫⟫ **postnuptially** *adv.*

post-obit /ˌpohst 'ohbit/ *adj* taking effect after death. [Latin *post obitum* after death]

post office *noun* **1** a national organization that runs a postal system. **2** a local branch of a national post office. **3** *NAmer* = POSTMAN'S KNOCK.

post office box *noun* a rented compartment in a post office where mail is kept for collection by the person or organization renting the compartment.

post-operative *adj* following a surgical operation.

postpaid *adv* with the postage paid, e.g. by the addressee or by a mail-order company sending goods.

postpartum /pohst'pahtəm/ *adj* relating to the period following birth. [scientific Latin *post partum* after birth]

postpone /pəˈspohn, pohs(t)ˈpohn/ *verb trans* to move (something) to a later time; to defer (it). ⟫⟫ **postponable** *adj*, **postponement** *noun*, **postponer** *noun.* [Latin *postponere* to place after, postpone, from POST- + *ponere* to place]

postpositive¹ *adj* said of a word: placed after or at the end of another word. ⟫⟫ **postpositively** *adv.* [late Latin *postpositivus*, from Latin *postponere*: see POSTPONE]

postpositive² *noun* a postpositive word.

postprandial *adj formal or humorous* following a meal: *He began to frequent another café, where more newspapers were taken, and his postprandial demitasse cost him a penny extra* — Henry James.

postscript /'pohs(ts)kript/ *noun* **1** a note added at the end of a letter, completed article, etc. **2** a subordinate or supplementary part. [Latin *postscriptum*, neuter past part. of *postscribere* to write after, from POST- + *scribere* to write]

post-structuralism *noun* a mode of literary criticism that revises and develops the theories of structuralism, revolving around the notion that there is no absolute meaning in language and therefore there are an indeterminate number of possible interpretations of any text.

Editorial note ⎯⎯⎯⎯⎯⎯⎯⎯⎯⎯⎯⎯⎯⎯⎯⎯
Post-structuralism challenges the binary oppositions characteristic of structuralism, emphasizing difference instead, while retaining the view that surfaces mask unrecognized meanings, motives, and processes which are decisive for culture and, indeed, individual identity. Its most influential practitioners have been Jacques Lacan in psychoanalysis, Roland Barthes in literary criticism, and Jacques Derrida in philosophy — Professor Catherine Belsey.

⟫⟫ **post-structural** *adj*, **post-structuralist** *noun and adj.*

post-traumatic stress disorder *noun* a condition in which the stress resulting from a traumatic experience persists for a long time after the event and causes symptoms such as emotional withdrawal, depression, and anxiety.

postulant /'postyoolənt/ *noun* a person seeking admission to a religious order. ⟫⟫ **postulancy** /-si/ *noun.* [French *postulant* petitioner, candidate, postulant, from Latin *postulant-, postulans*, present part. of *postulare* to ask]

postulate¹ /'postyoolayt/ *verb trans* **1** to assume or claim that (something) is true or that it exists, *esp* for the purposes of an argument. **2** to put forward (a candidate for ecclesiastical office) for the approval of a higher authority. ⟫⟫ **postulation** /-'laysh(ə)n/ *noun*, **postulator** *noun.* [Latin *postulatus*, past part. of *postulare* to ask, later 'to assume']

postulate² /'postyoolət/ *noun* **1** a hypothesis advanced as a premise in a train of reasoning. **2** a statement, e.g. in logic or mathematics, that is accepted without proof. [medieval Latin *postulatum*, neuter of *postulatus*: see POSTULATE¹]

posture¹ /'poschə/ *noun* **1** a position in which the body or a part of it is held. **2** a state or condition, *esp* in relation to other people or things: *events that put the country in a posture of defence.* **3** a frame of mind; an attitude: *a posture of moral superiority.* ⟫⟫ **postural** *adj.* [French *posture* via Italian *postura* from Latin *positura*, from *positus*, past part. of *ponere* to place]

posture² *verb intrans* **1** to assume a particular bodily posture. **2** to assume an affected posture that is designed to attract attention and impress others. **3** to assume an artificial or insincere attitude; to attitudinize. ⟫⟫ **posturer** *noun.*

postviral syndrome *noun* = CHRONIC FATIGUE SYNDROME.

postwar *adj* of or being the period after a war, *esp* World War I or II.

postwoman *noun* (*pl* **postwomen**) a woman who delivers the post.

posy[1] /'pohzi/ *noun* (*pl* **posies**) **1** a small bouquet of flowers. **2** *archaic* a brief sentiment, motto, or legend, *esp* one inscribed inside a ring. [alteration of POESY]

posy[2] /'pohzi/ *adj* see POSEY.

pot[1] /pot/ *noun* **1a** any of various usu rounded containers (e.g. of metal, glass, or earthenware) used for holding liquids or solids: *a cooking pot.* **b** a drinking vessel, e.g. of pewter, used *esp* for beer. **c** the contents of a pot: *a pot of coffee.* **2** = FLOWERPOT. **3** an enclosed framework for catching fish or lobsters. **4** = POTTY[2]. **5** *Brit* a shot in billiards or snooker in which a ball goes into a pocket. **6a** the total of the bets at stake at one time in a gambling game. **b** *chiefly NAmer* the common fund of a group. **7** *informal* (*usu in pl*) a large amount, *esp* of money. **8** *informal* = POTBELLY. **9** *informal* a trophy or cup awarded as a prize. ✳ **go to pot** *informal* to deteriorate or collapse: *All our plans went to pot.* **keep the pot boiling** to maintain an activity, *esp* at a vigorous level. ➤➤ **potful** (*pl* **potfuls**) *noun*. [Old English *pott*]

pot[2] *verb* (**potted, potting**) ➤ *verb trans* **1a** to place (something) in a pot. **b** to preserve (food) in a sealed pot, jar, or can: *potted chicken.* **c** to plant (e.g. a seedling) in a flowerpot. **2a** to shoot (an animal) for food. **b** to take a potshot at (somebody or something). **3** in billiards or snooker, to send (a ball) into a pocket. **4** to embed (e.g. electronic components) in a container with an insulating or protective material, e.g. plastic. **5** to sit (a young child) on a potty. ➤ *verb intrans* to make pottery.

pot[3] *noun slang* cannabis. [Mexican Spanish *potiguaya* cannabis leaves]

potable /'pohtəbl/ *adj* said of water: suitable for drinking. ➤➤ **potability** /-'biliti/ *noun*. [late Latin *potabilis* from Latin *potare* to drink]

potage /po'tahzh/ *noun* thick soup. [Old French *potage*: see POTTAGE]

potash /'potash/ *noun* **1a** = POTASSIUM CARBONATE. **b** = POTASSIUM HYDROXIDE. **2** potassium or a potassium compound, *esp* as used in agriculture or industry. [earlier *pot ashes*, because it was orig obtained by leaching wood ashes and evaporating the lye in iron pots]

potassium /pə'tasi·əm/ *noun* a silver-white metallic chemical element of the alkali metal group that is soft and light, occurs abundantly in nature, *esp* combined in minerals, is an essential element for all living organisms, and is used in medicine etc: symbol K, atomic number 19. ➤➤ **potassic** /-sik/ *adj*. [scientific Latin *potassium*, from POTASH]

potassium carbonate *noun* a chemical compound that can absorb water from the air to form a strongly alkaline solution and is used in making glass and soap: formula K_2CO_3. Also called POTASH.

potassium chlorate *noun* a chemical compound that is used as an oxidizing agent in matches, fireworks, and explosives: formula $KClO_3$.

potassium cyanide *noun* a very poisonous chemical compound used *esp* in extracting gold and silver from their ores: formula KCN.

potassium hydroxide *noun* a chemical compound that absorbs water from the air to form a strongly alkaline and caustic liquid and is used chiefly in making liquid soaps and detergents: formula KOH. Also called CAUSTIC POTASH, POTASH.

potassium nitrate *noun* a chemical compound that occurs naturally in fertile soils, is made commercially from potassium hydroxide and nitric acid, and is used as a fertilizer, in making gunpowder, and in preserving meat: formula KNO_3.

potassium permanganate *noun* a dark purple chemical compound used as an oxidizing agent and disinfectant: formula $KMnO_4$.

potassium sodium tartrate *noun* = ROCHELLE SALT.

potation /poh'taysh(ə)n/ *noun formal or humorous* **1** the act of drinking. **2** an alcoholic drink. [Middle English *potacioun* via French from Latin *potation-, potatio*, from *potare* to drink]

potato /pə'taytoh/ *noun* (*pl* **potatoes**) **1a** a plant of the nightshade family widely cultivated in temperate regions for its edible starchy tubers: *Solanum tuberosum.* **b** a tuber of this plant, used as a vegetable. **2** = SWEET POTATO. [Spanish *batata*, from Taino]

potato chip *noun NAmer* = CRISP[2].

potato crisp *noun chiefly Brit* = CRISP[2].

potbelly *noun* (*pl* **potbellies**) a protruding abdomen. ➤➤ **potbellied** *adj*.

potboiler *noun* a novel, painting, etc of little artistic merit and usu in a calculatedly popular style, produced to make a living.

pot-bound *adj* said of a potted plant: having roots that fill the available space in the pot, allowing no room for further growth.

poteen *or* **potheen** /po'cheen, po'teen/ *noun* Irish whiskey illicitly distilled, or any distilled alcoholic drink made at home. [Irish Gaelic *poitín*, dimin. of *pota* pot]

potent[1] /'poht(ə)nt/ *adj* **1** having or wielding great force, authority, or influence; powerful: *potent arguments.* **2** chemically or medicinally effective or powerful: *a potent vaccine.* **3** producing a powerful reaction, *esp* unexpectedly; strong: *This whisky is potent stuff.* **4** said of a man: able to have sexual intercourse, *esp* able to achieve erection. ➤➤ **potence** *noun*, **potency** /-si/ *noun*, **potently** *adv*. [Middle English from Latin *potent-, potens*, present part. of *posse* to be able, from *potis* able + *esse* to be]

potent[2] *adj* said of a heraldic cross: having flat bars across the ends of the arms. [obsolete *potent* crutch, from Middle English, modification of early French *potence* crutch, gibbet]

potentate /'poht(ə)ntayt/ *noun* somebody who wields great power; a ruler. [Middle English from Latin *potentatus*, from *potent-, potens*: see POTENT[1]]

potential[1] /pə'tensh(ə)l/ *adj* **1** existing in possibility; capable of coming into being or developing further: *potential benefits.* **2** said of a verb or verb phrase: expressing possibility. ➤➤ **potentially** *adv*. [Middle English from late Latin *potentialis*, from Latin *potentia* power, from *potent-, potens*: see POTENT[1]]

potential[2] *noun* **1** something that can develop or become actual; possible capacity or value: *a player with potential.* **2a** the work required to move a unit positive electrical charge from a reference point, e.g. infinity, to a point in question. **b** = POTENTIAL DIFFERENCE.

potential difference *noun* the voltage difference between two points that represents the work involved or the energy released in the transfer of a unit quantity of electricity from one point to another.

potential energy *noun* the energy that something has because of its position in a magnetic, electrical, or gravitational field, or because of the arrangement of parts.

potentiality /pə,tenshi'aliti/ *noun* **1** the ability to come into being or develop further. **2** = POTENTIAL[2] (1).

potentiate /pə'tenshiayt/ *verb trans* to make (something) effective or more effective; *specif* to make (two drugs or their action) more effective by administering them together. ➤➤ **potentiation** /-'aysh(ə)n/ *noun*, **potentiator** *noun*.

potentilla /poht(ə)n'tilə/ *noun* any of a large genus of plants and shrubs of the rose family that have usu yellow flowers with five petals: genus *Potentilla.* [from the Latin genus name, from medieval Latin *potentilla* garden heliotrope]

potentiometer /pə,tenshi'omitə/ *noun* **1** an instrument for measuring ELECTROMOTIVE FORCE (force driving a current round an electric circuit). **2** a device used to provide variable resistances in an electronic circuit, e.g. to control volume in a radio. ➤➤ **potentiometric** /-'metrik/ *adj*, **potentiometry** /-tri/ *noun*.

potheen /po'cheen, po'teen/ *noun* = POTEEN.

pother[1] /'podhə/ *noun* **1** a noisy disturbance; a commotion. **2** needless agitation over a trivial matter; fuss. [origin unknown]

pother[2] *verb* (**pothered, pothering**) ➤ *verb intrans* to fuss or worry. ➤ *verb trans* to cause (somebody) to fuss or worry.

pothole[1] *noun* **1** an unwanted hole in a road surface caused by wear, weathering, subsidence, etc. **2** a natural vertically descending hole in the ground or in the floor of a cave, or a system of these. **3** a circular hole worn in the rocky bed of a river by stones or gravel whirled round by the water. ➤➤ **potholed** *adj*.

pothole[2] *verb intrans* to explore underground pothole systems as a leisure activity. ➤➤ **potholer** *noun*, **potholing** *noun*.

pothook *noun* **1** a curved or S-shaped hook for hanging pots and kettles over an open fire or lifting them when hot. **2** a written character resembling a pothook.

potion /'pohsh(ə)n/ *noun* **1** a dose of medicine, poison, etc in liquid form. **2** a mixed drink intended to produce a specified effect: *a love potion*. [Middle English *pocioun* via French from Latin *potion-, potio* drink, potion, from *potare* to drink]

potlatch *noun* a ceremonial Native American feast marked by the lavish distribution of gifts as a display of wealth and prestige. [Chinook Jargon *potlatch*, from Nootka *patshatl* giving]

pot-luck *noun* whatever luck or chance may bring: *We must take pot-luck*. ✷ **take pot-luck** to share in whatever may be available to make a meal: *I hope Mr Lawford will take pot-luck with us, for it is just his own hour; and indeed we had something rather better than ordinary – lamb and spinach, and a veal Florentine* — Scott.

potoroo /pohtə'rooh/ *noun* (*pl* **potoroos**) = RAT KANGAROO. [from Dharuk, an Aboriginal language of New South Wales, Australia]

pot plant *noun* a plant grown in a flowerpot, usu for indoor ornament.

potpourri /pohpə'ree/ *noun* **1** a mixture of dried flowers, herbs, and spices, usu kept in a bowl for its fragrance. **2** a miscellaneous collection; a medley. [orig in the sense 'a stew made of various kinds of meat'; French *pot pourri*, literally 'rotten pot']

pot roast *noun* a joint of meat cooked by pot-roasting.

pot-roast *verb trans* to cook (a joint of meat) slowly by braising in a covered pot.

potsherd /'potshuhd/ *noun* a fragment of pottery. [Middle English *pot-sherd*, from POT¹ + *sherd* SHARD]

potshot /'potshot/ *noun* **1a** a shot taken at game without regard to the rules of sport. **b** a shot taken in a casual manner or at an easy target. **2** a critical remark made at random. [from the notion that such a shot is worthy only of somebody wishing to fill a cooking pot]

pot still *noun* a device used *esp* in the distillation of Irish grain whiskey and Scotch malt whisky, in which the heat of the fire is applied directly to the pot containing the fermenting grain or malt.

pottage /'potij/ *noun* a thick soup or stew of vegetables and meat. [Middle English from Old French *potage*, from *pot* pot, of Germanic origin]

potted *adj* **1** planted or grown in a flowerpot. **2** preserved in a sealed pot: *potted shrimps*. **3** *chiefly Brit* abridged or summarized, usu in a simplified or popular form: *potted biographies*.

potter¹ *noun* somebody who makes pottery. [Old English *pottere*, from *pott* POT¹]

potter² *verb intrans* (**pottered, pottering**) **1** (*often* + around/about) to spend time in aimless or leisurely activity: *He loves to potter around in the garden*. **2** to move or travel in a leisurely or random fashion: *pottering along country lanes*. [prob frequentative of English dialect *pote* to poke, from Old English *potian*]

potter's field *noun* a public burial place for paupers, unknown people, and criminals. [from the mention in Matthew 27:7 of the purchase of a potter's field for use as a graveyard]

potter's wheel *noun* a horizontal disc revolving on a vertical spindle, on which clay is shaped by a potter.

pottery *noun* (*pl* **potteries**) **1** a place where ceramic ware is made and fired. **2a** the art or craft of a potter. **b** the manufacture of pottery. **3** articles made of baked clay, *esp* earthenware.

potting compost *noun* a mixture of peat, loam, sand, etc used in place of soil for plants grown in flowerpots and other containers.

potting shed *noun* a garden shed used for potting seedlings, storing tools, etc.

pottle /'potl/ *noun* **1** a container holding half a gallon. **2** *archaic* a unit of liquid capacity equal to half a gallon (about 2.27l). **3** a container holding half a gallon. [Middle English *potel* from Old French, dimin. of *pot* pot]

potto /'potoh/ *noun* (*pl* **pottos**) a small nocturnal primate with a very short tail that lives in the forests of W Africa: *Perodicticus potto*. [of W African origin]

Pott's fracture *noun* a fracture near the lower end of the leg, involving a break of the tibia and fibula and a dislocation of the ankle. [named after Percival *Pott* d.1788, English surgeon, who described it]

potty¹ *adj* (**pottier, pottiest**) *Brit, informal* **1** slightly crazy: *That noise is driving me potty*. **2** foolish or silly: *a potty idea*. **3** (*usu* + about) having a great interest in or liking for something or somebody: *She's potty about her new boyfriend*. ⇒ **pottiness** *noun*. [prob from POT¹]

potty² *noun* (*pl* **potties**) a bowl-shaped receptacle used by a small child for urination and defecation.

pouch¹ /powch/ *noun* **1a** a small bag made of flexible material, often with a drawstring. **b** a bag of small or moderate size for storing or transporting goods; *specif* a lockable bag for mail or diplomatic dispatches. **2** a loose arrangement of cloth or other material in the shape of a pocket or bag. **3** an anatomical part resembling a pouch, e.g.: **a** a pocket of skin in the abdomen of marsupials for carrying their young. **b** a pocket of skin in the cheeks of some rodents used for storing food. **c** a loose fold of skin under the eyes. ⇒ **pouched** *adj*, **pouchy** *adj*. [Middle English from early French *pouche*, of Germanic origin]

pouch² *verb trans* **1** to put (something) into a pouch. **2** to form (something) into a pouch or a pouch-like shape. ⇒ *verb intrans* to form a pouch.

pouf /poof, poohf/ *noun* see POOF.

pouffe *or* **pouf** /poohf/ *noun* **1** a large firmly stuffed cushion that serves as a low seat or footrest. **2** a bouffant arrangement of the hair. [French *pouf* something inflated, of imitative origin]

poult¹ /pohlt/ *noun* a young turkey or other domestic fowl. [Middle English *polet*: see PULLET]

poult² *noun* a plain-weave silk fabric with slight crosswise ribs. [short for *poult-de-soie*, from French *pou-de-soie, poult-de-soie*, of unknown origin]

poulterer /'pohlt(ə)rə/ *noun* somebody who deals in poultry or game. [alteration of Middle English *pulter* from early French *pouletier*, from *poulet*: see PULLET]

poultice¹ /'pohltis/ *noun* a soft moist sometimes heated or medicated mass of clay, bread, mustard, etc spread on cloth and applied to inflamed or injured parts of the body. [medieval Latin *pultes* pap, from Latin *puls* porridge]

poultice² *verb trans* to apply a poultice to (e.g. a sore).

poultry /'pohltri/ *noun* chickens, ducks, and other domestic fowl kept for eggs or meat. [Middle English *pultrie* from Old French *poulet*: see PULLET]

pounce¹ /powns/ *verb intrans* **1** to swoop on and seize something with talons or claws. **2** (*often* + on) to seize something suddenly, eagerly, or with force: *She pounced on his offer*. **3** to make a sudden attack or approach. [Middle English *pounce* talon, sting, prob by shortening and alteration from *punson* pointed tool, dagger, from early French *poinçon*: see PUNCHEON²]

pounce² *noun* the act or an instance of pouncing.

pounce³ *noun* **1** a fine powder used in former times to prevent ink from running. **2** a fine powder for making stencilled patterns. [French *ponce* pumice, ultimately from Latin *pumic-, pumex*]

pounce⁴ *verb trans* **1** to apply pounce to (paper). **2** to stencil (a pattern) using pounce.

pouncet box /'pownsit/ *noun* a perforated box used in former times for carrying perfume or powder, e.g. for powdering hair. [early French *poncette* small pounce bag]

pound¹ /pownd/ *noun* (*pl* **pounds** *or* **pound**) **1a** an avoirdupois unit of weight equal to 16oz (about 0.454kg). **b** a troy unit of weight equal to 12oz (about 0.373kg). **2** the basic monetary unit of Britain, several Middle Eastern countries, the Sudan, and Cyprus. [Old English *pund*, from a prehistoric Germanic word borrowed from Latin *pondo* pound weight; (sense 2) from its being orig a pound weight of silver]

pound² *verb trans* **1** to reduce (something) to powder or pulp by beating or crushing it: *Pound the meat to a paste*. **2** to strike (something) heavily or repeatedly: *He pounded the door with his fists*. **3** to move along (a path or route) with heavy steps: *The policeman pounds his beat*. ⇒ *verb intrans* **1** to strike heavy repeated blows: *She pounded angrily on the table*. **2** to beat or throb with a heavy rhythm: *His heart was pounding with fear*. **3** to move with or make a dull repetitive sound: *They pounded down the road*. [Old English *pūnian*]

pound³ *noun* an act or sound of pounding.

pound⁴ *noun* **1** an enclosure for animals, *esp* stray or unlicensed animals. **2** a place where items of personal property, *esp* illegally parked vehicles, are held until redeemed by the owner. **3** a trap or prison. [Middle English *pounde* enclosure, from Old English *pund*-]

pound⁵ *verb trans* **1** to confine (*esp* animals) in an enclosure. **2** *archaic* to impound (something).

poundage /'powndij/ *noun* **1a** a fee, tax, or charge of so much per pound sterling. **b** the proportion of the takings of a business paid in wages. **2a** a charge per pound of weight. **b** weight expressed in pounds.

poundal *noun* a unit of force that gives a mass of one pound an acceleration of one foot per second per second. [POUND¹ + -*al* as in QUINTAL]

pounder *noun* **1** (*used in combinations*) something with a specified weight or value in pounds: *He caught a nine pounder with his new fishing rod.* **2** (*used in combinations*) a gun firing a projectile of a specified weight: *The artillery were using 25-pounders.*

pound out *verb trans informal* to produce (something) by or as if by striking repeated heavy blows: *She pounded out the story on an old typewriter.*

pound sterling *noun* the pound used as the monetary unit of Britain.

pour¹ /paw/ *verb trans* **1** to cause (a liquid or powder) to flow in a stream: *Pour the dirty water down the sink.* **2** to dispense (a drink) into a container: *Pour me a whisky.* **3** to supply or produce (something) freely or copiously: *She poured money into the firm.* ➤ *verb intrans* **1** to flow in a usu copious stream: *Blood poured from his nose.* **2** to move, come, or go with a continuous flow and in large quantities; to stream or flood: *People poured out of the offices at the end of the day.* **3** (*often* + down) to rain hard. ✳ **pour cold water on** to be critical of or unenthusiastic about (something): *He poured cold water on all their proposals.* **pour oil on troubled waters** to calm or defuse a heated situation. ➤➤ **pourable** *adj*, **pourer** *noun*. [Middle English *pouren*; earlier history unknown]

pour² *noun* something that pours or is poured: *a pour of concrete.*

pourboire /'pooəbwah/ *noun* a tip or gratuity. [French *pourboire*, from *pour boire* for drinking]

pour out *verb trans* to speak or express (e.g. feelings) volubly or at length: *He poured out his woes.*

pourparler /pooə'pahlay/ *noun* an informal discussion preliminary to negotiations. [French *pourparler*, literally 'in order to speak']

poussin /pooh'sanh (*French* pusē)/ *noun* a chicken that has been killed young for food. [French *poussin* via late Latin *pullicenus* from Latin *pullus* young bird, young of an animal]

pout¹ /powt/ *verb intrans* **1a** to show displeasure by thrusting out one's lips or wearing a sullen expression. **b** to thrust out one's lips in an expression of sexual provocativeness. **c** to sulk. **2** said of lips: to protrude. ➤ *verb trans* to thrust out (one's lips). ➤➤ **poutingly** *adv*. [Middle English *pouten*, perhaps of Scandinavian origin]

pout² *noun* **1** an act or an instance of pouting. **2a** a sullen expression. **b** (*usu* **the pouts**) a fit of pique.

pout³ *noun* (*pl* **pouts** or *collectively* **pout**) any of numerous species of large-headed fishes of the cod family, e.g. a bullhead or eelpout: family Zoarcidae. [Old English -*pūte*, prob from the same Scandinavian word as POUT¹]

pouter *noun* a domestic pigeon of a breed having a crop that can be inflated to an immense size.

poverty /'povəti/ *noun* **1a** the lack of sufficient money or material possessions for a life of moderate comfort. **b** the renunciation of individual property by a person entering a religious order.

Editorial note

Economists have tended to distinguish between conditions of absolute poverty, under which living standards are low according to an objective measure of human needs; or relative poverty under which living standards are low relative to the society in which they are sustained — Evan Davis.

2 *formal.* **a** a scarcity: *a poverty of ideas and images.* **b** the condition of lacking desirable elements; deficiency: *the poverty of our critical vocabulary.* [Middle English *poverte* via Old French from Latin *paupertat-, paupertas*, from *pauper*: see POOR]

poverty line *noun* an income below which an individual or family is officially regarded as living in poverty.

poverty-stricken *adj* very poor; destitute.

poverty trap *noun* a situation in which the total income of an individual or family fails to increase with earnings because of the resultant loss of state benefits.

POW *abbr* prisoner of war.

pow /pow/ *interj informal* an exclamation imitating the sound of a blow or explosion. [imitative]

powder¹ /'powdə/ *noun* **1** a solid substance that has been reduced to dry loose particles, e.g. by crushing or grinding. **2a** a substance, *esp* a cosmetic or a medicine, produced in the form of fine particles: *face powder.* **b** fine dry light snow. **3** gunpowder, or any of various explosives in powder form used in firearms and blasting. ✳ **keep one's powder dry** to remain alert and ready for action. **take a powder** *NAmer, informal* to leave in a hurry, *esp* from a difficult situation. ➤➤ **powdery** *adj*. [Middle English *poudre* via Old French from Latin *pulver-, pulvis* dust]

powder² *verb* (**powdered, powdering**) ➤ *verb trans* **1a** to sprinkle or cover (something) with or as if with powder. **b** to put cosmetic powder on (one's face, cheeks, etc). **2** to reduce or convert (a substance) to powder: *powdered chalk.* ➤ *verb intrans* to become powder. ➤➤ **powderer** *noun*.

powder blue *adj and noun* pale blue. [because the original pigment for this colour was composed of powdered smalt]

powder burn *noun* a burn on the skin or on a material caused by the firing of a handgun at very close range or by closeness to any sudden intense explosion.

powder horn *noun* a small container for carrying gunpowder, *esp* one made from the horn of an ox or cow.

powder keg *noun* **1** a small usu metal cask for holding gunpowder or blasting powder. **2** a place or situation with the potential to erupt into violence or produce a major disaster.

powder metallurgy *noun* the production of metallic objects from powdered metals.

powder monkey *noun* **1** somebody who works with or is in charge of explosives, e.g. in blasting operations. **2** a boy who in former times carried gunpowder from the magazine to the gunners on board a warship. [from the smallness and agility of the boys working on warships]

powder puff *noun* a small fluffy pad for applying cosmetic powder to the skin.

powder room *noun* a public toilet for women in a hotel, department store, etc.

power¹ /'powə/ *noun* **1a** the ability to do something or to produce an effect: *She was reputed to possess magic powers.* **b** legal or official authority, capacity, or right: *The police had no power to intervene.* **2** the possession of control, authority, or influence over others and the ability to determine the course of events: *Power tends to corrupt, and absolute power corrupts absolutely* — Lord Acton. **3** the position of being the ruler or government of a country or of exercising supreme political control: *the party in power.* **4a** somebody or something that possesses great authority or influence. **b** a sovereign state, especially from the point of view of its international influence and military strength: *a conference attended by representatives of all the great powers.* **5a** physical strength. **b** mental or moral incisiveness and effectiveness; vigour: *the power and insight of his analysis.* **6a** the energy supplied to a system or a machine to make it operate, *esp* electricity. **b** the energy or driving force generated by a motor or a similar machine. **c** (*used before a noun*) driven by such energy: *a power drill.* **7** in physics, the amount of work done or energy emitted or transferred per unit of time. **8** = MAGNIFICATION (2). **9a** the number of times a given number is to be multiplied by itself: *two to the power three = 2×2×2.* **b** = EXPONENT (2). **10** (*used before a noun*) involving or accompanied by high-powered discussion among business people: *a power breakfast.* ✳ **do somebody a power of good** to do somebody a great deal of good. **the powers that be** established authority or any controlling group [from Romans 13:1 'the powers that be are ordained by God']. [Middle English from Old French *poeir* to be able, ultimately from Latin *posse*: see POTENT¹]

power² *verb* (**powered, powering**) ➤ *verb trans* **1** to supply (a machine, vehicle, etc) with power. **2** to make (one's way) in a powerful and vigorous manner: *She powered her way to the top.* **3** (*often* + down/up) to switch an electrical device off or on. ➤ *verb intrans* to move in a powerful and vigorous manner: *He came powering down the back straight.*

power-assisted *adj* in which a power source is used to reinforce human muscular effort: *power-assisted steering.*

power base *noun* an area or group that provides the main support for a politician or other person in authority: *His power base is in the south of the country.*

powerboat *noun* a motorboat, *esp* a fast motorboat designed for racing. ⏵ **powerboating** *noun.*

power broker *noun* somebody who exerts a strong but usu covert political influence, e.g. on the choice of candidates for office. ⏵ **power-broking** *noun.*

power cut *noun* a failure in or reduction of the supply of electric power to an area.

power dive *noun* a dive by an aircraft accelerated by the power of its engine.

power-dive *verb intrans and trans* to make or cause (an aircraft) to make a power dive.

power dressing *noun* a smart or formal style of dressing by women intended to enhance their business and professional status by presenting an extremely businesslike and efficient image.

powerful /'powəf(ə)l/ *adj* **1** having great power, prestige, or influence. **2a** very strong or forceful: *a powerful blow; a powerful smell.* **b** extremely effective: *a powerful drug.* ⏵ **powerfully** *adv.*

powerhouse /'powəhows/ *noun* **1** = POWER STATION. **2** *informal* a dynamic individual who possesses great physical or mental force.

powerless *adj* **1** devoid of strength or resources; helpless. **2** lacking the authority or capacity to act: *The police were powerless to intervene.* ⏵ **powerlessly** *adv,* **powerlessness** *noun.*

power of attorney *noun* the legal authority to act for another person, temporarily or permanently, in certain specified ways, e.g. to sign cheques or act as agent.

power pack *noun* **1** a unit for converting a power supply, e.g. mains electricity, to a voltage suitable for an electronic circuit. **2** a compact, self-contained, and often portable unit that stores electrical power and supplies it to a machine.

power plant *noun* **1** = POWER STATION. **2** the engine and related equipment that supply power to a vehicle or a machine.

power play *noun* **1** a tactic in which a display of strength or the threat of force is used to gain an advantage. **2a** in team sports, an attacking manoeuvre that concentrates a large number of players in one particular area. **b** in ice hockey, a situation where one team has more players on the ice because one or more of the opposing team's players are temporarily suspended.

power point *noun Brit* an electric socket.

power politics *pl noun* (*treated as sing. or pl*) international politics characterized by attempts to advance national interests by force.

power sharing *noun* an arrangement that allows opposing groups or parties to share political power.

power shower *noun* a shower incorporating an electric pump to produce a powerful jet of water.

power station *noun* an electricity generating station.

power steering *noun* a form of steering for a motor vehicle in which power from the engine is used to reinforce the effort applied by the driver to the steering wheel.

powertrain *noun* the system of gears and shafts by which power is transmitted from an engine to e.g. the axles of a vehicle.

powwow[1] /'powwow/ *noun* **1** *informal* a meeting for discussion. **2** a traditional Native American ceremony with feasting and dancing. **3** among some Native Americans, a conference. **4** busy or noisy activity; a fuss or palaver: *Then we have several pages of romantic powwow and confusion dignifying nothing* — Mark Twain. [Narrangansett *powah, powwaw* shaman]

powwow[2] *verb intrans* to hold a powwow.

pox /poks/ *noun* (*pl* **pox** *or* **poxes**) **1** a viral disease, e.g. chickenpox, characterized by the formation of spots on the skin that may leave pockmarks after healing. **2a** *informal* syphilis. **b** *archaic* smallpox. ✲ **a pox on somebody/something** *archaic* used to express extreme annoyance with somebody or something. [alteration of *pocks,* pl of POCK]

poxy *adj* (**poxier, poxiest**) *chiefly Brit, informal* of very poor quality or little value; contemptible.

Pozidriv /'pozidriev/ *noun trademark* a screwdriver with a cross-shaped tip.

pozzolana /potsə'lahnə/ *noun* volcanic ash used in making hydraulic cement. ⏵ **pozzolanic** /-'lanik/ *adj.* [Italian *pozz(u)olana,* fem of *pozz(u)olano* of *Pozzuoli,* a town near Naples in Italy]

pozzuolana /potswə'lahnə/ *noun* = POZZOLANA.

pp *abbr* **1** pages. **2** past participle. **3** Latin *per procurationem:* used to indicate that a person is signing a letter or document on behalf of somebody else. **4** pianissimo.

PPE *abbr* Philosophy, Politics, and Economics.

ppi *abbr* in computing, pixels per inch.

ppm *abbr* parts per million.

PPP *abbr* **1** point to point protocol, software for connecting to the Internet using a modem. **2** purchasing power parity, an exchange rate that gives two currencies equal purchasing power within their own economies.

PPS *abbr* **1** Parliamentary Private Secretary. **2** Latin *post postscriptum:* used to introduce a second or further postscript.

PPV *abbr* pay-per-view.

PQ *abbr* **1** Parti Québécois. **2** Province of Quebec.

PR *abbr* **1** proportional representation. **2** public relations. **3** Puerto Rico.

Pr *abbr* the chemical symbol for praseodymium.

Pr. *abbr* **1** Priest. **2** Prince.

pr. *abbr* **1** pair. **2** present. **3** price. **4** pronoun.

praam /pram, prahm/ *noun* see PRAM[2].

practicable /'praktikabl/ *adj* **1** capable of being carried out; feasible. **2** usable. ⏵ **practicability** /-'biliti/ *noun,* **practicableness** *noun,* **practicably** *adv.* [French *praticable* from *pratiquer* to practise, put into practice, from *pratique:* see PRACTISE]

Usage note

practicable *or* practical? See note at PRACTICAL[1].

practical[1] /'praktikl/ *adj* **1** relating to the actual performance of tasks and to real-life experience rather than to theory. **2a** able to be put to use or put into effect in real situations: *He had a practical knowledge of French.* **b** adapted or suitable for a particular use: *It's not a very practical outfit to go hiking in.* **3** having or showing a realistic and down-to-earth approach to dealing with problems or situations. **4a** good at carrying out ordinary, *esp* manual tasks. **b** qualified by practice or practical training: *a good practical mechanic.* **5** very nearly as described, or as described in practice or effect if not in name; virtual: *It's a practical certainty that she will run for the Senate.* ✲ **for practical purposes** in real terms or situations; effectively; virtually. ⏵ **practicalness** *noun.* [via late Latin from Greek *praktikos:* see PRACTISE]

Usage note

practical *or* practicable? These two words are close together in meaning and sometimes confused. A *practical* plan or suggestion is one that is useful, realistic, and effective: the *practical* applications of a theory. A *practicable* plan is, simply, one that it is possible to carry out. A person can be described as *practical* ('good at ordinary tasks' or 'down-to-earth'), but not as *practicable.*

practical[2] *noun* an examination or lesson that tests or teaches the ability to put theory into practice.

practicality /prakti'kaliti/ *noun* (*pl* **practicalities**) **1** the practical nature of something or somebody. **2** the ability of something to be put into practice. **3** (*in pl*) the practical aspects of a situation or question: *He said a lot about the scheme's theoretical benefits, but little about the practicalities of implementing it.*

practical joke *noun* a trick or prank played on somebody to make them appear foolish: compare JOKE[1]. ⏵ **practical joker** *noun.*

practically *adv* **1** almost; nearly: *Practically everyone went to the party.* **2a** in a practical manner. **b** with regard to, or taking into account, actual realities: *There was, practically speaking, no way out for them.*

practice[1] /'praktis/ *noun* **1a** regular or repeated exercise in order to acquire skill in an activity. **b** a session devoted to such exercise: *Today's choir practice is cancelled.* **2** the actual carrying out of tasks, use of objects, or application of ideas or principles, as opposed to theory: *She was more renowned for the advocacy of strict moral principles than for their practice.* **3a** a repeated or customary action; a habit: *He made a practice of going to bed early.* **b** the usual way something is done by a specified group or at a specified place or time: *It is wise to conform to local practices.* **4a** work in a profession, *esp* law or medicine. **b** the business of a professional person, e.g. a doctor, or the building in which this business is carried on. ✳ **in practice 1** in real situations, as opposed to in theory. **2** currently able to do something well as a result of practising it. **3** working in a profession, *esp* law or medicine. **out of practice** currently unable to do something well as a result of not having practised it recently. [from PRACTISE, by analogy with the relationship between *advice* and *advise*]

Usage note
In British English *practice* is the correct spelling for the noun in all its senses: *do some piano practice; in theory and in practice; a veterinary practice.* The spelling for the equivalent verb is *practise*: *to practise the piano; to practise one's religion; a practising dental surgeon.* In American English, the spelling *practice* is used for both the noun and the verb.

practice² *verb NAmer* see PRACTISE.

practiced *adj NAmer* see PRACTISED.

practise (*NAmer* **practice**) /'praktis/ *verb trans* **1** to perform or work at (an activity) repeatedly so as to become proficient in it: *He practises the drums every day.* **2** to carry out or apply (something) in fact or in real situations, as opposed to talking or theorizing about it; to put (something) into practice: *They don't seem to practise what they preach.* **3a** to do (something) actively as part of one's regular behaviour or way of life: *to practise politeness.* **b** to be a committed follower of (a particular religion): *a practising Christian.* **4** to be professionally engaged in (a particular type of work): *to practise medicine.* ► *verb intrans* **1** to do repeated exercises for proficiency: *She practises at the skating rink every day.* **2** to pursue a profession, *esp* medicine or law, actively. **3** *formal* (+ on/upon) to take advantage of (someone or something): *He practised on their credulity with huge success* — Times Literary Supplement. ➤➤ **practiser** *noun.* [Middle English *practisen* from early French *practiser*, from *practique, pratique* practice, ultimately from Greek *praktikos* concerned with action, from *prattein* to act, do]

Usage note
practise *or* practice? See note at PRACTICE¹.

practised (*NAmer* **practiced**) *adj* **1** experienced or skilled. **2** *often derog* learned by practice: *a practised smile.*

practitioner /prak'tish(ə)nə/ *noun* **1** somebody who practises a profession, *esp* law or medicine. **2** somebody who practises a skill or art: *a practitioner of fiction.* [alteration of Middle English (Scots) *pratician,* from early French *practicien,* from *pratique:* see PRACTISE]

Prader-Willi syndrome /,prahdə 'vili/ *noun* a rare congenital disorder in which learning difficulties are accompanied by obsessive eating, obesity, and abnormal smallness of the genitals. [named after Andrea *Prader* b.1919 and Heinrich *Willi* d.1971, the Swiss paediatricians who first described it]

prae- *prefix* used especially in words taken directly from Latin or connected with ancient Rome: = PRE-: *praenomen; praesidium.* [Latin *prae* before]

praedial *or* **predial** /'preedi-əl/ *adj formal* relating to the land or to farming. [medieval Latin *praedialis* from Latin *praedium* landed property, from *praed-, praes* bondsman]

praesidium /pri'sidi-əm, pri'zid-/ *noun* see PRESIDIUM.

praetor (*NAmer also* **pretor**) /'preetə/ *noun* an ancient Roman magistrate ranking below a consul. ➤➤ **praetorial** /pree'tawri-əl/ *adj,* **praetorship** *noun.* [Middle English *pretor* from Latin *praetor*]

Praetorian Guard /pree'tawri-ən/ *noun* the Roman imperial bodyguard.

pragmatic /prag'matik/ *adj* **1** concerned with practicalities or expediency rather than theory or dogma; realistic. **2** relating to philosophical pragmatism. **3** relating to pragmatics. ➤➤ **pragmatically** *adv.* [via Latin from Greek *pragmatikos* skilled in law or business, from *pragmat-, pragma* deed, from *prattein* to do]

pragmatics *pl noun* (*treated as sing.*) a branch of linguistics dealing with the contexts in which people use language and the behaviour of speakers and listeners in relation to the process of communication.

pragmatic sanction *noun* a solemn decree of a sovereign on a matter of primary importance, e.g. the regulation of the succession, that has the force of fundamental law.

pragmatism /'pragmətiz(ə)m/ *noun* **1** a practical approach to problems and affairs: *They always try to strike a balance between principles and pragmatism.* **2** a philosophical movement asserting that the meaning or truth of a concept depends on its practical consequences.

Editorial note
William James, a leading pragmatist, argued that a belief is true when it puts us into a satisfactory relation to our experience, when it meets our needs and interests. Cognition is thus guided by our interests and values, he urged, and it is rational to give emotions a role in fixing what we should believe — Professor Christopher Hookway.

➤➤ **pragmatist** *adj and noun,* **pragmatistic** /-'tistik/ *adj.*

prairie /'preəri/ *noun* an extensive area of level or undulating and practically treeless grassland, *esp* in N America. [French *prairie* from Latin *pratum* meadow, prairie]

prairie chicken *noun* a grouse that lives mainly in the eastern part of the N American prairie. The male has an orange air sac on each side of its throat that it inflates during courtship displays: *Tympanuchus cupido.*

prairie dog *noun* any of several species of stout yellow-brown burrowing rodents that are related to the marmots, have a sharp barklike call, and live in colonies in the N American prairie: genus *Cynomys.*

prairie oyster *noun* a raw egg or yolk beaten with seasonings and swallowed whole, *esp* as a remedy for a hangover.

prairie schooner *noun* a horse-drawn covered wagon of the type used by the pioneers who settled the American West.

praise¹ /prayz/ *verb trans* **1** to express approval or admiration of (somebody or something). **2** to glorify or extol (e.g. God or a god). ➤➤ **praiser** *noun.* [Middle English *praisen* via early French *preisier* to prize, praise, from late Latin *pretiare* to prize, from Latin *pretium* PRICE¹]

praise² *noun* **1** admiration and approval, or words expressing this: *She won high praise for her efforts.* **2** worship.

praiseworthy *adj* deserving praise; laudable or commendable. ➤➤ **praiseworthily** *adv,* **praiseworthiness** *noun.*

Prakrit /'prahkrit/ *noun* any of the ancient or medieval Indic dialects other than Sanskrit. [Sanskrit *prākṛta* natural, vernacular]

praline /'prahleen/ *noun* a sweet substance made from nuts, *esp* almonds, caramelized in boiling sugar and ground, or a chocolate with a filling of this substance. [French *praline,* named after Count Plessis-*Praslin* d.1675, French soldier, whose cook invented it]

pralltriller /'prahltrilə/ *noun* in music, an ornament consisting of the rapid alternate playing or singing of the note required by the melody and the one immediately above it. [German *Pralltriller,* from *prallen* to rebound + *Triller* trill, from Italian *trillo:* see TRILL¹]

pram¹ /pram/ *noun chiefly Brit* a small four-wheeled carriage for a baby, pushed by a person on foot. [by shortening and alteration from *perambulator*]

pram² *or* **praam** /pram, prahm/ *noun* a small lightweight nearly flat-bottomed boat with a broad transom and usu a squared-off bow. [Dutch *praam*]

prana /'prahnə/ *noun* in yoga, controlled breathing considered as a spiritual exercise, or breath considered as a vital force. [Sanskrit *prāṇa* breathing out]

prance¹ /prahns/ *verb intrans* **1** to walk with high dancing steps in a lively and carefree or a silly, affected, and self-important manner: *prancing up and down, sublimely pleased with himself* — Norman Douglas. **2** said of a horse: **a** to move with a springy high-stepping gait. **b** to spring forward from the hind legs with the front legs in the air. ➤➤ **prancer** *noun,* **prancingly** *adv.* [Middle English *prauncen;* earlier history unknown]

prance² *noun* a prancing movement.

prandial /'prandi-əl/ *adj literary* relating to a meal. [Latin *prandium* late breakfast, luncheon]

prang¹ /prang/ *verb trans Brit, informal* to crash or damage (a vehicle or aircraft). [imitative]

prang² *noun Brit, informal* a crash involving a vehicle, aircraft, etc.

prank¹ /prangk/ *noun* a mildly mischievous act; a trick. [origin unknown]

prank² *verb trans formal* to dress or adorn (something) gaily or showily: *The field was pranked with flowers.* ► *verb intrans* to show oneself off. [prob from Dutch *pronken* to strut]

prankster /'prangkstə/ *noun* somebody who plays pranks.

prase /prayz/ *noun* a translucent form of CHALCEDONY (a type of quartz) that is light green in colour. [French *prase* from Latin *prasius* from Greek *prasios* leek green, from *prason* leek]

praseodymium /ˌprayzi·ohˈdimi·əm/ *noun* a silver-white metallic chemical element of the rare-earth group that is soft and ductile, occurs naturally in various minerals, and is used chiefly in making special alloys and in colouring glass: symbol Pr, atomic number 59. [scientific Latin *praseodymium*, from Greek *prasios* (see PRASE) + DIDYMIUM]

prat /prat/ *noun Brit, slang* a foolish or contemptible person. [orig in the sense 'a buttock, buttocks'; origin unknown]

prate /prayt/ *verb intrans* (*often* + about) to talk foolishly and excessively; to chatter. >> **prater** *noun*, **pratingly** *adv*. [Middle English from early Dutch *praten*; related to early Low German *pratelen* PRATTLE[1]]

pratfall *noun informal* **1** a fall on the buttocks. **2** a humiliating mishap or blunder.

pratie /ˈprayti/ *noun chiefly Irish* a potato. [Irish *prátai*, pl of *práta* potato]

pratincole /ˈpratingkohl/ *noun* any of several species of European, African, and Asian birds that have brownish plumage, short legs, long wings, and forked tails. They hunt dragonflies, grasshoppers, etc on the wing and generally live near water: genera *Glareola* and *Stiltia*. [Latin *pratum* meadow + *incola* inhabitant]

pratique /ˈprateek/ *noun* clearance given to an incoming ship by the health authority of a port. [French *pratique*: see PRACTISE]

prattle[1] /ˈpratl/ *verb intrans* to chatter in an artless, childish, or inconsequential manner. >> **prattler** *noun*, **prattlingly** *adv*. [Low German *pratelen*; related to early Dutch *praten* PRATE]

prattle[2] *noun* idle or childish talk.

prau /prow/ *noun* see PROA.

prawn /prawn/ *noun* any of numerous species of widely distributed edible ten-legged crustaceans that resemble large shrimps: genus *Leander* and other genera. [Middle English *prane*; earlier history unknown]

praxis /ˈpraksis/ *noun* (*pl* **praxes** /ˈprakseez/) **1** the exercise or practice of an art, science, or skill, as opposed to theory. **2** *formal* customary practice or conduct. [via medieval Latin from Greek *praxis* doing, action, from *prattein* to do, PRACTISE]

pray[1] /pray/ *verb intrans* **1** (*often* + for/to) to speak to God or a god aloud or in thought making a request or confession, giving thanks or praise, etc. **2** (*usu* + for) to wish or hope fervently. >> **verb trans 1** to appeal to (somebody) earnestly or humbly; *esp* to call on (God or a god) in a prayer: *I pray God they are safe.* **2** to wish or hope fervently for (something): *We all hope and pray it won't happen.* [Middle English *prayen* via Old French *preier* from Latin *precari*, from *prec-, prex* request, PRAYER]

pray[2] *adv formal* used as a polite, often ironically polite, formula accompanying a question, request, or plea: *And what, pray, is that supposed to mean?*

prayer /preə/ *noun* **1a** a personal request, confession, or expression of praise or thanksgiving, addressed to God or a god aloud or in thought: *We each said a prayer for the success and safety of the voyage.* **b** a set order of words used in praying. **2** the action or practice of praying to God or a god: *kneeling in prayer.* **3** (*in pl*) a religious service consisting chiefly of prayers. **4** an earnest request or devout wish. **5** something prayed or earnestly wished for: *My prayer is to see them all come home safely.* ✳ **not to have a prayer** to have no chance of success: *She tried hard but she didn't have a prayer.* [Middle English via Old French *preiere* from Latin *precaria*, fem of *precarius* obtained by entreaty, uncertain, from *prec-, prex* prayer]

prayer book *noun* **1** a book containing prayers for private use or for use in church services. **2** (*usu* **Prayer Book**) = BOOK OF COMMON PRAYER.

prayerful /ˈpreəf(ə)l/ *adj* **1** inclined to prayers; devout. **2** characterized by prayer. >> **prayerfully** *adv*, **prayerfulness** *noun*.

prayer mat *noun* a small Oriental rug used by Muslims to kneel on when praying.

prayer shawl *noun* = TALLITH.

prayer wheel *noun* a revolving cylinder to which written prayers may be attached, used by Tibetan Buddhists.

praying mantis *noun* a large green MANTIS (a predatory insect) that tends to stand half upright with its long forelegs folded in front of it as if in prayer: *Mantis religiosa.*

PRB *abbr* Pre-Raphaelite Brotherhood.

pre- *prefix* forming words, with the meanings: **1a** earlier than; prior to: *prehistoric.* **b** in advance; beforehand: *prefabricate.* **2** preparatory to: *premedical.* **3** situated in front of; anterior to: *premolar.* [Middle English via Old French from Latin *prae-*, from *prae* in front of, before]

preach /preech/ *verb intrans* **1** to deliver a sermon in the course of a religious service. **2** (*often* + at) to give advice, instructions, or warnings in an officious, tiresome, or highly moral manner. >> **verb trans 1a** to speak about, explain, or proclaim (a religious idea or system) in public: *to preach the gospel.* **b** to deliver (a sermon) publicly. **2** to advocate (something) earnestly. [Middle English *prechen* via Old French *prechier* from Latin *praedicare* to proclaim publicly, from PRAE- + *dicare* to proclaim]

preacher *noun* **1** somebody who preaches, *specif* the person who gives the sermon during a church service. **2** *chiefly NAmer* a Protestant clergyman.

preachify /ˈpreechifie/ *verb intrans* (**preachifies, preachified, preachifying**) *informal* to preach, *esp* to give advice or moralize in a long-winded and boring way.

preachment *noun* the act of preaching or a religious or moralizing sermon.

preachy *adj* (**preachier, preachiest**) *informal* characterized by or prone to moralizing. >> **preachily** *adv*, **preachiness** *noun*.

preamble /ˈpreeambl/ *noun* **1** an introductory statement; *specif* that of a constitution or statute. **2** an introductory or preliminary fact or circumstance. [Middle English via French from late Latin *preambulum*, neuter of *praeambulus* walking in front of, from Latin PRAE- + *ambulare* to walk]

preamp /ˈpreeamp/ *noun informal* = PREAMPLIFIER.

preamplifier /ˈpreeˈamplifie·ə/ *noun* an amplifier used to amplify a relatively weak signal, e.g. from a microphone or the pick-up of a record player, before feeding it to the main amplifier.

prearrange /pree·əˈraynj/ *verb trans* to arrange (something) beforehand: *at a prearranged signal.* >> **prearrangement** *noun*.

Preb. *abbr* Prebendary.

prebend /ˈprebənd/ *noun* **1** a stipend provided by a cathedral or collegiate church to a member of its chapter. **2** a clergyman who receives a prebend. >> **prebendal** /priˈbendl/ *adj*. [Middle English *prebende* via French from late Latin *praebenda* subsistence allowance granted by the state, from Latin *praebere* to grant, from PRAE- + *habere* to have, hold]

prebendary *noun* (*pl* **prebendaries**) **1** a canon in a cathedral chapter who receives a prebend. **2** a title given to an honorary canon in the Church of England.

prebiological /ˌpreebie·əˈlojikl/ *adj* relating to or existing at a time before life began, *esp* involved in originating life: *prebiological molecules.*

prebiotic /preebieˈotik/ *adj* = PREBIOLOGICAL.

prec. *abbr* preceding.

Precambrian /preeˈkambri·ən/ *adj* relating to or dating from the earliest aeon of geological history ending about 570 million years ago, during which the earth's crust solidified and the earliest life forms appeared. >> **Precambrian** *noun*.

precancerous /preeˈkansərəs/ *adj* said of a cell or a medical condition: likely to become cancerous or develop into cancer if not treated.

precarious /priˈkeəri·əs/ *adj* **1** characterized by a lack of security or stability, *esp* by the danger of falling. **2** dependent on chance or uncertain circumstances. >> **precariously** *adv*, **precariousness** *noun*. [Latin *precarius*: see PRAYER]

precast /preeˈkahst/ *adj* said of concrete or something made of concrete: cast in the form required before being placed in its final position.

precatory /ˈprekət(ə)ri/ *adj formal* expressing a wish. [late Latin *precatorius*, from Latin *precari*: see PRAY[1]]

precaution /priˈkawsh(ə)n/ *noun* **1** a measure taken beforehand to avoid possible harmful or undesirable consequences; a safeguard. **2** *informal* (*in pl*) contraceptive measures. **3** *formal* care taken in advance; foresight. >> **precautionary** *adj*. [French *précaution* from late Latin *praecaution-, praecautio*, from Latin *praecavēre* to guard against, from PRAE- + *cavēre* to be on one's guard]

precede /priˈseed/ *verb trans* **1a** to be, go, or come ahead or in front of (somebody or something). **b** to be earlier than (somebody or something). **2** (*usu* + with) to introduce or preface (something): *He preceded his address with a welcome to the visitors.* ➤➤ *verb intrans* to go or come before. ➤➤ **preceding** *adj*. [Middle English *preceden* via French from Latin *praecedere*, from PRAE- + *cedere* to go]

Usage note

precede *or* proceed? These two words are sometimes confused. To *precede* is to 'go before': *She preceded me into the room; The meeting had been held on the Tuesday preceding the Easter weekend.* To *proceed* means to 'go forward': *I was proceeding along the High Street; The work is proceeding well.* Only *proceed* can be followed by *to* and another verb: *She then proceeded to read the paragraph in question.*

precedence /'presid(ə)ns/ *noun* **1** greater importance or priority in being dealt with: *Give precedence to the jobs with the shorter deadlines.* **a** the right to be treated as ranking above others on a ceremonial or formal occasion: *A duke has precedence over an earl.* **b** the order of importance given to various ranks and titles on ceremonial occasions.

precedency /'presid(ə)nsi/ *noun* = PRECEDENCE.

precedent[1] /'presid(ə)nt/ *noun* **1** an earlier similar occurrence of something under consideration. **2** something done or said that may serve to justify a subsequent act or statement; *specif* a judicial decision that serves as a rule for similar cases.

precedent[2] /pri'seed(ə)nt, 'presid(ə)nt/ *adj* prior in time, order, arrangement, or significance.

precentor /pri'sentə/ *noun* **1** a leader of the singing of a choir or congregation. **2** a clergyman, *esp* a member of the staff of a cathedral, who directs choral services. ➤➤ **precentorial** /pree-sen'tawri-əl/ *adj*, **precentorship** *noun*. [late Latin *praecentor* from Latin *praecinere* to sing before, from PRAE- + *canere* to sing]

precept /'preesept/ *noun* a command or principle intended as a general rule of conduct. ➤➤ **preceptive** /pri'septiv/ *adj*. [Middle English from Latin *praeceptum*, neuter past part. of *praecipere* to take beforehand, instruct, from PRAE- + *capere* to take]

preceptor /pri'septə/ *noun* a teacher or tutor. ➤➤ **preceptorial** /preesep'tawri-əl/ *adj*.

precession /pri'sesh(ə)n/ *noun* a slow movement of the axis of rotation of a spinning body about another line intersecting it. ➤➤ **precessional** *adj*. [late Latin *praecession-, praecessio* act of preceding, from Latin *praecedere*: see PRECEDE]

precession of the equinoxes *noun* the slow westward motion of the equinoctial points along the ecliptic causing the earlier occurrence of the equinoxes in each successive sidereal year.

pre-Christian *adj* dating from before the beginning of the Christian era.

precinct /'preesingkt/ *noun* **1** (*in pl*) the region immediately surrounding a place; environs. **2** (*also in pl*). **a** an enclosure bounded by the walls surrounding a building. **b** a boundary: *a ruined tower within the precincts of the squire's grounds* — Thomas Love Peacock. **3** an area of a town or city not allowing access to traffic and usu with a specific function: *shopping precinct; university precinct.* **4** *NAmer* an administrative district for election purposes or police control. [Middle English from Latin *praecinctum*, neuter past part. of *praecingere* to gird about, from PRAE- + *cingere* to gird]

preciosity /preshi'ositi/ *noun* (*pl* **preciosities**) exaggerated delicacy and excessive refinement, e.g. in choice or use of language, or an example of this.

precious[1] /'preshəs/ *adj* **1** of great value or high price: *a precious stone.* **2** highly esteemed or cherished; dear: *His friendship was precious to her.* **3** excessively refined; affected. **4** used as an intensifier: highly valued by some but regarded with contempt by the speaker: *You can keep your precious Costa Brava: I prefer Blackpool!* ➤➤ **preciously** *adv*, **preciousness** *noun*. [Middle English via Old French from Latin *pretiosus*, from *pretium* PRICE[1]]

precious[2] *adv* very; extremely: *She has precious little to say on the subject.*

precious[3] *noun* a dear one; a darling: *my precious.*

precious metal *noun* gold, silver, or platinum.

precious stone *noun* a stone that has great value and is used as a jewel, e.g. a diamond, ruby, or emerald.

precipice /'presipis/ *noun* **1** a very steep or perpendicular slope, *esp* a sheer rockface or cliff. **2** disaster, or the brink of disaster. [early French *precipice* from Latin *praecipitium*, from *praecipit-, praeceps* steep, headlong, from PRAE- + *caput* head]

precipitant[1] /pri'sipit(ə)nt/ *adj* unduly hasty or sudden; precipitate. ➤➤ **precipitance** *noun*, **precipitancy** *noun*, **precipitantly** *adv*. [French *précipitant* from Latin *praecipitant-, praecipitans*, present part. of *praecipitare* to throw headlong, from *praecipit-, praeceps*: see PRECIPICE]

precipitant[2] *noun* **1** a chemical agent that causes the formation of a precipitate. **2** a causative factor that precipitates an action, event, or condition, e.g. an emotional state.

precipitate[1] /pri'sipitayt/ *verb trans* **1** to throw (something or somebody) violently; to hurl. **2** to bring about (an event or action) suddenly or unexpectedly: *The failure of government policy precipitated a general election.* **3a** to cause (a substance) to separate out from a solution or suspension. **b** to cause (vapour) to condense and fall as rain, snow, etc. ➤➤ *verb intrans* **1** to separate out from a solution or suspension. **2** to fall as rain, snow, etc. ➤➤ **precipitable** *adj*, **precipitative** /-tətiv/ *adj*, **precipitator** *noun*. [Latin *praecipitatus*, past part. of *praecipitare*: see PRECIPITANT[1]]

precipitate[2] /pri'sipitət/ *noun* a substance separated from a solution or suspension by chemical or physical change, usu as an insoluble or crystalline solid.

precipitate[3] /pri'sipitət/ *adj* **1** acting or carried out very suddenly or with undue haste: *a precipitate departure.* **2** lacking due care or consideration; rash. ➤➤ **precipitately** *adv*, **precipitateness** *noun*.

precipitation /pri,sipi'taysh(ə)n/ *noun* **1** rainfall, snowfall, hail, dew, or condensed moisture from the atmosphere in any other form, or the amount of it. **2** the process of precipitating something or of forming a precipitate. **3** a precipitate. **4** precipitate action.

precipitous /pri'sipitəs/ *adj* **1a** dangerously steep or high. **b** extremely sudden and very severe or calamitous in effect: *a precipitous fall in share prices.* **2** = PRECIPITATE[3] (1). ➤➤ **precipitously** *adv*, **precipitousness** *noun*. [French *précipiteux* from Latin *precipitium*: see PRECIPICE]

precis[1] /'praysee/ *noun* (*pl* **precis** /'praysee(z)/) a concise summary of the essential points, facts, etc of something. [French *précis* from early French *precis*: see PRECISE]

precis[2] *verb trans* (**precising** /'prayseeing/, **precised** /'prayseed/) to make a precis of (a text); to summarize.

precise /pri'sies/ *adj* **1** exact or accurate: *Can you give me a precise figure?* **2** specific or detailed with regard to the nature or facts of something: *I can't be absolutely precise yet about the time of death.* **3** carried out with great attention to accuracy: *precise timing.* **4** distinguished from every other; particular; very: *The door opened at that precise moment.* **5** strictly conforming to a rule, standard, convention, etc; punctilious. ➤➤ **precisely** *adv*, **preciseness** *noun*. [early French *precis* from Latin *praecisus*, past part. of *praecidere* to cut off, from PRAE- + *caedere* to cut]

precisian /pri'sizh(ə)n/ *noun* a person who stresses or practises scrupulous adherence to a strict standard, *esp* of religious observance or morality.

precision /pri'sizh(ə)n/ *noun* **1** the quality or state of being precise; exactness or accuracy. **2** the degree of accuracy with which an operation is performed, a measurement stated, etc. **3** (*used before a noun*) adapted for extremely accurate measurement or operation: *precision instruments.* **4** (*used before a noun*) marked by precision of execution: *precision bombing.* ➤➤ **precisionist** *noun*.

preclinical /pree'klinikl/ *adj* **1** relating to the period in the development of a medical condition before symptoms appear. **2** relating to a medical student's period of theoretical study before patients are encountered. ➤➤ **preclinical** *noun*.

preclude /pri'kloohd/ *verb trans* to make it impossible in advance to do (something) or for (somebody) to do something. ➤➤ **preclusion** /-zh(ə)n/ *noun*, **preclusive** /-siv/ *adj*. [Latin *praecludere*, from PRAE- + *claudere* to close]

precocial /pri'kohsh(ə)l/ *adj* said of the young of a bird: capable of a high degree of independent activity from birth: compare ALTRICIAL. **2** said of a species of bird: having precocial young. [scientific Latin *praecoces* precocial birds, from Latin, pl of *praecoc-, praecox*: see PRECOCIOUS]

precocious /pri'kohshəs/ *adj* **1a** showing or having mature qualities at an unusually early age. **b** *derog* said of a child: behaving, thinking, or speaking in an affectedly adult way. **2** occurring or developing at an exceptionally early time or stage. ➤➤ **precociously** *adv*, **precociousness** *noun*, **precocity** /pri'kositi/ *noun*. [Latin *praecoc-, praecox* early ripening, precocious, from PRAE- + *coquere* to cook]

precognition /preekəg'nish(ə)n/ *noun* the apparent ability to foresee future events; clairvoyance. ⟫ **precognitive** /pree'kognitiv/ *adj.* [late Latin *praecognition-, praecognitio* from Latin *praecognoscere* to know beforehand, from PRAE- + *cognoscere* to know]

pre-Columbian /preekə'lumbi-ən/ *adj* said *esp* of a culture or historical artefact: existing at, dating from, or relating to a time before the arrival of Columbus in America.

preconceive /preekən'seev/ *verb trans* to form (e.g. an opinion) prior to actual knowledge or experience.

preconception /preekən'sepsh(ə)n/ *noun* 1 a preconceived idea. 2 a prejudice.

preconcert /preekən'suht/ *verb trans formal* to organize (something) beforehand, often jointly with other people; to prearrange: *Her little plans and preconcerted speeches had all left her* — George Eliot.

precondition[1] /preekən'dish(ə)n/ *noun* something that must happen or be in existence to enable something else to happen or exist; a prerequisite.

precondition[2] *verb trans* 1 to put (something) into an appropriate condition for a process that is about to take place. 2 to influence or accustom (somebody) in advance to react to particular stimuli or situations in a particular way. ⟫ **preconditioning** *noun*.

preconscious[1] /pree'konshəs/ *adj* not present in the conscious mind but capable of being readily recalled to it. ⟫ **presciously** *adv*.

preconscious[2] *noun* the preconscious part of the mind.

precursor /pri'kuhsə/ *noun* 1a somebody or something that precedes and prepares the way for or signals the approach of somebody or something else; a forerunner. **b** a predecessor. 2 a substance from which another substance is formed. [Latin *praecursor*, from *praecurrere* to run before, from PRAE- + *currere* to run]

precursory *adj* having the character of a precursor; preliminary.

pred. *abbr* predicate.

predacious *or* **predaceous** /pri'dayshəs/ *adj* living by preying on other animals; predatory. [Latin *praedari* (see PREY[2]) + -ACEOUS or *acious* as in RAPACIOUS]

predate /pree'dayt/ *verb trans* 1 to exist at or date from a time before (something or somebody). 2 to assign an earlier date to (e.g. an event).

predation /pri'daysh(ə)n/ *noun* 1 the mode of life of animals that obtain their food primarily by hunting, killing, and eating other animals. 2 the act of preying or plundering; depredation. [Latin *praedation-, praedatio*, from *praedari*: see PREY[2]]

predator /'predətə/ *noun* 1 an animal that lives by hunting, killing, and eating other animals. **2a** somebody who exploits other people for personal gain. **b** a company that is actively seeking to take over other companies.

predatory *adj* 1 said of an animal: living by or adapted for hunting, killing, and eating other animals. 2 said of a person: likely to injure, rob, or exploit others for his or her own gain. 3 relating to or characterized by plunder or robbery. ⟫ **predatorily** *adv*.

predatory pricing *noun* the practice of selling goods at very low prices with the intention of forcing competitors out of the market.

predecease /preedi'sees/ *verb trans* to die before (another person). ⟫ **predecease** *noun*.

predecessor /'preedisesə/ *noun* 1 the previous occupant of a position or office to which another person has succeeded. 2 a person or thing that has been replaced or superseded by something else; a forerunner. 3 an ancestor. [Middle English *predecessour* via French from late Latin *praedecessor*, from PRAE- + *decessor* retiring governor, from *decedere* (see DECEASE[1]) in the sense 'retire from office']

predella /pri'delə/ *noun* 1 a low platform on which an altar stands in a church. 2 a row of small paintings or sculptures attached to or forming the base of an altarpiece. [Italian *predella*, literally 'stool']

predestinarian /ˌpreedesti'neəri-ən/ *noun* a person who believes in predestination. ⟫ **predestinarian** *adj*, **predestinarianism** *noun*. [PREDESTINATION + -ARIAN]

predestinate[1] /pree'destinət/ *adj* destined or determined beforehand. [Middle English from Latin *praedestinatus*, past part. of *praedestinare*: see PREDESTINE]

predestinate[2] /pree'destinayt/ *verb trans* to predestine. ⟫ **predestinator** *noun*.

predestination /ˌpreedesti'naysh(ə)n/ *noun* 1a the religious doctrine that God foreknows and foreordains all events. **b** a religious doctrine, *esp* associated with Calvinism, stating that from the beginning of time God has irrevocably destined some people for salvation and some for damnation. 2 the act of predestining or the fact of being predestined.

predestine /pree'destin/ *verb trans* to decide the fate of (somebody or something) irrevocably in advance. [Middle English *predestinen* via French from Latin *praedestinare*, from PRAE- + *destinare* to determine]

predetermine /preedi'tuhmin/ *verb trans* 1 to decide on or arrange (something) beforehand: *at a predetermined signal*. 2 to impose a direction or tendency on (something) beforehand: *The nature of the terrain predetermined the course the battle would take*. ⟫ **predetermination** /-'naysh(ə)n/ *noun*. [late Latin *praedeterminare*, from Latin PRAE- + *determinare*: see DETERMINE]

predeterminer /preedi'tuhminə/ *noun* in grammar, an adjective or adverb that can occur before a DETERMINER (word such as *the* or *her*) in a noun phrase, e.g. *both* in *both her hands*.

predial /'preedi-əl/ *adj* see PRAEDIAL.

predicable[1] /'predikəbl/ *adj* capable of being asserted. [late Latin *praedicabilis*, from *praedicare*: see PREDICATE[1]]

predicable[2] *noun* something that may be predicated, *esp* any of the five types of predicate in Aristotelian logic: genus, species, difference, property, and accident.

predicament /pri'dikəmənt/ *noun* a difficult, perplexing, or trying situation. [Middle English in the sense 'what is predicated', from late Latin *praedicamentum*, from *praedicare*: see PREDICATE[1]]

predicant[1] /'predikənt/ *adj* relating to preaching, or having preaching as a main activity. [Latin *praedicant-, praedicans*, present part. of *praedicare*: see PREDICATE[1]]

predicant[2] *noun* 1 a member of the Dominicans or any other religious order founded mainly in order to preach. 2 = PREDIKANT.

predicate[1] /'predikət/ *noun* 1 the part of a sentence or clause that contains the verb and says something about the subject. 2 something that is stated or denied of the subject in a logical proposition. [late Latin *praedicatum*, neuter past part. of *praedicare* to assert, predicate, preach, from PRAE- + *dicere* to state]

predicate[2] /'predikət/ *adj* relating to something that has been predicated.

predicate[3] /'predikayt/ *verb trans formal* 1 (+ on/upon) to base or found (something) on something else: *His theory is predicated on recent findings*. 2 to affirm or declare (something). 3 (*usu* + of) to assert (something) to be a quality or property of something or somebody. 4 to imply (something).

predicate calculus /'predikət/ *noun* a branch of symbolic logic in which symbols are used to represent names and predicates within propositions and to analyse their relationships.

predicative /pri'dikətiv/ *adj* 1 said of a modifying word: contained in the predicate of a sentence, e.g. *red* in *the dress is red*: compare ATTRIBUTIVE[1]. 2 relating to a predicate. ⟫ **predicatively** *adv*.

predict /pri'dikt/ *verb trans* to declare in advance that (something) will happen; *esp* to foretell (something) on the basis of observation, experience, or scientific reason. ⟫ **predictor** *noun*. [Latin *praedictus*, past part. of *praedicere*, from PRAE- + *dicere* to say]

predictable *adj* 1 capable of being predicted. 2 *derog* irritatingly obvious and easy to foresee, or always behaving or reacting in an easily foreseeable way. ⟫ **predictability** /-'biliti/ *noun*, **predictably** *adv*.

prediction /pri'diksh(ə)n/ *noun* 1 a statement of what will or is likely to happen in the future; a forecast. 2 the act of predicting. ⟫ **predictive** *adj*, **predictively** *adv*.

predigest /preedi'jest, preedie'jest/ *verb trans* 1 to treat (food) so as to make it easier to digest. 2 to prepare (a book or text) in simplified form to make it easier to understand. ⟫ **predigested** *adj*, **predigestion** *noun*.

predikant *or* **predicant** /predi'kant/ *noun* a minister in the Dutch Reformed Church of South Africa. [Dutch *predikant* via Old French *predicant*, ultimately from Latin *praedicare*: see PREDICATE[1]]

predilection /preedi'leksh(ə)n, predi-/ *noun* a liking or preference: *She admitted to herself that her old friend had still an uneradicated predilection for her society* — Henry James. [French *prédilection* from late Latin *praedilectus*, past part. of *praediligere* to love more, prefer, from PRAE- + *diligere*: see DILIGENT]

predispose /preedi'spohz/ *verb trans* **1** to make (somebody) more likely or more willing to do something: *A good teacher predisposes children to learn*. **2** (+ to) to make (somebody or something) susceptible to something: *Their diet predisposes them to heart disease*. ⮞⮞ **predisposition** /-'zish(ə)n/ *noun*.

prednisolone /pred'nisəlohn/ *noun* a synthetic steroid drug that is used to reduce inflammation and inhibit the action of the immune system, *esp* in the treatment of rheumatoid arthritis. [blend of PREDNISONE and -OL[1]]

prednisone /pred'nisohn/ *noun* a synthetic steroid drug, derived from cortisone, used to treat allergies and rheumatic conditions. [prob from *pregnane* (a saturated steroid hydrocarbon) + DIENE + CORTISONE]

predominant /pri'dominənt/ *adj* **1** constituting the largest part of or element in something; main. **2** having greater strength, influence, or authority than others. ⮞⮞ **predominance** *noun*, **predominantly** *adv*. [via French from late Latin *praedominant-, praedominans*, present part. of *praedominari* to predominate, from Latin PRAE- + *dominari*: see DOMINATE]

predominate /pri'dominayt/ *verb intrans* **1** to be greater in numbers or quantity or more common than any other. **2** to exert a controlling power or influence; to prevail. ⮞⮞ **predomination** /-'naysh(ə)n/ *noun*. [late Latin *praedominatus*, past part. of *praedominari*: see PREDOMINANT]

predynastic /preedi'nastik, preedie-/ *adj* relating to or dating from the period before the establishment of the recognized ruling dynasties in ancient Egypt in about 3000 BC.

preeclampsia /pree-i'klampsi-ə/ *noun* a serious abnormal condition that develops in late pregnancy and is characterized by a sudden rise in blood pressure and fluid retention.

preembryo /pree'embrioh/ *noun* (*pl* **preembryos**) a fertilized ovum in the period before embryonic tissue begins to be differentiated and before implantation in the womb.

preeminent /pri'eminənt/ *adj* superior to or more distinguished than all others, *esp* in a particular field of activity. ⮞⮞ **preeminence** *noun*, **preeminently** *adv*. [Latin *praeeminent-, praeeminens*, present part. of *praeeminere* to be outstanding, from PRAE- + *eminere*: see EMINENT]

preempt /pri'empt/ *verb trans* **1** to render (somebody else's action or intention) pointless or ineffective by acting first; to forestall (something): *The government's decision to build an airport preempted the council's plans*. **2** to take (something) over, *esp* to prevent others having it; to appropriate (something): *The movement was then preempted by a lunatic fringe*. **3** to acquire (something) by preemption. **4** to take the place of (something). ⮞ *verb intrans* to make a preemptive bid in bridge. ⮞⮞ **preemptor** *noun*. [back-formation from PREEMPTION]

preemption /pri'empsh(ə)n/ *noun* **1** acting first in order to forestall others. **2** a prior seizure or appropriation. **3a** the right of purchasing before others. **b** a purchase under this right. [late Latin *praeemption-, praeemptio*, from *praeemere* to buy before, from PRAE- + *emere* to buy]

preemptive /pri'emptiv/ *adj* **1** carried out in order to forestall intended action by others: *a preemptive attack that disabled the enemy*. **2** said of a bid in bridge: high enough to shut out bids by the opponents. **3** relating to or capable of preemption. ⮞⮞ **preemptively** *adv*.

preen /preen/ *verb trans* **1** said of a bird: to clean and smooth (its feathers) with its beak. **2** to dress or smarten (oneself) up. **3** *usu derog* (*often* + on) to pride or congratulate (oneself) on something, *esp* some imagined good quality. ⮞ *verb intrans* **1** to make oneself look smart or attractive in an ostentatious way. **2** to appear to be congratulating oneself; to gloat: *He couldn't help preening after his campaign victory*. **3** said of a bird: to preen its feathers. ⮞⮞ **preener** *noun*. [Middle English *preinen*; earlier history unknown]

preexist /pree-ig'zist/ *verb intrans* to exist in a former state or at a previous time.

preexistence *noun* existence in a former state or at a previous time, *esp* the existence of a soul before it enters a body. ⮞⮞ **preexistent** *adj*.

pref. *abbr* **1** preface. **2** preferred. **3** prefix.

prefab /'preefab/ *noun* a prefabricated structure or building.

prefabricate /pri'fabrikayt/ *verb trans* to make or manufacture the parts of (e.g. a building) at a factory ready for assembly elsewhere. ⮞⮞ **prefabrication** /-'kaysh(ə)n/ *noun*, **prefabricator** *noun*.

preface[1] /'prefəs/ *noun* **1** an introduction to a book, speech, etc. **2** something that precedes or heralds; a preliminary. [Middle English via French from Latin *praefation-, praefatio* foreword, from *praefari* to say beforehand, from PRAE- + *fari* to speak]

preface[2] *verb trans* **1** (*usu* + by/with) to provide a preface or introduction to (something said or written): *She prefaced her remarks with a toast to absent friends*. **2** to be a preliminary or preface to (something). ⮞⮞ **prefacer** *noun*.

prefatory /'prefət(ə)ri/ *adj* constituting or characteristic of a preface; introductory. ⮞⮞ **prefatorily** *adv*. [Latin *praefatus*, past part. of *praefari*: see PREFACE[1]]

prefect /'preefekt/ *noun* **1** *Brit, Aus, NZ* a senior student in a secondary school who is appointed to have some authority over other students. **2** in France, Italy, etc, the chief administrative officer of a department or region. **3** any of various high officials or magistrates in ancient Rome. [Middle English via French from Latin *praefectus*, past part. of *praeficere* to place at the head of, from PRAE- + *facere* to make]

prefecture /'preefekchə/ *noun* **1** the office or official residence of a prefect. **2** the district governed by a prefect. ⮞⮞ **prefectural** /pree'fekchoo(ə)rəl/ *adj*.

prefer /pri'fuh/ *verb trans* (**preferred, preferring**) **1** (*often* + to) to like (something or somebody) better than something or somebody else: *He prefers sports to reading*. **2** *formal* to bring (a charge) against somebody. **3** to give (somebody, *esp* a creditor) priority. **4** *archaic* to give promotion or advancement to (somebody): *Lo, Ambrose Philips is preferred for wit!* — Pope. ⮞⮞ **preferrer** *noun*. [Middle English *preferren* via French from Latin *praeferre* to put before, prefer, from PRAE- + *ferre* to carry]

preferable /'pref(ə)rəbl, prə'fuhrəbl/ *adj* preferred; more desirable: *I can come on either Tuesday or Wednesday, though Tuesday would be preferable*. ⮞⮞ **preferability** /-'biliti/ *noun*.

preferably *adv* as the best or most desirable option: *The box should preferably be lined with straw*.

preference /'pref(ə)rəns/ *noun* **1** (*usu* + for) greater liking for or a tendency to choose one thing rather than another: *He has always shown a preference for older women*. **2** a person, thing, or option preferred; a first choice: *Whisky, gin, or brandy? State your preference!* **3** special favour or consideration given to some over others: *Preference will be given to candidates with a qualification in maths*. **4** priority in the right to receive settlement of a debt. ✳ **for preference** as the preferred option; preferably. [French *préférence*, ultimately from Latin *praeferent-, praeferens*, present part. of *praeferre*: see PREFER]

preference share *noun* a share guaranteed priority over ordinary shares in the payment of dividends and usu in the distribution of assets: compare ORDINARY SHARE.

preferential /prefə'rensh(ə)l/ *adj* **1** showing special or undue favour and consideration: *He complained that the female employees had received preferential treatment*. **2** intended to give a special advantage to certain countries in trade relations. ⮞⮞ **preferentially** *adv*.

preferment *noun* advancement or promotion to a higher rank or office, *esp* in the Church: *A zealous High Churchman was I and so I got preferment* — Anonymous (The Vicar of Bray).

prefigure /pree'figə/ *verb trans* **1** to represent or suggest (something) in advance; to foreshadow (something). **2** to picture or imagine (something) beforehand; to foresee (something). ⮞⮞ **prefiguration** /-'raysh(ə)n/ *noun*, **prefigurative** /-rətiv/ *adj*, **prefigurement** *noun*. [Middle English *prefiguren* from late Latin *praefigurare*, from PRAE- + *figurare* to shape, picture, from *figura*: see FIGURE[1]]

prefix[1] /'preefiks/ *noun* **1** an affix, e.g. *un-* in *unhappy*, placed at the beginning of a word or before a word root: compare INFIX[2], SUFFIX[1]. **2** a title used before a person's name. ⮞⮞ **prefixal** *adj*, **prefixally** *adv*. [Latin *praefixum*, neuter past part. of *praefigere* to fasten before, from PRAE- + *figere* to fasten, FIX[1]]

prefix[2] *verb trans* **1** to attach (something) as a prefix to a word, etc. **2** to add (something) to the beginning: *She prefixed a brief introduction to the article*. **3** to add something to the beginning of (something): *He prefixed his speech with a few complimentary remarks*. [partly from Middle English *prefixen* to fix or appoint beforehand, from early French *prefixer*, from PRE- + *fixer* to fix, from Latin *fixus*: see FIX[1]; partly from PREFIX[1]]

preform /pree'fawm/ *verb trans* to form or shape (something) beforehand. ➤➤ **preform** *noun*, **preformation** /-'maysh(ə)n/ *noun*. [Latin *praeformare*, from PRAE- + *formare* to form, from *forma* FORM¹]

prefrontal /pree'fruntl/ *adj* **1** relating to or situated in the front part of a frontal lobe of the brain. **2** denoting or relating to a bone situated in front of the frontal bone. ➤➤ **prefrontal** *noun*.

preggers /'pregəz/ *adj Brit, informal* = PREGNANT (1). [by alteration]

preglacial /pree'glayshəl, -si-əl/ *adj* occurring before a period of glaciation.

pregnable /'pregnəbl/ *adj formal* capable of being successfully attacked and captured. ➤➤ **pregnability** /-'biliti/ *noun*. [Middle English from early French *prenable*: see IMPREGNABLE¹]

pregnancy /'pregnənsi/ *noun* (*pl* **pregnancies**) **1a** the state of carrying an unborn child or unborn young in the womb. **b** the period of time during which a foetus is carried in the womb. **2** a pregnant quality, *esp* mental inventiveness or richness in ideas or significance.

pregnant /'pregnənt/ *adj* **1** said of a woman or female animal: having an unborn child or unborn young in the womb. **2** rich in significance or implication; meaningful: *a pregnant pause*. **3** full of ideas or resourcefulness; inventive. **4** showing signs of the future; portentous: *the pregnant years of the prewar era*. **5** (+ with) full; teeming: *nature pregnant with life*. ➤➤ **pregnantly** *adv*. [Middle English from Latin *praegnant-*, *praegnans*, alteration of *praegnas*, from PRAE- + *gnatus* born, past part. of *nasci* to be born]

preheat /pree'heet/ *verb trans* to heat (something) before use; *esp* to heat (an oven) to the temperature required for cooking.

prehensile /pri'hensiel, pree-/ *adj* adapted for seizing or grasping, *esp* by wrapping round: *a prehensile tail*. ➤➤ **prehensility** /preehen'siliti/ *noun*. [French *préhensile* from Latin *prehensus*, past part. of *prehendere* to grasp firmly, from PRAE- + *hendere* to grasp]

prehension /pri'hensh(ə)n/ *noun formal* **1** the act of taking hold, seizing, or grasping. **2a** the act of perceiving with the senses. **b** the act of understanding something. [Latin *prehension-*, *prehensio*, from *prehendere*: see PREHENSILE]

prehistoric /preehi'storik/ *adj* **1** existing in, dating from, or relating to the period of human history before written records were made. **2** *informal* extremely old-fashioned or out of date. ➤➤ **prehistorically** *adv*.

prehistorical /preehi'storikl/ *adj* = PREHISTORIC.

prehistory /pree'histəri/ *noun* the prehistoric period of human existence, or the study of this period. ➤➤ **prehistorian** /-'stawri-ən/ *noun*.

preignition /pree-ig'nish(ə)n/ *noun* the detonation of the explosive fuel-air mixture in the cylinder of an internal-combustion engine too early for the engine to operate effectively.

preindustrial /pree-in'dustri-əl/ *adj* occurring in or relating to a period prior to the development of large-scale industry.

prejudge /pree'juj/ *verb trans* to pass judgment on (something or somebody) prematurely or before a full and proper examination: *I do not intend to prejudge the past* — William Whitelaw. ➤➤ **prejudger** *noun*, **prejudgment** *noun*. [early French *prejuger* from Latin *praejudicare*, from PRAE- + *judicare*: see JUDGE¹]

prejudice¹ /'prejoodis, 'prejədis/ *noun* **1a** a preconceived judgment or opinion, *esp* a biased and unfavourable one formed without sufficient reason or knowledge. **b** preconceived or biased judgments generally, or the attitude of mind that gives rise to them. **2** an irrational attitude of hostility directed against an individual, group, or race. **3** in law, disadvantage resulting from some judgment or action of another. ✳ **without prejudice** without affecting any legal right or claim. [Middle English via Old French from Latin *praejudicium* previous judgment, damage, from PRAE- + *judicium* judgment]

prejudice² *verb trans* **1** to cause (somebody) to have a prejudice. **2** to cause harm to (somebody or something) or put them at a disadvantage by some judgment or action.

prejudiced *adj* having or showing a prejudice, *esp* against somebody or something.

prejudicial /prejə'dish(ə)l/ *adj* **1** detrimental. **2** leading to prejudiced judgments. ➤➤ **prejudicially** *adv*.

prelacy /'preləsi/ *noun* (*pl* **prelacies**) **1a** the office of a prelate. **b** prelates considered as a group. **2** a form of church government in which authority rests with high-ranking clergymen.

prelapsarian /preelap'seəri-ən/ *adj* characteristic of or belonging to the time or state before the Fall of Man. [PRE- + Latin *lapsus*; see LAPSE¹]

prelate /'prelət/ *noun* a clergyman of high rank, e.g. a bishop or abbot. [Middle English *prelat* via Old French from medieval Latin *praelatus* one receiving preferment, from PRAE- + *latus*, past part. of *ferre* to carry]

prelim /'preelim/ *noun informal* **1** a preliminary, e.g. a preliminary round in a sports contest. **2** (*in pl*). **a** the first public examinations taken by students at some British universities. **b** in Scotland, school examinations held in order to prepare students for public examinations. **3** (*in pl*) all the pages or material preceding the main text of a published book.

preliminary¹ /pri'limin(ə)ri/ *noun* (*pl* **preliminaries**) **1** something that precedes or is introductory or preparatory to something else: *Let's dispense with the preliminaries and get straight down to business.* **2** a preliminary round in a sports contest. **3** (*in pl*) all the pages or material preceding the main text of a published book. [French *préliminaires* (pl) from medieval Latin *praeliminaris* (adj) preliminary, from Latin PRAE- + *limin-*, *limen* threshold]

preliminary² *adj* preceding and preparing for what is to follow; introductory. ➤➤ **preliminarily** *adv*.

preliterate /pree'litərət/ *adj* denoting a society or culture that has not yet developed the use of writing. ➤➤ **preliterate** *noun*.

prelude¹ /'prelyoohd/ *noun* **1** an introductory or preliminary performance, action, or event. **2a** a musical section or movement introducing the theme or chief subject or serving as an introduction, e.g. to an opera. **b** a short separate concert piece, usu for piano or orchestra. ➤➤ **preludial** /pri'l(y)oohdi-əl/ *adj*. [early French *prelude* from medieval Latin *praeludium*, from *praeludere* to play beforehand, from PRAE- + *ludere* to play]

prelude² *verb trans* to serve as prelude to (something). ➤➤ **preluder** *noun*.

premarital /pree'maritl/ *adj* occurring before marriage: *premarital sex*.

premature /premə'tyooə, 'premətyooə/ *adj* **1** happening, arriving, existing, or performed before the proper or usual time: *The question now is whether we should take a premature lunch here, or run our chance of starving before we reach the buffet at Newhaven* — Conan Doyle. **2** said of a human baby: born three or more weeks before the end of the normal gestation period. **3** hasty or impulsive. ➤➤ **prematurely** *adv*, **prematureness** *noun*, **prematurity** *noun*. [Latin *praematurus* too early, from PRAE- + *maturus* ripe, MATURE¹]

premaxilla /preemak'silə/ *noun* (*pl* **premaxillae** /-lee/) either of the pair of bones that form the front part of the upper jaw of most vertebrate animals and lie in front of the maxillae (see MAXILLA). ➤➤ **premaxillary** *adj* or *noun*. [scientific Latin]

premed /'pree'med, 'preemed/ *noun informal* **1** = PREMEDICATION. **2** a premedical student.

premedical /pree'medikl/ *adj* preceding or preparing for the professional study of medicine.

premedication /,preemedi'kaysh(ə)n/ *noun* the drugs that prepare a patient awaiting surgery to receive a general anaesthetic.

premeditate /pri'meditayt, pree-/ *verb trans* to think over and plan (something) beforehand: *premeditated murder*. ➤➤ **premeditative** /-tətiv/ *adj*, **premeditator** *noun*. [Latin *praemeditatus*, past part. of *praemeditari*, from PRAE- + *meditari* to MEDITATE]

premeditation /pri,medi'taysh(ə)n/ *noun* the planning of an act beforehand, *esp* as evidence of intent to commit that act.

premenstrual /pree'menstrooəl/ *adj* relating to or occurring in the period just before menstruation: *premenstrual tension*. ➤➤ **premenstrually** *adv*.

premenstrual syndrome *noun* a condition experienced by some women just before menstruation, involving emotional tension, mood swings, headaches, fluid retention, etc.

premier¹ /'premi-ə/ *adj* **1** first in position, rank, or importance; principal. **2** first in time; earliest. [Middle English *primier* via early French *premier* first, chief, from Latin *primarius*: see PRIMARY¹]

premier² *noun* **1** = PRIME MINISTER. **2** in Canada and Australia, the head of government in a province or state. [French, from *premier* (adj): see PREMIER¹]

premiere[1] /'premieə, 'premi·ə/ *noun* a first public performance of a play, film, opera, etc. [French *première*, fem of *premier*: see PREMIER[1]]

premiere[2] *verb trans* to give a first public performance of (a play, film, etc). ➤ *verb intrans* **1** to have a first public performance. **2** to appear for the first time as a star performer.

premiership *noun* **1** the position or office of a premier. **2a** a sports league or championship. **b** (**the Premiership**) the top division of the league competition for professional football clubs in England.

premillennial /preemi'leni·əl/ *adj* coming before a millennium. ➤➤ **premillennially** *adv*.

premillennialism *noun* the belief that Christ will return to earth for the Last Judgment before the beginning of the MILLENNIUM (a period of a thousand years of peace and happiness on earth). ➤➤ **premillennialist** *noun*.

premise[1] *or* **premiss** /'premis/ *noun* **1** a proposition stated or assumed as a basis of argument or inference; *specif* either of the first two propositions of a logical syllogism from which the conclusion is drawn. **2** something assumed or taken for granted; a presupposition. [Middle English *premisse* via French from Latin *praemissa*, fem past part. of *praemittere* to place ahead, from PRAE- + *mittere* to send]

premise[2] *verb trans* **1** to presuppose or postulate (something). **2** to state (something) as a premise or introduction to what follows.

premises *pl noun* **1a** a piece of land with the buildings on it. **b** a building or part of a building, *esp* as occupied and used for commercial purposes. **2** matters previously stated; *specif* the preliminary and explanatory part of a legal deed.

Word history ————————————————
(sense 1) because the buildings or parts of a building would be detailed in the preliminary part of a legal deed, and would then be referred to in the deed as 'the premises'. *Premises* actually entered English in the 14th cent. as a technical term for initial propositions in logic. The legal sense arose in the 15th cent., and the more general use for a building and grounds was established in the 18th cent.

premiss /'premis/ *noun* see PREMISE[1].

premium /'preemi·əm/ *noun* **1** the sum paid in order to obtain insurance for something or somebody. **2a** a sum added to the standard price, wage, etc, paid chiefly as an incentive; a bonus. **b** the amount by which the price at which something sells exceeds its nominal value. **3** a high value or a value in excess of that normally expected: *We put a premium on accuracy.* **4** *chiefly NAmer* (used before a noun) of exceptional quality or amount: *wine made from premium grapes.* ✳ **at a premium** valuable because rare or difficult to obtain: *Flats in Central London are at a premium.* [Latin *praemium* booty, profit, reward, from PRAE- + *emere* to take, buy]

Premium Bond *noun* a British government bond that is issued in units of £1 and which instead of earning interest is entered into a monthly draw for money prizes.

premolar /pree'mohlə/ *noun* a tooth situated between the canine and molar teeth. ➤➤ **premolar** *adj*.

premonition /premə'nish(ə)n/ *noun* **1** a strong feeling or intuition that something, *esp* something unpleasant, is going to happen; a presentiment: *She felt a premonition of danger.* **2** *formal* a warning of something to come; a forewarning: *a premonition of the troubles that lay in store.* ➤➤ **premonitory** /pri'monit(ə)ri/ *adj*. [via French from late Latin *praemonition-, praemonitio*, from Latin *praemonēre* to warn in advance, from PRAE- + *monēre* to warn]

Premonstratensian /ˌpreemonstrə'tensh(ə)n/ *noun* a member of a religious order founded by St Norbert at Prémontré in France in 1120. ➤➤ **Premonstratensian** *adj*. [medieval Latin *praemonstratensis* of *Prémontré*, an abbey in N France]

prenatal /pree'naytl/ *adj* occurring or being in a stage before birth. ➤➤ **prenatally** *adv*.

prenominal /pree'nomin(ə)l/ *adj* placed before a noun.

prentice /'prentis/ *noun archaic* = APPRENTICE[1].

prenuptial /pree'nupsh(ə)l/ *adj* occurring or made before marriage.

prenuptial agreement *noun* a contract made between a couple before they marry in which they set down how their assets are to be divided in the event of a divorce.

preoccupation /priˌokyoo'paysh(ə)n, pree-/ *noun* **1** (*often* + with) complete mental absorption or obsession. **2** something that absorbs all one's attention. [Latin *praeoccupation-, praeoccupatio* act of seizing beforehand, from *praeoccupare* to seize beforehand, from PRAE- + *occupare*: see OCCUPY]

preoccupied /pri'okyoopied/ *adj* (*often* + with) devoting all one's thoughts and attention to something, or lost in thought.

preoccupy /pri'okyoopie/ *verb trans* (**preoccupies, preoccupied, preoccupying**) **1** to engage the attention of (somebody) to the exclusion of other things. **2** to take possession of or occupy (something) in advance or before another person.

preoperative /pree'op(ə)rətiv/ *adj* occurring in the period preceding a surgical operation. ➤➤ **preoperatively** *adv*.

preordain /pree·aw'dayn/ *verb trans* to decree or decide (something) in advance. ➤➤ **preordainment** *noun*, **preordination** /-di'naysh(ə)n/ *noun*.

prep /prep/ *noun* **1** *Brit* homework done at or away from school. **2** *informal* = PREPARATORY SCHOOL. [short for PREPARATION]

prep. *abbr* **1** preparation. **2** preparatory. **3** preposition.

prepackage /pree'pakij/ *verb trans* to package (e.g. food) before offering it for sale to the consumer.

prepaid /pree'payd/ *verb* past tense and past part. of PREPAY.

preparation /prepə'raysh(ə)n/ *noun* **1** the work or activity of preparing. **2** (*usu in pl*) a preparatory act or measure: *He had made careful preparations for the journey.* **3** the state of being prepared; readiness. **4** something prepared, *esp* a medicine: *a preparation for colds.* **5** in music, lessening the impact of a dissonant note in a chord by including it in the previous chord as a consonant note. [Middle English *preparacion* via French from Latin *praeparation-, praeparatio*, from *praeparare*: see PREPARE]

preparative[1] /pri'parətiv/ *noun* something that prepares the way for or serves as a preliminary to something else.

preparative[2] *adj* = PREPARATORY.

preparatory /pri'parət(ə)ri/ *adj* **1** preparing or intended to prepare for something; introductory. **2** (+ to) in preparation for something: *He always takes a deep breath preparatory to drinking.* ➤➤ **preparatorily** *adv*.

preparatory school *noun* **1** *Brit* a private school preparing pupils for entrance to a public school. **2** *NAmer* a private school preparing pupils for college.

prepare /pri'peə/ *verb trans* **1a** to make (something) ready beforehand for some purpose, use, or activity: *The ground was prepared for sowing.* **b** to put (somebody) into a suitable frame of mind for something: *They prepared her gradually for the bad news.* **2** to work out the details of (something); to plan (something) in advance: *He was already preparing his strategy for the coming campaign.* **3a** to put (something) together: *prepare a prescription.* **b** to draw up (something) in written form: *prepare a report.* **4** in music, to moderate the effect of (a discordant note) by using it as a consonant note in the previous chord. ➤ *verb intrans* to get ready; to make preparations: *Whenever I prepare for a journey I prepare as though for death. Should I never return, all is in order* — Katherine Mansfield. ✳ **to be prepared to do something** to be willing to do something. ➤➤ **prepared** *adj*, **preparer** *noun*. [Middle English *preparen* via French from Latin *praeparare*, from PRAE- + *parare* to procure, prepare]

preparedness /pri'peəridnis, pri'peədnis/ *noun* a state of readiness to act or react, *esp* of having made adequate preparations for war.

prepay /pree'pay/ *verb trans* (*past tense and past part.* **prepaid** /pree'payd/) to pay for (something) in advance: *postage prepaid.* ➤➤ **prepayment** *noun*.

prepense /pri'pens/ *adj* in law, planned beforehand; premeditated: *malice prepense.* ➤➤ **prepensely** *adv.* [alteration (influenced by *pre-*) of Middle English *purpensed*, past part. of *purpensen* to deliberate, premeditate, from Old French *purpenser*, from *pur-* PRO-[1] + *penser* to think, from Latin *pensare*]

preponderant /pri'pond(ə)rənt/ *adj* **1** occurring in greater number or quantity. **2** having superior weight, force, or influence; predominant. ➤➤ **preponderance** *noun*, **preponderantly** *adv*.

preponderate /pri'pondərayt/ *verb intrans* **1** (*often* + over) to occur in greater or the greatest number or with greater or the greatest frequency. **2** to predominate in influence, power, or importance. ➤➤ **preponderation** /-'raysh(ə)n/ *noun.* [Latin *praeponderatus*, past part. of *praeponderare*, from PRAE- + *ponder-, pondus* weight]

prepone /pree'pohn/ *verb trans Indian* to move (something) forward to an earlier time. ➤➤ **preponement** *noun.* [PRE- + POSTPONE]

preposition /prepə'zish(ə)n/ *noun* a word or group of words, e.g. *by*, *on*, *from*, or *on account of*, that links a noun, pronoun, etc to another part of the sentence, as in 'Put it *on* the floor' and 'Where did they come *from*?' ⫸ **prepositional** *adj*, **prepositionally** *adv*. [Middle English *preposicioun* from Latin *praeposition-*, *praepositio*, from *praeponere* to put in front, from PRAE- + *ponere* to put]

prepositive /pri'pozətiv/ *adj* said of a word: placed in front of another word that it modifies or relates to. ⫸ **prepositively** *adv*. [late Latin *praepositivus* from Latin *praepositus* put before, from *praeponere*: see PREPOSITION]

prepossess /preepə'zes/ *verb trans* **1** *formal* to prejudice (somebody), *esp* in favour of somebody or something. **2** to cause (somebody) to be preoccupied with an idea, belief, or attitude.

prepossessing *adj* tending to create a favourable impression; attractive. ⫸ **prepossessingly** *adv*.

prepossession /preepə'zesh(ə)n/ *noun formal* **1** an opinion or impression formed beforehand; a prejudice. **2** an exclusive concern with one idea or object; a preoccupation.

preposterous /pri'post(ə)rəs/ *adj* ridiculous and absurd. ⫸ **preposterously** *adv*, **preposterousness** *noun*. [Latin *praeposterus*, literally 'with the hindside in front', from PRAE- + *posterus*: see POSTERIOR[1]]

prepotent /pree'poht(ə)nt/ *adj* **1** *formal* having great or the greatest power, authority, or influence; preeminent. **2** said of a parent: able to transmit more hereditary characteristics to its offspring than the other parent. ⫸ **prepotency** *noun*, **prepotently** *adv*. [Middle English from Latin *praepotent-*, *praepotens*, from PRAE- + *potens*: see POTENT[1]]

preppy[1] *or* **preppie** /'prepi/ *adj* (**preppier**, **preppiest**) *chiefly NAmer* **1** behaving like or typical of somebody educated at a preparatory school in the USA. **2** said of clothes or a person's way of dressing: neat, smart, and stylishly understated.

preppy[2] *or* **preppie** *noun chiefly NAmer* a person who is or resembles a student or former student at a preparatory school in the USA; a typical product of private secondary education.

preprandial /pree'prandi-əl/ *adj* suitable for or occurring in the time just before a meal: *a preprandial drink*.

preprint /pree'print/ *noun* the printing of a speech or paper before its formal publication or delivery.

prep school *noun* = PREPARATORY SCHOOL.

prepuce /'preepyoohs/ *noun* the foreskin, or a similar fold surrounding the clitoris. ⫸ **preputial** /pree'pyoohsh(ə)l/ *adj*. [Middle English via French from Latin *praeputium*]

prequel /'preekwəl/ *noun* a book, film, etc that portrays the events leading up to those described in an already existing work. [PRE- + -*quel* as in SEQUEL]

Pre-Raphaelite[1] /,pree 'rafəliet, -fi-əliet/ *noun* a member of the Pre-Raphaelite Brotherhood.

Pre-Raphaelite[2] *adj* **1** produced by or typical of the Pre-Raphaelite Brotherhood or any of its members. **2** said of a woman: having an appearance typical of Pre-Raphaelite painting, *esp* with a pale skin and abundant auburn hair. ⫸ **Pre-Raphaelitism** *noun*.

Pre-Raphaelite Brotherhood *noun* a group of English artists formed in 1848 who aimed to restore the artistic principles and practices of the early Renaissance and whose work is characterized by richness of colour and detail and religious and legendary subjects painted from nature. [named after *Raphael* (Raffaello Santi) d.1520, Italian painter]

prerecord /pree-ri'kawd/ *verb trans* to record (material for broadcasting) in advance of presentation or use.

pre-release *noun* something occurring or issued before the official date of release, e.g. a public showing of a film before its official date of release.

prerequisite /pri'rekwizit/ *noun* a requirement that must be satisfied in advance. ⫸ **prerequisite** *adj*.
Usage note
prerequisite *or* perquisite? See note at PERQUISITE.

prerogative[1] /pri'rogətiv/ *noun* **1** an exclusive or special right or privilege belonging to a person or group of people by virtue of rank or status. **2** any right or privilege. **3** the discretionary power possessed by the Crown. [Middle English via French from Latin *praerogativa*, Roman political division voting first in one of the

public assemblies, privilege, fem past part. of *praerogare* to ask for an opinion before another, from PRAE- + *rogare* to ask]

prerogative[2] *adj* having or relating to a prerogative.

Pres. *abbr* President.

pres. *abbr* present.

presage[1] /'presij/ *noun* **1** something that foreshadows or portends a future event; an omen. **2** an intuition of what is going to happen in the future; a presentiment. ⫸ **presageful** *adj*. [Middle English from Latin *praesagium*, from *praesagire* to forebode, from PRAE- + *sagire* to perceive keenly]

presage[2] /'presij, pri'sayj/ *verb trans* **1** to give an omen or warning of (something); to portend (something). **2** to forecast or predict (something). **3** to have a presentiment of (something).

Presb. *abbr* Presbyterian.

presby- *or* **presbyo-** *comb. form* forming words, denoting: old age: *presbyopia*. [medieval Latin from Greek *presby-* elder, from *presbys* old man]

presbyopia /prezbi'ohpi-ə/ *noun* a visual condition of old age in which loss of elasticity of the lens of the eye causes an inability to focus sharply for near vision. ⫸ **presbyopic** /-'opik/ *adj and noun*.

presbyter /'prezbitə/ *noun* **1** a member of the governing body of an early Christian Church. **2** = ELDER[2] (3). **3** in some episcopal churches, an official answerable to a bishop. ⫸ **presbyterate** /-'bitərət/ *noun*. [medieval Latin from Greek *presbyteros* elder, comparative of *presbys* old man, priest]

presbyterial /prezbi'tiəri-əl/ *adj* relating to presbyters or a presbytery.

Presbyterian[1] /prezbi'tiəri-ən/ *adj* relating to or constituting a Christian Church governed by elected representative bodies and traditionally Calvinistic in doctrine. ⫸ **Presbyterianism** *noun*.

Presbyterian[2] *noun* a member of a Presbyterian Church.

presbytery /'prezbit(ə)ri/ *noun* (*pl* **presbyteries**) **1** a local ruling body in Presbyterian Churches. **2** the house of a Roman Catholic parish priest. **3** the part of a church, east end of the chancel, reserved for the officiating clergy. [Middle English *presbytory* part of church reserved for clergy, via late Latin from Greek *presbyterion* group of presbyters, from *presbyteros*: see PRESBYTER]

preschool /pree'skoohl, 'preeskoohl/ *adj* relating to the period from infancy to first attendance at a primary school. ⫸ **preschooler** *noun*.

prescience /'presi-əns/ *noun* foreknowledge of events; foresight. ⫸ **prescient** *adj*, **presciently** *adv*. [Middle English from late Latin *praescientia*, from Latin *praescient-*, *praesciens*, present part. of *praescire* to know beforehand, from PRAE- + *scire* to know]

prescind /pri'sind/ *verb trans formal* (+ from) to separate (something) in the mind; to abstract (something). ⫸ *verb intrans formal* (+ from) to withdraw one's attention. [Latin *praescindere* to cut off in front, from PRAE- + *scindere* to cut]

prescribe /pri'skrieb/ *verb trans* **1a** said of a doctor: to order or recommend (a drug, medicine, or treatment) as a remedy for an illness. **b** to recommend (something) to somebody as likely to have a beneficial effect. **2** to give specific and authoritative instructions regarding (something); to lay (something) down: *the penalty prescribed by law*. ⫸ *verb intrans* **1** to write or give medical prescriptions. **2** to lay down a rule; to dictate. **3** to claim a title to something by right of prescription. ⫸ **prescriber** *noun*. [Latin *praescribere* to write at the beginning, dictate, order, from PRAE- + *scribere* to write]
Usage note
prescribe *or* proscribe? To *prescribe* is what doctors do – they specify a particular medicine for a patient. It means 'to lay down or order' positively that something should be done: *in the form prescribed by law*. To *proscribe* is a much rarer word and it has the opposite meaning - 'to forbid' or 'to ban': *Such practices were considered immoral and were proscribed by law*.

prescript /pri'skript, 'preeskript/ *noun formal* something laid down as a rule. [Middle English from Latin *praescriptus*, past part. of *praescribere*: see PRESCRIBE]

prescription /pri'skripsh(ə)n/ *noun* **1** a written direction or order for the preparation and use of a medicine, or the medicine prescribed. **2** written instructions for an optician specifying the corrective lenses required by somebody. **3** the action of laying down authoritative rules or directions. **4a** the establishment of a claim to something by use and enjoyment of it over a long period. **b** a claim founded on ancient or long-standing custom. [Middle

English via Old French from Latin *praescription-, praescriptio* from *praescribere*: see PRESCRIBE]

prescriptive /pri'skriptiv/ *adj* **1** giving instructions or laying down rules, e.g. regarding the correct use of language. **2** said of a right, title, claim, etc: established by, founded on, or arising from prescription. ➤➤ **prescriptively** *adv*.

preselector /preesi'lektə/ *noun* a system of gears, e.g. in a motor vehicle transmission, that enables a gear to be selected before it is actually engaged.

presence /'prez(ə)ns/ *noun* **1** the fact or condition of being present. **2** the immediate proximity of a person: *They never looked at ease in her presence*. **3** something non-physical that is felt to be present, such as a spirit. **4** a body of people playing an influential role in a place: *the withdrawal of the Soviet presence in eastern Europe*. **5a** a quality of poise, distinction, or personal magnetism that enables a person, *esp* a performer, to impress others: *She had great stage presence*. **b** a dignified bearing or appearance. ✳ **make one's presence felt** to compel attention and exert an influence on a situation.

presence of mind *noun* the ability to retain one's self-possession and act calmly in emergencies or difficult situations.

present[1] /'prez(ə)nt/ *noun* something presented; a gift. [Middle English from Old French *present* from *presenter*: see PRESENT[2]]

present[2] /pri'zent/ *verb trans* **1a** (+ to) to give (something) formally or ceremonially: *The Mayor will present the prizes this year*. **b** (+ with) to give or award something to (somebody) formally or ceremonially. **c** (+ with) to allow (somebody) to gain something without effort: *These circumstances presented them with their best opportunity*. **d** (+ with) to force (somebody) to deal with a problem or difficulty. **e** to introduce (somebody) formally. **2a** to bring (e.g. a play or performer) before the public. **b** to act as a presenter of (e.g. a television or radio programme). **c** to offer (a particular type of appearance) to the view of others; to show or exhibit (something). **3a** to submit (something written) for approval or consideration. **b** to describe or explain (e.g. a plan, idea, or policy) in a particular way. **c** to act the part of or perform (somebody or something), *esp* in a particular or distinctive way. **4** (*often* + to) to constitute or pose (a problem or difficulty). **5** *formal* to aim, point, or direct (e.g. a weapon) so as to face something or in a particular direction. **6** (+ to) to nominate (a clergyman) to a BENEFICE (ecclesiastical office). ➤ *verb intrans* **1** (*usu* + with) to come forward for medical examination, *esp* showing particular symptoms: *A patient rarely presents during the vesicular phase* — A B Wade. **2** to be seen, *esp* in a particular form; to appear: *a tumour that presents as an axillary mass*. ✳ **present arms** to hold a weapon, *esp* a rifle, upright in front of the body as a salute. **present itself** said *esp* of an opportunity or circumstance: to arise; to come about. **present oneself** to be present; to appear. [Middle English *presenten* via Old French *presenter* from Latin *praesentare*, from *praesent-, praesens*: see PRESENT[3]]

present[3] /'prez(ə)nt/ *adj* **1a** in or at a usu specified place: *He wasn't present at the meeting*. **b** existing in something mentioned or understood: *Methane and air have to be present in the right quantities for combustion to take place*. **2** now existing or in progress: *Time present and time past are both perhaps present in time future* — T S Eliot. **3** currently doing something or being discussed, dealt with, or considered: *as far as the present writer is concerned*. **4** denoting or relating to a verb tense that expresses present time or the time of speaking. ➤➤ **presentness** *noun*. [Middle English via Old French from Latin *praesent-, praesens*, present part. of *praeesse* to be before one, from PRAE- + *esse* to be]

present[4] /'prez(ə)nt/ *noun* **1** (**the present**) the time now in progress. **2** in language, a verb form describing a current event or state. **3** *formal* (*in pl*) the present words or statements. ✳ **at present** now. **for the present** now and for some time in the future; for the time being.

presentable /pri'zentəbl/ *adj* **1** fit to be seen or inspected. **2** fit in dress or manners to appear in company: *I must just make myself presentable for dinner*. ➤➤ **presentability** /-'biliti/ *noun*, **presentableness** *noun*, **presentably** *adv*.

presentation /prezən'taysh(ə)n/ *noun* **1a** the manner in which something is set forth, laid out, or presented. **b** the act or process of presenting something. **2a** something offered or given; a gift. **b** an occasion on which something, e.g. a gift or an award, is presented. **3a** an informative talk or lecture on a subject, often with illustrative material. **b** a descriptive or persuasive account, e.g. by somebody selling a product. **4** a formal introduction. **5** the

position in which the foetus lies in labour in relation to the mouth of the uterus. ➤➤ **presentational** *adj*.

presentationism *noun* in philosophy, the theory that the mind is directly aware of items in the external world: compare REPRESENTATIONALISM.

presentative /pri'zentətiv/ *adj* known or capable of being known directly rather than through cogitation.

present-day /'prez(ə)nt/ *adj* now existing or occurring; current or modern.

presenter /pri'zentə/ *noun* somebody who presents something; *specif* a broadcaster who introduces and provides comments during a programme.

presentient /pri'sensh(ə)nt, -ti·ənt, pri'zen-/ *adj formal* having a presentiment. [Latin *praesentient-, praesentiens*, present part. of *praesentire*: see PRESENTIMENT]

presentiment /pri'zentimənt/ *noun* a feeling that something is about to happen; a premonition: *Presentiments of strange discoveries hovered round me* — Herman Melville. ➤➤ **presentimental** /-'mentl/ *adj*. [French *pressentiment* from *pressentir* to have a presentiment, from Latin *praesentire* to feel beforehand, from PRAE- + *sentire* to feel]

presently /'prez(ə)ntli/ *adv* **1** before long; soon: *I'll be with you presently*. **2** at the present time; now: *She's presently unemployed*. **3** *archaic* immediately: *Dispatch it presently; the hour draws on* — Shakespeare.

Usage note

The standard British English meaning of *presently* used to be 'soon', 'in a minute': *I'll be with you presently*. What used to be thought of as an American or Scottish meaning 'now', 'at present', or 'currently' (*He's presently engaged with a client*) is becoming increasingly widely used in British English generally. The tense of the verb is usually an indicator of which sense is intended: used with the future tense the meaning is 'soon'; with the present tense the meaning is 'now'. Care should be taken to avoid the ambiguity in a sentence such as: *He's presently starting a new job*.

presentment /pri'zentmənt/ *noun* **1** the act of presenting a formal statement to an authority; *specif* a statement made on oath by a jury of a matter of fact within their own knowledge. **2** an act of offering a document that calls for acceptance or payment.

present participle /'prez(ə)nt/ *noun* a participle, e.g. *dancing, being*, expressing a current event or state.

present perfect /'prez(ə)nt/ *noun* a verb tense that expresses completion of an action at or before the time of speaking, e.g. *We have finished*.

preservationist /prezə'vaysh(ə)nist/ *noun* somebody who supports the preservation of historical or archaeological artefacts or sites; a conservationist.

preservation order /prezə'vaysh(ə)n/ *noun chiefly Brit* an order by a government or local authority requiring the owner of a historic building or a piece of land of special value or interest to preserve and maintain it.

preservative /pri'zuhvətiv/ *noun* something that preserves or has the power to preserve, *specif* a substance used to protect food, wood, etc against decay, discoloration, or spoilage. ➤➤ **preservative** *adj*.

preserve[1] /pri'zuhv/ *verb trans* **1a** to keep (something) in its original or present condition, in good condition, or free from decay. **b** to keep (something) in existence. **2** to maintain (an appearance or type of behaviour) in spite of adverse circumstances or provocation: *She preserves her habitual calm at all times*. **3** to keep (somebody or something) safe from injury, harm, or destruction; to protect. **4a** to can, pickle, or similarly prepare (a perishable food) to prevent decomposition and keep it for future use. **b** to make a preserve of (fruit). **5** to keep and protect (e.g. land or game) for private, *esp* sporting, use. ➤➤ **preservable** *adj*, **preservation** /prezə'vaysh(ə)n/ *noun*, **preserver** *noun*. [Middle English *preserven* via French from late Latin *praeservare* to guard beforehand, from Latin PRAE- + *servare* to keep, guard, observe]

preserve[2] *noun* **1** a preparation, e.g. a jam or jelly, consisting of fruit preserved by cooking whole or in pieces with sugar. **2** an area restricted for the preservation of natural resources, e.g. animals or trees, *esp* one used for regulated hunting or fishing. **3** something, e.g. a sphere of activity, reserved for certain people.

preset[1] /pree'set/ *verb trans* (**presetting**, *past tense and past part*. **preset**) to set (something) beforehand; *esp* to set a timing device on (an appliance) so that it switches itself on or off at a particular time. >>> **preset** *adj*, **presettable** *adj*.

preset[2] /'preeset/ *noun* a control or device that presets an appliance.

preshrunk /pree'shrungk/ *adj* said of a material: subjected to a process during manufacture designed to reduce later shrinking.

preside /pri'zied/ *verb intrans* **1** to occupy the place of authority, e.g. in a meeting or court. **2** (+ over) to exercise guidance, authority, or control. **3** (+ at) to perform as chief instrumentalist: *She presided at the organ.* **4** to be prominent: *the presiding genius of the company.* >>> **presider** *noun*. [Latin *praesidēre*, literally 'to sit in front or at the head of', from PRAE- + *sedēre* to sit]

presidency /'prezid(ə)nsi/ *noun* (*pl* **presidencies**) **1** the office of president. **2** the period during which a president holds office. **3** the action or function of somebody who presides; superintendence.

president /'prezid(ə)nt/ *noun* **1** (*often* **President**) an elected head of state in a republic. **2** *chiefly NAmer* the chief officer of an organization, e.g. a business corporation or university. **3** an official chosen to preside over a meeting or assembly. >>> **presidential** /-'densh(ə)l/ *adj*, **presidentially** /-'densh(ə)li/ *adv*. [Middle English via French from Latin *praesident-, praesidens*, present part. of *praesidēre*: see PRESIDE]

presiding officer *noun* the chairperson of a legislative assembly, e.g. the officer of the Scottish Parliament, the Northern Ireland Assembly, or the National Assembly for Wales corresponding in function to the Speaker of the House of Commons.

presidium *or* **praesidium** /pri'sidi·əm, pri'zi-/ *noun* (*pl* **presidia** /-di·ə/ *or* **presidiums**) a permanent executive committee in a Communist country. [Russian *prezidium* from Latin *praesidium* garrison, from *praesidēre*: see PRESIDE]

pre-Socratic *adj* denoting or relating to Greek philosophers or philosophy before Socrates. >>> **pre-Socratic** *noun*.

press[1] /pres/ *verb trans* **1a** to push firmly and steadily against (something). **b** to move (something) in a specified direction by pushing it. **2a** to squeeze out the juice or contents of (e.g. fruit). **b** to squeeze (something) to a desired density, smoothness, or shape: *pressed flowers*. **3** to iron (clothes, etc). **4a** to try hard to persuade (somebody); to entreat. **b** to harass or exert pressure on (somebody). **5** to lay emphasis or insist on (something): *He continued to press his point*. **6** to follow through (a course of action): *They decided not to press their claim*. **7** to clasp (e.g. somebody's hand or arm) in affection or courtesy. **8** to manufacture (e.g. a record) from a mould or matrix. > *verb intrans* **1** to exert pressure. **2** to force or push one's way, or make one's way determinedly. **3** to crowd closely; to mass. **4** (+ for) to make a strong effort to get something or persuade somebody to do something: *Car workers are pressing for salary increases*. **5** to require haste or speed in action: *Time is pressing*. **6** to come to a desired condition, *esp* of smoothness, by being pressed. >>> **presser** *noun*. [Middle English *pressen* via early French *presser* from Latin *pressare* to keep pressing, frequentative of *premere* to press]

press[2] *noun* **1** an apparatus or machine by which pressure is applied, e.g. for shaping material, extracting liquid, or compressing something. **2a** = PRINTING PRESS. **b** a publishing house or printing firm, or its premises. **3** (**the press**) (*treated as sing. or pl*). **a** newspapers and magazines collectively. **b** journalists collectively. **c** (*used before a noun*) by, for, or to do with newspapers and journalists: *press coverage*. **4** comment or notice in newspapers and magazines: *The proposal has so far received a bad press*. **5** an action of pressing or pushing; pressure. **6** a crowd of people; a throng. **7** a cupboard, *esp* one for books or clothes. ✳ **go to press** to be printed. [Middle English from Old French *presse*, from *presser*: see PRESS[1]]

press[3] *verb trans* in former times, to force (somebody) into military service, *esp* in an army or navy. ✳ **press into service** to force or persuade (somebody) to help, or use (something) for a specified purpose, *esp* temporarily at a time of great need or emergency: *The ironing board was pressed into service as an additional table*. [alteration, by association with PRESS[1], of obsolete *prest* to enlist by giving pay in advance, from Old French *prest* loan of money, advance on wages, from Latin *praestare* to stand surety for, from PRAE- + *stare* to stand]

press[4] *noun* the act of forcing people into military service, *esp* in a navy.

press agency *noun* = NEWS AGENCY.

press agent *noun* an agent employed to establish and maintain good public relations through publicity in the media.

press box *noun* a space reserved for reporters, e.g. at a sports stadium.

press button *noun* = PUSH BUTTON.

press conference *noun* an interview given by a public figure to journalists by appointment.

press cutting *noun Brit* a paragraph or article cut from a newspaper or magazine.

press fit *noun* a connection between two parts that involves forcing one into a slightly smaller hole in the other.

press gallery *noun* a usu raised area set aside for reporters, *esp* in a parliamentary assembly.

press gang *noun* (*treated as sing. or pl*) a detachment empowered to press men into military, *esp* naval service.

press-gang *verb trans* **1** to force (somebody) into service by a press gang. **2** to force (somebody) to do something unwillingly: *I was press-ganged into playing cricket in a charity match*.

pressie /'prezi/ *noun* see PREZZIE.

pressing[1] *adj* **1** very important or demanding immediate action or attention; urgent. **2** earnest or insistent: *those pressing prevailers, the ready-made tailors* — W S Gilbert. >>> **pressingly** *adv*.

pressing[2] *noun* one or more records or other objects produced from a single mould or matrix.

pressman *noun* (*pl* **pressmen**) **1** *Brit* a newspaper reporter. **2** the operator of a printing press.

pressmark *noun chiefly Brit* a combination of characters assigned to a book to indicate its place in a library.

press office *noun* an office of an organization, *esp* a government department, from which information concerning the organization's activities is released to the press.

press of sail *noun* the greatest amount of sail that a ship can use under given conditions.

press on *verb intrans* **1** to continue on one's way: *Press on along the Blackpool road until you come to a roundabout*. **2** to proceed in an urgent or resolute manner: *The firm is pressing on with its plans for expansion*.

pressor *adj* raising or tending to raise blood pressure, or tending to constrict the blood vessels. [late Latin *pressor* one who or that which presses, from Latin *premere* to press]

press release *noun* a prepared statement released to the news media.

pressroom *noun* the room in a printing works containing the printing presses.

press-stud *noun Brit* a usu metal fastener consisting of two parts joined by pressing.

press-up *noun* an exercise performed in a prone position by raising and lowering the body with the arms while supporting it only on the hands and toes.

pressure[1] /'preshə/ *noun* **1** the application of force to something by something else in direct contact with it; the force exerted by pressing or squeezing. **2** influence or compulsion directed towards achieving a particular end: *The unions put pressure on the government to increase wages*. **3** demands made by people or circumstances that necessitate a quick response or a sustained effort: *She's one of those people who work well under pressure*. **4** distress, trouble, or difficulty resulting from domestic, social, or economic factors: *under severe financial pressure*. **5** in physics, the force or thrust exerted over a surface divided by its area. **6** = ATMOSPHERIC PRESSURE. [Latin *pressura* from *pressus*, past part. of *premere* to press]

pressure[2] *verb trans* **1** to try to persuade or force (somebody) to do something. **2** *chiefly NAmer* = PRESSURIZE.

pressure cooker *noun* a metal vessel with an airtight lid in which superheated steam under pressure produces a very high temperature, used for cooking food quickly.

pressure gauge *noun* a gauge for indicating the pressure of a fluid.

pressure group *noun* an interest group organized to influence government policy or public opinion.

pressure point *noun* a point where a blood vessel may be compressed against a bone, e.g. to check bleeding.

pressure suit *noun* an inflatable suit to protect the body from low pressure.

pressurize *or* **pressurise** *verb trans* **1** to maintain near-normal atmospheric pressure in (e.g. an aircraft cabin). **2** to subject (somebody) to strong persuasion or coercion: *The prisoner's hunger strike pressurized the authorities into action.* **3** to design (something) to withstand pressure. ⨠ **pressurization** /-'zaysh(ə)n/ *noun*, **pressurizer** *noun*.

pressurized-water reactor *noun* a nuclear reactor in which water under high pressure is used as both the coolant and the moderator.

presswoman *noun* (*pl* **presswomen**) a woman working in journalism, *esp* as a reporter.

prestidigitation /ˌprestidiji'taysh(ə)n/ *noun* conjuring or sleight of hand. ⨠ **prestidigitator** /-'dijitaytə/ *noun*. [French *prestidigitation*, from *preste* nimble, quick (from Italian *presto*: see PRESTO[1]) + Latin *digitus* finger]

prestige /pre'steezh, pre'steej/ *noun* **1** high standing or esteem in the eyes of others, based on achievement or success. **2** an aura of glamour and desirability resulting from associations of social rank or material success. **3** (*used before a noun*) supposedly conferring or indicative of prestige: *a prestige executive suite.*

Word history
early French *prestige* conjuror's trick, illusion, from late Latin *praestigium*, irreg from Latin *praestringere* to tie up, blindfold, from PRAE- + *stringere* to bind tight. The early meaning, 'conjuror's trick' or 'illusion', gradually gave way to the sense 'glamour' in the early 19th cent., a sense it had earlier acquired in French (indeed, its importation into English may have come specifically from its application to Napoleon). 'Glamour' has since been interpreted more narrowly in the sense of social standing or wealth.

prestigious /pri'stijəs/ *adj* having or conferring prestige. ⨠ **prestigiously** *adv*, **prestigiousness** *noun*. [late Latin *praestigiosus* full of tricks, deceitful, from *praestigiae*, pl of *praestigium*: see PRESTIGE]

prestissimo /pre'stisimoh/ *adj and adv* said of a piece of music: to be performed at a very fast tempo. [Italian *prestissimo* superl of *presto*]

presto[1] /'prestoh/ *adj and adv* said of a piece of music: to be performed at a fast tempo. ⨠ **presto** *noun*. [Italian *presto* quick, quickly, from Latin *praestus* ready, from *praesto* (adv) on hand]

presto[2] *interj* = HEY PRESTO.

prestress /pree'stres/ *verb trans* to introduce internal stresses into (e.g. a structural beam) to counteract stresses that will result from an applied load. ⨠ **prestress** *noun*, **prestressed** *adj*.

presumably /pri'zyoohməbli/ *adv* it is reasonable to assume that; as one may reasonably assume: *Presumably Steve will marry Jane.*

presume /pri'zyoohm/ *verb trans* **1a** to suppose or assume (something), *esp* with some degree of certainty. **b** to take (something) for granted. **2** to undertake (to do something) without leave or justification; to dare: *I wouldn't presume to tell you how to do your job.* ⨠ *verb intrans* **1** to act or proceed on a presumption; to take something for granted. **2** to take liberties. **3** (+ on/upon) to take advantage, *esp* in an unscrupulous manner: *Don't presume on his kindness.* ⨠ **presumable** *adj*, **presumer** *noun*. [Middle English *presumen* via early French *presumer* to assume, from Latin *praesumere* to anticipate, assure, from PRAE- + *sumere* to take]

Usage note
presume *or* assume? See note at ASSUME.

presuming *adj* = PRESUMPTUOUS. ⨠ **presumingly** *adv*.

presumption /pri'zum(p)sh(ə)n/ *noun* **1** a presumptuous attitude or presumptuous conduct; effrontery. **2a** an attitude or belief based on reasonable evidence or grounds; an assumption. **b** a ground or reason for presuming something. **3** a legal inference as to the existence or truth of a fact. [Middle English *presumpcioun* via Old French from late Latin *praesumption-, praesumptio* presumptuous attitude, from Latin *praesumere*: see PRESUME]

presumptive /pri'zum(p)tiv/ *adj* **1** giving grounds for a reasonable opinion or belief: *presumptive evidence.* **2** based on probability or presumption: *heir presumptive.* ⨠ **presumptively** *adv*.

presumptuous /pri'zumptyooəs/ *adj* going beyond the limit of what is appropriate or acceptable; overconfident or forward. ⨠ **presumptuously** *adv*, **presumptuousness** *noun*. [Middle English via French from late Latin *praesumptuosus*, from *praesumptio*: see PRESUMPTION]

presuppose /preesə'pohz/ *verb trans* **1** to suppose (something) beforehand, usu without proof or justification. **2** to require (something) to exist or be the case in order that something else may exist or be true or valid: *A creation presupposes a creator.* ⨠ **presupposition** /ˌpreesupə'zish(ə)n/ *noun*. [Middle English *presupposen* via French from late Latin *praesupponere*, from PRAE- + *supponere*: see SUPPOSE]

presynaptic /preesi'naptik/ *adj* situated or occurring just before a nerve synapse. ⨠ **presynaptically** *adv*.

prêt-à-porter /ˌpret ah 'pawtay/ *adj* = OFF-THE-PEG. [French *prêt à porter* ready to wear]

pretax /pree'taks/ *adj* before tax has been deducted: *pretax profits.*

preteen /pree'teen/ *noun* a child under the age of 13.

pretence (*NAmer* **pretense**) /pri'tens/ *noun* **1** the act of attempting to appear to be or be doing something that one is not: *Sir, your wife, under pretence of keeping a bawdy-house, is a receiver of stolen goods* — Dr Johnson. **2** an outward and often insincere or inadequate display of something; a semblance: *The chairman was struggling to maintain some pretence of order in the meeting.* **3** (+ to) a claim made or implied, *esp* one not supported by fact: *He made no pretence to learning.* [Middle English from early French *pretensse*, ultimately from late Latin *praetensus*, past part. of Latin *praetendere*: see PRETEND[1]]

pretend[1] /pri'tend/ *verb trans* **1** to make it seem (that something is the case when it is not): *He's pretending to be deaf; She pretended that she didn't know.* **2** to act as if one were (somebody) or were doing (something) in a game of make-believe: *They're pretending to be doctors and nurses.* **3** to claim or make it appear that one has, thinks, or feels (something that one does not); to simulate (something): *He pretended an interest in politics just to get to know her better.* **4** to claim or assert (something): *I do not pretend to understand the theory fully.* ⨠ *verb intrans* **1** to act as if things were different from the way they really are, *esp* in play: *She was only pretending.* **2a** (+ to) to claim to have something: *He was not one who pretended to great learning.* **b** (+ to) to be ambitious for or suggest one has a right to something: *She did not pretend to high office.* [Middle English *pretenden* from Latin *praetendere* to stretch out, allege as an excuse, from PRAE- + *tendere* to stretch]

pretend[2] *adj* make-believe.

pretender *noun* **1** somebody who lays claim to something; *specif* a claimant, *esp* a false claimant, to a throne. **2** somebody who makes a false or hypocritical show: *a pretender to spirituality.*

pretense /pri'tens/ *noun NAmer* see PRETENCE.

pretension /pri'tensh(ə)n/ *noun* **1a** a claim, *esp* an unjustified one. **b** an ambition or aspiration. **2** vanity; pretentiousness. [late Latin *praetension-, praetensio*, from Latin *praetendere*: see PRETEND[1]]

pretentious /pri'tenshəs/ *adj* trying to appear impressive by an exaggerated and false display of importance or some otherwise admirable quality: *We are more afraid of being pretentious than of being dishonest* — Stephen Fry. ⨠ **pretentiously** *adv*, **pretentiousness** *noun*. [French *prétentieux* from *prétention* pretension, from late Latin *praetention-, praetentio*: see PRETENSION]

preterite (*NAmer* **preterit**) /'pretərit/ *adj* denoting a verb tense that expresses action in the past without reference to duration, continuance, or repetition. ⨠ **preterite** *noun*. [Middle English *preterit* via French from Latin *praeteritus*, past part. of *praeterire* to go by, pass, from *praeter* by, past + *ire* to go]

preterm /pree'tuhm/ *adj* occurring, born, or giving birth before the full time of a normal pregnancy has elapsed: *preterm labour.*

pretermit /preetə'mit/ *verb trans* (**pretermitted, pretermitting**) *formal* **1** to let (something) pass without mention or notice; to omit (something). **2** to leave (something) undone; to neglect (something). ⨠ **pretermission** /-'mish(ə)n/ *noun*. [Latin *praetermittere*, from *praeter* by, past + *mittere* to let go, send]

preternatural /preetə'nachərəl/ *adj formal* **1** exceeding what is natural or normal; extraordinary. **2** lying beyond or outside normal experience; supernatural. ⨠ **preternaturally** *adv*, **preternaturalness** *noun*. [medieval Latin *praeternaturalis*, from Latin *praeter naturam* beyond nature]

pretext /'preetekst/ *noun* a false reason given to disguise the real one; an excuse. [Latin *praetextus* show, display, past part. of *praetexere*, literally 'to weave in front', from PRAE- + *texere* to weave]

pretor /'preetə/ *noun NAmer* see PRAETOR.

prettify /'pritifie/ *verb trans* (**prettifies, prettified, prettifying**) to make (something) pretty or depict it prettily, *esp* in an inappropriate or superficial way. ➤➤ **prettification** /-fi'kaysh(ə)n/ *noun*.

pretty¹ /'priti/ *adj* (**prettier, prettiest**) **1a** attractive or aesthetically pleasing, *esp* in delicate or graceful ways, but less than beautiful: *a pretty girl*. **b** outwardly pleasant but lacking strength, purpose, or intensity: *pretty words that make no sense* — Elizabeth Barrett Browning. **2** used ironically: dreadful or terrible: *This is a pretty mess you've got us into*. **3** moderately large or considerable: *a very pretty profit*. ✱ **a pretty penny** *informal* a considerable amount of money: *That stamp collection will be worth a pretty penny one of these days*. ➤➤ **prettily** *adv*, **prettiness** *noun*, **prettyish** *adj*.

Word history

Middle English *praty, prety* artful, dainty, from Old English *prættig* tricky, from *prætt* trick. The Old English forerunner of *pretty* was a derogatory word meaning 'crafty'. But, reversing the semantic trend shown by *cunning, artful*, and *crafty*, by the 15th cent. it meant 'clever' or 'ingenious' in a usually approbatory sense, and thus became a generalized term of approval. Its use as an adverb meaning 'rather' dates from the 16th cent., and has become so well established and seemingly independent of the adjectival sense that few people would hesitate to say *pretty awful* or even *pretty ugly*.

pretty² *adv* **1a** to some degree; moderately: *pretty comfortable*. **b** very: *She felt pretty sick when she heard how much they were going to charge her*. **2** *informal* in a pretty manner; prettily. ✱ **be sitting pretty** to be in a strong position; to be well placed financially or in other respects. **pretty much/nearly/well** *informal* almost; very nearly: *That's pretty much what we expected*.

pretty³ *verb trans* (**pretties, prettied, prettying**) *informal* (*usu* + up) to make (something or somebody) pretty: *We need some nice curtains to pretty up the room*.

pretty⁴ *noun* (*pl* **pretties**) *archaic* a pretty person or thing, *esp* a dear or pretty child or young woman.

pretty-pretty *adj* pretty in an insipid or inappropriate way.

pretzel /'pretsl/ *noun* a brittle glazed and salted biscuit typically having the form of a loose knot. [German *Pretzel*, perhaps derived ultimately from Latin *brachiatus* having branches like arms, from *brachium, bracchium* arm]

prevail /pri'vayl/ *verb intrans* **1** (*often* + against/over) to gain a victory or the ascendancy through strength or superiority; to triumph. **2** (+ on/upon/with) to persuade somebody successfully: *She finally prevailed on him to sing*. **3** to be frequent; to predominate: *The west winds that prevail in the mountains*. **4** to be or continue in use or fashion; to persist: *a custom that still prevails*. [Middle English *prevailen* from Latin *praevalēre*, from PRAE- + *valēre* to be strong]

prevailing *adj* **1** most frequently occurring: *prevailing winds*. **2** currently widespread or predominant: *the prevailing fashion*. ➤➤ **prevailingly** *adv*.

prevalent /'prevələnt/ *adj* **1** generally or widely occurring or existing; widespread. **2** *archaic* predominant. ➤➤ **prevalence** *noun*, **prevalently** *adv*. [Latin *praevalent-, praevalens* very powerful, present part. of *praevalēre*: see PREVAIL]

prevaricate /pri'varikayt/ *verb intrans* to speak or act evasively so as to hide the truth; to equivocate. ➤➤ **prevarication** /-'kaysh(ə)n/ *noun*, **prevaricator** *noun*. [Latin *praevaricatus*, past part. of *praevaricari* to walk crookedly, from PRAE- + *varicare* to straddle]

Usage note

prevaricate *or* procrastinate? These words are close in meaning and therefore likely to be confused. However, there is a difference: to *prevaricate* is to dither or be evasive whereas to *procrastinate* is to put something off until tomorrow (literally or metaphorically). You will get no decision from a person who prevaricates, but with a little patience you will get one from a person who procrastinates. Of course, some people find ways of doing both.

prevenient /pri'veenyənt/ *adj formal* antecedent; preceding. ➤➤ **preveniently** *adv*. [Latin *praevenient-, praeveniens*, present part. of *praevenire*: see PREVENT]

prevent /pri'vent/ *verb trans* **1** to stop (something) from happening or existing: *Both sides took steps to prevent war*. **2** (*often* + from) to hold or keep (somebody or something) back; to stop (somebody or something) from doing something: *There's nothing to prevent you from going alone*. ➤➤ **preventability** /-'biliti/ *noun*, **preventable** *adj*, **preventer** *noun*, **preventible** *adj*, **prevention** /-sh(ə)n/ *noun*. [Middle English *preventen* to anticipate, from Latin *praeventus*, past part. of *praevenire* to come before, anticipate, forestall, from PRAE- + *venire* to come]

preventative¹ /pri'ventətiv/ *adj* = PREVENTIVE¹.

preventative² *noun* = PREVENTIVE².

preventive¹ /pri'ventiv/ *adj* **1** intended or serving to prevent something: *preventive medicine*. **2** undertaken to forestall an anticipated hostile action: *a preventive strike*. ➤➤ **preventively** *adv*, **preventiveness** *noun*.

preventive² *noun* something that prevents something, *esp* a drug or treatment that prevents disease.

preview¹ /'preevyooh/ *verb trans* **1** to view or show (e.g. a film or exhibition) in advance of public presentation. **2** to describe or report on (events, films, programmes, etc) that are to be presented in the near future.

preview² *noun* **1** an advance viewing, showing, or performance, e.g. of a film or exhibition. **2** a brief survey of something that is to come, *esp* a description of coming events or entertainments. **3** *chiefly NAmer* a film or television trailer.

previous /'preevi·əs/ *adj* **1** going before in time or order: *The previous occupants left the flat in a dreadful state*. **2** *informal* acting too soon; premature: *She was a bit previous when she said she'd got the job*. ✱ **previous to** before; prior to. ➤➤ **previously** *adv*, **previousness** *noun*. [Latin *praevius* leading the way, from PRAE- + *via* way]

previse /pri'viez/ *verb trans archaic or literary* to foresee or forecast (something). ➤➤ **prevision** /pree'vizh(ə)n/ *noun*. [Latin *praevisus*, past part. of *praevidere* to foresee, from PRAE- + *videre* to see]

prevue /'preevyooh/ *noun* = PREVIEW² (3).

prewar /pree'waw/ *adj* denoting the period preceding a war, *esp* World War I or II.

pre-wash¹ *noun* a preliminary wash before the main wash, *esp* in an automatic washing machine.

pre-wash² *verb trans* to give a pre-wash to (clothes, etc).

prey¹ /pray/ *noun* **1a** an animal taken by a predator as food. **b** somebody or something that is helpless or unable to resist attack; a victim. **2** the act or habit of preying: *a beast of prey*. [Middle English *preie* booty, prey, via Old French from Latin *praeda*]

prey² *verb intrans* **1a** (*often* + on/upon) to seize and devour prey: *Kestrels prey on mice*. **b** (*often* + on/upon) to live by extortion, deceit, or exerting undue influence: *Confidence tricksters prey on elderly women*. **2** (+ on/upon) to have a continuously oppressive or distressing effect: *There are a number of problems preying on my mind*. **3** (*usu* + on/upon) to make raids for booty: *Pirates preyed on the coast*. ➤➤ **preyer** /'prayə/ *noun*. [Middle English *preyen* via Old French from Latin *praedari*, from *praeda* PREY¹]

prezzie *or* **pressie** /'prezi/ *noun informal* a present. [by alteration from PRESENT¹]

priapic /prie'apik, prie'aypik/ *adj* = PHALLIC. [Latin *priapus* lecher, from *Priapus*, god of male generative power, from Greek *Priapos*]

priapism /'prie·əpiz(ə)m/ *noun* continuous, abnormal, and often painful erection of the penis.

price¹ /pries/ *noun* **1** the amount, *esp* of money, that is demanded by a seller of something or paid by a buyer. **2** something given or lost, or something undesirable gained, as a result of something else or in order to do or obtain something else: *The price of his carelessness was a broken window*. **3a** an amount sufficient to bribe somebody: *They believed that every man had his price*. **b** a reward for the catching or killing of somebody: *a man with a price on his head*. **4** the odds in betting. **5** *archaic* value; worth: *Who can find a virtuous woman? for her price is far above rubies* — Bible. ✱ **at any price** whatever the cost, effort, sacrifice, etc required. **at a price** paying a high price or at a heavy cost in terms of loss, sacrifice, etc. **what price ... ? 1** what are the chances of ... ? **2** what has become of ... ? [Middle English *pris* via Old French from Latin *pretium* price, money]

price² *verb trans* **1** to set a price for (something). **2** to find out the price of (something). ✱ **price oneself out of the market** to sell things at a higher price than most buyers are willing to pay. ➤➤ **pricer** *noun*.

price-cutting *noun* the practice of reducing prices, *esp* to a level designed to undermine competition.

price-earnings ratio *noun* a measure of the value of ordinary shares (shares in the equity capital of a business; see ORDINARY SHARE) determined as the ratio of their market price to their earnings per share.

price-fixing *noun* the practice of fixing the price of a product by agreement between its suppliers.

price index *noun* a number used to indicate changes in the level of prices from one period to another. It shows the level of the prices of a group of commodities relative to their level during an arbitrarily chosen base period. ➤➤ **price indexing** *noun*.

priceless *adj* **1** having a value that is too great to be calculated; invaluable. **2** *informal* particularly amusing or absurd: *She told me this priceless story.*

price ring *noun* a group of traders acting in agreement to maintain prices.

price-sensitive *adj* **1** highly responsive to changes in price: *price-sensitive consumers.* **2** likely to affect the price of something, *esp* stocks and shares: *price-sensitive information.*

price tag *noun* **1** a label on merchandise showing the price at which it is offered for sale. **2** price or cost: *The council was asked to put a price tag on the new nursery school.*

price war *noun* a period of commercial competition characterized by the repeated cutting of prices below those of competitors.

pricey or **pricy** *adj* (**pricier, priciest**) *chiefly Brit, informal* expensive.

prick¹ /prik/ *verb trans* **1** to pierce (somebody or something) slightly with a sharp point. **2** to puncture (something). **3** to affect (somebody) with sorrow or remorse: *His conscience began to prick him.* **4** (*often* + out) to mark or outline (something) with punctured holes or dots. **5** (*often* + up) said of an animal: to raise (its ears) so that they stand erect. **6** (*usu* + out) to transplant (seedlings) from the place where they germinate to a more permanent position, e.g. in a flower bed. ➤ *verb intrans* **1** to prick something or cause a pricking sensation. **2** to feel discomfort as if from being pricked. ✳ **prick up one's ears** to start to listen intently. ➤➤ **pricker** *noun*. [Old English *prica*]

prick² *noun* **1** the act of pricking something or the sensation of being pricked: *the prick of a needle.* **2a** a pointed instrument, weapon, etc. **b** a mark or shallow hole made by a pointed instrument. **3** a nagging or sharp feeling of sorrow or remorse: *the prick of conscience.* **4** *coarse slang* the penis. **5** *coarse slang* a disagreeable or contemptible person. ✳ **kick against the pricks** to harm oneself in a vain attempt to oppose or resist something [referring to an ox or horse kicking when goaded or spurred: the metaphorical use is from Acts 9:5, 26:14].

pricket /prikit/ *noun* **1** a spike on which a candle is stuck. **2** a buck, *esp* a male fallow deer, two years old. [Middle English *priket* from *prikke* PRICK²; (sense 2) prob from the straightness of its horns]

prickle¹ /prikl/ *noun* **1** a small sharp pointed spike sticking out from the leaf or stem of a plant or the skin of an animal. **2** a pricking, stinging, or tingling sensation. [Old English *pricle*]

prickle² *verb intrans and trans* to feel or cause (somebody or something) to feel a pricking, stinging, or tingling sensation.

prickly *adj* (**pricklier, prickliest**) **1** full of or covered with prickles. **2** causing or marked by prickling; stinging or tingling: *a prickly sensation.* **3a** troublesome or vexatious: *prickly issues.* **b** easily irritated: *a prickly disposition.* ➤➤ **prickliness** *noun*.

prickly heat *noun* a rash of red spots on the skin producing intense itching and tingling, caused by inflammation round the sweat ducts.

prickly pear *noun* **1** any of several species of cacti that have yellow flowers and spines or prickly hairs and bear an oval fruit: genus *Opuntia.* **2** the pulpy, pear-shaped, edible fruit of some of these cacti.

pricy /priesi/ *adj* see PRICEY.

pride¹ /pried/ *noun* **1** a feeling of delight or satisfaction arising from some action, achievement, possession, or relationship: *parental pride.* **2a** a consciousness of one's own worth and dignity; self-respect. **b** an excessive sense of one's own importance; conceit: *Pride was his downfall.* **3a** a source of pride. **b** (*treated as sing. or pl*) the best in a group or class: *This pup is the pride of the litter.* **4** (*treated as sing. or pl*) a group of lions. ✳ **pride of place** the most prominent or first position: *The trophy was given pride of place on the mantelpiece.* **somebody's pride and joy** a person or thing that is a particular source of pride and pleasure to somebody. ➤➤ **prideful** *adj*. [Old English *pryde* from *prūd*: see PROUD]

pride² *verb trans* (+ on/upon) to take pride in (oneself) for something: *He prided himself on his generosity.*

prie-dieu /pree dyuh/ *noun* (*pl* **prie-dieux** /pree dyuh/) **1** a kneeling bench with a raised shelf, designed for use by a person at prayer.

2 a low armless upholstered chair with a high straight back. [French *prie Dieu*, literally 'pray God']

prier or **pryer** /prie-ə/ *noun* an inquisitive person.

priest /preest/ *noun* a person authorized to perform the sacred rites of a religion, *specif* a clergyman ranking below a bishop and above a deacon, e.g. in the Anglican and Roman Catholic Churches: *It was manifest to me that there was something in the Roman Catholic religion which made the priests very dear to the people* — Trollope. ➤➤ **priestliness** *noun*, **priestly** *adj*. [Old English *prēost*, modification of late Latin *presbyter*, from Greek *presbyteros*: see PRESBYTER]

priestcraft *noun* **1** the knowledge and skills possessed by priests. **2** *derog* worldly intrigues or deceptions practised by priests, *esp* in politics: *in pious times ere priestcraft did begin* — Dryden.

priestess /pree'stes, 'preestis/ *noun* a female priest of a non-Christian religion.

priest hole *noun* a secret room or place of concealment for a priest, e.g. in a house during the persecution of Roman Catholic priests.

priesthood *noun* **1** the office or character of a priest. **2** (*treated as sing. or pl*) the whole body of priests.

priest's hole *noun* = PRIEST HOLE.

prig /prig/ *noun* somebody who is excessively self-righteous or affectedly precise about the observance of proprieties, e.g. of speech or manners. ➤➤ **priggery** *noun*, **priggish** *adj*, **priggishly** *adv*, **priggishness** *noun*. [origin unknown]

prim /prim/ *adj* (**primmer, primmest**) **1** stiffly formal and proper; decorous. **2** prudish. **3** said of features, *esp* the mouth: small and precise-looking: *How pleasant to meet Mr Eliot! with his features of clerical cut, and his brow so grim and his mouth so prim* — T S Eliot. ➤➤ **primly** *adv*, **primness** *noun*. [perhaps from Old French *prin*, *prime* excellent, delicate, from Latin *primus* first]

prima ballerina /'preemə/ *noun* (*pl* **prima ballerinas**) the principal female dancer in a ballet company. [Italian *prima ballerina*, literally 'first ballerina']

primacy /prieməsi/ *noun* **1** the office or rank of an ecclesiastical primate. **2** *formal* the state of being first, e.g. in importance, order, or rank; preeminence: *The primacy of the word ... that has in our age been used for mind-bending persuasion and brain-washing pulp ... remains a force for freedom that flies out between all bars* — Nadine Gordimer.

prima donna /,preemə 'donə/ *noun* (*pl* **prima donnas**) **1** a principal female singer, e.g. in an opera company. **2** an extremely sensitive or temperamental person. [Italian *prima donna*, literally 'first lady']

primaeval /prie'meevl/ *adj chiefly Brit* see PRIMEVAL.

prima facie¹ /,preemə 'fayshi/ *adv* at first impression: *The explanation seems, prima facie, implausible.* [Latin *prima facie* on first appearance]

prima facie² *adj* true, valid, or sufficient at first impression; apparent: *The theory offers a prima facie solution.*

primal /priem(ə)l/ *adj* **1** original or primitive: *Village life continues in its primal innocence* — Van Wyck Brookes. **2** first in importance; fundamental: *our primal concern.* ➤➤ **primality** /prie'maliti/ *noun*. [late Latin *primalis* from Latin *primus* first]

primarily /'priem(ə)rəli, prie'merəli/ *adv* **1** for the most part; chiefly. **2** in the first place; originally.

Usage note

The standard American pronunciation of *primarily* with the stress on the second syllable - *mar* - is now very widely used in Britain and accepted by modern dictionaries of British English. The traditional British English pronunciation, however, places the stress on the first syllable *pri*-.

primary¹ /'priem(ə)ri/ *adj* **1a** first in rank, importance, or value; principal. **b** basic or fundamental. **2** first in order of time or development; primitive. **3a** direct or first-hand: *primary sources of information.* **b** not derivable from other colours, odours, or tastes. **4a** preparatory to something else in a continuing process; elementary: *primary instruction.* **b** denoting or relating to the education of children aged between about five and eleven. **5** belonging to the first group or order in successive divisions, combinations, or ramifications: *primary nerves.* **6** denoting or relating to the usu nine or ten strong feathers on the joint of a bird's wing furthest from the body: compare SECONDARY¹. **7** denoting an industry that produces raw materials: compare SECONDARY¹, TERTIARY¹. **8** denoting the inducing current or its circuit in an induction coil or transformer. **9** in chemistry, denoting a carbon atom that is bonded to one other carbon atom only. **10** derived directly from the plant-forming tissue at a growing point on a plant: *primary tissue*; *primary growth*. **11** denoting the strongest degree of stress in speech: compare SECONDARY¹. **12** in geology, denoting formations of the Palaeozoic and earlier periods. [Latin *primarius* basic, of the first rank, from *primus* first]

primary² *noun* (*pl* **primaries**) **1** something that is first in rank, importance, or value; a fundamental. **2** in the USA, an election in which qualified voters nominate or express a preference for a particular candidate or group of candidates for political office, choose party officials, or select delegates for a party convention. **3** = PRIMARY SCHOOL. **4** = PRIMARY COLOUR. **5** any of the usu nine or ten strong feathers on the joint of a bird's wing furthest from the body: compare SECONDARY². **6a** in astronomy, a planet as distinguished from its satellites. **b** the brighter component of a double star: compare SECONDARY².

primary care *noun* the first level of health care provided in the community by general medical practitioners and specialist clinics.

primary cell *noun* a cell that converts chemical energy into electrical energy by irreversible chemical reactions.

primary colour *noun* **1** any of the three spectral bands red, green, and bluish violet from which all other colours can be obtained by suitable combinations. **2** any of the three coloured pigments red, yellow, and blue that cannot be matched by mixing other pigments.

primary consumer *noun* a herbivore: compare SECONDARY CONSUMER, TERTIARY CONSUMER.

primary school *noun* a school for pupils aged from about five to about eleven.

primary syphilis *noun* the first stage of syphilis, which is marked by the development of a deep ulcer and the spread of the causative bacterium in the tissues of the body: compare SECONDARY SYPHILIS, SYPHILIS, TERTIARY SYPHILIS.

primate¹ /'priemayt/ *noun* any of an order of mammals, including human beings, apes, monkeys, and lemurs, that have hands or feet adapted for grasping and a relatively large brain: order Primates. [from scientific Latin *primates*, pl of Latin *primas* principal, from *primus* first]

primate² /'priemayt, 'priemət/ *noun* a bishop who has precedence in a province, group of provinces, or nation. ✱ **Primate of England** the Archbishop of York. **Primate of All England** the Archbishop of Canterbury. ⟫⟫ **primateship** *noun*. [Middle English *primat* via Old French from medieval Latin *primat-*, *primas* archbishop, from Latin *primas* leader, from *primus* first]

primatology /priemə'toləji/ *noun* the branch of zoology dealing with primates, *esp* those other than modern human beings. ⟫⟫ **primatological** /-'lojikl/ *adj*, **primatologist** *noun*.

prime¹ /priem/ *noun* **1a** the most active, thriving, or successful stage or period, *esp* of one's life: *One's prime is elusive. You little girls, when you grow up, must be on the alert to recognise your prime at whatever time of your life it may occur* — Muriel Spark. **b** *archaic or literary* the earliest period; the dawn. **2** = PRIME NUMBER. **3** the symbol (') used in mathematics as a distinguishing mark, e.g. in denoting derivatives of a function, or as a symbol for feet or minutes. **4** in fencing, the first of eight parrying positions. **5** (*often* **Prime**) the second of the canonical hours, orig fixed for 6 a.m. [Old English *prīm*, from Latin *prima hora* first hour]

prime² *adj* **1** first in importance, significance, or authority; principal. **2a** first-rate or excellent. **b** of the highest grade or best quality. **3** first in time; original. **4** not deriving from something else; primary. ⟫⟫ **primely** *adv*, **primeness** *noun*. [Middle English via French from Latin *primus* first]

prime³ *verb trans* **1** to put (something) into working order by filling or charging it with something: *to prime a pump with water*. **2** to prepare (a surface), e.g. for painting, by applying a substance as a first coat. **3** to give (somebody) instructions or a warning beforehand. **4** to prepare (a firearm or charge) for firing by supplying it with priming or a primer. [prob from PRIME¹]

prime cost *noun* the combined total of raw material and direct labour costs incurred in production.

prime interest rate *noun* = PRIME RATE.

prime meridian *noun* the meridian at Greenwich of 0° longitude from which other longitudes E and W are reckoned.

prime minister *noun* **1** the chief executive of a parliamentary government. **2** the chief minister of a ruler or state. ⟫⟫ **prime ministership** *noun*.

prime mover *noun* **1** the original or most influential force in a development or undertaking: *He was the prime mover of the constitutional reform*. **2** an initial source of motive power, e.g. a windmill, water wheel, turbine, or internal-combustion engine. **3** God as the creator of and originator of all movement in the physical universe: compare FIRST CAUSE. [translation of medieval Latin *primus motor*]

prime number *noun* any positive whole number that can only be divided by itself and 1 to produce a whole number as the result.

primer¹ *noun* a book that provides a basic introduction to a subject; orig a book for teaching children to read. [Middle English from late Latin *primarium*, neuter of *primarius*: see PRIMARY¹]

primer² *noun* **1** material used in priming a surface, *esp* a type of paint used as a first coat on plaster, wood, etc. **2** a device, e.g. a percussion cap, used for igniting a charge.

prime rate *noun NAmer* an interest rate at which preferred customers can borrow from banks and which is the lowest commercial interest rate available at a particular time and place.

prime time *noun* the peak television viewing time, for which the highest rates are charged to advertisers.

primeval *or* **primaeval** /prie'meevl/ *adj* **1** dating from, existing in, or relating to the earliest age or ages. **2** existing in or persisting from the beginning, e.g. of the universe. ⟫⟫ **primevally** *adv*. [Latin *primaevus*, from *primus* first + *aevum* age]

primigravida /priemi'gravidə/ *noun* (*pl* **primigravidas** *or* **primigravidae** /-die/) a woman who is pregnant for the first time. [scientific Latin, from *primus* first + *gravida* pregnant]

priming /'prieming/ *noun* the explosive used for igniting a charge.

primipara /prie'mipərə/ *noun* (*pl* **primiparas** *or* **primiparae** /-ree/) **1** a woman who is giving birth for the first time. **2** a woman who has borne only one child. ⟫⟫ **primiparity** /-'pariti/ *noun*, **primiparous** *adj*. [scientific Latin, from *primus* first + *-para*, from Latin *parere* to give birth to]

primitive¹ /'primitiv/ *adj* **1a** belonging to or characteristic of an early stage of development; crude or rudimentary: *primitive technology*. **b** produced by or characteristic of a relatively simple, *esp* non-industrial or preliterate people or culture: *primitive art*. **2** *usu derog*. **a** said of accommodation or facilities: not up to the usual modern standards of comfort and hygiene. **b** said of people's behaviour: lacking in good manners, sophistication, or subtlety; crude or boorish. **3a** not having received any formal training in an art or craft; self-taught. **b** produced by a self-taught artist: *a primitive painting*. **4** denoting a painting or style of painting that deliberately imitates the work of artists without formal training. **5** of the earliest age or period; primeval: *the primitive church*. **6** original or primary. ⟫⟫ **primitively** *adv*, **primitiveness** *noun*. [Middle English *primitif* from Latin *primitivus* first of its kind, ultimately from *primus* first]

primitive² *noun* **1a** a member of a people with an undeveloped preindustrial way of life. **b** an unsophisticated person. **2a** an artist of an early, *esp* pre-Renaissance, period. **b** a later imitator of such an artist. **3a** an artist, *esp* a self-taught artist, whose work is marked by directness and naivety. **b** a primitive work of art. **4** a root word from which other words are derived.

primitivism *noun* **1** belief in the superiority of a simple way of life close to nature or without the acquisitions of modern civilization. **2** the style of art of primitive peoples or primitive artists. ⟫⟫ **primitivist** *noun and adj*, **primitivistic** /-'vistik/ *adj*.

primo /'preemoh/ *noun* (*pl* **primos**) in music, the first or leading part, e.g. in a duet or trio. [Italian *primo* first, from Latin *primus*]

primogenitor /priemoh'jenitə/ *noun* an ancestor or forefather, *esp* the earliest ancestor. [Latin *primus* first + *genitor* begetter, from *gignere* to beget]

primogeniture /priemoh'jenichə/ *noun* **1** the state or fact of being the firstborn of the children of the same parents. **2** the principle by which right of inheritance belongs to the eldest son. [late Latin *primogenitura*, from Latin *primus* + *genitura* birth, from *gignere* to beget]

primordia /prie'mawdi-ə/ *noun* pl of PRIMORDIUM.

primordial /prie'mawdi-əl/ *adj* **1a** existing from or at the beginning, *esp* from the beginning of time; primeval. **b** earliest formed in the development of an individual or structure. **2** fundamental or primary. ➤➤ **primordially** adv. [Middle English from late Latin primordialis, from Latin primordium origin, from primus first + ordiri to begin]

primordial soup noun the liquid mixture of chemical molecules, e.g. amino acids, fats, and sugars, from which life on earth is thought to have originated.

primordium /prie'mawdi·əm/ noun (pl **primordia** /-di·ə/) the earliest stage in the development of a part or organ. [Latin primordium: see PRIMORDIAL]

primp /primp/ verb trans and intrans chiefly NAmer to dress or adorn (oneself) or arrange (one's dress, hair, etc) in a careful or fastidious manner. [perhaps alteration of PRIM]

primrose /'primrohz/ noun **1** a small early-flowering perennial plant with pale yellow flowers: Primula vulgaris. **2** a pale yellow colour. [Middle English primerose via French from medieval Latin prima rosa first (early) rose]

primrose path noun a path of ease or pleasure, esp one leading to disaster.

primula /'primyoolə/ noun any of a genus of plants that includes the primrose, oxlip, cowslip, and polyanthus: genus Primula. [medieval Latin primula veris, literally 'firstling of spring']

primum mobile /,priemoom 'mohbili/ noun the outermost concentric sphere conceived in medieval astronomy as carrying the spheres of the fixed stars and the planets in its daily revolution. [Middle English from medieval Latin primum mobile, literally 'first moving thing']

Primus /'prieməs/ noun trademark a portable oil-burning stove used chiefly for cooking when camping. [Latin primus first]

primus inter pares /,prieməs intə 'peəreez/ noun first among equals. [Latin primus inter pares]

prince /prins/ noun **1** the son or grandson of a monarch. **2** a sovereign ruler, esp of a principality. **3** a title borne by noblemen of varying rank and status in various countries. **4** a man of high rank or standing in his class or profession: a prince among poets. ➤➤ **princedom** noun, **princeship** noun. [Middle English from Latin princip-, princeps chief, literally 'one taking the first part', from primus first + capere to take]

prince charming noun an ideal suitor. [named after Prince Charming, hero of the fairy tale Cinderella, a translation by the English writer Robert Samber fl.1729, of Cendrillon by Charles Perrault d.1703, French writer]

prince consort noun (pl **princes consort**) the husband of a reigning female sovereign.

princeling /'prinsling/ noun a petty or insignificant prince.

princely adj **1** belonging to or relating to a prince. **2** befitting a prince; noble: princely manners. **3** magnificent or lavish: a princely sum. ➤➤ **princeliness** noun, **princely** adv.

Prince of Darkness noun = SATAN.

Prince of Peace noun a title used by the prophet Isaiah to describe the coming Messiah and applied by Christians to Jesus Christ.

Prince of Wales /waylz/ noun the male heir apparent to the British throne.

prince's-feather noun a showy annual plant of the amaranth family often cultivated for its dense usu red flower spikes: Amaranthus hypochondriacus.

princess /prin'ses, before a name usu 'prinses/ noun **1** a daughter or granddaughter of a sovereign. **2** the wife or widow of a prince. **3** a woman who has the rank of a prince in her own right. **4** a woman, or something personified as female, that is outstanding in a specified respect.

princess royal noun the eldest daughter of a reigning king or queen.

principal[1] /'prinsipl/ adj **1** most important, consequential, or influential; chief. **2** denoting a capital sum placed at interest, due as a debt, or used as a fund. ➤➤ **principally** adv. [Middle English via Old French from Latin principalis, from princip-, princeps: see PRINCE]

Usage note

principal or principle? These two words, which are pronounced the same, are often confused. Principle is only ever a noun and has the basic sense of 'a fundamental truth or standard': it's the principle of the thing; I object to that on principle. Principal is most often used as an adjective meaning 'main': their principal aim in life. As a noun, principal means the 'head of an

educational establishment' (it is the American English word for a 'head teacher') or 'a leading actor or performer' (see PRINCIPAL[2]).

principal[2] noun **1** a person who has controlling authority or is in a leading position within an organization. **2a** the head of an educational institution. **b** NAmer a headteacher. **3** somebody who employs somebody else to act for him or her. **4** a person actually responsible for committing a crime. **5** the person ultimately liable on a legal obligation. **6** a leading performer in a play, opera, etc. **7** a capital sum placed at interest, due as a debt, or used as a fund. **8** a main rafter of a roof. **9** an organ stop, usu one sounding an octave above the diapason. ➤➤ **principalship** noun.

principal boy noun the role of the hero in British pantomime, traditionally played by a woman.

principality /prinsi'paliti/ noun (pl **principalities**) the office or territory of a prince.

principal parts pl noun the set of verb forms from which all the other forms can be derived.

principate /'prinsipət/ noun the regime characteristic of the early Roman emperors, in which some republican features survived. [Middle English, in the sense 'principality', from Latin principatus first place, from princeps: see PRINCE]

principle /'prinsipl/ noun **1** a universal and fundamental law, doctrine, or truth. **2a** a rule or code of conduct. **b** devotion to the rules of right conduct and morality; integrity: a man of principle. **3** the essence of or basic idea behind something: He objects to the principle of the thing, not the method. **4** a law or fact of nature underlying the working of an artificial phenomenon or an artificial system or device. **5** a primary source; a fundamental element: The ancients emphasized the opposing principles of heat and cold. **6** an ingredient, e.g. a chemical, that exhibits or imparts a characteristic quality. ✴ **in principle** with respect to fundamentals; in theory: She's prepared to accept the proposition in principle. **on principle** on the basis of one's beliefs or moral code: He refuses to give to charity on principle. [Middle English, modification of early French principe, from Latin principium beginning, from princip-, princeps: see PRINCE]

Usage note

principle or principal? See note at PRINCIPAL[1].

principled adj exhibiting, based on, or characterized by principle: her principled rejection of a shameful compromise.

prink /pringk/ verb trans and intrans to dress or groom (oneself) carefully. ➤➤ **prinker** noun. [prob alteration of prank to dress or adorn showily, prob from Dutch pronken to strut]

print[1] /print/ noun **1a** a mark made by pressure; an impression. **b** something impressed with a print or formed in a mould. **2** printed state or form. **3** printed matter or letters. **4** a copy made by printing, e.g.: **a** a photograph produced from a negative or transparency. **b** a reproduction of an original work of art, e.g. a painting. **c** an original work of art reproduced from a raised or engraved image on a wooden block, metal plate, etc. **5a** cloth or clothing with a pattern applied by printing. **b** a pattern of this kind. **c** (used before a noun) relating to or having a pattern of this kind: a print shirt. **6** (usu in pl) = FINGERPRINT[1]. ✴ **in print** said of a book: obtainable from the publisher. **out of print** said of a book: no longer obtainable from the publisher. [Middle English preinte from Old French preint, past part. of preindre to press, from Latin premere]

print[2] verb trans **1a** to stamp or impress (e.g. a mark or design) in or on something. **b** to stamp or impress (something) with a mark, design, etc. **2a** to make a copy of (something) by transferring ink to paper automatically, e.g. in a printing press or computer printer. **b** to publish (e.g. a book or newspaper) in print. **3** to make (a positive image) on a sensitized photographic surface from a negative or transparency. **4** to write (something) with each letter produced separately, not joined together. ➤ verb intrans **1a** to work as a printer. **b** to produce printed matter. **2** to use unjoined letters. ➤➤ **printability** /-'biliti/ noun, **printable** adj.

printed circuit noun an electronic circuit in which the components are connected by conductive material deposited in thin continuous paths on an insulating surface rather than by wires.

printer noun **1** somebody whose work is producing printed matter. **2** a machine that produces printed matter, e.g. computer printout, by mechanical, electronic, or photographic means.

printer's devil noun dated an apprentice or errand boy in a printing office.

printing *noun* **1** reproduction in printed form. **2** the art, practice, or business of a printer. **3** = IMPRESSION (7D). **4** handwriting with unjoined letters.

printing press *noun* a machine that produces printed matter, *esp* by pressing paper against an inked surface.

printmaker *noun* somebody, *esp* an artist, who designs and produces prints from blocks or plates. ➤➤ **printmaking** *noun*.

printout *noun* a printed record produced automatically, *esp* by a computer.

prion /'prie·on/ *noun* an infectious particle that is composed solely of protein and is thought to be responsible for brain diseases such as BSE and CJD. [proteinaceous infectious (particle) + -ON²]

prior¹ /'prie·ə/ *adj* **1** earlier in time or order. **2** taking precedence, e.g. in importance. ✳ **prior to** before in time. [Latin *prior* former, superior, compar of Old Latin *pri* before]

prior² *noun NAmer, informal* a previous conviction for a criminal offence: *He's got two priors for armed robbery.*

prior³ *noun* **1** the deputy head of a monastery ranking next below the abbot. **2** the head of a house of any of various religious communities. ➤➤ **priorate** /-rət/ *noun*, **priorship** *noun*. [Old English and early French, both from late Latin *prior* chief officer, administrator, from Latin *prior*: see PRIOR¹]

prioress /'prie·əris, -res/ *noun* a nun corresponding in rank to a prior.

prioritize *or* **prioritise** /prie'oritiez/ *verb trans* **1** to give priority to (something): *the offences which the public want to see prioritized.* **2** to arrange (things) in order of priority: *to organize and prioritize the workload.* ➤➤ **prioritization** /-'zaysh(ə)n/ *noun.*

priority /prie'oriti/ *noun* (*pl* **priorities**) **1a** the fact or condition of being prior. **b** superiority in rank. **c** the right to precede others: *Oncoming traffic has priority.* **2a** something meriting prior attention. **b** (*in pl*) the relative importance attached to each of a number of things: *get one's priorities right.* [Middle English via French from medieval Latin *prioritas*, from Latin *prior*: see PRIOR¹]

priory /'prie·əri/ *noun* (*pl* **priories**) a religious house under a prior or prioress.

prise *or* **prize** /priez/ *verb trans* **1** to press, force, or move (something) open or apart, e.g. with a lever. **2** to open, obtain, or remove (something) with difficulty: *prise information out of him.* [dialect *prise* a lever, from Old French *prise*: see PRIZE³]

prism /'priz(ə)m/ *noun* **1** a POLYHEDRON (three-dimensional figure) whose ends are similar, equal, and parallel polygons and whose sides are parallelograms. **2** a transparent prism, *esp* one with triangular ends, that is used to deviate or disperse a beam of light. [via late Latin from Greek *prismat-, prisma*, literally 'anything sawn', from *prizein* to saw]

prismatic /priz'matik/ *adj* **1** of, like, or being a prism. **2** formed, dispersed, or refracted by or as if by a prism: *prismatic colours.* ➤➤ **prismatically** *adv.*

prison /'priz(ə)n/ *noun* **1** a place of enforced confinement, *esp* a building in which people are confined while awaiting trial or for punishment after conviction: *To live in prison is to live without mirrors. To live without mirrors is to live without the self* — Margaret Atwood. **2** a state of confinement or captivity. [Middle English via Old French from Latin *prehension-, prehensio* act of seizing, from *prehendere*: see PREHENSILE]

prisoner *noun* **1** somebody kept in enforced confinement, *esp* somebody awaiting trial or convicted of an offence. **2** somebody who is trapped or restrained by a particular set of circumstances. ✳ **take somebody prisoner** to capture (somebody); to make (them) a prisoner.

prisoner of state *noun* (*pl* **prisoners of state**) a political prisoner.

prisoner of war *noun* somebody captured in war.

prisoner's base *noun* a children's game in which players try to catch and imprison members of the opposing team who have ventured out of their home territory.

prissy /'prisi/ *adj* (**prissier, prissiest**) prim and prudish, *esp* in a fussy way. ➤➤ **prissily** *adv*, **prissiness** *noun*. [prob blend of PRIM and SISSY¹]

pristine /'pristeen/ *adj* **1** belonging to the earliest period or state. **2** free from impurity or decay; fresh and clean as if new. ➤➤ **pristinely** *adv*. [Latin *pristinus* former]

Usage note

This word has been used since the 16th cent. to refer to a primeval condition. Because this sense often bears suggestions of freshness and newness, in the 20th cent. the word has been extended to mean not only 'pure, spotless' but (*esp* in the combination *pristine condition*) 'unused, mint'. This modern use is often regarded, however, as an unnecessary and confusing extension of the word.

prithee /'pridhee, 'pridhi/ *interj archaic* used to express a wish or request: please. [alteration of (*I*) *pray thee*]

privacy /'prievəsi, 'priv-/ *noun* **1** a state of being apart from the company or observation of others; seclusion. **2** freedom from undesirable intrusions, *esp* avoidance of publicity. [Middle English *privacie*, from *privat*: see PRIVATE¹]

private¹ /'prievit/ *adj* **1a** intended for or restricted to the use of a particular person, group, etc: *a private park.* **b** belonging to or concerning an individual person, company, or interest: *a private house.* **c** restricted to the individual or arising independently of others: *my private opinion.* **d** independent of the usual institutions: *private study.* **e** not general in effect: *a private statute.* **f** of or receiving medical treatment for which fees are charged. **g** of or administered by an individual or organization other than a governmental institution or agency: *a private pension scheme.* **2** not holding public office or employment: *a private citizen.* **3** not related to one's official position; personal: *private correspondence.* **4a** withdrawn from company or observation; sequestered: *a private retreat.* **b** not confiding in or seeking the companionship of others: *She was a very private person.* **c** not intended to be known publicly; secret: *private thoughts.* **5** having the rank of a private: *a private soldier.* ✳ **in private** without the presence or knowledge of others; confidentially. ➤➤ **privately** *adv*, **privateness** *noun*. [Middle English *privat*, from Latin *privatus*, past part. of *privare* to deprive, release, from *privus* private, set apart]

private² *noun* **1** somebody of the lowest rank in the British and US armies and the US marines. **2** *informal* (*in pl*) = PRIVATE PARTS.

private bill *noun* a legislative bill affecting a particular individual, class, or locality rather than the public at large: compare PUBLIC BILL.

private company *noun* a company that may place certain restrictions on the transfer of its shares which cannot be offered for sale to the general public: compare PUBLIC COMPANY.

private detective *noun* a person employed by an individual or organization other than the state to prevent crime, e.g. by catching shoplifters, or to investigate somebody's activities, e.g. in divorce cases.

private enterprise *noun* **1** business undertaken by private individuals or privately owned companies: compare PUBLIC ENTERPRISE. **2** = FREE ENTERPRISE.

privateer /prievə'tiə/ *noun* **1** a privately owned armed ship that can be commissioned by a government for use against an enemy in wartime. **2** the commander or any of the crew of a privateer. ➤➤ **privateering** *noun.*

privateersman *noun* (*pl* **privateersmen**) = PRIVATEER (2).

private eye *noun informal* = PRIVATE DETECTIVE.

private income *noun* income arising from investments or capital rather than from wages or a salary.

private investigator *noun* = PRIVATE DETECTIVE.

private law *noun* a branch of law concerned with the duties and rights of ordinary private individuals and their relations with one another: compare PUBLIC LAW.

private life *noun* the personal relationships, activities, etc of somebody, as distinct from their public or professional life.

private means *noun* = PRIVATE INCOME.

private member *noun* a Member of Parliament who does not hold a government appointment.

private member's bill *noun* a government bill introduced by a private member.

private parts *pl noun euphem* a person's genitalia.

private practice *noun* in Britain, a medical practice that is outside the National Health Service.

private school *noun Brit* a school that is supported by the fee-paying parents of pupils, not by the government.

private secretary *noun* **1** a secretary employed to assist with a person's individual and confidential business matters. **2** a civil servant who assists and advises a senior government official.

private sector *noun* the part of the economy that is not owned or directly controlled by the state: compare PUBLIC SECTOR.

privation /prie'vaysh(ə)n/ *noun* **1** the act or an instance of depriving; deprivation. **2** the condition of being deprived, *esp* in lacking the necessities of life. [Middle English *privacion* via French from Latin *privation-, privatio*, from *privare*: see PRIVATE¹]

privatise *verb trans* see PRIVATIZE.

privative /'privətiv/ *adj* marked by or expressing the lack or absence of a quality: *a-, un-, and non- are privative prefixes.* [Latin *privativus* indicating privation, from *privare*: see PRIVATE¹]

privatize *or* **privatise** *verb trans* to transfer or restore (a state-owned business, industry, etc) to private ownership. ➤➤ **privatization** /ˌ'zaysh(ə)n/ *noun*

privet /'privit/ *noun* an ornamental shrub that has evergreen leaves and small white flowers and is widely used as hedging: *Ligustrum vulgare* and *Ligustrum ovalifolium* and others. [origin unknown]

privilege¹ /'priv(i)lij/ *noun* **1** a right, immunity, or advantage granted exclusively to a particular person, class, or group, *esp* such an advantage attached to a position or office; a prerogative. **2** the possession of privileges, *esp* those conferred by rank or wealth. [Middle English via Old French from Latin *privilegium* law for or against a private person, from *privus* PRIVATE¹ + *leg-, lex* law]

privilege² *verb trans* **1** to grant a privilege to (somebody). **2** (+ from) to exempt (somebody) from a duty, liability, etc.

privileged *adj* **1** having or enjoying one or more privileges: *privileged classes.* **2** not subject to disclosure in court: *a privileged communication.* **3** (*usu* + from) exempt from (something, e.g. a liability or obligation).

privity /'priviti/ *noun* (*pl* **privities**) **1** joint, usu secret, knowledge of a private matter. **2** the relation between people who have a legal interest in the same transaction. [Middle English *privite* via Old French from late Latin *privitat-, privitas*, from Latin *privus* PRIVATE¹]

privy¹ /'privi/ *adj* **1** (+ to) sharing in the knowledge of something secret: *He claimed he was not privy to the conspiracy.* **2** *archaic* secret; private: *Is the banquet ready i' the privy chamber?* — Shakespeare; *This ... diviner ... told me what privy marks I had about me, as, the mark of my shoulder, the mole on my neck, the great wart on my left arm* — Shakespeare. ➤➤ **privily** *adv.* [Middle English *prive* via Old French from Latin *privatus*: see PRIVATE¹]

privy² *noun* (*pl* **privies**) **1** a small building containing a toilet. **2** somebody who shares a legal interest in a transaction.

Privy Council *noun* an advisory council nominally chosen by the British monarch and usu functioning through its committees. ➤➤ **Privy Councillor** *noun,* **Privy Counsellor** *noun.*

privy purse *noun* (*often* **Privy Purse**) in Britain, an allowance for the monarch's private expenses paid out of public revenues.

privy seal *noun* in Britain, a seal attached to certain state documents authorized by the monarch.

prize¹ /priez/ *noun* **1a** something offered or striven for in a competition, game of chance, etc. **b** (*used before a noun*) relating to or denoting a competition, game of chance, etc in which a prize is offered: *a prize draw.* **c** (*used before a noun*) awarded as, having received, or worthy of receiving a prize: *prize money; a prize marrow.* **2a** something exceptionally desirable or precious. **b** (*used before a noun*) highly valued: *a prize possession.* **c** often used ironically (*used before a noun*) excellent or outstanding; complete: *a prize idiot.* [Middle English *pris* prize, price: see PRICE¹]

prize² *verb trans* to value (something or somebody) highly; to esteem (them). [Middle English *prisen* via early French *prisier* from late Latin *pretiare*, from Latin *pretium* value, PRICE¹]

prize³ *noun* property or shipping lawfully captured at sea in time of war. [Middle English *prise* booty, from Old French *prise* act of taking, from *prendre* to take, from Latin *prehendere*: see PREHENSILE]

prize⁴ *verb trans* see PRISE.

prizefight *noun* a boxing match, *esp* an unlicensed one in which there is a prize, usu of money. ➤➤ **prizefighter** *noun,* **prizefighting** *noun.*

prize ring *noun* **1** a boxing ring where prizefighting takes place. **2** (**the prize ring**) the sport or practice of prizefighting.

PRO *abbr* **1** Public Records Office. **2** public relations officer.

pro¹ /proh/ *noun* (*pl* **pros**) **1** (*usu in pl*) an argument or piece of evidence in favour of a particular proposition or view: compare CON⁴: *an appraisal of the pros and cons.* **2** somebody who favours or

supports a particular proposition or view. [Middle English, from Latin *pro* (prep) for]

pro² *adv* in favour or affirmation: compare CON⁵: *Much has been written pro and con.*

pro³ *prep* for; in favour of.

pro⁴ *noun* (*pl* **pros**) *informal* = PROFESSIONAL².

pro⁵ *adj* = PROFESSIONAL¹: *He used to play pro football.*

pro⁶ *noun* (*pl* **pros**) *informal* = PROSTITUTE¹.

pro-¹ *prefix* forming words, with the meanings: **1** earlier than; prior to; before in time, place, order, etc: *prologue.* **2** projecting: *prognathous.* [Middle English via Old French and Latin from Greek *pro-* before, forward, forth, for, from *pro* for]

pro-² *prefix* forming words, with the meanings: **1** favouring; supporting; championing: *pro-American.* **2** taking the place of; substituting for: *pronoun.* **3** onward; forward: *progress; propel.* [French *pro-, por-, pur-* from Latin *pro* in front of, before, for]

proa /'proh-ə/ *or* **prau** /prow/ *noun* a fast Malay boat shaped like a canoe and equipped with oars, a large triangular sail, and an OUTRIGGER (stabilizing framework). [Malay *pĕrahu*]

proactive /proh'aktiv/ *adj* tending to take the initiative or to act in anticipation of events. [PRO-¹ + *-active* as in REACTIVE]

pro-am /ˌproh 'am/ *noun* **1** a competition, *esp* in golf, in which amateurs play professionals. **2** (*used before a noun*) relating to or denoting such a competition.

prob /prob/ *noun informal* a problem: *OK, no probs, I'll do that for you.*

probabilistic /probabi'listik/ *adj* of or based on probability.

probability /probə'biliti/ *noun* (*pl* **probabilities**) **1** the state of being probable. **2** something, e.g. an occurrence or circumstance, that is probable. **3** the likelihood that a given event will occur or a measure of this, usu expressed as the ratio of the number of times it occurs in a test series to the total number of trials in the series.

probable¹ /'probabl/ *adj* **1** supported by evidence strong enough to establish likelihood but not certainty. **2** likely to be or become true or real. ➤➤ **probably** *adv.* [Middle English via French from Latin *probabilis*, from *probare*: see PROVE]

probable² *noun* somebody or something probable, *esp* a person who will probably be selected for something: *She's a probable for the new post.*

probable cause *noun NAmer* in law, reasonable grounds or sufficient evidence for a person to be arrested or for an arrest warrant to be issued.

proband /'prohband/ *noun* in medicine, the first member of a family to be investigated in a genetic study. [Latin *probandus*, verbal noun from *probare*: see PROVE]

probang /'prohbang/ *noun* a slender flexible rod with a sponge on one end used *esp* for removing obstructions from or applying medication to the throat. [alteration (prob influenced by PROBE¹) of earlier *provang* (so named by the inventor), of unknown origin]

probate¹ /'prohbayt/ *noun* **1** the judicial determination of the validity of a will. **2** an official copy of a will certified as valid. [Middle English *probat*, from Latin *probatum*, neuter past part. of *probare*: see PROVE]

probate² *verb trans NAmer* to establish the validity of (a will) by probate.

probation /prə'baysh(ə)n/ *noun* **1a** subjection of an individual to a period of testing to ascertain suitability, e.g. for a job. **b** a method of dealing with offenders by which sentence is suspended subject to good behaviour and regular supervision by a probation officer. **2** the state or a period of being subject to probation: *on probation.* ➤➤ **probational** *adj,* **probationary** *adj.*

probationer *noun* **1** somebody whose suitability for a job is being tested during a trial period. **2** an offender on probation.

probation officer *noun* an officer appointed to supervise the conduct of offenders on probation.

probative /'prohbətiv/ *adj formal* chiefly in law, serving to prove; substantiating.

probe¹ /prohb/ *noun* **1** a slender surgical instrument for examining a cavity. **2a** a slender pointed metal conductor, e.g. of electricity or sound, that is temporarily connected to or inserted in something to be monitored or measured. **b** an unmanned spacecraft used to explore and send back information from space. **c** a flexible tube used in refuelling an aircraft in flight. **3a** the act or an instance of probing. **b** a tentative exploratory survey. **c** a penetrating or critical investigation, *esp* one carried out by a newspaper into corruption; an enquiry. [late Latin *proba* examination, from Latin *probare*: see PROVE]

probe² *verb trans* **1** to examine (something) with or as if with a probe. **2** to investigate (something) thoroughly. ➤ *verb intrans* to make an exploratory investigation. ➤➤ **prober** *noun*, **probing** *adj*, **probingly** *adv*.

probiotic /ˌprohbie'otik/ *noun* a preparation containing bacteria beneficial to health, especially to the healthy functioning of the gut. ➤➤ **probiotic** *adj*. [PRO-² + ANTIBIOTIC]

probit /'prohbit/ *noun* in statistics, a unit of measurement of probability based on deviations from the mean of a normal distribution. [short for *probability unit*]

probity /'prohbiti/ *noun formal* adherence to the highest principles and ideals; honesty or integrity: *No qualities were so likely to make a poor man's fortune as those of probity and integrity* — Benjamin Franklin. [early French *probité* from Latin *probitat-, probitas*, from *probus* honest]

problem /'problem/ *noun* **1a** a situation or question that is difficult to understand or resolve. **b** somebody who is difficult to deal with or understand. **c** (*used before a noun*) difficult to deal with; presenting a problem: *a problem child*. **2a** a question raised for enquiry, consideration, or solution. **b** a proposition in mathematics or physics for which a solution has to be found or from which a principle, etc can be demonstrated. **3** (*used before a noun*) dealing with a moral, social, or human problem: *a problem play*. [Middle English *probleme* via French and Latin from Greek *problēma*, literally 'something thrown forwards', from *proballein* to throw forward, from PRO-¹ + *ballein* to throw]

problematic /problə'matik/ *adj* **1** difficult to solve or decide; puzzling. **2** presenting a problem or problems. **3** open to question or debate; questionable. **4** said of a proposition in logic: asserted as possible. ➤➤ **problematically** *adv*.

problematical /problə'matikl/ *adj* = PROBLEMATIC.

pro bono publico /proh ˌbohnoh 'pooblikoh/ *adv and adj* **1** for the public good. **2** (*usu* **pro bono**) said of legal representation or the provision of legal services: free to the client, *esp* because they are on a low income. [Latin *pro bono publico*]

proboscidean *or* **proboscidian** /prohbə'sidi·ən/ *noun* any of an order of large mammals including the elephants and extinct related forms: order Proboscidea. ➤➤ **proboscidean** *adj*. [from the Latin order name, from *proboscid-, proboscis*: see PROBOSCIS]

proboscides /prə'bosideez/ *noun* pl of PROBOSCIS.

proboscidian /prohbə'sidi·ən/ *noun* = PROBOSCIDEAN.

proboscis /prə'bosis/ *noun* (*pl* **proboscises** /-seez/ *or* **proboscides** /-deez/) **1** a long flexible snout, e.g. the trunk of an elephant. **2** any of various elongated or extendable tubular mouthparts of an invertebrate animal, e.g. an insect, that are used *esp* for sucking. **3** *informal, humorous* the human nose. [via Latin from Greek *proboskis*, from PRO-¹ + *boskein* to feed]

proboscis monkey *noun* a large monkey of Borneo with a long fleshy nose: *Nasalis larvatus*.

procaine /'prohkayn, proh'kayn/ *noun* a synthetic drug that is used as a local anaesthetic. Also called NOVOCAINE. [PRO-² + *-caine* as in COCAINE]

procaryote /proh'karioht/ *noun* see PROKARYOTE.

procedure /prə'seejə/ *noun* **1** a particular way of acting or accomplishing something. **2** a series of ordered steps: *legal procedure*. **3** an established method of doing things: *a stickler for procedure*. **4** in computing, = SUBROUTINE. ➤➤ **procedural** *adj*, **procedurally** *adv*. [French *procédure*, from early French *proceder*: see PROCEED]

proceed /prə'seed/ *verb intrans* **1** to arise from a source; originate: *This trouble proceeded from a misunderstanding*. **2a** to begin and carry on an action, process, or movement. **b** to begin and carry on a legal action: *if they proceed against us*. **3** to continue after a pause or interruption. **4** to move along a course; to advance. [Middle English *proceden* via early French *proceder* from Latin *procedere*, from PRO-¹ + *cedere* to go]

Usage note
proceed or precede? See note at PRECEDE.

proceeding *noun* **1** a procedure. **2** (*in pl*) events; goings-on: *Through his drunken brain the whole memory of the evening's proceedings rushed back* — Liam O'Flaherty. **3** (*in pl*) legal action: *divorce*

proceedings. **4** (*in pl*) an official record of things said or done. **5** (*usu in pl*) an affair or transaction.

proceeds /'prohseedz/ *pl noun* **1** the total amount brought in: *the proceeds of the sale*. **2** the net amount received. [pl of obsolete *proceed* (noun) proceeds, from PROCEED]

process¹ /'prohses/ *noun* **1a** a moving forward, *esp* as part of a progression or development: *the historical process*. **b** something going on; a proceeding. **2a** a natural phenomenon marked by gradual changes that lead towards a particular result: *the process of growth*. **b** a series of actions or operations designed to achieve an end, *esp* a continuous operation or treatment, e.g. in manufacture. **3a** a whole course of legal proceedings. **b** a summons; a writ. **4** a prominent or projecting part of a living organism or anatomical structure: *a bony process*. ✳ **in the process of** while something is happening, being done, etc; during. [Middle English *proces* via French from Latin *processus*, past part. of *procedere*: see PROCEED]

process² *verb trans* **1** to subject (e.g. food, photographic film, etc) to a special process or treatment. **2** to take appropriate action on (something): *process an insurance claim*. **3** in computing, to operate on (data). ➤➤ **processable** *adj*.

process³ /prə'ses/ *verb intrans chiefly Brit* to move in a procession. [back-formation from PROCESSION]

procession /prə'sesh(ə)n/ *noun* **1a** a group of people, vehicles, etc, moving along in an orderly way, *esp* as part of a ceremony or demonstration. **b** the act or action of moving along in this way. **2** a succession or sequence. **3** in Christian theology, the emanation of the Holy Spirit. [Old English from Old French, from Latin *procession-, processio*, from *procedere*: see PROCEED]

processional¹ *noun* **1** a hymn, prayer, or other composition used in or intended for a procession. **2** a book containing such compositions.

processional² *adj* **1** of or moving in a procession. **2** used, intended, or suitable for a procession.

processor /'prohsesə/ *noun* **1** a person or device that processes something. **2** in computing, = CENTRAL PROCESSING UNIT.

process server /'prohses/ *noun* somebody who serves writs and other legal documents; a bailiff.

procès-verbal /ˌprohsay vuh'bal (*French* prɔsɛ verbal)/ *noun* (*pl* **procès-verbaux** /vuh'boh (*French* verbo)/) an official written record of an event, meeting, etc. [French *procès-verbal*, literally 'verbal trial']

pro-choice /proh/ *adj* said of a person, pressure group, etc: advocating or in favour of legally available abortion: compare PRO-LIFE. ➤➤ **pro-choicer** *noun*.

proclaim /prə'klaym/ *verb trans* **1** to declare (something) publicly and usu officially; to announce (it). **2** to give clear outward indication of (something). **3** to declare (somebody) to be something or to have a specified quality: *The press proclaimed him a racist liar*. ➤➤ **proclaimer** *noun*. [Middle English *proclamen* via French from Latin *proclamare*, from PRO-¹ + *clamare* to cry out]

proclamation /proklə'maysh(ə)n/ *noun* **1** the act or an instance of proclaiming or being proclaimed. **2** an official public announcement. ➤➤ **proclamatory** /prə'klamətəri, -tri/ *adj*. [Middle English *proclamacion* via French from Latin *proclamation-, proclamatio*, from *proclamare*: see PROCLAIM]

proclitic¹ /proh'klitik/ *adj* said of a word or part of a word: lacking independent stress and therefore pronounced with the following word as a phonetic unit, e.g. either occurrence of *to* in *to be or not to be*: compare ENCLITIC¹. ➤➤ **proclitically** *adv*. [Latin *procliticus*, from PRO-¹ + late Latin *-cliticus* as in *encliticus*: see ENCLITIC¹]

proclitic² *noun* a proclitic word or particle.

proclivity /prə'kliviti/ *noun* (*pl* **proclivities**) an inclination or predisposition towards something, *esp* something reprehensible: *Her free speech, her Continental ideas, and her proclivity for championing new causes ... made her an object of suspicion* — Willa Cather. [Latin *proclivitas* from *proclivis* sloping, prone, from PRO-² + *clivus* hill]

proconsul /proh'konsl/ *noun* **1** a governor or military commander of an ancient Roman province. **2** an administrator in a modern dependency or occupied area. ➤➤ **proconsular** /-syoolə/ *adj*, **proconsulate** /-syoolət/ *noun*, **proconsulship** *noun*. [Middle English, from Latin *pro consule* for a consul]

procrastinate /prə'krastinayt/ *verb intrans formal* to put off doing something until a later time; to delay or postpone. ➤➤ **procrastination** /-'naysh(ə)n/ *noun*, **procrastinator** *noun*. [Latin *procrastinatus*, past part. of *procrastinare*, from PRO-¹ + *crastinus* of tomorrow, from *cras* tomorrow]

Usage note ━━━━━━━━━━━━━━━━━━
procrastinate *or* **prevaricate?** See note at PREVARICATE.

procreate /'prohkriayt/ *verb trans and intrans formal* to conceive or produce (offspring); to reproduce. ⮞⮞ **procreant** *adj*, **procreation** /-'aysh(ə)n/ *noun*, **procreative** /-tiv/ *adj*, **procreator** *noun*. [Latin *procreatus*, past part. of *procreare*, from PRO-¹ + *creare* to create]

Procrustean /proh'krusti-ən/ *adj* seeking to enforce or establish conformity, e.g. to a policy or doctrine, by arbitrary and often violent means. [Latin *Procrustes*, name of a mythical robber of ancient Greece who forced his victims to fit a certain bed by stretching them or lopping off their legs, from Greek *Prokroustēs*, literally 'stretcher']

proctology /prok'toləji/ *noun* the branch of medicine that deals with the structure and diseases of the anus, rectum, and lower part of the large intestine. ⮞⮞ **proctological** /-'lojikl/ *adj*, **proctologist** *noun*. [Greek *prōktos* anus + -LOGY]

proctor /'proktə/ *noun* **1** an officer at certain universities, *esp* one appointed to maintain student discipline. **2** in the Church of England, an elected representative of the clergy at convocation. **3** in former times, a legal agent or attorney, *esp* at an ecclesiastical court. ⮞⮞ **proctorial** /-'tawri-əl/ *adj*, **proctorship** *noun*. [Middle English *procutour*, alteration of *procuratour*: see PROCURATOR]

procumbent /proh'kumbənt/ *adj* **1a** said of a stem: trailing along the ground without rooting. **b** said of a plant: having or producing such stems. **2** said *esp* of a heraldic figure: lying face down. [scientific Latin *procumbent-*, *procumbens*, present part. of *procumbere* to fall or lean forward, from PRO-¹ + -*cumbere* to lie down]

procuracy /'prokyoorəsi/ *noun* (*pl* **procuracies**) the office or position of a procurator.

procuration /prokyoo'raysh(ə)n/ *noun* **1** the appointment of or authority vested in an agent or attorney. **2** *formal* the action of obtaining something, e.g. supplies; procurement. [Middle English *procuratioun* via French from Latin *procuration-*, *procuratio*, from *procurare*: see PROCURE]

procurator /'prokyoorraytə/ *noun* **1** an agent or attorney. **2** an administrator of the Roman Empire entrusted with the financial management of a province. ⮞⮞ **procuratorial** /-rə'tawri-əl/ *adj*, **procuratorship** *noun*. [Middle English *procuratour* via French from Latin *procurator*, from *procurare*: see PROCURE]

procurator fiscal *noun* (*pl* **procurators fiscal** *or* **procurator fiscals**) a local coroner and public prosecutor in Scotland.

procure /prə'kyooə/ *verb trans* **1** to obtain (something), *esp* by particular care and effort. **2** to obtain (somebody) to act as a prostitute, *esp* on behalf of somebody else. **3** *formal* to achieve (something); to bring (it) about. ⮞ *verb intrans* to obtain prostitutes for other people. ⮞⮞ **procurable** *adj*, **procurement** *noun*. [Middle English *procuren* to contrive, obtain, from Latin *procurare* to take care of, from PRO-² + *cura* care]

procurer *or* **procuress** /-ris/ *noun* a man or a woman who obtains prostitutes for other people.

Prod /prod/ *noun* (*also* **Proddy, Proddie**) *informal, derog* a Protestant, *esp* in Ireland and as contrasted with a Roman Catholic.

prod¹ /prod/ *verb* (**prodded, prodding**) ⮞ *verb trans* **1** to poke or jab (somebody or something) with a finger, pointed instrument, etc. **2** to incite (somebody) to action; to stir or stimulate (them). ⮞ *verb intrans* to make a poking or jabbing movement, *esp* repeatedly. ⮞⮞ **prodder** *noun*. [perhaps alteration of dialect *brod* to goad]

prod² *noun* **1** a pointed instrument. **2** a prodding action; a jab. **3** an incitement to act; a stimulus.

Proddy *or* **Proddie** /'prodi/ *noun* see PROD.

prodigal¹ /'prodigl/ *adj* **1** recklessly extravagant or wasteful. **2** yielding abundantly; lavish: *prodigal of new ideas*. ⮞⮞ **prodigality** /-'galiti/ *noun*, **prodigally** *adv*. [Latin *prodigus*, from *prodigere* to drive away, squander, from PRO-¹ + *agere* to drive]

prodigal² *noun* **1** somebody who is recklessly extravagant or wasteful. **2** a repentant sinner or reformed spendthrift. [(sense 2) from the prodigal son in a biblical parable (Luke 15:11–32)]

prodigious /prə'dijəs/ *adj* **1** causing amazement or wonder. **2** remarkable in bulk, quantity, or degree; enormous: *If I had more room, I should take a prodigious delight in improving and planting* — Jane Austen. ⮞⮞ **prodigiously** *adv*, **prodigiousness** *noun*.

prodigy /'prodiji/ *noun* (*pl* **prodigies**) **1a** something extraordinary, inexplicable, or marvellous. **b** (+ of) an exceptional and wonderful example of a specified quality: *a prodigy of patience*. **2** somebody, *esp* a child, with extraordinary talents. [Latin *prodigium* omen, monster]

produce¹ /prə'dyoohs/ *verb trans* **1** to give being, form, or shape to (something); to make or manufacture (it). **2** to give birth or rise to (something). **3** to offer (something) to view or notice: *She produced her passport*. **4** to act as a producer of (e.g. a film, play, piece of recorded music, etc). **5** to cause (something) to accumulate. **6** *dated* in geometry, to extend (something) in length, area, or volume: *produce a side of a triangle*. ⮞ *verb intrans* to bear, make, or yield something. ⮞⮞ **producibility** /-'biliti/ *noun*, **producible** *adj*. [Middle English (Scots) *producen* from Latin *producere*, from PRO-² + *ducere* to lead]

produce² /'prodyoohs/ *noun* **1** agricultural products, *esp* fresh fruit and vegetables. **2** anything that is produced; a product or products.

producer /prə'dyoohsə/ *noun* **1** an individual or entity that grows agricultural products or manufactures articles. **2a** somebody who has responsibility for the administrative aspects of the production of a film, e.g. casting, schedules, and *esp* finance. **b** *Brit* somebody who has responsibility for the artistic or technical aspects of a play, broadcast, recording, etc: compare DIRECTOR.

producer gas *noun* a manufactured fuel gas consisting chiefly of carbon monoxide, hydrogen, and nitrogen.

product /'prodəkt, 'produkt/ *noun* **1** a saleable or marketable commodity: *Tourism should be regarded as a product*. **2a** something produced by a natural or artificial process. **b** a result of a combination of incidental causes or conditions: *a typical product of an arts education*. **3** the result of multiplying two or more numbers or expressions together. [Latin *productum* something produced, neuter past part. of *producere*: see PRODUCE¹]

production /prə'duksh(ə)n/ *noun* **1a** the act or process of producing. **b** the creation of exchange value, *esp* the making of goods to satisfy human wants. **2** total output, *esp* of a commodity or an industry. **3a** something produced; a product. **b** a literary or artistic work. **c** a work presented in the theatre or cinema or television or radio. **4** (*used before a noun*) manufactured in large numbers: *a production model*. ⮞⮞ **productional** *adj*.

production line *noun* = ASSEMBLY LINE.

productive /prə'duktiv/ *adj* **1** having the quality or power of producing, *esp* in abundance: *productive fishing waters*. **2a** yielding significant results or benefits: *a productive programme of education*. **b** yielding or devoted to the satisfaction of wants or the creation of exchange value. **3** (+ of) effective in bringing about or causing something: *laws that are productive of such hardship*. ⮞⮞ **productively** *adv*, **productiveness** *noun*.

productivity /produk'tiviti/ *noun* **1** the state or quality of being productive or the extent of this. **2** the relationship between the output of goods and services and the input used to produce them, *esp* the effectiveness of labour in terms of industrial output.

product placement *noun* a form of advertising in which companies pay to have their products featured in films, television programmes, etc.

proem /'proh·em/ *noun formal* **1** a preface or introduction, *esp* to a book or speech. **2** a prelude. ⮞⮞ **proemial** /proh'eemi-əl/ *adj*. [Middle English *proheme* via French and Latin from Greek *prooimion*, from PRO-¹ + *oimē* song]

Prof. *abbr* Professor.

prof /prof/ *noun informal* a professor.

profane¹ /prə'fayn/ *adj* **1** not concerned with religion or religious purposes. **2a** debasing or defiling what is holy; irreverent. **b** indecent, obscene, or blasphemous: *profane language*. **3a** not among the initiated. **b** not possessing esoteric or expert knowledge. ⮞⮞ **profanely** *adv*, **profaneness** *noun*. [Middle English *prophane* via French from Latin *profanus* profane, literally 'outside the temple', from PRO-¹ + *fanum* temple]

profane² *verb trans* **1** to treat (something sacred) with abuse, irreverence, or contempt; to desecrate (it). **2** to debase (something) by an unworthy or improper use. ⮞⮞ **profanation** /profə'naysh(ə)n/ *noun*, **profaner** *noun*.

profanity /prə'faniti/ *noun* (*pl* **profanities**) **1a** profane language. **b** a profane utterance; a swear word. **2** the state or quality of being profane.

profess /prə'fes/ *verb trans* **1a** to declare or admit (something) openly or freely; to affirm (it). **b** to declare (something) falsely; to claim or pretend (it). **2** to confess one's faith in or allegiance to (e.g. a religion). **3** to receive (somebody) formally into a religious community. **4** *archaic or humorous* to be a professor of (an academic discipline). ➤ *verb intrans* to make a profession or avowal. [Latin *professus*, past part. of *profitēri* to profess, confess, from PRO-¹ + *fatēri* to acknowledge; (sense 3) Middle English *profes* (adj) having professed one's vows, via French from Latin *professus*]

professed *adj* **1** openly and freely admitted or declared: *a professed atheist*. **2** claiming to be qualified: *a professed solicitor*. **3** pretended or false: *professed misery*. **4** having taken the vows of a religious community. ➤➤ **professedly** /-sidli/ *adv*.

profession /prə'fesh(ə)n/ *noun* **1a** an occupation requiring specialized knowledge and often long and intensive academic preparation. **b** (*treated as sing. or pl*) the whole body of people engaged in such an occupation. **2a** an act of openly declaring or claiming a faith, opinion, etc. **b** a protestation, declaration, or claim. **3** an avowed religious faith. **4** the act of taking the vows of a religious community.

professional¹ *adj* **1a** relating or belonging to or engaged in a profession. **b** characterized by or conforming to the technical or ethical standards of a profession: *Professional licence, if carried too far, your chance of promotion will certainly mar* — W S Gilbert. **c** characterized by conscientious workmanship: *He did a really professional job on the garden*. **2a** said of a person: taking part in an activity, *esp* a sport, as a paid occupation, as distinct from being an amateur: *a professional golfer*. **b** denoting or relating to an activity, *esp* a sport, in which the participants are paid: *professional football*. **3** *derog* said of a person: habitually engaging in something: *a professional agitator*. ➤➤ **professionally** *adv*.

professional² *noun* **1** somebody who engages in an occupation or activity professionally. **2** somebody with sufficient experience or skill in an occupation or activity to resemble a professional: *She's a real professional when it comes to mending cars*.

professional foul *noun* in sport, *esp* football, an intentional foul that prevents a member of the opposing side from gaining an advantage or scoring.

professionalism *noun* **1** the conduct, aims, or qualities, usu of a high and consistent standard, that characterize a profession or a professional person. **2** engagement in something that is usu regarded as an amateur activity for payment or as a livelihood.

professor /prə'fesə/ *noun* **1a** a staff member of the highest academic rank at a university; *esp* the head of a university department. **b** *NAmer* a teacher at a university or college. **2** somebody who professes or declares something, e.g. a faith or opinion. ➤➤ **professorate** /-rət/ *noun*, **professorial** /profi'sawri·əl/ *adj*, **professorially** /profi'sawri·əli/ *adv*, **professorship** *noun*.

professoriate *or* **professoriat** /profi'sawri·ət/ *noun* **1** (*treated as sing. or pl*) a body of professors. **2** a professorship. [modification of French *professorat*, from *professeur* professor, from Latin *professor*, from *profitēri*: see PROFESS]

proffer¹ /'profə/ *verb trans* (**proffered, proffering**) to present (something) for acceptance; to tender or offer (it). [Middle English *profren* via Anglo-French *profrer* from Old French *poroffrir*, from *por*-PRO-² + *offrir*: see OFFER¹]

proffer² *noun* the act or action or an instance of proffering.

proficient /prə'fish(ə)nt/ *adj* competent or expert in an art, skill, branch of knowledge, etc. ➤➤ **proficiency** /-si/ *noun*, **proficiently** *adv*. [Latin *proficient-*, *proficiens*, present part. of *proficere* to go forwards, accomplish, from PRO-² + *facere* to make]

profile¹ /'prohfiel/ *noun* **1** a side view, *esp* of the human face. **2** an outline seen or represented in sharp relief; a contour. **3** a side or sectional elevation, e.g.: **a** a drawing showing a vertical section of the ground. **b** a vertical section of a soil from the ground surface to the underlying material. **4** a set of data, often in graphic form, portraying the significant features of something. **5a** a concise written or spoken biographical or descriptive outline. **b** the extent to which somebody or something features in the media or attracts public attention. ✳ **in profile** as seen from one side; appearing side on. **keep a low profile** to take up or remain in a position that does not attract attention. [Italian *profilo*, from *profilare* to draw in outline, from *pro-* forwards (from Latin PRO-²) + *filare* to spin, from late Latin *filum* thread]

profile² *verb trans* **1** to produce a profile of (somebody or something), e.g. by drawing or writing. **2** to shape the outline of (something), *esp* by using a template. ➤➤ **profiler** *noun*.

profiling /'prohfieling/ *noun* **1** an analysis of a person's DNA to determine their physical characteristics, used *esp* in criminal investigations. **2** an analysis of a person's psychological make-up, e.g. through their responses to a comprehensive set of questions, *esp* to determine their suitability for a particular job or to see if they fit a known type of criminal offender.

profit¹ /'profit/ *noun* **1** a gain or benefit. **2** the excess of revenue over expenditure, *esp* in business. **3** compensation for the assumption of risk in business enterprise, as distinguished from wages or rent. ➤➤ **profitless** *adj*. [Middle English via Old French from Latin *profectus* advance, profit, past part. of *proficere*: see PROFICIENT]

profit² *verb* (**profited, profiting**) ➤ *verb intrans* (*often + from/by*) to derive benefit; to gain: *She profited greatly from these lessons*. ➤ *verb trans* to be of service to (somebody); to benefit (them): *It will not profit you to start an argument*.

profitable *adj* producing an advantage or financial or other gains. ➤➤ **profitability** /-'biliti/ *noun*, **profitably** *adv*.

profit and loss account *noun* a summary account used at the end of an accounting period to show income and expenditure and the resulting net profit or loss.

profiteer¹ /profi'tiə/ *verb intrans* to make an unreasonable profit, *esp* on the sale of scarce and essential goods. ➤➤ **profiteering** *noun*.

profiteer² *noun* somebody who profiteers.

profiterole /prə'fitərohl/ *noun* a small hollow ball of cooked choux pastry that has a sweet or savoury filling, *esp* one filled with whipped cream and covered with a chocolate sauce. [French *profiterole*, literally 'small profit', from *profiter* to profit, from Latin *profectus*: see PROFIT¹]

profit margin *noun* the amount by which a business's net income exceeds its outgoings or the difference between the selling price of a product and its cost price.

profit-sharing *noun* a system or process under which employees receive a part of the profits of an industrial or commercial enterprise.

profit-taking *noun* the sale of securities after a rise in price or before an expected fall in price.

profligate¹ /'profligət/ *adj* **1** utterly dissolute; immoral. **2** wildly extravagant; prodigal. ➤➤ **profligacy** /-si/ *noun*, **profligately** *adv*. [Latin *profligatus*, past part. of *profligare* to strike down, from PRO-² + *fligere* to strike]

profligate² *noun* a profligate person, *esp* one given to wildly extravagant and usu grossly self-indulgent expenditure.

pro forma¹ /,proh 'fawmə/ *adj* **1** made or carried out in a perfunctory manner or as a formality. **2** provided in advance to prescribe form or describe items: *a pro forma invoice*. [Latin *pro forma* for the sake of form]

pro forma² *adv* as a formality; as a matter of convention or politeness.

pro forma³ *noun* a standard form or document.

profound¹ /prə'fownd/ *adj* **1a** having intellectual depth and insight. **b** difficult to fathom or understand. **2a** extending far below a surface. **b** coming from, reaching to, or situated at a depth; deep-seated: *a profound sigh*. **3a** characterized by intensity of feeling or quality. **b** all encompassing; complete: *profound sleep*. ➤➤ **profoundly** *adv*, **profoundness** *noun*. [Middle English via French from Latin *profundus* deep, from PRO-¹ + *fundus* bottom]

profound² *noun* (**the profound**) *archaic or literary* something profound, *esp* the depth of the ocean or the unfathomableness of the mind.

profundity /prə'funditi/ *noun* (*pl* **profundities**) **1a** intellectual depth. **b** something profound or abstruse. **2** the state or quality of being profound or deep. [Middle English *profundite* via French from Latin *profunditat-*, *profunditas* depth, from *profundus*: see PROFOUND¹]

profuse /prə'fyoohs/ *adj* **1** liberal; extravagant: *profuse in their thanks*. **2** greatly abundant; bountiful: *a profuse harvest*. ➤➤ **profusely** *adv*, **profuseness** *noun*, **profusion** /-zh(ə)n/ *noun*. [Middle English from Latin *profusus*, past part. of *profundere* to pour forth, from PRO-¹ + *fundere* to pour]

prog¹ /prog/ *noun informal* a television or radio programme.

prog² *adj informal* said of rock music: progressive (see PROGRESSIVE ROCK).

progenitive /proh'jenitiv/ *adj* capable of reproducing.

progenitor /proh'jenitə/ *noun* **1a** a direct ancestor; a forefather. **b** a biologically ancestral form. **2** a precursor or originator: *progenitors of socialist ideas* — Times Literary Supplement. [Middle English via French from Latin *progenitor*, from *progignere* to beget, from PRO-¹ + *gignere* to beget]

progeny /'projini/ *noun* (*pl* **progenies**) **1** (*treated as sing. or pl*). **a** descendants or children. **b** offspring of animals or plants. **2** *formal* an outcome or product. [Middle English *progenie* via Old French from Latin *progenies*, from *progignere*: see PROGENITOR]

progesterone /prə'jestərohn/ *noun* a steroid hormone, that is secreted by the CORPUS LUTEUM and causes changes in the uterus in preparation for pregnancy. [PROGESTIN + STEROL + -ONE]

progestin /prə'jestin/ *noun* = PROGESTOGEN. [PRO-¹ + GESTATION + -IN¹]

progestogen /prə'jestəjin/ *noun* any of several steroid hormones involved in pregnancy and the prevention of ovulation. [PRO-¹ + GESTATION + -ogen as in OESTROGEN]

prognathic /prog'nathik/ *adj* = PROGNATHOUS.

prognathous /prog'naythəs/ *adj* having the lower jaw projecting beyond the upper part of the face: compare UNDERHUNG.

prognosis /prog'nohsis/ *noun* (*pl* **prognoses** /-seez/) **1** the prospect of recovery as anticipated from the usual course of disease or peculiarities of a particular case. **2** *formal* a forecast or prediction. [via Latin from Greek *prognōsis* foreknowledge, from *progignōskein* to know before, from PRO-¹ + *gignōskein* to know]

prognostic¹ /prog'nostik/ *noun formal* **1** something that foretells; a portent. **2** in medicine, a sign or symptom used to make a prognosis. [Middle English *pronostique* via French and Latin from Greek *prognōstikon*, neuter of *prognōstikos* foretelling, from *progignōskein*: see PROGNOSIS]

prognostic² *adj* used to make a prognosis.

prognosticate /prog'nostikayt/ *verb trans formal* **1** to foretell (something) from signs or symptoms; to predict (it). **2** to indicate (something) in advance; to presage (it). >> **prognostication** /-'kaysh(ə)n/ *noun*, **prognosticative** /-kətiv/ *adj*, **prognosticator** *noun*.

program¹ /'prohgram/ *noun* **1** a sequence of coded instructions that can be stored in a mechanism, e.g. a computer, enabling it to perform a specific operation. **2** *chiefly NAmer* see PROGRAMME¹.

Usage note
program *or* programme? British English has adopted the spelling *program* as standard in computer contexts: *a computer program*; *to program a computer*. In all other contexts the correct British English spelling is *programme*, while the correct American English spelling is *program*.

program² *verb trans* (**programmed, programming**, *NAmer* **programed, programing**) **1a** to work out a sequence of operations to be performed by (a computer or other mechanism); to provide (it) with a program. **b** to prepare or arrange (instructions, data, etc) for use by a computer or other mechanism. **2** *chiefly NAmer* see PROGRAMME². >> **programmability** /-'biliti/ *noun*, **programmable** /proh'graməbl/ *adj*, **programming** *noun*.

programer *noun NAmer* see PROGRAMMER.

programmatic /prohgrə'matik/ *adj* **1** of programme music. **2** of, resembling, or having a programme. >> **programmatically** *adv*.

programme¹ (*NAmer* **program**) /'prohgram/ *noun* **1a** a brief usu printed list of the features to be presented, the people participating, etc, in a public performance. **b** the performance of such a series of features. **c** a radio or television broadcast usu characterized by some theme or purpose giving it coherence and continuity. **2** a systematic plan of action: *a rehousing programme*. **3** a curriculum, prospectus, or syllabus: *a modular degree programme*. [French *programme* agenda, public notice, from Greek *programma*, from *prographein* to write before, from PRO-¹ + *graphein* to write]

Usage note
programme *or* program? See note at PROGRAM¹.

programme² (*NAmer* **program**) *verb trans* (**programmed, programming**, *NAmer* **programed, programing**) **1a** to arrange or provide a programme of or for (something). **b** to enter (something) in a programme; to schedule (it) as part of a programme. **2** to cause (something or somebody) to conform to a pattern, e.g. of thought or behaviour; to condition (them): *Their visions of marriage had been*

programmed by Hollywood. >> **programmability** /-'biliti/ *noun*, **programmable** /proh'graməbl/ *adj*, **programming** *noun*.

programme music *noun* music intended to suggest a sequence of images or incidents.

programmer (*NAmer* **programer**) *noun* **1** somebody who prepares and tests programs for computers and other mechanisms. **2** somebody or something that programs a mechanism, e.g. a computer.

progress¹ /'prohgres/ *noun* **1** forward or onward movement, e.g. towards a destination, objective, or goal; advance. **2** gradual improvement, *esp* a continuous development towards an improved, more modern, or more complete state: *But the skin of progress masks, unknown, the spotted wolf of sameness* — Wole Soyinka. **3** *archaic* a ceremonial journey, *esp* a monarch's tour of his or her dominions. ✳ **in progress** occurring; going on. [Middle English from Latin *progressus* advance, past part. of *progredi* to go forth, from PRO-¹ + *gradi* to go]

progress² /prə'gres/ *verb intrans* **1** to move forward; to proceed. **2** to develop to a higher, better, or more advanced stage. > *verb trans* to oversee and ensure the satisfactory progress or running of (e.g. a project): *The editor must progress articles from conception to publication.*

progression /prə'gresh(ə)n/ *noun* **1** the act or an instance of progressing; advance. **2a** a continuous and connected series; a sequence. **b** a sequence of numbers in which each term is related to its predecessor by a uniform law. **3** a succession of musical notes or chords. >> **progressional** *adj*.

progressive¹ /prə'gresiv/ *adj* **1a** of or characterized by progress or progression. **b** making use of or interested in new ideas, findings, or opportunities. **c** relating to or denoting an educational theory marked by an emphasis on the individual, informality, and self-expression. **2** moving forward continuously or in stages; advancing. **3** increasing in extent or severity: *a progressive disease*. **4** increasing in rate as the base increases: *a progressive tax*. **5** relating to or denoting a verb aspect or tense that expresses action in progress, e.g. *am working*. **6** said of a dance, card game, etc: involving successive changes of partner. >> **progressively** *adv*, **progressiveness** *noun*, **progressivism** *noun*, **progressivist** *noun and adj*.

progressive² *noun* **1a** somebody who advocates progressive ideas, e.g. in education. **b** somebody believing in moderate political change, *esp* social improvement. **2** a progressive verb aspect or tense, or a verb in this aspect or tense.

progressive rock *noun* a type of rock music that is characterized by extended, sometimes experimental, instrumentals usu featuring keyboard instruments, and often showing classical influences.

prohibit /prə'hibit, proh-/ *verb trans* (**prohibited, prohibiting**) **1** to forbid (something) by authority. **2a** to prevent (somebody) from doing something. **b** to prevent (something) from happening. >> **prohibiter** *noun*, **prohibitor** *noun*. [Middle English *prohibiten* from Latin *prohibitus*, past part. of *prohibēre* to hold away, from PRO-² + *habēre* to hold]

prohibition /proh·i'bish(ə)n/ *noun* **1** the act or an instance of prohibiting something. **2** an order that forbids or prevents something. **3** (*often* **Prohibition**). **a** the forbidding by law of the manufacture and sale of alcohol. **b** the period from 1920 to 1933 in the USA when a legal ban on the manufacture and sale of alcohol was in force. **4** a judicial writ forbidding a lower court from proceeding in a case beyond its jurisdiction. >> **prohibitionary** *adj*, **prohibitionist** *noun*.

prohibitive /prə'hibitiv/ *adj* **1** tending to prohibit or restrain. **2** said *esp* of a cost, charge, etc: tending to prevent or discourage the use or acquisition of something: *The running costs seemed prohibitive*. >> **prohibitively** *adv*, **prohibitiveness** *noun*.

prohibitory /prə'hibit(ə)ri/ *adj* = PROHIBITIVE.

project¹ /'projekt, 'prohjekt/ *noun* **1** a specific plan or design; a scheme. **2** a planned undertaking, e.g.: **a** a piece of research with a definite plan. **b** a large or complex piece of work, *esp* one involving joint effort. **c** a task or problem engaged in usu by a group of pupils, *esp* to supplement and apply classroom studies. **3** *NAmer*. **a** a group of houses for rent, usu with government subsidies. **b** (**the projects**) cheap, often run-down, rented housing; a poor or dilapidated neighbourhood, *esp* one where this type of accommodation is prevalent. [Latin *projectum*, literally 'something cast', neuter of *projectus*: see PROJECT²]

project² /prə'jekt/ *verb trans* **1a** to devise (something) in the mind; to design (it). **b** to plan, calculate, or estimate (something future) on the basis of known data or present trends. **c** to present (something) or transport (somebody) in imagination. **2** to throw (something or somebody) forward or upward, *esp* by mechanical means. **3** to cause (light or an image) to fall on a surface. **4** to cause (something) to protrude. **5a** to cause (one's voice) to be heard at a distance. **b** to communicate (something) vividly, *esp* to an audience. **c** to present or express (oneself) in a manner that wins approval. **6** to reproduce (e.g. a point, line, or area) on a surface by motion in a prescribed direction. **7** to attribute (something in one's own mind) to a person, group, or object: *A nation is an entity on which one can project many of the worst of one's instincts* — Times Literary Supplement. ➤ *verb intrans* **1** to jut out; to protrude. **2** to attribute something in one's own mind to a person, group, or object. [Latin *projectus*, past part. of *proicere* to throw forward, from PRO-² + *jacere* to throw]

projectile¹ /prə'jektiel/ *noun* **1** a body projected by external force and continuing in motion by its own inertia, *esp* a missile fired from a weapon. **2** a self-propelling weapon, e.g. a rocket.

projectile² *adj* **1** propelled with great force: *projectile vomiting*. **2** being or capable of being thrust forward.

projection /prə'jeksh(ə)n/ *noun* **1** the act of projecting something or somebody. **2a** a jutting out. **b** a part that juts out. **3** an estimate of future possibilities based on present trends. **4** the display of films or slides by projecting an image onto a screen. **5a** a systematic representation on a flat surface of latitude and longitude from the curved surface of the earth, the celestial sphere, etc. **b** the process of reproducing a spatial object on a surface by projecting its points or a reproduction formed by this process. **6** the act or an instance of perceiving a subjective mental image as objective, or something so perceived. **7** the attribution of one's own ideas, feelings, or attitudes to other people or to objects, *esp* as a defence against feelings of guilt or inadequacy. ➤ **projectional** *adj*.

projectionist *noun* the operator of a film projector.

projective /prə'jektiv/ *adj* of, produced by, or involving projection. ➤ **projectively** *adv*.

projective geometry *noun* a branch of geometry that deals with the properties of solids that are unaltered by projection.

projector /prə'jektə/ *noun* **1** an apparatus for projecting films or slides onto a surface. **2** *archaic* somebody who devises a project.

prokaryote *or* **procaryote** /proh'karioht/ *noun* a minute organism, e.g. a bacterium, that does not have a distinct nucleus: compare EUKARYOTE. ➤ **prokaryotic** /-'otik/ *adj*. [PRO-¹ + KARY- + -*ote* as in ZYGOTE]

prolactin /proh'laktin/ *noun* a protein hormone produced by the front lobe of the pituitary gland that is important in the reproduction of mammals and that stimulates milk production. [PRO-² + LACT- + -IN¹]

prolapse¹ /'prohlaps/ *noun* the falling down or slipping forward of a body part, e.g. the uterus, from its usual position. [late Latin *prolapsus* fallen, past part. of Latin *prolabi* to fall or slide forward, from PRO-¹ + *labi* to slide]

prolapse² *verb intrans* said of a body part: to fall down or slip forward from its usual position.

prolapsus /proh'lapsəs/ *noun* = PROLAPSE¹.

prolate /'prohlayt/ *adj* said of a spheroid: elongated in the direction of a line joining the poles: compare OBLATE. [Latin *prolatus*, past part. of *proferre* to bring forwards, extend, from PRO-¹ + *ferre* to carry]

prole /prohl/ *noun and adj informal, derog* = PROLETARIAN.

prolegomenon /prohli'gominən/ *noun* (*pl* **prolegomena** /-nə/) an introductory section, *esp* to a learned work. ➤ **prolegomenous** /-nəs/ *adj*. [Greek *prolegomenon*, literally 'something said beforehand', from *prolegein* to say beforehand, from PRO-¹ + *legein* to say]

prolepsis /proh'lepsis/ *noun* (*pl* **prolepses** /-seez/) **1** *formal* anticipation, *esp* the representation of a future act or development as if it already exists or has already been accomplished. **2** in rhetoric, the answering of anticipated objections. ➤ **proleptic** /-tik/ *adj*. [Greek *prolēpsis*, from *prolambanein* to take beforehand, from PRO-¹ + *lambanein* to take]

proletarian /prohli'teəri-ən/ *noun* a member of the proletariat. ➤ **proletarian** *adj*, **proletarianism** *noun*. [Latin *proletarius*,

member of the lowest social class who served the state by producing offspring, from *proles* progeny]

proletariat /prohli'teəri-ət/ *noun* (*treated as sing. or pl*) **1** the lowest social or economic class of a community: compare WORKING CLASS. **2** *esp* in Marxist theory, the working class, *esp* those workers who lack their own means of production and hence sell their labour to earn a living. **3** in ancient Rome, the lowest class of citizens: compare PATRICIAN (2). [French *prolétariat*, from Latin *proletarius*: see PROLETARIAN]

pro-life /proh/ *adj* said of a person, pressure group, etc: opposed to legally available abortion: compare PRO-CHOICE. ➤ **pro-lifer** *noun*.

proliferate /prə'lifərayt/ *verb intrans* **1** to grow or reproduce by rapid production of new parts, cells, buds, or offspring. **2** to increase rapidly in number or quantity. ➤ **proliferation** /-'raysh(ə)n/ *noun*, **proliferative** /-tiv/ *adj*. [earliest as *proliferation*, from French *prolifération*, from *proliférer* to proliferate, from *prolifère* proliferous, from Latin *proles* progeny + -FEROUS]

proliferous /prə'lif(ə)rəs/ *adj* **1** said of a plant: reproducing freely by vegetative means, e.g. by putting out runners or side-shoots. **2** said of an invertebrate animal: producing buds or branches, *esp* as a means of reproduction: *a proliferous coral*.

prolific /prə'lifik/ *adj* **1** producing offspring, fruit, etc freely. **2** marked by abundant inventiveness or productivity: *a prolific writer*. ➤ **prolificacy** /-kəsi/ *noun*, **prolifically** *adv*, **prolificness** *noun*. [French *prolifique*, ultimately from Latin *proles* progeny]

prolix /'prohliks/ *adj* **1** unduly or tediously prolonged or repetitious: *a prolix speech*. **2** given to using more words than are needed in speaking or writing; long-winded: *On important topics it is better to be a good deal prolix than even a little obscure* — Poe. ➤ **prolixity** /-'liksiti/ *noun*, **prolixly** *adv*. [Middle English via French from Latin *prolixus* extended, from PRO-¹ + *liquēre* to be fluid]

prolocutor /proh'lokyootə/ *noun* a person who chairs the lower house of a CONVOCATION (assembly) of the Anglican Church. [Latin *prolocutor* spokesman, from PRO-² + *locutor* speaker, from *loqui* to speak]

PROLOG *or* **Prolog** /'prohlog/ *noun* a computer programming language that is specially designed to handle logical relations between groups of data, *esp* in artificial intelligence and expert systems. [short for *programming logic*]

prologue (*NAmer* **prolog**) /'prohlog/ *noun* **1** the preface or introduction to a literary, cinematic, or musical work. **2** a speech, often in verse, addressed to the audience at the beginning of a play. **3** an introductory or preceding event or development. [Middle English *prolog* via Old French and Latin from Greek *prologos*, part of a Greek play preceding the entry of the chorus, from PRO-¹ + *legein* to speak]

prolong /prə'long/ *verb trans* **1** to lengthen (something) in time; to continue (it). **2** to lengthen (something) in space: *to prolong a line*. ➤ **prolongation** /prohlong'gaysh(ə)n/ *noun*, **prolonger** *noun*. [Middle English *prolongen* via French from late Latin *prolongare*, from PRO-¹ + Latin *longus* long]

prolusion /prə'l(y)oohzh(ə)n/ *noun formal* **1** a preliminary trial or exercise. **2** an introductory and often tentative discourse. ➤ **prolusory** /-zəri/ *adj*. [Latin *prolusion-, prolusio,* from *proludere* to play beforehand, from PRO-¹ + *ludere* to play]

PROM /prom/ *abbr* programmable read-only memory.

prom /prom/ *noun* **1** (*often* **Prom**) = PROMENADE CONCERT. **2** *Brit* = PROMENADE¹ (I). **3** *NAmer* a formal dance given for a high-school or college class, *esp* at the end of an academic year.

promenade¹ /'promənahd/ *noun* **1** a place for strolling, *esp* a paved walk along the seafront at a resort. **2** *dated* a leisurely stroll or ride taken for pleasure, usu in a public place and often as a social custom. **3** a figure in a square dance or country dance in which couples march usu anticlockwise in a circle. [French *promenade* from *promener* to take for a walk, from Latin *prominare* to drive forwards, from PRO-¹ + *minare* to drive]

promenade² *verb intrans* to take a promenade. ➤ *verb trans* **1** in dancing, to escort (one's partner) on a promenade. **2** *chiefly dated* to display (somebody or something) while strolling around: *promenading his new bicycle in front of his friends*.

promenade concert *noun* a concert of classical music at which some of the audience stand or walk about.

promenade deck *noun* an upper deck of a passenger ship where people can take a stroll.

promenader /promə'nahdə/ *noun* **1** somebody attending a promenade concert, *esp* a member of the audience in the area without seating. **2** somebody who takes a promenade.

promethazine /proh'methəzeen/ *noun* an antihistamine drug used to treat allergies and motion sickness. [PROPYL + *dimethylamine* (from DI-[1] + METHYL + AMINE) + PHENOTHIAZINE]

Promethean /prə'meethi·ən/ *adj* daringly original or creative. [from *Prometheus*, demigod of Greek mythology who stole fire from Zeus and gave it to the human race, via Latin from Greek *Promētheus*]

promethium /prə'meethi·əm/ *noun* a metallic chemical element of the rare-earth group obtained from the radioactive decay of uranium: symbol Pm, atomic number 61. [scientific Latin, named after *Prometheus*: see PROMETHEAN]

prominence /'prominəns/ *noun* **1** the state or quality of being prominent or conspicuous. **2** something prominent; a projection: *a rocky prominence*. **3** in astronomy, a large mass of incandescent gas arising from the lower solar atmosphere.

prominent /'prominənt/ *adj* **1a** widely and popularly known; famously eminent. **b** readily noticeable; conspicuous. **2** projecting beyond a surface or line; protuberant. ⟩⟩ **prominently** *adv*. [Latin *prominent-, prominens*, present part. of *prominēre* to jut forward, from PRO-[1] + *-minēre* to project]

promiscuous /prə'miskyoo·əs/ *adj* **1** indulging in or characterized by numerous casual and short-lived sexual relationships. **2** composed of a mixture of people or things. **3** not restricted to one class or person; indiscriminate: *a promiscuous and unprincipled attack on radicalism* — Arthur M Schlesinger. **4** casual; irregular: *promiscuous eating habits*. ⟩⟩ **promiscuity** /promi'skyooh·iti/ *noun*, **promiscuously** *adv*, **promiscuousness** *noun*. [Latin *promiscuus*, from PRO-[1] + *miscēre* to mix]

promise[1] /'promis/ *noun* **1** a declaration that one will or will not do something specified. **2** grounds for expectation usu of success, improvement, or excellence: *show promise*. **3** something promised. [Middle English *promis* from Latin *promissum*, neuter past part. of *promittere* to send forth, promise, from PRO-[1] + *mittere* to send]

promise[2] *verb trans* **1a** to pledge oneself to do, bring about, or provide (something): *She promised she would come*. **b** to make a promise to (somebody). **2** to give an assurance of (something to somebody): *It can be done, I promise you*. **3** *archaic* to betroth (somebody) to another. **4** to suggest (something) beforehand; to indicate (it): *dark clouds promising rain*. ⟩ *verb intrans* **1** to make a promise. **2** to give grounds for expectation, *esp* of something good. ⟩⟩ **promiser** *noun*.

promised land *noun* **1** (**the Promised Land**) the land of Canaan, which God promised Abraham that his descendants would possess (Genesis 12:7). **2** a place or condition believed to promise final satisfaction or realization of hopes.

promisee /promi'see/ *noun* a person to whom a promise is made.

promising *adj* full of promise; likely to succeed or to yield good results. ⟩⟩ **promisingly** *adv*.

promisor /promi'saw, 'promisə/ *noun* a person who makes a legally binding promise.

promissory /'promis(ə)ri/ *adj* containing or conveying a promise. [medieval Latin *promissorius*, from Latin *promissus*, past part. of *promittere*: see PROMISE[1]]

promissory note *noun* a written signed promise to pay, either on demand or at a fixed or determinable future time, a sum of money to a specified individual or to the bearer.

promo /'prohmoh/ *noun* (*pl* **promos**) *informal* an advertising promotion, *esp* a video or film. [short for PROMOTION]

promontory /'promənt(ə)ri/ *noun* (*pl* **promontories**) **1** a high point of land or rock projecting into a body of water; a headland. **2** a prominence or projection on a part of the body. [Latin *promunturium, promontorium*; prob related to *prominēre*: see PROMINENT]

promote /prə'moht/ *verb trans* **1a** to contribute to the growth or prosperity of (something); to further (it): *promote international understanding*. **b** to help bring (e.g. an enterprise) into being; to launch (it). **c** to present (e.g. merchandise) for public acceptance through advertising and publicity. **d** to contribute to (something) in a beneficial way: *Regular exercise promotes good health*. **2a** to cause (somebody) to advance in position, rank, or status. **b** to assign (a team) to a higher division of a sporting competition, e.g. a football league: compare RELEGATE. **c** in chess, to change (a pawn) into a more valuable piece when it reaches the end of the board. **d** *NAmer*

to cause (a student) to move to a higher class or grade. ⟩⟩ **promoter** *noun*, **promotive** /-tiv/ *adj*. [Latin *promotus*, past part. of *promovēre* to move forward, from PRO-[1] + *movēre* to MOVE[1]]

promotion /prə'mohsh(ə)n/ *noun* **1a** the act or fact of being raised in position or rank. **b** the act or fact of being assigned to a higher division of a sporting competition. **2a** the act of furthering the growth or development of something, *esp* sales or public awareness. **b** something, e.g. a price reduction or free sample, intended to promote something or increase sales. ⟩⟩ **promotional** *adj*.

prompt[1] /prompt/ *verb trans* **1** to move (somebody) to action; to incite (them): *Curiosity prompted him to ask the question*. **2** to serve as the inciting cause of (something); to urge (it): *These figures prompt serious anxiety about unemployment*. **3** to assist (somebody acting or speaking) by saying the next words of something forgotten or imperfectly learned. [Middle English *prompten* from late Latin *promptare*, from Latin *promptus*: see PROMPT[2]]

prompt[2] *adj* **1** performed readily or immediately: *prompt assistance*. **2a** ready and quick to act as occasion demands. **b** happening or arriving on time; punctual. ⟩⟩ **promptly** *adv*, **promptness** *noun*. [Middle English via French from Latin *promptus* ready, prompt, past part. of *promere* to bring forth, from PRO-[1] + *emere* to take]

prompt[3] *noun* **1a** the act or an instance of prompting or reminding somebody. **b** somebody or something that prompts or reminds somebody. **2a** a limit of time given for payment of an account for goods purchased. **b** a reminder of a limit of time given for payment. **3** in computing, any of various symbols on a VDU screen that indicate to the user the place where a command should go.

prompt[4] *adv informal* exactly; punctually: *The lecture will start at seven o'clock prompt*.

prompter /'promptə/ *noun* **1** a person who is positioned offstage during a performance of a play and who prompts actors when they forget their lines. **2** any person or device that prompts.

promptitude /'promptityoohd/ *noun formal* the quality or habit of being prompt; promptness or punctuality. [Middle English via French from late Latin *promptitudo*, from Latin *promptus*: see PROMPT[2]]

prompt note *noun* = PROMPT[3] (2B).

prompt side *noun* the side of the stage, usu to an actor's left in Britain and to an actor's right in the USA, where the prompter sits.

promulgate /'prom(ə)lgayt/ *verb trans* **1** to make (something) known by open declaration; to proclaim (it). **2** to put (a law, decree, etc) into action or force, *esp* by official proclamation. **3** to promote (something) publicly. ⟩⟩ **promulgation** /-'gaysh(ə)n/ *noun*, **promulgator** *noun*. [Latin *promulgatus*, past part. of *promulgare* to proclaim]

pron. *abbr* **1** pronoun. **2** pronounced. **3** pronunciation.

pronate /proh'nayt/ *verb trans* to rotate (the hand or foot) so that the palm or sole faces downward or backward: compare SUPINATE. ⟩⟩ **pronation** /-sh(ə)n/ *noun*. [late Latin *pronatus*, past part. of *pronare* to bend forward, from Latin *pronus*: see PRONE]

pronator /proh'naytə/ *noun* a muscle that is involved in pronating a hand or foot.

prone /prohn/ *adj* **1** (+ to) having a tendency or inclination to something: *He was not prone to rashness and precipitate action* — Jack London. **2a** having the front or lower surface downward: compare SUPINE[1] (1A). **b** lying flat on the ground. **3** (*used in combinations*) liable to suffer: *an accident-prone child; strike-prone industries*. **4** *archaic* sloping downward. ⟩⟩ **pronely** *adv*, **proneness** *noun*. [Middle English from Latin *pronus* bent forward, tending, from *pro* forwards]

prong[1] /prong/ *noun* **1** any of the slender sharp-pointed parts of a fork or similar instrument. **2** a subdivision of an argument, attacking force, etc. ⟩⟩ **pronged** *adj*. [Middle English *pronge, prange* fork; earlier history unknown]

prong[2] *verb trans* to stab, pierce, or spear (something) with or as if with a prong.

pronghorn *noun* (*pl* **pronghorns** or *collectively* **pronghorn**) a cud-chewing mammal of treeless parts of western N America that resembles an antelope: *Antilocapra americana*.

pronoid[1] /'prohnoyd/ *adj* showing undue optimism and happiness, and *esp* having a firm, and often unjustified, belief that one is liked by other people: *You're so pronoid, you think everybody* *likes you.* >> **pronoia** /proh'noyə/ *noun.* [PRO-² + *paranoid*: see PARANOIA]

pronoid² *noun* somebody who is pronoid.

pronominal /proh'nominl/ *adj* of, resembling, or constituting a pronoun. >> **pronominally** *adv.* [late Latin *pronominalis*, from Latin *pronomin-, pronomen*: see PRONOUN]

pronoun /'prohnown/ *noun* a word used as a substitute for a noun or noun phrase and referring to a previously named or an already understood person or thing, e.g. *I, he, that.* [Middle English *pronom* from Latin *pronomin-, pronomen*, from PRO-² + *nomin-, nomen* name]

pronounce /prə'nowns/ *verb trans* **1** to utter the sound or sounds of (a letter, syllable, word, etc), *esp* to say (it) correctly. **2** to declare (somebody or something) as being officially or ceremoniously in a specified state: *The priest pronounced them man and wife.* **3** to declare (somebody or something) as being authoritatively the case or as being an opinion: *The doctor pronounced him fit to work.* > *verb intrans* **1** (*often* + on/upon) to pass judgment; to declare one's opinion definitely or authoritatively. **2** to produce speech sounds. >> **pronounceable** *adj,* **pronouncer** *noun.* [Middle English *pronouncen* via French from Latin *pronuntiare*, from PRO-¹ + *nuntiare* to report, from *nuntius* messenger]

pronounced *adj* strongly marked or very conspicuous. >> **pronouncedly** /-sidli/ *adv.*

pronouncement *noun* **1** a usu formal declaration of opinion. **2** an authoritative announcement.

pronto /'prontoh/ *adv informal* without delay; quickly. [Spanish *pronto* from Latin *promptus*: see PROMPT²]

pronunciamento /prə,nunsi-ə'mentoh/ *noun* (*pl* **pronunciamentos**) a declaration, *esp* one made by the leaders of a revolt in a Spanish-speaking country, announcing a change of government or outlining political aims, etc. [Spanish *pronunciamiento* from *pronunciar* to pronounce, from Latin *pronuntiare*: see PRONOUNCE]

pronunciation /prə,nunsi'aysh(ə)n/ *noun* the act or manner of pronouncing a letter, syllable, word, etc. [Middle English *pronunciacion* via French from Latin *pronuntiation-, pronuntiatio*, from *pronuntiare*: see PRONOUNCE]

proof¹ /proohf/ *noun* **1a** evidence that compels acceptance of a truth or a fact. **b** the process of establishing the truth or validity of a statement. **c** an act, effort, or operation designed to establish or discover a fact or the truth; a test. **d** the body of evidence that determines the judgment of a tribunal. **2a** a sample printing of a piece of text, an engraving, etc, made for examination or correction. **b** a test photographic print. **3** a test of the quality of an article or substance. **4** the alcoholic content of a beverage compared with the standard for proof spirit. **5** in Scots law, a trial before a judge without a jury. [Middle English from Old French *preuve*, from late Latin *proba*, from Latin *probare*: see PROVE]

proof² *adj* **1** (*often used in combinations*) designed for or successful in resisting or repelling; impervious: *soundproof; proof against rain.* **2** used in proving, in testing, or as a standard of comparison. **3** of standard strength, quality, or alcoholic content. **4** serving as a sample, e.g. of printed text.

proof³ *verb trans* **1** to make or take a proof of (a typeset text, an engraving, etc). **2** (*often* + against) to give a resistant quality to (something), *esp* to make (it) waterproof. **3** = PROOFREAD. >> **proofer** *noun.*

proofread /'proohfreed/ *verb trans* to read and mark corrections on (a proof). >> **proofreader** *noun.* [earliest as *proofreader*]

proof spirit *noun* a mixture of alcohol and water containing a standard amount of alcohol, in Britain 57.1% by volume.

prop¹ /prop/ *noun* **1** a rigid usu auxiliary vertical support, e.g. a pole: *pit prop.* **2** a source of strength or support: *His daughter was his chief prop in his old age.* **3** = PROP FORWARD. [Middle English from early Dutch *proppe* stopper, support for vines]

prop² *verb trans* (**propped, propping**) **1** to support (something or somebody) by placing something under or against them: *I propped the window open with a stick.* **2** to support (something or somebody) by placing them against something: *I propped the ladder against the wall.*

prop³ *noun* any article or object used in a play or film other than painted scenery or costumes. [short for PROPERTY]

prop⁴ *noun informal* a propeller.

prop. *abbr* **1** proposition. **2** proprietor.

propaedeutic /prohpi'dyoohtik/ *adj formal* serving or needed as preparation for learning or further study. [Greek *propaideuein* to teach beforehand, from PRO-¹ + *paideuein* to teach, from *paid-, pais* child]

propaedeutical /prohpi'dyoohtikl/ *adj* = PROPAEDEUTIC.

propaganda /propə'gandə/ *noun* **1a** the usu organized spreading of ideas, information, or rumours designed to promote or damage an institution, movement, etc. **b** the ideas, information, etc so spread. **2** (**Propaganda**) a division of the Roman Catholic Church having jurisdiction over missionary territories and the training of priests for these.

Word history

from Latin *Congregatio de propaganda fide* Congregation for propagating the faith, organization established by Pope Gregory XV d.1623. This committee of cardinals was set up in 1622 to oversee the propagation of Roman Catholicism throughout the world.

propagandize *or* **propagandise** *verb intrans* to spread propaganda. > *verb trans* **1** to subject (somebody) to propaganda. **2** to spread (something) by propaganda. >> **propagandism** *noun,* **propagandist** *noun and adj,* **propagandistic** /-'distik/ *adj,* **propagandistically** /-'distikli/ *adv.*

propagate /'propəgayt/ *verb trans* **1** to cause (something, e.g. a plant) to reproduce or multiply by natural or artificial processes. **2** to pass down (e.g. a characteristic) to offspring. **3a** to cause (something) to spread out and affect a greater number or area; to disseminate (it). **b** to publicize (something): *propagate the Gospel.* **c** to transmit (*esp* energy) in the form of a wave. > *verb intrans* **1** to reproduce sexually or asexually. **2** to increase or extend. >> **propagation** /-'gaysh(ə)n/ *noun,* **propagative** /-gətiv/ *adj.* [Latin *propagatus*, past part. of *propagare* to propagate by cuttings, from *propages* cutting, shoot, offspring, from PRO-¹ + *pangere* to fasten]

propagator /'propəgaytə/ *noun* **1** a box, usu with a transparent lid and often capable of being heated, where germinating plants, young seedlings, and cuttings are kept until they have established root systems. **2** a person who spreads ideas, beliefs, information, etc to others.

propane /'prohpayn/ *noun* a heavy inflammable gas that is a member of the alkane series of organic chemical compounds, is found in crude petroleum and natural gas and is used *esp* as a fuel: formula C_3H_8. [*propionic* + -ANE]

propanoic acid /prohpə'noh·ik/ *noun* = PROPIONIC ACID. [PROPANE + -OIC]

propel /prə'pel/ *verb trans* (**propelled, propelling**) **1** to drive (something) forward by means of a force that imparts motion. **2** to urge (somebody) on; to motivate (them). [Middle English *propellen* from Latin *propellere*, from PRO-¹ + *pellere* to drive]

propellant *noun* **1** a gas in a pressurized container for expelling the contents when the pressure is released. **2** an explosive for propelling projectiles. **3** fuel plus oxidizer used by a rocket engine to provide thrust.

propellent *or* **propellant** *adj* capable of propelling.

propeller *noun* a device, consisting of a central hub with radiating twisted blades, that is used to propel a ship or aircraft.

propeller shaft *noun* a shaft that transmits mechanical power, *esp* from an engine to the wheels of a vehicle or the propeller of a ship or aircraft.

propelling pencil *noun Brit* a usu metal or plastic pencil with a thin replaceable lead that can be moved forward as it wears down by a screw device.

propene /'prohpeen/ *noun* = PROPYLENE. [*propionic* + -ENE]

propensity /prə'pensiti/ *noun* (*pl* **-ies,** *pl* **propensities**) *formal* a natural inclination or tendency. [archaic *propense* leaning towards, disposed, from Latin *propensus*, past part. of *propendere* to lean or incline towards, from PRO-¹ + *pendere* to hang]

proper¹ /'propə/ *adj* **1** suitable; appropriate. **2a** strictly accurate; correct. **b** strictly decorous; genteel: *prim and proper.* **3** (*often used after a noun*) being strictly so-called: *not part of the city proper.* **4** (+ to) belonging characteristically to a species or individual; peculiar to something or somebody: *ailments proper to tropical climates* — George Santayana. **5** *chiefly Brit, informal* thorough; complete: *I felt a proper idiot!* **6** (*often used after a noun*) said of a representation of something in heraldry: appearing in its natural colour. **7** appointed for the LITURGY (form of church service) of a particular day. **8** *archaic* belonging to oneself; own. **9** *archaic* very good.

>> **properness** *noun*. [Middle English *propre* proper, own, via Old French from Latin *proprius* one's own, special]

proper² *noun* in the Roman Catholic Church, the parts of the Mass that vary according to the particular day or time: compare ORDINARY².

proper³ *adv chiefly dialect* in a thorough manner; completely.

proper fraction *noun* a fraction in which the NUMERATOR (number above the line) is less than the DENOMINATOR (number below the line).

properly *adv* 1 in a fit manner; suitably: *properly dressed.* 2 in the required or appropriate way; correctly: *do it properly.* 3 strictly in accordance with fact: *properly speaking.* 4 *chiefly Brit, informal* to the full extent; completely.

proper motion *noun* in astronomy, a component of the true space velocity of a star relative to the sun that causes a change of apparent position on the celestial sphere.

proper name *noun* = PROPER NOUN.

proper noun *noun* a noun that designates a particular person, place, or thing and is usu capitalized, e.g. *Janet, London*: compare COMMON NOUN.

propertied /'propatid/ *adj* said of a person, class, etc: possessing property, *esp* land.

property /'propati/ *noun* (*pl* **properties**) **1a** something owned or possessed. **b** ownership. **c** something to which somebody has a legal title. **2** a piece of land and the building or buildings on it. **3a** a quality, attribute, or power inherent in something. **b** an attribute common to all members of a class. **4** *dated* = PROP³. >> **propertyless** *adj*. [Middle English *proprete* via early French *propreté, propriété* from Latin *proprietat-, proprietas*, from *proprius* one's own, characteristic]

prop forward *noun* in rugby, either of the two players on either side of the hooker in the front row of the scrum.

prophase /'prohfayz/ *noun* the initial stage of cell division in which the chromosomes become visible as paired chromatids and the nuclear membrane disappears: compare ANAPHASE, METAPHASE.

prophecy /'profisi/ *noun* (*pl* **prophecies**) **1** a prediction of an event. **2a** an inspired declaration of divine will and purpose. **b** the function or vocation of a prophet; the capacity to utter prophecies. [Middle English from Old French *prophecie*: see PROPHESY]

prophesy /'profisie/ *verb* (**prophesies, prophesied, prophesying**) > *verb trans* **1** to predict (something) with assurance or on the basis of mystic knowledge. **2** to utter (something) by, or as if by, divine inspiration. > *verb intrans* **1** to make a prediction. **2** to speak as if divinely inspired. >> **prophesier** /-sie-ə/ *noun*. [Middle English *prophesien*, from early French *prophesier*, from Old French *prophecie* prophecy, ultimately from Greek *prophētēs*: see PROPHET]

prophet /'profit/ *or* **prophetess** /-tes/ *noun* **1a** a man or woman who utters divinely inspired revelations. **b** the writer of any of the prophetic books of the Old Testament. **2** somebody who foretells future events; a predictor. **3** a spokesperson for a doctrine, movement, etc: *a prophet of socialism.* **4** (**the Prophet**). **a** in Islam, a name for Muhammad. **b** in the Mormon Church, a name for Joseph Smith, the founder of the Church. [Middle English *prophete* via Old French and Latin from Greek *prophētēs*, from PRO-¹ + *phētēs* speaker, from *phanai* to speak]

prophetic /prə'fetik/ *adj* **1** of or characteristic of a prophet or prophecy. **2** foretelling events; predictive. >> **prophetically** *adv*.

prophetical /prə'fetikl/ *adj* = PROPHETIC.

Prophets *pl noun* the second part of the Jewish scriptures.

prophylactic¹ /profi'laktik/ *adj* **1** guarding against, protecting from, or preventing disease. **2** *formal* tending to prevent or ward off; preventive. >> **prophylactically** *adv*. [Greek *prophylaktikos*, from *prophylassein* to keep guard before, from PRO-¹ + *phylassein* to guard, from *phylak-, phylax* guard]

prophylactic² *noun* **1** a prophylactic drug. **2** *chiefly NAmer* a contraceptive device, *esp* a condom.

prophylaxis /profi'laksis/ *noun* (*pl* **prophylaxes** /-seez/) action taken to preserve health and prevent the spread of disease. [via scientific Latin from Greek *prophylaktikos*: see PROPHYLACTIC¹]

propinquity /prə'pingkwiti/ *noun formal* **1** nearness in place or time; proximity. **2** nearness of relationship; kinship. [Middle English *propinquite*, from Latin *propinquitas* kinship, proximity, from *propinquus* near, related, from *prope* near]

propionic acid /prohpi'onik/ *noun* a rancid-smelling fatty acid found in milk and liquids obtained from the distillation of wood, coal, and petroleum and used *esp* in making flavourings and perfumes: formula $C_3H_6O_2$. [PRO-¹ + Greek *piōn* fat; because it is the first in the series of fatty acids]

propitiate /prə'pishiayt/ *verb trans* to gain or regain the favour or goodwill of (somebody); to appease (them). >> **propitiation** /-'aysh(ə)n/ *noun*, **propitiator** *noun*, **propitiatory** /-shət(ə)ri/ *adj*. [Latin *propitiatus*, past part. of *propitiare*, from *propitius*: see PROPITIOUS]

propitious /prə'pishəs/ *adj* **1** boding well; auspicious: *a propitious sign.* **2** tending to favour; opportune: *a propitious moment for the revolt to break out.* **3** favourably disposed; benevolent. >> **propitiously** *adv*, **propitiousness** *noun*. [Middle English *propicious* from Latin *propitius*, from PRO-¹ + *petere* to seek]

propjet *noun* = TURBOPROP.

propolis /'propəlis/ *noun* a brownish resinous material of waxy consistency collected by bees from the buds of trees and used as a glue in constructing and strengthening the hive. [via Latin from Greek *propolis* suburb, bee glue, from PRO-¹ + *polis* city]

proponent /prə'pohnənt/ *noun* somebody who argues in favour of something; an advocate. [Latin *proponent-, proponens*, present part. of *proponere*: see PROPOUND]

proportion¹ /prə'pawsh(ə)n/ *noun* **1** the relation of one part to another or to the whole with respect to magnitude, quantity, or degree. **2** harmonious relation of parts to each other or to the whole; balance. **3** a relationship of constant ratio: *Wages increased in proportion to the cost of living.* **4a** a proper or equal share: *Each did his proportion of the work.* **b** a fraction or percentage. **5** (*in pl*) size; dimensions. **6** a statement of equality of two ratios, e.g. 4/2=10/5. * **blow something out of (all) proportion** to attach too much importance or significance to something. **in proportion** having the correct or desirable relationship between constituent parts: *She may be short, but she's perfectly in proportion.* **out of proportion** lacking the correct or desirable relationship between constituent parts. **sense of proportion** an ability to assess the relative importance or significance of something or of things in general. >> **proportionability** *noun*, **proportionable** *adj*. [Middle English *proporcion* via French from Latin *proportion-, proportio*, from PRO-² + *portion-, portio* PORTION¹]

proportion² *verb trans* **1** to adjust (a part or thing) in proportion to other parts or things. **2** to make the parts of (something) harmonious or symmetrical.

proportional¹ *adj* **1a** (*often* +) being in a corresponding or appropriate relation with respect to size, shape, etc. **b** (*often* +) said of a mathematical variable: having the same or a constant ratio. **2** of or being a proportion. >> **proportionality** /-'naliti/ *noun*, **proportionally** *adv*.

proportional² *noun* in mathematics, a number or quantity in a proportion.

proportional representation *noun* an electoral system in which each political group gains a number of seats in a legislative assembly that is in proportion to the number of votes it wins.

proportionate¹ /prə'pawsh(ə)nət/ *adj* being in due proportion. >> **proportionately** *adv*.

proportionate² /prə'pawsh(ə)nayt/ *verb trans* to make (something) proportionate.

proposal /prə'pohzl/ *noun* **1** the act or an instance of putting something forward for consideration. **2a** a proposed idea or plan of action; a suggestion. **b** an offer of marriage. **3** an application for insurance.

propose /prə'pohz/ *verb trans* **1a** to present (an idea, a plan, etc) for consideration or adoption: *propose terms for peace.* **b** to establish (something) as an aim or intention: *I propose to spend the time working.* **2a** to recommend (somebody) to fill a place or vacancy; to nominate (them). **b** to announce (a toast): *I now propose the health of the bridesmaids.* > *verb intrans* **1** to form or put forward a plan or intention: *Man proposes, but God disposes.* **2** to make an offer of marriage. >> **proposer** *noun*. [Middle English *proposen* via French from Latin *proponere*: see PROPOUND]

propositi /prə'pozitie/ *noun pl* of PROPOSITUS.

proposition¹ /propə'zish(ə)n/ *noun* **1a** something offered for consideration or acceptance. **b** *informal* a proposal of sexual intercourse. **c** a formal mathematical statement to be proved. **d** in philosophy, an expression of something that can be either true or false. **2** somebody or something to be dealt with: *The firm is not a paying proposition.* ➤➤ **propositional** *adj.*

proposition² *verb trans* to make a proposal to (somebody); *specif* to propose sexual intercourse to (them).

propositus /prə'pozitəs/ *noun* (*pl* **propositi** /-tie/) = PROBAND. [Latin *propositus*, past part. of *proponere*: see PROPOUND]

propound /prə'pownd/ *verb trans formal* to offer (something) for discussion or consideration. ➤➤ **propounder** *noun*. [alteration of Middle English (Scots) *propone* from Latin *proponere* to display, propound, from PRO-¹ + *ponere* to put, place]

propranolol /proh'pranəlol/ *noun* a synthetic drug that blocks the action of adrenalin on beta-receptors in the heart and is used *esp* in the treatment of abnormal heart rhythms and to lower high blood pressure. [prob alteration of earlier *propanolol*, from *propanol* (propyl alcohol) + -OL¹]

proprietary¹ /prə'prie·ət(ə)ri/ *adj* **1** of or characteristic of a proprietor: *proprietary rights.* **2** made and marketed under a patent, trademark, etc: *a proprietary drug.* **3** privately owned and managed: *a proprietary clinic.* [late Latin *proprietarius*, from Latin *proprietas*: see PROPERTY]

proprietary² *noun* (*pl* **proprietaries**) **1** a body of proprietors. **2** a proprietary drug. [Middle English *proprietarie* owner, from late Latin *proprietarius*: see PROPRIETARY¹]

proprietary name *noun* a name that is registered as a trademark.

proprietor /prə'prie·ətə/ *or* **proprietress** /-tris/ *noun* **1** a man or woman having the legal right or exclusive title to something; an owner. **2** somebody having an interest less than absolute right, e.g. control or present use. ➤➤ **proprietorial** /-'tawri·əl/ *adj,* **proprietorship** *noun*. [alteration of PROPRIETARY²]

propriety /prə'prieiti/ *noun* (*pl* **proprieties**) **1** the quality or state of being proper; fitness. **2** the standard of what is socially or morally acceptable in conduct or speech; decorum. **3** (*in pl*) the conventions and manners of polite society. [Middle English *propriete* from early French *propriété*: see PROPERTY]

proprioceptive /ˌprohpri·ə'septiv/ *adj* of or being stimuli produced and received within an organism. ➤➤ **proprioception** /-sh(ə)n/ *noun*. [Latin *proprius* one's own + *-ceptive* as in RECEPTIVE]

proprioceptor /ˌprohpri·ə'septə/ *noun* a sense organ receiving or producing proprioceptive stimuli.

proptosis /prop'tohsis/ *noun* (*pl* **proptoses** /-seez/) forward projection or displacement of a body part, *esp* the eyeball. [via late Latin from Greek *proptōsis* falling forward, from *propiptein* to fall forwards, from PRO-¹ + *piptein* to fall]

propulsion /prə'pulsh(ə)n/ *noun* **1** the action or process of propelling. **2** something that propels. ➤➤ **propulsive** /-siv/ *adj*. [Latin *propulsus*, past part. of *propellere*: see PROPEL]

prop up *verb trans* to give e.g. moral or financial support to (something or somebody): *The government is propping up ailing industries.*

propyl /'prohpil, 'prohpiel/ *noun* **1** a chemical group with a valency of one that is derived from propane: formula C_3H_7. **2** (*used before a noun*) of or containing this chemical group. ➤➤ **propylic** /proh'pilik/ *adj*. [PROPIONIC ACID + -YL]

propyla /'propilə/ *pl noun* pl of PROPYLON.

propylaeum /propi'lee·əm/ *noun* (*pl* **propylaea** /-'lee·ə/) a vestibule or gateway of architectural importance in front of an ancient Greek temple. [via Latin from Greek *propylaion*, from PRO-¹ + *pylē* gate]

propylene /'propileen/ *noun* an inflammable gas obtained from petroleum and used chiefly in the synthesis of other chemical compounds: formula C_3H_6.

propylon /'propilon/ *noun* (*pl* **propylons** *or* **propyla** /-lə/) = PROPYLAEUM.

pro rata¹ /ˌproh 'rahtə/ *adj* proportional. [Latin *pro rata*, literally 'according to the rate']

pro rata² *adv* proportionally; in proportion.

prorate /proh'rayt, 'prohrayt/ *verb trans* to divide, distribute, or assess (something) pro rata. ➤➤ **proration** /proh'raysh(ə)n/ *noun*.

prorogue /prə'rohg, proh'rohg/ *verb* (**prorogues, prorogued, proroguing**) ➤ *verb trans* to terminate a session of (e.g. a parliament) without dissolving it. ➤ *verb intrans* to suspend a legislative session. ➤➤ **prorogation** /prohrə'gaysh(ə)n/ *noun*. [Middle English *prorogen* via French from Latin *prorogare*, from PRO-¹ + *rogare* to ask]

prosaic /prə'zayik/ *adj* **1** characteristic of prose as distinguished from poetry. **2** dull; unimaginative: *I am almost ashamed to say how tame and prosaic my dreams are grown* — Charles Lamb. **3** belonging to the everyday world; commonplace. ➤➤ **prosaically** *adv*. [late Latin *prosaicus* from Latin *prosa*: see PROSE¹]

prosaism /'prohzayiz(ə)m/ *noun formal* **1** a prosaic manner, style, or quality. **2** (*usu in pl*) a prosaic expression.

prosaist /proh'zayist/ *noun formal* **1** a writer of prose. **2** a prosaic person. [Latin *prosa*: see PROSE¹]

prosauropod /proh'sawrəpod/ *noun* a plant-eating dinosaur of the Triassic and Jurassic periods. [PRO-¹ + SAUROPOD]

proscenium /prə'seeni·əm/ *noun* (*pl* **proscenia** /-ni·ə/ *or* **prosceniums**) **1** the stage of an ancient Greek or Roman theatre. **2** the part of a stage in front of the curtain in a modern theatre. [via Latin from Greek *proskēnion*, from PRO-¹ + *skēnē* building forming the background for a dramatic performance]

proscenium arch *noun* the arch in a conventional theatre through which the spectator sees the stage.

prosciutto /prə'shootoh/ *noun* raw cured Italian ham, usu served in very thin slices as an ANTIPASTO (starter in an Italian meal). [Italian *prosciutto*, alteration of *presciutto*, from PRE- + *-sciutto* from Latin *exsuctus* dried up, past part. of *exsugere* to suck out, from EX-¹ + *sugere* to suck]

proscribe /proh'skrieb/ *verb trans* **1** to condemn or forbid (*esp* something considered harmful); to prohibit (it). **2** to outlaw or exile (somebody). ➤➤ **proscriber** *noun,* **proscription** /proh'skripsh(ə)n/ *noun,* **proscriptive** /proh'skriptiv/ *adj*. [Latin *proscribere* to publish, proscribe, from PRO-¹ + *scribere* to write]

Usage note
proscribe or **prescribe**? See note at PRESCRIBE.

prose¹ /prohz/ *noun* **1a** ordinary language without metrical structure. **b** a literary medium distinguished from poetry. **c** (*used before a noun*) written in prose. **2** a commonplace quality or character; ordinariness. [Middle English via French from Latin *prosa*, from *prosa oratio* straightforward speech, from *prorsus, prosus* straightforward, ultimately from *provertere* to turn forward, from PRO-¹ + *vertere* to turn]

prose² *verb intrans* **1** to write prose. **2** to write or speak in a dull prosaic manner. ➤ *verb trans* to turn (e.g. a poem) into prose.

prosecute /'prosikyooht/ *verb trans* **1a** to institute and pursue criminal proceedings against (somebody). **b** to institute legal proceedings with reference to (something): *prosecute a claim.* **2** *formal* to follow (something) through, to pursue (it): *determined to prosecute the investigation.* **3** *formal* to engage in (e.g. a trade). ➤ *verb intrans* to institute and carry on a prosecution. ➤➤ **prosecutable** *adj*. [Middle English *prosecuten* from Latin *prosecutus*, past part. of *prosequi*: see PURSUE]

prosecution /prosi'kyoohsh(ə)n/ *noun* **1** the act or an instance of prosecuting; *specif* the formal institution and pursuit of a criminal charge. **2** (*treated as sing. or pl*) the party that institutes or conducts criminal proceedings: *a witness for the prosecution.* **3** the act or an instance of doing something, *esp* until it is completed.

prosecutor *noun* somebody who institutes or conducts an official prosecution.

proselyte¹ /'prosiliet/ *noun* **1** a person who has been newly converted to a religion, political party, different way of thinking, etc. **2** a Gentile who has converted to Judaism. ➤➤ **proselytism** /-litiz(ə)m/ *noun*. [Middle English *proselite* via late Latin from Greek *prosēlytos* proselyte, alien resident, from *proserkesthai* to approach, from *pros* near + *erkesthai* to come]

proselyte² *verb trans and intrans chiefly NAmer* = PROSELYTIZE.

proselytize *or* **proselytise** /'prosilitiez/ *verb trans* to convert (somebody), *esp* to a new religion. ➤ *verb intrans* to make or try to make converts, *esp* to a new religion. ➤➤ **proselytization** /-'zaysh(ə)n/ *noun,* **proselytizer** *noun*.

prosencephalon /prosen'sefəlon/ *noun technical* = FOREBRAIN. [via Latin from Greek *prosō* forward + ENCEPHALON]

prosenchyma /pros'engkimə/ *noun* a plant tissue composed of elongated pointed cells, often with thickened cell walls, that occurs *esp* in the woody parts of a plant and is specialized for the conduction of water and food and for mechanical support. ➤➤ **prosenchymatous** /-'kimətəs/ *adj*. [via Latin from Greek *pros-* towards + *enkhuma* infusion]

prosimian /proh'simi-ən/ *noun* any of various lower primates such as the tree-shrews, the lemurs, and the lorises: suborder Prosimii. ➤➤ **prosimian** *adj.* [from the Latin suborder name, from PRO-¹ + Latin *simia* ape]

prosit /'prohzit/ *interj* used to wish somebody good health, *esp* before drinking. [German *prosit*, from Latin *prosit* may it be beneficial, from *prodesse*: see PROUD]

prosody /'prosədi/ *noun* **1a** the patterns of rhythm, metre, rhyme, and versification used in poetry. **b** the study of versification, *esp* of metrical structure. **2** the stress and intonation patterns in language. ➤➤ **prosodic** /prə'sodik/ *adj,* **prosodist** *noun.* [Middle English from Latin *prosodia* accent of a syllable, from Greek *prosōidia* song sung to instrumental music, accent, from *pros* in addition to + *ōide song*]

prosopopoeia /,prosəpə'pee-ə/ *noun* **1** a figure of speech in which an imaginary or absent person is represented as speaking or acting. **2** = PERSONIFICATION (1). [via Latin from Greek *prosōpopoiia*, from *prosōpon* mask, person + *poiein* to make]

prospect¹ /'prospekt/ *noun* **1** an extensive view; a scene. **2a** a mental picture of something to come: *the prospect of more examinations.* **b** expectation; possibility: *He has a fine career in prospect.* **c** (*in pl*) financial and social expectations. **d** (*in pl*) chances, *esp* of success. **3** a potential client, candidate, etc. **4a** a place showing signs of containing a mineral deposit. **b** a partly developed mine. **c** the mineral yield of a tested sample of ore or gravel. [Middle English from Latin *prospectus* view, prospect, past part. of *prospicere* to look forwards, from PRO-¹ + *specere* to look]

prospect² /prə'spekt/ *verb trans and intrans* to explore (an area), *esp* for mineral deposits. ➤➤ **prospector** *noun.*

prospective /prə'spektiv/ *adj* **1** likely to come about; expected. **2** likely to be or become: *prospective parents.* ➤➤ **prospectively** *adv.*

prospectus /prə'spektəs/ *noun* (*pl* **prospectuses**) a printed statement or brochure describing an organization or enterprise, e.g. an educational establishment or a share issue, and distributed to prospective students, customers, participants, etc. [Latin *prospectus*: see PROSPECT¹]

prosper /'prospə/ *verb* (**prospered, prospering**) ➤ *verb intrans* to succeed or thrive; *specif* to achieve economic success. ➤ *verb trans chiefly literary* to cause (something or somebody) to succeed or thrive: *May the gods prosper our city.* [Middle English *prosperen* via French from Latin *prosperare* to cause to succeed, from *prosperus* doing well]

prosperity /prə'speriti/ *noun* the condition of being successful or thriving, *esp* economic well-being.

prosperous /'prosp(ə)rəs/ *adj* marked by success, *esp* financial success. ➤➤ **prosperously** *adv.* [Middle English via French from Latin *prosperus* doing well]

prostaglandin /prostə'glandin/ *noun* any of a group of compounds derived from fatty acids that occur widely in body tissues and act locally to control various processes, e.g. the induction of labour and abortion. [PROSTATE¹ + -IN¹; from its occurrence in the sexual glands of animals]

prostate¹ /'prostayt/ *noun* in male mammals, a small mass of muscular and glandular tissue that is situated around the neck of the bladder and secretes an alkaline liquid constituting most of the volume of semen. [via Latin from Greek *prostatēs*, from *proïstanai* to put in front, from PRO-¹ + *histanai* to cause to stand]

prostate² *adj* relating to or in the region of the prostate gland.

prostate gland *noun* = PROSTATE¹.

prostatic /pro'statik/ *adj* = PROSTATE².

prosthesis /pros'theesis/ *noun* (*pl* **prostheses** /-seez/) **1a** an artificial device to replace a missing part of the body. **b** the surgical replacement of a missing or damaged body part with an artificial device. **2** = PROTHESIS. [via Latin from Greek *prosthesis* addition, from *prostithenai* to add to, from *pros-* in addition to + *tithenai* to put]

prosthetic /pros'thetik/ *adj* **1** of or being a prosthesis. **2** of prosthetics. **3** of or being a nonprotein group combined with a protein. ➤➤ **prosthetically** *adv.*

prosthetics *pl noun* (*treated as sing.*) the branch of surgery concerned with the replacement of missing or damaged body parts with artificial devices. **2** artificial body parts.

prostitute¹ /'prostityooht/ *noun* a person, *esp* a woman, who engages in sexual activities for money. [Latin *prostitutus*, past part.

of *prostituere* to offer for sale, to expose, from PRO-¹ + *statuere* to station]

prostitute² *verb trans* **1** to make a prostitute of (oneself or somebody else). **2** to devote (something) to corrupt or unworthy purposes; to debase (it): *prostitute one's talents.* ➤➤ **prostitution** /-'tyoohsh(ə)n/ *noun,* **prostitutor** *noun.*

prostrate¹ /'prostrayt/ *adj* **1a** lying full-length face downwards, *esp* in adoration or submission. **b** extended in a horizontal position; flat. **2** physically or emotionally weak or exhausted; overcome: *prostrate with grief.* **3** said of a plant: trailing on the ground. [Middle English *prostrat* from Latin *prostratus*, past part. of *prosternere*, from PRO-¹ + *sternere* to spread out, throw down]

prostrate² /prə'strayt/ *verb trans* **1** to throw or put (*esp* oneself) into a prostrate position. **2** to put (oneself) in a humble and submissive posture or state: *The whole team had to prostrate itself in official apology* — Claudia Cassidy. **3** to reduce (somebody) to submission, helplessness, or exhaustion; to overcome (them). ➤➤ **prostration** /-sh(ə)n/ *noun.*

prostyle¹ /'prohstiel/ *adj* said of a building, *esp* a classical Greek temple: having pillars or columns in front, forming a portico. [Latin *prostylos*, from PRO-¹ + Greek *stylos* pillar]

prostyle² *noun* a prostyle building or portico.

prosy /'prohzi/ *adj* (**prosier, prosiest**) said of speech or writing: dull, commonplace, or tedious. ➤➤ **prosily** *adv,* **prosiness** *noun.*

prot- *or* **proto-** *comb. form* forming words, with the meaning: **1** first in time; earliest; original: *prototype.* **2** first-formed; primary: *protozoan.* [Middle English *protho-*, from early French, from late Latin *proto-*, from Greek *prōt-, prōto-*, from *prōtos*]

protactinium /prohtak'tini-əm/ *noun* a shiny metallic radioactive chemical element of relatively short life: symbol Pa, atomic number 91. [PROT- + ACTINIUM; because it decays to form actinium]

protagonist /prə'tagənist/ *noun* **1** somebody who takes the leading part in a drama, novel, film, or story. **2** a leader or notable supporter of a cause. [Greek *prōtagōnistēs*, from PROT- + *agōnistēs* competitor at games, actor, from *agōnizesthai* to compete, from *agōn*: see AGONY]

Usage note

Strictly speaking, only dramas have *protagonists*. The word, which comes from Greek, originally meant 'first or main actor' and became extended to mean 'the main or a main character' in a drama, an artistic work, or a dramatic real-life situation: *By chapter three the protagonist is in conflict with all the other members of her family.* Protagonist is also frequently used to mean a 'supporter' (*a protagonist of the campaign/movement*). This use is based, it is suggested, on the mistaken assumption that the *pro-* at the beginning of the word is the common prefix meaning 'in favour of', whereas in fact the prefix involved is *prot(o)-* 'first', as in *prototype.* Given that it is based on a mistake and that it often represents an attempt to find a fancy substitute for 'supporter' or 'advocate', this use is best avoided.

protanopia /prohtə'nohpi-ə/ *noun* a form of colour blindness resulting in the inability to distinguish between reds, greens, and yellows. It is caused by insensitivity to red light: compare DEUTERANOPIA, TRITANOPIA. [PROT- + AN- + -OPIA]

protasis /'prohtəsis/ *noun* (*pl* **protases** /-seez/) the subordinate clause of a conditional sentence, e.g. *if I were you* in *I'd go if I were you:* compare APODOSIS. [via Latin from Greek *protasis* premise of a syllogism, conditional clause, from *proteinein* to stretch out before, put forwards, from PRO-¹ + *teinein* to stretch]

protea /'prohti-ə/ *noun* any of a genus of evergreen shrubs of the southern hemisphere grown for their dense flower heads surrounded by attractive coloured bracts (modified leaves; see BRACT (1)): genus *Protea.* [Latin genus name, from *Proteus*: see PROTEAN]

protean /'prohtee-ən/ *adj* **1** readily assuming different shapes or roles. **2** displaying great diversity or variety. [from Latin *Proteus*, mythological sea god with the power of assuming different shapes, from Greek *Prōteus*]

protease /'protiayz, -ays/ *noun* an enzyme that breaks down proteins. [PROTEIN + -ASE]

protect /prə'tekt/ *verb trans* **1a** to cover or shield (something or somebody) from injury or destruction. **b** to guard or defend (something or somebody) against attack, harm, danger, etc. **c** to take measures to save (an endangered species) from extinction. **2** to shield or foster (a home industry) by an import tariff. **3** to provide funds to guarantee payment of (e.g. a bill of exchange). [Latin *protectus*, past part. of *protegere*, from PRO-¹ + *tegere* to cover]

protectant *noun* something, *esp* a chemical substance, that provides protection.

protection /prəˈteksh(ə)n/ *noun* **1** the act or an instance of protecting or being protected. **2** something that protects. **3a** immunity from threatened violence, often purchased under duress. **b** money extorted by racketeers for such immunity. **4** insurance coverage. **5** = PROTECTIONISM.

protectionism *noun* the shielding of the producers of a country from foreign competition by import tariffs. ▶ **protectionist** *adj and noun*.

protective[1] /prəˈtektiv/ *adj* **1** providing or able to provide protection. **2** of or being an import tariff intended to protect domestic producers rather than to yield revenue. ▶ **protectively** *adv*, **protectiveness** *noun*.

protective[2] *noun* **1** something that provides protection. **2** *dated* a condom.

protective custody *noun* detention of somebody for their own safety.

protector *noun* **1** somebody or something that protects. **2a** (*often* **Protector**) somebody in charge of a kingdom during the minority or absence of the sovereign; a regent. **b** (**Protector**) the executive head of the Commonwealth of England, Scotland, and Ireland from 1653 to 1659, a title held by Oliver Cromwell (1653–8) and by Richard Cromwell (1658–9). ▶ **protectorship** *noun*.

protectorate /prəˈtekt(ə)rət/ *noun* **1a** a state that is partly controlled by and dependent on the protection of another more powerful state, without being fully annexed. **b** the relationship that exists between such a state and the one exerting control over it. **2a** (*often* **Protectorate**) government by a protector. **b** the rank, office, or period of rule of a protector. **c** (**Protectorate**) the government of the Commonwealth of England, Scotland, and Ireland from 1653 to 1659.

protectress /prəˈtektris/ *noun* a female protector.

protégé *or* **protégée** /ˈprotizhay (*French* prɔteʒe)/ *noun* somebody under the protection, guidance, or patronage of a more experienced or influential person. [French *protégé*, past part. of *protéger* to protect, from Latin *protegere*: see PROTECT]

protein /ˈprohteen/ *noun* any of numerous naturally occurring extremely complex organic chemical compounds that are essential constituents of all living cells and form an important part of the diet of human beings and other animals.

Editorial note ─────────
The human body contains some 100,000 distinct proteins. Each is a macromolecule consisting of long chains of amino acids. Several separate chains may be linked together and folded into complex three-dimensional configurations. Proteins are the organizing and working molecules of the cell. Fibrous insoluble proteins provide its shape and structure and soluble proteins include enzymes, controlling its metabolism — Professor Steven Rose.

▶ **proteinaceous** /prohtiˈnayshəs/ *adj*. [French *protéine* from late Greek *prōteios* primary, from Greek *prōtos* first]

pro tem /ˌproh ˈtem/ *adv and adj* for the time being. [short for Latin *pro tempore*]

proteolysis /prohtiˈoləsis/ *noun* the breakdown of proteins or peptides by the action of enzymes resulting in the formation of simpler products. ▶ **proteolytic** /-əˈlitik/ *adj*.

Proterozoic /ˌprohtərəˈzohˌik/ *adj* relating to or dating from the latter part of the Precambrian aeon, preceding the Palaeozoic era, lasting from about 2,500 to 570 million years ago, and marked by rocks containing a few fossils of algae and soft-bodied invertebrate animals. ▶ **Proterozoic** *noun*. [Greek *proteros* former, earlier (from *pro* before) + -ZOIC[2]]

protest[1] /prəˈtest/ *verb trans* **1** to make a formal or solemn declaration or affirmation of (something): *He protested his innocence.* **2** to execute or have executed a formal protest against (e.g. a bill or note). **3** *chiefly NAmer* to express usu strong objection to or disagreement with; to remonstrate against: *She was unwilling to protest the cost of her ticket.* ▶ *verb intrans* **1** to express usu strong disagreement or objection; to make a protest. **2** to engage in an organized public demonstration of disapproval. ▶ **protestant** *noun and adj*, **protester** *noun*, **protestingly** *adv*, **protestor** *noun*. [Middle English *protesten* via French from Latin *protestari*, from PRO-[1] + *testari*: see TESTAMENT]

protest[2] /ˈprohtest/ *noun* **1** a formal or solemn declaration of disapproval, disagreement, or objection. **2a** an organized public demonstration of disapproval. **b** (*used before a noun*) relating to or denoting such a demonstration: *a protest march.* **3** a display of unwillingness: *He went under protest.* **4** a sworn declaration that a note or bill has been duly presented and that payment has been refused.

Protestant[1] /ˈprotistənt/ *noun* an adherent of any of those Western Christian Churches that separated from the Roman Catholic Church at the Reformation or subsequently. ▶ **Protestantism** *noun*. [early French *protestant* from Latin *protestant-*, *protestans*, present part. of *protestari*: see PROTEST[1]]

Protestant[2] *adj* of Protestants or their religion.

Protestant ethic *noun* a belief that working hard and being thrifty is a person's duty and that living this way brings enough reward in itself.

Protestant work ethic *noun* = PROTESTANT ETHIC.

protestation /protəˈstaysh(ə)n/ *noun* **1** the act or an instance of protesting. **2** a solemn declaration or avowal.

prothalamion /prohthəˈlaymiˈən/ *or* **prothalamium** /-miˈəm/ *noun* (*pl* **prothalamia** /-miˈə/) a song or poem in celebration of a forthcoming marriage. [via Latin from PRO-[1] + Greek *-thalamion* as in *epithalamion* EPITHALAMIUM]

prothallium /prohˈthaliˈəm/ *noun* (*pl* **prothallia** /-liˈə/) = PROTHALLUS.

prothallus /prohˈthaləs/ *noun* (*pl* **prothalli** /-lie/) the small flat green plant body that develops from an asexually produced spore of a fern or related plant and bears sex organs that produce the reproductive cells; the gametophyte of a fern, horsetail, etc. ▶ **prothallial** *adj*. [PRO-[1] + THALLUS]

prothesis /ˈprothisis/ *noun* (*pl* **protheses** /-seez/) **1** the addition of a sound to the beginning of a word, e.g. in Old French *estat* from Latin *status*. **2** *esp* in the Eastern Orthodox Church: **a** the solemn preparation and presentation of the elements of the Eucharist. **b** the part of a church or the table where this is done. ▶ **prothetic** /prəˈthetik/ *adj*. [late Latin *prothesis*, alteration of Greek *prosthesis*: see PROSTHESIS]

prothonotary /prohthəˈnoht(ə)ri, prohˈthonət(ə)ri/ *noun* (*pl* **prothonotaries**) = PROTONOTARY.

prothrombin /prohˈthrombin/ *noun* a protein present in blood plasma that is produced in the liver in the presence of vitamin K and is converted into thrombin in the clotting of blood.

protist /ˈprohtist/ *noun* any of a major group of chiefly single-celled organisms including protozoans, single-celled algae, and simple fungi: kingdom Protista. ▶ **protistan** /-t(ə)n/ *adj and noun*. [via Latin from Greek *prōtistos* very first, primal, superl of *prōtos* first]

protium /ˈprohtiˈəm/ *noun* the ordinary, most common, and lightest isotope of hydrogen containing one proton in the atomic nucleus: compare DEUTERIUM, HYDROGEN, TRITIUM. [scientific Latin from Greek *prōtos* first]

proto- *comb. form* see PROT-.

protocol /ˈprohtəkol/ *noun* **1** a code of conduct, etiquette, and procedure, *esp* for official or ceremonial occasions: *You wonder whether the heat and the heavy robes will all be too much. What is the protocol for removing a collapsed Knight of the Garter?* — Jeremy Paxman. **2a** an original draft of a diplomatic document, e.g. a treaty. **b** an amendment or annexe to a treaty. **c** a signed record of agreement made at a diplomatic conference, internation negotiations, etc. **3** in computing, a set of rules relating to the form in which data must be presented, e.g. for transmission between computers. **4** the plan or a record of a scientific experiment or medical treatment. [early French *prothocole* via Latin from late Greek *prōtokollon* first part of a papyrus roll bearing details of manufacture or contents, from PROTO- + Greek *kollan* to glue together, from *kolla* glue]

Proto-Indo-European /ˈprohtoh/ *noun* the reconstructed hypothetical language that is the ancestor of all the Indo-European languages and has no recorded forms.

protomartyr /protohˈmahtə/ *noun* the first person to die for a cause; *specif* the first Christian martyr, St Stephen. [Middle English *prothomartir* via French and late Latin from late Greek *prōtomartyr-*, *prōtomartys*, from PROTO- + Greek *martyr-*, *martys* MARTYR[1]]

proton /ˈprohton/ *noun* an elementary particle that carries a single positive electrical charge and forms part of the nucleus of all known atoms, with the exception of the hydrogen atom of which it forms the entire nucleus. ➤➤ **protonic** /proh'tonik/ *adj.* [Greek *prōton*, neuter of *prōtos* first]

protonotary /'prohtə'noht(ə)ri, proh'tonət(ə)ri/ *noun* (*pl* **proto-notaries**) a chief clerk of any of various courts of law. [Middle English *prothonotarie* from late Latin *protonotarius*, from PROTO- + Latin *notarius*: see NOTARY]

protoplasm /'prohtəplaz(ə)m/ *noun* **1** the living material of a cell and its nucleus consisting of a complex of organic and inorganic substances, e.g. proteins and salts in solution. **2** the CYTOPLASM of a cell. ➤➤ **protoplasmic** /-'plazmik/ *adj.* [German *Protoplasma*, from PROTO- + PLASMA]

protoplast /'prohtəplast/ *noun* a living mass of protoplasm including a nucleus, considered as a single unit: *specif* a plant or bacterial cell without its surrounding cell wall. ➤➤ **protoplastic** /-'plastik/ *adj.* [early French *protoplaste* from late Latin *protoplastus* first man, from Greek *prōtoplastos* first formed, from PROTO- + *plastos* formed, from *plassein* to mould]

prototherian /prohtə'thiəri·ən/ *noun* any of a group of mammals comprising the monotremes: subclass Prototheria. ➤➤ **proto-therian** *adj.* [from the Latin name, from PROTO- + Greek *thēria*, pl of *thērion* wild animal]

prototype /'prohtətiep/ *noun* **1** an original model on which some-thing is based or from which it derives. **2** a first full-scale and usu operational form of a new type or design of a construction, e.g. an aeroplane. **3** somebody or something that exemplifies the essential features of a type. ➤➤ **prototypic** /-'tipik/ *adj*, **prototypical** /-'tipikl/ *adj.* [via French from Greek *prōtotypon*, neuter of *prōtotypos* archetypal, from PROTO- + *typos* type]

protozoan /prohtə'zoh·ən/ *or* **protozoon** /-'zoh·on/ *noun* (*pl* **protozoans** *or* **protozoa** /-'zoh·ə/) any of a group of minute single-celled animals that vary in structure and physiology, occur in almost every kind of habitat, and include some serious parasites of human beings and domestic animals: phylum Protozoa. ➤➤ **protozoal** *adj*, **protozoan** *adj*, **protozoic** /-ik/ *adj.* [Latin phylum name, from PROTO- + -ZOA]

protract /prə'trakt/ *verb trans* **1** to prolong (something) in time or space. **2** to lay down the lines and angles of (something) with a scale and protractor. **3** said of a muscle: to extend (a part of the body) forward or outward. ➤➤ **protracted** *adj*, **protractedly** *adv*, **protraction** /-sh(ə)n/ *noun.* [Latin *protractus*, past part. of *protrahere* to draw forward, from PRO-1 + *trahere* to draw]

protractile /prə'traktiel/ *adj* capable of being extended or thrust out: *protractile jaws.*

protractor *noun* **1** a usu flat semicircular instrument marked with degrees that is used for drawing or measuring angles. **2** a muscle that extends a body part: compare RETRACTOR.

protrude /prə'troohd/ *verb intrans* to project from or extend beyond the surrounding surface or place. ➤ *verb trans* to cause (something) to protrude. ➤➤ **protrusible** /-zibl/ *adj*, **protrusion** /-zh(ə)n/ *noun*, **protrusive** /-siv/ *adj.* [Latin *protrudere*, from PRO-1 + *trudere* to thrust]

protuberant /prə'tyoohb(ə)rənt/ *adj* projecting from a surround-ing or adjacent surface, often as a rounded mass; prominent or bulging. ➤➤ **protuberance** *noun.* [late Latin *protuberant-, protuber-ans*, present part. of *protuberare* to bulge out, from PRO-1 + Latin *tuber* hump, swelling]

proud /prowd/ *adj* **1** very pleased or satisfied, e.g. with some achievement, possession, or relationship: *proud of her son.* **2a** having or displaying excessive self-esteem. **b** having proper self-respect: *too proud to accept charity.* **3a** stately; magnificent. **b** giving reason for pride; glorious: *the proudest moment of her life.* **4** project-ing slightly from a surrounding surface. ✳ **do somebody proud 1** to treat somebody very well, *esp* to entertain them lavishly. **2** to give somebody cause for pride or gratification. ➤➤ **proudly** *adv*, **proudness** *noun.* [Old English *prūd*, prob from Old French *prod, prud, prou* capable, good, valiant, from late Latin *prode* advantage, back-formation from Latin *prodesse* to be advan-tageous, from PRO-2 + *esse* to be]

Prov. *abbr* **1** Proverbs (book of the Bible). **2** Province. **3** Provost.

prove /proohv/ *verb* (*past part.* **proved** *or* **proven** /'proohv(ə)n/) ➤ *verb trans* **1a** to establish the truth or validity of (something) by evidence or demonstration: *You must produce some documentation to prove your identity.* **b** to check the correctness of (e.g. an arithmet-ical operation). **2a** to test the quality of (something); to try (it) out. **b** to test (something) for conformity to a standard. **3** in law, to

verify the genuineness of (something), *esp* to obtain probate of (a will). **4** to show (oneself) to have the required or specified abilities, qualities, etc. ➤ *verb intrans* **1** to turn out, *esp* after trial: *The new drug proved to be effective.* **2** said of bread dough: to rise and become aerated before baking through the action of yeast. ➤➤ **provability** /-'biliti/ *noun*, **provable** *adj*, **provably** *adv.* [Middle English *proven* via Old French from Latin *probare* to test, approve, prove, from *probus* good, honest]

provenance /'provənəns/ *noun* a place of origin or record of ownership, e.g. of a work of art. [French *provenance* from *provenir* to come forth, originate, from Latin *provenire*, from PRO-1 + *venire* to come]

Provençal /provonh'sahl (*French* prɔvãsal)/ *noun* **1** a native or inhabitant of Provence, a region and former province of SE France. **2** the Romance language of the people of Provence or the variety of French they speak: compare OCCITAN. ➤➤ **Provençal** *adj.*

Word history
early French *provençal* of Provence, region of SE France. Words from the Provençal language that have passed into English, most of them coming by way of French and all being derived from Latin, include *career, cavalier, cocoon, funnel, noose, nougat,* and *nutmeg.*

provençale /provonh'sahl/ *adj* (*used after a noun*) said of food: cooked in a way that is typical of the French region of Provence, *esp* in a sauce made from tomatoes, garlic, and olive oil: *seafood provençale.*

provender /'provində/ *noun* **1** dry food for domestic animals. **2** *humorous* food; provisions. [Middle English via French from late Latin *provenda*, alteration of *praebenda*: see PREBEND]

proverb /'provuhb/ *noun* a brief pithy saying embodying a truth, a widely held belief, or a piece of advice: *Among the Ibo the art of conversation is regarded very highly, and proverbs are the palm-oil with which words are eaten* — Chinua Achebe. [Middle English *proverbe* via French from Latin *proverbium*, from PRO-1 + *verbum* word]

proverbial /prə'vuhbi·əl/ *adj* **1** of or resembling a proverb. **2** char-acteristic, stereotypical, or well-known: *the proverbial good humour of the pub landlord.* ➤➤ **proverbially** *adv.*

Proverbs *pl noun* (*treated as sing.*) the twentieth book of the Old Testament, a collection of wise sayings and moral stories, most of which are attributed to Solomon.

provide /prə'vied/ *verb intrans* **1** to supply what is needed for sus-tenance or support: *provide for a large family.* **2** to make adequate preparation; to take precautions: *provide against future loss.* **3** to make a proviso or stipulation: *The constitution provides for an elected president.* ➤ *verb trans* **1a** to furnish or equip (somebody with something): *Provide the children with new shoes.* **b** to supply or afford (something): *Curtains provide privacy.* **2** to state or stipulate (some-thing). ➤➤ **provider** *noun.* [Middle English *providen* from Latin *providēre*, literally 'to see ahead', from PRO-1 + *vidēre* to see]

provided *conj* = PROVIDING.

providence /'provid(ə)ns/ *noun* **1a** (*often* **Providence**) divine or superhuman guidance or care. **b** (**Providence**) God or nature con-ceived as the power sustaining and guiding human destiny. **2** ade-quate preparation or proper precautions taken in anticipation of future events. [Middle English via French from Latin *providentia*, from *provident-, providens*, present part. of *providēre*: see PROVIDE]

provident /'provid(ə)nt/ *adj* **1** showing foresight in providing for the future; prudent. **2** thrifty. ➤➤ **providently** *adv.* [Latin *provi-dent-, providens*: see PROVIDENCE]

providential /provi'densh(ə)l/ *adj* of or determined by or as if by providence; lucky. ➤➤ **providentially** *adv.*

provident society *noun* = FRIENDLY SOCIETY.

providing *conj* on condition; if and only if: *You may come providing you pay for yourself.*

province /'provins/ *noun* **1a** an administrative district or division of a country. **b** (**the provinces**) all of a country except the capital, *esp* when regarded as lacking sophistication. **2a** somebody's proper business, function, or activity: *It's outside my province.* **b** a field or sphere of knowledge or activity. **3** a territorial unit of religious administration, e.g. one under the jurisdiction of an archbishop or a subdivision of an order. **4** an area of the ancient Roman empire outside Italy and under the jurisdiction of a governor. [French *prov-ince* from Latin *provincia*]

provincial1 /prə'vinsh(ə)l/ *adj* **1a** of or coming from a province. **b** of or coming from the provinces. **2a** limited in outlook; narrow-minded. **b** lacking the sophistication or refinement associated with urban society: *He was imperfect, unfinished, inartistic; he was worse than provincial – he was parochial* — Henry James. ➤➤ **provinciality** /-shi'aliti/ *noun,* **provincially** *adv.*

provincial² *noun* **1** somebody living in or coming from a province or provinces. **2a** somebody with restricted interests or outlook. **b** somebody lacking sophistication or refinement. **3** the head of a religious province.

provincialism *noun* **1** the state or quality of being provincial. **2** concern for one's local area taking precedence over national affairs. **3** narrow-mindedness or lack of sophistication. **4** a dialectal or local word, phrase, or idiom.

proving ground /'proohving/ *noun* **1** a place designed for or used in testing equipment or scientific experimentation. **2** a place where something new is tried out.

provirus /'prohvie·ərəs/ *noun* a noninfectious form of a virus that reproduces itself inside a cell and is transmitted along with the genetic material of the host cell from one generation to the next. ➤➤ **proviral** *adj.*

provision¹ /prə'vizh(ə)n/ *noun* **1a** the act or an instance of providing something. **b** a measure taken beforehand; a preparation or precaution: *no provision made for delay.* **2** (*in pl*) a stock of food or other necessary supplies. **3** a proviso or stipulation, e.g. in a legal document. [Middle English via French from late Latin *provision-, provisio* act of providing, from Latin *providēre*: see PROVIDE]

provision² *verb trans* to supply (somebody or something) with provisions. ➤➤ **provisioner** *noun.*

Provisional *noun* a member of the unofficial wing of the IRA or of Sinn Fein.

provisional *adj* **1a** serving for the time being; *specif* requiring later confirmation: *provisional consent.* **b** *Brit* said of a driving licence: allowing the holder to drive under supervision until they have passed their driving test and a full licence has been issued. **2** (**Provisional**) relating to or denoting the unofficial wing of the IRA or of Sinn Fein. ➤➤ **provisionally** *adv.*

proviso /prə'viezoh/ *noun* (*pl* **provisos** *or* **provisoes**) **1** a clause in an unofficial document, contract, etc that introduces a condition. **2** a conditional stipulation. [Middle English, from late Latin *proviso quod* provided that]

provisory /prə'viez(ə)ri/ *adj* **1** conditional. **2** provisional.

provitamin /proh'vitamin/ *noun* a substance that can be converted in the body into a specific vitamin.

Provo /'prohvoh/ *noun* (*pl* **Provos**) *informal* = PROVISIONAL. [by shortening and alteration]

provocation /provə'kaysh(ə)n/ *noun* **1** the act or an instance of provoking; incitement. **2** something that provokes, usu to anger or irritation. [Middle English *provocacioun* via French from Latin *provocation-, provocatio,* from *provocare*: see PROVOKE]

provocative /prə'vokativ/ *adj* serving or tending to provoke or arouse to indignation, interest, sexual desire, etc. ➤➤ **provocatively** *adv,* **provocativeness** *noun.*

provoke /prə'vohk/ *verb trans* **1** to incite (a person or animal) to anger; to incense (them). **2** to cause (somebody or something) to behave in a specified way. **3** to stir up or evoke (something): *His candour provoked a storm of controversy* — Times Literary Supplement. **4** to provide the needed stimulus for (something). [Middle English *provoken* via early French *provoquer* from Latin *provocare,* from PRO-¹ + *vocare* to call]

provoking *adj* **1** (*used in combinations*) arousing a reaction of a specified kind: *a thought-provoking article.* **2** annoying; irritating; tiresome: *Emma, being now certain of her ball, began to adopt as the next vexation Mr Knightley's provoking indifference about it* — Jane Austen. ➤➤ **provokingly** *adv.*

provost /'provəst/ *noun* **1** the head of certain university colleges, public schools, etc. **2** the head of certain Scottish district councils. **3** the head of the CHAPTER (assembly of canons) in a cathedral or other church. [Old English *profost* via Old French from late Latin *propositus,* alteration of Latin *praepositus* one in charge, director, past part. of *praeponere*: see PREPOSITION]

provost marshal /prə'voh/ *noun* an officer who supervises military police.

prow /prow/ *noun* **1** the bow of a ship or boat. **2** a pointed projecting front part of something, e.g. a ski. [early French *proue,* prob via Old Italian dialect *prua* and Latin *prora* from Greek *prōira*]

prowess /'prowis/ *noun* **1** outstanding ability. **2** military valour and skill. [Middle English *prouesse* from Old French *proesse* from *prou*: see PROUD]

prowl¹ /prowl/ *verb intrans* (*often* + about/around) to move about or roam over a place in a stealthy or predatory manner: *Submarines were prowling along the coast.* ➤ *verb trans* to move about or roam over (a place) in a stealthy or predatory manner: *The cats prowled the garden every night.* [Middle English *prollen*; earlier history unknown]

prowl² *noun* the act or an instance of prowling. ✴ **on the prowl 1** engaged in prowling. **2** intent on finding a romantic or sexual partner.

prowler *noun* somebody that prowls, *esp* a person who creeps around a place stealthily with criminal intent, e.g. burglary or voyeurism.

prox. *abbr* proximo.

proximal /'proksim(ə)l/ *adj* said *esp* of an anatomical part: next to or nearest the point of attachment or origin: compare DISTAL. ➤➤ **proximally** *adv.* [Latin *proximus* nearest, next, superl of *prope* near]

proximate /'proksimət/ *adj formal* **1a** very near; close. **b** coming soon; imminent. **2a** next preceding or following. **b** next in a chain of cause and effect: *Ice on the road was the proximate cause of the accident, although other factors were involved.* **3** approximate. ➤➤ **proximately** *adv,* **proximateness** *noun.* [Latin *proximatus,* past part. of *proximare* to approach, from *proximus*: see PROXIMAL]

proximity /prok'simiti/ *noun* being close in space, time, or association; nearness. [early French *proximité* from Latin *proximitat-, proximitas,* from *proximus* nearest, next, superl of *prope* near]

proximity talks *noun* talks involving an intermediary passing between the main parties, when these decline to meet face to face.

proximo /'proksimoh/ *adj formal, dated* used in business correspondence: of or occurring in the next month after the present: compare INSTANT¹, ULTIMO. [Latin *proximo mense* in the next month]

proxy /'proksi/ *noun* (*pl* **proxies**) **1a** a deputy authorized to act as a substitute for another. **b** the agency, function, or office of such a deputy: *marriage by proxy.* **c** (*used before a noun*) of such a deputy: *a proxy vote.* **2** authority to act or vote for another, or a document giving this authority. [Middle English *procucie,* contraction of *procuracie,* via French from Latin *procuratio*: see PROCURATION]

Prozac /'prohzak/ *noun trademark* a drug taken as an antidepressant. It acts by slowing down the uptake of serotonin by the central nervous system.

PRP *abbr* **1** performance-related pay. **2** profit-related pay.

PRS *abbr* Performing Rights Society.

prude /proohd/ *noun* a person who shows or affects extreme modesty or propriety, *esp* in sexual matters. [French *prude* prudish woman, short for *prudefemme* good woman, from Old French *prode femme*]

prudence /'proohd(ə)ns/ *noun* **1** discretion or shrewdness in the management of affairs. **2** skill and good judgment in the use of resources; frugality. **3** caution or circumspection with regard to danger or risk.

prudent /'proohd(ə)nt/ *adj* characterized by, arising from, or showing prudence. ➤➤ **prudently** *adv.* [Middle English via French from Latin *prudent-, prudens,* contraction of *provident-, providens*: see PROVIDENCE]

prudential /prooh'densh(ə)l/ *adj* **1** of or proceeding from prudence. **2** exercising prudence, *esp* in business matters. ➤➤ **prudentially** *adv.*

prudery *noun* (*pl* **pruderies**) **1** the quality of being a prude. **2** a prudish act or remark.

prudish *adj* marked by prudery; priggish. ➤➤ **prudishly** *adv,* **prudishness** *noun.*

pruinose /'prooh·inohs/ *adj* said of part of a plant: covered with whitish dust or bloom: *pruinose stems.* [Latin *pruinosus* covered with hoarfrost, from *pruina* hoarfrost]

prune¹ /proohn/ *noun* **1** a dried plum. **2** *Brit, informal* a silly person. [Middle English from early French *prune* plum, via Latin *prunum* from Greek *proumnon*]

prune² *verb trans* **1** to cut off the dead or unwanted parts of (a woody plant or shrub). **2a** to reduce (text, etc) by eliminating superfluous matter: *You'll have to prune that speech a bit.* **b** to remove (something) as superfluous: *Prune away all ornamentation.* ➤ *verb intrans* to cut away what is unwanted. [Middle English *prouynen* from early French *proignier*]

prunella /prooh'nelə/ *noun* a strong woollen or silk fabric formerly used for gowns, e.g. for clergymen and barristers. [French *prunelle* sloe (from its dark colour), dimin. of *prune*: see PRUNE¹]

pruning hook *noun* a usu long-handled tool with a curved blade at the end for pruning trees and shrubs.

prurient /'prooəri·ənt/ *adj* inclined to, having, or arousing an excessive or unhealthy interest in sexual matters: *Knowledge of the structure of our bodies is the surest safeguard against prurient curiosity* — Marie Stopes. ➤ **prurience** *noun*, **pruriently** *adv*. [Latin *prurient-, pruriens*, present part. of *prurire* to itch, crave, be wanton]

prurigo /proo(ə)'riegoh/ *noun* a chronic inflammatory skin disease marked by raised itching spots. ➤ **pruriginous** /proo(ə)'rijənəs/ *adj*. [Latin *prurigo* itch, from *prurire* to itch]

pruritic /proo(ə)'ritik/ *adj* of or marked by itching. [Latin *prurire* to itch]

pruritus /proo(ə)'rietəs/ *noun* an intense sensation of itching, or any of various disorders, *esp* of the skin, that cause this. [Latin *pruritus*, past part. of *prurire* to itch]

Prussian /'prush(ə)n/ *noun* a native or inhabitant of Prussia, an area of eastern and central Europe originally inhabited by a Baltic-speaking people, but later a German kingdom, then a German state, and divided in 1947 between W Germany, E Germany, the USSR, and Poland. ➤ **Prussian** *adj*.

Prussian blue *noun* **1** any of numerous blue pigments consisting of iron cyanides. **2** a strong greenish blue colour.

prussic acid /'prusik/ *noun* an extremely poisonous weak acid, a solution of hydrogen cyanide in water; = HYDROCYANIC ACID. [partial translation of French *acide prussique*, from *acide* (see ACID¹) + *prussique* of Prussian blue]

pry¹ /prie/ *verb intrans* (**pries, pried, prying**) **1** (*usu* + into) to enquire in an overinquisitive or impertinent manner. **2** (*often* + into) to look closely or inquisitively at somebody's possessions, actions, etc: *His neighbours were always prying into his affairs.* ➤ **prying** *adj*, **pryingly** *adv*. [Middle English *prien*; earlier history unknown]

pry² *noun* (*pl* **pries**) **1** a person who pries into other people's business, etc. **2** the act or an instance of prying.

pry³ *verb trans* (**pries, pried, prying**) *chiefly NAmer* = PRISE. [by alteration]

pryer /'prie·ə/ *noun* see PRIER.

PS *abbr* **1** Passenger Steamer. **2** Police Sergeant. **3** (*also* **ps**) postscript. **4** Private Secretary. **5** used to designate part of the theatrical stage: prompt side.

Ps. *abbr* Psalms (book of the Bible).

PSA *abbr* **1** Property Services Agency. **2** prostatic specific antigen, an indicator of prostate cancer.

psalm /sahm/ *noun* **1** (*also* **Psalm**) a sacred song or poem used in worship, *esp* any of the biblical hymns attributed to King David of Israel and others and collected in the Book of Psalms. **2** (**Psalms**) (*treated as sing.*) the 19th book of the Old Testament, consisting of a collection of hymns. ➤ **psalmic** /'sahmik, 'salmik/ *adj*. [Old English *psealm* via late Latin from Greek *psalmos* song sung to a harp, from *psallein* to pluck, play a stringed instrument]

psalmist *noun* **1** a writer or composer of psalms, *esp* those in the Book of Psalms in the Old Testament. **2** (**the Psalmist**) a writer or composer of any of the psalms in the Book of Psalms; *specif* King David of Israel, to whom the whole book was traditionally attributed.

psalmody /'sahmədi, 'salmədi/ *noun* (*pl* **psalmodies**) **1** the practice or art of singing psalms in worship. **2** a collection of psalms. **3** the setting of psalms to music for singing. ➤ **psalmodic** /sal'modik/ *adj*, **psalmodist** *noun*. [Middle English *psalmodie* from late Latin *psalmodia* from late Greek *psalmōidia* singing to the harp, from *psalmos* (see PSALM) + *aidein* to sing]

Psalter /'sawltə/ *noun* a book containing a collection of biblical Psalms for liturgical or devotional use. [Old English *psalter* and Old French *psaltier*, both via late Latin *psalterium* from Greek *psaltērion*: see PSALTERY]

psalterium /sawl'tiəri·əm/ *noun* (*pl* **psalteria** /-ri·ə/) the third chamber of the stomach of a cow, sheep, etc; OMASUM. [late Latin *psalterium* (see PSALTER); from the resemblance of the folds to the pages of a book]

psaltery *noun* (*pl* **psalteries**) an ancient stringed musical instrument similar to the DULCIMER (instrument with strings stretched over a soundboard) but plucked. [Middle English *psalterie* via French and Latin from Greek *psaltērion*, from *psallein* to play on a stringed instrument]

p's and q's /,peez ən(d) 'kyoohz/ *pl noun informal* something, *esp* manners or language, that one should be mindful of: *Mind your p's and q's in front of your great-aunt.*

Word history

possibly alluding to the difficulty a child learning to write may have in distinguishing between *p* and *q*; a connection with *please* and *thank you* has also been suggested. Another suggestion is that the term derives from abbreviations for *pints* and *quarts* used when recording drinks to be paid for later.

PSBR *abbr* public sector borrowing requirement.

psephology /se'foləji/ *noun* the scientific study of elections. ➤ **psephological** /-'lojikl/ *adj*, **psephologically** /-'lojikli/ *adv*, **psephologist** *noun*. [Greek *psephos* pebble, ballot, vote + -LOGY; from the use of pebbles by the ancient Greeks in voting]

pseud¹ /s(y)oohd/ *noun informal* an intellectually or socially pretentious person. ➤ **pseudy** *adj*. [PSEUD-]

pseud² *adj informal* see PSEUDO (2).

pseud. *abbr* **1** pseudonym. **2** pseudonymous.

pseud- *or* **pseudo-** *comb. form* forming words, with the meanings: **1** false; sham; spurious: *pseudo-reds and crypto-fascists* — P J O'Rourke. **2** resembling closely; imitating: *pseudomorph*; *pseudo-intellectual*. [Middle English via Latin from Greek *pseudēs* false]

pseudepigrapha *or* **Pseudepigrapha** /s(y)oohdi'pigrəfə/ *noun* Jewish or Jewish-Christian religious writings mainly of the period 200 BC to AD 200 that are not included in any Scriptures but are biblical in style and are often purportedly written by a biblical character, e.g. the Psalms of Solomon, the Apocalypse of Abraham, the Testament of Adam, though some are anonymous: compare APOCRYPHA. ➤ **pseudepigraphal** *adj*, **pseudepigraphic** /,s(y)oohdepi'grafik/ *adj*, **pseudepigraphical** /,s(y)oohdepi'grafikl/ *adj*, **pseudepigraphous** /-'fəs/ *adj*. [Greek *pseudepigrapha*, neuter pl of *pseudepigraphos* falsely inscribed, written under a false name, from PSEUD- + *epigraphein* to inscribe, from EPI- + *graphein* to write]

pseudo /'s(y)oohdoh/ *adj* **1** apparent rather than actual; spurious: *There is an important distinction between true and pseudo freedom.* **2** *informal* false; pretentious. [Middle English, from PSEUD-]

pseudo- *comb. form* see PSEUD-.

pseudocarp /'s(y)oohdohkahp/ *noun* a fruit, such as an apple, pear, or strawberry, the major part of which consists of tissue other than that of the ripened ovary. ➤ **pseudocarpous** /-'kahpəs/ *adj*.

pseudocyesis /s(y)oohdohsie'eesis/ *noun* = PHANTOM PREGNANCY. [PSEUDO- + Greek *kyēsis* pregnancy, from *kyein* to be pregnant]

pseudomorph /'s(y)oohdəmawf, 's(y)oohdohmawf/ *noun* a mineral having the outward form of another mineral type. ➤ **pseudomorphic** /-'mawfik/ *adj*, **pseudomorphism** /-'mawfiz(ə)m/ *noun*, **pseudomorphous** /-'mawfəs/ *adj*.

pseudonym /'s(y)oohdənim/ *noun* a fictitious name, *esp* one used by an author. ➤ **pseudonymity** /-'nimiti/ *noun*, **pseudonymous** /s(y)ooh'doniməs/ *adj*, **pseudonymously** /s(y)ooh'doniməsli/ *adv*. [French *pseudonyme*, from Greek *pseudōnymos* bearing a false name, from PSEUD- + *onomos* name]

pseudopod /'s(y)oohdəpod/ *noun* a temporary protrusion of a single-celled animal, e.g. an amoeba, that serves to take in food, move the cell, etc.

pseudopodium /s(y)oohdə'pohdi·əm/ *noun* (*pl* **pseudopodia** /-'pohdi·ə/) = PSEUDOPOD.

pseudopregnancy /s(y)oohdoh'pregnənsi/ *noun* (*pl* **pseudopregnancies**) **1** = PHANTOM PREGNANCY. **2** a state resembling pregnancy that occurs in various mammals usu after an infertile copulation and during which oestrus does not occur. ➤ **pseudopregnant** *adj*.

psf *abbr* pounds per square foot.

pshaw /(p)shaw/ *interj* used to express irritation, disapproval, or disbelief.

psi[1] /sie, psie/ *noun* **1** the 23rd letter of the Greek alphabet (Ψ, ψ), equivalent to and transliterated as roman ps. **2** psychic or paranormal phenomena or abilities. [late Greek *psi* from Greek *psei*]

psi[2] *abbr* pounds per square inch.

psilocybin /sielə'siebin/ *noun* a hallucinogenic organic compound obtained from various mushrooms, such as the Mexican mushroom *Psilocybe mexicana*. [Latin genus name (from Greek *psilos* bald + *kybē* head) + -IN[1]]

psittacine[1] /'(p)sitəsien, -seen, -sin/ *adj* of the parrot family; like a parrot. [Latin *psittacinus* from *psittacus* parrot, from Greek *psittakos*]

psittacine[2] *noun* a bird of the parrot family.

psittacosis /(p)sitə'kohsis/ *noun* a severe infectious disease of parrots, pigeons, ducks, geese, and other birds that is caused by a parasitic micro-organism and that causes a serious form of pneumonia when transmitted to human beings. ▶ **psittacotic** /-'kotik/ *adj*. [scientific Latin, from Latin *psittacus* parrot + -OSIS]

psoas /'soh-əs/ *noun* (*pl* **psoai** /'soh-ie/ *or* **psoae** /'soh-ee/) either of two muscles in the groin that flex and rotate the hip joint. [Greek *psoa*; the accusative plural *psoās* was wrongly taken to be a nominative singular]

psoriasis /sə'rie-əsis/ *noun* a chronic skin condition characterized by distinct red patches covered by white scales. ▶ **psoriatic** /sori'atik/ *adj and noun*. [Greek *psōriasis*, from *psōrian* to have the itch, from *psōra* itch]

psst /pst/ *interj* used to attract somebody's attention quietly.

PST *abbr* Pacific Standard Time (time zone).

PSV *abbr Brit* public service vehicle.

psych *or* **psyche** /siek/ *verb trans informal* **1** *NAmer* to psychoanalyse (somebody). **2** *chiefly NAmer* to anticipate correctly the intentions or actions of (somebody); to outguess (them). **3** *chiefly NAmer* = PSYCH OUT. [by shortening from PSYCHOANALYSE, PSYCHOLOGY, etc]

psych- *or* **psycho-** *comb. form* forming words, with the meanings: **1a** mind; mental processes: *psychoactive*; *psychology*. **b** using psychoanalytical methods: *psychotherapy*. **c** brain: *psychosurgery*. **d** mental and: *psychosomatic*. **2** psyche: *psychic*. [Greek, from *psychē* breath, principle of life, life, soul]

psyche[1] /'sieki/ *noun* **1** the soul or self. **2** the mind. **3** the spirit; the underlying principle affecting a group's attitudes, etc: *the American psyche*. [Greek *psychē* breath, principle of life, life, soul]

psyche[2] /siek/ *verb trans* see PSYCH.

psychedelia /siekə'deeli-ə/ *noun* subculture of art, music, etc, associated with psychedelic drugs.

psychedelic /siekə'delik/ *adj* **1a** said of drugs: capable of producing altered states of consciousness that involve changed mental and sensory awareness, hallucinations, etc. **b** produced by or associated with the use of psychedelic drugs. **2a** imitating or reproducing effects, e.g. bright colours, or distorted or bizarre images or sounds associated with psychedelic drugs. **b** having colours and a swirling pattern. ▶ **psychedelically** *adv*. [Greek *psychē* soul + *dēloun* to show]

psychiatry /sie'kie-ətri/ *noun* a branch of medicine that deals with mental, emotional, or behavioural disorders. ▶ **psychiatric** /sieki'atrik/ *adj*, **psychiatrical** /sieki'atrik/ *adj*, **psychiatrically** /sieki'atrikli/ *adv*, **psychiatrist** *noun*. [PSYCH- + -IATRY]

psychic[1] /'siekik/ *adj* **1** lying outside the sphere of physical science or knowledge; involving telepathy, clairvoyance, or psychokinesis. **2** said of a person: **a** sensitive to nonphysical or supernatural forces or influences. **b** having a mysterious sensitivity, perception, or understanding; telepathic: *You must be psychic – I was just about to ring you*. **3** of or originating in the mind, soul, or spirit. ▶ **psychically** *adv*. [Greek *psychikos* of the soul, from *psychē*: see PSYCHE[1]]

psychic[2] *noun* **1** a psychic person. **2** a person through whom some people believe it is possible to communicate with the spirits of the dead; = MEDIUM[1] (5).

psychical /'siekikl/ *adj* = PSYCHIC[1].

psycho /'siekoh/ *noun* (*pl* **psychos**) *informal* a psychopath or psychotic person. ▶ **psycho** *adj*.

psycho- *comb. form* see PSYCH-.

psychoactive /siekoh'aktiv/ *adj* said of drugs: affecting the mind or behaviour.

psychoanalyse (*NAmer* **psychoanalyze**) /siekoh'anəliez/ *verb trans* to examine (somebody or something) or treat (somebody) by means of psychoanalysis.

psychoanalysis /,siekoh-ə'naləsis/ *noun* a method of analysing unconscious mental processes and treating mental disorders, *esp* by allowing the patient to talk freely about early childhood experiences, dreams, etc. ▶ **psychoanalyst** /-'anəlist/ *noun*, **psychoanalytic** /-anə'litik/ *adj*, **psychoanalytical** /-anə'litikl/ *adj*, **psychoanalytically** /-anə'litikli/ *adv*.

psychoanalyze /siekoh'anəliez/ *verb trans NAmer* see PSYCHOANALYSE.

psychobabble /'siekohbabl/ *noun informal* popularized psychological jargon used in a loose, trendy, or pretentious way to describe human feelings and relationships.

psychobiology /,siekohbie'oləji/ *noun* the study of mental processes and behaviour in relation to other biological processes and behaviour. ▶ **psychobiological** /-'lojikl/ *adj*, **psychobiologist** *noun*.

psychochemical[1] /siekoh'kemikl/ *adj* said of a chemical substance: that changes a person's state of consciousness.

psychochemical[2] *noun* a psychochemical substance.

psychodrama /'siekohdrahmə/ *noun* **1a** the playing of roles as a technique of psychotherapy or education. **b** an improvised dramatization of events from a patient's life designed to afford insight into and resolution of personal conflicts. **2** a drama in which the main interest is in the psychological behaviour and development of the characters. ▶ **psychodramatic** /-drə'matik/ *adj*.

psychodynamics /,siekohdie'namiks/ *pl noun* (*treated as sing. or pl*) the psychology of mental or emotional forces or processes and their effects on behaviour and mental states, or the explanation or interpretation of behaviour in terms of these forces. ▶ **psychodynamic** *adj*.

psychogenic /siekoh'jenik/ *adj* said of an illness: originating in the mind or in mental or emotional conflict rather than having a physical cause.

psychokinesis /,siekohki'neesis/ *noun* movement in physical objects produced by the power of the mind without physical contact. ▶ **psychokinetic** /-'netik/ *adj*.

psycholinguistics /,siekohling'gwistiks/ *pl noun* (*treated as sing. or pl*) the study of the interrelation between linguistic behaviour and the minds of speaker and hearer, e.g. in the production and comprehension of speech, language acquisition by children, and speech and language disorders. ▶ **psycholinguist** /-'linggwist/ *noun*, **psycholinguistic** *adj*.

psychological /siekə'lojikl/ *adj* **1a** of or relating to psychology. **b** mental; of the mind. **2** directed towards or intended to affect the will, morale, or mind: *psychological warfare*. ▶ **psychologically** *adv*.

psychological moment *noun* the occasion when conditions are most conducive to achieving a particular effect.

psychological profiling *noun* = PROFILING (2).

psychologize *or* **psychologise** /sie'koləjiez/ *verb trans* to explain or interpret (something) in psychological terms. ▶ *verb intrans* **1** to explain or interpret in psychological terms. **2** to study or use psychology.

psychology /sie'koləji/ *noun* (*pl* **psychologies**) **1** the science or study of mind and behaviour. **2** the mental or behavioural characteristics of an individual or group. ▶ **psychologist** *noun*.

psychometrics /siekə'metriks/ *pl noun* (*treated as sing. or pl*) the measurement of mental capacities and attributes, *esp* by the use of psychological tests, such as intelligence tests, or the branch of psychology concerned with this.

psychometry /sie'komətri/ *noun* **1** divination of facts concerning an object or its owner through physical contact with the object or proximity to it. **2** the psychological theory and technique of the measurement of mental capacities and attributes; = PSYCHOMETRICS. ▶ **psychometric** /-'metrik/ *adj*, **psychometrical** /-'metrikl/ *adj*, **psychometrically** /-'metrikli/ *adv*, **psychometrist** *noun*.

psychomotor /siekoh'mohtə/ *adj* relating to movement of a part of the body directly proceeding from mental activity: *a psychomotor seizure*.

psychoneurosis /ˌsiekohnyoo(ə)'rohsis/ *noun* (*pl* **psycho-neuroses** /-seez/) a neurosis, *esp* one based on emotional conflict. ➤➤ **psychoneurotic** /-'rotik/ *adj and noun*.

psychopath /'siekəpath/ *noun* **1** a person suffering from a severe emotional and behavioural disorder characterized by antisocial tendencies and usu the pursuit of immediate gratification through often violent acts. **2** a dangerously violent, mentally ill person. ➤➤ **psychopathic** /-'pathik/ *adj*, **psychopathically** /-'pathikli/ *adv*, **psychopathy** /sie'kopəthi/ *noun*.

psychopathology /ˌsiekohpə'tholəji/ *noun* psychological and behavioural aberrations occurring in mental disorder, or the study of such aberrations. ➤➤ **psychopathological** /-pathə'lojikl/ *adj*, **psychopathologist** *noun*.

psychopharmacology /ˌsiekohfahmə'koləji/ *noun* the study of the effect of drugs on the mind and behaviour. ➤➤ **psychopharmacological** /-'lojikl/ *adj*, **psychopharmacologist** *noun*.

psychophysics /siekoh'fiziks/ *pl noun* (*treated as sing. or pl*) a branch of psychology that deals with the relationship between the physical attributes of a stimulus and the characteristics of the resulting sensation or perception. ➤➤ **psychophysical** *adj*.

psychophysiology /ˌsiekohfizi'olǝji/ *noun* the physiology of psychological phenomena and mental processes. ➤➤ **psycho-physiological** /-'lojikl/ *adj*, **psychophysiologist** *noun*.

psychoses /sie'kohseez/ *noun* pl of PSYCHOSIS.

psychosexual /siekoh'seksy(oo)əl, -sh(ə)l/ *adj* of the emotional, mental, or behavioural aspects of sex. ➤➤ **psychosexuality** /-'aliti/ *noun*, **psychosexually** *adv*.

psychosis /sie'kohsis/ *noun* (*pl* **psychoses** /-seez/) severe mental derangement, e.g. schizophrenia, that results in the impairment or loss of contact with reality: *The evidence is overwhelming that there is some kind of genetic factor involved in the most serious forms of mental illness, the 'psychoses' like schizophrenia* — New Internationalist. ➤➤ **psychotic** /sie'kotik/ *adj and noun*, **psychotically** /sie'kotikli/ *adv*.

psychosocial /siekoh'sohsh(ə)l/ *adj* **1** relating social conditions to mental health: *psychosocial medicine*. **2** of or involving matters that are both psychological and social. ➤➤ **psychosocially** *adv*.

psychosomatic /ˌsiekohsə'matik/ *adj* of or resulting from the interaction of psychological and somatic factors, *esp* the production of physical symptoms or disorders by mental processes or psychological factors such as stress: *psychosomatic medicine; a psychosomatic illness*.

psychosurgery /siekoh'suhjəri/ *noun* brain surgery used to treat mental disorder. ➤➤ **psychosurgical** /-jikl/ *adj*.

psychotherapy /siekoh'therəpi/ *noun* treatment by psychological methods for mental, emotional, or psychosomatic disorders. ➤➤ **psychotherapeutic** /-'pyoohtik/ *adj*, **psychotherapeutically** /-'pyoohtikli/ *adv*, **psychotherapist** *noun*.

psychotic /sie'kotik/ *adj and noun* see PSYCHOSIS.

psychotropic /siekə'trohpik/ *adj* = PSYCHOACTIVE.

psych out *verb trans* **1** to intimidate or scare (somebody) by psychological means: *Their war dance at the beginning of a match is just an attempt to psych out the other team*. **2** to analyse or work out (a problem or course of action): *I psyched it all out by myself*.

psychro- *comb. form* forming words, denoting: cold: *psychrometer*. [Greek, from *psychros* cold, from *psychein* to cool]

psychrometer /sie'kromitə/ *noun* a HYGROMETER (instrument for measuring humidity) consisting of two similar thermometers with the bulb of one being kept wet so that the resulting cooling provides a measure of the dryness of the atmosphere. ➤➤ **psychrometric** /siekroh'metrik/ *adj*, **psychrometry** /-tri/ *noun*.

psych up *verb trans* to make (oneself) psychologically ready for doing something.

PT *abbr* physical training.

Pt *abbr* the chemical symbol for platinum.

pt *abbr* **1** part. **2** patient. **3** payment. **4** pint. **5** point. **6** port.

PTA *abbr* **1** Parent-Teacher Association. **2** *Brit* Passenger Transport Authority.

ptarmigan /'tahmigən/ *noun* (*pl* **ptarmigans** *or collectively* **ptarmigan**) a grouse of northern regions whose plumage turns white in winter: *Lagopus mutus*. [modification of Scottish Gaelic *tàrmachan* due to a supposed connection with Greek words beginning in *pt-*]

PTE *abbr* Passenger Transport Executive.

Pte *abbr* Private.

pter- *or* **ptero-** *comb. form* forming words, denoting: wing: *pteranodon*; *pterodactyl*. [Greek *pteron* wing, feather]

-ptera *comb. form* forming plural nouns, denoting: an order or suborder of insects, or the order of animals comprising the bats: *Diptera*; *Lepidoptera*. [Greek *ptera*, pl of *pteron* wing]

-pteran *comb. form* forming adjectives and nouns, with the meaning: of, or a member of, an order or suborder of insects, or the order of animals comprising the bats: *dipteran*; *lepidopteran*. [-PTERA]

pteranodon /te'ranədon/ *noun* any of a genus of pterosaurs (extinct flying reptiles; see PTEROSAUR) of the late Cretaceous period that had large toothless jaws, a hornlike crest, a small body, and very large membranous wings. [PTER- + AN- + Greek *odont-*, *odous* tooth]

pteridology /teri'dolǝji/ *noun* the study of ferns. ➤➤ **pteridological** /-'lojik(ə)l/ *adj*, **pteridologist** *noun*.

pteridophyte /'teridəfiet/ *noun* any of a group of ferns or other vascular plants that have roots, stems, and leaves but no flowers or seeds: division Pteridophyta. ➤➤ **pteridophytic** /-'fltik/ *adj*, **pteridophytous** /-'dofitəs/ *adj*.

ptero- *comb. form* see PTER-.

pterodactyl /terə'daktil/ *noun* any of a number of pterosaurs (extinct flying reptiles; see PTEROSAUR) of the Jurassic and Cretaceous periods that had toothed jaws and membranous wings. [PTERO- + Greek *daktylos* finger]

pteropod /'terəpod/ *noun* = SEA BUTTERFLY. ➤➤ **pteropodan** /-'pohdn/ *adj and noun*.

pterosaur /'terəsaw/ *noun* any of an order of extinct flying reptiles of the Jurassic and Cretaceous periods, having membranous wings that extended from the side of the body along the arm to the end of the greatly enlarged fourth digit. The pterosaurs included pteranodons and pterodactyls. [PTERO- + Greek *saurus* lizard]

-pterous *comb. form* forming adjectives, with the meanings: **1** having the type or number of wings specified: *apterous*; *dipterous*. **2** belonging to an order or suborder of insects: *lepidopterous*. [-PTERA]

pterygoid /'terigoyd/ *adj* of or lying in the region of the lower part of the wedge-shaped bone at the base of the vertebrate skull: *the pterygoid process*. [scientific Latin from Greek *pterygoeidēs*, literally 'shaped like a wing', from *pteryg-*, *pteryx* wing + *oeidēs* -OID]

PTFE *abbr* polytetrafluoroethylene.

PTN *abbr* public telephone network.

PTO *or* **pto** *abbr* please turn over.

Ptolemaic /toli'mayik/ *adj* **1** of Ptolemy, second-cent. Egyptian astronomer, mathematician, and geographer, or the PTOLEMAIC SYSTEM. **2** of the Graeco-Egyptian Ptolemies who ruled Egypt from 323 BC to 30 BC. [Greek *Ptolemaikos*]

Ptolemaic system *noun* the theoretical system of planetary movements according to which the sun, moon, and planets revolve round a stationary earth, as described by the second-cent. Egyptian astronomer Ptolemy: compare COPERNICAN SYSTEM. ➤➤ **Ptolemaist** *noun*.

ptomaine /'tohmayn/ *noun* any of various sometimes poisonous organic compounds formed by the action of putrefactive bacteria on nitrogen-containing matter. [Italian *ptomaina* from Greek *ptōma* fall, fallen body, corpse, from *piptein* to fall]

ptomaine poisoning *noun dated* = FOOD POISONING. It is now known that food poisoning is not caused by ptomaines.

ptosis /'tohsis/ *noun* (*pl* **ptoses** /-'tohseez/) a drooping of the upper eyelid. [Greek *ptōsis* act of falling, from *piptein* to fall]

PTSD *abbr* post-traumatic stress disorder.

P2P *abbr* peer-to-peer, denoting a system that allows computers to communicate directly with each other through the Internet without a central server.

Pty *abbr Aus, NZ, SAfr* Proprietary.

ptyalin /'tie·əlin/ *noun* an enzyme found in the saliva of many animals that breaks down starch into sugar. [Greek *ptyalon* saliva, from *ptyein* to spit]

p-type *adj* said of a semiconductor: having an excess of positively charged current carriers: compare N-TYPE. [short for *positive-type*]

Pu *abbr* the chemical symbol for plutonium.

pub /pub/ *noun* **1** *chiefly Brit* an establishment where alcoholic beverages are sold and consumed; = PUBLIC HOUSE. **2** *Aus, NZ* a hotel. [short for PUBLIC HOUSE]

pub. *or* **publ.** *abbr* **1** public. **2** publication. **3** published. **4** publisher. **5** publishing.

pubbing *noun informal* visiting pubs.

pubby *adj* (**pubbier, pubbiest**) having the atmosphere of a pub.

pub crawl *noun chiefly Brit, informal* a visit to a series of pubs, involving at least one drink at each.

pub-crawl *verb intrans chiefly Brit, informal* to go on a pub crawl.

puberty /'pyoohbəti/ *noun* **1** the condition of being or the period of becoming capable of reproducing sexually. **2** the age at which puberty occurs. >>> **pubertal** *adj.* [Middle English *puberte* from Latin *pubertas*, from *puber* adult]

pubes /'pyoohbeez/ *noun* (*pl* **pubes** /'pyoohbeez/) the pubic region or pubic hair. See also PUBIS. [Latin *pubis* manhood, body hair, pubic region]

pubescence /pyooh'bes(ə)ns/ *noun* **1** the state of being pubescent. **2** a pubescent covering or surface.

pubescent /pyooh'bes(ə)nt/ *adj* **1** arriving at or having reached puberty. **2** covered with fine soft short hairs: compare HISPID. [Latin *pubescent-, pubescens*, present part. of *pubescere* to reach puberty, become covered with hair, from *pubes*: see PUBES]

pubic /'pyoohbik/ *adj* of or situated in or near the region of the pubis, the external genital organs, or the pubic hair.

pubic hair *noun* the hair that appears at puberty round the genitals.

pubis /'pyoohbis/ *noun* (*pl* **pubes** /'pyoohbeez/) the bottom front of the three principal bones that form either half of the pelvis. [scientific Latin *os pubis* bone of the pubic region]

publ. *abbr* see PUB.

public[1] /'publik/ *adj* **1a** of or affecting all the people or the whole area of a nation or state: *public law.* **b** of or being in the service of the community: *public affairs.* **2** general or popular: *public awareness.* **3** of national or community concerns as opposed to private affairs; social. **4** accessible to or shared by all members of the community: *a public park.* **5a** exposed to general view; open: *a public quarrel.* **b** known to people in general: *He was threatening to make the information public.* **c** prominent; celebrated: *Sir, he is one of the many who have made themselves public without making themselves known* — Dr Johnson; *politicians, actors, and other public figures.* ✳ **go public 1** to become a public company. **2** to reveal information to the public. [Middle English *publique* via French from Latin *publicus*, alteration, by association of *pubes* adult, of *poplicus*, from *populus* the people]

public[2] *noun* **1** (**the public**) people as a whole; the populace. **2** a group or section of people having common interests or characteristics: *the motoring public.* **3** audience; fans: *He said he owed it to his public not to call off the show.* ✳ **in public** in the presence, sight, or hearing of strangers.

public-address system *noun* an apparatus including a microphone and loudspeakers used to address a large audience.

publican *noun* **1a** *chiefly Brit* the licensee of a public house. **b** *Aus, NZ* a person who keeps a hotel. **2** a private individual acting as a tax or revenue collector for the ancient Romans. [Middle English via French from Latin *publicanus* tax collector, from *publicum* public revenue, neuter of *publicus*: see PUBLIC[1]]

publication /publi'kaysh(ə)n/ *noun* **1** the act or process of publishing. **2** a published work. **3** the act or an instance of making information public. [Middle English *publicacioun* via French from late Latin *publication-, publicatio*, from Latin *publicare* to make public, publish, from *publicus*: see PUBLIC[1]]

public bar *noun Brit* a plainly furnished and often relatively cheap bar in a public house: compare SALOON (1A).

public bill *noun* a legislative bill affecting the public as a whole: compare PRIVATE BILL.

public company *noun* a company whose shares may be offered to the general public and apply for listing on the stock exchange: compare PRIVATE COMPANY.

public convenience *noun Brit* public toilet facilities.

public corporation *noun* a corporation responsible for running a nationalized service or industry.

public domain *noun* the status in law of property rights that are unprotected by copyright or patent and are subject to appropriation by anybody. ✳ **in the public domain** known by or obtainable by the general public.

public enemy *noun* a person, *esp* a notorious wanted criminal, who is a danger to the public.

public enterprise *noun* business or economic activity carried out by government departments or government-funded bodies: compare PRIVATE ENTERPRISE.

public expenditure *noun* spending by a government, local authorities, etc.

public health *noun* the protection and improvement of community health, *esp* sanitation, by government regulation and community effort, or the theory and practice relating to this.

public house /hows/ *noun* **1** *chiefly Brit* an establishment where alcoholic beverages are sold to be drunk on the premises. **2** *NAmer* an inn or hotel.

publicise /'publisiez/ *verb trans* see PUBLICIZE.

publicist /'publisist/ *noun* **1** a person whose job is to publicize something such as a book or organization; a press agent. **2** *dated* a journalist, *esp* one who is an expert or commentator on public affairs. **3** *dated* an expert on public or international law.

publicity /pu'blisiti/ *noun* **1a** information with news value issued as a means of gaining public attention or support. **b** paid advertising. **c** the dissemination of information or promotional material. **2** public attention or acclaim. **3** *formal* being public: *The whole sordid affair was subjected to the publicity of an open court.*

publicize *or* **publicise** /'publisiez/ *verb trans* to give publicity to (an event, organization, product, etc).

public law *noun* a branch of law regulating the relations of individuals with the government and the organization and conduct of the government itself: compare PRIVATE LAW.

public lending right *or* **Public Lending Right** *noun* the right of authors to a royalty on issues of their books from public libraries.

public limited company *noun* in Britain, a PUBLIC COMPANY whose shareholders have only a limited liability for any debts or losses created by the company.

publicly *adv* **1** in a manner observable by or in a place accessible to the public; openly. **2a** by the people generally; communally. **b** by a government: *publicly provided medical care.*

public nuisance *noun* **1** an illegal act that is harmful to the safety, comfort, or rights of the general public as a whole rather than of a particular individual: *Smoking on tube trains was declared a health hazard and a public nuisance.* **2** *informal* a person or group that is disruptive, harmful, or dangerous to the general public.

public opinion *noun* the opinions, views, or beliefs held by the general public, *esp* on an issue of national importance.

public prosecutor *noun* an official who conducts criminal prosecutions on behalf of the state.

Public Record Office *noun* in Britain, an institution containing an archive of official documents which are available for inspection or consultation by the general public.

public relations *pl noun* **1** the business of inducing the public to have understanding for and goodwill towards a famous person, organization, or institution. **2** the techniques involved in this. **3** the degree of understanding and goodwill achieved. **4** the relationship between a famous person, organization, or institution and the public.

public school *noun* **1** in Britain, an endowed independent, often single-sex, school, typically a large boarding school preparing pupils for higher education. **2** in N America and, *esp* formerly, in Scotland, a state school.

public sector *noun* the part of the economy owned or controlled by the national government or local authorities: compare PRIVATE SECTOR.

public servant *noun* **1** a person who belongs to or works for a government, state, local authority, etc. **2** *Aus, NZ* = CIVIL SERVANT.

public service *noun* **1** the business of supplying electricity, transport, etc to a community. **2** service rendered in the public interest. **3** employment in or for a government, state, local authority, etc. **4** *Aus, NZ* = CIVIL SERVICE.

public speaking *noun* **1** making speeches in public. **2** the art or science of effective oral communication with an audience: *She took a course in public speaking.* ➤➤ **public speaker** *noun*.

public-spirited *adj* motivated by concern for the general welfare.

public utility *noun* a business organization providing a public amenity, e.g. supplying water, gas, or electricity, and subject to special governmental regulation.

public works *pl noun* schools, roads, etc constructed for public use, *esp* by the government.

publish /'publish/ *verb trans* **1a** to produce (a book, newspaper, etc) or release (it) for sale or distribution to the public. **b** to print (information, an article, a letter, etc) in a book, newspaper, etc. **c** to issue the work of (an author). **2a** to make information generally known. **b** to announce (something) publicly. **3** to communicate (something libellous or defamatory about somebody) to another person. ➤ *verb intrans* **1** to have one's work produced or released for sale or distribution to the public. **2** to put out an edition of a newspaper, etc. ➤➤ **publishable** *adj*, **publishing** *noun*. [Middle English *publishen* via early French *publier* from Latin *publicare*, from *publicus*: see PUBLIC[1]]

publisher *noun* **1** a person or company whose business is publishing books, etc: *No publisher should ever express an opinion on the value of what he publishes* — Oscar Wilde. **2** *NAmer* a newspaper proprietor.

puce /pyoohs/ *adj* of a brownish purple colour. ➤➤ **puce** *noun*. [the noun from French *puce* flea, from Latin *pulic-, pulex*; the adj from the noun]

puck[1] /puk/ *noun* a vulcanized rubber disc used in ice hockey. [perhaps from English dialect *puck* to poke or hit, alteration of POKE[1]]

puck[2] *noun* a mischievous sprite. [Old English *pūca*]

pucka /'pukə/ *adj* see PUKKA.

pucker[1] /'pukə/ *verb* (**puckered, puckering**) ➤ *verb intrans* to become wrinkled or irregularly creased. ➤ *verb trans* to cause (material, etc) to pucker. [prob from POKE[3], alluding to the gathering up of the neck of a bag to close it]

pucker[2] *noun* a crease or wrinkle in a normally even surface.

puckish *adj* impish; whimsical. ➤➤ **puckishly** *adv*, **puckishness** *noun*. [PUCK[2] + -ISH]

pud /pood/ *noun Brit, informal* a pudding.

pudding /'pooding/ *noun* **1a** any of various sweet or savoury dishes of a soft to spongy or fairly firm consistency that are made from rice, tapioca, flour, etc and are cooked by boiling, steaming, or baking: *sponge pudding; steak and kidney pudding.* **b** dessert. **2** any of various sausage-like foods, e.g.: **a** = BLACK PUDDING. **b** = WHITE PUDDING. **3** *informal* a small podgy person. ✳ **in the pudding club** *informal* pregnant. ➤➤ **puddingy** /'poodingi/ *adj*.

Word history ⸻⸻
Middle English *poding* via French *boudin* black pudding, from Latin *botellus* sausage, small intestine. The word orig denoted a dish rather like haggis, consisting of minced meat, suet, and cereal boiled in an animal's stomach or intestine; later a sweet or savoury mixture enclosed in a crust and boiled or steamed, hence a cooked sweet dish forming part of a meal.

pudding stone *noun* = CONGLOMERATE[2] rock (rock composed of small stones embedded in a cement-like substance) in which the darker stones contrast with the lighter substance they are embedded in.

puddle[1] /'pudl/ *noun* **1** a small pool of liquid, *esp* one of rainwater. **2** a mixture, e.g. of clay, sand, and gravel, used as a waterproof covering. [Middle English *podel*, dimin. of Old English *pudd* ditch]

puddle[2] *verb trans* **1** to work (a wet mixture of earth or concrete) into a dense impervious mass. **2** to subject (iron) to puddling. ➤➤ **puddler** *noun*, **puddly** *adj*.

puddling *noun* the conversion of pig iron into wrought iron by heating and stirring with oxidizing substances.

pudency /'pyoohdənsi/ *noun formal* modesty; bashfulness. [Latin *pudentia*, from *pudent-, pudens*, present part. of *pudēre* to be ashamed]

pudendum /pyooh'dendəm/ *noun* (*pl* **pudenda** /-də/) (*usu in pl*) the external genital organs of a human being, *esp* of a female. ➤➤ **pudendal** *adj*. [sing. of Latin *pudenda*, literally 'the shameful parts', neuter pl of *pudendus*, from *pudēre* to be ashamed]

pudgy /'puji/ *adj* (**pudgier, pudgiest**) = PODGY. ➤➤ **pudgily** *adv*, **pudginess** *noun*. [origin unknown]

pueblo /'pwebloh, poo'ebloh/ *noun* (*pl* **pueblos**) **1a** a Native American village of Arizona, New Mexico, and adjacent areas, consisting of contiguous flat-roofed stone or clay houses in groups sometimes several storeys high. **b** (**Pueblo** *pl* **Pueblos** *or collectively* **Pueblo**) a member of any of the Native American peoples inhabiting such villages. **c** any Native American village of the south-west USA. **2** a small town or village in Spain or Spanish America. ➤➤ **Pueblo** *adj*. [Spanish *pueblo* village, people, from Latin *populus* PEOPLE[1]]

puerile /'pyooəriel/ *adj* **1** not befitting an adult; childish: *puerile remarks.* **2** juvenile. ➤➤ **puerilely** *adv*, **puerilism** /-riliz(ə)m/ *noun*, **puerility** /-'riliti/ *noun*. [French *puéril* from Latin *puerilis*, from *puer* boy, child]

puerperal /pyooh'uhp(ə)rəl/ *adj* of or occurring during childbirth or the period immediately following childbirth. [Latin *puerpera* woman in childbirth, from *puer* child + *parere* to give birth to]

puerperal fever *noun* an often serious and sometimes fatal infection of the female reproductive organs following childbirth or abortion, causing blood poisoning and inflammation.

Puerto Rican /,pwuhtoh 'reekən/ *noun* a native or inhabitant of Puerto Rico in the Caribbean. ➤➤ **Puerto Rican** *adj*.

puff[1] /puf/ *verb intrans* **1a** to exhale or blow forcibly: *He puffed into a blowpipe to shape the molten glass.* **b** to breathe hard and quickly; to pant. **c** to emit small whiffs or clouds, e.g. of smoke or steam. **d** to move while emitting puffs of smoke, etc: *The train puffed into the station.* **2** to blow in short gusts. **3** (*usu* + out/up) to become distended; to swell. ➤ *verb trans* **1a** to emit, propel, or blow (something) by puffs or as if by puffs; to waft (it). **b** to draw on (a pipe, cigarette, etc) with intermittent exhalations of smoke. **2a** (*usu* + out/up) to distend (something) with or as if with air or gas; to inflate (it). **b** (*usu* + up) to make (somebody) proud or conceited. **c** to praise (somebody or something) extravagantly and usu exaggeratedly, or to advertise (them) by this means. **3** to make (one's way) emitting puffs of breath or smoke. **4** (+ out) to extinguish (a candle, etc) by blowing. [Old English *pyffan*, of imitative origin]

puff[2] *noun* **1a** the act or an instance of puffing. **b** a slight explosive sound accompanying a puff. **c** a small cloud, e.g. of smoke, emitted in a puff. **d** a draw on a pipe or cigarette; a smoke. **2** a light round hollow pastry made of puff pastry: *a cream puff.* **3** *chiefly Brit, informal* one's breath: *She sat down until she got her puff back.* **4** a highly favourable notice or review, *esp* one that publicizes something or somebody. **5a** = POUFFE. **b** = POWDER PUFF. **6** *NAmer* a quilted bed cover; an eiderdown. **7** *informal* = POOF.

puff adder *noun* **1** a large venomous African viper that inflates its body and hisses loudly when disturbed: *Bitis arietans.* **2** = HOGNOSE SNAKE.

puffball *noun* **1** any of various spherical and often edible fungi that discharge a cloud of ripe spores when pressed or struck: family Lycoperdaceae. **2** a short skirt which is puffed out into a rounded outline and gathered in at the hem.

puffball skirt *noun* = PUFFBALL (2).

puffed *adj chiefly Brit, informal* out of breath.

puffed out *adj* = PUFFED.

puffed sleeve *noun* = PUFF SLEEVE.

puffer *noun* **1** a person or thing that puffs. **2** = GLOBEFISH (a fish that can inflate itself when disturbed). **3** *esp* in Scotland, a small coastal steamship that carries cargo.

puffer fish *noun* = PUFFER (2).

puffin /'pufin/ *noun* (*pl* **puffins** *or collectively* **puffin**) any of several species of seabirds of the auk family that have a short neck and a deep grooved multicoloured bill: genera *Fratercula* and *Lunda*. [Middle English *pophyn*, perhaps of Celtic origin]

puff pastry *noun* a type of light flaky pastry made with a rich dough containing a large quantity of butter.

puff sleeve *noun* a short full sleeve gathered at the upper and lower edges.

puffy *adj* (**puffier, puffiest**) said *esp* of the eyes or cheeks: swollen: *Her eyes were puffy from crying.* ➤➤ **puffily** *adv*, **puffiness** *noun*.

pug[1] /pug/ *noun* a dog of a breed with a small sturdy compact body, a tightly curled tail, and a broad wrinkled face. ➤➤ **puggish** *adj*, **puggy** *adj*.

Word history ⸻⸻
orig a term of endearment, perhaps of Dutch origin. Its use as a name for the dog may come from the obsolete senses 'monkey', and 'hobgoblin', which the dog's face was thought to resemble.

pug[2] *verb trans* (**pugged, pugging**) **1** to work and mix (clay, etc) when wet, *esp* to make it more homogeneous and easier to handle. **2** to plug or pack (a space) with a substance such as clay or mortar, *esp* to deaden sound. ➤➤ **pugging** *noun*. [perhaps alteration of POKE[1]]

pug[3] *noun informal* a boxer. [by shortening and alteration from *pugilist*]

puggaree *or* **pugaree** /'pugəri/ *or* **puggree** *or* **pugree** /'pugri/ *noun* **1** a turban. **2** a light turban or scarf wrapped round a sun helmet. [Hindi *pagṛī* turban]

pugilism /'pyoohjiliz(ə)m/ *noun formal* boxing. ➤➤ **pugilist** *noun*, **pugilistic** /-'listik/ *adj*, **pugilistically** /-'listikli/ *adv*. [Latin *pugil* boxer + -ISM]

pugnacious /pug'nayshəs/ *adj* inclined to fight or quarrel; belligerent. ➤➤ **pugnaciously** *adv*, **pugnaciousness** *noun*, **pugnacity** /pug'nasiti/ *noun*. [Latin *pugnac-, pugnax*, from *pugnare* to fight, from *pugnus* fist]

pug nose *noun* a nose having a slightly concave bridge and flattened nostrils. ➤➤ **pug-nosed** *adj*. [PUG[1]]

puisne /'pyoohni/ *adj* said *esp* of a judge: lower in rank. [early French *puisné*: see PUNY]

puissance /'pyooh·is(ə)ns, 'pwees(ə)ns (*French* pɥisɑ̃:s)/ *noun* **1** /'pweesanhs/ a showjumping competition which tests the horse's power to jump high obstacles. **2** *archaic or literary* strength or power. [Old French *puissance* from *puissant*: see PUISSANT]

puissant /'pyooh·is(ə)nt, 'pwees(ə)nt/ *adj archaic or literary* powerful: *a noble and puissant nation* — Milton. [Old French *puissant* powerful, from *poeir* to be able, be powerful, ultimately from Latin *posse*: see POTENT[1]]

puke[1] /pyoohk/ *verb trans and intrans informal* (*often* + up) to vomit (something). [perhaps imitative]

puke[2] *noun informal* **1** the act or an instance of vomiting. **2** vomit; something produced by vomiting.

pukka *or* **pucka** /'pukə/ *adj* **1** *informal*. **a** genuine or authentic. **b** first-class or excellent. **2** *chiefly Brit* stiffly formal or proper. [Hindi *pakkā* cooked, ripe, solid]

pul /poohl/ *noun* (*pl* **puls** *or* **puli** /'poohli, 'poohlee/) a unit of currency in Afghanistan, worth 100th of an afghani. [Persian *pūl* copper coin]

pula /'poolə/ *noun* the basic monetary unit of Botswana, divided into 100 thebe. [of Bantu origin]

pulchritude /'pulkrityoohd/ *noun formal* physical beauty. ➤➤ **pulchritudinous** /-'tyoohdinəs/ *adj*. [Middle English from Latin *pulchritudin-, pulchritudo*, from *pulcher* beautiful]

pule /pyoohl/ *verb intrans literary* to whine or whimper. ➤➤ **puler** *noun*. [prob imitative]

puli /'poohli, 'poohlee/ *noun* pl of PUL.

Pulitzer prize /'poolitsə/ *noun* any of various annual prizes for outstanding achievement in American journalism, literature, or music, established by the will of Joseph Pulitzer, Hungarian-born US newspaper publisher, d.1911.

pull[1] /pool/ *verb trans* **1a** to exert a force on (somebody or something) in such a way as to make them move towards oneself or the source of the force. **b** to draw (somebody or something) out of something in this way: *The cat had pulled some feathers from the bird's tail.* **c** to remove or extract (a nail, tooth, etc) by pulling. **d** to pluck (e.g. a flower) from a plant. **e** to lift (a plant) from the ground: *She sent the children out to pull turnips.* **f** to take out the entrails of (a chicken, duck, etc). **2** to make (something) come apart by force; to rend or tear (something): *Their little girl had pulled the books to pieces.* **3** to strain (a muscle, tendon, etc). **4** (*usu* + on) to bring out (a weapon) into the open in readiness for use: *Suddenly he pulled a knife on them.* **5** *informal* to draw the support or attention of (people); to attract (a crowd, audience, etc). **6** *informal*. **a** to commit (a crime): *They had been planning to pull a robbery the next day.* **b** (*often* + off) to carry out (a feat, action, etc) with daring and imagination: *They've pulled yet another financial coup.* **c** to attract (a sexual partner). **d** to do, perform, or say (something) with a deceptive intent: *She's been pulling these tricks for years.* **7** to draw (e.g. beer or cider) from the barrel, *esp* by pulling a pump handle. **8** *informal* to withdraw or remove (e.g. support, finance): *The company has decided to pull its share issue.* **9** to hit (a ball in e.g. cricket, golf, or baseball) towards the left from a right-handed swing or towards the right from a left-handed swing. **10** *informal* to arrest (somebody).

11 to hold back (a horse) from winning a race. **12** to work (an oar) by drawing back strongly; to row (a boat). **13** to print (e.g. a proof) by impression. **14** to retrieve information from (e.g. a database). **15** to stretch (e.g. a cooling humbug mixture) repeatedly. ➤➤ *verb intrans* **1a** to use force in drawing, dragging, or tugging. **b** to be capable of being pulled: *Soft wool pulls easily.* **c** (*often* + against/at/on) to try to move away from something that is resisting the movement. **2a** (*usu* + away/out/over) said of a vehicle: to move steadily: *A car pulled out of a driveway in front of me.* **b** said of a vehicle: to move through the exercise of mechanical energy. **3** (+ at/on) to draw hard or suck in smoking or drinking: *He pulled at his pipe and smiled enigmatically.* **4** said of a horse: to strain against the bit. **5** to row a boat. **6** to draw a gun. ✳ **pull a face** to grimace. **pull a fast one** *informal* to perpetrate a trick or fraud. **pull one's punches** to refrain from using all the force at one's disposal. **pull one's weight** to do one's full share of work [refers to a rower putting his full weight into the stroke]. **pull oneself together** to regain one's self-possession or self-control. **pull rank on** to assert one's authority over (somebody) in order to do something or get them to do something. **pull somebody's leg** to deceive or tease somebody playfully. **pull strings** to exert personal influence, *esp* secretly. **pull the plug** *informal* (*often* + on) to bring something to an end. **pull the strings** to be in control. **pull together** to work in harmony towards a common goal; to cooperate. ➤➤ **puller** *noun*. [Old English *pullian*]

pull[2] *noun* **1a** the act or an instance of pulling, or the force exerted by such an act. **b** a force that attracts, compels, or influences; an attraction. **c** force required to overcome resistance to pulling. **2** a device for pulling something, or for operating by pulling; a handle: *a drawer pull.* **3** a strain of a muscle, tendon, etc. **4a** a deep draught of liquid: *He took a long pull of his beer.* **b** an inhalation of smoke, e.g. from a cigarette. **5** the effort expended in moving: *It was a long pull uphill.* **6a** advantage: *the pull of a classical education.* **b** special influence exerted to obtain a privilege or advantage. **7a** an attacking stroke in cricket, made by hitting the ball to the LEG SIDE (same side of field as the batsman's legs are in relation to the middle stump) with a horizontal bat. **b** in golf or baseball, a hit towards the left from a right-handed swing or towards the right from a left-handed swing. **8** the act of holding a horse back from winning a race. **9a** a stroke with an oar. **b** a period of rowing. **10** in printing, a proof or impression.

pull apart *verb intrans* to separate or come to pieces when pulled. ➤ *verb trans* **1** to separate (something) or make it come to pieces by pulling. **2** to criticize (somebody or something) harshly.

pull away *verb intrans* **1** to draw oneself back or away. **2** to move off or ahead: *She pulled away from the leaders on the last lap.*

pull back *verb intrans* **1** to withdraw or retreat. **2** to improve one's position e.g. in a contest. ➤ *verb trans* **1** to cause (somebody, e.g. troops) to withdraw or retreat. **2** to withdraw (somebody or something) from a commitment or undertaking; = PULL OUT.

pull down *verb trans* to demolish or destroy (something).

pullet /'poolit/ *noun* a young female domestic fowl less than a year old. [Middle English *polet* young fowl, from early French *poulet*, ultimately from Latin *pullus* young of an animal, chicken, sprout]

pulley /'pooli/ *noun* (*pl* **pulleys**) **1a** a wheel with a grooved rim that is used with a rope or chain to change the direction and point of application of a pulling force. **b** one or more such wheels together with a block holding it or them. **2** a wheel used to transmit power or motion by means of a belt, rope, or chain passing over its rim. [Middle English *pouley* from early French *poulie*, prob ultimately from Greek *polos* axis, pole]

pull in *verb trans informal* **1** to attract (a crowd, etc). **2** to arrest (somebody). **3** to acquire (a sum of money) as payment or profit: *He pulls in £35,000 a year.* ➤ *verb intrans* **1** said *esp* of a train or road vehicle: to arrive at a destination or stopping place. **2** said of a vehicle or driver: to move to the side of or off the road in order to stop.

pull-in *noun chiefly Brit* a place where vehicles may pull in and stop, *esp* a roadside café.

Pullman /'poolmən/ *noun* (*pl* **Pullmans**) a railway passenger carriage with extra-comfortable furnishings. [named after George M *Pullman* d.1897, US inventor, who designed it]

Pullman car *noun* = PULLMAN.

pull off *verb trans* to carry out or accomplish (something) despite difficulties.

pullout *noun* **1** a removable section of a magazine, newspaper, or book: *See this week's handy TV guide pullout.* **2** a larger leaf in a book or magazine that when folded is the same size as the ordinary pages. **3** a military withdrawal.

pull out *verb intrans* **1** said *esp* of a train or road vehicle: to leave or depart. **2a** to withdraw from a military position. **b** to withdraw from a joint enterprise or agreement. **3** said of an aircraft: to resume horizontal flight after a dive. **4** said of a motor vehicle: to move out from behind a vehicle or into a stream of traffic. ✳ **pull out all the stops** to do everything possible to achieve an effect or action [refers to pulling out all the stops of an organ, thus bringing all the pipes into play].

pullover *noun* a sweater put on by being pulled over the head.

pull over *verb intrans* said of a driver or vehicle: to move towards the side of the road, *esp* in order to stop. ➤ *verb trans* to cause (a driver or vehicle) to pull over.

pull round *verb intrans* to return to good health or spirits. ➤ *verb trans* to cause or help (somebody) to pull round.

pull through *verb intrans* to survive or recover from a dangerous or difficult situation or illness. ➤ *verb trans* to cause (somebody) to pull through.

pullulate /'pulyoolayt/ *verb intrans* **1a** said of plants: to germinate or sprout. **b** to breed or produce rapidly and abundantly. **2** *formal* to swarm or teem. ➤➤ **pullulation** /-'laysh(ə)n/ *noun*. [Latin *pullulatus*, past part. of *pullulare*, from *pullulus*, dimin. of *pullus* chicken, young animal, sprout]

pull up *verb intrans* **1** to come to a halt; to stop. **2** (*often* + on/with) to draw even with or gain on others, e.g. in a race. ➤ *verb trans* **1** to bring (a vehicle) to a stop. **2** to reprimand or rebuke (somebody). ✳ **pull one's socks up** to make a greater effort or improve one's behaviour.

pull-up *noun* **1** an exercise performed by drawing oneself up while hanging by the hands until the chin is level with the support. **2** *chiefly Brit* = PULL-IN.

pulmonary /'poolmən(ə)ri, 'pul-/ *adj* of the lungs. [Latin *pulmonarius*, from *pulmon-, pulmo* lung]

pulmonary artery *noun* an artery that conveys deoxygenated blood from the heart to the lungs.

pulmonary valve *noun* the heart valve between the right ventricle and the pulmonary artery that stops blood flowing back into the right ventricle.

pulmonary vein *noun* a valveless vein that returns oxygenated blood from the lungs to the heart.

pulmonate *noun* a large order of gastropod molluscs including most land snails and slugs and many freshwater snails: class Pulmonata.

pulmonic /pool'monik, pul-/ *adj* = PULMONARY.

pulp[1] /pulp/ *noun* **1a** the soft juicy or fleshy part of a fruit or vegetable. **b** a soft mass of vegetable matter from which most of the water has been pressed. **c** the soft sensitive tissue that fills the central cavity of a tooth. **d** a material prepared by chemical or mechanical means from rags, wood, etc that is used in making paper. **2** a soft shapeless mass, *esp* one produced by crushing or beating: *They smashed his face to a pulp.* **3a** magazines or books cheaply produced on rough paper and containing sensational material. **b** (*used before a noun*) cheap and sensational: *pulp fiction.* **4** pulverized ore mixed with water. ➤➤ **pulpiness** *noun*, **pulpy** *adj*. [early French *poulpe* from Latin *pulpa* flesh, pulp]

pulp[2] *verb trans* **1** to reduce (something) to pulp. **2** to remove the pulp from (a fruit or vegetable). **3** to produce or reproduce (written matter) in pulp form. ➤ *verb intrans* to become pulp or pulpy. ➤➤ **pulper** *noun.*

pulpit /'poolpit/ *noun* **1a** a raised platform or high reading desk in church from which a sermon is preached. **b** (**the pulpit**) the clergy as a profession. **2** a means of getting one's opinions heard. [Middle English via late Latin from Latin *pulpitum* staging, platform]

pulpwood *noun* a wood, e.g. hemlock, pine, or spruce, used in making pulp for paper.

pulque /'poolkay, 'poolki/ *noun* a Mexican alcoholic drink made from the fermented juice of maguey plants. [Mexican Spanish *pulque* from Nahuatl *puliúhki* decomposed]

pulsar /'pulsah/ *noun* a celestial source, prob a rotating neutron star, of frequent intermittent bursts of radio waves. [PULSE[2] + -*ar* as in QUASAR]

pulsate /pul'sayt/ *verb intrans* **1** to beat with a pulse. **2** to throb or move rhythmically; to vibrate. **3** in physics and astronomy, to vary in brightness, magnitude, etc. ➤➤ **pulsatile** /'pulsətiel/ *adj,* **pulsation** /-sh(ə)n/ *noun,* **pulsative** /'pulsətiv/ *adj,* **pulsatory** /'pulsət(ə)ri, pul'saytəri/ *adj.* [Latin *pulsatus,* past part. of *pulsare,* from *pulsus,* past part. of *pellere* to drive, push, beat]

pulsatilla /pulsə'tilə/ *noun* (*pl* **pulsatillas**) any of a genus of perennial plants closely related to the anemones, with hairy and fernlike foliage: genus *Pulsatilla.* [Latin genus name, from *pulsatus* (see PULSATE), referring to the flowers being beaten about by the wind]

pulsator *noun* a device that works with a throbbing movement.

pulse[1] /puls/ *noun* **1a** a regular throbbing caused in the arteries by the contractions of the heart, palpable through the skin of the wrist or the neck. **b** the number of times a pulse beats in a specific period of time, as an indication, e.g., of fever: *The old doctor felt my pulse … and then with a certain eagerness, asked me whether I would let him measure my head* — Joseph Conrad. **2a** underlying sentiment or opinion, or an indication of this: *Opinion polls take the pulse of the nation.* **b** a feeling of liveliness; vitality. **3a** rhythmical vibrating or sounding. **b** a single beat or throb. **4a** a short-lived variation of electrical current, voltage, etc whose value is normally constant. **b** an electromagnetic wave or sound wave of brief duration. ➤➤ **pulseless** *adj.* [Middle English *puls* via French from Latin *pulsus:* see PULSATE]

pulse[2] *verb intrans* to pulsate or throb. ➤ *verb trans* **1** to drive (something) by or as if by a pulsation. **2** to cause (something) to pulsate. **3** to produce or modulate (electromagnetic waves, etc) in the form of pulses. **4** to operate (a device) with a pulse of energy. ➤➤ **pulser** *noun.*

pulse[3] *noun* the edible seeds of any of various leguminous crops, e.g. peas, beans, or lentils, or any plant yielding these. [Middle English *puls* via Old French *pouls* from Latin *pult-, puls* porridge of meat or pulses]

pulse code modulation *noun* a system of sound transmission in which the amplitude of the sound signal is sampled at regular intervals, and converted to a digital form in which it can be transmitted.

pulse modulation *noun* = PULSE CODE MODULATION.

pulverize *or* **pulverise** /'pulvəriez/ *verb trans* **1** to reduce (something) to very small particles, e.g. by crushing or grinding. **2** *informal* to annihilate or defeat (somebody) utterly. ➤ *verb intrans* to become pulverized. ➤➤ **pulverizable** *adj,* **pulverization** /-'zaysh(ə)n/ *noun,* **pulverizer** *noun.* [early French *pulveriser* from late Latin *pulverizare,* from Latin *pulver-, pulvis* dust, powder]

pulverulent /pul'ver(y)oolənt/ *adj formal* **1** consisting of or reducible to fine powder. **2** being or looking dusty. [Latin *pulverulentus* dusty, from *pulver-, pulvis* dust, powder]

puma /'pyoohmə/ *noun* (*pl* **pumas** *or collectively* **puma**) a powerful tawny big cat formerly widespread in the Americas but now extinct in many areas; = COUGAR, MOUNTAIN LION: *Felis concolor.* [Spanish *puma,* from Quechua]

pumice[1] /'pumis/ *noun* a light porous volcanic rock used *esp* as an abrasive and for polishing. ➤➤ **pumiceous** /pyoo'mishəs/ *adj.* [Middle English *pomis* via French from Latin *pumic-, pumex*]

pumice[2] *verb trans* to smooth or polish (something) with pumice.

pummel /'puml/ *verb trans* (**pummelled, pummelling,** *NAmer* **pummeled, pummeling**) to pound or strike (somebody or something) repeatedly, *esp* with the fists. [alteration of POMMEL[2]]

pump[1] /pump/ *noun* **1a** a device that raises, transfers, or compresses fluids or that reduces the density of gases, *esp* by suction or pressure or both. **b** a mechanism for transporting atoms, ions, or molecules across cell membranes. **2** the heart. **3** an act or the process of pumping. [Middle English *pumpe, pompe,* from early Low German *pumpe* or early Dutch *pompe,* prob from Spanish *bomba,* of imitative origin]

pump[2] *verb trans* **1a** to move (air, water, etc) with a pump. **b** to raise (water, etc) with a pump. **c** (*often* + out) to draw a gas or liquid out of (a container, etc) with a pump. **2a** (*usu* + up) to inflate (a tyre, etc) by means of a pump or bellows. **b** to supply (an organ, etc) with air by means of a pump or bellows. **3a** to give or inject (something) in large quantities or with force or enthusiasm: *Their solution was to pump money into the economy; She tried desperately to pump new life into the class.* **b** to fire (bullets) repeatedly into somebody or something. **c** *informal* to question (somebody) persistently and exhaustively: *They pumped her for information but she was giving* *nothing away.* **4** to move (something) rapidly up and down, as if working a pump handle: *She pumped his hand warmly.* **5** to transport (ions, etc) across a cell membrane by the expenditure of energy. ➤ *verb intrans* **1** to work a pump; to raise or move a liquid or gas with a pump. **2** to move in a manner that resembles the action of a pump handle. **3** to spurt out intermittently. * **pump iron** *informal* to exercise using weights.

pump³ *noun* **1** a flat shoe without fastenings that grips the foot chiefly at the toe and heel. **2** *chiefly N Eng* a plimsoll. [origin unknown]

pumpernickel /'pumpənikl/ *noun* a dark, coarse, slightly sour-tasting bread made from wholemeal rye. [German *Pumpernickel*, literally 'bumpkin', of unknown origin]

pumpkin /'pum(p)kin/ *noun* **1** a usu hairy prickly plant of the gourd family cultivated for its large usu round fruit with a deep yellow to orange rind and edible flesh: *Cucurbita pepo.* **2** a fruit of this plant, used as a vegetable. [alteration of *pumpion*, modification of French *popon, pompon* melon, pumpkin, ultimately from Greek *pepōn* ripened]

pump priming *noun* government investment expenditure designed to induce a self-sustaining expansion of economic activity.

pump room *noun* a room at a spa in which the water is distributed and drunk.

pun¹ /pun/ *noun* a humorous use of a word with more than one meaning or of words with the same or a similar sound but different meanings: *A good pun may be admitted among the smaller excellencies of lively conversation* — James Boswell. [prob short for obsolete *punnet, pundigrion*, perhaps alteration of Italian *puntiglio*: see PUNCTILIO]

pun² *verb intrans* (**punned, punning**) to make puns.

pun³ *verb trans* (**punned, punning**) to consolidate (earth, concrete, or hardcore) by repeated ramming or pounding. [Middle English *pounen* POUND²]

puna /'poohnə/ *noun* **1** a windswept tableland in the higher Andes. **2** = ALTITUDE SICKNESS. [American Spanish *puna*, from Quechua]

Punch /punch/ *noun* (*often* **Mr Punch**) a hook-nosed, hump backed, deceitful, and brutal man, the chief male character in a PUNCH-AND-JUDY SHOW. [based on the traditional clown character PUNCHINELLO]

punch¹ *verb trans* **1a** to hit (somebody or something), *esp* with a hard and quick thrust of the fist. **b** to create (something) with a punch or punches: *He accidentally punched a hole in the partition.* **c** to drive or push (something) forcibly by or as if by a punch. **d** to hit or push (something, e.g. a button or key), e.g. with one's finger: *I spend all day just punching the keys of a word processor.* **2** *NAmer.* **a** to poke or hit (somebody or something) with a stick. **b** to drive or herd (cattle). **3** to hit (a ball) with less than a full swing of a bat or racket. ➤ *verb intrans* to punch somebody or something. ➤➤ **puncher** *noun.* [Middle English *punchen* to prod, prick, from early French *poinçonner* to prick, stamp, from *poinçon* (see PUNCHEON²) in the sense 'pointed tool']

punch² *noun* **1** a blow with or as if with the fist. **2** *informal* effective energy or forcefulness: *You need an opening paragraph that packs a lot of punch.*

punch³ *noun* **1** a tool, usu in the form of a short steel rod, used *esp* for perforating, embossing, cutting, or driving the heads of nails below a surface, or a machine incorporating such a tool. **2** a device for cutting holes or notches in paper or cardboard. [prob short for PUNCHEON² in the sense 'pointed tool']

punch⁴ *verb trans* **1** to emboss, cut, perforate, or make (a hole or pattern) with a punch, or as if with a punch. **2** to make a hole in or pattern on (something) with a punch, or as if with a punch.

punch⁵ *noun* a drink made from wine or spirits mixed with fruit, spices, water, and occasionally tea: compare CUP¹. [perhaps from Hindi *pāc* five, from the traditional number of ingredients]

Punch-and-Judy show /,punch ən 'joohdi/ *noun* a traditional puppet show in which the hook-nosed hunchback Punch fights with and kills his wife Judy. Other traditional characters in the show include Toby the Dog, the Baby, the Beadle, the Doctor, the Hangman, and the Devil.

punchbag *noun* **1** an inflated or stuffed bag punched with the fists as a form of exercise or training, *esp* in boxing. **2** a person who serves as a stooge or butt for somebody else.

punchball *noun* **1** an inflated or stuffed ball on a flexible support that is punched with the fists as a form of exercise or training, *esp* in boxing. **2** a form of baseball adapted for play in small areas, characterized by the use of a rubber ball that is hit with a closed fist instead of a bat.

punch bowl *noun* **1** a large bowl in which a beverage, *esp* punch, is mixed and served. **2** *chiefly Brit* a bowl-shaped hollow among hills.

punch card *noun* = PUNCHED CARD.

punch-drunk *adj* **1** suffering brain damage as a result of repeated punches or blows to the head. **2** behaving as if punch-drunk; dazed.

punched card *noun* a card formerly used in data processing in which a pattern of holes or notches was cut to represent information or instructions.

punched tape *noun* a strip of paper having rows of holes punched across it which represent information or instructions used in computers and other machines.

puncheon¹ /'punch(ə)n/ *noun* a large cask of varying capacity, usu between 70 and 120 gall (318 and 545.5l). [Middle English *poncion*, from early French *ponchon, poinçon*, of unknown origin]

puncheon² *noun* **1a** a short upright timber for a frame, *esp* to carry a load, e.g. a roof. **b** a split log or heavy slab with the face smoothed. **2** a PUNCH³ (tool for embossing, perforating, etc), *esp* a die used by goldsmiths, cutlers, and engravers. [Middle English *ponson* pointed tool or weapon, king post, from early French *poinçon*, ultimately from Latin *punctus*, past part. of *pungere* to prick]

Punchinello /punchi'neloh/ *noun* (*pl* **Punchinellos** or **Punchinelloes**) **1** a short fat humpbacked clown or buffoon in traditional Italian puppet shows. **2** (*also* **punchinello**) *archaic* a short, fat, comical, or odd-looking person. [modification of Italian dialect *Polecenella*, perhaps from *pollecana* young turkey cock, from the resemblance between a turkey's beak and the clown character's hooked nose]

punch line *noun* a sentence or phrase that forms the climax to a joke, story, etc.

punch-up *noun* *chiefly Brit, informal* a fight, *esp* with the bare fists.

punchy *adj* (**punchier, punchiest**) **1** having punch; forceful. **2** *informal* = PUNCH-DRUNK. ➤➤ **punchily** *adv*, **punchiness** *noun.*

punctate /'pungktayt/ *adj* marked with minute spots or depressions: *a punctate leaf.* ➤➤ **punctation** /pungk'taysh(ə)n/ *noun.* [Latin *punctatus*, from *punctum*: see PUNCTILIO]

punctilio /pungk'tilioh/ *noun* (*pl* **punctilios**) **1** a minute and often petty detail of ceremony or observance. **2** careful observance of forms, e.g. in social conduct. [Italian *puntiglio* point of honour, scruple, quibble, from Spanish *puntillo*, dimin. of *punto* point, from Latin *punctum*, neuter past part. of *pungere* to prick]

punctilious /pungk'tili·əs/ *adj* **1** strict or precise in observing codes of conduct or conventions. **2** paying or showing careful attention to detail. ➤➤ **punctiliously** *adv*, **punctiliousness** *noun.* [French *pointilleux*, from *pointille*, dimin. of *pointe* point, from Latin *punctum*: see PUNCTILIO]

punctual /'pungktchooəl, 'pungktyooəl/ *adj* **1a** arriving, happening, performing, etc at the exact or agreed time. **b** having the habit of arriving, etc at agreed times. **2** in mathematics, relating to or having the nature of a point. ➤➤ **punctuality** /-'aliti/ *noun*, **punctually** *adv.* [medieval Latin *punctualis* from Latin *punctus* pricking, point, past part. of *pungere* to prick]

punctuate /'pungktchooayt, 'pungktyooayt/ *verb trans* **1** to mark or divide (a text) with punctuation marks. **2** to break into or interrupt (something) at intervals: *Our conversation was punctuated with coughs and sneezes.* ➤ *verb intrans* to use punctuation marks. ➤➤ **punctuator** *noun.* [medieval Latin *punctuatus*, past part. of *punctuare* to point, provide with punctuation marks, from Latin *punctus*: see PUNCTUAL]

punctuation /pungktchoo'aysh(ə)n, pungktyoo-/ *noun* **1** the dividing of writing with marks such as commas, colons, and full stops, in order to clarify meaning. **2** a system of punctuation, or the symbols used.

punctuation mark *noun* a standardized mark or sign such as a comma, colon, or full stop, used in punctuation.

puncture¹ /'pungkchə/ *noun* a hole or narrow wound made by piercing by or with a pointed object, *esp* a small hole made accidentally in a pneumatic tyre. [Latin *punctura*, from *punctus*: see PUNCTUAL]

puncture² *verb trans* **1** to pierce (the skin, a tyre, etc) with a pointed object. **2** to cause a puncture in (a tyre, etc). **3** to destroy (somebody's confidence, overconfidence, etc): *It is our business to puncture gasbags* — Virginia Woolf. ➤ *verb intrans* to become punctured.

pundit /'pundit/ *noun* **1** a person who gives opinions in an authoritative manner; an authority, or a person who believes that they are an authority. **2** a learned man or teacher; *specif* a PANDIT (a learned man in India). ➤➤ **punditry** /-tri/ *noun*. [Hindi *paṇḍit* from Sanskrit *paṇḍita* learned]

punga /'punga/ *noun* (*pl* **pungas**) see PONGA.

pungent /'punj(ə)nt/ *adj* **1** having a strong sharp smell or taste; acrid. **2a** marked by a sharp incisive quality: *pungent wit*. **b** to the point; highly expressive: *pungent prose*. **3** said of a leaf: having a stiff and sharp point. ➤➤ **pungency** /-si/ *noun*. [Latin *pungent-, pungens*, present part. of *pungere* to prick, sting]

Punic¹ /'pyoohnik/ *adj* **1** of or relating to Carthage, the Carthaginians, or their language. **2** treacherous; unfaithful. [Latin *punicus*, from *Poenus* inhabitant of Carthage, modification of Greek *Phoinix* Phoenician]

Punic² *noun* the Semitic language of ancient Carthage.

punish /'punish/ *verb trans* **1a** to impose a penalty on (an offender). **b** to impose a penalty for (an offence). **2** *informal* to treat (something) roughly or damagingly: *The way he drives fairly punishes his engine*. **3** *informal* to eat or drink (something) quickly, greedily, in large quantities, etc. ➤ *verb intrans* to inflict punishment. ➤➤ **punishable** *adj*, **punisher** *noun*. [Middle English *punisshen* via French from Latin *punire*, from *poena* penalty]

punishing *adj* very demanding or exhausting: *They were forced to walk at a punishing pace for hours on end*. ➤➤ **punishingly** *adv*.

punishment *noun* **1a** the act or an instance of punishing. **b** something done in order to punish; a judicial penalty: *No punishment has ever possessed enough power of deterrence to prevent the commission of crimes* — Hannah Arendt. **2** *informal* rough or damaging treatment: *The contenders both took plenty of punishment in the last round*.

punitive /'pyoohnətiv/ *adj* **1** inflicting or intended to inflict punishment: *a punitive expedition*. **2** punishing: *a punitive schedule*. [French *punitif* from medieval Latin *punitivus*, from Latin *punire*: see PUNISH]

punitive damages *pl noun* damages awarded in excess of normal compensation to the plaintiff in order to punish a defendant.

Punjabi /pun'jahbi, poon-/ *or* **Panjabi** /pun'jahbi/ *noun* **1** a native or inhabitant of the Punjab of NW India and NE Pakistan. **2** the Indic language spoken in the Punjab. ➤➤ **Punjabi** *adj*. [Hindi *pañjābī* of Punjab, from Persian *Pañjāb* Punjab, literally 'five waters', from the five rivers flowing through the area]

punk¹ /pungk/ *noun* **1a** a movement among young people originating in the late 1970s, characterized by a violent rejection of established society and expressed through punk rock and the wearing of aggressively outlandish clothes and hairstyles. **b** = PUNK ROCK. **c** a person following punk styles in music, dress, etc; a punk rocker.

Editorial note ━━━━━━━━━━━━━━━━
First coined as a collective term for white American groups playing rough, localised music in the 1960s, punk became a British youth movement in the late 1970s. It was originally a response to the perceived conventionality of mainstream rock, but subsequently became a lifestyle of anti-authoritarian attitudes to which the music was little more than a soundtrack — Richard Cook.

2 *chiefly NAmer, informal* a person who is considered worthless, degraded, or inferior, *esp* a petty criminal or thug. **3** *NAmer, informal* a young male homosexual partner of an older man. **4** *archaic* a prostitute. ➤➤ **punkish** *adj*, **punky** *adj*. [origin unknown]

punk² *adj* **1** *NAmer, informal* of very poor quality; inferior; worthless. **2** of punk or punk rock.

punk³ *noun* *chiefly NAmer* a dry spongy substance prepared from fungi and used to ignite fuses. [perhaps alteration of SPUNK]

punkah *or* **punka** /'pungkə/ *noun* a fan used *esp* formerly in India, consisting of a cloth-covered frame suspended from the ceiling and swung to and fro by means of a cord. [Hindi *pākhā*]

punk rock *noun* a style of rock music originating in the late 1970s, characterized by a driving tempo, crude or obscene lyrics, and an aggressive delivery. ➤➤ **punk rocker** *noun*.

punnet /'punit/ *noun Brit* a small basket of wood, plastic, etc, *esp* for soft fruit or vegetables. [perhaps a dimin. of dialect *pun* POUND¹]

punster /'punstə/ *noun* a person who is given to punning.

punt¹ /punt/ *noun* a long narrow flat-bottomed boat with square ends, usu propelled with a pole. [Old English from Latin *ponton-, ponto*: see PONTOON¹]

punt² *verb trans* **1** to propel (a punt) with a pole. **2** to transport (somebody or something) by punt. ➤ *verb intrans* to propel a punt; to go punting.

punt³ *verb intrans* **1** to play against the banker at a gambling game. **2** *Brit, informal* to bet or gamble. [French *ponter*, from *ponte* point in some games, play against the banker, from Spanish *punto*: see PUNCTILIO]

punt⁴ *verb trans and intrans* **1** in rugby, etc, to kick (a football) with the top or tip of the foot after the ball is dropped from the hands and before it hits the ground. **2** to give (a ball) a long high kick. [origin unknown]

punt⁵ *noun* the act or an instance of punting a football.

punt⁶ /poont/ *noun* the Irish pound, the former basic monetary unit of the Republic of Ireland (replaced by the euro in 2002). [Irish Gaelic *punt* pound]

punter /'puntə/ *noun* **1** *informal* a person who gambles, *esp* somebody who bets against a bookmaker. **2** *Brit, informal*. **a** a client, customer, or patron. **b** a prostitute's client. **3** *informal, esp dialect* a person. **4** *slang* a conman's victim or potential victim. **5** a player who punts a ball. **6** a person who uses a punt in boating.

puny /'pyoohni/ *adj* (**punier, puniest**) **1** slight or inferior in power, size, or importance; weak. **2** small in quantity. ➤➤ **puniness** *noun*. [early French *puisné* younger, literally 'born afterwards', from *puis* afterwards + *né* born]

pup¹ /pup/ *noun* **1** a young dog. **2** a young seal, rat, etc. **3** *chiefly Brit, dated* an arrogant or conceited young man. ✳ **in pup** going to produce pups; pregnant. **sell somebody a pup** *Brit, informal* to cheat somebody by selling them something worthless. [short for PUPPY]

pup² *verb intrans* (**pupped, pupping**) to give birth to a pup or pups.

pupa /'pyoohpə/ *noun* (*pl* **pupae** /'pyoohpee/ *or* **pupas**) the intermediate, usu inactive, form of an insect that undergoes metamorphism, e.g. a bee, moth, or beetle, that occurs between the LARVA, e.g. caterpillar, and the IMAGO (adult) stages. ➤➤ **pupal** *adj*. [Latin *pupa* girl, doll]

pupate /pyooh'payt/ *verb intrans* said of an insect: to become a pupa. ➤➤ **pupation** /-sh(ə)n/ *noun*.

pupil¹ /'pyoohpl/ *noun* **1** a child or young person at school or receiving tuition. **2** a person who has been taught or influenced by a distinguished person. **3** a person who is training to become a barrister. **4** in Roman and Scots law, a boy up to the age of 14 or a girl up to the age of 12 who is in the care of a guardian. [Middle English *pupille* minor, ward, via French from Latin *pupillus* male ward (from dimin. of *pupus* boy) and *pupilla* female ward, from dimin. of *pupa* girl, doll, puppet]

pupil² *noun* the round dark opening in the iris of the eye that varies in size to regulate the amount of light that passes to the retina. ➤➤ **pupilary** *adj*, **pupillary** *adj*. [early French *pupille* from Latin *pupilla*, dimin. of *pupa* girl, doll; from the tiny image of oneself seen reflected in another's eye]

pupillage /'pyoohpilij/ *or* **pupilage** *noun* **1** the state or period of being a pupil. **2** apprenticeship to a barrister.

pupil teacher *noun* formerly, a young person who taught in an elementary school while concurrently receiving education.

pupiparous /pyooh'pip(ə)rəs/ *adj* said of certain insects: producing mature larvae that are ready to pupate at birth. [PUPA + -PAROUS]

puppet /'pupit/ *noun* **1** a small-scale toy figure, e.g. of a person or animal, that is moved by strings, wires, or rods attached to the head, body, and limbs, or by movements of the hand and fingers inside the body. **2a** a person whose acts are controlled by an outside force or influence. **b** (*used before a noun*) controlled by an outside force or influence, *esp* another country: *a puppet government*. ➤➤ **puppeteer** /-'tiə/ *noun*, **puppetry** /-tri/ *noun*. [Middle

English *popet* from early French *poupette*, ultimately from Latin *pupa* girl, doll, puppet]

puppy /'pupi/ *noun* (*pl* **puppies**) **1** a young dog, *esp* one that is less than a year old. **2** *informal, dated* a conceited or ill-mannered young man. ⧫ **puppyhood** *noun*, **puppyish** *adj*. [Middle English *popi*, prob via early French *poupée* doll, toy, from Latin *pupa* girl, doll, puppet]

puppy fat *noun* temporary plumpness in children and adolescents.

puppy love *noun* short-lived romantic affection between adolescents.

Purana /poo'rahnə/ *noun* any of a class of Hindu sacred writings that date chiefly from AD 500 and are made up of traditional lore, including popular myths and legends. ⧫ **Puranic** /-'ranik/ *adj*. [Sanskrit *purāṇa* from *purāṇa* ancient, from *purā* formerly]

Purbeck marble /'puhbek/ *noun* = PURBECK STONE.

Purbeck stone *noun* a hard limestone used *esp* for building. [named after the Isle of *Purbeck*, district in Dorset, England, where it is found]

purblind /'puhbliend/ *adj* **1** partly blind. **2** lacking in vision or insight; obtuse. ⧫ **purblindly** *adv*, **purblindness** *noun*. [Middle English *pur blind* wholly blind, from *pur* purely, wholly, from *pur* (see PURE) + BLIND[1]]

purchase[1] /'puhchəs/ *verb trans* **1a** to obtain (something) by paying money or its equivalent; to buy (it). **b** to constitute the means for buying (something): *A pound seems to purchase less each year*. **c** to obtain (something) by labour, danger, or sacrifice: *I have purchased knowledge at the expense of all the common comforts of life* — Dr Johnson. **d** in law, to acquire (real estate) by means other than inheritance. **2** to move or raise (something) by a device such as a lever or pulley. ⧫ **purchasable** *adj*, **purchaser** *noun*. [Middle English *purchacen* from Old French *purchacier* to seek to obtain, from *por-, pur-* PRO-[2] + *chacier* to pursue, chase]

purchase[2] *noun* **1a** something obtained by payment of money or its equivalent. **b** the act or an instance of purchasing something. **2a** a mechanical hold or advantage, *esp* one applied through a pulley or lever. **b** an advantage used in applying power or influence. **c** a means, *esp* a mechanical device, by which one gains such an advantage. **3** a firm grip or contact, e.g. in climbing.

purchase tax *noun* formerly in Britain, a tax levied on the domestic sale of goods and usu calculated as a percentage of the purchase price.

purdah /'puhdə/ *noun* **1** the seclusion of women from public view among some Muslims and some Hindus, *esp* in India. **2** a screen used for this purpose. [Hindi and Urdu *parda* screen, veil]

pure /pyooə/ *adj* **1a** unmixed with any other matter: *pure gold*. **b** free from anything that vitiates or weakens: *He called for a return to the pure religion of our fathers*. **c** containing nothing that does not properly belong: *This is the pure text of the book, without the later additions*. **2** free from contamination: *All our oils are carefully refined and absolutely pure*. **3a** free from moral fault. **b** chaste. **c** ritually clean. **4** sheer or unmitigated: *It was pure folly to go out dressed like that*. **5** abstract or theoretical, as opposed to applied or practical: *pure mathematics*. **6a** said of an animal or plant: of unmixed ancestry. **b** said of an animal or plant: producing offspring of the same type; breeding true. **7a** said of a musical sound: being in tune and free from harshness. **b** said of a vowel: consisting of a single sound; not a diphthong. ⧫ **pureness** *noun*. [Middle English *pur* via French from Latin *purus*]

pureblood[1] *or* **pure-blooded** *adj* = PUREBRED[1].

pureblood[2] *noun* = PUREBRED[2].

purebred[1] *adj* said of an animal or plant: bred over many generations from members of a recognized breed, strain, or kind without mixture of other blood.

purebred[2] *noun* a purebred animal or, sometimes, plant.

puree[1] *or* **purée** /'pyooəray/ *noun* a thick pulp, e.g. of fruit or vegetables, produced by blending in a liquidizer or rubbing through a sieve. [early French *purée*, fem past part. of *purer* to purify, strain, from Latin *purare*, from *purus* PURE]

puree[2] *or* **purée** *verb trans* (**purees** *or* **purées**, **pureed** *or* **puréed**, **pureeing** *or* **puréeing**) to reduce (fruit, vegetables, etc) to a puree.

purely *adv* **1** without addition, *esp* of anything harmful. **2** simply; merely: *I read purely for relaxation*. **3** wholly or completely: *This was a selection based purely on merit*. **4** in a chaste or innocent manner.

purfle[1] /'puhfl/ *verb trans* to ornament the border or edges of (clothing or furniture) with a decorative ruffled band or (a violin, etc) with an inlaid decoration. [Middle English *purfilen* from early French *porfiler*, from PRO-[2] + late Latin *filare* to spin]

purfle[2] *noun* a decorative ruffled band or inlay.

purfling /'puhfling/ *noun* = PURFLE[2].

purgation /puh'gaysh(ə)n/ *noun* the act or result of purging.

purgative[1] /'puhgətiv/ *adj* causing evacuation of the bowels.

purgative[2] *noun* a purgative substance or medicine.

purgatory /'puhgət(ə)ri/ *noun* (*pl* **purgatories**) **1** a place or state of punishment in which, according to Roman Catholic doctrine, the souls of those who die in God's grace may make amends for past sins and so become fit for heaven. **2** *informal* a place or state of temporary suffering or misery: *The return trip was absolute purgatory*. ⧫ **purgatorial** /-'tawri-əl/ *adj*. [Middle English via French from medieval Latin *purgatorium*, from late Latin *purgatorius* purging, from Latin *purgare*: see PURGE[1]]

purge[1] /puhj/ *verb trans* **1** to rid (something) of impurities. **2a** to rid (a nation, party, etc) of unwanted or undesirable members, often summarily or by force. **b** to get rid of (undesirable people) by means of a purge. **3a** to clear (somebody) of guilt or of a charge. **b** to free (somebody) from moral impurity. **c** in law, to relieve oneself of (a legal offence, e.g. contempt of court, or the sentence for it) by some appropriate action. **4a** to cause evacuation of faeces from (the bowels). **b** to cause evacuation of faeces from the bowels of (somebody). ⧫ *verb intrans* to be purged or purified. [Middle English *purgen* via Old French from Latin *purgare* to purify, purge, from *purus* PURE + *agere* to drive, do]

purge[2] *noun* **1** the act or an instance of purging, *esp* of purging people from a group. **2** a purgative.

puri /'pooəri/ *noun* (*pl* **puris**) a deep-fried wheaten cake eaten *esp* with Indian curries. [Hindi *pūrī* from Sanskrit *pūrikā*]

purify /'pyooərifie/ *verb* (**purifies**, **purified**, **purifying**) ⧫ *verb trans* **1** to free (somebody) of guilt or moral impurity or imperfection. **2** to free (something) from undesirable elements. ⧫ *verb intrans* to grow or become pure or clean. ⧫ **purification** /-fi'kaysh(ə)n/ *noun*, **purificatory** /-fi'kayt(ə)ri/ *adj*, **purifier** *noun*. [Middle English *purifien* via French from Latin *purificare*, from Latin *purus* pure + *-ificare* -IFY]

Purim /'pooərim, pooh'reem/ *noun* a Jewish festival celebrated in February or March in commemoration of the deliverance of the Jews from the massacre plotted by Haman as recounted in the Old Testament book of Esther. [Hebrew *pūrīm* lots; from the casting of lots by Haman to decide on which day the massacre should take place (Esther 3:7 and 9:24–26)]

purine /'pyooəreen/ *or* **purin** /'pyooərin/ *noun* **1** a compound from which uric acid and related compounds are made in the body. **2** either of the bases, adenine or guanine, that are constituents of DNA and RNA and are derivatives of purine. [German *Purin*, from Latin *purus* pure + scientific Latin *uricum* uric acid]

purine base *noun* = PURINE (2).

purist /'pyooərist/ *noun* a person who keeps strictly and often excessively to established or traditional usage, *esp* in language. ⧫ **purism** *noun*, **puristic** /pyooə'ristik/ *adj*.

puritan /'pyooərit(ə)n/ *noun* **1** (**Puritan**) a member of a 16th- and 17th-cent., mainly Calvinist, Protestant group in England and New England which wished to purify the Church of England of all very ceremonial worship. **2** a person who practises or preaches a rigorous or severe moral code. ⧫ **Puritan** *adj*, **puritan** *adj*. [late Latin *puritas*: see PURITY]

puritanical /pyooəri'tanikl/ *adj* **1** of or characterized by a rigid morality; strict. **2** (*also* **Puritanical**) puritan or Puritan. ⧫ **puritanically** *adv*.

puritanism *noun* **1** (**Puritanism**) the beliefs and practices of the Puritans. **2** strictness and austerity, *esp* in matters of religion or conduct: *Puritanism — the haunting fear that someone, somewhere, may be happy* — H L Mencken.

purity *noun* **1** pureness. **2** the freedom, or relative freedom, of a colour from mixture with white. [Middle English *purete* via Old French from late Latin *puritat-, puritas*, from Latin *purus* PURE]

purl[1] /puhl/ *noun* **1** a basic knitting stitch made by inserting the needle into the back of a stitch that produces a raised pattern on the back of the work: compare KNIT[2]. **2** a thread of twisted gold or silver wire used for embroidering or edging. **3** *Brit* an ornamental edging of small loops or picots on lace, ribbon, or braid. [origin unknown]

purl[2] *verb trans* **1** to knit (a stitch) in purl. **2a** to decorate, edge, or border (a garment) with gold or silver thread. **b** to edge (lace, etc) with loops. ➤ *verb intrans* to do knitting in purl stitch.

purl[3] *noun* a gentle murmur or swirling movement of water in a brook, river, etc. [perhaps of Scandinavian origin]

purl[4] *verb intrans* said of a stream, brook, etc: to flow in eddies with a soft murmuring sound.

purler *noun Brit, informal* a heavy headlong fall. [PURL[4] in the sense 'to whirl, capsize']

purlieu /'puhlyooh/ *noun* (*pl* **purlieus**) **1** (*in pl*) environs or neighbourhood; **2** (*in pl*) confines or bounds. **3** a place frequently visited; a haunt. **4** land once part of, but later separated from, an English royal forest. [Middle English *purlewe* land on the border of an English royal forest, *esp* land formerly part of the forest, alteration of early French *puralé* inspection of a boundary by walking round it, from Old French *puraler* to go through, from *pur-* PRO-[2] + *aler* to go]

purlin *or* **purline** /'puhlin/ *noun* a horizontal beam in a roof bracing the rafters. [origin unknown]

purloin /pə'loyn/ *verb trans formal* to take (something) dishonestly; to steal (it). ➤➤ **purloiner** *noun*. [Middle English *purloinen* to put away, render ineffectual, from Old French *porloigner* to put off, delay, from *por-* PRO-[2] + *loing* at a distance, ultimately from Latin *longus* long]

purl stitch *noun* = PURL[1] (1).

purple[1] /'puhpl/ *noun* **1a** the colour between red and blue in hue. **b** a pigment or dye that colours purple. **c** cloth dyed purple. **d** a mollusc yielding a purple dye, *esp* the TYRIAN PURPLE of ancient times: genus *Purpura*. **2a** a purple robe worn as an emblem of rank or authority. **b** the red robes of a cardinal. **c** imperial, regal, or very high rank, e.g. in the Church: *He was born to the purple*. [Middle English *purpel, purper*, from Old English *purpure* via Latin *purpura* from Greek *porphyra* mollusc yielding purple dye, cloth dyed purple with this]

purple[2] *adj* **1** of the colour about midway between red and blue in hue. **2** said of writing: highly rhetorical; ornate: *purple prose*.

purple[3] *verb intrans* to become purple. ➤ *verb trans* to make (someone or something) purple.

purple heart *noun* **1** (**Purple Heart**) a US military decoration awarded to any member of the armed forces wounded in action. **2** *Brit, slang* a purplish blue heart-shaped tablet containing the drug phenobarbitone, formerly prescribed as a hypnotic or sedative and often abused by addicts. **3** (**purpleheart**). **a** a tropical tree native to north-east S America and Trinidad: *Peltogyne paniculata*. **b** the hard brown wood of this tree, which turns purple on exposure to the air.

purple passage *noun* = PURPLE PATCH (1).

purple patch *noun* **1** a piece of obtrusively ornate writing. **2** *informal* a period of good luck or success. [translation of Latin *pannus purpureus* purple patch; from the traditional splendour of purple cloth in contrast with more shabby materials]

purplish *adj* rather purple.

purport[1] /'puhpawt/ *noun formal* **1** professed or implied meaning; import. **2** purpose; intention. [Middle English from French *purport* content, tenor, from *purporter* to contain, from Old French *porporter* to convey, from *por-* PRO-[2] + *porter* to carry, from Latin *portare*]

purport[2] /pə'pawt/ *verb trans* **1** to claim (to be something); to seem, *esp* to be intended to seem (to be something): *The book purports to be an objective analysis but is nothing more than a string of prejudices.* **2** to mean or signify (something).

purpose[1] /'puhpəs/ *noun* **1** the object for which something exists or is done. **2** the reason or intention underlying some action. **3** resolution or determination: *Patience and tenacity of purpose are worth more than twice their weight of cleverness* — Thomas Huxley. **4** use, value, or advantage: *You mean we've done all this work to no purpose?* ✳ **on purpose** with intent; intentionally. **to the purpose** relevant. ➤➤ **purposeless** *adj*. [Middle English from Old French *purpos*, from *purposer* to purpose, from Latin *proponere*: see PROPOUND]

purpose[2] *verb trans formal* to have (something) as one's intention.

purpose-built *adj chiefly Brit* designed to meet a specific need: *a purpose-built conference centre.*

purposeful /'puhpəsf(ə)l/ *adj* **1** full of determination. **2** having a purpose or aim: *purposeful activities*. ➤➤ **purposefully** *adv*, **purposefulness** *noun*.

purposely *adv* with a deliberate or express purpose.

purposive /'puhpəsiv/ *adj formal* **1** serving or effecting a useful function though not necessarily as a result of deliberate intention. **2** having or tending to fulfil a conscious purpose; purposeful. ➤➤ **purposively** *adv*, **purposiveness** *noun*.

purpura /'puhpyoorə/ *noun* any of several conditions characterized by patches of purplish discoloration on the skin and mucous membranes and caused by abnormalities in the blood. ➤➤ **purpuric** /puh'pyooərik/ *adj*. [Latin *purpura*: see PURPLE[1]]

purpure /'puhpyooə/ *noun* used in heraldry: purple. [Old English *purpure*: see PURPLE[1]]

purr[1] /puh/ *verb intrans* **1** said of a cat: to make a low vibratory murmur. **2** to make a sound resembling a purr. [imitative]

purr[2] *noun* a purring sound.

purse[1] /puhs/ *noun* **1a** a small flattish bag for money, or a wallet with a compartment for holding change. **b** *NAmer* a handbag. **2a** resources; funds. **b** a sum of money offered as a prize or present, or the total amount of money offered in prizes for a given event. [Old English *purs*, modification of medieval Latin *bursa* bag, ultimately from Greek *byrsa* leather]

purse[2] *verb trans* to pucker or knit (the lips).

purser *noun* an officer on a ship who is responsible for documents and accounts and on a passenger ship for the comfort and welfare of passengers. [Middle English, from PURSE[1] + -ER[2]]

purse seine *noun* a large net designed to be set round a school of fish by two boats and so arranged that, after the ends have been brought together, the bottom can be closed. ➤➤ **purse seiner** *noun*.

purse strings *pl noun* control over expenditure: *He earns the money but she holds the purse strings.*

purslane /'puhslin/ *noun* **1** a fleshy-leaved trailing plant with tiny yellow flowers, sometimes eaten in salads: genus *Portulaca*. **2** any of numerous other plants of various genera. [Middle English from early French *porcelaine*, ultimately from Latin *porcillaca*, alteration of *portulaca*]

pursuance /pə's(y)ooh-əns/ *noun formal* a carrying out or into effect of a plan or order.

pursuant to /pə's(y)ooh-ənt/ *prep formal* in carrying out; in conformance to; according to. ➤➤ **pursuantly** *adv*.

pursue /pə's(y)ooh/ *verb* (**pursues**, **pursued**, **pursuing**) ➤ *verb trans* **1a** to follow (a fugitive, etc) in order to overtake, capture, kill, or defeat them. **b** to try persistently to form a relationship, *esp* a sexual relationship, with (somebody). **2** to find or employ measures to obtain or accomplish (a goal). **3a** to proceed along (a course): *The ship was pursuing a northerly course.* **b** to follow (a plan, etc). **4a** to engage in (some activity): *I only pursue gardening as a hobby.* **b** to follow up (an argument). **5** to continue to afflict (somebody); to haunt (them): *She was pursued by horrible memories.* ➤ *verb intrans* to go in pursuit. ➤➤ **pursuable** *adj*. [Middle English *pursuen* from Old French *poursuir*, from Latin *prosequi*, from PRO-[2] + *sequi* to follow]

pursuer *noun* **1** somebody or something that pursues or that is in pursuit. **2** in Scots law, a plaintiff or prosecutor.

pursuit /pə's(y)ooht/ *noun* **1a** the act or an instance of pursuing: *They set off in pursuit.* **b** (+ of) the deliberate quest for something: *the pursuit of wealth.* **2** an activity that one regularly engages in as a pastime or profession: *How difficult it was for women to avoid growing romantic, who have no active duties or pursuits* — Mary Wollstonecraft. **3** a bicycle race, usu over 3 to 5km (1.75 to 3mi), in which competitors, usu two at a time, start on opposite sides of a track and pursue each other round it. [Middle English from Old French *poursuite*, from *poursuir*: see PURSUE]

pursuivant /'puhs(w)iv(ə)nt/ *noun* **1** an OFFICER OF ARMS (official responsible for granting heraldic arms) ranking below a herald. **2** *archaic* a follower or attendant. **3** *formerly*, a royal messenger. [Middle English *pursevant* attendant of a herald, from early French *poursuivant* follower, from *poursuir, poursuivre*: see PURSUE]

purulent /'pyooərələnt/ *adj* **1** of or containing pus: *a purulent discharge.* **2** accompanied by suppuration. ➤➤ **purulence** *noun*. [Latin *purulentus*, from *pur-, pus* PUS]

purvey /pə'vay/ *verb trans* **1** to supply (provisions, etc), *esp* in the course of business. **2** to spread or pass on (information, *esp* gossip or scandal). [Middle English *purveien* via early French *porveeir* from Latin *providēre*: see PROVIDE]

purveyance *noun* **1** the act or an instance of purveying something, *esp* provisions. **2** formerly in Britain, the right of the sovereign when travelling through the country to requisition food, drink, and other supplies at less than their market price.

purveyor *noun* **1** a person who purveys something, *esp* provisions. **2** formerly in Britain, an official involved in PURVEYANCE for the sovereign.

purview /'puhvyooh/ *noun formal* **1** the range or limit of authority, responsibility, or concern. **2** the range of vision or understanding. **3** in law, the body or enacting part of a statute. [Middle English *purveu* from early French *purveu est* it is provided (the opening phrase of a statute)]

pus /pus/ *noun* thick opaque yellowish or greenish white fluid matter formed by suppuration, e.g. in an abscess. [Latin *pus*]

push¹ /poosh/ *verb trans* **1a** to apply a force to (somebody or something) in such a way as to make them move away from oneself or the source of the force. **b** to move (somebody or something) into or towards something in this way: *He pushed his glove back in his pocket.* **2** to make (one's way) by pushing. **3** to cause (something) to change in quantity or extent under pressure of some cause or force: *Scarcity of labour pushed up wages.* **4a** to press or urge (somebody) to do something: *They keep pushing us to go and see them.* **b** to urge (oneself, etc) to make great or greater efforts. **5a** to develop or promote (an idea or argument). **b** to make strong efforts to sell (a product, etc). **6** to force (somebody) towards or beyond the limits of capacity or endurance: *Poverty pushed them to breaking point.* **7** (*usu* **be pushing**) *informal* to approach in age or number: *The old man was already pushing 80.* **8** *slang* to engage in the illicit sale of (drugs). **9** to hit (a ball in e.g. cricket, golf, or baseball) towards the right from a right-handed swing or towards the left from a left-handed swing. ➤ *verb intrans* **1** to press against something with steady force in order to move it away or as if to do so. **2** to press forwards energetically against obstacles or opposition: *In the early 1900s explorers pushed out into the Antarctic.* **3** (+ for) to demand something strenuously: *MPs have been pushing for an official inquiry.* **4** to extend or stretch out to or into something: *There are fingers of dry land pushing into the swamp.* * **be pushed 1** to be too busy: *I'd love to stop and chat but I'm rather pushed this afternoon.* **2** to find it difficult: *They'd be pushed to finish the job by Friday.* **3** (+ for) to be almost unable to find enough (time, money, etc). **push one's luck** to take a further risk after being lucky in earlier risks. [Middle English *pusshen* from Old French *poulser* to beat, push, from Latin *pulsare*: see PULSATE]

push² *noun* **1a** the act or an instance of pushing. **b** a nonphysical pressure; an urge: *the push and pull of conflicting emotions.* **c** something, such as a button, that is pushed, e.g. to operate a device. **2a** a vigorous effort to attain an end; a drive. **b** a military assault or offensive. **c** an advance that overcomes obstacles. **3a** an exertion of influence to promote another's interests: *His father's push took him to the top.* **b** vigorous enterprise or energy: *She'll need a lot of push to get this business off the ground.* **c** stimulation to activity; an impetus. * **at a push** *chiefly Brit* if really necessary, although with some difficulty. **come to the push** *informal* to come to a time when some action is needed or carried out; to be necessary: *If it comes to the push, you can sleep here.* **get the push** *Brit, informal* to be dismissed, dropped, etc: *He got the push from his girlfriend last night.* **give somebody the push** *Brit, informal* to dismiss or drop (somebody): *His boss finally gave him the push.* **if/when push comes to shove** if or when a necessity arises, a difficulty must be faced, etc.

push ahead *verb trans* (*also* + with) to continue in a determined manner with an activity or undertaking.

push along *verb intrans Brit, informal* to leave; to go somewhere.

push around *verb trans* to bully (somebody).

push-bike *noun Brit, informal* a pedal cycle.

push button *noun* a small button or knob that when pushed operates or triggers something, *esp* by closing an electric circuit.

push-button *adj* **1** operated by means of a push button. **2** characterized by the use of long-range weapons rather than physical combat: *push-button warfare.*

pushcart *noun* a cart that is pushed or pulled by hand.

pushchair *noun Brit* a light folding chair on wheels in which very young children may be pushed.

pusher *noun informal* **1** a person who sells drugs illegally. **2** *informal* an aggressively ambitious or overassertive person. **3** a utensil used by a young child for pushing food onto a spoon or fork.

push in *verb intrans* to join a queue at a point in front of others already waiting, *esp* by pushing or jostling.

pushing¹ *adj* **1** aggressively ambitious. **2** aggressively or rudely self-assertive. ➤➤ **pushingly** *adv.*

pushing² *adv informal* said *esp* of ages: almost: *A man of pushing 60 shouldn't be doing that.*

push off *verb intrans Brit, informal* to go away, *esp* hastily or abruptly.

push on *verb intrans* (*also* + with) to continue on one's way, with an undertaking, etc in a determined manner.

pushover *noun informal* **1** an opponent who is easy to defeat or a victim who is incapable of effective resistance. **2** a person who is unable to resist a specified attraction: *He's a pushover for blondes.* **3** something accomplished without difficulty; a cinch.

push-pull *adj* of an arrangement of two thermionic valves (devices regulating electron flow; see THERMIONIC VALVE) or transistors in which an alternating input causes alternate valves or transistors to operate.

pushrod *noun* a rod put into action by a cam to open or close a valve in an internal-combustion engine.

push-start¹ *verb trans* to start (a motor vehicle) by pushing it along while it is in gear in order to turn the engine.

push-start² *noun* the act or an instance of push-starting a motor vehicle.

push through *verb trans* to force or persuade an executive or legislative body to accept (a proposal) or pass (legislation) in spite of opposition to it.

Pushtu /'pushtooh/ *noun and adj dated* = PASHTO.

push-up *noun chiefly NAmer* = PRESS-UP.

pushy *adj* (**pushier, pushiest**) self-assertive, often to an objectionable degree; forward. ➤➤ **pushily** *adv,* **pushiness** *noun.*

pusillanimous /pyoohsi'laniməs/ *adj* lacking courage and resolution; contemptibly timid. ➤➤ **pusillanimity** /-'nimiti/ *noun,* **pusillanimously** *adv.* [late Latin *pusillanimis*, from Latin *pusillus* very small + *animus* spirit]

puss /poos/ *noun informal* **1** used chiefly in addressing or calling to a cat: a cat. **2** a girl. [prob from early Low German *pūs*]

pussy¹ *noun* (*pl* **pussies**) **1** *informal* used chiefly by or to young children: a cat. **2** a catkin of the pussy willow. [orig a term of endearment for a girl or woman; from PUSS + -Y⁴]

pussy² *noun* (*pl* **pussies**) *coarse slang* **1** the vulva. **2** sexual intercourse with a woman. **3** women or a woman regarded sexually.

pussy³ /'pusi/ *adj* (**pussier, pussiest**) full of or resembling pus.

pussycat /'poosikat/ *noun* = PUSSY¹.

pussyfoot /'poosifoot/ *verb intrans* **1** to tread or move warily or stealthily. **2** to avoid committing oneself to a course of action. ➤➤ **pussyfooter** *noun.*

pussy willow /'poosi/ *noun* any of various willows having grey silky catkins.

pustulant¹ /'pustyoolənt/ *adj* inducing the formation of pustules.

pustulant² *noun* something, e.g. a chemical compound, that induces the formation of pustules.

pustular /'pustyoolə/ *adj* of, resembling, or covered with pustules.

pustulate¹ /'pustyoolayt/ *verb intrans* to form pustules. ➤ *verb trans* to cause (something) to form pustules.

pustulate² /'pustyoolət, -layt/ *adj* covered with pustules.

pustulated /'pustyoolaytid/ *adj* = PUSTULATE².

pustulation /pustyoo'laysh(ə)n/ *noun* **1** the act or an instance of producing pustules. **2** a pustule.

pustule /'pustyoohl/ *noun* **1** a small raised spot on the skin having an inflamed base and containing pus. **2** a small raised area like a blister or pimple. [Middle English, from Latin *pustula*]

put¹ /poot/ *verb* (**putting,** *past tense and past part.* **put**) ➤ *verb trans* **1a** to place (somebody or something) in or move them into a specified position or relationship: *Put the book on the table; He was put in prison for his beliefs.* **b** to write or inscribe (something). **2a** to bring (somebody or something) into a specified condition: *Our country right or wrong ... when wrong, to be put right* — Carl Schurz. **b** (*often* + to/on) to cause (somebody or something) to endure or undergo something specified: *We should at least put his ideas to the test; The doctor put her on a diet.* **c** (*often* + to/on) to impose or establish (something): *This is the Government putting yet another tax on travel; I intend to put an end to the argument once and for all.* **3a** to express, say, or state (something) in a certain way: *I don't quite know how to put this.* **b** to state or present (a proposition, question, etc) for consideration: *I put it to you that you are wrong.* **c** (+ into) to translate (prose or poetry) into another language. **d** (+ to) to adapt or set (words) to music. **e** (+ into) to express (e.g. a thought or emotion) in an explicit form: *He was unable to put his feelings into words.* **4a** (+ to) to devote or apply (something) to some purpose: *She put her mind to the problem; The money will be put to good use.* **b** (+ to) to assign (somebody) to do something: *Put them to work on the farm.* **c** to imagine (*esp* oneself) as being something or somewhere: *Put yourself in my place. What would you do?* **5a** (*usu* + in) to place (something) somewhere or attach it to something: *He puts his faith in reason alone.* **b** (*usu* + into) to invest (money): *He put all his money into steel.* **6a** (+ at) to estimate (something) at a certain level· *I'd put her age at about 40.* **b** (+ on) to attach or attribute (something): *She puts a high value on his friendship.* **c** (*usu* + on) to impute (something) to somebody or something: *She put all the blame on her husband.* **7** (+ on) to bet or wager (a sum of money, etc). **8** to throw (e.g. a shot or weight) with an overhand pushing motion, *esp* as an athletic contest. **9** to send, thrust, etc (e.g. a weapon or missile) into or through somebody or something. **10** (+ to) to bring together (an animal) with one of the opposite sex for breeding. ➤ *verb intrans* said of a ship: to take a specified course: *We immediately put into port.* * **be put to it** to have difficulty in achieving something: *They had been put to it to keep up with the rest of the class.* **not put it past somebody** to think somebody capable of doing or likely to do something. **put forth 1** to assert or propose. **2** to make public; to issue. **3** to bring into action; to exert. **4** said of a plant: to produce by growth. **put it there** an invitation to somebody to shake hands. **put on the map** to cause (a place) to be widely known. **put to bed 1** to settle (a child) in bed for the night. **2** to make the final preparations for printing (e.g. a newspaper). **put to death** to execute (somebody) or have them killed. **put together** to create as a united whole; to construct. **put to shame 1** to make (somebody) ashamed. **2** to disgrace (something) by comparison with something else: *Their garden certainly puts ours to shame.* **put two and two together** to draw the proper conclusion from given premises. **put upon 1** to impose on or take advantage of (somebody). **2** to cause (somebody) hardship. **stay put** to remain in the same position, situation, or condition. ➤➤ **putter** *noun.* [Old English *potian, pytan* to thrust, push]

put² *noun* **1** a throw made with an overhand pushing motion; *specif* the act or an instance of putting the shot. **2** = PUT OPTION.

put about *verb trans* **1** to spread (gossip, a false story, etc). **2** *chiefly N Eng* (*usu in passive*) to upset or disconcert (somebody). **3** to cause (a ship) to change direction. ➤ *verb intrans* said of a ship: to change direction.

put across *verb trans* to convey (the meaning or significance of something) effectively. * **put it/one across somebody** *Brit, informal* to trick or deceive somebody.

put aside *verb trans* **1** to place (something) to one side. **2** to save (money) for a later time. **3** to ignore or discard (something).

putative /'pyoohtǝtiv/ *adj formal* **1** commonly accepted or supposed. **2** assumed to exist or to have existed. ➤➤ **putatively** *adv.* [Middle English from late Latin *putativus,* from Latin *putare* to think]

put away *verb trans* **1a** to place (something) somewhere for storage when not in use or so that it is out of sight. **b** to save (money) for future use. **2** *informal* to confine (somebody), *esp* in a prison or a psychiatric institution. **3** *informal* to eat or drink (something), *esp* in large quantities. **4** to discard or renounce (something).

put back *verb trans* **1** to return (something) to its former or proper place after using it. **2** (*usu* + together) to join the parts or pieces of (something) to make it whole again. **3** to postpone or delay (an event, etc). **4** to set (a clock or watch) to an earlier time. ➤ *verb intrans* said of a ship: to return to port.

put by *verb trans* to save (money) for future use.

put down *verb trans* **1** to suppress (an illegal or hostile activity). **2** to kill (a sick or injured animal) painlessly. **3a** to put (an idea, thought, etc) in writing. **b** to enter (somebody or something) in a

list, e.g. of subscribers: *Put me down for £5.* **c** to put (a motion) on an agenda for discussion. **4** to pay (a sum of money) as a deposit. **5a** (+ as) to place (somebody) in a specified category: *I put him down as an eccentric.* **b** (+ to) to attribute (something) to a specified cause: *Just put it down to inexperience.* **6** *informal.* **a** to disparage or belittle (somebody or something): *For the most of us, if we do not talk of ourselves, or ... of the individual circles of which we are the centres, we can talk of nothing. I cannot hold with those who wish to put down the insignificant chatter of the world* — Trollope. **b** to humiliate or snub (somebody). **7** to put (a young child) to bed for the night. **8a** to let (a passenger) out of a vehicle, etc. **b** to land (an aircraft). **9** to store or set aside (wine, etc) for future use. ➤ *verb intrans* said of an aircraft or pilot: to land.

put-down *noun informal* a humiliating remark; a snub.

put forth *verb trans formal or literary* **1a** to assert or propose (an idea). **b** to make (something) known publicly. **2** to bring (effort) into action. **3** said of a plant: to produce or send out (leaves) by growth. ➤ *verb intrans formal or literary* said of a ship: to leave port.

put forward *verb trans* **1a** to propose (an idea, proposal, etc). **b** to nominate (a candidate) for election. **2** to set (a clock or watch) to a later time.

put in *verb trans* **1a** to submit (a claim, request, offer, etc). **b** to say (something) as a contribution to a conversation. **c** to spend (time) at an occupation or job. **2** to appoint or elect (somebody). **3** in cricket, to require (the opposing side) to bat first after winning the toss oneself. ➤ *verb intrans* **1** said of a ship, etc: to call at or enter a port, harbour, etc. **2** (+ for) to make an application, request, or offer for something.

put off *verb trans* **1a** to disconcert or repel (somebody). **b** to dissuade or discourage (somebody), or make them lose interest. **2a** to delay or postpone (an event or activity). **b** to get rid of (somebody) or persuade them to wait, *esp* by means of excuses or evasions. **3** to cause (an electrical device) to stop operating, e.g. by means of a switch.

put on *verb trans* **1a** to dress oneself in (an item of clothing). **b** to make (something) part of one's appearance or behaviour. **c** to feign or assume (a manner or feeling). **2** to switch on (an electric light or device). **3** to create or come to have an increased amount of (weight, etc). **4** to stage or produce (a play or other production). **5** to bet (a sum of money). **6** (*also* + to) to bring (somebody) to speak on the telephone. **7** (+ to) to inform (somebody) about something: *Don't forget it was me who put you on to them.* **8** *chiefly NAmer, informal* to mislead (somebody) deliberately, *esp* for amusement.

put-on¹ *adj* pretended; assumed.

put-on² *noun chiefly NAmer, informal* **1** an instance of deliberately misleading somebody. **2** a parody or spoof.

Putonghua /poohtoong'hwah/ *noun* the form of Chinese that is the standard language of the People's Republic of China; = MANDARIN (I). [Chinese *putonghua,* literally 'common spoken language']

put option *noun* an option to sell a specified amount of a security, e.g. a stock, or commodity, e.g. wheat, at a fixed price, at or within a specified time: compare CALL OPTION.

put out *verb trans* **1** to extend (something) or put it forward. **2** to extinguish (a fire, etc). **3a** to publish or issue (a leaflet, information, etc). **b** to broadcast (a report, etc). **4** to produce (a specified amount of power). **5a** to disconcert or confuse (somebody). **b** (*usu in passive*) to annoy or irritate (somebody). **c** to inconvenience (somebody): *Don't put yourself out for us.* **6** to dislocate (a part of the body). **7** to make (somebody) unconscious. **8** in baseball, cricket, etc, to cause (a player) to be out. **9** (*often* + to) to give or offer (a job of work) to be done by somebody outside the premises. **10** (*often* + to) to lend (money) for interest. **11** to make (an effort). ➤ *verb intrans* **1** said of a ship: to set out from shore. **2** *chiefly NAmer, informal* (*often* + for) said of a woman or girl: to be willing to have sexual intercourse with somebody.

put over *verb trans* **1** to communicate (information, etc). **2** *NAmer* to delay or postpone (an activity). * **put one over on somebody** *informal* to trick or deceive somebody.

put-put¹ /'putput/ *noun* a repeated popping sound made by a small motor.

put-put² /'putput/ *verb* (**put-putted, put-putting**) ➤ *verb intrans* **1** said of e.g. a motor: to make a repeated popping sound. **2** to move while put-putting. ➤ *verb trans* to make (its way) somewhere while put-putting: *The lawnmower put-putted its way across the grass.*

putrefaction /pyoohtri'faksh(ə)n/ *noun* **1** the decomposition of organic matter, *esp* the breakdown of proteins by bacteria and fungi, typically in the absence of oxygen, with the formation of foul-smelling, incompletely oxidized products. **2** the state of being putrefied; corruption. ➤➤ **putrefacient** /-'faysh(ə)nt/ *adj*, **putrefactive** /-tiv/ *adj*. [Middle English *putrefaccion* from late Latin *putrefaction-, putrefactio*, from Latin *putrefacere*: see PUTREFY]

putrefy /'pyoohtrifie/ *verb* (**putrefies, putrefied, putrefying**) ➤ *verb intrans* to become rotten or putrid. ➤ *verb trans* to cause (something) to become rotten or putrid. [Middle English *putrefien* via French from Latin *putrefacere* to make or become rotten, from *putrēre* (see PUTRID) + *facere* to make]

putrescent /pyooh'tres(ə)nt/ *adj* of or undergoing putrefaction. ➤➤ **putrescence** *noun*. [Latin *putrescent-, putrescens*, present part. of *putrescere* to become rotten, from *putrēre*: see PUTRID]

putrid /'pyoohtrid/ *adj* **1** said of organic matter: in a state of decomposition; decaying; rotten: *putrid meat*. **2** foul-smelling or corrupt as a result of putrefaction. **3** *archaic* said of a fever or sore throat: usu denoting respectively typhus fever or diphtheria: *A sore-throat! – I hope not infectious, I hope not of a putrid infectious sort* — Jane Austen. **4** *dated, informal*. **a** execrable: *putrid verse*. **b** used as an intensifier: *Some putrid fool sliced a ball ... and got me slap-bang in the eye* — Dorothy L Sayers. ➤➤ **putridity** /pyooh'triditi/ *noun*, **putridly** *adv*, **putridness** *noun*. [Latin *putridus* from *putrēre* to be rotten, from *puter, putris* rotten]

putsch /pooch/ *noun* a secretly plotted and suddenly executed attempt to overthrow a government. [Swiss German *Putsch* push]

putt[1] /put/ *noun* a gentle golf stroke made to roll the ball towards or into the hole. [alteration of PUT[2]]

putt[2] *verb trans* to hit (a golf ball) towards or into the hole with a gentle stroke. ➤ *verb intrans* to hit (golf balls) towards or into holes on a golf course or a putting green. ➤➤ **putting** *noun*.

puttee /'putee, pu'tee/ *noun* **1** a long cloth strip wrapped spirally round the leg from ankle to knee, *esp* as part of an army uniform. **2** *NAmer* a usu leather legging secured by a strap or catch or by laces. [Hindi *paṭṭi* strip of cloth]

putter[1] /'putə/ *noun* **1** a golf club used for putting. **2** a person who putts; a person considered with regard to their putting ability: *I'm a lousy putter but great with a 7 iron*.

putter[2] *verb intrans* (**puttered, puttering**) *NAmer* = POTTER[2]. [by alteration]

putter[3] /'pootə/ *noun* see PUT[1].

putter[4] /'putə/ *noun* a rapidly repeated popping sound made by a small motor.

putter[5] /'putə/ *verb* (**puttered, puttering**) ➤ *verb intrans* said of a motor: to make a rapidly repeated popping sound. ➤ *verb trans* to move along (a course) while puttering.

put through *verb trans* **1a** to carry (a plan, project, etc) into effect or to a successful conclusion. **b** to process or deal with (an application, etc). **2a** to make a telephone connection for (somebody). **b** to obtain a connection for (a telephone call). **3** to cause (somebody) to suffer (pain, unhappiness, etc).

putti /'pootee/ *noun* pl of PUTTO.

putting green /'puting/ *noun* **1** a smooth grassy area at the end of a golf fairway containing the hole into which the ball must be played. **2** an area of smooth grass laid out with a number of holes for putting as a game.

putto /'pootoh/ *noun* (*pl* **putti** /'pootee/) *esp* in Renaissance painting, a figure of a naked little boy, often with wings; a cherub or cupid. [Italian *putto* boy, from Latin *putus*]

putty[1] /'puti/ *noun* (*pl* **putties**) **1a** a doughlike cement, usu made of WHITING[2] (ground chalk) and linseed oil, used *esp* for fastening glass into windows and filling crevices in woodwork. **b** any of a number of similar mixtures of powder and linseed oil, with various uses. **c** a pasty substance consisting of hydrated lime and water, used as a finishing coat on plaster. **2** a greyish yellow colour. **3** a person who is easily manipulated: *He's just putty in her hands*. ➤➤ **putty** *adj*. [French *potée*, literally 'potful', from Old French *pot* pot, of Germanic origin]

putty[2] *verb trans* (**putties, puttied, puttying**) to use putty on (something), apply putty to (something), or fix (something) with putty.

put up *verb trans* **1** to build or erect (something). **2** to increase the amount of (a price, etc). **3** to give food and shelter to (somebody);

to accommodate. **4** to offer (something) for public sale. **5** (*often* + for) to contribute or offer (a sum of money, etc). **6a** to make a display of (a feeling, etc). **b** to offer (resistance). **7** to propose or offer (an idea) for consideration. **8** to nominate (somebody) for election. **9** to offer up (a prayer, etc). **10** to flush (game) from cover. **11** *archaic* to sheathe (a sword). ➤ *verb intrans* **1** to shelter or stay for a short time at a place. **2** (+ for) to present oneself as a candidate for office in an election. ✳ **put somebody up to something** to urge or incite somebody to do something. **put up or shut up** *informal* do something about what you are talking about or else stop talking about it. **put up with** to tolerate (somebody or something) with resignation: *It is because we put up with bad things that hotel-keepers continue to give them to us* — Anthony Trollope.

put-up *adj informal* contrived secretly beforehand: *The vote was obviously a put-up job.*

putz /puts/ *noun NAmer, informal* a stupid, worthless, or unpleasant person. [Yiddish *potz* fool, penis]

puzzle[1] /'puzl/ *verb trans* **1** to offer or represent to (a person or their mind) a problem that is difficult to solve or a situation that is difficult to understand or resolve; to confuse or perplex (them): *a schoolmaster puzzled by a hard sum* — Ralph Waldo Emerson. **2** to exert (oneself or one's mind) over a problem or situation; to make (oneself) think hard: *They puzzled their brains to find a solution*. ➤ *verb intrans* (*usu* + about/over) to be uncertain as to action, choice, or meaning: *We puzzled for days about whether or not to go.* ➤➤ **puzzled** *adj*, **puzzlement** *noun*, **puzzling** *adj*, **puzzlingly** *adv*. [origin unknown]

puzzle[2] *noun* **1a** somebody or something that puzzles. **b** a problem, toy, device, etc designed for testing one's ingenuity. **2** the state of being puzzled; perplexity.

puzzle out *verb trans* to find (a solution or meaning) by means of mental effort.

puzzler *noun* **1** something puzzling. **2** a person who enjoys solving puzzles for recreation.

PVA *abbr* polyvinyl acetate, a colourless synthetic resin used in paints and adhesives.

PVC *abbr* polyvinyl chloride, a colourless plastic vinyl used *esp* as a rubber substitute, e.g. in raincoats and wire covering.

PVS *abbr* **1** persistent vegetative state. **2** postviral syndrome.

Pvt *abbr chiefly NAmer* Private.

PW *abbr* policewoman.

pw *abbr* per week.

PWA *abbr* person with Aids.

PWR *abbr* pressurized water reactor.

pwr *abbr* power.

PY *abbr* Paraguay (international vehicle registration).

py- *or* **pyo-** *comb. form* forming words, denoting: pus: *pyaemia; pyorrhoea*. [Greek, from *pyon* pus]

pya /pyah, pi'ah/ *noun* a unit of currency in Myanmar, worth 100th of a kyat. [Burmese *pya*]

pyaemia (*NAmer* **pyemia**) /pie'eemi-ə/ *noun* blood poisoning accompanied by multiple abscesses. ➤➤ **pyaemic** /-mik/ *adj*.

pye-dog *or* **pie-dog** *or* **pi-dog** /pie/ *noun* a half-wild dog common in and around Asian villages. [prob by shortening and alteration from PARIAH DOG]

pyelitis /pie-ə'lietəs/ *noun* inflammation of the lining of the pelvis of the kidney. ➤➤ **pyelitic** /-'litik/ *adj*. [scientific Latin, from Greek *pyelos* trough, pan, used for 'pelvis']

pyemia /pie'eemi-ə/ *noun NAmer* see PYAEMIA.

pygidium /pie'jidi-əm, pie'gidiəm/ *noun* (*pl* **pygidia** /-di-ə/) the end structure, e.g. a tail, or end part of the body of various invertebrates. ➤➤ **pygidial** *adj*. [scientific Latin from Greek *pygidion*, dimin. of *pygē* rump]

pygmy *or* **pigmy** /'pigmi/ *noun* (*pl* **pygmies** *or* **pigmies**) **1** (**Pygmy**) a member of a people of equatorial Africa under 1.5m (about 5ft) in height. **2a** *derog* a very short person; a dwarf. **b** something that is a small example of its kind. **c** (*used before a noun*) being a small variety of something: *a pygmy chimpanzee*. **3** a person who is insignificant or inferior in a specified sphere or manner: *Who would pay attention to a political pygmy like him?* ➤➤ **pygmaean** /pig'mee-ən/ *adj*, **pygmean** /pig'mee-ən/ *adj*, **pygmoid** /'pigmoyd/ *adj*. [Middle English *pigmei* from Latin *pygmaeus* of a pygmy, dwarfish, from Greek *pygmaios*, from *pygmē* fist, measure of length]

pyjamas (*NAmer* **pajamas**) /pə'jahməz/ *pl noun* **1** a suit of loose lightweight jacket or top and trousers for sleeping in. **2** loose lightweight trousers traditionally worn in the East. ➤➤ **pyjama** *adj*. [Hindi *pājāma*, from Persian *pāi* leg + *jāma* garment]

pyknic /'piknik/ *adj* in anthropology, characterized by short stature and stocky build. [Greek *pyknos* dense, stocky]

pylon /'pielən, 'pielon/ *noun* **1** a tower for supporting either end of a wire, *esp* electricity power cables, over a long span. **2** a rigid structure on the outside of an aircraft for supporting something. **3** a post, tower, etc marking a prescribed course of flight for an aircraft. **4** either of two towers with sloping sides flanking the entrance to an ancient Egyptian temple. [Greek *pylōn*, from *pylē* gate]

pylorus /pie'lawrəs/ *noun* (*pl* **pylori** /-rie, -ree/) the opening from the vertebrate stomach into the intestine. ➤➤ **pyloric** /pie'lorik/ *adj*. [via late Latin from Greek *pylōros* gatekeeper, from *pylē* gate]

pyo- *comb. form* see PY-.

pyogenic /pie-ə'jenik/ *adj* producing pus.

pyorrhoea (*NAmer* **pyorrhea**) /pie-ə'riə/ *noun* an inflammation of the sockets of the teeth with a discharge of pus, usu leading to loosening of the teeth.

pyr- *or* **pyro-** *comb. form* forming words, with the meanings: **1** fire; heat: *pyrometer; pyromania.* **2** produced by or as if by the action of heat: *pyroelectricity.* [Greek *pyr* fire]

pyracantha /pierə'kanthə/ *noun* a Eurasian thorny shrub of the rose family with white or cream-coloured flowers and red, orange, or yellow berries: genus *Pyracantha*. [Latin genus name, from Greek *pyrakantha* an unidentified plant, from PYR- + *akantha* thorn]

pyramid[1] /'pirəmid/ *noun* **1a** a massive structure typically having a square ground plan, smooth or stepped outside walls in the form of four triangles that meet in a point at the top, and inner burial chambers, *esp* any of a number of such structures found in Egypt and enclosing the burial chambers of the pharaohs. **b** any structure or object of a similar form. **2a** a nonphysical structure or system, such as a social or organizational hierarchy, conceived of as having the form of a triangle or pyramid with a broad supporting base and narrowing gradually to an apex: *the forgotten man at the bottom of the economic pyramid* — Franklin D Roosevelt. **b** a business organization that consists of a number of holding companies and that is so structured that the company at the top of the hierarchy controls the entire group while having only a relatively small proportion of the total capital of the group. **3** in geometry, a polyhedron having a base that is a polygon and other faces that are triangles with a common vertex. **4** an anatomical structure resembling a pyramid, e.g.: **a** any of the conical masses that project from the MEDULLA (central portion) of the kidney into the kidney pelvis. **b** either of two large bundles of nerve fibres from the CEREBRUM (outer portion of the forebrain) that reach the MEDULLA OBLONGATA (rear portion) and are continuous with the pyramidal tracts of the spinal cord. **5** a crystal form having nonparallel faces that meet at a point. **6** (*in pl*) a game similar to billiards, played with 15 red balls and a cue ball. ➤➤ **pyramidal** /pi'ramidl/ *adj*, **pyramidally** /pi'ramidəli/ *adv*, **pyramidic** /-'midik/ *adj*, **pyramidical** /-'midikl/ *adj*, **pyramidically** /-'midikli/ *adv*. [Middle English via Latin from Greek *pyramid-, pyramis*]

pyramid[2] *verb* (**pyramided, pyramiding**) ➤ *verb intrans chiefly NAmer* **1** to increase rapidly and progressively step by step from a broad base. **2** to form a pyramid shape. ➤ *verb trans chiefly NAmer* to arrange (something) or build (it) up like a pyramid.

pyramid selling *noun* a system whereby agents for the sale of a product buy stock which they then recruit further agents to sell. This continues with agents at each level recruiting further agents.

pyre /'pie·ə/ *noun* **1** a heap of combustible material for burning a dead body as part of a funeral rite. **2** a pile of material to be burned. [via Latin from Greek *pyra*, from *pyr* fire]

Pyrenean /pirə'nee·ən/ *noun* a native or inhabitant of the Pyrenees, mountain range in SW Europe. ➤➤ **Pyrenean** *adj*.

pyrethrin /pie'reethrin/ *noun* either of two oily liquid insecticides that occur *esp* in pyrethrum flowers. [PYRETHRUM + -IN[1]]

pyrethrum /pie'reethrəm/ *noun* **1** any of several species of flowers of the daisy family with finely divided aromatic leaves and bright flowers: genus *Tanacetum* (formerly *Chrysanthemum* or *Pyrethrum*). **2** an insecticide made from the dried heads of some of these chrysanthemums. [via Latin from Greek *pyrethron* pellitory, from *pyr* fire]

pyretic /pie'retik/ *adj* of or relating to fever. [Greek *pyretikos*, from *pyretos* fever, from *pyr* fire]

Pyrex /'piereks/ *noun trademark* glass or glassware that is resistant to heat, chemicals, and electricity. [invented word based on PIE[1]; Pyrex was first used to make baking dishes]

pyrexia /pie'reksi·ə/ *noun technical* abnormal elevation of body temperature; fever. ➤➤ **pyrexial** *adj*, **pyrexic** /-sik/ *adj*. [scientific Latin *pyrexia*, from Greek *pyressein* to be feverish, from *pyretos*: see PYRETIC]

pyridine /'pirideen/ *noun* a pungent liquid that is an organic chemical base, is obtained from coal, and is used as a solvent and in the manufacture of medicines and waterproofing substances. [PYR- + ID[2] + -INE[2]]

pyridoxine /pieri'dokseen, -sin/ *noun* a vitamin of the vitamin B complex, found *esp* in cereal foods and convertible in the body into phosphate compounds that are important coenzymes; vitamin B_6. [PYRIDINE + OX- + -INE[2]]

pyrimidine /pie'rimideen, pi-, -din/ *noun* **1** an organic chemical compound with a penetrating smell. **2** any of the bases, cytosine, thymine, or uracil, that are constituents of DNA and RNA. [alteration of PYRIDINE]

pyrimidine base *noun* = PYRIMIDINE (2).

pyrite /'pieriet/ *noun* = IRON PYRITES. [Latin *pyrites*: see PYRITES]

pyrites /pie'rieteez, pi-/ *noun* (*pl* **pyrites**) any of various metallic-looking sulphide minerals, *esp* IRON PYRITES. ➤➤ **pyritic** /pie'ritik, pi-/ *adj*, **pyritous** /-təs/ *adj*. [Latin *pyrites* flint, from Greek *pyritēs* of or in fire, from *pyr* fire]

pyro- *comb. form* see PYR-.

pyroclastic /pierə'klastik/ *adj* formed from rock fragments or ash resulting from volcanic action, *esp* occurring as a fast-moving hot dense cloud: *pyroclastic flow*.

pyroelectricity /,pieroh·ilek'trisiti, -elek'trisiti/ *noun* a state of electrical polarization produced, e.g. in crystals, by a change of temperature. ➤➤ **pyroelectric** /-i'lektrik/ *adj*.

pyrogallol /pieroh'galol/ *noun* a phenol with weak acid properties that is used *esp* in photographic developers and in dye manufacture. [*pyrogallic* acid (from PYRO- + *gallic*: see GALLIC ACID) + -OL[1]]

pyrogen /'pierohjen, 'pierəjən/ *noun* a fever-producing substance.

pyrogenic /pierə'jenik/ *adj* **1** producing or produced by heat or fever. **2** said of a rock: = IGNEOUS. ➤➤ **pyrogenicity** /-'nisiti/ *noun*, **pyrogenous** /pie'rojinəs/ *adj*.

pyrography /pie'rogrəfi/ *noun* = POKERWORK (burning decorative designs into wood). ➤➤ **pyrographer** *noun*, **pyrographic** /-'grafik/ *adj*.

pyrolyse (*NAmer* **pyrolyze**) /'pierəliez/ *verb trans* to subject (something) to pyrolysis.

pyrolysis /pie'roləsis/ *noun* chemical change brought about by the action of heat. ➤➤ **pyrolytic** /-'litik/ *adj*.

pyrolyze *verb trans NAmer* see PYROLYSE.

pyromania /pierə'mayni·ə/ *noun* a compulsive urge to start fires. ➤➤ **pyromaniac** /-ak/ *noun*, **pyromaniacal** /-mə'nie·əkl/ *adj*.

pyrometer /pie'romitə/ *noun* an instrument for measuring temperatures, *esp* those beyond the range of mercury thermometers. ➤➤ **pyrometric** /-'metrik/ *adj*, **pyrometrical** /-'metrikl/ *adj*, **pyrometrically** /-'metrikli/ *adv*, **pyrometry** /-tri/ *noun*.

pyrope /'pierohp/ *noun* a deep red magnesium-aluminium garnet commonly used as a gem. [Middle English *pirope*, a red gem, via French and Latin from Greek *pyrōpos*, literally 'fiery-eyed', from PYR- + *ōp-, ōps* eye]

pyrophoric /pierə'forik/ *adj* **1** igniting spontaneously on contact with air. **2** said of an alloy: emitting sparks when scratched or struck, *esp* with steel. [Greek *pyrophoros* fire-bearing, from PYRO- + *-phoros -phorous*; see -PHORE]

pyrosis /pie'rohsis/ *noun technical* = HEARTBURN. [Greek *pyrōsis* burning, from *pyroun* to burn, from *pyr* fire]

pyrotechnics /pierə'tekniks/ *pl noun* **1** fireworks. **2** the art of making fireworks. **3** a brilliant or spectacular display: *Danny Baker's Morning Edition on BBC Radio Five is a stunning eruption of top-notch … rock, pop and country music, all of which comes second to non-stop verbal pyrotechnics from Danny* — The Scotsman. ➤➤ **pyrotechnic** *adj*, **pyrotechnical** *adj*, **pyrotechnist** *noun*. [earliest as *pyrotechnic* (adj), from French *pyrotechnique*, from Greek *pyr* fire + *technē* art]

pyroxene /'pierokseen, pie'rokseen/ *noun* any of a group of silicate minerals that commonly contain calcium, magnesium, or iron and are chief constituents of many igneous rocks. ➤➤ **pyroxenoid** /pie'roksinoyd/ *adj and noun.* [French *pyroxène*, from PYRO- + Greek *xenos* stranger, because the pyroxenes were formerly thought to be alien to igneous rocks]

pyroxylin /pie'roksilin/ *noun* an inflammable mixture of cellulose nitrates that is used *esp* in making plastics and coatings. [PYRO- + Greek *xylon* wood]

pyrrhic /'pirik/ *noun* a metrical foot consisting of two short or unaccented syllables. ➤➤ **pyrrhic** *adj.* [Latin *pyrrhichius*, from Greek *pous pyrrhichios* pyrrhic foot, the metre of a song which accompanied a *pyrrhichē*, a kind of war dance, named after *Pyrrhikos*, who invented it]

Pyrrhic victory *noun* a victory won at such great cost as to be barely a victory. [named after *Pyrrhus* d.272 BC, king of Epirus, who sustained heavy losses in defeating the Romans at the battle of Asculum in 279 BC]

Pyrrhonism /'pirəniz(ə)m/ *noun* total or radical scepticism, *esp* the sceptical doctrines of Pyrrho of Elis, Greek philosopher d.c.272 BC, and his followers. ➤➤ **Pyrrhonist** *noun.*

pyrrole /'pirohl/ *noun* a toxic liquid chemical compound that is the parent compound of many biologically important substances.

pyrrolidine /pi'rolideen/ *noun* a colourless alkaline liquid that is obtained naturally from tobacco leaves or produced synthetically from pyrrole: formula C_4H_9N. [Greek *pyrrhos* red]

pyruvate /pie'roohvayt/ *noun* a salt or ester of pyruvic acid.

pyruvic acid /pie'roohvik/ *noun* a liquid organic acid that smells like acetic acid and is an important intermediate compound in metabolism and fermentation: formula $CH_3COCOOH$. [PYR- + Latin *uva* grape; from its importance in fermentation]

Pythagoras' theorem /pie'thagərəs(iz)/ *noun* a theorem in geometry, according to which the square of the length of the hypotenuse of a right-angled triangle equals the sum of the squares of the lengths of the other two sides. [named after *Pythagoras* d.c.500 BC, philosopher and mathematician]

Pythagorean[1] /pie,thagə'ree-ən/ *adj* of or associated with the philosophy of Pythagoras and his followers, asserting the mystical significance of numbers and the transmigration of souls.

Pythagorean[2] *noun* a follower of Pythagoras and his teachings.

Pythian /'pithi-ən/ *adj* of Delphi or its oracle. [via Latin from Greek *pythios* of *Pythō* Pytho, former name of Delphi, town in Greece, from *Pythōn*: see PYTHON]

python /'pieth(ə)n/ *noun* any of several species of non-venomous snake found in Africa, Asia, and Australia, that kill their prey by constriction. Pythons include the largest living snakes, and can swallow animals up to the size of pigs, goats, and deer: family Pythonidae. ➤➤ **pythonic** /pie'thonik/ *adj,* **pythonine** /-nien, -neen/ *adj.* [via Latin from Greek *Pythōn*, the name of a monstrous serpent which guarded the oracle at Delphi and was killed by Apollo]

Pythonesque /piethə'nesk/ *adj* involving a crazy, surreal, and grotesque form of humour. [from the TV comedy series *Monty Python's Flying Circus* broadcast 1969–74]

pythoness /'piethənes, -nis, -'nes/ *noun* a woman who practises divination by means of a spirit that possesses her, *esp* an oracular priestess of Apollo at Delphi. [Middle English *Phitonesse* via French from late Latin *pythonissa* from Greek *Pythōn*, spirit of divination, from *Pythō*, seat of the Delphic oracle, from *Pythōn*: see PYTHON]

pyuria /pie'yooəri-ə/ *noun* pus in the urine, or a condition caused by it.

pyx *or* **pix** /piks/ *noun* **1** a container in which the bread used at Communion is kept, *esp* one used for carrying the Eucharist to the sick. **2** a box in a mint for deposit of sample coins reserved for testing. [Middle English via medieval Latin from Latin *pyxis*: see PYXIS]

pyxides /'piksideez/ *noun* pl of PYXIS.

pyxidium /pik'sidi-əm/ *noun* (*pl* **pyxidia** /-di-ə/) a capsular fruit that opens at maturity with the upper part falling off like a cap. [scientific Latin from Greek *pyxidion*, dimin. of *pyxis*: see PYXIS]

pyxis /'piksis/ *noun* (*pl* **pyxides** /-deez/) = PYXIDIUM. [via Latin from Greek *pyxis* box, from *pyxos* boxwood]

pzazz /pə'zaz/ *noun* see PIZZAZZ.

Q¹ *or* **q** *noun* (*pl* **Q's** *or* **Qs** *or* **q's**) **1a** the 17th letter of the English alphabet. **b** a written character or design denoting this letter. **c** the sound represented by this letter, one of the English consonants. **2** an item designated as Q, *esp* the 17th in a series.

Q² *noun* a source put forward by biblical critics for the material common to the gospels of Matthew and Luke that is not derived from that of Mark. [from initial letter of German *Quelle* source]

Q³ *abbr* **1** Qatar (international vehicle registration). **2** in chess, queen. **3** question.

q *abbr* **1** quarto. **2** question. **3** quintal. **4** quire.

qadi *or* **cadi** *or* **kadi** /'kahdi, 'kadi/ *noun* (*pl* **qadis** *or* **cadis** *or* **kadis**) a Muslim judge who administers the religious law. [Arabic *qāḍī*]

Qatari /ka'tahri/ *noun* a native or inhabitant of Qatar. ➤➤ **Qatari** *adj*.

qawwali /kə'vahli/ *noun* a type of Muslim religious music, sung *esp* by Sufis. [Arabic *qawwāli* from *qawwāl* singer]

QB *abbr* Queen's Bench.

QC *abbr* Queen's Counsel.

QED *abbr* **1** quantum electrodynamics. **2** used at the conclusion of a proof: which was to be demonstrated. [(sense 2) short for Latin *quod erat demonstrandum*]

Q fever *noun* a disease characterized by high fever, chills, and muscular pains that is caused by a rickettsial micro-organism and is transmitted to humans from sheep or cows by drinking raw milk, by contact, or by ticks. [Q short for QUERY¹; because its cause was orig unknown]

qi /chee/ *noun* see CHI².

qindar /kin'dah/ *or* **qintar** /kin'tah/ *noun* (*pl* **qindarka** /-kə/ *or* **qintars**) a unit of currency in Albania, worth 100th of a lek. [Albanian *qindar*, from *qind* a hundred]

Qld *abbr* Queensland.

QM *abbr* Quartermaster.

QMG *abbr* Quartermaster General.

QMS *abbr* Quartermaster Sergeant.

QPM *abbr* Queen's Police Medal.

qr *abbr* **1** quarter. **2** quire.

Q-ship *noun* an armed ship disguised as a merchant or fishing vessel and used chiefly in World War I to decoy enemy submarines into the range of its guns. [Q short for QUERY¹]

QSO *abbr* quasi-stellar object.

qt *abbr* quart.

q.t. ✳ **on the q.t.** *informal* secretly. [abbr of QUIET²]

qua /kwah, kway/ *prep* in the capacity or character of (somebody or something). [Latin *quaa* which way, as, ablative sing. fem of *qui* who]

quack¹ /kwak/ *verb intrans* to make the characteristic cry of a duck. [imitative]

quack² *noun* a quacking sound.

quack³ *noun* **1** somebody who pretends to have medical skills or qualifications. **2** *informal* a doctor. **3** somebody who pretends to have special knowledge or ability. **4** (*used before a noun*) of or characteristic of a quack: *quack medicines*. ➤➤ **quackish** *adj*. [short for *quacksalver* charlatan, from early Dutch *quacksalver*, literally 'salveseller', from *quacken* to prattle + *salf* salve]

quackery *noun* (*pl* **quackeries**) the practices or activities of a quack: *Mrs Renfrew … was … interesting on the ground of her complaint, which puzzled the doctors, and seemed clearly a case wherein the fullness of professional knowledge might need the supplement of quackery* — George Eliot.

quack grass *noun* *NAmer* = COUCH GRASS. [alteration of *quick grass*, alteration of *quitch grass*: see QUITCH]

quad¹ /kwod/ *noun* a quadrangle.

quad² *noun* in printing, a type-metal space block that is one en or more in width. [short for QUADRAT]

quad³ *noun* a quadruplet.

quad⁴ *adj* quadraphonic.

quad bike *noun* a vehicle resembling a motorcycle with four large wheels, designed for off-road use.

quadr- *comb. form* see QUADRI-.

quadragenarian /ˌkwodrəji'neəri-ən/ *noun* a person between 40 and 49 years old. ➤➤ **quadragenarian** *adj*. [Latin *quadragenarius* containing forty, from *quadraginta* forty]

Quadragesima /kwodrə'jesimə/ *noun* the first Sunday in Lent.

Word history
Latin *quadragesima*, fem of *quadragesimus* fortieth, from *quadraginta* forty. The word orig denoted the period of Lent, which begins forty days before Easter; the current sense is a shortening of *Quadragesima Sunday*.

quadragesimal *adj* (*also* **Quadragesimal**) of or characteristic of Lent.

quadrangle /'kwodranggl/ *noun* **1** = QUADRILATERAL¹. **2** a rectangular enclosure, *esp* a courtyard, with buildings on all four sides. ➤➤ **quadrangular** /kwo'dranggyoolə/ *adj*. [Middle English via French from Latin *quadriangulum*, neuter of *quadriangulus* quadrangular, from QUADRI- + *angulus* angle]

quadrant /'kwodrənt/ *noun* **1a** a quarter of the circumference of a circle. **b** the area of one quarter of a circle that is bounded by an arc containing an angle of 90°. **2** any of the four quarters into which something is divided by two real or imaginary lines that intersect each other at right angles. **3a** an instrument for measuring angles, usu consisting of a graduated arc of 90°. **b** a device or mechanical part shaped like or suggestive of the quadrant of a circle. ⟫ **quadrantal** /kwo'drantl/ *adj*. [Middle English from Latin *quadrant-*, *quadrans* fourth part, from *quattuor* four]

quadraphonic *or* **quadrophonic** /kwodrə'fonik/ *adj* of or being a system for recording or reproducing sound that uses four electrical channels between the source of the signal and its final point of use. ⟫ **quadraphonics** *pl noun*, **quadraphony** /kwo'drof(ə)ni/ *noun*. [irreg from QUADRI- + -PHONIC]

quadrat /'kwodrət, 'kwodrat/ *noun* **1** = QUAD². **2** a usu square plot of land used as a sample area for the ecological investigation of the plants or animals of a region. [alteration of QUADRATE²]

quadrate¹ /'kwodrət, 'kwodrayt/ *adj* **1** square or approximately square. **2** of or being a bone or cartilaginous structure on each side of the skull to which the lower jaw is hinged in birds, reptiles, fish, and amphibians. [Middle English from Latin *quadratus*, past part. of *quadrare* to make square, fit, from *quattuor* four]

quadrate² *noun* **1** a square or cube, or an approximately square or cubical space or object. **2** a quadrate bone.

quadrate³ /kwo'drayt/ *verb intrans archaic* (*usu* + with) to agree or correspond with something.

quadratic¹ /kwo'dratik/ *adj* in mathematics, relating to the power of two, or involving one or more terms of this but no higher power: *a quadratic equation.*

quadratic² *noun* a quadratic equation, curve, expression, etc.

quadrature /'kwodrəchə/ *noun* **1** in mathematics, the process of finding a square equal in area to a given surface or figure. **2** in astronomy, a configuration in which two celestial bodies form an angle of 90° with a third body, *esp* the earth. **3** in electronics, a phase difference of one quarter cycle or 90° between two waves, e.g. the current and voltage in an alternating current. [Latin *quadratura* square, act of squaring, from *quadrare*: see QUADRATE¹]

quadrennia /kwo'dreni·ə/ *noun* pl of QUADRENNIUM.

quadrennial /kwo'dreni·əl/ *adj* **1** consisting of or lasting for four years. **2** occurring every four years. ⟫ **quadrennially** *adv*.

quadrennium /kwo'dreni·əm/ *noun* (*pl* **quadrenniums** *or* **quadrennia** /-ni·ə/) a period of four years. [Latin *quadriennium*, from QUADRI- + *annus* year]

quadri- *or* **quadr-** *or* **quadru-** *comb. form* forming words, with the meanings: **1** four: *quadrilateral; quadrivalent.* **2** square: *quadric.* [Middle English from Latin *quadri-*, from *quattuor* four]

quadric¹ /'kwodrik/ *adj* in mathematics, of or involving a quadratic equation, expression, etc having more than two variables.

quadric² *noun* a quadric surface, curve, etc.

quadriceps /'kwodriseps/ *noun* (*pl* **quadriceps**) the large muscle at the front of the thigh that acts to extend and straighten the leg at the knee joint. [scientific Latin *quadricipit-*, *quadriceps*, from QUADRI- + -*cipit-*, -*ceps* as in *bicipit-*, *biceps* BICEPS]

quadrilateral¹ /kwodri'lat(ə)rəl/ *noun* a polygon having four sides. [Latin *quadrilaterus*, from QUADRI- + *later-*, *latus* side]

quadrilateral² *adj* having four sides.

quadrille /kwə'dril/ *noun* **1** a square dance for four couples made up of five or six figures, or a piece of music for this dance: *The musicians were securely confined in an elevated den, and quadrilles were being systematically got through by two or three sets of dancers —* Dickens. **2** a card game for four players, a variant of ombre, played with a pack of 40 cards and popular *esp* in the 18th cent: *Mrs Bates, the widow of a former vicar of Highbury, was a very old lady, almost past everything but tea and quadrille —* Jane Austen. [French *quadrille*, one of four groups of knights engaged in a tournament, from Spanish *cuadrilla* troop, or from Italian *quadriglia* band, troop, company, both from Latin *quadrum* square]

quadrillion /kwo'drilyən/ *noun* **1** *Brit* a million million million millions, the number one followed by 24 zeros (10²⁴). **2** *NAmer* a thousand million millions, the number one followed by 15 zeros (10¹⁵). ⟫ **quadrillion** *adj*, **quadrillionth** *adj and noun*. [French *quadrillion*, from QUADR- + -*illion* as in MILLION]

quadripartite /kwodri'pahtiet/ *adj* **1** consisting of or divided into four parts. **2** shared by or involving four parties or people: *a quadripartite agreement*. [Middle English from Latin *quadripartitus*, from QUADRI- + *partitus*, past part. of *partire* to divide, from *part-*, *pars* PART¹]

quadriplegia /kwodri'pleejə/ *noun* paralysis of both arms and both legs: compare HEMIPLEGIA, PARAPLEGIA. ⟫ **quadriplegic** /-jik/ *adj and noun*.

quadrivalent /kwodri'vaylənt/ *adj* = TETRAVALENT.

quadrivium /kwo'drivi·əm/ *noun* a group of studies consisting of arithmetic, music, geometry, and astronomy and forming the division of the seven liberal arts studied after the trivium in medieval universities: compare TRIVIUM. [Latin *quadrivium* crossroads, from QUADRI- + *via* way]

quadroon /kwo'droohn/ *noun* a person of one-quarter black ancestry. [modification of Spanish *cuarterón*, from *cuarto* a quarter, from Latin *quartus*: see QUARTER¹]

quadrophonic /kwodrə'fonik/ *adj* see QUADRAPHONIC.

quadru- *comb. form* see QUADRI-.

quadrumanous /kwo'droohmənəs/ *adj* said of monkeys and apes: having all four feet shaped like and functioning as hands. [scientific Latin *quadrumanus*, from QUADRU- + Latin *manus* hand]

quadruped /'kwodrooped/ *noun* an animal that walks on four legs or feet. ⟫ **quadruped** *adj*, **quadrupedal** /kwo'droopidl, -'peedl/ *adj*. [Latin *quadruped-*, *quadrupes* having four feet, from QUADRU- + *ped-*, *pes* foot]

quadruple¹ /'kwodroopl, kwo'droohpl/ *adj* **1** having four units or members. **2** being four times as great or as many. **3** in music, marked by four beats per bar: *quadruple time*. ⟫ **quadruply** /'kwodroopli/ *adv*. [early French *quadruple* from Latin *quadruplus*, from QUADRU- + -*plus* multiplied by]

quadruple² *verb trans* to make (something) four times as great or as many. ⟫ *verb intrans* to become four times as great or as many.

quadruple³ *noun* a number or amount four times as great as another.

quadruplet /'kwodrooplit, kwo'droohplit/ *noun* **1** any of four offspring born at one birth. **2** a combination of four of a kind. **3** in music, a group of four notes performed in the time of three notes of the same value. [from QUADRUPLE¹, by analogy with *double*, *doublet*]

quadruplicate¹ /kwo'droohplikat/ *adj* consisting of or existing in four corresponding or identical parts or examples: *quadruplicate invoices*. [Latin *quadruplicatus*, past part. of *quadruplicare* to quadruple, from *quadruplic-*, *quadruplex* fourfold, from QUADRU- + -*plex* -fold]

quadruplicate² /kwo'droohplikayt/ *verb trans* **1** to make (something) four times as great or as many; to multiply (it) by four. **2** to prepare (e.g. a document) in quadruplicate. ⟫ **quadruplication** /-'kaysh(ə)n/ *noun*.

quadruplicate³ /kwo'droohplikət/ *noun* any of four identical copies. ✴ **in quadruplicate** in the form of four identical copies.

quadruplicity /kwodroo'plisiti/ *noun* the state of being quadruple or quadruplicate.

quadrupole /'kwodroopohl/ *noun* a system composed of four equal electric charges or magnetic poles, each separated by a small distance from one of opposite sign or polarity.

quaestor /'kweestə/ *noun* any of numerous ancient Roman officials concerned chiefly with financial administration. ⟫ **quaestorial** /kwe'stawri·əl/ *adj*. [Latin *quaestor*, from *quaerere* to seek, ask]

quaff /kwof/ *verb chiefly literary* to drink (something), *esp* in long draughts or large amounts: *He quaffed off the wine, and he threw down the cup —* Scott. ⟫ **quaffer** *noun*. [origin unknown]

quag /kwag, kwog/ *noun archaic* a marsh or bog. ⟫ **quaggy** *adj*. [origin unknown]

quagga /'kwagə/ *noun* a recently extinct wild zebra of southern Africa with a brown back and striped head, neck, and forequarters: *Equus quagga*. [early Afrikaans *quagga* (modern *kwagga*), prob of Bantu origin]

quagmire /'kwagmie·ə, 'kwog-/ *noun* **1** an area of soft boggy land that yields under the foot. **2** a predicament from which it is difficult to extricate oneself.

quahog /'kwahhog/ *noun* an edible N American clam with a thick rounded shell: *Mercenaria mercenaria*. [Narraganset *poquaûhock*, from *pohkeni* dark, closed + *hogki* shell]

quaich *or* **quaigh** /kwayk, kwaykh/ *noun chiefly Scot* a small shallow drinking cup with two handles. [Scottish Gaelic *cuach*]

quail¹ /kwayl/ *noun* (*pl* **quails** *or collectively* **quail**) any of several species of game birds of Europe and Asia with rounded bodies and short tails that are related to but smaller than the partridge: genus *Coturnix* and other genera. [Middle English *quaille* via French from medieval Latin *quaccula*, of imitative origin]

quail[2] *verb intrans* to shrink back in fear; to cower: *The strongest quail before financial ruin* — Samuel Butler. [Middle English *quailen* to decline, fail, perhaps from early Dutch *quelen* to suffer]

quaint /kwaynt/ *adj* **1** pleasingly or strikingly old-fashioned or unusual. **2** unfamiliar or different in character or appearance; odd. ➤➤ **quaintly** *adv*, **quaintness** *noun*.

Word history
Middle English *cointe* skilled, elegant, fastidious, strange, via Old French from Latin *cognitus*, past part. of *cognoscere* to know. The meaning of *quaint* has undergone many developments since its introduction to English in the 13th cent. Its basic original meaning was 'knowing', 'clever', applied to people or their actions: *how quaint an orator you are* – Shakespeare, sometimes in later use with derogatory suggestions of cunning and guile. Transferred to objects, it first denoted ingenious or elaborate workmanship. It then came to mean 'pretty', 'fine', applied to objects or dress; or, applied to people, 'finely dressed', 'elegant', sometimes suggesting foppishness or fastidiousness and hence meaning 'elaborate', 'affected' in reference to language. By a further development, it acquired the sense 'unfamiliar', 'strange', which in turn shaded into the usual current sense 'attractively unusual'.

quake[1] /kwayk/ *verb intrans* **1** to shake or vibrate, usu from shock or instability. **2** to tremble or shudder, *esp* inwardly from fear. ➤➤ **quaky** *adj*. [Old English *cwacian*]

quake[2] *noun* **1** the act or an instance of quaking. **2** *informal* an earthquake.

Quaker *noun* a member of a pacifist Christian sect founded by George Fox (d.1691) that stresses INNER LIGHT (divine influence guiding the soul) and rejects sacraments and a formal ministry. ➤➤ **Quakerish** *adj*, **Quakerism** *noun*.

Word history
QUAKE[1] + -ER[2]. Orig derogatory, often said to come from the exhortation of its founder, George Fox, to his followers to 'tremble at the word of the Lord', but the term had been used earlier for various sects who expressed religious fervour by shaking or fits. The sect is properly called the Society of Friends; although it has never officially adopted the name *Quaker*, individual members often use it and it is not now regarded as insulting.

quaking grass *noun* any of several species of delicate grasses with branches that tremble in the wind: genus *Briza*.

qualifiable /ˈkwolifie·əbl/ *adj* capable of being qualified or modified.

qualification /ˌkwolifiˈkaysh(ə)n/ *noun* **1** an official record that a person has completed a course or passed an examination. **2** a quality or skill that makes a person suitable for a particular task or appointment. **3** a condition that must be complied with, e.g. for the attainment of a privilege: *a qualification for membership*. **4** a restriction in meaning or application; a limiting modification: *Their pleasure was complete, with only one qualification*. **5** the act of qualifying. [medieval Latin *qualification-*, *qualificatio*, from *qualificare*: see QUALIFY]

qualified /ˈkwolified/ *adj* **1a** having the training, experience, etc needed for a specified purpose; competent. **b** complying with the specific requirements or conditions for something; eligible. **2** limited or modified in some way: *qualified approval*.

qualifier /ˈkwolifie·ə/ *noun* **1** somebody or something that satisfies requirements or meets a specified standard. **2** in grammar, a word that restricts the meaning of another; a modifier. **3** a preliminary heat or contest; a qualifying round.

qualify /ˈkwolifie/ *verb* (**qualifies, qualified, qualifying**) ➤ *verb trans* **1a** to make (somebody or something) suitable by training, skill, etc for a particular purpose. **b** to render (somebody) legally capable or entitled. **2a** to reduce (something) from a general to a particular or restricted form: *He subsequently qualified the statement to exclude single parents*. **b** to make (something) less harsh or strict; to moderate (it). **c** in grammar, to have a subordinate relation to (a word or phrase); to modify (it). **3** (*often* + as) to characterize or describe (something): *cannot qualify it as … either glad or sorry* — T S Eliot. ➤ *verb intrans* **1** to be fit for an office or position: *He qualifies for the job by virtue of his greater experience*. **2** to reach an accredited level of competence: *She has just qualified as a lawyer*. **3** to exhibit a required degree of ability or achievement in a preliminary contest. [early French *qualifier* from medieval Latin *qualificare*, from Latin *qualis* of what kind]

qualitative /ˈkwolitətiv/ *adj* relating to or involving quality or kind. ➤➤ **qualitatively** *adv*.

qualitative analysis *noun* chemical analysis designed to identify the components of a substance or mixture.

quality /ˈkwoliti/ *noun* (*pl* **qualities**) **1a** degree of excellence; grade: *a decline in the quality of applicants*. **b** superiority in kind; high standard: *proclaimed the quality of his wife* — Compton Mackenzie. **c** *archaic* high social position. **2a** peculiar and essential character; nature: *The quality of mercy is not strained* — Shakespeare. **b** an inherent feature; a property. **3** a distinguishing attribute; a characteristic: *He listed all her good qualities*. **4** in phonetics, the identifying character of a vowel sound. **5** *archaic* a capacity or role: *By-and-by Celia would come in her quality of bridesmaid as well as sister* — George Eliot. **6** (*used before a noun*) superior in kind; of a high standard: *quality goods*; *a quality newspaper*. [Middle English *qualite* via Old French from Latin *qualitat-*, *qualitas*, from *qualis* of what kind]

quality control *noun* a system of ensuring adequate quality, *esp* in manufactured products, involving design analysis and the sampling of output with inspection for defects. ➤➤ **quality controller** *noun*.

quality time *noun* time in which one's attention is given entirely to a personal relationship, *esp* relatively short periods of time with one's child or children.

qualm /kwahm, kwawm/ *noun* **1** a scruple or feeling of uneasiness, *esp* about a point of conscience or honour. **2** a sudden feeling of anxiety or apprehension. **3** *archaic* a sudden and brief attack of illness, faintness, or nausea. ➤➤ **qualmish** *adj*. [origin unknown]

quandary /ˈkwond(ə)ri/ *noun* (*pl* **quandaries**) a state of perplexity or doubt; a dilemma. [origin unknown]

quango /ˈkwanggoh/ *noun* (*pl* **quangos**) *Brit* an autonomous body set up by the government and having statutory powers in a specific field. [acronym from *quasi-autonomous non-governmental organization*]

quant /kwont/ *noun* a long pole used for propelling a punt or barge. [perhaps via Latin from Greek *kontos* boat pole]

quanta /ˈkwontə/ *noun* pl of QUANTUM.

quantic /ˈkwontik/ *noun* in mathematics, a homogeneous function in a rational and integral form having two or more variables. [from Latin *quantus* how great, how much]

quantifier /ˈkwontifie·ə/ *noun* **1** in philosophy, a term that quantifies a logical proposition. **2** in grammar, a word or phrase expressing quantity, *esp* one other than a number, e.g. *many*, *several*, *lots of*.

quantify /ˈkwontifie/ *verb trans* (**quantifies, quantified, quantifying**) **1** to determine, express, or measure the quantity of (something). **2** in philosophy, to specify the universal, particular, or singular character of (a logical proposition). ➤➤ **quantifiable** *adj*, **quantification** /-fiˈkaysh(ə)n/ *noun*. [medieval Latin *quantificare*, from Latin *quantus* how much]

quantise /ˈkwontiez/ *verb trans* see QUANTIZE.

quantitative /ˈkwontitətiv/ *adj* **1** relating to or involving the measurement of quantity or amount. **2** expressed or expressible in terms of quantity. **3** said of metre in poetry: based on the length of syllables rather than their stress patterns: compare ACCENTUAL. ➤➤ **quantitatively** *adv*.

quantitative analysis *noun* chemical analysis designed to determine the amounts or proportions of the components of a substance.

quantitive /ˈkwontitiv/ *adj* = QUANTITATIVE. ➤➤ **quantitively** *adv*.

quantity /ˈkwontiti/ *noun* (*pl* **quantities**) **1** a specified or unspecified amount or number. **2** (*also in pl*) a considerable amount or number: *They wept like anything to see such quantities of sand* — Lewis Carroll. **3a** the aspect in which something is measurable in terms of magnitude. **b** a number, value, etc subjected to a mathematical operation. **c** somebody or something to take into account or be reckoned with: *He is an unknown quantity as military leader*. **4** in phonetics, the relative duration of a speech sound or sound sequence. **5** in philosophy, the character of a logical proposition as universal, particular, or singular. [Middle English *quantite* via Old French from Latin *quantitat-*, *quantitas*, from *quantus* how much, how large]

quantity surveyor *noun* somebody who estimates or measures quantities of materials and labour needed for a building project. ➤➤ **quantity surveying** *noun*.

quantize *or* **quantise** /ˈkwontiez/ *verb trans* **1** to subdivide (e.g. energy) into quanta. **2** to restrict (something) to a set of fixed values. ➤➤ **quantization** /-ˈzaysh(ə)n, kwonti-/ *noun,* **quantizer** *noun.* [QUANTITY + -IZE]

quantoid /ˈkwontoyd/ *noun informal* somebody who is very enthusiastic about statistics and quantitative methods of analysis. [QUANTITY + -OID]

quantum /ˈkwontəm/ *noun (pl* **quanta** /ˈkwontə/) **1** in physics, any of the discrete quantities that form the smallest units into which energy can be subdivided or by which it can increase or decrease. **2** *formal.* **a** a quantity, *esp* a total specified amount. **b** a portion or part. [Latin *quantum,* neuter of *quantus* how much]

quantum electrodynamics *pl noun (treated as sing. or pl)* a branch of physics dealing with the application of quantum mechanics to the interactions between particles having electrical charge and electromagnetic radiation.

quantum jump *noun* = QUANTUM LEAP.

quantum leap *noun* a sudden large increase or major advance. [orig a term in physics for an abrupt change of an electron or atom from one state to another, with the absorption or emission of a quantum; hence, strictly speaking, a sudden increase rather than a large one]

quantum mechanics *pl noun (treated as sing. or pl)* a branch of mechanics based on quantum theory that deals with the physical behaviour of atoms and particles of matter, e.g. their interactions with other particles or radiation, for which the laws of classical mechanics are inapplicable. ➤➤ **quantum mechanical** *adj.*

quantum number *noun* any of a set of integers or odd half integers that indicate the value of various properties, e.g. energy, of a particle or system and that define the state of the particle or system.

quantum theory *noun* a theory in physics based on the concept of the subdivision of energy into quanta.

quarantine[1] /ˈkworənteen/ *noun* **1a** a period of isolation imposed on people or animals, designed to prevent the spread of disease. **b** a place in which people, animals, vehicles, etc are kept during such a period. **2** any state of enforced isolation. [Italian *quarantina* period of forty days, from *quaranta* forty]

quarantine[2] *verb trans* **1** to put (a person or animal) into quarantine. **2** to isolate (somebody) from normal relations or communication.

quark[1] /kwahk/ *noun* in physics, a hypothetical particle that carries a fractional electric charge and is held to be a constituent of known elementary particles, e.g. the proton or neutron. [coined by Murray Gell-Mann b.1929, US physicist]

quark[2] *noun* a type of low-fat soft cheese made from skimmed milk curd. [German *Quark* curds]

quarrel[1] /ˈkworəl/ *noun* **1** a usu verbal conflict between people; an argument. **2** a reason for dispute or complaint: *I have no quarrel with his reasoning.* [early French *querele* complaint, from Latin *querela,* from *queri* to complain]

quarrel[2] *verb intrans* (**quarrelled, quarrelling,** NAmer **quarreled, quarreling**) **1** to have a quarrel; to argue. **2** (+ with) to find fault with something: *The teacher invariably found something to quarrel with in her essays.* ➤➤ **quarreller** *noun.*

quarrel[3] *noun* a short heavy arrow or bolt with a square head, *esp* for a crossbow. [Middle English via Old French *quarrel* square-headed arrow, building stone, from medieval Latin *quadrellum,* dimin. of Latin *quadrum* square]

quarrelsome /ˈkworəls(ə)m/ *adj* inclined or quick to quarrel, *esp* in a petty manner. ➤➤ **quarrelsomely** *adv,* **quarrelsomeness** *noun.*

quarrion *or* **quarrien** *or* **quarrian** /ˈkwori-ən/ *noun Aus* a cockatiel of inland Australia: *Leptolophus hollandicus.* [Wiradhuri *guwarraying*]

quarry[1] /ˈkwori/ *noun (pl* **quarries**) **1** an open excavation from which building materials, e.g. stone, slate, and sand, are obtained. **2** a source from which useful material, *esp* information, may be extracted. [Middle English *quarey* from early French *quarriere,* ultimately from Latin *quadrum* square]

quarry[2] *verb* (**quarries, quarried, quarrying**) ➤ *verb trans* **1** to obtain (e.g. stone) from a quarry. **2** to make a quarry in (e.g. land). **3** to obtain (e.g. information) from a source. ➤ *verb intrans* to dig in or as if in a quarry. ➤➤ **quarrier** *noun.*

quarry[3] *noun (pl* **quarries**) **1** the prey or game of a predator or hunter. **2** somebody or something pursued or sought. [Middle English *querre* entrails of game given to the hounds, from early

French *cuiree,* prob alteration of Old French *coree* entrails, from Latin *cor* heart]

quarryman *noun (pl* **quarrymen**) a worker in a quarry; a quarrier.

quarry tile *noun* a hardwearing unglazed floor tile.

quart /kwawt/ *noun* **1** a unit of liquid capacity equal to 2 pints (about 1.136l in Britain), (about 0.946l in the USA). **2** a unit of dry capacity equal to about 1.1l. **3** (*also* **quarte**) /kaht/ in fencing, the fourth of eight parrying positions. [Middle English *quart* one quarter of a gallon, via French from Latin *quartus:* see QUARTER[1]]

quartan /ˈkwawtn/ *adj* denoting an intermittent fever, *esp* malaria, that recurs at approximately 72-hour intervals. [Middle English *quarteyne* via French from Latin (*febris*) *quartana* (fever) of the fourth (day), from *quartanus* of the fourth, from *quartus:* see QUARTER[1]]

quarte /kaht/ *noun* see QUART (3).

quarter[1] /ˈkwawtə/ *noun* **1** any of four equal parts into which something is divisible or divided. **2** any of various units equal to or derived from a quarter of some larger unit; *specif* a quarter of a pound or hundredweight. **3** a quarter of a measure of time, e.g.: **a** any of four three-month divisions of a year. **b** a period of 15 minutes or a point of time marking this, *esp* before or after the hour: *at a quarter past four.* **4** a quarter of a US or Canadian dollar, or a coin of this value. **5** a limb of an animal or carcass together with the adjacent parts, *esp* a hindquarter. **6a** a compass point or the region around it. **b** a person, group, direction, or place not specifically identified: *We had financial help from many quarters.* **7** a division or district of a town or city: *the Chinese quarter.* **8a** (*usu in pl*) an assigned station or post: *battle quarters.* **b** (*in pl*) living accommodation or lodgings, e.g. for military personnel or domestic staff. **9** merciful consideration of an opponent; *specif* sparing the life of a defeated enemy: *The champion gave him no quarter.* **10a** a fourth part of the moon's periodic cycle of revolution around the earth. **b** a time when half the moon's lighted surface is visible from the earth. **11** any of the four or more divisions of a heraldic shield that are marked off by horizontal and vertical lines. **12** the part of a ship's side towards the stern, or any direction to the rear of the BEAM[1] (widest part) and from a specified side: *on the port quarter.* **13** any of the four equal periods into which the playing time of some games is divided. [Middle English via Old French *quartier* from Latin *quartarius,* from *quartus* fourth, from *quattuor* four]

quarter[2] *verb* (**quartered, quartering**) ➤ *verb trans* **1** to divide (something) into four equal or approximately equal parts. **2** to provide (somebody) with lodgings or shelter, *esp* to assign (a member of the armed forces) to accommodation: *The captain quartered his men on the villagers.* **3** said *esp* of a gundog: to crisscross (an area) in all directions in search of game, or in order to pick up an animal's scent. **4a** to arrange or bear (e.g. different coats of arms) in heraldic quarters on one shield. **b** to divide (a heraldic shield) into quarters. **5** in former times, to divide (a criminal's body) into four parts, usu after hanging, as a form of capital punishment. ➤ *verb intrans* **1** to lodge or dwell. **2** to strike on a ship's quarter: *The wind was quartering.*

quarter[3] *adj* consisting of or equal to a quarter.

quarterage /ˈkwawt(ə)rij/ *noun* a quarterly payment, tax, wage, or allowance.

quarterback *noun* in American football, a player usu positioned behind the centre who directs the attacking play of the team.

quarter-bound *adj* said of a book: bound in two materials with the better material on the spine only. ➤➤ **quarter binding** *noun.*

quarter day *noun* a day that begins a quarter of the year and on which a quarterly payment often falls due.

quarterdeck *noun* **1** the stern area of a ship's upper deck, traditionally used for official or ceremonial purposes. **2** (*treated as sing. or pl*) the officers of a ship or navy: compare LOWER DECK.

quarterfinal *noun* **1** any of four matches in a knockout competition, the winners of which go through to the semifinals. **2** (*in pl*) a round made up of such matches. ➤➤ **quarterfinalist** *noun.*

quarter horse *noun* NAmer a muscular horse capable of high speed for short distances. [from its high speed over distances up to a quarter of a mile]

quarter-hour *noun* = QUARTER[1] (3B).

quartering *noun* **1a** the division of a heraldic shield into four or more sections that usu contain coats of arms brought into a family by marriage. **b** any of the heraldic quarters so formed or the coat of arms it bears: *Shady? A nobleman shady, who can look back upon ninety-five quarterings?* — W S Gilbert. **2** the provision of lodgings, *esp* for military personnel.

quarter light *noun Brit* a small often triangular panel in the side window of a motor vehicle that can usu be opened for ventilation.

quarterly[1] *noun* (*pl* **quarterlies**) a periodical published at three-monthly intervals.

quarterly[2] *adj* **1** payable at three-monthly intervals: *a quarterly premium.* **2** recurring, issued, or spaced at three-monthly intervals.

quarterly[3] *adv* **1** at three-monthly intervals. **2** in heraldic quarters.

quartermaster *noun* **1** an army officer who provides supplies and quarters for a body of troops. **2** a petty officer or seaman who attends to a ship's compass, steering, and signals.

quartern /'kwawtən/ *noun* **1** *archaic* a quarter of any of various units of measurement, *esp* of a pint. **2** a loaf weighing 4lb or 1.6kg or having a 4in.-square cross-section. [Middle English from Old French *quarteron* quarter of a pound, quarter of a hundred, from *quartier*: see QUARTER[1]]

quarter note *noun NAmer* = CROTCHET.

quarter plate *noun* a photographic plate measuring 3¼ × 4¼in. (8.3 × 10.8cm).

quarter-pounder *noun informal* a hamburger weighing a quarter of a pound, usu served in a bread roll.

quarter sessions *pl noun* in former times, a local court in England and Wales with limited criminal and civil jurisdiction, held quarterly.

quarterstaff *noun* (*pl* **quarterstaves** /-stayvz/) a long stout staff formerly used as a weapon.

quarter tone *noun* in music, an interval of half a semitone.

quartet *or* **quartette** /kwaw'tet/ *noun* **1a** (*treated as sing. or pl*) in music, a group of four instruments, voices, or performers. **b** a musical composition for such a group. **2** (*treated as sing. or pl*) a group or set of four. [Italian *quartetto*, from *quarto* fourth, from Latin *quartus*: see QUARTER[1]]

quartic[1] /'kwawtik/ *adj* in mathematics, relating to the power of four, or involving one or more terms of this but no higher power. [Latin *quartus* fourth: see QUARTER[1]]

quartic[2] *noun* a quartic equation, curve, expression, etc.

quartile /'kwawtiel/ *noun* in statistics, any of three numbers that divide a frequency distribution into four groups with equal frequencies, or any of the groups of individuals, items, etc so formed. [medieval Latin *quartilis*, from Latin *quartus* (see QUARTER[1])]

quarto /'kwawtoh/ *noun* (*pl* **quartos**) **1** a book format in which a folded sheet forms four leaves. **2** a book in this format. **3** a size of paper corresponding to a leaf of such a book, usu 10 × 8in. (about 25 × 20cm). [Latin *quarto*, ablative of *quartus*: see QUARTER[1]]

quartz[1] /kwawts/ *noun* a crystalline mineral consisting of silicon dioxide that is a major constituent of many rocks, e.g. granite and sandstone, and occurs in colourless and coloured forms: formula SiO_2. [German *Quarz*, ultimately from a Slavic word meaning 'hard']

quartz[2] *adj* said of a clock or watch: controlled by the oscillations of a quartz crystal.

quartz glass *noun* a glass made of high purity silica prepared from quartz and noted for its transparency to ultraviolet radiation.

quartzite /'kwawtsiet/ *noun* a compact granular quartz rock derived from sandstone.

quasar /'kwaysah/ *noun* any of various unusually luminous very distant compact celestial objects thought to be supermassive black holes accreting matter in the centre of galaxies. [contraction of *quasi-stellar* radio source]

quash /kwosh/ *verb trans* **1a** to annul (e.g. a law or judgment). **b** to reject (a legal document) as invalid. **2** to suppress or crush (e.g. a rumour or rebellion). [Middle English *quassen* from early French *casser*, *quasser* to annul, from Latin *cassus* void, without effect; (sense 2) partly from Middle English *quashen* to smash, from early French *quasser*, *casser*]

quasi- *comb. form* forming words, with the meanings: **1** to some degree; partly: *quasi-officially.* **2a** having some resemblance to the specified thing. **b** seemingly: *quasi-stellar object.* [Latin *quasi* as if, as it were, approximately, from *quam* as + *si* if]

quasi-stellar object *noun* a quasar or similar astronomical body.

quassia /'kwoshə/ *noun* **1** a bitter substance obtained from the heartwood of various tropical trees, used medicinally and as an insecticide. **2** any of several species of trees from which this substance is obtained: genera *Quassia* and *Picrasma*. [from the Latin genus name, named after *Quassi*, 18th-cent. Surinamese slave who discovered its medicinal value]

quatercentenary /,kwatəsen'teenəri, -'tenəri/ *noun* (*pl* **quatercentenaries**) a 400th anniversary. [Latin *quater* (see QUATERNION) + CENTENARY[1]]

quaternary[1] /kwə'tuhnəri/ *adj* **1a** of or based on the number four. **b** fourth in a series. **2** (**Quaternary**) relating to or dating from a geological period, the second period of the Cenozoic era, lasting from about 1.64 million years ago to the present day, and marked by the first appearance of humans. **3** in chemistry, characterized by or resulting from the substitution of four atoms or groups in a molecule, *esp* being or containing an atom united by four bonds to four carbon atoms. >> **Quaternary** *noun.* [Latin *quaternarius* from *quaterni*: see QUATERNION]

quaternary[2] *noun* (*pl* **quaternaries**) a group of four or a member of such a group.

quaternion /kwə'tuhni·ən/ *noun* **1** a set of four parts, things, or people. **2** in mathematics, a generalized complex number that contains one real part and three imaginary parts. [Middle English *quaternyoun* from late Latin *quaternion-*, *quaternio*, from Latin *quaterni* four each, from *quater* four times, from *quattuor* four]

quatrain /'kwotrayn/ *noun* a stanza of four lines. [French *quatrain* from *quatre* four, from Latin *quattuor*]

quatrefoil /'katrəfoyl/ *noun* **1** a stylized figure or ornament in the form of a four-lobed leaf or flower. **2** a design enclosed by four joined foils (curves or arcs; see FOIL[1] (4)). [Middle English *quaterfoil* set of four leaves, from early French *quatre* + Middle English *-foil* as in TREFOIL]

quattrocento /,kwatroh'chentoh/ *noun* (*often* **Quattrocento**) the 15th cent., *esp* in Italian art. [Italian *quattrocento* four hundred, from *quattro* four + *cento* hundred: see CINQUECENTO]

quaver[1] /'kwayvə/ *verb* (**quavered, quavering**) > *verb intrans* **1** said *esp* of the voice: to tremble or shake. **2** to speak or sing in a trembling voice. > *verb trans* to say (something) in a trembling voice. >> **quavering** *adj*, **quaveringly** *adv*, **quavery** *adj*. [Middle English *quaveren*, frequentative of *quaven* to tremble]

quaver[2] *noun* **1** a musical note with the time value of half a crotchet or a quarter of a minim. *NAmer* Also called EIGHTH NOTE. **2** a tremulous sound.

quay /kee/ *noun* a landing place built beside navigable water for loading and unloading ships. >> **quayage** /'keeij/ *noun*. [alteration of Middle English *key* from Old French *kay*, of Celtic origin]

quayside *noun* a quay or the land bordering a quay.

Que. *abbr* Quebec.

quean /kween/ *noun* **1** *chiefly Scot* a woman, *esp* one who is young or unmarried. **2** *archaic* an impudent or disreputable woman; *specif* a prostitute. [Old English *cwene*]

queasy /'kweezi/ *adj* (**queasier, queasiest**) **1** causing or suffering from nausea. **2** causing or feeling anxiety or uneasiness. >> **queasily** *adv*, **queasiness** *noun*. [Middle English *coysy*, *qwesye*; earlier history unknown]

Quebecker *or* **Quebecer** /kwi'bekə/ *noun* a native or inhabitant of Quebec.

Quebecois *or* **Québecois** /kwibe'kwah, ki-/ *noun* (*pl* **Quebecois** *or* **Québecois** /-kwah/) a native or inhabitant of Quebec, *esp* a French-speaking one. [French *Québecois*, from *Québec* Quebec]

quebracho /kay'brahchoh/ *noun* (*pl* **quebrachos**) **1a** a tree of the sumach family that occurs *esp* in Argentina and has hard dense wood rich in substances used in tanning and dyeing: genus *Schinopsis.* **b** the hard dense wood of this tree. **2a** a S American tree of the periwinkle family with bark that was formerly used in the treatment of asthma: *Aspidosperma quebracho.* **b** the bark of this tree. [American Spanish *quebracho*, alteration of *quiebracha*, from Spanish *quiebra* it breaks + *hacha* axe, from the hardness of the wood]

Quechua /'kechwə/ *noun* (*pl* **Quechuas** *or collectively* **Quechua**) **1** a member of a Native American people of central Peru. **2** the language of the Quechua people and of the Inca Empire, spoken in Peru, Bolivia, and Ecuador. ➤➤ **Quechuan** *adj and noun*.

IDord history ━━━━━━━━━
Spanish *Quechua*, prob from Quechua *ghechwa* temperate valleys. Quechuan words that have passed into English, by way of Spanish, include *coca*, *condor*, *guano*, *llama*, *pampas*, *puma*, and *quinine*.

queen[1] /kween/ *noun* **1** a female monarch. **2** the wife or widow of a king. **3** a woman, or something personified as a woman, that is preeminent in a specified respect: *a beauty queen*; *Paris, queen of cities*. **4** in chess, the most powerful piece of each colour, which has the power to move any number of squares in any direction. **5** a playing card marked with a stylized figure of a queen and ranking usu below the king. **6** the fertile fully developed female in a colony of bees, wasps, ants, or termites. **7** a mature female cat. **8** *informal* an effeminate male homosexual. ➤➤ **queenly** *adj*. [Old English *cwēn* woman, wife, queen]

queen[2] *verb intrans* said of a pawn: to become a queen in chess. ➤ *verb trans* to promote (a pawn) to a queen in chess. ✳ **queen it** said of a woman: to behave in a domineering or arrogant manner.

Queen Anne /an/ *adj* **1** of or being a style of furniture prevalent in Britain *esp* during Queen Anne's reign (1707–14), marked by extensive use of upholstery and marquetry. **2** of or being a style of English architecture of the early 18th cent. characterized by restrained classical detail and the use of red brickwork. [named after *Queen Anne* of Britain, d.1714]

Queen Anne's lace *noun* = WILD CARROT.

queen bee *noun* **1** the reproductive female bee in a hive. **2** *informal* the dominant woman in a group or organization.

queen consort *noun* (*pl* **queens consort**) the wife of a reigning king.

queen dowager *noun* the widow of a king.

queen mother *noun* a woman who is the widow of a king and the mother of the reigning sovereign.

queen of puddings *noun* a dessert made from breadcrumbs, jam, and meringue.

queen post *noun* either of two vertical posts connecting the sides of a triangular framework supporting a roof or other structure with the base.

Queen's Bench *noun* used when the British monarch is a queen: a division of the High Court hearing both civil and criminal cases.

Queensberry rules /ˈkweenzb(ə)ri/ *pl noun* the basic rules of boxing. [named after the eighth Marquess of *Queensberry*, who sponsored the rules in 1867]

Queen's Counsel *noun* used when the British monarch is a queen: a senior barrister who has been appointed counsel to the Crown as a mark of professional distinction.

Queen's English *noun* used when the British monarch is a queen: standard or correct British English in speech or writing.

Queen's evidence *noun* used when the British monarch is a queen: evidence given for the Crown by an accomplice in a crime against the other people charged with that crime.

Queen's Guide *noun* used when the British monarch is a queen: a Guide who has reached the highest level of proficiency.

Queen's highway *noun* used when the British monarch is a queen: any public road.

queen-size *adj* said *esp* of a bed: larger or longer than the regular or standard size but smaller than king-size.

queen-sized /ˈkweensiezd/ *adj* = QUEEN-SIZE.

Queenslander /ˈkweenzləndə/ *noun* a native or inhabitant of Queensland.

Queen's Scout *noun* used when the British monarch is a queen: a Scout who has reached the highest level of proficiency.

Queen's speech *noun* used when the British monarch is a queen: a speech read by the sovereign at the opening of a new session of parliament, giving details of the government's proposed legislative programme.

queer[1] /kwiə/ *adj* **1a** odd or strange. **b** eccentric or mildly insane. **2** questionable or suspicious: *queer goings-on*. **3** *informal* slightly unwell; faint or queasy. **4** *informal*, *chiefly derog* homosexual. ➤➤ **queerish** *adj*, **queerly** *adv*, **queerness** *noun*. [perhaps from German *quer* athwart, oblique, perverse]

queer[2] *verb trans informal* to spoil or thwart (something): *That queered his plans*. ✳ **queer somebody's pitch** to prejudice or ruin somebody's chances in advance.

queer[3] *noun informal*, *chiefly derog* a male homosexual.

queer street *noun* (*often* **Queer Street**) *informal*, *dated* a condition of financial embarrassment or difficulty.

quell /kwel/ *verb trans* **1** to overwhelm (e.g. a rebellion) thoroughly; to suppress or subdue (it). **2** to overcome or alleviate (something): *The announcement did little to quell our fears*. ➤➤ **queller** *noun*. [Old English *cwellan* to kill]

quench /kwench/ *verb trans* **1** to relieve or satisfy (thirst) with liquid. **2** to bring (something) to an end, *esp* by satisfying, damping, or decreasing it: *the praise that quenches all desire to read the book* — T S Eliot. **3a** to put out (e.g. a fire); to extinguish (it). **b** to cool (e.g. hot metal) suddenly by immersion in oil, water, etc. ➤➤ **quenchable** *adj*, **quencher** *noun*, **quenchless** *adj*. [Old English *ācwencan* to extinguish]

quenelle /kəˈnel/ *noun* a small ball of a seasoned meat or fish mixture. [French *quenelle* from German *Knödel* dumpling, from Old High German *knodo*, *knoto*]

querist /ˈkwiərist/ *noun* somebody who enquires. [Latin *quaerere* to ask + -IST[1]]

quern /kwuhn/ *noun* a simple hand mill for grinding grain. [Old English *cweorn*]

quernstone *noun* either of two circular stones used in a quern.

querulous /ˈkwer(y)ooləs/ *adj* complaining, *esp* habitually; fretful or peevish. ➤➤ **querulously** *adv*, **querulousness** *noun*. [Latin *querulus*, from *queri* to complain]

query[1] /ˈkwiəri/ *noun* (*pl* **queries**) **1** a question, *esp* one expressing doubt or uncertainty. **2** = QUESTION MARK (1), (2). [alteration of *quere*, from Latin *quaere*, imperative of *quaerere* to ask]

query[2] *verb trans* (**queries**, **queried**, **querying**) **1a** to question the accuracy of (e.g. a statement). **b** to express doubt or uncertainty about (something). **2** to put (something) as a question: *'What's wrong?' she queried*. **3** *chiefly NAmer* to ask a question or questions of (somebody). ➤➤ **querier** *noun*.

query language *noun* a computer language designed for easy access and retrieval of information from a database.

quest[1] /kwest/ *noun* **1** the act or an instance of seeking; a pursuit or search: *in quest of happiness*. **2** the object of a quest; a goal. **3** an adventurous journey undertaken by a knight in medieval romance. [Middle English, in the sense 'search, pursuit, investigation', via French from Latin *quaesta*, fem past part. of *quaerere* to seek]

quest[2] *verb intrans* **1** said of a dog: to search for a trail or for game. **2** (*often* + for/after) to go on a quest: *explorers questing after gold*. ➤ *verb trans literary* to seek or search for (something).

question[1] /ˈkwesch(ə)n/ *noun* **1** a word, phrase, or sentence used to elicit information or test knowledge. **2** the act or an instance of asking; an enquiry. **3a** a subject or concern that is in dispute or at issue: *the abortion question*. **b** a matter: *It's only a question of time*. **c** a subject of debate or a proposition to be voted on in a meeting: *the question before the House*. **d** a problem to be resolved. **4a** doubt or objection: *Her integrity is beyond question*; *The evidence calls into question the veracity of his statement*. **b** chance or possibility: *no question of escape*. ✳ **in question** under discussion. **out of the question** preposterous or impossible. [Middle English via French from Latin *quaestion-*, *quaestio*, from *quaerere* to seek, ask]

question[2] *verb trans* **1a** to ask (somebody) a question. **b** to ask (somebody) a series of questions; to interrogate (them): *The police questioned her for six hours*. **2** to doubt or dispute (something): *I questioned the wisdom of his decision*. **3** to subject (facts or phenomena) to analysis; to examine (them). ➤ *verb intrans* to ask questions; to enquire. ➤➤ **questioner** *noun*, **questioning** *adj*, **questioningly** *adv*.

questionable *adj* **1** open to doubt or challenge; not certain or exact. **2** of doubtful morality or propriety; shady. ➤➤ **questionableness** *noun*, **questionably** *adv*.

question mark *noun* **1** a punctuation mark (?) used at the end of a sentence to indicate a direct question. **2** the sign (?) used to express uncertainty or doubt, e.g. before a date or in the margin of possibly inaccurate text.

question-master *noun* the person who asks the questions during a quiz.

questionnaire /kweshə'neə, *also* kes-/ *noun* a set of questions, usu on a form, to be asked of a number of people to obtain statistically useful information. [French *questionnaire*, from *questionner* to question, from Latin *quaestion-*, *quaestio*: see QUESTION¹]

question time *noun* a period during which members of a parliamentary body may put questions to a minister.

quetzal /'ketsl/ *noun* (*pl* **quetzals** *or* **quetzales** /ket'sahlays/) **1** a Central American bird that has brilliant blue, green, red, and gold plumage, a rounded hairlike crest on the head, and, in the male, very long upper tail feathers: *Pharomachrus mocinno*. **2** the basic monetary unit of Guatemala, divided into 100 centavos. [American Spanish *quetzal* from Nahuatl *quetzaltototl*, from *quetzalli* brilliant tail feather + *tototl* bird]

Quetzalcóatl /,ketslkoh'atl, -'kwahtl/ *noun* a Toltec and Aztec god identified with the air, sun, and civilization and represented as a feathered serpent. [Nahuatl *Quetzalcóatl*, from *quetzalli* brilliant tail feather + *cóatl* snake]

quetzales /ket'sahlays/ *noun* pl of QUETZAL.

queue¹ /kyooh/ *noun* **1a** a waiting line, *esp* of people or vehicles. **b** = WAITING LIST: *a housing queue.* **c** in computing, a list where items are inserted at one end and accessed or deleted at the other. **2** a pigtail. [French *queue* tail, from Latin *cauda*, *coda*]

queue² *verb* (**queues, queued, queuing** *or* **queueing**) ➤ *verb intrans* to line up or wait in a queue. ➤ *verb trans* in computing, to arrange (items) in a queue so that they can be accessed in order. ➤➤ **queuer** *noun.*

queue-jump *verb intrans* to join a queue at a point in front of those already waiting. ➤➤ **queue-jumper** *noun.*

quibble¹ /'kwibl/ *noun* **1** a minor objection or criticism, *esp* used as an equivocation. **2** *archaic* a pun. [dimin. of obsolete *quib*, in the same sense, prob from Latin *quibus*, dative and ablative pl of *qui* who, which]

quibble² *verb intrans* **1** to make minor or trivial objections. **2** to engage in petty argument; to bicker. ➤➤ **quibbler** *noun,* **quibbling** *adj.*

quiche /keesh/ *noun* a pastry shell filled with a rich savoury egg and cream custard and other ingredients such as ham, cheese, or vegetables. [French *quiche* from German dialect *Küchen* cake]

quick¹ /kwik/ *adj* **1a** fast in development or occurrence: *a quick succession of events.* **b** done with rapidity: *I gave the room a quick clean.* **c** lasting a short time; brief: *a quick look.* **d** marked by speed, readiness, or promptness of physical movement: *We walked with quick steps.* **e** inclined to hastiness, e.g. in action or response: *quick to find fault.* **f** capable of being easily and speedily prepared: *a quick and tasty dinner.* **2a** fast in understanding, thinking, or learning; mentally agile: *a quick mind.* **b** reacting with speed and keen sensitivity: *a quick temper.* **3** *archaic* alive. ✳ **quick as a flash** very quickly; instantaneously. **quick with child** *archaic* pregnant. ➤➤ **quickly** *adv,* **quickness** *noun.* [Old English *cwic* alive]

quick² *adv informal* in a quick manner; quickly.

quick³ *noun* **1** painfully sensitive flesh, *esp* under a fingernail or toenail. **2** the very centre of something; the heart. **3** (**the quick**) *archaic* (treated as pl) living people: *She was the first dead person he had ever seen … There was an immeasurable distance between the quick and the dead: they did not seem to belong to the same species —* Somerset Maugham. ✳ **cut to the quick** to make (somebody) feel deeply hurt or upset. [orig in the sense 'that which is alive'; from QUICK¹]

quicken *verb* (**quickened, quickening**) ➤ *verb trans* **1** to make (something) more rapid; to accelerate (it): *She quickened her steps.* **2** to enliven or stimulate (something). **3** to revive or give life to (somebody or something). ➤ *verb intrans* **1** to become more rapid: *His pulse quickened at the sight.* **2** to come to life. **3a** said of a pregnant woman: to reach the stage of pregnancy at which foetal motion is felt. **b** said of a foetus: to begin to show signs of life. ➤➤ **quickener** *noun.*

quickfire *adj* coming or operating quickly, *esp* in quick succession: *quickfire questions.*

quick-freeze *verb trans* (*past tense* **quick-froze**, *past part.* **quick-frozen**) to freeze (food) for preservation rapidly to minimize cell rupture, loss of flavour, etc.

quickie /'kwiki/ *noun informal* **1a** something done or made in a hurry, e.g. a brief act of sexual intercourse. **b** (*used before a noun*) done or made quickly: *a quickie divorce.* **2** an alcoholic drink consumed rapidly or in haste.

quicklime *noun* = LIME¹ (1A). [translation of Latin *calx viva* living lime]

quick march *noun* a military march in quick time.

quicksand *noun* a deep mass of loose wet sand into which heavy objects readily sink. [QUICK¹ in the sense 'alive, lively']

quickset *noun chiefly Brit* plant cuttings, *esp* hawthorn, set in the ground to grow into a hedge, or a hedge formed in this way. [QUICK¹ in the sense 'living']

quicksilver¹ *noun* = MERCURY¹. [translation of Latin *argentum viva* living silver, from the way it moves in its liquid state]

quicksilver² *adj* changeable in mood or rapid in movement.

quickstep¹ *noun* **1** a ballroom dance that is a fast foxtrot characterized by a combination of short rapid steps. **2** a piece of music composed for this dance.

quickstep² *verb intrans* (**quickstepped, quickstepping**) to dance the quickstep.

quick-tempered *adj* easily angered, irascible.

quickthorn *noun* = HAWTHORN. [from its rapid growth]

quick time *noun* a rate of marching of about 120 steps per minute.

quick-witted *adj* quick in understanding or response; mentally alert. ➤➤ **quick-wittedly** *adv,* **quick-wittedness** *noun.*

quid¹ /kwid/ *noun* (*pl* **quid**) *Brit, informal* a pound sterling: *I lent him ten quid.* ✳ **quids in** *Brit, informal* in the state of having made a usu large profit: *If we sell them at £5 each, we'll be quids in.* [perhaps from Latin *quid* what, anything, something]

quid² *noun* a wad of something, *esp* tobacco, for chewing. [dialect variation of CUD]

quiddity /'kwiditi/ *noun* (*pl* **quiddities**) **1** *formal* that which makes something what it is; essence. **2** a quibble. [medieval Latin *quidditas* essence, literally 'whatness', from Latin *quid* what]

quidnunc /'kwidnungk/ *noun archaic or literary* somebody who wants to know all the latest news or gossip. [Latin *quid nunc* what now]

quid pro quo /,kwid proh 'kwoh/ *noun* (*pl* **quid pro quos**) something given or received in exchange for something else. [Latin *quid pro quo*, literally 'something for something']

quiescent /kwi'es(ə)nt/ *adj* **1** causing no trouble. **2** at rest; inactive. ➤➤ **quiescence** *noun,* **quiescently** *adv.* [Latin *quiescent-*, *quiescens*, present part. of *quiescere*: see QUIET¹]

quiet¹ /'kwie·ət/ *adj* (**quieter, quietest**) **1a** making little or no noise: *Be quiet!* **b** free from noise or uproar; peaceful: *a quiet little village in the Cotswolds.* **c** marked by little or no motion, activity, or excitement; calm: *a quiet day at the office.* **d** enjoyed in peace and relaxation; undisturbed: *a quiet cup of tea.* **e** *informal* and usu involving small numbers of people: *a quiet wedding.* **2a** gentle or reserved: *a quiet temperament.* **b** unobtrusive or conservative: *quiet clothes.* **3** private or discreet: *Can I have a quiet word with you?* ➤➤ **quietly** *adv,* **quietness** *noun.* [Middle English via French from Latin *quietus*, past part. of *quiescere* to become quiet, rest, from *quiet-*, *quies* rest, QUIET²]

quiet² *noun* being quiet; tranquillity or silence. ✳ **on the quiet** without telling anyone; discreetly or secretly. [Middle English from Latin *quiet-*, *quies* rest, quiet]

quiet³ *adv* in a quiet manner.

quiet⁴ *verb* (**quieted, quieting**) ➤ *verb trans* **1** to calm or allay (something or somebody): *His words did nothing to quiet her fears.* **2** *chiefly NAmer* to make (somebody or something) quiet. ➤ *verb intrans chiefly NAmer* (+ down) to become quiet. ➤➤ **quieter** *noun.*

quieten *verb* (**quietened, quietening**) ➤ *verb intrans chiefly Brit* (*often* + down) to become quiet. ➤ *verb trans chiefly Brit* to make (somebody or something) quiet.

quietism *noun* **1** a system of religious mysticism teaching that perfection and spiritual peace are attained by annihilation of the will and passive absorption in contemplation of God and divine things. **2** a passive withdrawn attitude or policy towards the world or worldly affairs. ➤➤ **quietist** *adj and noun.*

quietude /'kwie·ətyoohd/ *noun formal* being quiet; repose. [early French *quietude* from late Latin *quietudo*, from Latin *quietus*: see QUIET¹]

quietus /kwie'eetəs, kwie'aytəs/ *noun* (*pl* **quietuses**) **1** *literary* death as a release from life: *Then he tried to close and give the quietus with his iron hook ... but Peter doubled under it* — J M Barrie. **2** final settlement, e.g. of a debt. [Middle English from medieval Latin *quietus est* he is quit, literally 'it is at rest', formula of discharge from obligation]

quiff /kwif/ *noun Brit* a lock of hair brushed so that it stands up over the forehead. [origin unknown]

quill¹ /kwil/ *noun* **1a** the hollow horny barrel of a feather. **b** any of the large stiff feathers of a bird's wing or tail. **c** any of the hollow sharp spines of a porcupine, hedgehog, etc. **2** a bird's feather fashioned into a writing pen: *the spasmodic scratching of a quill pen* — Hardy. **3a** a bobbin, spool, or spindle on which yarn is wound. **b** a hollow shaft often surrounding another shaft and used in various mechanical devices. **c** a roll of dried bark: *cinnamon quills*. [Middle English *quil* hollow reed, bobbin, prob from early Low German *quiele*]

quill² *verb trans* **1** to wind (thread or yarn) on a quill. **2** to make a series of small rounded ridges or fluted folds in (cloth).

quill pen *noun* = QUILL¹ (2).

quilt¹ /kwilt/ *noun* **1** a thick warm top cover for a bed consisting of padding held in place between two layers of cloth by usu crisscross lines of stitching. **2** a thin usu decorative top cover for a bed; a bedspread. **3** = DUVET. [Middle English *quilte* mattress, quilt, via Old French from Latin *culcita* mattress]

quilt² *verb trans* **1a** to fill, pad, or line (something) like a quilt: *a quilted jacket*. **b** to stitch, sew, or cover (something) with lines or patterns resembling those used in quilts. **2a** to stitch or sew (fabric) together in layers with padding in between. **b** to fasten (padding) between layers of fabric in this way. ➤ *verb intrans* to make quilts or quilted work. ➤ **quilter** *noun,* **quilting** *noun.*

quim /kwim/ *noun coarse slang* the female genitals. [origin unknown]

quin /kwin/ *noun Brit* a quintuplet.

quinary /'kwienəri/ *adj* **1** of or based on the number five. **2** fifth in a series. [Latin *quinarius* containing five, from *quinque* five]

quince /kwins/ *noun* **1** a round or pear-shaped fruit with hard acid flesh, used for marmalade, jelly, and preserves. **2** the Asian tree of the rose family that bears this fruit: *Cydonia oblonga*. [Middle English *quynce* quinces, pl of *coyn, quyn* quince, via early French *coin* and Latin *cotoneum* from Greek *melon Kydōnion* apple of Cydonia, ancient city in Crete]

quincentenary /kwinsen'teenəri, -'tenəri/ *noun* (*pl* **quincentenaries**) a 500th anniversary. ➤ **quincentennial** *adj* and *noun*. [Latin *quinque* five + CENTENARY¹]

quincunx /'kwinkungks/ *noun* an arrangement of five things, e.g. marks on a playing card, with one at each corner of a square or rectangle and one in the middle. ➤ **quincuncial** /kwin'kunsh(ə)l/ *adj*. [Latin *quincunc-, quincunx*, literally 'five-twelfths', from *quinque* five + *uncia* twelfth part]

quinella /ki'nelə, kwi-/ *noun* a bet, e.g. on a horse race, that involves predicting the first two finishers in either order. [American Spanish *quiniela*, a game of chance]

quinine /'kwineen, kwi'neen/ *noun* a bitter-tasting chemical compound that is obtained from cinchona bark, is an ingredient of tonic water, and has been widely used as a ·drug, *esp* in the treatment of malaria. [Spanish *quina* cinchona bark, from Quechua *kina* bark + -INE²]

quinoline /'kwinəleen, -lin/ *noun* a pungent oily liquid that is present in small amounts in coal tar, is obtained usu from aniline, and is used in the manufacture of many drugs and dyes: formula C_9H_7N. [Spanish *quina* (see QUININE) + -OL¹ + -INE²]

quinone /kwi'nohn, 'kwinohn/ *noun* **1** a chemical compound that is a derivative of benzene and is used in photography: formula $C_6H_4O_2$. **2** any of various related compounds including several that are biologically important as in energy-producing reactions inside cells. [Spanish *quina* (see QUININE) + -ONE]

quinqu- *comb. form* see QUINQUE-.

quinquagenarian /,kwingkwəji'neəri·ən/ *noun* a person between 50 and 59 years old. ➤ **quinquagenarian** *adj*. [Latin *quinquagenarius* containing fifty, from *quinquaginta* fifty]

Quinquagesima /kwingkwə'jesimə/ *noun* the Sunday before Lent. [Latin *quinquagesima*, fem of *quinquagesimus* fiftieth, from *quinquaginta* fifty; because Quinquagesima falls fifty days before Easter]

quinque- *or* **quinqu-** *comb. form* forming words, denoting: five: *quinquennium*. [Latin *quinque*]

quinquennia /kwing'kweni·ə, kwin-/ *noun* pl of QUINQUENNIUM.

quinquennial /kwing'kweni·əl, kwin-/ *adj* **1** consisting of or lasting for five years. **2** occurring or being done every five years. ➤ **quinquennially** *adv*.

quinquennium /kwing'kweni·əm, kwin-/ *noun* (*pl* **quinquenniums** *or* **quinquennia** /-ni·ə/) a period of five years. [Latin *quinquennium*, from QUINQUE- + *annus* year]

quinquereme /kwingkwi'reem/ *noun* an ancient Roman or Greek galley with five banks of oars. [early French *quinquereme* from Latin *quinqueremis*, from QUINQUE- + *remus* oar]

quinquevalent /kwingkwi'vaylənt, kwin'kwevələnt/ *adj* = PENTAVALENT.

quinsy /'kwinzi/ *noun* (*pl* **quinsies**) a severe inflammation of the tonsils, throat, or adjacent parts with swelling and fever. [Middle English *quinesie* via French and Latin from Greek *kynanchē* canine quinsy, from *kyn-, kyōn* dog + *anchein* to strangle]

quint¹ /kwint/ *noun NAmer* a quintuplet.

quint² /kint, kwint/ *noun* in piquet, a sequence of five cards of the same suit. [French *quinte* from Latin *quintus* fifth]

quintain /'kwintin/ *noun* a post with a revolving crosspiece having a target at one end and a sandbag at the other, used for tilting practice in medieval times. [Middle English *quintaine* via French from Latin *quintana* street in a Roman camp, separating the fifth maniple from the sixth, where military exercises were performed, fem of *quintanus* fifth in rank, from *quintus*: see QUINTE]

quintal /'kwintl/ *noun* **1** a unit of weight equal to 112lb (about 50.8kg) or 100lb (about 45.4kg); a hundredweight. **2** a metric unit of weight equal to 100kg (about 220.5lb). [Middle English via French and medieval Latin from Arabic *qinţār*, ultimately from Latin *centenarius* consisting of a hundred, from *centum* hundred]

quinte /kant/ *noun* in fencing, the fifth of eight parrying positions. [French *quinte* from Latin *quintus* fifth, from *quinque* five]

quintessence /kwin'tes(ə)ns/ *noun* **1** the pure and concentrated essence of something. **2** the most significant element in a whole. **3** the most typical example or perfect embodiment, e.g. of a quality or class: *the quintessence of pride*. **4** in ancient philosophy, the fifth and highest essence, which forms the heavenly bodies and permeates all nature. ➤ **quintessential** /kwinti'sensh(ə)l/ *adj,* **quintessentially** /kwinti'sensh(ə)li/ *adv*. [Middle English via French from medieval Latin *quinta essentia*, literally 'fifth essence']

quintet *or* **quintette** /kwin'tet/ *noun* **1a** (*treated as sing. or pl*) in music, a group of five instruments, voices, or performers. **b** a musical composition for such a group. **2** (*treated as sing. or pl*) a group or set of five. [Italian *quintetto*, from *quinto* fifth, from Latin *quintus*: see QUINTE]

quintillion /kwin'tilyən/ *noun* **1** *Brit* the number one followed by 30 zeros (10^{30}). **2** *NAmer* the number one followed by 18 zeros (10^{18}). ➤ **quintillion** *adj,* **quintillionth** *adj* and *noun*. [Latin *quintus* (see QUINTE) + *-illion* as in MILLION]

quintuple¹ /'kwintyoopl, kwin'tyoohpl/ *adj* **1** having five units or members. **2** being five times as great or as many. [early French *quintuple* from Latin *quintuplex*, from *quintus* (see QUINTE) + *-plex* -fold]

quintuple² *verb trans* to make (something) five times as great or as many. ➤ *verb intrans* to become five times as great or as many.

quintuple³ *noun* a number or amount five times as great as another.

quintuplet /'kwintyooplit, kwin'tyoohplit/ *noun* **1** any of five offspring born at one birth. **2** a combination of five of a kind. **3** in music, a group of five notes performed in the time of three or four notes of the same value. [from QUINTUPLE¹, by analogy with *double, doublet*]

quintuplicate¹ /kwin'tyoohplikət/ *adj* consisting of or existing in five corresponding or identical parts or examples: *quintuplicate invoices*. [Latin *quintuplicatus*, past part. of *quintuplicare* to quintuple, from *quintuplic-, quintuplex*: see QUINTUPLE¹]

quintuplicate² /kwin'tyoohplikayt/ *verb trans* **1** to make (something) five times as great or as many; to multiply (it) by five. **2** to prepare (e.g. a document) in quintuplicate.

quintuplicate³ /kwin'tyoohplikət/ *noun* any of five identical copies. ✳ **in quintuplicate** in the form of five identical copies.

quip¹ /kwip/ *noun* a clever, witty, or sarcastic observation or response. ➤➤ **quipster** /'kwipstə/ *noun*. [perhaps from Latin *quippe* indeed, to be sure]

quip² *verb intrans* (**quipped, quipping**) to make a quip.

quire¹ /kwie·ə/ *noun* **1** 24 or 25 sheets of paper of the same size and quality; one twentieth of a ream. **2** a set of folded sheets of paper, e.g. leaves or pages of a book, fitting one within another; *specif* four sheets of paper folded to form eight leaves or sixteen pages. [Middle English *quair* four sheets of paper folded once, collection of sheets, via French from Latin *quaterni*: see QUATERNION]

quire² *noun archaic* = CHOIR.

quirk /kwuhk/ *noun* **1** an odd or peculiar trait; an idiosyncrasy. **2** an accident or vagary: *by some quirk of fate*. **3** an abrupt twist or curve, e.g. in drawing or writing. **4** a groove separating an architectural moulding from adjoining members. ➤➤ **quirkiness** *noun*, **quirky** *adj*. [origin unknown]

quirt¹ /kwuht/ *noun* a riding whip with a short handle and a leather lash. [Mexican Spanish *cuarta* whip]

quirt² *verb trans* to hit (e.g. a horse) with a quirt.

quisling /'kwizling/ *noun* a traitor who collaborates with invaders. [named after Vidkun *Quisling* d.1945, Norwegian politician who collaborated with the Germans in World War II]

quit¹ /kwit/ *verb* (**quitting**, *past tense and past part*. **quitted** or **quit**) ➤ *verb trans* **1** to leave or depart from (a person or place): *Be ready to quit the building at a moment's notice*. **2** to relinquish (e.g. a way of thinking or acting); to stop (it): *Quit moaning!* **3** to give up (e.g. an activity or employment): *He quit his job*. **4** *archaic* to conduct (oneself) in a usu specified way: *They quit themselves with great courage*. ➤ *verb intrans* **1** to cease doing something; *specif* to give up one's job. **2** said of a tenant: to vacate occupied premises: *Their landlord gave them notice to quit*. **3** *informal* to admit defeat; to give up. [Middle English *quiten, quitten*, from Old French *quiter, quitter*, from *quite* free of, released, literally 'at rest', from Latin *quietus*: see QUIET¹]

quit² *adj* (+ of) released or free from obligation, charge, or penalty. [Middle English *quite, quit*, from Old French *quite*: see QUIT¹]

quitch /kwich/ *noun* = COUCH GRASS. [Old English *cwice*]

quitch grass *noun* = COUCH GRASS.

quitclaim /'kwitklaym/ *noun* a legal document by which one person renounces his or her right in favour of another. [Middle English *quite-claim* from early French *quiteclame*, from *quiteclamer*, literally 'to declare free']

quite /kwiet/ *adv and adj* **1a** wholly or completely: *not quite all; I'm quite sure*. **b** positively or certainly: *It's quite the best I've seen*. **2** more than usually; rather: *It took quite a while; That was quite some party!* **3** *chiefly Brit* to only a moderate degree: *quite good but not perfect*. ✳ **quite so** used to express agreement.

Word history
Middle English, from *quite*: see QUIT². From its original 14th-cent. meaning 'completely', used chiefly with verbs to signify the completion of an action, in the 18th cent. *quite* acquired the additional, weaker sense 'actually', 'really': *the widow, quite charmed with her new lodger* — Henry Fielding. By a further almost imperceptible process, in the mid-19th cent. the even weaker sense 'rather', 'fairly' developed.

quitrent /'kwitrent/ *noun* in former times, a fixed rent payable to a feudal superior in place of the performing of services. [Middle English *quiterent*, from *quite* (see QUIT²) + RENT¹]

quits /kwits/ *adj* on even terms as a result of repaying a debt or retaliating for an injury. ✳ **call it quits 1** to acknowledge that terms are now even or that neither side now has an advantage. **2** to call a halt to an activity. [Middle English, in the sense 'released from obligation', prob from medieval Latin *quittus*, alteration of Latin *quietus*: see QUIET¹]

quittance /'kwit(ə)ns/ *noun* **1** *archaic or literary* discharge or release from a debt or obligation. **2** a document that is evidence of this.

quitter *noun informal* a person who gives up too easily; a defeatist.

quiver¹ /'kwivə/ *noun* a case for carrying or holding arrows. [Middle English from Old French *quivre*, of Germanic origin]

quiver² *verb intrans* (**quivered, quivering**) to shake or move with a slight rapid trembling motion. ➤➤ **quivering** *adj*, **quivery** *adj*. [Middle English *quiveren*, prob from *quiver* agile, quick, from Old English *cwifer*]

quiver³ *noun* the act or an instance of quivering; a tremor.

qui vive /,kee 'veev/ ✳ **on the qui vive** on the alert or lookout. [French *qui-vive*, from *qui vive?* long live who?, challenge of a French sentry]

quixotic /kwik'sotik/ *adj* idealistic or chivalrous in a rash or impractical way. ➤➤ **quixotically** *adv*. [from Don *Quixote*, hero of the novel *Don Quixote de la Mancha* by Miguel de Cervantes Saavedra d.1616, Spanish novelist]

quixotical /kwik'sotikl/ *adj* = QUIXOTIC.

quiz¹ /kwiz/ *noun* (*pl* **quizzes**) **1** a public test of knowledge, *esp* as a form of entertainment. **2** a set of usu short quick questions. **3** *NAmer* an informal test given by a teacher to a student or class. **4** *archaic* an eccentric or quizzical person. **5** *archaic* a practical joke or hoax.

Word history
origin unknown. Sometimes said to have been coined by Richard Daly, an 18th-cent. Dublin theatre proprietor, who bet that he could introduce a nonsense word and that people would give a meaning to it. He had the word *quiz* written on walls all over the city, and it rapidly became part of the language. However, there is no evidence to support this story. The orig meaning was 'an odd or eccentric person', later 'a prank or witticism'; as a verb 'to make fun of somebody' (surviving in *quizzical*). The current senses of *quiz* arose much later, and may represent a different word.

quiz² *verb trans* (**quizzes, quizzed, quizzing**) **1** to question (somebody) closely. **2** *NAmer* to test (a student or class) informally. **3** *archaic* to look quizzically at (somebody), *esp* through an eyeglass. ➤➤ **quizzer** *noun*.

quizmaster *noun Brit* the person who asks the questions during a quiz.

quizzical /'kwizikl/ *adj* **1** indicating a state of puzzlement; questioning: *a quizzical glance*. **2** gently mocking; teasing. **3** *archaic* slightly or amusingly eccentric or odd. ➤➤ **quizzicality** /-'kaliti/ *noun*, **quizzically** *adv*. [see QUIZ¹]

quod /kwod/ *noun Brit, informal, dated* prison. [perhaps by shortening and alteration from QUADRANGLE]

quodlibet /'kwodlibet/ *noun* **1** a philosophical or theological point put forward for discussion, or a debate on such a point. **2** a light-hearted combination of familiar melodies. [from Latin *quod* what + *libet* it pleases]

quoin /koyn, kwoyn/ *noun* **1a** a solid exterior corner of a building. **b** a block used to form a quoin, usu distinguished visually from the adjoining surfaces. **2a** in printing, a wooden wedge or expandable metal device used to fasten type or plates in a CHASE⁵ (rectangular frame). **b** a wedge used for any of various purposes, e.g. to raise the level of a gun barrel. [alteration of COIN¹]

quoin² *verb trans* **1** to provide (part of a building) with quoins: *quoined walls*. **2** in printing, to fasten (e.g. type) with quoins.

quoit /koyt, kwoyt/ *noun* **1** a ring of rubber or iron used in a throwing game. **2** (*in pl, but treated as sing*.) a game in which quoits are thrown at an upright pin in an attempt to encircle the pin or land as near to it as possible. [Middle English *coite*; earlier history unknown]

quokka /'kwokə/ *noun* a small short-tailed wallaby of W Australia: *Setonix brachyurus*. [Nyungar *kwaka*]

quoll /kwol/ *noun* = DASYURE. [Guugu Yimidhirr *dhigul*]

quondam /'kwondam, 'kwondəm/ *adj formal* former; sometime: *But the quondam 'careless bachelor' begins to think he knows the answer to that ancient problem, 'how the money goes'* — Lewis Carroll. [Latin *quondam* at one time, formerly, from *quom, cum* when]

Quonset /'kwonsit/ *noun NAmer, trademark* a prefabricated shelter similar to a Nissen hut. [named after *Quonset* Point, Rhode Island, where they were first made]

quorate /'kwawrat, 'kwawrayt/ *adj formal* having a quorum: *Is this meeting quorate?*

Quorn /kwawn/ *noun trademark* a form of vegetable protein derived from fungi, used as a meat substitute. [named after the original manufacturer, *Quorn* Specialities Ltd, based in the village of Quorndon, Leicestershire]

quorum /'kwawrəm/ *noun* (*pl* **quorums**) the minimum number of members of a body that must be assembled for proceedings to be constitutionally valid. [Middle English, referring to certain usu eminent justices of the peace without whom the bench was not properly constituted, from Latin *quorum* of whom, genitive pl of *qui* who; from the wording of the commission formerly issued to justices of the peace]

quota /'kwohtə/ *noun* **1** a proportional part or share, *esp* the share or proportion to be either contributed or received by an individual or body: *Most factories fulfilled their production quota.* **2** the number or amount constituting a proportional share. **3** a numerical limit set on a class of people or things: *an immigration quota.* [medieval Latin *quota*, from Latin *quota pars* how great a part]

quotable /'kwohtəbl/ *adj* fit for or worth quoting. ➤➤ **quotability** /-'biliti/ *noun.*

quotation /kwoh'taysh(ə)n/ *noun* **1a** something quoted, *esp* a passage or phrase quoted from literature. **b** the use in music or art of material from an earlier work by somebody else or oneself. **2** the act of quoting. **3** a statement of the expected cost of a service or commodity; an estimate. **4a** the naming or publishing of current bids and offers for or prices of shares, securities, commodities, etc. **b** the current buying or selling price of a commodity, stock, share, etc.

quotation mark *noun* (*usu in pl*) either of a pair of punctuation marks (" " or ' ') used to indicate the beginning and end of a direct quotation or to enclose a word or phrase, e.g. a title or definition.

quote¹ /kwoht/ *verb trans* **1a** to repeat (a passage or phrase previously said or written, *esp* by another) in writing or speech, usu with an acknowledgment. **b** to repeat a passage or phrase from (a writer or work), *esp* in substantiation or illustration: *to quote Shakespeare.* **2** to make an estimate of or give exact information on (the price of a commodity or service). **3a** to name (the current buying or selling price) of a commodity, stock, share, etc. **b** to name the current buying or selling price of (a commodity, stock, share, etc). **c** to quote the shares of (a company) on a stock exchange. **4** to set off (a word or phrase) by quotation marks. ➤ *verb intrans* **1** to say or write something previously said or written, *esp* by another: *The Prime Minister said, and I quote, 'We have beaten inflation'.* **2** to give a

quotation for a service or commodity: *I asked him to quote for redecorating the house.* ✳ **quote ... unquote** *informal* used in speech at the beginning and end of a direct quotation, usu to emphasize that the intervening words are those actually used by the original speaker or writer. [medieval Latin *quotare* to mark the number of, number references, from Latin *quotus* of what number or quantity]

quote² *noun informal* **1** = QUOTATION (1A), (3). **2** = QUOTATION MARK.

quoth /kwohth/ *verb archaic* (*used only in first and third person sing.*) said: *quoth I.* [Middle English, past of *quethen* to say, from Old English *cwethan*]

quotidian /kwo'tidi-ən/ *adj* **1** occurring or recurring every day: *quotidian fever.* **2** commonplace or ordinary. [Middle English *cotidian* via French from Latin *quotidianus, cotidianus,* from *quotidie* every day, from *quot* (as) many as + *dies* day]

quotient /'kwohsh(ə)nt/ *noun* **1** the result of the division of one number or mathematical expression by another. **2** the ratio, usu multiplied by 100, between a test score and a measurement on which that score might be expected largely to depend. [Middle English *quocient*, modification of Latin *quotiens* how many times, from *quot* how many]

Qur'an /koo'rahn, koo'ran, kə'rahn, kə'ran/ *noun* see KORAN.

qursh /kooəsh/ *noun* (*pl* **qursh**) a unit of currency in Saudi Arabia, worth 20th of a rial. [Arabic *qirsh*]

q.v. *abbr* used to indicate a cross-reference: which see. [Latin *quod vide*]

qwerty /'kwuhti/ *adj* said of English-language computer and typewriter keyboards: having the conventional arrangement of keys, with the keys *q,w,e,r,t,y* on the left side of the top row of alphabetic characters: *Japanese computers use the qwerty keyboard to input Japanese to the system.*

R¹ *or* **r** *noun* (*pl* **R's** *or* **Rs** *or* **r's**) **1a** the 18th letter of the English alphabet. **b** a written character or design denoting this letter. **c** the sound represented by this letter, one of the English consonants. **2** an item designated as R, *esp* the 18th in a series.

R² *abbr* **1** rabbi. **2** in chemistry, radical. **3** rand. **4** Réaumur (scale of temperature). **5** rector. **6** regiment. **7** Regina. **8** registered (as a trademark). **9** Republican. **10** resistance. **11** reverse (gear). **12** Rex. **13** river. **14** Romania (international vehicle registration). **15** röntgen. **16** in chess, rook. **17** rouble. **18** Royal. **19** rupee.

R³ *noun* **1** in the USA and Australia, a film certified as suitable for people over the age of 18. **2** (*used before a noun*) of or being such a film. [short for RESTRICTED]

r *abbr* **1** radius. **2** railway. **3** rare. **4** recto. **5** right. **6** road. **7** ruled. **8** in cricket, runs.

-r¹ *suffix* forming the comparative degree of adjectives and adverbs of one syllable, and of some adjectives and adverbs of two or more syllables, that end in *e*: *truer; freer.*

-r² *suffix* forming nouns from words that end in *e*, denoting: a person who does a particular activity or is associated with something in particular: *old-timer; teenager; diner.*

RA *abbr* **1** Rear Admiral. **2** in astronomy, right ascension. **3** Royal Academician. **4** Royal Academy. **5** Royal Artillery. **6** República Argentina (international vehicle registration for Argentina).

Ra *abbr* the chemical symbol for radium.

ra /rah/ *interj* see RAH.

RAA *abbr* Royal Academy of Arts.

RAAF *abbr* Royal Australian Air Force.

rabbet¹ /ˈrabit/ *noun chiefly NAmer* = REBATE³.

rabbet² *verb trans* (**rabbeted, rabbeting**) *chiefly NAmer* = REBATE⁴.

rabbi /ˈrabie/ *noun* (*pl* **rabbis**) **1** a Jewish scholar qualified to teach and give advice on Jewish law. **2** a Jewish minister; *specif* the official leader of a Jewish congregation. [Middle English via late Latin from Greek *rhabbi* from Hebrew *rabbī* my master, from *rabh* master + *-ī* my]

rabbinate /ˈrabinət/ *noun* **1** the office or tenure of a rabbi. **2** the whole body of rabbis. [from obsolete *rabbin* rabbi, via French *rabbin* from medieval Latin *rabbinus*, ultimately from Hebrew *rabbī*: see RABBI]

rabbinic /rəˈbinik/ *adj* **1** of rabbis or their writings. **2** of Jewish law or teaching. ➤➤ **rabbinically** *adv.*

rabbinical /rəˈbinikl/ *adj* = RABBINIC.

rabbit¹ /ˈrabit/ *noun* (*pl* **rabbits** *or collectively* **rabbit**) **1a** any of several species of small long-eared mammals that are related to the hares but differ from them in producing naked young and in their burrowing habits: family Leporidae. **b** the soft fur of a rabbit. **c** *NAmer* a hare. **2** *informal* an unskilful player, e.g. in golf, cricket, or tennis. **3** *NAmer* a runner in a long-distance race who sets a fast pace for a teammate. **4** *Brit, informal* a chat. ➤➤ **rabbity** *adj.* [Middle English *rabet*, prob ultimately from early Dutch *robbe*; (sense 4) rhyming slang *rabbit and pork* talk]

rabbit² *verb intrans* (**rabbited, rabbiting**) **1** to hunt rabbits. **2** *Brit, informal* (*often* + on) to talk aimlessly or inconsequentially.

rabbit fever *noun informal* = TULARAEMIA.

rabbit punch *noun* a short chopping blow delivered to the back of the neck. [from the manner in which a rabbit is stunned before being killed]

rabble /ˈrabl/ *noun* **1** a disorganized or disorderly crowd of people; a mob. **2** (**the rabble**) the lowest class of society; the common people. [Middle English *rabel* pack of animals; earlier history unknown]

rabble-rouser *noun* somebody who stirs up anger or violence in a crowd; a demagogue. ➤➤ **rabble-rousing** *adj and noun.*

Rabelaisian /rabiˈlayzi-ən, -zhən/ *adj* marked by the robust humour, extravagant caricature, or bold naturalism characteristic of the French humorist and satirist François Rabelais (d.1553): *They were alone in the hotel but for a fat Frenchwoman of middle age, a Rabelaisian figure with a broad, obscene laugh* — Somerset Maugham.

rabid /ˈrabid, ˈraybid/ *adj* **1** unreasoning or fanatical in an opinion or feeling: *a rabid racist.* **2** of or affected with rabies. ➤➤ **rabidity** /rəˈbiditi/ *noun*, **rabidly** *adv*, **rabidness** *noun.* [Latin *rabidus* mad, from *rabere* to rave]

rabies /ˈraybeez, ˈraybiz/ *noun* a short-lasting usu fatal viral disease of the nervous system of warm-blooded animals, transmitted *esp* through the bite of an affected animal, and characterized by extreme fear of water and convulsions. [Latin *rabies* madness, from *rabere* to rave]

RAC *abbr Brit* **1** Royal Armoured Corps. **2** Royal Automobile Club.

raccoon *or* **racoon** /rəˈkoohn/ *noun* (*pl* **raccoons** *or* **racoons** *or collectively* **raccoon** *or* **racoon**) either of two species of small carnivorous mammals of N America that have a bushy ringed tail and live chiefly in trees: genus *Procyon.* [Virginian Algonquian *äräkhun*]

race¹ /rays/ *noun* **1a** a contest of speed, e.g. in running or riding. **b** (*in pl*) a meeting in which several races, *esp* for horses, are run. **c** a contest or rivalry for an ultimate prize or position: *the race for the league championship.* **2** a track or channel in which something rolls or slides; *specif* a groove for the balls in a ball bearing. **3a** a strong or rapid current of water in the sea, a river, etc. **b** a watercourse used industrially, e.g. to turn the wheel of a mill, or the current flowing in it. **4** *archaic.* **a** a set course, e.g. of the sun or moon, or duration of time. **b** the course of life. **5** a narrow enclosure through which animals pass individually, e.g. to be dipped or branded.

[Middle English *ras* rapid forward movement, also 'the regular course of the sun or moon', from Old Norse *rās*]

race² *verb intrans* **1** to compete in a race. **2** to go or move at top speed or out of control: *His pulse was racing*. **3** said of a motor, engine, etc: to run at a very high speed. ➤ *verb trans* **1** to have a race with (somebody): *She raced her brother to the garden gate*. **2** to enter (e.g. a horse or vehicle) in a race: *He always races his horses at Chepstow*. **3a** to drive (a car, etc) at high speed. **b** to transport or propel (something) at maximum speed. **c** to cause (e.g. an engine) to run at a very high speed.

race³ *noun* **1a** a division of humankind having physical characteristics that are transmissible by descent, e.g. skin colour. **b** the division of humankind into races; racial origin. **c** an ethnic group. **d** a group of people having a common ancestor. **2** an interbreeding group within a species of plants or animals; a subspecies. [early French *race* generation, from Old Italian *razza*]

racecard *noun* **1** the programme of events at a horse race meeting. **2** the printed list of this, showing runners, riders, trainers, and owners.

racecourse *noun* a place or track where races, *esp* horse races, are held.

racehorse *noun* a horse bred or kept for racing.

racemate /rə'seemayt, 'rasimayt/ *noun* in chemistry, a racemic compound or mixture.

raceme /rə'seem/ *noun* a simple stalk of flowers, e.g. that of the lily of the valley, in which the flowers are borne on short side-stalks of about equal length along a tall main stem: compare CYME. [Latin *racemus* bunch of grapes]

race meeting *noun Brit* an individual fixture for horse racing at a particular racecourse.

racemic /rə'seemik, rə'semik/ *adj* denoting a chemical compound or mixture that is composed of equal amounts of DEXTRO-ROTATORY (turning clockwise) and LAEVOROTATORY (turning anti-clockwise) forms of the same compound, and is optically inactive. [French *racémique* from Latin *racemus* bunch of grapes]

racemization *or* **racemisation** /,rasimie'zaysh(ə)n/ *noun* the action or process of changing from an optically active compound into a racemic compound or mixture.

racemose /'rasimohs/ *adj* in botany or anatomy, having racemes or growing in the form of a raceme. [Latin *racemosus* full of clusters, from *racemus* bunch of grapes]

racemose gland *noun* any of various glands in the body that have the appearance of a bunch of grapes.

racer /'raysə/ *noun* **1** a person, animal, or thing, e.g. a boat or car, that races or is used for racing. **2** a turntable on which a heavy gun can be moved. **3** a fast-moving snake of N America: genus *Coluber*.

race relations *pl noun* **1** relations between members of a country's different racial communities. **2** (*treated as sing. or pl*) the branch of sociology studying such relations.

race riot *noun* a riot caused by racial dissension.

racetrack *noun* a closed, usu oval track on which races, e.g. between cars or runners, are held.

raceway *noun chiefly NAmer* **1** a channel for a current of water, e.g. a millrace. **2** a tube protecting electric wires. **3** a racetrack, *esp* a track for harness racing.

rachis /'raykis/ *noun* (pl **rachises** *or* **rachides** /'rakideez, 'ray-/) **1a** the main stem of a plant's flower cluster. **b** an extension of the stalk of a compound leaf that bears the leaflets. **2** the spinal column. **3** the part of the shaft of a feather that bears the barbs. [scientific Latin *rachid-, rachis*, from Greek *rhachis* spine]

rachitis /ra'kietəs/ *noun* = RICKETS. ➤ **rachitic** /ra'kitik/ *adj*. [scientific Latin from Greek *rhachitis* disease of the spine, from *rhachis* spine]

Rachmanism /'rakməniz(ə)m/ *noun Brit* the unscrupulous exploitation of poor tenants by corrupt landlords.

Word history

named after Peter *Rachman* d.1962, English landlord. Rachman used intimidation to make tenants paying controlled rents leave so that he could let the properties for higher rents.

racial /'raysh(ə)l/ *adj* **1** of or based on a race: *racial characteristics*. **2** existing or occurring between people of different races: *racial harmony*. **3** directed towards a particular race or based on distinctions of race: *racial discrimination*. ➤ **racially** *adv*.

racialism *noun* = RACISM. ➤ **racialist** *noun and adj*.

racing *noun* the sport of competing in or organizing races, *esp* horse races.

racing car *noun* a car designed for use in the sport of motor racing.

racing demon *noun* a variation of the card game patience for several players.

racing driver *noun* a driver who takes part in the sport of motor racing.

racism *noun* **1** the belief that race is the primary determinant of human traits and capacities. **2** hostility towards or discrimination against people of races other than one's own. ➤ **racist** *noun and adj*.

rack¹ /rak/ *noun* **1** a framework, stand, or grating on which articles are placed: *a luggage rack*. **2** a bar with teeth on one face for meshing with a pinion or worm gear. **3** (**the rack**) an instrument of torture formerly used to stretch the victim's body. **4** a framework for holding fodder for livestock. **5a** a triangular frame used for arranging pool balls at the beginning of the game. **b** a single game of pool. **6** *NAmer, informal* a bed, or sleep. ✳ **on the rack** under great mental or emotional stress: *So much had her nerves been on the rack for her patron's safety* — Scott. [Middle English, prob from early Dutch *rec* framework]

rack² *verb trans* **1** to cause (somebody) to suffer torture, pain, or anguish: *She was racked by headaches*. **2** to torture (somebody) on the rack. **3** to raise (rents) oppressively. **4** to place (an object) in a rack.

rack³ *noun* a rapid flashy gait of a horse in which each foot touches the ground separately. [origin unknown]

rack⁴ *verb intrans* said of a horse: to move in a rack.

rack⁵ *noun* the front rib section of lamb used for chops or as a roast. [perhaps from RACK¹]

rack⁶ ✳ **rack and ruin/wrack and ruin** a state of destruction or extreme neglect. [Middle English from Old English *wræc* misery, punishment, something driven by the sea]

rack⁷ *verb trans* to draw off (wine or beer) from the lees or sediment. [Middle English *rakken* from Old Provençal *arracar*, from *raca* stems and husks of grapes after pressing]

rack⁸ *or* **wrack** *noun* a wind-driven mass of high, often broken clouds. [Middle English *rak*, prob of Scandinavian origin]

rack⁹ *verb intrans archaic* said of clouds: to fly or scud in high wind.

rack-and-pinion *adj* denoting a mechanism, *esp* a steering system, in which a toothed wheel engages with a notched bar or other shaft to convert linear into rotary motion or vice versa.

racket¹ *or* **racquet** /'rakit/ *noun* **1** a lightweight bat consisting of a netting stretched in an open frame with a handle attached, used in tennis, squash, badminton, and similar games. **2** (*in pl, but treated as sing.*) a game similar to squash for two or four players, played with a hard ball and rackets on a four-walled court. **3** *NAmer* a snowshoe shaped like a racket. [early French *raquette* via Italian *racchetta* from Arabic *rāḥah* palm of the hand]

racket² *noun* **1** a loud and confused noise; a din. **2** *informal*. **a** a fraudulent enterprise operated for profit, *esp* one involving bribery or intimidation. **b** an easy and lucrative means of earning a living. **c** a usu specified occupation or business: *He's in the publicity racket*. **3** *archaic* social whirl or excitement. [prob imitative]

racket³ *verb intrans* (**racketed, racketing**) **1** (+ about/around) to engage in an active, *esp* a dissipated, social life. **2** to move with or make a racket.

racketeer /raki'tiə/ *noun* a person who is involved in fraudulent schemes, *esp* somebody who extorts money or advantages by threats, blackmail, etc. ➤ **racketeering** *noun*.

rackety /'rakiti/ *adj* noisy or rowdy.

rack railway *noun* a railway that has a rack between its running rails that meshes with a gear wheel or pinion on a locomotive.

rack rent *noun* an excessive or unreasonably high rent. [RACK²]

rack-rent *verb trans dated* **1** to charge an excessive rent for (a property). **2** to charge (somebody) an excessive rent. ➤ **rack-renter** *noun*.

rack up *verb trans* to accumulate (a score or amount): *They had racked up 30 points in the first half; He had racked up a huge debt on his credit cards.*

raclette /ra'klet/ *noun* a dish of French or Swiss origin in which slices of potato are cooked with cheese or other toppings, traditionally over a fire but now usually under a grill. [French *raclette*, literally 'small scraper', from the scraping of the melted cheese onto the plate]

racon /'raykon/ *noun chiefly NAmer* a radar transmitter that upon receiving a radar signal emits a signal which reinforces the normal reflected signal or which introduces a code into the reflected signal, *esp* for identification purposes. [contraction of *radar beacon*]

raconteur /rakon'tuh/ *or* **raconteuse** /-'tuhz/ *noun* a man or woman who is very good at telling anecdotes: *He had stories and memories of escapades ... and was a colourful raconteur* — Penny Junor. [French *raconteur*, from Old French *raconter* to tell, from *ra-* RE- + *conter, compter*: see COUNT[1]]

racoon /rə'koohn/ *noun* see RACCOON.

racquet /'rakit/ *noun* see RACKET[1].

racy *adj* (**racier, raciest**) **1** slightly indecent; risqué. **2** full of zest or vigour. **3** said of a flavour: having a strongly marked quality; piquant. **4** having a body fitted for racing. >> **racily** *adv*, **raciness** *noun*. [RACE[3] in the archaic sense 'characteristic flavour or quality']

rad[1] /rad/ *noun* a unit of absorbed dose of ionizing radiation, e.g. X-rays, equal to an energy of 100 ergs per gram of irradiated material. [short for RADIATION]

rad[2] *adj chiefly NAmer, informal* excellent or admirable. [short for RADICAL[1]]

rad. *abbr* **1** radian. **2** radiator. **3** radius.

RADA /'rahdə/ *abbr Brit* Royal Academy of Dramatic Art.

radar /'raydah/ *noun* an electronic system that detects the presence, course, and speed of nearby ships, aircraft, etc by generating high-frequency radio waves and analysing the radio waves reflected back from the objects they strike. [acronym from *radio detection and ranging*]

radar gun *noun* a hand-held electronic device that uses radar technology to measure the speed of a moving object, used *esp* by the police to catch speeding drivers.

radar trap *noun* a stretch of road at which police officers regularly monitor drivers' speed using radar guns.

raddle[1] /'radl/ *noun* = REDDLE. [prob alteration of RUDDLE]

raddle[2] *verb trans* to colour (somebody or something) with reddle.

raddled *adj* said of a person: haggard with age or the effects of a dissipated lifestyle. [origin unknown]

radi- *comb. form* see RADIO-.

radial[1] /'raydi-əl/ *adj* **1** arranged like rays or radii from a central point or axis, or having parts that are arranged in this way. **2** denoting a tyre that has the cords of its fabric running at right angles to the circumference of the tyre: compare CROSSPLY. **3** said of a road: leading from the centre of a town outwards. **4** relating to or in the region of the RADIUS[1] (bone in the forearm). >> **radially** *adv*. [medieval Latin *radialis* from Latin *radius* RAY[1]]

radial[2] *noun* **1** a radial tyre. **2** a radial body part, e.g. an artery. **3** any line in a system of radial lines.

radial engine *noun* an internal-combustion engine with cylinders arranged radially round the crankshaft.

radial-ply *adj* = RADIAL[1] (2).

radial symmetry *noun* a pattern of symmetry, e.g. in animals, in which similar parts are arranged around a central axis: compare BILATERAL SYMMETRY, SYMMETRY.

radian /'raydi-ən/ *noun* a unit of angular measurement that is equal to the angle at the centre of a circle subtended (defined by extending from one side to the other; see SUBTEND) by a part of the circumference equal in length to the radius, taken as 57.3°.

radiant[1] /'raydi-ənt/ *adj* **1a** vividly bright and shining; glowing. **b** expressing love, affection, confidence, or happiness: *a radiant smile*. **c** radiating rays or reflecting beams of light. **2a** emitted or transmitted by radiation: *radiant energy*. **b** of or emitting radiant heat. >> **radiance** *noun*, **radiancy** *noun*, **radiantly** *adv*. [Middle English from Latin *radiant-, radians*, present part. of *radiare*: see RADIATE[1]]

radiant[2] *noun* **1** a point or object from which light or heat emanates; *specif* the part of a gas or electric heater that becomes incandescent. **2** in astronomy, the apparent point of origin on the celestial sphere of a meteor shower. [RADIATE[1] + -ANT[1]]

radiant energy *noun* energy in the form of electromagnetic waves, e.g. heat, light, or radio waves.

radiant flux *noun* the rate of emission or transmission of radiant energy.

radiant heat *noun* heat transmitted by radiation rather than by conduction or convection.

radiate[1] /'raydiayt/ *verb trans* **1a** to send (energy) out in rays or waves. **b** to show or display (a quality, feeling, etc) clearly; to manifest (it): *She radiates health and vitality.* **2** to disseminate (something) from a centre: *Aunt Alexandra sipped coffee and radiated waves of disapproval* — Harper Lee. >> *verb intrans* **1** to be given out in the form of rays. **2** to send out rays of light, heat, or any other form of radiation. **3** to proceed in a direct line from or towards a centre: *The foamy ridges that radiated from her bows suddenly disappeared* — Mark Twain. **4** said of a group of organisms: to spread into new areas and diversify. >> **radiative** *adj*. [Latin *radiatus*, past part. of *radiare*, from *radius* RAY[1]]

radiate[2] /'raydi-ət/ *adj* having rays or radial parts; *specif* having radial symmetry. >> **radiately** *adv*.

radiation /raydi'aysh(ə)n/ *noun* **1** the process of emitting radiant energy in the form of waves or particles. **2** energy radiated in the form of waves or particles, *esp* electromagnetic radiation, e.g. light, or emission from radioactive sources, e.g. alpha rays. **3** a radial arrangement of parts. >> **radiational** *adj*.

radiation sickness *noun* sickness that results from over-exposure to ionizing radiation, e.g. from X-rays or radioactive material, commonly marked by fatigue, nausea, vomiting, loss of teeth and hair, and, in more severe cases, leukaemia.

radiator /'raydiaytə/ *noun* **1** a room heater with a large surface area for radiating heat; *specif* one through which hot water or steam circulates as part of a central heating system. **2** a device with a large surface area used for cooling an internal-combustion engine by means of water circulating through it.

radical[1] /'radikl/ *adj* **1a** affecting or involving the basic nature or composition of something; fundamental: *We have made radical changes to the design.* **b** marked by a considerable departure from the usual or traditional; innovative. **2** designed to remove the root of a disease or all diseased tissue: *radical surgery.* **3a** favouring or tending to make extreme changes in existing views, habits, conditions, or institutions: *a radical reformer.* **b** of or being a political group associated with views, practices, and policies of extreme change. **c** advocating extreme measures to attain a political end: *the radical right.* **4** relating to or involving a mathematical root. **5** of or being a linguistic form from which others have derived. **6** of or growing from the root or the base of a stem. **7** belonging to the root of a musical power. **8** *chiefly NAmer, informal* excellent or admirable. >> **radicalism** *noun*, **radically** *adj*, **radicalness** *noun*. [Middle English from late Latin *radicalis*, from Latin *radic-, radix* root]

radical[2] *noun* **1** a person who is a member of a radical political party or who holds radical views. **2a** in chemistry, a group of atoms that is replaceable in a molecule by a single atom and is capable of remaining unchanged during a series of reactions. **b** = FREE RADICAL. **3a** a mathematical expression involving radical signs. **b** = RADICAL SIGN. **4** a root of a word. **5** a Chinese character used as the basis of other characters.

radical chic *noun derog* fashionable and usu superficial left-wing radicalism.

radicalize *or* **radicalise** /'radikəliez/ *verb trans* to make (somebody or something) radical, *esp* in politics. >> **radicalization** /,radikəlie'zaysh(ə)n/ *noun*.

radical sign *noun* the sign √ placed before a mathematical expression to denote that the square root, or some other root corresponding to an index number placed over the sign, is to be calculated.

radicchio /ra'dikioh/ *noun* (*pl* **radicchios**) a variety of chicory with red cabbage-like leaves, used *esp* in salads. [Italian *radicchio* chicory, from Latin *radicula*: see RADICLE]

radices /'raydiseez/ *noun* pl of RADIX.

radicle /'radikl/ *noun* **1** the lower part of a plant embryo or seedling that includes the embryonic root. **2** the rootlike beginning of a nerve, vein, or similar anatomical structure. **3** = RADICAL[2] (2). >> **radicular** /ra'dikyoolə/ *adj*. [Latin *radicula*, dimin. of *radic-, radix* root]

radii /'raydiie/ *noun* pl of RADIUS[1].

radio[1] /'raydioh/ *noun (pl* **radios**) **1** the transmission and reception of signals by means of electromagnetic waves. **2** a system that transmits and receives signals in this way, *esp* for the purposes of sound broadcasting or two-way communication. **3a** a device designed to receive sound broadcasts; a radio receiver. **b** a device designed to allow two-way communication by radio, e.g. in an aircraft. **4a** a radio broadcasting organization or station: *Radio London*. **b** the radio broadcasting industry. **c** the medium of radio communication. [short for RADIOTELEGRAPHY]

radio[2] *verb* (**radios, radioed, radioing**) ➤ *verb trans* **1** to send or communicate (a message) by radio. **2** to send a radio message to (somebody). ➤ *verb intrans* to send or communicate something by radio.

radio- *or* **radi-** *comb. form* forming words, with the meanings: **1** radio: *radiotelegraphy*. **2a** radiant energy or radiation: *radiobiology*. **b** radioactive: *radioelement*. **c** using ionizing radiation: *radiotherapy*. **d** radioactive isotopes of (a specified element): *radiocarbon*. **3** radius: *radio-ulna*. [French *radio-* from Latin *radius* RAY[1]]

radioactive *adj* of, caused by, or exhibiting radioactivity. ➤ **radioactively** *adv.*

radioactive decay *noun* the disintegration of the nucleus of an atom resulting in the formation of one or more new nuclei with the emission of alpha, beta, or gamma rays.

radioactive waste *noun* the radioactive by-products from the operation of a nuclear reactor or a nuclear fuel reprocessing plant.

radioactivity *noun* the property possessed by some elements, e.g. uranium, of spontaneously emitting alpha or beta rays and sometimes also gamma rays by the disintegration of the nuclei of atoms.

radio astronomy *noun* a branch of astronomy dealing with radio waves received from outside the earth's atmosphere.

radiobiology *noun* a branch of biology dealing with the effects of radiation on living organisms or the use of radioactive materials in biological and medical investigation. ➤ **radiobiological** /-'lojikl/ *adj,* **radiobiologically** /-'lojikli/ *adv,* **radiobiologist** *noun.*

radiocarbon *noun* any of various radioactive isotopes of carbon, *esp* carbon-14, used as a tracer element and in carbon dating.

radiochemistry *noun* a branch of chemistry dealing with radioactive substances and phenomena. ➤ **radiochemical** *adj,* **radiochemist** *noun.*

radio-controlled *adj* remotely controlled by means of a handset that makes use of radio technology.

radioelement *noun* a chemical element that is naturally radioactive.

radio frequency *noun* a frequency, e.g. of electromagnetic waves, intermediate between audio frequencies and infrared frequencies and used *esp* in radio and television transmission.

radiogenic /,raydi-ə'jenik/ *adj* produced by radioactivity.

radiogram /'raydi-əgram, 'raydiohgram/ *noun* **1** *Brit* a combined radio and record player. **2** = RADIOGRAPH[1]. **3** *dated* a telegram sent by radio.

radiograph[1] /'raydi-əgrahf, -graf/ *noun* a picture produced on a sensitive surface by a form of radiation other than light; *specif* an X-ray or gamma ray photograph. ➤ **radiographer** /-'ogrəfə/ *noun,* **radiographic** /-'grafik/ *adj,* **radiographically** /-'grafikli/ *adv,* **radiography** *noun.*

radiograph[2] *verb trans* to produce a radiograph of (something).

radioimmunoassay /,raydioh-imyoonoh'asay/ *noun* IMMUNO-ASSAY (technique for identifying and measuring the concentration of something) of a substance, e.g. insulin, that has been radioactively labelled.

radioimmunology *noun* immunology that makes use of radiological techniques.

radioisotope *noun* a radioactive isotope. ➤ **radioisotopic** /-'topik, -'tohpik/ *adj.*

radiolarian /,raydioh'leəri-ən/ *noun* any of a large order of marine protozoans (single-celled organisms; see PROTOZOAN) with a skeleton made of silica and radiating threadlike extensions for moving about and feeding: order Radiolaria. [Latin order name, from late Latin *radiolus* small sunbeam, dimin. of Latin *radius* RAY[1]]

radiology /raydi'oləji/ *noun* the study and use of radioactive substances and high-energy radiations, *esp* the use of radiant energy, e.g. X-rays and gamma rays, in the diagnosis and treatment of disease. ➤ **radiological** /-'lojikl/ *adj,* **radiologist** *noun.*

radiometer /raydi'omitə/ *noun* an instrument for measuring the intensity of radiant or sound energy. ➤ **radiometric** /-'metrik/ *adj,* **radiometry** /-tri/ *noun.*

radionics /raydi'oniks/ *pl noun* (*treated as sing. or pl*) a technique in complementary medicine that is based on the theory that all living things give off radiation.

radio-opaque *adj* = RADIOPAQUE.

radiopager *noun* a portable electronic device that receives a radio signal to alert the wearer that somebody is trying to contact him or her.

radiopaque /,raydioh'payk/ *adj* fully or nearly opaque to various forms of radiation, e.g. X-rays. ➤ **radiopacity** *noun.*

radiophonic /,raydi-ə'fonik, ,raydioh-/ *adj* denoting or creating sounds that are electronically produced. ➤ **radiophonically** *adv.*

radioscopy /raydi'oskəpi/ *noun* observation of objects opaque to light, *esp* by means of X-rays. ➤ **radioscopic** /-'skopik/ *adj.*

radiosonde /'raydiohsond/ *noun* a miniature radio transmitter carried into the atmosphere, e.g. by an unmanned balloon, together with instruments for broadcasting back details of humidity, temperature, air pressure, etc.

radiotelegraphy *noun* telegraphy carried out by means of radio waves. ➤ **radiotelegraphic** /-teli'grafik/ *adj.*

radiotelephone *noun* an apparatus for enabling telephone messages to be sent by radio, e.g. from a moving vehicle. ➤ **radiotelephonic** *adj,* **radiotelephony** *noun.*

radio telescope *noun* a radio receiver connected to a large aerial for recording and measuring radio waves from celestial bodies.

radiotherapy *noun* the treatment of disease, e.g. cancer, by means of X-rays or radiation from radioactive substances. ➤ **radiotherapeutic** /-'pyoohtik/ *adj,* **radiotherapist** *noun.*

radio-ulna *noun* a bone in the forelimb of an amphibian, e.g. a frog, that represents the fused radius and ulna of less primitive vertebrate animals, e.g. mammals.

radio wave *noun* an electromagnetic wave of radio frequency.

radish /'radish/ *noun* **1** a plant of the mustard family cultivated for its pungent fleshy typically dark red edible root: *Raphanus sativus*. **2** the root of this plant, eaten raw as a salad vegetable. [Middle English, alteration of Old English *rædic*, from Latin *radic-, radix* root, radish]

radium /'raydi-əm/ *noun* an intensely radioactive metallic chemical element of the alkaline-earth group that occurs in minute quantities in pitchblende and some other minerals, and is used chiefly in luminous materials and in the treatment of cancer: symbol Ra, atomic number 88. [Latin *radius* RAY[1] + -IUM]

radium therapy *noun* radiotherapy using radium.

radius[1] /'raydi-əs/ *noun (pl* **radii** /'raydi-ie/ *or* **radiuses**) **1** a straight line extending from the centre of a circle or sphere to the circumference or surface, or the length of this line. **2** a radial part, e.g. a spoke of a wheel. **3a** the circular area defined by a stated radius. **b** a bounded or circumscribed area: *I alerted all police cars within a two-mile radius*. **4** the bone on the thumb side of the human forearm, or a corresponding part in forms of vertebrate animals higher than fishes: compare ULNA. **5** the third and usu largest vein of an insect's wing. **6** an imaginary radial plane dividing the body of a radially symmetrical animal, e.g. a starfish, into similar parts. [Latin *radius* RAY[1], radius]

radius[2] *verb trans* (**radiused, radiusing**) to give a rounded edge to (e.g. a machine part).

radius vector *noun* **1** the length of a line segment from a fixed point, e.g. the origin in a polar coordinate system, to a variable point. **2** an imaginary straight line joining the centre of an attracting body, e.g. the sun, with that of a body, e.g. a planet, in orbit around it.

radix /'raydiks/ *noun (pl* **radices** /-seez/ *or* **radixes**) **1** the base of a number system. **2** a root or rootlike part. [Latin *radix* root]

R Adm. *abbr* Rear Admiral.

radome /'raydohm/ *noun* a housing sheltering a radar antenna, *esp* on an aircraft. [contraction of *radar dome*]

radon /'raydon/ *noun* a radioactive gaseous chemical element of the noble gas group that is used in radiotherapy: symbol Rn, atomic number 86. [from RADIUM + -*on* as in ARGON]

radula /'radyoolə/ *noun (pl* **radulae** /-lee/) a horny band covered with minute teeth found in some molluscs, e.g. snails, and used to tear up food and draw it into the mouth. ➤➤ **radular** *adj.* [Latin *radula* scraper, from *radere* to scrape]

Raelian /'rayli·ən/ *noun* a member of a religious movement believing that life on earth was created by extraterrestrial beings and having a particular interest in human cloning. ➤➤ **Raelian** *adj.* [from the name *Rael*, allegedly given by an extraterrestrial to the movement's founder, Claude Vorilhon, in 1973]

RAeS *abbr* Royal Aeronautical Society.

RAF /,ahr ay 'ef, raf/ *abbr Brit* Royal Air Force.

Rafferty's rules /'rafətiz/ *pl noun Aus, NZ, informal* the complete absence of rules. [from the Irish surname *Rafferty*, prob used as a humorous alteration of English dialect *raffety* irregular, from *raff*: see RAFFISH]

raffia *or* **raphia** /'rafi·ə/ *noun* **1** = RAFFIA PALM. **2** the fibre of the raffia palm used *esp* for making baskets, hats, and table mats. [Malagasy *rafia*]

raffia palm *noun* a palm tree of Madagascar with enormous fan-shaped leaves: *Raphia ruffia.*

raffish /'rafish/ *adj* marked by careless unconventionality; rakish. ➤➤ **raffishly** *adv*, **raffishness** *noun.* [obsolete *raff* jumble, rubbish, disreputable person, from Middle English *raf*, perhaps from early French *raffe, rafle* act of snatching]

raffle[1] /'rafl/ *noun* a lottery in which the prizes are usually goods. [Middle English in the sense 'kind of game with dice', from early French *rafle* act of snatching]

raffle[2] *verb trans* (*often* + off) to give (something) away as a prize in a raffle.

rafflesia /rə'fleezi·ə/ *noun* any of a genus of parasitic tropical plants that have no leaves and a single giant flower smelling of putrid meat: genus *Rafflesia.* [Latin genus name, named after Sir Thomas Stamford *Raffles* d.1826, English colonial administrator in SE Asia, who discovered it]

raft[1] /rahft/ *noun* **1a** a simple flat boat made by tying together a number of logs. **b** a flat usu wooden structure designed to float on water and used as a platform or vessel. **2** a floating cohesive mass, e.g. of seaweed or insect eggs. **3** a foundation slab for a building, usu made of reinforced concrete. [Middle English *rafte* rafter, raft, from Old Norse *raptr* rafter]

raft[2] *verb intrans* to travel by raft, or as if by raft. ➤ *verb trans* **1** to transport (something) by means of a raft. **2** to make (e.g. logs) into a raft to be transported. ➤➤ **rafting** *noun*, **raftsman** *noun.*

raft[3] *noun* a large collection or quantity: *Further delays in implementing the raft of legislation could cause real problems* — Guardian. [alteration of obsolete *raff*: see RAFFISH]

rafter[1] *noun* any of the parallel beams that form the framework of a roof. [Old English *ræfter*]

rafter[2] *noun* **1** a person who manoeuvres logs into position and binds them into rafts. **2** somebody who travels on a raft.

RAFVR *abbr Brit* Royal Air Force Volunteer Reserve.

rag[1] /rag/ *noun* **1a** a piece of old worn cloth. **b** (*in pl*) clothes that are in poor or ragged condition. **2** something resembling a rag, *esp* a scrap or unevenly shaped fragment of something: *a rag of cloud.* **3** *informal* a newspaper, *esp* one that is sensational or poorly written. **✷ lose one's rag** *informal* to lose one's temper. **on the rag** *chiefly NAmer, informal* menstruating. [Old English *ragg* from Old Norse *rögg* tuft, shagginess]

rag[2] *verb trans* (**ragged, ragging**) to apply paint to (e.g. a wall) using a rag to create a marbled effect.

rag[3] *noun* **1** a series of processions and stunts organized by students to raise money for charity. **2** *Brit, informal, dated* an outburst of boisterous fun; a prank.

rag[4] *verb trans* (**ragging, ragged**) **1** *Brit* to torment or tease (somebody). **2** to scold (somebody). [origin unknown]

rag[5] *noun* ragtime music, or a ragtime tune or dance. [short for RAGTIME]

rag[6] *noun* any of various hard rocks used in building. [origin unknown]

raga /'rahgə/ *noun* **1** any of the ancient traditional melodic patterns or modes in Indian music. **2** a musical composition based on one of these traditional patterns. [Sanskrit *rāga* colour, tone]

ragamuffin *or* **raggamuffin** /'ragəmufin/ *noun* **1** a ragged often disreputable person, *esp* a child. **2** = RAGGA. **3** somebody who performs or listens to ragga. [named after *Ragamoffyn*, a demon in the

poem *Piers Plowman* by William Langland d.1400, English poet, perhaps from RAG[1] + early Dutch *moffe* mitten]

rag-and-bone man *noun Brit* a usu itinerant dealer in old clothes, furniture, etc.

ragbag *noun* **1** a bag in which scraps of fabric are stored. **2** a miscellaneous collection: *a ragbag of prejudices.* **3** *informal* a dishevelled or slovenly person.

rag bolt *noun* a bolt that has barbs on its shank to grip the material in which it is set. [RAG[1] in the sense 'jagged projection on cast metal']

rag doll *noun* a stuffed cloth doll.

rage[1] /rayj/ *noun* **1a** violent and uncontrolled anger. **b** (*used in combinations*) anger caused by a particular situation: *road rage.* **c** violent action of a natural force, e.g. the wind or sea. **2** an intense feeling; a passion. **3** a fashionable and temporary enthusiasm, or the object of it: *Enormous hats were all the rage.* **4** *Aus, NZ, informal* a lively party with dancing. [Middle English from early French, from a variant of Latin *rabies* rage, madness, from *rabere* to be mad]

rage[2] *verb intrans* **1** to be in a rage. **2** to be violently stirred up or in tumult: *The wind raged outside.* **3** to be unchecked in violence or effect: *The controversy still rages.* **4** *Aus, NZ, informal* to have an enjoyable time.

ragga /'ragə/ *noun chiefly Brit* a style of reggae dance music with rap monologues. [from RAGAMUFFIN]

raggamuffin /'ragəmufin/ *noun* see RAGAMUFFIN.

ragged /'ragid/ *adj* **1a** said *esp* of clothes: torn or worn to tatters. **b** wearing tattered clothes. **2a** having an irregular edge or outline; jagged: *a ragged shoreline.* **b** executed or performed in an irregular, faulty, or uneven manner: *a rambling ragged book.* **c** said of a margin: not justified. **d** said of an animal: having a shaggy coat. **✷ run somebody ragged** to exhaust somebody. ➤➤ **raggedly** *adv*, **raggedness** *noun.*

ragged robin *noun* a perennial Eurasian plant of the pink family with ragged pink or white flowers: *Lychnis flos-cuculi.*

raggedy /'ragidi/ *adj chiefly NAmer, informal* ragged.

raggee /'rahgee, 'ra-/ *noun* see RAGI.

raggle-taggle /'ragl tagl/ *adj* unkempt or ragged. [from RAGTAG]

ragi *or* **raggee** /'rahgee, 'ragee/ *noun* **1** an E Indian cereal grass forming a staple food crop in E Asia. **2** the seeds of the ragi plant. [Hindi *rāgī*]

raging /'rayjing/ *adj* **1** causing great pain or distress: *raging toothache.* **2** violent or wild. **3** *informal* extraordinary or tremendous: *a raging success.*

raglan /'raglən/ *noun* a loose overcoat with raglan sleeves. [named after F J H Somerset, Baron *Raglan* d.1855, English field marshal, who wore such a coat]

raglan sleeve *noun* a sleeve that extends to the neckline with slanted seams from the underarm to the neck.

ragout /ra'gooh/ *noun* a well-seasoned stew, *esp* of meat and vegetables, cooked in a thick sauce. [French *ragoût*, from *ragoûter* to revive the taste, from *ra-* RE- + *goût* taste, from Latin *gustus*]

rag-rolling *noun* a technique of interior decorating in which a final coat of paint is textured by rubbing it with a cloth.

ragtag /'ragtag/ *adj* **1** scruffy. **2** consisting of a varied or odd mixture: *ragtag civilian militias.*

ragtime *noun* music with a rhythm characterized by strong syncopation in the melody and a regularly accented accompaniment, developed in America in about 1900 and usu played on the piano. [prob from RAGGED + TIME[1]]

rag trade *noun informal* the clothing trade.

ragweed *noun* a N American plant of the daisy family whose pollen is a major cause of hay fever: *Ambrosia artemisia.* [from its deeply-cut leaves]

ragworm *noun* any of several species of marine segmented worms that have pairs of bristly flat appendages used for locomotion and are used as bait by sea anglers: family Nereidae. [from its bristles, which give it a ragged appearance]

ragwort *noun* any of several species of yellow-flowered plants of the daisy family that have deeply cut leaves and are common weeds that are toxic to livestock: genus *Senecio.*

rah *or* **ra** /rah/ *interj chiefly NAmer, informal* a cheer of admiration or encouragement; hurrah.

rah-rah skirt /'rahrah/ *noun* a very short pleated skirt in a style typically worn by cheerleaders.

rai /rie/ *noun* a style of popular music that originated in Algeria and was influenced by traditional Bedouin music. [perhaps from Arabic *ha er-ray*, literally 'that's the opinion', a phrase used in the songs]

raid[1] /rayd/ *noun* **1a** a usu hostile incursion made in order to seize somebody or something: *a cattle raid.* **b** a surprise attack by a small force. **2** a sudden invasion by the police, e.g. in search of criminals or stolen goods. **3** on the Stock Exchange, an attempt to bring down share prices by concerted selling. **4** an act of robbery: *a bank raid.*

Word history
Middle English (Scottish) variant of ROAD in the early senses 'journey on horseback, mounted foray'. Both *raid* and *road* (in these senses) had become obsolete by the end of the 17th cent.; *raid* was revived in the early 19th cent. by the Scottish novelist Sir Walter Scott.

raid[2] *verb trans* **1** to make a raid on (a place or a person). **2** to take or steal something from (a place): *Who's been raiding the stationery cupboard?* ⧊ **raider** *noun.*

rail[1] /rayl/ *noun* **1** a horizontal bar, usu supported by posts, that serves as a barrier, e.g. across a balcony, or as a support on or from which something, e.g. a curtain, may be hung. **2** any of a number of vertical metal or wooden posts that form a fence; a railing. **3a** either of a pair of lengths of rolled steel forming a guide and running surface for trains or other wheeled vehicles. **b** the railway: *She always travels by rail.* **4** a horizontal structural support, e.g. in a door. **5** (*usu in pl*) either of the fences on each side of a horse-racing track. **6** an electrical conductor maintained at a constant voltage and used, e.g. on a printed circuit board, to supply a number of circuit elements with power at a fixed voltage. ✳ **be/go off the rails 1** *informal* to be or become mentally unbalanced; to behave strangely. **2** *informal* to be or become misguided or mistaken. [Middle English *raile* via early French *reille* from Latin *regula* ruler, from *regere* to keep straight, direct, rule]

rail[2] *verb trans* **1** (*often* + off) to enclose or separate (an area) with a rail or rails. **2** to transport (goods) by train.

rail[3] *noun* (*pl* **rails** *or collectively* **rail**) any of numerous wading birds of small or medium size, most of which have very long toes that enable them to run on soft wet ground: family Rallidae. [Middle English *raile* from early French *raale*, prob ultimately from Latin *radere* to scrape, because of the bird's harsh call]

rail[4] *verb intrans* (*often* + against/at) to utter angry complaints or abuse: *Some folks rail against other folks, because other folks have what some folks would be glad of* — Henry Fielding. ⧊ **railer** *noun.* [Middle English *railen* via early French *railler* to mock, and Old Provençal *ralhar* to babble, joke, ultimately from late Latin *ragere* to neigh]

railcar *noun Brit* a railway carriage fitted with its own engine.

railcard *noun Brit* any of various categories of card that entitle the holder to rail fares at reduced rates.

railhead *noun* **1** a point at which a railway meets important roads and other transport routes. **2** the farthest point reached by a railway; the terminal.

railing *noun* **1** a usu vertical rail in a fence or similar barrier. **2** a set of such rails, or the material used for making them.

raillery /'rayl(ə)ri/ *noun* (*pl* **railleries**) good-humoured teasing, or a teasing remark. [French *raillerie*, from early French *railler*: see RAIL[4]]

railroad[1] *noun NAmer* a railway.

railroad[2] *verb trans informal* **1a** to hustle (somebody) into taking action or making a decision: *He was not about to be railroaded by an officious committee-member.* **b** to push (e.g. a proposal) through hastily or without due consideration: *My hon. Friend … says that the Bill must be railroaded through the House, but I remind him that it is three long years since it was introduced* — Hansard. **2** *NAmer* to transport (people or things) by rail. **3** *NAmer* to convict (somebody) with undue haste or by unjust means. ➤ *verb intrans NAmer* to work or travel on the railways.

railway *noun chiefly Brit* **1a** a line of track usu having two parallel lines or rails fixed to sleepers on which trains run to transport goods and passengers. **b** such a track and its assets, e.g. rolling stock and buildings, constituting a single property. **2** a railway network or the organization that runs it: *She works on the railway.*

railwayman *noun* (*pl* **railwaymen**) *chiefly Brit* a man who works on a railway.

raiment /'raymənt/ *noun archaic or literary* clothing; dress: *young girls … who were dressed up in the brightest and lightest of raiment* — Hardy. [Middle English *rayment*, short for *arrayment*, from *arrayen*: see ARRAY[1]]

rain[1] /rayn/ *noun* **1a** water falling in drops condensed from vapour in the atmosphere. **b** a fall of rain; a rainstorm. **c** water that has fallen as rain; rainwater. **2** rainy weather. **3** (*in pl*) the rainy season, *esp* in tropical or sub-tropical climates. **4** a dense flow or fall of something: *There is nothing like a rain of bombs to start one trying to assess one's own achievement* — Patrick White. [Old English *regn*, *rēn*]

rain[2] *verb intrans* **1** said of rain: to fall in drops from the clouds. **2** to fall in profusion. ➤ *verb trans* **1** to send (things) down forcefully and in great numbers: *Heavy blows were rained down on his head.* **2** to bestow (e.g. gifts or compliments) abundantly. ✳ **rain cats and dogs** to rain heavily [possibly a corruption of Greek *katadupoi* cataract, but perhaps from the belief in Norse mythology that cats and dogs could foretell bad weather]. ➤ **rainless** *adj.*

rainbow /'raynboh/ *noun* **1** an arch in the sky consisting of a series of concentric arcs of the colours red, orange, yellow, green, blue, indigo, and violet, formed *esp* opposite the sun by the refraction, reflection, and interference of light rays in raindrops, spray, etc. **2** an array of bright colours. **3** a wide range of things of any kind.

rainbow coalition *noun* an alliance of numerous small political groups, often one that is short-lived and formed to address a particular issue.

rainbow-coloured *adj* of many colours.

rainbow nation *noun* a name given to modern S Africa, with reference to its multiracial population.

rainbow trout *noun* a large stout-bodied reddish trout of Europe and western N America: *Onchorhynchus mykiss.*

rain check *noun NAmer* **1** the stub of a ticket for an outdoor event, kept by a spectator to get free admission to a later performance if the event is interrupted by rain. **2** an assurance that an offer that cannot at present be accepted will remain open; *esp* an assurance that a customer can take advantage of a sale later if the item or service offered is not available, e.g. by being sold out: *If it's OK with you, I'll take a rain check on that.*

raincoat *noun* a long coat made from waterproof or water-resistant material.

raindrop *noun* a single drop of rain.

rainfall *noun* **1** a fall of rain; a shower. **2** the amount of rain that has fallen in a given area during a given time, usu measured by depth.

rainforest *noun* a dense tropical woodland with an annual rainfall of at least 2500mm (about 100in.) and containing lofty broad-leaved evergreen trees forming a continuous canopy.

rain gauge *noun* an instrument for measuring rainfall.

rainmaker *noun* **1** somebody who attempts to produce rain. **2** *NAmer, informal* a highly successful professional person, e.g. a lawyer or businessperson. ➤ **rainmaking** *noun.*

rain off *verb trans* (*usu in passive*) to interrupt or prevent (e.g. a sporting fixture) by rain.

rainproof *adj* said *esp* of clothes: impervious to rain.

rain shadow *noun* an area of relatively light rainfall in the lee of a mountain range.

rainstorm *noun* a storm of or with rain.

rainwater *noun* water that has fallen as rain and is therefore usu soft.

rainy *adj* (**rainier, rainiest**) **1** having or characterized by heavy rainfall: *the rainy season.* **2** wet with rain: *rainy streets.* ➤ **raininess** *noun.*

rainy day *noun* a future period when money or other things may be in short supply: *Keep the cash for a rainy day.*

raise[1] /rayz/ *verb trans* **1a** to lift (something or somebody) to a higher position. **b** to bring (somebody or something) to an upright or standing position. **2** to build or erect (something). **3a** to increase the strength, intensity, degree, or pitch of (something): *Don't raise your voice.* **b** to cause (something) to rise in level or amount: *They have raised the rent again.* **c** to place (somebody) higher in rank or dignity; to elevate (them). **4** to multiply (a quantity) by itself a number of times so as to produce a specified power. **5a** in poker, to increase the amount of (a bet). **b** to bet more than (a previous better). **c** in bridge, to make a higher bid in (a partner's suit). **d** to increase the bid of (one's partner). **6** to bring up (a subject) for consideration or debate: *Why did you have to raise that issue now?* **7** to get (things or people) together for a purpose; to collect (them): *raising funds; raising an army.* **8** to cause (something) to occur or appear: *My joke didn't even raise a smile.* **9a** to rear (a child or an animal). **b** to grow or cultivate (crops or other plants). **10a** to awaken (somebody). **b** to recall (somebody) from death, or as if from death. **11** to end or suspend the operation of (e.g. a siege); to abandon (it). **12** to cause (hunted game) to come out from concealment. **13** to bring (land) in sight on the horizon by approaching. **14** *Brit, informal* to establish radio or telephone communication with (a person or place): *He couldn't raise Melbourne.* **15a** to cause (e.g. a blister) to form on the skin. **b** to cause (e.g. an antibody) to be produced. **16** to bring up the nap of (cloth), esp by brushing. ✻ **raise an eyebrow/one's eyebrows** to show surprise, doubt, or disapproval. **raise Cain** *informal* to create a disturbance [Cain, the first murderer (Genesis 4:2–15); his name became a euphemism for the Devil]. **raise hell 1** *informal* to create a disturbance. **2** *informal* to complain angrily about something. **raise the roof** *informal* to make a loud noise, *esp* by cheering. >> **raisable** *adj,* **raiser** *noun.* [Middle English *raisen* from Old Norse *reisa*]

raise² *noun* **1** *chiefly NAmer* an increase in salary; a rise. **2** an increase of a bet or bid. **3** an act of raising or lifting something, e.g. a weight.

raised beach *noun* a beach formed by sea or lake and now above the present water level as a result of either local movements of the earth's crust or lowering of the sea level.

raisin /'rayz(ə)n/ *noun* a dried grape. >> **raisiny** *adj.* [Middle English from early French *raisin* grape, from Latin *racemus* cluster of grapes or berries]

raising agent *noun* any substance, e.g. yeast, that causes dough to rise; leaven.

raison d'être /,rayzon(h) 'detrə (*French* rezɔ̃ dɛtr)/ *noun* (*pl* **raisons d'être** /,rayzon(h) 'detrə (rezɔ̃ dɛtr)/) the main reason that something exists; its reason for being: *The clergyman is ... paid for this business of leading a stricter life than other people. It is his raison d'être* — Samuel Butler. [French *raison d'être*]

raita /'rietə/ *noun* an Indian side dish consisting of a chopped vegetable, e.g. onion or cucumber, mixed with yoghurt and served cold, usu as an accompaniment to a spiced dish. [Hindi *rāytā*]

Raj /rahj/ *noun* (**the Raj**) British rule in India before it gained independence in 1947. [Hindi *rāj* rule, from Sanskrit *rājya*]

rajah *or* **raja** /'rahjə/ *noun* **1** an Indian or Malayan prince or chief. **2** a person bearing a Hindu title of nobility. [Hindi *rājā* from Sanskrit *rājan* king]

Rajasthani /rahjə'stahni/ *noun* **1** a native or inhabitant of Rajasthan. **2** the Indic language of Rajasthan. >> **Rajasthani** *adj.* [Hindi *Rājasthānī* from *Rājasthān* Rajasthan, region in NW India]

Rajput *or* **Rajpoot** /'rahjpoot/ *noun* a member of a landowning military caste of N India. [Hindi *rājpūt* from Sanskrit *rājaputra* king's son, from *rājan* king + *putra* son]

rake¹ /rayk/ *noun* **1a** a long-handled implement with a head on which a row of projecting prongs is fixed for gathering hay, grass, etc or for loosening or levelling the surface of the ground. **b** any of several implements similar in shape or use, e.g. a tool used to draw together the money or chips on a gaming table. **c** a mechanical implement, usu with rotating pronged wheels, used for gathering hay. **2** an act of raking. [Old English *racu*]

rake² *verb trans* **1** to gather, loosen, or level (something) with or as if with a rake. **2** to scrape (something), e.g. in passing: *The thorns raked her arm.* **3** to sweep the length of (something), *esp* with gunfire. **4** to pull or drag (an object) through something: *He raked his fingers through his hair.* **5** (+ through) to search through (something): *She raked through her handbag and found the ticket.* >> **raker** *noun.*

rake³ *noun* **1** inclination from the perpendicular, *esp* the overhang of a ship's bow or stern. **2** the angle of inclination or slope, *esp* of a stage in a theatre. **3** the angle between the top cutting surface of a tool and a plane at right angles to the surface of the work. [origin unknown]

rake⁴ *verb trans and intrans* to incline, or cause (something) to incline from the perpendicular.

rake⁵ *noun* a dissolute man, *esp* in fashionable society. [short for archaic *rakehell* dissolute person, from RAKE² + HELL]

rake in *verb trans informal* to earn or gain (money) rapidly or in abundance.

rake off *verb trans informal* to collect a share of the profits from something, *esp* illegal profits.

rake-off *noun informal* a share of profits, *esp* those gained dishonestly. [from the use of a rake by a croupier to collect the losing chips in a gambling casino]

rake over *verb trans* = RAKE UP (I).

rake up *verb trans* **1** to revive (something long forgotten or eschewed): *It's no use raking up old grievances.* **2** to find or collect (something), *esp* with difficulty: *She managed to rake up enough money for the rent.*

raki /'rahki/ *noun* a strong grain-based spirit from Turkey and other parts of the Middle East. [Turkish *raki* from Arabic *'araq* sweat, juice, ARRACK]

rakish¹ /'raykish/ *adj* **1** said of a ship, boat, etc: having a smart stylish appearance suggestive of speed. **2** stylish or suggestive of a lively personality; dashing: *She wore her hat at a rakish angle.* >> **rakishly** *adv,* **rakishness** *noun.* [prob from RAKE³, from the raking masts of pirate ships]

rakish² *adj* of or living the dissolute life of a rake; licentious. >> **rakishly** *adv,* **rakishness** *noun.* [from RAKE⁵]

raku /'rahkooh/ *noun* a kind of earthenware fired at a low temperature with lead glazes to produce a dazzling metallic finish, used *esp* in the traditional Japanese tea ceremony. [Japanese *raku,* literally 'enjoyment']

rale /rahl/ *noun* (*usu in pl*) an abnormal wheezing sound that accompanies breathing, due *esp* to liquid in the lungs. [French *râle,* from *râler* to rattle]

rall. *abbr* rallentando.

rallentando /ralən'tandoh/ *adj and adv* in music, to be performed with a gradual decrease in tempo. [Italian *rallentando* slowing down, from *rallentare* to slow down]

rally¹ /'rali/ *verb* (**rallies, rallied, rallying**) > *verb trans* **1** to bring (people) together for a common cause. **2** to summon (personal qualities) in preparation for action: *We'll need to rally our wits.* > *verb intrans* **1** to come together again to renew an effort: *The troops rallied and drove back the enemy.* **2** to recover from illness, a state of depression or degeneration, etc: *After an earlier decline, share prices have begun to rally.* **3** to join in a common cause: *Thousands have rallied to the new party.* **4** to engage in a rally. **5** to drive in a rally. ✻ **rally round** to gather for the purpose of pooling practical or emotional support for somebody or something. >> **rallier** *noun.* [French *rallier* from Old French *ralier* to reunite, from *ra-* RE- + *alier* to unite, from Latin *alligare:* see ALLY¹]

rally² *noun* (*pl* **rallies**) **1** a mass meeting of people sharing a common interest or supporting a common, usu political, cause. **2** an event at which vehicles of a particular type are displayed. **3** a motor race over public roads, often countryside tracks, designed to test both speed and navigational skills. **4** a recovery of strength or courage. **5** a series of strokes interchanged between players, e.g. in tennis, before a point is won.

rally³ *verb trans* (**rallies, rallied, rallying**) *archaic* to ridicule or tease (somebody) in a good-humoured way. [French *railler* to mock]

rallycross *noun* a motor sport in which specially adapted saloon cars race round a one-mile circuit: compare AUTOCROSS, MOTOCROSS. [RALLY² + -*cross* as in CYCLO-CROSS]

RAM /ram/ *abbr* **1** random access memory. **2** *Brit* Royal Academy of Music.

ram¹ /ram/ *noun* **1** an uncastrated male sheep. **2** a battering ram. **3** the weight that strikes the blow in a pile driver. **4** the plunger of a press driven by the pressure exerted by a liquid or a force pump that draws or forces liquid through valves. **5a** a heavy beak on the prow of a warship, formerly used for piercing enemy vessels. **b** a warship equipped with a ram. **6** (**the Ram**) the constellation and sign of the zodiac Aries. [Old English *ramm*]

ram² *verb* (**rammed, ramming**) > *verb trans* **1** to force (something) down or in by driving, pressing, or pushing it: *He rammed his hat down over his ears.* **2** to force the passage or acceptance of (something): *The message had been rammed home.* **3** to strike against (something) violently and usu head-on. **4** to make (e.g. earth) firm and compact by pounding. > *verb intrans* to come into violent contact with something: *Her car rammed into a tree.* ✻ **ram**

something down somebody's throat to force somebody to accept or listen to something, *esp* by constant repetition. ≫ **rammer** noun.

Ramadan or **Ramadhan** /'ramədan, -dahn/ noun the ninth month of the Muslim year, during which fasting is practised daily from dawn to sunset. [Arabic *Ramaḍān*, literally 'the hot month', from *ramada* to be hot]

Raman effect /'rahmən/ noun in physics, a change in wavelength of some of the light that passes through a transparent medium, used when analysing the structure of molecules. [named after C V *Raman* d.1970, Indian physicist]

ramble[1] /'rambl/ verb intrans **1** to walk for pleasure, *esp* in the countryside and without a planned route. **2** to talk or write in a disconnected long-winded fashion. **3** to grow or extend irregularly: *a rambling old house*. ≫ **ramblingly** adv. [perhaps from Middle English *romblen*, frequentative of *romen* ROAM[1]]

ramble[2] noun a leisurely walk taken for pleasure, usu in the countryside and often without a planned route.

rambler noun **1** any of various climbing roses with small, often double, flowers in large clusters. **2** somebody who regularly walks in the countryside for pleasure, *esp* a member of an organization for such walkers.

Rambo /'ramboh/ noun (*pl* **Rambos**) a tough aggressive man who attempts to solve all problems by force or violence. ≫ **Rambo-esque** adj. [named after John *Rambo*, hero of books by David Morrell made into films in the 1980s]

rambunctious /ram'bungkshəs/ adj chiefly NAmer, informal full of youthful energy and boisterousness; rumbustious. ≫ **rambunctiously** adv, **rambunctiousness** noun. [prob alteration of RUMBUSTIOUS]

rambutan /ram'boohtn/ noun **1** a bright red spiny tropical fruit closely related to the lychee. **2** the Malaysian tree that bears this fruit: *Nephelium lappaceum*. [Malay *rambutan* from *rambut* hair]

RAMC abbr Brit Royal Army Medical Corps.

ramekin or **ramequin** /'ramikin, 'ramkin/ noun **1** an individual baking and serving dish. **2** a preparation of cheese with breadcrumbs, puff pastry, or eggs baked in an individual mould. [French *ramequin* from Low German *ramken*, dimin. of early Low German *rōm* cream]

rami /'raymi, 'rami, -ie/ noun pl of RAMUS.

ramie /'raymee, 'ramee/ noun **1** an Asian woody plant of the nettle family: *Boehmeria nivea*. **2** the strong shiny flexible flaxlike fibre yielded by the stem of this plant. [Malay *rami*]

ramification /,ramifi'kaysh(ə)n/ noun **1** (*usu in pl*) a wide-reaching and complex consequence: *The decision would have ramifications for the whole community*. **2a** the act or process of branching out. **b** the arrangement of branches, e.g. on a plant. **3a** a branch or subdivision of anything. **b** a branched structure.

ramify /'ramifie/ verb (**ramifies, ramified, ramifying**) ≻ verb intrans technical to separate into branches, divisions, or constituent parts; to spread out. ≻ verb trans to cause (something) to spread or branch out. [early French *ramifier* from medieval Latin *ramificare*, from Latin *ramus* branch]

ramjet noun a jet engine that uses the flow of compressed air produced by the forward movement of the aeroplane, rocket, etc to burn the fuel. [RAM[2] + JET[1]]

ramose /'raymohs/ adj consisting of or having branches: *a ramose sponge*. [Latin *ramosus* from *ramus* branch]

ramp[1] /ramp/ noun **1** a sloping floor, walk, or roadway leading from one level to another. **2** a stairway for entering or leaving an aircraft. **3** Brit a speedbump. **4** a point at which ongoing roadworks cause a sharp rise or fall in the level of the road. **5** a short usu vertical bend, slope, or curve where a handrail or the top course of a wall changes its direction. **6** Brit, informal on the Stock Exchange, a fraudulent scheme that involves the illicit raising of share prices. [French *rampe* from *ramper* to crawl, rear, of Germanic origin]

ramp[2] verb trans to add a ramp to (something). ≻ verb intrans **1** Brit, informal to inflate a price artificially and fraudulently. **2** said of a plant: to climb or spread vigorously. **3** archaic said of a heraldic animal: to stand or advance menacingly, with forelegs or arms raised. **4** archaic said of an animal: to move or act furiously; to rush around. [Middle English, orig in the senses 'to rear, rage, climb' from Old French *ramper*]

rampage[1] /ram'payj/ verb intrans to rush about wildly or violently. ≫ **rampager** noun. [Scottish, prob from RAMP[2] in the senses 'to rear, rage, climb' + RAGE[2]]

rampage[2] /'rampayj/ noun violent or uncontrolled behaviour. ✳ on the rampage behaving in a wild or violent way, *esp* carrying out a series of violent attacks. ≫ **rampageous** adj.

rampant /'rampənt/ adj **1a** characterized by wildness or absence of restraint, e.g. of opinion or action: *a rampant militarist*. **b** spreading or growing unchecked: *a rampant crime wave*. **2** (*usu used after a noun*) said of a heraldic animal: rearing up on one hind leg with forelegs extended: *a lion rampant*. ≫ **rampancy** /-si/ noun, **rampantly** adv. [Middle English from early French *rampant*, present part. of *ramper* to crawl]

rampart /'rampaht/ noun **1** a broad embankment or wall built as a fortification, e.g. around a fort or city, and usu surmounted by a parapet. **2** a protective barrier; a bulwark. [early French *rampart*, *rempart*, from *ramparer*, *remparer* to fortify, strengthen, from RE- + *emparer* to possess, defend, ultimately from Latin *parare* to prepare]

rampion /'rampi-ən/ noun **1** a European plant related to the harebell, with delicate blue flowers and a tuberous root that can be eaten in salads: genus *Campanula*. **2** a related plant, typically with blue flowers: genus Phyteuma. [prob modification of early French *raiponce* from Old Italian *raponzo*, ultimately from Latin *rapa*, *rapum* turnip, RAPE[3]]

ram raid noun a robbery in which entrance is gained to a building, e.g. a shop or bank, by driving a vehicle at speed through the front window. ≫ **ram-raider** noun, **ram-raiding** noun.

ramrod noun **1** a rod for ramming home the charge in a muzzle-loading firearm. **2** a rod for cleaning the barrels of rifles and other small arms. **3** somebody who is unyielding or rigid, *esp* a strict disciplinarian.

ramshackle adj badly constructed or needing repair; rickety: *The villa … looked to an English eye frail, ramshackle, and absurdly frivolous, more like a pagoda in a tea garden than a place where one slept* — Virginia Woolf. [alteration of *ransackled*, past part. of obsolete *ransackle*, frequentative of RANSACK]

ramsons /'ramsənz, 'ramzənz/ pl noun **1** (*treated as sing. or pl*) a broad-leaved variety of garlic plant found in Europe and Asia: *Allium ursinum*. **2** the bulbous root of this plant, eaten as a relish. [Old English *hramsan*, pl of *hramsa* wild garlic]

ramus /'rayməs, 'ram-/ noun (*pl* **rami** /-mi, -mie/) a projecting or elongated part or branch, e.g. a branch of a nerve. [from Latin *ramus* branch]

RAN abbr Royal Australian Navy.

ran /ran/ verb past tense of RUN[1].

ranch[1] /rahnch/ noun **1** a large farm for raising livestock, *esp* in N America and Australia. **2** chiefly NAmer a farm or area devoted to raising a particular crop or animal: *a poultry ranch*. **3** NAmer a ranch house. **4** NAmer ranch dressing. [Mexican Spanish *rancho* small ranch, from Spanish *rancho* camp, hut]

ranch[2] verb intrans to own, work, or live on a ranch. ≻ verb trans **1** to work as a rancher on (land). **2** to raise (a crop or animal) on a ranch. ≫ **rancher** noun.

ranch dressing noun NAmer a creamy white salad dressing containing milk or buttermilk, mayonnaise, garlic, and parsley.

ranchero /ran'cheəroh/ noun (*pl* **rancheros**) chiefly NAmer a person who works on a ranch in Mexico or the southwestern USA. [Mexican Spanish *ranchero*, from *rancho*: see RANCH[1]]

ranch house noun NAmer a large single-storey house, usu with a low-pitched roof and an open-plan interior.

rancid /'ransid/ adj said of food: smelling or tasting unpleasantly sour as a result of no longer being fresh. ≫ **rancidity** /ran'siditi/ noun, **rancidness** noun. [Latin *rancidus*, from *rancēre* to stink]

rancour (NAmer **rancor**) /'rangkə/ noun bitter and deep-seated ill will or hatred. ≫ **rancorous** /-rəs/ adj, **rancorously** adv. [Middle English *rancour* via French from late Latin *rancor*, from Latin *rancēre* to stink]

rand[1] /rand/ noun (*pl* **rand**) the basic monetary unit of S Africa, divided into 100 cents. [named after the *Rand*, gold-mining district of S Africa]

rand[2] noun a strip, usu of leather, put on a shoe before the layers in the heel are attached. [Middle English in the sense 'border', from Old English]

R & B *abbr* rhythm and blues.

R & D *abbr* research and development.

random[1] /'randəm/ *adj* **1** lacking a definite plan, purpose, or pattern. **2a** marked by absence of bias. **b** relating to, having, or being statistical elements or events with an ungoverned or unpredictable outcome, but with definite probability of occurrence. **c** being or relating to a statistical sample drawn from a population each member of which has equal probability of occurring in the sample. **d** characterized by procedures designed to obtain such samples. ➤➤ **randomly** *adv*, **randomness** *noun*. [Middle English, in the sense 'impetuosity, rush', from Old French *randon* great speed, from *randir* to run, of Germanic origin]

random[2] ✻ **at random** without a definite aim, direction, rule, or method.

random access memory *noun* the working memory of a computer, where programs are loaded before they can be used and in which data can be accessed directly and changed: compare READ-ONLY MEMORY.

randomize *or* **randomise** *verb trans* in statistics, to arrange (e.g. samples) so as to simulate a chance distribution, reduce interference by irrelevant variables, and yield unbiased statistical data. ➤➤ **randomization** /-mie'zaysh(ə)n/ *noun*, **randomizer** *noun*.

random walk *noun* a process, e.g. the random movement of molecules, consisting of a sequence of steps, each of whose characteristics, e.g. magnitude and direction, are determined by chance.

R and R *abbr* **1** rest and recreation. **2** rescue and resuscitation. **3** (*also* **R'n'R**) rock and roll.

randy /'randi/ *adj* (**randier, randiest**) **1** *chiefly Brit, informal* sexually aroused; lustful. **2** *chiefly Scot* rowdy or boisterous. ➤➤ **randily** *adv*, **randiness** *noun*. [prob from obsolete *rand* to rant, from obsolete Dutch *randen, ranten* RANT[1]]

ranee /'rahnee/ *noun archaic* = RANI.

rang /rang/ *verb* past tense of RING[3].

rangatira /rangga'tiərə/ *noun NZ* a Maori chief or noble. [Maori *rangatira*]

range[1] /'raynj/ *noun* **1a** a sequence, series, or scale between limits. **b** in mathematics, the set of values a function may take, *esp* the values that a dependent variable may have. **c** in statistics, the difference between the largest and smallest of a set of values. **2a** a number of individual people or objects forming a distinct class or series. **b** a line of products: *Come and see our new range of garden furniture.* **c** a variety or cross-section: *A wide range of people attended the course.* **3** the space or extent included, covered, or used for something; its scope. **4** the extent of pitch within a melody or within the capacity of a voice or instrument: *The E flat is below my range.* **5a** the distance to which a projectile can be propelled. **b** the distance between a weapon and target. **c** the distance between a camera and the object or person being photographed. **d** the maximum distance a vehicle can travel without refuelling. **e** the distance within which something, e.g. a sense, functions. **6a** a series of things in a line; a row. **b** a large connected group of mountains. **7a** an open region over which livestock may roam and feed, *esp* in N America. **b** the region throughout which a kind of living organism or community naturally lives or occurs. Home ranges, unlike territories, are undefended. **8a** a place where shooting, e.g. with bows, guns, or missiles, is practised. **b** a place where golf drives are practised. **9** a usu solid-fuel fired cooking stove that has one or more ovens and a flat metal, *esp* iron, top with one or more areas for heating pans. [Middle English in the sense 'row of persons', from Old French *renge*, from *rengier* see RANGE[2]]

range[2] *verb intrans* **1** to change or differ within limits: *Their ages ranged from 5 to 65.* **2** to travel or roam at large or freely: *Buffalo ranged the plains.* **3** to extend in a usu specified direction. **4** to include a large number of topics. **5** to live, occur in, or be native to, a specified region. **6** said of a gun or projectile: to have a usu specified range. **7** said *esp* of printing type: to correspond in direction or line; to align: *The lines should range right.* ➤ *verb trans* **1** to set (people or things) in a row or in the proper order: *Troops were ranged on either side.* **2** to place (something) among others in a specified position or situation: *He ranged himself with the radicals in the party.* **3** to roam over or through (an area). **4** to determine or give the elevation necessary for (a gun) to propel a projectile to a given distance. **5** to align (type). [Middle English *rangen* via early French *ranger* from Old French *rengier*, from *renc, reng*: see RANK[1]]

rangefinder *noun* a device for indicating or measuring the distance between a gun and a target or a camera and an object.

ranger /'raynjə/ *noun* **1a** a keeper of a park or forest. **b** an officer who patrols a N American national park or forest. **2a** a member of any of several bodies of law-enforcement officers in N America who patrol a usu specified region. **b** a soldier in the US army specially trained in close-range fighting and raiding tactics. **3** (**Ranger**) *Brit* a senior member of the Guide movement aged from 14 to 19.

Ranger Guide *noun* = RANGER (3).

ranging pole *noun* = RANGING ROD.

ranging rod /'raynjing/ *noun* a rod, usu painted with alternate red and white stripes, used in surveying to mark a straight line.

rangy /'raynji/ *adj* (**rangier, rangiest**) **1** said of a person: tall and slender. **2** said of an animal: long-limbed and long-bodied. ➤➤ **ranginess** *noun*.

rani /'rahnee/ *noun* (*pl* **ranis**) a Hindu queen or princess, *esp* the wife of a rajah. [Hindi *rānī* from Sanskrit *rājñī*, fem of *rājan* king]

rank[1] /rangk/ *noun* **1a** a degree or position in a hierarchy or order; *specif* an official position in the armed forces. **b** high social position: *the privileges of rank.* **2a** a row, line, or series of people or things: *ranks of trees.* **b** a line of soldiers standing side by side. **3** (**the ranks**) the ordinary members of an armed force as distinguished from the officers. **4** (*in pl*) the people belonging to a group or class: *The company announced that some new members would be joining its ranks.* **5** any of the eight rows of squares that extend across a chessboard: compare FILE[3] (2). **6** *Brit* a place where taxis wait to pick up passengers. **7** a complete set of organ pipes of the same type. [early French *renc, reng* line, place, row, of Germanic origin]

rank[2] *verb intrans* to take or have a position in relation to others. ➤ *verb trans* **1** to arrange (people or things) in lines or in a regular formation. **2** to determine the relative position of (somebody or something); to rate (them). **3** *NAmer* to outrank (e.g. an officer).

rank[3] *adj* **1** offensive in odour or flavour. **2** offensively gross or coarse. **3a** shockingly conspicuous; flagrant: *rank disloyalty.* **b** absolute or complete: *a rank outsider.* **4a** said of vegetation: excessively vigorous and often coarse in growth. **b** said of a place: covered in such vegetation. ➤➤ **rankly** *adv*, **rankness** *noun*. [Old English *ranc* overbearing, strong; related to Old English *riht* RIGHT[1]]

rank and file *noun* (*treated as sing. or pl*) **1** the ordinary members of an armed force as distinguished from the officers. **2** the ordinary members of an organization, society, or nation as distinguished from the leading or principal members: *rank and file members of the orchestra.*

ranker *noun* a person who serves or has served in the ranks, *esp* a commissioned officer promoted from the ranks.

ranking[1] *noun* a position in a hierarchy or on a scale.

ranking[2] *adj* **1** (*used in combinations*) having a rank of a specified kind: *high-ranking.* **2** *chiefly NAmer* having a high or the highest position.

rankle /'rangkl/ *verb intrans* to cause continuing anger, irritation, or bitterness: *But the slanders of the pen pierce to the heart; they rankle longest in the noblest spirits* — Washington Irving. [Middle English *ranclen* to fester, via early French *rancler* and Old French *draoncle, raoncle* festering sore, from Latin *dracunculus*, dimin. of *draco* serpent]

ransack /'ransak/ *verb trans* **1** to go through (a place) randomly stealing things and causing general chaos and destruction. **2** to search (a place) thoroughly. ➤➤ **ransacker** *noun*. [Middle English *ransaken* from Old Norse *rannsaka*, from *rann* house + *-saka* to search]

ransom[1] /'ransəm/ *noun* **1** a price paid or demanded for the release of a captured or kidnapped person. **2** the act of freeing a captive person by paying a ransom. ✻ **hold somebody to ransom 1** to kidnap somebody and demand money for their release. **2** to try to make somebody do something by threatening to hurt or damage them. [Middle English *ransoun* via Old French *rançon* from Latin *redemption-, redemptio*: see REDEMPTION]

ransom[2] *verb trans* **1** to free (somebody) from captivity or punishment by paying a ransom. **2** to deliver or redeem (somebody), *esp* from sin or its consequences.

rant[1] /rant/ *verb intrans* to talk in a noisy, excited, or declamatory manner. ➤ *verb trans* to say or announce (something) bombastically. ➤➤ **ranter** noun, **rantingly** adv. [obsolete Dutch ranten, randen]

rant² noun a loud, impassioned, or bombastic extravagant speech.

ranunculaceous /rə,nungkyoo'layshəs/ adj belonging to the buttercup family of plants: family Ranunculaceae. [from the Latin family name, from ranunculus: see RANUNCULUS]

ranunculus /rə'nungkyoolas/ noun (pl **ranunculuses** or **ranunculi** /-lie/) any of a large widely distributed genus of plants of the buttercup family that includes the buttercups and crowfoots and that typically have yellow flowers with five petals: genus Ranunculus. [Latin genus name, from ranunculus tadpole, crowfoot, dimin. of rana frog; perhaps because many species grow in water or in damp places where frogs may be found]

RAOC abbr Brit Royal Army Ordnance Corps.

rap¹ /rap/ noun **1** a sharp blow or knock, or the sound made by it. **2** a sharp rebuke or criticism. **3** informal the responsibility for or adverse consequences of an action: I ended up taking the rap. **4** chiefly NAmer, informal a charge, esp a criminal charge. **✳ a rap on/over the knuckles** informal a scolding. [Middle English rappe, prob of imitative origin]

rap² verb (**rapped, rapping**) ➤ verb trans **1** to strike (something hard) with a sharp blow. **2** to strike (something) against something hard. **3** (+ out) to utter (e.g. a command) abruptly and forcibly. **4** informal to criticize (somebody) sharply: Judge raps police over treatment of detainees. ➤ verb intrans to strike a quick sharp blow.

rap³ noun **1** chiefly NAmer, informal talk or conversation. **2** a type of pop music of black American origin characterized by rapidly chanted lyrics accompanied by electronic music with a heavy beat. [origin unknown]

rap⁴ verb intrans (**rapped, rapping**) **1** chiefly NAmer, informal to talk freely and frankly. **2** to sing or chant the lyrics to rap music. ➤➤ **rapper** noun.

rap⁵ ✳ **not care/give a rap** dated, informal not to care in the least: And all the while you are being built alive into a social structure you don't care a rap about — Willa Cather; After that I don't give a rap what happens — Jack London. [archaic rap counterfeit coin formerly common in Ireland, smallest coin, prob from Irish Gaelic ropaire robber]

rapacious /rə'payshəs/ adj **1** excessively grasping or covetous. **2** said of an animal: living on prey. ➤➤ **rapaciously** adv, **rapaciousness** noun, **rapacity** noun. [Latin rapac-, rapax, from rapere to seize]

rape¹ /rayp/ noun **1a** the crime of forcing somebody to have sexual intercourse against his or her will. **b** an instance of this crime. **2** the act or an instance of robbing or despoiling: the rape of the countryside. **3** an outrageous violation, e.g. of a principle or institution.

rape² verb trans **1** said of a man: to commit rape on (somebody). **2** to treat (something) in a violent or destructive way; to despoil (it). ➤➤ **raper** noun. [Middle English rapen to take by force, from Latin rapere]

rape³ noun **1** a European plant of the mustard family that has bright yellow flowers and is widely grown as a forage crop and for its seeds which yield rapeseed oil: Brassica napus. **2** any of several species of related plants: genus Brassica. [Middle English from Latin rapa, rapum turnip, rape]

rape⁴ noun the remains of grapes after they have been pressed, which are used for making vinegar. [French râpe grape stalk, prob of Germanic origin]

rapeseed noun the seed of the rape plant, used for making oil.

rapeseed oil noun an oil obtained from rapeseed and turnip seed and used chiefly as a cooking oil and lubricant.

raphe or **rhaphe** /'rayfee/ noun (pl **raphae** or **rhaphae** /'rayfi·ee/) a seam or ridge, e.g. at the union of the two halves of a part or organ of the body or on a seed. [Greek rhaphē seam, from rhaptein to sew]

raphia /'rafi·ə/ noun see RAFFIA.

raphide /'rafied/ noun (pl **raphides** /'rafideez/) any of the needle-shaped crystals, usu of calcium oxalate, that develop in some plant cells. [French raphide from Greek rhaphides, pl of rhaphid-, rhaphis needle]

rapid¹ /'rapid/ adj moving, acting, or occurring with speed; swift. ➤➤ **rapidity** /rə'piditi/ noun, **rapidly** adv, **rapidness** noun. [Latin rapidus seizing, sweeping, rapid, from rapere to seize, sweep away]

rapid² noun (usu in pl) a part of a river where the water flows swiftly over a steep usu rocky slope in the river bed.

rapid eye movement noun rapid movement of the eyes that occurs during the phases of sleep when dreaming is taking place.

rapid-fire adj **1** firing shots in rapid succession. **2** said esp of speech: proceeding with or characterized by rapidity, liveliness, or sharpness: rapid-fire interrogation.

rapier /'raypi·ə/ noun a straight two-edged sword with a narrow pointed blade. [early French (espee) rapiere rapier (sword), from râpe rasp, grater, because its perforated handle resembles a grater]

rapine /'rapien/ noun literary the forcible seizing and destroying of other people's property; pillage. [Middle English rapyne from Latin rapina, from rapere to seize, rob]

rapist /'raypist/ noun a man who commits rape.

rapparee /rapə'ree/ noun archaic a 17th-cent. Irish irregular soldier or bandit. [Irish Gaelic rapaire short pike]

rappee /ra'pee/ noun a pungent snuff made from dark tobacco leaves. [French (tabac) râpé, literally 'grated tobacco']

rappel¹ /rə'pel/ verb intrans (**rappelled, rappelling**) to abseil. [French rappel, literally 'recall', because the rope is looped around a firm object and brought back to the climber]

rappel² noun an act of abseiling.

rappen /'rahpən, 'rapən/ noun (pl **rappen**) a unit of currency in German-speaking parts of Switzerland and in Liechtenstein, worth 100th of a Swiss franc. [German Rappen, literally 'raven'; from the raven's head depicted on earlier German coins]

rapport /ra'paw/ noun a sympathetic or harmonious relationship. [French rapport from rapporter, literally 'to bring back', from RE- + aporter to bring, ultimately from Latin portare to carry]

rapporteur /rapaw'tuh/ noun a person responsible for preparing and presenting reports, e.g. from a committee to a higher body. [French rapporteur from rapporter: see RAPPORT]

rapprochement /ra'proshmonh/ noun the reestablishment of cordial relations, esp between nations. [French rapprochement from rapprocher to bring together, from RE- + Old French aprochier to approach, from Latin appropiare: see APPROACH¹]

rapscallion /rap'skalyən/ noun archaic a rascal. [alteration of rascallion, from RASCAL]

rapt /rapt/ adj **1** completely engrossed. **2** blissfully happy or joyful; enraptured. **3** Aus, informal = WRAPPED. ➤➤ **raptly** adv, **raptness** noun. [Middle English from Latin raptus, past part. of rapere to seize]

raptor /'raptə/ noun a bird of prey. [Latin raptor plunderer, from rapere to seize]

raptorial /rap'tawri·əl/ adj **1** said esp of a bird: living by hunting prey; predatory. **2** said of birds' feet: adapted for seizing prey.

rapture /'rapchə/ noun **1** a state or experience of being carried away by overwhelming emotion, esp joyous ecstasy. **2** (usu in pl) a state or expression of extreme happiness or enthusiasm: She went into raptures over the new car. **3** a mystical experience in which the spirit is exalted to a knowledge of divine things. ➤➤ **rapturous** /-rəs/ adj, **rapturously** /-rəsli/ adv, **rapturousness** /-rəsnis/ noun. [Latin raptus: see RAPT]

rara avis /,rahrə 'ayvis, ,reərə/ noun (pl **rara avises** or **rarae aves** /,rahri 'ayveez, ,reəri/) a rare or unusual person or thing. [Latin rara avis rare bird]

rare¹ /reə/ adj **1** seldom occurring or found: a rare moth. **2** marked by unusual quality, merit, or appeal: He showed rare tact. ➤➤ **rareness** noun. [Middle English from Latin rarus]

rare² adj said of red meat: cooked lightly so that the inside is still red. [alteration of Middle English rear from Old English hrēre boiled lightly]

rarebit noun = WELSH RAREBIT.

rare earth noun any of a series of metallic elements that includes the elements with atomic numbers from 58 to 71, usu lanthanum, and sometimes yttrium and scandium.

rare-earth element noun = RARE EARTH.

rare-earth metal noun = RARE EARTH.

raree show /'reeree/ noun archaic a side show or peep show. [alteration of rare show]

rarefaction /,reəri'faksh(ə)n/ noun **1** the act or an instance of rarefying. **2** a state or region of minimum pressure in a medium, e.g. the atmosphere, through which longitudinal waves, e.g. sound waves, pass. [French raréfaction from medieval Latin rarefaction-, rarefactio, from Latin rarefacere: see RAREFY]

rarefied /'reərifīed/ *adj* **1** said of air or the atmosphere: of a density that is lower than normal; thin. **2** very high or exalted, e.g. in rank: *She moved in rarefied political circles.* **3** intended for an elite or for the initiated only; esoteric or abstruse.

rarefy /'reərifie/ *verb* (**rarefies, rarefied, rarefying**) ➤ *verb trans* **1** to make (e.g. air or the atmosphere) less dense. **2** to make (something) more spiritual, refined, or abstruse. ➤ *verb intrans* to become less dense; to thin out. [Middle English *rarefien, rarifien* via French from Latin *rarefacere,* from *rarus* RARE¹ + *facere* to make]

rare gas *noun* = NOBLE GAS.

rarely *adv* **1** not often; seldom. **2** in an extreme or exceptional manner. **3** *archaic* with rare skill; excellently.

raring /'reəring/ *adj informal* full of enthusiasm or eagerness: *The horses were raring to go.* [present part. of English dialect *rare* to rear, alteration of REAR³]

rarity /'reəriti/ *noun* (*pl* **rarities**) **1** the quality, state, or fact of being rare. **2** somebody or something rare: *Notice Neptune, though, taming a sea-horse, thought a rarity, which Claus of Innsbruck cast in bronze for me*   Robert Browning.

rascal /'rahsk(ə)l/ *noun* **1** a mischievous person or animal. **2** an unprincipled or dishonest person. ➤➤ **rascality** /rah'skaliti/ *noun,* **rascally** *adj and adv.* [Middle English *rascaile* rabble, one of the rabble, prob from early French *rasque* mud]

raschel /rah'shel/ *noun* a type of warp-knitted fabric usu with open-work patterns: compare TRICOT. [shortening of *Raschel (machine)* a kind of loom, from German *Raschelmaschine,* named after *Rachel* (Elisa Félix) d.1858, French actress]

rase /rayz/ *verb trans* see RAZE.

rash¹ /rash/ *adj* acting with or resulting from undue haste or impetuosity. ➤➤ **rashly** *adv,* **rashness** *noun.* [Middle English *rasch* quick, of Germanic origin]

rash² *noun* **1** an outbreak of reddening or spots on the body. **2** a large number of instances of a specified thing during a short period: *There had been a rash of arrests.* [obsolete French *rache* scurf, from Latin *rasus,* past part. of *radere* to scrape]

rasher /'rashə/ *noun* a thin slice of bacon or ham. [perhaps from obsolete *rash* to cut, from Middle English *rashen*]

rasp¹ /rahsp/ *verb trans* **1** to rub (a surface) with something rough; *specif* to file (something) with a rasp. **2** to grate upon (somebody or their nerves); to irritate (them). **3** to say (something) in a grating tone. ➤ *verb intrans* to make a grating sound. ➤➤ **rasper** *noun,* **raspingly** *adv.* [Middle English *raspen,* of Germanic origin]

rasp² *noun* **1** a coarse file with rows of cutting teeth. **2** a rasping sound, sensation, or effect.

raspberry /'rahzb(ə)ri/ *noun* (*pl* **raspberries**) **1** any of various reddish pink edible berries that grow in clusters. **2** the low-growing shrub of the rose family that bears this berry: *Rubus idaeus.* **3** *informal* a rude sound made by sticking the tongue out and blowing noisily. [English dialect *rasp* raspberry + BERRY¹; (sense 3) rhyming slang *raspberry tart* fart]

Rasta /'rastə/ *noun and adj informal* = RASTAFARIAN.

Rastafarian /rastə'feəri·ən, -'fahri·ən/ *noun* a member of a religious and political movement among black W Indians that takes the former Emperor of Ethiopia, Haile Selassie, to be God, and looks for the redemption of the black race and the establishment of a homeland in Ethiopia. ➤➤ **Rastafarian** *adj,* **Rastafarianism** *noun.* [from *Ras Tafari,* literally 'Prince Tafari', the name of Haile Selassie d.1974, Emperor of Ethiopia, before his coronation]

Rastaman *noun* (*pl* **Rastamen**) *informal* a male Rastafarian.

raster /'rastə/ *noun* a pattern of parallel lines, the intensity of which is controlled to form an image on a television screen. [German *Raster* from Latin *raster, rastrum* rake, from *radere* to scrape]

rat¹ /rat/ *noun* **1** any of numerous species of rodents that resemble mice but are considerably larger and are widely regarded as pests and carriers of disease: genus *Rattus* and other genera. **2** *informal.* **a** a contemptible or wretched person; *specif* somebody who betrays or deserts friends or associates. **b** somebody who continues to work while colleagues are on strike; a blackleg. **3** *NAmer, informal* a person who spends a lot of time in a specified place: *a street rat.* ➤➤ **ratlike** *adj.* [Old English *ræt*]

rat² *verb intrans* (**ratted, ratting**) **1** to catch or hunt rats. **2** *informal* to desert e.g. one's party or cause. **3** *informal* (+ on) to betray or inform on one's associates. **4** *informal* (+ on) to default on an agreement. ➤➤ **ratting** *noun.*

rata /'rahtə/ *noun* any of several species of New Zealand trees of the myrtle family that bear bright red flowers and yield a hard dark red wood: genus *Metrosideros.* [Maori *rata*]

ratable /'raytabl/ *adj* see RATEABLE.

ratafia /ratə'fiə/ *noun* **1** any of various liqueurs flavoured with almonds or fruit. **2** a small sweet almond-flavoured biscuit or cake. [French *ratafia* liqueur flavoured with almonds]

rataplan /ratə'plan/ *noun* the sound of drumming. [French *rataplan,* of imitative origin]

rat-arsed *adj Brit, coarse slang* very drunk.

rat-a-tat /ˌrat ə 'tat/ *or* **rat-a-tat-tat** /ˌrat ə tat 'tat/ *noun* a sharp repeated knocking or tapping sound. [imitative]

ratatouille /ratə'tooh·i (*French* ratatuːj)/ *noun* a dish containing tomatoes, onions, and other vegetables, typically aubergines, courgettes, and peppers, stewed slowly in a vegetable stock until most of the liquid has evaporated. [French *ratatouille* from *touiller* to stir, from Latin *tudiculare;* see TOIL²]

ratbag *noun Brit, informal* an unpleasant or disagreeable person.

ratchet /'rachit/ *noun* **1** a mechanism that consists of a bar or wheel with angled teeth into which a cog, etc drops so that motion is allowed in one direction only. **2** a toothed wheel held in position or turned by a notched sliding bolt. [French *rochet* spool, ratchet, alteration of early French *rocquet* lance head, of Germanic origin]

ratchet wheel *noun* = RATCHET (2).

rate¹ /rayt/ *noun* **1** a quantity, amount, or degree of something measured per unit of something else. **2** a charge, payment, or price fixed according to a ratio, scale, or standard: *the rate of exchange; a good rate of interest.* **3** a fixed ratio between two things. **4** (*usu in pl*) a tax levied by a British local authority, based on property values. ✳ **at any rate** in any case; anyway. **at a rate of knots** *Brit, informal* very fast. [Middle English via French from medieval Latin *rata* from *ratus,* past part. of *reri* to determine, calculate, in the phrase (*pro*) *rata* (*parte*) according to a fixed proportion]

rate² *verb trans* **1** to assign (somebody or something) a relative rank or class. **2** to assign a rate to (e.g. a job or property). **3** to consider (somebody or something) to be of a particular standard: *She was rated an excellent pianist.* **4** to be worthy of (something); to deserve (it): *He now rates his own show.* **5** *informal* to think highly of (somebody or something): *I don't rate Spurs' chances of avoiding relegation.* ➤ *verb intrans* to be estimated at a specified level: *This rates as the best show ever staged in London.*

rate³ *verb trans archaic* to scold (somebody) angrily; to berate (them). [Middle English *raten;* earlier history unknown]

-rate *comb. form* forming adjectives, with the meaning: of the level of quality specified: *fifth-rate.*

rateable *or* **ratable** *adj* capable of being rated, estimated, or apportioned. ➤➤ **rateability** /-tə'biliti/ *noun,* **rateably** *adv.*

rateable value *noun* the estimated value of a British commercial property on which annual rate payments are calculated.

ratel /'raytl, 'raytel/ *noun* an African or Asiatic nocturnal carnivorous mammal resembling the badger: *Mellivora capensis.* [Afrikaans *ratel,* literally 'rattle', from early Dutch]

rate of exchange *noun* = EXCHANGE RATE.

ratepayer *noun* in Britain, an ordinary citizen regarded as a user of local or national services and somebody to whom local or national governments are accountable.

rather¹ /'rahdhə/ *adv* **1** more readily or willingly; sooner: *I left rather than cause trouble; I'd rather not go.* **2** to some degree; somewhat: *It's rather warm; The jacket is rather too big.* **3** somewhat excessively: *It's rather far for me.* **4** more properly, reasonably, or truly: *He is my father, or rather my stepfather.* **5** on the contrary; instead: *His health did not improve, but rather grew worse.* [Old English *hrathor,* compar of *hrathe* quickly]

rather² *interj Brit, dated* used to express enthusiastic approval or acceptance.

rathskeller /'rahtskelə (*German* ratskelər)/ *noun NAmer* a restaurant or beer cellar modelled on the cellar of a German town hall. [obsolete German *Rathskeller* restaurant in the basement of a town hall, from *Rat* council + *Keller* cellar]

ratify /'ratifie/ *verb trans* (**ratifies, ratified, ratifying**) to approve or confirm (e.g. a treaty) formally, so that it can come into force.

>> **ratifiable** *adj*, **ratification** /-fi'kaysh(ə)n/ *noun*, **ratifier** *noun*. [Middle English *ratifien* via French from medieval Latin *ratificare*, from Latin *ratus*: see RATE¹]

rating /'rayting/ *noun* **1** a classification according to grade. **2** a relative estimate or evaluation; standing: *The school has a good academic rating.* **3** (*in pl*) any of various indexes that list television programmes, new records, etc in order of popularity. **4** *Brit* a noncommissioned sailor, *esp* an ordinary seaman. **5** in sailing, a handicap given to a racing boat.

ratio /'rayshioh/ *noun* (*pl* **ratios**) **1** the relationship in quantity, number, or degree between one thing and another; proportion. **2** the indicated division of one mathematical expression by another. [Latin *ratio*: see REASON¹]

ratiocinate /rati'osinayt/ *verb intrans formal* to reason logically or formally. >> **ratiocination** /-'naysh(ə)n/ *noun*, **ratiocinative** /-tiv/ *adj*, **ratiocinator** *noun*. [Latin *ratiocinatus*, past part. of *ratiocinari* to reckon, from *ratio*: see REASON¹]

ration¹ /'rash(ə)n/ *noun* **1** a share or amount, e.g. of food, that somebody is allowed officially during a time of shortage, or that a person allows himself or herself. **2** (*in pl*) regular supplies of food given to troops in wartime. **3** (*in pl*) food supplies generally; provisions. [French *ration* from Latin *ration-, ratio*: see REASON¹]

ration² *verb trans* **1** to limit (a person or commodity) to a fixed ration: *Sugar was strictly rationed.* **2** to use (something) sparingly. **3** (*often* + out) to distribute or divide (e.g. commodities in short supply) in fixed quantities.

rational¹ *adj* **1** having, based on, or compatible with reason; reasonable: *rational behaviour.* **2** endowed with the ability to think logically: *rational beings.* **3** having a value that is a rational number. **4** denoting a mathematical expression that is the quotient of two polynomials with coefficients that are rational numbers. >> **rationality** /-'naliti/ *noun*, **rationally** *adv*. [Middle English *racional* from Latin *rationalis*, from *ration-, ratio*: see REASON¹]

rational² *noun* a number, e.g. 2/3, 4/1, or -0.16, that can be expressed as the result of dividing one integer by another: compare IRRATIONAL², SURD².

rationale /rashə'nahl/ *noun* **1** a logical basis for or explanation of beliefs, practices, or phenomena. **2** an underlying reason; a basis. [Latin *rationale*, neuter of *rationalis*: see RATIONAL¹]

rationalise *verb trans* see RATIONALIZE.

rationalism *noun* **1** the belief that reason, not emotion or intuition, should govern the actions that people take. **2** a theory that reason is a source of knowledge superior to and independent of sense perception.

Editorial note ———
Philosophical rationalists, such as Plato, Descartes, Leibniz, and Spinoza, rejected the empiricist claim that all our knowledge is grounded in experience. Treating mathematics as a model for other kinds of knowledge, they claimed that the exercise of reason could grasp the fundamental principles of nature and morality — Professor Christopher Hookway.

3 reliance on reason for the establishment of religious truth. >> **rationalist** *adj and noun*, **rationalistic** /-'listik/ *adj*, **rationalistically** /-'listikli/ *adv*.

rationalize *or* **rationalise** *verb trans* **1** to attribute (e.g. one's actions) to rational and creditable motives, without analysis of true, *esp* unconscious, motives, in order to provide plausible reasons for conduct: *Mankind has a powerful need to rationalize its actions* — Enoch Powell. **2** to increase the efficiency of (e.g. an industry) by more effective organization, usu entailing reductions in the workforce. **3** to free (a mathematical expression) from parts that are irrational numbers. >> *verb intrans* to provide plausible reasons for one's actions, opinions, etc: *His ability to rationalise verged on the psycopathic* — Guardian. >> **rationalization** /-'zaysh(ə)n/ *noun*, **rationalizer** *noun*.

rational number *noun* = RATIONAL².

ratite /'ratiet/ *noun* a bird, *esp* an ostrich, emu, moa, or kiwi, with a flat breastbone. >> **ratite** *adj*. [Latin *ratitus*, from *ratis* raft]

rat kangaroo *noun* any of several species of small ratlike Australian marsupials with long hind legs like those of the kangaroo: family Potoroidae. Also called POTOROO.

ratline /'ratlin/ *noun* any of the short transverse ropes attached to the shrouds of a ship to form rungs. [origin unknown]

ratoon¹ /ra'toohn/ *noun* a new shoot that develops from the root of the sugarcane or other perennial plant after cropping. [Spanish *retoño*, from *retoñar* to sprout, from RE- + *otoñar* to grow in autumn, from *otoño* autumn, from Latin *autumnus*]

ratoon² *verb intrans* said of a plant: to sprout from the root. >> *verb trans* to cause (a plant) to sprout from the root.

ratpack *noun informal* journalists and photographers who aggressively pursue the subjects of their stories, often as a group.

rat race *noun informal* a fiercely competitive and wearisome activity; *specif* the struggle to maintain one's position in a career or survive the pressures of modern urban life.

rat run *noun* **1** a path habitually taken by a rat. **2** *Brit, informal* a minor or side road used by drivers to avoid congestion in the rush hour.

ratsbane /'ratsbayn/ *noun literary* any kind of rat poison.

rattail *or* **rat's tail** *noun* **1** a horse's tail with little or no hair. **2** (*usu in pl*) something resembling the tail of a rat: *Her wet hair hung in rattails.*

rattan /rə'tan/ *noun* **1** a tropical climbing palm tree with very long tough stems: genus *Calamus*. **2** a part of the stem of a rattan used *esp* for walking sticks and wickerwork. [Malay *rotan*]

ratted *adj Brit, informal* drunk. [prob from the proverbial association of rats with drunkenness]

ratter *noun* a person or animal that catches rats, *esp* a dog or cat.

rattle¹ /'ratl/ *verb intrans* **1** to make a rapid succession of short sharp clinking or jangling sounds, usu as a result of being shaken or buffeted. **2** to move with a clatter or rattle. **3** (*often* + on) to chatter incessantly and aimlessly. **4** (+ about/around) to live in or occupy a house, building, etc that is too large. >> *verb trans* **1** to cause (something) to make a rattling sound. **2** *informal* to upset (somebody) to the point of loss of poise and composure: *The team allowed themselves to become rattled by the umpiring* — Guardian. **3** (+ off) to say or perform (something) in a brisk lively fashion: *She rattled off a long list of examples.* [Middle English *ratelen*, prob from early Low German, of imitative origin]

rattle² *noun* **1** a rattling sound. **2a** a child's toy consisting of loose pellets in a hollow container that rattles when shaken. **b** a device that consists of a springy tongue in contact with a revolving ratchet wheel which is rotated or shaken to produce a loud noise, used *esp* by football fans. **3** the sound-producing organ on a rattlesnake's tail. **4** a throat noise caused by air passing through mucus and heard *esp* at the approach of death. >> **rattly** *adj*.

rattler *noun* **1** something that rattles. **2** *NAmer, informal* a rattlesnake.

rattlesnake *noun* any of several species of American poisonous snakes with horny interlocking joints at the end of the tail that rattle when shaken: genera *Crotalus* and *Sistrurus*.

rattletrap *noun informal* a noisy old vehicle, *esp* a car.

rattling *adj* **1** making a rattle. **2** *informal, dated* quite fast; brisk: *The story moves at a rattling pace.* **3** *informal, dated* extremely good; excellent.

ratty *adj* (**rattier, rattiest**) **1** *Brit, informal* irritable. **2** *informal* in a state of very poor repair; dilapidated or shabby. **3** *Aus, informal* mentally unbalanced; mad. **4** resembling a rat. **5** infested with rats. >> **rattily** *adv*, **rattiness** *noun*.

raucous /'rawkəs/ *adj* disagreeably harsh or strident; noisy. >> **raucously** *adv*, **raucousness** *noun*. [Latin *raucus* hoarse]

raunch /rawnch/ *noun informal* sexual suggestiveness; earthiness. [back-formation from RAUNCHY]

raunchy /'rawnchi/ *adj* (**raunchier, raunchiest**) *informal* **1** energetic and sexually suggestive: *a pop group with a confident raunchy sound.* **2** *chiefly NAmer* having a dirty and untidy appearance; slovenly. >> **raunchily** *adv*, **raunchiness** *noun*. [origin unknown]

ravage¹ /'ravij/ *verb trans* to wreak havoc on (something); to devastate (it). >> **ravager** *noun*.

ravage² *noun* (*usu in pl*) damage resulting from ravaging: *the ravages of time.* [French *ravage* from early French *ravir*: see RAVISH]

rave¹ /rayv/ *verb intrans* **1** to talk irrationally, *esp* in delirium. **2** to talk or write with extreme or passionate enthusiasm about something: *All the papers are raving about her new film.* **3** *chiefly Brit, informal* to attend a rave. [Middle English *raven*, prob from Old French dialect *raver*, of Germanic origin]

rave² *noun* **1** *informal* an extravagantly favourable review of somebody or something: *The play opened to rave notices.* **2** *informal* a wild exciting period, experience, or event: *The party was a real rave.* **3** a very popular person or thing. **4** *chiefly Brit, informal* a very large organized party with dancing to loud electronic music. **5** any of various types of music, e.g. techno, with a fast hypnotic beat.

ravel[1] /'ravl/ *verb* (**ravelled, ravelling,** *NAmer* **raveled, raveling**) ⪢ *verb trans* **1** (+ out) to unravel or disentangle (something). **2** (*often* + up) to entangle or confuse (something). ⪢ *verb intrans* to become unwoven, untwisted, or unwound; to fray.

Word history
Dutch *rafelen*, from *rafel* loose thread; related to Old English *ræfter* RAFTER[1]. The seemingly contradictory senses of this verb, meaning both 'disentangle' and 'entangle', have coexisted ever since its earliest known occurrences in the 1580s. This is probably because, depending on one's point of view, threads running loose from woven material can be seen as either disentangling or entangling.

ravel[2] *noun* **1** a tangle or tangled mass. **2** a loose thread.

ravelin /'rav(ə)lin/ *noun* a temporary fortification in the form of two embankments built in the shape of an arrowhead. [early French *ravelin* from Old Italian *ravellino*, from Latin *ripa* bank]

raven[1] /'rayv(ə)n/ *noun* **1** a very large glossy black bird of the crow family, found throughout the northern hemisphere: *Corvus corax*. **2** any of several species of related birds: genus *Corvus*. [Old English *hræfn*]

raven[2] *adj* of a glossy black colour: *raven hair.* ⪢ **raven** *noun.*

raven[3] /'rav(ə)n/ *verb* (**ravened, ravening**) ⪢ *verb trans archaic* **1** to devour (something) greedily. **2** to spoil or destroy (something): *Men raven the earth, destroying its resources* — New Yorker. ⪢ *verb intrans archaic* to hunt for prey. ⪢ **ravening** *adj.* [early French *raviner* to rush, take by force, from *ravine*: see RAVINE]

ravenous /'rav(ə)nəs/ *adj* **1** fiercely eager for food; famished. **2** urgently seeking satisfaction, gratification, etc; insatiable. ⪢ **ravenously** *adv,* **ravenousness** *noun.*

raver *noun* **1** *informal* an energetic and uninhibited person who enjoys a wild social life. **2** *chiefly Brit, informal* somebody who often goes to raves or enjoys dancing to rave music. **3** somebody who raves, e.g. in delirium.

rave-up *noun* **1** *Brit, informal* a wild party. **2** *NAmer, informal* a loud and fast pop song that is good to dance to.

ravine /rə'veen/ *noun* a narrow steep-sided valley smaller than a canyon and usu worn by running water. ⪢ **ravined** *adj.* [French *ravine* violent rush (of water), in early French 'rapine, rush', from Latin *rapina*: see RAPINE]

raving[1] *noun* (*usu in pl*) a burst of speech that is irrational, incoherent, or wild.

raving[2] *adj and adv informal* used as an intensifier: great or greatly: *She was a raving beauty; He is raving mad.*

ravioli /ravi'ohli/ *pl noun* (*treated as sing. or pl*) pasta in the form of little cases containing meat, cheese, etc. [Italian *ravioli,* pl of Italian dialect *raviolo,* literally 'little turnip', ultimately from Latin *rapa* turnip, RAPE[3]]

ravish /'ravish/ *verb trans archaic or literary* **1** to fill (somebody) with joy, delight, etc: *He was ravished by the beauty of the scene.* **2** to take (somebody) away by force. **3** to rape (somebody). ⪢ **ravisher** *noun,* **ravishment** *noun.* [Middle English *ravisshen* from early French *ravir,* ultimately from Latin *rapere* to seize]

ravishing *adj* exceptionally attractive or pleasing. ⪢ **ravishingly** *adv.*

raw[1] /raw/ *adj* **1** not cooked. **2** not processed or purified and therefore still in its natural state: *raw fibres; raw sewage.* **3** not modified: *raw data.* **4** not having a hem. **5** having the surface abraded or chafed: *raw skin.* **6** sensitive: *She had hit a raw nerve with her remark.* **7** not refined or disguised in the least; crude: *raw emotion.* **8** lacking experience, training, etc; new: *a raw recruit.* **9** *NAmer, informal* vulgar or coarse: *raw language.* **10** disagreeably damp or cold. ⪢ **rawish** *adj,* **rawly** *adv,* **rawness** *noun.* [Old English *hrēaw*]

raw[2] *noun* (**the raw**) a sensitive place or state: *It touched her on the raw.* ✳ **in the raw 1** in the natural or crude state: *life in the raw.* **2** *informal* naked: *He slept in the raw.*

rawboned *adj* having a heavy or clumsy frame that seems inadequately covered with flesh.

raw deal *noun* an instance of unfair treatment.

rawhide *noun* **1** untanned leather. **2** *NAmer* a strip of rawhide used as a whip.

Rawlplug /'rawlplug/ *noun trademark* a plastic or metal sheath that fits into a hole drilled in a surface and expands to provide a secure fastening when a screw is inserted into it. [from the name of its inventor, John *Rawlings,* 20th cent. English engineer, + PLUG[1]]

raw material *noun* material that can be converted by manufacture, treatment, etc into a new and useful product.

raw sienna[1] *adj* of a yellowish brown colour.

raw sienna[2] *noun* **1** SIENNA (yellowish brown earthy substance used as a pigment) in its untreated state: compare BURNT SIENNA[2]. **2** the yellowish brown colour of this.

raw umber[1] *adj* of a dark yellowish brown colour.

raw umber[2] *noun* **1** UMBER (a naturally occurring earthy substance used as a pigment) in its natural state: compare BURNT UMBER[2]. **2** the dark yellowish brown colour of this.

ray[1] /ray/ *noun* **1a** any of the lines of light that appear to radiate from a bright object. **b** a narrow beam of radiant energy, e.g. light or X-rays. **c** a stream of particles, *esp* radioactive particles, travelling in the same line. **2a** a thin line suggesting a ray. **b** any of a group of lines diverging from a common centre. **3** *chiefly NAmer, informal* (*in pl*) sunlight considered as a tanning agent. **4** a slight manifestation or trace, e.g. of intelligence or hope. **5** = RAY FLOWER. **6a** any of the bony rods that support the fin of a fish. **b** any of the radiating parts of the body of a radially symmetrical animal, e.g. a starfish. ⪢ **rayed** *adj,* **rayless** *adj.* [Middle English via French from Latin *radius* rod, ray, radius]

ray[2] *verb intrans* **1** to radiate from a centre. **2** to shine in or as if in rays. ⪢ *verb trans literary* to emit (something) in rays; to radiate (it): *eyes that ray out intelligence* — Thomas Carlyle.

ray[3] *noun* any of numerous fishes with eyes on the upper surface of a flat body, large pectoral fins that look like wings, and a long narrow tail: order Batiformes. [Middle English *raye* via French from Latin *raia*]

ray[4] *noun* in music, the second note of a major scale in the tonic sol-fa system, or the note D in the fixed-doh system. [medieval Latin *re*: see GAMUT]

ray flower *noun* **1** any of the strap-shaped florets forming the outer ring of the head of a composite plant, e.g. an aster or daisy, that has central disc florets. **2** the entire flower head of a composite plant, e.g. a dandelion, that does not have disc florets: compare DISC FLOWER.

ray gun *noun* in science fiction, any of various weapons that stun or kill an enemy by directing at them a beam of energy of a kind that is usu only hazily defined.

Raynaud's disease /'raynohz/ *noun* a circulatory disorder in which spasms in the arteries or arterioles, usu in response to cold or vibration, produce numbness and discoloration in the fingers and toes. [named after Maurice *Raynaud* d.1881, French physician who first described it]

Raynaud's syndrome *noun* = RAYNAUD'S DISEASE.

rayon /'rayon, 'rayən/ *noun* a textile fibre produced by forcing and drawing cellulose through minute holes, or a fabric made from this fibre. [irreg from RAY[1], because of its sheen]

raze or **rase** /rayz/ *verb trans* to destroy or erase (something) completely; *specif* to lay (e.g. a town or building) level with the ground. [Middle English *rasen* via early French *raser* from Latin *rasus,* past part. of *radere* to scrape, shave]

razor[1] /'rayzə/ *noun* a sharp-edged cutting implement for shaving or cutting hair, *esp* facial hair. [Middle English *rasour* from Old French *raseor,* from *raser*: see RAZE]

razor[2] *verb trans* (**razored, razoring**) to cut or shave (hair) with a razor.

razorback *noun* **1** = RORQUAL. **2** a semiwild pig of the USA, with a narrow body and a ridged back.

razorbill *noun* a black and white N Atlantic auk with a flat sharp-edged bill: *Alca torda.*

razor blade *noun* a small thin flat piece of metal sharpened on one or two edges and used in a razor.

razor clam *noun* NAmer = RAZOR-SHELL.

razor-shell *noun* any of numerous marine bivalve molluscs that have a long narrow curved thin shell: family Solenidae.

razor wire *noun* fencing wire fitted at intervals with sharp-edged rectangular metal projections resembling razor blades.

razz[1] /raz/ *verb trans chiefly NAmer, informal* **1** to tease (somebody). **2** to heckle or deride (somebody).

razz[2] *noun chiefly NAmer, informal* = RASPBERRY (3). [short for *razzberry*, alteration of *raspberry*]

razzamatazz /razəˈtaz/ *noun* see RAZZMATAZZ.

razzle /ˈrazl/ * **on the razzle** *informal* enjoying a spell of partying or drinking. [short for RAZZLE-DAZZLE]

razzle-dazzle *noun* = RAZZMATAZZ. [irreg reduplication of DAZZLE[1]]

razzmatazz /ˈrazmətaz, -ˈtaz/ *or* **razzamatazz** /ˈrazəmətaz/ *noun informal* a noisy, colourful, and often gaudily showy atmosphere or activity: *the razzmatazz of professional sport.* [prob alteration of RAZZLE-DAZZLE]

RB *abbr* Republic of Botswana (international vehicle registration).

Rb *abbr* the chemical symbol for rubidium.

RC *abbr* **1** Red Cross. **2** reinforced concrete. **3** Republic of China (international vehicle registration for Taiwan). **4** Roman Catholic.

RCA *abbr* **1** Radio Corporation of America. **2** République Centrafricaine (international vehicle registration for Central African Republic). **3** *Brit* Royal College of Art.

RCAF *abbr* Royal Canadian Air Force.

RCB *abbr* République du Congo-Brazzaville (international vehicle registration for Republic of Congo).

RCD *abbr* residual current device.

RCH *abbr* Republic of Chile (international vehicle registration).

RCM *abbr Brit* Royal College of Music.

RCMP *abbr* Royal Canadian Mounted Police.

RCN *abbr* **1** Royal Canadian Navy. **2** *Brit* Royal College of Nursing.

RCP *abbr Brit* Royal College of Physicians.

RCS *abbr Brit* **1** Royal College of Science. **2** Royal College of Surgeons. **3** Royal Corps of Signals.

RCVS *abbr Brit* Royal College of Veterinary Surgeons.

RD *abbr* in banking, refer to drawer.

Rd *abbr* in street names, road.

RDA *abbr* **1** recommended daily allowance (of a food or drug). **2** *Brit* Regional Development Agency.

RDC *abbr Brit* formerly, Rural District Council.

RDF *abbr* radio direction-finder.

RE *abbr* **1** religious education. **2** *Brit* Royal Engineers.

Re *abbr* the chemical symbol for rhenium.

re[1] /ree/ *prep* with regard to or in the matter of; concerning. [Latin *re*, ablative of *res* thing, fact]

re[2] /ray, ree/ *noun* = RAY[4].

re- *prefix* forming verbs and their derivatives, with the meanings: **1** again or anew: *reborn; reprint.* **2** again in a new, altered, or improved way: *rehash; rewrite; rehouse.* **3** back or backwards: *recall; retract.* **4** away or down: *recede.* [Middle English via Old French *re-* from Latin *re-, red-* back, again, against]

Usage note
Most verbs that begin with the prefix *re-* meaning 'again' are spelt without a hyphen: *reboot the computer; recycle domestic waste.* Some people prefer to use a hyphen when the verb to which *re-* is attached begins with a vowel, especially *e*. However, spellings such as *reinsure* and *reuse* are shown in all modern British English dictionaries and forms such as *reentry* and *reexamine* in some. The hyphen is important, however, where two different meanings are involved, for example in distinguishing between *re-cover* (cover again) and *recover* ('recuperate'), *re-creation* ('creating anew') and *recreation* ('leisure'), or *re-form* ('form again') and *reform* ('change for the better').

're *contraction informal* are: *You're right.*

reach[1] /reech/ *verb trans* **1** (+ out) to stretch out (a part of the body): *Reach out your hand to her.* **2** to touch or grasp (something) by extending a part of the body, e.g. a hand, or an object: *I couldn't reach the apple.* **3** to extend to (something): *The shadow reached the wall.* **4** to get up to or as far as (something); to achieve or arrive at (it): *We took two days to reach the mountains; They hoped to reach an agreement.* **5** to contact or communicate with (somebody): *I managed to reach her by phone at the office.* **6** to pick up and draw (something) towards one; to pass (it): *Reach me my hat, will you?* **7** to make an impression on (somebody); to have an effect on (them). ▶ *verb intrans* **1a** to make a stretch with or as if with one's hand: *She reached towards the book on the top shelf.* **b** to strain after something: *Reaching above our nature does no good* — Dryden. **2a** to project or extend: *Her land reaches to the river.* **b** to arrive at or come to something: *as far as the eye could reach.* **3** to sail with the wind

blowing more or less from the side. ▶▶ **reachable** *adj.* [Old English *ræcan*]

reach[2] *noun* **1** the distance or extent of reaching or of ability to reach: *The book was out of my reach.* **2** range; *specif* the range of somebody's comprehension: *The idea was well beyond his reach.* **3** the action or an act of reaching: *He made a reach for his gun.* **4** (*usu in pl*) a continuous stretch or expanse, *esp* a straight uninterrupted portion of a river or canal. **5** (*in pl*) groups or levels in a usu specified activity or occupation; echelons: *the higher reaches of academic life.* **6** the tack sailed by a sailing ship with the wind blowing more or less from the side.

reach-me-down[1] *adj Brit, informal, dated* said *esp* of clothes: passed on from one person to another; second-hand.

reach-me-down[2] *noun Brit, informal, dated* a second-hand garment; a cast-off.

react /riˈakt/ *verb intrans* **1** to respond to something, e.g. a suggestion or proposal, in a particular way. **2** (+ against) to act in opposition to a force or influence. **3** to have a particular physiological response to a drug or other medical treatment. **4** to undergo chemical reaction or physical change. ▶ *verb trans* to cause (a substance) to react chemically. [medieval Latin *reactus*, past part. of *reagere*, from RE- + Latin *agere* to act]

reactance *noun* the part of the IMPEDANCE (total opposition) of an alternating-current circuit that is due to capacitance or inductance or both, expressed in ohms.

reactant *noun* a substance that takes part in a chemical reaction; *specif* a substance that is altered in the course of reacting chemically with another.

reaction /riˈaksh(ə)n/ *noun* **1** the act or an instance of reacting. **2** a mental or emotional response to circumstances. **3** a bodily response to a stimulus, e.g. the response of tissues to a foreign substance, e.g. a drug or an infective agent. **4** tendency towards a former and usu outmoded political or social order or policy. **5a** a chemical transformation or change; *specif* an action between atoms, molecules, etc to form one or more new substances. **b** a process involving change in atomic nuclei resulting from interaction with a particle or another nucleus. **6** in physics, the force that something subjected to the action of a force exerts equally in the opposite direction. ▶▶ **reactionist** *noun and adj.*

reactionary[1] *adj* opposing radical social change or favouring a return to a former political or social order: *the paradox of so many tough-talking, self-styled radicals uncritically accepting psychoanalytic ideas with their often politically reactionary consequences* — David E Stannard.

reactionary[2] *noun* (*pl* **reactionaries**) a reactionary person.

reaction engine *noun* an engine, e.g. a jet engine, that develops thrust by expelling a jet of fluid or a stream of particles.

reactivate /riˈaktivayt/ *verb trans* to make (something) active again. ▶▶ **reactivation** /-ˈvaysh(ə)n/ *noun.*

reactive /riˈaktiv/ *adj* **1** relating to reaction or reactance. **2** tending to or liable to react chemically: *highly reactive chemicals.* **3** tending to react passively to situations, instead of initiating or controlling them. **4** said of an illness, etc: caused by a reaction to a drug or other treatment: *reactive depression.* ▶▶ **reactivity** /reeakˈtiviti/ *noun.*

reactor /riˈaktə/ *noun* **1** an apparatus in which a chain reaction of fissile material, e.g. uranium or plutonium, is started and controlled, *esp* for the production of nuclear power or elementary particles; a nuclear reactor. **2** a vat in which an industrial chemical reaction takes place. **3** somebody who reacts, e.g. to a drug. **4** a device, e.g. a coil of wire, in an electrical circuit that introduces reactance into the circuit, e.g. for dimming a light.

read[1] /reed/ *verb* (*past tense and past part.* **read** /red/) ▶ *verb trans* **1a** to look at and understand (something written or printed) by recognizing the signs and symbols that it consists of. **b** to utter aloud the printed or written words of (something). **2a** to read the works of (an author or type of literature). **b** to read (a particular newspaper, magazine, etc) regularly. **3** to learn or find out (something) from written or printed matter: *I had read that the operation was dangerous.* **4a** to interpret the meaning or significance of (something): *You can read the situation in several ways.* **b** to learn or understand the nature of (something or somebody) by observing outward expression or signs: *I can read him like a book; I cannot read your thoughts.* **c** to foretell or predict (something): *She read his fortune.* **d** to interpret the action of or in (something) so as to anticipate what will happen or what needs doing: *A good canoeist reads the rapids.* **5** to proofread (a printed text). **6** to grant a reading to (a legislative bill). **7a** to look at the measurement shown on (e.g. a dial or gauge). **b** to indicate (a specified measurement): *The thermometer reads zero.* **8** *chiefly Brit* to study (a subject), *esp* for a degree: *He wants to read law.* **9** said of a computer: **a** to recognize and respond to (coded information recorded or stored). **b** to take (information) from a storage medium, e.g. a CD-ROM. **10** to receive and understand (a message) by radio. ➤ *verb intrans* **1** to perform the act of reading words; to read something. **2** (+ for) to study a subject in order to qualify for something: *She is reading for the Bar.* **3** to have particular qualities that affect comprehension when read: *Hebrew reads from right to left; The passage reads differently in older versions.* **✳ read between the lines** to work out the implicit meaning of something, rather than what is actually written. **take something as read** to accept something as agreed; to assume something. [Old English *rædan* to interpret, read]

read² /reed/ *noun* **1** *informal* something to read considered in terms of the interest, enjoyment, etc it provides: *The book is a good read.* **2** *chiefly Brit* a period or act of reading: *Have a quick read of this.*

read³ /red/ *adj* Instructed by or informed through reading. *He is widely read in contemporary literature.*

readable /'reedəbl/ *adj* **1** legible. **2** pleasurable or interesting to read. ➤➤ **readability** /-'biliti/ *noun*, **readably** *adv*.

reader /'reedə/ *noun* **1a** a person who reads, *esp* somebody regarded as a consumer of literature. **b** somebody who reads and corrects proofs; a proofreader. **c** somebody who evaluates manuscripts. **2** (**Reader**) a member of a British university staff between the ranks of lecturer and professor. **3** a lay reader. **4** a usu instructive and introductory book or anthology. **5** a device that reads or displays coded information on a tape, microfilm, etc.

readership *noun* **1** (*treated as sing. or pl*) a collective body of readers, *esp* the readers of a particular publication or author. **2** (**Readership**) the position or duties of a university Reader.

readily /'redəli/ *adv* **1** without hesitating; willingly: *He readily accepted advice.* **2** without much difficulty; easily: *I could readily understand her reasons.*

reading /'reeding/ *noun* **1a** an event at which a play, poetry, etc is read to an audience. **b** an act of formally reading a bill that constitutes any of three successive stages of approval by a legislature. **2** material read or intended for reading: *His biography makes fine reading.* **3** the extent to which a person has read: *a man of wide reading.* **4** a particular interpretation: *What is your reading of the situation?* **5** a particular performance of something, e.g. a musical work. **6** the value indicated or data produced by an instrument: *She examined the thermometer reading.*

reading age *noun* a child's reading ability expressed as the age of the average child with the same ability.

reading desk *noun* a desk designed to support a book in a convenient position for a reader, usu one who is standing.

reading room *noun* a room in a library, etc with facilities for reading or study.

readjust *verb intrans* to adapt to new or changing circumstances. ➤ *verb trans* to adjust (e.g. a control) to a new setting. ➤➤ **readjustment** *noun*.

read-only memory *noun* a memory in a computer system that is used for permanent storage of data and allows the user only to read the data and not to change it: compare RANDOM ACCESS MEMORY.

readout *noun* **1** the retrieval of information from a computer storage medium, e.g. computer memory or a CD-ROM. **2** the information retrieved from storage.

read out *verb trans* **1** to read (something) aloud. **2** to produce a readout of (something). **3** *NAmer* to expel (somebody) from an organization, e.g. a political party, often by a public reading of notice of dismissal.

read up *verb intrans* (*often* + on) to learn about something by reading.

read-write head *noun* in a computer, an electromagnetic device that allows data to be both read from and copied onto a disk or tape.

ready¹ /'redi/ *adj* (**readier, readiest**) **1a** prepared mentally or physically for an experience or action. **b** prepared or available for immediate use: *Dinner is ready.* **2** willingly disposed: *I'm ready to agree to his proposal.* **3** likely or about to do the specified thing: *I*

was ready to cry with vexation. **4** spontaneously prompt: *She always has a ready answer; a ready wit.* **5** presumptuously eager: *He is very ready with his criticism.* **✳ make ready** to prepare. ➤➤ **readiness** *noun*. [Old English *rǣde*]

ready² *verb trans* (**readies, readied, readying**) to make (something or somebody) ready.

ready³ *noun* (*pl* **readies**) (*also* **the ready**) *Brit, informal* (*in pl*) available money. **✳ at/to the ready 1** said of a gun: prepared and in the position for immediate aiming and firing. **2** available for immediate use.

ready cash *noun* = READY MONEY.

ready-made¹ *adj* **1** made beforehand, *esp* for general sale or use rather than to individual specifications: *ready-made suits; ready-made sandwiches.* **2** lacking originality or individuality: *ready-made opinions.* **3** readily available: *Her illness provided a ready-made excuse.*

ready-made² *noun* something ready-made, *esp* a garment.

ready-mixed *adj* **1** said of food: prepared for cooking, usu in the form of mixed dried ingredients to which only water, milk, etc needs to be added. **2** said of concrete: having ingredients already mixed.

ready money *noun* **1** immediately available cash. **2** payment on the spot: *I am greatly distressed, Aunt Augusta, about there being no cucumbers, not even for ready money* — Oscar Wilde.

ready reckoner *noun Brit* an arithmetical table, e.g. a list of numbers multiplied by a fixed per cent, or set of tables used as an aid in calculating.

ready-to-wear *adj* said of a garment: made in a standard size for general sale, rather than to an individual's measurements; off-the-peg.

reafforest /ree-ə'forist/ *verb trans chiefly Brit* = REFOREST. ➤➤ **reafforestation** /-'staysh(ə)n/ *noun*.

reagent /ri'ayj(ə)nt/ *noun* a substance that takes part in or brings about a particular chemical reaction. [medieval Latin *reagent-, reagens*, present part. of *reagere*: see REACT]

real¹ /'riəl/ *adj* **1a** not artificial, fraudulent, illusory, or fictional; actual or authentic: *Was Dick Turpin a real person?* **b** being precisely what the name implies; genuine: *Is this real butter?* **2** made according to traditional methods and implying a flavour superior to that produced by modern methods: *real ale; real bread.* **3** significant: *The heavy traffic poses a real problem.* **4** used chiefly for emphasis: complete or great: *Her visit was a real surprise.* **5** measured by purchasing power rather than the paper value of money: *real income.* **6** said of an image: formed by light rays converging at a point: compare VIRTUAL. **7** belonging to or concerned with the set of real numbers: *the real roots of an equation.* **✳ get real** *informal* (*usu in imperative*) to be realistic; to have some sense: *Listen Geoffrey, get real OK? People love cars, I love cars* — Ben Elton. ➤➤ **realness** *noun*. [Middle English in the senses 'real', 'ultimately relating to things' (in law), ultimately from Latin *res* thing, fact]

real² *noun* (**the real**) that which is real; reality. **✳ for real** *informal* in earnest; genuinely: *The children were fighting for real.*

real³ *adv chiefly NAmer, Scot, informal* very: *I'm real worried.*

real⁴ /ray'ahl/ *noun* (*pl* **reals** *or* **reales** /-lays/) **1** the basic monetary unit of Brazil, divided into 100 centavos. **2** a former monetary unit of Spain and Spanish colonies. [Spanish *real*, literally 'royal', from Latin *regalis*: see REGAL]

real estate /riəl/ *noun chiefly NAmer* property in buildings and land.

realgar /ri'algə/ *noun* an orange-red mineral consisting of arsenic sulphide. [Middle English via medieval Latin and Catalan from Arabic *rahj al-ghār* powder of the mine]

realign /ree-ə'lien/ *verb trans* to align (something) again, *esp* to reorganize (it) or form new groupings. ➤ *verb intrans* to change one's affiliations and become part of a different group, *esp* a political party or faction. ➤➤ **realignment** *noun*.

realise /'riəliez/ *verb trans* see REALIZE.

realism /'riəliz(ə)m/ *noun* **1** concern for fact or reality and rejection of things regarded as impractical or visionary. **2** representation of things in art and literature, in a way that is true to nature *esp* without idealization. **3a** in philosophy, the belief that objects of sense perception have real existence independent of the mind. **b** a doctrine that classes and universals exist independently of the mind. ➤➤ **realist** *adj and noun*.

realistic /ree·ə'listik/ *adj* **1** basing aims or opinions on known facts or acknowledged possibilities, rather than on ideals. **2** depicting things in a way that seems real. **3** based on what is reasonable or sensible; not excessive. **4** relating to philosophical realism. ➤ **realistically** *adv*.

reality /ri'aliti/ *noun* (*pl* **realities**) **1** the state of being real. **2a** a real event, entity, or state of affairs: *His dream became a reality.* **b** the totality of real things and events: *She was trying to escape from reality.* **3** in philosophy, something that exists independently of our perception or awareness of it. ✳ **in reality** in actual fact.

reality principle *noun* in Freudian psychoanalysis, the control by the ego of the pleasure-seeking tendencies of the id, as a response to social conventions or expectations.

reality TV *noun* a type of television programme in which ordinary people appear in natural or contrived real-life situations, usually involving difficult or unpleasant tasks and a strong element of competition between the participants.

realize *or* **realise** /'riəliez/ *verb trans* **1** to be or become fully aware of (something): *She did not realize the risk he was taking.* **2** to cause (something) to become a reality; to accomplish (it): *He finally realized his goal.* **3** to cause (something) to seem real: *In this book the characters are carefully realized.* **4a** to convert (property, assets, etc) into actual money. **b** to earn (money) by sale, investment, or effort: *The painting will realize several thousand pounds.* **5** to play or write (music) in full, e.g. from an incomplete composition. ➤ **realizable** *adj*, **realization** /-'zaysh(ə)n/ *noun*, **realizer** *noun*. [French *réaliser* from early French *real* REAL¹]

really¹ /'riəli/ *adv* **1** in reality; actually: *Did he really say that?; It's not very difficult really.* **2** without question; thoroughly: *He likes really cold weather; She really hates him.* **3** more correctly: *You should really have asked me first.*

really² *interj* used as an expression of surprise or indignation.

realm /relm/ *noun* **1** a kingdom. **2** (*also in pl*) a domain or sphere: *It is within the realms of possibility.* [Middle English from Old French *realme*, modification of Latin *regimen*: see REGIMEN]

real number /riəl/ *noun* a number, e.g. a square root of a positive number, an integer, or pi, that does not include a part that is a multiple of the square root of minus one.

realpolitik /ray'ahlpoliteek, ray'al-/ *noun* politics based on practical factors rather than on moral or ethical objectives, sometimes involving the flouting of civil liberties. [German *Realpolitik*, from *real* practical + *Politik* politics]

real presence /riəl/ *noun* the doctrine that Christ's body and blood are actually present in the Eucharist: compare CONSUBSTANTIATION.

real property *noun* property in buildings and land.

real tennis /riəl/ *noun* an early form of tennis, played with a racket and a solid ball in an irregularly-shaped indoor court divided by a net.

real-time /riəl'tiem/ *adj* said of a computer system: being constrained by the timing of events in the outside world, or collecting data from an external source, e.g. an air traffic control system.

realtor /'riəltə, 'riəltaw/ *noun NAmer* a real estate agent, *esp* a member of the National Association of Real Estate Boards.

realty /'riəlti/ *noun* real property: compare PERSONALTY. [REAL¹ + -*ty* as in PROPERTY]

ream¹ /reem/ *noun* **1** a quantity of paper equal to 20 quires or variously 480, 500, or 516 sheets. **2** (*usu in pl*) a great amount, e.g. of something written or printed: *She composed reams of poetry.* [Middle English *reme* via French from Arabic *rizmah* bundle]

ream² *verb trans* **1** to enlarge or widen (a hole) with a reamer. **2** to remove (something) by reaming. **3** *NAmer* to press the juice from (a citrus fruit). **4** *NAmer, coarse slang* to have anal intercourse with (somebody). **5** *NAmer, informal* to reprimand (somebody) severely; to upbraid (them). [perhaps ultimately from Old English dialect *rēman* to open up]

reamer *noun* **1** a rotating finishing tool with cutting edges used to enlarge or shape a hole. **2** *NAmer* a lemon squeezer.

reaming *noun coarse slang* anal intercourse.

reap /reep/ *verb trans* **1a** to cut or harvest (a crop), orig with a sickle or scythe but now using any method. **b** to clear (e.g. a field) of a crop by reaping. **2** to obtain or win (something), *esp* as the reward for effort: *You will reap lasting benefits from study.* ➤ *verb intrans* to cut or harvest crops. [Old English *reopan*; related to Old English *rāw* ROW¹]

reaper *noun* a person or machine that harvests crops. ✳ **the reaper/grim reaper** death, or the personification of death as a skeleton wielding a scythe.

reappear /ree·ə'piə/ *verb intrans* to appear again after being absent for a while. ➤ **reappearance** *noun*.

reappoint *verb trans* to appoint (somebody) again. ➤ **reappointment** *noun*.

reappraise /ree·ə'prayz/ *verb trans* to assess (something or somebody) again, and usu form a different opinion of their merit. ➤ **reappraisal** *noun*.

rear¹ /riə/ *noun* **1** the back part of something, e.g.: **a** the part of something located opposite its front: *the rear of a house.* **b** the part, e.g. of an army, that is furthest from the enemy. **c** *informal* the buttocks. **2** the space or position at the back: *He moved to the rear.* ✳ **bring up the rear** to be the last in a group, series, order, etc. [Middle English via Old French *rere* from Latin *retro*: see RETRO-]

rear² *adj* at the back: *a rear window.*

rear³ *verb trans* **1a** to breed and tend (an animal) or grow (e.g. a crop) for use or sale. **b** to bring up (a child). **2** to raise (something) into an upright position. **3** *formal* to build or construct (something). ➤ *verb intrans* **1** (*often* + up) said of a horse: to rise up on the hind legs. **2** (+ up) to react with strong emotion, usu anger, indignation, or resentment. **3** *literary* (*usu* + up/over) to rise to a height. ➤ **rearer** *noun*. [Old English *rǣran*; related to Old English *rīsan* RISE¹]

rear admiral *noun* a naval officer ranking above a commodore and below a vice admiral.

rear end *noun informal* the buttocks.

rear guard *noun* **1** a military detachment for guarding the rear of a main body or force, *esp* during a retreat. **2** the most conservative or reactionary faction within a group, *esp* a political party. [Middle English from Old French *reregarde*, from *rere* backward, behind (from RETRO-) + *garde* guard]

rearguard action *noun* vigorous resistance, *esp* in the face of defeat: *The workers fought a rearguard action against automation.*

rear lamp *noun* = REAR LIGHT.

rear light *noun chiefly Brit* either of the red lights on the rear of a motor vehicle.

rearm /ree'ahm/ *verb trans* to arm (e.g. a nation or military force) again, *esp* with new or better weapons. ➤ *verb intrans* to become armed again. ➤ **rearmament** *noun*.

rearmost *adj* farthest in the rear; last.

rearrange /ree·ə'raynj/ *verb trans* to arrange (something) differently.

rearview mirror *noun* a mirror in a motor vehicle that gives a view of the road and traffic behind the vehicle.

rearward¹ /'riəwəd/ *adj* located at or directed towards the rear. [REAR¹ + -WARD]

rearward² *noun archaic or literary* the rear, *esp* the rear division, e.g. of an army: *to rearward of the main column.* [Middle English from Anglo-French *rerewarde*, variant of Old French *reregarde*: see REAR GUARD]

rearward³ *adv* = REARWARDS.

rearwards *adv* at or towards the rear; backwards.

rear-wheel drive *noun* a transmission system in a motor vehicle that sends power to the rear wheels.

reason¹ /'reez(ə)n/ *noun* **1a** an explanation or justification: *She gave a good reason for being late.* **b** a rational ground or motive: *The last temptation is the greatest treason, to do the right deed for the wrong reason* — T S Eliot. **c** a fact, event, etc that brings something about; a cause: *What is the reason for earthquakes?* **2** the power of comprehending, inferring, or thinking, *esp* in orderly rational ways; intelligence.

Editorial note
Reason is the faculty of mind by which evidence is weighed, inferences are drawn, truth and falsity are judged, and explanations are sought and given. The exercise of reason is called rationality, and any means of arriving at judgments or beliefs which do not use reason, e.g. those purely emotionally based, are non-rational. Non-rational thought includes irrational thought, which involves judgments deliberately contrary to reason — Dr Anthony Grayling.

3 the ability to think or judge sensibly; sanity: *He seems to have lost all reason.* ✳ **it stands to reason** it is obvious or reasonable. **listen to reason** to be willing to accept advice to act sensibly. **within reason** within reasonable limits. **with reason** with good cause. [Middle English *resoun* via Old French *raison* from Latin *ration-, ratio* reason, computation, from Latin *reri* to calculate, determine, think]

Usage note ───────────────

It is argued by some traditionalists that when *reason* means 'cause' it already contains the idea expressed by causal words such as *because* and *why*, which means that it is unnecessary and incorrect to use them together with it. Strictly then, the sentence *The reason that the plan failed was that it overlooked two simple facts* is correct, and the sentence *The reason why the plan failed was because it overlooked two simple facts* is incorrect. Any problems in sentences involving *reason* can often be regarded by recasting and leaving out the word *reason* altogether: *The plan failed because it overlooked two simple facts.*

reason² *verb* (**reasoned, reasoning**) ➤ *verb intrans* **1** to use the faculty of reason so as to arrive at conclusions. **2** (+ with) to talk or argue with another person so as to influence his or her actions or opinions. ➤ *verb trans* **1** (*often* + out) to formulate, assume, analyse, or conclude (something) by the use of reason: *We had reasoned out a plan.* **2** to persuade or influence (somebody) by the use of reason: *I reasoned myself out of such fears.* ➤➤ **reasoner** *noun.*

reasonable *adj* **1a** moderate or fair: *a reasonable boss; reasonable weather.* **b** not extreme or excessive: *reasonable requests.* **c** in accord with reason; logical: *a reasonable theory.* **d** fairly inexpensive. **2a** sensible. **b** *archaic* having the faculty of reason; rational. ➤➤ **reasonableness** *noun,* **reasonably** *adv.*

reasoning *noun* **1** the drawing of inferences or conclusions through the use of reason. **2** a logical train of thought.

reasonless /'reezənləs/ *adj* **1** not reasoned; senseless: *reasonless hostility.* **2** not based on or supported by reasons: *a reasonless accusation.*

reassess *verb trans* to assess (somebody or something) again or in a new way. ➤➤ **reassessment** *noun.*

reassure /ree-ə'shooə, -'shaw/ *verb trans* to restore confidence to (somebody); to calm (them): *I was reassured by his promise.* ➤➤ **reassurance** *noun,* **reassuring** *adj,* **reassuringly** *adv.*

Réaumur scale /'rayoh'myooə/ *noun* a scale of temperature in which water freezes at 0° and boils at 80° under standard conditions. [named after René de *Réaumur* d.1757, French physicist, who invented it]

reave /reev/ *verb* (*past tense and past part.* **reft** /reft/) ➤ *verb intrans archaic* to plunder or rob. ➤ *verb trans archaic* **1** to deprive (somebody) of something; to rob (them). **2** to seize (something). ➤➤ **reaver** *noun.* [Old English *rēafian*]

rebarbative /ri'bahbətiv/ *adj formal* repellent or unattractive: *Still, everyone appeared to be extremely nice, except that that Dr. Greenfield man was a trifle rebarbative. (This was a word which Toby had recently learnt at school and could not now conceive of doing without.) — Iris Murdoch.* [French *rébarbatif* from early French *rebarber* to be repellent, ultimately from Latin *barba* beard, from the notion of two people facing each other aggressively, beard to beard]

rebate¹ /'reebayt/ *noun* **1** a return of part of a payment: *a tax rebate.* **2** a deduction from a sum before payment; a discount: *a 10% rebate.*

rebate² *verb trans* **1** to give (somebody) a rebate, e.g. on tax payments. **2** to make a rebate of (something). ➤➤ **rebatable** *adj.* [early French *rabattre* to beat down again, reduce, from RE- + *abattre* to fell, from Latin *battuere*]

rebate³ *noun* a groove or step cut into the edge of a piece of wood to which another piece is to be joined by means of a corresponding groove or step. [alteration of RABBET¹, via Middle English *rabat* from early French, literally 'act of beating down', from *rabattre*: see REBATE²]

rebate⁴ *verb trans* **1** to cut a rebate in (an edge). **2** to join (pieces) by means of a rebate.

rebec or **rebeck** /'reebek/ *noun* a medieval pear-shaped musical instrument, usu with three strings, played with a bow. [early French *rebec,* alteration of Old French *rebebe,* via Old Provençal from Arabic *rebāb*]

rebel¹ /'rebl/ *noun* somebody who rebels against a government, authority, convention, etc. [Middle English via Old French from Latin *rebellis,* from RE- + *bellum* war]

rebel² /ri'bel/ *verb intrans* (**rebelled, rebelling**) **1a** to oppose or disobey authority or control. **b** to carry out armed resistance to the authority of a government. **2a** to act in or show opposition: *She rebelled against the conventions of polite society.* **b** to feel or exhibit anger or revulsion: *It's no use rebelling at the injustice of life.*

rebellion /ri'belyən/ *noun* **1** opposition to authority or dominance. **2** open armed resistance to an established government, or an instance or campaign of such resistance.

rebellious /ri'belyəs/ *adj* **1** given to or engaged in rebellion: *rebellious troops.* **2** tending to oppose or defy authority or dominance: *a rebellious speech; a rebellious people.* ➤➤ **rebelliously** *adv,* **rebelliousness** *noun.*

rebirth /ree'buhth/ *noun* **1a** a new or second birth. **b** spiritual regeneration. **2** a renaissance or revival: *a rebirth of nationalism.*

reboot¹ /ree'booht/ *verb trans* to start up (a computer system) again. ➤ *verb intrans* said of a computer system: to start up.

reboot² *noun* the procedure of rebooting a computer system.

rebore¹ /ree'baw/ *verb trans* to enlarge and renew the bore of a cylinder in (an internal-combustion engine).

rebore² /'reebaw/ *noun* **1** the process of reboring a cylinder. **2** an engine that has rebored cylinders.

reborn /ree'bawn/ *adj* **1** brought back to life; born again. **2** regenerated; *specif* spiritually renewed.

rebound¹ /ri'bownd/ *verb intrans* **1** to spring back on collision or impact with another body. **2** to return to an original strong or healthy state after a setback, illness, etc. **3** (*often* + on) to return with an adverse effect to a source or starting point: *Their hatred rebounded on themselves.* [Middle English *rebounden* from Old French *rebondir,* from RE- + *bondir* to bound]

rebound² /'reebownd/ *noun* **1a** an instance of rebounding. **b** a recovery: *a sharp rebound in prices.* **2a** a shot, e.g. in basketball or football, that rebounds. **b** the act of gaining possession of a rebound, e.g. in basketball. ✳ **on the rebound** in, or whilst in, an unsettled or emotional state resulting from setback, frustration, or crisis: *She met him while on the rebound from an unhappy love affair.*

rebounder /ri'bowndə/ *noun* a small round trampoline used for fitness exercises.

rebozo /ri'bohzoh/ *noun* (*pl* **rebozos**) a long scarf that covers the head and shoulders, worn by Spanish and Spanish-American women. [Spanish *rebozo*]

rebrand /ree'brand/ *verb trans* **1** to change the brand name of (a product). **2** to update the image of (a company).

rebuff¹ /ri'buf/ *verb trans* to reject or refuse (somebody) sharply; to snub (them). [early French *rebuffer* from Old Italian *ribuffare* to reprimand, from *ri-* against + *buffo* gust, puff, of imitative origin]

rebuff² *noun* a curt rejection or refusal.

rebuild /ree'bild/ *verb trans* (*past tense and past part.* **rebuilt** /ree'bilt/) **1** to build (something) again, *esp* after severe damage to or destruction of the original: *The town hall was rebuilt after the war.* **2** to restore (something) to its previous good state: *She struggled to rebuild her life after the tragedy.* **3** to make extensive changes to (something); to remodel (it): *They set out to rebuild society.*

rebuke¹ /ri'byoohk/ *verb trans* to criticize (somebody) severely for doing something wrong; to reprimand (them). [Middle English *rebuken* to cut down, repress, from Old French *rebuker,* from RE- + *bukier* to beat]

rebuke² *noun* a reprimand.

rebus /'reebəs/ *noun* a representation of words or syllables by pictures that suggest the same sound, or a riddle that makes use of such representatives: *The ancient tiles which lined the porch were marked with the rebus of a cheese and a man after the original builder — Conan Doyle.* [Latin *rebus* by things, ablative pl of *res* thing]

rebut /ri'but/ *verb trans* (**rebutted, rebutting**) **1** to disprove or expose the falsity of (e.g. a claim); to refute (it). **2** *archaic* to drive (somebody) back; to repel (them). ➤➤ **rebuttable** *adj,* **rebuttal** *noun.* [Middle English *rebuten* from Old French *reboter,* from RE- + *boter* to butt]

rebutter *noun* **1** *archaic* in law, a defendant's answer to a plaintiff's SURREJOINDER. **2** somebody who rebuts something. [Old French *reboter:* see REBUT]

rec /rek/ *noun informal* **1** *Brit* a recreation ground. **2** *NAmer* recreation.

rec. *abbr* **1** receipt. **2** recommended.

recalcitrant[1] /ri'kalsitrənt/ *adj* **1** obstinately defiant of authority or restraint. **2** difficult to handle or control. >> **recalcitrance** *noun*, **recalcitrantly** *adv*. [late Latin *recalcitrant-, recalcitrans*, present part. of *recalcitrare* to be stubbornly disobedient, from Latin *recalcitrare* to kick back, from RE- + *calc-, calx* heel]

recalcitrant[2] *noun* somebody who is recalcitrant.

recalescence /reekə'lesəns/ *noun* an increase in the temperature of iron or a similar metal, occurring as the metal cools through a range of temperatures in which a change in crystal structure occurs. >> **recalescent** *adj*. [Latin *recalescere* to grow warm again, from RE- + *calescere* to grow warm]

recall[1] /ri'kawl/ *verb trans* **1a** to bring (something) back to mind; to remember (it): *In chapter one, he recalls his early years*. **b** to make somebody think of (something); to remind them of (it): *The film recalls early Hitchcock thrillers*. **2a** to call or summon (somebody) back officially: *They have recalled their ambassador*. **b** to request the return of (a faulty product) to the manufacturer. **3** to retrieve (stored material) in an information retrieval system. **4** to bring (someone) out of an absent-minded or inattentive state. **5** *archaic* to cancel or revoke (e.g. a decision). >> **recallable** *adj*.

recall[2] /ri'kawl, 'reekawl/ *noun* **1** a call or summons to return or return something: *There has been a recall of workers after the layoff*. **2** remembrance of what has been learned or experienced; recollection: *He has perfect visual recall*. **3** the act of revoking or the possibility of being revoked: *The matter is past recall*. **4** the ability (e.g. of an information retrieval system) to retrieve stored material. **5** *NAmer* the right or procedure by which an elected representative may be removed by the constituency or constituency party.

recant /ri'kant/ *verb trans* to withdraw or repudiate (a statement or belief) formally and publicly; to renounce (it). > *verb intrans* to make an open confession of error, *esp* to disavow a religious or political opinion or belief. >> **recantation** /reekan'taysh(ə)n/ *noun*, **recanter** *noun*. [Latin *recantare*, from RE- + *cantare*: see CHANT[1]]

recap[1] /'reekap, ri'kap/ *verb trans and intrans* (**recapped, recapping**) *informal* = RECAPITULATE. [by shortening from RECAPITULATE]

recap[2] /'reekap/ *noun informal* = RECAPITULATION.

recapitalize *or* **recapitalise** /ree'kapitəliez/ *verb trans* to reorganize the capital structure of (a business enterprise). >> **recapitalization** /-lie'zaysh(ə)n/ *noun*.

recapitulate /reekə'pityoolayt/ *verb trans* **1** to repeat the principal points of (an argument, etc); to sum (it) up. **2** in biology, said of an embryo: to undergo recapitulation. > *verb intrans* to sum up an argument or discourse. >> **recapitulatory** *adj*. [late Latin *recapitulatus*, past part. of *recapitulare* to restate under headings, sum up, from RE- + *capitulum*: see CHAPTER]

recapitulation /ˌreekəpityoo'laysh(ə)n/ *noun* **1** the act or an instance of recapitulating. **2** in embryology, the erroneous view that, in its development, an embryo passes through successive stages resembling adult ancestral types from which the organism has evolved. **3** in music, a modified repetition of the main themes forming the third section of a movement written in sonata form.

recapture[1] /ri'kapchə/ *verb trans* **1** to capture (somebody or something) again. **2** to experience (something) again: *The novel manages to recapture the atmosphere of the past*. **3** *NAmer* to take (excess earnings or profits) by law.

recapture[2] *noun* the act of recapturing something.

recast /ree'kahst/ *verb trans* (*past tense and past part.* **recast**) **1** to cast (something) again: *The bronzes were recast; They decided to recast the play*. **2** to remodel or refashion (something): *He recasts his political image to fit the times*.

recce[1] /'reki/ *noun chiefly Brit, informal* a reconnaissance. [by shortening and alteration]

recce[2] *verb* (**recced** *or* **recceed** /'rekid/, **recceing**) *chiefly Brit, informal* to reconnoitre.

recd *abbr* received.

recede[1] /ri'seed/ *verb intrans* **1a** to move back or away; to withdraw. **b** to slant backwards: *a receding chin*. **c** said of hair or a hairline: to stop growing around the temples and above the forehead. **2** to grow less, smaller, or more distant; to diminish: *There are fears that demand will recede; Hope receded*. [Latin *recedere* to go back, from RE- + *cedere* to go]

recede[2] /ree'seed/ *verb trans* to cede (e.g. land) back to a former possessor.

receipt[1] /ri'seet/ *noun* **1** a written or printed acknowledgment of having received goods or money. **2** the act or process of receiving: *Please acknowledge receipt of the goods*. **3** (*usu in pl*) something, e.g. goods or money, received: *She took the day's receipts to the bank*. **4** *archaic* a recipe. [Middle English *receite* via Old French from medieval Latin *recepta* received, fem past part. of *recipere*: see RECEIVE]

receipt[2] *verb trans* to acknowledge the payment or receipt of (a bill).

receivable /ri'seevəbl/ *adj* **1** capable of being received. **2** liable for payment: *accounts receivable*.

receivables /ri'seevəblz/ *pl noun* amounts of money owed to a company and thus part of its assets.

receive /ri'seev/ *verb trans* **1a** to come into possession of (something); to acquire or be given (it): *Please come up to receive your award*. **b** to take delivery of (something): *The prime minister received the petition; The radio station received thousands of complaints*. **c** to be provided with (something); to experience (it): *He had received his early education at home*. **d** *chiefly Brit, informal* to buy and sell (articles which have been stolen). **2** to convert (an incoming signal, *esp* radio waves) into a form suitable for human perception or for further electronic processing, e.g. amplification. **3a** to act in response to (something): *How did she receive the offer?* **b** to elicit (a particular response): *We had received nothing but hostility*. **4** to assimilate (e.g. ideas or impressions) through the mind or senses. **5** to eat or drink (the consecrated bread or wine of the Eucharist): *She received Communion*. **6** in tennis, squash, etc, to be the player who returns (the service of an opponent). **7a** to suffer the hurt or injury of (something): *He received a broken nose*. **b** to be forced to experience (something): *She received a life sentence for the murder*. **8** to take the force or pressure of (something); to bear (it): *These pillars receive the weight of the roof*. **9** to act as a receptacle or container for (something): *The cistern receives water from the roof*. **10** to accept (something) as authoritative or true; to believe (it): *received wisdom about the origins of the earth*. **11a** to welcome, greet, or entertain (somebody) formally. **b** to have a visit from (somebody). **c** to permit (somebody) to enter; to admit (them): *He was received into the priesthood*. > *verb intrans* **1** *formal* to be at home to visitors: *She receives on Tuesdays*. **2** *chiefly Brit, informal* to receive stolen goods; to act as an intermediary for thieves. [Middle English *receiven* via Anglo-French from Latin *recipere* to take back, from RE- + *capere* to take]

Received Pronunciation *noun* the form of British English pronunciation used by many educated British people, based on the pronunciation of people in southeastern England and widely regarded as the least regionally modified accent and suitable for adoption as the standard pronunciation.

receiver *noun* **1a** a radio, television, or other part of a communications system that receives the signal. **b** the part of a telephone that contains the mouthpiece and earpiece. **2** a person appointed to hold in trust and administer the property of a person declared bankrupt or insane person, or property that is the subject of a lawsuit. **3** *informal* somebody who receives stolen goods. **4a** in tennis, squash, etc, a person who returns service. **b** in American football, an offensive player who is eligible to catch a forward pass.

receivership *noun* **1** the office or function of a receiver. **2** the state of being in the hands of a receiver.

receiving order *noun Brit* a court order instructing a receiver to take control of the business or property of a person declared bankrupt.

recension /ri'sensh(ə)n/ *noun* **1** the critical revision of a text. **2** a revised text. [Latin *recension-, recensio* enumeration, from *recensēre* to review, from RE- + *censēre* to assess, tax]

recent /'rees(ə)nt/ *adj* **1a** of a time not long past: *the recent election*. **b** having lately come into existence: *the recent snow*. **2** (**Recent**) = HOLOCENE. >> **recency** /-si/ *noun*, **recently** *adv*, **recentness** *noun*. [Middle English via French from Latin *recent-, recens* fresh, recent]

receptacle /ri'septəkl/ *noun* **1** an object that receives and contains something. **2** the end of the flower stalk of a flowering plant which bears the petals and stamens. **3** in some brown algae, a swollen tip or the vegetative body containing reproductive structures. [Latin *receptaculum*, from *receptare* to receive, from *receptus*, past part. of *recipere*: see RECEIVE]

reception /ri'sepsh(ə)n/ *noun* **1** the action or process of receiving somebody or something. **2** a formal social gathering during which guests are received. **3** an office or desk where visitors or clients, e.g.

to an office, factory, or hotel, are received on arrival. **4** *Brit* a class for the youngest children in a primary school. **5** a response or reaction: *The play met with a mixed reception.* **6** an admission: *his reception into the Church.* **7** the receiving of a radio or television broadcast, or the quality of the signal received. [Middle English *recepcion* via French from Latin *reception-, receptio*, from *recipere*: see RECEIVE]

receptionist *noun* a person employed to greet and assist callers or clients, e.g. at an office or hotel.

reception room *noun* **1** a room used primarily for the reception of guests or visitors. **2** a room used for banquets and receptions in a hotel.

receptive /ri'septiv/ *adj* **1** able or inclined to receive, *esp* open and responsive to ideas, impressions, or suggestions: *a receptive mind.* **2** said of a nerve or nerve ending: able to receive and transmit stimuli; sensory. **3** said of a female animal: ready to mate. ➤ **receptively** *adv*, **receptiveness** *noun*, **receptivity** /reesep'tiviti/ *noun*.

receptor /ri'septə/ *noun* **1** a cell or group of cells that receives stimuli which are then transmitted as nerve impulses, *esp* a nerve ending, e.g. in the skin, or sense organ, e.g. a taste bud, that receives information about temperature, light, sound, etc from the environment. **2a** a chemical group on the surface of a cell that provides a site for a particular antibody or a virus to attach to. **b** a chemical structure, e.g. on an enzyme, that provides a site of attachment. **c** a chemical structure in or on the surface of a cell, to which a hormone, neurotransmitter, etc binds, triggering off a reaction, e.g. transmission of a nerve impulse, inside the cell.

recess¹ /ri'ses, 'reeses/ *noun* **1a** an alcove or niche: *a recess lined with books.* **b** an indentation or cleft: *a deep recess in the hill.* **2** (*in pl*) hidden, secret, or secluded places: *the dark recesses of the mind.* **3a** a suspension of usual business or activity, e.g. of a legislative body or law court, usu for a period of rest or relaxation. **b** *chiefly NAmer* a break between school classes. [Latin *recessus*, past part. of *recedere*: see RECEDE¹]

recess² *verb trans* **1** (*usu in passive*) to put or install (something) in a recess: *recessed lighting.* **2** to make a recess in (e.g. a wall). **3** *chiefly NAmer* to interrupt (e.g. a meeting) for a recess. ➤ *verb intrans chiefly NAmer* to take a break.

recession /ri'sesh(ə)n/ *noun* **1** a period of reduced economic activity and prosperity. **2** *formal* the act or an instance of receding; a withdrawal. **3** the withdrawal of clergy and choir at the end of a church service. ➤ **recessionary** *adj*.

recessional¹ *noun* a hymn or musical piece sung or played at the conclusion of a church service.

recessional² *adj* **1** of a withdrawal. **2** of a parliamentary recess.

recessive¹ /ri'sesiv/ *adj* **1** receding or tending to recede. **2** denoting the one of a pair of contrasting inherited characteristics that is suppressed if a dominant gene is present, or the gene that determines the characteristic: compare DOMINANT¹ (4). **3** in phonetics, denoting stress that falls on or near the first syllable of a word. ➤ **recessively** *adv*, **recessiveness** *noun*.

recessive² *noun* **1** a recessive gene or inherited characteristic. **2** an organism possessing one or more recessive characteristics.

recharge /ree'chahj/ *verb intrans* **1** to charge (something) again; *specif* to renew the active materials in (a storage battery). **2** to renew (one's energies or strength). ➤ **rechargeable** /ri'chahjəbl/ *adj*, **recharger** *noun*.

réchauffé /ray'shohfay (*French* reʃofe)/ *noun* **1** a warmed-up dish of food. **2** a rehash. [French *réchauffé* warmed up]

recherché /rə'sheəshay (*French* rəʃɛrʃe)/ *adj* **1** obscure or rare: *all manner of words – common, recherché, and slang —* New Yorker. **2** excessively refined or exaggeratedly self-important; pretentious or affected: *his recherché highbrow talk.* [French *recherché* sought out]

recidivist /ri'sidivist/ *noun* somebody who relapses, *esp* into criminal behaviour. ➤ **recidivism** *noun*, **recidivist** *adj*, **recidivistic** /-'vistik/ *adj*. [French *récidiviste*, from *récidiver* to relapse, via medieval Latin *recidivare* from Latin *recidivus* recurring, from *recidere* to fall back, from RE- + *cadere* to fall]

recipe /'resipi/ *noun* **1** a list of ingredients and instructions for making a food dish. **2** a procedure for doing or attaining something: *a recipe for success.* **3** *archaic* a doctor's prescription. [Latin *recipe* take, imperative of *recipere*: see RECEIVE]

recipient /ri'sipi·ənt/ *noun* somebody who or something that receives. ➤ **recipient** *adj*. [Latin *recipient-, recipiens*, present part. of *recipere*: see RECEIVE]

reciprocal¹ /ri'siprəkl/ *adj* **1** shared, felt, or shown by both sides; mutual: *The city's colleges extend reciprocal privileges to each other's students.* **2** given, shown, felt, or done in return: *the reciprocal devastation of nuclear war.* **3** marked by or based on reciprocity: *reciprocal trade agreements.* **4** said *esp* of mathematical functions: inversely related. ➤ **reciprocality** /-'kaliti/ *noun*, **reciprocally** *adv*. [Latin *reciprocus* returning the same way, from RE- + PRO-²]

Usage note

reciprocal, mutual, *or* common? See note at MUTUAL.

reciprocal² *noun* **1** a number which is such that when multiplied by a given number gives a product of one: *The reciprocal of 5 is 0.2.* **2** the inverse of a number under multiplication.

reciprocal pronoun *noun* a pronoun, e.g. *each other*, used to denote mutual action or relationship.

reciprocate /ri'siprəkayt/ *verb trans* **1** to give and take (something) mutually: *The two countries reciprocated pledges of friendship.* **2** to return (something) in kind or degree: *You should reciprocate a compliment gracefully.* ➤ *verb intrans* **1** to make a return for something: *He stroked the cat and it reciprocated by purring.* **2** to move forwards and backwards alternately: *a reciprocating valve.* ➤ **reciprocation** /-'kaysh(ə)n/ *noun*, **reciprocative** /-kətiv/ *adj*, **reciprocator** *noun*.

reciprocating engine *noun* an engine in which the to-and-fro motion of a piston is transformed into circular motion of the crankshaft.

reciprocity /resi'prositi/ *noun* **1** mutual dependence, action, or influence. **2** a mutual exchange of privileges, *esp* between countries or institutions.

recital /ri'sietl/ *noun* **1** a concert or public performance given by a musician, a small group of musicians, or a dancer. **2a** the act or an instance of reciting. **b** a detailed account. **c** a discourse or narration. **3** (*in pl*) in law, the details of the purpose and effect of a deed of sale, and of the history of the property that is being sold. ➤ **recitalist** *noun*.

recitative /,resitə'teev/ *noun* a rhythmically free style of singing used in opera and oratorio for dialogue and narration. [Italian *recitativo*, from *recitare* to recite, from Latin *recitare*: see RECITE]

recite /ri'siet/ *verb trans* **1** to repeat (something) from memory or read (it) aloud, *esp* before an audience. **2** to relate (things) in detail; to enumerate (them): *He recited a catalogue of offences.* ➤ *verb intrans* to repeat or read aloud something memorized or prepared. ➤ **recitation** /resi'taysh(ə)n/ *noun*, **reciter** *noun*. [Middle English *reciten* to state formally, via early French *reciter* to recite, from Latin *recitare*, from RE- + *citare*: see CITE]

reck /rek/ *verb trans archaic* **1** to take account of (something): *He little recked what the outcome might be.* **2** to matter to (somebody); to concern (them): *What recks it me that I shall die tomorrow?* [Old English *reccan* to take heed]

reckless /'reklis/ *adj* marked by lack of proper caution; careless of consequences: *reckless driving; reckless courage.* ➤ **recklessly** *adv*, **recklessness** *noun*.

reckon /'rek(ə)n/ *verb* (**reckoned, reckoning**) ➤ *verb trans* **1a** to estimate or calculate (something): *The cost was reckoned at £10,000.* **b** to determine (something) by reference to a fixed basis: *The Gregorian calendar is reckoned from the birth of Christ.* **c** (*often + up*) to count (things). **2** to consider or think of (something or somebody) in a specified way: *She is reckoned the leading expert on the subject.* **3** *informal* to suppose or think (something): *I reckon they're not coming.* **4** *informal* to have a high opinion of (something or somebody): *The boys reckon him because he's one of the lads.* ➤ *verb intrans* **1** (+ on) to place reliance on somebody or something: *I'm reckoning on your support.* **2** to make a calculation. **3** *archaic* (+ with) to settle accounts with somebody. **4** *informal* (+ on/to) to have a specified view of somebody or something: *I didn't reckon much to her new boyfriend.* **5** *informal* to expect to be able to do a particular thing: *We reckon to catch the last bus.* ✱ **reckon with** to take (somebody or something) into account. **reckon without** to fail to consider (somebody or something) or to ignore (them). [Middle English *rekenen* from Old English *gerecenian* to narrate]

reckoner *noun* any non-electrical calculating aid, e.g. an abacus.

reckoning *noun* **1** the act or an instance of reckoning. **2** a summing up; an appraisal: *My belief is that in life people will take you much at your own reckoning —* Trollope. **3a** a calculation or counting. **b** *archaic* an account or bill. **4** events regarded as retribution for earlier behaviour: *a day of reckoning.*

reclaim¹ /ri'klaym/ *verb trans* **1** to claim (something) back; to recover (it). **2** to make (*esp* land) available for human use by changing natural conditions. **3** to obtain (a useful substance) from a waste product. **4** *literary* to rescue or convert (somebody) from an undesirable state; to reform (them). ➤➤ **reclaimable** *adj*, **reclaimer** *noun*, **reclamation** /reklə'maysh(ə)n/ *noun*. [Middle English *reclamen* via Old French *reclamer* to call back, from Latin *reclamare* to cry out against, from RE- + *clamare* to cry out, CLAIM¹]

reclaim² *noun* **1** the act of reclaiming something. **2** the condition of being fit to be reclaimed: *beyond reclaim*.

réclame /ray'klahm (*French* rekla:m)/ *noun* public acclaim. [French *réclame* advertising, from *réclamer* to appeal, from Old French *reclamer*: see RECLAIM¹]

recline /ri'klien/ *verb trans and intrans* **1** to lean backwards, or cause (something) to lean backwards: *He reclined the seat a little.* **2** to be in, or place (something) in a relaxed position: *She reclines her head on the pillow.* ➤➤ **reclinable** *adj*. [Middle English *reclinen* via French from Latin *reclinare*, from RE- + *clinare* to bend]

recliner *noun* **1** a comfortable chair with a back that can be lowered to various angles for extra comfort. **2** a person who reclines.

recluse¹ /ri'kloohs/ *noun* somebody who leads a secluded or solitary life. ➤➤ **reclusion** /-zh(ə)n/ *noun*, **reclusive** /-siv/ *adj*, **reclusiveness** *noun*. [Old French *reclus* shut up, from late Latin *reclusus*, past part. of *recludere* to shut up, from RE- + Latin *claudere* to CLOSE¹]

recluse² *adj archaic* marked by a tendency to withdraw from society; solitary.

recognisance /ri'kogniz(ə)ns/ *noun* see RECOGNIZANCE.

recognisant /ri'kogniz(ə)nt/ *adj* see RECOGNIZANT.

recognise /'rekəgniez/ *verb trans* see RECOGNIZE.

recognition /rekəg'nish(ə)n/ *noun* the act of recognizing something or somebody, or the fact of being recognized. [Latin *recognition-, recognitio*, from *recognoscere*: see RECOGNIZE]

recognizance *or* **recognisance** /ri'kogniz(ə)ns/ *noun* in law, a bond entered into before a court or magistrate that requires a person to do something, e.g. pay a debt or appear in court at a later date. [alteration of Middle English *reconissaunce* from early French *reconoissance* recognition, from *reconoistre* to recognize, from Latin *recognoscere*: see RECOGNIZE]

recognizant *or* **recognisant** /ri'kogniz(ə)nt/ *adj formal* (+ of) recognizing or being aware of (something).

recognize *or* **recognise** /'rekəgniez/ *verb trans* **1a** to perceive (a thing or a person) to be something or somebody previously known or encountered. **b** to perceive (something) clearly: *He recognized his own inadequacy.* **2a** to admit (something or somebody) as being of a particular status or having validity: *They recognized her as legitimate representative.* **b** to acknowledge the de facto existence or the independence of (e.g. a government or state). **c** to admit that (something) is a fact: *He recognizes his obligation.* **3** to show appreciation of (something or somebody), e.g. by praise or reward: *Her bravery was recognized by a special award.* **4** said of somebody chairing a meeting: to allow (somebody) to speak. **5** said of e.g. a computer: to be able to identify correctly and deal with (e.g. a printed character). ➤➤ **recognizability** /-'biliti/ *noun*, **recognizable** *adj*, **recognizably** *adv*, **recognizer** *noun*. [Middle English via early French *reconoistre*, from Latin *recognoscere*, from RE- + *cognoscere* to know]

recoil¹ /ri'koyl/ *verb intrans* **1** to shrink back physically or emotionally, e.g. in horror, fear, or disgust. **2** said of a firearm: to move backwards sharply when fired. **3** to spring back into an uncompressed position; to rebound: *The spring recoiled.* **4** (+ on/upon) to return with an adverse effect to a source or starting point: *Their hatred recoiled on themselves.* [Middle English *reculen* from Old French *reculer* move backwards, from RE- + Latin *culus* buttocks]

recoil² /'reekoyl/ *noun* the act or an instance of recoiling, *esp* the backwards movement of a gun on firing.

recollect /rekə'lekt/ *verb trans* **1** to bring (something) back to the level of conscious awareness; to remember (it). **2** to bring (oneself) back to a state of composure or concentration. ➤ *verb intrans* to call something to mind. ➤➤ **recollection** *noun*, **recollective** /-tiv/ *adj*. [medieval Latin *recollectus*, past part. of *recolligere* to gather again, from RE- + Latin *colligere*: see COLLECT¹]

recombinant¹ /ri'kombinənt/ *adj* denoting DNA prepared by combining pieces of DNA from different organisms either of the same or different species.

recombinant² *noun* a recombinant organism, piece of genetic material, etc.

recombination /reekombi'naysh(ə)n/ *noun* **1** the act or process of recombining. **2** the formation in offspring of new combinations of genes that did not occur in the parents, by processes whereby sections of the chromosomes become interchanged, and genes coding for different forms of inheritable characteristics, e.g. blue or brown eyes and tallness or shortness, combine randomly. ➤➤ **recombinational** *adj*.

recommend /rekə'mend/ *verb trans* **1a** to endorse (something or somebody) as fit, worthy, or competent: *He recommends her for the position.* **b** to declare (something) to be worth accepting or trying: *The magazine recommended our restaurant.* **2** to advise (something): *We recommend that the matter be dropped; I recommend that you see a doctor.* **3** to make (something) acceptable or desirable: *The school has other things to recommend it.* **4** *archaic* to entrust or commit (something) to somebody: *We recommend his soul to God.* ➤➤ **recommendable** *adj*, **recommendation** /-'daysh(ə)n/ *noun*, **recommendatory** /-'mendət(ə)ri/ *adj*, **recommender** *noun*. [Middle English *recommenden* to praise, from medieval Latin *recommendare*, from Latin RE- + *commendare*: see COMMEND]

recompense¹ /'rekəmpens/ *verb trans* **1** to give something to (somebody) by way of compensation, e.g. for a service rendered or damage incurred: *We recompensed him for his losses.* **2** to amount to compensation for (something): *a pleasure that recompenses our trouble.* [Middle English *recompensen* via French from late Latin *recompensare*, from RE- + *compensare*: see COMPENSATE]

recompense² *noun* an equivalent or a return for something done, suffered, or given: *The sum was offered in recompense for injuries.*

reconcile /'rekənsiel/ *verb trans* **1a** to restore (e.g. opposing factions) to friendship or harmony. **b** to settle or resolve (e.g. differences of opinion). **2** (+ with) to make (something) consistent or congruous with something else: *How do you reconcile this ideal with reality.* **3** (+ to) to cause somebody to submit to or accept (something): *She was reconciled to hardship.* ➤➤ **reconcilable** *adj*, **reconcilement** *noun*, **reconciler** *noun*. [Middle English *reconcilen* via French from Latin *reconciliare*, from RE- + *conciliare*: see CONCILIATE]

reconciliation /ˌrekənsili'aysh(ə)n/ *noun* the act or an instance of reconciling, *esp* a renewed state of harmony or agreement that exists between previously opposing groups. ➤➤ **reconciliatory** /-'sili·ət(ə)ri/ *adj*. [Middle English from Latin *reconciliation-, reconciliatio*, from *reconciliare*: see RECONCILE]

recondite /'rekəndiet, ri'kondiet/ *adj* known only by or to a few people; obscure: *the recondite literature of the Middle Ages.* [Latin *reconditus*, past part. of *recondere* to conceal, from RE- + *condere* to put together, secrete]

recondition /reekən'dish(ə)n/ *verb trans Brit* to restore (something) to good working condition, e.g. by replacing parts: *a reconditioned washing machine.*

reconnaissance /ri'konəs(ə)ns/ *noun* **1** an exploratory military survey of enemy territory or positions. **2** any preliminary or exploratory survey. [French *reconnaissance*, literally 'recognition', from *reconnaître*, alteration of *reconnoître*: see RECONNOITRE¹]

reconnoitre¹ (*NAmer* **reconnoiter**) /rekə'noytə/ *verb trans and intrans* (**reconnoitres, reconnoitred, reconnoitring,** *NAmer* **reconnoiters, reconnoitered, reconnoitering**) to make an exploratory military survey of (e.g. an enemy position or a region of land). [obsolete French *reconnoître* to recognize, from early French *reconoistre*: see RECOGNIZE]

reconnoitre² *noun informal* a reconnaissance.

reconsider /reekən'sidə/ *verb* (**reconsidered, reconsidering**) to consider (something) again with a view to change, revision, or revocation. ➤➤ **reconsideration** /-'raysh(ə)n/ *noun*.

reconstitute /ree'konstityooht/ *verb trans* **1** to build or constitute (something) again or anew. **2** to restore (food etc) to its natural state by adding water, *esp* to dried ingredients. ➤➤ **reconstitution** /-'tyoohsh(ə)n/ *noun*.

reconstruct /reekən'strukt/ *verb trans* **1** to restore (something) to a previous condition; to rebuild (it): *They can reconstruct a dinosaur from its bones.* **2** to reorganize or reestablish (something): *Society had to be reconstructed after the war.* **3** to build up a mental image or physical representation of (e.g. a crime or a battle) from the available evidence. ➤➤ **reconstructable** *adj*, **reconstructible** *adj*, **reconstructive** *adj*.

reconstruction /reekən'struksh(ə)n/ *noun* **1** the act or an instance of reconstructing. **2** (*often* **Reconstruction**) the reorganization and reestablishment of the seceded states in the Union after the American Civil War.

reconvert /reekən'vuht/ *verb trans* to cause (somebody or something) to undergo conversion back to a former state. ➤➤ **reconversion** *noun.*

record[1] /ri'kawd/ *verb trans* **1a** to commit (something) to writing, print, film, etc so as to supply written evidence of it. **b** to state or indicate (something) for or as if for a record: *We want to record certain reservations.* **2a** to register (something) permanently by mechanical or other means: *The tremors were recorded by a seismograph.* **b** to indicate (a measurement on a scale); to read (it). **3** to give evidence of (something); to show (it): *The intensity of the explosion is recorded on the charred tree trunks.* **4** to convert (e.g. sound) into a permanent form fit for reproduction. ➤ *verb intrans* to record something. ➤➤ **recordable** *adj.* [Middle English *recorden* to recall, via Old French from Latin *recordari*, from RE- + *cord-, cor* heart]

record[2] /'rekawd, 'rekəd/ *noun* **1a** a permanent account of something that serves as evidence of it. **b** something that recalls, relates, or commemorates past events or feats. **c** an authentic official document. **d** the official copy of the papers used in a law case. **2** a body of known or recorded facts regarding something or somebody: *a criminal record; He has a fine record as a manager.* **3** a list of previous criminal convictions: *They couldn't employ her because she has a record.* **4** a performance, occurrence, or condition that goes beyond or is extraordinary among others of its kind; *specif* the best recorded performance in a competitive sport. **5a** a flat usu plastic disc with a spiral groove whose undulations encode musical or other sounds for reproduction on a record player. **b** the song, music, etc recorded on such a disc. **6** a unit making up a computer file. ✳ **for the record** to be reported as official. **off the record** not for publication. **on record** in or into the status of being known, published, or documented: *He is on record as saying this.* **put/set the record straight** to correct a mistake or misapprehension.

record-breaking /'rekawd, 'rekəd/ *adj* bettering all previous attempts or surpassing all previous totals. ➤➤ **record-breaker** *noun.*

record deck /'rekawd, 'rekəd/ *noun* the apparatus including a turntable and stylus on which a gramophone record is played.

recorded delivery /ri'kawdid/ *noun* a postal service available in Britain in which the delivery of a posted item is recorded.

recorder /ri'kawdə/ *noun* **1** something that records. **2** a person who keeps official records. **3a** (*often* **Recorder**) a magistrate formerly presiding over the court of quarter sessions. **b** (*often* **Recorder**) a barrister or solicitor who sits as a circuit judge or a part-time judge in the crown court. **4** a simple woodwind instrument consisting of a slightly tapering tube with usu eight finger holes and a fipple mouthpiece. ➤➤ **recordership** *noun.* [(sense 4) from RECORD[1] in an archaic sense 'to practise a tune']

recording /ri'kawding/ *noun* something, e.g. sound or a television programme, that has been recorded electronically.

recording angel *noun* an angel who supposedly keeps an account of an individual's misdemeanours.

recordist /ri'kawdist/ *noun* a person who makes recordings, *esp* sound recordings.

record player /'rekawd, 'rekəd/ *noun* an electronically operated system for playing records, consisting of a turntable, stylus, and amplifying equipment.

recount[1] /ri'kownt/ *verb trans* to relate (something) in detail. [Middle English *recounten* from early French *reconter*, from RE- + *conter, compter*: see COUNT[1]]

recount[2] /ree'kownt/ *verb trans* to count (something) again.

recount[3] /'reekownt/ *noun* a second or fresh counting, *esp* of votes.

recoup /ri'koohp/ *verb trans* **1** to regain (something lost): *He wrote the book in an attempt to recoup his fortune.* **2a** to get an equivalent for (e.g. losses); to make up for (them). **b** to pay (a person, organization, etc) back; to compensate (them). **3** in law, to rightfully withhold part of (a sum due). ➤ *verb intrans* to make up for something lost. ➤➤ **recoupable** *adj,* **recoupment** *noun.* [French *recouper* to cut back, from RE- + *couper* to cut]

recourse /ri'kaws/ *noun* **1a** a source of help or strength; a resort: *The only resource was prayer.* **b** the use of somebody or something for help or protection: *to have recourse to the law.* **2** in law, the right to demand payment from the maker or endorser of a negotiable

document, e.g. a cheque. ✳ **without recourse** used to indicate that the person who endorses e.g. a bill of exchange is not liable. [Middle English *recours* via early French and late Latin from Latin *recursus* act of running back, from *recurrere*: see RECUR]

recover /ri'kuvə/ *verb* (**recovered, recovering**) ➤ *verb trans* **1** to regain possession or use of (something): *She quickly recovered her senses.* **2** to bring (something or somebody) back to a normal position or condition: *He stumbled, then recovered himself.* **3a** to make up for (something): *We won't even recover our costs.* **b** to obtain (e.g. costs) by legal action. **4** to obtain (something) from an ore, waste product, or by-product. ➤ *verb intrans* **1** to regain a normal or stable position or condition, e.g. of health: *He's recovering from a cold.* **2** to obtain a final legal judgment in one's favour. ➤➤ **recoverability** /-'biliti/ *noun,* **recoverable** *adj,* **recoverer** *noun.* [Middle English *recoveren* via French from Latin *recuperare*: see RECUPERATE]

re-cover /ree'kuvə/ *verb trans* (**re-covered, re-covering**) to provide (e.g. a chair) with a new cover.

recovery /ri'kuv(ə)ri/ *noun* (*pl* **recoveries**) **1a** a return to normal health. **b** a regaining of balance or control, e.g. after a stumble or mistake. **c** an economic upturn, e.g. after a depression. **2** the recovering of something, e.g. a vehicle that has broken down. **3a** the bringing forward of the arm in swimming or an oar in rowing, in preparation for another stroke. **b** a golf shot that takes the ball out of the rough or a bunker.

recovery position *noun Brit* a position in which an unconscious person is placed to prevent choking, with the body lying face down and to the side.

recovery shot *noun* = RECOVERY (3B).

recreant /'rekri-ənt/ *adj archaic* **1** cowardly. **2** unfaithful to duty or allegiance. ➤➤ **recreancy** *noun,* **recreant** *noun,* **recreantly** *adv.* [Middle English from early French *recreant,* present part. of *recroire* to surrender, to abandon one's cause, ultimately from RE- + Latin *credere* to trust]

recreate /reekri'ayt/ *verb trans* **1** to reproduce (something) exactly: *They had to recreate an old frontier town for the film.* **2** to visualize or create (something that exists or has existed) in the imagination.

recreation /rekri'aysh(ə)n/ *noun* **1** a pleasurable activity engaged in for relaxation or enjoyment: *His favourite recreation was spying on his neighbours.* **2** the refreshment of the mind and spirits after work: *I profess myself one of those who consider intervals of recreation and amusement as desirable for everybody* — Jane Austen. [Middle English *recreacion* via French from Latin *recreation-, recreatio* restoration to health, from *recreare* to create anew, restore, refresh, from RE- + *creare* to CREATE]

re-creation /reekri'aysh(ə)n/ *noun* the act or an instance of recreating.

recreational /rekri'aysh(ə)nəl/ *adj* **1** of or for recreation: *The village has few recreational facilities.* **2** said of the use of drugs: taken for pleasure. ➤➤ **recreationally** *adv.*

recreation ground *noun Brit* an open space, e.g. a field, on which games can be played, usu provided by the local council for public use.

recriminate /ri'kriminayt/ *verb intrans* to make recriminations. ➤➤ **recriminative** /-nativ/ *adj,* **recriminatory** /-nət(ə)ri/ *adj.* [medieval Latin *recriminatus,* past part. of *recriminare,* from Latin RE- + *criminari* to accuse]

recrimination /ri,krimi'naysh(ə)n/ *noun* (*usu in pl*) an accusation of wrongdoing made against somebody who has made a similar accusation.

recrudesce /reekrooh'des/ *verb intrans formal* said of something undesirable, *esp* a disease: to break out or become active again. ➤➤ **recrudescence** *noun,* **recrudescent** *adj.* [Latin *recrudescere* to become raw again, from RE- + *crudescere* to become raw, from *crudus* raw, rough]

recruit[1] /ri'krooht/ *noun* a newcomer to a field or activity; *specif* a newly enlisted member of the armed forces. [French *recrute, recrue* fresh growth, new levy of soldiers, via early French *recroistre* from Latin *recrescere* to grow again, from RE- + *crescere* to grow]

recruit[2] *verb trans* **1a** to enlist (a person) as a recruit. **b** to obtain (somebody) as a member of a group, or obtain their help. **c** to secure the services of (somebody); to employ (them). **2** to enlist recruits for (e.g. an army, regiment, or society). ➤ *verb intrans* to enlist new members. ➤➤ **recruitable** *adj,* **recruiter** *noun,* **recruitment** *noun.*

rect- *or* **recto-** *comb. form* forming words, denoting: rectum: *rectal*. [Latin *rectum*]

recta /'rektə/ *noun* pl of RECTUM.

rectal /'rekt(ə)l/ *adj* relating to or in the region of the rectum. ➤ **rectally** *adv*.

rectangle /'rektanggl/ *noun* a polygon with four right angles and four sides, *esp* one with adjacent sides of different lengths. [medieval Latin *rectangulus* having a right angle, from Latin *rectus* right + *angulus* ANGLE[1]]

rectangular /rek'tanggyoolə/ *adj* **1** shaped like a rectangle: *a rectangular area*. **2** having faces or surfaces shaped like rectangles: *a rectangular solid*. **3** crossing, lying, or meeting at a right angle: *rectangular axes*. ➤ **rectangularity** /-'lariti/ *noun*, **rectangularly** *adv*.

rectangular coordinate *noun* = CARTESIAN COORDINATE.

rectangular hyperbola *noun* a hyperbola with rectangular asymptotes (straight line approached by a curve; see ASYMPTOTE).

recti /'rektie/ *noun* pl of RECTUS.

rectifier /'rektifie-ə/ *noun* a device for converting alternating current, e.g. from the mains, into direct current, e.g. for use in a radio.

rectify /'rektifie/ *verb trans* (**rectifies, rectified, rectifying**) **1** to set (something) right; to remedy (it): *Mistakes will have to be rectified*. **2** to correct (something) by removing errors: *We'll have to rectify the situation*. **3** to convert (alternating current) to direct current. **4** to purify (e.g. alcohol), *esp* by repeated or fractional distillation. **5** to determine the length of (an arc or curve). ➤ **rectifiable** *adj*, **rectification** /-fi'kaysh(ə)n/ *noun*. [Middle English *rectifien* via French from medieval Latin *rectificare*, from Latin *rectus* right]

rectilineal /rekti'lini-əl/ *adj* = RECTILINEAR.

rectilinear /rekti'lini-ə/ *adj* **1a** moving in or forming a straight line: *rectilinear motion*. **b** characterized by straight lines. **2** said of a lens: showing no distortion of parallel lines. ➤ **rectilinearity** /-'ariti/ *noun*, **rectilinearly** *adv*. [late Latin *rectilineus*, from Latin *rectus* straight + *linea*: see LINE[1]]

rectitude /'rektityoohd/ *noun formal* **1** moral integrity. **2** correctness in judgment or procedure. [Middle English via French from late Latin *rectitudo*, from Latin *rectus* straight, right]

recto /'rektoh/ *noun* (*pl* **rectos**) a right-hand page: compare VERSO. [Latin *recto (folio)* on the right-hand page]

recto- *comb. form* see RECT-.

rector /'rektə/ *noun* **1a** a person in charge of a parish; *specif* one in a Church of England parish where the tithes were formerly paid to the incumbent: compare VICAR. **b** a Roman Catholic priest directing a church with no pastor or one whose pastor has other duties. **2** the head of a university or college. **3** a student elected to serve on a Scottish university's governing body. ➤ **rectorate** /-rət/ *adj*, **rectorial** /rek'tawri-əl/ *adj*, **rectorship** *noun*. [Latin *rector* director, from *regere* to direct]

rectory *noun* (*pl* **rectories**) **1** a rector's residence. **2** a benefice held by a rector.

rectrix /'rektriks/ *noun* (*pl* **rectrices** /-seez/) any of a bird's tail feathers that are important in controlling flight direction. [Latin *rectrix*, fem of *rector*: see RECTOR]

rectum /'rektəm/ *noun* (*pl* **rectums** *or* **recta** /'rektə/) the last part of the intestine of a vertebrate animal, ending at the anus. [scientific Latin, from Latin *rectum intestinum* straight intestine]

rectus /'rektəs/ *noun* (*pl* **recti** /'rektie/) any of several straight abdominal muscles. [scientific Latin, from Latin *rectus musculus* straight muscle]

recumbent /ri'kumbənt/ *adj* **1** lying down or reclining: *Bernard enjoyed half an hour of that light and easy slumber which is apt to overtake idle people in recumbent attitudes in the open air on August afternoons* — Henry James. **2** said of a plant: growing close to the ground. **3** said of a bodily organ: resting against another organ. ➤ **recumbency** /-si/ *noun*, **recumbently** *adv*. [Latin *recumbent-, recumbens*, present part. of *recumbere* to lie down]

recuperate /ri'k(y)oohpərayt/ *verb intrans* to regain a former healthy state or condition; to recover. ➤ *verb trans* to regain (something lost): *The financial losses will not be recuperated*. ➤ **recuperable** *adj*, **recuperation** /-'raysh(ə)n/ *noun*, **recuperative** /-rətiv/ *adj*. [Latin *recuperatus*, past part. of *recuperare* to recover, from RE- + *capere* to take]

recur /ri'kuh/ *verb intrans* (**recurred, recurring**) **1** to occur again, *esp* repeatedly or after an interval: *I knew the difficulties would only recur*. **2** to come back to one's mind; to enter one's thoughts again. ➤ **recurrence** /ri'kurəns/ *noun*, **recurring** *adj*. [Middle English *recurren* to return, from Latin *recurrere*, literally 'to run back', from RE- + *currere* to run]

recurrent /ri'kurənt/ *adj* **1** returning or happening repeatedly or periodically: *recurrent complaints*. **2** said of nerves and blood vessels: running or turning back in a direction opposite to a former course. ➤ **recurrently** *adv*. [Latin *recurrent-, recurrens*, present part. of *recurrere*: see RECUR]

recurring decimal /ri'kuhring/ *noun* a decimal in which a particular digit or sequence of digits repeats itself indefinitely at some stage after the decimal point.

recursion /ri'kuhsh(ə)n/ *noun* **1** *formal* a return. **2** in mathematics, the repeated application of a particular procedure to the previous result, e.g. to determine a sequence of numbers or a more accurate approximation to a square root. [late Latin *recursion-, recursio*, from *recurrere*: see RECUR]

recursive /ri'kuhsiv/ *adj* **1** of or involving mathematical recursion. **2a** being a prescribed method that recurs indefinitely or until a specified condition is met: *a recursive rule in a grammar*. **b** being a computer program that calls itself into operation or calls other programs which in turn recall the original. ➤ **recursively** *adv*.

recurve /ri'kuhv/ *verb intrans* to bend backwards or inwards.

recusant /'rekyooz(ə)nt/ *noun* **1** a person who refuses to accept or obey established authority. **2** formerly, a Roman Catholic refusing to attend services of the Church of England, which was a statutory offence from about 1570 until 1791. ➤ **recusance** *noun*, **recusancy** *noun*, **recusant** *adj*. [Latin *recusant-, recusans*, present part. of *recusare* to refuse, from RE- + *causari* to give a reason, from *causa* CAUSE[1]]

recycle /ree'siekl, ri-/ *verb trans* **1** to return (a substance) to a previous stage in a cyclic process; *specif* to process (sewage, waste paper, glass, etc) for conversion back into a useful product. **2** to reclaim or re-use (something). ➤ *verb intrans* said *esp* of an electronic device: to return to an original condition so that operation can begin again. ➤ **recyclable** *adj*, **recycler** *noun*.

red[1] /red/ *adj* (**redder, reddest**) **1** of the colour of blood or a ruby, at the end of the spectrum next to orange. **2** said of hair or the coat of an animal: in the colour range between a medium orange and russet or bay. **3** tinged with or rather red: *a red sky*. **4a** said of the face: flushed, *esp* with anger or embarrassment. **b** said of the eyes: bloodshot. **5** said of wine: made from dark grapes and coloured by their skins. **6** failing to show a profit: compare BLACK[1] (7): *a red financial statement*. **7** *informal, derog* communist or socialist: compare WHITE[1] (13). **8** *archaic or literary* involving force, violence, or bloodshed: *red revolution*. ➤ **reddish** *adj*, **redly** *adv*, **redness** *noun*. [Old English *rēad*]

red[2] *noun* **1** the colour of blood or a ruby. **2** *informal, derog* a communist or socialist. ✳ **in the red** financially not in credit; insolvent; not making a profit. **see red** *informal* to become angry suddenly.

redact /ri'dakt/ *verb trans* to prepare (something) for publication; to edit (it). ➤ **redaction** /-sh(ə)n/ *noun*, **redactor** *noun*. [earliest as *redaction*, from French *rédaction*, ultimately from Latin *redigere* to bring down, reduce, from RE- + *agere* to do]

red admiral *noun* a common N American and European butterfly that has broad orange-red bands on the forewings and feeds on nettles in the larval stage: *Vanessa atalanta*.

red algae *pl noun* algae that are seaweeds with a predominantly red colour: division Rhodophyta.

redback *noun* a poisonous Australian spider that has a broad red stripe on its back: *Latrodectus mactans hasseltii*.

red biddy *noun Brit, informal, dated* a mixture for drinking consisting of red wine and methylated spirits.

red blood cell *noun* any of the haemoglobin-containing cells that carry oxygen to the tissues and are responsible for the red colour of vertebrate blood; an erythrocyte: compare WHITE BLOOD CELL.

red-blooded *adj* full of vigour; virile. ➤ **red-bloodedness** *noun*.

redbreast *noun chiefly Brit, informal* a robin.

redbrick *adj* denoting a British university founded between 1840 and World War II, as distinct from the ancient British universities: *His teachers threw scorn on the idea of going to a redbrick university when he could have chosen Oxford.* [from the common use of red brick in the buildings of such universities]

redbush *noun* = ROOIBOS (I).

redcap *noun* **1** *Brit, informal* a military police officer. **2** *NAmer* a railway porter.

red card *noun* a red card held up by a football referee to indicate the sending-off of a player: compare YELLOW CARD.

red-card *verb trans* to show a red card to (a player).

red carpet *noun* **1** a long piece of red carpet laid down for an important guest to walk on. **2** (*used before a noun*) marked by ceremonial courtesy: *red carpet treatment.*

red cedar *noun* **1** either of two American cedar trees with reddish brown bark: *Thuja plicata* and *Juniperus virginia.* **2** the hard wood of either of these trees, widely used in the building industry.

red cell *noun* = RED BLOOD CELL.

red cent *noun NAmer* **1** a one-cent coin. **2** a trivial amount: *It's not worth a red cent.*

redcoat *noun* **1** a British soldier, *esp* during the late 18th cent. and early 19th cent. when scarlet jackets were worn. **2** in Britain, a person who works as an entertainer at a Butlin's holiday camp.

red coral *noun* a gorgonian coral with a hard pinkish to red skeleton used for jewellery and ornaments: genus *Corallium.*

Red Crescent *noun* the Red Cross as it exists in Muslim countries, with the sign of a crescent substituted for the cross.

Red Cross *noun* an international humanitarian organization that has as its emblem a red Greek cross on a white background.

redcurrant *noun* **1** a small red edible berry. **2** the widely cultivated European bush that bears this berry: *Ribes rubrum.*

redd /red/ *verb trans* (*past tense and past part.* **redd** *or* **redded**) *NAmer, Scot, Irish* to set (something) in order; to make (it) tidy. [Middle English *redden* to clear, prob alteration of *ridden*: see RID]

red deer *noun* a large deer that is the common deer of temperate Europe and Asia and has a reddish brown coat in summer: *Cervus elaphus.*

Red Delicious *noun* a variety of eating apple with a red skin and soft sweet flesh.

redden *verb* (**reddened, reddening**) ➤ *verb trans* to make (something) red or reddish. ➤ *verb intrans* to become red, *esp* to blush.

reddle /'redl/ *noun* = RED OCHRE. [alteration of RUDDLE]

red duster *noun Brit, informal* the red ensign.

red dwarf *noun* a star with a low surface temperature and a mass about one tenth of that of the sun.

rede¹ /reed/ *noun archaic* counsel or advice: *Himself the primrose path of dalliance treads, and recks not his own rede* — Shakespeare. [Old English *ræd*, of Germanic origin]

rede² *verb trans archaic* **1** to give counsel to (somebody); to advise (them). **2** to interpret or explain (something).

redeem /ri'deem/ *verb trans* **1a** to offset the bad effect of (something): *Flashes of wit redeemed a dreary speech; The kitchen is the redeeming feature of the house.* **b** to atone for (a mistake, error of judgment, etc); to expiate (it). **c** to make (something) worthwhile; to retrieve (it): *No efforts of his could redeem such a hopeless undertaking.* **2a** to release (somebody) from blame or debt; to clear (them): *She redeemed herself by scoring a hat trick in the second half.* **b** to free (somebody) from the consequences of sin or evil. **3a** to get, win, or buy (something) back, *esp* to buy back (something used as security in return for a loan) by repaying the money loaned: *She went to redeem her pawned wedding ring.* **b** to recover possession of (something) by fulfilling an obligation, *esp* by payment of a debt. **c** to remove the obligation of (e.g. a bond) by making a stipulated payment: *The government redeem savings bonds on demand.* **d** to convert (trading stamps, tokens, etc) into money or goods. **4** to make (e.g. a promise) good; to fulfil (it). ➤ **redeemable** *adj,* **redeeming** *adj.* [Middle English *redemen,* modification of early French *redimer* from Latin *redimere,* from RE- + *emere* to take, buy]

Redeemer *noun* **1** (**the Redeemer**) Jesus Christ regarded as the saviour of humankind. **2** (**redeemer**) a person who redeems somebody or something.

redemption /ri'dem(p)sh(ə)n/ *noun* **1** the act of redeeming or the fact of being redeemed. **2** something that redeems, *esp* something that redeems somebody from sin or makes up for past offences. ➤➤ **redemptive** /-tiv/ *adj.* [Middle English *redempcioun* via French from Latin *redemption-, redemptio,* from *redimere:* see REDEEM]

red ensign *noun* the flag of the British merchant navy, consisting of a Union Jack in the upper corner on a red background.

redeploy /reedi'ploy/ *verb* to transfer (e.g. troops or workers) from one area or activity to another. ➤➤ **redeployment** *noun.*

redevelop /reedi'veləp/ *verb trans* to design, develop, or build (something) again; *specif* to renovate a deteriorating or depressed (urban) area. ➤➤ **redeveloper** *noun,* **redevelopment** *noun.*

red-eye *noun* **1** in photography, an effect that makes people seem to have red eyes, caused by the flash being held too close to the lens of the camera. **2** *chiefly NAmer, informal* a passenger aircraft making a long-distance overnight flight. **3** *NAmer, informal* cheap whisky. **4** a fish that has red eyes, e.g. the rudd.

red-faced *adj* embarrassed, or flushed with embarrassment.

redfish *noun* (*pl* **redfishes** *or collectively* **redfish**) **1** = KOKANEE. **2** *Brit* a male salmon that has just spawned.

red flag *noun* **1** an international symbol of danger. **2** the symbol of communism or socialism.

red fox *noun* a common reddish brown European fox that inhabits a range from the Mediterranean to the Arctic: *Vulpes vulpes.*

red giant *noun* a star that has a low surface temperature and a large diameter relative to the sun.

red grouse *noun* a dark reddish brown grouse that is important as a game bird and is found *esp* on the moors of N England and Scotland: *Lagopus lagopus scoticus.*

red gum *noun* **1** any of numerous species of Australian eucalyptus trees with smooth bark: genus *Eucalyptus.* **2** the hard reddish wood of these trees. **3** the reddish brown gum from some of these trees, used as an astringent.

red-handed *adj* in the act of committing a crime or misdeed: *I had been caught red-handed.*

red hat *noun* a broad-rimmed crimson hat that is the emblem of a cardinal's rank.

redhead *noun* a person with red hair. ➤➤ **redheaded** *adj.*

red heat *noun* the temperature at which a substance is red-hot.

red herring *noun* **1** a herring cured by salting and slow smoking to a dark brown colour. **2** something irrelevant that distracts attention from the real issue. [(sense 2) from the practice of drawing a red herring across a trail to confuse hunting dogs]

red-hot *adj* **1** glowing red with heat; extremely hot. **2** arousing enthusiasm; very popular: *a red-hot favourite.* **3** sensational; *specif* salacious: *a red-hot story.* **4** marked by intense emotion; ardent: *red-hot passion.*

red-hot poker *noun* a S African plant of the lily family with tall erect spikes of yellow flowers changing to bright red towards the top: *Kniphofia uvaria.*

redid /ree'did/ *verb* past tense of REDO.

Red Indian *noun dated, offensive* a Native American.

redingote /'redinggoht/ *noun* **1** an overcoat with a large collar worn, *esp* by men, in the 18th and 19th cents. **2** a woman's lightweight coat with a cut-away front below the waist. [French *redingote,* modification of English *riding coat*]

redintegrate /ri'dintigrayt/ *verb trans archaic* to restore (something or somebody) to a former sound state. ➤➤ **redintegration** /-'graysh(ə)n/ *noun,* **redintegrative** *adj.* [Middle English *redintegraten* from Latin *redintegratus* past part. of *redintegrare* from RE- + *integrare:* see INTEGRATE]

redirect /reedi'rekt, reedie'rekt/ *verb trans* to change the course or direction of (something); *specif* to send (post) to a different address. ➤➤ **redirection** /-sh(ə)n/ *noun.*

redistribution /,reedistri'byoohsh(ə)n/ *noun* the distribution of something, e.g. wealth, in different and usu more appropriate or fair proportions.

redivivus /redi'vievəs/ *adj* (*pl* **redivivi** /-vie/, *fem* **rediviva** /-və/, *pl* **redivivae** /-vee/) *literary* brought back to life; reborn. [Latin *redivivus* renovated, from RE- + *vivus* living]

red lead /led/ *noun* a red lead oxide formerly used in storage battery plates, in glass and ceramics, and as a paint pigment, now usually avoided because of its toxicity: formula Pb_3O_4.

Red Leicester *noun* = LEICESTER (I).

red-letter day *noun* a day of special significance, *esp* a particularly happy occasion. [from the practice of marking holy days in red letters in church calendars]

red light *noun* a red warning light, *esp* on a road or railway, commanding traffic to stop.

red-light district *noun* a district that has many brothels. [from the red lights that traditionally identified a prostitute's room or a brothel]

redline *verb trans chiefly NAmer, informal* **1** to refuse to lend money or to provide insurance cover to (somebody living in a high-risk area). **2** to drive (a vehicle) at its maximum rpm.

red meat *noun* dark-coloured meat, e.g. beef or lamb: compare WHITE MEAT.

red mullet *noun* any of several species of food fishes with reddish skin and long barbels (thin sensory projections; see BARBEL²) on its chin, found throughout the Mediterranean: *Muletus surmuletus* and other species.

redneck *noun NAmer, informal, derog* **1** a white member of the rural labouring class of the southern USA. **2** a bigoted reactionary. ➤➤ **redneck** *adj.* [from the sunburned necks of rural workers]

redo /ree'dooh/ *verb trans (third person sing. present tense* **redoes** /ree'duz/, *past tense* **redid** /ree'did/, *past part.* **redone** /ree'dun/) **1** to do (something) again or differently. **2** *informal* to decorate (a room or interior of a building) anew.

red ochre *noun* a red earthy HAEMATITE (iron oxide mineral) used as a pigment.

redolent /'redəlant/ *adj* **1** (+ of/with) suggesting a particular quality; evocative: *a city redolent of antiquity.* **2** (+ of/with) full of a specified fragrance: *air redolent of seaweed.* **3** *archaic or literary* having a pleasant smell. ➤➤ **redolence** *noun,* **redolently** *adv.* [Middle English via French, from Latin *redolent-, redolens,* present part. of *redolēre* to emit a scent, from RE- + *olēre* to smell]

redone /ree'dun/ *verb* past part. of REDO.

redouble¹ /ri'dubl/ *verb trans* to make (something) greater, more numerous, or more intense: *We redoubled our efforts.* ➤ *verb intrans* **1** to become redoubled. **2** /ree'dubl/ in bridge, to double an opponent's double.

redouble² /ree'dubl/ *noun* in bridge, a bid redoubling an opponent's bid.

redoubt /ri'dowt/ *noun* **1** a small usu temporary enclosed defensive fortified structure. **2** a secure place; a stronghold. [French *redoute* via Italian *ridotto* from Latin *reductus* withdrawn, from *reducere*: see REDUCE]

redoubtable *adj* **1** causing fear or alarm; formidable: *a redoubtable adversary.* **2** inspiring or worthy of awe or reverence. ➤➤ **redoubtably** *adv.* [Middle English *redoutable* from early French *redouter* to dread, from RE- + *douter* to doubt, from Latin *dubitare*: see DOUBT¹]

redound /ri'downd/ *verb intrans formal* **1** (+ to) to have a direct effect; to lead or contribute to something: *It can only redound to our advantage.* **2** *archaic* (+ on/upon) to rebound on or upon somebody: *The President's behaviour redounds on his party.* [Middle English *redounden* to overflow, via early French *redonder* from Latin *redundare,* from RE- + *unda* wave]

redox /'reedoks/ *noun (used before a noun)* of or involving both oxidation and reduction: *a redox reaction.* [blend of REDUCTION + OXIDATION]

red panda *noun* = PANDA (2).

red pepper *noun* the ripe red fruit of the capsicum or sweet pepper.

redpoll /'redpol/ *noun* any of several small finches that resemble and are closely related to the linnet: genus *Acanthis.* [POLL¹]

red poll /pohl/ *noun* an animal of a British breed of large red hornless dairy and beef cattle.

red rag *noun* something that arouses anger, *esp* something calculated to do so: *Behaviour which seems innocuous to one person can be a red rag to another.* [from the notion that bulls are enraged by the colour red]

redress¹ /ri'dres/ *verb trans* **1** to set (something) right; to remedy (it): *There were many social wrongs that needed to be redressed.* **2** to adjust (something) evenly, making it stable or equal again: *They had redressed the balance of power.* ➤➤ **redressable** *adj,* **redresser**

noun. [Middle English *redressen* from early French *redresser,* from RE- + *dresser*: see DRESS¹]

redress² *noun* **1** compensation for wrong or loss. **2** the putting right of what is wrong, or the means or possibility of putting it right.

re-dress /ree'dres/ *verb trans* to dress (e.g. a wound) again.

red rose *noun* **1** an emblem of the House of Lancaster. **2** a symbol of the Labour Party in Britain.

red salmon *noun* = SOCKEYE.

redshank *noun* either of two species of wading birds with pale red legs and feet, found throughout Europe and Asia: genus *Tringa.*

red shift *noun* a shift in the wavelengths of the light or other electromagnetic radiations emitted by a celestial body when seen from a distant point, e.g. the earth, from their normal positions in the spectrum towards longer wavelengths. This is a consequence of the Doppler effect or of the gravity of the body: compare BLUE SHIFT.

redskin *noun dated, offensive* a Native American.

red snapper *noun* any of various reddish fishes including many important as food that are common in warm seas: genus *Lutjanus.*

red spider *noun* any of several small mites that attack crop plants.

red squirrel *noun* a reddish brown Eurasian squirrel native to British woodlands that is gradually being replaced by the grey squirrel: *Sciurus vulgaris.*

redstart *noun* **1** any of several species of small songbirds with a chestnut tail and underparts, native to Europe: genus *Phoenicurus.* **2** an American warbler with conspicuous red or orange markings: genus *Setophaga.* **3** any of various related birds: family Turdidae. [RED¹ + obsolete *start* handle, tail]

red tape *noun* excessively complex bureaucratic routine that results in delay. [from the red tape used to bind legal documents in Britain]

red tide *noun* seawater discoloured and made toxic by the presence of large numbers of red protozoans.

reduce /ri'dyoohs/ *verb trans* **1** to make (something) less in size, amount, volume, extent, or number. **2** to make (a liquid) more concentrated, e.g. by boiling. **3** to make (something) less in strength, density, or value. **4** to lower the price of (something). **5a** to lower (somebody) in grade or rank; to demote. **b** to lower (somebody or something) in condition or status: *living in reduced circumstances.* **6** to bring or force (somebody) to a specified state or condition: *to be reduced to tears.* **7a** to change (something) from one form into another more simple or basic form. **b** to simplify the form of (e.g. a fraction or equation) without changing the value. **8** *archaic* to force (e.g. a city) to capitulate. **9a** to cause (something) to lose oxygen atoms; to remove oxygen from (a substance). **b** to combine (a chemical substance) with hydrogen; to add hydrogen atoms to (a substance). **c** to add one or more electrons to (e.g. an atom, molecule, or ion). **10** to correct (e.g. a fracture of a bone) by bringing the displaced or broken parts back into their normal positions. ➤ *verb intrans* **1** to become diminished or lessened. **2** *chiefly NAmer* to lose weight by dieting. **3** to become more concentrated, e.g. by boiling. **4** to become reduced: *Ferric iron reduces to ferrous iron.* ➤➤ **reducer** *noun,* **reducibility** /-sə'biliti/ *noun,* **reducible** *adj.* [Middle English *reducen* to lead back, from Latin *reducere,* from RE- + *ducere* to lead]

reducing agent *noun* a substance that reduces a chemical compound, usu by donating electrons: compare OXIDIZING AGENT.

reductant /ri'duktənt/ *noun* = REDUCING AGENT.

reductase /ri'duktayz/ *noun* any enzyme that increases the rate at which a biochemical reaction involving the chemical reduction of a compound occurs.

reductio ad absurdum /ri,duktioh ad ab'suhdəm/ *noun* proof of the falsity of a proposition by revealing the absurdity of its logical consequences. [late Latin *reductio ad absurdum,* literally 'reduction to the absurd']

reduction /ri'duksh(ə)n/ *noun* **1** the act or an instance of reducing. **2** the amount by which something is reduced. **3** a reproduction, e.g. of a picture, in a smaller size. **4** a liquid, e.g. a sauce, that has been reduced. ➤➤ **reductive** /-tiv/ *adj.* [Middle English *reduccion* restoration, via early French *reduction* and late Latin from Latin *reduction-, reductio,* from *reducere*: see REDUCE]

reductionism *noun* a procedure or theory that reduces complex data or phenomena to simple terms, *esp* oversimplification. ➤➤ **reductionist** *noun and adj*, **reductionistic** /-'nistik/ *adj*.

redundancy /ri'dundənsi/ *noun* (*pl* **redundancies**) **1** being redundant. **2** the part of a message that can be eliminated without loss of essential information. **3** *chiefly Brit* dismissal from a job.

redundant /ri'dundənt/ *adj* **1a** no longer useful or necessary; superfluous. **b** characterized by or containing an excess; *specif* excessively verbose: *a redundant literary style.* **c** serving as a backup so as to prevent failure of an entire system, e.g. a spacecraft, in the event of failure of a single component. **2** *chiefly Brit* no longer required for a job. ➤➤ **redundantly** *adv.* [Latin *redundant-, redundans*, present part. of *redundare*: see REDOUND]

reduplicate /ri'dyoohplikayt/ *verb trans* **1** to make or perform (something) again; to copy or repeat (it). **2** to form (a word) by reduplication. ➤ *verb intrans* to undergo reduplication. ➤➤ **reduplicate** *adj*.

reduplication /ri,reedyoohpli'kaysh(ə)n/ *noun* **1** the act or an instance of reduplicating. **2** the doubling of a word, or part of a word, with or without partial modification, e.g. in *hocus pocus* or *dilly-dally*. ➤➤ **reduplicative** /ree'dyoohplikətiv/ *adj*.

red water *noun* any of various diseases of cattle marked by the presence of blood or red blood cells in the urine.

red-water fever *noun* = RED WATER.

redwing *noun* a Eurasian thrush with red patches beneath its wings: *Turdus iliacus.*

redwood *noun* **1a** a commercially important Californian timber tree of the pine family that often reaches a height of 100m (about 300ft): *Sequoia sempervirens.* **b** the durable reddish wood of this tree. **2** a giant conifer native to Oregon: *Sequoiadendron giganteum.*

reebok /'reebok/ *noun* see RHEBOK.

re-echo /ree'ekoh/ *verb* (**re-echoes, re-echoed, re-echoing**) ➤ *verb intrans* to repeat or return an echo. ➤ *verb trans* to echo (something) back; to repeat (something said).

reed /reed/ *noun* **1** any of various tall grasses that grow in wet or marshy areas, or their thin, often prominently jointed stems: genera *Phragmites* and *Arundo*. **2a** a growth or mass of reeds; *specif* reeds used for thatching. **b** the stem of a reed. **3** a thin single tongue or flattened tube of cane, metal, or plastic, fastened over an air opening in a musical instrument, e.g. an organ, oboe, or clarinet, which causes an air column to vibrate. **4** a person or thing too weak to rely on; somebody or something easily swayed or overcome. **5** a device on a loom resembling a comb, used to space warp yarns evenly. **6** (*usu in pl*) a semicircular convex moulding that is usu one of several set parallel. **7** *literary* an arrow. [Old English *hrēod*]

reedbuck *noun* (*pl* **reedbucks** *or collectively* **reedbuck**) any of several species of fawn-coloured African antelopes of which the females are hornless: genus *Redunca*.

reed bunting *noun* a common Eurasian bunting that frequents marshy places: *Emberiza schoeniclus.*

reeding *noun* **1** a narrow semicircular convex moulding that is usu one of several set parallel as architectural decoration. **2** architectural decoration consisting of a series of reedings.

reedling /'reedling/ *noun* = BEARDED TIT.

redmace *noun* any of several species of tall reedy marsh plants with brown furry fruiting spikes: genus *Typha*. Also called CAT'S-TAIL. [MACE[1], which the plant was thought to resemble]

reed organ *noun* a keyboard instrument in which the wind acts on a set of freely vibrating reeds.

reed pipe *noun* an organ pipe producing its tone by the vibration of a beating reed in an air current: compare FLUE PIPE.

reedstop *noun* an organ stop that controls a rank of reed pipes.

re-educate /ree'edyookayt, ree'ejookayt/ *verb trans* **1** to cause (somebody) to think or behave in a different way. **2** to rehabilitate (e.g. offenders) through education. ➤➤ **re-education** /-'kaysh(ə)n/ *noun*.

reed warbler *noun* any of several species of Eurasian warblers that frequent marshy places: genus *Acrocephalus*.

reedy *adj* (**reedier, reediest**) **1** full of, covered with, or made of reeds. **2** slender or frail. **3** said of a voice: having the tonal quality of a reed instrument, *esp* thin and high: *Johnny's reedy tenor they knew well — Willa Cather.* ➤➤ **reediness** *noun*.

reef¹ /reef/ *noun* **1** a ridge of rocks, sand, or coral at or near the surface of water. **2** a vein of ore; a lode. [Dutch *rif*, prob of Scandinavian origin]

reef² *noun* a part of a sail taken in or let out to regulate the area exposed to the wind. [Middle English *riff* from Old Norse *rif*]

reef³ *verb trans* **1** to reduce the area of (a sail) exposed to the wind by rolling up or taking in a portion. **2** to shorten (a spar).

reefer¹ *noun* a close-fitting usu double-breasted jacket of thick cloth. [REEF³ + -ER²]

reefer² *noun informal* a cannabis cigarette, or cannabis. [prob from REEF² in the sense 'something rolled up' + -ER²]

reefer³ *noun* somebody who reefs a sail.

reefer jacket *noun* = REEFER¹.

reef knot *noun* a symmetrical knot made of two half-knots tied in opposite directions, commonly used for joining two ropes.

reefpoint *noun* any of various short lengths of line attached to a sail for the purpose of reefing.

reek¹ /reek/ *verb intrans* **1a** to give off or become permeated with a strong or offensive smell. **b** (+ of/with) to give a strong impression of some usu undesirable quality or feature: *The area reeks of poverty.* **2** *archaic* to give off smoke or vapour. ➤ *verb trans* to give (something) off; to exude (it): *He reeks charm.*

reek² *noun* **1** a strong or disagreeable smell. **2** *chiefly Scot, N Eng* smoke or vapour. ➤➤ **reeky** *adj*. [Old English *rēc* smoke]

reel¹ /reel, riəl/ *noun* **1** *chiefly Brit* a small spool for sewing thread. **2** a quantity of something wound on a reel. **3** a small wheel at the butt of a fishing rod for winding the line. **4** a spool with a projecting rim, e.g. for photographic film or magnetic tape. [Old English *hrēol*]

reel² *verb trans* **1** to wind (something) on or as if on a reel. **2** (+ in) to draw (a fish) out of the water by reeling a line. **3** (+ in) to entice (somebody) slowly and steadily.

reel³ *verb intrans* **1** to be giddy or bewildered: *His mind was reeling.* **2** to waver or fall back, e.g. from a blow: *She reeled back in horror.* **3** to walk or appear to move unsteadily, e.g. from dizziness or intoxication. ➤➤ **reeler** *noun*. [Middle English *relen*, prob from REEL¹]

reel⁴ *noun* a reeling motion.

reel⁵ *noun* a lively Scottish-Highland or Irish dance in which two or more couples perform a series of circular figures and winding movements, or the music for this dance. [prob from REEL⁴]

reel off *verb trans* **1** to tell or repeat (something) readily and without pause: *She reeled off all the facts and figures.* **2** to chalk (things) up, usu as a series: *They reeled off six wins in succession.*

reel-to-reel *adj* denoting or using magnetic tape passing between two reels that are unconnected and not in a cassette or cartridge: *a reel-to-reel tape recorder.*

re-entrant¹ /ree'entrənt/ *adj* said of an angle, point, etc: directed or pointing inwards: compare SALIENT¹.

re-entrant² *noun* a re-entrant angle.

re-entry /ree'entri/ *noun* (*pl* **re-entries**) **1** the return to and entry of the earth's atmosphere by a space vehicle. **2** a second or new entry, e.g. to a country: *a re-entry visa.* **3** in law, the retaking of possession of something.

reeve¹ /reev/ *noun* **1** the local administrative agent of an Anglo-Saxon king. **2** a medieval English manor officer with the job of ensuring that feudal obligations were discharged. **3** *Can* a council president in some municipalities. [Middle English *reve* from Old English *gerēfa*]

reeve² *verb trans* (*past tense and past part.* **rove** /rohv/ *or* **reeved**) **1** to pass (e.g. a rope) through a hole or opening. **2** to fasten (something) by passing it through a hole or round something. **3** to pass a rope through (e.g. a block). [prob from Dutch *reven* to reef a sail]

reeve³ *noun* a Eurasian bird, the female of the ruff. [prob alteration of RUFF¹]

re-export¹ /ri·ik'spawt, ri·ek'spawt/ *verb trans* to export (something that has been imported), e.g. after further processing. ➤➤ **re-exportation** /-'taysh(ə)n/ *noun*, **re-exporter** *noun*.

re-export² /ri'ekspawt/ *noun* the act of re-exporting, or something re-exported.

ref /ref/ *noun informal* the referee of a football match or other sporting contest.

ref. *abbr* **1** reference. **2** referred.

refection /ri'feksh(ə)n/ *noun literary* a light meal, or the taking of one. [Middle English *refeccioun* via French from Latin *refection-*, *refectio*, from *reficere* to restore, from RE- + *facere* to make]

refectory /ri'fekt(ə)ri/ *noun* (*pl* **refectories**) a dining hall in an institution, e.g. a monastery or college. [late Latin *refectorium*, ultimately from Latin *reficere*: see REFECTION]

refectory table *noun* a long narrow dining table with heavy legs.

refer /ri'fuh/ *verb* (**referred, referring**) ➤ *verb intrans* **1** (+ to) to direct attention to something by mentioning it; to allude to it: *The numbers refer to footnotes; No one referred to yesterday's quarrel.* **2** (+ to) to have recourse to something; to consult it: *He referred frequently to his notes while speaking.* ➤ *verb trans* **1** to send or direct (somebody) for treatment, aid, information, testimony, or decision: *She referred the patient to a specialist; I refer students to my other works.* **2** to explain (something) in terms of a general cause: *The doctor refers their depression to the weather.* **3** to allot (something) to a specified place, stage, period, or category: *Historians refer the fall of Rome to 410 AD.* **4** to experience (e.g. pain) as coming from or located in a different area from its source: *The pain in appendicitis may be referred to any area of the abdomen.* **5** to fail (somebody taking an examination). ✳ **refer to drawer** *Brit* used to inform the payee of a cheque that payment has been suspended. ➤➤ **referable** *adj*, **referral** *noun*, **referrer** *noun*. [Middle English *referren* from Latin *referre* to bring back, report, refer, from RE- + *ferre* to carry]

referee[1] /refə'ree/ *noun* **1** an official who supervises the play and enforces the laws in any of several sports, e.g. football and boxing. **2a** a person to whom a legal matter is referred for investigation or settlement. **b** a person who reviews an academic paper before publication. **c** a person who gives a professional or character reference to a candidate's prospective employer.

referee[2] *verb trans* (**referees, refereed, refereeing**) to act as a referee for (something or somebody).

reference[1] /'ref(ə)rəns/ *noun* **1** the act of referring to or consulting something or somebody for information, guidance, etc: *a manual designed for ready reference.* **2** bearing on or connection with a matter: *I'm ringing in reference to yesterday's incident.* **3a** an allusion or mention: *They made no reference to the problem.* **b** something that refers somebody to another source of information, e.g. a book or passage. **c** a source of information, e.g. a book or passage, to which a reader or inquirer is referred. **4a** a person to whom inquiries as to character or ability can be made; a referee. **b** a statement of the qualifications of a person seeking employment or appointment. **5** a standard for measuring, evaluating, etc. ➤➤ **referential** /-'rensh(ə)l/ *adj*.

reference[2] *verb trans* to provide (e.g. a book) with references to authorities and sources of information.

reference group *noun* a group to which somebody aspires or belongs that influences his or her attitudes and behaviour.

reference library *noun* a library in which the reference materials are for consultation only, not for loan.

referendum /refə'rendəm/ *noun* (*pl* **referendums** *or* **referenda** /-də/) **1** a vote by the whole electorate on a single question or measure proposed by a legislative body or by popular initiative: compare PLEBISCITE. **2** the process of submitting a measure to a vote of this kind. [Latin *referendum*, neuter of *referendus*, verbal noun from *referre*: see REFER]

referent /'ref(ə)rənt/ *noun* in linguistics, the thing that a symbol, e.g. a word or sign, stands for. [Latin *referent-*, *referens*, present part. of *referre*: see REFER]

referred pain *noun* pain that is not felt at the actual source but in another part of the body.

refill[1] /'reefil/ *noun* **1** a fresh supply of a drink in the same cup or glass: *You get a free refill with your coffee.* **2** a replacement for a container of a consumable substance, e.g. ink in a pen: *a refill for a ballpoint pen.*

refill[2] /ree'fil/ *verb trans* to make (something) full again. ➤ *verb intrans* to become full again. ➤➤ **refillable** *adj*.

refinance /ree'fienans, -'nans/ *verb trans* to renew or reorganize the financing of (something), e.g. at a lower rate of interest.

refine /ri'fien/ *verb trans* **1** to free (a raw material) from impurities. **2** to improve or perfect (e.g. a method) by pruning or polishing. ➤➤ **refiner** *noun*.

refined *adj* **1a** without crudeness or vulgarity; elegant, fastidious, or cultivated. **b** subtle and sophisticated. **2** said *esp* of food: processed industrially to remove impurities.

refinement *noun* **1** refining or being refined. **2a** a subtle feature, method, or distinction: *pursued the delicate art of suggestion to its furthest refinements* — C M Bowra. **b** a contrivance or device intended to improve or perfect: *The new model has many refinements.*

refinery /ri'fienəri/ *noun* (*pl* **refineries**) a plant where raw materials, e.g. metals, oil or sugar, are refined.

refit[1] /'ree'fit/ *verb trans* (**refitted, refitting**) to fit out (something) again with new fixtures and equipment; *esp* to renovate and modernize (a ship).

refit[2] /'reefit/ *noun* a repair or replacement of parts, fittings, etc.

reflate /ree'flayt/ *verb trans* to expand the volume of available money and credit or economic activity of (an economy).

reflation *noun* an expansion in the volume of available money and credit in the economy, *esp* as a result of government policy. ➤➤ **reflationary** *adj*. [RE- + *-flation* as in DEFLATION]

reflect /ri'flekt/ *verb trans* **1** to send or throw (light, sound, etc) back or at an angle: *A mirror reflects light.* **2** to show (something) as an image or likeness; to mirror (it): *The clouds were reflected in the water.* **3** to make (something) manifest or apparent; to give an idea of (it): *The pulse reflects the condition of the heart.* ➤ *verb intrans* **1** to throw back light or sound. **2** to think quietly and calmly. **3a** (+ on/upon) to tend to bring reproach or discredit: *The investigation reflects on all the members of the department.* **b** (+ on) to tend to bring about a specified appearance or impression: *This is not an act which reflects favourably on her.* [Middle English *reflecten* from Latin *reflectere* to bend back, from RE- + *flectere* to bend]

reflectance /ri'flekt(ə)ns/ *noun* a measure of the ability of a surface to reflect light or other radiant energy, e.g. heat, that is equal to the ratio of the rate of flow of energy reflected from the surface to the rate of flow of energy falling on the surface.

reflecting telescope *noun* a telescope that uses a mirror that reflects light rays as its principal focusing element rather than a lens.

reflection /ri'fleksh(ə)n/ *noun* **1** a reflecting of light, sound, etc. **2** something produced by reflecting, *esp*: **a** an image given back by or as if by a reflecting surface. **b** an effect produced by or related to a specified influence or cause: *A high crime rate is a reflection of an unstable society.* **3** (*usu* + on) an often obscure or indirect criticism: *'Devil's-foot root! No, I have never heard of it.' 'It is no reflection on your professional knowledge ... for ... there is no other specimen in Europe.'* — Conan Doyle. **4** consideration of some subject matter, idea, or purpose, or a thought formed by consideration: *On reflection it didn't seem such a good plan.* **5** in mathematics, a transformation of a figure with respect to a reference line or plane producing a mirror image of the figure. ➤➤ **reflectional** *adj*.

reflective /ri'flektiv/ *adj* **1** capable of reflecting light, images, or sound waves. **2** thoughtful or deliberative. **3** relating to or caused by reflection: *the reflective glare of the snow.* ➤➤ **reflectively** *adv*, **reflectiveness** *noun*, **reflectivity** /reeflek'tiviti/ *noun*.

reflector *noun* **1** a polished surface for reflecting radiation, *esp* light. **2** a reflecting telescope.

reflet /rə'flay/ *noun* an iridescent sheen, *esp* on ceramics. [French *reflet* reflection]

reflex[1] /'reefleks/ *noun* **1a** an action that takes place automatically in response to a stimulus and involves no conscious thought. **b** (*in pl*) the power of acting or responding with adequate speed: *A pilot needs good reflexes.* **c** an automatic way of behaving or responding: *Lying became a natural reflex for him.* **2** a reproduction or reflection that corresponds to some *usu* specified original. **3** a word or word element in a form determined by development from an earlier stage of the language. **4** *archaic* reflected heat, light, or colour. [Latin *reflexus*, past part. of *reflectere*: see REFLECT]

reflex[2] *adj* **1** said of an action: produced by a reflex without intervention of consciousness. **2** said of an angle: greater than 180° but less than 360°. **3** *archaic* said of light: reflected. **4** bent, turned, or directed back: *a stem with reflex leaves.* ➤➤ **reflexly** *adv*.

reflex arc *noun* the path through the nervous system travelled by a pulse in a reflex.

reflex camera *noun* a camera in which the image formed by the lens is reflected onto a ground-glass screen or is seen through the viewfinder for focusing and composition.

reflexion /ri'fleksh(ə)n/ *noun archaic* = REFLECTION.

reflexive[1] /ri'fleksiv/ *adj* **1a** of or being a member of a class of pronouns, e.g. *himself*, which refer back to the subject of a clause or sentence. **b** of or being a verb whose action is directed back on the doer or the grammatical subject, e.g. in *he perjured himself*. **2** relating to a physiological reflex. ➤➤ **reflexively** *adv*, **reflexiveness** *noun*, **reflexivity** /reeflek'siviti/ *noun*. [late Latin *reflexivus* from Latin *reflexus*: see REFLEX[1]]

reflexive[2] *noun* a reflexive verb or pronoun.

reflexology /reeflek'soləji/ *noun* a therapy used in alternative medicine for the treatment of various disorders, that involves massaging nerve endings in the feet to relieve tension, improve nerve and blood supplies, and stimulate the body's self-healing system. ➤➤ **reflexologist** *noun*.

reflux[1] /'reefluks/ *noun* **1** in chemistry, the process of heating a liquid to form vapours that cool and condense, and return to be heated again. **2** *technical* a flowing back; an ebb. [Middle English from late Latin, from RE- + *fluxus*: see FLUX[1]]

reflux[2] *verb intrans* **1** in chemistry, to undergo reflux. **2** *technical* to flow back or return.

refocus /ree'fohkəs/ *verb* (**refocused** *or* **refocussed, refocusing** *or* **refocussing**) ➤ *verb trans* **1** to focus (a lens or the eyes) again. **2** to change the emphasis or direction of (something). ➤ *verb intrans* **1** to focus something again. **2** to change emphasis or direction.

reforest /ree'forist/ *verb trans* to renew the forest cover of (an area) by seeding or planting. ➤➤ **reforestation** /-'staysh(ə)n/ *noun*.

reform[1] /ri'fawm/ *verb trans* **1** to amend or alter (something) for the better. **2** to put an end to (an evil) by enforcing or introducing a better method or course of action. **3** to induce or cause (somebody) to adopt a more virtuous, healthier, etc way of life. ➤ *verb intrans* to become changed for the better. ➤➤ **reformable** *adj*, **reformative** /-tiv/ *adj*, **reformatory** /-mət(ə)ri/ *adj*. [Middle English *reformen* via French from Latin *reformare*, from RE- + *formare* to form, from *forma* FORM[1]]

reform[2] *noun* **1** amendment of what is defective or corrupt: *educational reform*. **2a** a removal or correction of an abuse, a wrong, or errors. **b** a measure intended to effect this.

re-form /ree'fawm/ *verb trans* to form (something) again. ➤ *verb intrans* to take form again: *The ice re-formed on the lake.*

reformat /ree'fawmat/ *verb trans* (**reformatted, reformatting**) to arrange (something) in or put (it) into a new format: *We had to reformat the hard disk.*

reformation /refə'maysh(ə)n/ *noun* **1** reforming or being reformed. **2** (**the Reformation**) a 16th-cent. religious movement marked ultimately by the rejection of papal authority and some Roman Catholic doctrines and practices, and the establishment of the Protestant Churches. ➤➤ **reformational** *adj*.

reformatory /ri'fawmət(ə)ri/ *noun* (*pl* **reformatories**) *NAmer, dated* a penal institution to which young or first offenders or women are sent for reform.

Reformed *adj* Protestant; *specif* of the Calvinist Protestant Churches.

reformer *noun* **1** somebody who works for or urges reform. **2** (**Reformer**) a leader of the Protestant Reformation.

reformism *noun* a doctrine, policy, or movement of reform. ➤➤ **reformist** *noun and adj*.

Reform Judaism *noun* a liberalizing and modernizing branch of Judaism.

reform school *noun* an institution to which young offenders were formerly sent, instead of prison.

refract /ri'frakt/ *verb trans* **1** to deflect (light or another wave motion) from one straight path to another when passing from one medium, e.g. glass, to another, e.g. air, in which the velocity is different. **2** to determine the refracting power of (e.g. a lens). [Latin *refractus*, past part. of *refringere* to break open, break up, refract, from RE- + *frangere* to break]

refracting telescope *noun* a telescope that uses a lens that concentrates light rays as its principal focusing element rather than a mirror.

refraction /ri'fraksh(ə)n/ *noun* **1a** the deflection or deviation of a wave, e.g. a beam of light, from one straight path to another when passing from one medium, e.g. air, into another, e.g. glass, in which the speed of transmission of the wave is different. **b** the amount of deviation of a wave undergoing refraction. **2a** the

change in the apparent position of a celestial body due to bending of the light rays coming from it as they pass through the atmosphere. **b** the correction to be applied to the apparent position of a body because of this.

refractive /ri'fraktiv/ *adj* **1** said of a substance, lens, etc: having power to cause refraction. **2** relating or due to refraction. ➤➤ **refractively** *adv*, **refractivity** /reefrak'tiviti/ *noun*.

refractive index *noun* the ratio of the velocity of a radiation, e.g. light, in two adjacent mediums.

refractometer /reefrak'tomitə/ *noun* an instrument for measuring refractive indexes. ➤➤ **refractometric** /ri,fraktə'metrik/ *adj*, **refractometry** /-tri/ *noun*.

refractor *noun* **1** something that causes refraction, e.g. a lens. **2** = REFRACTING TELESCOPE.

refractory[1] *adj* **1** *formal* resisting control or authority; stubborn or unmanageable: *If I were attentive, I was called fawning, if refractory, an obstinate mule* — Mary Wollstonecraft. **2** resistant to treatment or cure: *a refractory cough*. **3** difficult to fuse, corrode, or draw out; *esp* capable of enduring high temperatures: *refractory metals*. ➤➤ **refractorily** *adv*, **refractoriness** *noun*. [alteration of *refractary* from Latin *refractarius*, from *refragari* to oppose, from RE- + *-fragari* as in *suffragari* to support with one's vote]

refractory[2] *noun* (*pl* **refractories**) a heat-resisting ceramic material.

refrain[1] /ri'frayn/ *verb intrans* (+ from) to keep oneself from doing, feeling, or indulging in something, *esp* from following a passing impulse. [Middle English *refreynen* via French from Latin *refrenare* to hold back, curb, from RE- + *frenum* bridle]

refrain[2] *noun* **1** a regularly recurring phrase or verse, *esp* at the end of each stanza or division of a poem or song; a chorus. **2** the musical setting of a refrain. [Middle English *refreyn* via French from Latin *refringere*: see REFRACT]

refrangible /ri'franjəbl/ *adj* capable of being refracted. ➤➤ **refrangibility** /-'biliti/ *noun*. [irreg from Latin *refringere*: see REFRACT]

refresh /ri'fresh/ *verb trans* **1a** to restore strength or vigour to (somebody); to revive (them), e.g. by food or rest. **b** to bring back the freshness or colour to (something stale or faded). **2** to restore or maintain (something) by a fresh supply; to replenish (it): *The waiter refreshed our glasses*. **3** to arouse or stimulate (e.g. the memory). **4** in computing, to update the data in (a file, Web page, etc). [Middle English *refresshen* from Old French *refreschir*, from RE- + *freis* FRESH[1]]

refresher *noun* **1** something, e.g. a drink, that refreshes. **2** a course of instruction designed to keep one abreast of developments in one's professional field.

refresher course *noun* = REFRESHER (2).

refreshing *adj* agreeably stimulating because of freshness or newness. ➤➤ **refreshingly** *adv*.

refreshment *noun* **1** refreshing or being refreshed. **2a** something, e.g. food or drink, that refreshes. **b** (*in pl*) assorted food and drink, *esp* for a light meal.

refried beans /'reefried/ *noun* dried beans that have been boiled, mashed, and fried with seasonings, *esp* in Mexican cookery. [translation of Spanish *frijoles refritos*]

refrigerant[1] /ri'frijərənt/ *noun* a substance used in refrigeration; *specif* one, e.g. a Freon, with the property of changing easily from a liquid to a gas, that is used in a refrigerator, freezer, etc to remove heat energy and transfer it to the surroundings.

refrigerant[2] *adj* causing cooling or freezing.

refrigerate /ri'frijərayt/ *verb trans* to make or keep (something) cold or cool; *specif* to freeze or chill (e.g. food) for preservation. ➤➤ **refrigeration** /-'raysh(ə)n/ *noun*, **refrigeratory** /-rat(ə)ri/ *adj*. [Latin *refrigeratus*, past part. of *refrigerare*, from RE- + *frigerare* to cool, from *frigor-, frigus* cold]

refrigerator *noun* an insulated appliance for keeping food, drink, etc cool.

refringent /ri'frinj(ə)nt/ *adj* refractive or refracting. ➤➤ **refringence** *noun*. [Latin *refringent-, refringens*, present part. of *refringere*: see REFRACT]

reft /reft/ *verb* past tense and past part. of REAVE.

refuel /ree'fyooh·əl/ *verb* (**refuelled, refuelling**, *NAmer* **refueled, refueling**) ⟩ *verb trans* to provide (a vehicle) with additional fuel. ⟩ *verb intrans* to take on additional fuel.

refuge /'refyoohj/ *noun* **1** a place that provides shelter or protection from danger or distress: *a mountain refuge*. **2** a person, thing, or course of action that offers protection or is resorted to in difficulties: *Patriotism is the last refuge of a scoundrel* — Dr Johnson. [Middle English via French from Latin *refugium*, from *refugere* to escape, from RE- + *fugere* to flee]

refugee /refyoo'jee/ *noun* somebody who flees for safety, *esp* to a foreign country to escape danger or avoid political, religious, or racial persecution. [French *réfugié*, past part. of *se réfugier* to take refuge, from Latin *refugium*: see REFUGE]

refugium /ri'fyoohji·əm/ *noun* (*pl* **refugia** /-ji·ə/) an area of relatively unaltered climate inhabited by plants and animals during a period of climatic change, e.g. a glaciation, affecting the surrounding regions, so that the surviving plants and animals are remnants of otherwise extinct forms. [Latin *refugium*: see REFUGE]

refulgence /ri'fulj(ə)ns/ *noun formal or literary* radiance or brilliance. ⟩⟩ **refulgent** *adj*, **refulgently** *adv*. [Latin *refulgentia* from *refulgent-*, *refulgens*, present part. of *refulgēre* to shine brightly, from RE- + *fulgēre* to shine]

refund[1] /ri'fund/ *verb trans* **1** to return (money) in restitution, repayment, or balancing of accounts. **2** to pay (somebody) back. ⟩⟩ **refundable** *adj*. [Middle English *refunden* via French from Latin *refundere* to pour back, from RE- + *fundere* to pour]

refund[2] /'reefund/ *noun* **1** the act or an instance of refunding. **2** a sum refunded.

refurbish /ree'fuhbish/ *verb trans* to repair, redecorate, and usu re-equip (e.g. a house). ⟩⟩ **refurbishment** *noun*.

refusal /ri'fyoohzl/ *noun* **1a** an expression of unwillingness to do something. **b** the fact of being denied something. **2** the right or option of refusing or accepting something before others.

refuse[1] /ri'fyoohz/ *verb trans* **1a** to express oneself as unwilling to accept (something): *They refused our offer of a loan*. **b** to show or express unwillingness to do (something): *The engine refused to start*. **2a** to be unwilling to allow or grant (something); to deny (it): *They refused admittance to anyone under 18*. **b** to be unwilling to allow or grant something to (somebody): *If he asks for more time, I can hardly refuse him*. **3** said of a horse: to decline to jump over (e.g. a fence). ⟩ *verb intrans* **1** to withhold acceptance, compliance, or permission. **2** said of a horse: to decline to jump a fence, wall, etc: *It refused at the third fence*. ⟩⟩ **refuser** *noun*. [Middle English *refusen* via French *refuser* from Latin *refusus*, past part. of *refundere*: see REFUND[1]]

refuse[2] /'refyoohs/ *noun* worthless or useless stuff that has been thrown away; rubbish. [Middle English from Old French *refus*, from *refuser*: see REFUSE[1]]

refusenik /ri'fyoohznik/ *noun* **1** formerly, a Soviet Jew who was refused permission to emigrate, *esp* to Israel. **2** somebody who refuses to accept a situation or proposal; a dissenter.

refute /ri'fyooht/ *verb trans* **1** to prove (somebody or something) wrong by argument or evidence. **2** to deny the truth or accuracy of (e.g. a claim). ⟩⟩ **refutable** /'refyootəbl, ri'fyooh-/ *adj*, **refutation** /refyoo'taysh(ə)n/ *noun*, **refuter** *noun*. [Latin *refutare*, from RE- + *-futare* to beat]

Usage note

To *refute* statements, accusations, or people is properly to prove them wrong by producing evidence or arguments against them, not merely to assert that they are wrong. The increasingly common use of phrases such as *refute the allegations*, where *refute* indicates merely a denial, is liable to criticism; *deny*, *reject* or *repudiate* are generally considered preferable to *refute* here.

regain /ri'gayn, ree'gayn/ *verb trans* to gain or reach (something) again; to recover (it).

regal /'reegl/ *adj* **1** relating to or suitable for a king or queen. **2** stately or splendid. ⟩⟩ **regality** /ree'galiti/ *noun*, **regally** *adv*. [Middle English via French from Latin *regalis*, from *reg-*, *rex* king]

regale /ri'gayl/ *verb trans* **1** to entertain (somebody) sumptuously. **2** to give pleasure or amusement to (somebody): *She regaled us with stories of her exploits*. [French *régaler*, from early French *gale* pleasure]

regalia /ri'gaylyə/ *pl noun* (*treated as sing. or pl*) **1** the ceremonial emblems or symbols indicative of royalty. **2** special dress, *esp*

official finery. [late Latin from Latin *regalia*, neuter pl of *regalis*: see REGAL]

regard[1] /ri'gahd/ *noun* **1** attention or consideration: *Due regard should be given to all facets of the question*. **2** a protective interest; care: *He ought to have more regard for his health*. **3** a feeling of respect and affection; esteem: *Her hard work won her the regard of her colleagues*. **4** (*in pl*) friendly greetings: *Give him my regards*. **5** an aspect to be taken into consideration; a respect: *The school was fortunate in that regard*. **6** a gaze or look. ✳ **in/with regard to** with respect to; concerning.

regard[2] *verb trans* **1** (*usu* + as/with) to think of or feel about (somebody or something) in a specified way; to consider (them): *He is highly regarded as a mechanic*; *I regarded the prospect with horror*. **2** to look steadily at (something). **3** to relate to (something); to concern (it). **4** to pay attention to (something); to take (it) into consideration or account. ✳ **as regards** in so far as it concerns. [Middle English *regarden* from Old French *regarder*, from RE- + *garder*: see GUARD[1]]

regardant /ri'gahd(ə)nt/ *adj* said of a heraldic animal: looking backwards. [Middle English from early French, present part. of *regarder* to look back]

regardful *adj formal* **1** (+ of) heedful or observant. **2** = RESPECTFUL.

regarding *prep* about; on the subject of.

regardless[1] *adj* (+ of) heedless or careless. ⟩⟩ **regardlessly** *adv*, **regardlessness** *noun*.

regardless[2] *adv* despite everything: *They went ahead with their plans regardless*.

regardless of *prep* in spite of: *regardless of our mistakes*.

regatta /ri'gatə/ *noun* a series of rowing, speedboat, or sailing races. [Italian *regatta*, literally 'contest']

regd *abbr* registered.

regelation /reeji'laysh(ə)n/ *noun technical* the refreezing of water derived from ice that has melted under high pressure when the pressure is relieved.

Regency /'reej(ə)nsi/ *adj* of or resembling the styles, e.g. of furniture or dress, prevalent during the time of the Prince Regent. [from the regency (1811–20) of George, Prince of Wales (afterwards George IV) d.1830]

regency *noun* (*pl* **regencies**) **1** the office, period of rule, or government of a regent or regents. **2** (*treated as sing. or pl*) a body of regents.

regenerate[1] /ri'jenərayt/ *verb trans* **1a** to generate or produce (something) anew; *esp* to replace (a body part or tissue) by new growth. **b** to produce (something) from a derivative or modified form, *esp* by chemical treatment: *regenerated cellulose*. **2a** to change (something) radically and for the better. **b** to subject (something) to spiritual or moral renewal or revival. ⟩ *verb intrans* said of a body, body part, or tissue: to undergo renewal, restoration, or regrowth, e.g. after injury. ⟩⟩ **regeneration** /-'raysh(ə)n/ *noun*, **regenerative** /-rətiv/ *adj*, **regeneratively** /-rətivli/ *adv*, **regenerator** *noun*. [Middle English from Latin *regenerare*, from RE- + *generare*: see GENERATE]

regenerate[2] /ri'jenərət/ *adj* spiritually reborn or converted.

regent /'reej(ə)nt/ *noun* **1** somebody who governs a kingdom in the minority, absence, or disability of the sovereign. **2** *NAmer* a school or college governor. ⟩⟩ **regent** *adj*. [Middle English via French or late Latin from Latin *regent-*, *regens*, present part. of *regere* to rule]

reggae /'regay/ *noun* popular music of West Indian origin, combining elements of rock, soul, and calypso, that is characterized by a strong accent on the usu unaccented second and fourth beats in a bar.

Editorial note

Reggae has become the catch-all term for a rich and complex Jamaican musical heritage. Originating in the friction between indigenous calypso traditions and post-World War II sound-systems playing black American rhythm and blues, it developed through bluebeat, ska, and rock-steady styles to take its most familiar 1970s form, as exported to a global audience by Bob Marley before his tragic early death from cancer in 1981 — Ben Thompson.

[Jamaican English *reggae* from *rege* RAG[1]]

regicide /'rejisied/ *noun* **1** the act of murdering a king. **2** a person who commits regicide. ⟩⟩ **regicidal** /-'siedl/ *adj*. [Latin *reg-*, *rex* king + *-cida* and *-cidium*: see -CIDE]

regime or **régime** /ray'zheem/ *noun* **1a** a form of management or government: *a socialist regime.* **b** a government in power. **2a** = REGIMEN. **b** a regular pattern of occurrence or action, e.g. of seasonal rainfall. [French *régime* from Latin *regimin-, regimen*: see REGIMEN]

regimen /'rejimən/ *noun* a systematic plan, e.g. of diet, exercise, or medical treatment, adopted *esp* to achieve some end. [Middle English from Latin *regimin-, regimen* rule, from *regere* to rule]

regiment[1] /'rejimənt/ *noun* **1** a permanent military unit consisting usu of a number of companies, troops, batteries, or sometimes battalions. **2** a large number or group. **3** *archaic* governmental rule. **>> regimental** /-'mentl/ *adj*, **regimentally** /-'mentəli/ *adv*. [Middle English, in the senses 'government', 'area governed', via French from late Latin *regimentum* rule, from Latin *regere* to rule]

regiment[2] /'rejiment/ *verb trans* **1** to subject (people or things) to strict and stultifying organization or control. **2** to form (troops) into a regiment. **>> regimentation** /-'taysh(ə)n/ *noun*.

regimentals /reji'mentlz/ *pl noun* formal military uniform or dress, *esp* that of a particular regiment: *They could talk of nothing but officers; and Mr Bingley's fortune, the mention of which gave animation to their mother, was worthless in their eyes when opposed to the regimentals of an ensign* — Jane Austen.

Regina /ri'jienə/ *noun* **1** a title given to a reigning queen and used after the first name, *esp* in its Latin form: *Elizabetha Regina*. **2** used in legal cases, when the British monarch is a queen, to denote the Crown as a party to the action. [Latin *regina* queen, fem of *reg-, rex* king]

region /'reej(ə)n/ *noun* **1a** an indefinite area of the world or universe. **b** a broadly uniform geographical or ecological area: *desert regions*. **2** an administrative area. **3** an indefinite area surrounding a specified body part: *the abdominal region*. **✳ in the region of** approximately: *She earns in the region of £200 a week*. [Middle English via French from Latin *region-, regio*, from *regere* to rule]

regional *adj* **1** relating to or characteristic of a region: *He has a regional accent*. **2** affecting a particular region; localized: *a regional assembly*. **>> regionally** *adv*.

regionalise *verb trans* see REGIONALIZE.

regionalism *noun* **1** development of an administrative system based on areas. **2** a characteristic feature, e.g. of speech, of a geographical area. **>> regionalist** *noun and adj*.

regionalize or **regionalise** *verb trans* to divide (something) into regions; *esp* to arrange (e.g. a country) in administrative regions. **>> regionalization** /-'zaysh(ə)n/ *noun*.

regisseur /rayzhi'suh (*French* reʒisœːr)/ *noun* a director responsible for staging a theatrical work, e.g. a ballet. [French *régisseur* from *régir* to direct, rule, from Latin *regere* to rule]

register[1] /'rejistə/ *noun* **1** a written record containing official entries of items, names, transactions, etc: *a hotel register*. **2a** a record of pupils' attendance at school. **b** a roster of qualified or available individuals: *the electoral register*. **3a** a part of the range of a human voice or musical instrument. **b** an organ stop. **4** in linguistics, the language style and vocabulary appropriate to particular circumstances or subject matter. **5** in printing, a condition of correct alignment or proper relative position, e.g. of the plates used in colour printing. **6** a device, e.g. in a computer, for temporarily storing and working on small amounts of data. **7a** a movable plate regulating admission of air, *esp* to solid fuel in a fire. **b** a grille, often with shutters, for admitting heated air or for ventilation. [Middle English *registre* via French and late Latin from Latin *regesta*, neuter pl past part. of *regerere*, literally 'to bring back', from RE- + *gerere* to bear]

register[2] *verb* (**registered, registering**) **>** *verb trans* **1a** to enter (information) officially in a register or to have (it) officially entered: *He registered the birth of his daughter*. **b** to enrol (somebody) formally. **c** to record (something) automatically; to indicate (it): *This dial registers speed*. **2** to secure special protection for (a piece of mail) by prepayment of a fee. **3** to show (an emotion) through facial expression or body language: *He registered surprise at the news*. **4a** to become aware of (something); to perceive (it). **b** to make a mental note of (something). **>** *verb intrans* **1a** to put one's name in a register: *They registered at the hotel*. **b** to enrol formally (as a student). **2a** to make or convey an impression: *The name didn't register*. **b** to be shown in somebody's facial expression or body language. **3a** to correspond exactly. **b** said of printed matter: to be in correct alignment. **>> registrable** /-strəbl/ *adj*.

Registered General Nurse *noun* a fully trained person who is officially allowed to practise as a nurse in Britain.

register office *noun* *Brit* a place where births, marriages, and deaths are recorded and civil marriages are conducted.

register ton *noun* see NET TON.

registrar /reji'strah, 'rej-/ *noun* **1a** an official recorder or keeper of records. **b** a senior administrative officer of a university. **c** a court official who deals with administrative and interlocutory matters and acts as a subordinate judge. **2** *Brit* a senior hospital doctor ranking below a consultant. [Middle English from medieval Latin *registrarius*, from *registrare*, from *registrum* register, neuter past part. of *regerere*: see REGISTER[1]]

registration /reji'straysh(ə)n/ *noun* **1** the act or an instance of registering or being registered. **2** an entry in a register.

registration document *noun* *Brit* an official document relating to a motor vehicle that gives the registration number, make, engine size, etc and details of the current ownership.

registration mark *noun* *Brit* an identifying combination of letters and numbers assigned to a motor vehicle.

registration number *noun* = REGISTRATION MARK.

registration plate *noun* = NUMBERPLATE.

registry /'rejistri/ *noun* (*pl* **registries**) **1** a place of registration; *specif* a register office. **2** registering or being registered.

registry office *noun* = REGISTER OFFICE.

Regius professor /'reejəs/ *noun* a holder of a professorship founded by royal subsidy at a British university. [Latin *regius* royal, from *reg-, rex* king]

regnal /'regnəl/ *adj* of a reign; *specif* calculated from a monarch's accession: *in his eighth regnal year*. [late Latin *regnalis* from Latin *regnum*: see REIGN[1]]

regnant /'regnənt/ *adj* reigning, usu as opposed to being a royal consort: *a queen regnant*. [Latin *regnant-, regnans*, present part. of *regnare* to reign, from *regnum*: see REIGN[1]]

regress[1] /'reegres/ *noun* **1** = REGRESSION. **2** the act of reasoning backwards from a conclusion. **3** *formal* an act of going or coming back.

regress[2] /ri'gres/ *verb intrans* to undergo or exhibit regression, decline, or backward movement, *esp* to an earlier state or condition. **>** *verb trans* **1** to induce, *esp* by hypnosis, a state of psychological regression in (somebody). **2** in statistics, to calculate the regression of (a variable). **>> regressor** *noun*. [Middle English from Latin *regressus*, from *regredi* to go back, from RE- + *gradi* to go]

regression /ri'gresh(ə)n/ *noun* **1** the act or an instance of regressing; *esp* a retrograde movement. **2a** a trend or shift towards a lower, less perfect, or earlier state or condition. **b** reversion to an earlier mental or behavioural level, *esp* to patterns of thought and behaviour typical of childhood or to a supposed previous life. **3** the statistical analysis of the association between two or more correlated variables, *esp* so that predictions, e.g. of sales over a future period of time, can be made.

regressive /ri'gresiv/ *adj* **1** tending to regress or produce regression. **2** characterized by, showing, or developing in the course of physiological, psychological, or evolutionary regression. **3** decreasing in rate as the base increases: *a regressive tax*. **>> regressively** *adv*, **regressiveness** *noun*.

regret[1] /ri'gret/ *verb trans* (**regretted, regretting**) **1a** to be very sorry about (something): *He regretted his mistakes*. **b** used in intimating an unwelcome ruling, etc: *The Principal regrets that she cannot reconsider her decision*. **2** to mourn the loss or death of (something or somebody). [Middle English *regretten* from Old French *regreter*, prob of Germanic origin]

regret[2] *noun* **1** the emotion arising from a wish that some matter or situation could be other than it is; *esp* grief or sorrow tinged with disappointment, longing, or remorse. **2** (*in pl*) a conventional expression of disappointment, *esp* on declining an invitation: *She couldn't come to tea, and sent her regrets*. **>> regretful** *adj*, **regretfulness** *noun*.

Usage note

regretful or **regrettable**? *Regretful* refers to the state of somebody's feelings: *Do you feel at all regretful about missing the opportunity? Regrettable*, on the other hand, comments on an event, an action, or a state of affairs: *It's most regrettable that she didn't see fit to come and answer these questions in person*.

regretfully /ri'gretfəli/ *adv* **1** in a regretful manner. **2** *non-standard* regrettably: *The obvious requirement of increased security has regretfully created the necessity of making an appointment.*

regrettable *adj* other than as one would wish; unwelcome.
Usage note
regrettable *or* regretful? See note at REGRET².

regrettably *adv* **1** in a regrettable manner; to a regrettable extent: *a regrettably steep decline in wages.* **2** it is regrettable that: *Regrettably, we had failed to consider alternatives.*

regroup /ree'groohp/ *verb trans* to form (people) into a new grouping; *specif* to alter the tactical formation of (military forces). ➤ *verb intrans* **1** to reorganize, e.g. after a setback, for renewed activity. **2** to alter the tactical formation of a military force.

regt *abbr* regiment.

regular¹ /'regyoolə/ *adj* **1** formed, built, arranged, or ordered harmoniously, symmetrically, or according to some rule, principle, or type: *regular verse; girl with regular features.* **2a** said of a polygon: having sides of equal length and angles of equal size. **b** said of a polyhedron: having faces that are identical regular polygons with identical angles between them. **3** said of a flower: having the petals, sepals, or other flower parts arranged in a radially symmetrical manner. **4a** steady or uniform in course, practice, or occurrence; habitual, usual, or constant: *regular habits; a regular visitor.* **b** recurring or functioning at fixed or uniform intervals: *a regular income.* **5** constituted, conducted, or done in conformity with established or prescribed usages, rules, or discipline: *a regular meeting of the council.* **6** in grammar, said of a word, *esp* a verb: conforming to the normal pattern of inflection: *Walk, paint, and dance are regular verbs.* **7** complete or absolute: *a regular fool.* **8** *NAmer* thinking or behaving in an acceptable manner; pleasant: *He wanted to prove he was a regular guy.* **9** *NAmer* standard or medium: *regular fries.* **10a** belonging to a religious order: compare SECULAR¹: *the regular clergy.* **b** being an officially qualified or approved member of a specified profession: *a regular solicitor.* **c** being or belonging to a permanent standing army: *a regular soldier.* ➤➤ **regularity** /-'lariti/ *noun,* **regularly** *adv.* [Middle English *reguler* via French and late Latin from Latin *regularis,* from *regula* rule]

regular² *noun* **1** somebody who is usu present or participating, *esp* somebody who habitually visits a particular place. **2a** a member of the regular clergy: compare SECULAR². **b** a soldier in a regular army.

regularize *or* **regularise** *verb trans* to make (something) regular. ➤➤ **regularization** /-'zaysh(ə)n/ *noun.*

regulate /'regyoolayt/ *verb trans* **1** to control or direct (something) according to rules. **2** to bring order, method, or uniformity to (something). **3** to fix or adjust the time, amount, degree, or rate of (something): *regulating the pressure of a tyre.* ➤➤ **regulable** *adj,* **regulative** /-lətiv/ *adj,* **regulator** *noun,* **regulatory** /-lət(ə)ri, -'layt(ə)ri/ *adj.* [late Latin *regulatus,* past part. of *regulare,* from Latin *regula* rule]

regulation /regyoo'laysh(ə)n/ *noun* **1** the act or an instance of regulating or being regulated. **2a** an authoritative rule dealing with details or procedure: *safety regulations in a factory.* **b** a rule or order having the force of law: *EU regulations.* **3** (used before a noun) conforming to regulations; official: *regulation uniform.*

reguli /'regyoolie/ *noun* pl of REGULUS.

regulo /'regyooloh/ *noun Brit* the temperature in a gas oven expressed as a specified number: *The meat needs to be cooked on regulo four.* [formerly a trademark: from REGULATE]

regulus /'regyooləs/ *noun* (pl **reguluses** *or* **reguli** /-lie/) the impure metallic mass formed in smelting ores. [late Latin *regulus* metallic antimony, from Latin *regulus* petty king, from *reg-, rex* king; perhaps so named because it readily combines with gold, which was regarded as a royal metal]

regurgitate /ri'guhjitayt/ *verb trans* **1** to bring (incompletely digested food) back from the stomach to the mouth. **2** to reproduce (something) in speech or writing with little or no alteration: *Ask them who will win the election and they can only guess, rely on anecdotal information or regurgitate polls or commentators they have read* — Daily Telegraph. ➤ *verb intrans* to be thrown or poured back. ➤➤ **regurgitation** /-'taysh(ə)n/ *noun.* [late Latin *regurgitatus,* past part. of *regurgitare,* from RE- + *gurgitare* to engulf, from Latin *gurgit-, gurges* whirlpool]

rehab /'reehab/ *noun informal* rehabilitation.

rehabilitate /ree(h)ə'bilitayt/ *verb trans* **1a** to restore (somebody) to a condition of health or useful and constructive activity, e.g.

after illness or imprisonment. **b** to restore (something) to a former capacity or state, e.g. of efficiency, soundness, or solvency: *rehabilitating slum areas.* **2** to reestablish the good name of (somebody). ➤➤ **rehabilitation** /-'taysh(ə)n/ *noun,* **rehabilitative** /-tiv/ *adj.* [late Latin *rehabilitatus,* past part. of *rehabilitare,* from RE- + *habilitare* to qualify, from Latin *habilitas:* see ABILITY]

rehash¹ /ree'hash/ *verb trans* to present or use (something) again in another form without substantial change or improvement.

rehash² /'reehash/ *noun* something presented in a new form without change of substance.

rehearsal /ri'huhsl/ *noun* **1** a practice session, *esp* of a play, concert, etc preparatory to a public performance. **2** the act or an instance of rehearsing.

rehearse /ri'huhs/ *verb trans* **1a** to hold a rehearsal of (e.g. a play); to practice (it). **b** to train or make (somebody) proficient by rehearsal. **2a** to present an account of (something) again: *He rehearsed the familiar story.* **b** to recount (points) in order: *They had rehearsed their grievances in a letter to the governor.* ➤ *verb intrans* to engage in a rehearsal of a play, concert, etc. ➤➤ **rehearser** *noun.* [Middle English *rehersen* from early French *rehercier,* literally 'to harrow again' from RE- + *hercier* to harrow, from *herce* harrow]

reheat¹ /'ree'heet/ *verb trans* to heat (e.g. cooked food) again. ➤➤ **reheater** *noun.*

reheat² *noun* the injection of fuel into the tailpipe of a turbojet engine to obtain extra thrust by combustion with uncombined air in the exhaust gases.

rehoboam /ree-ə'boh-əm/ *noun* a wine bottle, *esp* for champagne, that contains six times the amount of a standard bottle (about 4.8 litres or 8½ pints). [named after *Rehoboam* fl c.925 BC, a king of Judah, who fortified towns and laid in stocks of oil and wine (2 Chronicles 11:11)]

rehouse /ree'howz/ *verb trans* to establish (somebody) in new or better-quality housing.

rehydrate /ree'hiedrayt, reehie'drayt/ *verb trans* to restore fluid lost in dehydration to (something or somebody). ➤➤ **rehydration** /-'draysh(ə)n/ *noun.*

Reich /riekh/ *noun* the German empire: *the Third Reich.* [German *Reich* empire, kingdom]

reify /'reeifie/ *verb trans* (**reifies, reified, reifying**) to regard (something abstract) as a material thing. ➤➤ **reification** /-fi'kaysh(ə)n/ *noun,* **reificatory** /-fi'kaytəri/ *adj.* [Latin *res* thing + -FY]

reign¹ /rayn/ *noun* **1** the time during which somebody or something reigns. **2a** royal authority; sovereignty. **b** the dominion, sway, or influence of somebody resembling or likened to a monarch: *the reign of the military dictators.* [Middle English *regne* via Old French from Latin *regnum,* from *reg-, rex* king]

reign² *verb intrans* **1a** to possess or exercise sovereign power; to rule. **b** to hold office as head of state although possessing little governing power: *The queen reigns but does not rule.* **2** to be predominant or prevalent: *Chaos reigned in the classroom.* **3** to be the current holder of a trophy or title, *esp* in a sports event: *the reigning champion.*

reign of terror *noun* a period of ruthless violence committed by those in power. [*Reign of Terror,* a period of the French Revolution that was conspicuous for mass executions of political suspects]

reiki /'rayki/ *noun* a treatment for pain and stress using healing energy that is channelled from the therapist to the patient. [Japanese *reiki* universal life force energy]

reimburse /reeim'buhs/ *verb trans* **1** to pay back (money) to somebody: *We will reimburse your travel expenses.* **2** to make restoration or payment to (somebody): *I promise to reimburse you.* ➤➤ **reimbursable** *adj,* **reimbursement** *noun.* [RE- + obsolete *imburse* to put in the pocket, pay, from medieval Latin *imbursare,* from IN-² + *bursa:* see PURSE¹]

reimport /reeim'pawt/ *verb trans* to import (products made from raw materials that were exported). ➤➤ **reimportation** /-'taysh(ə)n/ *noun.*

rein¹ /rayn/ *noun* **1a** (usu in pl, but treated as sing. or pl) a long line fastened usu to both sides of a bit, by which a rider or driver controls an animal. **b** a similar device used to restrain a young child. **2** (in pl) controlling or guiding power: *the reins of government.* ✴ **draw rein** to bring a horse to a stop while riding. **give free rein to something** to allow something to proceed or function freely. [Middle English *reine* via French from Latin *retinēre:* see RETAIN]

rein[2] *verb trans* **1** (*often* + in) to check or stop (a horse) by pulling on the reins. **2** (*often* + in) to restrain or stop (something).

reincarnate /reein'kahnayt/ *verb trans* (*usu in passive*) to cause (a person or his or her soul) to be reborn in another body after death. ➤➤ **reincarnate** /-nət/ *adj.*

reincarnation /reeinkah'naysh(ə)n/ *noun* the rebirth of a soul in another body after death.

Editorial note ─────────────
Reincarnation is the process, described in several religions and philosophies, whereby some entity – the soul, the self, consciousness – departs the body upon death and is reborn as another form of life. Traditions differ as to whether this form may include plants, animals, ghosts, and gods in addition to humans. The final goal of several of the religions of ancient India is to escape from the cycle of reincarnation — Professor Donald Lopez.

reindeer /'rayndiə/ *noun* (*pl* **reindeers** *or collectively* **reindeer**) a deer that inhabits N Europe, Asia, and America, that has antlers in both sexes, and is often domesticated: *Rangifer tarandus*. [Middle English *reindere* from Old Norse *hreinn* reindeer + DEER]

reindeer moss *noun* a grey lichen that constitutes a large part of the food of reindeer: *Cladonia rangiferina*.

reinforce /reein'faws/ *verb trans* **1** to strengthen (something) with additional material or support; to make (it) stronger or more pronounced. **2** to strengthen or increase (e.g. an army) with additional forces. **3a** to stimulate (an experimental subject) with a reward following a correct or desired performance. **b** to encourage (a response) with a reward. ➤➤ **reinforcement** *noun,* **reinforcer** *noun.* [RE- + *inforce,* alteration of ENFORCE]

reinforced concrete *noun* concrete in which metal is embedded for strengthening.

reinstate /reein'stayt/ *verb trans* to restore (somebody or something) to a former position or state. ➤➤ **reinstatement** *noun.*

reinsure /reein'shooə, -'shaw/ *verb trans* said of an insurance company: to transfer (all or a part of a risk) to another insurance company. ➤➤ **reinsurance** *noun,* **reinsurer** *noun.*

reintegrate /ree'intigrayt/ *verb trans* **1** (*often* + into) to restore (something or somebody) to their place as part of a whole. **2** to restore (something) to a state of wholeness or unity. ➤➤ **reintegration** /-'graysh(ə)n/ *noun,* **reintegrative** *adj.* [medieval Latin *reintegratus,* past part. of *reintegrare* to renew, reinstate, from Latin RE- + *integrare* to integrate]

reinvent /reein'vent/ *verb trans* to remake or redo (something) completely. ✳ **reinvent the wheel** to waste time and effort making something that has already been invented. ➤➤ **reinvention** /-sh(ə)n/ *noun.*

reinvest /reein'vest/ *verb trans* to invest (e.g. earnings or investment income) rather than take or distribute the surplus as dividends or profits. ➤➤ **reinvestment** *noun.*

reissue /ree'ishooh, ree'isyooh/ *verb trans* (**reissues, reissued, reissuing**) to issue (something) again; *esp* to cause (it) to become available again: *The song has been reissued on a different record label.* ➤➤ **reissue** *noun.*

reiterate /ree'itərayt/ *verb trans* to say or do (something) over again or repeatedly, sometimes with wearying effect. ➤➤ **reiteration** /-'raysh(ə)n/ *noun,* **reiterative** /-tiv/ *adj.* [Latin *reiteratus,* past part. of *reiterare* to repeat, from RE- + *iterare:* see ITERATE]

reive /reev/ *verb chiefly Scot* to go raiding for the purpose of obtaining plunder. ➤➤ **reiver** *noun.* [variant of REAVE]

reject[1] /ri'jekt/ *verb trans* **1a** to refuse to accept, consider, submit to, or use (something). **b** to refuse to accept or admit (somebody): *The underprivileged feel rejected by society.* **2** to fail to accept (e.g. a skin graft or transplanted organ) as part of the organism because of immunological differences. ➤➤ **rejecter** *noun,* **rejection** /-sh(ə)n/ *noun,* **rejector** *noun.* [Middle English *rejecten* from Latin *rejectus,* past part. of *reicere* to throw back, from RE- + *jacere* to throw]

Usage note ─────
reject, deny, refute, *or* repudiate? See note at REFUTE

reject[2] /'reejekt/ *noun* a rejected person or thing; *esp* a substandard article of merchandise.

rejig /ree'jig/ *verb trans* (**rejigged, rejigging**) **1** to adjust or reorganize (something): *He recommended rejigging the timetable.* **2** to rearrange or reequip (e.g. a factory) so as to perform different work.

rejoice /ri'joys/ *verb intrans* **1** to feel or express joy or great delight. **2** (+ in) to have or enjoy (something noteworthy): *He rejoices in the name of Endeavour.* ➤ *verb trans archaic* to give joy to (somebody);

to gladden (them). ➤➤ **rejoicer** *noun,* **rejoicing** *noun and adj,* **rejoicingly** *adv.* [Middle English *rejoicen* from early French *rejoir,* from RE- + *joir* to rejoice, from Latin *gaudere*]

rejoin[1] /ri'joyn/ *verb trans* to say (something) in response, *esp* in a sharp or critical way. [Middle English *rejoinen* to answer to a legal charge, from French *rejoindre,* from RE- + *joindre:* see JOIN[1]]

rejoin[2] *verb trans* **1** to return to (something): *We rejoined the main carriageway; He rejoined his battalion.* **2** /ree'joyn/ to join (two things) together again; to reunite (them).

rejoinder /ri'joyndə/ *noun* **1** a reply, *esp* a sharp or critical answer. **2** *dated* in law, the answer made by the defendant in the second round of a legal action to the plaintiff's first reply. [Middle English *rejoiner* from early French *rejoindre:* see REJOIN[1]]

rejuvenate /ri'joohvənayt/ *verb trans* **1a** to make (somebody) young or youthful again; to reinvigorate (them): *Yet, though so plainly dressed, there was a certain rejuvenated appearance about her —* Hardy. **b** to restore (something) to an original or more vigorous state. **2a** to cause (a stream or river) to increase erosive activity, *esp* as a result of an increase in the height of the surrounding land. **b** to cause (land) to develop features, *esp* greater relief, characteristic of an earlier stage in a cycle of erosion. ➤➤ **rejuvenation** /-'naysh(ə)n/ *noun,* **rejuvenator** *noun.* [RE- + Latin *juvenis* young]

rejuvenescence /ri,joohvə'nes(ə)ns/ *noun* **1** a renewal of youthfulness or vigour; rejuvenation. **2** in biology, the reactivation of cells, causing new growth from old or injured parts. ➤➤ **rejuvenescent** *adj.* [late Latin *rejuvenescere* to become young again, from Latin RE- + *juvenescere* to become young, from *juvenis* young]

rekindle /ri'kindl, ree-/ *verb trans* **1** to arouse (e.g. an emotion) again. **2** to light (a fire) again.

rel. *abbr* **1** relating. **2** relative. **3** released. **4** religion. **5** religious.

relaid /ree'layd/ *verb trans* past tense and past part. of RELAY[3].

relapse[1] /ri'laps, 'reelaps/ *noun* a relapsing or backsliding; *esp* a recurrence of symptoms of a disease after a period of improvement. [Latin *relapsus,* past part. of *relabi* to slide back, from RE- + *labi* to slide]

relapse[2] /ri'laps/ *verb intrans* **1** to slip or fall back into a former worse state. **2** to sink or subside: *She relapsed into deep thought.*

relapsing fever *noun* a bacterial disease transmitted by lice and ticks that is marked by recurring high fever.

relate /ri'layt/ *verb trans* **1** to give an account of (something); to tell (it). **2** to show or establish logical or causal connection between (two or more things). ➤ *verb intrans* **1** to have relationship or connection: *I can't see how the two things relate.* **2** (+ to) to have or establish a relationship: *We discussed the way a child relates to a psychiatrist.* **3** (+ to) to respond, *esp* favourably: *I can't relate to that kind of music.* ➤➤ **relatable** *adj,* **relater** *noun.* [Latin *relatus* brought back, from RE- + *latus,* past part. of *ferre* to carry]

related *adj* **1** connected by reason of an established or discoverable relation. **2** connected by common ancestry or sometimes by marriage. ➤➤ **relatedness** *noun.*

relation /ri'laysh(ə)n/ *noun* **1a** a person connected by blood, marriage, or adoption; a relative. **b** relationship by blood, marriage, or adoption; kinship. **2** (*in pl*) **a** the attitude or behaviour which two or more people or groups show towards one another; interaction: *race relations.* **b** dealings or affairs: *foreign relations.* **c** communication or contact: *He broke off all relations with his family.* **d** *euphem* sexual intercourse. **3a** an aspect or quality, e.g. resemblance, that connects two or more things and enables them to be considered together in a meaningful way. **b** reference, respect, or connection: *Size bears little relation to ability.* **4a** the act of telling or recounting a story. **b** a story or an account of something. ✳ **in/with relation to** with regard to; concerning. ➤➤ **relational** *adj,* **relationally** *adv.*

relational database *noun* a computer database in which data is stored in a number of different tables which can be accessed simultaneously or individually using several routes.

relationship *noun* **1** the state or character of being related or interrelated. **2** a specific instance or type of kinship. **3** a state of affairs existing between those having relations or dealings: *He had a good relationship with his family.* **4** a close friendship or love affair.

relative[1] /'relətiv/ *noun* **1a** a person connected with another by blood relationship or marriage. **b** an animal or plant related to another by common descent. **2** in philosophy, something having or a term expressing a relation to, connection with, or necessary dependence on another thing. **3** a word referring grammatically to an antecedent.

relative[2] *adj* **1a** assessed or considered by comparison with something else; not absolute; comparative: *the relative isolation of life in the country.* **b** existing only in connection with or measurable only by reference to something else, e.g. a standard: *relative density*; *Supply is relative to demand.* **2a** introducing a subordinate clause qualifying an expressed or implied antecedent: *a relative pronoun.* **b** introduced by such a connective: *a relative clause.* **3** relevant or pertinent: *matters relative to world peace.* **4** said of major and minor keys and scales: having the same key signature. ➤➤ **relatively** *adv*, **relativeness** *noun.*

relative atomic mass *noun* the ratio of the average mass of an atom of an element to the mass of an atom of the most abundantly occurring isotope of carbon.

relative density *noun* the ratio of the density of a substance to the density of another substance, e.g. pure water or hydrogen, taken as a standard, when both densities are measured under the same conditions.

relative humidity *noun* the ratio of the actual water vapour present in the air to that when the air is saturated with water vapour at the same temperature: compare HUMIDITY.

relative molecular mass *noun* the weight of a molecule that may be calculated as the sum of the atomic weights of its constituent atoms.

relative to *prep* with regard to.

relativism *noun* a theory that knowledge and moral principles are relative and have no objective standard. ➤➤ **relativist** *noun.*

relativistic /relǝti'vistik/ *adj* **1** of or characterized by relativity or relativism. **2** in physics, moving at or being a velocity that causes a significant change in properties, e.g. mass, in accordance with the theory of relativity: *a relativistic electron.* ➤➤ **relativistically** *adv.*

relativity /relǝ'tiviti/ *noun* **1** the quality or state of being relative. **2** the state of being dependent for existence on, or determined in nature, value, or quality by, a relation to something else. **3a** a theory which is based on the two postulates (one) that the speed of light in a vacuum is constant and independent of the source or observer and (two) that the laws of physics, as expressed mathematically, are the same in all systems, leading to the assertion that mass and energy are equivalent and that mass, dimension, and time will change with increased velocity. **b** an extension of this theory to include gravitation and related acceleration phenomena.

relator /ri'laytǝ/ *noun* **1** somebody on whose suggestion or information a legal action is commenced. **2** somebody who relates; a narrator.

relaunch[1] /ree'lawnch/ *verb trans* to start (something) again, *esp* in a new form: *She tried to relaunch her career with a new single.*

relaunch[2] /'reelawnch/ *noun* the relaunching of something.

relax /ri'laks/ *verb trans* **1** to make (e.g. a muscle) less tense or rigid; to slacken (it). **2** to make (e.g. a rule) less severe or stringent. **3** to lessen the intensity, zeal, or energy of (something). **4** to relieve (somebody) from nervous tension: *The warm bath relaxed him.* ➤ *verb intrans* **1** to refrain from work or other activity and rest or enjoy leisure or recreation. **2** to cast off inhibition, nervous tension, or anxiety: *Relax, you're among friends.* **3** said of a muscle or muscle fibre: to stop contracting. **4** to become less intense or severe. **5** to become lax, weak, or loose. ➤➤ **relaxer** *noun.* [Middle English *relaxen* to make less compact, from Latin *relaxare*, from RE- + *laxare* to loosen, from *laxus* loose]

relaxant *noun* a substance, *esp* a drug, that produces relaxation or relieves muscular tension. ➤➤ **relaxant** *adj.*

relaxation /reelak'saysh(ǝ)n, relǝk-/ *noun* **1** the act or an instance of relaxing or the state of being relaxed. **2** a relaxing or recreational activity or pastime. **3** in physics, the attainment of an equilibrium state following the abrupt removal of some influence, e.g. light, high temperature, or stress.

relaxed *adj* **1** friendly and informal in manner or atmosphere. **2** feeling at rest or at ease. **3a** not strict or demanding: *They're fairly relaxed about timekeeping around here.* **b** characterized by a lack of precision or stringency; slack. ➤➤ **relaxedly** *adv.*

relaxin /ri'laksin/ *noun* a hormone produced by the CORPUS LUTEUM (hormone-producing tissue) in the ovary of a pregnant mammal that makes birth easier by causing relaxation of the pelvic ligaments.

relay[1] /'reelay/ *noun* **1a** a number of people who relieve others in some work: *The rescue workers working in relays around the clock.* **b** a fresh supply, e.g. of horses, arranged beforehand to take the place of others as they become tired. **2** a race between teams in which each team member covers a specified portion of the course and then is replaced by another. **3** a device set in operation by variation in an electric circuit and operating other devices in turn. **4a** the act of passing something along by stages. **b** such a stage. **c** something, *esp* a message, that is relayed.

relay[2] /'reelay, ri'lay/ *verb trans* **1** to pass (e.g. information) along by relays: *News was relayed to distant points.* **2** to control or operate (something) by a relay. **3a** to retransmit (a radio or television signal) by means of a relay. **b** to broadcast (a radio or television transmission), *esp* from a specified place: *This programme is being relayed by satellite from the USA.* **c** to send (a signal) by electronic means. [Middle English *relayen* from Old French *relaier*, from RE- + *laier* to leave, from Latin *laxare*: see RELAX]

relay[3] /ree'lay/ *verb trans* (*past tense and past part.* **relaid** /ree'layd/) to lay (something) again: *relaying track.*

release[1] /ri'lees/ *verb trans* **1a** to set (a person or animal) free from restraint, confinement, or servitude. **b** to free (somebody) from the constraints imposed by an obligation or responsibility: *She was released from her promise.* **2a** to give permission for the publication, performance, exhibition, or sale of (something). **b** to publish or issue (something): *The commission has released its findings.* **3** to operate or move (e.g. a handle or catch) in order to allow a mechanism free movement: *She released the hand brake.* **4** said of a cell, tissue, etc: to allow (e.g. a hormone) to pass from its place of origin or storage into the bloodstream, digestive tract, etc. **5** in law, to give up (a right, claim, etc) in favour of somebody else; to relinquish (it). ➤➤ **releasable** *adj*, **releaser** *noun.* [Middle English *relesen* via Old French *relessier* from Latin *relaxare*: see RELAX]

release[2] *noun* **1** the act or an instance of freeing or being freed: *an early release from jail.* **2** relief or deliverance from sorrow, suffering, or trouble. **3a** discharge from obligation or responsibility. **b** relinquishment or conveyance of a legal right or claim, or a document effecting this. **4** a device, e.g. a handle, used to release a mechanism as required. **5a** an item of news or information made publicly available; *esp* a statement prepared for the press. **b** a newly issued film, CD, etc.

relegate /'relǝgayt/ *verb trans* **1** to assign or move (somebody or something) to an inferior or insignificant place or status: *He relegated his old clothes to a box in the garage.* **2** *Brit* to demote (a team) to a lower division of a sporting competition, e.g. a football league: compare PROMOTE. ➤➤ **relegation** /-'gaysh(ǝ)n/ *noun.* [Latin *relegatus*, past part. of *relegare*, from RE- + *legare*: see LEGATE]

relent /ri'lent/ *verb intrans* **1** to become less severe, harsh, or strict, usu from reasons of humanity. **2** to become less intense or violent; to slacken or let up. [Middle English *relenten* to melt, dissolve, from Latin RE- + *lentare* to bend, from *lentus* flexible, slow]

relentless *adj* **1** said of a person: showing no sign of stopping or becoming less determined. **2** remaining constant at the same demanding level: *a relentless pace.* ➤➤ **relentlessly** *adv*, **relentlessness** *noun.*

relevant /'reliv(ǝ)nt/ *adj* **1** having a significant and demonstrable bearing on the matter at hand. **2** having practical application, *esp* to the real world: *Are traditional university courses still relevant?* ➤➤ **relevance** *noun*, **relevancy** /-si/ *noun*, **relevantly** *adv.* [late Latin *relevant-*, *relevans*, present part. of Latin *relevare*: see RELIEVE]

reliable /ri'lie-ǝbl/ *adj* suitable or fit to be relied on; dependable. ➤➤ **reliability** /-'biliti/ *noun*, **reliableness** *noun*, **reliably** *adv.*

reliance /ri'lie-ǝns/ *noun* **1** the act of relying. **2** the condition or attitude of somebody who relies: *Reliance on military power to achieve political ends seldom results in stable government.* ➤➤ **reliant** *adj.*

relic /'relik/ *noun* **1** something left behind after decay, disintegration, or disappearance: *relics of ancient cities.* **2** a trace of something past, *esp* an outmoded custom, belief, or practice. **3** a part of the body of or some object associated with a saint or martyr, that is preserved as an object of reverence. [Middle English *relik* via Old French from late Latin *reliquiae* (pl) remains of a martyr, from Latin *relinquere*: see RELINQUISH]

relict /'relikt/ *noun* **1** a group of plants or animals that is a surviving remnant of an otherwise extinct form. **2** a geological or geographical feature, e.g. a lake or mountain, or a rock remaining after other parts have disappeared or substantially altered. **3** *archaic* =

WIDOW[1]: *His landlady, Mrs Bardell – the relict and sole executrix of a deceased custom-house officer – was a comely woman of bustling manners and agreeable appearance* — Dickens. [(sense 1 and 2) from *relict* (adj) residual, from Latin *relictus*, past part. of *relinquere*: see RELINQUISH; (sense 3) early French *relicte* (woman) left behind, from late Latin *relicta*, fem of *relictus*]

relied /ri'lied/ *verb* past tense and past part. OF RELY.

relief /ri'leef/ *noun* **1** removal or lightening of something oppressive, painful, or distressing: *He sought relief from his asthma by moving to the coast.* **2** a feeling of happiness or comfort brought about by the removal of a burden: *Relief swept through me.* **3** a means of breaking or avoiding monotony or boredom; a diversion: *She read the Beano for light relief.* **4** aid in the form of money or necessities, *esp* for the poor. **5** somebody who takes over the post or duty of another: *a relief driver.* **6** a vehicle that is used at busy times to carry extra passengers: *a relief bus.* **7** release from a post or from the performance of a duty: *For this relief much thanks* — Shakespeare. **8** the liberation of a besieged city, castle, etc: *the relief of Mafeking.* **9** military assistance to an endangered or surrounded post or force. **10a** a method of sculpture in which forms and figures stand out from a surrounding flat surface. **b** a piece of sculpture done in relief. **c** projecting detail, ornament, or figures in sculpture. **11** sharpness of outline due to contrast: *The roof stood out in bold relief against the sky.* **12a** the differences in height of a land surface. **b** the representation of this on a map. * **on relief** *NAmer* said of a person: receiving money or other aid from the government because of need. [Middle English from Old French, from *relever*: see RELIEVE]

relief map *noun* a map representing topographical relief graphically by shading, hachures, etc, or by means of a three-dimensional scale model.

relief printing *noun* printing from raised letters.

relieve /ri'leev/ *verb trans* **1** (*often* + of). **a** to free (somebody) from a burden; to give aid or help to (them). **b** to set (somebody) free from an obligation, condition, or restriction. **2** to bring about the removal or alleviation of (something): *The aim is to relieve poverty in the Third World.* **3a** to release (somebody) from a post, station, or duty by substituting somebody else. **b** to take the place of (somebody who is presently on duty). **4a** (+ of) to dismiss (somebody) from a post: *He was relieved of his command and sent home in disgrace.* **b** *informal* to deprive (somebody); to rob (them): *Pickpockets swiftly relieved him of his wallet.* **5** to remove or lessen the monotony of (something): *His red robes relieved the drabness of the scene.* **6** *archaic* to raise (e.g. letters) in relief. * **relieve oneself** to urinate or defecate. ➤➤ **relievable** *adj.* [Middle English *releven* via Old French *relever* from Latin *relevare* to raise, relieve, from RE- + *levare* to raise]

relieved *adj* experiencing or showing relief, *esp* from anxiety or pent-up emotions. ➤➤ **relievedly** *adv.*

religion /ri'lij(ə)n/ *noun* **1** the organized service and worship of a god, gods, or the supernatural. **2** personal commitment or devotion to religious faith or observance. **3** a cause, principle, or system of beliefs held to with ardour and faith; something considered to be of supreme importance. * **get religion** *informal* to become a practising and zealous Christian or member of another religious faith, *esp* suddenly. [Middle English *religioun* from Latin *religion-, religio* reverence, religion, prob from *religare*: see RELY]

religionist *noun* a person adhering zealously to a religion. ➤➤ **religionism** *noun.*

religiose /ri'lijiohs/ *adj* excessively, obtrusively, or sentimentally religious. ➤➤ **religiosity** /-'ositi/ *noun.*

religious[1] /ri'lijəs/ *adj* **1** relating or devoted to the beliefs or observances of a religion. **2** showing faithful devotion to an acknowledged ultimate reality or deity; pious or devout: *a religious man.* **3** scrupulously and conscientiously faithful: *He is religious in his observance of rules of health.* **4** belonging or relating to a monastic order. ➤➤ **religiously** *adv,* **religiousness** *noun.*

religious[2] *noun* (*pl* **religious**) a member of a religious order under monastic vows.

relinquish /ri'lingkwish/ *verb trans* **1** to renounce or abandon (something); to give (it) up. **2a** to release (e.g. one's grip or hold) or to stop holding (something) physically: *He relinquished his grip.* **b** to give over possession or control of (something): *Few leaders willingly relinquish power.* ➤➤ **relinquishment** *noun.* [Middle English *relinquisshen* via French from Latin *relinquere* to leave behind, from RE- + *linquere* to leave]

reliquary /'relikwəri/ *noun* (*pl* **reliquaries**) a container or shrine in which sacred relics are kept. [French *reliquaire* from late Latin *reliquiarium,* from *reliquia* relic, from *reliquere*: see RELINQUISH]

reliquiae /ri'likwi·ee/ *pl noun* **1** fossil remains of plants or animals. **2** *formal* remains of the dead; *esp* relics. [Latin *reliquiae* remains, from *reliquere*: see RELINQUISH]

relish[1] /'relish/ *noun* **1** enjoyment of or delight in something that satisfies one's tastes, inclinations, or desires: *Mr Leopold Bloom ate with relish the inner organs of beasts and fowls* — James Joyce; *He had little relish for sports.* **2** something that adds an appetizing or savoury flavour; *esp* a highly seasoned sauce, e.g. of pickles or mustard, eaten with plainer food. **3** *archaic* characteristic, pleasing, or piquant flavour or quality: *The freshness and crispness of the raw onion, with the earthy taste, give it a great relish to one who has been a long time on salt provisions* — R H Dana. [alteration of Middle English *reles* taste, from Old French *reles* something left behind, release, from *relessier*: see RELEASE]

relish[2] *verb trans* **1** to enjoy (something); to have pleasure from (it). **2** to anticipate (something) with pleasure: *She didn't relish the prospect of her interview with the boss.* **3** *archaic* to add relish to (food). ➤➤ **relishable** *adj.*

relive /ree'liv/ *verb trans* to live (something) over again; *esp* to experience (it) again in the imagination.

relocate /reeloh'kayt, reelə'kayt/ *verb trans* **1** to locate (something) again. **2** to establish (something) in, lay (it) out in, or move (it) to a new place. ➤ *verb intrans* to move to a new place, *esp* to establish one's home or business in a new place. ➤➤ **relocation** /-sh(ə)n/ *noun.*

reluctance /ri'luktəns/ *noun* **1** a feeling or show of unwillingness. **2** in physics, the opposition offered by a magnetic substance to magnetic flux; *specif* the ratio of the magnetic potential difference to the corresponding flux.

reluctant /ri'luktənt/ *adj* neither quick nor eager to do something; unwilling: *She was reluctant to condemn him.* ➤➤ **reluctantly** *adv.* [Latin *reluctant-, reluctans,* present part. of *reluctari* to struggle against, from RE- + *luctari* to struggle]

rely /ri'lie/ *verb intrans* (**relies, relied, relying**) **1** (+ on/upon) to have confidence in; to trust: *Her husband was a man she could rely on.* **2** to be dependent on: *They rely on the spring for water.* [Middle English *relien* to rally, via French *relier* to bind together, from Latin *religare* to tie back, from RE- + *ligare* to tie]

REM /rem/ *abbr* rapid eye movement.

rem /rem/ *noun* a unit of ionizing radiation equal to the dosage that will cause the same biological effect as one röntgen of X-ray or gamma-ray radiation. [acronym from *röntgen equivalent man*]

remade /ree'mayd/ *verb* past tense and past part. of REMAKE[1].

remain /ri'mayn/ *verb intrans* **1a** to be neither destroyed, taken, nor used up; to survive: *Only a few ruins remain.* **b** to be something yet to be shown, done, or treated: *It remains to be seen.* **2** to stay in the same place or with the same person or group; *specif* to stay behind. **3** to continue to be: *She remained faithful.* [Middle English *remainen* via French from Latin *remanēre,* from RE- + *manēre* to stay]

remainder[1] /ri'mayndə/ *noun* **1a** a remaining group, part, or trace. **b** the number left after a subtraction. **c** the final undivided part after division, that is less than the divisor. **2** a book sold at a reduced price by the publisher after sales have fallen off. **3** in law, a future interest in property that is dependent upon the termination of a previous interest created at the same time. [Middle English from Anglo-French, from Latin *remanēre*: see REMAIN]

remainder[2] *verb trans* (**remaindered, remaindering**) to dispose of (copies of a book) as remainders.

remains *pl noun* **1** a remaining part or trace: *They threw away the remains of the meal.* **2** a dead body. **3** writings left unpublished at a writer's death.

remake[1] /ree'mayk/ *verb trans* (*past tense and past part.* **remade**) to make (something) anew or in a different form.

remake[2] /'reemayk/ *noun* a new version of a film.

remand[1] /ri'mahnd/ *verb trans* to return (a defendant or prisoner) to custody or release (them) on bail until they appear again in court. [Middle English *remaunden* via French and late Latin from Latin *remandere* to send back word, from RE- + *mandare*: see MANDATE[1]]

remand[2] *noun* the state of being remanded: *The prisoner was on remand.*

remanence /'remənəns/ *noun* the magnetic induction remaining in a magnetized substance when the magnetizing force has become zero.

remanent /'remənənt/ *adj* **1** of, being, or characterized by remanence. **2** *formal* residual or remaining. [Middle English from Latin *remanent-, remanens*, present part. of *remanēre*: see REMAIN]

remark¹ /ri'mahk/ *verb trans* **1** to express (something) as an observation or comment. **2** *formal* to take notice of (something); to observe (it). ➤ *verb intrans* (+ on/upon) to make a comment or observation. [French *remarquer*, from RE- + *marquer* to mark]

remark² *noun* **1** a casual expression of an opinion or judgment: *I'm heartily sick of his snide remarks*. **2** mention or notice: *The episode is barely worthy of remark*.

remarkable *adj* worthy of being, or likely to be, noticed; striking or extraordinary. ➤➤ **remarkableness** *noun*, **remarkably** *adv*.

remaster /ree'mahstə/ *verb trans* (**remastered, remastering**) to make a new master audio recording, *esp* one that is digital, in order to make a compact disc or stereo record with better sound quality.

rematch /'reemach/ *noun* a second match between the same contestants or teams.

REME /'reemi/ *abbr Brit* Royal Electrical and Mechanical Engineers.

remedial /ri'meedi-əl/ *adj* **1** intended as a remedy: *remedial treatment*. **2** denoting or relating to teaching methods or equipment designed to help people with learning difficulties: *remedial reading courses*. ➤➤ **remedially** *adv*.

remedy¹ /'remədi/ *noun* (*pl* **remedies**) **1** a medicine, application, or treatment that relieves or cures a disease. **2** something that corrects or counteracts an evil or deficiency: *The firing squad made a simple remedy for discontent*. **3** legal compensation or amends. [Middle English *remedie* via Anglo-French from Latin *remedium*, from RE- + *mederi* to heal]

remedy² *verb trans* (**remedies, remedied, remedying**) to provide or serve as a remedy for (something). ➤➤ **remediable** /ri'meedi-əbl/ *adj*.

remember /ri'membə/ *verb* (**remembered, remembering**) ➤ *verb trans* **1** to bring to mind or think of (something or somebody) again: *He remembers the old days; Remember me in your prayers*. **2** to retain (something) in the memory: *Try to remember the facts until the test is over*. **3** to give or leave (somebody) a present, tip, etc: *He was remembered in the will*. **4** to convey greetings from (somebody): *Please remember me to your mother*. **5** to record or commemorate (something or somebody): *History has not remembered their names*. ➤ *verb intrans* **1** to exercise or have the power of memory. **2** to have a recollection or remembrance. ➤➤ **rememberer** *noun*. [Middle English *remembren* via French from late Latin *rememorari*, from RE- + *memorari* to be mindful of, from Latin *memor* mindful]

remembrance /ri'membrəns/ *noun* **1** an act of recalling to mind: *Remembrance of the offence angered him all over again*. **2** a memory of a person, thing, or event: *She had only a dim remembrance of that night*. **3a** something that serves to keep in or bring to mind. **b** a commemoration or memorial. **c** a greeting or gift recalling or expressing friendship or affection.

Remembrance Day *noun* **1** = REMEMBRANCE SUNDAY. **2** = ARMISTICE DAY.

remembrancer *noun* **1** a person who or a thing that reminds. **2** (**Remembrancer**) any of several English officials originally having the duty of bringing a matter to the attention of the proper authority.

Remembrance Sunday *noun* the Sunday closest to 11 November, dedicated to the commemoration of the dead of both World Wars and of the end of hostilities in 1918 and 1945: compare VETERANS DAY.

remex /'reemeks/ *noun* (*pl* **remiges** /'remətjeez/) a large stiff feather of the wing of a bird. ➤➤ **remigial** /ri'mijiəl/ *adj*. [Latin *remig-, remex*, oarsman, from *remus* oar + *agere* to drive]

remind /ri'miend/ *verb trans* **1** to put (somebody) in mind of something; to cause (them) to remember. **2** (+ of) to appear to (somebody) to be like somebody else: *He reminded me very much of my brother*.

reminder *noun* **1** a thing that helps somebody to remember something. **2** a letter reminding somebody to do something, *esp* to pay a debt.

reminisce /remi'nis/ *verb intrans* to talk or write about events or people from one's own past. [back-formation from REMINISCENCE]

reminiscence *noun* **1** the process of thinking, talking, or writing about past experiences. **2a** a remembered experience. **b** (*usu in pl*) an account of a memorable experience: *the reminiscences of the old settler*. **3** something that recalls or is suggestive of something else. [late Latin *reminiscentia* from Latin *reminiscent-, reminiscens*, present part. of *reminisci* to remember]

reminiscent *adj* **1** tending to remind one, e.g. of something seen or known before: *a technology reminiscent of the Stone Age*. **2a** of the character of reminiscence. **b** marked by or given to reminiscence. ➤➤ **reminiscently** *adv*.

remiss /ri'mis/ *adj* **1** negligent in the performance of work or duty. **2** showing neglect or inattention: *Service was remiss in most of the hotels*. ➤➤ **remissly** *adv*, **remissness** *noun*. [Middle English from Latin *remissus*, past part. of *remittere*: see REMIT¹]

remissible *adj* capable of being forgiven: *remissible sins*.

remission /ri'mish(ə)n/ *noun* **1** the act or an instance of remitting. **2** a state or period during which something, e.g. the symptoms of a disease, is remitted. **3** *Brit* reduction of a prison sentence, *esp* because of the prisoner's good behaviour.

remit¹ /ri'mit/ *verb* (**remitted, remitting**) ➤ *verb trans* **1a** to refrain from inflicting or exacting (e.g. a debt): *remit a tax*. **b** to release somebody from the guilt or penalty of (sin). **2** to send (money) to a person or place. **3** to refer (something) for consideration; *specif* to return (a case) to a lower court. ➤ *verb intrans* to lessen in force or intensity; to moderate. ➤➤ **remittable** *adj*, **remitter** *noun*. [Middle English *remitten* from Latin *remittere* to send back, from RE- + *mittere* to send]

remit² /ri'mit, 'reemit/ *noun* **1** something remitted to another person or authority for consideration or judgment. **2** the area of responsibility or concern assigned to a person or authority: *Teachers seem to be stepping outside their remit*. **3** a proposal submitted, e.g. to a committee, for decision or action.

remittal /ri'mitl/ *noun* = REMISSION.

remittance /ri'mit(ə)ns/ *noun* **1a** a sum of money remitted. **b** a document by which money is remitted. **2** the act of remitting money.

remittance man *noun* a person living abroad on money sent from home, *esp* in the days of the British Empire.

remittent /ri'mit(ə)nt/ *adj* said of a disease: marked by alternating periods of abatement and increase of symptoms. [Latin *remittent-, remittens*, present part. of *remittere*: see REMIT¹]

remix¹ /ree'miks/ *verb trans* to change the balance of sounds of (a recording).

remix² /'reemiks/ *noun* a musical recording that has been remixed.

remnant /'remnənt/ *noun* **1** a usu small part or trace remaining. **2** an unsold or unused end of fabric. [Middle English, contraction of *remenant*, via French from Latin *remanēre*: see REMAIN]

remodel /ree'modl/ *verb trans* (**remodelled, remodelling**, *NAmer* **remodeled, remodeling**) to reconstruct (something); to alter the structure of (it).

remold¹ /ree'mohld/ *verb trans NAmer* see REMOULD¹.

remold² /'reemohld/ *noun NAmer* see REMOULD².

remonetize *or* **remonetise** /ree'munitiez/ *verb trans* to restore (e.g. silver) to use as legal tender. ➤➤ **remonetization** /-'za-ysh(ə)n/ *noun*. [RE- + *monetize* to coin money, establish as legal tender, from Latin *moneta* mint, MONEY]

remonstrance /ri'monstrəns/ *noun* an act or instance of remonstrating.

remonstrate /'remənstrayt, ri'monstrayt/ *verb intrans* (*usu* + with) to make one's objections or opposition to somebody's conduct, opinions, etc known forcefully. ➤ *verb trans* to say or plead (something) in protest, reproof, or opposition. ➤➤ **remonstration** /remən'straysh(ə)n/ *noun*, **remonstrative** /ri'monstrətiv/ *adj*, **remonstrator** /'remənstraytə/ *noun*. [late Latin *remonstratus*, past part. of *remonstrare* to demonstrate, from Latin RE- + *monstrare* to show]

remontant /ri'montənt/ *adj* said of a plant: flowering more than once in a season. ➤➤ **remontant** *noun*. [French *remontant*, present part. of *remonter* to come up again: see REMOUNT¹]

remora /'remərə/ *noun* any of several species of fishes that have a sucking disc on the head by means of which they cling to other fishes and to ships: family Echeneidae. [Latin *remora*, literally 'delay', from *remorari* to delay, from RE- + *morari* to delay; from a former belief that it held ships back]

remorse /ri'maws/ *noun* a deep and bitter distress arising from a sense of guilt for past wrongdoing. ⟫⟫ **remorseful** *adj*, **remorsefully** *adv*. [Middle English via French and late Latin from Latin *remorsus*, past part. of *remordēre* to bite again, from RE- + *mordēre* to bite]

remorseless *adj* **1** having no remorse; merciless: *Where were ye, Nymphs, when the remorseless deep closed o'er the head of your loved Lycidas?* — Milton. **2** persistent or indefatigable. ⟫⟫ **remorselessly** *adv*, **remorselessness** *noun*.

remortgage /ree'mawgij/ *verb trans* to take out another mortgage on (a property).

remote¹ /ri'moht/ *adj* **1** far removed in space, time, or relation: *the remote past; comments remote from the truth.* **2** situated far away from the main centres of activity or population; out-of-the-way or secluded. **3a** not arising from a direct or close action, *esp* involving an infrared or radio signal: *remote control.* **b** controlling something or being controlled indirectly or from a distance: *a computer with a hundred remote terminals.* **4** small in degree; slight: *a remote possibility.* **5** distant in manner; aloof. ⟫⟫ **remotely** *adv*, **remoteness** *noun*. [Latin *remotus*, past part. of *removēre*. see REMOVE¹]

remote² *noun informal* a remote-control device operating e.g. a television set.

remote control *noun* **1** control over an operation, e.g. of a machine or weapon, exercised from a distance usu by means of an electrical circuit or radio waves. **2** a device by which this is carried out.

remote sensing *noun* the act of studying the earth or another planet from space, e.g. for scientific purposes, collecting data, or making maps, *esp* by satellites using photographs, radar, etc.

remoulade /'remoolahd/ *noun* a mayonnaise sauce flavoured with mustard and herbs. [French *rémoulade*]

remould¹ (*NAmer* **remold**) /ree'mohld/ *verb trans* **1** to mould (something) again. **2** *Brit* to refashion the tread of (a worn tyre).

remould² (*NAmer* **remold**) /'reemohld/ *noun* a remoulded tyre.

remount¹ /ree'mownt/ *verb trans* **1** to mount (e.g. a horse) again. **2** to put (e.g. a picture) in a new mount. ⟫ *verb intrans* to mount again. [Middle English *remounten*; partly from RE- + *mounten*: see MOUNT¹; partly from early French *remonter*, from RE- + *monter*: see MOUNT¹]

remount² /'reemownt, ree'mownt/ *noun* a fresh riding horse; *esp* one used as a replacement for one which is exhausted.

removal /ri'moohvl/ *noun* **1** the act or an instance of removing. **2a** *Brit* the moving of household goods from one residence to another. **b** *Brit* (*used before a noun*) relating to or used in such a move: *removal expenses*; *a removal van.*

removalist *noun Aus* a person who owns or works for a removal company.

remove¹ /ri'moohv/ *verb trans* **1** to move (somebody or something) by lifting, pushing aside, or taking away or off: *He removed his hat*; *If all else fails, remove the child from the classroom.* **2** to get rid of (something); to eliminate (it): *The tumour had to be surgically removed.* **3** to dismiss (somebody) from office. ⟫ *verb intrans formal* to change location, station, or residence: *We are removing from the city to the suburbs.* ⟫⟫ **removability** /-'biliti/ *noun*, **removable** *adj*, **remover** *noun*. [Middle English *removen* via Old French from Latin *removēre*, from RE- + *movēre* to MOVE¹]

remove² *noun* **1a** a distance or interval separating one person or thing from another: *The poems that work best are at a slight remove from the personal.* **b** a degree or stage of separation: *It is a repetition, at many removes, of the theme of her first book.* **2** a form intermediate between two others in some British schools.

removed *adj* **1a** distant in degree of relationship. **b** of a younger or older generation: *A second cousin's child is a second cousin once removed.* **2** separate or remote in space, time, or character. ✳ **first cousin once removed** a child of one's first cousin.

REM sleep *noun* = PARADOXICAL SLEEP.

remunerate /ri'myoohnərayt/ *verb trans* to pay (somebody) for work done; to recompense (them). ⟫⟫ **remuneration** /-'raysh(ə)n/ *noun*, **remunerative** /-tiv/ *adj*. [Latin *remuneratus*, past part. of *remunerare* to recompense, from RE- + *munerare* to give, from *muner-, munus* gift]

renaissance /ri'nays(ə)ns, ri'nesonhs/ *noun* **1** (**Renaissance**) the humanistic revival of classical influence in Europe from the 14th to the 17th cent., expressed in a flowering of the arts, architecture,

and literature and by the beginnings of modern science. **2** (*often* **Renaissance**) a movement or period of vigorous artistic and intellectual activity. **3** a rebirth or revival. [early French *renaissance* rebirth, from *renaistre* to be born again, from Latin *renasci*, from RE- + *nasci* to be born]

Renaissance man *noun* a person of wide interests and expertise; *specif* a person equally at home in the arts and sciences.

renal /'reenl/ *adj* to do with or in the region of the kidneys. [French *rénal* or late Latin *renalis* from Latin *renes* kidneys]

renal pelvis *noun* = PELVIS (2).

renascence /ri'nays(ə)ns/ *noun* = RENAISSANCE.

renascent /ri'nays(ə)nt/ *adj formal* becoming active or vigorous again. [Latin *renascent-, renascens*, present part. of *renasci*. see RENAISSANCE]

rencounter¹ /ren'kowntə/ *noun archaic* **1** a chance meeting. **2a** a meeting between hostile forces; a conflict. **b** = DUEL¹: *Captain Falconer ... accepted a challenge from him, and in the rencounter received a mortal wound* — Scott. [early French *rencontre* from *rencontrer* to rencounter, from RE- + *encontrer*: see ENCOUNTER¹]

rencounter² *verb trans* (**rencountered, rencountering**) *archaic* to meet (somebody) by chance.

rend /rend/ *verb* (*past tense and past part.* **rent** /rent/) ⟫ *verb trans* **1** to wrest, split, or tear (something) apart or in pieces by violence. **2** to tear (the hair or clothing) as a sign of anger, grief, or despair. **3** to cause mental or emotional pain to (somebody). **4** to pierce (the silence) with sound. ⟫ *verb intrans* to become torn or split. [Old English *rendan*]

render¹ /'rendə/ *verb trans* (**rendered, rendering**) **1** to cause (something or somebody) to be or become something: *There was enough rain to render irrigation unnecessary.* **2a** to convey (something) to another; to deliver (it). **b** to give (something) up; to yield (it). **c** to deliver (e.g. an opinion or verdict) for consideration, approval, or information. **3a** to give (something) in acknowledgment of dependence or obligation: *Render therefore unto Caesar the things which are Caesar's* — Bible. **b** to do (a service) for another. **4a** to reproduce or represent (something) by artistic or verbal means; to depict (it). **b** to give a performance of (e.g. a piece of music). **c** to produce a copy or version of (something): *The documents are rendered in the original French.* **d** to translate (something). **5a** to melt down (fat). **b** to extract (e.g. fat from (meat) by melting. **6** to apply a coat of plaster or cement directly to (brickwork, stone, etc). ⟫⟫ **renderer** *noun*. [Middle English *rendren* to give up, give back, recite, translate, via early French *rendre* from an alteration of Latin *reddere*, partly from RE- + *dare* to give, and partly from RE- + *-dere* to put]

render² *noun* a material usu made of cement, sand, and a small percentage of lime, applied to form a protective or decorative covering for exterior walls.

rendering *noun* **1** = RENDITION. **2** plaster applied to a wall; render.

rendezvous¹ /'rondivooh, rondayvooh, 'ronh-/ *noun* (*pl* **rendezvous** /-vooh/) **1** a meeting at an appointed place and time. **2** a place appointed for assembling or meeting. [early French *rendezvous*, from *rendez-vous* present yourselves]

rendezvous² *verb intrans* (**rendezvouses** /-voohz/, **rendezvoused** /-voohd/, **rendezvousing** /-vooh·ing/) to come together at a rendezvous.

rendition /ren'dish(ə)n/ *noun* **1** = TRANSLATION (1). **2** a performance or interpretation. [obsolete French *rendition*, from *rendre*: see RENDER¹]

renegade /'renigayd/ *noun* **1** a deserter from one faith, cause, or allegiance to another. **2** an individual who rejects lawful or conventional behaviour. ⟫⟫ **renegade** *adj*. [Spanish *renegado* from late Latin *renegatus*, past part. of *renegare* to deny, from Latin RE- + *negare* to deny]

renege or **renegue** /ri'neeg, ri'nayg/ *verb intrans* **1** (*usu* + on) to go back on a promise or commitment: *She reneged on her contract.* **2** in cards, = REVOKE¹. ⟫⟫ **reneger** *noun*. [medieval Latin *renegare*: see RENEGADE]

renegotiate /reeni'gohshiayt/ *verb trans* to negotiate (something) again; *esp* to readjust (e.g. a price) by negotiation. ⟫⟫ **renegotiable** *adj*, **renegotiation** /-' aysh(ə)n/ *noun*.

renegue /ri'neeg, ri'nayg/ *verb intrans* see RENEGE.

renew /ri'nyooh/ *verb trans* **1** to begin (something) again; to resume (it): *There has been renewed fighting in Indonesia.* **2** to make (something) as if new; to restore (it) to freshness, vigour, or perfection. **3a** to grant or obtain an extension of or on (e.g. a subscription, lease, or licence). **b** to grant or obtain a further loan of (e.g. a library book). **4** to replace or replenish (something): *Renew the water in the tank weekly.* ➤➤ **renewer** *noun.*

renewable *adj* capable of being renewed; *esp* capable of being replaced by natural processes or correct management practices: *Sun, wind, and waves are renewable sources of energy.* ➤➤ **renewability** /-'biliti/ *noun,* **renewably** *adv.*

renewal *noun* **1** the act of renewing or the process of being renewed. **2** something, e.g. a subscription to a magazine, that is renewed. **3** something used for renewing; *specif* an expenditure that improves existing fixed assets.

reni- *or* **reno-** *comb. form* forming words, denoting: kidney: *reniform.* [Latin *renes* kidneys]

reniform /'renifawm, 'ree-/ *adj* kidney-shaped. [Latin *reniformis,* from RENI- + *-formis* -FORM]

renin /'reenin, 'renin/ *noun* an enzyme from the kidney that acts on proteins and plays a major role in the maintenance of blood pressure. [RENI- + -IN[1]]

rennet /'renit/ *noun* **1a** the membrane lining the stomach, *esp* the fourth stomach, of a young calf or related animal, used for curdling milk. **b** a prepared extract from the stomach or stomach lining of a young animal, that contains the enzyme rennin and is used for curdling milk to make cheese and junket. **2** any preparation containing rennin or a substance having the action of rennin on milk. [prob from an Old English word related to RUN[1]]

rennin /'renin/ *noun* any of several enzymes that coagulate milk and are used in making cheese and junkets, *esp* one from the mucous membrane of the stomach of a calf. [RENNET + -IN[1]]

reno- *comb. form* see RENI-.

renounce /ri'nowns/ *verb trans* **1** to give up, refuse, or resign (something), usu by formal declaration. **2** to refuse to follow, obey, or recognize (somebody) any further. ➤➤ **renouncement** *noun,* **renouncer** *noun.* [Middle English *renouncen* via Old French from Latin *renuntiare,* from RE- + *nuntiare* to report, from *nuntius* messenger]

renovate /'renəvayt/ *verb trans* **1** to restore (something) to a better state, e.g. by cleaning, repairing, or rebuilding. **2** *archaic* to restore (somebody) to life, vigour, or activity. ➤➤ **renovation** /-'vaysh(ə)n/ *noun,* **renovator** *noun.* [Latin *renovatus,* past part. of *renovare,* from RE- + *novare* to make new, from *novus* new]

renown /ri'nown/ *noun* the state of being widely known and admired; fame. [Middle English from Old French *renon,* from *renomer* to celebrate, from RE- + *nomer* to name, from Latin *nominare:* see NOMINATE[1]]

renowned *adj* celebrated or famous.

rent[1] /rent/ *noun* **1a** a usu fixed periodical payment made by a tenant or occupant of property or a user of goods to the owner. **b** an amount paid or collected as rent. **2** in economics, the portion of the income of an economy, e.g. of a nation, attributable to land as a factor of production in addition to capital and labour. [Middle English from Old French *rente* income, rent, ultimately from Latin *reddere:* see RENDER[1]]

rent[2] *verb trans* **1** to take and hold (e.g. a property) under an agreement to pay rent. **2** to grant the possession and use of (e.g. a property) for rent. ➤ *verb intrans NAmer* to be rented at a specified rate: *This car rents for $500 a week.* ➤➤ **rentable** *adj.*

rent[3] *noun* an opening or split; a tear. [English dialect *rent,* variant of REND]

rent[4] *verb* past tense and past part. of REND.

rent-a- *comb. form* forming words, with the meaning: rented or hired, or organized as if rented: *rent-a-mob.*

rental[1] *noun* **1** an amount paid or collected as rent. **2** an act of renting. **3** *NAmer* something, e.g. a house, that is rented.

rental[2] *adj* of or relating to rent or renting.

rent boy *noun Brit, informal* a young male prostitute.

renter *noun* **1** the lessee or tenant of property. **2** a distributor of cinema films. **3** something, e.g. a video cassette, that is rented.

rentier /'rontiay, 'ronh- (*French* rătje)/ *noun* somebody who lives mainly on unearned income, e.g. from land or shares. [Old French *rentier* from *rente:* see RENT[1]]

rent roll *noun* a register of a person's or company's lands and buildings showing the rents due and the total paid by each tenant.

renumber /ree'numbə/ *verb trans* (**renumbered, renumbering**) to number (something) again or differently.

renunciation /ri,nunsi'aysh(ə)n/ *noun* the act or practice of renouncing; *specif* self-denial practised for religious reasons. [Middle English from Latin *renuntiation-, renuntiatio,* from *renuntiare:* see RENOUNCE]

reopen /ree'ohp(ə)n/ *verb* (**reopened, reopening**) ➤ *verb trans* to open (something) again. ➤ *verb intrans* to open again: *School reopens in September.*

reorder /ree'awdə/ *verb trans* (**reordered, reordering**) **1** to order (something) again. **2** to arrange (something) in a different way.

reorganize *or* **reorganise** /ri'awgəniez/ *verb trans* to organize (something) again or in a different way. ➤➤ **reorganization** /-'zaysh(ə)n/ *noun,* **reorganizer** *noun.*

Rep. *abbr* **1** Republic. **2** Republican.

rep[1] /rep/ *noun informal* a representative; *specif* a sales representative.

rep[2] *noun informal* a repertory theatre or company.

rep[3] *or* **repp** *noun* a plain-weave fabric with raised crosswise ribs. [French *reps,* modification of English *ribs,* pl of RIB[1]]

rep[4] *noun NAmer, informal* reputation.

repaid /ri'payd, ree'payd/ *verb* past tense and past part. of REPAY.

repair[1] /ri'peə/ *verb trans* **1** to restore (something) by replacing a part or putting together what is torn or broken. **2** to restore (something) to a sound or healthy state; to renew (it). **3** to make (something) good; to remedy (it). ➤➤ **repairable** *adj,* **repairer** *noun.* [Middle English *repairen* via French from Latin *reparare,* from RE- + *parare* to prepare]

repair[2] *noun* **1** an instance or the act or process of repairing. **2** the relative condition of something with respect to soundness or need of repairing: *The car is in reasonably good repair.*

repair[3] *verb intrans formal* to betake oneself; to go: *He repaired to his home.* [Middle English *repairen* via French from late Latin *repatriare:* see REPATRIATE]

repair[4] *noun archaic* an abode.

reparable /'rep(ə)rəbl/ *adj* capable of being repaired.

reparation /repə'raysh(ə)n/ *noun* **1a** the act of making amends, offering expiation, or giving satisfaction for a wrong or injury. **b** something done or given as amends or satisfaction. **2** (*usu in pl*) damages; *specif* compensation payable by a defeated nation for war damages. ➤➤ **reparative** /ri'pərativ/ *adj.* [Middle English via French and late Latin from Latin *reparatus,* past part. of *reparare:* see REPAIR[1]]

repartee /repah'tee/ *noun* **1a** conversation involving the exchange of amusing and witty remarks. **b** skill in this. **2** a quick and witty reply. [French *repartie* from early French *repartir* to retort, from RE- + *partir:* see PART[2]]

repast /ri'pahst/ *noun formal* = MEAL[1]: *I saw a universal manifestation of discontent when the fumes of the repast met the nostrils of those destined to swallow it* — Charlotte Brontë. [Middle English from Old French *repast* from *repaistre* to feed, from RE- + *paistre* to feed, from Latin *pascere*]

repatriate /ree'patriayt, ree'pay-/ *verb trans* to restore (somebody) to his or her country of origin. ➤➤ **repatriate** /-tri·ət/ *noun,* **repatriation** /-'aysh(ə)n/ *noun.* [late Latin *repatriatus,* past part. of *repatriare* to go back to one's country, from RE- + *patria* native country, from *patr-, pater* father]

repay /ri'pay, ree'pay/ *verb trans* (*past tense and past part.* **repaid** /ri'payd, ree'payd/) **1a** to pay (something) back: *repay a loan.* **b** to give or inflict (something) in return or requital: *repay evil for evil.* **2** to compensate or requite (somebody). **3** to reward (something): *a company which repays hard work.* ➤➤ **repayable** *adj,* **repayment** *noun.*

repeal /ri'peel/ *verb trans* to revoke (a law). ➤➤ **repeal** *noun,* **repealable** *adj.* [Middle English *repelen* from Old French *repeler,* from RE- + *apeler* to appeal, call]

repeat[1] /ri'peet/ *verb trans* **1a** to say or state (something) again. **b** to say (something) through from memory. **c** to say (something) after somebody else: *Repeat these words after me.* **2a** to make, do, perform, present, or broadcast (something) again: *She repeated the experiment.* **b** to experience (something) again. **3** to express or present (oneself or itself) again in the same words, terms, or form. **>** *verb intrans* **1a** to say, do, or accomplish something again. **b** to occur more than once. **2** (*often* + *on*) said of food: to continue to be tasted intermittently after being swallowed. **>>** **repeatability** /-'biliti/ *noun*, **repeatable** *adj*. [Middle English *repeten* via French from Latin *repetere*, from RE- + *petere* to go to, seek]

repeat[2] *noun* **1** the act of repeating. **2** something repeated; *specif* a television or radio programme that has previously been broadcast at least once. **3a** a musical passage to be repeated in performance. **b** a sign placed before or after such a passage.

repeated *adj* **1** renewed or recurring again and again: *repeated changes of plan.* **2** said, done, or presented again.

repeatedly *adv* again and again.

repeater *noun* **1** a firearm that fires several times without having to be reloaded. **2** a watch that strikes the time when a catch is pressed.

repeating decimal *noun* = RECURRING DECIMAL.

repechage /repi'shahzh, 'repishahzh/ *noun* a heat, e.g. in rowing, in which losers from earlier heats are given another chance to qualify for the finals. [French *repêchage* second chance, reexamination for a candidate who has failed, from *repêcher* to fish out, rescue, from RE- + *pêcher* to fish]

repel /ri'pel/ *verb trans* (**repelled, repelling**) **1** to drive (something) back; to repulse (it). **2a** to drive (somebody) away: *Foul words and frowns must not repel a lover* — Shakespeare. **b** to be incapable of sticking to, mixing with, taking up, or holding (something): *The fabric repels moisture.* **c** said of a magnetic pole or an electric field: to tend to force (e.g. another magnet) away or apart by mutual action at a distance: *Two like electric charges repel one another.* **3** to cause aversion in (somebody); to disgust (them). [Middle English *repellen* from Latin *repellere*, from RE- + *pellere* to drive]

repellent[1] *or* **repellant** *adj* **1** serving or tending to drive away or ward off. **2** repulsive. **>>** **repellently** *adv*. [Latin *repellent-, repellens*, present part. of *repellere*: see REPEL]

repellent[2] *or* **repellant** *noun* something that repels, *esp* a substance used to prevent insect attacks.

repent /ri'pent/ *verb intrans* **1** to turn from sin and amend one's life. **2** to feel regret or contrition. **>** *verb trans* to feel sorrow, regret, or contrition for (something). **>>** **repentance** *noun*, **repentant** *adj*, **repenter** *noun*. [Middle English *repenten* from Old French *repentir*, from RE- + *pentir* to be sorry, from Latin *paenitēre* to repent]

repercussion /reepə'kush(ə)n/ *noun* **1** a widespread, indirect, or unforeseen effect of an act, action, or event. **2** *archaic* an echo or reverberation. **>>** **repercussive** /-siv/ *adj*. [Latin *repercussion-, repercussio*, from *repercutere* to drive back, from RE- + *percutere*: see PERCUSSION]

repertoire /'repətwah/ *noun* **1** a list or supply of dramas, operas, pieces, or parts that a company or person is prepared to perform. **2** a range of skills, techniques, or expedients. [French *répertoire* from late Latin *repertorium*: see REPERTORY]

repertory /'repət(ə)ri/ *noun* (*pl* **repertories**) **1a** the production and presentation of plays by a repertory company: *acting in repertory.* **b** a repertoire. **c** a company that presents several different plays in the course of a season at one theatre, or a theatre housing such a company. **2** = REPOSITORY (1A). [late Latin *repertorium* list, catalogue, from Latin *reperire* to find, from RE- + *parere* to produce]

repetend /'repitend, repi'tend/ *noun* in mathematics, the repeating digit in a recurring decimal fraction. [Latin *repetendum* something repeated, from *repetere*: see REPEAT[1]]

répétiteur /ri,peti'tuh/ *noun* somebody who coaches ballet dancers or opera singers. [French *répétiteur* from Latin *repetitus*, past part. of *repetere*: see REPEAT[1]]

repetition /repi'tish(ə)n/ *noun* **1** the act or an instance of repeating or being repeated. **2** a reproduction or copy. **>>** **repetitional** *adj*. [Latin *repetition-, repetitio*, from *repetere*: see REPEAT[1]]

repetitious /repi'tishəs/ *adj* characterized or marked by repetition; *esp* tediously repeating. **>>** **repetitiously** *adv*, **repetitiousness** *noun*.

repetitive /ri'petətiv/ *adj* = REPETITIOUS. **>>** **repetitively** *adv*, **repetitiveness** *noun*.

repetitive strain injury *noun* a medical condition characterized by pains in the wrists or arms, caused by making repeated awkward or jarring hand movements, and affecting mainly keyboard operators and musicians.

rephrase /ree'frayz/ *verb trans* to phrase (something) again; to put (it) in different words, *esp* to make the meaning clearer.

repine /ri'pien/ *verb intrans formal or literary* to feel or express dejection or discontent: *Speak thou, whose thoughts at humble peace repine, shall Wolsey's wealth, with Wolsey's end be thine?* — Dr Johnson. [RE- + PINE[2]]

replace /ri'plays/ *verb trans* **1** to restore (something) to a former place or position: *He replaced the cards in a file.* **2** to take the place of (somebody), *esp* as a substitute or successor. **3** (*often* + *with*) to put something new in the place of (something): *We wanted to replace the worn carpet.* **>>** **replaceable** *adj*, **replacer** *noun*.

Usage note

replace *or* substitute? These two words are close in meaning but differ somewhat in use. One *replaces* an old thing *with* a new thing, or one *substitutes* a new thing *for* an old thing. The meaning is essentially the same in both cases, but the prepositions are different (*replace … with* (or *by*); *substitute … for*) and the order in which 'old thing' and 'new thing' follow the verb is also different: *replace the House of Lords with an elected second chamber; substitute an elected second chamber for the House of Lords.*

replacement *noun* **1** the process of replacing or being replaced. **2** something or somebody that replaces something or somebody else; a substitute.

replant /ree'plahnt/ *verb trans* **1** to plant (something) again. **2** to provide (e.g. a garden) with new plants.

replay[1] /ree'play/ *verb trans* to play (something) again: *They had to replay the match.*

replay[2] /'reeplay/ *noun* **1a** the act or an instance of replaying. **b** the playing of a tape, e.g. a videotape. **2** a repetition or reenactment: *We don't want a replay of our old mistakes.* **3** a match played to resolve a tie in an earlier match.

replenish /ri'plenish/ *verb trans* to stock or fill (something) up again: *I replenished his glass.* **>>** **replenisher** *noun*, **replenishment** *noun*. [Middle English *replenisshen* from Old French *replenir* to fill, from RE- + *plein* full]

replete /ri'pleet/ *adj* **1** fully or abundantly provided or filled. **2** abundantly fed; sated. **>>** **repleteness** *noun*, **repletion** /-sh(ə)n/ *noun*. [Middle English via French from Latin *repletus*, past part. of *replēre* to fill up, from RE- + *plēre* to fill]

replevin /ri'plevin/ *noun* in law, the recovery of goods detained, upon security being given to try the matter in court. [Middle English from Anglo-French *replevine*, from Old French *replevir* to give security, from RE- + *plevir* to pledge]

replevy /ri'plevi/ *verb trans* (**replevies, replevied, replevying**) to get (goods) back by replevin. [Old French *replevir*: see REPLEVIN]

replica /'replikə/ *noun* **1** a close reproduction or facsimile, *esp* by the maker of the original. **2** a copy or duplicate. [Italian *replica* repetition, from *replicare* to repeat, ultimately from Latin *replicare*: see REPLY[1]]

replicate /'replikayt/ *verb trans* **1** to duplicate or repeat (something): *replicate a statistical experiment.* **2** to reproduce or make an exact copy of (something); to cause (it) to undergo replication. **3** to fold or bend (something) back: *a replicated leaf.* **>** *verb intrans* to produce a replica of itself: *Viruses replicate only under certain conditions.* **>>** **replicability** /-kə'biliti/ *noun*, **replicable** *adj*, **replicative** /-tiv/ *adj*. [late Latin *replicatus*, past part. of *replicare*: see REPLY[1]]

replication /repli'kaysh(ə)n/ *noun* **1a** a copy or reproduction. **b** the action or process of reproducing. **c** the process by which a complex molecule, virus, or cell structure, e.g. a MITOCHONDRION, is exactly reproduced or duplicated; *esp* the process by which an exact copy of a molecule of genetic material (DNA or RNA) is produced within a living cell. **2** performance of an experiment or procedure more than once; *esp* repetition of a complete experiment under the same conditions or the performance of an experiment on several samples at one time and place. **3** *dated.* **a** an answer or reply. **b** an answer to a reply; a rejoinder. **c** the reply made by the plaintiff in answer to the defendant's initial plea, answer, or opposing claim in a legal action.

reply[1] /ri'plie/ *verb intrans* (**replies, replied, replying**) **1** to respond in words or writing. **2** to do something in response. **>** *verb trans* to give (something) as an answer. [Middle English *replien* via French from Latin *replicare* to fold back, repeat, from RE- + *plicare* to fold]

reply[2] *noun* (*pl* **replies**) something said, written, or done in answer or response.

repo /'reepoh/ *noun* (*pl* **repos**) *NAmer, informal* a piece of property, e.g. a car, that has been repossessed.

repoint /ree'poynt/ *verb trans* to renew (e.g. brickwork) by adding mortar or cement.

report[1] /ri'pawt/ *noun* **1a** a usu detailed account or statement: *a news report*. **b** an account or statement of a judicial opinion or decision. **c** a usu formal record of the proceedings of a meeting or enquiry. **d** *Brit* a statement of a pupil's performance at school, sent to the pupil's parents or guardian. **2** common talk; rumour. **3** a loud explosive noise. **4** *formal* reputation or character: *of good report*. [Middle English via early French *reporter* from Latin *reportare*, from RE- + *portare* to carry]

report[2] *verb trans* **1a** to give information about (something); to relate (it). **b** to announce the presence, arrival, or sighting of (somebody or something). **2a** to convey news of (something). **b** to relate the words or sense of (something said). **c** to make a written record or summary of (something). **d** to watch for and present the newsworthy aspects or developments of (something), in writing or for broadcasting. **3a** to give a formal or official account or statement of (something). **b** to announce (something) as the result of examination or investigation: *The vet reported no sign of disease*. **4a** to make (something) known to the relevant authorities: *She ran to report a fire in the kitchen*. **b** to make a charge of misconduct against (somebody); to complain about (them): *I'll report you to the headmaster*. **5** said of a parliamentary committee: to return (a bill) to Parliament with conclusions or recommendations. ➤ *verb intrans* **1a** (*often* + on) to make, issue, or submit a report: *He reported on the company's financial situation*. **b** to act in the capacity of a news reporter. **2a** to present oneself: *Report at the main entrance*. **b** to account for oneself as specified: *She reported sick on Friday*. **3** (+ to) to be responsible to somebody superior: *You'll be reporting directly to the boss*. ➤➤ **reportable** *adj*.

reportage /repaw'tahzh, ri'pawtij/ *noun* **1** the act or process of reporting news. **2** writing intended to give a usu factual account of events. [French *reportage* from early French *reporter*: see REPORT[1]]

report card *noun NAmer* a school report.

reportedly *adv* according to report; reputedly: *She was reportedly seen leaving the party drunk.*

reported speech *noun* the words spoken by somebody grammatically adapted for inclusion in a sentence spoken or written by somebody else; indirect speech: *In reported speech, 'We are sorry' would become 'They said they were sorry'.*

reporter *noun* **1** a journalist who writes news stories. **2** somebody who gathers and broadcasts news. **3** somebody who makes a shorthand record of a proceeding.

report out *verb trans* to return (a bill) after consideration, and often with revision, to a legislative body for action.

report stage *noun* the stage in the British legislative process before the third reading of a bill.

repose[1] /ri'pohz/ *noun* **1** the state of resting after exertion or strain; *esp* rest in sleep: *the dear repose for limbs with travel tired* — Shakespeare. **2** composure of manner; poise. ➤➤ **reposeful** *adj*, **reposefully** *adv*.

repose[2] *verb intrans* **1** to be situated. **2** to lie resting. [Middle English *reposen* via French from late Latin *repausare*, from RE- + *pausare* to stop, from *pausa*: see PAUSE[1]]

repose[3] *verb trans formal* (+ in) to place (e.g. confidence or trust) in someone or something specified. [Middle English *reposen* to replace, from RE- + POSE[1]]

reposition /reepə'zish(ə)n/ *verb trans* to change the position of (something).

repository /ri'pozət(ə)ri/ *noun* (*pl* **repositories**) **1a** a place, room, or container where something is deposited or stored. **b** somebody or something that contains or stores a nonmaterial thing, *esp* in large quantities: *a repository of knowledge*. **2** a person to whom something is confided or entrusted. [Latin *repositorium* from *reponere* to replace, from RE- + *ponere* to place]

repossess /reepə'zes/ *verb trans* **1** to regain possession of (something). **2** to resume possession of (goods) in default of the payment of instalments due. ➤➤ **repossession** /-sh(ə)n/ *noun*, **repossessor** *noun*.

repoussé[1] /rə'poohsay/ *adj* said of sheet metal: decorated with patterns in relief made by hammering on the reverse side. [French *repoussé* past part. of *repousser* to press back, from RE- + *pousser* to push, thrust]

repoussé[2] *noun* repoussé metalwork.

repp /rep/ *noun* see REP[3].

repr. *abbr* **1** reprint. **2** reprinted.

reprehend /repri'hend/ *verb trans* to voice disapproval of (somebody); to censure (them). [Middle English *reprehenden* from Latin *reprehendere*, literally 'to hold back', from RE- + *prehendere*: see PREHENSILE]

reprehensible /repri'hensəbl/ *adj* deserving censure; culpable. ➤➤ **reprehensibility** /-'biliti/ *noun*, **reprehensibly** *adv*. [Middle English from late Latin *reprehensibilis*, from *reprehendere*: see REPREHEND]

represent /repri'zent/ *verb trans* **1a** to act for or in the place of (somebody): *He has represented his country at international level*. **b** to serve as the elected member of a legislative body for (a particular constituency or electorate): *the MP representing Leeds East*. **2** to take the place of (something) in some respect; to stand in for (it): *This orange represents the sun*. **3** to serve as a specimen, model, example, or instance of (something): *We chose ten people who represent the target audience*. **4** to serve as a sign or symbol of (something): *The snake represents Satan*. **5** to have the nature or effect of (something); to constitute (it): *This represents a flagrant breach of the rules*. **6** to portray or exhibit (something) in art; to depict (it). **7** to attribute a specified character or identity to (somebody or oneself), *esp* falsely: *He represents himself as a friend of the working man*. **8** to act the part or role of (somebody). **9** *formal* to point (something) out, *esp* in protest or remonstrance. ➤➤ **representability** /-'biliti/ *noun*, **representable** *adj*. [Middle English *representen* via French from Latin *repraesentare*, from RE- + *praesentare*: see PRESENT[2]]

re-present /reeprə'zent/ *verb trans* to present (something) again or in a new way. ➤➤ **re-presentation** /ˌreeprez(ə)n'taysh(ə)n/ *noun*.

representation /ˌreprizen'taysh(ə)n/ *noun* **1** somebody who or something that represents something else, e.g. an artistic likeness or image. **2** the act or an instance of representing or being represented. **3a** (*in pl*) a statement made to influence opinion. **b** a usu formal protest: *a representation in parliament*.

representational *adj* **1** relating to representation. **2** in the graphic or plastic arts, involving realistic depiction of physical objects or appearances.

representationalism *noun* in philosophy, the theory that the perceived object is an idea in the mind that represents an item in the external world: compare PRESENTATIONISM. ➤➤ **representationalist** *noun and adj*.

representationism *noun* = REPRESENTATIONALISM. ➤➤ **representationist** *noun and adj*.

representative[1] /repri'zentətiv/ *adj* **1a** serving as a typical or characteristic example: *a representative area*. **b** containing typical examples: *a representative sample of dishes from the menu*. **2a** acting on behalf of somebody else, *esp* through delegated authority. **b** based on or involving representation of the people in government or lawmaking, usu by election. **3** serving to represent: *The film wasn't representative of what life was really like then*. **4** said of art: = REPRESENTATIONAL. ➤➤ **representatively** *adv*, **representativeness** *noun*.

representative[2] *noun* **1a** somebody who represents a constituency, e.g. as a member of a parliament. **b** (*often* **Representative**) a member of the Australian or US House of Representatives or a US state legislature. **2a** somebody who represents somebody else as their agent, deputy, substitute, or delegate. **b** somebody who represents a business organization, *esp* a sales representative. **3** a typical example of a group, class, or quality; a specimen.

repress /ri'pres/ *verb trans* **1** to subdue (somebody or something) by force: *They moved quickly to repress the insurrection*. **2a** to prevent the natural or normal expression of (e.g. an emotion): *He repressed his anger*. **b** to exclude (e.g. a feeling) from consciousness by psychological repression: compare SUPPRESS. **c** to hold in (something showing emotion) by self-control: *She repressed a laugh*. **3** to prevent the normal activity or development of (somebody). **4** to hold (something) in check; to curb (it). **5** to inactivate (a gene) reversibly by inhibiting or blocking normal action. ➤➤ **represser** *noun*, **repressible** *adj*. [Middle English *repressen* from Latin *repressus*, past part. of *reprimere* to check, literally 'to press back', from RE- + *premere* to PRESS[1]]

repression /ri'presh(ə)n/ *noun* **1** the act or an instance of repressing or the state of being repressed: *the repression of unpopular* *opinions.* **2** a psychological process by which unacceptable desires or impulses are excluded from conscious awareness.

repressive /ri'presiv/ *adj* said of a government or regime: unjustly or unduly restricting people's freedom. ➤➤ **repressively** *adj*, **repressiveness** *noun*.

repressor *noun* something that represses, *esp* a protein, produced by a regulator gene, that indirectly inhibits the function of a gene responsible for protein synthesis.

reprieve¹ /ri'preev/ *verb trans* **1** to delay or remit the punishment of (e.g. a condemned prisoner). **2** to remove the threat of an unpleasant fate, e.g. demolition, closure, or dismissal, from (somebody or something) temporarily. [perhaps from early French *repris*, past part. of *reprendre*: see REPRISE¹]

reprieve² *noun* **1a** the act or an instance of reprieving. **b** a suspension or remission of a sentence, *esp* a death sentence, or the warrant for this. **2** a temporary removal of a threat to the existence or continuance of something.

reprimand¹ /'reprimahnd/ *noun* a severe and formal reproof. [French *réprimande* from Latin *reprimenda*, from *reprimere*: see REPRESS]

reprimand² /'reprimahnd, repri'mahnd/ *verb trans* to criticize (somebody) sharply or formally, usu from a position of authority.

reprint¹ /'reeprint/ *noun* **1** a subsequent impression of a book previously published in the same form. **2** the act or an instance of reprinting (e.g. a book).

reprint² /ree'print/ *verb trans* to print (something) again; to make a reprint of (it).

reprisal /ri'priezl/ *noun* **1** a retaliatory act. **2** a retaliation by force short of war. **3** the seizure of goods or citizens of a foreign country in retaliation for an injury. [Middle English *reprisail* via French from Old Italian *ripresaglia*, from *ripreso*, past part. of *riprendere* to take back, from *ri-* RE- + *prendere* to take, from Latin *prehendere*: see PREHENSILE]

reprise¹ /ri'preez/ *noun* a repetition of a musical passage, a musical number from a show, or a performance. [Middle English from early French *reprise*, from *reprendre* to take back, from RE- + *prendre* to take, from Latin *prehendere*: see PREHENSILE]

reprise² *verb trans* to repeat (a passage of music, a musical number, or a performance).

repro /'reeproh/ *noun* (*pl* **repros**) **1** a clear sharp proof made, *esp* from a raised and inked printing surface, to serve as photographic copy for a printing plate. **2** *informal* (*often used before a noun*) a reproduction, *esp* a copy of a work of art. [short for REPRODUCTION]

reproach¹ /ri'prohch/ *verb trans* to express disappointment and displeasure with (somebody) for conduct that is blameworthy or in need of improvement; to upbraid (them). ➤➤ **reproachable** *adj*, **reproacher** *noun*, **reproachingly** *adv*. [Middle English from Old French *reprochier* to reproach, ultimately from Latin RE- + *prope* near]

reproach² *noun* **1** an expression of rebuke or disapproval. **2** the act of reproaching or disapproving: *He was beyond reproach.* **3** discredit or disgrace: *Their methods brought reproach on them.* ➤➤ **reproachful** *adj*, **reproachfully** *adv*, **reproachfulness** *noun*.

reprobate¹ /'reprəbayt/ *noun* **1** somebody who is morally dissolute or unprincipled. **2** *archaic* in Calvinism, somebody who is condemned or predestined to eternal damnation.

reprobate² *adj* **1** morally dissolute; unprincipled. **2** *archaic* in Calvinism, predestined to damnation. [late Latin *reprobatus*: see REPROBATE³]

reprobate³ *verb trans archaic* to condemn strongly as unworthy, unacceptable, or evil. ➤➤ **reprobation** /-'baysh(ə)n/ *noun*. [Middle English *reprobaten* from late Latin *reprobatus*, past part. of *reprobare*: see REPROVE]

reprocess /ree'prohses/ *verb trans* to treat or process (something) again, so as to be suitable for reuse: *the reprocessing of nuclear waste.*

reproduce /reeprə'dyoohs/ *verb trans* **1** to produce (new living things of the same kind) by a sexual or asexual process. **2** to repeat, copy, or emulate (something): *She's been unable to reproduce the form she showed in the Australian Open.* **3** to imitate (something) closely: *A large metal sheet is shaken to reproduce the sound of thunder.* **4** to make an image or copy of (something). **5** to translate (a recording) into sound or an image. ➤ *verb intrans* **1** to undergo reproduction in a usu specified manner: *The picture reproduces well.* **2** to produce

offspring. ➤➤ **reproducer** *noun*, **reproducibility** /-'biliti/ *noun*, **reproducible** *adj*, **reproducibly** *adv*.

reproduction /reeprə'duksh(ə)n/ *noun* **1** the act or process of reproducing; *specif* the sexual or asexual process by which plants and animals give rise to offspring. **2a** something, e.g. a painting, that is reproduced; a copy. **b** (*used before a noun*) copied from an original or imitating the style of an earlier period. **3** the quality of sound or image produced by audio or video equipment.

reproductive /reeprə'duktiv/ *adj* relating to, involved in, or capable of reproduction. ➤➤ **reproductively** *adv*, **reproductiveness** *noun*.

reprogram *or* **reprogramme** /ree'prohgram/ *verb trans* (**reprogrammed, reprogramming,** NAmer **reprogramed, reprograming**) to alter the functioning of (e.g. a computer) by introducing a new program.

reprography /ri'prografi/ *noun* the science or practice of reproducing graphic matter, e.g. by photocopying. ➤➤ **reprographer** *noun*, **reprographic** /reprə'grafik/ *adj*. [REPRODUCTION + -GRAPHY]

reproof /ri'proohf/ *noun* criticism for a fault. [Middle English *reprof* from Old French *reprove*, from *reprover*: see REPROVE]

re-proof /ree'proohf/ *verb trans* **1** *Brit* to make (e.g. a garment) waterproof again. **2** to make a new proof of (e.g. a book).

reprove /ri'proohv/ *verb trans* to express disapproval of (somebody); to censure (them): *She reproved the child for her bad manners.* ➤➤ **reprover** *noun*, **reprovingly** *adv*. [Middle English *reproven* via Old French *reprover* from late Latin *reprobare* to disapprove, condemn, from Latin RE- + *probare* to test, approve]

reptile /'reptiel/ *noun* **1** any of a class of usu cold-blooded air-breathing vertebrates that include the alligators and crocodiles, lizards, snakes, turtles, and extinct related forms, e.g. the dinosaurs, and have a bony skeleton and a body usu covered with scales or bony plates: class Reptilia. **2** *informal* a grovelling or despicable person. [Middle English *reptil* via French or late Latin from Latin *reptus*, past part. of *repere* to creep]

reptilian¹ /rep'tilyən/ *adj* **1** resembling or having the characteristics of a reptile. **2** relating to reptiles.

reptilian² *noun* = REPTILE.

republic /ri'publik/ *noun* a state whose head is not a monarch and in which supreme power resides in the people and is exercised by their elected representatives governing according to law.

Editorial note ───────────────
The word 'republic' derives from the Latin res publica, meaning 'state'. Today it more commonly means a form of government in which the head of state is appointed or elected, as opposed to monarchy, in which the head of state is hereditary. The term may also refer to a style of politics – 'republican', emphasizing political participation and public spirit — Professor Vernon Bogdanor.

[French *république* from Latin *respublica*, from *res* thing, wealth + *publica*, fem of *publicus*: see PUBLIC¹]

republican¹ *adj* **1a** relating to or belonging to a republic. **b** advocating a republic. **2** (**Republican**) belonging or relating to a political party in the USA that is usu primarily associated with business, financial, and some agricultural interests and is held to favour a restricted governmental role in social and economic life. ➤➤ **republicanism** *noun*.

republican² *noun* **1** somebody who favours republican government. **2** (**Republican**) a member of the US Republican party. **3** (**Republican**) a supporter of the union of Northern Ireland with the Irish Republic.

repudiate /ri'pyoohdiayt/ *verb trans* **1** to refuse to have anything to do with (something); to disown (it). **2a** to refuse to accept (something); *esp* to reject (it) as unauthorized or as having no binding force. **b** to reject (e.g. a charge) as untrue or unjust. **3** to refuse to acknowledge or pay (e.g. a debt). **4** *archaic* to divorce or disown (a wife). ➤➤ **repudiation** /-'aysh(ə)n/ *noun*. [Latin *repudiatus*, past part. of *repudiare*, from *repudium* divorce]

Usage note ─────────────
repudiate, reject, deny, *or* **refute?** See note at REFUTE

repugnance /ri'pugnəns/ *noun* strong dislike, aversion, or antipathy. [Middle English, in the sense 'opposition' via Old French from Latin *repugnantia*, from *repugnare* to fight against, from RE- + *pugnare* to fight]

repugnant /ri'pugnənt/ *adj* **1** arousing strong dislike or aversion. **2** incompatible or inconsistent. ➤➤ **repugnantly** *adv*. [Middle English, in the senses 'opposed', 'contradictory', 'incompatible', via French from Latin *repugnant-, repugnans*, present part. of *repugnare*: see REPUGNANCE]

repulse[1] /ri'puls/ *verb trans* **1** to drive or beat (attackers) back. **2** to repel (somebody) by discourtesy, coldness, or denial. **3** to cause repulsion in (somebody). [Latin *repulsus*, past part. of *repellere*: see REPEL]

repulse[2] *noun* **1** a rebuff or rejection. **2** the act or an instance of repelling an assailant or the fact of being repelled.

repulsion /ri'pulsh(ə)n/ *noun* **1** a feeling of strong aversion. **2** in physics, a force, e.g. between like electric charges or like magnetic poles, tending to produce separation. **3** the act of repulsing or the fact of being repulsed.

repulsive /ri'pulsiv/ *adj* **1** arousing strong aversion or disgust. **2** serving or able to repulse. **3** *archaic* tending to repel or reject; forbidding. ⟫ **repulsively** *adv*, **repulsiveness** *noun*.

reputable /'repyootəbl/ *adj* held in good repute; well regarded. ⟫ **reputably** *adv*.

reputation /repyoo'taysh(ə)n/ *noun* **1a** overall quality or character as seen or judged by others. **b** fame; renown; celebrity: *a soldier ... seeking the bubble reputation even in the cannon's mouth —* Shakespeare. **c** recognition by other people of some characteristic or ability: *He has the reputation of being clever.* **2** a place in public esteem or regard; good name.

repute[1] /ri'pyooht/ *noun* **1** the character, quality, or status commonly ascribed to somebody or something. **2** the state of being favourably known or spoken of.

repute[2] *verb trans* (*usu in passive*) to believe or consider (somebody or something) to be as specified: *It is reputed to be the oldest specimen.* [Middle English *reputen* via French from Latin *reputare* to reckon up, think over, from RE- + *putare* to reckon]

reputed /ri'pyoohtid/ *adj* being such according to general or popular belief: *the reputed father of the child.* ⟫ **reputedly** *adv*.

request[1] /ri'kwest/ *noun* **1** the act or an instance of asking for something. **2** something asked for. **3** the condition or fact of being requested: *available on request.* **4** the state of being sought after: *a book in great request.* [Middle English *requeste* via French from (assumed) vulgar Latin *requaesta*, fem past part. of *requaerere*: see REQUIRE]

request[2] *verb trans* **1** to make a request to or of (somebody): *The tutor requested her to write a paper.* **2** to ask for (something): *The lawyer requested a brief delay.*

request stop *noun Brit* a point at which a public transport vehicle stops only by previous arrangement or when signalled.

requiem /'rekwi·əm, -em/ *noun* **1** a mass for the dead. **2** (*often* **Requiem**). **a** a musical setting of the mass for the dead. **b** a musical composition in honour of the dead. [Middle English from Latin *requiem*, first word of the introit of the requiem mass, accusative of *requies* rest, from RE- + *quies* quiet, rest]

requiescat /rekwi'eskat/ *noun* a prayer for the repose of a dead person. [Latin *requiescat* may he/she rest, from *requiescere* to rest, from RE- + *quiescere*: see QUIESCENT]

require /ri'kwie·ə/ *verb trans* **1a** to have to have (something) because it is necessary or essential; to need (it): *All living beings require food.* **b** to wish to have (something): *How many seats do you require?* **2** to call for (something) as suitable or appropriate: *The occasion requires formal dress.* **3** to regard (something) as obligatory; to demand (it): *required by law.* **4** to impose an obligation on (somebody); to compel (them): *You will be required to pass an examination before you can practise.* [Middle English *requeren* via French from (assumed) vulgar Latin *requaerere* to seek for, need, require, alteration of Latin *requirere*, from RE- + *quaerere* to seek, ask]

requirement *noun* **1** something wanted or needed. **2** a necessary precondition for something.

requisite[1] /'rekwizit/ *adj* necessary or required: *I made the requisite payment.* [Middle English from Latin *requisitus*, past part. of *requirere*: see REQUIRE]

requisite[2] *noun* **1** something that is required or necessary. **2** an article of the specified sort: *toilet requisites.*

requisition[1] /rekwi'zish(ə)n/ *noun* **1** the act of compulsorily taking over goods or property for official use. **2** a formal and authoritative written demand or application: *requisition for army supplies.* **3** the act of formally requesting somebody to perform an action. [Middle English via Old French from Latin *requisition-, requisitio*, from *requirere*: see REQUIRE]

requisition[2] *verb trans* to demand the use or supply of (something) formally or officially.

requite /ri'kwiet/ *verb trans* **1** *formal*. **a** to make suitable return to for (a benefit or service); to reward (it): *I should be guilty of great ingratitude if I omitted this honourable mention of her care and affection towards me, which I heartily wish it were in my power to requite as she deserves —* Jonathan Swift. **b** to compensate sufficiently for (an injury). **2** to make retaliation for (e.g. a wrong). ⟫ **requital** *noun*. [RE- + obsolete *quite* to quit, pay, from Middle English *quiten*: see QUIT[2]]

reran /ree'ran/ *verb* past tense of RERUN[1].

reread /ree'reed/ *verb trans* (*past tense and past part.* **reread** /ree'red/) to read (a piece of writing) again.

reredos /'riədos, 'riəridos, 'reərədos/ *noun* (*pl* **reredos** /-dos/) a usu ornamental wood or stone screen or partition wall behind an altar. [Middle English via Anglo-French, from Old French *arreredos*, from *arrere* behind + *dos* back, from Latin *dorsum*]

rerun[1] /ree'run/ *verb trans* (**rerunning**, *past tense* **reran** /-'ran/, *past part.* **rerun**) **1** to run (something, e.g. a race) again. **2** to show (e.g. a film or television programme) again.

rerun[2] /'reerun/ *noun* **1** the act or an instance of rerunning; a repetition. **2** a showing of a film, television programme, etc after its first run.

res. *abbr* **1** reserve. **2** residence. **3** resides. **4** resolution.

resale price maintenance /'reesayl/ *noun* the fixing by a manufacturer of a minimum price at which its goods may be sold to the public by a retailer, distributor, etc.

resat /ree'sat/ *verb* past tense and past part. of RESIT.

reschedule /ree'shedyool/ *verb trans* **1** to change the time that (an event) is to take place. **2** to set a new timetable for the repayment of (a debt).

rescind /ri'sind/ *verb trans* **1** to cancel or take back (e.g. an order). **2** to make (a law, contract, etc) void; to revoke or repeal (it). ⟫ **rescindable** *adj*, **rescinder** *noun*, **rescindment** *noun*. [Latin *rescindere*, from RE- + *scindere* to cut]

rescission /ri'sizh(ə)n/ *noun* the act or an instance of rescinding. [late Latin *rescission-, rescissio*, from Latin *rescindere*: see RESCIND]

rescript /'reeskript/ *noun* **1** a written answer to a legal enquiry or petition, *esp* the Pope's ruling on a point of Roman Catholic law. **2** an official or authoritative order, decree, or announcement. **3** an instance of rewriting; something rewritten. [Latin *rescriptum*, neuter past part. of *rescribere* to write in reply, from RE- + *scribere* to write]

rescue[1] /'reskyooh/ *verb trans* to free (somebody or something) from confinement, danger, harm, or difficulty; to save or deliver (them). ⟫ **rescuer** *noun*. [Middle English *rescuen* from Old French *rescoure*, from Latin RE- + *excutere*, from EX-[1] + *quatere* to shake]

rescue[2] *noun* the act or an instance of rescuing somebody or something: *The lifeboat came to their rescue.*

research[1] /ri'suhch, 'reesuhch/ *noun* **1** scientific or scholarly investigation, *esp* study or experiment aimed at the discovery, interpretation, or application of facts, theories, or laws. **2** careful or systematic searching or enquiry. [early French *recerche* from Old French *recerchier* to search thoroughly, from RE- + *cerchier*: see SEARCH[1]]

research[2] /ri'suhch/ *verb trans* **1a** to engage in research on (a subject): *We had to research the life of Chaucer.* **b** to engage in research for (e.g. a book or television programme): *The documentary was badly researched.* **2** to search or investigate (something) thoroughly: *They're researching the problem.* ⟫ *verb intrans* to carry out research. ⟫ **researchable** *adj*, **researcher** *noun*.

research and development *noun* the work done by a research body or commercial organization to increase knowledge or investigate the possibility of developing new products or services.

reseat /ree'seet/ *verb trans* **1** to show (somebody) to a different seat. **2** to make (a mechanical component, *esp* a valve) function correctly again by repairing wear or damage to it or to the part in which it is located. **3** to equip (something) with a new seat or seats.

resect /ri'sekt/ *verb trans* in surgery, to remove part of (an organ or other structure). ⟫ **resectable** *adj*, **resection** /-sh(ə)n/ *noun*, **resectional** /-sh(ə)nl/ *adj*. [Latin *resectus*, past part. of *resecare* to cut off, from RE- + *secare* to cut]

reseda /'residə/ *noun* any of a genus of flowering plants of the Mediterranean region that mostly have grey-green leaves: genus *Reseda*. [from the Latin genus name, from Latin *resedare* to allay; so called because the plant was used to treat tumours]

resemblance /ri'zembləns/ *noun* 1 the quality or state of resembling somebody or something else. 2 a point on which two people or things are similar. 3 a representation or image. ➤➤ **resemblant** *adj*.

resemble /ri'zembl/ *verb trans* to be similar to (something or somebody else), *esp* in appearance or superficial qualities. [Middle English *resemblen* from Old French *resembler*, from RE- + *sembler*: see SEMBLANCE]

resent /ri'zent/ *verb trans* to harbour or express ill will at (something considered wrong or unfair). ➤➤ **resentful** *adj*, **resentfully** *adv*, **resentfulness** *noun*, **resentment** *noun*. [Old French *ressentir* to feel strongly about, from RE- + Latin *sentire* to feel]

reserpine /'resəpin/ *noun* an alkaloid extracted from several related species of tropical shrub and sometimes used in the treatment of high blood pressure. [German *Reserpin*, prob irreg from scientific Latin *Rauwolfia serpentina* the Indian snakeroot, chief source of reserpine]

reservation /rezə'vaysh(ə)n/ *noun* 1a the act or an instance of reserving something, e.g. a seat or hotel room, or a record of this. b a reserved seat, hotel room, etc. 2 (*usu in pl*). a a specific doubt or objection: *We had reservations about the results.* b a limiting condition, or the specifying of such a condition: *They agreed, but with reservations.* 3 a strip of land separating carriageways on a major road. 4 an area of land set aside; *specif* one designated for the use of Native Americans by treaty. 5 *chiefly NAmer* an area in which hunting is not permitted, *esp* one set aside as a secure breeding place. 6 in law, a clause in a deed by which some right or interest is retained in a property being transferred to another, or the right or interest so retained.

reserve[1] /ri'zuhv/ *verb trans* 1 to retain (something) for future use; to keep (it) back: *Some of the grain is reserved for seed.* 2 to arrange that (a seat, hotel room, etc) be kept for one's own or another's use at a specified future time; to book (it). 3 to hold (something) over until later; to defer (it): *I'll reserve judgment until I've seen the report.* 4 to retain (e.g. a right). [Middle English *reserven* via early French *reserver* from Latin *reservare* to keep back, from RE- + *servare* to keep]

reserve[2] *noun* 1 a supply of something retained for future use or need. 2a *chiefly Brit* an area, e.g. of public land, set apart for the conservation of natural resources or rare plants and animals: *a nature reserve.* b an area of land used for regulated hunting or fishing: *a game reserve.* 3 = RESERVATION (4). 4 restraint, closeness, or caution in one's words and actions; reticence. 5 the act of making a qualification or expressing doubt: *She accepted without reserve.* 6a (*usu in pl*) a military force available as a support for regular forces when needed. b a member of a military reserve; a reservist. 7a in sport, a player or participant who has been selected to substitute for another if the need should arise, e.g. through injury. b (**the reserves**) a team made up of players who do not currently form part of the first team. 8 (*also in pl*) money, gold, foreign exchange, etc kept in hand or set apart, usu to meet liabilities. ✳ **in reserve** held back ready for use if needed.

re-serve /ree'suhv/ *verb trans* to serve (somebody or something) again.

reserve bank *noun* 1 a central bank that holds the reserves of other banks. 2 in the USA, a bank in the Federal Reserve System.

reserve currency *noun* foreign currency that a country's central bank holds in reserve as a means of payment of international debt.

reserved *adj* 1 restrained in speech and behaviour. 2a set apart or aside for future or special use. b kept for use by a particular person in accordance with a prior arrangement: *This table is reserved.* ➤➤ **reservedly** /-vidli/ *adv*, **reservedness** /-vidnis/ *noun*.

reserved occupation *noun* an occupation that excuses a person from military service in time of war.

reserve price *noun* a price announced at an auction as the lowest that will be considered.

reservist *noun* a member of a military reserve.

reservoir /'rezəvwah/ *noun* 1a a natural or artificial lake where water is collected and kept in quantity for use by a community. b a part of something, e.g. a machine, in which a liquid or gas is held. c a place in which liquid or gas gathers, e.g. in rock. d a cavity in an organism containing a bodily fluid or secretion. 2 an available

extra source or supply: *an untapped reservoir of ideas.* [French *réservoir* from early French *reserver*: see RESERVE[1]]

reset /ree'set/ *verb trans* (**resetting**, *past tense and past part.* **reset**) 1 to set (something) again or in a different way: *The bone will have to be reset.* 2 to change the reading of (e.g. a clock or meter); *specif* to restore (it) to zero. ➤➤ **resettable** *adj*.

res gestae /,reez 'jestee/ *pl noun* facts relevant to legal proceedings and admissible as evidence. [Latin *res gestae* things done]

reshape /ree'shayp/ *verb trans* to give a new form, structure, or orientation to (something).

reshuffle /ree'shufl/ *verb trans* 1 to rearrange (something) by altering the relative position or nature of its elements. 2 to reorganize (a group or team of people, *esp* government ministers) by a redistribution of roles. ➤➤ **reshuffle** *noun*.

reside /ri'zied/ *verb intrans* 1a to occupy a place as one's permanent home: *the people residing at this address.* b to make a place one's home for a time: *The King resided at Lincoln.* 2a (+ in) to lie in, or be associated or bound up with, a certain thing: *You pragmatists put the cart before the horse in making truth's being reside in verification-processes* — William James. b (+ in) to be vested as a right in a certain personage, etc: *the powers residing in the trustees.* [Middle English *residen* via French from Latin *residēre* to sit back, remain, abide, from RE- + *sedēre* to sit]

residence /'rezid(ə)ns/ *noun* 1 the act or fact of living in a place. 2 a dwelling, *esp* a large and impressive house or the official home of a government minister or other dignitary. 3 the period of living in a place: *after a residence of 30 years.* 4 = HALL OF RESIDENCE. ✳ **in residence** 1 said of a writer, artist, etc: serving in a regular capacity in a place, e.g. a college or gallery, and available to give instruction, advice, etc. 2 actually living in a usu specified place: *The Queen is in residence at Windsor.*

residency /'rezid(ə)nsi/ *noun* (*pl* **residencies**) 1 = RESIDENCE (1), (3). 2 a period of time spent as a writer or artist in residence, or the post itself. 3 *NAmer* a period of advanced training as a medical specialist. 4 a regular engagement at the same venue for a singer, band, etc. 5 in former times, the official home of a diplomatic agent residing at a foreign court or seat of government.

resident[1] /'rezid(ə)nt/ *adj* 1a living in a place, *esp* for some length of time. b serving in a regular or full-time capacity: *the resident engineer for the highway department.* c living at one's place of work: *a resident nanny.* 2 said of a quality: present or inherent. 3 said of an animal: not migratory. 4 said of a computer program: permanently present and available for use in the main memory, rather than having to be loaded separately. [Middle English from Latin *resident-, residens*, present part. of *residēre*: see RESIDE]

resident[2] *noun* 1a somebody who lives in a place. b a guest staying for one or more nights at a hotel. 2 an animal that does not migrate. 3 *NAmer* a doctor undergoing a residency. 4 in former times, a diplomatic agent residing at a foreign court or seat of government, *esp* a representative of the Crown in a British protectorate. ➤➤ **residentship** *noun*.

residential /rezi'densh(ə)l/ *adj* 1 used as a residence or by residents: *residential accommodation.* 2 relating to or involving residence: *a residential course.* 3 given over to private housing as distinct from industry or commerce: *a residential neighbourhood.* ➤➤ **residentially** *adv*.

residentiary[1] /rezi'denshəri/ *noun* (*pl* **residentiaries**) a member of the clergy who is required to live in the official residence of his or her place of appointment.

residentiary[2] *adj* 1 relating to or involving residence. 2 officially residing in a place.

residua /ri'zidyooə/ *noun* pl of RESIDUUM.

residual[1] /ri'zidyooəl/ *adj* 1a of or being a residue. b remaining as a residue, *esp* in a small quantity or for a short time. 2 leaving a residue that remains active or effective in air, soil, etc for some time: *residual pesticides.* ➤➤ **residually** *adv*. [Latin *residuum*: see RESIDUE]

residual[2] *noun* 1 something left over; a remainder. 2 in statistics, the difference between a result obtained by observation and one calculated from a formula, or between the MEAN[3] (average) of a set of observations and any one of them. 3 (*also in pl*) a payment made to an actor, musician, etc when a film, television programme, or other work they were involved in is rerun after the first showing.

residuary /ri'zidyooəri/ *adj* 1 of or being a residue; residual. 2 of or inheriting the residue of an estate: *a residuary legatee.*

residue /'rezidyooh/ *noun* **1** something that remains after a part, *esp* the greater part, is taken, separated, or designated; a remnant. **2** the part of a deceased person's estate that remains after the payment of all debts and bequests. **3** a substance remaining after chemical processing, e.g. distillation, or treatment to extract something useful or valuable. [Middle English via French from Latin *residuum*, neuter of *residuus* left over, from *residēre*: see RESIDE]

residuum /ri'zidyooəm/ *noun* (*pl* **residua** /-dyooə/) a residue, *esp* the residual product of a chemical reaction or process. [Latin *residuum*: see RESIDUE]

resign /ri'zien/ *verb intrans* to give up one's job or position. ➤ *verb trans* **1** to renounce (something) voluntarily, *esp* to relinquish (e.g. a right or position) by a formal act. **2** (+ to) to reconcile (oneself) to an unpleasant fact, circumstance, etc: *She resigned herself to her fate*. ➤➤ **resigner** *noun*. [Middle English *resignen* via French from Latin *resignare* to unseal, cancel, from RE- + *signare*: see SIGN²]

re-sign /ree'sien/ *verb trans* to sign (e.g. a document) again.

resignation /rezig'naysh(ə)n/ *noun* **1a** a formal notification of resigning: *She handed in her resignation*. **b** the act or an instance of resigning. **2** the quality or state of being resigned to something.

resigned *adj* marked by or expressing submission to something unpleasant regarded as inevitable: *a resigned look on his face*. ➤➤ **resignedly** /-nidli/ *adv*, **resignedness** /-nidnis/ *noun*.

resile /ri'ziel/ *verb intrans* to recoil or retract, *esp* to return resiliently to a prior position. [late Latin *resilire* to withdraw, from Latin: see RESILIENT]

resilient /ri'zilyənt/ *adj* **1a** capable of withstanding shock without permanent deformation or rupture. **b** able to return to shape after bending, stretching, squeezing, etc. **2** said *esp* of a person: able to recover from or adjust to misfortune, change, or disturbance. ➤➤ **resilience** *noun*, **resiliency** *noun*, **resiliently** *adv*. [Latin *resilient-, resiliens*, present part. of *resilire* to jump back, recoil, from RE- + *salire* to leap]

resin¹ /'rezin/ *noun* **1** any of various solid or semisolid yellowish to brown plant secretions, e.g. amber, that are insoluble in water and are used *esp* in varnishes, inks, and plastics. **2** any of numerous synthetic substances that have the qualities of natural resin. ➤➤ **resinous** /-nəs/ *adj*. [Middle English via early French *resine* and Latin *resina* from Greek *rhētinē* pine resin]

resin² *verb trans* (**resined**, **resining**) to treat (something) with resin.

resinate /'rezinayt/ *verb trans* to impregnate or flavour (something) with a resin or resinous product: *Retsina is a resinated wine*.

resist¹ /ri'zist/ *verb trans* **1** to withstand the force, action, or effect of (something). **2** to strive against or oppose (something or somebody): *resisting the enemy; those who resist change*. **3** to refrain from (something tempting): *I couldn't resist eating just one more cake.* ➤ *verb intrans* to exert force in opposition. ➤➤ **resister** *noun*, **resistibility** /-'biliti/ *noun*, **resistible** *adj*. [Middle English *resisten* via French from Latin *resistere*, from RE- + *sistere* to take a stand]

resist² *noun* a protective coating applied to a surface to cause it to resist the action of a particular agent, e.g. an acid or dye.

resistance *noun* **1** the act or an instance of resisting. **2** the ability to resist: *high resistance to infection*. **3** an opposing or retarding force. **4a** in physics, the opposition offered to the passage of a steady electric current through a body, circuit, or substance, usu measured in ohms. **b** = RESISTOR. **5** (*often* **Resistance**) an underground organization operating within an occupied country and engaging in secret operations against the occupying forces and those who collaborate with them.

resistance thermometer *noun* a scientific instrument that measures temperature by means of the changing electrical resistance in a wire.

resistant *adj* (*used in combinations*) capable of or offering resistance to a specified thing: *resistant to change; heat-resistant paint*.

resistivity /rezis'tiviti, ree-/ *noun* **1** resistance. **2** the ability of a substance to resist the passage through it of an electric current, equal to the electrical resistance of a unit volume of the substance. ➤➤ **resistive** /ri'zistiv/ *adj*.

resistless *adj archaic or literary* **1** too powerful to be resisted; irresistible: *This was the last sentence by which he could weary Catherine's attention, for he was just then borne off by the resistless pressure of a long string of passing ladies* — Jane Austen. **2** unable to resist. ➤➤ **resistlessly** *adv*, **resistlessness** *noun*.

resistor *noun* a component included in an electrical circuit to provide resistance.

resit /ree'sit/ *verb trans* (*past tense and past part.* **resat, resitting** /-'sat/) *Brit* to take (an examination) again after failing. ➤➤ **resit** /'reesit/ *noun*.

res judicata /,rayz yoohdi'kahtə, joohdi'kahtə, ,reez/ *noun* a matter finally decided by a court and not subject to being raised or contested in court again by the same parties unless the decision is amended on appeal to a higher court. [Latin *res judicata* judged matter]

resoluble /ri'zolyoobl/ *adj* capable of being resolved. [late Latin *resolubilis* from Latin *resolvere*: see RESOLVE¹]

re-soluble /ree'solyoobl/ *adj* able to be dissolved a second or subsequent time.

resolute /'rezəl(y)ooht/ *adj* **1** firmly resolved; determined. **2** showing resolution or determination: *a resolute statement*. ➤➤ **resolutely** *adv*, **resoluteness** *noun*. [Latin *resolutus*, past part. of *resolvere*: see RESOLVE¹]

resolution /rezə'l(y)oohsh(ə)n/ *noun* **1a** the act or process of solving or resolving something, e.g. a problem or dispute. **b** the act or process of reducing something to a simpler form. **2a** something that is resolved, *esp* a statement of firm intent: *New Year resolutions*. **b** firmness of resolve. **c** the act of making a firm decision. **d** a formal expression of opinion, will, or intent voted by a body or group. **3a** the capability, e.g. of a television or computer screen, to produce a clear and detailed image, or the degree of clarity of the image produced. **b** = RESOLVING POWER. **4** in medicine, the natural subsidence of a disease process or symptom, *esp* the disappearance of inflammation. **5** in chemistry, the separating of a compound or mixture into its constituents. **6** in music, the act of passing from a discordant to a concordant note or the progression of a chord from dissonance to agreeable harmony. **7** in mathematics, the analysis of a vector into two or more vectors of which it is the sum.

resolve¹ /ri'zolv/ *verb trans* **1a** to deal with (something, e.g. a dispute) successfully; to settle (it). **b** to find a solution to (a problem). **2a** to reach a firm decision about (something): *I resolved to try again.* **b** to declare or decide (something) by a formal resolution and vote. **3a** to break up or separate (something) into constituent parts: *O that this too too solid flesh would melt, thaw, and resolve itself into a dew* — Shakespeare. **b** to reduce (something) by analysis: *Try resolving the problem into simple elements.* **c** to express (e.g. a vector) as the sum of two or more components. **4** in medicine, to cause (a disease process or symptom) to subside or disappear. **5** in music, to make (notes or chords) progress from dissonance to agreeable harmony. **6** to separate (adjacent parts of an image) and make them distinguishable and independently visible. **7** to change (itself) gradually into a different apparent form: *The body floating in the water resolved itself into a lump of driftwood.* ➤ *verb intrans* **1** *formal* to form a resolution; to determine: *He resolved against overeating at Christmas.* **2** to become separated into constituent parts or become reduced by dissolving or analysis. **3** in music, to progress from dissonance to agreeable harmony. ➤➤ **resolvability** /-'biliti/ *noun*, **resolvable** *adj*, **resolved** *adj*, **resolvedly** /-vidli/ *adv*, **resolver** *noun*. [Latin *resolvere* to unloose, dissolve, from RE- + *solvere*: see SOLVE]

resolve² *noun* **1** the state of being determined or decided, or the degree to which somebody feels determined or decided. **2** a legal or official decision, *esp* a formal resolution. **3** something that is resolved.

resolvent *adj* having power to resolve, *esp* capable of reducing inflammation: *a resolvent drug*. ➤➤ **resolvent** *noun*. [Latin *resolvent-, resolvens*, present part. of *resolvere*: see RESOLVE¹]

resolving power *noun* **1** the ability of an optical system or apparatus to form distinct images of objects separated by small distances. **2** the ability of a photographic film or plate to reproduce the fine detail of an optical image.

resonance /'rezənəns/ *noun* **1** the quality or state of being resonant. **2a** a quality imparted to speech sounds by a buildup of vibrations in the vocal tract. **b** the intensification and enrichment of a musical tone by supplementary vibration. **c** strong vibration in a mechanical or electrical system caused by a relatively small vibration of the same or nearly the same frequency as that of the natural vibration of the system. **3** the possession by a molecule, chemical group, etc of two or more possible structures differing only in the distribution of electrons.

resonant /'rezənənt/ *adj* **1** continuing to sound; echoing. **2a** capable of inducing resonance. **b** relating to or exhibiting resonance.

3 intensified and enriched by resonance. **4** suggesting meanings or associations other than those that are immediately present. ⫸ **resonantly** adv.

resonate /'rezənayt/ verb intrans **1a** to produce or exhibit resonance. **b** to resound or reverberate. **2** to suggest meanings or associations beyond those that are immediately present: *The painting resonates with sexual imagery.* ⫸ verb trans to make (something) resonate. [Latin *resonatus*, past part. of *resonare*: see RESOUND]

resonator noun **1** something that resounds or resonates. **2** a device that responds to and can be used to detect a particular frequency. **3** a device for increasing the resonance or amplifying the sound of a musical instrument.

resorb /ri'sawb/ verb trans **1** to swallow, suck in, or absorb (something) again. **2** in physiology, to break down and incorporate (a previously differentiated tissue or structure) into the surrounding tissue. ⫸ verb intrans to be resorbed. ⫸ **resorbent** adj. [Latin *resorbēre*, from RE- + *sorbēre* to suck up]

resorcinol /ri'zawsinol/ noun a chemical compound that is obtained from various natural resins or produced artificially and is used in making dyes, medicines, and resins. [blend of RESIN¹ + *orcin* a natural or synthetic phenol + -OL¹]

resorption /ri'sawpsh(ə)n/ noun the process of resorbing or being resorbed. ⫸ **resorptive** /-tiv/ adj. [Latin *resorptus*, past part. of *resorbēre*: see RESORB]

resort¹ /ri'zawt/ noun **1** a frequently visited place providing accommodation and recreation, esp for holidaymakers: *a ski resort.* **2a** somebody or something that is turned to for help or protection; a refuge or resource: *They regarded the court as a last resort.* **b** formal the act of resorting to somebody or something; recourse: *We cannot win without resort to force.* [Middle English from Old French *resortir*, from RE- + *sortir* to go out, escape]

resort² verb intrans **1** (+ to) to turn to somebody or something or adopt a course of action to achieve an end: *They may resort to violence.* **2** formal to go, esp frequently or in large numbers. ⫸ **resorter** noun.

resound /ri'zownd/ verb intrans **1** to become filled with sound. **2** to produce a sonorous or echoing sound. **3** to become renowned: *a name to resound for ages* — Tennyson. [Middle English *resounen* via early French *resoner* from Latin *resonare*, from RE- + *sonare* to sound, from *sonus* SOUND¹]

resounding adj **1a** resonating. **b** impressively sonorous. **2** vigorously emphatic; unequivocal: *a resounding success.* ⫸ **resoundingly** adv.

resource¹ /ri'zaws, ri'saws/ noun **1a** (usu in pl) an available means of help, support, or provision. **b** (usu in pl) a source of wealth or revenue, e.g. minerals. **c** a source of information or expertise. **d** something to which one has recourse in difficulty; an expedient. **2** (usu in pl) the ability to deal with a difficult situation; resourcefulness. [obsolete French *ressourse* from Old French *resourdre* to rise again, from Latin *resurgere*: see RESURRECTION]

resource² verb trans to equip or supply (somebody or something, e.g. a school) with resources.

resourceful /ri'zawsf(ə)l, ri'sawsf(ə)l/ adj good at devising ways of dealing with difficult situations; enterprising. ⫸ **resourcefully** adv, **resourcefulness** noun.

respect¹ /ri'spekt/ noun **1a** high or special regard; esteem. **b** the quality or state of being esteemed: *achieving respect among connoisseurs.* **c** polite regard or deference. **d** (in pl) expressions of respect or politeness: *He paid his respects.* **e** slang used to express one's respect: *Respect to him! I couldn't do what he's doing.* **2** an aspect or detail: *a good plan in some respects.* **3** particular attention or consideration: *The piece was performed without respect to rhythm.* ✳ **in respect of 1** in relation to; concerning. **2** in payment of. **with respect to** in relation to; concerning. [Middle English from Latin *respectus*, past part. of *respicere* to look back at, regard, from RE- + *specere* to look]

respect² verb trans **1a** to consider (somebody or something) worthy of respect. **b** to refrain from violating or interfering with (something): *We must respect the sovereignty of a state.* **2** archaic to have reference to (something); to concern (it). ⫸ **respecter** noun.

respectable adj **1** worthy of respect. **2** decent or conventional in character or conduct. **3a** acceptable in size or quantity: *respectable amount.* **b** fairly good; tolerable. **4** fit to be seen; presentable:

respectable clothes. ⫸ **respectability** /-'biliti/ noun, **respectably** adv.

respectful /ri'spektf(ə)l/ adj marked by or showing respect or deference: *Oh, Chancellor unwary, it's highly necessary, your tongue to teach respectful speech, your attitude to vary* — W S Gilbert. ⫸ **respectfully** adv, **respectfulness** noun.

respecting prep with regard to; concerning.

respective /ri'spektiv/ adj belonging or relating to each; particular and separate: *They returned to their respective homes.* ⫸ **respectiveness** noun.

respectively adv **1** as distinct from others; separately. **2** in the order given: *Mary and Anne were 12 and 16 years old respectively.*

respell /ree'spel/ verb trans (**respelt** or **respelled**) to spell (a word) again or in another way, esp according to a particular phonetic system.

respirable /'respirəbl, ri'spie-ərəbl/ adj **1** fit for breathing. **2** capable of being taken in by breathing: *respirable particles of ash.*

respiration /respi'raysh(ə)n/ noun **1a** the physical process, e.g. breathing, by which air or dissolved gases are taken into the body and brought into contact with the blood or other liquid circulating in an organism. **b** the action of breathing. **c** a single act of breathing in and out. **2** the processes by which most organisms supply their cells and tissues with the oxygen needed for life-supporting processes and remove the carbon dioxide formed in energy-producing reactions. **3** any of various processes occurring in all living cells by which food substances are broken down to yield energy, and that in most animals and plants involve the use of oxygen and the production of carbon dioxide. ⫸ **respirational** adj, **respiratory** /'respirət(ə)ri, ri'spi-/ adj.

respirator /'respiraytə/ noun **1** a device worn over the mouth or nose to prevent the breathing of poisonous gases, harmful dusts, etc. **2** a device for maintaining artificial respiration, esp over a long period.

respiratory system noun a system of organs carrying out the function of respiration that consists typically of the lungs and the channels by which these are connected with the outer air.

respire /ri'spie-ə/ verb intrans **1a** formal to breathe. **b** to undergo respiration. **2** said loosely of a cell or tissue: to take up oxygen and produce carbon dioxide during respiration. ⫸ verb trans formal to breathe (something). [Middle English *respiren* from Latin *respirare* to breathe out, from RE- + *spirare* to blow, breathe]

respite¹ /'respiet, 'respit/ noun **1** a period of temporary delay, esp a reprieve. **2** a period of rest or relief. [Middle English from Old French *respit* refuge, ultimately from Latin *respectus*: see RESPECT¹]

respite² verb trans **1** formal to grant respite to (somebody). **2** to put off or delay (something).

respite care noun temporary care given to an elderly or disabled person so that their usual carer can have time off.

resplendent /ri'splend(ə)nt/ adj shining brilliantly; characterized by splendour. ⫸ **resplendence** noun, **resplendency** noun, **resplendently** adv. [Latin *resplendent-, resplendens*, present part. of *resplendēre* to shine out, from RE- + *splendēre* to shine]

respond¹ /ri'spond/ verb intrans **1a** to write or speak in reply; to answer. **b** to act in reply: *They responded to our appeal by sending blankets.* **2a** to react in response: *The plant will respond to a stimulus.* **b** to show a favourable reaction: *The disease does not normally respond to surgery.* ⫸ verb trans to write or say (something) in reply. ⫸ **responder** noun. [early French *respondre* from Latin *respondēre* to promise in return, answer, from RE- + *spondēre* to promise]

respond² noun **1** a pillar or pier that is attached to a wall and supports an arch or terminates a colonnade or arcade. **2** = RESPONSORY.

respondent¹ noun **1** a defendant, esp in an appeal or divorce case. **2** a person who replies to a survey, advertisement, etc. [Latin *respondent-, respondens*, present part. of *respondēre*: see RESPOND¹]

respondent² adj formal making a response; responsive.

responsa /ri'sponsə/ noun pl of RESPONSUM.

response /ri'spons/ noun **1** an act of responding. **2** something constituting a reply or reaction, e.g.: **a** something sung or said by the congregation or choir in reply to the priest or minister in a religious service. **b** a change in the activity of an organism or any of its parts resulting from stimulation. **c** the ratio of the power produced by an electrical system or device to the input. [Middle English *respounse* via early French *respons* from Latin *responsum* reply, neuter past part. of *respondēre*: see RESPOND¹]

responsibility /ri,sponsə'biliti/ *noun* (*pl* **responsibilities**) **1** the quality or state of being responsible, e.g.: **a** moral or legal obligation. **b** reliability or trustworthiness. **2** somebody or something for which one is responsible.

responsible *adj* **1a** liable to be called to account as the person who did something: *the officer responsible for the arrest*. **b** constituting the reason or cause of something: *Mechanical defects were responsible for the accident*. **2a** (*usu* + for) having charge, control, or care of something or somebody. **b** marked by or involving important duties, decision-making, control of others, accountability, etc: *a responsible job*. **3** able to discriminate between right and wrong and therefore accountable for one's own actions. **4** able to answer for one's own conduct; trustworthy or reliable. **5** having or showing sound judgment; sensible: *not a very responsible way to behave*. **6** (+ to) required to report or answer to the specified person or body. ➤➤ **responsibleness** *noun*, **responsibly** *adv*.

responsive /ri'sponsiv/ *adj* **1** quick to respond or react appropriately or sympathetically. **2** giving or constituting a response: *a responsive glance*; *responsive aggression*. ➤➤ **responsively** *adv*, **responsiveness** *noun*.

responsory /ri'spons(ə)ri/ *noun* (*pl* **responsories**) a set of phrases and responses sung or said after a reading in church.

responsum /ri'sponsəm/ *noun* (*pl* **responsa** /-sə/) a written decision from a rabbi or Jewish scholar in response to a submitted question or problem. [Latin *responsum*, in the sense 'formal opinion of a jurist': see RESPONSE]

respray /ree'spray/ *verb trans* to spray (something, e.g. a car) with a fresh coat of paint. ➤➤ **respray** /'reespray/ *noun*.

rest¹ /rest/ *noun* **1a** freedom or a break from activity or work. **b** a state of motionlessness or inactivity. **c** repose, relaxation, or sleep. **d** *literary* the repose of death. **2** peace of mind or spirit. **3a** in music, a silence of a specified duration, or a symbol representing this. **b** a brief pause in reading or speaking. **4** something used for support, e.g. a pole used in billiards or snooker to support the cue when playing a distant ball. **5** a place for resting, lodging, or taking refreshment: *a sailor's rest*. ✳ **at rest 1** resting or reposing, *esp* in sleep or death. **2** not moving. [Old English]

rest² *verb intrans* **1a** to relax the body or mind, e.g. by lying down or sleeping. **b** to lie dead: *rest in peace*. **2a** to stop working or exerting oneself. **b** said e.g. of a machine: to stop functioning or operating. **c** to stop moving. **3** to be free from anxiety or disturbance. **4a** to be set or lie supported: *A column rests on its pedestal*. **b** to be steadily directed: *Her gaze rested on the picture*. **5** (+ on) to be based or founded: *The verdict rested on several sound precedents*. **6** (+ with) to depend for action or accomplishment: *The answer rests with him*. **7** to be left without further attention: *We decided to let the matter rest*. **8** said of farmland: to remain idle or uncultivated. **9** to stop introducing evidence in a law case: *The defence rests*. ➤ *verb trans* **1** to give rest to (something or somebody): *We stopped to rest the horses*. **2** to place (something) on or against a support. **3a** to cause (something) to be firmly based or founded: *He rested all hope in his son*. **b** to stop presenting evidence pertinent to (a case). ✳ **rest on one's laurels** see LAUREL. ➤➤ **rester** *noun*.

rest³ *noun* **1** (**the rest**) the part, amount, or number that remains: *They ate the rest of the chocolate*. **2** (**the rest**) the other people or things: *Where is the rest of the money?* [Middle English from early French *reste*, from Latin *restare* to be left, to stand back, from RE- + *stare* to stand]

rest⁴ *verb intrans* to remain as specified: *Rest assured I won't tell a soul*.

restate /ree'stayt/ *verb trans* to state (something) again or in a different way, e.g. more emphatically. ➤➤ **restatement** *noun*.

restaurant /'rest(ə)ronh, -ront, -rənt/ *noun* a place where refreshments, *esp* meals, are sold usu to be eaten on the premises. [French *restaurant*, present part. of *restaurer* to restore, from Latin *restaurare*: see RESTORE]

restaurant car *noun* = DINING CAR.

restaurateur /,rest(ə)rə'tuh/ *noun* the manager or proprietor of a restaurant. [French *restaurateur* from late Latin *restaurator* restorer, from Latin *restaurare*: see RESTORE]

restful /'restf(ə)l/ *adj* **1** marked by, conducive to, or suggesting rest and repose: *a restful colour scheme*. **2** quiet and peaceful. ➤➤ **restfully** *adv*, **restfulness** *noun*.

restharrow /'rest·haroh/ *noun* a flowering creeping plant of the pea family that is native to Europe and Asia and has spines on its stems: genus *Ononis*. [from obsolete *rest* to arrest, stop + HARROW¹; because of its tough stems]

rest home *noun* a residential home for elderly people who need a degree of medical or nursing care.

resting /'resting/ *adj* **1** not moving or active; at rest. **2** *euphem* said *esp* of an actor: out of work. **3** of or characterized by dormancy or lack of growth, *esp* undergoing a period of dormancy before germination: *a resting spore*.

restitution /resti'tyoohsh(ə)n/ *noun* **1a** the returning of something, e.g. property, to its rightful owner. **b** compensation given for an injury or wrong. **2** the return or restoration of something to a former or its original state, shape, or position. [Middle English via Old French from Latin *restitution-, restitutio*, from *restituere* to restore, from RE- + *statuere*: see STATUTE]

restive /'restiv/ *adj* **1** stubbornly resisting authority or control. **2** restless and uneasy. ➤➤ **restively** *adv*, **restiveness** *noun*. [Middle English *restif* refusing to move, from early French, from *rester* to stop behind, remain, from Latin *restare*: see REST³]

Usage note

restive or **restless**? Because they are similar not only in form but also in meaning, these two words are difficult to keep apart. *Restive* means 'difficult to control or keep still': children and horses are commonly described as *restive* and the word is also applied to people who get impatient with restrictions placed on them: *The military were growing restive and kept urging the government to act*. *Restless* ('fidgety', 'unable to rest', or 'constantly moving') is applied much more widely than *restive* – not only to people, but also to movements and things: *restless pacing to and fro*; *a restless night*.

restless *adj* **1** characterized by or displaying inability to rest, *esp* due to mental agitation: *restless pacing to and fro*. **2** giving no rest: *a restless night*. **3** continuously moving or active: *the restless ocean*. **4** discontented with the present situation and anxious for change. ➤➤ **restlessly** *adv*, **restlessness** *noun*.

Usage note

restless or **restive**? See note at RESTIVE.

rest mass *noun* in physics, the mass of a body when it is at rest relative to the observer.

restoration /restə'raysh(ə)n/ *noun* **1** the process of restoring something to its former or original state. **2a** a reinstatement of somebody to a position previously held. **b** a handing back of something. **3** a representation or reconstruction of the original form, e.g. of a ruined building. **4** (**Restoration**) the reestablishment of the monarchy in England in 1660 under Charles II or the period that followed this.

restorative /ri'stawrətiv/ *adj* capable of restoring health or vigour: *restorative medicine*. ➤➤ **restorative** *noun*, **restoratively** *adv*.

restore /ri'staw/ *verb trans* **1** to bring (something) back to its former or original state, e.g. by repairing damage: *to restore a painting*. **2** to bring (something) back into existence, force, or use: *The police managed to restore order*. **3** *formal* to give (something) back; to return (it): *They restored the car to its owner*. **4** *formal* to put (somebody) in possession of something again: *newly restored to health*. ➤➤ **restorable** *adj*, **restorer** *noun*. [Middle English *restoren* via Old French *restorer* from Latin *restaurare* to renew, rebuild]

restrain /ri'strayn/ *verb trans* **1** to keep (something) under control; to limit, repress, or check (it): *She found it hard to restrain her anger*. **2** (*usu* + from) to prevent (somebody) from doing something: *They restrained the boy from jumping*. **3a** to hold onto and physically prevent (a person or animal) from moving, attacking, etc. **b** to deprive (somebody) of liberty, *esp* by placing them under arrest. ➤➤ **restrainable** *adj*, **restrainer** *noun*. [Middle English *restraynen* via early French *restraindre* from Latin *restringere* to restrain, restrict, from RE- + *stringere* to bind tight]

restrained *adj* characterized by restraint, *esp* not extravagant or emotional. ➤➤ **restrainedly** /-nidli/ *adv*.

restraint /ri'straynt/ *noun* **1** moderation of one's behaviour; self-restraint. **2** the absence of extravagance or indulgence. **3a** the act of restraining or the state of being restrained. **b** a restraining force or influence. **c** a device that prevents freedom of movement. [Middle English from early French *restrainte*, from *restraindre*: see RESTRAIN]

restraint of trade *noun* any action that prevents freedom of competition in a commercial market.

restrict /ri'strikt/ *verb trans* **1** to prevent (somebody or something) from moving or acting freely. **2** to confine (something) within bounds; to limit (it). [Latin *restrictus*, past part. of *restringere*: see RESTRAIN]

restricted *adj* **1a** not general; limited. **b** available only to particular groups or for a particular purpose. **c** subject to control, *esp* by law. **d** not intended for general circulation: *a restricted document*. **2** narrow or confined. ➤➤ **restrictedly** *adv*, **restrictedness** *noun*.

restriction /ri'striksh(ə)n/ *noun* **1** a regulation that restricts or restrains: *restrictions for motorists*. **2** the act of restricting or the state of being restricted. ➤➤ **restrictionist** *noun and adj*.

restrictive /ri'striktiv/ *adj* **1** restricting or tending to restrict: *restrictive regulations*. **2** in grammar, identifying rather than describing a modified word or phrase: compare NON RESTRICTIVE: *a restrictive clause*. ➤➤ **restrictively** *adv*, **restrictiveness** *noun*.

restrictive practice *noun* **1** an anti-competitive trading agreement between companies, e.g. as to conditions of sale or quantities to be manufactured, that is against the public interest. **2** a practice by the members of a trade union that limits the flexibility of management.

rest room *noun NAmer* public toilet facilities in a building, e.g. a restaurant.

restructure /ree'strukchə/ *verb trans* to change the make-up, organization, or pattern of (something, e.g. an institution or business).

result[1] /ri'zult/ *verb intrans* **1** to proceed or arise as a consequence, effect, or conclusion, usu from something specified: *damage resulting from negligence*. **2** (+ in) to have the specified outcome or end: *errors that result in tragedy*. [Middle English *resulten* via medieval Latin from Latin *resultare* to rebound, from RE- + *saltare* to leap]

result[2] *noun* **1** something that happens or follows as a consequence, effect, outcome, or conclusion. **2** something obtained by calculation, experiment, or investigation. **3a** the outcome or final score, mark, etc of a contest or examination. **b** *informal* a win in a sporting contest.

resultant[1] *adj* derived or resulting from something else. ➤➤ **resultantly** *adv*.

resultant[2] *noun technical* the single vector that is the sum of a given set of vectors.

resume /ri'zyoohm/ *verb trans* **1** to take, occupy, or assume (e.g. a position) again: *He … returned, resumed his seat by the fire, and proceeded to darn again* — Hardy. **2** to return to, continue, or begin again (e.g. work) after interruption. ➤➤ *verb intrans* to continue or begin again after an interruption: *The meeting will resume after lunch*. ➤➤ **resumable** *adj*. [Middle English *resumen* via early French *resumer* from Latin *resumere*, from RE- + *sumere* to take up, take]

résumé /'rez(y)oomay/ *noun* **1** a summary. **2** *NAmer* = CURRICULUM VITAE. [French *résumé*, past part. of *résumer* to resume, summarize, from early French *resumer*: see RESUME]

resumption /ri'zumpsh(ə)n/ *noun* the act or an instance of resuming. [Middle English via French from late Latin *resumption-, resumptio*, from Latin *resumere*: see RESUME]

resupinate /ri'syoohpinət/ *adj* said of a plant part: inverted, or appearing to be upside down. ➤➤ **resupination** /-'naysh(ə)n/ *noun*. [Latin *resupinatus*, past part. of *resupinare* to bend back to a supine position, from RE- + *supinare*: see SUPINATE]

resurface /ree'suhfis/ *verb trans* to provide (something, e.g. a road) with a new or fresh surface. ➤➤ *verb intrans* **1** to rise again to the surface *esp* of water. **2** to appear or show up again.

resurgence /ri'suhj(ə)ns/ *noun* a rising again into life, activity, or influence. ➤➤ **resurgent** *adj*. [earliest as *resurgent* in the sense 'somebody who has risen again', from Latin *resurgent-, resurgens*, present part. of *resurgere*: see RESURRECTION]

resurrect /rezə'rekt/ *verb trans* **1** to bring (somebody) back to life from the dead. **2** to bring (something) back into use or into a position of prominence or popularity. [back-formation from RESURRECTION]

resurrection /rezə'reksh(ə)n/ *noun* **1a** (**the Resurrection**) the rising of Christ from the dead. **b** (*often* **the Resurrection**) in the Christian faith, the rising again to life of all the human dead before the Last Judgment. **2** a resurgence, revival, or restoration. ➤➤ **resurrectional** *adj*. [Middle English from late Latin *resurrection-, resurrectio* act of rising from the dead, from Latin *resurgere* to rise again, from RE- + *surgere*: see SURGE[1]]

resurrectionist *noun* **1** somebody who believes that all dead people will be resurrected after the Last Judgment. **2** *archaic* a body-snatcher.

resuscitate /ri'susətayt/ *verb trans* **1** to revive (somebody) from unconsciousness or apparent death. **2** to impart new energy or vigour to (somebody or something); to revitalize (them). ➤➤ *verb intrans* to regain consciousness. ➤➤ **resuscitation** /-'taysh(ə)n/ *noun*, **resuscitative** /-tətiv/ *adj*, **resuscitator** *noun*. [Latin *resuscitatus*, past part. of *resuscitare*, literally 'to stir up again', from RE- + *suscitare* to stir up, from *sub-, sus-* up + *citare*: see CITE]

ret /ret/ *verb trans* (**retted, retting**) to soak (e.g. flax) so that the fibres are loosened from the woody tissue. [Middle English *reten* from early Dutch]

ret. *abbr* **1** retired. **2** return. **3** returned.

retable /ri'taybl/ *noun* a raised shelf or ledge above a church altar for the altar cross, the altar lights, and flowers. [French *retable* from Spanish *retablo*, from RETRO- + Latin *tabula* board, TABLE[1]]

retail[1] /'reetayl/ *verb trans* **1** to sell (goods) to final consumers who will not resell them. **2** /ri'tayl/ to relate or recount (e.g. gossip). ➤➤ *verb intrans* to be sold or available for sale to final customers: *This model retails at a higher price*. ➤➤ **retailer** *noun*. [Middle English *retailen* from Old French *retaillier* to cut back, divide, from RE- + *tailler* to cut]

retail[2] *noun* the sale of goods in small quantities to final consumers who will not resell them: compare WHOLESALE[1]. ➤➤ **retail** *adj and adv*.

retail price index *noun* a price index based on the retail prices of a range of selected essential commodities and used to show changes in the cost of living in Britain from month to month.

retail therapy *noun* = SHOPPING THERAPY.

retain /ri'tayn/ *verb trans* **1a** to continue to have or hold (something). **b** to continue to use or operate (something). **c** to keep (somebody) in one's pay or employment; *specif* to engage the services of (somebody) by paying them a retainer. **d** to keep (something) in one's mind or memory. **2a** to have the ability to hold or contain (something): *Lead retains heat*. **b** to hold (something) in place. ➤➤ **retainable** *adj*, **retainment** *noun*. [Middle English *reteinen, retainen* via early French *retenir* from Latin *retinēre* to hold back, keep, restrain, from RE- + *tenēre* to hold]

retainer *noun* **1** a fee paid to a lawyer or professional adviser in return for access to their services whenever they are required. **2** a reduced rent paid to reserve accommodation during the tenant's absence. **3a** an old and trusted domestic servant. **b** in former times, somebody who served a person of high rank.

retaining wall *noun* a wall built to hold back a mass of earth, water, etc.

retake[1] /ree'tayk/ *verb trans* (*past tense* **retook** /ree'took/, *past part.* **retaken** /-k(ə)n/) **1** to recapture (something or somebody). **2** to film, photograph, or record (something) again. **3** to sit (a test or examination) again.

retake[2] /'reetayk/ *noun* **1** a second filming, photographing, or recording of something. **2** a retaken test or examination.

retaliate /ri'taliayt/ *verb intrans* to take action that repays somebody, usu in kind, for some wrong they have done. ➤➤ **retaliation** /-'aysh(ə)n/ *noun*, **retaliative** /-yətiv/ *adj*, **retaliatory** /-yət(ə)ri/ *adj*. [late Latin *retaliatus*, past part. of *retaliare*, from RE- + *talio* punishment in kind]

retard /ri'tahd/ *verb trans* to slow down or delay (something), *esp* by preventing or hindering progress, development, or accomplishment. ➤➤ **retardation** /reetah'daysh(ə)n/ *noun*, **retarder** *noun*. [Latin *retardare*, from RE- + *tardus* slow]

retardant /ri'tahd(ə)nt/ *adj* slowing down or preventing something, *esp* a chemical reaction. ➤➤ **retardant** *noun*.

retarded /ri'tahdid/ *adj* slow or limited in intellectual or emotional development or academic progress.

retch /rech/ *verb intrans* to experience a vomiting spasm without actually vomiting anything. ➤➤ **retch** *noun*. [Old English *hræcan* to spit, hawk]

retd *abbr* **1** retired. **2** returned.

rete /'reeti/ *noun* (*pl* **retia** /'reeshi-ə, 'reeti-ə/) a network, *esp* a network of blood vessels or nerves. [Latin *rete* net]

retell /ree'tel/ *verb trans* (*past tense and past part.* **retold** /ree'tohld/) to tell (e.g. a story) again or in a different form.

retention /rɪ'tensh(ə)n/ *noun* **1a** the act of retaining or the state of being retained. **b** abnormal retaining within the body of something that should be eliminated, e.g. urine. **2** the ability or capacity to retain something, e.g. knowledge; retentiveness. [Middle English *retencioun* from Latin *retention-, retentio*, from *retinēre*: see RETAIN]

retentive /ri'tentiv/ *adj* able or tending to retain something, *esp* knowledge: *a retentive mind.* ➤➤ **retentively** *adv*, **retentiveness** *noun.*

rethink /ree'thingk/ *verb* (*past tense and past part.* **rethought** /ree'thawt/) to reconsider (a plan, attitude, etc) with a view to changing it. ➤➤ **rethink** /'reethingk/ *noun.*

retia /'reeshi-ə, 'reeti-ə/ *noun* pl of RETE.

reticent /'retis(ə)nt/ *adj* **1** inclined to be silent or reluctant to speak; reserved. **2** restrained in expression, presentation, or appearance: *The room has an aspect of reticent dignity* — A N Whitehead. ➤➤ **reticence** *noun*, **reticently** *adv.* [Latin *reticent-, reticens*, present part. of *reticēre* to keep silent, from RE- + *tacēre* to be silent]

reticle /'retikl/ *noun* = GRATICULE (1). [Latin *reticulum*: see RETICULE]

reticula *noun* pl of RETICULUM.

reticular /ri'tikyoolə/ *adj* = RETICULATE[1].

reticulate[1] /ri'tikyoolət/ *adj* having a network of veins, fibres, or lines. ➤➤ **reticulately** *adv.* [Latin *reticulatus*, from *reticulum*: see RETICULE]

reticulate[2] /ri'tikyoolayt/ *verb trans* to divide, mark, or arrange (something) so as to form a network. ➤➤ **reticulation** /-'laysh(ə)n/ *noun.* [back-formation from *reticulated* (adj), from Latin *reticulatus*: see RETICULATE[1]]

reticule /'retikyoohl/ *noun* **1** = GRATICULE (1). **2** a decorative drawstring bag used as a handbag by women in the 18th and 19th cents: *She saw her with a sort of anxious parade of mystery fold up a letter ... and return it into the purple and gold reticule by her side* — Jane Austen. [French *réticule* from Latin *reticulum* network, network bag, from dimin. of *rete* net]

reticulocyte /ri'tikyooləsiet/ *noun* a young red blood cell that has no nucleus. ➤➤ **reticulocytic** /-'sitik/ *adj.* [RETICULUM + -CYTE]

reticulum /ri'tikyooləm/ *noun* (*pl* **reticula** /-lə/) **1** the second stomach of a ruminant mammal in which folds of the lining form hexagonal cells. **2** a reticulate formation; a network. [Latin *reticulum*: see RETICULE]

retiform /'reetifawm, 'ret-/ *adj* having the structure of a net; reticulate. [Latin *rete* net + -IFORM]

retin- or **retino-** *comb. form* forming nouns and their derivatives, denoting: retina: *retinitis; retinol.*

retina /'retinə/ *noun* (*pl* **retinas** or **retinae** /-nee/) the light-sensitive membrane at the back of the eye that receives the image formed by the lens and is connected with the brain by the optic nerve. ➤➤ **retinal** *adj.* [Middle English *rethina* from medieval Latin *retina*, from Latin *rete* net]

retinal /'retinal, -'nal/ *noun* a derivative of vitamin A that, in combination with proteins, forms the pigments of the light-receiving parts of the retina. [RETIN- + -AL[3]]

retinitis /reti'nietəs/ *noun* inflammation of the retina often leading to blindness.

retinitis pigmentosa /pigmen'tohzə/ *noun* a hereditary disease causing a gradual degeneration of the retina and subsequent loss of vision. [scientific Latin, literally 'pigmented retinitis', because it is characterized by the occurrence of black pigment in the retina]

retino- *comb. form* see RETIN-.

retinol /'retinol/ *noun* a yellow chemical compound occurring *esp* in egg yolk, vegetables, and fish liver oil and essential for growth and vision; vitamin A. [RETIN- + -OL[1], because it is the source of retinal]

retinue /'retinyooh/ *noun* a group of attendants accompanying an important person, e.g. a head of state. [Middle English *retenue* from early French *retenue*, fem past part. of *retenir*: see RETAIN]

retiral /ri'tieərəl/ *noun chiefly Scot* retirement from work.

retire /ri'tie-ə/ *verb intrans* **1** to give up one's position or occupation permanently, *esp* at the end of one's working life: *She has retired from the civil service.* **2** *formal.* **a** to withdraw from a place: *They retired to the drawing room.* **b** to go to bed. **3** said of troops: to fall back or retreat. **4** to withdraw from a sporting contest: *The French*

driver retired on the penultimate lap. ➤ *verb trans* **1** to cause (somebody) to retire from a position or occupation. **2a** to order (a military force) to withdraw. **b** to withdraw (e.g. currency or shares) from circulation. ➤➤ **retirer** *noun.* [early French *retirer*, from RE- + *tirer* to draw]

retired *adj* **1** having concluded one's career: *a retired pilot.* **2** *archaic* remote from the world; secluded.

retirement *noun* **1a** withdrawal from one's position or occupation, *esp* permanent withdrawal from active working life. **b** the age at which one normally retires from work: *She reached retirement but was asked to work another year.* **c** the state of being retired. **2** the act or an instance of retiring. **3** *literary* a place of seclusion or privacy.

retirement pension *noun* a pension paid by the state to retired people who have reached a specified age.

retiring *adj* tending to avoid contact with other people; shy. ➤➤ **retiringly** *adv.*

retold /ree'tohld/ *verb* past tense and past part. of RETELL.

retook /ree'took/ *verb* past tense of RETAKE[1].

retool /ree'toohl/ *verb trans* **1** to equip (*esp* a factory) with new tools. **2** *chiefly NAmer* to reorganize (something), *esp* with a view to improving efficiency.

retort[1] /ri'tawt/ *verb trans* **1** to say (something) in reply or as a counter argument: *'I want the blacksmith.' 'And pray what might you be wanting with him?' retorted my sister, quick to resent his being wanted at all* — Dickens. **2** *archaic* to return (e.g. an argument or insult) in kind. ➤ *verb intrans* to answer back sharply or tersely. [Latin *retortus*, past part. of *retorquēre* to twist back, hurl back, from RE- + *torquēre* to twist]

retort[2] *noun* a terse, witty, angry, or cutting reply, *esp* one that turns the first speaker's words against them.

retort[3] *noun* **1** a container with a long neck bent downward, used for distillation and other chemical processes. **2** a container for the large-scale production of metal, gas, etc by heating a substance, e.g. ore or coal. [early French *retorte* via medieval Latin from Latin *retorta*, fem of *retortus*: see RETORT[1]; from its bent shape]

retort[4] *verb trans* to heat (something) in a retort.

retouch /ree'tuch/ *verb trans* **1** to restore or improve the appearance of (something) with small additions or changes; to touch (it) up. **2** to alter (a photographic negative or print) to produce a more acceptable appearance. ➤➤ **retouch** /'reetuch/ *noun*, **retoucher** *noun.* [early French *retoucher*, from RE- + *toucher*: see TOUCH[1]]

retrace /ree'trays/ *verb trans* **1** to go over (e.g. footsteps or a route) again, usu in the opposite direction. **2** to go back over (something) for the purposes of discovery or clarification. [French *retracer* from early French *retracier*, from RE- + *tracier*: see TRACE[2]]

retract /ri'trakt/ *verb trans* **1** to draw (something) back or in: *Cats can retract their claws.* **2a** to withdraw (something said or written); to take (it) back. **b** to refuse to abide by (e.g. a promise or agreement). ➤ *verb intrans* **1** to draw back. **2** to recant or disavow something. ➤➤ **retractable** *adj*, **retractive** *adj.* [Middle English *retracten* from Latin *retractus*, past part. of *retrahere*: see RETREAT[1]]

retractile /ri'traktiel/ *adj* capable of being retracted. ➤➤ **retractility** /reetrak'tiliti/ *noun.*

retraction /ri'traksh(ə)n/ *noun* the act or an instance of retracting; *specif* a statement that retracts an earlier one.

retractor *noun* **1** a surgical instrument for holding back organs or tissues, *esp* at the edges of an incision. **2** a muscle that draws in a body part: compare PROTRACTOR.

retrain /ree'trayn/ *verb intrans* to undergo a programme of training for work of a different kind. ➤ *verb trans* to teach (somebody) new skills.

retread[1] /ree'tred/ *verb trans* to renew the tread of (a worn tyre).

retread[2] /'reetred/ *noun* **1** a tyre with a new tread. **2** *informal.* **a** something brought back into use in a revised form. **b** somebody who returns to service after retirement or an absence.

retreat[1] /ri'treet/ *noun* **1a** the act or an instance of withdrawing, *esp* from something difficult, dangerous, or disagreeable; *specif* the forced withdrawal of troops from an enemy or an advanced position, or the signal to withdraw. **b** the process of receding from a position or state attained: *the retreat of a glacier.* **c** a military bugle call sounded at about sunset. **2** a place of peace, privacy, or safety; a refuge. **3** a period of withdrawal for prayer, meditation, and study. [Middle English *retret* via early French *retrait* from Latin *retrahere* to draw back, from RE- + *trahere* to draw]

retreat² *verb intrans* **1** to make a retreat; to withdraw. **2** *NAmer* to slope backward; to recede: *a retreating chin.* ➤ *verb trans* to draw or lead (something) back; *specif* to move (a piece) back in chess. ➤➤ **retreater** *noun.*

retrench /ri'trench/ *verb trans* **1** to reduce (something, *esp* costs or expenses). **2** *formal* to cut (something) out: *They had to retrench the offending paragraphs.* **3** *Aus* to make (a worker) redundant. ➤ *verb intrans* to make reductions, *esp* in expenses; to economize. ➤➤ **retrenchment** *noun.* [obsolete French *retrencher* from early French *retrenchier* to cut back, from RE- + *trenchier:* see TRENCH¹]

retrial /'reetrie-əl/ *noun* a second or subsequent legal trial.

retribution /retri'byoohrh(ə)n/ *noun* **1** punishment or retaliation for an insult or injury. **2** the dispensing of reward or punishment, *esp* by God. ➤➤ **retributive** /ri'tribyootiv/ *adj,* **retributively** /ri'tribyootivli/ *adv,* **retributory** /ri'tribyoot(ə)ri/ *adj.* [Middle English *retribucioun* via French from late Latin *retribution-, retributio,* from Latin *retribuere* to pay back, from RE- + *tribuere:* see TRIBUTE]

retrieve /ri'treev/ *verb trans* **1a** to get (something) back again; to recover (it): *He retrieved the documents he'd left on the bus.* **b** to rescue or save (somebody or something): *They tried to retrieve him from moral ruin.* **2** to remedy the ill effects of (something); to put (it) right: *She tried everything to retrieve the situation.* **3** to call (something) to mind again; to remember (it). **4** in sport, to return (e.g. a ball that is difficult to reach) successfully. **5** said of a dog: to find and bring in (killed or wounded game). **6** to recover (e.g. data) from a computer memory. ➤ *verb intrans* said of a dog: to retrieve game or bring back an object thrown by a person. ➤➤ **retrievability** /-'biliti/ *noun,* **retrievable** *adj,* **retrieval** *noun.* [Middle English *retreven,* modification of early French *retrouver* to find again, from RE- + *trouver* to find]

retriever *noun* a dog of a breed used to retrieve game in shooting.

retro¹ /'retroh/ *adj* in the style of an earlier period, usu in the recent past. [French *rétro,* short for *rétrograde* retrograde]

retro² *noun* objects, artworks, music, clothes, etc that imitate the style of an earlier period.

retro- *prefix* forming words, with the meanings: **1a** back towards the past: *retrograde.* **b** backward: *retroflex.* **2** situated behind: *retrochoir.* [Middle English from Latin *retro,* from RE- + *-tro* as in *intro* within]

retroaction /retroh'aksh(ə)n/ *noun* **1** a reciprocal action; a reaction. **2** retroactive operation, e.g. of a law or tax.

retroactive /retroh'aktiv/ *adj* extending in scope or effect to a prior time: *retroactive legislation; a retroactive tax.* ➤➤ **retroactively** *adv,* **retroactivity** /-'tiviti/ *noun.*

retrocede /retroh'seed/ *verb intrans* to go back; to recede. ➤ *verb trans* to cede back (e.g. a territory). ➤➤ **retrocession** /-'sesh(ə)n/ *noun.* [Latin *retrocedere,* from RETRO- + *cedere* to CEDE]

retrochoir /'retrohkwie·ə/ *noun* the part of a large church or cathedral behind the high altar.

retrofit /retroh'fit/ *verb trans* (**retrofitted, retrofitting**) to provide (a manufactured article) with new parts or equipment not available at the time of manufacture. ➤➤ **retrofit** /'ret-/ *noun.*

retroflex /'retrəfleks/ *adj* **1** said *esp* of a body part or plant part: turned or curved backward. **2** said of a speech sound: articulated with the tongue tip turned up or curled back just under the hard palate: *a retroflex consonant.* ➤➤ **retroflection** /-'fleksh(ə)n/ *noun,* **retroflexion** /-'fleksh(ə)n/ *noun.* [scientific Latin *retroflexus,* from RETRO- + Latin *flexus,* past part. of *flectere* to bend]

retroflexed /'retrəflekst/ *adj* = RETROFLEX.

retrograde¹ /'retrəgrayd/ *adj* **1** tending towards or resulting in a worse or less advanced state. **2** moving or directed backward. **3** ordered in a manner that is opposite to normal; reverse: *a retrograde alphabet.* **4** said of orbital or rotational movement: in a direction contrary to normal or contrary to that of neighbouring celestial bodies. ➤➤ **retrogradely** *adv.* [Middle English from Latin *retrogradus,* from RETRO- + *gradus* step]

retrograde² *verb intrans* **1** to move back; to recede. **2** to decline to a worse condition; to degenerate. ➤➤ **retrogradation** /-grə'daysh(ə)n, -gray'daysh(ə)n/ *noun.* [Latin *retrogradi,* from RETRO- + *gradi* to go]

retrogress /retrə'gres/ *verb intrans* **1a** to return to an earlier usu worse state. **b** to undergo retrogression. **2** to move backward; to

recede. ➤➤ **retrogressive** /-siv/ *adj,* **retrogressively** /-sivli/ *adv.* [Latin *retrogressus,* past part. of *retrogradi:* see RETROGRADE²]

retrogression /retrə'gresh(ə)n/ *noun* a reversal in development or condition, *esp* a return to a less advanced or specialized state during the development of an organism.

retro-rocket *noun* a rocket on an aircraft, spacecraft, etc that produces thrust in a direction opposite to or at an angle to its motion in order to slow it down or change its direction.

retrorse /ri'traws/ *adj* in biology, bent backward or downward. ➤➤ **retrorsely** *adv.* [Latin *retrorsus,* contraction of *retroversus:* see RETROVERSION]

retrospect /'retrəspekt/ *noun* a survey or review of past events. ✻ **in retrospect** when considering the past or a past event, *esp* in the light of present knowledge or experience, with hindsight. [RETRO- + -*spect* as in PROSPECT¹]

retrospection /retrə'speksh(ə)n/ *noun* the act or an instance of looking back over the past. [Latin *retrospectus,* past part. of *retrospicere* to look back at, from RETRO- + *specere* to look]

retrospective¹ /retrə'spektiv/ *adj* **1** relating to or affecting things in the past; retroactive. **2a** based on memory: *a retrospective report.* **b** of or given to retrospection. ➤➤ **retrospectively** *adv.*

retrospective² *noun* an exhibition showing the evolution of an artist's work over a period of years.

retroussé /rə'troohsay/ *adj* said of a nose: turned up at the end. [French *retroussé,* past part. of *retrousser* to tuck up, from RE- + *trousser:* see TRUSS²]

retroversion /retroh'vuhsh(ə)n/ *noun* **1** the act or process of turning back or regressing. **2** the bending backward of a body part or organ, *esp* the womb. ➤➤ **retroverted** /'retrohvuhtid/ *adj.* [Latin *retroversus* turned backward, from RETRO- + *versus,* past part. of *vertere* to turn]

retrovirus /'retrohvie·ərəs/ *noun* any of a family of RNA-containing viruses that possess the enzyme reverse transcriptase, many of which induce cancer and one of which causes Aids.

retsina /ret'seenə/ *noun* a white Greek wine flavoured with resin from pine trees. [modern Greek *retsina,* perhaps via Italian from Latin *resina:* see RESIN¹]

retune /ree'tyoon/ *verb trans* to tune (something, e.g. a musical instrument or television set) again.

return¹ /ri'tuhn/ *verb intrans* **1a** to go back or come back: *They returned home.* **b** (+ to) to go back to something in thought, conversation, or practice: *She soon returned to her old habits.* **2** (+ to) to pass back to an earlier owner: *The estate returned to a distant branch of the family.* **3** *formal* to reply, *esp* sharply or angrily. ➤ *verb trans* **1** to put (something) back in a former or proper place, position, or state: *He returned the book to the shelf.* **2** to give or send (something) back, *esp* to its owner. **3a** to state (something) officially, *esp* in answer to a formal demand: *She returned details of her income.* **b** to elect (a candidate). **c** to bring in (a verdict). **4** to bring in (e.g. a profit). **5** to repay (e.g. a compliment or favour). **6** in sport, to play (a ball or shuttlecock) hit by an opponent. **7** in card games, *esp* bridge, to lead (a card or suit) in response to one's partner's earlier action. **8** *formal* to say (something) in reply: *She returned a pretty sharp answer.* ➤➤ **returnable** *adj,* **returner** *noun.* [Middle English *returnen* from Old French *retourner,* from RE- + *tourner:* see TURN¹]

return² *noun* **1** the act or process of coming back to or from a place or condition. **2a** the act of returning something, *esp* to a former place, condition, or owner. **b** (*also in pl*) something returned, e.g. an unsold newspaper or unwanted ticket returned for a refund. **3** in sport, the returning of a ball or shuttlecock. **4** *Brit* a ticket bought for a trip to a place and back again: compare SINGLE² (4). **5** (*also in pl*) the profit from work, investment, or business. **6a** a financial account or formal report. **b** (*usu in pl*) a report or declaration of the results of an election. **7a** the continuation, usu at a right angle, of the facade of a building or of a moulding. **b** a means for conveying something, e.g. water or electric current, back to its starting point. **8** = CARRIAGE RETURN. ✻ **by return (of post)** by the next post to the sender of an item received. **in return** in compensation or repayment: *Those to whom evil is done do evil in return* — W H Auden. **many happy returns (of the day)** a birthday greeting.

return³ *adj* **1** relating to the act or process of returning: *the return journey.* **2a** done, delivered, or given in return: *a return visit.* **b** said of a game or match: played against the same opponent or opponents as before. **3** allowing something to return: *a return valve.* **4** doubled back on itself: *a return flue.*

return crease *noun* in cricket, any of the four lines at right angles to the bowling and popping creases from inside which the ball must be bowled.

returning officer *noun Brit* an official who presides over an election and declares the result.

return ticket *noun* = RETURN² (4).

retuse /ri'tyoohs/ *adj* said of a leaf: having a rounded end with a slight notch. [Latin *retusus* blunted, past part. of *retundere* to pound back, blunt, from RE- + *tundere* to beat, pound]

reunify /ree'yoohnifie/ *verb trans* (**reunifies, reunified, reunifying**) to restore the unity of (e.g. a previously divided country). ➤➤ **reunification** /-fi'kaysh(ə)n/ *noun*.

reunion /ree'yoohnyən/ *noun* a gathering of people, e.g. relatives or former associates, after a period of separation. **2a** the act or an instance of reuniting people or things. **b** the state of being reunited.

reunite /reeyoo'niet/ *verb trans* to bring (people or things) together again: *The child was reunited with its parents.* ➤ *verb intrans* to come together again. [medieval Latin *reunitus*, past part. of *reunire*, from RE- + late Latin *unire*: see UNITE]

reuse /ree'yoohz/ *verb trans* to use (something) again, *esp* after reclaiming or reprocessing it: *the need to reuse scarce resources.* ➤➤ **reusable** *adj*, **reuse** /ree'yoohs/ *noun*, **reuser** *noun*.

Rev. *abbr* **1** Revelation (book of the Bible). **2** Reverend.

rev[1] /rev/ *noun informal* (*usu in pl*) a revolution per minute of an engine. [short for REVOLUTION]

rev[2] *verb* (**revved, revving**) ➤ *verb trans informal* (*often* + up) to increase the number of revolutions per minute of (an engine), *esp* while stationary. ➤ *verb intrans informal* (*often* + up) to operate at an increased speed of revolution.

rev. *abbr* **1** revenue. **2** reverse. **3** review. **4** revised. **5** revision.

revaluate /ree'valyoohayt/ *verb trans* = REVALUE.

revalue /ree'valyooh/ *verb trans* **1** to change, *esp* to increase, the exchange value of (a currency). **2** to assess (something) again, *esp* arriving at a different conclusion; to reappraise (it). ➤➤ **revaluation** /-'aysh(ə)n/ *noun*.

revamp /ree'vamp/ *verb trans* to change and improve the appearance or structure of (something). ➤➤ **revamp** *noun*.

revanchism /ri'vahnshiz(ə)m/ *noun* a policy designed to recover lost territory or status. ➤➤ **revanchist** *noun and adj*. [French *revanche* from early French *revenche*: see REVENGE¹]

rev counter *noun* = TACHOMETER.

Revd *abbr* Reverend.

reveal[1] /ri'veel/ *verb trans* **1** to make known (something secret or hidden): *He rarely reveals his true feelings.* **2** to open (something) up to view: *The curtain rose to reveal an empty stage.* **3** to make (something) known through divine inspiration. ➤➤ **revealable** *adj*, **revealer** *noun*, **revealment** *noun*. [Middle English *revelen* via French from Latin *revelare* to uncover, reveal, from RE- + *velare* to cover, veil, from *velum* VEIL¹]

reveal[2] *noun* the side of an opening in a wall for a door or window, *esp* the part that lies between the frame and the outer surface of the wall. [alteration of *revail* from Middle English *revalen* to lower, from early French *revaler*, from RE- + *val*: see VALE¹]

revealed religion *noun* a religion that is based on teachings believed to be passed down directly by God.

revealing *adj* **1** exposing something usu concealed from view: *a revealing dress.* **2** providing significant or interesting information, often unintentionally: *The answer was revealing.*

reveille /ri'vali, ri'veli/ *noun* a call or signal to get up in the morning; *specif* a military bugle call. [modification of French *réveillez*, imperative pl of *réveiller* to awaken, ultimately from Latin *vigilare*: see VIGILANT]

revel[1] /'revl/ *verb intrans* (**revelled, revelling, NAmer reveled, reveling**) **1** (+ in) to derive intense satisfaction from something: *They revelled in his discomfiture.* **2** to enjoy oneself in a noisy and exuberant way. ➤➤ **reveller** *noun*. [Middle English *revelen* from early French *reveler* to rebel, from Latin *rebellare*, from RE- + *bellare* to make war, from *bellum* war]

revel[2] *noun* (*also in pl*) a riotous party or celebration.

revelation /revə'laysh(ə)n/ *noun* **1a** the act or an instance of revealing something. **b** something revealed, *esp* a sudden and illuminating disclosure. **2** a truth believed to be revealed by God to

man, or the communicating of it. **3** (**Revelation** *or* **Revelations**) a book of the New Testament in the form of a prophetic vision of the triumph of Christ as revealed to St John. [Middle English via French and late Latin from Latin *revelatus*, past part. of *revelare*: see REVEAL¹]

revelationist *noun* somebody who believes in the possibility or fact of divine revelation. ➤➤ **revelationist** *adj*.

revelatory /'revələt(ə)ri, revə'layt(ə)ri/ *adj* serving to reveal something.

revelry /'revlri/ *noun* (*pl* **revelries**) exuberant enjoyment or celebration.

revenant /'revinənt/ *noun literary* somebody who returns, *esp* from the dead. [French *revenant*, present part. of *revenir* to return, from Latin *revenire*: see REVENUE]

revenge[1] /ri'venj/ *noun* **1a** the act or an instance of retaliating in order to get even for a wrong or injury: *She took revenge on her former employers.* **b** a desire to retaliate in this way: *I saw revenge in his eyes.* **2** an opportunity for getting satisfaction or requital. [early French *revenge, revenche*, from *revengier, revenchier*: see REVENGE²]

revenge[2] *verb trans* **1** to retaliate for (an insult, injury, etc), *esp* by inflicting something similar on the perpetrators. **2** to take revenge on behalf of (oneself or somebody else). ➤➤ **revenger** *noun*. [Middle English *revengen* from early French *revengier*, from RE- + *vengier* to avenge, from Latin *vindicare*: see VINDICATE]

revengeful *adj* desiring or seeking revenge.

revenue /'revənyooh/ *noun* **1** the total income produced by a given source, e.g. an investment. **2** the total income of a business, usu before taxation and other deductions. **3a** the income, e.g. taxes or rates, that a government collects and receives into its treasury for public use. **b** a government department concerned with the collection of revenue. **4** (*also in pl*) an item of income. [Middle English from early French *revenue*, fem past part. of *revenir* to return, from Latin *revenire*, from RE- + *venire* to come]

reverb /ri'vuhb, 'reevuhb/ *noun* an artificial echo effect in recorded music, or an electronic device that produces it. [short for *reverberation*]

reverberate /ri'vuhbərayt/ *verb intrans* **1** said of a sound: to be reflected, *esp* many times; to continue in or as if in a series of echoes. **2** to have a continuing and powerful effect: *The scandal reverberated round the industry.* ➤ *verb trans* to reflect or return (light, heat, sound, etc). ➤➤ **reverberant** *adj*, **reverberantly** *adv*, **reverberation** /-'raysh(ə)n/ *noun*, **reverberative** /-rativ/ *adj*, **reverberator** *noun*, **reverberatory** /-b(ə)rət(ə)ri/ *adj*. [Latin *reverberatus*, past part. of *reverberare* to strike back, from RE- + *verberare* to lash]

reverberatory furnace /ri'vuhb(ə)rət(ə)ri/ *noun* a furnace or kiln in which heat is radiated or deflected from the curved roof onto the material to be treated.

revere /ri'viə/ *verb trans* to regard (somebody or something) with deep and devoted respect. [Latin *revereri*, from RE- + *vereri* to fear, respect]

reverence[1] /'rev(ə)rəns/ *noun* **1** honour or respect felt or shown, *esp* profound respect accorded to something sacred. **2** a gesture, e.g. a bow, denoting respect. **3** the state of being revered: *We hold her in reverence.* **4** (**Reverence**) used as a form of address to a member of the clergy: *thank you, Your Reverence.*

reverence[2] *verb trans* to regard or treat (somebody or something) with reverence.

reverend[1] /'rev(ə)rənd/ *adj* **1** worthy of reverence; revered. **2** (**Reverend**) used as a title for a member of the clergy: *the Reverend David Brown.* [Middle English via French from Latin *reverendus*, verbal noun from *revereri*: see REVERE]

Usage note
reverend *or* reverent? *Reverend* is a title used for a member of the clergy: *the Reverend William Hughes. Reverent* is an adjective meaning 'deeply respectful': *A reverent hush descended on the congregation.*

reverend[2] *noun informal* a member of the clergy.

Reverend Mother *noun* the title of the Mother Superior of a convent.

reverent /'rev(ə)rənt/ *adj* showing or characterized by reverence. ➤➤ **reverently** *adv*. [Middle English from Latin *reverent-, reverens*, present part. of *revereri*: see REVERE]

Usage note
reverent *or* reverend? See note at REVEREND¹.

reverential /revə'rensh(ə)l/ *adj* **1** expressing or having the quality of reverence: *a reverential biography.* **2** inspiring reverence. ➤➤ **reverentially** *adv.*

reverie /'revəri/ *noun* **1** a daydream. **2** the condition of being lost in thought or dreamlike fantasy. **3** a musical composition suggesting a dreamy state. **4** *archaic* a fanciful notion. [obsolete French *resverie* from early French *rêverie* delirium, from *resver, rever* to wander, be delirious]

revers /ri'viə/ *noun* (*pl* **revers** /ri'viəz/) a wide turned-back part or applied facing along the front edges of a garment; *specif* a lapel. [French *revers*, literally 'reverse', from early French *revers* (adj): see REVERSE[1]]

reversal /ri'vuhsl/ *noun* **1** the act or an instance of reversing, e.g.: a movement in an opposite direction, or the causing of such movement. **b** a change or overthrow of a legal proceeding or judgment, *esp* on appeal. **2** a conversion of a photographic positive into a negative or vice versa. **3** a change for the worse: *His condition suffered a reversal.*

reverse[1] /ri'vuhs/ *adj* **1a** opposite or contrary to a previous, normal, or usual condition or direction: *They announced the winners in reverse order.* **b** having the front turned away from an observer: *the reverse side of the fabric.* **2** causing backward movement: *reverse gear.* ➤➤ **reversely** *adv.* [Middle English *revers* via early French *revers* from Latin *reversus*, past part. of *revertere*: see REVERT]

reverse[2] *verb trans* **1a** to turn or change (something) to an opposite position or direction: *Reverse the order of the words.* **b** to turn (something) upside down or inside out. **2a** to overthrow or annul (a legal judgment). **b** to change (e.g. a decision or policy) to the contrary. **3** to cause (e.g. a motor vehicle) to go backward. ➤ *verb intrans* **1** to turn or move in the opposite direction. **2** to go or drive backward. **※ reverse the charges** *Brit* to arrange for the recipient of a telephone call to pay for it. ➤➤ **reverser** *noun.*

reverse[3] *noun* **1** the opposite of something: *Many ... think their own masters are better than the masters of other slaves ... when the very reverse is true* — Frederick Douglass. **2** the act of reversing or the state of being reversed. **3a** the side of a coin, medal, or currency note that does not bear the principal design and lettering: compare OBVERSE[2]. **b** the back part of something, e.g. the back cover of a book. **4** a gear that causes backward motion or reverses the direction of operation. **5** a change for the worse; a setback or misfortune. **※ in reverse 1** backward. **2** in the opposite direction.

reverse takeover *noun* the purchase of a large company, usu a public company, by a smaller company.

reverse transcriptase *noun* an enzyme found in retroviruses that catalyses the synthesis of DNA from RNA, the reverse of the usual sequence.

reversible[1] *adj* **1** capable of going through a sequence, e.g. of changes, in either direction: *a reversible chemical reaction.* **2** said of fabric or clothing: designed to be used with either side outward. **3** capable of being reversed: *a reversible decision.* ➤➤ **reversibility** /-'biliti/ *noun,* **reversibly** *adv.*

reversible[2] *noun* a reversible fabric or article of clothing.

reversing light *noun* a light on the rear of a vehicle that is switched on automatically when reverse gear is selected.

reversion /ri'vuhsh(ə)n/ *noun* **1** the act of reverting, *esp* a return to an earlier inferior state. **2a** a return to an ancestral type or reappearance of an ancestral characteristic; atavism. **b** an organism showing ancestral rather than parental characteristics; a throwback. **3** the right of future possession or enjoyment of something. **4a** the right to possess property at some future time, usu on the death of the present owner. **b** the property subject to such a right. **5** the sum to be paid on death in accordance with a life-insurance policy. ➤➤ **reversionary** *adj.* [Middle English via French from Latin *reversion-, reversio* act of returning, from *revertere*: see REVERT]

reversioner *noun* somebody who will come into possession of property by reversion.

revert /ri'vuht/ *verb intrans* **1a** to return to an earlier state, *esp* one considered lower, worse, or more primitive. **b** to return to a former practice, belief, etc. **c** said of an organism: to develop characteristics that were present in ancestors but have not been present in the species for some time. **d** to go back in thought or conversation: *They reverted to the subject of finance.* **2** said of property: to return to the original owner, or to the heirs of the original owner, after an interest previously granted to another or others has expired. ➤➤ **reverter** *noun,* **revertible** *adj.* [Middle English *reverten* via

French from Latin *revertere, reverti* to return, turn back, from RE- + *vertere, verti* to turn]

revet /ri'vet/ *verb trans* (**revetted, revetting**) to provide (an embankment, wall, etc) with a facing, *esp* of masonry. [French *revêtir* to clothe again, dress up, from Latin *revestire*, from RE- + *vestire*: see VEST[2]]

revetment *noun* **1** a facing of stone, concrete, etc built to protect a wall or retain an embankment. **2** a barricade to provide shelter, e.g. against bomb splinters.

review[1] /ri'vyooh/ *noun* **1** an act of inspecting or examining something, *esp* in order to decide if changes need to be made: *an annual pay review.* **2** a judicial reexamination of a case, e.g. by a higher court. **3a** a critical evaluation of a book, play, etc. **b** a magazine or newspaper, or part of one, devoted chiefly to critical articles. **4a** a general survey, e.g. of current affairs. **b** a retrospective view or survey, e.g. of somebody's life or work. **5** a formal military or naval inspection. **6** = REVUE. [obsolete French *reveue* from *revoir* to look over, from RE- + *voir* to see, from Latin *videre*]

review[2] *verb trans* **1a** to inspect or examine (something) critically or thoughtfully, often with a view to making changes: *They reviewed the results of the study.* **b** to examine or study (something) again. **2** to produce a review of (a book, play, etc). **3** to take a retrospective view of (something): *Let's review the past year.* **4** to hold a review of (troops, ships, etc).

reviewer *noun* a writer of critical reviews.

revile /ri'viel/ *verb trans* to criticize (somebody or something) very harshly or abusively. ➤➤ **revilement** *noun,* **reviler** *noun.* [Middle English *revilen* from early French *reviler* to despise, from RE- + *vil*: see VILE]

revise[1] /ri'viez/ *verb trans* **1** to look over (something) again in order to correct or improve it. **2** to make an amended, improved, or up-to-date version of (*esp* a text): *The dictionary is revised every four years.* **3** *Brit* to refresh one's knowledge of (e.g. a subject), *esp* before an examination: *She's busy revising her physics.* **4** to change (e.g. an opinion), *esp* in the light of further consideration or new information. ➤ *verb intrans Brit* to refresh one's knowledge of a subject, *esp* in preparation for an examination. ➤➤ **revisable** *adj,* **reviser** *noun,* **revisory** *adj.* [French *reviser* from Latin *revisere* to look at again, from RE- + *vidēre* to see]

revise[2] *noun* **1** the act of revising; revision. **2** a printing proof that incorporates changes marked in a previous proof.

Revised Standard Version *noun* a revised English translation of the Bible derived from the Revised Version and published in the USA in 1946 and 1952.

Revised Version *noun* a British revision of the Authorized Version of the Bible published in 1881 and 1885.

revision /ri'vizh(ə)n/ *noun* **1** the act of revising: *revision of a manuscript; revision for an examination.* **2** a revised version of something, *esp* a text. ➤➤ **revisionary** *adj.*

revisionism *noun* **1** the tendency or desire to revise politics, attitudes, etc. **2** *chiefly derog* a movement in Marxist socialism favouring an evolutionary rather than a revolutionary transition to socialism. ➤➤ **revisionist** *adj and noun.*

revitalize *or* **revitalise** /ree'vietəliez/ *verb trans* to impart new life or vigour to (somebody or something). ➤➤ **revitalization** /-'zaysh(ə)n/ *noun.*

revival /ri'vievl/ *noun* **1** renewed attention to or interest in something. **2** a new presentation or production, e.g. of a play. **3a** a period of renewed religious fervour. **b** an often emotional evangelistic meeting or series of meetings. **4** restoration of an earlier fashion, style, or practice. **5** the act of reviving or the state of being revived.

revivalism *noun* **1** the spirit or methods characteristic of religious revivals. **2** the desire or tendency to revive earlier fashions, styles, or practices. ➤➤ **revivalist** *noun and adj,* **revivalistic** /-'listik/ *adj.*

revive /ri'viev/ *verb trans* **1** to bring (somebody) back to a state of consciousness, health, or strength. **2** to bring (something) back into an active state or current use: *They revive old musicals.* ➤ *verb intrans* to return to a state of consciousness, health, or strength. ➤➤ **revivable** *adj,* **reviver** *noun.* [Middle English *reviven* via French from Latin *revivere* to live again, from RE- + *vivere* to live]

revivify /ree'vivifie/ *verb trans* (**revivifies, revivified, revivifying**) to give (somebody or something) new life or vigour; to revitalize (them): *Cessation in his love-making had revivified her love* — Hardy.

⋙ revivification /-fi'kaysh(ə)n/ *noun*. [French *révivifier* from late Latin *revivificare*, from RE- + *vivificare*: see VIVIFY]

revocable *or* **revokable** /'revəkəbl, ri'voh-/ *adj* capable of being revoked: *a revocable clause*. [Middle English via French from Latin *revocabilis*, from *revocare*: see REVOKE[1]]

revocation /revə'kaysh(ə)n/ *noun* the act or an instance of revoking something, e.g. an offer or a contract. [Middle English via French from Latin *revocation-, revocatio*, from *revocare*: see REVOKE[1]]

revokable /'revəkəbl, ri'voh-/ *adj* see REVOCABLE.

revoke[1] /ri'vohk/ *verb trans* to declare (something) to be no longer valid or operative; to annul (it): *The will has been revoked*. ⋙ *verb intrans* in card games, to fail to follow suit when able to do so, in violation of the rules. ⋙ **revoker** *noun*. [Middle English *revoken* via French from Latin *revocare*, from RE- + *vocare* to call]

revoke[2] *noun* the act or an instance of revoking in a card game.

revolt[1] /ri'vohlt/ *verb intrans* **1** to reject or refuse to acknowledge the authority or control of a government, employer, etc; to rebel. **2** to feel or recoil in disgust or loathing: *We revolted at their behaviour*. ⋙ *verb trans* to cause (somebody) to feel or recoil in disgust or loathing; to nauseate (them). ⋙ **revolter** *noun*. [early French *revolter* via Old Italian *rivoltare* to overthrow, from Latin *revolvere*: see REVOLVE[1]]

revolt[2] *noun* **1** a rebellion, *esp* a determined and armed one. **2** a movement or expression of vigorous opposition.

revolting *adj* extremely offensive; nauseating. ⋙ **revoltingly** *adv*.

revolute /'revəl(y)ooht/ *adj* said *esp* of the edges of a leaf: rolled backward or downward. [Latin *revolutus*, past part. of *revolvere*: see REVOLVE[1]]

revolution /revə'loohsh(ə)n/ *noun* **1a** the movement of an object round a central point or axis; rotation. **b** one complete turn made in this way: *2000 revolutions per minute*. **c** movement in a circular course; *specif* the action by a planet or other celestial body of going round in an orbit. **d** one complete round made in this way. **e** a single recurrence of a cyclical process or succession of related events. **2a** a sudden or far-reaching change. **b** a fundamental political change, *esp* the overthrow of one government and the substitution of another. **c** in Marxism, the class struggle and violent transitional period leading to the triumph of socialism. [Middle English *revolucioun* via French from late Latin *revolution-, revolutio*, from Latin *revolvere*: see REVOLVE[1]]

revolutionary[1] *adj* **1** completely new and different. **2a** of or being a revolution: *revolutionary war*. **b** promoting or engaging in revolution: *a revolutionary speech*.

revolutionary[2] *noun* (*pl* **revolutionaries**) somebody who advocates or is engaged in a revolution.

revolutionise *verb trans* see REVOLUTIONIZE.

revolutionist *noun chiefly NAmer* = REVOLUTIONARY[2].

revolutionize *or* **revolutionise** *verb trans* to change (something) fundamentally or completely: *an idea that has revolutionized the steel industry*.

revolve[1] /ri'volv/ *verb intrans* **1** to move in a circular course or round a central point or axis. **2** (+ around) to be centred on a specified theme or main point: *The dispute revolved around wages*. **3** to be considered in turn: *All sorts of ideas revolved in her head*. **4** to recur: *as the seasons revolved*. ⋙ *verb trans* **1** to cause (something) to turn round on or as if on an axis. **2** *literary* to ponder (something): *He revolved the scheme in his mind*. ⋙ **revolvable** *adj*, **revolving** *adj*. [Middle English *revolven* from Latin *revolvere* to roll back, cause to return, from RE- + *volvere* to roll]

revolve[2] *noun Brit* a device used on a stage to allow a set or piece of scenery to be rotated.

revolver *noun* a handgun with a revolving cylinder of several chambers each holding one cartridge and allowing several shots to be fired without reloading.

revolving credit *noun* a credit facility that may be used repeatedly up to the limit specified after partial or total repayments have been made.

revolving door *noun* a door with usu four sections that pivot on a central axis, e.g. at the entrance to a public building.

revue /ri'vyooh/ *noun* a theatrical production consisting typically of brief often satirical sketches, songs, and dances. [French *revue* from obsolete French *reveue*: see REVIEW[1]]

revulsion /ri'vulsh(ə)n/ *noun* **1** a feeling of utter distaste or repugnance. **2** a sudden or violent reaction or change: *For many years we enacted a perfect farce of subserviency to the dicta of Great Britain. At last a revulsion of feeling, with self-disgust, necessarily ensued —* Poe. **3** in medicine, *esp* in former times, the process of drawing disease from one part of the body to another, e.g. by the use of counter-irritants. ⋙ **revulsive** /-siv/ *adj*. [Latin *revulsion-, revulsio* act of tearing away, from *revellere* to pluck away, from RE- + *vellere* to pluck]

reward[1] /ri'wawd/ *verb trans* **1** to give a reward to (somebody). **2** to give a reward to somebody for (something): *Her persistence was finally rewarded*. ⋙ **rewardable** *adj*, **rewarder** *noun*. [Middle English *rewarden* from Anglo-French *rewarder* to regard, reward, from Old French *regarder*: see REGARD[2]]

reward[2] *noun* **1** something offered or given for service, effort, or achievement. **2** a sum of money offered in return for the capture of a criminal or the recovery of lost or stolen property, or for information leading to either. **3** something that is justly received as a consequence of good or bad behaviour; deserts. ⋙ **rewardless** *adj*.

rewarding *adj* yielding a reward; personally satisfying: *a very rewarding experience*.

rewa-rewa /'raywəraywə/ *noun* a tall New Zealand tree with reddish wood: *Knightia excelsa*. [Maori *rewa-rewa*]

rewind /ree'wiend/ *verb trans* (*past tense and past part.* **rewound** /ree'wownd/) to wind (film, tape, etc) back to the beginning or to an earlier point. ⋙ **rewind** /'reewiend/ *noun*.

rewire /ree'wie-ə/ *verb trans* to provide (e.g. a house) with new electric wiring. ⋙ **rewirable** *adj*.

reword /ree'wuhd/ *verb trans* to alter the wording of (something); to rewrite or restate (it) in different words.

rework /ree'wuhk/ *verb trans* **1** to revise or rewrite (something). **2** to reprocess (e.g. used material) for further use.

rewound /ree'wownd/ *verb* past tense and past part. of REWIND.

rewrite[1] /ree'riet/ *verb* (*past tense* **rewrote** /ree'roht/, *past part.* **rewritten** /ree'ritn/) to write (something) again, *esp* differently: *She rewrote the ending of the story*. ⋙ **rewriter** *noun*.

rewrite[2] /'reeriet/ *noun* **1** the act or an instance of rewriting. **2** something rewritten.

rewritten /ree'ritn/ *verb* past part. of REWRITE[1].

rewrote /ree'roht/ *verb* past tense of REWRITE[1].

Rex /reks/ *noun* **1** a title given to a reigning king and used after the first name, *esp* in its Latin form: *Georgius Rex*. **2** used in legal cases, when the British monarch is a king, to denote the Crown as a party to the action. [Latin *rex* king]

Reye's syndrome /'reez, 'rayz/ *noun* a rare often fatal metabolic disease that occurs primarily in children after a viral illness, is characterized by vomiting, fever, and coma, and involves swelling of the brain and fatty degeneration of the liver. [named after R D K *Reye* d.1978, Australian paediatrician, who first described it]

Reynard /'raynahd, 'renahd/ *noun literary* a fox. [Middle English *Renard, Renart*, name of the fox who is hero of the 13th-cent. French poem *Roman de Renart*]

RF *abbr* radio frequency.

Rf *abbr* the chemical symbol for rutherfordium.

RFC *abbr* **1** formerly, Royal Flying Corps. **2** Rugby Football Club.

RG *abbr* Republic of Guinea (international vehicle registration).

RGN *abbr* Registered General Nurse.

RGS *abbr* Royal Geographical Society.

RH *abbr* **1** Republic of Haiti (international vehicle registration). **2** right hand.

Rh[1] *abbr* rhesus (factor).

Rh[2] *abbr* the chemical symbol for rhodium.

rh *abbr* right hand.

RHA *abbr Brit* **1** Regional Health Authority. **2** Royal Horse Artillery.

rhabdomancy /'rabdəmansi/ *noun formal* the use of a rod or stick to divine for water or minerals. [Greek *rhabdomanteia*, from *rhabdos* rod + *manteia* -MANCY]

rhadamanthine /radə'manthien/ *adj* (*often* **Rhadamanthine**) *literary* rigorously just or uncompromising: *He accordingly addressed a carefully considered epistle to Sue, and, knowing her emotional temperament, threw a Rhadamanthine strictness into the lines here and* *there* — Hardy. [from *Rhadamanthus*, according to Greek mythology the judge of souls in the underworld]

Rhaeto-Romance /ˌreetoh rohˈmans/ *noun* = RHAETO-ROMANIC. ⟫ **Rhaeto-Romance** *adj*.

Rhaeto-Romanic /roh'manik/ *noun* any of a group of Romance languages of E Switzerland and the Tyrol that includes Romansch. ⟫ **Rhaeto-Romanic** *adj*. [Latin *Rhaetus* of *Rhaetia*, ancient Roman province + ROMANIC]

rhaphe /ˈrayfee/ *noun* (*pl* **rhaphae** /ˈrayfi·ee/) see RAPHE.

rhapsodic /rapˈsodik/ *adj* **1** resembling a rhapsody. **2** extravagantly emotional; rapturous. ⟫ **rhapsodically** *adv*.

rhapsodize *or* **rhapsodise** /ˈrapsədiez/ *verb intrans* **1** to speak or write with ardent enthusiasm or deep emotion. **2** to write or recite epic poems. ⟫ **rhapsodist** *noun*.

rhapsody /ˈrapsədi/ *noun* (*pl* **rhapsodies**) **1** a musical composition in one continuous movement, usu a free fantasy, often based on an epic, heroic, or national idea. **2a** an expression in speech or writing of ardent enthusiasm or deep emotion. **b** a state of rapture or ecstasy. **3** an epic poem, or part of one, that is short enough to be recited in a single sitting. [via Latin from Greek *rhapsōidia* recitation of selections from epic poetry, rhapsody, from *rhaptein* to sew, stitch together]

rhatany /ˈratəni/ *noun* (*pl* **rhatanies**) **1** the dried root of a S American shrub, used in medicine as an astringent. **2** the shrub that yields this root: genus *Krameria*. [Spanish *ratania* from Quechua *ratánya*]

rhea /ˈriə/ *noun* either of two species of large flightless S American birds that are similar to but smaller than the ostrich: *Rhea americana* and *Pterocnemia pennata*. [from the Latin genus name, named after *Rhea*, mother of Zeus in mythology]

rhebok *or* **reebok** /ˈreebok/ *or* **rhebuck** /ˈreebuk/ *noun* a small antelope of S Africa with a woolly coat of brownish grey hair and short horns: *Pelea capreolus*. [Dutch *reebok* roebuck]

Rhenish /ˈrenish, ˈreenish/ *adj* of the river Rhine or the adjoining regions. [Latin *Rhenus* the river Rhine]

rhenium /ˈreeni·əm/ *noun* a silver-grey metallic chemical element similar to manganese that occurs naturally in molybdenum ores, and is used *esp* in catalysts and thermocouples: symbol Re, atomic number 75. [scientific Latin *rhenium*, from Latin *Rhenus* the river Rhine]

rheo- *comb. form* forming words, denoting: flow or current: *rheostat*. [Greek *rhein* to flow]

rheology /riˈoləji/ *noun* a branch of physics dealing with the deformation and flow of matter. ⟫ **rheological** /ree·əˈlojik/ *adj*, **rheologist** *noun*.

rheostat /ˈriəstat, ˈree·əstat/ *noun* a device that regulates an electric current by varying resistance. ⟫ **rheostatic** /-ˈstatik/ *adj*.

rhesus baby /ˈreesəs/ *noun* a baby born with the blood disease erythroblastosis foetalis, caused by the presence of antibodies in its mother's Rh-negative blood that act on and destroy the cells of its own Rh-positive blood.

rhesus factor *noun* any of several substances present in red blood cells that are used to define blood groups and can provoke intense allergic reactions when incompatible blood types are mixed, e.g. during pregnancy or in blood transfusions. [because it was first detected in rhesus monkeys]

rhesus monkey *noun* a small pale brown monkey of S Asia that is a macaque: *Macaca mulatta*. [named after *Rhesus*, a mythical king of Thrace]

rhesus negative *adj* lacking rhesus factor in the red blood cells.

rhesus positive *adj* having rhesus factor in the red blood cells.

rhetoric /ˈretərik/ *noun* **1** the art of speaking or writing effectively; *specif* the principles and rules of composition, or the study of them. **2a** skill in the effective use of speech. **b** insincere or exaggerated language that is calculated to produce an effect. [Middle English *rethorik* via French and Latin from Greek *rhētorikē* art of oratory, from *rhētōr* orator, rhetorician, from *eirein* to say, speak]

rhetorical /riˈtorikl/ *adj* **1a** relating to or involving rhetoric. **b** used merely for rhetorical effect. **2** tending to speak in an impressive or exaggerated way; grandiloquent. ⟫ **rhetorically** *adv*.

rhetorical question *noun* a question to which no answer is expected, used to make a statement with dramatic effect.

rhetorician /retəˈrish(ə)n/ *noun* **1** an eloquent or pretentious writer or speaker. **2** an expert in or teacher of rhetoric.

rheum /roohm/ *noun* a watery discharge from the eyes, nose, etc. ⟫ **rheumy** *adj*. [Middle English *reume* via French and Latin from Greek *rheuma* flow, flux, from *rhein* to flow]

rheumatic[1] /roohˈmatik, roo-/ *adj* **1** relating to or characteristic of rheumatism. **2** suffering from or affected by rheumatism. ⟫ **rheumatically** *adv*. [Middle English *rewmatik* characterized by watery discharge, via Latin from Greek *rheumatikos*, from *rheumat-*, *rheuma*: see RHEUM]

rheumatic[2] *noun* somebody suffering from rheumatism.

rheumatic fever *noun* an acute disease that occurs chiefly in children and young adults and is characterized by fever, inflammation and pain in the joints, and sometimes damage to the heart valves.

rheumaticky *adj informal* suffering from or affected by rheumatism; rheumatic.

rheumatics *pl noun informal* (*treated as sing. or pl*) rheumatism.

rheumatism /ˈroohmətiz(ə)m/ *noun* **1** any of various conditions characterized by inflammation and pain in muscles, joints, or fibrous tissue. **2** = RHEUMATOID ARTHRITIS.

Word history ——
via Latin from Greek *rheumatismos* flux, rheum, from *rheumatizesthai* to suffer from a flux, from *rheumat-*, *rheuma*: see RHEUM. The disease was orig thought to be caused by watery humours flowing within the body.

rheumatoid /ˈroohmətoyd/ *adj* characteristic of or affected by rheumatism or rheumatoid arthritis.

rheumatoid arthritis *noun* a progressively worsening disease of unknown cause that is characterized by painful inflammation and swelling of joint structures.

rheumatology /roohmə'toləji/ *noun* a branch of medicine dealing with rheumatic diseases. ⟫ **rheumatological** /-ˈlojikl/ *adj*, **rheumatologist** *noun*.

rhin- *or* **rhino-** *comb. form* forming words, denoting: nose: *rhinoplasty*; *rhinal*. [scientific Latin *rhin-*, *rhino-*, from Greek *rhin-*, *rhis*]

rhinal /ˈrienl/ *adj* of or relating to the nose; nasal.

rhine /rien/ *noun Brit, dialect* a wide drainage ditch or watercourse. [prob ultimately from Old English *ryne* flow, watercourse]

rhinestone *noun* a colourless artificial gemstone made of glass, paste, quartz, etc. [translation of French *caillou du Rhin* pebble of the *Rhine*, river in W Europe]

rhinitis /rieˈnietis/ *noun* in medicine, inflammation of the mucous membrane of the nose.

rhino /ˈrienoh/ *noun* (*pl* **rhinos** *or collectively* **rhino**) *informal* a rhinoceros.

rhino- *comb. form* see RHIN-.

rhinoceros /rieˈnos(ə)rəs/ *noun* (*pl* **rhinoceroses** *or collectively* **rhinoceros**) any of several species of large plant-eating hoofed mammals of Africa and Asia with very thick skin and either one or two horns on the snout: family Rhinocerotidae: *For an actress to be a success, she must have the face of a Venus, the brains of a Minerva, the grace of Terpsichore, the memory of a Macaulay, the figure of Juno, and the hide of a rhinoceros* — Ethel Barrymore. [Middle English *rinoceros* via Latin from Greek *rhinokerōt-*, *rhinokerōs*, from *rhin-* nose + *keras* horn]

rhinoplasty /ˈrienohplasti/ *noun* plastic surgery of the nose. ⟫ **rhinoplastic** /-ˈplastik/ *adj*.

rhiz- *or* **rhizo-** *comb. form* forming words, denoting: root: *rhizocarp*. [scientific Latin *rhiz-*, *rhizo-*, from Greek *rhiza* root]

-rhiza *or* **-rrhiza** *comb. form* (*pl* **-rhizae** *or* **-rhizas**) forming nouns, denoting: a root or a part resembling or connected with a root: *mycorrhiza*. [scientific Latin *-rhiza*, from Greek *rhiza* root]

rhizo- *comb. form* see RHIZ-.

rhizocarp /ˈriezohkahp/ *noun* a plant with perennial underground parts but annual stems and foliage. ⟫ **rhizocarpic** /-ˈkahpik/ *adj*, **rhizocarpous** /-pəs/ *adj*.

rhizoid /ˈriezoyd/ *noun* a rootlike structure in mosses, fungi, and ferns. ⟫ **rhizoidal** *adj*.

rhizome /ˈriezohm/ *noun* a long thick horizontal underground plant stem distinguished from a true root in having buds and usu scalelike leaves. ⟫ **rhizomatous** /rieˈzohmətəs/ *adj*. [via scientific

Latin from Greek *rhizōmat-*, *rhizoma* mass of roots, from *rhizoun* to cause to take root, from *rhiza* root]

rhizopod /'riezohpod/ *noun* any of various single-celled organisms, e.g. the amoeba, with lobed rootlike pseudopods (projections enabling movement, feeding, etc; see PSEUDOPOD).

rho /roh/ *noun* the 17th letter of the Greek alphabet (P, ρ), equivalent to and transliterated as roman rh. [Greek *rhō*, of Semitic origin; related to Hebrew *rēsh*, 20th letter of the Hebrew alphabet]

rhod- *or* **rhodo-** *comb. form* forming words, with the meaning: rose or rose-coloured: *rhodium*. [Latin *rhod-*, *rhodo*, from Greek *rhodon* rose]

rhodamine /'rohdəmeen, -min/ *noun* any of a group of bright yellowish red to bluish red fluorescent dyes.

Rhode Island Red /rohd/ *noun* a domestic fowl of a breed originating in the USA, having brownish red plumage. [named after *Rhode Island*, state of the USA, where the breed originated]

Rhodesian /roh'deesh(ə)n, roh'deezh(ə)n/ *noun* a native or inhabitant of Rhodesia (now Zimbabwe). ➤➤ **Rhodesian** *adj*.

Rhodes scholarship /rohdz/ *noun* any of numerous scholarships available at Oxford University to candidates from the Commonwealth and the USA. ➤➤ **Rhodes scholar** *noun*. [named after Cecil *Rhodes* d.1902, English statesman and financier in S Africa, who founded them]

rhodium /'rohdi-əm/ *noun* a white hard metallic chemical element of the platinum group that occurs naturally in platinum ores, and is used in alloys and to plate jewellery: symbol Rh, atomic number 45. [scientific Latin *rhodium*, from Greek *rhodon* rose, from the pink colour of its salts in solution]

rhodo- *comb. form* see RHOD-.

rhodochrosite /rohdoh'krohsiet, roh'dokrəsiet/ *noun* a rose-coloured mineral consisting essentially of the chemical compound manganese carbonate. [German *Rhodocrosit* from Greek *rhodochrōs* rose-coloured, from *rhodon* rose + *chrōs* colour]

rhododendron /rohdə'dendrən/ *noun* any of a genus of shrubs and trees of the heather family that have clusters of showy red, pink, purple, or white flowers and usu large leathery evergreen leaves: genus *Rhododendron*: *We had passed between the white posts of a gate and up a curving drive, lined with rhododendron bushes —* Conan Doyle. [from the Latin genus name, from Greek *rhododendron* rosebay, from *rhodon* rose + *dendron* tree]

rhodolite /'rohdəliet/ *noun* a pink or purple garnet used as a gem.

rhodonite /'rohdəniet/ *noun* a pale red mineral that consists essentially of the chemical compound manganese silicate and is used as an ornamental stone. [German *Rhodonit* from Greek *rhodon* rose]

rhodopsin /roh'dopsin/ *noun* = VISUAL PURPLE. [RHOD- + Greek *opsis* sight, vision + -IN[1]]

rhomb /rom/ *noun* **1** a rhombus. **2** a rhombohedron. [early French *rhombe* via Latin from Greek *rhombos* RHOMBUS]

rhomb- *or* **rhombo-** *comb. form* forming words, denoting: rhombus: *rhombohedron*. [early French *rhomb-* via Latin from Greek *rhombos* RHOMBUS]

rhombencephalon /romben'sefələn/ *noun* = HINDBRAIN (2).

rhombi /'rombie/ *noun* pl of RHOMBUS.

rhombic /'rombik/ *adj* shaped like a rhombus.

rhombo- *comb. form* see RHOMB-.

rhombohedron /romboh'heedrən/ *noun* (pl **rhombohedrons** or **rhombohedra** /-drə/) a six-sided solid whose faces are rhombuses. ➤➤ **rhombohedral** *adj*.

rhomboid[1] /'romboyd/ *noun* a parallelogram with adjacent sides of unequal length. [early French *rhomboïde* via Latin from Greek *rhomboeidēs* resembling a rhombus, from *rhombos* RHOMBUS]

rhomboid[2] *adj* shaped like a rhombus or rhomboid.

rhomboidal /'romboydl/ *adj* = RHOMBOID[2].

rhombus /'rombəs/ *noun* (pl **rhombuses** or **rhombi** /'rombie/) a parallelogram with equal sides but unequal angles; a diamond-shaped figure. [via Latin from Greek *rhombos*]

rhotic /'rohtik/ *adj* denoting a dialect in which /r/ sounds are pronounced both at the ends of words and before consonants. [RHO + -OTIC[1]]

RHS *abbr* **1** Royal Historical Society. **2** Royal Horticultural Society. **3** Royal Humane Society.

rhubarb /'roohbahb/ *noun* **1a** any of several species of plants of the dock family that have large fleshy leaves with edible stalks: genus *Rheum*. **b** the thick succulent greenish red leafstalks of this plant, usu cooked with sugar and eaten as a dessert. **2** *Brit* a noise made by actors, traditionally by repeating the word *rhubarb* in a low voice, to suggest the sound of background conversation. **3** *chiefly Brit, informal* nonsense or rubbish. **4** *chiefly NAmer, informal* a heated or noisy dispute. [Middle English *rubarbe* via French from medieval Latin *reubarbarum*, alteration of *rha barbarum*, literally 'foreign rhubarb']

rhumb /rum/ *noun* **1** any of the 32 points of the compass. **2** = RHUMB LINE. [Spanish *rumbo* rhumb, rhumb line]

rhumba /'rumbə/ *noun* see RUMBA.

rhumb line *noun* an imaginary line on the surface of the earth that crosses each MERIDIAN (imaginary circle passing through both poles) at the same oblique angle and is the course sailed by a ship following a single compass direction.

rhyme[1] /riem/ *noun* **1a** correspondence in the sound of words or their final syllables, *esp* those at the ends of consecutive or alternate lines of verse. **b** a word that corresponds with another in this way: '*Bought*' *is a rhyme for* '*taut*'. **2** rhyming verse, or a poem written in such verse. ✳ **rhyme or reason** good sense, reasonableness, or logic: *without rhyme or reason*. ➤➤ **rhymeless** *adj*. [alteration of Middle English *rime* from Old French, from Latin *rhythmus*: see RHYTHM]

rhyme[2] *verb intrans* **1a** said of a word or syllable: to constitute a rhyme: '*Date*' *rhymes with* '*eight*'. **b** said of a line of verse: to end with a rhyming word or syllable: *The second line rhymes with the fourth*. **c** said of verse: containing or made up of rhyming lines. **2** to compose rhymes. ➤➤ **verb trans 1** to use (a word) as a rhyme: *You can't rhyme* '*gas*' *with* '*farce*'. **2** to write or rewrite (something) in rhyming verse. ➤➤ **rhymer** *noun*.

rhyme scheme *noun* the pattern of rhymes in a stanza or poem.

rhymester /'riemstə/ *noun* a poet, *esp* one regarded as inferior; a poetaster: *Tennyson a poet! Why, he's only a rhymester! —* James Joyce.

rhyming slang *noun* slang in which a word is replaced by a rhyming phrase that is usu subsequently reduced to the first element, e.g. *head* becomes *loaf of bread* and then *loaf*.

Editorial note
First noted around 1800, rhyming slang has spread from its native London to Australia and the US. Not merely doggerel, the best such slang offers an internal joke as well as the simple rhyme, e.g. 'trouble and strife', for wife. Arguably no longer a dialect of London's East End, rhyming slang is for many the only slang, as much a tourist attraction as black cabs and red buses — Jonathon Green.

rhyolite /'rie-əliet/ *noun* a fine-grained acid volcanic rock similar to granite but formed from lava. ➤➤ **rhyolitic** /-'litik/ *adj*. [German *Rhyolith*, from Greek *rhyax* stream, stream of lava + *lithos* stone]

rhythm /'ridh(ə)m/ *noun* **1a** the pattern or recurrent alternation of strong and weak or long and short elements in the flow of sound, *esp* in speech. **b** the pattern of stresses on the words used in poetry; metre. **2a** in music, the regular recurrence of a pattern of stress and length of notes. **b** a characteristic pattern of this kind: *music in rumba rhythm*. **3** movement or fluctuation marked by a regular recurrence or pattern of elements. **4** a regularly recurrent change in a biological process or state. **5** the effect created by the harmonious interaction of elements in a play, novel, film, painting, etc. [early French *rhythme* via Latin *rhythmus* from Greek *rhythmos*, from *rhein* to flow]

rhythm and blues *noun* popular music with elements of blues and jazz, developed by black American musicians.

rhythmic /'ridhmik/ *adj* **1** of or involving rhythm. **2** moving or progressing with a pronounced or flowing rhythm. **3** regularly recurring. ➤➤ **rhythmically** *adv*, **rhythmicity** /ridh'misiti/ *noun*.

rhythmical /'ridhmikl/ *adj* = RHYTHMIC.

rhythm method *noun* a method of birth control that involves not having sexual intercourse on those days in the woman's menstrual cycle when conception is most likely to occur.

rhythm section *noun* the group of instruments in a band that supply the rhythm, *esp* the drums and the bass.

RI *abbr* **1** Regina et Imperatrix (Queen and Empress). **2** religious instruction. **3** Republic of Indonesia (international vehicle registration). **4** Rex et Imperator (King and Emperor). **5** Rhode Island (US postal abbreviation). **6** Royal Institution.

ria /riə/ *noun* a narrow inlet caused by the submergence of a river valley, or part of one. [Spanish *ría* from *río* river, from Latin *rivus* stream]

rial /ri'ahl/ *noun* **1** the basic monetary unit of Iran, Oman, and Yemen. **2** = RIYAL (1). [Persian *rial* via Arabic *riyāl* from Spanish *real* royal]

rib[1] /rib/ *noun* **1a** any of the paired curved rods of bone or cartilage that stiffen the body walls of most vertebrate animals and protect the heart, lungs, etc. **b** a cut of meat that includes a rib. **2** something resembling a rib in shape or function: e.g. **a** a transverse member of the frame of a ship that runs from keel to deck. **b** a structural member of the wing of an aircraft that runs from the leading edge to the trailing edge. **c** any of the rods supporting the fabric of an umbrella. **d** an arched support or ornamental band in vaulting. **3** an elongated ridge, e.g.: **a** a vein of a leaf or an insect's wing. **b** any of a series of narrow ridges in a knitted or woven fabric. **4** a ribbed part of a piece of knitting, or the pattern of stitches used to produce it. [Old English]

rib[2] *verb trans* (**ribbed, ribbing**) **1** to provide or enclose (something) with ribs: *ribbed vaulting.* **2** to form (something) into ribs or ridges; *specif* to form a pattern of vertical ridges in (a piece of knitting) by alternating knit stitches and purl stitches.

rib[3] *verb trans* (**ribbed, ribbing**) *informal* to tease (somebody). ⟫ **ribbing** *noun.* [prob from RIB[1], from the tickling of the ribs to cause laughter]

RIBA *abbr* Royal Institute of British Architects.

ribald /'rib(ə)ld, 'riebawld/ *adj* **1** said of stories, language, etc: crudely or obscenely humorous. **2** said of a person: inclined to indulge in coarse or indecent humour: *Over the mantel was the familiar picture … of a young lady having her shoes shined by a ribald small boy* — Christopher Morley. ⟫ **ribaldry** /'ribaldri, 'rie-/ *noun.* [Middle English, in the sense 'menial retainer, rascal', from Old French *ribaut, ribauld* wanton, rascal, from *riber* to be wanton, of Germanic origin]

riband /'ribənd/ *noun* a ribbon used *esp* as an award for achievement. [Middle English, alteration of *riban*: see RIBBON[1]]

ribbing *noun* **1** an arrangement of ribs. **2** a ribbed part of a piece of knitting.

ribbon[1] /'ribən/ *noun* **1a** a narrow band of fabric used for decorative effect, e.g. in fastening the hair, tying parcels, etc. **b** a piece of usu multicoloured ribbon worn as a military decoration or in place of a medal. **2a** a long narrow ribbonlike strip. **b** a strip of inked material used in a typewriter or computer printer. **3** (*in pl*) tatters or shreds: *Her coat was in ribbons.* ⟫ **ribbonlike** *adj.* [Middle English *riban* from early French *riban, ruban*, prob of Germanic origin]

ribbon[2] *verb* (**ribboned, ribboning**) ⟩ *verb trans* to adorn (something) with ribbons. ⟩ *verb intrans* to extend in a long narrow ribbonlike strip.

ribbon development *noun* the development of a row of buildings, *esp* housing, along a main road.

ribbonfish *noun* any of various fish with long thin bodies.

ribbon worm *noun* = NEMERTEAN.

ribcage *noun* the enclosing wall of the chest consisting chiefly of the ribs and their connective tissue.

ribgrass *noun chiefly NAmer* = RIBWORT.

riboflavin /rieboh'flayvin/ *noun* a yellow chemical compound of the vitamin B complex occurring *esp* in green vegetables, milk, eggs, and liver and often used to give a yellow or orange colour to processed food. Also called VITAMIN B$_2$, VITAMIN G. [RIBOSE + Latin *flavus* yellow]

ribonucleic acid /,riebohnyooh'kleeik, -'klayik/ *noun* = RNA. [RIBOSE + NUCLEIC ACID]

ribose /'riebohs, 'riebohz/ *noun* a sugar containing five carbon atoms in the molecule that occurs in riboflavin, RNA, etc. [contraction of *arabinose* a sugar obtained from gums]

ribosome /'riebəsohm/ *noun* any of the minute granules containing RNA and protein that occur in cells and are the sites where proteins are synthesized. ⟫ **ribosomal** /-'sohml/ *adj.* [RIBONUCLEIC ACID + -SOME[1]]

rib-tickler *noun* an amusing joke, story, etc. ⟫ **rib-tickling** *adj.*

ribwort *noun* a species of plantain with long narrow ribbed leaves: *Plantago lanceolata.*

rice[1] /ries/ *noun* **1** any of several species of cereal grasses that are widely cultivated in warm climates: genus *Oryza.* **2** the grains of this plant used as food. [Middle English *rys* via Old French *ris* and Old Italian *riso* from Greek *oryza, oryzon*]

rice[2] *verb trans* to press (soft food, e.g. cooked potato) through a ricer or similar utensil.

rice bowl *noun* **1** a bowl for eating rice or rice-based dishes, usu small enough to hold in one hand. **2** a region in which rice is produced.

rice paper *noun* **1** a very thin edible material resembling paper made from various plant sources, e.g. rice straw, used *esp* to prevent small cakes or biscuits from sticking to the tin in which they are baked. **2** a very thin paper made from the pith of a Chinese tree or shrub of the ivy family, used *esp* for painting.

ricer *noun* a kitchen utensil in which soft foods, e.g. cooked potato, are pressed through perforations to produce strings or particles about the size of rice grains.

ricercar /'reechəkah/ *or* **ricercare** /-'kahray/ *noun* (*pl* **ricercars** *or* **ricercari** /-ree/) any of various forms of instrumental music of the 16th and 17th cents, usu contrapuntal in style. [Italian *ricercare* to seek again, from *ri-* RE- + late Latin *circare*: see SEARCH[1]; from the disguising of the themes by various alterations]

rich /rich/ *adj* **1a** having abundant possessions, *esp* material and financial wealth. **b** said of a country or area: having abundant natural resources, successful industries, a strong economy, etc. **2a** having high worth, value, or quality: *a rich crop.* **b** (*often* + in) well supplied or endowed: *rich in natural talent.* **3** impressively lavish; sumptuous. **4a** vivid and deep in colour: *a rich red.* **b** full and mellow in tone or quality: *a rich voice.* **c** strong or pungent: *rich odours.* **5** highly productive or remunerative; high-yielding: *a rich mine.* **6a** said of soil: having abundant plant nutrients. **b** said of food: highly seasoned, fatty, oily, or sweet. **c** said of a fuel–air mixture, *esp* in an internal combustion engine: containing a higher proportion of fuel than normal. **7** *informal* highly amusing or irritating, *esp* because ironic or ridiculous: *That's rich, coming from him!* ⟫ **richness** *noun.* [Old English *rīce* and Old French *riche* powerful, wealthy, both from prehistoric Germanic words borrowed from Celtic]

riches *pl noun* great wealth. [Middle English, from *richesse* richness, from Old French *riche*: see RICH]

richly *adv* **1** in a rich manner: *richly decorated.* **2** in full measure; amply: *praise richly deserved.*

Richter scale /'riktə, 'rikhtə/ *noun* a logarithmic scale for expressing the magnitude of a seismic disturbance, e.g. an earthquake. [named after Charles *Richter* d.1985, US seismologist, who devised it]

ricin /'riesin, 'risin/ *noun* a poisonous protein in the bean of the castor-oil plant. [Latin *ricinus* castor-oil plant]

rick[1] /rik/ *noun* a stack of hay, corn, etc in the open air, *esp* one constructed in a regular shape, often with a thatched top. [Old English *hrēac*]

rick[2] *verb trans* to stack (e.g. hay) in ricks.

rick[3] *verb trans chiefly Brit* to wrench or sprain (e.g. one's neck). ⟫ **rick** *noun.* [perhaps from Middle English *wrikken* to move unsteadily, of Low German or Dutch origin]

rickets /'rikits/ *pl noun* (*treated as sing.*) a disease, *esp* of children, characterized by softening and deformation of bones resulting from a failure to assimilate calcium and vitamin D, usu due to a lack of sunlight or vitamin D. [perhaps an alteration of RACHITIS]

rickettsia /ri'ketsi-ə/ *noun* (*pl* **rickettsias** *or* **rickettsiae** /-si-ee/) any of a group of micro-organisms similar to bacteria that live as parasites in cells and cause various diseases, e.g. typhus: genus *Rickettsia.* ⟫ **rickettsial** *adj.* [from the Latin genus name, named after Howard T *Ricketts* d.1910, US pathologist, who first described these organisms and died of typhus caused by them]

rickety /'rikiti/ *adj* **1** likely to collapse, *esp* because badly made or old and worn; unsound: *rickety stairs.* **2** feeble in the joints: *a rickety old man.* **3** suffering from rickets. ⟫ **ricketiness** *noun.*

rickrack *or* **ricrac** /'rikrak/ *noun* a flat braid woven to form zigzags and used *esp* as trimming on clothing. [reduplication of RACK[2]]

rickshaw *or* **ricksha** /'rikshaw/ *noun* a small covered two-wheeled vehicle pulled by one or more people, used *esp* in SE Asia. [modification of Japanese *jinrikisha*, from *jin* man + *riki* strength + *sha* vehicle]

ricochet[1] /'rikəshay, -shet/ *noun* **1** the rebound of a projectile (e.g. a bullet) that strikes a hard or flat surface at an angle. **2** the sound of such a rebound. **3** something that rebounds in this way. [French *ricochet*, of unknown origin]

ricochet[2] *verb intrans* (**ricocheted** /-shayd/ *or* **ricochetted** /-shetid/, **ricocheting** /-shaying/ *or* **ricochetting** /-sheting/) said of e.g. a bullet: to rebound off one or more hard or flat surfaces.

ricotta /ri'kotə/ *noun* a soft white unsalted Italian cheese made from sheep's milk. [Italian *ricotta*, fem past part. of *ricuocere* to cook again, from Latin *recoquere*, from RE- + *coquere* to cook]

ricrac /'rikrak/ *noun* see RICKRACK.

RICS *abbr* Royal Institution of Chartered Surveyors.

rictus /'riktəs/ *noun* **1** an unnatural gaping grin or grimace. **2** the size of the opening of a bird's beak or a fish's mouth. ⪢ **rictal** *adj*. [Latin *rictus* open mouth, past part. of *ringi* to open the mouth]

rid /rid/ *verb trans* (**ridding**, *past tense and past part.* **rid** *or* **ridded**) (+ of) to relieve (somebody or something) of something unwanted: *He wanted to rid himself of his troubles*. ✽ **get rid of** to free oneself of (something unwanted). [Middle English *ridden* to clear, from Old Norse *rythja*]

riddance /'rid(ə)ns/ *noun* deliverance from something or somebody unwanted. ✽ **good riddance** an expression of relief at becoming free of something or somebody unwanted. [RID + -ANCE]

ridden /'rid(ə)n/ *verb* past part. of RIDE[1].

-ridden *comb. form* forming adjectives, with the meanings: **1** afflicted or excessively concerned with: *conscience-ridden*. **2** excessively full of or supplied with: *slum-ridden*.

riddle[1] /'ridl/ *noun* **1** a short and *esp* humorous verbal puzzle. **2** a mystifying phenomenon: *the riddle of her disappearance*. **3** something or somebody difficult to understand. [Old English *rædelse* opinion, conjecture, riddle]

riddle[2] *verb intrans* to speak in riddles. ⪢ *verb trans* to explain or solve (a riddle). ⪢ **riddler** *noun*.

riddle[3] *noun* a large coarse sieve, e.g. for sifting grain or gravel. [Old English *hriddel*]

riddle[4] *verb trans* **1** to separate (e.g. grain from chaff) with a riddle; to sift (it). **2** to pierce (something) with many holes: *riddled with bullets*. **3** to spread through (something), *esp* as an affliction: *The state … was riddled with poverty* — Thomas Wood.

ride[1] /ried/ *verb* (*past tense* **rode** /rohd/, *past part.* **ridden** /'rid(ə)n/) ⪢ *verb intrans* **1a** to sit and travel mounted on and usu controlling an animal. **b** to travel on or in a vehicle. **2** to be sustained: *They rode on a wave of popularity*. **3** (+ on) to be contingent or depend on something: *Everything rides on her initial success*. **4a** said of a ship: to be moored or anchored. **b** to appear to float: *The moon rode in the sky*. **5** to continue without interference or change: *Let things ride for a while*. **6a** to move from a correct or usual position: *The screwdriver tends to ride out of the slot*. **b** (+ up) said of clothing: to work up the body as one moves. **7** to be bet: *A lot of money is riding on the favourite*. ⪢ *verb trans* **1a** to sit and travel mounted on and in control of (e.g. a horse or a bicycle). **b** to ride a horse, motorcycle, etc in (a race). **c** to travel across or patrol (an area) by car, horse, etc. **d** to move with or float on (e.g. waves). **2** (*often* + out) to survive (a danger or difficulty) without great damage or loss. **3** to yield to (a punch) so as to soften the impact. **4a** said of a male animal: to mount (a female) in copulation. **b** *coarse slang* to have sexual intercourse with (a woman). **5a** (*usu in passive*) to obsess or oppress (somebody): *They were ridden by anxiety*. **b** *NAmer* to harass (somebody) persistently. ✽ **be riding for a fall** to act in such a way that failure or disaster seems inevitable. **ride high** to experience success. ⪢ **ridable** *adj*, **rideable** *adj*. [Old English *rīdan*]

ride[2] *noun* **1** an act of travelling on horseback or by vehicle as an outing or a journey. **2** any of various mechanical devices, e.g. at a funfair, for riding on. **3** a usu straight road or path in a wood, forest, etc used for riding, for access, or as a firebreak. **4** *coarse slang*. **a** a sexual partner, *esp* a woman. **b** an act of sexual intercourse. ✽ **take for a ride 1** *informal* to deceive or trick (somebody). **2** *chiefly NAmer, informal* to take (somebody) away in a car in order to kill them.

rider *noun* **1** somebody who rides; *specif* somebody who rides a horse, a bicycle, or a motorcycle. **2** something added by way of qualification or amendment, e.g.: **a** a clause appended to a legal document, *esp* a legislative bill at its third reading in the British Parliament. **b** a statement, e.g. a recommendation for mercy,

appended to a jury's verdict. **3** a part of something that overlies, moves along, or reinforces another. ⪢ **riderless** *adj*.

ridge[1] /rij/ *noun* **1a** a range of hills or mountains. **b** a long narrow stretch of elevated land. **2** the line along which two upward-sloping surfaces meet; *specif* the top of a roof at the intersection of two sloping sides. **3** an elongated part that is raised above a surrounding surface, e.g. the raised part between furrows on ploughed ground. **4** in meteorology, an elongated area of high barometric pressure: compare TROUGH. ⪢ **ridgy** *adj*. [Old English *hrycg*]

ridge[2] *verb trans* to form (something) into a ridge or ridges. ⪢ *verb intrans* to form a ridge or ridges.

ridgepiece *noun* a horizontal beam in a roof that supports the upper ends of the rafters.

ridgepole *noun* **1** the horizontal pole at the top of a tent. **2** = RIDGEPIECE.

ridgeway *noun* *Brit* a path or road along the ridge of a hill.

ridicule[1] /'ridikyoohl/ *noun* scornful or contemptuous words or actions; derision. [French *ridicule* from Latin *ridiculum* jest, neuter of *ridiculus*: see RIDICULOUS]

ridicule[2] *verb trans* to treat (somebody or something) with ridicule; to mock (them).

ridiculous /ri'dikyooləs/ *adj* arousing or deserving ridicule; absurd or preposterous. ⪢ **ridiculously** *adv*, **ridiculousness** *noun*. [Latin *ridiculosus* from *ridiculus* laughable, from *ridēre* to laugh]

riding[1] *noun* **1** the riding of horses as a sport or pastime. **2** a path used for horse riding; a bridle path.

riding[2] *noun* **1** (*often* **Riding**) any of three former administrative jurisdictions of Yorkshire. **2** an administrative or electoral district of a Commonwealth dominion, e.g. Canada. [Old English *thrithing*, from Old Norse *thrithjungr* third part, from *thrithi* third]

riding crop *noun* a short whip that a rider uses to urge a horse on.

riding light *noun* a light indicating that a boat or ship is at anchor.

riel /'ree-əl/ *noun* the basic monetary unit of Cambodia, divided into 100 sen. [Khmer *riel*]

riem /reem/ *noun* *SAfr* a soft pliable strip of leather. [Afrikaans *riem* strap, belt, from early Dutch *rieme*]

riempie /'reempi/ *noun* *SAfr* a narrow leather thong used *esp* in furniture construction. [Afrikaans *riempje*, dimin. of *riem*: see RIEM]

Riesling /'reezling/ *noun* **1** a variety of grape grown *esp* in Germany and used in the production of white wine. **2** a usu medium-dry white wine produced from this grape. [German *Riesling*]

rife /rief/ *adj* **1** occurring everywhere or to a great degree; prevalent: *Fear was rife in the city*. **2** (+ with) abundantly supplied with or full of something: *The city was rife with rumours*. [Old English *rȳfe*, perhaps from Old Norse *rīfr* abundant]

riff[1] /rif/ *noun* a constantly repeated phrase in jazz or rock music, typically played as a background to a solo improvisation. [prob by shortening and alteration from REFRAIN[2]]

riff[2] *verb intrans* to play riffs.

riffle[1] /'rifl/ *verb* (**riffling**) ⪢ *verb intrans* (*often* + through) to leaf or thumb rapidly or cursorily: *riffle through files*. ⪢ *verb trans* **1** to ruffle (something) slightly: *The wind riffled the water*. **2a** to leaf through (something) rapidly; *specif* to leaf through (e.g. a pile of papers) by running a thumb over the edges of the leaves. **b** to shuffle (playing cards) by separating the deck into two parts and running the thumbs over the edges of the cards to interleave them. [perhaps alteration of RUFFLE[1]]

riffle[2] *noun* **1a** the act or an instance of riffling. **b** the sound of shuffling or leafing through something. **2a** *NAmer* a shallow stretch of rough water in a stream. **b** *NAmer* a ripple on water.

riffle[3] *noun* **1** a series of blocks, rails, etc laid on the bottom of a sluice to form grooves to catch and retain a mineral, e.g. gold. **2** a groove formed in this way. [prob from RIFFLE[2]]

riffraff /'rifraf/ *noun* disreputable or worthless people; rabble: *Don't you deceive yourself by supposing for a moment that I am a man of family. I am a bit of dirty riffraff* — Dickens. [Middle English *riffe raffe*, from *rif and raf* every single one, from early French *rif et raf* completely, from *rifler* to plunder + *raffe* act of snatching]

rifle[1] /'riefl/ *noun* **1** a firearm, usu held at shoulder level, with a long barrel that has spiral grooves cut inside it to spin the bullet and produce a straight trajectory. **2** (*in pl*) a body of soldiers armed with rifles.

rifle² *verb trans* **1** to cut spiral grooves inside the barrel of (a rifle, cannon, etc). **2** to propel (e.g. a ball) with great force or speed. [early French *rifler*: see RIFLE³]

rifle³ *verb trans* **1** to search through (something, e.g. a drawer or safe), *esp* in order to find and steal something. **2** to steal (something). ➤➤ **rifler** *noun*. [Middle English *riflen* from early French *rifler* to scratch, file, plunder, of Germanic origin]

rifleman *noun* (*pl* **riflemen**) **1** a soldier armed with a rifle. **2** a small New Zealand songbird with greenish yellow plumage: *Acanthisitta chloris*.

rifle range *noun* a place for shooting practice with rifles.

rifling *noun* **1** the act or process of making spiral grooves, *esp* inside the barrel of a gun. **2** a system of spiral grooves inside the barrel of a gun.

rift¹ /rift/ *noun* **1** a fissure or crack, *esp* in the earth. **2** an opening made by splitting or tearing something apart. **3** a disruption of friendly relations between individuals, nations, etc. [Middle English, of Scandinavian origin]

rift² *verb trans* to tear (something) apart; to split (it).

rift valley *noun* a valley formed by the subsidence of the earth's crust between two or more parallel faults.

rig¹ /rig/ *verb trans* (**rigged, rigging**) **1a** to fit out (e.g. a ship) with rigging, sails, etc. **b** to prepare (rigging, sails, etc) for use: *rig the spinnaker*. **2** (*usu* + out) to clothe or dress (somebody). **3** (*often* + out) to supply (somebody or something) with equipment for a particular use. **4** (*often* + up) to make, assemble, or erect (something), *esp* for temporary use. [Middle English *riggen*, prob of Scandinavian origin]

rig² *noun* **1** the distinctive shape, number, and arrangement of sails and masts of a boat or ship. **2** an outfit of clothing worn for a particular occasion or activity: *in ceremonial rig*. **3** an installation, equipment, or machinery fitted for a usu specified purpose: *an oil rig; a CB radio rig*. **4** *chiefly NAmer* a truck.

rig³ *verb trans* (**rigged, rigging**) to manipulate, influence, or control (something) for dishonest purposes: *The election has been rigged*. [orig as a noun meaning 'ridicule, trick, swindle', of unknown origin]

rigadoon /rigə'doohn/ *noun* a lively dance in duple or quadruple time that was popular in the 17th and 18th cents, or a piece of music for this dance. [French *rigaudon*, said to be named after a dancing master called *Rigaud* who invented it]

rigatoni /rigə'tohni/ *pl noun* (*treated as sing. or pl*) pasta in the form of short, ridged, and sometimes curved tubes. [Italian *rigatoni*, from *rigato*, past part. of *rigare* to furrow, flute, from *riga* line, of Germanic origin]

rigger *noun* **1** (*used in combinations*) a ship of a specified rig: *a square-rigger*. **2a** somebody who rigs boats, ships, etc. **b** somebody who works on an oil rig. **c** somebody skilled in operating cranes, erecting scaffolding, etc. **3** a projecting support for a rowlock, *esp* on a racing boat.

rigging *noun* **1a** the ropes and chains used aboard a boat or ship, *esp* for controlling sails and supporting masts. **b** the ropes, wires, and struts used to support the structure of a biplane, hang-glider, etc. **2** any similar system used for support and manipulation, e.g. of theatrical scenery.

right¹ /riet/ *adj* **1** in accordance with what is morally good, just, or proper. **2** conforming to facts or truth: *the right answer*. **3** suitable or appropriate: *the right woman for the job*. **4** acting or judging in accordance with truth or fact; not mistaken. **5** in a correct, proper, or healthy state: *not in his right mind*. **6** conforming to what is socially favoured or acceptable. **7** being the side of fabric that is intended to be seen, e.g. on a finished garment. **8a** of, on, or being the side of somebody or something that is nearer the east when the front faces north. **b** of, on, or being the side of something that is closer to the right hand of an observer positioned directly in front: *the bottom right corner of the screen*. **c** located on the right side when facing downstream: *the right bank of a river*. **9** (*often* **Right**) of the right or right wing in politics. **10** in geometry, having its axis perpendicular to the base: *a right cone*. **11** *chiefly Brit, informal* real or utter: *a right mess*. ✳ **as right as rain** fine and healthy. **on the right side of 1** in favour with: *trying to get on the right side of the boss*. **2** less than the specified age: *I'm still on the right side of fifty*. ➤➤ **rightness** *noun*. [Old English *riht*; (sense 9) see word history at LEFT¹]

right² *noun* **1** qualities that together constitute the ideal of moral conduct or merit moral approval. **2a** a power, privilege, interest, etc to which one has a just claim. **b** (*also in pl*) a legal claim to land, property, etc or its contents: *mineral rights*. **3** something one may legitimately claim as due. **4** the cause of truth or justice: *We trust that right may prevail*. **5** the quality or state of being factually or morally correct: *You are in the right*. **6a** the part on the right side. **b** the location or direction of the right side. **c** the right hand, or a blow struck with it. **7** (*often* **the Right**) (*treated as sing. or pl*). **a** those professing conservative or reactionary political views. **b** = RIGHT WING (1A), (1B). ✳ **by rights** with reason or justice; properly. **in one's own right** by virtue of one's own qualifications or attributes, rather than by association with somebody or something else. **2** correct in what one says or does. **to rights** into proper order.

right³ *adv* **1** in a proper or correct manner: *You guessed right; I knew he wasn't doing it right*. **2** in the exact location or position: *right in the middle of the floor*. **3** in a direct line or course; straight: *Go right home*. **4** all the way; completely: *It blew right out of the window*. **5** without delay; immediately: *right after lunch; right now*. **6** to the full: *We were right royally entertained*. **7** on or towards the right: *She looked left and right*.

right⁴ *verb trans* **1** to adjust or restore (something) to the proper state or condition; to correct (it). **2** to bring or restore (e.g. a boat) to an upright position. **3** to compensate for or avenge (a wrong, an injustice, etc). ➤➤ **rightable** *adj*, **righter** *noun*.

right⁵ *interj informal* an expression of agreement or compliance.

right angle *noun* an angle of 90°; any of the four angles formed at the centre of a circle divided into four equal parts. ✳ **at right angles** forming a right angle. ➤➤ **right-angled** *adj*.

right ascension *noun* in astronomy, the distance measured eastward along the CELESTIAL EQUATOR (circle around the imaginary sphere representing the universe) between the point where the sun crosses it in spring and the point where it is cut by a line drawn from the CELESTIAL POLE (point around which stars appear to rotate) through a given celestial object.

right away *adv* without delay or hesitation.

right-back *noun* in football, hockey, etc, a defensive player on the right wing.

righteous /'riechəs/ *adj* **1** acting in accord with divine or moral law; free from guilt or sin. **2a** morally right or justified. **b** arising from an outraged sense of justice: *righteous indignation*. ➤➤ **righteously** *adv*, **righteousness** *noun*. [alteration of Middle English *rightwise, rightwos* from Old English *rihtwīs*, from *riht* RIGHT¹ + *wise* WISE¹]

rightful /'rietf(ə)l/ *adj* **1** in accordance with notions of fairness; equitable. **2a** having a just claim; legitimate: *the rightful owner*. **b** held by right; legal: *rightful authority*. **3** fitting or proper: *her rightful place*. ➤➤ **rightfully** *adv*, **rightfulness** *noun*.

right hand *noun* **1** the hand on the right side of the body. **2** a reliable or indispensable person. **3** a place of honour.

right-hand *adj* **1** situated on the right: *the right-hand side*. **2** of, designed for, or done with the right hand. **3** chiefly or constantly relied on: *my right-hand man*.

right-handed¹ *adj* **1** using the right hand habitually or more easily than the left: *a right-handed batsman*. **2** of, designed for, or done with the right hand. **3** said of a rotary motion or spiral curve: clockwise. ➤➤ **right-handedly** *adv*, **right-handedness** *noun*.

right-handed² *adv* using the right hand.

right-hander *noun* **1** a right-handed person. **2** a blow struck with the right hand.

Right Honourable *adj* used as a title for certain dignitaries, e.g. privy councillors and senior government ministers.

rightism *noun* (*often* **Rightism**) right-wing principles and policy, or advocacy of these. ➤➤ **rightist** *noun and adj*.

rightly *adv* **1** in accordance with right conduct; fairly or legitimately. **2** in the right manner; properly. **3** according to truth or fact; correctly. **4** *informal* with certainty: *I can't rightly say*.

right-minded *adj* thinking and acting by just or honest principles.

righto /rie'toh/ *interj chiefly Brit, dated* an expression of agreement or compliance.

right off *adv informal* without delay or hesitation.

right of search *noun* in time of war, the right to stop and search a merchant vessel on the high seas to ascertain whether it is carrying goods that are liable to seizure.

right of way *noun* (*pl* **rights of way**) **1a** a legal right of passage over another person's property. **b** the course along which a right of way exists. **2** a precedence accorded to one vehicle, vessel, etc over another by custom or law. **3** *chiefly NAmer* the strip of land over which a public road, railway, power line, etc is built or installed.

right on *interj informal* an expression of agreement or approval.

right-on *adj informal* conforming to current trends in social or political thinking.

Right Reverend *adj* used as a title for high ecclesiastical officials.

rights issue *noun* an issue of new shares available to existing shareholders only.

rightsize *verb trans* to change the size of (a business company) in order to maximize efficiency, usu by cutting the workforce.

right-thinking *adj* = RIGHT-MINDED.

right-to-life *adj* = PRO-LIFE.

right triangle *noun NAmer* a right-angled triangle.

rightward /'rietwəd/ *adj* towards or on the right.

rightwards (*NAmer* **rightward**) *adv* towards the right.

right whale *noun* any of several species of large whalebone whales with no dorsal fin, very long whalebone plates instead of teeth, and a large head: family Balaenidae. [because some species were formerly considered the right whales to hunt because of their value and slow speed]

right wing *noun* **1** (*often* **Right Wing**). **a** the more conservative division of a group or party. **b** the members of a European legislative body holding more reactionary political views and occupying the right side of a legislative chamber: compare LEFT WING, WING[1]. **2** in sport, the right side of the field when facing towards the opposing team, or the players positioned on this side. ⮞ **right-winger** *noun*.

right-wing *adj* **1** belonging to or characteristic of the right wing in politics. **2** professing conservative or reactionary political views.

rigid /'rijid/ *adj* **1a** unable to bend or be bent; stiff. **b** fixed in appearance: *Her face was rigid with pain.* **c** having the outer shape maintained by a fixed framework. **2** inflexibly set in opinions or habits. **3** strictly maintained; unable to be changed: *a rigid schedule.* **4** precise and accurate in procedure. ⮞ **rigidity** /ri'jiditi/ *noun*, **rigidly** *adv*, **rigidness** *noun*. [Middle English via French from Latin *rigidus*, from *rigēre* to be stiff]

rigidify /ri'jidifie/ *verb* (**rigidifies, rigidified, rigidifying**) ⮞ *verb trans* to make (something) rigid. ⮞ *verb intrans* to become rigid.

rigmarole /'rigmərohl/ *noun* **1** an absurdly long and complex procedure. **2** a confused or nonsensical account or explanation: *I was wondering, Watson, what on earth could be the object of this man in telling us such a rigmarole of lies* — Conan Doyle. [alteration of obsolete *ragman roll* long list, catalogue]

rigor /'rigə/ *noun* **1** a sense of chilliness accompanied by muscle contraction and convulsive shuddering or tremor, e.g. preceding a fever. **2a** rigidity of a muscle or other tissue. **b** = RIGOR MORTIS. **3** *NAmer* see RIGOUR. [Latin *rigor*: see RIGOUR]

rigor mortis /'mawtis/ *noun* the temporary rigidity of muscles that occurs after death. [Latin *rigor mortis* stiffness of death]

rigorous /'rigərəs/ *adj* **1** manifesting, exercising, or favouring rigour; very strict: *rigorous standards of hygiene.* **2** harsh or severe: *a rigorous climate.* **3** scrupulously accurate; precise. ⮞ **rigorously** *adv*.

rigour (*NAmer* **rigor**) /'rigə/ *noun* **1** harsh inflexibility in opinion, temper, or judgment. **2** the quality of being unyielding or inflexible; strictness. **3** severity of life; austerity. **4** (*also in pl*) a condition that makes life difficult or unpleasant. **5** strict mathematical or logical precision. [Middle English via early French *rigueur* from Latin *rigor* stiffness, from *rigēre* to be stiff]

rigout /'rigowt/ *noun informal* a complete outfit of clothing.

rile /riel/ *verb trans* **1** to make (somebody) angry or resentful. **2** *NAmer* = ROIL (1). [alteration of ROIL]

rill[1] /ril/ *noun* **1** a small brook: *For we were nursed upon the self-same hill, fed the same flock, by fountain, shade, and rill* — Milton. **2** a small channel formed in soil or rock. [Dutch *ril* or Low German *rille*]

rill[2] *or* **rille** *noun* a long narrow valley on the moon's surface. [German *Rille* channel made by a small stream, from Low German *rille* RILL[1]]

RIM *abbr* Mauritania (international vehicle registration). [French *République Islamique de Mauritanie* Islamic Republic of Mauritania]

rim[1] /rim/ *noun* **1** an outer edge or border, *esp* of something circular or curved. **2** the outer ring of a wheel not including the tyre. **3** an outer edge or boundary. ⮞ **rimless** *adj*. [Old English *rima*]

rim[2] *verb trans* (**rimmed, rimming**) **1** to serve as a rim for (something); to border (it). **2** *coarse slang* to lick, suck, or kiss the anus of (somebody) to stimulate them sexually.

rime[1] /riem/ *noun* **1** frost. **2** an accumulation of granular ice tufts on the windward sides of exposed objects at low temperatures. [Old English *hrīm*]

rime[2] *verb trans* to cover (something) with or as if with rime.

rime[3] *noun archaic* = RHYME[1].

rime[4] *verb archaic* = RHYME[2].

rimfire *adj* **1** said of a cartridge: having the primer in the rim of the base rather than in the centre. **2** said of a gun: designed for firing rimfire cartridges.

rimmed *adj* (*usu used in combinations*) having a rim: *gold-rimmed spectacles.*

rimu /'reemooh/ *noun* **1** a large coniferous tree of New Zealand: *Dacrydium cupressinum.* **2** the soft wood of this tree. [Maori *rimu*]

rimy /'riemi/ *adj* (**rimier, rimiest**) covered in frost.

rind[1] /riend/ *noun* **1** a hard or tough outer layer of fruit, cheese, bacon, etc. **2** the bark of a tree. [Old English]

rind[2] *verb trans* to remove the rind from (a fruit, etc) or the bark from (a tree).

rinderpest /'rindəpest/ *noun* an infectious fever, *esp* of cattle. [German *Rinderpest*, from *Rinder* (pl) cattle + *Pest* pestilence]

ring[1] /ring/ *noun* **1a** a circular band usu of precious metal, worn on the finger for adornment, etc. **b** a circular band for holding, connecting, hanging, moving or fastening, or for identification. **2a** a circular line, figure, arrangement, or object: *Everybody join hands and form a ring.* **b** an encircling arrangement. **c** a circular or spiral course. **3** an electric element or gas burner in the shape of a circle, set into the top of a cooker, etc, which provides a source of heat for cooking: compare GAS RING. **4a** a space, often a circular one, for exhibitions or competitions, *esp* such a space at a circus. **b** a square enclosure in which boxing or wrestling matches are held. **c** (**the ring**) boxing as a profession: *He retired after nine years in the ring.* **d** an enclosed area for betting at a racecourse. **5** any of the concentric bands of e.g. ice and rock that revolve round some planets, e.g. Saturn or Uranus. **6a** = ANNUAL RING. **b** a ridge or marking on a fish scale that represents one year's growth. **7** (*treated as sing. or pl*) an exclusive association of people, often for a corrupt purpose: *a drug ring.* **8** a closed chain of atoms in a molecule. Also called CLOSED CHAIN. **9** in mathematics, a set of elements that is closed under two binary operations, e.g. addition and multiplication, in a group with respect to the first operation and in which the second operation is associative and distributive relative to the first: *The ring of all integers.* ✳ **run rings round somebody** *informal* to surpass or outdo somebody, *esp* in a way that makes them appear foolish. [Old English *hring*]

ring[2] *verb trans* (*past tense and past part.* **ringed**) **1** to place or form a ring round (somebody or something); to encircle (them). **2** to attach a ring to (a bird or animal). **3** to cut a GIRDLE[1] (ring formed by cutting away bark) round (a tree), usu in order to kill it; GIRDLE[2]. ⮞ **ringed** *adj*.

ring[3] *verb* (*past tense* **rang** /rang/, *past part.* **rung** /rung/) ⮞ *verb intrans* **1a** to make the sound of a bell or something similar: *The doorbell rang.* **b** (+ for) to sound a bell as a summons: *She rang for the butler.* **2a** to sound resonantly: *Cheers rang through the building.* **b** (*often* + with) to be filled with resonant sound; to resound: *The room rang with laughter.* **3** said of one's ears: to have the sensation of a continuous humming sound. **4a** to be filled with talk or report. **b** to sound repeatedly: *Praise rang in her ears.* **5** *chiefly Brit* (*often* + up) to telephone: *I rang up and ordered a taxi.* ⮞ *verb trans* **1** to cause (something, *esp* a bell) to ring. **2** to sound (something) by, or as if by, ringing a bell. **3** (*often* + in/out) to announce (something) by, or as if by, ringing. **4** *chiefly Brit* (*often* + up) to telephone (somebody). **5** *slang* to alter the numberplate, serial number, etc of (a stolen motor vehicle). ✳ **ring a bell** to sound familiar. **ring the changes** to vary the manner of doing or arranging something [orig referring to changes in bell-ringing: see CHANGE² (4)]. **ring true** to appear to be true or authentic. **ring up/down the curtain 1** to raise the curtain at the start, or lower it at the end, of a theatrical show. **2** (*often* + *on*) to start, or finish, something. [Old English *hringan*]

ring⁴ *noun* **1a** the act or an instance of ringing. **b** *Brit, informal* a telephone call: *Give me a ring if you want to go out.* **2** a clear resonant sound made by vibrating metal, or a similar sound. **3** resonant tone. **4** a set of bells. **5** a loud sound continued, repeated, or reverberated. **6** a sound or character suggestive of a particular quality or feeling: *This story has a familiar ring to it.*

ringhark *verb trans* to cut a GIRDLE¹ (ring formed by cutting away bark) round (a tree), usu in order to kill it; = GIRDLE⁹ (2).

ring binder *noun* a loose-leaf binder in which split metal rings attached to a metal back hold perforated sheets of paper in place.

ringbolt *noun* an eyebolt with a ring through its loop.

ringbone *noun* a bony outgrowth on a horse's pastern bones, usu causing lameness.

ringdove *noun* **1** *Brit* a woodpigeon. **2** *NAmer* an African dove with a black band round its neck, related to the collared dove: *Streptelia decaocto roseogrisea.* [(sense 1) from the white patch on each side of its neck]

ringed *adj* encircled or marked with or as if with rings.

ringer *noun* **1** *informal* somebody or something that strongly resembles another: *She's a dead ringer for her sister.* **2** *informal* a horse entered in a race under false representations. **3** *slang* a stolen motor vehicle with a false numberplate, serial number, etc. **4** somebody who rings bells, e.g. at a church. **5** *Aus, NZ.* **a** the shearer who has shorn the most sheep in a shed. **b** somebody who owns or works with livestock.

ring fence *noun* **1** a fence that surrounds an area completely. **2** a prohibition against using money intended for a specific purpose for any other purpose.

ring-fence *verb trans* **1** to surround (an area) with a ring fence. **2** to prohibit (money intended for a specific purpose) from being used for any other purpose.

ring finger *noun* the third finger, *esp* of the left hand, counting the index finger as the first, on which the wedding ring is usu worn.

ringgit /'ringgit/ *noun* (*pl* **ringgit** *or* **ringgits**) the basic monetary unit of Malaysia and Brunei, divided into 100 sen. [Malay *ringgit*]

ringhals /'ring·hals/ *noun* SEE RINKHALS.

ring in *verb intrans* to call in, e.g. to an office, by telephone. ➤ *verb trans* to mark or accompany the start of something, *esp* a new year, by or as if by ringing bells.

ringing *adj* **1** resounding: *Far on the ringing plains of windy Troy* — Tennyson. **2** vigorously unequivocal: *a ringing condemnation.* ➤➤ **ringingly** *adv.*

ringleader *noun* a leader of a group that engages in illegal or objectionable activities.

ringlet /'ringlit/ *noun* **1** a long lock of hair curled in a spiral. **2** any of several species of dark brown butterflies with eyespots on the wings: genus *Aphantopus* and other genera.

ring main *noun Brit* a domestic wiring circuit in which a number of power points are connected to supply cables which form a closed loop.

ringmaster *noun* the person in charge of performances in a circus ring.

ringneck *noun* a bird or animal with a ring of colour round its neck, e.g. the ring-necked pheasant.

ring-necked *adj* said of a bird, snake, etc: having a ring of colour about the neck.

ring-necked pheasant *noun* a pheasant with a white neck ring, a variety of the common pheasant that was introduced in temperate regions as a game bird: *Phasianus colchicus.*

ring off *verb intrans Brit* to terminate a telephone conversation.

ring out *verb intrans* to sound resonantly. ➤ *verb trans* to mark or accompany the end of something, *esp* the end of a year, by or as if by ringing bells.

ring ouzel *noun* an Old World thrush, the male of which is black with a broad white bar across the breast: *Turdus torquatus.*

ring-pull *noun* a built-in device for opening a tin consisting of a ring that, when pulled, removes a hermetically sealed tab or lid.

ring road *noun* a road round a town or town centre designed to relieve traffic congestion.

ringside *noun* **1** the area surrounding a ring, *esp* providing a close view of a contest. **2** a place that gives a close view. **3** (*used before a noun*). **a** at the ringside: *a ringside seat at a circus.* **b** giving a close view: *I want to have a ringside view of the proceedings.*

ringtail *noun* an animal having a tail marked with rings of differing colours.

ring-tail *adj* having a tail marked with rings of differing colours.

ring-tailed *adj* = RING-TAIL.

ringtone *noun* a tune or song that is played by a mobile phone handset when it receives a call.

ring up *verb trans* **1** to record (a sale) by means of a cash register. **2** to record or achieve (something). [from the bell that rings when a sum is recorded by a cash register]

ringworm *noun* a contagious fungous disease of the skin, hair, or nails in which ring-shaped discoloured patches form on the skin.

rink /ringk/ *noun* **1a** a surface of ice for ice-skating, ice hockey, or curling, or a building containing such an ice surface. **b** an enclosure for roller-skating. **2a** part of a bowling green being used for a match. **b** part of an ice rink being used for a match in curling. **3** (*treated as sing. or pl*) a team in bowls, curling, or quoits. [Middle English (Scots) *rinc* area in which a contest takes place, from early French *renc*: see RANK¹]

rinkhals /'ringk·hals/ *or* **ringhals** /'ring·hals/ *noun* (*pl* **rinkhalses** *or* **ringhalses** *or collectively* **rinkhals** *or* **ringhals**) a venomous spitting cobra of southern Africa, with one or two white rings around its throat: *Hemachatus haemachatus.* [Afrikaans *rinkhals* (formerly *ringhals*), from *ring* ring + *hals* neck]

rink rat *noun NAmer, informal* a young person who frequents an ice-hockey rink.

rinse¹ /rins/ *verb trans* **1** (*often* + *out*) to remove soap from (washed clothing) with clean water. **2** (*often* + *out*) to remove (dirt, impurities, or unwanted matter) by washing lightly. ➤➤ **rinser** *noun.* [Middle English *rincen* from Old French *rincer*, from Latin *recent-, recens* fresh, recent]

rinse² *noun* **1** the act or an instance of rinsing. **2a** liquid used for rinsing. **b** a solution that temporarily tints the hair.

Rioja /ri'oh·hə/ *noun* a dry red or white wine produced in La Rioja, N Spain.

riot¹ /'rie·ət/ *noun* **1** violent public disorder; *specif* a disturbance of the peace by three or more people. **2** a profuse and random display: *The woods were a riot of colour.* **3** *informal* somebody or something wildly funny. **4** *archaic* unrestrained revelry or boisterous behaviour. **5** *archaic* lascivious behaviour. ✳ **read the riot act** to give somebody a severe warning or reprimand. **run riot 1** to act or function wildly or without restraint: *You're letting your imagination run riot.* **2** to grow or occur in profusion. [Middle English from Old French *riot* dispute, from *rioter* to argue]

riot² *verb intrans* (**rioted, rioting**) **1** to participate in a riot. **2** to behave in an unrestrained way. **3** *archaic* to behave lasciviously. ➤➤ **rioter** *noun.*

riotous /'rie·ətəs/ *adj* **1** wild and disorderly; wanton: *riotous behaviour; riotous living.* **2** exciting; exuberant: *a riotous party.* **3** profuse; bright: *a riotous display of tulips.* ➤➤ **riotously** *adv,* **riotousness** *noun.*

RIP *abbr* may he/she/they rest in peace. [Latin *requiescat* (sing.)/*requiescant* (pl) *in pace*]

rip¹ /rip/ *verb* (**ripped, ripping**) ➤ *verb intrans* **1** to become torn; to rend. **2** to rush along: *He ripped past the finishing post.* ➤ *verb trans* **1a** to tear or split (something) apart, *esp* in a violent manner. **b** to saw or split (wood) along the grain. **2** (+ out/off) to remove (something) by force: *The previous owners had ripped out the fireplace.* ✳ **let rip** *informal* to do something without restraint: *The audience let rip with loud screams when the band appeared on stage.* **rip into** to criticize (somebody) fiercely. ➤➤ **ripper** *noun.* [prob from Flemish *rippen* to strip off roughly]

rip² *noun* a tear or torn split.

rip³ *noun* a body of rough water formed by the meeting of opposing currents, winds, etc, or by passing over ridges. [perhaps from RIP²]

rip⁴ *noun informal, dated* **1a** a mischievous young person. **b** a debauched person. **2** a worn-out worthless horse. [perhaps by shortening and alteration from REPROBATE¹]

riparian /rie'peəri·ən/ *adj* of or occurring on the bank of a river. [Latin *riparius*, from *ripa* bank]

rip cord *noun* a cord or wire for releasing a parachute from its pack.

rip current *noun* = RIPTIDE.

ripe /riep/ *adj* **1** said of fruit or grain: fully grown and developed; mature. **2** said of a cheese or wine: brought by ageing to full flavour or the best state; mellow. **3** (*often* + with) ruddy, plump, or full like ripened fruit. **4** mature in knowledge, understanding, or judgment. **5a** (*often* + for) fully arrived; propitious: *The time seemed ripe for the experiment.* **b** (+ for) fully prepared or ready for (something): *The firm was ripe for change.* **6** *informal* smutty or indecent. ✳ **a ripe old age** a very great age: *He lived to a ripe old age despite being a smoker.* ➤ **ripely** *adv*, **ripeness** *noun*. [Old English *rīpe*]

ripen /'riepən/ *verb* (**ripened, ripening**) ➤ *verb intrans* to become ripe. ➤ *verb trans* to make (something) ripe.

ripieno /ripi'aynoh/ *noun* (*pl* **ripienos** *or* **ripieni** /-nee/) a supplementary or accompanying group of instruments or voices, *esp* all the instruments or musical parts as distinct from the soloists. [Italian *ripieno* filled up, from *ri-* RE- + *pieno* full, from Latin *plenus*]

rip off *verb trans informal* **1** to defraud (somebody). **2a** to steal (something). **b** to rob (somebody).

rip-off *noun informal* **1** an instance of financial exploitation, *esp* the charging of an exorbitant price. **2** an illegal or poor-quality imitation or copy, e.g. of a film or book. **3** the act or an instance of stealing.

riposte[1] /ri'post/ *noun* **1** a piece of retaliatory banter. **2** a fencer's quick return thrust following a parry. [French *riposte* from Italian *risposta* answer, from *rispondere* to respond, from Latin *respondēre*: see RESPOND[1]]

riposte[2] *verb intrans* to make a riposte.

ripper /'ripə/ *noun* **1** somebody or something that rips, e.g.: **a** a machine used to break up rock, ore, etc. **b** a murderer who kills and mutilates with a knife. **2** *chiefly Aus, informal* an excellent example or instance of something. **3** a program that allows sound to be loaded from a CD onto the hard drive of a computer.

ripping *adj Brit, informal, dated* extremely good; excellent: *She tells some ripping yarns.* ➤➤ **rippingly** *adv*. [prob from present part of RIP[1]]

ripple[1] /'ripl/ *noun* **1** a small wave or a succession of small waves. **2a** = RIPPLE MARK. **b** a sound like that of rippling water: *a ripple of laughter.* **c** a feeling or emotion that spreads through a person, place, etc. **3** a small periodic fluctuation or variation in an otherwise steady current or voltage. **4** *NAmer* = RIFFLE[2] (2). ➤➤ **ripply** *adj*.

ripple[2] *verb intrans* **1a** to become covered with small waves. **b** to flow in small waves or undulations. **2** to flow with a light rise and fall of sound or inflection. **3** to proceed with an undulating motion, so as to cause ripples. **4** to spread irregularly outwards, *esp* from a central point. ➤ *verb trans* **1** to stir up small waves on (water). **2** to impart a wavy motion or appearance to (something): *He was rippling his muscles.* ➤➤ **rippler** *noun*. [perhaps frequentative of RIP[1]]

ripple mark *noun* any of a series of small ridges produced, *esp* on sand, by wind or water.

riprap[1] /'riprap/ *noun NAmer* stone used for a foundation or a protecting mass of loose stones. [orig in the sense 'the sound of rapping'; reduplication of RAP[1]]

riprap[2] *verb trans* (**riprapped, riprapping**) *NAmer* to build (something) with riprap.

rip-roaring *adj* noisily excited or exciting; exuberant.

ripsaw *noun* a coarse-toothed saw designed to cut wood in the direction of the grain: compare CROSSCUT SAW.

ripsnorter *noun chiefly NAmer, informal* somebody or something exceptionally powerful, unusual, or exciting: *The finale was a ripsnorter.* ➤➤ **ripsnorting** *adj*.

riptide *noun* **1** = RIP[3]. **2** a strong surface current flowing outwards from a shore.

RISC /risk/ *abbr* reduced instruction set computer.

rise[1] /riez/ *verb intrans* (*past tense* **rose** /rohz/, *past part.* **risen** /'riz(ə)n/) **1a** to move upwards; to ascend. **b** to slope upwards. **2a** to assume an upright position, *esp* from lying, kneeling, or sitting. **b** to get up from sleep or from one's bed. **3** said of the sun, moon, etc: to appear above the horizon. **4a** to extend above other objects or people. **b** said of dough or other mixture: to increase in height or volume by cooking. **5a** to increase in amount or number. **b** to attain a higher office or rank: *No man rises so high as he knows not whither he goes* — Oliver Cromwell. **6a** to occur or come into being. **b** said of a river: to have its source: *The Rhine rises in Switzerland.* **c** to be built. **7** (+ to) to show oneself equal to (a challenge). **8a** to become cheered or encouraged: *Her spirits rose when she heard the news.* **b** to increase in fervour or intensity. **9** *chiefly Brit* to end a session; to adjourn. **10** (*often* + up) to rebel; to take up arms. **11** to return to life. **12** said of a fish: to come to the surface of a river, lake, etc. **13** said of hair or fur: become erect. ✳ **rise above** to overcome or not be affected or constrained by (difficulties, unworthy feelings, etc). **rise to the bait** to react with annoyance to unpleasant words or behaviour. [Old English *rīsan*]

rise[2] *noun* **1** the act or an instance of rising or having risen, e.g.: **a** a movement upwards. **b** emergence, e.g. of the sun, above the horizon. **c** the upward movement of a fish to seize food or bait. **2a** an upward slope or gradient. **b** a spot higher than surrounding ground. **3a** an increase, *esp* in amount, number, value, or intensity. **b** *Brit* an increase in pay. **4** the vertical height of something; *specif* the vertical height of a step. ✳ **get/take a rise out of** to provoke (somebody) to annoyance by teasing them. **give rise to** to be the origin or cause of (something).

riser *noun* **1** somebody who rises in a specified manner: *an early riser.* **2** the upright part between two consecutive stair treads. **3** a vertical pipe conveying liquid or gas upwards.

risible /'rizibl/ *adj* **1** arousing or provoking laughter. **2** inclined or susceptible to laughter. ➤➤ **risibility** /-'biliti/ *noun*, **risibly** *adv*. [late Latin *risibilis*, from Latin *ridēre* to laugh]

rising[1] *adj* **1** approaching a specified age: *He's rising forty.* **2** achieving a higher rank or greater influence: *She's a rising young barrister in London.*

rising[2] *noun* an insurrection or uprising.

rising damp *noun Brit* moisture that has entered the floor of a building and moved up a wall.

risk[1] /risk/ *noun* **1** a dangerous element or factor; a hazard. **2** possibility of loss, injury, or damage: *The man who knows it can't be done counts the risk, not the reward* — Elbert Hubbard. **3a** the chance of loss or the dangers to that which is insured in an insurance contract. **b** somebody or something that is a specified hazard to an insurer: *a poor insurance risk.* **c** an insurance hazard from a specified cause: *a war risk.* ✳ **at risk** (*often* + of) in danger: *Children are at risk of infection if they don't wash their hands after touching animals.* **at somebody's (own) risk** with the person concerned accepting responsibility for any possible harm to themselves, damage to or loss of their possessions, etc: *Cars are parked here at their owners' risk.* [French *risque* from early Italian *risco* danger]

risk[2] *verb trans* **1** to expose (something, e.g. one's life) to hazard or danger. **2** to incur the risk or danger of (something unpleasant happening): *He risked being dismissed if he was caught altering the records.*

risk capital *noun* capital invested in a new enterprise.

risky *adj* (**riskier, riskiest**) involving danger or the possibility of loss or failure. ➤➤ **riskily** *adv*, **riskiness** *noun*.

risotto /ri'zotoh/ *noun* (*pl* **risottos**) an Italian dish of rice cooked in stock and flavoured with vegetables, shellfish, etc. [Italian *risotto* from *riso*: see RICE[1]]

risqué /'ri:skay, 'riskay/ *adj* verging on impropriety or indecency. [French *risqué*, past part. of *risquer* to risk, from *risque*: see RISK[1]]

rissole /'risohl/ *noun* a small fried cake or ball of cooked minced food, *esp* meat. [French *rissole* from early French *roissole* from Latin *russeolus* reddish, from *russus* red]

rit. *abbr* ritardando.

ritardando /ritah'dandoh/ *adj and adv* said of a piece of music: to be performed with a gradual decrease in tempo. ➤➤ **ritardando** *noun*. [Italian *ritardando* from Latin *retardandum*, verbal noun from *retardare*: see RETARD]

rite /riet/ *noun* **1** a ceremonial act or action, or a prescribed form of words or actions for this purpose. **2** the characteristic liturgy of a church or group of churches. [Middle English from Latin *ritus*]

ritenuto /rita'nyoohtoh/ *adj and adv* said of a piece of music: to be performed with an immediate decrease in tempo. ➤➤ **ritenuto** *noun*. [Italian *ritenuto*, past part. of *ritenere* to hold back, retain, from Latin *retinēre*: see RETAIN]

rite of passage *noun* (*usu in pl*) a ritual associated with a change of status, e.g. assuming adult status and responsibilities, in the life of an individual. [translation of French *rite de passage*]

ritornello /ritaw'neloh/ *noun* (*pl* **ritornellos** *or* **ritornelli** /-lee/) a short recurrent instrumental passage in a vocal composition or concerto. [Italian *ritornello*, dimin. of *ritorno* return, from *ritornare* to return]

ritual[1] /'rityooəl/ *noun* **1** the form or order of words prescribed for a religious ceremony. **2a** a ritual observance. **b** any formal and customary act or series of acts.

ritual[2] *adj* **1** of rites or a ritual; ceremonial: *a ritual dance*. **2** according to religious law or social custom. >>> **ritually** *adv*. [Latin *ritualis* from *ritus* RITE]

ritual abuse *noun* **1** the sexual and physical abuse of people, *esp* children, as a satanic ritual. Also called SATANIC ABUSE. **2** the physical abuse of children by adults taking part in supposed satanic rituals.

ritualise *verb trans and intrans* see RITUALIZE.

ritualism *noun* the use of ritual, or excessive devotion to it. >>> **ritualist** *noun*, **ritualistic** /-'listik/ *adj*, **ritualistically** /-'listikli/ *adv*.

ritualize *or* **ritualise** *verb trans* to convert (an act) into a ritual. >> *verb intrans* to practise ritualism. >>> **ritualization** /-'zaysh(ə)n/ *noun*, **ritualized** *adj*.

ritz /rits/ * **put on the ritz** *informal*, *dated* to put on a show of glamour and luxury. [back-formation from RITZY]

ritzy /'ritsi/ *adj* (**ritzier, ritziest**) *informal* ostentatiously smart. >>> **ritzily** *adv*, **ritziness** *noun*. [from the *Ritz* hotels, noted for their opulence]

rival[1] /'rievl/ *noun* **1a** any of two or more people competing for a single goal. **b** somebody who tries to compete with and be superior to another. **2** somebody or something that equals another in desirable qualities. **3** (*used before a noun*) having comparable pretensions or claims: *a rival company*. >>> **rivalry** /-ri/ *noun*. [French from Latin *rivalis* a person using the same stream as another, a rival in love, from *rivus* stream]

rival[2] *verb trans* (**rivalled, rivalling**, *NAmer* **rivaled, rivaling**) **1** to possess qualities that approach or equal (those of another). **2** to strive to equal or excel (somebody or something).

rive /riev/ *verb* (*past tense* **rived**, *past part.* **riven** /'riv(ə)n/) >> *verb trans* (*usu in passive*) **1a** to wrench (something) open or tear (it) apart or to pieces. **b** *archaic* to split (wood or stone) with force or violence; to cleave (it): *They unpacked their basket under an aged walnut with a riven trunk out of which bumblebees darted* — Edith Wharton. **2** to rend (a country, etc) with distress or dispute. >> *verb intrans archaic* said of wood or stone: to become split. [Middle English *riven* from Old Norse *rifa*]

river /'rivə/ *noun* **1** a natural stream of water of considerable volume. **2a** a flow that matches a river in volume: *a river of lava*. **b** (*in pl*) a copious or overwhelming quantity: *He cried rivers of tears when she left.* **3** (*used before a noun*) inhabiting or relating to a river: *a river dolphin.* * **sell down the river** to betray (somebody) or destroy their faith or expectations. >>> **riverless** *adj*. [Middle English from Old French *rivere*, ultimately from Latin *riparius* riparian, from *ripa* bank]

river blindness *noun* = ONCHOCERCIASIS.

riverine /'rivərien/ *adj literary* **1** of, formed by, or resembling a river. **2** living or situated on the banks of a river.

rivet[1] /'rivit/ *noun* a headed metal pin used to unite two or more pieces by passing the shank through a hole in each piece and then beating or pressing down the plain end so as to make a second head. [Middle English *rivette*, from early French *river* to be attached]

rivet[2] *verb trans* (**riveted, riveting**) **1** to fasten (something) with or as if with rivets. **2** (*usu in passive*) to attract and hold (the attention, etc) completely. **3** to fix (something) firmly. >>> **riveter** *noun*.

riveting *adj* holding the attention; fascinating.

riviera /rivi'eərə/ *noun* (*also* **Riviera**) a coastal region, usu with a mild climate, frequented as a resort. [named after the *Riviera*, region in SE France and NW Italy, from Italian *riviera* seashore]

rivière /rivi'eə/ *noun* a necklace of precious stones, e.g. diamonds, usu having one large stone at the centre. [French *rivière* river, from Old French *rivere*: see RIVER]

rivulet /'rivyoolit/ *noun* a small stream. [Italian *rivoletto*, dimin. of *rivolo*, from Latin *rivulus*, dimin. of *rivus* stream]

riyal /ri'ahl/ *noun* **1** the basic monetary unit of Qatar and of Saudi Arabia. **2** = RIAL (1). [Arabic *riyāl* from Spanish *real* ROYAL[1]]

RL *abbr* **1** Republic of Lebanon (international vehicle registration). **2** Rugby League.

rly *abbr* railway.

RM *abbr* **1** Republic of Madagascar (international vehicle registration). **2** *Brit* Royal Mail. **3** *Brit* Royal Marines.

rm *abbr* **1** ream. **2** room.

RMA *abbr Brit* Royal Military Academy (Sandhurst).

RMM *abbr* Republic of Mali (international vehicle registration).

rms *abbr* root-mean-square.

RN *abbr* **1** *chiefly NAmer* registered nurse. **2** Republic of Niger (international vehicle registration). **3** *Brit* Royal Navy.

Rn *abbr* the chemical symbol for radon.

RNA *noun* a nucleic acid similar to DNA that contains ribose and uracil as structural components instead of deoxyribose and thymine, and is associated with the control of cellular chemical activities. [contraction of *ribonucleic acid*]

RNAS *abbr Brit* Royal Naval Air Service.

RNIB *abbr Brit* Royal National Institute for the Blind.

RNLI *abbr Brit* Royal National Lifeboat Institution.

RNR *abbr* Royal Naval Reserve.

RNZAF *abbr* Royal New Zealand Air Force.

RNZN *abbr* Royal New Zealand Navy.

RO *abbr* Romania (international vehicle registration).

r.o. *abbr* in cricket, run out.

roach[1] /rohch/ *noun* (*pl* **roaches** *or collectively* **roach**) a silver-white European freshwater fish of the carp family: *Rutilus rutilus*. [Middle English from early French *roche*]

roach[2] *noun informal* **1** *chiefly NAmer* a cockroach. **2** the butt of a cannabis cigarette.

roach[3] *noun* a concave or convex curvature in the edge of a sail. [origin unknown]

roach clip *noun informal* a small device used to hold the butt of a cannabis cigarette.

road /rohd/ *noun* **1a** an open way, usu a paved one, for the passage of vehicles, people, and animals. **b** the part of a paved surface used by vehicles. **2a** a route or path: *He's on the road to ruin.* **b** space or room, *esp* for forward movement: *Can you move that, please? It's in my road; Let's get some of these minor details out of the road first.* **3** (*also in pl, but treated as sing.*) a relatively sheltered stretch of water near the shore where ships may ride at anchor. **4** *NAmer* a railway. **5** a passage in a mine. * **one for the road** *informal* a last alcoholic drink before leaving. **on the road** travelling or touring, e.g. on business. >>> **roadless** *adj*. [Old English *rād* ride, journey, RAID[1]]

roadbed *noun* **1** the earth foundation of a road prepared for surfacing. **2** the bed on which the sleepers, rails, and ballast of a railway rest.

roadblock *noun* a road barricade set up by an army, the police, etc.

road-fund licence *noun* = TAX DISC.

road hog *noun informal* a reckless driver of a motor vehicle who obstructs or intimidates others.

roadholding *noun* the ability of a moving vehicle to remain stable, *esp* when cornering.

roadhouse /'rohd·hows/ *noun* a pub or restaurant situated on a main road in a country area.

road hump *noun* = SLEEPING POLICEMAN.

roadie /'rohdi/ *noun informal* a person who looks after the transport and setting up of equipment of entertainers, *esp* a rock group.

roadman /'rohdmən/ *noun* (*pl* **roadmen**) a man who mends or builds roads.

road metal *noun* broken stone used in making and repairing roads or ballasting railways.

road movie *noun* a film portraying various episodes involving characters during a long journey by road.

road pricing *noun* the practice of charging motorists for the use of certain busy roads, in order to relieve congestion.

road rage *noun* violent and aggressive behaviour by a motorist towards another road user.

roadroller *noun* a machine equipped with heavy wide smooth rollers for compacting road surfaces during construction.

roadrunner *noun* either of two species of fast-running American birds of the cuckoo family that rarely fly: genus *Geococcyx*.

road show *noun* 1 a group of touring entertainers, *esp* pop musicians, or a performance given by them. 2 a public-relations or government information unit that travels from place to place to give displays or demonstrations. 3 a radio or television programme broadcast from different locations.

roadstead /'rohdsted/ *noun* a sheltered stretch of water; = ROAD (3).

roadster /'rohdstə/ *noun* 1a an open sports car that seats two people. b a sturdy bicycle for ordinary use on common roads. 2 a horse for riding or driving on roads.

road tax *noun* = VEHICLE EXCISE DUTY.

road test *noun* 1 a test of a vehicle taken under practical operating conditions on the road. 2 a test of any piece of equipment in use.

road-test *verb trans* to test (a vehicle or other piece of equipment) under practical operating conditions.

road train *noun chiefly Aus* a truck that pulls one or more trailers.

roadway *noun* 1 a road. 2 the part of a road used by vehicles.

roadwork *noun* 1 *Brit* (*in pl*) the repair or construction of roads, or the site of such work. 2 conditioning for an athletic contest, e.g. a boxing match, consisting mainly of long runs.

roadworthy *adj* said of a vehicle: in a fit condition to be used on the roads; in proper working order. ⋙ **roadworthiness** *noun*.

roam¹ /rohm/ *verb intrans* to go aimlessly from place to place; to wander. ⋙ *verb trans* to range or wander over (an area). ⋙ **roamer** *noun*. [Middle English *romen*; earlier history unknown]

roam² *noun* the act or an instance of wandering from place to place.

roan¹ /rohn/ *adj* said of horses and cattle: having a coat of a reddish brown base colour that is muted and lightened by some white hairs. [early French *roan* from Old Spanish *roano*]

roan² *noun* an animal, e.g. a horse, with a roan coat.

roan³ *noun* a sheepskin tanned with powder made from the leaves of the sumach tree and coloured and finished to imitate morocco leather. [origin unknown]

roar¹ /raw/ *noun* 1 the deep prolonged cry characteristic of a wild animal. 2 a loud cry, call, etc, e.g. of pain, anger, or laughter. 3 a loud continuous confused sound: *the roar of the waves*.

roar² *verb intrans* 1a to give a roar. b to sing or shout with full force. 2a to laugh loudly and deeply. b to do something while emitting or making a loud roaring sound: *The car roared along the road.* c said of a fire: to burn fiercely and noisily. 3 to happen or progress rapidly: *She joined the firm in 1997 and was soon roaring to the top.* 4 said of a horse suffering from roaring: to make a loud noise in breathing. ⋙ *verb trans* 1 to utter (something) with a roar. 2 to cause (oneself) to become (something) by roaring: *He roared himself hoarse at the match.* ⋙ **roarer** *noun*. [Old English *rārian*]

roaring¹ *adj* 1 *informal* marked by energetic or successful activity: *We did a roaring trade in home-made scones.* 2 making or characterized by a sound resembling a roar: *a roaring fire.* ⋙ **roaringly** *adv*.

roaring² *noun* noisy breathing in a horse occurring during exertion and caused by muscular paralysis.

roaring³ *adv informal* extremely or thoroughly: *They went out and got roaring drunk.*

roaring forties *pl noun* (**the roaring forties**) either of two areas of stormy westerly winds between latitudes 40° and 50° N and S.

roast¹ /rohst/ *verb trans* 1a to cook (food, *esp* meat) by exposing it to dry heat, e.g. in an oven or by surrounding it with hot embers. b to dry and brown (something) slightly by exposure to heat: *Coffee beans are roasted.* 2 to heat (ore or other inorganic material) with air to cause the removal of volatile material, oxidation, etc. 3 to heat (somebody or something) to excess. 4 to criticize (somebody) severely. ⋙ *verb intrans* 1 to cook food by roasting. 2 to be excessively hot. ⋙ **roaster** *noun*. [Middle English *rosten* from Old French *rostir*, of Germanic origin]

roast² *noun* 1 a piece of meat roasted or suitable for roasting. 2 *NAmer* a party at which food is roasted, *esp* in the open air.

roast³ *adj* said of food, *esp* meat: roasted.

roasting¹ *adj informal* extremely hot.

roasting² *noun informal* a severe scolding.

rob /rob/ *verb* (**robbed, robbing**) ⋙ *verb trans* 1 to steal something from (a person or place), *esp* by violence or threat. 2 (+ of) to deprive (somebody) of something due, expected, or desired: *A Cherokee is too smart to put anything in the contribution box of a race that's robbed him of his birthright* — Howard Estabrook. ⋙ *verb intrans* to commit robbery. ⋙ **robber** *noun*. [Middle English *robben* from Old French *rober*, of Germanic origin]

robbery /'robəri/ *noun* (*pl* **robberies**) the act or an instance of robbing; *specif* theft accompanied by violence or threats.

robe¹ /rohb/ *noun* 1 (*also in pl*) a long flowing outer garment, *esp* one used for ceremonial occasions or as a symbol of office or profession. 2 *NAmer* a dressing gown. [Middle English from Old French *robe* booty, robe (clothes being often taken as booty), of Germanic origin]

robe² *verb trans* (*usu in passive*) to clothe or cover (somebody) with or as if with a robe. ⋙ *verb intrans* to put on a robe. ⋙ **robed** *adj*.

robin /'robin/ *noun* 1 a small brownish European bird of the thrush family, having an orange-red throat and breast: *Erithacus rubecula*. 2 a large N American thrush with a dull reddish breast and underparts: *Turdus migratorius*. [Middle English *robin redbrest*, from *Robin*, nickname for *Robert*]

robinia /rə'bini-ə/ *noun* any of a genus of deciduous trees or shrubs of the pea family having pinnate leaves and pealike flowers, *esp* LOCUST (2B): genus *Robinia*. [Latin genus name, named after Jean *Robin* d.1629, French botanist and gardener to the royal family in Paris, who introduced some species to Europe]

robin redbreast /'redbrest/ *noun* = ROBIN.

robot /'rohbot/ *noun* 1 an automatic apparatus or device that performs functions ordinarily ascribed to human beings or operates with what appears to be almost human intelligence. 2a a humanoid machine that walks and talks. b somebody efficient or clever who lacks human warmth or sensitivity. 3 *SAfr* a set of traffic lights. [Czech *robot*, from *robota* forced labour; coined by Karel Čapek d.1938, Czech writer]

robotic /rə'botik/ *adj* 1 relating to or resembling a robot: *robotic dancing*. 2 said of a person: efficient or clever but lacking in human warmth or sensitivity.

robotics *pl noun* (*treated as sing. or pl*) a field of interest concerned with the construction, maintenance, and behaviour of robots: *Robotics is a major science-fiction theme.*

robust /rə'bust/ *adj* 1a having or exhibiting vigorous health or stamina. b strongly formed or constructed. c firm in purpose or outlook. 2 earthy, rude. 3 requiring strenuous exertion. 4 full-bodied: *a robust red wine.* ⋙ **robustly** *adv*, **robustness** *noun*. [Latin *robustus* oaken, strong, from *robor-, robur* oak, strength]

robusta /roh'bustə/ *noun* 1 a variety of coffee bean, or coffee prepared from such beans. 2 a variety of coffee tree that is indigenous to Central Africa but has been introduced elsewhere, e.g. in Java: *Coffea canephora*. [Latin *robusta*, fem. of *robustus*: see ROBUST; *Coffea canephora* was formerly called *Coffea robusta*]

ROC *abbr Brit* formerly, Royal Observer Corps.

roc /rok/ *noun* a mythical bird of gigantic size. [Arabic *rukhkh* from Persian *ruk*]

rocaille /roh'kie, rə-/ *noun* 1 an 18th-cent. style of decorative art and architecture involving stylized shell-like, rocklike, and scroll-like motifs and others resembling ferns, flowers, and coral; = ROCOCO¹. 2 decorative ornamentation with shells and stones, *esp* on fountains and artificial grottoes in gardens of the late Renaissance. [French *rocaille* loose stones, stony ground, from *roc* rock]

rocambole /'rokəmbohl/ *noun* a European leek used for flavouring: *Allium scorodoprasum*. [French *rocambole* from German *Rockenbolle*, from *Rocken, Roggen* rye + *Bolle* bulb]

Rochelle salt /ro'shel/ *noun* sodium potassium tartrate, used *esp* in baking powders and in piezoelectric crystals. [named after La *Rochelle*, city in W France where it is mined]

roche moutonnée /ˌrosh mooh'tonay/ *noun* (*pl* **roches moutonnées** /ˌrosh mooh'tonay/) a long rounded rock mound shaped and ridged by the movement of an ice sheet. [French *roche moutonnée*, literally 'fleecy rock']

rochet /'rochit/ *noun* a white ceremonial vestment resembling a surplice, worn *esp* by bishops. [Middle English from Old French, dimin. of *roc* coat, of Germanic origin]

rock¹ /rok/ *noun* **1** a large mass of stone forming a cliff, promontory, or peak. **2** a large concreted mass of stony material. **3** consolidated or unconsolidated solid mineral matter. **4** *NAmer* a stone. **5** something like a rock in firmness; a firm or solid foundation or support. **6** a coloured and flavoured sweet, usu produced in the form of a cylindrical stick. **7** *informal* a gem, *esp* a diamond. **8** *informal* crack cocaine, or a piece of crack cocaine. ✳ **on the rocks 1** *informal* in or into a state of destruction or wreckage: *Their marriage was on the rocks.* **2** served over ice cubes: *Scotch on the rocks.* ➤➤ **rocklike** *adj.* [Middle English *rokke* via Old French *rocque* from medieval Latin *rocca*]

rock² *verb trans* **1** to move (somebody or something) gently back and forth in or as if in a cradle. **2a** said of an explosion, etc: to cause (something) to sway back and forth. **b** to daze or stun (somebody). **c** said of a piece of news, etc: to disturb or upset (somebody). ➤ *verb intrans* **1** to become moved rapidly or violently backward and forward, e.g. under impact. **2** to move rhythmically back and forth. **3** to dance to or play rock music. ✳ **rock the boat** to disturb the equilibrium of a situation [popularized by the hit song 'Sit Down, You're Rocking the Boat' in the 1950s musical *Guys and Dolls*]. [Old English *roccian*]

rock³ *noun* **1** = ROCK 'N' ROLL. **2** a style of popular music derived from rock and roll that is usu played on electronically amplified instruments and characterized by a persistent, heavily accented beat.

rockabilly /'rokəbili/ *noun* rock music with a strong country-and-western influence. [blend of ROCK³ + HILLBILLY]

rock and roll *noun* see ROCK 'N' ROLL.

rock bottom *noun* the lowest or most fundamental part or level.

rock-bottom *adj* the lowest possible: *rock-bottom prices.*

rockbound *adj* said of a shore, etc: surrounded or strewn with rocks; rocky.

rock cake *noun* a small cake with a rough irregular surface, containing currants and sometimes spice.

rock chick *noun informal* a female rock musician, or a woman who is involved in the rock-music industry in some other capacity.

rock cress *noun* = ARABIS.

rock crystal *noun* transparent colourless quartz.

rock dove *noun* a bluish grey Old World wild pigeon that is the ancestor of the domestic pigeons: *Columba livia.*

rocker *noun* **1a** a rock musician or fan. **b** a rock song. **2** *Brit* a member of a group of leather-jacketed young British motorcyclists in the 1960s who waged war on the mods: compare MOD². **3a** either of the two curved pieces of wood or metal on which an object, e.g. a cradle, rocks. **b** something mounted on rockers; *specif* a rocking chair. **c** any object resembling a rocker or with parts resembling a rocker. **4** a device that works with a rocking motion. ✳ **off one's rocker** *informal* crazy, mad.

rocker switch *noun* a switch that operates by means of a spring-loaded rocker.

rockery *noun* (*pl* **rockeries**) a bank or mound of rocks and earth where rock plants are grown.

rocket¹ /'rokit/ *noun* **1a** a firework consisting of a long case filled with a combustible material fastened to a guiding stick and projected through the air by the rearward discharge of gases released in combustion. **b** such a device used as an incendiary weapon or as a propelling unit, e.g. for a lifesaving line or whaling harpoon. **2** a jet engine that carries with it everything necessary for its operation and is thus independent of the oxygen in the air. **3** a rocket-propelled bomb, missile, or projectile. **4** *Brit, informal* a sharp reprimand. [Italian *rocchetta*, dimin. of *rocca* distaff, of Germanic origin]

rocket² *verb intrans* (**rocketed, rocketing**) **1** said of prices, etc: to rise or increase rapidly or spectacularly. **2** to travel with the speed of a rocket.

rocket³ *noun* **1** a Mediterranean plant of the cabbage family, the larger leaves of which are used when young in salad: *Eruca vesicaria.* **2** a plant of the cabbage family with yellow flowers that grows as a weed in most parts of the world: genera *Sisymbrium* and *Barbarea.* [early French *roquette* from Italian *ruchetta*, ultimately from Latin *eruca* downy-stemmed plant]

rocketeer /roki'tiə/ *noun* somebody who designs or travels in space rockets.

rocketry /'rokitri/ *noun* the study of, experimentation with, or use of rockets.

rocket science *noun* **1** = ROCKETRY. **2** *chiefly NAmer, informal* something that requires intelligence to do or understand.

rocket scientist *noun* **1** a scientist involved in rocketry. **2** *chiefly NAmer, informal* a highly intelligent person: *It doesn't take a rocket scientist to work that out.*

rockfall /'rokfawl/ *noun* a mass of falling or fallen rocks.

rockfish *noun* (*pl* **rockfishes** or *collectively* **rockfish**) **1** any of various fish that live among rocks or on rocky bottoms. **2** = ROCK SALMON.

rock garden *noun* **1** a garden containing one or more rockeries. **2** a rockery.

rockhopper *noun* a medium-sized penguin found in New Zealand, Antarctica, and the Falkland Islands, having a stout bill and yellow crests on the side of the head: *Eudyptes crestatus.*

rocking chair *noun* a chair mounted on rockers.

rocking horse *noun* a toy horse mounted on rockers.

rocking stone *noun* a large stone that is balanced in such a way that it can be easily rocked.

rockling /'rokling/ *noun* any of several species of rather small elongated marine fishes of the cod family: genera *Ciliata* and *Rhinomenus.*

rock lobster *noun* = SPINY LOBSTER.

rock music *noun* = ROCK³ (2).

rock 'n' roll /,rok (ə)n 'rohl/ *or* **rock and roll** *noun* **1** a style of popular music that originated in the 1950s, characterized by a heavy beat, much repetition of simple phrases, and often country, folk, and blues elements: *Rock 'n' roll is instant coffee* — Bob Geldof.

Editorial note
Synthesized out of black rhythm-and-blues of the 1940s and white country music of the same era, rock 'n' roll became the youth music of choice in America – and subsequently the rest of the developed world – in the mid 1950s. The full term is still used to describe the pop music of that period, but the more abbreviated 'rock' is an unspecific generic for most subsequent styles of popular music — Richard Cook.

2 a style of dancing to this music.

rock pigeon *noun* = ROCK DOVE.

rock plant *noun* a small plant, *esp* an alpine plant, that grows among rocks or in rockeries.

rock rabbit *noun* a pika.

rockrose *noun* a woody plant or shrub with showy flowers: family Cistaceae.

rock salmon *noun Brit, not now used technically* a dogfish or wolffish when used as food.

rock salt *noun* common salt occurring as a solid mineral.

rockshaft *noun* a shaft, e.g. in a steam engine, that rocks on its bearings instead of revolving.

rockslide *noun* = ROCKFALL.

rock solid *adj* **1** completely firm, fixed, or stable. **2** unwavering; committed: *a rock-solid Conservative.*

rocksteady *noun* a type of Jamaican popular music originating in the early 1960s, a precursor of reggae.

rockumentary /rokyoo'mentəri/ *noun* (*pl* **rockumentaries**) *informal* a documentary on the subject of rock music or a particular rock band or musician. [blend of ROCK³ + DOCUMENTARY²]

rock wool *noun* mineral wool made from limestone or siliceous rock.

rocky¹ *adj* (**rockier, rockiest**) **1** full of or consisting of rocks. **2** filled with obstacles; difficult: *The firm is going through a rocky patch at the moment.* ➤➤ **rockiness** *noun.* [ROCK¹]

rocky² *adj* (**rockier, rockiest**) unsteady; tottering. ➤➤ **rockily** *adv,* **rockiness** *noun.* [ROCK²]

Rocky Mountain goat *noun* = MOUNTAIN GOAT (2).

rococo¹ /rə'kohkoh/ *adj* **1a** of or typical of a style of architecture and decoration in 18th-cent. Europe characterized by elaborate sometimes asymmetrical curved forms and shell motifs. **b** of an 18th-cent. musical style marked by much light ornamentation. **2** excessively ornate or florid. [French *rococo*, irreg from *rocaille* from *roc* ROCK¹]

rococo² *noun* rococo work or style: *He thought of her ... as he might have thought of a Dresden-china shepherdess. Miss Osmond, indeed, in the bloom of her juvenility, had a hint of the rococo* — Henry James.

rod /rod/ *noun* **1a** a slender bar, e.g. of wood or metal. **b** a pole with a line for fishing. **c** a wand or staff carried as a sign of office, power, or authority. **2** a straight slender stick. **3a** a stick or bundle of twigs used for corporal punishment. **b** (**the rod**) punishment with such a rod. **4** *chiefly Brit* formerly, a unit of length equal to about 5m (5½yd). **5** any of the relatively long rod-shaped light receptors in the retina that are sensitive to faint light: compare CONE¹ (6). **6** *NAmer, slang* a pistol. ➤➤ **rodless** *adj*, **rodlike** *adj*. [Old English *rodd*]

rode /rohd/ *verb* past tense of RIDE¹.

rodent /'rohd(ə)nt/ *noun* any of an order of gnawing mammals including the mice, rats, squirrels, and beavers: order Rodentia. [Latin *rodent-, rodens,* present part. of *rodere* to gnaw]

rodenticide /roh'dentisied/ *noun* something, *esp* a poison, that kills, repels, or controls rodents.

rodent ulcer *noun* a malignant tumour that appears as an ulcer of exposed skin on the face, and spreads slowly outwards destroying other tissue. [Latin *rodent-, rodens:* see RODENT]

rodeo /'rohdioh, rə'dayoh/ *noun* (*pl* **rodeos**) **1** a public performance featuring the riding skills of cowboys. **2** a roundup. [Spanish *rodeo* from *rodear* to surround, from *rueda* wheel, from Latin *rota*]

rodomontade /,rodəmon'tayd/ *noun* **1** a bragging speech. **2** vain boasting or bluster; bombast. [early French *rodomontade* from Italian *Rodomonte,* character in *Orlando Innamorato* by Matteo Boiardo d.1494, Italian poet]

roe¹ /roh/ *noun* **1** the eggs of a female fish, *esp* when still enclosed in a membrane, or the corresponding part of a male fish. **2** the eggs or ovaries of an invertebrate, e.g. a lobster. [Middle English, of Germanic origin]

roe² *noun* = ROE DEER.

roebuck /'rohbuk/ *noun* (*pl* **roebucks** *or collectively* **roebuck**) a male roe deer.

roe deer *noun* a small Eurasian deer with erect cylindrical antlers that is noted for its nimbleness and grace: *Capreolus capreolus.* [*roe* from Old English *rā* roe deer]

roentgen /'runtyən, 'rəntyən/ *noun* see RÖNTGEN.

roentgenogram /'runtyənohgram, 'rən-/ *noun* see RÖNTGEN-OGRAM.

roentgenology /runtyə'noləji, rən-/ *noun* see RÖNTGENOLOGY.

roentgen ray *noun* see RÖNTGEN RAY.

rogan josh /,rohgən 'johsh/ *noun* an Indian dish of curried meat, prawns, or vegetables, in a tomato and capsicum sauce. [Urdu *rogan josh,* literally 'stewed in ghee']

Rogation Day *noun* any of the days of prayer, *esp* for the harvest, observed on the three days before Ascension Day and, by Roman Catholics, also on 25 April.

rogations /roh'gaysh(ə)nz/ *pl noun* the religious observance of the Rogation Days marked *esp* by solemn supplication. [Middle English *rogacion* litany, supplication, from late Latin *rogation-, rogatio,* from Latin *rogare* to ask]

roger¹ /'rojə/ *interj* used in radio and signalling to indicate that a message has been received and understood. [the name *Roger,* former communications codeword for the letter *r*]

roger² *verb trans and intrans* (**rogered, rogering**) *Brit, coarse slang* said of a man: to have sexual intercourse with (somebody). [obsolete *roger* (penis), from the name *Roger*]

rogue¹ /rohg/ *noun* **1** a wilfully dishonest or corrupt person. **2** a mischievous person; a scamp. **3** a plant or an animal that displays a chance variation making it different to and sometimes inferior to others. **4** (*used before a noun*) said of an animal: roaming alone and vicious and destructive: *a rogue elephant.* [orig denoting a vagrant or beggar; prob from Latin *rogare* to ask]

rogue² *verb trans* (**roguing, rogueing**) to weed out inferior, diseased, etc plants from (a field or crop).

roguery /'rohg(ə)ri/ *noun* (*pl* **rogueries**) an act characteristic of a rogue.

rogues' gallery *noun informal* a collection of pictures of people arrested as criminals.

roguish *adj* **1** wilfully dishonest or corrupt. **2** mischievous. ➤➤➤ **roguishly** *adv*, **roguishness** *noun*.

roil /royl/ *verb trans* **1** to make (a liquid) muddy or opaque by stirring up the sediment in it. **2** *NAmer* to annoy or rile (somebody). ➤ *verb intrans* said of a liquid: to become muddy or opaque with sediment. [origin unknown]

roister /'roystə/ *verb intrans* (**roistered, roistering**) to engage in noisy revelry. ➤➤ **roisterer** *noun*, **roisterous** /-rəs/ *adj*. [archaic *roister* roisterer, from French *ruistre* boor, from Latin *rusticus:* see RUSTIC¹]

ROK *abbr* Republic of Korea (international vehicle registration).

role *or* **rôle** /rohl/ *noun* **1a** a part played by an actor. **b** a socially expected behaviour pattern, usu determined by an individual's status in a particular society. **2** a function. [French *rôle* roll (originally referring to the roll of paper on which the actor's part was written), from Old French *rolle:* see ROLL²]

role model *noun* somebody who serves as an example to others of how to behave in a particular role.

role playing *noun* behaving in a way typical of another or of a stereotype, often for therapeutic or educational purposes.

roll¹ /rohl/ *verb intrans* **1a** to move along by turning over and over. **b** said of a vehicle, etc: to move on wheels. **c** to revolve on an axis. **2** (*often + up*) to form a round shape: *The hedgehog had rolled into a ball.* **3a** said of liquid: to flow in an abundant stream; to pour. **b** said of clouds, etc: to flow with an undulating motion. **c** to extend in broad undulations: *rolling hills.* **4** to move onward in a regular cycle or succession. **5** said of the eyes: to rotate in their sockets. **6** to become carried on a stream. **7** said of thunder, etc: to reverberate. **8a** said of a ship, aircraft, etc: to rock gently from side to side as it moves forward. **b** to walk with a swinging gait. **c** to move so as to reduce the impact of a blow. **9a** said of a machine: to begin to move or operate: *The presses started to roll.* **b** said of film or television credits: to be displayed by moving up the screen. **c** to move forward or begin to make progress: *We finally got the business rolling.* ➤ *verb trans* **1a** to move (something or somebody) forward by causing them to turn over and over. **b** to move (something) on rollers or wheels: *Roll the trolley over here.* **2** to carry (something) forward with an easy continuous motion: *The river rolls its waters to the sea.* **3a** to cause (something fixed) to revolve on or as if on an axis. **b** to cause (something) to move in a circular manner. **4a** to put a wrapping round (something). **b** (*often + up*) to wrap (something) round on itself or shape it into a round mass: *Roll up that map; it will not be wanted these ten years* — William Pitt. **5** to press, spread, or level (something) with a roller. **6a** to sound (something) with a full reverberating tone. **b** to make a continuous beating sound on (a drum, etc). **c** to utter (the letter *r*) with a trill. **7** *informal* to rob (somebody sleeping or unconscious). ✳ **be rolling in money/ rolling in it** *informal* to be very wealthy. [Middle English from Old French *roller,* ultimately from Latin *rotula:* see ROLL²]

roll² *noun* **1** something rolled up to resemble a cylinder or ball, e.g.: **a** a quantity, e.g. of fabric or paper, rolled up to form a single package. **b** any of various food preparations rolled or rolled up for cooking or serving: *a sausage roll.* **c** a small piece of baked yeast dough, usu eaten with a filling of meat, cheese, salad, etc. **d** anything of a similar shape: *You could see the rolls of fat on his body through his clothes.* **2a** a written document that may be rolled up; *specif* one bearing an official or formal record. **b** a list of names or related items; a catalogue. **c** an official list of people, e.g. members of a school or of a legislative body. **3** = ROLLER¹ (1), (2). **4** *NAmer, Aus* paper money folded or rolled into a wad. [Middle English via Old French *rolle* from Latin *rotula,* dimin. of *rota* wheel]

roll³ *noun* **1** a rolling movement, e.g.: **a** a swaying movement of the body, e.g. in walking or dancing. **b** a side-to-side movement, e.g. of a ship. **c** a flight manoeuvre in which a complete revolution about the longitudinal axis of an aircraft is made with the horizontal direction of flight being approximately maintained. **2a** a sound produced by rapid strokes on a drum. **b** a rhythmic sonorous flow, *esp* of speech. **c** a reverberating sound. ✳ **a roll in the hay/sack** *informal* amorous activity, *esp* an act of sexual intercourse. **on a roll** *informal* having a period of success. [from ROLL¹]

roll back *verb trans* to slow or reverse (a process).

roll bar *noun* a metal bar in a car that is designed to strengthen the frame and act as overhead protection if the car rolls over.

roll by *verb intrans* said of time: to pass quickly: *The years roll by.*

roll call *noun* **1** the calling out of a list of names, e.g. for checking attendance. **2** a comprehensive survey: *Workers from Yarrow and trade unionists from England and Scotland carried banners which were a roll call of industrial struggles past and present* — Scotsman.

rolled gold *noun* metal, e.g. brass, coated with a thin layer of gold.

rolled oats *pl noun* oats that have been husked and flattened.

roller[1] *noun* **1** a revolving cylinder over or on which something is moved or which is used to press, shape, or apply something. **2a** a hair curler. **b** a cylinder or rod on which something, e.g. a blind, is rolled up. **3** a long strip of bandage rolled up. **4** a long heavy wave.

roller[2] *noun* **1** any of several species of brightly coloured Old World birds noted for performing aerial rolls in their nuptial display: family Coraciidae. **2a** a canary with a soft trilling song. **b** a variety of tumbler pigeon. [German *Roller* from *rollen* to roll, reverberate, via French from Latin *rotula*: see ROLL[2]]

rollerball *noun* a pen whose writing tip is a small movable ball.

roller bearing *noun* a bearing in which the rotating part turns on rollers held in a cylindrical housing.

Rollerblade *noun trademark* (*usu in pl*) an in-line skate (see IN-LINE SKATES).

rollerblade *verb intrans* to skate on Rollerblades. ⋙ **rollerblader** *noun*.

roller coaster *noun* **1** an elevated railway in a funfair, constructed with curves and inclines on which the cars roll. **2** a situation in which one experiences highs and lows: *an emotional roller coaster*.

roller-coaster *verb intrans* (**roller-coastered, rollercoastering**) **1** to ride on a roller coaster. **2** to experience a roller coaster, e.g. in one's emotions or fortunes.

roller skate *noun* a metal frame holding usu four small wheels that allows the wearer to glide over hard surfaces, or a shoe fitted with such a frame.

roller-skate *verb intrans* to skate on roller skates. ⋙ **roller skater** *noun*, **roller skating** *noun*.

roller towel *noun* a continuous towel hung from a roller.

rollick /'rolik/ *verb intrans* to move or behave in a carefree boisterous manner; to frolic. [perhaps a blend of ROMP[1] or ROLL[1] and FROLIC[1]]

rollicking[1] *adj* boisterously carefree.

rollicking[2] *noun Brit, informal* a severe scolding. [prob alteration of BOLLOCKING]

roll in *verb intrans informal* **1** to be received in large quantities. **2** to arrive casually, *esp* when late.

rolling mill *noun* an establishment or machine in which metal is rolled into plates and bars.

rolling pin *noun* a long cylinder for rolling out dough.

rolling stock *noun* **1** the vehicles owned and used by a railway. **2** *NAmer* the road vehicles owned and used by a haulage company.

rolling stone *noun* somebody who leads a wandering or unsettled life.

rollmop *noun* a herring fillet rolled up and pickled by being marinated in spiced vinegar or brine. [back-formation from *rollmops* (taken to be plural) from German *Rollmops*, from *rollen* to roll + *Mops* simpleton, pug-nosed dog, from Low German]

roll neck *noun* a loose high collar, *esp* on a jumper, worn rolled over.

roll on *interj Brit* used to urge on a desired event: *Roll on summer!*

roll-on *noun* **1** a liquid preparation, e.g. deodorant, applied to the skin by means of a rolling ball in the neck of the container. **2** *Brit* a woman's elasticated girdle without fastenings. **3** (*used before a noun*) applied by means of a rolling ball in the neck of the container: *a roll-on deodorant*.

roll-on roll-off *adj* allowing vehicles to drive on or off: *a roll-on roll-off ferry*.

rollout *noun* the public introduction or unveiling of a new aircraft.

roll out *verb trans* **1** to spread something out by unrolling it. **2** to introduce or unveil (a new product).

rollover *noun* **1** the extension of a loan or debt for a longer period. **2** in a lottery, the carrying-over of unwon prize money to be added to prize money for the following draw.

roll over *verb intrans* **1a** to move by a rolling motion: *Could you roll over onto your side, please.* **b** said of a boat, etc: to capsize or overturn. **c** said of e.g. a dog: to roll into the position of lying on its back with its legs in the air. **2** said of unwon prize money in a

lottery: to be added to the jackpot for the next draw. ⋙ *verb trans* **1** to transfer (funds) from one investment to a similar investment. **2** to negotiate new terms for (a financial contract), e.g. to allow (a loan) to continue to a later date than orig contracted. **3** to add (unwon prize money in a lottery) to the jackpot for the next draw. **4** to defeat (somebody) overwhelmingly.

rolltop desk *noun* a writing desk with a sliding cover often of parallel slats fastened to a flexible backing.

roll up *verb intrans informal* to arrive.

roll-up *noun informal* **1** *Brit* a hand-rolled cigarette. **2** *Aus* the people attending a meeting.

Rolodex /'rohlədeks/ *noun NAmer, trademark* a rotary index file, usu used for names, addresses, etc. [invented name based on ROLLER[1] + INDEX[1]]

roly-poly[1] /,rohli 'pohli/ *noun* (*pl* **roly-polies**) a pudding consisting of pastry spread with a filling, e.g. jam, rolled, and baked or steamed. [reduplication of *roly*, from ROLL[1] + -Y[3]]

roly-poly[2] *adj informal* short and plump.

ROM /rom/ *abbr* read-only memory.

Rom. *abbr* Romans (book of the Bible).

rom. *abbr* roman (type).

Romaic /roh'may·ik/ *noun* the modern Greek vernacular. ⋙ **Romaic** *adj*. [modern Greek *Rhōmaiikos* from Greek *Rhōmaïkos* Roman, from *Rhōmē* Rome, capital city of Italy]

romaine lettuce /roh'mayn, rə'mayn/ *noun chiefly NAmer* a cos lettuce. [French *romaine*, fem. of *romain* Roman, from Latin *Romanus*: see ROMANCE[1]]

Roman[1] /'rohmən/ *adj* **1** of Rome or the Romans. **2** (**roman**) said of numbers or letters: not slanted; perpendicular. **3** of the see of Rome or the Roman Catholic Church. [Old English from Latin *Romanus*: see ROMANCE[1]]

Roman[2] *noun* **1** a native or inhabitant of ancient or modern Rome. **2** (**roman**) roman letters or type.

roman à clef /,rohmonh a 'klay (*French* rɔmã a kle)/ *noun* (*pl* **romans à clef** /,rohmonh (*French* rɔmã)/) a novel in which real people or actual events are fictionally disguised. [French *roman à clef*, literally 'novel with a key']

Roman alphabet *noun* the alphabet used for writing most European languages, based on the alphabet developed in ancient Rome from the Etruscan alphabet.

Roman blind *noun* a window blind in which the material can be drawn up into horizontal folds or pleats.

Roman candle *noun* a cylindrical firework that discharges balls or stars of fire at intervals.

Roman Catholic[1] *noun* a member of the Roman Catholic Church. ⋙ **Roman Catholicism** /kə'tholisiz(ə)m/ *noun*.

Roman Catholic[2] *adj* relating or belonging to the Roman Catholic Church.

Roman Catholic Church *noun* a Christian church headed by the pope, who is Bishop of Rome, and having a hierarchy of priests and bishops under the pope, a form of service centred on the Mass, and a body of dogma formulated by the Church as the interpreter of revealed truth.

Romance /roh'mans, rə'mans/ *noun* the family of languages that developed from Latin and that includes e.g. French, Spanish, and Italian. ⋙ **Romance** *adj*.

Word history
Middle English from Old French *romanz*: see ROMANCE[1]. The word originally referred to the vernacular language of France, as opposed to Latin.

romance[1] *noun* **1** romantic love: *Are you looking for romance?* **2** a love affair. **3a** a story or film about romantic love. **b** such stories or films collectively. **4** a medieval verse tale dealing with chivalric love and adventure. **5** a prose narrative dealing with imaginary characters involved in heroic, adventurous, or mysterious events that are remote in time or place. **6** an emotional aura attaching to an enthralling era, adventure, or pursuit. **7** something lacking any basis in fact.

Word history
Middle English *romauns* via Old French *romanz* from Latin *romanice* in the Roman manner, later 'in the vernacular', from *romanicus* Romance, from *Romanus* (adj and noun) Roman, from *Roma* Rome. The word originally referred to a narrative written in the vernacular, as opposed to Latin, many of which were about chivalrous deeds or courtly love.

romance[2] *verb intrans* **1** to exaggerate or invent detail or incident. **2a** to entertain romantic thoughts or ideas. **b** said of a couple: to spend time together in a romantic way, e.g. dancing or kissing. ➤ *verb trans* **1** to have a love affair with (somebody). **2** to behave amorously towards (somebody), sometimes with ulterior motives.

romance[3] *noun* a short instrumental or social piece of music orig in ballad style but later a more general lyric or sentimental genre. [French *romance* via Spanish from Latin *romanice*: see ROMANCE[1]]

romancer *noun* **1** somebody prone to romancing. **2** a writer of romance.

Roman Empire *noun* (**the Roman Empire**) the empire ruled by the Roman emperors from 27 BC until AD 395.

Romanesque[1] /rohmə'nesk/ *noun* a style of architecture developed in Italy and western Europe and characterized after AD 1000 by the use of the round arch and vault, and in its mature form decorative arcading, and elaborate mouldings: compare NORMAN.

Editorial note
The term 'Romanesque' is used to describe Western European architecture and art of the 11th and 12th cents, and is associated especially with the expansion of monasticism and the building of large stone churches. It is characterized by massive masonry, round-headed arches, and vaulting inspired by ancient Roman precedent and by the use of stylized ornament — Bridget Cherry.

[French *Romanesque* from *roman* Romance, from Old French *romanz*: see ROMANCE[1]]

Romanesque[2] *adj* relating to the style of architecture called Romanesque.

roman-fleuve /,rohmonh 'fluhv (*French* rɔmã flœv)/ *noun* (*pl* **romans-fleuves** /,rohmonh 'fluhv (*French* rɔmã flœv)/) a novel or series of novels in the form of a long and leisurely chronicle of a family or community; = SAGA (2). [French *roman-fleuve*, literally 'river novel']

Roman holiday *noun* an entertainment at the expense of others' suffering. [from the bloody combats staged as entertainment in ancient Rome]

Romani /'rohmoni/ *noun and adj* (*pl* **Romanis**) see ROMANY.

Romanian *or* **Rumanian** *or* **Roumanian** /roo'mayni·ən, roh-, rə-/ *noun* **1** a native or inhabitant of Romania in E Europe. **2** the Romance language of Romania and Moldova. ➤➤ **Romanian** *adj*.

Romanic /roh'manik/ *noun and adj* = ROMANCE. [Latin *Romanicus*: see ROMANCE[1]]

romanise /'rohmoniez/ *verb trans* see ROMANIZE.

Romanism *noun dated* Roman Catholicism.

Romanist *noun* **1** a specialist in the language, culture, or law of ancient Rome. **2** *chiefly derog* Roman Catholic.

romanize *or* **romanise** /'rohmoniez/ *verb trans* **1** (*often* **Romanize**) formerly, to make (a people or country) Roman; to Latinize (them). **2** to make (somebody) Roman Catholic. **3** to write or print (text, etc) in the roman alphabet or in roman type. ➤➤ **romanization** /-'zaysh(ə)n/ *noun*.

roman law /'rohmən/ *noun* (*also* **Roman law**) the legal system of the ancient Romans, which forms the basis of many modern legal codes.

Roman nose *noun* a nose with a prominent, slightly aquiline bridge.

Roman numeral *noun* a numeral in a system of notation based on the ancient Roman system using the symbols i, v, x, l, c, d, m.

Romano- *comb. form* relating to the Romans or the Roman Empire: *Romano-British*.

romans à clef /,rohmonh a 'klay/ *noun* pl of ROMAN À CLEF.

Romansch *or* **Romansh** /roh'mansh/ *noun* the Rhaeto-Romanic dialects spoken in parts of southern Switzerland. ➤➤ **Romansch** *adj*. [Romansch *rumantsch* from Latin *romanice*: see ROMANCE[1]]

romans-fleuves /,rohmonh 'fluhv/ *noun* pl of ROMAN-FLEUVE.

Romansh /roh'mansh/ *noun* see ROMANSCH.

romantic[1] /roh'mantik, rə-/ *adj* **1a** having an inclination for romance. **b** marked by or constituting strong feeling, *esp* love. **2** consisting of or like a romance. **3** impractical or fantastic in conception or plan. **4** having no basis in real life. **5** (*often* **Romantic**) of or having the characteristics of romanticism. ➤➤ **romantically** *adv*. [French *romantique* from obsolete French *romant* romance, from Old French *romanz*: see ROMANCE[1]]

romantic[2] *noun* **1** a romantic person: *I'm a romantic – a sentimental person thinks things will last – a romantic person hopes against hope that they won't* — F Scott Fitzgerald. **2** (**Romantic**) a Romantic writer, artist, or composer.

romanticise /roh'mantisiez, rə-/ *verb trans and intrans* see ROMANTICIZE.

romanticism /roh'mantisiz(ə)m, rə-/ *noun* (*also* **Romanticism**) a chiefly late 18th- and early 19th-cent. literary, artistic, and philosophical movement that reacted against neoclassicism by emphasizing individual aspirations, nature, the emotions, and the remote and exotic. ➤➤ **romanticist** *noun*.

romanticize *or* **romanticise** /roh'mantisiez, rə-/ *verb trans* to present (a person or incident) in a misleadingly romantic way. ➤ *verb intrans* to hold romantic ideas. ➤➤ **romanticization** /-'zaysh(ə)n/ *noun*.

Romany *or* **Romani** /'rohmoni/ *noun* (*pl* **Romanies** *or* **Romanis**) **1** the Indic language of the gypsies. **2** a gypsy. ➤➤ **Romani** *adj*, **Romany** *adj*.

Word history
Romany *romani* (adj) gypsy, from *rom* gypsy man, from Sanskrit *ḍomba* man of a low caste of musicians. Romany words which have passed into English include *cosh, didicoi, nark, pal*, and *rum* (strange). It is likely that further research would provide evidence that the contribution of Romany to English cant and slang is larger than has been recognized.

Romeo /'rohmioh/ *noun* (*pl* **Romeos**) a romantic male lover. [named after *Romeo*, hero of the play *Romeo and Juliet* by William Shakespeare d.1616, English poet and dramatist]

Romish /'rohmish/ *adj chiefly derog* Roman Catholic.

romp[1] /romp/ *verb intrans* **1** to play in a boisterous manner. **2** *informal* to engage in light-hearted sexual activity. ✳ **romp home** *informal* to win easily. [alteration of RAMP[2] in the senses 'to rear, rage, climb']

romp[2] *noun* **1** boisterous or bawdy entertainment or play. **2** *informal* an effortless winning pace. **3** *informal* a period of light-hearted sexual activity.

rompers *pl noun* a one-piece child's garment combining a top or bib and short trousers.

romper suit *noun* = ROMPERS.

rondavel /ron'dahvl/ *noun SAfr* a circular one-roomed hut in the grounds of a house, used as a guest room or for storage. [Afrikaans *rondawel*]

rondeau /'rondoh/ *noun* (*pl* **rondeaux** /'rondoh(z)/) a 13-line poem in three stanzas with only two rhymes, in which the opening words of the first line are used as a refrain to the second and third stanzas. [early French *rondeau* from Old French *rondel*: see RONDEL]

rondel /'rondl/ *noun* a rondeau usu consisting of 13 lines of eight or ten syllables, in which the first two lines are repeated as a refrain in the middle of the poem and the first line is again repeated as the last line. [Middle English *rondel, rondelle*, from French *rondel*, literally 'small circle', dimin. of *round-, roont*: see ROUND[1]]

rondo /'rondoh/ *noun* (*pl* **rondos**) an instrumental composition, often the last movement in a concerto or sonata, usu having an opening section that recurs in the form ABACADA. [Italian *rondò* from early French *rondeau*, from Old French *rondel*: see RONDEL]

rondo form *noun* a musical form in which the main section is alternated with contrasting sections, thus ABACADA.

rone /rohn/ *noun Scot* a gutter along the eaves of a house to catch and carry rainwater. [perhaps related to *run*]

röntgen *or* **roentgen** /'runtyən, 'rəntyən/ *noun* a unit of ionizing radiation equal to the amount that produces ions of one sign carrying a charge of 2.58×10^{-4} coulomb in 1kg of air. [named after Wilhelm Conrad *Röntgen* d.1923, German physicist, discoverer of X-rays]

röntgenogram *or* **roentgenogram** /'runtyənohgram, 'rən-/ *noun* an X-ray photograph.

röntgenography /runtyə'nogrəfi, rən-/ *noun* photography by means of X-rays. ➤➤ **röntgenographic** /-'grafik/ *adj*, **röntgenographically** /-'grafikli/ *adv*.

röntgenology *or* **roentgenology** /runtyə'noləji, rən-/ *noun* radiology involving the use of X-rays for diagnosis or treatment of disease.

röntgen ray *or* **roentgen ray** *noun* = X-RAY[1].

roo /rooh/ *noun* (*pl* **roos** *or collectively* **roo**) *Aus, informal* a kangaroo.

rood /roohd/ *noun* **1** a cross or crucifix; *specif* a large crucifix on a beam or screen at the entrance to the chancel of a church. **2** *chiefly Brit* a former unit of land area equal to about 1011m² (a quarter of an acre). [Old English *rōd* rod, rood]

roof /roohf/ *noun* (*pl* **roofs**) **1a** the upper rigid cover of a building. **b** a dwelling or home: *Why not … share the same roof* — Virginia Woolf. **2a** the highest point or level. **b** something resembling a roof in form or function. **3** the vaulted or covering part of the mouth, skull, etc. ➤➤ **roofless** *adj.* [Old English *hrōf*]

roof² *verb trans* **1** (*usu in passive*) to cover (something) with or as if with a roof. **2** to serve as a roof over (a building). ➤➤ **roofed** *adj*, **roofer** *noun*, **roofing** *noun.*

roofline *noun* **1** the line formed by the soffits, fascias, and other features below the roof of a building. **2** the shape of the roof of a vehicle.

roof rack *noun chiefly Brit* a metal frame fixed on top of a car roof, for carrying things.

rooftree *noun* = RIDGEPIECE.

rooibos /'roybos/ *noun* **1** a S African evergreen shrub with red leaves, which are used to make a form of tea: genus *Aspalathus*. **2** a S African shrub or tree with red leaves and yellow flowers: genus *Combretum*. [Afrikaans *rooibos*, literally 'red bush']

rooinek /'roynek/ *noun SAfr, chiefly derog or humorous* a British person, *esp* a British immigrant. [Afrikaans *rooinek*, from *rooi* red + *nek* neck]

rook¹ /rook/ *noun* a common Old World bird with black plumage, similar to the related carrion crow but having a bare grey face: *Corvus frugilegus*. [Old English *hrōc*]

rook² *verb trans informal* to defraud (somebody) by cheating them. [ROOK¹ in the archaic senses 'cheat, swindler']

rook³ *noun* in chess, either of two pieces of each colour that have the power to move along the ranks or files across any number of consecutive unoccupied squares; = CASTLE¹ (3). [Middle English *rok* via French from Arabic *rukhkh*, from Persian]

rookery *noun* (*pl* **rookeries**) **1a** the nests, usu built in the upper branches of trees, of a colony of rooks. **b** a breeding ground or haunt of a colony of penguins, seals, etc. **2** a crowded dilapidated tenement or maze of dwellings.

rookie /'rooki/ *noun informal* **1** a recruit, *esp* in the armed forces or the police force. **2** a novice. [alteration of RECRUIT¹]

room¹ /roohm, room/ *noun* **1** an extent of space occupied by, or sufficient or available for, something: *There's room for another person on the couch*. **2a** a partitioned part of the inside of a building. **b** (*also in pl*) a set of rooms used as a separate lodging. **3** (+ *for*) suitable or fit occasion for (something); opportunity for (something): *Your work is good, but there's room for improvement*. ➤➤ **roomful** (*pl* **roomfuls**) *noun.* [Old English *rūm*]

room² *verb intrans NAmer* (*often* + with) to occupy a room or rooms, often paying rent; to share lodgings: *Julie rooms with her friend Rachael.*

roomed *adj* (*used in combinations*) containing rooms of the number or kind specified: *a six-roomed house.*

roomer /'roohmə/ *noun NAmer* a lodger: *Why, I'll build me a little house and take me a couple of roomers* — Harper Lee.

roomie /'roohmi/ *noun chiefly NAmer, informal* a roommate.

rooming house /'roohming hows/ *noun chiefly NAmer* a lodging house.

roommate /'roohmmayt/ *noun* **1** any of two or more people sharing the same room, e.g. in a university hall of residence. **2** *NAmer* a flatmate.

room service *noun* the facility by which a hotel guest can have food, drinks, etc brought to their room.

roomy /'roohmi/ *adj* (**roomier, roomiest**) having ample room; spacious. ➤➤ **roomily** *adv*, **roominess** *noun.*

roost¹ /roohst/ *noun* a support or place where birds roost. [Old English *hrōst*]

roost² *verb intrans* said of a bird or bat: to settle down for rest or sleep; to perch.

rooster *noun chiefly NAmer* the adult male of the domestic fowl; = COCK¹ (IA).

root¹ /rooht/ *noun* **1a** the underground part of a flowering plant that anchors and supports it and absorbs and stores food. **b** a fleshy and edible root, bulb, or tuber, e.g. a carrot or turnip. **2a** the end

of a nerve nearest the brain and spinal cord. **b** the part of a tooth, hair, the tongue, etc by which it is attached to the body. **3a** something that is an underlying cause or basis, e.g. of a condition or quality. **b** *archaic* in e.g. the Authorized Version of the Bible, an ancestor or progenitor. **c** the essential core, the heart. **d** (*in pl*) a feeling of belonging established through close familiarity or family ties with a particular place: *roots in Scotland.* **4** in grammar, the base element from which a word is derived. **5** the tone from the overtones of which a chord is composed; the lowest note of a chord in normal position. **6a** a number which produces a given number when taken an indicated number of times as a factor: *Two is the fourth root of 16.* **b** a number that satisfies an equation to an identity when it is substituted for the variable. **7** *Aus, NZ, coarse slang* an act of sexual intercourse. ✷ **take root 1** said of a plant: to become rooted. **2** to become fixed or established. ➤➤ **rootlet** /'roohtlit/ *noun*, **rootlike** *adj*, **rooty** *adj.* [Old English *rōt* from Old Norse *rót*]

root² *verb trans* **1** to enable (a plant) to develop roots. **2** to fix or implant (somebody) as if by roots: *rooted to the spot with fear.* **3** *Aus, NZ, coarse slang* to have sexual intercourse with (somebody). ➤ *verb intrans* said of a plant: to grow roots or take root. ✷ **be rooted in** to originate or have developed from (something). ➤➤ **rooted** *adj*, **rootedness** *noun.*

root³ *verb intrans* **1** said of a pig: to dig with the snout. **2** (+ about/in) to poke or dig about in something; to search unsystematically for something. [Old English *wrōtan*]

root⁴ *verb intrans informal* (+ for) to lend vociferous or enthusiastic support to (somebody or something). ➤➤ **rooter** *noun.* [perhaps alteration of Scots or northern English dialect *rout* to bellow, from Old Norse *rauta*]

root and branch *adv* so as to leave no remnant; completely. ➤➤ **root-and-branch** *adj.* [from Malachi 4:1 '… all that do wickedly shall be stubble, and the day that cometh shall burn them up … it shall leave them neither root nor branch']

root beer *noun chiefly NAmer* a sweetened effervescent drink flavoured with extracts of roots and herbs.

root canal *noun* the part of the central cavity of a tooth, containing blood vessels and nerves, lying in the root of a tooth.

root crop *noun* a crop, e.g. turnips or sugar beet, grown for its enlarged roots.

root ginger *noun* = GINGER (IC).

rootle /'roohtl/ *verb intrans Brit, informal* = ROOT³. [frequentative of ROOT³]

rootless *adj* said of a person: not being tied, e.g. by family commitments, to a particular place. ➤➤ **rootlessness** *noun.*

root-mean-square *noun* the square root of the arithmetic mean of the squares of a set of numbers.

root nodule *noun* a bacteria-containing swelling on a plant root; = NODULE (3).

root out *verb trans* to get rid of or destroy (somebody or something) completely.

roots music *noun* popular music inspired by local folk and traditional music.

rootstock *noun* **1** an underground plant part formed from several stems. **2a** a stock for grafting consisting of a piece of root. **b** a plant or plant part consisting of roots and lower trunk onto which a scion is grafted. **c** a plant from which cuttings are taken.

root vegetable *noun* a ROOT CROP or the edible root of such a crop.

ropable /rohpəbl/ *adj* see ROPEABLE.

rope¹ /rohp/ *noun* **1a** a strong thick cord composed of strands of fibres or wire twisted or braided together. **b** a long slender strip of material resembling or used like rope. **c** (**the rope**) execution by hanging. **2** a row or string consisting of things united by or as if by braiding, twining, or threading: *a rope of pearls.* **3** (**the ropes**) methods or procedures: *The boss asked me to show the new girl the ropes.* ✷ **on the ropes 1** in boxing, having been forced against the ropes that enclose the ring. **2** close to defeat. [Old English *rāp*]

rope² *verb trans* **1a** to bind, fasten, or tie (something or somebody) with a rope. **b** to catch (e.g. cattle) with a lasso. **2** (*usu* + off) to enclose, separate, or divide (something) by a rope. **3** to connect (a party of climbers) with a rope. ➤ *verb intrans* **1** said of a party of climbers: to put on a rope for climbing. **2** (+ down/up) to climb down or up.

ropeable or **ropable** /'rohpəbl/ adj 1 able to be roped. 2 Aus, informal violently angry. [(sense 2) from the notion of an angry person needing to be restrained by tying with ropes]

rope in verb trans to enlist (somebody, esp somebody reluctant) in a group or activity.

rope ladder noun a ladder having rope sides and rope, wood, or metal rungs.

rope's end noun formerly, a piece of rope used for flogging, esp in the navy.

ropewalk noun formerly, a long covered area where ropes were made.

ropewalker noun dated an acrobat who walks along a rope high in the air.

ropeway noun an endless aerial cable moved by a stationary engine and used to transport goods, e.g. logs and ore.

ropy or **ropey** /'rohpi/ adj (**ropier, ropiest**) 1 like rope in texture or appearance. 2 Brit, informal. a of poor quality; shoddy. b somewhat unwell. 3a gelatinous or slimy from bacterial or fungal contamination: ropy milk; ropy flour. b capable of being drawn out into a thread. ➤➤ **ropiness** noun.

Roquefort /'rok(ə)faw/ noun trademark a strong-flavoured crumbly French cheese with bluish green veins, made from the curds of ewes' milk. [named after Roquefort, village in SW France, where it is made]

roquet[1] /'rohkay/ verb trans and intrans (**roqueted, roqueting**) said of a croquet ball or the player who strikes it: to hit (another ball). [prob alteration of CROQUET[2]]

roquet[2] noun the act or an instance of roqueting.

ro-ro /'rohroh/ adj roll-on roll-off.

rorqual /'rawkwəl/ noun any of several species of large whalebone whales with the skin of the throat marked with deep longitudinal furrows: family Balaenopteridae. [French rorqual via Norwegian from Old Norse reytharhvalr, from reythr rorqual + hvalr whale]

Rorschach test /'rawshahk, 'rawshahkh/ noun a personality test based on the interpretation of a person's reactions to a set of standard inkblot designs. [named after Hermann Rorschach d.1922, Swiss psychiatrist, who devised it]

rort[1] /rawt/ noun Aus, informal 1 a fraud or swindle. 2 a boisterous social gathering. [origin unknown]

rort[2] verb intrans Aus, informal 1 to swindle. 2 to roister. ➤ verb trans Aus, informal = RIG[3]. ➤➤ **rorter** noun.

rosace /'rohzays/ noun 1 a rose window. 2 a rosette. [French rosace from Latin rosaceus, from rosa ROSE[1]]

rosacea /roh'zayshi·ə/ noun a disorder of the skin of the face in which blood vessels enlarge, so giving the face a flushed rosy appearance.

rosaceous /roh'zayshəs/ adj of or belonging to the rose family. [Latin rosa ROSE[1] + -ACEOUS]

rosaniline /roh'zanilin, -lien/ noun an organic chemical compound from which many dyes are derived. [Latin rosa ROSE[1] + ANILINE]

rosaria /roh'zeəri·ə/ noun pl of ROSARIUM.

rosarian /roh'zeəri·ən/ noun somebody who specializes in the cultivation of roses.

rosarium /roh'zeəri·əm/ noun (pl **rosariums** or **rosaria** /-ri·ə/) formal a rose garden. [Latin rosarium: see ROSARY]

rosary /'rohz(ə)ri/ noun (pl **rosaries**) 1 a series of prayers in Roman Catholicism. 2 a string of beads used in counting the prayers of the rosary while they are being recited. [medieval Latin from Latin rosarium rose garden, neuter of rosarius of roses, from rosa ROSE[1]]

rose[1] /rohz/ noun 1a a widely cultivated prickly shrub: genus Rosa. b the showy fragrant flower of this shrub. c a roselike flowering plant, e.g. a Christmas rose. 2 something resembling a rose in form, e.g.: a a circular design, e.g. on a lute. b a perforated outlet for water, e.g. from a shower or watering can. c a circular fitting that anchors the flex of a light bulb to a ceiling. d the form of a gem, esp a diamond, with a flat base and triangular facets rising to a point. 3 a pale to dark pinkish colour. ✳ **under the rose** archaic = SUB ROSA. ➤➤ **roselike** adj. [Old English rōse and Old French rose, both ultimately from Latin rosa]

rose[2] adj 1a of, containing, or used for roses. b flavoured, sweetly scented, or coloured with or like roses. 2 of the colour rose.

rose[3] verb past tense of RISE[1].

rosé /'rohzay/ noun a light pink table wine made from red grapes by removing the skins after fermentation has begun. [French rosé pink, from Old French rose: see ROSE[1]]

roseate /'rohzi·ət/ adj 1 resembling a rose, esp in colour. 2 marked by unrealistic optimism. [Latin roseus rosy, from rosa ROSE[1]]

rosebay noun 1 = ROSEBAY WILLOWHERB. 2 an azalea of N America: Rhododendron lapponicum. [ROSE[1] + BAY[3]]

rosebay willowherb /'wilohhuhb/ noun a tall Eurasian and N American plant of the evening primrose family with long spikes of pinkish purple flowers: Epilobium angustifolium.

rosebud noun 1 the bud of a rose. 2 Brit, dated a pretty girl or young woman.

rose chafer noun a metallic green European beetle that feeds on rose leaves and flowers as an adult: Cetonia aurata.

rose-coloured adj of a pale to dark pinkish colour. ✳ **look/ see/etc through rose-coloured glasses/spectacles** to view (a person, situation, etc) in an overoptimistic unrealistic light.

rose-cut adj said of gems, esp diamonds: cut with a flat circular base and triangular facets rising to a point.

rosehip noun see HIP[2].

rosella /roh'zelə/ noun any of several species of brightly coloured parakeets of Australia: genus Platycercus. [irreg from Rosehill, district of SE Australia, where the bird was first seen]

rose mallow noun a hibiscus with large rose-coloured flowers: genus Hibiscus.

rosemary /'rohzməri/ noun a fragrant shrubby Eurasian plant the leaves of which are used as a cooking herb: Rosmarinus officinalis: There's rosemary, that's for remembrance — Shakespeare.

Word history

Middle English rosmarine from Latin rosmarinus, from ror-, ros dew + marinus of the sea, perhaps because of its small blue flowers. The change in spelling came about by association with ROSE[1] and the name Mary, either from or giving rise to the legend that the Virgin Mary washed her robe and hung it on a rosemary bush to dry; the dye ran and coloured the flowers.

rose of Sharon /'sharən/ noun a Eurasian Saint-John's-wort often grown for its large yellow flowers: Hypericum calycinum. [named after the Plain of Sharon, region in Palestine]

roseola /roh'zee·ələ/ noun a rash of pink spots occurring in German measles or a similar virus disease, esp of children. ➤➤ **roseolar** adj. [scientific Latin roseola from Latin roseus rosy, from rosa ROSE[1]]

rose-tinted adj = ROSE-COLOURED.

rosette /roh'zet/ noun 1 an ornament usu made of material gathered so as to resemble a rose and worn as a badge, trophy, or trimming. 2 a stylized carved or moulded rose used as a decorative motif in architecture. 3 a cluster of leaves in crowded circles or spirals, e.g. in the dandelion. [French rosette small rose, from Old French rose: see ROSE[1]]

rose water noun a solution of rose oils in water, used as a perfume.

rose window noun a circular window filled with tracery radiating from its centre.

rosewood noun 1 any of several species of leguminous tropical trees: genus Dalbergia. 2 the valuable dark red or purplish wood of this tree, streaked and variegated with black.

Rosh Hashanah or **Rosh Hashana** /,rosh hə'shahnə/ noun the Jewish New Year. [Late Hebrew rōsh hashshānāh, literally 'beginning of the year']

Rosicrucian /rozi'kroohsh(ə)n/ noun an adherent or member of any of various organizations derived from a 17th- and 18th-cent. movement devoted to occult or esoteric wisdom. ➤➤ **Rosicrucian** adj, **Rosicrucianism** noun. [from Rosa Crucis, Latinized form of the name of Christian Rosenkreuz, reputed 15th-cent. founder of the movement]

rosin[1] /'rozin/ noun a translucent resin that is the residue from the distillation of turpentine, used in making varnish and soldering flux and for rubbing on violin bows. ➤➤ **rosiny** adj. [Middle English, modification of early French resine: see RESIN[1]]

rosin[2] verb trans (**rosined, rosining**) to rub or treat (the bow of a violin, etc) with rosin.

RoSPA /'rospə/ abbr Brit Royal Society for the Prevention of Accidents.

roster[1] /'rostə/ *noun* **1** a list or register giving the order in which personnel are to perform a duty, go on leave, etc. **2** an itemized list, *esp* of people available for a particular task or duty. [Dutch *rooster* list, literally 'gridiron', from *roosten* to roast; from the parallel lines in which it is written]

roster[2] *verb trans* (**rostered, rostering**) (*usu in passive*) to place (somebody or something) on a roster.

rösti /'rosti, 'ruhsti/ *noun* a Swiss dish of grated potato, and sometimes onion, formed into a cake and fried. [Swiss German *Rösti*]

rostrum /'rostrəm/ *noun* (*pl* **rostra** /'rostrə/ *or* **rostrums**) **1a** a stage for public speaking. **b** a raised platform on a stage. **c** a platform supporting a film or television camera. **2** a body part, e.g. an insect's snout or beak, shaped like a bird's bill. ➤➤ **rostral** *adj*.

Word history
Latin *rostrum* beak, ship's beak, from *rodere* to gnaw. The word, in the plural *rostra*, was originally applied to a platform for public speakers in the forum in Rome, which was decorated with the beaks of captured ships.

rosy /'rohzi/ *adj* (**rosier, rosiest**) **1a** rose-pink. **b** (*often in combination*) having a rosy complexion: *rosy-cheeked youngsters*. **2** characterized by or encouraging optimism: *a rosy future*. ➤➤ **rosily** *adv*, **rosiness** *noun*.

rot[1] /rot/ *verb* (**rotted, rotting**) ➤ *verb intrans* **1** to undergo decomposition, *esp* from the action of bacteria or fungi. **2a** to go to ruin. **b** to become morally corrupt. ➤ *verb trans* to cause (something) to decompose or deteriorate. [Old English *rotian*]

rot[2] *noun* **1a** the state of rotting or being rotten; decay. **b** something rotting or rotten. **c** = DRY ROT. **d** = WET ROT. **2** any of several plant or animal diseases, *esp* of sheep, that cause breakdown and death of tissues. **3** *informal* nonsense or rubbish: *You're talking rot*.

rota /'rohtə/ *noun* **1** *chiefly Brit* a list specifying a fixed order of rotation, e.g. of people or duties. **2** (**the Rota**) a tribunal of the governing body of the Roman Catholic Church (papal CURIA). [Latin *rota* wheel]

Rotarian[1] /roh'teəri·ən/ *noun* a member of a Rotary Club.

Rotarian[2] *adj* relating to Rotarians, Rotary Clubs, or Rotary International.

rotary[1] /'roht(ə)ri/ *adj* **1a** turning on an axis like a wheel. **b** proceeding about an axis: *rotary motion*. **2** having a principal part that turns on an axis. **3** characterized by rotation. **4** denoting a printing press using a rotating curved printing surface. [medieval Latin *rotarius* from Latin *rota* wheel]

rotary[2] *noun* (*pl* **rotaries**) **1** a rotary machine. **2** *NAmer* a traffic roundabout.

Rotary Club *noun* a club belonging to Rotary International, an organization of business and professional men and women devoted to serving the community and advancing world peace. [so named because meetings were orig held in members' offices in rotation]

rotary press *noun* a printing press that prints from curved plates on a revolving cylinder onto paper pressed against them by another revolving cylinder, e.g. as used for printing newspapers on paper fed from large rolls.

rotate[1] /roh'tayt/ *verb intrans* **1** to turn about an axis or a centre; to revolve. **2a** to take turns at performing an act or operation. **b** to perform an ordered series of actions or functions. ➤ *verb trans* **1** to cause (something) to turn about an axis or centre. **2a** to order (something) in a recurring sequence. **b** to cause (a crop or crops) to grow in rotation. **c** to exchange (individuals or units) with others. ➤➤ **rotatable** *adj*, **rotative** /'rohtətiv/ *adj*, **rotatory** /'rohtət(ə)ri, roh'tayt(ə)ri/ *adj*. [Latin *rotatus*, past part. of *rotare*, from *rota* wheel]

rotate[2] /'rohtayt/ *adj* said of a flower: having petals or sepals radiating like the spokes of a wheel. [Latin *rota* wheel]

rotation /roh'taysh(ə)n/ *noun* **1** the act or an instance of rotating, or being rotated on or as if on an axis or centre. **2a** the act or an instance of rotating something. **b** one complete turn; the angular displacement required to return a rotating body or figure to its original orientation. **3a** recurrence in a regular series. **b** the growing of different crops in succession in one field, usu in a regular sequence. **4** the turning of a limb about its long axis. ➤➤ **rotational** *adj*.

rotator *noun* something that rotates or causes rotation, e.g.: **a** a muscle that partially rotates a body part on its axis. **b** a rotating planet or galaxy.

rotavator *or* **rotovator** /'rohtəvaytə/ *noun trademark* an implement with blades or claws that revolve rapidly and till or break up the soil. [contraction of *rotary cultivator*]

ROTC *abbr NAmer* Reserve Officers' Training Corps.

rote /roht/ *noun* the mechanical use of the memory: *He learned the speech by rote*. [Middle English, in the sense 'habit, custom'; earlier history unknown]

rotenone /'rohtinohn/ *noun* an insecticide extracted from the roots of various tropical plants, *esp* those of genera *Derris* and *Lonchocarpus*. [Japanese *roten* derris + -ONE]

rotgut *noun informal* alcoholic spirits of low quality.

roti /'rohti/ *noun* (*pl* **rotis**) in Indian cookery, a flat cake of unleavened bread. [Hindi *roti*]

rotifer /'rohtifə/ *noun* any of a phylum of minute aquatic invertebrate animals with circles of cilia at the front that look like rapidly revolving wheels: phylum Rotifera. [Latin *rota* wheel + -FER]

rotisserie /roh'tisəri, roh'tees-/ *noun* **1** a restaurant specializing in roast and barbecued meats. **2** an appliance fitted with a spit on which food is cooked. [French *rôtisserie*, from early French *rostisserie*, from *rostir* to roast, of Germanic origin]

rotogravure /ˌrohtohgrə'vyooə/ *noun* a type of photogravure in which the impression is produced by a rotary press. [Latin *rota* wheel + -O- + GRAVURE]

rotor /'rohtə/ *noun* **1** a part that revolves in a machine, *esp* the rotating member of an electrical machine. **2** a complete system of more or less horizontal blades that supplies all or nearly all the force supporting an aircraft, e.g. a helicopter, in flight. [contraction of ROTATOR]

rotovator /'rohtəvaytə/ *noun* see ROTAVATOR.

rotten[1] /'rot(ə)n/ *adj* **1** having rotted; putrid. **2** morally or politically corrupt: *The system is rotten through and through*. **3a** *informal* extremely unpleasant: *I've had a rotten day at work*. **b** unhappy; ashamed: *I felt rotten about having to lie to her*. **c** inferior; useless; not good: *That was a rotten idea!* **d** suffering or marked by illness or discomfort: *I felt rotten after eating that curry*. ➤➤ **rottenly** *adv*, **rottenness** *noun*. [Middle English *roten* from Old Norse *rotinn*]

rotten[2] *adv informal* very much: *She fancies him rotten*.

rotten borough *noun* said *esp* of certain English constituencies before 1832: an election district with very few voters.

rottenstone *noun* a much-weathered limestone rich in silica, used for polishing.

rotter /'rotə/ *noun informal, dated* a thoroughly objectionable person.

rottweiler /'rotvielə, 'rotwielə/ *noun* a tall strongly-built black-and-tan dog with short hair. [German *Rottweiler* from *Rottweil*, town in SW Germany]

rotund /rə'tund/ *adj* **1** markedly plump. **2** rounded. **3** high-flown or sonorous. ➤➤ **rotundity** *noun*, **rotundly** *adv*. [Latin *rotundus*, from *rotare*: see ROTATE[1]]

rotunda /rə'tundə/ *noun* (*pl* **rotundas**) a round building, *esp* one covered by a dome. [Italian *rotonda* from Latin *rotunda*, fem of *rotundus*: see ROTUND]

ROU *abbr* Republic of Uruguay (international vehicle registration).

rouble *or* **ruble** /'roohbl/ *noun* the basic monetary unit of Russia, Belarus, and Tajikistan. [Russian *rubl'*]

roué /'rooh·ay/ *noun* a debauched man, *esp* one past his prime: *I knew him for a young roué of a vicomte – a brainless and vicious youth* — Charlotte Brontë.

Word history
French *roué*, literally 'broken on the wheel', past part. of *rouer* to break on the wheel (see WHEEL[1] (6)), ultimately from Latin *rotare* to rotate. The implication is that such a person deserves this punishment.

rouge[1] /roohzh/ *noun* **1** a red cosmetic, *esp* for the cheeks. **2** ferric oxide as a red powder, used as a pigment and in polishing glass, metal, or gems. [French *rouge*, literally 'red', from Latin *rubeus* reddish]

rouge[2] *verb trans* to apply rouge to (the cheeks or lips).

rough[1] /ruf/ *adj* **1** having an irregular or uneven surface, e.g.: **a** not smooth. **b** covered with or made up of coarse hair. **c** said of terrain: covered with boulders, bushes, etc. **2a** said of the weather, etc: turbulent, stormy. **b** harsh, violent. **c** requiring strenuous effort: *I've had a rough day*. **d** (*often* + on) unfortunate and hard to bear: *His illness is rather rough on his wife*. **3** coarse or rugged in character or appearance, e.g.: **a** said of a voice: harsh to the ear. **b** crude in style or expression. **c** ill-mannered; uncouth. **4a** crude; unfinished. **b** executed hastily or approximately: *a rough draft.* **5** *Brit, informal* ill or exhausted, *esp* through lack of sleep or heavy drinking: *I felt rough after staying up all night.* ✳ **the rough edge/side of somebody's tongue** *informal* harsh words; a scolding. ➤➤ **roughish** *adj,* **roughness** *noun.* [Old English *rūh*]

rough² *noun* **1** *chiefly Brit, informal* a hooligan or ruffian. **2** (**the rough**) uneven ground covered with high grass, brush, and stones; *specif* such ground bordering a golf fairway. **3a** a quick preliminary drawing or layout. **b** something, *esp* written or illustrated, in a crude or preliminary state. **c** broad outline. **4** (**the rough**) the rugged or disagreeable side or aspect: *You have to take the rough with the smooth.*

rough³ *adv Brit* in want of material comforts; without proper lodging: *He's been sleeping rough.*

rough⁴ *verb trans* to roughen (something). ✳ **rough it** *informal* to live in uncomfortable or primitive conditions.

roughage /'rufij/ *noun* coarse bulky food, e.g. bran, that is relatively high in fibre and low in digestible nutrients and that by its bulk stimulates intestinal peristalsis.

rough-and-ready *adj* **1** said of a method, etc: crudely or hastily constructed or conceived; makeshift. **2** said of a person: uncouth or unsophisticated.

rough-and-tumble¹ *noun* disorderly unrestrained fighting or physical play.

rough-and-tumble² *adj* **1** disorderly and unrestrained. **2** rough, rowdy, or disorganized.

roughcast¹ /'rufkahst/ *noun* a plaster of lime mixed with shells or pebbles used for covering buildings: *Some man or other must present Wall; and let him have some plaster, or some loam, or some rough-cast about him, to signify wall* — Shakespeare.

roughcast² *verb trans* (*past tense and past part.* **roughcast**) to plaster (a wall) with roughcast.

rough cut *noun* a print of a film after only preliminary editing.

rough diamond *noun* **1** an uncut diamond. **2** a person without social graces but of an upright or amiable nature.

rough-dry¹ *adj* said of laundry: dried but not ironed or pressed.

rough-dry² *verb trans* (**rough-dries, rough-dried, rough-drying**) to dry (laundry) without ironing or pressing it.

roughen *verb* (**roughened, roughening**) ➤ *verb trans* to make (something) rough. ➤ *verb intrans* to become rough.

rough-hew *verb trans* (*past part.* **rough-hewed** or **rough-hewn** /hjoohn/) to hew (timber or stone) coarsely without smoothing or finishing.

rough-hewn *adj* said of a person: lacking refinement.

roughhouse¹ /'rufhows/ *noun chiefly NAmer, informal* an instance of brawling or excessively boisterous play.

roughhouse² *verb intrans* to engage in a roughhouse. ➤ *verb trans informal* to treat (somebody) in a boisterously rough manner.

roughly *adv* **1a** with insolence or violence. **b** in primitive fashion; crudely. **2** without claim to completeness or exactness; approximately.

roughneck *noun* **1** *informal* a ruffian or tough. **2** a worker who handles the heavy drilling equipment of an oil rig.

rough out *verb trans* **1** to shape or plan (a sketch, etc) in a preliminary way. **2** to outline (a plan, etc).

roughrider *noun* a person who is accustomed to riding unbroken or little-trained horses.

roughshod ✳ **ride roughshod over** to treat (a person or their rights) forcefully and without justice or consideration.

rough shooting *noun* the sport of shooting game, e.g. pigeons or rabbits, on unprepared ground with no beaters.

rough stuff *noun informal* violent behaviour; violence.

rough trade *noun informal* **1** male homosexual prostitution involving violence or brutality. **2** male homosexuals, *esp* prostitutes, who engage in such acts.

rough up *verb trans informal* to beat (somebody) up.

roulade /rooh'lahd/ *noun* **1** a roll of food, e.g. a rolled and cooked slice of stuffed meat or a pudding consisting of a roll of sponge and cream. **2** an elaborate vocal embellishment sung to one syllable.

[French *roulade*, literally 'act of rolling', from *rouler* to roll, from Old French *roller*: see ROLL¹]

rouleau /'roohloh/ *noun* (*pl* **rouleaux** or **rouleaus** /'roohlohz/) **1** a little roll, *esp* a roll of coins in paper. **2** a decorative piping or rolled strip used as a trimming. [French *rouleau*, dimin. of *roule* roll, from Old French *rolle*: see ROLL²]

roulette¹ /rooh'let/ *noun* **1** a gambling game in which players bet on which compartment of a revolving wheel a small ball will come to rest in. **2** a toothed wheel or disc, e.g. for producing rows of dots on engraved plates or for perforating paper. [French *roulette* small wheel, ultimately from late Latin *rotella*, dimin. of Latin *rota* wheel]

roulette² *verb trans* to mark or perforate (paper, etc) with a roulette.

Roumanian /roo'mayni·ən/ *noun and adj* see ROMANIAN.

round¹ /rownd/ *adj* **1a** having every part of the surface or circumference equidistant from the centre. **b** cylindrical: *a round peg.* **c** approximately round: *a round face.* **2** well filled out; plump: *round cheeks.* **3a** moving in or forming a ring or circle. **b** following a roughly circular route: *a round tour of the Cotswolds.* **4a** complete, full: *a round dozen.* **b** said of a number: approximately correct, *esp* exact only to a specific decimal. **c** *archaic* substantial in amount: *a good round sum.* **d** said of pace: brisk. **5** direct in expression: *a round oath.* **6a** said of a voice: having full resonance or tone. **b** said of a vowel: pronounced with rounded lips; labialized. **7** presented with lifelike fullness. ➤➤ **roundish** *adj,* **roundness** *noun.* [Middle English from Old French *round-, roont* from Latin *rotundus,* from *rotare*: see ROTATE¹]

round² *adv chiefly Brit* **1a** in a circular or curved path. **b** with revolving or rotating motion: *The wheels go round.* **c** in circumference: *a tree five feet round.* **d** in, along, or through a circuitous or indirect route: *The road goes round by the lake.* **e** in an encircling position: *a field with a fence all round.* **2a** in close from all sides so as to surround: *The children crowded round.* **b** near; about. **c** here and there in various places. **3a** in rotation or recurrence: *Your birthday will soon be round again.* **b** from beginning to end; through: *all year round.* **c** in or to the other or a specified direction: *Turn round; Try to talk her round.* **d** back to consciousness or awareness; = TO² (3). **e** in the specified order or relationship: *She got the story the wrong way round.* **4** about, approximately: *round 1900.* **5** to a particular person or place: *I invited them round for drinks.* ✳ **round about 1** approximately; more or less. **2** in a ring round; on all sides of.

Usage note

round, around, *or* about? See note at AROUND¹.

round³ *prep chiefly Brit* **1a** so as to revolve or progress about (a centre). **b** so as to encircle or enclose (something): *We were all seated round the table.* **c** so as to avoid or get past (something); beyond the obstacle of (something): *We got round his objections.* **d** in a position on the other side of: *She lives just round the corner.* **e** near to (something); about (something): *She looked round her.* **2a** in all directions outwards from (something or somebody): *She looked round her.* **b** here and there in or throughout: *I want to travel round Europe.* **3** so as to have a centre or basis in: *Rotary International is a movement organized round the idea of service.*

round⁴ *noun* ✳ **go/make the round(s)** to be passed from person to person: *There's a story going the rounds that the factory's going to be shut down.* **in the round 1** in full sculptured form unattached to a background. **2** with a central stage surrounded by an audience: *theatre in the round.* **3a** something round, e.g. a circle, curve, or ring. **b** a circle of people or things. **4** a rounded or curved part. **5a** a circling or circuitous path or course. **b** motion in a circle or a curving path. **6a** a route or assigned territory habitually traversed, e.g. by a paper boy or police officer. **b** (*usu in pl*) a series of visits made by a general practitioner to patients in their homes. **c** (*usu in pl*) a series of visits made by a hospital doctor to the patients under their care: *She doesn't like to be interrupted when she's making her rounds.* **d** (*usu in pl*) a series of customary social calls: *She's been doing the rounds of her friends.* **7** one of a recurring sequence of actions or events: *a round of talks.* **8** a fixed succession of actions, etc that recur over a period of time: *That's all part of my daily round.* **9a** any of a series of units of action in a game or sport, e.g. covering a prescribed time or distance, or allowing each player one turn. **b** a division of a tournament in which each contestant plays one other. **c** the action of playing all the holes of a golf course or putting green once. **10** an unaccompanied canon sung in unison or at the octave in which the parts are identical. **11** a set of drinks served at one time to each person in a group. **12a** *Brit* a single slice of bread or toast. **b** a sandwich made with two whole slices of bread. **c** a cut of beef between the rump and the lower leg. **13a** a single shot from a gun, or from each of a number of guns. **b** a unit of ammunition consisting of the parts necessary to fire one shot. **14** a prolonged burst, e.g. of applause.

round[5] *verb trans* **1** to go round (a bend or corner): *The ship rounded the headland.* **2** to encircle or encompass (something). **3** (*often* + *off/ up/down*) to express (a figure) as a round number: *11.3572 rounded off to three decimal places becomes 11.357.* **4a** to make (something) round or rounded. **b** to make (the lips) round and protruded. **c** to produce (a vowel) with rounded lips; to labialize (it). **5** (*often* + *off/ out*) to bring (something) to completion or perfection. ➤ *verb intrans* **1a** to become round, plump, or smooth in outline. **b** (+ *off/ out*) to reach fullness or completion. **2** to follow a winding or circular course: *They were rounding into the home stretch.*

roundabout[1] *noun* **1** a road junction formed round a central island about which traffic moves in one direction only, or a paved or planted circle in the middle of this. **2** *Brit.* **a** a merry-go-round. **b** a rotatable platform that is an amusement in a children's playground.

roundabout[2] *adj* circuitous; indirect.

round dance *noun* **1** a folk dance in which participants form a ring. **2** a ballroom dance in which couples progress round the room.

rounded *adj* **1** made round; smoothly curved. **2** fully developed; mature.

roundel /'rowndl/ *noun* **1** a round figure or object, e.g.: **a** a circular panel, window, etc. **b** a circular mark identifying the nationality of an aircraft, *esp* a warplane. **2** an English modification of the rondeau. [Middle English from Old French *rondel*, from *round-, roont*: see ROUND[1]]

roundelay /'rowndilay/ *noun literary* **1** a simple song with a refrain. **2** a poem with a refrain recurring frequently or at fixed intervals. [modification of early French *rondelet*, dimin. of Old French *rondel*: see ROUNDEL]

rounders *pl noun* (*treated as sing.*) a field game between two teams with bat and ball that resembles baseball, where players try to score 'rounders' by running round all four bases before the ball is fielded. [so called because the batter tries to score a *rounder* by running round all the bases before the ball is returned to the bowler]

Roundhead *noun* an adherent of Parliament in the English Civil War. [from the short-cropped hair of some of the Parliamentarians]

roundhouse /'rowndhows/ *noun* **1** a circular building for housing and repairing locomotives. **2** *informal* a blow in boxing delivered with a wide swing. **3** formerly, a cabin or apartment on the after part of a quarterdeck.

roundly *adv* **1a** in a blunt or severe manner: *She roundly rebuked him.* **b** thoroughly. **2** in a round or circular form or manner.

round on *verb trans* to turn against (somebody) and attack them, *esp* to suddenly scold (somebody).

round robin *noun* **1** a tournament in which every contestant plays every other contestant in turn. **2** a written petition or protest, *esp* one on which the signatures are arranged in a circle so that no name heads the list. [prob from the name *Robin*]

round-shouldered *adj* having stooping or rounded shoulders: compare SQUARE-SHOULDERED.

roundsman *noun* (*pl* **roundsmen**) **1** *Brit* somebody, e.g. a milkman, who takes, orders, sells, or delivers goods on an assigned route. **2** *Aus, NZ* a journalist covering a particular subject.

round table *noun* a meeting or conference of several people on equal terms. ➤➤ **round-table** *adj*.

round-the-clock *adj* lasting or continuing 24 hours a day; constant.

round trip *noun* a trip to a place and back, usu over the same route.

roundup *noun* **1a** the collecting in of cattle by riding round them and driving them. **b** a gathering in of scattered people or things. **2** a summary of information, e.g. from news bulletins.

round up *verb trans* **1** to collect (cattle) by a roundup. **2** to gather in or bring together (people or things) from various quarters.

roundworm *noun* = NEMATODE.

roup[1] /roohp/ *noun* a virus disease of poultry in which soft whitish lesions form on the mouth, throat, and eyes. [origin unknown]

roup[2] /rowp/ *noun chiefly Scot, N Eng* an auction.

roup[3] *verb trans chiefly Scot, N Eng* to sell (something) by auction. [Middle English, in the senses 'to roar, croak'; of Scandinavian origin]

rouse /rowz/ *verb trans* **1** to arouse (somebody) from sleep or apathy. **2** to stir up (somebody's curiosity); to provoke (it). ➤ *verb intrans* **1** to become stirred. ➤➤ **rouser** *noun*. [Middle English *rousen*; earlier history unknown]

rouseabout /'rowsəbowt/ *noun Aus, NZ* a handyman on a sheep farm; a labourer.

rousing *adj* giving rise to enthusiasm; stirring. ➤➤ **rousingly** *adv.*

roust /rowst/ *verb trans* **1** to rouse (somebody), *esp* out of bed. **2** *NAmer, informal* to treat (somebody) roughly. [perhaps by alteration of ROUSE]

roustabout /'rowstəbowt/ *noun* an unskilled or semiskilled labourer, *esp* in an oilfield or refinery. [ROUST]

rout[1] /rowt/ *noun* **1** a state of wild confusion; *specif* a confused retreat; headlong flight. **2** a disastrous defeat. [early French *route* dispersal, troop, defeat, prob via Italian from Latin *rupta*: see ROUTE[1]]

rout[2] *verb trans* **1** to defeat (an army, team, etc) decisively or disastrously. **2** to put (an army) to headlong flight.

rout[3] *noun archaic* **1** a disorderly crowd of people; a mob. **2** a fashionable social gathering: *He was obliged to go … to Lady Harrington's before he came, it being her Rout Day* — Fanny Burney. [Middle English *route* via French from Latin *rupta*: see ROUTE[1]]

rout[4] *verb trans* to gouge out or make a furrow in (a surface). ➤ *verb intrans* said of a pig: to dig with the snout; = ROOT[3] (I). [alteration of ROOT[3]]

route[1] /rooht/ *noun* **1a** a regularly travelled way: *Follow the trunk route north; We're very close to a bus route.* **b** *NAmer* a main highway: *Route 66.* **c** a means of access; a path: *There's no easy route to success.* **2** a line of travel; a course: *There's a danger of flooding from rivers that have changed their route.* **3** an itinerary. **4** *NAmer* = ROUND[4] (6a). [Middle English via French from Latin *rupta* (in *rupta via* broken or worn path), fem past part. of *rumpere* to break]

route[2] *verb trans* (**routeing** *or* **routing**) **1** to divert (vehicles or people) in a specified direction: *All business was routed through his colleague.* **2** to send (something) by a selected route; to direct (it).

routeman *noun* (*pl* **routemen**) *NAmer* a roundsman.

route march *noun* a long and tiring march, *esp* as military training.

router[1] /'rowtə/ *noun* something that routs, e.g.: **a** a plane for cutting a groove. **b** a machine with a cutter set on a revolving spindle for milling out the surface of wood or metal.

router[2] /'roohtə/ *noun* somebody or something that routes, e.g. a device in computing that directs data around a network.

routine[1] /rooh'teen/ *noun* **1a** a regular course of procedure. **b** habitual or mechanical performance of an established procedure. **2** a fixed piece of entertainment often repeated: *a dance routine.* **3** a particular sequence of computer instructions for carrying out a given task. [French *routine* from early French *route*: see ROUTE[1]]

routine[2] *adj* **1** of or in accordance with established procedure. **2** commonplace or repetitious in character. ➤➤ **routinely** *adv.*

rout out *verb trans* = ROOT OUT.

roux /rooh/ *noun* (*pl* **roux** /rooh/) a cooked mixture of fat and flour used as a thickening agent in a sauce. [French *roux*, from (*beurre*) *roux* browned (butter)]

rove[1] /rohv/ *verb intrans* **1** to wander aimlessly or idly. **2** said of the eyes: to stray and change direction without concentration. ➤ *verb trans* to wander aimlessly through or over (a place). [Middle English *roven* to shoot at rovers (random targets in archery), prob of Scandinavian origin]

rove[2] *verb* past tense and past part. of REEVE[2].

rove[3] *verb trans* to join (textile fibres) with a slight twist and draw out into roving. [origin unknown]

rove[4] *noun* the act or an instance of roving.

rove beetle *noun* any of numerous predatory beetles with long bodies and small wing cases: family Staphylinidae. [perhaps from ROVE[1]]

rover[1] *noun* **1** a wanderer. **2** in Australian Rules football, one of the players who form the ruck. **3** (*usu in pl*) in archery, a randomly chosen or long-distance target. [Middle English, in the sense 'random target in archery', from *roven*: see ROVE[1]]

rover[2] *noun archaic* a pirate. [Middle English from early Dutch, from *roven* to rob]

roving[1] *adj* **1** not restricted as to location or area of concern. **2** inclined to ramble or stray: *a roving fancy*. [ROVE[1]]

roving[2] *noun* a slightly twisted roll or strand of textile fibres. [ROVE[3]]

roving commission *noun Brit* authority given without rigidly defined terms.

roving eye *noun* promiscuous sexual interests. [ROVING[1]]

row[1] /roh/ *noun* **1** a number of objects or people arranged in a straight line, or the line along which they are arranged. **2** *chiefly Brit* a way or street. ✳ **in a row** *informal* one after another; successively. [Old English *rāw*]

row[2] *verb intrans* **1** to propel a boat by means of oars. **2** to engage in the sport of rowing. ➤ *verb trans* **1a** to propel (a boat) with or as if with oars. **b** to compete against (a person or team) in rowing. **2** to transport (a person or goods) in a boat propelled by oars. ➤➤ **rower** *noun*. [Old English *rōwan*]

row[3] *noun* the act or an instance of rowing a boat.

row[4] /row/ *noun informal* **1** *chiefly Brit* a noisy quarrel or stormy dispute. **2** *chiefly Brit* excessive or unpleasant noise. **3** *Brit* a reprimand. [origin unknown]

row[5] /row/ *verb intrans chiefly Brit, informal* to engage in quarrelling.

rowan /'roh·ən, 'rowən/ *noun* any of several species of small Eurasian trees of the rose family that bear white flowers and red berries: genus *Sorbus*. [of Scandinavian origin]

rowdy[1] /'rowdi/ *adj* (**rowdier, rowdiest**) coarse or boisterous. ➤➤ **rowdily** *adv*, **rowdiness** *noun*. [perhaps irreg from ROW[4]]

rowdy[2] *noun* (*pl* **rowdies**) a rowdy person; a tough. ➤➤ **rowdyism** *noun*.

rowel[1] /'rowəl/ *noun* a revolving disc with sharp marginal points at the end of a spur. [Middle English *rowelle* from early French *rouelle* small wheel, ultimately from late Latin *rotella*: see ROULETTE[1]]

rowel[2] *verb trans* (**rowelled, rowelling**, *NAmer* **roweled, roweling**) to goad (something) with or as if with a rowel.

rowing boat /'roh·ing/ *noun chiefly Brit* a small boat designed to be rowed.

rowing machine /'roh·ing/ *noun* an exercise machine that works all the major muscle groups by simulating rowing movements.

rowlock /'rolək/ *noun* a device for holding an oar in place and providing a fulcrum for its action. [prob alteration of OARLOCK]

royal[1] /'roy(ə)l/ *adj* **1a** of monarchical ancestry: *the royal family*. **b** of the crown: *the royal estates*. **c** in the crown's service: *the Royal Air Force*. **2** suitable for royalty; regal or magnificent. **3** of superior size, magnitude, or quality. **4** of or being a part of the rigging of a sailing ship next above the topgallant. ➤➤ **royally** *adv*. [Middle English via early French *roial* from Latin *regalis*, from *reg-, rex* king]

royal[2] *noun* **1** *informal* somebody of royal blood. **2** a size of paper usu 635 × 508mm (25 × 20in.). **3** a stag of eight years or more having antlers with at least twelve points. **4** a royal sail or mast.

Royal Assent *noun* (**the Royal Assent**) formal ratification of a parliamentary bill by a British sovereign.

royal blue *noun* rich purplish blue. ➤➤ **royal-blue** *adj*.

Royal Commission *noun* in Britain, a committee of enquiry appointed by the Crown.

royal fern *noun* a large fern with tall spreading fronds: *Osmunda regalis*.

royal flush *noun* in poker, a straight flush having an ace as the highest card.

Royal Gala *noun* a variety of eating apple with a red and yellow skin.

royalist[1] *noun* (*also* **Royalist**) a supporter of a king or queen or of monarchical government, e.g. a Cavalier. ➤➤ **royalism** *noun*.

royalist[2] *or* **Royalist** *adj* **1** supporting a king or queen or monarchical government in general. **2** of Royalists, e.g. Cavaliers.

royal jelly *noun* a highly nutritious secretion of the honeybee that is fed to the very young larvae and to all larvae that will develop into queens.

royal palm *noun* any of several species of tropical American palms with a tall naked trunk: genus *Roystonea*.

royal standard *noun* a banner bearing the royal coat of arms.

royal tennis *noun* = REAL TENNIS. [by alteration]

royalty /'royəlti/ *noun* (*pl* **royalties**) **1a** people of royal blood. **b** a privileged class of a specified type: *show-business royalty*. **2a** royal sovereignty. **b** a monetary benefit received by a sovereign, e.g. a percentage of minerals. **3** regal character or bearing. **4** a right of jurisdiction granted by a sovereign. **5a** a payment made to an author, composer, or inventor for each copy or example of their work sold. **b** a share of the product or profit reserved by one who grants an oil or mining lease. [Middle English *roialte* from early French *roialté*, from *roial*: see ROYAL[1]]

royal warrant *noun* a warrant authorizing a company to supply goods to a royal household.

rozzer /'rozə/ *noun Brit, informal* a police officer. [origin unknown]

RP *abbr* **1** Received Pronunciation. **2** Republic of the Philippines (international vehicle registration).

RPG *noun* a high-level computer language that generates programs from the user's specifications and is used *esp* to produce business reports. [abbr of *report program generator*]

RPI *abbr* retail price index.

rpm *abbr* **1** resale price maintenance. **2** revolutions per minute.

rpt *abbr* report.

RPV *abbr* remotely piloted vehicle.

RR *abbr* **1** Right Reverend. **2** *NAmer* rural route.

-rrhagia *comb. form* forming nouns, denoting: abnormal or excessive discharge or flow: *menorrhagia*. [scientific Latin from Greek, from *rhēgnynai* to break, burst]

-rrhea *comb. form NAmer* see -RRHOEA.

-rrhiza *comb. form* see -RHIZA.

-rrhoea (*NAmer* **-rrhea**) *comb. form* forming nouns, denoting: flow; discharge: *leucorrhoea*. [Middle English *-ria* via Latin from Greek *-rrhoia*, from *rhein* to flow]

RS *abbr Brit* Royal Society.

Rs *abbr* rupee.

RSA *abbr* **1** Republic of South Africa. **2** Royal Scottish Academician or Academy. **3** Royal Society of Arts.

RSC *abbr* Royal Shakespeare Company.

RSFSR *abbr* formerly, Russian Soviet Federated Socialist Republic. [Russian *Rossiiskaya Sovetskaya Federativnaya Sotsialisticheskaya Respublika*]

RSI *abbr* repetitive strain injury.

RSM *abbr* **1** *Brit* Regimental Sergeant Major. **2** Republic of San Marino (international vehicle registration). **3** *Brit* Royal Society of Medicine.

RSPB *abbr Brit* Royal Society for the Protection of Birds.

RSPCA *abbr Brit* Royal Society for the Prevention of Cruelty to Animals.

RSV *abbr* Revised Standard Version (of the Bible).

RSVP *abbr* please reply. [short for French *répondez s'il vous plaît*]

RT *abbr* radiotelephony.

rt *abbr* right.

RTA *abbr Brit* road traffic accident.

RTE *abbr* Irish Radio and Television. [short for Irish Gaelic *Radio Telefís Éireann*]

Rt Hon. *abbr Brit* Right Honourable.

RU *abbr* **1** Republic of Urundi (international vehicle registration for Burundi). **2** Rugby Union.

Ru[1] *abbr* the chemical symbol for ruthenium.

Ru[2] *abbr* Ruth (book of the Bible).

RU486 *noun trademark* = MIFEPRISTONE.

rub[1] /rub/ *verb* (**rubbed, rubbing**) ➤ *verb trans* **1** to subject (something) to pressure and friction, *esp* with a back-and-forth motion. **2a** to cause (an object) to move with pressure and friction along a surface. **b** to treat (something) in any of various ways by rubbing. **c** to apply (a substance) to a surface by rubbing: *Rub some ointment on your skin*. **3** to bring (objects) into reciprocal back-and-forth or rotary contact. ➤ *verb intrans* **1** to move along a surface with pressure. **2a** to move with friction so as to become worn down or sore. **b** to cause vexation or anger. ✳ **rub shoulders** to associate closely; to mix socially. **rub/rub up the wrong way** to irritate or displease (somebody): *Sentimentality is only sentiment that rubs you up the wrong way* — Somerset Maugham. **rub somebody's nose in something** see NOSE[1]. [Middle English *rubben*, perhaps from Low German]

rub[2] *noun* **1** the act or an instance of rubbing; the application of friction and pressure. **2** a cream or ointment for rubbing on a painful body part. **3** (**the rub**). **a** an obstacle or difficulty: *To die, to sleep; to sleep: perchance to dream: ay, there's the rub* — Shakespeare. **b** something grating to the feelings, e.g. a gibe or harsh criticism. **4** in bowls, an unevenness of the surface of the green, or the effect this has on the movement of a bowl.

rub along *verb intrans Brit, informal* **1** to continue coping in a difficult situation. **2** to remain on friendly terms.

rubato /roo'bahtoh/ *noun* (*pl* **rubatos** *or* **rubati** /-tee/) expressive fluctuation of speed within a musical phrase. [Italian *rubato*, past part. of *rubare* to rob, of Germanic origin]

rubber[1] /'rubə/ *noun* **1a** an elastic substance obtained by coagulating the milky juice of the rubber tree or other plant that is used, *esp* when toughened by chemical treatment, in car tyres, waterproof materials, etc. **b** any of various synthetic substances resembling rubber. **2a** *Brit* a small piece of rubber or plastic used for rubbing out pencil marks on paper, card, etc. **b** an instrument or object used in rubbing, polishing, or cleaning. **3** something like or made of rubber, e.g.: **a** *NAmer, informal* a condom. **b** *NAmer* (*usu in pl*) a galosh. ➤➤ **rubbery** *adj*. [RUB[1]]

rubber[2] *noun* **1** a contest consisting of an odd number of games or matches won by the side that takes a majority, *esp* a three- or five-game match in bridge or whist. **2** an extra game played to decide a match after a tie. [origin unknown]

rubber band *noun* a continuous band of rubber used for holding small objects together.

rubber bullet *noun* a solid rubber projectile that is designed to be fired from a special gun to control rioters: compare PLASTIC BULLET.

rubber cement *noun* an adhesive consisting typically of vulcanized rubber dispersed in an organic chemical solvent, e.g. toluene.

rubberize *or* **rubberise** *verb trans* to coat or impregnate (something) with rubber.

rubberneck[1] *noun informal* **1** an overinquisitive person. **2** a tourist or sightseer, *esp* one on a guided tour. [from the idea of stretching one's neck to see]

rubberneck[2] *verb intrans informal* **1** to show exaggerated curiosity. **2** to engage in sightseeing.

rubbernecker *noun* = RUBBERNECK[1].

rubber plant *noun* a plant that yields rubber, *esp* a tall Asian tree of the fig family with glossy leathery leaves, also grown as a houseplant: *Ficus elastica*.

rubber stamp *noun* **1** a stamp of rubber for making imprints. **2** somebody who unthinkingly assents to the actions or policies of others. **3** a routine endorsement or approval.

rubber-stamp *verb trans* **1** to imprint (something) with a rubber stamp: *Now, an engineer can look at the car, say it's okay and rubber-stamp the paperwork* — Autocar and Motor. **2** to approve, endorse, or dispose of (a plan, etc) as a matter of routine or at the dictate of another.

rubber tree *noun* a S American tree of the spurge family that is cultivated in plantations and is the chief source of rubber: *Hevea brasiliensis*.

rubbing *noun* an image of a raised surface obtained by placing paper over it and rubbing the paper with charcoal, chalk, etc: *a brass rubbing.*

rubbish[1] /'rubish/ *noun* **1** *chiefly Brit* worthless or rejected articles; trash. **2** often used as an exclamation: something worthless; nonsense. ➤➤ **rubbishy** *adj*. [Middle English *robys* from Anglo-French *rubbous*, perhaps from Old French *robe*: see ROBE[1]]

rubbish[2] *verb trans Brit, informal* to condemn (a person or their work) as rubbish.

rubbish[3] *adj* (*often* + at) worthless or very bad: *I'm rubbish at maths.*

rubble /'rubl/ *noun* **1** broken fragments of building material, e.g. brick, stone, etc. **2** rough broken stones or bricks used in coarse masonry or in filling courses of walls. [Middle English *robyl*, perhaps ultimately from Old French *robe*: see ROBE[1]]

rubdown *noun* the act or an instance of rubbing something down, e.g. a brisk rubbing of the body, usu with a towel or cloth.

rub down *verb trans* to clean, smooth, or dry (something) by rubbing it.

rube /roohb/ *noun NAmer, informal* an unsophisticated rustic; a bumpkin. [*Rube*, nickname for *Reuben*]

rubella /rooh'belə/ *noun* a virus disease that is milder than typical measles but is damaging to the foetus when occurring early in pregnancy; = GERMAN MEASLES. [Latin *rubella*, fem of *rubellus* reddish, from *ruber* red]

rubellite /'roohbəliet/ *noun* a pink to red tourmaline used as a gem. [Latin *rubellus*: see RUBELLA]

rubeola /rooh'bee·ələ/ *noun* = MEASLES (1). [scientific Latin *rubeola*, neuter pl of *rubeolus* reddish, from Latin *rubeus*]

Rubicon /'roohbikən, -kon/ *noun* a bounding or limiting line, *esp* one that when crossed commits somebody irrevocably. [Latin *Rubicon-*, *Rubico*, river of N Italy, forming part of the boundary between Cisalpine Gaul and Italy, the crossing of which by Julius Caesar in 49 BC began a civil war]

rubicund /'roohbikənd/ *adj* ruddy: *a small inn, designated by a rubicund portrait of his majesty George the Third* — Washington Irving. ➤➤ **rubicundity** /-'kunditi/ *noun*. [Latin *rubicundus*, from *rubēre* to be red]

rubidium /rooh'bidi·əm/ *noun* a silver-white metallic chemical element of the alkali metal group that occurs naturally in various minerals, and is used in photocells: symbol Rb, atomic number 37. [scientific Latin *rubidium* from Latin *rubidus* red, from *rubēre* to be red]

rubiginous /rooh'bijinəs/ *adj literary* rust-coloured. [Latin *robiginosus*, *rubiginosus* rusty, from *robigin-*, *robigo* rust]

Rubik's cube /'roohbiks/ *or* **Rubik cube** *noun* a puzzle consisting of a usu plastic cube having each face divided into nine small coloured or distinctively marked square segments and rotatable about a central square, that must be restored to an initial condition in which each face shows nine identical squares. [named after Ernö Rubik b.1944, Hungarian designer, who invented it]

rub in ✳ **rub it in** *informal* to dwell on something unpleasant or embarrassing.

ruble /'roohbl/ *noun* see ROUBLE.

rub off *verb intrans* **1** to come off or disappear as the result of rubbing. **2** (*often* + on) to exert an influence through contact or example: *Her enthusiasm rubbed off on the rest of the group.* ➤ *verb trans* to remove (something) by rubbing.

rub out *verb trans* **1** to remove (pencil marks, etc) with a rubber. **2** *chiefly NAmer, slang* to kill or murder (somebody). ➤ *verb intrans* to be removable with a rubber.

rubric /'roohbrik/ *noun* **1** a heading, e.g. in a book or manuscript, written or printed in a distinctive colour or style. **2a** a heading under which something is classed. **b** an authoritative rule, *esp* a rule for the conduct of church ceremonial. **c** an explanatory or introductory commentary. ➤➤ **rubrical** *adj*. [Middle English *rubrike* red ochre, heading in red letters of part of a book, via French from Latin *rubrica*, from *rubr-*, *ruber* red]

rubricate /'roohbrikayt/ *verb trans* to provide rubrics for (a book or manuscript). ➤➤ **rubrication** /-'kaysh(ə)n/ *noun*, **rubricator** *noun*.

rub up *verb trans* **1** to polish (something) by rubbing. **2** to revive or refresh one's knowledge of (a subject). ✳ **rub up the wrong way** see RUB[1].

ruby /'roohbi/ *noun* (*pl* **rubies**) **1** a red corundum used as a precious gem. **2a** the dark red colour of the ruby. **b** something like a ruby in colour. **3** (*used before a noun*) of or marking a 40th anniversary: *a ruby wedding.* [Middle English via French from Latin *rubeus* reddish]

RUC *abbr* Royal Ulster Constabulary.

ruche /roohsh/ *noun* a pleated or gathered strip of fabric used for trimming. ➤➤ **ruched** *adj*. [French *ruche* from medieval Latin *rusca* bark of a tree, of Celtic origin]

ruching /'roohshing/ *noun* = RUCHE.

ruck[1] /ruk/ *noun* **1** a situation in Rugby Union in which one or more players from each team close round the ball when it is on the ground and try to kick the ball out to their own team: compare MAUL[2]. **2** in Australian Rules football, three players who do not have fixed positions. **3a** an indistinguishable mass of people or things. **b** (**the ruck**) the usual run of people or things. [Middle English *ruke* pile of combustible material, of Scandinavian origin]

ruck² *verb intrans* in Rugby Union or Australian Rules football, to be part of a ruck.

ruck³ *verb* (*often* + up) to wrinkle or crease.

ruck⁴ *noun* a wrinkle or crease. [of Scandinavian origin]

ruck⁵ *noun Brit, informal* a fight. [perhaps by shortening of RUCKUS]

rucksack *noun* a lightweight bag carried on the back and fastened by straps over the shoulders, used *esp* by walkers and climbers. [German *Rucksack*, from *Rucken* (alteration of *Rücken* back) + *Sack* bag]

ruckus /'rukəs/ *noun* a row or disturbance. [prob a blend of RUC-TION and RUMPUS]

ruction /'rukʃ(ə)n/ *noun informal* **1** (*in pl*) a violent dispute. **2** a disturbance or uproar. [perhaps by shortening and alteration from INSURRECTION]

rudbeckia /roohd'beki·ə/ *noun* a N American composite plant with showy yellow to orange flower heads with dark cone-shaped centres: genus *Rudbeckia*. [Latin genus name, named after Olof *Rudbeck* d.1702, Swedish scientist]

rudd /rud/ *noun* (*pl* **rudd**) a silver-coloured freshwater European fish of the carp family resembling the roach: *Rutilus erythrophthalmus*. [prob from archaic *rud*: see RUDDLE]

rudder /'rudə/ *noun* **1** a flat piece hinged vertically to a ship's stern for changing course with. **2** a movable auxiliary aerofoil attached to the fin that serves to control direction of flight of an aircraft in the horizontal plane. **3** somebody or something that gives guidance or direction, e.g. in life. [Middle English *rother* from Old English *rōther* paddle]

rudderless *adj* **1** lacking a rudder. **2a** lacking direction. **b** lacking a strong leader.

ruddle /'rudl/ *noun* RED OCHRE (natural red earthy substance), *esp* when used for marking sheep. [dimin. of English dialect *rud* redness, red ochre, from Old English *rudu* redness]

ruddy /'rudi/ *adj* (**ruddier, ruddiest**) **1** said of a complexion: having a healthy reddish colour. **2** red; reddish. **3** *Brit, euphem* = BLOODY³. ⋙ **ruddily** *adv*, **ruddiness** *noun*. [Old English *rudig*, from *rudu* redness]

rude /roohd/ *adj* **1** lacking refinement or propriety, e.g.: **a** discourteous. **b** vulgar; indecent. **c** ignorant; unlearned. **2** sudden and unpleasant; abrupt: *a rude awakening*. **3** robust; vigorous: *in rude health*. **4a** in a rough or unfinished state. **b** primitive; undeveloped. ⋙ **rudely** *adv*, **rudeness** *noun*, **rudery** /'roohd(ə)ri/ *noun*. [Middle English via French from Latin *rudis* crude, raw]

ruderal¹ /'roohdərəl/ *adj* said of a plant: growing where the natural cover of vegetation has been disturbed by human activity, *esp* growing on waste ground or among debris. [scientific Latin *ruderalis* from Latin *ruder-, rudus* rubble]

ruderal² *noun* a ruderal plant.

rudiment /'roohdimənt/ *noun* **1** (*usu in pl*) a basic principle or element or a fundamental skill. **2a** (*usu in pl*) something as yet unformed or undeveloped: *the rudiments of a plan*. **b** a deficiently developed body part or organ; = VESTIGE (2). **c** a body part or organ in its earliest stage of development or when just beginning to develop; = PRIMORDIUM. ⋙ **rudimental** /-'mentl/ *adj*. [Latin *rudimentum* beginning, from *rudis* raw, RUDE]

rudimentary /roohdi'ment(ə)ri/ *adj* **1** basic; fundamental. **2** of a primitive kind; crude. **3** very poorly developed or represented only by a vestige: *A hyrax has a rudimentary tail*. ⋙ **rudimentarily** *adv*.

rue¹ /rooh/ *verb trans* to feel penitence or bitter regret for (e.g. a past deed): *I rue the day I met her*. [Old English *hrēowan*]

rue² *noun archaic* **1** deep regret; bitter sorrow. **2** compassion; pity.

rue³ *noun* a strong-scented woody plant with bitter leaves formerly used in medicine: *Ruta graveolens*: *He had hanging in the attic great bunches of dried herbs: wormwood, rue, horehound ... Usually there was a jug of one or other decoction standing on the hob* — D H Lawrence. [Middle English via French from Latin *ruta* from Greek *rhytē*]

rueful /'roohf(ə)l/ *adj* **1a** mournful or regretful. **b** feigning sorrow. **2** arousing pity or compassion. ⋙ **ruefully** *adv*, **ruefulness** *noun*.

ruff¹ /ruf/ *noun* **1** a broad starched collar of fluted linen or muslin worn in the late 16th and early 17th cents. **2** a fringe or frill of long hairs or feathers growing round the neck of a bird or other animal.

3 (*fem* **reeve**) a Eurasian sandpiper the male of which has a large ruff of erectable feathers during the breeding season: *Philomachus pugnax*. ⋙ **ruffed** *adj*. [prob back-formation from RUFFLE²]

ruff² *verb trans* = TRUMP² (1). [*ruff* (noun) a former card game, kind of trump, from early French *roffle, ronfle*]

ruff³ *noun* the act or an instance of trumping in cards.

ruff⁴ *or* **ruffe** *noun* a small freshwater European perch with a greenish brown body: *Gymnocephalus cernua*. Also called POPE. [Middle English *ruf*, perhaps a variant spelling of ROUGH¹]

ruffian /'rufi·ən/ *noun* a brutal and lawless person. ⋙ **ruffianism** *noun*, **ruffianly** *adj*. [early French *rufian* from Italian *ruffiano*, ultimately of Germanic origin]

ruffle¹ /'rufl/ *verb trans* **1a** to disturb the smoothness of (something). **b** to trouble or vex (somebody). **2** said of a bird: to erect (its feathers) as if in a ruff. **3** to make (fabric) into a ruffle. **4a** to flip through (e.g. pages). **b** to shuffle (playing cards). ⋙ *verb intrans* to become ruffled. ⋙ **ruffled** *adj*. [Middle English *ruffelen*; earlier history unknown]

ruffle² *noun* **1a** a strip of fabric gathered or pleated on one edge. **b** a fringe or frill of long hairs or feathers growing round the neck of a bird, etc; = RUFF¹. **2** a disturbance of surface evenness, e.g. a ripple or crumple. **3** the act or an instance of ruffling e.g. cards.

rufiyaa /'roohfieyah/ *noun* (*pl* **rufiyaa**) the basic monetary unit of the Maldives, divided into 100 laris. [via Maldivian from Hindi *rūpaiyā* rupee]

rufous /'roohfəs/ *adj* said of an animal: reddish brown. [Latin *rufus* red]

rug /rug/ *noun* **1** a heavy mat, usu smaller than a carpet and with a thick pile, which is used as a floor covering. **2** *chiefly Brit* a woollen blanket, often with fringes on two opposite edges, used as a wrap, *esp* when travelling. **3** *chiefly NAmer, informal* a wig or toupee. [prob of Scandinavian origin]

rugby *or* **Rugby** /'rugbi/ *noun* a football game played between two teams with an oval ball, which features kicking, lateral hand-to-hand passing, and tackling.

Word history

named after *Rugby* School, in Warwickshire, England, where it was first played. According to tradition, this game originated when a Rugby schoolboy named William Webb Ellis picked up a football and ran with it, despite the rules forbidding this, in 1823. The evidence for this exploit is dubious. It is clear, however, that handling and running with the ball had become a feature of football at Rugby School by the late 1830s, and it was formalized in the set of rules published in 1846.

Rugby League *noun* a form of rugby originating in the north of England, played by teams of 13 players each, featuring a six-player scrum, and permitting professionals to play.

Rugby Union *noun* a form of rugby played by teams of 15 players each and featuring an eight-player scrum, which was restricted to amateurs until 1995.

rugged /'rugid/ *adj* **1** said of terrain: having a rough uneven surface or outline. **2a** presenting a severe test of ability or stamina. **b** strongly built or constituted; sturdy. **3** said of a man: having attractively strong masculine features. **4** said of a face: seamed with wrinkles and furrows: *a rugged face*. **5a** austere; stern. **b** uncompromising: *rugged individualism*. ⋙ **ruggedly** *adv*, **ruggedness** *noun*. [Middle English, from RUG]

rugger /'rugə/ *noun Brit, informal* rugby. [by alteration]

rugose /'roohgohs/ *adj* in biology, wrinkled or ridged: *rugose leaves*. ⋙ **rugosely** *adv*, **rugosity** /rooh'gositi/ *noun*. [Latin *rugosus*, from *ruga* wrinkle]

rug rat *noun NAmer, informal* a very young child.

ruin¹ /'rooh·in/ *noun* **1** physical, moral, economic, or social collapse. **2** a ruined person or structure. **3** destruction: *The repeated air of sad Electra's poet had the power to save the Athenian walls from ruin bare* — Milton. **4** a person's downfall, or the cause of it: *Whisky was his ruin*. **5** (*usu in pl*). **a** the state of being wrecked or decayed: *The city lay in ruins*. **b** the remains of something destroyed: *She stared at the ruins of her pudding lying on the kitchen floor*. [Middle English *ruine* via French from Latin *ruina* from *ruere* to fall]

ruin² *verb trans* **1a** to damage (something) irreparably; to spoil (it). **b** to reduce (somebody) to financial ruin. **c** *archaic* to ravish or deflower (a virgin): *For many innocent girls ... are, as it may emphatically be termed, ruined before they know the difference between virtue and vice* — Mary Wollstonecraft. **2** to reduce (a building, etc) to ruins.

ruination /rooh·i'naysh(ə)n/ *noun* the act or an instance of ruining or being ruined, or a cause of it.

ruinous /'rooh·inəs/ *adj* **1** causing ruin or the likelihood of ruin: *The company won't survive with that ruinous sales performance.* **2** dilapidated or ruined. >> **ruinously** *adv*, **ruinousness** *noun*.

rule¹ /roohl/ *noun* **1a** a prescriptive specification of conduct or action. **b** the laws or regulations prescribed by the founder of a religious order for observance by its members. **c** an established procedure, custom, or habit. **2a** a generally prevailing quality, state, or form. **b** a standard of judgment. **c** a regulating principle, *esp* of a system: *the rules of grammar.* **3** the exercise or a period of dominion by a particular ruler or government. **4** a usually valid generalization. **5** a strip or set of jointed strips of metal, wood, or plastic marked off in units and used for measuring or marking off lengths or drawing straight lines. **6** a printed or written line or dash. **7** (**Rules**) = AUSTRALIAN RULES FOOTBALL. * **as a rule** generally; for the most part. [Middle English *reule* via French from Latin *regula* straight edge, rule, from *regere* to lead straight]

rule² *verb trans* **1a** to exert control, direction, or influence on (a people). **b** to exercise control over (something), *esp* by restraining it: *She ruled her appetites firmly.* **2** to exercise power or firm authority over (somebody). **3** to lay down (a decision) authoritatively, *esp* judicially. **4a** to mark with lines drawn along or as if along the straight edge of a ruler. **b** to mark (a line) on something with a ruler. > *verb intrans* **1** to exercise supreme authority: *It is an axiom, enforced by all the experience of the ages, that they who rule industrially will rule politically* — Aneurin Bevan. **2** to make a judicial decision. **3a** to be predominant. **b** to prevail. * **rule the roost** to be in charge. >> **ruled** *adj.*

rule of thumb *noun* a rough practical or common-sense method rather than a precise or technical one. [said to derive from the use of the thumb as a rough measure]

rule out *verb trans* **1a** to exclude or eliminate (something). **b** to deny the possibility of (something): *The chairman ruled out further discussion.* **2** to make (something) impossible; to prevent (it).

ruler *noun* **1** somebody, *specif* a sovereign, who rules. **2** a smooth-edged strip of metal, wood, plastic, etc that is marked off in units, e.g. centimetres, and is used for drawing straight lines, for measuring, or for marking off lengths. >> **rulership** *noun.*

ruling¹ *noun* an official or authoritative decision.

ruling² *adj* **1** exerting power or authority. **2** chief; predominant.

rum¹ /rum/ *noun* **1** an alcoholic spirit made by distilling a fermented cane product, e.g. molasses. **2** a glass or measure of rum. [prob short for obsolete *rumbullion* rum, of unknown origin]

rum² *adj* (**rummer, rummest**) *Brit, informal, dated* peculiar; strange: *She's a rum customer.* >> **rumly** *adv*, **rumness** *noun*. [earlier *rome*, perhaps from Romany *rom*: see ROMANY]

Rumanian /rooh'mayni·ən/ *noun and adj* see ROMANIAN.

rumba *or* **rhumba** /'rumbə/ *noun* a ballroom dance of Cuban origin marked by steps with a delayed transfer of weight and pronounced hip movements, or the music for this dance. [American Spanish *rumba*]

rum baba *noun* = BABA.

rumble¹ /'rumbl/ *verb intrans* **1** to make a low heavy rolling sound. **2** *NAmer, informal* to engage in a street fight. > *verb trans* **1** to utter or emit (something) with a low rolling sound. **2** *Brit, informal* to reveal or discover the true character of (something or somebody). >> **rumbler** *noun*, **rumbling** *adj.* [Middle English *rumblen*, prob from obsolete Dutch *rommelen*]

rumble² *noun* **1** a rumbling sound. **2** *NAmer, informal* a street fight, *esp* between gangs.

rumble seat *noun NAmer* = DICKEY (2B).

rumbustious /rum'buschəs/ *adj chiefly Brit, informal* irrepressibly or coarsely exuberant. >> **rumbustiously** *adv*, **rumbustiousness** *noun*. [alteration of *robustious*, from ROBUST]

rumen /'roohmen/ *noun* (*pl* **rumens** *or* **rumina** /'roohminə/) the large first compartment of the stomach of a ruminant mammal in which cellulose is broken down, *esp* by the action of symbiotic bacteria. [Latin *rumin-, rumen* gullet]

ruminant¹ /'roohminənt/ *adj* **1a** of or being a member of a group of hoofed mammals including the cattle, sheep, and camels that chew the cud and have a complex three- or four-chambered stomach. **b** cud-chewing. **2** meditative; contemplative.

ruminant² *noun* a ruminant mammal.

ruminate /'roohminayt/ *verb intrans* **1** to engage in contemplation. **2** said of a ruminant: to chew again what has been chewed slightly and swallowed. > *verb intrans* **1** to contemplate (something). **2** said of a ruminant: to chew the cud. >> **rumination** /-'naysh(ə)n/ *noun*, **ruminative** /-nativ/ *adj*, **ruminatively** /-nativli/ *adv*, **ruminator** *noun*. [Latin *ruminatus*, past part. of *ruminari* to chew the cud, muse upon, from *rumin-, rumen* gullet]

rummage¹ /'rumij/ *verb intrans* to engage in a haphazard search. > *verb trans* **1** to make a thorough search of (an untidy or congested place). **2** (+ out) to uncover (something) by searching. >> **rummager** *noun*. [obsolete *rummage* in the sense 'act of packing cargo', modification of early French *arrumage*, from *arrumer* to stow, from early Dutch *ruim* room]

rummage² *noun* **1** a thorough search, *esp* among a jumbled assortment of objects. **2a** *chiefly NAmer* = JUMBLE² (2). **b** *NAmer* a miscellaneous or confused accumulation.

rummage sale *noun chiefly NAmer* a jumble sale.

rummer *noun* a tall drinking glass, used *esp* for wine. [German *Römer* from Dutch *roemer*]

rummy /'rumi/ *noun* a card game in which each player tries to assemble combinations of related cards and to be the first to turn all their cards into such combinations. [perhaps from *rummy* queer, strange, from RUM² + -Y¹]

rumour¹ (*NAmer* **rumor**) /'roohmə/ *noun* **1** a statement or report circulated without confirmation of its truth. **2** talk or opinion widely disseminated but with no identifiable source. [Middle English *rumour* via French from Latin *rumor* noise]

rumour² (*NAmer* **rumor**) *verb trans* (*usu in passive*) to tell or spread (something) by rumour: *It's rumoured that he's moving to London.*

rump /rump/ *noun* **1** the rear part of a quadruped mammal, bird, etc; the buttocks. **2** *humorous* a person's buttocks. **3** a cut of beef from between the loin and round. **4** a small or inferior remnant of a larger group, e.g. a parliament. >> **rumpless** *adj.* [Middle English, prob of Scandinavian origin]

rumple¹ /'rumpl/ *verb trans* (*usu in passive*) **1** to wrinkle or crumple (clothing, etc). **2** to make (somebody's hair) unkempt; to tousle (it). > *verb intrans* to become rumpled. >> **rumpled** *adj*, **rumply** /'rumpli/ *adj.* [Dutch *rompelen*]

rumple² *noun* a fold or wrinkle.

rumpus /'rumpəs/ *noun* a noisy commotion: *'Such a rumpus everywhere!' continued the Otter. 'All the world seems out on the river to-day.'* — Kenneth Grahame. [perhaps alteration of RUMBLE²]

rumpus room *noun NAmer* a room, usu in the basement of a house, that is used for recreation, e.g. hobbies and games.

rumpy-pumpy /,rumpi 'pumpi/ *noun informal* sexual activity. [reduplication of RUMP]

run¹ /run/ *verb* (**running**, *past tense* **ran** /ran/, *past part.* **run**) > *verb intrans* **1a** to go at a speed faster than a walk, with only one foot on the ground at any time. **b** said of a horse: to move at a fast gallop. **2a** to hasten or move quickly or erratically. **b** to flee or escape. **c** to hasten with a specified purpose: *Run and fetch the doctor.* **d** to make a quick, easy, or casual trip or visit: *I'm going to run up to town for the day.* **3a** to compete in a race. **b** to be a candidate in an election. **4a** to move in a certain way: *a chair that runs on castors.* **b** to pass or slide freely or cursorily: *A thought ran through my mind.* **5** to sing or play quickly: *She ran up the scale.* **6** said of a boat: to sail before the wind as distinct from reaching or sailing close-hauled. **7a** said of a bus, train, or ferry: to go back and forth; to ply: *The trains don't always run on time.* **b** said of fish: to ascend a river to spawn. **8** said of a machine, engine, etc: to function or operate. **9a** said of an agreement, contract, etc: to continue in force. **b** said of interest, a debt, etc: to continue to accumulate. **10** to have a specified tendency; to pass to a specified state: *to run to fat; Money ran low.* **11** to flow or course: *running water.* **12a** to become by flowing: *The water ran cold.* **b** to reach a specified state by discharging liquid: *The well ran dry.* **13** said of a tap, etc: to discharge liquid. **14a** to melt or turn to liquid. **b** said of colours: to spread or dissolve when wet. **c** said of a sore: to discharge pus or serum. **15a** to lie or extend in a specified position, direction, or relation to something: *The road runs through a tunnel.* **b** to have a certain form or expression: *The letter runs as follows.* **16a** to occur persistently: *A note of despair runs through the narrative.* **b** to reach a specified level: *Inflation is running at 4 per cent.* **c** to play or be featured continuously, e.g. in a theatre or newspaper. **17** (+ to). **a** to extend to (a specified size or amount): *The book runs to 500 pages.* **b** to be adequate for or be able to afford (a purchase, expense, etc): *My salary won't run to a car.* **18** to spread quickly from point to point: *Chills ran up his spine.* **19** (+ on) to be concerned with or dwell on (something). **20** *chiefly NAmer* said of tights or stockings: to ladder. ➤ *verb trans* **1a** to carry on, manage, or control (a business, etc). **b** to operate (a machine, etc). **c** to put (a computer program) into operation. **d** to subject (something) to a treatment or process. **e** to make oneself liable to (a risk). **2a** to own, maintain, and use (a motor vehicle). **b** to cause (a bus, train, or ferry) to ply or travel along a regular route. **c** to convey (somebody) in a vehicle. **3a** to cause (something) to pass lightly, freely, or cursorily: *She ran a comb through her hair.* **b** to cause (something) to lie or extend in a specified position or direction: *You could run a wire in from the aerial.* **c** to cause (something) to pass forcibly into a certain state, often by accident: *He ran his car off the road.* **4a** to cause (water, etc) to move or flow in a specified way or into a specified position. **b** to cause (a tap) to pour out liquid. **c** to fill (a bath, etc) from a tap. **5** to publish (a story) or show (a film, play) etc to the public. **6** to register or enrol (somebody) as a contestant or candidate. **7a** to cover (a distance) by running: *She ran ten miles.* **b** to bring (oneself or somebody else) to a specified condition by or as if by running: *He ran himself almost to death.* **8a** to pursue or trace (something or somebody) to their source. **b** to drive or chase (somebody) away: *They ran him out of town.* **9a** to slip through or past (a blockade, etc). **b** to smuggle (goods). **10a** to drive (livestock), *esp* to a grazing place. **b** to provide pasturage for (livestock). ✳ **run across** to meet with or discover (somebody or something) by chance. **run after 1** to pursue or chase (somebody). **2** to seek the company of (somebody). **run a temperature** to be feverish. **run into 1** to collide with (something or somebody). **2** to encounter or meet (somebody or something). **3** to amount to (a specified figure). **run short 1** to become insufficient. **2** (+ of) to come near the end of (available supplies). **run through 1** to squander (money). **2** to perform (something), *esp* for practice or instruction. **3** to read through (something) quickly. **run to earth/ground** to find (a person or an animal) after a protracted search. [Old English *rinnan* and Old Norse *rinna* (verb intrans), *renna* (verb trans)]

run² *noun* **1a** the act or an instance of running; continued rapid movement. **b** a running race. **c** a quickened gallop. **d** the gait of a runner. **e** a school of fish migrating or ascending a river to spawn. **2a** a short excursion in a car. **b** the distance covered in a period of continuous journeying. **c** a regularly travelled course or route: *esp of identical or similar things; a run of bad luck.* **d** a rapid passage up or down a musical scale. **e** an unbroken course of performances or showings. **f** a persistent and heavy commercial or financial demand: *a run on gilt-edged securities.* **g** three or more playing cards of the same suit in consecutive order of rank. **3** general tendency or direction: *You need to watch the run of the stock market.* **4** the average or prevailing kind or class: *the general run of students.* **5a** a way, track, etc frequented by animals. **b** an enclosure for domestic animals where they may feed or exercise. **6** an inclined course, e.g. for skiing. **7** in cricket, a unit of scoring made typically by each batsman running the full length of the wicket. **8** a ladder in tights or a stocking. **9** (**the runs**) *informal* diarrhoea. ✳ **give somebody a run for their money** to present a serious challenge to (somebody). **on the run 1** in haste; without pausing. **2** in hiding or running away, *esp* from lawful authority.

runabout *noun* a light motor car, aeroplane, or motorboat.

run along *verb intrans informal* often used as an order or request: to leave or go away.

runaround *noun* (**the runaround**) *informal* delaying action, *esp* in response to a request: *When I phoned to complain, they just gave me the runaround.*

run around *verb intrans* **1** to make a number of short trips. **2** (+ with) to associate casually with (somebody). **3** *informal* to have a series of sexual encounters.

runaway *noun* **1** a fugitive. **2** something, e.g. a horse, that is running out of control. **3** (*used before a noun*). **a** running out of control: *a runaway train.* **b** won by a long lead; decisive: *a runaway victory.*

run away *verb intrans* ✳ **run away with 1** to take (something) away in haste or secretly, *esp* to steal it. **2** to go beyond the control of (somebody): *His imagination ran away with him.* **3** to believe (something) too easily: *Don't run away with the idea that you can stay.* **4** to flee or escape. **5** to avoid or escape from one's responsibilities.

runcible spoon /'runsibl/ *noun* a sharp-edged fork with three broad curved prongs. [coined with indefinite meaning by Edward Lear d.1888, English writer and painter]

rundown *noun* **1** an item-by-item report; a résumé. **2** the gradual decline of something: *the rundown of the steel industry.*

run down *verb trans* **1a** to knock (a person or animal) down with a vehicle. **b** to run against (a vessel) and cause it to sink. **2a** to chase (a person or animal) to exhaustion or until captured. **b** to find (something) by extensive searching. **3** to disparage (somebody) meanly or unfairly. **4** to allow the gradual decline or closure of (an industry, etc). ➤ *verb intrans* **1** to deteriorate or cease to function. **2** to decline in physical condition.

run-down *adj* **1** in a state of disrepair. **2** in poor health.

rune /roohn/ *noun* **1** any of the characters of an alphabet probably derived from Latin and Greek and used in medieval times, *esp* in carved inscriptions, by the Germanic peoples. **2** a magical or cryptic utterance or inscription. ⋙ **runic** /'roohnik/ *adj*. [orig from Old English *rūn* mystery, runic character, writing, becoming obsolete in the Middle English period. Reintroduced in the 17th cent. from Old Norse *rúnar* hidden lore]

rung¹ /rung/ *noun* **1a** any of the crosspieces of a ladder. **b** a rounded part placed as a crosspiece between the legs of a chair. **2** a level or stage in something that can be ascended: *We're still on the bottom rung of the social scale.* [Old English *hrung*]

rung² *verb past part.* of RING³.

run in *verb trans* **1** *Brit* to use (a vehicle) carefully when it is new. **2** *informal* to arrest (somebody), *esp* for a minor offence.

run-in *noun* **1** *informal* a quarrel. **2** the final part of a race or racetrack.

runnel /'runl/ *noun* a small stream; a brook. [Old English *rynel*]

runner *noun* **1** an entrant for a race that actually competes in it. **2a** a bank or stockbroker's messenger. **b** (*usu in combination*) somebody who smuggles or distributes illicit or contraband goods: *a gun-runner.* **3** a straight piece on which something slides, e.g.: **a** a longitudinal piece on which a sledge or ice skate slides. **b** a groove or bar along which something, e.g. a drawer or sliding door, slides. **4** a horizontal stem from the base of a plant that buds to produce new plants; = STOLON. **5a** a long narrow carpet, e.g. for a hall or staircase. **b** a narrow decorative cloth for a table or dresser top. ✳ **do a runner** *Brit, informal* to leave in haste, *esp* to avoid paying for something or to escape the scene of a crime.

runner bean *noun* **1** *chiefly Brit* a tropical American climbing bean with large bright red flowers widely cultivated for its long green edible pods: *Phaseolus coccineus.* **2** a pod of this plant, used as a vegetable.

runner-up *noun* (*pl* **runners-up**) a competitor or team that comes second in a contest or race.

running¹ *noun* **1** the act or an instance of running. **2** management; operation: *There's quite a lot to the running of a small business.* ✳ **in/out of the running** having a good/poor chance of winning. **make the running** to set the pace.

running² *adj* **1** runny. **2a** having stages that follow in rapid succession: *a running battle.* **b** made during the course of a process or activity: *a running commentary.* **3** cursive; flowing. **4** designed or used for running: *a running track.*

running³ *adv* in succession: *You've been late three days running.*

running board *noun* a footboard, *esp* at the side of a motor car.

running head *noun* a headline repeated on consecutive pages of a book.

running knot *noun* a knot that slips along the rope or line round which it is tied.

running light *noun* any of the lights carried by a moving ship, aeroplane, car, etc, *esp* at night, that indicate size, position, and direction of movement.

running mate *noun* **1** a candidate standing for a subordinate place in a US election. **2** *chiefly NAmer* a horse that is entered in a race as a pacesetter for another horse.

running repairs *pl noun* repairs, usu minor or temporary ones, made to machinery that is in operation without shutting it down.

running stitch *noun* a small even sewing stitch run in and out of cloth, e.g. for gathering.

runny *adj* (**runnier, runniest**) having a tendency to run: *a runny nose.*

runoff *noun* **1** a final decisive race, contest, or election. **2** the portion of the rainfall that ultimately reaches streams. **3** *NZ* an area of grazing land for young animals.

run off *verb intrans* to run away. ➤ *verb trans* **1a** to produce (copies) with a printing press or copier. **b** to compose or produce (something) quickly. **c** to decide (a race or contest) by a runoff. **2** to drain off (a liquid). ✳ **run off with** to run away with (somebody or something).

run-of-the-mill *adj* average; commonplace: *Your aunt has asked me to try and impress upon you … that you are not from run-of-the-mill people, that you are the product of several generations' gentle breeding* — Harper Lee.

run on *verb intrans* **1** to continue without interruption. **2** to talk or narrate at length. ➤ *verb trans* to continue (something) without a break.

run-on *noun* something, e.g. a dictionary entry, run on.

run out *verb intrans* said of a supply, etc: to become depleted or used up. ➤ *verb trans* in cricket, to dismiss (a batsman who is outside his crease and attempting a run) by breaking the wicket with the ball. ✳ **run out of** to use up the available supply of (something). **run out on** *informal* to desert (somebody).

run over *verb intrans* **1** to overflow. **2** to exceed a limit. ➤ *verb trans* **1** to injure or kill (a person or animal) with a motor vehicle. **2** to read through (something) quickly.

runt /runt/ *noun* **1** an animal unusually small of its kind, *esp* the smallest of a litter of pigs. **2** *derog* a puny person. **3** a large domestic pigeon. ➤➤ **runty** *adj*. [origin unknown]

run through *verb trans* to pierce (somebody) with a weapon, e.g. a sword.

run-through *noun* **1** a sequence of actions performed for practice. **2** a cursory reading, summary, or rehearsal.

run-time *noun* **1** the time that a computer program takes to run. **2** the time when a computer program is being run by a user as opposed to when it is being created by a programmer.

run up *verb trans* **1** to accumulate or incur (debts). **2** to make (a piece of clothing) quickly. **3a** to hoist (a flag). **b** to erect (something) hastily. ✳ **run up against** to encounter (a difficulty, etc).

run-up *noun* **1** a period that immediately precedes an action or event: *There were riots during the run-up to the last election.* **2** an approach run to provide momentum, e.g. for a jump or throw.

runway *noun* **1** an artificially surfaced strip of ground on an airfield for the landing and takeoff of aeroplanes. **2** a narrow stage in the centre of a room on which fashion shows are held; = CATWALK (1). **3** a path made by or for animals.

rupee /rooh'pee/ *noun* the basic monetary unit of various countries of the Indian subcontinent and the Indian Ocean, i.e. India, Mauritius, Nepal, Pakistan, the Seychelles, and Sri Lanka. [Hindi *rūpaiyā* from Sanskrit *rūpya* coined silver]

rupiah /rooh'pee-ə/ *noun* the basic monetary unit of Indonesia. [Hindi *rūpaiyā*: see RUPEE]

rupture[1] /'rupchə/ *noun* **1a** the act or an instance of breaking apart or bursting. **b** the state of being broken apart or burst. **2** breach of peace or concord; *specif* open hostility between nations. **3a** a hernia. **b** the tearing apart of a tissue, *esp* muscle. [Middle English *ruptur* via French from Latin *ruptura* fracture, from *rumpere* to break]

rupture[2] *verb trans* **1a** to part (something) by violence; to break or burst (it). **b** to create a breach of (a peaceful situation, etc). **2** to cause a rupture in (oneself or a body part). ➤ *verb intrans* to have or undergo a rupture.

rural /'rooərəl/ *adj* of the country, country people or life, or agriculture: compare URBAN. ➤➤ **ruralism** *noun*, **ruralist** *noun*, **rurality** /rooh'raliti/ *noun*, **rurally** *adv*. [Middle English via French from Latin *ruralis*, from *rur-, rus* open land]

rural dean *noun chiefly Brit* a priest supervising one district of a diocese.

Ruritanian /,rooəri'tayni·ən/ *adj* of or characteristic of an imaginary Central European country used as a setting for adventure stories of romance and intrigue, *esp* contemporary cloak-and-dagger court intrigues. [from *Ruritania*, fictional kingdom in the novel *The Prisoner of Zenda* by Anthony Hope (Sir Anthony Hope Hawkins) d.1933, English writer]

RUS *abbr* Russia (international vehicle registration).

ruse /roohz/ *noun* a wily subterfuge. [Middle English from early French, from *ruser* to dodge, deceive]

rush[1] /rush/ *verb intrans* **1** to move forward, progress, or act quickly or eagerly or without preparation. **2** to follow strongly and quickly.

➤ *verb trans* **1** to push or impel (somebody or something) forward with speed or violence. **2** to perform or finish (something) in a short time or at high speed: *He rushed his breakfast.* **3** to urge (somebody) to an excessive speed. **4** to run against (somebody or something) in attack, often with an element of surprise; to charge (them). **5** *Brit, informal* to cheat or overcharge (somebody). ➤➤ **rusher** *noun*. [Middle English *russhen* via French from Latin *recusare*: see RECUSANT]

rush[2] *noun* **1a** a rapid and violent forward motion. **b** a sudden onset of emotion: *a quick rush of sympathy.* **2a** a surge of activity, or busy or hurried activity: *the bank holiday rush.* **b** a burst of productivity or speed. **c** a sudden demand for something. **3** a great movement of people, *esp* in search of wealth. **4** (*usu in pl*) the unedited print of a film scene processed directly after shooting. **5** an immediate brief pleasurable feeling, *esp* one resulting from an intravenous injection of a drug such as heroin. **6** (*used before a noun*) requiring or marked by special speed or urgency: *a rush job.*

rush[3] *noun* a tufted marsh plant with cylindrical hollow leaves, used for the seats of chairs and for plaiting mats: genus *Juncus*. ➤➤ **rushy** *adj*. [Old English *risc*]

rush hour *noun* a period of the day when traffic is at a peak.

rushlight *noun* formerly, a candle that consisted of the pith of a rush dipped in grease.

rusk /rusk/ *noun* a piece of sliced bread baked again until dry and crisp, or a light dry biscuit similar to this. [modification of Spanish and Portuguese *rosca* coil, twisted roll, roll of bread]

russet[1] /'rusit/ *noun* **1** a reddish to yellowish brown. **2** a russet-coloured winter eating apple. **3** formerly, a coarse homespun reddish brown or grey fabric used for clothing. [Middle English from Old French *rousset*, ultimately from Latin *russus* red]

russet[2] *adj* **1** reddish to yellowish brown: *But look, where the morn, in russet mantle clad, walks o'er the dew of yon high eastward hill* — Shakespeare. **2** *archaic* rustic or homely.

Russia leather /,rushə/ *noun* leather used *esp* for bookbinding, made by tanning skin with willow, birch, or oak bark and then rubbing the flesh side with a birch oil. [named after *Russia*, country in E Europe]

Russian /'rush(ə)n/ *noun* **1** a native or inhabitant of Russia. **2** the Slavonic language of Russia, also widely spoken in E Europe and central Asia. ➤➤ **Russian** *adj*.

Word history

Of the Russian words which have passed into English, most of the best-known fall into four groups: politics and sociology (*agitprop, Bolshevik, commissar, glasnost, intelligentsia, perestroika, pogrom*); aeronautics (*cosmonaut, sputnik*); fauna and natural features of Russia (*mammoth, steppe, tundra*); and domestic items (*balalaika, kaftan, samovar, vodka*).

Russian doll *noun* any of a series of progressively smaller, brightly painted dolls that fit inside each other.

Russianize or **Russianise** /'rushəniez/ *verb trans* to make (something) Russian in nature. ➤➤ **Russianization** /-'zaysh(ə)n/ *noun*.

Russian Orthodox Church *noun* (**the Russian Orthodox Church**) the largest branch of the Orthodox Church, and the national church in Russia.

Russian roulette *noun* **1** an act of bravado consisting of spinning the cylinder of a revolver loaded with one cartridge, pointing the muzzle at one's own head, and pulling the trigger. **2** a potentially risky or suicidal venture.

Russian salad *noun* a salad of cold diced cooked vegetables, e.g. carrot and potato, in mayonnaise.

Russki or **Russky** /'ruski/ *noun* (*pl* **Russkis** or **Russkies**) *derog* a Russian. [Russian *Russkiĭ* (adj and noun) from *Rus*, old name for Russia]

Russo- *comb. form* forming words, with the meanings: **1** the Russian nation, people, or culture: *Russophobia*. **2** Russian; Russian and: *Russo-Japanese*. [*Russia* and *Russian*]

rust[1] /rust/ *noun* **1a** brittle reddish hydrated ferric oxide that forms as a coating on iron, *esp* iron chemically attacked by moist air. **b** a comparable coating produced on another metal, or anything similar. **2** a destructive fungal disease of plants in which reddish brown pustular lesions form. **3** a reddish brown to orange colour. **4** corrosive or injurious influence or effect. ➤➤ **rustless** *adj*. [Old English *rūst*]

rust² *verb intrans* **1** to form rust; to become oxidized: *Iron rusts.* **2** to degenerate, *esp* through lack of use or advancing age. ➤ *verb trans* to cause (a metal) to form rust.

rustbelt *noun informal* an area of the northern USA marked by the prevalence of heavy industry which is now in decline.

rustic¹ /'rustik/ *adj* **1** of or suitable for the country. **2** characteristic of country people. **3a** made of the rough branches of trees: *rustic furniture.* **b** finished by rusticating: *a rustic joint in masonry.* ➤ **rustically** *adv*, **rusticity** /ru'stisiti/ *noun*. [Middle English *rustik* via French from Latin *rusticus*, from *rus* open land]

rustic² *noun often derog* an unsophisticated rural person.

rusticate /'rustikayt/ *verb trans* **1** *Brit* to suspend (a student) from college or university. **2** to bevel or cut a groove, channel, etc, in (the edges of stone blocks, etc) to make the joints conspicuous: *a rusticated stone wall.* **3** to impart a rustic character to (something). ➤ *verb intrans dated* to go into or reside in the country. ➤ **rustication** /-'kaysh(ə)n/ *noun*, **rusticator** *noun*.

rustle¹ /'rusl/ *verb intrans* **1a** to make or cause a rustle. **b** to move with a rustling sound. **2** to steal cattle or horses. ➤ *verb trans* **1** to cause (something) to make a rustle. **2** to steal (cattle or horses). ➤ **rustler** *noun*. [Middle English *rustelen*, of imitative origin]

rustle² *noun* a quick succession or confusion of faint sounds.

rustle up *verb trans informal* to produce (food, etc) adeptly or at short notice.

rustproof¹ *adj* able to resist rust.

rustproof² *verb trans* to make (something) incapable of rusting; to treat (it) so as to make it able to resist rust.

rusty *adj* (**rustier, rustiest**) **1** affected by or as if by rust, *esp* stiff with or as if with rust: *the creaking of rusty hinges.* **2a** of the colour rust. **b** dulled in colour by age and use; shabby: *a rusty old suit of clothes.* **3a** slow or lacking skill through lack of practice or advanced age. **b** showing lack of practice: *My French is a bit rusty now.* ➤ **rustily** *adv*, **rustiness** *noun*.

rut¹ /rut/ *noun* **1** a track worn by habitual passage, *esp* of wheels on soft or uneven ground. **2** an established practice, *esp* a tedious routine: *I feel I've just got into a rut.* [perhaps modification of early French *route*: see ROUTE¹]

rut² *verb trans* (**rutted, rutting**) to make a rut in (soft or uneven ground). ➤ **rutted** *adj*.

rut³ *noun* **1a** an annually recurrent state of readiness to copulate, in the male deer or other mammal. **b** oestrus; heat. **2** (*often* **the**

rut) the period during which rut normally occurs. [Middle English *rutte* via French from Latin *rugitus*, past part. of *rugire* to roar]

rut⁴ *verb intrans* (**rutted, rutting**) to be in a state of rut.

rutabaga /roohtə'baygə/ *noun NAmer* a swede. [Swedish dialect *rotabagge*, from *rot* root + *bagge* bag]

ruth /roohth/ *noun archaic* **1** pity; compassion. **2** sorrow for one's own faults; remorse. [Middle English *ruthe* from *ruen* RUE¹]

ruthenium /rooh'theeni·əm/ *noun* a rare white chemical element of the platinum group that occurs naturally in platinum ores, and is used in hardening platinum alloys and in catalysts: symbol Ru, atomic number 44. [scientific Latin *ruthenium* from medieval Latin *Ruthenia* Russia]

rutherfordium /rudhə'fawdyəm, -di·əm/ *noun* an artificially produced radioactive chemical element: symbol Rf, atomic number 104. [named after Ernest *Rutherford* died 1937, New Zealand-born British physicist]

ruthless /'roohthlis/ *adj* showing no pity or compassion. ➤ **ruthlessly** *adv*, **ruthlessness** *noun*.

rutile /'roohtil, 'roohtiel/ *noun* a reddish brown or black lustrous mineral consisting of titanium dioxide. [German *Rutil* from Latin *rutilus* reddish]

ruttish *adj* lustful.

RV *abbr* **1** *NAmer* recreational vehicle. **2** Revised Version (of the Bible).

RWA *abbr* Rwanda (international vehicle registration).

Rwandan /roo'andən/ *or* **Rwandese** /-'deez/ *noun* a native or inhabitant of Rwanda. ➤ **Rwandan** *adj*, **Rwandese** *adj*.

-ry *suffix* see -ERY: *citizenry; wizardry.* [Middle English -*rie* from Old French, short for -*erie* -ERY]

rye /rie/ *noun* **1a** a hardy grass widely grown for grain: *Secale cereale.* **b** the seeds of this grass, from which a wholemeal flour is made. **2** = RYE WHISKY. **3** = RYE BREAD. [Old English *ryge*]

rye bread *noun* bread made wholly or in part of rye flour and usu containing caraway seeds.

ryegrass *noun* any of several species of grasses used *esp* for pasture: genus *Lolium.* [alteration of obsolete *raygrass*, from obsolete *ray* darnel, of unknown origin]

rye whisky *noun* a whisky distilled from rye or from rye and malt.

ryot /'rie·ət/ *noun* an Indian peasant or tenant farmer. [Hindi *raiyat*, from Persian, from Arabic *ra'iyah* flock, herd]

S¹ *or* **s** *noun* (*pl* **S's** *or* **Ss** *or* **s's**) **1a** the 19th letter of the English alphabet. **b** a written character or design denoting this letter. **c** the sound represented by this letter, one of the English consonants. **2** an item designated as S, *esp* the 19th in a series.

S² *abbr* **1** in chemistry, entropy. **2** saint. **3** siemens. **4** Signor. **5** small. **6** society. **7** South. **8** Southern. **9** Sweden (international vehicle registration).

S³ *abbr* the chemical symbol for sulphur.

s *abbr* **1** second. **2** shilling. **3** singular. **4** son. **5** succeeded.

's *contraction informal* **1** is: *She's here.* **2** has: *He's seen them.* **3** used in questions: does: *What's he want?* **4** us: *Let's go.*

-s¹ *suffix* **1** forming the plural of most nouns that do not end in *s, z, sh, ch,* or *y* after a consonant: *cats; boys; beliefs.* **2** (*also* **-'s**) forming the plural of abbreviations, numbers, letters, and symbols used as nouns: *MCs; the 1940s; £s; B's.* [Old English *-as*, nominative and accusative ending of some masc nouns]

-s² *suffix* forming the third person sing. present of most verbs that do not end in *s, z, sh, ch,* or *y* after a consonant: *falls; takes; plays.* [Old English (Northumbrian) *-es, -as*, prob from Old English *-es, -as*, second person sing. present indicative ending]

-'s¹ *suffix* forming the possessive of singular nouns, plural nouns not ending in *s*, and some pronouns: *boy's; children's; anyone's.* [Old English *-es*, genitive sing. ending]

-'s² *suffix* see -s¹ (2).

SA *abbr* **1** Salvation Army. **2** Saudi Arabia (international vehicle registration). **3** South Africa. **4** South America. **5** South Australia.

saag /sahg/ *noun Indian* spinach, *esp* when used in Indian cooking. [Hindi *sāg*]

sabadilla /sabə'dilə/ *noun* **1** a Mexican plant of the lily family: *Schoenocaulon officinale.* **2** the bitter seeds of this plant, which are a source of veratrine, a substance used in medicine and insecticides. [Spanish *cebadilla*, dimin. of *cebada* barley, from *cebo* feed, from Latin *cibus* food]

Sabaean /sə'bee-ən/ *noun* **1** a native or inhabitant of ancient Saba (Sheba) in SW Arabia. **2** the Semitic language of the Sabaeans. ⫸ **Sabaean** *adj.* [via Latin from Greek *Sabaios*, from *Saba*, from Arabic *Sabā'*]

sabbat /'sabət, 'sabat/ *noun* = SABBATH (3). [French *sabbat* sabbath, from Latin *sabbatum*: see SABBATH]

Sabbatarian¹ /sabə'teəri-ən/ *noun* **1** somebody who observes the sabbath, *esp* on Saturday, in strict conformity with the fourth commandment. **2** somebody who advocates abstinence from work, sporting activities, etc on Sunday. ⫸ **Sabbatarianism** *noun.* [Latin *sabbatarius*, from *sabbatum*: see SABBATH]

Sabbatarian² *adj* **1** of the sabbath. **2** of or being a Sabbatarian or Sabbatarians.

sabbath /'sabəth/ *noun* **1** (*usu* **the Sabbath**) the seventh day of the week observed from Friday evening to Saturday evening as a day of rest and worship, *esp* by Jews. **2** (*often* **the Sabbath**) Sunday observed among Christians as a day of rest and worship: *Anybody can observe the Sabbath, but making it holy surely takes the rest of the week* — Alice Walker. **3** a midnight assembly of witches. [Old English *sabat* via Latin *sabbatum* from Greek *sabbaton*, from Hebrew *shabbāth*, literally 'rest']

sabbatical¹ /sə'batikl/ *noun* a period of leave, often with pay, granted *usu* every seventh year, e.g. to a university teacher: *on sabbatical.* [via late Latin from Greek *sabbatikos*, from *sabbaton*: see SABBATH]

sabbatical² *adj* **1** (*often* **Sabbatical**) *archaic* of the sabbath: *sabbatical laws.* **2** of or being a sabbatical.

sabbatical year *noun* **1** a year of sabbatical leave. **2** (*often* **Sabbatical year**) a year of rest for the land observed every seventh year in ancient Judaea.

saber¹ /'saybə/ *noun NAmer* see SABRE¹.

saber² *verb trans NAmer* see SABRE².

Sabine /'sabien, 'saybien/ *noun* a member of an ancient people of the Apennines in central Italy. ⫸ **Sabine** *adj.* [Middle English *Sabin* from Latin *Sabinus*]

sabkha /'sabkhə, 'sabkə/ *noun* an area of flat land in coastal regions of N Africa and Arabia that is regularly flooded, causing an accumulation of salt and other products of evaporation. [Arabic *sabkha*]

sable¹ /'saybl/ *noun* (*pl* **sables** *or collectively* **sable**) **1a** a mammal related to the martens and weasels that is found in the forests of N Asia and feeds on small animals and eggs: *Martes zibellina.* **b** the valuable dark brown fur of the sable. **2** in heraldry, the colour black. **3** = SABLE ANTELOPE. [Middle English via French from early High German *zobel*, of Slavonic origin]

sable² *adj* **1** (*often used after a noun*) in heraldry, black. **2** *literary* black, dark, or gloomy.

sable antelope *noun* a large black antelope that lives in the forests of S Africa and has large parallel curved horns, an erect mane, and long hair at the throat: *Hippotragus niger.*

sabot /'saboh/ *noun* **1** a wooden shoe worn in various European countries. **2** a thrust-transmitting carrier that positions a projectile in a gun barrel or launching tube and increases its speed on firing. [French *sabot*, alteration of early French *savate* old shoe]

sabotage¹ /'sabətahzh/ *noun* **1** destructive or obstructive action by enemy agents, discontented workers, etc that is intended to hinder military or industrial activity. **2** deliberate subversion, e.g. of a plan or project. [French *sabotage* from *saboter* to clatter with sabots, botch, sabotage, from *sabot*: see SABOT]

sabotage² *verb trans* to destroy, obstruct, or subvert (something) by sabotage.

saboteur /sabə'tuh/ *noun* somebody who commits sabotage. [French *saboteur* from *saboter*: see SABOTAGE¹]

sabra /'sabrə/ *noun* (*often* **Sabra**) a native-born Israeli Jew.

Word history
New Hebrew *ṣabbār*, literally 'prickly pear'. The prickly pear is a common plant in coastal areas of Israel.

sabre¹ (*NAmer* **saber**) /'saybə/ *noun* **1** a heavy cavalry sword with a curved single-edged blade. **2** a light fencing or duelling sword with an arched guard that covers the back of the hand and a tapering flexible blade: compare ÉPÉE, FOIL⁵. [French *sabre*, modification of German dialect *Sabel*, ultimately from Hungarian *szabilya*]

sabre² (*NAmer* **saber**) *verb trans* to strike, wound, or kill (somebody) with a sabre.

sabre-rattling *noun* the display of military power, *esp* in an aggressively intimidating way.

sabre-toothed tiger *noun* any of various extinct large members of the cat family with long curved upper canines: genus *Smilodon* and other genera.

sabreur /sa'bruh/ *noun* somebody who carries, fights, or fences with a sabre. [French *sabreur* from *sabrer* to strike with a sabre, from *sabre*: see SABRE¹]

sac /sak/ *noun* a pouch, often filled with fluid, within an animal or plant. ≫ **saclike** *adj*. [early French *sac* bag, from Latin *saccus*: see SACK¹]

saccade /sa'kahd/ *noun* a small rapid jerky movement of the eye, *esp* as it jumps from one point of fixation to another, e.g. in reading. ≫ **saccadic** /sa'kadik/ *adj*. [French *saccade* twitch, jerk, from early French *saquer* to pull, draw, from *sac* bag, from Latin *saccus*: see SACK¹]

saccate /'sakayt, 'sakət/ *adj* having the form of a sac or pouch: *a saccate corolla*.

sacchar- *or* **sacchari-** *or* **saccharo-** *comb. form* forming words, denoting: sugar: *saccharide*. [via Latin from Greek *sakcharon*, via Pali from Sanskrit *śarkarā* gravel, sugar]

saccharide /'sakəried/ *noun* a simple sugar or a combination of simple sugars.

saccharimeter /sakə'rimitə/ *noun* a device for measuring the amount of sugar in a solution.

saccharin /'sakərin/ *noun* a chemical compound that is several hundred times sweeter than sugar and is used e.g. in low-calorie diets.

saccharine /'sakərin, -reen/ *adj* **1** of, like, or containing sugar: *saccharine taste*. **2** excessively sweet; mawkish: *saccharine sentiment*.

saccharo- *comb. form* see SACCHAR-.

saccharometer /sakə'romitə/ *noun* = SACCHARIMETER.

saccharose /'sakərohs, -rohz/ *noun* = SUCROSE.

saccular /'sakyoolə/ *adj* resembling a sac or saccule.

sacculate /'sakyoolət, -layt/ *or* **sacculated** /-laytid/ *adj* having or formed from a series of saccules or saclike expansions. ≫ **sacculation** /-'laysh(ə)n/ *noun*.

saccule /'sakyoohl/ *or* **sacculus** /-ləs/ *noun* (*pl* **saccules** *or* **sacculi** /-lee, -lie/) a little sac; *specif* the smaller of the two connected chambers in the membranous LABYRINTH (sensory structures of the inner ear): compare UTRICLE. [Latin *sacculus*, dimin. of *saccus*: see SACK¹]

sacerdotal /sasə'dohtl/ *adj* of priests or the priesthood. ≫ **sacerdotally** *adv*. [Middle English via French from Latin *sacerdotalis*, from *sacerdot-, sacerdos* priest, from *sacer* SACRED]

sacerdotalism *noun* a religious belief emphasizing the powers of priests as essential mediators between God and human beings. ≫ **sacerdotalist** *noun*.

sachem /'saych(ə)m, 'sach(ə)m/ *noun* **1** a Native American chief. **2** *NAmer, informal* a political leader or a head of an organization, etc. [Narraganset and Pequot *sachima*]

Sachertorte /'sakətohtə, 'zakə- (*German* 'zaxətortə)/ *noun* (*pl* **Sachertorten**) a rich dark chocolate cake, usu of two layers with apricot jam sandwiching them together and smothered in chocolate icing. [named after Franz *Sacher*, the 19th cent. German pastry chef who invented it + German *Torte* cake or pastry]

sachet /'sashay/ *noun* **1** a small sealed plastic or paper bag or packet usu holding just enough of something, e.g. shampoo or sugar, for use at one time. **2** a small bag containing a perfumed powder used to scent clothes and linens. [French *sachet* from Old French, dimin. of *sac* bag: see SAC]

sack¹ /sak/ *noun* **1** a usu rectangular large bag, e.g. of paper or canvas. **2** the amount contained in a sack. **3** a garment without shaping, *esp* a loosely fitting dress, coat, or jacket. **4** (**the sack**) *informal* dismissal from employment: *get the sack*. **5** (**the sack**) *chiefly NAmer, informal* bed: *still in the sack at midday*. **6** in American football, a tackle that prevents a quarterback from passing the ball. ✱ **hit the sack** *informal* to go to bed. ≫ **sackful** *noun*. [from Old English *sacc* bag, sackcloth, via Latin *saccus* from Greek *sakkos*, of Semitic origin]

sack² *verb trans* **1** to place (something) in a sack. **2** *informal* to dismiss (somebody) from a job. **3** in American football, to tackle (the quarterback) behind the line of scrimmage before a pass can be thrown. ≫ **sacker** *noun*.

sack³ *noun* any of various dry white wines formerly imported to Britain from S Europe. [modification of early French *sec* dry, from Latin *siccus*]

sack⁴ *noun* the plundering of a place captured in war. [early French *sac* from Old Italian *sacco*, literally 'bag (of loot)', from Latin *saccus*: see SACK¹]

sack⁵ *verb trans* **1** to plunder (e.g. a town) after capture. **2** to strip (a place) of valuables. ≫ **sacker** *noun*.

sackbut /'sakbut/ *noun* an early form of trombone used in the Renaissance. [early French *saqueboute* hooked lance, from Old French *saquer* (see SACCADE) + *bouter, boter* to push, of Germanic origin]

sackcloth *noun* **1** a coarse fabric used as sacking. **2** a garment of sackcloth worn as a sign of mourning or penitence. ✱ **sackcloth and ashes** a usu public display of mourning or penitence.

sacking *noun* material for sacks, *esp* a coarse fabric such as hessian.

sack race *noun* a race in which each contestant has their legs enclosed in a sack and progresses by jumping.

sacra /'saykrə/ *noun* pl of SACRUM.

sacral¹ /'saykrəl/ *adj* relating to or in the region of the sacrum.

sacral² *adj* relating to, used in, or denoting sacred rites or symbols.

sacrament /'sakrəmənt/ *noun* **1** a formal religious act, e.g. baptism, regarded as conferring divine grace on the recipient. **2** (**the Sacrament**) the bread and wine used in the Eucharist; *specif* the consecrated bread. **3** something considered to have sacred or religious significance. [Middle English *sacrement, sacrament* via Old French and late Latin from Latin *sacramentum* oath of allegiance, obligation, from *sacrare*: see SACRED]

sacramental¹ /sakrə'mentl/ *adj* of or having the character of a sacrament. ≫ **sacramentally** /-'taliti/ *noun*, **sacramentally** *adv*.

sacramental² *noun* a sacrament-like action or object of devotion in Roman Catholic practice.

sacramentalism *noun* belief in or use of sacramental rites, acts, or objects; *specif* belief that the sacraments bring about and are necessary for salvation.

sacrarium /sa'kreəri·əm/ *noun* (*pl* **sacraria** /-ri·ə/) **1a** = SANCTUARY (1). **b** = PISCINA. **2** an ancient Roman shrine in a temple or a home. [late Latin *sacrarium* from Latin *sacr-, sacer* SACRED]

sacred /'saykrid/ *adj* **1a** dedicated or set apart for the service or worship of a god or gods. **b** dedicated as a memorial: *sacred to his memory*. **2a** worthy of religious veneration; holy. **b** commanding reverence and respect. **3** relating to, used in, or suitable for religion; not secular or profane: *sacred music*. ≫ **sacredly** *adv*, **sacredness** *noun*. [Middle English, past part. of *sacren* to consecrate, via Old French from Latin *sacrare*, from *sacr-, sacer* holy, cursed]

sacred cow *noun* somebody or something granted unreasonable immunity from criticism: *Sacred cows make the best hamburgers* — attributed to Abbie Hoffman. [from the veneration of the cow by the Hindus]

sacrifice¹ /'sakrifies/ *noun* **1a** an act of making an offering to a deity, *esp* the killing of a victim on an altar. **b** something or somebody offered in sacrifice. **2a** the losing or surrender of one thing for the sake of a greater: *It seemed inconceivable to those who had made such sacrifices during the war, that you, as their King, refused a lesser sacrifice* — Queen Mary, mother of Edward VIII. **b** something forgone or done without: *the sacrifices made by parents*. [Middle English via Old French from Latin *sacrificium*, from *sacr-*, *sacer* SACRED + *facere* to make]

sacrifice² *verb trans* **1** to offer (something or somebody) as a sacrifice. **2** to give up or lose (something) for the sake of an ideal or end. **3** in chess, to allow (a specified piece) to be captured, *esp* in order to gain a later advantage. ➤ *verb intrans* to offer up or perform the rites of a sacrifice. ➤➤ **sacrificer** *noun*.

sacrificial /sakri'fish(ə)l/ *adj* involving or involved in sacrifice. ➤➤ **sacrificially** *adv*.

sacrilege /'sakrilij/ *noun* **1** a violation of what is sacred, e.g. the improper or secular use of a sacred object. **2** gross irreverence towards somebody or something sacred. ➤➤ **sacrilegious** /-'lijəs/ *adj*, **sacrilegiously** /-'lijəsli/ *adv*. [Middle English via Old French from Latin *sacrilegium*, from *sacrilegus* one who steals sacred things, from *sacr-*, *sacer* SACRED + *legere* to gather, steal]

sacring bell /'saykring/ *noun* a small bell rung during the Eucharist or Mass, *esp* at the elevation of the consecrated bread and wine.

sacristan /'sakristən/ *or* **sacrist** /'sakrist, 'saykrist/ *noun* **1** somebody in charge of the sacristy and ceremonial equipment of a church. **2** a sexton. [Middle English from late Latin *sacristanus* from *sacrista*: see SACRISTY]

sacristy /'sakristi/ *noun* (*pl* **sacristies**) a room in a church where sacred vessels and vestments are kept and where the clergy put on their vestments. [late Latin *sacristia* from *sacrista* sacristan, from Latin *sacr-*, *sacer* SACRED]

sacroiliac /sakroh'iliak, say-/ *adj* relating to or in the region of the sacrum and the ILIUM (part of the pelvis) or the joint between them.

sacrosanct /'sakrəsangkt, 'sakroh-/ *adj* accorded the highest reverence and respect. ➤➤ **sacrosanctity** /-'sangktiti/ *noun*. [Latin *sacrosanctus*, prob from *sacro sanctus* hallowed by a sacred rite]

sacrum /'saykrəm/ *noun* (*pl* **sacra** /'saykrə/) the part of the spinal column that is directly connected with or forms part of the pelvis and in human beings consists of five fused vertebrae. [scientific Latin *sacrum* from late Latin *os sacrum* last bone of the spine, literally 'holy bone'; from the belief that the soul resided there]

SAD /sad/ *abbr* seasonal affective disorder.

sad /sad/ *adj* (**sadder, saddest**) **1a** affected with or expressing unhappiness. **b** causing or associated with unhappiness. **c** deplorable; regrettable: *a sad decline in standards*. **2** *informal* pathetic or contemptible. ➤➤ **sadness** *noun*. [Old English *sæd* satisfied, sated, weary, also 'weighty, dense, firmly fixed', hence in Middle English 'steadfast, serious, grave', later 'pensive, sorrowful']

sadden *verb* (**saddened, saddening**) ➤ *verb trans* to make (somebody) sad. ➤ *verb intrans* to become sad.

saddhu /'sahdooh/ *noun* see SADHU.

saddle¹ /'sadl/ *noun* **1** a usu padded and leather-covered seat secured to the back of a horse, donkey, etc for the rider to sit on. **2** a similar seat on certain vehicles, e.g. a bicycle or tractor. **3** something like a saddle in shape, position, or function, e.g. a marking on the back of an animal. **4** a ridge connecting two peaks. **5** a part of a harness for a draught animal that is used to keep the strap that passes under the animal's tail in place. **6** a large cut of meat from a sheep, hare, rabbit, deer, etc consisting of both sides of the unsplit back including both loins. **7** the rear part of a male fowl's back extending to the tail. ✳ **in the saddle** in control. ➤➤ **saddleless** *adj*. [Old English *sadol*]

saddle² *verb trans* **1** to put a saddle on (e.g. a horse). **2** to burden or encumber (somebody): *She saddled me with the paperwork*.

saddleback *noun* any of several animals with saddle-shaped markings on the back, *esp* a medium-sized black pig with a white band crossing the back. ➤➤ **saddlebacked** *adj*.

saddlebag *noun* a pouch or bag attached to the back of a saddle, or either of a pair laid across behind the saddle of a horse or hanging over the rear wheel of a bicycle or motorcycle.

saddlebow /'sadlboh/ *noun* the curved or raised front part of a saddle.

saddlecloth *noun* a piece of cloth, leather, etc placed under a horse's saddle to prevent rubbing.

saddle horse *noun* a horse suited or trained for riding.

saddler *noun* somebody who makes, repairs, or sells saddles and other leather equipment for horses.

saddlery /'sadləri/ *noun* (*pl* **saddleries**) **1** the usu leather equipment, e.g. saddles, bridles, etc, used for riding and controlling a horse. **2a** the making, repair, or sale of saddlery. **b** a saddler's place of work or trade.

saddle soap *noun* a mild oily soap used for cleansing and conditioning leather.

saddle-stitched *adj* fastened by stitches or staples through the fold: *a saddle-stitched magazine*.

saddletree *noun* the frame of a saddle.

saddo /'sadoh/ *noun* (*pl* **saddos**) *Brit, informal* a pathetic or contemptible person. [from SAD]

Sadducee /'sadyoosee/ *noun* a member of a Jewish aristocratic and priestly sect noted at the time of Jesus Christ for rejecting various beliefs of the Pharisees, e.g. resurrection and the existence of angels. ➤➤ **Sadducean** /-'see-ən/ *adj*. [Old English *sadduce* via late Latin *sadducaeus* from Greek *saddoukaios*, from late Hebrew *ṣāddûqi* descendant of Zadok, high priest and supposed founder]

sadhu *or* **saddhu** /'sahdooh/ *noun* an Indian ascetic, usu a wandering holy man. [Sanskrit *sādhu*]

sadiron /'sadie-ən/ *noun* a heavy iron that is pointed at both ends, used *esp* in former times for pressing clothes and linen. [SAD in the obsolete sense 'compact, heavy' + IRON¹]

sadism /'saydiz(ə)m/ *noun* **1a** the act or an instance of obtaining sexual pleasure or gratification by inflicting physical pain or emotional or mental torture, *esp* through humiliation, on another person: compare MASOCHISM: *Sadism is the necessary outcome of the belief that one sex is passive and suffers sex at the hands of another —* Germaine Greer. **b** an inclination towards sadism. **2a** delight in inflicting pain or suffering. **b** extreme cruelty. ➤➤ **sadist** *noun*, **sadistic** /sə'distik/ *adj*, **sadistically** /sə'distikli/ *adv*. [named after the Marquis de *Sade* d.1814, French writer frequently imprisoned for sexual crimes and acts of wanton cruelty]

sadly *adv* **1** in a sad manner. **2** it is sad or regrettable that; unfortunately: *Sadly, we were too late.*

sadomasochism /saydoh'masəkiz(ə)m/ *noun* **1** the act or an instance of obtaining sexual pleasure or gratification through sadism and masochism. **2** an inclination towards sadism and masochism. ➤➤ **sadomasochist** *noun*, **sadomasochistic** /-'kistik/ *adj*.

SADS /sadz/ *abbr* = SUDDEN ADULT DEATH SYNDROME.

sad sack *noun NAmer, informal* an inept or clumsy person.

sae *abbr* stamped addressed envelope.

safari /sə'fahri/ *noun* (*pl* **safaris**) **1** an overland expedition, *esp* in E Africa, to observe, hunt, or scientifically study wild animals in their natural habitat. **2** the people, animals, vehicles, etc involved in such an expedition. [Swahili *safari* from Arabic *safar* journey]

safari jacket *noun* a jacket made of lightweight material, *esp* cotton, and typically having short sleeves, two breast pockets, and a belt.

safari park *noun* a large tract of land where wild animals, e.g. lions, are kept so that visitors can drive through and observe them in their natural habitat or conditions that are close to this.

safari suit *noun* a suit comprising a safari jacket and matching shorts, trousers, or skirt.

safe¹ /sayf/ *adj* **1** secure from threat of danger, harm, or loss. **2** free from harm or risk; no longer in danger. **3** providing protection or security from danger. **4a** not threatening or entailing danger: *Is your dog safe?* **b** unlikely to cause controversy: *keeping to safe subjects*. **5a** not liable to take risks. **b** trustworthy; reliable. ✳ **safe as houses** very secure. **to be on the safe side** as a precaution. ➤➤ **safely** *adv*, **safeness** *noun*. [Middle English via early French *sauf* from Latin *salvus* safe, healthy]

safe² *noun* **1** a reinforced usu fireproof room or cabinet, often with a complex lock or locking system, where money, valuables, etc are stored. **2** a receptacle, *esp* a cupboard, for the temporary storage of fresh and cooked foods. [from SAVE¹]

safe³ *adv* in a safe manner or condition; safely.

safe-blower *noun* a safe-breaker who uses explosives.

safe-breaker *noun* somebody who breaks open safes to steal the contents.

safe-conduct *noun* **1** an official guarantee of protection given to a person, e.g. when passing through a military zone or occupied area. **2** an official document that guarantees safe-conduct.

safe-cracker *noun* = SAFE-BREAKER.

safe-deposit *noun* **1** a place, e.g. the vault of a bank, for the safe storage of valuables. **2** (*used before a noun*) used for the safe storage of valuables: *a safe-deposit box.*

safeguard[1] *noun* **1** a precautionary measure or stipulation. **2** a pass; a safe-conduct. [Middle English *saufgarde* from early French, from Old French *sauf* (see SAFETY) + *garde* guard, of Germanic origin]

safeguard[2] *verb trans* to provide a safeguard for (something or somebody); to protect (them).

safe house *noun* a place used for concealment and safety, e.g. a meeting place for spies or terrorists or a shelter for people threatened with violence.

safekeeping *noun* protection or the state of being kept safe: *I left it with her for safekeeping.*

safelight *noun* a darkroom lamp with a filter to screen out rays that are harmful to photographic film or paper.

safe period *noun* the time during a woman's menstrual cycle when conception is least likely to occur, usu just before or just after her period.

safe seat *noun* a parliamentary seat that was won with a large majority by one party at an election and is likely to be retained by that party in a subsequent election: compare MARGINAL[2] (I).

safe sex *noun* sexual activity in which precautions are taken to prevent the transmission of Aids and similar diseases, e.g. sexual intercourse with the protection of a condom.

safety /'sayfti/ *noun* (*pl* **safeties**) **1** the condition of being safe from causing or suffering harm or loss. **2a** (*used before a noun*) designed to prevent injury, damage, or accidental use. **b** a safety device, *esp* a safety catch. **3** a billiard or snooker shot made with no attempt to score or so as to leave the balls in an unfavourable position for the opponent. **4** in American football, a defensive back who lines up far behind the line of scrimmage to guard against breakaway movements. [Middle English from early French *sauveté*, from Old French *sauve*, fem of *sauf*: see SAFE[1]]

safety belt *noun* **1** = SEAT BELT. **2** a belt fastening somebody to something to prevent falling or injury.

safety catch *noun* a device, e.g. on a gun or a machine, designed to prevent accidental use.

safety curtain *noun* a fireproof curtain in a theatre that can isolate the stage from the auditorium in case of fire.

safety-deposit *noun* = SAFE-DEPOSIT.

safety factor *noun* the ratio of the strength of a material to the maximum stress expected in use.

safety glass *noun* glass that has been strengthened or laminated so that it will not shatter into dangerously sharp pieces.

safety lamp *noun* a miner's lamp constructed to avoid ignition of inflammable gas, usu by enclosing the flame in wire gauze.

safety match *noun* a match capable of being ignited only on a specially prepared surface, usu the side of its own matchbox.

safety net *noun* **1** a net designed to protect people working or performing in high places by catching them if they fall. **2** a measure intended to provide protection or assistance in times of hardship or difficulty: *the safety net of unemployment benefit.*

safety pin *noun* a pin in the form of a clasp with a guard covering its point when fastened.

safety razor *noun* a razor with a guard for the blade to prevent users from cutting their skin.

safety valve *noun* **1** an automatic escape or pressure-relief valve, e.g. for a steam boiler. **2** an outlet for pent-up energy or emotion: *Playing computer games can act as a safety valve for life's frustrations.*

safflower /'saflowə/ *noun* **1** a widely grown SW Asian and N African plant of the daisy family with seeds rich in edible oil: *Carthamus tinctorius.* **2** a red dye prepared from the large orange or red flower heads of this plant. [early French *saffleur* via Old Italian *saffiore* from Arabic *asfar* yellow, a yellow plant]

saffron /'safron, 'safrən/ *noun* **1a** a deep gold aromatic pungent spice made from the dried stigmas (flower parts; see STIGMA) of a type of crocus and used to colour and flavour foods. **b** an autumn-flowering crocus with purple or white flowers from which this spice is derived: *Crocus sativus.* **c** (*used before a noun*) coloured or flavoured with saffron: *saffron rice.* **2** an orange-yellow colour.

[Middle English from Old French *safran* via late Latin from Arabic *za'farān*]

safranine /'safrənin, -neen/ *or* **safranin** /-nin/ *noun* any of various usu red synthetic dyes used for textiles and in staining specimens for study under a microscope. [French *safran* (see SAFFRON) + -INE[2]]

sag[1] /sag/ *verb intrans* (**sagged, sagging**) **1** to droop, sink, or settle from or as if from weight, pressure, or loss of tautness. **2a** to lose strength or vigour: *His spirits were sagging from overwork.* **b** to decline from a thriving state: *sagging industrial production.* [Middle English *saggen*, prob of Scandinavian origin]

sag[2] *noun* **1** a part that sags: *the sag in a rope.* **2** an instance or amount of sagging: *Sag is inevitable in a heavy unsupported span.* **3** a temporary economic decline. **⟫ saggy** *adj.*

saga /'sahgə/ *noun* **1a** a medieval Icelandic or Norse narrative dealing with historic or legendary figures and events. **b** a modern heroic narrative resembling this. **2** a novel or series of novels in the form of a long and leisurely chronicle of a family or community. **3** *informal* a long detailed account, often of a series of related events: *the ongoing saga of their feud with the neighbours.* [Old Norse *saga* narrative]

sagacious /sə'gayshəs/ *adj* **1** having sound judgment or perception: *a sagacious judge of character.* **2** prompted by or indicating keen discernment or foresight: *sagacious purchase of stock.* **⟫ sagaciously** *adv,* **sagacity** /sə'gasiti/ *noun.* [Latin *sagac-, sagax* wise]

sagamore /'sagəmaw/ *noun* a subordinate chief of certain Native American peoples, *esp* the Algonquians. [Abnaki *sāgimau*, literally 'he prevails over']

sage[1] /sayj/ *noun* somebody, e.g. a great philosopher, renowned or revered for wise teachings or sound judgment. [Middle English from Old French, ultimately from Latin *sapere* to taste, have good taste, be wise]

sage[2] *adj* **1** having great wisdom derived from reflection and experience. **2** proceeding from or indicating wisdom and sound judgment: *sage counsel.* **⟫ sagely** *adv,* **sageness** *noun.*

sage[3] *noun* **1a** a plant of the mint family whose greyish green aromatic leaves are used in cooking for flavouring: *Salvia officinalis.* **b** the leaves of this plant used as a culinary herb. **2** = SAGEBRUSH. [Middle English via early French *sauge* from Latin *salvia* healing plant, from *salvus* healthy; from its use as a medicinal herb]

sagebrush *noun* any of several species of aromatic low-growing shrubs of the daisy family that cover large areas of plains in the W USA: genus *Artemisia.*

sage green *adj* of a greyish green colour. **⟫ sage green** *noun.*

saggar *or* **sagger** /'sagə/ *noun* a box made of fireclay in which delicate ceramic pieces are baked. [prob alteration of SAFEGUARD[1]]

sagittal /'sajitl/ *adj* **1** relating to or in the region of the suture between the parietal bones that stretches from the front to the back of the top of the skull. **2** relating to or in the region of the middle plane or a plane parallel to the midline of the body. **⟫ sagittally** *adv.* [Latin *sagitta* arrow]

Sagittarius /saji'teəri·əs/ *noun* **1** in astronomy, a constellation (the Archer) depicted as a centaur shooting an arrow. **2a** in astrology, the ninth sign of the zodiac. **b** a person born under this sign. **⟫ Sagittarian** *adj and noun.* [Latin *sagittarius* archer, from *sagitta* arrow]

sagittate /'sajitayt/ *adj* said of a plant or animal part, *esp* a leaf: shaped like an arrowhead. [Latin *sagitta* arrow]

sago /'saygoh/ *noun* (*pl* **sagos**) **1** a dry powdered starch prepared from the pith of a sago palm and used *esp* as a food, e.g. in a milk pudding. **2** a dessert made with sago. [Malay *sagu* sago palm]

sago palm *noun* any of various tall Indian and Malaysian palms that yield sago: *Metroxylon sagu* and other species.

saguaro /sə'gwahroh/ *noun* (*pl* **saguaros**) a huge treelike cactus of the southwestern US and Mexico that has upward curving branches, white flowers, and an edible fruit: *Carnegiea gigantea.* [Mexican Spanish *saguaro*]

Saharan /sə'hahrən/ *noun* of the Sahara desert.

sahib /'sah(h)ib/ *noun* a term of address used in India, *esp* among the indigenous population in colonial times, as a mark of respect to a European man. [Urdu *ṣāḥib* via Persian from Arabic *ṣāḥib* friend, master]

Sahiwal /'sah·hival, -wal/ *noun* an animal of a breed of cattle with a distinctive hump on the back of its neck and used in tropical regions, *esp* for pulling ploughs.

said[1] /sed/ *verb* past tense and past part. of SAY[1].

said[2] *adj* aforementioned.

saiga /'sieɡə/ *noun* either of two antelopes that have enlarged snouts and live on the steppes around the Volga river and Caspian sea: *Saiga tartarica* and *Saiga mongolia*. [Russian *saïga*]

sail[1] /sayl/ *noun* **1a** an expanse of fabric that is spread to catch or deflect the wind as a means of propelling a ship, boat, etc. **b** the sails of a vessel considered collectively. **c** (*pl* **sails** *or* **sail**) a vessel equipped with sails. **2** something resembling a sail in function or form: *the sails of a windmill*. **3a** a voyage by ship or boat: *a five-day sail from the nearest port*. **b** an excursion in a sailing vessel: *go for a sail on the river*. ✳ **under sail** with sails set and not propelled by an engine. ⫸ **sailed** *adj*. [Old English *segl*]

sail[2] *verb intrans* **1a** to travel in a boat or ship. **b** to travel in or handle a sailing boat as a sporting or leisure activity. **2a** to travel on water, *esp* by the action of wind on sails. **b** to move without visible effort or in a stately manner: *She sailed gracefully into the room*. **3** to begin a journey by water: *sail with the tide*. ⫸ *verb trans* **1** to travel over (a body of water) in a ship or boat: *sail the seven seas*. **2** to direct or manage the operation of (a ship or boat). ✳ **sail close to the wind 1** to sail as close as possible to the direction from which the wind is blowing. **2** to be near to a point of danger or to a limit that it is unwise to cross. **sail into** to attack (somebody or something) vigorously or sharply: *She sailed into me for being late*. **sail through** to succeed in (something) with ease: *He sailed through the exam*. ⫸ **sailable** *adj*, **sailing** *noun*.

sailboard *noun* a flat buoyant board with a mast and a sail, used in the sport of windsurfing. ⫸ **sailboarder** *noun*, **sailboarding** *noun*.

sailboat *noun chiefly NAmer* = SAILING BOAT.

sailcloth *noun* **1** a heavy canvas used for sails, tents, or upholstery. **2** a lightweight canvas used for clothing.

sailer *noun* a sailing vessel considered with reference to characteristics such as speed, handling, etc: *a good sailer*.

sailfish *noun* (*pl* **sailfishes** *or collectively* **sailfish**) any of several species of large marine fishes related to the swordfish but having a very large sail-like fin along the back that can be lowered to give increased speed: genus *Istiophorus*.

sailing boat *noun* a boat fitted with sails for propulsion.

sailing ship *noun* a ship fitted with sails for propulsion.

sailor *noun* **1a** somebody who sails a ship or boat; a mariner. **b** a member of a ship's crew, *esp* one below the rank of officer. **c** somebody who sails as a sporting or leisure activity. **2** a person who travels by water, *esp* one considered with reference to their susceptibility to seasickness: *a bad sailor*.

sailor collar *noun* a broad collar that has a square flap across the back and tapers to a V in the front.

sailplane *noun* a glider designed for sustained soaring flights.

sainfoin /'sanfoyn/ *noun* a Eurasian red- or pink-flowered plant of the pea family widely grown for hay and pasture on chalk and dry soils because it has long strong roots that can penetrate considerable depths in search of water: *Onobrychis viciifolia*. [French *sainfoin* from early French *sain* healthy (from Latin *sanus*) + *foin* hay (from Latin *fenum*); because of its medicinal properties]

saint[1] /saynt; *before a name usu* s(ə)nt/ *noun* **1** a person officially recognized by the Christian Church, *esp* through canonization, as being outstandingly holy and so worthy of veneration: *I'll give my … subjects for a pair of carvèd saints, and my large kingdom for a little grave* — Shakespeare. **2a** any of the spirits of the dead in heaven. **b** = ANGEL (1A). **3** any of a member of various Christian groups regarding themselves as God's chosen people. **4** a person of outstanding piety or virtue. ⫸ **sainthood** *noun*, **saintlike** *adj*, **saintliness** *noun*, **saintly** *adj*. [Middle English via French from Latin *sanctus* sacred, past part. of *sancire* to make sacred]

saint[2] *verb trans* to recognize or designate (somebody) as a saint; *specif* to canonize (them).

Saint Agnes' Eve /'aɡnis(iz)/ *noun* the night of 20 January, when a girl or woman is traditionally able to see her future husband in a dream. [named after *St Agnes* d.304, virgin martyr and patron saint of virgins, whose feast day is on 21 January]

Saint Andrew's cross /'androohz/ *noun* **1** a cross consisting of two intersecting diagonal bars. **2** a cross formed by two white diagonals on a blue background, e.g. on a flag, *esp* the national flag of Scotland. [named after *St Andrew* d.c.60, one of the twelve apostles, who was crucified on such a cross]

Saint Anthony's fire /'antəniz/ *noun* any of several inflammations or gangrenous conditions of the skin, e.g. erysipelas or ergotism. [named after *St Anthony* d.356, Egyptian monk, whom victims prayed to for relief]

Saint Bernard /'buhnəd/ *noun* a large powerful dog of a breed originating in the Swiss Alps, having a thick shaggy coat and orig kept to rescue travellers who got into difficulty in the snow, traditionally having a small barrel of brandy attached to the collar. [named after the hospice of Grand *St Bernard*, Switzerland, where such dogs were first bred]

sainted *adj* **1** relating to or denoting a saint; canonized. **2** saintly; pious. **3a** having entered into heaven; dead: *my sainted mother*. **b** *dated* used in exclamations: *Oh, my sainted aunt!*

Saint Elmo's fire /'elmohz/ *noun* a flamelike electrical discharge sometimes seen in stormy weather at prominent points, e.g. on an aeroplane, ship, or building. [named after *St Elmo* Erasmus d.303, Italian bishop and patron saint of sailors; St Elmo's fire was believed to be a sign of his protection]

Saint George's Cross /'jawjiz/ *noun* **1** a cross consisting of two intersecting bars that form the shape of a plus sign (+). **2** a red cross of this kind on a white background, e.g. on a flag, *esp* the national flag of England. [named after *St George* d.c.303, a Christian martyr who supposedly killed a ferocious dragon]

Saint John's wort /jonz/ *noun* **1** any of numerous species of plants and shrubs with attractive five-petalled yellow flowers: genus *Hypericum*. **2** a preparation made from this plant and used as a natural antidepressant. [named after *St John* the Baptist fl c.27, prophet, because some species flower around the time of his feast day, 24 June]

saintpaulia /s(ə)nt'pawli·ə/ *noun* = AFRICAN VIOLET. [named after Baron W von *Saint Paul* d.1910, German explorer who discovered it]

saint's day *noun* a day in the calendar of the Christian Church on which a saint is commemorated.

Saint Swithin's Day /'swidh(ə)nz/ *noun* 15 July observed in honour of St Swithin and traditionally held to be a day on which, if it rains, it will continue to rain for the next 40 days. [named after *St Swithin* d.862, English bishop]

Saint Vitus's dance /'vietəs(iz)/ *noun dated* = SYDENHAM'S CHOREA. [named after *St Vitus*, third-cent. Christian child martyr, because victims visited his shrine to seek a cure]

saith /seth/ *verb* archaic third person sing. present of SAY[1].

saithe /sayth/ *noun* (*pl* **saithes** *or collectively* **saithe**) = COLEY. [of Scandinavian origin]

Saiva /'shievə, 'sievə/ *noun* a member of a famous Hindu sect devoted to the cult of the god Siva. ⫸ **Saivism** *noun*. [Sanskrit *śaiva* from *śiva* Siva]

sake[1] /sayk/ *noun* benefit, purpose, or interest. ✳ **for God's/ goodness/heaven's sake** used as an exclamation of protest, impatience, etc. **for old times' sake** because of or as an acknowledgment of a shared past; in memory of something in the past: *They went for a drink for old times' sake*. **for the sake of 1** in order to help or please (somebody); for the benefit of (them): *We moved to the country for the sake of the children*. **2** for the purpose of (something); in the interest of (it): *OK, for the sake of peace, you can have the last of the ice cream*. **3** so as to get, keep, or improve (something): *You should relax more for the sake of your health*. [Old English *sacu* guilt, contention, in Middle English 'accusation, one side's case in a legal action'; the current phrases date from the 13th cent. and prob come from Old Norse]

sake[2] *or* **saki** /'sahki/ *noun* a Japanese alcoholic drink made from fermented rice. [Japanese *sake*]

saker /'saykə/ *noun* a large falcon that has dark plumage and winters in the Balkans, Asia Minor, and Egypt: *Falco cherrug*. [Middle English *sagre* via French from Arabic *şaqr*]

saki[1] /'sahki/ *noun* (*pl* **sakis**) any of several species of monkeys that live in the forests of S America, have thick curly hair and usu a long bushy tail, and feed on fruit: genera *Pithecia* and *Chiropotes*. [French *saki* from Tupi *saqui*]

saki² /'sahki/ *noun* see SAKE².

Sakti /'sahkti, 'shahkti/ *noun* see SHAKTI.

sal /sal/ *noun* **1** an Indian tree valued for its wood and resin: *Shorea robusta*. **2** the teak-like wood of this tree. [Hindi *sāl* from Sanskrit *śāla*]

salaam¹ /sə'lahm/ *noun* a ceremonial greeting or gesture of respect performed in Arab-speaking and Muslim countries by bowing low and placing the right palm on the forehead. [Arabic *salām*, literally 'peace']

salaam² *verb intrans* to perform a salaam.

salable /'sayləbl/ *adj* see SALEABLE.

salacious /sə'layshəs/ *adj* **1** arousing sexual desire; lewd. **2** lecherous; lustful. ➤➤ **salaciously** *adv*, **salaciousness** *noun*. [Latin *salac-, salax* fond of leaping, lustful, from *salire* to leap]

salad /'saləd/ *noun* **1a** mixed raw vegetables, e.g. lettuce, cucumber, and tomato, served usu with a dressing as a side dish or with cold meat, fish, cheese, etc as a main course. **b** a dish of raw or cold cooked foods cut into small pieces and sometimes combined with a dressing: *fruit salad*. **2** a vegetable or herb eaten raw in salad, *esp* lettuce. [Middle English *salade* via French from Old Provençal *salada*, from *salar* to salt, from Latin *sal* salt]

salad days *pl noun* a time of youthful inexperience or indiscretion: *my salad days when I was green in judgment* — Shakespeare.

salamander /'saləmandə/ *noun* **1** any of numerous species of amphibians that superficially resemble lizards but are scaleless and covered with a soft moist skin: order Urodela. **2a** a mythical animal that lives in fire or that can withstand the effects of fire. **b** an elemental being said to inhabit fire. **3** a metal plate that is heated and held over food to brown the top. ➤➤ **salamandrine** /-drin/ *adj*. [Middle English *salamandre* via French and Latin from Greek *salamandra*]

salami /sə'lahmi/ *noun* (*pl* **salamis**) a highly seasoned sausage, often containing garlic, that is usu thinly sliced and eaten cold. [Italian *salami*, pl of *salame* salami, from *salare* to salt, from *sale* salt, from Latin *sal*]

sal ammoniac /,sal ə'mohniak/ *noun dated* = AMMONIUM CHLORIDE. [Middle English from Latin *sal ammoniacus*: see AMMONIA]

salary¹ /'saləri/ *noun* (*pl* **salaries**) a fixed usu monthly payment made to an employee, *esp* a professional or office worker: compare WAGE¹. [Middle English *salarie* from Latin *salarium* money for the purchase of salt, salary, from *sal* salt]

salary² *verb trans* (**salaries, salaried, salarying**) to pay a salary to (somebody). ➤➤ **salaried** *adj*.

salbutamol /sal'byoohtəmol/ *noun* a synthetic drug used in the treatment of asthma to relax the muscles of the bronchioles of the lungs and make breathing easier. [Latin *sal* salt + BUTYL + AMINE + -OL¹]

salchow /'salkow/ *noun* in ice-skating, a jump from the inside backward edge of one skate to the outside backward edge of the other skate with one or more turns in the air. [named after Ulrich Salchow d.1949, Swedish skating champion, who first performed it]

sale /sayl/ *noun* **1** the act or an instance of selling; *specif* the transfer of ownership of and title to property or goods from one person to another for a price. **2a** an event at which goods are offered for sale: *an antiques sale*. **b** an opportunity to buy or a period of selling goods at bargain prices. **c** a public disposal of goods to the highest bidder; an auction. **3a** (*in pl*) operations and activities involved in promoting and selling goods or services: *Joe is the manager in charge of sales.* **b** (*in pl, used before a noun*) of, involved in, or used in selling: *sales talk; sales department.* **4a** an opportunity of selling or being sold; demand: *We are counting on a large sale for the new product.* **b** (*also in pl*) a quantity sold: *Total sales rose last year.* **c** (*in pl*) gross receipts obtained from selling. ✳ **on/for sale** available for purchase. [Old English *sala*, from Old Norse]

saleable *or* **salable** *adj* capable of being or fit to be sold. ➤➤ **saleability** /-'biliti/ *noun*.

sale or return *noun* an arrangement by which a buyer, *esp* a retail outlet, pays only for the goods that are sold and may return what is unsold.

saleratus /salə'raytəs/ *noun NAmer* a raising agent used in baking consisting of potassium bicarbonate or sodium bicarbonate. [scientific Latin *sal aeratus* aerated salt]

saleroom *noun chiefly Brit* a place where goods are displayed for sale, *esp* by auction.

salesclerk /'saylzklahk; *NAmer* 'saylzkluhk/ *noun chiefly NAmer* = SHOP ASSISTANT.

salesman *or* **saleswoman** *noun* (*pl* **salesmen** *or* **saleswomen**) a salesperson. ➤➤ **salesmanship** *noun*.

salesperson *noun* (*pl* **salespersons** *or* **salespeople**) somebody employed to sell goods or services, e.g. in a shop or within an assigned territory.

Salian /'sayli·ən/ *noun* a member of a Frankish people that settled in an area bordering on the Ijssel river in the Netherlands early in the fourth cent. ➤➤ **Salian** *adj*. [late Latin *Salii* Salian Franks]

Salic /'saylik, 'salik/ *adj* relating to or denoting a Salian or the Salian people. [early French *salique* from late Latin *Salicus*, from *Salii* Salian Franks]

salicin /'salisin/ *noun* a bitter compound found in the bark and leaves of several willows and poplars and used in medicine as salicylic acid. [French *salicine*, from Latin *salic-, salix* willow + -INE²]

Salic law /'salik/ *noun* **1** the legal code of the Salian people. **2** a rule, held to derive from this code, that excludes females from succession to a throne: *My learned lord, we pray you to proceed, and justly and religiously unfold, why the law Salique, which they have in France, or should, or should not, bar us in our claim* — Shakespeare.

salicylic acid /sali'silik/ *noun* an acid used as a fungicide and to make chemical compounds, e.g. aspirin, that are used to relieve pain and fever and in the treatment of rheumatism: formula $C_7H_6O_3$. [French *salicyle* the radical of the acid, from *salicine*: see SALICIN]

salient¹ /'sayli·ənt/ *adj* **1a** standing out conspicuously: *salient characteristics.* **b** most noticeable or important: *the salient points of a theory.* **2** projecting beyond a line or level. **3** said of an angle, point, etc: pointing upward or outward: compare RE-ENTRANT¹. **4a** said of an animal: moving by leaps or springs. **b** said of a heraldic representation of an animal, e.g. a frog: depicted as if leaping or bounding. ➤➤ **salience** *noun*, **saliency** /-si/ *noun*, **saliently** *adv*. [Latin *salient-, saliens*, present part. of *salire* to leap]

salient² *noun* something, e.g. a promontory, that projects outward or upward from its surroundings; *specif* an outwardly projecting part of a fortification, trench system, or line of defence.

salientian /sayli'enshi·ən/ *noun* any of various amphibians, including frogs and toads, that lack a tail as adults and have long hind limbs suited to leaping and swimming: order Salientia. ➤➤ **salientian** *adj*. [Latin *salient-, saliens*: see SALIENT¹ + -IAN]

salina /sə'lienə/ *noun* a salt marsh, lake, spring, etc. [Spanish *salina* from Latin *salinae* saltworks, fem pl of *salinus*: see SALINE¹]

saline¹ /'saylien/ *adj* **1** of, containing, or resembling salt: *a saline solution.* **2** said of a laxative: containing salts of potassium, sodium, or magnesium. ➤➤ **salinity** /sə'liniti/ *noun*. [Middle English from Latin *salinus*, from *sal* salt]

saline² *noun* a saline solution, *esp* one similar in its concentration of ions to body fluids.

salinometer /sali'nomətə/ *noun* an instrument, e.g. a hydrometer, for measuring the amount of salt in a solution. [SALINE¹ + -O- + -METER²]

saliva /sə'lievə/ *noun* a slightly alkaline mixture of water, protein, salts, and often enzymes that is secreted into the mouth by salivary glands, providing lubrication to make chewing food easier, often beginning the breakdown of starches. ➤➤ **salivary** /sə'lievəri, 'saliv(ə)ri/ *adj*. [Middle English from Latin *saliva*]

salivary gland *noun* any of the mammalian glands that secrete saliva either when food is in the mouth or as a reflex response to the smell, sight, or thought of food.

salivate /'salivayt/ *verb intrans* **1** to have a flow of saliva, *esp* in anticipation of food. **2** to show great or excessive eagerness or excitement: *They were salivating at the prospect of huge profits.* ➤ *verb trans* to cause (*esp* an animal) to produce large amounts of saliva. ➤➤ **salivation** /-'vaysh(ə)n/ *noun*.

Salk vaccine /sawlk/ *noun* an injectable vaccine against poliomyelitis. [named after Jonas Salk d.1995, US microbiologist who developed it]

sallee /'sali/ *noun* see SALLY³.

sallet /'salit/ *noun* a light 15th-cent. helmet with a projection over the back of the neck, part of a medieval suit of armour. [Middle English from early French *sallade*, ultimately from Latin *caelare* to engrave, from *caelum* chisel]

sallow¹ /'saloh/ *noun* any of several species of Eurasian broad-leaved willows, some of which are important sources of charcoal: genus *Salix*. [Old English *sealh*]

sallow² *adj* of a sickly yellowish colour: *a sallow complexion*. ➤ **sallowish** *adj*, **sallowness** *noun*. [Old English *salu*]

sallow³ *verb trans* to make (somebody or something) sallow.

sally¹ /'sali/ *noun* (*pl* **sallies**) **1** a rushing forth; *esp* a sortie of troops from a besieged position. **2a** a brief outbreak: *a sally of rage*. **b** a witty remark or retort. **3** a short excursion; a jaunt. [early French *saillie* from Old French *saillir* to rush forward, from Latin *salire* to leap]

sally² *verb intrans* (**sallies, sallied, sallying**) **1** to rush out or issue forth suddenly. **2** (*usu + forth*) to set out, e.g. on a journey.

sally³ *or* **sallee** *noun* (*pl* **sallies** *or* **sallees**) an Australian eucalyptus or acacia tree. [prob alteration of SALLOW¹]

Sally Lunn /sali 'lun/ *noun* a bread or teacake made from sweetened yeast dough and typically served in toasted buttered slices. [said to be named after *Sally Lunn*, a woman who either baked or sold such bread in the English city of Bath]

salmagundi /salmə'gundi/ *noun* (*pl* **salmagundis**) **1** a dish of chopped meats, anchovies, eggs, and vegetables often arranged in rows for contrast and served with a dressing. **2** a mixture composed of many usu unrelated elements. [French *salmigondis*]

salmi /'salmi/ *noun* (*pl* **salmis**) a dish consisting of partly roasted game stewed in a rich wine sauce. [French *salmis*, short for *salmigondis* SALMAGUNDI]

salmon /'samən/ *noun* (*pl* **salmons** *or collectively* **salmon**) **1a** a large soft-finned game and food fish of the N Atlantic that is highly valued for its pink flesh: *Salmo salar*. **b** any of several species of related soft-finned fishes: family Salmonidae. **c** the flesh of a salmon used as food. **2** an orange-pink colour. [Middle English *samon* via French from Latin *salmon-, salmo*]

salmonella /salmə'nelə/ *noun* (*pl* **salmonellae** /-lee/) **1** any of various bacteria that cause diseases, *esp* food poisoning, in human beings and other warm-blooded animals: genus *Salmonella*. **2** an illness caused by this, *esp* food poisoning. ➤ **salmonellosis** /-'lohsis/ *noun*. [named after Daniel E *Salmon* d.1914, US veterinary surgeon, who first isolated a strain of the genus]

salmon ladder *noun* = FISH LADDER.

salmon trout *noun* = SEA TROUT.

salon /'saloh, 'salon/ *noun* **1** a commercial establishment where hairdressers, beauticians, couturiers, etc see their clients: *a beauty salon*. **2** an elegant reception room or living room. **3** formerly, a gathering of literary figures, artists, and the socially or politically prominent, held regularly in a fashionable home: *She tried to found a salon, and only succeeded in opening a restaurant* — Oscar Wilde. **4** (**Salon**) an exhibition, *esp* in France, of works of art by living artists. [French *salon*: see SALOON]

saloon /sə'loohn/ *noun* **1a** *Brit* a comfortable, well-furnished, and often relatively expensive bar in a public house: compare PUBLIC BAR. **b** *NAmer* a room or establishment in which alcoholic beverages are sold and consumed. **2** a public room or hall, e.g. a ballroom, an exhibition room, or a lounge on a passenger ship. **3** *Brit* an enclosed car with two or four doors and a separate boot. **4** a well-appointed railway carriage with no compartments. [French *salon* from Italian *salone* large hall, from *sala* hall, of Germanic origin]

saloon bar *noun* = SALOON (1A).

saloon car *noun* = SALOON (3).

salopettes /salə'pets/ *pl noun* high-waisted usu padded or quilted trousers with shoulder straps worn for skiing. [French *salopette* salopettes + -s¹ as in *trousers*, etc]

salpiglossis /salpi'glosis/ *noun* any of various plants of the nightshade family usu cultivated for their brightly coloured funnel-shaped flowers: genus *Salpiglossis*. [Latin genus name, from Greek *salpinx* trumpet + *glōssa* tongue]

salping- *or* **salpingo-** *comb. form* forming nouns, denoting: the Fallopian tubes: *salpingitis*; *salpingostomy*. [scientific Latin, from Greek *salping-, salpinx* trumpet]

salpingectomy /salping'jektəmi/ *noun* (*pl* **salpingectomies**) the surgical removal of the Fallopian tubes. [SALPING- + -ECTOMY]

salpingitis /salping'jietis/ *noun* inflammation of the Fallopian tubes. [SALPING- + -ITIS]

salpingo- *comb. form* see SALPING-.

salpingostomy /salping'gostəmi/ *noun* (*pl* **salpingostomies**) a surgical procedure to unblock a Fallopian tube or to reverse a sterilization operation in which the Fallopian tubes have been surgically tied. [SALPINGO- + -STOMY]

salpinx /'salpingks/ *noun* (*pl* **salpinges** /sal'pinjeez/) **1** = FALLOPIAN TUBE. **2** = EUSTACHIAN TUBE. [scientific Latin from Greek *salping-, salpinx* trumpet]

salsa /'salsə/ *noun* **1a** a type of Latin American popular music of Cuban origin that is lively, rhythmic, and sensuous. **b** dancing performed to this music. **2** a spicy Mexican relish of chopped mixed vegetables, usu tomatoes and onions, with chillies. [Spanish *salsa* sauce, from Latin *salsus*; see SAUCE¹]

salsify /'salsifie, -fi/ *noun* (*pl* **salsifies**) **1** a European plant of the daisy family cultivated for its long tapering edible roots: *Tragopogon porrifolius*. **2** the root of this plant, used as a vegetable. [French *salsifis* from obsolete Italian *salsifica*, prob from late Latin *saxifica* any of various herbs, from Latin *saxum* rock + *fricare* to rub]

SALT /sawlt/ *abbr* Strategic Arms Limitation Talks.

salt¹ /sawlt, solt/ *noun* **1** (*also* **common salt**) sodium chloride occurring naturally, e.g. as a mineral deposit, and dissolved in sea water and used *esp* in the form of white powder or crystals for seasoning or preserving food. **2a** any of numerous chemical compounds resulting from replacement of all or part of the hydrogen atoms of an acid by a metal atom or other chemical group. **b** (*in pl*) a mixture of the salts of usu sodium, potassium, or magnesium used as a laxative: *Epsom salts*. **c** (*in pl*) = SMELLING SALTS. **3a** an ingredient that imparts savour, piquancy, or zest: *add salt to the debate*. **b** sharpness of wit. **4** an experienced sailor: *a tale worthy of an old salt*. **5** = SALTCELLAR. ✳ **below the salt** in a socially disadvantageous position. **rub salt into the wound/somebody's wounds** to make something that is already painful, embarrassing, humiliating, etc even worse. **the salt of the earth** a person or group whose goodness, kindness, honesty, etc makes them worthy of respect and admiration: *one of those happy souls which are the salt of the earth, and without whom, this world would smell like what it is – a tomb* — Shelley. **with a pinch/grain of salt** with doubts or reservations as to the truth: *We take what he says with a pinch of salt*. **worth one's salt** worthy of respect; competent or effective, *esp* in doing one's work [from the money paid to soldiers in Roman times to buy salt; compare SALARY¹]. ➤ **saltlike** *adj*. [Old English *sealt*]

salt² *verb trans* **1** to treat, season, or preserve (something) with common salt or brine: *salted peanuts*. **2** to give flavour or piquancy to (e.g. a story). **3** to sprinkle (something) with or as if with salt; *specif* to sprinkle salt on (a road or path) to melt ice or snow. **4** to enrich (e.g. a mine) fraudulently by adding valuable matter, *esp* mineral ores. ➤ **salter** *noun*.

salt³ *adj* **1a** containing or impregnated with salt; saline or salty: *salt water*. **b** being or inducing a taste similar to that of common salt, one of the four basic taste sensations: compare BITTER¹, SOUR¹, SWEET¹. **2** cured or seasoned with salt; salted: *salt pork*. **3** containing, overflowed by, or growing in salt water: *a salt marsh*. **4** said of wit: sharp or pungent. ➤ **saltness** *noun*.

saltarello /saltə'reloh/ *noun* (*pl* **saltarellos** *or* **saltarelli** /-lee/) an Italian dance characterized by lively hopping or leaping steps. [Italian *saltarello* from *saltare* to leap, from Latin: see SALTATION]

saltation /sal'taysh(ə)n/ *noun* **1** the direct transformation of one form of an organism into another that is suggested by some evolutionary theories. **2** in geology, the jumping movement of particles transported in turbulent air or water. **3** *formal* the action or process of leaping. [Latin *saltation-, saltatio* dancing, dance, from *saltare* to leap, dance, frequentative of *salire* to leap]

saltatorial /saltə'tawri·al/ *adj* of, marked by, or adapted for leaping: *the saltatorial leap of a grasshopper*.

salt away *verb trans* to put (*esp* money) by in reserve; to save or hoard (it).

saltbush *noun* any of several species of shrubby plants of the goosefoot family that thrive in dry alkaline soil and are often important grazing plants in dry regions: genus *Atriplex*.

saltcellar *noun* a cruet for salt, *esp* a small open dish or a shaker with one or more holes in the top used for salt at table. [alteration (influenced by *cellar*) of Middle English *salt saler*, from SALT¹ + *saler* cruet for salt, via French from Latin *salarius* of salt, from *sal* salt]

salt dome *noun* a dome-shaped arch in sedimentary rock that has a mass of rock salt as its core.

saltern /'sawltən, 'soltən/ *noun* a place where salt is made, e.g. by boiling sea water or leaving it to evaporate. [Old English *sealtern*, from *sealt* SALT¹ + *ærn* house]

salt flat *noun* (*usu in pl*) a salt-encrusted flat area resulting from evaporation of a former body of water.

salting *noun chiefly Brit* (*usu in pl*) a marshy coastal area flooded regularly by tides.

saltire /'saltie-ə/ *noun* a diagonal cross, one of the ordinaries (basic designs; see ORDINARY² (2)) used in heraldry. [Middle English *sautire* from early French *saultoir* stile, saltire, from *saulter* to jump, from Latin *saltare*: see SALTATION]

salt lick *noun* a place to which animals regularly go to lick a salt deposit, or a block of selected minerals provided for animals to lick.

salt marsh *noun* flat land that is frequently flooded by seawater and supports a characteristic community of plants able to survive under these conditions.

salt out *verb trans* to precipitate or separate (a dissolved substance) from a solution by the addition of salt.

saltpan *noun* a natural or artificial basin where salt is produced by the evaporation of salt water.

saltpetre (*NAmer* **saltpeter**) /'sawlt'peetə, solt-/ *noun* 1 = POTASSIUM NITRATE. 2 = CHILE SALTPETRE. [alteration of Middle English *salpeter* from early French *salpetre* from late Latin *sal petrae* salt of the rock]

saltus /'saltəs/ *noun* (*pl* **saltuses**) a sudden transition, e.g. to a conclusion in logic; a jump. [Latin *saltus* leap, past part. of *salire* to leap]

saltwater *adj* of, living in, or being salt water.

saltwort *noun* a plant of the goosefoot family that has prickly leaves and small greenish flowers and grows *esp* in salty habitats: genus *Salsola*.

salty *adj* (**saltier, saltiest**) 1 of, seasoned with, or containing salt. 2 having a usu strong taste of salt. 3a piquant; witty: *a salty retort*. b earthy; coarse: *salty language*. >> **saltily** *adv*, **saltiness** *noun*.

salubrious /sə'loohbri-əs/ *adj* 1 favourable to or promoting health or well-being: *a salubrious climate*. 2 pleasant; respectable: *not a very salubrious district*. >> **salubriously** *adv*, **salubriousness** *noun*, **salubrity** *noun*. [Latin *salubris* from *salus* health]

saluki /sə'loohki/ *noun* (*pl* **salukis**) a dog of a breed originating in N Africa, having a smooth silky coat, a tall slender build, long droopy ears, and fringed feet. [Arabic *salūqiy* of *Saluq*, ancient city in Arabia]

salutary /'salyoot(ə)ri/ *adj* 1a having a beneficial or edifying effect: *salutary advice*. b said *esp* of a bad experience: offering an opportunity to learn or improve. 2 *archaic* promoting health. >> **salutarily** *adv*. [early French *salutaire* from Latin *salutaris*, from *salut-*, *salus* health]

salutation /salyoo'taysh(ə)n/ *noun* 1 an expression of greeting or courtesy by word or gesture: *And the angel … said, Hail thou that art highly favoured, the Lord is with thee: blessed art thou among women. And … she was troubled at his saying, and cast in her mind what manner of salutation this should be* — Bible. 2 a word or phrase of greeting, e.g. *Dear Sir* or *Ladies and Gentlemen*, that conventionally opens a letter or speech. >> **salutational** *adj*.

salutatory /sə'lyoohtət(ə)ri/ *adj* relating to, in the form of, or resembling a salutation.

salute¹ /sə'looht/ *verb trans* 1 to address (somebody) with expressions of greeting, goodwill, or respect. 2a to show respect and recognition to (e.g. a military superior) by assuming a prescribed position, *esp* by raising the hand to the side of the head. b to honour (somebody) by a conventional military or naval ceremony, *esp* by the firing of a gun or guns into the air. c to praise (something or somebody): *They saluted her courage*. > *verb intrans* to make a salute. >> **saluter** *noun*. [Middle English *saluten* from Latin *salutare*, from *salut-*, *salus* health, safety, greeting]

salute² *noun* 1 a greeting or salutation. 2 a sign or ceremony expressing goodwill or respect: *The festival was a salute to the arts*. 3 an act of saluting somebody, *esp* a military superior, or the prescribed position, gesture, etc for this. 4 a firing of guns into the air as a ceremonial sign of respect, honour, or celebration. ✳ **take the salute** said e.g. of a senior officer in the armed forces or a non-military dignitary: to be the person honoured by a military parade, to whom the parade salutes in marching past.

Salvadorean *or* **Salvadorian** /salvə'dawri-ən/ *noun* a native or inhabitant of El Salvador, a republic in Central America. >> **Salvadorean** *adj*, **Salvadorian** *adj*.

salvage¹ /'salvij/ *noun* 1a the act or an instance of saving or rescuing a ship or its cargo from loss at sea. b the act or an instance of saving or rescuing property, e.g. from fire. c in law, payment made to somebody who saves or rescues something, *esp* a ship or its cargo, from loss or damage. 2a property saved or rescued from a calamity, e.g. a wreck or fire. b something of use or value extracted from waste material. [French *salvage* from early French *salver*: see SAVE¹]

salvage² *verb trans* 1 to save or rescue (something, e.g. a ship or its cargo) from loss or damage. 2 to extract or preserve (something of use or value) from destruction or failure. >> **salvageable** *adj*, **salvager** *noun*.

salvation /sal'vaysh(ə)n/ *noun* 1 deliverance from danger, difficulty, or destruction. 2 (*often* **one's salvation**) somebody or something that brings about salvation. 3 in Christian theology, deliverance from the power and effects of sin brought about by faith in Christ. >> **salvational** *adj*. [Middle English via Old French from late Latin *salvation-*, *salvatio*, from Latin *salvare*: see SAVE¹]

Salvation Army *noun* an international evangelical and charitable Christian group organized on military lines and founded in 1865 by William Booth for performing welfare and missionary work among the poor.

salvationism *noun* religious teaching emphasizing the saving of the soul. >> **salvationist** *adj and noun*.

Salvationist *noun* a member of the Salvation Army.

salve¹ /salv, sahv/ *noun* 1 an ointment for soothing wounds or sores. 2 a soothing influence or agency: *a salve to their wounded pride*. [Old English *sealf*]

salve² *verb trans* 1 to apply a salve to (e.g. a wound or sore). 2 to soothe or assuage (something): *salve a troubled conscience*.

salver /'salvə/ *noun* a tray, *esp* an ornamental silver one, on which food and drinks are served or letters and visiting cards are presented. [modification of French *salve* from Spanish *salva* sampling of food to detect poison, tray, from *salvar* to save, from Latin *salvare*: see SAVE¹]

salvia /'salvi-ə/ *noun* 1 any of various widely distributed plants or shrubs of the mint family, including sage: genus *Salvia*. 2 an ornamental species of salvia grown for its scarlet or purple flowers: *Salvia splendens*. [Latin *salvia*: see SAGE³]

salvo /'salvoh/ *noun* (*pl* **salvos** *or* **salvoes**) 1 a simultaneous discharge of two or more guns or missiles in military or naval action or as a salute. 2 a sudden or emphatic burst, e.g. of criticism or applause. [Italian *salva* via French from Latin *salve* hail!, imperative of *salvēre* to be healthy, from *salvus* healthy]

sal volatile /ˌsal və'latili/ *noun* an aromatic solution of ammonium carbonate in alcohol or aqueous ammonia used as smelling salts: *'And here is the second volume of The Sentimental Journey.' … 'Very well – give me the sal volatile.' 'Is it in a blue cover, Ma'am?' 'My smelling bottle, you simpleton!'* — Sheridan. [scientific Latin *sal volatile*, literally 'volatile salt']

salwar /sul'wah, -'vah/ *or* **shalwar** /shul'wah, -'vah/ *noun* light trousers that are loose-fitting around the waist and hips, tapering to a close fit at the ankle, traditionally worn under a kameez by women in N India, Pakistan, and Bangladesh and by women of N Indian, Pakistani, and Bangladeshi descent. [Urdu from Persian *salwār*]

SAM /sam/ *abbr* surface-to-air missile.

Sam. *abbr* Samuel (books of the Bible).

samara /sə'mahrə/ *noun* a dry one-seeded fruit with one or more winglike projections that is produced by various trees, e.g. the ash, maple, and sycamore; a key. [Latin *samara* elm seed]

Samaritan /sə'marit(ə)n/ *noun* 1 a native or inhabitant of ancient Samaria. 2a somebody who selflessly gives aid to those in distress. b (**the Samaritans**) *Brit* an organization that offers a telephone counselling service to people in despair. c a person who is a member of the Samaritans, *esp* somebody who counsels people who phone for help or advice. >> **Samaritan** *adj*.

Word history

Middle English via late Latin from Greek *samaritēs* inhabitant of *Samaria*, district and city of ancient Palestine; (sense 2) from the parable of the good Samaritan, Luke 10:30–7. The common modern use of *Samaritan* for a selfless helper misses some of the point of Christ's parable of the Samaritan who stopped to help a man robbed and wounded by the roadside. To Christ's Jewish audience, a Samaritan was an enemy and an outcast, as appears in the incident of Christ's visit to a Samaritan village: 'the Jews have no dealings with the Samaritans' (John 4:9). The Samaritans had split from mainstream Judaism several centuries before Christ's birth; furthermore, the Jews despised them for being of mixed blood.

samarium /sə'meəri·əm/ *noun* a pale grey metallic chemical element of the lanthanide series, that is used *esp* in alloys that form permanent magnets: symbol Sm, atomic number 62.

Word history
scientific Latin *samarium* from French *samarskite*, mineral named after Colonel von *Samarski*, 19th-cent. Russian mine official. Samarium was first seen in the spectrum of samarskite.

samba[1] /'sambə/ *noun* **1** a Brazilian dance of African origin characterized by a dip and spring upward at each beat of the music. **2** the music for this dance. [Portuguese *samba*, of African origin]

samba[2] *verb intrans* (**sambas, sambaed, sambaing**) to dance the samba.

sambar *or* **sambur** /'sambə/ *noun* (*pl* **sambars** *or* **samburs** *or collectively* **sambar** *or* **sambur**) a large Asian deer with three-pointed antlers and long coarse hair on the throat: *Cervus unicolor*. [Hindi *sābar* from Sanskrit *śambara*]

Sam Browne belt /,sam 'brown/ *noun* a leather belt supported by a light strap passing over the right shoulder and worn by certain military and police officers. [named after Sir *Sam*uel James *Browne* d.1901, British army officer, who invented it]

sambur /'sambə/ *noun* see SAMBAR.

same[1] /saym/ *adj* **1a** being one single thing, person, or group: *sitting at the same table*. **b** used as an intensive: *born in this very same house*. **2** being the specified one or ones: *make the same mistake as last time*. **3** identical in appearance, quantity, type, etc: *two women wearing the same dress*. [Middle English from Old Norse *samr*]

same[2] *pronoun* **1** the same thing, person, or group: *do the same for you*. **2** something previously mentioned: *He ordered a drink and refused to pay for same*. ✳ **all/just the same** nevertheless.

Usage note
The use of *same* as a pronoun (*To installing one electric shower and connecting and testing same: £170*) is a commercial or legal use. It should not be used in informal speech or writing.

same[3] *adv* (*usu* **the same**) in the same manner: *two words spelt the same*.

sameness *noun* **1** identity or similarity. **2** monotonous uniformity.

samey /'saymi/ *adj* (**samier, samiest**) *Brit, informal* lacking individuality or originality; boringly monotonous: *I don't like their new album – the songs are all too samey*.

samfu /'samfooh/ *noun* an outfit of loose trousers with a matching high-necked jacket or blouse worn by Chinese women. [Chinese (Cantonese) from *saam* dress, coat + *foo* trousers]

Sami /'sahmi/ *noun* (*pl* **Samis** *or collectively* **Sami**) **1** a member of an indigenous people inhabiting Lapland, a region covering northern Scandinavia and the Kola Peninsula of northwestern European Russia. **2** the Finno-Ugric language spoken by these people. ⏩ **Sami** *adj*. [the local name for this people; origin unknown]

Samian /'saymi·ən/ *noun* a native or inhabitant of Samos, Greek island in the Aegean. ⏩ **Samian** *adj*. [via Latin from Greek *samios* of *Samos*]

Samian ware *noun* a fine glossy red earthenware pottery produced mainly in Roman Gaul in the first three cents AD.

samisen /'samisen/ *noun* a three-stringed Japanese musical instrument with a long neck and a rectangular body, played by plucking using a large plectrum. [Japanese *samisen* from Chinese (Pekingese) *sanxian*, from *san* three + *xian* string]

samite /'samiet, 'saymiet/ *noun* a rich medieval silk fabric interwoven with gold or silver and used for clothing: *An arm rose up from out the bosom of the lake, clothed in white samite, mystic, wonderful, holding the sword* — Tennyson. [Middle English *samit* via French from late Latin *examitum*, *samitum* from Greek *hexamiton*, neuter of *hexamitos* of six threads, from HEXA- + *mitos* thread]

samizdat /'samizdat/ *noun* in the former USSR and some countries of eastern Europe, a system by which literature suppressed by the government was clandestinely printed and distributed. [Russian *samizdat*, literally 'self-publishing house']

Samoan /sə'moh·ən/ *noun* **1** a native or inhabitant of Samoa, group of islands in the S Pacific Ocean. **2** the Polynesian language of the people of Samoa. ⏩ **Samoan** *adj*.

samosa /sə'mohsə/ *noun* (*pl* **samosas** *or* **samosa**) a small triangular pastry case filled with spiced minced meat, vegetables, etc and deep-fried, served *esp* as an appetizer or a starter to an Indian meal. [Persian and Urdu *samosa*]

samovar /'saməvah/ *noun* a metal urn with a tap at its base and an interior heating tube that is used, *esp* in Russia, to boil water for tea. [Russian *samovar*, from *samo-* self + *varit'* to boil]

Samoyed /samə'yed, sə'moy·ed/ *noun* (*pl* **Samoyeds** *or collectively* **Samoyed**) **1a** a member of a group of indigenous, mainly nomadic, peoples inhabiting northeastern parts of European Russia and northwestern parts of Siberia. **b** any of a group of Uralic languages spoken by these peoples. **2** a dog of a breed originating in Siberia, having a very thick whitish or creamish coat and used *orig* for pulling sledges. ⏩ **Samoyed** *adj*, **Samoyedic** /samə'yedik/ *adj*. [Russian *samoed*]

samp /samp/ *noun NAmer* coarsely ground maize, or a porridge made from this. [Narraganset *nasaump* corn mush]

sampan /'sampan/ *noun* a small flat-bottomed boat used in rivers and harbours in the Far East and usu propelled by an oar or oars at the stern. [Chinese (Cantonese) *saambaan*, from *saam* three + *baan* board, plank]

samphire /'samfie·ə/ *noun* **1** a European rock plant of the carrot family that grows near the sea and has fleshy edible leaves: *Crithmum maritimum*. **2** = GLASSWORT. [alteration of earlier *sampiere*, from early French (*herbe de*) *Saint Pierre* St Peter's (herb)]

sample[1] /'sahmpl/ *noun* **1a** a part or item serving to show the character or quality of a larger whole or group. **b** (*used before a noun*) intended as or used for a sample. **2** a selection of items or individuals from a statistical population whose properties are studied to gain information about the whole. **3** a specimen, e.g. of blood, urine, etc, taken for scientific testing or analysis. **4a** a sound created by electronic sampling. **b** a piece of recorded music incorporated into another piece of usu electronic music by sampling. [Middle English via French from Latin *exemplum*: see EXAMPLE[1]]

sample[2] *verb trans* **1** to take a sample of or from (something), e.g. for testing or analysis. **2** to experience or get a taste of (something): *And then we went out to sample the resort's nightlife*. **3** to take an extract from (a recording) and mix it into a new recording.

sampler *noun* **1** a decorative piece of needlework typically having letters or verses embroidered on it in various stitches as an example of skill. **2** a collection of representative specimens, extracts, or examples. **3** somebody or something that collects, prepares, or examines samples. **4** in recording, a piece of equipment used for sampling, *esp* a computer with special software.

sampling *noun* **1** a statistical sample. **2** the act, process, or technique of selecting or taking a sample. **3** a technique in which recorded sounds or extracts are incorporated into a new recording.

samsara /sam'sahrə/ *noun* in Hinduism and Buddhism, the indefinitely repeated cycle of birth, life, death, and reincarnation. ⏩ **samsaric** *adj*. [Sanskrit *saṁsāra*, literally 'passing through']

samurai /'sam(y)oorie/ *noun* (*pl* **samurai**) **1** the warrior aristocracy of feudal Japan. **2** a member of the samurai. [Japanese *samurai*]

san /san/ *noun informal* = SANATORIUM.

sanative /'sanətiv/ *adj formal, archaic* having the power to heal; curative. [Middle English *sanatif* via French from late Latin *sanativus*, from Latin *sanare* to cure, from *sanus* healthy]

sanatorium /sanə'tawri·əm/ *noun* (*pl* **sanatoriums** *or* **sanatoria** /-ri·ə/) **1** an establishment where people suffering or recovering from long-term illnesses receive medical treatment or care. **2** *Brit* a room, *esp* in a boarding school, where sick people are looked after. [Latin *sanatorium*, neuter of *sanatorius* curative, from *sanare*: see SANATIVE]

sancta /'sangktə/ *noun* pl of SANCTUM.

sancta sanctorum /sangk'tawrəm/ *noun* pl of SANCTUM SANCTORUM.

sanctify /'sangktifie/ *verb trans* (**sanctifies, sanctified, sanctifying**) **1** to set (something) apart for a sacred purpose or for religious use. **2** to free (somebody) from sin. **3** to give moral, social, or religious sanction to (something). **4** to make or declare (something) productive of holiness or piety: *Keep the sabbath day to sanctify it* — Bible. ⏩ **sanctification** /-fi'kaysh(ə)n/ *noun*, **sanctifier** *noun*.

[Middle English *sanctifien* via French from late Latin *sanctificare*, from Latin *sanctus*: see SAINT[1]]

sanctimonious /sangkti'mohni·əs/ *adj* 1 making a show or pretence of piety. 2 assured of one's own rightness, virtue, or moral superiority; self-righteous. ➤➤ **sanctimoniously** *adv*, **sanctimoniousness** *noun*, **sanctimony** /'sangktiməni/ *noun*. [Latin *sanctimonia* devoutness, from *sanctus*: see SAINT[1]]

sanction[1] /'sangksh(ə)n/ *noun* 1 official permission or authoritative ratification. 2 something, e.g. a moral principle, that makes an oath or rule binding. 3a a penalty attached to an offence. b (*usu in pl*) an economic or military measure adopted to force a nation to change some policy or comply with international law. 4a a consideration that determines moral action or judgment. b a mechanism of social control for enforcing a society's standards. 5 a formal ecclesiastical decree. [via French from Latin *sanction-, sanctio*, from *sancire* to make holy]

sanction[2] *verb trans* 1 to give authoritative approval or consent to (something). 2 to make (something) valid or binding; to ratify (it). ➤➤ **sanctionable** *adj*.

sanctitude /'sangktityoohd/ *noun formal* saintliness or holiness.

sanctity /'sangktiti/ *noun* (*pl* **sanctities**) 1 holiness of life and character. 2 the quality or state of being holy or inviolable: *the sanctity of marriage*. 3 (*usu in pl*) a sacred object, obligation, etc. [Middle English *saunctite* via French from Latin *sanctitat-, sanctitas*, from *sanctus*: see SAINT[1]]

sanctuary /'sangktyoo(ə)ri, -chəri/ *noun* (*pl* **sanctuaries**) 1 a consecrated place, e.g.: a the ancient temple at Jerusalem or its HOLY OF HOLIES (sacred inner chamber). b the most sacred part of a religious building, *esp* the part of a Christian church in which the altar is placed. c a place for worship, e.g. a church or a temple. 2 a place of refuge and protection. 3a a refuge for wildlife where predators are controlled and hunting is illegal: *a bird sanctuary*. b a refuge for animals that have been injured, neglected, ill-treated, etc: *a donkey sanctuary*. 4 the immunity from punishment by law formerly extended to somebody taking refuge in a church or other sacred building. [Middle English *sanctuarie* via French from late Latin *sanctuarium*, from Latin *sanctus*: see SAINT[1]]

sanctum /'sangktəm/ *noun* (*pl* **sanctums** or **sancta** /'sangktə/) 1 a sacred place. 2 a place of private privacy and security, e.g. a study. [Latin *sanctum*, neuter of *sanctus*: see SAINT[1]]

sanctum sanctorum /sangk'tawrəm/ *noun* (*pl* **sanctum sanctorums** or **sancta sanctorum**) 1 = HOLY OF HOLIES. 2 *humorous* = SANCTUM. [late Latin *sanctum sanctorum* holy of holies]

Sanctus /'sangktəs/ *noun* in the Christian Church, a hymn of adoration sung or said before the prayer of consecration in the celebration of the Eucharist. [Middle English, from late Latin *Sanctus, sanctus, sanctus* Holy, holy, holy, opening of a hymn sung by the angels in Isaiah 6:3]

Sanctus bell *noun* = SACRING BELL.

sand[1] /sand/ *noun* 1 loose granular particles smaller than gravel and coarser than silt that result from the disintegration of rock, *esp* quartz, forming the main constituent of beaches and the beds of seas and rivers. 2 (*usu in pl*) an area of sand, *esp* on the seashore. 3 (*in pl*) the grainy material that passes through an hourglass, as representing an ever-diminishing allocation of time for something: *The sands of this government run out very fast* — Harold Laski. 4a a yellowish grey colour. b (*used before a noun*) of this colour. [Old English *sand*]

sand[2] *verb trans* 1 (*often* + down) to smooth or prepare (a surface, floor, etc) by grinding or rubbing with an abrasive, e.g. sandpaper. 2 to sprinkle (something, e.g. an icy road surface) with or as if with sand. 3 (*often* + up) to cover or choke (something) with sand.

sandal[1] /'sandl/ *noun* a light shoe typically consisting of a sole held on the foot by straps or thongs. ➤➤ **sandalled** *adj*. [Middle English *sandalie* via Latin from Greek *sandalion*, dimin. of *sandalon* wooden shoe]

sandal[2] *noun* = SANDALWOOD.

sandalwood *noun* 1a an Indo-Malayan tree with close-grained fragrant yellowish HEARTWOOD (hard central wood): *Santalum album*. b the wood of this tree, used *esp* in ornamental carving and cabinetwork. c an aromatic oil obtained from this tree, used *esp* in perfumes and soaps. 2 any of various trees that resemble the sandalwood and yield similar wood. [Middle English via French from late Latin *sandalum*, from late Greek *santalon*, derivative of Sanskrit *candana*, of Dravidian origin]

sandarac /'sandərak/ *noun* a resin obtained *esp* from an African tree of the pine family and used in making varnish and incense. [Latin *sandaraca* red colouring, from Greek *sandarakē* realgar, red pigment from realgar]

sandbag[1] *noun* a bag filled with sand and used as ballast in a boat or balloon, as a means of preventing flood water entering a property, or as protection in a temporary fortification such as a trench.

sandbag[2] *verb trans* (**sandbagged, sandbagging**) 1 to barricade, stop up, or weight (something) with sandbags. 2 to hit or stun (somebody) with a sandbag, or as if with a sandbag. ➤➤ **sandbagger** *noun*.

sandbank *noun* a large deposit of sand, *esp* one that becomes visible at low tide or forms a shallow area in a river or coastal waters.

sandbar *noun* a ridge of sand built up by currents in a river or sea.

sandblast[1] *verb trans* to treat (a surface) with a high-speed jet of sand propelled by air or steam, e.g. in engraving or cleaning glass or stone. ➤➤ **sandblaster** *noun*.

sandblast[2] *noun* a jet of sand used in sandblasting.

sand-blind *adj archaic* having poor eyesight: compare STONE-BLIND. [Middle English, prob from Old English *sam-* half + BLIND[1]]

sandbox *noun* 1 a box carried on a train from which sand may be scattered on the rails to prevent slipping. 2 a shaker formerly used for sprinkling sand on wet ink. 3 *NAmer* a box that contains sand for children to play in.

sandboy *noun archaic* a boy who sold sand. ✳ **happy as a sandboy** cheerfully absorbed or engrossed; very happy or carefree. [orig in the sense 'pedlar of sand']

sandcastle *noun* a model of a castle or other structure made in damp sand, *esp* at the seaside.

sand dollar *noun* any of numerous flat circular invertebrate animals related to the sea urchins that live chiefly on sandy seabeds in shallow water: order Clypeasteroidea.

sand eel *noun* any of several species of silvery eel-like sea fishes that have a single fin along the back and are often found buried or burrowing in sand: family Ammodytidae.

sander *noun* a machine or device, *esp* a power tool, that smooths, polishes, or scours by means of abrasive material usu in the form of a disc or belt.

sanderling /'sandəling/ *noun* a small plump sandpiper with largely grey-and-white plumage: *Calidris alba*. [perhaps irreg from SAND[1] + -LING]

sand flea *noun* 1 = CHIGOE. 2 = SANDHOPPER.

sandfly *noun* (*pl* **sandflies**) 1 any of various small biting flies that transmit disease: genus *Phlebotomus* and others. 2 any of various other small flies, *esp* a name given in Australia and New Zealand to the BLACKFLY (I).

sandgrouse *noun* (*pl* **sandgrouse**) any of several species of birds of dry parts of Europe, Asia, and Africa that have long pointed wings and tail, grey or brown plumage, and short feet: family Pteroclidae.

sandhi /'sandi/ *noun* the modification of a speech sound or word form according to context, e.g. the change of the indefinite article *a* to *an* before a vowel. [Sanskrit *saṃdhi*, literally 'placing together']

sandhopper *noun* any of numerous flattened shrimplike invertebrate animals that live on beaches and leap like fleas: genus *Orchestia* and other genera.

Sandinista /sandi'neestə/ *noun* a member of the Sandinista National Liberation Front, the ruling political group in Nicaragua from 1979 to 1990. [Augusto César *Sandino* d.1934, Nicaraguan guerrilla leader who organized an uprising against US marines in 1927]

sandman *noun* (**the sandman**) a mythical figure who supposedly sends children to sleep by sprinkling sand in their eyes.

sand martin *noun* a small brown-and-white martin of the N hemisphere that usu nests in colonies in holes bored into banks of sand: *Riparia riparia*.

sandpaper[1] *noun* paper that has a thin layer of sand glued to it, used in smoothing wood, etc. ➤➤ **sandpapery** *adj*.

sandpaper[2] *verb trans* (**sandpapered, sandpapering**) to rub or smooth (a surface) with or as if with sandpaper.

sandpiper *noun* any of numerous small wading birds with long slender legs and longer bills than the related plovers: genus *Calidris*.

sandpit *noun* **1** an enclosure containing sand for children to play in. **2** a pit from which sand is extracted.

sandshoe *noun* a light canvas shoe; a plimsoll.

sandstone *noun* a sedimentary rock consisting of sand grains, usu of quartz, held together by silica, calcium carbonate, or other cement.

sandstorm *noun* a strong wind driving clouds of sand, *esp* in a desert.

sandwich[1] /'san(d)wich, 'san(d)wij/ *noun* **1a** two slices of usu buttered bread containing any of various fillings, e.g. cold meat, cheese, or jam: *Professor McGonagall raised her wand … A large plate of sandwiches, two silver goblets and a jug of iced pumpkin juice appeared with a pop* — J K Rowling. **b** a sponge cake with jam, cream, etc between its two or more layers. **2** something resembling a sandwich in being layered or having a filling. [named after John Montagu, fourth Earl of *Sandwich* d.1792, for whom this snack was devised so that he could eat without leaving the gambling table]

sandwich[2] *verb trans* **1** (+ between) to insert (something) between two things of a different quality or character. **2** (*often* + in) to create room or time for (something or somebody): *I can sandwich you in at 5.30.* **3** (+ together) to put (things) together in layers.

sandwich board *noun* either of two boards hung in front of and behind the body by straps from a person's shoulders and used *esp* for advertising.

sandwich course *noun Brit* a vocational course consisting of alternate periods of study and employment or practical experience.

sandwort *noun* any of several genera of usu low-growing plants of the pink family that have white or pink flowers and grow in tufts in dry sandy regions: genus *Arenaria* and other genera.

sandy *adj* (**sandier, sandiest**) **1** consisting of, containing, or sprinkled with sand. **2** resembling sand in texture. **3** said *esp* of hair: having a yellowish brown or gingerish colour. ➤➤ **sandiness** *noun.*

sand yacht *noun* a light wheeled vehicle that is propelled by sails and used *esp* for racing on sand as a sport or pastime.

sandy blight *noun Aus, informal* an irritation or inflammation of the eye.

sane /sayn/ *adj* **1** mentally sound; able to anticipate and assess the effect of one's actions. **2** proceeding from a sound mind; rational. ➤➤ **sanely** *adv,* **saneness** *noun.* [Latin *sanus* healthy, sane]

Sanforized *or* **Sanforised** /'sanfəriezd/ *adj trademark* said of cotton or another fabric: having already been shrunk by a mechanical process before being manufactured into clothing etc. [named after *Sanford* L Clivett d.1968, US inventor of the process]

San Franciscan /ˌsan frənˈsiskən/ *noun* a native or inhabitant of the Californian city of San Francisco. ➤➤ **San Franciscan** *adj.*

sang /sang/ *verb* past tense of SING[1].

sangfroid /song'frwah/ *noun* self-possession or coolness, *esp* under strain. [French *sang-froid,* literally 'cold blood']

Sangiovese /sanjoh'vayzi/ *noun* **1** a variety of grape used in the production of red wine, e.g. Chianti. **2** a wine produced from this grape. [Italian *Sangiovese*]

sangoma /sang'gohmə, sang'gawmə/ *noun* (*pl* **sangomas**) *SAfr* a witch doctor. [Zulu *isangoma*]

Sangrail /sang'grayl/ *or* **Sangreal** /'sanggri·əl/ *noun* = HOLY GRAIL. [Middle English from Old French *saint graal*]

sangria /sang'gree·ə/ *noun* a Spanish drink made of red wine, fruit juice, and soda water or lemonade, often with pieces of fruit in it. [Spanish *sangría,* literally 'bleeding', from *sangre* blood, from Latin *sanguis*]

sanguinary /'sanggwin(ə)ri/ *adj formal* **1** bloodthirsty; murderous. **2** causing or accompanied by bloodshed. [Latin *sanguinarius,* from *sanguin-, sanguis* blood]

sanguine[1] /'sanggwin/ *adj* **1a** in medieval physiology, having blood as the predominating HUMOUR[1] (7) (body fluid believed to determine a person's disposition). **b** having the bodily form and temperament held to be characteristic of such predominance and marked by sturdiness, high colour, and cheerfulness. **2** confident; optimistic: *disappointed in a very sanguine hope* — Jane Austen. **3** ruddy: *a sanguine complexion.* **4** *chiefly literary* of a blood-red colour: *like to that sanguine flower inscribed with woe* — Milton. **5** *formal* bloody or bloodthirsty. ➤➤ **sanguinely** *adv,* **sanguineness** *noun.*

[Middle English *sanguin* via French from Latin *sanguineus,* from *sanguin-, sanguis* blood]

sanguine[2] *noun* **1** a blood-red colour. **2** a pencil used in drawing to produce such a colour.

sanguineous /sang'gwini·əs/ *adj* **1** of or containing blood. **2** = SANGUINARY. **3** = SANGUINE[1]. [Latin *sanguineus:* see SANGUINE[1]]

Sanhedrin /san'heedrin, 'sanidrin/ *noun* the supreme council and tribunal of the Jews before AD 70, having religious, civil, and criminal jurisdiction. [late Hebrew *sanhedhrīn gĕdhōlāh* great council]

sanicle /'sanikl/ *noun* any of a genus of plants of the carrot family having fruits covered in hooked bristles and roots that were formerly used in medicine, *esp* as an astringent: genus *Sanicula.* [Middle English via French from late Latin *sanicula,* prob from Latin *sanus* healthy]

sanitarium /sani'teəri·əm/ *noun* (*pl* **sanitariums** *or* **sanitaria** /-ri·ə/) *NAmer* = SANATORIUM. [from Latin *sanitat-, sanitas:* see SANITY]

sanitary /'sanit(ə)ri/ *adj* **1** of or promoting health: *sanitary measures.* **2** free from dirt, germs, etc and so posing no danger to health; hygienic. ➤➤ **sanitarian** *noun,* **sanitariness** *noun.* [French *sanitaire* from Latin *sanitas:* see SANITY]

sanitary napkin *noun NAmer* = SANITARY TOWEL.

sanitary towel *noun* a disposable absorbent pad worn externally during menstruation to absorb the flow of blood.

sanitary ware *noun* bathroom plumbing fixtures, e.g. sinks, toilet bowls, baths, etc.

sanitation /sani'taysh(ə)n/ *noun* **1** the maintenance or improvement of sanitary conditions to promote hygiene and prevent disease. **2** facilities and measures that are involved in the promotion of hygiene and prevention of disease, *esp* the disposal of sewage and collection of rubbish.

sanitize *or* **sanitise** /'sanitiez/ *verb trans* **1** to make (something) sanitary by cleaning, sterilizing, etc. **2** to make (something) more acceptable by removing offensive or undesirable features: *a sanitized version of the story.* ➤➤ **sanitization** /-'zaysh(ə)n/ *noun.*

sanity /'saniti/ *noun* **1** the state or quality of being sane; soundness or health of mind. **2** rational or sensible behaviour or judgment. [Middle English *sanite* from Latin *sanitat-, sanitas* health, sanity, from *sanus* healthy, sane]

sank /sangk/ *verb* past tense of SINK[1].

sans /sanz/ *prep archaic* without: *My love to thee is sound, sans crack or flaw* — Shakespeare. [Middle English from early French *san, sans,* modification of Latin *sine* without]

sans-culotte /sanzkyoo'lot (*French* sɔ̃kylɔt)/ *noun* **1** an extreme radical republican of the French Revolution, *esp* one belonging to the lower classes. **2** a radical or revolutionary political extremist. ➤➤ **sans-culottism** *noun.* [French *sans-culotte,* literally 'without knee breeches', because sans-culottes typically wore long trousers rather than the knee breeches worn by the upper classes]

Sanskrit /'sanskrit/ *noun* the ancient Indic language of the people of India, now only used as a language of religion and scholarship. It is the ancestor of many Indo-European languages. ➤➤ **Sanskrit** *adj,* **Sanskritic** /san'skritik/ *adj,* **Sanskritist** *noun.* [Sanskrit *saṃskṛta,* literally 'perfected', from *sam* together + *karoti* he makes]

sans serif *or* **sanserif** /ˌsan 'serif/ *noun* a letter or typeface with no serifs (short lines at upper and lower ends of strokes; see SERIF).

Santa Claus *or* **Santa** /'santə klawz/ *noun* = FATHER CHRISTMAS. [US modification of Dutch *Sinterklaas,* alteration of *Sint Nikolaas* Saint Nicholas fl fourth cent., bishop of Myra in Asia Minor and patron saint of children, who was known for his benevolence and generosity]

santim /'santeem/ *noun* a unit of currency in Latvia, worth 100th of a lat. [Latvian *santims* from French *centime* CENTIME]

santolina /santə'leenə/ *noun* any of various low-growing aromatic Mediterranean shrubs of the daisy family that have finely cut leaves and flower heads on long stalks: genus *Santolina.* [Latin genus name, alteration of SANTONICA]

santonica /san'tonikə/ *noun* the dried unopened flower heads of a wormwood plant, containing santonin. [scientific Latin *santonica* from Latin *herba santonica* plant of the Santoni, a people of SW Gaul]

santonin /'santənin/ *noun* a chemical compound found in wormwood plants and used *esp* formerly to treat infections with parasitic intestinal worms. [SANTONICA + -IN¹]

sap¹ /sap/ *noun* **1a** a watery solution containing dissolved sugars, mineral salts, etc that circulates through the conducting system of a plant. **b** a body fluid essential to life, health, or vigour. **c** vitality; vigour. **2** *informal* a foolish or gullible person. ⟫⟫ **sapless** *adj*. [Old English *sæp*]

sap² *verb trans* (**sapped, sapping**) to drain (something or somebody) of sap or vitality.

sap³ *noun* the extension of a trench to a point beneath or near an enemy's fortifications. [early French *sappe* hoe, from Old Italian *zappa* spade, spadework, prob of Asian origin]

sap⁴ *verb* (**sapped, sapping**) ⟫ *verb intrans* to proceed by or dig a sap. ⟫ *verb trans* **1** to destroy (something) by undermining, or as if by undermining: *sap their morale*. **2** to weaken or exhaust (somebody) gradually. **3** to operate against (somebody or something) by a sap.

sapele /sə'peeli/ *noun* **1** any of several W African trees with hard cedar-scented wood resembling mahogany: genus *Entandrophragma*. **2** the hard reddish brown often striped wood of this tree, used *esp* for making furniture. [named after *Sapele*, a port on the Benin river in Nigeria, from which it was exported]

saphenous /sə'feenəs/ *adj* relating to or in the region of either of the two superficial veins in the leg. The longer of the two, running from the foot, up the inside of the leg, to the groin, is the longest vein in the human body. [late Latin *saphena* saphenous vein, from Arabic *sāfin*]

sapid /'sapid/ *adj* **1** having a usu strong pleasant flavour. **2** agreeable; engaging. ⟫⟫ **sapidity** /sə'piditi/ *noun*. [Latin *sapidus* tasty, from *sapere* to taste]

sapient /'saypi·ənt/ *adj formal* possessing or expressing great wisdom or discernment. ⟫⟫ **sapience** *noun*, **sapiently** *adv*. [Middle English via French from Latin *sapient-, sapiens*, present part. of *sapere* to taste, have a good taste, be wise]

sapiential /sapi'ensh(ə)l/ *adj* relating to, providing, having, or showing wisdom. [Old French *sapiential* from Latin *sapientia* wisdom, from *sapere* to taste, have good taste, be wise]

sapling /'sapling/ *noun* **1** a young tree. **2** *literary* a youth. **3** a young greyhound. [Middle English, from SAP¹ + -LING]

sapodilla /sapə'dilə/ *noun* **1** a round edible fruit with a brownish bristly skin and sweet yellowish brown flesh. **2** the large American evergreen tree that bears this fruit and that also yields CHICLE (a substance used in chewing gum): *Manilkara zapota*. **3** the hard durable reddish wood of this tree. [Spanish *zapotillo*, dimin. of *zapote*, from Nahuatl *tzapotl*]

saponaceous /sapə'nayshəs/ *adj* resembling or containing soap. [scientific Latin *saponaceus*, from Latin *sapon-, sapo* soap, of Germanic origin]

saponify /sə'ponifie/ *verb* (**saponifies, saponified, saponifying**) ⟫ *verb trans* **1** to convert (e.g. fat, oil, etc) into soap by decomposition with an alkali. **2** to break down (an ester) into an acid and alcohol by hydrolysis. ⟫ *verb intrans* said of a fat, ester, etc: to undergo this kind of conversion or breakdown. ⟫⟫ **saponifiable** *adj*, **saponification** /-fi'kaysh(ə)n/ *noun*. [French *saponifier*, from Latin *sapon-, sapo*: see SAPONACEOUS]

saponin /'sapənin/ *noun* any of various chemical compounds, obtained from plants, that produce a soapy lather and are used *esp* in detergents. [French *saponine*, from Latin *sapon-, sapo*: see SAPONACEOUS]

sappanwood /'sapənwood/ *noun* **1** an E Indian tree of the pea family: *Caesalpina sappan*. **2** the wood of this tree, from which a red dye is obtained. [Malay *sapang* heartwood of sappanwood + WOOD¹]

sapper /'sapə/ *noun* **1** a soldier specializing in battlefield construction, e.g. digging trenches and laying mines. **2** in the British army, a soldier of the Royal Engineers. [SAP⁴ + -ER²]

sapphic /'safik/ *adj* **1** of or being a four-line stanza made up chiefly of trochees and dactyls. **2** (**Sapphic**) characteristic of the ancient Greek lyric poetry of Sappho (6th cent. BC), *esp* in relation to her erotic descriptions of love between women. **3** lesbian.

sapphics *pl noun* verse in sapphic stanzas.

sapphire /'safie·ə/ *noun* **1** any transparent or translucent variety of the mineral corundum of a colour other than red, *esp* a transparent rich blue variety used as a gem. **2** a deep brilliant blue colour. ⟫⟫ **sapphire** *adj*, **sapphirine** /'safirien/ *adj*. [Middle English *safir* via Old French and Latin from Greek *sappheiros*, prob ultimately from Sanskrit *śanipriya*, literally 'dear to the planet Saturn', from *śani* Saturn + *priya* dear]

sapphism /'safiz(ə)m/ *noun* lesbianism. ⟫⟫ **sapphist** *noun*. [from *Sappho* d.6th cent. BC, female Greek poet whose work was erroneously believed to be about lesbian relationships, + -ISM]

sappy *adj* (**sappier, sappiest**) **1** said of a plant: containing a lot of sap. **2** *chiefly NAmer, informal* foolishly sentimental. ⟫⟫ **sappiness** *noun*.

sapr- or **sapro-** *comb. form* forming words, denoting: **1** dead or decaying organic matter: *saprophyte*. **2** putrefaction: *saprogenic*. [Greek *sapros* rotten]

saprogenic /saproh'jenik/ *adj* of, causing, or resulting from putrefaction.

saprophagous /sa'profəgəs, sə-/ *adj* feeding on decaying matter.

saprophyte /'saprohfiet/ *noun* a plant, fungus, or bacterium that lives on or obtains nourishment from dead or decaying plant and animal tissues. ⟫⟫ **saprophytic** /-'fitik/ *adj*, **saprophytically** /-'fitikli/ *adv*.

saprotrophic /saproh'trohfik/ *adj* feeding on dead or decaying plant and animal tissues.

sapsucker *noun* any of several species of N American woodpeckers that feed on the sap of trees: genus *Sphyrapicus*.

sapwood *noun* the younger softer outer wood of a tree trunk or branch that lies between the bark and the heartwood and consists of living tissue.

saraband or **sarabande** /'sarəband/ *noun* **1** a stately court dance of the 17th and 18th cents resembling the minuet. **2** a musical composition or movement in slow triple time with the accent on the second beat. [French *sarabande* from Spanish *zarabanda*]

Saracen /'sarəs(ə)n/ *noun* **1** a member of a nomadic people of the desert area between Syria and Arabia, *esp* in classical Roman times. **2** a Muslim at the time of the Crusades. **3** an Arab. ⟫⟫ **Saracen** *adj*, **Saracenic** /-'senik/ *adj*. [Middle English via late Latin from late Greek *Sarakēnos*]

sarc- or **sarco-** *comb. form* forming words, denoting: **1** flesh: *sarcophagus*. **2** striated muscle: *sarcoplasm*. [Greek *sark-, sarko-*, from *sark-, sarx* flesh]

sarcasm /'sahkaz(ə)m/ *noun* **1** caustic and ironic language used to express contempt or bitterness, *esp* towards an individual. **2** the use of such language. ⟫⟫ **sarcastic** /sah'kastik/ *adj*, **sarcastically** /sah'kastikli/ *adv*. [French *sarcasme* via late Latin from Greek *sarkasmos*, from *sarkazein* to tear flesh, bite the lips in rage, sneer, from *sark-, sarx* flesh]

sarcenet or **sarsenet** /'sahsnit/ *noun* a soft thin silk used for dresses, veilings, or trimmings. [Middle English *sarcenet* from Anglo-French *sarzinett*, prob from *Sarzin* Saracen, ultimately from late Greek *Sarakēnos*]

sarco- *comb. form* see SARC-.

sarcoma /sah'kohmə/ *noun* (*pl* **sarcomas** or **sarcomata** /-tə/) a usu cancerous tumour arising *esp* in connective tissue, e.g. muscle, ligaments or tendons. ⟫⟫ **sarcomatous** /-təs/ *adj*. [scientific Latin *sarcoma* from Greek *sarkōmat-, sarkōma* fleshy growth, from *sarkoun* to grow flesh, from *sark-, sarx* flesh]

sarcomatosis /sah,kohmə'tohsis/ *noun* (*pl* **sarcomatoses** /-seez/) a disease characterized by the presence and spread of sarcomas.

sarcophagus /sah'kofəgəs/ *noun* (*pl* **sarcophagi** /-gie/ or **sarcophaguses**) a stone coffin, *esp* one with a carved decoration or inscription.

Word history

Latin *sarcophagus lapis* limestone used for coffins, from Greek *lithos sarkophagos*, literally 'flesh-eating stone', from SARCO- + *phagein* to eat. The stone used to make a sarcophagus was believed to destroy the flesh of the corpse inside it.

sarcoplasm /'sahkohplaz(ə)m/ *noun* the cytoplasm of a striated muscle fibre. ⟫⟫ **sarcoplasmic** /-'plazmik/ *adj*. [SARCO- + PLASMA]

sard /sahd/ *noun* a deep orange-red variety of chalcedony used as a gemstone. Also called SARDINE², SARDIUS. [French *sarde* via Latin *sarda* from Greek *sardios*, perhaps from *Sardō* Sardinia]

sardar /'suhdah, suh'dah/ *noun* see SIRDAR.

sardine¹ /sah'deen/ *noun* (*pl* **sardines** *or collectively* **sardine**) a small or immature fish of the herring family, *esp* the young of the European pilchard of a size suitable for preserving for food: *When the seagulls follow a trawler, it is because they think sardines will be thrown into the sea* — Eric Cantona. ✳ **like sardines** very closely packed or crowded together. [Middle English *sardeine* via French from Latin *sardina*, ultimately from Greek *Sardō* Sardinia]

sardine² /'sahdein/ *noun* = SARD. [variant form of SARDIUS]

Sardinian /sah'dini·ən/ *noun* **1** a native or inhabitant of Sardinia, island in the Mediterranean. **2** the Romance language of the people of Sardinia. ➤➤ **Sardinian** *adj.*

sardius /'sahdi·əs/ *noun* **1** = SARD. **2** a precious stone worn by the Jewish high priest. [via late Latin from Greek *sardios*: see SARD]

sardonic /sah'donik/ *adj* disdainfully or cynically humorous; derisively mocking. ➤➤ **sardonically** *adv*, **sardonicism** *noun*.

Word history
French *sardonique* via Latin from Greek *sardonios* Sardinian, alteration of *sardanios* scornful. The alteration came about by association with a Sardinian plant reputed to cause convulsive grimaces.

sardonyx /'sahdəniks/ *noun* a quartz mineral consisting of parallel layers of orange-red sard and milky-white chalcedony, used as a gemstone. [Middle English *sardonix* via Latin from Greek *sardonyx*, prob from *sardius* (see SARD) + *onyx* ONYX]

saree /'sahri/ *noun* see SARI.

sargasso /sah'gasoh/ *noun* (*pl* **sargassos**) a large mass of floating vegetation, *esp* sargassum, in the sea. [Portuguese *sargaço*]

sargassum /sah'gasəm/ *noun* a brown seaweed that has small air bladders enabling it to float, often in large masses, on the surface of the water: genus *Sargassum*. [Latin genus name, from SARGASSO]

sarge /sahj/ *noun informal* a sergeant. [by shortening]

sari *or* **saree** /'sahri/ *noun* (*pl* **saris** *or* **sarees**) a garment made from a length of lightweight cloth draped so that one end forms a long skirt and the other a covering for the shoulder or head and is traditionally worn by women of the Indian subcontinent and by women of Indian, Pakistani, etc descent. [Hindi *sāṛī* from Sanskrit *śāṭī*]

sarking /'sahking/ *noun Brit* boards or felt fixed between rafters and roofing material, e.g. slates or tiles. [Middle English (Scots), from *serk* shirt, from Old English *serc*]

sarky /'sahki/ *adj* (**sarkier**, **sarkiest**) *Brit*, *informal* sarcastic. ➤➤ **sarkily** *adv*, **sarkiness** *noun*. [by shortening and alteration]

sarnie /'sahni/ *noun Brit*, *informal* a sandwich. [by shortening and alteration]

sarod /sə'rohd/ *noun* a lute used in classical music of N India. [Urdu *sarod* from Persian *surod* melody]

sarong /sə'rong, 'sahrong/ *noun* **1a** a loose skirt made of a long strip of cloth wrapped round the body and traditionally worn by men and women in Malaysia and the Pacific islands. **b** a similar garment now worn, usu tied at the waist, *esp* on top of a bikini or swimsuit at the beach. **2** cloth for sarongs. [Malay *sarong*, literally 'sheath', from *kain sarong* cloth sheath]

saros /'sayros/ *noun* a cycle of about 6585 days during which a particular sequence of eclipses occurs and after which the centres of the sun and moon return to the same relative positions.

Word history
Greek *saros* from Babylonian *šaru* period of 3600 years. The modern meaning prob arises from a misinterpretation of the Babylonian word.

sarrusophone /sə'roohzəfohn, sə'rus-/ *noun* a woodwind musical instrument of the oboe family that is made of metal and is used *esp* in military bands. [named after its inventor, W *Sarrus*, 19th-cent. French bandmaster + -O- + -PHONE]

Sars *or* **SARS** /sahz/ *noun* severe acute respiratory syndrome, a severe form of respiratory disease that first developed in southern China.

sarsaparilla /sahs(ə)pə'rilə/ *noun* **1a** any of several species of tropical American trailing or climbing plants of the lily family with prickly stems: genus *Smilax*. **b** the dried roots of this plant, or an extract of these, used *esp* as a flavouring. **2** a sweetened non-alcoholic fizzy drink flavoured with sarsaparilla. [Spanish *zarzaparilla*, from *zarza* bush + *parrilla*, dimin. of *parra* vine]

sarsen /'sahs(ə)n/ *noun* a large mass of very hard siliceous sandstone left after the erosion of a continuous bed or layer and used in prehistoric monuments such as Stonehenge. [short for *sarsen stone*, prob alteration of *Saracen stone*, i.e. a pagan stone or monument]

sarsenet /'sahsnit/ *noun* see SARCENET.

sartorial /sah'tawri·əl/ *adj* relating to tailoring or clothing, *esp* men's clothing: *sartorial elegance*. ➤➤ **sartorially** *adv*. [Latin *sartor* tailor: see SARTORIUS]

sartorius /sah'tawri·əs/ *noun* (*pl* **sartorii** /-ri·ie/) a long muscle that crosses the front of the thigh obliquely and is involved in bending and unbending the knee.

Word history
scientific Latin *sartorius* from Latin *sartor* tailor, from *sarcire* to mend. The muscle assists in rotating the leg to the cross-legged sitting position associated with tailors.

SAS *abbr* Special Air Service.

sash¹ /sash/ *noun* a band of cloth worn round the waist or over one shoulder as part of a uniform or official dress, a symbol of rank, etc. ➤➤ **sashed** *adj.* [Arabic *shāsh* muslin]

sash² *noun* **1** a frame in which panes of glass are set in a window or door. **2** such a frame together with its panes forming a usu sliding part of a sash window. ➤➤ **sashed** *adj.* [prob modification of French *châssis* (see CHASSIS), taken as pl]

sashay¹ /'sashay/ *verb intrans chiefly NAmer, informal* **1a** to walk casually; to saunter. **b** to strut ostentatiously, *esp* with exaggerated swaying movements of the hips and shoulders. **2a** to proceed in a zigzag manner. **b** in square dancing, to perform a sashay. [alteration of CHASSÉ²]

sashay² *noun* a square dance figure in which partners sidestep in a circle round each other with the man moving behind the woman.

sash cord *noun* a cord used to connect a sash weight to a window sash.

sashimi /'sashimi/ *noun* a Japanese dish consisting of thinly sliced raw fish served in bite-sized pieces with a spicy dip, usu of soy sauce. [Japanese *sashimi*]

sash weight *noun* either of two counterweights for balancing a window sash in a desired position.

sash window *noun* a window having one or two sashes that slide vertically in a frame to open it.

Sask. *abbr* Saskatchewan.

Sasquatch /'saskwach/ *noun* a hairy humanlike animal that is supposed to live in the mountain areas of W Canada where it is said to leave huge footprints. [of Salishan (an Algonquian language) origin]

sass¹ /sas/ *noun NAmer, informal* impudent talk; backchat. [back-formation from SASSY]

sass² *verb trans NAmer, informal* to talk impudently or disrespectfully to (somebody).

sassafras /'sasəfras/ *noun* **1** a tall eastern N American tree of the laurel family with aromatic leaves, small clusters of yellow flowers, and dark blue berries: *Sassafras albidum*. **2** the dried aromatic root bark of this tree, used for flavouring and as the source of a yellowish oil used in perfumery. [Spanish *sasafrás*, ultimately from Latin *saxifraga*: see SAXIFRAGE]

Sassanian¹ /sə'sayni·ən/ *adj* = SASSANID¹. [from *Sassan* (see SASSANID¹) + -IAN]

Sassanian² *noun* = SASSANID².

Sassanid¹ /'sasənid/ *adj* relating to or associated with the dynasty that ruled in Persia from about AD 224 to AD 651. [from *Sassan*, name of the grandfather of the founder of the dynasty, + -ID¹ (4)]

Sassanid² *noun* a member of the Sassanid dynasty.

Sassenach /'sasənakh/ *noun Scot, Irish, derog* an English person. [Irish Gaelic *Sasanach* and Scottish Gaelic *Sasunnach*, of Germanic origin and related to Old English *Seaxan* Saxons]

sassy /'sasi/ *adj* (**sassier**, **sassiest**) *chiefly NAmer, informal* **1** impudent; cheeky. **2** vigorous; lively: *I'm sickly but sassy* — Joel Chandler Harris. **3** stylishly elegant; chic. ➤➤ **sassily** *adv*, **sassiness** *noun*. [alteration of SAUCY]

Sat. *abbr* Saturday.

sat /sat/ *verb* past tense and past part. of SIT¹.

Satan /'sayt(ə)n/ *noun* the adversary of God and lord of evil in Judaism and Christianity. [Old English via late Latin and Greek from Hebrew *śāṭān* adversary, plotter]

satang *noun* (*pl* **satang** *or* **satangs**) a unit of currency in Thailand, worth 100th of a baht. [Thai *satang* from Pali *sata* hundred]

satanic /sə'tanik/ *adj* **1** of Satan or satanism: *satanic pride; satanic rites*. **2** extremely cruel or malevolent. ⟫ **satanically** *adv*.

satanic abuse *noun* = RITUAL ABUSE.

satanism /'sayt(ə)niz(ə)m/ *noun* **1** the worship of Satan, typically marked by the travesty of Christian ceremonies. **2** innate or calculated wickedness. ⟫ **satanist** *noun and adj*.

satay /'satay/ *noun* a dish of southeast Asia, *esp* Indonesia and Malaysia, consisting of pieces of marinated spiced meat that are skewered, barbecued, and usu served with a peanut-flavoured sauce. [Malay *satai*]

SATB *abbr* soprano, alto, tenor, bass, denoting the singing voices of a choir or the voices required for a particular piece of music, *esp* choral music.

satchel /'sachəl/ *noun* a usu stiff rectangular bag often with a shoulder strap, *esp* one used by schoolchildren for carrying books, etc. [Middle English *sachel* via French from Latin *sacellus*, dimin. of *saccus*: see SACK¹]

sate¹ /sayt/ *verb trans* **1** to satisfy (e.g. a thirst or appetite) by indulging it to the full. **2** to supply (somebody or something) with more than is needed or desired. [prob by shortening and alteration from SATIATE]

sate² /sayt, sat/ *verb* archaic past tense of SIT¹.

sateen /sa'teen/ *noun* a smooth durable shiny linen or cotton fabric resembling satin. [alteration of SATIN]

satellite /'satəliet/ *noun* **1a** a celestial body orbiting another of larger size. **b** an artificial device that orbits the earth, the moon, or another celestial body, *esp* one that collects astronomical or other scientific information or one that is used in transmitting and receiving communication or television signals. **c** (*used before a noun*) of or involving an artificial satellite or satellites: *satellite communications*. **2a** somebody or something attendant, subordinate, or dependent, *esp* a country subject to another more powerful country. **b** (*used before a noun*) subordinate or dependent: *a satellite nation*. **3** an urban community that is physically separate from an adjacent city but dependent on it, e.g. as a source of employment. **4** an obsequious follower. ⟫ **satellite** *adj*. [early French *satellite* from Latin *satellit-*, *satelles* attendant]

satellite dish *noun* a dish-shaped aerial used to transmit and receive signals in satellite communications, *esp* satellite television.

satellite television *noun* a system of broadcasting television signals using satellites in space to transmit and receive signals.

satiable /'saysh(y)əbl/ *adj formal* capable of being satisfied.

satiate /'sayshiayt/ *verb trans* = SATE¹. ⟫ **satiation** /-'aysh(ə)n/ *noun*. [Latin *satiatus*, past part. of *satiare*, from *satis* enough]

satiety /sə'tie-iti/ *noun* the feeling or state of being fed or gratified to or beyond capacity. [early French *satieté* from Latin *satietat-*, *satietas*, from *satis* enough]

satin /'satin/ *noun* **1** a fabric, orig made from silk, in which the warp threads predominate on the face to produce a smooth shiny front and a dull back. **2** (*used before a noun*) made of or resembling satin: *paint with a satin finish*. ⟫ **satiny** *adj*. [Middle English via French from Arabic *zaytūnī* from *Zaytūn*, Chinese *Tseutung*, former name of a seaport in China]

satinet *or* **satinette** /sati'net/ *noun* **1** an imitation satin made from cotton or synthetic fibre as opposed to silk. **2** a thin inferior type of satin.

satin stitch *noun* a long embroidery stitch nearly alike on both sides and worked in straight parallel lines so closely as to resemble satin.

satinwood *noun* **1** a deciduous tree of the mahogany family that grows in India and Sri Lanka: *Chloroxylon swietenia*. **2** a related tree that grows in the islands of the Caribbean and in southern Florida: *Zanthoxylum flava*. **3** the shiny yellowish brown wood of either of these trees, used in furniture making, marquetry, etc.

satire /'satie-ə/ *noun* **1a** a literary work that holds up human vices and follies to ridicule or scorn. **b** the genre of such literature: *Satire is moral outrage transformed into comic art* — Philip Roth. **2** biting wit, irony, or sarcasm intended to expose foolishness or vice. [French *satire* from Latin *satira*, alteration of *satura* verse on many subjects, medley]

satirical /sə'tirikl/ *or* **satiric** *adj* **1** characterized by or involving the use of satire. **2** bitingly sarcastic or humorously critical. ⟫ **satirically** *adv*.

satirise /'satiriez/ *verb trans and intrans* see SATIRIZE.

satirist /'satirist/ *noun* somebody who satirizes, *esp* a writer of satires.

satirize *or* **satirise** /'satiriez/ *verb trans* to censure or ridicule (somebody or something) by means of satire. ⟫ *verb intrans* to write or use satire. ⟫ **satirization** *noun*.

satisfaction /satis'faksh(ə)n/ *noun* **1a** the fulfilment of something that is necessary, expected, or desired, or the good feeling experienced when this happens: *Restoring the old car gave him great satisfaction*. **b** a source or means of such fulfilment. **2a** compensation for a loss, insult, or injury; atonement or restitution. **b** the discharge of a legal obligation or claim, e.g. by payment of a debt. **c** an opportunity to vindicate one's honour, *esp* through a duel. **3a** in Christian theology, atonement for sin achieved through Christ's death. **b** in the Roman Catholic and Anglican Churches, a penance. [Middle English via French from Latin *satisfaction-*, *satisfactio*, from *satisfacere*: see SATISFY]

satisfactory /satis'fakt(ə)ri/ *adj* **1a** fulfilling a need, expectation, or desire: *I hope your meal was satisfactory*. **b** adequate, but not exceptionally good: *Lucy has made satisfactory progress in maths this year*. **2** said of a patient's condition or recovery: progressing in an acceptable way or progressing as expected. **3** said of a legal verdict or evidence given in a law court: sound or acceptable for the purposes of the case in question. ⟫ **satisfactorily** *adv*, **satisfactoriness** *noun*.

satisfice /'satisfies/ *verb intrans formal* to do or spend as little as possible in the achievement of a specified objective. [alteration of SATISFY, influenced by Latin *satisfacere*: see SATISFY]

satisfy /'satisfie/ *verb* (**satisfies, satisfied, satisfying**) ⟫ *verb trans* **1** to fulfil the needs, expectations, or desires of (somebody or something): *Finding a job that satisfies you can be difficult*. **2** to meet or comply with (the requirements of something or somebody). **3** to provide (somebody) with reassurance, proof, etc; to convince: *We are satisfied that he is innocent*. **4** to pay off (a debt or a creditor). **5** said of a mathematical quantity: to make (an equation) true. ⟫ *verb intrans* **1** to be sufficient or adequate. **2** to give pleasure or contentment. ⟫ **satisfiable** *adj*, **satisfied** *adj*, **satisfying** *adj*, **satisfyingly** *adv*. [Middle English via French from Latin *satisfacere* to content, do enough, from *satis* enough + *facere* to make]

satori /sə'tawri/ *noun* a state of intuitive enlightenment achieved or sought in Zen Buddhism. [Japanese *satori*, literally 'awakening']

satrap /'satrap/ *noun* **1** a governor of a province in ancient Persia. **2** a subordinate ruler, *esp* a despotic one. [Middle English via Latin from Greek *satrapēs*, from early Persian *khshathra* province + *pāavan* protector]

satrapy /'satrəpi/ *noun* (*pl* **satrapies**) the territory or jurisdiction of a satrap.

satsuma /sat'soohmə/ *noun* **1** a sweet seedless type of tangerine with a loose skin. **2** the small citrus tree, orig cultivated in Japan, that bears this fruit. [named after *Satsuma*, former province of Japan]

saturable /'sachoorəbl/ *adj* capable of saturation. ⟫ **saturability** /-'biliti/ *noun*.

saturate /'sachoorayt/ *verb trans* **1a** to treat, provide, or fill (a substance) with another substance to the point where no more of it can be absorbed, dissolved, or retained: *water saturated with salt*. **b** to cause (two or more substances) to combine chemically until there is no further ability or tendency to combine. **2** to cause (something or somebody) to become thoroughly wet. **3a** to fill (something) completely with a permeating or suffusing effect or substance: *Moonglow saturates an empty sky* — Henry Miller. **b** to fill (something) to capacity. **4** to supply (a market) with all the goods it will absorb. **5** to overwhelm (an area) with military forces or firepower. [Latin *saturatus*, past part. of *saturare*, from *satur* sated, full]

saturated *adj* **1a** said of a solution: not capable of absorbing or dissolving any more of the substance it contains. **b** said of a chemical compound: unable or not tending to form products by chemical addition or by uniting directly with another compound; *esp* containing no double bonds or triple bonds between carbon atoms. **2** said of a colour: free from dilution with white; bright and rich.

saturation /satchoo'raysh(ə)n/ *noun* **1** the action of saturating or the state of being saturated. **2** (*used before a noun*) denoting maximum concentration.

saturation point *noun* the stage at which no more of something can be absorbed or tolerated.

Saturday /'satəday/ *noun* the seventh day of the week, following Friday. [Old English *sæterndæg*, translation of *Saturni dies* day of Saturn, the Roman god of agriculture]

Saturnalia /satə'nayli·ə/ *noun* (*pl* **Saturnalias** *or* **Saturnalia**) **1** (*treated as sing. or pl*) the festival of Saturn in ancient Rome, beginning on 17 December, a time of general and unrestrained merrymaking. **2** (*often* **saturnalia**) a wild party or an occasion when a great amount of alcohol is consumed, leading to unrestrained behaviour; an orgy. ➤➤ **saturnalian** *adj*. [Latin *Saturnalis* relating to Saturn, from *Saturnus* Saturn, Roman god of agriculture]

Saturnian /sə'tuhni·ən/ *adj* **1** of or influenced by the planet Saturn. **2** saturnine.

saturniid /sə'tuhniid/ *noun* any of a family of mainly tropical moths, including the giant silk moth and giant peacock moth, with stout hairy bodies and strong usu brightly coloured wings: family Saturniidae. [scientific Latin *Saturniidae* (pl) from the genus name *Saturnia*, from Latin *Saturnus* Saturn, Roman god of agriculture]

saturnine /'satənien/ *adj* **1a** said of a person or their temperament: gloomy or sullen. **b** dark and brooding: *a saturnine expression*. **2** *archaic* related to lead or affected by lead poisoning. ➤➤ **saturninely** *adv*. [Middle English, literally 'born under or influenced by Saturn', the planet that was believed by astrologers to induce a tendency to be gloomy or melancholic]

satyagraha /'sutyəgrahhə, su'tyəgrəhə/ *noun* passive resistance as practised by Mahatma Gandhi against British rule in India; nonviolent non-cooperation. [Sanskrit *satyāgraha*, literally 'insistence on truth']

satyr /'satə/ *noun* **1** (*also* **Satyr**) in classical mythology, a woodland god associated with drunken revelry and lustfulness. In Greek representations, the satyr was a man with a horse's ears and tail, and in Roman representations he was a man with the tail, legs, and horns of a goat. **2** a lecherous man, *esp* one affected by satyriasis. **3** any of various butterflies, most of which have brown wings with small eyespots: genus *Satyrus*. ➤➤ **satyric** /sə'tirik/ *adj*. [Middle English via French and Latin from Greek *satyros*]

satyriasis /satə'rie·əsis/ *noun* excessive sexual desire in a male: compare NYMPHOMANIA. [via Latin from Greek *satyriasis* from *satyros* SATYR]

sauce¹ /saws/ *noun* **1** a liquid or semiliquid substance used as a relish, dressing, or accompaniment to food: *tomato sauce*. **2** *NAmer* stewed fruit eaten as a dessert. **3** something that adds zest or piquancy. **4** *chiefly Brit, informal* cheek or impudence. **5** (**the sauce**) *chiefly NAmer, informal* alcoholic drink: *She lost her job and hit the sauce*. [Middle English via French from Latin *salsus* salted, past part. of *sallere* to salt, from *sal* salt]

sauce² *verb trans* **1** to dress or prepare (food) with a sauce. **2** to make (something) more interesting. **3** *informal* to be impudent to (somebody).

sauce boat *noun* a shallow jug with a handle for serving sauce, gravy, etc at the table.

sauced *adj chiefly NAmer, informal* very drunk.

saucepan /'sawspən/ *noun* a deep usu cylindrical cooking pan typically with a long handle and a lid. ➤➤ **saucepanful** (*pl* **saucepanfuls**) *noun*.

saucer /'sawsə/ *noun* a small usu circular shallow dish with a central depression in which a cup is placed. ➤➤ **saucerful** (*pl* **saucerfuls**) *noun*. [Middle English from early French *saussier* a dish for sauce]

saucier /'sawsiay/ *noun* a chef who specializes in making sauces. [French *saucier* from *sauce*: see SAUCE¹]

saucy *adj* (**saucier, sauciest**) *informal* **1** *chiefly Brit* mildly titillating or sexually suggestive, *esp* in a humorous way: *saucy jokes*. **2** cheeky or impudent. **3** *chiefly NAmer* engagingly lively, forward, or high-spirited. ➤➤ **saucily** *adv*, **sauciness** *noun*.

Saudi /'sowdi/ *noun* (*pl* **Saudis**) **1** a native or inhabitant of Saudi Arabia. **2** a member of the ruling dynasty of Saudi Arabia. ➤➤ **Saudi** *adj*. [named after *Sa'ūd*, founder of the ruling dynasty]

Saudi Arabian *noun* a native or inhabitant of Saudi Arabia. ➤➤ **Saudi Arabian** *adj*.

sauerkraut /'sowəkrowt/ *noun* finely chopped pickled cabbage. [German *sauer* sour + *Kraut* cabbage]

sauger /'sawgə/ *noun* a small N American freshwater game fish, related to the wall-eyed pike, with a distinctive spotted dorsal fin: *Stizostedion canadense*. [origin unknown]

sault /sooh/ *noun Can* a waterfall or rapids. [Canadian French *sault* from early French *saut* a leap or jump, from Latin *saltus*: see SALTUS]

sauna /'sawnə/ *noun* **1** a small room where people go to invigorate their bodies in extremely hot dry air or steam produced by throwing water over hot stones. **2** a session in such a room. [Finnish *sauna*]

saunter¹ /'sawntə/ *verb intrans* (**sauntered, sauntering**) to walk about in an idle or casual manner; to stroll. ➤➤ **saunterer** *noun*. [prob from Middle English *santren* to muse, of unknown origin]

saunter² *noun* a casual stroll.

-saur *comb. form* forming nouns, denoting: the names of reptiles, *esp* extinct ones: *ichthyosaur; dinosaur*. [via Latin from Greek *sauros* lizard]

saurian¹ /'sawri·ən/ *adj* relating to or resembling a lizard. [Greek *sauros* a lizard + *-ian* -AN²]

saurian² *noun* any of a group of reptiles that includes the lizards and, in older classifications, the crocodiles and various extinct forms, such as the dinosaurs: group Sauria.

saurischian /saw'riski·ən/ *noun* a dinosaur with a pelvic structure with three branches, similar to that of a lizard: compare ORNITHISCHIAN. ➤➤ **saurischian** *adj*. [Greek *sauros* lizard + *ischion* hip joint + -AN¹]

sauropod /'sawrəpod/ *noun* a plant-eating dinosaur with a long neck and tail, a small head, and very large limbs, e.g. an apatosaurus. [scientific Latin *Sauropoda* (pl), from Greek *sauros* lizard + *pous* foot]

-saurus *comb. form* forming nouns, denoting: the genus name of reptiles, *esp* extinct ones: *stegosaurus; megalosaurus*. [via Latin from Greek *sauros* lizard]

saury /'sawri/ *noun* (*pl* **sauries**) any of several species of slender long-jawed edible marine fish of tropical and temperate waters: family Scomberesocidae. [via Latin from Greek *sauros* horse mackerel]

sausage /'sosij/ *NAmer* 'sawsij/ *noun* **1** a food made from finely chopped raw meat, or a meat substitute, often mixed with cereal and seasonings, and put in a tubular casing, orig one made from animal intestines. **2** a similar food made from cooked or cured meat, often with the addition of spices, and usu eaten cold in thin slices. **3** something tube-shaped. ✱ **not a sausage** *Brit, informal* nothing at all or not a bit. [Middle English via French from Latin *salsus*: see SAUCE¹]

sausage dog *noun Brit, informal* = DACHSHUND.

sausage meat *noun* seasoned minced meat, usu pork, mixed with cereal, used to fill sausages and sausage rolls, as a poultry stuffing, etc.

sausage roll *noun* a small piece of sausage meat wrapped in pastry.

sausage tree *noun* a tropical African tree with clusters of scarlet flowers and long fruits suspended on stalks: *Kigelia pinnata*.

sauté¹ /'sawtay, 'sohtay/ *verb trans* (**sautés, sautéed** *or* **sautéd, sautéing**) to fry (*esp* potatoes) in a small amount of hot oil or fat. [French *sauté*, past part. of *sauter* to jump]

sauté² *adj* fried quickly in shallow hot oil or fat.

sauté³ *noun* **1** a dish of food that has been fried quickly in a small amount of hot oil or fat. **2** in ballet, a move in which the dancer jumps from both feet and lands in the starting position.

Sauternes /soh'tuhn/ *noun* **1** a sweet golden-coloured Bordeaux wine made in the commune of Sauternes in France. **2** (*also* **Sauterne**) a medium sweet white wine produced in California.

Sauvignon /'sohvinyanh/ *noun* **1** a variety of grape used in the production of white wine. **2** a wine produced from this grape. [French *Sauvignon; Sauvignon blanc*, literally 'white Sauvignon']

savage¹ /'savij/ *adj* **1** not domesticated or under human control; untamed: *savage beasts*. **2a** very severe: *savage criticism*. **b** wild; cruel; violent; ferocious: *Music has charms to soothe a savage breast* — Congreve. **3** said of a place or landscape: rugged and usu uncultivated. **4** *offensive* said of a people: lacking a developed culture. ➤➤ **savagely** *adv*, **savageness** *noun*, **savagery** *noun*. [Middle English *sauvage* via French from Latin *salvaticus*, alteration of Latin *silvaticus* of the woods, wild, from *silva* a wood]

savage² *noun* **1** *offensive* a member of a society or people regarded as lacking a developed culture. **2a** a brutal, rude, or unmannerly person. **b** a fierce animal.

savage³ *verb trans* **1** to attack or treat (somebody or something) brutally or ferociously. **2** to criticize (somebody or something) severely: *Her latest play was savaged by the critics.*

savanna or **savannah** /sə'vanə/ *noun* a tropical or subtropical grassland with scattered trees. [Spanish *zavana* from Taino *zabana*]

savant or **savante** /'sav(ə)nt/ *noun* a man or woman who has exceptional knowledge of a particular field, *esp* science or literature. [French *savant*, literally 'knowing', present part. of *savoir* to know]

savarin /'sav(ə)rin/ *noun* **1** a rich yeast-leavened cake baked in a ring mould and soaked with a liqueur-flavoured syrup. **2** the mould used for making this cake. [named after Anthelme Brillat-*Savarin* d.1826, French politician and gourmet]

savate /sə'vat/ *noun* a French form of boxing in which blows are delivered with the hands or feet. [French *savate*, literally 'an ill-fitting or old shoe']

save¹ /sayv/ *verb trans* **1a** to rescue or deliver (somebody or something) from danger or harm. **b** to prevent (somebody) from dying. **c** to preserve or guard (somebody or something) from injury, destruction, or loss. **d** in Christianity, to preserve (somebody's soul) from damnation. **2** to put (something) aside as a store or reserve or for a particular use: *She saves her newspapers for recycling.* **3** in computing, to preserve (e.g. a file) by copying and storing it in the computer's memory or on a disk. **4a** to economize in the use of (something); to conserve: *Driving like this saves petrol.* **b** to keep (something) from being spent, wasted, or lost: *I saved time by taking a short cut.* **5** to make (something) unnecessary; to avoid or obviate: *That would save me going into town.* **6a** to prevent (a match) from being lost to an opponent. **b** to prevent an opponent from scoring or winning (e.g. a trick, goal, or point). **c** in baseball, to keep (a team's winning position) that another pitcher has created. **7** to maintain or preserve (something): *She lied to save appearances.* ➤ *verb intrans* **1** (*often* + up) to put aside money. **2** in sport, to make a save: *The fullback saved on the line.* ✳ **save face** to avoid being humiliated. **save one's breath** to refrain from saying something because it would be pointless. **save somebody's skin/neck/ bacon** to rescue or help somebody in difficulty. **save the day/ situation** to come up with a solution to a problem, *esp* at the last moment. ➤➤ **savable** *adj,* **saveable** *adj.* [Middle English *saven* via early French *salver* from Latin *salvare,* from *salvus* SAFE¹]

save² *noun* **1** in sport, *esp* football and hockey, an act of preventing an opponent from scoring. **2** in baseball, an instance of maintaining another pitcher's winning position. **3** in computing, a command to copy and store material in memory or on a disk.

save³ *prep formal or literary* except or other than (somebody or something): *Nobody was home save Clio the cat.* [early French *sauf*: see SAFE¹]

save⁴ *conj formal or literary* were it not; only: *We would have protested save that he was a friend.*

save as you earn *noun Brit* a government-run saving scheme, with tax benefits, involving regular contributions that are usu deducted directly from a person's pay.

saveloy /'savəloy/ *noun Brit* a highly seasoned red cooked sausage made from smoked pork. [French *cervela* from Italian *cervellata* sausage]

saver *noun* **1** a person who regularly saves money, *esp* in a bank or through a saving scheme. **2** (*used in combinations*) something that helps to reduce the consumption of a commodity: *The offer is a great money-saver.* **3** a type of ticket for travelling by bus, train, or aeroplane that is cheaper than the usual fare, but often has special conditions for its use.

savin /'savin/ *noun* **1** a bushy variety of juniper with dark spreading foliage and small yellowish green berries: *Juniperus sabina.* **2** an oil extracted from this plant, formerly used medicinally, *esp* in treating rheumatism and inducing abortions. [Middle English from early French *savine,* from Latin *herba sabina* Sabine herb]

saving¹ *noun* **1** an economy or reduction, e.g. in money or time. **2a** (*in pl*) money that has been put aside for future use, *esp* in a bank or through a saving scheme. **b** (*often in pl, used before a noun*) involving the putting aside of money, *esp* on a regular basis: *a saving scheme.* **3** a legal reservation or exemption.

saving² *adj* (*used in combinations*) preventing waste or loss: *time-saving appliances.*

saving³ *prep* **1** except (something or somebody). **2** *archaic* without disrespect to (something or somebody).

saving grace *noun* **1** a redeeming or compensatory quality or feature: *It is rather an absurd business, this ritual of ours ... But it has at least the saving grace of antiquity to excuse it* — Conan Doyle. **2** God's redeeming grace.

savings account *noun* a type of bank or building society account in which interest is earned on money that is saved.

savings and loan association *noun NAmer* an institution for saving money at interest and borrowing money for house purchases and other major expenses.

savings bank *noun* a bank for savings accounts only.

Savings Bond *noun* **1** *Brit* = PREMIUM BOND. **2** *NAmer* a nontransferable registered bond issued by the government in denominations of $25 to $10,000.

savings certificate *noun Brit* a government certificate guaranteeing that the interest paid on savings will be at a fixed rate, usu for a term of five years.

saviour (*NAmer* **savior**) /'sayvyə/ *noun* **1** a person who saves somebody or something from danger or destruction. **2** (**the/our Saviour**) in Christianity, Jesus Christ or God. [Middle English *saveour* via French from Latin *salvator,* from *salvare*: see SAVE¹]

savoir faire /,savwah 'feə/ *noun* the ability to behave appropriately in social situations. [French *savoir-faire,* literally 'knowing how to do']

savor¹ /'sayvə/ *verb trans and intrans NAmer* see SAVOUR¹.

savor² *noun NAmer* see SAVOUR².

savory¹ /'sayv(ə)ri/ *noun* (*pl* **savories**) any of several species of aromatic plants of the mint family used as herbs: genus *Satureja.* [Middle English *saverey,* prob ultimately from Latin *satureia*]

savory² *adj NAmer* see SAVOURY¹.

savory³ *noun NAmer* see SAVOURY².

savour¹ (*NAmer* **savor**) /'sayvə/ *verb trans* **1** to appreciate (something, *esp* the taste or smell of food or drink) with relish. **2** to enjoy and appreciate (something) to the full: *She savours, for a moment, her feelings about her lover* — Penelope Lively. ➤ *verb intrans* (+ of) to have a specified smell, taste, or quality: *Their arguments savour of cynicism.* [Middle English via French from Latin *sapor,* from *sapere* to taste]

savour² (*NAmer* **savor**) *noun* **1** a characteristic taste or smell. **2** a pleasantly stimulating distinctive quality: *He always felt that being controversial added savour to conversation.* **3** a slight hint or trace. ➤➤ **savourless** *adj.*

savoury¹ (*NAmer* **savory**) /'sayv(ə)ri/ *adj* **1** said of food: having a salty or spicy flavour, often in contrast to being sweet. **2** morally wholesome or respectable: *He's not the most savoury of characters.* ➤➤ **savourily** *adv,* **savouriness** *noun.*

savoury² (*NAmer* **savory**) *noun* (*pl* **savouries**, *NAmer* **savories**) *chiefly Brit* a salty or spicy snack or a savoury dish.

savoy /sə'voy, 'savoy/ *noun* a hardy cabbage with a compact head of wrinkled and curled leaves. [named after *Savoy,* a region of SE France]

Savoyard /sə'voyahd/ *noun* **1** a native or inhabitant of the Savoy region of SE France. **2** the French dialect of the people of Savoy. ➤➤ **Savoyard** *adj.*

savvy¹ /'savi/ *verb trans and intrans* (**savvies, savvied, savvying**) *informal* to know or understand (something). [modification of Spanish *sabe usted* you know]

savvy² *noun informal* practical know-how or shrewd judgment: *political savvy.*

savvy³ *adj* (**savvier, savviest**) *informal* shrewd or knowledgeable.

saw¹ /saw/ *verb* past tense of SEE¹.

saw² *noun* **1a** a hand tool with a toothed blade, used for cutting hard material, e.g. wood, metal, or bone, by moving the blade backwards and forwards. **b** a power tool with a toothed disc or rotating band. **2** a serrated organ or body part. ➤➤ **sawlike** *adj.* [Old English *saga*]

saw³ *verb* (*past part.* **sawn** /sawn/, *NAmer* **sawed**) ➤ *verb trans* **1** to cut (wood, etc) with or as if with a saw. **2** to make or shape (something) by cutting with a saw. **3** to cut through or sever (something) with or as if with a saw. ➤ *verb intrans* **1** to use a saw. **2** to undergo cutting with a saw: *This wood saws easily.* **3** to make sawing motions: *The horse sawed at the reins.*

saw⁴ *noun* a maxim, proverb, or well-known saying. [Old English *sagu* a saying or discourse]

sawbill *noun* = MERGANSER.

sawbones *noun* (*pl* **sawbones**) *informal, dated* a doctor or surgeon.

sawdust *noun* fine particles of wood produced in sawing.

sawed-off *adj chiefly NAmer* see SAWN-OFF.

sawfish *noun* (*pl* **sawfishes** *or collectively* **sawfish**) any of several species of large fishes related to the rays, *esp* of tropical America and Africa, with a long body and a long flattened snout that has large teeth on each side, giving a serrated effect: family Pristidae.

sawfly *noun* (*pl* **sawflies**) any of numerous insects related to the wasps that lay their eggs in plant tissue, which they penetrate by means of a pair of serrated blades in the egg-laying organ of the female: suborder Symphyta.

sawhorse *noun* a rack on which wood is laid for sawing.

sawmill *noun* a factory or machine in which wood is cut, e.g. into planks.

sawn /sawn/ *verb* past part. of SAW[3].

sawn-off (*NAmer* **sawed-off**) *adj* **1** said of a shotgun: having the end of the barrel shortened to make it easier to use or conceal. **2** *informal* said of a garment, *esp* a skirt: shortened. **3** *NAmer, informal* said of a person or animal: shorter than average in height.

saw set *noun* an instrument used to set the teeth of a saw at an angle.

sawtooth *or* **sawtoothed** *adj* **1** shaped or arranged like the teeth of a saw; serrated: *a sawtooth roof*. **2** said of a waveform: characterized by a slow linear rise and a rapid linear fall or a rapid linear rise and a slow linear fall.

sawyer /'sawyə/ *noun* a person who saws timber, *esp* for a living.

sax[1] /saks/ *noun informal* a saxophone or saxophone player.

sax[2] *noun* see ZAX.

saxe /saks/ *adj* of a light blue colour with a greenish or greyish tinge. ➤➤ **saxe** *noun*. [French *Saxe* Saxony, the German region where a dye of this colour was produced]

saxe blue *adj* = SAXE. ➤➤ **saxe blue** *noun*.

saxhorn *noun* a valved brass instrument usu played upright like a tuba and used *esp* in brass and military bands. [named after Adolphe *Sax* d.1894, Belgian maker of musical instruments]

saxicolous /sak'sikələs/ *adj* said of plants: inhabiting or growing among rocks: *saxicolous lichens*. [Latin *saxum* rock + *colere* to inhabit]

saxifrage /'saksifrij, -frayj/ *noun* any of a genus of low-growing plants with showy flowers and often tufted leaves, many of which are grown in rock gardens: genus *Saxifraga*. [Middle English via French from Latin *saxifraga*, from *saxum* rock + *frangere* to break]

Saxon /'saks(ə)n/ *noun* **1** a member of a Germanic people that invaded England along with the Angles and Jutes in the fifth and sixth cents AD. **2** a native or inhabitant of modern Saxony in Germany. **3** = OLD SAXON. **4** = OLD ENGLISH. ➤➤ **Saxon** *adj*. [Middle English from Latin *Saxones* Saxons, of Germanic origin and related to Old English *Seaxan* Saxons]

saxony /'saksəni/ *noun* **1** a fine soft woollen fabric. **2** a fine closely twisted knitting yarn. [named after the German region of *Saxony* where it was orig produced]

saxophone /'saksəfohn/ *noun* a brass instrument of a family played with a single reed like a clarinet but with a conical bore like an oboe and finger keys, used *esp* in jazz and popular music. ➤➤ **saxophonic** /-'fonik/ *adj*, **saxophonist** /sak'sofənist/ *noun*. [French *saxophone*, named after Adolphe *Sax* (see SAXHORN)]

say[1] /say/ *verb* (*third person sing. present tense* **says** /sez/, *past tense and past part.* **said** /sed/) ➤ *verb trans* **1** to state (something) in spoken words. **2** to utter or pronounce (a sound, word, sentence, etc): *She has difficulty saying her r's*. **3** to recite or repeat (a prayer, list, etc). **4a** said of a clock, watch, gauge, etc: to indicate or show (information). **b** said of a look, expression, etc: to give expression to or communicate (a feeling, sense, etc). **5a** (usu in passive) to report or allege (something) to be the case: *The house is said to be three hundred years old*. **b** to form an opinion about or remember (something): *I can't say when I last saw him*. **c** to assume (something) for the purposes of discussion: *Say she's telling the truth*. ➤ *verb intrans* to express oneself; to speak: *You may start when I say*. ✳ **go without saying** to be obvious. **how say you?** used in asking the jury in a court of law to declare its verdict. **I say!** *Brit, dated* used to express surprise or to attract attention. **not to say** *chiefly Brit* and

indeed; or perhaps even: *He's rather impolite, not to say downright rude at times*. **say fairer** *Brit* to express oneself any more generously: *You can't say fairer than that*. **say the word** to give permission for something to go ahead. **say when** used to tell somebody when to stop, *esp* when a drink is being poured: *The Right Hon. was a tubby little chap who looked as if he had been poured into his clothes and forgotten to say 'When'* — P G Wodehouse. **that is to say 1** in other words; in effect. **2** or at least: *He is coming, that is to say he promised he would*. **there is no saying** it is impossible to know or form an opinion. **they say** it is proposed or rumoured. **to say nothing of** without even considering; not to mention. **when all is said and done** when everything has been taken into consideration. **wouldn't say boo to a goose** used to describe somebody who is very timid. **you don't say** used to express surprise, approval, dismay, etc. ➤➤ **sayable** *adj*, **sayer** *noun*. [Old English *secgan*]

say[2] *noun* **1** an expression of opinion or a chance to speak: *I will have my say*. **2** a right or power to influence something: *They had no say in the matter*.

say[3] *adv* **1** at a rough estimate; about: *The picture is worth, say, £2000*. **2** for example: *We could leave next week, say on Monday*.

say[4] *interj NAmer, informal* used to express surprise or to attract attention: *Say, that's a cute kid you've got there!*

SAYE *abbr* save as you earn.

saying *noun* a maxim or proverb.

say-so *noun informal* **1** a person's unsupported assertion. **2** the right of final decision.

sayyid /'sie·id/ *noun* **1** used as an honorary title for a high-ranking Muslim. **2** a Muslim who claims direct descent from Muhammad's grandson Husain. [Arabic *sayyid*, literally 'lord']

Sb *abbr* the chemical symbol for antimony. [from Latin *stibium* antimony trisulphide]

SBS *abbr* Special Boat Service.

s.c. *abbr* small capitals.

SC *abbr* **1** South Carolina (US postal abbreviation). **2** *Brit* special constable.

Sc *abbr* the chemical symbol for scandium.

sc. *abbr* **1** scene. **2** scilicet.

s/c *abbr* self-contained.

scab[1] /skab/ *noun* **1** a crust of hardened blood and serum over a wound. **2** mange or scabies of domestic animals, *esp* mange of sheep caused by a parasitic mite. **3** any of various plant diseases characterized by crusted spots, or one of these spots itself. **4** *informal*. **a** a contemptible person. **b** a strikebreaker or a person brought in to replace striking employees. [Middle English from Old Norse *skab*; (sense 4) prob by association with early Dutch *schabbe* slut]

scab[2] *verb intrans* (**scabbed, scabbing**) **1** (*often* + over) said of a cut or graze: to become covered with a scab. **2** said of somebody during an industrial dispute: to act or work as a scab.

scabbard /'skabəd/ *noun* a sheath for a sword, dagger, or bayonet. [Middle English *scaubert* from Anglo-French *escauberge*, of Germanic origin]

scabbardfish *noun* (*pl* **scabbardfishes** *or collectively* **scabbardfish**) any of several species of widely distributed marine fishes that have a long narrow body and sharp pointed dagger-like teeth: genus *Lepidopus* and other genera.

scabby /'skabi/ *adj* (**scabbier, scabbiest**) **1a** covered with scabs. **b** diseased with scab. **2** mean or contemptible: *a scabby trick*. **3** squalid or shabby: *scabby tenements*. ➤➤ **scabbily** *adv*, **scabbiness** *noun*.

scabies /'skaybiz/ *noun* a contagious skin disease caused by a parasitic mite that burrows in the skin, usu characterized by intense itchiness and inflammation. [Latin *scabies* scurf, mange, itch, from *scabere* to scratch]

scabious[1] /'skaybi·əs/ *noun* any of several species of Mediterranean and temperate European and Asian plants with blue or violet flowers in dense heads at the end of long stalks: genus *Scabiosa* and other genera. [Middle English *scabiose* from Latin *scabiosa herba* the scabies plant, because it was formerly used in treating skin diseases]

scabious[2] *adj* **1** affected with mange; scabby. **2** relating to, affected with, or resembling scabies. [Latin *scabiosus* from *scabies*: see SCABIES]

scabrous /'skaybrəs/ *adj* **1** rough to the touch with scales, scabs, raised patches, etc. **2** dealing with indecent or offensive themes;

salacious. **3** *formal* said of a person, problem, etc: difficult to deal with; intractable. ➤➤ **scabrously** *adv*, **scabrousness** *noun*. [late Latin *scabrosus* from Latin *scaber* rough]

scad /skad/ *noun* (*pl* **scads** *or collectively* **scad**) any of various spiny-finned fishes, *esp* the horse mackerel. [origin unknown]

scads *pl noun chiefly NAmer, informal* a large number or quantity: *scads of money.* [origin unknown]

scaffold[1] /'skafəld/ *noun* **1** a raised platform formerly used in public executions for hanging or beheading criminals: *It is always your moralist that makes assassination a duty, on the scaffold or off it* — George Bernard Shaw. **2** a structure made from scaffolding. **3** a platform above ground or floor level. [Middle English from early French *escafaut*, ultimately from CATA- + Latin *fala* siege tower]

scaffold[2] *verb trans* to erect scaffolding around (a building). ➤➤ **scaffolder** *noun*.

scaffolding *noun* **1** a temporary structure consisting of connected poles and planks, erected on the outside of a building that is being built or repaired. **2** the poles and planks used for this.

scag /skag/ *noun* see SKAG.

scagliola /skal'yohlə/ *noun* imitation marble consisting of finely ground gypsum mixed with glue. [Italian *scagliola*, literally 'little chip', of Germanic origin]

scalable /'skayləbl/ *adj* **1** capable of being climbed. **2** able to be changed in size or scale. **3** *technical* able to be measured on a given scale. ➤➤ **scalability** /-'biliti/ *noun*.

scalar[1] /'skaylə/ *adj* said of a quantity: having magnitude but not direction. [Latin *scalaris* of or like a ladder, from *scala* staircase, ladder]

scalar[2] *noun* **1** a real number rather than a vector. **2** a quantity that has magnitude but no direction: compare PHASOR, VECTOR[1].

scalare /skə'lahri/ *noun* (*pl* **scalares** *or collectively* **scalare**) a freshwater fish that lives in the rivers of tropical S America. It has a laterally compressed body, often with black and silver stripes, and is a popular aquarium fish: *Pterophyllum scalare*. Also called ANGELFISH. [Latin *scalaris* of or like a ladder, from *scala* staircase, ladder]

scalariform /skə'larifawm/ *adj* said *esp* of the water-conducting cell walls of certain plants: having thickened bands or markings arranged like the rungs of a ladder. [Latin *scalariformis*, from *scalaris* (see SCALAR[1]) + -IFORM]

scalar product *noun* a real number obtained by multiplying together the lengths of two vectors and the cosine of the angle between them.

scalawag /'skaləwag/ *noun NAmer* see SCALLYWAG.

scald[1] /skawld/ *verb trans* **1** to injure or burn (something or somebody) with hot liquid or steam. **2** to bring (a liquid, *esp* milk) almost to boiling point. **3** to subject (something) to brief immersion in boiling water. **4** *archaic* to rinse (something) in boiling water. *** like a scalded cat** very quickly. [Middle English *scalden* via early French *escalder* from late Latin *excaldare* to wash in warm water, from EX-[1] + Latin *calidus* hot, warm]

scald[2] *noun* **1** an injury or burn to the body caused by scalding. **2** any of various abnormal plant conditions that result from overexposure to sunlight or atmospheric pollution, causing brown patches that look similar to burns.

scald[3] /skawld, skald/ *noun* see SKALD. ➤➤ **scaldic** *adj*.

scaldfish *noun* (*pl* **scaldfishes** *or collectively* **scaldfish**) a small edible European flatfish with large easily damaged scales that leave a mark like a burn if removed: *Arnoglossus laterna.*

scalding *adj* **1** boiling hot. **2** said *esp* of a remark or review: biting or scathing.

scale[1] /skayl/ *noun* **1a** any of the numerous small overlapping plates that cover and protect the skin of fish, reptiles, etc. **b** a small thin plate resembling this, *esp* a naturally occurring one: *scales of mica; the scales on a moth's wing.* **2** a dry flake of dead skin, *esp* one caused by disease. **3a** a white deposit of lime formed on the inside of a kettle, iron, hot water pipe, etc caused by the evaporation or constant passage of hard water. **b** a deposit of tartar on teeth. **4a** a black scaly coating of oxide that forms on the surface of iron when heated and that must be removed before further processing can take place. **b** a similar coating that forms on other metals when heated. **5** = SCALE LEAF. **6** = SCALE INSECT. ➤➤ **scaled** *adj*, **scaleless** *adj*. [Middle English from French *escale*, of Germanic origin]

scale[2] *verb trans* **1** to remove the scale or scales from (something), usu by scraping. **2** to cover (something) with scale. ➤ *verb intrans*

1 to separate and come off in scales; to peel or flake off. **2** to shed scales. **3** to form scale or scales. ➤➤ **scaler** *noun*.

scale[3] *noun* **1** (*usu in pl*) any of various instruments or machines for weighing, orig one consisting of a simple balance, but now usu a device with an internal mechanism. **2** either pan or tray of a balance. **3** (**the Scales**) the constellation and sign of the zodiac Libra. *** tip the scales 1** to register weight. **2** to shift the balance of power or influence; to be a deciding factor in something: *His fluency in French tipped the scales in his favour.* [Middle English, literally 'bowl', from Old Norse *skál*]

scale[4] *verb trans* to weigh (something or somebody) on or as if on scales. ➤ *verb intrans* to have a specified weight on scales.

scale[5] *noun* **1a** a graduated range of values used in measuring something. **b** a measuring instrument with such a range of values marked on it. **2** the relative size, degree, or extent of something: *The scale of the damage was much worse than we had originally thought.* **3a** the ratio between the size of an existing object and a model or representation of the object. **b** a graduated line on a map or chart indicating the length used to represent a larger unit, e.g. one centimetre = one kilometre. **4** in music, a series of rising or falling notes with a regular pattern of intervals between them: *Down the road someone is practising scales* — Louis MacNeice. **5** in mathematics, the notation of a specified number system: *the binary scale.* **6** a graduated system: *a scale of taxation; a pay scale.* *** to scale** said of a map, model, or representation of something: produced with a uniform size ratio between it and the original: *The floor plans were drawn to scale.* ➤➤ **scaler** *noun*. [Middle English from Latin *scala* ladder, staircase]

scale[6] *verb trans* **1** to climb up or over, or reach the top of (something high): *The attackers managed to scale the wall.* **2** to make a map, model, or representation of (something) using a uniform size ratio. **3** to measure (something) using a specified scale. **4** to arrange (something) in a graduated series. **5** to regulate, set, or estimate (something) according to a rate or standard: *The production schedule is scaled to projected need.* **6** (*usu* + up) to increase (something): *The company scaled up production to meet the extra demand.* **7** (*usu* + down/back) to decrease (something): *We are now scaling down imports.* ➤ *verb intrans* to vary according to a scale. ➤➤ **scaler** *noun*.

scale armour *noun* armour that consists of small overlapping pieces of leather or metal fastened on leather or cloth.

scaleboard *noun* very thin wood used in making bookbindings and backings for pictures.

scale insect *noun* any of various small bugs that attach themselves by their mouthparts to plants and then produce a protective scale about their bodies. They can be severe crop pests in large numbers: superfamily Coccoidea.

scale leaf *noun* a small and scaly leaf, *esp* one that is modified to protect a bud or that forms the outer covering of a bulb.

scalene /'skayleen/ *adj* **1** said of a triangle: having sides of unequal length. **2** relating to or in the region of the scalenus. [Latin *scalenus* from Greek *skalēnos* uneven]

scalenus /skə'leenəs/ *noun* (*pl* **scaleni** /-nie/) any one of four paired muscles that extend from the neck vertebrae to the first or second ribs. They are involved in neck movement and chest movements associated with breathing. [from Latin *scalenus musculus* uneven muscle, so called because the paired muscles are of unequal lengths: see SCALENE]

scallion /'skalyən/ *noun* an onion with a small bulb, such as the spring onion or shallot. [Middle English *scaloun* from Anglo-French *scalun*, from Latin *Ascalonia* (*caepa*) (onion) of *Ascalon*, seaport in southern Palestine]

scallop[1] /'skoləp, 'skaləp/ *noun* **1a** any of various edible marine molluscs that have a shell consisting of two wavy-edged halves, each with a fan-shaped pattern of ridges, and that swim by opening and closing the halves of the shell: genus *Chlamys* and other genera. **b** the large muscle of a scallop used as food. **2** one half of a scallop shell or a similarly shaped dish used for baking and serving food, *esp* seafood. **3** any of a continuous series of rounded or angular projections forming a decorative border on material, clothes, linen, etc. **4** = ESCALOPE. [Middle English from early French *escalope* shell, of Germanic origin]

scallop[2] *verb* (**scalloped, scalloping**) ➤ *verb trans* **1** to shape, cut, or finish (an edge or border) in decorative scallops. **2** to bake (food, *esp* potatoes) in a scallop shell or shallow baking dish, usu with a sauce. ➤ *verb intrans* *NAmer* to gather or dredge for scallops. ➤➤ **scalloper** *noun*.

scally /'skali/ *noun* (*pl* **scallies**) *NW English dialect, informal* a rogue or rascal. [shortening of SCALLYWAG]

scallywag /'skaliwag/ (*NAmer* **scalawag** /'skaləwag/) *noun informal* a mischievous but likable person; a rascal. [origin unknown]

scalp[1] /skalp/ *noun* **1a** the skin and underlying tissue at the top and back of the human head, usu including the hair. **b** a part of this with the hair attached, cut or torn from an enemy and taken as a battle trophy, *esp* formerly by Native American warriors. **2** any trophy of victory. **3** *Scot* a bare rocky mound, *esp* one surrounded by water or vegetation. [Middle English, prob of Scandinavian origin]

scalp[2] *verb trans* **1** to remove the scalp of (somebody, *esp* a dead enemy). **2** *informal* to punish or defeat (somebody). **3** *chiefly NAmer, informal*. **a** to buy and sell (securities or shares) to make small quick profits. **b** to obtain (tickets) cheaply for resale at greatly increased prices. ➤➤ **scalper** *noun*.

scalpel /'skalpl/ *noun* a small very sharp thin-bladed knife used *esp* in surgery. [Latin *scalpellum*, dimin. of *scalper* knife, from *scalpere* to scrape]

scalpel safari *noun informal* = MEDICAL TOURISM.

scaly /'skayli/ *adj* (**scalier, scaliest**) **1** covered with or composed of scale or scales. **2** flaky. ➤➤ **scaliness** *noun*.

scaly anteater *noun* = PANGOLIN.

scam[1] /skam/ *noun informal* a scheme for obtaining money dishonestly; a swindle. [origin unknown]

scam[2] *verb trans* (**scammed, scamming**) *informal* to swindle (somebody or something). ➤➤ **scammer** *noun*.

scammony /'skaməni/ *noun* (*pl* **scammonies**) **1** either of two species of twining plants found in Asia and Mexico: *Convolvulus scammonia* and *Ipomoea orizabensis*. **2** the dried root of this plant, used in the production of a strong laxative. [Middle English *scamonie* via Latin from Greek *skammōnia*]

scamp[1] /skamp/ *noun* an impish or playful person, *esp* a child. ➤➤ **scampish** *adj*. [from obsolete *scamp* to act as a highway robber]

scamp[2] *verb trans dated* to perform (work or an activity) in a hasty, careless, or haphazard manner. [perhaps related to SKIMP]

scamper[1] /'skampə/ *verb intrans* (**scampered, scampering**) to run nimbly, lightly, and playfully: *The rabbits scampered off as we approached*. [prob from SCAMP[2]]

scamper[2] *noun* a dash or scurry.

scampi /'skampi/ *noun* (*treated as sing. or pl*) Norway lobsters or large prawns, prepared and cooked, e.g. in batter or breadcrumbs. [Italian *scampi*, pl of *scampo* a European lobster, ultimately from Greek *kampē* bending, from its shape]

scan[1] /skan/ *verb* (**scanned, scanning**) ➤ *verb trans* **1** to glance at (something, *esp* written matter) hastily, casually, or in search of a particular item: *He scanned the newspaper for suitable job adverts*. **2** to examine (something) with attention to detail: *Our technicians scan each photograph thoroughly*; *Police scanned the hills with binoculars in search of the crash site*. **3a** to examine successive portions of (an object) with a sensing device, such as a photometer or a beam of radiation. **b** to make a detailed examination of (part or all of the body) in this way, using ultrasonic waves, X-rays, etc. **4a** to change (an image) into an electrical signal by moving an electron beam across it according to a predetermined pattern for television transmission. **b** to reproduce (an image) from an electrical signal, *esp* on a television screen. **c** to convert (data, graphics, an image, etc) into a digital format for electronic purposes. **d** to examine (a section of magnetic tape or computer disk) for the presence of recorded data. **5** to examine or search (an object or region) using a radar scanner. **6** to read or mark (a piece of verse) in order to show metrical structure. ➤ *verb intrans* said of verse: to conform to a metrical pattern: *The third line doesn't scan*. ➤➤ **scannable** *adj*. [Middle English *scannen* from Latin *scandere* to climb, to scan a verse; prob from the idea of stamping the feet as a way of showing a metrical beat]

scan[2] *noun* **1** the act or an instance of scanning. **2a** a medical examination of a part of the body using a scanner. **b** an image produced by a medical scanner. **3** a radar or television trace.

scandal /'skandl/ *noun* **1** an act or event that is generally regarded as morally or legally unacceptable or utterly disgraceful: *Considering that knowledgeable scientists had expressed skepticism about Pilt-*

down Man from the time of its discovery, this concealment of the evidence is a greater scandal than the original fraud — Phillip E Johnson. **2** a person, thing, or event that causes or should cause public outcry. **3** malicious or damaging rumour, or the gossip that arises from this: *Love and scandal are the best sweeteners of tea* — Henry Fielding. ➤➤ **scandalous** *adj*, **scandalously** *adv*, **scandalousness** *noun*. [Latin *scandalum* a cause of offence, from Greek *skandalon* a stumbling block]

scandalize *or* **scandalise** *verb trans* to shock or offend (somebody) by immoral or disgraceful behaviour.

scandalmonger /'skandəlmunggə/ *noun* somebody who spreads or revels in scandal or gossip.

Scandinavian /skandi'nayvi·ən/ *noun* **1** a native or inhabitant of Scandinavia, a region of N Europe including Norway, Sweden, and neighbouring countries. **2** = NORTH GERMANIC. ➤➤ **Scandinavian** *adj*.

scandium /'skandi·əm/ *noun* a rare silver-white metallic chemical element: symbol Sc, atomic number 21. [Latin *Scandia*, ancient name of the southern Scandinavian peninsula + -IUM]

scanner *noun* **1** a device used to scan the human body with X-rays, ultrasonic waves, etc. **2** a device that converts data, graphics, an image, etc into a digital format for electronic purposes. **3** a device for sensing recorded data. **4** the rotating aerial of a radar set.

scanning electronic microscope *noun* an electron microscope in which the specimen is examined directly in a moving electron beam, and electrons reflected by the specimen are used to form a magnified three-dimensional image.

scansion /'skansh(ə)n/ *noun* **1** the analysis of verse to show its metre. **2** the way in which a particular piece of verse scans. [Latin *scansion-, scansio*, from *scandere* to climb]

scant[1] /skant/ *adj* **1** barely sufficient; inadequate: *Mick has always paid scant regard to conventions*. **2a** falling short of or being made up a specified amount, measurement, etc: *We had a scant five pounds left*. **b** (*usu* + of) having an inadequate supply of something: *He's fat, and scant of breath* — Shakespeare. ➤➤ **scantly** *adv*, **scantness** *noun*. [Middle English from Old Norse *skamt*, neuter of *skammr* short]

scant[2] *verb trans chiefly NAmer* **1** to restrict or withhold the supply of (something). **2** to deprive (somebody or something) of a sufficient or the expected amount of something. **3** to pay little or no attention to (somebody or something).

scant[3] *adv* scarcely or hardly: *I can scant believe it*.

scantling /'skantling/ *noun* **1** a small piece of timber, e.g. an upright piece in the framework of a house. **2** (*also in pl*). **a** the dimensions of timber and stone used in building. **b** the dimensions of a frame or STRAKE (band of hull planking or plates) used in shipbuilding. **3** *archaic* a small amount. [alteration of Middle English *scantilon* mason's or carpenter's gauge, from early French *escantillon* sample]

scanty *adj* (**scantier, scantiest**) **1** small or insufficient in quantity. **2** said of clothing: skimpy and revealing. ➤➤ **scantily** *adv*, **scantiness** *noun*.

scape /skayp/ *noun* **1** the shaft of an animal part, *esp* an antenna or feather. **2** a leafless flower stalk arising directly from the root of a plant, as in the dandelion. [Latin *scapus* shaft, stalk, from Greek *skapos* rod]

-scape *comb. form* forming nouns, denoting: a pictorial representation of a view: *a seascape*. [from LANDSCAPE[1]]

scapegoat[1] *noun* **1** a person who is made to take the blame for somebody else's wrongdoing or mistake. **2** in the Bible, a goat that was sent out into the wilderness after the chief priest of the Jews had symbolically placed the sins of the Israelites on it. [from *scape*, a short form of ESCAPE[1] + GOAT]

scapegoat[2] *verb trans* to make a scapegoat of (somebody).

scapegrace *noun archaic* an incorrigible rascal. [from *scape*, a short form of ESCAPE[1] + GRACE[1]]

scaphoid /'skafoyd/ *noun and adj dated* = NAVICULAR. [via Latin from Greek *skaphoeidēs*, from *skaphos* boat]

scapula /'skapyoolə/ *noun* (*pl* **scapulae** /-lee/ *or* **scapulas**) a large flat triangular bone on each side of the vertebrate pectoral girdle; the shoulder blade in mammals. [Latin *scapula* shoulder blade]

scapular[1] *noun* **1a** a long wide band of cloth with an opening for the head, worn front and back over the shoulders as part of a monastic habit. **b** a pair of small cloth squares joined by shoulder tapes, worn as a symbol of affiliation to a religious order. **2** a scapular feather. [Latin *scapula* shoulder, shoulder blade]

scapular² *adj* **1** relating to or in the region of the shoulder or the shoulder blade. **2** denoting any of the feathers covering the base of a bird's wing.

scapulary /'skapyoʊləri/ *noun* (*pl* **scapularies**) = SCAPULAR¹.

scar¹ /skah/ *noun* **1** a mark left on the skin or other body tissue by an injury, *esp* one that has healed or is healing: *He jests at scars, that never felt a wound* — Shakespeare. **2** a mark left on a plant stem, *esp* one where a leaf formerly grew. **3** a mark of damage or wear. **4** a lasting ill effect, *esp* a psychological one caused by trauma: *One of his men had been killed … in a manner that left a scar upon his mind* — H G Wells. ➤➤ **scarless** *adj*. [Middle English *escare* via French and Latin from Greek *eskhard* scab]

scar² *verb* (**scarred, scarring**) ➤ *verb trans* **1** to mark (something) with or as if with a scar: *quarries that scar the landscape*. **2** to do lasting injury or psychological damage to (somebody): *The tragedy scarred her for life*. ➤ *verb intrans* **1** to form a scar. **2** to become scarred.

scar³ *noun* a steep rocky cliff on a mountainside. [Middle English *skere* from Norse *sker* low reef]

scarab /'skarəb/ *noun* **1a** a large dung beetle that the ancient Egyptians held sacred: *Scarabaeus sacer*. **b** a representation of this sacred beetle, e.g. carved on an amulet or formed from a gemstone, used as a talisman. **2** any similar beetle, *esp* a scarabaeid. [via Latin from Greek *skarabeios* beetle]

scarabaeid /skarə'beeid/ *noun* any of a large group of stout-bodied beetles including the dung beetles and the tropical Goliath and Hercules beetles: superfamily Scarabaeoidea. ➤➤ **scarabaeid** *adj*.

Scaramouch or **Scaramouche** /'skarəmoohsh, -mowch/ *noun* a stock character in the COMMEDIA DELL'ARTE (Italian comedy of the 16th–18th cents) who is a portrayal of a Spanish don characterized by boastfulness and cowardice. [Italian *Scaramuccia*, from *scaramuccia*: see SKIRMISH¹]

scarce¹ /skeəs/ *adj* **1** not plentiful or abundant, *esp* not sufficient to meet demand. **2** few in number; rare. ✳ **make oneself scarce** *informal* to disappear or leave a place, *esp* to avoid trouble, recriminations, etc. ➤➤ **scarceness** *noun*, **scarcity** *noun*. [Middle English *scars* from early French *escars*, prob from Latin *excerpere*: see EXCERPT¹]

scarce² *adv* *archaic* scarcely or hardly.

scarcely *adv* **1a** only just: *We had scarcely finished eating*. **b** almost not: *There are scarcely any left*. **2** certainly or probably not: *I could scarcely disagree with an expert*.

scare¹ /skeə/ *verb trans* **1** to frighten (a person or animal) suddenly; to alarm. **2** (+ off/away) to drive (a person or animal) away by frightening them. ➤ *verb intrans* to become afraid: *I don't scare easily*. ➤➤ **scarer** *noun*. [Middle English *skerren* from Old Norse *skerra*, from *skjarr* shy, timid]

scare² *noun* **1** a sudden or unwarranted fright. **2** a widespread state of alarm or panic: *a bomb scare*.

scarecrow *noun* **1** an object, usu suggesting a human figure, set up to frighten birds away from crops. **2** *informal* a very thin or ragged person.

scared *adj* thrown into or living in a state of fear, fright, or panic; afraid.

scaredy-cat *noun* *informal* somebody who is easily frightened, cowardly, or over-cautious.

scaremonger /'skeəmunggə/ *noun* somebody who encourages panic, *esp* without reason. ➤➤ **scaremongering** *noun*.

scare tactics *pl noun* the use of fear to intimidate or influence somebody.

scare up *verb trans* *chiefly NAmer, informal* to produce (something) hastily or with difficulty: *Can we scare up a few more people for the quiz team?*

scarf¹ /skahf/ *noun* (*pl* **scarves** /skahvz/ *or* **scarfs**) a strip or square of cloth worn round the neck or over the head for decoration or warmth. [early French *escarpe* sash, sling]

scarf² *noun* (*pl* **scarfs**) **1** a method of joining two pieces of timber to form one continuous straight piece without any variation in width, in which the ends of the two pieces are chamfered, notched, or halved to fit each other. **2** either of the ends of pieces of timber that fit together to form a scarf joint. **3** an incision made in a whale so that the blubber can be removed. [Middle English *skarf*, prob of Scandinavian origin]

scarf³ *verb trans* **1** to join the ends of (two pieces of wood) with a scarf joint. **2** to form a scarf on (a piece of wood). **3** to cut a scarf in (a whale).

scarf joint *noun* = SCARF² (1).

scarfskin *noun* *archaic* the EPIDERMIS (outer layer of the skin), *esp* that forming the cuticle of a nail. [SCARF¹]

scarify /'skeərifie, 'ska-/ *verb trans* (**scarifies, scarified, scarifying**) **1** to scrape (a lawn) in order to remove moss, dead leaves, and other debris. **2** to break up and loosen the surface of (e.g. soil or a road). **3** to make scratches or small cuts in (the skin or other tissue) as a medical treatment or in certain traditional forms of skin decoration. **4** to injure the feelings of (somebody), e.g. by harsh criticism. ➤➤ **scarification** /-fi'kaysh(ə)n/ *noun*, **scarifier** *noun*. [early French *scarifier* via late Latin from Greek *skariphasthai* to scratch an outline, sketch, from *skariphos* stylus]

scarlatina /skahlə'teenə/ *noun* = SCARLET FEVER. [scientific Latin *scarlatina* via Italian from Latin *scarlata*: see SCARLET]

scarlet /'skahlət/ *adj* of a vivid red colour tinged with orange. ➤➤ **scarlet** *noun*. [Middle English *scarlat* brightly coloured cloth, via French from medieval Latin *scarlata*, from Persian *saqalāt* a kind of rich cloth, ultimately via late Latin *sigillatus* adorned with small figures, from *sigillum*, dimin. of Latin *signum* image, SIGN¹]

scarlet fever *noun* an infectious fever caused by a bacterium that attacks the red blood cells, characterized by a red rash and inflammation of the nose, throat, and mouth.

scarlet pimpernel *noun* a common creeping plant with usu red flowers that close in cloudy weather: *Anagallis arvensis*.

scarlet runner *noun* = RUNNER BEAN.

scarlet woman *noun* **1** *euphem* a woman who is sexually promiscuous; *esp* a prostitute. **2** used by some extreme Protestant sects: the Roman Catholic Church. [from the description of 'the great whore' in Revelation 17:1–6]

scarp¹ /skahp/ *noun* **1** a steep slope, *esp* a cliff face, produced by faulting or erosion; an escarpment. **2** the inner side of a ditch below the parapet of a fortification. [Italian *scarpa*]

scarp² *verb trans* to cut down or erode (something) to form a vertical or steep slope.

scarper /'skahpə/ *verb intrans* (**scarpered, scarpering**) *Brit, informal* to run away. [perhaps from Italian *scappare* to escape]

Scart /skaht/ *noun* (*also* **SCART**) a 21-pin socket used *esp* to connect different pieces of home entertainment equipment, e.g. to connect a stereo system to a television or video recorder to give better sound quality. [acronym from French *Syndicat des constructeurs des Appareils Radiorécepteurs et Téléviseurs*, the committee that designed it]

scarves /skahvz/ *noun* pl of SCARF¹.

scary /'skeəri/ *adj* (**scarier, scariest**) *informal* **1** causing fear or alarm; frightening or daunting: *like an American car … great on the straights but scary on the corners* — Guitarist. **2** weird; spooky: *a scary resemblance*. ➤➤ **scarily** *adv*, **scariness** *noun*.

scat¹ /skat/ *verb intrans* (**scatted, scatting**) *informal* to depart rapidly. [orig used as an interjection to drive away a cat, perhaps short for *scatter*]

scat² *noun* jazz singing with improvised vocals that sound like a musical instrument rather than conventional lyrics. [perhaps imitative]

scat³ *verb intrans* (**scatted, scatting**) to sing using improvised vocal sounds.

scat⁴ *noun* animal droppings, *esp* from a carnivore. [from Greek *skat-, skōr* excrement]

scathe¹ /skaydh/ *noun* *archaic* harm or injury. ➤➤ **scatheless** *adj*. [Middle English *skathe* from Old Norse *skathi* injury]

scathe² *verb trans* **1** *archaic* to denounce (somebody). **2** *literary* to harm (something).

scathing *adj* bitterly severe; scornful: *a scathing condemnation*. ➤➤ **scathingly** *adv*.

scatology /skə'tolǝji/ *noun* **1** the scientific study of excrement, *esp* in determining the diet, e.g. of extinct animals or prehistoric peoples. **2** an obsession or preoccupation with excrement or excretion, or literature, comedy, etc that displays this. ➤➤ **scatological** /skatə'lojikl/ *adj*. [Greek *skat-, skōr* dung + -OLOGY]

scatter¹ /'skatə/ *verb* (**scattered, scattering**) ➤ *verb trans* **1** to cause (a group or collection) to separate widely: *The dog scattered the flock of sheep.* **2** to distribute (something) carelessly or at irregular intervals: *Do you have to scatter your toys all over the house?* **3** to sow (seed) by casting in all directions. **4a** to reflect (e.g. a beam of light particles) irregularly and diffusely. **b** to diffuse or disperse (a beam of radiation). ➤ *verb intrans* to separate and go in various directions. ➤➤ **scatterer** *noun.* [Middle English *scateren*, prob a variant of SHATTER]

scatter² *noun* **1** the act of scattering. **2** a small amount or number of things irregularly distributed: *a scatter of orange lights.* **3** the state or extent of being scattered.

scatterbrain *noun* somebody who is disorganized or incapable of concentration. ➤➤ **scatterbrained** *adj.*

scatter diagram *noun* in statistics, a two-dimensional graph consisting of points whose positions represent values of two variables under study.

scattergun *noun* **1** *chiefly NAmer* a shotgun. **2** (*used before a noun*) targeting or covering a wide range or area, usu at random: *a scattergun approach.*

scattering *noun* **1** an act in which, or the process by which, something scatters or is scattered. **2** a small number or quantity interspersed here and there: *a scattering of visitors.*

scattershot *noun* = SCATTERGUN (2).

scatty /'skati/ *adj* (**scattier, scattiest**) *Brit, informal* forgetful or disorganized, *esp* in a slightly eccentric way. ➤➤ **scattily** *adv,* **scattiness** *noun.* [from SCATTERBRAIN]

scaup /skawp/ *noun* (*pl* **scaups** or collectively **scaup**) any of several species of diving ducks, the males of which have glossy greenish or purplish heads: genus *Aythya.* [perhaps alteration of Scottish *scalp* bed of shellfish, from its fondness for shellfish]

scavenge /'skavinj/ *verb trans* **1** to search for (something that could be of use), *esp* among rubbish or discarded items. **2** said of certain animals, birds, and fish: to search for and feed on (carrion or refuse). **3a** to remove (burned gases) from the cylinder of an internal-combustion engine after a working stroke. **b** to remove (an undesirable constituent) from a substance or region by chemical or physical means. **c** to clean and purify (molten metal) by causing impurities to form compounds that can be easily removed. ➤ *verb intrans* **1** to work or act as a scavenger. **2** to obtain food by scavenging. [back-formation from SCAVENGER]

scavenger *noun* **1** somebody who scavenges. **2** an animal that feeds habitually on refuse or carrion. **3** a chemical that removes something unwanted or makes an undesirable substance harmless. [alteration of Middle English *scavager* a person who collected *scavage,* a toll on goods sold by non-resident merchants (from Old French *escauwage* inspection, ultimately of Germanic origin), and who was later made responsible for keeping the streets clean]

scazon /'skayzon/ *noun* a line of poetry with a faltering rhythm, *esp* one consisting of iambic feet but with a TROCHEE (long or stressed syllable followed by short or unstressed syllable) or SPONDEE (two long or stressed syllables) at the end. [via Latin from Greek *skazōn,* from *skazein* to limp]

ScD *abbr* Doctor of Science. [Latin *scientiae doctor*]

SCE *abbr* Scottish Certificate of Education.

scena /'shaynə/ *noun* **1** a scene in an opera. **2** an elaborate vocal solo, *esp* an extended dramatic one in opera. [Italian *scena,* literally 'scene']

scenario /si'nahrioh/ *noun* (*pl* **scenarios**) **1** an outline or synopsis of a dramatic work, novel, or film, including details of the plot, characters, and settings. **2** an account or synopsis of a projected course of action: *According to this scenario, unemployment could fall to a few thousand in five years.* **3** a background or scene: *Oxford is not an obvious scenario for dramatic confrontation* — Isis. [Italian *scenario* from Latin *scaenarium,* from *scaena:* see SCENE]

scenarist /si'nahrist/ *noun* a writer of scenarios, *esp* for films.

scend¹ /send/ *verb intrans archaic* said of a ship: to rise upwards on a wave. [alteration of SEND]

scend² *noun archaic* **1** the lifting motion of a wave. **2** the rising and falling motion of a ship that this causes.

scene /seen/ *noun* **1** a place or setting in which something real or imaginary happens or happened: *the scene of the crime.* **2** a landscape or view, *esp* an attractive one. **3a** a division of an act in a play: *an attendant lord, one that will do to swell a progress, start a scene or two* — T S Eliot. **b** a single situation, unit of dialogue, or sequence in a play, film, or television programme. **c** a stage setting or the items of scenery in a play, opera, ballet, etc. **4** a public display of violent or unrestrained feeling: *Please don't make a scene.* **5a** a sphere of activity or interest: *the drug scene.* **b** *informal* something in which a person is particularly interested, involved, or concerned: *Philosophy's not really my scene.* **c** the people active in a particular sphere: *The poets are very much a different scene from the novelists* — Margaret Drabble. ❋ **behind the scenes** out of the public view. **set the scene** to provide the necessary background information for something. [Latin *scaena* a stage, from Greek *skēnē* a temporary shelter]

scene dock *noun* a space near the stage in a theatre where scenery is stored.

scenery /'seenəri/ *noun* **1** the natural features of a landscape, *esp* when considered attractive. **2** the painted scenes or hangings and accessories used on a theatre stage or film set. [Italian *scenario:* see SCENARIO]

scenic /'seenik/ *adj* **1** of or displaying natural scenery, *esp* when considered impressive or attractive. **2** of the stage, a stage setting, or stage representation. **3** said of a painting, photograph, etc: representing an action or event. ➤➤ **scenically** *adv.*

scenic railway *noun* a miniature railway, e.g. at a fun fair, with artificial scenery and sometimes natural landscape features along the way.

scent¹ /sent/ *noun* **1** a characteristic or particular smell, *esp* a pleasant one: *I love the scent of freesias.* **2** a light perfume worn on the skin. **3** a smell left by an animal on a surface that it has passed over, by which the animal may be traced: *The hounds followed the fox's scent.* **4** a trail of evidence that can be followed in a search or investigation: *She tried to throw the detectives off the scent.* **5** *archaic* the sense of smell: *Bears have a keen scent.* ➤➤ **scentless** *adj.*

scent² *verb trans* **1** to give a usu pleasant smell to (something): *Exotic candles scented the room.* **2** to perceive (something) by the sense of smell. **3** to get or have an inkling of (something): *I think I scent trouble.* ➤ *verb intrans* to use the sense of smell in seeking or tracking prey: *The hounds were scenting in the undergrowth.* ➤➤ **scented** *adj.* [Middle English from early French *sentir* to feel, perceive, smell, from Latin *sentire* to perceive, SENSE¹]

scent gland *noun* a specially modified animal gland that secretes a PHEROMONE (chemical substance stimulating a response) or other strong-smelling substance, used for marking territory, for defence, etc.

scent mark *noun* a strong-smelling substance secreted by an animal in urine or faeces, or from a scent gland, as a means of marking its territory.

scent-mark *verb intrans* said of an animal: to leave scent marks on its territory.

scent marking *noun* = SCENT MARK.

scepter /'septə/ *noun NAmer* see SCEPTRE.

sceptic (*NAmer* **skeptic**) /'skeptik/ *noun* **1** a person with a mistrustful attitude to accepted opinions. **2** a person who doubts basic religious principles, e.g. eternal life and divine guidance; an atheist. **3** in philosophy, somebody who denies the possibility of absolute knowledge, believing that even the most rigorous enquiry can only lead to an approximation of certainty. ➤➤ **sceptical** *adj,* **sceptically** *adv,* **scepticism** /-siz(ə)m/ *noun.* [via Latin from Greek *skeptikos,* from *skepsis* enquiry or doubt]

sceptre (*NAmer* **scepter**) /'septə/ *noun* **1** a staff carried by a ruler as a symbol of sovereignty. **2** royal or imperial authority; sovereignty. ➤➤ **sceptred** *adj.* [early French *ceptre* via Latin from Greek *skēptron* staff]

sch. *abbr* school.

Schadenfreude /'shahdənfroydə/ *noun* enjoyment obtained from the misfortunes of somebody else. [German *Schadenfreude,* from *Schaden* damage + *Freude* joy]

schappe /'shapə/ *noun* (*also* **schappe silk**) fabric or yarn spun from silk waste. [German *Schappe* waste silk]

schedule¹ /'shedyool, *NAmer* 'skedyool/ *noun* **1a** a plan of things to be done and the order in which to do them: *This project is running to a very tight schedule.* **b** a programme of all the appointments, tasks, etc that a person or group has arranged; an agenda: *There cannot be a crisis next week. My schedule is already full* — Henry Kissinger. **2** a timetable or the times fixed in a timetable: *The trains are running behind schedule again.* **3a** a statement of supplementary details appended to a legal or legislative document, often in the form of a list, table, or inventory. **b** any list, catalogue, or inventory: *Here is a schedule of the contents of the flat.* * **on/to/according to schedule** as planned or on time. ➤➤ **schedular** *adj.*

Word history

Middle English *sedule* a scroll or note, via French from late Latin *schedula* a slip of paper, from Greek *skhedē* papyrus leaf. The Middle English spelling was reflected in the original pronunciation /'sedyool/. The pronunciation /'skedyool/ arose in the 17th cent., along with the current spelling. The usual British pronunciation /'shedyool/, based on the French, dates from the early 19th cent., but did not catch on in the USA, where the lexicographer Noah Webster recommended that 'the pronunciation ought to follow the analogy of *scheme*'. The influence of American English has now reintroduced /'skedyool/ as an alternative in British English.

schedule[2] *verb trans* **1** to appoint or designate (something) to occur at a fixed time: *We've scheduled the new edition for release in July.* **2** to include (somebody or something) in a schedule. **3** *Brit* to place (a property) on a list of the buildings or historical sites to be preserved or protected by law. ➤➤ **scheduler** *noun.*

scheduled *adj* **1** relating to, forming, or placed on a schedule. **2** said of an aeroplane or flight: operating or occurring as part of a regular timetable, as distinct from being specially chartered. **3** said of a building or historical site: listed as being legally preserved or protected.

scheduled caste *noun* in India, the official name for any of the inferior classes who, in recognition of their lowly status, have special rights and concessions: compare DALIT, UNTOUCHABLE[2].

scheelite /'sheeliet/ *noun* a yellowish brown mineral that consists of calcium tungstate and is an important source of tungsten. [named after Karl *Scheele* d.1786, Swedish chemist, who first isolated tungstic acid from it]

schefflera /'sheflərə/ *noun* = UMBRELLA TREE (1). [Latin genus name, named after J C *Scheffler* d.1786, German botanist]

schema /'skeemə/ *noun* (*pl* **schemata** /-tə/ *or* **schemas**) **1** a representation of something in the form of a diagram, plan, theory, or outline. **2** in logic, a syllogistic figure. **3** in Kantian philosophy, a rule or principle that allows the understanding to unify experience. [via Latin from Greek *skhēma* a form or figure]

schematic[1] /ski'matik/ *adj* **1** representing something in a simplified or diagrammatic way: *a schematic layout.* **2** relating to a philosophical schema. **3** said of thinking, understanding, an idea, or a response: unsophisticated or formulaic: *This book will appeal to lovers of military history, but its characterisations often seem thin and schematic* — Daily Telegraph. ➤➤ **schematically** *adv.*

schematic[2] *noun* a schematic drawing or diagram, *esp* of an electric or electronic circuit.

schematise *verb trans* see SCHEMATIZE.

schematism /'skeemətiz(ə)m/ *noun* the arrangement of parts in a pattern or according to a scheme or schema.

schematize *or* **schematise** /'skeemətiez/ *verb trans* **1** to express or depict (something) schematically. **2** to form (something) into a systematic arrangement. ➤➤ **schematization** /-'zaysh(ə)n/ *noun.*

scheme[1] /skeem/ *noun* **1** a systematic plan or programme for a course of action or for putting an idea, project, etc into practice: *a recycling scheme.* **2** a systematic arrangement of parts or elements; a design: *a colour scheme.* **3** an organized system of financial investment, insurance, etc: *a company pension scheme.* **4** a secret plan, *esp* one that involves something illegal, dishonest, or wrong. **5** *chiefly Scot* a housing estate run by a local authority. [from Latin *schema* a figure of speech or a representation, orig of the position of the celestial bodies, from Greek *skhēma* form, figure]

scheme[2] *verb intrans* to make a plan to do something, *esp* something illegal, dishonest, or wrong. ➤ *verb trans* to plan (something) according to a scheme. ➤➤ **schemer** *noun.*

scheming *adj* shrewdly devious or cunning. ➤➤ **schemingly** *adv.*

schemozzle /shi'mozl/ *noun* see SHEMOZZLE.

scherzando /skeət'sandoh/ *adj and adv* said of a piece of music: to be performed in a sprightly or playful manner. ➤➤ **scherzando** *noun.* [Italian *scherzando*, literally 'joking']

scherzo /'skeatsoh/ *noun* (*pl* **scherzos** *or* **scherzi** /'skeatsi/) a lively instrumental musical composition or movement in quick, usu triple, time. [Italian *scherzo*, literally 'joke']

Schick test /shik/ *noun* a test of a person's susceptibility to diphtheria in which a diluted diphtheria toxin is injected into the skin, causing an inflamed red patch in those who are at risk.

[named after Bela *Schick* d.1967, Hungarian-born US paediatrician, who devised it]

schilling /'shiling/ *noun* the former basic monetary unit of Austria, divided into 100 groschen (replaced by the euro in 2002). [German *Schilling* a gold coin; related to Old English *scilling* SHILLING]

schipperke /'shipəki/ *noun* a small black dog of a tailless breed with erect triangular ears and a ruff of longer hair round its neck. [Flemish *schipperke*, literally 'little boatman', dimin. of early Dutch *schipper* (see SKIPPER[1]), because of its use as a watchdog on boats]

schism /'siz(ə)m, 'skiz(ə)m/ *noun* **1** the separation of a group into opposing factions, *esp* because of different ideologies. **2** the formal division of a Church or religious body, either into two entities or with one faction breaking away, usu caused by ideological or doctrinal differences. [Middle English *scisme* via French and Latin from Greek *skhisma* cleft, from *skhizein* to split]

schismatic[1] /siz'matik, skiz-/ *adj* relating to, characteristic of, or advocating schism. ➤➤ **schismatically** *adv.*

schismatic[2] *noun* a person who creates, promotes, or takes part in schism, *esp* formerly in the Christian Church.

schist /shist/ *noun* a metamorphic crystalline rock composed of thin layers of different minerals, *esp* mica, and capable of being split into thin flaky planes. ➤➤ **schistose** /'shistohs/ *adj.* [French *schiste* from Latin *schistos lapis* fissile stone, from Greek *schizein* to split]

schistosome /'shistəsohm/ *noun* a parasitic blood fluke that infests snails, birds, and mammals, causing disease: genus *Schistosoma.* [Latin genus name, from Greek *schistos* divided + *sōma* body]

schistosomiasis /,shistəsoh'mie·əsis/ *noun* a tropical disease caused by infestation with schistosomes, characterized by anaemia, inflammation of the blood vessels, and severe diarrhoea. Also called BILHARZIA.

schiz- *or* **schizo-** *comb. form* forming words, with the meanings: **1** split or divided: *schizocarp.* **2** schizophrenia: *schizoid.* [from Greek *schizein* to split]

schizanthus /skit'santhəs/ *noun* a S American plant with attractively variegated lobed flowers: genus *Schizanthus.* [SCHIZ- + Greek *anthos* flower]

schizo /'skitsoh/ *noun* (*pl* **schizos**) *informal, offensive* a person with schizophrenia. ➤➤ **schizo** *adj.*

schizo- *comb. form* see SCHIZ-.

schizocarp /'shiezohkahp, 'skitsoh-/ *noun* a dry compound fruit, e.g. of the hollyhock or the geranium, that splits into several single-seeded parts when it is ripe. [SCHIZO- + Greek *karpos* fruit]

schizogenous /shie'zojənəs, skit'soj-/ *adj* said of a space between plant cells: formed when a cell wall splits. ➤➤ **schizogenic** /shiezə'jenik, skitsə-/ *adj.* [from SCHIZO- + -GEN + -OUS]

schizogony /shie'zogəni, skit'sog-/ *noun* a form of asexual reproduction by dividing many times into identical spores that is characteristic of single-celled parasitic organisms, e.g. the malaria parasite. ➤➤ **schizogonous** *adj.* [SCHIZO- + Greek *-gonia* production]

schizoid[1] /'skitsoyd/ *adj* **1** in psychiatry, said of a personality type: characterized by extreme shyness and an inability to cope in social situations. **2** *informal* resembling schizophrenia, *esp* in showing conflicting or contradictory attitudes. **3** *informal* mad or crazy.

schizoid[2] *noun* somebody with a schizoid personality.

schizomycete /skitsoh'mieseet/ *noun* any of a class of microscopic organisms, e.g. a bacterium: class *Schizomycetes.* [SCHIZO- + *mykēs* fungus]

schizont /'skitsont/ *noun* a stage in the life cycle of a SPOROZOAN (single-celled parasitic organism) that contains many nuclei and reproduces by schizogony. [SCHIZ- + -ONT]

schizophrenia /skitsə'freeni·ə/ *noun* any of several mental disorders characterized by loss of contact with reality and disintegration of personality, usu with hallucinations, behavioural and emotional conflict, etc. ➤➤ **schizophrenic** /-'frenik/ *adj and noun,* **schizophrenically** /-'frenikli/ *adv.* [SCHIZO- + Greek *phrēn* mind]

schlemiel /shlə'miəl/ *noun NAmer, informal* an unlucky bungling person, *esp* one who is easily victimized. [Yiddish *shlemiel*]

schlep[1] *or* **schlepp** /shlep/ *verb trans chiefly NAmer, informal* to carry or haul (something) with difficulty. ➤ *verb intrans chiefly NAmer, informal* to move with difficulty. [Yiddish *shlep* from High German *sleppen* to drag]

schlep² or **schlepp** *noun chiefly NAmer, informal* **1** a difficult or trying journey. **2** somebody who is regarded as clumsy, stupid, or useless.

schlepper /'shlepə/ *noun chiefly NAmer, informal* = SCHLEP² (2).

schlieren /'shliərən/ *pl noun* **1** regions of varying density in a transparent medium, often caused by pressure or temperature differences or flaws, and appearing as streaks on a photograph when a beam of light is passed through the medium. **2** small masses or streaks in IGNEOUS rock (rock formed by cooling and solidification of molten rock material) that differ in composition from the main body. [German *Schlieren*, plural of *Schliere* a streak]

schlock /shlok/ *noun chiefly NAmer, informal* **1** cheap, inferior, or shoddy goods, literature, etc; trash. **2** (*used before a noun*) worthless or tasteless: *Hammersmith Road and its schlock architecture is proof that conservationists are not as powerful as the architectural profession likes to believe* — Independent. ⟫ **schlocky** *adj.* [Yiddish *shlak* apoplexy, from *shlog* wretch]

schloss /shlos/ *noun* a German or Austrian castle. [German *Schloss* castle]

schmaltz or **schmalz** /shmawlts/ *noun* excessive sentimentalism, *esp* in music or art. ⟫ **schmaltzy** *adj.* [Yiddish *shmalts* rendered fat, from German *Schmalz* lard]

schmear or **schmeer** or **shmear** or **shmeer** /shmiə/ *noun NAmer, informal* fat or grease. ✳ **the whole schmear** *NAmer* all that is possible or available: *We had champagne, caviar, the whole schmear.* [Yiddish *shmirn* grease]

Schmidt telescope or **Schmidt camera** /shmit/ *noun* a telescope or camera with an objective image-forming lens system that has a concave spherical mirror with a transparent plate in front of it for minimizing distortion. Such devices are used *esp* in astronomy, enabling wide areas of sky to be seen or photographed. [named after Bernhard *Schmidt* d.1935, Estonian-born German optical scientist, who invented the system]

schmo or **schmoe** or **shmo** /shmoh/ *noun* (*pl* **schmoes** or **shmoes**) *NAmer, informal* a stupid or useless person. [prob an alteration of SCHMUCK]

schmooze¹ or **shmooze** /shmoohz/ *verb intrans and trans chiefly NAmer* to chat or gossip with (somebody), *esp* in order to obtain something or to make a useful contact: *Britain's best-known film producer is leaving showbiz for politics because he's tired of schmoozing* — Independent. ⟫ **schmoozer** *noun*, **schmoozy** *adj.* [Yiddish *shmuesn* to chat]

schmooze² or **shmooze** *noun chiefly NAmer* a chat or gossip.

schmuck or **shmuck** /shmuk/ *noun NAmer, informal* a stupid or utterly despicable person. [Yiddish *shmok* penis]

schnapps /shnaps/ *noun* (*pl* **schnapps**) **1** a strong alcoholic drink; *esp* strong gin as orig made in the Netherlands. **2** a glass or measure of schnapps. [German *Schnaps* dram of liquor, from Low German and Dutch *snaps* mouthful]

schnauzer /'shnowzə, 'shnowtsə/ *noun* a dog of a German breed with a long head, wiry coat, and prominent whiskers. [German *Schnauze* snout, muzzle]

schnitzel /'shnits(ə)l/ *noun* a thin slice of meat, *esp* veal, coated in breadcrumbs and fried. [German *Schnitzel* slice]

schnook /shnook/ *noun NAmer, informal* a stupid person, *esp* somebody who is gullible or easily duped. [prob from Yiddish *shnuk* snout]

schnorrer /'shnawrə/ *noun chiefly NAmer, informal* a beggar, *esp* a habitual sponger. [Yiddish *shnorer* a beggar, prob related to German *schnurren* to hum, because of the musical instruments beggars played in the hope of getting a handout]

schnozz /shnoz/ *noun NAmer, informal* = SCHNOZZLE.

schnozzle /'shnozl/ *noun NAmer, informal* a person's nose. [prob via Yiddish *shnoyts* from German *Schnauze* snout]

scholar /'skolə/ *noun* **1a** a person who specializes in or has knowledge of a particular subject, *esp* in the arts: *a world-renowned classical scholar.* **b** *chiefly archaic or literary* a person of learning and academic interests: *He was a scholar, and a ripe and good one; exceeding wise, fair-spoken and persuading* — Shakespeare. **2** a university student who holds a scholarship. **3** somebody who attends a school or studies under a teacher. [Old English *scolere* from late Latin *scholaris*, from Latin *schola*: see SCHOOL¹]

scholarly *adj* characteristic of or suitable for learned people; academic. ⟫⟫ **scholarliness** *noun.*

scholarship *noun* **1** the character, methods, or attainments of a scholar; learning. **2** a grant of money awarded, e.g. by a college or foundation, to a student of academic merit to pay for education, books, upkeep while studying, etc.

scholastic¹ /skə'lastik/ *adj* **1** relating to education or schools. **2** suggestive or characteristic of scholasticism, *esp* in unnecessary subtlety or dryness; pedantic. **3** (*often* **Scholastic**) relating to or denoting medieval scholasticism. ⟫⟫ **scholastically** *adv.* [via Latin from Greek *skholastikos* studious or relating to learning, from *skholē* SCHOOL¹]

scholastic² *noun* **1** (*often* **Scholastic**) an advocate or adherent of medieval scholasticism. **2** in the Roman Catholic Church, a person who is undergoing preparatory study before entering the priesthood, *esp* a member of the Society of Jesus. **3** somebody who is fond of using logic subtly, *esp* in philosophical or theological debate. **4** a student or pupil.

scholasticism /skə'lastisiz(ə)m/ *noun* **1** (*often* **Scholasticism**) a philosophical movement dominant in W Christian civilization, *esp* between the 12th and 14th cents, that combined religious dogma with the tradition of the writings of the authoritative early Christian writers, *esp* St Augustine, and later with the philosophy of Aristotle. **2** close or pedantic adherence to the traditional teachings or methods of a school or sect.

scholia /'skoli·ə/ *noun* pl of SCHOLIUM.

scholiast /'skohliast/ *noun* a medieval annotator of ancient texts, *esp* Greek texts. ⟫⟫ **scholiastic** /-'astik/ *adj.* [medieval Greek *skholiastēs*, from *skholiazein* to write scholia: see SCHOLIUM]

scholium /'skoli·əm/ *noun* (*pl* **scholia** /'skoli·ə/) a marginal annotation or comment made by a scholiast. [via Latin from Greek *skholion* comment, from *skholē* lecture, SCHOOL¹]

school¹ /skoohl/ *noun* **1a** a building or organization for educating children. **b** the pupils, staff, activities, etc of such a building or organization considered collectively. **c** a session of a school. **d** (*used before a noun*) relating to or denoting such an educational establishment, or its pupils, staff, activities, etc: *school uniforms; The school day begins at nine o'clock.* **2** any institution primarily concerned with education, *esp* an establishment or organization dedicated to teaching a specified subject or skill: *a driving school.* **3a** a department or faculty in a university: *the School of Linguistics.* **b** *NAmer, informal* a university. **4a** a group of people who share the same approach to a subject or who adhere to the same doctrine, *esp* in the arts, philosophy, or theology: *the Frankfurt school.* **b** a way of thinking about or approaching something: *the current school of feminist thought.* **5** a source of knowledge: *All my experience was gained at the school of life.* **6** *Brit* a group of people who gamble or drink together, *esp* on a regular basis: *a poker school.* [Old English *scōl* via Latin *schola* from Greek *skholē* leisure, discussion, place for lectures]

school² *verb trans* **1** *NAmer or formal* to educate (somebody) in an institution of learning: *He had been schooled in Paris.* **2** to train or drill (a person or animal) in a specified field of knowledge, skill, or ability: *She had been schooled in chess by her father; to school a horse.*

school³ *noun* a large number of fish or aquatic animals of one kind swimming together. [Middle English *scole* from early Dutch *schole*; related to Old English *scolu* SHOAL³]

school⁴ *verb intrans* said of fish or sea mammals: to form a school.

school board *noun* **1** *Brit* an elected committee formerly in charge of providing and overseeing the running of local state schools, *esp* elementary schools. **2** *NAmer* a group of citizens who oversee the running of local schools.

schoolboy *noun* a boy who attends school.

schoolchild *noun* (*pl* **schoolchildren**) a child who attends school.

schoolgirl *noun* a girl who attends school.

schoolhouse /'skoohlhows/ *noun* **1** a building used as a school, *esp* a country primary school. **2** *Brit* a house attached to or near a school, where the teacher of the school lives.

schoolie /'skoohli/ *noun Aus or dialect, informal* a school pupil or schoolteacher.

schooling *noun* **1a** education or instruction received in school. **b** training or guidance from practical experience. **2** the training of a horse, *esp* in the formal techniques of show jumping, dressage, etc.

schoolman *noun* (*pl* **schoolmen**) **1** a teacher at a medieval W European university. **2** a scholastic philosopher or theologian.

schoolmarm /'skoolmahm/ *noun* **1** *chiefly NAmer* a female school-teacher, *esp* a rural or small-town schoolmistress regarded as prim or strict. **2** a prim woman with old-fashioned or traditional views. ➤➤ **schoolmarmish** *adj*.

schoolmaster *noun* **1** a man who is a schoolteacher. **2** an experienced person or thing, e.g. a horse used to give training or confidence to riders or other horses. ➤➤ **schoolmastering** *noun*, **schoolmasterly** *adv*.

schoolmate *noun informal* a companion at school.

schoolmistress *noun* a woman who is a schoolteacher.

schoolteacher *noun* a person who teaches in a school. ➤➤ **schoolteaching** *noun*.

schooner /'skoohnə/ *noun* **1** a fore-and-aft rigged sailing vessel with two or more masts. **2a** *Brit* a large sherry glass. **b** *NAmer, Aus, NZ* a tall beer glass. [origin unknown]

schorl /shawl/ *noun* a black variety of tourmaline containing a high percentage of iron. [German *Schörl*, of unknown origin]

schottische /sho'teesh/ *noun* a round dance in duple time resembling a slow polka, or a piece of music for this. [German *schottische Tanz* Scottish dance]

schtuck /shtook/ *noun* see SHTOOK.

schtum /shtoom/ *adj* see SHTUM.

schtup /shtoop/ *verb trans* see SHTUP.

schuss[1] /shoos/ *verb intrans* to ski down a straight high-speed ski run.

schuss[2] *noun* **1** a straight high-speed ski run. **2** the act or an instance of schussing. [German *Schuss* shot]

schwa /shwah/ *noun* **1** the symbol /ə/ used to represent an unstressed vowel, such as the first and last vowels of *banana*, in the International Phonetic Alphabet. **2** an unstressed vowel of this kind. [German *Schwa* from Hebrew *shĕwā*]

sci. *abbr* **1** science. **2** scientific.

sciatic /sie'atik/ *adj* **1** relating to or in the region of the hip. **2** relating to, affected with, or caused by sciatica: *sciatic pains*. ➤➤ **sciatically** *adv*. [early French *sciatique* via late Latin *sciaticus* from Greek *ischiadikos* relating to the hips or hip joints, from *ischion* hip joint]

sciatica /sie'atikə/ *noun* pain in the back of the thigh, buttocks, and lower back caused *esp* by pressure on the sciatic nerve. [late Latin *sciatica*, fem of *sciaticus*: see SCIATIC]

sciatic nerve *noun* either of the two largest nerves in the body that run from the lower spine down the back of each thigh to the calf.

SCID *abbr* severe combined immune deficiency, a rare disorder of the immune system that manifests during the first three months of life, causing very low resistance to infections and diseases.

science /'sie-əns/ *noun* **1** the study, description, experimental investigation, and theoretical explanation of the nature and behaviour of phenomena in the physical and natural world.

Editorial note
Nowadays, the unqualified word 'science' usually refers to natural and physical science, excluding not only metaphysics and theology but even technology. Technology uses science for human purposes, but science itself is the disinterested study of the real world. Science transcends nations and cultures, and normally proceeds by inventing hypotheses and systematically testing them against observation and, especially, experiment — Professor Richard Dawkins.

2 a branch of systematized knowledge as an object of study: *Moral philosophy, or the science of human nature, may be treated after two different manners* — David Hume. **3** something, e.g. a skill or technique, that may be studied or learned systematically: *the science of boxing*. **4** *archaic* knowledge or the possession of knowledge, *esp* as distinct from ignorance or misunderstanding: *For between true science and erroneous doctrines, ignorance is in the middle* — Hobbes. [Middle English via French from Latin *scientia* knowledge, from *scire* to know]

science fiction *noun* the genre of novels, films, etc involving the imaginative use of science and technology, usu set in the future.

science park *noun* an area with a concentration of businesses involved in scientific and technological study, research, and manufacturing.

scienter /sie'entə/ *adv* in law, used to describe the committing of an offence: knowingly or wilfully. [Latin *scienter* from *scire* to know]

sciential /sie'ensh(ə)l/ *adj archaic* **1** relating to or producing knowledge. **2** knowledgeable or skilful. [Middle English from late Latin *scientialis*, from Latin *scientia*: see SCIENCE]

scientific /sie-ən'tifik/ *adj* **1** relating to, based on, or using the methods of science. **2** systematic. ➤➤ **scientifically** *adv*. [Latin *scientificus* producing knowledge, from *scientia*: see SCIENCE]

scientism /'sie-əntiz(ə)m/ *noun* **1** methods and attitudes regarded as typical of scientists. **2** an exaggerated trust or belief in the power of scientific methods and knowledge, e.g. to explain psychological phenomena or solve human problems. ➤➤ **scientistic** /-'tistik/ *adj*.

scientist /'sie-əntist/ *noun* a person who is an expert in or who studies one of the natural or physical sciences, or who puts scientific methods into practice.

Word history
The earliest known use of this word occurs in a report (1834) of a meeting of the British Association for the Advancement of Science, where it was proposed – but rejected – that it should be adopted as a general name for a student of natural science. It was introduced, apparently independently, by William Whewell in 1840. The word did not win widespread acceptance for many years; as late as 1890 it was criticized as 'an ignoble Americanism'. The form *scientist* was recorded earlier, in 1785, but in the sense 'a person employing scientific principles'. Earlier terms for a person practising science include *philosopher*, *natural philosopher*, and *naturalist*, but none of these is precisely equivalent to the modern term.

Scientology /sie-ən'toləji/ *noun trademark* a disputedly religious and psychotherapeutic movement, begun in 1952 by L Ron Hubbard, that advocates self-knowledge as a means of spiritual fulfilment. ➤➤ **Scientologist** *noun*. [SCIENCE + -OLOGY]

sci-fi /'sie fie/ *noun informal* = SCIENCE FICTION.

scilicet /'sieliset/ *adv* used to introduce a missing word or in clarifying something obscure: namely. [Latin *scire* to know + *licet* it is permitted]

scilla /'silə/ *noun* a bulbous plant of the lily family, similar to the bluebell, with clusters of pink, blue, or white flowers: genus *Scilla*. [via Latin from Greek *skilla* SQUILL]

Scillonian /si'lohni-ən/ *noun* a native or inhabitant of the Scilly Isles off SW England. ➤➤ **Scillonian** *adj*.

scimitar /'simitə, -tah/ *noun* a short sword with a curved blade that narrows towards the hilt, orig used in the Middle East. [Italian *scimitarra*, perhaps from Persian *shimshīr*]

scintigram /'sintigram/ *noun* an image of an internal part of the body produced by scintigraphy.

scintigraphy /sin'tigrəfi/ *noun* a diagnostic technique in which a two-dimensional picture of a body part is obtained after the administration of a radioactive substance by detecting and measuring the emitted radiation. ➤➤ **scintigraphic** /-'grafik/ *adj*. [SCINTILLATION + -GRAPHY, from the scintillation counter used to record radiation on the picture]

scintilla /sin'tilə/ *noun* an iota or trace: *She showed not a scintilla of remorse*. [Latin *scintilla* spark]

scintillate /'sintilayt/ *verb intrans* **1** to emit sparks. **2** to sparkle or twinkle. **3** in physics, said of a substance: to fluoresce briefly as a result of having been struck by a charged particle or photon. [Latin *scintillare* to sparkle, from *scintilla* spark]

scintillating *adj* **1** shining, sparkling, or flashing. **2a** ingeniously witty: *This novel … is all scintillating word-play, dazzling but lifeless* — New Statesman. **b** captivatingly brilliant or vivacious in conversation: *Their hostess was at her most scintillating*. ➤➤ **scintillatingly** *adv*.

scintillation /sinti'laysh(ə)n/ *noun* **1** the act of scintillating. **2** a spark or flash of light. **3** in physics, a flash of light produced when a photon, alpha particle, or other form of radiation hits a substance that is capable of fluorescence. **4** the twinkling of stars, a phenomenon caused by the strata of the earth's atmosphere deflecting the rays of light.

scintillation counter *noun* a device for measuring the amount of radioactivity in a sample by detecting and counting the flashes of light in a crystal or PHOSPHOR (substance showing phosphorescence) that result from the emission of radioactive particles from the sample.

scintillator *noun* **1** a substance that scintillates. **2** a scintillation counter.

sciolism /'sie-əliz(ə)m/ *noun archaic* a superficial pretence of learning. ➤➤ **sciolist** *adj and noun*, **sciolistic** /-'listik/ *adj*. [Latin *sciolus* smatter, dimin. of *scius* knowing, from *scire* to know]

scion /'sie·ən/ *noun* **1** (*NAmer also* **cion**) a detached living part of a plant used in grafting and rooting. **2** a descendant or offspring, *esp* of a notable family. [Middle English from early French *cion* young shoot]

scirocco /shi'rokoh, si-/ *noun* see SIROCCO.

scirrhus /'sirəs/ *noun* (*pl* **scirrhi** /'sirie/) a hard slow-growing malignant tumour, *esp* in the breast, consisting mostly of fibrous tissue. ➤➤ **scirrhous** /'sirəs/ *adj.* [via Latin from Greek *skiros* hard]

scissile /'sisiel/ *adj* said *esp* of a chemical bond: capable of being split easily. [Latin *scissilis*, from *scindere* to split]

scission /'sizh(ə)n/ *noun* **1** a division, split, or cut. **2** the act or an instance of splitting; *esp* the splitting of a chemical bond. [Latin *scission-, scissio*, from *scindere* to split]

scissor /'sizə/ *verb* (**scissored, scissoring**) ➤ *verb trans* **1** to cut (an object or shape) with scissors. **2** to move (e.g. the legs) in a manner resembling the action of cutting with scissors. ➤ *verb intrans* said of the legs: to move like scissors.

scissors *pl noun* **1** a cutting instrument with two blades pivoted so that their cutting edges slide past each other. **2** a gymnastic or athletic feat in which the leg movements suggest the opening and closing of scissors. [Middle English *sisoures* from early French *cisoires*, ultimately from Latin *caedere* to cut]

scissors hold *noun* a wrestling hold in which the legs are locked round the head or body of an opponent.

scissors kick *noun* a swimming kick in which the legs move from the hip and come together like scissor blades.

sciurine /'sieyoorin, -rien/ *adj* of or belonging to a family of rodents that includes squirrels, chipmunks, and marmots: family Sciuridae. [Latin *sciurus* from Greek *skiouros* (see SQUIRREL[1]) + -INE[1]]

scler- *or* **sclero-** *comb. form* forming words, with the meaning: hard: *scleroderma.* [via Latin from Greek *skleros* hard]

sclera /'skliərə/ *noun* the opaque white outer coat that encloses the eyeball except for the part covered by the cornea. ➤➤ **scleral** /'skliərəl, 'sklerəl/ *adj.* [scientific Latin from Greek *skleros* hard]

sclerenchyma /sklie'rengkimə/ *noun* a supporting tissue in more evolutionarily advanced plants composed of cells with thickened and woody walls: compare COLLENCHYMA, PARENCHYMA. ➤➤ **sclerenchymatous** /-'kimətəs/ *adj.* [scientific Latin, from Greek *skleros* hard + *enkhuma* infusion]

sclero- *comb. form* see SCLER-.

scleroderma /skliəroh'duhmə/ *noun* chronic thickening and hardening of the lower tissue layers of the skin, affecting localized patches or the whole body. [from SCLERO- + -DERMA]

scleroprotein /skliəroh'prohteen/ *noun* any of various fibrous proteins, such as the collagens found in ligaments, tendons, and cartilage, and the keratins found in hair, horns, and nails.

sclerose /'skliərohs, 'sklerohs/ *verb trans and intrans* to undergo or cause (body tissue) to undergo sclerosis.

sclerosis /sklə'rohsis/ *noun* **1** abnormal hardening of tissue, *esp* from overgrowth of fibrous tissue. **2** a disease characterized by the hardening of tissue, *esp* multiple sclerosis. **3** the natural hardening of plant cell walls usu by the formation of lignin. [Middle English *sclirosis* via Latin from Greek *sklērōsis* hardening, from *sklēroun* to harden, from *skleros* hard]

sclerotia *noun pl* of SCLEROTIUM.

sclerotic[1] /sklə'rotik/ *adj* **1** relating to or in the region of the sclera. **2** relating to or affected with sclerosis.

sclerotic[2] *noun* = SCLERA. [medieval Latin *sclerotica*, ultimately from Greek *sklēroun*: see SCLEROSIS]

sclerotin /'sklerətin, 'skliərətin/ *noun* an insoluble protein found in the hard outer covering of insects, spiders, crabs, etc. [SCLERO- + *tin* as in KERATIN]

sclerotium /sklə'rohti·əm/ *noun* (*pl* **sclerotia** /-ti·ə/) a compact mass of hardened fungal threads that in some fungi becomes detached and remains dormant until a favourable opportunity for growth occurs. [scientific Latin, from Greek *skleros* hard]

sclerotized /'sklerətiezd/ *adj* said of the outer covering of an insect: hardened by substances other than chitin.

sclerous /'skliərəs/ *adj* hard or bony.

SCM *abbr Brit* **1** State Certified Midwife. **2** Student Christian Movement.

scoff[1] /skof/ *verb intrans* (*often* + at) to show contempt for something or speak contemptuously about it: *Truth from his lips prevailed with double sway, and those that came to scoff remained to pray —* Goldsmith. ➤➤ **scoffer** *noun*, **scoffing** *adj and noun*, **scoffingly** *adv.*

scoff[2] *noun* **1** an expression of scorn, derision, or contempt; a jeer. **2** *archaic* an object of mockery or derision. [Middle English *scof* mockery, scorn, prob of Scandinavian origin]

scoff[3] *verb trans chiefly Brit, informal* to eat (food) greedily, rapidly, or in an ill-mannered way. [prob alteration of Scots and N English *scaff*, of unknown origin]

scoff[4] *noun chiefly Brit, informal* food. [partly from SCOFF[3], partly from Afrikaans *skof* quarter of a day, meal, from Dutch *schoft*]

scold[1] /skohld/ *verb trans* to reprove or find fault with (somebody) angrily. ➤➤ **scolder** *noun.*

scold[2] *noun archaic* a woman who habitually nags or quarrels. [Middle English *scald*, prob from Old Norse *skāld* poet, SKALD]

scolex /'skohleks/ *noun* (*pl* **scolices** /sko'leeseez/) the anterior end of a tapeworm, bearing suckers or hooks with which it attaches itself to a host. [via Latin from Greek *skōlēx* worm]

scoliosis /skoli'ohsis/ *noun* (*pl* **scolioses** /-seez/) an abnormal sideways curvature of the spine: compare KYPHOSIS, LORDOSIS. ➤➤ **scoliotic** /-'otik/ *adj.* [scientific Latin, from Greek *skolios* crooked + -OSIS]

scollop[1] /'skoləp/ *noun archaic* = SCALLOP[1].

scollop[2] *verb trans and intrans archaic* = SCALLOP[2].

scombroid /'skombroyd/ *noun* any of a suborder of spiny-finned sea fishes, such as the mackerel, used for food: suborder Scombroidea. ➤➤ **scombroid** *adj.* [Greek *skombros* mackerel + -OID]

sconce[1] /skons/ *noun* **1** a bracket, often an ornamental one, attached to a wall for holding a candle or light. **2** a flat candlestick that has a handle. [Middle English from early French *esconse* screened lantern, from Latin *abscondere*: see ABSCOND]

sconce[2] *noun archaic* a detached defensive earthwork, such as a fort or mound. [Dutch *schans* brushwood, from German *Schanze*]

scone /skon, skohn/ *noun* a small light cake made from a dough or batter containing a raising agent and baked in a hot oven or on a griddle. [perhaps from Dutch *schoonbroot* fine white bread]

scoop[1] /skoohp/ *noun* **1a** a large ladle for taking up or skimming liquids. **b** a utensil with a handle and a small bowl used for spooning out soft food, *esp* ice cream. **c** a small spoon-shaped utensil for cutting or gouging, e.g. in surgical operations. **2** a deep bucket forming part of a mechanical digger or dredger, used for lifting and moving building materials, grain, etc. **3** the act or an instance of scooping. **4** the amount held by a scoop: *three scoops of mashed potato.* **5** *informal* a story or item of news secured for publication or broadcast, *esp* exclusively or ahead of rival journalists. **6** (**the scoop**) *NAmer* the latest news or information. **7** *informal* something, *esp* money, that is obtained by acting quickly or through sudden good fortune. **8** a cavity or small hole. ➤➤ **scoopful** (*pl* **scoopfuls**) *noun.* [Middle English from Dutch or Low German *schōpe* bucket for bailing water, waterwheel bucket]

scoop[2] *verb trans* **1** (*often* + out/up) to take (something) out or up with or as if with a scoop: *She scooped out the last of the mayonnaise from the jar; He scooped up the little boy and carried him off to bed.* **2** (*often* + out) to make (a hollow) with or as if with a scoop. **3** *informal* to report a news item in advance of (a competitor). **4** *informal* to obtain (something, *esp* money) by swift action or sudden good fortune: *We scooped the lottery jackpot.* ➤➤ **scooper** *noun.*

scoop neck *noun* a low-cut rounded neckline, or a woman's garment with such a neckline. ➤➤ **scoop-necked** *adj.*

scoosh[1] /skoohsh/ *noun Scot* a squirt of liquid.

scoosh[2] *verb trans Scot* to squirt (liquid). [imitating the sound]

scoot /skooht/ *verb intrans informal* to go or move suddenly and swiftly; to dart: *The children scooted up the stairs.* [prob from Old Norse *skjóta* to shoot]

scooter *noun* **1** a child's toy consisting of a narrow board with usu one wheel at each end and an upright steering handle, propelled by pressing one foot against the ground. **2** = MOTOR SCOOTER.

scope[1] /skohp/ *noun* **1** space or opportunity for action, thought, or development: *The garden had plenty of scope for improvement.* **2a** extent of treatment, activity, or influence: *That issue is beyond the scope of this enquiry.* **b** extent of understanding or perception: *a mind remarkable for its scope —* John Buchan. **3** *archaic* a purpose or intention. **4** the amount of anchor cable extended when a ship rides at anchor. [orig in the sense 'target': Italian *scopo* purpose, goal, from Greek *skopos* target, from *skeptesthai* to look out]

scope² *noun informal* a periscope, telescope, oscilloscope, etc. [independent use of -SCOPE]

scope³ *verb trans NAmer, informal* **1** to look at or examine (something) carefully. **2** to assess (something). [from SCOPE¹]

-scope *comb. form* forming nouns, denoting: an instrument for viewing or observing: *microscope*. [Latin *-scopium* from Greek *skopien* to look at]

-scopic *comb. form* forming adjectives, with the meaning: relating to a viewing instrument: *microscopic*.

scopolamine /skoh'poləmeen/ *noun* = HYOSCINE. [Latin *Scopolia*, genus name of the plants it comes from + AMINE]

scops owl /skops/ *noun* any of several species of very small brown owls with tufted ears: genus *Otus*. [Latin *Scops*, former genus name, from Greek *skops*]

-scopy *comb. form* forming nouns, denoting: viewing or observation: *radioscopy*. [from Greek *skopien* to look at]

scorbutic /skaw'byoohtik/ *adj* relating to, resembling, or affected with scurvy. [Latin *scorbuticus*, from *scorbutus* scurvy]

scorch¹ /skawch/ *verb trans* **1** to burn (something) in such a way that a change in colour or texture is produced. **2** to cause (something, *esp* land or vegetation) to become completely dried up because of the effects of intense heat; to parch. ➤ *verb intrans* **1** to become burned or dried up. **2** *informal* to move or travel at great and usu excessive speed. [Middle English, prob from Old Norse *skorpna* to shrivel up]

scorch² *noun* **1** a mark resulting from scorching. **2** a browning of plant tissues usu caused by disease or intense heat.

scorched earth policy *noun* **1** a strategy during a military campaign in which anything that an invading army might use is deliberately destroyed. **2** a strategy in business in which a company that fears a hostile take-over bid temporarily reduces its apparent assets in order to make it seem like a less attractive proposition.

scorcher *noun* **1** *informal* a very hot day or a period of very hot weather. **2** *Brit, informal* something that is regarded as remarkable: *He played an absolute scorcher of a game*. **3** somebody or something that scorches.

scorching *adj* **1** very hot: *a scorching summer afternoon*. **2** *informal* very fast: *at a scorching pace*. ➤➤ **scorchingly** *adv*.

score¹ /skaw/ *noun* **1** the number of points, goals, runs etc a team or individual makes in a game, competition, etc, or a record of this: *The half-time score was two nil; Who's keeping the score?* **2** a result of a test or examination, usu expressed in numbers or letters. **3** (*pl* **score**) twenty or a group or set of twenty people or things: *Three score plus ten equals seventy*. **4** an unspecified large number or quantity: *We've had scores of applications for the job; Donna has shoes by the score*. **5** (**the score**) *informal* the way things are; the state of affairs: *What's the score then? Did you buy the car or not?* **6a** the written or printed representation of all the parts for a musical composition. **b** a musical composition, *esp* the music for a film or theatrical production. **c** a complete description of a dance composition with the dancers' moves written in symbolic form. **7a** a line, scratch, or incision made with a sharp instrument. **b** a mark or notch formerly used as a means of keeping an account or tally, e.g. in a pub. **8** a grievance or grudge: *I have a score to settle with him*. **9** a subject or topic: *We have no doubts on that score*. **10** *informal*. **a** the act of successfully obtaining illegal drugs. **b** an amount of an illegal drug obtained. **c** anything obtained illegally, *esp* stolen goods. **d** a sexual conquest. ✳ **know the score** *informal* to know what is happening, or what the facts are. **on the score of** *Brit* because of: *The director refused to stage the play on the score of its controversial subject matter*. **over the score** beyond what is considered usual or acceptable; excessive or unfair: *Once he starts drinking, Phil tends to go over the score*. **pay/settle a/the score 1** to take revenge. **2** *dated* to pay a bill or debt. ➤➤ **scoreless** *adj*. [Old English *scoru* a set of twenty, from Old Norse *skor* notch, tally, twenty]

score² *verb trans* **1a** to gain (e.g. points) in a game, competition, etc: *I scored eight runs*. **b** to have (a specified number of points) as a value in a game or contest: *The ace scores twelve points in this game*. **2** *informal*. **a** to gain or win (something): *He scored a huge success with his new novel*. **b** to succeed in obtaining (something, *esp* illegal drugs). **3a** to arrange (music) for specific voice or instrumental parts or a combination of both. **b** to arrange (music) for an

orchestra; to orchestrate. **4** to mark (a surface) with lines, grooves, scratches, or notches. **5** (+ out/through) to delete or cancel something written or printed by putting a line through it. **6** to keep a record of (amounts, expenditure, etc) using notches on a tally. ➤ *verb intrans* **1** to make a score in a game or contest. **2** to keep score in a game or contest. **3** to obtain a rating or grade: *She scored highly in her tests*. **4** *informal*. **a** to obtain illicit drugs. **b** to succeed in having sexual intercourse. ✳ **score (points) off somebody** *Brit, informal* to humiliate somebody or get the better of them in a debate or argument. ➤➤ **scorer** *noun*.

scoreboard *noun* a large board at a sports ground that shows spectators the current score in a game or match.

scorecard *noun* **1** a card for recording a score, *esp* in golf. **2** a card listing the names of the players in a game, *esp* in cricket.

scoreline *noun* the result of a game or match: *The half-time score-line was one all*.

scoresheet *noun* **1** a sheet of paper for recording the scores in a game. **2** the record of goals scored and the names of the scorers in a match.

scoria /'skawri·ə/ *noun* (*pl* **scoriae** /-ee/) **1** rough cindery lava; volcanic slag. **2** the refuse from smelting ores or melting metals. ➤➤ **scoriaceous** /-'ayshəs/ *adj*. [via Latin from Greek *skōria* rubbish, from *skōr* excrement]

scorn¹ /skawn/ *noun* **1** vigorous contempt; disdain. **2** an open expression of extreme contempt: *He poured scorn on the whole affair*. **3** an object of extreme disdain or derision. ✳ **laugh to scorn** *archaic or literary* to jeer at (something or somebody) or hold them in contempt: *Laugh to scorn the power of man, for none of woman born shall harm Macbeth* — Shakespeare. ➤➤ **scornful** *adj*, **scornfully** *adv*, **scornfulness** *noun*. [Middle English from early French *escarn* contempt, of Germanic origin]

scorn² *verb trans* **1** to treat (something or somebody) with outspoken or angry contempt: *Heaven has no rage, like love to hatred turned, nor Hell a fury, like a woman scorned* — Congreve. **2** to refuse or reject (something) out of contempt: *Teachers are now scorning the old methods*. ➤➤ **scorner** *noun*.

Scorpio /'skawpioh/ *noun* **1a** in astrology, the eighth sign of the zodiac. **b** a person born under this sign. **2** = SCORPIUS. ➤➤ **Scorpian** *adj and noun*. [Latin *scorpio* scorpion]

scorpion /'skawpi·ən/ *noun* **1a** any of an order of arachnids that have an elongated body and a narrow tail bearing a venomous sting at the tip: order Scorpiones. **b** any of various similar, but unrelated, arachnids and insects. **2** (**the Scorpion**) the constellation Scorpius or sign of the zodiac Scorpio. **3** *literary* (*in pl*) a whip studded with metal spikes. [Middle English via French from Latin *scorpio*, from Greek *skorpios* sea fish, scorpion; (sense 3) with reference to 1 Kings 12:11]

scorpion fish *noun* any of various spiny-finned sea fishes, some of which have a venomous spine on the dorsal fin: family Scorpaenidae.

scorpion fly *noun* any of a family of flesh-eating insects that have cylindrical bodies and the male genitalia enlarged into a swollen bulb: order Mecoptera.

Scorpius /'skawpi·əs/ *noun* a constellation (the Scorpion) that contains the first-magnitude star Antares. [via Latin from Greek *skorpios* SCORPION]

scorzonera /skawzə'niərə/ *noun* a European composite plant with a black edible root similar to that of salsify: *Scorzonera hispanica*. [Latin genus name, from Italian *scorzone*, from medieval Latin *curtio* venomous snake, prob because the roots were used as an antidote to snake bites]

Scot /skot/ *noun* **1** a native or inhabitant of Scotland. **2** a member of a Gaelic people orig of N Ireland that settled in Scotland during the fifth cent. AD. [Old English *Scottas* Irishmen, from Latin *Scotus* Irishman]

Scot. *abbr* **1** Scotland. **2** Scottish.

scot *noun archaic* a municipal tax, or the payment or levying of this. ✳ **scot and lot** a former municipal tax that qualified those paying it to have a vote in parliamentary elections. [Middle English from Old Norse *skot* a shot or contribution]

Scotch¹ /skoch/ *adj dated* = SCOTTISH. [contraction of SCOTTISH]

Usage note

Scotch, Scots, *or* Scottish? *Scotch* is, for general purposes, an outdated adjective and disliked by many Scots. It should only be used in the specific combinations where it is familiar and established: *a Scotch egg; Scotch whisky*. *Scottish* is an all-purpose adjective that can be used for people, places and things in or relating to Scotland: *a Scottish soldier; a Scottish tourist resort; the Scottish education system*. *Scots* may be used to describe people (*a Scots politician, the Scots Guards*), but its use seems to be becoming less common.

Scotch[2] *noun* **1** = SCOTCH WHISKY. **2** (**the Scotch**) *dated* the people of Scotland. **3** *dated* the form of English spoken in Scotland, *esp* in the Lowlands.

scotch[1] *verb trans* **1** to put an end to (something, e.g. a rebellion or rumour); to crush or repudiate. **2** *archaic* to temporarily disable (something) or make it harmless. **3** to block or prop (something or somebody) with or as if with a wedge. [Middle English *scocchen* to gash; earlier history unknown]

scotch[2] *noun archaic* a wedge used to prevent a wheel, etc from rolling.

scotch[3] *verb trans archaic* to make a cut or score on the surface of (something, *esp* the skin). [Middle English, of unknown origin]

scotch[4] *noun archaic* a cut or score on the surface of something, *esp* the skin.

Scotch bonnet *noun* a variety of very hot chilli pepper. [so called because it resembles a TAM-O'-SHANTER]

Scotch broth *noun* soup made from beef or mutton, vegetables, and barley.

Scotch catch *noun* = SCOTCH SNAP.

Scotch egg *noun* a hard-boiled egg covered with sausage meat, coated with breadcrumbs, and deep-fried, usu eaten cold.

Scotchman *or* **Scotchwoman** *noun* (*pl* **Scotchmen** *or* **Scotchwomen**) *dated* a Scottish man or woman.

Scotch mist *noun* **1** a heavy wet mist of the type that is characteristically found in the Scottish Highlands. **3** a light drizzle. **3** used ironically to refer to something that does not exist, or something obvious that another person cannot see: *I thought you said you'd lost your glasses. What's that on the top of your head then, Scotch mist?*

Scotch pancake *noun* = DROP SCONE.

Scotch snap *noun* a rhythmical pattern, used *esp* in the STRATH-SPEY (Scottish dance), consisting of a short note followed by a lengthened one.

Scotch tape *noun chiefly NAmer, trademark* a type of clear adhesive tape.

Scotch whisky *noun* whisky distilled in Scotland, *esp* from malted barley.

Scotchwoman *noun* see SCOTCHMAN.

scoter /'skohtə/ *noun* (*pl* **scoters** *or collectively* **scoter**) any of several species of sea ducks, with dark brown or black feathers, living mainly in northern regions: genus *Melanitta*. [origin unknown]

scot-free *adj* without any penalty, payment, or injury. [see *scot* and *lot* at SCOT]

scotia /'skohshə/ *noun* in classical architecture, a deep concave moulding, *esp* on the base of a column. [via Latin from Greek *skotia*, from *skotos* darkness, from the shadow it casts]

Scotland Yard /'skotlənd/ *noun* (*treated as sing. or pl*) the criminal investigation department of the London metropolitan police force. [named after *Scotland Yard*, a street in London formerly the site of the headquarters of the metropolitan police]

scotoma /skə'tohmə/ *noun* (*pl* **scotomas** *or* **scotomata** /-tə-/) a blind or dark spot in the visual field. [via late Latin from Greek *skotoma*, from *skotoun* to darken, from *skotos* darkness]

Scots[1] /skots/ *adj* used *esp* of the people and language: Scottish.

Usage note
Scots, Scotch, or Scottish? See note at SCOTCH[1].

Scots[2] *noun* the form of the English language spoken in Scotland, and the literary language based on it.

Scotsman *or* **Scotswoman** *noun* (*pl* **Scotsmen** *or* **Scotswomen**) a man or woman who is a native or inhabitant of Scotland: *There are few more impressive sights in the world than a Scotsman on the make* — J M Barrie.

Scots pine *noun* a N European and Asian pine tree with spreading branches, bluish green needles, and hard yellow wood used for timber: *Pinus sylvestris*.

Scotswoman *noun* see SCOTSMAN.

Scotticism /'skotisiz(ə)m/ *noun* a characteristic feature of Scottish English, *esp* as contrasted with standard English.

Scottie /'skoti/ *noun informal* **1** (*also* **Scottie dog**) = SCOTTISH TERRIER. **2** used as a nickname: a Scotsman or a man of Scottish descent.

Scottish *noun* (**the Scottish**) (*treated as pl*) the people of Scotland. ➤ **Scottish** *adj*, **Scottishness** *noun*.

Usage note
Scottish, Scots, or Scotch? See note at SCOTCH[1].

Scottish Gaelic /'gahlik, 'gaylik/ *noun* the Gaelic language spoken in Scotland.

Word history
Words from Scottish Gaelic that have passed into common use in English include *banshee, cairn, clan, loch, plaid, spunk*, and *trousers*.

Scottish Nationalist Party *noun* the political party of Scotland that advocates complete independence for the country. ➤ **Scottish Nationalist** *noun*.

Scottish terrier *noun* a terrier of a Scottish breed having short legs and a very wiry coat of usu black hair.

scoundrel /'skowndrəl/ *noun* an unscrupulous or dishonest person. ➤ **scoundrelly** *adj*. [origin unknown]

scour[1] *verb trans* **1a** to clean (something) by vigorous rubbing, *esp* with abrasive material. **b** to remove (e.g. dirt) by rubbing. **2** to clear (e.g. a pipe or ditch) by removing dirt and debris. **3a** said of running water or a glacier: to create an eroded channel in (something). **b** to erode (a channel or pool). **4** to clean out (the bowels) by purging. ➤ *verb intrans* said of livestock, *esp* cattle: to suffer from diarrhoea. ➤ **scourer** *noun*. [Middle English *scouren* from early Dutch or early Low German *schüren*, via early French *escurer* from Latin *excurare* to clean off, from EX-[1] + *curare* to take care of, clean, from *cura* care]

scour[2] *noun* **1** the act or process of scouring or the state of being scoured. **2** a place that has been scoured, e.g. by running water. **3** (*also in pl*) diarrhoea affecting livestock, *esp* cattle or pigs.

scour[3] /'skowə/ *verb trans* to search (something) thoroughly: *Police were scouring the countryside for the missing toddler*. ➤ *verb intrans* to hurry about, *esp* with the aim of finding something. [Middle English *scuren*, prob of Scandinavian origin]

scourge[1] /skuhj/ *noun* **1** somebody or something that is the source or cause of trouble or distress. **2** a whip formerly used to inflict punishment.

scourge[2] *verb trans* **1** to cause great distress to (somebody). **2** to flog (somebody) with a scourge. ➤ **scourger** *noun*. [early French *escorgier* to whip, from EX-[1] (2) + Latin *corrigia* whip]

scouring rush *noun* a plant with stems covered in hard granules of silica, such as the horsetail, formerly used for scouring: genus *Equisetum*.

scourings *noun* material removed by scouring or cleaning.

scours *noun* see SCOUR[2] (3).

Scouse /skows/ *noun Brit, informal* **1** the dialect or accent of Liverpool. **2** (*also* **Scouser**) a native or inhabitant of Liverpool. ➤ **Scouse** *adj*. [short for LOBSCOUSE, because of the popularity of this dish in Merseyside]

scout[1] /skowt/ *noun* **1a** a person who is sent ahead to obtain information, *esp* a soldier sent out to survey land or assess an enemy's position or strength. **b** a ship or aircraft on reconnaissance duties. **2** (**Scout**) a member of the Scout Association, a worldwide movement for young people that stresses qualities of leadership, responsibility, and helpfulness. **3** = TALENT SCOUT. **4** *dated* a man or boy; a chap. **5** an Oxford University college servant or domestic worker: compare GYP[3] (1). **6** the act or an instance of looking at, searching for, or assessing something.

scout[2] *verb intrans* **1** to make an advance survey, e.g. to obtain military information; to reconnoitre. **2** to look for something: *I scouted around for a suitable picnic spot; She was scouting for new talent*. ➤ *verb trans* to observe or explore (a place) in order to obtain information: *They were scouting the hills for guerrillas*. ➤ **scouter** *noun*. [Middle English *scouten* via Old French *escouter* to listen, from Latin *auscultare* to listen attentively]

scout[3] *verb trans archaic* to reject (somebody or something) with contempt or ridicule: *Academics scouted the new theory*. ➤ *verb intrans archaic* to scoff. [prob of Scandinavian origin]

scout car *noun chiefly NAmer* a fast armoured military reconnaissance vehicle.

Scouter *noun* an adult leader in the Scout movement.

Scouting *noun* the activities of the Scout movement.

scow /skow/ *noun* a large flat-bottomed usu unpowered boat used chiefly for transporting ore, sand, refuse, etc. [Dutch *schouw* ferry boat]

scowl[1] /skowl/ *verb intrans* to frown or wrinkle the brows in expression of anger or displeasure. ⨠ **scowler** *noun*. [Middle English *skoulen*, prob of Scandinavian origin]

scowl[2] *noun* a facial expression of annoyance or displeasure; an angry frown.

SCPO *abbr* Senior Chief Petty Officer.

SCPS *abbr* Brit Society of Civil and Public Servants.

SCR *abbr* Brit senior common room.

Scrabble /'skrabl/ *noun trademark* a board game in which individual letters on small tiles are used to form words that are arranged as in a crossword puzzle: *Playing 'Bop' is like scrabble with all the vowels missing* — Duke Ellington. [perhaps from SCRABBLE[1] in an earlier sense 'to scrawl or scribble']

scrabble[1] *verb intrans* **1** to scratch or scrape about, e.g. in an attempt to find or catch hold of something: *The dog scrabbled at the pile of earth.* **2** to scramble or clamber: *We scrabbled up the rocky hillside.* **3** (*often* + for) to struggle frantically to get something: *The children were scrabbling for leftovers.* [Dutch *schrabbelen* to scratch]

scrabble[2] *noun* **1** the act or an instance of scrabbling. **2** a disorderly movement or struggle. **3** a persistent scratching or clawing.

scrag[1] /skrag/ *noun* **1** a thin or scrawny person or animal. **2** *informal, archaic* a person's neck. **3** = SCRAG-END. [perhaps alteration of CRAG in the sense 'neck']

scrag[2] *verb trans* (**scragged, scragging**) *informal* **1** *chiefly Brit* to seize and beat (somebody). **2** *NAmer* to kill (somebody), *esp* by strangling.

scrag-end *noun Brit* the bony end nearest the head of a neck of mutton or veal.

scraggly /'skragli/ *adj* (**scragglier, scraggliest**) *chiefly NAmer, informal* irregular or ragged: *a scraggly beard.*

scraggy *adj* (**scraggier, scraggiest**) lean and lanky; scrawny. ⨠ **scraggily** *adv*, **scragginess** *noun*.

scram /skram/ *verb intrans* (**scrammed, scramming**) *informal* to go away quickly or immediately. [shortened form of SCRAMBLE[1]]

scramble[1] /'skrambl/ *verb intrans* **1** to move or climb, e.g. up a steep slope or over uneven ground, using the hands as well as the feet. **2** to move with haste, urgency, or panic. **3** to compete eagerly or chaotically for possession of something: *The fans were scrambling for front-row seats.* **4** to become muddled or jumbled up. **5** said *esp* of an aircraft or its crew: to take off quickly, e.g. in response to an alert. **6** in American football, said of a quarterback: to run with the ball behind the line of scrimmage, or to run forward with the ball, having been unable to pass it. ➤ *verb trans* **1** to cause (something) to become muddled or jumbled up: *All this technology scrambles my brain.* **2** to prepare (eggs) in a pan by stirring during cooking. **3** to cause or order (an aircraft) to scramble. **4** to make (a message, etc) unintelligible to those without the means to decode it, *esp* by using an electronic device: *The company scrambles the signal so that only subscribers to cable television can access it.* [perhaps alteration of SCRABBLE[1]]

scramble[2] *noun* **1** the act or an instance of scrambling. **2** a climb over rough ground. **3** *Brit* a motorcycle race over rough ground, *esp* a motocross race. **4** a disordered mess; a muddle or jumble. **5** a rapid emergency takeoff of fighter aircraft.

scrambled egg *noun* **1** (*also in pl*) a dish made by beating eggs with a little liquid, usu milk, and cooking gently while stirring. **2** *informal* gold braid behind the peak of a senior military officer's cap.

scrambler *noun* **1** an electronic device that makes telephone, television, or radio signals impossible to access without the appropriate decoding equipment. **2** a motorcycle designed for racing over rough ground, *esp* motocross. **3** somebody who scrambles, *esp* a person who enjoys hillwalking over rough terrain.

scrambling *noun* = MOTOCROSS.

scramjet *noun* a RAMJET (type of jet engine) in which combustion takes place in a stream of air that is itself moving at supersonic speed. [from *supersonic* + *combustion* + RAMJET]

scran /skran/ *noun dialect* food. [origin unknown]

scrap[1] /skrap/ *noun* **1** a small detached fragment; a bit: *a scrap of paper.* **2** (*in pl*) discarded or leftover food. **3a** the residue from a manufacturing process. **b** manufactured articles or parts, *esp* of metal, or other material rejected or discarded and useful only for reprocessing. [Middle English from Old Norse *skrap* scraps]

scrap[2] *verb trans* (**scrapped, scrapping**) **1** to abandon, discard, or get rid of (something): *We need to scrap that idea and start again.* **2** to convert (something) into scrap: *The navy decided to scrap the battleship.*

scrap[3] *verb intrans* (**scrapped, scrapping**) *informal* **1** to fight or quarrel: *The kids were scrapping in the playground.* **2** (*usu* + for) to struggle or compete: *Several players are scrapping for a place in the team.* ⨠ **scrapper** *noun*. [origin unknown]

scrap[4] *noun informal* **1** a fight or quarrel. **2** a struggle: *There was a scrap for third place.*

scrapbook *noun* a blank book in which miscellaneous items, such as newspaper cuttings or postcards, may be pasted.

scrape[1] /skrayp/ *verb trans* **1a** to grate harshly over or against (something): *The keel scraped the stony bottom.* **b** to damage or injure (something) by contact with a rough surface: *She scraped her shins on the rocks.* **c** to draw (something) roughly or noisily over a surface: *He scraped his fingernails across the blackboard.* **2a** to remove (clinging matter) from a surface by usu repeated strokes of an edged instrument: *I scraped the snow off the windscreen.* **b** to make (a surface) smooth or clean with strokes of an edged or rough instrument. **3** to draw and fasten (hair) back from the face: *Her thin grey hair was scraped into a bun.* **4** to achieve (e.g. an exam grade or a pass) by a narrow margin. ➤ *verb intrans* **1** to move in sliding contact with a rough or abrasive surface: *I heard his bike scrape against the side of the shed.* **2** to accumulate money by small but difficult economies. ✳ **scrape the barrel/bottom of the barrel** to resort to the weakest resources at one's disposal, usu because they are all that remain available. ⨠ **scraper** *noun*, **scraping** *adj and noun*. [Old English *scrapian* to scratch with the fingernails]

scrape[2] *noun* **1a** an act of scraping. **b** the sound of scraping. **c** an injury or mark caused by scraping. **2** *Brit* a thin layer, *esp* of butter, jam, etc. **3** *informal* an awkward or embarrassing predicament, *esp* as a result of foolish behaviour. **4** *archaic* an act of bowing obsequiously in which the foot is drawn back along the ground.

scrape by *verb intrans* to manage with meagre resources.

scraperboard *noun* specially prepared cardboard with a layer of china clay below a layer of Indian ink. The ink can be removed using a sharp tool to produce a design or picture composed of white lines.

scrape through *verb intrans* to get by with difficulty or succeed by a narrow margin.

scrape together *verb trans* to collect or procure (money or other resources) with difficulty.

scrape up *verb trans* = SCRAPE TOGETHER.

scrap heap *noun* a pile of discarded materials, *esp* metal. ✳ **on the scrapheap** said of somebody or something: no longer wanted or useful.

scrapie /'skraypi/ *noun* a usu fatal disease of sheep that affects the central nervous system, characterized by twitching, intense itching, emaciation, and finally paralysis. [from SCRAPE[1]]

scrapple /'skrapl/ *noun NAmer* a seasoned mixture of minced meat, usu pork, and maize meal set in a mould and served sliced and fried. [dimin. of SCRAP[1]]

scrappy *adj* (**scrappier, scrappiest**) **1** disjointed or incomplete. **2** *NAmer, informal* argumentative. ⨠ **scrappily** *adv*, **scrappiness** *noun*.

scrapyard *noun Brit* a yard where scrap metal and other discarded materials are collected or processed.

scratch[1] /skrach/ *verb trans* **1a** to mark, scrape, or cut the surface of (something) with or on a sharp or jagged object. **b** to make a superficial wound on (somebody or something): *Scratch a lover, and find a foe* — Dorothy Parker. **2** to scrape or rub (a body part), *esp* to relieve itching. **3** to scrape or dig (the ground, etc) with the claws or nails. **4** to write or draw (something) by scoring a surface: *He scratched his initials on the desk.* **5** to scribble (a note, etc) quickly. **6** to manage to do (something), *esp* with great difficulty: *He scratched a living selling his stories.* **7a** to cancel or erase (something) with or as if with a line: *Please scratch that last remark from the minutes; We'll have to scratch the fixture if any more players drop out.* **b** to withdraw (an entry) from a competition. **8** said of a disc jockey: to move (a vinyl record) manually backwards and forwards on a rotating turntable to create rhythmic effects, *esp* in modern dance music. ➤ *verb intrans* **1** to scrape or rub part of the body, *esp* to relieve itching. **2** to mark, scrape, or cut a surface with something sharp: *She scratched at the blob of paint.* **3** said of a bird or animal: to use the beak or claws, *esp* to dig around for food. **4** to make a grating sound: *The cat was scratching at the door.* **5** (+ for) to look around for something: *He was scratching around for people to invite.* **6** to cancel or withdraw from a contest or engagement. * **scratch the surface** to deal with something inadequately or superficially: *These measures don't even scratch the surface of the problem.* ➤➤ **scratcher** *noun.* [prob a blend of English dialect *scrat* and *cratch*, both meaning 'to scratch']

scratch² *noun* **1** a mark or injury produced by scratching. **2** *informal* a slight wound. **3** an act or sound of scratching. **4** a scrawl or scribble. **5** the starting line in a race for competitors not receiving a handicap. **6** a contestant or team whose name is withdrawn from an event, etc. **7** in billiards, snooker, etc, a lucky shot. **8** = SCRATCHING. * **from scratch** from the very beginning: *We had to abandon the idea and start from scratch.* **up to scratch** reaching a satisfactory, suitable, or adequate standard or level: *His work wasn't up to scratch.*

scratch³ *adj* **1** arranged or put together haphazardly or hastily: *a scratch team.* **2** made or done by chance and not as intended: *a scratch shot.* **3** without handicap or allowance: *a scratch golfer.*

scratchcard *noun* a small card with a coated section or sections on it, which are scratched off to reveal symbols that indicate whether a prize has been won.

scratch file *noun* in computing, a temporary file used for storing data while a program is in use.

scratching *noun* an effect in modern dance music achieved by manually interfering with the rotation of a vinyl record on a turntable.

scratch pad *noun* **1** *chiefly NAmer* a small notebook, usu with detachable pages. **2** a section of a computer's memory devoted to the temporary storage of files and data.

scratchy *adj* (**scratchier, scratchiest**) **1** tending to scratch or irritate: *scratchy wool.* **2** making a scratching noise: *a scratchy pen.* **3** made with or as if with scratches: *scratchy drawing.* ➤➤ **scratchily** *adv,* **scratchiness** *noun.*

scrawl¹ /skrawl/ *verb trans and intrans* to write or draw (something) awkwardly, hastily, or carelessly. ➤➤ **scrawly** *adj.* [origin unknown]

scrawl² *noun* an untidy or careless piece of writing or drawing: *The signature was just a scrawl.*

scrawny /'skrawni/ *adj* (**scrawnier, scrawniest**) exceptionally and often unhealthily thin; bony: *scrawny cattle.* ➤➤ **scrawniness** *noun.* [variant spelling of dialect *scranny*, prob of Scandinavian origin]

scream¹ /skreem/ *verb intrans* **1** to make a sudden loud piercing cry, *esp* in fear or pain. **2** to produce harsh high noises: *Chain saws screamed in the forest.* **3** to move with a shrill noise resembling a scream: *A strong wind screamed through the trees.* **4** to laugh uncontrollably or dementedly. ➤ *verb trans* **1** to say (something) in a loud, shrill, or hysterical voice. **2** to bring (oneself) to a specified state by screaming: *The young fans screamed themselves hoarse.* [origin unknown]

scream² *noun* **1** a loud shrill cry or noise. **2** *informal* somebody or something that is very amusing.

screamer *noun* **1** somebody or something that screams. **2** any of several species of S American waterbirds similar to the geese and noted for their loud raucous cry: family Anhimidae. **3** *informal* something that is regarded as remarkable, *esp* in terms of its speed: *Owen struck a screamer into the top corner of the net.* **4** *chiefly NAmer, informal* a sensational headline in a newspaper, *esp* one set in very large bold type. **5** *informal* in printing, an exclamation mark. **6** *informal, dated* somebody or something that causes screams of laughter.

screamingly *adv* extremely: *screamingly funny; screamingly obvious.*

scree /skree/ *noun* loose stones or rocky debris on a hillside or mountain slope, or a hill or slope formed from an accumulation of stones or rocks. [prob ultimately from Old Norse *skritha* landslide]

screech¹ /skreech/ *verb intrans* **1** to utter a shrill piercing cry; to cry out, *esp* in terror or pain. **2** to make a shrill piercing sound: *The*

car screeched to a halt. ➤➤ **screecher** *noun,* **screechy** *adj.* [Middle English *scrichen,* of imitative origin]

screech² *noun* a shrill sound or cry.

screech owl *noun* **1** *Brit* = BARN OWL. **2** *NAmer* any of several species of small owls with tufted ears and distinctive screeching calls: genus *Otus.*

screed /skreed/ *noun* **1** an overlong speech or piece of writing, *esp* one that is dull. **2** a mixture of cement applied to a floor to give it a level surface. **3** a strip of plaster or other material used as a guide to the thickness of a coat of plaster, cement, etc. ➤➤ **screeding** *noun.* [Middle English *screde* fragment, later 'strip', prob a spelling variant of SHRED¹]

screen¹ /skreen/ *noun* **1a** a fixed or movable partition or curtain used as a room divider or to give protection, concealment, or privacy. **b** an ornamental frame or panel, *esp* one used to hide something: *a fire screen.* **2** a windscreen on a motor vehicle. **3** something that shelters, protects, or conceals: *The garden is bordered by a screen of trees.* **4** fine netting set in a frame and used in a window or door to keep insects out. **5a** the part of a television set, radar receiver, video display unit, etc on which images or data are displayed. **b** a blank surface on which photographic images, cinematic films, etc are projected or reflected. **c** a glass plate ruled with crossing opaque lines through which an image is photographed in making a HALFTONE (etched plate used for printing). **6** the medium of films or television: *He's been a star of both stage and screen.* **7** a sieve or plate of perforated material, often set in a frame, used to separate coarser from finer parts. **8** any of various devices that prevent interference, e.g. from electrical or magnetic fields. **9** anything used as a front or disguise, e.g. for secret or illegal practices: *The shop was just a screen for his drug-dealing business.* **10** a manoeuvre in various sports whereby an opponent is legally cut off from the play, *esp* the act of impeding a defensive player in basketball. **11** an act of screening, e.g. for the presence of disease. [Middle English *screne* from early French *escren,* of Germanic origin]

screen² *verb trans* **1a** to shelter or protect (somebody or something) with a screen. **b** to guard (somebody or something) from injury, danger, or punishment. **c** (*also* + off) to separate or enclose (somebody or something) with a screen. **2** to show or broadcast (a film, television programme, etc) on a screen. **3a** to investigate (somebody or something) systematically, *esp* in order to ascertain qualification or suitability: *His job is to screen visa applications.* **b** to carry out a test on (somebody) for the presence of disease. **c** to test or check (somebody or something) for the presence of weapons, etc. **4** to pass (coal, gravel, or ashes) through a screen to separate the finer parts from the coarser ones. ➤ *verb intrans* to provide a screen in a game or sport. ➤➤ **screenable** *adj,* **screener** *noun,* **screenful** (*pl* **screenfuls**) *noun.*

screening *noun* **1** a showing of a film or television programme. **2** the act or process of evaluating, investigating, or testing for something. **3** screens used to protect or separate. **4** (*in pl*) material, e.g. waste or fine coal, separated by using a screen.

screenplay *noun* the script of a film including description of characters, details of scenes and settings, dialogue, and stage directions.

screen-print *verb trans* to print (something) through silk or other material treated so as to make some areas impervious. ➤➤ **screen print** *noun,* **screen-printed** *adj.*

screen saver *noun* a computer program that generates a blank screen or moving screen images after the image on the screen has remained unchanged for a time, to prevent damage to the screen that a static image can cause.

screen test *noun* a short filmed performance used to assess an actor's suitability for a film role.

screen-test *verb trans* to subject (an actor) to a screen test.

screenwriter *noun* a writer of screenplays. ➤➤ **screenwriting** *noun.*

screw¹ /skrooh/ *noun* **1a** a sharp-pointed tapering metal pin with a raised spiral thread running round it and a slotted head turned by a screwdriver to fasten parts together. **b** a cylinder with a raised spiral thread running round the outside of it; a male screw. **c** a cylinder with a raised spiral thread running round the inside of it, used with a male screw to form a seal, etc; a female screw. **2** the act or an instance of turning a screw or something similar. **3** *Brit* a twisted paper packet containing a small amount of salt, tobacco, etc. **4** the propeller of a ship or aircraft. **5** (*usu* **the screw**) an instrument of torture acting like a screw, e.g. a thumbscrew. **6** *informal* a prison warder. **7** *coarse slang.* **a** an act of sexual intercourse. **b** a partner in sexual intercourse. **8** *Brit, informal, dated* a salary, wage, or payment. **9** *Brit, informal, archaic* a mean or miserly person. **10** *Brit, informal* an old or worn-out horse. **✳ have a screw loose** *informal* to be slightly mad or eccentric. **put the screws on** *informal* to exert pressure on (somebody), *esp* psychological pressure. [Middle English from early French *escrue* a female screw or nut, from Latin *scrofa*, literally 'sow']

screw² *verb trans* **1** to attach, fasten, or close (something) by means of a screw or something similar: *He screwed the handle of the door back on; Screw the cap on tightly.* **2** to unite (parts) by means of a screw or a twisting motion: *Screw the two pieces together.* **3a** to operate, tighten, or adjust (something) by means of a screw. **b** to cause (something) to rotate spirally about an axis. **4** to twist or crush (something) out of shape: *He screwed the letter into a ball and threw it away.* **5** to give backwards spin to (a billiard or snooker ball). **6** *informal* to make oppressive demands on (somebody): *She screwed him for every penny he had.* **7** *informal* used to express annoyance, contempt, or frustration: *Screw the lot of you!* **8** *informal* to cheat or defraud (somebody). **9** *coarse slang* to have sexual intercourse with (somebody). **➤** *verb intrans* **1** (*often* + in/on/together). **a** to rotate like or as a screw. **b** to become attached or secured by screwing: *These panels just screw on.* **2** (*often* + round/around) to move with a twisting or writhing motion. **3** *coarse slang* to have sexual intercourse. **✳ have one's head screwed on (the right way)** *informal* to have plenty of common sense or act in a sensible way. **➤➤ screwable** *adj*, **screwer** *noun*.

screw around *verb intrans* **1** *coarse slang* to have sexual intercourse with many partners. **2** *informal* to waste time; to mess about.

screwball¹ *adj chiefly NAmer, informal* **1** crazily eccentric or whimsical. **2** said of a film comedy: involving eccentric characters in absurd situations, usu with a fast-moving but implausible plot.

screwball² *noun chiefly NAmer* **1** a baseball pitch that swerves in the opposite direction to a curve ball. **2** *informal* a whimsical, eccentric, or mad person.

screw cap *noun* = SCREW TOP (1).

screwdriver *noun* **1** a tool for turning screws, usu with a tip that fits into the head of the screw. **2** a cocktail made from vodka and orange juice.

screwed *adj* **1** twisted or distorted. **2** *informal* drunk. **3** *informal* ruined or finished. [past part. of SCREW²]

screw eye *noun* a device with a pointed threaded shaft and a head in the form of a loop.

screw pine *noun* = PANDANUS. [from its twisted stems]

screw propeller *noun* = PROPELLER.

screw thread *noun* the projecting spiral rib of a screw.

screw top *noun* **1** a lid or cover for a bottle, jar, etc with a spiral thread inside. **2** a bottle, jar, etc with this type of lid or cover. **➤➤ screw-top** *adj*.

screw up *verb trans* **1** to tighten, fasten, or lock (something) with a screw or a device like a screw. **2** to crush or crumple (something): *She screwed up his letter.* **3** to twist or distort (something): *She screwed up her eyes in the bright sunlight.* **4** *informal* to cause (somebody) to become anxious, neurotic, or emotionally disturbed. **5** *informal* to cause (something) to go badly wrong. **6** *chiefly NAmer, informal* to ruin (something) completely. **7** to summon up (one's courage). **➤** *verb intrans informal* to bungle a task completely: *For the Prime Minister to be personally involved in the Damage Control operation showed just how seriously Digby had screwed up* — Ben Elton.

screwy *adj* (**screwier**, **screwiest**) *chiefly NAmer, informal* absurd, eccentric, or mad. **➤➤ screwiness** *noun*.

scribble¹ /'skribl/ *verb trans* to write or draw (something) hurriedly without regard for legibility or coherence. **➤** *verb intrans* **1** to make random or meaningless marks with a pen, pencil, etc: *The baby scribbled on my homework.* **2** *informal* to write novels, poetry, etc. **➤➤ scribbler** *noun*, **scribbly** *adj*. [Middle English *scriblen* from medieval Latin *scribillare*, dimin. of Latin *scribere* to write]

scribble² *noun* an untidy drawing or piece of writing, *esp* one that has been hastily done.

scribe¹ /skrieb/ *noun* **1** a person who copied manuscripts in ancient and medieval times. **2** *informal* an author; a journalist. **3a** a Jewish record-keeper and interpreter of the law in ancient Israel. **b** a professional Jewish theologian and jurist. **4** = SCRIBER. **➤➤ scribal** *adj*. [Latin *scriba* official writer, from *scribere* to write]

scribe² *verb trans* **1** to mark a line on (a surface) by scoring with a pointed instrument. **2** to make (a line or other mark) by scratching or gouging. **➤** *verb intrans literary* to work as a scribe; to write. [prob shortening of DESCRIBE]

scriber *noun* a sharp-pointed tool for making marks, *esp* for marking out material, e.g. metal, to be cut.

scrim /skrim/ *noun* **1** a durable plain-woven usu cotton fabric used for upholstery, curtain lining, etc. **2** a transparent sheet of fabric used in theatre sets as a backcloth or screen. [origin unknown]

scrimmage¹ /'skrimij/ *noun* **1** a disorderly struggle or fight. **2** in American football, the interplay between two teams that begins with the passing back of the ball from the ground. [alteration of SKIRMISH¹]

scrimmage² *verb intrans* in American football, to take part in a scrimmage. **➤** *verb trans* in American football, to put (the ball) into a scrimmage. **➤➤ scrimmager** *noun*.

scrimp /skrimp/ *verb intrans* (*often* + on) to be frugal or sparing with something; to skimp. **✳ scrimp and save** to economize wherever possible: *We have to scrimp and save just to pay the rent.* [Scots *scrimp* meagre, prob of Scandinavian origin]

scrimshank /'skrimshangk/ *verb intrans Brit, informal* said *esp* of somebody in the armed forces: to avoid duties or obligations. **➤➤ scrimshanker** *noun*. [origin unknown]

scrimshaw¹ /'skrimshaw/ *noun* **1** carved or coloured work made from ivory or whalebone, *esp* by sailors. **2** the art or process of producing this. [origin unknown]

scrimshaw² *verb trans* to carve or engrave designs on (ivory, bones, shells, etc).

scrip¹ /skrip/ *noun* **1a** a certificate entitling the holder to a particular number of shares, bonds, etc. **b** such certificates collectively. **c** any of various documents entitling the holder to receive something, such as an allotment of land. **2** a brief written list, etc. **3** a scrap, *esp* a small piece of paper with writing on it. [contraction of *subscription receipt*]

scrip² *noun* a small bag or pouch, *esp* one formerly carried by a beggar or pilgrim. [Latin *scrippum* pilgrim's knapsack]

scrip³ *noun* a doctor's prescription.

scripophily /skri'pofəli/ *noun* the pursuit or hobby of collecting old bond and share certificates. **➤➤ scripophilist** *noun*. [from SCRIP¹ + -PHILE + -Y²]

script¹ /skript/ *noun* **1a** written characters; handwriting. **b** printed lettering resembling handwriting. **c** the characters used in writing a particular language; an alphabet: *Russian script.* **2a** something written; a text. **b** a manuscript. **c** the written text of a play, film, or broadcast, *esp* the one used in a production or performance. **d** *Brit* a person's written answers in an examination. [Latin *scriptum* something written, from *scribere* to write]

script² *verb trans* to prepare a script for (something): *a speech scripted by one of his advisers.*

script³ *noun informal* a prescription for medicine, etc. [contraction of PRESCRIPTION]

scriptorium /skrip'tawri-əm/ *noun* (*pl* **scriptoria** /-ri-ə/ *or* **scriptoriums**) a room where scribes in a medieval monastery did their work of copying manuscripts. [medieval Latin *scriptorium* from Latin *scribere* to write]

scripture /'skripchə/ *noun* **1a** (*also in pl*) the sacred writings of the Christian religion as contained in the Bible: *You cannot name any example from any heathen author but I will better it in Scripture* — James I (VI of Scotland). **b** a passage from the Bible. **2** the sacred writings of another religion. **➤➤ scriptural** *adj*, **scripturally** *adv*. [Latin *scriptura* written material, from *scribere* to write]

scriptwriter *noun* a person who writes a script for a film or play, or for a radio or television programme. **➤➤ scriptwriting** *noun*.

scrivener /'skriv(ə)nə/ *noun* **1a** a notary. **b** formerly, a professional copyist or scribe. **2** in former times, a person who received money for investment at interest and arranged loans on security; a broker. [early French *escrivein* from Latin *scriba*: see SCRIBE¹]

scrod /skrod/ *noun NAmer* a young fish, e.g. a cod or haddock, *esp* one split and boned for cooking. [origin unknown]

scrofula /'skrofyoolə/ *noun no longer in technical use* tuberculosis of the lymph glands, *esp* in the neck. **➤➤ scrofulous** *adj*. [medieval Latin *scrofula* swelling of the lymph glands, from Latin *scrofa* breeding sow, perhaps because sows were prone to such swellings]

scroll[1] /skrohl/ *noun* **1a** a roll of parchment, etc, usu with writing or a drawing on it. **b** an ancient book, manuscript, or document on a roll of parchment, etc. **2** a stylized ornamental design imitating the spiral curves of a scroll, e.g. on a column in classical architecture. [Middle English *scrowle* from early French *escroue* scrap, scroll, of Germanic origin]

scroll[2] *verb trans* **1** in computing, to cause (text or graphics displayed on a screen) to move vertically or horizontally in order to display and view other parts. **2** to roll (something) up into a scroll. ➤ *verb intrans* **1** said of computer text or graphics displayed on a screen: to move vertically or horizontally. **2** to move computer text or graphics vertically or horizontally. ➤➤ **scrollable** *adj,* **scroller** *noun,* **scrolling** *noun.*

scroll bar *noun* a narrow panel at the edge of a computer screen that allows a user to scroll through text or graphics using a mouse.

scroll saw *noun* a thin handsaw for cutting curves or irregular designs.

scrollwork *noun* decoration made up of scroll-like patterns.

Scrooge /skroohj/ *noun* a miserly person. [named after Ebenezer *Scrooge,* a grumpy miser in *A Christmas Carol* by Charles Dickens d.1870, English writer]

scrotum /'skrohtəm/ *noun* (*pl* **scrota** /'skrohtə/ *or* **scrotums**) in most male mammals, an external pouch of skin that contains the testes. ➤➤ **scrotal** *adj.* [Latin *scrotum*]

scrounge[1] /skrownj/ *verb trans and intrans informal* to try to obtain (something) free or at another person's expense: *She's always scrounging cigarettes*; *He lived by scrounging off his relatives.* ➤➤ **scrounger** *noun.* [alteration of English dialect *scrunge* to steal]

scrounge[2] *noun informal* an act of scrounging: *I'm on the scrounge again.*

scrub[1] /skrub/ *verb* (**scrubbed, scrubbing**) ➤ *verb trans* **1** to clean (something) by hard rubbing, *esp* with a stiff brush. **2** to remove (dirt, etc) by hard rubbing. **3** to purify (a gas or vapour) using a liquid. **4** *informal* to cancel or abandon (something): *Let's scrub that idea.* ➤ *verb intrans* (*usu* + up) said of a surgeon: to spend time thoroughly washing the hands and forearms before performing an operation. [prob from Dutch *schrubben* to rub hard or scrub]

scrub[2] *noun* **1** an act of scrubbing. **2** a gently abrasive skin cream. **3** (*in pl*) sterile clothing worn by staff in an operating theatre.

scrub[3] *noun* **1a** vegetation consisting chiefly of stunted trees or shrubs. **b** (*also in pl*) an area covered with such vegetation. **c** *chiefly Aus* remote countryside; the bush. **2** *chiefly NAmer* a domestic animal of mixed or unknown parentage and usu inferior type. **3** a small or stunted person or thing. **4** *chiefly NAmer.* **a** a sports player who does not have a regular team place. **b** a team composed of such players. [Middle English, in the sense 'stunted tree'; alteration of SHRUB[1]]

scrubber *noun* **1** a person or thing that scrubs. **2** an apparatus for removing impurities, *esp* from gases. **3** *chiefly Brit, informal* a promiscuous woman or a prostitute.

scrubby *adj* (**scrubbier, scrubbiest**) **1** inferior in size or quality; stunted: *scrubby cattle.* **2** covered with or consisting of scrub. [from SCRUB[3]]

scrub turkey *noun* = BRUSH TURKEY.

scrub typhus *noun* an acute infectious disease caused by a RICKETTSIA (micro-organism resembling a bacterium), transmitted by mites, and characterized by sudden fever, severe headache, skin rash and lesions, and painful swelling of the lymph glands.

scruff[1] /skruf/ *noun* the back of the neck; the nape. [origin unknown]

scruff[2] *noun Brit, informal* an untidily dressed or grubby person. [English dialect *scruff* dandruff, something worthless, alteration of SCURF]

scruffy *adj* (**scruffier, scruffiest**) slovenly and untidy, *esp* in personal appearance: *scruffy jeans.* ➤➤ **scruffily** *adv,* **scruffiness** *noun.*

scrum[1] /skrum/ *noun* **1** in rugby, a set piece in which the forwards of each side crouch in a tight formation with the two front rows of each team meeting shoulder to shoulder so that the ball can be put in play between them. **2** *Brit, informal* a disorderly struggle; a jostle: *the morning scrum to board the bus.* [shortened form of SCRUMMAGE[1]]

scrum[2] *verb intrans* (**scrummed, scrumming**) **1** to take part in a rugby scrum. **2** *informal* to crowd or jostle for position.

scrum down *verb intrans* to form a rugby scrum.

scrum half *noun* **1** the player in rugby who puts the ball into the scrum. **2** the position of this player.

scrummage[1] /'skrumij/ *noun* = SCRUM[1]. [alteration of SCRIMMAGE[1]]

scrummage[2] *verb intrans* = SCRUM[2]. ➤➤ **scrummager** *noun.*

scrummy *adj* (**scrummier, scrummiest**) *informal* delicious. [from SCRUMPTIOUS]

scrump /skrump/ *verb trans Brit, informal* to steal (fruit, *esp* apples) from an orchard. [from English dialect *scrump* withered apple]

scrumple /'skrumpl/ *verb trans Brit* to crumple (something). [alteration of CRUMPLE[1]]

scrumptious /'skrum(p)shəs/ *adj informal* said *esp* of food: delicious or delightful. ➤➤ **scrumptiously** *adv,* **scrumptiousness** *noun.* [prob alteration of SUMPTUOUS]

scrumpy *noun Brit* dry rough cider, *esp* as traditionally brewed in the English West Country. [English dialect *scrump* something shrivelled, *esp* a shrivelled apple of the kind used to make this type of cider]

scrunch[1] /skrunch/ *verb trans* **1** to crunch, crush, or crumple (something): *He had scrunched his handkerchief into a ball.* **2** *chiefly NAmer* (*often* + up) to contract or hunch (e.g. the shoulders). ➤ *verb intrans* **1** to move with or make a crunching sound: *Her boots scrunched in the snow.* **2** *chiefly NAmer* to hunch up; to crouch: *The children scrunched closer.* [alteration of CRUNCH[1]]

scrunch[2] *noun* a crunching sound.

scrunch-dry *verb trans* (**scrunch-dries, scrunch-dried, scrunch-drying**) to use the fingers and a hairdryer to dry (hair) to give it a tousled look.

scrunchie *or* **scrunchy** /'skrunchi/ *noun* (*pl* **scrunchies**) *chiefly Brit* a loop of elastic, loosely covered in fabric, used for tying hair up or back.

scruple[1] /'skroohpl/ *noun* **1a** a moral consideration that raises a doubt or discourages an action. **b** an uneasy feeling that arises from a doubt about the morality of something: *I'd have no scruples about telling your manager what she did.* **2** a unit of weight equal to 20 grains (1.296 grams), formerly used by apothecaries. **3** *archaic* a very small amount. [Middle English via French from Latin *scrupulus* small weight, small sharp stone, dimin. of *scrupus* rough pebble or, figuratively, a source or cause of mental discomfort]

scruple[2] *verb intrans* to hesitate or be reluctant to do something on grounds of conscience: *he who wouldn't scruple to defend a known criminal.*

scrupulous /'skroohpyooləs/ *adj* **1** painstakingly exact. **2** having a strong desire to avoid doing anything wrong or immoral. ➤➤ **scrupulosity** /-'lositi/ *noun,* **scrupulously** *adv,* **scrupulousness** *noun.* [Middle English from Latin *scrupulosus,* from *scrupulus:* see SCRUPLE[1]]

scrutineer /skroohti'niə/ *noun* **1** a person who examines or observes something. **2** *Brit* a person who takes or counts votes at an election.

scrutinize *or* **scrutinise** /'skroohtiniez/ *verb trans* to examine (something) painstakingly or in minute detail. ➤➤ **scrutinizer** *noun.*

scrutiny /'skroohtini/ *noun* (*pl* **scrutinies**) **1** a searching study, enquiry, or inspection. **2** surveillance: *The prisoners must be kept under close scrutiny.* [Latin *scrutinium* from *scrutari* to search, sort rubbish, from *scruta* rubbish]

scry /skrie/ *verb intrans* (**scries, scried, scrying**) to predict events, e.g. by crystal gazing. [shortened form of DESCRY]

SCSI *abbr* small computer systems interface, a system for connecting a computer to a peripheral device.

scuba /'sk(y)oohbə/ *noun* an aqualung. [acronym from *self-contained underwater breathing apparatus*]

scuba-dive *verb intrans* to swim underwater with an aqualung, *esp* in a sea with interesting or unusual marine life. ➤➤ **scuba-diver** *noun,* **scuba-diving** *noun.*

scud[1] /skud/ *verb intrans* (**scudded, scudding**) **1** to move or run swiftly, *esp* as if being swept along: *Fluffy clouds scudded along the breeze.* **2** said of a ship: to run before a gale. [prob of Scandinavian origin]

scud[2] *noun* **1** a sudden shower or gust of wind. **2** ocean spray or masses of cloud driven swiftly by the wind. **3** the act of scudding.

scuff[1] /skuf/ *verb trans* **1** to scratch, chip, or damage the surface of (something, *esp* shoes). **2** to drag or shuffle (the feet) along while walking or back and forth while standing. ➤ *verb intrans* **1** to slouch along without lifting the feet. **2** to become scratched or roughened by wear: *Patent leather soon scuffs.* [prob of Scandinavian origin]

scuff[2] *noun* a mark or damage caused by scuffing.

scuffle[1] /'skufl/ *noun* **1** a confused, impromptu, and usu brief fight. **2** a shuffling sound or movement. [prob of Scandinavian origin]

scuffle[2] *verb intrans* **1** to struggle or fight at close quarters, often in a confused way. **2** to move in a quick but shuffling way.

scull[1] /skul/ *noun* **1a** an oar moved to and fro over the stern of a boat as a means of propulsion. **b** either of a pair of light oars used by a single rower. **2** a narrow light racing boat propelled by a scull or sculls. [Middle English, of unknown origin]

scull[2] *verb intrans* to propel a boat by a scull or sculls. ➤➤ **sculler** *noun.*

scullery /'skuləri/ *noun* (*pl* **sculleries**) a small kitchen or a room where kitchen work, such as washing dishes and preparing vegetables, is done. [Middle English from early French *escuelerie*, from *escuelle* bowl, from Latin *scutella*: see SCUTTLE[1]]

scullion /'skulyən/ *noun archaic* a kitchen servant, *esp* one who does the most menial jobs. [Middle English from early French *escouillon* dishcloth, swab, from Latin *scōpa* broom, twig]

sculp /skulp/ *verb trans and intrans* = SCULPT. [Latin *sculpere* to carve]

sculpin /'skulpin/ *noun* (*pl* **sculpins** *or collectively* **sculpin**) any of numerous species of spiny marine and freshwater fishes, many of which are scaleless: genus *Cottus* and other genera. [origin unknown]

sculpt /skulpt/ *verb trans* to create (something) by sculpture. ➤ *verb intrans* to work as a sculptor. [French *sculpter* from Latin *sculpere* to carve, or a humorous back-formation from SCULPTURE[1]]

sculptor /'skulptə/ *noun* a man or woman who creates sculptures, *esp* an artist who does this for a living.

sculptress /'skulptris/ *noun* a female sculptor.

sculpture[1] /'skulpchə/ *noun* **1a** the art of creating three-dimensional works of art, *esp* by carving, modelling, or casting hard or mouldable materials. **b** a piece of work produced by sculpture, or such works as an artistic genre. **2** impressed or raised marks, *esp* on a plant or animal part, or a pattern formed by these. ➤➤ **sculptural** *adj*, **sculpturally** *adv*, **sculpturesque** /-'resk/ *adj*. [Middle English from Latin *sculptura*, from *sculpere* to carve]

sculpture[2] *verb trans* **1a** to form an image or representation of (something) from solid material, e.g. wood or stone. **b** to form (e.g. wood or stone) into a three-dimensional work of art. **2** to change (the form of the earth's surface) by natural processes, e.g. erosion and deposition. **3** to shape (something) by or as if by carving or moulding: *She was proud of her beautifully sculptured nose.*

scum[1] /skum/ *noun* **1** pollutants or impurities that have risen to or collected on the surface of a liquid. **2** *informal* an utterly corrupt or despicable person, or a group of such people: *The rich are the scum of the earth in every country* — G K Chesterton. ➤➤ **scummy** *adj*. [Middle English from early Dutch *schum*]

scum[2] *verb trans and intrans* (**scummed, scumming**) to become or cause (something) to become covered with scum.

scumbag *noun informal* a despicable or obnoxious person. [from an earlier US sense 'condom', from SCUM[1] in the sense 'semen' + BAG[1]]

scumble[1] /'skumbl/ *verb trans* **1** to soften the lines or colours of (a drawing or painting) by light rubbing or by applying a thin coat of opaque colouring or paint. **2** to produce an effect of broken colour on (a painted surface) by exposing some of the lower layers of paint. [prob from SCUM[2]]

scumble[2] *noun* **1** a coat of paint or layer of colouring applied in scumbling. **2** the effect of scumbling.

scuncheon /'skunsh(ə)n/ *noun* an inner face of a door jamb or window frame. [early French *escoinson*, from *coin*: see COIN[1]]

scungy /'skunji/ *adj* (**scungier, scungiest**) *Aus, NZ, informal* disgusting or of poor quality. [perhaps from Scots *scunge* a sly or vicious person]

scunner[1] /'skunə/ *noun chiefly Scot* **1** an unreasonable dislike or prejudice: *She took a scunner to him.* **2** somebody or something that is regarded as irritating; a nuisance. [Middle English (Scots) *skunniren* to be annoyed]

scunner[2] *verb trans and intrans* (**scunnered, scunnering**) *chiefly Scot* to become or cause (somebody) to become disgusted or exasperated: *It scunners me to think of them treating that poor dog so badly.*

scunnered /'skunərt/ *adj chiefly Scot* extremely fed up, disgusted, or exasperated.

scup /skup/ *noun* (*pl* **scup**) a common edible marine fish that lives in American Atlantic coastal waters: *Stenotomus chrysops.* [Narraganset *mishcup*, from *mishe* big + *cuppi* close together, from the size and shape of its scales]

scupper[1] /'skupə/ *noun* an opening in a ship's side for draining water from the deck. [Middle English *skopper*, perhaps from Old French *escopir* to spit]

scupper[2] *verb trans* (**scuppered, scuppering**) **1** *chiefly Brit, informal* to prevent (something) from working, happening, etc: *The bad weather scuppered our plans for a picnic.* **2** to sink (a ship) deliberately. [origin unknown]

scurf /skuhf/ *noun* **1** thin dry scales flaking from the skin, e.g. dandruff. **2** scaly pieces that have come off or that are peeling from a surface, e.g. flaky paint. **3a** a scaly deposit or covering on some plant parts. **b** a plant disease characterized by scurf. ➤➤ **scurfy** *adj*. [Old English *sceorf*]

scurrilous /'skuriləs/ *adj* **1** said of a person, report, etc: making defamatory remarks, *esp* with the intention of damaging somebody's reputation. **2** using or containing coarse or abusive humour. **3** wicked and unscrupulous: *They are scurrilous impostors who rob vulnerable people.* ➤➤ **scurrility** /sku'riliti/ *noun*, **scurrilously** *adv*, **scurrilousness** *noun*. [Latin *scurrilis* jeering, from *scurra* buffoon, jester]

scurry[1] /'skuri/ *verb intrans* (**scurries, scurried, scurrying**) to move with short hurried steps, often in an agitated or confused state; to scamper. [shortened form of *hurry-scurry*, reduplication of HURRY[1]]

scurry[2] *noun* (*pl* **scurries**) **1** an act or the sound of scurrying. **2** a flurry of snow.

scurvy[1] /'skuhvi/ *noun* a disease caused by a lack of vitamin C and marked by spongy gums, loosening of the teeth, and bleeding under the skin. [from SCURF + -Y[2]]

scurvy[2] *adj* (**scurvier, scurviest**) *archaic* disgustingly mean or contemptible: *a scurvy trick.* ➤➤ **scurvily** *adv*, **scurviness** *noun*.

scurvy grass *noun* any of several species of plants whose leaves were formerly eaten to prevent scurvy: genus *Cochlearia.*

scut /skut/ *noun* a short erect tail, *esp* that of a rabbit, hare, or deer. [origin unknown]

scuta /'skyoohtə/ *noun* pl of SCUTUM.

scutage /'skyoohtij/ *noun* in feudal times, a tax levied on a tenant of a knight's estate in place of military service. [Middle English from Latin *scutagium* shield tax, from *scutum* shield]

scutch /skuch/ *verb trans* to separate the woody fibre from (flax or hemp) by beating. ➤➤ **scutcher** *noun*. [French *escoucher* to beat, ultimately from Latin *excutere* to shake out, from EX-[1] + *quatere* to shake]

scutcheon /'skutchən/ *noun archaic* = ESCUTCHEON.

scute /skyooht/ *noun* a hard bony plate, *esp* one that forms part of the EXOSKELETON (external covering) of some reptiles, or the shell of a turtle. [Latin *scutum* shield]

scutellum /skyooh'teləm/ *noun* (*pl* **scutella** /-lə/) **1** any of several small usu hard shield-shaped plates or scales on an animal, e.g. on the feet of a bird. **2** an intermediate absorbing organ between the embryo and the ENDOSPERM (nutritive tissue) in a grass seed. ➤➤ **scutellar** *adj*, **scutellate** /'skyoohtilayt, -lət/ *adj*. [Latin *scutellum*, dimin. of *scutum* shield]

scutter[1] /'skutə/ *verb intrans* (**scuttered, scuttering**) *chiefly Brit* to move with small quick steps or actions; to scurry or scamper. [prob from SCUTTLE[2]]

scutter[2] *noun chiefly Brit* an act or the sound of scuttering.

scuttle[1] /'skutl/ *noun* **1** = COAL SCUTTLE. **2** *Brit* the top part of the body of a car behind the bonnet, to which the windscreen and instrument panel are attached. [Old English *scutel* dish, platter, via Old Norse from Latin *scutella* drinking bowl, dimin. of *scutra* platter]

scuttle[2] *verb intrans* to scurry or scamper. [prob blend of SCUD[1] and SHUTTLE[2]]

scuttle[3] *noun* **1** a quick shuffling pace. **2** a short dash, *esp* a quick departure.

scuttle[4] *verb trans* **1** to sink (one's own ship) deliberately, e.g. by making holes in the hull. **2** to destroy or wreck (something): *Protesters tried to scuttle attempts to reach agreement.*

scuttle[5] *noun* a small opening or hatchway with a movable lid on the deck of a ship, or the movable lid itself. [prob via early French *escoutille* from Spanish *escotilla* hatchway, of Germanic origin]

scuttlebutt *noun* **1** a cask on a ship's deck containing fresh water. **2** *chiefly NAmer, informal* gossip or rumour. [SCUTTLE[5] + BUTT[6]]

scutum /'skyoohtəm/ *noun* (*pl* **scuta** /'skyoohtə/) **1** = SCUTE. **2** in insects, the middle one of three thoracic segments. [Latin *scutum* shield]

scuzz /skuz/ *noun chiefly NAmer, informal* **1** something that is regarded as disreputable, tasteless, disgusting, or squalid. **2** a disreputable or obnoxious person. [prob a shortened form of *disgusting*, from DISGUST[2]]

scuzzbag *noun* = SCUZZBALL.

scuzzball *noun chiefly NAmer, informal* a despicable or obnoxious person.

scuzzy *adj* (**scuzzier, scuzziest**) *chiefly NAmer, informal* **1** dirty or squalid: *I'm not going to sit on that scuzzy seat.* **2** disreputable or tasteless; sleazy: *They sell scuzzy books and magazines.*

scythe[1] /siedh/ *noun* a long curving blade fastened at an angle to a long handle, for cutting crops, *esp* grass, corn, etc, or for cutting back overgrown vegetation: *The even mead, that erst brought sweetly forth the freckled cowslip, burnet, and green clover, wanting the scythe, all uncorrected, rank, conceives by idleness, and nothing teems but hateful docks, rough thistles … burs* — Shakespeare. [Old English *sithe*]

scythe[2] *verb trans* to cut (grass, corn, etc) with a scythe. ➤ *verb intrans* to move rapidly and devastatingly through something: *Their army scythed through our troops.*

Scythian /'sidhi-ən/ *noun* **1** a member of an ancient nomadic people inhabiting Scythia, a region north of the Black Sea, now part of the Ukraine. **2** the extinct Iranian language of the people of Scythia. ➤➤ **Scythian** *adj.*

SD *abbr* **1** Social Democrat. **2** South Dakota (US postal abbreviation). **3** standard deviation. **4** Swaziland (international vehicle registration).

SDak *abbr* South Dakota.

SDI *abbr NAmer* Strategic Defense Initiative.

SDLP *abbr* in Northern Ireland, Social Democratic and Labour Party.

SDP *abbr Brit* Social Democratic Party.

SDR *abbr* special drawing right.

SE *abbr* **1** Southeast. **2** Southeast (London postcode). **3** Southeastern. **4** Stock Exchange.

Se *abbr* the chemical symbol for selenium.

sea /see/ *noun* **1a** the great body of salt water that covers much of the earth. **b** the waters of the earth as distinguished from the land and air. **c** a large more or less landlocked body of salt water: *the Mediterranean Sea.* **2** (*also in pl*) heavy swell or turbulent waves, *esp* in contrast to calm water: *The fishing boat sank in rough seas.* **3** something vast or overwhelming likened to the sea: *a sea of mud; a sea of faces.* **4** the seafaring life: *He had run away to sea.* **5** = MARE[2]. ✳ **at sea 1** on the sea in a ship or boat. **2** unable to understand; lost or bewildered. **go to sea** to become a sailor. **put (out) to sea** to start out on a journey by sea. [Old English *sæ*]

sea anchor *noun* a device, typically a canvas bag, thrown overboard and dragged behind a ship or seaplane to slow it, reduce drifting, and keep its head to the wind.

sea anemone *noun* a solitary and brightly coloured POLYP (cylindrical organism attached at one end) with a cluster of tentacles superficially resembling a flower: order Actiniaria.

seabag *noun chiefly NAmer* a bag, usu made of canvas with a drawstring neck, used by a sailor for clothes and personal things.

sea bass /bas/ *noun* any of various marine fishes that live in American coastal waters and are related to the groupers: family Serranidae.

seabed *noun* the floor of the sea.

seabird *noun* a bird, such as a gull or albatross, that lives on the sea or coast.

seaboard[1] *noun chiefly NAmer* land beside or near the sea.

seaboard[2] *adj chiefly NAmer* **1** situated on or near the coast: *Several seaboard strongholds were attacked at the start of the war.* **2** relating to the coast or coastal waters: *The coast guard is a special naval force assigned to seaboard duties.*

seaborgium /see'bawgi-əm, 'seebaw-/ *noun* a radioactive transuranic chemical element that is artificially produced: symbol Sg, atomic number 106. [named after Glenn *Seaborg* d.1999, US nuclear chemist]

seaborne *adj* **1** conveyed on or over the sea. **2** carried on by sea and ships: *seaborne trade.*

sea bream *noun* any of numerous marine spiny-finned food fishes: family Sparidae.

sea breeze *noun* a cool breeze blowing inland from the sea, usu during the day.

sea butterfly *noun* any of a group of small marine gastropod molluscs with the foot expanded into broad winglike swimming organs. Some species are shell-less, others have delicate shells: subclass Opisthobranchia.

SEAC /'seeak/ *abbr* Brit School Examinations and Assessment Council.

sea change *noun* a complete transformation. [orig a change brought about by the sea; Shakespeare, *The Tempest* I:ii:403]

sea chest *noun* a sailor's personal storage chest.

sea coal *noun archaic* mineral coal as opposed to charcoal.

seacock *noun* a valve in the hull of a vessel through which water may be let in or pumped out.

sea cow *noun* either of two aquatic plant-eating mammals, the dugong or the manatee.

sea cucumber *noun* any of several species of holothurians (sea animals with a long flexible muscular body; see HOLOTHURIAN), *esp* one whose body is cucumber-shaped, some species of which are used as food: class Holothuroidea.

sea dog *noun informal* a veteran sailor.

sea eagle *noun* any of several species of fish-eating eagles that live near the sea: genus *Haliaeetus.*

sea-ear *noun* = ABALONE.

sea elephant *noun* = ELEPHANT SEAL.

sea fan *noun* any of various corals with a fan-shaped skeleton: genus *Gorgonis* and other genera.

seafarer /'seefeərə/ *noun* **1** a sailor. **2** a person who travels by sea. [SEA + FARE[2] + -ER[2]]

seafaring[1] /'seefeəring/ *noun* travel by sea, *esp* the occupation of a sailor.

seafaring[2] *adj* frequently travelling by sea, *esp* while working as a sailor.

seafood *noun* edible marine fish, shellfish, crustaceans, etc.

seafront *noun* the part of a seaside town immediately beside the sea.

sea-girt *adj literary* surrounded by the sea.

seagoing *adj* of or designed for travel on the sea.

sea gooseberry *noun* a CTENOPHORE (jellyfish-like sea creature) with a transparent, more or less spherical body and two long sticky tentacles: *Pleurobrachia pileus.*

sea-green *adj* of a light bluish green colour. ➤➤ **sea green** *noun.*

sea gull *noun* = GULL[1].

sea hare *noun* any of various large shell-less molluscs with tentacles that project like rabbit ears: genus *Aplysia* and other genera.

sea holly *noun* a European coastal plant of the carrot family with bluish spiny leaves and pale blue flowers: *Eryngium maritimum.*

sea horse *noun* **1** any of numerous species of small fishes with a head and body shaped like the head and neck of a horse. Their bodies are covered in rings of bony plates and end in curled tails. Sea horses swim in an upright position, and are notable in that, when breeding, it is the males that carry the eggs until they hatch: genus Hippocampus. **2** a mythical creature that is half horse and half fish.

sea-island cotton *noun* **1** a tropical American variety of cotton plant with fine long-staple fibres: *Gossypium barbadense.* **2** the cotton fibre from this plant. **3** fabric woven from this fibre. [named after the Sea Islands, a chain of islands off the coast of South Carolina, Georgia, and Florida, where it is grown]

sea kale *noun* **1** a fleshy European plant of the mustard family used as a herb in cooking: *Crambe maritima*. **2** = CHARD.

sea kale beet *noun* = CHARD.

seal[1] /seel/ *noun* **1a** a closure, e.g. a strip of paper over the cork or cap of a bottle or jar, or a wax seal on a document, that must be broken in order to give access, and so when unbroken guarantees that the item so closed has not been opened or tampered with. **b** a tight and effective closure, e.g. against the passage of air, water, etc. **c** the water in a TRAP[1] (water-filled bend) in a pipe that prevents foul-smelling gases coming out of the pipe. **2a** something that confirms, ratifies, or makes secure; a guarantee or assurance: *a seal of authenticity*. **b** an emblem or word impressed or stamped on a document as a mark of authenticity. **c** a device used to impress such a word or emblem, e.g. on wax or moist clay. **d** a disc, *esp* of wax, bearing such an impression. **e** an ornamental adhesive stamp that may be used to close a letter or package. **3** a seal that is a symbol of authority or mark of office: *He was appointed Keeper of the Seals*. **4** (**the seal, the seal of confession, the seal of the confession**) the obligation a priest is under never to reveal what is said in a person's confession. ✳ **set/put one's seal on/to something 1** to seal something with one's personal seal. **2** to give one's approval and endorsement to something. **set/put the/a seal on something** to conclude a deal, confirm an arrangement or fact, etc: *His death merely set a seal on the fact that he had never existed —* Hannah Arendt. **under seal** with an authenticating seal attached. [Middle English *seel* via Old French from Latin *sigillum*, dimin. of *signum* sign, seal]

seal[2] *verb trans* **1a** to close (something) so as to prevent anything getting in or out, *esp* to make it airtight or watertight: *The jars must be tightly sealed if the jam is to keep*. **b** to close (a document, envelope, bottle, etc), with or without a seal, e.g. to prevent anybody opening it or tampering with the contents. **c** to roast the outer surface of (meat) very rapidly and briefly so that the meat's juices remain in the meat when it is cooking. **d** to cover (something porous, e.g. a plaster wall) with a coating of a nonporous substance: *Seal the wall with size before papering it.* **e** to fix (something) in position or close breaks in it with a filling, e.g. of plaster. **f** to stick (one thing) fast to another: *But ah! she gave me never a look, for her eyes were sealed to the holy book —* Matthew Arnold. **2** to confirm (an arrangement, etc) or make it secure by or as if by a seal: *The agreement was sealed with a public handshake.* **3a** to set or affix an authenticating seal to (something such as a document). **b** to authenticate or ratify (something). **c** to mark (something) with a stamp or seal, e.g. as evidence of size, weight, capacity, or quality. **4** to determine (something) irrevocably: *Her answer sealed our fate.* ✳ **my lips are sealed** I can be trusted to keep my mouth shut. ➤➤ **sealable** *adj*.

seal[3] *noun* (*pl* **seals** *or collectively* **seal**) **1** any of numerous marine carnivorous mammals chiefly of cold regions with limbs modified into webbed flippers for swimming: families Otariidae, Phocidae. **2** sealskin. [Old English *seolh*]

seal[4] *verb intrans* to hunt seal. ➤➤ **sealing** *noun*.

sea-lane *noun* an established sea route.

sealant *noun* a sealing agent for closing, waterproofing, etc.

sea lavender *noun* a chiefly maritime plant with bluish purple flowers: genus *Limonium*.

sealed-beam *adj* said of an electric light, *esp* a car headlight: having a light-emitting filament, a reflector, and often a lens, contained in one sealed unit.

sealed road *noun* *Aus, NZ* a road with a solid surface, e.g. of bitumen.

sea legs *pl noun* bodily adjustment to the motion of a ship, indicated *esp* by ability to walk steadily and by freedom from seasickness.

sea leopard *noun* = LEOPARD SEAL.

sealer[1] *noun* **1** a coat, e.g. of size, applied to prevent subsequent coats of paint, varnish, or wallpaper paste from being too readily absorbed. **2** *chiefly NAmer* an official who certifies conformity to a standard of correctness. [SEAL[1]]

sealer[2] *noun* a person or ship engaged in hunting seals.

sea level *noun* the mean level of the surface of the sea midway between high and low tide.

sea lily *noun* a CRINOID (marine invertebrate related to starfish and sea urchins) with long frond-like tentacles, *esp* one that remains attached to the sea bottom by means of a stalk throughout its life: class Crinoidea.

seal in *verb trans* **1** to prevent (somebody or something) getting out, being affected by outside conditions, etc, by putting them in something and sealing it tightly: *Once we're sealed in, we can take our breathing apparatus off.* **2** to prevent (something) coming through to the surface, e.g. of a wall or ceiling, by covering it with a coat of sealer, etc.

sealing wax *noun* a resinous composition that becomes soft when heated and is used for sealing letters, parcels, etc.

sea lion *noun* any of several large species of seals found in the Pacific Ocean that have visible external ears, short coarse fur, and large flippers by means of which they can move around on land: family Otariidae.

sea loch *noun* a loch connecting with the sea.

seal off *verb trans* to close or surround (something) securely, *esp* in order to prevent movement in or out: *Troops sealed off the airport.*

Sea Lord *noun* either of two senior naval officers who are members of the Admiralty Board of the Ministry of Defence.

seal ring *noun* a signet ring engraved with a seal.

sealskin[1] *noun* **1** the skin of a seal, or leather made from it. **2** a garment made of sealskin.

sealskin[2] *adj* made of sealskin.

seal up *verb trans* to close or enclose (something) tightly.

Sealyham terrier /'seeli·əm/ *noun* a terrier of a breed originating in Wales, having a wiry, usu white, coat and short legs. [named after *Sealyham*, estate in Pembrokeshire, SW Wales, where it was first bred]

seam[1] /seem/ *noun* **1** a line of stitching joining two pieces of fabric, *esp* along their edges: *I never cared for fashion much, amusing little seams and witty little pleats —* David Bailey. **2a** a line, groove, or ridge formed at the meeting of two edges. **b** a layer or stratum of coal, rock, etc. **c** a scar left by a cut or wound. **d** a wrinkle. **3** the space between adjacent planks or plates of a ship. ✳ **be bursting/bulging at the seams** to be as full as somebody or something can be. **come/fall apart at the seams** to break up, disintegrate, fail, etc: *After the first act, the play just fell apart at the seams.* [Old English *sēam*; related to Old English *siwian* to SEW]

seam[2] *verb trans* **1** to join (something) by sewing or as if by sewing. **2** to mark (something) with a seam, furrow, or scar.

seaman *noun* (*pl* **seamen**) a sailor or mariner. ➤➤ **seamanlike** *adj*, **seamanly** *adj*, **seamanship** *noun*.

seam bowling *noun* in cricket, fast bowling in which the ball is made to bounce on its seam and thereby deviate from a straight line. ➤➤ **seam bowler** *noun*.

seamer *noun* **1** in cricket, a seam bowler. **2** in cricket, a delivery bowled by a seam bowler. **3** a person or machine that seams clothing, etc.

sea mile *noun* a unit of length used in sea and air navigation, being the length of one MINUTE[1] (angular distance) of a GREAT CIRCLE (theoretical circle on surface of earth). The length varies with latitude, from about 1842m at the equator to 1861m at the North and South Poles: compare NAUTICAL MILE.

seamless *adj* **1** without seams. **2** without breaks, gaps, or discontinuities.

seamount *noun* an undersea mountain.

sea mouse *noun* a large broad marine worm with a broad segmented body covered on the back with hairlike bristles: genus *Aphrodite*.

seamstress /'seemstris/ *noun* a woman whose occupation is sewing. [fem of *seamster* a person who sews, from Middle English *semester, semster*, from Old English *sēamestre* seamstress, tailor, from *sēam* SEAM[1]]

seamy *adj* (**seamier, seamiest**) unpleasant; sordid: *This book reveals the seamy side of the building trade.* ➤➤ **seaminess** *noun*. [SEAM[1] + -Y[1]; orig in the sense of having the rough side of the seam showing]

Seanad Éireann /ˌshanəd 'eərən, ˌshanədh/ *noun* the upper house of parliament in the Republic of Ireland: compare DÁIL. [Irish Gaelic *Seanad Éireann* Irish senate]

séance *or* **seance** /'sayons, 'sayonhs/ *noun* a meeting at which people attempt to communicate with the dead. [French *séance* from *seoir* to sit, from Latin *sedēre*]

sea otter *noun* a rare large marine otter of N Pacific coasts that feeds largely on shellfish: *Enhydra lutris*.

sea pen *noun* any of numerous colonial sea invertebrates related to the corals, many of which have a feathery form: order Pennatulacea.

sea-pink *noun* a variety of THRIFT (coast and mountain plant): *Armeria maritima*.

seaplane *noun* an aeroplane designed to take off from and land on the water, with floats or skis in place of wheels.

seaport *noun* a port, harbour, or town accessible to seagoing ships.

sea purse *noun* the horny egg case of skates and some sharks.

SEAQ /'see-ak/ *abbr* Stock Exchange Automated Quotations.

seaquake *noun* an underwater earthquake. [SEA + -*quake* as in EARTHQUAKE]

sear[1] /sie/ *verb trans* **1a** to burn, scorch, or injure (somebody or something) with a sudden application of intense heat. **b** to brown the surface of (meat) by frying it quickly in hot fat. **2a** to mark (something) with a branding iron. **b** to fix (something) in a person's mind as if with a branding iron: *It was a sight which was seared on my memory for ever.* **3** to make (somebody) callous or insensitive: *Their consciences had been seared by the violence of their environment.* **4** to make (a plant, etc) withered and dried up. [Old English *sēarian* to become withered, from *sēar* withered, SERE[1]]

sear[2] *noun* a mark or scar left by burning or scorching.

sear[3] *adj* see SERE[1].

search[1] /suhch/ *verb trans* **1a** (*often* + for) to look through or over (something) carefully or thoroughly in order to find or discover something: *The police searched the house for clues.* **b** to examine (a person) for concealed articles, e.g. weapons or drugs. **c** to examine (one's conscience, etc), *esp* in order to discover intention or nature: *She searched her heart for her true motives.* **d** to make a thorough scrutiny of (public records, etc) to check on or find information. **e** to investigate (a computer file, database, etc) to find certain information. **2** to cover (an area) with gunfire. ➤ *verb intrans* **1** (*usu* + for) to look or enquire carefully or thoroughly: *She searched for the relevant papers.* **2** (*usu* + into) to make painstaking investigation or examination: *We searched into the matter very thoroughly.* ✷ **search me!** *informal* used to express ignorance of the answer to a question. ➤➤ **searchable** *adj,* **searcher** *noun.* [Middle English *cerchen* from early French *cerchier* to go about, survey, search, from late Latin *circare* to go about, from Latin *circum* round about]

search[2] *noun* **1** the act or an instance of searching, *esp* an organized act of searching. **2** an exercise of the RIGHT OF SEARCH (right to stop and search ships). ✷ **in search of** looking for (something).

search engine *noun* software that searches the Internet for information, or a service that uses such software.

searching *adj* trying to find information, e.g. about somebody's opinions, feelings, etc: *a searching gaze.* ➤➤ **searchingly** *adv.*

searchlight *noun* an apparatus for projecting a movable beam of light, or the beam of light itself.

search out *verb trans* to uncover, find, or ascertain (something) by investigation or searching: *We could hunt through old newspapers to search out the relevant facts.*

search party *noun* a group of people organized to search for a missing person, etc.

search warrant *noun* a warrant authorizing a search of premises by police officers.

searing *adj* **1** very hot: *the searing heat of the desert.* **2** very strong, angry, forceful, etc: *a searing indictment of the government's policies.* ➤➤ **searingly** *adv.*

sea room *noun* room for a ship to manoeuvre at sea.

seascape /'seeskayp/ *noun* a picture representing a view of the sea.

Sea Scout *noun* a member of a Scout troop that specializes in sea and water activities.

sea serpent *noun* a large sea monster resembling a serpent, often reported to have been seen but never proved to exist.

sea shanty *noun* = SHANTY[2].

seashell *noun* the empty shell of a sea mollusc.

seashore *noun* **1** land next to the sea. **2** in law, land between the high- and low-water marks.

seasick *adj* suffering from the motion sickness associated with travelling by ship, boat, or hovercraft. ➤➤ **seasickness** *noun.*

seaside *noun* land bordering the sea, *esp* a holiday resort or beach beside the sea.

sea slug *noun* a shell-less marine gastropod mollusc: order Nudibranchia.

sea snail *noun* **1** a creeping spiral-shelled marine gastropod mollusc: subclass Prosobranchia. **2** any of numerous species of small slimy marine fishes that are found in cold seas and that usu have the pelvic fins modified to form a sucker: genus *Liparis*.

sea snake *noun* **1** = SEA SERPENT. **2** any of several species of often highly poisonous aquatic snakes of the Pacific regions with a tail shaped like an oar: subfamily Hydrophiinae.

season[1] /'seez(ə)n/ *noun* **1a** any of the four parts, often quarters, into which the year is commonly divided according to the prevailing weather conditions, etc: *season of mists and mellow fruitfulness* — Keats. **b** a period characterized by a particular kind of weather: *the dry season.* **c** a period of the year characterized by or associated with a particular activity or phenomenon: *the holiday season.* **d** a time when an animal, bird, or fish may, or may not, legally be caught or killed. **e** a series of performances of works by a playwright, composer, etc, films by a given director or with a particular star, etc: *a Sean Connery season.* **f** the time of year when a place is most frequented: *It's difficult to find accommodation there at the height of the season.* **g** the time of a major holiday; *specif* the Christmas season: *Season's Greetings.* **2** *archaic* an indefinite length of time: *We are here for a season, and then gone for ever.* **3** *archaic* an appropriate time: *To every thing there is a season, and a time to every purpose* — Bible. ✷ **in season 1** said of food: readily available and in the best condition for eating. **2** said of game: legally available to be hunted or caught. **3** said of a female animal: on heat; ready to mate and produce offspring. **4** said *esp* of advice: given when most needed or most welcome: *a word in season.* **out of season** not in season. [Middle English via Old French *saison* from Latin *sation-, satio* action of sowing, from *serere* to sow]

season[2] *verb trans* (**seasoned, seasoning**) **1a** to give (food) more flavour by adding seasoning. **b** to make (something) less harsh or unpleasant. **c** to enliven (something): *conversation seasoned with wit.* **2a** to treat or expose (timber) over a period so as to prepare it for use. **b** to make (somebody) fit or expert by experience: *a seasoned veteran.* ➤➤ **seasoner** *noun.* [Middle English *sesounen* from early French *assaisoner* to ripen, season, from Old French *as-* (see AD-) + *saison*: see SEASON[1]]

seasonable *adj* **1** suitable to the season or circumstances. **2** *archaic* occurring in good or proper time; opportune. ➤➤ **seasonableness** *noun,* **seasonably** *adv.*

seasonal *adj* **1** of, occurring, or produced at a particular season: *seasonal rainfall.* **2** determined by seasonal need or availability: *seasonal employment.* ➤➤ **seasonally** *adv.*

seasonal affective disorder *noun* a tendency to depression and lethargy during the winter months, apparently brought on by biochemical changes caused by lack of sunlight.

seasoning *noun* something such as salt, pepper, a spice, or a herb, added to food primarily for the savour that it imparts.

season ticket *noun* Brit a ticket sold, usu at a reduced price, for an unlimited number of trips over the same route during a limited period, admittance to a series of events, etc.

sea squill *noun* = SQUILL (1A).

sea squirt *noun* any of various small primitive sea animals that exist as free-swimming tadpole-like larvae but as adults are potato-shaped creatures with a tough outer membrane and are permanently attached to a surface, such as a rock: class Ascidiacea.

sea stack *noun* = STACK[1] (II).

seat[1] /seet/ *noun* **1a** a piece of furniture, e.g. a chair, stool, or bench, for sitting in or on. **b** the part of something on which one rests when sitting: *the seat of a chair.* **c** the buttocks, or the part of an item of clothing that covers the buttocks. **d** a place for sitting: *He took his seat next to her.* **e** a unit of seating accommodation, or a ticket for this: *I've got a seat for the show.* **2a** a special chair, e.g. a throne, of somebody in authority, or the status symbolized by it. **b** a right of sitting, e.g. in parliament or on an elected committee: *She lost her seat in the Commons in the last election.* **c** Brit a parliamentary constituency. **3a** a place where something is established or practised: *As a youth, he attended various ancient seats of learning.* **b** a place from which authority is exercised: *the seat of government.* **4** a large country mansion: *a country seat.* **5** a bodily part in which a particular function, disease, etc is centred. **6a** a part at or forming the base of something. **b** a part or surface on or in which another part or surface rests: *a valve seat.* **7** posture in or a way of sitting on horseback. [Middle English *sete* from Old Norse *sæti*; related to Old English *sittan* SIT[1]]

seat[2] *verb trans* **1a** to cause (somebody) to sit or assist (them) in finding a seat: *They seated her next to the door.* **b** to provide seats for (a number of people): *They're building a new theatre that will seat over 4000 people.* **c** to put (oneself or another person) in a sitting position. **2** (*usu in passive*) to place or settle (something) somewhere. **3** to fit (something) to or with a seat; to position (it). **4** to install (somebody) in a position of authority. ⮞ *verb intrans* **1** said of a garment: to become baggy in the area covering the buttocks: *Your woollen dress has seated badly.* **2** to fit correctly on a seat. ⮞ **seater** *noun.*

seat belt *noun* an arrangement of straps designed to secure a person in a seat in an aeroplane, vehicle, etc.

-seater *comb. form* forming nouns and adjectives, with the meaning: designed to seat the number specified: *a 200-seater airliner.*

seating *noun* **1a** the act or an instance of providing with seats. **b** the arrangement of seats, e.g. in a theatre. **2a** material for upholstering seats. **b** a base on or in which something rests: *a valve seating.*

SEATO /'seetoh/ *abbr* Southeast Asia Treaty Organization.

sea trout *noun* a European and N African fish related to the salmon that migrates into fresh water to spawn: *Salmo trutta trutta.*

sea urchin *noun* an ECHINODERM (sea creatures including starfish) usu with a thin spherical shell covered with movable spines: class Echinoidea.

seawall *noun* a wall or embankment to protect the shore from erosion or to act as a breakwater.

seaward /'seewəd/ *adj* **1** facing or directed towards the sea. **2** coming in off the sea: *a seaward wind.*

seawards *or* **seaward** *adv* towards the sea.

seaway *noun* **1** the sea as a route for travel. **2** a deep inland waterway that admits ocean shipping. **3** a ship's progress. **4** a moderate or rough sea.

seaweed *noun* **1** an alga growing in the sea, typically having thick slimy fronds. **2** an abundant growth of this plant.

seaworthy *adj* said of a ship: fit or safe for a sea voyage. ⮞ **seaworthiness** *noun.*

sebaceous /si'bayshəs/ *adj* of or secreting sebum or other fatty material. [Latin *sebaceus* made of tallow, from *sebum* tallow]

sebaceous cyst *noun* a fatty swelling in a sebaceous gland.

sebaceous gland *noun* a gland in the skin that secretes sebum. Sebaceous glands are found on all parts of the body except the soles of the feet and the palms of the hands. Blockage of the gland outlets is a cause of acne.

seborrhoea (*NAmer* **seborrhea**) /sebə'riə/ *noun* excessive discharge of sebum, e.g. on the scalp. [scientific Latin, from SEBUM + -RRHOEA]

sebum /'seebəm/ *noun* fatty lubricant matter secreted by the sebaceous glands of the skin. [Latin *sebum* tallow, grease]

SEC *abbr* Securities and Exchange Commission.

sec[1] /sek/ *noun Brit, informal* a second or moment: *Hang on a sec!*

sec[2] *adj* said of wine: not sweet; dry. [French *sec* dry, from Latin *siccus*]

sec. *abbr* **1** secant. **2** second. **3** secondary. **4** secretary. **5** section. **6** sector.

secant /'seekənt/ *noun* **1** a straight line cutting a curve at two or more points. **2** the trigonometric function that is the reciprocal of the cosine. [Latin *secant-, secans*, present part. of *secare* to cut]

secateurs /'sekətuhz, -'tuhz/ *pl noun chiefly Brit* small pruning shears. [French *sécateur* cutter, from Latin *secare* to cut]

secede /si'seed/ *verb intrans* to withdraw from an organization, federation, etc. ⮞ **seceder** *noun.* [Latin *secedere*, from *sed-, se-* apart + *cedere* to go]

secession /si'sesh(ə)n/ *noun* the act or an instance of seceding. ⮞ **secessionism** *noun,* **secessionist** *noun.* [Latin *secession-, secessio,* from *secedere*: see SECEDE]

sech /sesh, sech, shek, sek'aych/ *noun* a hyperbolic secant: compare HYPERBOLIC FUNCTION.

seclude /si'kloohd/ *verb trans* **1** to remove or separate (oneself or another person) from contact with others. **2** to make (something) hidden from view. [Middle English *secluden* to keep away, from Latin *secludere* to separate, seclude, from *se-* apart + *claudere* to close]

secluded *adj* **1** screened or hidden from view. **2** living in seclusion. ⮞ **secludedly** *adv,* **secludedness** *noun.*

seclusion /si'kloohzh(ə)n/ *noun* **1** the act or an instance of secluding or being secluded. **2** a secluded or isolated place. ⮞ **seclusive** /-siv/ *adj,* **seclusively** /-sivli/ *adv,* **seclusiveness** /-sivnis/ *noun.* [medieval Latin *seclusion-, seclusio,* from Latin *secludere*: see SECLUDE]

Seconal /'sekənal/ *noun trademark* a barbiturate drug used as a sedative.

second[1] /'sekənd/ *adj* **1a** denoting a person or thing having the position in a sequence corresponding to the number two: *A bride at her second marriage does not wear a veil. She wants to see what she is getting* — Helen Rowland. **b** next to the first in value, quality, or degree. **c** (+ to) inferior; subordinate: *As a musician, he was second to none.* **d** standing next below the top in authority or importance: *second mate.* **2** alternate; other: *The city elects a mayor every second year.* **3** another; one more: *Would you like a second cup?* **4** resembling or suggesting a prototype: *He saw himself as a second Napoleon.* **5** in music, denoting one of two parts for the same instrument or voice, usu lower in pitch or subordinate to the first part: *the second violins.* **6** denoting the second forward gear of a motor vehicle. ✴ **at second hand** from or through an intermediary: *I heard the news at second hand.* [Middle English via French from Latin *secundus* second, following, favourable, from *sequi* to follow]

second[2] *noun* **1a** somebody or something that is next after the first in rank, order, time, position, authority, or precedence: *He was the second to resign.* **b** a Cub Scout or Brownie Guide second in rank to a sixer. **2** a person who aids, supports, or stands in for another, *esp* the assistant of a duellist or boxer. **3a** a place next below the first in a contest or examination. **b** in Britain, a second-class honours degree: *an upper second.* **4** the second forward gear of a motor vehicle. **5** (*usu in pl*) a slightly flawed or inferior article, e.g. of merchandise. **6** *informal* (*in pl*) a second helping of food or second course of a meal. **7a** in music, an interval of two degrees of a diatonic scale, or the combination of two notes at such an interval. **b** = SUPERTONIC. **8** a speech seconding a motion.

second[3] *adv* = SECONDLY.

second[4] *noun* **1a** a 60th part of a minute of time or of a minute of angular measure. **b** the basic SI unit of time, equal to the duration of 9,192,631,770 periods of vibration of a specific radiation of a particular caesium isotope, caesium-133. **2** a moment: *The bird, meanwhile, had become a fireball ... and next second there was nothing but a smouldering pile of ash on the floor* — J K Rowling. [Middle English *secunde* from medieval Latin *secunda,* fem of Latin *secundus*: see SECOND[1]; because it is the second sexagesimal division of a unit, as a minute is the first]

second[5] *verb trans* **1** to give support or encouragement to (somebody). **2** to endorse (a motion or nomination). ⮞ **seconder** *noun.* [Latin *secundare,* from *secundus*: see SECOND[1]]

second[6] /si'kond/ *verb trans chiefly Brit* to release (a teacher, businessman, military officer, etc) from a regularly assigned position for temporary duty with another organization or at another post. ⮞ **secondee** /-'dee/ *noun,* **secondment** *noun.* [French *second* second position, from *second*: see SECOND[1]]

secondary[1] /'sekənd(ə)ri/ *adj* **1a** of second rank or importance: *secondary streams.* **b** of or constituting the second strongest degree of stress in speech: compare PRIMARY[1]. **2a** immediately derived from something primary or basic; derivative: *secondary sources.* **b** of or being the induced current or its circuit in an induction coil or transformer: *a secondary coil; secondary voltage.* **3a** not first in order of occurrence or development. **b** of the second order or stage in a series or sequence. **4** of a level of education between primary and tertiary: *a secondary school.* **5** of or being a manufacturing industry: compare PRIMARY[1], TERTIARY[1]. **6** of the second segment of the wing of a bird or the feathers growing on it: compare PRIMARY[1]. **7** produced away from a growing point by the activity of plant formative tissue, *esp* cambium: *secondary growth; secondary phloem.* **8a** characterized by or resulting from the replacement of two atoms or chemical groups in a molecule by other atoms or groups. **b** of or containing a carbon atom united to two other carbon atoms: *a secondary compound.* **c** of a chemical group attached to a secondary carbon atom. **d** said of an amine: having the nitrogen atom attached to two carbon atoms and one hydrogen atom; containing the group NH. ➤ **secondarily** *adv,* **secondariness** *noun.*

secondary² *noun* (*pl* **secondaries**) **1a** somebody or something that is secondary. **b** somebody who occupies a subordinate or auxiliary position; a deputy. **2** a malignant tumour at a site that is distant from the original tumour. **3** a secondary electrical circuit or coil. **4** any of the main feathers of the forearm of a bird: compare PRIMARY². **5a** the fainter component of a double star. **b** a heavenly body that orbits another body: compare PRIMARY².

secondary cell *noun* an electric cell that converts chemical energy into electrical energy by reversible chemical reactions and that may be recharged by the passing of an appropriate current.

secondary colour *noun* a colour formed by mixing primary colours in equal or equivalent quantities.

secondary consumer *noun* a carnivore that eats herbivores: compare PRIMARY CONSUMER, TERTIARY CONSUMER.

secondary emission *noun* the emission of electrons from a surface as a result of bombardment of the surface by particles, e.g. electrons or ions, from another source.

secondary modern *noun* formerly in Britain, a secondary school providing a practical rather than academic type of education.

secondary picketing *noun chiefly Brit* picketing by members of a trade union and others at a place where there is an industrial dispute in which they are not directly involved.

secondary school *noun* a school usu for pupils aged from about 11 to about 18.

secondary sexual characteristic *noun* a physical or mental attribute characteristic of a particular sex, e.g. the breasts of a female mammal, that appears at puberty or in the breeding season, and is not directly concerned with reproduction.

secondary syphilis *noun* the second stage of syphilis, from two to six months after infection, in which a long-lasting skin rash appears: compare PRIMARY SYPHILIS, SYPHILIS, TERTIARY SYPHILIS.

second ballot *noun* a second round of voting in an election in which no candidate received enough votes to win in the first round, generally with the candidate or candidates who were at the bottom of the poll in the first round having been dropped for the second vote.

second best *noun* somebody or something that comes after the best in quality or worth: *It is the best of all trades, to make songs, and the second best to sing them* — Hilaire Belloc. ➤ **second-best** *adj.*

second chamber *noun* the upper chamber of a legislative assembly that has two chambers, such as the British Parliament or the US Congress.

second childhood *noun* the period of life when one's mental faculties decline; one's dotage.

second class *noun* the second and next to highest group in a classification.

second-class¹ *adj* **1** of a second class: *a second-class honours degree.* **2** inferior or mediocre. **3** socially, politically, or economically deprived: *second-class citizens.* **4** said of mail in the UK: handled less quickly than first-class mail but more cheaply.

second-class² *adv* **1** in accommodation, next below the best: *I always travel second-class.* **2** by second-class mail: *Just send the letters second-class.*

Second Coming *noun* (**the Second Coming**) in Christianity, the return of Christ to judge the world on the last day.

second cousin *noun* a child of a first cousin of either of one's parents.

second-degree burn *noun* a burn characterized by blistering and surface destruction of the skin: compare FIRST-DEGREE BURN, THIRD-DEGREE BURN.

seconde /si'kond, sə'gonhd/ *noun* one of eight parrying positions in fencing. [French *seconde* second (position), fem of *second:* see SECOND¹]

Second Empire *adj* of a style, e.g. of furniture, popular in mid-19th-cent. France and marked by heavy ornate modification of Empire styles.

second fiddle *noun* a secondary or subordinate role or function: *I won't play second fiddle to your wife.*

second floor *noun* **1** *Brit* the floor two levels above the ground floor. **2** *NAmer* the floor immediately above the ground floor.

second-generation *adj* **1** denoting the children of immigrants to a particular country. **2** *esp* in computer science, relating to a second stage of technical development in which improvements are made to earlier models, or to the improved models themselves.

second growth *noun* forest trees that regenerate naturally after removal of the first growth by felling or by fire.

second-guess *verb trans* **1** to try to guess the actions of (somebody else). **2** to foretell or predict (something).

secondhand¹ /sekənd'hand/ *adj* **1a** acquired after being owned by another: *a secondhand car.* **b** dealing in secondhand goods: *a secondhand bookshop.* **2a** received from or through an intermediary: *secondhand information.* **b** not original; derivative.

secondhand² *adv* **1** from a dealer in secondhand goods; from among things that have been previously owned. **2** through an intermediary; indirectly.

second hand /'sekənd hand/ *noun* the hand marking seconds on the face of a watch or clock.

secondi *noun pl* of SECONDO.

second-in-command *noun* an officer who is immediately subordinate to a commander; a deputy commander.

second language *noun* **1** a language that has official recognition in a country although it is not the, or a, main national language. **2** a language used by a person or community for business, education, etc although it is not the mother tongue of that person or community.

second lieutenant *noun* the lowest rank of commissioned officer in some armed forces, or a person of that rank.

secondly *adv* used to introduce a second point; second.

second man *noun Brit* a train driver's assistant.

second nature *noun* an action or ability that practice has made instinctive.

secondo /se'kondoh/ *noun* (*pl* **secondi** /-dee/) in music, the second, usu lower, part in a duet. [Italian *secondo* second, from Latin *secundus:* see SECOND¹]

second person *noun* a grammatical category referring to the person or thing addressed or any of the verb-forms or pronouns belonging to this category, e.g. *are* or *you:* compare FIRST PERSON, PERSON, THIRD PERSON.

second-rate *adj* of inferior quality or value. ➤ **second-rater** *noun.*

second reading *noun* **1** the stage in the British legislative process providing for debate on the principal features of a bill. **2** the stage in the US legislative process that occurs when a bill has been reported back from committee and that provides an opportunity for full debate and amendment.

second sight *noun* the ability to see future events, things happening elsewhere, etc. ➤ **second-sighted** *adj.*

second string *noun chiefly NAmer* a substitute player or team, e.g. in football. ✳ **a second string to one's bow** a person, thing, or course of action available or planned as an alternative should a first choice fail. ➤ **second-string** *adj.* [from the reserve bowstring carried by an archer in case the first breaks]

second thoughts *pl noun* a reconsideration of a previous decision: *You don't have to go ahead with it if you're having second thoughts.*

second wind /wind/ *noun* renewed energy or endurance after a period of severe exertion: *I don't want to stop now. I'm just getting my second wind.*

Second World *noun* the countries of the former communist bloc, including those of the former Soviet Union and many Eastern European countries, e.g. Poland and Romania: compare FIRST WORLD, THIRD WORLD (1).

secrecy /'seekrəsi/ *noun* **1** the habit or practice of keeping secrets or maintaining privacy or concealment. **2** the condition of being hidden or concealed: *Complete secrecy surrounded the conference.* [Middle English *secretee,* from SECRET¹]

secret¹ /'seekrit/ *adj* **1a** kept or hidden from knowledge or view: *He was determined to keep his mission secret.* **b** marked by the practice of discretion; secretive. **c** *archaic* said of a person: discreet; keeping the lips sealed: *Indeed, this counsellor is now most still, most secret,* and most grave, who was in life a foolish prating knave — Shakespeare. **d** conducted or operating in secret: *secret negotiations.* **2** retired or secluded. **3** revealed only to the initiated; esoteric: *secret rites.* **4** containing information whose unauthorized disclosure could endanger national security. ➤➤ **secretly** *adv.* [Middle English via French from Latin *secretus,* past part. of *secernere* to separate, distinguish, from *se-* apart + *cernere* to sift]

secret² *noun* **1a** something kept hidden or unexplained. **b** a fact concealed from others or shared confidentially with a few: *Three may keep a secret, if two of them are dead* — Benjamin Franklin. **2** something taken to be the means of attaining a desired end: *the secret of longevity.* **3** something that is not understood; a mystery. **4** a prayer said inaudibly by the priest just before the first part of the mass. ✳ **in secret** in a private place or manner; in secrecy.

secret agent *noun* a spy.

secretaire /sekrə'teə/ *noun* a writing desk with a top section for books. [French *secrétaire* escritoire, secretary, from early French *secretaire* secretary, from medieval Latin *secretarius:* see SECRETARY]

secretariat /sekrə'teəri·ət/ *noun* **1** a government administrative department or its staff. **2** the administrative section of an organization or its staff. **3** the position or place of work of a secretary. [French *secrétariat* from medieval Latin *secretariatus,* from *secretarius:* see SECRETARY]

secretary /'sekrətri, -teri/ *noun* (*pl* **secretaries**) **1** a person who is employed to handle correspondence and manage routine administrative work for an individual or organization. **2a** = COMPANY SECRETARY. **b** an officebearer of an organization or society responsible for its records and correspondence. **3a** in Britain, a senior civil servant who acts as assistant to a minister or ambassador. **b** = SECRETARY OF STATE: *the Home Secretary.* **c** in the USA, an officer of state who superintends a government administrative department. **4** = SECRETAIRE. ➤➤ **secretarial** /-'teəri·əl/ *adj,* **secretaryship** *noun.* [Middle English *secretarie* person entrusted with a secret, from medieval Latin *secretarius* confidential employee, secretary, from Latin *secretum* a secret, neuter of *secretus:* see SECRET¹]

secretary bird *noun* a large long-legged African bird of prey that feeds largely on reptiles: *Sagittarius serpentarius.* [prob from the resemblance of its crest to a bunch of quill pens stuck behind the ear]

secretary-general *noun* (*pl* **secretaries-general**) a principal administrative officer, e.g. of the United Nations.

secretary of state *noun* **1** in Britain, a member of the government who is the head of any of various government departments. **2** in the USA, the head of the government department responsible for foreign affairs.

secret ballot *noun* an official ballot that is marked in secret.

secrete¹ /si'kreet/ *verb trans* to form and give off (a secretion). ➤➤ **secretor** *noun,* **secretory** /-təri/ *adj.* [back-formation from SECRETION]

secrete² *verb trans* to deposit (something) in a hidden place: *He was found to have secreted heroin about his person.* ➤➤ **secreter** *noun.* [alteration of obsolete *secret* to keep secret, from SECRET¹]

secretion /si'kreesh(ə)n/ *noun* **1a** the bodily process of making and releasing some material either functionally specialized, e.g. a hormone, saliva, latex, or resin, or isolated for excretion, e.g. urine. **b** a product formed by this process. **2** the act or an instance of hiding something. ➤➤ **secretionary** *adj.* [(sense 1) from French *sécrétion,* from Latin *secretion-, secretio* separation, from *secernere:* see SECRET¹; (sense 2) from SECRETE²]

secretive /'seekrətiv/ *adj* inclined to secrecy; not open or outgoing in speech or behaviour. ➤➤ **secretively** *adv,* **secretiveness** *noun.* [back-formation from *secretiveness,* partial translation of French *secrétivité,* from *secret:* see SECRET¹]

secret police *noun* a police organization operating largely in secrecy, *esp* for the political purposes of a government.

secret service *noun* **1** a governmental agency concerned with national security, operating largely in secrecy. **2** (**Secret Service**) a British government intelligence department.

secret society *noun* a society, *esp* one with moral or political purposes, whose members keep their activities secret from others.

sect /sekt/ *noun* **1a** *usu derog* a dissenting or schismatic religious body, *esp* if smaller in numbers than established denominations and regarded by them as heretical or extreme. **b** *derog* a denomination. **2a** a group maintaining strict allegiance to a doctrine or leader. **b** a party or faction. [Middle English *secte* via French from

late Latin *secta* organized ecclesiastical body, from Latin *secta* way of life, class of persons, from *sequi* to follow]

sect. *abbr* **1** section. **2** sectional.

-sect *comb. form* forming verbs, with the meaning: cut; divide: *bisect.* [Latin *sectus,* past part. of *secare* to cut]

sectarian¹ /sek'teəri·ən/ *noun* **1** an adherent of a sect, *esp* if fanatical or intolerant of others. **2** a bigoted person.

sectarian² *adj* **1** of or characteristic of a sect or sectarian. **2** limited in character or scope; parochial. ➤➤ **sectarianism** *noun.*

sectarianize *or* **sectarianise** *verb trans* to make (somebody or something) sectarian.

sectary /'sektəri/ *noun* (*pl* **sectaries**) *archaic* a member of a sect. [medieval Latin *sectarius,* from late Latin *secta:* see SECT]

section¹ /'seksh(ə)n/ *noun* **1a** a part of something considered in isolation: *the northern section of the route.* **b** a distinct part or portion of something written, *esp* a subdivision of a chapter or a part of a newspaper, etc dealing with one particular topic: *the sports section.* **c** any of several component parts that may be separated and reassembled: *The bookcase comes in sections for home assembly.* **d** a segment of a citrus fruit. **2a** a distinct part of a community or group of people. **b** a group having a distinct status or pursuing a special interest within an organization such as a political party. **c** a division of an orchestra composed of one class of instruments: *the percussion section.* **d** (*treated as sing. or pl*) a subdivision of a platoon, troop, or battery that is the smallest tactical military unit. **3a** a distinct part of a territorial or political area. **b** a piece of land one square mile, or about 2.6 square km, in area forming one of the 36 subdivisions of a US township. **c** *chiefly NZ* a designated plot of land, *esp* for building. **4** the action or an instance of cutting or separating by cutting; *esp* the action of dividing tissues, etc surgically: *a caesarean section.* **5a** a part removed or separated by or as if by cutting. **b** a very thin slice, e.g. of tissue, suitable for examination under a microscope. **6a** a shape or area as it would appear if a solid form were cut through by one plane. **b** the plane figure resulting from the cutting through of a solid form by one plane. **7a** a section of railway track controlled by one set of signals. **b** a length of railway track under the care of a particular set of workers. **8** a printed sheet that is folded to form part, e.g. eight leaves, of a book; = SIGNATURE. **9** a sign (§) commonly used in printing as a mark for the beginning of a section and as a reference mark. [Latin *section-, sectio,* from *secare* to cut]

section² *verb trans* **1** to cut or separate (something) into sections. **2** to represent (something) in sections, e.g. by a drawing. **3** to cut (a specimen, etc) so as to show a section of it. **4** *Brit* to confine (somebody) to a psychiatric institution in accordance with a section of a mental health act.

sectional *adj* **1** of a section or sections. **2** composed of or divided into sections: *sectional furniture.* **3** restricted to or concerned with a particular group or locality: *sectional interests.* ➤➤ **sectionally** *adv.*

sectionalise *verb trans* see SECTIONALIZE.

sectionalism *noun* an excessive concern for the interests of a region or group. ➤➤ **sectionalist** *adj* and *noun.*

sectionalize *or* **sectionalise** *verb trans* to divide (a region, etc) into sections.

section mark *noun* = SECTION¹ (9).

sector /'sektə/ *noun* **1a** a part of a field of activity, *esp* of business, trade, etc: *employment in the public sector.* **b** a portion of a military area of operation. **2** a part of a circle consisting of two radii and the portion of the circumference between them: compare SEGMENT¹. **3** in computing, a section of a storage device such as a floppy disk that forms the smallest unit of storage. **4** a mathematical measuring device with two graduated arms hinged at one end. [late Latin from Latin *sector* cutter, from *secare* to cut]

sectorial /sek'tawri·əl/ *adj* of or having the shape of a sector of a circle.

secular¹ /'sekyoolə/ *adj* **1a** of this world rather than the heavenly or spiritual. **b** not overtly or specifically religious or concerned with religion. **c** not controlled by a religious body, such as the Church. **2** not bound by monastic vows or rules; *specif* of clergy not belonging to a particular religious order: compare REGULAR¹. **3a** taking place once in an age or a century. **b** surviving or recurring through ages or centuries. **c** occurring very slowly over a long period of time. ➤➤ **secularity** /-'lariti/ *noun,* **secularly** *adv.* [Middle English via Old French and late Latin from Latin *saecularis* coming once in an age, from *saeculum* breed, generation, age, used by early Christians to mean 'the world', as opposed to the Church]

secular² *noun* **1** a member of the secular clergy: compare REGULAR². **2** a layperson.

secularise *verb trans* see SECULARIZE.

secularism *noun* disregard for or rejection or exclusion of religious beliefs and practices, e.g. in ethics, politics, or education. ➤➤ **secularist** *noun and adj*, **secularistic** /-'ristik/ *adj*.

secularize *or* **secularise** *verb trans* **1** to convert (somebody or something) to or imbue (them) with secularism. **2** to change (something) from a religious to a secular function or form. **3** to transfer (property, etc) from ecclesiastical to civil use. **4** to release (somebody) from monastic vows. ➤➤ **secularization** /-'zaysh(ə)n/ *noun*, **secularizer** *noun*.

secund /si'kund/ *adj* said of leaves or flowers: growing on only one side of the stem. [Latin *secundus*: see SECOND¹]

secure¹ /si'kyooə/ *adj* **1a** free from danger. **b** free from risk of loss: *Only freedom can make security secure* — Karl Popper. **c** affording safety: *a secure hideaway*. **d** firm; dependable. **e** firmly fixed or fastened: *a secure foundation*. **f** free from risk of escape. **2a** calm in mind. **b** confident in opinion or hope. **3** assured or certain: *When the reinforcements arrived, victory was secure*. **4** *archaic* overconfident. ➤➤ **securely** *adv*, **secureness** *noun*. [Latin *securus* safe, secure, from *se* without + *cura* care]

secure² *verb trans* **1** to fix or fasten (something) firmly; to shut (it) tightly. **2** to make (something or somebody) safe from risk or danger; to protect (them) against intrusion or disturbance: *We must secure our supply lines from enemy raids*. **3** to guarantee (something) against loss or denial: *He plans to present a bill to secure the rights of strikers*. **4a** to guarantee payment to (a creditor). **b** to guarantee payment of (a debt). **5** to obtain (something), *esp* as the result of effort: *They managed to secure a port cabin for the return voyage*. **6** to effect (something); to bring (it) about: *They secured the release of the prisoner*. ➤ *verb intrans* **1** (+ against) to make somebody or something secure against risk, danger, or uncertainty. **2** to obtain something: *First offer over £500 secures*. ➤➤ **securable** *adj*, **securement** *noun*, **securer** *noun*.

securitize *or* **securitise** /si'kyooərətiez/ *verb trans* to make (a debt, e.g. a mortgage, or an asset, e.g. land) marketable in the form of securities. ➤➤ **securitization** /-'zaysh(ə)n/ *noun*, **securitizer** *noun*.

security /si'kyooəriti/ *noun* (*pl* **securities**) **1a** freedom from danger, fear, anxiety, destitution, etc. **b** stability or dependability: *There's no job security any more*. **2a** protection. **b** measures taken to protect against *esp* espionage, theft, sabotage, unauthorized use, etc. **c** (*treated as sing. or pl*) an organization or department whose task is to maintain security. **3a** something pledged to guarantee the fulfilment of an obligation. **b** a person who undertakes to fulfil another person's obligation if that person cannot or does not. **4a** an evidence of debt or of ownership, e.g. a stock certificate. **b** the asset represented by such a certificate.

security blanket *noun* **1a** a blanket or anything similar to which a baby or young child becomes attached as a source of comfort and security. **b** any source of comfort or security: *I know I won't need these notes in the meeting. They're just a security blanket*. **2** *Brit* a withholding or suppression of information by those in authority for the sake of security: *A security blanket was thrown over the talks lest premature media reports jeopardized the outcome*.

Security Council *noun* a permanent council of the United Nations responsible for the maintenance of peace and security.

security guard *noun* a person employed to guard a building, person, etc: *We now in the United States have more security guards for the rich than we have police services for the poor districts* — J K Galbraith.

security risk *noun* somebody or something that is considered a threat to the security of a country, organization, etc, e.g. because of the person's beliefs, the possibility of subversion, etc.

secy *or* **sec'y** *abbr* secretary.

sedan /si'dan/ *noun* **1** *NAmer, Aus, NZ* = SALOON (3). **2** = SEDAN CHAIR.

sedan chair *noun* a portable enclosed chair, *esp* of the 17th and 18th cents, designed to seat one person and be carried on poles by two people. [*sedan* perhaps via an Italian dialect word from Latin *sella* saddle, from *sedēre* to sit]

sedate¹ /si'dayt/ *adj* calm and even in temper or pace. ➤➤ **sedately** *adv*, **sedateness** *noun*. [Latin *sedatus*, past part. of *sedare* to calm, settle, from *sedēre* to sit]

sedate² *verb trans* to give a sedative to (a person or animal). [back-formation from SEDATIVE²]

sedation /si'daysh(ə)n/ *noun* **1** the induction, *esp* with a sedative, of a relaxed easy state. **2** the condition of being in such a state: *She was kept under sedation for a while*.

sedative¹ /'sedətiv/ *adj* tending to calm or to tranquillize nervousness or excitement. [Middle English from early French *sedatif*, from Latin *sedare*: see SEDATE¹]

sedative² *noun* something that has a sedative effect, *esp* a sedative drug.

sedentary /'sed(ə)ntri/ *adj* **1** doing or involving much sitting: *a sedentary occupation*. **2** said *esp* of birds: not migratory. **3** said of animals: permanently attached to a surface, e.g. a rock: *sedentary barnacles*. [early French *sedentaire* from Latin *sedentarius*, from *sedent-, sedens*, present part. of *sedēre* to sit]

Seder /'saydə/ *noun* a Jewish domestic ceremonial dinner held on the first evening or first two evenings of the Passover in commemoration of the exodus from Egypt. [Hebrew *sēdher* order]

sedge /sej/ *noun* any of a family of marsh plants differing from grasses *esp* in having solid stems, usu triangular in cross-section: family Cyperaceae, *esp* genus *Carex*. ➤➤ **sedgy** *adj*. [Old English *secg*]

sedge warbler *noun* a small European songbird that breeds in marshy places and has streaked brown upper parts, a reddish brown rump, and a pale stripe above the eye: *Acrocephalus schoenobaenus*.

sedilia /sə'dili·ə/ *pl noun* (*sing.* **sedile** /sə'dielee/) (*treated as sing. or pl*) a set of three seats of masonry on the south side of the chancel of a church for the celebrant, deacon, and subdeacon. [Latin *sedilia*, pl of *sedile* seat, from *sedēre* to sit]

sediment /'sedimənt/ *noun* **1** the matter that settles to the bottom of a liquid. **2** material deposited by water, wind, or glaciers. [early French *sediment* from Latin *sedimentum* settling, from *sedēre* to sit, sink down]

sedimentary /sedi'ment(ə)ri/ *adj* **1** of or containing sediment: *sedimentary deposits*. **2** said of rock: formed by or from deposits of sediment. ➤➤ **sedimentarily** *adv*.

sedimentation /,sedimen'taysh(ə)n/ *noun* the forming or depositing of sediment.

sedition /si'dish(ə)n/ *noun* incitement to defy or rise up against the government. ➤➤ **seditionary** *adj*. [Middle English via French from Latin *sedition-, seditio*, literally 'separation', from *se-* apart + *ition-, itio* act of going, from *ire* to go]

seditious /si'dishəs/ *adj* **1** tending to arouse or take part in sedition; guilty of sedition. **2** of or constituting sedition. ➤➤ **seditiously** *adv*, **seditiousness** *noun*.

seduce /si'dyoohs/ *verb trans* **1** to persuade (somebody) to have sexual intercourse. **2** to lead (somebody) astray, *esp* by false promises. **3** to incite (somebody) to disobedience or disloyalty. ➤➤ **seducer** *noun*, **seducible** *adj*. [Latin *seducere* to lead away, from *se-* apart + *ducere* to lead]

seduction /si'duksh(ə)n/ *noun* **1** the act or an instance of seducing, *esp* enticement to sexual intercourse. **2** the power of attracting or luring; charm: *the delusive seduction of martial music* — Fanny Burney. [via French from late Latin *seduction-, seductio*, from Latin *seducere*: see SEDUCE]

seductive /si'duktiv/ *adj* tending to seduce; alluring; attractive: *literature, the most seductive ... of professions* — John Morley. ➤➤ **seductively** *adv*, **seductiveness** *noun*.

seductress /si'duktris/ *noun* a female seducer. [obsolete *seductor* male seducer (from late Latin, from Latin *seducere*: see SEDUCE) + -ESS]

sedulous /'sedyooləs/ *adj formal* **1** involving or accomplished with steady perseverance: *sedulous craftsmanship*. **2** diligent in application or pursuit: *a sedulous student*. ➤➤ **sedulity** /si'dyoohliti/ *noun*, **sedulously** *adv*, **sedulousness** *noun*. [Latin *sedulus*, from *sedulo* sincerely, diligently, from *se* without + *dolus* guile]

sedum /'seedəm/ *noun* any of a widely distributed genus of fleshy-leaved plants that includes the stonecrops: genus *Sedum*. [Latin *sedum* houseleek]

see¹ /see/ *verb* (*past tense* **saw** /saw/, *past part.* **seen** /seen/) ➤ *verb trans* **1a** to perceive (somebody or something) with the eyes. **b** to look at or inspect (something): *Can I see your ticket please?* **2a** to experience or be aware of (something): *I hate to see animals mis-*

treated. **b** to allow something to happen to (somebody): *I won't stand by and see you bullied*. **3** to read (something): *I saw it in the paper*. **4** to watch or look at (e.g. a play, film, television programme, etc). **5a** to imagine or foresee (something): *I can't see him objecting*. **b** (*often* + *as*) to regard (somebody or something) in a certain way: *She sees me as a friend*. **6** to perceive or deduce (something): *We couldn't see the point of it*. **7** to undergo or have experience of (something): *His shoes had seen a lot of wear*. **8** said of a period of time: to be marked by (certain events or characteristics): *The next century saw a wave of revolutions*. **9** to determine or decide (something): *See if you can come*. **10** to make sure of (something): *See that you finish it today*. **11** to find (something acceptable or attractive) in somebody or something: *I can't understand what he sees in her*. **12** to call on or visit (somebody). **13** to keep company with (somebody), *esp* in an amorous relationship. **14** to grant a meeting, etc to (somebody): *The president will see you now*. **15** to accompany or escort (somebody): *I'll see you home now*. **16** to meet (a bet) in poker or equal the bet of (a player). ➤ *verb intrans* **1a** to have the power of sight. **b** to perceive objects by sight: *It's too dark to see*. **2** to give or pay attention: *See here!* **3** to consider something. ✳ **as far as I can see** judging as well as I can. **be seeing you** *informal* goodbye. **let me see** used as an introduction to a tentative opinion. **see about 1** to deal with or consider (a matter): *We'll see about that*. **2** to consult or visit somebody about (a job, purchase, etc). **see one's way to** to feel capable of doing (something). **see somebody through** to provide for somebody until the end of (a time of difficulty): *We've enough supplies to see us through the winter*. **see somebody right 1** to make sure that somebody does not suffer loss. **2** to protect and reward e.g. a protégé. **see the back of** to be rid of (somebody or something). **see through** to grasp the true nature of (somebody or something); to penetrate (a deception). **see to** to attend to (something) or care for (somebody). **see you/see you later** *informal* goodbye. [Old English *sēon*]

see² *noun* a bishopric. [Middle English *se* via French from Latin *sedes* seat, from *sedēre* to sit]

seed¹ /seed/ *noun* (*pl* **seeds** *or collectively* **seed**) **1** the grains or ripened fertilized ovules of plants used for sowing. **2a** the fertilized ripened ovule of a flowering plant or conifer that contains an embryo and is capable of germination to produce a new plant. **b** said of a plant: the condition or stage of bearing seed: *in seed*. **3** a source of development or growth: *This defeat sowed the seeds of discord*. **4** a competitor who has been seeded in a tournament. **5a** something, e.g. a tiny particle, that resembles a seed in shape or size. **b** a crystal introduced into a solution to induce crystallization. **6** (*used before a noun*) **a** acting as a seed: *a seed crystal*. **b** used for planting: *a seed potato*. **7** *archaic or literary*. **a** semen, sperm, or milt. **b** offspring; progeny. ✳ **go/run to seed 1** said of a plant: to develop seed. **2a** to decay. **b** to become unattractive by being shabby or careless about appearance. ➤➤ **seeded** *adj*, **seedless** *adj*, **seedlike** *adj*. [Old English *sǣd*; related to Old English *sāwan* SOW²]

seed² *verb intrans* **1** to sow seed. **2** said of a plant: to produce or shed seeds. ➤ *verb trans* **1a** to plant seeds in (a field, plot, etc). **b** to sow (seeds). **2** to extract the seeds from (raisins, etc). **3a** to schedule (tournament players or teams) so that superior ones will not meet in early rounds. **b** to rank (a contestant) relative to others on the basis of previous record. **4a** to treat (a solution, etc) with solid particles to stimulate crystallization, condensation, etc. **b** to treat (a cloud) in this way to produce rain, snow, etc.

seedbed *noun* **1** a bed of fine soil prepared for planting seed and growing young plants. **2** a place where something specified develops: *the seedbed of revolution*.

seedcake *noun* a sweet cake containing aromatic seeds, e.g. caraway seeds.

seed capital *noun* money required to set up an enterprise, fund preliminary research, etc.

seed corn *noun* **1** corn of good quality that is used for sowing. **2** *Brit* an invaluable resource for future development.

seedeater *noun* a bird, e.g. a finch, whose diet consists basically of seeds.

seeder *noun* **1** an implement for sowing or planting seeds. **2** a device for seeding fruit. **3** somebody or something that seeds clouds to produce precipitation.

seed leaf *noun* = COTYLEDON.

seedling /'seedling/ *noun* **1** a plant grown from seed rather than from a cutting. **2** a young plant, *esp* a nursery plant before permanent transplantation.

seed money *noun* = SEED CAPITAL.

seed oyster *noun* a young oyster, *esp* of a size suitable for transferring to another bed to start a new colony.

seed pearl *noun* a very small often imperfect pearl.

seedpod *noun* a pod, e.g. of a pea or bean plant, that contains seeds.

seedsman *noun* (*pl* **seedsmen**) a person who sows or deals in seeds.

seedtime *noun* the sowing season.

seed vessel *noun* = PERICARP.

seedy *adj* (**seedier**, **seediest**) **1** containing or full of seeds: *a seedy fruit*. **2a** shabby or grubby: *children in seedy clothes*. **b** somewhat disreputable; run-down: *a seedy district*. **c** *informal*, *dated* slightly unwell. ➤➤ **seedily** *adv*, **seediness** *noun*.

see in *verb trans* to celebrate the beginning of (something): *They stayed up to see the New Year in*.

seeing¹ *conj* (*often* + *that*) in view of the fact; since. [present part. of SEE¹]

Usage note

It is permissible in modern English to use *seeing* as a conjunction meaning 'since' or 'in view of the fact that': *Seeing we're late anyway, another five minutes probably won't make any difference*. The correct way to use it, however, is on its own or followed by *that*. The form *seeing as how* is considered non-standard by most modern authorities. Care should also be taken to ensure that the conjunction *seeing* cannot be confused with the present participle of *to see*. *Seeing that he was in trouble, she decided to help him* is ambiguous to the extent that it is not entirely clear whether or not she was an eyewitness to the fact that he was in trouble.

seeing² *noun* in astronomy, the quality of image obtained through a telescope.

seek /seek/ *verb* (*past tense and past part.* **sought** /sawt/) ➤ *verb trans* **1** to resort to or go to (a place, etc): *I have to seek the shade on a hot day*. **2a** (*often* + *out*) to go in search of (something or somebody). **b** to try to discover (something): *They are seeking a solution to the problem*. **3** to ask for (advice, etc). **4** to try to acquire or gain (something): *He set out to seek fame and fortune*. **5** to make an effort (to do something); to try or aim (to do it): *We seek to cater for every taste*. ➤ *verb intrans* (*often* + *for/after*) to make a search or enquiry. ➤➤ **seeker** *noun*. [Old English *sēcan*]

seem /seem/ *verb intrans* **1** to give the impression, whether true or false, of being or doing something: *He seemed enthusiastic at the time*; *It seemed a longer wait than usual*; *You seem to be undecided*; *The noise seemed to come from the broom cupboard*. **2** used in reporting from observed or available facts: *Well, you seem to have won*; *It seems that he lost his passport*; *There seems to be a hold-up at Junction 7*. **3** used to express one's own opinion, or ask or note somebody else's: *'Why seems it so particular with you?' 'Seems, madam! Nay, it is. I know not seems.'* — Shakespeare. **4** used in registering fanciful impressions: *It only seems like yesterday*. **5** used merely to add tentativeness in saying that one knows or recalls something: *That name seems to ring a bell*. ✳ **not seem** used for 'seem not': *He doesn't seem to understand*; *I can't seem to throw off this flu*. **would seem** used ironically for 'seem': *It would seem to be raining*. [Middle English *semen* to suit, be appropriate, seem, from Old Norse *soema* to honour, from *soemr* fitting, suitable]

seeming *adj* apparent rather than real: *Cannot you imagine with what unwilling feelings the former belles of the house of Rushworth did many a time repair to this chapel … starched into seeming piety, but with their heads full of something very different?* — Jane Austen. [present part. of SEEM]

seemingly *adv* **1** so far as can be seen or judged. **2** to outward appearance only.

seemly *adj* (**seemlier**, **seemliest**) in accord with good taste or propriety. ➤➤ **seemliness** *noun*. [Middle English *semely* from Old Norse *soemiligr*, from *soemr* fitting, suitable]

seen /seen/ *verb* past part. of SEE¹.

see off *verb trans* **1** to be present at the departure of (somebody): *I'll come to the airport to see you off*. **2** *Brit*, *informal* to chase (somebody or something) away.

see out *verb trans* **1** to escort (somebody) to the outside of a room or building. **2** to last until the end of (a period of time): *We have enough fuel to see the winter out*.

seep¹ /seep/ *verb intrans* to pass slowly through or as if through fine pores or small openings: *Water seeped in through a crack*. ➤➤ **seepage** *noun*. [Old English *sipian*]

seep² *noun* **1** a spot where a fluid, e.g. water, oil, or gas, contained in the ground oozes slowly to the surface and often forms a pool. **2** *NAmer* a spring.

seer¹ /siə/ *noun* **1a** a person who predicts future events. **b** a person who is credited with exceptional moral and spiritual insight. **c** a person who practises divination. **2** a person who sees.

seer² *noun* (*pl* **seers** *or* **seer**) any of various Indian units of weight; *esp* a unit equal to about one kilogram or about two pounds. [Hindi *ser*]

seersucker /'siəsukə/ *noun* a light, slightly puckered fabric of linen, cotton, or rayon. [Hindi *sīrśakar*, from Persian *shīr-o-shakar* striped cotton garment, literally 'milk and sugar']

seesaw¹ /'seesaw/ *noun* **1a** a plank balanced in the middle so that one end goes up as the other goes down, or any similar device. **b** the game or activity played by two or more people riding on opposite ends of a seesaw and alternately rising in the air and sinking to the ground. **2a** an alternating up-and-down or backward-and-forward movement. **b** anything, e.g. a process or movement, that alternates: *He swung on a seesaw of shame and defiance.*

Word history
reduplication of SAW³. Orig used by sawyers as a rhythmical refrain in work chants; the nursery rhyme *Seesaw, Margery Daw* comes from such a chant.

seesaw² *verb intrans* **1a** to move backward and forward or up and down. **b** to play at seesaw. **2a** to alternate. **b** to vacillate. ➤ *verb trans* to cause (something) to move with a seesaw motion.

seesaw³ *adj and adv* moving backward and forward or up and down.

seethe /seedh/ *verb intrans* **1a** to be in a state of agitated confused movement. **b** to churn or foam as if boiling. **2** to feel or express violent emotion: *He was seething with rage.* [Old English *sēothan*]

seething *adj* **1** intensely hot: *a seething inferno.* **2** constantly moving or active. **3** very angry. ➤➤ **seethingly** *adv*.

see through *verb trans* to undergo or endure (something) to the end: *We've agreed to help and we're going to see it through.*

see-through *adj* said *esp* of clothing: transparent or almost so, *esp* in a sexually arousing way.

segment¹ /'segmənt/ *noun* **1a** a separate piece of something: *Chop the stalks into short segments.* **b** any of the constituent parts into which a body, entity, or quantity is divided or marked off: *Language can only deal meaningfully with a special, restricted segment of reality* — George Steiner. **2** in mathematics, a portion cut off from a geometrical figure by one or more points, lines, or planes, e.g.: **a** a part of a circular area bounded by a chord of that circle and the arc subtended by it: compare SECTOR. **b** a part of a sphere cut off by a plane or included between two parallel planes. **c** the part of a line between two points in the line. **3** in linguistics, any of the series of vowels and consonants into which an utterance can be divided. ➤➤ **segmental** /seg'mentl/ *adj*, **segmentally** /seg'mentəli/ *adv*, **segmentary** *adj*. [Latin *segmentum*, from *secare* to cut]

segment² /seg'ment/ *verb trans* to separate or divide (something) into segments. ➤ *verb intrans* to separate or divide into segments.

segmentation /segmən'taysh(ə)n, segmen-/ *noun* **1** the act or process of segmenting. **2** the formation of many cells from a single cell, e.g. in a developing egg. **3** the condition of having a body or body part made up of a series of similarly structured segments, or the form this takes.

segregate /'segrigayt/ *verb trans* **1** to separate (somebody or something) from others; to set (them) apart. **2a** to cause or force separation of (a racial group, etc) from the rest of a community. **b** to cause or force separation, *esp* of racial groups, within (a community, etc). **3** to cause (genes) to undergo genetic segregation. ➤ *verb intrans* **1** to withdraw. **2** to undergo separation or segregation. **3** to undergo genetic segregation. ➤➤ **segregative** /-tiv/ *adj*, **segregator** *noun*. [Latin *segregatus*, past part. of *segregare*, from *se-* apart + *greg-*, *grex* herd]

segregated *adj* **1** set apart from others of the same kind. **2** administered separately for different groups or races: *segregated education.*

segregation /segri'gaysh(ə)n/ *noun* **1a** the separation or isolation of a race, class, or ethnic group. **b** the separation for special treatment or observation of individuals or items from a larger group: *The government approved measures for the segregation of political prisoners from common criminals.* **2** the separation of pairs of genes controlling the same hereditary characteristic that occurs during meiotic cell division. ➤➤ **segregational** *adj*, **segregationist** *noun and adj*.

segue¹ /'segway, 'saygway/ *verb intrans* (**segues, segued, segueing**) **1** to proceed without pause from one musical number or theme to another. **2** used as a direction in music to instruct a performer to perform the music that follows in the same manner as the music that has preceded it. [Italian *segue* there follows, from *seguire* to follow, from Latin *sequi*]

segue² *noun* a request to join one musical number or theme to another without a break.

seguidilla /segi'dilyə, -'deelyə/ *noun* **1** a Spanish dance in quick triple time. **2** music for this dance. [Spanish *seguidilla*, dimin. of *seguida* sequence, from *seguir* to follow, from Latin *sequi*]

seiche /saysh/ *noun* a tide-like oscillation of the surface of a lake or landlocked sea. [Swiss French *seiche*, perhaps from German *Seiche* sinking]

Seidlitz powder /'sedlits/ *noun* a mild laxative consisting of one powder of sodium bicarbonate and sodium potassium tartrate and another of tartaric acid that are mixed in water and drunk while effervescing. [named after *Seidlitz* (Sedlčany), village in the Czech Republic; from the similarity of its effect to that of the water of the village]

seif /sayf, seef/ *noun* (*also* **seif dune**) a long narrow sand dune or chain of sand dunes in a desert, generally running parallel to the direction of the prevailing wind. [Arabic *sayf* sword]

seigneur /say'nyuh/ *or* **seignior** /'saynjə/ *noun* a feudal lord. ➤➤ **seigneurial** *adj*, **seigniorial** /say'nyaw-/ *adj*. [early French *seigneur* from medieval Latin *senior* superior, lord, from Latin *senior*: see SENIOR¹]

seigneury /'saynyəri/ *noun* see SEIGNIORY.

seignior /'saynyə/ *noun* see SEIGNEUR.

seigniorage *or* **seignorage** /'saynyərij/ *noun* a government revenue from the manufacture of coins calculated as being the difference between the face value and the metal value of the coins. [Middle English from early French *seigneurage* in the sense 'right of the lord' (*esp* to coin money), from *seigneur*: see SEIGNEUR]

seigniory *or* **seignory** *or* **seigneury** *noun* (*pl* **seigniories** *or* **seign-ories** *or* **seigneuries**) the territory or authority of a feudal lord.

seine¹ /sayn/ *noun* a large net with weights on one edge and floats on the other that hangs vertically in the water and is used to enclose fish when its ends are pulled together or drawn ashore. [Old English *segne* via a prehistoric Germanic word and Latin from Greek *sagēnē*]

seine² *verb intrans* to fish with a seine. ➤ *verb trans* to catch or try to catch (fish) with a seine. ➤➤ **seiner** *noun*.

seise /seez/ *verb trans* see SEIZE (5).

seisin *or* **seizin** /'seezin/ *noun* **1** the possession of land in feudal times by the person occupying and using it. **2** the possession of a freehold estate in land. [Middle English *seisine, sesin*, from Old French *saisine*, from *saisir*: see SEIZE]

seism- *or* **seismo-** *comb. form* forming words, denoting: earthquake; vibration: *seismometer*. [Greek, from *seismos*: see SEISMIC]

seismic /'siezmik/ *or* **seismal** *adj* **1** of or caused by an earth vibration, *esp* an earthquake. **2** of a vibration on the moon or other celestial body comparable to a seismic event on earth. ➤➤ **seismicity** /siez'misiti/ *noun*. [Greek *seismos* shock, earthquake, from *seiein* to shake]

seismo- *comb. form* see SEISM-.

seismogram /'siezməgram/ *noun* a record made by a seismograph.

seismograph /'siezməgrahf, -graf/ *noun* an apparatus to measure and record earth tremors. ➤➤ **seismographer** /siez'mogrəfə/ *noun*, **seismographic** /-'grafik/ *adj*, **seismography** /siez'mogrəfi/ *noun*.

seismology /siez'moləji/ *noun* the science that deals with earth vibrations, *esp* earthquakes. ➤➤ **seismologic** /-'lojik/ *adj*, **seismological** *adj*, **seismologically** /-'lojikli/ *adv*, **seismologist** *noun*.

seismometry /siez'momitri/ *noun* the scientific study and measurement of earthquakes.

seize /seez/ *verb trans* **1** to take hold of (somebody or something) abruptly or eagerly. **2a** to take possession of (something or somebody) by force. **b** to take (somebody) prisoner. **3** to confiscate (something), *esp* by legal authority. **4a** to attack or afflict (somebody) physically: *She was seized with an attack of arthritis.* **b** to possess (the mind) completely or overwhelmingly. **5** (*also* **seise**) in law, to give (somebody) ownership or possession of property, *esp* land. **6** to bind or fasten (ropes or spars) together with cord or twine. ➤ **verb intrans 1** (+ on/upon) to lay hold of something suddenly, forcibly, or eagerly: *The company seized on her idea for a new TV series*. **2a** (*often* + up) said of brakes, pistons, etc: to become jammed through excessive pressure, temperature, or friction. **b** (*often* + up) said of an engine: to fail to operate owing to the seizing of a part. ➤ **seizable** *adj*. [Middle English *saisen* from Old French *saisir* to put in possession of, from medieval Latin *sacire*, of Germanic origin]

seizin /ˈseezin/ *noun* see SEISIN.

seizure /ˈseezhə/ *noun* **1** the taking possession of somebody or something by legal process. **2** a sudden attack, e.g. of disease.

selachian /siˈlayki·ən/ *noun* any of an order of cartilaginous fishes usu considered to include the sharks and dogfishes and sometimes the rays: formerly order Selachii. [scientific Latin from Greek *selachos* shark]

seldom[1] /ˈseldəm/ *adv* in few instances; rarely or infrequently: *What appears in newspapers is often new but seldom true* — Peter Kavanagh. [Old English *seldan*]

seldom[2] *adj dated* rare or infrequent.

select[1] /siˈlekt/ *adj* **1** picked out in preference to others. **2a** of special value or quality. **b** exclusively or fastidiously chosen, *esp* on the basis of social characteristics: *The club has a very select membership*. **3** judicious in choice: *select appreciation*. ➤➤ **selectness** *noun*. [Latin *selectus*, past part. of *seligere* to select, from *se-* apart + *legere* to gather, select]

select[2] *verb trans* to take (somebody or something) according to preference from among a number; to pick out or choose (them). ➤ **verb intrans** to make a selection or choice. ➤➤ **selected** *adj*.

select committee *noun* a temporary committee of a legislative body, established to examine one particular matter.

selectee /silekˈtee/ *noun NAmer* a conscript.

selection /siˈleksh(ə)n/ *noun* **1** the act or an instance of selecting. **2a** somebody or something selected. **b** a collection of selected items. **3** a range of things from which to choose. **4** a natural or artificially imposed process that results in the survival and propagation only of organisms with desired or suitable attributes so that their heritable characteristics only are perpetuated in succeeding generations: compare NATURAL SELECTION, STRUGGLE FOR EXISTENCE.

selective /siˈlektiv/ *adj* **1** of or characterized by selection. **2** selecting or tending to select. **3** said of an electronic circuit or apparatus: having the ability to respond to a particular frequency or band of frequencies. ➤➤ **selectively** *adv*, **selectiveness** *noun*, **selectivity** /seelekˈtiviti/ *noun*.

selector *noun Brit* a person who chooses the members of a sports team.

selen-[1] *or* **seleno-** *comb. form* forming words, denoting: moon: *selenography*. [Latin *selen-*, from Greek *selēn-*, from *selēnē* moon]

selen-[2] *or* **seleni-** *or* **seleno-** *comb. form* forming words, denoting: selenium: *selenic*.

selenite /ˈseliniet/ *noun* calcium sulphate occurring in transparent crystals or crystalline masses. [Latin *selenites* from Greek *selēnitēs lithos* stone of the moon, from *selēnē* moon, from the belief that it waxed and waned with the moon]

selenium /siˈleeni·əm/ *noun* a grey non-metallic chemical element chemically resembling sulphur and tellurium that occurs naturally in various sulphide ores, and is used in electronic devices such as solar cells: symbol Se, atomic number 34. ➤➤ **selenic** /-nik/ *adj*. [scientific Latin from Greek *selēnē* moon]

selenium cell *noun* a strip of selenium used as a light-sensitive element in a photoelectric cell.

seleno-[1] *comb. form* see SELEN-[1].

seleno-[2] *comb. form* see SELEN-[2].

selenography /seliˈnogrəfi/ *noun* the study and description of the physical features of the moon. ➤➤ **selenographer** *noun*, **selenographic** /-ˈgrafik/ *adj*.

selenology /seliˈnoləji/ *noun* a branch of astronomy dealing with the moon. ➤➤ **selenological** /-ˈlojikl/ *adj*, **selenologist** *noun*.

Seleucid /siˈloohsid/ *noun* a member of a third-cent. BC Syrian and W Asian dynasty under which Greek language and culture were introduced into Syria. ➤➤ **Seleucid** *adj*. [named after *Seleucus I*

d.280 BC, Macedonian general under Alexander the Great and founder of the dynasty + Latin *-ides* masc patronymic suffix]

self[1] /self/ *noun* (*pl* **selves** /selvz/) **1a** the entire being of an individual. **b** a person's individual character, or one part or aspect of it: *A person's true self is revealed in adversity*. **c** the body, emotions, thoughts, sensations, etc that constitute the individuality and identity of a person: *I have no self ... What I have instead is a variety of impersonations I can do* — Philip Roth. **2** personal interest, advantage, or welfare: *All I have done I have done with no thought of self*. **3** a bird or animal that is of one single colour. [Old English]

self[2] *pronoun* myself; himself; herself.

self[3] *adj* identical throughout, e.g. in colour or material.

self- *comb. form* forming words, with the meanings: **1a** oneself; itself: *self-supporting*. **b** of oneself or itself: *self-abasement*. **c** by oneself or itself: *self-propelled*; *self-starting*. **d** automatically: *self-regulating*. **2a** to, with, for, or in oneself or itself: *self-confident*; *self-addressed*. **b** of or in oneself or itself inherently: *self-evident*; *self-explanatory*.

self-abandonment *noun* **1** a surrender of selfish interests or desires. **2** a lack of self-restraint.

self-abasement *noun* humiliation of oneself, *esp* in response to a sense of guilt.

self-abnegating *adj* self-denying. ➤➤ **self-abnegation** *noun*.

self-absorbed *adj* preoccupied with one's own thoughts, activities, or welfare. ➤➤ **self-absorption** *noun*.

self-abuse /ə'byoohs/ *noun* **1** = SELF-REPROACH. **2** misuse of one's talents and abilities. **3** *euphem* masturbation.

self-acting *adj* acting of or by itself, or capable of doing so; automatic.

self-addressed *adj* **1** addressed for return to the sender: *a self-addressed envelope*. **2** spoken to and intended for oneself: *self-addressed criticisms*.

self-adjusting *adj* adjusting automatically by itself.

self-aggrandizing *adj* acting or seeking to enhance one's power or status. ➤➤ **self-aggrandizement** /-dizmənt/ *noun*.

self-appointed *adj* assuming a position of authority not ratified by others: *I've no time for these self-appointed guardians of public morals*.

self-approbation *noun* satisfaction, *esp* excessive satisfaction, with one's own actions and achievements.

self-assembly *noun* **1** the putting together of furniture, etc by oneself from a set of components bought in a shop. **2** (*used before a noun*) designed for self-assembly: *self-assembly bunk beds*.

self-assertion *noun* the act or an instance of firmly asserting oneself or one's own rights, claims, or opinions. ➤➤ **self-asserting** *adj*, **self-assertive** /-tiv/ *adj*.

self-assurance *noun* = SELF-CONFIDENCE. ➤➤ **self-assured** *adj*, **self-assuredly** /-ridli/ *adv*.

self-catering *adj* provided with lodging and kitchen facilities but not meals: *a self-catering holiday*.

self-centred *adj* concerned excessively with one's own desires or needs. ➤➤ **self-centredly** *adv*, **self-centredness** *noun*.

self-certification *noun* in Britain, the system by which an employee who has been absent from work for no more than six days because of illness or incapacitation can fill in a form stating the reason for their absence rather than having to produce a certificate signed by a doctor.

self-cocking *adj* said of a gun: cocked by the operation of some part of the mechanism rather than by hand.

self-collected *adj* = SELF-POSSESSED.

self-coloured *adj* **1** of a single colour: *a self-coloured flower*. **2** in its natural colour; not dyed.

self-command *noun* = SELF-CONTROL.

self-composed *adj* having or showing mental or spiritual composure.

self-confessed *adj* openly acknowledged: *He was a self-confessed debauchee*. ➤➤ **self-confessedly** /-sidli/ *adv*.

self-confidence *noun* confidence in oneself and one's own powers and abilities. ➤➤ **self-confident** *adj*, **self-confidently** *adv*.

self-congratulation *noun* a complacent acknowledgment of one's own superiority or good fortune. ➤➤ **self-congratulatory** /-lət(ə)ri/ *adj*.

self-conscious *adj* **1** uncomfortably conscious of oneself as an object of notice; ill at ease. **2a** conscious of oneself as a possessor of mental states and originator of actions. **b** intensely aware of oneself. ⋙ **self-consciously** *adv*, **self-consciousness** *noun*.

self-consistent *adj* having each element logically consistent with the rest; internally consistent. ⋙ **self-consistency** /-si/ *noun*.

self-contained *adj* **1** complete in itself: *Each episode of the series is self-contained.* **2** said of accommodation: including within itself a kitchen, bathroom, etc, and usu a separate front door; not sharing facilities. **3a** showing self-possession. **b** formal and reserved in manner. ⋙ **self-containedly** /-nidli/ *adv*, **self-containedness** /ˈkən'wyndnls, -nidnls/ *noun*.

self-content *noun* a feeling or expression of self-satisfaction. ⋙ **self-contented** *adj*, **self-contentedly** *adv*, **self-contentedness** *noun*, **self-contentment** *noun*.

self-contradiction *noun* **1** contradiction of oneself. **2** a statement that contains two contradictory elements or ideas. ⋙ **self-contradictory** *adj*.

self-control *noun* restraint of one's own impulses or emotions. ⋙ **self-controlled** *adj*.

self-critical *adj* **1** unduly critical of oneself. **2** able to judge one's own motives or actions impartially.

self-criticism *noun* the act of or capacity for criticizing one's own faults or shortcomings.

self-deception *noun* the act of deceiving oneself, or the state of being deceived by oneself, e.g. about one's character or motives. ⋙ **self-deceit** /diˈseet/ *noun*, **self-deceptive** /-tiv/ *adj*.

self-defeating *adj* said of a plan or action: having the effect of preventing its own success.

self-defence *noun* **1** the act of defending or justifying oneself. **2** the legal right to defend oneself with reasonable force. ⋙ **self-defensive** *adj*.

self-denial *noun* the restraint or limitation of one's desires or their gratification: *Self-denial is not a virtue; it is only the effect of prudence on rascality* — George Bernard Shaw. ⋙ **self-denying** *adj*.

self-deprecating *adj* given to self-depreciation. ⋙ **self-deprecatingly** *adv*, **self-deprecation** /-ˈkaysh(ə)n/ *noun*.

self-depreciation *noun* disparagement or understatement of oneself. ⋙ **self-depreciating** *adj*, **self-depreciatory** /-shət(ə)ri/ *adj*.

self-destruct *verb intrans* to destroy oneself or itself. ⋙ **self-destruction** *noun*, **self-destructive** /-tiv/ *adj*.

self-determination *noun* **1** free choice of one's own actions or states without outside influence. **2** determination by the people of a place of its own political status; the right to choose one's own government, etc. ⋙ **self-determined** /diˈtuhmind/ *adj*, **self-determining** *adj*.

self-discipline *noun* the power to discipline one's thoughts and actions, usu for the sake of improvement. ⋙ **self-disciplined** *adj*.

self-doubt *noun* a lack of confidence in oneself; diffidence. ⋙ **self-doubting** *adj*.

self-drive *adj chiefly Brit* said of a hired vehicle: intended to be driven by the hirer.

self-educated *adj* having taught oneself from books, etc rather than having followed a course of education in school, college, etc or with a tutor.

self-effacement *noun* the act of making oneself inconspicuous, *esp* because of modesty; humility. ⋙ **self-effacing** *adj*, **self-effacingly** *adv*.

self-employed *adj* earning income directly from one's own business, trade, or profession rather than as salary or wages from an employer. ⋙ **self-employment** *noun*.

self-esteem *noun* **1** confidence and satisfaction in oneself; self-respect. **2** vanity.

self-evident *adj* requiring no proof; obvious. ⋙ **self-evidence** *noun*, **self-evidently** *adv*.

self-examination *noun* **1** the analysis of one's conduct, motives, etc. **2** the examination of one's body in order to detect early signs of disease.

self-existent *adj* existing independently of any cause or agency. ⋙ **self-existence** *noun*.

self-explanatory *adj* capable of being understood without explanation.

self-expression *noun* **1** the expression of one's individual characteristics, e.g. through painting or poetry. **2** the assertion of one's own character through uninhibited behaviour. ⋙ **self-expressive** /-siv/ *adj*.

self-fertilization *or* **self-fertilisation** *noun* fertilization by the union of ova with pollen or sperm from the same individual: compare CROSS-FERTILIZATION. ⋙ **self-fertile** /ˈfuhtiel/ *adj*, **self-fertility** /fəˈtiliti/ *noun*, **self-fertilized** /ˈfuhtiliezd/ *adj*, **self-fertilizing** /ˈfuhtiliezing/ *adj*.

self-fulfilling *adj* **1** coming true, or likely to do so, because the fact that it has been asserted or assumed causes actions or behaviour that are bound to make it come true: *Telling a child it's a loser can be a self-fulfilling prophecy.* **2** marked by or achieving self-fulfilment: *Writing is a self-fulfilling hobby.*

self-fulfilment *noun* **1** making oneself feel content and fulfilled. **2** fulfilling itself.

self-generated *adj* generated or originated from within oneself.

self-giving *adj* self-sacrificing or unselfish.

self-governed *adj* not influenced or controlled by others; *specif* having self-government.

self-governing *adj* having control over oneself; *specif* having self-government.

self-government *noun* **1** control of one's own political affairs: compare HOME RULE. **2** = SELF-CONTROL.

self-harming *noun* the act or an instance of deliberately injuring oneself, e.g. by cutting one's arm, as a symptom of a psychiatric disorder.

self-hatred *or* **self-hate** *noun* hatred of oneself; *specif* hatred redirected towards oneself in frustration or despair. ⋙ **self-hating** *adj*.

self-heal *noun* a small violet-flowered plant of the mint family held to possess healing properties: *Prunella vulgaris.*

self-help *noun* **1** the bettering or helping of oneself without dependence on others. **2a** a method of, or the practice of, solving personal or community problems by forming a group for action and mutual support. **b** (*used before a noun*) promoting self-help: *a self-help book.*

selfhood *noun* **1a** the state of existing as a unique individual. **b** personality. **2** selfishness.

self-image *noun* one's conception of oneself or of one's role.

self-importance *noun* **1** an exaggerated sense of one's own importance. **2** arrogant or pompous behaviour. ⋙ **self-important** *adj*, **self-importantly** *adv*.

self-induced *adj* **1** induced by oneself or itself. **2** produced by self-inductance.

self-inductance *noun* inductance due to self-induction.

self-induction *noun* induction of an electromotive force in a circuit by a varying current in the same circuit.

self-indulgence *noun* excessive or unrestrained gratification of one's own appetites, desires, or whims. ⋙ **self-indulgent** *adj*.

self-interest *noun* a concern for one's own advantage and well-being: *People often act out of self-interest and fear.* ⋙ **self-interested** *adj*.

selfish *adj* concerned with or directed towards one's own advantage, pleasure, or well-being without regard for others. ⋙ **selfishly** *adv*, **selfishness** *noun*. [SELF¹ + -ISH]

self-justification *noun* the act or an instance of making excuses for oneself. ⋙ **self-justificatory** *adj*.

self-justifying *adj* automatically justifying its existence or occurrence: *self-justifying extravagance.*

self-knowledge *noun* knowledge or understanding of one's own capabilities, character, feelings, or motives.

selfless *adj* having no concern for self; unselfish. ⋙ **selflessly** *adv*, **selflessness** *noun*.

self-loading *adj* said of a firearm: automatically ejecting the empty cartridge case after a shot and loading the next cartridge from the magazine; = SEMIAUTOMATIC¹. ⋙ **self-loader** *noun*.

self-love *noun* **1** conceit; narcissism. **2** an *esp* selfish concern for one's own happiness or advantage. ⋙ **self-loving** *adj*.

self-made *adj* **1** having risen from poverty or obscurity by one's own efforts: *A self-made man is one who believes in luck and sends his son to Oxford* — Christina Stead. **2** made by oneself.

self-mastery *noun* = SELF-CONTROL.

self-motivated *adj* driven by one's own internal impetus; self-starting. ➤ **self-motivation** /-'vaysh(ə)n/ *noun*.

self-opinionated *adj* **1** conceited. **2** stubbornly holding to one's own opinion; opinionated.

self-perception *noun* an appraisal of oneself, *esp* a self-image.

self-perpetuating *adj* continuing or renewing oneself or itself indefinitely, or capable of doing so: *Quarrels like that tend to be self-perpetuating.*

self-pity *noun* a self-indulgent dwelling on one's own sorrows or misfortunes. ➤ **self-pitying** *adj*, **self-pityingly** *adv.*

self-pollination *noun* the transfer of pollen from the anther of a flower to the stigma of the same or a genetically identical flower: compare CROSS-POLLINATION. ➤ **self-pollinated** /'pol-/ *adj*, **self-pollinating** /'pol-/ *adj.*

self-portrait *noun* **1** a portrait of an artist done by himself or herself. **2** a description of one's character or personality given by oneself.

self-possessed *adj* having or showing self-possession; composed in mind or manner; calm. ➤ **self-possessedly** /-sidli/ *adv.*

self-possession *noun* control of one's emotions or behaviour, *esp* when under stress; composure.

self-preservation *noun* an instinctive tendency to act so as to safeguard one's own existence.

self-proclaimed *adj* = SELF-STYLED.

self-propelled *adj* **1** propelled by one's or its own power; *specif* containing within itself the means for its own propulsion: *A car is a self-propelled vehicle.* **2** mounted on a vehicle rather than towed: *a self-propelled artillery piece.* ➤ **self-propelling** *adj.*

self-questioning *noun* examination of one's own actions and motives.

self-raising flour (*NAmer* **self-rising flour**) *noun* a commercially prepared mixture of flour containing a raising agent: compare PLAIN FLOUR.

self-realization *or* **self-realisation** *noun* fulfilment by oneself of the possibilities inherent in one's nature.

self-recording *adj* said of an instrument: making an automatic record.

self-regard *noun* **1** concern or consideration for oneself or one's own interests. **2** = SELF-RESPECT. ➤ **self-regarding** *adj.*

self-regulating *adj* **1** regulating itself, *esp* automatically: *a self-regulating mechanism.* **2** regulating its own activities without interference from outside bodies or the law. ➤ **self-regulation** /-'laysh(ə)n/ *noun*, **self-regulative** /-lətiv/ *adj*, **self-regulator** *noun*, **self-regulatory** /-lət(ə)ri/ *adj.*

self-reliance *noun* reliance on one's own efforts and abilities; independence: *Bathsheba loved Troy in the way that only self-reliant women love when they abandon their self-reliance* — Hardy. ➤ **self-reliant** *adj.*

self-reproach *noun* the act of blaming or censuring oneself. ➤ **self-reproachful** *adj*, **self-reproaching** *adj.*

self-respect *noun* a proper respect for one's human dignity: *No one who has any self-respect stays in Ireland* — James Joyce.

self-respecting *adj* having or characterized by self-respect or integrity.

self-restraint *noun* restraint imposed on oneself, *esp* on the expression of one's feelings.

self-righteous *adj* sure of one's own righteousness, *esp* in contrast with the actions and beliefs of others; narrow-mindedly moralistic. ➤ **self-righteously** *adv*, **self-righteousness** *noun.*

self-righting *adj* said of a boat: capable of righting itself when capsized.

self-rising flour *noun NAmer* see SELF-RAISING FLOUR.

self-rule *noun* = SELF-GOVERNMENT.

self-sacrifice *noun* sacrifice of oneself or one's well-being for the sake of an ideal or for the benefit of others: *Self-sacrifice enables us to sacrifice other people without blushing* — George Bernard Shaw. ➤ **self-sacrificing** *adj.*

selfsame /'selfsaym/ *adj* precisely the same; identical: *He left the selfsame day.*

self-satisfaction *noun* a smug satisfaction with oneself or one's position or achievements.

self-satisfied *adj* feeling or showing self-satisfaction: *She had a self-satisfied smile on her face.*

self-sealing *adj* **1** capable of sealing itself, e.g. after puncture: *The engine is fitted with a self-sealing fuel tank.* **2** said of an envelope, etc: capable of being sealed by pressure without the addition of moisture or use of gum.

self-seeded *adj* said of a plant: self-sowing.

self-seeking[1] *adj* seeking only to safeguard or further one's own interests; selfish. ➤ **self-seeker** *noun.*

self-seeking[2] *noun* self-seeking behaviour; selfishness.

self-service[1] *noun* **1** the act or an instance of serving oneself, e.g. in a cafeteria or supermarket, with items to be paid for at a cashier's desk. **2** a shop or cafeteria where customers serve themselves.

self-service[2] *adj* said of a shop, cafeteria, etc: where customers serve themselves.

self-serving *adj* serving one's own interests, *esp* at the expense of honesty or the welfare of others.

self-sow /soh/ *verb intrans* (*past tense* **self-sowed**, *past part.* **self-sown** /sohn/ *or* **self-sowed**) said of a plant: to grow from seeds spread naturally, e.g. by wind or water.

self-starter *noun* **1** a person with initiative, *esp* one who is able to work without supervision. **2** an electric motor used to start an internal-combustion engine without a crank, or the switch that starts this motor. ➤ **self-starting** *adj.*

self-styled *adj* called by oneself, *esp* without justification: *He's one of those self-styled experts on interpersonal relationships.*

self-sufficient *adj* **1** able to maintain oneself or itself without outside aid; capable of providing for one's own needs: *This community is self-sufficient in dairy products.* **2** having unwarranted assurance of one's own ability or worth. ➤ **self-sufficiency** /-si/ *noun*, **self-sufficiently** *adv.*

self-sufficing *adj* = SELF-SUFFICIENT. ➤ **self-sufficingly** *adv.*

self-supporting *adj* **1** meeting one's needs by one's own labour or income. **2** said of a wall: supporting itself or its own weight.

self-sustaining *adj* **1** maintaining or able to maintain oneself by independent effort. **2** maintaining or able to maintain itself once started: *a self-sustaining nuclear reaction.* ➤ **self-sustained** *adj.*

self-tapping screw *noun* a screw made of hard metal which cuts its own thread when driven in.

self-taught *adj* **1** having knowledge or skills acquired by one's own efforts: *She's a self-taught pianist.* **2** learned by oneself without formal instruction.

self-tender *noun* an offer made by a company to its shareholders to buy back its own shares, e.g. in order to prevent a takeover bid.

self-timer *noun* a device on a camera that delays the operation of the shutter, so allowing the photographer to move to a position where they can be included in the photograph.

self-will *noun* stubborn or wilful adherence to one's own desires or ideas; obstinacy. ➤ **self-willed** *adj.*

self-winding /'wiending/ *adj* not needing to be wound by hand: *a self-winding watch.*

self-worth *noun* = SELF-ESTEEM.

Seljuk /sel'joohk/ *noun* a member of any of several Turkish dynasties ruling over a great part of western Asia in the 11th, 12th, and 13th cents. ➤ **Seljukian** *adj.*

sell[1] /sel/ *verb* (*past tense and past part.* **sold** /sohld/) ➤ *verb trans* **1a** to give (goods or property) in exchange for money, other goods, etc. **b** to deal in (a commodity or service): *Her father sells insurance.* **c** to cause or promote the sale of (something): *Advertising sells newspapers.* **d** to achieve a sale of (a certain number): *Her books have sold a million copies.* **2** to give up (something worthwhile) dishonourably: *You sold the firm's good name for the sake of quick profits.* **3a** to persuade somebody about (an idea, etc). **b** *informal* (+ on) to persuade (somebody) to accept or enjoy something: *The purpose of the project is to sell children on reading.* **4** *informal* (*usu in passive*) to deceive or cheat (somebody). ➤ *verb intrans* **1** to transfer something to another's ownership by sale. **2** to be sold or achieve sales. **3** (+ at/for) to have a specified price. ✱ **sell short 1** to belittle or disparage (somebody or something). **2** to sell (stocks) one does not own, in the hope of buying them more cheaply before the time comes to sell them. ➤➤ **sellable** *adj*. [Old English *sellan*]

sell² *noun informal* **1** the act or an instance of selling. **2** a deliberate deception; a hoax.

sell-by date *noun* **1** a date after which a perishable food product must not be offered for sale: compare USE-BY DATE. **2** *informal* the time beyond which somebody or something begins to deteriorate or decline; one's prime: *He used to be a bit of a heart-throb but he's past his sell-by date now.*

seller *noun* **1** a person who sells something. **2** a product offered for sale and selling in a specified manner: *Her first book was a poor seller.*

seller's market *noun* a market in which demand exceeds supply: compare BUYER'S MARKET.

selling plate *noun* a race in which the winning horse is auctioned. [*plate* in the sense 'a race for which the prize is a gold or silver cup or similar trophy', from PLATE¹]

selling-plater *noun* **1** a horse that runs chiefly in selling plates. **2** an inferior racehorse.

selling point *noun* a particularly good, beneficial, or notable aspect or detail of something that is emphasized, e.g. in selling or promoting it.

selling race *noun* = SELLING PLATE.

sell off *verb trans* to dispose of (something) completely by selling it until all stock is gone, *esp* at a reduced price. ➤➤ **sell-off** *noun*.

Sellotape /'selǝtayp/ *noun trademark* adhesive tape. [blend of CELLULOSE + TAPE¹]

sellotape *verb trans* to fix (something) with Sellotape or any similar tape.

sell out *verb trans* **1** to dispose of (something) entirely by sale. **2** to betray or be unfaithful to (e.g. one's cause or associates), *esp* for profit. ➤ *verb intrans* **1** = SELL UP. **2** (*often* + on) to betray one's cause or associates.

sell-out *noun* **1** a performance, exhibition, or contest for which all tickets or seats are sold. **2** *informal* a betrayal.

sell-through *noun* **1** the ratio of the quantity of particular goods sold by a retailer to the quantity of those goods bought by it from a wholesaler. **2** the selling of (something, *esp* video cassettes) as opposed to renting them out or without first renting them out. **3** (*used before a noun*) available for sale without first having been available for renting: *a sell-through video.*

sell up *verb intrans and trans chiefly Brit* to sell (a business or property) completely.

seltzer /'seltsǝ/ *noun dated* a natural or artificially prepared mineral water containing carbon dioxide. [modification of German *Selterser Wasser* water of Selters, from Nieder-*Selters*, village in Hesse, Germany where there are mineral springs]

selva /'selvǝ/ *noun* dense tropical rainforest, *esp* in the Amazon basin in S America. [Spanish or Portuguese *selva* from Latin *silva* a wood]

selvage *or* **selvedge** /'selvij/ *noun* **1a** the edge on either side of a woven fabric, so finished as to prevent unravelling; *specif* a narrow border often of different or heavier threads than the fabric and sometimes in a different weave. **b** an edge, e.g. of wallpaper, meant to be cut off and discarded. **2** a border or edge. [Middle English *selvage* prob from Middle Flemish *selvegge*, *selvage*, from *selv* self + *egge* edge]

selves /selvz/ *noun* pl of SELF¹.

Sem. *abbr* Semitic.

sem. *abbr* seminary.

semantic /si'mantik/ *adj* **1** of semantics. **2** of meaning in language. ➤➤ **semantically** *adv*. [Greek *sēmantikos* significant, from *sēmainein* to signify, mean, from *sēma* sign, token]

semantics *pl noun* **1** (*treated as sing. or pl*). **a** a branch of linguistics concerned with meaning. **b** a branch of semiotics dealing with the relation between signs and the objects they refer to. **c** a branch of philosophy concerned with the interpretation of sentences or other terms in natural or formal artificial languages.

Editorial note
Much of semantics focuses on the structure of vocabulary, analysing the way individual words change their meaning, relate to each other in sense (e.g. as synonyms or antonyms), and are grouped into different fields. But meaning is also conveyed through grammar, intonation, and social inter-

action, and the multi-faceted nature of the subject continues to provide linguistics with a major challenge — Professor David Crystal.

2a (*treated as sing.*) the meaning of a sentence, word, etc, or the interpretation of it: *There are real differences between the two proposals — it's not just a matter of semantics.* **b** (*treated as sing. or pl*) a branch of semiotics dealing with the relation between signs and the objects they refer to. ➤➤ **semanticist** /-sist/ *noun*.

semaphore¹ /'semǝfaw/ *noun* **1** an apparatus for conveying information by visual signals, e.g. by the position of one or more pivoted arms. **2** a system of visual signalling by two flags held one in each hand. [Greek *sēma* sign, signal + -PHORE]

semaphore² *verb trans* to convey (information) by or as if by semaphore. ➤ *verb intrans* to send signals by or as if by semaphore.

semasiology /si,maysi'olǝji/ *noun* the study of meaning and the relationship between signs and the things they represent; = SEMANTICS. ➤➤ **semasiological** /-'lojikl/ *adj*, **semasiologist** *noun*. [German *Semasiologie*, from Greek *sēmasia* meaning, from *sēmainein*: see SEMANTIC]

sematic /si'matik/ *adj* said of the colours, *esp* bright coloration, of a poisonous or unpleasant animal: warning of danger. One example of sematic coloration is that of the skunk. [Greek *sēmat-*, *sēma* sign]

semblance /'semblǝns/ *noun* **1** outward and often deceptive appearance; a show: *He was pure evil wrapped in a semblance of piety.* **2** *archaic* resemblance; similarity. [Middle English from early French *sembler* to be like, seem, from Latin *simulare*: see SIMULATE]

sememe /'semeem/ *noun* a minimal unit of meaning in language; *specif* in some theories, the meaning of a morpheme. [SEMANTIC + -EME]

semen /'seemǝn/ *noun* a suspension of spermatozoa (male reproductive cells: see SPERMATOZOON) in the secretions of various glands, produced by the male reproductive glands and conveyed to the female reproductive tract during coitus. [Latin *semen* seed, from *serere* to sow]

semester /si'mestǝ/ *noun* an academic term lasting half a year, *esp* in N America and Germany. [German *Semester* from Latin *semestris* half-yearly, from *sex* six + *mensis* month]

semi /'semi/ *noun* (*pl* **semis**) *informal* **1** *Brit* a semidetached house. **2** a semifinal.

semi- *prefix* forming words, with the meanings: **1a** half of: *semicircle*. **b** occurring halfway through or twice within a specified period of time: compare BI-¹: *semiannual*; *semicentenary*. **2** to some extent; partly; incompletely: *semicivilized*; *semi-independent*. **3a** partial; incomplete: *semiconsciousness*; *semidarkness*. **b** having some of the characteristics of: *semimetal*. **c** quasi: *semijudicial*. [Middle English from Latin *semi-* half]

semiannual /semi'anyoo(ǝ)l/ *adj* **1** occurring every six months or twice a year. **2** lasting for half a year. ➤➤ **semiannually** *adv*.

semiarid /semi'arid/ *adj* characteristic of a climactic zone, marginal to deserts, where the limited rainfall is unable to sustain a continuous cover of vegetation. ➤➤ **semiaridity** /-'riditi/ *noun*.

semiautomatic¹ /,semiawtǝ'matik/ *adj* **1** operated partly automatically and partly by hand. **2** said of a firearm: using gas pressure or force of recoil and mechanical spring action to eject the empty cartridge case after each first shot and to load the next cartridge from the magazine, but requiring release and another press of the trigger for each successive shot. ➤➤ **semiautomatically** *adv*.

semiautomatic² *noun* a semiautomatic weapon.

semibreve /'semibreev/ *noun* a musical note with the time value of two minims or four crotchets.

semicentenary /,semisen'teenǝri, -'tenǝri/ *noun* (*pl* **semicentenaries**) a 50th anniversary, or the celebration of it.

semicentennial /,semisen'teni-ǝl/ *noun chiefly NAmer* = SEMICENTENARY.

semicircle /'semisuhkl/ *noun* a half circle, or an object or arrangement in the form of a half circle. ➤➤ **semicircular** /-'suhkyoolǝ/ *adj*. [Latin *semicirculus*, from SEMI- + *circulus* circle]

semicircular canal *noun* any of the three loop-shaped tubular parts of the inner ear that together constitute a sensory organ associated with the maintenance of bodily equilibrium.

semicolon /'semi'kohlon/ *noun* a punctuation mark (;) used chiefly to mark a break or pause between sentence elements, such as clauses, that is greater than the break or pause indicated by a comma and less than that indicated by a full stop: *'He has no good red blood in his body.' … 'No. Somebody put a drop under a magnifying-glass and it was all semicolons and parentheses.'* — George Eliot.

semiconductor /ˌsemikənˈduktə/ *noun* **1** a substance, e.g. silicon or germanium, whose electrical conductivity at room temperature is between that of a conductor and that of an insulator, and whose conductivity increases with a rise in temperature or the presence of certain impurities. Semiconductors are used extensively in transistors and many other electronic devices. **2** (*also* **semiconductor device**) a device incorporating a semiconductor. ⟫ **semiconducting** *adj.*

semiconscious /semiˈkonshəs/ *adj* not fully aware or responsive. ⟫ **semiconsciously** *adv*, **semiconsciousness** *noun*.

semicylindrical /ˌsemisiˈlindrikl/ *adj* having the shape of a longitudinal half of a cylinder.

semidarkness /semiˈdahknis/ *noun* partial darkness; shade.

semidetached[1] /ˌsemidiˈtacht/ *adj* forming one of a pair of residences joined by a common wall.

semidetached[2] *noun* one of a pair of houses joined by a common wall.

semifinal[1] /semiˈfienl/ *adj* **1** next to the last in a knockout competition. **2** of or participating in a semifinal.

semifinal[2] *noun* a semifinal match or round. ⟫ **semifinalist** *noun*.

semifitted /semiˈfitid/ *adj* said of an item of clothing: conforming roughly to the lines of the body.

semifluid[1] /semiˈflooh-id/ *adj* having qualities intermediate between those of a liquid and a solid; viscous.

semifluid[2] *noun* a semifluid substance.

semiliquid[1] /semiˈlikwid/ *adj* = SEMIFLUID[1].

semiliquid[2] *noun* = SEMIFLUID[2].

semiliterate /semiˈlit(ə)rət/ *adj* **1** able to read and write on an elementary level. **2** able to read, but unable to write.

Sémillon /saymiˈyonh/ *noun* **1** a variety of grape used in the production of white wine, e.g. Sauternes. **2** a wine produced from this grape. [via French from Latin *semen* seed]

semilunar /semiˈloohnə/ *adj* crescent-shaped. [scientific Latin *semilunaris*, from SEMI- + Latin *lunaris*: see LUNAR]

semilunar valve *noun* any of the crescent-shaped pocket-like flaps that occur in two sets of three to form the aortic or pulmonary valves that prevent blood flowing backward into the heart.

semimetal /semiˈmetl/ *noun* an element such as arsenic that has some metallic properties. ⟫ **semimetallic** /-miˈtalik/ *adj*.

semimonthly[1] /semiˈmunthli/ *adj* done, appearing, etc twice a month.

semimonthly[2] *adv* twice a month.

semimonthly[3] *noun* (*pl* **semimonthlies**) a semimonthly publication.

seminal /ˈseminl/ *adj* **1a** original and influential: *a seminal book.* **b** containing or contributing the seeds of future development. **c** in a rudimentary, uncompleted form. **2** of, storing, or conveying seed or semen: *a seminal vesicle.* ⟫ **seminally** *adv.* [Middle English via French from Latin *seminalis*, from *semin-, semen*: see SEMEN]

seminar /ˈseminah/ *noun* **1** a group of students studying with a university or college teacher, or a meeting of such a group; = TUTORIAL[1]. **2** an advanced or graduate class, often a group of research students, meeting to exchange and discuss results, or a meeting of such a group. **3** a meeting for exchanging and discussing information. [German *Seminar* from Latin *seminarium*: see SEMINARY]

seminarian /semiˈneəri·ən/ *noun* a student in a seminary, *esp* of the Roman Catholic Church.

seminarist /ˈseminərist/ *noun* = SEMINARIAN.

seminary /ˈsemin(ə)ri/ *noun* (*pl* **seminaries**) **1** an institution for the training of the clergy, *esp* Roman Catholic priests and rabbis. **2** *archaic* a private school, *esp* for girls: *It seems that she's a fairy from Andersen's library, and I took her for the proprietor of a Ladies' Seminary* — W S Gilbert. [Middle English *seminary* seedbed, nursery, seminary, from Latin *seminarium*, from *semin-, semen*: see SEMEN]

seminiferous /semiˈnif(ə)rəs, see-/ *adj* producing or bearing seed or semen. [Latin *semin-, semen* (see SEMEN) + -IFEROUS]

semiofficial /ˌsemi·əˈfish(ə)l/ *adj* having some but not complete official authority or standing: *a semiofficial statement.* ⟫ **semiofficially** *adv.*

semiology /semiˈoləji, see-/ *noun* the study of signs, *esp* semiotics. ⟫ **semiological** /-ˈlojikl/ *adj*, **semiologist** *noun*. [Greek *sēmeion* sign + -LOGY]

semiotics /semiˈotiks, see-/ *pl noun* (*treated as sing. or pl*) the study and general theory of signs and symbols in artificial and natural languages with regard to their relationship to the things they represent, to each other, and to their use.

Editorial note
In addition to philosophical interest in semiotics, the 20th cent. has seen the emergence of anthropological and linguistic dimensions to the subject. These view semiotic behaviour as patterned human communication in all modalities – sound, vision, touch, smell, taste. The techniques have applications in several domains (e.g. psychiatry, social psychology), and have been extended to the study of animal communication (zoosemiotics) — Professor David Crystal.

⟫ **semiotic** *adj*. [Greek *sēmeiōtikos* observant of signs, from *sēmeiousthai* to interpret signs, from *sēmeion* sign]

semipermanent /semiˈpuhmənənt/ *adj* **1** lasting or intended to last for a long time but not permanent. **2** having the characteristics of something permanent but subject to change or review: *a semipermanent agreement.* ⟫ **semipermanently** *adv.*

semipermeable /semiˈpuhmi-əbl/ *adj* said *esp* of a membrane: permeable to small molecules but not to larger ones. ⟫ **semipermeability** /-ˈbiliti/ *noun.*

semiprecious /semiˈpreshəs/ *adj* said of a gemstone: of less commercial value than a precious stone.

semipro[1] /semiˈproh/ *adj informal* = SEMIPROFESSIONAL[1].

semipro[2] *noun* (*pl* **semipros**) = SEMIPROFESSIONAL[2].

semiprofessional[1] /ˌsemiprəˈfesh(ə)nl/ *adj* **1** engaging in an activity for pay or gain but not as a full-time occupation: *My father used to play in a semiprofessional dance band.* **2** engaged in by semiprofessional players. **3** not fully professional. ⟫ **semiprofessionally** *adv.*

semiprofessional[2] *noun* a person who engages in an activity, e.g. a sport, semiprofessionally.

semiquaver /ˈsemikwayvə/ *noun* a musical note with the time value of half a quaver or a quarter of a crotchet. *NAmer* Also called SIXTEENTH NOTE.

semirigid /semiˈrijid/ *adj* **1** not completely rigid. **2** having a flexible cylindrical gas container with an attached stiffening keel that carries the load: *a semirigid airship.*

semiskilled /semiˈskild/ *adj* of, being, or requiring workers who have less training than skilled workers and more than unskilled workers.

semiskimmed *adj* said of milk: with some of its cream removed.

semisolid[1] /semiˈsolid/ *adj* having the qualities of both a solid and a liquid; highly viscous.

semisolid[2] *noun* a semisolid substance.

Semite /ˈseemiet, ˈsemiet/ *noun* a member of any of a group of peoples of SW Asia chiefly represented now by the Jews and Arabs. [French *sémite* from late Latin *sēmita* descendant of *Shem*, eldest son of Noah]

Semitic[1] /siˈmitik/ *adj* **1** of the Semites, *esp* the Arabs and Jews; *specif* Jewish. **2** of a branch of the Afro-Asiatic language family that includes Hebrew, Aramaic, Arabic, and Amharic.

Semitic[2] *noun* the Semitic languages, or any Semitic language.

semitone /ˈsemitohn/ *noun* the smallest interval between two notes in European classical music; half a tone; the interval, e.g. E-F or C-C sharp between two adjacent keys on a keyboard instrument. ⟫ **semitonal** *adj*, **semitonic** /-ˈtonik/ *adj*.

semitrailer /semiˈtraylə/ *noun chiefly NAmer* a trailer having rear wheels but supported by a towing vehicle at the front.

semitropical /semiˈtropikl/ *adj* = SUBTROPICAL.

semivowel /ˈsemivowl/ *noun* a speech sound, e.g. /y/ or /w/, formed in the same way as a vowel but functioning as a consonant, or a letter representing such a sound.

semiweekly /semiˈweekli/ *adj and adv* appearing or taking place twice a week: *a semiweekly news bulletin; She goes to the gym semiweekly.*

semolina /semə'leenə/ *noun* the purified hard parts left after milling of wheat, used to make pasta and in milk puddings. [Italian *semolino*, dimin. of *semola* bran, from Latin *simila* finest wheat flour]

sempervivum /sempə'veevəm, -'vievəm/ *noun* (*pl* **sempervivums**) any of a genus of African and Eurasian plants with fleshy pointed-tipped leaves that grow in close rosettes, often planted in rock gardens: genus *Sempervivum*. [Latin genus name, neuter of *sempervivus* ever-living, from *semper* ever, always + *vivus* living]

sempiternal /sempi'tuhnl/ *adj chiefly literary* everlasting; eternal. ➤➤ **sempiternally** *adv.* [Middle English from late Latin *sempiternalis* from Latin *sempiternus*, from *semper* ever, always + *aeternus* ETERNAL[1]]

semplice /'semplichi/ *adj and adv* said of a piece of music: to be performed in a simple unaffected manner. [Italian *semplice* simply, from Latin *simplic-, simplex*: see SIMPLE[1]]

sempre /'sempri, 'sempray/ *adv* in music, always. [Italian *sempre* from Latin *semper*]

sempstress /'sem(p)stris/ *noun* = SEAMSTRESS. [fem of *sempster*, variant of *seamster*: see SEAMSTRESS]

Semtex /'semteks/ *noun trademark* a plastic explosive manufactured in Czechoslovakia. [prob from *Semtin*, a village in the Czech Republic near which it was produced, + EXPLOSIVE[2]]

SEN *abbr Brit* State Enrolled Nurse.

sen[1] /sen/ *noun* (*pl* **sen**) a former unit of currency in Japan, worth 100th of a yen. [Japanese *sen*, ultimately from Chinese (Pekingese) *qian* money]

sen[2] *noun* (*pl* **sen**) **1** a unit of currency in Cambodia, worth 100th of a new riel. **2** a unit of currency in Indonesia, worth 100th of a rupiah. **3** a unit of currency in Malaysia and Brunei, worth 100th of a ringgit. [modification of CENT]

sen. *abbr* **1** senate. **2** senator. **3** senior.

senate /'senit/ *noun* (*treated as sing. or pl*) **1a** the supreme council of the ancient Roman republic and empire. **b** the upper chamber in some legislatures that consist of two houses. **2** the governing body of some universities. [Middle English *senat* via French from Latin *senatus*, literally 'council of elders', from *sen-, senex* old, old man]

senator *noun* a member of a senate. ➤➤ **senatorial** /-'tawri-əl/ *adj*, **senatorship** *noun.* [Middle English *senatour* via Old French from Latin *senator*, from *senatus*: see SENATE]

send /send/ *verb* (*past tense and past part.* **sent** /sent/) ➤ *verb trans* **1** to cause or direct (somebody or something) to go to a place: *An Ambassador is an honest man sent to lie abroad for the good of his country* — Henry Wotton. **2** to cause (somebody or something) to go or move quickly or violently: *The blow sent him half across the room.* **3** to cause (a message or communication) to be delivered or transmitted: *You could send a fax.* **4** (*often + out*) to emit or discharge (something): *The kitchen sent out delicious aromas.* **5** to cause (somebody) to be in a specified state: *The remark sent him into a rage.* **6** *informal* to delight or move (somebody). ➤ *verb intrans* (*usu + for*) to summon or order somebody or something: *We had better send for a doctor.* ✳ **send away for** to send an order for (something) by post. **send packing** to dismiss (somebody) roughly or in disgrace. ➤➤ **sendable** *adj*, **sender** *noun.* [Old English *sendan*]

send down *verb trans* **1** *Brit* to suspend or expel (a student) from a university. **2** *informal* to send (a convicted person) to prison.

send forth *verb trans* **1** to discharge (e.g. rain). **2** to emit (a sound or cry).

send in *verb trans* **1** to cause (something) to be delivered to an authority, group, or organization. **2** to appoint (somebody) to deal with a difficulty: *They'll need to send a receiver in to deal with the bankruptcy.*

send off *verb trans* **1** to dispatch (somebody or something). **2** to attend to the departure of (somebody). **3** said of a referee: to order (a player) to leave the playing field because of a misdemeanour.

send-off *noun* an enthusiastic demonstration of goodwill at the beginning of a trip, etc.

send on *verb trans* **1** to dispatch (e.g. luggage) in advance. **2** to forward (mail).

send out *verb trans* **1** to circulate (something) or issue it for delivery, e.g. by post: *I've sent the invitations out.* **2** to dispatch (e.g. an order) from a shop or place of storage.

send round *verb trans* to circulate (a communication).

send up *verb trans* **1** *chiefly Brit* to mock or ridicule (somebody or something). **2** *chiefly NAmer* to send (somebody) to prison.

send-up *noun informal* a satirical imitation, *esp* on stage or television; a parody.

sene /'saynay/ *noun* a unit of currency in Western Samoa, worth 100th of a tala. [Samoan *sene*, modification of CENT]

senectitude /si'nektityoohd/ *noun formal* old age. [medieval Latin *senectitudo*, alteration of Latin *senectus* old age, from *sen-, senex* old, old man]

Senegalese /,senigə'leez/ *noun* (*pl* **Senegalese**) a native or inhabitant of Senegal in W Africa. ➤➤ **Senegalese** *adj*.

senescence /si'nes(ə)ns/ *noun* the condition or process of being or becoming old or withered. ➤➤ **senescent** *adj.* [Latin *senescent-, senescens*, present part. of *senescere* to grow old, from *sen-, senex* old]

seneschal /'senish(ə)l/ *noun* formerly, the agent or bailiff of a feudal lord's estate. [Middle English via French from medieval Latin *seniscalus*, of Germanic origin]

sengi /'senggi/ *noun* (*pl* **sengi**) a unit of currency in the Democratic Republic of Congo, worth 100th of a likuta or 10,000th of a new zaïre. [Kikongo *sengi, senki*, from French *cinq* five]

senhor /se'nyaw/ *noun* (*pl* **senhors** or **senhores** /-rees, -reez/) in Portugal and Brazil, a title equivalent to *Mr*, also used as a generalized term of direct address to a man. [Portuguese from medieval Latin *senior* superior, lord, from Latin: see SENIOR[1]]

senhora /se'nyawrə/ *noun* in Portugal and Brazil, a title equivalent to *Mrs*, also used as a generalized term of direct address to a married woman. [Portuguese *senhora*, fem of *senhor*: see SENHOR]

senhores *noun* pl of SENHOR.

senhorita /senyə'reetə/ *noun* in Portugal and Brazil, a title equivalent to *Miss*, also used as a generalized term of direct address to a girl or unmarried woman. [Portuguese *senhorita*, dimin. of *senhora*, fem of *senhor*: see SENHOR]

senile /'seeniel/ *adj* of, exhibiting, or characteristic of old age, or the mental or physical weakness associated with it: *No trace of the rifle's deadly work could be found on the tiger ... Evidently the beast of prey had succumbed to heart-failure, caused by the sudden report of the rifle, accelerated by senile decay* — Saki. ➤➤ **senility** /si'niliti/ *noun.* [Latin *senilis*, from *sen-, senex* old, old man]

senile dementia *noun* progressive deterioration of mental faculties occurring in old age.

senior[1] /'seenyə/ *adj* **1** higher in standing or rank: *senior officers.* **2a** older: *senior citizens.* **b** relating to old age and older people. **3a** *Brit* relating to students in the upper years of secondary school. **b** *NAmer* relating to students in the final year preceding graduation from secondary or higher education. **4** used to distinguish a father with the same name as his son; elder. [Middle English from Latin *senior* older, older man, elder, compar of *sen-, senex* old, old man]

senior[2] *noun* **1** a person who is older than another specified person: *She's five years his senior.* **2** in sporting competitions, etc, an adult as opposed to a junior, or a more advanced player as opposed to a less advanced one: *The seniors' race was won by a 56-year-old mother of four.* **3** an elderly person. **4a** *Brit* a student in the upper years of secondary school. **b** *NAmer* a student in the final year preceding graduation from secondary or higher education. **c** a person of higher standing or rank: *Always be considerate to your juniors; some day they may be your seniors.*

senior aircraftman or **senior aircraftwoman** *noun* a rank of the Royal Air Force below junior technician, approximately equivalent to the rank of private in the army.

senior citizen *noun* an elderly person, *esp* an old age pensioner.

senior common room *noun* **1** a common room for teachers, lecturers, etc. **2** (*treated as sing. or pl*) the staff community in a college or university.

senior high school *noun NAmer* a high school covering grades nine to twelve or ten to twelve.

seniority /seeni'oriti/ *noun* **1** relative status, rank, etc. **2** a privileged status attained by length of continuous service, e.g. in a company.

senior moment *noun* a moment of forgetfulness or absent-mindedness, *esp* in the elderly.

senior nursing officer *noun Brit* a person who is in charge of the nursing staff in a hospital.

senior registrar *noun Brit* a doctor holding the grade of hospital doctor senior to registrar.

Senior Service *noun* (**the Senior Service**) *Brit* the Royal Navy, *esp* as opposed to the army.

seniti /'seniti/ *noun* (*pl* **seniti**) a unit of currency in Tonga, worth 100th of a pa'anga. [Tongan *seniti*, modification of CENT]

senna /'senə/ *noun* 1 any of a genus of leguminous plants, shrubs, and trees of warm regions: genus *Cassia*. Also called CASSIA. 2 the dried leaflets or pods of certain of these plants, used as a laxative. [medieval Latin *sena* from Arabic *sanā*]

sennet /'senit/ *noun* in Elizabethan drama, a signal call on a trumpet or cornet for stage entrances or exits. [prob alteration of SIGNET in the obsolete sense 'signal']

sennight *or* **se'nnight** /'seniet/ *noun archaic* a week. [Old English *seofon nihta* seven nights]

sennit /'senit/ *noun* a braided cord or fabric, e.g. of plaited rope yarns. [perhaps from French *coussinet*, dimin. of early French *cossin*: see CUSHION[1]; from its use to protect cables from fraying]

senor *or* **señor** /se'nyaw/ *noun* (*pl* **senors** *or* **señores** /-rays/) in Spanish-speaking countries, a title equivalent to *Mr*, also used as a generalized term of direct address to a man. [Spanish *señor* from medieval Latin *senior* superior, lord, from Latin: see SENIOR[1]]

senora *or* **señora** /se'nyawrə/ *noun* (*pl* **senoras** *or* **señoras**) in Spanish-speaking countries, a title equivalent to *Mrs*, also used as a generalized term of direct address to a married woman. [Spanish *señora*, fem of *señor*: see SENOR]

señores *noun* pl of SENOR.

senorita *or* **señorita** /senyə'reetə/ *noun* (*pl* **senoritas** *or* **señoritas**) in Spanish-speaking countries, a title equivalent to *Miss*, also used as a generalized term of direct address to a girl or an unmarried woman. [Spanish *señorita*, dimin. of *señora*, fem of *señor*: see SENOR]

sensate /'sensayt/ *adj* 1 endowed with bodily senses: *a sensate being*. 2 relating to or apprehended through the senses. ⋙ **sensately** *adv*. [late Latin *sensatus* from Latin *sensus*: see SENSE[1]]

sensation /sen'saysh(ə)n/ *noun* 1a a mental process, e.g. seeing or hearing, resulting from stimulation of a sense organ. b a state of awareness of a specified type resulting from internal bodily conditions or external factors; a feeling or sense: *sensations of fatigue*. 2a a surge of intense interest or excitement: *Their elopement caused a sensation*. b a cause of such excitement, *esp* somebody or something that is in some respect remarkable or outstanding. [medieval Latin *sensation-, sensatio*, from Latin *sensus*: see SENSE[1]]

sensational *adj* 1 arousing an immediate, intense, and usu superficial interest or emotional reaction. 2 *informal* exceptionally or unexpectedly excellent or impressive. 3 of the mental process of sensation. ⋙ **sensationally** *adv*.

sensationalise *verb trans* see SENSATIONALIZE.

sensationalism *noun* 1 the use of sensational subject matter or style, or the sensational material itself. 2 a theory that limits the source of knowledge to sensation or sense perceptions. ⋙ **sensationalist** *noun and adj*, **sensationalistic** /-'listik/ *adj*.

sensationalize *or* **sensationalise** *verb trans* to report (a story, etc) in sensationalist terms.

sense[1] /sens/ *noun* 1 a meaning conveyed or intended, *esp* any of a range of meanings a word or phrase may bear, e.g. as isolated in a dictionary entry. 2a the faculty of perceiving the external world or internal bodily conditions by means of feeling, hearing, sight, smell, taste, etc. b any of these individual faculties of perception. 3a an ability to use the senses for a specified purpose: *She had a good sense of balance*. b a definite but often vague awareness or impression: *a sense of insecurity*. c an awareness that motivates action or judgment: *It was done out of a sense of justice*. d a capacity for discernment and appreciation: *I admired her for her sense of humour*. 4 (*usu in pl, but treated as sing.*) soundness of mind or judgment: *Have you taken leave of your senses?* 5 the prevailing view; a consensus: *It is the role of the moderator to take the sense of the meeting.* 6 an ability to put the mind to effective use; practical intelligence. 7 point or reason: *What's the sense in doing that?* 8 in mathematics, either of two opposite directions of motion. ✳ **make sense** 1 to be understandable. 2 to seem reasonable. [Middle English from early French *sens* sensation, feeling, mechanism of perception, meaning, from Latin *sensus*, past part. of *sentire* to perceive, feel]

sense[2] *verb trans* 1a to perceive (something) by the senses. b to be or become conscious of (something): *The deer could sense danger.* 2 to grasp or comprehend (something): *I sense the import of the remark.* 3 to detect (a symbol, radiation, etc) automatically.

sense-datum *noun* (*pl* **sense-data**) a sensation resulting from the stimulation of any of the senses.

sensei /'sensay, sen'say/ *noun* (*pl* **sensei**) a martial arts instructor. [Japanese *sensei* teacher, master, from *sen* previous, before + *sei* life, birth, generation]

senseless *adj* 1 unconscious: *He was knocked senseless by the blow.* 2 foolish or stupid: *It was some senseless practical joke* — Conan Doyle. 3 meaningless; purposeless: *a senseless motiveless murder.* ⋙ **senselessly** *adv*, **senselessness** *noun*.

sense organ *noun* a bodily structure that responds to a stimulus, e.g. heat or sound waves, by initiating impulses in nerves that convey them to the central nervous system where they are interpreted as sensations.

sensibility /sensi'biliti/ *noun* (*pl* **sensibilities**) 1 (*usu in pl*). a refined or exaggerated sensitiveness in feelings and tastes. b feelings, *esp* moral feelings or scruples. c heightened susceptibility to feelings of pleasure or pain, e.g. in response to praise or blame. d the ability to discern and respond freely to something, e.g. emotion in another person. 2 the ability to have sensations.

sensible *adj* 1a having, containing, or indicative of good sense or sound reason: *sensible, temperate, sober, well-judging persons* — J H Newman. b plain and practical: *Wear sensible shoes for the walk.* 2 (+ of/to) capable of sensing something: *sensible to pain.* 3 *archaic*. a perceptible to the senses or to understanding: *His distress was sensible from his manner.* b large enough to be observed or noticed; considerable: *There has been a sensible decrease in crime this year.* 4 (+ of) aware or conscious of something. ⋙ **sensibleness** *noun*, **sensibly** *adv*. [Middle English via French from Latin *sensibilis*, from *sensus*: see SENSE[1]]

sensitise /'sensitiez/ *verb trans and intrans* see SENSITIZE.

sensitive /'sensitiv/ *adj* 1 (+ to) capable of being stimulated or excited by external agents such as light, gravity, or contact: *This film is coated with a photographic emulsion sensitive to red light.* 2 (*often* + to) highly responsive or susceptible, e.g.: a easily provoked or hurt emotionally. b finely aware of the attitudes and feelings of others or of the subtleties of a work of art. c abnormally sensitive; allergic: *The baby was found to be sensitive to cow's milk.* d capable of registering minute differences; delicate: *These are very sensitive scales.* e readily affected or changed by external agents, e.g. light or chemical stimulation. f said of a radio receiving set: highly responsive to incoming waves. 3a needing careful or tactful handling; tricky: *People's weight is a very sensitive issue.* b concerned with highly classified information: *These documents are highly sensitive.* ⋙ **sensitively** *adv*, **sensitiveness** *noun*, **sensitivity** /-'tiviti/ *noun*. [Middle English via French from medieval Latin *sensitivus*, from Latin *sensus*: see SENSE[1]]

sensitive plant *noun* a mimosa with leaves that fold or droop when touched: *Mimosa pudica.*

sensitize *or* **sensitise** /'sensitiez/ *verb trans* to make (somebody or something) sensitive or abnormally sensitive. ⋙ *verb intrans* to become sensitive or abnormally sensitive. ⋙ **sensitization** /-'zaysh(ə)n/ *noun*, **sensitizer** *noun*.

sensor *noun* a device that responds to heat, light, sound, pressure, magnetism, etc and transmits a resulting impulse, e.g. for measurement or operating a control. [Latin *sensus*: see SENSE[1]]

sensoria *noun* pl of SENSORIUM.

sensorial /sen'sawri-əl/ *adj* = SENSORY.

sensorimotor /ˌsensəri'mohtə/ *adj* of or functioning in both sensory and motor aspects of bodily activity.

sensorium /sen'sawri-əm/ *noun* (*pl* **sensoriums** *or* **sensoria** /-ri-ə/) 1 the sensory apparatus of the body. 2 the parts of the brain or the mind concerned with the reception and interpretation of stimuli from the sensory apparatus. [late Latin *sensorium* sense organ, from Latin *sensus*: see SENSE[1]]

sensory /'sens(ə)ri/ *adj* of sensation or the senses.

sensual /'sensyooəl, 'senshooəl/ *adj* 1a relating to or consisting in the gratification of the senses or the indulgence of appetites. b devoted to or preoccupied with the senses or appetites, rather than the intellect or spirit. c voluptuous. 2 = SENSORY. ⋙ **sensualism** *noun*, **sensualist** *noun*, **sensuality** /-'aliti/ *noun*, **sensually** *adv*.

[Middle English from late Latin *sensualis*, from Latin *sensus*: see SENSE[1]]

Usage note

sensual or *sensuous*? *Sensual* is the more common word and the one that frequently carries overtones of sexual desire or pleasure: *pouting sensual lips*; *sensual pleasures*. *Sensuous* is the more neutral word: it also means 'appealing to the senses' but without the feeling of self-indulgence or sexiness associated with *sensual*: *the artist's sensuous use of colour and texture.*

sensuous /'sensyooəs, 'senshooəs/ *adj* **1a** providing or characterized by gratification of the senses; appealing strongly to the senses: *sensuous pleasure.* **b** suggesting or producing rich imagery or sense impressions: *sensuous verse.* **2** of the senses or objects perceived by the senses. **3** readily influenced by sense perception. ≫ **sensuosity** /-'ositi/ *noun*, **sensuously** *adv*, **sensuousness** *noun*. [Latin *sensus* (see SENSE[1]) + -OUS]

Usage note

sensuous or *sensual*? See note at SENSUAL.

sent[1] /sent/ *verb* past tense and past part. of SEND.

sent[2] *noun* (*pl* **sentee** /'senti/) a unit of currency in Estonia, worth 100th of a kroon. [Estonian *sent*, modification of CENT]

sente /'senti/ *noun* (*pl* **lisente** /li'senti/) a unit of currency in Lesotho, worth 100th of a loti. [Sotho *sente*, modification of CENT]

sentee *noun* pl of SENT[2].

sentence[1] /'sentəns/ *noun* **1** a grammatically self-contained speech unit that expresses an assertion, a question, a command, a wish, or an exclamation, and is shown in writing with a capital letter at the beginning and with appropriate punctuation, usu a full stop, at the end. **2a** a judgment formally pronounced by a court and specifying a punishment: *Marriage isn't a word — it's a sentence* — King Vidor. **b** the punishment so imposed: *He served his sentence in a maximum-security prison.* **3** *archaic* a maxim or saying. [Middle English via French from Latin *sententia* feeling, opinion, sentence, from *sentire* to feel]

sentence[2] *verb trans* **1** (*often* + to) to impose a judicial sentence on (a criminal). **2** to consign (somebody or something) to an unpleasant fate: *This development sentences rural industries to extinction.*

sentence adverb *noun* in grammar, an adverbial expression such as *frankly* or *by the way*, which stands outside the construction. Also called DISJUNCT.

sentential /sen'tenshl/ *adj* relating to grammatical sentences.

sententious /sen'tenshəs/ *adj* **1** terse; pithy. **2a** full of terse or pithy sayings. **b** given to pompous moralizing. ≫ **sententiously** *adv*, **sententiousness** *noun*. [Middle English from Latin *sententiosus*, from *sententia*: see SENTENCE[1]]

senti /'senti/ *noun* (*pl* **senti**) a unit of currency in Kenya, Uganda, and Tanzania, worth 100th of a shilling. [Swahili *senti*, modification of CENT]

sentience /'sensh(ə)ns/ *noun* **1** a sentient quality or state. **2** rudimentary feeling and perception as distinguished from thought and the higher emotions.

sentient /'sensh(ə)nt/ *adj* **1** capable of perceiving through the senses; conscious. **2** keenly sensitive in perception or feeling. ≫ **sentiently** *adv*. [Latin *sentient-, sentiens*, present part. of *sentire* to perceive, feel]

sentiment /'sentimənt/ *noun* **1a** emotion or sentimentality, or an attitude, thought, or judgment prompted or coloured by feeling or emotion. **b** (*usu in pl*) a specific view or opinion: *We held similar sentiments on the matter.* **c** a feeling or attitude: *They were elected on a wave of nationalistic sentiment.* **2a** sensitive feeling; refined sensibility, *esp* as expressed in a work of art. **b** indulgently romantic or nostalgic feeling. **3** the underlying intended meaning of a communication as distinguished from its overt expression: *The sentiment is admirable, though it is clumsily put.* [Middle English via Old French from medieval Latin *sentimentum*, from Latin *sentire* to feel]

sentimental /senti'mentl/ *adj* **1** appealing to or resulting from feeling rather than reason: *Ugly as it was, we kept her gift for its sentimental value.* **2** having an excess of superficial sentiment. ≫ **sentimentalism** *noun*, **sentimentalist** *noun*, **sentimentality** /-'taliti/ *noun*, **sentimentally** *adv*.

sentimentalize or **sentimentalise** *verb intrans* to indulge in sentiment. ≫ *verb trans* to make (somebody or something) an object of usu superficial sentiment; to romanticize (them). ≫ **sentimentalization** /-'zaysh(ə)n/ *noun*.

sentinel[1] /'sentinl/ *noun* somebody or something that keeps guard; a sentry. [early French *sentinelle* from Old Italian *sentinella*, from *sentina* vigilance, from *sentire* to perceive, from Latin]

sentinel[2] *verb trans* (**sentinelled, sentinelling**, *NAmer* **sentineled, sentineling**) **1** to watch over (somebody or something) as a sentinel. **2** to post (somebody) as a sentinel.

sentry /'sentri/ *noun* (*pl* **sentries**) a guard or watch, *esp* a soldier standing guard at a gate, door, etc. [perhaps from obsolete *sentrinel*, variant spelling of SENTINEL[1]]

sentry box *noun* a shelter for a standing sentry.

senza /'sentsə/ *prep* in music, without. [Italian *senza*]

SEO *abbr* Senior Executive Officer.

Sep. *abbr* **1** September. **2** Septuagint.

sepal /'sepl/ *noun* any of the modified leaves comprising the CALYX (green outer part) of a flower. ≫ **sepaloid** /'seepəloyd, 'sep-/ *adj*. [scientific Latin *sepalum*, from Greek *skepē* covering + -*lum* as in *petalum* petal]

-sepalous *comb. form* forming adjectives, with the meaning: having a stated number or type of sepals.

separable /'sep(ə)rəbl/ *adj* capable of being separated or dissociated. ≫ **separability** /-'biliti/ *noun*, **separableness** *noun*, **separably** *adv*. [Middle English from Latin *separabilis*, from *separare*: see SEPARATE[1]]

separate[1] /'sepərayt/ *verb trans* **1a** to set or keep apart (two or more people or things); to divide (them) or stand between (them). **b** (*often* + from) to make a distinction between (two or more people or things); to distinguish (them): *It is sometimes hard to separate religion from magic.* **c** to disperse (people or things) in space or time; to scatter (them): *The population lived in widely separated hamlets.* **d** to detach (somebody or something) from a larger group: *The wolves tried to separate a calf from the herd.* **e** to sever (something). **2** (*usu in passive*) to part (a married couple) by separation: *They are not divorced but they are separated.* **3** to isolate or segregate (somebody). **4a** (*often* + out) to isolate (something) from a mixture or compound: *This process separates the cream from the milk.* **b** (*often* + out) to divide (something) into constituent parts or types. **5** *NAmer* to discharge (somebody): *After five years, he was separated from the army.* ≫ *verb intrans* **1** to become divided or detached; to move or come apart. **2a** (*often* + from) to sever an association; to withdraw: *Eventually, the party separated from the federation.* **b** to cease to live together as husband and wife, *esp* by formal arrangement. **3** to go in different directions. **4** (*often* + out) to become isolated from a mixture. ≫ **separative** /'sep(ə)rətiv/ *adj*. [Middle English *separaten* from Latin *separatus*, past part. of *separare*, from *se-* apart + *parare* to prepare, procure]

Usage note

Separate is spelt with two *a*'s and only two *e*'s. It may help to remember that it is related etymologically to the words *pare* and *prepare*.

separate[2] /'sep(ə)rət/ *adj* **1** set or kept apart; detached or separated. **2** not shared with another; individual: *You'll all be in separate rooms.* **3a** existing independently; autonomous. **b** unconnected. **c** different in kind; distinct: *We have our own separate ways of doing things.* **4** belonging to each individually: *Their separate achievements are very different.* **5** solitary; alone; apart: *I like my separate existence.* ≫ **separately** *adv*, **separateness** *noun*.

separates /'sep(ə)rəts/ *pl noun* garments, e.g. skirts, blouses, and trousers, that are designed to be worn together to form an interchangeable outfit.

separation /sepə'raysh(ə)n/ *noun* **1** the act or an instance of separating. **2a** a point, line, or means of division. **b** an intervening space; a gap or break. **3** cessation of cohabitation between husband and wife by mutual agreement or judicial decree.

separatism /'sep(ə)rətiz(ə)m/ *noun* a belief or movement advocating separation, e.g. schism, secession, or racial segregation. ≫ **separatist** *noun* and *adj*.

separator /'sepəraytə/ *noun* a person or thing that separates; *specif* a device for separating liquids of different specific gravities, e.g. cream from milk, or liquids from solids.

Sephardi /si'fahdi/ *noun* (*pl* **Sephardim** /-dim/) a member or descendant of the non-Yiddish-speaking branch of European Jews that settled in Spain and Portugal: compare ASHKENAZI. ≫ **Sephardic** /-dik/ *adj*. [late Hebrew *sĕphāradhī*, from Hebrew *sĕphāradh*, denoting a region where Jews were once exiled (Obadiah 20), later taken to be Spain]

sepia[1] /'seepi·ə/ *noun* **1** the inky secretion of cuttlefishes, or a brown pigment obtained from this. **2** a rich dark brown, as seen in early photographic prints. **3** a print or photograph of a brown colour. [Latin *sēpia* cuttlefish, from Greek]

sepia[2] *adj* **1** of the colour sepia. **2** made of or done in sepia: *a sepia print*.

sepoy /'seepoy/ *noun* an Indian soldier employed by a European power, *esp* Britain. [Portuguese *sipai* from Urdu *sipāhī* cavalryman, from Persian]

seppuku /se'poohkooh/ *noun* = HARA-KIRI. [Japanese *seppu* to cut + *ku* abdomen]

sepsis /'sepsis/ *noun* (*pl* **sepses** /'sepseez/) the spread of bacteria from a focus of infection, *esp* septicaemia. [scientific Latin from Greek *sēpsis* decay, from *sēpein* to make putrid]

Sept. *abbr* **1** September. **2** Septuagint.

sept /sept/ *noun* a branch of a clan. [prob alteration of SECT]

septa /'septə/ *noun* pl of SEPTUM.

septate /'septayt/ *adj* divided by or having a septum.

September /sep'tembə, səp-/ *noun* the ninth month of the year.

Word history

Middle English *Septembre* via French from Latin *September* the seventh month, from *septem* seven. The early Roman calendar consisted of ten months, March to December, plus apparently an uncounted winter period. The months January and February were added to fill this gap, traditionally by Numa Pompilius fl.c.700 BC, second King of Rome.

septenary[1] /'septinəri/ *adj* **1** of the number seven. **2** consisting of seven people or things. [Middle English from Latin *septenarius*, from *septeni* in sevens, from *septem* seven]

septenary[2] *noun* (*pl* **septenaries**) **1** a group of seven people or things. **2** seven years.

septennial /sep'teni·əl/ *adj* **1** consisting of or lasting for seven years. **2** occurring or performed every seven years. ⫸ **septennially** *adv*. [late Latin *septennium* period of seven years, from Latin *septem* + *-ennium* as in BIENNIUM]

septet /sep'tet/ *noun* **1** a musical composition for seven instruments, voices, or performers. **2** (*treated as sing. or pl*) a group or set of seven, *esp* the performers of a septet. [German *Septett* from Latin *septem* seven]

septic /'septik/ *adj* **1** putrefactive. **2** relating to, involving, or characteristic of sepsis. ⫸ **septically** *adv*, **septicity** /sep'tisiti/ *noun*. [Latin *septicus* from Greek *sēptikos*, from *sēpein* to make putrid]

septicaemia (*NAmer* **septicemia**) /septi'seemi·ə/ *noun* invasion of the bloodstream by micro-organisms from a focus of infection, with chills, fever, etc; blood poisoning. [scientific Latin, from Latin *septicus* (see SEPTIC) + -AEMIA]

septic tank *noun* a tank in which the solid matter of continuously flowing sewage is disintegrated by bacteria.

septillion /sep'tilyən/ *noun* **1** *Brit* the number one followed by 42 zeros (10⁴²). **2** *NAmer* the number one followed by 24 zeros (10²⁴). ⫸ **septillionth** *noun and adj*. [French *septillion* from Latin *septem* seven + *-illion* as in MILLION]

septime /sep'teem/ *noun* in fencing, the seventh of eight parrying positions. [Latin *septimus* seventh, from *septem* seven]

septuagenarian[1] /,sepchooəji'neəri·ən, ,septwə-/ *adj* aged between 70 and 79 years old. [Latin *septuagenarius* of or containing seventy, from Latin *septuageni* seventy each, from *septuaginta* seventy]

septuagenarian[2] *noun* a person between 70 and 79 years old.

Septuagesima /,sepchooə'jesimə, ,septwə-/ *noun* the third Sunday before Lent. [Middle English from Latin *septuagesima*, fem of *septuagesimus* 70th, from *septuaginta* 70; because it is the 70th day before Easter]

Septuagint /'sepchooəjint, 'septwəjint/ *noun* a pre-Christian Greek version of the Jewish Scriptures arranged and edited by Jewish scholars about 300 BC. [late Latin *Septuaginta* from Latin *septuaginta* 70; from the approximate number of its translators]

septum /'septəm/ *noun* (*pl* **septa** /'septə/) a dividing wall or membrane, *esp* between bodily spaces or masses of soft tissue. ⫸ **septal** *adj*. [scientific Latin, from Latin *saeptum* enclosure, fence, wall, from *sepire* to enclose, from *sepes* hedge]

septuple[1] /sep'tyoohpl/ *adj* **1** having seven units or members. **2** seven times as great or as many. [late Latin *septuplus*, from Latin *septem* seven + *-plus* multiplied by]

septuple[2] *verb intrans* to become seven times as much or as many. ▶ *verb trans* to make (something) seven times as much or as many.

septuplet /'septyooplit, sep'tyoohplit/ *noun* **1** any of seven offspring born at one birth. **2** a combination of seven of a kind. [Latin *septuplus* (see SEPTUPLE[1]), on the pattern of words such as *triplet*]

sepulcher[1] /'sepəlkə/ *noun* *NAmer* see SEPULCHRE[1].

sepulcher[2] *verb trans* *NAmer* see SEPULCHRE[2].

sepulchral /si'pulkrəl/ *adj* **1** suited to or suggestive of a tomb; sombre, gloomy, or dismal; funereal. **2** relating to the burial of the dead. ⫸ **sepulchrally** *adv*.

sepulchre[1] (*NAmer* **sepulcher**) /'sepəlkə/ *noun* a place of burial; a tomb. [Middle English *sepulcre* via French from Latin *sepulcrum*, *sepulchrum*, from *sepelire* to bury]

sepulchre[2] (*NAmer* **sepulcher**) *verb trans* *chiefly literary* to place or enclose (somebody) in a sepulchre.

sepulture /'sep(ə)lchə/ *noun* *formal* burial; interment. [Middle English via French from Latin *sepultura*, from *sepultus*, past part. of *sepelire* to bury]

seq. *abbr* **1** sequel. **2** (*pl* **seqq.**) the following. [Latin *sequens*, plural *sequentes*, *sequentia*, from *sequi* to follow]

sequel /'seekwəl/ *noun* **1a** a play, film, or literary work continuing the course of a narrative begun in a preceding one. **b** subsequent development or course of events. **2** a consequence or result. [Middle English via French from Latin *sequela*, from *sequi* to follow]

sequela /si'kweelə/ *noun* (*pl* **sequelae** /-lee/) an aftereffect of disease or injury. [Latin *sequela*: see SEQUEL]

sequence[1] /'seekwəns/ *noun* **1** a continuous or connected series: *a strange sequence of events*. **2** a continuous progression. **3** the order of succession of things, events, etc. **4** a subsequent but not resultant occurrence or course. **5** an extended series of poems united by their theme: *a sonnet sequence*. **6** in music, a succession of not necessarily exact repetitions: compare OSTINATO, IMITATION (3). **7a** a succession of related shots or scenes developing a single subject or phase of a film story. **b** an episode, *esp* in a film: *This sequence was cut out of the 1963 version*. **8** a succession of mathematical terms formed according to some rule or law, e.g. *2, 4, 8, 16 …*. **9** in card games, three or more consecutive playing cards, usu of the same suit. **10** the order of structural units, e.g. amino acids in a protein or chemical bases in DNA or RNA, in a complex biological molecule. [Middle English from late Latin *sequentia* what follows, from Latin *sequent-*, *sequens*, present part. of *sequi* to follow]

sequence[2] *verb trans* **1** to place (people, things, etc) in ordered sequence. **2** to determine the amino acid sequence of (a protein), nucleotide sequence of (a nucleic acid), etc. ⫸ **sequencing** *noun*.

sequence of tenses *noun* the dependence of the tense of a verb in a subordinate clause on that of the verb in the main clause, as in *He says he can* and *He said he could*.

sequencer *noun* any of various devices for arranging things, e.g. informational items or the events in the launching of a rocket, into a sequence, or for separating things, e.g. amino acids into protein, in a sequence.

sequent[1] /'seekwənt/ *adj formal* **1** consecutive; succeeding. **2** consequent; resultant. ⫸ **sequently** *adv*. [Latin *sequent-*, *sequens*: see SEQUENCE[1]]

sequent[2] *noun* something that follows; a consequence or result.

sequential /si'kwensh(ə)l/ *adj* **1** of or arranged in a sequence; serial. **2** following in sequence. ⫸ **sequentiality** /-shi'aliti/ *noun*, **sequentially** *adv*.

sequential access *noun* in computing, a method of accessing data from a file by reading through the file from the beginning: compare DIRECT ACCESS.

sequester /si'kwestə/ *verb trans* (**sequestered, sequestering**) **1** *chiefly literary* (*usu in passive or reflexive*) to segregate (somebody) from the company of others: *He that travelleth into a country … let him sequester himself from the company of his countrymen* — Bacon; *The jurors were sequestered throughout the weekend in sealed hotel rooms*. **2a** in law, to seize (a person's property) and hold it temporarily until a debt is paid or a dispute is settled. **b** in international law, to seize (the property of an enemy). **3** to hold (a metallic ion, etc) in solution, usu by inclusion in an appropriate complex. [Middle English *sequestren* via French from late Latin *sequestrare* to surrender for safekeeping, set apart, from Latin *sequester* agent, depositary, bailee]

sequestered *adj* secluded; screened from other people's view; free from disturbance: *Their walk, which was not above two miles long, lay through shady lanes and sequestered footpaths* — Dickens.

sequestrate /'seekwistrayt, 'sek-/ *verb trans* **1** in law, = SEQUESTER (2A). **2** in Scots law, to declare (somebody) bankrupt, or to hand over (a bankrupt's property) to pay a debt. ➤➤ **sequestration** /-'straysh(ə)n/ *noun*, **sequestrator** *noun*. [late Latin *sequestratus*, past part. of *sequestrare* : see SEQUESTER]

sequin /'seekwin/ *noun* **1** a very small disc of shining metal or plastic used for ornamentation, *esp* on clothing. **2** a former gold coin of Italy and Turkey. [French *sequin* from Italian *zecchino*, from *zecca* a mint, from Arabic *sikkah* die, coin]

sequoia /si'kwoyə/ *noun* either of two huge coniferous Californian trees: genus *Sequoia*. [named after *Sequoyah* d.1843, Cherokee who created a writing system for the Cherokee language]

sera /'siərə/ *noun* pl of SERUM.

serac /'serak, se'rak/ *noun* a pinnacle, sharp ridge, or block of ice among the crevasses of a glacier. [French *sérac* a kind of white cheese, from medieval Latin *seracium* whey, from Latin *serum*]

seraglio /se'rahlioh, -lyoh/ *noun* (*pl* **seraglios**) **1** = HAREM. **2** a sultan's palace. [Italian *serraglio* enclosure, seraglio; partly from medieval Latin *serraculum* bar of a door, bolt, from late Latin *serare* to bolt; partly from Turkish *saray*: see SERAI]

serai /se'rie/ *noun* = CARAVANSERAI. [Turkish *saray* mansion, palace, from Persian *sarāi* mansion, inn]

serape /sə'rahpi/ *noun* a brightly coloured woollen shawl worn over the shoulders, *esp* by Mexican men. [Mexican Spanish *sarape*]

seraph /'serəf/ *noun* (*pl* **seraphim** /-fim/ or **seraphs**) any of the six-winged angels standing in the presence of God. In the traditional hierarchy of angels, the seraphim are the highest of the nine orders of angels. ➤➤ **seraphic** /si'rafik/ *adj*. [late Latin *seraphim* seraphs, from Hebrew *šĕrāphīm*]

Serb /suhb/ *noun* **1a** a native or inhabitant of Serbia. **b** a member of the ethnic community whose language is Serbo-Croatian, written in the Cyrillic alphabet, and whose religion is Eastern Orthodox Christianity. **2** the Serbo-Croatian language, as spoken in Serbia and elsewhere and written in the Cyrillic alphabet: compare BOSNIAN, CROATIAN. ➤➤ **Serb** *adj*, **Serbian** *adj*. [Serbian *Srb* Serbian, *Srbija* Serbia]

Serbian /'suhbi·ən/ *noun* = SERB.

Serbo-Croat /,suhboh'kroh·at/ *noun* = SERBO-CROATIAN.

Serbo-Croatian /,suhbohkroh'aysh(ə)n/ *noun* **1** the Slavonic language of the Serbs, Croats, Bosnians, and Montenegrins. **2** a person whose native language is Serbo-Croatian. ➤➤ **Serbo-Croatian** *adj*.

SERC *abbr* Science and Engineering Research Council.

sere¹ or **sear** /siə/ *adj archaic or literary* shrivelled; withered. [Old English *sēar* dry]

sere² *noun* a series of successive ecological communities established in one area. ➤➤ **seral** *adj*. [Latin *series*: see SERIES]

serenade¹ /serə'nayd/ *noun* **1** a complimentary vocal or instrumental performance, *esp* one given outdoors at night by a man for a woman who is the object of his desire, or any musical piece suggestive of this. **2** an instrumental composition in several movements written for a small ensemble. [French *sérénade* from Italian *serenata*, from *sereno* clear, calm (of weather), from Latin *serenus*]

serenade² *verb intrans* to perform a serenade. ➤ *verb trans* to perform a serenade in honour of (somebody). ➤➤ **serenader** *noun*.

serendipity /serən'dipiti/ *noun* the faculty of discovering pleasing or valuable things by chance. ➤➤ **serendipitous** /-təs/ *adj*. [from its possession by the heroes of the Persian fairy tale *The Three Princes of Serendip*; *Serendip* was an ancient name for Sri Lanka]

serene /sə'reen/ *adj* **1** free of storms or adverse changes; clear or fine: *serene skies*; *serene weather*. **2** having or showing tranquillity and peace of mind: *a serene smile*. **3** used as part of a title of royalty, etc: august; honoured: *Her Serene Highness Princess Marie of Liechtenstein*. ➤➤ **serenely** *adv*, **sereneness** *noun*, **serenity** /sə'reniti/ *noun*. [Latin *serenus*]

serf /suhf/ *noun* a member of a class of agricultural labourers in a feudal society, bound in service to a lord, and often transferred with the land they worked if its ownership changed hands. ➤➤ **serfage** /'suhfij/ *noun*, **serfdom** *noun*, **serfhood** *noun*. [early French *serf* from Latin *servus* slave, servant, serf]

serge /suhj/ *noun* a durable twilled fabric having a smooth clear face and a pronounced diagonal rib on the front and the back. [Middle English *sarge* via French from Latin *serica*, fem of *sericus*: see SILK]

sergeant or **serjeant** /'sahj(ə)nt/ *noun* **1** a police officer ranking in Britain between constable and inspector and in the USA below a lieutenant. **2** a non-commissioned officer in the army, air force, or marines, ranking above a corporal. **3** = SERGEANT-AT-ARMS. [Middle English in the senses 'servant', 'attendant', 'common soldier', from Old French *sergent, serjant*, from Latin *servient-, serviens*, present part. of *servire* to serve]

sergeant-at-arms or **serjeant-at-arms** *noun* (*pl* **sergeants-at-arms** or **serjeants-at-arms**) an officer attending the British Speaker or Lord Chancellor, or a similar officer in other legislatures.

sergeant major *noun* (*pl* **sergeant majors**) **1** a warrant officer in the British army or Royal Marines. **2** the highest rank of non-commissioned officer in the US navy and marines.

serial¹ /'siəri·əl/ *noun* **1** a work appearing, e.g. in a magazine or on television, in parts, usu at regular intervals. **2** a publication issued as one of a consecutively numbered continuing series.
Usage note
serial or **cereal**? See note at CEREAL.

serial² *adj* **1** of, in, or constituting a series, rank, or row: *serial order*. **2** appearing in successive instalments: *An autobiography is an obituary in serial form with the last instalment missing* — Quentin Crisp. **3** of or being music based on a series of notes in an arbitrary but fixed order without regard for traditional tonality. **4** in computing, transferring data one bit at a time. ➤➤ **serially** *adv*. [SERIES + -AL¹]
Usage note
serial or **cereal**? See note at CEREAL.

serialise *verb trans* see SERIALIZE.

serialism *noun* serial music, or the theory or practice of composing it.
Editorial note
Serialism is a compositional method in which one or more musical parameters – pitch, duration, dynamic level – is ordered in a fixed series and repeated (at different pitch levels, or in inversion or retrograde) throughout the course of a work. For composers writing atonal music in the first decades of the 20th cent., total freedom proved hard to sustain, and Arnold Schoenberg in particular looked for a way of systematizing this language. His system, using 'twelve notes only related to each other', first introduced in 1923, was to prove hugely influential (and increasingly dogmatically prescriptive) in Western music for more than 50 years — Andrew Clements.

serialist *noun* a person who writes serials or who composes serial music.

serialize or **serialise** *verb trans* to arrange or publish (a story) in serial form. ➤➤ **serialization** /-'zaysh(ə)n/ *noun*.

serial killer *noun* a person who kills a number of people over a period of time, *esp* if using the same method of killing or involving a given category of victim.

serial monogamy *noun* the practice of having a series of long-term monogamous sexual relationships.

serial number *noun* a number used as a means of identification that indicates position in a series.

seriate¹ /'siəriayt/ *adj formal* arranged in a series. [from SERIES]

seriate² *verb trans formal* to arrange (something) in a series.

seriatim /siəri'atim/ *adv and adj* in regular order; one after the other. [medieval Latin *seriatim* from Latin *series*: see SERIES]

sericeous /si'rishəs/ *adj* said of part of an animal or plant: silky; covered in fine hairs. [late Latin *sericeus* silken, from Latin *sericum*: see SILK]

sericulture /'serikulchə/ *noun* the production of raw silk by breeding silkworms. ➤➤ **sericultural** /-'kulchərəl/ *adj*, **sericulturist** *noun*. [Latin *sericum* (see SILK) + CULTURE¹]

series /'siəriz, 'siəreez/ *noun* (*pl* **series**) **1** a number of things or events of the same kind following one another in spatial or temporal succession: *a concert series; a series of small rooms*. **2** any group of systematically related items: *What passes for identity in America is a series of myths about one's heroic ancestors* — James Baldwin. **3** a succession of issues of volumes published with continuous numbering or related subjects or authors and format. **4** a number of radio or television programmes involving the same characters in different stories or with the same topic and/or presenters. **5** a number of games, e.g. of cricket, played between two teams: *We*

*will be providing coverage of next month's five-match series between Eng-
land and Australia.* **6** the coins or currency of a particular country
and period. **7** an arrangement of devices in an electrical circuit in
which the whole current passes through each device: compare
PARALLEL². **8** a usu infinite mathematical sequence whose terms
are to be added together. **9** a division of rock formations that is
smaller than a system and comprises rocks deposited during an
epoch. **10** a group of chemical compounds or elements related in
structure and properties. [Latin *series*, from *serere* to join, link
together]

serif /'serif/ *noun* a tiny decorative line added at the tip of the stroke
of a printed letter. ➤➤ **seriffed** *adj.* [prob from Dutch *schreef*
stroke, line, from *schriven* to write, from Latin *scribere*]

serigraph /'serigrahf, -graf/ *noun* a print made by a silk-screen
process. ➤➤ **serigrapher** /sə'rigrəfə/ *noun,* **serigraphy** /sə'rigrəfi/
noun. [Latin *sericum* (see SILK) + Greek *graphein* to write, draw]

serin /'serin/ *noun* any of a genus of small Old World finches,
including the canaries, with yellowish or brownish feathers: genus
Serinus. [French *serin* canary, of unknown origin]

serine /'sereen, 'siəreen/ *noun* an amino acid found in most proteins. [*sericin,* gelatinous protein in silk fibre (from Latin *sericum*
SILK) + -INE²]

seriocomic /,siərioh'komik/ *adj* containing a mixture of the serious
and the comic. ➤➤ **seriocomically** *adv.*

serious /'siəri-əs/ *adj* **1** grave or thoughtful in appearance or manner; sober. **2a** sincere and in earnest; not joking or pretending: *Is
she serious about giving up her job?* **b** deeply interested or committed:
No serious fisherman would use a rod like that. **3a** having or possibly
leading to important or dangerous consequences; severe: *a serious
injury.* **b** *informal* substantial in size or quantity: *earning serious
money.* **4a** involving or requiring careful attention and concentration: *serious study.* **b** relating to a weighty or important matter: *a
serious play.* ➤➤ **seriousness** *noun.* [Middle English *seryows* via
French from late Latin *seriosus,* alteration of Latin *serius* earnest,
serious]

seriously *adv* **1a** in a sincere or purposeful manner; earnestly: *I'm
seriously thinking of emigrating to Australia.* **b** used to indicate that
the speaker is not or no longer joking: *Seriously, you should be more
careful.* **2a** to a serious extent; severely: *seriously injured.* **b** *informal*
extremely: *These people are seriously weird.* ✳ **take something/
somebody seriously** to regard something or somebody as worthy
of careful attention and a considered response.

serious-minded *adj* having a serious outlook on life.
➤➤ **serious-mindedly** *adv.*

serjeant /'sahj(ə)nt/ *noun* see SERGEANT.

serjeant-at-arms *noun* (*pl* **serjeants-at-arms**) see SERGEANT-
AT-ARMS.

serjeant-at-law *noun* (*pl* **serjeants-at-law**) a member of a
former class of barristers of the highest rank.

sermon /'suhmən/ *noun* **1** a religious discourse delivered in public,
usu by a clergyman as a part of a religious service. **2** a speech on
conduct or duty, *esp* one that is unduly long or tedious. [Middle
English via Old French from Latin *sermon-, sermo* speech, conversation, from *serere* to link together]

sermonize *or* **sermonise** *verb intrans* to give moral advice in an
officious or dogmatic manner. ➤➤ **sermonizer** *noun.*

sero- *comb. form* forming words, denoting: serum: *serology.* [Latin
serum whey, SERUM]

serology /si'roləji/ *noun* the medical study of the reactions and
properties of serum, *esp* blood serum. ➤➤ **serological** /siərə'lojikl/
adj, **serologist** *noun.*

seronegative /,siəroh'negətiv/ *adj* giving a negative result in serological tests; *specif* not having a significant level of serum antibodies, thus indicating no previous exposure to the infectious
agent being tested.

seropositive /,siəroh'pozətiv/ *adj* giving a positive result in serological tests; *specif* having a significant level of serum antibodies,
thus indicating previous exposure to the infectious agent being
tested.

serosa /si'rohsə, -zə/ *noun* = SEROUS MEMBRANE. ➤➤ **serosal** *adj.*
[scientific Latin, fem of medieval Latin *serosus:* see SEROUS]

serotine /'serətien/ *noun* an insect-eating bat common in southern
and central Europe: *Vespertilio serotinus.* [French *sérotine* from Latin

serotina, fem of *serotinus* coming late; because it flies late in the
evening]

serotonin /serə'tohnin/ *noun* a chemical compound that causes
constriction of small blood vessels and occurs *esp* in blood platelets
and as a neurotransmitter in the brain. [SERO- + TONIC¹ + -IN¹]

serous /'siərəs/ *adj* **1** relating to or producing serum. **2** resembling
serum, *esp* in being thin and watery: *a serous exudate.* [early French
sereux from medieval Latin *serosus,* from Latin *serum* SERUM]

serous membrane *noun* a thin membrane, e.g. the peritoneum,
with cells that secrete a watery liquid.

serow /'seroh/ *noun* either of two species of goat antelopes found
in eastern Asia that are usu rather dark-coloured and heavily built:
genus *Capricornis.* [Lepcha *sā-ro* long-haired Tibetan goat]

serpent /'suhpənt/ *noun* **1** *literary* a large snake. **2** (**the Serpent**)
the Devil. **3** a wily treacherous person. **4** an obsolete bass woodwind instrument with an S-shaped barrel. [Middle English via
French from Latin *serpent-, serpens,* present part. of *serpere* to creep]

serpentine¹ /'suhpəntien/ *adj* **1** winding or turning first one way
and then another. **2** relating to or like a serpent, e.g. in form or
movement. **3** subtly tempting; wily or artful. [Middle English via
French from late Latin *serpentinus,* from Latin *serpent-, serpens:* see
SERPENT]

serpentine² *noun* something wavy or winding; *specif* a movement
with semicircular turns to right and left in dressage.

serpentine³ *noun* a usu dull green mottled mineral consisting
mainly of hydrated magnesium silicate. [Middle English from late
Latin *serpentina, serpentinum,* fem and neuter of *serpentinus:* see
SERPENTINE¹]

serpiginous /suh'pijinəs/ *adj* said of an ulcer, ringworm, etc:
having an uneven edge, or tending to spread. [medieval Latin
serpigin-, serpigo creeping skin disease, from Latin *serpere* to creep]

SERPS /suhps/ *abbr Brit* state earnings-related pension scheme.

serrate /'serət, 'serayt/ *adj* **1** with a notched or toothed edge. **2** said
of a leaf: with toothlike projections pointing forwards or towards
the tip. [late Latin *serratus,* past part. of *serrare* to saw, from Latin
serra saw]

serrated /sə'raytid/ *adj* having projections like the teeth of a saw;
jagged.

serration /sə'raysh(ə)n/ *noun* **1** any of the points of a serrated edge.
2 a row of projections resembling the teeth of a saw.

serried /'serid/ *adj* crowded or pressed together; compact: *The
crowd collected in a serried mass* — Somerset Maugham. [past part.
of archaic *serry* to press close, from early French *serré,* past part. of
serrer to press, crowd, ultimately from Latin *sera* lock, bolt]

serum /'siərəm/ *noun* (*pl* **serums** *or* **sera** /'siərə/) **1** the watery part
of a body fluid remaining after clotting or curdling, *esp* the protein-
rich fluid constituent of blood. **2** blood serum obtained from inoc-
ulated animals and containing specific antibodies. **3** = WHEY.
[Latin *serum* whey, serum]

serum albumin *noun* the ALBUMIN (a type of protein) that normally makes up more than half of the protein in blood serum.

serum hepatitis *noun* = HEPATITIS B.

serval /'suhv(ə)l/ *noun* an African wildcat with long ears, long legs,
and a tawny black-spotted coat: *Felis serval.* [French *serval* from
Portuguese *cerval* deerlike, from *cervo* deer, from Latin *cervus*]

servant /'suhv(ə)nt/ *noun* somebody who or something that serves
others; *specif* somebody employed to perform personal or domestic
duties for somebody else. [Middle English from Old French, present
part. of *servir:* see SERVE¹]

serve¹ /suhv/ *verb trans* **1a** to act in such a way as to help or benefit
(something or somebody): *The citizen's duty is to serve society.* **b** to
be a useful possession or attribute to (somebody): *This watch has
served me well over the years.* **2** to attend to or provide for (a customer)
in a shop, bar, etc. **3a** to supply (food or drink) to guests or diners.
b to wait on (somebody) at table. **4a** to act as a servant to (somebody). **b** to give due honour and obedience to (God). **5** to be
employed or spend time as a member of the armed forces of (a
country). **6** in the Christian Church: to assist the officiating priest
at (the Mass or Eucharist). **7a** (*often + as*) to work in a particular
capacity or hold office for (a period of time): *He served seven years
as an apprentice.* **b** to be imprisoned for (a period of time). **8** said of
a school or other institution: be available for use by the people of
(an area). **9** (*often + as/for*) to be useful to (somebody) in a particular
capacity: *The males had great canine teeth, which served them as*

formidable weapons — Darwin; *A great stone that I happened to find ... served me for an anchor* — Jonathan Swift. **10** to put (the ball or shuttlecock) into play in tennis, badminton, and similar games. **11** (*often* + *on*) to deliver or execute (e.g. a writ or summons) as required by law. **12** said of a male animal: to copulate with (a female). **13** to wind yarn or wire tightly round (a rope or stay) for protection. **14** *formal* to behave towards or treat (somebody) in a specified way: *He served me very ill.* ➤ *verb intrans* **1a** to hold a post or office or to discharge a duty: *She served on a jury for three weeks.* **b** to be employed or spend time as a member of the armed forces. **2** to attend to customers in a shop, bar, etc. **3a** to distribute drinks or helpings of food during a meal. **b** to act as a waiter. **4** in the Christian Church: to assist the officiating priest at Mass or the Eucharist. **5** to act as a servant. **6** (*often* + *as/for*) to be of use in a particular capacity, fulfil a particular purpose, or have particular effect: *The blanket box also served as a window seat; This may serve to remind us that we are all fallible.* **7** to be adequate or satisfactory; to suffice. **8a** in tennis, badminton, and similar games, to hit the ball or shuttle to an opponent in order to begin a period of play. **b** (+ *out*) to win a set or match after serving for and winning the final game. ✳ **if memory serves** if I remember correctly. **serve a purpose** to assist in performing a task or achieving a goal. **serve somebody right** to be the fate or punishment that somebody deserves. **serve somebody's turn** to be useful to somebody. [Middle English *serven* via Old French *servir* from Latin *servire* to be a slave, serve, from *servus* slave, servant]

serve² *noun* the act of hitting the ball or shuttlecock to begin a period of play in tennis, badminton, and similar games.

server *noun* **1** the player who serves, e.g. in tennis. **2a** something used in serving food or drink: *a pair of salad servers.* **b** somebody who serves food or drink. **3** somebody who assists the priest at Mass. **4** a computer or program that connects users in a network to a centralized resource or store of data.

servery *noun* (*pl* **serveries**) a room, counter, or hatch, e.g. in a public house, from which food is served.

serve up *verb trans* **1** to serve (food) at a table. **2** *informal* to offer or supply (something): *They're serving up the same old excuses.*

Servian /'suhvi-ən/ *adj and noun archaic* = SERB.

service¹ /'suhvis/ *noun* **1a** (*often* + *to*) work or duty carried out for a person, organization, country, etc, *esp* when considered as contributing to the welfare of others rather than being for personal gain. **b** help, use, or benefit: *These shoes have given me good service.* **2** an operation, system, or facility designed to meet a public need: *a bus service.* **3a** the work of attending to customers in a shop, bar, hotel, etc, or the manner in which this work is done: *The service in the restaurant was dreadful.* **b** employment as a servant: *I entered his lordship's service as a boy of sixteen.* **c** (*used before a noun*) used in serving or delivering: *a service entrance.* **4a** (*in pl*) useful work that does not produce a tangible commodity. **b** (*used before a noun*) carrying out useful work of this kind: *the service sector.* **5** a helpful action; a favour: *You did him a service by warning him about the inspection.* **6a** a religious ceremony, *esp* in a Christian church, or a meeting for worship. **b** the form prescribed for a particular religious ceremony: *the burial service.* **7** a routine operation carried out to inspect, repair, and maintain a machine or motor vehicle. **8** a set of articles for a particular use; *specif* a set of matching tableware for serving a specified meal, food, or drink: *a 24-piece dinner service.* **9** an administrative division, e.g. of a government or business: *the consular service.* **10a** (*usu in pl*) any of a nation's military forces, e.g. the army or navy. **b** (*used before a noun*) belonging or relating to the armed forces: *service personnel.* **11** *chiefly Brit* (*in pl, but sometimes treated as sing.*) facilities, e.g. restaurants, toilets, and petrol stations, provided for the users of a motorway. **12** (*in pl*) utilities, e.g. gas, water, sewage, or electricity, available or connected to a building. **13** a serve in tennis, badminton, etc. **14** the act of delivering a legal writ, process, or summons to somebody as prescribed by law. **15** the act of copulating with a female animal. ✳ **be at somebody's service** to be available, whenever required, to help somebody or to be used by them. **be of service to somebody** to help, benefit, or be of use to somebody. **in service 1** said of a machine or vehicle: currently being used or operated. **2** said of a person: working as a domestic servant. **out of service 1** not currently being used or operated. **2** broken down. [Middle English via Old French from Latin *servitium* condition of a slave, body of slaves, from *servus* slave]

service² *verb trans* **1** to provide a service or services to (somebody or something). **2** to carry out routine repairs and maintenance on

(a machine or vehicle). **3** to meet interest payments on and provide for the eventual repayment of the capital of (a debt). **4** said of a male animal: to copulate with (a female). ➤➤ **servicer** *noun.*

service³ *noun* either of two species of Old World trees of the rose family resembling the mountain ash but with larger flowers and larger edible fruits: *Sorbus domestica* and *Sorbus torminalis.* [Old English *syrfe* from Latin *sorbus*]

serviceable *adj* **1** fit and ready to use; in working order. **2** giving good service; durable. ➤➤ **serviceability** /-'biliti/ *noun,* **serviceableness** *noun,* **serviceably** *adv.*

service area *noun chiefly Brit* an area at the side of a motorway or other road where there are various facilities, e.g. toilets, restaurants, and a filling station, for travellers.

serviceberry /'suhvisb(ə)ri/ *noun* (*pl* **serviceberries**) any of numerous species of N American trees and shrubs of the rose family with showy white flowers and edible purple or red fruits: genus *Amelanchier.*

service book *noun* a book containing forms of worship used in religious services.

service box *noun* a rectangular area 1.6m (5ft 3in.) square on each side of a squash court, inside which a player must stand to serve.

service car *noun NZ* a coach or bus.

service charge *noun* a percentage of a bill added to the total to pay for service, usu instead of a tip.

service flat *noun Brit* a flat with a charge for certain services, e.g. cleaning, included in its rent.

service industry *noun* an industry that does work or provides goods or materials for other industries, but does not manufacture anything.

service line *noun* a line on the court in various games, e.g. tennis, marking the boundary of the area within which the ball must land when it is served.

serviceman *noun* (*pl* **servicemen**) **1** a male member of the armed forces. **2** *chiefly NAmer* somebody employed to repair or maintain equipment.

service mark *noun* a mark or logo used to identify a particular type of commercial service.

service module *noun* a spacecraft module that contains propellant tanks, fuel cells, and the main rocket engine.

service provider *noun* a company that provides computer users with access to the Internet.

service road *noun* a small road that usu runs parallel to a major road and provides access to the houses, shops, etc along it.

service station *noun* a commercial establishment at the roadside that sells petrol, oil, etc and sometimes carries out maintenance and repair work on vehicles.

servicewoman *noun* (*pl* **servicewomen**) **1** a female member of the armed forces. **2** *chiefly NAmer* a woman employed to repair or maintain equipment.

serviette /suhvi'et/ *noun chiefly Brit* a table napkin. [French *serviette* from *servir*: see SERVE¹]

servile /'suhviel/ *adj* **1** slavishly or unctuously submissive; abject or obsequious. **2** characteristic of or befitting a slave or a menial: *a servile task.* ➤➤ **servilely** *adv,* **servility** /suh'viliti/ *noun.* [Middle English from Latin *servilis,* from *servus* slave]

serving *noun* a single portion of food or drink; a helping.

servitor /'suhvita/ *noun archaic or formal* a servant. [Middle English *servitour* via French from late Latin *servitor* from Latin *servire*: see SERVE¹]

servitude /'suhvityoohd/ *noun* **1** the state of being a slave or completely subject to somebody or something else. **2** a right by which something owned by one person is subject to a specified use or enjoyment by another. [Middle English via French from Latin *servitudo* slavery, from *servus* slave]

servo /'suhvoh/ *noun* (*pl* **servos**) a servomotor or servomechanism.

servomechanism /'suhvohmekəniz(ə)m/ *noun* an automatic device that enables a large power output to be controlled by relatively small power input, as in the power-assisted steering and braking systems of vehicles. [*servo-* as in SERVOMOTOR + MECHANISM]

servomotor /'suhvohmohtə/ *noun* a motor that provides the power in a servomechanism. [French *servo-moteur* from Latin *servus* slave, servant + -O- + French *moteur* motor]

sesame /'sesəmi/ *noun* **1** a plant grown in tropical Asia that produces small flattish seeds used as a source of oil and as a flavouring agent: *Sesamum indicum*. **2** the seeds of the sesame plant. [alteration of *sesam*, *sesama*, via Latin *sesamum*, *sesama*, from Greek *sēsamon*, *sēsamē*, of Semitic origin]

sesamoid /'sesəmoyd/ *noun* a small round mass of bone or cartilage in a tendon, *esp* at a joint or bony prominence. ➤➤ **sesamoid** *adj*. [Greek *sēsamoeidēs* resembling sesame seed, from *sēsamon*: see SESAME]

sesqui- *comb. form* forming words, with the meanings: **1** one and a half times: *sesquicentennial*. **2** *dated* containing three atoms or equivalents of a specified element or radical, *esp* combined with two of another: *sesquioxide*. [Latin *sesqui-* one and a half, literally 'and a half', from *semis* a half (from SEMI-) + *-que* and]

sesquicentenary /,seskwisen'teenəri, -'tenəri/ *noun* (*pl* **sesquicentenaries**) = SESQUICENTENNIAL.

sesquicentennial /,seskwisen'teni-əl/ *noun* a 150th anniversary, or its celebration. ➤➤ **sesquicentennial** *adj*.

sesquipedalian /,seskwipə'dayli-ən/ *adj* **1** many-syllabled. **2** fond of or characterized by the use of long words, usu to excess: *a sesquipedalian style*. [Latin *sesquipedalis* a foot and a half long, from SESQUI- + *ped-*, *pes* foot]

sessile /'sesiel/ *adj* **1** attached directly by the base without a stalk: *a sessile leaf*. **2** permanently attached or established and not free to move about: *sessile polyps*. ➤➤ **sessility** /se'siliti/ *noun*. [Latin *sessilis* relating to sitting, from *sedēre* to sit]

sessile oak *noun* = DURMAST.

session /'sesh(ə)n/ *noun* **1** a period devoted to a particular activity, *esp* by a group of people: *a recording session*. **2a** a meeting or series of meetings of a body such as a court or council for the transaction of business; a sitting. **b** the period between the first meeting of a legislative or judicial body and its final adjournment. **3** the period of the day or year during which a school conducts classes. **4** the governing body of a Presbyterian congregation consisting of the minister and elders. ➤➤ **sessional** *adj*. [Middle English via French from Latin *session-*, *sessio*, act of sitting, from *sedēre* to sit]

sesterce /'sestuhs/ *noun* an ancient Roman coin worth one quarter of a denarius. [Latin *sestertius* two and a half times as great (from its being equal orig to two and a half asses: see AS⁴), from *semis* half (from SEMI-) + *tertius* third]

sestertium /se'stuhti-əm/ *noun* (*pl* **sestertia** /-ti-ə/) a monetary unit in ancient Rome worth 1000 sesterces. [Latin *sestertium*, genitive pl of *sestertius* (in the phrase *milia sestertium* thousands of sesterces)]

sestertius /se'stuhti-əs/ *noun* (*pl* **sestertii** /-ti-ie/) = SESTERCE.

sestet /ses'tet/ *noun* a group of six lines of verse, *esp* the last six lines of a sonnet. [Italian *sestetto*, from *sesto* sixth, from Latin *sextus*, from *sex* six]

sestina /se'steenə/ *noun* a lyrical poem consisting of six six-line stanzas and a three-line ENVOY¹ (short final stanza), in which the same six words are used, each time in a different order, to end the lines of all the stanzas. [Italian *sestina*, from *sesto*: see SESTET]

set¹ /set/ *verb* (**setting**, *past tense and past part.* **set**) ➤ *verb trans* **1a** to put (something) in a particular position, *esp* to place it carefully or deliberately: *They set the ladder against the wall*. **b** to make (something) fixed and rigid: *We set the fence posts in concrete*. **2** to place (one person or thing) in relation to another: *She set duty before pleasure*. **3a** to put (something or somebody) into a specified condition: *Thank you for setting my mind at rest*; *The slaves were set free*. **b** to put (somebody or something) into activity or motion, or start them doing something: *The remark set me thinking*. **4** to decide on and fix (an amount, time, etc): *Have you set a date for the wedding?* **5** to create or provide (something) as a model or challenge: *You must set an example to your brothers and sisters*; *She's just set a new record for the 5000 metres*. **6a** to give somebody (a task) to perform. **b** to prescribe (a course, text, etc) for study by students at a certain level or for a particular examination. **7** to instruct (somebody) to do something: *They set us to collect wood for the fire*. **8a** to prepare or adjust (a device) ready for use: *I'll set the alarm for seven o'clock*. **b** to prepare (a table) for a meal. **9** to bring (something) into contact with something else: *I need to marshal my thoughts before I set pen to paper*; *She set a match to the fire*. **10a** to describe (an event, story, etc) as taking place in a specified historical period or geographical location. **b** to provide music or instrumentation for (a song, poem, etc). **11** to plant (seedlings). **12** to unfurl (a sail) so that it catches the wind. **13a** to arrange (type) for printing. **b** to put (text) into type or its equivalent. **14a** to fix (the hair) in a desired style by waving, curling, or arranging it, usu while wet. **b** to restore (a bone or limb) to its normal position when dislocated or fractured. **15a** to fix (a gem) in a border of metal: *this precious stone set in the silver sea* — Shakespeare. **b** (*usu* + with) to cover or surround (something) with decorative objects; to stud or dot (something): *a clear sky set with stars*. **16a** to bend the tooth points of (a saw) alternately in opposite directions. **b** to sink (the head of a nail) below the surface. **17** to cause (e.g. fruit) to develop. **18a** to divide (a year group of pupils) into sets. **b** to teach (a school subject) by dividing the pupils into sets. ➤ *verb intrans* **1** said of the sun, moon, etc: to pass below the horizon; to go down. **2a** to become solid or thickened by chemical or physical alteration: *The cement sets rapidly*. **b** said of a broken bone: to become whole again by knitting together. **3** used as a command to runners to put themselves into the starting position immediately before the starting signal for a race. **4** said of fruit or seeds: to develop, usu as a result of pollination. **5** to have or take a specified direction in motion; to flow or tend: *The wind was setting south*. **6** said of a gun dog: to indicate the position of game by crouching or pointing. **7** to dance face to face with somebody in a square dance: *Set to your partner and turn*. **8** *chiefly dialect* to sit. ✳ **set about 1** to start on (a task or undertaking) with determination. **2** to attack (somebody) physically or verbally. **set on 1** to attack (somebody) violently. **2** to urge (a person or an animal) to attack or pursue somebody: *He set his dog on the intruders*. **3** to incite (somebody) to action. **set sail** to begin a voyage. **set the pace** to determine the speed or rate which others must match to keep up. **set to work** to start to do something: *He set to work to undermine their confidence*. [Old English *settan*]

set² *adj* **1** arranged or laid down in advance, or fixed by authority; prescribed or specified: *There are three set books for the examination*. **2** (*usu* + on/upon) resolutely intending to do something; determined: *She's set on going*. **3** said of a meal: consisting of a specified combination of dishes available at a fixed price. **4** unchanging and immovable or rigid: *a set frown*. **5** ready: *We're all set for an early morning start*. **6** conventional or stereotyped: *Her speech was full of set phrases*. ✳ **set in one's ways** reluctant to change one's habits. [Middle English *sett*, past part. of *setten* to set, from Old English *settan*]

set³ *noun* **1** a number of things, usu of the same kind, that belong or are used together or that form a unit: *a chess set*; *a good set of teeth*. **2** (*treated as sing. or pl*) a group of people associated by common interests: *the smart set*. **3** (*treated as sing. or pl*) a group of pupils of roughly equal ability in a particular subject who are taught together: compare STREAM¹ (5), BAND¹ (7). **4** an apparatus made up of electronic components assembled so as to function as a unit: *a television set*. **5** a collection of mathematical elements, e.g. numbers or points. **6** in tennis and similar sports, a division of a match comprising a number of games. **7a** the artificial scenery used for a play or for a particular scene in a play. **b** the place where a scene from a film is shot. **8** a session of jazz or rock music, usu followed by an intermission, or the music played during such a session. **9** the basic formation in a country dance or square dance. **10a** a young plant or rooted cutting ready for transplanting. **b** a small bulb, corm, or tuber used for propagation: *onion sets*. **11** the manner in which something is positioned; bearing or posture: *the graceful set of his head*. **12** direction of flow: *the set of the wind*. **13a** a mental inclination, tendency, or habit. **b** predisposition to act in a certain way in response to an anticipated stimulus or situation. **14** the fact of becoming firm or solid. **15** a way of styling the hair by curling or waving. **16** permanent change of form due to repeated or excessive stress. **17** the amount of deviation from a straight line; *specif* the degree to which the teeth of a saw have been set. **18** = SETT. ✳ **make a dead set at** *Brit* to try very hard to win the attention and affection of (somebody).

Word history

partly from SET¹, partly from Middle English via French from Latin *secta*: see SECT. As a general rule the senses referring to the way something is arranged or inclined came from the former, and senses referring to a group of people or things from the latter. Some dictionaries treat this word as two separate nouns, but as they seldom agree on which senses come from each source it seems more sensible to accept that the two have become inextricably entwined.

seta /'seetə/ *noun* (*pl* **setae** /'seetee/) a slender bristle or similar part of an animal or plant. ➤➤ **setaceous** /si'tayshəs/ *adj*, **setal** *adj*. [Latin *saeta, seta* bristle]

set apart *verb trans* (*often* + from) to make (somebody or something) noticeable or outstanding.

set aside *verb trans* **1** to put (something) to one side; to discard (something). **2** to keep or save (something) for a particular purpose. **3** to annul or override (a verdict or decision).

set-aside *noun* **1** an agricultural policy whereby farmers are paid to take some of their land out of production, e.g. by leaving it fallow or by turning it to forestry, thus reducing agricultural surpluses. **2** the land so left unused. ➤➤ **set-aside** *adj*.

setback *noun* **1** something that causes problems or delays and holds up the progress of something or somebody. **2** a recessed part in a wall or building. **3** the placing of a building, or part of a building, behind the building line to allow ventilation and light to nearby areas.

set back *verb trans* **1** to prevent or hinder the progress of (somebody or something), to impede or delay. **2** *informal* to cost (somebody) a specified amount.

set by *verb trans* to put (something) aside for future use.

set down *verb trans* **1** to place (something or somebody) at rest on a surface or on the ground. **2a** to allow (a passenger) to alight from a vehicle. **b** to land (an aircraft) on the ground or water. **3** to record (something) in writing: *You could, for a need, study a speech of some dozen or sixteen lines which I would set down … could you not?* — Shakespeare. **4a** (+ as) to regard or consider (somebody or something) in a particular way: *They set him down as a liar.* **b** (+ to) to attribute or ascribe (something): *She set her success down to sheer perseverance.*

set forth *verb trans* to give an account or description of (something). ➤ *verb intrans* to start on a journey.

SETI /'seti/ *abbr* search for extraterrestrial intelligence.

set in *verb intrans* **1** said of something unwelcome: to become established: *The rot has set in.* **2** said of the wind or tide: to blow or flow towards the shore. **3** to insert (something); *esp* to stitch (a sleeve) into a garment.

set-in *adj* cut separately and stitched in: *set-in sleeves.*

setline *noun* *NAmer* a long heavy fishing line to which several hooks are attached in series.

set off *verb intrans* to start on a journey. ➤ *verb trans* **1a** to cause (somebody or something) to start doing something. **b** to cause (a bomb, firework, etc) to explode. **2a** to put (something) into relief, or show it up by contrast. **b** to adorn, embellish, or enhance (something or somebody). **3** *chiefly NAmer* to compensate for or offset (something). **4** in accountancy, to regard a credit on (an account) as cancelling out a debit in another.

set-off *noun* **1** something that sets off another thing; a contrast: **2** something that counterbalances or compensates for something else. **3** the discharge of a debt by setting against it a sum owed by the creditor to the debtor. **4** in printing, the accidental transference of ink from one sheet to another.

setose /'seetohs/ *adj* covered with setae; bristly. [Latin *setosus, saetosus*, from *seta, saeta* bristle]

set out *verb intrans* to start on a course, journey, or career. ➤ *verb trans* **1** to state or describe (something) at length. **2** to begin (to do something) with a definite purpose. **3a** to arrange and present (something) graphically or systematically. **b** to create or construct (something) according to a plan or design.

set piece *noun* **1** a work of art, literature, etc, or part of one, that has a formal pattern or style. **2** any of various moves in football or rugby, e.g. a corner kick or free kick, by which the ball is put back into play after a stoppage. **3** an arrangement of fireworks that forms a pattern or picture while burning.

set point *noun* in tennis, etc, a point that will enable one player or side to win the set, or a situation in which one player or side can win the set by winning the next point.

setscrew *noun* **1** a screw that is tightened to prevent relative movement between parts, e.g. of a machine, and keep them in a set position. **2** a screw that serves to adjust a machine.

set square *noun* *chiefly Brit* a flat triangular instrument with one right angle and two other angles of known size, usu 45° or 30° and 60°, used to mark out or test angles.

Setswana /se'tswahnə/ *noun* = TSWANA (2). [the Tswana name]

sett /set/ *noun* **1** the burrow of a badger. **2** a usu rectangular block of stone or wood formerly used for paving streets. **3a** the particular pattern of squares and stripes used for a tartan. **b** a square in a tartan. [alteration of SET³]

settee /se'tee/ *noun* a long upholstered seat with a back and usu two arms for seating more than one person; a sofa. [alteration of SETTLE²]

setter *noun* a large gundog trained to point on finding game.

set theory *noun* a branch of mathematics or of symbolic logic that deals with the nature and relations of sets.

setting *noun* **1a** the background or surroundings of an object or event. **b** the time and place in which the action of a literary, dramatic, or cinematic work is supposed to occur. **2** the scenery used in a theatrical or film production. **3** the position on a scale, dial, etc at which a control mechanism is set and that governs the level at which a machine operates. **4** the music composed for a text, e.g. a poem. **5** = PLACE SETTING. **6** the frame in which a gem is mounted.

settle¹ /'setl/ *verb trans* **1** to find an answer to or reach agreement about (a difficulty, disagreement, etc). **2** to pay (an account, debt, etc). **3** to place (somebody or something) firmly or comfortably: *He settled himself in an armchair.* **4a** to provide (somebody) with a place to live in a particular area. **b** to supply (an area) with inhabitants; to colonize (a place). **5a** to cause (something) to sink and become compacted: *The rain settled the dust.* **b** to clarify (a liquid) by causing the sediment to sink. **6a** to make (somebody or something) less anxious, agitated, uncomfortable, or disturbed; to calm (one's nerves). **b** *dated* to make (somebody) subdued or well-behaved: *One word from the referee settled him.* **7** (+ on) to bestow (property or money) on somebody for their lifetime by means of a legal document such as a will: *She settled her estate on her son.* **8** to put (one's affairs) in order or to make a final disposition of them. ➤ *verb intrans* **1a** to come to rest. **b** to descend gradually to the ground or onto or over an area or surface. **2a** said of a building, the ground, etc: to sink slowly to a lower level; to subside. **b** said of a ship: to become lower in the water, usu before sinking. **3** said of a liquid: to become clearer by depositing sediment or scum. **4a** to become established in a specified place, or as a permanent condition: *His mood settled into apathy.* **b** to establish a home or a colony in a place. **5a** (*often* + down) to become calm or orderly. **b** (*usu* + down) to adopt an ordered or stable lifestyle. **6a** (+ on) to make a decision or choice regarding something: *Have they settled on a name for the baby yet?* **b** (+ for) to be content with or accept something less than one originally hoped for. **7a** (*usu* + up/with) to pay what is owing to or adjust accounts with somebody. **b** to end a legal dispute by the agreement of both parties, without court action. ✳ **settle down to** to begin to do (something) in a concentrated and purposeful way. [Old English *setlan* from *setl* seat, SETTLE²]

settle² *noun* a wooden bench with arms, a high solid back, and often an enclosed base which can be used as a chest. [Old English *setl* seat]

settle in *verb intrans* to become comfortably established in a new environment. ➤ *verb trans* to help (somebody) to become comfortably established.

settlement *noun* **1** the act or process of settling or of settling something. **2** an agreement resolving differences: *Management and unions have reached a settlement.* **3a** a place or region where a new community has been recently established. **b** a small village, *esp* an isolated one. **4a** the act of bestowing property, money, etc on somebody, by means of a deed or will. **b** the sum, property, or income secured to a person by such a settlement. **5** a building providing various community services, e.g. educational, recreational, and cultural facilities, in an underprivileged area.

settler *noun* somebody who settles in an area that was previously uninhabited or sparsely inhabited.

settlings *pl noun* sediment; dregs.

settlor *noun* somebody who makes a legal settlement, *esp* of money or property.

set to *verb intrans* **1** to make an eager or determined start on a job or activity. **2** to begin fighting.

set-to *noun* (*pl* **set-tos**) *informal* a usu brief and vigorous conflict.

set up *verb trans* **1a** to raise (something) into position; to erect (something). **b** to assemble (something) and prepare it for use or operation. **2a** to bring (something) into existence; to create, found, or institute (something). **b** to make the preparations and plans for (a meeting, event, etc); to organize (something). **c** to put forward (an idea, theory, etc) for acceptance. **d** to cause or bring about (a feeling, state, etc): *These issues can set up strong personal tensions between party members.* **3** to produce or give voice to (a loud noise). **4a** (*often* + as) to place (somebody) in a high office or powerful position. **b** (*often* + as/in) to provide (somebody) with an independent livelihood. **c** to bring or restore (somebody) to health or success. **d** (*usu* + for/with) to provide (somebody) with what is necessary or useful: *We're well set up with logs for the winter.* **5** *informal* to cause (somebody) to appear guilty; to incriminate or frame (somebody). ➤ *verb intrans* (*often* + as/in) to start in business. ✳ **set oneself up as** to claim to be (something). **set up house** to live together as a household. **set up shop** to establish one's business.

set-up *noun* **1** the way in which something is organized or arranged. **2** a particular arrangement of apparatus required to perform a task. **3** *informal* an attempt to incriminate or deceive somebody. **4** *chiefly NAmer, informal* a contest with a prearranged outcome.

seven /'sev(ə)n/ *noun* **1** the number 7, or the quantity represented by it. **2** something having seven parts or members. **3a** the age of 7 years. **b** the hour five hours before midday or midnight. **4** (*in pl, but treated as sing. or pl*) a rugby game played with teams of seven players each. ➤ **seven** *adj*, **sevenfold** *adj and adv*. [Old English *seofon*]

seven seas *pl noun* all the oceans of the world.

seventeen /sev(ə)n'teen/ *adj and noun* the number 17, or the quantity represented by it. ➤ **seventeenth** *adj and noun*. [Old English *seofontiēne*, from *seofon* SEVEN + *tiēne* ten]

seventh *adj and noun* **1** denoting a person or thing having the position in a sequence corresponding to the number seven. **2** one of seven equal parts of something. **3a** in music, an interval of seven degrees of a diatonic scale, or the combination of two notes at such an interval. **b** = SUBTONIC. ➤ **seventhly** *adv*. [Old English *seofotha*, from *seofon* SEVEN + -TH[1]]

Seventh-Day Adventist *noun* a member of a group of Adventist Christians who advocate or observe Saturday as the Christian Sabbath.

seventh heaven *noun* a state of supreme rapture or bliss: *She was in seventh heaven when she found she was pregnant.* [because the seventh is the highest of the seven heavens of Muslim and cabalist doctrine]

seventy *adj and noun* (*pl* **seventies**) **1** the number 70, or the quantity represented by it. **2** (*in pl*) the numbers 70 to 79; *specif* a range of temperatures, ages, or dates within a century represented by these numbers. ➤ **seventieth** *adj and noun*. [Old English *seofontig*, short for *hundseofontig* group of seventy, from *hund* hundred + *seofon* seven + -*tig* group of ten]

seventy-eight *noun* a gramophone record that plays at 78 revolutions per minute.

Seven Wonders of the World *pl noun* the seven structures considered to be the most magnificent of the ancient world.

seven-year itch *noun* marital discontent allegedly leading to infidelity after about seven years of marriage.

sever /'sevə/ *verb trans* (**severed, severing**) **1a** to divide (something) by cutting it. **b** to remove (a part or portion) by or as if by cutting. **2** to put or keep apart (two or more things or people); to separate: *Here are severed lips, parted with sugar breath* — Shakespeare; *Lover and friend thou hast removed and severed from me far* — Milton. **3** to break off or terminate (a relationship or connection): *The two countries have severed economic links.* ➤ **severable** *adj*. [Middle English *severen* via early French *severer* from Latin *separare*: see SEPARATE[1]]

several[1] /'sev(ə)rəl/ *adj* **1** more than two or a few, but fewer than many: *several hundred times*. **2** *formal* separate or distinct from one another; respective: *They are all specialists in their several fields.* **3** relating separately to each individual involved: *a several judgment.* [Middle English in the sense 'separate', 'different', via Anglo-French *several* from medieval Latin *separalis*, from Latin *separ* separate, back-formation from *separare*: see SEPARATE[1]]

several[2] *pronoun* (*treated as pl*) an indefinite number more than two and fewer than many: *several of the guests.*

severally *adv formal* each in turn; separately or singly: *Having thus addressed you severally, I conclude by addressing you collectively* — Thomas Paine.

severalty *noun* (*pl* **severalties**) **1** possession of property by an individual in his or her own right, as opposed to joint possession: *tenants in severalty.* **2** *formal* the quality or state of being several or distinct. [early French *severalte*, from Anglo-French *severalté*, from *several*: see SEVERAL[1]]

severance /'sevərəns/ *noun* **1a** the act of separating something by cutting or of cutting something off. **b** the state of being separated from something or somebody. **2** the act of putting an end to a connection or relationship with somebody. **3a** discharge from employment. **b** *informal* = SEVERANCE PAY.

severance pay *noun* an amount payable to an employee on termination of employment.

severe /si'viə/ *adj* **1** having a stern expression or character; austere. **2** rigorous in judgment, requirements, or punishment; stringent. **3** strongly critical or condemnatory; censorious. **4** sober or restrained in decoration or manner; plain. **5** marked by harsh or extreme conditions: *severe winters.* **6** requiring much effort; arduous: *a severe test.* **7** having a powerful and dangerous effect; serious; grave: *severe depression.* ➤ **severely** *adv*, **severity** /si'veriti/ *noun*. [French *sévère* from Latin *severus* grave, serious, strict]

Seville orange /se'vil/ *noun* a reddish orange fruit with a bitter rind and sour flesh, used *esp* for making marmalade. [named after *Seville*, a province and city in SW Spain famous for its oranges]

Sèvres /'sevrə/ *noun* an elaborately decorated fine porcelain. [named after *Sèvres*, the town in France near Paris where it is made]

sew /soh/ *verb trans* (*past tense* **sewed**, *past part.* **sewn** /sohn/ *or* **sewed**) **1a** to unite, fasten, or attach (something) by stitches made with a needle and thread. **b** to close or enclose (something) by sewing: *She sewed the money into the lining of her dress.* **2** to make or mend (something) by sewing. [Old English *sīwian*]

sewage /'s(y)ooij/ *noun* waste matter carried off by sewers.

sewage farm *noun* a place where sewage is treated, *esp* to be made into fertilizer.

sewer[1] /'s(y)ooə/ *noun* an artificial usu underground drain or pipe used to carry off waste matter, *esp* excrement, from houses, towns, etc and surface water from roads and paved areas. [Middle English from early French *esseweur, seweur*, from *essewer* to drain, ultimately from EX-[1] + Latin *aqua* water]

sewer[2] /'soh·ə/ *noun* somebody who or something that sews.

sewerage /'s(y)ooərij/ *noun* **1** a system of sewers. **2** the removal and disposal of surface water by sewers. **3** sewage.

sewing /'soh·ing/ *noun* **1** the activity or work of somebody who sews something. **2** work, such as a piece or pieces of cloth or clothing, that has been or is to be sewn.

sewn /sohn/ *verb* past part. of SEW.

sew up *verb trans* **1** to mend or close (e.g. a hole, opening, or tear) by sewing. **2** *informal* to bring (something) to a successful or satisfactory conclusion: *We managed to sew up the pay negotiations.* ✳ **have something sewn up 1** to be certain of winning or achieving something. **2** to have complete and exclusive control over something.

sex[1] /seks/ *noun* **1** either of two categories, male or female, into which organisms are divided on the basis of their reproductive role. **2** the structural, functional, and behavioural characteristics that are involved in reproduction and that distinguish males and females. **3a** = SEXUAL INTERCOURSE. **b** sexual activity in general. **4** *euphem* the genitals. **5** (*used before a noun*). **a** to do with sexual function and activity: *sex drive.* **b** based on differences between the sexes: *sex discrimination.* **6** the biological process of recombination of genetic material. [Middle English from Latin *sexus*]

Usage note

sex *and* gender See note at GENDER.

sex[2] *verb trans* **1** to identify the sex of (a young animal). **2** *informal* (+ up) to arouse (somebody) sexually.

sex- *or* **sexi-** *comb. form* forming words with the meaning: six: *sexivalent; sexpartite.* [Latin *sex* six]

sexagenarian /,seksəji'neəri·ən/ *noun* a person between 60 and 69 years old. ➤ **sexagenarian** *adj*. [Latin *sexagenarius* of or containing 60, 60 years old, from *sexageni* 60 each, from *sexaginta* 60]

Sexagesima /seksə'jesimə/ *noun* the second Sunday before Lent. [Latin *Sexagesima*, fem of *sexagesimus* 60th, from *sexaginta* 60; because it falls 60 days before Easter]

sexagesimal *adj* relating to or based on the number 60. [Latin *sexagesimus*: see SEXAGESIMA]

sex-and-shopping *adj* denoting a type of novel in which interest centres on graphic descriptions of the sexual experiences of the main character, usu a woman, and on the various upmarket brand names mentioned as contributing to her lifestyle.

sex appeal *noun* sexual attractiveness.

sex bomb *noun informal* a person, *esp* a woman, with extraordinary sex appeal.

sexcentenary /seksen'teenəri, -'tenəri/ *noun* (*pl* **sexcentenaries**) the 600th anniversary of something, or its celebration. ➤➤ **sexcentenary** *adj*. [from Latin *sexcenteni* 600 each, from *sexcenti* 600]

sex chromosome *noun* a chromosome concerned directly with the inheritance of male or female sex.

sexed *adj* having sex, sex appeal, or sexual desires, *esp* to a specified degree: *highly sexed*.

sex hormone *noun* a hormone that affects the growth or function of the reproductive organs or the development of secondary sex characteristics, e.g. facial hair in men.

sexi- *comb. form* see SEX-.

sexism *noun* **1** a belief that sex determines a person's intrinsic capacities and role in society. **2** discrimination on the basis of sex; *esp* prejudice against women on the part of men. ➤➤ **sexist** *adj and noun*.

sex kitten *noun informal* a woman who makes a display of her sex appeal.

sexless *adj* **1** lacking sexuality or sexual intercourse: *sexless marriage*. **2** lacking sex appeal or the sexual urge: *Because Mildred was indifferent to him he had thought her sexless* — Somerset Maugham.

sex life *noun* a person's sexual activity and relationships.

sex-linked *adj* **1** said of a gene: located on a non-homologous region of a pair of XY chromosomes. **2** said of an inheritable characteristic, e.g. colour blindness: determined by a sex-linked gene and therefore much commoner in one sex than in the other. ➤➤ **sex-linkage** *noun*.

sex object *noun* a person regarded exclusively as a means of sexual satisfaction.

sexology /sek'soləji/ *noun* the study of human sexual behaviour. ➤➤ **sexological** /-'lojikl/ *adj*, **sexologist** *noun*.

sexpartite /'sekspahtiet/ *adj* **1** consisting of or divided into six parts. **2** involving six participants.

sexploitation /seksploy'taysh(ə)n/ *noun* the use of sex for commercial gain, *esp* in films and publications. [blend of SEX[1] and *exploitation*]

sexpot *noun informal* an extremely sexy person.

sex shop *noun* a shop that sells objects that contribute to sexual arousal or pleasure, pornographic books and magazines, etc.

sex symbol *noun* a famous person who embodies male or female sex appeal.

sext /sekst/ *noun* the fourth of the canonical hours, orig fixed for twelve noon. [Middle English *sexte* from late Latin *sexta (hora)* sixth hour of the day (counting from 6am), fem of *sextus* sixth, from *sex* six]

sextant /'sekstənt/ *noun* an instrument for measuring angles that is used, *esp* in navigation, to observe the altitudes of celestial bodies and so determine the observer's position on the earth's surface. [scientific Latin *sextant-, sextans* sixth part of a circle, from Latin, sixth part, from *sextus* sixth, from *sex* six]

sextet /sek'stet/ *noun* **1a** a group of six instruments, voices, or performers. **b** a musical composition for such a group. **2** (*treated as sing. or pl*) a group or set of six. [alteration of SESTET]

sextillion /sek'stilyən/ *noun* (*pl* **sextillions** or **sextillion**) **1** the number one followed by 21 zeros (10^{21}). **2** *Brit, dated* the number one followed by 36 zeros (10^{36}). [French *sextillion*, irreg from SEX- + -*illion* as in MILLION]

sextodecimo *noun* = SIXTEENMO.

sexton /'sekstən/ *noun* a church officer who takes care of the church property and is often also the gravedigger. [Middle English *secresteyn, sexteyn* via early French *secrestain* from medieval Latin *sacristanus*: see SACRISTAN]

sex tourism *noun* tourism that specifically aims to take advantage of less stringent laws or rules regarding sexual behaviour in foreign countries.

sextuple[1] /'sekstyoopl/ *adj* **1** being six times as much or as many. **2** having six units or members. ➤➤ **sextuple** *noun*. [prob from medieval Latin *sextuplus*, from Latin *sextus* sixth (from *sex* six) + -*plus* multiplied by]

sextuple[2] *verb trans and intrans* to become or make (something) six times as much or as many.

sextuplet /'sekstyooplit, sek'styoohplit/ *noun* **1** a combination of six of a kind. **2** any of six offspring born at one birth. **3** a group of six equal musical notes performed in the time ordinarily given to four of the same value. [medieval Latin *sextupius* (see SEXTUPLE[1]), on the pattern of such words as *triplet*]

sexual /'seksyoo(ə)l, 'seksh(ə)l/ *adj* **1** relating to or involving physical attraction and contact between individuals ultimately associated with the desire to reproduce. **2** associated with being a member of one or the other sex or with relations between the two sexes. *sexual conflict*. **3** said of reproduction: involving the fusion of male and female gametes (reproductive cells; see GAMETE). ➤➤ **sexually** *adv*. [late Latin *sexualis*, from Latin *sexus* SEX[1]]

sexual harassment *noun* repeated unwelcome physical contact or sexual suggestions and remarks directed at somebody, *esp* in the workplace.

sexual intercourse *noun* sexual activity with genital contact involving penetration, *esp* of the vagina by the penis.

sexualise *verb trans* see SEXUALIZE.

sexuality /seksyoo'aliti/ *noun* (*pl* **sexualities**) **1** the condition of having a sexual nature and experiencing sexual desires. **2** a person's sexual orientation, as a heterosexual or a homosexual, or sexual preferences. **3** sexual activity.

sexualize *or* **sexualise** *verb trans* to make (something) sexual; to endow (something) with a sexual character or significance.

sexually transmitted disease *noun* any disease that is transmitted through sexual intercourse, e.g. syphilis or gonorrhoea.

sexual selection *noun* an evolutionary process in which the preference by one sex of certain characteristics in the other leads to the preservation of these characteristics in the species.

sex worker *noun euphem* = PROSTITUTE[1].

sexy *adj* (**sexier, sexiest**) **1a** sexually attractive. **b** sexually suggestive or stimulating; erotic. **2** sexually aroused. **3a** capable of arousing interest and excitement; enjoyable: *History, to the French, is sexy in a way that just is not true here* — Daily Telegraph. **b** trendy or fashionable: *For the first time in anyone's memory, pensions are a sexy subject* — The Times. ➤➤ **sexily** *adv*, **sexiness** *noun*.

Seyfert galaxy /'seefət, 'siefət/ *noun* any of a class of spiral galaxies with small compact bright nuclei that send out radio waves. [named after Carl K *Seyfert* d.1960, US astronomer, who first called attention to them]

SF *abbr* **1** science fiction. **2** Sinn Fein.

sf *abbr* sforzando.

SFA *abbr* **1** Scottish Football Association. **2** *Brit, informal* sweet Fanny Adams.

SFO *abbr* Serious Fraud Office.

sforzando /sfawt'sandoh/ *adj and adv* said of a note or chord in music: to be performed with a heavy stress or accent. ➤➤ **sforzando** *noun*. [Italian *sforzando* using force, verbal noun and present part. of *sforzare* to force]

SG *abbr* **1** Solicitor General. **2** (*often* **sg**) specific gravity.

Sg *abbr* the chemical symbol for seaborgium.

sgd *abbr* signed.

SGML *abbr* standard generalized mark-up language; an international standard method used in publishing for representing texts in electronic form so that their formatting is not dependent on any one particular system.

SGP *abbr* Singapore (international vehicle registration).

sgraffito /sgra'feetoh/ *noun* (*pl* **sgraffiti** /-tee/) decoration in which parts of a surface layer, e.g. of plaster, are cut or scratched away to expose a different coloured background. [Italian *sgraffito*, past part. of *sgraffire* to scratch]

Sgt *abbr* Sergeant.

Sgt Maj. *abbr* Sergeant Major.

sh /sh/ *interj* used to request or command silence. [alteration of HUSH[1]]

Shabbat /sha'baht/ *noun* (*pl* **Shabbatim** /-tim/) the Jewish Sabbath. [Hebrew *shabbāth* sabbath, literally 'rest']

shabby /'shabi/ *adj* (**shabbier, shabbiest**) **1a** threadbare or faded from wear: *a shabby sofa*. **b** dilapidated; run-down: *a shabby district*. **2** dressed in worn or grubby clothes; seedy: *a shabby tramp*. **3** shameful or despicable: *What a shabby trick, driving off and leaving me to walk home!* ⟫⟫ **shabbily** *adv*, **shabbiness** *noun*. [from English *shab* scab, a low fellow, from Old English *sceabb*]

Shabuoth or **Shavuot** /shah'vooh·oth, -as/ *noun* a Jewish festival observed in May or June in commemoration of the revelation of the Ten Commandments at Mount Sinai (Exodus 19). [Hebrew *shābhū'ō'th* weeks]

shack /shak/ *noun* a small crudely built dwelling or shelter. [perhaps via Mexican Spanish *jacal* from Nahuatl *xacatli* wooden hut]

shackle[1] /'shakl/ *noun* **1** a pair of metal rings joined by a chain used to fasten a prisoner's hands or legs. **2** (*usu in pl*) something that restricts or prevents free action or expression. **3** a U-shaped piece of metal with a pin or bolt to close the opening. [Old English *sceacul*]

shackle[2] *verb trans* **1a** to bind (somebody) with shackles; to fetter. **b** to fasten or secure (something) with shackles. **2** to deprive (a person, group, organization, etc) of freedom of thought or action by means of restrictions or handicaps; to impede.

shack up *verb intrans informal* (*usu* + together/with) to live with and have a sexual relationship with somebody.

shad /shad/ *noun* (*pl* **shads** or *collectively* **shad**) any of several species of fishes of the herring family found in European and N American waters that have a relatively deep body and swim up rivers from the sea to breed: genera *Alosa* and *Caspialosa*. [Old English *sceadd*]

shaddock /'shadək/ *noun* **1** a very large usu pear-shaped citrus fruit closely related to the grapefruit but often with coarse dry pulp. Also called POMELO. **2** the tree that bears this fruit: *Citrus grandis*. [named after Captain *Shaddock*, the 17th-cent. English ship commander who brought the seed to Barbados]

shade[1] /shayd/ *noun* **1a** partial darkness caused when something stands in the path of rays of light. **b** a place sheltered, e.g. by foliage, from the direct heat and glare of the sun. **2** (*usu* **the shade**) relative obscurity or insignificance. **3a** something that intercepts or diffuses light or heat, e.g. a lampshade. **b** *chiefly NAmer* a window blind. **4** *informal* (*in pl*) sunglasses. **5** the reproduction of shade in a picture. **6** a particular variety of a colour, usu with respect to its darkness or lightness: *a shade of pink*. **7** a minute difference or amount: *the shades of meaning in a poem*. **8a** a transitory or illusory appearance. **b** = GHOST[1] (I). **9** *literary* (*in pl*) the shadows that gather as night falls. **10** (**the Shades**) *literary* the underworld; the home of the dead. **✳ a shade** a tiny bit; somewhat: *a shade too much salt*. **shades of** used to indicate that one is reminded of or struck by a resemblance to a specified person or thing: *And – shades of Robin Hood – he only did it to help the poor!* [Old English *sceadu*]

shade[2] *verb trans* **1a** to shelter or screen (somebody or something) by intercepting light or heat. **b** to cover (somebody or something) with a shade. **2** to darken or obscure (something) with or as if with a shadow. **3a** to represent the effect of shade on (something). **b** to mark (a picture or drawing) with shading or gradations of colour. **4** to change (something) by gradual transition. **5** to reduce (a price) by a small amount. **6** *informal* to win or have the advantage in (a contest) by a very narrow margin. ⟫ *verb intrans* (+ into) to pass by slight changes or imperceptible degrees.

shade tree *noun* a tree grown primarily to produce shade.

shading /'shayding/ *noun* lines, dots, or colour used to suggest three-dimensionality, shadow, or degrees of light and dark in a picture.

shadoof or **shaduf** /sha'doof/ *noun* a counterbalanced pole on a pivot used since ancient times, *esp* in Egypt, for raising water, e.g. for irrigation. [Arabic *shādūf*]

shadow[1] /'shadoh/ *noun* **1a** a dark shape made upon a surface by an object positioned between it and a source of light: *The trees cast their shadows on the wall*. **b** (*used before a noun*) used to cast a shadow on a screen, or in which shadows appear on a screen: *shadow puppet*. **2a** partial darkness caused when an opaque object cuts off the light from a light source: *The light from a stair window shone behind her, and her features were in shadow* — Christopher Morley. **b** a dark area

on an X-ray film. **c** a dark area resembling shadow: *He had shadows under his eyes from fatigue*. **3** a shaded or darker portion of a picture. **4** a small degree or portion; a trace: *without a shadow of doubt*. **5** a much reduced and weakened form of somebody or something; a vestige: *After his illness he was only a shadow of his former self*. **6** a source of gloom or disquiet: *His death cast a shadow on the festivities*. **7** a pervasive and often disabling influence: *He had to govern under the shadow of his mighty predecessor*. **8a** an inseparable companion or follower. **b** someone, e.g. a spy or detective, who follows and observes somebody else closely. **9a** (*used before a noun*) denoting the leaders of a parliamentary opposition who would constitute the cabinet if their party were in power: *the shadow cabinet*. **b** (*used before a noun*) denoting the member of the opposition who holds the equivalent position in the shadow cabinet to a particular government minister: *the shadow chancellor*. [Old English *sceaduw-, sceadu* shade, shadow]

shadow[2] *verb trans* **1** to cast a shadow over (something or somebody). **2** to follow (somebody) secretly; to keep (somebody) under surveillance. **3a** to follow and observe (an experienced worker) in order to learn how to do a job. **b** to be the equivalent in the shadow cabinet of (a particular government minister).

shadow-box *verb intrans* to box with an imaginary opponent, *esp* as a form of training. ⟫⟫ **shadow-boxing** *noun*.

shadowgraph /'shadohgrahf, -graf/ *noun* **1** an image made by casting the shadow of an object onto a surface or screen. **2** = RADIOGRAPH[1].

shadow play *noun* a theatrical performance in which the shadows of the performers, actors or puppets, are shown on a lighted screen.

shadowy *adj* (**shadowier, shadowiest**) **1a** of the nature of or resembling a shadow; insubstantial: *You are the only person I have to care for, and you are so shadowy. You're just an imaginary man I've made up* — Jean Webster. **b** scarcely perceptible; indistinct. **2** lying in or obscured by shadow: *deep shadowy interiors*. ⟫⟫ **shadowiness** *noun*.

shaduf /sha'doof/ *noun* see SHADOOF.

shady /'shaydi/ *adj* (**shadier, shadiest**) **1** producing or giving shade: *a shady tree*. **2** sheltered from the direct heat or light of the sun: *a shady spot*. **3** *informal*. **a** of questionable legality: *a shady deal*. **b** of doubtful integrity; disreputable: *She's a shady character*. ⟫⟫ **shadily** *adv*, **shadiness** *noun*.

shaft[1] /shahft/ *noun* **1a** the long narrow body of a spear, arrow, lance, or similar weapon, or the weapon itself. **b** the handle of a tool or implement, e.g. a hammer or golf club. **2** a usu cylindrical bar used to support rotating pieces in a machine or to transmit power or motion by rotation. **3a** a vertical or inclined opening leading underground to a mine, well, etc. **b** a vertical opening or passage through the floors of a building: *a lift shaft*. **4** a sharply delineated beam of light shining from an opening. **5** the cylindrical pillar between the capital and the base of a column. **6** in medieval architecture, a cylindrical or polygonal vertical member attached to a wall or flanking an aperture. **7** a pole; *specif* either of two poles between which a horse is hitched to a vehicle. **8** a scornful, satirical, or pithily critical remark; a barb. **9** the central stem of a feather. **10** the straight middle part of a long bone between the enlarged ends. **✳ get the shaft** *NAmer, informal* to be treated unfairly. **give somebody the shaft** *NAmer, informal* to treat somebody unfairly. [Old English *sceaft* handle, pole]

shaft[2] *verb trans* **1** *informal* to treat (somebody) unfairly, dishonestly, or harshly. **2** *Brit, coarse slang* said of a man: to have sexual intercourse with (somebody).

shafting *noun* an arrangement of shafts in a power-transmission system.

shag[1] /shag/ *noun* **1a** an unkempt or uneven tangled mass or covering, e.g. of hair. **b** long coarse or matted fibre or nap: *a shag pile carpet*. **2** a strong coarse tobacco cut into fine shreds. **3** a European bird related and similar to but smaller than the cormorant: *Phalacrocorax aristotelis*. [Old English *sceacga* rough or matted hair; (sense 3) perhaps from the bird's shaggy crest]

shag[2] *verb trans* (**shagged, shagging**) **1** *Brit, coarse slang* to have sexual intercourse with (somebody). **2** *Brit, slang* (+ out) to make (somebody) utterly exhausted. [origin unknown]

shag[3] *noun Brit, coarse slang* an act of sexual intercourse.

shagbark *noun* **1** a N American hickory tree with a grey shaggy outer bark that peels off in long strips. **2** the wood of this tree.

shaggy *adj* (**shaggier, shaggiest**) **1a** covered with or consisting of long, coarse, or matted hair. **b** said of a fabric: having a rough nap, texture, or surface. **2** unkempt. ➤➤ **shaggily** *adv*, **shagginess** *noun*.

shaggy-dog story *noun* a protracted and inconsequential funny story whose humour lies in the pointlessness or irrelevance of the conclusion.

shagreen /shaˈgreen/ *noun* **1** an untanned leather covered with small round granulations and usu dyed green. **2** the rough skin of various sharks and rays. ➤➤ **shagreen** *adj*. [by folk etymology from French *chagrin* untanned leather, from Turkish *sagr* horse's rump]

shah /shah/ *noun* a sovereign of Iran. ➤➤ **shahdom** *noun*. [Persian *shāh* king]

shahtoosh /shaˈtoohsh/ *noun* see SHATOOSH.

shake¹ /shayk/ *verb* (*past tense* **shook** /shook/, *past part.* **shaken** /ˈshaykən/) ➤ *verb intrans* **1** to move back and forth or up and down with short rapid movements. **2** to vibrate, *esp* from the impact of a blow or shock. **3** to tremble as a result of physical or emotional disturbance. **4** (*often* + on) to shake hands: *If you agree let's shake on it.* ➤ *verb trans* **1** to cause (something or somebody) to shake or tremble. **2** to brandish or flourish (something, e.g. one's fist), *esp* in a threatening manner. **3** to put (somebody or something) in a specified state by quick jerky movements: *He shook himself free from the man's grasp.* **4** to dislodge or eject (something) with quick jerky movements: *He shook the dust from the cloth.* **5** to cause (one's confidence, etc) to weaken: *It tends to shake one's faith in human nature.* **6** to shock or upset (somebody): *The news shook him.* **7** to clasp (hands) in greeting or farewell or to convey goodwill or agreement. ✲ **shake a leg** *informal* to hurry up. **shake one's head** to move one's head from side to side to indicate disagreement, denial, disapproval, etc. ➤➤ **shakable** *adj*, **shakeable** *adj*. [Old English *sceacan*]

shake² *noun* **1** an act of shaking: *She indicated her disapproval with a shake of the head.* **2** (*usu* **the shakes**) a condition of trembling, e.g. from chill or fever; *specif* DELIRIUM TREMENS. **3** a wavering, vibrating, or alternating motion caused by a blow or shock. **4** = TRILL¹ (1). **5** = MILK SHAKE. **6** *chiefly NAmer, informal* an earthquake. **7** *informal* a moment: *I'll be round in two shakes.* ✲ **a fair shake** *NAmer, informal* fair treatment. **no great shakes** *informal* not very good or proficient.

shakedown *noun* **1** a makeshift bed, e.g. one made up on the floor. **2** *NAmer* an act or instance of shaking somebody down; *esp* extortion. **3** *NAmer* a thorough search. **4a** *NAmer* a trial period or trial run intended to bring to light any faults in or problems with new equipment and to familiarize its users with it. **b** (*used before a noun*) designed to test a new ship, aircraft, etc and allow the crew to become familiar with it: *a shakedown cruise.*

shake down *verb intrans* **1** to settle for the night, *esp* in a makeshift bed. **2** to become comfortably established, *esp* in a new place or occupation. ➤ *verb trans* **1** to settle (something) by or as if by shaking it. **2** to submit (a piece of equipment) to a trial period. **3** *NAmer* to extort money from (somebody). **4** *NAmer* to make a thorough search of (somebody).

shake off *verb trans* **1** to free oneself from (something unwelcome): *Johnson's extraordinary facility of composition, when he shook off his constitutional indolence, and resolutely sat down to write, is admirably described* — James Boswell. **2** to escape from (a pursuer).

shaker *noun* **1** a container or utensil used to sprinkle or mix a substance by shaking: *a flour shaker; a cocktail shaker.* **2** (**Shaker**) a member of an American sect practising celibacy and a self-denying communal life. ➤➤ **Shaker** *adj*, **Shakerism** *noun*. [SHAKE¹ + -ER²; (sense 2) from a dance with shaking movements performed as part of worship]

Shakespearean¹ *or* **Shakespearian** /shaykˈspiəri·ən/ *adj* characteristic of the plays and poetry of the English dramatist and poet William Shakespeare (d.1616).

Shakespearean² *or* **Shakespearian** *noun* an authority on or devotee of Shakespeare and his works.

Shakespeareana *or* **Shakespeariana** /shaykˌspiəri·ahnə/ *pl noun* collected items by, about, or associated with Shakespeare.

shake up *verb trans* **1** to mix (something) by shaking it. **2** to shock or upset (somebody). **3** to rouse (somebody) from a state of inactivity or complacency. **4** *informal* to reorganize (something, e.g. a

company or institution) drastically. **5** to restore (e.g. a pillow or cushion) to its proper shape by shaking it.

shake-up *noun informal* an act of shaking up; *specif* an extensive and often drastic reorganization, e.g. of a company.

shako /ˈshahkoh, ˈshakoh/ *noun* (*pl* **shakos** *or* **shakoes**) a stiff military hat with a high crown and plume. [French *shako* from Hungarian *csákó*]

Shakta /ˈshuktə/ *noun* an adherent of Shaktism. [Sanskrit *Śākta*, from *Śakti*]

Shakti /ˈshukti/ *or* **Sakti** /ˈsahkti, ˈshakti/ *noun* the dynamic energy of a Hindu god personified as his female consort; *broadly* cosmic energy as conceived in Hindu thought. [Sanskrit *Śakti*]

Shaktism /ˈshuktiz(ə)m/ *noun* a Hindu cult of devotion to the female principle: compare VAISHNAVA.

shaky *adj* (**shakier, shakiest**) **1** not firm, still, or stable; likely to wobble or shake. **2a** unlikely to withstand pressure, opposition, etc; precarious: *a shaky coalition.* **b** said e.g. of beliefs or principles: not held with great conviction or commitment. **3a** unsound in health; poorly. **b** characterized by or affected with shaking or trembling. ➤➤ **shakily** *adv*, **shakiness** *noun*.

shale /shayl/ *noun* a finely stratified or laminated rock formed by the consolidation of clay, mud, or silt. [perhaps ultimately from Old English *scealu* shell]

shale oil *noun* a crude dark oil obtained from oil shale by heating.

shall /shəl, *strong* shal/ *verb aux* (*third person sing. present tense* **shall**, *past tense* **should** /shəd, *strong* shood/) **1** used in the first person to express an action or state in the future: *We shall try to be there.* **2** used to express determination or insistence: *They shall not prevent us.* **3** used to express a polite request or suggestion: *Shall I open a window?* **4** *formal* used to express a requirement or command: *It shall be unlawful to carry firearms.* [Old English *sceal*]

Usage note
shall or **will**? Traditionally *shall* was used to form the future tense for the first person singular and plural (*I/we shall go tomorrow*) and to state a firm intention if used with any other personal pronoun (*You shall go to the ball*; *Britons never, never, never shall be slaves*). Conversely *will* formed the future tense for the second and third person (*You/they will know soon enough*) and expressed a firm intention if used with *I* or *we* (*I will not put up with this*). This distinction has largely died out, with *I will* or *we will* being used in informal usage and the general use of the contraction *'ll*, e.g. *I'll, we'll*. See also note at SHOULD.

shallop /ˈshaləp/ *noun* a small open boat propelled by oars or sails and used chiefly in shallow waters. [early French *chaloupe*, alteration of Dutch *sloep* SLOOP]

shallot /shəˈlot/ *noun* **1** a perennial plant that is cultivated for its small edible onion-like bulbs: *Allium ascalonicum.* **2** a bulb of this plant, used *esp* for pickling and in seasoning. [modification of French *échalote*, prob from Latin *Ascalonia*: see SCALLION]

shallow¹ /ˈshaloh/ *adj* **1** having little depth: *shallow water.* **2** superficial in knowledge, thought, or feeling. **3** not marked or accentuated: *The plane went into a shallow dive.* ➤➤ **shallowly** *adv*, **shallowness** *noun*. [Middle English *schalowe*, of Germanic origin]

shallow² *verb intrans* to become shallow.

shallow³ *noun* (*usu in pl*) a shallow place in a body of water.

shalom /shəˈlohm, shəˈlom/ *interj* used as a Jewish greeting and farewell. [Hebrew *shālōm* peace]

shalom aleichem /əˈlaykəm, -khəm/ *interj* used as a traditional Jewish greeting. [Hebrew *shālōm 'alēkhem* peace unto you]

shalt /shalt/ *verb archaic* second person sing. present tense of SHALL.

shalwar *noun* see SALWAR.

sham¹ /sham/ *noun* **1a** an imitation or counterfeit object purporting to be genuine. **b** a person who shams. **2a** a trick intended to delude; a hoax. **b** cheap falseness or hypocrisy: *Tonight, for the first time in my life, I saw through the hollowness, the sham, the silliness of the empty pageant in which I had always played* — Oscar Wilde. [perhaps from English dialect *sham* shame, alteration of SHAME¹]

sham² *adj* **1** not genuine; imitation: *sham pearls.* **2** pretended or feigned: *sham indignation.*

sham³ *verb* (**shammed, shamming**) ➤ *verb trans* to pretend to have or feel (something); to counterfeit: *I shammed a headache to get away.* ➤ *verb intrans* to create a deliberately false impression; to pretend: *Is she really hurt or just shamming?*

shaman /'shahmən, 'shaymən/ noun (pl **shamans**) a priest believed to exercise magic power, e.g. for healing and divination, esp through ecstatic trances. ⨠⨠ **shamanism** noun, **shamanist** noun. [Russian shaman from Tungus šaman]

shamateur /'shamətə, shamə'tuh/ noun derog a sports player who is officially classed as amateur but who takes payment. ⨠⨠ **shamateurism** noun. [blend of SHAM¹ and AMATEUR¹]

shamble¹ /'shambl/ verb intrans to walk awkwardly with dragging feet; to shuffle. [prob from English dialect shamble malformed, ungainly, perhaps from obsolete shamble legs, referring to the rickety legs of a stall in a meat market: see SHAMBLES]

shamble² noun a shambling gait.

shambles noun (pl **shambles**) **1** a scene or a state of great destruction, chaos, or confusion; a mess: The place was left a shambles by hooligans. **2a** archaic a slaughterhouse. **b** a place of carnage. [obsolete shamble meat market, stall selling meat, from Old English scamul, sceamul stool, table]

shambolic /sham'bolik/ adj Brit, informal utterly chaotic or confused. [irreg from SHAMBLES]

shame¹ /shaym/ noun **1a** a painful emotion caused by consciousness of guilt, shortcomings, impropriety, or disgrace. **b** susceptibility to such emotion: How dare you tell lies to my face? Have you no shame? **2a** humiliating disgrace or disrepute; ignominy. **b** a cause of disgrace. **3** a cause of regret; a pity: It's a shame you weren't there. ✳ **put to shame 1** to cause (somebody) to feel shame, esp by outdoing them. **2** to show (something) to be considerably inferior. **shame on you** you ought to feel ashamed. [Old English scamu]

shame² verb trans **1** to bring shame to (somebody); to disgrace. **2** to put (somebody) to shame by outdoing them. **3** to fill (somebody) with a sense of shame. **4** (usu + into) to compel (somebody) to do something by causing them to feel guilty: They were shamed into confessing.

shamefaced adj **1** showing modesty; bashful. **2** showing shame; ashamed. ⨠⨠ **shamefacedly** /shaym'faysidli, shaym'faystli/ adv, **shamefacedness** /shaym'faysidnis, shaym'faystnis/ noun. [alteration of archaic shamefast bound by shame, from Old English scamfæst, from scamu SHAME¹ + fæst fixed, FAST¹]

shameful adj **1** bringing disrepute or ignominy; disgraceful. **2** arousing a feeling of shame. ⨠⨠ **shamefully** adv, **shamefulness** noun.

shameless adj **1** not feeling shame, esp in situations where other people would; brazen. **2** done with a complete disregard for the usual proprieties. ⨠⨠ **shamelessly** adv, **shamelessness** noun.

shammy /'shami/ noun (pl **shammies**) informal = CHAMOIS (2). [by alteration]

shampoo¹ /sham'pooh/ noun (pl **shampoos**) **1a** a usu foaming liquid soap, detergent, etc used for washing the hair. **b** a similar cleaning agent used on a carpet, car, etc. **2** a washing of the hair, car, carpet, etc with shampoo.

shampoo² verb trans (**shampoos, shampooed, shampooing**) **1** to wash or clean (esp the hair or a carpet) with shampoo. **2** to wash the hair of (somebody). ⨠⨠ **shampooist** noun. [orig in the sense 'to massage', esp as part of a Turkish bath; from Hindi cāmpo press!, imperative of cāmpnā to press]

shamrock /'shamrok/ noun **1** a type of clover with leaves that consist of three leaflets, used as the national emblem of Ireland: Trifolium minus and other species. **2** any of various similar three-leaved plants. [Irish Gaelic seamróg]

shandy /'shandi/ noun (pl **shandies**) a drink consisting of beer mixed with lemonade or ginger beer. [short for shandygaff, of unknown origin]

shanghai /shang'hie/ verb trans (**shanghais, shanghaied, shanghaiing**) **1** to compel (somebody) to join a ship's crew, esp with the help of drink or drugs. **2** informal to trick or force (somebody) into doing something. [from Shanghai, seaport in China; from the formerly widespread use of this method to procure sailors for voyages to the Orient]

Shangri-la /,shanggri 'lah/ noun a remote imaginary place where life approaches perfection. [named after Shangri-La, imaginary land depicted in the novel Lost Horizon by James Hilton d.1954, English novelist]

shank /shangk/ noun **1a** a leg; specif the part of the leg between the knee and the ankle in human beings or the corresponding part in various other vertebrates. **b** a cut of beef, veal, mutton, or lamb from the leg, esp the lower part of the leg. **2a** a straight narrow part of an object, e.g. a nail or pin, an anchor, or a key. **b** the narrow part of the sole of a shoe beneath the instep. **3a** a part of an object by which it can be attached to something else, e.g. a projection on the back of a solid button. **b** a short stem of thread that holds a sewn button away from the cloth. **4** the end, e.g. of a drill bit, that is gripped in a chuck. **5** the band of a ring. [Old English scanca]

shanks's mare /'shangksiz/ noun chiefly NAmer = SHANKS'S PONY.

shanks's pony noun one's own feet or legs considered as a means of transport: We all went home by shanks's pony. [shanks, pl of SHANK]

shanny /'shani/ noun (pl **shannies**) a small greenish brown European blenny: Blennius pholis. [origin unknown]

shan't /shahnt/ contraction shall not.

shantung /shan'tung/ noun a silk fabric in plain weave with a slightly irregular surface. [named after Shandong, also written Shantung, a province in NE China where it was first made]

shanty¹ /'shanti/ noun (pl **shanties**) a small crudely built or dilapidated dwelling or shelter; a shack. [Canadian French chantier cabin in a lumber camp, ultimately from Latin cantherius trellis]

shanty² noun (pl **shanties**) a song sung by sailors in rhythm with their work. [modification of French chanter to sing]

shantytown noun a town, or an area of a town, consisting mainly of shanties.

SHAPE /shayp/ abbr Supreme Headquarters Allied Powers Europe.

shape¹ /shayp/ verb trans **1** to give a particular form or shape to (something): She shaped the clay into a cube. **2** to adapt the form or outline of (something) so as to fit neatly and closely: The dress is shaped to cling to your hips. **3** to determine the nature or course of (e.g. events or a person's life). ⨠ verb intrans (often + up) to develop or proceed: How are your plans shaping now? ⨠⨠ **shapable** adj, **shapeable** adj, **shaper** noun. [Old English scieppan]

shape² noun **1** the visible or tactile form of a particular thing or kind of thing, esp its outline or outer surface. **2** the contour of the human body, esp of the trunk; a person's figure. **3a** a circle, square, or other standard geometrical form. **b** a piece of paper or any other material cut or made into a particular esp geometrical form. **4** an appearance adopted or assumed by somebody or something; a guise: The devil appeared to Eve in the shape of a serpent. **5a** definite form, whether physical, structural, verbal, or mental. **b** a general structure or plan: Economics determines the final shape of any society. **6a** the condition of a person or thing, esp at a particular time: He's in excellent shape for his age. **b** a satisfactory condition: It took a lot of work to get the car into shape. **7** a phantom or apparition. ✳ **in shape** in good condition, esp physically. **in the shape of** as a form of; by way of. **lick/knock/whip into shape** to bring (somebody or something) into a satisfactory condition. **out of shape** in poor condition, esp physically. **take shape** to become more clearly defined; to take on a definite or distinctive form. ⨠⨠ **shaped** adj.

shapeless adj **1** having no definite shape. **2** deprived of its usual or proper shape; misshapen: a shapeless old hat. ⨠⨠ **shapelessly** adv, **shapelessness** noun.

shapely adj (**shapelier, shapeliest**) having a pleasing shape; well-proportioned: He had … tender shapely strong freckled hands — James Joyce. ⨠⨠ **shapeliness** noun.

shape up verb intrans **1** to proceed satisfactorily. **2** said of a person: to become physically fit. **3** to develop in a particular way: This is shaping up to be an enthralling contest.

shard /shahd/ noun **1** a piece or fragment of something brittle, e.g. earthenware or glass. **2** = SHERD (2). [Old English sceard]

share¹ /sheə/ noun **1a** a portion belonging to, due to, or contributed by an individual. **b** a full or fair portion: She's had her share of fun. **2a** the part allotted or belonging to any member of a group owning property together. **b** any of the equal portions into which the invested capital of a company is divided. ✳ **go shares** informal to divide or share something. [Old English scearu cutting, tonsure; related to Old English scieran SHEAR¹]

share² verb trans **1** to partake of, use, experience, or enjoy (something) with others. **2** (+ out) to divide and distribute (something) in shares; to apportion. **3** to tell somebody about (something). ⨠ verb intrans (often + in) to have a share or part. ⨠⨠ **sharable** adj, **shareable** adj, **sharer** noun.

share³ noun a ploughshare. [Old English scear]

sharecropper *noun NAmer* a tenant farmer, *esp* in the southern USA, who gives the landlord an agreed share of the crop as rent. ➤ **sharecropping** *adj and noun.*

share-farmer *noun Aus, NZ* a tenant farmer who pays a share of the crop in rent and receives a share of the profits from the landlord.

shareholder *noun* a holder or owner of one or more shares in a company. ➤ **shareholding** *adj and noun.*

share index *noun* an index showing the trend in share prices on a stock exchange.

share option *noun* a scheme that enables employees of a company to buy shares in it at a fixed price at some date in the future.

shareware *noun* computer software that is made available free or at a token cost to any user.

sharia *or* **sheria** /shə'ree-ə/ *noun* the body of divine law in Islam that governs the religious and secular life of Muslims. [Arabic *sharīah*]

sharif /sha'reef/ *noun* **1** a descendant of the prophet Muhammad through his daughter Fatima. **2** somebody of noble ancestry or political preeminence in a predominantly Islamic country. ➤ **sharifian** *adj.* [Arabic *sharif*, literally 'illustrious']

shark[1] /shahk/ *noun* (*pl* **sharks** *or collectively* **shark**) any of a large number of mostly large, typically grey marine fishes that are usu active and voracious predators and have gill slits at the sides and a mouth on the under part of the body: subclass Elasmobranchii. [origin unknown]

shark[2] *noun* **1** a greedy unscrupulous person who exploits others by usury, extortion, or trickery. **2** *NAmer, informal* somebody who is an expert, *esp* in a specified field. [prob modification (influenced in form and meaning by SHARK[1]) of German *Schurke* scoundrel]

sharkskin *noun* **1** leather made from the hide of a shark. **2** a smooth stiff durable fabric in twill or basket weave with small woven designs.

sharon fruit /'sharən/ *noun* a persimmon, *esp* a variety with a tough bright orange skin, no seeds, and sweet pulpy orange flesh. [named after the Plain of *Sharon*, in western Israel, where it is grown]

sharp[1] /shahp/ *adj* **1** well adapted to cutting or piercing, usu by having a thin edge or fine point. **2a** characterized by hard lines and angles: *sharp features.* **b** involving an abrupt change in direction: *a sharp turn.* **3a** clear in outline or detail; distinct: *a sharp image.* **b** conspicuously clear; marked: *sharp contrast.* **4a** sudden and vigorous or violent: *a sharp tap.* **b** capable of acting or reacting quickly: *sharp reflexes.* **5a** said of the senses: able to perceive clearly and distinctly. **b** intellectually alert and penetrating. **6a** causing intense usu sudden anguish: *a sharp pain.* **b** verbally hurtful: *a sharp rebuke.* **7a** affecting the senses or sense organs intensely, e.g. pungent, tart, or acid in flavour. **b** said of a sound: shrill or piercing. **8** bitingly cold; icy: *a sharp wind.* **9a** said of a musical note: raised one semitone in pitch. **b** slightly higher than the true or desired pitch. **10** *informal* stylish or dressy. **11** paying shrewd usu selfish attention to personal gain: *a sharp trader.* ✱ **at the sharp end** involved in the most active, difficult, or dangerous aspect of a situation. ➤➤ **sharply** *adv*, **sharpness** *noun.* [Old English *scearp*]

sharp[2] *adv* **1** in an abrupt manner: *The car pulled up sharp*; *Turn sharp right.* **2** exactly or precisely: *four o'clock sharp.* **3** above the proper musical pitch: *He's singing sharp.*

sharp[3] *noun* **1a** a musical note one semitone higher than the note at that position on the staff. **b** the character (#) that indicates such a note. **2** a relatively long needle with a sharp point and a small rounded eye for use in general sewing. **3** *chiefly NAmer* a swindler or sharper.

sharp[4] *verb trans NAmer* to raise the pitch of (a note) by one semitone.

sharpen *verb trans and intrans* (**sharpened, sharpening**) to make (something) or become sharp or sharper. ➤➤ **sharpener** *noun.*

sharpening stone *noun* = WHETSTONE.

sharper *noun* a cheat or swindler; *esp* a gambler who habitually cheats.

sharpish[1] *adv Brit, informal* with haste; somewhat quickly.

sharpish[2] *adj* fairly sharp.

sharp practice *noun* unscrupulous dealings.

sharp-set *adj* **1** set at a sharp angle or so as to present a sharp edge. **2** eager for food; very hungry.

sharpshooter *noun* a good marksman. ➤➤ **sharpshooting** *noun.*

sharp-tongued *adj* cutting or sarcastic in speech; quick to rebuke.

sharp-witted *adj* having or showing mental alertness or acute perceptions and intelligence.

shashlik *or* **shashlick** /'shashlik/ *noun* = KEBAB. [Russian *shashlyk*, of Turkic origin]

Shasta daisy /'shastə/ *noun* a tall plant orig from the Pyrenees that bears a single large white flower resembling a daisy: *Leucanthemum maximum.* [named after Mount *Shasta* in California, USA, where it grows]

shastra /'shastrə/ *noun* any of the sacred scriptures of the Hindu religion. [Sanskrit *sāstra*]

shat /shat/ *verb* past tense of SHIT[1].

shatoosh *or* **shahtoosh** /sha'toohsh/ *noun* **1** wool from an endangered species of Tibetan antelope. **2** a fine scarf or shawl made of this wool.

shatter /'shatə/ *verb* (**shattered, shattering**) ➤ *verb trans* **1a** to break (something) into pieces, e.g. by a sudden blow. **b** to cause (something) to break down; to impair or destroy: *His nerves were shattered*; *The accident shattered my confidence.* **2** to have a forceful or violent effect on the feelings of (somebody): *She was absolutely shattered by the news.* **3** *informal* to cause (somebody) to be utterly exhausted: *She felt shattered by the long train journey.* ➤ *verb intrans* to break apart suddenly; to disintegrate. ➤➤ **shattered** *adj*, **shattering** *adj*, **shatteringly** *adv.* [Middle English *schateren*, prob of Germanic origin]

shatterproof *adj* made so as not to shatter: *shatterproof glass.*

shave[1] /shayv/ *verb* (*past tense* **shaved**, *past part.* **shaved** *or* **shaven** /'shayv(ə)n/) ➤ *verb trans* **1a** to remove the hair from (somebody or something) by cutting close to the roots, *esp* with a razor. **b** to cut off (hair, a moustache, or a beard) in this way. **2** to cut or trim (something) closely. **3** (*often* + off) to remove (something) in thin layers, slices, or shreds: *He shaved off a sliver of cheese.* **4** to reduce (e.g. a price) by a small amount: *She shaved two seconds off the world record.* **5** to come very close to or brush against (something) in passing. ➤ *verb intrans* to shave hair, *esp* facial hair. [Old English *scafan*]

shave[2] *noun* **1** an act or the process of shaving. **2** a tool or machine for shaving wood, etc. **3** a thin slice; a shaving.

shavehook *noun* a tool for scraping that has a usu triangular blade set at right angles to a shaft.

shaveling /'shayvling/ *noun archaic* **1** *derog* a tonsured clergyman; a priest. **2** a young man; a stripling.

shaven /'shayv(ə)n/ *verb* past part. of SHAVE[1].

shaver *noun* **1** an electric-powered razor. **2** *informal, dated* a boy or youngster.

shavetail *noun NAmer, informal* an inexperienced person, *esp* a newly commissioned officer in the armed forces. [from the practice of shaving the tails of newly broken in mules to distinguish them from experienced ones]

Shavian /'shayvi-ən/ *adj* characteristic of the plays and writings of the Irish-born author and socialist George Bernard Shaw (d.1950). [modern Latin *Shavius*, latinized form of the name Shaw]

shaving *noun* **1** (*usu in pl*) a thin layer or shred shaved off: *wood shavings.* **2** (*used before a noun*) used in the process of shaving one's face, legs, etc: *shaving foam.*

Shavuot /shah'vooh·oth, -əs/ *noun* see SHABUOTH.

shaw /shaw/ *noun chiefly Brit* the stalks and leaves of a cultivated crop, e.g. potatoes or turnips. [prob alteration of SHOW[2]]

shawl /shawl/ *noun* a usu decorative square, oblong, or triangular piece of fabric that is worn to cover the head or shoulders. [Urdu and Persian *shāl*]

shawl collar *noun* a collar that is rolled back and follows a continuous line round the neck and down the front edges of a garment.

shawm /shawm/ *noun* an early woodwind musical instrument with a DOUBLE REED (two flat pieces of cane that vibrate to make the sound when blown across), a precursor of the oboe. [Middle English *schalme* from early French *chalemie*, modification of late Latin *calamellus*, dimin. of Latin *calamus* reed, from Greek *kalamos*]

Shawnee /shaw'nee/ *noun* (*pl* **Shawnees** *or collectively* **Shawnee**) **1** a member of a Native American people orig of the central Ohio valley. **2** the Algonquian language of this people. [back-formation from obsolete *Shawnese*, from Shawnee *Shaawanwaaki*, literally 'those in the south']

shay /shay/ *noun* = CHAISE (I). [from CHAISE, taken as pl]

she[1] /shi, *strong* shee/ *pronoun* **1** used to refer to a female person or creature, previously mentioned, who is neither the speaker nor hearer: *She is my mother.* **2** used to refer to something regarded as feminine, e.g. by personification: *She was a fine ship.* **3** *Aus, NZ* used instead of *it*, *esp* when referring to a situation in general terms. [Middle English, prob alteration of Old English *hēo*, fem of *hē* HE[1]]

she[2] /shee/ *noun* **1** a female person or creature: *Is the kitten a he or a she?* **2** (*used before a noun*) female: *a she-wolf.*

shea /shiə/ *noun* a tropical African tree of the sapodilla family with fatty nuts that yield shea butter: *Vitellaria paradoxa* or *Butyrospermum parkii.*

shea butter *noun* a pale solid fat from the seeds of the shea tree used in food, soap, and candles.

sheaf[1] /sheef/ *noun* (*pl* **sheaves** /sheevz/) **1** a quantity of plant material, *esp* the stalks and ears of a cereal grass, bound together. **2** a collection of items laid or tied together: *a sheaf of papers.* [Old English *scēaf*]

sheaf[2] *verb trans* to tie or bind (something) into a sheaf or sheaves.

shear[1] /shiə/ *verb* (*past tense* **sheared**, *past part.* **sheared** *or* **shorn** /shawn/) ➤ *verb trans* **1a** to cut off the hair, wool, fleece, etc from (somebody, an animal, or a part of the body). **b** to cut or clip (hair, wool, a fleece, etc) from somebody or something. **2a** to cut (something) with or as if with shears. **b** (*often* + off) to cut or break (something) off something else. **3** to subject (something) to a shear force. ➤ *verb intrans* **1** to become divided or separated under the action of a shear force: *The bolt may shear off.* **2** *chiefly Scot* to reap crops with a sickle. ✳ **be shorn of** to be deprived of (something); to have (something) taken away from one: *She has been shorn of her authority.* ➤➤ **shearer** *noun*, **shearing** *noun*. [Old English *scieran*]

shear[2] *noun* **1** (*in pl*). **a** a cutting implement similar to a pair of scissors but typically larger. **b** any of various cutting tools or machines operating by the action of opposed cutting edges of metal. **2** *Brit* an instance of shearing sheep: *a sheep of two shears.* **3** a force that causes or tends to cause two adjacent layers in a body to slide on each other in a direction parallel to their plane of contact.

shearling /'shiəling/ *noun chiefly Brit* a sheep after its first shearing.

shear pin *noun* an easily replaceable pin inserted at a critical point in a machine, designed to break and stop the machine when subjected to excess stress.

shearwater *noun* any of numerous species of dark-coloured seabirds with long wings that usu skim close to the waves in flight: genus *Puffinus* and other genera.

sheatfish /'sheetfish/ *noun* = WELS. [alteration of *sheathfish*, from SHEATH + FISH[1]]

sheath /sheeth/ *noun* (*pl* **sheaths** /sheedhz/) **1** a case or cover for a blade, e.g. of a knife or sword. **2** a cover or case of a plant or animal body, or part of one: *The leaves of grasses form a sheath round the main stalk.* **3** a close-fitting protective casing or covering, e.g. around an electric cable. **4** a condom. **5** a woman's very close-fitting dress. [Old English *scēath*]

sheathe /sheedh/ *verb trans* **1** to insert (a sword, dagger, etc) into its sheath: *Patricians, draw your swords, and sheathe them not till Saturninus be Rome's Emperor* — Shakespeare. **2** said of an animal, *esp* a cat: to retract (its claws). **3** to cover or encase (something) in or as if in a sheath: *Her eyes, like marigolds, had sheathed their light* — Shakespeare; *his legs ... being sheathed in bulging leggings* — Hardy; *I had its big door sheathed with boiler iron* — Mark Twain. [Middle English *shethen*, from *shethe* SHEATH]

sheathing /'sheedhing/ *noun* material used to sheathe something, e.g. a covering of boards or waterproof material on a timber roof or the metal plates on a ship's hull.

sheath knife *noun* a knife that has a fixed blade and is carried in a sheath.

sheave[1] /sheev/ *noun* a grooved wheel, e.g. in a pulley block. [Middle English *sheve*, of Germanic origin]

sheave[2] *verb trans* to gather and bind (*esp* corn) into a sheaf. [from SHEAF[1]]

sheaves *noun* pl of SHEAF[1].

shebang /shi'bang/ *noun chiefly NAmer, informal* an affair or business: *She's head of the whole shebang.* [perhaps alteration of SHEBEEN]

shebeen /shi'been/ *noun esp* in Ireland, Scotland, or South Africa, an unlicensed or illegally operated drinking establishment. [Irish Gaelic *síbín* little mug, bad ale]

shed[1] /shed/ *verb trans* (**shedding**, *past tense and past part.* **shed**) **1a** to cast off or let fall (a natural covering such as leaves, hair, or a skin). **b** to take off (an item of clothing). **2** to get rid of (something or somebody); to discard or do away with: *The firm is shedding another 100 workers.* **3a** to cause (blood) to flow by wounding or killing. **b** to let (tears) flow. **c** to cast, spread, or diffuse (light, brightness, etc): *boys who sought for shells along the shore, their white feet shedding pallor in the sea* — W J Turner. **4** to drop (a load) accidentally. **5** to be incapable of holding or absorbing (a liquid); to repel: *A duck's plumage sheds water.* ✳ **shed light on something** to help to clarify something: *Recent fossil discoveries ... shed light on the environments in which the various groups of hominoid emerged* — Nature. [Old English *scēadan* to separate, divide, scatter, in Middle English 'to pour out', later 'to cast off or let fall']

shed[2] *noun* = WATERSHED (I).

shed[3] *noun* **1** a usu single-storeyed building for shelter, storage, etc. **2** a large roofed structure, usu open on all sides, for storing or repairing vehicles, machinery, etc. [variant spelling of SHADE[1]]

she'd /shid, sheed/ *contraction* **1** she had. **2** she would.

shedder *noun* **1** an animal that sheds its skin or its coat, e.g. a snake or llama. **2** a female salmon after it has spawned.

she-devil *noun* an extremely cruel, spiteful, or malicious woman.

shedload /'shedlohd/ *noun informal* (*also in pl*) a large amount: *She spends shedloads on designer clothes.*

sheen /sheen/ *noun* **1** a bright or shining quality or condition; brightness or lustre. **2** a subdued shininess on a surface. **3** a lustrous surface imparted to textiles through finishing processes or use of shiny yarns. ➤➤ **sheeny** *adj.* [obsolete *sheen* beautiful, from Old English *scīene*]

sheeny /'sheeni/ *noun* (*pl* **sheenies**) *NAmer, derog* a Jewish person. [origin unknown]

sheep /sheep/ *noun* (*pl* **sheep**) **1** a ruminant mammal with a thick woolly coat, related to the goat; *specif* one domesticated for its flesh and wool. **2** an inane or docile person; *esp* one easily influenced or led. ✳ **separate the sheep from the goats** to identify and distinguish between those members of a group that are superior and those that are inferior. [Old English *scēap*]

sheepcote /'sheepkot, 'sheepkoht/ *noun chiefly Brit* = SHEEPFOLD.

sheep-dip *noun* a liquid preparation into which sheep are plunged, *esp* to destroy parasites.

sheepdog *noun* a dog used to tend, drive, or guard sheep; *esp* a Border collie.

sheepdog trials *pl noun* a competition in which sheepdogs are judged on their ability to perform tasks such as rounding up and penning sheep.

sheepfold *noun* a pen or shelter for sheep.

sheepish *adj* embarrassed by consciousness of a fault: *a sheepish look.* ➤➤ **sheepishly** *adv*, **sheepishness** *noun.*

sheep's eyes *pl noun* wistful amorous glances: *He kept making sheep's eyes at her.*

sheepshank /'sheepshangk/ *noun* a knot for shortening a rope.

sheepskin *noun* **1** the skin of a sheep with the wool on: *a sheepskin coat.* **2** the skin of a sheep with the wool removed, or leather made from it.

sheep tick *noun* a bloodsucking tick whose young cling to bushes and readily attach themselves to passing animals.

sheep walk *noun chiefly Brit* a tract of land on which sheep are pastured.

sheer[1] /shiə/ *adj* **1** not mixed or mingled with anything else; utter: *sheer ignorance.* **2** forming a vertical or almost vertical surface to or from a great height; precipitous: *a sheer cliff.* **3** transparently fine; diaphanous: *sheer tights.* [Middle English *schere* freed from guilt, prob alteration of *skere* pure, from Old Norse *skœrr*]

sheer[2] *adv* **1** altogether or completely: *His name went sheer out of my head.* **2** straight up or down without a break: *Rugged cliffs rose sheer out of the sea.*

sheer³ *verb trans and intrans* to deviate or cause (something) to deviate from a course. [perhaps alteration of SHEAR¹]

sheer⁴ *noun* a turn, deviation, or change in a course, e.g. of a ship.

sheer⁵ *noun* the curvature from front to rear of a ship's deck as observed when looking from the side. [perhaps alteration of SHEAR²]

sheerlegs *pl noun* (*treated as sing. or pl*) a hoisting apparatus consisting of two or more upright beams fastened together at their upper ends and having tackle for lifting heavy loads, e.g. masts or guns.

sheer off *verb intrans chiefly Brit* to depart or turn away abruptly, *esp* in order to avoid something.

sheet¹ /sheet/ *noun* **1** a broad piece of cloth; *specif* a rectangle of cotton or other fabric used as an article of bed linen. **2a** a usu rectangular piece of paper. **b** (*usu in pl*) a printed section for a book, *esp* before it has been folded, cut, or bound. **3** a broad usu flat expanse: *a sheet of ice*. **4** a suspended or moving expanse: *a sheet of flame; sheets of rain*. **5a** a piece of something that is thin in comparison to its length and breadth. **b** a flat metal baking utensil. **6** (*used before a noun*) rolled or spread out in a sheet: *sheet steel*. **7** the unseparated postage stamps printed by one impression of a plate on a single piece of paper. **8** a newspaper, periodical, or pamphlet. [Old English *scȳte*; related to Old English *scēotan* SHOOT¹]

sheet² *verb trans* **1** to form (something) into a sheet or sheets. **2** to provide or cover (something) with a sheet or sheets. ➤ *verb intrans* to come down in sheets: *The rain sheeted against the windows*.

sheet³ *noun* **1** a rope that regulates the angle at which a sail is set in relation to the wind. **2** (*in pl*) the spaces at either end of an open boat. [Old English *scēata* lower corner of a sail]

sheet anchor *noun* **1** an emergency anchor formerly carried in the broadest part of a ship. **2** a principal support or a person or thing to be depended on, *esp* in danger; a mainstay. [alteration (prob influenced by SHEET³) of *shoot anchor*, perhaps from Middle English *shot* two cables spliced together, of unknown origin]

sheet bend *noun* a knot or hitch used for temporarily fastening one rope to a loop in another.

sheet glass *noun* glass made in large sheets directly from the furnace.

sheeting *noun* **1** material in the form of sheets: *plastic sheeting*. **2** material suitable for making into sheets.

sheet lightning *noun* lightning in diffused or sheet form due to reflection and diffusion by clouds: compare FORKED LIGHTNING.

sheet metal *noun* metal in the form of a thin sheet.

sheet music *noun* **1** music in its printed form. **2** a printed copy of a piece of music.

sheikh *or* **sheik** /shayk, sheek/ *noun* **1** an Arab leader, *esp* the head of a clan or community. **2** a Muslim religious or community leader. ➤➤ **sheikhdom** *noun*. [Arabic *shaykh* old man, leader, from *šāka* to be or grow old]

sheila *or* **sheilah** /'sheelə/ *noun Aus, NZ, informal* a young woman; a girl. [alteration (influenced by girl's name *Sheila*) of English dialect *shaler*]

shekel /'shekl/ *noun* **1** the basic monetary unit of Israel, divided into 100 agorot. **2** an ancient Hebrew gold or silver coin. **3** *informal* (*in pl*) money. [Hebrew *sheqel*, from *shāqal* to weigh]

sheldrake /'sheldrayk/ *noun* (*pl* **sheldrakes** *or collectively* **sheldrake**) a male shelduck. [Middle English, from English dialect *sheld-* pied + DRAKE¹]

shelduck /'shelduk/ *noun* (*pl* **shelducks** *or collectively* **shelduck**) any of several species of Old World ducks; *esp* a common mostly black and white duck slightly larger than the mallard: genus *Tadorna*. [*shel-* as in SHELDRAKE + DUCK¹]

shelf /shelf/ *noun* (*pl* **shelves** /shelvz/) **1** a thin flat usu long and narrow piece of a solid material fastened horizontally at a distance from the floor, e.g. on a wall or in a cupboard, bookcase, etc, to hold objects. **2** something resembling a shelf in form or position, e.g.: **a** a partially submerged sandbank or ledge of rocks. **b** a flat projecting layer of rock. **c** = CONTINENTAL SHELF. ✳ **off the shelf** available from stock, not made to order. **on the shelf 1** in a state of inactivity or uselessness. **2** considered unlikely to marry, *esp* because of being too old. [Middle English *schelfe* from early Low German *schelf*]

shelf-life *noun* the length of time for which a product, e.g. a tinned or packaged food, may be stored or displayed without serious deterioration.

shell¹ /shel/ *noun* **1a** a hard rigid covering of an animal, e.g. a turtle, oyster, or beetle, often largely made up of calcium. **b** the hard or tough outer covering of an egg, *esp* a bird's egg. **2** a seashell. **3** shell material or shells: *an ornament made of shell*. **4** the covering or outside part of a fruit or seed, *esp* when hard or fibrous. **5** something resembling a shell, e.g.: **a** a framework or exterior structure; *esp* the outer frame of a building that is unfinished or has been destroyed, or the bodywork of a vehicle. **b** an edible case for holding a filling: *a pastry shell*. **6a** a projectile for a large gun containing an explosive bursting charge. **b** a metal or paper case that holds the charge in cartridges, fireworks, etc. **7** ?*Amer* a cartridge. **8** a narrow light racing boat propelled by one or more rowers. **9** any of various spherical regions surrounding the nucleus of an atom at various distances from it and each occupied by a group of electrons of approximately equal energy. **10** a hollow form devoid of substance: *mere effigies and shells of men* — Thomas Carlyle. ✳ **come out of one's shell** to become less shy or reserved and more communicative. **go/retreat into one's shell** to become reserved and uncommunicative. ➤➤ **shelly** *adj*. [Old English *sciell*]

shell² *verb trans* **1** to take (something) out of its natural enclosing cover, e.g. a shell, husk, pod, or capsule: *shell peanuts*. **2** to fire shells at, on, or into (a target). ➤ *verb intrans* **1** to fall or scale off in thin pieces. **2** to fall out of the pod or husk: *nuts that shell on falling from the tree*.

she'll /shil, *strong* sheel/ *contraction* **1** she will. **2** she shall.

shellac¹ /shə'lak/ *noun* **1** the purified form of a resin produced by various insects, usu obtained as yellow or orange flakes. **2** a solution of this in alcohol used *esp* in making varnish. [SHELL¹ + LAC¹; translation of French *laque en écailles* lac in thin flakes]

shellac² *verb trans* (**shellacked, shellacking**) **1** to treat or coat (something) with shellac. **2** *NAmer* to defeat (somebody) conclusively; to thrash.

shellback *noun* an old or very experienced sailor.

shell company *noun* a company with no assets or trading operations of its own that is used by its owners as a means of controlling other companies or conducting various financial operations.

shellfire *noun* the firing of large guns or the shells discharged from them.

shellfish *noun* an aquatic invertebrate animal with a shell or carapace, *esp* an edible mollusc or crustacean.

shell game *noun NAmer* **1** = THIMBLERIG. **2** any deceptive trick or manoeuvre.

shell jacket *noun* a short tight military jacket worn buttoned up the front.

shell out *verb trans and intrans informal* to pay (money).

shell pink *adj* of a light yellowish pink colour. ➤➤ **shell pink** *noun*.

shell program *noun* a computer program that provides a basic framework within which users can run or develop their own programs.

shellproof *adj* constructed so as to resist attack by shells or bombs.

shell shock *noun* a mental disorder characterized by neurotic and often hysterical symptoms, resulting from exposure to conditions that cause intense stress, such as wartime combat. ➤➤ **shell-shocked** *adj*.

shell suit *noun* a lightweight tracksuit with a warm cotton lining and a typically shiny nylon covering.

Shelta /'sheltə/ *noun* a secret language based on Gaelic used by some travelling people in the British Isles. [origin unknown]

shelter¹ /'sheltə/ *noun* **1** something, *esp* a structure, providing cover or protection: *an air-raid shelter*. **2** the state of being covered and protected; refuge: *We took shelter in a shop doorway*. [perhaps from obsolete *sheltron* (phalanx), from Old English *scieldtruma*, from *scield* SHIELD¹ + *truma* troop]

shelter² *verb* (**sheltered, sheltering**) ➤ *verb trans* **1** to serve as a shelter for (something or somebody): *A thick hedge sheltered the orchard*. **2** to keep (somebody or something) concealed or protected: *Local peasants sheltered her family in a mountain cave*. ➤ *verb intrans* to take cover or find refuge: *We sheltered under the awning*.

sheltered *adj* **1** protected from hardship or unpleasant realities: *a sheltered life.* **2** said of accommodation: designed for elderly or disabled people to live safely and as independently as possible, under the care of a resident warden: *sheltered housing.*

shelty *or* **sheltie** /'shelti/ *noun* (*pl* **shelties**) a Shetland pony or sheepdog. [prob ultimately from Old Norse *Hjalti* Shetlander]

shelve /shelv/ *verb trans* **1** to provide (a space or piece of furniture) with shelves. **2** to place (something) on a shelf. **3a** to put (something) off or aside: *We decided to shelve the project.* **b** to remove (somebody) from active service; to dismiss. ➤ *verb intrans* to slope gently. [from SHELVES]

shelves *noun* pl of SHELF.

shelving *noun* shelves, or material for constructing shelves.

shemozzle *or* **schemozzle** /shi'mozl/ *noun informal* a scene of confusion, dispute, or uproar; a to-do or mix-up. [Yiddish *shlimazel* bad luck, difficulty, misfortune, from *shlim* bad, ill + *mazel* luck]

shenanigan /shi'nanigən/ *noun informal* (*usu in pl*) **1** deliberate deception; trickery. **2** boisterous mischief; high jinks. [origin unknown]

she-oak *noun* = CASUARINA.

Sheol /'sheeohl, 'sheeol/ *noun* the abode of the dead in early Hebrew thought. [Hebrew *Sh̆e'ōl*]

shepherd[1] /'shepəd/ *noun* **1** somebody who tends sheep. **2** a pastor. [Old English *scēaphyrde*, from *scēap* SHEEP + *hierde* herdsman]

shepherd[2] *verb trans* **1** to tend (sheep) as a shepherd. **2** to guide, marshal, or conduct (people) like sheep: *The teachers shepherded the children onto the train.*

shepherd dog *noun* a sheepdog.

shepherdess /'shepədis/ *noun* a woman or girl who tends sheep, *esp* as depicted in stories or paintings.

shepherd's crook *noun* a shepherd's long staff with one end formed into a large hook.

shepherd's pie *noun* a hot dish of minced meat, *esp* lamb, with a mashed potato topping: compare COTTAGE PIE.

shepherd's purse *noun* a white-flowered annual plant of the mustard family that has small flat heart-shaped seed pods and is a common weed: *Capsella bursa-pastoris.*

sherardize *or* **sherardise** /'sherədiez/ *verb trans* to coat (e.g. iron or steel) with zinc by heating it with zinc dust. [named after *Sherard Cowper-Coles* d.1936, English inventor]

Sheraton /'sherət(ə)n/ *adj* denoting a style of furniture that originated in England around 1800 and is characterized by straight lines and graceful proportions. [named after Thomas *Sheraton* d.1806, English furniture designer]

sherbet /'shuhbət/ *noun* **1a** a sweet powder that effervesces in liquid and is eaten dry or used to make fizzy drinks. **b** a drink made with this powder. **2** *NAmer* = SORBET (1). **3** a Middle Eastern cold drink of sweetened and diluted fruit juice. [Turkish *şerbet* from Persian *sharbat*, from Arabic *sharbah* drink]

sherd /shuhd, shahd/ *noun* **1** = SHARD (1). **2** fragments of pottery vessels.

sheria /shə'ree·ə/ *noun* see SHARIA.

sheriff /'sherif/ *noun* **1** the honorary chief executive officer of the Crown in an English county, who has mainly judicial and ceremonial duties. **2** the chief judge of a Scottish county or district. **3** a county law enforcement officer in the USA. ➤➤ **sheriffdom** *noun*. [Old English *scīrgerēfa*, from *scīr* SHIRE + *gerēfa* REEVE[1]]

sheriff court *noun* the main inferior court in Scotland, dealing with both civil and criminal cases, and having appeal to the High Court of Justiciary.

Sherpa /'shuhpə/ *noun* (*pl* **Sherpa** *or* **Sherpas**) a member of a Tibetan people living on the high southern slopes of the Himalayas. ➤➤ **Sherpa** *adj*. [Tibetan *sharpa* somebody who lives in the east]

sherry /'sheri/ *noun* (*pl* **sherries**) **1** a blended fortified wine from S Spain that varies in colour from very light to dark brown. **2** a glass or measure of sherry. [alteration of *sherris* (taken as pl), from *Xeres* (now *Jerez*), a city in Spain where it was first produced]

she's /shiz, *strong* sheez/ *contraction* **1** she is. **2** she has.

Shetland /'shetlənd/ *noun* **1** a Shetland pony or sheepdog. **2** (*often* **shetland**) a lightweight loosely twisted yarn of Shetland wool used

for knitting and weaving, or a garment made from this. [named after the *Shetland* Islands off N Scotland]

Shetland pony *noun* an animal of a breed of small stocky shaggy ponies that originated in the Shetland Islands of Scotland.

Shetland sheepdog *noun* an animal of a breed of small dogs that resemble miniature collies.

Shetland wool *noun* fine wool from sheep raised in the Shetland Islands, or yarn spun from it.

shew /show/ *verb trans and intrans Brit, archaic* = SHOW[1].

shewbread *or* **showbread** *noun* consecrated unleavened bread ritually placed by the Jewish priests of ancient Israel on a table in the sanctuary of the Tabernacle on the Sabbath. [translation of German *Schaubrot*, translation of Greek *artoi enōpioi* bread facing (God), translation of Hebrew *lehem pānīm* bread in the divine presence]

Shia /'shee·ə/ *noun* (*pl* **Shias** *or collectively* **Shia**) **1** the branch of Islam deriving authority from Muhammad's cousin and son-in-law Ali and his appointed successors, the Imams: compare SUNNI. **2** a member of this branch of Islam. [Arabic *shī'ah* sect]

shiatsu /shee'atsooh, shi-/ *noun* = ACUPRESSURE. [Japanese *shiatsuryōhō*, from *shi* finger + *atsu-* pressure + *ryōhō* therapy]

shibboleth /'shibəleth/ *noun* **1a** a commonplace belief or saying: *the shibboleth that crime does not pay.* **b** a catchword or slogan. **2** a custom or particular use of language that characterizes the members of a particular group.

Word history

Hebrew *shibbōleth* stream; from the use of this word as a test to distinguish Gileadites from Ephraimites, who pronounced it *sibbōleth*. In the biblical account (Judges 12:4–6) of a battle between the Ephraimites and Gileadites, the Ephraimites were defeated, and those of their forces who escaped the battlefield tried to pass themselves off as Gileadites and cross the river Jordan to safety. To identify them, everyone crossing the river was asked to pronounce the word *shibboleth*. The Ephraimites, who spoke a different dialect, could not cope with the /sh/ sound but could only pronounce it as /s/; thus they were found out, and 42,000 of them were killed. The metaphorical senses of the word entered English in the mid-17th cent.

---

shickered /'shikəd/ *adj Aus, NZ, informal* drunk. [Yiddish *shiker* from Hebrew *shikkōr*, from *shikhar* to be drunk]

shield[1] /sheeld/ *noun* **1** a piece of armour, e.g. of wood, metal, or leather, carried on the arm or in the hand and used *esp* for warding off blows. **2** somebody or something that protects or defends. **3** something designed to protect people from injury from moving parts of machinery, live electrical conductors, etc. **4** an armoured screen protecting an otherwise exposed gun. **5** a protective structure, e.g. a carapace, scale, or plate, of some animals. **6** a defined area on which heraldic arms are displayed; *esp* one that is wide at the top and rounds to a point at the bottom. **7** something resembling a shield, e.g.: **a** a trophy awarded in recognition of achievement, e.g. in a sporting event. **b** a decorative or identifying emblem, *esp* a US police officer's official badge. **8** the Precambrian central rock mass of a continent. [Old English *scield*]

shield[2] *verb trans* **1** to protect (something or somebody) with or as if with a shield; to provide with a protective cover or shelter. **2** to prevent (somebody or something) from being seen; to hide or screen. **3** to prevent harmful radiation, light, sound, etc escaping from (something).

shieldbug *noun* any of various bugs that emit a disagreeable odour. [from the shield-like shape of its scutellum]

shield volcano *noun* a volcano with a very broad low dome and gently sloping sides.

shieling /'sheeling/ *noun* **1** *Brit, dialect* a mountain hut used as a shelter by shepherds. **2** a summer pasture in the mountains. [Scots *shiel* shed, hut, from Middle English (northern) *schele, shale*]

shift[1] /shift/ *verb trans* **1** to change the place, position, or direction of (something or somebody); to move: *I can't shift the grand piano.* **2** to exchange (one thing) for or replace it by another; to change: *The traitor had again shifted his allegiance.* **3** *Brit* to remove (e.g. a stain) by cleaning, rubbing, etc. **4** *informal* to sell or dispose of (something), *esp* quickly or in large quantities. **5** *informal* to consume (food or drink), *esp* in large quantities: *I shifted a few pints last night.* ➤ *verb intrans* **1a** to change place or position: *He was shifting uneasily in his chair.* **b** to change direction: *The wind shifted round to the east.* **2** *NAmer* to change gear in a motor vehicle. **3** *Brit, informal* to move fast: *We'd better shift if we don't want to miss the train.* **4** said of a sound: to become changed phonetically as a language evolves. ✳ **shift for oneself** to assume responsibility for providing for oneself. **shift oneself** *Brit, informal* to start moving fast; to hurry up. ➤➤ **shiftable** *adj*, **shifter** *noun*. [Old English *sciftan* to divide, arrange]

shift² *noun* **1a** a change in direction: *a shift in the wind*. **b** a change in emphasis, judgment, or attitude. **2a** (*treated as sing. or pl*) a group who work, e.g. in a factory, in alternation with other groups. **b** a scheduled period of work or duty: *on the night shift*. **3** a change in place or position, e.g.: **a** the relative displacement of rock masses on opposite sides of a fault. **b** a change in position of a line or band in a spectrum: compare DOPPLER EFFECT. **4** systematic sound change as a language evolves. **5a** *archaic* a deceitful or underhand scheme or method; a subterfuge or dodge. **b** (*usu in pl*) an expedient tried in difficult circumstances. **6** a loose unfitted dress or slip. **7** *NAmer* the gear change in a motor vehicle.

shift key *noun* a key on a typewriter or computer keyboard that is held down to produce a different set of characters, *esp* the capitals.

shiftless *adj* **1** lacking resourcefulness; inefficient. **2** lacking ambition or motivation; lazy. ➤➤ **shiftlessly** *adv*, **shiftlessness** *noun*.

shifty *adj* (**shiftier**, **shiftiest**) **1** given to deception, evasion, or fraud. **2** indicative of a furtive or devious nature: *shifty eyes*. ➤➤ **shiftily** *adv*, **shiftiness** *noun*.

shigella /shi'gelə/ *noun* (*pl* **shigellae** /-lee/ *or* **shigellas**) any of a genus of bacteria that cause dysentery, *esp* in human beings: genus *Shigella*. [named after Kiyoshi *Shiga* d.1957, the Japanese bacteriologist who discovered them]

shih-tzu /shee'tsooh/ *noun* a small dog of an old Chinese breed with a square short unwrinkled muzzle, short muscular legs, and massive amounts of long dense hair. [Chinese (Pekingese) *shīzgǒu*, literally 'lion dog']

Shiite /'shee·iet/ *noun* an adherent of Islam as taught by the Shia. ➤➤ **Shiism** *noun*, **Shiite** *adj*.

shikari /shi'kahri/ *noun* (*pl* **shikaris**) *Indian* a big-game hunter, *esp* a professional hunter or guide. [Urdu *shikari* from Persian, from *sikār*]

shiksa *or* **shikse** /'shiksə/ *noun* *derog* a non-Jewish girl. [Yiddish *shikse*, fem of *sheykets*, *sheygets* non-Jewish boy, from Hebrew *šeqeṣ* blemish, abomination]

shill¹ /shil/ *noun* *NAmer, informal* a person who poses, e.g. as a customer or gambler, so as to entice others. [prob short for *shillaber* of unknown origin]

shill² *verb intrans* *NAmer, informal* to act as a shill.

shillelagh /shi'layli/ *noun* an Irish cudgel. [named after *Shillelagh*, a town in County Wicklow, Ireland, famed for its oak trees]

shilling /'shiling/ *noun* **1a** a former monetary unit in Britain and various Commonwealth countries, worth one 20th of a pound or twelve old pence. **b** a coin representing one shilling. **2** the basic monetary unit of Kenya, Somalia, Tanzania, and Uganda. [Old English *scilling*]

shilly-shally /'shili shali/ *verb intrans* (**shilly-shallies**, **shilly-shallied**, **shilly-shallying**) to show hesitation or lack of decisiveness. ➤➤ **shilly-shally** *noun*. [orig *shill I*, *shall I*, reduplication of *shall I*]

shim¹ /shim/ *noun* a thin piece of wood, metal, etc used to fill in the space between things, e.g. for support or adjustment of fit. [origin unknown]

shim² *verb trans* (**shimmed**, **shimming**) to fill out or level up (something) by the use of one or more shims.

shimmer¹ /'shimə/ *verb intrans* **1** to shine with a softly tremulous or wavering light; to glimmer. **2** to appear in a fluctuating wavy form: *the shimmering heat from the pavement*. **3** to move with an unobtrusiveness suggestive of the play of light: *Jeeves shimmered out and came back with a telegram* — P G Wodehouse. [Old English *scimerian*]

shimmer² *noun* **1** a shimmering light. **2** a wavering and distortion of the visual image of a far object usu resulting from heat-induced changes in atmospheric refraction. ➤➤ **shimmery** *adj*.

shimmy¹ /'shimi/ *noun* (*pl* **shimmies**) **1** a chemise. **2** a jazz dance characterized by a shaking of the body from the shoulders downwards. [(sense 1) by alteration; (sense 2) short for *shimmy-shake* and *shimmy-shiver*]

shimmy² *verb intrans* (**shimmies**, **shimmied**, **shimmying**) **1** to dance the shimmy. **2** to shake, quiver, or tremble.

shin¹ /shin/ *noun* **1** the front part of the leg of a vertebrate animal below the knee. **2** a cut of meat from this part, *esp* from the front leg of a quadruped: *a shin of beef*. [Old English *scinu*]

shin² *verb* (**shinned**, **shinning**) ➤ *verb intrans* (*usu* + up/down) to climb by gripping with the hands or arms and the legs and hauling oneself up or lowering oneself down: *The boy shinned up the tree*. ➤ *verb trans* **1** to kick (somebody) on the shins. **2** to climb (something) by shinning.

shinbone *noun* = TIBIA (1).

shindig /'shindig/ *noun informal* a usu boisterous social gathering. [alteration of SHINDY]

shindy /'shindi/ *noun* (*pl* **shindys** *or* **shindies**) *informal* a quarrel or brawl. [prob alteration of *shinny*. see SHINTY]

shine¹ /shien/ *verb* (*past tense and past part.* **shone** /shon/) ➤ *verb intrans* **1** to emit light. **2** to be bright with reflected light. **3** to be outstanding or distinguished: *She always shines in mathematics*. **4** to have a radiant or lively appearance: *His face shone with enthusiasm*. ➤ *verb trans* **1** to direct the light of (e.g. a lamp or torch). **2** (*past tense and past part.* **chined**) to make (something) bright by polishing: *He decided to get his shoes shined*. [Old English *scīnan*]

shine² *noun* **1** brightness caused by the emission or reflection of light. **2** brilliance or splendour: *Pageantry that has kept its shine over the centuries*. **3** fine weather; sunshine: *come rain, come shine*. **4** an act of polishing shoes. **⁕ take a shine to** *informal* to like (somebody or something) immediately. **take the shine off** to make (something) less enjoyable, exciting, etc.

shiner *noun* **1** *informal* = BLACK EYE. **2** any of several species of small N American freshwater fishes with a silvery skin: genus *Notropis* and other genera. **3** a thing that shines or that can be used to shine something.

shingle¹ /'shinggl/ *noun* **1** a small thin piece of building material, usu wood, for laying in overlapping rows as a covering for the roof or sides of a building. **2** *dated* a woman's short haircut in which the hair is shaped into the nape of the neck. **3** *NAmer* a small signboard, *esp* one indicating the office of a doctor, lawyer, etc: *Laitner ... permitted Arobin's name to decorate the firm's letterheads and to appear upon a shingle that graced Perdido Street* — Kate Chopin. [Middle English *schingel*, from Latin *scindula*, *scandula* split piece of wood]

shingle² *verb trans* **1** to cover (a roof, etc) with shingles: *The cabin's plank walls were supplemented with sheets of corrugated iron, its roof shingled with tin cans hammered flat* — Harper Lee. **2** to cut (hair) in a shingle: *It had been necessary to shingle the hair as closely as possible* — L M Montgomery.

shingle³ *noun* small rounded pebbles, or an area, *esp* on the seashore, that is covered with them. ➤➤ **shingly** *adj*. [prob of Scandinavian origin]

shingles *pl noun* (*treated as sing.*) severe short-lasting inflammation of certain nerve endings, caused by a virus and associated with a rash of blisters and often intense pain. [Middle English *schingles*, alteration of medieval Latin *cingulus* girdle, from Latin *cingere* to gird; because the rash may encircle the body]

shining /'shiening/ *adj* **1** emitting or reflecting light; bright. **2** possessing an especially noteworthy or remarkable quality; outstanding: *a shining example of bravery*.

shin pad *noun* a pad worn to protect the shin when playing games such as football or hockey.

shinsplints *pl noun* (*treated as sing.*) a painful muscular swelling of the lower leg that is a common injury in athletes who regularly run on hard surfaces.

Shinto /'shintoh/ *noun* the indigenous animistic religion of Japan, including the veneration of the Emperor as a descendant of the sun goddess.

Editorial note
The Japanese word 'shinto' means, literally, 'the way of the gods'. Although commonly defined as the indigenous (that is, pre-Buddhist) religion of Japan, such a meaning is the product of Japanese modernists who sought to identify a native religious heritage for Japan existing prior to the introduction of foreign elements. Shinto only became a separate religion during the 19th cent. and has continued as such — Professor Donald Lopez

➤➤ **Shinto** *adj*, **Shintoism** *noun*, **Shintoist** *noun and adj*, **Shintoistic** /-'istik/ *adj*. [Japanese *shintō*]

shinty /'shinti/ *noun* a variation of hurling played in Scotland. [alteration of *shinny*, a kind of hockey, perhaps from SHIN¹ + -Y¹]

shiny /'shieni/ *adj* (**shinier, shiniest**) **1** bright or glossy in appearance; lustrous or polished: *shiny new shoes.* **2** having worn to a smooth surface that reflects light. ➤➤ **shininess** *noun.*

ship[1] /ship/ *noun* **1a** a floating vessel, usu propelled by an engine, for travelling over water, *esp* a large seagoing one. **b** a square-rigged sailing vessel having a bowsprit and usu three masts. **2** (*treated as sing. or pl*) a ship's crew. **3a** a spacecraft. **b** an airship or other aircraft. ✳ **when one's ship comes in** when one becomes rich. [Old English *scip*]

ship[2] *verb* (**shipped, shipping**) ➤ *verb trans* **1a** to transport (e.g. goods) on board a ship. **b** to transport (e.g. goods) by another means, e.g. road or rail. **2** *informal* (*often* + off) to send (somebody or something) somewhere: *His parents shipped him off to boarding school.* **3** to put (a piece of equipment) in place on a boat ready for use. **4** to take (something) into a ship or boat: *The crew had already shipped the gangplank.* **5** said of a boat or ship: to take in (water) over the side. **6** to engage (somebody or a crew) for service on a ship. ➤ *verb intrans* to go or travel by ship. ➤➤ **shippable** *adj.*

-ship *suffix* forming nouns, denoting: **1** state, condition, or quality: *friendship.* **2a** the office, status, or profession: *professorship.* **b** the period during which the specified office or position is held: *during his dictatorship.* **3** art or skill: *horsemanship; scholarship.* **4** (*treated as sing. or pl*) the whole group or body sharing the specified state: *readership; membership.* **5** somebody entitled to the specified rank, title, or appellation: *his Lordship.* [Old English *-scipe*]

ship biscuit *noun* = SHIP'S BISCUIT.

shipboard[1] ✳ **on shipboard** on board a ship.

shipboard[2] *adj* existing or taking place on board a ship.

ship-breaker *noun* a person or company that dismantles and scraps old ships.

shipbuilder *noun* a person or company that designs or constructs ships. ➤➤ **shipbuilding** *noun.*

ship canal *noun* a canal large enough to allow the passage of seagoing vessels.

ship chandler *noun* a person or company that provides supplies for boats or ships.

shipload *noun* as much or as many as a ship will carry.

shipmate *noun* a fellow sailor.

shipment *noun* **1** the act or process of shipping. **2** a consignment or quantity of goods shipped: *a shipment of oranges.*

ship money *noun* a tax levied at various times in England until 1640, to provide ships for the national defence.

ship of the line *noun* a ship of war large enough to have a place in the line of battle.

shipowner *noun* the owner of a ship or a share in a ship.

shipper *noun* a person or company that ships goods.

shipping *noun* **1** ships, *esp* those sailing in a particular area or belonging to one port or country. **2** the activity or business of a shipper.

ship-rigged *adj* square-rigged.

ship's biscuit *noun chiefly Brit* a type of hard biscuit orig for eating on board ship.

shipshape *adj* neat; tidy. [shortening of *shipshapen*, from SHIP[1] + *shapen*, archaic past part. of SHAPE[1]]

shipway *noun* the structure on which a ship is built and from which it is launched.

shipworm *noun* any of various elongated marine clams that resemble worms and burrow in submerged wood: *Teredo navalis* and other species.

shipwreck[1] *noun* **1** a wrecked ship or its remains. **2** the destruction or loss of a ship. **3** an irrevocable collapse or destruction. [alteration of *shipwrack* from Old English *scipwrœc*, from *scip* SHIP[1] + *wrœc* something driven by the sea, from *wrecan* to drive]

shipwreck[2] *verb trans* **1** to cause (somebody or a ship) to undergo shipwreck. **2** to ruin (somebody or something).

shipwright /'shipriet/ *noun* a person skilled in ship construction and repair.

shipyard *noun* a yard, place, or enclosure where ships are built or repaired.

Shiraz /shi'raz, shiə'rahz/ *noun* **1** a variety of grape used in the production of dark full-bodied red wine. **2** a wine produced from this grape. [named after *Shiraz*, city in Iran, from where the vine is said to have originated]

shire /shie-ə/ *noun* **1a** an administrative subdivision; *specif* an English county, *esp* one with a name ending in *-shire.* **b** (*usu* **the Shires**) an English rural district consisting chiefly of Leicestershire and Northamptonshire. **2** = SHIRE HORSE. [Old English *scīr* office, shire]

shire horse *noun* an animal of a British breed of large heavy draught horses with long hair on their fetlocks. [because the breed originated in the Shires]

shirk[1] /shuhk/ *verb trans and intrans* to evade or dodge (a duty, responsibility, etc). ➤➤ **shirker** *noun.* [orig in the sense 'to trick, swindle', prob ultimately from German *Schurke* scoundrel]

shirk[2] *noun archaic* a person who shirks.

shirr /shuh/ *verb trans* (**shirred, shirring**) **1** to draw (e.g. cloth) together by means of shirring. **2** *chiefly NAmer* to bake (eggs removed from the shell) in a small dish until set. [origin unknown]

shirring /'shuhring/ *noun* a decorative gathering, *esp* in cloth, made by drawing up the material along two or more parallel lines of stitching or rows of elastic thread.

shirt /shuht/ *noun* a garment for the upper body, usu one that opens the full length of the centre front and has sleeves and a collar. ✳ **have/take the shirt off somebody's back** *informal* to take somebody's last remaining possessions. **keep one's shirt on** *informal* to remain calm; not to lose one's temper. **lose one's shirt** *informal* to lose a large amount of money or everything one has, *esp* in gambling. **put one's shirt on** *Brit, informal* to bet all the money one has on (something).

Word history

Old English *scyrte*, related to Old Norse *skyrta* shirt, kirtle, ancestor of SKIRT[1]. Both prob come from the same prehistoric Germanic word as SHORT[1], literally meaning 'short garment'.

shirting *noun* fabric suitable for shirts.

shirt-lifter *noun Brit, slang, derog* a male homosexual.

shirtsleeve *noun* the sleeve of a shirt. ✳ **in shirtsleeves** said of a man: not wearing a jacket over his shirt.

shirt-sleeve *or* **shirt-sleeved** *adj* **1** not wearing a jacket, or consisting of people in shirtsleeves: *a shirt-sleeve audience.* **2** marked by informality and directness: *shirt-sleeve diplomacy.*

shirtwaister (*NAmer* **shirtwaist**) *noun* a fitted dress that fastens down the centre front to just below the waist or to the hem.

shirty *adj* (**shirtier, shirtiest**) *informal* bad-tempered or annoyed. [from the obsolete phrase *to get someone's shirt out* to cause somebody to lose his or her temper, probably from the idea of stripping off the shirt in preparation for a fight]

shish kebab /'shish ki,bab/ *noun* a kebab cooked on a skewer. [Turkish *şiş kebap*, from *şiş* skewer + *kebap* roast meat]

shit[1] /shit/ *verb trans and intrans* (**shitting**, past tense and past part. **shitted** *or* **shit** *or* **shat** /shat/) *coarse slang* to defecate on or in (something). ✳ **shit oneself 1** *coarse slang* to defecate in one's clothing. **2** *coarse slang* to be extremely frightened or anxious. [Middle English *shiten*, prob from Old English *bescītan* to smear with excrement]

shit[2] *noun coarse slang* **1** faeces. **2** an act of defecation. **3a** nonsense or foolishness. **b** a despicable person. **4** a narcotic drug, *esp* cannabis. ✳ **be in the shit** *coarse slang* to be in serious trouble. **be up shit creek (without a paddle)** *coarse slang* to be in a very difficult situation. **not to give a shit** *coarse slang* to be totally unconcerned. **when the shit hits the fan** *coarse slang* when the real trouble begins, e.g. when somebody in authority finds out about a mistake, or its disastrous consequences make themselves felt. [Old English *scitte* diarrhoea]

shit[3] *interj coarse slang* used to express annoyance or impatience.

shite /shiet/ *noun and interj Brit, coarse slang* = SHIT[2], SHIT[3].

shit-eating *adj NAmer, coarse slang* complacent or smug: *a shit-eating grin.*

shit-hot *adj coarse slang* really good or brilliant.

shitless ✳ **be scared shitless** *coarse slang* to be extremely scared.

shitlist *noun NAmer, coarse slang* a list of disliked people or things or of people that one intends harm to.

shitload *noun coarse slang* a very large number or quantity.

shit-scared *adj coarse slang* completely terrified.

shitty *adj* (**shittier, shittiest**) *coarse slang* **1a** nasty or unpleasant. **b** contemptible. **2** covered in excrement.

Shiva /'sheevə/ *noun* see SIVA.

shivaree /shivə'ree/ *noun NAmer* = CHARIVARI.

shiver[1] /'shivə/ *verb intrans* (**shivered, shivering**) to tremble, *esp* with cold or fever. [Middle English *shiveren*, of unknown origin]

shiver[2] *noun* **1** an instance of shivering; a tremor. **2** (**the shivers**) a fit of shivering. ⟫ **shivery** *adj*.

shiver[3] *noun* any of the small pieces that result from the shattering of something brittle. [Middle English *schivre*, of Germanic origin]

shiver[4] *verb trans and intrans* (**shivered, shivering**) to break into many small fragments, or to cause (something) to do this.

shmear /shmiə/ *noun* see SCHMEAR.

shmeer /shmiə/ *noun* see SCHMEAR.

shmo /shmoh/ *noun* see SCHMO.

shmooze[1] /shmoohz/ *verb trans and intrans* see SCHMOOZE[1].

shmooze[2] *noun* see SCHMOOZE[2].

shmuck /shmuk/ *noun* see SCHMUCK.

shoal[1] /shohl/ *noun* **1** an underwater sandbank, *esp* one exposed at low tide. **2** an area of shallow water. [alteration of Middle English *shold, shoald*, from Old English *sceald* shallow]

shoal[2] *verb intrans* to become shallow or less deep.

shoal[3] *noun* a large group, *esp* of fish. [Old English *scolu* multitude]

shock[1] /shok/ *noun* **1a** a sudden or violent disturbance of a person's thoughts or emotions. **b** something that causes a disturbance of this kind: *The news came as a terrible shock.* **2** a state in which most bodily functions temporarily cease to operate as normal that is associated with reduced blood volume and pressure and caused usu by severe injuries, bleeding, burns, or psychological trauma. **3** sudden stimulation of the nerves and convulsive contraction of the muscles caused by the passage of electricity through the body. **4a** a violent impact or collision. **b** a violent shaking or jarring: *an earthquake shock.* **5** *informal* = SHOCK ABSORBER. [early French *choc* from *choquer* to strike against, from Old French *choquier*]

shock[2] *verb trans* **1a** to cause (somebody) to feel sudden surprise, terror, horror, or offence. **b** to cause (somebody) to undergo a physical or nervous shock. **2** to cause (e.g. an animal) to experience an electric shock. **3** to impel (somebody) by or as if by a shock: *His expression shocked her into realizing her selfishness.* ⟫ **shockable** *adj*.

shock[3] *noun* a pile of sheaves of grain or stalks of maize set upright in a field. [Middle English, prob from early Dutch or early Low German *schok*]

shock[4] *verb trans* to arrange (sheaves of grain) in shocks.

shock[5] *noun* a thick bushy mass, usu of hair. [perhaps from SHOCK[3]]

shock absorber *noun* a device for absorbing the energy of sudden jolts or shocks, *esp* fitted to a motor vehicle to give a smoother ride.

shocker *noun informal* **1** something horrifying or offensive, e.g. a sensational work of fiction or drama. **2** an incorrigible or naughty person.

shock-headed *adj* having a thick bushy mass of hair.

shocking *adj* **1** giving cause for indignation or offence. **2** *Brit, informal* very bad: *She had a shocking cold.* ⟫ **shockingly** *adv*.

shocking pink *adj* of a striking, vivid, bright, or intense pink colour. ⟫ **shocking pink** *noun*.

shock jock *noun chiefly NAmer, informal* a radio disc jockey or chat show host noted for the offensive or provocative nature of their comments or opinions.

shockproof *adj* resistant to shock; constructed so as to absorb shock without damage: *a shockproof watch.*

shock therapy *noun* a treatment for some serious mental disorders that involves artificially inducing a coma or convulsions.

shock treatment *noun* = SHOCK THERAPY.

shock troops *pl noun* troops trained and selected for assault.

shock wave *noun* **1** = BLAST[1] (1B). **2** a compressional wave formed whenever the speed of a body, e.g. an aircraft, relative to a medium, e.g. the air, exceeds that at which the medium can transmit sound.

shod /shod/ *verb* past tense and past part. of SHOE[2].

shoddy[1] /'shodi/ *adj* (**shoddier, shoddiest**) **1** hastily or poorly done; inferior. **2** cheaply imitating things of better quality, *esp* in a vulgarly pretentious way. **3** discreditable or despicable. ⟫ **shoddily** *adv*, **shoddiness** *noun*. [origin unknown]

shoddy[2] *noun* a fabric, often of inferior quality, manufactured wholly or partly from reclaimed wool: *When you have nothing else to wear but cloth of gold and satins rare, for cloth of gold you cease to care – up goes the price of shoddy* — W S Gilbert.

shoe[1] /shooh/ *noun* **1a** an outer covering for the human foot that does not extend above the ankle and has a thick or stiff sole and often an attached heel. **b** a metal plate or rim for the hoof of an animal. **2** something resembling a shoe in shape or function. **3** the part of a vehicle braking system that presses on the brake drum. ✳ **be in somebody's shoes** to be in somebody else's situation or position. **dead men's shoes** a situation in which a job, position, or property can only be obtained through the death or voluntary withdrawal of somebody else. [Old English *scōh*]

shoe[2] *verb trans* (**shoes, shoed, shoeing**, *past tense and past part.* **shod**) **1** to fit (e.g. a horse) with a shoe. **2** to protect or reinforce (something) with a usu metal shoe. **3** (*usu in passive*) to equip (somebody) with shoes.

shoeblack *noun dated* = BOOTBLACK.

shoehorn *noun* a curved piece of metal, plastic, etc used to ease the heel into the back of a shoe.

shoe-horn *verb trans* to force (somebody or something) into a limited space: *They were shoe-horning passengers into the trains.*

shoelace *noun* a lace or string for fastening a shoe.

shoemaker *noun* somebody whose occupation is making or repairing footwear.

shoeshine *noun* an act of polishing shoes.

shoestring *noun* **1** *NAmer* = SHOELACE. **2** *informal* an amount of money inadequate or barely adequate to meet one's needs: *She was trying to run a business on a shoestring.* [(sense 2) because shoestrings were a typical item sold by pedlars]

shoetree *noun* a roughly foot-shaped device made of wood or plastic and metal, inserted in a shoe to keep it in shape when not being worn.

shofar /'shohfah, 'shohfə/ *noun* (*pl* **shofars** or **shofroth** /shoh'frohth, -'froht/) a ram's-horn trumpet used in synagogues before and during Rosh Hashanah and at the conclusion of Yom Kippur. [Hebrew *shōphār*]

shogun /'shohgən/ *noun* any of a line of Japanese military governors who effectively ruled the country before the revolution of 1867–68. ⟫ **shogunate** /-nayt/ *noun*. [Japanese *shōgun* general]

Shona /'shohnə/ *noun* (*pl* **Shonas** *or collectively* **Shona**) **1** a member of a group of peoples inhabiting parts of southern Africa. **2** any of the Bantu languages of the Shona. ⟫ **Shona** *adj*. [a Bantu name]

shone /shon/ *verb* past tense and past part. of SHINE[1].

shoo[1] /shooh/ *interj* used in frightening away an animal. [Middle English *schowe*]

shoo[2] *verb trans* (**shoos, shooed, shooing**) to drive (an animal) away by crying 'Shoo!'

shoo-in *noun NAmer, informal* somebody, e.g. a contestant, who is a certain and easy winner.

shook[1] /shook/ *verb* past tense of SHAKE[1].

shook[2] *noun NAmer* a set of wooden staves and end pieces for making a hogshead, cask, or barrel. [origin unknown]

shoot[1] /shooht/ *verb* (*past tense and past part.* **shot** /shot/) ⟫ *verb trans* **1a** to strike and wound or kill (a person or an animal) with a bullet from a gun, arrow from a bow, or similar missile: *When I came back to Dublin I was courtmartialled in my absence and sentenced to death in my absence, so I said they could shoot me in my absence* — Brendan Behan. **b** to fire (a gun) or release an arrow from (a bow). **c** to fire (bullets, blanks, arrows) from a gun or bow. **2a** to hunt (game) with a firearm or bow for food or sport. **b** to hunt over (an area) with a gun or bow. **c** to remove or destroy (something) firing a bullet or arrow at it. **3a** to cause (something) to move suddenly or swiftly forward. **b** to throw (somebody or something) off or out, *esp* with force: *The horse shot its rider out of the saddle.* **c** (*often + out*) to thrust (something) forwards; to stick (something) out: *The toad shot out its tongue.* **d** to emit (e.g. light or flame) suddenly and rapidly. **4a** to drive (e.g. a ball or puck) *esp* towards a goal or hole, by striking it with the arm, hand, foot, or an implement. **b** to engage in (a sport or game that involves shooting): *shoot pool; shoot* a round of golf. **c** to score (something) by shooting. **5a** to utter (e.g. words or sounds) rapidly, suddenly, or violently: *shooting staccato inquiries* — Angus Wilson. **b** to direct (e.g. a glance) at somebody with suddenness or intensity: *She shot a look of anger at him.* **6a** to photograph or film (somebody or something). **b** to make (a film, videotape, etc). **7a** to push or slide (e.g. the bolt of a door or lock) into or out of a fastening. **b** to pass (a shuttle) through the warp threads in weaving. **8a** said of a boat: to pass swiftly by, over, or along (a bridge, waterfall, or rapids). **b** *informal* said of a vehicle or driver: to pass through (a road junction or traffic lights) without slowing down or stopping. **9** *slang* to take (a drug) by hypodermic needle. **10** to plane (e.g. the edge of a board) straight or true. **11** *informal* to place or offer (a bet) on the result of casting dice. ➤ *verb intrans* **1a** to cause a weapon to discharge a missile, *esp* to fire a gun. **b** to use a firearm or bow for sport or hunting. **2a** to propel an object, e.g. a ball, in a particular way. **b** to drive the ball or puck in football, hockey, etc towards the goal. **3a** to move or to be emitted or ejected rapidly or violently: *Sparks were shooting up from the burning timbers*; *His feet shot out from under him.* **b** to stream out suddenly; to spurt: *Blood shot from the wound.* **c** to produce a piercing sensation that moves rapidly through part of the body: *Pain shot up his arm.* **d** to slide into or out of a fastening. **4a** to record a series of visual images, e.g. on cinefilm or videotape; to make a film or videotape. **b** to operate a camera or set cameras in operation; to film. **5** to grow or sprout by putting out shoots. **6** (*often* + out) to protrude or project. **7** to throw dice. ✷ **shoot a line** *informal* to lie about something, or to embroider an account of it in romantic or boastful detail. **shoot craps** to play a game of craps. **shoot one's cuffs** to pull one's shirt cuffs down. **shoot oneself in the foot** to act inadvertently to one's own disadvantage; to bring about one's own downfall. **shoot one's mouth off** *informal* to talk foolishly or indiscreetly. **shoot the breeze** *NAmer, informal* to chat. **the whole shooting match** *informal* everything. [Old English *scēotan*]

shoot² *noun* **1a** a stem or branch with its leaves, buds, etc, *esp* when not yet mature. **b** = OFFSHOOT. **2a** a shooting trip or party. **b** land over which somebody holds the right to shoot game. **c** a shooting match. **3a** a rush of water down a descent in a stream. **b** = CHUTE. **4** a session during which a photographer takes photographs or a film or video is shot.

shoot down *verb trans* **1a** to kill or incapacitate (somebody) by shooting them. **b** to bring down (an aircraft or missile) by shooting. **2** *informal* to dismiss or reject (a proposal or other person making it).

shooter *noun* **1** a person empowered to score goals in netball. **2** (*usu in combination*) a repeating pistol: *a six-shooter.*

shooting box *noun Brit* a small country house used by a shooting party.

shooting brake *noun Brit, dated* = ESTATE CAR.

shooting gallery *noun* a usu covered range equipped with targets for practice in shooting with firearms.

shooting star *noun* a meteor appearing as a temporary streak of light in the night sky.

shooting stick *noun* a spiked stick with a handle that opens out into a seat.

shoot-out *noun* **1** *informal* a usu decisive battle fought with handguns or rifles. **2** = PENALTY SHOOT-OUT.

shoot through *verb intrans Aus, NZ, informal* to leave; *specif* to make a hasty departure.

shoot up *verb intrans* **1** to grow or increase rapidly. **2** *informal* to inject a narcotic drug into a vein.

shop¹ /shop/ *noun* **1** a building or room for the retail sale of merchandise or for the sale of services. **2** a place or part of a factory where a particular manufacturing or repair process takes place. **3** the jargon or subject matter peculiar to an occupation or sphere of interest. **4** *informal* an act of shopping. ✷ **talk shop** to talk about one's business or profession, *esp* outside working hours. [Old English *sceoppa* booth]

shop² *verb* (**shopped, shopping**) ➤ *verb intrans* **1** to visit a shop in order to purchase goods. **2** to try to find (something), usu in order to purchase (it): *City are shopping for a new striker.* ➤ *verb trans informal* to inform on (somebody); to betray (them): *The police tried to get him to shop his mates.*

shopaholic /shopə'holik/ *noun informal* somebody who shops obsessively.

shop around *verb intrans* to investigate a market or situation in search of the best buy or alternative.

shop assistant *noun Brit* somebody employed to sell goods in a retail shop.

shopfitter *noun* somebody who equips a shop with fittings, e.g. shelves. ➤➤ **shopfitting** *noun.*

shopfloor *noun* **1** *Brit* the area in which machinery or workbenches are located in a factory or mill, *esp* considered as a place of work. **2** (*treated as sing. or pl*) the workers in an establishment as distinct from the management.

shopfront *noun* the front side of a shop facing the street.

shopkeeper *noun* somebody who runs a retail shop. ➤➤ **shopkeeping** *noun.*

shoplift *verb trans and intrans* to steal (something) from a shop. ➤➤ **shoplifting** *noun.* [back-formation from SHOPLIFTER]

shoplifter *noun* somebody who steals from a shop while pretending to be a customer.

shopper *noun* **1** somebody who is shopping. **2** *Brit* a bag used for shopping, *esp* a square bag on wheels that can be pulled along. **3** a bicycle that has small wheels and a basket.

shopping *noun* **1** the act of purchasing goods from shops. **2** goods purchased on a shopping trip.

shopping centre *noun* a group of retail shops and service establishments of different types, often designed to serve a community or neighbourhood.

shopping mall *noun* a large enclosed shopping centre, usu with space for car parking.

shopping therapy *noun* shopping undertaken as a release from the stresses and strains of everyday life.

shopsoiled *adj chiefly Brit* soiled, faded, or in less than perfect condition through excessive handling or display in a shop.

shop steward *noun* a union member elected to represent usu manual workers.

shopwalker *noun Brit* somebody employed in a large shop to oversee the shop assistants and aid customers.

shopwindow *noun* **1** a usu large window in which a shop displays merchandise. **2** a place where something or somebody can be exhibited to best advantage; a showcase.

shopworn *adj chiefly NAmer* = SHOPSOILED.

shoran /'shawran/ *noun* a system of short-range aircraft navigation in which radar signals are sent out and returned by two ground stations of known position. [contraction of *short-range navigation*]

shore¹ /shaw/ *noun* **1** the land bordering the sea or another large body of water. **2** land as distinguished from the sea. **3** in law, coastland that lies between ordinary high- and low-water marks. [Middle English from early Dutch or early Low German *schōre*]

shore² *verb trans* to support (something) with a beam or prop, *esp* to prevent its sinking or sagging; to prop (it) up. [Middle English *shoren* from early Dutch or early Low German *shore* prop]

shore³ *noun* a beam or prop used to shore something.

shore⁴ *verb archaic or Aus, NZ* past tense of SHEAR¹.

shore leave *noun* time granted to members of a ship's crew to go ashore.

shoreline *noun* **1** the line where a body of water and the shore meet. **2** the strip of land along this line.

shorewards /'shawwədz/ *adv* towards the shore.

shoring *noun* **1** the act of supporting with or as if with shores. **2** a system or quantity of shores.

shorn /shawn/ *verb* past part. of SHEAR¹.

short¹ /shawt/ *adj* **1** having little or insufficient length or height. **2** not extended in time; brief: *a short vacation.* **3** limited in distance: *a short walk.* **4** seeming to pass quickly: *She made great progress in just a few short years.* **5a** not coming up to a measure or requirement: *in short supply.* **b** not reaching far enough: *The throw was short by five metres.* **c** (*often* + of) insufficiently supplied: *short of cash.* **6a** not lengthy or protracted; concise. **b** made briefer; abbreviated: *Sue is short for Susan.* **7a** abrupt or curt. **b** quickly provoked: *a short temper.* **8a** said of a speech sound: having a relatively short duration. **b** said of one of a pair of similarly spelt vowel sounds: shorter in duration than the other. **c** said of a syllable in verse: of relatively brief duration. **d** said of a syllable in verse: unstressed. **9** said of odds in betting: almost even. **10** payable at an early date; short-term. **11a** said of a seller: not yet possessing the goods or property that he or she has contracted to sell because their price is expected to fall before the delivery date. **b** relating to the sale of securities or commodities that the seller does not possess or has not contracted for at the time of the sale. **12** said of pastry: crisp and easily broken owing to the presence of fat; crumbly. **13** in cricket: **a** denoting or occupying a fielding position near the batsman. **b** said of a bowled ball: bouncing relatively far from the batsman. ✳ **get/have somebody by the short and curlies** *informal* to have somebody totally at one's mercy. **in short order** quickly. **in the short run** for the immediate future. **make short work of something** to get through something quickly: *The children made short work of the plate of cakes.* **short and sweet** brief and not too unpleasant: *Let's keep the meeting short and sweet.* **short for** an abbreviation for. ➤➤ **shortish** *adj*, **shortness** *noun*. [Old English *scort*|

short² *adv* **1** in an abrupt manner; suddenly: *The car stopped short.* **2** before reaching a specified or intended point or target: *The shells fell short.* **3** in a curt manner. **4** said of a financial deal: by a short sale. ✳ **be taken/caught short** *Brit, informal* to feel a sudden embarrassing need to defecate or urinate. **bring/pull somebody up short** to make somebody stop or pause suddenly. **short of 1** less than. *Nothing short of a miracle can save them now.* **2** before reaching (an extreme): *He stopped short of murder.*

short³ *noun* **1** *Brit, informal* a drink of spirits; *esp* such a drink as opposed to beer. **2** a brief film, often a documentary or educational film. **3a** a short syllable or vowel. **b** a short sound or signal, e.g. in Morse code. **4** = SHORT CIRCUIT. **5a** somebody who operates on the short side of the market. **b** (*in pl*) short-term bonds. **6** (*in pl*) a byproduct of wheat milling that includes the germ, bran, and some flour. ✳ **for short** as an abbreviation. **in short** by way of summary; briefly.

short⁴ *verb trans and intrans* to short-circuit or cause (something) to short-circuit.

short-acting *adj* said of a drug: effective for a short time.

shortage /'shawtij/ *noun* a lack or deficit.

short back and sides *noun Brit* a man's hairstyle in which the hair round the ears and at the neck is cut very short.

shortbread *noun* a thick crumbly biscuit made from flour, sugar, and fat.

shortcake *noun* **1** = SHORTBREAD. **2** a thick short cake resembling biscuit that is usu sandwiched with a layer of fruit and cream and eaten as a dessert.

shortchange *verb trans* **1** to give less than the correct amount of change to (somebody). **2** *informal* to cheat (somebody): *If the author doesn't show a mastery of psychological theory and trace the murderer's little foibles back to problems with toilet-training, the reader feels shortchanged* — Daily Telegraph.

short circuit *noun* the accidental or deliberate joining of two parts of an electric circuit by a conductor of less resistance that allows an excessive current to flow, usu blowing a fuse.

short-circuit *verb trans* (**short-circuited, short-circuiting**) **1** to apply a short circuit to or cause a short circuit in (something) so as to render it inoperative. **2** to bypass or circumvent (something).

shortcoming *noun* a deficiency or defect: *They felt his shortcomings made him unsuited to management.*

shortcrust pastry *noun* a basic pastry used for pies, flans, and tarts and made with half as much fat as flour.

shortcut *noun* a route or procedure quicker and more direct than one customarily followed.

short-dated *adj* said of a stock or bond: having a short time to run before redemption.

short-day *adj* producing flowers on exposure to short periods of daylight.

short division *noun* arithmetic division in which the successive steps can be worked out mentally.

shorten *verb trans* (**shortened, shortening**) **1** to make (something) short or shorter. **2** to add fat to (e.g. pastry dough). **3** to reduce the area or amount of (sail that is set).

shortening *noun* an edible fat, e.g. butter or lard, used to shorten pastry, biscuits, etc.

shortfall *noun* = DEFICIT.

shorthand *noun* **1** a method of rapid writing that substitutes symbols and abbreviations for letters, words, or phrases. **2** a system or instance of rapid or abbreviated communication: *verbal shorthand.*

shorthanded *adj* short of the usual or requisite number of staff; understaffed.

shorthand typist *noun* somebody who takes shorthand notes, *esp* from dictation, then transcribes them using a typewriter.

short head *noun* in horse racing, a distance less than the length of a horse's head.

shorthorn *noun* an animal of a breed of beef cattle with short horns originating in the N of England and including good milk-producing strains.

shortie /'shawti/ *noun* see SHORTY.

short list *noun Brit* a list of selected candidates, e.g. for a job, from whom a final choice must be made.

short list *verb trans Brit* to place (somebody) on a short list.

short-lived /'livd/ *adj* not living or lasting long.

shortly *adv* **1a** in a short time: *We will be there shortly.* **b** at a short interval: *shortly after sunset.* **2a** in a few words; briefly. **b** in an abrupt manner.

short measure *noun* a measured quantity, e.g. of alcohol, that is smaller than the amount paid for.

short-order *adj NAmer* denoting or to do with food that can be quickly cooked.

short-range *adj* **1** relating to, suitable for, or capable of travelling only short distances: *a short-range missile.* **2** involving a relatively short period of time.

shorts *pl noun* **1** knee-length or less than knee-length trousers. **2** *NAmer* men's underpants.

short shrift *noun* **1** summary or inconsiderate treatment. **2** a brief respite for confession before execution.

short sight *noun* = MYOPIA.

short-sighted *adj* **1** able to see near objects more clearly than distant objects; myopic. **2** lacking foresight. ➤➤ **short-sightedly** *adv*, **short-sightedness** *noun*.

short-staffed *adj* having fewer than the usual number of workers.

shortstop *noun* in baseball, the fielder defending the area between second and third base.

short story *noun* a short piece of prose fiction usu dealing with only a few characters and incidents.

Editorial note ⎯⎯⎯⎯⎯⎯⎯
The short story originally goes back to the legend of the fairy tale. In the Romantic period it was refined, above all by Edgar Allen Poe, as a 'poetic' concentrated form. Now it suggests a tale about a single incident told from a single perspective in a single sitting, in a distinct voice, without a word wasted. Great practitioners include Tolstoy, Chekhov, Joyce, Maupassant, James, Mann, Hemingway, and Lawrence — Professor Malcolm Bradbury.

short-tempered *adj* quickly or easily made angry.

short-term *adj* **1** involving a relatively short period of time: *short-term plans.* **2** involving a financial operation or obligation lasting for a brief period, *esp* one of less than a year.

short-termism *noun* a tendency to concentrate on immediate results or prospects, and to neglect long-term strategy: *Britain's poor record of investment both in new machinery and in research and development is surely linked to short-termism in share investment* — The Guardian.

short time *noun* reduced working hours because of a lack of work.

short ton *noun* a US unit of weight that is equal to 2000lb (about 907.19kg).

short-waisted *adj* said of a garment: with an unusually high waist.

short wave *noun* a band of radio waves having wavelengths between about 10m and 100m and typically used for amateur transmissions or long-range broadcasting.

short-winded /'windid/ *adj* **1** affected with or characterized by shortness of breath. **2** brief or concise in speaking or writing.

shorty *or* **shortie** /'shawti/ *noun* (*pl* **shorties**) *informal* a short person or thing, *esp* a nightdress.

Shoshone /shə'shohni/ *noun* (*pl* **Shoshones** *or collectively* **Shoshone**) **1** a member of any of a group of Native American peoples, orig ranging through California, Colorado, Idaho, Utah, and Wyoming. **2** the Uto-Aztecan language of these peoples.

shot¹ /shot/ *noun* **1** the act of firing a gun, bow, etc, or of discharging a bullet, arrow, etc at a target. **2** somebody who shoots, *esp* with regard to their ability: *Luckily she was a terrible shot and the pen missed him completely.* **3a** a stroke or throw in a game, e.g. tennis, billiards, or basketball. **b** a kick aimed at the goal in football. **4** *informal* an attempt or try: *I had a shot at mending the puncture.* **5** a wild guess or conjecture. **6a** (*pl* **shot**) something propelled by shooting; *esp* small lead or steel pellets forming a charge for a shotgun. **b** (*pl* **shot**) a single non-explosive projectile for a gun or cannon. **7a** a metal sphere that is thrown for distance as an athletic field event. **b** this event. **8** the distance that a missile is or can be projected; range or reach. **9a** a single photographic exposure; *esp* a snapshot. **b** a single sequence of a film or a television programme taken by one camera without interruption. **10a** a hypodermic injection of a drug or vaccine: *I needed a shot of morphine to deaden the pain; Has he had his tetanus shot?* **b** *informal* a small amount applied at one time; a dose: *a shot of oxygen.* **c** *informal* a single drink of spirits: *a shot of bourbon.* **11** a pointed or telling remark. **12** the launch of a rocket into space: *a moon shot.* ✴ **a shot in the dark** a wild guess. **a shot in the arm** *informal* a stimulus or boost: *The money will provide a much-needed shot in the arm for the industry.* **give it/something one's best shot** to try to do something as well as one possibly can. **like a shot** *informal* very rapidly. [Old English *scot*]

shot² *adj* **1** said of a fabric: having colour effects which change with the light; iridescent: *shot silk.* **2** suffused or streaked with colour: *hair shot with grey; shot enamel.* **3** (+ with) infused or permeated with a quality or element: *shot through with wit.* **4** *informal* utterly exhausted or ruined: *His nerves are shot.* ✴ **be/get shot of somebody/something** *chiefly Brit, informal* to be or get rid of somebody or something.

shot³ *verb* past tense and past part. of SHOOT¹.

shotgun *noun* **1** an often double-barrelled smoothbore shoulder weapon for firing quantities of metal shot at short ranges. **2** (*used before a noun*) denoting something that is enforced or done in a hurry: *a shotgun merger.*

shotgun wedding *noun informal* a wedding that is forced or required, *esp* because of the bride's pregnancy.

shot put /poot/ *noun* an athletic field event involving the throwing of a SHOT¹ (heavy metal sphere). ⟫⟫ **shot-putter** *noun,* **shot-putting** *noun.*

shotten /'shot(ə)n/ *adj* said of a fish: having ejected its spawn and so of inferior food value. [archaic past part. of SHOOT¹]

should /shəd, *strong* shood/ *verb aux* the past tense of SHALL, used: **1** to introduce a possibility or presumption: *I should be surprised if he wrote.* **2** to introduce a fact that is the object of comment: *It's odd that you should mention that.* **3** to express obligation or recommendation: *You should take a bus to Marble Arch.* **4** in reported speech to express an action or state in the future: *She banged on the door and said we should be late.* **5** to express probability or expectation: *They should be here by noon.* **6** to express a polite form of direct statement: *I should have thought it was colder than that.* [Old English *sceolde* owed, was obliged to; past tense of *sceal* SHALL]

Usage note ⸻

should *or* **would**? Traditionally, *should* and *would* were used in reported speech in the same way as *shall* and *will* were used in direct speech; *should* for the first person singular and plural, *would* for the second and third persons: *I said I should be there; She told me she would be there.* This distinction is now made more rarely, and *would* is generally used instead of *should.* In spoken and informal contexts any distinction between *should* and *would* is hidden by the use of the contraction *'d; I'd; we'd,* etc. Note, however, that only *should* is used with the meaning 'ought to' as in: *I should go, but I don't particularly want to.* See also note at SHALL.

shoulder¹ /'shohldə/ *noun* **1a** the part of the human body that connects the arm to the trunk. **b** a corresponding part of a lower vertebrate. **c** the part of a garment that covers the wearer's shoulder. **2** (*in pl*). **a** the two shoulders and the upper part of the back: *He shrugged his shoulders.* **b** capacity for bearing a burden, e.g. of blame or responsibility: *She placed the guilt squarely on his shoulders.* **3** a cut of meat including the upper joint of the foreleg and adjacent parts. **4** an area adjacent to a higher, more prominent, or more important part, e.g. the slope of a mountain near the top. **5** that part of a road to the side of the surface on which vehicles travel; the hard shoulder. **6** a rounded or sloping part, e.g. of a stringed instrument or a bottle, where the neck joins the body. ✴ **put one's shoulder to the wheel** to make an effort, *esp* a cooperative effort. **shoulder to shoulder** side by side or united. [Old English *sculdor*]

shoulder² *verb trans* (**shouldered, shouldering**) **1a** to place or carry (something) on one's shoulder or shoulders: *She shouldered her rucksack.* **b** to assume the burden or responsibility of (something): *We would have to shoulder the costs.* **2** to push or thrust (somebody or something) with one's shoulder. **3** to push (one's way) aggressively: *He shouldered his way through the crowd.*

shoulder bag *noun* a bag that has a strap attached at each side of sufficient length for the bag to be hung over the shoulder.

shoulder blade *noun* = SCAPULA.

shoulder pad *noun* a shaped pad sewn into the shoulder of a garment.

shoulder strap *noun* a strap that passes across the shoulder and holds up a garment or supports a bag.

shoulder surfing *noun* the practice of watching a person key in their PIN number at a cash dispenser, in order to use the information fraudulently: compare IDENTITY THEFT.

shouldest /'shoodist/ *or* **shouldst** /shoodst/ *verb* archaic past second person sing. of SHALL.

shouldn't /'shoodnt/ *contraction* should not.

shout¹ /showt/ *verb intrans* **1** to utter a sudden loud cry. **2** *Aus, NZ, informal* to buy a round of drinks. ⟫ *verb trans* **1** to utter (something) in a loud voice. **2a** *Aus, NZ, informal* to buy something, *esp* a drink, for (another person). **b** *Aus, NZ, informal* to buy (something, *esp* a drink) for somebody else: *I dropped in to see if you'd shout an old friend a drink.* ⟫⟫ **shouter** *noun.* [Middle English *shouten,* of Germanic origin]

shout² *noun* **1** a loud cry or call. **2** *Brit, informal* a round of drinks, or one's turn to buy a round.

shout down *verb trans* to drown the words of (a speaker) by shouting.

shove¹ /shuv/ *verb trans* **1** to push (something) along with steady force. **2** to push (somebody or something) in a rough, careless, or hasty manner: *Of other care they little reckoning make, than how to scramble at the shearers' feast and shove away the worthy bidden guest* — Milton. ⟫ *verb intrans* **1** to force a way forwards: *Bargain hunters shoved towards the counter.* **2** to move something by pushing: *You pull and I'll shove.* [Old English *scūfan* to thrust away]

shove² *noun* a hard push.

shove-halfpenny *noun* a game played on a special flat board on which players shove discs, e.g. coins, into marked scoring areas.

shovel¹ /'shuvl/ *noun* an implement consisting of a broad scoop or a dished blade with a handle, used to lift and throw loose material. [Old English *scofl*]

shovel² *verb* (**shovelled, shovelling,** *NAmer* **shoveled, shoveling**) ⟫ *verb trans* **1** to dig, clear, or shift (e.g. snow) with a shovel. **2** to convey (something) clumsily or in a mass as if with a shovel: *He shovelled his food into his mouth.*

shoveler *noun* see SHOVELLER.

shovelful /'shuvlf(ə)l/ *noun* (*pl* **shovelfuls**) as much as a shovel will hold.

shovel hat *noun* a shallow-crowned hat with a wide brim turned up at the sides, formerly often worn by clergymen.

shoveller *or* **shoveler** *noun* any of several species of dabbling ducks that have a large and very broad beak: genus *Anas, esp Anas clypeata.* [Middle English, in the sense 'spoonbill'; alteration of *shovelard,* from SHOVEL¹]

shove off *verb intrans informal* to go away; to leave.

shove up *verb intrans informal* to move so that there is room for another person.

show¹ /shoh/ *verb* (*past part.* **shown** *or* **showed**) ⟫ *verb trans* **1** to cause or permit (something) to be seen. **2** to exhibit (something) or put it on display. **3** to present (a film or television programme) for people to watch. **4** to reveal or display (a feeling or emotion). **5** to demonstrate or display (a quality or characteristic): *They show great courage; The trade figures showed a large deficit.* **6** to point out (something) to somebody: *I showed him where I lived.* **7** to conduct or usher (somebody): *A young woman showed me to my seat.* **8a** to establish or prove (something): *Tests showed that the painting was a fake.* **b** to inform or instruct (somebody): *He showed me how to solve the problem.* **9** to present (an animal) for judging in a show. **10** in law, to allege or plead (something): *show cause.* ⟫ *verb intrans* **1** to be visible or noticeable: *Anger showed in his face.* **2** to be staged or presented: *The new film is now showing.* **3** *chiefly NAmer* to put in an appearance: *The star failed to show for the award ceremony.* **4** *NAmer* to finish among the first three in a race. ✳ **show one's face** to let oneself be seen; to appear: *But I must have this money, or else I can never show my face inside the club again* — Conan Doyle. **show one's hand** to declare one's intentions or reveal one's sources. **show one's teeth** to show that one has power or authority. **show one's true colours** to show one's real nature or opinions. **show the door to** to tell (somebody) to leave. ➤➤ **shower** *noun*. [Old English *scēawian* to look, look at, see]

show² *noun* **1** an act of making something visible or noticeable. **2a** a false appearance or demonstration of something; a pretence: *a show of friendship*. **b** a more or less true appearance of something; a sign: *a show of reason*. **c** an impressive display: *a show of strength*. **3** a theatrical presentation. **b** a radio or television programme. **4** a large display or exhibition arranged to arouse interest or stimulate sales: *the Boat Show*. **5** a competitive exhibition of animals, plants, etc to demonstrate quality in breeding. **6** something exhibited, *esp* for wonder or ridicule; a spectacle. **7** *informal* an enterprise or affair: *She was running the whole show*. **8** *NAmer, Aus, NZ, informal* a chance. **9** a bloodstained vaginal discharge indicating the onset of labour. ✳ **for show** simply in order to impress or attract attention. **good/bad/poor show!** *Brit, informal, dated* used to express approval or disapproval: *a good, bad, or poor state of affairs*. **on show 1** on display in an exhibition. **2** noticeable or being shown, e.g. in somebody's behaviour. **show of hands** a vote where people raise their hands to indicate assent or dissent, etc.

show biz /biz/ *noun informal* = SHOW BUSINESS. ➤➤ **showbizzy** *adj*.

showboat *noun* a paddle-wheel river steamship containing a theatre and carrying a troupe of actors who present plays for riverside communities.

showbread *noun* see SHEWBREAD.

show business *noun* the arts, occupations, and businesses, e.g. theatre, films, and television, that comprise the entertainment industry.

showcase¹ *noun* **1** a case, box, or cabinet with a transparent usu glass front or top used for displaying and protecting articles in a shop or museum. **2** a setting or surround for exhibiting something to best advantage.

showcase² *verb trans* to exhibit (something): *The programme showcases the talents of an extraordinary actress.*

showdown *noun* **1** the final settlement of a contested issue or the confrontation by which it is settled. **2** in poker, the placing of hands face up on the table to determine the winner of a round.

shower¹ /'showə/ *noun* **1** a fall of rain, snow, etc of short duration. **2** something like a rain shower: *a shower of tears; showers of sparks from a bonfire*. **3a** an apparatus that provides a stream of water for spraying on the body. **b** an act of washing oneself using such an apparatus. **4** *chiefly NAmer* a party for a bride-to-be or expectant mother, when gifts are given. **5** *Brit, informal* a motley or inferior collection of people. **6** a large number of particles produced when a cosmic-ray particle collides with the upper atmosphere. ➤➤ **showery** *adj*. [Old English *scūr*]

shower² *verb* (**showered, showering**) ➤ *verb intrans* **1** to descend in or as if in a shower: *Letters showered on him in praise and protest*. **2** to take a shower. ➤ *verb trans* **1a** to wet (somebody or something) copiously, e.g. with water, in a spray, fine stream, or drops. **b** to cause (something) to fall in a shower: *Factory chimneys showered soot on the neighbourhood*. **c** to cover (somebody or something) with or as if with a shower. **2** to present (somebody) with something in abundance: *They showered him with honours*.

showerproof *adj* said of a fabric or garment: treated so as to give protection from a slight wetting.

showgirl *noun* a young woman who dances or sings in the chorus of a theatrical production.

show home *noun* = SHOW HOUSE.

show house /hows/ *noun* a decorated and furnished house shown to prospective buyers of new houses on a development.

showing *noun* **1** an act of putting something on view; a display, exhibition, or presentation. **2** performance in competition: *He made a good showing in the finals*. **3** a statement or presentation of a case; evidence.

showjumping *noun* the competitive riding of horses one at a time over a set course of obstacles in which the winner is judged according to ability and speed. ➤➤ **showjumper** *noun*.

showman *noun* (*pl* **showmen**) **1a** somebody who presents a theatrical show. **b** the manager of a circus or fairground. **2** a person with a flair for dramatically effective presentation. ➤➤ **showmanship** *noun*.

shown /shohn/ *verb past part*. of SHOW¹.

show off *verb intrans* to behave boastfully or ostentatiously. ➤ *verb trans* to display (something) proudly.

show-off *noun* somebody who shows off; an exhibitionist.

showpiece *noun* a prime or outstanding example used for exhibition.

showplace *noun* a place, e.g. an estate or building, regarded as an example of beauty or excellence.

showroom *noun* a room where goods for sale are displayed.

show-stopper *noun* an act, song, or performer that wins applause so prolonged as to interrupt a performance. ➤➤ **show-stopping** *adj*.

show trial *noun* a trial conducted by a state, *esp* a totalitarian one, to make an impression at home or abroad.

show up *verb intrans* **1** to be evident or conspicuous. **2** *informal* to arrive, *esp* unexpectedly. ➤ *verb trans* **1** to reveal the shortcomings of (somebody or something) by comparison. **2** *informal* to embarrass (somebody).

showy *adj* (**showier, showiest**) **1** making an attractive show; striking: *showy blossoms*. **2** given to or marked by pretentious display; gaudy. ➤➤ **showily** *adv*, **showiness** *noun*.

shoyu /'shohyooh/ *noun* a soy sauce made from fermented soya beans with barley or wheat, used as a flavouring in oriental cooking. [Japanese *shōyu*]

shrank /shrangk/ *verb past tense* of SHRINK¹.

shrapnel /'shrapnəl/ *noun* **1** a hollow projectile that contains bullets or pieces of metal and that is exploded by a bursting charge to produce a shower of fragments. **2** bomb, mine, or shell fragments thrown out during explosion. [named after Henry *Shrapnel* d.1842, English artillery officer, who invented the shell]

shred¹ /shred/ *noun* **1** a narrow strip cut or torn off. **2** a fragment or scrap. [Old English *scrēade*]

shred² *verb* (**shredded, shredding**) ➤ *verb trans* to cut or tear (something) into shreds. ➤ *verb intrans* to come apart in or be reduced to shreds.

shredder *noun* a machine for shredding paper.

shrew /shrooh/ *noun* **1** any of numerous species of small chiefly nocturnal mammals with a long pointed snout, very small eyes, and velvety fur: family Soricidae. **2** an ill-tempered nagging woman; a scold. [Old English *scrēawa*; (sense 2) from the belief that the shrew's bite was poisonous]

shrewd /shroohd/ *adj* **1** marked by keen discernment and hard-headed practicality: *shrewd common sense*. **2** wily or artful: *a shrewd operator*. **3a** said of a blow: severe or hard. **b** *literary* said of wind or weather: bitter or piercing. ➤➤ **shrewdly** *adv*, **shrewdness** *noun*. [Middle English *shrewed* wicked, mischievous, from *shrewe* SHREW (2)]

shrewish *adj* bad-tempered, aggressive, or nagging. ➤➤ **shrewishly** *adv*, **shrewishness** *noun*.

shrewmouse *noun* = SHREW.

shriek¹ /shreek/ *verb intrans* to utter or make a shrill piercing cry; to screech: *She shrieked with laughter; Jets shrieked overhead*. ➤ *verb trans* (*often* + out) to utter (something) with a shriek or sharply and shrilly. ➤➤ **shrieker** *noun*. [Middle English *shriken*, of imitative origin]

shriek² *noun* **1** a shrill usu wild cry. **2** a sound similar to this: *The shriek of chalk on the blackboard*.

shrieval /'shreevl/ *adj* of a sheriff. [*shrieve*, obsolete variant of SHERIFF]

shrievalty *noun* (*pl* **shrievalties**) *chiefly Brit* the office, term of office, or jurisdiction of a sheriff.

shrift /shrift/ *noun* **1** *archaic* the act of shriving; confession. **2** a remission of sins pronounced by a priest in the sacrament of penance. [Old English *scrift* from *scrīfan* to SHRIVE]

shrike /shreek/ *noun* any of numerous species of usu largely grey or brownish songbirds that often impale their prey on thorns: family Laniidae. [perhaps from Old English *scrīc* thrush]

shrill[1] /shril/ *adj* **1** having, making, or being a sharp high-pitched sound; piercing. **2** said *esp* of complaints or protests: made in a loud, insistent way. ⟫ **shrillness** *noun*, **shrilly** *adv*.

shrill[2] *verb intrans* to utter or emit a high-pitched piercing sound: *Alarm bells shrilled as the robbers raced away.* ⟫ *verb trans* to scream (something). [Middle English *shrillen*, of Germanic origin]

shrimp[1] /shrimp/ *noun* (*pl* **shrimps** *or collectively* **shrimp**) **1** any of numerous mostly small marine crustaceans with a long slender body, compressed abdomen, and ten long legs: class Crustacea. **2** *informal, humorous* a very small or puny person. [Middle English *shrimpe*, of Germanic origin]

shrimp[2] *verb intrans* to fish for or catch shrimps. ⟫ **shrimper** *noun*.

shrine[1] /shrien/ *noun* **1a** a place in which devotion is paid to a saint or deity. **b** a receptacle for sacred relics. **c** a niche containing a religious image. **2** a receptacle, e.g. a tomb, for the dead. **3** a place or object hallowed by its history or associations: *Oxford is a shrine of learning.* [Old English *scrīn*, via a prehistoric Germanic word from Latin *scrinum* book chest]

shrine[2] *verb trans literary* to enshrine (something).

shrink[1] /shringk/ *verb* (*past tense* **shrank** /shrangk/, *past part.* **shrunk** /shrungk/ *or* **shrunken** /'shrungk(ə)n/) ⟫ *verb intrans* **1** to contract to a smaller volume or extent, e.g. as a result of heat or moisture. **2** to draw back or cower away, e.g. from something painful or horrible. **3** to show reluctance, e.g. before a difficult or unpleasant duty; to recoil. ⟫ *verb trans* to cause (something) to contract; *specif* to compact (cloth) by a treatment, e.g. with water or steam, that results in contraction. ⟫ **shrinkable** *adj*, **shrinker** *noun*. [Old English *scrincan*]

shrink[2] *noun informal* a psychoanalyst or psychiatrist. [short for HEADSHRINKER]

shrinkage /'shringkij/ *noun* **1a** the act or process of shrinking. **b** the degree of shrinking: *The material suffered a 10% shrinkage in transit.* **2** the loss in weight of carcasses during shipment and storage, *esp* if frozen, and in the process of preparing the meat for consumption. **3** loss of merchandise from a shop by shoplifting.

shrinking violet *noun informal* a meek or very shy person.

shrink wrap *noun* tough clear plastic film that is wrapped around an object and then shrunk, e.g. by heating, to make a tight-fitting, sealed package.

shrink-wrap *verb trans* (**shrink-wrapped, shrink-wrapping**) to wrap (e.g. a book or meat) in shrink wrap.

shrive /shriev/ *verb trans* (*past tense* **shrove** /shrohv/, *past part.* **shriven** /'shriv(ə)n/) *archaic* to hear the confession of (somebody) and absolve them. [Old English *scrīfan* to shrive, impose as a penance]

shrivel /'shrivl/ *verb* (**shrivelled, shrivelling,** *NAmer* **shriveled, shriveling**) ⟫ *verb intrans* **1** to contract and become dry and wrinkled, *esp* through loss of moisture. **2a** said of a person: to become weak, cowed, or ineffective. **b** to become smaller or disappear almost entirely. ⟫ *verb trans* to cause (something or somebody) to shrivel. [perhaps of Scandinavian origin]

shriven /'shriv(ə)n/ *verb* past part. of SHRIVE.

shroud[1] /shrowd/ *noun* **1** a burial garment, e.g. a winding-sheet. **2** something that covers, conceals, or guards: *a shroud of smoke.* **3** any of the ropes or wires giving support, usu in pairs, to a ship's mast. **4** a protective cover or guard, *esp* a streamlined shield protecting part of a spacecraft from the heat of launching. [Old English *scrūd* clothing]

shroud[2] *verb trans* **1a** to envelop and conceal (something): *The landscape was shrouded in a thick mist.* **b** to obscure or disguise (something or somebody). **2** to dress (a body) for burial.

shroud-laid *adj* said of a rope: having four strands and a core.

shrove /shrohv/ *verb* past tense of SHRIVE.

Shrovetide /'shrohvtied/ *noun* the period immediately before Ash Wednesday.

Shrove Tuesday *noun* the Tuesday before Ash Wednesday; pancake day. [from the practice of being shriven before Lent]

shrub[1] /shrub/ *noun* a low-growing woody plant that usu has several stems. ⟫ **shrubby** *adj*. [Old English *scrybb* brushwood]

shrub[2] *noun* a drink made of sweetened fruit juice and spirits, *esp* rum. [Arabic *sharāb* drink]

shrubbery /'shrub(ə)ri/ *noun* (*pl* **shrubberies**) a planting or growth of shrubs.

shrug[1] /shrug/ *verb* (**shrugged, shrugging**) ⟫ *verb trans* to lift and contract (one's shoulders) as an expression of e.g. uncertainty, unconcern, or resignation. ⟫ *verb intrans* to raise the shoulders expressively in doubt, dismissiveness, or resignation. [Middle English *schruggen* to fidget; earlier history unknown]

shrug[2] *noun* **1** an act of shrugging the shoulders, e.g. in resignation: *Still have I borne it with a patient shrug* — Shakespeare. **2** a short frontless cardigan covering the arms, shoulders, and back.

shrug off *verb trans* to brush (something) aside; to disregard or belittle (it): *He shrugged the problem off.*

shrunk /shrungk/ *verb* past part. of SHRINK[1].

shrunken *verb* past part. of SHRINK[1].

shtetl /'shtetl/ *noun* (*pl* **shtetlach** /'shtetlahkh/ *or* **shtetls**) a small Jewish town or village formerly found in E Europe. [Yiddish *shtetl*, of Germanic origin]

shtick /shtik/ *noun informal* an entertainer's routine or gimmick; a turn. [Yiddish *shtik* piece, from German *Stück*]

shtook *or* **schtuck** /shtook/ *noun informal* a bad or awkward situation; trouble; the lurch: *I realized that he had gone off and left me in shtook.* [origin unknown]

shtum *or* **schtum** /shtoom/ *adj informal* silent or dumb: *He told me to keep shtum.* [Yiddish *shtum* from German *stumm*]

shtup *or* **schtup** /shtoop/ *verb trans* (**shtupped** *or* **schtupped, shtupping** *or* **schtupping**) *coarse slang* to have sexual intercourse with (somebody). [Yiddish *shtup* from German *stupsen* to push]

shubunkin /shə'bungkin/ *noun* a goldfish that is mottled, *esp* with blue, and is often kept in aquaria. [Japanese *shubunkin*]

shuck[1] /shuk/ *noun NAmer* **1** a pod or husk, e.g. the outer covering of a nut or of maize. **2** the shell of an oyster or clam. **3** (*in pl*) something of no value: *not worth shucks.* **4** *informal* (*in pl*) used as an interjection to express disappointment, surprise, or self-deprecation: *Shucks, it was nothing.* [origin unknown]

shuck[2] *verb trans NAmer* **1** to strip (something) of shucks. **2** (*often* + off) to remove or dispose of (something) like a shuck: *shuck off clothing; shuck off bad habits.* ⟫ **shucker** *noun*.

shudder[1] /'shudə/ *verb intrans* (**shuddered, shuddering**) **1** to tremble with a sudden brief convulsive movement. **2** to quiver or vibrate. ⟫ **shuddering** *adj*, **shudderingly** *adv*, **shuddery** *adj*. [Middle English *shoddren* from early Dutch *schüderen*]

shudder[2] *noun* an act of shuddering; a shiver.

shuffle[1] /'shufl/ *verb trans* **1** to move (the feet) along, or back and forth, without lifting them. **2a** to rearrange (e.g. playing cards or dominoes) to produce a random order. **b** to move (things or people) about between various different positions or locations, *esp* so as to create disorder or confusion: *They had shuffled funds among various accounts.* **3** to mix (things) together in a confused mass; to jumble (them). ⟫ *verb intrans* **1a** to move or walk by sliding or dragging the feet. **b** to dance in a lazy nonchalant manner with scraping and tapping motions of the feet. **2** to mix playing cards by shuffling. **3** to behave in an evasive or underhand way. ⟫ **shuffler** *noun*. [origin unknown]

shuffle[2] *noun* **1a** a shuffling, e.g. of cards. **b** a right or turn to shuffle: *It's your shuffle.* **2** a rearrangement of things or people; a reshuffle. **3a** a dragging sliding movement of the feet. **b** a dance characterized by such movement.

shuffleboard *noun* a game in which players use long-handled cues to shove wooden discs into scoring areas of a diagram marked on a smooth surface. [alteration of obsolete *shove-board*]

shufti /'shufti/ *noun* (*pl* **shuftis**) *Brit, informal* a look or glance: *Have a shufti at the radar screen.* [orig military slang; from Arabic *shāfa* to try to see]

shul /shool/ *noun* = SYNAGOGUE. [Yiddish *shul* from early High German *schuol* school]

shun /shun/ *verb trans* (**shunned, shunning**) to avoid (somebody or something) deliberately, *esp* habitually: *Few actors shun publicity.* [Old English *scunian*]

shunt[1] /shunt/ *verb trans* **1a** to move (e.g. a train) from one track to another. **b** *Brit* to move (railway vehicles) to different positions on the same track within terminal areas. **2a** to provide (an electrical circuit) with or divert it by means of an electrical shunt. **b** to divert (blood) by means of a surgical shunt. **3a** (*often* + off/onto) to avoid (e.g. a task, responsibility) by transferring it to somebody else. **b** to move (something or somebody) to a less important position. ➤ *verb intrans* **1** to move into a side track. **2** to travel back and forth: *The investigators shunted between the two towns.* ➤➤ **shunter** *noun*. [Middle English *shunten* to flinch, perhaps from SHUN]

shunt² *noun* **1** an act of shunting. **2a** a conductor joining two points in an electrical circuit so as to form a parallel path through which a portion of the current may pass. **b** a surgical passage created between two blood vessels to divert blood from one part to another. **c** *chiefly Brit* = SIDING (1). **3** *informal* a minor collision of motor vehicles, *esp* one in which one vehicle runs into the back of another.

shush¹ /shoosh, shush/ *interj* used to demand silence. [imitative]

shush² *verb trans informal* to tell (somebody) to be quiet, *esp* by saying 'Shush!'

shut¹ /shut/ *verb* (**shutting**, *past tense and past part.* **shut**) ➤ *verb trans* **1** to place (something) in position to close an opening. **2** to fasten (something) with a lock or bolt. **3** to prevent entrance to or exit from (e.g. a building or street). **4** to confine (somebody or something) by enclosure or as if by enclosure: *The cat got shut in a cupboard.* **5** to close (something) by bringing enclosing or covering parts together: *She shut her eyes.* **6** to cause (something) to cease or suspend operation: *The shops had been shut for hours.* ➤ *verb intrans* **1** to become closed. **2** to cease or suspend operation. [Old English *scyttan*]

shut² *adj* **1** in the closed position, or fastened in place. **2** not open for business.

shut away *verb trans* to remove or isolate (somebody or something) from others.

shutdown *noun* the cessation or suspension of an activity, e.g. work in a mine or factory.

shut down *verb trans* to cease or suspend the operation of (a machine, business, etc). ➤ *verb intrans* to cease or suspend operation.

shut-eye *noun informal* = SLEEP¹ (1).

shutoff *noun chiefly NAmer* a stoppage or interruption.

shut off *verb trans* **1a** to cut off or stop the flow of (something). **b** to stop the operation of (e.g. a machine). **2** (+ from) to isolate or separate (somebody or something): *a village shut off from the rest of the world.* ➤ *verb intrans* to cease operating: *The heater shuts off automatically.*

shut out *verb trans* **1** to exclude (somebody or something). **2** *chiefly NAmer* to prevent (an opponent) from scoring in a game or contest.

shut-out *noun chiefly NAmer* **1** a sporting contest in which one side fails to score any goals, points, etc. **2** the act of preventing an opposing side from scoring.

shutter¹ *noun* **1a** a usu hinged outside cover for a window, often fitted as one of a pair. **b** a usu movable cover or screen, e.g. over a door or as part of stage scenery. **2** a device that opens and closes the lens aperture of a camera. **3** the movable slots in the box enclosing the swell organ part of a pipe organ, which are opened to increase the volume of the sound. ➤➤ **shutterless** *adj*.

shutter² *verb trans* (**shuttered, shuttering**) to provide or close (something) with shutters.

shuttering *noun* a temporary mould placed to support concrete while setting.

shuttle¹ /'shutl/ *noun* **1a** a usu spindle-shaped device that holds a bobbin and is used in weaving for passing the thread of the weft between the threads of the warp. **b** a sliding thread holder that carries the lower thread in a sewing machine through a loop of the upper thread to make a stitch. **2a** a vehicle that regularly travels back and forth over a usu short route. **b** a reusable space vehicle; a space shuttle. **3** = SHUTTLECOCK. [Old English *scytel* bar, bolt]

shuttle² *verb intrans* to travel to and fro rapidly or frequently. ➤ *verb trans* to transport (somebody) in or by a shuttle: *Crewmen were shuttled to the shore in dinghies.*

shuttlecock *noun* the object hit back and forth between players in badminton, orig consisting of a cork with feathers stuck in it, now usu a lightweight hollow plastic cone with a solid, heavier rounded end. [SHUTTLE¹ + COCK¹]

shuttle diplomacy *noun* diplomacy carried out by an intermediary who travels frequently between the countries concerned.

shut up *verb trans* **1** to lock and prevent access to (a building). **2** to imprison or confine (somebody or something). **3** *informal* to cause (somebody) to be silent, *esp* to force (a speaker) to stop talking. ➤ *verb intrans* **1** to cease or suspend operation. **2** *informal* to become silent, *esp* to stop talking.

shy¹ /shie/ *adj* (**shyer, shyest**) **1** easily alarmed; timid. **2a** sensitively reserved or retiring; bashful: *I was too shy to give a speech.* **b** expressive of such a state or nature: *He spoke in a shy voice.* **3** (*often used in combinations*) tending to avoid a person or thing; distrustful: *camera-shy.* **4** (*often + of*) wary of committing oneself; circumspect or reluctant: *She was shy of disclosing her income.* **5** *chiefly NAmer, informal* lacking or short: *We're three points shy of what we need to win.* ➤➤ **shyly** *adv*, **shyness** *noun*. [Old English *scēoh*]

shy² *verb intrans* (**shies, shied, shying**) **1** said *esp* of a horse: to start suddenly aside in fright or alarm; to recoil. **2** (*usu + away/away from*) to avoid facing or committing oneself to something, *esp* through nervousness: *They shied away from buying the flat when they learned the full price.*

shy³ *noun* (*pl* **shies**) a sudden movement, *esp* made in fright.

shy⁴ *verb trans* (**shies, shied, shying**) *dated* to throw (e.g. a stone) with a jerking movement; to fling (it). [perhaps from SHY¹]

shy⁵ *noun* (*pl* **shies**) the act of shying; a toss or throw.

shyster /'shiestə/ *noun chiefly NAmer, informal* somebody, *esp* a lawyer, who is professionally unscrupulous. [prob from *Scheuster*, the name of a US attorney fl 1840, who was frequently rebuked in a New York court for pettifoggery]

SI¹ *noun* a system of units whose basic units are the metre, kilogram, second, ampere, kelvin, candela, and mole and which uses prefixes, e.g. micro-, kilo-, and mega-, to indicate multiples or fractions of ten: compare SI². [short for French *Système International d'Unités* international system of units]

SI² *abbr* **1** Statutory Instrument. **2** Système International (d'Unités): compare SI¹.

Si *abbr* the chemical symbol for silicon.

si /see/ *noun* in music, te. [see GAMUT]

sial /'sie-əl/ *noun* the outer layers of the earth, composed chiefly of relatively light rock rich in silica and alumina. ➤➤ **sialic** /sie'alik/ *adj*. [blend of SILICA + ALUMINA]

sialagogue /sie'aləgog/ *noun* a drug that promotes the flow of saliva. [Latin *sialagogus* promoting the expulsion of saliva, from Greek *sialon* saliva + late Latin *-agogus* -AGOGUE]

sialic acid /sie'alik/ *noun* any of a group of amino sugars found as glycoproteins (components of blood; see GLYCOPROTEIN) and mucoproteins (complex substances containing protein and carbohydrate; see MUCOPROTEIN). [Greek *sialon* saliva]

siamang /'sie-əmang/ *noun* a large black gibbon found in the forests of Sumatra and Malaysia that has a resonant booming call and feeds chiefly on fruit: *Hylobates syndactylus.* [Malay *siamang*]

Siamese /sie-ə'meez/ *noun* (*pl* **Siamese**) **1** *dated* a native or inhabitant of Siam (now Thailand). **2** *dated* the Thai language. **3** = SIAMESE CAT. ➤➤ **Siamese** *adj*.

Siamese cat *noun* a cat of a domestic breed of oriental origin, with blue eyes, short hair, and a pale fawn or grey body with darker ears, paws, tail, and face.

Siamese fighting fish *noun* see FIGHTING FISH

Siamese twin *noun* either of a pair of congenitally joined twins. [named after Chang and Eng d.1874, congenitally joined twins born in Siam (Thailand), who became celebrities in Europe and the US]

SIB *abbr* Securities and Investments Board.

sib /sib/ *noun* **1** a blood relation; a kinsman or kinswoman. **2** a brother or sister considered irrespective of sex; *broadly* any of two or more individuals having a parent in common. **3** a group of people descended on one side from a real or supposed ancestor. [Old English *sibb*]

Siberian /sie'biəri-ən/ *noun* a native or inhabitant of Siberia. ➤➤ **Siberian** *adj*.

sibilant¹ /'sibilənt/ *adj* having, containing, or producing a hissing sound, e.g. /sh, zh, s, z/. ➤➤ **sibilance** *noun*. [Latin *sibilant-, sibilans*, present part. of *sibilare* to hiss, whistle, of imitative origin]

sibilant² *noun* in phonetics, a sibilant speech sound.

sibling /'sibling/ *noun* any of two or more individuals having one or both parents in common; a brother or sister.

sibyl /'sibil/ *noun* any of several female prophets credited to widely separate parts of the ancient world; *broadly* any female prophet. ➤➤ **sibylline** /-lien/ *adj.* [Middle English *sibile*, *sybylle* via Old French and Latin from Greek *Sibylla*]

sic /sik/ *adv* used after a printed word or passage to indicate that it is intended exactly as printed or that it exactly reproduces an original: intentionally so written. [Latin *sic* so, thus]

Usage note
Sic is used when quoting someone else's words exactly to show that a mistake or oddity in them comes from the person quoted, not from the person quoting: *According to the chairman, 'These figures apply only to the months of Febuary [sic] and March'*.

siccative /'sikətiv/ *noun* a substance used to accelerate the drying of paints, inks, etc. [late Latin *siccativus* making dry, from Latin *siccare* to dry, from *siccus* dry]

sick[1] /sik/ *adj* **1** affected by a disease or medical condition; ill or ailing: *a sick child.* **2** (*often used in combinations*) likely to vomit; queasy or nauseated: *He felt sick in the car; airsick.* **3a** (*often + with*) sickened by intense emotion, e.g. shame or fear: *sick with fear; worried sick.* **b** (+ of) having a strong aversion because of surfeit; satiated: *sick of flattery.* **c** filled with disgust or chagrin: *That sort of gossip makes one sick.* **4** *informal* disappointed or upset: *She was sick when she found out that she had missed his phone call.* **5a** mentally or emotionally disturbed; morbid: *She had a sick relationship with a destructive man.* **b** said of humour: macabre or sadistic. **6** *archaic* distressed and longing for something that one has lost or been parted from: *sick for one's home.* ✳ **be sick 1** *chiefly Brit* to vomit. **2** to be ill. ➤➤ **sickish** *adj.* [Old English *sēoc*]

sick[2] *noun Brit, informal* vomit.

sick[3] *verb trans Brit, informal* (*usu + up*) to vomit (something).

sick and tired *adj* thoroughly bored or sated; fed up: *I'm sick and tired of you nattering.*

sickbay *noun* a compartment or room, e.g. in a ship, used as a dispensary and hospital.

sickbed *noun* the bed on which somebody lies sick.

sick building syndrome *noun* a condition affecting workers in buildings with sealed windows and humidification systems, characterized by headache, eye irritation, flu-like symptoms, and lethargy.

sicken *verb* (**sickened, sickening**) ➤ *verb trans* **1** to cause (somebody) to feel ill or nauseous. **2** to drive (somebody) to the point of disgust or loathing. ➤ *verb intrans* **1** to become ill. **2** (+ for) to begin to show signs of illness: *The baby looked as if she was sickening for a cold.*

sickening *adj* **1** causing a feeling of nausea: *a sickening smell.* **2** very horrible or repugnant: *He fell to the floor with a sickening thud.* **3** *informal* very irritating or annoying. ➤➤ **sickeningly** *adv.*

sick headache *noun chiefly NAmer* = MIGRAINE.

sickie /'siki/ *noun informal* a day's absence from work claimed as sick leave.

sickle /'sikl/ *noun* an agricultural implement for cutting plants or hedges, consisting of a curved metal blade with a short handle. [Old English *sicol*]

sick leave *noun* absence from work because of illness.

sickle cell *noun* an abnormal red blood cell of crescent shape that occurs in the blood of people affected with sickle-cell anaemia.

sickle-cell anaemia *noun* a hereditary anaemia in which most of the red blood cells become crescent-shaped, causing recurrent short periods of fever and pain.

sickly *adj* (**sicklier, sickliest**) **1a** susceptible to illness and often unwell. **b** feeble or weak: *a sickly plant.* **2a** associated with sickness: *a sickly complexion.* **b** producing or tending to produce disease: *a sickly climate.* **3** showing aversion, reluctance, or unease: *a sickly smile.* **4a** tending to produce nausea or feelings of repugnance: *a sickly taste.* **b** mawkish or saccharine: *sickly sentiment.* ➤➤ **sickliness** *noun.*

sick-making *adj informal* = SICKENING.

sickness *noun* **1** ill health. **2** a specific disease. **3** nausea or queasiness.

sicko /'sikoh/ *noun* (*pl* **sickos**) *informal* somebody who is mentally ill or perverted.

sick pay *noun* salary or wages paid to an employee while on sick leave.

sickroom *noun* a room set aside for or occupied by sick people.

sidalcea /si'dalsi-ə/ *noun* any of a genus of plants of the mallow family with pink flowers: genus *Sidalcea.* [Latin genus name, blend of *Sida* + *Alcea*, related genera]

side[1] /sied/ *noun* **1a** a surface forming a face of an object, *esp* one that is neither the front nor back, top nor bottom. **b** either surface of a thin object: *the other side of the page; the right side of the cloth.* **c** a boundary line of a geometrical figure. **2a** a position next to and to the right or left of something, somebody, or a reference point. **b** a region or direction considered in relation to a centre or line of division: *the south side of the city; surrounded on all sides.* **3a** the right or left part of the trunk of the body: *a pain in the side.* **b** the right or left half of the animal body or of a meat carcass: *a side of beef.* **4** a slope of a hill, ridge, etc. **5a** a sports team. **b** a person or group in competition or dispute with another: *Which side are you on?* **c** the attitude or opinions of a person or group in competition or dispute with another; a part: *He took my side in the argument.* **6a** an aspect or part of something viewed in contrast with some other aspect or part: *the better side of his nature.* **b** a position viewed as opposite to or contrasted with another: *It would be an indifferent question, my dear Major, that hadn't two sides to it; and I've known many that had three* — J Fenimore Cooper. **7** a line of descent traced through a parent: *my grandfather on my mother's side.* **8** *Brit, informal* a television channel: *What's on the other side?* **9** = SIDESPIN. ✳ **get on the right side of** *informal* to be viewed in a favourable or friendly way by (somebody). **on the side 1** in addition to a principal occupation; *specif* as a dishonest or illegal secondary activity: *The art teacher does a bit of plumbing on the side.* **2** *chiefly NAmer* in addition to the main portion: *a pizza with coleslaw on the side.* **take sides** to give one's support to one of the people or parties in a dispute. [Old English *sīde* side of the body]

side[2] *adj* **1a** forming or relating to a side. **b** situated on the side: *a side window.* **2** directed towards or from the side: *side thrust; a side wind.* **3** additional to the main part or portion: *a side order of French fries.* **4** incidental or subordinate: *side issue.*

side[3] *verb intrans* (+ with/against) to take sides; to join or form sides: *They sided with the rebels.*

side[4] *noun Brit, informal* a swaggering or self-important manner; arrogance or pretentiousness: *She's got no side, that's one thing in her favour.* [obsolete *side* proud, boastful, from Old English *sīd* wide, capacious, prob related to *sīde* SIDE[1]]

side arm *noun* a weapon, e.g. a sword, revolver, or bayonet, worn at the side or in the belt.

sideband *noun* a band of frequencies resulting from modulation, e.g. of radio waves, close to but either greater than or less than the carrier frequency.

sidebar *noun chiefly NAmer* **1** an additional newspaper article dealing with a particular aspect of a story appearing in a main article. **2** something additional or complementary. **3** in a law court, a private conversation between the lawyers and the judge.

sideboard *noun* **1** a usu flat-topped piece of dining room furniture with compartments and shelves for holding plates, glasses, etc. **2** *Brit* (*in pl*) = SIDEBURNS.

sideburns *pl noun* hair on the side of the face that extends from the hairline to below the ears. [alteration of earlier *burnsides*, named after Ambrose *Burnside* d.1881, US general, who wore them]

side by side *adv* beside one another: *The couple walked side by side down the aisle.*

sidecar *noun* **1** a small vehicle with a single wheel, attached to the side of a motorcycle or motor scooter to carry one or more passengers. **2** a cocktail made of brandy, orange liqueur, and lemon juice.

side chain *noun* in chemistry, a group of atoms that is attached to an atom in a chain or to a ring in a molecule.

sided *adj* (*usu used in combinations*) having sides, usu of a specified number or kind: *one-sided; glass-sided.*

side dish *noun* any of the foods accompanying and subordinate to the main dish of a course.

side drum *noun* a small double-headed drum with one or more snares stretched across its lower head.

side effect *noun* a secondary and usu adverse effect, e.g. of a drug.

side-foot *verb trans* to kick (a ball) using the inside of the foot.

sidekick *noun informal* somebody closely associated with another, *esp* as a subordinate.

sidelight *noun* **1a** a light at the side of a motor vehicle. **b** the red port light or the green starboard light carried by ships travelling at night. **2** a window at the side of a door or a larger window. **3** incidental or additional information.

sideline[1] *noun* **1a** a line of goods manufactured or sold in addition to one's principal line. **b** a business or activity pursued in addition to a full-time occupation. **2** a line at right angles to a goal line or end line and marking a side of a court or field of play. **3** (**the sidelines**) the standpoint of people not immediately participating.

sideline[2] *verb trans* to put (somebody) out of action; to put (them) on the sidelines.

sidelong[1] *adv* towards the side; obliquely. [alteration of *sideling* sideways, from SIDE[1] + adverbial suffix *-ling*]

sidelong[2] *adj* **1** inclining or directed to one side: *sidelong glances.* **2** indirect rather than straightforward.

sideman *noun* (*pl* **sidemen**) a member of a band or orchestra, *esp* a jazz or swing orchestra, other than the leader or featured performer.

side-on *adv* **1** with one side facing in a given direction. **2** in profile.

sidereal /sie'diəri-əl/ *adj* of, or expressed in relation to, stars or constellations. [Latin *sidereus* from *sider-*, *sidus* star, constellation]

sidereal day *noun* the interval between two successive transits of the March equinox over the upper meridian of a particular place; 23h, 56min, 4.09s of solar time.

sidereal period *noun* the period of revolution of one celestial body, e.g. the moon or a planet, about another, with reference to the stars.

sidereal time *noun* time based on the sidereal day.

sidereal year *noun* the time in which the earth completes one revolution in its orbit round the sun measured with respect to the fixed stars; 365 days, 6h, 9min, and 9.54s of solar time.

siderite /'siedəriet/ *noun* **1** a naturally occurring yellow or brown ferrous carbonate that is a valuable iron ore: formula FeCO₃. **2** a nickel–iron meteorite. ⧉ **sideritic** /-'ritik/ *adj.* [German *Siderit* from Greek *sidēros* iron]

sidesaddle[1] *noun* a saddle for women riders in skirts in which the rider sits with both legs on the same side of the horse.

sidesaddle[2] *adv* on or as if on a sidesaddle.

sideshow *noun* **1a** a minor show offered in addition to a main exhibition, e.g. of a circus. **b** a fairground booth or counter offering a game of luck or skill. **2** an incidental diversion.

sideslip[1] *verb intrans* (**sideslipped, sideslipping**) **1** to move sideways through the air in a downward direction. **2** to skid sideways.

sideslip[2] *noun* a sideways skid or movement.

sidesman *noun* (*pl* **sidesmen**) any of a group of people in an Anglican church who assist the churchwardens, *esp* in taking the collection in services.

sidespin *noun* sideways spin imparted to a ball.

sidesplitting *adj informal* extremely funny.

sidestep *verb* (**sidestepped, sidestepping**) ⧉ *verb intrans* **1** to step sideways or to one side. **2** to evade an issue or decision. ⧉ *verb trans* **1** to move quickly out of the way of (something): *sidestep a blow.* **2** to bypass or evade (something): *He is adept at sidestepping awkward questions.*

side step *noun* **1** a step aside, e.g. in boxing to avoid a punch. **2** a step taken sideways, e.g. when climbing on skis.

side street *noun* a minor street branching off a main thoroughfare.

sidestroke *noun* a swimming stroke executed while lying on one's side.

sideswipe[1] *noun* **1** an incidental deprecatory remark, allusion, or reference. **2** *chiefly NAmer* an act or instance of sideswiping; a glancing blow.

sideswipe[2] *verb trans chiefly NAmer* to strike (somebody or something) with a glancing blow along the side: *She sideswiped a parked car.*

sidetrack[1] *verb trans* to divert (somebody) from a course or purpose; to distract (them): *Following the lake shore, through moist native bush and along sandy beaches, we were continually sidetracked by whistling birds, strange tree growths and inviting rivers* — Outdoor Action.

sidetrack[2] *noun* **1** an unimportant line of thinking that is followed instead of a more important one. **2** *NAmer* = SIDING.

sidewalk *noun NAmer* = PAVEMENT.

sidewall *noun* the part of a tyre between the tread and the rim.

sideward /'siedwəd/ *adj* = SIDEWAYS.

sidewards (*NAmer* **sideward**) *adv* towards one side.

sideways (*NAmer* **sideway**) *adv and adj* **1** to or from the side: *a sideways movement.* **2** with one side forward: *Turn it sideways.* **3** to a position of equivalent rank: *a sideways career move.*

side whiskers *pl noun* long sideburns.

sidewinder[1] /'siedwiendə/ *noun* a rattlesnake of N America that moves over sand by looping its body into S-shaped curves: *Crotalus cerastes.* [SIDE[2] + *winder* from WIND[3]]

sidewinder[2] /'siedwiendə/ *noun NAmer* a heavy swinging blow from the side. [SIDE[2] + *winder* from WIND[2]]

sidewise *adv and adj* = SIDEWAYS.

siding *noun* **1** a short length of railway track connected with and usu running beside a main track. **2** *NAmer* material, e.g. boards or metal sheets, forming the exposed surface of the outside walls of wooden framed buildings

sidle /'siedl/ *verb intrans* **1** to move obliquely. **2** (+ up) to walk timidly, hesitantly, or furtively; to edge along. [back-formation from *sideling*: see SIDELONG[1]]

SIDS *abbr* sudden infant death syndrome.

siege /seej/ *noun* **1** a military operation in which a city or fortified place is surrounded, blockaded, and bombarded to compel it to surrender. **2** a similar operation, e.g. by a police force, to force somebody to surrender. ✳ **lay siege to 1** to besiege (e.g. a city) militarily: *laid siege to the town.* **2** to pursue (somebody or something) diligently or persistently. [Middle English *sege* from Old French, ultimately from Latin *sedēre* to sit]

siege mentality *noun* a state of mind in which a person thinks that he or she is being attacked.

siemens /'seemənz/ *noun* (*pl* **siemens**) the SI unit of conductance. [named after Werner von *Siemens* d.1892, German electrical engineer]

sienna /si'enə/ *noun* an earthy substance containing oxides of iron and usu of manganese. It is brownish yellow when raw and orange red or reddish brown when burned and is used as a pigment. [Italian *terra di Siena* Siena earth, from *Siena, Sienna,* a town in Italy]

sierra /si'eərə/ *noun* a range of mountains, *esp* with a serrated or irregular outline. [Spanish *sierra* saw, from Latin *serra*]

Sierra Leonean /li'ohni-ən/ *noun* a native or inhabitant of Sierra Leone in W Africa. ⧉ **Sierra Leonean** *adj.*

siesta /si'estə/ *noun* an afternoon nap or rest: *But Englishmen detest a siesta* — Noël Coward. [Spanish *siesta* from late Latin *sexta (hora)* noon: see SEXT]

sieve[1] /siv/ *noun* a device with a meshed or perforated bottom that will allow the passage of liquids or fine solids while retaining coarser material or solids. [Old English *sife*]

sieve[2] *verb trans* to sift (something).

sievert /'seevət/ *noun* a unit of ionizing radiation equal to the dose equivalent of one joule per kilogram. [named after Rolf *Sievert* d.1966, Swedish physicist]

sift /sift/ *verb trans* **1a** to put (e.g. flour) through a sieve to remove lumps or coarse particles. **b** to scatter (something) with a sieve, or as if with a sieve: *I sifted icing sugar onto the cake.* **2** (*often* + out) to separate or remove (something) from a mixture using a sieve. **3a** to study or investigate (something) thoroughly; to probe or scrutinize (it). **b** (*often* + through) to study or examine (things) so as to pick out the best or most valuable; to screen (them). ⧉ *verb intrans* to move or fall like the fine powder produced by a sieve. [Old English *siftan*]

sifter *noun* something used for sifting, *esp* a castor.

Sig. *abbr* Signor.

sig. *abbr* signature.

sigh[1] /sie/ *verb intrans* **1** to take a long deep audible breath, e.g. in weariness or grief. **2** *said esp of the wind*: to make a sound like sighing. **3** (+ for) to grieve or yearn: *He's still sighing for the days of his youth.* ⧉ *verb trans* to express (something) by or with sighs. [Old English *sīcan*]

sigh[2] *noun* **1** an act of sighing, *esp* when expressing an emotion or feeling, e.g. weariness or relief. **2** a sound of or resembling sighing: *sighs of the summer breeze.*

sight¹ /siet/ *noun* **1** the process, power, or function of seeing; *specif* the one of the five basic physical senses by which light received by the eye is interpreted by the brain as a representation of the forms, brightness, and colour of the objects of the real world.

Editorial note

Sight – one of the five senses – is the process by which light received by the eye is interpreted by the brain as a representation of the forms, brightness and colour of the objects of the real world. Light received by the eye is refracted by the cornea before passing through the lens where the image is focused onto the retina and inverted. A coded form of the image is then transmitted from the retina via the optic nerve to the cerebral cortex of the brain — Dr John Cormack.

2a the act of looking at or beholding: *She fainted at the sight of blood.* **b** the perception of an object by the eye; a view or glimpse: *We got a sight of the Queen.* **3** the range of vision; the distance or area one can see. **4** something seen, *esp* a spectacle: *the familiar sight of the postman coming along the street.* **5a** (*in pl*) the things, e.g. impressive or historic buildings in a particular place, regarded as worth seeing: *We spent a day in London seeing the sights.* **b** *informal* something ridiculous or displeasing in appearance: *You must get some sleep, you look a sight.* **6a** a device for guiding the eye, e.g. in aiming a firearm or bomb. **b** a device with a small aperture through which objects are to be seen and by which their direction is ascertained. **7** an observation, e.g. by a navigator, to determine direction or position. **8** *informal* a great deal; a lot: *She got a sight more working freelance.* **✳ at first sight** when viewed without proper investigation: *At first sight the place seemed very dull.* **at/on sight** as soon as seen or presented to view: *Instructions were given that the gunman should be shot on sight.* **in sight 1** able to be seen, within visual range, or under observation. **2** able to be reached or achieved in a relatively short time. **know by sight** to be able to recognize (somebody) if one sees them. **lose sight of 1** to be no longer able to see (somebody or something). **2** to be no longer aware of or paying attention to (something). **out of sight 1** in such a place or at such a distance as to be or become invisible. **2** beyond all expectation or reason: *Prices have risen out of sight during the past year.* **3** (*also* **outasight**) *chiefly NAmer, informal, dated* marvellous or wonderful: *The party was out of sight!* **raise/lower one's sights** to become more/less ambitious. **set one's sights on** to aim to achieve (something); to have (it) as one's goal or ambition. **sight for sore eyes** *informal* somebody or something whose appearance or arrival is an occasion for joy or relief. [Old English *gesiht* thing seen]

sight² *verb trans* **1** to get or catch sight of (something): *Several whales had been sighted.* **2** to look at (something) through a sight, or as if through a sight; *esp* to test for straightness. **3** to aim (e.g. a weapon) by means of sights. **4a** to equip (e.g. a gun) with sights. **b** to adjust the sights of (e.g. a gun). **➤** *verb intrans* to take aim, e.g. in shooting.

sighted *adj* (*usu used in combinations*) having sight, *esp* of a specified kind: *clear-sighted; short-sighted.*

sighting *noun* **1** a view or glimpse, *esp* of something that is not often seen: *That was the last known sighting of the missing man.* **2** an observation made with a sight, e.g. of a gun.

sighting shot *noun* a shot made by shooters to help them adjust their sights.

sightless *adj* **1** lacking sight; blind. **2** *literary* = INVISIBLE¹. **➤➤ sightlessly** *adv*, **sightlessness** *noun*.

sightline *noun* a line of sight from a member of a theatre audience to some part of the stage; *specif* a line behind which an actor is not visible to the audience or some portion of the audience: *The wide auditorium and narrow proscenium arch gave the theatre very poor sightlines.*

sightly *adj* (**sightlier, sightliest**) **1** pleasing to the eye; attractive. **2** *chiefly NAmer* affording a fine view: *homes in a sightly location.* **➤➤ sightliness** *noun*.

sight-read /'siet reed/ *verb* (*past tense and past part.* **sight-read** /red/) **➤** *verb trans* to read (e.g. a foreign language) or perform (music) without previous preparation or study. **➤** *verb intrans* to read at sight; *esp* to perform music at sight. **➤➤ sight-reader** *noun*.

sight screen *noun* in cricket, a screen placed on the boundary of a field behind the bowler to improve the batsman's view of the ball.

sightsee *verb intrans* to make a tour of interesting or attractive sights. **➤➤ sightseeing** *noun*, **sightseer** *noun*.

sight unseen *adv* without previous inspection or appraisal: *He bought the car sight unseen.*

siglum /'sigləm/ *noun* (*pl* **sigla** /'siglə/) an abbreviation, e.g. a special character, used on a manuscript, coin, or seal. [late Latin *siglum*, perhaps from Latin *sigillum* little figure, dimin. of *signum* mark, token, SIGN¹]

sigma /'sigmə/ *noun* **1** the 18th letter of the Greek alphabet (Σ, σ, or at the end of a word ς), equivalent to and transliterated as roman s. **2** in mathematics, the symbol (Σ), usu denoting a summation. [Greek *sigma*, of Semitic origin]

sigmoid /'sigmoyd/ *adj* **1** curved like the letter C or S. **2** relating to the sigmoid flexure of the intestine. **➤➤ sigmoidally** /sig'moydəli/ *adv*. [Greek *sigmoeidēs* from *sigma*: see SIGMA; from a common form of sigma shaped like the Roman letter C]

sigmoidal /sig'moydl/ *adj* = SIGMOID.

sigmoid flexure *noun* the contracted and crooked part of the large intestine occurring at the end of the colon immediately above the rectum.

sign¹ /sien/ *noun* **1a** something serving to indicate the presence or existence of something: *We saw no sign of him anywhere.* **b** a presage or portent: *signs of an early spring.* **c** something material or external that stands for or signifies something spiritual. **d** objective evidence of plant or animal disease that usu causes no perceptible disability. **2** a board or notice carrying advertising matter or giving warning, command, information or direction. **3a** a motion or gesture by which a thought, command, or wish is made known; a signal. **b** a mark with a conventional meaning, used to replace or supplement words. **c** a meaningful unit of language, e.g. a word. **4a** a character, e.g. a flat or sharp, used in musical notation. **b** a segno (musical repeat sign). **c** a character, e.g. (÷), indicating a mathematical operation. **d** either of two characters (+) and (−) that form part of the symbol of a number and characterize it as positive or negative. **5** a remarkable event indicating the will of a deity. **6** any of the twelve divisions of the zodiac. [Middle English *signe* via early French *signe* from Latin *signum* mark, token, sign, image, seal]

sign² *verb trans* **1a** to put a signature to (something); to ratify or attest (it) by hand or seal: *I forgot to sign the cheque; The prisoner signed a confession.* **b** to write down (one's name). **c** (*often* + over) to assign (something) formally: *He signed over his property to his brother.* **2** to engage or hire (somebody) by securing a signature on a contract of employment: *We have signed a new striker from Arsenal.* **3** to indicate, represent, or express (something) by a sign. **4** to make the sign of the cross on or over (something). **5** to place a sign on (something). **➤** *verb intrans* **1** to write one's signature, *esp* in token of assent, responsibility, or obligation: *Sign here.* **2** to make a sign or signal. **3** to use sign language. **➤➤ signed** *adj*, **signer** *noun*. [Middle English *signen* via French from Latin *signare* to mark, sign, seal, from *signum* SIGN¹]

signage /'sienij/ *noun chiefly NAmer* signs collectively.

signal¹ /'signəl/ *noun* **1a** an action, gesture, event, or watchword that has been agreed on as the occasion for a concerted action: *They waited for the signal to begin the attack.* **b** anything that prompts a particular action or event to take place: *His scolding was a signal for the little girl to start crying.* **2** a conventional sign that conveys a particular piece of information or gives a warning or command: *a signal that warns of an air raid.* **3** a sign consisting of a set of coloured lights or a vertical post with a moving arm that regulates the flow of traffic, *esp* on a railway line. **4** the sound or image conveyed by telegraph, telephone, radio, radar, or television. **5** the variations of a physical quantity, e.g. pressure, current, or voltage, by which information may be transmitted in an electronic circuit or system, e.g.: **a** the wave that is used to modulate a CARRIER (wave carrying information to be transmitted): *the video signal.* **b** the wave produced by the modulation of a carrier by a signal: *a radio signal.* [Middle English via French from late Latin *signale* from Latin *signum* SIGN¹]

signal² *verb* (**signalled, signalling,** *NAmer* **signaled, signaling**) **➤** *verb intrans* to make or send a signal: *I signalled and turned left.* **➤** *verb trans* **1** to warn, order, or request (somebody) to do something by a signal: *He signalled the children to wait.* **2** to communicate (something) by signals: *They signalled their refusal.* **3** to be a sign of (something); to mark (it): *Her resignation signalled the end of a long career.* **➤➤ signaller** *noun*.

signal³ *adj* markedly different from the ordinary; conspicuous or outstanding: *a signal achievement.* **➤➤ signally** *adv*. [French *signalé*, past part. of *signaler* to distinguish, via Old Italian from late Latin *signale*: see SIGNAL¹]

signal box *noun Brit* a raised building above a railway line from which signals and points are worked.

signalize *or* **signalise** *verb trans* **1** *chiefly NAmer* to point out (something) carefully or distinctly; to draw attention to (it). **2** to make (something) noteworthy; to distinguish (it): *a performance signalized by consummate artistry.* ➤➤ **signalization** /-'zaysh(ə)n/ *noun.*

signalman *noun* (*pl* **signalmen**) somebody employed to operate signals, e.g. for a railway.

signal-to-noise ratio *noun* the ratio of a wanted signal to that of unwanted random interference, usu expressed in decibels.

signatory /'signət(ə)ri/ *noun* (*pl* **signatories**) somebody who signs a document along with another or others; *esp* a government bound with others by a signed convention. [Latin *signatorius* of sealing, from *signare*: see SIGN²]

signature /'signəchə/ *noun* **1a** the name of a person written with his or her own hand, usu in a distinctive way, to serve as a means of identification or authorization. **b** the act of signing one's name. **2a** in printing, a letter or figure placed usu at the bottom of the first page on each sheet of printed pages, e.g. of a book, as a direction to the binder in gathering the sheets. **b** the sheet itself. **3a** = KEY SIGNATURE. **b** = TIME SIGNATURE. **4** *NAmer* the part of a medical prescription that contains the directions to the patient. **5** a distinguishing or identifying mark, feature, or quality. [early French or late Latin *signature*, from Latin *signare*: see SIGN²]

signature tune *noun* a melody, passage, or song used to identify a programme, entertainer, etc.

signboard *noun* a sign on a board, e.g. to advertise a product.

signee /sie'nee/ *noun* somebody who has signed a document.

signet /'signit/ *noun* **1** a personal seal used officially in lieu of signature. **2** the impression made by a signet. **3** a small intaglio seal, e.g. in a finger ring. [Middle English from early French *signet*, dimin. of *signe*: see SIGN¹]

signet ring *noun* a finger ring engraved with a signet, seal, or monogram.

significance /sig'nifikəns/ *noun* **1a** something conveyed as a meaning, often latently or indirectly. **b** the quality of conveying or implying. **2a** the quality of being important; consequence. **b** the quality of being statistically significant.

significant /sig'nifikənt/ *adj* **1** having meaning; *esp* expressive: *The painter's task is to pick out the significant details* — Herbert Read. **2** suggesting or containing a veiled or special meaning: *Perhaps her glance was significant.* **3a** having or likely to have influence or effect; important: *The budget brought no significant changes.* **b** probably caused by something other than chance: *There is a statistically significant correlation between vitamin deficiency and disease.* ➤➤ **significantly** *adv.* [Latin *significant-, significans*, present part. of *significare*: see SIGNIFY]

significant figures *pl noun* the specified number of digits in a number that are considered to give correct or sufficient information on its accuracy, and are read from the first non-zero digit on the left to the last non-zero digit on the right, unless a final zero expresses greater accuracy.

significant other *noun chiefly NAmer* a person who has a particularly close and important relationship with somebody, *esp* a spouse or lover.

signification /ˌsignifi'kaysh(ə)n/ *noun* **1** signifying by symbolic means, e.g. signs. **2** the meaning that a term, symbol, or character normally conveys or is intended to convey.

signify /'signifie/ *verb* (**signifies, signified, signifying**) ➤ *verb trans* **1a** to mean or denote (something). **b** to be an indication of or imply (something). **2** to show (something), *esp* by a conventional token, e.g. a word, signal, or gesture. ➤ *verb intrans* to have significance; to matter. [Middle English *signifien* via Old French from Latin *significare* to indicate, signify, from *signum* SIGN¹]

sign in *verb intrans* to record one's arrival by signing a register or punching a card. ➤ *verb trans* to record the arrival of (a person) or receipt of (an article) by signing: *All deliveries must be signed in at the main gate.*

signing *noun* **1** somebody who is signed, e.g. by a football club. **2** sign language for the deaf.

sign language *noun* **1** a system of hand gestures used for communication, e.g. by the deaf. **2** unsystematic communication chiefly by gesture between people speaking different languages.

sign off *verb intrans* **1** to announce the end of a message, programme, or broadcast and finish broadcasting. **2** to end a letter, e.g. with a signature. **3** *Brit* to end the receipt of medical treatment, unemployment benefit, etc, by signing a document. ➤ *verb trans* said of a doctor: to declare (somebody) unfit for work because of illness.

sign on *verb intrans* **1** to commit oneself to a job by signature or agreement: *I signed on as a member of the crew.* **2** *Brit* to register as unemployed.

signor /'seenyaw, see'nyaw/ *noun* (*pl* **signors** *or* **signori** /-ree/) used of or to an Italian-speaking man as a title equivalent to *Mr*. [Italian *signore, signor* from medieval Latin *senior* superior, lord, from Latin *senior*: see SENIOR¹]

signora /seen'yawrə/ *noun* (*pl* **signoras** *or* **signore** /-ray/) used of or to an Italian-speaking married woman as a title equivalent to *Mrs* or as a generalized term of direct address. [Italian *signora*, fem of *signore, signor*: see SIGNOR]

signore /seen'yawray/ *noun* (*pl* **signori** /-ree/) used as a generalized term of direct address equivalent to *sir* when speaking to an Italian man. [Italian *signore*: see SIGNOR]

signori *noun* pl of SIGNOR, SIGNORE.

signorina /seenyaw'reenə/ *noun* (*pl* **signorinas** *or* **signorine** /-nay/) used to or of an unmarried Italian-speaking girl or woman as a title equivalent to *Miss*, or as a generalized term of direct address. [Italian *signorina*, dimin. of *signora* married woman, fem of *signor*: see SIGNOR]

signory /'seenyəri/ *noun* (*pl* **signories**) = SEIGNIORY. [Middle English *signorie* from early French *seigneurie*, from *seigneur*: see SEIGNEUR]

sign out *verb intrans* to indicate one's departure by signing in a register. ➤ *verb trans* to record or approve the release or withdrawal of (something or somebody).

signpost¹ *noun* a post, e.g. at a road junction, with signs on it to direct travellers.

signpost² *verb trans* **1a** to provide (an area) with signposts or guides. **b** to indicate the presence or direction of (something) with a signpost: *The turn-off isn't signposted.* **2** to indicate or mark (something).

sign up *verb intrans* to join an organization or accept an obligation by signing a contract; *esp* to enlist in the armed services. ➤ *verb trans* to cause (somebody) to sign a contract.

signwriter *noun* somebody who designs and paints signs, *esp* for commercial premises.

sika /'seekə/ *noun* (*pl* **sikas** *or collectively* **sika**) a small reddish brown deer introduced into Britain from Japan and now living wild in many areas: *Sika nippon.* [Japanese *shika*]

Sikh /seek/ *noun* an adherent of Sikhism. ➤➤ **Sikh** *adj.* [Punjabi *Sikh*, literally 'disciple', from Sanskrit *śisya*]

Sikhism /'seekiz(ə)m/ *noun* a monotheistic religion of India, founded by the Guru Nanak (1469–1539).

Editorial note

Punjabi for 'disciple', Sikhism is an Indian religion founded by Guru Nanak (1469–1539), who spoke of one god beyond Hindu and Muslim sectarian notions. Since the death of the tenth guru in 1708, authority has resided in the Sikh holy book. Male members of the community often show allegiance to the faith by never cutting their beard or hair, concealing the latter in a turban — Professor Donald Lopez.

silage /'sielij/ *noun* fodder converted, *esp* in a silo, into succulent feed for livestock. [short for ENSILAGE]

silane /'silayn, 'sielayn/ *noun* any of various compounds of silicon and hydrogen that are analogous to hydrocarbons of the methane series. [blend of SILICON + METHANE]

sild /sild/ *noun* (*pl* **silds** *or collectively* **sild**) a young herring other than a brisling, *esp* one that is canned in Norway. [Danish and Norwegian *sild*]

silence¹ /'sieləns/ *noun* **1** absence of sound or noise; stillness. **2** a state of not speaking or making a noise. **3** failure to mention a particular thing: *I can't understand the government's silence on such an important topic.* [Middle English via French from Latin *silentium*, from *silent-, silens*: see SILENT]

silence² *verb trans* **1** to make (something) silent or substantially reduce the amount of noise it makes. **2** to prevent (somebody) from speaking, writing, or expressing an opinion; to suppress (them). **3**

to cause (a gun, mortar, etc) to cease firing by return fire, bombing, etc.

silencer *noun* **1** a silencing device for a small firearm. **2** *chiefly Brit* a device for deadening the noise of the exhaust gas release of an internal-combustion engine.

silent /'sielənt/ *adj* **1** free from sound or noise; still. **2a** saying nothing; mute or speechless. **b** disinclined to speak; not talkative. **3a** endured without speaking or making verbal complaints: *silent grief*. **b** conveyed by refraining from reaction or comment; tacit: *silent assent*. **4a** making no mention; uninformative: *History is silent about this man*. **b** said of a business partner: taking no active part in the conduct of a business. **5** said of a letter: not pronounced, e.g. the *b* in *doubt*. **6** said of a film: without spoken dialogue. >> **silently** *adv*. [Latin *silent-, silens* present part. of *silēre* to be silent]

silent majority *noun* (*treated as sing. or pl*) a majority who do not assert their views, which are believed to be moderate.

Silesian /sie'leezi·ən/ *noun* a native or inhabitant of Silesia in central Europe. >> **Silesian** *adj*.

silex /'sieleks/ *noun* a heat-resistant glass made from fused quartz. [Latin *silic-, silex* flint, quartz]

silhouette[1] /siloo'et/ *noun* **1** the shape of a body as it appears against a lighter background. **2** a portrait in profile cut from dark material and mounted on a light background.

Word history
French *silhouette*, named after Étienne de *Silhouette* d.1767, French controller-general of finances. One suggestion is that Silhouette was notorious for his parsimony in matters of public expenditure, and that his name was first applied to things made cheaply. It then became attached to 'silhouettes' because they were not painted portraits but were cut out of paper.

silhouette[2] *verb trans* to cause (something) to appear in silhouette: *The film ends with the lovers silhouetted against the sunset*.

silica /'silikə/ *noun* silicon dioxide occurring in many rocks and minerals, e.g. quartz, opal, and sand: formula SiO_2. [Latin *silic-, silex* flint, quartz]

silica gel *noun* silica resembling coarse white sand in appearance but possessing many fine pores and therefore extremely adsorbent.

silicate /'silikət, -kayt/ *noun* any of numerous insoluble often complex compounds that contain silicon and oxygen, constitute the largest class of minerals, and are used in building materials, e.g. cement, bricks, and glass.

siliceous *or* **silicious** /si'lishəs/ *adj* **1** relating to or containing silica or a silicate. **2** said of plants: needing a soil rich in silica. [Latin *siliceus* of flint, from *silic-, silex* flint, quartz]

silicic /si'lisik/ *adj* derived from or containing silica or silicon.

silicic acid *noun* any of various weakly acid substances obtained as gelatinous masses by treating silicates with acids.

silicide /'silisied/ *noun* a chemical compound composed of silicon and another chemical element or a chemical group.

silicify /si'lisifie/ *verb* (**silicifies, silicified, silicifying**) > *verb trans* to convert (something) into or impregnate it with silica. > *verb intrans* to become silicified. >> **silicification** /-fi'kaysh(ə)n/ *noun*.

silicious /si'lishəs/ *adj* see SILICEOUS.

silicon /'silikən/ *noun* **1** a grey non-metallic chemical element that occurs, in combination with other elements, as the most abundant element next to oxygen in the earth's crust, and is used in alloys and in the manufacture of glass: symbol Si, atomic number 14. **2** (*usu* **Silicon**) (*used before a noun*) indicating an area where a group of high-tech companies or industries are clustered. [Latin *silica* silica + *-on* as in CARBON]

silicon carbide *noun* a very hard dark chemical compound of silicon and carbon that is used as an abrasive, as a heat-resisting material, and in electrical resistors: formula SiC.

silicon chip *noun* = CHIP[1] (5).

silicone /'silikohn/ *noun* any of various polymeric organic silicon compounds obtained as oils, greases, or plastics and used for water-resistant and heat-resistant lubricants, varnishes, and electrical insulators.

silicosis /sili'kohsis/ *noun* a disease of the lungs marked by hardening of the tissue and shortness of breath and caused by prolonged inhalation of silica dusts: compare PNEUMOCONIOSIS. >> **silicotic** /-'kotik/ *adj*.

siliqua /'silikwə/ *or* **silique** /si'leek/ *noun* (*pl* **siliquae** /-kwee/ *or* **siliques**) a long narrow seed capsule that is characteristic of plants of the mustard family. [Latin *siliqua* pod, husk]

silk /silk/ *noun* **1** a fine continuous protein fibre produced by various insect larvae, usu for cocoons; *esp* a lustrous tough elastic fibre produced by silkworms and used for textiles. **2** thread, yarn, or fabric made from silk filaments. **3** *Brit, informal* a King's or Queen's Counsel. **4** (*in pl*) the cap and shirt of a jockey made in the registered racing colour of his or her stable. **5a** a silky material or filament, e.g. that produced by a spider. **b** the tuft of fine fibres at the tip of an ear of maize. ❉ **take silk** *Brit* to become a Queen's or King's Counsel. [Old English *seolc* from late Latin *sericum*, neuter of *sericus* silken, ultimately from Greek *Sēres*, the inhabitants of the Far Eastern countries where silk was first made; (sense 3) from the silk gown that they wear]

silk cotton *noun* kapok or another silky or cottony seed covering.

silk-cotton tree *noun* either of two tropical trees of the baobab family with lobed leaves and large fruits with the seeds enveloped by silk cotton: *Bombax ceiba* and *Ceiba pentandra*.

silken *adj* **1** made of silk. **2** resembling silk, *esp* in softness or lustre.

silk gland *noun* a gland, e.g. in an insect larva or spider, that produces a sticky fluid that is extruded in filaments and hardens into silk on exposure to air.

silk hat *noun* a hat with a tall cylindrical crown and a silk-plush finish worn by men as a dress hat.

silk moth *noun* a large Asiatic moth whose rough wrinkled hairless yellowish caterpillar produces the silk used commercially: *Bombyx mori*.

silk screen *noun* a prepared silk or organdie screen used in screen-printing.

silk-screen *verb trans* to produce (e.g. a print) using a silk screen.

silkworm *noun* the larva of a silk moth, which spins a large amount of strong silk in constructing its cocoon.

silky *adj* (**silkier, silkiest**) **1** resembling or consisting of silk; silken. **2** said of a voice: suave or ingratiating. >> **silkily** *adv*, **silkiness** *noun*.

sill /sil/ *noun* **1a** a horizontal piece, e.g. a timber, that forms the lowest member, or one of the lowest members, of a framework or supporting structure, e.g. a window frame or door frame. **b** a narrow shelf projecting from the base of a window frame, *esp* inside a room. **2** in geology, a horizontal sheet of intrusive igneous rock running between strata of other rocks. **3** a submerged ridge at relatively shallow depth separating two deeper bodies of water. [Old English *syll*]

sillabub /'siləbub/ *noun archaic* = SYLLABUB.

sillimanite /'siləmaniet/ *noun* a brown, greyish, or pale green mineral consisting of an aluminium silicate. [named after Benjamin *Silliman* d.1864, US geologist]

silly[1] /'sili/ *adj* (**sillier, silliest**) **1a** showing a lack of common sense or sound judgment: *'I am astonished … that you should be so ready to think your own children silly.' … 'If my own children are silly, I must hope to be always sensible of it.'* — Jane Austen. **b** trifling or frivolous: *a silly remark*. **2** stunned or dazed: *I was scared silly*; *The blow knocked me silly*. **3** in cricket, denoting or occupying a fielding position in front of and dangerously near the batsman: *silly mid-off*. **4** *archaic*. **a** simple and unsophisticated: *Perhaps their loves, or else their sheep, was all that did their silly thoughts so busie keep* — Milton. **b** feeble-minded: *Davie's no just like other folk … but he's no sae silly as folk tak him for* — Scott. >> **sillily** *adv*, **silliness** *noun*.

Word history
Old English *sǣlig* happy, fortunate, blessed by God, from Old English *sǣl* happiness. During the Middle English period the word came to mean 'holy, pious', hence 'innocent, harmless, defenceless, pathetic', also, by the 15th cent. 'ignorant, simple, foolish'.

silly[2] *noun* (*pl* **sillies**) *informal* a silly person: *She is what is called a silly, still she answers pretty well* — W S Gilbert.

silly-billy *noun* (*pl* **silly-billies**) *chiefly Brit, informal* somebody absurd or silly.

silly season *noun chiefly Brit* a period when newspapers resort to reporting trivial or frivolous matters through lack of important news.

silo /'sieloh/ *noun* (*pl* **silos**) **1** a trench, pit, or tall cylinder, e.g. of wood or concrete, usu sealed to exclude air and used for making and storing silage. **2** an underground structure for housing a guided missile. [Spanish *silo* via Latin from Greek *siros* grain pit]

silt[1] /silt/ *noun* a deposit of sediment, e.g. at the bottom of a river. ➤➤ **silty** *adj*. [Middle English *cylte*, prob of Scandinavian origin]

silt[2] *verb trans and intrans* (*often* + up) to become, or to cause (e.g. a river, harbour) to become, choked or obstructed with silt. ➤➤ **siltation** /sil'taysh(ə)n/ *noun*.

siltstone *noun* a rock composed chiefly of hardened silt.

Silurian /sie'l(y)ooəri·ən, si-/ *adj* relating to or dating from a geological period, the third period of the Palaeozoic era, lasting from about 439 million to about 409 million years ago, and marked by the first appearance of land plants. ➤➤ **Silurian** *noun*. [Latin *Silures* an ancient British tribe who lived in Wales, where rocks of this period can be easily seen]

silvan /'silvən/ *adj* see SYLVAN.

silver[1] /'silvə/ *noun* **1a** a white metallic chemical element that is ductile and malleable, takes a very high degree of polish, is chiefly univalent in compounds, has the highest thermal and electrical conductivity of any substance, and is used in jewellery, ornaments, etc: symbol Ag, atomic number 47. **b** (*used before a noun*) made of silver. **2a** coins made of silver or cupro-nickel. **b** articles, *esp* tableware, made of or plated with silver. **c** cutlery made of other metals. **d** silver as a commodity. **3** *informal* = SILVER MEDAL. ✻ **be born with a silver spoon in one's mouth** to be born into a wealthy, *esp* upper-class, family. [Old English *seolfor*]

silver[2] *adj* **1a** of a whitish grey colour. **b** resembling silver, *esp* in having a white lustrous sheen. **2a** giving a soft, clear, ringing sound. **b** eloquently persuasive: *a silver tongue*. **3** marking a 25th anniversary: *a silver wedding*. ➤➤ **silver** *noun*.

silver[3] *verb* (**silvered, silvering**) ➤ *verb trans* **1** to cover or coat (something) with silver or a substance resembling silver. **2** to impart a silvery lustre or whiteness to (something). ➤ *verb intrans* to become silver or grey in colour.

silver age *noun* a period that, although quite productive or prosperous, marks a decline from a previous golden age and, in the arts, may see form and technique prevailing over more inward and substantial qualities.

silver birch *noun* a common Eurasian birch tree with silvery-white peeling bark: *Betula pendula*.

silver disc *noun* a music award in the form of a framed silver record given to an artist, group, etc in Britain for selling 60,000 copies of an album or 200,000 copies of a single.

silver fern *noun* **1** = PONGA. **2** a silver fern leaf used as an emblem of New Zealand.

silver fir *noun* any of various firs with leaves that have a white or silvery white undersurface.

silverfish *noun* (*pl* **silverfishes** *or collectively* **silverfish**) **1** any of various small wingless insects; *esp* one found in houses that is sometimes injurious to sized paper, e.g. wallpaper, or starched fabrics: *Lepisma saccharina*. **2** any of various silvery fishes.

silver foil *noun* = TINFOIL.

silver fox *noun* **1** a genetically determined colour phase of the common red fox in which the pelt is black tipped with white. **2** a pelt or fur from a fox in this colour phase.

silver gilt *noun* silver that has been covered with a thin layer of gold.

silver jubilee *noun* the 25th anniversary of a special event, e.g. the accession of a sovereign.

silver lining *noun* a consoling or hopeful prospect. [from metaphorical use of the phrase *every cloud has a silver lining*, i.e. a white edge]

silver medal *noun* a medal of silver awarded to somebody who comes second in a competition. ➤➤ **silver medallist** *noun*.

silver plate *noun* **1** a plating of silver. **2** tableware and cutlery of silver or a silver-plated metal.

silver-plate *verb trans* to coat (e.g. metal) with a thin layer of silver.

silver screen *noun* (**the silver screen**) the film industry.

Editorial note
The 'silver' in 'silver screen' is a throwback to the days when black-and-white was the norm, silver being the photosensitive metal in film emulsion. The 'silver screen' generally applies to movies made before about 1940 (when colour began to dominate), and to the increasingly archaic style of that era. The term sometimes applies to the whole picture business, and

the ethos of publicity, and so there is a suggestion of fraudulence with the fun — David Thomson.

silver service *noun* a style of serving food to diners in a restaurant or hotel, using a silver spoon and fork.

silverside *noun* **1** *Brit* a cut of beef from the outer part of the top of the leg below the aitchbone, that is boned and often salted. **2** (*also* **silversides**) any of numerous species of small fishes that have a silvery stripe along each side: family Atherinidae. [(sense 1) from its being considered the best cut]

silversmith *noun* a craft worker who makes objects in silver.

silver-tongued *adj* eloquent or persuasive.

silverware *noun* tableware and cutlery of silver or a silver-plated metal.

silverweed *noun* any of various somewhat silvery plants; *esp* a cinquefoil with leaves covered in a dense mat of silvery hairs on the underside: *Potentilla anserina*.

silvery *adj* **1** having the lustre or whiteness of silver. **2** containing or consisting of silver. **3** having a soft clear musical tone. ➤➤ **silveriness** *noun*.

silviculture /'silvikulchə/ *noun* a branch of forestry dealing with the development and care of forests. ➤➤ **silvicultural** /-'kulch(ə)rəl/ *adj*, **silviculturist** /-'kulchərist/ *noun*. [French *silviculture*, from Latin *silva, sylva* forest + *cultura*: see CULTURE[1]]

sim /sim/ *noun informal* a computer or video game that involves simulating an activity: *a sad lack of choice for Mac gamers when it comes to good racing sims* — Macformat. [short for *simulation*: see SIMULATE]

simian[1] /'simi·ən/ *adj* of or resembling a monkey or ape. [Latin *simia* ape, perhaps from *simus* snub-nosed, from Greek *simos*]

simian[2] *noun* a monkey or ape.

similar /'similə/ *adj* **1** marked by correspondence or resemblance, *esp* of a general kind: *The houses are similar but not identical*. **2** said of geometric figures: having corresponding angles, and corresponding sides in the same ratio, so that they have the same shape but differ in size: *similar triangles*. ➤➤ **similarity** /-'lariti/ *noun*, **similarly** *adv*. [French *similaire* from Latin *similis* like, similar]

simile /'simili/ *noun* a figure of speech explicitly comparing two unlike things, e.g. in *cheeks like roses*: compare METAPHOR. [Latin *simile* comparison, neuter of *similis* like, SIMILAR]

similitude /si'milityoohd/ *noun* **1** correspondence in kind, quality, or appearance. **2** *archaic*. **a** a counterpart or double. **b** a comparison or simile. [Middle English via French from Latin *similitudo*, from *similis* like, SIMILAR]

simmer /'simə/ *verb* (**simmered, simmering**) ➤ *verb intrans* **1a** said of a liquid: to bubble gently below or just at the boiling point. **b** said of food: to cook in a simmering liquid. **2a** to develop or ferment: *He had ideas simmering in the back of his mind*. **b** to be agitated by suppressed emotion: *simmering with anger*. ➤ *verb trans* to cook (food) in a simmering liquid. [alteration of English dialect *simper* from Middle English *simperen*, of imitative origin]

simmer down *verb intrans* to become calm or less excited.

simnel cake /'simnəl/ *noun Brit* a rich fruit cake traditionally filled with a layer of almond paste and baked for mid-Lent and Easter. [Middle English *simenel* via Old French from Latin *simila* fine wheat flour]

simony /'siməni, 'sie-/ *noun* the buying or selling of a church office or ecclesiastical promotion. ➤➤ **simoniac** /si'mohniak/ *adj and noun*, **simoniacal** /siemə'nie·əkl/ *adj*. [late Latin *simonia*, named after *Simon* Magus first cent. AD, Samaritan sorcerer, who tried to buy the gift of healing from the Apostle Peter (Acts 8:9–24)]

simoom /si'moohm/ *or* **simoon** /si'moohn/ *noun* a hot dry violent dust-laden wind blowing from an Asian or African desert. [Arabic *samūm*]

simp /simp/ *noun chiefly NAmer, informal* = SIMPLETON.

simpatico /sim'patikoh, sim'pah-/ *adj* **1** congenial or likeable. **2** having similar interests; compatible. [Italian *simpatico* and Spanish *simpático*, both from Latin *sympathia*: see SYMPATHY]

simper[1] /'simpə/ *verb* (**simpered, simpering**) ➤ *verb intrans* to smile in a foolish self-conscious manner. ➤ *verb trans* to say (something) with a simper: *She simpered her apologies*. ➤➤ **simpering** *adj*, **simperingly** *adv*. [perhaps of Scandinavian origin]

simper[2] *noun* a foolish self-conscious smile.

simple[1] /'simpl/ *adj* **1** easily understood or performed; straightforward: *a simple task*. **2a** lacking ornamentation; basic or plain: *dressed in simple garments*. **b** free from elaboration or showiness; unpretentious: *She wrote in a simple style*. **3a** free from guile or vanity; innocent or unassuming. **b** lacking experience or sophistication; naive. **4** lacking intelligence; feeble-minded. **5** of humble birth or lowly position: *a simple farmer*. **6** sheer or unqualified: *the simple truth of the matter*. **7** not made up of many like units; not compound, e.g.: **a** said of a fruit: developing from a single ovary. **b** said of a leaf: not subdivided into branches or leaflets. **c** said of a sentence: consisting of only one main clause and no subordinate clauses. **d** in chemistry, composed essentially of one basic substance or element; fundamental. **8** said of a statistical hypothesis: specifying exact values for the stated statistical conditions. ⫸ **simpleness** *noun*. [Middle English via Old French from Latin *simplus* simple, single (from *sem-*, *sim-* one + *-plus* multiplied by), and *simplic-*, *simplex* plain, unmixed (from *sem-*, *sim-* + *-plic-*, *-plex* -fold)]

simple[2] *noun archaic* a medicinal plant. [SIMPLE[1], in the sense 'not compound']

simple eye *noun* an eye, e.g. of an insect, with only one lens.

simple fraction *noun* = COMMON FRACTION.

simple fracture *noun* a bone fracture produced in such a way as to leave the surrounding skin and tissue undamaged.

simple harmonic motion *noun* a vibratory motion, e.g. the swing of a pendulum, in which the acceleration is proportional and opposite to the displacement of the body from an equilibrium position.

simple-hearted *adj* having a sincere and unassuming nature; artless.

simple interest *noun* interest paid or calculated only on the original capital sum of a loan.

simple machine *noun* any of various elementary mechanisms formerly considered as the elements of which all machines are composed and including the lever, the wheel and axle, the pulley, the inclined plane, the wedge, and the screw.

simple-minded *adj* **1** lacking in intelligence or judgment; stupid or foolish. **2** devoid of subtlety; unsophisticated. ⫸ **simple-mindedly** *adv*, **simple-mindedness** *noun*.

simple time *noun* in music, time in which there are two, three, or four beats to a bar, each beat divisible by two, four, etc: compare COMPOUND TIME.

simpleton /'simplt(ə)n/ *noun* somebody who is mentally deficient or who lacks common sense or intelligence. [SIMPLE[1] + -*ton* as in surnames such as *Washington*]

simplex[1] /'simpleks/ *adj* **1** consisting of a single part or structure; simple. **2** allowing telecommunication in only one direction at a time. [Latin *simplic-*, *simplex* plain, unmixed: see SIMPLE[1]]

simplex[2] *noun* in linguistics, a simple, non-compound word.

simplicity /sim'plisiti/ *noun* **1** the state or quality of being simple. **2a** directness of expression; clarity. **b** restraint in ornamentation; austerity or plainness. **3a** freedom from affectation or guile; sincerity or straightforwardness. **b** lack of subtlety or penetration; naivety. [Middle English *simplicite* via French from Latin *simplicitat-*, *simplicitas*, from *simplic-*, *simplex*: see SIMPLE[1]]

simplify /'simplifie/ *verb trans* (**simplifies, simplified, simplifying**) to make (something) simple or simpler. ⫸ **simplification** /-fi'kaysh(ə)n/ *noun*. [French *simplifier* via medieval Latin *simplificare*, from Latin *simplus*: see SIMPLE[1]]

simplistic /sim'plistik/ *adj* deliberately or naively uncomplicated, *esp* where a more complex approach is appropriate; oversimplified: *It's too simplistic to pretend that one way is better than the other because the comparison isn't between like and like* — Caterer & Hotelkeeper. ⫸ **simplistically** *adv*.

simply *adv* **1a** without ambiguity; clearly: *a simply worded reply*. **b** without ornamentation or show: *simply furnished*. **c** without affectation or subterfuge; candidly. **2a** solely or merely: *He eats simply to keep alive*. **b** without any question: *The concert was simply marvellous*.

simulacrum /simyoo'laykrəm/ *noun* (*pl* **simulacra** /-krə/ *or* **simulacrums**) *formal* **1** an image or representation of something or somebody. **2** a vague or superficial likeness or an imperfect imitation. [Latin *simulacrum* from *simulare*: see SIMULATE]

simulate /'simyoolayt/ *verb trans* **1** to assume the outward qualities or appearance of (something), usu with the intent to deceive. **2** to make a functioning model of (a system, device, or process), e.g. by using a computer. ⫸ **simulation** /-'laysh(ə)n/ *noun*, **simulative** /-tiv/ *adj*. [Latin *simulatus*, past part. of *simulare* to copy, represent, feign, from *similis* like, SIMILAR]

simulator *noun* a device that simulates various conditions or the mechanisms involved in operating a system, in order to train operators or for the purposes of research.

simulcast[1] /'siməlkahst/ *noun* a simultaneous broadcast on television and radio, or on two or more channels or networks. [blend of SIMULTANEOUS + BROADCAST[2]]

simulcast[2] *verb trans* to broadcast simultaneously on television and radio, or on two or more channels or networks.

simultaneous /simǝl'tayni·ǝs/ *adj* existing, occurring, or functioning at the same time. ⫸ **simultaneity** /-tǝ'nayiti, -tǝ'nee·iti/ *noun*, **simultaneously** *adv*, **simultaneousness** *noun*. [(assumed) late Latin *simultaneus* from Latin *simul* at the same time]

simultaneous equations *pl noun* a set of equations that are satisfied by the same values of the variables.

sin[1] /sin/ *noun* **1** an offence against moral or religious law or divine commandments.

Editorial note
Usually taken to refer to moral (and especially sexual) misconduct, the term 'sin' implies a state in which a person has chosen to separate himself or herself from God. Since breaking religious or moral rules is believed to be a sign of such separation, sin has come to refer more generally to the action rather than the spiritual state — Dr Mel Thompson.

2 an action considered highly reprehensible: *It's a sin to waste food*. ✱ **live in sin** to cohabit. ⫸ **sinless** *adj*, **sinlessly** *adv*, **sinlessness** *noun*. [Old English *synn*]

sin[2] *verb intrans* (**sinned, sinning**) **1** to commit a sin. **2** (*often* + against) to violate a law or principle; to offend: *writers who sin against good taste*. ⫸ **sinner** *noun*.

sin[3] *abbr* sine.

sin bin *noun* **1** *informal* an enclosure occupied by a player, e.g. in ice hockey, who has been temporarily sent off. **2** *Brit* a place where an offender, e.g. a persistently disruptive pupil in a school, is segregated.

since[1] /sins/ *adv* **1** continuously from then until now: *She has stayed there ever since*. **2** before now; ago: *He should have done it long since*. **3** between then and now; subsequently: *They have since become rich*. [Middle English *sins*, contraction of *sithens*, from *sithen*, from Old English *siththan*, from *sith tham* after that, from *sith* since + *tham*, dative of *thæt* THAT[1]]

since[2] *prep* **1** in the period between (a specified past time) and now: *We haven't met since 1973*. **2** from (a specified past time) until now: *It's a long time since breakfast*.

since[3] *conj* **1** between now and the past time when: *He has held two jobs since he left school*. **2** continuously from the past time when: *ever since he was a child*. **3** in view of the fact that; because: *Since it was raining he wore a hat*; *This stamp is more interesting, since rarer*.

sincere /sin'siǝ/ *adj* free from deceit or hypocrisy; honest or genuine: *The missionaries were prompted by a sincere desire for good* — Herman Melville. ⫸ **sincereness** *noun*, **sincerity** /sin'seriti/ *noun*. [early French *sincere* from Latin *sincerus* clean, pure]

sincerely /sin'siǝli/ *adv* in a sincere way. ✱ **yours sincerely** used to end a formal letter when the writer has addressed the recipient by name.

sinciput /'sinsiput/ *noun* (*pl* **sinciputs** *or* **sincipita** /sin'sipitǝ/) **1** = FOREHEAD. **2** the upper half of the skull. [Latin *sincipit-*, *sinciput*, from SEMI- + *caput* head]

sine /sien/ *noun* in mathematics, the trigonometric function that for an acute angle in a right-angled triangle is the ratio between the side opposite the angle and the hypotenuse: compare COSINE, TANGENT[1]. [Latin *sinus* curve, later 'fold in a garment', used in medieval Latin to translate Arabic *jayb* pocket, sine]

sinecure /'sinikyooǝ, 'sie-/ *noun* an office or position that provides an income while requiring little or no work. ⫸ **sinecurism** *noun*, **sinecurist** *noun*. [late Latin (*beneficium*) *sine cura* (benefice) without cure of souls]

sine curve *noun* the continuous S-shaped graph of the equation $y = a\sin bx$ where a and b are constants.

sine die /ˌsieni 'deeay, 'die, ˌsini/ *adv* without any future date being designated, e.g. for resumption: *The meeting adjourned sine die.* [Latin *sine die*, literally 'without a day']

sine qua non /ˌsini kway 'non, kwah, 'nohn, ˌsieni/ *noun* an absolutely indispensable or essential thing. [late Latin *sine qua non* without which not]

sinew /'sinyooh/ *noun* **1** = TENDON. **2a** solid resilient strength; vigour: *intellectual and moral sinew.* **b** (*usu in pl*) the chief means of support; mainstay: *the sinews of political stability.* ⟩⟩ **sinewless** *adj.* [Old English *sinwe, sinewe* tendon]

sine wave *noun* a wave form that represents periodic oscillations in which the amount of vertical displacement at each point is proportional to the sine of the horizontal distance from a reference point.

sinewy /'sinyooi/ *adj* **1a** having or resembling sinews. **b** possessing great muscular strength, usu in a lean and supple body: *The smith, a mighty man is he, with large and sinewy hands* — Longfellow. **c** said e.g. of a writing style: powerful and dynamic, but without harshness. **2** said of meat: tough and chewy.

sinfonia /sin'fohni-ə/ *noun* (*pl* **sinfonie** /-neeay/ *or* **sinfonias**) **1** = SYMPHONY. **2a** an orchestral composition used as an introduction to vocal works, e.g. opera, *esp* in the 18th cent.; an overture. **b** an instrumental interlude in baroque opera. **3** a symphony orchestra. [Italian *sinfonia* from Latin *symphonia*: see SYMPHONY]

sinfonietta /ˌsinfohni'etə, sinfo'nyetə/ *noun* **1** a short or lightly orchestrated symphony. **2a** a small symphony orchestra. **b** a small orchestra of strings only. [Italian *sinfonietta*, dimin. of *sinfonia*: see SINFONIA]

sinful /'sinf(ə)l/ *adj* tainted with, marked by, or full of sin; wicked. ⟩⟩ **sinfully** *adv,* **sinfulness** *noun.*

sing[1] /sing/ *verb* (*past tense* **sang** /sang/, *past part.* **sung** /sung/) ⟩ *verb intrans* **1a** to produce musical sounds by means of the voice. **b** to utter words in musical notes with changes in the tone, pitch, or loudness of the voice to convey meaning. **c** to work or spend time as a singer: *He sings in the church choir.* **d** (+ along) to join in and accompany somebody else who is singing. **2** to make a shrill whining or whistling sound: *A kettle was singing on the fire.* **3** to produce musical or melodious sounds: *The birds were singing in the trees.* **4** to buzz or ring: *The punch made his ears sing.* **5a** (*usu* + out) to make a loud clear utterance: *He sang out in the darkness.* **b** *informal* (+ out) to call or shout: *Sing out if you need a hand.* **6** *informal* to give information or evidence. ⟩ *verb trans* **1** to produce (musical sounds) by means of the voice; *esp* to utter (words, musical scales, etc) in musical notes. **2a** to relate or celebrate (something) in verse. **b** to express (something) vividly or enthusiastically: *They sang his praises.* **3** to chant or intone (e.g. a mass). **4** to bring (somebody) to a specified state by singing: *He sang the child to sleep.* ⟩⟩ **singable** *adj,* **singer** *noun,* **singing** *noun.* [Old English *singan*]

sing[2] *noun informal* a session of singing; a singsong.

sing. *abbr* singular.

singalong /'singəlong/ *noun informal* = SINGSONG (2).

Singaporean /ˌsinggə'pawri-ən/ *noun* a native or inhabitant of Singapore in SE Asia. ⟩⟩ **Singaporean** *adj.*

singe[1] /sinj/ *verb trans* (**singed, singeing**) to burn (something) superficially or slightly; to scorch (it); *esp* to remove the hair, down, or nap from (something) by brief exposure to a flame. [Old English *sencgan*]

singe[2] *noun* a superficial burn; a scorch.

Singh /sing/ *noun* a title used by a Sikh boy or man to show that he belongs to the fraternity of warriors. [Punjabi *singh* from Sanskrit *simha* lion]

Singhalese /singgə'leez/ *noun see* SINHALESE.

single[1] /'singgl/ *adj* **1** not accompanied by others; one, solitary, or sole: *the single survivor of the disaster.* **2** consisting of a separate unique whole; individual or distinct: *every single citizen; Food is our most important single need.* **3a** of, suitable for, or involving only one person: *a single portion of chips; a single room.* **b** consisting of or having only one part or feature: *single thread.* **c** having one aspect as opposed to two or more; uniform: *a single standard for men and women.* **4** (*in negative contexts*) even one: *I didn't know a single person there.* **5a** not married. **b** of the unmarried state: *the single life.* **6** said of a plant or flower: having one set or whorl of petals: compare DOUBLE[1] (8). **7** said of combat: involving only two people. **8** *archaic* honest or sincere: *a single devotion.* ⟩⟩ **singleness** *noun,* **singly** *adv.* [Middle English via French from Latin *singulus* one only]

single[2] *noun* **1** a CD or gramophone record, *esp* of popular music, with a single short track, or one on each side. **2** a single thing or amount; *esp* a single measure of spirits. **3a** in cricket, a single run scored. **b** in baseball, a hit that enables the batter to reach first base. **4** *Brit* a ticket bought for a trip to a place but not back again: compare RETURN[2] (4). **5** (*usu in pl*) an unmarried adult: *a singles club.* **6a** *Brit* formerly, a one-pound note. **b** *NAmer* a one-dollar note.

single[3] *verb trans* (+ out) to select or distinguish (somebody or something) from a number or group.

single-action *adj* said of a firearm: that requires the hammer to be cocked before firing.

single-blind *adj* of or being an experimental procedure which is designed to eliminate false results, in which the experimenters, but not the subjects, know the make-up of the test and control groups during the actual course of the experiments: compare DOUBLE-BLIND.

single-breasted *adj* said of a coat or jacket: having a centre fastening with one row of buttons: compare DOUBLE-BREASTED.

single cream *noun Brit* cream that is thinner and lighter than double cream, contains 18% butterfat, and is suitable for pouring: compare DOUBLE CREAM.

single-decker *noun Brit* a bus that has a single deck.

singledom *noun* the state of being maritally single or romantically unattached.

single entry *noun* a method of bookkeeping that records business transactions in a single account and usu consists only of a record of cash flow and personal accounts with debtors and creditors.

single file *noun* a line, e.g. of people, moving one behind the other.

single-handed *adj* **1** performed or achieved by one person or with one on a side: *a single-handed crossing of the Atlantic.* **2** working or managing alone or unassisted by others. **3** using or requiring the use of only one hand: *He hit a powerful single-handed backhand shot.* ⟩⟩ **single-handed** *adv,* **single-handedly** *adv.*

single-lens reflex *noun* a camera in which the image is viewed using a mirror behind the lens and a five-sided prism in front of the eyepiece.

single malt *noun* a high quality unblended Scottish malt whisky.

single-minded *adj* having a single overriding purpose. ⟩⟩ **single-mindedly** *adv,* **single-mindedness** *noun.*

single parent *noun* a man or woman who is bringing up a child or children without a permanent partner.

singles *noun* (*pl* **singles**) a game, e.g. of tennis, with one player on each side.

singlestick *noun* **1** one-handed fighting or fencing with a wooden stick. **2** the stick used for this.

singlet /'singglit/ *noun chiefly Brit* a vest, or a similar garment worn by athletes. [because it has only one thickness of cloth]

single ticket *noun* = SINGLE[2] (4).

singleton /'singglt(ə)n/ *noun* **1** a card that is the only one of its suit in a dealt hand. **2** an individual as opposed to a pair or group; *specif* an offspring born singly. **3** in mathematics, a set containing only one member. [SINGLE[1] + -*ton* as in SIMPLETON]

single transferable vote *noun* a system of voting in a constituency with more than one member; candidates are listed in order of preference, and votes are redistributed until enough members have been chosen.

singletree *noun NAmer* a bar to which the straps of a horse's harness are fastened; a swingletree. [alteration of SWINGLETREE by association with *double-tree*, the crosspiece to which the swingletrees of two horses pulling abreast are hitched]

singsong /'singsong/ *noun* **1** a voice delivery characterized by a monotonous cadence or rhythm or rising and falling inflection. **2** *Brit* a session of group singing. ⟩⟩ **singsong** *adj.*

singular[1] /'singgyoolə/ *adj* **1** superior; exceptional: *a man of singular attainments.* **2** very unusual or strange; peculiar: *the singular events leading up to the murder.* **3a** of a separate person or thing; individual. **b** said of a word or word form: denoting one person, thing, or instance: compare DUAL[1] (2), PLURAL[1] (1). **4** said of a mathematical matrix: having a determinant equal to zero. **5** not general: *a singular proposition in logic.* ⟩⟩ **singularly** *adv.* [Middle English *singuler* via Old French from Latin *singularis*, from *singulus* only one]

singular[2] *noun* in grammar, the singular number, the inflectional form denoting it, or a word in that form.

singularise /'singgyoolǝriez/ *verb trans* see SINGULARIZE.

singularity /singgyoo'lariti/ *noun* (*pl* **singularities**) **1** something singular, e.g.: **a** a separate unit. **b** an unusual or distinctive trait; a peculiarity: *Her eyes were dark, and they had the singularity of seeming at once dull and restless* — Henry James. **2** the state or quality of being singular. **3** in mathematics, a point at which a function is undefined, e.g. by reason of division by zero or non-existence of a derivative. **4** in astronomy, a point of infinite density at the centre of a black hole.

singularize or **singularise** /'singgyoolǝriez/ *verb trans* **1** to make (something) exceptional or distinctive. **2** in grammar, to make (a word) singular. ➤➤ **singularization** /-'zaysh(ǝ)n/ *noun.*

sinh /shien, sinch/ *abbr* hyperbolic sine. [SINE + *h* for HYPERBOLIC[2]]

Sinhalese or **Singhalese** /sin(h)ǝ'leez/ or **Sinhala** /sin'hahlǝ/ *noun* (*pl* **Sinhalese** or **Singhalese** or **Sinhala**) **1** a member of a people that inhabit Sri Lanka, an island in the Indian Ocean, and form the major part of its population. **2** the Indic language of the Sinhalese. ➤➤ **Sinhalese** *adj.* [Sanskrit *Simṅhala* Sri Lanka]

sinister /'sinistǝ/ *adj* **1** darkly or insidiously evil or productive of vice. **2** threatening evil or ill fortune; ominous. **3** of or on the left-hand side of a heraldic shield from the bearer's point of view: compare DEXTER. ➤➤ **sinisterly** *adv,* **sinisterness** *noun.* [Middle English *sinistre* from Latin *sinistr-, sinister* on the left side, unlucky, inauspicious]

sinistral /'sinistrǝl/ *adj* **1** of or inclined to the left. **2a** left-handed. **b** said of the shell of a gastropod mollusc: having whorls that turn in a clockwise direction from the top to the bottom: compare DEXTRAL. ➤➤ **sinistrality** /-'straliti/ *noun,* **sinistrally** *adv.*

sinistrorse /'sinistraws, sini'straws/ *adj* said of a plant: twining spirally upward round an axis from right to left: compare DEXTRORSE. ➤➤ **sinistrorsely** *adv.* [Latin *sinistrorsus* turned towards the left, from *sinistr-, sinister* on the left side + *versus,* past part. of *vertere* to turn]

Sinitic /si'nitik/ *adj* of the Chinese, their language, or their culture; *specif* of the group of Sino-Tibetan languages that comprises the various forms of Chinese. [late Latin *Sinae* (see SINO-) + *-itic* as in SEMITIC[1]]

sink[1] /singk/ *verb* (*past tense* **sank** /sangk/, *past part.* **sunk** /sungk/) ➤ *verb intrans* **1a** to go down below the surface of liquid or a soft substance. **b** said of a ship: to fall to the bottom of a body of water. **c** (*usu* + in/into) to penetrate a solid through the surface: *The ink sinks into the paper.* **2a** to fall or drop to a lower place or level: *He sank to his knees; Her voice sank to a whisper.* **b** to disappear below the horizon. **c** said of a cooking mixture: to fail to rise in the middle. **3** to become deeply absorbed or pass into a state of lowered consciousness: *He sank into a doze.* **4** to go downwards in quality, condition, amount, or worth: *Munro had again sunk into that sort of apathy which had beset him since his late overwhelming misfortunes* — J Fenimore Cooper; *Tess seemed ... pleased to hear that she had won high opinion from a stranger when, in her own esteem, she had sunk so low* — Hardy. **5** to deteriorate physically: *The patient was sinking fast and hadn't long to live.* ➤ *verb trans* **1a** to cause (a ship) to sink. **b** to force (something) down, *esp* into the ground. **c** to cause (something) to penetrate deeply. **d** to dig or bore (a well or shaft) in the earth. **2** (*usu in passive*) to overwhelm or defeat (somebody): *If we don't reach the frontier by midnight we're sunk.* **3** to pay no heed to (something); to ignore or suppress (something): *They sank their differences.* **4** to invest (money or energy) in something. **5** *informal* to consume (a drink), *esp* quickly. **6a** to hit (a golf ball) into the hole. **b** in snooker, billiards, etc, to hit (a ball) into a pocket. ✳ **sink or swim** to succeed or fail through one's own efforts. ➤➤ **sinkable** *adj,* **sinkage** /'singkij/ *noun.* [Old English *sincan*]

sink[2] *noun* **1** a basin, *esp* in a kitchen, connected to a drain and a water supply and used for washing. **2a** = SINK HOLE. **b** a depression in which water, e.g. from a river, collects and becomes absorbed or evaporated. **3** *technical* a body or process that stores or dissipates something, e.g. energy. **4** a place of vice or corruption. **5** (*used before a noun*) said of a school or a housing estate: located in a deprived area.

sinker *noun* a weight for sinking a fishing line, sounding line, etc.

sink estate *noun* a run-down local-authority housing estate in which poverty, crime, and other social problems are rife.

sink hole *noun* **1** a hollow, *esp* in a limestone region, through which surface water disappears into a connecting underground cavern or passage. **2** a hollow place or depression in which drainage collects.

sink in *verb intrans* said of information etc: to enter the mind or understanding.

sinking feeling *noun* an uncomfortable feeling in the stomach, caused by hunger, fear, or anticipation of something unpleasant.

sinking fund *noun* a fund built up by regular deposits for paying off the original capital sum of a debt when it falls due.

Sino- *comb. form* forming words, with the meanings: **1** the Chinese nation, people, or culture: *Sinophile.* **2** Chinese and: *Sino-Tibetan.* [via French from late Latin *Sinae* (pl) Chinese, via Greek from Arabic *Sīn* China]

sinologue /'sienǝlog, 'sin-/ *noun* a sinologist.

sinology /sie'nolǝji, si-/ *noun* the study of the Chinese and their language, literature, history, and culture. ➤➤ **sinological** /sienǝ'lojikl, sin-/ *adj,* **sinologist** *noun.* [prob from French *sinologie,* from SINO- + *-logie* -LOGY]

Sino-Tibetan /,sienoh ti'bet(ǝ)n/ *noun* a language family that includes Chinese, Tibetan, and Burmese. ➤➤ **Sino-Tibetan** *adj.*

sinsemilla /sinsǝ'meel(y)ǝ/ *noun* a high-grade and very potent form of marijuana. [Mexican Spanish *sinsemilla,* from *sin* without + *semilla* seed]

sinter[1] /'sintǝ/ *noun* **1** a deposit containing silica or calcium, formed by the evaporation of hot spring water. **2** material that has been sintered. [German *Sinter* from Old High German *sintar* slag]

sinter[2] *verb* (**sintered, sintering**) ➤ *verb trans* to make (metal powders) into a coherent mass by heating and usu compressing them. ➤ *verb intrans* to become a coherent mass by this process.

sinuate /'sinyooayt/ *adj* said *esp* of a leaf: having a wavy edge with strong indentations. ➤➤ **sinuately** *adv.* [Latin *sinuatus,* past part. of *sinuare* to bend, from *sinus* curve]

sinuous /'sinyoo·ǝs/ *adj* **1a** having a serpentine or wavy form; winding. **b** lithe; supple: *dancers with a sinuous grace.* **2** intricate or tortuous: *sinuous argumentation.* ➤➤ **sinuosity** /-'ositi/ *noun,* **sinuously** *adv,* **sinuousness** *noun.* [Latin *sinuosus,* from *sinus* curve]

sinus /'sienǝs/ *noun* **1** any of several cavities in the bones of the skull that communicate with the nostrils and contain air. **2** a channel for blood from the veins. **3** a wider part in a body duct or tube, e.g. a blood vessel. **4** a narrow passage by which pus is discharged from a deep abscess or boil. **5** a cleft or indentation between adjoining lobes, e.g. of a leaf. [Latin *sinus* curve, fold, hollow]

sinusitis /sienǝ'sietǝs/ *noun* inflammation of a nasal sinus.

sinusoid /'sienǝsoyd/ *noun* **1** = SINE CURVE. **2** a minute space or passage for blood in the tissues of an organ, e.g. the liver. ➤➤ **sinusoidal** /-'soydl/ *adj.* [medieval Latin *sinus:* see SINE]

Sion /'sie·ǝn/ *noun* see ZION.

Siouan /'sooh·ǝn/ *noun* a family of Native American languages of central and eastern N America, including Choctaw, Crow, and Dakota. ➤➤ **Siouan** *adj.*

Sioux /sooh/ *noun* (*pl* **Sioux** /sooh(z)/) **1** a member of a group of Native American peoples. **2** any of the Siouan languages of these peoples. [French *Sioux,* short for *Nadowessioux,* from Ojibwa *Nadoweisiw*]

sip[1] /sip/ *verb trans and intrans* (**sipped, sipping**) to drink (something) delicately or a little at a time. ➤➤ **sipper** *noun.* [Middle English *sippen,* prob alteration of *suppen:* see SUP[1]]

sip[2] *noun* a small quantity, *esp* of a drink, taken by sipping.

siphon[1] or **syphon** /'siefǝn/ *noun* **1a** a tube by which a liquid can be transferred up over the side of a container then down to a lower level by using atmospheric pressure. **b** a bottle containing aerated water that is driven out through a tube by the pressure of the gas when a valve in the tube is opened. **2** in zoology, a tubular organ in an animal, *esp* a mollusc, that is used to take in or expel liquid. ➤➤ **siphonal** *adj,* **siphonic** /sie'fonik/ *adj.* [French *siphon* from Latin *siphon-, sipho* tube, pipe, siphon, from Greek *siphōn*]

siphon[2] or **syphon** *verb trans* (**siphoned** or **syphoned, siphoning** or **syphoning**) **1** (*also* + off) to convey, draw off, or empty (liquid) by a siphon. **2** (*also* + off) to draw off (money) gradually from a fund.

siphonophore /sie'fonəfaw/ *noun* any of an order of marine invertebrate animals resembling jellyfish that swim or float on the open sea and live in colonies: order Siphonophora. [Greek *siphōn* + -o- + -PHORE]

SIPP /sip/ *noun* self-invested personal pension, a pension scheme in which the person purchasing the pension is able to specify the investments made.

sippet /'sipit/ *noun archaic* a small triangular piece of dry toast or fried bread used as a garnish or dipped into soup, gravy, etc. [dimin. of SOP¹]

sir /sə, *strong* suh/ *noun* **1a** used without a name as a form of respectful or polite address to a man: *Can I help you, sir?* **b** (**Sir**) used with *Dear* as a conventional form of address at the beginning of a letter. **2a** (**Sir**) used as a title before the forename of a knight or baronet: *Sir Walter Scott.* **b** a man of rank or position. [Middle English, from SIRE¹]

sirdar *or* **sardar** /'suhdah, suh'dah/ *noun* **1** a person of high rank or authority, e.g. a hereditary noble or military chief, *esp* in India. **2** a Sikh. [Hindi *sardar*, from Persian]

sire¹ /sie·ə/ *noun* **1** the male parent of a domestic animal. **2a** a father. **b** a male ancestor. **3** *archaic* used as a title and form of address to a man of rank or authority, *esp* a king. [Middle English in the senses 'father', 'master', via Old French from Latin *senior*: see SENIOR¹]

sire² *verb trans* said *esp* of a male domestic animal: to beget (offspring).

siree /sə'ree/ *noun NAmer, informal* see SIRREE.

siren /'sierən/ *noun* **1a** an electrically operated device for producing a penetrating warning sound: *an ambulance siren.* **b** an apparatus producing musical tones by the rapid interruption of a current of air, steam, etc by a perforated rotating disc. **2** (*often* **Siren**) in Greek mythology, any of a group of women or winged creatures that lured sailors to destruction by their singing. **3** a dangerously alluring or seductive woman; a temptress. **4** any of a genus of eel-shaped amphibians with small forelimbs but no hind limbs and with external gills as well as lungs: genus *Siren.* [Middle English via French from Latin *Sirena,* fem of *Siren,* from Greek *Seirēn*]

sirenian /sie'reeni·ən/ *noun* any of an order of aquatic plant-eating mammals including the manatee and dugong: order Sirenia. ⟫⟫ **sirenian** *adj.* [from the Latin order name, from Latin *Siren:* see SIREN]

sirloin /'suhloyn/ *noun* a cut of beef from the upper part of the hind loin just in front of the rump.

Word history
alteration of earlier *surloin,* modification of early French *surlonge,* from SUR-¹ + *loigne, longe:* see LOIN. Ever since the mid-17th cent., it has commonly been claimed that the word *sirloin* originated when an English king (variously identified as Henry VIII, James I, and Charles II) facetiously knighted a particularly large and succulent loin of beef as *Sir Loin.* The story cannot give the true origin of the word, for the etymology shown here is unquestionable; if it is true, it can only be that the king was punning on the existing word. The story may well have been responsible, however, for the introduction of the spelling *sirloin* in the 17th cent. to replace the earlier *surloin* (the occasional use of *surloin* as late as the end of the 19th cent. was probably due to pedantry); probably it also gave rise to the use of *baron* for a joint of beef including two sirloins.

sirocco *or* **scirocco** /si'rokoh/ *noun* (*pl* **siroccos** *or* **sciroccos**) a hot dust-laden wind from the N African deserts that blows onto the Mediterranean coast of S Europe. [Italian *scirocco, sirocco,* from Arabic *sharq* east]

sirrah *or* **sirra** /'sirə/ *noun archaic* used as a form of address implying inferiority in the person addressed. [alteration of SIR]

sirree *or* **siree** /sə'ree/ *noun NAmer, informal* used for emphasis, usu after *yes* or *no:* sir. [by alteration]

sirup /'sirəp/ *noun NAmer* see SYRUP. ⟫⟫ **sirupy** *adj.*

SIS *abbr* Secret Intelligence Service.

sis /sis/ *noun informal* used *esp* in direct address: sister.

sisal /'siesl/ *noun* **1** a widely cultivated Mexican plant of the amaryllis family with leaves that yield a strong fibre: *Agave sisalana.* **2** the strong durable white fibre obtained from the leaves of this plant, used for ropes, matting, etc. [Mexican Spanish *sisal,* named after *Sisal,* port in Yucatán, Mexico]

siskin /'siskin/ *noun* a small greenish yellow finch of temperate Europe and Asia that is related to the goldfinch. [German dialect *Sisschen,* dimin. of early High German *zīse* siskin, of Slavonic origin]

sissy¹ /'sisi/ *noun* see CISSY¹.

sissy² *adj* see CISSY².

sister /'sistə/ *noun* **1** a woman or girl having the same parents as another person: *Mary and I are sisters.* **2a** (*often* **Sister**) a member of a women's religious order; *specif* a Roman Catholic nun. **b** a fellow female member of a Christian Church. **3** a woman who shares a common tie or interest, e.g. adherence to feminist principles. **4** (*often* **Sister**) *Brit* a female nurse in charge of a hospital ward or a small department: compare CHARGE NURSE. **5** *informal* used in direct address: a girl or woman. **6** (*used before a noun*) related as if by sisterhood; of the same class, type, etc: *sister ships.* ⟫⟫ **sisterliness** *noun,* **sisterly** *adj.* [Old English *sweostor*]

sisterhood *noun* **1** the state of being sisters. **2a** a society or community of women bound by religious vows. **b** a group of women bound by a common tie or interest, e.g. the feminist movement.

sister-in-law *noun* (*pl* **sisters-in-law**) **1** the sister of one's husband or wife. **2** the wife of one's brother.

sistrum /'sistrəm/ *noun* (*pl* **sistra** /'sistrə/) an ancient percussion instrument, used *esp* in Egypt, consisting of a thin metal frame with loose metal rods or loops that jingle when shaken. [Middle English via Latin from Greek *seistron,* from *seiein* to shake]

Sisyphean /sisi'fee·ən/ *adj* both endless and fruitless: *a Sisyphean task.* [named after *Sisyphus,* mythical king condemned in Hades to roll uphill a heavy stone that constantly rolled down again]

sit¹ /sit/ *verb* (**sitting,** *past tense and past part.* **sat** /sat/) ⟫ *verb intrans* **1a** to rest in a position supported by the buttocks and with the back upright. **b** to perch or roost. **2** to occupy a place as a member of an official body: *She sits on the parish council.* **3** to be in session for official business: *We visited London when Parliament was sitting.* **4** said of a bird: to cover eggs for hatching. **5** (+ for) to pose or act as a model for an artist or photographer. **6** to lie or hang in a specified manner relative to a wearer: *The collar sits awkwardly.* **7** to lie or rest: *a kettle sitting on the stove.* **8** to baby-sit. ⟫ *verb trans* **1** to cause (somebody) to be seated; to place (them) on or in a seat. **2** said of a bird: to sit on (eggs). **3** *Brit* to take part in (an examination) as a candidate. ✽ **sit on 1** to delay action or decision concerning (something). **2** *informal* to repress or squash (somebody). **sit tight** *informal* to maintain one's position. [Old English *sittan*]

sit² *noun* an act or period of sitting: *I had a long sit at the station between trains.*

sitar /'sitah, si'tah/ *noun* an Indian lute with a long neck, movable frets, and a varying number of strings. ⟫⟫ **sitarist** /si'tahrist/ *noun.* [Urdu *sitār* from Persian, from *sih* three + *tār* string]

sit back *verb intrans* to relinquish one's efforts or responsibility: *magistrates who sit back and accept police objections* — Yorkshire Post.

sitcom /'sitkom/ *noun informal* = SITUATION COMEDY. [shortening]

sit-down *noun* **1a** = SIT-DOWN STRIKE. **b** a form of protest in which people sit down in a public place, e.g. in the street, and refuse to move. **2** *informal* a period of sitting, *esp* for rest: *After our long walk we needed a sit-down.* **3** (*used before a noun*) denoting a meal eaten while seated at a table: *a sit-down dinner for 50 guests.*

sit-down strike *noun* a strike by workers while continuing to occupy their place of employment as a protest and a means of forcing their employer to comply with their demands.

site¹ /siet/ *noun* **1a** an area of ground that was, is, or will be occupied by a building, town, etc: *an archaeological site.* **b** an area of ground for or scene of some specified activity: *a caravan site; a building site.* **2** the place or point of something: *the site of the wound.* **3** = WEBSITE. [Middle English in the senses 'place, position', via Anglo-French from Latin *situs,* past part. of *sinere* to leave, place, or lay]

site² *verb trans* to place (e.g. a building) on a site or in position; to locate (it).

sit in *verb intrans* **1** to stage a sit-in. **2** (*often* + on) to participate as a visitor or observer: *He sat in on our group discussion.* **3** (+ for) to stand in for somebody.

sit-in *noun* a continuous occupation of a building by a body of people as a protest and means of forcing compliance with demands.

Sitka spruce /'sitkə/ *noun* a tall spruce tree native to N America with reddish brown bark, thin needles, and strong lightweight wood: *Picea sitchensis.* [named after *Sitka,* town in Alaska]

sit out *verb trans* **1** to remain until the end of (something) or the departure of (somebody): *I was determined to sit the film out.* **2** to refrain from participating in (a dance, etc).

sitter *noun* **1** a person who sits, e.g. as an artist's model: *Every portrait that is painted with feeling is a portrait of the artist, not of the sitter* — Oscar Wilde. **2** a hen that is sitting on eggs. **3** *NAmer* a baby-sitter. **4** *informal* in sport, an easy shot, catch, etc.

sitting[1] *noun* **1a** a single period of continuous sitting, e.g. for a portrait: *I read the book at one sitting.* **b** a period in which a group of people are served a meal, e.g. in a restaurant or canteen: *Dinner is served in two sittings.* **2** a session, *esp* of an official body. **3** a batch of eggs for incubation or the period when the hen sits on them.

sitting[2] *adj* **1** that is sitting: *a sitting hen.* **2** in office or actual possession: *the sitting member for Leeds East.*

sitting duck *noun informal* an easy or defenceless target for attack, criticism, or exploitation.

sitting room *noun chiefly Brit* a room, *esp* in a private house, used for recreation and relaxation.

sitting target *noun informal* = SITTING DUCK.

sitting tenant *noun Brit* a tenant who is at the present time in occupation, e.g. of a house or flat.

situate[1] /'sityooayt, 'sich-/ *verb trans* to place (something or somebody) in a site, situation, context, or category; to locate (them) there. [medieval Latin *situatus*, past part. of *situare* to place, from Latin *situs*: see SITE[1]]

situate[2] /'sityoo-ət, 'sich-/ *adj formal* having a site; situated or located.

situated /'sityooaytid, 'sich-/ *adj* **1** located: *conveniently situated.* **2** supplied to the specified extent with money or possessions: *comfortably situated.* **3** being in the specified circumstances: *rather awkwardly situated.*

situation /sityoo'aysh(ə)n, sich-/ *noun* **1a** the way in which something is placed in relation to its surroundings. **b** a locality: *a house in a windswept situation.* **2** position with respect to conditions and circumstances: *The military situation remains obscure.* **3a** the circumstances at a particular moment, *esp* a critical or problematic state of affairs: *The situation called for swift action.* **b** a complicated or critical state of affairs at a stage in the action of a narrative or drama. **4** a position of employment; a post: *He found a situation as a gardener.* >> **situational** *adj.*

situation comedy *noun* a television or radio comedy series that involves the same basic cast of characters in a succession of connected or unconnected episodes.

sit up *verb intrans* **1a** to rise from a reclining to a sitting position. **b** to sit with the back straight. **2** to stay up after the usual time for going to bed. **3** *informal* to show interest, alertness, or surprise.

sit-up *noun* the movement of raising the upper body into a sitting position from a position lying flat on the back, without bending the legs, performed repeatedly as an exercise to improve physical fitness.

situs /'sietəs/ *noun chiefly NAmer* the place where something exists or originates; *specif* the place where something, e.g. a right, is held to be located in law. [Latin *situs*: see SITE[1]]

sitz bath /sits/ *noun* a bath in which one remains in a sitting posture, immersed only up to the hips, or a bath taken in this manner, *esp* for therapeutic purposes. [part translation of German *Sitzbad*, from *Sitz* act of sitting + *Bad* bath]

Siva *or* **Shiva** /'sheevə/ *noun* the god of destruction and regeneration in the Hindu sacred triad: compare BRAHMA, VISHNU. [Sanskrit *Śiva*]

six /siks/ *noun* **1** the number 6, or the quantity represented by it. **2** something having six parts or members, e.g. the smallest unit in a pack of Cub Scouts or Brownie Guides. **3a** the age of 6 years. **b** the hour halfway between midday and midnight. **4** a shot in cricket that crosses the boundary before it bounces and scores six runs. ✱ **at sixes and sevens** in disorder, confused, or in a muddle [said to derive from a 15th-cent. dispute between two livery companies over which should come sixth and which seventh in ceremonial processions; they eventually agreed to take turns]. **for six** *Brit, informal* so as to be totally wrecked, overwhelmed, or defeated: *Trade balance went for six* — The Economist. **six of one and half a dozen of the other** a situation in which a choice must be made between alternatives that are almost or effectively the same. >> **six** *adj,* **sixfold** *adj and adv.* [Old English *siex*]

sixer *noun* the leader of a six in a pack of Cub Scouts or Brownie Guides.

six-gun *noun* = SIX-SHOOTER.

six-pack *noun* **1** a pack of six bottles or cans, *esp* of beer, bought together. **2** *informal* highly developed abdominal muscles.

sixpence /'sikspəns/ *noun* a small silver-coloured coin worth six old pence (2.5p).

six-shooter *noun* a six-chambered revolver.

sixte /sikst/ *noun* in fencing, the sixth of eight parrying positions.

sixteen /sik'steen/ *adj and noun* the number 16, or the quantity represented by it. >> **sixteenth** *adj and noun.* [Old English *sixtȳne*, from *siex* SIX + *tȳne, tien* ten]

sixteenmo /sik'steenmoh/ *noun* (*pl* **sixteenmos**) **1** the size of a piece of paper cut from a sheet of standard size divided into 16 parts. **2** a book format in which a folded sheet forms 16 leaves, or a book in this format. [SIXTEEN + *-mo* as in DUODECIMO]

sixteenth note *noun chiefly NAmer* = SEMIQUAVER.

sixth /siksth/ *adj and noun* **1** denoting a person or thing having the position in a sequence corresponding to the number six. **2** one of six equal parts of something. **3a** in music, an interval of six degrees of a diatonic scale, or the combination of two notes at such an interval. **b** = SUBMEDIANT. >> **sixthly** *adv.* [Old English *siexta*]
Usage note
Care should be taken to ensure that the *-th* is pronounced at the end of *sixth*, to avoid confusion with *six*.

sixth form *noun* in England and Wales, the highest classes of a secondary school in which pupils study for A levels. >> **sixth-former** *noun.*

sixth-form college *noun* in England and Wales, a state school for pupils beyond GCSE level.

sixth sense *noun* a keen intuitive power viewed as analogous to the five physical senses.

sixty *adj and noun* (*pl* **sixties**) **1** the number 60, or the quantity represented by it. **2** (*in pl*) the numbers 60 to 69; *specif* a range of temperatures, ages, or dates within a century characterized by these numbers. >> **sixtieth** *adj and noun.* [Old English *siextig* (noun) group of sixty, from *siex* SIX + *-tig* group of ten]

sixty-fourmo /'fawrmoh/ *noun* (*pl* **sixty-fourmos**) **1** the size of a piece of paper cut from a sheet of standard size divided into 64 parts. **2** a book format in which a folded sheet forms 64 leaves, or a book in this format.

sixty-fourth note *noun NAmer* = HEMIDEMISEMIQUAVER.

sixty-nine *noun* = SOIXANTE-NEUF.

sizable *or* **sizeable** /'siezəbl/ *adj* fairly large; considerable. >> **sizably** *adv.*

sizar /'siezə/ *noun* a poor student, e.g. at Cambridge University, who paid lower fees and orig acted as a servant to other students in return. [alteration of *sizer*, from SIZE[1] in the obsolete sense 'a fixed portion of food and drink', prob because sizars were given a ration of bread and ale]

size[1] /siez/ *noun* **1a** physical magnitude, extent, or bulk; overall dimensions. **b** bigness: *You should have seen the size of their house.* **2** any of a series of graduated measures, *esp* of clothing, conventionally identified by numbers or letters: *a size 12 dress.* ✱ **that's (about) the size of it** *informal* that is the actual state of affairs. [Middle English *sise* assize, from Old French *assise*, short for *assise*: see ASSIZE]

size[2] *verb trans* **1** to arrange or grade (things) according to size. **2** to make (something) in a particular size: *systems sized to fit your living room.* >> **sizer** *noun.*

size[3] *adj* (*used in combinations*) = SIZED (I): *a bite-size biscuit.*

size[4] *noun* a thick sticky material, e.g. a preparation of glue, flour, varnish, or resins, used for filling the pores in surfaces, e.g. of paper, textiles, or plaster. [perhaps the same word as SIZE[1]]

size[5] *verb trans* to cover, stiffen, or glaze (something) with or as if with size.

sizeable *adj* see SIZABLE.

sized *adj* **1** (*used in combinations*) having a specified size: *a medium-sized car.* **2** arranged or graded according to size.

sizeism *or* **sizism** *noun* discrimination on the grounds of a person's physical size. >> **sizeist** *noun and adj.*

size up *verb trans* **1** to form an opinion of (somebody or something). **2** to estimate the size of (something). ➤ *verb intrans* to conform to requirements or specifications.

sizism *noun* see SIZEISM.

sizzle[1] /'sizl/ *verb intrans* **1** to make a hissing sound while or as if while frying. **2** *informal* to be very hot. **3** *informal* to be very passionate, angry, etc. ➤➤ **sizzler** *noun*, **sizzling** *adj*. [imitative]

sizzle[2] *noun* a sizzling sound.

SJ *abbr* Society of Jesus.

sjambok /'shambok/ *noun* in S Africa, a whip of rhinoceros hide. [Afrikaans *sambok, sjambok*, from Malay *cambok* large whip, from Urdu *cābuk*]

SK[1] *abbr* Saskatchewan (US postal abbreviation).

SK[2] *abbr* Slovakia (international vehicle registration).

ska /skah/ *noun* popular music of W Indian origin that is a forerunner of and similar to reggae. [Jamaican English *ska*, of imitative origin]

skag *or* **scag** /skag/ *noun slang* heroin. [origin unknown]

skald *or* **scald** /skawld, skald/ *noun* a composer and reciter of heroic poetry of ancient Scandinavia. ➤➤ **skaldic** *adj*. [Old Norse *skáld*, of unknown origin]

skat /skat/ *noun* a card game played with 32 cards by three players who bid for the privilege of attempting to win a specified number of tricks. [German *Skat*, modification of Italian *scarto* discard, from *scartare* to discard, from *s-* (from EX-[1]) + Latin *carta*: see CARD[1]]

skate[1] /skayt/ *noun* **1** an ice skate or a roller skate. **2** a period of skating. ✳ **get/put one's skates on** *informal* to hurry up. [modification of Dutch *schaats* stilt, skate, from early French *escache* stilt]

skate[2] *verb intrans* **1** to glide along on skates by sliding the feet forward alternately. **2** to glide or slide as if on skates. ✳ **skate over/round** to avoid dealing with (problems, controversial issues, etc). **skate on thin ice** to be in a dangerous or delicate situation. **skate through** to accomplish (something) rapidly or easily. ➤➤ **skater** *noun*, **skating** *noun*.

skate[3] *noun* (*pl* **skates** *or collectively* **skate**) any of several species of rays with large flat pectoral fins that are an important food fish: genus *Raja*. [Middle English *scate* from Old Norse *skata*]

skateboard[1] *noun* a narrow board about 60cm (2ft) long mounted on roller-skate wheels and ridden, usu standing up, for recreation.

skateboard[2] *verb intrans* to ride on a skateboard. ➤➤ **skateboarder** *noun*, **skateboarding** *noun*.

skean dhu /ˌskee·ən 'dhooh/ *noun* a dagger worn in the stocking by Scottish Highlanders in full dress. [Scottish Gaelic *sgian dubh*, literally 'black dagger']

skedaddle /ski'dadl/ *verb intrans informal* to run away; to depart in haste. [origin unknown]

skeet /skeet/ *noun* a form of clay-pigeon shooting in which targets are hurled across the shooting range from traps on either side. [modification of Old Norse *skjóta* to shoot]

skeg /skeg/ *noun* **1** a small fin fixed to the rear end of a yacht's keel. **2** a fin situated underneath the rear end of a surfboard that is used for steering and to give stability. [Dutch *scheg*; akin to Old Slavonic *skokū* leap]

skein /skayn/ *noun* **1** a loosely coiled length of yarn or thread; a hank. **2** something suggesting the twists or coils of a skein; a tangle: *They unravelled the skein of evidence*. **3** a flock of wildfowl, e.g. geese, in flight. [Middle English *skeyne* from early French *escaigne*]

skeletal /'skelitl/ *adj* of, forming, attached to, or resembling a skeleton. ➤➤ **skeletally** *adv*.

skeleton /'skelitn/ *noun* **1a** a supportive or protective rigid structure or framework of an organism, *esp* the bony or cartilaginous framework supporting the soft tissues and protecting the internal organs of a vertebrate animal. **b** a set of real or replica bones of a human being or animal joined together in their current positions, e.g. for medical study. **2** something reduced to its bare essentials. **3** an emaciated person or animal. **4** a basic structural framework. **5** (*used before a noun*) reduced to the bare minimum: *a skeleton staff*. ✳ **skeleton in the cupboard** a secret cause of shame, *esp* in a family. **skeleton in the closet** *NAmer* a secret cause of shame, *esp* in a family. [via scientific Latin from Greek *skeleton*, neuter of *skeletos* dried up, from *skellein* to dry up]

skeletonize *or* **skeletonise** *verb trans* **1** to reduce (something) to skeleton form: *a skeletonized leaf*. **2** to produce (something) in skeleton form: *skeletonize a news story*.

skeleton key *noun* a key, *esp* one with most or all of the serrations absent, that is able to open many simple locks.

skelp /skelp/ *verb trans Scot, N Eng* to slap or spank (somebody). [Middle English, prob of imitative origin]

skep /skep/ *noun* **1** a farm basket used *esp* in mucking out stables. **2** a beehive, *esp* a domed hive made of twisted straw. [Old English *sceppe* basket, basketful, from Old Norse *skeppa* bushel]

skeptic /'skeptik/ *noun NAmer* see SCEPTIC. ➤➤ **skeptical** *adj*, **skeptically** *adv*, **skepticism** *noun*.

skerrick /'skerik/ *noun chiefly Aus, NZ* a very small amount; a scrap: *We didn't have a skerrick of meat to eat*. [origin unknown]

skerry /'skeri/ *noun* (*pl* **skerries**) *chiefly Scot* a rocky island; a reef. [Orcadian dialect *skerry* from Old Norse *sker*]

sketch[1] /skech/ *noun* **1** a preliminary study or draft, *esp* a rough drawing representing the chief features of an object or scene. **2** a brief description or outline: *a sketch of his personality*. **3a** a short theatrical piece having a single scene, *esp* a comic act. **b** a short discursive literary composition: *one of Poe's sketches, in which a close reasoner follows the unspoken thoughts of his companion* — Conan Doyle. **c** a short musical composition, usu for piano. [Dutch *schets* from Italian *schizzo*, from *schizzare* to make a sketch, ultimately via Latin from Greek *skhedios* extempore, on the spur of the moment]

sketch[2] *verb trans* **1** to make a sketch of (something). **2** (*often + out*) to describe (something) briefly; to outline (it): *They sketched out their business plan*. ➤ *verb intrans* to make a sketch. ➤➤ **sketcher** *noun*.

sketchbook *noun* a book of sheets of plain paper used for sketching.

sketchy *adj* (**sketchier, sketchiest**) lacking completeness, clarity, or substance; superficial or scanty. ➤➤ **sketchily** *adv*, **sketchiness** *noun*.

skew[1] /skyooh/ *adj* **1** set, placed, or running obliquely. **2** said e.g. of a statistical distribution: more developed on one side or in one direction than another; not symmetrical. **3** said of two lines: neither parallel nor intersecting. **4** distorted or biased. ➤➤ **skewness** *noun*.

skew[2] *noun* **1** obliqueness or slant: *on the skew*. **2** a deviation from a straight line or symmetrical form.

skew[3] *verb intrans* to take an oblique course; to twist or swerve. ➤ *verb trans* **1** to cause (something) to skew. **2a** to distort or bias (something). **b** to cause (something, e.g. statistical data) to deviate from a true or expected value or a symmetrical form. [Middle English *skewen* to escape, skew, from a dialect variant of early French *eschiuver*: see ESCHEW]

skewback *noun* a stone or course of masonry with an inclined face against which either end of a segmental arch abuts.

skewbald[1] *adj* said of a horse: marked with spots and patches of white and another colour, *esp* not black. [obsolete *skewed* skewbald, of unknown origin + *bald* as in PIEBALD[1]]

skewbald[2] *noun* a skewbald horse.

skewer[1] /'skyooh·ə/ *noun* **1** a long pin of wood or metal used to hold a large piece of meat together while roasting or to hold small pieces of meat, vegetables, etc together for grilling. **2** something resembling this in form or function. [alteration of English dialect *skiver*, of unknown origin]

skewer[2] *verb trans* (**skewered, skewering**) to fasten or pierce (something) with or as if with a skewer.

skew-whiff *adj chiefly Brit, informal* not straight; askew.

ski[1] /skee/ *noun* (*pl* **skis**) **1a** a long narrow strip of wood, metal, or plastic that curves upward in front and is usu one of a pair attached to the feet for gliding over snow. **b** = WATER SKI. **2** a runner shaped like a ski attached to the bottom of a vehicle, aircraft, etc. [Norwegian *ski* from Old Norse *skíth* stick of wood, ski]

ski[2] *verb intrans* (**skis, skied, skiing** *or* **ski-ing**) to glide on skis as a way of travelling, for recreation, or as a sport. ➤➤ **skiable** *adj*, **skier** *noun*, **skiing** *noun*.

skibob /'skeebob/ *noun* a bicycle-like vehicle with short skis in place of wheels that is used for gliding downhill over snow. ➤➤ **skibobber** *noun*. [SKI[1] + *bob* as in BOBSLEIGH]

skid¹ /skid/ *verb* (**skidded, skidding**) ➤ *verb intrans* said of a vehicle: to slip or slide, usu sideways and out of the driver's control. ➤ *verb trans* to apply a brake or skid to (a wheel).

skid² *noun* **1** the act or an instance of skidding. **2** a runner used as part of the landing gear of an aircraft. **3** a plank or roller used to support, lift or move a structure or object. **4** a device placed under a wheel to act as a brake, e.g. on a hill. **5** (**the skids**) *informal* the road to defeat or downfall: *The company hit the skids in 1995.* [orig in the sense 'supporting beam', perhaps of Scandinavian origin and related to SKI¹]

skiddoo *or* **skidoo** /ski'dooh/ *verb intrans* (**skiddoos** *or* **skidoos, skiddoed** *or* **skidooed, skiddooing** *or* **skidooing**) *chiefly NAmer, informal* to run away; to depart in haste. [prob alteration of SKEDADDLE]

skid-lid *noun Brit, informal* a motorcyclist's crash helmet.

Skidoo /ski'dooh/ *noun* (*pl* **Skidoos**) *chiefly NAmer, trademark* a snowmobile.

skidoo *verb intrans* see SKIDDOO.

skidpan *noun* a slippery surface on which vehicle drivers may practise the control of skids.

skid road *noun* = SKID ROW.

skid row /roh/ *noun chiefly NAmer, informal* a district frequented by down-and-outs and alcoholics. [orig *skid road*, a road along which logs are moved on skids, hence a part of town frequented by lumberjacks]

skiff /skif/ *noun* a light rowing or sailing boat. [early French *esquif* from Old Italian *schifo*, of Germanic origin]

skiffle /'skifl/ *noun* a style of popular music of the 1950s played by a group on guitars accompanied by improvised instruments, e.g. washboards. [perhaps imitative]

skijoring /skee'jawring/ *noun* a winter sport in which a person wearing skis is drawn over snow or ice by a horse or vehicle. ➤➤ **skijorer** *noun.* [Norwegian *skikjøring*, from *ski* SKI¹ + *kjøring* driving]

ski jump¹ *noun* **1** a steep high ramp overhanging a slope, used for competitive ski jumping. **2** a jump made by a skier from such a ramp.

ski jump² *verb intrans* to make a ski jump. ➤➤ **ski jumper** *noun,* **ski jumping** *noun.*

skilful (*NAmer* **skillful**) /'skilf(ə)l/ *adj* possessing or displaying skill; expert. ➤➤ **skilfully** *adv.*

ski lift *noun* a power-driven conveyor consisting of a series of bars or seats suspended from a continuous overhead moving cable and used for transporting skiers or sightseers up and down a mountainside.

skill /skil/ *noun* **1** special ability in a particular field, *esp* acquired by learning and practice. **2** a task, technique, trade, etc requiring skill. ➤➤ **skill-less** *adj.* [Middle English *scele* distinction, knowledge, from Old Norse *skil*]

skilled *adj* **1** having mastery of or proficiency in something, e.g. a technique or trade. **2** of, being, or requiring workers with skill and training in a particular occupation or craft.

skillet /'skilit/ *noun* **1** a small frying pan. **2** *chiefly Brit* a small saucepan with three or four legs, used in former times for cooking on the hearth. [Middle English *skelet*, perhaps from early French *escuelete* small platter, dimin. of *escuele* platter, from Latin *scutella*]

skillful /'skilf(ə)l/ *adj NAmer* see SKILFUL.

skilly /'skili/ *noun Brit* a thin gruel or broth, often served in prisons and workhouses in former times. [by shortening and alteration from *skilligalee*, of unknown origin]

skim¹ /skim/ *verb* (**skimmed, skimming**) ➤ *verb trans* **1a** to clear (a liquid) of floating matter. **b** to remove (e.g. fat or scum) from the surface of a liquid. **2** to pass swiftly or lightly over (a surface). **3** to throw (a flat stone) so that it bounces along the surface of water. **4** to read (something) cursorily and rapidly; to glance through (it) for the most important points. ➤ *verb intrans* **1** to glide lightly or smoothly along or just above a surface. **2** (*usu* + through/over) to give something a cursory glance or consideration. [Middle English *skimmen*, back-formation from SKIMMER]

skim² *noun* **1** a thin layer, coating, or film. **2** the act or an instance of skimming.

ski mask *noun* a knitted protective covering for the head and face, worn *esp* by skiers.

skimmed milk *noun* milk with the cream removed.

skimmer *noun* **1** somebody or something that skims. **2** any of several species of seabirds with long wings that feed by flying with the elongated lower part of the beak immersed in the water: genus *Rynchops.* **3** a flat perforated scoop or spoon used for skimming liquid. [Middle English from Old French *escumoir*, from *escumer* to remove scum from, from *escume* scum]

skimmia /'skimi-ə/ *noun* a shrub of the orange family that is grown for its red berries and evergreen foliage: genus *Skimmia.* [from the Latin genus name, prob from Japanese *shikimi*, a similar plant, *Illicium anisatum*]

skim milk *noun NAmer* = SKIMMED MILK.

skimp /skimp/ *verb intrans* (*usu* + on) to spend too little on, use less than enough of, or give insufficient attention to something. ➤ *verb trans* to skimp on (something). [*skimp* barely sufficient, perhaps an alteration of *scrimp* (meagre): see SCRIMP]

skimpy *adj* (**skimpier, skimpiest**) inadequate in quality, size, etc; scanty: *She was wearing a skimpy top.* ➤➤ **skimpily** *adv,* **skimpiness** *noun.*

skin¹ /skin/ *noun* **1a** the external layer of the body of a person or animal, *esp* when forming a tough but flexible cover: *a marvellously old man, whose skin seemed so much too large for his body that it would not stay in position* — Hardy. **b** any of various outer layers, e.g. the rind of a fruit or vegetable or the casing of a sausage. **2a** the external covering of an animal, e.g. a fur-bearing mammal, separated from the body; a pelt. **b** the skin of an animal prepared for use, e.g. in a garment; a hide. **c** a container for wine or water made of animal skin. **3** a person's complexion. **4** a covering or casing forming the outside surface of a ship, aircraft, etc. **5** a film that forms on the surface of some liquids, *esp* as they cool. **6** *Brit, informal* = SKINHEAD (1). **7** *informal* a drum. **8** *informal* a cover for an MP3 player. ✳ **by the skin of one's teeth** by a very narrow margin. **get under somebody's skin** *informal* to irritate, provoke, or interest somebody intensely. **no skin off somebody's nose** *informal* no disadvantage to somebody: *It's no skin off my nose if you don't come to the party.* **skin and bone** very thin; emaciated. **under the skin** beneath apparent or surface differences; fundamentally. ➤➤ **skinless** *adj.* [Old English *scinn* from Old Norse *skinn*]

skin² *verb* (**skinned, skinning**) ➤ *verb trans* **1a** to strip, scrape, or peel away an outer covering, e.g. the skin or rind, of (something). **b** to scrape or graze the surface of (a part of the body): *He fell and skinned his knee.* **2** to cover (something) with or as if with skin. **3** *informal* to strip (somebody) of money or property; to fleece (them). ➤ *verb intrans* (+ over) to become covered with or as if with skin: *The wound had skinned over within a week.*

skin-deep *adj* **1** as deep as the skin. **2** superficial: *Beauty is only skin-deep.*

skin diving *noun* swimming under water with a face mask, flippers, and sometimes an aqualung. ➤➤ **skin diver** *noun.*

skin flick *noun informal* a film involving nudity and explicit sexual activity.

skinflint *noun informal* a miser or niggardly person.

skinful /'skinf(ə)l/ *noun Brit, informal* a large amount, *esp* of alcoholic drink.

skin game *noun NAmer, informal* a swindling game or trick.

skin graft *noun* a piece of skin that is surgically removed from one area of the body to replace skin in a defective or damaged area.

skinhead *noun* **1** any of a group of young people with extremely short hair, a distinctive way of dressing, and often an aggressive racist attitude. **2** an extremely short haircut.

skink /skingk/ *noun* a small lizard of tropical Africa and Asia that has smooth scales: family Scincidae. [via Latin from Greek *skinkos*]

skinned *adj* (*used in combinations*) having skin of a specified kind: *dark-skinned.*

skinner *noun* a person who deals in skins, pelts, or hides.

skinny¹ *adj* (**skinnier, skinniest**) *informal* **1** very thin. **2** made with skimmed milk: *a skinny latte.* ➤➤ **skinniness** *noun.*

skinny² *noun* (*pl* **skinnies**) *informal* **1** a coffee made with skimmed milk. **2** *chiefly NAmer* inside information or gossip.

skinny-dipping *noun chiefly NAmer, informal* swimming in the nude. ➤➤ **skinny-dipper** *noun.*

skin peel *noun* see PEEL² (2).

skint /skint/ *adj Brit, informal* having no money; penniless. [alteration of *skinned*, past part. of SKIN²]

skin test *noun* a test in which a substance is applied to or introduced beneath the skin, used in detecting allergies or immunity to disease.

skintight *adj* fitting extremely closely to the body: *skintight jeans*.

skip¹ /skip/ *verb* (**skipped, skipping**) ➤ *verb intrans* **1a** to move with light leaps and bounds; to gambol. **b** to proceed by hopping on alternate feet. **2** to jump repeatedly over a rope swung round the body over the head and under the feet. **3** to bounce across a surface. **4** to pass over or omit an interval, section, or step: *The story skips to the present day*. **5** (+ about) to flit about unmethodically. **6** (+ through) to deal with something in a hasty or cursory manner. ➤ *verb trans* **1** to leave out (a step in a progression or series); to omit (it). **2** to fail to attend (something); to miss (it): *We decided to skip church that Sunday*. **3** to cause (a stone) to bounce across a surface; to skim (it). **4** *informal* to depart from (a place) quickly and secretly: *The gang skipped town*. [Middle English *skippen*, perhaps of Scandinavian origin]

skip² *noun* **1** a light bounding step or gait; a skipping movement. **2** an act of omission, e.g. in reading.

skip³ *noun* **1** a large open container for waste or rubble. **2** a bucket or cage for raising or lowering workers and materials, e.g. in mining or quarrying. **3** = SKEP (1). [alteration of SKEP]

skip⁴ *noun* the captain of a team in some games, e.g. curling or bowls. [short for SKIPPER¹]

skip⁵ *verb trans* (**skipped, skipping**) to act as captain of (a team).

ski pants *pl noun* trousers made of stretchy fabric with a strap under the foot, worn by women for skiing or leisure.

skipjack *noun* **1** a tuna with a striped body that is an important food fish: *Katsuwonus pelamis*. **2** = CLICK BEETLE. [from SKIP¹ + JACK¹; (sense 1) from its habit of jumping above the surface of the water; (sense 2) from its habit of suddenly springing into the air]

ski-plane *noun* an aircraft with skis fitted to its undercarriage for landing on snow.

skipper¹ *noun informal* **1** the captain of a ship or boat. **2** the captain or first pilot of an aircraft. **3** *Brit* the captain of a sports team. [Middle English from early Dutch *schipper*, from *schip* ship]

skipper² *verb trans* (**skippered, skippering**) to act as skipper of (a boat, aircraft, etc).

skipper³ *noun* **1** somebody or something that skips. **2** any of numerous small butterflies with a stout hairy body and a darting flight: family Hesperiidae.

skipping-rope *noun* a length of rope that is swung round the body from head to toe and jumped over as it passes under the feet as an exercise or game.

skirl¹ /skuhl/ *verb intrans* to emit the high shrill sound of the bagpipes. [Middle English (Scots) *skrillen, skirlen*, of Scandinavian origin]

skirl² *noun* a skirling sound.

skirmish¹ /'skuhmish/ *noun* **1** a minor or irregular military engagement, usu between small outlying detachments. **2a** a brief clash or fight. **b** any minor or petty dispute. [Middle English *skyrmissh*, alteration of *skarmish*, via French from Old Italian *scaramuccia*, of Germanic origin]

skirmish² *verb intrans* to engage in a skirmish. ➤➤ **skirmisher** *noun*.

skirr /skuh/ *verb intrans* to move rapidly, *esp* with a whirring or grating sound: *Birds skirred off from the bushes* — D H Lawrence. [perhaps alteration of SCOUR¹]

skirt¹ /skuht/ *noun* **1a** a garment worn by women and girls that hangs from and fits closely round the waist. **b** a free-hanging part of a garment, e.g. a dress or coat, extending from the waist down. **c** a flexible wall containing the air cushion of a hovercraft. **d** either of two flaps on a saddle covering the bars from which the stirrups are hung. **2** *Brit* a membranous gristly cut of beef from the flank. **3** (*also in pl*) the borders or outer edge of an area or group. **4** *archaic* a part or attachment serving as a rim, border, or edging. ✱ **bit of skirt** *informal* a woman regarded as a sex object. ➤➤ **skirted** *adj*. [Middle English from Old Norse *skyrta* shirt, kirtle: see SHIRT]

skirt² *verb trans* **1** to go or pass round (a place or thing); *specif* to avoid (something) through fear of difficulty, danger, or dispute: *The tanks skirted the minefield; His article skirted the crucial issues*. **2**

to extend along or form the border or edge of (something). ➤ *verb intrans* (*often* + along/around) to lie or move along an edge, border, or margin: *We skirted round the coast*. ➤➤ **skirted** *adj*.

skirting *noun* **1** *Brit* = SKIRTING BOARD. **2** fabric suitable for skirts.

skirting board *noun Brit* a board, often with decorative moulding, that is fixed along the base of an interior wall and covers its joint with the floor.

skit /skit/ *noun* a satirical or humorous sketch or story: *She did a skit on Queen Victoria*. [origin unknown]

skite¹ /skiet/ *verb intrans chiefly Scot* to slip or slide obliquely. [prob of Scandinavian origin]

skite² /skiet/ *verb intrans Aus, NZ, informal* to brag or boast. [perhaps from English dialect *skite* to defecate, from Middle English *skyten*, from Old Norse *skīta*]

skite³ *noun Aus, NZ, informal* **1** a boast or boastful talk. **2** a boaster or braggart.

skitter /'skitə/ *verb* (**skittered, skittering**) ➤ *verb intrans* **1a** to glide or skip lightly or swiftly. **b** to skim along a surface. **2** to twitch a fishing lure or baited hook through or along the surface of water. ➤ *verb trans* to cause (something) to skitter. [prob frequentative of archaic *skite* to move quickly, prob of Scandinavian origin]

skittish /'skitish/ *adj* **1** easily frightened; restive: *a skittish horse*. **2a** lively or frisky in behaviour. **b** variable or fickle. ➤➤ **skittishly** *adv*, **skittishness** *noun*. [Middle English, prob of Scandinavian origin and related to SKITTER]

skittle /'skitl/ *noun* **1** (*in pl, but treated as sing.*) a bowling game played by rolling a wooden ball at a standing group of nine pins in order to knock over as many as possible. **2** a pin used in skittles. [perhaps of Scandinavian origin]

skittle out *verb trans* in cricket, to dismiss (a batting side) for a low score.

skive¹ /skiev/ *verb intrans Brit, informal* (*often* + off) to evade work or duty, *esp* out of laziness; to shirk. ➤➤ **skiver** *noun*. [prob from French *esquiver* to slink away]

skive² *verb trans* to cut off (leather or rubber) in thin layers or pieces; to pare (it). [Old Norse *skifa*]

skivvy¹ /'skivi/ *noun* (*pl* **skivvies**) **1** *Brit, informal* a female domestic servant. **2** *chiefly Aus, NZ* a knitted cotton jumper with long sleeves and a high neck. [origin unknown]

skivvy² *verb intrans* (**skivvies, skivvied, skivvying**) *informal* to perform menial domestic tasks; to act as a skivvy.

skoal /skohl/ *or* **skol** /skol/ *interj* used as a toast: cheers or good health. [Danish *skaal*, literally 'cup']

skookum /'skoohkəm/ *adj NAmer, informal* big and strong. [Chinook Jargon *skookum*]

skua /'skyooh·ə/ *noun* any of several species of large dark-coloured seabirds that tend to harass weaker birds until they drop or disgorge the fish they have caught: genera *Catharacta* and *Stercorarius*. [scientific Latin *skua* from Faeroese *skūgvur*]

skulduggery *or* **skullduggery** /skul'dugəri/ *noun* devious trickery, *esp* underhand or unscrupulous behaviour. [alteration of *sculduddery* gross or lewd conduct, of unknown origin]

skulk /skulk/ *verb intrans* **1** to move in a stealthy or furtive manner; to slink. **2** to hide or conceal oneself, *esp* out of cowardice or for a sinister purpose; to lurk. ➤➤ **skulker** *noun*. [Middle English *skulken*, of Scandinavian origin]

skull /skul/ *noun* **1** the skeleton of the head of a vertebrate animal forming a bony or cartilaginous case that encloses and protects the brain and chief sense organs and supports the jaws: *That skull had a tongue in it, and could sing once* — Shakespeare. **2** *informal* the seat of understanding or intelligence; the brain: *Can't you get that fact into your thick skull?* ➤➤ **skulled** *adj*. [Middle English *skulle*, of Scandinavian origin]

skull and crossbones /'krosbohnz/ *noun* a representation of a human skull over two crossed thigh bones, usu used as a warning of danger to life and formerly displayed on pirate flags: compare CROSSBONES.

skullcap *noun* **1** a closely fitting cap, *esp* a light brimless cap fitting over the crown of the head. **2** the upper portion of the skull. **3** a plant of the mint family with a helmet-shaped CALYX (circle of leaflike structures supporting the flower): genus *Scutellaria*.

skullduggery /skul'dugəri/ *noun* see SKULDUGGERY.

skunk /skungk/ *noun* **1** any of several species of common black-and-white American mammals of the weasel family with a pair of anal glands from which a foul-smelling secretion is ejected: genus *Mephitis*. **2** *informal* a thoroughly obnoxious person. [Abnaki *segankw*]

skunk cabbage *noun* either of two N American plants of the arum family with evil-smelling flowers: *Lysichiton americanum* and *Symplocarpus foetidus*.

sky¹ /skie/ *noun* (*pl* **skies**) **1** the upper atmosphere as seen from the earth; the heavens. **2** *literary* heaven. **3** (*also in pl*) weather as manifested by the condition of the sky: *clear skies*. **✳ praise to the skies** to praise (somebody or something) very highly. **the sky's the limit** *informal* there is no limit to what can be achieved, won, etc. [Middle English in the senses 'cloud', 'sky', from Old Norse *skȳ* cloud]

sky² *verb trans* (**skies, skied, skying**) *informal* to throw or hit (a ball) high in the air.

sky blue *adj* of the light blue colour of the sky on a clear day. **➤➤ sky blue** *noun*.

skydive *verb intrans* to take part in the sport of skydiving. **➤➤ skydiver** *noun*.

skydiving *noun* the sport of jumping from an aircraft and executing body manoeuvres in the air before opening one's parachute.

Skye terrier /skie/ *noun* a terrier of a breed originating in Scotland, having short legs and long wiry hair. [named after *Skye*, island of Inner Hebrides, Scotland, where the breed originated]

skyey /'skie·i/ *adj literary* **1** relating to the sky; ethereal. **2** relating to the stars as controlling human destiny: *Reason thus with life. If I do lose thee, I do lose a thing that none but fools would keep. A breath thou art, servile to all the skyey influences* — Shakespeare.

sky-high *adv and adj* **1** very high into the air. **2** to a very high level or degree: *Prices rose sky-high*. **✳ blow sky-high** to blow (something) to bits; to destroy (it) completely.

skyjack /'skiejak/ *verb trans* to hijack (an aircraft). **➤➤ skyjacker** *noun*. [SKY¹ + -*jack* as in HIJACK¹]

skylark¹ *noun* a common brown lark noted for its song, *esp* as uttered in vertical flight or while hovering: *Alauda arvensis*.

skylark² *verb intrans* to act in a high-spirited or mischievous manner.

skylight *noun* a window in a roof or ceiling.

skyline *noun* **1** an outline, e.g. of buildings or a mountain range, against the background of the sky. **2** the apparent juncture of earth and sky; the horizon.

sky marshal *noun* = AIR MARSHAL (2).

sky pilot *noun slang* a clergyman; *specif* a military chaplain.

skyrocket¹ *noun* = ROCKET¹ (1A).

skyrocket² *verb intrans* (**skyrocketed, skyrocketing**) to shoot up abruptly: *Prices are skyrocketing*.

skysail /'skiesayl, 'skiesl/ *noun* a sail set above the ROYAL² (sail above topgallant) on a square-rigged ship.

skyscape /'skieskayp/ *noun* an expanse of sky, *esp* as depicted by an artist.

skyscraper *noun* a very tall many-storeyed building, usu constructed with a steel frame, *esp* one containing offices.

skyward /'skiewəd/ *adj and adv* towards the sky; upward.

skywards *adv* = SKYWARD.

skyway *noun chiefly NAmer* a route used by aircraft.

skywriting *noun* writing in the sky by means of a visible substance, e.g. smoke, emitted from an aircraft. **➤➤ skywriter** *noun*.

slab¹ /slab/ *noun* **1** a large thick flat piece or slice, e.g. of stone, wood, cake, or bread. **2** the rough outside piece cut from a log when squaring it. **3** *Brit, informal* a mortuary table. [Middle English *slabbe*; earlier history unknown]

slab² *verb trans* (**slabbed, slabbing**) **1** to divide or form (something) into slabs. **2** to cut slabs from (a log).

slack¹ /slak/ *adj* **1a** not taut; loose: *a slack rope*. **b** lacking in usual or normal firmness: *slack muscles*. **2** characterized by slowness or indolence; sluggish: *a slack pace*. **3** insufficiently prompt, diligent, or careful; negligent or lax: *slack supervision*. **4** lacking in activity; not busy: *a slack market*. **➤➤ slackly** *adv*, **slackness** *noun*. [Old English *sleac*]

slack² *noun* **1** a part of something, e.g. a rope, that hangs loose. **2** (*in pl*) trousers, *esp* for casual wear. **3** *informal* a lull or decrease in activity; a quiet season or period.

slack³ *verb trans* **1a** to be sluggish or negligent in performing or doing (something). **b** to lessen or moderate (something): *He slacked his pace as the sun grew hot*. **2** (*often* + off) to release tension in (something); to loosen (it). **3a** to cause (something) to abate or moderate. **b** to slake (lime). **➤ verb intrans 1** (+ off/up) to be or become slack: *Trade has slacked off*. **2** *Brit, informal* to shirk or evade work or duty. **➤➤ slacker** *noun*.

slack⁴ *noun* coal in very small pieces. [Middle English *sleck*, of Germanic origin]

slacken *verb* (**slackened, slackening**) **➤ verb intrans 1** (*often* + off) to become slack. **2** (*often* + off) to become less active, rapid, or intense. **➤ verb trans 1** (*often* + off) to make (something) slack. **2** (*often* + off) to make (something) less active, rapid, or intense.

slack water *noun* the period around the turn of the tide when there is no apparent tidal motion.

slag¹ /slag/ *noun* **1** waste matter from the smelting of metal ores. **2** the rough cindery lava from a volcano. **3** *Brit* waste material from coal mining, e.g. shale or coal dust. **4** *Brit, informal, derog* a promiscuous or coarse woman or girl. **➤➤ slaggy** *adj*. [early Low German *slagge*]

slag² *verb trans* (**slagged, slagging**) *Brit, informal* (*also* + off) to criticize or make abusive comments about (somebody).

slagheap *noun Brit* a high mound of waste material, e.g. from coal mining.

slain /slayn/ *verb* past part. of SLAY.

slainte /'slahnzhə/ *interj Irish, Scot* used as a drinking toast. [Irish Gaelic *sláinte*, Scottish Gaelic *slàinte* health]

slake /slayk/ *verb trans* **1** to satisfy or quench (one's thirst or desire). **2** to cause (caustic lime) to react with water to produce calcium hydroxide. [Middle English *slaken* to abate, allay, loosen, from Old English *slacian* to slacken, from *sleac* SLACK¹]

slaked lime *noun* a dry white powder consisting essentially of the chemical compound calcium hydroxide that is made by treating caustic lime with water.

slalom /'slahləm/ *noun* a skiing or canoeing race on a zigzag or winding course between obstacles. [Norwegian *slalom* sloping track]

slam¹ /slam/ *verb* (**slammed, slamming**) **➤ verb trans 1** to shut (e.g. a door) forcibly and noisily; to bang (it). **2a** to put or throw (something) down noisily and violently: *He slammed his books on the table and stormed out*. **b** to force (something) into sudden and violent action: *I slammed on the brakes*. **3** to strike (somebody or something) vigorously: *She slammed the ball into the net*. **4** *informal* to criticize (somebody or something) harshly. **5** *informal* to defeat (somebody) easily. **➤ verb intrans 1** to make a banging noise: *The door slammed behind him*. **2** (*usu* + into) to strike or crash into something violently. **3** *informal* to move violently or angrily: *She slammed out of the office*. [prob of Scandinavian origin]

slam² *noun* a banging noise, *esp* one made by a door in closing.

slam³ *noun* in bridge, the winning of all tricks or all tricks but one. [orig the name of a card game: origin unknown]

slam-dance *verb intrans chiefly NAmer* to dance to rock music in a style that involves intentionally bumping into other dancers. **➤➤ slam-dancing** *noun*.

slam dunk *noun* in basketball, an unusually forceful DUNK² (goal scored from above the hoop).

slammer *noun* (**the slammer**) *slang* a prison.

slander¹ /'slahndə/ *noun* **1** false spoken charges that do damage to another's reputation, or the utterance of such charges: compare LIBEL¹. **2** a false defamatory oral statement: *The common argument that crime is caused by poverty is a kind of slander on the poor* — H L Mencken. **➤➤ slanderous** /-rəs/ *adj*, **slanderously** /-rəsli/ *adv*. [Middle English *sclaundre, slaundre*, via Old French from late Latin *scandalum*: see SCANDAL]

slander² *verb trans* (**slandered, slandering**) to utter slander against or about (somebody). **➤➤ slanderer** *noun*.

slang¹ /slang/ *noun* **1** informal vocabulary that is composed typically of new words or meanings, impolite or vulgar references, etc, and that belongs to familiar conversation rather than written language: *In the detestable slang of the day we were now both 'at a deadlock'* — Wilkie Collins. **2** language peculiar to a particular group;

argot or jargon: *prison slang.* **3** (*used before a noun*) of or belonging to such vocabulary or language: *a slang term.* ➤➤ **slangily** *adv*, **slanginess** *noun*, **slangy** *adj.* [origin unknown]

slang² *verb trans informal* to abuse (somebody) with harsh or coarse language: *The two drivers were slanging each other.* ➤ *verb intrans informal* to use harsh or vulgar abusive language.

slanging match *noun chiefly Brit, informal* an angry and abusive exchange between two or more people.

slant¹ /slahnt/ *verb intrans* **1** to turn or incline from a horizontal or vertical line or level; to slope. **2** to take a diagonal or oblique course, direction, or path. ➤ *verb trans* **1** to give an oblique or sloping direction to (something). **2** to interpret or present (e.g. information) in a biased way or from a particular point of view. ➤➤ **slanting** *adj.* [Middle English *slenten* to fall obliquely, of Scandinavian origin]

slant² *noun* **1** a slanting direction, line, or plane; a slope: *She placed the mirror at a slant.* **2a** a particular or personal point of view, attitude, or opinion. **b** an unfair bias or distortion, e.g. in a piece of writing. ➤➤ **slantways** *adv and adj*, **slantwise** *adv and adj.*

slant³ *adj* sloping.

slant height *noun* the length of a line from the edge of the base to the point of a cone.

slap¹ /slap/ *noun* **1a** a quick sharp blow, *esp* with the open hand. **b** a noise that suggests a slap. **2** *informal* make-up. ✴ **slap in the face** a rebuff or insult. **slap on the back** an expression of congratulations. [Low German *slapp*, of imitative origin]

slap² *verb* (**slapped, slapping**) ➤ *verb trans* **1** to strike (somebody or something) sharply with the open hand or a flat object. **2** (*usu + on*) to put, place, or throw (something) somewhere with careless haste or force: *She slapped paint on the wall.* ➤ *verb intrans* (*usu + against*) to hit something with the sound of a slap: *waves slapping against the wall.*

slap³ *adv informal* directly or with force: *The ball landed slap on top of a holly bush.* [prob from Low German *slapp*, from *slapp* (noun)]

slap and tickle *noun Brit, informal* playful lovemaking.

slap-bang *adv informal* **1** in a highly abrupt or forceful manner. **2** precisely: *slap-bang in the middle.*

slapdash¹ *adj* haphazard or slipshod.

slapdash² *adv* in a haphazard or slipshod manner.

slap down *verb trans informal* to restrain or quash the initiative of (somebody) rudely or forcefully.

slaphappy *adj informal* **1** irresponsibly casual: *the slaphappy state of our democracies* — Alistair Cooke. **2** buoyantly carefree; happy-go-lucky. **3** = PUNCH-DRUNK (1).

slaphead *noun Brit, informal, derog* a bald man.

slapper *noun Brit, informal, derog* a promiscuous or coarse woman.

slapstick *noun* **1** a form of comedy characterized by farce and horseplay; knockabout comedy. **2** a device comprising two flat pieces of wood fastened at one end and making a loud noise when used, *esp* in former times, by an actor or clown to strike somebody.

slap-up *adj chiefly Brit, informal* said *esp* of a meal: lavish or luxurious.

slash¹ /slash/ *verb trans* **1a** to cut (something or somebody) with violent sweeping strokes. **b** to make (one's way) by or as if by cutting down obstacles. **2** to cut slits in (e.g. a garment), *esp* so as to reveal an underlying fabric or colour. **3** *informal* to reduce (e.g. a price) drastically; to cut (it). **4** to criticize (somebody) cuttingly. **5** *archaic* to whip or scourge (somebody): *Drag him to the marketplace – slash him with bridle-reins and dog-whips!* — Scott. ➤ *verb intrans* **1** to cut or hit recklessly or savagely. **2** said of rain: to fall hard and obliquely. [Middle English *slaschen*, prob from early French *eslachier* to break]

slash² *noun* **1a** a long cut or stroke made by or as if by slashing. **b** the act or an instance of slashing. **2** an ornamental slit in a garment. **3** = SOLIDUS (1). **4** *Brit, informal* an act of urinating. **5** *NAmer* wood chips and other debris remaining after trees have been felled.

slash-and-burn *adj* of or being a method of agriculture involving the felling and burning of shrubs or trees to make land available, usu temporarily, for arable crops.

slasher *noun* somebody or something that slashes, *esp* a billhook.

slasher movie *noun informal* a horror film, *esp* one in which victims are slashed with knives.

slashing *adj* incisively satirical or critical.

slat /slat/ *noun* a thin narrow flat strip, *esp* of wood or metal, e.g. a lath or louvre. ➤➤ **slatted** *adj.* [Middle English in the sense 'slate', from Old French *esclat* splinter, from *esclater* to burst, splinter]

slate¹ /slayt/ *noun* **1** a fine-grained metamorphic rock consisting of compressed clay, shale, etc and easily split into thin layers. **2** a piece of such rock used as roofing material. **3** a tablet of slate or similar material used for writing on, *esp* in former times. **4** a dark bluish grey or greenish grey colour. **5** a list of candidates for nomination or election. ✴ **on the slate** *Brit* on credit. ➤➤ **slaty** *adj.* [Middle English from Old French *esclat*: see SLAT]

slate² *verb trans* **1** to cover (a roof) with slates. **2** *chiefly NAmer.* **a** to schedule (something) for action. **b** to nominate (somebody) for election or appointment.

slate³ *adj* **1** made of slate. **2** of a dark bluish grey or greenish grey colour.

slate⁴ *verb trans chiefly Brit, informal* to criticize (something or somebody) severely. [prob alteration of Middle English *slat* to hurl or throw smartly, prob of Scandinavian origin]

slater *noun* **1** a person who slates roofs. **2a** a woodlouse. **b** any of various marine animals related to the woodlice. [SLATE¹; (senses 2a and 2b) from its colour]

slather /'sladhə/ *noun chiefly NAmer, informal* (*usu in pl*) a great quantity. ✴ **open slather** *Aus, NZ, informal* unrestricted freedom of action for all. [origin unknown]

slattern /'slatən/ *noun dated* an untidy slovenly woman or girl. ➤➤ **slatternliness** *noun*, **slatternly** *adj.* [prob from German *schlottern* to hang loosely, slouch]

slaughter¹ /'slawtə/ *noun* **1** the act of killing; *specif* the butchering of livestock for market. **2** the killing of many people, e.g. in battle; carnage. ➤➤ **slaughterous** /-rəs/ *adj.* [Middle English from Old Norse *slátr* butcher's meat]

slaughter² *verb trans* (**slaughtered, slaughtering**) **1** to kill (animals) for food. **2** to kill (people) violently or in large numbers. **3** *informal* to defeat (opposing players) decisively; to thrash (them). ➤➤ **slaughterer** *noun.*

slaughterhouse /'slawtəhows/ *noun* an establishment where animals are killed for food.

Slav /slahv/ *noun* a member of any of the peoples, *esp* of E Europe, who speak a Slavonic language as their native tongue. [Middle English *Sclav* via medieval Latin *Schlavus, Sclavus* from late Greek *Sklabos*, from *Sklabēnoi* Slavs, of Slavonic origin]

slave¹ /slayv/ *noun* **1** a person held in servitude as the property of another. **2** a person who is dominated by a specified thing or person: *a slave to fashion.* **3** a device that is directly controlled by and often copies the actions of another: compare MASTER¹ (10). **4** a drudge: *women who are merely kitchen slaves.*

Word history

Middle English *sclave* via French from medieval Latin *sclavus* captive, from *Sclavus*: see SLAV. The Slavonic peoples were conquered in the ninth cent. and many were enslaved.

slave² *verb intrans* **1** to work hard, like a slave; to toil. **2** to traffic in slaves.

slave bangle *noun* a bangle worn round the upper arm.

slave driver *noun* **1** *informal* a harsh taskmaster. **2** an overseer of slaves.

slave labour *noun* hard work for little reward.

slaver¹ /'slayvə/ *noun* **1** a person engaged in the slave trade. **2** a ship used in the slave trade.

slaver² /'slavə/ *verb intrans* (**slavered, slavering**) **1** to drool or slobber. **2** (*usu + over*) to show great or excessive desire for something or somebody. [Middle English *slaveren*, of Germanic origin]

slaver³ /'slavə/ *noun* saliva dribbling from the mouth.

slavery /'slayv(ə)ri/ *noun* **1a** the state of being a slave. **b** the practice of owning slaves. **2** drudgery; toil.

slave state *noun* a state of the USA in which slavery was legal until the American Civil War.

slave trade *noun* traffic in slaves, *esp* the transportation of black Africans to America for profit before the American Civil War. ➤➤ **slave trader** *noun.*

slavey /'slayvi/ *noun Brit, informal, dated* a hard-working female domestic servant; a drudge.

Slavic /'slahvik, 'slavik/ *noun* = SLAVONIC. ➤➤ **Slavic** *adj.*

slavish /'slayvish/ *adj* **1** obsequiously imitative; devoid of original-ity. **2** abjectly servile. ➤➤ **slavishly** *adv*, **slavishness** *noun*.

Slavonic /slə'vonik/ *noun* a branch of the Indo-European language family including Bulgarian, Czech, Polish, Russian, and Serbo-Croatian. ➤➤ **Slavonic** *adj*. [medieval Latin *slavonicus* from *Sclavonia, Slavonia* land of the Slavs, from *Sclavus*: see SLAV]

slaw /slaw/ *noun NAmer* coleslaw.

slay /slay/ *verb trans* (*past tense* **slew** /slooh/, *past part*. **slain** /slayn/) **1** *archaic or literary* to kill (a person or animal) violently or with great bloodshed; to slaughter (them). **2** *NAmer* to murder (some-body). **3** *informal* to affect (somebody) overpoweringly, e.g. with awe or delight; to overwhelm (them). ➤➤ **slayer** *noun*. [Old Eng-lish *slēan* to strike, slay]

SLD *abbr* Social and Liberal Democrats.

sleaze /'sleez/ *noun informal* **1** a sleazy quality; sleaziness. **2** *chiefly NAmer* a sleazy thing or person. [back-formation from SLEAZY]

sleazebag *or* **sleazeball** *noun chiefly NAmer, informal* a despicable or obnoxious person.

sleazy *adj* (**sleazier, sleaziest**) **1a** said of a place: squalid and dis-reputable. **b** said of behaviour: corrupt or immoral. **2** *dated* said of cloth or clothing: flimsy. ➤➤ **sleazily** *adv*, **sleaziness** *noun*. [origin unknown]

sled[1] /sled/ *noun NAmer* = SLEDGE[1]. [Middle English *sledde* from early Low German *sledde*]

sled[2] *verb* (**sledded, sledding**) *NAmer* = SLEDGE[2].

sledge[1] /slej/ *noun* **1** a vehicle with runners that is pulled by reindeer, dogs, etc over snow or ice. **2** *Brit* = TOBOGGAN[1]. [early Dutch *sleedse*]

sledge[2] *verb intrans* to ride or be conveyed in a sledge. ➤ *verb trans* to transport (somebody or something) by sledge. [orig in the sense 'to use a sledgehammer': from SLEDGE[3]]

sledge[3] *noun* = SLEDGEHAMMER. [Old English *slecg*]

sledge[4] *verb trans* said of a fielder in cricket: to break the concen-tration of (an opposing batsman) by making provocative remarks.

sledgehammer *noun* **1** a large heavy hammer that is wielded with both hands. **2** (*used before a noun*) clumsy or heavy-handed: *a sledgehammer package of spending cuts*. [SLEDGE[3]]

sleek[1] /sleek/ *adj* **1a** smooth and glossy as if polished: *sleek dark hair*. **b** having a smooth well-groomed look: *a sleek cat*. **c** said of a person: having a well-fed or flourishing appearance. **2** elegant, styl-ish, or streamlined. **3** excessively or artfully suave; ingratiating. ➤➤ **sleekly** *adv*, **sleekness** *noun*, **sleeky** *adj*. [alteration of SLICK[1]]

sleek[2] *verb trans* to make (the hair) sleek or smooth. [Middle English *sleken*, alteration of *sliken*: see SLICK[3]]

sleep[1] /sleep/ *noun* **1** the natural periodic suspension of conscious-ness that is essential for the physical and mental well-being of higher animals: *What hath night to do with sleep?* — Milton. **2a** a sleeplike state; torpor or inactivity. **b** the state of an animal during hibernation. **c** *euphem* death: *The vet put the cat to sleep*. **3** a period spent sleeping: *I need a good long sleep*. **4** *informal* dried mucus that sometimes collects in the eye corners when sleeping. ✳ **go to sleep 1** to fall asleep. **2** to lose sensation; to become numb: *My foot has gone to sleep*. [Old English *slæp*]

sleep[2] *verb* (*past tense and past part*. **slept** /slept/) ➤ *verb intrans* **1** to rest in a state of sleep. **2** to be in a state, e.g. of quiescence or death, resembling sleep. **3** *informal* (+ with/together) to have sexual intercourse or a sexual relationship. ➤ *verb trans* **1** to provide sleeping accommodation for (a specified number of people): *The boat sleeps six*. **2a** (+ away) to spend (time) in sleep: *He slept away the hours*. **b** (+ off) to get rid of or recover from (something) by sleep-ing: *sleep off a headache*. ✳ **sleep on** to consider (something) more fully, *esp* overnight, before making a decision. **sleep rough** to sleep out of doors, *esp* in uncomfortable conditions: *homeless people sleep-ing rough on the streets*.

sleep around *verb intrans* to be sexually promiscuous.

sleeper *noun* **1** = SLEEPING CAR. **2** somebody or something unpromising or unnoticed that suddenly attains prominence or value. **3** a spy who infiltrates an organization but remains inactive until required to fulfil a particular task. **4** *Brit* a ring or stud worn in a pierced ear to keep the hole open. **5** a timber, concrete, or steel transverse support to which railway rails are fixed.

sleep in *verb intrans* **1** to sleep late, either intentionally or acci-dentally. **2** = LIVE IN.

sleeping bag *noun* a large thick bag of warm material for sleeping in, *esp* when camping.

sleeping car *noun* a railway carriage divided into compartments having berths for sleeping.

sleeping partner *noun* a partner who takes no active part in the running of a firm's business.

sleeping pill *noun* a drug in the form of a tablet or capsule that is taken to induce sleep.

sleeping policeman *noun* a hump in a road designed to slow vehicles to a low speed.

sleeping sickness *noun* **1** a serious disease that is prevalent in tropical Africa, is marked by protracted lethargy, and is caused by a TRYPANOSOME (single-celled parasite) and transmitted by tsetse flies. **2** *NAmer* = SLEEPY SICKNESS.

sleepless *adj* **1** not able to sleep. **2** marked by lack of sleep: *a sleep-less night*. **3** *literary* unceasingly active. ➤➤ **sleeplessly** *adv*, **sleep-lessness** *noun*.

sleep out *verb intrans* **1** to sleep out of doors. **2** = LIVE OUT.

sleepover *noun* an occasion of staying overnight as a guest at somebody's home.

sleepsuit *noun Brit* an all-in-one garment worn by a baby for sleep-ing in.

sleepwalk *verb intrans* to walk in one's sleep. ➤➤ **sleepwalker** *noun*.

sleepy *adj* (**sleepier, sleepiest**) **1a** ready to fall asleep. **b** charac-teristic of sleep. **2** lacking alertness; sluggish or lethargic. **3** sleep-inducing; soporific. **4** having little activity; tranquil: *a sleepy little village*. ➤➤ **sleepily** *adv*, **sleepiness** *noun*.

sleepyhead *noun informal* a sleepy person.

sleepy sickness *noun* a form of ENCEPHALITIS (inflammation of the brain) caused by a viral infection and characterized by extreme drowsiness. Also called ENCEPHALITIS LETHARGICA.

sleet[1] /sleet/ *noun* **1** partly frozen falling rain, or snow and rain fall-ing together. **2** *chiefly NAmer* a thin coating of ice. ➤➤ **sleety** *adj*. [Middle English *slete*, of Germanic origin]

sleet[2] *verb intrans* to send down sleet: *It's sleeting*.

sleeve /sleev/ *noun* **1** a part of a garment covering the arm or upper arm. **2** a paper or cardboard covering that protects a gramophone record when not in use. **3** a tubular machine part designed to fit over another part, e.g. to form a connection. ✳ **have up one's sleeve** to have (something) as an undeclared resource: *He has some new ideas up his sleeve*. ➤➤ **sleeved** *adj*, **sleeveless** *adj*. [Old English *slīefe*]

sleeving *noun Brit* the covering of an insulated electric cable.

sleigh[1] /slay/ *noun* a large sledge drawn by horses or reindeer. [Dutch *slee*, alteration of *slede*]

sleigh[2] *verb intrans* to drive or travel in a sleigh.

sleigh bell *noun* a bell attached to the harness of a horse drawing a sleigh.

sleight /sliet/ *noun literary* **1** deceitful craftiness. **2** a stratagem. [Middle English from Old Norse *slœgth*, from *slœgr* sly]

sleight of hand *noun* **1** manual skill and dexterity in conjuring or juggling. **2** adroitness in deception.

slender /'slendə/ *adj* **1a** gracefully slim. **b** small or narrow in cir-cumference or width in proportion to length or height. **2a** flimsy or tenuous: *a slender hope*. **b** limited or inadequate in amount; meagre: *a man of slender means*. ➤➤ **slenderly** *adv*, **slenderness** *noun*. [Middle English *sclendre, slendre*; earlier history unknown]

slenderize *or* **slenderise** /'slendəriez/ *verb intrans chiefly NAmer* to become slender. ➤ *verb trans chiefly NAmer* to make (something or somebody) slender.

slept /slept/ *verb* past tense and past part. of SLEEP[2].

sleuth[1] /sloohth/ *noun informal* a detective. [short for SLEUTH-HOUND]

sleuth[2] *verb intrans informal* to act as a detective.

sleuthhound *noun* **1** *dated* a bloodhound. **2** *informal* a detective. [Middle English, from *sleuth* track of an animal or person (from Old Norse *slōth*) + HOUND[1]]

S level *noun* **1** an examination in any of various subjects at a higher level than A level and usu taken at the same time. **2** a pass in this examination. [abbreviation of *Special level*]

slew[1] /slooh/ *verb trans* to turn or twist (something) about a fixed point that is usu the axis. ➤ *verb intrans* **1** to turn, twist, or swing about. **2** to skid. [origin unknown]

slew[2] *noun* **1** a slewing movement. **2** the position or inclination of something after slewing.

slew[3] *verb* past tense of SLAY.

slew[4] *or* **slue** *noun chiefly NAmer, informal* a large number or quantity: *a whole slew of complaints.* [Irish Gaelic *sluagh*]

slice[1] /slies/ *noun* **1a** a thin broad flat piece cut from a larger whole: *a slice of ham.* **b** a wedge-shaped piece, e.g. of pie or cake. **2a** a portion or share: *a slice of the profits.* **b** a part or section of a larger whole: *a sizable slice of the public.* **3** an implement with a broad blade used for lifting, turning, or serving food: *a fish slice.* **4a** in golf, the flight of a ball that deviates from a straight course in the direction of the dominant hand of the player propelling it: compare HOOK[1]. **b** a similar shot in other sports, e.g. tennis. [Middle English from Old French *esclice* splinter, from *esclicier* to splinter, of Germanic origin]

slice[2] *verb trans* **1** to cut through (something) with or as if with a knife: *I sliced the melon in two.* **2** to cut (something) into slices: *sliced bread.* **3** to hit (a ball) so that a slice results. ➤ *verb intrans* **1** to slice something. **2** to move rapidly or effortlessly: *slicing through the water.* ➤➤ **sliceable** *adj,* **slicer** *noun.*

slick[1] /slik/ *adj* **1a** cleverly and effectively executed: *a slick operation.* **b** deft or skilful: *slick goal-keeping.* **2** superficially plausible or impressive; glib. **3** smooth or slippery. **4** said of a tyre: having no tread. ➤➤ **slickly** *adv,* **slickness** *noun.* [Middle English *slike,* of Germanic origin]

slick[2] *noun* **1a** something having a smooth or slippery surface. **b** = OIL SLICK. **2** a slick tyre, *esp* one used for motor racing on a dry track.

slick[3] *verb trans* to make (something) sleek or smooth. [Middle English *slicken,* of Germanic origin]

slickenside /'slikənsied/ *noun* a smooth grooved surface on rock, produced by the movement of one surface over another. [English dialect *slicken* smooth (alteration of SLICK[1]) + SIDE[1]]

slicker *noun NAmer* **1** a raincoat with a smooth surface, *esp* an oilskin. **2** *informal.* **a** an artful crook; a swindler. **b** a city dweller, *esp* one with sophisticated mannerisms. [SLICK[3]; (sense 2) from obsolete sense 'to make plausible, to deceive']

slide[1] /slied/ *verb* (*past tense and past part.* **slid** /slid/) ➤ *verb intrans* **1a** to move in continuous contact with a smooth surface. **b** to glide over a slippery surface, e.g. snow or ice. **2** to slip or fall by losing one's grip or footing. **3** to pass quietly and unobtrusively. **4** to move smoothly and easily. **5** to pass by smooth or imperceptible gradations, *esp* to a lower level or worse state: *The economy slid from recession to depression.* ➤ *verb trans* **1** to cause (something) to slide: *I slid the book along the table.* **2** to place or introduce (something) unobtrusively or stealthily: *She slid the note into his hand.* ➤➤ **slidable** *adj,* **slider** *noun.* [Old English *slīdan*]

slide[2] *noun* **1a** a structure with a narrow sloping smooth or slippery surface down which children slide in play. **b** a channel or track down or along which something is slid. **c** a track or slope suitable for sliding or tobogganing. **2a** the act or an instance of sliding. **b** = PORTAMENTO. **c** a technique in guitar playing in which a tube-shaped device is moved over the frets to produce a gliding effect between notes. **3** a sliding part or mechanism, e.g.: **a** a moving piece of a mechanism that is guided by a part along which it slides. **b** a U-shaped section of tube in the trombone that is pushed out and in to produce notes of different pitch. **4a** a flat piece of glass on which an object is mounted for examination under a microscope. **b** a photographic transparency suitably mounted for projection. **5** *Brit* = HAIR-SLIDE. **6** a landslide or avalanche.

slide rule *noun* a ruler having a central sliding strip with graduations that enable calculations to be made.

slide valve *noun* a valve that opens and closes a passageway by sliding over a hole.

sliding scale *noun* a flexible scale, e.g. of fees or subsidies, that can be adjusted according to changes or variation in some other factor, e.g. individual income.

slight[1] /sliet/ *adj* **1** small in amount or degree: *a slight chance of rain.* **2a** having a slim or frail build. **b** lacking strength or bulk; flimsy. **c** unimportant; trivial. **d** not serious; minor: *caught a slight chill.* ➤➤ **slightly** *adv,* **slightness** *noun.* [Middle English, in the

senses 'smooth', 'sleek', 'slight', from Old Norse *sléttr* level, smooth]

slight[2] *verb trans* **1** to treat (somebody) with disdain or pointed indifference; to snub (them). **2** to treat (something) as slight or unimportant: *In hastily forming and giving his opinion of other people … and in slighting too easily the forms of worldly propriety, he displayed a want of caution which Eleanor could not approve* — Jane Austen. **3** *NAmer* to perform or attend to (a task or duty) carelessly or inadequately.

slight[3] *noun* an act of slighting, e.g. a humiliating affront.

slighting *adj* characterized by disregard or disrespect; disparaging: *a slighting remark.* ➤➤ **slightingly** *adv.*

slily /'slieli/ *adv* slyly.

Slim /slim/ *noun* an African name for Aids. [from its wasting effect]

slim[1] *adj* (**slimmer, slimmest**) **1** slender in build; attractively thin. **2** of small or narrow circumference or width, *esp* in proportion to length or height. **3** scanty or slight: *a slim chance of success.* ➤➤ **slimly** *adv,* **slimness** *noun.* [orig as a noun, in the sense 'lazy or worthless person': Dutch *slim* bad, inferior, from Middle Dutch *slimp* crooked, bad]

slim[2] *verb* (**slimmed, slimming**) ➤ *verb intrans* to become thinner, *esp* by dieting. ➤ *verb trans* **1** to cause (something or somebody) to become or appear slender: *a style that slims the waist.* **2** (*often* + down) to reduce the workforce of (a company, organization, etc). ➤➤ **slimmer** *noun,* **slimming** *noun.*

Slim disease *noun* = SLIM.

slime[1] /sliem/ *noun* **1** soft wet mud. **2** a thick slippery substance often forming an unpleasant layer on a surface: *The pond was covered with green slime.* **3** mucus or a similar substance secreted by various animals, e.g. slugs. [Old English *slīm*]

slime[2] *verb trans* to smear or cover (something or somebody) with slime.

slimeball *noun informal* an unpleasant obsequious person, *esp* a man.

slime mould *noun* any of a group of single-celled organisms that may aggregate into a mobile mass of fused cells and reproduce by spores: division Myxomycota.

slimline *adj* **1** having a slim shape: *a slimline pen.* **2** said of food and drinks: low-calorie: *slimline tonic.*

slimy /'sliemi/ *adj* (**-ier, -iest, slimier, slimiest**) **1a** of or resembling slime; viscous. **b** covered with or yielding slime. **2** *informal* characterized by obsequious flattery; offensively ingratiating. **3** *chiefly NAmer, informal* vile or offensive. ➤➤ **slimily** *adv,* **sliminess** *noun.*

sling[1] /sling/ *noun* **1a** a looped line used to hoist, lower, or carry something, e.g. a rifle. **b** a bandage suspended from the neck to support an injured arm or hand, *esp* a triangular bandage folded in half and knotted behind the neck. **c** a device resembling a sling for carrying a baby. **2** a simple weapon for throwing stones, usu consisting of a short strap that is looped round the missile, whirled round, and then released at one end. **3** an act of slinging or hurling something, *esp* a stone or other missile.

sling[2] *verb trans* (*past tense and past part.* **slung** /slung/) **1** to cast (something) with a careless and usu sweeping or whirling motion; to fling (it): *She slung the coat over her shoulder.* **2** to throw (a stone) with a sling. **3** to hoist, lower, or carry (something) in or as if in a sling. **4** *Brit, informal* (+ out) to remove or expel (somebody) unceremoniously: *He was slung out of the team for misconduct.* ✳ **sling one's hook** see HOOK[1]. ➤➤ **slinger** *noun.* [Middle English *slingen,* prob from Old Norse *slyngva* to hurl]

sling[3] *noun* a drink made of gin with water or fruit juice and sugar. [origin unknown]

slingback *noun* a backless shoe that is held on at the heel by a strap passing round the back of the ankle.

sling off *verb intrans chiefly Aus, informal* (*often* + at) to jeer or mock.

slingshot *noun NAmer* = CATAPULT[1] (1).

slink[1] /slingk/ *verb* (*past tense and past part.* **slunk** /slungk/) ➤ *verb intrans* **1** to move in a graceful provocative manner. **2** to go or move stealthily or furtively, e.g. in fear or shame. ➤ *verb trans* said of an animal: to give premature birth to (young). [Old English *slincan* to creep]

slink[2] *noun* **1** the prematurely born young of an animal. **2** an act of slinking.

slinky *adj* (**slinkier, slinkiest**) *informal* **1** sleek and flowing in movement or outline, *esp* following the lines of the body in a flowing and sensual manner: *a slinky catsuit.* **2** characterized by slinking; stealthily quiet: *slinky movements.* ➤➤ **slinkily** *adv,* **slinkiness** *noun.*

slip[1] /slip/ *verb* (**slipped, slipping**) ➤ *verb intrans* **1a** to slide out of place or away from one's grasp. **b** to slide on or down a slippery surface: *She slipped on the stairs.* **2** to decline from a standard or accustomed level by degrees. **3** to make a mistake; to blunder. **4a** to move with a smooth sliding motion. **b** to move quietly and cautiously; to steal. **c** to pass gently, smoothly, or imperceptibly, e.g. from one state or condition into another: *She gradually slipped into unconsciousness.* **5** (+ into/out of) to get quickly or easily into or out of clothing: *He slipped into something more casual.* **6** said of time: to elapse or pass: *The hours slipped away.* **7** = SIDESLIP[1]. ➤ *verb trans* **1** to cause (something) to move easily and smoothly; to slide (something). **2** to free oneself from (a restraint): *The dog slipped his collar.* **3a** to let (an animal) loose from a restraining leash or grasp. **b** to let go of (something, e.g. a mooring line). **4** (+ on/off) to put on or take off (a piece of clothing) quickly or easily: *She slipped off her shoes.* **5** to place or pass (something) quietly or secretly: *I slipped him a fiver.* **6** said of an animal: to give birth to (dead young) prematurely. **7** in knitting, to transfer (a stitch) from one needle to another without working it. **8** to leave (the clutch of a vehicle) partially engaged by keeping the pedal slightly depressed. ✳ **let slip 1** to say (something) casually or accidentally. **2** to fail to take (e.g. a chance). **slip one's mind/memory** to be forgotten or overlooked. ➤➤ **slippage** /'slipij/ *noun.* [Middle English *slippen* from early Dutch or early Low German *slippen*]

slip[2] *noun* **1a** the act or an instance of slipping. **b** a small geological fault, or a movement producing one. **c** a type of landslide. **d** a movement of a glacier over its rock floor. **2** a minor mistake or error. **3a** a woman's undergarment that resembles a light skirt or sleeveless dress. **b** a case into which something is slipped; *specif* a pillowcase. **4** in cricket, a fielding position close to the batsman and just to the off side of the wicketkeeper. **5** = SLIPWAY. **6** a dog's leash that can be quickly unfastened. **7** = SIDESLIP[2]. ✳ **give somebody the slip** *informal* to elude or evade somebody in pursuit. **slip of the tongue/pen** a minor or inadvertent mistake in speaking or writing.

slip[3] *noun* **1a** a small piece of paper; *specif* a printed form. **b** a long narrow strip of material, e.g. paper or wood. **2** a young and slim person: *a mere slip of a girl.* **3** = GALLEY (4B). **4** a small shoot or twig cut for planting or grafting. [Middle English, prob from early Dutch or early Low German *slippe* split, slit, flap]

slip[4] *verb trans* (**slipped, slipping**) to take cuttings from (a plant); to divide (it) into slips.

slip[5] *noun* a semifluid mixture of clay and water used by potters for coating or decorating ceramic ware. [Old English *slypa* slime, paste]

slip carriage *noun* a railway carriage that can be detached without stopping the train.

slipcase *noun* a protective container with one open end for one or more books.

slip coach *noun* = SLIP CARRIAGE.

slipcover *noun* **1** = LOOSE COVER. **2** = DUST JACKET.

slipknot *noun* **1** a knot that can be untied by pulling. **2** = RUNNING KNOT.

slip-on[1] *adj* said *esp* of shoes: having no fastenings and therefore easily slipped on or off.

slip-on[2] *noun* a slip-on shoe.

slipover *noun* a sleeveless pullover.

slipped disc *noun* a protrusion of one of the cartilage discs that separate the spinal vertebrae, producing pressure on spinal nerves and resulting in intense back pain.

slipper[1] *noun* **1** a flat-heeled comfortable shoe that is worn while relaxing at home: *He was clad but lightly in his slippers, dressing gown, and nightcap* — Dickens. **2** a light shoe that is easily slipped on or off the foot, *esp* one worn for dancing. ➤➤ **slippered** *adj.* [Middle English, from *slippen*: see SLIP[1]]

slipper[2] *verb trans* (**slippered, slippering**) to beat (a child) with a slipper as a punishment.

slipper bath *noun Brit* in former times, a bath covered over at the end at which the feet and legs go.

slippery *adj* (**slipperier, slipperiest**) **1a** tending to cause sliding, *esp* because icy, greasy, wet, or polished: *slippery roads.* **b** tending to slip from the grasp. **2** said of a person: not to be trusted; shifty. **3** said of a situation: not firmly fixed; unstable. ✳ **slippery slope** a course of action that is bound to lead to trouble. ➤➤ **slipperiness** *noun.* [alteration of Middle English *slipper,* from Old English *slipor*]

slippery elm *noun* a N American elm with hard wood and a slimy inner bark that was formerly used medicinally: *Ulmus fulva.*

slippy *adj* (**slippier, slippiest**) *informal* slippery. ✳ **be/look slippy** *Brit, dated* to be quick; to hurry up. ➤➤ **slippiness** *noun.*

slip road *noun Brit* a short one-way road providing access to or exit from a major road, e.g. a motorway.

slipshod *adj* **1** careless or slovenly: *slipshod reasoning.* **2** *archaic* down-at-heel. [orig in the sense 'wearing loose shoes'; from SLIP[1] + SHOD]

slipstitch *verb trans* to sew (something) with slip stitches.

slip stitch *noun* **1** a concealed stitch for sewing folded edges, e.g. hems, made by alternately running the needle inside the fold and picking up a thread or two from the body of the article. **2** a knitting stitch that is transferred from one needle to another without working it.

slipstream[1] *noun* **1** a stream of air or water driven backward by a propeller. **2** an area of reduced air pressure and forward suction immediately behind a rapidly moving vehicle. **3** something that sweeps one along in its course.

slipstream[2] *verb intrans* to drive or ride in a slipstream and so gain the advantage of reduced air resistance, e.g. in a race.

slip up *verb intrans* to make a mistake; to blunder.

slip-up *noun informal* a mistake or oversight.

slipware *noun* pottery decorated or coated with slip.

slipway *noun* a sloping ramp extending out into the water to serve as a place for launching, landing, building, or repairing ships or boats.

slit[1] /slit/ *verb trans* (**slitting,** *past tense and past part.* **slit**) **1** to make a slit in (something). **2** to cut or tear (something) into long narrow strips. ➤➤ **slitter** *noun.* [Middle English *slitten,* alteration of dialect *slidder,* frequentative of SLIDE[1]]

slit[2] *noun* a long narrow cut or opening.

slither[1] /'slidhə/ *verb intrans* (**slithered, slithering**) **1** to move smoothly with a sliding or snakelike motion. **2** to slide unsteadily, *esp* on or as if on a slippery surface. ➤➤ **slithery** *adj.* [Old English *slidrian,* frequentative of *slīdan* SLIDE[1]]

slither[2] *noun* a slithering movement.

slit trench *noun* a narrow trench, *esp* for shelter in battle.

sliver[1] /'slivə/ *noun* **1** a small slender piece cut, torn, or broken off something; a splinter. **2** an untwisted strand or rope of textile fibre produced by a combing machine. [Middle English *slivere,* from *sliven* to slice off, from Old English *slīfan* to cleave, split]

sliver[2] *verb* (**slivered, slivering**) ➤ *verb trans* **1** to cut or break (something) into slivers. **2** to form (textile fibre) into slivers. ➤ *verb intrans* to become split into slivers; to splinter.

slivovitz /'slivəvits/ *noun* a dry colourless plum brandy. [Serbo-Croatian *šljivovica,* from *šljiva, sliva* plum]

SLO *abbr* Slovenia (international vehicle registration).

Sloane Ranger /slohn/ *noun Brit, informal* a young upper-class person of conventional outlook and dress, *esp* one who leads an active social life with friends of the same type. ➤➤ **Sloaney** *adj.* [blend of *Sloane* Square, a fashionable address in London, and *Lone Ranger,* a hero of cowboy stories and films]

slob /slob/ *noun* **1** *informal* a slovenly or uncouth person. **2** *Irish* muddy or miry land. ➤➤ **slobbish** *adj.* [Irish *slab* mud]

slobber[1] /'slobə/ *verb* (**slobbered, slobbering**) ➤ *verb intrans* **1** to let saliva dribble from the mouth; to drool. **2** (*often* + over) to express emotion effusively and excessively. ➤ *verb trans* to smear (something) with or as if with food or saliva dribbling from the mouth: *The baby slobbered his bib.* ➤➤ **slobberer** *noun.* [Middle English *sloberen,* prob from early Dutch *slobberen* to walk through mud, to feed noisily]

slobber[2] *noun* **1** saliva dribbled from the mouth. **2** oversentimental language or conduct. ➤➤ **slobbery** *adj.*

sloe /sloh/ *noun* **1** = BLACKTHORN. **2** the small spherical fruit of the blackthorn, which is blue-black in colour and has an acid taste. [Old English *slāh*]

sloe-eyed *adj* having soft dark almond-shaped or slanted eyes.

sloe gin *noun* a liqueur consisting of gin in which sloes have been steeped.

slog[1] /slog/ *verb* (**slogged, slogging**) ➤ *verb intrans* **1** to walk, move, or travel slowly and laboriously: *They slogged through the snow.* **2** to work laboriously; to toil. ➤ *verb trans* **1** to hit (e.g. a cricket ball or a boxing opponent) hard and often wildly. **2** to plod (one's way) with determination, *esp* in the face of difficulty. ✳ **slog it out** to compete fiercely for success. ➤➤ **slogger** *noun.* [origin unknown]

slog[2] *noun* **1** persistent hard work. **2** an arduous march or tramp. **3** a hard and often wild blow.

slogan /'slohgən/ *noun* **1** a phrase used to express and make public a particular view, position, or aim. **2** a brief catchy phrase used in advertising or promotion. **3** a war cry or rallying cry formerly used by a Scottish clan.

Word history
alteration of earlier *slogorn*, from Scottish Gaelic *sluagh-ghairm* army cry. From the early 16th cent. to the early 19th cent., *slogan* is known only in the works of Scottish writers. Its wider familiarity is almost certainly due to its use by Sir Walter Scott (see also note at DERRING-DO), and by the mid-19th cent. it was in common use in a metaphorical sense. Archaic forms such as *slogorne*, *sloghorne*, and *slughorne* gave rise to the misapprehension by the poets Thomas Chatterton and Robert Browning that there was a type of trumpet called a 'slughorn'.

slo-mo /'sloh moh/ *noun* = SLOW MOTION.

sloop /sloohp/ *noun* a fore-and-aft rigged sailing vessel with one mast and a single foresail: *And where but from Nantucket, too, did that first adventurous little sloop put forth, partly laden with imported cobblestones – so goes the story – to throw at the whales? — Herman Melville.* [Dutch *sloep*]

sloop of war *noun* a small warship carrying guns on one deck only.

sloot /slooht/ *noun SAfr* a small watercourse or irrigation channel. [Afrikaans *sloot* from Dutch, a ditch]

slop[1] /slop/ *verb* (**slopped, slopping**) ➤ *verb trans* **1a** to cause (a liquid) to spill over the side of a container. **b** to splash or spill liquid on (something). **2** to serve (food or drink) messily: *He slopped soup into the bowl.* **3** to feed slops to (an animal). ➤ *verb intrans* **1** said of a liquid: to become spilt or splashed. **2** (+ through) to tramp through mud or slush. **3** (+ around/about) to slouch or flop around: *He spends his whole day slopping around the house.* **4** *chiefly NAmer* to show mawkish sentiment; to gush.

slop[2] *noun* **1a** (*usu in pl*) waste food or a thin gruel fed to animals. **b** (*usu in pl*) liquid household refuse, e.g. dirty water or urine. **2** (*usu in pl*) thin tasteless drink or liquid food. **3** liquid spilt or splashed. **4** *NAmer* mawkish sentiment in speech or writing; gush. [Middle English *sloppe* slush, mud, prob from Old English *sloppe* dung]

slop[3] *noun archaic* **1** a loose smock or overall. **2** (*in pl*). **a** clothing and other articles sold on board a ship to sailors. **b** cheap or shoddy clothing. [Middle English *sloppe*, prob from early Dutch *slop*]

slop basin *noun* a bowl for receiving the dregs left in tea or coffee cups at table.

slope[1] /slohp/ *verb intrans* **1** to lie at a slant; to incline. **2** to take an oblique course. ➤ *verb trans* **1** to cause (something) to incline or slant. **2** in military drill, to hold (a rifle) in the slope position: *slope arms.* ➤➤ **sloping** *adj.* [Middle English *slope* obliquely, of Germanic origin]

slope[2] *noun* **1** upward or downward inclination or slant; gradient. **2a** a piece of inclined ground. **b** (*usu in pl*) the side of a mountain or hill. **3** an inclined surface. **4** in military drill, a position in which the rifle rests on the shoulder with the butt in the hand.

slope off *verb intrans informal* to go away, *esp* furtively; to sneak off.

slop out *verb intrans* said of a prisoner: to empty slops from a chamber pot.

sloppy /'slopi/ *adj* (**sloppier, sloppiest**) **1a** wet so as to splash; slushy: *a sloppy racetrack.* **b** wet or smeared with or as if with spilt or splashed liquid. **c** disagreeably wet; watery: *sloppy porridge.* **2** slovenly or careless: *sloppy work.* **3** excessively or mawkishly sentimental. **4** said of a garment: loose-fitting and casual. ➤➤ **sloppily** *adv*, **sloppiness** *noun.*

slosh[1] /slosh/ *noun* **1** the slap or splash of liquid. **2** watery snow or liquid mud; slush. **3** *Brit, informal* a heavy blow. ➤➤ **sloshy** *adj.* [prob blend of SLOP[2] and SLUSH[1]]

slosh[2] *verb intrans* **1** said of liquid: to flow or move with a splashing motion or sound: *Water sloshing about in the bottom of the bucket.* **2** to flounder or splash through water, mud, etc. ➤ *verb trans* **1** to splash (something) about in liquid. **2** to splash (a liquid) on or into something. **3** to make (something) wet by splashing. **4** *Brit, informal* to hit or beat (somebody): *She sloshed him on the head with a bucket.* ➤➤ **sloshy** *adj.*

sloshed *adj informal* drunk.

slot[1] /slot/ *noun* **1** a narrow opening or slit, e.g. for inserting a coin. **2** a place or position in an organization, sequence, or schedule. [Middle English, denoting the hollow of the breastbone, from early French *esclot*, of unknown origin]

slot[2] *verb* (**slotted, slotting**) ➤ *verb trans* **1a** (*often* + in/into) to place (something) in a slot: *The shelves are slotted into the sides.* **b** (*often* + in/into) to assign (something or somebody) to a slot: *I can slot in a short meeting after lunch.* **2** to cut a slot in (something). ➤ *verb intrans* **1** (*often* + in/into) to be fitted by means of a slot or slots: *a do-it-yourself bookcase that slots together in seconds.* **2** (*often* + in/into) to have or take a place in an organization, schedule, etc: *Jim's visit slots in between Christmas and New Year.*

slot[3] *noun* the track of an animal, e.g. a deer. [early French *esclot* hoofprint, track, prob of Scandinavian origin]

sloth /slohth/ *noun* **1** disinclination to action or work; indolence. **2** any of several species of slow-moving mammals that inhabit tropical forests of S and Central America, hanging face upward from the branches and feeding on leaves, shoots, and fruits: genera *Bradypus* and *Choloepus*. ➤➤ **slothful** *adj*, **slothfully** *adv*, **slothfulness** *noun*. [Middle English *slouthe*, from SLOW[1]]

sloth bear *noun* a common bear of India and Sri Lanka with a long snout: *Melursus ursinus.*

slot machine *noun* **1** *Brit* = VENDING MACHINE. **2** = FRUIT MACHINE.

slouch[1] /slowch/ *verb intrans* **1** to sit, stand, or walk with a slouch: *He slouched behind the wheel.* **2** to hang down limply; to droop. ➤ *verb trans* **1** to cause (the shoulders) to droop. **2** *dated* to turn down one side of the brim of (a hat). ➤➤ **sloucher** *noun*. [origin unknown]

slouch[2] *noun* **1** a gait or posture characterized by stooping or excessive relaxation of body muscles. **2** *informal* a lazy, incompetent, or awkward person: *He's no slouch at DIY.* ➤➤ **slouchy** *adj.*

slouch hat *noun* a soft felt hat with a wide flexible brim.

slough[1] /slow/ *noun* **1a** a swamp. **b** a place of deep mud or mire. **c** *NAmer* a marshy inlet or backwater. **2** a state of dejection, hopelessness, or degradation: *a slough of self-pity.* ➤➤ **sloughy** *adj.* [Old English *slōh*]

slough[2] /sluf/ *noun* **1** the cast-off skin of a snake. **2** a mass of dead tissue separating from a wound, an ulcer, etc. ➤➤ **sloughy** *adj.* [Middle English *slughe*, of Germanic origin]

slough[3] /sluf/ *verb trans* **1** to cast off (e.g. a skin or shell). **2** (+ off) to get rid of or discard (something) as irksome or objectionable. ➤ *verb intrans* **1** said e.g. of a skin: to become shed or cast off. **2** said e.g. of a snake: to cast off a skin.

Slovak /'slohvak/ *noun* **1** a native or inhabitant of Slovakia in E central Europe. **2** the Slavonic language of the Slovaks. ➤➤ **Slovak** *adj*, **Slovakian** /sloh'vaki·ən, slə'vahki·ən/ *adj and noun*. [Slovak *Slovák* Slavonic]

sloven /'sluvn/ *noun dated* a person who is habitually negligent of neatness or cleanliness. [Middle English *slovevn* rascal, perhaps from Flemish *sloovin* woman of low character]

Slovene /'slohveen/ *noun* **1** a native or inhabitant of Slovenia in E Europe. **2** the Slavonic language of the Slovenes. ➤➤ **Slovene** *adj*, **Slovenian** /slə'veeni·ən/ *adj and noun*. [German *Slovene* from Slovene *Sloven*]

slovenly *adj* **1** untidy or dirty, *esp* in personal appearance. **2** lazily slipshod; careless. ➤➤ **slovenliness** *noun.*

slow[1] /sloh/ *adj* **1a** moving or proceeding with little or less than usual speed: *Traffic was slow.* **b** exhibiting or marked by lack of speed or haste: *He moved with slow deliberation.* **2** requiring or taking a long time; gradual: *a slow convalescence.* **3a** designed or used for slow movement: *the slow lane.* **b** having qualities that hinder or prevent rapid movement: *a slow putting green.* **4** said of a clock or watch: registering a time earlier than the correct one. **5a** lacking in intelligence; dull. **b** naturally inert or sluggish: *a slow imagination*. **6a** lacking in interest or variety; boring. **b** lacking in activity; slack: *Business is always slow after Christmas*. **7a** lacking in readiness, promptness, or willingness: *a shop with slow service*. **b** not quickly aroused or excited: *She was slow to anger*. **8** said of an oven: set at a low temperature. **9** in photography, requiring a relatively long period of exposure: *slow film*. ➤ **slowish** *adj*, **slowly** *adv*, **slowness** *noun*. [Old English *slāw*]

slow² *adv* in a slow manner; slowly. ✳ **go slow** to hold or take part in a go-slow.

slow³ *verb intrans* (*often* + down/up) to become slow or slower: *Production of new cars slowed*. ➤ *verb trans* (*often* + down/up) to make (something or somebody) slow or slower.

slowcoach *noun Brit, informal* a person who thinks, moves, or acts slowly.

slow handclap *noun* a slow rhythmic clapping used by an audience to express annoyance or impatience.

slow march *noun* a slow marching pace of about 60 or 70 paces a minute.

slow match *noun* a slow-burning match or fuse used *esp* in former times for firing explosives.

slow motion *noun* a technique that makes filmed or televised action appear unnaturally slow, e.g. by increasing the amount of film exposed in a given time and then projecting it at the standard speed or by playing back a video recording at less than the standard speed. ➤ **slow-motion** *adj*.

slowpoke *noun NAmer, informal* = SLOWCOACH.

slow virus *noun* a virus or virus-like organism that produces infection and symptoms only after a long latent period and is the cause of some neurological disorders, e.g. Creutzfeldt-Jakob disease.

slowworm *noun* a legless European lizard with a grey-brown snakelike body: *Anguis fragilis*. [Old English *slāwyrm*, from *slā-* (related to Swedish *slå* earthworm) + *wyrm* serpent, WORM¹]

SLR *abbr* single-lens reflex.

slub¹ /slub/ *noun* **1a** a small thickened section in a yarn or thread. **b** fabric woven from yarn containing slubs. **c** (*used before a noun*) having a knobbly effect caused by slubs: *slub fabric*. **2** slubbed wool fibres. [origin unknown]

slub² *verb trans* (**slubbed, slubbing**) to draw out and twist (fibres of wool) slightly in preparation for spinning. [earliest as *slubbing*: origin unknown]

sludge /sluj/ *noun* **1** mud or ooze. **2** a slimy or slushy mass, deposit, or sediment, e.g.: **a** precipitated solid matter produced by sewage treatment processes. **b** a precipitate from a mineral oil, e.g. in an internal-combustion engine. **3** new sea ice forming in thin detached crystals. ➤➤ **sludgy** *adj*. [prob alteration of SLUSH¹]

slue¹ /slooh/ *verb* (**slues, slued, sluing**) = SLEW¹.

slue² *noun* = SLEW².

slue³ *noun* see SLEW⁴.

slug¹ /slug/ *noun* a slimy elongated invertebrate animal with no shell that is related to the snail and is found in most damp parts of the world: family Limacidae. [Middle English *slugge* sluggard, of Scandinavian origin]

slug² *noun* **1** a quantity of alcoholic drink, *esp* spirits, swallowed at a single gulp. **2** a lump, disc, or cylinder of metal, plastic, or other material, e.g.: **a** a bullet. **b** *NAmer* a disc for insertion in a slot machine. **3a** in printing, a line of type cast as one piece. **b** a strip of metal used for spacing that is thicker than a lead. **4** a unit of mass that will acquire an acceleration of one foot per second per second when acted on by a force of one pound; about 14.6kg (32.174lb). [prob from SLUG¹]

slug³ *verb trans* (**slugged, slugging**) to swallow (an alcoholic drink) at a single gulp; to swig (it).

slug⁴ *verb trans* (**slugged, slugging**) *chiefly NAmer, informal* to hit (somebody or something) hard, *esp* with the fist or a bat. ✳ **slug it out** to compete fiercely for success. ➤➤ **slugger** *noun*. [prob variant of SLOG¹]

slug⁵ *noun chiefly NAmer, informal* a heavy blow, *esp* with the fist.

sluggard¹ /ˈslugəd/ *noun* a habitually lazy person. ➤➤ **sluggardly** *adj*. [Middle English *sluggart* from *slug* to be lazy or slow, prob of Scandinavian origin]

sluggard² *adj* habitually lazy.

sluggish *adj* **1** slow in movement, flow, or growth. **2a** averse to activity or exertion; indolent. **b** lacking energy or activity; torpid. **3** slow to respond, e.g. to stimulation or treatment: *a sluggish engine*. ➤➤ **sluggishly** *adv*, **sluggishness** *noun*.

sluice¹ /sloohs/ *noun* **1a** an artificial passage for water, e.g. in a millstream, fitted with a valve or gate for stopping or regulating flow. **b** a body of water pent up behind a floodgate. **2** = SLUICE GATE. **3** a channel to drain or carry off surplus water. **4** a long inclined trough for washing ores or gold-bearing earth. **5** an act of sluicing. [alteration of Middle English *scluse* via French from Latin *exclusa*, fem past part. of *excludere*: see EXCLUDE]

sluice² *verb trans* **1a** to wash (something) with or in running water. **b** to drench (something) with a sudden vigorous flow; to flush (it). **2** to draw off (water) by or through a sluice. ➤ *verb intrans* said of water: to pour from or as if from a sluice.

sluice gate *noun* a small gate for emptying the chamber of a lock or regulating the amount of water passing through a channel.

sluiceway *noun* an artificial channel into which water is let by a sluice.

slum¹ /slum/ *noun* **1a** (*usu in pl*) a poor overcrowded run-down area, *esp* in a city. **b** a house in such an area. **2** a squalid disagreeable place to live. ➤➤ **slummy** *adj*. [origin unknown]

slum² *verb intrans* (**slummed, slumming**) **1** to live in squalor or on very slender means. **2** to visit a place on a much lower social level, *esp* out of curiosity or for amusement. ✳ **slum it** *informal* to live temporarily in conditions inferior to those to which one is accustomed. ➤➤ **slummer** *noun*.

slumber¹ /ˈslumbə/ *verb intrans* (**slumbered, slumbering**) *literary* **1** to sleep: *But your slumbering teems with such horrible dreams that you'd very much better be waking* — W S Gilbert. **2** to lie dormant or latent: *a slumbering volcano*. ➤➤ **slumberer** *noun*. [Middle English *slumberen*, frequentative of *slumen* to doze, prob from Old English *slūma* slumber]

slumber² *noun literary* sleep.

slumbrous *or* **slumberous** /ˈslumbrəs/ *adj literary* **1** heavy with sleep; sleepy: *slumbrous eyelids*. **2** inducing sleep; soporific.

slump¹ /slump/ *verb intrans* **1a** to drop down suddenly and heavily; to collapse: *She slumped to the floor*. **b** to fall or sink abruptly: *Morale slumped with news of the defeat*. **2** to go into a marked or sustained decline: *Sales slumped last year*. **3** to assume a drooping posture or carriage; to slouch. [prob of Scandinavian origin]

slump² *noun* **1** the act or an instance of slumping. **2** a marked or sustained decline, *esp* in economic activity or prices.

slung /slung/ *verb* past tense and past part. of SLING².

slunk /slungk/ *verb* past tense and past part. of SLINK¹.

slur¹ /sluh/ *verb* (**slurred, slurring**) ➤ *verb intrans* **1** (+ over) to pass over something without due mention, consideration, or emphasis: *He slurred over certain facts*. **2** to pronounce words unclearly by running together and omission of sounds. ➤ *verb trans* **1a** to run together, omit, or pronounce unclearly (words, sounds, etc). **b** to utter (speech) in this manner. **2** in music, to perform (successive notes of different pitch) in a smooth or connected manner. [prob from Low German *slurrn* to shuffle]

slur² *noun* **1** a slurred utterance or manner of speech. **2** in music, a curved line connecting notes to be slurred.

slur³ *verb trans* (**slurred, slurring**) to cast aspersions on (somebody or something); to disparage (them). [obsolete English dialect *slur* thin mud, from Middle English *sloor*]

slur⁴ *noun* an insulting or disparaging remark; a slight.

slurp¹ /sluhp/ *verb* to eat or drink (something) noisily or with a sucking sound. [Dutch *slurpen*]

slurp² *noun* a slurping sound.

slurry /ˈsluri/ *noun* (*pl* **slurries**) a watery mixture of insoluble matter, e.g. mud, manure, or lime. [Middle English *slory*, prob related to SLUR³]

slush¹ /slush/ *noun* **1** partly melted or watery snow. **2** liquid mud; mire. **3** *informal* excessively sentimental language, literature, etc. ➤➤ **slushiness** *noun*, **slushy** *adj*. [prob imitative]

slush² *verb intrans* to splash in or through slush.

slush fund *noun* a fund for bribing officials or financing other corrupt practices.

slut /slut/ *noun* a promiscuous or slovenly woman: *'I am not a slut, though I thank the gods I am foul.' 'Well, praised be the gods for thy* *foulness. Sluttishness may come hereafter.'* — Shakespeare. **>> sluttish** *adj*, **sluttishness** *noun*. [Middle English *slutte*; earlier history unknown]

sly /slie/ *adj* (**slyer, slyest**) **1a** clever in concealing one's intentions; furtive. **b** lacking in integrity and candour; crafty. **2** humorously mischievous; roguish: *He gave me a sly glance*. **✳ on the sly** in a manner intended to avoid notice; secretly. **>> slyly** *adv*, **slyness** *noun*. [Middle English *sli* from Old Norse *slœgr*]

slype /sliep/ *noun* a narrow passage; *specif* one between the transept and chapter house or deanery in an English cathedral or abbey. [prob from Flemish *slijpe* place for slipping in and out]

SM *abbr* **1** sadomasochism. **2** Sergeant Major.

Sm *abbr* the chemical symbol for samarium.

smack¹ /smak/ *noun* **1a** a sharp blow, *esp* from something flat; a slap. **b** the sound of such a blow. **2** a loud kiss. **3** a noisy parting of the lips. **✳ smack in the eye** *informal* a setback or rebuff.

smack² *verb trans* **1** to hit (somebody) smartly, *esp* with the open hand in punishment. **2a** to strike (something) with a smack or with the sound of a smack. **b** to put (something) down forcefully or noisily. **3** to open (the lips) with a sudden sharp sound, *esp* in anticipation of food or drink. **>** *verb intrans* to make or give a smack. [early Dutch *smacken* to strike, of imitative origin]

smack³ *adv informal* squarely and with force; directly: *He drove smack into the car parked opposite*.

smack⁴ *verb intrans* **1** (+ of) to have the taste or smell of something. **2** (+ of) to have a trace or suggestion of something: *This appointment smacks of nepotism*.

smack⁵ *noun* **1** a characteristic taste or smell. **2** a slight trace or suggestion. [Old English *smæc* taste]

smack⁶ *noun* a small coastal fishing vessel. [Dutch *smak* or Low German *smack*]

smack⁷ *noun slang* heroin. [perhaps from Yiddish *shmek* sniff, whiff, pinch of snuff]

smacker *noun informal* **1** a loud kiss. **2a** *Brit* a pound sterling. **b** *NAmer* a dollar.

small¹ /smawl/ *adj* **1a** of less than normal, usual, or average size; not large. **b** immature or young: *small children*. **2a** not great in quantity, value, amount, etc. **b** made up of few individuals or units: *a small audience*. **3a** said of written or printed letters: lower-case, not capital. **b** said of words: without a capital letter, so used in a general sense rather than to refer to the movement or political party that the capital denotes: *My philosophy is a liberal one, with a small 'l'* — Reg Prentice. **4** lacking in strength: *a small voice*. **5a** operating on a limited scale: *a small farmer*. **b** minor in power, influence, etc: *She only has a small say in the matter*. **c** limited in degree: *I paid small heed to his warning*. **d** humble or modest: *a small beginning*. **6** of little consequence; trivial: *a small matter*. **7a** mean or petty. **b** reduced to a humiliating position: *They made me feel small*. **>> smallish** *adj*, **smallness** *noun*. [Old English *smæl*]

small² *noun* **1** a part smaller than the remainder; *specif* the narrowest part of the back. **2** *Brit, informal* (*in pl*) small articles of underwear.

small³ *adv* **1** in or into small pieces: *Cut the onion up small*. **2** in a small manner or size: *Write small*.

small arm *noun* (*usu in pl*) a portable firearm.

small beer *noun chiefly Brit* people or matters of small importance.

small-bore *adj* said of a firearm: having a relatively small calibre, *esp* 5.6mm (0.22in).

small calorie *noun* = CALORIE (1A).

small capital *noun* a letter that has the form of a capital but the height of lower-case *e*, *n*, *x*, etc.

small change *noun* **1** coins of low denomination. **2** something trifling or commonplace.

small circle *noun* a circle formed on the surface of a sphere by the intersection of a plane that does not pass through the centre of the sphere.

small-claims court *noun* a special court intended to simplify and speed up the process of handling claims for small sums of money.

small fry *pl noun* **1** small fish. **2** insignificant people or things; *specif* young children.

smallgoods *pl noun Aus, NZ* meat, e.g. bacon or sausages, sold prepared for eating.

smallholding *noun Brit* a small farm. **>> smallholder** *noun*.

small hours *pl noun* (**the small hours**) the hours immediately following midnight.

small intestine *noun* the part of the intestine that lies between the stomach and colon, consisting of the duodenum, jejunum, and ileum.

small-minded *adj* **1** having narrow interests or outlook. **2** characterized by petty meanness. **>> small-mindedly** *adv*, **small-mindedness** *noun*.

smallpox *noun* an acute infectious viral disease characterized by fever and pustules that dry up and form scabs, eventually leaving permanent scars.

small print *noun* something made deliberately obscure; *specif* a part of a document containing important but unattractive conditions that is often confusingly worded or printed in small type.

small-scale *adj* relatively small in scope or extent: *a small-scale undertaking*.

small screen *noun* (**the small screen**) television.

small slam *noun* in bridge, the winning of 12 of the 13 tricks by one player or side.

smallsword /'smawlsawd/ *noun* a light tapering sword used for thrusting in former times.

small talk *noun* light or casual conversation; chitchat.

small-time *adj informal* insignificant in operation and status; petty: *small-time hoodlums*. **>> small-timer** *noun*.

smalt /smawlt, smolt/ *noun* a deep blue pigment made from glass coloured with cobalt oxide and used in enamels and ceramics. [early French *smalt* from Old Italian *smalto*, of Germanic origin]

smarm /smahm/ *verb trans* **1** to make (one's way) by obsequiousness or fawning. **2a** to plaster or smear (a substance): *She smarmed on a thick layer of make-up*. **b** to flatten or smooth (one's hair) with an oily or greasy substance. **>** *verb intrans* to seek favour by servile behaviour; to ingratiate oneself. [origin unknown]

smarmy *adj* (**smarmier, smarmiest**) *informal* marked by flattery, obsequiousness, or smugness; unctuous. **>> smarmily** *adv*, **smarminess** *noun*.

smart¹ /smaht/ *adj* **1a** neat, stylish, or elegant in dress or appearance. **b** said of a place: characteristic of or frequented by fashionable society: *a smart restaurant*. **2** *informal*. **a** mentally alert; bright. **b** clever or shrewd: *a smart investment*. **3** witty or persuasive: *a smart talker*. **4a** of or using the most modern technology; *specif* operating in a way that emulates human intelligence, behaviour, etc. **b** said of a bomb or missile: containing a device that guides it to its target. **5** brisk or spirited: *walking at a smart pace*. **6** causing a sharp stinging pain: *She gave him a smart blow with the ruler*. **7** forceful or vigorous. **>> smartly** *adv*, **smartness** *noun*.

smart² *verb intrans* **1a** to be the cause of a sharp stinging pain. **b** to feel or have such a pain. **2** to feel or endure mental distress: *smarting from a rebuke*. **3** (*often* + for) to pay a heavy penalty: *He would have to smart for this foolishness*. [Old English *smeortan*]

smart³ *adv archaic* in a smart manner; smartly.

smart⁴ *noun* **1** *NAmer, informal* (*in pl*) intelligence or shrewdness. **2** a smarting pain.

smart alec or **smart aleck** /'alik/ *noun informal* **1** an arrogant person with pretensions to knowledge or cleverness. **2** (*used before a noun*) showing pretensions to knowledge or cleverness: *smart-alec answers*. **>> smart-alecky** *adj*. [*Alec*, nickname for *Alexander*]

smart-arse *noun slang* = SMART ALEC.

smart-ass *noun NAmer* = SMART-ARSE.

smart card *noun* a credit or debit card with an inbuilt memory chip that keeps a record of transactions conducted with the card.

smarten *verb* (**smartened, smartening**) **>** *verb intrans* (*often* + up) to make one's appearance smarter. **>** *verb trans* (*often* + up) to make (e.g. oneself or a place) smart or smarter.

smartish *adv chiefly Brit, informal* in a rapid manner; quickly: *You'd better get dressed smartish*.

smart money *noun* people with inside information or much experience, or money ventured by such people: *The smart money is talking of an economic recovery*.

smart set *noun* (**the smart set**) fashionable society.

smash[1] /smash/ *verb trans* **1** to break (something) to pieces by violence; to shatter (it). **2a** to drive, throw, or hit (something) violently, *esp* causing breaking or shattering. **b** to hit (a ball or shuttlecock) downward with a forceful overhand stroke. **3** (*often* + up) to destroy (something) utterly; to wreck (it). ➤ *verb intrans* **1** to break to pieces suddenly under collision or pressure. **2a** (+ into) to crash into something; to collide with it: *The car smashed into a tree.* **b** (*usu* + against/through) to strike something violently, *esp* causing breakage or damage. **3** said of a business: to fail. [perhaps blend of SMACK[2] and MASH[2]]

smash[2] *noun* **1a** the action or sound of smashing; crash. **b** utter collapse or ruin, *esp* bankruptcy. **2a** a violent blow, attack, or collision: *a five-car smash.* **b** the result of smashing, *esp* a wreck due to collision. **3** a forceful overhand downward stroke in tennis or badminton. **4** the condition of being smashed or shattered. **5** *informal* = SMASH HIT.

smash[3] *adv* with a resounding crash.

smash-and-grab *adj* denoting a robbery committed by smashing a shop window and snatching the goods on display.

smashed *adj informal* extremely drunk.

smasher *noun Brit, informal* somebody or something that is very impressive or attractive.

smash hit *noun informal* an outstanding success: *His latest play is a smash hit.*

smashing *adj chiefly Brit, informal* extremely good; excellent: *a smashing film.* ➤➤ **smashingly** *adv.*

smash-up *noun informal* a serious accident; a crash: *a ten-car smash-up on the M1.*

smatter /'smatə/ *noun* = SMATTERING.

smattering /'smat(ə)ring/ *noun* **1** (*usu* + of) a limited or superficial knowledge of a subject. **2** a small amount. [verbal noun from *smatter* to spatter, speak with superficial knowledge, dabble in, from Middle English *smateren*, of unknown origin]

SME *abbr* Surinam (international vehicle registration).

smear[1] /smiə/ *verb trans* **1a** to spread (something) with a sticky, greasy, or viscous substance; to daub (it). **b** to spread (a substance) thickly over a surface. **2a** to stain or dirty (something) by or as if by smearing. **b** to blacken the reputation of (somebody). **3** to obscure or blur (something) by or as if by smearing; to smudge (it). ➤ *verb intrans* to become smeared: *Don't touch the paint or it will smear.* ➤➤ **smearer** *noun,* **smeary** *adj.*

smear[2] *noun* **1** a mark made by or as if by smearing a substance. **2** an unsubstantiated accusation: *She took the article as a personal smear.* **3a** material smeared on a surface. **b** material taken or prepared for microscopic examination by smearing on a slide: *a vaginal smear.* [Middle English *smere* from Old English *smeoru* grease, ointment]

smear test *noun* = CERVICAL SMEAR.

smectic /'smektik/ *adj* of or being a type of LIQUID CRYSTAL (liquid having properties of a crystalline solid) that has molecules arranged in layers with the longest axes perpendicular to the plane of the layers: compare CHOLESTERIC, NEMATIC. [Latin *smecticus* cleansing, having the properties of soap, from Greek *smēktikos,* from *smēchein* to clean]

smegma /'smegmə/ *noun* the secretion of a sebaceous gland; *specif* the sebaceous matter that collects beneath the foreskin of the penis. [via Latin from Greek *smēgma,* from *smēchein* to wash off, clean]

smell[1] /smel/ *verb* (*past tense and past part.* **smelt** /smelt/ *or* **smelled**) ➤ *verb trans* **1a** to perceive the odour of (something) by the sense of smell. **b** to sniff (something) in order to perceive its odour. **2** to detect or become aware of (something) by instinct: *I could smell trouble.* ➤ *verb intrans* **1** to exercise the sense of smell. **2** to have a specified smell: *These clothes smell damp.* **3** (+ of) to have a characteristic aura of something; to be suggestive of it: *Reports of survivors seemed to smell of truth.* **4** to have an offensive smell; to stink. ✳ **smell a rat** *informal* to have a suspicion of something wrong. ➤➤ **smeller** *noun.* [Middle English *smellen;* earlier history unknown]

smell[2] *noun* **1** the one of the five basic physical senses by which the qualities of substances in contact with sensitive areas in the nose are interpreted by the brain as characteristic odours.
Editorial note
Smell – one of the five senses – is the ability to detect, for example, gases, vapours, and airborne particles by stimulation of nerve endings in the nose;

the nerve endings responsible for the sensation of smell, or 'olfaction', are restricted to a small area lying high in the nasal passages. 'Sniffing' carries air directly to these receptors, although substances usually travel to the receptors in 'eddy currents' from the main air stream — Dr John Cormack.

2a the quality of something as perceived by this sense; an odour. **b** an unpleasant odour. **3** a pervading quality; an aura: *the smell of corruption.* **4a** the process, function, or power of smelling. **b** the act or an instance of smelling.

smelling salts *pl noun* (*treated as sing. or pl*) a usu scented preparation of ammonium carbonate and aqueous ammonia sniffed as a stimulant to relieve faintness.

smell out *verb trans* **1** to detect or discover (somebody or something) by or as if by smelling: *The dog smelt out the criminal.* **2** to fill (a place) with an *esp* offensive smell: *The cigarettes smelt out the room.*

smelly *adj* (**smellier, smelliest**) having a strong, often unpleasant smell.

smelt[1] /smelt/ *noun* (*pl* **smelts** *or collectively* **smelt**) any of various small fishes that closely resemble the trouts and have delicate oily flesh with a distinctive smell and taste: family Osmeridae. [Old English]

smelt[2] *verb trans* **1** to melt (ore) to separate the metal. **2** to separate (metal) by smelting ore. ➤➤ **smelter** *noun,* **smeltery** *noun.* [Dutch or Low German *smelten*]

smelt[3] *verb* past part. of SMELL[1].

smew /smyooh/ *noun* a MERGANSER (type of duck) of N Europe and Asia, the male of which is mostly white with black patches round the eyes: *Mergus albellus.* [ultimately of Germanic origin]

smidgin *or* **smidgen** /'smijin/ *noun informal* a small amount; a bit. [prob alteration of English dialect *smitch* smudge]

smilax /'smielaks/ *noun* **1** = SARSAPARILLA. **2** a tender climbing vinelike plant that has glossy bright green leaves and is often grown for ornament: *Asparagus asparagoides.* [via Latin from Greek *smilax* bindweed, yew]

smile[1] /smiel/ *verb intrans* **1** to have or assume a smile: *O villain, villain, smiling, damned villain … Meet it is I set it down, that one may smile and smile, and be a villain* — Shakespeare. **2a** (*often* + at) to look with amusement or scorn: *He smiled at his own weakness.* **b** (*often* + at) to remain stoically cheerful in the face of sorrow, etc. **c** (*often* + on) to bestow approval or favour: *Fortune smiled on their venture.* **d** to appear pleasant or agreeable: *a green and smiling landscape.* ➤ *verb trans* **1** to utter or express (something) with a smile: *She smiled her thanks.* **2** (*also* + away/off) to dispel (awkwardness, etc) or effect any other end by smiling: *He smiled away his embarrassment.* ➤➤ **smiler** *noun,* **smilingly** *adv.* [Middle English *smilen,* of Germanic origin]

smile[2] *noun* **1** a change of facial expression in which the corners of the mouth curve slightly upwards to express *esp* amusement, friendliness, pleasure, or approval: *Who passed without much the same smile? This grew; I gave commands; then all smiles stopped together* — Robert Browning. **2** a pleasant or encouraging appearance.

smiley[1] *adj* smiling.

smiley[2] *noun* a symbol used to represent a smiling face, *esp* in email.

smirch[1] /smuhch/ *verb trans* **1** to make (something) dirty or stained, *esp* by smearing. **2** to bring discredit or disgrace on (e.g. somebody's reputation). [Middle English *smorchen;* earlier history unknown]

smirch[2] *noun* **1** a dirty mark; a smear or stain. **2** a blemish or flaw, e.g. on somebody's reputation.

smirk[1] /smuhk/ *verb intrans* to smile in a fatuous, smug, or scornful manner. ➤➤ **smirker** *noun,* **smirkingly** *adv.* [Old English *smearcian* to smile]

smirk[2] *noun* a fatuous, smug, or scornful smile.

smit /smit/ *verb archaic* past part. of SMITE.

smite /smiet/ *verb* (*past tense* **smote** /smoht/, *past part.* **smitten** /'smit(ə)n/) ➤ *verb trans* **1** *archaic or literary.* **a** to strike (something or somebody) sharply or heavily, *esp* with an implement held in the hand. **b** to kill, injure, or damage (somebody or something), *esp* with sharp or heavy blows. **2a** to attack or afflict (somebody or something) suddenly and injuriously: *smitten by disease.* **b** to have a sudden powerful effect on (somebody or something): *smitten with grief.* **c** to attract (somebody) strongly: *smitten by her beauty.* ➤ *verb*

intrans *archaic, literary* (*often* + on/upon) to beat down or come forcibly. ➤➤ **smiter** *noun*. [Old English *smītan*]

smith /smith/ *noun* **1** a person who works in metal, *esp* a blacksmith. **2** (*used in combinations*) a person who works with a specified material or who produces a specified type of article: *goldsmith*; *songsmith*. [Old English]

smithereens /smidhə'reenz/ *pl noun* small fragments; bits: *The house was blown to smithereens by the explosion.* [Irish Gaelic *smidirín*, dimin. of *smiodar* fragment]

smithery *noun* the work, art, or trade of a smith.

smithy /'smidhi/ *noun* (*pl* **smithies**) the workshop of a smith; *specif* a blacksmith's forge.

smitten /'smit(ə)n/ *verb* past part. of SMITE.

smock[1] /smok/ *noun* **1a** a protective outer garment worn e.g. by artists. **b** a garment resembling a long loose shirt gathered into a yoke and decorated with smocking, formerly worn by farm labourers. **2a** a light loose garment resembling this, *esp* in being gathered into a yoke, worn by pregnant women. **b** *dated* a garment of this kind. [Old English *smoc* woman's loose undergarment]

smock[2] *verb trans* to decorate (e.g. a garment) with smocking.

smock frock *noun* = SMOCK[1] (1B).

smocking *noun* a decorative effect, *esp* on a garment, made by gathering cloth in regularly spaced tucks held in place with ornamental stitching that often forms a diamond or honeycomb effect.

smog /smog/ *noun* a fog made heavier and darker by smoke and chemical fumes. ➤➤ **smoggy** *adj*. [blend of SMOKE[1] and FOG[1]]

smoke[1] /smohk/ *noun* **1a** the gaseous products of burning carbon-containing materials, made visible by the presence of small particles of carbon. **b** a suspension of particles in a gas. **2** fumes or vapour resembling smoke. **3** something of little substance, permanence, or value. **4** something that obscures. **5a** an act or spell of smoking, *esp* tobacco. **b** *informal* something, e.g. a cigarette, that is smoked. **6** = BIG SMOKE. ✱ **go up in smoke** to come to nothing; to disappear: *All his plans went up in smoke.* [Old English *smoca*]

smoke[2] *verb intrans* **1** to emit smoke, often excessively or faultily. **2a** to inhale and exhale the fumes of tobacco, cannabis, heroin, etc. **b** to use cigarettes, cigars, a pipe, etc, *esp* habitually. ➤ *verb trans* **1** to inhale and exhale the smoke of (e.g. a cigarette). **2** to cure (e.g. meat or fish) by exposure to smoke, traditionally from wood or peat. **3** to colour or darken (e.g. glass) with or as if with smoke. **4a** to fumigate (a place). **b** to drive (something or somebody) out or away by smoke: *smoke a fox from its den.* ➤➤ **smokable** *adj*, **smokeable** *adj*, **smoked** *adj*, **smoking** *noun and adj*.

smokehouse /'smohkhows/ *noun* a building or room where meat, fish, etc is cured in a dense wood smoke.

smokeless *adj* producing little or no smoke: *smokeless fuel.*

smokeless zone *noun Brit* a designated neighbourhood where the emission of smoke, *esp* from domestic coal fires, is forbidden or where the use of smokeless fuel is the only fuel allowed.

smoke out *verb trans* **1** to drive (something or somebody) out or away by smoke. **2** to bring (something) to public view or knowledge.

smoker *noun* **1** somebody who regularly or habitually smokes tobacco. **2** a railway carriage or compartment in which smoking is allowed. **3** an informal gathering for men only.

smoke screen *noun* **1** a screen of smoke to hinder observation of a military force, area, or activity. **2** something said or done in order to conceal, confuse, or deceive.

smokestack *noun* a chimney or funnel through which smoke and gases are discharged, e.g. from a locomotive, ship, or factory.

smoking jacket *noun* a man's loosely fitting usu velvet jacket formerly worn while smoking, *esp* at home after a meal.

smoko /'smohkoh/ *noun* (*pl* **smokos**) *Aus, NZ, informal* a short rest period from work, e.g. for a cup of tea, a cigarette, etc: *Many stevedores don't leave the hold during smoko; they just curl up on the softest bit of cargo they can find and go to sleep* — John Morrison.

smoky *adj* (**smokier, smokiest**) **1** emitting smoke, *esp* in large quantities: *a smoky fire.* **2a** having the characteristics or appearance of smoke. **b** suggestive of smoke, *esp* in flavour, smell, or colour. **3a** filled with smoke. **b** made black or grimy by smoke. ➤➤ **smokily** *adv*, **smokiness** *noun*.

smolder[1] /'smohldə/ *verb intrans NAmer* see SMOULDER[1].

smolder[2] *noun NAmer* see SMOULDER[2].

smolt /smohlt/ *noun* (*pl* **smolts** *or collectively* **smolt**) a young salmon or trout that is about two years old and is assuming the silvery colour of the adult in anticipation of its first migration from fresh water to the sea. [Middle English (Scots); earlier history unknown]

smooch[1] /smoohch/ *verb intrans informal* **1** to kiss and cuddle. **2** *Brit* to dance slowly, holding one's partner in a close embrace. ➤➤ **smoocher** *noun*, **smoochy** *adj*. [alteration of English dialect *smouch* to kiss loudly, of imitative origin]

smooch[2] *noun informal* the act or an instance of smooching.

smoodge *or* **smooge** /smoohj/ *verb intrans Aus, NZ, informal* **1** to kiss and cuddle. **2** to try to ingratiate oneself. [prob alteration of SMOOCH[1]]

smooth[1] /smoohdh/ *adj* **1a** having a continuous even surface. **b** free from hair or hairlike projections. **c** said of liquid: of an even consistency; free from lumps. **d** giving no resistance to sliding; frictionless. **2** free from difficulties or obstructions. **3** even and uninterrupted in movement or flow: *a smooth ride.* **4a** equable; composed: *a smooth disposition.* **b** urbane; courteous. **c** excessively and often artfully suave; ingratiating: *a smooth salesman.* **5** not sharp or acid: *a smooth sherry.* ➤➤ **smoothly** *adv*, **smoothness** *noun*. [Old English *smōth*]

smooth[2] *verb trans* **1** to make (something) smooth. **2** (*often* + out) to press (something) flat. **3** (*often* + down) to cause (something) to lie evenly and in order: *He smoothed down his hair.* **4** (*often* + away/over) to dispel or alleviate (e.g. enmity or perplexity). **5** to free (something) from obstruction or difficulty: *smooth the way.* **6** to free (something) from what is harsh or disagreeable. ➤ *verb intrans* to become smooth. ➤➤ **smoother** *noun*.

smooth[3] *noun* **1** a smooth or agreeable side or aspect: *take the rough with the smooth.* **2** the act or an instance of smoothing.

smooth[4] *adv archaic* in a smooth manner; without irregularities or difficulties.

smoothbore *adj* said of a firearm: lacking spiral grooves in its barrel; not rifled.

smoothen *verb trans and intrans* (**smoothened, smoothening**) = SMOOTH[2].

smooth hound *noun* either of two species of small sharks of shallow N Atlantic waters: genus *Mustelus*.

smoothie *or* **smoothy** /'smoohdhi/ *noun* (*pl* **smoothies**) **1** *informal* a person who behaves with suave self-assurance, *esp* a man with an ingratiating manner. **2** a non-alcoholic drink made from fresh fruit purée mixed with milk, yoghurt, or ice cream.

smoothing iron *noun* an old-fashioned type of iron for pressing clothes, etc, *esp* one that was heated on a fire or on top of a stove.

smooth muscle *noun* muscle tissue that is made up of elongated cells in thin sheets and performs involuntary functions, e.g. in abdominal structures of vertebrate animals: compare STRIATED MUSCLE.

smooth snake *noun* a European nonpoisonous snake that is reddish brown in colour and has smooth scales: *Coronella austriaca*.

smooth-talking *adj* ingratiating and persuasive in speech.

smooth-tongued *adj* = SMOOTH-TALKING.

smoothy *noun* see SMOOTHIE.

smorgasbord /'smawgəsbawd/ *noun* **1** a variety of foods and dishes, e.g. hors d'oeuvres, hot and cold meat or fish, cheeses, salads, etc. **2** a meal or buffet at which this is served. [Swedish *smörgåsbord*, from *smörgås* open sandwich + *bord* table]

smorzando /smawt'sandoh/ *adj and adv* said of a piece of music: to be performed with gradually decreasing intensity of tone, so that the sound dies away. [Italian *smorzando*, literally 'extinguishing']

smote /smoht/ *verb* past tense of SMITE.

smother[1] /'smudhə/ *verb* (**smothered, smothering**) ➤ *verb trans* **1a** to kill (somebody or something) by covering the nose and mouth in order to cut off the supply of air. **b** to overcome or cause discomfort to (somebody) through or as if through lack of air. **c** to suppress (a fire) by excluding oxygen. **2a** to suppress the expression of (e.g. a feeling). **b** to conceal (something): *smother a yawn.* **c** to prevent the growth or development of (something or somebody). **d** to cause (somebody) to experience feelings of being oppressed. **3a** to cover (something) thickly; to blanket (it): *Snow smothered the trees and hedgerows.* **b** to overwhelm (somebody): *She smothered him* *with kisses.* ➤ *verb intrans* to become smothered. [Old English *smorian* to suffocate]

smother² *noun* **1** a dense cloud of gas, smoke, dust, etc. **2** a confused mass of things. ➤➤ **smothery** *adj.*

smothered mate *noun* in chess, a situation in which a king is checkmated by a knight and unable to move because all adjoining squares are occupied.

smoulder¹ (*NAmer* **smolder**) /'smohldə/ *verb intrans* (**smouldered, smouldering,** *NAmer* **smoldered, smoldering**) **1** to burn feebly with little flame and often much smoke. **2** to exist in a state of suppressed ferment: *Resentment smouldered in her.* **3** to show suppressed anger, hate, jealousy, etc: *eyes smouldering with hate.* [Middle English *smolder*, of Germanic origin]

smoulder² (*NAmer* **smolder**) *noun* a slow burning fire or thick smoke coming from it.

SMP *abbr* statutory maternity pay.

SMS *abbr* Short Message (or Messaging) Service, a system that permits the sending of text messages of up to 160 characters to and from mobile telephones.

smudge¹ /smuj/ *verb trans* **1a** to smear or daub (something): *He accidentally smudged ink onto the clean desk.* **b** to make (e.g. writing) indistinct; to blur (it): *Rain had smudged the address.* **2** to soil (something) with or as if with a smudge. **3** *NAmer* to disinfect or protect (something) by means of smoke. ➤ *verb intrans* **1** to make a smudge. **2** to become smudged. [Middle English *smogen*; earlier history unknown]

smudge² *noun* **1** a blurry spot or streak. **2** an indistinct mass; a blur: *Soon the boat was just a smudge on the horizon.* **3** *NAmer* a smouldering smoky fire lit on the windward side of a crop for protection, e.g. from frost or insects. ➤➤ **smudgily** *adv,* **smudginess** *noun,* **smudgy** *adj.*

smug /smug/ *adj* (**smugger, smuggest**) **1** looking or feeling excessively pleased or satisfied with oneself or one's actions. **2** highly self-satisfied and complacent: *the constant prying and peeping, the hypocritical lectures, the heavy doses of smug morality* — David Graham Phillips; *Some say that only people can think, and that computers cannot be people; they then sit back and look smug* — K Eric Drexler. ➤➤ **smugly** *adv,* **smugness** *noun.* [prob from Low German *smuck* neat, from early Low German *smucken* to dress]

smuggle /'smugl/ *verb trans* **1** to import or export (goods) secretly, *esp* illegally in order to avoid paying duties. **2** to convey or introduce (something) surreptitiously and illicitly: *He smuggled his notes into the examination.* ➤ *verb intrans* to import or export goods in violation of the law, *esp* customs laws. ➤➤ **smuggler** *noun,* **smuggling** *noun.* [Low German *smuggeln* and Dutch *smokkelen*]

smut¹ /smut/ *noun* **1** a particle of soot or other matter that soils or blackens something. **2a** any of various destructive fungal diseases, *esp* of cereal grasses, marked by a transformation of plant organs, *esp* cereal ears, into dark masses of spores. **b** a parasitic fungus causing such a disease: order Ustilaginales. **3** obscene language, writing, pictures, etc. ➤➤ **smuttily** *adv,* **smuttiness** *noun,* **smutty** *adj.*

smut² *verb* (**smutted, smutting**) ➤ *verb trans* **1** to mark or taint (something) with smuts. **2** to affect (a crop or plant) with smut. ➤ *verb intrans* to become affected by smut. [Middle English *smotten* to defile, corrupt, of Germanic origin]

SN *abbr* Senegal (international vehicle registration).

Sn *abbr* the chemical symbol for tin. [Latin *stannum* tin]

snack¹ /snak/ *noun* a light meal; food eaten between regular meals.

snack² *verb intrans* to eat a snack. [Middle English *snaken* to bite, prob from early Dutch *snacken* to snap at, bite]

snaffle¹ /'snafl/ *noun* a simple usu jointed bit for a bridle. [prob from Low German or Dutch]

snaffle² *verb trans informal* to take possession of (something), *esp* by devious means; to steal (it). [origin unknown]

snafu¹ /sna'fooh/ *noun chiefly NAmer, informal* a state of total confusion. [short for *situation normal all fucked up*]

snafu² *verb trans* (**snafus, snafued, snafuing**) *chiefly NAmer, informal* to bring (something) into a state of total confusion.

snafu³ *adj chiefly NAmer, informal* utterly confused or awry.

snag¹ /snag/ *noun* **1** a concealed or unexpected difficulty or obstacle: *The snag is, there's no train on Sundays.* **2** a sharp or jagged projecting part. **3** an irregular tear or flaw made by or as if by catching on a snag: *a snag in her tights.* **4a** a stub or stump remaining

after a branch has been chopped or torn off. **b** a tree or branch embedded in a lake or stream bed and constituting a hazard to navigation. ➤➤ **snaggy** *adj.* [of Scandinavian origin]

snag² *verb* (**snagged, snagging**) ➤ *verb trans* **1** to catch (something) on or as if on a snag. **2** to clear (e.g. a river) of snags. **3** *chiefly NAmer* to halt or impede (something). **4** *chiefly NAmer* to catch or obtain (something) by quick action: *I snagged a taxi.* ➤ *verb intrans* to become snagged.

snag³ *noun Aus, informal* a sausage. [prob from English dialect *snag* morsel, snack]

snaggle-toothed /'snag(ə)l,tootht/ *adj* said of a person or animal: having irregular, broken, or prominently projecting teeth. [frequentative of SNAG²]

snail /snayl/ *noun* **1** any of numerous species of invertebrate animals that live on land or in freshwater and have a soft body enclosed in an external spiral shell: class Gastropoda. **2** a slow-moving or sluggish person or thing. [Old English *snægl*]

snail mail *noun informal* the ordinary postal system as opposed to email.

snail's pace *noun* a very slow speed or rate of progress.

snake¹ /snayk/ *noun* **1** any of numerous limbless scaly reptiles with a long tapering body and with salivary glands often modified to produce venom that is injected through grooved or tubular fangs: suborder Ophidia. **2** a sly treacherous person. **3** something long, slender, and flexible; *specif* a flexible rod for clearing blocked pipes. **4** in former times, a system in which the values of the currencies of countries in the European Union were allowed to vary against each other within narrow limits. ✳ **snake in the grass** a secretly treacherous friend or associate. [Old English *snaca*]

snake² *verb trans* to wind (e.g. one's way) in the manner of a snake. ➤ *verb intrans* to move or extend silently, secretly, or windingly: *The path snaked down to the sea.*

snakebird *noun* = DARTER. [from its snakelike neck]

snakebite *noun* **1** the bite of a snake, *esp* a venomous snake. **2** a drink consisting of cider mixed with an equal quantity of lager.

snake charmer *noun* an entertainer who exhibits the power to control venomous snakes supposedly by magic, usu using music and rhythmical movements.

snake eyes *pl noun* (*treated as sing.*) in a game of chance using a pair of dice, a throw in which both dice show one spot each. ✳ **come up snake eyes** to be a complete failure; to have the worst possible outcome.

snakehead *noun* a member, or the leader, of a Chinese gang involved in smuggling illegal Chinese immigrants into other countries.

snakeroot *noun* any of numerous plants that have roots believed to cure snakebites: *Cimieifuga racemosa, Polygala senega,* and others.

snakes and ladders *pl noun* (*treated as sing.*) a board game in which players move counters along numbered squares on a chequered board, sometimes advancing rapidly up a ladder or being forced backward down a snake.

snake's head *noun* a European plant of the lily family that grows in damp meadowland and has a purple-and-white chequered bell-shaped flower on a slender drooping stem: *Fritillaria meleagris.*

snakeskin *noun* the skin of a snake or leather made from this.

snaky *adj* (**snakier, snakiest**) **1** formed of or entwined with snakes: *the Gorgon with the snaky hair* — Joseph Addison. **2** resembling a snake; serpentine: *the snaky arms of an octopus.* **3** slyly venomous or treacherous: *oiliness and snaky insinuation* — De Quincey. **4** full of snakes. **5** *Aus, NZ* bad-tempered or angry. ➤➤ **snakily** *adv,* **snakiness** *noun.*

snap¹ /snap/ *verb* (**snapped, snapping**) ➤ *verb intrans* **1a** to make a sudden closing of the jaws; to seize something sharply with the mouth: *fish snapping at the bait.* **b** to grasp or snatch at something eagerly: *snap at any chance.* **2** to utter sharp biting words; to give an irritable retort: *He snapped at his wife.* **3a** to make a sharp or cracking sound. **b** to break suddenly, *esp* with a sharp cracking sound. **c** to close or fit in place with an abrupt movement or sharp sound: *The catch snapped shut.* **4** to collapse under strain or lose self-control, *esp* suddenly. ➤ *verb trans* **1** to seize (something) with or as if with a sudden closing of the jaws. **2** (+ up) to take possession or advantage of (something) suddenly or eagerly: *shoppers snapping up bargains.* **3** to utter (something) curtly or abruptly: *He snapped an answer.* **4a** to cause (something) to make a snapping sound: *She* *snapped her fingers.* **b** to cause to break suddenly, *esp* with a sharp cracking sound: *I snapped the end off the twig.* **c** to put (something) into a particular position with a sudden movement or sharp sound: *snap the lid shut.* **5a** to take (a picture) with a camera. **b** to photograph (somebody or something). **6** in American football, to put (the ball) into play with a backward movement. * **snap out of something** *informal* to free oneself from a mood, habit, etc by an effort of will. ⟫ **snappingly** *adv.* [Dutch or Low German *snappen*]

snap² *noun* **1** an abrupt closing, e.g. of the mouth in biting. **2** the act or an instance of seizing something abruptly; a sudden snatch. **3** a brief usu curt retort. **4a** a sound made by snapping. **b** a sudden sharp breaking of something thin or brittle. **5** a sudden spell of harsh weather: *a cold snap.* **6** a thin brittle biscuit: *a ginger snap.* **7** a catch or fastening that closes with a click. **8** = SNAPSHOT. **9** vigour; energy. **10** a card game in which each player tries to be the first to shout '*snap*' when two cards of identical value are laid successively. **11** *dialect.* **a** a small meal or snack, *esp* elevenses. **b** food, *esp* food taken to eat at work. **12** *NAmer, informal* something that is easy and presents no problems; a cinch.

snap³ *interj* **1** used in the card game snap when two cards of identical value are laid successively. **2** used to draw attention to an identity or similarity: *Snap! You're reading the same book as me.*

snap⁴ *adv* with a snap or the sound of a snap.

snap⁵ *adj* **1** performed suddenly, unexpectedly, or without deliberation: *a snap judgment.* **2** shutting or fastening with a click. **3** *NAmer* very easy or simple: *a snap course.*

snapdragon *noun* a garden plant of the foxglove family with attractive white, red, or yellow two-lipped flowers: *Antirrhinum majus.* [from the fancied resemblance of the flowers to the face of a dragon]

snap fastener *noun chiefly NAmer* = PRESS-STUD.

snapper *noun* **1** (*pl* **snappers** *or collectively* **snapper**) any of numerous species of flesh-eating fishes of warm seas caught for food or sport: chiefly in family Lutjanidae. **2** = SNAPPING TURTLE. **3** somebody or something that snaps.

snapping turtle *noun* a large American turtle that has powerful jaws: *Chelydra serpentina.*

snappish *adj* **1a** given to curt irritable speech. **b** arising from annoyance or irritability: *a snappish reply.* **2** said of a dog: inclined to snap or bite. ⟫ **snappishly** *adv*, **snappishness** *noun.*

snappy *adj* (**snappier, snappiest**) **1** = SNAPPISH. **2a** quickly or hurriedly made or performed. **b** lively; animated: *snappy repartee.* **c** stylish; smart: *a snappy dresser.* * **make it snappy!** *informal* be quick!; hurry up! ⟫ **snappily** *adv*, **snappiness** *noun.*

snap roll *noun* an aircraft manoeuvre in which a plane quickly turns a complete circle about its longitudinal axis while flying horizontally.

snapshot *noun* a casual photograph taken typically by an amateur with a simple camera and without regard to technique.

snap shot *noun* a quick shot, e.g. in football, hockey, or rifle-shooting.

snare¹ /snea/ *noun* **1a** a trap, often consisting of a noose that pulls tight, for catching birds or small animals. **b** something designed or intended to trap or deceive. **2** any of the catgut strings or metal spirals placed over the skin of a snare drum to produce a rattling sound. **3** a surgical instrument consisting usu of a wire loop constricted by a mechanism in the handle and used for removing tissue masses, e.g. tonsils, polyps, etc. [Old English *snearu* from Old Norse *snara*]

snare² *verb trans* **1a** to capture (something or somebody) by or as if by a snare. **b** to gain (something) by artful or skilful actions: *snare a top job.* **2** to entangle or hold (something or somebody) as if in a snare. ⟫ **snarer** *noun.*

snare drum *noun* a small double-headed drum with one or more snares stretched across its lower head.

snarl¹ /snahl/ *noun* **1** a tangle, *esp* of hair or thread; a knot. **2** a confused or complicated situation, *esp* a snarl-up. ⟫ **snarly** *adj.* [Middle English *snarle*, prob dimin. of SNARE¹]

snarl² *verb trans* **1** (*often* + up) to cause (something) to become knotted and intertwined; to tangle (it). **2** (*often* + up) to make (something) excessively confused or complicated. **3** to decorate (metal) by hammering a tool against the underside to form raised shapes on the upper surface. ⟫ *verb intrans* (*often* + up) to become snarled. ⟫ **snarler** *noun.*

snarl³ *verb intrans* **1** to growl with bared teeth. **2** to speak in a vicious or bad-tempered manner. ⟫ *verb trans* to utter or express (something) with a snarl or in a snarling manner. ⟫ **snarler** *noun*, **snarling** *adj*, **snarlingly** *adv.* [frequentative of obsolete *snar* to growl, of imitative origin]

snarl⁴ *noun* the act or sound of snarling.

snarl-up *noun* a state of confusion, disorder, or obstruction; *specif* a traffic jam.

snatch¹ /snach/ *verb intrans* **1** (*often* + at) to attempt to seize something suddenly: *snatch at a rope.* ⟫ *verb trans* **1** to seize or grab (something or somebody) suddenly and usu forcibly, wrongfully, or with difficulty. **2** to take or grasp (something) abruptly or hastily: *snatch a quick glance.* ⟫ **snatcher** *noun.* [Middle English *snacchen* to give a sudden snap, seize, of Germanic origin]

snatch² *noun* **1** a snatching at or of something. **2a** a brief period of time or activity: *snatches of sleep.* **b** something fragmentary or hurried: *I caught a brief snatch of their conversation.* **3** *informal* a robbery. **4** in weight-lifting, a lift in which the weight is raised from the floor directly to an overhead position.

snatchy *adj* (**snatchier, snatchiest**) marked by breaks in continuity; spasmodic. ⟫ **snatchily** *adv.*

snazzy /'snazi/ *adj* (**snazzier, snazziest**) *informal* stylishly or flashily attractive. [perhaps blend of SNAPPY and JAZZY]

sneak¹ /sneek/ *verb* (*past tense and past part.* **sneaked** *or NAmer informal* **snuck** /snuk/) ⟫ *verb intrans* **1** to go stealthily or furtively; to slink: *boys sneaking over the orchard wall.* **2** to behave in a furtive or servile manner. **3** *Brit, informal* to tell somebody in authority of another's wrongdoing: *sneak on your classmates.* ⟫ *verb trans* to put, bring, or take (something) in a furtive or artful manner: *She sneaked a glance at the report.* * **sneak up on** to approach (somebody or something) stealthily. [prob from English dialect *snike*, from Old English *snican* to sneak along]

sneak² *noun* **1a** the act or an instance of sneaking. **b** (*used before a noun*) done stealthily, furtively, or without warning: *a sneak attack.* **2** somebody who acts in a stealthy or furtive manner. **3** *Brit, informal* somebody, *esp* a schoolchild, who informs on others. ⟫ **sneakily** *adv*, **sneakiness** *noun*, **sneaky** *adj.*

sneaker *noun chiefly NAmer* (*usu in pl*) a soft casual or sports shoe; a trainer.

sneaking *adj* **1** furtive; underhand. **2** mean; contemptible. **3a** not openly expressed; secret: *a sneaking desire for publicity.* **b** instinctively felt but unverified: *a sneaking suspicion.* ⟫ **sneakingly** *adv.*

sneak thief *noun* a thief who steals opportunistically and without using violence or breaking into buildings.

sneck¹ /snek/ *noun NEng, Scot, dialect* a latch. [Middle English *snekke*, of Germanic origin]

sneck² *verb trans NEng, Scot, dialect* to close or fasten (a door or window) with a sneck.

sneer¹ /snia/ *verb intrans* **1** to smile or laugh with a curl of the lips to express scorn or contempt. **2** to speak or write in a scornfully jeering manner. ⟫ *verb trans* to utter (something) with a sneer. ⟫ **sneerer** *noun*, **sneering** *adj*, **sneeringly** *adv.* [Middle English, prob of Germanic origin]

sneer² *noun* a sneering expression or remark.

sneeze¹ /sneez/ *verb intrans* to make a sudden violent involuntary audible expiration of breath from the nose and mouth, *esp* as a result of irritation to the nasal passages. * **sneeze at** to make light of (something): *The idea is not to be sneezed at.* ⟫ **sneezer** *noun*, **sneezy** *adj.* [Old English *fnēosan*]

sneeze² *noun* the act or sound of sneezing: *I like to write when I feel spiteful; it's like having a good sneeze* — D H Lawrence.

sneezewort *noun* a strong-scented Eurasian plant of the daisy family found in damp and shady places that has clusters of small white flowers and long greyish green leaves that induce sneezing when dried and powdered: *Achillea ptarmica.*

snick¹ /snik/ *verb trans* **1** to cut (something) slightly; to nick (it). **2** in cricket, to hit (the ball) with the edge of the bat. [prob from obsolete *snick or snee* to engage in cut-and-thrust fighting, alteration of earlier *steake or snye*, from Dutch *steken* to stab and *snijden* to cut]

snick² *noun* **1** a small cut; a nick. **2** in cricket, a blow with the edge of the bat or the resulting deflection of the ball.

snicker¹ /'snika/ *verb intrans* (**snickered, snickering**) **1** to snigger. **2** said of a horse: to whinny. [imitative]

snicker² *noun* **1** a snigger. **2** a whinny.

snide /snied/ *adj* **1** slyly disparaging; insinuating: *snide remarks.* **2** *chiefly NAmer* mean; low: *a snide trick.* **3** counterfeit; bogus. ➤➤ **snidely** *adv,* **snideness** *noun,* **snidey** *adj.* [origin unknown]

sniff¹ /snif/ *verb intrans* to draw air audibly up the nose, *esp* for smelling or for clearing the nasal passages. ➤ *verb trans* **1** to smell or inhale (something) through the nose. **2** (+ out) to detect or become aware of (something) by or as if by smelling. ✳ **sniff at** to regard or treat (something) with contempt or disdain: *The offer is not to be sniffed at.* ➤➤ **sniffer** *noun.* [Middle English *sniffen,* of imitative origin]

sniff² *noun* **1** the act or sound of sniffing. **2** a quantity that is sniffed: *a good sniff of sea air.* **3** *informal* a trace or hint.

sniffer dog *noun* a police dog trained to detect drugs or explosives by smell.

sniffle¹ /'snifl/ *verb intrans* to sniff repeatedly. ➤➤ **sniffler** *noun.* [frequentative of SNIFF¹]

sniffle² *noun* **1** the act or sound of sniffling. **2** (*also in pl*) a head cold marked by a runny discharge from the nose: *He's got the sniffles.* ➤➤ **sniffly** *adj.*

sniffy *adj* (**sniffier, sniffiest**) *informal* having or expressing a haughty attitude; supercilious. ➤➤ **sniffily** *adv,* **sniffiness** *noun.*

snifter /'sniftə/ *noun informal* **1** a small drink of spirits. **2** *chiefly NAmer* = BALLOON GLASS. [English dialect *snift* to sniff, snort, of imitative origin]

snig /snig/ *verb trans* (**snigged, snigging**) *Aus, NZ* to drag (logs) with chains or ropes. [origin unknown]

snigger¹ /'snigə/ *verb intrans* (**sniggered, sniggering**) to laugh in a partly suppressed and often derisive manner. ➤➤ **sniggerer** *noun,* **sniggering** *adj and noun.* [alteration of SNICKER¹]

snigger² *noun* the act or sound of sniggering.

snip¹ /snip/ *noun* **1a** a small piece, *esp* one snipped off; a fragment or bit. **b** a cut or notch made by snipping. **c** the act or sound of snipping. **2** *Brit, informal* a bargain. **3** *Brit, informal* something easy to do; a cinch. **4** (*in pl*) shears used *esp* for cutting sheet metal by hand. [from Dutch and Low German *snip*]

snip² *verb* (**snipped, snipping**) ➤ *verb trans* (*often* + off) to cut (something) with, or as if with, shears or scissors, *esp* with short rapid strokes: *I snipped off a corner of the fabric.* ➤ *verb intrans* to make a short rapid cut with, or as if with, shears or scissors: *snipping away at her hair.*

snipe¹ /sniep/ *noun* (*pl* **snipes** *or collectively* **snipe**) any of several species of wading birds that have long slender straight bills and inhabit *esp* marshy areas: genus *Gallinago.* [Middle English, of Scandinavian origin]

snipe² *verb intrans* **1** (*often* + at) to shoot at exposed individuals usu from a hiding place at long range. **2** (*usu* + at) to aim a snide or obliquely critical attack at somebody. ➤➤ **sniper** *noun.* [from the sense 'to shoot or hunt snipe']

snipefish *noun* (*pl* **snipefishes** *or collectively* **snipefish**) a fish that lives in temperate and tropical seas and has a long thin snout: family Macrorhamphosidae.

snippet /'snipit/ *noun* a small part, piece, or item, *esp* a fragment of writing or conversation. ➤➤ **snippety** *adj.* [dimin. of SNIP¹]

snippy /'snipi/ *adj* (**snippier, snippiest**) *informal* abrupt, *esp* in a rude way. ➤➤ **snippily** *adv,* **snippiness** *noun.* [from SNIP¹]

snit /snit/ *noun NAmer, Aus, NZ, informal* a bad or sulky mood: *She's been in a snit all day.* [origin unknown]

snitch¹ /snich/ *verb intrans informal* to inform on somebody. ➤ *verb trans informal* to steal (something). [prob from SNITCH²; verb trans prob influenced by SNATCH¹]

snitch² *noun informal* an informer.

snivel¹ /'snivl/ *verb intrans* (**snivelled, snivelling,** *NAmer* **sniveled, sniveling**) **1** to have a runny nose. **2** to sniff mucus up the nose audibly. **3** to complain in a whining way. **4** to speak or act in a whining, tearful, or weakly emotional manner. ➤➤ **sniveller** *noun,* **snivelling** *adj.* [Middle English *snivelen,* from (assumed) Old English *snyflan*]

snivel² *noun* the act or instance of snivelling.

snob /snob/ *noun* **1** somebody who tends to patronize or avoid those regarded as social inferiors. **2** somebody who blatantly attempts to cultivate or imitate those admired as social superiors: *Tom had no handkerchief, and he looked on boys who had, as snobs —*

Mark Twain. **3** somebody who has an air of smug superiority in matters of knowledge or taste: *a cultural snob.* **4** *archaic* a lowly person of vulgar tastes: *my impression being that your family are, in the aggregate, impertinent snobs; and, in detail, unmitigated ruffians —* Dickens. ➤➤ **snobbery** *noun,* **snobbish** *adj,* **snobbishly** *adv,* **snobbishness** *noun,* **snobbism** *noun,* **snobby** *adj.*

Word history

origin unknown; often said to be from *s.nob.,* short for Latin *sine nobilitate* without nobility, used in various contexts to distinguish persons not of noble birth, but there is no evidence to link such an abbreviation with the word *snob.* This originally meant a shoemaker, later any member of the lower classes; hence somebody who despises their own class and aspires to membership of a higher one.

SNOBOL /'snohbol/ *noun* a high-level computer language for handling strings of symbols. [short for *string oriented symbolic language*]

snoek /snoohk/ *noun* (*pl* **snoeks** *or collectively* **snoek**) *SAfr* any of several vigorous active marine fishes, e.g. the barracouta or barracuda. [via Afrikaans from Dutch *snoek* pike]

snog¹ /snog/ *verb intrans* (**snogged, snogging**) *Brit, informal* to kiss and cuddle. [perhaps alteration of SNUG²]

snog² *noun informal* the act or an instance or period of snogging.

snood /snoohd/ *noun* **1** a net or fabric bag worn at the back of a woman's head to hold the hair, *esp* in former times. **2** *Scot* a hair ribbon or band formerly worn by unmarried women. **3** a broad tubular knitted garment worn as a hood or scarf. [Old English *snōd*]

snook¹ /snoohk/ *noun* a gesture of derision made by putting the thumb to the nose and spreading the fingers out: *cock a snook.* [origin unknown]

snook² *noun* (*pl* **snooks** *or collectively* **snook**) a large Caribbean fish caught for food or sport: *Centropomus undecimalis.* [Dutch *snoek* pike]

snooker¹ /'snoohkə/ *noun* **1** a game played on a billiard table in which players hit a white ball with a cue in order to strike one of 21 coloured balls and send them in a set order into the pockets around the table: compare BILLIARDS, POOL². **2** a position of the balls in the game of snooker in which a direct shot would lose points.

Word history

said to be from British army slang *snooker* new military cadet, of unknown origin. The game was devised by army officers in India in the 1870s and is supposed to have been named by one of them because of the inept play of another.

snooker² *verb trans* (**snookered, snookering**) **1** to prevent (an opponent) from making a direct shot in snooker by playing the cue ball so that another ball lies between it and the target ball. **2a** *informal* to present an obstacle to (somebody or something): *The rain snookered our plans to have a picnic.* **b** to put (somebody or something) in a difficult or impossible position. ➤➤ **snookered** *adj..*

snoop¹ /snoohp/ *verb intrans* to look or pry in a sneaking or interfering manner. ➤➤ **snooper** *noun,* **snoopy** *adj.* [Dutch *snoepen* to buy or eat on the sly]

snoop² *noun* **1** somebody who snoops. **2** the act or an instance of snooping.

snoot /snooht/ *noun informal* a snout or nose. [Middle English *snute:* see SNOUT]

snooty *adj* (**snootier, snootiest**) *informal* **1** haughty; disdainful. **2** characterized by snobbish attitudes: *a snooty neighbourhood.* ➤➤ **snootily** *adv,* **snootiness** *noun.*

snooze¹ /snoohz/ *verb intrans informal* to sleep lightly for a short time; to take a nap. ➤➤ **snoozer** *noun.* [origin unknown]

snooze² *noun informal* a short light sleep; a nap. ➤➤ **snoozy** *adj.*

snore¹ /snaw/ *verb intrans* to breathe with a rough hoarse noise due to vibration of the soft palate during sleep. ➤➤ **snorer** *noun.* [Middle English *snoren* to snort; prob imitative]

snore² *noun* the act or sound of snoring.

snorkel¹ /'snawkl/ *noun* **1** a J-shaped tube allowing a swimmer or diver to breathe while face down in the water. **2** a tube that houses air intake and exhaust pipes and can be extended above the surface of the water from a submerged submarine. [German *Schnorchel*]

snorkel² *verb intrans* (**snorkelled, snorkelling,** *NAmer* **snorkeled, snorkeling**) to swim or operate submerged using a snorkel. ➤➤ **snorkeller** *noun.*

snort¹ /snawt/ *verb intrans* **1** to force air violently through the nose with a rough harsh sound. **2** to express scorn, anger, or surprise by a snort. ➤ *verb trans* **1a** to express (something) by a snort: *He snorted his contempt.* **b** to utter (something) with a snort. **2** *informal* to inhale (a drug): *snort coke.* [Middle English *snorten* to snort, snore; prob imitative]

snort² *noun* **1** an act or sound of snorting. **2** *informal* a small drink, usu of spirits. **3** *informal.* **a** the act or an instance of inhaling a drug. **b** an amount of a drug inhaled or to be inhaled.

snorter *noun* **1** somebody or something that snorts. **2** *informal* something extremely powerful, difficult, or impressive.

snot /snot/ *noun informal* **1** mucus from the nose. **2** a contemptible or unpleasant person. [Old English *gesnot*]

snotty *adj* (**snottier, snottiest**) *informal* **1** soiled or covered with nasal mucus. **2** arrogantly or snobbishly unpleasant. **3** contemptible; despicable.

snout /snowt/ *noun* **1** a long projecting nose, e.g. of a pig. **2a** a forward prolongation of the head of various animals. **b** the human nose, *esp* when large or grotesque. **3** something resembling an animal's snout in position, function, or shape, e.g. a nozzle. **4** *informal* a cigarette or tobacco. **5** *informal* an informer. ➤➤ **snouted** *adj,* **snouty** *adj.* [Middle English *snute* from early Dutch or early Low German *snūt*]

snow¹ /snoh/ *noun* **1a** white flakes falling from the sky that consist of small ice crystals formed directly from vapour in the atmosphere. **b** fallen snow. **c** (*also in pl*) a fall of snow. **2a** any of various congealed or crystallized substances resembling snow in appearance. **b** small transient light spots on a television or radar screen, usu caused by weakness or absence of a signal. **c** *informal* cocaine. ➤➤ **snowless** *adj.* [Old English *snāw*]

snow² *verb intrans* **1** to send down snow: *It snowed all day.* **2** to fall like snow. ➤ *verb trans* **1** to cause (something) to fall like snow. **2** (+ in/up) to cover, shut in, or block (something or somebody) with or as if with snow: *They found themselves snowed in after the blizzard.* **3** *chiefly NAmer* to deceive, persuade, or charm (somebody) glibly.

snowball¹ *noun* **1** a round mass of snow pressed or rolled together for throwing. **2** a cocktail drink made of advocaat with lemonade.

snowball² *verb trans* **1** to throw snowballs at (somebody or something). ➤ *verb intrans* **1** to throw snowballs. **2** to increase or expand at a rapidly accelerating rate.

snowberry /'snohb(ə)ri/ *noun* (*pl* **snowberries**) a low-growing shrub of the honeysuckle family with white berries and pink flowers in small clusters that is commonly planted in gardens: *Symphoricarpos albus.*

snow blindness *noun* painful sensitiveness to light or temporarily impaired vision caused by exposure of the eyes to ultraviolet rays reflected from snow or ice. ➤➤ **snow-blind** *adj.*

snowblink *noun* a white glare in the sky over an expanse of snow.

snowboard *noun* a board resembling a large skateboard or a short wide ski used to descend a snow-covered slope in a standing position. ➤➤ **snowboarder** *noun,* **snowboarding** *noun.*

snowbound *adj* confined or surrounded by snow.

snow bunting *noun* a Eurasian and N American BUNTING¹ (finchlike bird) that breeds in the arctic regions and is a winter visitor to Europe: *Plectrophenax nivalis.*

snowcap *noun* a covering of snow on a mountain top. ➤➤ **snowcapped** *adj.*

snowdrift *noun* a bank of snow blown together by the wind.

snowdrop *noun* a European plant of the daffodil family that grows from a bulb and bears nodding white flowers that appear in late winter or very early spring: *Galanthus nivalis.*

snowfall *noun* the amount of snow falling at one time or in a given period.

snowfield *noun* a broad level expanse of snow, *esp* a permanent mass of snow.

snowflake *noun* **1** a flake or crystal of snow. **2** any of several species of European plants with white flowers resembling those of the snowdrop: genus *Leucojum.*

snow goose *noun* a large white goose with black-tipped wings, that breeds chiefly in N America: *Anser caerulescens.*

snow-in-summer *noun* **1** a white-flowered creeping European plant of the pink family commonly grown in rock gardens: *Cerastium tomentosum.* **2** an Australian evergreen shrub: *Helichrysum rosmarinifolium.*

snow job *noun chiefly NAmer, informal* an attempt to persuade or deceive somebody by overwhelming them with information or flattery.

snow leopard *noun* a large mammal of the cat family of upland central Asia with long heavy fur that is irregularly blotched with brownish black in summer and almost pure white in winter: *Panthera uncia.* Also called OUNCE².

snow line *noun* the level, e.g. height above sea level or line of latitude, beyond which land is permanently covered in snow.

snowman *noun* (*pl* **snowmen**) a pile of snow shaped to resemble a human figure.

snowmobile /'snohməbeel/ *noun* any of various motor-powered vehicles for travel on snow. [SNOW¹ + AUTOMOBILE]

snowplough¹ (*NAmer* **snowplow**) *noun* **1** any of various vehicles or devices used for clearing snow. **2** in skiing, the act or an instance of snowploughing.

snowplough² (*NAmer* **snowplow**) *verb intrans* to force the heels of one's skis outward, keeping the tips together, in order to descend slowly, stop, or turn.

snowshoe¹ /'snohshooh/ *noun* a light oval wooden frame strung with thongs that is attached to the foot to enable a person to walk on soft snow without sinking.

snowshoe² *verb intrans* to walk or proceed in snowshoes. ➤➤ **snowshoer** *noun.*

snowstorm *noun* a storm of or with snow.

snow under *verb trans* (*usu in passive*) to overwhelm (somebody or something), *esp* with more than can be handled or absorbed: *We were snowed under with applications for the job.*

snow-white *adj* spotlessly white.

snowy *adj* (**snowier, snowiest**) **1a** composed of snow. **b** characterized by or covered with snow. **2** resembling snow, *esp* in whiteness. ➤➤ **snowily** *adv,* **snowiness** *noun.*

snowy owl *noun* a very large white arctic owl that is a winter visitor to Europe and N America: *Nyctea scandiaca.*

SNP *abbr* Scottish National Party.

snr *abbr* senior.

snub¹ /snub/ *verb trans* (**snubbed, snubbing**) **1** to treat (somebody or something) with contempt, *esp* by deliberately ignoring them or it: *Five dressy girls, of thirty-one or more: so gracious to the shy young men they snubbed so much before* — Lewis Carroll. **2a** to check (e.g. a rope) suddenly while running out, *esp* by winding it around a fixed object. **b** to halt or restrict the motion of (e.g. a boat) by snubbing a line. [Middle English *snubben* to rebuke sharply, from Old Norse *snubba* to rebuke or check]

snub² *noun* the act or an instance of snubbing, *esp* a slight.

snub³ *adj* said of a nose: short and slightly turned-up.

snub-nosed *adj* **1** having a short and slightly turned-up nose. **2** having a very short barrel: *a snub-nosed revolver.*

snuck /snuk/ *verb NAmer, informal* past tense and past part. of SNEAK¹: *'Where's Ruthie an' Winfiel'?' 'They snuck off after Pa.'* — John Steinbeck.

snuff¹ /snuf/ *verb trans* **1** to extinguish (a flame or candle), *esp* by the use of a snuffer. **2** (+ out) to make (something) extinct; to put an end to (it), *esp* suddenly or unexpectedly: *an accident that snuffed out a life.* **3** to trim the snuff of (a candle), *esp* by the use of snuffers. *** snuff it** *informal* to die.

snuff² *noun* the charred part of a candle wick. [Middle English *snoffe,* of unknown origin]

snuff³ *noun* a preparation of powdered often scented tobacco usu inhaled through the nostrils. *** up to snuff 1** *informal* up to standard. **2** *informal* in good health or condition. **3** *Brit, dated, informal* not easily deceived. [Dutch *snuf,* short for *snuftabak,* from *snuffen* to snuff + *tabak* tobacco]

snuff⁴ *verb trans* to inhale, smell, or sniff at (something). ➤ *verb intrans* **1** to inhale or sniff. **2** to take snuff. [Middle English from early Dutch *snuffen* to sniff, snuff]

snuffbox *noun* a small often ornate box for holding snuff.

snuffer *noun* **1** an implement consisting of a small hollow cone attached to a handle, used for extinguishing candles. **2** (*in pl*) an implement resembling a pair of scissors, used for trimming the wick of a candle.

snuffle¹ /'snufl/ *verb intrans* **1a** to sniff, usu audibly and repeatedly. **b** to draw air through an obstructed nose with a sniffing sound. **2** to speak in nasal or whining tones. *▶ verb trans* to utter (something) with a sniffing sound or in nasal tones. *▶▶* **snuffler** *noun*. [prob from Low German and Dutch *snuffelen*]

snuffle² *noun* **1** the act or sound of snuffling. **2** a nasal twang. **3** (**the snuffles**) a cold in the nose. *▶▶* **snuffly** *adj*.

snuff movie *noun informal* a pornographic film in which one of the participants is actually murdered during filming. [from *snuff* it: see SNUFF¹]

snuffy¹ /'snufi/ *adj* (**snuffier, snuffiest**) **1** quick to become annoyed; huffy. **2** supercilious; disdainful.

snuffy² *adj* (**snuffier, snuffiest**) **1** resembling snuff. **2** addicted to the use of snuff. **3** soiled with snuff.

snug¹ /snug/ *adj* (**snugger, snuggest**) **1** enjoying or giving warm secure comfort or shelter; cosy. **2a** fitting closely and usu comfortably: *a snug coat*. **b** tight or figure-hugging: *a snug fit*. **3** *archaic* offering or having a degree of comfort and ease: *a snug income*. *▶▶* **snugly** *adv*, **snugness** *noun*. [orig in the sense 'shipshape', perhaps of Scandinavian origin]

snug² *verb* (**snugged, snugging**) *▶ verb intrans* to snuggle. *▶ verb trans* to make (something or somebody) snug.

snug³ *noun Brit* a small private room or compartment in a pub. [short for SNUGGERY]

snuggery *noun* (*pl* **snuggeries**) **1** *chiefly Brit* a snug cosy place, *esp* a small private room. **2** = SNUG³.

snuggle /'snugl/ *verb intrans* **1** to curl up comfortably or cosily; to nestle. **2** to draw close, *esp* for comfort or in affection: *She snuggled up to her father*. [frequentative of SNUG²]

SO *abbr* Somalia (international vehicle registration).

So. *abbr* south.

so¹ /soh/ *adv* **1a** in this way; thus: *while she was so employed*. **b** used as a substitute for a preceding word or word group: *Do you really think so?* **c** in the same way; also: *I worked hard and so did she*. **d** correspondingly: *As the wind increased, so the sea grew rougher*. **e** in such a way: *The book is so written that a child could understand it*. **f** used to introduce the idea of purpose: *He hid so as not to get caught*. **2a** to such an extreme degree: *had never been so happy*. **b** used to introduce a comparison: *not so fast as mine*. **c** used to introduce a result: *so fast that I couldn't keep up*. **d** very: *I'm so glad you could come*. **e** to a definite but unspecified extent or degree: *We can only do so much in a day*. **f** most certainly; indeed: *I hope to win and so I shall*. **3** therefore; consequently: *The witness is biased and so unreliable*. **4** then; subsequently: *and so to bed*. **5** *chiefly dialect* used to counter a negative charge: *You did so!* ✳ **and so forth/and so on 1** and others or more of the same kind. **2** and further in the same manner. **3** and the rest. **so be it** used to express often resigned acceptance. **so many 1** a certain number of: *read so many chapters each night*. **2** used as an intensive before plurals: *behaved like so many animals*. **so much 1** to the degree indicated or suggested: *If they lose their way, so much the better for us*. **2** a certain amount of: *I can only spend so much time on it*. **3** used as an intensive before mass nouns: *It sounded like so much nonsense*. **4** an unspecified or undetermined amount, price, etc: *charge so much a mile*. **5** all that can or need be said or done: *so much for the history of the case*. **so much as** even: *I can't so much as remember his name now*. [Old English *swā*]

so² *conj* **1** with the result that: *Her diction is good, so every word is clear*. **2** in order that: *Be quiet so he can sleep*. **3** for that reason; therefore: *I don't want to go, so I won't*. **4a** used as an introductory particle: *So here we are*. **b** used to belittle a point under discussion: *So what?* **c** used to indicate awareness of a discovery: *so, that's who did it*.

so³ *adj* **1** conforming with actual facts; true: *She said things that were not so*. **2** disposed in a definite order: *His books are always exactly so*.

so⁴ *pronoun* such as has been specified or suggested; the same: *He became chairman and remained so*. ✳ **or so** used to indicate an approximation or conjecture: *I've known her 20 years or so*.

so⁵ *noun* see SOH.

soak¹ /sohk/ *verb intrans* **1** to lie immersed in liquid, e.g. water, *esp* so as to become saturated or softened: *put the clothes to soak*. **2a** (*usu* + in/into/through) to enter or pass through something by or as if by pores or small openings; to permeate. **b** (+ in) to become fully felt or appreciated. *▶ verb trans* **1** to make (something or somebody) thoroughly wet. **2a** to immerse (something) in a liquid to wet or permeate it thoroughly. **b** to immerse the mind and feelings of (oneself or somebody else): *soak yourself in history*. **3** to extract

(something) by or as if by immersion in a liquid: *soak the dirt out*. **4a** (*often* + up) to draw (something) in by or as if by absorption: *soaked up the sunshine*. **b** *informal, archaic* to intoxicate (oneself) with alcohol. **5** *informal* to charge (somebody) an excessive amount of money: *soak the taxpayers*. *▶▶* **soakage** /'sohkij/ *noun*, **soaked** *adj*, **soaker** *noun*, **soaking** *adj and noun*. [Old English *socian*; related to Old English *sūcan* to suck]

soak² *noun* **1a** the act or an instance or period of soaking or being soaked. **b** the liquid, etc in which something is soaked. **2** *informal* a person who drinks alcohol to excess, *esp* habitually. **3** *Aus* a natural depression where rainwater collects.

soakaway *noun Brit* a hole dug in the ground into which rain or waste water flows and naturally drains away.

so-and-so *noun* (*pl* **so-and-sos**) **1** an unnamed or unspecified person or thing: *Miss So-and-so*. **2** *euphem* a disliked or unpleasant person: *the cheeky so-and-so!*

soap¹ /sohp/ *noun* **1** a substance used to cleanse and EMULSIFY (stabilize oil-and-water mixtures) that lathers when rubbed in water and consists essentially of chemical salts formed by the combination of sodium or potassium with fatty acids: *I write letters blatant on medicines patent … and vow my complexion derives its perfection from somebody's soap – which it doesn't* — W S Gilbert. **2** a chemical salt formed by the combination of a fatty acid with a metal. **3** = SOAP OPERA. ✳ **no soap** *informal* no chance; not possible. *▶▶* **soapless** *adj*. [Old English *sāpe*]

soap² *verb trans* **1** to rub soap over or into (something or somebody). **2** *informal* (*often* + up) to flatter (somebody).

soapberry /'sohpb(ə)ri, 'sohpberi/ *noun* (*pl* **soapberries**) **1** a berry-like fruit that has a high saponin content, produces a frothy lather when crushed, and is used as a soap substitute. **2** any of several species of tropical trees or shrubs that bear this fruit: chiefly in genus *Sapindus*.

soapbox *noun* **1** an improvised platform used by an informal orator. **2** any public forum that allows people to express their views, exchange ideas, etc: *Internet newsgroups act as modern day soapboxes*.

soap opera *noun* a serialized radio or television drama usu dealing with the domestic lives of a group of characters who live or work in the same place. [because such programmes were formerly sponsored in the USA by soap manufacturers]

soapstone *noun* a soft greyish green or brown stone having a soapy feel and composed mainly of talc.

soapwort *noun* a European plant of the pink family that has clusters of pink or white flowers and leaves that yield a detergent when bruised: *Saponaria officinalis*.

soapy *adj* (**-ier, -iest, soapier, soapiest**) **1a** covered with soap; lathered. **b** containing or combined with soap. **2a** smooth and slippery. **b** suave; ingratiating. *▶▶* **soapily** *adv*, **soapiness** *noun*.

soar¹ /saw/ *verb intrans* **1a** to fly or rise high into the air. **b** to sail, glide, or hover in the air, often at a great height. **c** said *esp* of a glider: to fly using thermals (upward currents of hot air; see THERMAL²) to maintain or gain height. **2** to rise rapidly or to a very high level: *The temperature soared*. **3** to rise upward in position or status: *a soaring reputation*. **4** to be of imposing height or stature; to tower: *Mountains soared above us*. *▶▶* **soarer** *noun*, **soaring** *adj and noun*, **soaringly** *adv*. [Middle English *soren* from early French *essorer* to air, soar, from EX-¹ + Latin *aura* air]

soar² *noun* **1** the act or an instance of soaring; upward flight. **2** the range, distance, or height attained in soaring.

sob¹ /sob/ *verb* (**sobbed, sobbing**) *▶ verb intrans* **1** to weep with convulsive catching of the breath. **2** to make a sound like that of a sob or sobbing. *▶ verb trans* **1** to bring (e.g. oneself) to a specified state by sobbing: *He sobbed himself to sleep*. **2** to express or utter (something) with sobs: *She sobbed her grief*. *▶▶* **sobbing** *adj and noun*. [Middle English *sobben*, of Germanic origin]

sob² *noun* the act or an instance, bout, or sound of sobbing.

s.o.b. *abbr NAmer, informal* son of a bitch.

sober¹ /'sohbə/ *adj* **1a** not drunk. **b** not addicted to alcohol. **2** gravely or earnestly thoughtful. **3** calmly self-controlled; sedate. **4a** well balanced; realistic: *the sober truth*. **b** sane; rational. **5** subdued in tone or colour. *▶▶* **soberly** *adv*, **soberness** *noun*. [Middle English *sobre* via French from Latin *sobrius*]

sober[2] *verb* (**sobered, sobering**) ➤ *verb intrans* (*usu* + up) to become sober. ➤ *verb trans* (*usu* + up) to make (somebody) sober. ➤➤ **sobering** *adj*.

sobriety /sə'brieiti/ *noun formal* the state, quality, or fact of being sober. [Middle English *sobrietie* via French from Latin *sobrietat-, sobrietas*, from *sobrius* SOBER]

sobriquet /'sohbrikay/ *or* **soubriquet** /'sooh-, 'soh-/ *noun* a nick-name: *The Useless Quack joined the Navy and grew a gingery beard, which enabled Lewis (always anxious to invent fresh sobriquets for his friends) to label him the Red Admiral* — A N Wilson. [French *sobriquet* from early French *soubriquet* tap under the chin, nickname]

sob story *noun informal* a sentimental story or account intended to elicit sympathy, esp for the person telling it.

Soc. *abbr* **1** socialist. **2** society.

soca /'sohkə/ *noun* a style of popular music, associated particularly with Trinidad, blending elements of soul and calypso. [blend of SOUL + CALYPSO]

socage *or* **soccage** /'sokij/ *noun* feudal tenure of land usu in return for agricultural service or payment of rent and without any duty to perform military service. [Middle English, from *soc*: see SOKE]

so-called *adj* **1** commonly named; popularly so termed: *involved in so-called campus politics.* **2** falsely or improperly so named: *deceived by his so-called friend.*

soccage /'sokij/ *noun* see SOCAGE.

soccer /'sokə/ *noun* = ASSOCIATION FOOTBALL. [by shortening and alteration of ASSOCIATION FOOTBALL]

sociable[1] /'sohshəbl/ *adj* **1** inclined to seek or enjoy companion-ship; companionable. **2** marked by or conducive to friendliness or cordial social relations: *We spent a sociable evening at the club.* ➤➤ **sociability** /-'biliti/ *noun,* **sociableness** *noun,* **sociably** *adv.* [via French from Latin *sociabilis,* from *sociare* to join, associate, from *socius* companion, associate]

Usage note
sociable or **social**? See note at SOCIAL[1].

sociable[2] *noun* **1** *NAmer* = SOCIAL[2]. **2** a type of open carriage with two inward facing seats positioned opposite each other.

social[1] /'sohsh(ə)l/ *adj* **1** of human society: *social institutions.* **2a** of or based on status in a particular society: *his social set.* **b** of the upper classes: *a column of social gossip.* **3a** sociable. **b** of, involving, or pro-moting companionship or friendly interaction with others: *a social evening.* **4a** tending to form cooperative relationships; gregarious: *Humans are social beings.* **b** living and breeding in more or less organized communities: *social insects.* **c** said of a plant: tending to grow thickly in patches or clumps. ➤➤ **socially** *adv.* [Latin *socialis,* from *socius* companion, ally, associate]

Usage note
social or **sociable**? *Social,* as an adjective, is an all-purpose neutral word meaning 'connected with society': *social conditions; social work. Sociable* is a complimentary term used mainly to describe people meaning 'fond of company' or 'friendly': *She's feeling very sociable this evening.*

social[2] *noun* a social gathering, usu connected with a church or club.

social anthropology *noun* the branch of anthropology that deals with the development of and comparison between human societies and cultures.

social climber *noun derog* somebody who strives to gain a higher social position or acceptance in fashionable society. ➤➤ **social climbing** *noun.*

social compact *noun* = SOCIAL CONTRACT.

social contract *noun* an actual or supposed agreement among individuals forming an organized society or between the commu-nity and the governing power that defines and limits the rights and duties of each, *esp* one under which certain individual freedoms are surrendered in return for state protection. [translation of French *contrat social*]

social democracy *noun* a political movement advocating a gradual and peaceful transition from capitalism to socialism by democratic means. ➤➤ **social democratic** *adj,* **social democrat** *noun.*

social exclusion *noun* a situation in which a person or social group lacks the opportunity to participate fully in the social, polit-ical, and cultural life of their community, for example because of unemployment, low income, or a low level of education: compare SOCIAL INCLUSION.

social fund *noun* in the UK, a fund set up as part of the social security system from which people in need may receive money as a grant or loan for a specified purpose.

social inclusion *noun* a situation that provides a person or social group with the opportunity to have a reasonable quality of life and participate fully in the social, political, and cultural life of their community, etc: compare SOCIAL EXCLUSION.

social insurance *noun* a compulsory state insurance system, usu funded by contributions from employers and employees, that pro-vides assistance for the sick, the old, the unemployed, etc.

socialise *verb trans* see SOCIALIZE.

socialism *noun* **1a** an economic and political theory advocating collective or state ownership and administration of the means of production and distribution of goods. **b** an economic or political system based on this.

Editorial note
The social emphasis in socialism is shown by the fact that, in the 19th cent., it was contrasted often with individualism rather than with capitalism. The democratic state apparently offered a means of achieving socialism by con-sent – a strategy to which social democrats adhered, despite electoral set-backs, while Communists instead opted for the shortcut of revolution and autocracy — Professor Peter Clarke.

2 in Marxist theory, a transitional stage of society in which the means of production is under collective control but goods are dis-tributed according to work done.

socialist[1] *noun* **1** somebody who advocates or practises socialism. **2** (**Socialist**) a member of a party that advocates socialism.

socialist[2] *adj* **1** of socialism. **2** (**Socialist**) of or being a party that advocates socialism.

socialistic /sohshəl'istik/ *adj* of or tending towards socialism. ➤➤ **socialistically** *adv.*

socialist realism *noun* **1** in Communist countries, *esp* the former Soviet Union under Stalin, a theory of the role and function of the arts in an evolving socialist state that evaluates artistic pro-duction according to the extent to which it reaffirms the ideals and goals of Communism. **2** crudely propagandistic art produced in Communist countries exalting the dignity of labour, the wisdom of the leadership, etc.

socialite /'sohshəliet/ *noun* somebody who is socially active or prominent, *esp* in fashionable society.

sociality /sohshi'aliti/ *noun* **1** the tendency to associate in or form social groups. **2** the state or quality of being sociable or social.

socialize *or* **socialise** *verb intrans* to behave or interact in a soci-able manner: *He likes to socialize with his colleagues.* ➤ *verb trans* **1a** to make (somebody) fit or prepared for life in society. **b** to train (an animal, *esp* a dog) to behave well in public, *esp* to make (it) interact well with other animals. **2** to adapt (something) to social needs or uses: *socialize science.* **3** to constitute (something) on a socialist basis: *socialize industry.* ➤➤ **socialization** /-'zaysh(ə)n/ *noun,* **socializer** *noun.*

social market *noun* an economic system in which a free market operates with equality of opportunity and social responsibility, supplemented by state assistance for the old, the unemployed, etc.

social realism *noun* the use of realism in art for the purpose of social or political comment.

social science *noun* **1** the scientific study of human society and the relationships between its members. **2** a subject, e.g. economics or politics, dealing with a particular aspect of human society. ➤➤ **social scientist** *noun.*

social secretary *noun* somebody who arranges and handles the social engagements of a person or group.

social security *noun* **1** state provision, e.g. through retirement, etc pensions, unemployment benefit, sickness benefit, etc, for the economic security and social welfare of individuals. **2** a social security allowance made to help people to meet the basic costs of living.

social service *noun* **1** activity or assistance designed to promote social welfare. **2** (*in pl*) organized services, e.g. education or hous-ing, provided by the state for this purpose.

social studies *pl noun* (*treated as sing.*) a branch of study relating to social relationships and the functioning of human society.

social work *noun* the activities of any of various professional agencies concerned with the aid of underprivileged or disadvan-taged members of society. ➤➤ **social worker** *noun.*

societal /sə'sie-ətl/ *adj* of society: *societal forces*. ⟫ **societally** *adv*.

society /sə'sieiti/ *noun* (*pl* **societies**) **1** the human race considered in terms of its structure of social institutions: *Society cannot tolerate lawlessness*. **2** a community having common traditions, institutions, and collective interests: *There is no such thing as society; there are individual men and women, and there are families* — Margaret Thatcher. **3a** a clearly identifiable social circle: *literary society*. **b** a class of wealthy or privileged people regarded as arbiters of fashion or manners. **c** (*used before a noun*) of this class of people: *a society wedding*. **4** (*often* **Society**) an organized group working together or periodically meeting because of common interests, beliefs, or profession: *the Royal Society; He joined the local society of creative writers*. **5** companionship or association with others; company: *She prefers the society of other women*. **6** a natural group of plants or animals, usu of a single species. [early French *société* from Latin *societat-, societas*, from *socius* companion]

socio- *comb. form* **1** forming words, denoting: society and: *socioeconomic*. **2** forming words, with the meanings: **a** social: *sociolinguistics*. **b** social and: *sociopolitical*. [French *socio-* from Latin *socius* companion]

sociobiology /ˌsohsiohbie'oləji, ˌsohshi-/ *noun* the scientific study of animal behaviour from the point of view that all behaviour has evolved by natural selection. ⟫ **sociobiological** /-'lojikl/ *adj*, **sociobiologically** /-'lojikli/ *adv*, **sociobiologist** *noun*.

socioeconomic /ˌsohsiohekə'nomik, -eekə'nomik, ˌsohshi-/ *adj* of or involving a combination of social and economic factors.

sociolinguistics /ˌsohsiohling'gwistiks, ˌsohshi-/ *pl noun* (*treated as sing.*) the study of language as determined by social and cultural factors. ⟫ **sociolinguist** /-'ling-gwist/ *noun*, **sociolinguistic** /-'tik/ *adj*, **sociolinguistically** /-'tikli/ *adv*.

sociology /sohsi'oləji, sohshi-/ *noun* the scientific study of social institutions and relationships, *esp* the development and behaviour of organized human groups. ⟫ **sociological** /-'lojikl/ *adj*, **sociologically** /-'lojikli/ *adv*, **sociologist** *noun*.

sociometry /sohsi'omətri, sohshi-/ *noun* the scientific study and measurement of social relationships within a particular group of people. ⟫ **sociometric** /-'metrik/ *adj*, **sociometrist** *noun*.

sociopath /'sohsiohpath, 'sohshi-/ *noun* somebody suffering from an emotional and behavioural disorder characterized by asocial or antisocial behaviour; *broadly* a psychopath. ⟫ **sociopathic** /-'pathik/ *adj*, **sociopathy** /-'opəthi/ *noun*.

sock¹ /sok/ *noun* **1** a usu knitted covering for the foot extending above the ankle and sometimes to the knee. **2** an insole for a shoe. **3** a light shoe worn by actors in comedy in ancient Greece and Rome: *then to the well-trod stage anon, if Jonson's learned sock be on* — Milton. ✳ **pull one's socks up** *informal* to make a determined effort to do better. **put a sock in it** *Brit, informal* to stop talking. [Old English *socc* light shoe, via Latin *soccus* from Greek *sukkhos*]

sock² *verb trans informal* to hit (somebody or something) forcefully. ✳ **sock it to** *informal, dated* to impress or astound (somebody) by doing something very well or vigorously. [prob of Scandinavian origin]

sock³ *noun informal* a vigorous or forceful blow; a punch: *I gave him a sock on the chin*.

socket¹ /'sokit/ *noun* **1** an opening or hollow that forms a holder for something or into which something fits, e.g. any of various bony hollows in the body: *the eye socket*. **2** a device in an electrical circuit into which a plug, bulb, etc can be fitted. **3** a short tube that is shaped at one end to fit over a nut or bolt and has a square hole at the other end to receive the driving shaft of a tool. [Middle English *soket* from Anglo-French, dimin of Old French *soc* ploughshare, of Celtic origin]

socket² *verb trans* (**socketed, socketing**) **1** to provide (something) with a socket. **2** to place (something) in a socket.

sockeye *noun* (*pl* **sockeyes** *or collectively* **sockeye**) a small but commercially important Pacific salmon that swims up rivers of the N USA and Canada to spawn in spring: *Oncorhynchus nerka*. [by folk etymology from Salish, an Algonquian language, dialect *suk-kegh*, literally 'fish of fishes']

socking *adv chiefly Brit, informal* extremely: *a socking great pile of bricks*.

socle /'sokl/ *noun* a plain projecting part at the base of a wall or column. [French *socle* from Italian *zoccolo* wooden shoe, socle, from Latin *socculus*, dimin of *soccus*: see SOCK¹]

Socratic¹ /so'kratik/ *adj* characteristic of the philosophy of Socrates (d.399 BC), *esp* in relation to his method of achieving knowledge through question-and-answer sessions and deliberately casting doubt on accepted beliefs. ⟫ **Socratically** *adv*.

Socratic² *noun* a follower of Socrates.

Socratic irony *noun* a pretence of ignorance in order to entice others into exposing their pretensions of knowledge through skilful questioning.

sod¹ /sod/ *noun* **1** a clump of grass together with the roots and surrounding soil; a piece of turf. **2** *literary* the grass-covered surface of the ground. [Middle English from early Dutch or early Low German *sode*]

sod² *noun chiefly Brit* **1** *slang* an objectionable person. **2** *informal, chiefly humorous* a person: *He's not a bad little sod taken by and large* — Noel Coward. **3** *informal* something difficult, trying, or unpleasant. ✳ **sod all** *Brit, slang* nothing at all. [short for SODOMITE]

sod³ *verb trans* (**sodded, sodding**) *Brit, slang* usu used in the imperative as an oath: to damn: *Sod you!*

soda /'sohdə/ *noun* **1** any of several chemical compounds containing sodium, e.g. sodium carbonate, sodium bicarbonate, or sodium hydroxide. **2a** = SODA WATER. **b** *chiefly NAmer* a sweet fizzy drink. [via Italian from medieval Latin *soda* barilla plant, formerly burned as a source of sodium carbonate, from Arabic *suwwad* saltwort]

soda ash *noun* commercial sodium carbonate in a form that does not contain water.

soda bread *noun* a bread raised with sodium bicarbonate and cream of tartar as distinct from yeast-leavened bread.

soda fountain *noun* **1** *chiefly NAmer* an apparatus with a delivery tube and taps for dispensing soda water. **2** *NAmer* a shop or counter where sodas, ice cream, etc are prepared and served.

sodality /soh'daliti/ *noun* (*pl* **sodalities**) **1** a brotherhood or community. **2** an organized society or fellowship; *specif* a devotional or charitable association of lay Roman Catholics. [Latin *sodalitat-, sodalitas* comradeship, club, from *sodalis* comrade]

soda siphon *noun* = SIPHON¹ (bottle for aerated water).

soda water *noun* **1** water containing carbon dioxide under pressure causing it to fizz. **2** a drink of this.

sodden¹ /'sod(ə)n/ *adj* **1** full of moisture or water; saturated: *the sodden ground*. **2** heavy, damp, or doughy because of imperfect cooking: *sodden bread*. **3** (*usu used in combinations*). **a** said of a person: having drunk an excessive amount of a specified type of alcohol. **b** said of a person's mind, speech, etc: impaired because of this: *his whisky-sodden brain*. ⟫ **soddenly** *adv*, **soddenness** *noun*. [Middle English *soden* boiled, archaic past part. of *sethen* to SEETHE]

sodden² *verb* (**soddened, soddening**) ⟫ *verb trans* to make (something) sodden. ⟫ *verb intrans* to become sodden.

sodding /'soding/ *adj and adv Brit, slang* used as an intensifier to express annoyance, exasperation, etc: *Shut the sodding door!*

sodium /'sohdi-əm/ *noun* a silver-white metallic chemical element of the alkali metal group that is soft, waxy, and easily worked, occurs abundantly in nature in combination with other chemical compounds, is very reactive chemically, is an essential element for living organisms, and is used in industry: symbol Na, atomic number 11. [scientific Latin, from SODA + -IUM]

sodium bicarbonate *noun* a white weakly alkaline chemical compound used *esp* in baking powders, in fire extinguishers, and in medicine to neutralize stomach acidity: formula $NaHCO_3$. Also called BAKING SODA, SODIUM HYDROGENCARBONATE.

sodium carbonate *noun* a chemical compound used *esp* in making soaps and chemicals, in water softening, in cleaning and bleaching, and in photography: formula Na_2CO_3.

sodium chloride *noun* a chemical compound used *esp* as a seasoning for food; common salt: formula NaCl.

sodium hydrogencarbonate *noun technical* = SODIUM BICARBONATE.

sodium hydroxide *noun* a white brittle caustic solid chemical compound used *esp* in making soap, rayon, and paper: formula NaOH. Also called CAUSTIC SODA.

sodium lamp *noun* = SODIUM-VAPOUR LAMP.

sodium thiosulphate /thie-oh'sulfayt/ *noun* a chemical compound used *esp* as a photographic fixing agent and as a bleach: formula $Na_2S_2O_3$.

sodium-vapour lamp *noun* an electric lamp used *esp* for street lighting in which the discharge takes place through sodium vapour causing a characteristic yellow-orange light.

sod off *verb intrans Brit, slang* to go away.

Sodom /'sodəm/ *noun* a place that is noted for its depravity, corruption, wickedness, etc. [from *Sodom*, a city in ancient Palestine that, together with Gomorrah, was destroyed by God as a punishment for the depravity of its citizens (Gen. 19:24)]

sodomise /'sodəmiez/ *verb trans* see SODOMIZE.

sodomite /'sodəmiet/ *noun* somebody who practises sodomy.

sodomize *or* **sodomise** /'sodəmiez/ *verb trans* to have anal intercourse with (somebody).

sodomy /'sodəmi/ *noun* sexual intercourse other than normal vaginal intercourse between a man and a woman, *esp* the penetration of the penis into the anus of another male or a female. [Middle English from Old French *sodomie*, from late Latin *Sodoma* Sodom, city of ancient Palestine; from the homosexual desires of the men of Sodom (Genesis 19:1–11)]

sod's law *or* **Sod's Law** *noun* = MURPHY'S LAW. [SOD²]

soever /soh'evə/ *adv literary* to any possible or known extent: *how fair soever she may be.*

-soever *comb. form* forming words, with the meaning: of any kind; at all: *whatsoever; howsoever.*

sofa /'sohfə/ *noun* a long upholstered seat with a back and two arms or raised ends that typically seats two to four people. [Arabic *ṣuffah* long bench]

sofa bed *noun* a sofa that can be converted into a bed, *esp* by unfolding the seat part.

soffit /'sofit/ *noun* the underside of an overhanging part of a building, a staircase, an arch, etc. [French *soffite* from Italian *soffitto*, from Latin *suffixus*, past part. of Latin *suffigere*: see SUFFIX¹]

S. of Sol. *abbr* Song of Solomon (book of the Bible).

soft¹ /soft/ *adj* **1a** yielding to physical pressure: *a soft mattress; soft ground.* **b** of a consistency that may be shaped, moulded, spread, or easily cut: *soft dough; soft cheese.* **c** relatively lacking in hardness: *soft wood.* **2a** pleasing or agreeable to the senses; bringing ease or comfort. **b** smooth or delicate in texture; not rough: *soft cashmere.* **c** not bright or glaring; subdued: *a soft glow.* **d** quiet in pitch or volume; not harsh. **e** said of the consonants *c* and *g*: pronounced /s/ and /j/ respectively, e.g. in *acid* and *age.* **3** deficient in or free from substances, e.g. chemical compounds containing calcium or magnesium, that prevent lathering of soap: *soft water.* **4a** falling, blowing, etc with slight force; not violent: *soft breezes.* **b** balmy or mild in weather or temperature. **c** marked by restraint; not of the most extreme kind: *soft porn.* **d** said of a drug: not of the most addictive or harmful kind. **5a** marked by kindness, leniency, or moderation. **b** based on negotiation and conciliation rather than on a show of power or on threats: *take a soft line.* **c** *informal* demanding little effort; easy. **6a** lacking resilience or strength, *esp* as a result of pampering or luxury. **b** not protected against enemy attack; vulnerable. **c** *informal* mentally deficient; foolish: *soft in the head.* **7a** easily affected with tender emotions; impressionable. **b** readily influenced or imposed upon; compliant. **c** lacking firmness or strength of character; feeble. **8a** said of radiation: having relatively low energy. **b** said *esp* of iron: easily magnetized and demagnetized. **c** not sharply outlined, *esp* having a slight intentional blurring: *a photograph in soft focus.* **9** marked by a gradually declining trend: *Wool prices are increasingly soft.* ✴ **have a soft spot for** to have a fondness or sentimental weakness for (somebody or something). **soft on 1** amorously attracted to (somebody), *esp* secretly. **2** taking a lenient or compassionate view of (something or somebody); reacting to or treating (them) without severity: *It's not our policy to be soft on truants.* ➤➤ **softish** *adj*, **softly** *adv*, **softness** *noun*. [Old English *sōfte* calm, gentle, agreeable]

soft² *noun* a soft object, material, or part: *the soft of the thumb.*

soft³ *adv* **1** in a soft or gentle manner: *How soft the poplars sigh* — A E Housman. **2** in a weak or foolish manner: *Don't talk so soft.* **3** *archaic (as an interjection)* used to interrupt oneself or break into a conversation: *But soft! methinks I do digress too much* — Shakespeare.

softa /'softə/ *noun* a Muslim student of divinity and sacred law. [Turkish *softa* from Persian *sōkhtah* on fire]

softball *noun* a game similar to baseball played on a smaller field with a larger softer ball.

soft-boiled *adj* said of an egg: cooked to the point at which the white solidifies but the yolk remains unset.

soft coal *noun* = BITUMINOUS COAL.

soft copy *noun* information stored in a computer's memory or shown on a screen and not in physical form: compare HARD COPY.

soft-core *adj* said of pornography: mildly titillating; excluding highly explicit pictures or descriptions of sexual acts.

soft-cover *adj* said of a book: bound in flexible covers; *specif* paperback.

soft drink *noun* a non-alcoholic drink that is usu served cold.

soften /'sof(ə)n/ *verb* (**softened, softening**) ➤ *verb trans* **1** to make (something or somebody) soft or softer. **2** (*often* + up) to impair the strength or resistance of (somebody or something): *She tried to soften him up with compliments.* ➤ *verb intrans* to become soft or softer. ➤➤ **softener** *noun.*

soft fruit *noun chiefly Brit* an edible fruit, e.g. a strawberry, raspberry, or blackcurrant, that is small, stoneless, and grows on low bushes.

soft furnishings *pl noun chiefly Brit* articles made of cloth, e.g. curtains or chair covers, that increase the comfort or improve the appearance of a room or piece of furniture.

soft goods *pl noun* textiles and textile products, e.g. clothing.

soft-headed *adj* foolish; stupid. ➤➤ **soft-headedness** *noun.*

soft-hearted *adj* kind; compassionate. ➤➤ **soft-heartedly** *adv*, **soft-heartedness** *noun.*

softie *or* **softy** /'softi/ *noun* (*pl* **softies**) **1** *informal* a sentimental or soft-hearted person. **2** a feeble person. **3** a foolish or gullible person.

softly-softly *adj Brit* characterized by caution, patience, or guile: *a softly-softly approach to delicate problems.* [from the proverb *softly softly catchee monkey*]

soft option *noun* (**the soft option**) the choice, out of a number of alternatives, that is easiest or that seems to involve the least difficulty.

soft palate *noun* the fleshy part at the back of the HARD PALATE (roof of the mouth) that partially separates the mouth and throat.

soft-paste porcelain *noun* a type of artificial porcelain, usu containing some glass or clay and fired at a lower temperature than genuine porcelain.

soft pedal *noun* a foot pedal on a piano that reduces the volume of sound.

soft-pedal *verb trans* (**soft-pedalled, soft-pedalling**, *NAmer* **soft-pedaled, soft-pedaling**) **1** to attempt to minimize the importance of (something), *esp* by talking cleverly or evasively; to play (it) down: *soft-pedal the issue of arms sales.* **2** to use the soft pedal in playing (a piano).

soft sell *noun* the use of suggestion or gentle persuasion in selling rather than aggressive pressure: compare HARD SELL.

soft-shell clam *noun* an edible N American clam with a long thin shell: *Mya arenaria.* Also called STEAMER CLAM.

soft-shoe *adj* relating to or denoting tap dancing done in soft-soled shoes without metal taps.

soft shoulder *noun chiefly NAmer* an unsurfaced strip of land at the edge of a road.

soft soap *noun* **1** a semifluid soap. **2** *informal* flattery.

soft-soap *verb trans informal* to persuade or mollify (somebody) with flattery or smooth talk.

soft-spoken *adj* **1** having a soft or gentle voice. **2** suave.

soft touch *noun informal* a person who is easily imposed on or taken advantage of, *esp* somebody who is known to be willing to lend money.

software *noun* the entire set of programs, procedures, and related documentation associated with a computer system: compare HARDWARE (I).

Editorial note ━━━━━━━━━━━━━━━━━━━━━━━━━━━━━
Essentially there are three types of software. Application software performs useful tasks for the computer's user, such as word processing, accounting, or drawing. System software, like an operating system, performs tasks that control the computer. Development software (e.g. a language compiler) is used by programmers to write more software — Dick Pountain.

softwood *noun* the wood of a coniferous tree.

softy *noun* see SOFTIE.

soggy /'sogi/ *adj* (**soggier, soggiest**) **1a** waterlogged; soaked: *a soggy lawn*. **b** heavy, damp, or doughy because of imperfect cooking: *soggy pastry*. **2** heavily dull: *soggy prose*. >> **soggily** *adv*, **sogginess** *noun*. [English dialect *sog* marsh + -Y[1]]

soh *or* **so** /soh/ *noun* in music, the fifth note of a major scale in the tonic sol-fa system, or the note G in the fixed-doh system. [Middle English *sol* from medieval Latin: see GAMUT]

soi-disant /swah 'deezonh (*French* swa dizã)/ *adj* self-styled; so-called: *a soi-disant artist*. [French *soi-disant*, literally 'calling oneself']

soigné *or* **soignée** /'swahnyay/ *adj* said of a man or woman: well-groomed; elegant. [French *soigné*, past part. of *soigner* to take care of, from late Latin *soniare*]

soil[1] /soyl/ *noun* **1a** loose material composed of weathered rock fragments and usu decayed plant and animal matter that covers large parts of the land surface of the earth. **b** the upper layer of such material that may be dug and in which plants grow. **c** a layer of soil with a characteristic PROFILE[1] (series of layers or zones) that develops from a certain type of rock or other material. **2** country; land: *It's good to be back on home soil*. **3** (**the soil**) agricultural life or work. **4** a medium in which something takes hold and develops. >> **soilless** *adj*. [Middle English via Anglo-French from Latin *solium* seat, prob confused with Latin *solum* ground]

soil[2] *verb trans* **1a** to make (something) dirty, *esp* superficially. **b** to defecate on or in (something): *soiled nappies*. **2** to defile (something or somebody) morally; to corrupt (them). **3** to blacken or tarnish (e.g. somebody's reputation). >> *verb intrans* to become soiled or dirty. [Middle English *soilen* from Old French *soiller* to wallow, soil, ultimately from Latin *suculus*, dimin. of *sus* pig]

soil[3] *noun* **1** dirt or defilement. **2** refuse or sewage.

soil[4] *verb trans* to feed (farm animals, *esp* cattle) on green fodder as a means of fattening or purging. [prob from SOIL[3]]

soil pipe *noun* a pipe for carrying off wastes from toilets.

soil science *noun* the scientific study of soils.

soiree *or* **soirée** /'swahray/ *noun* (*pl* **soirees** *or* **soirées** /-rayz/) a party or reception held in the evening, *esp* in a private house. [French *soirée* evening period, evening party, from early French *soir* evening, from Latin *sero* at a late hour, from *serus* late]

soixante-neuf /,swasont 'nuhf/ *noun* a sexual activity involving mutual stimulation of the genitals by the partners' lips and tongues. [French *soixante-neuf*, literally 'sixty-nine'; from the position adopted by the partners in this activity]

sojourn[1] /'sojən/ *noun formal* a temporary stay: *a sojourn in the country*. [Middle English *sojorn*, from Old French *sojorner* to stay temporarily, ultimately from Latin *sub* under, during + late Latin *diurnum* day]

sojourn[2] *verb intrans formal* to stay as a temporary resident. >> **sojourner** *noun*. [Middle English *sojornen* from Old French *sojorner*: see SOJOURN[1]]

soke /sohk/ *noun* **1** the right in Anglo-Saxon and early English law to hold a local court of justice and receive certain fees and fines. **2** the district that is under the jurisdiction of a particular court. [Middle English *soc, soke*, from late Latin *soca*, from Old English *sōcn* enquiry, jurisdiction]

sol[1] /sol/ *noun* = SOH.

sol[2] *noun* (*pl* **soles** /'solez, 'solez/) the basic monetary unit of Peru, divided into 100 centimos. [American Spanish *sol*, literally 'sun', via Spanish from Latin]

sol[3] *noun* a colloidal solution composed of solid particles dispersed in a liquid medium: compare GEL[1] (2). [short for SOLUTION]

sol. *abbr* **1** solicitor. **2** soluble. **3** solution.

sola /'sohla/ *adj* see SOLUS.

solace[1] /'soləs/ *noun* **1** consolation or comfort in grief or anxiety. **2** somebody or something that is a source of this. [Middle English *solas* via Old French from Latin *solacium*, from *solari* to console]

solace[2] *verb trans* **1** to give solace to (somebody); to console (them). **2** to alleviate or relieve (grief etc). >> **solacer** *noun*.

solanaceous /solə'nayshəs/ *adj* relating to or denoting a plant of a family of flowering plants, which includes the potato, tobacco, and some of the nightshades. [scientific Latin *Solanaceae*, family name, from *solanum* nightshade, from *sol* sun]

solan goose /'sohlən/ *noun archaic* = GANNET. [Middle English *soland*, from Old Norse *sūla* gannet + *önd* duck]

solanine /'solənin, -neen/ *or* **solanin** /-nin/ *noun* a bitter poisonous ALKALOID (chemical compound) found in several plants of the potato family, *esp* tomatoes and green potatoes. [French *solanine*, from Latin *solanum*: see SOLANACEOUS]

solar[1] /'sohlə/ *adj* **1** of or derived from the sun, *esp* as affecting the earth: *solar eclipse*. **2** measured by the earth's course in relation to the sun: *solar time*. **3** produced or operated by the action of the sun's light or heat: *solar heating*. [Middle English from Latin *solaris*, from *sol* sun]

solar[2] *noun* an upper room in a medieval house. [Old English, ultimately from Latin *solarium*: see SOLARIUM]

solar cell *noun* a device, e.g. a photovoltaic cell, that is able to convert the energy of sunlight into electrical energy and is used as a power source.

solar constant *noun* the quantity of radiant solar heat received by a given area of the earth's surface in a given time.

solar day *noun* the interval between two crossings of the meridian by the sun.

solar eclipse *noun* an eclipse in which the moon wholly or partially obscures the sun.

solar energy *noun* **1** radiant energy from the sun. **2** = SOLAR POWER.

solar flare *noun* = FLARE[2] (4A).

solarium /sə'leəri·əm/ *noun* (*pl* **solaria** /-ri·ə/ *or* **solariums**) **1** a room with extensive areas of glass allowing the warmth and light of the sun to stream in, e.g. for relaxation or treatment of illness. **2** a bed, room, or establishment equipped with sunbeds, sunlamps, etc. [Latin *solarium*, from *sol* sun]

solar panel *noun* **1** a large number of solar cells grouped together, e.g. on a spacecraft. **2** a panel, e.g. on the roof of a building, that is used to generate heat or electricity from sunlight.

solar plexus /'pleksəs/ *noun* **1** *technical* an interlacing network of nerves in the abdomen behind the stomach. **2** the pit of the stomach. [from the radiating nerve fibres, likened to the sun's rays]

solar power *noun* power derived from solar energy, used to generate electricity, heat, etc.

solar system *noun* the sun together with the planets and other celestial bodies that are held by its attraction and revolve round it.

solar wind /wind/ *noun* the continuous flow of electrically charged particles from the sun's surface into and through space.

solar year *noun* the time taken by the earth to move once round the sun, about 365¼ solar days.

solatium /sə'laynshi·əm/ *noun* (*pl* **solatia** /-shi·ə/) a compensation, e.g. a sum of money, given as solace for suffering, loss, hurt feelings, etc. [Latin *solacium, solatium*: see SOLACE[1]]

sold /sohld/ *verb* past tense and past part. of SELL[1].

solder[1] /'sohldə, 'soldə/ *noun* **1** an alloy, *esp* of tin and lead, used when melted to join metallic surfaces. **2** something that unites or cements. [Middle English *soudure* from early French *souder* to solder, from Latin *solidare* to make solid, from *solidus* SOLID[1]]

solder[2] *verb* (**soldered, soldering**) >> *verb trans* **1** to unite or repair (something) by solder. **2** to bring or restore (something) to firm union: *a friendship soldered by common interests*. >> *verb intrans* to become united or repaired by or as if by solder. >> **solderable** *adj*, **solderer** *noun*.

soldering iron *noun* a usu electrically heated device with a pointed or wedge-shaped end that is used for melting and applying solder.

soldier[1] /'sohljə/ *noun* **1a** a person who is engaged in military service, *esp* in the army. **b** an enlisted man or woman, as opposed to a commissioned officer. **c** a person who works tirelessly for a cause: *a soldier in the green movement*. **2** any of a CASTE (specialized form) of ants or wingless termites that have large heads and long jaws and are *esp* involved in defending and feeding other members of the colony. >> **soldierly** *adj*, **soldiership** *noun*. [Middle English *soudier* from Old French *soldier*, from *soulde* soldier's pay, from late Latin *solidus* gold coin: see SOLIDUS]

soldier[2] *verb intrans* (**soldiered, soldiering**) **1** to serve as a soldier. **2** (+ on) to press doggedly forward; to persevere in the face of difficulties etc.

soldier beetle *noun* any of various brightly coloured soft-bodied beetles: family Cantharidae.

soldier of fortune *noun* a person who engages in military service for financial gain or for the love of adventure; a mercenary.

soldiery *noun* (*pl* **soldieries**) **1** (*treated as sing. or pl*) a body of soldiers: *The Emperor's drunken soldiery are abed* — W B Yeats. **2** the profession of being a soldier.

sole[1] /sohl/ *noun* **1a** the undersurface of a foot. **b** the part of a garment or article of footwear on which the sole rests. **2** the usu flat bottom or lower part of something or the base on which something rests. >> **soled** *adj.* [Middle English via French from Latin *solea* sandal, from Latin *solum* base, ground, soil]

sole[2] *verb trans* to provide (a shoe) with a sole.

sole[3] *noun* (*pl* **soles** *or collectively* **sole**) any of several species of marine flatfishes that have small mouths and small eyes placed close together, including some valued as superior food fishes: family Soleidae and other families. [Middle English via French from Old Provençal *sola*, from Latin *solea*: see SOLE[1]]

sole[4] *adj* **1** being the only one; only: *She was her mother's sole confidante.* **2** belonging or relating exclusively to one individual or group: *sole rights of publication.* **3** *archaic* said *esp* of a woman: not married. **4** *archaic* solitary; alone. >> **soleness** *noun.* [Middle English, in the sense 'alone', via early French *seul* from Latin *solus*]

solecism /'solisiz(ə)m/ *noun* **1** a minor blunder in speech or writing, e.g. a grammatical error. **2** a deviation from what is proper or normal, *esp* a breach of etiquette or decorum. >> **solecistic** /-'sistik/ *adj.* [Latin *soloecismus* from Greek *soloikismos*, from *soloikos* speaking incorrectly, literally 'inhabitant of *Soloi*', a city in ancient Cilicia where a substandard form of Attic was spoken]

solely /'sohl(l)i/ *adv* **1** without another; singly: *He was solely responsible.* **2** to the exclusion of all else; only: *done solely for money.*

solemn /'soləm/ *adj* **1** performed or uttered with sincerity, *esp* so as to be legally binding: *a solemn oath.* **2** marked by the observance of established form or ceremony; *specif* celebrated with full religious rites. **3a** marked by seriousness and sobriety. **b** sombre; gloomy. **c** conveying a deep sense of reverence or exaltation: *stirred by the solemn music.* >> **solemnly** *adv,* **solemnness** *noun.* [Middle English *solemne* via Old French from Latin *sollemnis* ceremonial, customary, from *sollus* whole]

solemnise /'soləmniez/ *verb trans* see SOLEMNIZE.

solemnity /sə'lemniti/ *noun* (*pl* **solemnities**) **1** the quality or state of being solemn: *the solemnity of his words.* **2** formal or ceremonious observance of an occasion or event. **3** a solemn event or occasion.

solemnize *or* **solemnise** /'soləmniez/ *verb trans* **1** to observe or honour (something) with solemnity. **2** to perform (something) with pomp or ceremony, *esp* to celebrate (a marriage) with religious rites. **3** to make (something) solemn or serious; to dignify (it). >> **solemnization** /-'zaysh(ə)n/ *noun.*

solenoid /'solənoyd/ *noun* a coil of wire commonly in the form of a long cylinder that, when carrying a current, produces a magnetic field and draws in a movable usu iron rod. >> **solenoidal** /-'noydl/ *adj.* [French *solénoïde* from Greek *sōlēnoeidēs* pipe-shaped, from *sōlēn* pipe]

soleplate *noun* **1** the undersurface of an iron used for pressing cloth or clothing. **2** the lower part of a wall built around a frame on which the bases of the studs (upright parts of the framework; see STUD[1]) stand.

sol-fa[1] /'sol fah, sol 'fah/ *noun* **1** the syllables *doh, ray, me,* etc used in singing the notes of the scale. **2** = TONIC SOL-FA. [medieval Latin *sol* + *fa*: see GAMUT]

sol-fa[2] *verb trans and intrans* (**sol-fas, sol-faed, sol-faing**) to sing (something) using sol-fa syllables.

solfatara /solfa'tahra/ *noun* a volcanic vent that yields only hot vapours and sulphurous gases. [Italian *solfatara* sulphur mine, from *solfo* sulphur, from Latin *sulfur*]

solfège /sol'fezh/ *noun* (*pl* **solfèges** /sol'fezh/) **1** a singing exercise using *esp* the sol-fa syllables. **2** the application of syllables, *esp* the sol-fa syllables, to a musical scale or a melody; solmization. [French from Italian SOLFEGGIO]

solfeggio /sol'fejioh/ *noun* (*pl* **solfeggi** /-jee/ *or* **solfeggios**) = SOLFÈGE. [Italian, from *sol-fa* SOL-FA[1]]

soli /'sohlee/ *noun* pl of SOLO[1].

solicit /sə'lisit/ *verb* (**solicited, soliciting**) >> *verb trans* **1a** to make a formal or earnest appeal or request to (somebody); to entreat (them). **b** to make a play for (something), or try to obtain (it) by urgent requests or pleas: *With the capercailzie, the females flit around the male whilst he is parading ... and try to solicit his attention* — Darwin. **2a** said *esp* of a prostitute: to accost (somebody) publicly with an offer of sex for money. **b** to attempt to lure or entice (somebody), *esp* into evil. >> *verb intrans* **1** (*usu* + for) to ask earnestly for something. **2** said *esp* of a prostitute: to accost somebody publicly with an offer of sex for money. >>> **solicitation** /-'taysh(ə)n/ *noun.* [Middle English *soliciten* to disturb, take charge of, via early French *solliciter* from Latin *sollicitare* to disturb, from *sollicitus* anxious, from *sollus* whole + *citus*, past part. of *ciēre* to move]

solicitor *noun* **1** a qualified lawyer who advises clients, represents them in the lower courts, and prepares cases for barristers to try in the higher courts: compare BARRISTER. **2** in the USA, the chief law officer of a municipality, county, or government department. >> **solicitorship** *noun.*

solicitor general *noun* (*pl* **solicitors general**) **1** (**Solicitor General**) a Crown law officer ranking below the Attorney General or, in Scotland, the Lord Advocate. **2** a federally appointed assistant to the US attorney general. [Middle English, in the sense 'a representative, agent, or petitioner', from early French *solliciteur*, from *solliciter*: see SOLICIT]

solicitous /sə'lisitəs/ *adj* **1** showing concern or anxiety: *solicitous about the future.* **2** full of desire; eager: *solicitous of approval.* **3** showing meticulous or excessive care, attention, or consideration. >> **solicitously** *adv,* **solicitousness** *noun.* [Latin *sollicitus*: see SOLICIT]

solicitude /sə'lisityoohd/ *noun* **1a** the state or quality of being solicitous; concern. **b** excessive care or attention. **2** (*also in pl*) a cause of care or concern.

solid[1] /'solid/ *adj* **1a** without an internal cavity: *a solid ball of rubber.* **b** having no opening or division: *a solid wall.* **c** composed of or having a single substance or character: *solid rock.* **d** of uniform colour or tone. **2a** three-dimensional. **b** of or dealing with three-dimensional objects or solids. **3a** neither liquid nor gas; retaining shape without needing external support. **b** of uniformly close and coherent texture; compact. **4a** set in type or printed with minimum spacing between lines. **b** joined without a hyphen: *a solid compound.* **5** of good substantial quality or kind, e.g.: *a well constructed from durable materials: solid furniture.* **b** sound; convincing: *solid reasons.* **6a** without break or interruption: *I waited three solid hours.* **b** unanimous: *He had the solid support of his party.* **7a** reliable or reputable. **b** financially secure: *a solid investment.* **c** good but not exceptional; sound: *a solid worker.* **d** serious in character or intent: *He sent the President a solid memorandum.* **8** *chiefly NAmer, informal* in staunch or intimate association: *solid with his boss.* **9** *Aus, NZ, informal* excessively or unreasonably severe. >> **solidity** /sə'liditi/ *noun,* **solidly** *adv,* **solidness** *noun.* [Middle English *solide* via French from Latin *solidus*]

solid[2] *noun* **1a** a substance that does not flow perceptibly under moderate stress. **b** (*usu in pl*) the part of a solution or suspension that when freed from a solvent or suspending medium has the qualities of a solid: *milk solids.* **2** a geometrical figure, e.g. a cube or sphere, with three dimensions. **3** something solid, e.g. a solid colour.

solid angle *noun* a three-dimensional spread of directions from a point, e.g. from the vertex of a cone or at the intersection of three planes, that is usu measured in steradians.

solidarity /soli'dariti/ *noun* unity based on shared interests, objectives, and standards. [French *solidarité*, from *solidaire* characterized by solidarity, from Latin *solidum* whole sum, neuter of *solidus* SOLID[1]]

solid geometry *noun* a branch of geometry that deals with figures of three-dimensional space.

solidi /'solidie/ *noun* pl of SOLIDUS.

solidify /sə'lidifie/ *verb* (**solidifies, solidified, solidifying**) >> *verb intrans* to become solid. >> *verb trans* to make (something) solid. >> **solidification** /-fi'kaysh(ə)n/ *noun,* **solidifier** *noun.*

solid-state *adj* **1** relating to the properties, structure, or reactivity of solid material, *esp* relating to the arrangement or behaviour of ions, molecules, nucleons, electrons, and holes in the crystals of a substance, e.g. a semiconductor, or to the effect of crystal imperfections on the properties of a solid substance: *solid-state physics.* **2** using the electric, magnetic, or PHOTIC (involving light) properties of solid materials; not using thermionic valves: *a solid-state stereo system.*

solidus /'solidəs/ *noun* (*pl* **solidi** /-die/) **1** a punctuation mark (/) used *esp* to denote 'per' (e.g. in *metres/second*), 'or' (e.g. in *and/or*), to separate the terms of a fraction (e.g. in *19/20*), or the components of a date (e.g. in *19/10/99*). **2** a curve, usu on a graph showing the relationship between temperature and composition for a mixture, below which only the solid phase can exist. **3** an ancient Roman gold coin introduced by Constantine and used until the fall of the Byzantine Empire. [Middle English via late Latin from Latin *solidus* SOLID¹; (sense 1) late Latin *solidus* shilling, from its former use as a symbol for shillings]

solifluction /soli'fluksh(ə)n/ *noun* the slow creeping *esp* of saturated soil down a gentle slope that usu occurs in regions of permafrost. [Latin *solum* soil + *fluction-, fluctio* act of flowing, from *fluere* to flow]

soliloquize *or* **soliloquise** /sə'liləkwiez/ *verb intrans* **1** to talk to oneself. **2** to perform a soliloquy. ➤➤ **soliloquist** *noun*.

soliloquy /sə'liləkwi/ *noun* (*pl* **soliloquies**) **1** the act of speaking one's thoughts aloud while alone. **2** a dramatic device of this kind, used *esp* to let the audience know the thoughts and motivations of a character. [late Latin *soliloquium*, from Latin *solus* alone + *loqui* to speak]

solipsism /'solipsiz(ə)m/ *noun* the philosophical belief or theory that the only thing that can be known to exist is the self. It is an extreme form of scepticism. ➤➤ **solipsist** *noun*, **solipsistic** /-'sistik/ *adj*. [Latin *solus* alone + *ipse* self + -ISM]

solitaire /'solitea, soli'tea/ *noun* **1a** a game played by one person in which a number of pieces, e.g. pegs or balls, are removed from a cross-shaped pattern by jumping one over another, the aim being to leave a single piece on the board. **b** *chiefly NAmer* = PATIENCE (card game). **2a** a single gem, *esp* a diamond, set alone, usu in a ring. **b** a ring with a single gem. **3a** either of two extinct flightless birds of the Indian Ocean related to the dodo: *Pezophaps solitaria* or *Ornithaptera solitaria*. **b** any of several species of N American songbirds of the thrush family with dull grey plumage: genus *Myadestes*. [French *solitaire* solitary, from Latin *solitarius*: see SOLITARY¹]

solitary¹ /'solit(ə)ri/ *adj* **1a** fond of being alone: *of a solitary disposition*. **b** lonely: *He was left solitary by his wife's death*. **c** performed or spent without companions: *a solitary weekend*. **2a** said e.g. of insects: living alone; not gregarious, colonial, or social. **b** said e.g. of flowers: occurring singly and not as part of a cluster. **3** being the only one; sole: *the solitary example*. **4** unfrequented; remote: *living in a solitary place*. ➤➤ **solitarily** *adv*, **solitariness** *noun*. [Middle English from Latin *solitarius*, from *solitas* aloneness, from *solus* alone]

solitary² *noun* (*pl* **solitaries**) **1** somebody who habitually seeks solitude; a recluse or hermit. **2** *informal* = SOLITARY CONFINEMENT.

solitary confinement *noun* the state of being confined in isolation, *esp* as a punishment for a prisoner.

solitude /'solityoohd/ *noun* **1** the state of being alone or remote from society; seclusion. **2** a lonely or unfrequented place. [Middle English via French from Latin *solitudin-, solitudo*, from *solus* alone]

solmization *or* **solmisation** /solmie'zaysh(ə)n/ *noun* the act, practice, or system of using syllables, *esp* the sol-fa syllables, to denote musical notes or the degrees of a musical scale. [French *solmisation*, from *solmiser* to sol-fa, from *sol* soh + *mi* me + -*iser* -IZE]

solo¹ /'sohloh/ *noun* (*pl* **solos** *or* **soli** /'sohlee/) **1a** a musical composition, song, or dance for a single performer. **b** the performance of a solo. **2** a flight by one person alone in an aircraft. **3** any of various card games in which a player elects to play without a partner against the other players. ➤➤ **soloist** *noun*. [Italian *solo* alone, from Latin *solus*]

solo² *adv* without a companion; alone: *fly solo*.

solo³ *adj* **1** being done or performed alone; unaccompanied: *a solo flight; a piece for piano solo*. **2** being a single parent: *a solo father*.

solo⁴ *verb intrans* (**soloes, soloed, soloing**) to perform by oneself, *esp* to fly solo in an aircraft.

Solomonic /solə'monik/ *adj* having or showing great wisdom. [from *Solomon* d.c.933 BC, king of Israel renowned for his wisdom]

Solomon's seal /'soləmənz/ *noun* **1** an emblem consisting of two interlaced triangles forming a six-pointed star and formerly used as an amulet, *esp* against fever; STAR OF DAVID. **2** any of numerous species of plants of the lily family with drooping usu greenish white bell-shaped flowers, long smooth fleshy leaves, and gnarled rhizomes (underground stems; see RHIZOME): genus *Polygonatum*.

Word history
named after *Solomon* d.c.933 BC, king of Israel. The plant name is prob from the fancied resemblance of scars on the rhizome to the emblem.

so long *interj informal* used to express farewell: *'So long,' he said, and pushed his way out* — John Steinbeck. [prob by folk etymology from Irish Gaelic *slán*, literally 'health', from Old Irish *slán*]

solo whist *noun* a game of whist in which one player attempts to win by a previously declared margin against the other players.

solstice /'solstis/ *noun* **1** either of the two points on the ECLIPTIC¹ (apparent path of the sun) at which the distance from the celestial equator is greatest, passed by the sun each year about 22 June and 22 December. **2** either of the two times, the longest and shortest days of the year, when the sun passes one of these points. ➤➤ **solstitial** /sol'stish(ə)l/ *adj*. [Middle English via Old French from Latin *solstitium*, from *sol* sun + *stitus*, past part. of *sistere* to come to a stop, cause to stand]

solubilize *or* **solubilise** /'solyoobiliez/ *verb trans* to make (something) soluble. ➤➤ **solubilization** /-'zaysh(ə)n/ *noun*.

soluble /'solyoobl/ *adj* **1** said of a substance: capable of being dissolved in or as if in a liquid. **2** capable of being solved or explained: *soluble questions*. ➤➤ **solubility** /-'biliti/ *noun*, **solubly** *adv*. [Middle English via French from late Latin *solubilis*, from Latin *solvere*: see SOLVE]

solus /'sohləs/ *adj* **1** said of the position of an advertisement: set apart from others. **2** (*also fem* **sola**) used in stage directions: alone. [Latin *sōlus* alone]

solute /'solyooht, so'lyooht/ *noun* a dissolved substance. [Latin *solutus*, past part. of *solvere*: see SOLVE]

solution /sə'loohsh(ə)n/ *noun* **1a** the act or the process by which a solid, liquid, or gaseous substance is uniformly mixed usu with a liquid. **b** a usu liquid uniform mixture formed by this process. **c** the condition of being dissolved. **2a** an answer to a problem. **b** the act or process of solving a problem. [Middle English via French from Latin *solution-, solutio*, from *solvere*: see SOLVE]

Solutrean /solyoo'tree-ən, sə'lyoohtriən/ *adj* of an Upper Palaeolithic culture of Europe characterized by finely flaked stone implements. [from *Solutré*, village in E France where remains of the culture were found]

solvate¹ /'solvayt/ *noun* a complex formed by the chemical combination of a solute with a solvent. [SOLVENT¹ + -ATE¹]

solvate² *verb trans* to combine with (a solute or solvent molecule) to form a solvate. ➤➤ **solvation** /sol'vaysh(ə)n/ *noun*.

solve /solv/ *verb trans* to find an answer to or explanation for (a problem, mystery, etc). ➤ *verb intrans* to solve something: *substitute the known values of the constants and solve for x*. ➤➤ **solvable** *adj*, **solver** *noun*. [Middle English *solven* to loosen, dissolve, untie, from Latin *solvere*, from *sed-, se-* apart + *luere* to release]

solvent¹ /'solvənt/ *adj* **1** able to pay all debts, *esp* with money in hand. **2** said of a substance, *esp* a liquid: able to dissolve other substances: *solvent fluids*. ➤➤ **solvency** /-si/ *noun*, **solvently** *adv*. [Latin *solvent-, solvens*, present part. of *solvere*: see SOLVE]

solvent² *noun* a substance, *esp* a liquid, that is capable of dissolving or dispersing one or more other substances.

solvent abuse *noun* the practice of inhaling the intoxicating fumes from solvents, cleaning fluids, glues, etc.

solvolysis /sol'voləsis/ *noun* a chemical reaction, e.g. hydrolysis if the solvent is water, of a solvent and solute that results in the formation of new compounds. ➤➤ **solvolytic** /-'litik/ *adj*. [SOLVENT² + -O- + -LYSIS]

Som. *abbr* Somerset.

som /sohm/ *noun* (*pl* **som**) the basic monetary unit of Kyrgystan and Uzbekistan, divided into 100 tiyin.

soma¹ /'sohmə/ *noun* an intoxicating plant juice used in ancient India as an offering to the gods and as a drink of immortality in Vedic ritual. [Sanskrit *soma*]

soma² *noun* **1** all of an organism except the reproductive cells. **2** the body of an organism. **3** the cell body of a neuron. [via Latin from Greek *sōmat-, sōma* body]

Somali /sə'mahli/ *noun* (*pl* **Somalis** *or collectively* **Somali**) **1** a member of an indigenous people inhabiting Somalia in NE Africa. **2** the Cushitic language spoken by this people, also spoken in parts of Ethiopia, Kenya, and Djibouti. ➤➤ **Somali** *adj*.

Somalian /sə'mahli-ən/ *noun* a native or inhabitant of Somalia in NE Africa. ➤➤ **Somalian** *adj.*

somat- or **somato-** *comb. form* forming words, denoting: soma: *somatotype*. [via Latin from Greek *sōmat-, sōmato-* from *sōmat-, sōma* body]

somatic /soh'matik, sə-/ *adj* **1** of the body, *esp* as distinguished from the mind. **2** of the wall of the body, *esp* excluding the limbs and head. ➤➤ **somatically** *adv.* [Greek *sōmatikos*, from *sōmat-, sōma* body]

somatic cell *noun* any of the cells of the body that compose its tissues, organs, and parts other than the reproductive cells.

somato- *comb. form* see SOMAT-.

somatotrophic hormone /soh,matə'trohfik/ or **somatotrophin** /-fin/ or **somatotropin** /-pin/ *noun* = GROWTH HORMONE (1).

somatotype /soh'matətiep/ *noun* a classification of human body build, the main ones being endomorph, mesomorph, and ectomorph.

sombre (*NAmer* **somber**) /'sombə/ *adj* **1** dark; gloomy. **2** of a dull or dark colour. **3a** serious, grave. **b** depressing, melancholy. *sombre thoughts.* ➤➤ **sombrely** *adv*, **sombreness** *noun*. [French *sombre*, ultimately from SUB- + Latin *umbria* shade]

sombrero /som'breəroh/ *noun* (*pl* **sombreros**) a hat of felt or straw with a very wide brim, worn *esp* in Mexico. [Spanish *sombrero* from *sombra* shade]

some¹ /səm, *strong* sum/ *adj* **1a** being an unknown, undetermined, or unspecified unit or thing: *some film or other.* **b** being an unspecified member of a group or part of a class: *Some birds cannot fly.* **2a** being of an unspecified amount or number: *Give me some water.* **b** being of an appreciable or considerable amount or number: *It may take some time.* **3** *chiefly informal.* **a** important, striking, or excellent: *That was some party!* **b** no kind of: *Some friend you are!* [Old English *sum*]

some² /sum/ *pronoun* **1** some part, amount, or number but not all: *some of my friends.* **2** *chiefly NAmer* an indefinite additional amount: *She ran a mile and then some.*

some³ /sum/ *adv* **1** approximately; about: *some 80 houses.* **2** *chiefly NAmer, informal* somewhat.

-some¹ *suffix* forming adjectives, with the meaning: characterized by the thing, quality, state, or action specified: *awesome; burdensome; cuddlesome.* [Old English *-sum*]

-some² *suffix* forming nouns, denoting: a group with the number of members, *esp* people, specified: *foursome.* [Old English *sum* (pronoun) one, some]

-some³ *comb. form* forming nouns, denoting: intracellular particle: *chromosome.* [via Latin from Greek *sōmat-, sōma* body]

somebody¹ /'sumbədi/ *pronoun* some indefinite or unspecified person.

somebody² *noun* (*pl* **somebodies**) a person of position or importance.

some day *adv* at some unknown or unspecified future time; sometime.

somehow *adv* **1a** by some means not known or designated. **b** no matter how. **2** for some mysterious reason: *I don't think so, somehow.*

someone /'sumwən, 'sumwun/ *pronoun* = SOMEBODY¹.

someplace *adv chiefly NAmer* = SOMEWHERE¹.

somersault¹ /'suməsawlt/ *noun* **1** a leaping or rolling movement in which a person turns forward or backward in a complete revolution bringing the feet over the head. **2** a complete reversal of policy or opinion; a U-turn. [early French *sombresaut* leap, from SUPER- + Latin *saltus* leap, past part. of *salire* to leap]

somersault² *verb intrans* to perform a somersault.

something¹ *pronoun* **1a** some indeterminate or unspecified thing: *look for something cheaper.* **b** used to replace forgotten matter or to express vagueness: *He's something or other in the Foreign Office.* **c** some part; a certain amount: *I've seen something of her work.* **2a** a thing or person of consequence: *make something of one's life; The child is quite something.* **b** some truth or value: *There's something in what you say.* ✲ **something else** *informal* something or somebody that makes others pall in comparison: *Her apple pie is something else.* **something of a** a fairly notable: *something of a raconteur.*

something² *adv* **1a** in some degree; somewhat: *shaped something like a funnel.* **b** used to suggest approximation: *There were something*

like a thousand people there. **2** *informal* to an extreme degree: *He swears something awful.*

-something *comb. form informal* forming nouns, denoting: somebody of an age within the specified decade: *fortysomething.*

sometime¹ *adv* **1** at some unknown or unspecified future time: *I'll do it sometime.* **2** at some unknown or unspecified point of time in a specified period: *sometime last night.*

sometime² *adj* having been formerly: *the sometime chairman.*

sometimes *adv* at intervals; occasionally.

someway or **someways** *adv chiefly NAmer* by some unknown or unspecified means; somehow.

somewhat *adv* to some degree; slightly.

somewhere¹ *adv* **1** in, at, or to some unknown or unspecified place. **2** to a place or state symbolizing positive accomplishment or progress: *At last we're getting somewhere.* **3** at an approximate or unspecified point: *somewhere between eight and nine o'clock.*

somewhere² *noun* an undetermined or unnamed place.

somite /'sohmiet/ *noun* any of the longitudinal series of segments into which the body of many invertebrate animals, e.g. earthworms, and the embryos of vertebrate animals are divided. [Greek *sōma* body + -ITE¹]

sommelier /'suməlyay, 'som-/ *noun* a waiter in charge of wines and their service, *esp* in a restaurant. [early French *sommelier* court official charged with transportation of supplies, pack-animal driver, from Old Provençal *saumalier* pack-animal driver, from *sauma* pack animal, load of a pack animal, via late Latin from Greek *sagma* packsaddle]

somnambulate /som'nambyoolayt/ *verb intrans* to walk while sleeping. ➤➤ **somnambulant** *adj and noun*, **somnambulation** /-'laysh(ə)n/ *noun.*

somnambulist /som'nambyoolist/ *noun* somebody who walks in their sleep. ➤➤ **somnambulism** *noun*, **somnambulistic** /-'listik/ *adj*, **somnambulistically** /-'listikli/ *adv.* [Latin *somnus* sleep + *ambulare* to walk]

somniferous /som'nifərəs/ *adj* inducing sleep; soporific. ➤➤ **somniferously** *adv.* [Latin *somnifer*, from *somnus* sleep + *-fer* -FEROUS]

somnolent /'somnələnt/ *adj* **1** inclined to or heavy with sleep; drowsy. **2** tending to induce sleep: *a somnolent sermon.* ➤➤ **somnolence** *noun*, **somnolency** /-si/ *noun*, **somnolently** *adv.* [Middle English *sompnolent* via French from Latin *somnolentus*, from *somnus* sleep]

son /sun/ *noun* **1a** a male offspring, *esp* of human beings. **b** a male adopted child. **c** (*also in pl*) a male descendant. **2** (**Son** or **the Son**) the second person of the Trinity; Christ. **3** somebody closely associated with or deriving from a specified background, place, etc: *a son of the welfare state.* **4** an informal form of address used *esp* to a boy or a younger man. ➤➤ **sonless** *adj*, **sonship** *noun.* [Old English *sunu*]

sonar /'sohnah/ *noun* **1a** a system for detecting the presence and location of a submerged object by means of reflected sound waves. **b** the apparatus or a device used for this. **2** a method of echolocation used in water, e.g. by whales, or in air, e.g. by bats. [short for *sound navigation ranging*]

sonata /sə'nahtə/ *noun* a musical composition typically for one instrument, often with piano accompaniment, and of three or four movements in contrasting forms and keys. [Italian *sonata* from *sonare* to sound, from Latin]

sonata form *noun* a musical form that is used for the first movement of a sonata, symphony, concerto, etc and consists basically of an exposition, a development, and a recapitulation in which usu two themes are introduced, developed, and then repeated.

Editorial note

The preeminent instrumental form of the 18th, 19th and early 20th cents, sonata form relies upon the contrast between two musical keys (conventionally tonic and dominant). Classical sonata form is built on two main themes and consists of three parts – an exposition that begins with the first theme in the tonic and moves to the dominant for the statement of the second, a development that develops the two themes, often ranging through a variety of keys, and eventually a return to the tonic for the recapitulation in which both themes are heard in the tonic key. As the form evolved, however, the archetype was subjected to far more elaboration — Andrew Clements.

sonatina /sonə'teenə/ *noun* a short usu simplified sonata. [Italian *sonatina*, dimin. of *sonata*: see SONATA]

sonde /sond/ *noun* any of various devices for testing and usu transmitting information about physical conditions, e.g. at high altitudes. [French *sonde*, literally 'sounding line': see SOUND⁶]

sone /sohn/ *noun* a subjective unit of loudness equal to 40 phons for an average listener. [Latin *sonus* sound]

son et lumière /,son ay looh'myeə/ *noun* an entertainment held at night at a historical site, e.g. a cathedral or stately home, that uses lighting and recorded sound to present the place's history. [French *son et lumière*, literally 'sound and light']

song /song/ *noun* **1** the act, art, or sound of singing with the human voice. **2a** a short musical composition usu with words. **b** such compositions considered collectively.

Editorial note

A song is a vocal piece of music nearly always with words and accompaniment that expresses a human situation or emotion; no other musical genre has older roots or encompasses a wider repertoire of traditional sub-species. Folk songs evoke national characteristics yet can show a startling similarity of melody or rhythm, suggesting archetypes. The more sophisticated 'art' songs began with the chansons of medieval minstrels and reached a pinnacle in the 19th cent. Lieder of Schubert and Schumann — Amanda Holden.

3 poetry: *famous in song and story.* **4** the usu melodious sounds made by birds and some other animals. **5** *informal* a very small sum: *sold for a song.* ✳ **on song 1** *Brit, informal* in good form or condition. **2** *Brit, informal* in peak working order. [Old English *sang*; related to Old English *singan* to SING¹]

song and dance *noun informal* **1** *chiefly Brit* a fuss or commotion: *Don't make a song and dance about it.* **2** *NAmer* an involved explanation designed to confuse or mislead.

songbird *noun* **1** a bird that utters a succession of musical tones. **2** *technical* any group of passerine birds that have highly developed vocal organs: suborder Oscines.

song cycle *noun* a group of related songs designed to form a musical entity.

Song of Songs *noun* a collection of love poems forming a book in canonical Jewish and Christian Scripture. [translation of Hebrew *shīr hashshīrīm*]

songster /'songstə/ *noun* **1** a skilled singer. **2** a writer of songs or poetry. **3** a songbird.

songstress /'songstris/ *noun* a female songster.

song thrush *noun* a common African and Eurasian thrush that has a brown back and wings and a pale breast with small dark spots: *Turdus philomelos.*

songwriter *noun* somebody who writes words or music for songs, *esp* popular songs. ➤➤ **songwriting** *noun.*

sonic /'sonik/ *adj* **1** using, produced by, or relating to sound waves: *sonic altimeter.* **2** of or being the speed of sound in air at sea level, about 340 metres per second (741mph): compare HYPERSONIC. **3** said of a wave or vibration: having a frequency within the audibility range of the human ear. ➤➤ **sonically** *adv.* [Latin *sonus* sound]

sonic barrier *noun* = SOUND BARRIER.

sonic boom *noun* a sound resembling an explosion produced when a shock wave formed at the nose of an aircraft travelling at supersonic speed reaches the ground.

sonics /'soniks/ *pl noun* (*treated as sing.*) the scientific study of the properties of sound, *esp* the study of vibrations in matter.

son-in-law *noun* (*pl* **sons-in-law**) the husband of one's daughter.

sonnet¹ /'sonit/ *noun* **1** a fixed verse form with any of various rhyming schemes and consisting typically of 14 lines of ten syllables each. **2** a poem in this form. [Italian *sonetto* from Old Provençal *sonet* little song, dimin. of *son* sound, song, from Latin *sonus* sound]

sonnet² *verb* (**sonneted, sonneting**) ➤ *verb intrans* to write sonnets. ➤ *verb trans* to write about, celebrate, or praise (something or somebody) in a sonnet.

sonneteer /soni'tiə/ *noun* a composer of sonnets, *esp* without high standards.

sonny /'suni/ *noun* an informal form of address used *esp* to a young boy.

sonobuoy /'sohnohboy/ *noun* a buoy equipped with apparatus for detecting underwater sounds and transmitting them by radio. [Latin *sonus* sound + BUOY¹]

son of a bitch *noun* (*pl* **sons of bitches**) *informal* an offensive or disagreeable person, often used as a term of abuse.

Son of Man *noun* according to the gospels, a title used by Christ to describe his earthly ministry and his role in the final judgment; humankind; Christ.

sonorant /'sonərənt/ *noun* a letter or speech sound that can function as a consonant or a vowel.

sonorous /'sonərəs/ *adj* **1** giving out sound, e.g. when struck. **2** pleasantly loud, rich, or deep in sound. **3** impressive in effect or style: *She made a sonorous speech to the assembly.* ➤➤ **sonority** /sə'noriti/ *noun,* **sonorously** *adv,* **sonorousness** *noun.* [Latin *sonorus* from *sonor* sound, noise]

sonsy or **sonsie** /'sunzi/ *adj* (**sonsier, sonsiest**) **1** bringing good fortune; lucky. **2a** said of a person's face: having a healthy glow. **b** *chiefly Scot* said of a woman: buxom and attractive. **3** cheerful and friendly. [Scots *sons* health, from Scottish and Irish Gaelic *sonas* good fortune]

sook /sook/ *noun chiefly Aus, informal* a cowardly or timid person. [variant of SUCK² in the sense 'stupid person']

sool /soohl/ *verb trans Aus, NZ* **1** (*often* + on) to incite or urge (a person or animal), *esp* to attack. **2** said *esp* of a dog: to attack (e.g. another animal). ➤➤ **sooler** *noun.* [English dialect *sowl* to pull by the ears, of unknown origin]

soon /soohn/ *adv* **1** before long; without undue time lapse: *soon after sunrise.* **2** in a prompt manner; speedily: *as soon as possible; the sooner the better.* **3** used in comparisons: in preference; willingly: *I'd sooner walk than drive; I'd just as soon not.* ✳ **no sooner ... than** at the very moment that or immediately after: *no sooner had I sat down than the phone rang.* **sooner or later** at some uncertain future time; eventually. [Old English *sōna*]

Usage note

When the phrase *no sooner* starts a sentence, the normal order of the verb and subject following it should be reversed: *No sooner had she said this, than the telephone rang.* Note that the correct word to use after *no sooner* is *than*, not *when*: *I had no sooner sat down than Mary started calling for me from the garden.*

soot¹ /soot/ *noun* a fine black powder or flaky substance that consists chiefly of carbon and is formed by the incomplete burning of organic matter, e.g. coal. [Old English *sōt*]

soot² *verb trans* to coat, cover, or clog (something) with soot.

sooth¹ /soohth/ *adj archaic* true or real. [Old English *sōth*]

sooth² *noun archaic* truth, fact, or reality. ✳ **in sooth** *archaic* truly.

soothe /soohdh/ *verb trans* **1** to calm (somebody) by or as if by showing attention or concern; to placate (them). **2** to relieve or alleviate (e.g. pain). **3** to bring comfort or reassurance to (somebody). ➤ *verb intrans* to bring peace or ease. ➤➤ **soother** *noun,* **soothing** *adj,* **soothingly** *adv.*

Word history

Old English *sōthian* to prove the truth, from *sōth* true. Sense 1 arose in the 17th cent. from the earlier meanings 'to support or encourage somebody in an assertion' and 'to flatter'.

soothsayer /'soohthsayə/ *noun* somebody who predicts the future; a prophet. ➤➤ **soothsaying** *noun.* [Middle English *sothseyer* somebody who speaks the truth, from *soth* SOOTH² + SAY¹]

sooty /'sooti/ *adj* (**sootier, sootiest**) **1a** producing soot: *sooty fires.* **b** covered or soiled with soot. **2** of the colour of soot; black. ➤➤ **sootily** *adv,* **sootiness** *noun.*

sop¹ /sop/ *noun* **1** a piece of food, *esp* bread, dipped or soaked in a liquid, e.g. soup. **2** something offered or done as a concession, appeasement, or bribe. [Old English *sopp*; related to Old English *sūpan* to swallow, SUP¹]

sop² *verb trans* (**sopped, sopping**) **1** to soak or dip (something) in or as if in liquid: *bread sopped in gravy.* **2** (*usu* + up) to mop up (e.g. water) so as to leave a dry surface. **3** *archaic* to wet (something) thoroughly; to soak (it).

sop. *abbr* soprano.

sophism /'sofiz(ə)m/ *noun* **1** an argument that is apparently correct but actually false, *esp* such an argument used to deceive. **2** = SOPHISTRY (1). [via Latin from Greek *sophisma*, from *sophizesthai*: see SOPHIST]

sophist /'sofist/ *noun* **1** any of various ancient Greek teachers of rhetoric, philosophy, and the art of successful living noted for their subtle and often specious reasoning. **2** a false reasoner; a user of sophistry. ➤➤ **sophistic** /so'fistik/ *adj,* **sophistical** /so'fistikl/ *adj,* **sophistically** /so'fistikli/ *adv.* [Latin *sophista* from Greek *sophistēs,* literally 'expert, wise man', from *sophizesthai* to become wise, deceive, from *sophos* clever, wise]

sophisticate[1] /sə'fistikayt/ *verb trans* **1a** to make (somebody) refined, cultured, or knowledgeable. **b** to deprive (somebody) of naivety; to make (them) worldly-wise. **2** to make (something) more highly developed, elaborate, or complex. **3** to mislead (somebody) by sophistry. **4** to alter (something) so as to deceive. ⟫ **sophistication** /-'kaysh(ə)n/ *noun*. [Middle English *sophisticaten* from late Latin *sophisticatus*, past part. of *sophisticare*, via Latin from Greek *sophistikos* sophistic, from *sophistēs* sophist]

sophisticate[2] /sə'fistikat/ *noun* a sophisticated person.

sophisticated /sə'fistikaytid/ *adj* **1** highly developed; complex: *sophisticated electronic devices*. **2a** having refined tastes; cultured. **b** worldly-wise; knowing: *a sophisticated adolescent*. **3** intellectually subtle or refined: *a sophisticated novel*. **4** not in a natural, pure, or original state; adulterated: *a sophisticated oil*. ⟫ **sophisticatedly** *adv*.

sophistry /'sofistri/ *noun* (*pl* **sophistries**) **1** seemingly true but unsound subtle reasoning or argument. **2** = SOPHISM (1).

sophomore /'sofəmaw/ *noun NAmer* a second-year student at university, college, or high school. ⟫ **sophomoric** /-'morik/ *adj*. [from *sophom*, obsolete variant of SOPHISM + -OR[1]]

Sophy /'sohfy/ *noun* (*pl* **Sophies**) in former times, a title for the sovereign of Persia. [Persian *Safī* from Arabic *Safi-al-dīn* pure of religion]

-sophy *comb. form* forming nouns, denoting: knowledge; wisdom; science: *theosophy*. [Middle English *-sophie* via Old French and Latin from Greek *-sophia*, from *sophia* wisdom, from *sophos* wise]

soporific[1] /sopə'rifik/ *adj* **1** causing or tending to cause sleep: *It is said that the effect of eating too much lettuce is 'soporific'* — Beatrix Potter. **2** of or marked by sleepiness or lethargy. [prob from French *soporifique*, from Latin *sopor* deep sleep]

soporific[2] *noun* something that induces sleep, e.g. a soporific drug.

sopping /'soping/ *adj* wet through; soaking. [present part. of SOP[2]]

sopping wet *adj* = SOPPING.

soppy /'sopi/ *adj* (**soppier, soppiest**) *informal* **1** weakly sentimental; mawkish: *You get so soppy about couples* — Iris Murdoch. **2** *chiefly Brit, informal* silly; inane. **3** = SOPPING. ⟫ **soppily** *adv*, **soppiness** *noun*. [orig in the sense 'soaking wet'; from SOP[2] + -Y[1]]

sopranino /soprə'neenoh/ *noun* (*pl* **sopraninos**) a musical instrument, e.g. a recorder or saxophone, higher in pitch than soprano. [Italian *sopranino*, dimin. of *soprano*: see SOPRANO]

soprano /sə'prahnoh/ *noun* (*pl* **sopranos**) **1** the highest singing voice of women or boys, or a singer with this voice. **2** (*used before a noun*) a musical instrument having the highest or second highest range. **3** the highest singing part in conventional four-part harmony. [Italian *soprano* from *sopra* above, from Latin *supra*]

soprano clef *noun* in music, a clef with middle C on the lowest line of the stave.

Sorb /sawb/ *noun* **1** a member of an indigenous people formerly inhabiting a region now in eastern Germany and western Poland and descended from the Wends (see WEND). **2** the Slavonic language spoken by this people, now with only a small number of speakers in eastern Germany. ⟫ **Sorbian** *adj and noun*. [German *Sorbe*, from Sorb *Serb*]

sorb *noun* **1** = SERVICE[3]. **2** any of several African and Eurasian trees of the rose family related to the service. **3** the fruit of any of these trees, *esp* the fruit of the service. [French *sorbe* fruit of the service tree, from Latin *sorbum*]

sorbet /'sawbay, 'sawbit/ *noun* **1** a water ice, *esp* one made with fruit juice and sometimes egg whites. **2** = SHERBET (sweet powder or drink). [early French *sorbet* a fruit drink, from Old Italian *sorbetto*, from Turkish *şerbet*: see SHERBET]

sorbitol /'sawbitol/ *noun* a crystalline chemical compound found in some fruits and used as a sweetener. [SORB + -ITE[3] + -OL[1]]

sorcerer /'saws(ə)rə/ *noun* a man or woman who uses sorcery; a wizard or witch.

sorceress /'saws(ə)ris/ *noun* a female sorcerer.

sorcery /'saws(ə)ri/ *noun* the art and practice of using magical power, *esp* with the aid of evil spirits. [Middle English *sorcerie* from Old French *sorcier* sorcerer, ultimately from Latin *sort-, sors* chance, lot]

sordid /'sawdid/ *adj* **1a** dirty; filthy. **b** wretched; squalid. **2** base; vile: *sordid motives*. **3** meanly greedy; niggardly. ⟫ **sordidly** *adv*, **sordidness** *noun*. [Latin *sordidus*, from *sordes* dirt]

sordino /saw'deenoh/ *noun* (*pl* **sordini** /-nee/) **1** = MUTE[2] (2). **2** (*usu in pl*) = DAMPER (1). [Italian *sordino* from *sordo* silent, from Latin *surdus*]

sore[1] /saw/ *adj* **1a** causing or suffering pain. **b** painfully sensitive; tender: *sore muscles*. **c** hurt or inflamed so as to be or seem painful: *sore runny eyes*. **2a** causing difficulty, annoyance, anxiety, or distress: *Overtime is a sore point with him*. **b** severe; urgent: *a sore need for change*. **3** *chiefly NAmer* angry; upset. ⟫ **soreness** *noun*. [Old English *sār*]

sore[2] *noun* **1** a localized sore spot on the body, *esp* one with the tissues ruptured and usu infected. **2** a source of pain, distress, or vexation; an affliction.

sore[3] *adv archaic* greatly or extremely: *John Barleycorn got up again and sore surpris'd them all* — Robert Burns.

sorehead *noun NAmer, informal* a person easily angered or disgruntled.

sorely *adv* **1** much; extremely: *sorely tempted*. **2** painfully; grievously.

sorghum /'sawgəm/ *noun* any of various economically important African and Eurasian tropical grasses similar to maize but with the seed-bearing spikes in pairs on a hairy stalk: genus *Sorghum*. [Latin genus name, from Italian *sorgo*]

sori /'sawrie/ *noun* pl of SORUS.

SORN /sawn/ *abbr Brit* Statutory Off Road Notification, the requirement that a vehicle owner intending to keep a vehicle off the road and unlicensed must inform the DVLA of this intention.

sorority /sə'roriti/ *noun* (*pl* **sororities**) a social club of girls or women, *esp* at a N American university or college: compare FRATERNITY (1B). [late Latin *sororitas* sisterhood, from Latin *soror* sister]

sorption /'sawpsh(ə)n/ *noun* absorption or adsorption, or both together considered as a single chemical process. [back-formation from ABSORPTION and ADSORPTION]

sorrel[1] /'sorəl/ *noun* **1** a brownish orange to light brown colour. **2** a sorrel-coloured animal, *esp* a horse. ⟫ **sorrel** *adj*. [Middle English *sorelle* from early French *sorel*, from *sor* reddish brown]

sorrel[2] *noun* **1** any of several species of plants of the dock family with acidic-flavoured leaves that are eaten in salads: genus *Rumex*. **2** = WOOD SORREL. [Middle English *sorel* from early French *surele*, from Old French *sur* sour, of Germanic origin]

sorrow[1] /'soroh/ *noun* **1** deep distress and regret, e.g. over the loss of something precious. **2** a cause of grief or sadness. **3** the outward expression of grief or sadness. ⟫ **sorrowful** *adj*, **sorrowfully** *adv*, **sorrowfulness** *noun*. [Old English *sorg*]

sorrow[2] *verb intrans* to feel or express sorrow.

sorry[1] /'sori/ *adj* (**sorrier, sorriest**) **1** full of regret, penitence, or pity: *I'm sorry if I hurt your feelings; She felt sorry for the poor wretch*. **2** inspiring sorrow, pity, or scorn: *He looked a sorry sight in his torn clothes*. **3** bad or regrettable: *a sorry state of affairs*. ⟫ **sorrily** *adv*, **sorriness** *noun*.

Word history
Old English *sārig* from *sār* SORE[1]. The modern forms of the word may have developed through association with SORROW[1].

sorry[2] *interj* an exclamation used to apologize.

sort[1] /sawt/ *noun* **1a** a group constituted on the basis of any common characteristic; a class or kind. **b** an instance of a kind: *a sort of herbal medicine*. **2** nature; disposition: *people of an evil sort*. **3** a letter or character in a FOUNT[2] (set of printing type). **4** *informal* a person; an individual: *He's not a bad sort*. **5** *archaic* way; manner: *Every reader had in some sort to be a student* — G M Trevelyan. ✳ **of sorts/of a sort** of an inconsequential or mediocre quality. **out of sorts 1** somewhat ill. **2** grouchy; irritable. **sort of** *informal* to a moderate degree; somewhat; in a way: *It's sort of hard to describe*. [Middle English from early French *sorte*, ultimately from Latin *sort-, sors* chance, lot]

Usage note
See note at KIND[1].

sort[2] *verb trans* **1a** to put (things) in groups according to kind, class, or quality: *sort the good apples from the bad*. **b** to arrange (things) in an orderly manner; to put (them) in order: *The data is sorted by computer*. **2** *chiefly Scot* to put (something) into good or working order;

to repair (it). ✳ **sort with** *archaic, formal* to correspond to (something); to agree with (it). ➤➤ **sortable** *adj*, **sorter** *noun*.

sorted /'sawtid/ *adj Brit, informal* **1** organized; ready for use. **2** supplied with illegal drugs. **3** emotionally stable or well-adjusted.

sortie[1] /'sawti/ *noun* **1** a sudden emergence of troops from a defensive position against the enemy. **2** a single mission or attack by one aircraft. **3** a brief trip, *esp* to a hostile or unfamiliar place. [French *sortie* from *sortir* to go out, escape]

sortie[2] *verb intrans* (**sorties, sortied, sortieing**) to make a sortie.

sortilege /'sawtilij/ *noun* prediction of the future or fortune-telling by drawing lots. [Middle English from late Latin *sortilegium*, from Latin *sortilegus* foretelling, from *sort-, sors* lot + *legere* to gather]

sort out *verb trans* **1** to clarify or resolve (e.g. a problem), *esp* by thoughtful consideration. **2a** to separate (something) from a mass or group: *Sort out the important papers and throw the rest away.* **b** to clear up or tidy (something): *It will take ages to sort out this mess.* **3** *chiefly Brit, informal* to punish or take vengeance on (somebody), *esp* by violent means.

sorus /'sawrəs/ *noun* (*pl* **sori** /'sawrie/) a cluster of reproductive bodies of a fungus, fern, alga, or other lower plant, *esp* any of the dots on the underside of a fertile fern frond consisting of a cluster of spore-producing capsules. [via Latin from Greek *sōros* heap]

SOS *noun* **1** an internationally recognized signal of distress which is rendered in Morse code as ··· – – – ···. **2** a call or request for help or rescue. [often said to stand for *Save Our Souls*, but the letters were actually chosen because they are simple to transmit and recognize in Morse code]

so-so[1] /'soh soh/ *adj* neither very good nor very bad; middling: *His leg is but so-so* — Shakespeare.

so-so[2] *adv* moderately well; tolerably.

sostenuto /sostə'nyoohtoh/ *adj and adv* said of a piece of music: to be performed in a sustained or prolonged manner. ➤➤ **sostenuto** *noun*. [Italian *sostenuto*, past part. of *sostenere* to sustain, from Latin *sustinēre*: see SUSTAIN[1]]

sot /sot/ *noun* a habitual drunkard. ➤➤ **sottish** *adj*. [Old English *sott* fool]

soteriology /soh,tiəri'oləji/ *noun* in Christian theology, the doctrine of salvation. ➤➤ **soteriological** /-'lojikl/ *adj*. [Greek *sōtērion* salvation, from *sōtēr* saviour, from *sōzein* to save]

Sotho /'sootoo/ *noun* (*pl* **Sothos** or collectively **Sotho**) **1** a member of a group of indigenous peoples inhabiting Botswana, Lesotho, and South Africa. **2** a group of Bantu languages spoken by these peoples, including Tswana. ➤➤ **Sotho** *adj*.

sotto voce /,sotoh 'vohchi/ *adv and adj* in a quiet voice; in an undertone. [Italian *sotto voce*, literally 'under the voice']

sou /sooh/ *noun* (*pl* **sous** /sooh(z)/) **1** any of various former French coins of low value. **2** *informal* the smallest amount of money: *He hadn't a sou to his name.* [French *sou* via Old French *sol* from late Latin *solidus* gold coin: see SOLIDUS]

soubrette /sooh'bret/ *noun* in traditional stage comedy, the role of a coquettish maid or frivolous young woman. [French *soubrette* from Provençal *soubreto*, fem of *soubret* coy, from *soubra* to surmount, exceed, from Latin *superare* to be above, from *super* above]

soubriquet /'soohbrikay/ *noun* see SOBRIQUET.

souchong /sooh'chong, sooh'shong/ *noun* a large-leaved black variety of China tea. [Chinese (Cantonese) *siu* small *chung* sort]

soufflé /'soohflay/ *noun* a light fluffy baked dish made by carefully folding egg yolks and sometimes other ingredients into stiffly beaten egg whites. [French *soufflé*, past part. of *souffler* to blow, puff up, from Latin *sufflare*, from SUB- + *flare* to blow]

sough[1] /sow/ *verb intrans* said of the wind, waves, etc: to make a soft moaning, sighing, or rustling sound. [Old English *swōgan*]

sough[2] *noun* a soft moaning or sighing sound.

sought /sawt/ *verb* past tense and past part. of SEEK.

sought-after *adj* greatly desired or courted; much in demand: *the world's most sought-after concert entertainers.*

souk /soohk/ *noun* an open-air bazaar or market in a Muslim country. [Arabic *sūq* market]

soukous /'sookoos/ *noun* a style of dance music originating in Central Africa and influenced by Latin American rhythms. [perhaps from French *secouer* to shake]

soul /sohl/ *noun* **1** the immaterial essence or animating principle of an individual life. **2** the spiritual principle embodied in human beings, all rational and spiritual beings, or the universe. **3** all that constitutes a person's self. **4a** an active or essential part: *Minorities are the very soul of democracy.* **b** a moving spirit; a leader: *the soul of the rebellion.* **5** spiritual vitality; fervour. **6** a person: *She's a kind old soul.* **7** exemplification or personification: *He's the soul of integrity.* **8a** music that originated in black American gospel singing, is closely related to rhythm and blues, and is characterized by intensity of feeling and earthiness. **b** (*used before a noun*) relating to or denoting this kind of music: *a soul singer.* **c** a strong positive feeling, *esp* of intense sensitivity and emotional fervour. **d** (*used before a noun*) characteristic of black Americans or their culture: *soul food.*

Editorial note

Descriptive of both a quality of innate spirituality and intensity in music, and of the black pop music of the 1960s in particular, soul centred on performers whose style and delivery was closely linked to gospel music but was applied to secular material: rhythm and blues infused with more tenderness and sophistication — Richard Cook.

➤➤➤ **souled** *adj*. [Old English *sāwol*]

soul-destroying *adj* said *esp* of a task, job, etc: giving no chance for the mind to work; very uninteresting.

soul food *noun* food, e.g. chitterlings and ham hocks, traditionally eaten by black Americans, *esp* in the southern states.

soulful /'sohlf(ə)l/ *adj* full of or expressing intense or excessive feeling: *a soulful look.* ➤➤ **soulfully** *adv*, **soulfulness** *noun*.

soulless *adj* **1** having no soul or no warmth of feeling; lacking sensitivity or compassion. **2** bleak or uninviting: *a soulless room.* ➤➤ **soullessly** *adv*, **soullessness** *noun*.

soul mate *noun* a person with whom one has a close affinity; a lover.

soul-searching *noun* scrutiny of one's mind and conscience, *esp* with regard to aims and motives.

sound[1] /sownd/ *noun* **1a** the effect resulting from stimulation of the specialized cells and groups of cells that receive auditory stimuli; the sensation perceived by the sense of hearing. **b** a particular auditory impression or quality; a noise or tone: *the sound of children laughing.* **c** energy that is produced by a vibrating body, is transmitted by longitudinal waves of pressure that travel outwards from the source through a medium, e.g. air, and is the objective cause of hearing. **2** hearing distance; earshot. **3** an impression conveyed, e.g. by a report: *He's having a rough time by the sound of it.* **4a** recorded sounds, e.g. on records or film soundtracks. **b** radio broadcasting as opposed to television. **c** that part of television equipment that processes sound signals. **5a** a characteristic musical style: *the big band sound; the Liverpool sound of the 1960s.* **b** *informal* (*in pl*) music, *esp* popular music: *cool big beat sounds.* **6** a minimal segment of spoken language. ➤➤ **soundless** *adj*, **soundlessly** *adv*, **soundlessness** *noun*. [Middle English *soun* via Old French from Latin *sonus*]

sound[2] *verb intrans* **1a** to make a sound. **b** to resound. **2** to have a specified import when heard; to seem: *His story sounds incredible.* ➤ *verb trans* **1a** to cause (e.g. a musical instrument) to emit sound. **b** to give out (a sound). **2** to put (something) into words; to voice (it). **3a** to make (something) known; to proclaim (it): *They sounded his praises far and wide.* **b** to order, signal, or indicate (something) by a sound: *Sound the alarm!; The clock sounded the hour.* **4** to examine or test the condition of (e.g. the chest or lungs) by tapping.

sound[3] *adj* **1a** free from injury or disease; healthy. **b** free from flaw, defect, or decay: *sound timber.* **2** solid or firm; stable. **3a** free from error, fallacy, or misapprehension: *sound reasoning.* **b** showing or grounded in thorough knowledge and experience: *sound scholarship.* **4** showing integrity and good judgment. **5** deep and undisturbed: *a sound sleep.* **6** thorough or severe: *a sound whipping.* **7** *Brit, informal* very good: *Thanks for the meal, it was sound!* ➤➤ **soundly** *adv*, **soundness** *noun*. [Old English *gesund*]

sound[4] *adv* fully or thoroughly: *sound asleep.*

sound[5] *noun* **1a** a long broad sea inlet. **b** a long passage of water connecting two larger bodies or separating a mainland and an island. **2** the air bladder of a fish. [Old English *sund* swimming, sea, and Old Norse *sund* swimming, strait]

sound[6] *verb trans* **1** to measure (the depth of water in something): *sound a well.* **2** to explore or examine (a body cavity) with a probe. ➤ *verb intrans* said of a fish or whale: to dive down suddenly. [Middle English *sounden* from early French *sonder*, from *sonde* sounding line, prob of Germanic origin]

sound[7] *noun* a probe for exploring or sounding body cavities. [French *sonde* from early French: see SOUND[6]]

soundalike *noun* a person or thing that sounds like another: *a Frank Sinatra soundalike.*

sound barrier *noun* a sudden large increase in aerodynamic drag that occurs as an aircraft nears the speed of sound.

sound bite *noun* **1** a short excerpt from a speech or statement, *esp* one chosen for its aptness or pithiness and used as a means of encapsulating a political stance or policy on a television or radio broadcast. Its use is often seen as a cynical attempt to deceive or mislead the public. **2** (*used before a noun*) relating to or denoting a sound bite or its use: *sound bite television; sound bite culture.*

soundboard *noun* **1** a thin resonant board placed in a musical instrument to reinforce its sound by sympathetic vibration. **2** a structure behind or over a pulpit, rostrum, or platform to direct sound forwards.

sound box *noun* the hollow resonating chamber in the body of a musical instrument, e.g. a violin.

sound card *noun* a printed circuit board used in a personal computer to produce good quality sound, e.g. for multimedia applications.

sound effect *noun* a sound, other than speech or music, used to create an effect in a play, radio programme, film, etc, *esp* an artificially produced one which imitates an effect, e.g. the shaking of a metal sheet to sound like thunder.

sounder *noun* a device for making soundings.

sound hole *noun* an opening in the body of a musical instrument for increasing resonance.

sounding[1] *noun* **1a** the act or process or an instance of ascertaining the depth of water in something. **b** a measurement taken by sounding. **c** the depth so determined. **2** the measurement of atmospheric conditions. **3** (*in pl*) a place or part of a body of water where a sounding line will reach the bottom. **4** (*also in pl*) a probe, test, or sampling of opinion or intention.

sounding[2] *adj* **1** *archaic* sonorous or resounding. **2** imposing or pompous.

sounding board *noun* **1a** someone whose reaction serves as a test for new ideas. **b** a device or agency that helps spread opinions or ideas. **2** = SOUNDBOARD.

sounding line *noun* a line or wire weighted at one end for sounding.

sound off *verb intrans informal* **1** to voice opinions freely and vigorously. **2** *chiefly NAmer* to speak loudly.

sound out *verb trans* to attempt to find out the views or intentions of (somebody): *We'll sound him out about the new proposals.*

sound post *noun* a post in an instrument of the viol or violin family set nearly under the bridge for support and for transmitting sound vibrations to the back.

soundproof[1] *adj* designed or intended to prevent or minimize sound penetration: *a soundproof booth.*

soundproof[2] *verb trans* to make (e.g. a room) soundproof.

sound shift *noun* in linguistics, a systematic sound change as a language evolves.

sound spectrograph *noun* an instrument used for analysing and recording the frequencies and intensities of the components of a sound.

sound system *noun* electronic equipment for reproducing and amplifying sound.

sound track *noun* **1** the narrow strip at the edge of a film that carries the sound recording. **2** the recorded music accompanying a film.

sound wave *noun* a wave by which sound is propagated.

soup /soohp/ *noun* **1** a liquid food typically having a meat, fish, or vegetable stock as a base and often thickened and containing pieces of solid food. **2** *NAmer, informal* nitroglycerine. **3** *informal* chemicals for developing film. ✱ **in the soup** *informal* in an awkward or embarrassing predicament. [French *soupe* sop, soup, of Germanic origin]

soupçon /'soohpson, 'soohpsonh/ *noun* (*pl* **soupçons** /-sonz/) a small amount; a dash. [French *soupçon* suspicion, ultimately from Latin *suspicere*: see SUSPECT[1]]

soup kitchen *noun* an establishment where food, e.g. soup and bread, is given to the needy or homeless, often for free.

soup up *verb trans informal* **1** to increase the power of (an engine or car). **2** to make (something) more attractive, interesting, etc. [prob from English slang *soup* a drug injected into a racehorse to stimulate it]

soupy *adj* (**soupier, soupiest**) **1** having the consistency of soup. **2** *informal* sentimental or mawkish.

sour[1] /sowa/ *adj* **1** being or inducing an acid taste similar to that of vinegar, lemons, etc, one of the four basic taste sensations: compare BITTER[1], SALT[3], SWEET[1]: *sour pickles.* **2** having the acid taste or smell of fermentation; turned: *sour milk.* **3** smelling or tasting of decay; rancid or rotten: *sour breath.* **4** disenchanted or embittered: *a sour woman.* **5** said of soil: excessively acidic. **6** said of petroleum products: containing foul-smelling sulphur compounds ✱ **go/turn sour 1** to turn out wrong or badly: *The project had gone sour.* **2** to become unpleasant or less harmonious: *Their relationship turned sour.* ➤➤ **sourish** *adj*, **sourly** *adv*, **sourness** *noun*. [Old English *sūr*]

sour[2] *noun chiefly NAmer* a cocktail made with a usu specified spirit, lemon or lime juice, sugar, and sometimes soda water: *a whisky sour.*

sour[3] *verb trans* to make (something) sour. ➤ *verb intrans* to become sour.

source[1] /saws/ *noun* **1a** a means of supply: *a secret source of wealth.* **b** a place of origin; a beginning. **c** somebody or something that initiates or inspires. **d** a person, publication, etc that supplies information, *esp* at first hand. **2** the point of origin of a stream of water. **3** a generative force; a cause. **4** *archaic* a spring or fountain. ✱ **at source** at the point of origin or issue. [Middle English *sours* via French from Latin *surgere*: see SURGE[1]]

source[2] *verb trans* **1** to obtain (materials or components) for a manufacturing process: *All the timber for its products will now be sourced from countries with a recognized reafforestation programme — Daily Telegraph.* **2** to trace (something) to a source.

source code *noun* a list of commands in text form that can be converted into machine code by a compiler to execute a computer program.

sour cream *noun* cream that has been deliberately made sour by the addition of lactic acid-forming bacteria, for use in cooking, salads, etc.

sourdough *noun* **1a** bread dough in which the yeast is still active, that is reserved from one baking for use as a leaven in the next. **b** bread made from this. **2** *NAmer* a veteran inhabitant, *esp* an old-time prospector, of Alaska or northwestern Canada. [(sense 2) from the use of sourdough for making bread in prospectors' camps]

soured cream *noun* = SOUR CREAM.

sour grapes *pl noun* (*treated as sing.*) an attitude of disparagement towards something achieved or owned by another because one is unable to attain it oneself. [from the fable, ascribed to Aesop, of the fox who, finding himself unable to reach some grapes, disparaged them as sour]

sourpuss *noun informal* a gloomy, bitter, or bad-tempered person. [SOUR[1] + *puss* face, from Irish Gaelic *pus* mouth]

sousaphone /'soohzəfohn/ *noun* a large tuba that has a flared adjustable bell and is designed to encircle the player and rest on the left shoulder. ➤➤ **sousaphonist** *noun*. [named after John Philip *Sousa* d.1932, US bandmaster and composer]

sous chef /'sooh shef/ *noun* an assistant cook in a restaurant or hotel. [French *sous chef*, literally 'under chef']

souse[1] /sows/ *verb trans* **1** to pickle (something): *soused herring.* **2a** to plunge (something) in liquid; to immerse (it). **b** to drench or saturate (something). **3** *informal* to make (somebody) drunk. ➤ *verb intrans* to become immersed or drenched. [Middle English *sousen* from early French *souz, souce* pickling solution, of Germanic origin]

souse[2] *noun* **1** brine or vinegar in which foods are preserved. **2** *chiefly NAmer* something pickled, *esp* seasoned and chopped pork trimmings, fish, or shellfish. **3** *informal* a drunkard.

souslik /'soohslik/ *noun* = SUSLIK.

soutane /sooh'tan/ *noun* a cassock, *esp* one worn by a Roman Catholic priest. [French *soutane* from Italian *sottana*, from *sotto* under, from Latin *subtus*]

souterrain /'soohtərayn/ *noun* a prehistoric underground stone-built passage or chamber, commonly associated with stone forts in Ireland and Scotland. [French *souterrain*, from *sous* under + *terrain* ground]

south[1] /sowth/ *noun* **1** the direction 90° clockwise from east. **2** (*often* **South**) regions or countries lying to the south of a specified or implied point of orientation. [Old English *sūth*]

south[2] *adj and adv* **1** at, towards, or coming from the south. **2** said of the wind: blowing from the south. ✳ **south by east** in a position or direction between south and south-southeast. **south by west** in a position or direction between south and south-southwest.

South African *noun* a native or inhabitant of the Republic of South Africa. ➤➤ **South African** *adj.*

South American *noun* a native or inhabitant of South America. ➤➤ **South American** *adj.*

southbound *adj and adv* going or moving south.

Southdown *noun* an animal of an English breed of small hornless meat-producing sheep with medium-length wool. [named after the *South Downs*, hills in SE England where the breed originated]

southeast[1] *noun* **1** the direction midway between south and east. **2** (*often* **Southeast**) regions or countries lying to the southeast of a specified or implied point of orientation. ➤➤ **southeastward** /-wəd/ *adj and adv*, **southeastwards** /-wədz/ *adv.*

southeast[2] *adj and adv* **1** at, towards, or coming from the southeast. **2** said of the wind: blowing from the southeast.

southeaster *noun* a wind blowing from the southeast.

southeasterly[1] *adj and adv* **1** in a southeastern position or direction. **2** said of a wind: blowing from the southeast.

southeasterly[2] *noun* (*pl* **southeasterlies**) a wind blowing from the southeast.

southeastern *adj* in or towards the southeast; inhabiting the southeast.

southerly[1] /'sudhəli/ *adj and adv* **1** in a southern position or direction. **2** said of a wind: blowing from the south.

southerly[2] *noun* (*pl* **southerlies**) a wind blowing from the south.

southern /'sudhən/ *adj* in or towards the south; inhabiting the south. ➤➤ **southernmost** *adj.*

Southerner *noun* (*also* **southerner**) a native or inhabitant of the South.

southern-fried *adj* said of food, *esp* chicken: coated in a spicy batter and deep fried.

Southern lights *pl noun* = AURORA AUSTRALIS.

southernwood *noun* a shrubby fragrant European wormwood with bitter foliage: *Artemisia abrotanum*.

southing /'sowdhing, 'sowthing/ *noun* **1** distance due south in latitude from the preceding point of measurement, used *esp* in navigation at sea. **2** southerly progress. **3** in astronomy, the transit of a celestial body, *esp* the sun, across the meridian due south of the observer.

South Korean *noun* a native or inhabitant of South Korea. ➤➤ **South Korean** *adj.*

southpaw *noun* **1** a left-handed boxer who leads with the right hand and guards with the left. **2** *chiefly NAmer* a left-handed person.

south pole *noun* **1a** (*often* **South Pole**) the southernmost point of the rotational axis of the earth or another celestial body. **b** the southernmost point on the celestial sphere, about which the stars seem to revolve. **2** the southward-pointing pole of a magnet.

south-southeast[1] *noun* the direction midway between south and southeast.

south-southeast[2] *adj and adv* at, towards, or coming from the south-southeast.

south-southwest[1] *noun* the direction midway between south and southwest.

south-southwest[2] *adj and adv* at, towards, or coming from the south-southwest.

southward /'sowthwəd/ *adj and adv* towards the south; in a direction going south.

southwards *adv* towards the south; southward.

southwest[1] *noun* **1** the direction midway between south and west. **2** (*often* **Southwest**) regions or countries lying to the southwest of a specified or implied point of orientation. ➤➤ **southwestward** /-wəd/ *adj and adv*, **southwestwards** /-wədz/ *adv.*

southwest[2] *adj and adv* **1** at, towards, or coming from the southwest. **2** said of the wind: blowing from the southwest.

southwester *noun* a wind blowing from the southwest.

southwesterly[1] *adj and adv* **1** in a southwestern position or direction. **2** said of a wind: blowing from the southwest.

southwesterly[2] *noun* (*pl* **southwesterlies**) a wind blowing from the southwest.

southwestern *adj* in or towards the southwest; inhabiting the southwest.

souvenir /soohvə'niə/ *noun* something that serves as a reminder, e.g. of a person, place, or past event; a memento. [French *souvenir*, literally 'act of remembering', from *se souvenir* to remember, from Latin *subvenire* to come up, come to mind, from SUB- + *venire* to come]

souvlaki /sooh'vlahki/ *noun* (*pl* **souvlakia** /-kiə/ *or* **souvlakis**) a Greek dish of meat, usu lamb, grilled on a skewer. [Greek *souvlakia* small skewers, from *souvla* skewer]

sou'wester /sow'westə/ *noun* a waterproof hat with a wide slanting brim longer at the back than in front. [orig in the sense 'gale blowing from the southwest'; contraction of SOUTHWESTER]

sovereign[1] /'sovrin/ *noun* **1** somebody possessing supreme power, *esp* a monarch. **2** a former British gold coin worth one pound. [Middle English *soverain* from Old French, ultimately from Latin *super* above; the spelling changed in the 15th cent. by association with REIGN[1]]

sovereign[2] *adj* **1a** possessing supreme power: *sovereign ruler.* **b** unlimited in extent; absolute: *sovereign power.* **c** enjoying political autonomy: *a sovereign state.* **2a** of outstanding excellence or importance: *their sovereign sense of humour* — Winston Churchill. **b** of an unqualified nature; utmost: *sovereign contempt.* **3** of, relating to, or befitting a sovereign. ➤➤ **sovereignly** *adv.*

sovereignty *noun* (*pl* **sovereignties**) **1a** supreme power, *esp* over a politically organized body. **b** freedom from external influence or control; autonomy. **c** controlling influence. **2** an autonomous state.

Soviet /'sohvi·ət, 'so-/ *adj* inhabiting, belonging or relating to, or characteristic of the former USSR.

soviet *noun* **1a** an elected governmental or administrative council in the former USSR. **b** a meeting of such a council. **2** (**Soviets**) the people, *esp* the political and military leaders, of the former USSR. [Russian *soviet* council]

sovietize *or* **sovietise** *verb trans* **1** to bring (a person or a country) under Soviet control. **2** to force (a country) into conformity with Soviet cultural patterns or government policies. ➤➤ **sovietization** /-'zaysh(ə)n/ *noun.*

sow[1] /sow/ *noun* **1a** an adult female pig. **b** the adult female of various other animals, e.g. the grizzly bear. **2** a mass of metal solidified in a channel that conducts molten metal, *esp* iron, to moulds. [Old English *sugu*]

sow[2] /soh/ *verb* (*past tense* **sowed**, *past part.* **sown** /sohn/ *or* **sowed**) ➤ *verb trans* **1a** to scatter (seed) on the earth to enable plants to grow, or to scatter the seed of (a particular plant). **b** to strew (an area) with seed. **2** to implant or initiate (something): *sow suspicion.* **3** to disperse or disseminate (something). ➤ *verb intrans* to plant seed for growth, *esp* by scattering. ✳ **sow one's wild oats** to indulge in the wildness and promiscuity of youth, before settling down to a steady life. ➤➤ **sower** *noun.* [Old English *sāwan*]

sow thistle /sow/ *noun* any of several species of plants of the daisy family that have fleshy stems, milky juice, prickly leaves, and yellow flower heads: genus *Sonchus.*

soy /soy/ *noun* **1** a brown liquid sauce made by subjecting soya beans to long fermentation and to digestion in brine, used in oriental cookery. **2** = SOYA. [Japanese *shōyu* from Chinese (Cantonese) *shi-yau* soya bean oil]

soya /'soyə/ *noun* **1** an Asian plant of the pea family widely grown for its seeds and for forage and soil improvement: *Glycine max.* **2** protein from the edible seed of this plant. **3** *chiefly Brit* soy sauce. [Dutch *soja* from Japanese *shōyu*: see SOY]

soya bean (*NAmer* **soybean** /'soybeen/) *noun* the edible oil-rich and protein-rich seed of the soya plant.

soya milk *noun* a milk substitute made from soya bean flour.

soybean *noun NAmer* see SOYA BEAN.

soy sauce *noun* = SOY (1).

sozzled /ˈsoz(ə)ld/ *adj informal* very drunk. [dialect *sozzle* to splash, souse, intoxicate, prob imitative]

SP *abbr* starting price.

sp. *abbr* **1** species. **2** specific. **3** spelling.

spa /spah/ *noun* **1** a spring of mineral water. **2** a usu fashionable resort with mineral springs. **3** a commercial establishment providing health and beauty treatments. **4** a bathtub with an apparatus for producing a whirlpool effect with jets of aerated water. [named after *Spa*, a town in Belgium famous for its mineral springs]

spa bath *noun* = SPA (4).

space[1] /spays/ *noun* **1a** the limitless three-dimensional extent in which objects and events occur and have relative position and direction. **b** physical space independent of what occupies it. **2** the region beyond the earth's atmosphere or beyond the solar system. **3a** continuous, unoccupied, or unimpeded distance, area, or volume: *There's space in the trunk for a few more things*. **b** an amount of room set apart or available for something: *a parking space*. **4** freedom for personal development and fulfilment: *She walked out, saying she needed some space*. **5** a period of time; or its duration: *in the space of 20 minutes*. **6** a blank area on a page, e.g. separating words or lines. **7** a seat, berth, or standing room on a public vehicle. **8** a set of mathematical entities, e.g. the theoretical positions occupied by all the points on a straight line, that obey a set of axioms: *Euclidean space*. **9** any of the degrees between or above or below the lines of a musical stave. **10** a brief interval during which a telegraph key is not causing electrical contact to be made. [Middle English via Old French from Latin *spatium* area, room, interval of space or time]

space[2] *verb trans* (*often* + out) to place (two or more things) at intervals or arrange (them) with space between. ⪢ **spacer** *noun*.

space age *noun* (**the space age**) the era in which the exploration of space and space travel have become possible.

space-age *adj* suggestive of the technology of the space age; ultramodern or futuristic.

space bar *noun* the horizontal bar below the lowest row of keys on a typewriter or computer keyboard, which is pressed to make a space.

space capsule *noun* a small spacecraft, or the part of a larger spacecraft containing the crew, that is designed to be returned to earth.

spacecraft *noun* (*pl* **spacecraft**) a vehicle designed to travel beyond the earth's atmosphere.

spaced out *adj informal* dazed or stupefied, *esp* by a narcotic substance.

space heating *noun* the heating of relatively small, usu enclosed spaces, e.g. rooms in a building, *esp* for human comfort, with the heater either within the space or external to it. ⪢ **space heater** *noun*.

spaceman *or* **spacewoman** *noun* (*pl* **spacemen** *or* **spacewomen**) **1** somebody who travels outside the earth's atmosphere. **2** a visitor to earth from outer space.

space platform *noun* = SPACE STATION.

spaceport *noun* an installation for testing and launching spacecraft.

space probe *noun* = PROBE[1] (2B).

spaceship *noun* a manned spacecraft.

space shuttle *noun* a vehicle designed to serve as a reusable transport between the earth and destinations in space, *esp* a US space vehicle launched by rocket but able to land like an aircraft.

space station *noun* a manned artificial satellite designed for a fixed orbit about the earth and to serve as a base.

space suit *noun* a suit equipped to make life in space possible for its wearer.

space-time *noun* a system of one temporal and three spatial coordinates by which any physical object or event can be located.

space-time continuum *noun* = SPACE-TIME.

space walk *noun* a trip outside a spacecraft made by an astronaut in space.

spacey *or* **spacy** *adj* (**spacier, spaciest**) *informal* of or in a spaced-out state: *music with a spacey effect*.

spacial /ˈspaysh(ə)l/ *adj* see SPATIAL.

spacing *noun* **1a** the act of providing something with spaces or placing things at intervals. **b** an arrangement in space: *Alter the spacing of the chairs*. **2** the distance between any two objects in a usu regularly arranged series.

spacious /ˈspayshəs/ *adj* containing ample space; roomy. ⪢ **spaciously** *adv*, **spaciousness** *noun*. [Middle English via French from Latin *spatiosus*, from *spatium* SPACE[1]]

spacy *adj* see SPACEY.

spade[1] /spayd/ *noun* a digging implement with a flat, usu rectangular, metal blade that can be pushed into the ground with the foot and is attached to a long handle. ✳ **call a spade a spade** to speak frankly and usu bluntly: *'When I see a spade I call it a spade.' 'I am glad to say that I have never seen a spade.'* Oscar Wilde. ⪢ **spadeful** (*pl* **spadefuls**) *noun*. [Old English *spadu*]

spade[2] *verb trans* to dig up, shape, or work (something) with a spade.

spade[3] *noun* **1a** a playing card marked with one or more black figures in the shape of a spearhead. **b** (*in pl*) the suit comprising cards identified by this figure. **2** *informal, offensive* a black person. ✳ **in spades** *informal* in the extreme. [Italian *spada* or Spanish *espada* broad sword (used as a mark on playing cards); both via Latin from Greek *spathē* blade]

spadework *noun* the routine preparatory work for an undertaking.

spadix /ˈspaydiks/ *noun* (*pl* **spadices** /-seez/) a spike of crowded flowers, e.g. in an arum, with a fleshy or succulent axis usu enclosed in a spathe. [via Latin from Greek *spadik-, spadix* frond torn from a palm tree, from *span* to draw, pull]

spaghetti /spəˈgeti/ *pl noun* (*treated as sing. or pl*) pasta in the form of thin solid strings of varying widths. [Italian *spaghetti*, pl of *spaghetto*, dimin. of *spago* cord, string]

spaghetti western *noun informal* a western film made cheaply in Europe.

spahi /ˈspah(h)ee/ *noun* (*pl* **spahis**) **1** a member of a former corps of irregular Turkish cavalry. **2** a member of a former corps of Algerian native cavalry in the French Army. [early French *spahi* via Turkish from Persian *sipāhī* cavalryman]

spake /spayk/ *verb archaic* past tense of SPEAK.

spall[1] /spawl/ *noun* a small splinter or chip, *esp* of stone. [Middle English *spalle*; earlier history unknown]

spall[2] *verb trans* to break up (stone, ore, etc) into fragments. ⪢ *verb intrans* **1** to break off in fragments; to chip. **2** to undergo spallation.

spallation /spəˈlaysh(ə)n/ *noun* a nuclear reaction in which the bombardment of an atomic nucleus with high-energy particles or photons (particles of radiant energy; see PHOTON) results in the ejection of protons, neutrons, etc from the nucleus. [SPALL[2]]

Spam /spam/ *noun trademark* a tinned pork luncheon meat. [shortening of *spiced ham*]

spam[1] *noun* messages, *esp* inappropriate or unsolicited ones, sent to a large number of users or newsgroups on the Internet. [from a Monty Python sketch featuring Spam]

spam[2] *verb trans* (**spammed, spamming**) to send a message to (many people) on the Internet. ⪢ **spammer** *noun*.

span[1] /span/ *noun* **1** an extent, distance, or spread between two limits, e.g.: **a** a limited stretch of time, *esp* an individual's lifetime. **b** the full reach or extent: *the remarkable span of his memory*. **c** distance or extent between abutments or supports, e.g. of a bridge. **d** a part of a bridge between supports. **e** = WINGSPAN. **2a** the distance from the end of the thumb to the end of the little finger of a spread hand. **b** a former English unit of length equal to 9in. (about 0.23m). [Old English *spann*]

span[2] *verb trans* (**spanned, spanning**) **1a** to extend across (something) in space or time: *His career spanned four decades*. **b** to form an arch over (something): *A small bridge spanned the pond*. **2** to measure (something) by the hand with fingers and thumb extended.

span[3] *verb archaic* past tense of SPIN[1].

span[4] *noun* a pair of animals, e.g. oxen, usu matched in appearance and action and driven together. [Dutch *span* from early Dutch *spannen* to hitch up]

Spandex /ˈspandeks/ *noun trademark* an elastic textile fibre made largely from polyurethane. [alteration of EXPAND]

spandrel /'spandrǝl/ *noun* the space between the right or left exterior curve of an arch and an enclosing right angle. [Middle English *spandrell* via Anglo-French from Old French *espandre* to spread out, from Latin *expandere*: see EXPAND]

spangle¹ /'spanggl/ *noun* **1** = SEQUIN (1). **2** a small glittering object or particle: *gold spangles of dew* — Edith Sitwell. ➤➤ **spangly** *adj*. [Middle English *spangel*, dimin. of *spang* shiny ornament, from early Dutch *spange* buckle]

spangle² *verb trans* to set or sprinkle (something) with or as if with spangles. ➤ *verb intrans* to glitter as if covered with spangles; to sparkle.

Spaniard /'spanyǝd/ *noun* a native or inhabitant of Spain. [Middle English *Spaignard* from early French *Espaignart*, from *Espaigne* Spain]

spaniel /'spanyǝl/ *noun* a dog of a small or medium-sized breed with short legs, long wavy hair, feathered legs and tail, and large drooping ears. [Middle English *spaniell* from Old French *espaigneul* Spanish (dog), from Latin *Hispania* Spain, where it originated]

Spanish /'spanish/ *noun* the official Romance language of the people of Spain and of the countries colonized by Spaniards. ➤➤ **Spanish** *adj*.

Word history
Spanish (adj) from Middle English *Spainish* from *Spain*. The many Spanish words that have passed into English include *alligator, armadillo, armada, bonanza, cargo, embargo, garrotte, guerrilla, gusto, intransigent, macho, mosquito, patio, peccadillo, ranch, silo, stevedore, stockade, tornado, vanilla,* and *vigilante*. Many of the best-known ones reflect Spanish exploration and involvement in America. Further words (such as *cafeteria, canyon, lariat,* and *stampede*) were first borrowed in American English from words specific to the varieties of Spanish that have evolved in America, and it seems likely that the growing Hispanic population in the USA will increasingly influence the language. In addition, Spanish has been the medium through which many loanwords from Central and South American languages (such as *potato* and *tobacco*) have entered English.

Spanish American *noun* a native or inhabitant of any of the Spanish-speaking countries of America, or a citizen of the USA of Spanish descent. ➤➤ **Spanish-American** *adj*.

Spanish fly *noun* **1** a green blister beetle of S Europe: *Lytta vesicatoria*. **2** a preparation of Spanish flies used as an aphrodisiac. Also called CANTHARIDES.

Spanish guitar *noun* a guitar of the classical acoustic type, *esp* as distinct from an electric guitar.

Spanish moss *noun* a plant of the pineapple family that hangs in long tufts of greyish green strands from the branches of trees in the S USA and the W Indies: *Tillandsia usneoides*.

Spanish omelette *noun* an omelette containing cooked chopped vegetables, e.g. onions, potatoes, and green peppers: compare OMELETTE.

Spanish onion *noun* a large mild-flavoured onion.

spank¹ /spangk/ *verb trans* to strike (somebody), *esp* on the buttocks, with the open hand or something flat. [imitative]

spank² *noun* a slap or a series of slaps.

spanker *noun* **1** a fore-and-aft sail set on the aftermost mast of a square-rigged ship. **2** *informal* something impressive. [origin unknown]

spanking¹ *adj* **1** vigorous or brisk: *They rode off at a spanking pace.* **2** remarkable of its kind; striking. [origin unknown]

spanking² *noun* a series of spanks: *He said the child needed a good spanking.*

spanner /'spanǝ/ *noun chiefly Brit* a tool consisting of a flat metal bar with one or both ends shaped for holding or turning nuts or bolts with geometrically shaped heads. ✷ **spanner in the works** *informal* an obstruction or hindrance, e.g. to a plan or operation. [German *Spanner* instrument for winding springs, from *spannen* to stretch, draw tight]

spar¹ /spah/ *noun* **1** a stout pole. **2a** a mast, boom, gaff, yard, etc used to support or control a sail. **b** any of the main longitudinal members of the wing or fuselage of an aircraft. [Middle English *sparre*; earlier history unknown]

spar² *verb intrans* (**sparred, sparring**) **1a** to box without putting full force into one's blows, *esp* in practice. **b** to engage in a practice bout of boxing. **2** to argue or wrangle: *The public quite enjoys watching politicians sparring at the Dispatch Box.* **3** to strike or fight with feet or spurs in the manner of a gamecock. [Old English *sperran, spyrran* to hit out]

spar³ *noun* a sparring match or session.

spar⁴ *noun* any of various non-metallic minerals which usu split easily. [Low German *spar*]

sparaxis /spǝ'raksis/ *noun* (*pl* **sparaxis**) a South African plant of the iris family with showy multicoloured flowers: genus *Sparaxis*. [Latin genus name, from Greek *sparassō* to tear]

spare¹ /speǝ/ *adj* **1** not in use; *esp* reserved for use in emergency: *a spare tyre.* **2a** in excess of what is required; surplus. **b** not taken up with work or duties; free: *spare time.* **3** plain and unelaborate, uncluttered, or concise: *a spare prose style.* **4** healthily lean; wiry. **5** *informal* not abundant; meagre. ✷ **go spare** *Brit, informal* to become extremely angry or distraught: *I was late home and my father went spare.* ➤➤ **sparely** *adv*, **spareness** *noun*. [Old English *spær* scarce, meagre, frugal, hence in Middle English 'thriftily set aside for future use', leading in the 16th cent. to 'left over, surplus']

spare² *verb trans* **1** to make (something) available for others' use, or give (it) up as surplus to requirements: *I can only spare five minutes, I'm afraid.* **2** to refrain from destroying, punishing, or harming (somebody or something). **3** to refrain from using (something): *Spare the rod and spoil the child.* **4** to relieve (somebody) of the necessity of doing or undergoing something: *Spare yourself the trouble.* **5** (*usu in negative contexts*) to use or dispense (something) frugally: *Don't spare the butter.* ➤ *verb intrans archaic* to be frugal: *Some will spend and some will spare* — Burns. ✷ **spare no expense** to pay as much as is needed. **to spare** above and beyond what is needed; available; left: *We arrived at the station with two minutes to spare.* [Old English *sparian*]

spare³ *noun* **1a** a spare or duplicate item or part; *specif* a spare part for a motor vehicle. **b** = SPARE TYRE. **2** in tenpin bowling, the knocking down of all ten pins with the first two balls in a frame.

sparerib *noun* a pork rib with most of the surrounding meat removed for use as bacon. [by folk etymology from Low German *ribbesper* pickled pork ribs roasted on a spit, from early Low German *ribbesper*, from *ribbe* rib + *sper* spear, spit]

spare tyre *noun* **1** an extra tyre carried by a motor vehicle as a spare. **2** *informal* a roll of fat at the waist.

sparge /spahj/ *verb trans esp* in brewing, to moisten or rinse (something) by sprinkling; to spray (it). ➤➤ **sparge** *noun*. [prob from early French *espargier* sprinkle, from Latin *spargere* to scatter]

sparing /'speǝring/ *adj* **1** not wasteful; frugal: *We must be sparing with the butter.* **2** meagre or scant. ➤➤ **sparingly** *adv*, **sparingness** *noun*.

spark¹ /spahk/ *noun* **1a** a small particle of a burning substance thrown out by something that is on fire or remaining when combustion is nearly completed. **b** a hot glowing particle struck from a larger mass: *sparks flying from under a hammer.* **2a** a luminous disruptive electrical discharge of very short duration between two conductors of opposite high potential separated by a gas, e.g. air. **b** an electrical discharge of this kind produced by a spark plug in an internal-combustion engine. **3** a sparkle or flash. **4** something that sets off or stimulates an event, development, etc. **5** a trace, *esp* one which may develop; a germ: *a spark of decency.* **6** *informal.* **a** (*in pl*) a radio operator on a ship. **b** (*in pl*) an electrician. [Old English *spearca*]

spark² *verb intrans* to produce or give off sparks; *specif* to produce a spark to provide ignition in an internal-combustion engine. ➤ *verb trans* **1** (+ off) to prompt or precipitate (something): *The question sparked off a lively discussion.* **2** to stir (somebody) to activity; to incite (them): *A player can spark his team to victory.*

spark³ *noun archaic* **1** a foppish young man; a gallant. **2** a lover or beau. ➤➤ **sparkish** *adj*. [perhaps of Scandinavian origin and related to Old Norse *sparkr* sprightly, prob influenced by SPARK¹]

spark chamber *noun* a device that is used to detect the path of a high-energy particle by observable electric discharges.

spark gap *noun* a usu air-filled space between two electrical conductors, e.g. in a sparking plug, in which electric sparks occur.

sparking plug *noun* = SPARK PLUG.

sparkle¹ /'spahkl/ *verb intrans* **1a** to give off or reflect glittering points of light; to scintillate. **b** to give off sparks. **2** to show brilliance or animation: *The dialogue sparkles with wit.* [Middle English *sparklen*, frequentative of *sparken* to spark, from SPARK¹]

sparkle² *noun* **1** a little spark; a flash of light. **2** vivacity or gaiety. ➤➤ **sparkly** *adj*.

sparkler *noun* **1** a hand-held firework that throws off brilliant sparks on burning. **2** *informal* a cut and polished diamond or other gem.

sparkling wine *noun* wine that is fizzy, either through natural processes of fermentation or by having gas added.

spark plug *noun* a part that fits into the cylinder head of an internal-combustion engine, e.g. of a car, and produces the electric spark that ignites the air–fuel mixture.

sparring partner *noun* **1** a boxer's companion for practice in sparring during training. **2** a habitual opponent, e.g. in friendly argument.

sparrow /'sparoh/ *noun* any of several small dull-coloured song-birds related to the finches; *esp* the house sparrow: *Passer domesticus*. [Old English *spearwa*]

sparrowgrass *noun chiefly dialect* = ASPARAGUS. [by folk etymology from ASPARAGUS]

sparrow hawk *noun* a small Eurasian and N African hawk that has a long tail and short rounded wings and preys on smaller birds: *Accipiter nisus*.

sparse /spahs/ *adj* consisting of few and scattered elements; *esp* not thickly grown or settled. ➤ **sparsely** *adv*, **sparseness** *noun*, **sparsity** *noun*. [Latin *sparsus* spread out, past part. of *spargere* to scatter]

Spartan /'spaht(ə)n/ *noun* **1** a native or inhabitant of ancient Sparta, a city in ancient Greece. **2** (*also* **spartan**) a person of great courage and endurance. ➤ **Spartan** *adj*.

Word history
Middle English from Latin *Spartanus* (adj and noun), from *Sparta*. The ancient citizens of Sparta were famed for their courage, self-discipline, and austere lifestyle.

spartan *adj* **1** not offering or designed for ease and comfort, or indifferent to them; austere. **2** having or showing courage and endurance.

spasm /'spaz(ə)m/ *noun* **1** an involuntary and abnormal muscular contraction. **2** a sudden violent and brief effort or emotion: *spasms of helpless mirth*. [Middle English *spasme* via French and Latin from Greek *spasmos*, from *span* to draw, pull]

spasmodic /spaz'modik/ *adj* **1** occurring at intervals and usu suddenly and unpredictably; intermittent: *He made spasmodic attempts at studying.* **2a** resembling a spasm, *esp* in sudden violence: *a spasmodic jerk.* **b** relating to, or affected or characterized by spasms. ➤ **spasmodically** *adv*. [Latin *spasmodicus* from Greek *spasmōdēs*, from *spasmos*: see SPASM]

spastic[1] /'spastik/ *adj* **1** of or characterized by spasm: *a spastic colon.* **2** *dated, sometimes offensive* affected by cerebral palsy. **3** *informal, offensive* ineffectual or incompetent. ➤ **spastically** *adv*, **spasticity** /spa'stisiti/ *noun*. [Latin *spasticus* from Greek *spastikos* drawing in, from *span* to draw, pull]

spastic[2] *noun* **1** *dated, sometimes offensive* somebody who has cerebral palsy or a similar condition that involves paralysis and muscular incoordination from birth. **2** *informal, offensive* a clumsy or ineffectual person.

spastic paralysis *noun* paralysis with involuntary contraction or uncontrolled movements of the affected muscles: compare CEREBRAL PALSY.

spat[1] /spat/ *verb* past tense and past part. of SPIT[1].

spat[2] *noun* a cloth or leather gaiter covering the instep and ankle. [short for SPATTERDASH]

spat[3] *noun informal* a small-scale or petty argument. [prob imitative]

spat[4] *verb intrans* (**spatted, spatting**) to quarrel pettily or briefly.

spat[5] *noun* (*pl* **spats** *or collectively* **spat**) a young oyster or other bivalve mollusc. [origin unknown]

spatchcock[1] /'spachkok/ *verb trans* **1** to cook (a fowl or small game bird) by splitting along the backbone and frying or grilling. **2** to insert (words) into a passage or put (them) together in a forced or incongruous way. [prob alteration of *spitchcock* split and grilled eel, of unknown origin]

spatchcock[2] *noun* a fowl that is dressed, split open, and cooked by frying or grilling immediately after its slaughter.

spate /spayt/ *noun* **1** a large number or amount, *esp* occurring in a short space of time: *the recent spate of fire bombs.* **2** a state of flood: *a river in full spate.* [Middle English (Scots and Northern English); earlier history unknown]

spathe /spaydh/ *noun* a sheath consisting of a bract or pair of bracts enclosing the cluster of flowers on a plant: *the spathe of cuckoopint.* [Latin *spatha* broad sword, from Greek *spathē* blade]

spathic /'spathik/ *adj* resembling spar. [German *Spath, Spat* spar]

spathulate /'spathyoolət/ *adj* see SPATULATE.

spatial *or* **spacial** /'spaysh(ə)l/ *adj* relating to, occupying, or occurring in space. ➤ **spatiality** /spayshi'aliti/ *noun*, **spatially** *adv*. [Latin *spatium* SPACE[1]]

spatiotemporal /,spayshioh'temp(ə)rəl/ *adj* **1** having both spatial and temporal qualities. **2** of space-time. ➤ **spatiotemporally** *adv*. [Latin *spatium* SPACE[1] + *tempor-, tempus* time]

Spätlese /'shpaytlayzə/ *noun* (*pl* **Spätleses** *or* **Spätlesen** /-layzən/) a white wine produced *esp* in Germany from late-gathered and therefore riper grapes. [German *spät* late + *Lese* picking]

spatter[1] /'spatə/ *verb* (**spattered, spattering**) ➤ *verb trans* **1** to splash or sprinkle (something or somebody) with drops of liquid, or as if with drops of liquid: *His coat was spattered with mud.* **2** to scatter (something) by splashing or sprinkling, or as if by splashing or sprinkling. ➤ *verb intrans* to spurt out in scattered drops: *Blood spattered everywhere.* [prob from a prehistoric Germanic word, of imitative origin]

spatter[2] *noun* **1** the sound of spattering. **2** a drop spattered on something or a stain due to spattering.

spatterdash *noun* a long leather gaiter formerly worn when riding.

spatula /'spatyoolə/ *noun* an implement with a flat, thin, blunt-edged, usu rectangular blade at the end of a short handle, used for spreading, mixing, etc soft substances or powders. [late Latin *spatula* spoon, spatula, dimin. of Latin *spatha*: see SPATHE]

spatulate /'spatyoolət/ *or* **spathulate** /'spathyoolət/ *adj* shaped like a spatula: *spatulate spines of a caterpillar.*

spavin /'spavin/ *noun* a bony enlargement or soft swelling of the hock of a horse associated with strain. ➤ **spavined** *adj*. [Middle English *spavayne* from early French *espavain*, of Germanic origin]

spawn[1] /spawn/ *verb trans* **1** said of an aquatic animal: to produce or deposit (eggs). **2** to produce (something) or cause (something) to appear, *esp* abundantly: *A successful pop group spawns a host of imitators.* ➤ *verb intrans* **1** to deposit spawn. **2** to produce young, *esp* in large numbers. ➤ **spawner** *noun*. [Middle English *spawnen* via Anglo-French from Old French *espardre* to pour out, from Latin *expandere*: see EXPAND]

spawn[2] *noun* **1** the large number of eggs produced by frogs, oysters, fish, etc. **2** (*treated as sing. or pl*) = OFFSPRING. **3** mycelium, *esp* for propagating mushrooms.

spay /spay/ *verb trans* to remove the ovaries of (a female animal). [Middle English *spayen* from Old French *espeer* to cut with a sword, ultimately from Latin *spatha*: see SPATHE]

SPCK *abbr* Society for Promoting Christian Knowledge.

speak /speek/ *verb* (*past tense* **spoke** /spohk/, *past part.* **spoken** /'spohk(ə)n/) ➤ *verb intrans* **1a** to utter words or articulate sounds with the voice; to talk. **b** to express thoughts or feelings in this way. **c** to exchange remarks with someone, *esp* in greeting. **d** to greet and have normal or polite relations with somebody or each other: *We're not speaking at the moment.* **2a** to make a formal speech or address. **b** *formal* (+ to) to comment on or deal with a particular point in the course of a speech, etc: *I shall speak to that issue shortly.* **c** (+ for) to act as spokesman for somebody else: *I am speaking for the whole group.* **3** to express thoughts or feelings in writing: *The article speaks about recent discoveries.* **4a** to express thoughts or feelings by other than verbal means: *Actions speak louder than words.* **b** to make a communication; to convey meaning or significance. **c** (+ of) to be indicative or suggestive of a fact or circumstance: *His battered shoes spoke of a long journey.* **5** to make a characteristic or natural sound: *All at once the thunder spoke* — George Meredith. **6** said of a hunting hound: to bark. ➤ *verb trans* **1** to use or be able to use (a language) in oral communication: *He speaks good Spanish.* **2a** to utter (e.g. a word) with the speaking voice. **b** to express (something) with the voice. **3a** to make (something) known in writing. **b** to convey (something) by other than verbal means; to reveal: *His eyes spoke affection.* ✷ **so to speak** used as an apologetic qualification for an unusual, accidentally punning, or ambiguous phrase: *The ball is, so to speak, back in the manager's court.* **speak in tongues** to speak in an unintelligible language when ecstatic during religious worship. **speak one's mind** to say frankly what one thinks. **speak volumes** to convey a great deal of information by means other than words: *a frown that spoke volumes*. **to speak of** (*usu in negative contexts*) worthy of mention or notice: *no talent to speak of*. ➤➤ **speakable** *adj*. [Old English *sprecan, specan*]

-speak *comb. form* forming nouns, denoting: language peculiar to or characteristic of a specified person, group, subject, or place, *esp* when considered to be clumsy, hypocritical, or deliberately obscure: *computerspeak*; *teenspeak*.

speakeasy *noun* (*pl* **speakeasies**) *informal* a place where alcoholic drinks were illegally sold during Prohibition in the USA in the 1920s and 1930s. [from the need to *speak easy* (softly) in ordering illicit goods]

speaker *noun* **1a** somebody who speaks, *esp* at public functions. **b** somebody who speaks a specified language: *an Italian-speaker*. **2** the presiding officer of a deliberative or legislative assembly. **3** = LOUDSPEAKER.

speakership *noun* the position of speaker, *esp* of a lawmaking body.

speaking *adj* **1a** capable of speech. **b** (*usu used in combinations*) containing chiefly native speakers of the language specified: *English-speaking countries*. **2** highly significant or expressive; eloquent: *a speaking look*. **3** able to speak a specified language: *French-speaking*.

speaking clock *noun Brit* a recorded message giving the correct time to telephone callers.

speaking tube *noun* a pipe through which conversation may be conducted, e.g. between different parts of a building.

speak out *verb intrans* to speak loudly or boldly; to state one's opinion frankly.

speak up *verb intrans* **1** to speak more loudly. **2** to state one's opinion frankly. **3** (+ for) to speak in defence of somebody.

spear[1] /spiə/ *noun* **1** a thrusting or throwing weapon with a long shaft and sharp head or blade used by hunters or foot soldiers. **2** a sharp-pointed instrument with barbs used in spearing fish. [Old English *spere*]

spear[2] *verb trans* to pierce, strike, or take hold of (something) with or as if with a spear: *He speared a sausage from the dish*.

spear[3] *noun* a usu young blade, shoot, or sprout, e.g. of asparagus or broccoli. [alteration of SPIRE[1]]

spearfish *noun* (*pl* **spearfishes** or collectively **spearfish**) any of several species of large powerful oceanic fishes related to the marlins and sail fishes: genus *Tetrapturus*.

speargrass *noun* any of various grasses that have sharp leaves or seeds: genera *Heteropogon, Stipa* and other genera.

speargun *noun* a device used for firing a spear in underwater fishing.

spearhead[1] *noun* **1** the sharp-pointed head of a spear. **2** a leading element or force in a development, course of action, etc.

spearhead[2] *verb trans* to serve as the leader of or a leading force in (e.g. an attack).

spearmint *noun* a common mint grown for its aromatic oil: *Mentha spicata*.

spear side *noun* the male branch of a family.

spec[1] /spek/ *noun informal* a speculation: *one company worth trying as a spec* — The Economist. ✱ **on spec 1** *informal* as a speculation, with no certainty of sale or gain: *houses built on spec*. **2** *informal* in the hope of finding or obtaining something desired: *I rang up on spec, doubting whether there'd be anyone at home*.

spec[2] *noun informal* = SPECIFICATION: *He always went for the machine with the best spec*.

special[1] /'spesh(ə)l/ *adj* **1** distinguished from others of the same category, *esp* because in some way superior. **2** held in particular esteem: *a special friend*. **3** other than or in addition to the usual: *a special edition of a newspaper*. **4** designed or undertaken for a particular end, occasion, or need: *a special method of restoring paintings*. **5** for the use or education of children who have learning difficulties, emotional difficulties, or a physical disability: *special schools*. ➤➤➤ **specialness** *noun*. [Middle English via Old French from Latin *specialis* individual, particular, from Latin *species*: see SPECIES]
Usage note
specially *or* especially? See note at ESPECIALLY.

special[2] *noun* **1** a special person or thing. **2** a dish in a restaurant that is not normally on the menu. **3** a special offer in a shop. **4** *Brit* = SPECIAL CONSTABLE.

Special Branch *noun* in Britain, the branch of the police force concerned with political security.

special constable *noun Brit* somebody employed as an extra policeman, e.g. in times of emergency.

special delivery *noun Brit* a service that offers the delivery of a letter or parcel by a guaranteed time.

special drawing right *noun* a right to buy additional foreign currency from the International Monetary Fund.

special effect *noun* (*usu in pl*) an unusual visual or acoustic effect; *esp* one introduced into a film or prerecorded television production by special processing.
Editorial note
Special effects are those not possible in mere photography or sound recording. They included matte work, split screens, models, stop motion, and so on. They were the work of specialists (like Willis O'Brien on King Kong), but in the 1980s, with the computer and digitalization, special effects has come to mean the electronic semblance of photography with 'impossible' subjects (e.g. in Jurassic Park) — David Thomson.

specialise *verb trans and intrans* see SPECIALIZE.

specialised *adj* see SPECIALIZED.

specialism *noun* **1** specialization in an occupation or branch of knowledge. **2** a field of specialization; a speciality.

specialist *noun* **1** somebody who specializes in a special occupation or branch of knowledge. **2** a medical practitioner who specializes in a specific group of complaints: *an ear, nose, and throat specialist*. ➤➤ **specialist** *adj*.

speciality /speshi'aliti/ (*NAmer* **specialty** /'spesh(ə)lti/) *noun* (*pl* **specialities**, *NAmer* **specialties**) **1a** a special aptitude or skill. **b** a particular occupation or branch of knowledge. **c** (*usu* **specialty**) a branch of medicine. **2** a product, service, etc that a person, place, or establishment specializes in: *The cheese is a speciality of this region*.
Usage note
speciality *or* specialty? The subject that a person specializes in is their *speciality* in British English, but *specialty* in American English. The branch of medicine that a doctor specializes in, however, is usually a specialty in both varieties of English.

specialize or **specialise** *verb intrans* **1** (*often* + in) to concentrate one's efforts in a special or limited activity or field: *The firm specializes in children's books*. **2** to undergo biological specialization; *esp* to change so as to adapt to a particular mode of life or environment, e.g. in the course of evolution. ➤ *verb trans* to apply or adapt (something) to a specific end or use. ➤➤ **specialization** /-'zaysh(ə)n/ *noun*.

specialized or **specialised** *adj* intended or fitted for a specific purpose or occupation: *specialized personnel*.

special licence *noun* a British form of marriage licence permitting marriage without the publication of banns or at a time and place other than those prescribed by law.

specially *adv* **1** for a particular purpose. **2** in a special way.
Usage note
specially *or* especially? See note at ESPECIALLY.

special needs *pl noun* in education, special requirements that a pupil has because of a physical disability, emotional or behavioural problems, or a learning difficulty.

special pleading *noun* **1** the allegation of special or new matter in a legal action, as distinguished from a direct denial of the matter pleaded by the opposite side. **2** an argument that ignores the damaging or unfavourable aspects of a case.

special school *noun Brit* a school for children who have special needs.

special team *noun* in American football, a group of players within a team who play in a particular situation, e.g. a kick-off or penalty.

specialty /'spesh(ə)lti/ *noun* (*pl* **specialties**) **1** chiefly *NAmer* see SPECIALITY. **2** the particular branch of medicine in which a doctor specializes. **3** a legal agreement embodied in a sealed document. [Middle English *specialte* from Old French *especialte*, ultimately from Latin *specialis*: see SPECIAL[1]]
Usage note
specialty *or* speciality? See note at SPECIALITY.

speciation /speeshi'aysh(ə)n/ *noun* the evolutionary development of new biological species; the process, involving physical separation of some organisms from a main interbreeding group, by which a new species is formed.

specie /'speeshiz/ *noun* money in coins rather than notes. ✳ **in specie 1** in the same or similar form or kind: *ready to return insult in specie*. **2** in coin. [from Latin *in specie* in kind]

species /'speeshiz/ *noun* (*pl* **species** /'speeshiz/) **1a** a class of individuals having common attributes and designated by a common name. **b** a category in the biological classification of living things that ranks immediately below a genus, comprises related organisms or populations potentially capable of interbreeding, and is designated by a name, e.g. *Homo sapiens*, that consists of the name of a genus followed by a Latin or latinized uncapitalized noun or adjective. **c** an individual or kind belonging to a biological species. **d** a particular kind of atomic nucleus, atom, molecule, or ion. **e** (*used before a noun*) denoting a plant belonging to a biological species as distinct from a horticultural variety: *a species rose*.

Editorial note
Biologists distinguish species criteria from species concepts. Species criteria describe how to recognize members of a species. Species concepts explain why the living world is organized into discrete species. Some species (particularly animals) exist because of interbreeding, but others (such as some plants and microbes) may not. The rise of the theory of evolution made species more difficult to define because species can change and blur into one another — Dr Mark Ridley.

2 a kind or sort: *a dangerous species of criminal*. **3** the consecrated bread and wine of the Roman Catholic or Eastern Orthodox Eucharist. [Latin *species* appearance, form, kind, species, from *specere* to look]

speciesism *noun* human disregard of the needs of other animals. ⟫⟫ **speciesist** *adj and noun*.

specif. *abbr* specifically.

specific[1] /spə'sifik/ *adj* **1a** distinct from others, clearly and individually identified: *In this specific instance, there may be grounds for making an exception*. **b** being or relating to those properties of something that allow it to be assigned to a particular category: *the specific qualities of a drug*. **2** free from ambiguity; explicit or particular: *specific instructions*. **3a** (*usu* + to) confined to a particular individual, group, or circumstance: *a disease specific to horses*. **b** having a particular rather than a general influence, e.g. on a body part, disease, or chemical reaction: *antibodies specific for the smallpox virus*. **4** in biology, of or constituting a species, *esp* a biological species. **5** in physics, being any of various arbitrary physical constants; *esp* one relating an expression of quantity to unit mass, volume, or area: *specific heat capacity*. **6** said of a tax or duty: imposed at a fixed rate per unit, e.g. of weight or count. ⟫⟫ **specifically** *adv*, **specificity** /spesi'fisiti/ *noun*. [late Latin *specificus* from Latin *species*: see SPECIES]

specific[2] *noun* **1** a drug or remedy having a specific effect on a disease. **2a** a characteristic quality or trait. **b** (*in pl*) particulars: *haggling over the legal and financial specifics* — Time.

specification /,spesifi'kaysh(ə)n/ *noun* **1** the act or an instance of specifying. **2** (*usu in pl*). **a** a detailed description of something, e.g. a building or car, *esp* in the form of a plan. **b** a written description of an invention for which a patent is sought.

specific charge *noun* in physics, the ratio of electric charge to mass of an elementary particle.

specific gravity *noun* the ratio of the density of any substance to the density of a substance taken as a standard, e.g. pure water or hydrogen, when both densities are obtained by weighing in air; relative density.

specific heat capacity *noun* the heat, usu measured in joules, required to raise the temperature of a unit mass, e.g. one kilogram, of a substance by a unit temperature, e.g. one degree kelvin.

specific performance *noun* in law, performance of a legal contract according to its terms, ordered where damages would be inadequate.

specify /'spesifie/ *verb trans* (**specifies, specified, specifying**) **1a** to identify (something) clearly and individually. **b** to state (something) explicitly or in detail. **2** to include (something) as an item in a specification: *We specified oak flooring*. ⟫⟫ **specifiable** *adj*, **specifier** *noun*. [Middle English *specifien* via Old French from late Latin *specificare* to describe, from *specificus*: see SPECIFIC[1]]

specimen /'spesimin/ *noun* **1a** an item or part typical of a group or whole; a sample. **b** a sample of urine, blood, tissue, etc taken for medical examination. **2a** a distinct individual within a particular

category. **b** *informal* a person or individual. [Latin *specimen* pattern, model, from *specere* to look at, look]

specious /'speeshəs/ *adj* **1** superficially persuasive or apparently sound but fallacious: *specious reasoning*. **2** having a deceptive attraction or fascination. ⟫⟫ **speciously** *adv*, **speciousness** *noun*. [Middle English from Latin *speciosus* beautiful, plausible, from *species*: see SPECIES]

speck[1] /spek/ *noun* **1** a small spot or blemish. **2** a small particle: *a speck of sawdust*. [Old English *specca*]

speck[2] *verb trans* to mark (something) with specks.

speckle[1] /'spekl/ *noun* a little speck, e.g. of colour. [Middle English from early Dutch *spekked*]

speckle[2] *verb trans* to mark (something) with speckles. ⟫⟫ **speckled** *adj*.

specs /speks/ *pl noun informal* = SPECTACLES.

spectacle /'spektəkl/ *noun* **1** something exhibited as unusual, noteworthy, or entertaining; *esp* a striking or dramatic public display or show. **2** an object of scorn or ridicule, *esp* due to odd appearance or behaviour: *He made a spectacle of himself*. [Middle English via French from Latin *spectaculum*, from *spectare* to watch, from *spectus*, past part. of *specere* to look, look at]

spectacled *adj* **1** wearing a pair of spectacles. **2** having markings suggesting a pair of spectacles: *the spectacled salamander*.

spectacles *pl noun* a pair of lenses in a frame worn in front of the eyes to correct or improve one's vision; = GLASSES.

spectacular[1] /spek'takyoolə/ *adj* extremely impressive, *esp* in being very large, colourful, exciting, and dramatic: *a spectacular display of fireworks*. ⟫⟫ **spectacularly** *adv*.

spectacular[2] *noun* something, e.g. a stage show, that is spectacular.

spectate /spek'tayt, 'spektayt/ *verb intrans* to be present as a spectator, e.g. at a sports event. [back-formation from SPECTATOR]

spectator /spek'taytə/ *noun* **1** somebody who attends an event or activity in order to watch. **2** somebody who looks on without participating; an onlooker: *Rescuers were hampered by spectators*. [Latin *spectator* from *spectare*: see SPECTACLE]

specter /'spektə/ *noun NAmer* see SPECTRE.

spectra /'spektrə/ *noun* pl of SPECTRUM.

spectral /'spektrəl/ *adj* **1** of or suggesting a spectre. **2** of or made by a spectrum. ⟫⟫ **spectrally** *adv*.

spectre (*NAmer* **specter**) /'spektə/ *noun* **1** a visible ghost. **2** something that haunts or perturbs the mind; a phantasm: *the spectre of hunger*. [French *spectre* from Latin *spectrum* appearance, spectre, from *specere* to look, look at]

spectro- *comb. form* forming words, denoting: a spectrum: *spectroscope*. [Latin *spectrum*: see SPECTRE]

spectrogram /'spektrəgram/ *noun* a photograph or diagram of a spectrum.

spectrograph /'spektrəgrahf, -graf/ *noun* an instrument for dispersing light, sound waves, etc into a spectrum and recording or mapping it. ⟫⟫ **spectrographic** /-'grafik/ *adj*, **spectrographically** /-'grafikli/ *adv*, **spectrography** /spek'trogrəfi/ *noun*.

spectroheliograph /spektroh'heeli·əgrahf, -graf/ *noun* an apparatus for making photographs of the sun at one wavelength showing its bright regions and prominences.

spectrohelioscope /spektroh'heeli·əskohp/ *noun* **1** = SPECTROHELIOGRAPH. **2** an instrument similar to a spectroheliograph used for visual as distinguished from photographic observations.

spectrometer /spek'tromitə/ *noun* a spectroscope fitted for measurements of the spectra observed with it. ⟫⟫ **spectrometric** /-'metrik/ *adj*, **spectrometry** /-tri/ *noun*.

spectrophotometer /,spektrohfoh'tomitə/ *noun* an instrument for measuring the intensity of light at various wavelengths, or a substance's absorption of light. ⟫⟫ **spectrophotometric** /-'metrik/ *adj*, **spectrophotometrically** /-'metrikli/ *adv*, **spectrophotometry** /-tri/ *noun*.

spectroscope /'spektrəskohp/ *noun* an instrument for forming and examining optical spectra. ⟫⟫ **spectroscopic** /-'skopik/ *adj*, **spectroscopically** /-'skipikli/ *adv*, **spectroscopist** /spek'troskəpist/ *noun*, **spectroscopy** /spek'troskəpi/ *noun*.

spectrum /'spektrəm/ *noun* (*pl* **spectra** /spektrə/) **1** the series of colours ranging from red, having the longest wavelength, to violet, with the shortest wavelength, that is produced when a beam of white light is dispersed, e.g. by a prism. **2** a series of images formed when a beam of a particular type of electromagnetic radiation, e.g. X-rays, ultraviolet radiation, or radio waves, is dispersed and then brought to a focus so that the components of the beam are arranged in the order of their wavelengths. **3** = ELECTROMAGNETIC SPECTRUM. **4** the range of frequencies of sound waves. **5** an interrelated sequence or range: *a wide spectrum of interests.* [Latin *spectrum*: see SPECTRE]

specula /'spekyoolə/ *noun* pl of SPECULUM.

specular /'spekyoolə/ *adj* **1** of or having the qualities of a mirror. **2** conducted with the aid of a medical speculum. [Latin *specularis* of a mirror, from *speculum* mirror]

speculate /'spekyoolayt/ *verb intrans* **1** to form an opinion or theory about something in advance of the evidence to support it; to conjecture. **2** to assume a business risk in the hope of gain; *esp* to buy or sell in expectation of profiting from market fluctuations. **3** to meditate on or ponder about something; to reflect. ➤➤ **speculation** /-'laysh(ə)n/ *noun,* **speculator** *noun.* [Latin *speculatus,* past part. of *speculari* to spy out, examine, from *specula* watchtower, from *specere* to look, look at]

speculative /'spekyoolətiv/ *adj* **1** involving, based on, or constituting speculation; theoretical rather than demonstrable. **2** questioning or enquiring: *a speculative glance.* ➤➤ **speculatively** *adv.*

speculum /'spekyooləm/ *noun* (*pl* **specula** /-lə/ *or* **speculums**) **1** an instrument inserted into a body passage for medical inspection or treatment. **2** a reflector in an optical instrument. **3** a patch of colour on the secondary feathers of many birds, *esp* ducks. [Latin *speculum* mirror, from *specere* to look, look at]

sped /sped/ *verb* past tense and past part. of SPEED².

speech /speech/ *noun* **1a** the communication or expression of thoughts in spoken words. **b** the ability to express or communicate thoughts by speaking. **c** = CONVERSATION. **2** a public discourse; an address. **3a** a language or dialect: *It is systematically ungrammatical colloquial speech which embeds people in their feudal ancestry* — Independent. **b** an individual manner of speaking. **4** a unit of one or more lines to be spoken by a character in a play. [Old English *sprǣc, spǣc*]

speech day *noun Brit* an annual ceremonial day at some schools when prizes are presented.

speechify /'speechifie/ *verb intrans* (**speechifies, speechified, speechifying**) to speak or make a speech in a pompous manner. ➤➤ **speechifier** *noun.*

speechless *adj* **1a** unable to speak; dumb. **b** deprived of speech, e.g. through horror or rage. **2** refraining from speech; silent. **3** incapable of being expressed in words: *a shape of speechless beauty* — Shelley. ➤➤ **speechlessly** *adv,* **speechlessness** *noun.*

speech recognition *noun* a computer system that converts speech into text.

speech therapy *noun* therapy for people who have problems with speaking and language. ➤➤ **speech therapist** *noun.*

speed¹ /speed/ *noun* **1a** the act or state of moving swiftly; swiftness. **b** rate of motion; *specif* the magnitude of a velocity irrespective of direction. **c** power of motion; impetus. **2** rate of performance or execution: *He tried to increase his reading speed.* **3a** the sensitivity to light of a photographic film, plate, or paper expressed numerically. **b** the power of a lens or optical system, e.g. in a camera, to admit more or less light. **c** the duration of a photographic exposure. **4** each of the gear ratios of a bicycle. **5** *slang* methamphetamine, or any of several chemically related stimulant amphetamine drugs. **6** *archaic* good fortune; success. * **at speed** while moving fast. **up to speed** having all the relevant information: *She brought me up to speed on the latest developments.* [Old English *spēd*]

speed² *verb* (*past tense and past part.* **sped** /sped/ *or* **speeded**) ➤ *verb intrans* **1** to move or go quickly: *He sped to her bedside.* **2** to travel at excessive or illegal speed: *She was fined for speeding.* **3** *slang* to be under the influence of amphetamines. **4** *archaic* to meet with success or prosperity. ➤ *verb trans* to cause (something or somebody) to move quickly; to hasten (them): *She tried to speed the parting guests.* ➤➤ **speeder** *noun.*

speedball *noun slang* cocaine mixed with heroin or morphine or an amphetamine and usu taken by injection.

speedboat *noun* a fast motorboat.

speedbump *noun* a hump in a road designed to make vehicles travel at a slow speed.

speed camera *noun* a camera placed at the side of a road to take photographs of vehicles that are speeding.

speed hump *noun Brit* = SPEEDBUMP.

speed limit *noun* the maximum speed permitted by law in a given area or under specified circumstances.

speedo /'speedoh/ *noun* (*pl* **speedos**) *informal* = SPEEDOMETER.

speedometer /spi'domitə/ *noun* an instrument for indicating speed; a tachometer.

speed up *verb intrans* to move or work faster; to accelerate. ➤ *verb trans* to cause (somebody or something) to move faster.

speedway *noun* **1** a usu oval racecourse for motorcycles. **2** the sport of racing motorcycles usu belonging to professional teams on closed cinder or dirt tracks. **3** *NAmer* a fast road.

speedwell *noun* any of several species of plants that mostly have slender stems and small blue or whitish flowers: genus *Veronica.*

speedy *adj* (**speedier, speediest**) swift or quick. ➤➤ **speedily** *adv,* **speediness** *noun.*

speiss /spies/ *noun* a mixture of metallic arsenic compounds produced when smelting certain ores. [German *Speise* food, speiss, ultimately from late Latin *expensa*: see EXPENSE]

speleology /speeli'oləji/ *noun* **1** the scientific study of caves. **2** the sport of exploring caves; potholing. ➤➤ **speleological** /-'lojikl/ *adj,* **speleologist** *noun.* [Latin *speleum* cave (from Greek *spēlaion*) + -O- + -LOGY]

spell¹ /spel/ *noun* **1a** a spoken word or form of words held to have magic power: *Fain would I have a book wherein I might behold all spells and incantations, that I might raise up spirits when I please* — Marlowe. **b** a state of enchantment. **2** a compelling influence or attraction. [Old English *spel* speech, talk, story]

spell² *verb* (*past tense and past part.* **spelt** /spelt/ *or* **spelled**) ➤ *verb trans* **1a** to name, write, or print the letters of (a word) in order or in a specified manner: *She spelt my name wrong.* **b** said of letters: to form (a word): *C-a-t spells cat.* **2** to amount to or mean (something): *Crop failure would spell famine for the whole region.* ➤ *verb intrans* **1** to form words with letters. **2** to write words correctly: *Many graduates can't spell.* [Middle English *spellen* from Old French *espeller,* of Germanic origin]

spell³ *noun* **1** a short or indefinite period or phase: *There will be cold spells throughout April.* **2** a period spent in a job or occupation: *Then I did a spell in catering.* **3a** a period of illness, depression, or other abnormal physical or mental state: *She's having one of her bad spells.* **b** a sudden brief attack or fit of dizziness, shivering, coughing, etc. **4** *chiefly Aus* a period of rest from work, activity, or use. [from SPELL⁴]

spell⁴ *verb* (*past tense and past part.* **spelled**) ➤ *verb trans* **1** to give a brief rest to (somebody). **2** *chiefly NAmer* to relieve (somebody) for a time; to stand in for (them): *The two guards spelled each other.* ➤ *verb intrans* *chiefly Aus* to rest from work or activity for a time. [Old English *spelian* to take somebody's place]

spellbind /'spelbiend/ *verb trans* (*past tense and past part.* **spellbound** /'spelbownd/) to bind or hold (somebody) as if by a spell or charm; to bewitch (them). ➤➤ **spellbinder** *noun,* **spellbinding** *adj,* **spellbindingly** *adv.* [back-formation from SPELLBOUND]

spellbound *adj* held as if by a spell: *a spellbound audience.*

spellcheck *verb trans* to check the spelling in (a document) with a spellchecker.

spellchecker *noun* a computer program used in word processing to check the spelling in a document by comparing each word with a dictionary held on disk.

speller *noun* **1** somebody who spells words, *esp* in a specified way: *He is a good speller.* **2** *chiefly NAmer* a book with exercises for teaching spelling.

spelling *noun* **1** the act of forming or the ability to form words from letters. **2** the sequence of letters that make up a particular word: *Her name had an unusual spelling.*

spelling bee *noun* a spelling competition.

spelling checker *noun* = SPELLCHECKER.

spell out *verb trans* **1** to read (words) slowly and haltingly. **2** to explain (something) clearly and in detail. **3** to come to understand (something); to discern (it): *I tried in vain to spell out his meaning.*

spelt¹ /spelt/ *noun* a primitive wheat whose ears contain two light red kernels: *Triticum spelta.* [Old English from late Latin *spelta,* of Germanic origin]

spelt[2] *verb* past tense and past part. of SPELL[2].

spelter /'speltə/ *noun* zinc, *esp* cast in slabs for commercial use. [prob modification of early Dutch *speauter*]

spelunker /spi'lungkə/ *noun NAmer* somebody who makes a hobby of exploring and studying caves. ➤➤ **spelunking** *noun*. [Latin *spelunca* cave, from Greek *spēlynx*]

spencer /'spensə/ *noun* **1** a woman's thin woollen vest. **2** a short waist-length jacket. [named after George John, second Earl *Spencer* d.1834, English politician]

spend[1] /spend/ *verb* (*past tense and past part.* **spent** /spent/) ➤ *verb trans* **1** to use up or pay out (money): *She spent £90 on a new suit.* **2** to wear (something) out; to exhaust (it): *The storm gradually spent itself.* **3** to cause or permit (time) to elapse; to pass (it): *They spent the summer at the beach.* ➤ *verb intrans* to pay out resources, *esp* money. ✳ **spend a penny** *Brit, informal, euphem* to urinate. ➤➤ **spendable** *adj*, **spender** *noun*. [Old English *spendan*, from Latin *expendere*: see EXPEND, and Old French *despendre* from Latin *dispendere*: see DISPENSE]

spend[2] *noun informal* an amount of money spent: *The paper's advertising spend will reach £7million.*

spending money *noun* an allowance; pocket money.

spendthrift *noun* somebody who spends carelessly or wastefully. ➤➤ **spendthrift** *adj*. [SPEND[1] + THRIFT in the obsolete sense 'accumulated wealth']

Spenserian /spen'siəri·ən/ *adj* relating to or in the style of the poet Edmund Spenser (d.1599) or his works. ➤➤ **Spenserian** *noun*.

Spenserian stanza *noun* a poetic stanza consisting of eight lines of iambic pentameter and an Alexandrine, with a rhyme scheme *ababbcbcc*. [named after Edmund *Spenser*, who used it in his allegorical romance *The Faerie Queene*]

spent[1] /spent/ *adj* **1a** used up; consumed. **b** exhausted of useful components or qualities: *spent matches.* **2** drained of energy; exhausted: *He was spent after his nightlong vigil.* **3** exhausted of spawn or sperm: *a spent salmon.*

spent[2] *verb* past tense and past part. of SPEND[1].

sperm /spuhm/ *noun* (*pl* **sperms** *or collectively* **sperm**) **1a** the male fertilizing fluid; semen. **b** a male gamete; spermatozoon. **2a** = SPERM WHALE. **b** spermaceti or sperm oil from the sperm whale. [Middle English via French and late Latin from Greek *sperma* seed]

sperm- *comb. form* see SPERMATO-.

spermaceti /spuhmə'seeti, -'seti/ *noun* a waxy solid obtained from the oil of whales, *esp* sperm whales, and used in ointments, cosmetics, and candles. [Middle English *sperma cete* from late Latin *sperma ceti* whale sperm]

spermat- *comb. form* see SPERMATO-.

spermatheca /spuhmə'theekə/ *noun* (*pl* **spermathecae** /'kee/) a sac for sperm storage in the female reproductive tract of many lower animals. [scientific Latin *spermatheca*, from *sperma* SPERM + THECA]

spermatic /spuh'matik/ *adj* relating to, resembling, carrying, or full of sperm.

spermatic cord *noun* a cord that suspends the testis within the scrotum.

spermatid /'spuhmətid/ *noun* any of the cells that form spermatozoa.

spermato- *or* **sperm-** *or* **spermat-** *or* **spermo-** *comb. form* forming words, denoting: sperm or seeds: *spermatid; spermatocyte.* [via French and late Latin from Greek *spermat-, sperma*]

spermatocyte /spuh'matəsiet/ *noun* a cell giving rise to sperm cells; *esp* a cell of the last or next to last generation preceding the spermatozoon.

spermatogenesis /spuh,matə'jenəsis/ *noun* the process of male gamete formation including meiotic cell division and transformation of the four resulting spermatids into spermatozoa. ➤➤ **spermatogenetic** /-'netik/ *adj*.

spermatogonium /spuh,matə'gohni·əm/ *noun* (*pl* **spermatogonia** /-ni·ə/) a male germ cell that constitutes the earliest stage in the developmental process that leads to the formation of spermatozoa. ➤➤ **spermatogonial** *adj*. [Latin *spermatogonium*, from SPERMATO- + *gonium*, from Greek *gonos* seed]

spermatophore /spuh'matəfaw/ *noun* a capsule, packet, or mass enclosing spermatozoa produced by the male and conveyed to the female in the insemination of various invertebrates, e.g. the spider.

spermatophyte /spuh'matəfiet/ *noun* any of a group of higher plants constituting those that produce seeds.

spermatozoid /,spuhmətə'zoh·id/ *noun* a motile male gamete of a plant, usu produced in an antheridium.

spermatozoon /,spuhmətə'zoh·ən/ *noun* (*pl* **spermatozoa** /-'zoh·ə/) **1** a motile male gamete of an animal, usu with rounded or elongated head and a long tail-like FLAGELLUM (whiplike structure). **2** = SPERMATOZOID. ➤➤ **spermatozoal** *adj*, **spermatozoan** *adj*.

sperm bank *noun* a place where semen for artificial insemination is stored.

sperm count *noun* an indication of how fertile a man is, obtained by measuring the concentration of sperm in a given volume of seminal fluid.

spermicide /'spuhmisied/ *noun* something that kills sperm, *esp* a substance, e.g. a cream or gel used as a contraceptive. ➤➤ **spermicidal** /-'siedl/ *adj*. [SPERM + -I- + -CIDE]

spermo- *comb. form* see SPERMATO-.

sperm oil *noun* a pale yellow oil obtained from the sperm whale.

sperm whale *noun* a large toothed whale that has a vast blunt head with a cavity in the front part containing a fluid mixture of spermaceti and oil: *Physeter macrocephalus.* Also called CACHALOT. [short for *spermaceti whale*]

spew[1] /spyooh/ *verb intrans* **1** to vomit. **2** to come forth in a flood or gush. ➤ *verb trans* to propel or eject (something) with violence or in great quantity: *a volcano spewing ash and lava.* ➤➤ **spewer** *noun*. [Old English *spīwan*]

spew[2] *noun* **1** vomit. **2** material that gushes or is ejected from a source.

SPF *abbr* sun protection factor.

sp. gr. *abbr* specific gravity.

sphagnum /'sfagnəm, 'spagnəm/ *noun* any of a large genus of atypical mosses that grow only in wet acid areas, e.g. bogs, where their remains become compacted with other plant debris to form peat: genus *Sphagnum.* [Latin genus name, from Greek *sphagnos*, a moss]

sphalerite /'sfaləriet/ *noun* zinc sulphide occurring as a mineral. [German *Sphalerit* from Greek *sphaleros* deceitful, from *sphallein* to cause to fall; from its often being mistaken for galena]

sphene /sfeen/ *noun* a black or brown mineral that is a silicate of calcium and titanium and often contains varying amounts of other chemical elements, e.g. manganese and iron. [French *sphène* from Greek *sphēn* wedge; from the shape of its crystals]

sphenoid /'sfenoyd/ *noun* a bone at the base of the skull shaped like a wedge. ➤➤ **sphenoidal** /sfə'noydl/ *adj*. [via Latin from Greek *sphēnoeidēs* wedge-shaped, from *sphēn* wedge]

sphere[1] /sfiə/ *noun* **1** a space or solid enclosed by a surface, all points of which are equidistant from the centre; a globe or ball. **2a** the apparent surface of the heavens forming the dome of the visible sky. **b** any of the revolving spherical transparent shells in which, according to ancient astronomy, the celestial bodies are set. **c** *literary* a planet or star. **3** the area covered by somebody's knowledge or expertise, or the milieu in which they exist or have influence. **4** the natural or proper place for somebody or something; *esp* social position or class: *It is obvious that our social spheres have been widely different* — Oscar Wilde. ➤➤ **spheral** *adj*, **spheric** /'sferik/ *adj*, **sphericity** /sfi'risiti/ *noun*. [Middle English *spere* globe, celestial sphere, via Old French from Latin *sphaera*, from Greek *sphaira* ball]

sphere[2] *verb trans archaic* **1** to place or enclose (something) in a sphere. **2** to form (something) into a sphere.

-sphere *comb. form* forming nouns, denoting: something with the shape of a sphere: *hemisphere.*

spherical /'sferikl/ *adj* **1** having the form of a sphere. **2** relating to or dealing with a sphere or the properties of a sphere. ➤➤ **spherically** *adv*.

spherical aberration *noun* aberration that is caused by the spherical form of a lens or mirror and that gives different foci for central and marginal rays.

spherical angle *noun* the angle between two intersecting arcs of the great circles of a sphere.

spherical coordinate *noun* any of three coordinates that are used to locate a point in space and that comprise one length and two angles.

spheroid /'sfiəroyd/ *noun* a figure resembling a sphere. ➤➤ **spheroidal** /sfə'roydl/ *adj*, **spheroidicity** /-'disiti/ *noun*.

spherometer /sfiə'romitə/ *noun* an instrument for measuring the curvature of a surface.

spherule /'sfiər(y)oohl, 'sfer(y)oohl/ *noun* a little sphere or spherical body. [late Latin *sphaerula*, dimin. of Latin *sphaera*: see SPHERE¹]

spherulite /'sfiər(y)ooliet, 'sfe-/ *noun* a spherical body of radiating crystal fibres found in some volcanic rocks. ➤➤ **spherulitic** /-'litik/ *adj*. [SPHERULE + -ITE¹]

sphincter /'sfingktə/ *noun* a muscular ring, surrounding and able to contract or close a bodily opening. ➤➤ **sphincteral** *adj*. [late Latin *sphincter* from Greek *sphinktēr* band, from *sphingein* to bind tight]

sphinx /sfinks/ *noun* (*pl* **sphinxes** or **sphinges** /'sfinjeez/) **1a** (**the Sphinx**) a female monster in Greek mythology, with a lion's body and a human head, that killed those who failed to answer a riddle it set them. **b** an enigmatic or mysterious person. **2** an ancient Egyptian image in the form of a recumbent lion, usu with a human head. **3** = HAWKMOTH. [via Latin from Greek *sphinx*, from *sphingein* to bind tight, said to be because the Sphinx sometimes killed by strangulation]

sphygmograph /'sfigməgrahf, -graf/ *noun* an instrument that records graphically the movements or character of the pulse in the arteries. [Greek *sphygmos* pulse + -GRAPH]

sphygmomanometer /,sfigmohmə'nomitə/ *noun* an instrument for measuring arterial blood pressure. ➤➤ **sphygmomanometry** /-tri/ *noun*. [Greek *sphygmos* pulse + MANOMETER]

spic /spik/ *noun* NAmer, *offensive* a Spanish-speaking Latin American person. [alteration of *spig*, short for *spigotty*, prob from the broken English phrase *no speaka de English* (I don't speak English), supposed to be much used by Spanish Americans]

spic-and-span *adj* see SPICK-AND-SPAN.

spiccato /spi'kahtoh/ *noun* (*pl* **spiccatos**) in music, a technique used by string players in which a short sound is produced by bouncing the bow on the string, or a passage or note played in this way. [Italian *spiccato*, past part. of *spiccare* to detach, pick off]

spice¹ /spies/ *noun* **1a** any of various aromatic vegetable products, e.g. pepper, ginger, or nutmeg, used to season or flavour foods. **b** such products collectively. **2** something that adds zest or relish: *Variety's the very spice of life* — Cowper. [Middle English via Old French and late Latin *species* goods, wares, from Latin: see SPECIES]

spice² *verb trans* **1** to season (something) with spice. **2** (*often* + up) to add zest or relish to (something): *cynicism spiced with wit*.

spicebush *noun* an aromatic N American shrub of the laurel family: *Lindera benzoin*.

spick-and-span or **spic-and-span** /,spik ən(d) 'span/ *adj* spotlessly clean and tidy; spruce. [short for *spick-and-span-new*, extension of *span-new* brand-new, from Middle English, partial translation of Old Norse *spānnȳr*, from *spānn* chip of wood + *nȳr* new, influenced by early Dutch *spiksplinternieuw*, literally 'splinter-new']

spicule /'spikyoohl, 'spiekyoohl/ *noun* **1** a tiny pointed usu hard structure; *esp* any of the minute structures composed of calcium carbonate or silica that together support the tissue of various invertebrates, e.g. a sponge. **2** a jet of relatively cool gas rising through the lower atmosphere of the sun. ➤➤ **spiculate** /-lət/ *adj*. [late Latin *spicula* arrowhead, alteration of Latin *spiculum*, dimin. of *spica* spike of grain]

spicy /'spiesi/ *adj* (**spicier, spiciest**) **1a** having the quality, flavour, or fragrance of spice. **b** strongly seasoned with spices; piquant. **2** somewhat scandalous or racy: *spicy gossip*. ➤➤ **spicily** *adv*, **spiciness** *noun*.

spider /'spiedə/ *noun* **1** any member of an order of usu small invertebrate animals with eight legs, and two or more pairs of spinnerets (specialized organs; see SPINNERET) for spinning threads of silk that they use to make cocoons for their eggs, nests for themselves, or webs for entangling their prey: order Araneae. **2** any of various devices consisting of a frame or skeleton with radiating arms or spokes. **3** Brit a bundle of elastic straps with hooks, used to attach a load to a bicycle or motor vehicle. **4** a support for a snooker cue that is raised on legs to enable the player to hit the ball from above when other balls are in the way. [Old English *spīthra* from *spinnan* SPIN¹]

spider crab *noun* any of numerous crabs with extremely long legs and nearly triangular bodies: genus *Macropodia* and other genera.

spider mite *noun* any of several species of small mites that spin webs, *esp* the red spider mite that attacks crop plants: family Tetranychidae.

spider monkey *noun* any of several species of S American monkeys with long slender limbs, a rudimentary or absent thumb, and a very long prehensile tail: genus *Brachyteles*.

spider plant *noun* any of various house plants with long narrow leaves, e.g. a tradescantia. [because some have clusters of plantlets hanging down on long stems, resembling a spider on a thread]

spiderwort *noun* any of various American plants that are grown as house plants: *Tradescantia virginiana* and other species. [because its stamens resemble a spider's legs]

spidery *adj* **1a** resembling a spider in form or manner; *specif* long, thin, and sharply angular like the legs of a spider: *spidery handwriting*. **b** resembling a spider's web; *esp* composed of fine threads or lines in a weblike arrangement: *spidery lace*. **2** infested with spiders.

spiegeleisen /'shpeegəliez(ə)n, 'spee-/ *noun* pig iron containing 15–30% manganese. [German *Spiegeleisen*, from *Spiegel* mirror (from its lustre) + *Eisen* iron]

spiel¹ /shpeel, speel/ *noun informal* a glib line of talk, usu designed to influence or persuade; patter. [German *Spiel* a game]

spiel² *verb intrans informal* to talk volubly or glibly. ➤ *verb trans informal* (*usu* + off) to tell or describe (something) glibly and at length. ➤➤ **spieler** *noun*.

spiffing /'spifing/ *adj Brit, informal, dated* extremely good; excellent: *Auntie is a spiffing cook*. [English dialect *spiff* dandified, of unknown origin]

spifflicate /'splifikayt/ *verb trans Brit, informal* to defeat or destroy (something) utterly; to flatten (it). [origin unknown]

spiffy /'spifi/ *adj* (**spiffier, spiffiest**) NAmer, *informal* smart or spruce. [English dialect *spiff* dandified]

spigot /'spigət/ *noun* **1** a small plug used to stop up the vent of a cask. **2** the part of a tap, *esp* on a barrel, which controls the flow. **3** a projection on the end of a piece of piping or guttering that fits into an adjoining piece. [Middle English, prob ultimately from Latin *spica* spike of grain]

spike¹ /spiek/ *noun* **1** a pointed object or projection usu made of metal, e.g.: **a** any of a row of pointed iron projections on the top of a wall or fence. **b** an upright metal rod on which rejected copy is impaled in a newspaper office. **c** any of several metal projections set in the sole and heel of a running shoe to improve grip. **2** a very large nail. **3** (*in pl*) track shoes. **4** a voltage pulse in a stimulated nerve. **5a** a pointed element in a graph or tracing. **b** an unusually high and sharply defined maximum, e.g. on a graph. **6** Brit, *informal* a hostel for homeless people. [Middle English, prob from early Dutch *spiker*]

spike² *verb trans* **1** to pierce (something) with or impale (it) on a spike. **2** to reject (newspaper copy) by impaling on a spike, or as if by impaling on a spike. **3a** to add spirits to (a non-alcoholic drink). **b** to add something, e.g. a drug, to (food). **4** to fasten, attach, or provide (something) with spikes: *spike the soles of climbing boots*. **5** in volleyball, to drive (a ball) from a front-line position sharply downwards into an opponent's court. **6** to suppress or thwart (something) completely: *They spiked the rumour*. **7** to disable (a cannon loaded at the discharging end) temporarily by driving a spike into the hole through which the charge is ignited. **✲ spike somebody's guns** to foil an opponent's plan. ➤➤ **spiker** *noun*.

spike³ *noun* **1** an elongated cluster of flowers growing directly without stalks, from a single main stem. **2** an ear of grain. [Middle English *spik* ear of corn, from Latin *spica*]

spiked *adj* **1** having a sharp projecting point. **2** said of a plant: having flowers that grow in a spike.

spikelet /'spieklit/ *noun* in botany, a small or secondary spike; *specif* any of the small spikes that make up the compound inflorescence of a grass or sedge.

spikenard /'spieknahd/ *noun* **1** a fragrant ancient ointment believed to have been derived from an E Indian aromatic plant of the valerian family. **2** the plant that produces a rhizome from which this ointment is made: *Nardostachys grandiflora*. [Middle English via early French *spicanarde* from late Latin *spica nardi* spike of nard]

spiky *adj* (**spikier, spikiest**) **1** having a sharp projecting point or points. **2** *informal* easily upset or annoyed.

spile[1] /spiel/ *noun* **1** a spigot or plug. **2** *NAmer* a spout inserted in a tree to draw off sap. [Dutch *spijl* stake, from early Dutch or early Low German *spile* splinter, wooden pin]

spile[2] *verb trans* to supply (e.g. a cask) with a spile.

spill[1] /spil/ *verb* (*past tense and past part.* **spilt** /spilt/ *or* **spilled**) ⟩ *verb trans* **1** to cause or allow (usu liquid) to fall, flow, or run out of a container so as to be lost or wasted, *esp* accidentally: *He spilt his tea all over the table.* **2** to cause (blood) to be shed. **3** to empty or discharge (something): *The train spilt its passengers onto the platform.* **4** *informal* to let (information) out; to divulge or disclose (it). **5** to empty (a sail) of wind. ⟩ *verb intrans* **1** to flow or fall out, over, or off and become wasted, scattered, or lost. **2** to spread profusely or beyond limits: *Crowds spilt into the streets.* ✳ **spill the beans** *informal* to divulge information, *esp* indiscreetly. ⟩⟩ **spillage** /'spilij/ *noun*, **spiller** *noun*. [Old English *spillan* to kill, destroy, squander]

spill[2] *noun* **1** a quantity spilt. **2** a fall from a horse or vehicle.

spill[3] *noun* a thin twist of paper or sliver of wood used for lighting a fire, pipe, etc. [Middle English *spille* splinter, from early Low German *spile* splinter, wooden pin]

spillikin /'spilikin/ *noun* **1** (*in pl, but treated as sing.*) a game in which a set of thin rods or straws is allowed to fall in a heap with each player in turn trying to remove them one at a time without disturbing the rest. **2** any of the pieces used in spillikins. [SPILL[2] + -KIN]

spillover *noun* **1** the act or an instance of spilling over. **2** a quantity that spills over.

spill over *verb intrans* to overflow, e.g. into an adjacent or related area.

spillway *noun* a passage for surplus water from a dam.

spilt /spilt/ *verb* past tense and past part. of SPILL[1].

spin[1] /spin/ *verb* (**spinning**, *past tense and past part.* **spun** /spun/) ⟩ *verb intrans* **1a** to revolve rapidly; to whirl. **b** said of wheels: to revolve rapidly without gripping, e.g. in mud or wet grass. **c** said of a ball: to revolve in the air and deviate from a straight line on bouncing. **d** to have the sensation of spinning; to reel: *My head is spinning.* **2a** to draw out and twist fibre into yarn or thread. **b** said of a spider, silkworm, or insect: to form a thread by extruding a sticky rapidly hardening liquid. **3a** said of an aircraft: to fall in a spin. **b** to plunge helplessly and out of control. **4** to fish with a spinner. ⟩ *verb trans* **1a** to cause (something) to revolve rapidly: *spin a top.* **b** to project (a ball) so that it revolves in the air and deviates from a straight line on bouncing. **2a** to draw out and twist (fibre) into yarns or threads. **b** to produce (yarn or thread) by drawing out and twisting a fibrous material. **3** to form (e.g. a web or cocoon) by spinning. **4** to shape (something) into threadlike form in manufacture, or to manufacture (something) by a whirling process. **5** to spin-dry (clothes). **6** to compose and tell (a usu long involved tale). **7** *informal* to present (information, news, etc) in a way that highlights certain aspects of it and creates an impression favourable to a particular political party, politician, or other organization or individual. [Old English *spinnan*]

spin[2] *noun* **1a** the act or an instance of spinning or twirling. **b** the whirling motion imparted, e.g. to a ball, by spinning. **2a** an aerial manoeuvre or flight condition in which an aircraft stalls and plunges steeply downwards out of control rotating about its longitudinal or vertical axis as it goes. **b** a plunging descent or downward spiral. **3** *informal* a particular interpretation or slant given to a proposal, policy, piece of information, etc; *esp* a favourable interpretation given by a spin doctor. **4a** in physics, the property of an ELEMENTARY PARTICLE (minute particle of matter) that corresponds to intrinsic ANGULAR MOMENTUM (quantity of rotational motion), that can be thought of as rotation of the particle about an axis through its centre, and that is mainly responsible for magnetic properties. **b** a measure of this. **5** *informal* a short excursion, *esp* by motor vehicle: *They went for a spin in the Rolls.* ✳ **in a spin** *informal* in a state of mental confusion; in a panic: *The news put us all in a spin.* ⟩⟩ **spinning** *noun and adj.*

spina bifida /,spienə 'bifidə/ *noun* a congenital condition in which there is a defect in the formation of the spine allowing the membranes surrounding the spinal cord to protrude and usu associated with disorder of the nerves supplying the lower part of the body. [Latin *spina bifida* bifid spinal column]

spinach /'spinij, 'spinich/ *noun* **1** a plant of the goosefoot family cultivated for its large dark green edible leaves: *Spinacia oleracea.* **2** the leaves of this plant, used as a vegetable. [early French *espinache*, *espinage* via Old Spanish and Arabic from Persian *isfānākh*]

spinach beet *noun* **1** a beet that lacks a fleshy root and is cultivated solely for its leaves that resemble spinach in flavour. **2** the leaves of this plant, used as a vegetable.

spinal /'spienəl/ *adj* relating to or in the region of the backbone. ⟩⟩ **spinally** *adv.*

spinal canal *noun* the passage through the vertebrae of the spinal column that contains the spinal cord.

spinal column *noun* the elongated structure of bone running the length of the trunk and tail of a vertebrate, which consists of a jointed series of vertebrae and protects the spinal cord; the backbone.

spinal cord *noun* the cord of nervous tissue that extends from the brain lengthways along the back in the spinal canal, carries impulses to and from the brain, and serves as a centre for initiating and coordinating many reflex actions.

spinal tap *noun NAmer* a lumbar puncture.

spin bowling *noun* in cricket, bowling in which the ball is made to spin by the bowler and so deviate from a straight line as it bounces. ⟩⟩ **spin bowler** *noun.*

spindle[1] /'spindl/ *noun* **1a** a round stick with tapered ends used to form and twist the yarn in hand spinning. **b** the long slender pin by which the thread is twisted in a spinning wheel. **c** any of various rods or pins holding a bobbin in a textile machine, e.g. a spinning frame. **d** the pin in a loom shuttle. **2a** a turned often decorative piece, e.g. in a baluster. **b** = NEWEL. **3a** a pin or axis about which something turns. **b** a spike on which papers can be impaled. **4** the bar or shaft, usu of square section, that carries the knobs and actuates the latch or bolt of a lock. **5** a spindle-shaped figure seen in microscopic sections of dividing cells along which the chromosomes are distributed. [Old English *spinel*]

spindle[2] *verb intrans* said of a plant or stem: to grow into or have a long slender stalk.

spindleshanks *pl noun informal, dated* **1** long thin legs. **2** (*treated as sing.*) a person with long thin legs.

spindle tree *noun* any of several species of shrubs, small trees, or climbing plants that typically have red fruits and a hard wood formerly used for spindle making: *Euonymus europaea* and other species.

spindly *adj* (**spindlier, spindliest**) having an unnaturally tall or slender appearance, *esp* suggestive of physical weakness: *spindly legs.*

spin doctor *noun informal* somebody whose job is to make sure that the media report political events and policies in a way that creates a favourable impression for a particular politician or political party: *The election was won despite the spin doctors* — Daily Telegraph.

spin-drier *or* **spin-dryer** *noun* a machine for spin-drying clothes.

spindrift *noun* sea spray. [alteration of Scots *speendrift*, from *speen* to drive before a strong wind + DRIFT[2]]

spin-dry *verb trans* (**spin-dries, spin-dried, spin-drying**) to remove water by placing (wet laundry) in a rapidly rotating drum.

spin-dryer *noun* see SPIN-DRIER.

spine /spien/ *noun* **1a** = SPINAL COLUMN. **b** something like a spinal column or constituting a central axis or chief support. **c** the back of a book, usu lettered with the title and author's name. **2** a stiff pointed plant part, *esp* one that is a modified leaf or leaf part. **3** a sharp rigid part of an animal or fish; or a pointed prominence on a bone. ⟩⟩ **spined** *adj.* [Middle English, in the senses 'thorn', 'spinal column', from Latin *spina*]

spine-chiller *noun* a book, film, etc that is terrifying in a sinister way.

spine-chilling *adj* causing fear or terror.

spinel /spi'nel/ *noun* any of a group of hard minerals that have a similar crystal structure and are oxides of two metals; *esp* a colourless to ruby-red or black oxide of magnesium and aluminium used as a gem. [Italian *spinella*, dimin. of *spina* thorn, from Latin *spina*]

spineless *adj* **1a** having no spinal column; invertebrate. **b** lacking strength of character. **2** free from spines, thorns, or prickles. ⟩⟩ **spinelessly** *adv*, **spinelessness** *noun.*

spinet /'spinit, spi'net/ *noun* a small harpsichord that has the strings at an angle to the keyboard. [Italian *spinetta*, prob named after Giovanni *Spinetti* fl 1503, its reputed inventor]

spine-tingling *adj informal* causing pleasurable nervous excitement; thrilling.

spinifex /'spienifeks/ *noun* any of a genus of Australian grasses with spiny seeds or stiff sharp leaves: genus *Spinifex*. [from the Latin genus name, from Latin *spina* + *facere* to make]

spinnaker /'spinəkə/ *noun* a large triangular sail set forward of a yacht's mast on a long light pole and used when running before the wind. [said to be a contraction of *Sphinx's acre*, *Sphinx* being the name of the first yacht to have one]

spinner *noun* **1** somebody or something that spins. **2** a fisherman's lure consisting of a spoon, blade, or set of wings that revolves when drawn through the water. **3** a conical fairing attached to an aircraft propeller hub and revolving with it. **4** a bowler of spin bowling, or a ball delivered with spin.

spinneret /spinə'ret/ *noun* **1** an organ, *esp* of a spider or caterpillar, for producing threads of silk from the secretion of silk glands. **2** a small metal plate, thimble, or cap with fine holes through which a chemical solution, e.g. of cellulose, is forced in the spinning of man-made filaments.

spinney /'spini/ *noun* (*pl* **spinneys**) *Brit* a small wood with undergrowth. [early French *espinaye* thorny thicket, from *espine* thorn, from Latin *spina* thorn, spinal column]

spinning jenny /'jeni/ *noun* an early multiple-spindle machine for spinning wool or cotton.

spinning mule *noun* = MULE[1] (3).

spinning wheel *noun* a small domestic machine for spinning yarn or thread by means of a spindle driven by a hand- or foot-operated wheel.

spin-off *noun* **1** a by-product: *household products that are spin-offs of space research*. **2** something which is a further development of some idea or product: *a spin-off from a successful TV series*.

spinose /'spienohs, 'spienohz/ *adj* having spines: *a fly with black spinose legs*.

spinous /'spienəs/ *adj* **1** covered with spines: *spinous appendages*. **2** slender like a spine: *a spinous larva*.

spin out *verb trans* **1** to cause (something) to last longer, *esp* by thrift: *There was a limit to how far they could spin out their meagre rations*. **2** to extend or prolong (something): *The report should have taken five minutes and she spun it out to half an hour*. **3** to dismiss (a batsman or batswoman in cricket) by spin bowling.

spinster /'spinstə/ *noun* an unmarried woman, *esp* a woman who is past the usual age for marrying or who seems unlikely to marry. ⟩⟩ **spinsterhood** *noun*, **spinsterish** *adj*. [Middle English *spinnestere* woman engaged in spinning, from *spinnen* to spin + *-estere* -STER]

spiny /'spieni/ *adj* (**spinier, spiniest**) **1** covered or armed with spines; bearing spines, prickles, or thorns. **2** slender and pointed like a spine. **3** *informal* full of difficulties or annoyances; puzzling: *spiny problems*. ⟩⟩ **spininess** *noun*.

spiny anteater *noun* = ECHIDNA.

spiny lobster *noun* any of several species of edible crustaceans distinguished from the true lobster by having a simple unenlarged first pair of legs and a spiny carapace: family Palinuridae.

spiracle /'spierəkl, 'spirakl/ *noun* a breathing orifice, e.g. the blowhole of a whale or a tracheal opening in an insect. ⟩⟩ **spiracular** /spie'rakyoolə, spi-/ *adj*. [Latin *spiraculum*, from *spirare* to breathe]

spiraea (*NAmer* **spirea**) /spie'riə/ *noun* any of a genus of herbaceous plants or shrubs of the rose family that have small white or pink flowers in dense clusters and are commonly grown in gardens: genus *Spiraea*. [Latin genus name, from Greek *speiraia*, prob from *speira* spiral, coil]

spiral[1] /'spierəl/ *adj* **1a** winding round a centre or pole and gradually approaching or receding from it: *the spiral curve of a watch spring*. **b** winding round a centre or pole and remaining at a constant distance from it; helical: *a spiral staircase*. **2** involving an advance to higher levels through a series of cyclical movements: *a spiral theory of social development*. ⟩⟩ **spirally** *adv*. [late Latin *spiralis* from Latin *spira* coil, from Greek *speira*]

spiral[2] *noun* **1a** the path of a point in a plane moving round a central point while continuously receding from or approaching it. **b** a three-dimensional curve, e.g. a helix, with one or more turns about an axis. **2** a single turn or coil in a spiral object. **3a** something with a spiral form. **b** a spiral flight. **4** a continuously expanding and accelerating increase or decrease: *wage spirals*.

spiral[3] *verb* (**spiralled, spiralling**, *NAmer* **spiraled, spiraling**)
⟩ *verb intrans* to go, *esp* to rise, in a spiral course: *Prices spiralled*.
⟩ *verb trans* to cause (something) to take a spiral form or course.

spiral binding *noun* a book or notebook binding in which a continuous spiral wire or plastic strip is passed through holes along one edge. ⟩⟩ **spiral-bound** *adj*.

spiral galaxy *noun* a galaxy with a nucleus from which extend usu two spiral arms.

spirant /'spierənt/ *noun* in phonetics, = FRICATIVE. ⟩⟩ **spirant** *adj*. [Latin *spirant-, spirans*, present part. of *spirare* to breathe]

spire[1] /spie-ə/ *noun* **1** a tall slim structure that tapers to a point on top of a tower: compare STEEPLE. **2** the upper tapering part of something, e.g. a tree or antler. **3** a slender tapering blade or stalk, e.g. of grass. ⟩⟩ **spired** *adj*, **spiry** *adj*. [Old English *spīr*]

spire[2] *verb intrans* to taper up to a point like a spire.

spire[3] *noun* **1** a spiral or coil. **2** the inner or upper part of a spiral gastropod shell. ⟩⟩ **spired** *adj*. [Latin *spira*: see SPIRAL[1]]

spirea /spie'riə/ *noun NAmer* see SPIRAEA.

spirillum /spi'riləm/ *noun* (*pl* **spirilla** /-lə/) any of a genus of long curved bacteria; broadly a spirochaete or other spiral filamentous bacterium: genus *Spirillum*. [Latin genus name, from dimin. of *spira*: see SPIRAL[1]]

spirit[1] /'spirit/ *noun* **1** the animating or vital force of living organisms. **2** (*in pl*) temper or state of mind, *esp* when lively or excited: *in high spirits*. **3** liveliness, energy, or courage in a person or their actions: *She showed great spirit during her imprisonment*. **4** the immaterial intelligent or conscious part of a person. **5** enthusiastic loyalty: *team spirit*. **6** the motivating principle or attitude influencing or characterizing something: *undertaken in a spirit of fun*. **7** a person of a specified kind or character: *a kindred spirit*. **8a** prevailing characteristic or feeling: *the spirit of the age*. **b** the true meaning of something, e.g. a rule or instruction, in contrast to its verbal expression: *spirit of the law*. **9** a supernatural being or essence, e.g.: **a** the soul. **b** a being that is bodiless but can become visible; *specif* a ghost. **c** a malevolent being that enters and possesses a person. **d** (**the Spirit**) the Holy Spirit. **10** (*also in pl*) distilled liquor of high alcoholic content, e.g. gin, whisky, and rum. **11** (*in pl*) any of various readily vaporizing liquids obtained by distillation or breakdown of petroleum, wood, etc. **12a** = ALCOHOL (1). **b** a usu readily vaporizing solvent, e.g. an alcohol, ester, or hydrocarbon. **c** an alcoholic solution of a readily vaporizing substance: *spirit of camphor*. ✱ **in spirit** sympathetically involved in an event or situation if not physically present. **in spirits** in a cheerful or lively frame of mind. **out of spirits** in a gloomy or depressed frame of mind. ⟩⟩ **spiritless** *adj*. [Middle English via Old French from Latin *spiritus*, literally 'breath']

spirit[2] *verb trans* (**spirited, spiriting**) **1** (*often* + away) to carry (somebody or something) off, *esp* secretly or mysteriously: *She was spirited away to a mountain hideout*. **2** *archaic* (*often* + up) to infuse (somebody) with spirit; *esp* to animate or inspire (them): *Hope and apprehension of feasibleness spirits all industry* — John Goodman.

spirited *adj* **1** full of energy, animation, or courage: *a spirited discussion*. **2** (*usu used in combinations*) having the frame of mind specified: *low-spirited*. ⟩⟩ **spiritedly** *adv*, **spiritedness** *noun*.

spirit gum *noun* a solution, e.g. of gum arabic in ether, used by actors for attaching false hair to the skin.

spiritism *noun* a belief that spirits of the dead communicate with the living; spiritualism. ⟩⟩ **spiritist** *noun and adj*, **spiritistic** /-'tistik/ *adj*.

spirit lamp *noun* a lamp in which a vaporizing liquid fuel, e.g. methylated spirits, is burned.

spirit level *noun* a device that uses the position of a bubble in a curved transparent tube of liquid to indicate whether a surface is level.

spirit of hartshorn /'hahts·hawn/ *or* **spirits of hartshorn** *noun* a solution of ammonia in water.

spiritous /'spiritəs/ *adj* see SPIRITUOUS.

spirits of turpentine *noun* (*treated as sing. or pl*) = TURPENTINE[1] (1B).

spiritual[1] /'spirichoo(ə)l/ *adj* **1** relating to one's spirit and higher consciousness, as distinct from one's earthbound body and nature;

non-corporeal: *I wish to set forth my faith as particularly answering this double spiritual need* — G K Chesterton. **2a** relating to religious matters or values: *spiritual songs.* **b** ecclesiastical rather than lay or temporal: *spiritual authority.* **3** based on or related through sympathy of thought or feeling: *our spiritual home.* **4a** existing as spirit; incorporeal. **b** relating to supernatural beings or phenomena. ➤➤ **spiritually** *adv.* [Middle English via early French *spirituel* from Latin *spiritualis* of breathing, of wind, of the spirit, breath, from *spiritus* SPIRIT[1]]

spiritual[2] *noun* a usu emotional religious song of a kind developed among black Christians in the southern USA.

spiritualise *verb trans* see SPIRITUALIZE.

spiritualism *noun* **1** a belief that spirits of the dead communicate with the living, *esp* through a medium or at a séance. **2** in philosophy, the doctrine that spirit is the ultimate reality. ➤➤ **spiritualist** *noun*, **spiritualistic** /-'listik/ *adj.*

spirituality /ˌspirichoo'aliti/ *noun* **1** sensitivity or attachment to religious values: *a man of deep spirituality.* **2** a practice of personal devotion and prayer: *a study of Byzantine spirituality.* [Middle English *spiritualte* via French from Latin *spiritualis*: see SPIRITUAL[1]]

spiritualize *or* **spiritualise** *verb trans* **1** to make (something) spiritual; to elevate (it) to a spiritual plane: *Illness and solitude did much to spiritualize his mind.* **2** to give a spiritual meaning to (something) or understand (it) in a spiritual sense. ➤➤ **spiritualization** /-'zaysh(ə)n/ *noun.*

spirituous /'spirichooəs/ *or* **spiritous** /'spiritəs/ *adj formal or archaic* containing or impregnated with alcohol obtained by distillation: *spirituous liquors.* [French *spiritueux* from Latin *spiritus* SPIRIT[1]]

spiro-[1] *comb. form* forming words, denoting: coil or twist: *spirochaete.* [late Latin *spir-* from Latin *spira*: see SPIRAL[1]]

spiro-[2] *comb. form* forming words, denoting: breathing: *spirograph.* [Latin *spirare* to breathe]

spirochaete (*NAmer* **spirochete**) /'spierohkeet/ *noun* any of an order of slender spirally undulating bacteria including those causing syphilis and relapsing fever: order Spirochaetales. [from the Latin genus name *Spirochaeta*, from *spira* (see SPIRAL[1]) + Greek *chaitē* long hair]

spirograph /'spierəgrahf, -graf/ *noun* **1** an instrument for recording respiratory movements. **2** (**Spirograph**) *trademark* a toy consisting of a set of toothed rings with small holes in them which are moved around a frame to draw patterns. ➤➤ **spirographic** /-'grafik/ *adj.*

spirogyra /spierə'jierə/ *noun* any of a genus of freshwater conjugating green algae whose cells contain spiral chlorophyll bands: genus *Spirogyra.* [Latin genus name, from Greek *speira* coil + *gyros* ring, circle]

spirometer /spie'romitə/ *noun* an instrument for measuring the air entering and leaving the lungs. ➤➤ **spirometry** /-tri/ *noun.*

spirt[1] /spuht/ *verb trans and intrans* see SPURT[1].

spirt[2] *noun* see SPURT[2].

spit[1] /spit/ *verb* (**spitting**, *past tense and past part.* **spat** /spat/ *or* **spit**) ➤ *verb intrans* **1a** to eject saliva from the mouth. **b** (*usu* + at/on) to eject saliva as an expression of aversion or contempt. **2** said of a cat: to make a characteristic rasping noise to show hostility. **3** to rain very lightly. **4** to sputter: *The sausages were spitting in the pan.* ➤ *verb trans* **1** to eject (e.g. saliva) from the mouth. **2a** to express (hostile or malicious feelings) by spitting, or as if by spitting: *He spat his contempt.* **b** (*often* + out) to utter (words) vehemently or with a spitting sound: *She spat out the words.* **3** to emit (something) as if by spitting: *The guns spat fire.* ✳ **not trust somebody as far as one can spit** to distrust them utterly: *He trusted neither of them as far as he could spit, and he was a poor spitter, lacking both distance and control* — P G Wodehouse. **spit chips** *Aus, informal* to be very angry. **spit it out** (*usu in imperative*) to say what is on one's mind without further delay. ➤➤ **spitter** *noun.* [Old English *spittan*, of imitative origin]

spit[2] *noun* **1** spittle or saliva. **2** the act of spitting. **3** = SPITTING IMAGE.

spit[3] *noun* **1** a slender pointed rod for holding meat over a source of heat, e.g. an open fire. **2** an elongated often hooked strip of sand or shingle extending from the coast. [Old English *spitu*]

spit[4] *verb trans* (**spitted**, **spitting**) to fix (meat) on a spit; to impale (it).

spit and polish *noun* extreme attention to cleanliness and orderliness. [from the practice of cleaning objects such as shoes by spitting on them before polishing them]

spite[1] /spiet/ *noun* petty ill will or malice. ✳ **in spite of** regardless of; in defiance or contempt of: *They decided to play the match in spite of the rain.* **in spite of oneself** in spite of one's intentions, wishes, character, etc: *He felt sorry in spite of himself.* ➤➤ **spiteful** *adj*, **spitefully** *adv*, **spitefulness** *noun.* [Middle English, short for DESPITE[2]]

spite[2] *verb trans* to annoy, harm, or hinder (somebody) out of spite: *She went on playing the radio at full volume just to spite them.*

spitfire *noun* a quick-tempered or volatile person.

spitting cobra *noun* either of two venomous African snakes that eject their venom towards the victim without striking: *Naja nigricollis* or the rinkhals: *Hemachatus hemachatus.*

spitting image *noun* (**the spitting image**) the exact likeness. [alteration of *spit and image*]

spittle /'spitl/ *noun* **1** saliva ejected from the mouth. **2** a frothy secretion exuded by some insects. [Old English *spætl*]

spittlebug *noun* – FROGHOPPER.

spittoon /spi'toohn/ *noun* a receptacle for spit. [SPIT[2] + *-oon* as in BALLOON[1]]

spit up *verb intrans informal* said *esp* of a baby: to vomit.

spitz /spits/ *noun* a dog of a stocky heavy-coated breed with a pointed muzzle and ears. [German *Spitz* from *spitz* pointed; from the shape of its ears and muzzle]

spiv /spiv/ *noun Brit, informal* a slick individual who lives by sharp practice or petty fraud; *specif* a black marketeer operating after World War II. ➤➤ **spivvy** *adj.* [alteration of English dialect *spiff* flashy dresser, from *spiffy* dandified]

splanchnic /'splangknik/ *adj* to do with or in the region of the internal organs. [via Latin from Greek *splanchnikos*, from *splanchna* (pl) *viscera*]

splash[1] /splash/ *verb intrans* **1a** to move about vigorously in a liquid, *esp* striking the surface, causing it to fly up and spatter: *The baby splashed about in the bath.* **b** to move through or into a liquid and cause it to spatter: *The boy splashed through the puddle.* **2** to become spattered about: *Milk splashed all over the floor.* **3a** to spread or scatter in the manner of splashed liquid: *Sunlight splashed over the lawn.* **b** to flow, fall, or strike with a splashing sound: *a brook splashing over rocks.* **4** *chiefly Brit, informal* (+ out) to spend money liberally; to splurge: *We splashed out on a new dinner service.* ➤ *verb trans* **1** to dash a liquid or semiliquid substance on or against (something). **2** to soil or stain (something) with splashed liquid. **3a** to cause (a liquid or semiliquid substance) to spatter about, *esp* with force. **b** to scatter (something) in the manner of a splashed liquid: *Sunset splashed its colours across the sky.* **4** to mark or overlay (something) with patches of contrasting colour. **5** to display (something) prominently; *specif* to print (an item) in a conspicuous position in a newspaper or magazine: *The affair was splashed all over the local papers.* [alteration of PLASH[2]]

splash[2] *noun* **1** the action or sound of splashing. **2a** a spot or daub from splashed liquid, or as if from splashed liquid: *a mud splash on the wing.* **b** a usu vivid patch of colour or of something coloured: *splashes of yellow tulips.* **3** a small but usu significant amount of liquid; a dash: *a splash of soda in the whisky.* **4** *informal* a conspicuously featured item in a newspaper or magazine. ✳ **make a splash** to attract attention or make a vivid impression. ➤➤ **splashy** *adj.*

splashback *noun* a panel or screen, e.g. behind a sink or cooker, to protect the wall from splashes.

splashdown *noun* the landing of a spacecraft in the ocean.

splash down *verb intrans* said of a spacecraft: to land in the ocean.

splat[1] /splat/ *noun* a single flat often ornamental piece of wood forming the centre of a chair back. [obsolete *splat* to spread flat, from Middle English *splatten*, of imitative origin]

splat[2] *noun* a splattering or slapping sound, as of the noise of the impact when something falls and is flattened. ➤➤ **splat** *adv.* [imitative]

splatter[1] /'splatə/ *verb* (**splattered**, **splattering**) ➤ *verb trans* to spatter heavy drops of (something). ➤ *verb intrans* to scatter or fall in or as if in heavy drops: *Rain splattered against the windscreen.* [prob blend of SPLASH[1] and SPATTER[1]]

splatter[2] *noun* a splash of something in heavy drops.

splatter movie *noun informal* a film in which many people die in gruesome ways.

splay[1] /splay/ *verb trans* **1** to spread or open (something) out, *esp* in a V or fan shape. **2** to make (e.g. the edges of an opening) slanting. ➤ *verb intrans* **1** to become splayed. **2** to slope or slant. [Middle English *splayen*, short for *displayen*: see DISPLAY[1]]

splay[2] *adj* turned outwards: *splay knees*.

splay[3] *noun* **1** a slope or bevel, *esp* of the sides of a door or window. **2** a spread or expansion.

splayfoot *noun* a foot abnormally flattened and spread out. ➤➤ **splayfoot** *adj*, **splayfooted** /splay'footid/ *adj*.

spleen /spleen/ *noun* **1** a ductless organ near the stomach or intestine of most vertebrates that is concerned in the final destruction of blood cells, storage of blood, and production of lymphocytes. **2** bad temper; spite. ➤➤ **spleenful** *adj*. [Middle English *splen* via French and Latin from Greek *splēn*; (sense 1) from the former belief that such feelings originated in the spleen]

spleenwort *noun* any of various ferns that have spore clusters borne obliquely on the upper side of a leaf vein: genus *Asplenium*. [from the belief in its power to cure disorders of the spleen]

splen- *or* **spleno-** *comb. form* forming words, denoting: the spleen: *splenectomy*; *splenomegaly*. [Latin *splen-*, *spleno-* from Greek *splēn-*, *splēno-*, from *splēn* spleen]

splendent /'splendant/ *adj archaic* shining or glossy. [Middle English via late Latin from Latin *splendent-*, *splendens*, present part. of *splendēre* to shine]

splendid /'splendid/ *adj* **1a** magnificent or sumptuous. **b** shining or brilliant. **2** illustrious or distinguished. **3** of the best or most enjoyable kind; excellent: *a splendid picnic*. ➤➤ **splendidly** *adv*, **splendidness** *noun*. [Latin *splendidus*, from *splendēre* to shine]

splendiferous /splen'dif(ə)rəs/ *adj informal, humorous* = SPLENDID: *his splendiferous eruption of eloquence* — Times Literary Supplement. ➤➤ **splendiferously** *adv*, **splendiferousness** *noun*. [SPLENDOUR + -IFEROUS]

splendour (*NAmer* **splendor**) /'splendə/ *noun* **1** great brightness or lustre; brilliance. **2** grandeur or pomp. [Middle English *splendure* via Anglo-French from Latin *splendor*, from *splendēre* to shine]

splenectomy /spli'nektəmi/ *noun* (*pl* **splenectomies**) the surgical removal of the spleen.

splenetic /spli'netik/ *adj* **1** bad tempered or spiteful. **2** *archaic* given to melancholy. ➤➤ **splenetically** *adv*. [late Latin *spleneticus* from Latin *splen*: see SPLEEN]

splenic /'spleenik, 'splenik/ *adj* to do with or in the region of the spleen: *splenic blood flow*. [Latin *splenicus* from Greek *splēnikos*, from *splēn* spleen]

splenius /'spleeni-əs/ *noun* (*pl* **splenii** /'spleeniie/) a flat oblique muscle on each side of the back of the neck. [Latin *splenius* from *splenium* plaster, compress, from Greek *splēnion*, from *splēn* SPLEEN]

spleno- *comb. form* see SPLEN-.

splenomegaly /spleenoh'megəli/ *noun* enlargement of the spleen. [SPLENO- + Greek *megal-*, *megas* large]

splice[1] /splies/ *verb trans* **1a** to join (e.g. ropes) by interweaving the strands. **b** to unite (e.g. film, magnetic tape, or timber) by overlapping the ends or binding with adhesive tape. **2** *Brit, informal* (*usu in passive*) to unite (two people) in marriage. ✳ **splice the mainbrace** to serve rum on a ship. ➤➤ **splicer** *noun*. [obsolete Dutch *splissen*]

splice[2] *noun* **1** a joining or joint made by splicing. **2** a wedge-shaped projection on a cricket-bat handle that is fitted into the blade.

spliff /splif/ *noun slang* a marijuana cigarette; a joint. [origin unknown]

spline /splien/ *noun* **1** a thin wood or metal strip used in building construction. **2** a piece, ridge, or groove that prevents a shaft from turning freely in a surrounding tubular part but usu allows lengthways motion. ➤➤ **splined** *adj*. [origin unknown]

splint[1] /splint/ *noun* **1** material or a device used to protect and immobilize a body part, e.g. a broken arm. **2** a thin strip of wood suitable for interweaving, e.g. into baskets. **3** a thin strip of wood used for lighting a fire. **4** a bony enlargement on the upper part of the cannon bone of a horse, usu on the inside of the leg. [Middle English from early Low German *splinte*, *splente* metal plate or pin]

splint[2] *verb trans* to support and immobilize (e.g. a broken arm) with a splint.

splint bone *noun* either of the two slender rudimentary bones on either side of the cannon bone in the limbs of horses and related animals.

splinter[1] /'splintə/ *noun* a sharp thin piece, *esp* of wood or glass, split or broken off lengthways. ➤➤ **splintery** *adj*. [Middle English from early Dutch *splinter*]

splinter[2] *verb* (**splintered**, **splintering**) ➤ *verb trans* **1** to split or rend (something) into long thin pieces; to shatter (it). **2** to split (e.g. a group or party) into fragments, parts, or factions. ➤ *verb intrans* to become splintered.

splinter group *noun* a small group or faction broken away from a parent organization.

split[1] /split/ *verb* (**splitting**, *past tense and past part.* **split**) ➤ *verb trans* **1** to divide or separate (something) , usu lengthways along a grain or seam or by layers. **2** to separate (constituent parts) by putting something in between. **3** to tear (something) apart; to burst (something). **4** to subject (an atom or atomic nucleus) to artificial disintegration, *esp* by fission. **5** to affect (something) as if by shattering or tearing apart: *a roar that split the air*. **6a** to divide or share (something) between people. **b** to divide (e.g. a political party) into opposing factions, parties, or groups. **7** *NAmer* to mark (a ballot) or cast (a vote) so as to vote for candidates of different parties. ➤ *verb intrans* **1** to become split lengthways or into layers. **2** to break apart; to burst or rupture. **3** to become divided up or separated off into smaller groups or parts. **4** (*often* + up) to end a relationship or connection. **5** *informal* to leave, *esp* hurriedly or abruptly. **6** *informal* (*often* + with) to share something, e.g. loot or profits, with others. **7** *Brit, informal* (*often* + on) to let out a secret; to act as an informer. ✳ **split hairs** to make oversubtle or trivial distinctions. **split one's sides** to laugh heartily. **split the difference** to compromise by taking the average of two amounts. **split the vote** to cause the votes for a particular political tendency to be divided among two or more candidates, allowing a candidate of opposed views to win. ➤➤ **splitter** *noun*. [early Dutch *splitten*]

split[2] *noun* **1a** a narrow break made by splitting; a tear or crack. **b** a piece or section split off. **2a** the act or an instance of splitting. **b** a division into divergent or opposing groups or elements; a breach: *a split in party ranks*. **3** (**the splits**) in gymnastics, the act of lowering oneself to the floor or leaping into the air with the legs extended at right angles to the trunk either to the front and rear or on each side. **4** a sweet dish made of sliced fruit, *esp* a banana, with ice cream, syrup, and often nuts and whipped cream. **5** a wine bottle holding a quarter of the usual amount, or a small bottle of mineral water, tonic water, etc.

split[3] *adj* **1** prepared for use by splitting: *split bamboo*; *split hides*. **2** divided or fractured.

split end *noun* **1** (*usu in pl*) an end of a human hair that has split into two or more strands. **2** in American football, an offensive player who lines up several yards outside the tackle.

split infinitive *noun* an infinitive with a word, usu an adverb, between *to* and the verb, as in *to fully agree*: *Asked about grammar, the panellists strongly resisted confusions of singular and plural ... But half agreed to tolerate split infinitives – as in Star Trek's 'to boldly go'* — The Guardian.

split-level *adj* **1** said of a room, house, etc: divided so that the floor level in one part is less than a full storey higher than an adjoining part. **2** said of a cooker: divided so that the hob and the oven are separate units. ➤➤ **split-level** *noun*.

split pea *noun* a dried pea in which the cotyledons are usu split apart.

split personality *noun* a personality composed of two or more internally consistent groups of behaviour tendencies and attitudes each acting more or less independently of the other.

split pin *noun* a strip of metal folded double that can be used as a fastener by inserting it through a hole and then bending back the ends.

split ring *noun* a metal ring of two flat turns on which keys may be kept.

split screen *noun* **1** an effect in which two juxtaposed images are displayed simultaneously on a film or television screen. **2** in computing, a display in which the screen is used for two or more documents or activities at the same time.

split second *noun* a fractional part of a second; a flash. ➤ **split-second** *adj*.

split shift *noun* a shift of working hours divided into two or more widely-separated working periods.

split ticket *noun NAmer* a ballot cast by a voter who votes for candidates of more than one party: compare STRAIGHT TICKET.

splitting *adj* causing a piercing sensation: *a splitting headache.*

splodge[1] /sploj/ *noun Brit, informal* a splotch or blot. [prob alteration of SPLOTCH[1]]

splodge[2] *verb trans Brit, informal* to mark (something) with a large irregular blot. ➤ **splodgy** *adj*.

splosh[1] /splosh/ *verb informal* to splash (something). [by alteration]

splosh[2] *noun informal* = SPLASH[2].

splotch[1] /sploch/ *noun informal* a large irregular spot or smear; a blotch. ➤ **splotchy** *adj*. [perhaps blend of SPOT[1] and BLOTCH[1]]

splotch[2] *verb trans informal* to mark (something) with a splotch or splotches.

splurge[1] /spluhj/ *noun informal* **1a** a large amount of something used extravagantly or ostentatiously. **b** an ostentatious display of something. **2** an extravagant spending spree. [perhaps blend of SPLASH[2] and SURGE[2]]

splurge[2] *verb intrans informal* **1** to make a splurge. **2** (*often* + on) to spend money extravagantly: *They splurged on a slap-up meal.* ➤ *verb trans informal* **1** (*often* + on) to spend (money) extravagantly or ostentatiously: *She splurged all her allowance on new clothes.* **2** to use or display (something) in large amounts or ostentatiously: *I simply splurge paint all over the canvas.*

splutter[1] /spluta/ *verb* (**spluttered, spluttering**) ➤ *verb intrans* **1** to spit out bits of food, saliva, etc noisily, e.g. when choking or laughing. **2** to eject small fragments or splashes with a crackling or popping sound: *a fire spluttering in the grate.* **3** to speak hastily and confusedly; to sputter. ➤ *verb trans* to utter (something) hastily and confusedly. ➤ **splutterer** *noun*, **spluttering** *adj*, **spluttery** *adj*. [prob alteration of SPUTTER[1]]

splutter[2] *noun* a spluttering sound.

Spode /spohd/ *noun* fine ceramic ware, e.g. bone china, made at the works established by Josiah Spode at Stoke-on-Trent in Staffordshire. [named after Josiah *Spode* d.1827, English potter]

spodumene /spodyoomeen/ *noun* a mineral that is a lithium aluminium silicate occurring as very large variously coloured crystals. [French *spodumène* via German from Greek *spodoumenos*, present part. of *spodousthai* to be burned to ashes, from *spodos* ashes]

spoil[1] /spoyl/ *verb* (*past tense and past part.* **spoilt** /spoylt/ *or* **spoiled**) ➤ *verb trans* **1a** to damage (something) seriously; to ruin (it): *Heavy rain spoilt the crops.* **b** to impair the enjoyment of (something); to mar (it): *A quarrel spoilt the celebration.* **c** to fill in (e.g. a voting paper) wrongly so as to render it invalid. **2a** to impair the character of (somebody) by overindulgence: *He spoils his son.* **b** to treat (somebody) indulgently; to pamper (them): *Spoil your guests with fresh lobster.* **3** *archaic* to rob (somebody) or steal (property) by force. ➤ *verb intrans* to become unfit for use or consumption, usu as a result of decay: *Fruit soon spoils in warm weather.* ✳ **be spoilt for choice** *Brit* to have so many choices that one cannot decide. **spoiling for a fight** having an eager desire for a fight. [Middle English *spoilen* via French from Latin *spoliare* to strip, plunder, rob, from *spolium* booty, SPOIL[2]]

spoil[2] *noun* **1** (*usu in pl*) plunder taken from an enemy in war or a victim in robbery; loot. **2** (*usu in pl*) something gained by special effort or skill. **3** earth and rock excavated or dredged. [Middle English *spoile* via Old French from Latin *spolia*, pl of *spolium* spoil, booty]

spoilage /spoylij/ *noun* **1** something spoilt or wasted. **2** loss by being spoilt.

spoiler *noun* **1** a long narrow plate along the upper surface of an aircraft wing that may be raised for reducing lift and increasing drag. **2** an air deflector at the front or rear of a motor vehicle to reduce the tendency to lift off the road at high speeds. **3** somebody or something that spoils, *esp* a story published in a newspaper to spoil another paper's sales.

spoilsman *noun* (*pl* **spoilsmen**) *NAmer* somebody who serves a political party for a share of the spoils, or somebody who sanctions such practice.

spoilsport *noun* somebody who spoils the fun of others.

spoils system *noun chiefly NAmer* the practice of distributing public offices and their financial rewards to members of the victorious party and their friends after an election.

spoilt /spoylt/ *verb* past tense and past part. of SPOIL[1].

spoke[1] /spohk/ *verb* past tense of SPEAK.

spoke[2] *noun* **1a** any of the small radiating bars inserted in the hub of a wheel to support the rim. **b** any of the protruding knobs around the circumference of a ship's steering wheel. **2** a rung of a ladder. ✳ **put a spoke in somebody's wheel** to prevent somebody's plans from succeeding [from the 'spoke' or pin put through a hole in a solid cartwheel to slow it down when going downhill]. [Old English *spāca*]

spoken[1] /spohk(ə)n/ *adj* **1a** delivered by word of mouth; oral: *a spoken request.* **b** used in speaking or conversation; uttered: *the spoken word.* **2** (*used in combinations*) characterized by speaking in a specified manner: *soft-spoken; plainspoken.* [past part. of SPEAK]

spoken[2] *verb* past part. of SPEAK.

spoken-for *adj* reserved or taken; *specif* engaged to be married.

spokeshave *noun* a plane with a blade set between two handles, used for shaping curved surfaces. [SPOKE[2]]

spokesman /spohksmən/ *or* **spokeswoman** *noun* (*pl* **spokesmen** *or* **spokeswomen**) somebody who speaks on behalf of somebody else or a group of people. [prob irreg from *spoke*, obsolete past part. of SPEAK]

spokesperson *noun* (*pl* **spokespersons** *or* **spokespeople**) a spokesman or spokeswoman.

spokeswoman *noun* see SPOKESMAN.

spoliation /spohli'aysh(ə)n/ *noun* **1a** the act of plundering. **b** the state of being plundered, *esp* in war. **2a** the act of damaging or injuring, *esp* irreparably. **b** the changing or mutilation of a legal document to render it invalid. ➤ **spoliator** *noun*. [Middle English from Latin *spoliation-, spoliatio*, from *spoliare*: see SPOIL[1]]

spondee /spondee/ *noun* a metrical foot consisting of two long or stressed syllables. ➤ **spondaic** /spon'dayik/ *adj*. [Middle English *sponde* via French from Latin *spondeum*, from Greek *spondeios* of a libation, from *spondē* libation; from its use in music accompanying libations]

spondulicks /spon'dyoohliks/ *pl noun Brit, informal* funds or money. [perhaps from Greek *spondylikos* (adj), from *spondylos* species of shell sometimes used as currency]

spondylitis /spondi'lietis/ *noun* inflammation of the spinal vertebrae. [Latin *spondylitis*, from Greek *sphondylos, spondylos* vertebra + -ITIS]

sponge[1] /spunj, spunzh/ *noun* **1** an elastic porous mass of interlacing horny fibres that forms the internal skeleton of various marine animals and is able when wetted to absorb water. **2a** a piece of sponge, e.g. for cleaning. **b** a porous rubber or cellulose product used as a sponge. **c** a piece of sponge used with spermicide as a barrier contraceptive. **3** any of a phylum of aquatic lower invertebrate animals that are essentially double-walled cell colonies and permanently attached as adults: phylum Porifera. **4** a sponge cake or sponge pudding. **5** a metal, e.g. platinum, in the form of a porous solid composed of fine particles. **6** *informal* a sponger. **7** *informal* a heavy drinker: *I will do anything, Nerissa, ere I will be married to a sponge* — Shakespeare. [Old English via Latin from Greek *spongia*]

sponge[2] *verb trans* **1** (*often* + down/off) to cleanse, wipe, or moisten (something) with a sponge, or as if with a sponge. **2** (*often* + out) to erase or destroy (something) with a sponge, or as if with a sponge: *Whole paragraphs had been sponged out.* **3** *informal* to obtain (e.g. money) by sponging on another: *She tried to sponge the price of a coffee.* **4** to decorate (e.g. a wall) using paint on a sponge. ➤ *verb intrans informal* (*often* + on/off) to obtain *esp* financial assistance by exploiting people's natural generosity or organized welfare facilities: *He wasn't going to sponge off the state for ever.* ➤➤ **spongeable** *adj*.

sponge bag *noun Brit* a small waterproof usu plastic bag for holding toilet articles.

sponge bath *noun NAmer* = BLANKET BATH.

sponge cake *noun* a light sweet cake made with approximately equal quantities of sugar, flour, and eggs but no shortening.

sponge pudding *noun Brit* a sweet steamed or baked pudding made with sugar, flour, and eggs.

sponger *noun* somebody who lives off others, *esp* by exploiting their natural generosity.

sponge rubber *noun* cellular rubber resembling a natural sponge in structure.

spongiform /'spunjifawm/ *adj* resembling a sponge in appearance or texture.

spongy *adj* (**spongier, spongiest**) 1 resembling a sponge, *esp* in being soft, porous, absorbent, or moist. 2 said of a metal: in the form of a sponge. >>> **sponginess** *noun*.

sponson /'spuns(ə)n/ *noun* 1a a projection from the side of a ship or tank enabling a gun to fire forwards. b an air chamber along the side of a canoe to increase stability and buoyancy. 2 a light air-filled structure protruding from the hull of a seaplane to steady it on water. 3 a triangular platform on a paddle steamer that supports the paddle wheel. [prob by shortening and alteration from EXPANSION]

sponsor¹ /'sp_onsə/ *noun* 1 a person or organization that pays for a project or activity, e.g.: a somebody who pays the cost, or part of the cost, of a cultural or sporting event. b somebody who contributes towards a charity by giving money for a participant's efforts in an organized fund-raising event, e.g. a sponsored walk. c *chiefly NAmer* somebody who pays the cost of a radio or television programme, usu in return for limited advertising time during its course. 2 a person who presents a candidate for baptism or confirmation and undertakes responsibility for his or her religious education or spiritual welfare; a godparent. 3 somebody who introduces and supports a bill, motion, etc in parliament. 4 somebody who assumes responsibility for some other person or thing. >>> **sponsorial** /spon'sawri·əl/ *adj*, **sponsorship** *noun*. [Latin *sponsor* guarantor, surety, from *spondēre* to promise]

sponsor² *verb trans* (**sponsored, sponsoring**) to be or stand as sponsor for (somebody or something).

spontaneous /spon'tayni·əs/ *adj* 1 proceeding from natural feeling or innate tendency without external constraint: *a spontaneous expression of gratitude*. 2 springing from a sudden impulse: *a spontaneous offer of help*. 3 controlled and directed internally. 4 developing without apparent external influence, force, cause, or treatment: *spontaneous recovery from a severe illness*. 5 *archaic* said of plants: indigenous; natural. >>> **spontaneity** /sponta'nayiti, -'neeiti/ *noun*, **spontaneously** *adv*, **spontaneousness** *noun*. [late Latin *spontaneus* from Latin *sponte* of one's free will, voluntarily]

spontaneous combustion *noun* self-ignition of combustible material through chemical action, e.g. oxidation, of its constituents: *He lay upon his bed, the very core and centre of a blaze of ruddy light ... apprehensive that he might be at that very moment an interesting case of spontaneous combustion* — Dickens.

spontaneous generation *noun* = ABIOGENESIS.

spoof¹ /spoohf/ *noun informal* 1 a light, humorous, but usu telling parody. 2 a hoax or deception. [named after *Spoof*, a hoaxing game invented by Arthur Roberts d.1933, English comedian]

spoof² *verb trans informal* 1 to make good-natured fun of (somebody); to lampoon (them): *a comedy that spoofs travelling salesmen*. 2 to deceive or hoax (somebody).

spook¹ /spoohk/ *noun* 1 *informal* a ghost or spectre. 2 *chiefly NAmer* = SPY². [Dutch *spook*]

spook² *verb trans* to make (an animal or a person) frightened or frantic; *esp* to startle (them) into violent activity, e.g. stampeding: *The noise spooked the herd of horses.* > *verb intrans* to become frightened: *They don't spook easily.*

spooky *adj* (**spookier, spookiest**) *informal* causing irrational fear, *esp* because suggestive of supernatural presences; eerie. >>> **spookily** *adv*, **spookiness** *noun*.

spool¹ /spoohl/ *noun* 1 a cylindrical device which has a rim or ridge at each end and a hole, usu through the middle, for a pin or spindle and on which thread, wire, tape, etc is wound. 2 material or the amount of material wound on a spool. 3 *chiefly NAmer* a reel for cotton, thread, etc. [Middle English *spole* from early French *espole* or early Dutch *spoele*, both of Germanic origin]

spool² *verb trans* to wind (e.g. yarn or film) onto a spool. > *verb intrans* to be wound onto or off a spool.

spool³ *verb trans* in computing, to transfer (data intended for a peripheral device) to an intermediate storage, e.g. for output at a later time. [acronym from *simultaneous peripheral operation online*]

spoon¹ /spoohn/ *noun* 1a an eating, cooking, or serving implement consisting of a small shallow round or oval bowl with a handle. b = SPOONFUL. 2 something curved like the bowl of a spoon, e.g.: a a usu metal or shell fishing lure. b an oar with a curved blade and tip. [Old English *spōn* splinter, chip]

spoon² *verb trans* 1 to take up and usu transfer (e.g. a liquid) in a spoon: *She spooned soup into his mouth.* 2 to propel (a ball) weakly upwards. > *verb intrans dated, informal* to indulge in caressing and amorous talk. [verb intrans from SPOON¹ in the obsolete sense 'simpleton, doting lover, sweetheart']

spoon bait *noun* = SPOON¹ (2A).

spoonbill *noun* any of several species of wading birds with a bill that is greatly expanded and flattened at the tip: genera *Platalea* and *Ajaia*.

spoon bread *noun NAmer* soft bread made of maize mixed with milk, eggs, and fat and served with a spoon.

spoonerism /'spoohnəriz(ə)m/ *noun* a transposition of the initial sounds or letters of two or more words, e.g. in *tons of soil* for *sons of toil*. [named after William *Spooner* d.1930, English clergyman and scholar, who was known for such errors]

spoon-feed *verb trans* 1 to feed (somebody) by means of a spoon. 2a to present (e.g. information or entertainment) in an easily assimilable form that precludes independent thought or critical judgment: *spoon-feeding political theory to students*. b to present information to (somebody) in this manner.

spoonful /'spoohnf(ə)l/ *noun* (*pl* **spoonfuls**) as much as a spoon will hold.

spoony¹ *adj* (**spoonier, spooniest**) 1 *informal, dated* sentimentally in love; besotted. 2 *informal, archaic* silly or foolish; *esp* excessively sentimental.

spoony² *noun* (*pl* **spoonies**) *informal, archaic* somebody who is silly or foolish; *esp* a doting lover. [SPOON¹: see SPOON²]

spoor¹ /spooə, spaw/ *noun* a track, a trail, or droppings, *esp* of a wild animal. [Afrikaans *spoor* from early Dutch]

spoor² *verb* to track (an animal) by a spoor.

spor- *or* **spori-** *or* **sporo-** *comb. form* forming words, denoting: seed; spore: *sporangium*; *sporogenous*. [Greek *spora* seed, sowing]

sporadic /spə'radik/ *adj* occurring occasionally or in scattered instances: *sporadic outbreaks of violence*. >>> **sporadically** *adv*. [via late Latin from Greek *sporadikos*, from *sporad-, sporas* scattered]

sporangiophore /spə'ranji·əfaw/ *noun* a stalk or receptacle bearing sporangia.

sporangium /spə'ranji·əm/ *noun* (*pl* **sporangia** /-ji·ə/) a case or cell within which asexual spores are produced. >>> **sporangial** *adj*. [scientific Latin, from SPOR- + Greek *angeion* vessel]

spore¹ /spaw/ *noun* a primitive hardy reproductive body, usu with a single cell, produced by plants, algae, fungi, protozoans (primitive single-celled animals; see PROTOZOAN), bacteria, etc and capable of development into a new individual either on its own or after fusion with another spore. >>> **spored** *adj*, **sporiferous** /spaw'rifərəs, spə-/ *adj*. [scientific Latin *spora* seed, spore, from Greek *spora* act of sowing, seed, from *speirein* to sow]

spore² *verb intrans* to produce or reproduce by spores.

spori- *or* **sporo-** *comb. form* see SPOR-.

sporocyst /'spawrohsist, 'spawrəsist/ *noun* a resting cell, e.g. in slime moulds and algae, that may give rise to asexual spores. >>> **sporocystic** /-'sistik/ *adj*.

sporogenesis /spawroh'jenəsis/ *noun* reproduction by or formation of spores.

sporogenous /spə'rojinəs/ *adj* relating to, involving, or reproducing by sporogenesis.

sporogonium /spawrə'gohni·əm, sporə-/ *noun* (*pl* **sporogonia** /-ni·ə/) the SPOROPHYTE (asexual generation) of a moss or liverwort consisting typically of a stalk bearing a capsule in which spores are produced, and remaining permanently attached to the plant body. [scientific Latin, from SPOR- + *-gonium* on the pattern of ARCHEGONIUM]

sporogony /spə'rogəni/ *noun* reproduction by spores; *specif* spore formation in a type of parasitic single-celled animal (SPOROZOAN) by development of a cyst and subsequent division of a ZYGOTE (reproductive cell formed after fertilization). >>> **sporogonic** /spora'gonik/ *adj*, **sporogonous** /-nəs/ *adj*.

sporophore /'spawrəfaw, 'spo-/ *noun* a spore-bearing stem or other structure in a fungus.

sporophyll *or* **sporophyl** /'spawrəfil, 'spo-/ *noun* a spore-bearing leaf, e.g. that of a fern.

sporophyte /'spawrəfiet, 'spo-/ *noun* the generation of a plant exhibiting alternation of generations that bears asexual spores, or a member of such a generation. ➤➤ **sporophytic** /-'fitik/ *adj.*

-sporous *comb. form* forming adjectives, with the meaning: having spores of the kind or quantity specified: *homosporous.* ➤➤ **-spory** *comb. form.*

sporozoan /spawrə'zoh·ən/ *noun* any of a phylum of strictly parasitic protozoans (single-celled animals; see PROTOZOAN) that have a complicated life cycle usu involving both asexual and sexual generations often in different hosts and include important pathogens (disease-causing organisms; see PATHOGEN), e.g. malaria parasites and coccidia: phylum Sporozoa. ➤➤ **sporozoan** *adj.* [Latin class name *Sporozoa*, from SPOR- + -ZOA]

sporozoite /spawrə'zoh·iet/ *noun* an infectious form of some sporozoans that is a product of sporogony and initiates an asexual cycle in the new host. [Latin *Sporozoa* (see SPOROZOAN) + -ITE¹]

sporran /'sporən/ *noun* a leather pouch sometimes trimmed with fur, that is worn hanging in front of the kilt with men's traditional Highland dress. [Scottish Gaelic *sporan* purse]

sport¹ /spawt/ *noun* **1** (*often used in pl before another noun*) an activity or game requiring physical skill and having a set of rules or code of practice, that is engaged in either individually or as one of a team, for exercise or recreation or as a profession: *Football is my favourite sport.* **2** such activities collectively: *I enjoy sport.* **3** the activities of hunting, shooting, or fishing; the catch or kill from these: *Boat anglers enjoyed good sport with cod, a few dogfish and rays —* Anglers' Mail. **4** *archaic* a source of diversion or recreation; a pastime: *to have his fireside enlivened by the sports and nonsense … of a child —* Jane Austen; *The transition to the sport of window-breaking … was easy and natural —* Dickens. **5** *archaic* sexual play: *When the blood is made dull with the act of sport —* Shakespeare. **6** *literary* (+ of) something tossed about like a plaything: *Men are the sport of circumstances, when the circumstances seem the sport of men —* Byron. **7** a laughing stock: *A single woman, with a very narrow income, must be a ridiculous, disagreeable old maid, the proper sport of boys and girls —* Jane Austen. **8** a person who is a good loser, is generous-minded, and does not mind being laughed at: *She's used to people taking the mickey – she's a good sport.* **9** *chiefly NAmer* a playboy or gambler. **10** *Aus, NZ, informal* used as a form of familiar address, chiefly to men. **11** a biological individual, or a part of one, exhibiting a sudden deviation from type beyond the normal limits of variation, usu as a result of mutation; a freak of nature. ✳ **in sport** for fun; in fun: *I know there is a proverb, 'Love me, love my dog': but that is not always so very practicable … if the dog be set upon you to … snap at you in sport —* Charles Lamb. **make sport of/at** *archaic* to make fun of (somebody or something): *If I suspect without cause, why then make sport at me, then let me be your jest —* Shakespeare; *He may, indeed, love to make sport of people by vexing their vanity —* James Boswell. **the sport of kings** horse racing. ➤➤ **sportful** *adj,* **sportfully** *adv,* **sportfulness** *noun.* [Middle English *sporte* via Anglo-French from Old French *desport* pastime, recreation, sport, from *se desporter*: see SPORT²]

sport² *verb trans* to wear (something, *esp* something distinctive): *He was sporting a bright yellow tie.* ➤ *verb intrans* **1** *literary* to play about happily; to frolic: *lambs sporting in the meadow.* **2** (*often + with*) to dally or trifle amorously: *to sport with Amaryllis in the shade, or with the tangles of Neaera's hair —* Milton. **3** in biology, to deviate or vary abruptly from type, e.g. by bud variation; to mutate. ➤➤ **sporter** *noun.* [Middle English *sporten* from Old French *se desporter* to divert or amuse oneself, from DIS- + Latin *portare* to carry]

sportif /spaw'teef/ *adj* **1** fond of sports; athletic; sporty. **2** said of clothes: informal, casual, or suitable as sportswear: *She describes her style as sportif for work, more dressy when she's with family or friends —* Daily Telegraph. [French *sportif* relating to sport, sporty]

sporting *adj* **1** concerned with sport: *sporting activities.* **2** fond of or taking part in sports: *sporting nations.* **3** like a good sport; generous-minded: *It's very sporting of you to let us kip down here.* ✳ **a sporting chance** a reasonable chance of success, victory, or recovery. ➤➤ **sportingly** *adv.*

sportive /'spawtiv/ *adj literary* frolicsome; playful: *I am not in a sportive humour now —* Shakespeare. ➤➤ **sportively** *adv,* **sportiveness** *noun.*

sports bar *noun* a public bar where customers can watch non-stop televised sport.

sports car *noun* a low fast motor car, usu having seats for two people.

sportscast *noun chiefly NAmer* a news broadcast reporting on sport. ➤➤ **sportscaster** *noun.* [from BROADCAST², on the pattern of NEWSCAST]

sports coat *noun NAmer* = SPORTS JACKET.

sports jacket *noun* a man's jacket for informal wear, usu made of tweed or other thick fabric.

sportsman *or* **sportswoman** *noun* (*pl* **sportsmen** *or* **sportswomen**) **1** a man or woman who engages in sports. **2** a man or woman who is fair, a good loser, and a gracious winner. ➤➤ **sportsmanlike** *adj,* **sportsmanly** *adj.*

sportsmanship *noun* conduct becoming to a sportsperson.

sports medicine *noun* the branch of medicine specializing in the treatment of injuries and medical disorders related to sport, and to the assessment and enhancement of fitness.

sportsperson *noun* (*pl* **sportspeople** *or* **sportspersons**) a sportsman or sportswoman.

sportster /'spawtstə/ *noun* a sports car.

sports utility *noun NAmer* a powerful four-wheel-drive vehicle.

sportswear *noun* clothes worn for sport or for casual wear, *esp* out of doors.

sportswoman *noun* see SPORTSMAN.

sporty *adj* (**sportier, sportiest**) **1** said of a person: fond of sport and athletic activities. **2** said of clothes: designed for sporting activities or casual wear. **3** said of a car: like a sports car in appearance or performance. ➤➤ **sportily** *adv,* **sportiness** *noun.*

sporulate /'spor(y)oolayt/ *verb intrans* to form spores.

sporulation /spor(y)oo'laysh(ə)n/ *noun* **1** the formation of spores. **2** division into many small spores. ➤➤ **sporulative** /'spor(y)oolətiv/ *adj.* [scientific Latin *sporula*: see SPORULE]

sporule /'sporyoohl/ *noun* a very small spore. [scientific Latin *sporula*, dimin. of *spora*: see SPORE¹]

spot¹ /spot/ *noun* **1** a small roundish area different in colour or texture from the surrounding surface. **2** a dirty mark; a small stain. **3** a pimple or any small red blemish on the skin. **4** *chiefly NAmer.* **a** = PIP⁵ (1A), (1B). **b** used with a number to designate something, e.g. a banknote, that has a specified number of pips, units, etc: *He played the three-spot into the corner pocket; You'll pay a five-spot for overnight parking.* **5** *chiefly Brit, informal* a small amount; a bit: *a spot of bother.* **6** a place or area: *a nice spot for a picnic.* **7** (*used before a noun*) on-the-spot: *spot coverage of the news.* **8** (*used before a noun*) denoting a system of trading in which goods are paid for and delivered immediately after sale: *a spot sale.* **9** (*used in combinations*) a location, aspect, or point: *the city's nightspots; one of the high spots of the holiday.* **10** a place allocated to a person on a broadcast programme or show; = SLOT¹ (2): *She has a regular spot on 'Yesterday in Parliament'.* **11** (*often before a noun*) a brief space between broadcast television or radio programmes used for an announcement or advertising: *spot announcements.* **12** = SPOTLIGHT¹ (1). **13** = SPOT BOARD. ✳ **change one's spots** (*usu in negative contexts*) to alter one's character for the better [Jeremiah 13:23 'Can the Ethiopian change his skin, or a leopard his spots? Then may ye also do good, that are accustomed to do evil']. **hit the spot** said *esp* of food or drink: to be just what one requires: *Would a dram hit the spot?* **in a spot/in a tight spot** *informal* in difficulties. **on the spot 1** immediately; at once: *I paid on the spot.* **2** at the place of action: *We had no doctor on the spot.* **3** in one place, without progressing: *running on the spot.* **put somebody on the spot** to place somebody in a situation where they must give an answer or react appropriately without being fully prepared. [Middle English, in the sense 'speck, stain', of Germanic origin]

spot² *verb* (**spotted, spotting**) ➤ *verb trans* **1** to notice or detect (somebody or something): *I spotted Cindy in the back row; She spotted a mistake.* **2** to single out or identify (somebody or something promising). **3** to watch for and record the sighting of (wildlife species, trains, etc). **4** to locate (the enemy's position, etc) accurately. **5** to mark (a material, etc) with spots: *spotted with mould.* **6** to sully (somebody's reputation). **7** in billiards, to place (the ball) on its starting point. **8** *NAmer* to lend (somebody) a specified sum of money: *I can spot you $50.* **9** to allow (a fellow competitor or rival team) an advantage in a game, etc. ➤ *verb intrans* **1** said of a fabric: to be susceptible to staining or discoloration in spots. **2** said of a liquid, etc: to leave spots or stains. **3** said of an aircraft or pilot: to act as a spotter, *esp* to locate targets. **4** *chiefly Brit* (with 'it' as subject) to fall lightly in scattered drops: *It's spotting with rain.* ➤➤ **spottable** *adj.* [Middle English, in the sense 'to mark, stain'; (senses 1–4) from a 19th-cent. sense 'to mark or note somebody as a criminal']

spot ball *noun* in billiards, the one of a pair of white cue balls that is marked with two black spots.

spot board *noun* in building work, etc, a board on which to mix and work plaster before applying it.

spot check *noun* a random check made to test overall quality, accuracy, etc.

spot-check *verb trans and intrans* to sample or investigate (something) on the spot and usu at random.

spot height *noun* the height of a point above sea level, e.g. as recorded on a map.

spot kick *noun* in football, a penalty kick.

spotlamp *noun* = SPOTLIGHT[1] (1).

spotless *adj* **1** free from dirt or stains; immaculate. **2** pure or unblemished: *a spotless reputation.* ➤➤ **spotlessly** *adv,* **spotlessness** *noun.*

spotlight[1] *noun* **1a** a narrow intense beam of light focused on and brightly illuminating a thing or person, *esp* an actor or other performer on stage. **b** the lamp from which such a beam is projected. **2** (**the spotlight**) full public attention: *Their domestic tragedy suddenly thrust them into the media spotlight.*

spotlight[2] *verb trans* (**spotlighting,** *past tense and past part.* **spotlighted** *or* **spotlit** /'spotlit/) **1** to illuminate (somebody or something) by focusing a spotlight on them. **2** to direct public attention towards (somebody or something): *The incident had spotlighted a major flaw in the system.*

spot-on *or* **spot on** *adj Brit, informal* **1** absolutely correct or accurate: *Your diagnosis was spot on.* **2** exactly right: *Thanks for the spot-on birthday present.* ➤➤ **spot on** *adv.*

spotted *adj* **1** marked or patterned with spots. **2** *literary* sullied or tarnished: *He inherited a spotted name.*

spotted dick *noun Brit* a steamed or boiled sweet suet pudding containing dried fruit, *esp* currants. [arbitrary use of *Dick,* nickname for *Richard*]

spotted dog *noun* **1** = DALMATIAN (1). **2** = SPOTTED DICK.

spotted fever *noun* **1** a bacterial infection transmitted by ticks, accompanied by a fever and skin rash. **2** any of various other severe feverish illnesses accompanied by a skin rash.

spotted gum *noun* an Australian eucalyptus tree, the bark of which peels off in patches, presenting a mottled appearance, and is used for shipbuilding, making railway sleepers, etc: *Eucalyptus maculata.*

spotter *noun* **1** (*used in combinations*). **a** a person who makes a hobby of watching for and recording the occurrence of things of a certain class: *trainspotters.* **b** a person on the lookout for a certain thing: *a talent-spotter.* **2** (*often used before a noun*) a pilot or aircraft detailed to spot enemy positions: *a spotter plane.* **3** in the army, a member of a battery who advises on the adjustment of the line of fire.

spotting *noun* (*used in combinations*) the activity of watching out for something: *trainspotting; talent-spotting.*

spotty *adj* (**spottier, spottiest**) **1a** marked with spots. **b** said of a person or a part of the body: having spots. **2** *chiefly NAmer* lacking evenness or regularity, *esp* in quality: *spotty attendance.* ➤➤ **spottily** *adv,* **spottiness** *noun.*

spot-weld *verb trans* to join together (metal parts) with small circular welds, executed at scattered points using electrical heat and pressure.

spousal[1] /'spowzl/ *adj chiefly NAmer or archaic or literary* relating to marriage or to a spouse: *spousal embraces* — Milton; *They may also have benefited from spousal comfort* — David E Stannard. ➤➤ **spousally** *adv.*

spousal[2] *noun archaic or literary* (*also in pl*) the marriage ceremony; a nuptial: *My nobler fate shall knit our spousals with a tie, too strong for Roman laws to break* — Shakespeare.

spousal equivalent *noun NAmer* a partner who is the equivalent of one's husband or wife, including a same-sex partner, *esp* with regard to tax and benefits.

spouse /spows, spowz/ *noun* a married person; a husband or wife. [Middle English via Old French *espous* (masc), *espouse* (fem), from

Latin *sponsus* betrothed man, groom, and *sponsa* betrothed woman, bride, from *sponsus,* past part. of *spondēre* to promise, betroth]

spouse equivalent *noun NAmer* = SPOUSAL EQUIVALENT.

spout[1] /spowt/ *verb trans* **1** to eject (liquid, etc) in a copious stream: *wells spouting oil.* **2** *informal.* **a** to speak or utter (*esp* something platitudinous) in a strident or pompous manner: *spouting party slogans.* **b** to declaim or recite (poetry, etc). ➤ *verb intrans* **1** to issue with force or in a jet; to spurt: *Water was spouting from the rock.* **2** to eject material, *esp* liquid, in a jet: *spouting wounds.* **3** *informal* to discourse, *esp* pompously; to speechify. ➤➤ **spouter** *noun.* [Middle English from early Dutch *spouten* to spout, of imitative origin]

spout[2] *noun* **1** a projecting tube, e.g. on a teapot or kettle, or lip, e.g. on a jug, to facilitate pouring. **2** a downpipe conveying water from a roof gutter. **3** a chute for conveying grain. **4** a sudden downpour, or a gush or jet of water; = WATERSPOUT. **5** formerly, a lift at a pawnbroker's, for taking pawned goods up to a storage room. **✳ up the spout 1** *informal* ruined; scuppered: *Basically my holiday plans are up the spout.* **2** *informal* said of a woman: pregnant. **3** said of a cartridge or bullet: in the barrel ready to fire. **4** *archaic* in the keeping of a pawnbroker; pawned: *Please to put that up the spout, ma'am, with my pins, and rings, and watch and chain, and things* — Thackeray. ➤➤ **spouted** *adj,* **spoutless** *adj.*

spp. *abbr* species (pl).

SPQR *abbr* senatus populusque Romanus. [Latin, the Senate and the people of Rome]

SPR *abbr* Society for Psychical Research.

Spr *abbr Brit* Sapper.

Sprachgefühl /'shprahkhgəfoohl (*German* /ʃpraːxgəfyːl/) *noun* an instinctive aptitude for a language and understanding of its typical usage. [German *Sprachgefühl,* from *Sprache* language + *Gefühl* feeling]

spraddle /'spradl/ *verb trans chiefly NAmer, W Indian* to spread (one's legs) out wide. [orig in sense 'sprawl', perhaps from *sprad,* dialect past part. of SPREAD[1]]

sprag /sprag/ *noun* **1** a pointed stake or steel bar for locking the wheel of a stationary vehicle. **2** a timber support in the workings of a coalmine; a pit prop (see PROP[1] (1)). [perhaps of Scandinavian origin]

sprain[1] /sprayn/ *verb trans* to wrench or twist (a joint) violently so as to stretch or tear the ligaments and cause swelling and bruising. [origin unknown]

sprain[2] *noun* **1** the act or an instance of spraining a joint. **2** a sprained condition.

spraing /sprayng/ *noun* a viral disease of potatoes characterized by arc-shaped lesions in the flesh of the tuber and ring-shaped marks on the leaves. [orig Scots in the sense 'streak', 'stripe', prob of Scandinavian origin]

sprang /sprang/ *verb* past tense of SPRING[1].

sprat /sprat/ *noun* **1** any of several species of small sea fishes of the herring family; = BRISLING: *Sprattus sprattus* and other species. **2** *informal* any young or small fish, *esp* a herring. **✳ a sprat to catch a mackerel** *Brit* a small outlay made, or minor risk taken, in the hope of attracting a major catch. [Old English *sprott*]

sprauncy /'sprawnsi/ *or* **sproncy** /'spronsi/ *adj* (**sprauncier** *or* **sproncier, sprauncist** *or* **sproncist**) *Brit, informal* smart, stylish, or showy: *She's bought new sprauncy clothes for the children and herself* — L P Hartley. [prob related to dialect *sprouncey* cheerful]

sprawl[1] /sprawl/ *verb intrans* **1** to lie or sit with arms and legs spread out carelessly or awkwardly: *sprawling in an armchair.* **2** to spread or develop irregularly over a landscape, etc: *The city sprawls all over the hillside.* ➤ *verb trans* (*often + out*) to cause (one's limbs or body) to spread out: *She glowered at the rows of feckless bodies that lay sprawled in the chairs* — Willa Cather. ➤➤ **sprawling** *adj,* **sprawlingly** *adv,* **sprawly** *adj.* [Old English *sprēawlian* to move convulsively]

sprawl[2] *noun* **1** a sprawling position: *She landed in an undignified sprawl.* **2** an irregular spreading mass or group: *the sprawl of holiday chalets.*

spray[1] /spray/ *verb trans* **1** to discharge, disperse, or apply (a fluid) as a spray: *He sprayed paint on the wall.* **2** to direct a spray of something onto (a surface) or throughout (a place): *We sprayed the wall with paint; They sprayed the room with machine-gun fire.* **3** said of a male cat: to mark out its territory by urinating throughout (an area) or over (an object). **➤ verb intrans** to be dispersed in the form of a spray: *White foam sprayed into the air each time a wave broke.* **➤➤ sprayer** *noun.* [early Dutch *spra(e)yen* to sprinkle]

spray² *noun* **1** fine droplets of water blown or falling through the air: *the spray from the waterfall.* **2** a jet of vapour or finely divided liquid. **3** a device, e.g. an aerosol, atomizer, or hose attachment for a tap, by which liquid is discharged or applied in a spray. **4a** the action of spraying or of applying a spray: *Give the roses a spray.* **b** a substance, e.g. paint or insecticide, so applied. **5** a shower of small flying objects: *a spray of bullets.*

spray³ *noun* **1** a flowering branch or shoot of a plant. **2** a bouquet of cut flowers and foliage. **3** a small decorative arrangement of flowers and leaves, e.g. for attaching to a wedding outfit; = COR-SAGE (1). **4** a brooch resembling a spray. [Middle English, developed from Old English (*e*)*sprei* found in personal and place names]

spraycan *noun* an aerosol container.

spraydeck *noun* on a kayak, a cover fitted to the opening in the deck so as to make a waterproof seal round the canoeist's waist.

spray-dry *verb trans* to produce a powdered form of (a liquid substance, e.g. milk or other foodstuffs, ceramic materials, fertilizers, etc), by spraying it into a flow of hot air.

spray gun *noun* an apparatus resembling a gun for dispensing a substance, e.g. paint or insecticide, in the form of a spray.

sprayskirt *noun* = SPRAYDECK.

spread¹ /spred/ *verb* (**spreading**, *past tense and past part.* **spread**) **➤ verb trans 1** (*often* + out) to open or extend (something contracted or folded): *The bird spread its wings for flight; Spread out the map.* **2** to distribute (something) over an area: *spreading manure; He spread butter on his toast.* **3** (*often* + with) to cover (a surface) with an even layer of something: *She spread her toast with marmalade.* **4** (*often* + out) to divide out (work, etc) over a period or among a number of people. **5** to prepare (a table) for a meal; to set (a table). **6** to communicate (something) to an ever-widening group: *Spread the news; They spread alarm and despondency.* **7** to extend the range or incidence of (an infectious disease, etc). **8** said of a locomotive, etc: to force (rails, etc) apart. **➤ verb intrans 1** to be distributed over, or cover, an ever-widening area: *The fire spread rapidly.* **2** to be communicated to more and more people: *Panic spread among the population.* **3** to be applicable in a thin layer: *soft margarines that spread easily.* **4** said of rails: to be forced apart by pressure or weight. **✳ spread oneself too thin** to divide oneself between too many jobs or activities, so that one does nothing effectively. **➤➤ spreadability** /-'biliti/ *noun,* **spreadable** *adj.* [Old English *sprædan*]

spread² *noun* **1** the distribution or expansion of something, or the extent of this: *the spread of Christianity.* **2** an expanse or stretch of something: *the spread of a bird's wings.* **3** the two facing pages forming an opening in a newspaper or magazine, or the matter occupying such an opening, *esp* if continuous across the fold. **4** a wide obstacle for a horse to jump. **5** *NAmer, dialect* a ranch. **6** a food product designed to be spread, e.g. on bread or biscuits: *cheese spread.* **7** *informal* a sumptuous meal; a feast. **8** (*used in combinations*) a cloth cover: *a bedspread.* **9a** the distance between two points; a gap or span. **b** the difference between the buying price and selling price of shares. **c** the difference between the cost price and the selling price of a product.

spread betting *noun* the laying of bets on the number of points, etc to be scored, rather than on the simple outcome of a contest, winnings being calculated according to the margin of difference between the spread of points quoted by the bookmaker and those represented in the result.

spread-eagle¹ *verb trans* **1** to cause (somebody) to be stretched out into the position of a spread-eagle. **2** *informal* to defeat or rout (an opponent) utterly. **➤ verb intrans 1** in skating, to perform a spread-eagle. **2** to stand or lie with arms and legs stretched out wide; to sprawl.

spread-eagle² *noun* **1** a representation of an eagle with wings raised and legs extended, used as a symbol of the USA. **2** a skating movement executed with the skates heel to heel in a straight line.

spreader *noun* **1** in sailing, a bar fixed to the mast to spread the angle of the upper rigging. **2** any device for spreading something, e.g. a machine for distributing manure over an area, or for keeping things apart, e.g. a bar on which to space out the parallel wires of a multiwire antenna.

spreadsheet *noun* a software system in which large groups of numerical data can be displayed on a VDU in a set format, e.g. in rows and columns, and rapid automatic calculations and adjustments can be made.

Sprechgesang /'shprekhgəzang (*German* ʃpreçgəzaŋ)/ *noun* a voice delivery halfway between speaking and singing. [German *Sprechgesang* speaking song, from *sprechen* to speak + *Gesang* song]

Sprechstimme /'shprekhshtimə (*German* ʃpreçʃtimə)/ *noun* **1** the kind of voice delivery used in SPRECHGESANG. **2** = SPRECHGESANG. [German *Sprechstimme* speaking voice, from *sprechen* to speak + *Stimme* voice]

spree¹ /spree/ *noun* (*used in combinations*) a bout of unrestrained indulgence in an activity: *a spending spree; a drinking spree.* **✳ go on the spree 1** *dated* to indulge in a spell of wild behaviour; to go out on the town. **2** *dated* to have a bout of unrestrained drinking.

Word history

origin uncertain. It has been suggested that *spree* is an alteration of Scots *spreath* cattle raid, foray, from Scottish Gaelic *spréidh* cattle, from Latin *praeda* booty, PREY¹.

spree² *verb intrans* (**sprees, spreed, spreeing**) *dated* to indulge in a spree.

sprezzatura /spretsə'tooərə, -'tyooərə/ *noun* a deliberately cultivated appearance of well-bred insouciance or *esp,* in artistic or literary performance, of careless assurance. [Italian *sprezzatura* unconcern, ultimately from Latin *spretion-, spretio* disdain, from *spernere* to disdain]

sprig¹ /sprig/ *noun* **1** a small shoot or twig. **2** an ornament in the form of a sprig, *esp* a moulded decoration for applying to a pot before firing. **3** a small headless nail. **4** *chiefly derog, informal* a young offspring; *specif* a youth. **➤➤ spriggy** *adj.* [Middle English *sprigge,* of Germanic origin]

sprig² *verb trans* (**sprigged, sprigging**) to decorate (pottery) with sprigs. **➤➤ sprigger** *noun.*

sprigged *adj* said of a fabric or wallpaper: patterned with sprigs of flowers or leaves: *Wore my sprigged muslin robe with blue trimmings* — Jane Austen.

sprightly *or* **spritely** /'sprietli/ *adj* (**sprightlier** *or* **spritelier, sprightliest** *or* **spriteliest**) said usu of an elderly person: full of vitality and liveliness; spirited. **➤➤ sprightliness** *noun.* [obsolete *spright,* variant of SPRITE]

spring¹ /spring/ *verb* (**springing,** *past tense* **sprang** /sprang/, *past part.* **sprung** /sprung/) **➤ verb intrans 1** to move suddenly with a jumping action; to dart or bound: *She sprang to her feet; He sprang at her.* **2** to move by elastic force: *The lid sprang shut.* **3** said of planking, etc: to become warped or split: *The boards sprang as the wood dried.* **4** said of an arch: to begin its curve from its vertical side support. **5** to issue suddenly; to well up: *Tears sprang into her eyes.* **6** (*often* + up) said of plants or buildings: to appear suddenly: *New housing estates were springing up everywhere.* **7** (*usu* + from) to appear suddenly or unexpectedly: *Where did you spring from?* **8** (*usu* + from) to originate or arise: *the lethargy which springs from despair* — Conan Doyle. **9** *archaic or literary* said of the dawn or day: to break: *ere day began to spring* — Dryden. **10** (+ up) said of a wind: to begin to blow. **11** *NAmer, Aus, informal* (+ for) to pay for something. **➤ verb trans 1** to cause (something with a spring mechanism) to operate: *They sprang the trap.* **2** to manoeuvre (something) into position by pressing and bending: *He sprang the bar into place.* **3** (*usu in passive*) to provide (furniture, etc) with springs, or impart elasticity to (a wooden floor). **4** to cause (a game bird) to rise from cover. **5** *informal* to contrive the release or escape of (a prisoner). **✳ spring something/a surprise on somebody** to amaze somebody with unexpected news. [Old English *springan* to jump]

spring² *noun* **1a** a source of supply; *esp* a source of water issuing from the ground. **b** (*also in pl*) a place where water with specific properties, e.g. medicinal, rises naturally to the ground surface: *hot springs; pure spring water.* **c** *literary* (*in pl*) the sources of energy, motivation, inspiration, etc: *When old age approaches … the springs of life dry up* — Encyclopaedia Britannica. **2a** the season of new growth between winter and summer, in the N hemisphere the months of March, April, and May; = SPRINGTIME: *spring weather.* **b** in astronomy, the period in the N hemisphere extending from the March EQUINOX (time when day and night are of equal length) to the June SOLSTICE (longest day of the year). **c** (*used before a noun*) denoting a cereal crop sown in the spring and harvested the same year as sown: *spring barley.* **3** a mechanical part, e.g. of bent or coiled metal, that recovers its original shape when released after deformation. **4** the mechanism of springing back to normal position when tension is released. **5** capacity for springing; resilience or bounce: *There is* *no spring left in the mattress; He walks with a spring in his step.* **6** the act or an instance of springing; a jump or bound. **7** in architecture, the point at which an arch begins its curve from its vertical side support; = SPRINGING. **8** a mooring line. ⨠ **springless** *adj,* **springlike** *adj.* [Old English *spring* source, well]

spring balance *noun* a device using a spiral spring for measuring weight or force.

Spring Bank Holiday *noun* = SPRING HOLIDAY.

springboard *noun* **1** a flexible board on which a diver or gymnast springs to gain extra height before a dive or vault. **2** something that provides an initial stimulus or impetus: *She could be seeing this gig as the springboard to a comeback.* **3** *Aus, Can* a platform secured to a tree trunk for the use of a lumberjack working well above the ground.

springbok /'springbok/ *noun* (*pl* **springboks** *or collectively* **springbok**) **1** a swift and graceful southern African gazelle noted for its habit of springing lightly and suddenly into the air: *Antidorcas marsupialis.* **2** (*often* **Springbok**) a sportsman or sportswoman representing S Africa in an international match or tour abroad. [Afrikaans *springbok,* from Dutch *springen* to jump + *bok* antelope, goat]

spring chicken *noun chiefly NAmer* a young and tender chicken suitable for the table, orig only available in the spring. ✴ **be no spring chicken** *humorous* said of a person: to be no longer young.

spring-clean[1] *verb trans* **1** to give a thorough cleaning to (a house or furnishings), typically in the springtime. **2** to put (an organization, etc) into a proper or more satisfactory order. ⨠ *verb intrans* to spring-clean a house. [back-formation from *spring-cleaning*]

spring-clean[2] *noun* the act or an instance of spring-cleaning.

springe /sprinj, sprinzh/ *noun* a snare for catching small animals: *Why, as a woodcock to mine own springe ... I am justly kill'd with mine own treachery* — Shakespeare. [Middle English *sprenge, springe;* related to Old English *springan* SPRING[1]]

springer /'springə/ *noun* **1** = SPRINGER SPANIEL. **2** in architecture, the lowest of the stones in the SPRINGING (initial curve) of an arch. **3** a cow that is about to calve.

springer spaniel *noun* a small spaniel of either of two breeds that was once used chiefly for finding and flushing small game. [SPRING[1] in the sense 'to flush game']

spring fever *noun* a feeling of restlessness, excitement, or desire for adventure and novelty, felt in spring.

spring greens *pl noun* a young green cabbage that is picked before the heart has fully developed.

springhaas /'springhahs/ *or* **springhare** /'springheə/ *noun* (*pl* **springhase** *or collectively* **springhaas** /'springhahzə/) a nocturnal burrowing rodent of E and S Africa, of kangaroo-like appearance, having long hind legs, a long bushy tail, and rabbit-like head: *Pedetes capensis.* [Afrikaans *springhaas* jumping hare, from Dutch *springen* to jump + *haas* hare]

Spring Holiday *noun* the last Monday in May, observed as a public holiday in England, Wales, and N Ireland.

springing *noun* in architecture, the incipient curvature of an arch or vault as it rises out of its vertical side support.

spring line *noun* = SPRING[2] (8).

spring-loaded *adj* loaded or secured by means of spring tension or compression: *a spring-loaded bolt.*

spring lock *noun* a lock whose bolt is spring-loaded, so that it locks automatically and a key is required only to open it.

spring onion *noun chiefly Brit* an onion with a small mild-flavoured thin-skinned bulb and long green shoots that is chiefly eaten raw in salads.

spring peeper *noun* = PEEPER[2].

spring roll *noun* in Chinese cuisine, a small thin pancake filled with bamboo shoots, prawns, meat, etc rolled into a cylinder and deep-fried.

springtail *noun* any of various small primitive wingless insects with a springlike organ enabling it to leap: order Collembola.

springtide *noun literary* springtime: *and spread rich odors through our springtide air* — Oscar Wilde.

spring tide *noun* a tide of maximum height occurring at new and full moon.

springtime *noun* **1** the season of spring. **2** *literary* one's youth: *And bitter is my misery to think that in the springtime of my being, I must leave this pleasant land* — William Cullen Bryant.

springy /'springi/ *adj* (**springier, springiest**) having an elastic or bouncy quality; resilient: *She walks with a springy step; The turf was dry and springy.* ⨠ **springily** *adv,* **springiness** *noun.*

sprinkle[1] /'springkl/ *verb trans* **1** to scatter (a liquid) in fine drops or (a substance) in the form of a powder or fine particles: *Sprinkle icing sugar over the cake.* **2** to scatter a liquid or fine particles over (a surface); to wet (it) slightly: *Sprinkle the shirt before ironing; Sprinkle the cake with icing sugar.* **3** (*usu in passive*) to dot (something) here and there: *meadows sprinkled with flowers.* ⨠ *verb intrans NAmer* to rain lightly in scattered drops. [Middle English *sprenklen, sprinclen,* of Germanic origin]

sprinkle[2] *noun* **1** an instance of sprinkling. **2** a light fall of rain. **3** a light covering; = SPRINKLING. **4** *NAmer* (*in pl*) small thin sugar strands that are used as a decoration on iced cakes, ice cream, etc.

sprinkler *noun* **1** any of the series of nozzles in a SPRINKLER SYSTEM that release water in a spray in response to heat or smoke. **2** an apparatus for watering a lawn by spraying. ⨠ **sprinklered** *adj.*

sprinkler system *noun* a fire-extinguishing system consisting of a series of nozzles installed in the ceilings of a building that release water in response to the presence of smoke or a rise in temperature.

sprinkling *noun* a small quantity or number, *esp* falling in scattered drops or particles or distributed randomly: *a sprinkling of snow.*

sprint[1] /sprint/ *verb intrans* **1** to run at top speed, *esp* over a short distance in competitive athletics. **2** *informal* to run; to dash: *Sprint round to the chemist's.* ⨠ **sprinter** *noun,* **sprinting** *noun.* [of Scandinavian origin]

sprint[2] *noun* **1** the act or an instance of sprinting. **2** a running race of no more than 400m. **3a** a short fast swimming or cycling race. **b** a burst of speed: *He found the energy for a final sprint.*

sprit /sprit/ *noun* a spar that crosses a four-cornered fore-and-aft sail diagonally to support the peak. [Old English *spréot* pole, spear]

sprite /spriet/ *noun* **1** a fairy or elf, *esp* one associated with water. **2** a computer graphic that can be manipulated as a unit on screen. **3** a red flash seen in the upper atmosphere above a thunderstorm. [Middle English *sprit,* contraction of SPIRIT[1], or via Old French *esprit, espirit* from Latin *spiritus* SPIRIT[1]]

spritely *adj* see SPRIGHTLY.

spritsail /'sprits(ə)l, 'spritsayl/ *noun* a sail extended by a sprit.

spritz[1] /sprits/ *verb trans* to squirt or spray (something) briefly. [German *spritzen* to squirt]

spritz[2] *noun* a brief spray or squirt of something: *a spritz of soda water.*

spritzer *noun* a long drink consisting of wine diluted with soda water, sparkling water, or lemonade. [German *Spritzer* a splash]

sprocket /'sprokit/ *noun* **1** a tooth or projection on the rim of a wheel, shaped so as to engage the links of a chain. **2** a wheel or cylinder having sprockets, e.g. to engage a bicycle chain. [origin unknown]

sprog[1] /sprog/ *noun Brit* **1** *informal* a baby. **2** *slang* an army recruit; a tyro. [orig World War II RAF slang, perhaps a perversion of FROGSPAWN, or from obsolete *sprag* a young cod or salmon, a lively youngster, of unknown origin]

sprog[2] *verb intrans* (**sprogged, sprogging**) *informal* said of a woman: to have a baby.

sproncy /'spronsi/ *adj* see SPRAUNCY.

sprout[1] /sprowt/ *verb intrans* **1** said of a shoot, etc: to grow, spring up, or come forth. **2** said of a plant: to send out shoots or new growth. ⨠ *verb trans* **1** said of a plant: to send out (shoots, leaves, new growth, etc). **2** to develop or grow (something): *The boy has sprouted a few hairs on his chin.* [Middle English *sprouten,* of Germanic origin]

sprout[2] *noun* **1** a shoot, e.g. from a seed or root. **2** = BRUSSELS SPROUT.

spruce[1] /sproohs/ *noun* any of numerous species of evergreen coniferous trees with a conical head of dense foliage and soft light wood: genus *Picea.* [Middle English *Spruce* Prussia, Prussian, alteration of *Pruce,* from Old French]

spruce² *adj* neat or smart in dress or appearance; trim: *his spruce black coat and his bowler hat* — Somerset Maugham. ⇒ **sprucely** *adv*, **spruceness** *noun*.

Word history

perhaps from obsolete *Spruce leather* leather imported from Prussia: see SPRUCE¹. Spruce leather was a fashionable leather imported in the 16th cent.

spruce³ *verb trans* (+ up) to make (oneself or another person) spruce. ➤ *verb intrans* (+ up) to make oneself spruce: *Better spruce up for dinner.*

spruce⁴ *verb intrans* *Brit, dated, informal* to pretend or feign, *esp* to malinger or feign illness. ➤ *verb trans* to deceive (somebody). ⇒ **sprucer** *noun*. [origin unknown]

spruce beer *noun* an alcoholic drink flavoured with spruce; *esp* one made from spruce twigs and needles boiled with molasses or sugar and fermented with yeast.

sprue¹ /sprooh/ *noun* a chronic disease suffered by visitors to the tropics, with diarrhoea, ulceration of the mouth, and other symptoms of food malabsorption and vitamin deficiency. [Dutch *spruw* thrush]

sprue² *noun* 1 the hole through which molten metal or plastic enters a mould. 2 a piece of metal or plastic that has solidified in such a hole. [origin unknown]

spruik /'sproohk, 'sprooh·ik/ *verb intrans* *Aus, informal* to give a public harangue, e.g. advertising a show. ⇒ **spruiker** *noun*. [origin unknown]

spruit /sprayt/ *noun* *SAfr* a small watercourse that is usu dry except in the rainy season. [Afrikaans *spruit* small stream, tributary, from Dutch *spruit* offshoot, scion, sprig]

sprung¹ *verb* past part. of SPRING¹.

sprung² /sprung/ *adj* fitted with springs, or possessed of springiness: *a sprung mattress; a well-sprung floor.*

sprung rhythm *noun* a poetic rhythm designed to approximate the natural rhythm of speech, each metrical foot having one stressed syllable followed by a varying number of unstressed syllables. [coined by Gerard Manley Hopkins d.1889, English poet and leading exponent of the metre]

spry /sprie/ *adj* (**sprier** *or* **spryer**, **spriest** *or* **spryest**) vigorously active; nimble. ⇒ **spryly** *adv*, **spryness** *noun*. [prob of Scandinavian origin]

spud¹ /spud/ *noun* 1 *informal* a potato. 2 a small narrow spade. 3 a piece of piping connecting two plumbing fittings. 4 *NAmer, informal* an incompetent person. [Middle English *spudde* dagger, of uncertain origin]

spud² *verb* (**spudded**, **spudding**) ➤ *verb trans* 1 to dig up or remove (weeds) with a spud. 2 to begin to drill (an oil well). ➤ *verb intrans* to begin to drill an oil well.

spud-bashing *noun* *informal* the peeling of potatoes, *esp* when done as a punishment in a military camp.

spud wrench *noun* a bar ending in a socket, used for tightening bolts.

spue /spyooh/ *verb trans and intrans* (**spues**, **spued**, **spuing**) *archaic* = SPEW¹.

spumante /spooh'mantay/ *noun* any of various white Italian sparkling wines. [Italian *spumànte* sparkling, sparkling wine, present part. of *spumare* to foam, from *spùma* foam, from Latin *spuma*]

spume¹ /spyoohm/ *noun* *literary* froth or foam. ⇒ **spumous** /'spyoohmǝs/ *adj*, **spumy** *adj*. [Middle English via French from Latin *spuma* foam, froth, scum]

spume² *verb intrans* said of a torrent, etc: to foam or froth.

spumone /spoo'mohnay, -ni/ *or* **spumoni** /spoo'mohni/ *noun* an Italian dessert of fine soft ice cream containing layers of various colours and flavours, with chopped fruit and nuts. [Italian *spumone*, augmentation of *spùma*: see SPUMANTE]

spun /spun/ *verb* past tense and past part. of SPIN¹.

spun glass *noun* fibreglass.

spunk /spungk/ *noun* 1 *informal* spirit; pluck. 2 *Brit, coarse slang* semen. 3 *Aus, informal* a sexually attractive person. 4 any of various fungi used to make tinder. ⇒ **spunkily** *adv*, **spunky** *adj*. [perhaps Scottish Gaelic *spong* and Irish Gaelic *sponc* sponge, tinder, ultimately from Greek *spongia* SPONGE¹]

spun silk *noun* a yarn or fabric made from silk waste that has been boiled to remove the natural gum.

spun sugar *noun* sugar boiled until it forms long threads on cooling, then shaped and used to decorate cold desserts or heaped on a stick as CANDY FLOSS.

spun yarn *noun* 1 a textile yarn spun from staple fibres. 2 a small rope or cord formed of two or more rope yarns loosely twisted together.

spur¹ /spuh/ *noun* 1 a pointed or wheel-shaped metal device secured to the heel of a rider's boot and used to prick the horse's flank in order to urge it on. 2 a goad to action; a stimulus or incentive: *Natural concupiscence seemeth as a spur to marriage* — Bacon. 3 something projecting like or suggesting a spur, e.g.: **a** a projecting root or branch of a tree. **b** a fruit-bearing side shoot. **c** a tubular projection of a plant flower head, e.g. in larkspur, columbine, and some orchids, often containing nectar. **d** a stiff sharp spine, e.g. on the wings or legs of a bird or insect, *esp* one on a cock's leg. **e** a metal spike fitted to a fighting cock's leg. 4 a ridge that extends sideways from a mountain or range of mountains. **5a** a short length of railway connecting with a major line. **b** a short road connecting with a major route, *esp* a motorway. 6 a support for ceramic products in a kiln. 7 a protective wall or jetty built out from a riverbank or seashore; = GROYNE. ✳ **on the spur of the moment** suddenly; on impulse. **win one's spurs** to prove oneself or become recognized as competent in some activity [from the chivalric tradition of acquiring spurs on achieving knighthood]: *Pocock won his spurs as a slave-driver* — Jack London. ⇒ **spurless** *adj*. [Old English *spura*]

spur² *verb* (**spurred**, **spurring**) ➤ *verb trans* 1 to urge (a horse) on with spurs. 2 (*often* + on) to incite or encourage (somebody) to make a greater effort. 3 (*usu in passive*) to fit (somebody) with spurs. 4 to prune back (a side shoot) close to the stem. ➤ *verb intrans* to urge a horse on; to ride hard. ✳ **booted and spurred** *humorous* dressed for outdoors; ready to stir forth.

spurdog *noun* a large grey dogfish found in shoals in the N Atlantic and Mediterranean, with white spots on its skin and poisonous spines in front of its dorsal fins: *Squalus acanthias*.

spurge /spuhj/ *noun* any of numerous species of a genus of mostly shrubby plants with a bitter milky juice and greenish flowers: genus *Euphorbia*. [Middle English from Old French *espurge*, from *espurgier* to purge, from Latin *expurgare* to cleanse, from EX-¹ + *purgare* (see PURGE¹), in reference to the purgative properties of the juice]

spur gear *noun* a gear wheel with teeth projecting away from its axis.

spurge laurel *noun* a low-growing Eurasian shrub with leathery oblong evergreen leaves, small green flowers, and poisonous black berries: *Daphne laureoloa*.

spurious /'spyooǝri·ǝs/ *adj* 1 false; fake; invented: *a spurious excuse.* 2 said of argument or reasoning: apparently sound but containing flaws. 3 said of a material, biological part, etc: not the thing in question though superficially resembling it: *German miners found a spurious copper ore which they called Kupfernickel, or 'copper devil'.* 4 *archaic* said of a child: illegitimate: *adultery by the wife followed by the birth of a spurious child* — Law Report, Queen's Bench Division, 1885. [late Latin *spurius* false, earlier 'illegitimate', 'a bastard']

spurn /spuhn/ *verb trans* 1 to reject (something or somebody) with disdain: *They spurned my suggestion.* 2 *archaic* to kick (a dog, etc) away: *you that did … foot me as you spurn a stranger cur over your threshold* — Shakespeare. ⇒ **spurner** *noun*. [Old English *spurnan* to kick, spurn]

spurrey *or* **spurry** /'spuri/ *noun* (*pl* **spurreys** *or* **spurries**) any of several species of small plants of the pink family, with white or pink flowers: genera *Spergula* and *Spergularia*. [Dutch *spurrie*, prob ultimately from late Latin *spergula*]

spurrier /'spuri·ǝ, 'spuh-/ *noun* a maker of spurs.

spur royal *noun* a gold 15-shilling piece of James I (VI of Scotland) bearing a sun with rays, resembling the wheel or rowel of a spur.

spurry *noun* see SPURREY.

spurt¹ *or* **spirt** /spuht/ *verb intrans* 1 to gush out in a jet: *Blood was spurting from the wound.* 2 to put on speed or increase effort. ➤ *verb trans* to cause (liquid) to gush out in a jet: *The bottle lay on its side spurting pricey champagne.* [prob imitative]

spurt² *or* **spirt** *noun* 1 a sudden forceful gush; a jet. 2 a sudden increase in effort or speed: *She put on a spurt for the finish.*

spurtle /'spuhtl/ *noun chiefly Scot* a wooden stick for stirring porridge. [origin unknown]

spur track *noun* = SPUR¹ (5A).

spur wheel *noun* = SPUR GEAR.

sputa /'spyootə/ *noun* pl of SPUTUM.

sputnik /'sputnik, 'spootnik/ *noun* any of a series of artificial satellites put into orbit by the former USSR, *esp* the first of all such satellites, launched in October 1957. [Russian *sputnik*, literally 'travelling companion', from *s*- together + *put* way, path, route + -NIK]

sputter¹ /'sputə/ *verb* (**sputtered, sputtering**) ➤ *verb trans* **1** to utter (something) hastily or explosively in confusion, anger, or excitement; = SPLUTTER¹. **2a** to dislodge (atoms) from the surface of a material by collision with high-energy particles, e.g. electrons. **b** to deposit (a metallic film) by such a process. ➤ *verb intrans* **1** to eject particles of food or saliva noisily from the mouth. **2** to speak in an explosive or incoherent manner. **3** to make explosive popping sounds: *bacon sputtering in the frying pan.* ➤➤ **sputterer** *noun*. [Dutch *sputteren*, of imitative origin]

sputter² *noun* **1** confused and excited speech. **2** the act or an instance of sputtering, or the sound of sputtering.

sputum /'spyoohtəm/ *noun* (*pl* **sputa** /'spyoohtə/) matter, made up of discharges from the respiratory passages and saliva, that is coughed up. [Latin *sputum* spittle, neuter past part. of *spuere* to spit]

spy¹ /spie/ *verb* (**spies, spied, spying**) ➤ *verb intrans* **1** (*often* + for) to work for a government or other organization by secretly gathering data about enemies or rivals; to serve as a spy: *When did he start spying for the Russians?* **2** (+ on) to watch somebody secretly: *You were spying on me!* ➤ *verb trans* **1** to catch sight of or spot (somebody or something): *At length I spied her in the crowd.* **2** (+ out) to find (something) out by spying or observation: *You naughty, sneaking, wicked boy! I'll teach you to spy out my secrets … and to make fun of me!* — Frank L Baum. ✳ **spy out the land** to investigate how things stand before making any definite move. [Middle English *spien* from Old French *espier*, of Germanic origin]

spy² *noun* (*pl* **spies**) **1** a person who keeps secret watch on somebody or something. **2** a person who attempts to gain information in one country, company, etc and communicate it to another, usu hostile, one. **3** the act or an instance of spying.

spyglass *noun* a small telescope.

spyhole *noun Brit* = PEEPHOLE.

Sq *abbr* **1** in street names, square. **2** Squadron.

sq. *abbr* square.

SQL *abbr* structured query language, a computer language used in database management and manipulation.

Sqn Ldr *abbr* Squadron Leader.

squab¹ /skwob/ *noun* (*pl* **squabs** *or collectively* **squab**) **1** a fledgling bird, *esp* a pigeon. **2** *Brit* a thick upholstery cushion for a chair, car seat, etc. ➤➤ **squabby** *adj.* [prob of Scandinavian origin]

squab² *adj* (**squabber, squabbest**) *archaic* squarish and plump; squat: *And so we rode quietly on, the squab little notary taking the lead* — Washington Irving.

squabble¹ /'skwobl/ *verb intrans* to quarrel noisily, *esp* over trifles. ➤➤ **squabbler** *noun.* [prob of Scandinavian origin]

squabble² *noun* a noisy quarrel.

squab pie *noun Brit* **1** pigeon pie. **2** *archaic* a mutton or pork pie with a thick pastry crust, containing onions and apples.

squacco /'skwakoh/ *noun* (*pl* **squaccos**) a small beige and white heron of S Europe, Asia, and Africa, with a short neck and a crest: *Ardeola ralloides.* [Italian dialect *squacco, sguacco*]

squad /skwod/ *noun* (*treated as sing. or pl*) **1** a small group of military personnel assembled for a purpose: *a drill squad.* **2** a small group working as a team: *a flying squad.* **3** a sports team: *the England squad.* [French *esquade, escouade* from Italian *squadra* square, ultimately from Latin *quadra*]

squad car *noun chiefly NAmer* a police car having radio communication with headquarters.

squaddy *or* **squaddie** /'skwodi/ *noun* (*pl* **squaddies**) *Brit, informal* a private in the armed forces. [prob alteration (influenced by *squad*) of dialect *swaddy* a country lad, lout, prob of Scandinavian origin]

squadron /'skwodrən/ *noun* (*treated as sing. or pl*) **1** a unit of cavalry or of an armoured regiment, usu consisting of three or more troops. **2** a variable naval unit consisting of a number of warships on a particular operation. **3** a unit of an air force consisting usu of between 10 and 18 aircraft. [Italian *squadrone*, orig a group of soldiers drawn up in a square, from *squadra*: see SQUAD]

squadron leader *noun* an officer in the British air force senior in rank to a flight lieutenant, and junior to a wing commander.

squalene /'skwayleen/ *noun* a chemical compound of the TERPENE group (unsaturated hydrocarbons), $C_{30}H_{50}$, that is widely distributed in nature, e.g. in seeds, human sebum, and *esp* in shark-liver oils, and is an important intermediate in the reaction to produce sterols, e.g. cholesterol. [scientific Latin *Squalus*, name of a genus of sharks + -ENE]

squalid /'skwolid/ *adj* **1** filthy and degraded from neglect or poverty: *living in squalid conditions.* **2** sordid; disreputable: *No doubt he had his own squalid reasons for keeping quiet.* ➤➤ **squalidly** *adv*, **squalidness** *noun.* [Latin *squalidus* filthy, squalid, from *squalēre* to be rough and dirty, from *squalus* dirty]

squall¹ /skwawl/ *verb* said of a baby: to cry raucously; to scream. ➤➤ **squaller** *noun.* [prob of Scandinavian origin]

squall² *noun* a raucous cry; a scream.

squall³ *noun* **1** a sudden violent wind, often with rain or snow. **2** a short-lived commotion: *a minor domestic squall.* ➤➤ **squally** *adj.* [prob of Scandinavian origin]

squall line *noun* in meteorology, a band of stormy weather with squally winds accompanying a cold front.

squalor /'skwolə/ *noun* the quality or state of being squalid: *living in squalor.* [Latin *squalor* from *squalēre*: see SQUALID]

squam- *or* **squamo-** *comb. form* forming words, denoting: scale; squama: *squamous.* [Latin *squama* fish scale]

squama /'skwaymə, 'skwahmə/ *noun* (*pl* **squamae** /'skwaymee, 'skwahmee/) a scale, or a structure resembling one. [Latin *squama* fish scale]

squamate¹ /'skwaymayt/ *adj* scaly: *squamate reptiles.* [Latin *squamatus* scaly, from *squama* scale]

squamate² *noun* any of an order of reptiles including the snakes and lizards: order Squamata. [Latin *squamatus*: see SQUAMATE¹]

squamo- *comb. form* see SQUAM-.

squamous /'skwayməs, 'skwahməs/ *or* **squamose** /'skwaymohs, 'skwahmohs/ *adj* **1** covered with or consisting of scales; scaly. **2** denoting a surface tissue consisting of a single layer of flat scalelike cells. [Latin *squamosus* scaly, from *squama* scale]

squamule /'skwaymyoohl/ *noun* a minute scale, as found covering the stems of certain plants or the skins of certain animals. ➤➤ **squamulose** /-lohs/ *adj.* [Latin *squamula*, dimin. of *squama* scale]

squander /'skwondə/ *verb trans* (**squandered, squandering**) **1** to waste, dissipate, or misuse (something, e.g. money, time, or talents): *He squandered his earnings on drink.* **2** *archaic* to scatter or disperse (a quantity of things): *He hath a third [ship] at Mexico, a fourth for England, and other ventures he hath, squandered abroad* — Shakespeare. [origin unknown]

square¹ /skweə/ *noun* **1** a plane figure with all four sides equal and four right angles. **2** an open space in a town or city, formed at the meeting of two or more streets, and often laid out with grass and trees. **3** *NAmer* a block of buildings surrounded by four streets. **4** the drilling area at a military barracks. **5** formerly, a body of foot soldiers drawn up in a rectangle. **6** a closely trimmed area at the centre of a cricket ground, any oblong strip of which may be selected as the wicket. **7** a woman's headscarf. **8** an arrangement of letters, numbers, etc in a square; compare MAGIC SQUARE. **9** any of the quadrilateral spaces marked out on a board, used for playing games. **10** a T-shaped or L-shaped instrument used to draw, measure, or test right angles. **11** in astrology, a 90° ASPECT (quarter) of a circle. **12** the product of a number multiplied by itself. **13** a unit of 100 square feet used to measure flooring, roofing, etc. **14** *informal, dated* a person who is excessively conventional or conservative in tastes or outlook. ✳ **back to/at square one** back where one started without the least progress having been made. **on the square 1** at right angles. **2** *informal* fair and open; honest. **out of square** not at an exact right angle. [Middle English from Old French *esquare*, ultimately from Latin *quadra*]

square² *adj* **1** having four equal sides and four right angles, or approximating to this shape. **2a** forming a right angle: *a square corner.* **b** at right angles. **c** level or parallel. **3** approximating to a cube: *a square cabinet.* **4** of a shape or build suggesting strength and solidity; broad in relation to length or height: *square shoulders; a square jaw.* **5** square in cross section: *a square tower.* **6** used before a unit of length: denoting an area equal to that of a square whose sides are of the specified unit: *a square metre; six square feet.* **7** placed after a length measurement: denoting the area of a square expanse or object whose sides are of the specified measurement: *a table roughly three metres square.* **8** exactly adjusted, arranged, or aligned; neat and orderly: *It took a while to get the room square again.* **9** fair, honest, or straightforward: *He has been square in all his dealings.* **10** (*usu* **all square**) leaving no balance; settled: *The accounts are all square.* **11** in a competition, even, tied: *After four games they were square.* **12** said of the spars of a square-rigged ship: set at right angles with the mast and keel. **13** in cricket, relating to a fielding position at right angles to the line between the wickets and level with the batsman's or batswoman's wicket: *square leg.* **14** *informal, dated* excessively conservative; dully conventional. **15** said of a rhythm: simple; uncomplicated. ✴ **square peg in a round hole** a person in an environment incompatible with their personality or abilities. ➤➤ **squareness** *noun,* **squarish** *adj.*

square³ *verb trans* **1** (*often* + off) to make (something) square or rectangular: *Square off the corners.* **2** (*often* + off) to mark off (a surface) into squares or rectangles. **3** to adjust (one's shoulders) so as to present a rectangular outline suggestive of resolution or determination. **4** to multiply (a number) by itself or raise it to the second power: *Five squared is 25.* **5** to adjust (something) so as to make it compatible with a standard or principle: *square our actions by the opinions of others* — Milton. **6** (*often* + with) to bring (one thing) into agreement with (another), or reconcile them: *How do astrophysicists square such discoveries with Christian belief?* **7** to balance or settle (an account). **8** to even the score of (a contest). **9** *informal* to bribe (somebody) into acquiescence: *I'll square the caretaker.* ➤ *verb intrans* (+ with) to match or agree precisely: *Her story doesn't square with the facts.* ✴ **square the circle** to contrive something impossible [in reference to the hopeless mathematical task of constructing a square that is exactly equal in area to a given circle using only a ruler and compass]. ➤➤ **squarer** *noun.*

square⁴ *adv* **1** directly; precisely: *I hit the nail square on the head.* **2** in a directly challenging manner: *I looked him square in the eye.* **3** *informal* in a straightforward or honest manner: *It might have been OK if you'd acted square with me.* **4** so as to face something directly: *The house stands square on to the road.* **5** transversely across a cricket pitch or football field: *He hit the ball square to the right.*

square away *verb intrans* to set the yards (spars; see YARD¹) of a square-rigged ship at right angles to the mast and keel so as to sail before the wind. ➤ *verb trans* **1** *NAmer, informal* to tidy up (some business, etc) or deal with (it) satisfactorily: *I have to square away all this work before the weekend.* **2** to set (the yards) of a square-rigged ship at right angles to the mast: *At four bells the order was given to square away the yards* — R H Dana.

square-bashing *noun chiefly Brit* military drill, *esp* marching, on a barrack square.

square bracket *noun* either of two written or printed marks [ ] used to enclose a mathematical expression or other written or printed matter.

square dance *noun* a dance for four couples who form a hollow square. ➤➤ **square dancer** *noun,* **square dancing** *noun.*

square deal *noun* an honest and fair arrangement or transaction: *I got a square deal on the trade-in.*

square-eyed *adj humorous* having developed eyes the shape of a television screen, from too much viewing. ➤➤ **square eyes** *pl noun.*

square go *noun Scot* a stand-up fist fight; an unarmed scrap.

squarehead *noun NAmer, derog* a German, Dutch, or Scandinavian, *esp* an immigrant.

square knot *noun* = REEF KNOT.

square leg *noun* in cricket, a fielding position halfway to the boundary on the leg side, level with the batsman.

squarely *adv* directly, firmly, or unequivocally: *Teilhard aimed to bring Christianity up to date by founding it squarely upon the rock of evolution* — Phillip E Johnson.

square meal *noun* a nutritionally balanced and satisfying meal.

square measure *noun* a system of units for measuring areas, or a unit in such a system.

square number *noun* a number that is the square of another number, that is, the product of another number multiplied by itself, e.g. 1, 4, 9, 16.

square off *verb intrans* **1** *NAmer* to assume a fighting stance; = SQUARE UP. **2** *Aus, NZ* to settle a disagreement. ➤ *verb trans Aus, NZ* to placate (somebody) or make things right with them.

square of opposition *noun* in logic, a diagram representing the four types of proposition that can occur in a syllogism.

square piano *noun* a small early piano, oblong and flat-topped, being horizontally strung.

square rig *noun* a sailing-ship rig in which the principal sails are square sails. ➤➤ **square-rigged** *adj,* **square-rigger** *noun.*

square root *noun* the number which, when multiplied by itself, gives the number in question: *The square root of nine is three.*

square sail *noun* a four-sided sail held open by a rod that is suspended at its centre from a mast.

square shooter *noun chiefly NAmer, informal* a frank, honest, or just person. ➤➤ **square-shooting** *adj.*

square shouldered *adj* having shoulders that present a rect angular outline: compare ROUND-SHOULDERED: *She was a tall, square-shouldered person* — Samuel Butler.

square-toed *adj* **1** said of shoes: shaped square over the toes. **2** *archaic* conservative or old-fashioned: *We old people must retain some square-toed predilection for the fashions of our youth* — Edmund Burke.

square up *verb intrans* **1** to settle a bill or pay somebody what one owes them. **2** said of opponents: to face each other ready to fight. ✴ **square up to 1** to prepare oneself to meet (a challenge). **2** to assume a fighting stance towards (an opponent).

square wave *noun* the rectangular wave form of a quantity that varies periodically and abruptly from one to the other of two constant values.

squark /skwahk/ *noun* the partner or counterpart of a quark in the SUPERSYMMETRY theory (that for every elementary particle there is a corresponding particle with complementary qualities). [SUPER¹ + QUARK¹]

squarrose /'skwarohz, 'skworohz/ *adj* **1** said of an animal's skin or plant surface: rough through being hairy or scaly. **2** said of scales: curving outward at right angles to the surface they cover. [Latin *squarrosus* scurfy, scabby]

squash¹ /skwosh/ *verb trans* **1** to press or crush (something) into a flat mass: *Somebody sat on my hat and squashed it.* **2** to apply pressure to (somebody or something) by pushing or squeezing: *We were all squashed together in one small room.* **3** to put down (a rebellion, etc); = QUASH. **4** to humiliate (somebody) or reduce them to silence, e.g. with a cutting remark. ➤ *verb intrans* **1** said *esp* of something resilient: to flatten out under pressure or impact. **2** to squeeze or press oneself into a space: *We all squashed into the front row.* ➤➤ **squasher** *noun.* [alteration of QUASH]

squash² *noun* **1** the condition of being squashed, e.g. against other people in a crowd. **2** *dated* a social gathering: *the Freshers' squash.* **3** an indoor game played usu by two people in a four-walled court with light long-handled rackets and a small rubber ball (from whose squashy nature the game gets its name) that can be played off any wall. **4** *Brit* a soft drink made from the sweetened and concentrated juice of citrus fruits, usu diluted for drinking.

squash³ *adv* with a squash or a squashing sound: *The pudding slipped and landed squash on the kitchen floor.*

squash⁴ *noun* (*pl* **squashes** *or collectively* **squash**) **1** any of several species of plants of the cucumber family bearing edible gourds: genus *Cucurbita.* **2** any of various types of gourd whose flesh is cooked and eaten as a vegetable, or used for livestock feed. [shortening of *isquoutersquash,* from Natick and Narraganset *askútasquash*]

squash rackets *pl noun* (*treated as sing.*) = SQUASH² (3).

squash tennis *noun* a game similar to SQUASH RACKETS but played with larger rackets and a larger pneumatic ball.

squat¹ /skwot/ *verb intrans* (**squatted, squatting**) **1** to crouch close to the ground as if to escape detection. **2** (*also* + down) to assume or maintain a position in which the body is supported on the feet and the knees are bent, so that the haunches rest on or near the heels. **3** to occupy property as a squatter. [Middle English *squatten* from Old French *esquatir* to flatten, ultimately from Latin EX-¹ + *coactus,* past part. of *cogere:* see COGENT]

squat² *noun* **1a** the act or an instance of squatting. **b** the posture of a person or animal that squats. **2a** an empty building occupied by or available to squatters. **b** the act or an instance of squatting in an uninhabited building.

squat³ *adj* (**squatter, squattest**) disproportionately short or low and broad: *I caught one glimpse of his short, squat, strongly built figure* — Conan Doyle. ➤➤ **squatly** *adv*, **squatness** *noun*.

squatocracy *noun* see SQUATTOCRACY.

squatt /skwot/ *noun* the larva of the housefly, used as bait in angling. [perhaps from SQUAT³]

squatter *noun* **1** a person who occupies otherwise empty property without rights of ownership or payment of rent. **2** *Aus* a person who owns large tracts of grazing land.

squat thrust *noun* a strenuous physical exercise in which one starts in a squatting position and thrusts one's legs out backward at full stretch.

squattocracy *or* **squatocracy** /skwo'tokrasi/ *noun* (*pl* **squattocracies** *or* **squatocracies**) *Aus* squatters (see SQUATTER (2)) collectively, as an affluent and powerful lobby. ➤➤ **squattocratic** /-'kratik/ *adj*. [SQUATTER (sense 2) + -CRACY]

squatty *adj* (**squattier, squattiest**) *chiefly NAmer* dumpy; thickset; = SQUAT³.

squaw /skwaw/ *noun* **1** *offensive* a Native N American woman or wife. **2** *humorous* a woman; one's wife. [Massachuset *squa, ussqua* woman]

squawfish *noun* (*pl* **squawfishes** *or collectively* **squawfish**) a large predatory freshwater carp of west N America: *esp Ptychocheilus oregonensis*. [from SQUAW, with reference to its former importance to Native Americans]

squawk¹ /skwawk/ *verb intrans* **1** to utter a harsh abrupt scream. **2** *informal* to make a loud or vehement protest. ➤➤ **squawker** *noun*. [of imitative origin]

squawk² *noun* the act or an instance of squawking.

squawk box *noun chiefly NAmer, informal* a loudspeaker, *esp* as part of an intercom system.

squaw man *noun NAmer, offensive* a white man married to a Native N American woman.

squeak¹ /skweek/ *verb intrans* **1** to utter or make a squeak: *The floorboards squeak.* **2** *informal* to turn informer; = SQUEAL¹. **3** (+ through) to pass an examination or otherwise succeed, by the narrowest of margins. ➤ *verb trans* to utter (something) in a squeak. [Middle English, of imitative origin]

squeak² *noun* a short shrill cry or noise. ✱ **a narrow/near squeak** an escape barely managed. **not a squeak** not the slightest sound: *There hasn't been a squeak from the baby.* ➤➤ **squeakily** *adv*, **squeakiness** *noun*, **squeaky** *adj*.

squeaker *noun* **1** a squeaking device, e.g. inside a toy animal. **2** a person or thing that squeaks. **3** *chiefly NAmer, informal* a victory won by a narrow squeak. **4** *chiefly Brit* an unfledged pigeon.

squeaky-clean *adj informal* **1** said orig of newly washed hair: so clean that it squeaks when rubbed. **2** absolutely clean: *in squeaky-clean laboratory conditions.* **3** morally unassailable; goody-goody: *a squeaky-clean public image.*

squeal¹ /skweel/ *verb intrans* **1** to utter or make a squeal: *squealing with pain.* **2** *informal* to turn informer: *He was bribed to squeal on his boss.* **3** *informal* to complain or protest. ➤ *verb trans* to utter (something) with a squeal. ➤➤ **squealer** *noun*. [Middle English, of imitative origin]

squeal² *noun* a shrill sharp cry or noise: *squeals of delight.*

squeamish /'skweemish/ *adj* **1** easily made to feel faint or nauseous, e.g. at the sight of blood. **2** nauseous: *feeling squeamish.* **3** fastidious in manners, scruples, or convictions: *She wasn't squeamish about telling the odd lie.* **4** easily shocked or offended. ➤➤ **squeamishly** *adv*, **squeamishness** *noun*. [Middle English *squeimous* from Anglo-French *escoimous* squeamish, disdainful]

squeegee¹ /'skweejee/ *noun* (*pl* **squeegees** /-jeez/) **1** a tool with a rubber blade used for spreading liquid on or removing it from a surface, e.g. a window. **2** a roller or other device used similarly in lithography or photography. [from archaic *squeege* to press, alteration of SQUEEZE¹]

squeegee² *verb trans* (**squeegees, squeegeed, squeegeeing**) to smooth, wipe, or treat (a surface, etc) with a squeegee.

squeeze¹ /skweez/ *verb trans* **1** to compress (something) *esp* by applying physical pressure to its sides: *He squeezed her hand.* **2** to extract (liquid, etc) from something by pressure: *Squeeze the juice from a lemon.* **3** to force, thrust, or cram (something) into a restricted space: *She squeezed lots of clothes into her suitcase.* **4** to extract (money or information) from somebody, *esp* by threats or extortion. **5** to pressurize (somebody) into parting with money or information. **6** to cause economic hardship to (a business, etc). **7** to crowd (people or things) into a restricted area: *small houses squeezed between railway and canal.* **8** (+ in/into) to fit (a person or task) into a tight schedule: *Dr White will squeeze you in at three o'clock.* **9** (+ out) to force (somebody) out of their job, area of activity, etc: *We are being squeezed out by the competition.* **10** in bridge, to force (another player) to discard a card to their disadvantage. ➤ *verb intrans* (+ through/into, etc) to force one's way somewhere: *He squeezed through the window.* ➤➤ **squeezability** /-'biliti/ *noun*, **squeezable** *adj*, **squeezer** *noun*. [Old English *cwȳsan*]

squeeze² *noun* **1** the act or an instance of squeezing; a compression: *She gave his hand a squeeze.* **2** a quick hug or embrace. **3** a quantity squeezed out from something: *a squeeze of lemon.* **4** *informal* a condition of being crowded together; a crush: *It'll be a bit of a squeeze if we travel in the same car.* **5** *dated* a crowded social gathering; = SQUASH²: *The weather is getting terribly hot for squeezes* — Lady Sarah Lyttelton. **6** financial pressure caused by restricting credit, used *esp* by a government to reduce price inflation: *a credit squeeze.* **7** in bridge, a forced act of discarding a valuable card. **8** in baseball, the batting of a ball gently to the infield, so that a runner on third base can start for home as soon as the ball is pitched. **9** *NAmer, informal* one's boyfriend or girlfriend: *my main squeeze.* ✱ **put the squeeze on** *informal* to put pressure on (somebody), e.g. to part with money, information, etc.

squeeze-box *noun informal* an accordion.

squeeze off *verb trans informal* **1** to shoot (a round or shot) from a gun: *He squeezed off a shot or two.* **2** to take (a photograph): *He squeezed off some shots of the baby.*

squeeze play *noun* = SQUEEZE² (8).

squeezy *adj* (**squeezier, squeeziest**) **1** said of a plastic container: flexible, so as to dispense its contents when squeezed. **2** *archaic* crowded or constricted: *and then another squeezy quadrille* — Thomas Lister.

squelch¹ /skwelch/ *verb intrans* to make the sucking sound typically produced by somebody walking through mud: *… squelch through a miry farm gateway* — Adrian Bell. ➤ *verb trans informal* to crush or suppress (opposition, etc). ➤➤ **squelcher** *noun*, **squelchy** *adj*. [of imitative origin]

squelch² *noun* a squelching sound.

squib¹ /skwib/ *noun* **1** a small firework that burns with a fizz and finishes with a small explosion. **2** a short witty or satirical speech or piece of writing. [prob of imitative origin]

squib² *verb* (**squibbed, squibbing**) ➤ *verb intrans* **1** *chiefly archaic* to utter or publish squibs: *It is a sport now to taunt and squib and deride at other men's virtues* — Bunyan. **2** *Aus, informal.* **a** to back down; to chicken out. **b** (+ on) to betray somebody. ➤ *verb trans* **1** to produce squibs against (somebody) or lampoon (them): *I have been squibbing him for these two years* — Disraeli. **2** (*often* + off) to shoot or fire (a gun): *squibbing off all six barrels* — Kipling. **3** *Aus, informal* to back down from (a challenge): *Don't squib it!*

SQUID /skwid/ *abbr* used in magnetometers: superconducting quantum interference device.

squid¹ /skwid/ *noun* (*pl* **squids** *or collectively* **squid**) any of numerous species of cephalopod molluscs (class including octopuses and cuttlefish; see CEPHALOPOD) that have eight arms, two long tentacles, a long tapered body and a tail fin on each side: genus *Loligo* and other genera. [origin unknown]

squid² *verb intrans* (**squidded, squidding**) to fish with squid as bait.

squidgy /'skwiji/ *adj* (**squidgier, squidgiest**) *chiefly Brit, informal* soft and squashy. [of imitative origin]

squiffy /'skwifi/ *or* **squiffed** *adj* (**squiffier, squiffiest**) *chiefly Brit, informal* slightly drunk; tipsy. [origin unknown]

squiggle¹ /'skwigl/ *noun* a short wavy twist or line, *esp* in handwriting or drawing. ➤➤ **squiggly** *adj*.

squiggle² *verb intrans chiefly NAmer* to wriggle or squirm. ➤ *verb trans chiefly NAmer* to squeeze (something) from a tube, etc onto a surface: *She squiggled butter icing onto the cake.* [blend of SQUIRM[1] and WRIGGLE[1] or WIGGLE[1]]

squilgee /'skwiljee/ *noun* = SQUEEGEE[1].

squill /skwil/ *noun* **1a** a Mediterranean plant of the lily family with white flowers and broad leaves, that reproduces by bulbs: *Drimia maritima.* **b** (*also in pl, but treated as sing.*) an extract of this bulb, used medicinally, e.g. as an expectorant. **2** any of several species of plants resembling the hyacinth, with violet or blue-striped flowers: *Scilla verna, Puschkinia scilloides,* and other species. **3** = SQUILLA. [Middle English via Latin *squilla, scilla* sea onion, shrimp, from Greek *skilla*]

squilla /'skwilə/ *noun* (*pl* **squillas** or **squillae** /'skwilee/) a shrimp-like crustacean that burrows in mud or beneath stones in shallow water along the seashore: genus *Squilla.* [Latin genus name, from Latin *squilla*: see SQUILL]

squillion /'skwilyən/ *noun informal* an enormously high but unspecified quantity or number: *Schemes like that cost squillions.* [modelled fancifully on MILLION, TRILLION]

squinancywort /'skwinənsiwuht/ *noun* a small plant with fragrant white or purple flowers and narrow leaves, formerly used for treating quinsy: *Asperula cynanchica.* [late Latin *squinantia,* variant of *quinantia* quinsy, sore throat (prob a blend of Greek *kynanchē* (see QUINSY) and *synanchē* sore throat) + WORT[1]]

squinch[1] /skwinch/ *noun* an arch, lintel, etc placed across the interior corner of a square to support a dome. [alteration of *scunch* back part of the side of an opening, shortened from SCUNCHEON]

squinch[2] *verb trans chiefly NAmer* to screw up (one's eyes or face). ➤ *verb intrans* **1** said of the eyes: to close or screw up tightly. **2** to crouch down in a tightly curled-up position. [perhaps blend of SQUEEZE[1] or SQUINT[1], and PINCH[1]]

squint[1] /skwint/ *verb intrans* **1** to have a squint in the eye. **2** to look or peer with eyes partly closed: *squinting at the telephone directory.* ➤➤ **squinter** *noun,* **squintingly** *adv.*

squint[2] *noun* **1** abnormal alignment of an eye, so that it turns permanently towards or away from the nose, because of an imbalance of the muscles of the eyeball; = STRABISMUS. **2** an oblique opening in an interior wall or column of a church, allowing a view of the altar from a side aisle; = HAGIOSCOPE. **3** *informal* a quick glance: *Have a squint at this.* ➤➤ **squinty** *adj.* [Middle English, short for *asquint* sidelong (adv), of Germanic origin]

squint[3] *adj* **1** *chiefly Scot* crooked; skew: *That picture's squint.* **2** *chiefly archaic* said of the eyes: having a squint; squinting.

squint-eyed *adj* **1** having a squint. **2** *archaic* malevolent: *squint-eyed jealousy.*

squirarchy *noun* see SQUIREARCHY.

squire[1] /skwie-ə/ *noun* **1** formerly, the shield-bearer or armour-bearer of a knight, typically a young nobleman training for knighthood. **2** an owner of a country estate, *esp* the principal local landowner. **3** *NAmer, archaic* a title accorded to a lawyer, judge, or magistrate. **4** *Brit, informal* a form of address used by one man to another. ➤➤ **squiredom** *noun,* **squireship** *noun.* [Middle English *squier* from Old French *esquier*: see ESQUIRE]

squire[2] *verb trans* to escort (a woman): *He squired her to the ball.*

squirearchy or **squirarchy** /'skwie-ərahki/ *noun* (*pl* **squirearchies** or **squirarchies**) the gentry or landed-proprietor class. ➤➤ **squirearch** *noun,* **squirearchal** *adj,* **squirearchical** /skwie-ə'rahkikl/ *adj.*

squireen /skwie-ə'reen/ *noun Anglo-Irish* a petty squire or lesser landowner, *esp* in Ireland. [SQUIRE[1] + *-een,* dimin. suffix from Irish Gaelic *-ín*]

squirm[1] /skwuhm/ *verb intrans* **1** to twist about like a worm; to wriggle. **2** to feel or show acute discomfort at something embarrassing, shameful, or unpleasant: *squirming with embarrassment.* ➤➤ **squirmer** *noun,* **squirmy** *adj.* [perhaps imitative]

squirm[2] *noun* the act or an instance of squirming.

squirrel[1] /'skwirəl/ *noun* **1** any of numerous species of tree-dwelling rodents that have a long bushy tail and strong hind legs, and feed chiefly on nuts and seeds: genus *Sciurus* and other genera. **2** used in the names of other members of the family Sciuridae, e.g. GROUND SQUIRREL. **3** the fur of any of these animals. **4** *informal* a person who hoards things, from the squirrel's proverbial habit of hoarding nuts. [Middle English via Old French *esquireul,* ultimately from Greek *skiouros* squirrel, from *skia* shadow + *oura* tail]

squirrel[2] *verb trans* (**squirrelled, squirrelling,** *NAmer* **squirreled, squirreling**) (*usu* + away) to secrete (something) somewhere or hoard (it) for future use.

squirrel cage *noun* **1** a cylindrical exercise cage for a small animal that rotates on the principle of a treadmill. **2** a type of induction motor having a rotor with cylindrically arranged metal bars like those on an animal's treadmill. **3** a monotonous existence; a repetitive piece of drudgery.

squirrelfish *noun* (*pl* **squirrelfishes** or *collectively* **squirrelfish**) any of several species of brightly coloured fishes with large eyes, inhabiting warm seas around coral reefs: family Holocentridae.

squirrelly *adj* **1** like a squirrel in appearance or habit. **2** *chiefly NAmer.* **a** restless; nervous. **b** eccentric or unpredictable.

squirrel monkey *noun* a small soft-haired S American monkey with a long tail, that leaps from tree to tree: *Saimiri sciureus.*

squirt[1] /skwuht/ *verb intrans* said of a liquid: to issue in a sudden forceful stream from a narrow opening. ➤ *verb trans* **1** to cause (a liquid) to squirt: *He squirted water from the hosepipe.* **2** to direct a jet or stream of liquid at (somebody or something): *squirting people with a water pistol.* ➤➤ **squirter** *noun.* [Middle English, of imitative origin]

squirt[2] *noun* **1** a small rapid stream of liquid; a jet: *a squirt of soda water.* **2** *informal* a small, insignificant, or impudent person.

squirting cucumber *noun* a Mediterranean plant of the gourd family with a cucumber-like fruit that falls when ripe and explosively discharges a pulp containing its seeds: *Ecballium elaterium.*

squish[1] /skwish/ *verb intrans* to make a slight squelching or sucking sound. ➤ *verb trans informal* to squash (something or somebody). [alteration of SQUASH[1]]

squish[2] *noun* the act or an instance of squishing.

squishy *adj* (**squishier, squishiest**) soft and moist. ➤➤ **squishiness** *noun.*

squit /sqwit/ *noun Brit, informal* **1** a small insignificant person. **2** (**the squits**) diarrhoea. [prob from dialect *squit* to squirt]

squitters /'skwitəz/ *pl noun informal* diarrhoea. [dialect *squit* to squirt]

squiz /skwiz/ *noun* (*pl* **squizzes**) *Aus, NZ, informal* a curious glance or look. [perhaps blend of SQUINT[2] and QUIZ[1]]

Sr[1] *abbr* **1** senior. **2** Señor. **3** Sir. **4** Sister.

Sr[2] *abbr* the chemical symbol for strontium.

sr *abbr* steradian or steradians.

Sra *abbr* Señora.

SRAM *abbr* static random-access memory.

SRC *abbr* Science Research Council.

Sri /shree, sree/ *noun* used as a conventional title of respect when addressing or referring to an Indian male. [Sanskrit *śrī* majesty, holiness]

Sri Lankan /shri 'langkən, sri/ *noun* a native or inhabitant of Sri Lanka. ➤➤ **Sri Lankan** *adj.*

SRN *abbr* State Registered Nurse.

SRO *abbr* **1** Self-Regulatory Organization. **2** standing room only. **3** Statutory Rules and Orders.

Srta *abbr* Señorita.

SS[1] *noun* (*treated as sing. or pl*) Adolf Hitler's bodyguard and special police force within the Nazi party. [abbr for German *Schutzstaffel* defence squad]

SS[2] *abbr* **1** saints. **2** steamship. **3** Song of Songs (book of the Bible).

SSAFA *abbr Brit* Soldiers', Sailors', and Airmen's Families Association.

SSC *abbr* **1** Solicitor in the Supreme Court (a Scottish legal officer). **2** in physics, superconducting super collider.

SSE *abbr* south-southeast.

SSP *abbr Brit* statutory sick pay.

ssp. *abbr* (*pl* **sssp.**) subspecies.

SSR *abbr* formerly, Soviet Socialist Republic.

SSRC *abbr Brit* Social Science Research Council.

SSRI *abbr* selective serotonin reuptake inhibitor (any of various antidepressants).

SSSI *abbr Brit* site of special scientific interest.

SST *abbr* supersonic transport.

SSW *abbr* south-southwest.

St *abbr* **1** Saint. **2** in street names, street. **3** in physics, stokes.

st. *abbr* **1** stanza. **2** stitch. **3** stone. **4** in cricket, stumped by.

s.t. *abbr* short ton.

-st¹ *suffix* forming the superlative degree of adjectives and adverbs of one syllable, and of some adjectives and adverbs of two or more syllables, that end in *e*: *surest*; *completest*.

-st² *suffix* forming the archaic second person singular present (the form used with *thou*) of verbs that end in *e*: *comest*; *forgivest*.

-st³ *suffix* used after the figure one to indicate the ordinal number *first*: *61st*; *691st*.

Sta *abbr* in place names or church names, Santa.

sta. *abbr* station.

stab¹ /stab/ *noun* **1** a wound produced by a pointed weapon. **2** a thrust with a pointed weapon or other pointed object: *He made little stabs with his umbrella.* **3** a sharp spasm: *a stab of pain.* **4** a pang of intense emotion: *a stab of remorse.* ✴ **a stab in the back** an act of treachery that causes somebody's downfall. **have/make a stab at** *informal* to make an attempt at (something): *I'm going to have a stab at writing a novel.* [Middle English *stabbe* wound, of unknown origin]

stab² *verb* (**stabbed, stabbing**) ➤ *verb trans* **1** to pierce or wound (a person or animal) with or as if with a pointed weapon. **2** to thrust or jab (a pointed object) somewhere: *He stabbed his finger at the page.* ➤ *verb intrans* (+ at) to thrust at somebody or something with a pointed weapon or other pointed object. ✴ **stab somebody in the back** to betray somebody. ➤➤ **stabber** *noun*, **stabbing** *adj and noun*.

Stabat Mater /ˌstahbat ˈmahtə/ *noun* **1** a medieval Latin hymn about the suffering of the Virgin Mary at the crucifixion, with the first line *Stabat mater dolorosa* (the mother stood sorrowing). **2** a musical setting for this hymn.

stabilator /ˈstaybəlaytə/ *noun* a device in the tail of an aircraft combining the functions of a stabilizer and elevator.

stabile¹ /ˈstaybiel/ *noun* an abstract sculpture or construction similar to a mobile but stationary. [Latin *stabilis* (see STABLE³), on the model of MOBILE²]

stabile² *adj* **1** stationary; fixed. **2** not subject to chemical change. [Latin *stabilis*: see STABLE³]

stabilise /ˈstaybəliez/ *verb trans and intrans* see STABILIZE.

stabiliser *noun* see STABILIZER.

stability /stəˈbiliti/ *noun* (*pl* **stabilities**) **1** the quality of being stable: *mental stability*; *political stability.* **2** the quality of being firmly based and evenly balanced. **3** in physics, the property of a body to recover equilibrium after being disturbed. **4** in chemistry, resistance to chemical change or to physical disintegration. **5** in meteorology, the condition of an air mass which has no upward movement. **6** a vow taken by a Benedictine monk or nun to remain in the religious house into which they are received.

stabilize *or* **stabilise** /ˈstaybəliez/ *verb trans* **1** to make (something) stable or firm: *stabilizing the economy.* **2** to maintain the stability of (an aircraft, etc) by means of a stabilizer. **3** to limit fluctuations of (prices, etc). ➤ *verb intrans* to become stable: *His condition has stabilized.* ➤➤ **stabilization** *noun*.

stabilizer *or* **stabiliser** *noun* **1** a chemical substance added to another substance or to a system to prevent or retard an unwanted alteration of physical state. **2** a gyroscopic device to keep ships steady in a rough sea. **3** *chiefly NAmer* the horizontal tailplane of an aircraft. **4** (*in pl*) a pair of small wheels fitted either side of a child's bicycle to give support.

stable¹ /ˈstaybl/ *noun* **1** (*also in pl*) a building in which domestic animals, *esp* horses, are sheltered and fed, usu with stalls or compartments. **2** (*treated as sing. or pl*). **a** the racehorses or racing cars owned by one person or organization. **b** a group of holdings of any other kind: *the owner of a stable of newspapers.* **c** a group of sportspersons or performers under one management. **d** the team or organization behind a certain range of products, productions, etc: *Tom Conti makes his comedy debut in a new seven-part drama 'Old Boy Network', from the same stable as 'Porridge' and 'Yes, Minister'* — Good Housekeeping. ➤➤ **stableful** *noun*, **stableman** *noun*. [Middle English via Old French from Latin *stabulum*, from *stare* to stand]

stable² *verb trans* **1** to put or keep (a horse) in a stable. **2** to base or keep (a train) in a depot. ➤ *verb intrans* to be accommodated in a stable.

stable³ *adj* **1** likely to remain firmly upright; not likely to collapse, overturn, etc. **2** well-founded or securely established so as to endure and be dependable: *a stable relationship.* **3** not subject to change or fluctuation; unvarying: *a stable currency.* **4** not subject to feelings of mental or emotional insecurity; sane, well-adjusted: *a stable personality.* **5** in physics, of such a nature as to return after disturbance to normal position, equilibrium, or steady motion. **6** able to resist alteration in chemical, physical, or biological properties: *stable emulsions.* **7** said of an atomic nucleus, elementary particle, etc: not spontaneously radioactive: *a stable isotope.* ➤➤ **stableness** *noun*, **stably** *adv.* [Middle English via Old French from Latin *stabilis*, from *stare* to stand]

stable boy *or* **stable girl** *or* **stable man** *noun* an assistant employed in a stable.

stable companion *noun* = STABLEMATE.

stable door *noun* a door of the kind typical for a stable, horizontally divided so that the upper half may be opened leaving the lower half closed.

stable fly *noun* a two-winged fly that sucks the blood of large animals including humans and is common around stables, often entering houses, *esp* in autumn: *Stomoxys calcitrans.*

Stableford /ˈstayblfəd/ *noun* in golf, a form of play in which points are scored according to the number of strokes taken to play each hole. [named after its inventor, Frank *Stableford* d.1959, American amateur golfer]

stable girl *noun* see STABLE BOY.

stable lad *noun* *Brit* a boy or man who works in a stable.

stable man *noun* see STABLE BOY.

stablemate *noun* **1** a horse stabled with the one in question. **2** a person or thing having the same source, work place, trainer, etc as the one specified: *the Daily Mirror and its Scottish stablemate, the Record.*

stabling *noun* indoor accommodation for animals.

stablish /ˈstablish/ *verb trans archaic* = ESTABLISH: *The God of all grace … make you perfect, stablish, strengthen, settle you* — Bible.

staccato¹ /stəˈkahtoh/ *adj and adv* **1** said of a piece of music: to be performed with each note produced in a clear, abrupt, detached style. **2** said of speech: with a jerky delivery rather than flowing smoothly with natural cadences: *She spoke in the dry, staccato tone of one who repeats a French exercise* — Saki. [Italian *staccato* detached, past part. of *staccare* to detach]

staccato² *noun* (*pl* **staccatos**) **1** in music, a staccato passage. **2** in speech, a staccato style of delivery.

staccato mark *noun* a dot or a pointed vertical stroke placed over or under a musical note to be produced staccato.

stachys /ˈstakis/ *noun* any of a genus of LABIATE plants (of the mint family), including lamb's ears, betony, and the woundworts, typically with flowers in spikes: genus *Stachys.* [Latin genus name, from Greek *stachys* ear of corn]

stack¹ /stak/ *noun* **1** a pile, *esp* an orderly one. **2** a cone-shaped, rectangular, or cylindrical pile of hay or straw, left standing in the field for storage. **3** a pyramid of three rifles interlocked. **4** a pile of chips sold to or won by a poker player. **5** a store of data, e.g. in a computer, from which the most recently stored item must be the first retrieved. **6** a number of aircraft circling an airport at allocated altitudes, waiting their turn to land. **7** (*also in pl*) compact shelving for books at a library, not usu accessible to the public. **8** a group of loudspeakers for a public-address sound system. **9** *Brit* a unit of measure, *esp* for firewood, that is equal to 108 cubic feet (about 3.06 cubic metres). **10** a chimney or vertical exhaust pipe: *a smokestack.* **11** *Brit* a pillar-shaped rocky islet near a cliffy shore that has been detached from the mainland by wave erosion. **12** *informal* (*also in pl*) a large quantity or number: *They've got stacks of money*; *a stack of jobs still to do.* [Middle English *stak* from Old Norse *stakkr* haystack]

stack² *verb trans* **1** to pile (things) into a stack. **2** to fill (spaces) with stacks of things: *stacking shelves in the supermarket.* **3** to assign (an aircraft) to a particular altitude and position within a group of aircraft circling before landing. **4** to shuffle (a pack of cards) in such a way as to enable one to cheat. ➤ *verb intrans* **1** to form a stack: *The tables are designed to stack.* **2** said of a snowboarder: to fall over. ✴ **be stacked against/in favour of** said of conditions, etc: to be highly likely to produce an unfavourable/favourable result for (somebody or something) [from card games, in which a skilful cheat can 'stack' or place a deck in an order which suits them]. **▶▶ stackable** adj, **stacker** noun.

stacked adj **1** said of a heel: made from narrow layers of leather or wood glued together. **2** informal said of a woman: having large breasts.

stack up verb intrans NAmer **1** to accumulate into a queue or back-log: Cars stack up every time the bus in front stops to let passengers on or off. **2** informal (often + against) to measure up or compare: Our products stack up well against the competition. **3** informal (usu in negative contexts) to make sense or be plausible; to add up: Their explanation doesn't stack up.

staddle /'stadl/ noun a base or framework for a stack of hay or straw. [Old English stathol base, support]

stadholder /'stad·hohldə/ noun see STADTHOLDER.

stadia /'staydi·ə/ noun **1** a surveying method for determination of distances and differences of height by means of a telescopic instrument having two horizontal lines through which the marks on a graduated staff are observed. **2** the instrument or staff used. [Italian stadia, prob from Latin, pl of STADIUM]

stadium /'staydi·əm/ noun (pl **stadiums** or **stadia** /'staydi·ə/) **1** a sports ground surrounded by tiers of seats for spectators. **2** in ancient Greece and Rome, a course for foot races or chariot races, surrounded by tiered seats. **3** (pl stadia) any of various ancient Greek and Roman units of length, usu of about 185m (about 202yd). **4** a stage or period of development, e.g. between successive moults in the development of an insect, or in the progress of a disease. [Middle English via Latin stadium from Greek stadion race-course, unit of length, alteration of spadion, from span to pull]

stadtholder /'stat·hohldə/ or **stadholder** /'stad-/ noun **1** the chief magistrate, effectively the hereditary head, of the Dutch republic during the period 1580–1802, the title in origin acknowledging the sovereignty of the Spanish king. **2** a viceroy in any of the provinces of the Netherlands. **▶▶ stadtholderate** /-rət/ noun, **stadtholdership** noun. [partly translating Dutch stadhouder, from stad place + houder holder]

staff¹ /stahf/ noun **1** (treated as sing. or pl). **a** the body of people in charge of the internal operations of an institution, business, etc. **b** the body of teachers at a school or university. **c** a group of officers appointed to assist a commanding officer. **d** the personnel who assist a superior, e.g. a director, in carrying out an assigned task. **2** (usu **Staff**) = STAFF SERGEANT. **3** (pl **staves**) a long stick carried in the hand for support in walking or as a weapon. **4** a supporting pole or shaft: a flagstaff. **5** a rod carried as a symbol of office or authority. **6** a crosier. **7** Brit a rod given to a train driver as a token of authorization to proceed along a single-track line. **8** (pl **staves**) in music, the STAVE¹ (5). **✱ the staff of life** literary bread or some other staple food. [Old English stæf]

staff² verb trans to supply (an organization, etc) with a staff or with workers.

staff³ noun a mixture of plaster, hair, cement, etc used to cover the surface of temporary buildings. [origin unknown]

staffage /stə'fahzh/ noun extra items added to a painting for verisimilitude or decoration, esp the figures of humans or animals inserted into a landscape. [pseudo-French staffage from German staffieren to decorate, prob from Old French estoffer: see STUFF¹]

staff college noun a college that trains military officers for staff appointments.

staff corporal noun a non-commissioned rank in the British army senior to STAFF SERGEANT and subordinate to WARRANT OFFICER.

staffer noun chiefly NAmer a member of a staff, e.g. of a newspaper.

staff notation noun musical notation using the five-line stave, as distinct from tonic sol-fa.

staff nurse noun Brit a qualified nurse on the staff of a hospital who is next in rank below a sister or charge nurse.

staff officer noun a commissioned officer assigned to a military commander's staff.

Staffordshire bull terrier /'stafədshə/ noun a terrier of a breed originating in Staffordshire, having a thickset muscular frame, broad head with long muzzle and dropped ears, and a short coat, usu white with markings.

staffroom noun a common room for the use of teachers in a school or college.

Staffs /stafs/ abbr Staffordshire.

staff sergeant noun **1** a non-commissioned army officer of a rank senior to a sergeant and junior to a warrant officer. **2** a non-commissioned US air-force officer of a rank senior to an airman and junior to a technical sergeant.

stag¹ /stag/ noun **1a** an adult male red deer. **b** the male of any of various deer. **2** chiefly NAmer an unaccompanied man at a social gathering. **3** (used before a noun) for men only: a stag do. **4** Brit a person who buys newly issued shares in the hope of selling them to make a quick profit. [Old English stagga]

stag² verb (**stagged**, **stagging**) **▶** verb trans **1** to buy or apply for (shares in a new issue) with the intention of selling them immediately at a profit. **2** NAmer to cut (a pair of trousers) off short leaving rough jagged edges: stagged denims. **▶** verb intrans NAmer said of a man: to attend a social event without a female companion.

stag beetle noun any of numerous large beetles the males of which have long and often branched mandibles suggesting the antlers of a stag: genus Lucanus.

stage¹ /stayj/ noun **1** a period or step in a progress, activity, or development, e.g. any of the distinguishable periods of growth and development of a child, plant, or animal: the larval stage of an insect. **2** a connected group of components in an electrical circuit that performs some well-defined function, e.g. amplification, and that forms part of a larger electrical circuit. **3** any of two or more propulsion sections of a rocket that are jettisoned when their fuel is exhausted. **4** any of the divisions of a journey, e.g. one day's riding or driving between predetermined points of a race or rally that is extended over several days. **5** chiefly Brit a bus stop from which or to which fares are calculated; = FARE STAGE. **6** a place of rest formerly provided for those travelling by stagecoach; a station. **7** the distance between two stopping places on a road. **8** a stagecoach. **9** a raised platform. **10** the area of a theatre where the acting takes place, including the wings and storage space. **11** (**the stage**) the acting profession. **12** an arena of action or forum of discussion: our role on the international stage. **13** a scaffold for workmen. **14** a floor of a building. **15** the small platform of a microscope on which an object is placed for examination. **16** a range of rock strata corresponding to an age in geological time. **✱ hold the stage** to dominate discussion and hold public attention. **in easy stages** without hurry; step by step. **on the stage** in or with the acting profession. **set the stage for** to provide the necessary basis or preparation for (a particular scenario): The stage was all set for a grand reconciliation. **stage left/right** on the left or right of the stage from the point of view of an actor facing the audience. [Middle English via Old French estage dwelling, stay, situation, literally 'a place to stop or stand', ultimately from Latin stare to stand]

stage² verb trans **1** to produce (a theatrical production) on a stage. **2** to produce and organize (a public event). **3** to set (a play, film, etc) in a specified historical period or place: It was staged in Venice in the time of Casanova. **4** to contrive (something dramatic), esp with maximum publicity: He staged a comeback with a TV special. **5** in medicine, to diagnose (a patient or disease) as having reached a certain stage. **▶▶ stageability** /-'biliti/ noun, **stageable** adj.

stagecoach noun formerly, a horse-drawn passenger and mail coach that ran on a regular schedule between established stops.

stagecraft noun **1** competence in writing or staging plays. **2** the effective management of theatrical devices or techniques.

stage direction noun a description, e.g. of a character or setting, or direction, e.g. to indicate sound effects or the movement or positioning of actors, provided in the text of a play.

stage door noun the entrance to a theatre that is used by the people who work there.

stage fright noun nervousness felt at appearing before an audience.

stagehand noun a theatre worker who handles scenery, props, or lights.

stage-manage verb trans **1** to be the stage manager of (a play, etc). **2** to arrange (an event, etc) so as to achieve a desired result. **▶▶ stage management** noun. [back-formation from STAGE MANAGER]

stage manager noun a person who is in charge of the stage during a performance and supervises related matters beforehand.

stage name noun the name used professionally by an actor.

stager noun **1** = OLD STAGER. **2** archaic an actor.

stagestruck /'stayjstruk/ adj **1** fascinated by the stage. **2** having an ardent desire to become an actor or actress.

stage whisper *noun* **1** a loud whisper by an actor, audible to the audience, but supposedly inaudible to others on stage. **2** a whisper that is deliberately made audible.

stagey *adj* see STAGY.

stagflation /stag'flaysh(ə)n/ *noun* a state of affairs in which inflation in the economy is accompanied by zero growth in industrial production. [blend of *stagnation* (see STAGNATE) and INFLATION]

stagger¹ /'stagə/ *verb* (**staggered, staggering**) ⮞ *verb intrans* to reel from side to side, usu while moving; to totter. ⮞ *verb trans* **1** to dumbfound or astonish (somebody). **2** *archaic* to knock (somebody) off balance with a blow. **3** to arrange (a set of things) in any of various alternating or overlapping positions or times: *The staff's holidays are staggered.* ⮞⮞ **staggerer** *noun*. [alteration of Middle English *stacker*, from Old Norse *stakra*, frequentative of *staka* to push]

stagger² *noun* **1** (*in pl, but treated as sing.*) an abnormal condition of domestic animals and birds associated with damage to the brain and spinal cord, causing loss of muscular coordination and a staggering gait. **2** (**the staggers**) (*in pl, but treated as sing.*). **a** an inability to stand or walk steadily. **b** a form of vertigo occurring in association with decompression sickness. **3** (**the stagger**) the staggered disposition of runners on the track at the start of a distance race. **4** a design feature of biplanes whereby the front edges of their wings are not in line.

staggered directorships *pl noun* a system in a business company of appointing directors for staggered terms, to prevent the long-term domination of the board by a potential, *esp* unwelcome, bidder to take over the company.

staggering *adj* astonishing or overwhelming. ⮞⮞ **staggeringly** *adv.*

staging /'stayjing/ *noun* **1a** a platform serving as a stage. **b** a set of temporary platforms supported by scaffolding. **2** *Brit* shelving in a greenhouse. **3** *archaic* the business of running stagecoaches.

staging area *noun* an assembly point or checkpoint for groups, *esp* military formations, en route for a destination.

staging post *noun* a regular stopping place for vehicles, *esp* aircraft, between their point of departure and their destination.

stagnant /'stagnənt/ *adj* **1** said of an expanse of water: not flowing in a current or stream; motionless. **2** stale: *Long disuse had made the air stagnant and foul* — Bram Stoker. **3** dull or inactive: *a stagnant economy.* ⮞⮞ **stagnancy** /-si/ *noun*, **stagnantly** *adv.*

stagnate /stag'nayt/ *verb intrans* to become or remain stagnant: *I'm not going to stay at home and let my brain stagnate.* ⮞⮞ **stagnation** /-sh(ə)n/ *noun*. [Latin *stagnatus*, past part. of *stagnare* to stagnate, from *stagnum* body of standing water]

stag night *noun* an exclusively male celebration, *esp* one held for a man about to be married: compare HEN NIGHT.

stag party *noun* = STAG NIGHT.

stagy *or* **stagey** /'stayji/ *adj* (**stagier, stagiest**) said of behaviour, speech, gestures, etc: artificially dramatic; consciously theatrical. ⮞⮞ **stagily** *adv*, **staginess** *noun*.

staid /stayd/ *adj* sedate; starchily old-fashioned in attitude. ⮞⮞ **staidly** *adv*, **staidness** *noun*. [archaic past part. of STAY¹]

stain¹ /stayn/ *verb trans* **1** to mark, discolour, or soil (something). **2** *literary* to suffuse (an area) with colour: *A blush stained her white throat.* **3** *literary* to taint or dishonour (a person or their character, reputation, etc) through guilt, vice, corruption, etc: *a mother stained* — Shakespeare; *An incident occurred that was to stain the family name.* **4** to colour (wood or a biological specimen) by using processes or dyes affecting the material itself. ⮞ *verb intrans* **1** to become stained: *Silk stains easily.* **2** to cause staining: *Blackberries stain.* ⮞⮞ **stainability** /-'biliti/ *noun*, **stainable** *adj*, **stainer** *noun*. [Middle English *steynen*, shortened from *disteynen*, from Old French *desteindre* to discolour, from DIS- + Latin *tingere* to wet, dye]

stain² *noun* **1** a soiled or discoloured spot. **2** a moral taint or blemish: *He came through the business with not a stain on his reputation.* **3a** a preparation, e.g. of dye or pigment, used in staining; *esp* one capable of penetrating the pores of wood. **b** a dye or mixture of dyes used in microscopy to make minute and transparent structures visible, to differentiate tissue elements, or to produce specific chemical reactions.

stained glass *noun* glass coloured or stained, usu for use in leaded windows.

stainless *adj* **1** free from stain or stigma: *a stainless reputation.* **2** resistant to stain; rust-resistant. ⮞⮞ **stainlessly** *adv*, **stainlessness** *noun.*

stainless steel *noun* steel containing chromium and highly resistant to rusting and corrosion.

stair /steə/ *noun* **1** (*usu in pl*) a flight of steps or a series of flights for passing from one level to another. **2** any step of a stairway. ✳ **below stairs** *Brit* in the servants' quarters. [Old English *stæger*]

staircase *noun* **1** the structure or part of a building containing a stairway. **2** a flight of stairs with the supporting framework, casing, and balusters.

stairhead *noun* a landing at the top of a flight of stairs.

stairlift *noun* a lift in the form of a chair, fitted at the edge of a domestic stair to carry an infirm or elderly person from one floor to the next.

stair rod *noun* a rod holding a stair carpet into the angle between two stairs, itself secured by catches on either side. ✳ **coming down like stair rods** *informal* said of rain: falling vertically and very heavily.

stairway *noun* one or more flights of stairs, usu with intermediate landings.

stairwell *noun* a vertical shaft in which stairs are located.

staithe /staydh/ *noun* *Brit* a wharf from which coal may be loaded on a vessel. [Middle English *stathe* from Old Norse *stöth* landing stage]

stake¹ /stayk/ *noun* **1** a pointed wooden or iron post used for driving into the ground as a marker or support. **2a** a post to which a person, *esp* a religious heretic, was formerly bound for execution by burning. **b** (**the stake**) execution by this method. **3** a group of wards forming an administrative district in the Mormon Church. ✳ **go to the stake for** to die for (one's convictions or another person): *He'd go to the stake for his beliefs.* **pull up stakes** *NAmer* to leave; to move out. [Old English *staca* pin, stake]

stake² *verb trans* **1a** (*often* + off/out) to mark out (an area) with stakes. **b** (*often* + off/out) to claim ownership of (a plot of land, etc) by this means. **2** to support (a plant) with a stake. **3** to tether (an animal) to a stake. ✳ **stake one's claim** to assert one's ownership of, or right to, something, orig with reference to mining claims in the N American gold rush.

stake³ *verb trans* **1** to bet or hazard (a sum of money, one's reputation, etc): *I'll stake my good name … that the track is a fresh one* — Conan Doyle. **2** *chiefly NAmer* to back (a person or business concern) financially. ⮞⮞ **staker** *noun.*

stake⁴ *noun* **1** something, *esp* a sum of money, that is staked. **2** an interest or share in an undertaking, e.g. a commercial venture. **3** (*also in pl*) the prize in a contest, *esp* a horse race. **4** (*often* **Stakes**) (*in pl, treated as pl or sing.*) used in the names of horse races to denote a race in which all the owners of the competing horses contribute equally to the prize money. **5** (*in pl*) the competitive world of something: *It was normal to develop a comfortable middle-aged spread and to withdraw from the sex and beauty stakes* — Mary Batchelor. ✳ **at stake** at issue; in jeopardy: *Our reputation is at stake.* [Middle English, perhaps from STAKE¹, from the idea of a thing to be wagered being put on a stake]

stake boat *noun* an anchored boat marking the course for a boat race.

stake body *noun* *NAmer* a lorry trailer having a flat platform with removable posts along the sides.

stakebuilding *noun* the process of accumulating shares in a company.

stakeholder *noun* **1** an individual or group holding a substantial proportion of a company's shares. **2** a person without shares in a company but with an interest in how it fares, such as an employee, customer, or member of the local community.

stakeholder pension *noun* a low-cost flexible personal pension scheme intended *esp* for people on low incomes.

stake net *noun* a fishing net that is draped from stakes.

stake out *verb trans informal* to conduct a surveillance of (a suspected area, person, etc). ⮞⮞ **stakeout** *noun.*

Stakhanovite /sta'kanəviet/ *noun* an industrial worker, *esp* in the former USSR, awarded recognition and privileges for outstanding productivity. ⮞⮞ **Stakhanovism** *noun*, **Stakhanovist** *noun*. [named after Alexei German *Stakhanov* d.1977, Russian miner who used innovative methods to increase his productivity]

stalactite /'staləktiet/ *noun* an icicle-like deposit of calcium carbonate hanging from the roof or sides of a cave. ➤➤ **stalactiform** /sta'laktifawm/ *adj*, **stalactitic** /-'titik/ *adj*. [scientific Latin *stalactites*, from Greek *stalaktos* dripping, from *stalassein* to let drip]

Stalag /'stahlag/ *noun* in World War II, a German prison camp for non-commissioned officers and lower ranks. [German *Stalag*, contraction of *Stammlager* base camp, from *Stamm* base + *Lager* camp]

stalagmite /'stalagmiet/ *noun* a deposit of calcium carbonate like an inverted stalactite, growing upward from the floor of a cave, formed by drips from the ceiling. ➤➤ **stalagmitic** /-'mitik/ *adj*. [scientific Latin *stalagmites*, from Greek *stalagma* a drop or *stalagmos* dripping, both from *stalassein* to let drip]

stale[1] /stayl/ *adj* 1 said of food: tasteless or unpalatable from age. 2 said of air: musty or foul. 3a said of news: no longer fresh or interesting. b tedious from familiarity: *stale jokes*. 4 said of a cheque or debt: no longer valid because out of date. 5 impaired in vigour or effectiveness, from overexertion or repetitiveness. ➤➤ **stalely** *adv*, **staleness** *noun*. [Middle English, orig describing ale which had become clear and strong with standing, prob via Anglo-French from Old French *estaler* to come to a standstill, from *estal* place, position, of Germanic origin]

stale[2] *verb intrans* to become stale. ➤ *verb trans* to cause (something) to become stale: *Age cannot wither her, nor custom stale her infinite variety —* Shakespeare.

stale[3] *verb intrans* said *esp* of horses and cattle: to urinate. [Middle English *stalen*, perhaps ultimately from Old French *estaler*: see STALE[1]]

stale[4] *noun* the urine of cattle or horses.

stale[5] *noun archaic* a prostitute: *I stand dishonoured that have gone about to link my dear friend to a common stale —* Shakespeare. [orig denoting a bird used as a decoy to attract others into a net; prob from Anglo-French *estale* decoy, something fixed, from Old French *estal*: see STALE[1]]

stale bull *noun* in the stock market, a dealer who can neither get rid of unsold stock in the wake of a price rise nor afford to buy new stock.

stalemate *noun* 1 a position in chess representing a draw, in which only the king can move and although not in check can move only into check. 2 any position of deadlock. [obsolete *stale* stalemate (via Anglo-French *estale* fixed position, from Old French *estal*: see STALE[1]) + MATE[3]]

Stalinism /'stahliniz(ə)m, 'sta-/ *noun* the theory and practice of communism developed by Stalin from Marxism-Leninism and characterized by rigid authoritarianism. ➤➤ **Stalinist** *noun and adj*. [Joseph *Stalin* d.1953, Russian political leader]

stalk[1] /stawk/ *verb trans* 1 to pursue (a prey or quarry) stealthily, so as eventually to effect a kill. 2 to follow and watch (a person, often a celebrity, with whom one has become obsessed), to the point of persecution. 3 *literary* said of illness, death, or terror, etc: to sweep through (a population, etc): *A new and virulent pestilence stalked the ranks of besiegers and besieged alike.* ➤ *verb intrans* 1 to pursue a prey or quarry stealthily, for food or for sport. 2 to walk in a stiff haughty fashion: *She stalked out in a huff.* ➤➤ **stalking** *noun*. [Old English *-stealcian* in *bistealcian* to walk stealthily; related to Old English *stelan* STEAL[1]]

stalk[2] *noun* 1a the act or an instance of stalking quarry or prey. b a stalking expedition: *They took part in a Highland deerstalk.* 2 a stiff or haughty walk: *With martial stalk hath he gone by our watch —* Shakespeare.

stalk[3] *noun* 1a the main stem of a herbaceous plant, often with its attached parts. b the stem of a leaf or fruit: *cherry stalks*. 2 a slender upright supporting or connecting structure, *esp* in an animal: *eyes projecting on stalks*. ➤➤ **stalked** *adj*, **stalkless** *adj*, **stalklike** *adj*, **stalky** *adj*. [Middle English, perhaps from Old English *stalu* upright length of wood]

stalk-and-slash movie *noun* = SLASHER MOVIE.

stalker *noun* 1 a person who stalks game. 2 a person who, to the point of persecution, follows and watches somebody, often a celebrity, with whom they have become obsessed.

stalk-eyed *adj* said *esp* of crustaceans: having the eyes raised on stalks.

stalking-horse *noun* 1 a screen shaped like a horse for a hunter to hide behind when stalking prey. 2 something used to mask a purpose. 3 in politics, a person who stands for the leadership of

their party solely to bring about an election and allow a stronger and more likely contender to stand.

stall[1] /stawl/ *noun* 1a any of several compartments for domestic animals in a stable or barn. b (*in pl*) = STARTING STALLS. 2a a wholly or partly enclosed seat in the chancel of a church. b a church pew. 3a a booth, stand, or counter at which articles are displayed or offered for sale, e.g. in a market place. b a sideshow at a fair, etc, where one can compete for prizes: *a hoopla stall*. 4 a small compartment: *a shower stall*. 5 *Brit* (*in pl*) the seats on the main floor of an auditorium, e.g. in a theatre. 6 *NAmer* an individually marked-out parking space. 7 a protective sheath for a finger or toe. 8a the cutting-out of a vehicle engine. b the condition of an aircraft when airflow is so obstructed, e.g. from moving forward too slowly, that lift is lost. [Old English *steall* cattleshed, stable]

stall[2] *verb trans* 1 to put or keep (an animal) in a stall, e.g. to fatten it. 2 to cause (a vehicle or its engine) to stop running, usu by mistake. 3 to cause (an aircraft) to lose speed dangerously so that it cannot be controlled and begins to drop. 4 (*usu in passive*) to prevent the progress of (a transaction, etc): *The peace process has been temporarily stalled.* ➤ *verb intrans* 1 said of a vehicle, engine, or driver: to suffer a stall: *I stalled at the traffic lights.* 2 said of an aircraft or pilot: to experience a stall in flying.

stall[3] *verb intrans* to play for time; to delay: *You're stalling for time.* ➤ *verb trans* to divert or delay (somebody), *esp* by evasion, prevarication, or deception: *Try to stall them till we have more facts.* [from STALL[4]]

stall[4] *noun* a delaying tactic; a ploy intended to divert or distract somebody. [alteration of STALL[5] in an obsolete sense 'pickpocket's accomplice']

stallage /'stawlij/ *noun Brit* 1 *esp* formerly, a fee charged for setting up a market stall, or rent paid for the use of one. 2 *esp* formerly, the right to hold a market stall.

stall-feed *verb trans* (**stall-feeding**, past tense and past part. **stall-fed**) to confine (an animal) to a stall in order to feed it intensively, *esp* as a means of fattening it for slaughter.

stallholder *noun* a person who runs a stall, *esp* in a market place.

stallion /'stalyən/ *noun* an uncastrated male horse, *esp* one kept for breeding. [Middle English *stalion* from Old French *estalon*, of Germanic origin]

stalwart[1] /'stawlwət/ *adj* 1 strong in body, mind, or spirit: *our prisoner breathing hard, with a stalwart constable on each side of him —* Conan Doyle. 2 dependable; staunch: *a stalwart defender of old-fashioned values.* ➤➤ **stalwartly** *adv*, **stalwartness** *noun*. [Middle English, alteration of *stalworth*, from Old English *stælwierthe* serviceable]

stalwart[2] *noun* a stalwart person, *esp* a staunch supporter: *the party stalwarts.*

stamen /'staymən/ *noun* the organ of a flower that produces the male GAMETE (reproductive cell) enclosed in a pollen grain, and consists of an ANTHER (pollen-containing part) and a filament. [Latin *stamen* warp thread, applied by Pliny to the stamens of the lily]

stamin- *or* **stamini-** *comb. form* forming words, denoting: stamen: *staminode*. [Latin *stamin-, stamen*: see STAMEN]

stamina /'staminə/ *noun* the capacity for sustained mental and physical effort.

Word history
Latin *stamina*, pl of *stamen* warp thread. Originally in the sense 'the essentials or rudiments' of something, likened to the warp threads of cloth; the current sense comes from the use of Latin *stamen* to refer to the thread of a person's life spun by the Fates, hence the life force each person possesses at birth, the strength of which, barring accidents, determines the length of their life.

staminate /'staminət, -nayt/ *adj* 1 said of plants: having or producing stamens. 2 said of plants: having stamens but no carpels (female reproductive organs; see CARPEL); male: compare PISTILLATE.

stamini- *comb. form* see STAMIN-.

staminode /'staminohd/ *noun* an abortive or sterile stamen. [scientific Latin *staminodium*, from STAMIN- + Greek *-ōdēs* -like]

stammer[1] /'stamə/ *verb* (**stammered**, **stammering**) ➤ *verb intrans* to speak or utter with involuntary stops and repetitions, *esp* of initial consonants, and often prolongation of vowel sounds; to stutter. ➤ *verb trans* to utter (something) in a stammering voice, e.g. in fright. ➤➤➤ **stammerer** *noun*. [Old English *stamerian* to stammer]

stammer² *noun* a tendency to stammer.

stamp¹ /stamp/ *verb trans* **1** to bring down (one's foot) forcibly in angry insistence. **2** to grind (something) with the sole of the foot: *He stamped his cigarette end into the ground.* **3** to pound or crush (ore, etc) with a pestle or a heavy instrument. **4** to impress or imprint (words, etc) on something: *The serial number is stamped on the frame.* **5** to leave (a permanent or indelible image) in someone's mind, etc: *The scene was stamped on his memory.* **6** to imprint or impress words, etc on (something): *Their personal papers were stamped with the label 'Jude'.* **7** said of a quality, etc: to characterize (something): *the defeatism that stamps all his writings from this period.* **8** to leave (a characteristic mark) on something: *He managed to stamp his personality on everything he touched.* **9** to attach a postage stamp to (an envelope, etc). **10** to cut out, bend, or form (something) using a stamp or DIE² (moulding device): *The tokens had been stamped from lead sheets, 84 at a time.* ➤ *verb intrans* **1** to thrust the foot forcibly or noisily downward. **2** (+ on) to crush something by or as if by stamping: *I stamped on the cigarette end; Individualism was firmly stamped on.* ➤➤➤ **stamper** *noun*. [Middle English *stampen* to crush, pulverize, of Germanic origin]

stamp² *noun* **1** a device or instrument for stamping a mark, etc on a surface. **2** the impression or mark made by stamping or imprinting. **3** a characteristic quality: *The correspondence somehow had the stamp of authenticity.* **4** distinctive type: *racists and people of that stamp.* **5** a lasting mark: *Hardship had left its stamp on her.* **6** the act of stamping, or the noise made by this: *with a stamp of her foot.* **7** a printed adhesive piece of paper used as a token of credit, etc; = POSTAGE STAMP or TRADING STAMP. **8** a block for crushing ore at a stamp mill.

stamp duty *noun* a tax on the legal recognition of certain documents.

stampede¹ /stam'peed/ *noun* **1** a wild headlong rush or flight of frightened animals. **2** a sudden mass movement of people: *a stampede towards the exits.* [via American Spanish from Spanish *estampida* a crash or din, from *estampar* to stamp, of Germanic origin]

stampede² *verb intrans* to run away or rush in panic or on impulse. ➤ *verb trans* to panic (animals) into rushing headlong, or (people) into doing something precipitately: *The shot stampeded the herd; We must not be stampeded into accepting what is a highly suspect package.*

stamp hinge *noun* a piece of transparent gummed paper designed for attaching stamps to the page of an album.

stamping ground *noun* one's favourite or habitual haunt: *We visited the site of the Cavern, the Beatles' old stamping ground.*

stamp mill *or* **stamping mill** *noun* a mill in which ore is crushed.

stamp out *verb trans* **1** to suppress or smother (a fire) by stamping on it. **2** to eradicate or destroy (something): *The government means to stamp out benefit fraud.*

stamp tax *noun* = STAMP DUTY.

stance /stahns, stans/ *noun* **1** a way of standing: *He adopted a belligerent stance.* **2** an intellectual or emotional attitude: *They took an anti-union stance.* **3** the position of body or feet from which a sportsperson, e.g. a batsman or golfer, plays. **4** *Scot* a site for a taxi rank or street stall. **5** in climbing, a foothold. [Middle English via French from Italian *stanza*: see STANZA]

stanch¹ /stawnch, stahnch/ *verb trans NAmer* see STAUNCH¹.

stanch² /stawnch/ *adj* see STAUNCH² (3).

stanchion /'stahnsh(ə)n, 'stansh(ə)n/ *noun* an upright bar, post, or support, e.g. for a roof. ➤➤➤ **stanchioned** *adj*. [Middle English *stanchon* from Old French *estanchon*, from *estance* stay, support, prob ultimately from Latin *stant-, stans*: see STANZA]

stand¹ /stand/ *verb* (*past tense and past part.* **stood**) ➤ *verb intrans* **1** to support oneself on one's feet in an erect position. **2** to get to one's feet: *Everyone stood.* **3** to be a specified height when fully erect: *stand six feet two.* **4** to rest upright on a base or lower end: *A clock stood on the shelf.* **5** to occupy a place or location: *The house stands on a hill.* **6** to be upright as distinct from flattened or destroyed: *The bombing left few buildings standing.* **7** to remain stationary or inactive: *The car stood in the garage for a week; the train now standing at Platform 5.* **8** said of water: to accumulate and remain motionless: *standing water; Tears stood in their eyes.* **9** said of ingredients in cooking: to remain undisturbed: *Leave the mixture to stand for an hour.* **10** to be, with regard to state, development, etc: *copy the passage*

exactly as it stands; How do things stand at present? **11** to be in a specified state: *stand empty; stand idle.* **12** to take a particular attitude: *How do you stand on equal pay?* **13** to be in a certain position as a result of something said or done to one: *to stand accused.* **14** to remain valid or efficacious: *The present arrangement stands till further notice.* **15** to have or maintain a relative position in or as if in a graded scale: *It stands first in its class.* **16** to qualify for or be likely to gain something: *She stands to inherit at least £100, 000.* **17** *chiefly Brit* (*often* + for) to be a candidate in an election: *to stand for Parliament.* **18** (*also* **stand at stud**) said of a male animal, *esp* a stallion: to be available as a stud. **19** said of a ship: to be moving steadily in a certain direction: *stand due east.* ➤ *verb trans* **1** to set (something) upright or place it somewhere. **2** to endure or withstand (a testing experience): *I don't know how she stands the strain; shoes that stand a lot of hard wear.* **3** to undergo (an ordeal): *stand trial.* **4** (*usu in negative contexts*) to bear (a person or thing): *I can't stand her husband.* **5** to perform the duty of (*esp* a guard): *stand sentinel.* **6** *informal* to treat (somebody) to a meal, etc: *I'll stand you dinner.* ✷ **leave standing** to surpass somebody spectacularly. **stand a chance** to have a chance. **stand alone** to be unequalled. **stand and deliver** a highwayman's order to hand over valuables. **stand aside 1** to stand clear of something. **2** to resign from a position. **stand back** to distance oneself from a situation in order to assess it more objectively. **stand by 1** to support or remain loyal to (somebody). **2** to honour (a promise). **stand firm/fast** to remain steadfast in the face of opposition. **stand for 1** to represent or mean (something): *What does 'lb' stand for?* **2** (*usu in negative contexts*) to permit or put up with (something). **stand on ceremony** to insist on correct procedure. **stand on end** said of hair: to be erect as a result of fear: *I could a tale unfold whose lightest word would … make … thy knotted and combined locks to part, and each particular hair to stand on end —* Shakespeare. **stand one's ground** to maintain one's position against opposition. **stand on one's own feet/one's own two feet** to be self-reliant. **stand over** to watch or supervise (somebody) closely or oppressively. **stand still for** *NAmer* (*usu in negative contexts*) to tolerate (something). **stand to reason** to follow logically. ➤➤➤ **stander** *noun*. [Old English *standan*]

stand² *noun* **1** an act, position, or place of standing: *He took up a stand near the exit.* **2** *archaic* a halt or standstill: *He made a sudden stand —* Wordsworth. **3** a definite attitude taken towards something: *The school takes a tough stand on drugs.* **4** an effort to fight for or resist something: *They made a stand for equality of treatment.* **5** in cricket, a partnership of two batsmen or batswomen, or the runs scored by them: *a stand of over 100.* **6** a stop made by a touring theatre company, rock group, etc to give a performance, or a town where such a stop is made: *a one-night stand.* **7** (*also in pl*) a structure of tiered seats for spectators of a sport or spectacle: *cheering from the stands.* **8** a raised platform for a band, speaker, etc. **9** a small temporary outdoor stall selling food or other goods: *a hot-dog stand.* **10** a usu temporary structure erected, e.g. at a trade exhibition, to display or demonstrate wares. **11** a place where taxis await hire. **12** a frame or rack on or in which to place things: *an umbrella stand.* **13** (**the stand**) *NAmer* the witness-box: *The defendant took the stand.* **14** *Aus, NZ.* **a** a shearer's position on the floor of the shearing shed. **b** a shearer's equipment. **15** a compact group of plants or trees: *a stand of horse chestnuts.* **16** *SAfr* a plot of building land.

stand-alone *adj* said of a piece of computer hardware or software: operating independently of other software or hardware.

standard¹ /'standəd/ *noun* **1** a level of quality or achievement: *a high standard of workmanship.* **2** (*also in pl*) a requisite level of quality: *Some restaurant kitchens fail to meet minimum standards of cleanliness.* **3** (*also in pl*) a norm used for comparison: *Travel was slow by today's standards.* **4** (*in pl*) principles of behaviour based on ideas of integrity or honour: *moral standards.* **5a** the fineness and legally fixed weight of the metal used in coins. **b** a system whereby a currency is valued in terms of gold: *the gold standard.* **6** a measure of timber equal to 162 cubic ft (4.67 cubic metres). **7** a flag or banner, e.g.: **a** a long narrow tapering flag that is personal to an individual or corporation and bears heraldic insignia. **b** the personal flag of a member of a royal family or of a head of state. **c** a distinctive flag carried by cavalry or armoured regiments. **8** a stanchion or support. **9a** a shrub or soft-stemmed plant grown with an erect main stalk so that it forms or resembles a tree. **b** a fruit tree grafted on a stock that does not induce dwarfing. **10a** the large irregular upper petal of a flower of a pea, bean, clover, etc. **b** any of the three inner erect and incurved petals of an iris. **11** something standard, e.g.: **a** a musical composition, *esp* a popular song, that has become a part of the established repertoire. **b** a model of a car supplied without optional extras. **12** *SAfr* a class or year in a high school. ✳ **raise the/one's standard** to take up arms; to prepare to make a stand for or against something. [Middle English from Old French *estandard* rallying point, standard, of Germanic origin]

standard² *adj* **1** denoting or conforming to a standard, *esp* as established by law or custom: *of standard weight.* **2** sound and usable but not of top quality: *the standard model.* **3** denoting the smallest size of a range of marketed products: *available in standard, family, super, and mega packs.* **4** regularly and widely used, available, or supplied: *a standard socket.* **5** well established and very familiar: *the standard weekend television programmes.* **6** recognized as authoritative and of lasting value: *a standard reference work.* **7** said of language: uniform and well established by usage in the speech and writing of educated people and widely accepted as a norm: *Standard English.* ➤➤ **standardly** *adv.*

standard assessment tasks *pl noun* in Britain, a series of standard tests given to schoolchildren at particular stages to assess their progress against the attainment targets (see ATTAINMENT TARGET) specified for core subjects in the National Curriculum.

standard-bearer *noun* **1** a person, e.g. a soldier, who carries a standard or banner. **2** a conspicuous figure at the forefront of an organization, movement, or party.

standardbred *noun* an animal of an American breed of light trotting and pacing horses bred for speed and noted for endurance. [because a horse could be entered in the studbook only if it reached a certain standard of speed]

standard cost *noun* the cost of a manufacturing process projected in its budget, as against the actual final cost.

standard deviation *noun* a measure of the extent to which values of a variable are scattered about the mean value in a frequency distribution and equal to the square root of the mean of the squared deviations of the values from the mean.

standard error *noun* the standard deviation of the distribution of values of a statistic, e.g. the mean, obtained from a large number of samples.

standard gauge *noun* a railway gauge of 4ft 8½in. (1.435m), used on most railways. ➤ **standard-gauge** *adj.*

Standard Grade *noun* in Scotland, an examination that is equivalent to English GCSE, designed to test the application of knowledge as much as its acquisition.

standardize *or* **standardise** *verb trans* **1** to make (things) conform to a standard: *Examiners meet beforehand to standardize their marking principles.* **2** to test (a substance, etc) or ascertain the properties of (it) by comparison with a standard. ➤ *verb intrans* (+ on) to adopt a certain brand or make as standard equipment, etc. ➤➤ **standardization** /-'zaysh(ə)n/ *noun.*

standard lamp *noun* a lamp with a tall support that stands on the floor.

standard model *noun* a mathematical representation of the electromagnetic, weak, and strong interactions between the elementary particles of matter.

standard of living *noun* a level of welfare or subsistence maintained by an individual, group, or community and shown *esp* by the level of consumption of necessities, comforts, and luxuries.

standard time *noun* the officially established time, with reference to Greenwich Mean Time, of a region or country.

standby *noun* (*pl* **standbys**) **1a** a person or thing that is held in reserve and can be relied on in case of necessity. **b** a state of readiness for duty or use. **c** (*used before a noun*) held in reserve and ready for use or duty: *standby equipment.* **2** (*used before a noun*) of tickets: unreserved and becoming available for sale shortly before e.g. a performance or the departure of a flight: *standby tickets.*

stand by *verb intrans* **1** to be present but remain aloof or inactive. **2** to wait in a state of readiness: *Stand by for action.*

stand down *verb intrans* **1** *chiefly Brit* to relinquish an office or position. **2** *chiefly Brit* said of a witness: to go off duty. **3** to leave the witness-box. ➤ *verb trans chiefly Brit* **1** to send (soldiers) off duty. **2** to dismiss or lay off (workers).

standee /stan'dee/ *noun* (*pl* **standees** /-'deez/) a person standing when the norm is to be seated, e.g. as a passenger on a bus, audience member, spectator, etc.

stand in *verb intrans* **1** (+ for) to act as substitute for somebody. **2** said of a ship: to sail close to the shore.

stand-in *noun* **1** a person who is employed to occupy an actor's place while lights and camera are made ready, or at other times when the actor is not required in person. **2** a substitute.

standing¹ *adj* **1** said of timber or grain: not yet cut down or harvested. **2** said of water: not flowing; stagnant. **3** said of an offer, etc: permanently in force or available. **4** said of printing type: set up ready and stored for use. ✳ **all standing** used in reference to the stopping of a ship: with no time to lower the sails.

standing² *noun* **1** status, position, or reputation: *people of high standing in the community.* **2** length of existence or duration: *an MP of many years' standing.* ✳ **in good standing** (+ with) on good terms with somebody: *She was in good standing with her boss.*

standing army *noun* a permanent army of paid soldiers.

standing committee *noun* a permanent committee appointed, *esp* by a legislative body such as Parliament, to consider a particular subject.

standing joke *noun* something that is a regular source of amusement or target of derision.

standing jump *noun* a jump performed from a stationary start, without a run-up.

standing order *noun* **1** *Brit.* **a** an order to a bank to pay a specified sum of money to another named account at specified times: compare DIRECT DEBIT. **b** an instruction, e.g. to a supplier, in force until specifically changed. **2** (*in pl*) rules governing the procedure of an organization, which remain in force until specifically changed.

standing ovation *noun* a prolonged burst of applause for a speaker or performer, during which the audience rise to their feet in enthusiasm.

standing rigging *noun* permanent rigging, e.g. stays and shrouds, used primarily to secure the masts and fixed spars of a vessel or to support radio, radar, and other equipment carried aloft.

standing room *noun* space for standing, *esp* accommodation available for spectators or passengers after all seats are filled.

standing start *noun* the starting of a race from a stationary position.

standing stone *noun* any of many large stones fixed erect in prehistoric times, some with carvings, some evidently of funerary or religious significance: = MENHIR.

standing wave *noun* a vibration of a body or physical system in which the amplitude varies from point to point but is constant at any particular point.

standish /'standish/ *noun esp* formerly, an inkstand, or a stand for pens and ink: *Amy laid a bit of red tape, with sealing-wax, a taper, and a standish before him* — Louisa M Alcott. [prob formed from STAND¹, but sometimes said to be a blend of STAND¹ + DISH¹]

standoff *noun* **1** a state of deadlock or stalemate between opponents. **2** = STAND-OFF HALF.

stand off *verb intrans* **1** in sailing, to keep a distance from the shore. **2** to reach deadlock. **3** said of a horse: to take off early for a jump.

stand-off half *noun* in rugby, the player positioned between the scrum-half and the three-quarter backs.

standoffish *adj derog* reserved; aloof. ➤➤ **standoffishly** *adv,* **standoffishness** *noun.*

standoff weapon *noun* a missile or bomb that can be directed towards its target from a safe distance.

stand on *verb intrans* in sailing, to keep steering in the same direction.

standout *noun chiefly NAmer, informal* a prominent, *esp* strikingly splendid, person or thing.

stand out *verb intrans* **1** to be especially visible. **2** to be obvious or noteworthy: *Two factors stand out.* **3** (+ for/against) to be stubborn in insisting on something or resisting it: *Stand out for better working conditions.*

standover *adj Aus, informal* denoting a criminal, gang, etc using intimidation to extort money, etc: *a standover man.*

stand over *verb intrans* to be postponed.

standpipe *noun* a pipe fitted with a tap and used for an outdoor water supply.

standpoint *noun* **1** the position from which one views a scene or object: *Perspective varies according to your standpoint.* **2** one's point of view with regard to some issue: *Consider it from the disabled child's standpoint.*

standstill *noun* a state in which motion or progress is absent; a stop or impasse: *Traffic was at a standstill in the city centre; Negotiations had come to a standstill.*

stand to *verb intrans* to take up a position of readiness (e.g. for action or inspection): *Order the men to stand to.* ➤➤ **stand-to** *noun.*

stand-to *noun* the act or an instance of standing to.

stand up *verb intrans* **1** to rise to or maintain a standing or upright position. **2** (*usu in negative contexts*) said of reasoning, evidence, etc: to bear close scrutiny: *That argument won't stand up.* ➤ *verb trans informal* to fail to keep an appointment with (somebody): *I was beginning to think he'd stood me up.* ✳ **stand up and be counted** to make one's views known. **stand up for** to defend (a person or thing) against attack or criticism. **stand up to 1** to withstand the damaging effects of (something): *clothes that stand up to hard wear.* **2** to confront or prepare to resist (aggressors or their activities) boldly.

stand-up¹ *adj* **1a** said of a comedian: performing solo in front of an audience by telling stories and jokes. **b** said of a comic act: performed by a stand-up comedian: *stand-up comedy.* **2** denoting a formal white collar worn with evening dress, etc, starched so as to stand upright. **3** denoting a meal at a reception, etc, that is taken standing up.

stand-up² *noun* **1** a stand-up comedian. **2** stand-up comedy.

Stanford-Binet test /ˌstanfəd ˈbiˈnay/ *noun* an intelligence test prepared at Stanford University as a revision of the Binet-Simon scale, measuring a person's mental ability against the average for their age group. [Stanford University, California, USA]

stanhope /ˈstanəp, ˈstanhohp/ *noun* formerly, a light horsedrawn carriage for a single occupant, with two or four wheels: *The vehicle was not exactly a gig, neither was it a stanhope* — Dickens. [named after Fitzroy *Stanhope* d.1864, English clergyman for whom the first one was made]

stank /stangk/ *verb* past tense of STINK¹.

Stanley knife /ˈstanli/ *noun trademark* a knife with a hollow handle and a short sharp replaceable blade, used for trimming carpets, hardboard, etc. [named after F T *Stanley*, US businessman, founder of the Stanley Rule and Level Company in 1843]

stann- *comb. form* forming words, denoting: tin: *stannous.* [late Latin *stannum* tin]

stannary /ˈstanəri/ *noun* (*pl* **stannaries**) (*also in pl*) *esp* formerly, a tin-mining region of Cornwall or Devon. [medieval Latin *stannaria* (pl) tin mine, from late Latin *stannum* tin]

stannary court *noun* formerly, any of the independent courts set up for the regulation of miners' affairs in Cornwall and Devon.

stannic /ˈstanik/ *adj* **1** relating to or containing tin with a valency of four. **2** denoting a compound of tin with this valency: *stannic sulphide.* [prob from French *stannique*, from late Latin *stannum* tin]

stannite /ˈstaniet/ *noun* a steel-grey or iron-black mineral that is a sulphide of copper, iron, and tin, has a metallic lustre, and is used as a source of tin.

stannous /ˈstanəs/ *adj* **1** relating to or containing tin with a valency of two. **2** denoting a compound of tin with this valency: *stannous fluoride.*

stanza /ˈstanzə/ *noun* **1** a division of a poem consisting of a series of lines arranged together in a recurring pattern of metre and rhyme; = VERSE¹. **2** in Greek and Latin prosody, a unit of four lines in certain metres. ➤➤ **stanza'd** *adj*, **stanzaed** *adj*, **stanzaic** /stanˈzayik/ *adj*. [Italian *stanza* standing place, stanza, ultimately from Latin *stant-*, *stans* present part. of *stare* to stand]

stapedes /ˈstaypideez/ *noun* pl of STAPES.

stapelia /stəˈpeeli-ə/ *noun* a cactus-like succulent plant of S Africa with large star-shaped flowers that smell of carrion: genus *Stapelia*. [Latin genus name, named after J B van *Stapel* d.1636, Dutch botanist]

stapes /ˈstaypeez/ *noun* (*pl* **stapes** or **stapedes** /ˈstaypideez/) the innermost of the chain of three small bones in the ear of a mammal, shaped like a stirrup and transmitting vibrations from the INCUS (middle bone) to the inner ear; stirrup bone: compare INCUS, MALLEUS. [medieval Latin *stapes* stirrup]

staph /staf/ *noun informal* = STAPHYLOCOCCUS. ➤➤ **staph** *adj.*

staphyl- *or* **staphylo-** *comb. form* forming words, with the meanings: **1** the uvula: *staphyloplasty.* **2** resembling a bunch of grapes: *staphylococcus.* [Greek *staphylē* a bunch of grapes]

staphylococcus /ˌstafilohˈkokəs/ *noun* (*pl* **staphylococci** /-ˈkok(s)ie, -ˈkok(s)ee/) any of various spherical bacteria that include parasites of skin and mucous membranes and cause boils, septic infections of wounds, etc. ➤➤ **staphylococcal** *adj*, **staphylococcic** /-ˈkok(s)ik/ *adj.*

staphyloplasty /ˌstafilohˈplasti/ *noun* plastic surgery to the soft palate or uvula.

staple¹ /ˈstaypl/ *noun* **1** a small piece of wire with ends bent at right angles which can be driven through thin sheets of material, *esp* paper, and clinched to secure the items. **2** a U-shaped metal loop, both ends of which can be driven into a surface, e.g. to secure something to it. [Old English *stapol* post]

staple² *verb trans* to fasten (things) together, or (one thing) to another, with staples.

staple³ *noun* **1a** a food constituting the main nourishment of a community, etc: *Maize flour was the staple of the local diet.* **b** the main constituent of something: *that train of meteorological questions and answers which forms the great staple of polite English conversation* — Sidney Smith. **2** the main trading commodity or raw material of a region: *Coffee rapidly became the staple of the economy.* **3** the fibre of cotton or wool graded for length and fineness: *wool of a short staple.* **4** in the Middle Ages, a town appointed, usu by royal authority, to be the centre for merchants involved in the sale or export of commodities in bulk. [Middle English from Old French *estaple* market, from early Dutch and early Low German *stapel* emporium, pillar]

staple⁴ *adj* **1** denoting a leading commodity in the economy of a region: *staple crops such as wheat and rice.* **2** main; principal; chief: *Our staple drink has been at times tea, at times coffee.*

staple gun *noun* a hand-held mechanical device that propels staples into a hard surface, used for fixing posters to walls, etc.

stapler *noun* a small hand-operated device for inserting wire staples.

star¹ /stah/ *noun* **1** any natural luminous body visible in the sky, *esp* at night. **2** any of millions of gaseous bodies of great mass, heat, and light, such as the sun, that radiate energy. **3** (*also in pl*). **a** in astrology, a configuration of the planets that is held to influence a person's destiny, character, etc: *The fault, dear Brutus, is not in our stars, but in ourselves, that we are underlings* — Shakespeare. **b** (**the stars**) an astrological forecast; a horoscope. **4** a stylized figure with five or more points that represents a star. **5** a star-shaped ornament or medal worn as a badge of honour, authority, or rank or as the insignia of an order. **6** an asterisk. **7** a star-shaped symbol used to indicate degree of excellence: *a four-star hotel.* **8** a white patch on the forehead of a horse or other animal. **9** used in the names of certain echinoderms (phylum including starfish; see ECHINODERM): *cushion star.* **10** any famous performer or celebrity of stage, screen, or television, or sports personality: *a star of the running track.* **11** the leading performer of a group: *the star of the ballet troupe.* **12** a person who stands out among their fellows: *She was the star of her year.* **13** *informal* a kind or generous person: *Thanks, Mum, you're a star.* **14** (*used before a noun*) denoting outstanding quality, etc: *have star quality.* ✳ **my stars!** *informal, dated* an expression of astonishment. **see stars** *informal* to see dots and flashes before one's eyes, as when stunned or dazed. **somebody's star is rising** somebody is becoming successful. ➤➤ **starless** *adj*, **starlike** *adj.* [Old English *steorra*]

star² *verb* (**starred, starring**) ➤ *verb trans* **1** said of a film, play, etc: to feature (a certain star) in a leading role. **2** to mark (something) with a star or asterisk, for particular commendation or notice: *starred items.* **3** to spangle or adorn (a surface) with star-shaped decorations, etc. ➤ *verb intrans* to play a leading role in a production: *now starring in a West End musical.*

star anise *noun* **1** a star-shaped fruit with a seed in each point, used unripened in Asian cuisine. **2** the tree, native to China, that bears this fruit: *Illicium verum.*

star apple *noun* **1** an apple-shaped edible purple fruit with its seeds arranged star-fashion. **2** the tropical American evergreen tree that bears this fruit: *Chrysophyllum cainito.*

starboard¹ /ˈstahbəd/ *noun* the right side of a ship or aircraft looking forward: compare PORT². ➤➤ **starboard** *adj.* [Old English *stēorbord*, from *stēor-* steering oar + *bord* ship's side]

starboard² *verb trans* to turn or put (a helm or rudder) to the right.

starburst *noun* **1** a pattern of rays or lines radiating from a point or source of light. **2** a lens attachment for a camera that produces a starburst effect around the image of a light source. **3** an explosion that takes place with this effect. **4** a burst of star formation within a galaxy.

starch¹ /stahch/ *verb trans* **1** to stiffen (clothes or fabric) with starch. **2** *NAmer, informal* said of a boxer: to defeat (one's opponent) by a knockout. ➤➤ **starcher** *noun*. [Old English *sterced* stiffened]

starch² *noun* **1** an odourless tasteless complex carbohydrate that is the chief storage form of carbohydrate in plants, is an important foodstuff, being obtained chiefly from cereals and potatoes, and is also used in pharmacy and medicine. **2** a material prepared from this, used in adhesives and sizes, and in the form of a powder or spray to stiffen fabric. **3** *dated* formality, stiffness, or pomposity.

Star Chamber *noun* **1** a court in England that was abolished in 1641, had both civil and criminal jurisdiction, and was noted for its arbitrary and oppressive procedures. **2** (**star chamber**) any oppressive tribunal. **3** *Brit* during a Conservative regime, a committee of senior ministers who vet the spending of each government department. [from the painted stars on the ceiling of the original courtroom]

starch-reduced *adj* said of bread, etc: containing less than the usual proportion of starch, so as to be suitable for slimmers.

starchy *adj* (**starchier, starchiest**) **1** said of foods or other substances: containing a lot of starch. **2** said of a social atmosphere, somebody's manner, etc: stiff and formal. ➤➤ **starchily** *adv*, **starchiness** *noun*.

star connection *noun* a Y-shaped electrical connection in motors, etc, where one end of each winding in a three-phase system is connected to a common point, and the other to a separate terminal. ➤➤ **star-connected** *adj*.

star-crossed *adj literary* ill-fated: *From forth the fatal loins of these two foes a pair of star-crossed lovers take their life* — Shakespeare.

stardom *noun* the status or position of a celebrity or star.

stardust *noun* **1** *dated* a magical romance-bearing influence, sometimes imagined as a starry mist: *They had stardust in their eyes.* **2** a cluster of far-distant stars apparently forming a bright cloud.

stare¹ /stea/ *verb intrans* **1** to look fixedly, often with wide-open eyes: *She stared at him in astonishment.* **2** to stand out conspicuously: *The name stared from the list.* **3** said of an animal's fur or a bird's plumage: to bristle or stand on end, *esp* with illness or fear. ➤ *verb trans* (+ into) to cow (somebody) into submissive behaviour by staring intimidatingly at them. ✳ **be staring death/defeat, etc in the face** to face imminent death, defeat, etc. **stare somebody in the face** said of a solution, etc: to be only too obvious. **stare somebody in the eye** to return somebody's look boldly. ➤➤ **starer** *noun*. [Old English *starian* to stare, gaze]

stare² *noun* a staring look or expression: *a blank stare.*

stare down *verb trans* = STARE OUT.

stare out *verb trans* to cause (somebody) to look away by staring fixedly into their eyes.

starfish /'stahfish/ *noun* (*pl* **starfishes** or *collectively* **starfish**) any of numerous species of marine echinoderms (phylum including starfish and sea urchins; see ECHINODERM) that have a body consisting of a central disc surrounded by five equally spaced arms with tube feet on the underside, and feeds largely on molluscs, e.g. oysters: class Asteroidea.

starflower *noun* any of several plants with star-shaped flowers, *esp* STAR-OF-BETHLEHEM.

starfruit *noun* = CARAMBOLA (1).

stargaze *verb intrans informal* **1** to observe or examine the stars. **2** to gaze raptly, contemplatively, or absentmindedly; to daydream. ➤➤ **stargazing** *noun*. [back-formation from STARGAZER]

stargazer *noun* **1** *informal* an astrologer. **2** *informal* an astronomer. **3** *Aus, informal* a horse that turns its head while galloping. **4** a tropical marine fish with eyes and mouth on top of its head, which buries itself in the sand of the ocean floor with only its eyes showing: families Uranoscopidae and Dactyloscopidae.

stark /stahk/ *adj* **1** said of a landscape, surroundings, etc: bleak or bare; desolate: *a stark white room.* **2** harshly clear or plain: *the stark reality; in stark contrast.* **3** sheer; utter: *stark terror.* **4** short for STARK-NAKED. **5** *archaic or literary.* **a** rigid in or as if in death: *lying stiff and*

stark. **b** strong; robust. ✳ **stark mad/stark staring mad** *informal* utterly mad. ➤➤ **starkly** *adv*, **starkness** *noun*. [Old English *stearc* hard, unyielding, rigid]

Stark effect *noun* the splitting of lines in the spectrums of atoms in the presence of a strong electric field. [named after Johannes Stark d.1957, German physicist, who discovered the effect in 1913]

starkers /'stahkəz/ *adj Brit, informal* completely naked: *He was sunbathing starkers.* [STARK-NAKED + -ers on the pattern of such words as *preggers* for *pregnant*]

stark-naked *adj* completely naked. [alteration of *start-naked*, from Old English *steort* tail]

starlet /'stahlit/ *noun* **1** a young film actress being coached for starring roles and given prominent billing. **2** a rising young female athlete.

starlight *noun* the light of the stars. ➤➤ **starlit** *adj*.

starling¹ /'stahling/ *noun* any of various species of gregarious European birds with dark brown, or in summer glossy greenish black, plumage: *Sturnus vulgaris* and other species. [Old English *stærlinc*, from *stær* starling + -*ling*, -*linc* -LING]

starling² *noun* one of a series of wooden piles erected round the pier of a bridge to protect it from the current, from contact with vessels, and from floating debris. [prob alteration of dialect *staddling*, from STADDLE]

star network *noun* a type of computer network in which all nodes (terminals; see NODE) are individually connected to the central unit.

star-of-Bethlehem /'bethlihem/ *noun* any of a genus of plants of the lily family with grasslike leaves and white or yellow star-shaped flowers: *esp Ornithogalum angustifolium.* Also called STAR-FLOWER.

Star of David /'dayvid/ *noun* a six-pointed star made from two superimposed equilateral triangles that is a symbol of Judaism and the State of Israel. [named after David, King of Judah in biblical accounts]

star route *noun NAmer, dated* the former name for HIGHWAY CONTRACT ROUTE.

starry /'stahri/ *adj* (**starrier, starriest**) **1** said of the sky: adorned or studded with stars: *a starry night.* **2** shining like stars; sparkling: *starry eyes.* **3** said of flowers: star-shaped; STELLATE. **4** *informal* relating to the stars of the entertainment world, or to celebrities generally: *The company was powerful ... well stocked with effective programme-makers, valuable copyrights, excellent sales force, but perhaps ... a bit short on starry names* — Melvyn Bragg.

starry-eyed *adj* given to thinking in a dreamy, impractical, or overoptimistic manner.

Stars and Bars *pl noun* (*usu treated as sing.*) the first flag adopted by the Confederates at the time of the American Civil War, having two red bars and one white, and a circle of white stars, one for every Confederate state.

Stars and Stripes *pl noun* (**the Stars and Stripes**) (*treated as sing.*) the flag of the USA, having 13 alternately red and white horizontal stripes and a blue rectangle in the top left-hand corner with white stars representing the states.

star sapphire *noun* a sapphire that reflects light in the form of a star-shaped figure, *esp* when cut with a convex surface.

star shell *noun* a shell that on bursting releases a brilliant light for illumination and signalling.

starship *noun* in science fiction, a large spaceship carrying personnel on interstellar journeys.

star sign *noun* a sign of the zodiac: *My star sign is Sagittarius.*

star-spangled *adj literary* studded with stars. ✳ **the Star-Spangled Banner 1** the national anthem of the USA. **2** = STARS AND STRIPES.

star stream *noun* a stream of stars drifting in the same general direction in a galaxy, or, in the case of the Milky Way, either of two main streams of stars seeming to be drifting in opposite directions.

star-struck *adj* fascinated by celebrities, *esp* film stars.

star-studded *adj* **1** covered with stars: *a star-studded uniform.* **2** *informal* featuring a large number of well-known stars: *a star-studded cast.*

START /staht/ *abbr* Strategic Arms Reduction Talks.

start¹ /staht/ *verb intrans* **1** to come into operation or existence: *When does the film start?* **2** to begin functioning: *The car won't start.*

3 to begin an activity or undertaking, e.g. eating or working: *We started with soup.* **4** to begin a course or journey: *They started at dawn.* **5** to begin moving; to make as if to move: *She started towards the door.* **6** (+ from/at) said of prices: to range from a specified amount: *Holiday-cottage rents start from £300 per week.* **7** to be a participant at the start of a sporting contest: *Fifteen horses started and ten finished.* **8** to move suddenly and violently; to spring: *He started angrily to his feet.* **9** to react with a sudden brief involuntary movement: *The bell rang and she started.* **10** to issue with sudden force: *Tears started in her eyes.* **11** to protrude, or seem to protrude: *His eyes were starting from their sockets.* **12** said of timbers, rivets, etc: to become loosened or forced out of place. ➤ *verb trans* **1** to begin (to do something): *Hilary started playing the piano at the age of three; He started to hum; Shall we start work?* **2** to set (something) going: *start a fire; start a rumour.* **3** to cause (machinery, etc) to begin operating: *I can't start the car.* **4** to initiate (a venture): *He plans to start a business.* **5** to set (somebody) up in business, etc: *Her parents lent her £1000 just to start her.* **6** to set (people) working: *We start four new machinists on Monday.* **7** to cause (somebody) to begin doing something: *That started us all laughing.* **8** to give the signal for (a race) to begin or (the competitors) to set off. **9** to begin tackling (a job), eating (a meal), etc. **10** to embark on or begin to use (another of something): *She started another chapter.* **11** *informal* to conceive (a baby). **12** to flush (game) or cause (an animal) to leave a place of concealment. **13** to cause (rivets or timbers) to become loosened or displaced. **14** *archaic* to startle (somebody) or make them start. ❋ **start on 1** to embark on (a task, journey, etc). **2** *informal* to begin attacking (somebody) verbally: *Don't start on me now.* **start something** *informal* to cause trouble or complications, *esp* unintentionally. **to start with 1** at the beginning; initially: *I wasn't too keen to start with.* **2** in the first place; for a start: *He should never have had access to that file to start with.* [Old English *styrtan* to caper or leap, later senses developing from the notion of sudden movement]

start[2] *noun* **1** the beginning of a movement, activity, journey, etc: *at the start of the project.* **2** a starting place, e.g. for a race. **3** a lead or handicap conceded to a competitor at the start of a race or competition, or the amount of this: *a 15-second start.* **4** an advantage or lead; a head start: *His background gave him a good start in politics.* **5** a sudden involuntary bodily movement or reaction, e.g. from surprise or alarm: *You gave me a start.* ❋ **for a start** in the first place; to start with: *For a start you need special permission.*

starter *noun* **1** the person who gives the signal to start a race. **2** a runner or other competitor at the start of a race or competition: *There are twelve starters.* **3** in baseball, the pitcher who opens the game. **4** a person who begins to engage in some activity, etc; a beginner: *a late starter.* **5** an automatic device that activates machinery, *esp* a vehicle engine: *the self-starter.* **6a** material containing micro-organisms, e.g. yeasts, used to induce fermentation, e.g. in milk or beer. **b** a chemical compound used to start a chemical reaction. **7** *chiefly Brit* (*also in pl*) the first course of a meal. ❋ **for starters** *chiefly Brit, informal* in the first place; to start with: *She's too old for the part for starters.* **under starter's orders** said of runners in a horse race, etc: awaiting the signal to start.

starter home *noun* a flat or house of a size and price to suit a first-time home-buyer.

start in *verb intrans informal* to begin doing something, *esp* talking: *Then she started in about the kids' lack of consideration.* ❋ **start in on 1** *NAmer* to begin to tackle (something). **2** *NAmer* to begin attacking or criticizing (somebody); to start on (somebody).

starting block *noun* either of two angled supports mounted on a frame, against which a sprinter braces their feet when in a crouched position at the start of a race.

starting gate *noun* **1** a mechanically operated barrier raised at the start of a race, e.g. a horse race. **2** a barrier that when knocked aside by a competitor, e.g. a skier, starts an electronic timing device.

starting grid *noun* a system of lines on a racetrack marking the starting positions of cars or motorcycles; = GRID (4).

starting handle *noun Brit esp* formerly, a crank used to start an internal-combustion engine.

starting pistol *noun* a pistol fired as the starting signal for a race.

starting price *noun esp* in horse racing, the betting odds as they stand at the start of a race.

starting stalls *pl noun* a line of stalls or traps in which horses or dogs are enclosed at the beginning of a race and from which they are released simultaneously by the opening of the mechanical barriers at the front of each stall.

startle /'stahtl/ *verb trans* **1** to cause (somebody) to start in alarm, etc: *The noise startled the baby, who began to howl.* **2** to alarm (somebody): *I was startled to see a stranger coming out of the house.* ➤➤ **startler** *noun*, **startling** *adj*, **startlingly** *adv*. [Old English *steartlian* to kick, struggle]

start off *verb intrans* **1** to begin: *Let's start off by introducing ourselves.* **2** to set out or begin a journey. ➤ *verb trans* **1** to set (something) in motion: *a question to start the discussion off with.* **2** to set (somebody) up in business, etc: *We needed a bank loan to start us off.*

start out *verb intrans* **1** to begin a journey. **2** to launch into a venture, etc: *We started out with £5 and a typewriter.*

start over *verb intrans chiefly NAmer* to begin all over again.

start up *verb intrans* to arise or come into being. ➤ *verb trans* to set (something) going or operating: *I would like to start up a business; Start up the computer.*

star turn *noun* the most prominently billed or impressive act in a show, etc.

starve /stahv/ *verb intrans* **1** to suffer severely from hunger or lack of nourishment. **2** to die of hunger. **3** to be in dire need. **4a** *informal* to be ravenous: *I'm starving.* **b** *archaic* to be very cold. ➤ *verb trans* **1** to cause (a person or animal) to suffer acutely, or to die of, hunger. **2** (+ of) to deprive (a person or animal) of something: *starved of affection.* **3** (+ into/out of) to force (people) into surrender or out of a place by starving them. ➤➤ **starvation** /stah'vaysh(ə)n/ *noun.* [Old English *steorfan* to die]

starveling /'stahvling/ *noun archaic* a person or animal that is thin from or as if from lack of food: *If I hang … Sir John [Falstaff] hangs with me, and thou knowest he is no starveling* — Shakespeare.

Star Wars *pl noun* (*treated as sing. or pl*) = STRATEGIC DEFENCE INITIATIVE. [nickname drawn from 1977 film *Star Wars*]

starwort *noun* **1** any of several species of plants with star-shaped flowers: genus *Stellaria* and other genera. **2** any of several species of aquatic plants with a floating rosette of leaves: genus *Callitriche*.

stash[1] /stash/ *verb trans informal* (*often + away*) to store (something) in a secret place for future use. [origin unknown]

stash[2] *noun informal* **1** a secret store of drugs, weapons, etc. **2** *dated* a hiding place; a cache.

stasis /'staysis/ *noun* (*pl* **stases** /'stayseez/) **1** a slowing or stoppage of the normal flow of body fluids, e.g.: **a** a slowing of the current of circulating blood. **b** reduced movement of material through the intestines, causing constipation. **2** a state of static balance or equilibrium; stagnation. [scientific Latin from Greek *stasis* act or condition of standing or stopping, from *histasthai* to stand]

-stasis *comb. form* (*pl* **-stases**) forming nouns, denoting: **1** stoppage; slowing down; inhibition: *haemostasis; bacteriostasis.* **2** stable state: *homoeostasis.* [scientific Latin, from Greek *stasis*: see STASIS]

stat[1] /stat/ *abbr informal* **1** photostat. **2** statistic. **3** statistics. **4** thermostat.

stat[2] *abbr* used in prescriptions, etc: straight away. [short for Latin *statim* immediately]

-stat *comb. form* forming nouns, denoting: agent or device for regulating: *thermostat; rheostat.* [scientific Latin from Greek *-statēs* that which stops or steadies, from *histanai* to cause to stand]

statant /'staytənt/ *adj* said of a heraldic animal: standing with all four feet on the ground. [formed irregularly from Latin *status*, past part. of *stare* to stand]

state[1] /stayt/ *noun* **1** the condition or situation of somebody or something: *in an unsound state of mind.* **2a** a condition of nervous tension: *She got in a state about the exam.* **b** a squalid or confused condition: *What a state the room was in!* **3** any of the stages that an organism can have during development: *insects in the larval state.* **4** physical condition in terms of molecular structure: *water in its gaseous state.* **5a** *formal or literary* social position; status; = ESTATE (6): *You should be content with your state.* **b** elaborate or luxurious style of living: *travelling in state.* **c** formal dignity; pomp: *The coffin was borne in state to Westminster Abbey.* **6** *archaic or literary* any of the three divisions of society, clergy, nobility, or commons; = ESTATE (5). **7** (*often* **State**) (*treated as sing. or pl*) a politically organized community usu occupying a definite territory; *esp* one that is sovereign. **8** (*often* **the State**) the body politic of such a community. **9** the operations or concerns of the central government of a country: *matters of state.* **10a** (*often* **State**) a constituent unit of a nation having a federal government: *the United States of America.* **b** (**the States**) the United States of America. **11** (*used before a noun*).

a (often **State**) relating to the State or the body politic: *state secrets*. **b** (often **State**) involving ceremony, or relating to ceremonial occasions: *the state opening of Parliament; a state visit*. **12a** any of the printed versions of the same edition of a book. **b** an impression taken from an etched or engraved plate at any stage. ✴ **lie in state** said of a deceased person, *esp* a head of state: to be placed on public view before burial so that people may pay their respects. **state of emergency** a situation involving national danger or extreme disaster, during which the government assumes special powers and suspends normal procedure. **state of affairs** (*also* **state of things**) a situation; the present or current situation. **state of grace** the state of being free of sin, *esp* after spiritually administered forgiveness. **state of play 1** *Brit* the current score in a cricket or football match. **2** *Brit* the current situation. ➤➤ **statehood** *noun* [Middle English *stat*, shortened from *estat* estate, via Old French from Latin *status* standing, condition: see STATUS; (sense 8) from the phrase *status rei publicae* 'condition of the republic']

state² *verb trans* **1** to declare (something) formally. **2** to present the facts of (a legal case) for consideration. **3** to specify (something): *The library may be used only at stated times*. **4** to present (a theme) in a musical composition so that the listener becomes acquainted with it. ➤➤ **statable** *adj*, **stateable** *adj*.

state bank *noun* in the USA, a bank that is incorporated under the charter of a state and is not required to join the Federal Reserve System.

state capitalism *noun* an economic system in which the state controls production and the deployment of capital.

statecraft *noun* the art of conducting state affairs.

State Department *noun* in the USA, the government department in charge of foreign affairs.

State Duma *noun* the lower house of the Russian parliament.

State Enrolled Nurse *noun* in Britain, a nurse who is qualified to perform most of the tasks involved in practical nursing, junior in rank to a STATE REGISTERED NURSE.

statehouse /'stayt·hows/ *noun* **1** the building in which a US state legislature sits. **2** *NZ* a private house owned and rented out by the government.

stateless *adj* not recognized as a citizen of any country; having no nationality: *a stateless person*. ➤➤ **statelessness** *noun*.

stately *adj* (**statelier, stateliest**) **1** imposing; dignified: *stately language; stately bearing*. **2** impressive in size or proportions: *Here are still to be seen stately porticos; imposing staircases* — Charles Lamb. ➤➤ **stateliness** *noun*.

stately home *noun* *Brit* a large country residence, usu of historical or architectural interest and open to the public.

statement¹ *noun* **1** the act or an instance of stating something orally or in writing. **2** something that is stated; a declaration. **3** a formal account or narration: *I made a statement to the police*. **4** in grammar or linguistics, an assertion as distinct from a question, command, interjection, etc. **5** in philosophy, a PROPOSITION¹. **6** the presentation of a theme in a musical composition. **7** a summary of a financial account: *a monthly bank statement*. **8** a deliberate outward manifestation of a firm expression of feeling or attitude: *a fashion statement*. **9** the smallest meaningful self-contained unit of text in a computer program. **10** in Britain, an official assessment made of a child's special educational needs.

statement² *verb trans* to designate (a child) officially as having special educational needs.

statement-making *adj* said of style, fashion, etc: definitive, deliberately individual, and with a degree of panache.

statement of attainment *noun* *Brit* an individual programme of objectives in particular subjects designed to be achievable within a pupil's attainment levels.

statement of claim *noun* the initial pleading of the plaintiff in a High Court action, in which the allegation against the defendant is made.

state-of-the-art *adj* using the most advanced technology available at the present time: *a state-of-the-art hi-fi system*.

state prisoner *noun* a person imprisoned for political reasons; = PRISONER OF STATE.

stater /'staytə/ *noun* any of various ancient gold or silver coins of the Greek city-states. [Middle English via late Latin from Greek *statēr*, literally 'a unit of weight', from *histanai* to cause to stand, weigh]

State Registered Nurse *noun* in Britain, a nurse who is fully qualified to perform all the tasks involved in nursing, senior in rank to a STATE ENROLLED NURSE: compare REGISTERED GENERAL NURSE.

stateroom *noun* **1** a large room in a palace or similar building for use on ceremonial occasions. **2** a private cabin in a ship, *esp* a large comfortable one.

States *pl noun* (**the States**) (*treated as sing. or pl*) the USA.

state school *noun* a British school that is publicly financed and provides compulsory free education.

state's evidence *noun* *NAmer* evidence for the prosecution in criminal proceedings, given by a participant or accomplice in the crime.

States General *pl noun* **1** the assembly of the three French estates, that is, clergy, nobility, and burghers, before 1789 and the Revolution. **2** the legislature of the Netherlands from the 15th cent. to 1796.

stateside *adj and adv* chiefly *NAmer, informal* in or to the USA: *Cajun chicken and other delights of stateside cuisine; The band is causing a buzz stateside*.

statesman *or* **stateswoman** *noun* (*pl* **statesmen** *or* **stateswomen**) an experienced political leader, *esp* one who has come to be respected for shrewd judgment uncontaminated by party political considerations. ➤➤ **statesmanlike** *adj*, **statesmanly** *adj*, **statesmanship** *noun*.

state socialism *noun* a political system in which the government controls industry and services. ➤➤ **state socialist** *noun*.

states' rights *pl noun* in the USA, all rights not vested by the Constitution in the federal government nor forbidden by it to the individual states.

state trial *noun* a trial brought by the state for offences against it.

state trooper *noun* in the USA, a state police officer.

statewide *adj and adv* in the USA, throughout the state in question: *a statewide contest; Statewide, he got 50% of the Republican vote*.

static¹ /'statik/ *adj* **1** characterized by a lack of movement, animation, progression, or change: *a static population; a rather static performance*. **2** standing or fixed in one place; stationary. **3** exerting force by reason of weight alone without motion: *static load; static pressure*. **4** of or relating to bodies at rest or forces in equilibrium: compare DYNAMIC¹ (1A). **5** relating to or producing stationary charges of electricity; electrostatic. **6** said of computer memory: using devices that will preserve the stored information indefinitely without the need for any periodic attention or adjustment. ➤➤ **statically** *adv*. [scientific Latin *staticus* from Greek *statikos* causing to stand, skilled in weighing, from *histanai* to cause to stand, weigh]

static² *noun* **1** electrical disturbances causing unwanted signals in a radio or television system; atmospherics. **2** short for STATIC ELECTRICITY. **3** *NAmer* angry interchanges or behaviour.

-static *comb. form* forming adjectives, with the meanings: **1** causing the slowing or inhibition of something: *bacteriostatic*. **2** regulating something or maintaining it in a steady state: *thermostatic; homoeostatic*.

statice /'statisi/ *noun* = SEA LAVENDER. [Latin *statice*, former genus name, ultimately from Greek *statikē*, fem of *statikos* causing to stand, astringent (see STATIC¹); because the plant was used to staunch blood]

static electricity *noun* a stationary electrical charge as distinct from a current, usu caused by friction, producing sparks or crackling, and attracting hair and dust.

static line *noun* a cord attaching a parachute pack to an aircraft, to open the parachute after the person jumping is clear of the craft, as an alternative to a RIP CORD.

statics *pl noun* (*treated as sing. or pl*) a branch of mechanics dealing with the relations of forces that produce equilibrium among solid bodies.

statin /'statin/ *noun* any of a group of drugs designed to lower cholesterol levels in the blood.

station¹ /'staysh(ə)n/ *noun* **1** a regular or major stopping place for trains, buses, etc,, with e.g. platforms for boarding and alighting, and associated buildings with passenger facilities, etc. **2** the place or position in which something or somebody stands or is assigned to stand or remain: *Remain at your stations*. **3** a post or sphere of duty or occupation. **4** a post or area to which a military or naval force is assigned. **5** *Aus, NZ* a stock farm or ranch. **6** *dated* standing; rank: *your station in life.* **7** a place for specialized observation and study of scientific phenomena: *a marine biology station.* **8** a place established to provide a public service: *a petrol station.* **9** a fire station or police station. **10** an establishment equipped for radio or television transmission or reception. **11** a radio or television channel. ✻ **stations of the cross** a series of representations in painting, sculpture, etc, of incidents in the progress of Christ as he carried his cross from Pilate's house to Calvary. [Middle English via Old French from Latin *station-, statio* a standing still, a place where one stands, from *stare* to stand]

station² *verb trans* to assign (somebody) to a post or station: *He is stationed in Bahrain.*

stationary /'stayshən(ə)ri/ *adj* **1** having a fixed position; immobile: *a stationary caravan.* **2** = GEOSTATIONARY. **3** unchanging in condition; neither progressing nor deteriorating: *In learning and development children tend to alternate between stationary phases and phases of rapid progress.* [Latin *stationarius* stationed at a post, from *station-, statio*: see STATION¹]

Usage note
stationary or stationery? These two words, which are pronounced the same, are often confused. *Stationary* is the adjective meaning 'standing still': *a stationary vehicle. Stationery* refers to the type of goods sold by a *stationer* (which is perhaps the easiest way of remembering the difference in spelling): paper, envelopes and the like.

stationary bicycle *noun* = EXERCISE BIKE.

stationary orbit *noun* the orbit of a GEOSTATIONARY satellite in the plane of the orbited body's equator, the path and speed of which keep it above the same point on the orbited body.

stationary point *noun* on a graph, a point on a curve where the tangent is parallel to the horizontal axis, that is, where the gradient is zero, as at a turning point.

stationary wave *noun* = STANDING WAVE.

station bill *noun* a list assigning members of a ship's crew to their official stations.

station break *noun NAmer* a break between broadcast programmes during which an announcement naming the transmitting station is made.

stationer *noun* a shopkeeper who deals in stationery. [via Middle English *staciouner* from late Latin *stationarius* a tradesman at a fixed stall, from *station-, statio* stall: see STATION¹]

stationery /'stayshən(ə)ri/ *noun* **1** materials used for writing, typing, etc; office supplies. **2** paper and envelopes for letter writing: *personalized stationery.* [from STATIONER]

Usage note
stationery or stationary? See note at STATIONARY.

station hand *noun Aus, NZ* a worker on a large sheep farm or cattle ranch.

station house *noun NAmer* the main building of a police station or fire station.

station-keeping *noun* the act or an instance of maintaining a ship's allotted position in a fleet that is on the move.

stationmaster *noun* an official in charge of a railway station.

station-pointer *noun* a navigational device that determines a ship's position relative to two prominent objects, e.g. two landmarks.

station wagon *noun chiefly NAmer* = ESTATE CAR.

statism /'staytiz(ə)m/ *noun* concentration of economic controls and planning in the hands of the state. ➤➤ **statist** *noun and adj.*

statistic /stə'tistik/ *noun* **1** a single term or quantity in or computed from a collection of statistics. **2** a numerical value, e.g. the standard deviation or mean, used in describing and analysing data. [back-formation from STATISTICS]

statistical *adj* relating to statistics. ➤➤ **statistically** *adv.*

statistical mechanics *pl noun (treated as sing. or pl)* a branch of mechanics dealing with the application of the principles of statistics to the mechanics of a system consisting of a large number of particles having motions that differ only in discrete steps over a large range.

statistical significance *noun* the extent to which the result of a statistical investigation can be held genuinely to represent a trend as distinct from reflecting mere random variation or disproportionate sampling.

statistician /stati'stish(ə)n/ *noun* **1** a person who compiles statistics. **2** a specialist in the principles and methods of statistics.

statistics *pl noun* **1** *(treated as sing. or pl)* a branch of mathematics dealing with the collection, analysis, interpretation, and presentation of masses of numerical data. **2** *(treated as pl)* a collection of quantitative data. [German *Statistik* study of political facts and figures, from modern Latin *statisticus* relating to politics, from Latin *status* state]

stative /'staytiv/ *adj* denoting a verb that expresses a bodily or mental state, and typically is not used in the continuous tenses, such as *be, like, hate, believe, know,* as opposed to one expressing an action or event, such as *go, fly, happen.* [Latin *stativus* standing still, from *status* past part. of *stare* to stand]

stato- *comb. form* forming words, denoting: equilibrium or statics: *statolith.* [Greek *statos* stationary, from *histasthai* to stand]

statocyst /'statohsist/ *noun* an organ of balance occurring *esp* in invertebrate animals and consisting usu of a liquid-filled sac in which are suspended chalky particles.

statolith /'statohlith/ *noun* **1** any of the chalky particles in a statocyst. **2** any of various solid bodies, e.g. starch grains, in the CYTOPLASM (jellylike material) of plant cells that may be responsible by changes in their position for changes in orientation of a part or organ.

stator /'staytə/ *noun* a stationary part in a machine in or about which a rotor revolves. [from STATIONARY on the model of ROTOR]

statoscope /'statəskohp/ *noun* an instrument for indicating small changes in the altitude of an aircraft.

stats /stats/ *pl noun informal* statistics.

statuary¹ /'statyooəri/ *noun (pl* **statuaries)** **1** statues collectively. **2** *formal* the fashioning of statues. **3** *archaic* a sculptor.

statuary² *adj* relating to or suitable for statues: *statuary marble.*

statue /'statyooh, 'stachooh/ *noun* a likeness, e.g. of a person or animal, sculptured, cast, or modelled in a solid material, e.g. bronze or stone. [Middle English via Old French from Latin *statua,* from *statuere* to set up, from *status*: see STATUS]

statuesque /statyoo'esk/ *adj* resembling a statue in dignity, formal beauty, or stately size or deportment: *Though long and expansive, her neck certainly showed more cords and cavities than consorted with his vague ideal of statuesque beauty* — Harold Frederic. ➤➤ **statuesquely** *adv,* **statuesqueness** *noun.*

statuette /statyoo'et/ *noun* a small statue: *He found in a curiosity shop a grotesque little statuette in ivory* — Henry James.

stature /'stachə/ *noun* **1** the natural height of a person when standing upright: *a man of middling stature.* **2** standing or reputation: *her growing political stature.* **3** status: *an essay on the scientific stature of psychoanalysis.* [Middle English, via Old French from Latin *statura* height, growth, from *status*: see STATUS]

status /'staytəs/ *noun* **1** the condition or standing of a person, territory, etc in the eyes of the law: *The status of the Isle of Man could best be described as intermediate between a colony and a dominion.* **2** position or rank in relation to others in a hierarchy or social structure: *The century has seen a significant improvement in the status of women.* **3** high social position; prestige: *In their own country they had enjoyed status and prosperity.* **4** a state of affairs; the situation in regard to something: *marital status.* [Latin *status* standing, condition, past part. of *stare* to stand]

status epilepticus /epi'leptikəs/ *noun* a condition in which epileptic fits follow one after the other without the patient recovering consciousness between them. [scientific Latin, from Latin *status* condition (see STATUS) + Greek *epilēpticus* from *epilēpsia*: see EPILEPSY]

status quo /kwoh/ *noun* the existing state of affairs: *Accept the status quo.* [Latin *status quo,* literally 'the state in which']

status quo ante /'anti/ *noun* the previous situation; things as they were before. [Latin *status quo ante,* literally 'the state in which formerly']

status symbol *noun* a possession recognized as indicating high social status or wealth: *A jet-ski was the current must-have status symbol.*

statutable /'statyootəbl/ *adj dated* recognized in statute law; legally punishable; = STATUTORY: *Hoaxing is not a statutable offence* — Daily Telegraph.

statute /'statyooht/ *noun* **1** a law passed by a legislative body: *the statutes on immigration.* **2** any of the permanent rules of an organization: *the statutes of the University of Oxford.* **3** *archaic* a decree of God or of a king: *Abraham ... kept ... my commandments, my statutes, and my laws* — Bible. [Middle English, via Old French *statut* from late Latin *statutum* law, regulation, neuter past part. of *statuere* to set up, from *status*: see STATUS]

statute-barred *adj* in the English legal system, said *esp* of a debt claim: no longer enforceable because the prescribed period of time for enforcement has elapsed.

statute book *noun* (**the statute book**) the whole body of legislation of a given jurisdiction.

statute law *noun* enacted written law: compare COMMON LAW, EQUITY (2).

statute mile *noun* a legal term for a MILE of 1760yds.

statute of limitations *noun* a statute stipulating a time after which rights cannot be enforced or offences punished.

statutes at large *pl noun chiefly NAmer* the country's statutes as originally drawn up.

statutory /'statyoot(ə)ri/ *adj* **1** recognized by statute. **2** established, regulated, or imposed by or in conformity to statute: *a statutory age limit.* **3** *humorous* obligatory through long use or tradition: *statutory Christmas fare.* ⟫ **statutorily** /-t(ə)rəli/ *adv.*

statutory instrument *or formerly* **statutory order** *noun* an official document recording any law which has been made by a minister exercising their delegated legislative powers and which has not gone through parliament.

statutory rape *noun* in US law, sexual intercourse with a girl who is below the statutory age of consent.

statutory tenant *noun* a person legally permitted to remain in a property after the lapse of their tenancy.

staunch[1] (*NAmer* **stanch**) /stawnch, stahnch/ *verb trans* **1** to stop the flow of (blood, etc). **2** to stop the flow of blood from (a wound). ⟫ **staunchable** *adj,* **stauncher** *noun.* [Middle English from Old French *estanchier* to stop the flow of, from *estanc* dried up]

staunch[2] *adj* **1** steadfast in loyalty or principle: *staunch supporters.* **2** said of a wall: sturdily constructed. **3** (*also* **stanch** /stahnch, stawnch/) *archaic* said of a ship: watertight. ⟫ **staunchly** *adv,* **staunchness** *noun.* [Middle English from Old French *estanche*, fem of *estanc* dried up]

stave[1] /stayv/ *noun* **1** an iron pole or wooden stick; = STAFF[1] (3). **2** any of the narrow strips of wood or iron placed edge to edge to form the sides, covering, or lining of a barrel, bucket, or other vessel or structure. **3** a supporting bar, e.g. a crosspiece in a chair, or the rung of a ladder. **4** a verse or stanza of a poem. **5** a set of five horizontal spaced lines on and between which music is written. [back-formation from *staves*, pl of STAFF[1]]

stave[2] *verb trans* (*past tense and past part.* **staved** *or* **stove** /stohv/) **1** (+ in) to crush or break (a hard casing, etc) inward: *The steering wheel stove his chest in.* **2** to fit (a chair, etc) with staves.

stave off *verb trans* to ward or fend off (a threatening ill), *esp* temporarily: *This chocolate bar will stave off hunger.*

staves *noun* pl of STAFF[1] (3), (8).

stavesacre /'stayvzaykə/ *noun* **1** a Eurasian larkspur, once used as an insecticide: *Delphinium staphisagria.* **2** the poisonous seeds of this plant, which have an emetic and laxative effect. [by folk etymology from Middle English *staphisagre*, via late Latin from Greek *staphis agria* wild raisin, from *staphis* dried grapes, raisins + *agrios* wild]

stay[1] /stay/ *verb intrans* **1** to remain in a place and not move. **2** to remain in a particular state and not change: *Stay calm.* **3** to reside temporarily somewhere: *I'm staying with my aunt.* **4** *Scot, SAfr* to dwell permanently somewhere: *He stays in Edinburgh.* **5** to remain somewhere so as to be included in some activity: *Stay for dinner.* **6** in racing, to keep going, or keep up: *He's staying with the leaders.* **7** *archaic* to stop or pause. **8** *archaic* to wait: *He will stay till you come* — Shakespeare. ⟩ *verb trans* **1** to remain (a certain time) somewhere: *Stay the night.* **2** to last out (a race or the course). **3** *archaic* to halt the progress of (a disease). **4** to delay or prevent (a judicial procedure, such as an execution). **5** *archaic or literary* to stop (a person) from doing something. ✳ **stay put** to stay where placed or left. **stay somebody's hand** *literary* to stop somebody acting: *the childish dread which had hitherto stayed my hand* — Poe. [Middle English via Old French *ester* from Latin *stare* to stand]

stay[2] *noun* **1** a period of residing at a place. **2** the suspension of a judicial procedure: *a stay of execution.*

stay[3] *noun* a strong rope, now usu of wire, used to support a ship's mast or similar tall structure, e.g. a flagstaff. ✳ **be in stays** said of a sailing ship: to have its head into the wind while tacking. **miss stays** said of a sailing ship: to fail in going about from one tack to another. [Old English *stæg*]

stay[4] *verb trans* to support (a mast, chimney, etc) with stays.

stay[5] *noun* **1** *literary* somebody or something that serves as a prop; a support: *Who like thyself my guide and stay can be?* — H F Lyle. **2** (*in pl*) formerly, a corset stiffened with bones. [Old French *estaie* wooden brace, of Germanic origin]

stay[6] *verb trans* to sustain or provide physical or moral support for (somebody): *Stay me with flagons* — Bible.

stay-at-home *noun* **1** a person who prefers to remain in their own home, locality, or country. **2** (*used before a noun*) denoting such a person: *a stay-at-home mum.*

stayer *noun* **1** a racehorse that habitually stays the course. **2** a person who has the stamina and willpower to keep going.

staying power *noun informal* stamina.

stay on *verb intrans* to remain in a place, *esp* after the expected time limit, or after others have left.

stay over *verb intrans* to stay the night.

staysail /'staysayl, 'stays(ə)l/ *noun* a FORE-AND-AFT sail (one aligned from bow to stern) hoisted on a stay.

stay stitching *noun* a line of stitches sewn round an edge, e.g. a neckline, before making up a garment in order to prevent the cloth from stretching.

stay up *verb intrans* not to go to bed.

stay-ups *pl noun* hold-ups (see HOLDUP (3)).

STD *abbr* **1** Doctor of Sacred Theology. **2** sexually transmitted disease. **3** subscriber trunk dialling. [(sense 1) Latin *sacrae theologiae doctor*]

std *abbr* standard.

STD code *noun* a set of four or more digits dialled before the subscriber's local telephone number, that determine the routeing of a call.

Ste *abbr* used with female names in French: Sainte.

stead[1] /sted/ *noun* the office, place, or function ordinarily or formerly occupied or carried out by somebody or something else: *A new chairman was appointed in his stead.* ✳ **stand somebody in good stead** to be an advantage to somebody: *My languages stood me in good stead in my job abroad.* [Old English *stede* place]

stead[2] *verb trans archaic* to be of service to (somebody): *May you stead me? Will you pleasure me?* — Shakespeare.

steadfast /'stedfahst, 'stedfəst/ *adj* **1** firmly fixed; steady or immovable: *a steadfast gaze.* **2** not subject to change: *steadfast determination.* **3** said of a person: loyal or unwavering: *her steadfast supporters.* ⟫ **steadfastly** *adv,* **steadfastness** *noun.* [Old English *stedefæst* standing firm]

Steadicam /'stedikam/ *noun trademark* a body harness with weights, on which to mount a hand-held film camera to keep it steady.

steading /'steding/ *noun Scot, N Eng* a small farm; a farmstead. [Middle English *steding*, from Old English *stede* place, farm]

steady[1] /'stedi/ *adj* (**steadier, steadiest**) **1** firmly positioned or balanced; not shaking, rocking, etc. **2** direct or sure in movement; unfaltering: *a steady hand.* **3** showing or continuing with little variation or fluctuation; stable or uniform: *a steady breeze; steady prices.* **4** not easily moved or upset; calm: *steady nerves.* **5** constant and dependable; consistent; not erratic: *a steady worker; steady progress.* **6** *dated* not given to dissipation; sober: *a steady lad.* ⟫ **steadily** *adv,* **steadiness** *noun.* [Middle English, from STEAD[1] + -Y[1]]

steady[2] *verb* (**steadies, steadied, steadying**) ⟩ *verb intrans* to keep or become steady: *Her racing heart slowed and steadied.* ⟩ *verb trans* to make (somebody or something) steady or steadier: *She put a hand on the banister to steady herself.* ⟫ **steadier** *noun.*

steady[3] *adv* used *esp* by sailors: in a steady manner; steadily: *Steady as she goes!* ✳ **go steady** *informal* to have a long-term relationship with a boyfriend or girlfriend. **steady on!** used to tell somebody to calm down.

steady[4] *noun* (*pl* **steadies**) *informal* a boyfriend or girlfriend with whom one has a long-term relationship.

steady-going *adj* said of a person: level-headed, sober, and sensible: *The life of a quiet, steady-going undergraduate has been told in a score of novels* — Samuel Butler.

steady state *noun* in physics, a dynamically balanced state or condition of a system or process that tends to remain when once achieved.

steady-state theory *noun* a theory of the universe postulating that it has always existed and has always been expanding with CONTINUOUS CREATION of matter: compare BIG BANG THEORY.

steak /stayk/ *noun* **1a** a slice of meat cut from a fleshy part, e.g. the rump, of a beef carcass and suitable for grilling or frying. **b** a poorer-quality, less tender beef cut, usu from the neck and shoulder, suitable for braising or stewing. **2** a thick slice of any meat, *esp* pork or gammon. **3** a cross-sectional slice from between the centre and tail of a large fish: compare CUTLET (2). [Middle English *steke* from Old Norse *steik*]

steakhouse /'stayk·hows/ *noun* a restaurant where the speciality is steaks.

steak tartare /tah'tah/ *noun* uncooked steak mince mixed with raw egg and onion and seasoned. [French *tartare* Tartar-style]

steal[1] /steel/ *verb* (*past tense* **stole** /stohl/, *past part.* **stolen** /'stohlən/) ➤ *verb trans* **1** to take (something) without permission or illegally, with no intention of returning it. **2** to use (someone else's ideas, work, material, etc) without acknowledgment, so passing them off as one's own. **3** to take (a look, etc) surreptitiously: *He stole a glance at his wristwatch.* **4a** to gain (an advantage over a rival, etc) by getting the better of them. **b** in sport, to get (the ball or possession of it, a run, point, goal, etc) by catching one's opponent out. **5** in baseball, to run and get to (a base) while the pitcher is delivering the ball to the batter. ➤ *verb intrans* **1** to take someone else's property dishonestly or illegally: *accused of stealing.* **2** to come or go stealthily or unobtrusively: *He had stolen into the room without her noticing.* ✳ **steal a march on** to outdo (somebody) without their realizing what is happening till too late: *He evidently intended to steal a march upon me, and smuggle a fine picture to New York, under my very nose; expecting me to know nothing of the matter* — Poe. **steal somebody's thunder** to anticipate or preempt somebody's words or actions, thus lessening or destroying their effect. **steal somebody's heart** *literary* to charm or beguile somebody, *esp* into falling in love with one. **steal the show** to make a bigger and better impression than other ostensibly more prominent participants. ➤➤ **stealer** *noun*. [Old English *stelan*]

steal[2] *noun* **1** *informal* a bargain: *It's a steal at £55.* **2** *chiefly NAmer.* **a** a theft. **b** something stolen, e.g. an idea: *The device was an obvious steal from Stoppard's 'Rosencrantz and Guildenstern'.* **3** in baseball, the act or an instance of stealing a base.

stealth /stelth/ *noun* **1** caution and surreptitiousness in movement or activity on the part of somebody trying to avoid detection. **2** (*used before a noun*) denoting aircraft or missiles so designed technologically as to be able to avoid acoustic or radar detection. [Middle English in the sense 'theft'; related to Old English *stelan* STEAL[1]]

stealth bomber *noun* a US military aircraft the design and advanced technology of which enable it to escape detection by radar or infra-red sensors.

stealthy *adj* (**stealthier, stealthiest**) characterized by stealth; cautious and furtive, so as to avoid detection: *stealthy footsteps; a stealthy glance at the clock.* ➤➤ **stealthily** *adv*, **stealthiness** *noun*.

steam[1] /steem/ *noun* **1** the vapour into which water is converted when heated to its boiling point. **2** the mist formed by the condensation of water vapour when cooled. **3** energy or power generated by steam under pressure. ✳ **full steam ahead** at maximum speed or pressure: *The conversion work is going full steam ahead.* **gather/get up/pick up steam** said of an activity: to gain speed and impetus. **have steam coming out of one's ears** *informal* to be absolutely furious. **let off/blow off steam** *informal* to release one's pent-up energy, emotional tension, etc. **under one's own steam** said of somebody journeying somewhere: using one's own means of travel or transport; not relying on a lift from somebody else; independently. [Old English *stēam*]

steam[2] *verb intrans* **1** to give off steam or vapour: *The pavements steamed in the sun.* **2** to move by means of steam power: *The 2.30 Cambridge-to-Ely steamed past; We steamed out of the harbour.* **3** *informal* to move or progress quickly: *She's steaming ahead with her research.* **4** to undergo cooking by steam: *The Christmas pudding was steaming on the stove.* **5** (+ up) said of a glass surface: to become

covered with condensed steam: *Her glasses steamed up in the hot kitchen.* ➤ *verb trans* **1** to cook (food) in steam from boiling water. **2** (+ off/open) to apply steam to (something stuck with gum, etc) in order to soften the adhesive and release its hold: *She steamed the stamp off the envelope; He steamed open her letter.* **3** to expose (something, e.g. clothes for pressing) to steam. ✳ **get steamed up 1** said of glass, etc: to become covered with condensation. **2** *informal* to get angry or agitated: *There's no need to get steamed up about it.*

steam age *noun* (**the steam age**) the period during which trains were drawn by steam locomotives.

steam bath *noun* **1** a room, e.g. at a fitness centre, that can be filled with hot steam to induce sweating and clean and refresh the body. **2** a session in a steam bath.

steamboat *noun* a boat propelled by steam power, *esp* a US paddle-wheel river boat of the 19th cent.

steam boiler *noun* a vessel in which water is boiled to produce steam, *esp* in a steam engine.

steam chest *noun* the chamber from which steam is distributed to a cylinder of a steam engine.

steam distillation *noun* the act or an instance of distilling a liquid in a current of steam.

steamed *adj* **1** said of food: cooked by steaming: *steamed fish.* **2** *Brit, informal* helplessly drunk. **3** *chiefly NAmer, informal* irked or upset.

steam engine *noun* a stationary or locomotive engine driven or worked by steam.

steamer *noun* **1** a ship powered by steam. **2a** a saucepan for steaming food in. **b** a perforated metal device placed inside a saucepan for steaming food in. **3** a device for directing steam at clothing, etc, to remove creasing. **4** *informal* a diver's or canoeist's wetsuit.

steamer clam *noun* = SOFT-SHELL CLAM.

steamer duck *noun* a stocky grey, usu flightless, S American duck that uses its wings to churn up the water when it is escaping from danger: *Tachyeres brachypterus.*

steamer rug *noun NAmer, dated* a travelling rug, orig one for the use of steamer passengers sitting on deck.

steamer trunk *noun* a solidly constructed trunk of the kind formerly taken on board ship by steamer passengers.

steaming[1] *adj* **1** giving off steam: *plates of steaming soup.* **2** very hot or humid. **3** *Brit, informal* helplessly drunk. **4** *Brit, informal* furiously angry.

steaming[2] *noun informal* a method of robbery whereby a gang of thieves rush through a crowded public place stealing what they can from people on the way.

steam iron *noun* an electric iron with a compartment holding water that is converted to steam by the iron's heat and emitted through the soleplate onto the fabric being pressed.

steam jacket *noun* a hollow steam-filled casing for a cylinder, used to heat its contents.

steam organ *noun* a fairground organ operated by steam, played either by a keyboard or by a punched tape that feeds itself through.

steam point *noun* the temperature (100°C) at which the maximum vapour pressure of water is equal to one atmosphere.

steam radio *noun humorous* radio regarded as antiquated in comparison with television.

steamroll *verb trans* see STEAMROLLER[2].

steamroller[1] *noun* a machine equipped with wide heavy rollers for compacting newly laid tarmacadam, etc.

steamroller[2] *or* **steamroll** *verb trans* (**steamrollered** *or* **steamrolled, steamrollering** *or* **steamrolling**) **1** said of a legislative body, etc: to force acceptance of (a measure) by crushing opposition or curtailing discussion. **2** to force (somebody) into acquiescence or into doing something: *Don't let them steamroller you into making a decision before you're ready.*

steamship *noun* a steam-powered ship; a steamer.

steam shovel *noun* a steam-driven mechanical excavator consisting of a bucket operating from a long beam.

steam turbine *noun* a turbine driven by the pressure of steam against the turbine blades.

steamy *adj* (**steamier, steamiest**) **1** full of steam. **2** hot and humid: *a steamy atmosphere.* **3** *informal* said of fiction, films, etc:

portraying sexual activity; erotic: *a steamy thriller.* ➤➤ **steamily** *adv,* **steaminess** *noun.*

steapsin /sti'apsin/ *noun* the LIPASE (enzyme that promotes the breakdown of fats) in the digestive juice produced by the pancreas. [Greek *stear* fat + *-psin* on the pattern of PEPSIN]

stearate /'stiərayt/ *noun* a salt or ESTER (compound produced by reaction between acid and alcohol) of stearic acid.

stearic /'stiərik, sti'arik/ *adj* **1** relating to, obtained from, or resembling stearin or tallow. **2** of stearic acid: *stearic esters.* [French *stéarique,* from Greek *stear* fat]

stearic acid *noun* a fatty acid that is obtained from hard fat, e.g. tallow, with salts that are used in soap manufacture; formula $C_{18}H_{36}O_2$. [French *stéarique,* from Greek *stear* fat]

stearin *or* **stearine** /'stiərin/ *noun* **1** an ESTER (compound produced by reaction between acid and alcohol) of glycerol and stearic acid. **2** the solid portion of a fat. [French *stéarine,* from Greek *stear* fat]

steat- *or* **steato-** *comb. form* forming words, denoting: fat: *steatopygia.* [Greek *steat-, stear* fat]

steatite /'stee-ətiet/ *noun* the mineral TALC[1] in solid form; = SOAPSTONE. ➤➤ **steatitic** /-'titik/ *adj.* [via Latin from Greek *steatitis* or *steatitēs* (*lithos*) tallow-like (stone), from *steat-, stear* fat]

steato- *comb. form* see STEAT-.

steatolysis /stee-ə'toləsis/ *noun* the digestive process by which fats are emulsified and converted into glycerine and fatty acids.

steatopygia /,stee-ətoh'piji-ə/ *noun* a substantial development of fat on the buttocks, common among the Khoikhoi people, and other peoples of arid areas of S Africa. ➤➤ **steatopygic** /-jik/ *adj,* **steatopygous** /-'topigəs, -'piegəs/ *adj.* [STEATO- + Greek *pygē* rump, buttocks]

steatorrhoea *or* **steatorrhea** /,stee-ətə'riə/ *noun* an excess of fat in the faeces.

steatosis /stee-ə'tohsis/ *noun* a metabolic disorder resulting in the infiltration of the liver cells with fat.

steed /steed/ *noun archaic or literary* a swift or spirited horse, *esp* as a mount: *the Duke, great Bolingbroke, mounted upon a hot and fiery steed* — Shakespeare. [Old English *stēda* stallion; related to *stōd* STUD[3]]

steel[1] /steel, stiəl/ *noun* **1** a bluish grey alloy of iron with carbon, notable for its strength and hardness, distinguished from cast iron by its malleability under certain conditions, and widely used in construction work. **2** cold hardness or unyielding strength: *a heart of steel; nerves of steel.* **3** an instrument or implement of steel, e.g.: **a** a tool, e.g. a ridged rod with a handle, for sharpening knives. **b** a piece of steel for striking sparks from flint. **c** *literary* a sword or dagger: *And as he plucked his cursed steel away, mark how the blood of Caesar follow'd it* — Shakespeare. **4** *literary* a suit of armour: *clad in compleat steel* — Milton. [Old English *stýle, stēle*]

steel[2] *adj* **1** made of steel: *steel girders.* **2** like steel in being cold and hard: *thy steel bosom* — Shakespeare.

steel[3] *verb trans* **1** to overlay, point, or edge (something) with steel. **2** (*often* + against) to harden (one's heart, etc): *She looked so irresistibly beautiful … that no man alive could have steeled his heart against her* — Wilkie Collins. **3** to fill (somebody's heart) with resolve: *O God of battles, steel my soldiers' hearts* — Shakespeare. **4** to nerve (oneself) to do something: *I had steeled myself to brazen it out* — Jack London.

steel band *noun* a band of Caribbean origin that plays steel drums. ➤➤ **steelbandsman** *noun.*

steel blue *noun* **1** a dark greyish blue colour. **2** any of the blue colours assumed by steel at various temperatures in tempering. ➤➤ **steel-blue** *adj.*

steel drum *noun* a drum-like percussion instrument, orig made in Trinidad, consisting of an oil drum with one end beaten into facets giving a range of notes.

steel engraving *noun* **1** the engraving of a design into a steel plate. **2** a print taken from an engraved steel plate.

steel grey *noun* a dark bluish grey colour. ➤➤ **steel-grey** *adj.*

steel guitar *noun* a guitar with steel strings on which a glissando effect is produced by sliding a metal bar along the strings while plucking them; = HAWAIIAN GUITAR.

steelhead *noun* a large N American migratory rainbow trout: *Salmo gairdneri.*

steel pan *noun* = STEEL DRUM.

steel wool *noun* long fine loosely compacted steel fibres used for scouring and burnishing.

steelworks *pl noun* (*treated as sing. or pl*) a factory where steel is made. ➤➤ **steelworker** *noun.*

steely /'steeli/ *adj* (**steelier, steeliest**) *chiefly literary* resembling steel in hardness, strength, colour, or brightness: *the steely sea* — Joseph Conrad; *His eyes shone out with a steely glitter* — Conan Doyle. ➤➤ **steeliness** *noun.*

steelyard *noun* a balance in which an object to be weighed is suspended from the shorter arm of a lever and the weight determined by moving a counterbalance along a graduated scale on the longer arm until equilibrium is attained. [STEEL[2] + YARD[1] in the sense 'rod']

steenbok /'steenbok, 'staynbok/ *or* **steinbok** /'stienbok, 'steenbok/ *or* **steenbuck** /'steenbuk, 'staynbuk/ *noun* a small antelope of S and E Africa with straight upright horns, a reddish brown coat, and a small tail and ears: *Raphiceros campestris.* [Afrikaans *steenbok,* from Dutch *steen* stone + *bok* buck]

steep[1] /steep/ *adj* **1** sloping sharply, or nearly vertical: *a steep hill.* **2** said of a rise or fall in an amount, level, etc: substantial and rapid: *a steep drop in living standards.* **3** *informal* said of a price: unreasonably high. **4** *informal.* **a** said of a request, condition, etc: excessive; difficult to comply with: *That's a bit steep.* **b** said of a story: difficult to credit; far-fetched. ➤➤ **steepish** *adj,* **steeply** *adv,* **steepness** *noun.* [Old English *stēap* high, steep, deep]

steep[2] *noun chiefly literary* a steep mountain slope; a precipice: *the almost inaccessible steeps which form the base of the vast and rugged mountain of Cruachan* — Scott.

steep[3] *verb trans* **1** to soak (something) in a liquid, e.g. for softening, cleansing, bleaching, or extracting an essence: *Steep the whites before washing.* **2** (*usu in passive,* + in) to imbue (somebody) thoroughly with a subject, influence, etc: *The most fecundating minds … have been steeped in and saturated with Greek literature* — J R Lowell. ➤ *verb intrans* to undergo the process of soaking in a liquid: *Leave the shirt to steep overnight.* ➤➤ **steeper** *noun.* [Middle English, of Germanic origin]

steep[4] *noun* **1** the act or an instance of steeping. **2** a liquid for steeping things in, or a tank containing this.

steepen *verb* (**steepened, steepening**) ➤ *verb intrans* to become steeper. ➤ *verb trans* to make (an incline, etc) steeper.

steeple /'steepl/ *noun* **1** a church tower with a spire. **2** a spire surmounting the tower of a church, or rising directly from its roof: compare SPIRE[1]. **3** *archaic* a tower on a church or other building. ➤➤ **steepled** *adj.* [Old English *stēpel* tower]

steeplechase *noun* **1a** a horse race over a racecourse with hedges and ditches for jumping: compare FLAT RACE, HURDLE[1] (2B). **b** *archaic* a horse race across country with hedges, walls, ditches, etc to jump. **2** a middle-distance running race over obstacles, strictly one of 3000m over 28 hurdles and seven water jumps. ➤➤ **steeplechaser** *noun,* **steeplechasing** *noun.* [from the use of church steeples as landmarks to guide the riders]

steeple-crowned *adj* said of a hat: having a tall pointed crown.

steeplejack *noun* a person who climbs chimneys, towers, etc to paint, repair, or demolish them.

steer[1] /stiə/ *verb trans* **1** to guide or control the course or direction of (a vehicle or ship): *He steered the ship into harbour.* **2** to guide or channel (people or things) in a certain direction: *She steered the guests into the dining room; Try to steer the conversation away from sensitive topics.* ➤ *verb intrans* **1** to direct the course of a vehicle or ship. **2** (*usu* + for) to pursue a particular course: *We decided to steer for home.* **3** said of a vehicle: to be easy, difficult, etc to steer: *The new car steers wonderfully.* ✱ **steer a/one's course for** to navigate in the direction of (a place): *steering a course for Lisbon.* **steer clear of** to keep well away from (somebody or something) or give (them) a wide berth: *Wear strong colours – steer clear of pastel shades.* ➤➤ **steerability** /-'biliti/ *noun,* **steerable** *adj,* **steerer** *noun,* **steering** *noun.* [Old English *stīeran*]

steer[2] *noun informal* a piece of guidance or advice. ✱ **a bum steer** a misleading recommendation.

steer[3] *noun* an ox or bull castrated before sexual maturity; = BULLOCK. [Old English *stēor* young ox]

steerage /'stiərij/ *noun* **1** *archaic or literary* the act or an instance of steering a ship, or its direction: *But he that hath the steerage of my course direct my sail!* — Shakespeare. **2** formerly, a large section in a passenger ship for passengers paying the lowest fares: *To me it was … of no great consequence, whether I went in the cabin or in the steerage*

— Frederick Douglass. [(sense 2) from its orig being located near the rudder]

steerage-way *noun* a rate of forward motion sufficient to make a ship or boat respond to movements of the rudder.

steer-by-wire *noun* computer-assisted semi-automatic management of the engine and controls of a motor vehicle.

steering column *noun* the column that encloses the links between the steering wheel and the steering gear of a vehicle.

steering committee *noun* a committee that determines the order in which business will be taken up, e.g. in Parliament.

steering gear *noun* a mechanism by which something is steered.

steering group *noun* = STEERING COMMITTEE.

steering wheel *noun* a wheel that is turned by hand by a driver or helmsman to steer a motor vehicle, ship, etc.

steersman /'stiəzmən/ *noun* (*pl* **steersmen**) a helmsman.

steeve[1] /steev/ *noun* the angle that the bowsprit of a sailing vessel makes with the horizontal. [origin unknown]

steeve[2] *verb trans* to angle (the bowsprit).

steeve[3] *noun* a long spar used in stowing cargo. [French *estivar* or Spanish *estibar* to stow cargo, both from Latin *stipare* to pack tight]

stegosaur /'stegəsawr/ *or* **stegosaurus** /-'sawrəs/ *noun* (*pl* **stegosaurs** *or* **stegosauruses**) any of a large group of dinosaurs of the Jurassic and early Cretaceous periods, with a double row of strongly developed bony plates along the back. [scientific Latin *Stegosaurus*, from Greek *stegos* roof + *sauros* lizard]

stein /stien, shtien/ *noun* a large earthenware beer mug traditionally of German design, often with a hinged lid. [German *Stein* stone]

steinbok /'stienbok, 'steenbok/ *noun* see STEENBOK.

stela /'steelə/ *noun* (*pl* **stelae** /'steelie, 'steelee/) = STELE. [via Latin from Greek *stēlē*: see STELE]

stele /'steeli, steel/ *noun* 1 a usu carved or inscribed stone slab or pillar, sometimes used as a gravestone. 2 the cylindrical central region of food- and water-conducting tissue in the stem of a plant. ➤➤ **stelar** *adj*. [Greek *stēlē* standing block, gravestone]

stellar /'stelə/ *adj* 1 relating to a star or stars. 2 *chiefly NAmer, informal* relating to or featuring star performers: *a stellar line-up*. 3 *informal* said of profits, etc: enormous; astronomical. [late Latin *stellaris* from Latin *stella* star]

stellar wind *noun* a stream of charged particles flowing continuously from a star.

stellate /'stelət, 'stelayt/ *or* **stellated** /ste'laytid/ *adj* said of a flower or its petals: having a radiating shape, like a stylized star. [Latin *stella* star]

stelliform /'stelifawm/ *adj* star-shaped: *stelliform marine animals*. [Latin *stella* star + -IFORM]

stellular /'stelyoolə/ *adj esp* in mineralogy, having the form of a small star or small stars. ➤➤ **stellularly** *adv*. [late Latin *stellula*, dimin. of Latin *stella* star]

stem[1] /stem/ *noun* 1 the main stalk or trunk of a plant or shrub, from which the leaves and flowers develop. 2 the slender stalk of a flower, leaf, or fruit; = PEDICEL, PETIOLE. 3 a bunch of bananas. 4a the upright timber at the prow of a ship to which the sides are fixed. b the prow of a ship: compare STERN[2]. 5 a genealogical stock or line of ancestry, *esp* a main line from which others have branched: *And there shall come forth a rod out of the stem of Jesse* — Bible. 6 the main unchanging part of a word to which inflectional endings or other formative affixes are added. 7 a vertical stroke of a letter or musical note. 8 the tube of a tobacco pipe. 9 the slender support between the base and bowl of a wineglass. 10 a shaft of a watch used for winding. 11 the shaft of a bolt. ✳ **from stem to stern** with reference to a ship: from end to end: *A shudder shook the vessel from stem to stern*. ➤➤ **stemless** *adj*, **stemlike** *adj*. [Old English *stefn, stemn* stem of a plant or ship]

stem[2] *verb* (**stemmed, stemming**) ➤ *verb intrans formal* (+ from) to originate or arise from something: *Naturalistic evolution belongs to the category of knowledge ... and so resistance to it stems from ignorance* — Phillip E Johnson. ➤ *verb trans* 1 to remove the stems from (fruit, etc). 2 said of a ship: to make headway against (the tide or current). ➤➤ **stemmer** *noun*.

stem[3] *verb* (**stemmed, stemming**) ➤ *verb trans* 1 to stop (something flowing); STAUNCH[1]: *She tried to stem the bleeding*. 2 to stop (the onward progress of something): *They aim to stem the rising tide of crime*. 3 to turn (one's skis) heel outward in stemming. ➤ *verb*

intrans to retard oneself by forcing the heel of one or both skis outward from the line of progress. [Middle English *stemmen* to dam up, from Old Norse *stemma* to dam]

stem[4] *noun* in skiing, the action of forcing the heel of one or both skis outward in order to slow down.

stem cell *noun* an unspecialized cell, e.g. in bone marrow, that gives rise to differentiated cells, e.g. blood cells.

stem christie /'kristi/ *noun* a turn in skiing in which the back end of one ski is forced outward from the line of progress and the other ski is then brought parallel to it. [*christie* shortened from *Christiania*, former name of Oslo, capital of Norway]

stem ginger *noun* the underground part of the stem of a ginger plant, *esp* cut up and preserved in syrup or as crystallized pieces.

stemma /'stemə/ *noun* (*pl* **stemmata** /-tə/) 1 the recorded genealogy of a family; a family tree. 2 a diagram showing how a text relates to its various manuscript versions. 3 a simple eye present in some insects; = OCELLUS. [via Latin from Greek *stemma* wreath, pedigree (from the wreaths placed on ancestral images), from *stephein* to crown, enwreathe]

stemmatics /ste'matiks/ *pl noun* (*treated as sing.*) the study of the relationship between variant surviving texts of a work, *esp* so as to reconstruct a missing original.

stemmed *adj* (*used in combinations*) having a stem of the kind specified: *a thick-stemmed variety; long-stemmed glasses*.

stemple /'stempl/ *noun archaic* any of the crossbars serving as steps or supports in a mineshaft. [origin unknown]

stem stitch *noun* an embroidery stitch executed by overlapping stitches lengthways so as to form a narrow line, used for depicting plant stems.

stem turn *noun* a skiing turn executed by stemming the outside ski.

stemware *noun NAmer* wine glasses or other glasses with a stem.

stem-winder /'wiendə/ *noun NAmer* 1 a watch that can be wound by turning a knob on a stem, as distinct from one needing a key. 2 *informal* a rousing or inspiring speech.

Sten /sten/ *noun* a lightweight British submachine gun. [coined from the initials of the inventors, R V *Shepherd* and H J *Turpin*, and *Enfield*, district of London, site of the Royal Small Arms Factory, on the model of BREN GUN]

sten- *or* **steno-** *comb. form* forming words, with the meaning: narrow; contracted: *stenography*; *stenosis*. [Greek *stenos* narrow, close, scanty]

stench /stench/ *noun* a stink. [Old English *stenc* smell]

stencil[1] /'stens(ə)l/ *noun* 1 an impervious material, e.g. a sheet of paper or metal, perforated with a design or lettering through which a substance, e.g. ink or paint, is forced onto the surface below. 2 a sheet of strong tissue paper impregnated or coated, e.g. with paraffin or wax, for use *esp* in typing a stencil of a text, from which to produce copies. [Middle English *stanselen* to ornament with sparkling colours, from Old French *estanceler*, from *estancele* spark, ultimately from Latin *scintilla*]

stencil[2] *verb trans* (**stencilled, stencilling**, *NAmer* **stenciled, stenciling**) 1 to produce (a design, etc) by means of a stencil. 2 to decorate (a surface) with a stencil. ➤➤ **stenciller** *noun*.

steno- *comb. form* see STEN-.

stenography /stə'nogrəfi/ *noun* the writing and transcription of shorthand. ➤➤ **stenographer** *noun*, **stenographic** /stenə'grafik/ *adj*, **stenographically** /stenə'grafikli/ *adv*.

stenohaline /stenoh'haylien, -leen/ *adj* said of an aquatic organism: unable to withstand wide variation in the amount of salt present in the surrounding water. [STENO- + Greek *halinos* of salt, from *hals* salt]

stenosis /sti'nohsis/ *noun* (*pl* **stenoses** /-seez/) a narrowing or constriction of the diameter of a bodily passage or orifice. ➤➤ **stenosed** /'stenohzd, 'stenohst/ *adj*, **stenotic** /sti'notik/ *adj*. [scientific Latin from Greek *stenōsis* act of narrowing, from *stenoun* to narrow, from *stenos* narrow]

stenothermal /stenoh'thuhml/ *adj* said of an organism: unable to withstand a wide variation in temperature.

stenotype /'stenətiep/ *noun trademark* a small machine rather like a typewriter, used to record speech by means of shorthand characters representing phonemes. ➤➤ **stenotypist** *noun*, **stenotypy** /-pi, stə'notipi/ *noun*.

stent[1] /stent/ *noun* a splint fitted inside a vessel of the body, e.g. a duct or blood vessel, to ease obstruction or expedite healing. [orig denoting a substance invented by Charles *Stent* d.1885, English dentist, used to make dental impressions, also a cast or impression of a bodily cavity made with it, and used to maintain shape or pressure while healing; the current sense dates from the 1960s]

stent[2] *noun Scot* an assessment of property for tax purposes. [Middle English, from Old French *estente* valuation, related to *extente*: see EXTENT]

stent[3] *verb trans Scot* to assess (property) for tax purposes.

stenter /'stentə/ *noun* = TENTER. [from Middle English *stenten* to stretch out, set up a tent, shortened from *extenden*: see EXTEND]

stentor /'stentə/ *noun* **1** *literary* a person with a loud voice. **2** the name of a genus of sedentary protozoans (single-celled organisms; see PROTOZOAN) with a trumpet-shaped mouth: genus *Stentor*.

Word history
named after *Stentōr*, the Greek herald in the Trojan War. Homer claimed that Stentor could shout as loudly as 50 men put together.

stentorian /sten'tawri·ən/ *adj* said of a person's voice or delivery: extremely loud. [see STENTOR]

step[1] /step/ *noun* **1a** a movement made by raising one foot and bringing it down in front of the other in walking or running. **b** the space passed over in one step: *three steps to the left*. **c** a short distance: *just a step from the beach*. **d** in dancing, etc, a combination of foot movements constituting a unit or a repeated pattern: *Today we're going to learn a new step*. **e** one's manner of walking; one's stride: *He had a spring in his step*. **f** the sound of a footstep: *I heard steps in the hall*. **g** (*in pl*) one's course or way: *To the Three Jolly Bargemen, therefore, I directed my steps* — Dickens; *A solicitor ... kindly and carefully guided my steps, whenever the course of the narrative led me into the labyrinth of the law* — Wilkie Collins. **2a** (*also in pl*) a flat supporting surface for the foot in ascending or descending, *esp* one in a series; a stair: *a flight of steps; the bottom step*. **b** a rung of a ladder. **c** (*in pl*) a stepladder: *Could I borrow your steps?* **d** a doorstep: *The milk and papers were on the front step*. **e** in climbing, a foothold cut in an ice slope. **3a** a degree, grade, or rank in a scale: *It'll be another step up in my career*. **b** a stage in the progress of something: *Every step in the process was carefully monitored*. **c** (*also in pl*) an action, proceeding, or measure: *Marriage is a serious step; We are taking steps to improve the situation*. **4** in a yacht, etc, a socket designed to receive an upright spar; *esp* a block for supporting the base of a mast. **5** in physics, a sudden change in amount, e.g. of a voltage. **6** *chiefly NAmer* in music, an interval of one note in a scale; = TONE[1]. **7** = STEP AEROBICS. ✳ **in step 1** (*often* + with) with each foot moving to the same time as the corresponding foot of others, or in time to music. **2** (*often* + with) in harmony or agreement: *keep in step with fashion*. **out of step** (*often* + with) not in step: *She was out of step with her generation*. **step by step** little by little; gradually. **watch/mind one's step** to behave or proceed with caution. ➤➤ **steplike** *adj*. [Old English *stæpe, stepe*]

step[2] *verb* (**stepped, stepping**) ➤ *verb intrans* **1** to move by raising one foot and bringing it down in front of the other, or in another position. **2** (+ on) to tread hard on something: *to step on the brake*. **3** (*often* + into) to progress as though in one simple step: *step into a good job*. ➤ *verb trans* **1** to take (a certain number of paces): *Step three paces to the right*. **2** to erect (a spar, mast, flagstaff, etc) by fixing the lower end into a socket. **3** to cut steps or notches, etc in (a key). ✳ **step aside 1** to stand clear of something. **2** to resign from a position. **step back** to distance oneself from a situation in order to assess it more objectively. **step forward** to volunteer one's services. **step into somebody's shoes** to take over their role or job. **step it** *dated, informal* to dance. **step on it/the gas** *informal* to drive or move faster; to hurry up. **step out of line** to fail to conform. [Old English *stæppan, steppan*]

step- *comb. form* forming words, denoting: a relationship by remarriage and not by blood: *stepfather; stepsister*. [Old English *stēop-*, related to *bestēpan* to deprive or bereave]

step aerobics *pl noun* (*treated as sing. or pl*) a kind of aerobics that involves stepping up onto and down from a portable plastic block.

stepbrother *noun* a son of one's stepparent by a former marriage.

step-by-step *adj* said of progress, etc: marked by successive degrees, usu of limited extent; gradual.

stepchild *noun* (*pl* **stepchildren**) a child of one's wife or husband by a former marriage.

stepdaughter *noun* a daughter of one's wife or husband by a former marriage.

step down *verb trans* to lower (the voltage at which an alternating current is operating) by means of a transformer. ➤ *verb intrans* to retire or resign. ➤➤ **step-down** *adj*.

stepfamily *noun* (*pl* **stepfamilies**) a family that includes one or more stepchildren.

stepfather *noun* the husband of one's mother by a subsequent marriage.

stephanotis /stefə'nohtis/ *noun* any of a genus of climbing plants of Madagascar and Malaya, with fragrant waxy white flowers: genus *Stephanotis*. [Latin genus name, from Greek *stephanōtis* fit for a crown, from *stephanos* crown, wreath, from *stephein* to crown, wreathe]

step in *verb intrans* **1** to make a brief informal visit. **2** to intervene in an affair or dispute. **3** to take somebody's place in an emergency.

step-in *adj* **1** said of clothes: put on by being stepped into. **2** denoting ski bindings that click into place automatically when the boot is positioned on the ski.

step-ins *pl noun* **1** a pair of shoes that are slipped on without fastening; = slip-ons (see SLIP-ON[2]). **2** *chiefly NAmer, dated* a pair of women's briefs.

stepladder *noun* a hinged ladder with flat rungs and often a platform.

stepmother *noun* the wife of one's father by a subsequent marriage.

step out *verb intrans* **1** to begin to walk faster. **2** *NAmer, informal* to withdraw from involvement. **3** *dated, informal* (*often* + with) to go out with somebody, as in a romantic involvement. ➤ *verb trans* to measure out (a certain distance) by stepping: *step out 100 yards*.

stepparent *noun* the husband or wife of one's parent by a subsequent marriage. ➤➤ **stepparenting** *noun*.

steppe /step/ *noun* a vast grassy treeless plain, *esp* in SE Europe or Asia. [Russian *step'* lowland]

stepped *adj* **1** said of a surface: cut into steps. **2** said of an arrangement or disposition of things, etc: set out in a series of steps so as to avoid unwanted symmetry or coinciding; = staggered (see STAGGER[1]). **3** *archaic or literary* advanced or far on: *a man far stepped in years; I am in blood stepped in so far* — Shakespeare.

steppe lemming *noun* a rodent of central Asia similar to a vole, with a black stripe down its back, which burrows and is sometimes a threat to crops and pasture: *Lagurus lagurus*.

stepper *noun* **1** an electric motor or other mechanical device whose movement or rotation is in small distinct steps. **2** the plastic block used for step aerobics. **3** (*used in combinations*) a person, horse, etc, that steps a certain way: *a high-stepper*.

stepping-stone *noun* **1** a stone on which to step, e.g. in crossing a stream, swampy or muddy patch, etc. **2** something regarded as a means of progress or advancement.

stepsister *noun* a daughter of one's stepparent by a former marriage.

stepson *noun* a son of one's wife or husband by a former marriage.

step up *verb trans* **1** to increase (the voltage at which an alternating current is operating) by means of a transformer. **2** to increase, augment, or advance (an operation, output, etc) by one or more steps: *step up production*. ➤➤ **step-up** *adj*.

stepwise *adj and adv* arranged in or proceeding in steps: *a stepwise introduction of variables*.

-ster *suffix* forming nouns, denoting: **1** a person who handles or operates something: *tapster; teamster*. **2** a person who goes in for the activity specified: *songster; punster*. **3** a person characterized by being something: *youngster; oldster*. **4** a sporty type of car: *roadster; sportster*. [Old English *-estre, -istre*]

steradian /stə'raydi·ən/ *noun* the SI unit of solid angular measurement that is equal to the solid angle at the centre of a sphere subtended by an area on the surface of the sphere equal to the square of the radius of the sphere. [STERE- + RADIAN]

stercoraceous /stuhkə'rayshəs/ *adj* **1** denoting, containing, or relating to excrement. **2** foul; revolting. [Latin *stercor-, stercus* dung + -ACEOUS]

stere /stiə/ *noun* a metric unit of volume equal to one cubic metre (about 1.3 cubic yd). [French *stère* from Greek *stereos* solid]

stere- *or* **stereo-** *comb. form* forming words, with the meaning: relating to or having solidity or three dimensions: *stereography; stereochemistry*. [Greek *stereos* solid]

stereo¹ /'sterioh, 'stiərioh/ *noun* (*pl* **stereos**) **1a** stereophonic sound: *recorded in stereo*. **b** a stereophonic record-player, etc. **2a** stereoscopic photography. **b** a stereoscopic photograph. **3** in printing, = STEREOTYPE¹.

stereo² *adj* **1** stereoscopic. **2** stereophonic.

stereo- *comb. form* see STERE-.

stereobate /'steriohbayt, 'stiəri-/ *noun* a solid structure of masonry used as a foundation. [French *stéréobate* via Latin from Greek *stereobatēs* foundation course, from STEREO- + *bainein* to go]

stereochemistry /ˌsterioh'kemistri, ˌstiəri-/ *noun* a branch of chemistry that deals with the spatial arrangement of atoms and groups in molecules. ⯮ **stereochemical** *adj*, **stereochemically** *adv*.

stereogram /'steriohgram, 'stiəri-/ *noun* an image of an object that gives the impression of being three-dimensional, *esp* one generated by computer.

stereography /steri'ogrəfi, stiəri-/ *noun* the art, process, or technique of drawing solid bodies on a plane surface. ⯮ **stereographic** /-'grafik/ *adj*, **stereographically** /-'grafikli/ *adv*.

stereoisomer /ˌsterioh'iesəmə, ˌstiəri-/ *noun* any of a group of related isomers of a molecule in which atoms are linked in the same order but differ in their spatial arrangement. ⯮ **stereoisomeric** /-soh'merik/ *adj*, **stereoisomerism** /-'soməriz(ə)m/ *noun*.

stereolithography /ˌsteriohli'thogrəfi, ˌstiəri-/ *noun* the formation of a three-dimensional object layer by layer from a computer-generated design, using a liquid polymer that is hardened by a moving laser beam. ⯮ **stereolithographic** /-'grafik/ *adj*.

stereophonic /ˌsteri·ə'fonik, ˌstiəri-/ *adj* relating to or denoting sound reproduction or a system of sound reproduction in which the sound is split into and reproduced by two different channels to give spatial effect: compare MONOPHONIC (1). ⯮ **stereophonically** *adv*, **stereophony** /-'ofəni/ *noun*.

stereopsis /steri'opsis, stiəri-/ *noun* stereoscopic or binocular vision resulting from the reception of visual stimuli from both eyes in combination. ⯮ **stereoptic** *adj*.

stereopticon /steri'optikon, stiəri-/ *noun* a double slide-projector that combines two images to produce a three-dimensional effect. [STEREO- + Greek *optikon*, neuter of *optikos*: see OPTIC¹]

stereoscope /'steri·əskohp, 'stiəri-/ *noun* an optical instrument with two eyepieces through which the observer views two pictures taken from points of view a little way apart to get the effect of a single three-dimensional picture.

stereoscopy /steri'oskəpi, stiəri-/ *noun* the seeing of objects in three dimensions; binocular vision; = STEREOPSIS. ⯮ **stereoscopic** /-'skopik/ *adj*, **stereoscopically** /-'skopikli/ *adv*.

stereoselective /ˌsteriohsi'lektiv, ˌstiəri-/ *adj* said of a chemical reaction: designed to produce a particular stereoisomeric (see STEREOISOMER) form of the product; = STEREOSPECIFIC. ⯮ **stereoselectivity** /-'tiviti/ *noun*.

stereospecific /ˌsteriohspə'sifik, ˌstiəri-/ *adj* **1** relating to the spatial arrangement of the atoms of a specific STEREOISOMER. **2** = STEREOSELECTIVE. ⯮ **stereospecifically** *adv*, **stereospecificity** /-spesi'fisiti/ *noun*.

stereotaxic /ˌsterioh'taksik, ˌstiəri-/ *or* **stereotactic** /-'taktik/ *adj* relating to or denoting a technique or apparatus used in research or surgery of the nervous system for directing the tip of a delicate instrument, e.g. a needle or an electrode, in three planes into a predetermined area of the brain. ⯮ **stereotactically** /-'taktikli/ *adv*.

stereotype¹ /'steri·ətiep, 'stiəri-/ *noun* **1** a person or thing that conforms to a fixed or general pattern; a standardized simplistic image: *Hollywood stereotypes*. **2** a relief printing plate made by making a cast from a mould of composed type. ⯮ **stereotypic** /-'tipik/ *adj*, **stereotypical** /-'tipikl/ *adj*, **stereotypically** /-'tipikli/ *adv*. [French *stéréotype* (adj), from STEREO- + *type* TYPE¹]

stereotype² *verb trans* **1** to have a conventionalized mental image of, or represent (a person or thing) as a stereotype. **2** to make a stereotype from (a mould of a composed page of type, etc). ⯮ **stereotyper** *noun*, **stereotypy** /-pi/ *noun*.

stereotyped *adj* lacking originality or individuality: *stereotyped notions of racial characteristics*.

stereovision /'steriohvizh(ə)n, 'stiəri-/ *noun* the perception or presentation of three-dimensional objects in three dimensions.

steric /'sterik, 'stiərik/ *adj* relating to or involving the arrangement of atoms in space. ⯮ **sterically** *adv*. [irregularly formed from Greek *stereos* solid]

sterilant /'sterilənt/ *noun* a substance used as an agent for destroying pathogenic micro-organisms, or soil pests.

sterile /'steriel/ *adj* **1** said of a person or animal: unable to produce young. **2** said of a plant: unable to produce fruit or seeds. **3** said of land: unable to produce crops; impoverished; barren. **4** deficient in ideas or originality: *sterile minds; sterile academic treatises*. **5** free from living organisms, *esp* micro-organisms: *a sterile environment; sterile conditions*. **6** bringing no rewards or results; not productive: *the sterile search for jobs*. ⯮ **sterilely** *adv*, **sterility** /stə'riliti/ *noun*. [Middle English via Old French from Latin *sterilis*]

sterilize *or* **sterilise** /'steriliez/ *verb trans* **1** to make (instruments, an environment, etc) sterile by destroying micro-organisms. **2** to make (a person or animal) unable to produce young by removing or blocking the organs of reproduction. ⯮ **sterilization** /-'zaysh(ə)n/ *noun*.

sterilizer *or* **steriliser** *noun* an apparatus in which medical instruments, etc are heated to a temperature that destroys micro-organisms.

sterlet /'stuhlət/ *noun* (*pl* **sterlets** *or collectively* **sterlet**) a small sturgeon of the Caspian Sea and the Danube, fished for its flesh and its caviar: *Acipenser ruthenus*. [via French from Russian *sterlyad'*]

sterling¹ /'stuhling/ *noun* British money: *Prices are given in sterling*. [Middle English, of uncertain origin; perhaps from Old English *steorra* star + -LING, because a small star appeared on certain Norman coins]

sterling² *adj* **1** made of sterling silver: *Are the spoons all sterling?* **2** said of a person's character or efforts: of genuine worth or quality: *Thank the committee for their sterling work*.

sterling area *noun* a group of countries, chiefly of the British Commonwealth, whose currencies were formerly tied to British sterling, and whose reserves were in sterling rather than gold or dollars.

sterling silver *noun* silver that is at least 92.25% pure.

stern¹ /stuhn/ *adj* **1** harsh, strict, or severe, *esp* in imposing discipline or exercising authority: *a stern regime; The nuns were surprisingly stern with the kids*. **2** tough; hardhearted: *When the poor have cried, Caesar hath wept; ambition should be made of sterner stuff* — Shakespeare. **3** firm; uncompromising: *Nothing would shake their stern resolve*. **4** said of a landscape or environment: hostile; austere. ⯮ **sternly** *adv*, **sternness** *noun*. [Old English *styrne*]

stern² *noun* **1** the rear end of a ship: compare STEM¹. **2** *humorous* one's bottom. ⯮ **sternmost** *adj*, **sternwards** /'stuhnwədz/ *adv*. [Middle English, prob from Old Norse *stjórn* steering]

sterna /'stuhnə/ *noun* pl of STERNUM.

sternal rib *noun* any of the seven upper ribs on either side of the breastbone that are connected to it by cartilage; = TRUE RIB.

sternebra /'stuhnibrə/ *noun* (*pl* **sternebrae** /-bri/) any of the fused segments that make up the breastbone. [STERNUM + -*ebra* as in VERTEBRA]

sternforemost /stuhn'fawmohst/ *adv* in nautical reference, backward.

sternocleidomastoid /ˌstuhnohkliedoh'mastoyd/ *noun* either of two long muscles on each side of the neck that connect the MASTOID PROCESS (prominence behind the ear) with the CLAVICLE (collarbone) and STERNUM (breastbone), used in rotating the neck and nodding. [Greek *sternon* STERNUM + *cleid-*, *cleis* key, clavicle + MASTOID¹]

sternpost *noun* the principal supporting structure at the stern of a ship extending from keel to deck.

sternsheets *pl noun* the flooring in a ship's after section or, in an open boat, the part between the stern and the aftermost THWART² (rowing bench).

sternum /'stuhnəm/ *noun* (*pl* **sternums** *or* **sterna** /'stuhnə/) **1** a narrow flat vertical bone in the centre of the thorax, to which the collarbones and the upper seven ribs are attached. Also called BREASTBONE. **2** in arthropods (insects, crustaceans, etc; see ARTHROPOD), a ventral plate on each section of the body. ⯮ **sternal** *adj*. [scientific Latin from Greek *sternon* chest, breastbone]

sternutation /stuhnyoo'taysh(ə)n/ *noun formal* the action of sneezing. ➤➤ **sternutatory** /stuh'nyoohtət(ə)ri/ *adj.* [Latin *sternutation-*, *sternutatio*, from *sternutare*, frequentative of *sternuere* to sneeze]

sternutator /'stuhnyootaytə/ *noun* something, e.g. an irritant gas, that induces sneezing and often tears and vomiting.

sternway *noun* backward movement of a ship.

stern-wheeler *noun* a steamer having a paddle wheel at the stern.

steroid /'steroyd, 'stiəroyd/ *noun* any of numerous chemical compounds containing the ring of carbon atoms characteristic of the sterols and including the sterols and various hormones, e.g. testosterone, and glycosides, e.g. digitalis, which have important physiological effects. ➤➤ **steroidal** *adj.* [STEROL + -OID]

sterol /'sterol/ *noun* any of various solid CYCLIC (containing a ring of carbon atoms) alcohols, e.g. cholesterol, widely distributed in animal and plant fats. [*-sterol* extracted from CHOLESTEROL]

stertorous /'stuhtərəs/ *adj* said of breathing: characterized by a harsh snoring or gasping sound. ➤➤ **stertorously** *adv.* [scientific Latin *stertor* snoring sound, from Latin *stertere* to snore]

stet /stet/ *verb trans* (**stetted, stetting**) to direct retention of (a word or passage previously ordered to be deleted or omitted) by marking with a tick or the word *stet*. [Latin *stet* let it stand, from *stare* to stand]

stethoscope /'stethəskohp/ *noun* an instrument used to detect and study sounds produced in the body, *esp* by the heart and lungs, consisting of a sound-transmitting disc connected by a pair of tubes to earpieces. ➤➤ **stethoscopic** /-'skopik/ *adj*, **stethoscopically** /-'skopikli/ *adv*, **stethoscopy** /ste'thoskəpi/ *noun.* [French *stéthoscope*, from Greek *stēthos* chest + -SCOPE]

stetson /'stets(ə)n/ *noun NAmer* trademark a broad-brimmed high-crowned felt hat. [named after John B. *Stetson* d.1906, American hat manufacturer]

stevedore[1] /'steevədaw/ *noun* a person employed to load and unload ships; = DOCKER. [Spanish *estibador*, from *estibar* to stow cargo, from Latin *stipare* to pack tight]

stevedore[2] *verb trans and intrans* **1** to handle (cargo) as a stevedore. **2** to load or unload the cargo of (a ship) in port.

Stevengraph /'steev(ə)ngrahf, -graf/ *or* **Stevensgraph** /'steev(ə)nzgrahf, -graf/ *noun* a woven silk picture. [named after Thomas *Stevens* d.1888, English weaver, whose company produced them]

stew[1] /styooh/ *noun* **1** a dish of meat, vegetables, or both, cooked in liquid in a closed pan or casserole. **2** *informal* an agitated state; a panic: *She got in a stew over the interview.* **3** *archaic* a public room providing steam baths. **4** *dated* a brothel. [Middle English from Old French *estuve*, from *estuver* to heat in steam, prob ultimately from Greek *typhos* smoke]

stew[2] *verb trans* to cook (meat, fruit, etc) in liquid in a closed vessel: *stewed apples.* ➤ *verb intrans* **1** said of food: to cook slowly in a closed vessel. **2** said of tea: to become over-strong and bitter from prolonged brewing. **3** *informal* to be in a state of agitation: *They just left us here to stew.* ✳ **stew in one's own juice** *informal* to be left to suffer the consequences of one's own stupidity.

stew[3] *noun Brit* **1** a fishtank. **2** an artificial oyster bed. [Middle English from Old French *estui*, from *estoier* to confine]

stew[4] *noun NAmer, informal* an air stewardess or steward.

steward[1] /'styooh-əd/ *noun* **1** a person who manages the provisioning of food and attends to the needs of passengers, e.g. on an airliner, ship, or train. **2** a person who supervises the provision and distribution of food and drink in a club, college, etc. **3** an official in charge of arrangements and proceedings at a large public event, e.g. a race meeting. **4a** *esp* formerly, a person employed to manage a large house or estate: *If my lady have not call'd up her steward Malvolio and bid him turn you out of doors, never trust me*—Shakespeare. **b** *esp* formerly, an administrator of the Crown estates, attached to the British royal household. **5** = SHOP STEWARD. ➤➤ **stewardship** *noun.* [Old English *stīweard*, from *stig* home, hall + *weard* WARD[1]]

steward[2] *verb trans* to serve as steward of (an estate, etc) or manage (a public event, etc). ➤ *verb intrans* to do the duties of steward. ➤➤ **stewarding** *noun.*

stewardess /'styooh-ədis, styooh-ə'des/ *noun* a woman who attends to the needs of passengers aboard an airliner or ship.

stewed *adj* **1** said of tea: bitter-tasting as a result of infusing for too long. **2** *informal* drunk.

stewpot *noun* a large pan for cooking stew in.

stg *abbr* sterling.

sth *abbr* **1** something. **2** south.

sthenic /'sthenik/ *adj dated* having abounding or even excessive strength and energy; very strong and active. [Greek *sthenos* strength]

stibine /'stibien/ *noun* a colourless poisonous flammable gas, formerly used as a fumigating agent. [Latin *stibium* antimony + -INE[2]]

stibnite /'stibniet/ *noun* a mineral consisting of antimony trisulphide, that occurs in lead-grey crystals of metallic lustre and is the chief source of antimony. [from STIBINE in its former sense 'stibnite' + -ITE[1]]

stichomythia /stikoh'mithi-ə/ *or* **stichomythy** /sti'komithi/ *noun* a form of dialogue, *esp* in classical Greek drama, in which the interlocutors speak alternate lines. ➤➤ **stichomythic** /-thik/ *adj.* [Greek *stichomythia* from *stichomythein* to speak dialogue in alternate lines, from *stichos* line, verse + *mythos* speech]

-stichous *comb. form* forming adjectives, with the meaning: having so many lines, rows, sections, etc: *distichous.* [Greek *stichos* row]

stick[1] /stik/ *noun* **1** a twig or slender branch from a tree or shrub, *esp* gathered or cut for a purpose, e.g. as fuel or for the construction of something. **2** a long slender piece of wood specially fashioned for use, e.g.: **a** a club or staff used as a weapon; a stave. **b** a walking stick. **c** a mast or spar on a ship. **d** an implement used for striking or propelling a ball or other object in a game: *a hockey stick; a lacrosse stick.* **3** (*usu in combinations*) any of various implements resembling a stick in shape, origin, or use, e.g. a gear stick (= GEAR LEVER), JOYSTICK (aircraft control column or lever for controlling computer image). **4** a conductor's baton. **5** something prepared, e.g. by cutting, moulding, or rolling, in a long, slender, often cylindrical form: *a stick of Blackpool rock; a stick of dynamite.* **6** a thick plant stalk: *a stick of celery.* **7a** a number of bombs arranged for release from a plane at intervals across a target. **b** a number of parachutists dropping together. **c** a small group of soldiers detailed to perform a particular task. **8** *informal.* **a** *dated* a person: *a decent old stick.* **b** a dull, stiff, or spiritless person. **9** the cane used as a punishment; *also* a caning or beating: *We got the stick for the slightest spelling mistake.* **10** the threat of punishment as a means of obtaining compliance, often contrasted with a CARROT representing an inducement: *Carrot-and-stick methods may work with some children.* **11** *informal* critical disapproving comment: *I got plenty of stick from orthodox teachers for not including spelling rules.* **12** (*in pl*) **a** in hockey, the raising of a player's stick above shoulder level, constituting a foul. **b** (**the sticks**) *informal* goalposts or cricket stumps. **c** (**the sticks**) *informal, derog* remote or backward rural areas: *living out in the sticks.* **13** a piece of furniture: *The bailiffs took every last stick.* **14** *informal* a marijuana cigarette; = JOINT[1] (8). **15** in commerce, the stock of unsold shares left from an unsuccessful issue to be bought up by underwriters. ✳ **up sticks** *Brit, informal* to move out; to go and live elsewhere. [Old English *sticca* stick, peg, spoon]

stick[2] *verb* (*past tense and past part.* **stuck**) ➤ *verb trans* **1a** (*usu* + in/into/through) to thrust (a sharp or pointed object) into or through something. **b** to impale (something) on a pointed object. **2** *informal* to poke (something) somewhere: *She stuck her head round the door.* **3a** *informal* to put (something) somewhere, *esp* temporarily: *Stick your bags in that corner.* **b** *informal* used to express scornful rejection: *They can stick their job.* **4** to attach (one thing) to another, or fix (several pieces) together. **5** *informal* (*in passive*) to become fixed or unable to move: *The wheels were stuck in the mud; We got stuck in a traffic jam for two hours.* **6** *chiefly Brit, informal* (*usu in negative contexts*) to bear or stand (a person or thing): *I can't stick his voice.* **7** to pierce or stab (an animal): *squealing like a stuck pig.* ➤ *verb intrans* **1** (*often* + into) said of something sharp or pointed: to be fixed in something. **2** (+ out/out of/up) to protrude or project: *Your collar's sticking up.* **3** to become fixed or immovable: *The drawer stuck fast.* **4** *informal* to remain somewhere: *She had to stick at home all week.* **5** (+ at) to persist at a task, etc. **6** (+ with) to persevere with something: *He decided to stick with science and train as a doctor.* **7** (+ to) not to deviate from something: *stick to the path; stick to the truth.* **8** to become fixed or attached to a surface, etc: *The burrs stuck to her clothes; The stamp wouldn't stick.* **9** said of a charge, etc: to be recognized as valid, being supported by evidence, etc: *They'd never get an accusation like that to stick.* **10** in pontoon, to decline another card from the dealer: compare TWIST[1]. ✳ **be stuck for** to lack or need (something): *I'm temporarily stuck for cash.* **be stuck on** *informal* to be infatuated with (somebody): *I'm dead stuck on you – and that's a God's fact. You've taken me clean off my feet* — David Graham Phillips. **be stuck with 1** to be obliged to deal with (something). **2** to be unable to escape from (somebody or something). **get stuck in/into** *informal* to involve oneself wholeheartedly in a task, etc. **not stick at** to go well beyond (a certain course) to achieve an end: *Don't think they'd stick at blackmail.* **stick by 1** to continue to support (somebody). **2** to honour (a promise, etc). **stick one's neck out** *informal* to take an initiative or risk that leaves one vulnerable. **stick something on somebody** *informal* to get somebody blamed for something. **stick together** to continue to support each other; to remain united. [Old English *stician* to stab, prick]

stick³ *verb trans* (**sticked, sticking**) **1** to provide a stick as a support for (something), *esp* to stake (a plant). **2** in printing, to set or compose (type) in a composing stick.

stick⁴ *noun* adhesive quality: *These stamps have lost their stick.*

stickability /stikə'biliti/ *noun informal* a capacity for perseverance; staying power.

stick around *verb intrans informal* to linger somewhere, *esp* in the hope or expectation of something occurring to one's advantage.

stickball *noun NAmer* an informal street game played with a stick and ball, on the lines of baseball.

sticker *noun* **1** an adhesive label or notice: *They had one of those 'baby-on-board' stickers in the back window.* **2** *informal* a tenacious or persevering person.

stick figure *noun* a simplified drawing of a human being with single lines for the body and limbs.

stickhandle *verb trans* in ice hockey, to manoeuvre (the puck) dexterously.

sticking plaster *noun* an adhesive dressing for covering superficial wounds.

sticking point *noun* a point at which an obstacle to progress or agreement arises; the obstacle itself.

stick insect *noun* any of numerous species of insects with a long thin body resembling a stick: family Phasmatidae.

stick-in-the-mud *noun* (*pl* **stick-in-the-muds**) *informal* a person who dislikes and avoids change.

stickleback /'stiklbak/ *noun* any of several small scaleless freshwater or coastal fishes that have two or more spines in front of the dorsal fin: *Gasterosteus aculeatus* and other species. [Middle English, from Old English *sticel* goad, thorn, sting + BACK¹]

stickler /'stiklə/ *noun* (*often* + for) a person who insists on exactness or completeness in the observance of something: *a stickler for accuracy.* [obsolete *stickle* to act as umpire, from Middle English *stightlen* to control, ultimately from Old English *stihtan* to put in order]

stick out *verb intrans* **1** to jut out; to project. **2** to be prominent or conspicuous; to stand out. ✲ **stick it out** *informal* to endure something unwelcome or arduous to the end. **stick out for** to insist on or persist in demanding (something).

stickpin *noun NAmer* a straight pin with an ornamental head and sheathed point, used to keep a necktie in place.

stick shift *noun NAmer* **1** a manually operated TRANSMISSION (gear-change) system in a motor vehicle. **2** a vehicle that has manual transmission. **3** a gear lever.

stickup *noun chiefly NAmer, informal* an armed robbery or holdup.

stick up *verb intrans* to stand upright or on end; to protrude. ➤ *verb trans chiefly NAmer, informal* to rob (somebody) at gunpoint. ✲ **stick up for** to defend (somebody or something) against attack or criticism.

sticky *adj* (**stickier, stickiest**) **1a** adhesive: *sticky tape.* **b** viscous; gluey: *a sticky mess.* **c** coated with a sticky substance: *sticky hands.* **2a** said of the weather: humid or muggy. **b** sweaty or clammy: *I'm feeling hot and sticky.* **3a** awkward; stiff: *After a sticky beginning they became good friends.* **b** difficult; problematic: *a sticky situation.* ✲ **come to a sticky end** *informal* to meet with ruin, disaster, a nasty death, etc, through one's own folly or wickedness. ➤➤ **stickily** *adv*, **stickiness** *noun*.

stickybeak¹ *noun Aus, NZ, informal* an inquisitive person.

stickybeak² *verb intrans Aus, NZ, informal* to be inquisitive; to pry.

sticky-fingered *adj informal* inclined to steal things.

sticky wicket *noun* a cricket pitch drying after rain and therefore difficult to bat on. ✲ **on a sticky wicket** *informal* in a situation where one cannot be certain of one's ground.

stiction /'stiksh(ə)n/ *noun* the frictional force that is overcome to set one surface in motion when it is in contact with another. [blend of STATIC¹ + FRICTION]

stifado /sti'fahdoh/ *noun* a Greek dish of meat stewed with onions and often tomatoes. [modern Greek *stiphado*]

stiff¹ /stif/ *adj* **1** not easily bent; rigid: *a piece of stiff card.* **2** said of a handle, lever, lock, or other mechanism: hard to operate or turn. **3a** said of the body or a part of it: not moving freely: *I'm getting old and stiff.* **b** said of the body or a part of it: painful to move as a result of intensive or unwonted exercise, or of strain: *stiff muscles; a stiff neck.* **4** said of a mixture: thick: *Mix ingredients till they form a stiff paste.* **5a** said of social relations: formal; not relaxed and friendly: *a stiff and distant politeness.* **b** lacking in ease or grace: *He felt stiff and awkward.* **6a** said of a contest: hard fought. **b** said of a wind: strong. **c** said of an alcoholic drink: strong. **d** said of a punishment: harsh or severe. **e** said of a physical challenge: arduous: *a stiff climb.* **f** said of a price: high. **7** *chiefly NAmer, informal* drunk. **8** *informal* used to intensify certain past participles used as adjectives: *scared stiff; bored stiff.* ✲ **a stiff upper lip** a stoical, dry-eyed self-control. **stiff with something** full of it: *The place was stiff with uniformed police.* ➤➤ **stiffish** *adj*, **stiffly** *adv*, **stiffness** *noun*. [Old English *stif*]

stiff² *adv* stiffly: *The supervisor stood up straight and stiff, and told his story like a lesson* — Stevenson.

stiff³ *noun informal* **1** a corpse. **2** *dated* a fellow. **3** *chiefly NAmer* a priggish boring person. **4** a sure loser; a bad bet. **5** a failure; a flop.

stiff⁴ *verb trans informal* **1** *NAmer* to cheat (somebody). **2** *NAmer* to fail to tip (somebody). **3** *NAmer* to snub (somebody). **4** to kill (somebody). ➤ *verb intrans informal* to be a failure; to flop.

stiff-arm *verb trans* in games, to tackle or fend off (an opponent) by extending an arm rigidly: compare STRAIGHT-ARM.

stiffen *verb* (**stiffened, stiffening**) ➤ *verb trans* to make (something) stiff or stiffer: *stiffened collars.* ➤ *verb intrans* to become stiffer: *He stiffened when he caught sight of her; The breeze stiffened from the west.* ➤➤ **stiffener** *noun*, **stiffening** *noun*.

stiff-necked *adj chiefly archaic* haughty; stubborn; opinionated: *She had ideas of her own, and was stiff-necked enough to set the fashions themselves at defiance, if the fashions didn't suit her views* — Wilkie Collins.

stifftail *noun* any of various genera of diving ducks with pointed tail feathers that they habitually hold upright: family Anatidae.

stiffy *noun* (*pl* **stiffies**) *coarse slang* an erection of the penis.

stifle¹ /'stiefl/ *verb trans* **1** to suffocate (a person or animal) or prevent (them) from breathing freely: *We were nearly stifled, it was so hot in there.* **2** to suppress (a yawn, a giggle, etc). **3** to curb or repress (something), or prevent its development: *They seemed bent on stifling individual talent and initiative; They tried to stifle the rebellion.* ➤ *verb intrans* to be unable to breathe freely; to suffocate. ➤➤ **stifling** *adj*, **stiflingly** *adv*. [alteration of Middle English *stuflen*, perhaps from Old French *estouffer* to smother]

stifle² *noun* the joint next above the hock in the hind leg of a horse or other four-legged animal corresponding to the knee in human beings. [Middle English; earlier history unknown]

stifle bone *noun* the bone in front of a horse's STIFLE² (hind knee joint).

stigma /'stigmə/ *noun* (*pl* **stigmas** *or* **stigmata** /-tə, stig'mahtə/) **1** a connotation of disgrace associated with certain things: *the stigma of redundancy.* **2** (*pl* **stigmata**) (*in pl*) in Christianity, *esp* Roman Catholicism, marks resembling those left on Christ's body by the crucifixion appearing on the bodies, *esp* the palms, of saintly or particularly blessed people. **3** a small spot or opening on a plant, animal, or insect. **4** in medicine, a visible sign of a disease. **5** in flowers, the part of the PISTIL (female organ) that receives the pollen. [via Latin from Greek *stigma* a brand or mark made by a pointed instrument]

stigmatic¹ /stig'matik/ *adj* **1** relating to a stigma, stigmas, or stigmata. **2** anastigmatic; see ANASTIGMAT. ➤➤ **stigmatically** *adv*.

stigmatic² *or* **stigmatist** /'stigmətist, stig'mahtist/ *noun* a person marked with the stigmata of Christ.

stigmatize *or* **stigmatise** /'stigmətiez/ *verb trans* **1** to describe or identify (somebody or something) in disapproving terms: *Grammarians stigmatize certain usages as incorrect; stigmatized sexual* *minorities.* **2** to mark (a person) with the stigmata of Christ. ➤➤ **stigmatization** /-'zaysh(ə)n/ *noun.*

stilb /stilb/ *noun* a unit of luminance in physics, etc, equivalent to one candela per square centimetre. [French *stilb* from Greek *stilbein* to gleam]

stilbene /'stilbeen/ *noun* a synthetic HYDROCARBON (class of compound found in petroleum, etc) that forms phosphorescent crystals and is used in making dyes. [Greek *stilbein* to gleam + -ENE]

stilboestrol (*NAmer* **stilbestrol**) /stil'beestrəl/ *noun* a synthetic compound similar to oestrogen, used in hormone treatments, taken post-coitally as a contraceptive, and given to livestock to promote growth. [a blend of STILBENE, OESTRUS + -OL¹]

stile¹ /stiel/ *noun* **1** a step or set of steps for climbing over a fence or wall. **2** a turnstile. [Old English *stigel*]

stile² *noun* any of the vertical members in a door frame, window frame, or panel. [prob from Dutch *stijl* post]

stiletto /sti'letoh/ *noun* (*pl* **stilettos** *or* **stilettoes**) **1** a slender rod-like dagger. **2** a pointed instrument for piercing holes, e.g. for eyelets, in leather, cloth, etc. **3** *Brit.* **a** an extremely narrow tapering high heel on a woman's shoe. **b** a shoe with such a heel. [Italian *stiletto*, dimin. of *stilo* stylus, dagger, from Latin *stilus* stake, STYLUS]

still¹ /stil/ *adj* **1a** not moving: *still water.* **b** calm or tranquil: *the still air; a still evening.* **c** *archaic or literary* said of a sound, voice, etc: quiet and contained: *I shall follow the guiding of that still small voice which interprets the dictates of conscience* — Charlotte Brontë. **2** said of drinks: not carbonated; not effervescent: *still orange.* **3** denoting or relating to static photographs as distinct from moving pictures: *a still photographer.* ➤➤ **stillness** *noun.* [Old English *stille*]

still² *adj and adv* without movement; not stirring: *Be still; Sit still.*

still³ *verb trans chiefly archaic or literary* to calm or quieten (somebody or something): *If you hear a child cry in the night, you must call to the nurse and bid her still it* — Shakespeare; *Instead of trying to still his fears, he encouraged them* — George Eliot. ➤ *verb intrans* to become calm, quiet, or motionless. [Old English *stillan* to calm, appease]

still⁴ *adv* **1** as before; even now or even then: *Drink it while it's still hot; You aren't still worrying about the key, are you?* **2** in spite of that; nevertheless: *I still think it's immoral.* **3** however; looking on the bright side: *Still, we've nearly finished.* **4** (*in negative contexts*) yet: *I still haven't written to thank them.* **5** *archaic or literary* always; continually: *And I will love thee still, my dear, till a' the seas gang dry* — Burns. **6** (*used with comparatives*) even; yet: *I've thought of a still nicer idea.*

still⁵ *noun* **1** a still photograph, *esp* a photograph of actors or a scene from a film reproduced for publicity or documentary purposes. **2** *chiefly literary* quiet; silence: *in the still of the night.*

still⁶ *noun* an apparatus used in distillation, *esp* of spirits, comprising either the chamber in which the vaporization is carried out or the entire equipment. [from *still* (verb), shortened from DISTIL]

stillage /'stilij/ *noun* a stand or frame on which articles are kept off the floor, e.g. while drying or awaiting packing. [Dutch *stellage* scaffolding, from *stellen* to place]

stillbirth *noun* the birth of a dead infant.

stillborn *adj* **1** said of a baby: dead at birth. **2** said of an idea, etc: failing from the start; abortive: *Her plan for a weekly discussion group was stillborn.*

still hunt *noun NAmer* the act or an instance of hunting game by stealthy means such as stalking or ambush.

still-hunt *verb trans chiefly NAmer* to hunt (game) by stealthy means such as stalking or ambush. ➤ *verb intrans chiefly NAmer* to hunt game by stalking, ambush, or other stealthy means.

stillicide /'stiliside/ *noun* **1** *archaic* a continual dripping of water. **2** in Scots law, a right whereby rainwater dripping from one's eaves may fall on one's neighbour's land. [Latin *stillicidium*, from *stilla* drop + *cadere* to fall]

still life *noun* (*pl* **still lifes**) a picture showing an arrangement of inanimate objects, e.g. fruit or flowers.

still room *noun esp* formerly, a room in a large household where provisions are stored and tea and coffee are prepared: *learning the mysteries of the kitchen and the still-room* — Charles Kingsley. [orig denoting a room in which there was a STILL⁶]

stilly¹ /'stilli/ *adv* in a calm, still, quiet, or contained manner: *The hum of either army stilly sounds* — Shakespeare. [STILL¹ + -LY²]

stilly² /'stili/ *adj literary* still; quiet: *the stilly twilight of the place* — William Cullen Bryant. [STILL¹ + -Y¹]

stilt /stilt/ *noun* (*pl* **stilts** *or collectively* **stilt**) **1a** either of two poles each with a rest or strap for the foot, that enable the user to walk along above the ground. **b** any of a set of piles, posts, etc that support a building above ground or water level. **c** a support for a ceramic vessel being fixed in a kiln. **2** any of several long-legged wading birds with three toes and mainly black and white plumage: genera *Cladorhynchus* and *Himantopus*. [Middle English *stilte*, of Germanic origin]

stilted /'stiltid/ *adj* **1** said of writing or speech: stiffly formal and unnatural. **2** denoting an arch that continues the vertical line of its side supports before curving inward. ➤➤ **stiltedly** *adv*, **stiltedness** *noun.* [past part. of *stilt* to raise on stilts, from STILT]

Stilton /'stilt(ə)n/ *noun* either of two varieties of a white cheese with a wrinkled rind, enriched with cream: Blue Stilton, with blue veins, and White Stilton. [named after *Stilton*, village in Cambridgeshire, England, where it was orig sold]

stimulant¹ /'stimyoolənt/ *noun* **1** a drug, etc that produces a temporary increase in the functional activity or efficiency of an organism. **2** anything that promotes interest or activity: *The company of young people was an invariable stimulant and would rouse him from his lethargy.*

Usage note

stimulant *or* **stimulus?** A *stimulus* (plural *stimuli*) is anything that stimulates a reaction from somebody or something: a prod with a stick, a promise of more pay, or the threat of dismissal might act as a *stimulus* to somebody making them work harder. A *stimulant*, on the other hand, is primarily a substance, especially a drink or drug, that temporarily makes somebody more energetic or alert.

stimulant² *adj* having a stimulating effect.

stimulate /'stimyoolayt/ *verb trans* **1** to promote (a physiological process) or increase the activity of (an organ): *Chewing stimulates the production of saliva; Fertility drugs were used to stimulate the ovaries.* **2** to give mental nourishment or encouragement to (a person, their mind, etc): *You have stimulated my curiosity; I was stimulated to carry out my own researches.* ➤ *verb intrans* to serve as a mental or physiological stimulant or stimulus: *His lectures failed to stimulate.* ➤➤ **stimulating** *adj*, **stimulation** /-'laysh(ə)n/ *noun*, **stimulative** /-lətiv/ *adj*, **stimulator** *noun*, **stimulatory** /-lat(ə)ri/ *adj.* [Latin *stimulatus*, past part. of *stimulare* to goad, urge, from *stimulus* goad]

stimulus /'stimyooləs/ *noun* (*pl* **stimuli** /-lee, -lie/) **1** something, e.g. an environmental change, that directly influences the activity of living organisms, e.g. by exciting a sensory organ or evoking muscular contraction or glandular secretion: *Light acts as a stimulus to the brain.* **2** something that rouses or incites to activity; an incentive: *Students tend to need the stimulus of exams to concentrate their attention on their work.* [Latin *stimulus* goad, spur]

Usage note

stimulus *or* **stimulant?** See note at STIMULANT¹.

sting¹ /sting/ *verb* (*past tense and past part.* **stung** /stung/) ➤ *verb trans* **1** said *esp* of a plant, insect, or fish: to give an irritating or poisonous wound to (a person or animal): *I was stung by a bee.* **2** said of rain, wind, etc: to inflict pain on (somebody) as though by whipping or lashing: *Hail stung their faces.* **3a** to cause a pang of bitterness or pain in (somebody): *stung by his remark; stung with remorse.* **b** (*usu* + into) to goad (somebody) into doing or feeling something: *Her taunts stung him into action.* **4** *informal* to overcharge or cheat (somebody): *The tourists didn't apparently mind getting stung by the street traders.* ➤ *verb intrans* **1a** said of a plant or insect: to have a sting or use it: *Nettles sting.* **b** said of taunts, bitter thoughts, etc: to cause a pang: *Remembered folly stings* — Dr Johnson. **2** said of a part of the body: to smart: *The smoke made my eyes sting.* ➤➤ **stingingly** *adv.* [Old English *stingan*]

sting² *noun* **1a** a sharp organ, typically in certain plants, insects, or fish, that can wound by piercing and injecting a poisonous secretion. **b** the act or an instance of stinging; the thrust of a sting into the flesh. **c** a wound or pain caused by stinging. **2** pain inflicted as if by stinging: *the sting of the whip; the sting of the wind and rain.* **3** a pang of emotional or mental pain, or the act or an instance of inflicting it: *She could still feel the sting of his remark.* **4** *informal.* **a** a confidence trick. **b** an elaborate deception mounted by law-enforcement officers to trap criminals. ✱ **a sting in the tail** a telling and unexpected climax to a story, etc. ➤➤ **stingless** *adj.* [Old English *sting*]

stingaree /stingə'ree, 'sting-/ *noun* **1** a cinnamon-coloured sting-ray found in shallow waters around Australia: *Urolophus testaceus*. **2** *NAmer, Aus* any stingray. [alteration of STINGRAY]

stinging nettle *noun* = NETTLE¹ (1).

stingo /'stinggoh/ *noun* a strong kind of English beer, orig brewed in Yorkshire. [STING², from its sharp taste]

stingray *noun* any of several species of ray with a whiplike tail bearing a long poisonous serrated spine capable of inflicting severe wounds: families Dasyatidae and Urolophidae.

stingy /'stinji/ *adj* (**stingier, stingiest**) *informal* **1** mean or ungenerous in giving or spending: *stingy employers*. **2** said of an allotted share or portion: scanty or small: *a stingy helping*. ➤➤ **stingily** *adv*, **stinginess** *noun*. [perhaps from a dialect variant of STING¹ or STING²]

stink¹ /stingk/ *verb intrans* (*past tense* **stank** /stangk/ *or* **stunk** /stungk/, *past part.* **stunk**) **1** (*also* + of) to give off a strong offensive smell: *The place stank of urine*. **2** *informal*. **a** (*also* + of) to be highly suspect, or suggestive of dishonest practice: *This appointment stinks of nepotism*. **b** to be contemptible or beneath consideration: *Her proposal stinks*. **c** to be in bad repute: *That name stank around here*. **d** (+ of/with) to possess money to an offensive degree: *He positively stinks of money*. [Old English *stincan*]

stink² *noun* **1** (*also* + of) a strong offensive smell; a stench: *the stink of stale vomit*. **2** *informal* a row or scandal: *There was a big stink over her promotion*. **3** *informal*, dated (in *pl*, *treated as sing*.) chemistry as a school subject. ✳ **like stink** *informal* very hard or intensively: *We worked like stink to finish on time*. **raise a stink** *informal* to cause a row or fuss, e.g. over something perceived as an abuse. ➤➤ **stinky** *adj*.

stink bomb *noun* a small capsule which emits a foul smell when broken.

stink bug *noun* a type of SHIELDBUG that emits a foul smell when handled.

stinker *noun informal* **1** an offensive or contemptible person. **2** something extremely difficult or unpleasant: *The examination was a stinker*.

stinkhorn *noun* a fungus noted for its foul smell: family Phallaceae.

stinking¹ *adj informal* **1** severe and unpleasant: *I've got a stinking cold*. **2** offensively drunk. **3** contemptible or inadequate: *He was a stinking father*. ➤➤ **stinkingly** *adv*.

stinking² *adv informal* used as an intensifier expressing disapproval or contempt: *They're stinking rich; He got stinking drunk*.

stinking mayweed /'mayweed/ *noun* a foul-smelling Eurasian plant of the daisy family with white and yellow flowers: *Anthemis cotula*. [*mayweed* from Old English *mayethe*, a plant of the daisy family + WEED¹]

stinko /'stingkoh/ *adj informal* very drunk.

stink out *verb trans* **1** to cause (a place) to be filled with a stench: *Kippers always stink the house out*. **2** to drive (somebody) out of a place by filling it with an offensive or suffocating smell.

stinkpot *noun* **1** *chiefly NAmer, informal*. **a** a contemptible or inadequate person. **b** a motor vehicle with smelly exhaust fumes. **2** formerly, a hand-thrown missile filled with combustible material emitting a suffocating smoke: *A piratical fleet closed round her, threw a stinkpot into the engine-room, and overpowered the crew* — Westminster Gazette. **3** an American turtle inhabiting muddy waters that gives off a foul smell when disturbed: *Kinosternon odoratum*.

stinkweed *noun* any of various strong-scented or foetid plants, e.g. THORN APPLE: *esp Diplotaxis muralis*.

stinkwood *noun* **1** any of several species of trees yielding unpleasant-smelling wood: *Ocotea bullata* and other species. **2** the wood of such trees.

stint¹ /stint/ *verb trans* **1** to restrict (somebody, *esp* oneself) to a small share or allowance: *Had he been wise he would have … stinted himself to one bottle at a meal* — Macaulay. **2** to be sparing with (a commodity): *She stinted neither time nor effort in the search for a cure*. ➤ *verb intrans* (*often* + on) to be sparing or frugal: *They never stinted on entertaining*. ➤➤ **stinter** *noun*. [Middle English *stinten* to stop, from Old English *styntan* to blunt, dull]

stint² *noun* **1** one's quota or round of duty or work: *I've done my stint*. **2** restraint; limitation: *Mrs Kohler made him soups and broths without stint* — Willa Cather.

stint³ *noun* (*pl* **stints** *or collectively* **stint**) any of several species of small sandpipers: *Calidris minuta* and other species. [Middle English *stynte*; earlier history unknown]

stipe /stiep/ *noun* a usu short plant stalk, *esp* supporting a seaweed, fern frond, or the cap of a fungus. ➤➤ **stiped** *adj*. [French *stipe* from Latin *stipes* stalk, literally 'tree trunk']

stipel /'stiepl/ *noun* a pair of small leaflike structures growing at the base of a leaflet; a secondary STIPULE. ➤➤ **stipellate** /stie'pelayt, -lət/ *adj*. [scientific Latin *stipella*, dimin. of *stipula*: see STIPULE]

stipend /'stiepend/ *noun* a fixed sum of money paid periodically, e.g. to a clergyman, as a salary or to meet expenses. [alteration of Middle English *stipendy*, from Latin *stipendium*, from *stip-, stips* gift + *pendere* to weigh, pay]

stipendiary¹ /stie'pendyəri, sti-/ *adj* **1** receiving a stipend, as distinct from working voluntarily. **2** relating to, or in the nature of, a stipend.

stipendiary² *noun* (*pl* **stipendiaries**) a person who receives a stipend.

stipendiary magistrate *noun* a legally qualified paid magistrate.

stipes /'stiepeez/ *noun* (*pl* **stipites** /'stipiteez/) **1** a PEDUNCLE (stalk) of a fern frond, seaweed, or fungus; = STIPE. **2** a PEDUNCLE (stalklike structure) in an animal, etc, *esp* the second joint of an insect's MAXILLA (mouthpart). ➤➤ **stipitate** /'stipitayt/ *adj*. [Latin *stipit-, stipes*, literally 'tree trunk']

stipple¹ /'stipl/ *verb intrans* to paint, draw, or engrave using small dots or dabs of colour. ➤ *verb trans* **1a** to portray or represent (flesh, a landscape, etc) by stippling. **b** to apply (paint, etc) in stipple. **c** to texture or roughen (a painted or cemented surface). **2** to dapple, speckle, or fleck (a surface): *Sunlight stippled the courtyard*. ➤➤ **stippler** *noun*, **stippling** *noun*. [Dutch *stippelen* to spot, dot]

stipple² *noun* a method of painting using small points, dots, dabs, or strokes to represent degrees of light, shade, and tone.

stipulate /'stipyoolayt/ *verb trans* **1** to specify (something) as a condition or requirement of an agreement or offer: *The number of female members was stipulated in the constitution*. **2** to demand, promise, or agree (something) in making an agreement: *It was stipulated that weapons were to be handed in before peace negotiations commenced*. ➤ *verb intrans* (+ for) to demand something as an express term in an agreement: *We stipulated for marble*. ➤➤ **stipulator** *noun*, **stipulatory** /-lət(ə)ri/ *adj*. [Latin *stipulatus*, past part. of *stipulari* to demand some term in an agreement]

stipulation /stipyoo'laysh(ə)n/ *noun* something, e.g. a condition, stipulated: *I was given a temporary reader's ticket with the stipulation that it was for my use only*.

stipule /'stipyoohl/ *noun* a small paired leaflike appendage at the base of a leaf or leaf stalk. ➤➤ **stipular** *adj*, **stipulate** /-lət, -layt/ *adj*, **stipulated** /-laytid/ *adj*. [Latin *stipula* straw, stalk, dimin. of Latin *stipes* tree trunk]

stir¹ /stuh/ *verb* (**stirred, stirring**) ➤ *verb trans* **1a** to move (a liquid or semiliquid) around by means of repeated circular movement with a spoon or other implement, usu in order to blend the ingredients. **b** (+ in/into) to blend (an ingredient) into a mixture by stirring: *Stir a dollop of cream into each bowl of soup*. **2** to cause a slight movement in (something): *The breeze stirred the leaves*. **3** (*often* + up) to disturb or agitate (something lying still): *Their feet stirred up the mud on the river bed*. **4** to move or exert (oneself): *I promised to stir myself sufficiently to cut the grass*. **5** to rouse (somebody) to activity: *Suddenly we were stirred into active and energetic debate*. **6** to evoke (feelings, memories, etc): *The story had stirred his sympathy*. **7** (*usu* + up) to provoke (trouble, etc): *stirring up strife*. ➤ *verb intrans* **1** to make a slight movement: *Not a leaf stirred*. **2** to wake and begin to move: *Nobody in the household was stirring yet*. **3** to move oneself: *An hour later she had still not stirred from the arm-chair*. **4** *Brit, informal* to create trouble or ill-feeling between people by gossip, tale-bearing, etc. ✳ **stir one's stumps** *informal* to bestir oneself. [Old English *styrian* to rouse, agitate]

stir² *noun* **1** the act or an instance of stirring with a spoon, etc: *Give the mince an occasional stir*. **2** a sensation or commotion; a flurry in the media: *Their engagement created quite a stir*.

stir³ *noun informal* prison. [perhaps from Romany *sturbin* jail]

stirabout *noun chiefly Irish* porridge prepared by stirring oatmeal into boiling water or milk.

stir-crazy *adj chiefly NAmer, informal* crazy or insane as, or as if as, a result of prolonged confinement in prison.

stir-fry[1] *verb trans and intrans* (**stir-fries, stir-fried, stir-frying**) to cook small pieces of food by stirring them together while rapidly frying them in hot oil. ➤➤ **stir-fried** *adj*.

stir-fry[2] *noun* (*pl* **stir-fries**) a stir-fried dish.

stirk /stuhk/ *noun dialect* a YEARLING (between one and two years old) bullock or heifer. [Old English *stirc*]

Stirling engine /'stuhling/ *noun* an external-combustion engine used to provide power e.g. for refrigeration, operating on a closed-cycle system whereby air or an inert gas is by turns cooled and compressed and then heated and expanded. [named after Robert *Stirling* d.1878, Scottish clergyman and engineer, who invented it]

stirps /stuhps/ *noun* (*pl* **stirpes** /'stuhpeez/) **1** a branch of a family or the person from whom it is descended. **2a** in BIOLOGY, a group of animals equivalent to a superfamily. **b** in biology, a race or sub-species of plants with characteristics retained by cultivation. [Latin *stirps* stem, stock]

stirrer *noun* **1** a utensil for stirring. **2** *informal*. **a** a person who deliberately stirs up feeling; a troublemaker. **b** *Aus, NZ* a political agitator or activist.

stirring *adj* rousing; inspiring: *stirring tales of adventure*.

stirrup /'stirəp/ *noun* **1** either of a pair of D-shaped metal frames or hoops in which a horse-rider's foot is placed, attached by a strap to a saddle and used to assist mounting and as a support while riding. **2** (*also* **lithotomy stirrup**) either of a pair of suspended supports for the ankles, used during childbirth, gynaecological examination, etc. **3** = STAPES. **4** a U-shaped clamp or support used in carpentry and machinery. **5** on a sailing ship, any of a series of short ropes suspending a rope for sailors to walk along from the YARD[1] (spar from which sail hangs). [Old English *stigrāp*, from *stige* ascent, descent + *rāp* rope]

stirrup bone *noun* = STAPES.

stirrup cup *noun* a farewell alcoholic drink, formerly one taken by somebody already mounted.

stirrup iron *noun* = STIRRUP (1).

stirrup leather *noun* the strap by which a stirrup is suspended from a saddle.

stirrup pants *pl noun NAmer* = SKI PANTS.

stirrup pump *noun* a portable hand pump held in position by a foot bracket and used *esp* in firefighting.

stirrup strap *noun* = STIRRUP LEATHER.

stishie /'stishi/ *noun* see STOOSHIE.

stishovite /'stishəviet/ *noun* a dense type of silica formed at high temperatures or under very high pressure, found e.g. in meteorite craters. [named after S M *Stishov*, 20th-cent. Russian chemist, who synthesized it before it was discovered as a natural material]

stitch[1] /stich/ *noun* **1a** a single in-and-out movement of a threaded needle in sewing, embroidering, etc. **b** a portion of thread left in the material after one such movement. **c** in surgery, etc, a tied loop of thread used to close a wound; a SUTURE[1]. **d** a single loop of thread or yarn round a knitting needle, crochet hook, etc. **e** such a loop after being worked to form one of a series of links in a fabric. **2a** a series of stitches that are formed in a particular manner or constitute a complete step or design. **b** a method of stitching. **3** a local sharp and sudden pain in the side brought on by running or exercise. **4** *informal* (*usu in negative contexts*) the least scrap of clothing: *not wearing a stitch*. ✳ **in stitches** laughing uncontrollably. [Old English *stice* prick, stitch in the side]

stitch[2] *verb trans* **1** to sew (fabric, a garment, etc). **2** to work on or decorate (fabric, etc) with stitches. **3** to bind together the pages of (a book or pamphlet) with staples or thread. ➤ *verb intrans* to make stitches; to sew. ➤➤ **stitcher** *noun*, **stitchery** *noun*, **stitching** *noun*.

stitch up *verb trans Brit, informal* **1** to tamper with evidence, etc so as to incriminate (somebody). **2** to cheat or defraud (somebody). **3** to conclude (a deal, etc) to one's own advantage usu by dishonest manipulation.

stitchwort *noun* any of several species of large chickweeds, with white starlike flowers, formerly used to cure a stitch in the side: genus *Stellaria*. [Old English *sticwyrt* agrimony, from *stice* STITCH[1] + WORT[1]]

stithy /'stidhi/ *noun* (*pl* **stithies**) *archaic* an anvil or a smithy: *My imaginations are as foul as Vulcan's stithy* — Shakespeare. [Middle English from Old Norse *stethi*]

stiver /'stievə/ *noun* (*usu in negative contexts*) a former Dutch coin worth one twentieth of a guilder, proverbial as a negligible amount of money: *not to speak of my three years' beef and board, for which I would not have to pay one stiver* — Herman Melville. [Dutch *stuiver*]

STM *abbr* scanning tunnelling microscope.

stoa /'stoh·ə/ *noun* (*pl* **stoas** *or* **stoae** /'stoh·ee, 'stoh·ie/) in classical Greek architecture, a portico, roofed colonnade, or colonnaded walk. [Greek *stoa*]

stoat /stoht/ *noun* (*pl* **stoats** *or collectively* **stoat**) a European weasel with a brown coat, turning white in winter in northern regions, and a long black-tipped tail: *Mustela erminea*. [Middle English *stote*: earlier history unknown]

stob /stob/ *noun* **1** *chiefly Scot, NAmer* a stump of broken branch. **2** *chiefly Scot, NAmer* a stake for fencing. **3** *Scot* a thorn or splinter, *esp* when driven into the skin. [variant of STUB[1]]

stochastic /stə'kastik/ *adj* **1** in statistics, relating to or denoting random sequential processes in which the probabilities at each step depend on the outcome of previous steps: *stochastic models*. **2** in statistics, random. ➤➤ **stochastically** *adv*. [Greek *stochastikos* skilful in aiming, from *stochazesthai* to aim at, guess at, from *stochos* target, aim, guess]

stock[1] /stok/ *noun* **1a** the equipment, materials, or supplies of an establishment. **b** a store or supply of raw materials or finished goods. **c** (*also in pl*) one's store or supply of anything: *We could do with more wine – our stocks are running low.* **d** (treated as sing. *or pl*) farm animals kept for their milk or for slaughter; livestock. **2a** the capital raised by a company through the issue and subscription of shares: *The value of the company's stock doubled within two years.* **b** (*also in pl*) the proportion of this capital held in the form of shares by an individual or company, entitling the holder to dividends, partial ownership, and voting rights. **c** (*in pl*) the shares of a particular company or type of company: *blue-chip stocks*. **d** government securities issued at a fixed rate of interest in fixed units: *gilt-edged stock*. **e** one's standing or reputation: *I proved a lot more knowledgeable on constitutional law than the others and I felt my stock had risen.* **3a** the raw material from which something is made. **b** the liquid in which meat, fish, or vegetables have been simmered that is used as a basis for soup, gravy, or sauce. **c** the portion of a pack of cards not distributed to the players at the beginning of a game. **d** unexposed photographic film. **e** a drama company's repertoire of plays. **4a** the trunk or main stem of a plant, *esp* one into which a shoot (SCION) is inserted for grafting. **b** the RHIZOME (thickened underground stem) of a plant. **c** a plant from which cuttings are taken. **d** any of several species of plants or shrubs of the cabbage family grown for their sweet-scented flowers: genus *Matthiola*. **5a** a person's line of descent; their family or lineage: *Silvana comes of Italian stock; I'm from working-class stock.* **b** a breed or variety of a plant or animal, or the population representing it. **6** the crosspiece of an anchor. **7** a neckband or cravat, usu white with flowing ends, worn by men, *esp* clergymen, in the 18th and early 19th cents, still occasionally worn as part of formal hunting costume. **8** a supporting framework or structure, e.g.: **a** (*in pl*) the frame or timbers holding a ship during construction. **b** (*in pl*) formerly, a device consisting of a wooden frame with holes in which the feet, or feet and hands, can be locked, in which petty criminals were held for public punishment: *The Lord High Bishop orthodox – the Lord High Coachman on the box – the Lord High Vagabond in the stocks – they all shall equal be* — W S Gilbert. **c** the part to which the barrel and firing mechanism of a rifle or pistol are attached. **d** the butt of an implement, e.g. a whip or fishing rod. **e** = BRACE[1] (8). **f** a long beam on a field gun forming the third support point in firing. **g** the beam of a plough to which handles, cutting blades, and mouldboard are secured. ✳ **in stock** in the shop or warehouse and available for delivery. **on the stocks** in preparation but unfinished: *a new play on the stocks*. **out of stock** sold out; having none available for delivery. **put stock in** to attach importance to (something) or set store by (it). **take stock** (*often* + of) to review a situation, etc dispassionately: *Many people approaching 40 take stock of their lives.* ➤➤ **stockless** *adj*. [Old English *stocc* tree trunk, stump, block of wood]

stock[2] *verb trans* **1** to supply (a place) with a stock of something: *He is stocking shelves in the supermarket.* **2** to start or keep a stock of (something): *We don't stock that brand.* **3** to fit (an implement, etc) to or with a stock. ➤ *verb intrans* said of a plant: to send out new shoots. ✳ **stock up** (*often* + on) to lay in a supply of something: *Better stock up on spirits for the Christmas period.*

stock[3] *adj* **1a** kept in stock regularly: *clearance sale of stock goods.* **b** regularly and widely available or supplied: *dresses in all the stock* sizes. **2** kept for breeding purposes; = BROOD³: *a stock mare.* **3** *informal* commonly used or brought forward; standard: *the stock answer.*

stockade¹ /stoʹkayd/ *noun* **1** a line of stout posts set vertically to form a defence. **2** an enclosure or pen made with posts and stakes. **3** *chiefly NAmer* a military prison. [obsolete French *estocade* from Spanish *estacada*, from *estaca* stake, pale, of Germanic origin]

stockade² *verb trans* to fortify or surround (a homestead, encampment, etc) with a stockade. ⟫⟫ **stockaded** *adj.*

stockbreeder *noun* a person who breeds livestock. ⟫⟫ **stockbreeding** *noun.*

stockbroker *noun* a broker who buys and sells securities. ⟫⟫ **stockbrokerage** /-rij/ *noun,* **stockbroking** *noun.*

stockbroker belt *noun Brit* an area on the outskirts of a large town or city that is inhabited chiefly by wealthy middle-class people.

stock car *noun* **1** a racing car having the strengthened chassis of a commercially produced assembly-line model. **2** *NAmer* a covered latticed railway wagon for livestock.

stock company *noun* **1** *NAmer* a drama company based in one theatre; = REPERTORY (1C). **2** = JOINT-STOCK COMPANY.

stock cube *noun* a cube of compressed dehydrated meat, fish, or vegetable stock, used for flavouring stews, gravies, etc.

stock dove *noun* a dove of Europe and Asia, similar to but smaller and darker than a woodpigeon, that nests in hollow trees: *Columba oenas.* [Middle English, prob from STOCK¹ in the sense 'tree trunk', from its nesting habits]

stocker *noun* **1** *NAmer* a farm animal being matured and fattened for slaughter. **2** *NAmer, informal* a stock car. **3** a person who stocks shelves in a supermarket, etc.

stock exchange *noun* **1** an association of people organized to provide an auction market among themselves for the purchase and sale of securities. **2** the building occupied by such a group.

stockfish *noun* (*pl* **stockfishes** *or collectively* **stockfish**) **1** a hake found in S African coastal waters: *Merluccius capensis.* **2** cod, haddock, etc dried in the open air without salt. [Middle English from early Dutch *stocvisch,* from *stoc* stick + *visch* fish]

stockholder *noun* **1** a person who stocks supplies for a manufacturer. **2** *NAmer* = SHAREHOLDER. ⟫⟫ **stockholding** *noun.*

stockinet *or* **stockinette** /stokiʹnet/ *noun* a soft elastic knitted fabric used for bandages, wrapping, etc, and formerly for underwear. [alteration of *stocking net*]

stocking /ʹstoking/ *noun* **1** a woman's closely fitting garment for the foot and leg, typically of fine knitted nylon and held up by suspenders or an elasticated strip that grips the thigh. **2** *NAmer or archaic* a man's long sock: *He was dressed in knickerbockers, with red stockings* — Henry James. **3** a cylindrical knitted bandage for the leg. **4** (**Christmas stocking**) an ornamental stocking hung up by children on Christmas Eve, to be filled with presents. **5** a band of white extending up to a horse's knee or hock. ⟫⟫ **stockinged** *adj,* **stockingless** *adj.* [from STOCK¹ in the obsolete sense 'stocking']

stocking cap *noun* a conical knitted cap tapering to a long point that hangs down.

stocking-filler *noun Brit* a small inexpensive present for putting in somebody's Christmas stocking.

stocking mask *noun* a nylon stocking pulled down over the face to distort and disguise the features, used by criminals.

stocking stitch *noun* a knitting stitch made by alternately knitting and purling rows of stitches to form a fabric with an even surface and uniform pattern.

stock-in-trade *noun* **1** the equipment necessary to or used in a trade or business. **2** the range of skills typically on tap to a person in any particular line: *the tact and charm that are the stock-in-trade of a successful society hostess.*

stockist *noun Brit* a retailer who stocks goods, *esp* of a particular kind or brand: *your local stockist.*

stockjobber *noun dated* a stock-exchange member who deals only with brokers or other jobbers. ⟫⟫ **stockjobbery** *noun,* **stockjobbing** *noun.*

stockman *noun* (*pl* **stockmen**) *NAmer, Aus* a person who owns or takes care of livestock.

stock market *noun* a stock exchange or the transactions made on it.

stock option *noun* = SHARE OPTION.

stockpile¹ *noun* an accumulated store, *esp* a reserve supply of something essential accumulated for use during a shortage.

stockpile² *verb trans* to accumulate a stockpile of (an essential commodity, etc). ⟫⟫ **stockpiler** *noun.*

stockpot *noun* a pot in which stock is prepared or kept as a basis for stews, soup, etc.

stockroom *noun* a storage place for supplies or goods used in a business.

stock saddle *noun* a deep-seated saddle with a high pommel used orig by cattlemen.

stock split *noun NAmer* a fresh issue of shares to existing shareholders in proportion to their current holding.

stock-still *adv* completely motionless: *standing stock-still.*

stocktaking *noun* **1** the checking or taking of an inventory of goods or supplies held e.g. in a shop. **2** the activity of appraising a situation at a given moment, e.g. by considering past progress and resources.

stock-watering *noun* the creating of new shares in a company whose assets are not sufficient to justify it.

stock whip *noun* a short-handled whip with a long lash, used for herding cattle, etc.

stocky /ʹstoki/ *adj* (**stockier, stockiest**) said *esp* of a person: short, sturdy, and relatively thick in build. ⟫⟫ **stockily** *adv,* **stockiness** *noun.*

stockyard *noun chiefly NAmer* a yard in which cattle, pigs, horses, etc are kept temporarily for slaughter, market, or shipping.

stodge¹ /stoj/ *noun chiefly Brit, informal* **1** heavy filling starchy food, such as steamed pudding. **2** solid indigestible reading matter. [from STODGE²]

stodge² *verb trans informal, dated* to cram (oneself) with food or information: *He … leaves me to stodge myself with his Times* — George Bernard Shaw. ⟫ *verb intrans informal, dated* to cram oneself with food: *Peter … could eat, really eat … but he could not stodge just to feel stodgy* — J M Barrie. [perhaps from STUFF² influenced by PODGE]

stodgy *adj* (**stodgier, stodgiest**) **1** said of food: heavy and filling. **2** *informal* dull; boring; over-conventional: *a stodgy novel.* ⟫⟫ **stodgily** *adv,* **stodginess** *noun.*

stoep /stoohp/ *noun SAfr* a raised veranda or open porch. [Afrikaans *stoep,* from Dutch]

stogie *or* **stogy** /ʹstohgi/ *noun* (*pl* **stogies**) *chiefly NAmer* a roughly made, slender, inexpensive cigar. [orig *stoga,* short for *Conestoga,* town in Pennsylvania, USA]

stoic¹ /ʹstoh·ik/ *noun* **1** (**Stoic**) a member of an ancient Greek or Roman school of philosophy, founded at Athens by Zeno of Citium, equating happiness with knowledge and holding that wisdom consists in self-mastery, submission to natural law, and indifference to pain, pleasure, and the caprices of fortune. **2** a person who bears pain, hardship, and sorrow without showing their feelings or complaining. [via Latin from Greek *stōikos* of the portico, from *Stoa Poikilē* the Painted Portico, portico at Athens where Zeno taught]

stoic² *adj* **1** (**Stoic**) relating to the Stoics or Stoicism. **2** = STOICAL.

stoical *adj* bearing pain, hardship, and sorrow without complaining or showing one's feelings. ⟫⟫ **stoically** *adv.*

stoichiometry /stoykiʹomətri/ *noun* **1** the quantitative relationship between two or more chemically or physically reacting substances. **2** the analysis or determination of this relationship. ⟫⟫ **stoichiometric** /-ohʹmetrik/ *adj.* [Greek *stoicheion* element + -METRY]

stoicism /ʹstoh·isiz(ə)m/ *noun* **1** (**Stoicism**) the philosophy of the Stoics. **2** stoical behaviour: *They put up with the privations of camp life with stoicism and good humour.*

stoke /stohk/ *verb trans* **1** to stir up or tend (a fire or furnace) and supply it with fuel. **2** to feed or encourage (an emotion): *There was no shortage of injustices to stoke their resentment.* ⟫ *verb intrans informal* (+ up) to eat plentifully in preparation for effort. [back-formation from STOKER]

stokehold *noun* a compartment containing a steamship's boilers and furnaces.

stokehole *noun* the space in which stokers work when tending a ship's furnaces.

stoker *noun* a person employed to tend a furnace, *esp* on a ship, and supply it with fuel. [Dutch *stoker* from *stoken* to fuel a furnace, earlier 'to push, poke']

stokes /stohks/ *noun* (*pl* **stokes**) a unit of kinematic viscosity in the centimetre-gram-second system used in fluid mechanics and equivalent to 10⁻⁴ square metres per second. [named after Sir George *Stokes* d.1903, British physicist]

STOL /stol/ *abbr* short takeoff and landing.

stole¹ /stohl/ *verb* past tense of STEAL¹.

stole² *noun* **1** a large rectangular scarf or shawl in a light fabric or fur, worn by women across the shoulders, *esp* with evening dress. **2** an ecclesiastical vestment consisting of a long silk band worn traditionally over both shoulders and hanging down in front by bishops and priests, and over the left shoulder by deacons. [Old English via Latin from Greek *stolē* robe, from *stellein* to array]

stolen /'stohlən/ *verb* past part. of STEAL¹.

stolid /'stolid/ *adj* difficult to arouse emotionally or mentally; unemotional. **▶▶ stolidity** /stə'liditi/ *noun*, **stolidly** *adv*, **stolidness** *noun*. [Latin *stolidus* dull, stupid]

stollen /'stolən (*German* ʃtɔlən)/ *noun* (*pl* **stollen** or **stollens**) a sweet spicy yeast bread made to an orig German recipe, containing fruit and nuts and coated with icing sugar. [German *Stollen*, from Old High German *stollo* post, support]

stolon /'stohlon/ *noun* **1** a horizontal branch from the base of a plant, e.g. the strawberry, which produces new plants; = RUNNER. **2** the branching structure that anchors a colony of lower invertebrates to its SUBSTRATE (surface on which it lives and feeds). **▶▶ stolonate** /-nayt/ *adj*, **stoloniferous** /-'nif(ə)rəs/ *adj*. [Latin *stolon-*, *stolo* branch, sucker]

stoma /'stohmə/ *noun* (*pl* **stomas** or **stomata** /-tə, stoh'mahtə/) **1** any of various small simple bodily openings, *esp* in a lower animal. **2** any of the minute openings in the epidermis of a plant organ, e.g. a leaf, through which gases pass. **3** a permanent surgically made opening, e.g. through the abdominal wall into the bowel, or into the trachea. **▶▶ stomal** *adj*, **stomatal** *adj*. [via Latin from Greek *stomat-*, *stoma* mouth]

stomach¹ /'stumək/ *noun* **1a** in a vertebrate, a saclike organ formed by a widening of the alimentary canal between the oesophagus at the top and the duodenum at the bottom, in which the first stages of digestion occur. **b** any of four such organs in ruminants (cattle, sheep, deer, etc; see RUMINANT¹). **2** the part of the body that contains the stomach; the belly or abdomen. **3a** desire or capacity for food; appetite: *His eyes were bigger than his stomach*. **b** (*usu in negative contexts*) inclination or desire: *I had no stomach for an argument*. **✳ a strong stomach** a lack of squeamishness. **on an empty stomach** not having eaten anything. **turn somebody's stomach 1** to disgust somebody completely: *That sort of conduct turns my stomach*. **2** to sicken or nauseate somebody: *The foul smell turned his stomach*. **▶▶ stomachful** *noun*. [Middle English via Old French from Latin *stomachus* gullet, oesophagus, stomach, from Greek *stomachos*, from *stoma* mouth]

stomach² *verb trans* (*usu in negative contexts*) **1** to find (a specified food) palatable or digestible: *He can't stomach rich food*. **2** to bear (something irksome) without protest or resentment: *I couldn't stomach his attitude*.

stomachache *noun* a pain in the area of the stomach or in the abdomen generally.

stomacher *noun* a separate panel, often of richly embroidered or jewelled fabric, covering the chest and ending in a point at or below the waist, worn from the 15th cent. by men and women, and by women, as the centre front of a bodice, into the 18th cent.

stomachic¹ /stə'makik/ *adj* **1** relating to the stomach. **2** denoting a medicine stimulating the function of the stomach or improving digestion. **▶▶ stomachically** *adv*.

stomachic² *noun* a stomachic medicine.

stomach pump *noun* a suction pump with a flexible tube for removing liquids from the stomach or injecting liquids into it.

stomat- or **stomato-** *comb. form* forming words, denoting: a mouth; a stoma: *stomatitis*; *stomatology*. [Greek *stomat-*, *stoma* mouth]

stomata /'stohmətə, stoh'mahtə/ *noun* pl of STOMA.

stomate /'stohmayt/ *noun* = STOMA (2). **▶▶ stomatal** /'stohmətl/ *adj*. [apparently devised as sing. of STOMATA]

stomatitis /stohmə'tietəs/ *noun* any of numerous inflammatory diseases of the mouth. **▶▶ stomatitic** /-'titik/ *adj*.

stomato- *comb. form* see STOMAT-.

stomatology /stohmə'toləji/ *noun* the branch of medicine dealing with the mouth and its disorders. **▶▶ stomatological** /-'lojikl/ *adj*, **stomatologist** *noun*.

-stome *comb. form* forming nouns, denoting: a mouth or mouthlike opening: *peristome*. [Greek *stoma* mouth, or *stomion*, dimin. of *stoma*]

-stomous *comb. form* forming adjectives, with the meaning: having a mouth or mouths of the kind or number specified: *monostomous*. [Greek *stoma* mouth]

stomp¹ /stomp/ *verb intrans informal* to walk or dance with a heavy step. **▶▶ stomper** *noun*, **stomping** *noun and adj*, **stompy** *adj*. [alteration of STAMP¹]

stomp² *noun* a jazz dance characterized by heavy stamping.

stomping ground *noun NAmer* = STAMPING GROUND.

-stomy *comb. form* (*pl* **-stomies**) forming nouns, denoting: a surgical operation to create an artificial opening in some part: *colostomy*. [Greek *stoma* mouth]

stone¹ /stohn/ *noun* **1a** the hard compacted non-metallic earthy or mineral matter of which rock is composed. **b** this material as proverbially cold, hard, immobile, etc: *I … felt them [Falstaff's feet] and they were as cold as any stone* — Shakespeare; *The widow's lamentations … would have pierced a heart of stone* — Dickens; *Every animal was motionless, as though turned to stone* — Jack London. **2** a piece of rock; a pebble. **3** a gem. **4** (*used in combinations*) a piece of stone adapted to a particular function: *a paving stone*; *a gravestone*. **5** a greyish beige colour. **6** a meteorite composed of stone as distinct from metal. **7** a smooth flat metal surface on which a printing forme is made up from type or blocks. **8** a hard accretion of mineral particles in an organ or duct; = CALCULUS: *a kidney stone*. **9** the hard seed in a peach, cherry, plum, etc. **10** (*pl usu* **stone**) *Brit* a unit of weight equal to 14 pounds (about 6.35 kilograms). **11a** a heavy round flat-bottomed stone with a gooseneck handle used in the game of curling. **b** a playing piece used in various games, e.g. backgammon. **✳ a stone's throw** no very great distance. **leave no stone unturned** to make every possible effort to find or obtain something. [Old English *stān*]

stone² *verb trans* **1** formerly, to hurl stones at (somebody), *esp* to kill (them) by this means: *Cowards were stoned to death* — Gibbon. **2** to remove the stones or seeds of (a fruit): *stoned raisins*. **✳ stone me/stone the crows!** *Brit, informal* an exclamation of amazement. **▶▶ stoner** *noun*.

stone³ *adj* **1** made of stone: *stone steps*. **2** of a greyish beige colour.

Stone Age *noun* (**the Stone Age**) the first known period of prehistoric human culture characterized by the use of stone tools and weapons, covering about 2.5 million years and subdivided into the Palaeolithic, Mesolithic, and Neolithic periods.

Editorial note

The Stone Age is the first and longest stage of human technology, beginning with the first recognizable stone tools around 2.5 million years ago (in Africa, on present evidence) and continuing until the advent of metals. Its duration varies in different parts of the world. It is generally divided into three stages: the Palaeolithic (Old Stone Age), Mesolithic (Middle), and Neolithic (New). The concept arose because stone tools, being virtually indestructible, dominate the archaeological record throughout this period, but it is known that many of them were in fact used in the procurement and use of long-vanished organic materials, such as wood — Dr Paul Bahn.

stone-blind *adj* completely blind: compare SAND-BLIND: *He walked right into me as though he had been stone-blind* — Joseph Conrad.

stone-broke *adj chiefly NAmer, informal* = STONY-BROKE.

stonechat *noun* any of various species of common small thrushes of Europe and Asia, the male of which has a black head and chestnut underparts: *Saxicola torquata* and other species. [from its call, suggestive of stones being knocked together]

stone circle *noun* a circle of megaliths (large upright stones; see MEGALITH) of prehistoric, *esp* Bronze-Age, construction, having a presumed ritual function.

stone-cold *adj* absolutely cold: *This soup is stone-cold*. **✳ stone-cold sober** utterly sober; not in the least drunk.

stonecrop *noun* any of numerous species of plants with fleshy leaves that grow on rocks and walls: genus *Sedum*.

stone curlew *noun* any of various species of large wading birds of Europe, Asia, and tropical America, with a large head and yellow eyes, found in stony or sandy habitats: *Burhinus oedicnemus* and other species.

stone-cutter *noun* **1** a person who cuts and carves stone. **2** a machine for dressing stone. ➤➤ **stone-cutting** *noun*.

stoned *adj informal* intoxicated by a drug, e.g. marijuana, or alcohol.

stone-dead *adj* completely dead.

stone-deaf *adj* completely deaf; having no residual hearing.

stonefish *noun* (*pl* **stonefishes** *or collectively* **stonefish**) a tropical fish of the Indian and Pacific Oceans with venomous dorsal spines, that lies motionless on the sea bed resembling a lump of rock: *Synanceia verrucosa* and other species.

stone fly *noun* any of several families of insects with aquatic flesh-eating larvae, the adult being used by anglers for bait: order Plecoptera.

stone fruit *noun* a fruit with a stone, such as a peach, plum, or cherry; = DRUPE.

stone-ground *adj* said of flour: ground with millstones.

stone lily *noun* a fossil CRINOID (primitive marine animal related to the starfish).

stonemason *noun* a person who prepares stone for building.

stone pine *noun* a S European pine tree with branches that radiate into the shape of an umbrella, the seeds of which are eaten as pine nuts (see PINE NUT): *Pinus pinea*.

stonewall *verb intrans* **1** to obstruct or delay parliamentary debate. **2** to be evasive or obstructive. **3** *chiefly Brit* to bat excessively defensively and cautiously in cricket. ➤ *verb trans* to block (a request, etc) by means of evasive replies, *esp* in politics. ➤➤ **stonewaller** *noun*, **stonewalling** *noun*.

stoneware *noun* opaque ceramic ware that is fired at a high temperature and is nonporous: compare EARTHENWARE.

stonewashed *or* **stonewash** *adj* said of *esp* denim clothing: washed with abrasive materials, e.g. pumice, so as to produce a worn and faded appearance.

stonework *noun* **1** masonry. **2** those parts of a building that are constructed of stone. ➤➤ **stoneworker** *noun*.

stonewort *noun* any of various genera of a family of freshwater green algae often encrusted with chalky deposits: genus *Chara* and other genera.

stoney /'stohni/ *noun* see STONY.

stonk[1] /stongk/ *noun slang esp* in World War II: a concentrated artillery bombardment: *Our gunners were preparing for a stonk.* [said to be formed from *standard concentration*]

stonk[2] *verb trans slang esp* in World War II, to subject (a place) to a concentrated artillery bombardment.

stonker *noun informal* something or somebody that is pretty amazing. ➤➤ **stonking** *adj*.

stonkered *adj Aus, NZ, informal* **1** totally exhausted or defeated. **2** drunk. [perhaps from Scots and N English dialect *stonk* a marbles game]

stony *or* **stoney** /'stohni/ *adj* (**stonier, stoniest**) **1a** full of stones: *a stony beach*. **b** resembling stone: *a stony accretion*. **2** cold or unresponsive; without compassion: *stony silence; a stony heart*. **3** *informal* stony-broke. ✱ **fall on stony ground** said of good advice, etc: to go unheeded [in reference to Matthew 13:5]. ➤➤ **stonily** *adv*, **stoniness** *noun*.

stony-broke *adj Brit, informal* completely without funds; = BROKE[2].

stonyhearted *adj* unfeeling; cruel. ➤➤ **stonyheartedness** *noun*.

stood /stood/ *verb* past tense and past part. of STAND[1].

stooge[1] /stoohj/ *noun* **1a** a person being used by somebody more powerful to do unpleasant or distasteful jobs. **b** *chiefly NAmer, informal* a decoy or police informer; = NARK[1], STOOL PIGEON. **2** the member of a comedy duo who speaks the feed lines and is the butt of the other's jokes. [origin unknown]

stooge[2] *verb intrans* **1** (+ for) to act as stooge for a comedian. **2** *informal* (+ around/about) to move aimlessly to and fro.

stook[1] /stook/ *noun chiefly Brit* a group of sheaves of grain set upright against one another to dry; = SHOCK[3]. [Middle English, of Germanic origin]

stook[2] *verb trans* to put (sheaves of grain) into stooks.

stool[1] /stoohl/ *noun* **1a** a seat usu without back or arms supported by three or four legs or a central pedestal. **b** a low bench or portable support for the feet or for kneeling on; a footstool. **2** *esp* in medicine, a discharge of faecal matter. **3a** a tree stump or plant crown from which shoots grow out. **b** a growth of shoots from such a base. **4** *NAmer* a decoy bird used by hunters. ✱ **fall between two stools** **1** to have elements of two categories and so belong satisfactorily to neither. **2** to fail through hesitation, etc to avail oneself of either of two possibilities. [Old English *stōl*]

stool[2] *verb intrans* said of a plant: to throw out shoots from a stump or crown. ➤ *verb trans* to cut back (a plant) to or almost to ground level to promote new growth.

stoolball *noun* a game resembling cricket that is played chiefly in S England, *esp* by women, and is characterized by underarm bowling.

stoolie /'stoohli/ *noun NAmer, informal* = STOOL PIGEON. [shortened from STOOL PIGEON]

stool pigeon *noun chiefly NAmer* **1** a police informer. **2** a person acting as a decoy. [prob from the early practice of fastening a decoy bird to a stool]

stoop[1] /stoohp/ *verb intrans* **1a** to bend the body forward and downward, sometimes simultaneously bending the knees: *She stooped to pick up the child*. **b** to stand or walk with a temporary or habitual forward inclination of the head, body, or shoulders: *He was getting old and beginning to stoop*. **2a** to condescend: *The gods stoop to intervene in the affairs of men*. **b** (*usu in negative contexts*) to lower oneself morally: *I hope I would not stoop to spying on a friend*. **3** said of a bird: to fly or dive down swiftly, usu to attack prey. ➤ *verb trans* to bend (one's head or shoulders) forward and downward: *He had to stoop his head to catch her stifled whisper* — Edith Wharton. [Old English *stūpian*]

stoop[2] *noun* **1** a stooping position or posture: *He walks with a stoop*. **2** the descent of a bird, *esp* on its prey.

stoop[3] *noun chiefly NAmer* a porch, platform, entrance stairway, or small veranda at a house door. [Dutch *stoep*]

stooped *adj* having a stooping shape or posture: *stooped shoulders*.

stooshie /'stooshi/ *or* **stishie** /'stishi/ *noun Scot, informal* a fuss or commotion, *esp* an unnecessary one. [perhaps an alteration of ECSTASY]

stop[1] /stop/ *verb* (**stopped, stopping**) ➤ *verb intrans* **1** to come to an end; to discontinue moving or operating. **2** said of a bus or train: to call at a place to take on or let off passengers. **3** to break one's journey; to stay somewhere: *We could stop for a night or two in Paris*. **4** *Brit, informal* to remain somewhere: *Shall we stop at home?* ➤ *verb trans* **1a** (*often* + from) not to let (somebody or something) do something, or prevent (them) from continuing: *She tried to stop me from applying*. **b** to check or suppress (something) or cause (it) to cease: *stop the bleeding*. **c** to cease or discontinue (an activity): *stop writing now; stop work at five*. **2a** to halt the progress of (a person, vehicle, etc). **b** to interrupt the functioning of (a mechanism). **3a** to parry (a blow, sword stroke, etc). **b** *informal* to get in the way of (a bullet, blow, etc) *esp* so as to be hurt or killed. **4** to beat (one's opponent) in a boxing match by a knockout. **5** to pinch out the growing tip of (a plant). **6a** to obstruct the passage of (something). **b** to close up, block off, or plug (an opening). **c** (*often* + up) to choke or obstruct (a channel, etc). **d** to cover over or fill in (a hole or crevice), e.g. to fill (a hole in a tooth) with amalgam, etc. **7a** to deduct or withhold (a sum due). **b** to instruct one's bank not to honour or pay (a cheque). **8** in music: **a** to change the pitch of (a string) by pressing it with a finger. **b** to close (a hole) on a wind instrument with a finger. **c** to close the upper end of (an organ pipe) to lower its note by an octave. **9** to hold a high card and enough protecting cards in bridge to be able to block (an opponent's scoring run). ✱ **stop at nothing** to be unscrupulous in achieving one's ends. **stop dead** to come to a sudden and complete halt. ➤➤ **stoppable** *adj*. [Old English *stoppian* to block up]

stop[2] *noun* **1a** the act or an instance of stopping; a halt: *Wait till the bus comes to a stop before you get off*. **b** a place where a train or bus halts to let passengers on or off: *I'm getting off at the next stop*. **2** a device or mechanism that prevents movement: *a doorstop*. **3** a plug or stopper. **4a** a knob or lever on an organ or harpsichord that brings into play a set of organ pipes or strings of a particular tone quality and range of pitch. **b** a means of regulating the pitch of a musical instrument, e.g. any of the holes in a wind instrument: *You would play upon me; you would seem to know my stops* — Shakespeare. **5** in phonetics, a consonant during the articulation of which there is a stage, e.g. in the *p* of *apt* or the *g* of *tiger*, when the breath passage is completely closed. **6a** in photography, the APERTURE (circular opening) of an optical system, e.g. a camera lens. **b** in photography, a marking of a series, e.g. of f-numbers, on a camera for indicating settings of the DIAPHRAGM (adjustable light-controlling disc). **7** *Brit.* **a** a punctuation mark. **b** *dated* used in telegrams: a full stop. **✴ put a stop to something** to prevent something from continuing.

stopbank *noun Aus, NZ* an embankment built to prevent flooding.

stop bath *noun* an acid bath used to stop photographic development of a negative or print before immersing it in a fixer.

stop by *verb intrans chiefly NAmer* to make a brief visit somewhere.

stopcock *noun* a valve for stopping or regulating flow, e.g. of fluid through a pipe.

stop down *verb trans* to reduce the effective aperture of (a lens) by means of a diaphragm.

stope /stohp/ *noun* a steplike underground excavation formed as ore is removed. ⟫⟫ **stoping** *noun*. [prob from Low German *stope* step]

stopgap *noun* a temporary expedient; a makeshift.

stop-go *adj* **1** continually stopping and restarting. **2** *Brit* said of economic policy: characterized by an alternation between stimulating and restricting demand.

stop knob *noun* = STOP² (4A).

stop light *noun* a red traffic signal.

stop list *noun* **1** a list, issued by an association, etc, of people banned from doing business with it. **2** a set of words, typically the commonest, that in the interests of rapidity are automatically excluded from computer-generated indexes or concordances.

stop-loss *adj* denoting an order to a broker to sell a security or commodity at a stated price, to limit loss.

stop-motion *noun* the technique in cinematic animation of repeatedly stopping and restarting the camera, to create an illusion of movement in animated figures.

stop off *verb intrans* to break one's journey somewhere, *esp* overnight.

stop-off *noun* a break in a journey; = STOPOVER.

stop out *verb intrans Brit, informal* not to come home. ⟫ *verb trans* in printing, etc to mask (the area not to be printed or etched).

stopover *noun* a stop at an intermediate point in a journey; = STOP-OFF.

stop over *verb intrans* = STOP OFF.

stoppage /stopij/ *noun* **1** the act or an instance of stopping. **2** a blockage. **3** a concerted cessation of work by a group of employees that is usu more spontaneous and less serious than a strike. **4** *Brit* a deduction from pay by an employer for the payment of National Insurance, etc.

stoppage time *noun* = INJURY TIME.

stopped *adj* said of an organ pipe, etc: closed at one end and so sounding an octave lower than it would open.

stopper¹ *noun* **1** a plug or bung, *esp* one fitting into the neck of a bottle. **2** in baseball, a pitcher who prevents batters in the opposing team from scoring well. **3** in football or American football, a player who protects the goal from attacks initiated in midfield. **4** a clamp or other device that prevents a rope, e.g. in climbing or sailing, from running out completely.

stopper² *verb trans* (**stoppered, stoppering**) to close or secure (something) with or as if with a stopper. ⟫⟫ **stoppered** *adj*.

stopping *adj* denoting a train that stops at most intermediate stations.

stopple¹ /stopl/ *noun NAmer* a plug or bung; = STOPPER¹: *dispute about whether the stopple of a departed Buon Retiro scent bottle was genuine or spurious* — Mark Twain. [Middle English, partly from Old French *estouppail* bung, partly from STOP¹]

stopple² *verb trans NAmer* to seal (a bottle or other container) with a stopper; = STOPPER².

stop press *noun* **1** late news added to a newspaper after printing has begun. **2** the space reserved for this.

stop signal *noun* = STOP LIGHT.

stop up *verb trans* to block (a hole, passage, etc). ⟫ *verb intrans Brit, informal* not to go to bed.

stop volley *noun* in tennis, a volley played close to the net and only partially followed through, so that the ball drops just over the net.

stopwatch *noun* a watch with a hand that can be started and stopped at will for exact timing of races, etc.

storage /stawrij/ *noun* **1** the act or an instance of storing. **2a** the safekeeping of goods in a depository such as a warehouse: *They put their furniture into storage when they went to Australia for two years.* **b** the fee paid for warehousing property. **3** space available for storing things. **4** the act or an instance of storing data in a computer memory or on disk. **5** the production, by means of electric energy, of chemical reactions that when allowed to reverse themselves generate electricity again without serious loss.

storage battery *noun* a battery used for storing electrical energy; = ACCUMULATOR.

storage cell *noun* = STORAGE BATTERY.

storage heater *noun Brit* an electric device that is used for storing heat when electricity is cheaply available, e.g. at night, and for radiating heat when electricity is expensive, e.g. in the daytime.

storax /stawraks/ *noun* **1a** an aromatic gum resin used in incense, perfumery, and medicine. **b** = LIQUIDAMBAR. **2** any of several species of tree yielding storax, with clusters of white flowers: *Styrax officinalis* and other species. [Middle English from Latin *storax*, alteration of *styrax*, from Greek]

store¹ /staw/ *verb trans* **1** to supply (a place) with a store of something for future use. **2** (*often* + up/away) to accumulate (something) as a reserve supply: *They store vegetables for winter use.* **3** to place (property, furniture, etc) in a warehouse, etc for later use or disposal. **4** to enter (data) in a computer memory, on a diskette, etc, for future access. **5** to have storage room for (goods, data, etc): *Some zip disks store up to 250 megabytes of data.* **✴ be stored with something** to have a rich supply of something: *Her mind was stored with information on this and that.* ⟫⟫ **storable** *adj*, **storer** *noun*. [Middle English via Old French *estorer* from Latin *instaurare* to renew, restore]

store² *noun* **1** a quantity of things kept for future use. **2** (*in pl*) in the armed forces, etc, a supply of food, equipment, ammunition, etc: *military stores.* **3** a collection or accumulation: *a great store of anecdotes.* **4** storage: *furniture kept in store.* **5a** (*also* **department store**) a large shop selling a variety of goods. **b** *chiefly NAmer* a shop. **6** a young meat animal suitable for fattening. **✴ in store** awaiting one in the future: *There's a nasty surprise in store for him if he goes on like this.* **set store by something** to put faith in something or regard it as important and worthwhile: *She set great store by her daily ten-minute exercise routine.* [Middle English from Old French *estore*, from *estorer*: see STORE¹]

store card *noun* a credit card issued by a chain store, etc, that allows customers to purchase goods and services for which they pay by monthly account.

storefront *noun chiefly NAmer* **1** = SHOPFRONT. **2** one or more rooms on the ground floor of a commercial building facing onto the street and used as a shop.

storehouse /stawhows/ *noun* **1** a warehouse. **2** an abundant supply or source; a treasury: *This is memory, which is as it were the storehouse of our ideas* — John Locke.

storekeeper *noun* **1** a person who keeps and records stock, e.g. in a warehouse. **2** *NAmer* a shopkeeper.

storeman *noun* (*pl* **storemen**) *Brit* a person who is employed to organize and handle stored goods or parts, *esp* in industry.

store of value *noun* in economics, the function of money that enables goods and services to be paid for some time after they have been acquired or made use of.

storeroom *noun* a place for the storing of goods or supplies.

storey (*NAmer* **story**) /stawri/ *noun* (*pl* **storeys** *or NAmer* **stories**) **1** a horizontal division or level of a building. **2** the set of rooms occupying one level of a building. [Middle English from late Latin *historia* picture, in Anglo-Latin 'storey of a building', perhaps from the architectural device of decorating a façade with tiers of sculptures]

storeyed (*NAmer* **storied**) *adj* (*used in combinations*) having the number of storeys specified: *a two-storeyed house*.

storiated /'stawriaytid/ *adj* ornamented with elaborate designs. [late Latin *historiatus*, past part. of *historiare* to relate, to tell a story in pictures, via Latin from Greek *historia*: see HISTORY]

storied[1] /'stawrid/ *adj literary* **1** celebrated in story or history: *Of all the world's storied thoroughfares, it must be confessed that none produces quite the effect of Hollywood Boulevard* — S J Perelman. **2** ornamented with historical scenes or inscribed with a memorial record: *Can storied urn or animated bust back to its mansion call the fleeting breath?* — Gray.

storied[2] *adj NAmer* see STOREYED.

stork /stawk/ *noun* any of various species of large wading birds of Europe, Asia, and Africa that have long stout bills and typically black and white plumage, and are related to the ibises and herons: *Ciconia ciconia* and other species. [Old English *storc*]

storksbill *noun* a plant of the geranium family with elongated pointed fruits: genus *Erodium*.

storm[1] /stawm/ *noun* **1** a violent disturbance of the weather marked by high winds and usu by rain, snow, hail, sleet, or thunder and lightning. **2** a heavy fall of rain, snow, or hail. **3** a wind having a speed of 103–117km/h (about 64–72mph). **4** a violent shower of objects, e.g. missiles. **5** a tumultuous outburst: *a storm of abuse; a storm of weeping*. **6** a violent assault on a defended position. **✳ go down a storm** *informal* said of a performance, etc: to be rapturously received. **storm and stress** = STURM UND DRANG. **storm in a teacup** a disproportionate fuss about something relatively minor. **take by storm 1** said of troops: to capture (a position, stronghold, etc) by a sudden violent attack. **2** to bowl over (an audience, etc): *a novel that took the world by storm*. [Old English]

storm[2] *verb intrans* **1** to shout angrily; to rage: *Why look you, how you storm!* — Shakespeare. **2** to rush furiously: *She stormed out of the room*. **3** said of troops: to move in a sudden assault or attack: *They stormed ashore at zero hour*. **4** to be stormy: *It stormed all day*. ➤ *verb trans* to attack or take (a fortified place, etc) by storm.

stormbound *adj* confined or delayed by a storm or its effects: *The little bay was full of stormbound ships*.

storm centre *noun* **1** the point of lowest pressure at the centre of a cyclonic storm. **2** the place, thing, etc at the centre of a row, disturbance, or trouble: *Chicago had always been the storm-centre of the conflict between labor and capital* — Jack London; *The unfortunate Deplis ... found himself ... once more the storm-centre of a furious controversy* — Saki.

storm cloud *noun* **1** a heavy dark cloud bringing rain or presaging a storm. **2** a build-up of circumstances likely to lead to trouble or conflict.

stormcock *noun* = MISTLE THRUSH. [from the belief that its singing heralds a storm]

storm cone *noun* in Britain, a tarred canvas cone hoisted by coastguards as a gale warning, the number and position of the cones conveying information about the direction and strength of the wind.

storm cuff *noun* a close-fitting or elasticated inner cuff, *esp* on an anorak or waterproof jacket.

storm door *noun chiefly NAmer* a door placed outside an ordinary external door for protection against severe weather.

storm drain *noun* a drain built to take away the extra water during a particularly heavy downfall.

stormer *noun Brit, informal* something that is remarkably impressive.

storm flap *noun* a flap attached to a tent opening, or the opening of a coat or jacket, to protect it from rain.

storm glass *noun* formerly, a sealed tube containing a solution which was supposed to change in appearance when storms were approaching.

storming *adj informal* said usu of a sporting or musical performance: wonderfully fast and furious.

storm lantern *noun chiefly Brit* = HURRICANE LAMP.

storm petrel *noun* a small sooty black and white petrel frequenting the N Atlantic and Mediterranean, whose appearance was formerly thought to presage bad weather: *Hydrobates pelagicus* and other species.

storm sail *noun* a substitute sail for stormy weather, of smaller size and tougher fabric than the normal one.

storm sewer *noun* = STORM DRAIN.

storm trooper *noun* **1** a member of the Nazi militia, the SA (*Sturmabteilung*). **2** a member of a force of SHOCK TROOPS.

storm troops *pl noun* = SHOCK TROOPS.

stormwater *noun* surface water produced by heavy rain or snow.

storm window *noun chiefly NAmer* an extra window fitted to the outside of a window frame for protection from stormy or wintry weather.

stormy *adj* (**stormier**, **stormiest**) **1** wild, windy, characterized by thunderstorms, or in a state or of an appearance associated with storms: *a stormy day; stormy seas*. **2** full of turmoil or fury: *a stormy marriage*. ➤➤ **stormily** *adv*, **storminess** *noun*.

stormy petrel *noun* **1** = STORM PETREL. **2** a person who is fond of arguing.

story[1] /'stawri/ *noun* (*pl* **stories**) **1** an account of incidents or events. **2** a statement of the facts of a situation in question: *according to their story*. **3** an anecdote; *esp* an amusing one. **4** = SHORT STORY. **5** the plot of a literary or dramatic work. **6** a rumour. **7** used to children: a lie; a falsehood. **8** a legend or romance. **9** a news article or broadcast. **✳ the same old story** the familiar scenario, unsatisfactory as ever. **the story goes** they say; apparently. **the story of one's life** something that has befallen one all too frequently. **to cut a long story short** to get quickly to the point. [Middle English, in the sense 'true narrative', via Old French and Latin from Greek *historia*: see HISTORY]

story[2] *noun* (*pl* **stories**) *NAmer* see STOREY.

storyboard *noun* a series of drawings or photographs showing the shots planned for a television or cinema film.

storybook *noun* **1** a book of fairy tales. **2** (*used before a noun*) denoting romance of the kind associated with fairy tales; = FAIRY TALE.

story editor *noun* an editor who advises on the content of film and television scripts.

storyline *noun* the plot of a novel, play, film, etc.

storyteller *noun* **1** a relater of tales or anecdotes. **2** *informal* a liar.

stot /stot, stoht/ *verb* (**stotted, stotting**) ➤ *verb trans Scot, informal* to bounce (a ball, etc). ➤ *verb intrans Scot, informal* **1** to bounce. **2** to walk bouncily. **3** to stagger drunkenly. [origin unknown]

stotin /sto'teen/ *noun* a unit of currency in Slovenia, worth 100th of a tolar. [Slovene *stotin*, literally 'one hundredth']

stotinka /sto'tingkə, stoh-/ *noun* (*pl* **stotinki** /-kee/) a unit of currency in Bulgaria, worth 100th of a lev. [Bulgarian *stotinka*, literally 'one hundredth']

stoup /stoohp/ *noun* **1** a basin for holy water at the entrance of a church. **2** a flagon or large drinking mug or glass. [Middle English, in the senses 'cask', 'pail', from Old Norse *staup* cup]

stour /stooə/ *noun Scot* dust rising in a cloud or deposited in a thick layer. ➤➤ **stoury** *adj*. [Middle English, perhaps from Anglo-French *estur* turmoil]

stoush[1] /stowsh/ *verb trans Aus, NZ, informal* to hit (somebody) or fight (them). [origin unknown]

stoush[2] *noun Aus, NZ, informal* a fight or quarrel.

stout[1] /stowt/ *adj* **1** heavily built; corpulent; fat. **2** strong and thick; sturdily made: *stout walking boots*. **3** bold and brave; stalwart; not easily daunted: *a stout fighter*. **4** firm; resolute: *They put up a stout resistance*. ➤➤ **stoutish** *adj*, **stoutly** *adv*, **stoutness** *noun*. [Middle English from Old French *estout*, of Germanic origin]

stout[2] *noun* a dark sweet heavy-bodied beer brewed with roasted malt or barley. [STOUT[1]; prob short for *stout ale*]

stouthearted *adj* courageous; valiant. ➤➤ **stoutheartedly** *adv*.

stove[1] /stohv/ *noun* **1a** an enclosed appliance that burns fuel or uses electricity to provide heat chiefly for domestic purposes. **b** a cooker. **2** *chiefly Brit* a hothouse. [Middle English, in the sense 'heated room, steam room', from early Dutch or early Low German *stove*]

stove[2] *verb trans* **1** to force (plants) in a hothouse. **2** to treat (metalwork, ceramics, etc) by heating in a stove.

stove[3] *verb* a past tense and past part. of STAVE[2].

stove enamel *noun* a type of enamel treated in a stove to make it heatproof.

stovepipe *noun* metal piping used as a stove chimney or to connect a stove with a flue: *Near one wall there was a black cast-iron stove, its stovepipe going straight up through the ceiling* — John Steinbeck.

stovepipe hat *noun* a silk hat of the mid-to-late 19th cent., similar to a top hat but considerably taller.

stovies /'stohviz/ *pl noun Scot* a dish of stewed potatoes with onions. [Scot *stove* to stew]

stow /stoh/ *verb trans* **1** to put (something) away or into store: *Stow the camping gear in the attic.* **2** to pack away (something) in an orderly fashion in an enclosed space: *Stow the sails.* **3** to fill (a ship's hold, etc) with cargo. **4** *informal* (+ away) to cram in (food): *We stowed away a huge dinner.* * **stow it!** *informal* shut up! [Old English *stōwigan* to retain, from *stōw* place]

stowage /'stowij/ *noun* **1** the action of stowing something or the process of being stowed: *The mate ... has the charge of the stowage ... of the cargo* — R H Dana. **2** storage capacity. **3** a place for storage. **4** goods in storage or to be stowed.

stowaway¹ *noun* a person who stows away, *esp* on a ship.

stowaway² *adj* designed to be dismantled or folded for storage: *stowaway tables and chairs.*

stow away *verb intrans* to hide oneself aboard a vehicle, *esp* a ship, as a means of travelling without payment or escaping from a place undetected.

STP *abbr* **1** professor of sacred theology. **2** short-term potentiation. **3** standard temperature and pressure. [(sense 1) Latin *Sanctae Theologiae Professor*]

str. *abbr* **1** strait. **2** used in rowing: stroke.

strabismus /strə'bizməs/ *noun* the condition of having a squint in one's eye. ⋙ **strabismic** /-mik/ *adj.* [scientific Latin from Greek *strabismos* condition of squinting, from *strabizein* to squint]

Strad /strad/ *noun* = STRADIVARIUS.

straddle¹ /'stradl/ *verb trans* **1** to stand, sit, or be astride (something). **2** to bracket (a target) with missiles, e.g. shells or bombs. **3** to be on land on either side of (something): *The village straddles the frontier.* **4** *NAmer* to come down in favour of both sides of (the thing at issue). ➤ *verb intrans archaic* to stand or *esp* sit with the legs wide apart: *A great pile of living embers diffused a strong and ruddy glow from the arched chimney. Before this straddled Dom Nicolas* — Stevenson. ⋙ **straddler** *noun.* [alteration of English dialect *striddle*, ultimately from STRIDE¹]

straddle² *noun* **1** a straddling stance or position. **2** a financial contract or option giving the holder the double privilege of selling securities to or buying securities from the maker of the contract.

Stradivarius /stradi'veəri-əs/ *noun* (*pl* **Stradivariuses**) a violin made by the Italian violin-maker Antonio Stradivari (d.1737) or his family or followers. [Latinized form of *Stradivari*]

strafe¹ /strahf, strayf/ *verb trans* to rake (ground troops, etc) with fire at close range, *esp* with machine-gun fire from low-flying aircraft. ⋙ **strafer** *noun.* [German *Gott strafe England* God punish England, slogan of the Germans in World War I]

strafe² *noun* the act or an instance of strafing.

straggle¹ /'stragl/ *verb intrans* **1** to lag behind or stray away from the main body, *esp* from a line of march. **2** to move or spread untidily away from the main body of something: *straggling branches.* ⋙ **straggler** *noun.* [Middle English *straglen*, of unknown origin]

straggle² *noun* a straggling group, e.g. of people or objects: *a little straggle of mourners* — Elizabeth Bowen.

straggly /'stragli/ *adj* (**stragglier, straggliest**) loosely spread out or scattered irregularly: *a straggly beard.*

straight¹ /strayt/ *adj* **1a** extending in one direction without bends or curves: *a straight road.* **b** in geometry, said of a line: lying on the shortest path between any two points on it. **c** said of hair: not wavy or curly. **d** said of a course, route, aim, etc: going direct to its destination or target. **e** said of a garment, *esp* a skirt: not gathered or flared. **2a** level, upright, or symmetrically positioned; not skew: *That picture's not straight.* **b** in a proper or tidy state: *I'll never get this room straight.* **3a** honest or fair: *straight dealing.* **b** accurately sorted out; correct: *Get your facts straight.* **4a** clear, simple, or logical: *straight thinking; a straight choice.* **b** candid; frank; not evasive: *Give me a straight answer; straight talking.* **c** said of a tip: from a trustworthy source. **5** said of successes: following consecutively or uninterruptedly: *her seventh straight win; She got straight As in her*

exams. **6** said of an alcoholic drink: unmixed; neat. **7a** in the theatre, denoting a conventional play as distinct from e.g. a farce or musical. **b** *informal* conventional in appearance, habits, opinions, etc; = SQUARE². **c** *informal* not using or under the influence of drugs. **d** *informal* heterosexual as distinct from homosexual or bisexual. * **keep a straight face** to refrain from laughing. **set somebody straight on something** to give somebody the facts about something and clear up any misunderstanding. ⋙ **straightish** *adj,* **straightly** *adv,* **straightness** *noun.* [Middle English, old past part. of STRETCH¹]

straight² *adv* **1** upright: *Sit up straight.* **2** directly; in a straight line: *He was looking straight at me; Go straight on.* **3** without delay or hesitation; immediately: *straight after breakfast; Go straight home.* **4** *archaic* at once: *I'll be with you straight.* **5** honestly; without evasion: *I tell you straight.* **6** clearly; accurately: *I couldn't think straight.* * **go straight** to leave one's life of crime and live honestly. **straight off/out** without hesitation: *She gave me his number straight off.* **straight up 1** *Brit, informal* honestly: *I'm telling you it's all right. Straight up.* **2** *NAmer* neat; unmixed: *bourbon straight up.*

straight³ *noun* **1** (**the straight**) a straight line or arrangement: *Keep it on the straight.* **2** a straight part or piece of something, e.g. the HOME STRAIGHT on a race course. **3** a poker hand containing five cards in sequence but not of the same suit. **4** *informal.* **a** a conventional person. **b** a heterosexual. * **the straight and narrow** a strictly honest or moral way of life [in reference to *Strait is the gate and narrow is the way which leadeth unto life* in Matthew 7:14].

straight angle *noun* an angle of 180°.

straight-arm *verb trans NAmer* to ward (a person) off or push away (an obstacle) with a stiffly outstretched arm: compare STIFF-ARM.

straightaway *or* **straight away** *adv* without hesitation or delay; immediately.

straightbred *adj* produced from a single breed, strain, or type: compare CROSSBRED: *a straightbred Angus heifer.*

straight chain *noun* an open chain of atoms having no side chains.

straight-cut *adj* said of tobacco: cut lengthways into long fibres.

straightedge *noun* **1** a piece of wood, metal, etc with an accurate straight edge for testing surfaces, drawing straight lines, etc. **2** a piece of one of the straight sides of a jigsaw puzzle.

straight-eight *noun* an internal-combustion engine with eight cylinders in line.

straighten *verb* (**straightened, straightening**) ➤ *verb intrans* **1** (+ up) to sit or stand. **2** (+ up) said of a vehicle, ship, etc: to stop turning and travel in a straight line. ➤ *verb trans* **1** (+ up) to set (something) straight. **2a** (*also* + out) to make (something) smooth or tidy. **b** (+ out) to sort out (a difficulty, etc). ⋙ **straightener** *noun.*

straight-faced *adj* betraying no amusement.

straight fight *noun chiefly Brit* a contest, *esp* an election contest, between two candidates only.

straight flush *noun* a poker hand containing five cards of the same suit in sequence.

straightforward *adj* **1** said of a person: truthful; frank; easy to deal with. **2** free from evasiveness or ambiguity; direct; candid: *a straightforward account.* **3** presenting no hidden difficulties: *a perfectly straightforward case.* **4** said of language: simple; clear-cut; precise. ⋙ **straightforwardly** *adv,* **straightforwardness** *noun.*

straightjacket¹ *noun* see STRAITJACKET¹.

straightjacket² *verb trans* = STRAITJACKET².

straightlaced *adj* see STRAITLACED.

straight-line *adj* in finance, spread uniformly or spreading accumulation or payments uniformly, *esp* in equal parts, over a given term: *straight-line depreciation.*

straight man *noun* a straight actor serving as foil to a clown or comedian; = STOOGE¹.

straight-out *adj NAmer* **1** forthright; blunt: *a straight-out answer.* **2** outright; thoroughgoing: *a straight-out Democrat.*

straight razor *noun NAmer* = CUTTHROAT RAZOR.

straight ticket *noun NAmer* a ballot cast for the candidates of one party: compare SPLIT TICKET.

straightway *adv archaic* immediately; forthwith: *Faithful ... straightway was carried up through the clouds* — Bunyan.

strain¹ /strayn/ *verb trans* **1a** to exert (a part of one's body) to the maximum: *He strained his ears to hear the faint sounds.* **b** to wrench or sprain (a part of one's body) through over-exertion: *I've strained my back.* **2** to make great or excessive demands on (something): *a story that strains one's credulity.* **3** to stretch (fabric, etc) to maximum extension and tautness. **4** *literary* to hug (somebody) tightly: *Eliza … strained the child closer to her bosom* — Harriet Beecher Stowe. **5a** to pass (a liquid) through a sieve or filter: *Strain the meat stock before re-using it.* **b** (+ off) to separate or drain off (liquid) by this means. **c** (+ out/out of) to remove (solid matter) from liquid by this means: *Strain the lumps out of the gravy.* ➤ *verb intrans* **1** to make strenuous efforts to do something; to strive: *She has to strain to reach the high notes now.* **2** (*often* + at) to pull violently: *The dog was straining at its leash.* **3** to labour or struggle: *straining under the weight of their packs.* **4** to contract the muscles strenuously in attempting to pass faeces. ➤➤ **strainable** *adj.* [Middle English via Old French *estreindre* from Latin *stringere* to bind or draw tight, press together]

strain² *noun* **1** a force being exerted on something: *the strain on the rope; His back and shoulders took the strain.* **2a** in physics, the deformation of a material body subjected to stress. **b** in physics, the amount of such deformation, usu equal to the change in a dimension, e.g. length or volume, divided by the original dimension. **3a** mental or emotional stress or tension, or something that causes this: *He is suffering from strain; the stresses and strains of combining a career with having a family.* **b** a wrench, sprain, or other bodily injury caused by excessive tension, effort, or use: *back strain.* **4a** (*also in pl*) a tune, air, or passage of music: *That strain again! It had a dying fall* — Shakespeare; *the strains of a Strauss waltz.* **b** the tone, manner, or content of an utterance: *He continued in that strain for some time.*

strain³ *noun* **1a** a breed, race, or variety of an animal or plant: *a high-yielding strain of winter wheat.* **b** a particular type of a bacterium or virus: *a new and distinct strain of Asian flu.* **2** an inherited but not dominant characteristic, quality, or disposition: *a strain of madness in the family.* **3** a variation on something such as a philosophy, movement, etc: *a slightly different strain of logical positivism.* [Old English *strēon* gain, acquisition, in Middle English 'offspring, progeny']

strained *adj* **1** done or produced with excessive effort; not spontaneous: *a strained smile.* **2** tense; uneasy: *strained relations; a strained silence.* **3** showing the effects of strain: *a strained expression.* **4** said e.g. of an instance or example cited: far-fetched.

strainer *noun* a device, e.g. a sieve, to retain solid pieces while a liquid passes through: *a tea-strainer.*

strain gauge *noun* = EXTENSOMETER.

strait¹ /strayt/ *adj archaic* narrow: *Strait is the gate … which leadeth unto life* — Bible. ➤➤ **straitly** *adv*, **straitness** *noun*. [Middle English via Old French *estreit* from Latin *strictus* constricted, past part. of *stringere* to bind tightly]

strait² *noun* **1** (*also in pl*) a narrow channel connecting two large bodies of water: *the Straits of Messina.* **2** (*in pl*) a situation of difficulty or distress: *in dire straits.*

straiten *verb trans* (**straitened, straitening**) *archaic* **1** (*usu in passive*) to subject (somebody) to severely restricting difficulties, *esp* of a financial kind: *a woman straitened both in means and in reputation* — Hardy. **2** to restrict (something) in range or scope: *those natural dilations of the youthful spirit, which circumstances cannot straiten* — Charles Lamb.

straitened *adj literary* denoting poverty-stricken circumstances in which severe economies must be made.

straitjacket¹ *or* **straightjacket** *noun* **1** a cover or outer garment of strong material used to bind the body and *esp* the arms closely, in restraining a violent prisoner or psychiatric patient. **2** something that restricts or confines like a straitjacket: *the straitjacket of convention.*

straitjacket² *or* **straightjacket** *verb trans* (**straitjacketed** *or* **straightjacketed, straitjacketing** *or* **straightjacketing**) to restrain (a person, their spirit, etc) with or as if with a straitjacket: *old straitjacketing teaching methods that don't allow for diversity.*

straitlaced *or* **straightlaced** *adj* excessively strict in manners or morals.

strake /strayk/ *noun* **1** a continuous band of hull planking or plates running from stem to stern on a ship, or the width of this. **2** a projecting ridge added to an aircraft or other vehicle to increase stability. **3** any of the metal plates forming the rim of a wooden tyre. [Middle English from late Latin *straca, stracus* rim, prob. related to Old English *streccan* STRETCH¹]

stramash /strə'mash/ *noun Scot* a row or commotion. [prob imitative]

stramonium /strə'mohni·əm/ *noun* a medicine prepared from the leaves and poisonous seeds of the THORN APPLE, used e.g. to treat nervous disorders. [scientific Latin *stramonium*, perhaps coined from Tartar *turman* a medicine for horses]

strand¹ /strand/ *verb trans* (*usu in passive*) **1** to run, drive, or cause (a ship) to drift onto a shore. **2** to leave (a person) in a strange or unfavourable place, *esp* without funds or means to depart.

strand² *noun literary* a shore or beach. [Old English, of unknown origin]

strand³ *noun* **1a** any of the threads, strings, or wires twisted or laid parallel to make a cord, rope, or cable. **b** something, e.g. a molecular chain, resembling this. **2** a string of beads: *a strand of pearls.* **3** any of the elements interwoven in a complex whole: *follow the strands of the story.* [Middle English; earlier history unknown]

strand⁴ *verb trans* **1** to break a strand of (a rope) accidentally. **2** to form (a rope) by winding strands together. ➤➤ **stranded** *adj.*

strange /straynj/ *adj* **1** not native to or naturally belonging in a place; of external origin, kind, or character: *strange species.* **2** not known, heard, seen, or visited before: *a strange man at the door; strange places.* **3** exciting wonder or surprise: *strange doings.* **4** *archaic* (+ to) lacking experience or acquaintance of something; unaccustomed to it: *We were strange to the experience.* ✱ **strange to say/tell** it is odd that; surprisingly. ➤➤ **strangely** *adv.* [Middle English via Old French *estrange* from Latin *extraneus* foreign, external, from *extra* outside, fem. of *exter*: see EXTERIOR¹]

strangeness *noun* **1** the state or fact of being strange. **2** in physics, the quantum property that explains the unexpectedly long lifetime possessed by certain elementary particles, e.g. kaons.

strange particle *noun* an elementary particle, e.g. a kaon, with a strangeness quantum number different from zero.

stranger *noun* **1** a person who is unknown or with whom one is unacquainted: *She was a stranger to me.* **2** a person unfamiliar in the place in question; a foreigner or alien. **3** (+ to) a person who is ignorant of or unacquainted with something: *a stranger to books.* **4** in Britain, a person who is not a member or official of the House of Commons: *the Strangers' Gallery.* [Middle English via Old French *estrangier* foreign, foreigner, from Latin *extraneus*: see STRANGE]

strangle /'stranggl/ *verb trans* **1** to choke (a person or animal), *esp* to death, by compressing their throat; = THROTTLE². **2** to suppress (a groan, cry, etc): *a strangled sob.* **3** to hinder the development of (something): *The boarding-school ethic tended to strangle initiative.* ➤ *verb intrans* to die from or as if from being strangled. ➤➤ **strangler** *noun.* [Middle English via Old French from Latin *strangulare*, from Greek *strangalan*, from *strangalē* halter]

stranglehold *noun* **1** a grip round the neck that can lead to strangulation. **2** a total control or monopoly of something: *The corporation was acquiring a stranglehold over the market.*

strangles *pl noun* (*usu treated as sing.*) a contagious feverish disease of horses, with nasal discharge, inflammation, and abscesses between the jawbones.

strangulate /'stranggyoolayt/ *verb trans* **1** (*usu as past part.*) to constrict or compress (a blood vessel, loop of intestine, etc) in a way that interrupts the ability to act as a passage: *a strangulated hernia.* **2** *informal* to strangle (somebody). ➤➤ **strangulation** /-'laysh(ə)n/ *noun.* [Latin *strangulatus*, past part. of *strangulare*: see STRANGLE]

strangury /'stranggyoori/ *noun* slow and painful urination. [Middle English via Latin from Greek *strangouria*, from *strang-, stranx* drop squeezed out + *ouron* urine]

strap¹ /strap/ *noun* **1** (*often used in combinations*) a strip of leather, cloth, or other flexible material used for fastening, securing, holding together, or carrying, often with a buckle: *a watchstrap.* **2** a narrow strip forming part of a garment and holding it in position on the body: *shoulder straps.* **3** a band, plate, or loop of metal for binding objects together or for clamping an object in position. **4** a strip of wood screwed into a wall to take the weight of a hanging fixture such as a cupboard. **5** a leather or rubber loop hanging from the roof of a bus or train for standing passengers to hold onto. **6a** a strip of leather used for flogging, *esp* formerly in schools. **b** (*the* **strap**) punishment by this means: *I got the strap for talking in class.* **7** *Irish, informal, derog* an immoral or immodest woman. ➤➤ **strapless** *adj*, **strappy** *adj.* [variant of STROP¹]

strap[2] *verb trans* (**strapped, strapping**) **1** to secure (something) with or attach (it) by means of a strap. **2** *Brit* (*also* + *up*) to support (a sprained joint, etc) with overlapping strips of adhesive plaster. **3** to beat (somebody) with a strap.

straphanger *noun* a passenger in a train, bus, etc who has to hold a strap or handle for support while standing. ➤➤ **straphanging** *noun.*

strap hinge *noun* a hinge with long flat extensions for screwing onto the surface of a door, gate, etc.

strapline *noun* a secondary heading or caption in a newspaper, etc.

strappado /strə'pahdoh, strə'paydoh/ *noun* (*pl* **strappadoes** or **strappados**) a former torture consisting of hoisting the victim by a rope and letting them fall almost to the ground. [modification of Italian *strappata*, literally 'sharp pull']

strapped *adj informal* (*often* + *for*) short of money: *strapped for cash.*

strapping[1] *adj* said of a person: big, strong, and sturdy in build.

strapping[2] *noun* **1** adhesive bandaging for wounds or injuries. **2** metal or leather straps collectively.

strapwork *noun* architectural or sculptural ornamentation imitating interlaced straps.

strass /stras/ *noun* = PASTE[1] (3). [German *Strass*, named after Josef Strasser, 18th-cent. German jeweller, who invented it]

strata /'strahtə/ *noun* pl of STRATUM.

stratagem /'stratəjəm, -jem/ *noun* **1** an artifice or trick for deceiving and outwitting an opponent. **2** a cleverly contrived trick or scheme. **3** *archaic* cunning; guile. [French *stratagème* via Latin from Greek *stratēgēma* a trick, from *stratēgein* to be a general, manoeuvre, from *stratēgos* general, from *stratos* army + *agein* to lead]

stratal /'straytl, 'strahtl/ *adj* relating to strata or a stratum.

strategic /strə'teejik/ *adj* **1** relating to the long-term pursuit of objectives: *strategic planning.* **2** relating to military effectiveness: *the strategic importance of Malta and Gibraltar to the British.* **3** said of weapons, missiles, etc: designed to disrupt industry and communications in the enemy homeland, rather than for use on the battlefield: compare TACTICAL. **4** said of materials and resources: required for the conduct of war. **5** *often humorous* relating to the discreet handling of a situation: *I placed myself at a strategic distance, hoping to eavesdrop on the conversation.* ➤➤ **strategically** *adv.*

strategical /strə'teejik(ə)l/ *adj* = STRATEGIC.

Strategic Defence Initiative *noun* a US government programme, launched by President Reagan, aimed at providing an effective defence against nuclear attack by means of a computer-linked network of detecting and anti-missile systems, many of them satellite-based.

strategise /'stratijiez/ *verb intrans* see STRATEGIZE.

strategist /'stratijist/ *noun* a person who is skilled in strategy.

strategize or **strategise** /'stratijiez/ *verb intrans NAmer* to devise strategies.

strategy /'stratiji/ *noun* (*pl* **strategies**) **1a** the science and art of employing all the resources of a nation or group of nations to carry out agreed policies in peace or war. **b** the science and art of military command exercised to meet the enemy in combat under advantageous conditions: compare TACTICS. **c** an instance of the application of this: *His strategy had succeeded, enabling the Allied advance to broaden out.* **2a** long-term planning in the pursuit of objectives, or the art of this: *our strategy for the next financial year.* **b** a plan or method devised to meet a need: *strategies for dealing with dissatisfied customers.* [Greek *stratēgia* generalship, from *stratēgos*: see STRATEGY]

strath /strath/ *noun* a flat wide river valley, *esp* in Scotland. [Scottish Gaelic *srath*]

strathspey /strath'spay/ *noun* a Scottish dance that is similar to a reel but has a slower tempo and a more gliding step. [named after *Strath Spey*, district of Scotland]

strati /'strahtie, 'straytie/ *noun* pl of STRATUS.

strati- *comb. form* forming words, denoting: stratum: *stratify.* [scientific Latin *stratum*: see STRATUM]

straticulate /strə'tikyoolət, -layt/ *adj* having thin parallel strata. [from scientific Latin *straticulum*, dimin. of *stratum*: see STRATUM]

stratify /'stratifie/ *verb* (**stratifies, stratified, stratifying**) ➤ *verb trans* **1** to form, deposit, or arrange (material, etc) in strata. **2** to divide (a population, etc) into status groups or social strata. **3** to store (seeds) in layers in a moist medium. ➤ *verb intrans* to become arranged in strata. ➤➤ **stratification** /-fi'kaysh(ə)n/ *noun.*

stratigraphy /strə'tigrəfi/ *noun* **1a** the origin, distribution, and succession of rock strata. **b** the branch of geology concerned with this. **2** the analysis of the chronological order of archaeological remains and deposits: *the stratigraphy of the site.* ➤➤ **stratigraphic** /strati'grafik/ *adj.*

strato- *comb. form* forming words, denoting: **1** in cloud classification, stratus and: *stratocumulus.* **2** layer; stratum: *stratovolcano; stratosphere.* [(sense 1) from Latin *stratus*, past part. of *sternere* to strew; (sense 2) see STRATUM]

stratocracy /strə'tokrəsi/ *noun* (*pl* **stratocracies**) a military government. [Greek *stratos* army + -CRACY]

stratocumulus /strahtoh'kyoohmyoolǝs, stray-/ *noun* stratified cumulus consisting of large dark clouds often covering the whole sky, *esp* in winter, occurring at low altitude, between about 350 and 2000m (about 1200 and 7000ft).

stratopause /'stratəpawz/ *noun* the upper boundary of the STRATOSPHERE, dividing it from the IONOSPHERE. [STRATOSPHERE + Greek *pausis* cessation, from *pauein* to stop]

stratosphere /'stratəsfiə/ *noun* **1** the layer of the earth's atmosphere between the TROPOSPHERE and the MESOSPHERE (that is, above about 6–18km (4–11mi) and up to 50km (30mi)) in which temperature increases with height. **2** *informal* the highest levels of something: *the stratosphere of English society* — New Yorker. ➤➤ **stratospheric** /-'sferik/ *adj*, **stratospherical** /-'sferikl/ *adj.*

stratovolcano /,stratohvol'kaynoh/ *noun* (*pl* **stratovolcanoes**) a volcano composed of alternating layers of ash and lava.

stratum /'strahtəm, 'straytəm/ *noun* (*pl* **strata** /'strahtə, 'straytə/) **1** a horizontal layer or series of layers of any homogeneous material, e.g.: **a** a sheetlike mass of rock or earth deposited between beds of other rock. **b** a layer of the sea or atmosphere. **c** a layer of tissue. **d** a layer in which archaeological remains are found on excavation. **2** a socioeconomic level of society: *the higher social strata.* [scientific Latin *stratum* layer, from Latin *stratum* bed, coverlet, literally 'something laid down', neuter past part. of *sternere* to strew, spread out]

stratum corneum /,stratəm 'kawni·əm, ,strahtəm/ *noun* the comparatively tough outer layer of the skin. [scientific Latin *stratum corneum* horny layer, from *stratum* (see STRATUM) + Latin *corneus* horny, from *cornu* horn]

stratus /'strahtəs, 'straytəs/ *noun* (*pl* **strati** /'strahtie, 'straytie/) a cloud formation consisting of massive broad uniformly thick cloud, occurring at low altitude, between the surface and about 450m (about 1500ft). [scientific Latin *stratus*, past part. of Latin *sternere* to spread, strew]

stravaig /strə'vayg/ *verb intrans Scot, Irish* to wander about or abroad, *esp* without a sensible purpose. [prob alteration of obsolete *extravage* to ramble, from late Latin *extravagari* to wander away, stray, from EXTRA- + *vagari* to wander]

straw /straw/ *noun* **1a** dry stalky plant residue, *esp* stalks of grain after threshing, used for bedding, thatching, fodder, making hats, etc. **b** a single stalk from such residue. **2** a dry coarse stem, *esp* of a cereal grass. **3** a tube of paper, plastic, etc for sucking up a drink. **4** a pale yellow colour: *Those straw-coloured women have dreadful tempers* — Oscar Wilde. ✳ **catch/clutch/grasp at straws** to turn in desperation to any, even a manifestly inadequate, means of saving the situation. **draw the short straw** to be the person chosen to do something unpleasant. **not care a straw for** to be totally indifferent to (somebody or something). **straw in the wind** a hint or apparently insignificant fact that is an indication of a coming event. ➤➤ **strawy** *adj.* [Old English *strēaw*]

strawberry /'strawb(ə)ri/ *noun* (*pl* **strawberries**) **1a** a small sweet red fruit covered with seeds. **b** the creeping plant of the rose family that bears this fruit, with runners and white flowers: genus *Fragaria*. **2** a deep pinkish red colour. [Old English, from STRAW + BERRY[1], perhaps with reference to the chaff-like appearance of the seeds]

strawberry blonde *noun* **1** a reddish blonde hair colour. **2** a woman with this hair colour.

strawberry mark *noun* a red elevated birthmark composed of small blood vessels.

strawberry roan *noun* a roan horse with a light red ground colour.

strawberry tomato *noun* = CAPE GOOSEBERRY.

strawberry tree *noun* a European evergreen tree of the heath family with clustered white flowers and fruits like strawberries: *Arbutus unedo*.

strawboard *noun* coarse cardboard made of straw pulp and used usu for boxes and book covers.

straw boss *noun NAmer, informal* a low-grade manager or supervisor with little authority.

strawflower *noun* an everlasting flower of Australia, of the daisy family: *Helichrysum bracteatum*.

straw man *noun* = MAN OF STRAW.

straw poll *noun* an unofficial ballot carried out to test opinion on some issue. [prob from the phrase *a straw in the wind*]

straw vote *noun NAmer, NZ* = STRAW POLL.

strawweight *noun* a weight in professional boxing of no more than 47.6kg (105lbs).

stray[1] /stray/ *verb intrans* **1** to wander away from the main group, or from the proper place or route. **2** to wander or move about aimlessly: *She happened to stray into the library one day.* **3** *dated or humorous* to deviate from the path of moral rectitude, *esp* to be unfaithful to one's spouse. **4** said of an eye or hand: to move apparently casually in some direction: *Her eye strayed towards the clock.* ➤➤ **strayer** *noun.* [Middle English from Old French *estraier* to stray, ultimately from Latin EXTRA- + *vagari* to wander]

stray[2] *noun* **1** a domestic animal wandering at large or lost. **2** *dated* a lost or homeless person, *esp* a child: *waifs and strays.* **3** (*in pl*). **a** interference in radio or television reception; = STATIC[2]. **b** undesired CAPACITANCE (storage of an electric charge) in a piece of equipment.

stray[3] *adj* **1** said of a domestic animal: having strayed; wandering; lost: *a stray dog.* **2** said of hair: having escaped from an arrangement: *She tucked a stray lock behind her ear.* **3** occurring at random or sporadically: *a few stray instances.* **4** said of an electric charge, etc: unwanted; causing interference: *stray voltages.*

streak[1] /streek/ *noun* **1** a line or band of a different colour from the background. **2** a sample containing micro-organisms, e.g. bacteria, implanted in a line on a solid culture medium, e.g. agar jelly, for growth. **3** an inherent quality, *esp* one that is only occasionally manifested: *He had a mean streak in him.* ✳ **like a streak** *informal* without a moment's hesitation: *He was off like a streak.* **on a winning streak** enjoying a series of successes or lucky breaks. **streak of lightning** a flash of lightning. [Old English *strica*]

streak[2] *verb trans* (*usu in passive*) to make streaks on or in (something): *a face streaked with tears.* ➤ *verb intrans* **1** to move swiftly: *a jet streaking across the sky.* **2** *informal* to run naked through a public place for fun, as a challenge, or as a statement-making gesture. ➤➤ **streaked** *adj,* **streaker** *noun,* **streaking** *noun.*

streaky *adj* (**streakier, streakiest**) **1** marked with streaks. **2** said of bacon: having lines of fat and lean. **3** said of a shot in cricket: hit off the edge of the bat. **4** *chiefly NAmer, informal* varying in quality or effectiveness; unreliable. ➤➤ **streakily** *adv,* **streakiness** *noun.*

stream[1] /streem/ *noun* **1** a body of running water, typically one narrower than a river. **2a** a body of flowing liquid or gas. **b** an unbroken flow, e.g. of gas or particles of matter. **3** a steady succession: *She kept up an endless stream of chatter; a steady stream of applicants.* **4** a continuous moving procession: *a stream of traffic.* **5** *Brit* any of a graded range of groups in a school to which pupils of the same age group are assigned according to their general academic ability: compare BAND[1] (7), SET[3] (3): *the A stream.* ✳ **go with/against the stream** to conform to, or be opposed to, a general trend. **on/off stream** operational or available, or not so: *lots of new software coming on stream.* [Old English *strēam*]

stream[2] *verb intrans* **1** to flow in a stream: *Water streamed along the gutters.* **2** to flood or pour in great quantity: *Sunlight streamed into the room; People were streaming out of the bingo hall.* **3** to trail, or extend in a trail: *with her hair streaming out behind her.* **4** to run profusely with liquid: *walls streaming with condensation.* **5** *Brit* to practise the division of pupils into streams. ➤ *verb trans* **1** to emit (liquid) freely or in a stream. **2** *Brit* to divide (a school or an age group of pupils) into streams.

streamer *noun* **1** a coiled strip of coloured paper for throwing at a party. **2** a pennant. **3** a long ribbon-like appendage, as on a jellyfish. **4** a banner headline in a newspaper. **5** a long extension of the sun's corona visible only during a total eclipse. **6** = TAPE STREAMER.

streamer weed *noun* any of various water plants with fronds that waft in the current.

streaming *adj* **1** said of a cold: causing the eyes and nose to run uncontrollably. **2** denoting a tape drive on a computer for transferring data in bulk while the tape is running.

streamline[1] *noun* **1** the path of a fluid, e.g. air or water, relative to a solid body past which the fluid is moving smoothly without turbulence. **2** a contour given to a car, aeroplane, etc so as to minimize resistance to motion, e.g. through air.

streamline[2] *verb trans* **1** to design or construct (a vehicle, etc) with a streamline. **2** to make (an organization) simpler, more efficient, or better integrated.

streamlined *adj* **1a** having a streamline contour. **b** effectively integrated; organized. **2** having flowing lines.

stream of consciousness *noun* **1** in psychology, individual conscious experience considered as a continuous flow of reactions and experiences. **2** a literary technique used to convey this.

streel /streel/ *verb intrans Irish* **1** to walk about idly; to saunter. **2** to trail like a streamer. [Irish Gaelic *straoilleán* loiterer]

streeler *noun Irish* a slovenly person: *an ugly young streeler with a murderous gob on him* — J M Synge.

street /street/ *noun* **1** a public thoroughfare in a city, town, or village, typically with buildings, *esp* including shops, along both sides, and pavements. **2** (*treated as sing. or pl*) the inhabitants or temporary occupants of a street: *There's no need to tell the whole street.* **3** (*used before a noun*). **a** homeless; living and sleeping in the streets: *street kids.* **b** relating to the culture of those adept at surviving in the urban environment: *street chic.* ✳ **on the street** homeless; vagrant. **on the streets** earning one's living as a prostitute. **streets ahead/better** *informal* immeasurably better: *streets ahead of the other candidates.* **up/down one's street** suited to one's abilities or tastes. [Old English *strǣt* via a prehistoric Germanic word from Latin *strata* (*via*) paved (way), fem past part. of *sternere* to strew, spread]

street Arab *noun dated* a homeless ragged child wandering the streets; an urchin.

streetcar *noun NAmer* a tram.

street cred *noun* = STREET CREDIBILITY.

street credibility *noun* a convincing knowledge of what goes on in the urban subculture.

street cry *noun* any of the cries of hawkers selling wares in the street.

street door *noun* the main door of a house opening onto the street.

street furniture *noun* street fittings such as lamps, litter bins, road signs, and postboxes, installed for public use or convenience.

street lamp *noun* = STREET LIGHT.

street-legal *adj* said of a vehicle: fully licensed for use on the road.

street light *noun* any of the lamps lighting a street, usu mounted on a tall post. ➤➤ **streetlighting** *noun.*

street name *noun NAmer* a name under which a purchaser holds stock, usu that of a bank, dealer, or stockbroking firm.

street-smart *adj chiefly NAmer, informal* = STREETWISE.

street theatre *noun* drama or acts, *esp* of an improvised nature, performed in shopping areas, etc, often as part of a local festival.

street value *noun* the likely price that something, *esp* a quantity of drugs, could command if sold illegally on the street.

streetwalker *noun* a prostitute who solicits in the streets: compare CALL GIRL. ➤➤ **streetwalking** *noun.*

streetwise *adj informal* **1** familiar with the life of city streets, *esp* with its disreputable or criminal underworld. **2** resourceful at surviving and prospering in modern urban conditions.

Strega /'straygə/ *noun trademark* an orange-flavoured Italian liqueur. [Italian *strēga* witch, hag]

strelitzia /strə'litsi-ə/ *noun* any of a genus of S African plants with showy flowers, including the bird-of-paradise flower: genus *Strelitzia*. [Latin genus name, in honour of Charlotte of Mecklenberg-Strelitz d.1818, queen of George III]

strength /strength/ *noun* **1a** the physical power one has in one's body; muscle power: *You don't know your own strength.* **b** one's health and energy: *She has regained her strength after a bout of* shingles. **c** moral courage: *He didn't have the strength to resist.* **2** in a material object, ability to withstand pressure, prolonged use, etc; durability; toughness; solidity: *Nylon is preferred for climbing ropes because of its strength.* **3** the intensity of something, or the degree to which it is present or exists: *The strength of feeling on the issue was evident.* **4** used with reference to solutions, alcoholic drinks, etc: the amount contained of the effective ingredient. **5** the force, effectiveness, or convincing quality of an argument, etc: *the strength of their case.* **6** impregnability: *acting from a position of strength.* **7** force measured in membership, or members present: *at full strength; below strength.* **8** a good point: *Know your own strengths and weaknesses.* **9** *Aus, NZ* meaning or point: *What's the strength of it all?* *** gather strength** to get stronger or larger, increase numerically, etc: *The movement was gathering strength.* **go from strength to strength** to become ever more successful. **on the strength of** on the basis of (something): *They offered him a place straight away on the strength of his interview.* **⟩⟩⟩ strengthless** *adj.* [Old English *strengthu*]

strengthen /'strength(ə)n/ *verb* (**strengthened, strengthening**) **⟩** *verb trans* to make (something or somebody) stronger **⟩** *verb intrans* to become stronger. **⟩⟩⟩ strengthener** *noun.*

strenuous /'strenyoo·əs/ *adj* **1** vigorous and wholehearted: *He made strenuous efforts to have her reinstated.* **2** requiring effort or stamina: *strenuous exercise.* **⟩⟩⟩ strenuosity** /-'ositi/ *noun,* **strenuously** *adv,* **strenuousness** *noun.* [Latin *strenuus* brisk]

strep /strep/ *noun informal* = STREPTOCOCCUS. **⟩⟩⟩ strep** *adj.*

strepto- *comb. form* forming words, with the meanings: **1** twisted; twisted chain: *streptococcus.* **2** relating to streptococci or streptomycetes: *streptokinase.* [Greek *streptos* twisted, from *strephein* to twist]

streptocarpus /streptoh'kahpəs/ *noun* a S African plant with funnel-shaped flowers and spirally twisted fruits: genus *Streptocarpus.* [Latin genus name, from STREPTO- + Greek *karpos* fruit]

streptococcus /streptə'kokəs/ *noun* (*pl* **streptococci** /-'kok(s)ie/) any of a genus of chiefly parasitic bacteria that occur in pairs or chains and include some that cause diseases in human beings and domestic animals: genus *Streptococcus.* **⟩⟩⟩ streptococcal** *adj,* **streptococcic** /-'kok(s)ik/ *adj.* [Latin genus name, from STREPTO- + COCCUS]

streptokinase /streptoh'kienayz, -nays/ *noun* an enzyme produced by some streptococcal bacteria that breaks down blood clots. [STREPTO- + *kinase* (an enzyme), from KINETIC]

streptomycete /streptə'mieseet/ *noun* any of a family of rod-shaped bacteria found chiefly in the soil feeding on dead and decaying plant and animal matter in the soil, some having antibiotic properties: genus *Streptomyces,* etc. [Latin genus name *Streptomycet-, Streptomyces,* from STREPTO- + Greek *mycēt-, mykēs* fungus]

streptomycin /streptə'miesin/ *noun* an antibiotic obtained from a soil bacterium and used *esp* in the treatment of tuberculosis. [Latin *Streptomyces,* genus name of bacteria]

streptothricin /streptə'thriesin, -'thrisin/ *noun* an antibiotic that is obtained from a bacterium, *Streptomyces lavendulae,* and is used in the treatment of diseases, e.g. hepatitis. [Latin genus name *Streptothric-, Streptothrix,* from STREPTO- + *-thrix* having hairlike filaments, from Greek *trich-, thrix* hair]

stress¹ /stres/ *noun* **1a** pressure exerted on a physical object: *the part of the beam that takes most of the stress.* **b** the force of this per unit area. **2** mental or emotional tension; strain: *suffering from stress.* **3a** intensity of utterance given to a speech sound, syllable, or word so as to produce relative loudness; accent: *The stress comes on the second syllable.* **b** such force or prominence given to a syllable in verse or a note in music, as part of the rhythm. *** lay stress on** to emphasize (a point). **⟩⟩⟩ stressful** *adj,* **stressfully** *adv,* **stressless** *adj.* [Middle English, in the sense 'constraint', shortened from DISTRESS¹]

stress² *verb trans* **1** to emphasize (a point, etc): *I have to stress the need for confidentiality.* **2** to accent or emphasize (a word, syllable, etc): *In Czech most words are stressed on the first syllable.* **3** (*usu in passive, also* + out) to subject (somebody) to emotional or mental stress: *too stressed to be sociable; feeling stressed out.*

stress mark *noun* in phonetics, a mark to show where the stress comes in a word, typically a short vertical superscript stroke placed before the stressed syllable, or a sloping one after it.

stretch¹ /strech/ *verb trans* **1a** (+ out) to lay (oneself) down at full length: *He stretched himself out on the couch.* **b** (+ out) to hold out or extend (an arm or leg): *Stretch your arms out to the sides.* **c** *informal* (+ out) to knock down or fell (somebody): *The blow stretched him out full length on the carpet.* **2a** to pull, extend, or expand (material) till it becomes taut: *Stretch the canvas over the frame.* **b** to extend (oneself or one's limbs) to maximum height, length, etc, to relieve muscle stiffness, etc: *The cat got up and stretched itself.* **3a** to enlarge (something) by force: *I'm going to have my shoes stretched.* **b** to provide adequate challenge for (a person or their mind): *I'm not being stretched in this job.* **c** to strain (some resource, etc): *Cash supplies were already stretched to their utmost.* **d** to supplement or expand (something) beyond normal limits: *I stretch my pay packet with a spot of overtime. The rules can be stretched this once.* **⟩** *verb intrans* **1a** to extend in space; to reach or spread: *broad plains stretching to the sea.* **b** to extend over a period of time: *The summer holidays stretched ahead of her.* **2a** (+ out) to lie at full length: *I stretched out on the sofa.* **b** to extend one's body or limbs to full length to relieve muscle stiffness, etc: *Stand up and stretch.* **3** to elongate oneself in trying to reach something; to reach out: *She stretched over and switched off the bedside light.* **4a** said of material, garments, etc: to have an elastic quality: *These jeans stretch.* **b** said of materials, garments, etc: to become permanently enlarged: *My jumper stretched in the wash.* *** stretch a point** to distort the rules slightly so as to accommodate a need, etc. **stretch one's legs** to go for a walk. **⟩⟩⟩ stretchable** *adj,* **stretchiness** *noun,* **stretchy** *adj.* [Old English *streccan*]

stretch² *noun* **1** the act or an instance of extending the body and limbs to full length: *Get up and have a good stretch.* **2** the quality of elasticity in a material, etc. **3** an extent or area: *a stretch of water; a fine stretch of coastline.* **4** a leg of a journey, course, track, etc: *the home stretch.* **5** a period of time: *She was left by herself for long stretches.* **6** *informal* a period in prison: *He did a stretch in Parkhurst.* *** at a stretch** continuously: *I work twelve hours at a stretch.* **at full stretch** to full capacity: *Hospital resources are at full stretch to meet the emergency.* **not by any stretch of the imagination** not conceivably: *The play could not be described as entertaining by any stretch of the imagination.*

stretcher¹ *noun* **1** a light portable bed for carrying a sick, injured, or dead person, typically consisting of a sheet of canvas or other fabric stretched between two poles. **2** (*often used in combinations*) a person or thing that stretches; *esp* a mechanism for stretching or expanding something: *a glove-stretcher.* **3** in bricklaying, a brick or stone laid with its length parallel to the face of the wall: compare HEADER (3). **4** a timber or rod used, *esp* when horizontal, as a tie in a structural framework, e.g. for building. **5** a wooden frame over which a canvas for painting is stretched and fastened. **6** a rod or bar extending between two legs of a chair or table. **7** a board in a rowing boat that serves as a rest for a rower's feet.

stretcher² *verb trans* (**stretchered, stretchering**) to carry (an injured or sick person) on a stretcher: *He was stretchered off the field.*

stretcher-bearer *noun* a person who helps to carry stretchers, *esp* in a war.

stretch limo *noun informal* = STRETCH LIMOUSINE.

stretch limousine *noun informal* a custom-built limousine that has been lengthened to provide extra seating.

stretch marks *pl noun* permanent marks on the skin caused by significant, usu rapid, weight gain or loss, *esp* those on the abdomen resulting from pregnancy.

stretto /'stretoh/ *noun* (*pl* **stretti** /'stretee/) **1 a** the overlapping of answer with subject in a musical fugue. **b** the part of a fugue characterized by this overlapping. **2** (*also*) **stretta** /'stretə/ a concluding musical passage performed in a quicker tempo. [Italian *stretto* (masc) and *stretta* (fem) narrow, close, from Latin *strictus,* past part. of *stringere* to compress]

streusel /'shtroyzl, 'stroohzl/ *noun* a crumble topping for a pie, pastry, etc made of flour, fat and sugar, and sometimes cinnamon. [German *Streusel* from *streuen* to strew, sprinkle]

strew /strooh/ *verb trans* (*past tense* **strewed**, *past part.* **strewn** /stroohn/) **1** to spread (something) by scattering: *She strewed clean sand on the floor* — Kipling. **2** (+ with) to cover (a place) with or as if with something scattered: *areas strewn with large turves* — Hardy. **3** to become dispersed over (a place): *the great variety of buoyant matter that strewed the coast of Lofoden* — Poe. [Old English *strewian, strēowian*]

strewth /stroohth/ *interj* see STRUTH.

stria /'strie·ə/ *noun* (*pl* **striae** /'strie·ee/) **1** a minute groove on the surface of a rock, crystal, etc. **2** a narrow groove, ridge, line of colours, etc, *esp* when one of a parallel series. [Latin *stria* furrow, channel]

striate¹ /'strieayt/ *verb trans* to mark (something) with striae.

striate² /'strie·ət/ *adj* = STRIATED.

striated /'strieaytid/ *adj* **1** marked with striae. **2** of or being striated muscle.

striated muscle *noun* muscle that is marked by alternate light and dark bands, is made up of long fibres, and comprises the voluntary muscle of vertebrates: compare SMOOTH MUSCLE.

striation /strie'aysh(ə)n/ *noun* **1a** the condition of being striated. **b** an arrangement or pattern of striae. **2** = STRIA.

stricken¹ /'strikən/ *adj* **1** said of somebody's face or expression: horrified or distressed. **2a** (*often* + by/with) badly hurt or hit by illness: *His companion lay stricken and bleeding; stricken with multiple sclerosis*. **b** (*used in combinations*) hit by the calamity, emotion, etc specified: *poverty-stricken; panic-stricken*. ✷ **stricken in age/years** *archaic* advanced into old age: *Abraham and Sara were ... well stricken in age* — Bible. [past part. of STRIKE¹]

stricken² *verb* past part. of STRIKE¹: *She was actually stricken dumb for five seconds* — L M Montgomery.

strickle /'strikl/ *noun* **1** an instrument for levelling off measures of grain. **2** a tool for sharpening scythes. [Old English *stricel*]

strict /strikt/ *adj* **1a** stringent in requirement or control: *under strict orders*. **b** severe in discipline: *a strict teacher*. **2a** inflexibly maintained or adhered to; complete: *strict secrecy*. **b** rigorously conforming to rules or standards: *a strict teetotaller*. **3** narrowly construed; restricted: *a strict interpretation of the Act*. **4** exact or precise: *in the strict sense of the word*. ➤➤ **strictly** *adv*, **strictness** *noun*. [Middle English, in the sense 'restricted, narrow', from Latin *strictus*, past part. of *stringere* to bind tight]

strict construction *noun* in law, the literal interpretation of a statute, etc by a court.

strict implication *noun* in logic, implication of the kind where the proposition 'if A then B' is true only if B can be deduced from A.

strict liability *noun* in law, liability that is not dependent on culpability resulting from actual negligence, etc.

stricture /'strikchə/ *noun* **1** a restraint or restriction: *moral strictures*. **2** (*usu* + on) an adverse criticism; a censure: *The self-importance of all those people! What I would give to hear your strictures on them!* — Jane Austen. **3a** an abnormal narrowing of a bodily passage. **b** the part so narrowed. [Middle English from late Latin *strictura*, from Latin *stringere* to bind tight]

stride¹ /stried/ *verb* (*past tense* **strode** /strohd/, *past part.* **stridden** /'strid(ə)n/) ➤ *verb intrans* to walk with long steps, usu with energy or firmness of purpose. ➤ *verb trans* **1** to move over or along (an area, place, or distance) by or as if by striding. **2** to cross (an obstacle) with a single long step. **3** *literary* to bestride or straddle (something). ➤➤ **strider** *noun*. [Old English *stridan*]

stride² *noun* **1a** a long step. **b** the distance covered in a single stride. **2** a striding way of walking: *her loose-limbed stride*. **3a** the most effective natural pace. **b** a state of maximum competence or capability: *get into one's stride*. **4** *chiefly Aus, NZ, informal* (*in pl*) trousers. **5** = STRIDE PIANO. ✷ **make strides** to make good progress; to advance rapidly: *Technology has made great strides*. **take something in one's stride** to confront or deal with something difficult or unpleasant without becoming flustered or upset: *She took the dangers in her stride*.

strident /'stried(ə)nt/ *adj* **1** loud and obtrusive: *strident voices*. **2** expressing opinions, demands, etc loudly or urgently. ➤➤ **stridence** *noun*, **stridency** /-si/ *noun*, **stridently** *adv*. [Latin *strident-, stridens*, present part. of *stridere, stridēre* to make a harsh noise]

stride piano *noun* a style of jazz piano playing in which the right hand plays the melody while the left hand alternates between a single note and a chord played an octave or more higher. [from the repeated 'strides' taken by the left hand]

stridor /'striedaw/ *noun* **1** in medicine, a harsh vibrating sound heard during breathing when the air passages are obstructed. **2** a strident sound. [Latin *stridor* a squeak, hiss, shriek, from *stridēre* to make a harsh noise]

stridulate /'stridyoolayt/ *verb intrans* said *esp* of crickets, grasshoppers, etc: to make a shrill creaking noise by rubbing together specialized body parts. ➤➤ **stridulation** /-'laysh(ə)n/ *noun*,

stridulatory /-lət(ə)ri/ *adj*. [earliest as *stridulation* from French, from Latin *stridulus* shrill, squeaky, from *stridere, stridēre* to make a harsh noise]

strife /strief/ *noun* **1** bitter conflict or dissension. **2** *Aus, NZ* trouble of any kind. ➤➤ **strifeless** *adj*. [Middle English *strif* from Old French *estrif*, prob from *estriver* to STRIVE]

strigil /'strijil/ *noun* an instrument used by ancient Greeks and Romans for scraping moisture, sweat, dirt, etc off the skin after bathing or exercising. [Latin *strigilis* from *stringere* to touch lightly]

strigose /'striegohs/ *adj* **1** in botany, having bristles or scales lying against a surface: *a strigose leaf*. **2** in zoology, marked with fine grooves: *the strigose wing cases of a beetle*. [scientific Latin *strigosus*, from Latin *striga* bristle, furrow]

strike¹ /striek/ *verb* (*past tense* **struck** /struk/, *past part.* **struck** or *NAmer* **stricken** /'strikən/) ➤ *verb trans* **1a** to hit (somebody or something) with one's hand, a weapon, etc. **b** to inflict (something): *She struck a blow for feminism*. **2** to afflict (somebody) suddenly: *He was stricken by a heart attack*. **3** to delete or cancel (something): *Her name was struck from a list*. **4a** to make a mental impact on (somebody): *They were struck by its speed; How does that strike you?* **b** to occur suddenly to (somebody). **5** to make and ratify (a bargain). **6** to indicate (the time) by sounding: *The clock struck seven*. **7** to create (a particular mood, atmosphere, etc): *The speech struck a gloomy note*. **8a** to send (something) down or out: *Trees struck roots deep into the soil*. **b** to penetrate (something) painfully: *The news struck him to the heart*. **9a** said of light: to fall on (something). **b** said of a sound: to become audible to (somebody). **10** to put (somebody) suddenly in a particular state: *The blow struck him unconscious*. **11a** to take down the tents of (a camp). **b** to dismantle (e.g. a stage set). **c** to haul down (a flag). **12a** to cause (a match) to ignite. **b** to produce (fire) by striking. **13** to produce (an object) by stamping: *strike a medal*. **14** to assume (a pose). **15** to arrive at (a balance). **16** to discover (something, *esp* minerals): *strike gold*. **17** to cause (an arc) to form, e.g. between electrodes of an arc lamp. **18a** to hook (a fish) by a sharp pull on the line. **b** said of a fish: to snatch at (bait). **19** to play or produce (a note, chord, etc) on keys or strings. **20a** to place (a plant cutting) in a medium for growth and rooting. **b** to propagate (a plant) in this manner. **21** *NAmer* to engage in a strike against (an employer). ➤ *verb intrans* **1** (+ off/out) to embark on a journey, *esp* in a particular direction: *They struck off across the field*. **2a** to aim a blow. **b** to make an attack. **3** (*often* + against) to collide forcefully. **4a** said of the time: to be indicated by a clock, bell, or chime: *The hour had just struck*. **b** to make known the time by sounding: *The clock struck*. **5** said of a fish: to seize bait or a lure. **6** said of a plant cutting: to take root. **7** to withdraw one's labour in protest against an employer. ✷ **strike back** to respond to an attack by attacking in return; to retaliate. **strike oil** to achieve financial success. [Old English *strican* to stroke, go]

strike² *noun* **1** an act of hitting or colliding with something or somebody. **2** a stoppage of work, *esp* by members of a trade union, in order to make a protest or to force an employer to comply with demands. **3** a success in finding or hitting something, *esp* a discovery of a valuable mineral deposit: *a lucky oil strike*. **4** a military air attack, *esp* an air attack on a target. **5** in baseball, a pitched ball that is not hit by the batter. **6** in tenpin bowling, the knocking down of all ten pins with the first bowl in a frame. **7** in cricket, the opportunity to receive the bowling by being at the appropriate wicket. **8** a pull on a line by a fish. **9** the direction of a horizontal line formed at the angle of intersection of an upward-sloping stratum of rock and a horizontal plane.

strikebound *adj* said e.g. of a factory: subjected to or disabled by a strike.

strikebreaker *noun* somebody who works during a strike, *esp* somebody hired to replace a striking worker.

strikebreaking *noun* action designed to break up a strike.

strike down *verb trans* said of death or a disease: to afflict (somebody) suddenly.

strike force *noun* a military force established for the purpose of making sudden attacks.

strike off *verb trans* **1** to forbid (somebody) to continue in professional practice usu because of misconduct or incompetence. **2** to remove or cancel (e.g. names on a list).

strike out *verb trans* **1** to delete (something). **2** in baseball, to put (a batter) out by means of three strikes. ➤ *verb intrans* **1** in baseball, to be put out by failing to hit three balls pitched. **2** *chiefly NAmer, informal* to be unsuccessful.

strike pay *noun* an allowance paid by a trade union to its members on strike.

striker *noun* **1** a player who strikes, *esp* a football player whose main role is to score goals. **2** a worker on strike. **3** a device that strikes the firing pin of a gun.

strike rate *noun* the number of goals or points scored by a player or team, *esp* an average number.

strike up *verb intrans* to begin to sing or play. ➤ *verb trans* **1** to cause (e.g. a band) to begin singing or playing. **2** to cause (something) to begin: *We struck up a conversation.*

striking *adj* attracting attention, *esp* because of unusual or impressive qualities. ➤➤ **strikingly** *adv.*

striking circle *noun* in hockey, the semicircle in front of the goal, from within which the ball must be hit to score a goal.

Strimmer /'strimə/ *noun trademark* a machine for trimming the edges of a lawn, etc, held above the ground and fitted with a length of strong cord that cuts by rotating at high speed. [blend of STRING¹ + TRIMMER]

Strine /strien/ *noun informal* Australian English, *esp* as represented in humorous transliterations of phrases that supposedly reflect Australian pronunciation, e.g. *egg nishing* for *air conditioning.* [alteration of AUSTRALIAN¹]

string¹ /string/ *noun* **1** a narrow cord used *esp* to tie, hang, or fasten things. **2a** a length of gut, wire, etc used to produce notes in certain musical instruments, e.g. the violin and piano. **b** (*usu in pl*) a stringed instrument of an orchestra. **c** (*used before a noun*) relating to, consisting of, or performed on stringed instruments: *a string quintet.* **3a** a group of objects threaded on a string: *a string of beads.* **b** a set of things arranged in a sequence. **c** a succession or sequence: *the author of a string of bestsellers.* **d** in computing, a sequence of characters treated as a unit. **e** a group of usu scattered business concerns under one ownership: *a string of shops.* **f** the animals, *esp* racehorses, belonging to or used by somebody. **4** a plant fibre, e.g. a leaf vein. **5** (*treated as sing. or pl*) any of several teams of players ranked at different levels: *a second-string player.* **6a** any of the interwoven lengths of nylon, gut, etc stretched across the head of a sports racket. **b** = BOWSTRING. **7a** = STRINGBOARD. **b** = STRING COURSE. **8** (*in pl*) conditions or obligations attached to something: *a relationship with no strings attached.* **9** in physics, a hypothetical one-dimensional entity that is a fundamental component of matter. **10** (*used before a noun*) made with threads woven in wide meshes: *a string vest; a string bag.* ✲ **have two/several strings to one's bow** to have more than one resource to call on. **on a string** under one's control: *She kept him on a string.* ➤➤ **stringed** *adj*, **stringless** *adj.* [Old English *streng*]

string² *verb trans* (*past tense and past part.* **strung** /strung/) **1** to equip (something) with strings. **2a** to thread (things) on a string, or as if on a string. **b** to tie, hang, or fasten (something) with string. **3** to remove the strings of (e.g. beans). **4** (*often* + out) to extend or stretch (something) like a string.

string along *verb intrans informal* **1** to accompany somebody, *esp* reluctantly: *They decided to string along with the crowd.* **2** (+ with) to agree with somebody. ➤ *verb trans informal* to deceive or fool (somebody), *esp* as a delaying tactic: *They strung him along with false promises.*

string bean *noun* a bean with stringy fibres between the sides of the pods, *esp* a French bean or runner bean.

stringboard *noun* either of the inclined sides of a staircase supporting or covering the ends of the steps.

string course *noun* a horizontal projecting band in a wall.

stringendo /strin'jendoh/ *adj and adv* said of a piece of music: to be performed with increasing intensity and speed. [Italian *stringendo* from *stringere* to press, from Latin *stringere* to bind tight]

stringent /'strinj(ə)nt/ *adj* **1** rigorous or strict, *esp* with regard to rules or standards. **2** said of economic conditions: marked by money scarcity and credit strictness. ➤➤ **stringency** /-si/ *noun*, **stringently** *adv.* [Latin *stringent-, stringens*, present part. of *stringere* to bind tight]

stringer *noun* **1a** a horizontal structural support. **b** = STRINGBOARD. **2** a longitudinal structural part, e.g. in an aircraft's fuselage or ship's hull. **3** a correspondent employed by a publication or news agency on a part-time or casual basis to provide reports from a particular place.

stringhalt *noun* lameness in the hind legs of a horse caused by muscular spasms. [STRING¹ in the sense 'sinew, tendon' + HALT³]

stringpiece *noun* a long horizontal timber that supports, connects, or reinforces the parts of a wooden structure; *specif* the heavy squared timber lying along the top of the piles forming a dock front or wooden pier.

string quartet *noun* **1** a group of four musicians playing stringed instruments, usu comprising two violins, a viola, and a cello. **2** a composition for string quartet.

string tie *noun* a narrow tie.

string up *verb trans* to kill (somebody) by hanging.

stringy *adj* (**stringier, stringiest**) **1** containing or resembling fibrous matter or string: *stringy hair; stringy meat.* **2** slim and muscular; wiry. **3** said of a liquid or sticky substance: capable of being drawn out to form a string. ➤➤ **stringiness** *noun.*

stringybark *noun* any of several Australian eucalyptus trees with thick fibrous bark.

strip¹ /strip/ *verb* (**stripped, stripping**) ➤ *verb trans* **1a** to remove clothing, covering, or surface material from (something or somebody). **b** to remove (wallpaper, paint, etc) from a surface. **c** to deprive (somebody) of possessions, privileges, or rank. **2a** to remove furniture, equipment, or accessories from (e.g. a house or ship). **b** to dismantle (e.g. an engine). **3** to damage the thread or teeth of (a screw, cog, etc). **4a** to remove cured leaves from the stalks of (tobacco). **b** to remove the midrib from (tobacco leaves). **5** to press the last available milk from the teats of (*esp* a cow). **6** to sell off (a company's assets). ➤ *verb intrans* **1** to undress. **2** to perform a striptease. [Old English *strīpan*]

strip² *noun* the act or an instance of undressing, *esp* a striptease.

strip³ *noun* **1a** a long narrow piece of material. **b** a long narrow area of land or water. **2** *Brit* the distinctive clothes worn by a sports team. **3** = LANDING STRIP. [Middle English; perhaps from early Low German *strippe* strap]

strip cartoon *noun* a series of drawings, e.g. in a magazine, forming a usu humorous narrative.

strip club *noun* a club that features striptease artists.

stripe¹ /striep/ *noun* **1** a line or narrow band differing in colour or texture from adjacent parts, *esp* any of a series of parallel bands of this type. **2** a bar, chevron, etc of braid or embroidery worn usu on the sleeve of a uniform to indicate rank or length of service. **3** *chiefly NAmer* a distinct variety or sort; a type: *men of the same political stripe.* ➤➤ **stripeless** *adj.* [Middle English, prob from early Dutch or early Low German]

stripe² *verb trans* to mark stripes on (something). ➤➤ **striped** *adj.*

stripe³ *noun* a blow with a rod or lash. [Middle English]

striped muscle *noun* = STRIATED MUSCLE.

stripey *adj* see STRIPY.

strip farming *noun* the growing of crops in separate strips of land allotted to individual farmers so that good and bad land is fairly distributed.

strip light *noun* a long tubular fluorescent lamp. ➤➤ **strip lighting** *noun.*

stripling /'stripling/ *noun archaic or humorous* an adolescent boy. [Middle English, from STRIP³ + -LING]

strip mining *noun chiefly NAmer* opencast mining. ➤➤ **strip miner** *noun.*

stripper *noun* **1** somebody who performs a striptease. **2** a tool or solvent for removing something, *esp* paint.

strippergram *noun* a message, e.g. birthday greetings, delivered by somebody hired to accompany it with a striptease.

strip poker *noun* a poker game in which players pay their losses by removing articles of clothing.

strip-search *verb trans* to undress and search (a person) for forbidden objects, e.g. drugs or weapons, concealed about the body. ➤➤ **strip search** *noun.*

striptease *noun* **1** an act or entertainment in which a performer undresses gradually in an erotic manner in front of the audience. **2** (*used before a noun*) involving or performing striptease: *a striptease artist.* ➤➤ **stripteaser** *noun.*

stripy *or* **stripey** /'striepi/ *adj* (**stripier, stripiest**) marked or coloured with stripes; striped.

strive /striev/ *verb intrans* (*past tense* **strove** /strohv/ *or* **strived,** *past part.* **striven** /'striv(ə)n/ *or* **strived**) **1** to endeavour; to try hard. **2** to struggle in opposition; to contend. ▶▶ **striver** *noun.* [Middle English *striven* from Old French *estriver*, of Germanic origin]

strobe /strohb/ *noun* = STROBOSCOPE. [by shortening and alteration]

strobe lighting *noun* flashing intermittent lights, e.g. at a disco, produced by a stroboscope.

strobile /'strohbiel/ *noun* = STROBILUS.

strobilus /stroh'bieləs/ *noun* (*pl* **strobili** /-lie/) = CONE¹ (IA). [late Latin *strobilus* pinecone, from Greek *strobilos* twisted object, top, pinecone, from *strobos* action of whirling]

stroboscope /'strohbəskohp/ *noun* an instrument for measuring or observing motion, *esp* rotation or vibration, by allowing successive views of very short duration so that the motion appears slowed or stopped, e.g. a lamp that flashes intermittently at varying frequencies. ▶▶ **stroboscopic** /-'skopik/ *adj*, **stroboscopically** /-'skopikli/ *adv.* [Greek *strobos* whirling + -SCOPE]

strode /strohd/ *verb* past tense of STRIDE¹.

stroganoff /'strogənof/ *noun* a dish of strips of meat, e.g. beef, cooked in a rich sauce with sour cream. [named after Count Paul *Stroganoff* d.1817, Russian diplomat]

stroke¹ /strohk/ *verb trans* **1** to pass the hand over (something) gently in one direction. **2** *NAmer* to flatter (somebody), *esp* in order to persuade or deceive them. ▶▶ **stroker** *noun.* [Old English *strācian*]

stroke² *noun* an act of stroking or caressing.

stroke³ *noun* **1** the act of striking, *esp* a blow with a weapon or implement. **2** a single unbroken movement, *esp* one that is repeated. **3** a striking of the ball in a game, e.g. cricket or tennis; *specif* a striking of the ball that constitutes the scoring unit in golf. **4a** an action by which something is done, produced, or achieved: *a stroke of genius.* **b** an unexpected occurrence: *a stroke of luck.* **5** a sudden reduction or loss of consciousness, sensation, and voluntary motion caused by rupture or obstruction of an artery of the brain. **6a** a technique for propelling the body or a boat through water: *Crawl is the fastest swimming stroke.* **b** in rowing, an oarsman who sits at the back of a racing boat and sets the pace for the rest of the crew. **7** the slightest amount of effort or work: *She never does a stroke.* **8** the movement in either direction of a mechanical part, e.g. a piston rod, or the distance it travels. **9** the sound of a striking clock: *at the stroke of twelve.* **10a** a mark made by a single movement of a pen, brush, etc. **b** *Brit* = SOLIDUS (I). ✳ **at a stroke** by a single action. **off one's stroke** performing below one's usual standard. **on the stroke** precisely: *He left on the stroke of ten.* [Middle English, from STRIKE¹]

stroke⁴ *verb trans* **1** to set the pace for (a rowing crew or boat). **2** to hit (a ball) with a controlled swinging blow. ▶ *verb intrans* to row at a specified number of strokes a minute.

stroke play *noun* a golf competition scored by the total number of strokes: compare MATCH PLAY.

stroll¹ /strohl/ *verb intrans* to walk in a leisurely manner. [prob from German dialect *strollen*]

stroll² *noun* a leisurely walk.

stroller *noun NAmer* = PUSHCHAIR.

strolling *adj* going from place to place, *esp* in search of work: *strolling players.*

stroma /'strohmə/ *noun* (*pl* **stromata** /-tə/) **1** the supporting framework of some animal organs and cells. **2a** a compact mass of fungal hyphae (threadlike filaments; see HYPHA) giving rise to a spore-producing body. **b** the colourless material of a CHLOROPLAST (specialized plant cell part) in which the chlorophyll-containing layers are embedded. ▶▶ **stromal** *adj*, **stromatic** /stroh'matik/ *adj.* [scientific Latin *stromat-*, *stroma* via Latin from Greek *strōmat-*, *strōma* bed covering, from *stornynai* to spread out]

strong /strong/ *adj* **1** having or marked by great physical power. **2** having moral or intellectual power. **3** having great resources of wealth, talent, etc: *a film with a strong cast.* **4** of a specified number: *an army ten thousand strong.* **5a** striking or superior of its kind: *a strong resemblance.* **b** effective or efficient, *esp* in a specified area: *strong on logic.* **6** forceful or cogent: *strong evidence.* **7a** rich in some active agent, e.g. a flavour or extract; concentrated: *strong beer; strong tea.* **b** said of a colour: intense. **c** said of an acid or base: forming electrically charged atoms or groups of atoms freely in solution.

d magnifying by refracting greatly: *a strong lens.* **8** moving with vigour or force: *a strong wind.* **9** full of passion or enthusiasm; ardent: *a strong supporter.* **10** well established; firm: *strong beliefs.* **11** not easily upset or nauseated: *a strong stomach.* **12** having a pungent or offensive smell or flavour. **13** tending towards steady or higher prices: *a strong market.* **14** in grammar, of or being a verb or verb conjugation that forms the past tense and past participle by internal vowel change, e.g. *drink, drank, drunk*: compare WEAK. ✳ **come on strong** *informal* to behave in a forceful or aggressive manner. **(still) going strong** *informal* continuing to be active, effective, successful, etc. ▶▶ **strongish** *adj*, **strongly** *adv.* [Old English *strang*]

strongarm *adj* using or involving undue force: *strongarm tactics.*

strongbox *noun* a strongly made chest for money or valuables.

strong breeze *noun* a wind having a speed of 39 to 49km/h (25 to 31mph).

strong drink *noun* intoxicating liquor.

strong force *noun* = STRONG INTERACTION.

strong gale *noun* a wind having a speed of 75 to 88km/h (47 to 54mph).

stronghold *noun* **1** a fortified place. **2a** a place of refuge or survival: *one of the last strongholds of the Gaelic language.* **b** a place dominated by a specified group: *a Tory stronghold.*

strong interaction *noun* in physics, an interaction between elementary particles that is more powerful than any other known force and is responsible for binding protons and neutrons in atomic nuclei: compare WEAK INTERACTION.

strong language *noun* offensive language, *esp* swearing.

strong man *noun* **1** a man who performs feats of muscular strength. **2** *informal* an autocratic leader.

strong-minded *adj* marked by firmness and independence of thought and judgment. ▶▶ **strong-mindedly** *adv*, **strong-mindedness** *noun.*

strongpoint *noun* a small fortified defensive position.

strong point *noun* something in which one excels.

strong room *noun* a room in which money and valuables are stored, typically a fireproof room that cannot be broken into.

strong suit *noun* **1** in card games, a suit of which a player holds a number of cards of high value. **2** = STRONG POINT: *By prearrangement the debate was limited to foreign and defence matters, which Mr Ford considered his strong suit* — Independent.

strontia /'stronti·ə/ *noun* a white solid chemical compound resembling lime that is an oxide of strontium: formula SrO. [scientific Latin *strontia* from obsolete English *strontian*, named after *Strontian* village in Scotland where it was discovered]

strontium /'stronti·əm/ *noun* a silver-white metallic chemical element of the alkaline-earth group, chemically similar to calcium, that occurs naturally in various minerals and is used to produce red flames in fireworks and flares: symbol Sr, atomic number 38. [scientific Latin *strontium*, from STRONTIA]

strontium-90 *noun* a radioactive isotope of strontium present in the fallout from nuclear explosions and hazardous because it can replace calcium in bone.

strop¹ /strop/ *noun* **1** a strip of material, *esp* a leather band, used for sharpening a razor. **2** a band or loop of rope or metal used on a ship or boat to hold or lift heavy objects. [Middle English *strop* thong, prob via a prehistoric Germanic word from Latin *stroppus*, from Greek *strophos* twisted cord]

strop² *verb trans* (**stropped, stropping**) to sharpen (a razor) on a strop.

strop³ *noun Brit, informal* an angry mood; a temper. [prob a backformation from STROPPY]

strophanthin /stroh'fanthin/ *noun* any of several poisonous glycosides (chemical compounds containing sugars; see GLYCOSIDE) or mixtures of glycosides obtained from African plants of the periwinkle family and used as heart stimulants. [Latin *Strophanthus*, genus name of the plants]

strophe /'strohfi/ *noun* **1** in classical Greek drama, the first of two turning movements made by the chorus while a choral ode is sung, or the part of the ode that accompanies this movement: compare ANTISTROPHE. **2** in poetry, a rhythmic system composed of two or more lines repeated as a unit. [Greek *strophē*, literally 'act of turning', from *strephein* to turn, twist]

strophic /'strofik, 'strohfik/ *adj* **1** of, containing, or consisting of strophes. **2** using the same music for successive stanzas of a song.

stroppy *adj* (**stroppier, stroppiest**) *Brit, informal* quarrelsome or angrily uncooperative. [perhaps by shortening and alteration from OBSTREPEROUS]

strove /strohv/ *verb* past tense of STRIVE.

strow /stroh/ *verb trans* (*past part.* **strown** /strohn/ *or* **strowed**) *archaic* = STREW. [variant of STREW]

struck /struk/ *verb* past tense and past part. of STRIKE¹.

structural /'strukch(ə)rəl/ *adj* **1a** of or affecting structure. **b** forming part of a structure. **c** used in or suitable for building structures: *structural steel.* **2** of the physical make-up of a plant or animal body. ⟫ **structurally** *adv.*

structural formula *noun* a chemical formula showing the arrangement of atoms and bonds in the molecule: compare MOLECULAR FORMULA.

structuralism *noun* a method or approach used in anthropology, literary criticism, etc that seeks to analyse data in terms of the significance of underlying relationships and patterns of organization.

Editorial note ─────────────────────
Structuralism proposed that the products of the human mind (stories, myths, societies, for example) were the effect of structures that escaped our awareness. However diverse their surfaces, artefacts and even whole cultures were all ultimately reducible to a single structure, commonly understood as a binary opposition between antithetical values. In the 1960s structuralism was largely superseded by poststructuralism — Professor Catherine Belsey.

⟫ **structuralist** *noun and adj.*

structural linguistics *pl noun* (*treated as sing. or pl*) an approach to linguistics that emphasizes the underlying structures in language.

structural unemployment *noun* unemployment that results from a shift in a country's commercial and industrial base, rather than from a falling demand for workers.

structure¹ /'strukchə/ *noun* **1a** something that is constructed, e.g. a building. **b** something that is organized in a definite pattern. **2** the way in which something is constructed or organized. **3a** the arrangement of particles or parts in a substance or body: *soil structure; molecular structure.* **b** arrangement or interrelation of elements: *economic structure.* ⟫ **structureless** *adj.* [Middle English from Latin *structura*, from *struere* to heap up, build]

structure² *verb trans* to construct or organize (something) in a particular way.

strudel /'stroohdl/ *noun* a pastry made from a thin sheet of dough rolled up with filling and baked: *apple strudel.* [German *Strudel*, literally 'whirlpool']

struggle¹ /'strugl/ *verb intrans* **1** to proceed with difficulty or great effort: *struggling to make ends meet.* **2** to make violent or strenuous efforts against opposition or confinement. **3** to compete. ⟫ **struggler** *noun.* [Middle English *struglen*, perhaps of imitative origin]

struggle² *noun* **1** a violent effort or exertion. **2** a determined attempt in adverse circumstances. **3** a hard-fought contest. **4** a difficult task.

struggle for existence *noun* the competition for food, space, etc that tends to eliminate less efficient individuals of a population, thereby increasing the chance of inherited traits being passed on from the more efficient survivors: compare NATURAL SELECTION, SELECTION.

strum /strum/ *verb* (**strummed, strumming**) ⟫ *verb trans* **1** to play (a musical instrument, e.g. a guitar) by brushing the thumb, the fingertips, or a plectrum over the strings. **2** to play (music) in this way. ⟫ *verb intrans* to strum a stringed instrument. ⟫ **strummer** *noun.* [imitative]

struma /'stroohmə/ *noun* (*pl* **strumae** /'stroohmee/ *or* **strumas**) **1** = GOITRE. **2** a swelling at the base of the capsule in many mosses. **3** *archaic* = SCROFULA. ⟫ **strumose** /'stroohmohs/ *adj,* **strumous** *adj.* [Latin *struma* tumour]

strumpet /'strumpit/ *noun archaic or humorous* a prostitute or promiscuous woman: *I am no strumpet, but of life as honest as you that thus abuse me* — Shakespeare. [Middle English; earlier history unknown]

strung /strung/ *verb* past tense and past part. of STRING¹.

strung-up *adj* extremely nervous or tense.

strut¹ /strut/ *verb* (**strutted, strutting**) ⟫ *verb intrans* **1** to walk with a proud or erect gait. **2** to walk with a pompous air; to swagger. ⟫ *verb trans* to provide, support, or stiffen (something) with a strut. ⟫⟫ **strutter** *noun.* [Middle English *strouten* to swell, protrude stiffly, swagger, from Old English *strūtian* to exert oneself]

strut² *noun* **1** a structural piece designed to support or strengthen a framework by resisting pressure in the direction of its length. **2** a strutting step or walk.

struth *or* **strewth** /strooth/ *interj* an expression of surprise, alarm, or annoyance. [short for *God's truth*]

struthious /'stroohthi-əs/ *adj* of or resembling an ostrich. [late Latin *struthio* ostrich, from Greek *strouthos*]

strychnine /'strikneen/ *noun* a bitter poisonous chemical compound obtained from nux vomica and related plants and used as a poison, e.g. for rodents, and medicinally in small amounts as a stimulant to the central nervous system. [Latin *Strychnos*, genus name of nux vomica, from Latin *strychnos* nightshade, from Greek]

Stuart¹ /'styoo-ət/ *adj* relating or belonging to the royal house that ruled Scotland from 1371 to 1603 and Britain from 1603 to 1649 and from 1660 to 1714. [Robert *Stewart* (Robert II of Scotland) d.1390]

Stuart² *noun* a member or supporter of the Stuart royal house.

stub¹ /stub/ *noun* **1a** a small part of a page, e.g. of a chequebook, left on the spine as a record of the contents of the part torn away. **b** the part of a ticket returned to the user after inspection. **2** a short blunt part of a pencil, cigarette, etc left after a larger part has been used up or broken off. **3** the part of a plant remaining after the stem or trunk has been cut; the stump. **4** something cut short, stunted, or blunted. [Old English *stybb*]

stub² *verb trans* (**stubbed, stubbing**) **1** to strike (one's foot or toe) against a hard object or surface accidentally. **2** (+ out) to extinguish (e.g. a cigarette) by crushing the end. **3a** to grub (a plant) up by the roots. **b** to clear (land) by uprooting stumps.

stub axle *noun* a short axle bearing one wheel, e.g. one of the front wheels of a car.

stubble /'stubl/ *noun* **1** the stalky remnants of plants, *esp* cereal crops, that remain rooted in the soil after harvest. **2** a rough growth of short bristly hairs on a man's face. ⟫ **stubbled** *adj,* **stubbly** *adj.* [Middle English *stuble* via Old French *estuble* from Latin *stupula* stalk, straw, alteration of *stipula*: see STIPULE]

stubborn /'stubən/ *adj* **1** unyielding or determined, *esp* unreasonably so. **2** difficult to get rid of: *a stubborn cold.* ⟫ **stubbornly** *adv,* **stubbornness** *noun.* [Middle English *stuborn*; earlier history unknown]

stubby¹ *adj* (**stubbier, stubbiest**) short and thick: *stubby fingers.* ⟫ **stubbiness** *noun.*

stubby² *noun* (*pl* **stubbies**) *Aus, informal* a small beer bottle.

stucco¹ /'stukoh/ *noun* (*pl* **stuccos** *or* **stuccoes**) *esp* formerly, a cement or fine plaster used to coat or decorate ceilings and interior and exterior walls: *There might be some ground for offence ... there might be some reason for the glance his father gave towards the ceiling and stucco* — Jane Austen. [Italian *stucco*, of Germanic origin]

stucco² *verb trans* (**stuccoes** *or* **stuccos, stuccoed, stuccoing**) to coat or decorate (a wall or building) with stucco.

stuck /stuk/ *verb* past tense and past part. of STICK¹.

stuck-up *adj informal* superciliously self-important or conceited.

stud¹ /stud/ *noun* **1a** a solid button with a shank or eye on the back inserted through an eyelet in a garment as a fastener or ornament. **b** a rivet or nail with a large head used for ornament or protection. **c** a small piece of jewellery for a pierced ear. **2a** a piece, e.g. a rod or pin, projecting from a machine and serving chiefly as a support or axis. **b** a projecting piece, e.g. on a boot or tyre, to increase grip. **3** any of the smaller upright posts in a timber frame, wall, or partition of a building. **4** *NAmer* the height of a room from floor to ceiling. **5** a crosspiece in each link of a heavy chain. [Old English *studu*]

stud² *verb trans* (**studded, studding**) **1** to decorate, cover, or protect (something) with studs. **2** to set (something) thickly with a number of prominent objects: *a sky studded with stars.* **3** to provide (e.g. a building or wall) with studs.

stud³ *noun* **1a** (*treated as sing. or pl*) a group of animals, *esp* horses, kept primarily for breeding. **b** a place, e.g. a farm, where such animals are kept. **2a** a male animal, *esp* a stallion, kept for breeding.

b *informal* a sexually active man. **3** the state of being kept for breeding. [Old English *stōd*]

studbook *noun* an official record of the pedigree of purebred horses, dogs, etc.

studding sail *noun* an additional light sail set at the side of a square sail in light winds. [*studding* prob from early Dutch or early Low German *stotinge* thrusting]

student /'styood(ə)nt/ *noun* **1a** somebody who undertakes a course of study, *esp* somebody who attends a college or university. **b** (*used before a noun*) denoting somebody training for a profession: *a student nurse*. **2** an attentive and systematic observer: *a student of human nature*. [Middle English from Latin *student-, studens*, present part. of *studēre* to study]

studentship *noun* **1** *Brit* a grant for study, *esp* at a university. **2** the state of being a student.

Student's t test *noun* in statistics, a probability density function that is used *esp* in testing whether a statistical sample is likely to have come from a larger sample of known statistical properties. [*Student*, pseudonym of W S Gossett d.1937, Brit statistician, who formulated it]

studhorse *noun* a stallion kept *esp* for breeding.

studied /'studid/ *adj* **1** carefully considered or prepared. **2** produced or adopted for effect; deliberate: *studied indifference*. ➤➤ **studiedly** *adv*.

studio /'styoohdioh/ *noun* (*pl* **studios**) **1a** the workroom of a painter, sculptor, or photographer. **b** a place for the study of an art, e.g. dancing, singing, or acting. **2a** a place where films are made. **b** (*also in pl*) a film production company including its premises and employees. **3** a room equipped for the production of radio or television programmes. **4** = STUDIO FLAT. [Italian *studio* study, from Latin *studium*]

studio couch *noun* a backless couch that can be converted into a double bed by sliding from underneath it the frame of a single bed.

studio flat *noun* a small flat consisting typically of one main room with a small kitchen and bathroom.

studious /'styoohdi-əs/ *adj* **1** pursuing studies seriously and with commitment. **2a** marked by or suggesting serious thoughtfulness or diligence: *a studious effort; a studious expression on his face*. **b** deliberate. ➤➤ **studiously** *adv*, **studiousness** *noun*.

stud poker *noun* a form of poker in which each player's first card is dealt face down and the next four face up, with a round of betting taking place after each of the last four rounds of dealing.

studwork *noun* work supported, strengthened, held together, or ornamented by studs.

study¹ /'studi/ *noun* (*pl* **studies**) **1a** the application of the mind to acquiring knowledge, *esp* by reading: *the study of Latin*. **b** a careful examination or analysis of a subject. **2** a branch of learning. **3** a room devoted to study, writing, reading, etc. **4** a literary or artistic work intended as a preliminary or experimental interpretation. **5** a musical composition intended for improvement of technique. ✳ **in a brown study** *dated* lost in thought or contemplation. [Middle English *studie* via Old French *estudie* from Latin *studium* zeal, application]

study² *verb* (**studies, studied, studying**) ➤ *verb intrans* to engage in study. ➤ *verb trans* **1** to engage in the study of (a subject); to learn about (it): *study medicine*. **2** to read, observe, or consider (something) attentively or in detail. **3** to try to memorize (something): *actors studying their lines*.

stuff¹ /stuf/ *noun* **1a** materials, supplies, or equipment used in various activities: *The plumber left some of his stuff behind*. **b** personal property; possessions. **2a** an unspecified material substance: *We sold tons of the stuff*. **b** a group of miscellaneous objects: *Pick that stuff up off the floor*. **c** *informal* alcoholic drink or addictive drugs. **d** *informal* money. **3** subject matter or expertise: *a teacher who knows his stuff*. **4** the essence of a usu abstract thing: *the stuff of greatness*. **5** a finished textile suitable for clothing, *esp* wool or worsted fabric. **6** *informal* worthless ideas, opinions, or writing; rubbish. ✳ **do one's stuff** *informal* to perform to the best of one's capabilities. **that's the stuff** *informal* that is what is needed. [Middle English from Old French *estoffe*, from *estoffer* to equip, stock, prob ultimately from Old High German *stopfōn* to stop up, stuff]

stuff² *verb trans* **1a** to fill (something) by packing things in. **b** to gorge (oneself) with food. **c** to fill (e.g. meat or vegetables) with a stuffing. **d** to fill (e.g. upholstered furniture) with soft material or

padding. **e** to fill out the skin of (an animal) for mounting. **f** to stop up (a hole) by packing in material; to plug (it). **2** to force or thrust (something) into a confined space: *He stuffed the papers into his briefcase*. **3** (*usu* + up) to choke or block up (the nasal passages). **4** *Brit, coarse slang, dated* said of a man: to have sexual intercourse with (a woman). **5** *Brit, informal* to defeat or thwart (somebody or something). **6** *NAmer* to put fraudulent votes in (a ballot box). ✳ **get stuffed!** *Brit, informal* a forceful expression of disagreement or anger. ➤➤ **stuffer** *noun*.

stuffed shirt *noun informal* a smug, pompous, and usu reactionary person.

stuff gown *noun* the woollen gown worn in court by a barrister who is not a QC.

stuffing *noun* **1** material used to stuff something, *esp* upholstered furniture, soft toys, etc. **2** a seasoned mixture of ingredients used to stuff meat, vegetables, etc. ✳ **knock the stuffing out of somebody 1** to beat somebody severely. **2** to cause somebody to lose vigour or vitality.

stuffing box *noun* a device that prevents leakage along a moving part passing through a hole in a vessel containing steam, water, or oil and that consists of a casing of compressed material arranged round the moving part.

stuff sack *noun* a cloth bag into which a sleeping bag, clothing, etc is stored by stuffing rather than rolling or folding.

stuffy *adj* (**stuffier, stuffiest**) **1a** badly ventilated; close. **b** blocked or congested: *a stuffy nose*. **2** lacking interest or inspiration; dull. **3** narrowly conventional in behaviour; straitlaced. ➤➤ **stuffily** *adv*, **stuffiness** *noun*.

stultify /'stultifie/ *verb trans* (**stultifies, stultified, stultifying**) **1** to bore (somebody) by being tedious or repetitive. **2** to cause (something) to appear foolish or absurd. **3** to make (something) futile or useless, *esp* through enfeeblement or repression: *Centralization stultifies local initiative*. ➤➤ **stultification** /-fi'kaysh(ə)n/ *noun*, **stultifier** *noun*, **stultifying** *adj*. [late Latin *stultificare* to make foolish, from Latin *stultus* foolish]

stum¹ /stum/ *noun* in winemaking, unfermented grape juice or partly fermented juice added to wine as a preservative. [Dutch *stom* dumb]

stum² *verb trans* (**stummed, stumming**) to preserve (wine) by adding stum.

stumble¹ /'stumbl/ *verb intrans* **1** to trip in walking or running. **2a** to walk unsteadily or clumsily. **b** to speak or act in a hesitant or faltering manner. **b** (+ upon/on/across) to find or discover something or somebody unexpectedly or by chance. ➤➤ **stumbler** *noun*, **stumbling** *adj*, **stumblingly** *adv*. [Middle English *stumblen*, prob of Scandinavian origin]

stumble² *noun* an act of stumbling.

stumbling block *noun* an obstacle to progress or understanding.

stumer /'styoohmə/ *noun Brit, slang* **1** a sham or fraud. **2** a worthless or forged coin, note, or cheque. [origin unknown]

stump¹ /stump/ *noun* **1** the part of a plant, *esp* a tree, remaining in the ground attached to the root after the stem is cut. **2a** the part of an arm, leg, etc remaining attached to the body after the rest is removed. **b** a rudimentary or vestigial bodily part. **3** a remaining part; a stub. **4** any of the three upright wooden rods that together with the bails form the wicket in cricket. **5** a heavy tread; noisy footsteps. **6** *chiefly NAmer* a place or occasion for political public speaking. ✳ **draw stumps** to end play in a cricket match. [Middle English *stumpe* from early Low German *stump* or early Dutch *stomp*]

stump² *verb trans* **1** *informal* (*usu in passive*) to baffle or bewilder (somebody): *I was stumped by her question*. **2** said of a wicketkeeper: to dismiss (a batsman who is out of the crease but not running) by breaking the wicket with the ball. **3** *NAmer* to travel over (a region) making political speeches or supporting a cause. ➤ *verb intrans* **1** to walk heavily or noisily. **2** *chiefly NAmer* to travel about making political speeches or supporting a cause.

stump³ *noun* a short thick roll of leather, paper, etc, usu pointed at both ends and used to soften lines in a drawing. [French *estompe*, from Flemish *stomp* stub]

stump⁴ *verb trans* to use a stump on (a drawing).

stumper *noun informal* a puzzling question; a teaser.

stump up *verb trans and intrans chiefly Brit, informal* to pay (what is due), *esp* unwillingly.

stumpy *adj* (**stumpier, stumpiest**) short and thick; stubby. ⨠ **stumpiness** *noun*.

stun /stun/ *verb trans* (**stunned, stunning**) **1** to make (somebody) dazed or briefly unconscious, e.g. by a blow. **2** to overcome (somebody), *esp* with astonishment or disbelief. [Middle English *stunen*, modification of Old French *estoner*: see ASTONISH]

stung /stung/ *verb* past tense and past part. of STING¹.

stun gun *noun* a weapon that discharges high-voltage electricity or missiles to immobilize a human target without inflicting lasting injury.

stunk /stunk/ *verb* past tense and past part. of STINK¹.

stunner *noun informal* an unusually attractive or impressive person or thing: *Rossetti and Burne-Jones had one night been at the theatre, where they had made the acquaintance ... of two girls sitting behind them. The girls were 'stunners', and the elder of them, Jane Burden, was a particularly striking beauty* — Timothy Hilton.

stunning *adj informal* strikingly attractive or impressive. ⨠ **stunningly** *adv*.

stunsail *or* **stuns'l** /'stuns(ə)l/ *noun* = STUDDING SAIL. [by contraction]

stunt¹ /stunt/ *verb trans* to hinder or arrest the growth or development of (something or somebody). ⨠ **stunted** *adj*, **stuntedness** *noun*. [English dialect *stunt* stubborn, stunted, abrupt, prob of Scandinavian origin]

stunt² *noun* **1** an unusual or difficult feat, *esp* one displaying physical or acrobatic prowess. **2** something done purely as a way of attracting attention or publicity. **3** a foolish scheme or action. [orig US college slang; origin unknown]

stunt³ *verb intrans* to perform stunts.

stuntman *or* **stuntwoman** *noun* (*pl* **stuntmen** *or* **stuntwomen**) a man or woman employed, *esp* as a substitute for an actor, to perform dangerous feats.

stupa /'stoohpə/ *noun* a Buddhist monument in the form of a dome- or bell-shaped building. [Sanskrit *stūpa*]

stupe /styoohp/ *noun* a hot, wet, often medicated cloth applied to the body, e.g. to stimulate circulation or relieve pain. [Middle English via Latin *stuppa* coarse part of flax, tow, from Greek *styppē*]

stupefacient /st(y)oohpi'fayshənt/ *adj* said of a drug: causing a state of semi-consciousness. ⨠ **stupefacient** *noun*.

stupefy /'st(y)oohpifie/ *verb trans* (**stupefies, stupefied, stupefying**) **1** to make (somebody) groggy or insensible. **2** to astonish (somebody). ⨠ **stupefaction** /-'faksh(ə)n/ *noun*, **stupefying** *adj*. [early French *stupefier* from Latin *stupefacere*, from *stupēre* to be astonished + *facere* to make, do]

stupendous /styooh'pendəs/ *adj* **1** causing astonishment or wonder; marvellous. **2** of astonishing size or greatness; tremendous. ⨠ **stupendously** *adv*, **stupendousness** *noun*. [Latin *stupendus*, from *stupēre* to be astonished]

stupid /'styoohpid/ *adj* **1** lacking common sense or intelligence; slow-witted. **2** dulled in feeling or perception; torpid. **3** *informal* annoying or exasperating: *This stupid torch won't work.* ⨠ **stupidity** /styooh'piditi/ *noun*, **stupidly** *adv*, **stupidness** *noun*. [early French *stupide* from Latin *stupidus*, from *stupēre* to be benumbed, be astonished]

stupor /'styoohpə/ *noun* **1** a condition characterized by reduction or suspension of sense or feeling. **2** a state of extreme apathy or torpor. ⨠ **stuporous** /-rəs/ *adj*. [Middle English from Latin *stupor*, from *stupēre* to be benumbed, be astonished]

sturdy /'stuhdi/ *adj* (**sturdier, sturdiest**) **1** strongly built or constructed. **2a** having physical strength or vigour; robust. **b** showing determination or firmness of purpose; resolute. ⨠ **sturdily** *adv*, **sturdiness** *noun*.

Word history

Middle English in the senses 'fierce, reckless, stubborn', via Old French *estourdi* stunned, ultimately from Latin *turdus* thrush. The bird was formerly associated with drunkenness, prob because it can become intoxicated from eating overripe fruit.

sturgeon /'stuhj(ə)n/ *noun* any of several species of usu large edible fishes whose roe is made into caviar: family Acipenseridae. [Middle English from Old French *estourjon*, of Germanic origin]

Sturm und Drang /,stuhm ənt 'drang, ,shtuhm oont/ *noun* a German literary and artistic movement of the late 18th cent. characterized by high emotion and often dealing with the individual's revolt against society. [German *Sturm und Drang* (Storm and Stress), drama by Friedrich von Klinger d.1831, German writer]

stutter¹ /'stutə/ *verb* (**stuttered, stuttering**) ⨠ *verb intrans* **1** to speak with involuntary hesitation or disruption of speech, e.g. by spasmodic repetition or prolongation of vocal sounds. **2** to make a series of abrupt sounds or movements. ⨠ *verb trans* to say (something) with a stutter. ⨠ **stutterer** *noun*, **stuttering** *adj*, **stutteringly** *adv*. [frequentative of English dialect *stut* to stutter, from Middle English *stutten*, of Germanic origin]

stutter² *noun* **1** the act or an instance of stuttering. **2** a speech disorder that produces stuttering.

sty¹ /stie/ *noun* (*pl* **sties**) = PIGSTY. [Old English *stig*]

sty² *verb trans* (**sties, stied, stying**) to put or keep (a pig) in a sty.

sty³ *or* **stye** *noun* (*pl* **sties** *or* **styes**) an inflamed swelling of a sebaceous gland at the edge of an eyelid. [short for obsolete *styan*, alteration of Old English *stīgend* riser, from *stīgan* to go up]

Stygian /'stiji·ən/ *adj formal or literary* extremely dark or gloomy. [via Latin from Greek *stygios*, from *Styg-, Styx* Styx, mythical river of the underworld]

styl-¹ *or* **stylo-** *comb. form* forming words, denoting: a pillar: *stylobate*. [Latin *styl-, stylo-*, from Greek *stylos* pillar]

styl-² *or* **stylo-** *comb. form* forming words, denoting: a style: *styloid*. [Latin *stilus* stake, stalk, stylus]

style¹ /stiel/ *noun* **1a** a distinctive or characteristic manner of doing something: *a room decorated in a sober style*. **b** a distinctive way of presenting oneself, speaking, etc: *He doesn't shout: that's not his style*. **c** elegance or sophistication in dress, social behaviour, etc: *people with style*. **2a** a manner of expression in writing, painting, music, etc, *esp* when characteristic of an individual, period, etc: *Style is not neutral; it gives moral directions* — Martin Amis. **b** the procedures followed by a particular publishing house regarding spelling, capitalization, punctuation, etc. **3** a title or mode of address. **4a** a slender elongated part, e.g. a bristle, on an animal. **b** a prolongation of a plant OVARY (seed-producing organ) bearing a STIGMA (pollen-receiving structure) at the top. **c** = STYLUS (2), (3). ✳ **in style** with much elegance or extravagance: *She celebrated her birthday in style*. ⨠ **stylar** *adj*, **styleless** *adj*. [Middle English *stile, style* via Old French from Latin *stilus* stake, stylus, style of writing]

style² *verb trans* **1** to design or arrange (something) in a particular style. **2** to designate (somebody or something) by an identifying term; to name or call (them): *They styled themselves freedom fighters*. ⨠ **styler** *noun*.

-style *comb. form* **1** forming adjectives, with the meaning: resembling: *a leather-style briefcase*. **2** forming adverbs, with the meaning: in the style or manner of: *She bowed Japanese-style*.

stylet /'stielit/ *noun* **1a** a slender surgical probe. **b** a thin wire inserted into a catheter to maintain rigidity or into a hollow needle to keep it clear of obstruction. **2** a relatively rigid elongated organ or part, e.g. a piercing mouthpart, of an animal. **3** = STILETTO (1), (2). [French *stylet* via early French *stilet* stiletto, from Old Italian *stiletto*: see STILETTO]

styli /'stielie/ *noun* pl of STYLUS.

stylise *verb trans* see STYLIZE.

stylish *adj* fashionably elegant. ⨠ **stylishly** *adv*, **stylishness** *noun*.

stylist *noun* **1** a hairdresser, *esp* one of the more senior hairdressers in a salon. **2** somebody who develops, designs, or advises on styles. **3** a writer who cultivates a fine literary style. **4** somebody who performs with style.

stylistic /stie'listik/ *adj* relating to style, *esp* literary or artistic style. ⨠ **stylistically** *adv*.

stylistics *pl noun* (*treated as sing. or pl*) the study of style, *esp* in literature.

stylite /'stieliet/ *noun* any of a number of early Christian hermits who lived on the tops of pillars. ⨠ **stylitic** /stie'litik/ *adj*. [late Greek *stylitēs* from Greek *stylos* pillar]

stylize *or* **stylise** *verb trans* to represent or design (something) according to a conventional style or pattern rather than according to nature. ⨠ **stylization** /-'zaysh(ə)n/ *noun*.

stylo-¹ *comb. form* see STYL-¹.

stylo-² *comb. form* see STYL-².

stylobate /'stieləbayt/ *noun* a continuous flat step or pavement on which a row of architectural columns is placed. [via Latin from

Greek *stylobatēs*, from *stylos* pillar + *batēs* base, from *bainein* to walk, go]

stylograph /'stieləgrahf, -graf/ *noun* a type of fountain pen that has a fine tube in place of a nib.

styloid /'stieloyd/ *adj* denoting a long slender pointed part projecting from a bone, e.g. at the end of the ULNA (bone of lower arm).

stylops /'stielops/ *noun* (*pl* **stylops**) any of various tiny insects that live as parasites inside the bodies of other insects, *esp* bees and wasps: order Strepsiptera. [Greek *stylos* column + *ops* eye]

stylus /'stieləs/ *noun* (*pl* **styli** /'stielie/ *or* **styluses**) **1** a tiny piece of material, e.g. diamond, with a rounded tip used in a gramophone to follow the groove on a record and transmit the sound. **2** a pointed instrument used in ancient times for writing on clay or waxed tablets. **3** any of various instruments for marking or incising a surface. [modification of Latin *stilus* stake, stylus]

stymie[1] /'stiemi/ *noun* in golf, a condition on a green where the path of a ball to the hole is blocked by another player's ball. [perhaps from Scots *stymie* person with poor eyesight]

stymie[2] *verb trans* (**stymies, stymied, stymying** *or* **stymieing**) to present an obstacle to (somebody or something); to thwart (them).

styptic /'stiptik/ *adj* tending to contract tissues, *esp* to check bleeding. >>> **styptic** *noun*. [Middle English *stiptik* via Latin from Greek *styptikos*, from *styphein* to contract]

styrax /'stieraks/ *noun* = STORAX. [Latin *styrax*: see STORAX]

styrene /'stiereen/ *noun* a colourless liquid chemical compound used chiefly in making rubber, plastics, etc. [from Latin *styrax* STORAX, from which it was orig obtained]

suable /'s(y)ooh·əbl/ *adj* liable to be sued. >>> **suability** /-'biliti/ *noun*.

suasion /'swayzh(ə)n/ *noun formal* the act of influencing or persuading. >>> **suasive** /'swaysiv/ *adj*. [Middle English from Latin *suasion-, suasio*, from *suadēre* to urge, persuade]

suave /swahv/ *adj* **1** smoothly though often superficially charming and polite. **2** said *esp* of men: elegant and sophisticated. >>> **suavely** *adv*, **suaveness** *noun*, **suavity** *noun*. [early French *suave* pleasant, sweet, from Latin *suavis* pleasant]

sub[1] /sub/ *noun informal* **1** a submarine. **2** a subscription. **3** a substitute, *esp* in a sport. **4** a subsistence allowance, an advance of money. **5** a subeditor.

sub[2] *verb* (**subbed, subbing**) >> *verb intrans informal* to act as a substitute. >> *verb trans informal* **1** to lend or advance money to (somebody). **2** to subedit (a newspaper, etc).

sub- *or* **suc-** *or* **suf-** *or* **sug-** *or* **sup-** *or* **sur-** *or* **sus-** *prefix* forming words, with the meanings: **1** under, beneath, or below: *subsoil; submarine*. **2a** next in rank below; subordinate: *subdeacon*. **b** a subordinate portion or subdivision of something: *subcommittee*. **c** a repeated or further instance of a specified action or process: *subcontract; sublet*. **3** bearing an incomplete, partial, or inferior resemblance to; approximately: *subhuman*. **4** adjacent to or bordering on: *subarctic*. **5** said of a chemical compound: containing less than the normal or usual amount of a specified element: *suboxide*. [Middle English from Latin *sub-* under, below, secretly, from below, up, near, from *sub* under, close to, during]

subacid *adj* **1** moderately acid: *subacid fruit juices*. **2** rather tart: *subacid comments*. >>> **subacidity** *noun*, **subacidness** *noun*. [Latin *subacidus*, from SUB- + *acidus* acid]

subalpine *adj* **1** of the lower slopes of the Alps. **2** of or growing on high upland slopes below the treeline.

subaltern[1] /'subalt(ə)n/ *adj* **1** low in rank or status; subordinate. **2** in logic, denoting a particular proposition that may be inferred from a universal proposition. [late Latin *subalternus*, from Latin SUB- + *alternus* alternate, from *alter* other (of two)]

subaltern[2] *noun* somebody holding a subordinate position; *specif* a commissioned officer in the British Army ranking below a captain.

subantarctic *adj* relating to or denoting a region just outside the Antarctic Circle.

sub-aqua /,sub 'akwə/ *adj* relating to underwater sports or explorations, *esp* those requiring underwater breathing apparatus.

subaquatic *adj* = SUBAQUEOUS.

subaqueous *adj* existing, formed, or taking place in or under water.

subarctic *adj* relating to or denoting a region just outside the Arctic Circle.

subassembly *noun* an assembled unit designed to be incorporated with other units in a finished product.

subatomic *adj* **1** occurring within an atom: *a subatomic process*. **2** smaller than an atom: *a subatomic particle*.

subbasement *noun* a basement below the main basement of a building.

subclass *noun* **1** a category in the biological classification of living things below a class and above an order. **2** a subdivision of a class. **3** = SUBSET.

subclavian *adj* relating to or denoting an artery, nerve, etc situated under the CLAVICLE (collarbone). >>> **subclavian** *noun*. [scientific Latin *subclavius*, from SUB- + *clavicula*: see CLAVICLE]

subclinical *adj* having undetectable symptoms, *esp* because the condition has not developed sufficiently: *a subclinical infection*. >>> **subclinically** *adv*.

subcommittee *noun* a subdivision of a committee usu organized for a specific purpose.

subconscious[1] *adj* **1** existing in the mind but not admitted to consciousness: *his subconscious motive*. **2** imperfectly or incompletely conscious: *a subconscious state*. >>> **subconsciously** *adv*, **subconsciousness** *noun*.

subconscious[2] *noun* (**the subconscious**) the part of the mind in which mental activity takes place below the threshold of consciousness.

Editorial note

Subconscious is the active mind 'below' but affecting the conscious mind. The notion of subconscious wishes and fears is the essential idea of Freud, and also Jung. This is different from the current neurological view that most of the physiological processing is unconscious. Indeed, in Freud's time the unconscious was mysterious; now it is consciousness that is so puzzling — Professor Richard Gregory.

subcontinent *noun* **1** a vast discernible subdivision of a continent; *specif* the part of Asia comprising India, Pakistan, and Bangladesh. **2** a landmass of great size but smaller than any of the generally recognized continents. >>> **subcontinental** /-'nentl/ *adj*.

subcontract[1] /subkən'trakt/ *verb trans and intrans* **1** to engage a third party to perform under a separate contract all or part of (work included in an original contract). **2** to undertake (work) under such a contract. >>> **subcontractor** /-'traktə, 'sub-/ *noun*.

subcontract[2] /sub'kontrakt/ *noun* a contract between a party to an original contract and a third party, *esp* one to provide all or a specified part of the work or materials required in the original contract.

subcontrary /sub'kontrəri/ *noun* (*pl* **subcontraries**) in logic, either of a pair of propositions related to each other in such a way that both may be true but both cannot be false. >>> **subcontrary** *adj*.

subcritical *adj* in nuclear physics, being or using a mass of fissile material of insufficient size to sustain a chain reaction: *a subcritical mass; a subcritical reactor*.

subculture *noun* **1** a sector of society whose members have a shared pattern of behaviour and values distinguishable from the mainstream culture. **2** a culture, e.g. of bacteria, derived from another culture. >>> **subcultural** /sub'kul-/ *adj*.

subcutaneous *adj* being, situated, used, or applied under the skin: *subcutaneous fat*. >>> **subcutaneously** *adv*. [late Latin *subcutaneus*, from Latin SUB- + *cutis* skin]

subdeacon *noun* a cleric ranking below a deacon in some Christian Churches.

subdiaconate *noun* the office or rank of a subdeacon.

subdivide *verb trans* to divide (something already divided, or one or more of its parts) into more and smaller parts. >> *verb intrans* to become subdivided.

subdivision *noun* **1** any of the parts into which something is subdivided. **2** the act of subdividing.

subdominant *noun* in music, the fourth note of a diatonic scale.

subdue /səb'dyooh/ *verb trans* (**subdues, subdued, subduing**) **1** to reduce the intensity or degree of (e.g. light or colour). **2** to bring (something) under control; to curb (it): *His words subdued her fears*. **3** to conquer and bring (e.g. a people) into subjection. **4** *archaic* to bring (land) under cultivation. >>> **subduable** *adj*, **subduer** *noun*. [Middle English *sodewen, subduen*, via early French *soduire* to seduce, from Latin *subducere*, literally 'to draw from below', from SUB- + *ducere* to lead]

subdued *adj* **1** lacking normal cheerfulness or liveliness; low-spirited. **2** reduced or lacking in force, intensity, or strength. **3** brought under control by or as if by military conquest. ➤➤ **subduedly** *adv*.

subdural /sub'dyooərəl/ *adj* located between the DURA MATER and the ARACHNOID (respectively the outermost and middle of the three membranes covering the brain and spinal cord).

subedit *verb trans* (**subedited, subediting**) **1** *chiefly Brit* to edit (e.g. a newspaper article) in preparation for printing; to copy-edit (it). **2** to be assistant editor of (e.g. a newspaper).

subeditor *noun* **1** *chiefly Brit* somebody who edits the text of a newspaper, magazine, etc in preparation for printing. **2** an assistant editor. ➤➤ **subeditorial** /-'tawri·əl/ *adj*.

suberin /'syoohbərin/ *noun* a complex waxy substance that is the basis of cork. [French *subérine* from Latin *suber* cork tree, cork]

subfamily *noun* (*pl* **subfamilies**) **1** a category in the biological classification of living things below a family and above a genus. **2** a major subgroup of languages within a language family; *specif* one including more than one branch.

subfusc[1] /'subfusk/ *adj literary* drab or gloomy. [Latin *subfuscus* brownish, dusky, from SUB- + *fuscus* dark brown]

subfusc[2] *noun formal* academic dress for members of a university, *esp* Oxford University.

subgenus *noun* (*pl* **subgenera**) a category in the biological classification of living things below a genus and above a species. ➤➤ **subgeneric** *adj*.

subhead *or* **subheading** *noun* **1** a subordinate caption, title, or headline. **2** the heading of a subdivision, e.g. in a document.

subhuman *adj* **1** below the level expected of or appropriate to normal human beings; debased: *subhuman behaviour*. **2** said of animals: lower than human beings in terms of evolutionary development, *esp* only slightly lower.

subj. *abbr* **1** subject. **2** subjunctive.

subjacent /sub'jays(ə)nt/ *adj formal* **1** situated under or below something. **2** underlying: *subjacent causes*. ➤➤ **subjacency** /-si/ *noun*. [Latin *subjacent-, subjacens*, present part. of *subjacēre* to lie under, from SUB- + *jacēre* to lie]

subject[1] /'subjikt/ *noun* **1a** a branch of knowledge or learning, *esp* one taught or studied at school, college, or university. **b** a person or thing concerning which something is said or done: *a subject of dispute*. **c** a matter dealt with in an article, speech, etc. **2a** somebody or something represented in a work of art. **b** an individual whose reactions are studied, e.g. in a psychological experiment. **c** a dead body for anatomical study and dissection. **3a** in grammar, the word or phrase in a sentence or clause denoting the person or thing about which something is stated or that performs the action of a verb. **b** in logic, the term of a proposition denoting the thing about which something is stated, denied, or predicated. **c** a principal phrase of a musical composition or movement. **4** somebody owing obedience or allegiance to another, *esp* to a ruler or sovereign power. **5** in philosophy, the entity that sustains or assumes the form of thought or consciousness, e.g. the mind or ego. ➤➤ **subjectless** *adj*. [Middle English via French from Latin *subjectus* one under authority and *subjectum* subject of a proposition, masc and neuter of the past part. of *subicere* to subject, from SUB- + *jacere* to throw]

subject[2] *adj* **1** (*often* + to) owing obedience or allegiance to another: *subject nations*; *They are subject to higher authority*. **2** (+ to) dependent or conditional on something: *The plan is subject to approval*. **3a** (+ to) liable or exposed to something: *subject to temptation*. **b** (+ to) having a tendency or inclination to something; prone to it: *subject to colds*.

subject[3] /səb'jekt/ *verb trans* **1** (+ to) to cause (somebody or something) to undergo something. **2** (+ to) to make (somebody or something) liable to something; to expose (them) to it. **3** (*often* + to) to bring (e.g. a people) under control or rule. ➤➤ **subjection** /-sh(ə)n/ *noun*.

subjective[1] /səb'jektiv/ *adj* **1a** peculiar to a particular individual; personal. **b** arising from conditions within the brain or sense organs and not directly caused by external stimuli: *subjective sensations*. **c** relating to, determined by, or arising from the mind or self: *subjective reality*. **d** characteristic of or belonging to reality as perceived by the observer rather than as independent of the

observer. **2** lacking in reality or substance; illusory. **3** said of a case of nouns and pronouns: relating to or denoting a grammatical subject. ➤➤ **subjectively** *adv*, **subjectiveness** *noun*, **subjectivity** /subjek'tiviti/ *noun*.

subjective[2] *noun* in grammar, the subjective case.

subjectivism *noun* **1** the doctrine that individual feelings or reactions form the basis of moral or aesthetic judgments and that there are no absolute values. **2** a theory holding that all knowledge is subjective and that there is no objective reality. ➤➤ **subjectivist** *noun*.

subject matter *noun* that which is represented or dealt with in speech, writing, or art.

subject to *prep* depending on (something): *Subject to your approval, I will go*.

subjoin *verb trans formal* to add (e.g. comments or extra information) to the end of a speech, text, etc; to append (it). [early French *subjoindre* from Latin *subjungere* to join beneath, add, from SUB- + *jungere* to JOIN[1]]

sub judice /'joohdisl/ *adv* currently being considered by a court and therefore not open to discussion. [Latin *sub judice* under a judge]

subjugate /'subjoogayt/ *verb trans* to bring (somebody or something) under the control of another authority. ➤➤ **subjugation** /-'gaysh(ə)n/ *noun*, **subjugator** *noun*. [Middle English *subjugaten* from Latin *subjugatus*, past part. of *subjugare*, literally 'to bring under the yoke', from SUB- + *jugum* yoke]

subjunctive[1] /səb'jungktiv/ *adj* in grammar, of or being a verb mood that represents an act or state not as a fact but as a possibility or wish. ➤➤ **subjunctively** *adv*. [late Latin *subjunctivus* from Latin *subjunctus*, past part. of *subjungere*: see SUBJOIN]

subjunctive[2] *noun* the subjunctive mood, or a verb form expressing it.

sublease[1] *noun* a lease by a tenant of leased property to a subtenant, usu for a shorter term than the tenant's own.

sublease[2] *verb trans* to lease (a property) to a subtenant. ➤➤ **sublessee** *noun*, **sublessor** *noun*.

sublet[1] *verb trans and intrans* (*past tense and past part.* **sublet, subletting**) said of a tenant: to lease or rent (all or part of a property) to a subtenant.

sublet[2] *noun* a property obtained by or available for subletting.

sublieutenant *noun* a Royal Navy rank above midshipman and below lieutenant, or an officer holding this rank.

sublimate[1] /'sublimayt/ *verb trans* **1** in psychology, to divert the expression of (an instinctual desire or impulse) from a primitive form to a socially or culturally acceptable one. **2** = SUBLIME[2] (I), (2). ➤➤ **sublimation** /-'maysh(ə)n/ *noun*. [medieval Latin *sublimatus*, past part. of *sublimare* to raise, from *sublimis*: see SUBLIME[1]]

sublimate[2] /'sublimayt, 'sublimət/ *noun* in chemistry, a solid obtained by sublimation.

sublime[1] /sə'bliem/ *adj* **1** of the highest moral or spiritual worth; exalted. **2** astoundingly beautiful or grand. **3** outstanding or extreme: *sublime indifference*. **4** *informal* excellent: *The meal was sublime*. ➤➤ **sublimely** *adv*, **sublimity** /su'blimiti/ *noun*. [Latin *sublimis* to or in a high position, from SUB- + *limen* threshold, lintel]

sublime[2] *verb trans* **1** in chemistry, to cause (a substance) to sublime. **2** to make (something) finer or of higher worth. ➤ *verb intrans* in chemistry, to pass directly from the solid to the vapour state, without passing through the liquid state, and usu to pass directly back to the solid state.

subliminal /sə'bliminl/ *adj* **1** said of a stimulus: inadequate to produce a conscious sensation or perception. **2** existing or functioning below the level of conscious awareness: *the subliminal mind*. ➤➤ **subliminally** *adv*. [SUB- + Latin *limin-, limen* threshold, lintel]

subliminal advertising *noun* screen advertising in which persuasive images are shown so fleetingly that they are registered only by the subconscious mind.

sublingual *adj* situated, occurring, or administered under the tongue. ➤➤ **sublingually** *adv*.

sublittoral *adj* situated, occurring, or growing between the high and low watermarks.

sublunar *adj* between the moon and the earth, *esp* within the moon's orbit.

sublunary *adj chiefly literary* belonging to the material world, *esp* as distinct from the spiritual world and subordinate to it; earthly. [late Latin *sublunaris*, from Latin SUB- + *luna* moon]

submachine gun *noun* an automatic or semiautomatic portable rapid-firing gun of limited range using pistol-type ammunition.

submarginal *adj* **1** next to a margin or a marginal part: *submarginal spots on an insect wing.* **2** falling below a minimum necessary for some purpose, e.g. economic exploitation: *submarginal hill farms.* ⏵⏵ **submarginally** *adv.*

submarine¹ /'submareen, submə'reen/ *noun* a vessel designed for undersea operations, *esp* a warship armed with torpedoes or missiles.

submarine² *adj* situated, occurring, or growing under water, *esp* in the sea: *submarine plants.*

submariner /sub'marinə/ *noun* a crew member of a submarine.

submaxilla *noun* (*pl* **submaxillae** *or* **submaxillas**) the lower jaw or jawbone, *esp* in human beings. ⏵⏵ **submaxillary** *adj.*

submediant *noun* in music, the sixth note of a diatonic scale.

submerge /səb'muhj/ *verb trans* **1** to put (something) under water. **2** to cover (something) with water; to flood (it). **3a** to cover (something) completely; to obscure (it). **b** to bury or suppress (something, e.g. feelings). **4** to give (somebody) an overwhelming amount, e.g. of work, to deal with; to inundate (them). ⏵ *verb intrans* to go under water. ⏵⏵ **submerged** *adj*, **submergence** *noun*. [Latin *submergere*, from SUB- + *mergere* to plunge]

submerse /səb'muhs/ *verb trans and intrans technical* to submerge. ⏵⏵ **submersed** *adj*, **submersion** /-sh(ə)n/ *noun*. [Latin *submersus*, past part. of *submergere*: see SUBMERGE]

submersible¹ /səb'muhsəbl/ *adj* capable of going or operating under water.

submersible² *noun* something submersible, *esp* a vessel used for undersea exploration and construction work.

submicroscopic *adj* too small to be seen using an ordinary microscope.

submission /səb'mish(ə)n/ *noun* **1a** the act or an instance of submitting something for consideration, inspection, etc. **b** something submitted for consideration, inspection, etc. **2** the state of being submissive, humble, or compliant. **3** the act or an instance of submitting to the authority or control of another. **4** in wrestling, an act of submitting to the superiority of an opponent's hold. [Middle English via French from Latin *submission-, submissio* act of lowering, from *submittere*: see SUBMIT]

submissive /səb'misiv/ *adj* willing or tending to submit to others. ⏵⏵ **submissively** *adv*, **submissiveness** *noun.*

submit /səb'mit/ *verb* (**submitted, submitting**) ⏵ *verb trans* **1a** to send or commit (something) to another person or authority for consideration, inspection, judgment, etc. **b** to put (something) forward as an opinion; to suggest (it): *We submit that the charge is not proved.* **2a** to subject (something or somebody) to a process or practice. **b** to yield (something or somebody) to the authority or will of another. ⏵ *verb intrans* **1** to yield oneself to the authority or will of another. **2** to allow oneself to be subjected to something. ⏵⏵ **submitter** *noun*. [Middle English *submitten* from Latin *submittere* to lower, submit, from SUB- + *mittere* to send]

submucosa /submyooh'kohzə/ *noun* (*pl* **submucosae** /-sie/) a supporting layer of loose connective tissue directly under a mucous membrane. ⏵⏵ **submucosal** *adj*. [scientific Latin *submucosa (membrana)* (membrane) beneath the mucous membrane]

submultiple *noun* a number that can divide another number exactly, without a remainder: *8 is a submultiple of 72.*

subnormal *adj* **1** lower or smaller than normal. **2** having less of something, *esp* intelligence, than is normal. ⏵⏵ **subnormality** /-'maliti/ *noun*, **subnormally** *adv.*

subnuclear *adj* **1** below the level of organization of the nucleus of a living cell. **2a** smaller than the nucleus of an atom. **b** occurring in an atomic nucleus.

suborbital *adj* **1** situated beneath the ORBIT¹ (socket) of the eye. **2a** being or involving less than one complete orbit: *a spacecraft's suborbital flight.* **b** intended for suborbital flight: *a suborbital rocket.*

suborder *noun* a division of an order; *specif* a category in the biological classification of living things below an order and above a family.

subordinate¹ /sə'bawd(ə)nət/ *adj* **1a** occupying a lower class, rank, or position; inferior. **b** of secondary importance. **2** subject to or controlled by authority. ⏵⏵ **subordinately** *adv*. [Middle English *subordinat* from medieval Latin *subordinatus*, from Latin SUB- + *ordinare* to order]

subordinate² *noun* a subordinate person or thing, *esp* a person of lower rank.

subordinate³ /sə'bawd(ə)nayt/ *verb trans* **1** to place (somebody or something) in a subordinate position. **2** to make (e.g. a people) subject or subservient; to subdue (them). ⏵⏵ **subordination** /-'naysh(ə)n/ *noun*, **subordinative** /-nətiv/ *adj.*

subordinate clause *noun* a clause that functions as a noun, adjective, or adverb in a complex sentence and is dependent on the main clause, e.g. *when he heard* in *He laughed when he heard.*

subordinating conjunction *noun* a conjunction such as *because* or *although* that introduces a subordinate clause: compare COORDINATING CONJUNCTION.

suborn /sə'bawn/ *verb trans* to induce (somebody) to commit perjury or another illegal act, *esp* by bribery. ⏵⏵ **subornation** /subaw'naysh(ə)n/ *noun*, **suborner** *noun*. [early French *suborner* from Latin *subornare*, from SUB- secretly + *ornare* to furnish, equip]

suboxide *noun* an oxide containing a relatively small proportion of oxygen.

subplot *noun* a subordinate plot in fiction or drama.

subpoena¹ /sə'peenə/ *noun* a writ commanding somebody to appear in court. [Middle English *suppena* from Latin *sub poena* under penalty (the first words of the writ)]

subpoena² *verb trans* (**subpoenas, subpoenaed, subpoenaing**) to serve (somebody) with a subpoena.

subpolar *adj* subantarctic or subarctic.

sub-post office *noun* in Britain, a local post office offering a smaller range of services than a main post office and often located inside a larger shop.

subrogate /'subrəgayt/ *verb trans* in law, to substitute (somebody or something) for another, *esp* in respect of claims, rights, etc. [Latin *subrogatus*, past part. of *subrogare, surrogare*, from SUB- in place of + *rogare* to ask]

subrogation /subrə'gaysh(ə)n/ *noun* in law, the substitution of one person for another, *esp* as a creditor, together with the transfer of associated rights.

sub rosa /'rohzə/ *adv* in strict confidence; secretly.

⎯⎯⎯ **Word history** ⎯⎯⎯
Latin *sub rosa*, literally 'under the rose', from the ancient custom of hanging a rose over the council table to indicate that all present were sworn to secrecy. According to one tradition, the rose is the emblem of silence because Cupid gave the god Harpocrates a rose to bribe him not to reveal Venus' love affairs.
⎯⎯⎯⎯⎯⎯⎯⎯⎯⎯⎯⎯⎯⎯⎯⎯⎯⎯

subroutine *noun* a sequence of computer instructions that can be used repeatedly in a program.

sub-Saharan *adj* relating or belonging to the regions of Africa that lie south of the Sahara desert.

subscribe /səb'skrieb/ *verb intrans* **1a** (+ to) to pay regularly in order to receive a periodical or service. **b** (+ to) to give money, e.g. to charity, *esp* in the form of regular donations or payments. **c** (+ to) to give consent or approval to something written by signing it. **2** (*usu* + for) to agree to purchase and pay for shares, *esp* of a new issue. **3** (+ to) to feel favourably disposed to something; to agree with it. ⏵ *verb trans* **1a** to give a written pledge to contribute (an amount of money). **b** to sign (e.g. a document) with one's own hand. **2** to write (one's name) underneath something. ⏵⏵ **subscriber** *noun*. [Middle English *subscriben* from Latin *subscribere* to write beneath, from SUB- + *scribere* to write]

subscriber trunk dialling *noun* Brit the system by which a telephone user can dial direct to any telephone within the system without being connected by an operator.

subscript /'subskript/ *adj* said of a letter, number, or symbol: written or printed, usu in smaller type, below and to the right or left of another character. ⏵⏵ **subscript** *noun*. [Latin *subscriptus*, past part. of *subscribere*: see SUBSCRIBE]

subscription /səb'skripsh(ə)n/ *noun* **1a** a purchase by prepayment of something, *esp* a certain number of issues of a periodical. **b** Brit membership fees paid regularly. **c** an application to purchase shares of a new issue. **2** a sum of money pledged. **3** formal a signature. **4** the act or an instance of subscribing to something.

[Middle English *subscripcioun* signature, from Latin *subscription-, subscriptio*, from *subscribere*: see SUBSCRIBE]

subscription concert *noun* any of a series of concerts for which tickets are bought in advance.

subsection *noun* a subdivision of a section.

subsequence /'subsikwəns/ *noun formal* **1** the state of being subsequent. **2** a subsequent event.

subsequent /'subsikwənt/ *adj* following in time or order; succeeding. ➤➤ **subsequently** *adv*. [Middle English from Latin *subsequent-, subsequens*, present part. of *subsequi* to follow closely, from SUB- + *sequi* to follow]

subserve /səb'suhv/ *verb trans formal* to serve as a means of furthering (e.g. a purpose or action). [Latin *subservire* to serve, be subservient, from SUB- + *servire* to serve]

subservient /səb'suhvi·ənt/ *adj* **1** obsequiously submissive; servile. **2** useful in an inferior capacity; subordinate. ➤➤ **subservience** *noun*, **subserviently** *adv*. [Latin *subservient-, subserviens*, present part. of *subservire*: see SUBSERVE]

subset *noun* a set contained within a larger set, *esp* a mathematical set each of whose elements is an element of a given set.

subshrub *noun* a usu low-growing bush or shrub having woody stems or branches with tips that die back annually. ➤➤ **subshrubby** *adj*.

subside /səb'sied/ *verb intrans* **1** to become less forceful or intense; to abate: *The storm subsided*. **2a** said of ground: to cave in; to collapse. **b** to sink so as to form a depression. **c** to fall to a lower level or return to a normal level: *The floods subsided*. **3** to sink or fall to the bottom; to settle. **4** *informal* to collapse into a sitting or lying position, usu through exhaustion: *He subsided into a chair*. [Latin *subsidere*, from SUB- + *sidere* to sit down, sink]

subsidence /'subsidəns, sub'siedəns/ *noun* the act or an instance of subsiding, *esp* the slow sinking of an area of land.

subsidiarity /səb'sidiariti/ *noun* the principle that a central authority should control only those activities that cannot be satisfactorily controlled at a more immediate or local level.

subsidiary¹ /səb'sidyəri/ *adj* **1** serving to assist or supplement; auxiliary. **2** of secondary importance. [Latin *subsidiarius*, from *subsidium*: see SUBSIDY]

subsidiary² *noun* (*pl* **subsidiaries**) somebody or something subsidiary, *esp* a company that is wholly controlled by another.

subsidize *or* **subsidise** /'subsidiez/ *verb trans* **1** to provide (somebody or something) with a subsidy, *esp* to aid or promote (e.g. a private enterprise) with public money. **2** to pay part of the cost of (a product or service), making it cheaper for those who buy or use it: *Why should we subsidize their children's education?* **3** to purchase the assistance of (a person or company) by payment of a subsidy. ➤➤ **subsidization** /-'zaysh(ə)n/ *noun*, **subsidizer** *noun*.

subsidy /'subsidi/ *noun* (*pl* **subsidies**) **1** a grant or gift of money, e.g. one made by a government to a person or organization to assist an enterprise deemed advantageous to the public. **2** in former times, a sum of money granted by Parliament to the Crown and raised by special taxation. [Middle English from Latin *subsidium* reserve troops, support, assistance, from SUB- near + *sedēre* to sit]

subsist /səb'sist/ *verb intrans* **1** to have only the basic necessities of life. **2** to continue to exist. **3** (+ in) to be present as an element or quality in something; to reside in it. [late Latin *subsistere* to exist, from Latin *subsistere* to come to a halt, remain, from SUB- + *sistere* to set, stand]

subsistence *noun* **1** the state of subsisting. **2** the minimum, e.g. of food and shelter, necessary to support life. ➤➤ **subsistent** *adj*. [Middle English from late Latin *subsistentia*, from *subsistent-, subsistens*, present part. of *subsistere*: see SUBSIST]

subsistence allowance *noun* an award of money intended to cover basic living costs, often in the form of an advance on wages.

subsistence farming *noun* farming that provides enough food for the farm household, usu without significant surplus for sale.

subsistence level *noun* a standard of living in which one has no more than the basic necessities of life.

subsistence wage *noun* a wage just sufficient to provide the basic necessities of life.

subsoil¹ *noun* the layer of weathered material that lies under the surface soil.

subsoil² *verb trans* to turn, break, or stir the subsoil of (land). ➤➤ **subsoiler** *noun*.

subsonic *adj* **1** being or travelling at a speed less than that of sound in air. **2** = INFRASONIC. ➤➤ **subsonically** *adv*.

subspace *noun* in mathematics, a subset of a space, *esp* one that has the properties, e.g. those of a vector space, of the including space.

sub specie aeternitatis /sub ˌspekiay ie,tuhni'tahtis/ *adv* seen in its essential or universal form. [Latin *sub specie aeternitatis*, literally 'under the aspect of eternity']

subspecies *noun* (*pl* **subspecies**) a category in the biological classification of living things that ranks immediately below a species. ➤➤ **subspecific** /subspi'sifik/ *adj*.

substance /'substəns/ *noun* **1a** a physical material from which something is made or formed: *an oily substance*. **b** matter of particular or definite chemical constitution. **2a** the fundamental or essential part or import: *the substance of his argument*. **b** correspondence with reality: *The allegations were without substance*. **c** solid quality. **3** material possessions; property: *a man of substance*. **4** in philosophy, ultimate underlying reality. ✳ **in substance** in respect to essentials; essentially. [Middle English via Old French from Latin *substantia*, from *substant-, substans*, present part. of *substare* to stand under, from SUB- + *stare* to stand]

substandard *adj* **1** of a quality lower than that expected or prescribed. **2** = NON-STANDARD.

substantial /səb'stansh(ə)l/ *adj* **1** considerable in size or quantity; significantly large: *a substantial income*. **2** ample to satisfy and nourish: *a substantial meal*. **3** firmly constructed; solid. **4** being largely but not wholly the specified thing: *a substantial lie*. **5** having material existence; real. **6** well-to-do; prosperous. **7** relating to the fundamental substance or essence of something. ➤➤ **substantiality** /-shi'aliti/ *noun*, **substantially** *adv*. [Middle English via Old French *substantiel* from late Latin *substantialis*, from Latin *substantia*: see SUBSTANCE]

substantialism *noun* in philosophy, the doctrine that all phenomena have an underlying and substantial reality. ➤➤ **substantialist** *noun*.

substantiate /səb'stanshiayt/ *verb trans* to establish (e.g. a statement or claim) by proof or evidence; to verify (it). ➤➤ **substantiation** /-'aysh(ə)n/ *noun*, **substantiative** /-shi·ətiv/ *adj*.

substantive¹ /səb'stantiv, 'substəntiv/ *adj* **1** having substance or significance; substantial. **2** being a totally independent entity. **3** defining rights and duties: *substantive law*. **4** said of a rank or position: permanent and definite rather than temporary or acting. **5** in grammar, relating to or functioning as a noun. **6** said of a dye: not requiring a mordant. ➤➤ **substantively** *adv*. [Middle English from late Latin *substantivus*, from Latin *substantia*: see SUBSTANCE]

substantive² /'substəntiv/ *noun* a noun, or a word or phrase that functions syntactically as a noun. ➤➤ **substantival** /-'tievl/ *adj*. [Middle English *substantif* via early French *substantif* from late Latin *substantivus*: see SUBSTANTIVE¹]

substation *noun* **1** an installation where the voltage of an electric current from a power station is transformed for distribution to consumers within a particular district. **2** a subsidiary station.

substituent /sub'stityoo·ənt/ *noun* in chemistry, an atom or group that replaces another atom or group in a molecule. ➤➤ **substituent** *adj*. [Latin *substituent-, substituens*, present part. of *substituere*: see SUBSTITUTE¹]

substitute¹ /'substityooht/ *noun* somebody or something that takes the place of another, e.g. a player who may replace another withdrawn from a game. ➤➤ **substitute** *adj*, **substitutive** /-tiv/ *adj*. [Middle English from Latin *substitutus*, past part. of *substituere* to put in place of, from SUB- + *statuere* to set up, place, from *status*: see STATUS]

substitute² *verb trans* **1** (*usu* + for) to put (one thing) in the place of another: *You can substitute yogurt for cream to make the sauce less rich*. **2** in sport, to introduce a substitute for (somebody): *They substituted their centre forward in the second half*. **3a** to introduce (an atom or group) as a substituent. **b** to replace (an atom or group) with a substituent. ➤ *verb intrans* to serve as a substitute. ➤➤ **substitutable** /-'tyoohtəbl/ *adj*, **substitution** /-'tyoohsh(ə)n/ *noun*, **substitutional** /-'tyooshənl/ *adj*, **substitutionary** /-'tyooshən(ə)ri/ *adj*.

Usage note

substitute *or* replace? See note at REPLACE.

substrate /'substrayt/ *noun* **1** = SUBSTRATUM (1). **2** the base on which an organism lives: *Limpets live on a rocky substrate*. **3** a substance acted on chemically, e.g. by an enzyme. [Latin *substratum*: see SUBSTRATUM]

substratum *noun* (*pl* **substrata** /-tə/) **1** a layer of rock or soil that lies immediately below the surface. **2** a foundation or basis: *His argument has a substratum of truth*. **3** an underlying support. [Latin *substratum*, neuter past part. of *substernere* to spread under, from SUB- + *sternere* to spread out]

substructure *noun* any structure that forms the foundation or framework on which something is constructed. ➤➤ **substructural** /sub'struk-/ *adj*.

subsume /səb'syoohm/ *verb trans* to include (something) as a member of a group or type; to incorporate (it). ➤➤ **subsumable** *adj*, **subsumption** /səb'sum(p)sh(ə)n/ *noun*. [medieval Latin *subsumere*, from Latin SUB- + *sumere* to take up]

subtenant *noun* somebody who rents all or part of a property from a tenant. ➤➤ **subtenancy** *noun*.

subtend /səb'tend/ *verb trans* **1a** to extend between the end points of the lines that converge to form (an angle): *A hypotenuse subtends a right angle*. **b** to extend between the end points of (an arc): *an arc subtended by a chord*. **2** said of a plant part: to be lower than (something), *esp* so as to embrace or enclose it: *a bract that subtends a flower*. [Latin *subtendere* to stretch beneath, from SUB- + *tendere* to stretch]

subterfuge /'subtəfyoohj/ *noun* **1** deception or trickery used as a means of concealment or evasion. **2** a trick or ruse. [late Latin *subterfugium* from Latin *subterfugere* to escape, evade, from *subter-* secretly + *fugere* to flee]

subterminal *adj* situated or occurring near an end: *a subterminal band of colour*.

subterranean /subtə'rayni·ən/ *or* **subterraneous** /-ni·əs/ *adj* **1** existing, occurring, or operating under the surface of the earth. **2** hidden or out of sight. ➤➤ **subterraneanly** *adv*, **subterraneously** *adv*. [Latin *subterraneus*, from SUB- + *terra* earth]

subtext *noun* **1** the underlying meaning or theme of a text. **2** any underlying message.

subtilize *or* **subtilise** /'sutiliez/ *verb trans* to make (something) subtle. ➤ *verb intrans* to act or think subtly. ➤➤ **subtilization** /-'zaysh(ə)n/ *noun*.

subtitle¹ *noun* **1** (*also in pl*) a printed text, e.g. a translation or transcription of dialogue, that appears at the bottom of the screen during a film or television broadcast. **2** a secondary or explanatory title, e.g. of a book or article.

subtitle² *verb trans* **1** to provide subtitles for (e.g. a film or television broadcast). **2** to provide a subtitle for (e.g. a book or article). ➤➤ **subtitled** *adj*.

subtle /'sutl/ *adj* **1a** pleasantly or tastefully delicate; understated: *a subtle fragrance*. **b** difficult to understand, analyse, or distinguish: *subtle differences*. **2** showing keen insight and perception. **3** cleverly contrived; ingenious. **4** *archaic* artful or cunning. ➤➤ **subtleness** *noun*, **subtly** *adv*. [Middle English *sutil, sotil* via Old French from Latin *subtilis* finely woven, from SUB- + *tela* web]

subtlety *noun* (*pl* **subtleties**) **1** the quality of being subtle. **2** something subtle, *esp* a fine distinction. [Middle English *sutilte* via Old French from Latin *subtilitat-, subtilitas*, from *subtilis*: see SUBTLE]

subtonic *noun* in music, the seventh note of a diatonic scale.

subtopia /sub'tohpi·ə/ *noun* **1** a suburban residential area regarded as an ideal place in which to live. **2** an area of unattractive and sprawling development on the outskirts of a town. [blend of SUBURB + UTOPIA; (sense 2) influenced by SUB-]

subtotal¹ *noun* the sum of part of a series of figures to be added.

subtotal² *verb trans* (**subtotalled, subtotalling**, *NAmer* **subtotaled, subtotaling**) to add (figures) in order to arrive at a subtotal.

subtract /səb'trakt/ *verb trans* **1** to take (one number) away from another in calculating the difference between them. **2** to remove (a part) from a whole. ➤ *verb intrans* to perform a subtraction. ➤➤ **subtracter** *noun*, **subtractive** *adj*. [Latin *subtractus*, past part. of *subtrahere* to draw from beneath, withdraw, from SUB- + *trahere* to draw]

subtraction /səb'traksh(ə)n/ *noun* **1** the operation of calculating the difference between two given numbers. **2** the removal of a part from a whole.

subtrahend /'subtrə'hend/ *noun* a number that is to be subtracted from another. [Latin *subtrahendus*, verbal noun from *subtrahere*: see SUBTRACT]

subtropic *adj* = SUBTROPICAL.

subtropical *adj* of or denoting the regions bordering on the tropics.

subtropics *pl noun* subtropical regions.

subulate /'syoohbyoolət, -layt/ *adj technical* narrow and tapering to a fine point: *a subulate leaf*. [scientific Latin *subulatus* from Latin *subula* awl]

subunit *noun* a unit that forms a discrete part of a more comprehensive unit.

suburb /'subuhb/ *noun* (*also in pl*) an outlying part of a city or large town, *esp* a residential district. [Middle English from Latin *suburbium*, from SUB- + *urbs* city]

suburban /sə'buhbən/ *adj* **1** relating to or located in a suburb. **2** typical of suburbs or the people who live in them, *esp* limited and unadventurous in outlook.

suburbanise *verb trans* see SUBURBANIZE.

suburbanite /sə'buhbəniet/ *noun* a person who lives in a suburb.

suburbanize *or* **suburbanise** *verb trans* **1** to make (an area) into a suburb. **2** to make (somebody or something) suburban. ➤➤ **suburbanization** /-'zaysh(ə)n/ *noun*.

suburbia /sə'buhbi·ə/ *noun* the suburbs of a city, or their inhabitants.

subvention /səb'vensh(ə)n/ *noun* **1** the provision of financial assistance or support. **2** an endowment or subsidy, *esp* a government grant. [late Latin *subvention-, subventio* assistance, from Latin *subvenire* to come up, come to the rescue, from SUB- + *venire* to come]

subversion /səb'vuhsh(ə)n/ *noun* the act or an instance of subverting, *esp* a systematic attempt to overthrow or undermine a government or political system by people working within the country concerned. [Middle English via French from late Latin *subversion-, subversio*, from Latin *subvertere*: see SUBVERT]

subversive¹ /sub'vuhsiv/ *adj* **1** tending to undermine the established system, e.g. of government: *Whatever is funny is subversive, every joke is ultimately a custard pie* — George Orwell. **2** engaging in subversive activities. ➤➤ **subversively** *adv*, **subversiveness** *noun*.

subversive² *noun* a subversive person.

subvert /səb'vuht/ *verb trans* **1** to overthrow or undermine the power of (e.g. a government or institution). **2** to pervert or corrupt (somebody) by undermining their morals, allegiance, or faith. ➤➤ **subverter** *noun*. [Middle English *subverten* via French from Latin *subvertere* to turn from beneath, from SUB- + *vertere* to turn]

subway /'subway/ *noun* **1** *Brit* a passage under a street for pedestrians. **2** *chiefly NAmer* an underground railway system: compare TUBE¹.

suc- *prefix* see SUB-.

succedaneum /suksə'dayni·əm/ *noun* (*pl* **succedaneums** *or* **succedanea** /-ni·ə/) *archaic* a substitute, *esp* a medical treatment or drug used in place of another. ➤➤ **succedaneous** *adj*. [scientific Latin *succedaneum*, neuter of Latin *succedaneus* substituted, from *succedere*: see SUCCEED]

succeed /sək'seed/ *verb intrans* **1a** to have a favourable result; to turn out well. **b** to achieve a desired object or end. **c** to attain wealth or fame. **2a** (+ to) to inherit something, *esp* sovereignty, rank, or title. **b** to follow after another in order. ➤ *verb trans* **1** to follow (something) in sequence. **2** to come after (somebody) as heir or successor. ➤➤ **succeeder** *noun*. [Middle English *succeden* from Latin *succedere* to go up, follow after, succeed, from SUB- + *cedere* to go]

succès de scandale /ˌsooksay də skon'dahl (*French* syksɛ də skādal)/ *noun* **1** something, e.g. a work of art, that wins popularity or notoriety because of its scandalous nature rather than its merits. **2** the reception given to such a piece. [French *succès de scandale*, literally 'success of scandal']

success /sək'ses/ *noun* **1a** a favourable outcome to an undertaking. **b** the achievement of a desired object or end. **c** the attainment of wealth or fame. **2** somebody or something that succeeds: *The band* *was an overnight success.* [Latin *successus* outcome, past part. of *succedere*: see SUCCEED]

successful *adj* **1** resulting in success: *a successful experiment.* **2** having succeeded: *the successful candidate.* **3** having gained wealth, fame, professional or social standing, etc: *a successful banker.* ➤➤ **successfully** *adv*, **successfulness** *noun*.

succession /sək'sesh(ə)n/ *noun* **1a** the order or right of succeeding to a property, title, office, or throne. **b** the line having such a right. **2a** the act of following in order; sequence. **b** (*treated as sing. or pl*) a number of people or things that follow each other in sequence. **3** the act or process of becoming entitled to a deceased person's property or title. **4** the change in the composition of an ecological community as the competing organisms respond to and modify the environment. ✷ **in succession** following one another without interruption. ➤➤ **successional** *adj*. [Middle English via French from Latin *succession-, successio*, from *succedere*: see SUCCEED]

successive *adj* following one after the other in succession. ➤➤ **successively** *adv*, **successiveness** *noun*.

successor *noun* somebody or something that follows another, *esp* a person who succeeds to a throne, title, or office. [Middle English *successour* via Old French from Latin *successor*, from *succedere*: see SUCCEED]

success story *noun* **1** the progress of somebody or something from obscurity or poverty to fame or wealth, or an account of such progress. **2** *informal* somebody or something that is successful.

succinct /sək'singkt/ *adj* clearly expressed in few words; concise. ➤➤ **succinctly** *adv*, **succinctness** *noun*. [Middle English from Latin *succinctus*, past part. of *succingere* to tuck up, from SUB- + *cingere* to gird]

succinic acid /sək'sinik/ *noun* an acid found widely in nature and active in energy-yielding chemical reactions in organisms: formula $C_4H_6O_4$. [French *succinique* from Latin *succinum* amber, from which it was first obtained]

succor[1] /'sukə/ *noun NAmer* see SUCCOUR[1].

succor[2] /'sukə/ *verb trans NAmer* see SUCCOUR[2].

succory /'suk(ə)ri/ *noun* = CHICORY. [alteration of Middle English *cicoree*: see CHICORY]

succotash /'sukətash/ *noun* a dish of beans, green maize, and other ingredients. [of Algonquian origin; related to Narraganset *msikwatâs* succotash]

Succoth /'sukoht, 'sukohth/ *noun* see SUKKOTH.

succour[1] (*NAmer* **succor**) /'sukə/ *noun* **1** relief from trouble, pain, etc. **2** assistance in time of difficulty. **3** somebody or something that provides succour. [Middle English *succur* via Old French and medieval Latin from Latin *succursus*, past part. of *succurrere* to run up, run to help, from SUB- + *currere* to run]

succour[2] (*NAmer* **succor**) *verb trans* to go to the aid of (somebody in need or distress).

succubus /'sukyoobəs/ *noun* (*pl* **succubi** /-bie/) a female demon believed to have sexual intercourse with men in their sleep: compare INCUBUS (1). [Middle English from medieval Latin *succubus*, alteration of late Latin *succuba* prostitute, from Latin *succubare* to lie under, from SUB- + *cubare* to lie]

succulent[1] /'sukyoolənt/ *adj* **1** said of food: full of juice and flavour. **2** said of a plant: having juicy fleshy tissues. ➤➤ **succulence** *noun*, **succulently** *adv*. [Latin *suculentus*, from *sucus* juice, sap]

succulent[2] *noun* a succulent plant, e.g. a cactus.

succumb /sə'kum/ *verb intrans* **1** (+ to) to yield or give in to something or somebody with superior strength or overpowering appeal. **2** to die from disease or injury. [French *succomber* from Latin *succumbere*, from SUB- + *-cumbere* to lie down]

succursal /sə'kuhsəl/ *adj* said of a monastery or other religious establishment: subsidiary. [French *succursale* from medieval Latin *succursus*, from Latin *succurrere*: see SUCCOUR[1]]

such[1] /such/ *adj and adv* **1a** of the kind, quality, or extent: *His schedule is such that we rarely meet.* **b** used with *as* to introduce an example or comparison: *such trees as spruce or pine.* **c** of that or the same sort: *There's no such place.* **2** of so extreme a degree or extraordinary a nature: *ever such a lot of people; in such a hurry.* ✷ **such as 1** for example: *reptiles, such as lizards.* **2** the same kind as; like: *women such as my sister.* **3** used to suggest lack of merit, worth, quantity, etc: *We forced down the soup, such as it was.* [Old English *swilc*]

---

such[2] *pronoun* (*pl* **such**) **1** that thing, fact, or action: *Such was the result.* **2** (*in pl*) similar people or things: *tin and glass and such.* **3** (*in pl*) such people; those: *Such as wish to leave may do so.* ✷ **as such** in himself, herself, itself, or themselves; intrinsically: *As such the gift was worth little.*

such and such *adj informal* not named or specified.

suchlike[1] *adj* of the kind mentioned; similar.

suchlike[2] *pronoun* (*pl* **suchlike**) a similar person or thing.

suck[1] /suk/ *verb trans* **1a** to draw (e.g. liquid) into the mouth by creating a partial vacuum with the contracted lips and tongue. **b** to draw liquid from (something) in this way: *suck an orange.* **c** to take (something) into the mouth as if sucking a liquid from it: *She sucked the end of her pencil.* **d** to eat (e.g. a sweet) by means of sucking movements of the lips and tongue. **2** to draw (something) in or up by or as if by suction: *plants sucking moisture from the soil.* **3** to draw (somebody) by irresistible force: *He was sucked into the conspiracy.* ➤ *verb intrans* **1** to draw something in or up by suction, *esp* to draw milk from a breast or udder with the mouth. **2** said of a pump: to draw air instead of water. **3** *chiefly NAmer, slang* to be worthless or objectionable. [Old English *sūcan*]

suck[2] *noun* **1** the act of sucking. **2** a sucking movement, sound, or force. ✷ **give suck to** *archaic* to suckle (a baby or young animal).

sucker[1] *noun* **1a** a cup-shaped device, *esp* of rubber, that can cling to a surface by suction. **b** a mouth, e.g. of a leech, or other animal organ adapted for sucking or clinging to a surface. **c** a pipe or tube through which something is drawn by suction. **d** a device for creating or regulating suction, e.g. a piston or valve in a pump. **2** a shoot from the roots or stem of a plant that can grow into an independent plant if it becomes detached. **3** any of numerous freshwater fishes closely related to the carps and usu having thick soft lips: family Catostomidae. **4** *informal.* **a** a gullible person. **b** a person irresistibly attracted by something specified: *a sucker for chocolate.* **5** *archaic* a human infant or young animal that sucks, *esp* at a breast or udder; a suckling.

sucker[2] *verb* (**suckered, suckering**) ➤ *verb trans* **1** to remove suckers from (a plant). **2** *chiefly NAmer, informal* to cheat or deceive (somebody). ➤ *verb intrans* said of a plant: to send out suckers.

sucker punch *noun informal* a devastating blow delivered unexpectedly.

sucking *adj* said *esp* of a pig: not yet weaned; *broadly* very young.

suckle /'sukl/ *verb trans* **1** to give milk to (a baby or young animal) from the breast or udder. **2** to suck milk from the breast or udder of (a mother or female animal): *lambs suckling the ewes.*

suckling /'sukling/ *noun* an unweaned baby or young animal.

suck off *verb trans coarse slang* to stimulate (somebody, *esp* a man) to orgasm with the mouth or tongue.

sucks *interj informal* an expression of defiance or derision.

suck up *verb intrans informal* to act in an obsequious manner: *You should see them sucking up to the director in the hope of getting good parts.*

sucrase /'s(y)oohkrayz/ *noun* = INVERTASE. [French *sucre* sugar + -ASE]

sucre /'soohkray/ *noun* the basic monetary unit of Ecuador, divided into 100 centavos. [Spanish *sucre*, named after Antonio José de Sucre d.1830, S American liberator]

sucrose /'s(y)oohkrohs, 's(y)oohkrohz/ *noun* the form of sugar obtained from sugarcane and sugar beet and occurring in most plants. [French *sucre* sugar + -OSE[2]]

suction /'suksh(ə)n/ *noun* **1a** the act of exerting a force on a solid, liquid, or gaseous body that draws it in or causes adherence by means of reduced air pressure over part of its surface. **b** the force so exerted. **2** the act of sucking. ➤➤ **suctional** *adj*. [late Latin *suction-, suctio* from Latin *sugere* to suck]

suction pump *noun* a pump in which liquid is drawn by suction into the partial vacuum left when a piston is drawn out.

suctorial /suk'tawri·əl/ *adj* in zoology, adapted for sucking up fluids or adhering by suction: *a suctorial mouth.* [scientific Latin *suctorius*, from Latin *sugere* to suck]

SUD *abbr* Sudan (international vehicle registration).

Sudanese /soohdə'neez, 'sooh-/ *noun* (*pl* **Sudanese**) a native or inhabitant of Sudan in NE Africa. ➤➤ **Sudanese** *adj*.

sudatorium /s(y)oohdə'tawri·əm/ *noun* (*pl* **sudatoria** /-ri·ə/) a room, *esp* in an ancient Roman bathhouse, where steam or hot air is used to induce sweating. [Latin *sudatorium*, neuter of *sudatorius*: see SUDATORY]

sudatory /'s(y)oohdət(ə)ri/ *adj* relating to or inducing sweating. [Latin *sudatorius*, from *sudare* to sweat]

sudd /sud/ *noun* floating vegetation that forms obstructive masses in the upper White Nile. [Arabic *sudd* obstruction]

sudden¹ /'sud(ə)n/ *adj* **1a** happening or coming unexpectedly: *a sudden shower.* **b** falling away sharply; steep. **2** marked by or showing haste; abrupt. ➤➤ **suddenly** *adv*, **suddenness** *noun*. [Middle English *sodain* via French from Latin *subitaneus*, from *subitus* sudden, past part. of *subire* to come up, from SUB- + *ire* to go]

sudden² ✱ **all of a sudden** without warning; suddenly.

sudden adult death syndrome *or* **sudden death syndrome** *noun* sudden fatal heart failure, *esp* in fit and active young adults between the ages of 15 and 35.

sudden death *noun* **1** an extra period of play to break a tie that ends the moment one player or side gains the lead. **2** unexpected death or death occurring within minutes from any cause other than violence, e.g. a heart attack.

sudden infant death syndrome *noun* = COT DEATH.

sudden wealth syndrome *noun* psychological and other problems experienced by those who unexpectedly acquire large sums of money.

sudoriferous /s(y)oohdə'rif(ə)rəs/ *adj* producing or carrying sweat: *sudoriferous glands; a sudoriferous duct.* [late Latin *sudorifer*, from Latin *sudor* sweat + -*ifer* -IFEROUS]

sudorific¹ /s(y)oohdə'rifik/ *adj* causing sweating; diaphoretic. [scientific Latin *sudorificus* from Latin *sudor* sweat]

sudorific² *noun* a drug that induces sweating.

Sudra /'s(y)oohdrə/ *noun* a Hindu of the lowest caste traditionally restricted to menial occupations: compare BRAHMAN, KSHATRIYA, VAISYA. [Sanskrit *śūdra*]

suds /sudz/ *pl noun* the lather on soapy water. [prob from early Dutch *sudse* marsh]

sudsy *adj* frothy or foamy.

sue /s(y)ooh/ *verb trans* **1** to bring a legal action against (a person, institution, etc). **2** (*usu* + for) to appeal to (somebody) for something. ➤ *verb intrans* **1** to take legal proceedings in court. **2** (*usu* + for/to) to make a formal request or application to somebody for something. ➤➤ **suer** *noun*. [Middle English *suen* to follow, make legal claim to, bring legal action against, via Old French *suivre* from Latin *sequi* to follow, pursue]

suede /swayd/ *noun* leather with a velvety surface produced by rubbing the flesh side to make a soft nap of short fibres. [French (*gants de*) *Suède* Swedish (gloves)]

suet /'s(y)ooh·it/ *noun* the hard fat round the kidneys and loins in cattle or sheep, which yields tallow and is used in cooking. [Middle English *sewet*, dimin. of Anglo-French *sue*, from Latin *sebum* tallow, grease, suet]

suet pudding *noun* a boiled or steamed sweet or savoury pudding containing suet.

suf- *prefix* see SUB-.

suffer /'sufə/ *verb* (**suffered, suffering**) ➤ *verb trans* **1** to be forced to endure (something unpleasant, *esp* pain, illness, etc). **2** to experience (something unpleasant): *We've suffered a setback.* **3** *archaic*. **a** to allow (somebody to do something): *Suffer the little children to come unto me.* **b** to tolerate (somebody or something). ➤ *verb intrans* **1** to endure pain, distress, or death. **2** to sustain loss or damage. **3** to be put at a disadvantage. **4a** (+ from) to be affected by something, *esp* an illness. **b** (+ from) to be subject to something. ➤➤ **sufferable** *adj*, **sufferer** *noun*. [Middle English *suffren* via Old French from Latin *sufferre* to bear up, from SUB- + *ferre* to bear]

sufferance *noun* **1** tolerance implied by a lack of interference or objection rather than actual approval: *He was only there on sufferance.* **2** capacity to withstand; endurance.

suffering *noun* the state of somebody who suffers, *esp* somebody who is in pain.

suffice /sə'fies/ *verb intrans* to meet a need; to be enough: *A brief note will suffice.* ➤ *verb trans archaic* to be enough for (somebody or something). ✱ **suffice (it) to say** used to indicate that further information has been withheld, e.g. for the sake of brevity or discretion: *Suffice it to say he has resigned.* [Middle English *sufficen* via French from Latin *sufficere* to put under, meet the need of, from SUB- + *facere* to make, do]

sufficiency /sə'fish(ə)nsi/ *noun* (*pl* **sufficiencies**) **1** a sufficient amount. **2** the quality of being sufficient; adequacy.

sufficient /sə'fish(ə)nt/ *adj* enough to meet the needs of a situation; adequate. ➤➤ **sufficiently** *adv*. [Middle English from Latin *sufficient-, sufficiens*, present part. of *sufficere*: see SUFFICE]

suffix¹ /'sufiks/ *noun* an affix, e.g. -*ness* in *happiness*, placed at the end of a word or after a root: compare INFIX², PREFIX¹. [Latin *suffixum* neuter past part. of *suffigere* to fasten underneath, from SUB- + *figere* to fasten]

suffix² *verb trans* to attach (an affix) as a suffix. ➤➤ **suffixation** /-'saysh(ə)n/ *noun*.

suffocate /'sufəkayt/ *verb trans* **1** to stop the breathing of (somebody), e.g. by strangling or asphyxiation. **2** to deprive (a person, animal, plant, etc) of oxygen. **3** to make (somebody) uncomfortable by lack of cool fresh air. ➤ *verb intrans* **1** to die from being unable to breathe. **2** to be uncomfortable through lack of air. ➤➤ **suffocating** *adj*, **suffocatingly** *adv*, **suffocation** /-'kaysh(ə)n/ *noun*. [Latin *suffocatus*, past part. of *suffocare* to choke, stifle, from SUB- + *fauces* throat]

Suffolk /'sufək/ *noun* **1** an animal of an English breed of black-faced hornless sheep. **2** an animal of an English breed of chestnut-coloured draught horses. [named after *Suffolk*, county of England where the breeds originated]

Suffolk punch *noun* = SUFFOLK (2).

suffragan /'sufrəgən/ *noun* **1** a diocesan bishop subordinate to a METROPOLITAN² (bishop of a province). **2** a bishop assisting a diocesan bishop and having no right of succession. [Middle English via French from medieval Latin *suffraganeus*, from Latin *suffragium* support, prayer]

suffrage /'sufrij/ *noun* **1** the right to vote in political elections; franchise. **2** *archaic* a vote given in favour of a question or in the choice of somebody for an office. **3** a short prayer of intercession, usu in a series. [Latin *suffragium* vote, political support]

suffragette /sufrə'jet/ *noun* a woman campaigning for the right to vote to be extended to women, *esp* any of a group of militant campaigners in Britain in the early 20th cent.

suffragist /'sufrəjist/ *noun* somebody who advocates extending the right to vote, *esp* to women. ➤➤ **suffragism** *noun*.

suffuse /sə'fyoohz/ *verb trans* (*usu in passive*) to spread over or through (something); to permeate (it). ➤➤ **suffusion** /-zh(ə)n/ *noun*, **suffusive** /-siv/ *adj*. [Latin *suffusus*, past part. of *suffundere* to pour beneath, from SUB- + *fundere* to pour]

Sufi /'soohfi/ *noun* (*pl* **Sufis**) a Muslim mystic. ➤➤ **Sufic** /'soohfik/ *adj*, **Sufism** *noun*. [Arabic *ṣūfiy*, literally '(man) of wool', because of their woollen clothing]

sug- *prefix* see SUB-.

sugar¹ /'shoogə/ *noun* **1a** a sweet usu crystalline substance that consists essentially of sucrose, is colourless or white when pure, tending to brown when less refined, is obtained *esp* from sugarcane or sugar beet, and is important as a source of dietary carbohydrate and as a sweetener and preservative of other foods. **b** any of a class of water-soluble carbohydrates that are of varying sweetness and include glucose, ribose, and sucrose. **2** *chiefly NAmer, informal* a term of endearment. **3** *slang, dated* heroin, LSD, or any similar drug.

Word history
Middle English *sucre* via medieval Latin *zuccarum*, Old Italian *zucchero*, Arabic *sukkar*, and Persian *shakar* from Sanskrit *śarkarā*. The history of this word reflects the route by which the product was originally transmitted to England: from India to Persia, then through Arab territories to Italy and thence to the rest of Europe. Sugarcane, the only commercial source of sugar until extraction from sugar beet was developed in the early 19th cent., may well have originated in India; in any case, the production of sugar began in India, by about 3000 BC, and the ultimate source of the word is a Sanskrit word probably originally meaning 'grit' or 'gravel', reflecting the granular appearance of sugar. From India, sugar spread both eastwards and westwards. To the west, the major region of early sugarcane cultivation was Khūzistān in Persia. Arab traders, often acting as intermediaries between India and Europe, developed the art of sugar refining and introduced sugar in the Middle Ages to Egypt, Italy, and southern Spain. Venice became the European centre of the sugar trade; a Venetian invented loaf sugar, and in 1319 100,000lb of sugar was shipped to London by a Venetian merchant. The earliest references to sugar in England date from the late 13th cent.; early English records are very variable in spelling

but most seem to reflect the French form *sucre*, itself a derivative of the Italian *zucchero*.

sugar² *verb trans* (**sugared, sugaring**) **1** to make (something) palatable or attractive. **2** to sprinkle, coat, or sweeten (something) with sugar. ➤➤ **sugared** *adj*.

sugar beet *noun* a variety of beet grown for the sugar in its white roots.

sugar candy *noun* **1** crystals of sugar formed by crystallizing a sugar solution and used as a sweetener, e.g. for coffee. **2** *NAmer* = CANDY¹ (2).

sugarcane *noun* a tall grass with stout stems that is widely grown in warm regions as a source of sugar: *Saccharum officinarum*.

sugar-coated *adj* **1** covered with a hard coat of sugar. **2** superficially attractive; having its unpleasantness concealed.

sugar daddy *noun informal* a usu elderly man who lavishes gifts and money on a young woman in return for sex or companionship.

sugar diabetes *noun informal* = DIABETES MELLITUS.

sugar glider *noun* a flying PHALANGER (tree-dwelling marsupial) that feeds on the sap of eucalyptus trees: *Petaurus breviceps*.

sugaring *noun* **1** a method of hair removal using a sugar paste. **2** *chiefly Can* the process of boiling maple sap to make syrup and sugar.

sugarloaf *noun* a moulded cone of refined sugar.

sugar maple *noun* a N American maple tree with a sweet sap that is the chief source of maple syrup and maple sugar: *Acer saccharum*.

sugarplum *noun archaic* a small round sweet usu of flavoured and coloured boiled sugar.

sugar snap pea *noun* a variety of mangetout pea that has a thick rounded pod.

sugar soap *noun* a substance consisting of soap and washing soda used for stripping paint or cleaning surfaces prior to painting.

sugary *adj* **1** containing, resembling, or tasting of sugar. **2** exaggeratedly or cloyingly cute or sentimental.

suggest /sə'jest/ *verb trans* **1** to put (something) forward as a possibility or for consideration. **2** to call (something) to mind by thought or association; to evoke (it). **3** to express (something) indirectly; to imply (it): *Her look suggested irritation*. ➤➤ **suggester** *noun*. [Latin *suggestus*, past part. of *suggerere* to put under, furnish, suggest, from SUB- + *gerere* to carry]

suggestible *adj* easily influenced by suggestion. ➤➤ **suggestibility** /-'biliti/ *noun*.

suggestion /sə'jesch(ə)n/ *noun* **1a** the act of suggesting. **b** something suggested. **2a** indirect means, e.g. the natural association of ideas, used to evoke ideas or feelings. **b** the impressing of an idea, attitude, desired action, etc on the mind of another. **3** a slight indication; a trace: *the suggestion of a smile*.

suggestive /sə'jestiv/ *adj* **1a** (*often* + of) tending to suggest; indicative. **b** (*often* + of) stirring mental associations; evocative. **2** suggesting something improper or indecent; risqué. ➤➤ **suggestively** *adv*, **suggestiveness** *noun*.

suicidal /s(y)ooh-i'siedl/ *adj* **1** relating to or involving suicide. **2** marked by an impulse to commit suicide. **3a** dangerous, *esp* to life. **b** harmful to one's own interests. ➤➤ **suicidally** *adv*.

suicide /'s(y)ooh-isied/ *noun* **1a** the act of killing oneself intentionally. **b** the ruining of one's own interests: *political suicide*. **2** somebody who commits suicide. **3** (*used before a noun*) denoting action that will result in the death of the person undertaking it, usu an attack intended to kill others: *a suicide bombing*. [Latin *sui* of oneself + -CIDE]

suicide pact *noun* an agreement between two or more people to commit suicide together.

sui generis /,sooh-ie 'jenəris, ,sooh-i/ *adj* unique. [Latin *sui generis* of its own kind]

sui juris /'jooəris/ *adj* having full legal rights or capacity. [Latin *sui juris* of one's own right]

suint /'sooh-int, swint/ *noun* the dried sweat of sheep deposited in the wool, rich in potassium-containing chemical compounds. [French *suint* from *suer* to sweat, from Latin *sudare*]

suit¹ /s(y)ooht/ *noun* **1a** an outer costume of two or more matching articles of clothing, *esp* a jacket and trousers or a skirt, that are designed to be worn together. **b** a costume to be worn for a specified purpose or under particular conditions: *a diving suit; a suit of*

armour. **2a** all the playing cards in a pack bearing the same symbol, i.e. hearts, clubs, diamonds, or spades. **b** all the cards in a particular suit held by one player: *a five-card suit*. **c** the suit led in card games: *follow suit*. **3** a group of things forming a unit or constituting a collection: *a suit of sails*. **4** a legal action; a lawsuit. **5** *informal* a business executive or bureaucrat, *esp* one considered as faceless but influential. **6** *formal or archaic*. **a** a petition or appeal. **b** courtship. [Middle English *sute* act of following, retinue, lawsuit, set, from Old French *siute*, ultimately from Latin *sequi* to follow, pursue]

Usage note

suit *or* **suite?** Both these words mean a 'set' of things, but different things are involved. A *suit* is a set of clothes or armour, or one of the four sets of playing cards making up a pack (hearts, clubs, spades, or diamonds): *follow suit*. *Suit* can also mean 'a court action' or 'a request or appeal': *grant somebody's suit*. A *suite* is a set of matching furniture, of rooms, or related pieces of music (Holst's *Planet Suite*), or of computer software. It can also mean the retinue of servants or staff attending a grandee or high-ranking official.

suit² *verb trans* **1a** to be becoming to or look right with (somebody or something). **b** to be good for the health or well-being of (somebody). **2** to accommodate or adapt (something) to a particular situation, circumstances, etc. **3** to satisfy, please, or be convenient to (somebody or oneself): *That suits me fine*. ➤ *verb intrans* **1** to be appropriate or satisfactory: *These prices don't suit*. **2** (+ up) put on specially required clothing, e.g. a uniform or protective outfit. ✳ **suit somebody down to the ground** to suit somebody extremely well. ➤➤ **suited** *adj*.

suitable *adj* appropriate for a particular person, situation, etc; fitting. ➤➤ **suitability** /-'biliti/ *noun*, **suitableness** *noun*, **suitably** *adv*.

suitcase *noun* a rectangular usu rigid case with a hinged lid and a handle, used for carrying clothes and other personal items when travelling.

suite /sweet/ *noun* **1** a group of rooms occupied as a unit. **2** a set of matching furniture, e.g. a settee and two armchairs, for a room: *a three-piece suite*. **3** a set of computer software. **4a** an instrumental musical form consisting of a series of dance-related pieces. **b** a modern instrumental composition in several movements of different character. **c** an orchestral arrangement of material drawn from a longer work, e.g. a ballet, in the form of a suite. **5** *formal* (*treated as sing. or pl*) a retinue, *esp* the personal staff accompanying an official or dignitary on business. [French *suite*, alteration of Old French *siute*: see SUIT¹]

Usage note

suite *or* **suit?** See note at SUIT¹.

suiting *noun* fabric suitable for making suits.

suitor /'s(y)oohtə/ *noun* **1** *dated* somebody who courts a woman with a view to marriage. **2** somebody who is looking to buy or take over a business. [Middle English, in the sense 'follower, pleader', via Anglo-French from Latin *secutor* follower, from *sequi* to follow]

sukiyaki /soohki'yaki, -'yahki/ *noun* a Japanese dish of thin slices of meat, soya-bean curd, and vegetables cooked in soy sauce, sake, and sugar. [Japanese *sukiyaki*]

Sukkoth *or* **Succoth** /'sukoht, 'sukohth/ *noun* a Jewish harvest festival celebrated in September or October to commemorate the temporary shelters used by the Israelites during their wandering in the wilderness after leaving Egypt (Exodus 13). [Hebrew *Sukkōth*, pl of *sukkāh* hut, temporary shelter]

sulcate /'sulkayt/ *adj* said of a plant or animal part: marked with parallel grooves running lengthways. [Latin *sulcatus*, past part. of *sulcare* to furrow, from *sulcus* furrow]

sulcus /'sulkəs/ *noun* (*pl* **sulci** /'sulsie/) a shallow furrow on a body part, *esp* between the ridges on the surface of the brain. [Latin *sulcus* furrow]

sulf- *or* **sulfo-** *comb. form NAmer see* SULPH-.

sulfa drug *noun NAmer see* SULPHA DRUG.

sulfanilamide /sulfə'niləmied/ *noun NAmer see* SULPHANILAMIDE.

sulfate /'sulfayt/ *noun NAmer see* SULPHATE.

sulfide /'sulfied/ *noun NAmer see* SULPHIDE.

sulfite /'sulfiet/ *noun NAmer see* SULPHITE.

sulfonamide /sul'fonəmied/ *noun NAmer see* SULPHONAMIDE.

sulfonate /'sulfənayt/ *noun NAmer see* SULPHONATE.

sulfone /'sulfohn/ *noun NAmer see* SULPHONE.

sulfonic /sul'fonik, sul'fohnik/ *adj NAmer see* SULPHONIC.

sulfur¹ /'sulfə/ *noun NAmer see* SULPHUR¹.

sulfur² *verb trans NAmer* see SULPHUR².

sulfurate /'sulfyoorayt/ *verb trans NAmer* see SULPHURATE.

sulfureted hydrogen /'sulfyooretid/ *noun NAmer, dated* see SULPHURETTED HYDROGEN.

sulfuric /sul'fyooərik/ *adj NAmer* see SULPHURIC.

sulfurize *verb trans NAmer* see SULPHURIZE.

sulfurous /'sulf(ə)rəs, sul'fyooərəs/ *adj NAmer* see SULPHUROUS.

sulk¹ /sulk/ *verb intrans* to be moodily silent, *esp* through resentment or disappointment. [back-formation from SULKY¹]

sulk² *noun* (*usu in pl*) a fit of sulking.

sulky¹ *adj* (**sulkier, sulkiest**) sulking or given to fits of sulking. ⧄ **sulkily** *adv*, **sulkiness** *noun*. [prob alteration of obsolete *sulke* sluggish]

sulky² *noun* (*pl* **sulkies**) a light two-wheeled one-horse vehicle for one person, used *esp* in trotting races: *He just wanted to see those green Tennesseans stare and gawk when they saw him come a-ripping along in a sulky* — Mark Twain. [prob from SULKY¹, from its holding a solitary person]

sullage /'sulij/ *noun* **1a** refuse or sewage. **b** waste water from a household. **2** solid matter deposited by running water; silt. [prob from early French *soiller, souiller*: see SOIL²]

sullen /'sulən/ *adj* **1** silently gloomy or resentful; unsociable. **2** dismal or gloomy. ⧄ **sullenly** *adv*, **sullenness** *noun*. [Middle English *solain* sullen, solitary, ultimately from Latin *solus* alone]

sully /'suli/ *verb trans* (**sullies, sullied, sullying**) to mar the purity of (something, e.g. a reputation); to defile or tarnish (it). [prob from early French *soiller*: see SOIL²]

sulph- *or* **sulpho-** (*NAmer* **sulf-** *or* **sulfo-**) *comb. form* forming words, with the meaning: sulphur, or containing sulphur in the molecular structure: *sulphanilamide*. [French *sulf-, sulfo-* from Latin *sulphur, sulfur*]

sulpha drug (*NAmer* **sulfa drug**) /'sulfə/ *noun* any of various synthetic drugs chemically related to sulphanilamide that are used to kill or inhibit the growth of bacteria. [*sulpha* short for SULPHANILAMIDE]

sulphanilamide (*NAmer* **sulfanilamide**) /sulfə'niləmied/ *noun* a chemical compound that is a sulphonamide and to which most of the sulpha drugs are related. [*sulphanilic* (SULPH- + ANILINE + -IC¹) + AMIDE]

sulphate (*NAmer* **sulfate**) /'sulfayt/ *noun* a chemical compound that is a salt or ester of sulphuric acid. [modification of French *sulfate*, from Latin *sulphur, sulfur*]

sulphide (*NAmer* **sulfide**) /'sulfied/ *noun* a compound containing sulphur and a less electronegative element.

sulphite (*NAmer* **sulfite**) /'sulfiet/ *noun* a chemical compound that is a salt or ester of sulphurous acid. [modification of French *sulfite*, alteration of *sulfate*: see SULPHATE]

sulpho- *comb. form* see SULPH-.

sulphonamide (*NAmer* **sulfonamide**) /sul'fonəmied/ *noun* any of a group of chemical compounds that are amides of a sulphonic acid, including sulpha drugs.

sulphonate (*NAmer* **sulfonate**) /'sulfənayt/ *noun* a chemical compound that is a salt or ester of a sulphonic acid.

sulphone (*NAmer* **sulfone**) /'sulfohn/ *noun* any of various compounds containing the chemical group SO_2 with two chemical bonds between its sulphur atom and usu a carbon atom.

sulphonic (*NAmer* **sulfonic**) /sul'fonik, sul'fohnik/ *adj* of, being, or derived from the acid group $-SO_2OH$: *sulphonic acid*.

sulphur¹ (*NAmer* **sulfur**) /'sulfə/ *noun* **1** a non-metallic chemical element chemically resembling oxygen that occurs naturally *esp* as yellow crystals, and is used *esp* in rubber vulcanization and in medicine for treating skin diseases: symbol S, atomic number 16. **2** a pale greenish yellow colour. [Middle English *sulphur* brimstone, via Old French from Latin *sulpur, sulphur, sulfur*]

sulphur² (*NAmer* **sulfur**) *verb trans* (**sulphured, sulphuring**, *NAmer* **sulfured, sulfuring**) to treat (something) with sulphur or a compound of sulphur; to sulphurate (it).

sulphurate (*NAmer* **sulfurate**) /'sulfyoorayt/ *verb trans* to treat (something) with sulphur or a compound of sulphur. ⧄ **sulphuration** /-'raysh(ə)n/ *noun*.

sulphur bottom whale *noun dated* = BLUE WHALE. [from the yellowish splotches on its belly]

sulphur dioxide *noun* a pungent toxic gas that is a major air pollutant and is used in making sulphuric acid, in bleaching, and as a food preservative: formula SO_2.

sulphuretted hydrogen (*NAmer* **sulfureted hydrogen**) /'sulfyooretid/ *noun dated* = HYDROGEN SULPHIDE.

sulphuric (*NAmer* **sulfuric**) /sul'fyooərik/ *adj* of or containing sulphur, *esp* high valency sulphur.

sulphuric acid *noun* a heavy corrosive oily acid that is a vigorous oxidizing and dehydrating agent: formula H_2SO_4.

sulphurize *or* **sulphurise** (*NAmer* **sulfurize**) *verb trans* to treat (something) with sulphur or a compound of sulphur. ⧄ **sulphurization** /-'zaysh(ə)n/ *noun*.

sulphurous (*NAmer* **sulfurous**) /'sulf(ə)rəs, sul'fyooərəs/ *adj* **1** of or containing sulphur, *esp* low valency sulphur. **2** resembling or derived from sulphur. **3** *literary* relating to or coming from hell; hellish. **4** *literary* marked by violent passion or strong language; fiery.

sulphurous acid /sul'fyooərəs/ *noun* a weak unstable acid used for bleaching and as a reducing agent: formula H_2SO_3.

sultan /'sult(ə)n/ *noun* **1** a sovereign of a Muslim state, *esp* the former Ottoman Empire. **2** a small domestic hen of a breed originating in Turkey. ⧄ **sultanate** /-nət/ *noun*. [early French *sultan* via medieval Latin from Arabic *sulṭān* power, ruler]

sultana /səl'tahnə/ *noun* **1** the light brown raisin of a pale yellow seedless grape. **2** a female member of a sultan's family, *esp* a sultan's wife. [Italian *sultana*, fem of *sultano* sultan, from Arabic *sulṭān* power, ruler]

sultry /'sultri/ *adj* (**sultrier, sultriest**) **1** oppressively hot and humid. **2** exciting strong sexual desire; sensual. ⧄ **sultrily** *adv*, **sultriness** *noun*. [obsolete *sulter* to swelter, alteration of SWELTER¹]

sum¹ /sum/ *noun* **1** an amount of money. **2** the result of adding numbers: *The sum of five and seven is twelve.* **3** the whole amount of anything; the total. **4** numbers to be added, subtracted, multiplied, or divided; a simple arithmetical problem. **5** in mathematics, the limit of the sum of the first n terms of an infinite series as n increases indefinitely. ✳ **in sum** briefly. [Middle English *summe* via Old French from Latin *summa* total, sum of money, fem of *summus* highest, chief]

sum² *verb trans* (**summed, summing**) to calculate the sum of (several numbers or amounts).

sumach *or* **sumac** /'soohmak, 'shoomak/ *noun* **1** any of several species of trees, shrubs, and climbing plants, e.g. poison ivy, with feathery leaves that turn to brilliant colours in the autumn and loose clusters of red or whitish berries: genera *Rhus* and *Cotinus*. **2** the dried powdered leaves and flowers of a sumach, used in tanning and dyeing. [Middle English *sumac* via French from Arabic *summāq*]

Sumatran /soo'mahtrən/ *noun* a native or inhabitant of Sumatra. ⧄ **Sumatran** *adj*.

Sumerian /sooh'miəri·ən, sooh'meə-/ *noun* **1** a native or inhabitant of Sumer, an ancient region of Babylonia. **2** the extinct language of the Sumerians, which has no known relationship with any other language. ⧄ **Sumerian** *adj*.

summa cum laude /,soomə koom 'lowday/ *adv and adj* graduating with the highest class of university degree, *esp* from a N American university. [Latin *summa cum laude* with highest praise]

summarize *or* **summarise** /'suməriez/ *verb trans* to reduce (something) to a summary; to express (it) in concise terms. ⧄ **summarization** /-'zaysh(ə)n/ *noun*, **summarizer** *noun*.

summary¹ /'suməri/ *noun* (*pl* **summaries**) a brief account covering the main points of something. [Middle English via medieval Latin *summarius* from Latin *summa*: see SUM¹]

summary² *adj* **1a** done quickly without delay or formality: *a summary dismissal*. **b** of or using a summary proceeding; *specif* tried or triable in a magistrates' court. **2** concise but comprehensive: *a summary report*. ⧄ **summarily** *adv*, **summariness** *noun*.

summary jurisdiction *noun* the authority of a court to make an immediate judgment on a case.

summary offence *noun* an offence that may be tried in a lower court, e.g. a magistrate's court, without full legal proceedings.

summat /'sumət/ *pronoun N Eng dialect* something. [alteration of the obsolete pronoun *somewhat* something]

summation /su'maysh(ə)n/ *noun* **1** the act or process of adding numbers. **2** a total. **3** cumulative action or effect. **4** the act or an instance of summing up. **5** a summary. ➤➤ **summational** *adj*, **summative** *adj*. [medieval Latin *summation-*, *summatio*, from *summare* to add, from Latin *summa*: see SUM¹]

summer¹ /'sumə/ *noun* **1a** the season between spring and autumn, the warmest part of the year, in the N hemisphere the months of June, July, and August; = SUMMERTIME. **b** in astronomy, the period in the N hemisphere extending from the June SOLSTICE (longest day of the year) to the September EQUINOX (time when day and night are of equal length). **2** a period of maturity. **3** *literary* (*usu in pl*) a year: *a girl of 17 summers.* **4** (*used before a noun*) of, during, or suitable for summer: *a summer dress.* [Old English *sumor*]

summer² *adj* said of crops: sown in the spring and harvested in the same year as sown: compare WINTER²: *summer wheat.*

summer³ *verb* (**summered, summering**) ➤ *verb intrans* (+ in) to spend the summer in a particular place. ➤ *verb trans* to provide (e.g. cattle or sheep) with pasture during the summer.

summer⁴ *noun archaic* a large horizontal beam or stone used in building. [Middle English, in the senses 'packhorse, beam', via early French *somier* and late Latin from Greek *sagma* packsaddle]

summerhouse /'suməhows/ *noun* a small building in a garden designed to provide a shady place in summer.

summer pudding *noun* a cold dessert consisting of soft fruits, e.g. raspberries and blackcurrants, encased by a basin-shaped mould of white bread.

summersault¹ /'suməsawlt/ *noun archaic* = SOMERSAULT¹.

summersault² *verb intrans archaic* = SOMERSAULT².

summer school *noun* a course of teaching held during the summer vacation, *esp* on university premises.

Summer Time *noun* = BRITISH SUMMER TIME.

summertime *noun* the season of summer.

summer-weight *adj* said *esp* of clothing: lightweight and therefore suitable for summer.

summery *adj* of, suggesting, or suitable for summer.

summing-up *noun* **1** a concluding summary. **2** a survey of the evidence in a case given by a judge to the jury before it considers its verdict.

summit /'sumit/ *noun* **1** the highest point or peak of a hill or mountain. **2** the topmost level attainable: *the summit of her career.* **3** a conference of highest-level officials or heads of government. [Middle English *somete* via Old French from Latin *summum*, neuter of *summus* highest]

summiteer /sumi'tiə/ *noun* a person participating in a summit conference.

summon /'sumən/ *verb trans* (**summoned, summoning**) **1** to order (somebody) to come; to send for (them): *I was summoned to her office.* **2** to command (somebody) by a summons to appear in court. **3** (*often* + up) to call up or muster (a particular quality): *He summoned up his courage.* **4** to call people to attend (a meeting); to convene (it). ➤➤ **summoner** *noun.* [Middle English *somonen* via Old French *somondre* from Latin *summonēre* to remind secretly, from SUB- + *monēre* to warn]

summons¹ /'sumənz/ *noun* (*pl* **summonses**) **1** a written notification ordering somebody to appear in court. **2** a call or order by authority to appear at a particular place or to attend to something. [Middle English *somouns* from Old French *somonse*, past part. of *somondre*: see SUMMON]

summons² *verb trans* to serve (somebody) with a summons; to summon (them).

summum bonum /,suməm 'bohnəm, ,soomoom 'bonoom/ *noun formal* the supreme good from which all others are derived. [Latin *summum bonum* highest good]

sumo /'s(y)oohmoh/ *noun* Japanese wrestling between two contestants of immense build who lose if they are forced out of the contest area or if any part of their body other than the soles of their feet touches the ground. [Japanese *sumō*]

sump /sump/ *noun* **1** *chiefly Brit* the lower section of the crankcase of an internal-combustion engine used as a reservoir for lubricating oil. **2** the lowest part of a mine shaft, into which water drains. **3** any pit or reservoir serving as a drain or receptacle for *esp* waste liquids. **4** = CESSPOOL (1). [Middle English *sompe* swamp, from early High German *sumpf* marsh]

sumpter /'sumptə/ *noun archaic* a pack animal. [short for obsolete *sumpter horse*, from Middle English *sumpter* packhorse driver, via French and late Latin from Greek *sagma* packsaddle]

sumptuary /'sumptyoo·əri/ *adj* designed to regulate personal expenditure and prevent extravagance and luxury: *sumptuary laws.* [Latin *sumptuarius*, from *sumptus* expense, past part. of *sumere* to take, spend]

sumptuous /'sumpchoo·əs, 'sumptyoo·əs/ *adj* lavishly rich, costly, or luxurious. ➤➤ **sumptuously** *adv*, **sumptuousness** *noun.* [early French *sumptueux* from Latin *sumptuosus*, from *sumptus*: see SUMPTUARY]

sum total *noun* **1** a total arrived at through the counting of sums. **2** the whole amount; the totality.

sum up *verb trans* **1** to summarize (something). **2** to form or express a rapid or concise appraisal of (something or somebody). ➤ *verb intrans* to present a summary.

Sun. *abbr* Sunday.

sun¹ /sun/ *noun* **1a** (*often* **Sun**) the star nearest to the earth, round which the earth and other planets revolve. **b** a star or other celestial body that emits its own light. **2** the heat or light radiated from the sun. **3** *literary* a day or a year. ✳ **catch the sun** to become suntanned or sunburnt. **under the sun** in the world: *He was the last person under the sun I expected to see.* ➤➤ **sunless** *adj*, **sunward** *adj and adv*, **sunwards** *adv.* [Old English *sunne*]

sun² *verb trans* (**sunned, sunning**) to expose (*esp* oneself) to the rays of the sun.

sunbaked *adj* dried or baked hard by exposure to sunshine.

sunbath *noun* a period of sunbathing.

sunbathe *verb intrans* to lie or sit in the sun or under a sunlamp, *esp* in order to get a suntan. ➤➤ **sunbather** *noun.*

sunbeam *noun* a ray of light from the sun.

sunbed *noun* **1** a folding portable bed, usu made from canvas on a metal frame and sometimes padded, used for sunbathing, as a garden seat, etc. **2** a unit consisting of a couch and an array of sunlamps.

sunbelt *noun* an area with a warm sunny climate, *esp* one in which people prefer to live and work so as to be able to enjoy superior recreational opportunities.

sunbird *noun* any of numerous species of small brilliantly coloured tropical birds of Africa and Asia that resemble hummingbirds: family Nectariniidae.

sunblind *noun chiefly Brit* a shade on a window, e.g. a venetian blind or awning, that gives protection from the sun's rays.

sunblock *noun* a cosmetic preparation that protects exposed skin from the ultraviolet rays in sunlight.

sunbonnet *noun* a bonnet with a wide brim framing the face and usu having a ruffle at the back to protect the neck from the sun.

sunbow *noun* an arch resembling a rainbow made by the sun shining through vapour or mist.

sunburn¹ *noun* inflammation of the skin caused by overexposure to sunlight.

sunburn² *verb* (**sunburned** *or* **sunburnt**) ➤ *verb trans* (*usu in passive*) to burn or tan (somebody) by exposure to sunlight. ➤ *verb intrans* to become sunburnt.

sunburst *noun* **1** a sudden and dazzling appearance of the sun from behind a cloud. **2** an ornament or jewelled brooch representing a sun surrounded by rays.

suncream *noun* cream applied to protect the skin from the sun's ultraviolet rays.

sundae /'sunday/ *noun* a dish of ice cream served with a topping of fruit, nuts, syrup, etc. [prob alteration of SUNDAY¹, perhaps because it was, or was believed to be, made from ice cream left over at the end of the week, or because it was sold only on Sundays, perhaps because of laws concerning what could be sold on the sabbath]

sun dance *noun* a Native N American religious ceremony held in honour of the sun.

Sundanese /sundə'neez/ *noun* (*pl* **Sundanese**) **1** a member of a chiefly Muslim people of western Java. **2** the language of this people. ➤➤ **Sundanese** *adj.* [Sundanese *Sunda* western Java + -ESE²]

Sunday[1] /'sunday, 'sundi/ *noun* **1** the first day of the week, following Saturday, observed by Christians as a day of worship. **2** a newspaper published on Sundays: *further scandal in the Sundays.* [Old English *sunnandæg* day of the sun, translation of Latin *solis dies*]

Sunday[2] *adj* **1** of or associated with Sunday. **2** amateur or unskilful: *Sunday painters; Sunday drivers.*

Sunday best *noun informal* one's best clothes. [best clothes were traditionally worn on Sunday to attend church]

Sunday school *noun* a class of religious instruction held, *esp* for children, on Sundays.

sunder /'sundə/ *verb trans* (**sundered, sundering**) *archaic or literary* to break (something) apart or in two; to sever (it). [Old English *gesundrian, syndrian*]

sundew *noun* any of several species of bog plants with long glistening sticky hairs on the leaves that attract and trap insects: genus *Drosera*.

sundial *noun* an instrument that shows the time of day by the shadow of a pointer on a graduated plate or cylindrical surface.

sun disc *noun* an ancient symbol consisting of a disc with stylized wings emblematic of a sun-god, e.g. Ra in ancient Egypt.

sun dog *noun* = PARHELION.

sundown *noun chiefly NAmer* = SUNSET.

sundowner *noun* **1** *Brit, dated, informal* an alcoholic drink taken at sunset, or the first drink of an evening. **2** *Aus, informal* a homeless itinerant person; a tramp. [(sense 2) from their habit of arriving at sundown, too late to do any work, at a place where they hope to obtain food and lodging]

sundrenched *adj* where the sun almost always shines: *its sundrenched coastline.*

sundress *noun* a lightweight dress designed for sunny weather, typically sleeveless and with shoulder straps.

sun-dried *adj* dried and preserved by exposure to sunlight.

sundry[1] /'sundri/ *adj* of various kinds; miscellaneous: *sundry articles.* [Old English *syndrig* separate, distinct]

sundry[2] * **all and sundry** everybody.

sundry[3] *noun* (*pl* **sundries**) **1** (*in pl*) miscellaneous small articles or items. **2** *Aus* = EXTRA[2] (4).

sunfast *adj* resistant to fading by sunlight: *sunfast dyes.*

sunfish *noun* (*pl* **sunfishes** *or collectively* **sunfish**) **1** any of several species of large marine fishes with a nearly oval body, a bony skeleton, long pointed fins on their backs, and a length of up to 3m (about 10ft): *Mola mola* and other species. **2** any of several species of brightly coloured freshwater fishes of N America: family Centrarchidae.

sunflower *noun* a tall plant of the daisy family with large yellow-rayed flower heads bearing edible seeds that are often used as animal feed and yield an edible oil: *Helianthus annus.*

sung /sung/ *verb* past part. of SING[1].

sunglasses *pl noun* tinted glasses worn to protect the eyes from the sun.

sunhat *noun* a large-brimmed hat worn to protect the head and face from the sun.

sunk /sungk/ *verb* past part. of SINK[1].

sunken /'sungk(ə)n/ *adj* **1** submerged, *esp* lying at the bottom of a body of water. **2** lying or constructed below the surrounding or normal level: *a sunken bath.* **3** hollow or recessed: *sunken cheeks; sunken eyes.* [obsolete past part. of SINK[1]]

sunk fence *noun* = HA-HA[2].

sunlamp *noun* **1** an electric lamp that emits *esp* ultraviolet light and is used for tanning the skin, muscular therapy, etc. **2** a large lamp used in film-making that has parabolic reflectors to produce an intense beam of light.

sunlight *noun* light emitted by the sun; sunshine.

sunlit *adj* lit by the sun.

sunlounge *noun Brit* a room with large windows positioned to admit a lot of sunlight.

Sunna /'soonə, 'sunə/ *noun* the body of Islamic custom and practice based on Muhammad's words and deeds. [Arabic *sunnah*, literally 'way, course, rule']

Sunni /'sooni/ *noun* (*pl* **Sunni** *or* **Sunnis**) **1** the major branch of Islam that keeps to the orthodox tradition and acknowledges the first four caliphs as rightful successors of Muhammad: compare SHIA. **2** a Sunnite. **>>> Sunni** *adj.* [Arabic *sunnīy*, from *sunnah*: see SUNNA]

Sunnite /'sooniet/ *noun* an adherent of the Sunni branch of Islam. **>>> Sunnite** *adj.*

sunny *adj* (**sunnier, sunniest**) **1** bright with sunshine. **2** cheerful, optimistic: *a sunny disposition.* **3** exposed to or warmed by the sun. **>>> sunnily** *adv,* **sunniness** *noun.*

sunray pleats *pl noun* a series of pleats in fabric, *esp* in a skirt, that are usu wider at the bottom than at the top.

sunrise *noun* the rising of the topmost part of the sun above the horizon as a result of the rotation of the earth, or the time when this happens.

sunrise economy *noun* an economy based on sunrise industries, or a country, etc having such an economy.

sunrise industry *noun* a comparatively new and expanding industry.

sunroof *noun* an opening or removable panel in the roof of a car.

sunscreen *noun* **1** a substance used in suntan preparations, e.g. sunblocks and suncreams, to protect the skin from excessive ultraviolet radiation. **2** a preparation containing such a substance.

sunset *noun* **1** the descent of the topmost part of the sun below the horizon as a result of the rotation of the earth, or the time when this happens. **2** the period in which something declines or draws to a close.

sunshade *noun* **1** a parasol. **2** an awning.

sunshine *noun* **1** the sun's light or direct rays. **2** a place receiving the warmth and light of the sun: *sat in the sunshine.* **3** used as an informal and often ironic form of address. **>>> sunshiny** *adj.*

sun sign *noun* a sign of the zodiac.

sunspot *noun* **1** a transient dark marking on the visible surface of the sun caused by a relatively cooler area. **2** *informal* a sunny holiday destination.

sunstroke *noun* heatstroke caused by direct exposure to the sun.

sunsuit *noun dated* a child's outfit, e.g. of top and shorts, worn for playing in sunny weather.

suntan *noun* a browning of the skin from exposure to the sun. **>>> suntanned** *adj.*

suntrap *noun* a sheltered place that receives a large amount of sunshine.

sunup *noun chiefly NAmer* = SUNRISE.

Suomi /'sooh-əmi/ *pl noun* the Finnish people. [Finnish *Suomi* Finland, the Finns]

sup[1] /sup/ *verb trans and intrans* (**supped, supping**) *chiefly dialect* to drink (liquid) in small mouthfuls. [Old English *sūpan, suppan*]

sup[2] *noun chiefly dialect* a mouthful, *esp* of liquid; a sip.

sup[3] *verb intrans* (**supped, supping**) *dated* to eat one's evening meal. [Middle English *soupen, suppen* from Old French *souper*, from *soupe*: see SOUP]

sup. *abbr* **1** superior. **2** superlative. **3** supplement. **4** supplementary. **5** supra.

sup- *prefix* see SUB-.

super[1] /'s(y)oohpə/ *adj informal* a general term of approval: *a super time.* [short for SUPERFINE]

super[2] *noun* **1** a superfine grade or extra large size of a manufactured product or substance. **2** *informal* a superintendent or supervisor, *esp* a police superintendent. **3** *informal* a superphosphate.

super- *prefix* forming words, with the meanings: **1** higher in quantity, quality, or degree than; more than: *superhuman.* **2a** in addition; extra: *supertax.* **b** exceeding or so as to exceed a norm: *superheat; supersaturate.* **c** to an excessive degree: *superabundant.* **d** surpassing all or most others of its kind, e.g. in size or power: *supertanker.* **3** situated or placed above, on, or at the top of something: *superlunary; superscript.* **4** in chemistry, having the specified atom or group of atoms present in an unusually large proportion: *superphosphate.* **5** constituting a wider category: *superfamily.* **6** superior in status, title, or position: *superpower.* [Latin *super-* over, above, in addition, from *super* over, above, on top of]

superabundant *adj* more than ample; excessive. **>>> superabundance** *noun,* **superabundantly** *adv.* [Middle English from late Latin *superabundant-, superabundans,* present part. of *superabundare* to exist in more than ample quantities, from SUPER- + *abundare*: see ABOUND]

superadd *verb trans formal* to add (something) over and above something else. ➤➤ **superaddition** /-'dish(ə)n/ *noun*. [Middle English *superadden* from Latin *superaddere*, from SUPER- + *addere*: see ADD]

superannuable /s(y)oohpə'ranyooəbl/ *adj* offering or providing a pension on retirement: *a superannuable post*.

superannuate /s(y)oohpə'ranyooayt/ *verb trans* 1 to make or declare (something) obsolete or out-of-date. 2 to retire (somebody) on a pension, *esp* because of age or infirmity. [back-formation from SUPERANNUATED]

superannuated *adj* 1 retired on a pension. 2 obsolete. [medieval Latin *superannuatus*, past part. of *superannuari* to be too old, from Latin SUPER- + *annus* year]

superannuation /,s(y)ooparanyoo'aysh(ə)n/ *noun* 1a the regular contribution made by employees to their pension scheme, deducted from wages or salary. b a retirement pension funded in this way. 2 the act of superannuating or the state of being superannuated.

superb /s(y)ooh'puhb/ *adj* 1 of excellent quality: *The meal was superb*. 2 marked by grandeur or magnificence. ➤➤ **superbly** *adv*, **superbness** *noun*. [Latin *superbus* excellent, proud, from *super* over, above]

superbug *noun* a bacterium that has developed resistance to antibiotics.

supercalender[1] *noun* a stack of highly polished rollers used to give a very smooth finish to paper.

supercalender[2] *verb trans* (**supercalendered, supercalendering**) to process (paper) in a supercalender.

supercargo *noun* (*pl* **supercargoes** *or* **supercargos**) an officer on a merchant ship in charge of the commercial concerns of the voyage. [Spanish *sobrecargo*, from *sobre-* over (from SUPER-) + *cargo*: see CARGO]

supercharge /'s(y)oohpəchahj/ *verb trans* 1 to increase the efficiency of (an engine) by means of a supercharger. 2 to charge (e.g. a remark) with an excessive amount of energy, emotion, or tension: *supercharged rhetoric*.

supercharger *noun* a device, e.g. a compressor, supplying fuel and air to an internal-combustion engine at a pressure higher than normal for greater efficiency.

superciliary /s(y)oohpə'sili·əri/ *adj* relating to or in the region of the eyebrow or the part of the face above the eye. [scientific Latin *superciliaris* from Latin *supercilium*: see SUPERCILIOUS]

supercilious /s(y)oohpə'sili·əs/ *adj* coolly disdainful; haughty: *Arabella went in, nodding good-bye to him with a supercilious, affronted air — Hardy*. ➤➤ **superciliously** *adv*, **superciliousness** *noun*. [Latin *superciliosus*, from *supercilium* eyebrow, haughtiness, from SUPER- + *cilium* eyelid]

superclass *noun* a category in the biological classification of living things ranking between a phylum or division and a class.

supercomputer *noun* any of a class of very powerful computers that are capable of performing at great speed and are used for repeated calculation cycles on vast amounts of data.

superconductivity *noun* a complete disappearance of resistance to the passage of an electric current in various metals and alloys, usu at temperatures near ABSOLUTE ZERO (hypothetical temperature at which there is complete absence of heat). ➤➤ **superconducting** *adj*, **superconductive** *adj*.

superconductor *noun* a substance that exhibits superconductivity.

supercontinent *noun* any of the large landmasses that are thought to have existed in the geological past and to have divided to form the present continents.

supercool *verb trans* to cool (a liquid) below its freezing point without solidification or crystallization. ➤ *verb intrans* to become supercooled.

supercritical *adj* 1 in nuclear physics, having more than the critical mass. 2 said of a flow of liquid: faster than the speed of waves in the liquid. 3 said of an aerofoil, *esp* a wing: having supersonic airflow while travelling at subsonic speeds and therefore giving increased lift and speed.

super-duper /'doohpə/ *adj informal* of exceedingly great value or superiority: *a super-duper racing bike*. [reduplication of SUPER[1]]

superego *noun* (*pl* **superegos**) the one of the three divisions of the mind in psychoanalytic theory that is only partly conscious, reflects social rules, and functions as a conscience to reward and punish: compare EGO, ID.

superelevation *noun* the vertical difference between the heights of the inner and outer edges of a road, pavement, or railway track.

supererogation /s(y)oohpə·erə'gaysh(ə)n/ *noun* 1 the act of performing more than is required by duty, obligation, or need. 2 in the Roman Catholic Church, prayers, good works, etc that are performed in addition to those that are obligatory. [medieval Latin *supererogation-*, *supererogatio*, from *supererogare*: see SUPEREROGATORY]

supererogatory /,s(y)oohpəri'rogət(ə)ri/ *adj* 1 performed to an extent beyond that needed or required. 2 superfluous or nonessential. [medieval Latin *supererogatorius* from Latin *supererogare* to expend in addition, from SUPER- + *erogare* to pay out]

superfamily *noun* (*pl* **superfamilies**) 1 a category in the biological classification of living things ranking above a family and below an order or suborder. 2 a similar category sometimes used in classifying languages.

superfecundation /,s(y)oohpəfeekən'daysh(ə)n/ *noun* = SUPERFETATION.

superfetation /,s(y)oohpəfee'taysh(ə)n/ *noun* successive fertilization of two or more ova of different ovulations resulting in the presence of embryos of different ages in the same uterus. [medieval Latin *superfetation-*, *superfetatio*, from Latin *superfetare* to conceive while already pregnant, from SUPER- + *fetus* act of bearing young, offspring]

superficial /s(y)oohpə'fish(ə)l/ *adj* 1 lying on, not penetrating below, or affecting only the surface: *a superficial wound*. 2 apparent rather than real: *The government has made some superficial changes*. 3 said of a person: not capable of serious thought; shallow. 4 not careful, thorough, or deep: *She carried out a superficial inspection of the room*. 5 not significant; trivial: *The book had the same plot, apart from a few superficial differences*. ➤➤ **superficiality** /-fishi'aliti/ *noun*, **superficially** *adv*, **superficialness** *noun*. [Middle English from late Latin *superficialis*, from Latin *superficies*: see SUPERFICIES]

superficies /s(y)oohpə'fisheez/ *noun* (*pl* **superficies**) *archaic* 1 a surface. 2 the external aspect or appearance of a thing. [Latin *superficies* surface, from SUPER- + *facies*: see FACE[1]]

superfine *adj* 1 of extremely fine size or texture: *superfine toothbrush bristles*. 2 said *esp* of merchandise: of high quality or grade.

superfluid *noun* a liquid that flows with negligible internal friction and carries heat extremely readily, e.g. helium below about $-271°C$. ➤➤ **superfluid** *adj*, **superfluidity** *noun*.

superfluity /s(y)oohpə'flooh·iti/ *noun* (*pl* **superfluities**) 1 an excess; a supply exceeding what is required. 2 something unnecessary or superfluous. [Middle English *superfluitee* via French and late Latin from Latin *superfluus*: see SUPERFLUOUS]

superfluous /s(y)ooh'puhfloo·əs/ *adj* exceeding what is sufficient or necessary; extra. ➤➤ **superfluously** *adv*, **superfluousness** *noun*. [Middle English from Latin *superfluus* running over, from *superfluere* to overflow, from SUPER- + *fluere* to flow]

supergiant *noun* a rare type of star that may be five hundred times larger than the sun and thousands of times more luminous.

superglue *noun* an adhesive that sets quickly to make a very strong bond.

supergrass *noun Brit, informal* a police informer who gives information about a large number of criminals.

superheat *verb trans* 1 to heat (a liquid) above its boiling point without conversion into vapour. 2 to heat (a vapour) so that it remains a gas without condensation: *superheated steam*. ➤➤ **superheater** *noun*.

superhero *noun* (*pl* **superheroes**) a character in a cartoon, film, etc with extraordinary powers such as great strength or the ability to fly that they use to fight crime or rescue people from danger.

superheterodyne[1] /s(y)oohpə'hetərədien/ *adj* of or using a form of radio or television reception in which the radio frequency signal is combined with a wave of a frequency such that the result is a signal superimposed on a carrier wave of intermediate frequency. [blend of SUPERSONIC + HETERODYNE[1]]

superheterodyne[2] *noun* a superheterodyne receiver.

superhighway *noun NAmer* a motorway.

superhuman *adj* **1** being above the human; divine: *superhuman beings.* **2** exceeding normal human power, size, or capability: *a superhuman effort.* ➤➤ **superhumanly** *adv.*

superimpose /ˌs(y)oohpərim'pohz/ *verb trans* to place or lay (one thing) over or above something else, usu without concealing it: *The speech had been superimposed on the recorded music.* ➤➤ **superimposable** *adj,* **superimposition** /-pə'zish(ə)n/ *noun.*

superincumbent /ˌs(y)oohpərin'kumbənt/ *adj literary* lying and usu exerting pressure on something else. [Latin *superincumbent-, superincumbens,* present part. of *superincumbere* to lie on top of, from SUPER- + *incumbere* to lie down on]

superinduce /ˌs(y)oohpə'indyoohs/ *verb trans* to introduce (something) as an addition over or above something already existing. ➤➤ **superinduction** *noun.* [Latin *superinducere,* from SUPER- + *inducere* to lead in]

superintend /ˌs(y)oohpərin'tend/ *verb trans* to be in charge of (somebody or something); to supervise or direct. ➤➤ **superintendence** *noun.* [late Latin *superintendere,* from Latin SUPER- + *intendere* (see INTEND), in the sense 'direct attention to']

superintendency /ˌs(y)oohpərin'tend(ə)nsi/ *noun* (*pl* **superintendencies**) **1** the office or jurisdiction of a superintendent. **2** the act or function of superintending; supervision.

superintendent *noun* **1** a person who supervises or manages something. **2** a British police officer ranking next above a chief inspector. **3** the chief of a US police department. **4** *NAmer* a caretaker. ➤➤ **superintendent** *adj.* [medieval Latin *superintendent-, superintendens,* from late Latin, present part. of *superintendere:* see SUPERINTEND]

superior[1] /s(y)ooh'piəri·ə/ *adj* **1a** of higher rank, quality, or importance: *Her accent was far superior to a maid's* — John Fowles. **b** excellent of its kind. **2a** better: *Man is not much superior to a rat in finding his way in a maze* — Michael Polanyi. **b** greater in quantity or number. **3** situated higher up; upper: *the superior laryngeal nerve.* **4a** said of the ovary of a flower: free from a surrounding part, e.g. the calyx. **b** said of the calyx of a flower: attached to and apparently arising from the ovary. **5** in printing, denoting a letter or symbol printed above the line; superscript. **6** courageously or serenely indifferent or unyielding, e.g. to something painful or disheartening. **7** affecting or assuming a haughty or conceited air; supercilious. ➤➤ **superiority** /-'oriti/ *noun,* **superiorly** *adv.* [Middle English via French from Latin *superior,* compar of *superus* upper, from *super* over, above]

superior[2] *noun* **1** a person who is above another in rank or office; *specif* the head of a religious house or order. **2** somebody or something that surpasses another in quality or merit. **3** in printing, a letter or symbol printed above the line or above another.

superior court *noun* **1** a court whose decisions have the power to settle points of law; *esp* the High Court or Court of Appeal in England and Wales. **2** a court of general jurisdiction in some US states.

superiority complex *noun* an exaggeratedly high opinion of oneself: compare MEGALOMANIA (2).

superior planet *noun* any of the six planets Mars, Jupiter, Saturn, Uranus, Neptune, and Pluto, which orbit further from the sun than the earth does.

superjacent /ˌs(y)oohpə'jays(ə)nt/ *adj technical* lying above or on something: *superjacent rocks.* [Latin *superjacent-, superjacens,* present part. of *superjacēre* to lie over or upon, from SUPER- + *jacēre* to lie]

superl. *abbr* superlative.

superlative[1] /s(y)ooh'puhlətiv/ *adj* **1** surpassing all others; of the highest degree: *He spoke with superlative ease.* **2** in grammar, of or constituting the degree of comparison expressing an extreme or unsurpassed level or extent: compare COMPARATIVE[1] (3): *The superlative of 'hot' is 'hottest'.* ➤➤ **superlatively** *adv,* **superlativeness** *noun.* [Middle English *superlatif* via French from late Latin *superlativus,* from Latin *superlatus,* past part. of *superferre* to carry over, raise high, from SUPER- + *ferre* to carry]

superlative[2] *noun* **1** the superlative degree or form in a language. **2** an exaggerated expression, *esp* of praise: *The review was full of superlatives.*

superlunary /ˌs(y)oohpə'loohnəri/ *adj literary* beyond the moon; celestial. [SUPER- + Latin *luna* moon]

superman *noun* (*pl* **supermen**) **1** in Nietzschean philosophy, a superior type of man that has learnt to renounce fleeting pleasures and attain fulfilment and dominance through the use of creative power. **2** *informal* a man of extraordinary or superhuman power or achievements. [translation of German *Übermensch*]

supermarket /'s(y)oohpəmahkit/ *noun* a usu large self-service retail shop selling foods and household merchandise: *There should be supermarkets that sell things and supermarkets that buy things back* — Andy Warhol.

supermodel *noun* a very successful fashion model who has become a celebrity.

supermundane /ˌs(y)oohpə'mundayn/ *adj* elevated above ordinary worldly concerns.

supernal /s(y)ooh'puhn(ə)l/ *adj* **1** *literary* belonging to or coming from a celestial realm; heavenly. **2** located in or belonging to the sky. ➤➤ **supernally** *adv.* [Middle English via French from Latin *supernus,* from *super* over, above]

supernatant /ˌs(y)oohpə'nayt(ə)nt/ *adj* **1** floating on the surface of something. **2** *technical* said of a liquid: lying above settled solid material. [Latin *supernatant-, supernatans,* present part. of *supernatare* to float, from SUPER- + *natare* to swim]

supernatural[1] /ˌs(y)oohpə'nach(ə)rəl/ *adj* **1** departing from what is usual or normal, *esp* so as to appear to transcend the laws of nature. **2** of an order of existence beyond the visible observable universe; *esp* of God or a god, spirit, or devil. **3** attributed to an invisible agent, e.g. a ghost. ➤➤ **supernaturally** *adv.* [medieval Latin *supernaturalis,* from SUPER- + Latin *natura:* see NATURE]

supernatural[2] *noun* (**the supernatural**) supernatural forces, beings, or manifestations.

supernaturalism *noun* **1** the quality or state of being supernatural. **2** belief in a supernatural power and order of existence. ➤➤ **supernaturalist** *noun.*

supernormal *adj* exceeding the normal or average. ➤➤ **supernormality** *noun,* **supernormally** *adv.*

supernova /ˌs(y)oohpə'nohvə/ *noun* (*pl* **supernovae** /-'nohvi/ *or* **supernovas**) a star that explodes, increasing in brightness by millions of times for a few weeks or months and throwing off most of its mass.

supernumerary[1] /ˌs(y)oohpə'nyoohmərəri/ *adj* **1** exceeding the usual or stated number: *a supernumerary tooth.* **2** not listed among the regular components of a group, *esp* a military organization. [late Latin *supernumerarius,* from SUPER- + Latin *numerus* NUMBER[1]]

supernumerary[2] *noun* (*pl* **supernumeraries**) **1** a person employed as an extra assistant or substitute. **2** an actor employed to play a non-speaking part in a play or film; an extra.

superorder *noun* a category in the biological classification of living things between an order and a class or subclass.

superordinate[1] /ˌs(y)oohpə'rawdinət/ *adj* superior in rank, class, or status. [SUPER- + -*ordinate* as in SUBORDINATE[1]]

superordinate[2] *noun* **1** a superordinate thing in a system of classification. **2** a person who is superior in rank, class, or status. **3** a word with a meaning that includes the meaning of another word or words.

superphosphate *noun* a fertilizer made from insoluble mineral phosphates by treatment with sulphuric acid.

superpose /ˌs(y)oohpə'pohz/ *verb trans* **1** to place or lay (one thing) over or above something else. **2** to lay (e.g. a geometric figure) on another in such a way that all like parts coincide. ➤➤ **superposed** *adj,* **superposition** /-pə'zish(ə)n/ *noun.* [prob from French *superposer,* ultimately from Latin *superponere,* from SUPER- + *ponere* to place]

superpower *noun* an extremely powerful nation; *specif* any of a very few dominant states in the world.

supersaturated *adj* **1** said of a solution: containing more dissolved substance than a saturated solution. **2** said of a vapour: containing more molecules than a saturated vapour. ➤➤ **supersaturation** *noun.*

superscribe /ˌs(y)oohpə'skrieb/ *verb trans* **1** to write (an inscription) above or on the outside of something. **2** to write (e.g. a word) above existing text. [Latin *superscribere,* from SUPER- + *scribere* to write]

superscript /'s(y)oohpəskript/ *adj* said of a letter, number, or symbol: written or printed, usu in smaller type, above and to the right or left of another character. ➤➤ **superscript** noun. [Latin superscriptus, past part. of superscribere: see SUPERSCRIBE]

superscription /s(y)oohpə'skripsh(ə)n/ noun 1 the act or an instance of superscribing. 2 words written on the surface of, outside, or above something else. [Middle English via French from late Latin superscription-, superscriptio, from Latin superscribere: see SUPERSCRIBE]

supersede /s(y)oohpə'seed/ verb trans to take the place of (esp something inferior or outmoded); to replace or supplant: Buses superseded trams in many cities. ➤➤ **supersedure** /-'seejə/ noun, **supersession** /-'sesh(ə)n/ noun. [early French superseder to refrain from, from Latin supersedēre to be superior to, refrain from, from SUPER- + sedēre to sit]

Usage note ————
Supersede has no c in it and no double e. It comes from a Latin verb supersedēre, which literally means 'to sit above someone'.

supersonic /s(y)oohpə'sonik/ adj 1 denoting or using a speed from one to five times the speed of sound in air. 2 to do with supersonic aircraft or missiles: the supersonic age. 3 = ULTRASONIC[1]. ➤➤ **supersonically** adv

supersonics pl noun (treated as sing. or pl) = ULTRASONICS.

superstar noun a performer or entertainer in sport, cinema, pop music, etc who is extremely popular and successful. ➤➤ **superstardom** noun.

superstition /s(y)oohpə'stish(ə)n/ noun 1 excessive belief in supernatural or irrational forces in human affairs: It is the customary fate of new truths to begin as heresies and to end as superstitions — T H Huxley. 2 a widely held belief or widely practised act that has no rational basis, esp one associated with supposedly supernatural influences and thought to bring good or bad luck. ➤➤ **superstitious** adj, **superstitiously** adv, **superstitiousness** noun. [Middle English supersticion via French from Latin superstition-, superstitio, from SUPER- + stare to stand]

superstore noun a very large supermarket, often situated on the outskirts of a town.

superstratum noun (pl **superstrata**) an overlying stratum or layer. [SUPER- + -stratum as in SUBSTRATUM]

superstring noun in physics, a form of one-dimensional subatomic particle according to theories of elementary-particle interactions that involve supersymmetry.

superstructure noun 1a the part of a building above the ground. b the structural part of a ship above the main deck. 2 an entity, concept, or complex based on a more fundamental one. 3 in Marxist theory, social institutions, e.g. law or politics, that are built on the economic base. ➤➤ **superstructural** adj.

supersymmetry noun in physics, a theory of elementary-particle interactions that relates every particle to a partner with a different spin and a much greater mass. ➤➤ **supersymmetric** adj.

supertanker noun a very large tanker.

supertax noun a tax paid in addition to normal tax.

supertonic noun in music, the second note of a diatonic scale.

supervene /s(y)oohpə'veen/ verb intrans to happen in a way that interrupts some plan or process. ➤➤ **supervenience** noun, **supervenient** adj, **supervention** noun. [Latin supervenire, from SUPER- + venire to come]

supervise /'s(y)oohpəviez/ verb trans to oversee (e.g. a task or workers). ➤➤ **supervisor** noun, **supervisory** adj. [medieval Latin supervisus, past part. of supervidēre, from SUPER- + Latin vidēre to see]

supervision /s(y)oohpə'vizh(ə)n/ noun a critical watching and directing, e.g. of activities or an operation.

superweed noun a plant that has been accidentally crosspollinated by a genetically modified, herbicide-resistant crop plant, and which has therefore itself become resistant to herbicides.

superwoman noun (pl **superwomen**) informal a woman of extraordinary or superhuman power or achievements.

supinate /'s(y)oohpinayt/ verb trans to rotate (the hand or foot) so that the palm or sole faces forwards or upwards: compare PRONATE. ➤➤ **supination** /-'naysh(ə)n/ noun. [Latin supinatus, past part. of supinare to lay backwards or on the back, from supinus SUPINE[1]]

supinator /'s(y)oohpinaytə/ noun a muscle that produces the motion of supination.

supine[1] /'s(y)oohpien, s(y)ooh'pien/ adj 1a lying on the back or with the face upwards: compare PRONE (2A). b with the palm of the hand facing upwards. 2 mentally or morally weak or slack. ➤➤ **supinely** adv, **supineness** noun. [Latin supinus]

supine[2] noun a Latin verbal noun formed from the stem of the past participle. [Middle English supyn from Latin supinum, neuter of supinus SUPINE[1]]

supper /'supə/ noun 1 an evening meal or snack. 2 a fund-raising social affair featuring a light or informal evening meal. ✳ **sing for one's supper** to do something in return for food, etc. ➤➤ **supperless** adj. [Middle English from Old French souper, from souper: see SUP[3]]

supplant /sə'plahnt/ verb trans to take the place of (somebody or something else); to oust or supersede. ➤➤ **supplanter** noun. [Middle English supplanten via French from Latin supplantare to overthrow by tripping up, from SUB- + planta sole of the foot]

supple /'supl/ adj 1a capable of being bent or folded without creases, cracks, or breaks; pliant: supple leather. b able to perform bending or twisting movements with ease and grace; lithe: the supple legs of a dancer. 2 compliant, often to the point of submissiveness. ➤➤ **supplely** /'supli/ adv, **suppleness** noun, **supply** /'supli/ adv [Middle English souple via Old French from Latin supplic-, supplex submissive, suppliant, bending under, from SUB- + plicare to fold]

supplejack /'supljak/ noun a climbing plant with strong supple stems: Berchemia scandens, Paullinia plumieri, and other species.

supplement[1] /'suplimənt/ noun 1 something that completes, makes good a deficiency, or makes a useful addition: He took various dietary supplements. 2 a part issued to update or extend a book or periodical. 3 an extra charge payable for something: a single room supplement. 4 an angle or arc that when added to a given angle or arc equals 180°. [Middle English from Latin supplementum, from supplēre: see SUPPLY[1]]

Usage note ————
See note at COMPLEMENT[1].

supplement[2] /'supliment, -'ment/ verb trans to add a supplement to (something): She supplemented her income by doing some home tuition. ➤➤ **supplementation** /-'taysh(ə)n/ noun.

supplemental /supli'mentl/ adj serving to supplement something. ➤➤ **supplementally** adv.

supplementary /supli'ment(ə)ri/ adj 1 added as a supplement; additional. 2 being or relating to a supplementary angle.

supplementary angle noun either of two angles whose sum is 180°.

supplementary benefit noun Brit a social security benefit formerly paid to those who did not qualify for unemployment benefit, replaced in 1988 by income support.

suppletion /sə'pleesh(ə)n/ noun the occurrence of a word form as a member of the set of inflections of another totally different form, e.g. went as the past tense of go, or better as the comparative form of good. ➤➤ **suppletive** /-tiv/ adj. [medieval Latin suppletion-, suppletio act of supplementing, from Latin supplēre: see SUPPLY[1]]

suppliant[1] /'supli·ənt/ adj humbly imploring or entreating. ➤➤ **suppliantly** adv. [early French suppliant, present part. of supplier to supplicate, from Latin supplicare: see SUPPLICATE]

suppliant[2] noun = SUPPLICANT[1].

supplicant[1] /'suplikənt/ noun a person who supplicates.

supplicant[2] adj = SUPPLIANT[1].

supplicate /'suplikayt/ verb intrans to beg humbly; esp to pray to God. ➤ verb trans 1 to ask (somebody) humbly and earnestly for something. 2 to ask humbly and earnestly for (something). ➤➤ **supplication** /-'kaysh(ə)n/ noun, **supplicatory** /-kət(ə)ri/ adj. [Middle English supplicaten from Latin supplicatus, past part. of supplicare, from supplic-, supplex: see SUPPLE]

supply[1] /sə'plie/ verb trans (**supplies, supplied, supplying**) 1 to provide (something that is needed), esp on a regular basis: They supply components to the motor industry. 2 to provide (somebody) with something: She supplied him with all the details. 3 to provide for or satisfy (something): This book supplies a long-felt need. 4 archaic to substitute for somebody else in (a place or role); specif to replace a clergyman in (a church or pulpit). ➤➤ **supplier** noun. [Middle English supplien via French from Latin supplēre to fill up, supplement, supply, from SUB- + plēre to fill]

supply[2] noun (pl **supplies**) 1a the quantity or amount, e.g. of a commodity, needed or available: a fresh supply of towels; Beer was in short supply in that hot weather — Nevil Shute. b (usu in pl) provisions or stores. **2** the act or process of supplying something: *the supply of fuel to the engine.* **3** in economics, the quantity of a commodity or service available or offered for sale at a specified price and time: compare DEMAND¹. **4** (*used before a noun*) denoting a teacher who is on call to fill temporary vacancies in schools. **5a** *Brit* (*in pl*) money voted by a legislature to pay for costs. **b** (*used before a noun*) of or for the raising of government revenue: *a supply bill.*

supply-side *adj* of or being an economic theory that reduced taxation stimulates economic activity by encouraging productivity and investment, and so increases tax revenues. ➤➤ **supply-sider** *noun.*

support¹ /sə'pawt/ *verb trans* **1** to hold up or serve as a foundation or prop for (something): *Steel girders support the building.* **2a** to provide (somebody) with a home, food, clothes, etc; to maintain: *We have three children to support.* **b** to provide a basis for the existence or subsistence of (somebody or something): *The planet could not support life.* **3** to endure (something) bravely or quietly; to bear or tolerate. **4** to assist or help (somebody or something), e.g. by giving money or sustaining morale: *Her best friend had always supported her when she was in trouble.* **5** to approve of or encourage (something or somebody). **6** to uphold or defend (something or somebody) as valid or right; to advocate. **7** to provide (something) with substantiation; to corroborate: *Unfortunately, our findings do not support your claim.* **8a** to argue or vote for (e.g. a political party). **b** to be an enthusiastic or loyal follower of (e.g. a football team). **9a** to act with (a principal actor). **b** to perform before (the main act at a concert). **10** in computing, to work with (e.g. a program or device), or to enable it to work. ➤➤ **supportable** *adj*, **supportably** *adv*. [Middle English *supporten* via French from Latin *supportare* to carry, from SUB- + *portare* to carry]

support² *noun* **1** the act or an instance of supporting somebody or something. **2** the condition of being supported: *Having no other means of support, prostitution becomes her only refuge* — Mary Wollstonecraft. **3** something that holds something up or serves as a prop. **4** somebody who offers help, encouragement, etc. **5** a supporting act in a concert. **6** an appliance or garment worn to relieve pressure on or protect an injured part of the body.

supporter *noun* **1** somebody who supports something: *supporters of the local football team; a supporter of capital punishment.* **2** either of two figures, e.g. of animals, placed one on each side of a heraldic shield as if holding or guarding it. **3** = SUPPORT² (6).

supporting *adj* **1** that supports something: *a supporting wall.* **2** said of an actor or role: subordinate.

supportive /sə'pawtiv/ *adj* providing support; *esp* sustaining morale: *The Prime Minister's husband has always been supportive.* ➤➤ **supportively** *adv,* **supportiveness** *noun.*

suppose /sə'pohz/ *verb trans* **1a** to lay (something) down tentatively as a hypothesis, assumption, or proposal: *Suppose a fire broke out; Suppose we wait a bit.* **b** to hold (something) as an opinion; to believe: *She supposed it wouldn't matter.* **c** to think (something) probable or in keeping with the facts: *It seemed reasonable to suppose that they would make a profit.* **d** to conjecture or think (something): *When do you suppose he'll arrive?* **2** to assume or presuppose (something): *These plans suppose the measurements to be accurate.* ✳ **be supposed to do something** to be expected, intended, or allowed to do something: *Drivers are supposed to wear seat belts; You're not supposed to go in there.* ➤➤ **supposable** *adj.* [Middle English *supposen* via French from Latin *supponere* to put under, substitute, from SUB- + *ponere* to put]

supposed /sə'pohzd, sə'pohzid/ *adj* believed or imagined to be such: *the sight which makes supposed terror true* — Shakespeare. ➤➤ **supposedly** /-zidli/ *adv.*

supposing *conj* if by way of hypothesis: *Supposing they saw you … ?*

supposition /supə'zish(ə)n/ *noun* **1** the act or an instance of supposing. **2** something that is supposed; a hypothesis. ➤➤ **suppositional** *adj.* [Middle English from Latin *supposition-, suppositio* act of placing beneath, from *supponere*: see SUPPOSE]

supposititious /'supəzishəs/ *adj* of the nature of or based on a supposition; hypothetical. ➤➤ **supposititiously** *adv,* **suppositiousness** *noun.*

supposititious /sə,pozi'tishəs/ *adj* **1** fraudulently substituted; spurious. **2** falsely presented as a genuine heir; illegitimate. ➤➤ **supposititiously** *adv,* **supposititiousness** *noun.* [Latin *suppositicius, from supponere*: see SUPPOSE]

suppository /sə'pozit(ə)ri/ *noun* (*pl* **suppositories**) a cone or cylinder of medicated material intended to melt after insertion into a bodily passage or cavity, e.g. the rectum. [medieval Latin *suppositorium* from Latin *supponere*: see SUPPOSE]

suppress /sə'pres/ *verb trans* **1** to put an end to (something) by force; to subdue. **2** to stop the publication or revelation of (something). **3a** to hold (something) back; to restrain: *He managed to suppress a yawn.* **b** to arrest, check, or inhibit (something). **4** to deliberately exclude (a thought, feeling, etc) from consciousness: compare REPRESS. ➤➤ **suppressible** *adj,* **suppression** *noun,* **suppressive** *adj.* [Middle English *suppressen* from Latin *suppressus,* past part. of *supprimere* to press down, from SUB- + *premere* to press]

suppressant *noun* a substance, *esp* a drug, that tends to suppress rather than eliminate something undesirable.

suppressor *noun* **1** somebody or something that suppresses. **2** an electrical component, e.g. a capacitor, added to a circuit to suppress oscillations that would otherwise cause radio interference.

suppurate /'supyoorayt/ *verb intrans* to form or discharge pus. ➤➤ **suppuration** /-'raysh(ə)n/ *noun,* **suppurative** /-rətiv/ *adj.* [Latin *suppuratus,* past part. of *suppurare,* from SUB- + *pur-, pus* PUS]

supra /'s(y)oohprə/ *adv formal* earlier in this writing; above. [Latin *supra* above, beyond, earlier]

supra- *prefix* forming words, with the meaning: **1** above or on top: *supraorbital.* **2** beyond or transcending: *supranational.* [Latin, from *supra* above, beyond, earlier]

supranational /s(y)oohprə'nash(ə)nl/ *adj* transcending national boundaries or interests. ➤➤ **supranationalism** *noun.*

supraorbital /s(y)oohprə'awbitl/ *adj* situated above the orbit of the eye. [scientific Latin *supraorbitalis,* from SUPRA- + medieval Latin *orbita*: see ORBIT¹]

suprarenal /s(y)oohprə'reenl/ *adj* situated above or in front of the kidneys: *a suprarenal gland.* [scientific Latin *suprarenalis,* from SUPRA- + Latin *renes* kidneys]

supremacist /s(y)ooh'preməsist/ *noun* an advocate or adherent of group supremacy, *esp* somebody who believes in the superiority of one race over another: *a white supremacist.* ➤➤ **supremacist** *adj.*

supremacy /s(y)ooh'preməsi/ *noun* the state of being supreme; supreme authority, power, or position. [SUPREME + -*acy* as in PRIMACY]

suprematism /s(y)ooh'prematiz(ə)m/ *noun* a Russian art movement dating from about 1913 that was essentially an extreme form of cubism, characterized by abstract works using simple geometric shapes. ➤➤ **suprematist** *noun and adj.* [French *suprématie* supremacy]

supreme /s(y)ooh'preem/ *adj* **1** highest in rank or authority: *the supreme commander.* **2** greatest, strongest, or most important: *a place where justice reigned supreme.* **3** highest in degree or quality; extreme: *He received an award for supreme endurance and bravery in battle.* **4** ultimate; *specif* involving death: *They were called upon to make the supreme sacrifice.* ➤➤ **supremely** *adv.* [Latin *supremus,* superl of *superus*: see SUPERIOR¹]

Supreme Being *noun* (**the Supreme Being**) God; *specif* the superior deity of the Gnostics.

Supreme Court *noun* the highest judicial tribunal in a nation or state.

Supreme Court of Judicature *noun* a court in England and Wales formed by the amalgamation of several superior courts and consisting of the High Court, Court of Appeal, and Crown Court.

Supreme Soviet *noun* the highest legislative body of the former Soviet Union or a former Soviet republic.

supremo /s(y)ooh'preemoh/ *noun* (*pl* **supremos**) *Brit, informal* **1** a ruler, leader, or director: *England's new football supremo.* **2** an administrator with a particular responsibility: *A water supremo had been appointed to cope with the drought.* [Spanish and Italian *supremo* supreme, from Latin *supremus*: see SUPREME]

Supt *abbr* superintendent.

sur-¹ *prefix* forming words, with the meaning: above, over, or beyond: *surtax; surreal; surface.* [Middle English via Old French from Latin *super-*]

sur-² *prefix* see SUB-.

sura /'soorə/ *noun* a chapter of the Koran. [Arabic *sūrah,* literally 'row']

surah /'soorə/ *noun* a soft twilled fabric of silk or rayon. [alteration of *surat* a type of cotton, named after *Surat*, city in W India where it was first made]

sural /'sooərəl/ *adj* relating to or in the region of the calf of the leg. [Latin *suralis*, from *sura* calf]

surcease[1] /suh'sees/ *verb intrans NAmer or archaic* **1** to desist from action. **2** to come to an end. ➤ *verb trans NAmer or archaic* to put an end to (something). [Middle English *sursesen, surcesen* from early French *sursis*, past part. of *surseoir*, from Latin *supersedēre*: see SUPERSEDE]

surcease[2] /'suhsees/ *noun NAmer or archaic* a cessation; *esp* a temporary respite or end.

surcharge[1] /'suhchahj/ *noun* **1** an additional charge, tax, or cost. **2** *Brit.* **a** an omission in an account for which credit ought to have been given. **b** the showing of such an omission. **3** an overprint on a stamp, *esp* one that alters the value.

surcharge[2] *verb trans* **1a** to subject (somebody) to an additional charge. **b** to overcharge (somebody). **2** to mark a surcharge on (a stamp). [Middle English *surchargen* from early French *surchargier*, from SUR-[1] + *chargier* to charge]

surcingle /'suhsinggl/ *noun* a band passing round a horse's body usu to bind a saddle, rug, or pack to its back. [Middle English *sursengle* via early French *surcengle*, from SUR-[1] + *cengle* girdle, from Latin *cingulum*, from *cingere* to gird]

surcoat /'suhkoht/ *noun* an outer coat or cloak; *specif* a loose tunic formerly worn over armour. [Middle English from early French *surcote*, from SUR-[1] + *cote*: see COAT[1]]

surd[1] /suhd/ *adj* said of a speech sound: uttered without vibration of the vocal chords; voiceless. [Latin *surdus* deaf, silent, stupid]

surd[2] *noun* **1** an irrational root, e.g. √2, or an expression containing irrational roots: compare IRRATIONAL[2], RATIONAL[2]: $5 + 3 \sqrt{3}$ *is a surd*. **2** a surd speech sound.

sure[1] /shooə, shaw/ *adj* **1** marked by or given to feelings of confident certainty: *Are you sure you're right?* **2** (+ of) confident that something is true, will happen, etc: *She wasn't sure of his feelings.* **3** certain; bound: *She is sure to win; The train is sure to be late.* **4** not in any doubt; true: *One thing is sure, I won't be inviting them again!* **5** reliable: *Feeling sick is a sure sign that you're nervous.* ✳ **for sure** as a certainty. **to be sure** it must be acknowledged; admittedly. ➤➤ **sureness** *noun.* [Middle English via French *sur* from Latin *securus*: see SECURE[1]]

sure[2] *adv chiefly NAmer, informal* **1** willingly; of course: *Sure, I'll come.* **2** certainly: *I sure am tired.*

sure enough *adv informal* as one might confidently expect.

sure-fire *adj informal* certain to succeed: *a sure-fire recipe.*

sure-footed *adj* **1** not liable to stumble or fall. **2** not liable to err; confident. ➤➤ **sure-footedly** *adv,* **sure-footedness** *noun.*

surely *adv* **1** it is to be believed, hoped, or expected that: *Surely it won't rain.* **2** without doubt; certainly. **3** without danger; safely: *He drove slowly but surely.* **4** as if inevitably: *Slowly but surely the ship went down.* **5** *chiefly NAmer, informal* willingly; of course.

sure thing *noun informal* **1** something that is certain or guaranteed. **2** *chiefly NAmer* certainly; of course.

surety /'shooəriti/ *noun* (*pl* **sureties**) **1** a person who assumes legal liability for the debt, default, or failure, e.g. to appear in court, of somebody else. **2** a formal engagement, e.g. a pledge, given for the fulfilment of an undertaking; a guarantee. **3** the state of being certain or confident. ➤➤ **suretyship** *noun.* [Middle English *surte* via French *surté* from Latin *securitat-, securitas* security, from *securus*: see SECURE[1]]

surf[1] /suhf/ *noun* the foam and swell of waves breaking on the shore. [origin unknown]

surf[2] *verb intrans* to stand or lie on a surfboard and ride on the waves towards the shore. ➤ *verb trans* to browse through (e.g. the Internet or TV channels) randomly. ➤➤ **surfer** *noun,* **surfing** *noun.*

surface[1] /'suhfis/ *noun* **1** the exterior or upper boundary or layer of an object or body: *the surface of the earth; Make sure all surfaces are clean and dry.* **2** the area of a surface. **3** the uppermost level of a body of liquid: *She swam up to the surface.* **4** the external or superficial aspect of something. **5** in geometry, a plane or curved two-dimensional set of points, e.g. the boundary of a three-dimensional region: *the surface of a sphere.* ✳ **on the surface** to all outward appearances; superficially. [French *surface*, from SUR-[1]+ *face*: see FACE[1]]

surface[2] *adj* **1** of, located on, or designed for use at the surface of something. **2** situated or employed on the surface of the earth: *miners and surface workers.*

surface[3] *verb intrans* **1** to come to the surface, *esp* of water. **2** to become apparent: *We were waiting for the next scandal to surface.* **3** *informal* to wake up or get out of bed: *He never surfaces before ten.* ➤ *verb trans* **1** to give a surface to (something). **2** to apply the surface layer to (e.g. a road). **3** to bring (e.g. a submarine) to the surface. ➤➤ **surfacer** *noun.*

surface-active *adj* capable of lowering the surface tension of a liquid.

surface area *noun* = SURFACE[1] (2).

surface mail *noun* mail sent by land or sea.

surface structure *noun* in structural linguistics, the simple syntactic form of a sentence.

surface tension *noun* a property of liquids that produces an effect such that the surface in contact with air or another gas tends to have the smallest possible area and acts like an elastic skin under tension.

surface-to-air missile *noun* a usu guided missile launched from the ground against a target in the air.

surface-to-surface missile *noun* a usu guided missile launched from the ground against a target on the ground.

surfactant /suh'fakt(ə)nt/ *noun* a surface-active substance, e.g. a detergent. ➤➤ **surfactant** *adj.* [contraction of SURFACE-ACTIVE + -ANT[1]]

surfboard *noun* a long narrow buoyant board used in surfing.

surfboat *noun* a boat for use in heavy surf.

surfcasting *noun* fishing from the shore by casting a line into the surf. ➤➤ **surfcaster** *noun.*

surfeit[1] /'suhfit/ *noun* **1** an excessive amount. **2** *archaic* an illness caused by excessive indulgence in food, drink, etc. [Middle English from early French *surfait*, from *surfaire* to overdo, from SUR-[1] + *faire* to do, from Latin *facere*]

surfeit[2] *verb* (**surfeited, surfeiting**) ➤ *verb trans* to feed or supply (somebody) to excess; to satiate. ➤ *verb intrans archaic* to overindulge in something to the point of disgust or nausea: *They are as sick that surfeit with too much as they that starve with nothing* — Shakespeare.

surficial /suh'fish(ə)l/ *adj* to do with a surface, *esp* the surface of the earth. [SURFACE[1] + -icial as in SUPERFICIAL]

surfie /'suhfi/ *noun chiefly Aus, NZ, informal* somebody whose way of life centres on surfing.

surg. *abbr* **1** surgeon. **2** surgery. **3** surgical.

surge[1] /suhj/ *noun* **1** the motion of swelling, rolling, or sweeping forwards like that of a wave or series of waves: *They hear like Ocean on a western beach the surge and thunder of the Odyssey* — Andrew Lang. **2a** a large wave or billow; a swell. **b** a series of swells or large billow. **3** a sudden increase: *a surge in share prices.* **4** a short-lived sudden rise of current in an electrical circuit.

surge[2] *verb intrans* **1** to move with a surge or in surges: *The crowd surged past us.* **2** to increase suddenly. **3** said of an electrical current or voltage: to rise suddenly to an excessive or abnormal value. **4** to rise and fall; to toss: *The ship surged in heavy seas.* **5** said of a rope: to loosen round a windlass, capstan, or other winding device. [early French *sourge-*, stem of *sourdre* to rise, surge, from Latin *surgere* to go straight up, rise, from SUR-[2] + *regere* to lead straight]

surgeon /'suhj(ə)n/ *noun* **1** a medical specialist who practises surgery. **2** a medical officer in the navy. [Middle English *surgien* via Anglo-French from Old French *cirurgien*, from *cirurgie*: see SURGERY]

surgeon fish *noun* any of numerous species of tropical fishes with one or more sharp movable spines near the base of the tail: family Acanthuridae. [from the spines suggesting a surgeon's instruments]

surgeon general *noun* (*pl* **surgeons general**) the chief medical officer of a branch of the US armed services or of a US public health service.

surgeon's knot *noun* a reef knot with a double turn in the first loop.

surgery /'suhj(ə)ri/ *noun* (*pl* **surgeries**) **1** the branch of medicine that deals with diseases and conditions requiring or amenable to operative or manipulative procedures. **2a** the work done by a surgeon. **b** a surgical operation. **3** *Brit* a place where a doctor or dentist treats patients. **4** *Brit* a session at which a lawyer, MP, or other professional person is available for usu informal consultation. [Middle English *surgerie* via French *cirurgie*, *surgerie* and Latin *chirurgia*, ultimately from Greek *cheirourgia*, from *cheirourgos* working with the hand, from *cheir* hand + *ergon* work]

surgical /'suhjikl/ *adj* **1** relating to surgeons or surgery. **2** used in or in connection with surgery: *a surgical stocking.* **3** following or resulting from surgery. **4** involving precision bombing: *surgical strikes.* ➤➤ **surgically** *adv.* [French *chirugical* from *cirurgie*: see SURGERY]

surgical spirit *noun Brit* a mixture consisting mainly of methylated spirits and used *esp* as a skin disinfectant.

suricate /'syooərikayt/ *noun* a meerkat of southern Africa with dark bands on its back and a dark tail tip: *Suricata suricatta.* [French *surikate*, prob from a native name in S Africa]

surly /'suhli/ *adj* (**surlier**, **surliest**) irritably sullen and bad-tempered. ➤➤ **surlily** *adv*, **surliness** *noun.* [alteration of Middle English *sirly* lordly, imperious, from SIR]

surmise[1] /sə'miez/ *verb trans* to imagine or infer (something) on scanty evidence; to guess. [Middle English *surmisen* to accuse, via French from Latin *supermittere* to throw on, from SUPER- + *mittere* to send]

surmise[2] /sə'miez, 'suhmiez/ *noun* a conjecture or guess: *He stared at the Pacific – and all his men looked at each other with a wild surmise* — Keats.

surmount /sə'mownt/ *verb trans* **1** to overcome (a difficulty or obstacle). **2** to get over or above (something). **3** to stand or lie on the top of (something). ➤➤ **surmountable** *adj.* [Middle English *surmounten* from early French *surmonter*, from SUR-[1] + *monter*: see MOUNT[1]]

surname[1] /'suhnaym/ *noun* **1** the name shared in common by members of a family. **2** *archaic* a descriptive name given to somebody; a nickname. [translation of Old French *surnom*, literally 'over name', from SUR-[1] + *nom* name]

surname[2] *verb trans* to give a surname to (somebody).

surpass /sə'pahs/ *verb trans* **1** to go beyond (something) in quality, degree, or performance; to exceed. **2** to transcend the reach, capacity, or powers of (something): *Her beauty surpasses description.* ➤➤ **surpassable** *adj.* [early French *surpasser*, from SUR-[1] + *passer*: see PASS[1]]

surpassing *adj archaic or literary* greatly exceeding others. ➤➤ **surpassingly** *adv.*

surplice /'suhplis/ *noun* a loose white outer ecclesiastical vestment, usu of knee length, with large open sleeves.

Word history
Middle English *surplis* via Old French from medieval Latin *superpellicium*, from SUPER- + *pellicium* coat of skins, from *pellis* skin. A surplice was originally put on over the fur garments that were worn in church to keep out the cold.

surplus /'suhpləs/ *noun* **1** an amount that remains over and above what is used or needed. **2** an excess of income over expenditure. **3** the excess of a company's net worth over the value of its capital stock. ➤➤ **surplus** *adj.* [Middle English via French from medieval Latin *superplus*, from SUPER- + Latin *plus* more]

surplus value *noun* in Marxist theory, the difference between the value of work done or of commodities produced by employees and the wages paid by the employer.

surprise[1] /sə'priez/ *noun* **1** the feeling caused by an unexpected event; astonishment. **2** something unexpected or surprising. **✳ take somebody by surprise 1** to come upon somebody without warning. **2** to capture somebody suddenly. **3** to astonish somebody. [Middle English from early French, fem past part. of *surprendre* to take over, surprise, from SUR-[1] + *prendre* to take, from Latin *prehendere*: see PREHENSILE]

surprise[2] *verb trans* **1** to fill (somebody) with wonder or amazement. **2** to take (somebody) unawares: *We surprised them in the act.* **3** to attack or capture (somebody or something) unexpectedly. ➤➤ **surprised** *adj*, **surprisedly** *adv.*

surprising *adj* causing surprise; unexpected. ➤➤ **surprisingly** *adv.*

surra /'sooərə/ *noun* a severe disease of domestic animals that is transmitted by insect bites and characterized by fever and internal bleeding. [Marathi *sūra* wheezing sound]

surreal /sə'riəl/ *adj* **1** having a strange dreamlike irrational quality or atmosphere. **2** relating to surrealism. [back-formation from SURREALISM]

surrealism *noun* a movement in art, literature, and film dating from the 1920s that reflected the influence of psychoanalysis, seeking to use the incongruous images formed by the unconscious to transcend reality as perceived by the conscious mind. Surrealist artists include Joan Miró, René Magritte, and Salvador Dalì, who also collaborated with the Spanish film director Luis Buñuel to make surrealist films.

Editorial note
Surrealism was a movement which aimed at the transformation of humanity as well as the arts, replacing arid bourgeois normality with the spontaneous freedom of the irrational and unconscious (nonetheless there were fierce disputes over ideological orthodoxy). Many of its leading figures were poets, but artists – including Dali and Ernst – and the film director Luis Buñuel were also members — Martin Gayford.

➤➤ **surrealist** *noun and adj.* [French *surréalisme*, from SUR-[1] + *réalisme* realism]

surrealistic /sə,riə'listik/ *adj* **1** relating to surrealism. **2** = SURREAL (I). ➤➤ **surrealistically** *adv.*

surrebuttal /suhri'butəl/ *noun* = SURREBUTTER.

surrebutter /suhri'butə/ *noun archaic* in law, the reply made by the plaintiff in the fourth round of PLEADING[1] (allegations and counter-allegations in a legal action) to the defendant's REBUTTER (answer to the surrejoinder). [SUR-[1] + REBUTTER]

surrejoinder /suhri'joyndə/ *noun archaic* in law, a plaintiff's reply to a defendant's rejoinder. [SUR-[1] + REJOINDER]

surrender[1] /sə'rendə/ *verb* (**surrendered, surrendering**) ➤ *verb intrans* to give oneself up into the power of somebody else, *esp* after fighting or resisting for a time. ➤ *verb trans* **1** to hand (something) over to the power, control, or possession of somebody else, *esp* under compulsion: *They were made to surrender their weapons.* **2** to give (oneself) up into the power of somebody else, *esp* as a prisoner. **3** to give up (something, e.g. a right) completely; to agree to forgo (something), *esp* in favour of somebody else. **4** said of a tenant: to give up (a lease) to a landlord. **5** to give (oneself) over to something, e.g. an influence or course of action. **✳ surrender to bail** to appear in court having been released on bail. [Middle English *surrenderen* from early French *surrendre*, from SUR-[1] + *rendre*: see RENDER[1]]

surrender[2] *noun* **1** the act or an instance of surrendering. **2** the voluntary cancellation of an insurance policy by the party insured in return for a payment.

surreptitious /surəp'tishəs/ *adj* done, made, or acquired by stealth; clandestine. ➤➤ **surreptitiously** *adv*, **surreptitiousness** *noun.* [Middle English from Latin *surrepticius*, from *surripere* to snatch secretly, from SUR-[2] + *rapere* to seize]

surrey /'suri/ *noun* (*pl* **surreys**) *NAmer* a four-wheeled horse-drawn carriage with two seats, used for pleasure trips. [short for *Surrey cart*, from which the surrey was adapted, which was first made in *Surrey*, county of England]

surrogacy /'surəgəsi/ *noun* (*pl* **surrogacies**) **1** the act or state of being a surrogate mother. **2** the act or state of being a surrogate.

surrogate[1] /'surəgət/ *noun* **1** a person appointed to act in place of another; a substitute or deputy. **2** a deputy appointed to act for a bishop in granting marriage licences. **3** a local judicial officer in some states of the USA, e.g. New York, who has jurisdiction over the validation of wills, the settlement of estates, and the appointment and supervision of guardians. [Latin *surrogatus*, past part. of *surrogare* to choose in place of another, substitute, from SUR-[2] + *rogare* to ask]

surrogate[2] *adj* involving surrogate motherhood: *surrogate births* – *Daily Telegraph*; *surrogate contracts* – *New Scientist*.

surrogate mother *noun* a woman who carries and bears a child for a couple, who provide either a fertilized egg for implantation or semen for artificial insemination. ➤➤ **surrogate motherhood** *noun.*

surround[1] /sə'rownd/ *verb trans* **1** to enclose (something) on all sides: *The garden was surrounded by a wall.* **2** to be present all round (somebody or something) as part of their environment: *She grew up surrounded by luxury.* **3** to cause (somebody or something) to be encircled or enclosed by something: *She surrounded herself with talented advisers.* [Middle English *surrounden* to overflow, via French from late Latin *superundare*, from SUPER- + Latin *unda* wave]

surround² *noun* **1** a border or edging. **2** (*in pl*) surroundings.

surroundings *pl noun* the circumstances, conditions, objects, etc by which one is surrounded; one's environment.

surtax /'suhtaks/ *noun* a graduated income tax formerly imposed in Britain in addition to the normal income tax for people whose net income exceeded a specified sum.

surtitle¹ /'suhtietl/ *noun* a translation of the dialogue of an opera or play that is projected onto a screen above the stage.

surtitle² *verb trans* to provide surtitles for (an opera or play).

surtout /'suhtooh/ *noun* a man's long close-fitting overcoat, worn *esp* in the late 19th cent. [French *surtout*, from SUR-¹ + *tout* all, from Latin *totus* whole]

surveillance /sə'vayləns/ *noun* close watch kept over somebody or something, e.g. by a detective. [French *surveillance* from *surveiller* to watch over, from SUR-¹ + *veiller* to watch, from Latin *vigilare*: see VIGILANT]

survey¹ /sə'vay, 'suhvay/ *verb trans* **1** to look over and examine (something) closely. **2** to view (something) from or as if from a height, or contemplate it as a whole: *Let Observation with extensive view, survey mankind from China to Peru* — Dr Johnson. **3** to determine and portray the form, extent, and position of (e.g. a tract of land). **4** *Brit* to examine and report on the condition of (a building, e.g. a house for sale). **5** to conduct a statistical survey on (a group of people). [Middle English *surveyen* from early French *surveeir* to look over, from SUR-¹ + *veeir* to see]

survey² /'suhvay/ *noun* **1** a statistical enquiry into the opinions, preferences, etc of a group of people. **2** an act of surveying, e.g. an examination of a building to determine its condition. **3** a report drawn up by a surveyor.

sur·vey·or /sə'vay·ə/ *noun* a person whose occupation is surveying land or buildings. ⏵ **surveyorship** *noun*.

survivable /sə'vievəbl/ *adj* **1** not liable to be destroyed or damaged; *esp* capable of surviving military attack: *The US has traditionally relied on survivable second-strike weapons* — Christian Science Monitor. **2** that can be survived: *a survivable air crash*.

survival /sə'vievl/ *noun* **1** the act or fact of continuing to live or exist: *Ultimately there is no test of literary merit except survival* — George Orwell. **2** somebody or something that survives, *esp* after others of their kind have disappeared.

survivalism *noun* the policy or practice of ensuring one's own survival in the event of war or other catastrophe, e.g. by learning to handle weapons and live off the land. ⏵ **survivalist** *noun and adj*.

survival of the fittest *noun* = NATURAL SELECTION.

survival sex *noun* prostitution undertaken to secure a person's basic needs in life.

survive /sə'viev/ *verb intrans* to remain alive or in existence; to live on: *Education is what survives when what has been learnt has been forgotten* — B F Skinner; *She managed to survive on bread and water.* ⏵ *verb trans* **1** to continue to exist or live after (something): *Nobody survived the crash.* **2** to remain alive or in being after the death of (somebody): *His son survived him.* [Middle English *surviven* via French from Latin *supervivere* to outlive, from SUPER- + *vivere* to live]

survivor /sə'vievə/ *noun* somebody who survives.

sus¹ /sus/ *noun Brit, informal* suspicion of loitering with intent to commit a crime: *sus laws; She was arrested on sus.* [short for SUSPICION]

sus² *noun* = SUSS² (1).

sus- *prefix* see SUB-.

susceptibility /sə,septə'biliti/ *noun* (*pl* **susceptibilities**) **1** being susceptible. **2** an inability to resist an outside agent, e.g. a disease-causing agent or a drug; sensitivity. **3** (*in pl*) feelings or sensibilities. **4** the ratio of the magnetization in a substance to the corresponding magnetizing force.

susceptible /sə'septəbl/ *adj* **1** open, subject, or unresistant to some stimulus, influence, or agency: *In her weakened state she was susceptible to infection.* **2** easily moved or emotionally affected; impressionable. **3** capable of submitting to an action, process, or operation: *a theory susceptible of proof.* ⏵ **susceptibly** *adv.* [late Latin *susceptibilis* from Latin *suscipere* to take up, admit, from SUS- + *capere* to take]

susceptive /sə'septiv/ *adj archaic* susceptible.

sushi /'soohshi, 'sooshi/ *noun* a Japanese dish of balls or slices of cold vinegar-flavoured boiled rice garnished with raw fish or other ingredients. [Japanese *sushi*]

suslik /'suslik/ *noun* any of several species of large short-tailed E European and Asian burrowing rodents: genus *Spermophilus*. [Russian *suslik*]

suspect¹ /sə'spekt/ *verb trans* **1** to imagine (something) to be true, likely, or probable: *I suspect that you are right.* **2** to believe (somebody) to be guilty without conclusive proof: *They suspected her of giving false information.* **3** to distrust or have doubts about (something): *They suspected his motives.* [Middle English *suspecten*, from Latin *suspectus*, past part. of *suspicere* to look up at, regard with awe, suspect, from SUS- up, secretly + *specere* to look at]

suspect² /'suspekt/ *noun* somebody who is suspected, e.g. of a crime.

suspect³ /'suspekt/ *adj* regarded with suspicion; likely to be false or dangerous.

suspend /sə'spend/ *verb trans* **1** to hang (something), *esp* so that it is free on all sides except at the point of support: *The chandelier was suspended on a chain.* **2** to keep (something) from falling or sinking by some invisible support, e.g. buoyancy: *We could see dust suspended in the air.* **3** to cause (something) to stop temporarily: *The bus service has been suspended.* **4** to set (something) aside, or make it temporarily inoperative: *They agreed to suspend the rules.* **5** to defer (a prison sentence) on particular conditions. **6** to hold (something) in an undetermined or undecided state awaiting fuller information: *I ask you to suspend judgment.* **7** to debar (somebody) temporarily from office, membership, or employment: *He was suspended on full pay while the allegations were investigated.* **8** to hold (a musical note) over into the following chord. [Middle English *suspenden* via Old French *suspendre* from Latin *suspendere* to hang up, interrupt, from SUB- + *pendere* to cause to hang, weigh]

suspended animation *noun* temporary suspension of the vital body functions, e.g. in people nearly drowned.

suspender *noun* **1** *Brit* any of the straps with fastening devices on a suspender belt or corset that hold up a woman's stockings. **2** an elasticated band with a fastening device for holding up a sock. **3** *NAmer* (*in pl*) = BRACES.

suspender belt *noun Brit* a garment consisting of two pairs of short straps hanging from a belt or girdle to which are attached fastening devices for holding up a woman's stockings.

suspense /sə'spens/ *noun* **1** a state of uncertain expectation as to a decision or outcome, often causing excitement or anxiety. **2** the condition of being suspended. ⏵ **suspenseful** *adj.* [Middle English from early French *suspens*, from *suspendre*: see SUSPEND]

suspense account *noun* in bookkeeping, an account in which items are temporarily recorded before it is decided where they will ultimately be entered.

suspension /sə'spensh(ə)n/ *noun* **1** suspending or being suspended. **2** the system of devices, e.g. springs, supporting the upper part of a vehicle on the axles. **3a** the state of a substance when it exists as particles mixed with but undissolved in a liquid, gas, or solid. **b** a substance in this state. **4a** in music, the holding over of one or more notes of a chord into the following chord, producing a momentary discord; *specif* such a dissonance in which the note or notes suspended are then moved downwards to create concord. **b** a note held over in this way. **5** stoppage of payment of business obligations through insolvency or financial failure. [late Latin *suspension-, suspensio*, from Latin *suspendere*: see SUSPEND]

suspension bridge *noun* a type of bridge that has its roadway suspended from two or more cables.

suspensive /sə'spensiv/ *adj* **1** stopping temporarily; suspending. **2** characterized by suspense. ⏵ **suspensively** *adv,* **suspensiveness** *noun.*

suspensory¹ /sə'spens(ə)ri/ *adj* **1** serving to suspend. **2** relating to suspension.

suspensory² *noun* (*pl* **suspensories**) something, e.g. a ligament or muscle, that suspends or holds up something, e.g. an organ.

suspicion /sə'spish(ə)n/ *noun* **1** the act or an instance of thinking that somebody is guilty, dishonest, etc, or that something is wrong, false, etc, without proof or on slight evidence; mistrust. **2** a state of mental uneasiness and uncertainty; doubt. **3** a slight touch or trace: *There was just a suspicion of garlic in the sauce.* ✳ **above suspicion** too honest or virtuous to be suspected of having done something wrong. **on suspicion** suspected: *They were arrested on suspicion of spying*. **under suspicion** suspected of having done something wrong. [Middle English from Latin *suspicion-, suspicio*, from *suspicere*: see SUSPECT[1]]

suspicious /sə'spishəs/ *adj* **1** tending to arouse suspicion; dubious: *The bodies were found in suspicious circumstances*. **2** inclined to suspect; distrustful: *He is suspicious of strangers*. **3** expressing or indicating suspicion: *She gave them a suspicious glance*. ⟫⟫ **suspiciously** *adv*, **suspiciousness** *noun*.

suss[1] /sus/ *verb trans Brit, informal* to uncover the truth about (something); to realize: *I soon sussed that he was lying*. [by shortening and alteration from SUSPECT[1]]

suss[2] *noun Brit, informal* **1** a suspect in a police enquiry. **2** knowledge or know-how.

sussed /sust/ *adj Brit, informal* said of a person: knowledgeable; aware.

Sussex /'susiks/ *noun* a chicken of an English breed with white and black plumage. [named after *Sussex*, county of England, where the breed originated]

suss out *verb trans Brit, informal* **1** to investigate (e.g. a place). **2** to realize (something); to work (something) out. **3** to uncover the true nature of (somebody or something).

sustain[1] /sə'stayn/ *verb trans* **1** to support the weight of (something). **2** to give support, sustenance, or relief to (somebody or something): *Hope sustained them until they were rescued*. **3** to cause (something) to continue; to prolong. **4** to suffer or undergo (something): *We sustained heavy losses*. **5** to allow or admit (something) as valid: *The court sustained the motion*. **6** to support (something) by adequate proof; to confirm: *This testimony sustains our contention*. ⟫⟫ **sustained** *adj*, **sustainedly** *adv*, **sustainer** *noun*, **sustainment** *noun*. [Middle English *sustenen* via Old French *sustenir* from Latin *sustinēre* to hold up, sustain, from SUS- + *tenēre* to hold]

sustain[2] *noun* the prolonging of a musical note, e.g. on a keyboard, or the facility that allows this.

sustainable *adj* **1** able to be sustained. **2** able to be maintained at a fixed level without exhausting natural resources or damaging the environment: *sustainable development*. ⟫⟫ **sustainability** /-'biliti/ *noun*, **sustainably** *adv*.

sustenance /'sustinəns/ *noun* **1a** means of support, maintenance, or subsistence; a living. **b** food or provisions; nourishment. **2** sustaining or being sustained. [Middle English from Old French, from *sustenir*: see SUSTAIN[1]]

sustentation /susten'taysh(ə)n/ *noun formal* sustaining or being sustained; *esp* maintenance or upkeep. [Middle English via French from Latin *sustentation-, sustentatio* act of holding up, from *sustentare* to hold up, from *sustentus*, past part. of *sustinēre*: see SUSTAIN[1]]

susurration /syoohsə'raysh(ə)n/ *noun literary* a whispering or rustling sound. [Middle English from late Latin *susurration-, susurratio*, from Latin *susurrare* to whisper, from *susurrus* whisper, hum]

susurrus /syooh'surəs/ *noun* = SUSURRATION.

sutler /'sutlə/ *noun* formerly, a person who sold provisions to an army, often established in a shop or an army post. [obsolete Dutch *soeteler*, from Low German *suteler* sloppy worker, camp cook]

sutra /'soohtrə/ *noun* **1** a Hindu, *esp* Vedic, sacred writing or saying, or a collection of these. **2** a discourse of the Buddha. [Sanskrit *sūtra* thread, string of precepts, sutra]

suttee /'sutee, su'tee/ *noun* **1** the former custom of a Hindu widow being cremated on the funeral pyre of her husband, as an indication of her devotion to him. **2** a widow being cremated in this way. [Sanskrit *satī* wife who performs suttee, literally 'good woman', fem of *sat* true, good]

suture[1] /'soohchə/ *noun* **1a** a strand or fibre used in the sewing together of parts of the living body. **b** a stitch made with a suture. **c** the act or process of sewing with sutures. **2** the solid join between two bones, e.g. of the skull. **3** a furrow at the junction of animal or plant parts; *esp* a line along which a fruit, etc will split to release the seed. ⟫⟫ **sutural** *adj*. [early French *suture* from Latin *sutura* seam, suture, from *suere* to sew]

suture[2] *verb trans* to unite, close, or secure (e.g. a wound) with sutures.

SUV *abbr* sport utility vehicle, a powerful four-wheel-drive vehicle suitable for off-road driving.

suzerain /'soohz(ə)rayn/ *noun* **1** a dominant state controlling the foreign relations of an internally autonomous vassal state. **2** a feudal overlord. ⟫⟫ **suzerainty** /-rənti/ *noun*. [Old French *suserain*, from *sus* up (from Latin *sursum*, from SUB- up + *versum* -wards) + *-erain* as in *soverain* SOVEREIGN[1]]

Sv *abbr* sievert.

s.v. *abbr* used to indicate that a reference will be found under the word or heading given. [Latin *sub verbo* under the word; *sub voce* under that heading]

svelte /sfelt, svelt/ *adj* slender or lithe in an elegant and attractive way. [French *svelte* from Italian *svelto*, past part. of *svellere* to pluck out, modification of Latin *evellere*, from EX-[1] + *vellere* to pull]

Svengali /sven'gahli, sveng-/ *noun* somebody who attempts, often with sinister motives, to influence or mould another person.

Word history

named after *Svengali*, sinister hypnotist in the novel *Trilby* by George Du Maurier d.1896, English artist and writer. In the novel Svengali trains Trilby's singing voice by hypnosis.

SVGA *abbr* super video graphics array.

SW *abbr* **1** short wave. **2** Southwest. **3** Southwest (London postcode). **4** Southwestern.

SWA *abbr* Namibia (international vehicle registration). [South West Africa]

swab[1] *or* **swob** /swob/ *noun* **1** a wad of absorbent material used for applying medication, cleaning wounds, taking specimens, etc. **2** a specimen taken with a swab. **3** a mop or sponge. **4** *archaic* a useless or contemptible person.

swab[2] *or* **swob** *verb trans* (**swabbed** *or* **swobbed, swabbing** *or* **swobbing**) **1** to clean (a wound) with a swab. **2** to apply medication to (a part of the body) with a swab. **3** (*often* + down) to clean (a surface, *esp* a deck) by washing, *esp* with a mop. ⟫⟫ **swabber** *noun*. [back-formation from *swabber* sailor whose job was to swab decks, from Dutch *zwabber*, from *zwabberen* to mop]

swaddle /'swodl/ *verb trans* **1** to wrap (a baby) in swaddling clothes. **2** to swathe or envelop (something). [Middle English *swadelen, swathelen*, from Old English *swathian* SWATHE[2]]

swaddling clothes *pl noun* narrow strips of cloth formerly wrapped round a baby to restrict movement.

swag[1] /swag/ *noun* **1a** something, e.g. a moulded decoration, hanging in a curve between two points. **b** a suspended cluster, e.g. of flowers. **c** an arrangement of fabric hanging in a heavy curve or fold. **2** *informal* goods acquired, *esp* by unlawful means; loot. **3** *Aus, NZ* a pack or roll of personal belongings. **4** *Aus, NZ, informal* (*usu in pl*) a large amount or number: *They collected a swag of prizes*. [Middle English, in the sense 'bulging bag'; prob of Scandinavian origin]

swag[2] *verb* (**swagged, swagging**) ⟫ *verb trans* to hang (e.g. curtains) in heavy curves or folds. ⟫ *verb intrans* to hang heavily; to sag.

swage[1] /swayj/ *noun* a tool for shaping metal by hammering. [Middle English *swage* ornamental border, from early French *souage*]

swage[2] *verb trans* to shape (something) by means of a swage.

swage block *noun* a perforated cast-iron or steel block with a variety of grooved sides that is used in shaping metal.

swagger[1] /'swagə/ *verb intrans* (**swaggered, swaggering**) to behave in an arrogant or pompous manner; *esp* to walk with an air of overbearing self-confidence or self-satisfaction. ⟫⟫ **swaggerer** *noun*, **swaggering** *adj*, **swaggeringly** *adv*. [prob from SWAG[2]]

swagger[2] *noun* **1** a self-confident or self-satisfied gait. **2** arrogant or conceitedly self-assured behaviour.

swagger[3] *adj Brit, informal, dated* fashionable; elegant.

swagger stick *noun* a short light *usu* leather-covered stick, carried *esp* by army officers.

swaggie /'swagi/ *noun Aus, NZ, informal* a swagman.

swagman *noun* (*pl* **swagmen**) *Aus, NZ* a tramp or itinerant worker who carries his possessions with him.

Swahili /swə'heeli/ *noun* (*pl* **Swahilis** *or collectively* **Swahili**) **1** a member of a Bantu-speaking people of Zanzibar and the adjacent coast. **2** a Bantu language used in trade and government in E Africa and the Congo region. ⟫⟫ **Swahili** *adj*. [Arabic *sawāḥil*, pl of *sāḥil* coast]

swain /swayn/ *noun* **1** *archaic* a peasant; *specif* a shepherd. **2** *literary* a male admirer or suitor. [Middle English *swein* boy, servant, from Old Norse *sveinn*]

swallow¹ /'swoloh/ *noun* any of numerous species of small migratory birds that are noted for their graceful flight, have a short bill, long wings, and a forked tail, and feed on insects caught while flying: family Hirundinidae. [Old English *swealwe*]

swallow² *verb trans* **1** to cause (e.g. food or drink) to pass from the mouth through the oesophagus into the stomach. **2** to envelop or engulf (something): *They were swallowed up by the shadows.* **3** to accept (something) without question or protest. **4** to believe (something) naively. **5** to refrain from expressing or showing (something): *She swallowed her anger.* **6** to utter (something) indistinctly. ➤ *verb intrans* **1** to cause something to pass from the mouth through the oesophagus. **2** to perform the action of swallowing something, *esp* under emotional stress. ➤➤ **swallowable** *adj*, **swallower** *noun*. [Old English *swelgan*]

swallow³ *noun* **1** an act of swallowing. **2** an amount that can be swallowed at one time.

swallow dive *noun Brit* a forward dive executed with the back arched and arms spread sideways.

swallow hole *noun* = SINK HOLE (1).

swallowtail *noun* **1** a deeply forked and tapering tail, e.g. of a swallow. **2** a tailcoat. **3** any of several species of large butterflies with the hind wing lengthened to resemble a tail: *esp* genus *Papilio*. ➤➤ **swallow-tailed** *adj*.

swam /swam/ *verb* past tense of SWIM¹.

swami /'swahmi/ *noun* (*pl* **swamis**) used as a title: a Hindu ascetic or religious teacher. [Hindi *svāmī* from Sanskrit *svāmin* owner, lord, from *sva* one's own]

swamp¹ /swomp/ *noun* an area of wet spongy land sometimes partially or intermittently covered with water; a marsh. ➤➤ **swampy** *adj*. [alteration of Middle English *sompe*, from early Dutch *somp* morass]

swamp² *verb trans* **1** to flood or submerge (something). **2** to overwhelm (somebody) with too much of something. ➤ *verb intrans* said of a boat: to become submerged.

swamp fever *noun* a contagious viral disease of horses.

swan¹ /swon/ *noun* any of several species of large long-necked aquatic birds usu with pure white plumage that are graceful swimmers: *esp* genus *Cygnus*. ➤➤ **swanlike** *adj*. [Old English *swan*]

swan² *verb intrans* (**swanned, swanning**) *Brit, informal* to wander or travel aimlessly or ostentatiously, usu for pleasure: *She went swanning round Europe for a month.*

swan dive *noun NAmer* = SWALLOW DIVE.

swank¹ /swangk/ *verb intrans informal* to swagger; to show off. [perhaps from early High German *swanken* to sway]

swank² *noun informal* **1** arrogance or ostentation of dress or manner. **2** a conceited person.

swank³ *adj NAmer* swanky.

swanky *adj* (**swankier, swankiest**) *informal* **1** fashionably elegant; smart: *a swanky restaurant.* **2** showy or ostentatious: *a swanky car.* **3** inclined to show off; conceited. ➤➤ **swankily** *adv*, **swankiness** *noun*.

swan neck *noun* an S-shaped curve in a pipe or tube.

swannery *noun* (*pl* **swanneries**) *Brit* a place where swans are bred or kept.

swansdown *noun* **1** the soft downy feathers of the swan used *esp* as trimming on clothing. **2** a heavy cotton flannel that has a thick nap on the face. **3** a soft woollen fabric containing silk, cotton, or rayon, used for baby clothes.

swan song *noun* **1** a farewell appearance or performance, or a final work or pronouncement. **2** a song said to be sung by a dying swan.

swan-upping /'uping/ *noun Brit* the annual inspection and marking of royal swans on the River Thames. [*upping* from UP³ in the sense 'to drive up and catch']

swap¹ *or* **swop** /swop/ *verb* (**swapped** *or* **swopped, swapping** *or* **swopping**) ➤ *verb trans* to exchange (things), usu with another person: *The children were swapping football cards in the playground*; *We sat around swapping stories.* ➤ *verb intrans* to make an exchange or substitution: *They have swapped over to a metric system.* ➤➤ **swapper** *noun*. [Middle English *swappen* to strike; from the practice of striking hands in closing a business deal]

swap² *or* **swop** *noun* **1** an act of exchanging things. **2** something exchanged for another. **3** a duplicate copy of something that is being collected, e.g. a stamp.

SWAPO /'swahpoh/ *abbr* South-West Africa People's Organization.

swaraj /swə'rahj/ *noun* Indian national or local self-government. ➤➤ **swarajist** *noun and adj*. [Sanskrit *svarāj* self-ruling, from *sva* one's self + *rājya* rule]

sward /swawd/ *noun* a surface of short grass, or a piece of ground covered with this. ➤➤ **swarded** *adj*. [Old English *sweard, swearth* skin, rind]

swarf /swawf/ *noun* material, e.g. metallic particles and abrasive fragments, produced by a cutting or grinding tool. [prob of Scandinavian origin]

swarm¹ /swawm/ *noun* **1a** a large mass of flying insects. **b** a large number of honeybees, *esp* when emigrating from a hive with a queen bee to start a new colony elsewhere. **c** a cluster of free-floating or free-swimming single-celled organisms. **2** a group of people or things, *esp* when massing together: *There were swarms of sightseers.* [Old English *swearm*]

swarm² *verb intrans* **1** said of bees: to collect together and depart from a hive. **2** to move or assemble in a crowd; to throng. **3** (+ with) to contain a swarm; to teem with something: *The streets were swarming with cars.* **4** (+ up) to climb rapidly by gripping with the hands and feet. ➤➤ **swarmer** *noun*.

swart /swawt/ *adj archaic or literary* swarthy. [Old English *sweart*]

swarthy /'swawdhi/ *adj* (**swarthier, swarthiest**) of a dark colour or complexion. ➤➤ **swarthily** *adv*, **swarthiness** *noun*. [alteration of obsolete *swarty*, from SWART]

swash¹ /swosh/ *verb intrans* **1** said of water: to move with a splashing sound. **2** *archaic* to swagger. [prob imitative]

swash² *noun* **1** a body of splashing water, *esp* seawater rushing up a beach when a wave breaks. **2** a dashing of water against or on something. **3** a narrow channel of water lying within a sandbank or between a sandbank and the shore.

swash³ /swosh/ *adj* in printing, said of a letter: having strokes ending in a flourish. [origin unknown]

swashbuckler /'swoshbuklə/ *noun* a swaggering adventurer or daredevil. ➤➤ **swashbuckling** *adj*. [SWASH¹ + BUCKLER]

swastika /'swostikə/ *noun* **1** an ancient symbol in the shape of a cross with the ends of the arms extended at right angles in a clockwise or anticlockwise direction. **2** this symbol with arms extended clockwise as the emblem of the German Nazi Party and Third Reich. [Sanskrit *svastika*, from *svasti* welfare, from *su-* well + *asti* he is]

swat¹ /swot/ *verb trans* (**swatted, swatting**) to hit (e.g. an insect) with a sharp slapping blow. [N English and US alteration of SQUAT¹, the original sense]

swat² *noun* **1** a quick crushing blow. **2** a swatter.

swatch /swoch/ *noun* **1** a sample piece of fabric or other material. **2** a collection of sample pieces bound together. [origin unknown]

swath /swoth/ *noun chiefly NAmer* = SWATHE¹. [Old English *swæth* footstep, trace]

swathe¹ /swoth, swawth, swaydh/ *noun* **1** a row of cut grain or grass left by a scythe or mowing machine. **2** a long broad strip. **3** a space cleared as if by a scythe: *The article cut a swathe through all the intricate arguments.*

swathe² /swaydh/ *verb trans* **1** to bind or wrap (something) with a bandage or strip of material. **2** to envelop (something). ➤➤ **swather** *noun*. [Old English *swathian*]

swathe³ *noun* **1** a band used in swathing. **2** something that envelops.

swatter *noun* = FLYSWATTER.

sway¹ /sway/ *verb intrans* **1** to move slowly and rhythmically back and forth or from side to side. **2** to walk in a swaying manner. **3** to move gently from an upright to a leaning position. **4** to fluctuate or alternate between one attitude or position and another. ➤ *verb trans* **1** to make (something) swing, rock, or oscillate. **2a** to exert a controlling influence on (somebody): *He had been too much swayed by ambition.* **b** to change the opinions of (somebody), *esp* by eloquence or argument: *She couldn't sway the hostile crowd.* **3** *literary* to rule or govern (somebody). [Middle English *sweyen* to go down, fall, of Germanic origin]

sway² *noun* **1** swaying or being swayed. **2a** controlling influence or power; dominance. **b** rule or dominion. ✴ **hold sway** to have influence or power.

swayback *noun* the abnormal condition, *esp* in horses, of having a sagging back. ➤➤ **swaybacked** *adj*.

Swazi /'swahzi/ *noun* (*pl* **Swazis** *or collectively* **Swazi**) **1** a native or inhabitant of Swaziland in southern Africa. **2** a member of a people inhabiting Swaziland and parts of South Africa. **3** the Nguni language of this people. ➤➤ **Swazi** *adj*. [*Mswati*, a 19th-cent. Swazi king]

swear /swea/ *verb* (*past tense* **swore** /swaw/, *past part.* **sworn** /swawn/) ➤ *verb trans* **1** to utter or take (an oath) solemnly. **2** to assert (something) as true, often under oath: *a sworn affidavit*. **3** to promise (something) emphatically or earnestly: *She swore not to be late*. **4** to administer an oath to (somebody). **5** to bind (somebody) by an oath: *I swore him to secrecy*. ➤ *verb intrans* **1** to use profane or obscene language: *Money doesn't talk, it swears* — Bob Dylan. **2** to take an oath. ✴ **swear by** to place great confidence in (something): *He swore by garlic as a remedy for colds*. **swear off** *informal* to vow to abstain from (something). **swear to** to express certainty about (something): *She couldn't swear to his being the same man*. ➤➤ **swearer** *noun*. [Old English *swerian*]

swear in *verb trans* to induct (somebody) into office by administration of an oath.

swear out *verb trans NAmer* to procure (a warrant for arrest) by making a sworn accusation.

swearword *noun* a profane or obscene oath or word.

sweat¹ /swet/ *noun* **1** the fluid excreted from the sweat glands of the skin; perspiration. **2** moisture issuing from or gathering in drops on a surface. **3** *informal* a state of anxiety or impatience. **4** *informal* hard work; drudgery. ✴ **break sweat** *informal* to make a great physical effort: *He finished first without breaking sweat*. **by the sweat of one's brow** by one's own hard work. **in a cold sweat** *informal* in a state of anxiety. **no sweat** *informal* not a problem or difficulty: *I can do that all right, no sweat!* [Old English *swāt*]

sweat² *verb* (*past tense and past part.* **sweated** *or NAmer* **sweat**) ➤ *verb intrans* **1** to excrete moisture in visible quantities through the openings of the sweat glands, *esp* as a result of heat, exertion, or anxiety. **2a** to emit or exude moisture: *Cheese sweats in ripening*. **b** to gather surface moisture in beads as a result of condensation. **3** to exert oneself so as to cause perspiration; to work hard: *She had been sweating over her letter of application for hours*. **4** to undergo mental or emotional tension or anxiety: *I thought I'd leave him to sweat for a while*. **5** said of vegetables: to cook gently in melted fat until the juices run out. ➤ *verb trans* **1** to emit (sweat) from pores. **2** to cause (a person or animal) to sweat. **3** to cook (vegetables) gently in melted fat until the juices run out. **4a** to melt (e.g. solder) by heating so as to cause a flow, *esp* between surfaces to join them. **b** to join (surfaces) by such means. **c** to heat (metal) so as to extract a constituent that will melt easily. **5** *NAmer, informal* to worry about (something). ✴ **sweat blood** *informal* to work or worry intensely. [Old English *swǣtan*]

sweatband *noun* a band of material worn round the head or wrist or inserted in a hat or cap to absorb sweat.

sweated *adj* done or produced under a sweatshop system: *sweated labour; sweated goods*.

sweater *noun* **1** = JUMPER¹ (I). **2** a person who causes sweating; *specif* an employer in a sweatshop. [SWEAT² + -ER²]

sweat gland *noun* a tubular gland in the skin that secretes fluid through a minute pore on the surface of the skin.

sweating sickness *noun* an epidemic fever characterized by profuse sweating and rapid death that appeared in Britain in the 15th and 16th cents.

sweat off *verb trans* to lose (weight) by exercise or sweating.

sweat out *verb trans* **1** to cure or relieve (an illness) by sweating. **2** *informal* to endure (something unpleasant).

sweatpants *pl noun* loose-fitting trousers worn by athletes or for leisure.

sweats *pl noun chiefly NAmer, informal* a sweatsuit or sweatpants.

sweatshirt *noun* a loose collarless pullover of heavy cotton jersey.

sweatshop *noun* a place of work in which people are employed for long hours at low wages and under poor conditions.

sweatsuit *noun* a loose-fitting suit made up of a sweatshirt and sweatpants.

sweaty *adj* (**sweatier, sweatiest**) **1** covered with or smelling of sweat. **2** causing sweating. ➤➤ **sweatily** *adv*, **sweatiness** *noun*.

Swede /sweed/ *noun* a native or inhabitant of Sweden. [Low German or obsolete Dutch *Swēde*]

swede /sweed/ *noun* **1** a Eurasian plant cultivated for its bulbous yellow-fleshed root: *Brassica napobrassica*. **2** a root of this plant, used as a vegetable and for cattle fodder. [from its having been introduced into Scotland from Sweden]

Swedish /'sweedish/ *noun* the N Germanic language spoken in Sweden and Finland. ➤➤ **Swedish** *adj*.

Word history
Sweden, country of NW Europe. Modern Swedish words that have passed into English include *gauntlet* (in 'run the gauntlet'), *moped*, *ombudsman*, *orienteering*, and *tungsten*.

sweep¹ /sweep/ *verb* (*past tense and past part.* **swept** /swept/) ➤ *verb trans* **1a** to clean (something) by brushing: *He swept the kitchen floor*. **b** to remove (something) by brushing: *She was sweeping up the leaves*. **2** to remove or take (something) with a single forceful action: *He swept the books off the desk*. **3** to drive or carry along (somebody or something) with irresistible force: *They were swept into office by the wave of protest*. **4** to move through or along (a place) with overwhelming speed or violence: *A new craze is sweeping the country*. **5** (+ away) to destroy (something) completely; to wipe out. **6** to cover the entire range of (something): *His eyes swept the horizon*. **7** to move lightly over (something) with a rapid continuous movement: *His fingers swept the keyboard*. **8** to trace or describe the path or extent of (e.g. a line or circle). **9** *NAmer* to win an overwhelming victory in (something): *They swept the polls*. **10** in cricket, to play a sweep at (a ball). ➤ *verb intrans* **1** to clean a surface by brushing. **2** to move swiftly, forcefully, or devastatingly: *Fire swept through the business quarter*. **3** to go with stately or sweeping movements: *She swept out of the room*. **4** to move or extend in a wide curve: *The hills sweep down to the sea*. **5** in cricket, to play a sweep. ✴ **sweep somebody off their feet** to cause somebody to fall in love with one. **sweep something under the carpet** to conceal something in the hope that it will be ignored. **sweep the board** to win everything in a contest. [Middle English *swepen* from Old English *swāpan*]

sweep² *noun* **1** an act of sweeping. **2** a chimney sweep. **3a** a curving or circular course or line. **b** a broad extent: *an unbroken sweep of woodland*. **c** the extent of a sweeping movement; scope. **d** a movement of great range and force: *the great sweep of the industrial revolution*. **4** deviation from parallelism or perpendicularity with respect to a reference line: *the sweep of an aeroplane wing*. **5** in electronics, the movement of an electron beam across the surface of a cathode-ray tube. **6** *informal* a sweepstake. **7** *NAmer* an overwhelming victory. **8** a windmill sail. **9** a long oar. **10** a long pole or timber pivoted on a tall post and used to raise and lower a bucket in a well. **11** in cricket, an attacking stroke played on bended knee with a horizontal bat designed to send the ball behind the batsman on the leg side and usu played against slower bowlers.

sweepback *noun* the backward slant of an aircraft wing.

sweeper *noun* **1** a person or thing that sweeps. **2** in soccer, a defensive player who plays behind the backs as a last line of defence before the goalkeeper.

sweeping *adj* **1** extending in a wide curve or over a wide area. **2a** extensive; wide-ranging: *sweeping reforms*. **b** marked by wholesale and indiscriminate inclusion: *sweeping generalities*. ➤➤ **sweepingly** *adv*, **sweepingness** *noun*.

sweepings *pl noun* refuse, rubbish, etc collected by sweeping.

sweepstake *noun* (*also in pl*) a lottery or other form of gambling, e.g. on a horse race, in which all the stakes are awarded to one winner or divided among the winners. [Middle English *swepestake* somebody who wins all the stakes in a game, from SWEEP¹ + STAKE⁴]

sweet¹ /sweet/ *adj* **1** being or inducing a taste similar to that of sugar, one of the four basic taste sensations: compare BITTER¹, SALT³, SOUR¹. **2a** not sour, rancid, decaying, or stale. **b** not salt or salted. **c** free from noxious gases or other pollutants. **d** free from excess of acid, sulphur, or corrosive salts: *sweet petroleum*. **e** having a pleasant smell or taste. **3a** delightful or charming. **b** marked by gentle good humour or kindliness. **c** pleasing to the ear or eye. **4** much loved; dear. **5** working or moving smoothly. **6** said of jazz: performed with little improvisation and at a steady rhythm. **7** *archaic* used as a form of address: *sweet sir*. ✴ **keep somebody sweet** *informal* to keep somebody happy and cooperative. **sweet on somebody** *informal, dated* in love with somebody.

sweetish *adj*, **sweetly** *adv*, **sweetness** *noun*. [Old English *swēte*]

sweet² *noun* **1** *Brit* a small piece of confectionery prepared with sugar or chocolate, *esp* one made chiefly of boiled and crystallized sugar. **2** *Brit* a pudding or dessert. **3** used as a form of address: a darling or sweetheart. **4** (*in pl*) pleasures; delights.

sweet-and-sour *adj* seasoned with a sauce containing sugar and vinegar or lemon juice: *sweet-and-sour pork*.

sweetbread *noun* the pancreas or thymus of a young animal, e.g. a calf, used for food.

sweetbrier *or* **sweetbriar** *noun* a wild rose with stout prickles and white or pink flowers: *Rosa rubiginosa*.

sweet cherry *noun* **1** a large sweet cherry. **2** the white-flowered Eurasian tree that bears this fruit: *Prunus avium*.

sweet cicely *noun* **1** a European plant of the carrot family with a strong aniseed smell: *Myrrhis odorata*. **2** the leaves of this plant, used as a herb. [*cicely* by folk etymology from *seseli* a genus of perennial herbs, via Latin from Greek *seselis*]

sweet corn *noun* **1** a variety of maize cultivated for its kernels, which contain a high percentage of sugar. **2** the kernels of young tender ears of sweet corn, used as a vegetable.

sweeten *verb* (**sweetened, sweetening**) ➤ *verb trans* **1** to make (something) sweet or sweeter. **2** *informal* to improve the mood or attitude of (somebody). **3** to make (something) less painful or trying. **4** to free (something) from something undesirable, *esp* to remove sulphur compounds from it. ➤ *verb intrans* to become sweet.

sweetener *noun* **1** a substance added to food or drink to sweeten it, *esp* one used instead of sugar. **2** *chiefly Brit, informal* a bribe.

sweet Fanny Adams *noun* see FANNY ADAMS.

sweet flag *noun* a marsh plant of the arum family with long leaves and an aromatic root: *Acorus calamus*. Also called CALAMUS.

sweet gale *noun* = BOG MYRTLE. [Old English *gagel*]

sweet gum *noun* **1** a N American tree of the witch hazel family with corky branches and hard wood: *Liquidambar styraciflua*. **2** the HEARTWOOD (older harder non-living wood in a tree trunk) of the sweet gum or a reddish brown timber prepared from it.

sweetheart *noun* **1** a person that one loves; a darling. **2** used as an affectionate form of address. **3** *informal* (*used before a noun*) relating to or constituting an agreement or transaction between two parties that has benefits for both of them but is disadvantageous to an unrepresented third party.

sweetie /'sweeti/ *noun informal* **1** *Brit* used by or to children: a sweet. **2** used as a term of endearment. **3** a pleasing or attractive person or animal. **4** a variety of grapefruit with a green skin and a sweet taste.

sweetie pie *noun informal* **1** used as a term of endearment. **2** a pleasing or attractive person.

sweeting *noun* **1** a sweet apple. **2** *archaic* sweetheart; darling: *Trip no further, pretty sweeting* — Shakespeare. [Middle English *sweting*, from *swete* SWEET¹ + *-ing* (of such) a kind, from Old English *-ing*, *-ung*]

sweetmeat *noun archaic* a crystallized fruit, sugar-coated nut, or other sweet or delicacy rich in sugar.

sweet pea *noun* any of several species of garden plants of the pea family with slender climbing stems and colourful fragrant flowers: *Lathyrus odoratus* and other species.

sweet pepper *noun* **1** a large mild thick-skinned capsicum fruit. **2** a pepper plant bearing this fruit.

sweet potato *noun* **1** a tropical climbing plant of the bindweed family with purplish flowers that is cultivated for its large sweet tubers: *Ipomoea batatas*. **2** a tuber of this plant, used as a vegetable.

sweetsop *noun* **1** a custard apple with a thick green skin and sweet edible pulp. **2** the tropical American evergreen tree that bears this fruit: *Annona squamosa*.

sweet talk *noun informal* flattery.

sweet-talk *verb trans informal* to persuade (somebody) to do something by flattering them.

sweet tooth *noun* a fondness for sweet food.

sweet william /'wilyəm/ *noun* a widely cultivated Eurasian plant of the pink family with small white to deep red or purple flowers, often mottled or striped: *Dianthus barbatus*. [from the name *William*]

swell¹ /swel/ *verb* (*past tense* **swelled**, *past part.* **swollen** /'swohlən/, **swelled**) ➤ *verb intrans* **1a** to expand gradually beyond a normal or original limit: *The population of the town has swelled*. **b** to be distended or puffed up: *Her ankle was already swelling*. **c** to curve outwards or upwards; to bulge. **2** to become charged with emotion: *His heart swelled with pride*. ➤ *verb trans* to increase the size, number, volume, or intensity of (something). [Old English *swellan*]

swell² *noun* **1** a rounded protuberance or bulge. **2** the act or process of swelling. **3a** a gradual increase and decrease of the volume in music. **b** a device used in an organ for controlling volume of sound. **4** a surging or undulating movement of water, often continuing beyond or after its cause. **5** *informal, dated* a person of fashion or high social position.

swell³ *adj* **1** *NAmer, informal, dated* excellent. **2** *archaic* stylish or socially prominent.

swell box *noun* a chamber in an organ containing a set of pipes and having shutters that open or shut to regulate the volume of sound.

swelling *noun* **1** something swollen; *specif* an abnormal bodily protuberance or enlargement. **2** the condition of being swollen.

swell organ *noun* a division of an organ in which the pipes are enclosed in a swell box.

swelter¹ /'sweltə/ *verb intrans* (**sweltered, sweltering**) to suffer, sweat, or be faint from heat. [Middle English *sweltren*, frequentative of *swelten* to die, be overcome by heat, from Old English *sweltan* to die]

swelter² *noun* a state of oppressive heat.

sweltering *adj* oppressively hot. ➤➤ **swelteringly** *adv*.

swept /swept/ *verb* past tense and past part. of SWEEP¹.

swept-back /swept/ *adj* said of an aircraft wing: slanting backwards.

swept-wing *adj* said of an aircraft: having swept-back wings.

swerve¹ /swuhv/ *verb intrans* to turn aside abruptly from a straight line or course; to deviate. ➤ *verb trans* to make (something) turn aside or deviate. ➤➤ **swerver** *noun*. [Old English *sweorfan* to wipe, turn away]

swerve² *noun* the act or an instance of swerving: *from swerve of shore to bend of bay* — James Joyce.

SWG *abbr Brit* standard wire gauge.

swift¹ /swift/ *adj* **1** moving or capable of moving at great speed: *a swift horse; a swift gallop*. **2** occurring suddenly or lasting a very short time: *a swift visit*. **3** quick to respond; ready: *a swift temper; The government was swift to act*. ➤➤ **swiftly** *adv*, **swiftness** *noun*. [Old English]

swift² *adv* swiftly: *a swift-flowing river*.

swift³ *noun* **1** any of numerous dark-coloured birds noted for their fast darting flight in pursuit of insects. They have long narrow pointed wings and a forked tail and spend most of their lives on the wing: family Apodidae. **2** any of several lizards that run swiftly: *esp* genus *Sceloporus*. **3** a reel for winding yarn or thread. **4** any of the large cylinders that carry forward the material in a carding machine.

swiftlet /'swiftlit/ *noun* a small cave-dwelling swift of SE Asia and Australasia: genera *Collocalia* and *Aerodramus*.

swig¹ /swig/ *noun* a quantity drunk in one swallow: *An' I'll get a swig in hell from Gunga Din!* — Kipling. [origin unknown]

swig² *verb trans* (**swigged, swigging**) to drink (something) in long draughts. ➤➤ **swigger** *noun*.

swill¹ /swil/ *verb trans* **1** *Brit* (*often* + out) to wash (something), *esp* by flushing with water. **2** *informal* to drink (something) greedily. ➤ *verb intrans Brit, informal* to drink or eat freely or greedily. ➤➤ **swiller** *noun*. [Old English *swillan*]

swill² *noun* **1** a semiliquid food for animals such as pigs, composed of edible refuse mixed with water or skimmed or sour milk. **2** *informal* a swig. **3** *informal* disgusting food or drink. **4** rubbish; waste.

swim¹ /swim/ *verb* (**swimming**, *past tense* **swam** /swam/, *past part.* **swum** /swum/) ➤ *verb intrans* **1** to propel the body in water by bodily movements, e.g. of the limbs, fins, or tail. **2** to float on a liquid. **3** to be immersed in or flooded with a liquid: *The sausages were swimming in gravy*. **4** to have a floating, whirling, or dizzy effect or sensation: *Her head was swimming*. ➤ *verb trans* **1a** to cross (a stretch of water) by swimming. **b** to use (a stroke) in swimming. **2** to cause (a person or animal) to swim or float. ✳ **swim against**

the tide to move counter to the prevailing or popular trend. ➤➤ **swimmer** *noun*. [Old English *swimman*]

swim² *noun* **1** an act or period of swimming. **2** an area frequented by fish. * **in the swim** active or involved in activities, current affairs, etc.

swim bladder *noun* the air bladder of a fish that serves as a buoyancy mechanism.

swimmable *adj* capable of being swum.

swimmeret /'swimərit/ *noun* any of a series of small unspecialized appendages under the abdomen of many crustaceans that are used for swimming or carrying eggs.

swimming *noun* the act, skill, or sport of somebody who swims.

swimming bath *noun Brit* (*also in pl*) an indoor swimming pool.

swimming cap *noun* a tight-fitting rubber cap worn when swimming to cover the hair.

swimming costume *noun Brit* a close-fitting garment worn for swimming.

swimmingly *adv informal* very well; splendidly: *Everything went swimmingly.*

swimming pool *noun* an artificial pool for people to swim in.

swimming trunks *pl noun* shorts worn for swimming by men or boys.

swimsuit *noun* = SWIMMING COSTUME.

swimwear *noun* clothing suitable for swimming.

swindle¹ /'swindl/ *verb trans* **1** to take money or property from (somebody) by fraud or deceit. **2** to obtain (money or property) by fraud or deceit. ➤➤ **swindler** *noun*. [earliest as *swindler*, from German *Schwindler* giddy person, cheat, from *schwindeln* to be dizzy, from Old High German *swintilōn*, frequentative of *swintan* to diminish, vanish]

swindle² *noun* an act of fraud or deceit.

swine /swien/ *noun* **1** (*pl* **swine**) *formal or NAmer* a pig. **2** (*pl* **swine** *or* **swines**) *informal* a contemptible person. **3** *informal* something unpleasant: *It was a swine of a job.* ➤➤ **swinish** *adj*, **swinishly** *adv*, **swinishness** *noun*. [Old English *swīn*]

swine fever *noun* a highly infectious often fatal viral disease of pigs.

swineherd *noun* a person who tends pigs.

swing¹ /swing/ *verb* (*past tense and past part.* **swung** /swung/) ➤ *verb intrans* **1a** to move freely to and fro when suspended or as if suspended. **b** to hang freely from a support. **2a** to move in or describe a circle or arc. **b** to turn on, or as if on, a hinge or pivot; to move in a gentle curve. **c** to turn and face the opposite direction. **3** to move into a new position by grasping a fixed support. **4** in cricket, said of a bowled ball: to deviate from a straight path before reaching the batsman. **5** *informal* to be executed by hanging. **6** (*often* + out) to hit or aim at somebody or something with a sweeping arm movement. **7** to fluctuate from one condition, position, or object of attention to another: *He swings between optimism and pessimism.* **8a** said of music: to have a steady pulsing rhythm. **b** to play or sing with a lively compelling rhythm; *specif* to play swing. **9a** to move along rhythmically: *I saw her swinging down the street.* **b** to start up in a smooth vigorous manner: *We were ready to swing into action.* **10** *informal* to be lively and exciting. **11** *informal* to be sexually promiscuous, *esp* by swapping sexual partners. ➤ *verb trans* **1a** to move (something) from one point to another by suspension: *The cranes swing cargo over the ship's side.* **b** to suspend (something) between two points so that it can sway or turn. **2a** to cause (a hammer, axe, etc) to move vigorously through a wide curve or circle. **b** to cause (something) to sway or pivot. **3** to cause (something) to face or move in another direction: *I swung the car into a side road.* **4** in cricket, to make (a delivery of a ball) deviate from a straight path. **5** to deliver (a punch) with a sweeping arm movement. **6a** to bring (somebody) round by influence. **b** to influence (a decision, vote, etc) decisively. **c** *informal* to succeed in achieving or obtaining (something). * **swing the lead** *Brit, informal* to neglect one's work, *esp* by inventing excuses; to malinger. [Old English *swingan* to beat, fling oneself, rush]

swing² *noun* **1** a suspended seat on which a person can swing to and fro. **2** an act or the motion of swinging, e.g.: **a** a stroke or blow delivered with a sweeping movement. **b** a sweeping or rhythmic movement of the body or a body part. **c** the regular movement of a freely suspended object, e.g. a pendulum, to and fro along an arc. **d** the arc or range through which something swings. **e** a curving

course or outline. **3** in cricket, deviation of the ball from a straight path while travelling through the air before reaching the batsman. **4** a shift from one condition or state to another, *esp* a change in public opinion or political preference: *a 10% swing to Labour.* **5** jazz played with a steady lively rhythm and simple harmony. * **get into the swing of things** *informal* to accustom oneself to a situation or undertaking. **go with a swing** *informal* to be enjoyable and successful. **in full swing** at the height of activity. **swings and roundabouts** *Brit, informal* a situation in which a loss or disadvantage is balanced by a gain or advantage of another kind.

swingbin *noun Brit* a rubbish bin with a lid that is pushed open and swings shut.

swing bridge *noun* a bridge that can be swung aside to let ships through.

swing door *noun* a door that can be pushed open from either side and that swings closed when released.

swinge /swinj/ *verb trans literary* to beat or punish (somebody). [Old English *swengan* to move violently, shake]

swingeing /'swinjing/ *adj chiefly Brit* severe or drastic: *They have made swingeing cuts in public expenditure.*

swinger /'swing-ə/ *noun informal* **1** *dated* a lively or fashionable person. **2** a person who engages freely in sex, *esp* in swapping sexual partners.

swinging /'swinging/ *adj informal* **1** lively and exciting. **2** sexually liberated. [present part. of SWING¹]

swingle¹ /'swing-gl/ *noun* a wooden instrument like a large knife that is used for beating and cleaning flax. [Middle English *swingel* from early Dutch *swinghel*]

swingle² *verb trans* to clean (flax) by beating it with a swingle.

swingletree *noun chiefly Brit* the pivoted swinging bar to which the traces of a harness are attached and by which a vehicle or plough is drawn. [SWINGLE¹ + TREE¹]

swingometer /swing'omitə/ *noun informal* a device for representing statistical movements, *esp* in the electoral support of a political party, by means of an adjustable pointer attached to a dial.

swing shift *noun NAmer* a shift worked from afternoon to late evening, before the night shift.

swing-wing *adj* said of an aircraft: having movable wings giving the best angles of sweepback for both low and high speeds. ➤➤ **swing-wing** *noun*.

swipe¹ /swiep/ *verb intrans informal* to strike or hit out with a sweeping motion. ➤ *verb trans* **1** *informal* to strike (something) with a sweeping motion. **2** *informal* to steal (something). **3** *informal* to pass (a card) through a machine that can read information encoded in its magnetic strip. ➤➤ **swiper** *noun*. [prob alteration of SWEEP¹]

swipe² *noun informal* **1** a strong sweeping blow. **2** an unexpected criticism.

swipe card *noun* a plastic card containing a magnetic strip encoded with information that can be read when the card is passed through a special machine.

swirl¹ /swuhl/ *noun* **1** a whirling mass or motion. **2** a twisting shape, mark, or pattern. ➤➤ **swirly** *adj*. [Middle English (Scottish) in the sense 'whirlpool', prob of Low German or Dutch origin]

swirl² *verb intrans and trans* to move or cause (something) to move in eddies or whirls.

swish¹ /swish/ *noun* **1a** a sharp hissing or rushing sound: *the swish of a whip.* **b** a light sweeping or brushing sound: *the swish of long skirts on the ground.* **2** a movement causing either of these sounds. ➤➤ **swishy** *adj*. [imitative]

swish² *verb intrans and trans* to move or cause (something) to move with a swish: *The horse swished its tail.*

swish³ *adj Brit, informal* smart and fashionable. [origin unknown]

Swiss /swis/ *noun* (*pl* **Swiss**) a native or inhabitant of Switzerland in central Europe. ➤➤ **Swiss** *adj*. [early French *Suisse*, from early High German *Swizer*, from *Swiz* Switzerland]

Swiss chard *noun* = CHARD.

Swiss cheese plant *noun* an evergreen climbing plant of the arum family that has large dark green leaves with deep notches and many perforations and is widely cultivated as a houseplant: *Monstera deliciosa.* [from the holes in the leaves resembling those in some Swiss cheeses]

Swiss roll *noun Brit* a thin sheet of sponge cake spread with jam, cream, etc and rolled up.

switch[1] /swich/ *noun* **1** a device for making, breaking, or changing the connections in an electrical circuit. **2** a shift or change, *esp* a sudden one. **3** a slender flexible twig or rod. **4** *NAmer* a set of railway points. **5** a tress of hair attached to augment a hairstyle. **6** a tuft of long hairs at the end of the tail of an animal, e.g. a cow. [perhaps from early Dutch *swijch* twig]

switch[2] *verb trans* **1** to make a sudden change in (something): *They had to switch the venue at the last minute.* **2** to exchange (things): *Can I switch places with you?* **3** to cause (an electric current) to flow, stop flowing, or change path by means of a switch. **4** *chiefly NAmer* to turn (rolling stock) from one railway track to another; to shunt. **5** *archaic* to strike or beat (somebody or something) with or as if with a switch. ➤ *verb intrans* to make a change or exchange: *You can switch to a different course after your first year.* ➤➤ **switchable** *adj,* **switcher** *noun.*

switchback *noun* **1** *Brit.* **a** a zigzag road or railway in a mountainous region. **b** a road with many alternating ascents and descents. **2** a roller coaster.

switchblade *noun chiefly NAmer* a flick knife.

switchboard *noun* an apparatus consisting of a panel or frame on which switching devices are mounted; *specif* an arrangement for the manual switching of telephone calls.

switched-on *adj Brit, informal* responsive, alert, or aware.

switchgear *noun* equipment used for the switching of electrical currents.

switch-hitter *noun* **1** in baseball, a player who can bat either right-handed or left-handed. **2** *NAmer, informal* somebody who is bisexual.

switchman *noun* (*pl* **switchmen**) *NAmer* a person who works a switch, e.g. on a railway.

switch off *verb trans* to turn off (e.g. a light or machine) by operating an electrical switch. ➤ *verb intrans informal* to lose interest.

switch on *verb trans* to turn on (e.g. a light or machine) by operating an electrical switch.

swither[1] /'swidhə/ *verb intrans* (**swithered, swithering**) *Scot* to be indecisive. [origin unknown]

swither[2] *noun Scot* a state of indecision or uncertainty.

swivel[1] /'swivl/ *noun* a device joining two parts so that one part can pivot freely. [Old English *swīfan* to revolve]

swivel[2] *verb* (**swivelled, swivelling,** *NAmer* **swiveled, swiveling**) ➤ *verb intrans* to turn on or as if on a swivel. ➤ *verb trans* to turn (something) about a point or axis: *She swivelled her eyes.*

swivel chair *noun* a chair that swivels on its base.

swiz /swiz/ *noun* (*pl* **swizzes**) *Brit, informal* **1** something that does not live up to one's hopes or expectations. **2** a swindle or fraud. [prob short for SWIZZLE[1]]

swizzle[1] /'swizl/ *noun Brit, informal* a swiz. [prob alteration of SWINDLE[2]]

swizzle[2] *noun* an alcoholic cocktail. [origin unknown]

swizzle[3] *verb trans* to mix or stir (a drink) with a swizzle stick.

swizzle[4] *verb trans Brit, informal* to cheat or swindle (somebody).

swizzle stick *noun* a thin rod used to stir mixed drinks.

swob[1] /swob/ *noun* see SWAB[1].

swob[2] *verb trans* see SWAB[2].

swollen /'swohlən/ *verb* past part. of SWELL[1].

swoon[1] /swoohn/ *verb intrans* to faint: *Home they brought her warrior dead: She nor swooned, not uttered cry —* Tennyson. [Middle English *swounen,* from obsolete *swoun* fainting, from Old English *geswōgen* overcome, suffocated]

swoon[2] *noun* a partial or total loss of consciousness.

swoop[1] /swoohp/ *verb intrans* to move abruptly with a sweeping or diving motion; *esp* to make a sudden attack or raid: *The eagle swooped down on its prey.* ➤ *verb trans informal* to carry (somebody or something) off abruptly. [alteration of Middle English *swepen*: see SWEEP[1]]

swoop[2] *noun* an act of swooping: *Three men were arrested in a drug-squad swoop.* ✱ **at one fell swoop** see FELL[5].

swoosh[1] /swoosh, swoohsh/ *noun* a rushing or swirling sound. [imitative]

swoosh[2] *verb intrans* to make or move with a swoosh.

swop[1] /swop/ *verb trans and intrans* see SWAP[1].

swop[2] *noun* see SWAP[2].

sword /sawd/ *noun* **1** a cutting or thrusting weapon with a long usu sharp-pointed and sharp-edged blade. **2** (**the sword**) *literary* the use of force, e.g. in war: *The pen is mightier than the sword —* E G Bulwer-Lytton. **3** something, e.g. the beak of a swordfish, that resembles a sword. ✱ **cross swords** to fight or argue. **put somebody to the sword** to kill somebody with a sword. [Old English *sweord*]

sword-bearer *noun* an official who carries a ceremonial sword on formal occasions.

sword dance *noun* a dance performed with swords; *esp* a Scottish solo dance performed in the angles formed by two swords crossed on the ground. ➤➤ **sword dancer** *noun.*

swordfish *noun* (*pl* **swordfishes** *or collectively* **swordfish**) a very large oceanic food fish that has a very long beak formed by the bones of the upper jaw: *Xiphias gladius.*

sword grass *noun* any of various grasses or sedges having leaves with a sharp or toothed edge.

sword knot *noun* an ornamental cord or tassel tied to the hilt of a sword.

sword of Damocles /'daməkleez/ *noun* an impending disaster. [from the legend of the sword suspended by a single hair over the head of Damocles, a courtier of ancient Syracuse, as a reminder of the insecurity of a tyrant's happiness]

swordplay *noun* the art, skill, or practice of wielding a sword.

swordsman *noun* (*pl* **swordsmen**) a person skilled in swordplay. ➤➤ **swordsmanship** *noun.*

swordstick *noun* a walking stick in which a sword blade is concealed.

swordtail *noun* a small brightly marked Central American fish often kept in tropical aquariums: *Xiphophorus helleri.* [so called because of its long thin tail]

swore /swaw/ *verb* past tense of SWEAR.

sworn[1] /swawn/ *verb* past part. of SWEAR.

sworn[2] *adj* **1** made under oath, or as if under oath: *a sworn statement.* **2** determined to remain as specified: *The two boys were sworn enemies.*

SWOT /swot/ *abbr* used in the analysis of a product: strengths, weaknesses, opportunities, and threats.

swot[1] /swot/ *noun Brit, informal* a person who studies hard or excessively. [alteration of SWEAT[1]]

swot[2] *verb intrans* (**swotted, swotting**) *Brit, informal* to study hard, e.g. for an exam.

swum /swum/ *verb* past part. of SWIM[1].

swung /swung/ *verb* past tense and past part. of SWING[1].

swung dash *noun* a character (~) used chiefly to represent part or all of a previously spelt-out word.

swy /swie/ *noun Aus, NZ* = TWO-UP. [German *zwei* two]

SY *abbr* Seychelles (international vehicle registration).

sybarite /'sibəriet/ *noun* somebody who likes to indulge in sensual pleasures. ➤➤ **sybaritic** /-'ritik/ *adj,* **sybaritism** *noun.* [from the notorious luxury of the people of the ancient city of Sybaris in Italy]

sycamore /'sikəmaw/ *noun* **1** a Eurasian maple widely planted as a shade tree: *Acer pseudoplatanus.* **2** *NAmer* a plane tree, *esp* a very large spreading tree: *Platanus occidentalis.* **3** = SYCOMORE. [Middle English *sicamour* via French and Latin from Greek *sykomoros,* from *sykon* fig + *moron* mulberry]

sycomore /'sikəmaw/ *noun* a tree of the Middle East that is grown as a shade tree and has sweet edible fruit similar to the common fig: *Ficus sycomorus.*

syconium /sie'kohni·əm/ *noun* (*pl* **syconia** /-ni·ə/) a multiple fleshy fruit, such as a fig, in which the ovaries are borne within an enlarged succulent receptacle. [scientific Latin from Greek *sykon* fig + -IUM]

sycophant /'sikəfant/ *noun* a self-seeking flatterer; a toady. ➤➤ **sycophancy** *noun,* **sycophantic** /-'fantik/ *adj,* **sycophantically** /-'fantikli/ *adv.*

Word history

Latin *sycophanta* informer, swindler, sycophant, from Greek *sykophantēs* informer, from *sykon* fig + *phainein* to show. The origin and development of the meaning is not clear; the most popular theory, put forward by Plutarch, was that the word referred to a person who informed on those who illegally exported figs or who stole the fruit of sacred fig trees; others claimed that a sycophant was an official connected with sacred fig trees who denounced those who were not worthy to belong to the cult, or one who metaphorically 'made a fig' (an obscene gesture) at the person they accused. None of these theories is now thought to be true. In English the word originally meant 'an informer', later 'a bearer of false or malicious tales'; the sense 'flatterer' may be due to the idea of currying favour by slandering others or flattering the listener. The sense 'swindler, impostor', from Latin, was also used in English from the late 16th to the early 18th cents.

sycosis /sie'kohsis/ *noun* an inflammatory disorder of the hair follicles marked by raised spots. [orig denoting an ulcer resembling a fig: scientific Latin from Greek *sykōsis*, from *sykon* fig]

Sydenham's chorea /'sidnəmz/ *noun* a nervous disorder mainly affecting children, marked by spasmodic movements of the limbs and facial muscles and by lack of coordination, associated with rheumatic fever. [named after Thomas Sydenham d.1689, English physician, who first described it]

syenite /'sie·əniet/ *noun* an igneous rock composed chiefly of feldspar. ➤ **syenitic** /-'nitik/ *adj*. [Latin *Syenites* (*lapis*) (stone) of *Syene*, ancient city in Egypt]

syl- *prefix* see SYN-.

syllabary /'siləbari/ *noun* (*pl* **syllabaries**) a table or list of syllables; *specif* a set of written characters each one of which represents a syllable. [scientific Latin *syllabarium* from Latin *syllaba*: see SYLLABLE]

syllabi /'siləbie/ *noun* pl of SYLLABUS.

syllabic¹ /si'labik/ *adj* **1** enunciated with separation of syllables. **2** said of a consonant: constituting a syllable; *esp* not accompanied in the same syllable by a vowel sound. **3** of or constituting a type of verse in which the metre is based on a count of syllables. ➤ **syllabically** *adv*. [via late Latin from Greek *syllabikos*, from *syllabē*: see SYLLABLE]

syllabic² *noun* a syllabic character or sound.

syllabify /si'labifie/ *verb trans* (**syllabifies, syllabified, syllabifying**) to form or divide (words) into syllables. ➤ **syllabification** /-fi'kaysh(ə)n/ *noun*.

syllable /'siləbl/ *noun* **1** an uninterruptible unit of spoken language that usu consists of one vowel sound either alone or with a consonant sound preceding or following. **2** a letter or symbol representing a syllable. ➤ **syllabled** *adj*. [Middle English via early French *sillabe* and Latin *syllaba* from Greek *syllabē*, from *syllambanein* to gather together, from SYN- + *lambanein* to take]

syllabub /'siləbub/ *noun* a cold dessert usu made by curdling sweetened cream or milk with wine, cider, or other acidic liquid. [origin unknown]

syllabus /'siləbəs/ *noun* (*pl* **syllabi** /-bie/ or **syllabuses**) a summary of a course of study or of examination requirements. [late Latin *syllabus*, alteration of Latin *sittybas* label for a book, from Greek *sittyba* index, label]

syllepsis /si'lepsis/ *noun* (*pl* **syllepses** /-seez/) **1** the use of a word in a syntactic relationship with two or more words, only one of which it formally agrees with, e.g. in 'neither he nor I knows'. **2** = ZEUGMA. ➤ **sylleptic** /si'leptik/ *adj*. [via Latin from Greek *syllēpsis*, from *syllambanein*: see SYLLABLE]

syllogise *verb intrans* see SYLLOGIZE.

syllogism /'siləjiz(ə)m/ *noun* a pattern of deductive reasoning consisting of two premises and a conclusion, e.g. 'all men are mortal; Socrates is a man; therefore Socrates is mortal'. ➤ **syllogistic** /-'jistik/ *adj*, **syllogistically** /-'jistikli/ *adv*. [Middle English *silogisme* via French and Latin from Greek *syllogismos*, from *syllogizesthai* to syllogize, from SYN- + *logizesthai* to calculate, from *logos* reckoning, word]

syllogize or **syllogise** /'siləjiez/ *verb intrans* to reason by means of syllogisms. [Middle English *sylogysen* via late Latin from Greek *syllogizesthai*: see SYLLOGISM]

sylph /silf/ *noun* **1** a slender graceful woman or girl. **2** an imaginary being inhabiting the air. ➤ **sylphlike** *adj*. [Latin *sylpha*]

sylvan or **silvan** /'silvən/ *adj* **1** of, located in, or characteristic of the woods or forest. **2** full of woods or trees. [medieval Latin *silvanus*, *sylvanus*, from Latin *silva*, *sylva* wood]

sylvine /'silveen/ *noun* a mineral that is a natural potassium chloride and occurs in colourless cubes or crystalline masses: formula KCl. [French *sylvine* from scientific Latin *sal digestivus Sylvii* digestive salt of *Sylvius*, latinized name of Jacques Dubois d.1555, French physician]

sylvite /'silviet/ *noun* = SYLVINE.

sym- *prefix* see SYN-.

symbiont /'simbiont/ *noun* an organism living in symbiosis. [Greek *symbiount-*, *symbiōn*, present part. of *symbioun*: see SYMBIOSIS]

symbiosis /simbi'ohsis, simbie-/ *noun* (*pl* **symbioses** /-seez/) the living together of two dissimilar organisms in intimate association, usu to the benefit of both: compare ANTIBIOSIS. ➤ **symbiotic** /-'otik/ *adj*, **symbiotically** /-'otikli/ *adv*. [scientific Latin via German *symbiose* from Greek *symbiōsis* state of living together, from *symbioun* to live together, from *symbios* companion, from SYM- + *bios* life]

symbol /'simbl/ *noun* **1** something that stands for or suggests something else by reason of association, convention, etc; *esp* a visible sign of something invisible: *The lion is a symbol of courage.* **2** a sign used in writing or printing to represent operations, quantities, elements, relations, or qualities in a particular field, e.g. chemistry or music. [Latin *symbolum* token, sign, symbol, from Greek *symbolon*, literally 'token of identity verified by comparing its other half', from *symballein* to throw together, compare, from SYM- + *ballein* to throw]

symbolic /sim'bolik/ *adj* of, using, or constituting a symbol or symbols. ➤ **symbolical** *adj*, **symbolically** *adv*.

symbolic logic *noun* a method of developing and representing logical principles using a formalized system of symbols.

symbolise *verb trans* see SYMBOLIZE.

symbolism *noun* **1** the art or practice of representing things by symbols or giving things a symbolic meaning. **2** a system of symbols. **3** the literary and artistic mode of expression of the symbolists. ➤ **symbolistic** /-'listik/ *adj*.

symbolist *noun* **1** somebody who uses symbols or symbolism. **2** any of a group of *esp* 19th-cent. French writers and artists who used symbols to convey a subjective view of reality and immaterial or intangible states or truths, e.g. by exploiting the figurative resources of language. ➤ **symbolist** *adj*.

symbolize or **symbolise** *verb trans* **1** to serve as a symbol of (something). **2** to represent, express, or identify (something) by means of symbols. ➤ **symbolization** /-'zaysh(ə)n/ *noun*.

symbology /sim'boləji/ *noun* **1** the art of expression by symbols. **2** the study or interpretation of symbols. **3** a system of symbols.

symmetric *adj* = SYMMETRICAL.

symmetrical /si'metrikl/ *adj* **1** having the same proportions, design, shape, etc on both sides; *specif* capable of division by a longitudinal plane into similar halves. **2** said of a flower: having the same number of members in each whorl of floral leaves. **3** said of a chemical compound: having symmetry in the molecular structure. ➤ **symmetrically** *adv*.

symmetrize or **symmetrise** /'simitriez/ *verb trans* to make (something) symmetrical.

symmetry /'simitri/ *noun* (*pl* **symmetries**) **1** the property of being symmetrical; *esp* correspondence in size, shape, and relative position of parts on opposite sides of a dividing line or median plane or about a centre or axis: compare BILATERAL SYMMETRY, RADIAL SYMMETRY. **2** balanced proportions, or beauty of form arising from balanced proportions. **3** the property possessed by a physical phenomenon whereby it remains unaffected by certain changes, e.g. of orientation in space or of the sign of the electric charge. [via Latin from Greek *symmetria*, from *symmetros* symmetrical, from SYN- + *metron* measure]

sympathectomy /simpə'thektəmi/ *noun* (*pl* **sympathectomies**) the surgical removal of a sympathetic nerve.

sympathetic /simpə'thetik/ *adj* **1** given to, showing, or arising from compassion and sensitivity to others' feelings: *I told her my problems but she wasn't very sympathetic.* **2** favourably inclined: *My parents were not sympathetic to the idea.* **3** appropriate to one's mood or temperament; congenial. **4** existing or operating through an affinity, association, or relationship in which each of two or more people or things is simultaneously affected in a similar way. **5a** belonging or relating to the sympathetic nervous system. **b**

mediated by or acting on the sympathetic nerves. **6** denoting musical sounds produced, or strings sounded, by sympathetic vibration. ➤➤ **sympathetically** *adv.* [scientific Latin *sympatheticus*, from Latin *sympathia*: see SYMPATHY]

sympathetic magic *noun* magic in which an action performed in one place is thought to cause or influence a similar event in another place.

sympathetic nervous system *noun* the part of the autonomic nervous system that tends to depress secretion, e.g. of digestive juices in the gut, decrease the tension and elasticity of smooth muscle, and cause the contraction of blood vessels.

sympathetic vibration *noun* a vibration produced in one body by the vibrations of exactly the same frequency in a neighbouring body.

sympathize *or* **sympathise** /'simpǝthiez/ *verb intrans* **1** to share in distress or suffering; to commiserate: *I can sympathize with everything, except suffering* — Oscar Wilde. **2** to agree with somebody or something; to be in sympathy with them. ➤➤ **sympathizer** *noun*.

sympathomimetic[1] /,simpǝthohmi'metik/ *adj* simulating sympathetic nervous action in physiological effect: *sympathomimetic drugs*. [SYMPATHETIC + -O- + MIMETIC]

sympathomimetic[2] *noun* a sympathomimetic drug.

sympathy /'simpǝthi/ *noun* (*pl* **sympathies**) **1a** the act or capacity of entering into or sharing the feelings of another: *He had no sympathy for the poor.* **b** a feeling or the expression of pity for the distress or suffering of another: *a few words of sympathy.* **2a** inclination to think or feel alike; emotional or intellectual accord. **b** (*also in pl*) a feeling of loyalty; a tendency to give favour or support: *The Labour party can draw on a general tradition of sympathy for women's rights* — Angela Carter; *They suspected her of having Tory sympathies.* **c** an affinity, association, or relationship between people or things in which each is simultaneously affected in a similar way. **d** unity or harmony in action or effect. [Latin *sympathia* from Greek *sympatheia*, from *sympathēs* having common feelings, sympathetic, from SYM- + *pathos* feelings, emotion, experience]

sympetalous /sim'petǝlǝs/ *adj* = GAMOPETALOUS.

symphonic /sim'fonik/ *adj* relating to or having the form or character of a symphony. ➤➤ **symphonically** *adv.*

symphonic poem *noun* an extended orchestral composition, based on a legend, tale, etc.

symphonist /'simfǝnist/ *noun* a composer of symphonies.

symphony /'simfǝni/ *noun* (*pl* **symphonies**) **1a** an extended piece for orchestra, typically in four contrasting movements. **b** a composition of similar proportions.

Editorial note ⸻
Now exclusively used to designate a large-scale work for full orchestra conventionally in four contrasted movements, the term symphony originally had a variety of meanings: in the baroque, for instance, it described vocal music with instruments or the orchestral introductions or interludes in an opera. Its development as a preeminent genre in its own right began in the 18th cent. and reached its classical peak in the 104 symphonies of Haydn. It was taken into wholly new territory by Beethoven, who in his nine symphonies expanded the genre which culminated in the massive, all-embracing works of Mahler in the 1900s — Andrew Clements.

2 something of great harmonious complexity or variety: *The room was a symphony in blue.* **3** *chiefly NAmer* = SYMPHONY ORCHESTRA. [Middle English *symphonie* harmony, via Old French and Latin from Greek *symphōnia*, from *symphōnos* concordant in sound, from SYM- + *phōnē* voice, sound]

symphony orchestra *noun* a large orchestra comprising string, wind, brass, and percussion instruments.

symphysis /'simfisis/ *noun* (*pl* **symphyses** /-seez/) an immovable joint between bones, *esp* where the surfaces are connected by fibrous cartilage in a narrow joint membrane: *pubic symphysis.* ➤➤ **symphyseal** /-'zee-ǝl/ *adj*, **symphysial** /sim'fizi-ǝl/ *adj*. [scientific Latin from Greek *symphysis* state of growing together, from *symphyesthai* to grow together, from SYM- + *phyein* to make grow, bring forth]

sympodium /sim'pohdi-ǝm/ *noun* (*pl* **sympodia** /-di-ǝ/) in botany, an apparent main axis or stem that is formed from secondary axes. ➤➤ **sympodial** *adj*. [scientific Latin *sympodium*, from SYM- + Greek *podion* base]

symposium /sim'pohzi-ǝm/ *noun* (*pl* **symposia** /-zi-ǝ/ *or* **symposiums**) **1a** a formal meeting at which several specialists deliver short addresses on a topic. **b** a published collection of opinions on

a subject, *esp* in a periodical. **2** a party with music and conversation, e.g. one held after a banquet in ancient Greece. [via Latin from Greek *symposion*, from *sympinein* to drink together, from SYM- + *pinein* to drink]

symptom /'simptǝm/ *noun* **1** something giving evidence or indication of a disease or other physical disorder: *Here am I, dying of a hundred good symptoms* — Alexander Pope. **2** something that indicates the existence of something else, *esp* something undesirable: *Crumbling classrooms are a symptom of the lack of investment in education.* ➤➤ **symptomless** *adj*. [via late Latin from Greek *symptōmat-*, *symptōma* happening, attribute, symptom, from *sympiptein* to happen, from SYM- + *piptein* to fall]

symptomatic /simptǝ'matik/ *adj* **1** being a symptom of a disease. **2** concerned with, affecting, or acting on symptoms. **3** characteristic or indicative: *Such behaviour is symptomatic of the decline in moral standards.* ➤➤ **symptomatically** *adv*.

symptomatology /,simptǝmǝ'tolǝji/ *noun* **1** a branch of medical science concerned with the symptoms of diseases. **2** the symptoms characteristic of a disease.

syn. *abbr* **1** synonym. **2** synonymous.

syn- *or* **syl-** *or* **sym-** *prefix* forming words, with the meaning: with, along with, or together: *syllogism*; *sympathy*; *synthesis*. [Middle English via Old French and Latin from Greek, from *syn* with, together with]

synaeresis /si'niǝrisis/ *noun* see SYNERESIS.

synaesthesia (*NAmer* **synesthesia**) /sinǝs'theezyǝ, -zh(y)ǝ/ *noun* a sensation in one part of the body accompanying or brought about by a stimulus in a different part, *esp* a subjective sensation or image of a sense other than the one being stimulated, e.g. an impression of colour produced by a sound. ➤➤ **synaesthetic** /-'thetik/ *adj*. [scientific Latin, from SYN- + *-aesthesia* as in ANAESTHESIA]

synagogue /'sinǝgog/ *noun* **1** the house of worship and communal centre of a Jewish congregation. **2** a Jewish congregation. ➤➤ **synagogal** /-'gogl/ *adj*, **synagogical** /-'gojikl/ *adj*. [Middle English *synagoge* via Old French and late Latin from Greek *synagōgē* assembly, synagogue, from *synagein* to bring together, from SYN- + *agein* to lead]

synapse /'sienaps/ *noun* the point between two nerves across which a nervous impulse is transmitted. ➤➤ **synaptic** /si'naptik/ *adj*, **synaptically** /-'naptikli/ *adv*. [scientific Latin from Greek *synapsis* juncture, from *synaptein* to fasten together, from SYN- + *haptein* to fasten]

synapsis /si'napsis/ *noun* (*pl* **synapses**) the pairing of corresponding chromosomes resulting in their ultimate association and the formation of cross-shaped areas of contact that is characteristic of the first phase of MEIOSIS (cell division producing the sex cells). [scientific Latin from Greek *synapsis*: see SYNAPSE]

synarthrosis /sinah'throhsis/ *noun* (*pl* **synarthroses** /-seez/) an immovable joint between bones united by fibrous tissue, e.g. symphyses. [Greek *synarthrōsis*, from SYN- + *arthrōsis* joint between two bones, from *arthron* joint]

sync[1] *or* **synch** /singk/ *noun informal* synchronization: *The film was out of sync.*

sync[2] *or* **synch** *verb trans informal* (*often* + up) to match (film and sound track) so that they run exactly in synchronization.

syncarpous /sin'kahpǝs/ *adj* said of a flower, fruit, etc: having the carpels united in a compound ovary.

synch[1] /singk/ *noun* see SYNC[1].

synch[2] *verb trans* see SYNC[2].

synchro /'singkroh/ *noun* **1** synchronized swimming. **2** synchromesh.

synchro- *comb. form* forming words, with the meaning: synchronized or synchronous: *synchromesh.* [*synchronized*, past part. of SYNCHRONIZE and SYNCHRONOUS]

synchromesh /'singkrǝmesh/ *noun* a gear system designed to synchronize the speeds of the different moving parts involved in a gear change so that it can be effected smoothly.

synchronic /sing'kronik/ *adj* of or dealing with phenomena, *esp* of language, at one point in time, ignoring historical antecedents: compare DIACHRONIC. ➤➤ **synchronically** *adv*.

synchronicity /,singkrǝ'nisiti/ *noun* the coincidence in a person's life of two or more events which seem to be linked in significance but which have no causal connection.

synchronise *verb trans and intrans* see SYNCHRONIZE.

synchronism /'singkrəniz(ə)m/ *noun* **1** the quality of being synchronous; simultaneousness. **2** chronological arrangement of historical events so as to indicate coincidence or coexistence, or a table showing such an arrangement. >> **synchronistic** /-'nistik/ *adj*, **synchronistically** /-'nistikli/ *adv*.

synchronize *or* **synchronise** /'singkrəniez/ *verb trans* **1** to make (two or more things) synchronous in occurrence or operation: *Let's synchronize watches.* **2** to arrange (events) so as to indicate coincidence or coexistence. **3** to make (sound) exactly simultaneous with the action in a film or a television programme. > *verb intrans* to happen at the same time. >> **synchronization** /-'zaysh(ə)n/ *noun*, **synchronizer** *noun*.

synchronized swimming *noun* exhibition or competitive swimming in which the movements of one or more swimmers are synchronized with a musical accompaniment so as to form changing patterns.

synchronous /'singkrənəs/ *adj* **1** happening, existing, or arising at precisely the same time. **2a** going on or operating together at exactly the same rate. **b** recurring together. **3** involving or indicating synchronism. **4** in physics, having the same PERIOD (time taken to complete one cycle or repeating event). **5** said of an orbit: taking the same time as a rotation of the earth, so that a satellite appears fixed. >> **synchronously** *adv*. [via late Latin from Greek *synchronos*, from SYN- + *chronos* time]

synchronous motor *noun* an electric motor having a speed strictly proportional to the frequency of the operating current.

synchrony /'singkrəni/ *noun* synchronistic occurrence, arrangement, or treatment.

synchrotron /'singkrətron/ *noun* an apparatus that imparts very high speeds to charged particles by combining a high-frequency electric field and a low-frequency magnetic field.

syncline /'singklien/ *noun* a trough of stratified rock in which the layers dip towards each other from either side: compare ANTICLINE. >> **synclinal** /sing'klienl/ *adj*. [earliest as *synclinal*, from SYN- + Greek *klinein* to lean]

syncopate /'singkəpayt/ *verb trans* to modify or affect (musical rhythm) by syncopation. >> **syncopator** *noun*. [medieval Latin *syncopatus*, past part. of *syncopare*, from late Latin *syncope*: see SYNCOPE]

syncopation /singkə'paysh(ə)n/ *noun* a temporary displacement of the regular metrical accent in music caused typically by stressing a weak beat or omitting the strong beat. >> **syncopative** /'singkəpaytiv/ *adj*.

syncope /'singkəpi/ *noun* **1** temporary loss of consciousness; fainting. **2** the dropping of one or more sounds or letters in a word, e.g. in *fo'c'sle* for *forecastle*. >> **syncopal** *adj*. [late Latin *syncope* from Greek *synkopē*, literally 'cutting short', from *synkoptein* to cut short, from SYN- + *koptein* to cut]

syncretise *verb trans and intrans* see SYNCRETIZE.

syncretism /'singkritiz(ə)m/ *noun* **1** the combination of different forms of belief, *esp* religious belief, or practice. **2** the fusion of two or more orig different inflectional forms of words, e.g. the use of *was* for pl and second person sing. subjects in nonstandard English as well as for first and third person sing. >> **syncretic** /sing'kretik/ *adj*, **syncretist** *noun and adj*, **syncretistic** /-'tistik/ *adj*. [scientific Latin from Greek *synkrētismos* federation of Cretan cities, from SYN- + *Krēt-*, *Krēs* Cretan]

syncretize *or* **syncretise** /'singkrietiez/ *verb trans and intrans* to attempt to unify or reconcile (e.g. principles or sects), or to become unified or reconciled. >> **syncretization** /-'zaysh(ə)n/ *noun*.

syncytium /sin'siti-əm/ *noun* (*pl* **syncytia** /-ti-ə/) **1** a mass of living material with many nuclei resulting from fusion of cells. **2** an organism consisting of such a structure. >> **syncytial** /sin'sishəl/ *adj*. [scientific Latin, from SYN- + CYT- + -IUM]

syndactyly /sin'daktili/ *noun* a union of two or more digits that occurs normally, e.g. in many birds, and occasionally as an inherited abnormality in human beings. >> **syndactyl** *adj*, **syndactylism** *noun*. [scientific Latin *syndactylia*, from SYN- + Greek *daktylos* finger]

syndesmosis /sindes'mohsis/ *noun* (*pl* **syndesmoses** /-seez/) a joint in which the touching surfaces of the bones are rough and are bound together by a ligament. >> **syndesmotic** /-'motik/ *adj*. [scientific Latin from Greek *syndesmos* fastening, ligament, from *syndein* to bind together, from SYN- + *dein* to bind]

syndetic /sin'detik/ *adj* **1** using conjunctions to join clauses. **2** said of a clause: connected by means of a conjunction. >> **syndetical** *adj*, **syndetically** *adv*. [Greek *syndetikos* from *syndein* to bind together]

syndic /'sindik/ *noun* **1** an agent who transacts business for a university or corporation. **2** a government administrator in some countries. >> **syndical** *adj*. [French *syndic* via late Latin *syndicus* representative of a corporation, from Greek *syndikos* assistant at law, advocate, representative of a state, from SYN- + *dikē* judgment, case at law]

syndicalism /'sindikəliz(ə)m/ *noun* **1** a system of economic organization in which industries are owned and managed by the workers. **2** a revolutionary doctrine according to which workers should seize control of the economy and the government by direct means, such as a general strike. >> **syndicalist** *adj and noun*. [French *syndicalisme*, from *chambre syndicale* trade union]

syndicate¹ /'sindikət/ *noun* **1** (*treated as sing. or pl*) a group of people or concerns who combine to carry out a particular transaction, e.g. buying or renting property, or to promote a common interest. **2** a business concern that supplies material for simultaneous publication in many newspapers or periodicals. **3a** the office of a syndic. **b** (*treated as sing. or pl*) a council or body of syndics. [French *syndicat*, from *syndic*: see SYNDIC]

syndicate² /'sindikayt/ *verb trans* **1** to sell (e.g. a cartoon) to a syndicate for simultaneous publication in many newspapers or periodicals. **2** to manage (something) by a syndicate. >> **syndication** /-'kaysh(ə)n/ *noun*.

syndrome /'sindrohm/ *noun* **1** a group of signs and symptoms that occur together and characterize a particular medical disorder. **2** a set of concurrent emotions, actions, etc that usu form an identifiable pattern. >> **syndromic** /-'dromik/ *adj*. [scientific Latin, from Greek *syndromē* combination, syndrome, from SYN- + *dramein* to run]

syne¹ /sien, zien/ *adv Scot* since then; ago: *I would have told ye this long syne* — Stevenson. [Middle English (northern and Scottish), contraction of *sithen*: see SINCE¹]

syne² *conj and prep Scot* since.

synecdoche /si'nekdəki/ *noun* a figure of speech in which a word for a part is used to mean the whole, e.g. *50 sail* instead of *50 ships*, or the whole to mean a part, e.g. in 'Leeds defeated Stoke'. >> **synecdochic** /-'dokik/ *adj*, **synecdochical** /-'dokikl/ *adj*, **synecdochically** /-'dokikli/ *adv*. [via Latin from Greek *synekdochē*, from SYN- + *ekdochē* sense, interpretation, from *ekdechesthai* to receive, understand, from EX-² + *dechesthai* to receive]

synecology /sini'koləji/ *noun* a branch of ecology that deals with the structure and development of ecological communities. >> **synecological** /sin,ekə'lojikl/ *adj*. [German *Synökologie*, from SYN- + *Ökologie* ecology]

syneresis *or* **synaeresis** /si'niərisis/ *noun* (*pl* **synereses** /-seez/ *or* **synaereses**) **1** the contraction of two vowels into a diphthong or single vowel. **2** the separation of liquid from a gel caused by contraction. [via late Latin from Greek *synairesis*, from *synairein* to contract, from SYN- + *hairein* to take]

synergic /si'nuhjik/ *adj* working together; cooperating: *synergic muscles*. [scientific Latin *synergicus*, from *synergia*: see SYNERGISM]

synergism /'sinəjiz(ə)m, si'nuh-/ *noun* cooperative action between two or more agencies, e.g. drugs or muscles, whose combined effect is greater than the sum of their separate effects. >> **synergistic** /-'jistik/ *adj*. [scientific Latin *synergismus* and *synergia*, from Greek *synergos* working together, from SYN- + *ergon* work]

synergist /'sinəjist/ *noun* something, e.g. a chemical or muscle, that enhances the effectiveness of an active agent.

synergy /'sinəji, si'nuhji/ *noun* **1** synergism. **2** cooperation between two organizations, e.g. business companies or research laboratories, that achieves more than both would achieve if they worked separately. [scientific Latin *synergia*: see SYNERGISM]

synesthesia /sinees'theezyə, -zh(y)ə/ *noun NAmer* see SYNAESTHESIA.

syngamy /'singgəmi/ *noun* sexual reproduction by union of gametes (reproductive cells; see GAMETE).

synod /'sinəd, 'sinod/ *noun* **1a** the governing assembly of an Anglican PROVINCE (division under an archbishop), diocese, or deanery. **b** a Presbyterian governing body ranking above the PRESBYTERY (local ruling body) and below the general assembly. **c** a regional or national organization of Lutheran congregations. **2** a formal meeting to decide ecclesiastical matters. **3** the ecclesiastical district governed by a synod. ▶ **synodal** *adj.* [via late Latin from Greek *synodos* meeting, assembly, from SYN- + *hodos* way, journey]

synodic /si'nodik/ *adj* relating to a CONJUNCTION (apparent meeting or passing of two stars, planets, or satellites) or the period between two successive conjunctions of the same celestial bodies. [Greek *synodikos*, from *synodos*: see SYNOD]

synodical /si'nodikl/ *adj* **1** of or relating to a synod. **2** = SYNODIC.

synodic month *noun* = LUNAR MONTH.

synonym /'sinənim/ *noun* any of two or more words or expressions in a language that are used with the same meaning, e.g. *begin* and *start*. ▶ **synonymic** /-'nimik/ *adj*, **synonymical** /-'nimikl/ *adj*, **synonymity** /-'nimiti/ *noun*. [Middle English *sinonyme* via Latin from Greek *synōnymon*, neuter of *synōnymos* synonymous, from SYN- + *onyma* name]

synonymous /si'noniməs/ *adj* **1** having the character of a synonym. **2** alike in meaning or significance; closely associated: *brand names that are synonymous with quality.* ▶ **synonymously** *adv*, **synonymousness** *noun*.

synonymy /si'nonimi/ *noun* (*pl* **synonymies**) **1** the character of being synonymous. **2** the study or distinguishing of synonyms. **3** a list or collection of synonyms.

synopsis /si'nopsis/ *noun* (*pl* **synopses** /-seez/) a condensed statement or outline, e.g. of a narrative. [via late Latin from Greek *synopsis* comprehensive view, from *synopsesthai* to be going to see together, from SYN- + *opsesthai* to be going to see]

synopsize *or* **synopsise** /si'nopsiez/ *verb trans* to make a synopsis of (e.g. a novel).

synoptic[1] /si'noptik/ *adj* **1** providing a comprehensive view of a whole. **2** (**Synoptic**) of or being the first three Gospels of the New Testament. **3** relating to or displaying meteorological conditions that exist simultaneously over a broad area. ▶ **synoptical** *adj*, **synoptically** *adv*. [Greek *synoptikos*, from *synopsesthai*: see SYNOPSIS]

synoptic[2] *noun* any of the first three Gospels of the New Testament, or their authors.

synovia /si'nohvi-ə, sie-/ *noun* a transparent viscous lubricating fluid secreted by a joint or tendon membrane. ▶ **synovial** *adj*. [scientific Latin *sinovia*]

synovitis /sienə'vietəs/ *noun* inflammation of a synovial membrane.

syntactic /sin'taktik/ *adj* of or conforming to the rules of syntax or syntactics. ▶ **syntactical** *adj*, **syntactically** *adv*. [scientific Latin from Greek *syntaktikos* arranging together, from *syntassein*: see SYNTAX]

syntactics *pl noun* (*treated as sing. or pl*) a branch of SEMIOTICS (study of signs and symbols in languages) dealing with the formal relations between signs in abstraction from what they signify.

Editorial note
The philosophical background of 'syntactics' is what distinguishes it from syntax, which is the standard usage within linguistics. Most linguists think of syntax as the study of sentence structure, but some also use the term to include the analysis of word structure (otherwise known as morphology), and some extend it to larger stretches of language, such as conversational dialogues — Professor David Crystal.

syntagm /'sintag(ə)m/ *noun* a syntactic sequence of linguistic forms; a linguistic construction. ▶ **syntagmatic** /-'matik/ *adj*. [scientific Latin *syntagma* collection of statements, from Greek, from *syntassein*: see SYNTAX]

syntagma /sin'tagmə/ *noun* (*pl* **syntagmas** *or* **syntagmata** /-'mahtə/) = SYNTAGM.

syntax /'sintaks/ *noun* **1a** the way in which words are put together to form phrases, clauses, or sentences. **b** the part of grammar dealing with this. **c** a set of rules for this. **2** in computing, the set of rules governing a programming language. [French *syntaxe* via late Latin from Greek *syntaxis*, from *syntassein* to arrange together, from SYN- + *tassein* to arrange]

synth /sinth/ *noun informal* = SYNTHESIZER.

synthesis /'sinthəsis/ *noun* (*pl* **syntheses** /-seez/) **1** the composition or combination of separate or diverse elements into a coherent whole: compare ANALYSIS. **2** the artificial production of a substance by chemical reaction. **3** in philosophy, the third and final stage of a reasoned argument: compare ANTITHESIS, THESIS.

▶ **synthesist** *noun*. [via Latin from Greek *synthesis*, from *syntithenai* to put together, from SYN- + *tithenai* to put, place]

synthesize *or* **synthesise** /'sinthisiez/ *verb trans* **1** to produce (something) by synthesis. **2** to combine (things) to form a whole. **3** to produce (sound) electronically.

synthesizer *noun* an electronic musical instrument that produces a sound that can be altered in many ways, e.g. to mimic other instruments, and is usu played by means of a keyboard.

synthetic[1] /sin'thetik/ *adj* **1** produced by chemical reaction, *esp* as an imitation of something natural: *synthetic drugs*; *synthetic silk*. **2** not genuine or sincere. **3** in philosophy, relating to or involving synthesis; not analytic. **4** said of a language: characterized by the addition of inflections, e.g. the English possessive *-'s*, rather than by the use of separate words, e.g. the preposition *of*, to show the function of a word in a sentence. ▶ **synthetical** *adj*, **synthetically** *adv*. [Greek *synthetikos* of composition, component, from *syntithenai*: see SYNTHESIS]

synthetic[2] *noun* a product of chemical synthesis, *esp* a textile fibre.

synthetize *or* **synthetise** /'sinthitiez/ *verb trans* = SYNTHESIZE.

syphilis /'sifəlis/ *noun* a contagious usu sexually transmitted and often congenital disease caused by a spirochaetal bacterium: compare PRIMARY SYPHILIS, SECONDARY SYPHILIS, TERTIARY SYPHILIS. ▶ **syphilitic** /-'litik/ *adj and noun*. [scientific Latin, named after *Syphilus*, hero of the poem *Syphilis sive Morbus Gallicus* (*Syphilis or the French disease*) by Girolamo Fracastoro d.1553, Italian physician and poet]

syphon[1] /'siefən/ *noun* see SIPHON[1].

syphon[2] *verb trans* see SIPHON[2].

SYR *abbr* Syria (international vehicle registration).

Syrah /si'rah/ *noun* = SHIRAZ (1), (2). [French *Syrah* SHIRAZ]

Syriac /'siriak/ *noun* a literary and liturgical language that is a form of Aramaic, *esp* used by eastern Christian Churches. [via Latin from Greek *syriakos* Syrian, from *Syria*, ancient country in Asia]

Syrian /'siri-ən/ *noun* a native or inhabitant of Syria in SW Asia. ▶ **Syrian** *adj*.

syringe[1] /sə'rinj/ *noun* a device used to inject fluids into or withdraw them from the body or its cavities; *esp* one that consists of a hollow barrel fitted with a plunger and a hollow needle. [Middle English *syring* via medieval Latin from Greek *syring-*, *syrinx* panpipe, tube]

syringe[2] *verb trans* to flush out or spray (something) with a syringe.

syrinx /'siringks/ *noun* (*pl* **syringes** /si'rinjeez/ *or* **syrinxes**) **1** a set of panpipes. **2** a vocal organ of birds that is a modification of the lower trachea, bronchi, or both. [scientific Latin from Greek *syrinx* panpipe]

syrup (*NAmer* **sirup**) /'sirəp/ *noun* **1a** a thick sticky solution of sugar and water, often flavoured or mixed with medicinal substances. **b** the concentrated juice of a fruit or plant; *esp* the thick sticky liquid obtained from crushed sugarcane after evaporation and before crystallization in sugar manufacture. **2** cloying sweetness or sentimentality. ▶ **syrupy** *adj*. [Middle English *sirup* via early French *sirop* and medieval Latin *syrupus* from Arabic *sharāb* beverage]

systaltic /si'staltik, si'stawltik/ *adj* alternately and regularly contracting and dilating; pulsating. [Greek *systaltos* from *systellein*: see SYSTOLE]

system /'sistəm/ *noun* **1a** a regularly interacting or interdependent group of items forming a unified whole: *the solar system.* **b** a group of body organs that together perform one or more usu specified functions: *the digestive system.* **c** a group of devices or an organization forming a network, *esp* for distributing something or serving a common purpose: *a heating system.* **2** a form of social, economic, or political organization: *the capitalist system.* **3** an organized set of doctrines, ideas, or principles, usu intended to explain the arrangement or working of a systematic whole: *the Newtonian system of mechanics.* **4a** an organized or established procedure: *a filing system.* **b** a manner of classifying, symbolizing, or formalizing things: *a taxonomic system.* **5** harmonious arrangement or pattern; order. **6** a major division of rocks usu larger than a series and including all those formed during a geological period or era. **7** the body considered as a functional unit: *Overeating is bad for the system.* **8** (**the system**) an organized society or social situation regarded as stultifying or restrictive: *You can't beat the system.* ✱ **get something out**

of one's system *informal* to stop thinking or worrying about something. ➤ **systemless** *adj.* [via late Latin from Greek *systēmat-*, *systēma*, from *synistanai* to combine, from SYN- + *histanai* to cause to stand]

systematic /sistə'matik/ *adj* **1** relating to or consisting of a system. **2** methodical in procedure or plan; thorough: *The investigation was systematic.* **3** of or concerned with classification; *specif* taxonomic. ➤ **systematically** *adv.* [via late Latin from Greek *systēmatikos*, from *systēmat-*, *systēma*: see SYSTEM]

systematic error *noun* a statistical error that is not determined by chance but by an effect that distorts the information in a definite direction.

systematics *pl noun* (*treated as sing. or pl*) the branch of biology dealing with the classification and study of living things with regard to their natural relationships.

systematise *verb trans* see SYSTEMATIZE.

systematist /'sistəmətist, si'stem-, si'stee-/ *noun* **1** a maker or follower of a system. **2** a taxonomist.

systematize *or* **systematise** /'sistəmətiez/ *verb trans* to arrange (e.g. information) according to a set method; to order systematically. ➤ **systematization** /-'zaysh(ə)n/ *noun,* **systematizer** *noun.*

systemic[1] /si'steemik, si'stemik/ *adj* **1** of or common to a system, e.g. affecting the body generally. **2** said of an insecticide, pesticide, etc: making the organism, *esp* a plant, toxic to a pest by entering the tissues. ➤ **systemically** *adv.*

systemic[2] *noun* a systemic pesticide.

systemize *or* **systemise** *verb trans* to systematize (something). ➤ **systemization** /-'zaysh(ə)n/ *noun,* **systemizer** *noun.*

systems analysis *noun* the analysis of a complex task or procedure by computer in order to discover ways of accomplishing it more efficiently. ➤ **systems analyst** *noun.*

systole /'sistəli/ *noun* a rhythmically recurrent contraction; *esp* the contraction of the heart by which the blood is forced onwards and the circulation kept up: compare DIASTOLE. ➤ **systolic** /si'stolik/ *adj.* [Greek *systolē*, from *systellein* to contract, from SYN- + *stellein* to send]

syzygy /'siziji/ *noun* (*pl* **syzygies**) **1** a configuration in which three celestial bodies, e.g. the sun, moon, and earth, lie in a straight line. **2** any pair of things. ➤ **syzygial** /si'ziji-əl/ *adj.* [via late Latin from Greek *syzygia* conjunction, from *syzygos* yoked together, from SYN- + *zygon* yoke]

T¹ *or* **t** *noun* (*pl* **T's** *or* **Ts** *or* **t's**) **1a** the 20th letter of the English alphabet. **b** a written character or design denoting this letter. **c** the sound represented by this letter, one of the English consonants. **2** an item designated as T, *esp* the 20th in a series. ✳ **to a T** to perfection; exactly.

T² *abbr* **1** temperature. **2** tenor. **3** tera-. **4** tesla. **5** Thailand (international vehicle registration). **6** true.

T³ *symbol* surface tension.

T⁴ *abbr* the chemical symbol for tritium.

t¹ *abbr* **1** tare. **2** teaspoon or teaspoonful. **3** temperature. **4** tempo. **5** in grammar, tense. **6** time. **7** ton. **8** tonne. **9** transitive. **10** troy or troy weight.

t² *symbol* in statistics, distribution.

't *pronoun archaic or literary* it: *'Tis strange what a man may do; The worst of 't is we now have no horse.*

-t *suffix* forming the past tense and past part. of some verbs: *meant; spoilt.*

TA *abbr* Territorial Army.

Ta *abbr* the chemical symbol for tantalum.

ta /tah/ *interj Brit, informal* thanks. [orig baby talk]

TAB *abbr* **1** *Aus, NZ* Totalizator Agency Board. **2** typhoid-paratyphoid A and B vaccine.

tab¹ /tab/ *noun* **1** a flap or loop of material by which something can be held or lifted. **2** a projection from a card or file, or something fitted to a file, that gives information about its contents. **3** an appendage or extension, e.g. any of a series of small pendants forming a decorative border or edge of a garment. **4** *chiefly NAmer* a bill, *esp* for a meal or drinks. **5** a small auxiliary AEROFOIL (winglike part) hinged to one of the main movable controlling surfaces of an aircraft to help stabilize the aircraft in flight. **6** *Brit* an insignia or marking on the collar of a military uniform that denotes a high-ranking officer. ✳ **keep tabs on** *informal* to keep (somebody or something) under close surveillance. **pick up the tab** *informal* to pay a bill, e.g. in a restaurant, or other expenses: *If you go on this course, the company will pick up the tab.* [perhaps related to TAG¹]

tab² *verb trans* (**tabbed, tabbing**) **1** to provide or ornament (something) with tabs. **2** *NAmer* to single (somebody or something) out; to designate (them).

tab³ *noun* = TABULATOR. [by shortening]

tab⁴ *verb* (**tabbed, tabbing**) ➤ *verb trans* to arrange (data, etc) in tabular form; to tabulate (it). ➤ *verb intrans* to move or place something by means of a tabulator: *Tab across to the third column.*

tab⁵ *noun informal* a tablet, *esp* one containing an illegal drug. [short for TABLET]

tab⁶ *noun* **1** (*usu in pl*) a narrow curtain used *esp* for masking offstage space in a theatre. **2** (*in pl*) = TABLEAU CURTAINS.

tabard /'tabəd/ *noun* **1** a short emblazoned tunic worn by a knight over his armour. **2** a herald's official cape or coat emblazoned with the arms of his lord or sovereign. **3** a straight-hanging sleeveless outer garment, *esp* one with slits at the sides for part or all of its length, worn by women. [Middle English from Old French *tabart*]

tabaret /'tabərit/ *noun* a hard-wearing upholstery fabric with alternate satin and watered silk stripes. [prob alteration of TABBY¹]

Tabasco /tə'baskoh/ *noun trademark* a hot pungent condiment sauce made from capsicums. [from *Tabasco*, a state in Mexico]

tabbouleh /tə'boohlay, 'taboohlay/ *noun* a Middle Eastern salad dish made from bulgur wheat mixed with tomatoes, olive oil, mint, and parsley and usu served with lettuce. [Arabic *tabbūla*]

tabby¹ /'tabi/ *noun* (*pl* **tabbies**) **1a** a domestic cat with a usu brownish, grey, or yellow coat striped and mottled with darker shades. **b** a female domestic cat. **2a** a plain-weave fabric. **b** *archaic* a plain silk taffeta fabric, *esp* with an irregular wavy finish. [French *tabis* via medieval Latin from Arabic *'attābī*, from *Al-' Attābīya*, quarter in Baghdad where the silk fabric was manufactured]

tabby² *adj* said of a cat: striped and mottled with darker colours; brindled.

tabernacle /'tabənakl/ *noun* **1a** (*often* **Tabernacle**) a tent sanctuary used by the Israelites during the Exodus. **b** the name in some denominations of Christianity, e.g. the Nonconformists and Mormons, for their meeting place or church. **2a** a receptacle for the consecrated bread and wine used at Communion, often forming part of an altar. **b** a niche in a church wall, e.g. for a statue. **3** a support in which a mast is stepped and pivoted so that it can be lowered, e.g. to negotiate a bridge. ➤➤ **tabernacular** /-'nakyoolə/ *adj*. [Middle English via French from Latin *tabernaculum* tent, dimin. of *taberna* hut, TAVERN]

tabes /'taybeez/ *noun* (*pl* **tabes**) **1** *technical* emaciation, *esp* a wasting of the flesh or a body part that accompanies a chronic disease. **2** = TABES DORSALIS. ➤➤ **tabetic** /tə'betik/ *adj and noun*. [Latin *tabes*, literally 'wasting away']

tabescent /tə'besənt/ *adj* affected or characterized by or causing progressive wasting.

tabes dorsalis /daw'sahlis/ *noun* a form of late stage syphilis that affects the sensory nerves and is characterized by progressive degeneration of the nerve fibres, causing severe stabbing pains in the legs and abdomen, unsteady walking movements, and often the loss of control of the bladder. [scientific Latin *tabes dorsalis* dorsal tabes]

tabla /'tahblə/ *noun* a pair of small hand drums of different sizes used *esp* in Indian classical music. [Persian and Urdu *tablah* and Hindi *tablā*, all from Arabic *ṭabl* drum]

tablature /'tablǝchǝ/ *noun* an instrumental notation indicating the string, fret, keys, or fingering to be used instead of the note to be sounded. [early French *tablature* from Italian *tavolatura*, from *tavolare* to enclose with boards, also 'to set to music', ultimately from Latin *tabula* board, TABLE¹]

table¹ /'taybl/ *noun* **1a** a piece of furniture consisting of a smooth flat slab of wood, etc fixed on legs or some other support. **b** any similar object, such as a BIRD TABLE or OPERATING TABLE: *when the evening is spread out against the sky like a patient etherized upon a table* — T S Eliot. **2a** the food served at a meal: *He always keeps a good table.* **b** the act or instance of assembling to eat; a meal: *We rarely all sit down at table together.* **c** (*used before a noun*) suitable for a table or for use at table: *table manners; table linen.* **3a** a group of people assembled at, or as if at, a table: *a famous poker table, which challenged all comers* — Harvey Fergusson. **b** a meeting for negotiation: *They strove to bring the warring nations to the peace table.* **4a** a systematic arrangement of data, usu in rows and columns, for ready reference. **b** a systematically arranged list of figures, information, etc: *There should be a table of contents at the front of the book.* **c** = MULTIPLICATION TABLE: *The trouble is, kids don't learn their tables at school like we used to.* **5a** the upper flat surface of a precious stone. **b** a broad area of land elevated on all sides; a plateau or tableland. **c** a horizontal stratum of rock. **d** the upper or front surface of a stringed musical instrument. **6a** a STRING COURSE. **b** a raised or inset rectangular panel on a wall, bearing decoration or an inscription. **7** either of the two leaves of a backgammon board, or either half of a leaf. *** lay something on the table** to put something forward for discussion. **on the table** *chiefly Brit* under discussion or put forward for discussion: *There are several items on the table, so we'd better get started.* **turn the tables** to bring about a reversal of the relative conditions or fortunes of two contending parties [from the idea of turning the board or table round in games such as chess, so reversing the opponents' positions]. **under the table** into a stupor: *My mother could drink you under the table, you wimp.* [Old English *tabule* and Old French *table*, both from Latin *tabula* board, tablet, list]

table² *verb trans* **1** to enter (e.g. information) in a table, or to present (it) in the form of a table. **2a** *Brit* to place (a matter) on the agenda. **b** *NAmer* to remove (a matter) from consideration indefinitely.

tableau /'tabloh/ *noun* (*pl* **tableaux** *or* **tableaus** /'tabloh(z)/) **1** a graphic description or representation of a scene. **2** a dramatic or artistic grouping of figures. **3a** a depiction of a scene usu presented on a stage by silent and motionless costumed participants. **b** a point in a stage performance when those on stage briefly remain motionless. [French *tableau* picture, from early French *tablel*, dimin. of *table*: see TABLE¹]

tableau curtains *pl noun* stage curtains that have diagonal cords attached to the lower ends allowing them to be drawn upwards and towards the wings.

tableau vivant /,tabloh vee'vonh (*French* tablo vivã) / *noun* (*pl* **tableaux vivants** /,tabloh vee'vonh/) = TABLEAU (3A). [French *tableau vivant* living picture]

tablecloth *noun* a cloth that is spread over a dining table before the places are set.

table dancing *noun* erotic dancing performed for customers in nightclubs at their tables. ➤➤ **table dancer** *noun*.

table d'hôte /,tahble 'doht/ *noun* (*pl* **tables d'hôte** /,tahblǝ/ *or* **table d'hôtes** /'doht/) a meal consisting of a fixed number of courses with a limited choice or no choice of dishes, provided at a fixed price: compare À LA CARTE. ➤➤ **table d'hôte** *adj and adv.* [French *table d'hôte*, literally 'host's table']

tableland *noun* a broad level area of land elevated on all sides; a PLATEAU¹.

table licence *noun Brit* a licence that allows alcoholic drinks to be served in a restaurant only to patrons who are having a meal.

table manners *pl noun* the conventional polite behaviour expected when one is eating a meal at table.

table mat *noun* a small often decorative mat placed under a hot dish to protect the surface of a table from heat.

table salt *noun* fine-grained free-flowing salt suitable for use at the table and in cooking.

tablespoon *noun* **1** a large spoon used for serving. **2** = TABLESPOONFUL.

tablespoonful *noun* (*pl* **tablespoonfuls**) **1** as much as a tablespoon can hold. **2** a unit of measure equal to about 15ml (about 0.5fl oz).

tablet /'tablit/ *noun* **1a** a small solid shaped mass or capsule of medicinal material. **b** a compressed block of a solid material: *a tablet of soap.* **2** a flat slab or plaque suitable for or bearing an inscription. **3** a pad or block of paper for writing on. **4** in Scotland, a hard fudge made from butter, sugar, and condensed milk, sometimes with other flavourings or ingredients, usu cut into small squares. [Middle English *tablett* from early French *tablete*, dimin. of *table*: see TABLE¹]

table talk *noun* informal conversations that are carried on during meal times.

table tennis *noun* a game based on tennis and played with round wooden bats and a small hollow plastic ball on an indoor table divided by a low net.

tableware *noun* utensils, e.g. glasses, dishes, plates, and cutlery, for serving and eating food at the table.

table wine *noun* a wine considered suitable for drinking with food, often one that is relatively inexpensive.

tabloid /'tabloyd/ *noun* **1** a newspaper of a type having a relatively small page size, usu 30cm x 40cm (12in. x 16in.), and containing news stories in condensed form and informal language, often of a sensational nature or written in a sensationalist style, and with many photographs: compare BROADSHEET. **2** (*used before a noun*). **a** relating to, denoting, suitable for, or characteristic of a tabloid or tabloids: *tabloid journalism.* **b** dealing with material similar to that contained in tabloids, and doing so in a similar style: *tabloid television.* [TABLET + -OID; orig a trademark for a concentrated form of drugs and chemicals; the current senses come from the idea of condensation and compression]

taboo¹ *or* **tabu** /tǝ'booh, ta'booh/ *adj* **1a** too sacred or evil to be touched, named, or used. **b** set apart as unclean or accursed. **2** forbidden, *esp* on grounds of morality, tradition, or social usage rather than being illegal.

Word history
Tongan *tabu* set apart, forbidden. The word is believed to have been introduced into English by the English explorer Captain James Cook during his voyages in the 1760s and 1770s.

taboo² *or* **tabu** *noun* (*pl* **taboos** *or* **tabus**) **1** a prohibition imposed by social custom: *Whenever a taboo is broken, something good happens, something vitalizing* — Henry Miller. **2** a prohibition, *esp* in Polynesia, against touching, saying, or doing something for fear of harm from a supernatural force. **3** an object, word, behaviour, etc that is prohibited.

taboo³ *or* **tabu** *verb trans* (**taboos** *or* **tabus, tabooed** *or* **tabued, tabooing** *or* **tabuing**) **1** to set (something) apart as taboo. **2** to avoid or ban (something) as taboo.

tabor *or* **tabour** /'taybǝ/ *noun* a small drum with one head of soft calfskin used, *esp* formerly, to accompany a pipe or fife played by the same person. [Middle English from Old French *tabour* drum]

tabouret (*NAmer* **taboret**) /'tabǝrit/ *noun* **1** a cylindrical seat or stool without arms or back. **2** in sewing, = TAMBOUR¹ (2A). **3** a small tabor. [French *tabouret*, literally 'small drum', dimin. of *tabour* drum]

tabu¹ /tǝ'booh, ta'booh/ *adj* see TABOO¹.

tabu² *noun* see TABOO².

tabu³ *verb trans* see TABOO³.

tabular /'tabyoolǝ/ *adj* **1a** said of data, statistics, etc: arranged in a table. **b** said of quantities: computed by means of a table. **2a** having a broad flat surface. **b** laminar. **c** said of a crystal: having two parallel flat faces. ➤➤ **tabularly** *adv.* [Latin *tabularis* of boards, from *tabula* board, tablet, TABLE¹]

tabula rasa /,tabyoolǝ 'rahsǝ/ *noun* (*pl* **tabulae rasae** /,tabyoolee 'rahsee/) **1** a person's mind, *esp* at birth, thought of as blank or empty before receiving outside impressions. **2** the state of having no preconceived notions. **3** a chance for a fresh start, with nothing carried over from the past. [Latin *tabula rasa* smoothed or erased tablet]

tabularize *or* **tabularise** /'tabyoolǝriez/ *verb trans* = TABULATE¹. ➤➤ **tabularization** /-'zaysh(ǝ)n/ *noun.* [Latin *tabula* tablet, TABLE¹]

tabulate¹ /'tabyoolayt/ *verb trans* to arrange (data, etc) in tabular form. ➤➤ **tabulable** /'tabyoolǝbl/ *adj*, **tabulation** /-'laysh(ǝ)n/ *noun.* [Latin *tabula* tablet, TABLE¹]

tabulate[2] /'tabyoolit, -layt/ *or* **tabulated** /-laytid/ *adj* having a flat surface.

tabulator /'tabyoolaytə/ *noun* **1** a business machine that sorts and selects information from marked or perforated cards. **2** an attachment to a typewriter or software on a computer that is used for arranging data in columns, or the key operating this.

tacamahac /'takəməhak/ *or* **tacmahack** /'takməhak/ *noun* **1** any of several aromatic gum resins used *esp* for incense. **2** any of various trees that produce these gums, e.g. the BALSAM POPLAR. [Spanish *tacamahaca* from Nahuatl *tecamaca*]

tacet /'tayset, 'taset/ *verb intrans* used in music to indicate that a particular instrument or voice is to remain silent during a movement or long section. [Latin *tacet* (it) is silent, from *tacēre* to be silent]

tacheometer /taki'omitə/ *noun* = TACHYMETER. [French *tachéomètre*, from Greek *tachys* swift + French *-mètre* -METER[2]]

tachism *or* **tachisme** /'tashiz(ə)m/ *noun* a form of ACTION PAINTING (painting by spattering or smearing paint on canvas) that originated in the 1940s in France and was seen as a way of expressing the unconscious. ➤➤ **Tachist** *adj and noun*, **tachist** *adj and noun*. [French *tachisme*, from *tache* stain, spot, blob]

tachistoscope /tə'kistəskohp/ *noun* an apparatus for briefly exposing visual stimuli, used in the study of learning, attention, and perception. ➤➤ **tachistoscopic** /-'skopik/ *adj*. [Greek *tachistos*, superl of *tachys* swift + -SCOPE]

tacho /'takoh/ *noun* (*pl* **tachos**) *informal* **1** = TACHOGRAPH. **2** = TACHOMETER.

tacho- *comb. form* forming words, denoting: speed: *tachometer*.

tachograph /'takəgrahf, -graf/ *noun* a device for automatically recording the speed and time of travel of a vehicle, *esp* a lorry.

tachometer /ta'komitə/ *noun* a device for indicating speed of rotation, e.g. of a vehicle engine.

tachy- *comb. form* forming words, with the meaning: rapid; accelerated: *tachycardia*. [Greek, from *tachys* rapid]

tachycardia /taki'kahdi·ə/ *noun* relatively rapid heart action, whether normal, e.g. after exercise, or abnormal and indicative of disease: compare BRADYCARDIA.

tachygraphy /ta'kigrəfi/ *noun* shorthand, *esp* as used by the ancient Greeks and Romans and in medieval Greek and Latin writing. ➤➤ **tachygraphic** /-'grafik/ *adj*, **tachygraphical** /-'grafikl/ *adj*. [Greek *tachygraphos* stenographer, from TACHY- + *graphein* to write]

tachymeter /ta'kimitə/ *noun* a surveying instrument for determining distance, bearings, etc quickly.

tachyon /'taki·on/ *noun* a hypothetical ELEMENTARY PARTICLE (particle smaller than atom) that travels faster than light. [TACHY- + -ON[2]]

tachyphylaxis /ˌtakifi'laksis/ *noun* (*pl* **tachyphylaxes** /-seez/) **1** a rapid decrease in a patient's response to a drug. **2** a rapid loss of sensitivity to a toxic substance produced e.g. by repeated inoculations of small doses of it. [TACHY- + *phylaxis* as in PROPHYLAXIS]

tacit /'tasit/ *adj* implied or understood but not actually expressed. ➤➤ **tacitly** *adv*. [French *tacite* from Latin *tacitus* silent, past part. of *tacēre* to be silent]

taciturn /'tasituhn/ *adj* not communicative or talkative: *a terrible, beetle-browed, mastiff-mouthed, yellow-skinned, broad-bottomed, grim-taciturn individual* — Thomas Carlyle. ➤➤ **taciturnity** /-'tuhniti/ *noun*, **taciturnly** *adv*. [French *taciturne* from Latin *taciturnus*, from *tacitus*: see TACIT]

tack[1] /tak/ *noun* **1** a small short sharp-pointed nail, usu with a broad flat head. **2** a long loose straight stitch usu used to hold two or more layers of fabric together temporarily. **3a** the direction of a sailing vessel with respect to the direction of the wind. **b** the run of a sailing vessel on one tack. **c** a change of course from one tack to another. **d** a course of action: *He's off on a new tack*. **e** an approach to something; a way of thinking or dealing with something: *They're on completely the wrong tack*. **4** the lower forward corner of a fore-and-aft sail. **5** a sticky or adhesive quality. [Middle English *tak* something that attaches, prob from Old French *tache* big nail, clasp, of Germanic origin]

tack[2] *verb trans* **1a** to fasten or attach (something) with tacks. **b** to sew (something) with long loose stitches, often temporarily. **2** (*often* + on) to add (something) as a supplement. **3** to change the course of (a sailing vessel) from one tack to the other by turning the bow towards the wind. ➤ *verb intrans* **1a** to tack a sailing vessel.

b said of a sailing vessel: to undergo being tacked. **2a** to follow a zigzag course. **b** to change one's policy or attitude abruptly. ➤➤ **tacker** *noun*.

tack[3] *noun* equipment, e.g. saddles, stirrups, harnesses, etc, used in horse riding. [shortening of TACKLE[1]]

tack[4] *noun* cheap, poorly made, worthless, or rubbishy things or material. [back-formation from TACKY[2]]

tackle[1] /'takl/ *noun* **1** a set of equipment used in a particular activity: *fishing tackle*. **2a** a ship's rigging. **b** an assembly of ropes and pulleys arranged to gain mechanical advantage for hoisting and pulling. **3a** the act or an instance of tackling in sport. **b** in American football, either of the players second from the end of the front line of a defensive or offensive formation. [Middle English *takel*, prob from early Dutch or Low German *takel* ship's rigging, from *taken* to get hold of]

tackle[2] *verb trans* **1a** to take hold of or grapple with (somebody or something), *esp* in an attempt to stop or restrain (them or it). **b** to take or attempt to take the ball from (an opposing player) in hockey or football. **c** to seize and pull down or stop (an opposing player with the ball) in rugby or American football. **2a** to set about dealing with (a problem, etc). **b** to speak to (somebody) about a difficult matter: *Someone is going to have to tackle her about her attitude some day*. **3** (*often* + up) to attach or secure (something) with or as if with tackle. **4** (*often* + up) to harness (a horse). ➤ *verb intrans* to tackle an opposing player. ➤➤ **tackler** *noun*.

tacky[1] *adj* (**tackier, tackiest**) slightly sticky to the touch: *The varnish is nearly dry, but it's still a bit tacky*. ➤➤ **tackiness** *noun*. [TACK[1]]

tacky[2] *adj* (**tackier, tackiest**) *informal* **1** shabby; shoddy. **2** in poor taste; vulgar. ➤➤ **tackily** *adv*, **tackiness** *noun*. [US *tacky* an inferior horse or person, of unknown origin]

tacmahack /'takməhak/ *noun* see TACAMAHAC.

taco /'takoh, 'tahkoh/ *noun* (*pl* **tacos**) a tortilla that is filled, e.g. with meat, then rolled or folded and fried. [Mexican Spanish from Spanish *taco* bung, snack]

tact /takt/ *noun* a keen sense of how to handle people or affairs so as to avoid friction or giving offence: *It is tact that is golden, not silence* — Samuel Butler. ➤➤ **tactful** *adj*, **tactfully** *adv*, **tactfulness** *noun*, **tactless** *adj*, **tactlessly** *adv*, **tactlessness** *noun*. [French *tact* sense of touch, from Latin *tactus*, past part. of *tangere* to touch]

tactic /'taktik/ *noun* **1** a method of employing forces in combat. **2** a device for achieving an end. [Greek *taktikē*, fem of *taktikos*: see TACTICS]

-tactic *comb. form* see -TAXIS.

tactical *adj* **1** of tactics in general or a tactic, e.g.: **a** denoting small-scale actions serving a larger purpose: compare STRATEGIC. **b** made or carried out with only a limited or immediate end in view. **c** characterized by adroit planning or manoeuvring to accomplish a purpose. **d** said of voting or a vote: made in favour of the candidate most likely to defeat the candidate one least wants to win rather than for the candidate one prefers but who has little chance of winning. **2** of combat tactics, e.g.: **a** involving operations of local importance or brief duration: compare STRATEGIC. **b** said e.g. of nuclear weapons: of or designed for air attack in close support of ground forces: compare STRATEGIC. ➤➤ **tactically** *adv*.

tactician /tak'tish(ə)n/ *noun* somebody skilled in tactics.

tactics *pl noun* (*treated as sing. or pl*) **1a** the science and art of disposing and manoeuvring forces in combat: compare STRATEGY. **b** the art or skill of employing available means to accomplish an end. **2** a system or mode of procedure. [Greek *taktika*, neuter pl of *taktikos* of order, of tactics, fit for arranging, from *tassein* to arrange, place in battle formation]

tactile /'taktiel/ *adj* **1** of or perceptible by the sense of touch. **2** said of a person: in the habit of touching people in a friendly way. ➤➤ **tactilely** *adv*, **tactility** /tak'tiliti/ *noun*. [French *tactile* from Latin *tactilis*, from *tangere* to touch]

tactual /'takchooəl/ *adj formal* = TACTILE. ➤➤ **tactually** *adv*. [Latin *tactus*: see TACT]

tad /tad/ *noun informal* a small amount. ✳ **a tad** somewhat, rather: *It's a tad difficult to explain*. [prob from English dialect *tad* TOAD]

tadger /'tajə/ *or* **todger** /'tojə/ *noun Brit, informal* a penis. [origin unknown]

tadpole /'tadpohl/ *noun* the larva of an amphibian, such as a frog or toad, having in the early stage a rounded body, a long tail, no legs, and external gills. As it matures, the tail shrinks and legs and internal gills develop. [Middle English *taddepol*, from *tode* toad + *polle* head]

Tadzhik /tah'jik, 'tahjik/ *noun* see TAJIK.

taedium vitae /ˌteedi·əm 'veetie, 'vietee/ *noun* weariness or loathing of life. [Latin *taedium vitae*]

tae kwon do /ˌtie kwon 'doh, ˌtay/ *noun* an Oriental system of self-defence, developed in Korea, that features kicking and punching and resembles karate. [Korean *tae kwon do* kick fist method]

tael /tayl/ *noun* **1** any of various units of weight of E Asia, *esp* a Chinese unit of weight of approximately 38 grams (1.75oz). **2** any of various Chinese units of currency based on the value of a tael weight of silver. [Portuguese *tael* from Malay *tahil* weight]

taenia (*NAmer* **tenia**) /'teeni·ə/ *noun* (*pl* **taeniae** /'teeni·ee/ *or* **taenias**) **1** any of various bandlike anatomical structures, e.g. a band of nervous tissue or muscle. **2** any of a genus of tapeworms: genus *Taenia*. **3** in the ENTABLATURE (upper facade) of a classical building or building in classical style, a narrow band between the ARCHITRAVE (lowest part) and the FRIEZE¹ (middle section). **4** in ancient Greece, a narrow decorative headband. [via Latin from Greek *tainia* band, ribbon]

taeniasis (*NAmer* **teniasis**) /tee'nie·əsis/ *noun* infestation with or disease caused by tapeworms. [TAENIA + -IASIS]

taffeta /'tafitə/ *noun* a crisp plain-woven lustrous fabric of various fibres used *esp* for women's clothing. [Middle English from early French *taffetas* via Old Italian and Turkish from Persian *tāftah*, from *tāftan* to shine]

taffia /'tafi·ə/ *noun* see TAFIA.

taffrail /'tafrayl, 'tafrəl/ *noun* a rail round the stern of a ship.

Word history
alteration of *tafferel* from Dutch *tafereel* panel, picture, dimin. of *tavel* table. *Tafferel* orig meant 'carved panel', later the flat part of a ship's stern above the transom, which was often decorated with carvings, or the rail along the top of it; hence the alteration *taffrail*, by association with RAIL¹.

Taffy /'tafi/ *noun* (*pl* **Taffies**) *Brit, chiefly derog* a Welshman. [modification of Welsh *Dafydd* David, a common Welsh forename]

taffy *noun* (*pl* **taffies**) *NAmer* a toffee-like sweet made from molasses or brown sugar. [earlier form of TOFFEE; origin unknown]

tafia *or* **taffia** /'tafi·ə/ *noun* a type of cheap W Indian rum distilled from molasses or the waste byproducts from brown sugar refining. [French *tafia*, from W Indian Creole, alteration of RATAFIA]

tag¹ /tag/ *noun* **1a** a piece of hanging or attached material; *specif* a flap or loop on a garment by which to hang it up, or that carries information such as washing instructions. **b** a cardboard, plastic, metal, etc marker used for identification or classification: *The price tags were hidden under the boxes the rings were in.* **c** in computing, a label attached to data. **2** = ELECTRONIC TAG. **3a** a saying or maxim; a trite quotation used for superficial effect: *How does that old Latin tag go? Quis custodiet ipsos custodes?* **b** a recurrent or characteristic verbal expression. **c** a final speech or line, e.g. in a play or joke, *esp* one that serves to clarify a point, sum up a moral point, or create a dramatic effect. **d** the refrain of a song. **4a** a loose hanging piece of torn cloth; a tatter. **b** a piece of matted wool or hair. **5** a rigid binding on an end of a shoelace. **6a** a descriptive or identifying word or phrase accompanying or replacing a name. **b** a personal symbol, typically a pseudonym, sprayed in paint in a public place by a graffiti writer. **7** a decorative elaboration or flourish, e.g. in a person's signature; a PARAPH. **8** the tip of an animal's tail, *esp* if of a different colour to the rest of the tail. **9** a small piece of bright material, e.g. tinsel, round the shank of the hook at the end of the body of an artificial fishing fly. [Middle English *tagge*, perhaps of Scandinavian origin]

tag² *verb* (**tagged, tagging**) ➤ *verb trans* **1** to provide or mark (somebody or something) with a tag or as if with a tag: e.g. **a** to supply (something) with an identifying marker, price label, etc: *He tagged every item in his shop.* **b** to label or brand (somebody or something) as something: *We had him tagged as a chauvinist from the start.* **c** to fit (somebody) with an ELECTRONIC TAG (device for tracking where a person is). **d** to distinguish (a chemical compound or substance) by making it radioactive; to label it. **2** (*often* + on) to attach (something) as an addition; to append (it). **3** to remove tags of wool or hair from (e.g. an animal). ➤ *verb intrans* (*usu* + along/on) to go with somebody, keeping close to them: *We're going off on an adventure and we don't want you little ones tagging along with us.*

tag³ *noun* **1** a game in which one player chases others and tries to make one the next chaser by touching them. **2** the act of tagging (one's partner) in TAG WRESTLING. [origin unknown]

tag⁴ *verb trans* (**tagged, tagging**) **1** to touch (somebody) in or as if in a game of tag. **2** to touch the hand of (one's partner) in TAG WRESTLING in order to change over active and inactive roles in the contest.

Tagalog /tə'gahlog/ *noun* (*pl* **Tagalogs** *or collectively* **Tagalog**) **1** a member of an indigenous people inhabiting central Luzon in the Philippines. **2** the Austronesian language spoken by this people. ➤➤ **Tagalog** *adj*. [Tagalog, from *tagá* native + *ilog* river]

tag day *noun NAmer* = FLAG DAY.

tag end *noun* **1** the last part: *the tag end of the day.* **2** a loose end of thread.

tagetes /'tajitəs/ *noun* (*pl* **tagetes**) any of a genus of marigold: genus *Tagetes*. [Latin genus name; named after *Tages*, an Etruscan god who sprang from the ploughed earth]

tagliatelle /talyə'teli/ *pl noun* (*treated as sing. or pl*) pasta in the form of narrow ribbons. [Italian *tagliatelle*, pl of *tagliatella*, from *tagliare* to cut, from late Latin *taliare*]

tag line *noun* = TAG¹ (3C).

tag question *noun* an interrogative phrase or clause, e.g. *didn't she?, did he?*, attached to the end of a statement, usu to invite agreement with what has been said.

tag team *noun* a team of two wrestlers in TAG WRESTLING.

tag wrestling *noun* a form of wrestling involving two teams of two wrestlers, in which only one member of each team is in the ring at any one time. A wrestler may ask his partner to replace him at any time by touching his hand.

tahini /tə'heeni/ *noun* a thick oily paste made from sesame seeds, used as a seasoning *esp* in Middle Eastern cookery. [Arabic *ṭaḥana* to crush]

Tahitian /tə'heesh(ə)n/ *noun* **1** a native or inhabitant of Tahiti, island in the S Pacific. **2** the Polynesian language of the people of Tahiti. ➤➤ **Tahitian** *adj*.

tahr /tah/ *noun* see THAR.

tahsil /tə'seel/ *noun* an administrative or tax district of certain states in India. [Persian and Urdu *taḥsil*, from Arabic, literally 'collection of revenue']

tahsildar /tah'seeldah/ *noun* a collector of revenues in India. [Persian and Urdu *taḥsildār*, from *taḥsil*: see TAHSIL]

Tai /tie/ *noun* **1** a member of a group of peoples of SE Asia, including the Thai. **2** a group of Sino-Tibetan languages including Lao and Thai. ➤➤ **Tai** *adj*. [variant of THAI]

t'ai chi /ˌtie 'jee, ˌtie 'chee/ *or* **t'ai chi ch'uan** /'chwahn/ *noun* an Oriental system of physical exercise, based on a sequence of slow controlled movements, and thought to relieve stress and develop an inner spiritual force. [Chinese *t'ai chi ch'üan*, also written *taijiquan*, from *t'ai* extreme + *chi* limit + *ch'üan* fist, boxing]

taiga /'tiegə/ *noun* moist coniferous forest that begins where the tundra ends and is dominated by spruces and firs. [Russian *taïga*]

tail¹ /tayl/ *noun* **1a** the rear end of the body of an animal. **b** an extension from this, e.g. a usu flexible extension of the backbone of a vertebrate or the feathers at the rear end of a bird. **2a** the rear part of an aircraft consisting of horizontal and vertical stabilizing surfaces with attached control surfaces. **b** the luminous trail of gas and dust behind a comet. **c** a line or queue of people or things. **d** a long section of braided hair; = PIGTAIL. **e** the back or last part of something. **3a** the lower or inferior part of something. **b** the bottom edge or margin of a printed page. **4** (*in pl*). **a** = COAT TAILS. **b** = TAILCOAT; *specif* formal evening dress for men including a tailcoat and a white bow tie. **5** (*in pl, but treated as sing. or pl*) the reverse of a coin: compare HEAD¹ (4): *Heads you win, tails you lose.* **6** *informal*. **a** a person, e.g. a detective, who follows or keeps watch on somebody: *We'll put a tail on him this evening.* **b** the trail of a fugitive: *He soon had the police on his tail.* **7** *chiefly NAmer, informal* the buttocks. **8** *informal* women considered sexually: *He's out chasing tail.* ✳ **bit/piece of tail** a woman regarded in terms of her sexual attractiveness. **turn tail** *informal* to reverse direction and run away. **with one's tail between one's legs** having been totally defeated or confounded. ➤➤ **tailed** *adj*, **tailless** *adj*, **tail-like** *adj*. [Old English *tægel*]

tail² *verb trans* **1** *informal* to follow (somebody) for purposes of surveillance. **2a** to remove the tail of (an animal). **b** to remove the stalk of (e.g. a gooseberry): compare TOP² (3C). **3** to fasten an end of (a tile, brick, or timber) into a wall or other support. **4** to connect (something) at an end or (things) end to end. ➤ *verb intrans* **1** (often + back) to form a long queue: *Traffic is tailing back all the way to junction17*. **2** (+ off/away) to diminish gradually in strength, volume, quantity, etc.

tail³ *adj* in law, limited as to TENURE (right or term of holding something); entailed (see ENTAIL¹ (2)). [Middle English *taille* from Old French *taillié*, past part. of *taillier*: see TAILOR¹]

tail⁴ *noun* in law, = ENTAIL²: *in tail*.

tailback *noun* a long queue of motor vehicles, *esp* when caused by an obstruction that blocks the road.

tailboard *noun* a hinged or removable board or gate at the rear of a vehicle.

tailcoat *noun* a coat with tails, *esp* a man's formal evening coat with two long tapering skirts at the back. ➤➤ **tailcoated** *adj*.

tail end *noun* **1** the back or rear end. **2** the concluding period.

tailender *noun* **1** in cricket, a relatively inexpert batsman who bats towards the end of a side's innings. **2** somebody or something that finishes or arrives later than others; a straggler.

tailgate¹ *noun* **1** *esp NAmer* = TAILBOARD. **2** a door at the rear of a car, *esp* one that opens upwards.

tailgate² *verb intrans and trans* to drive dangerously close behind (another vehicle).

tailing *noun* **1** the part of a projecting stone or brick that is inserted in a wall. **2** (*usu in pl, but treated as sing.*) residue separated in the preparation of grain, ore, etc.

tail light *noun* a usu red warning light mounted at the rear of a vehicle; a REAR LIGHT.

tailor¹ /'taylə/ *noun* somebody whose occupation is making or altering clothes, *esp* men's suits and other made-to-measure outer garments. [Middle English *taillour* from Old French *tailleur*, from *taillier* to cut, limit, from late Latin *taliare*, from Latin *talea* twig, cutting]

tailor² *verb* (**tailored, tailoring**) ➤ *verb trans* **1** said of a tailor: to make (a garment) for a particular customer. **2** (+ for/to) to make or adapt (something) to suit a special need or purpose. ➤ *verb intrans* to do the work of a tailor.

tailorbird *noun* any of several species of Asiatic, E Indian, and African warblers that stitch leaves together to support and hide their nests: genus *Orthotomus*.

tailored *adj* **1** said of clothing: **a** made by a tailor. **b** fashioned or fitted; cut so as to fit the figure well. **2a** wearing well-fitted clothing. **b** neat; well-cared for: *tailored lawns*.

tailoring *noun* **1** the business or occupation of a tailor. **2** the work or workmanship of a tailor.

tailor-made *adj* **1** said of clothes: made by a tailor to fit a particular customer. **2** made or fitted for a particular use or purpose.

tailpiece *noun* **1** a piece added at the end; an appendage. **2** a triangular piece from which the strings of a stringed instrument are stretched to the pegs. **3** an ornament placed below the text on a page, e.g. at the end of a chapter: *Well … if I am to turn over a new page, this may figure as a tail-piece to the old* — Henry James. **4** a short beam or rafter with one end fastened in a wall and the other end supported by a beam across an opening.

tailpipe *noun* **1** the exit pipe of the exhaust system of a motor vehicle's engine. **2** the part of a jet engine that carries the exhaust gases rearwards and discharges them through an outlet.

tailplane *noun* the horizontal stabilizing projection of an aircraft's tail.

tailrace *noun* **1** the stream of a MILLRACE (channel in which water flows to and from a watermill) beyond the mill wheel. **2** a channel in which mine tailings (residues separated from ore; see TAILING) are floated off.

tail rotor *noun* a small stabilizing propeller on the tail of a helicopter.

tailskid *noun* **1** a runner used as part of the landing gear of an aircraft and attached to the underside of the aircraft's tail. **2** a skid that starts with a vehicle's rear wheels.

tailspin *noun* **1** a spiralling, often uncontrolled, dive by an aircraft. **2** *informal* a mental or emotional collapse; a loss of capacity to cope or react. **3** *informal* a state of chaos or panic: *Problems in Eastern markets could tip the Western economies into a tailspin*.

tailstock *noun* an adjustable part of a lathe that holds the fixed spindle.

tailwind *noun* a wind blowing in the same general direction as a vehicle, aircraft, or ship, is travelling.

Taino /'tienoh/ *noun* (*pl* **Tainos** *or collectively* **Taino**) **1** a member of an extinct people formerly inhabiting the Antilles and Bahamas. **2** the Arawakan language of this people. ➤➤ **Taino** *adj*.

Word history

Taino *taino* noble, lord. Words from the Taino language that have passed into English, mostly by way of Spanish, include *barbecue, cassava, hammock, hurricane, maize, potato,* and *tobacco*.

taint¹ /taynt/ *verb trans* **1** to touch or affect (somebody or something) slightly with something bad: *So many people round here are tainted with prejudice*. **2** to affect (something) with putrefaction; to spoil (it). **3** to contaminate (somebody) morally; to corrupt (them). ➤ *verb intrans archaic* said *esp* of food or water: to become affected with putrefaction; to spoil or go bad. [partly from Middle English *tainten* to colour, from early French *teint*, past part. of *teindre*, from Latin *tingere* to dip, moisten, tinge; partly from Middle English *tuynten* from early French *atuint*, past part. of *ataindre*: see ATTAIN]

taint² *noun* **1** a contaminating mark or influence. **2** a defect or flaw. **3** a slight trace of contamination or of something bad or undesirable. ➤➤ **taintless** *adj*.

taipan /'tiepan/ *noun* a large, brown, extremely venomous snake of Australia and New Guinea: *Oxyuranus scutellatus*. [Wik Munkan (extinct Aboriginal language) *dhayban*]

Taiwanese /tiewə'neez/ *noun* (*pl* **Taiwanese**) a native or inhabitant of Taiwan. ➤➤ **Taiwanese** *adj*.

taj /tahj/ *noun* a tall conical hat worn in some Muslim countries. [via Arabic from Persian *taj* crown, crest, cap]

Tajik *or* **Tadzhik** /tah'jik, 'tahjik/ *noun* (*pl* **Tajiks** *or* **Tadzhiks** *or collectively* **Tajik** *or* **Tadzhik**) **1** a member of an indigenous people inhabiting Tajikistan, Afghanistan, Uzbekistan, and China. **2** (*also* **Tajiki, Tadzhiki** /tah'jeeki/) the Iranian language spoken by this people. ➤➤ **Tadzhik** *adj*, **Tajik** *adj*. [Persian *tajik*]

taka /'tahkə, 'tahkah/ *noun* (*pl* **taka**) the basic monetary unit of Bangladesh, divided into 100 paisa. [Bengali *ṭākā* rupee, from Sanskrit *ṭaṅka* a stamped coin]

takahe /'tahkahee/ *noun* a rare flightless New Zealand bird related to the rails: *Notornis mantelli* and *Porphyrio mantelli*. [Maori *takahe*]

take¹ /tayk/ *verb* (*past tense* **took** /took/, *past part.* **taken** /'taykən/) ➤ *verb trans* **1** to reach for (something) and hold it. **2** to grasp or grip (something): *He took her arm and led her across the road*. **3a** to get (somebody or something) into one's possession or control. **b** to seize or capture (somebody or something) physically: *They took no prisoners*. **4** to acquire or use (something) without authority or right. **5a** to capture (an opponent's piece in a board game). **b** to win (cards) in a card game. **6a** to lead or carry (somebody or something) to another place: *The bus will take you into town; Shall I take him some tea?* **b** to use (something) as a route or means of transport: *I'll take the train; Which road shall we take?* **7** to bring (somebody or something) to a particular state: *His ability will take him to the top*. **8** to choose (somebody or something). **9** to remove or subtract (something). **10a** to remove (somebody) by death: *He was taken in his prime*. **b** to end (somebody's life). **11** to choose or make use of (something): *She decided to take the green one*. **12a** to eat or drink (something): *Do you take sugar in your tea?* **b** to expose oneself to (e.g. sun or air) for pleasure or physical benefit. **13** to undertake or perform (an action, etc): *to take a walk; to take aim; to take legal action*. **14** to be affected by (a feeling): *She took pity on him and gave him some money*. **15** to commit oneself to (somebody or something): *He had taken a vow of silence; Her mother always took his side*. **16** to adopt or advance (a point of view, opinion, etc): *I'd take a more lenient view now*. **17** to do or use (something) for some purpose: e.g. **a** to have recourse to (something) as an instrument for doing something: *to take measures*. **b** to find (safety or refuge) somewhere. **18** to assume or gain (a certain form or attribute). **19** to proceed to occupy or hold (something): *to take a seat; to take office; to take possession*. **20** to claim (something) as rightfully one's own: *You can't take all the credit for our success*. **21a** to need or require (something): *It takes two to speak the truth – one to speak and another to hear* — Henry David Thoreau. **b** to use or accept (something) as a necessary component: *The camera takes a special cartridge*. **c** to wear (a certain size of clothing). **d** in grammar, to have or require (something) as the typical pattern: *Transitive verbs take an object*. **22** to derive or draw (something) from somebody or something: *The* book takes its title from the name of the hero. **23** to accept (an action, etc): *I don't think the table would take a polish*. **24a** to obtain or ascertain (something, e.g. information) as the result of a special procedure: *The police took his fingerprints; They take a census every twenty years*. **b** to get or record (something) in writing: *Who's going to take notes?* **c** to get or record (somebody or something) by photography; to make (a photograph, etc). **25** to receive or accept (something), whether willingly or reluctantly: *She was accused of taking a bribe; Are you willing to take a bet?* **26** to accept (a risk, etc) or use (an opportunity, etc). **27a** to apply oneself to the study of (a subject). **b** to study for and receive (a degree, etc). **28** to secure (a position, etc) in a contest, etc: *The following year he took second place.* **29a** to submit to or undergo (something unpleasant): *They took a lot of criticism*. **b** to put up with or endure (something). **30** to support or withstand (something): *I wonder if the rope will take my weight*. **31a** to accept (something) as true. **b** to follow (advice). **c** to accept (something) with the mind in a specified way: *She took the news calmly*. **32a** to have (something), *esp* for enjoyment: *You need to take a holiday*. **b** to feel or experience (something): *I take no pleasure in this; She's very quick to take offence*. **33a** to accept (money, etc) in payment: *They won't take dollars here*. **b** to receive (something) in compensation. **34** to accommodate or hold (something): *The suitcase wouldn't take another thing*. **35a** to apprehend or understand (something): *They were slow to take his meaning*. **b** to consider (somebody or something) in a certain way: *We can take that as settled, then; Do you take me for a fool?* **c** to consider or use (somebody or something) as an example: *Take Shakespeare, now*. **36a** to deal with (something): *Let's take the comments one at a time*. **b** to consider or view (something) in a specified relation: *Taken together, the details were significant*. **37** to go round, into, over, etc (something, e.g. a corner, street, etc): *She took the corner on two wheels; The third turning on the right*. **38** to catch or come upon (somebody) in a specified situation, action, or way: *His arrival took us by surprise.* **39** to delight or win the approval of (somebody): *He was quite taken with her at their first meeting.* **40** to perform or conduct (e.g. a class or service) as a duty or task. **41a** to strike or hit (somebody or something) in or on a specified part: *The blow took him full on the chin*. **b** to be struck or hit by (something): *He took the blow full on the chin*. **42** to cheat or swindle (somebody). **43** to bring into or receive in a particular human relationship or connection: *She was reduced to taking lodgers; It's time he took a wife.* **44** to have sexual intercourse with (somebody). **45a** to catch (a ball) in basketball or cricket. **b** in cricket, to cause the batting side to lose (a wicket). **46** to let in (something): *The boat was taking water fast.* **47** said of a horse: to jump (a fence). ➤ *verb intrans* **1** said of a plant or seed: to begin to grow; to form a root. **2** to work or mix well: *This is a glue that takes well on cloth*. **3** to win favour; to be popular. **4** to burn effectively. **5** said of a fish: to catch hold of a lure or bait. **6** to admit of being photographed. ✳ **be taken ill/sick** to fall ill. **take after** to resemble (an older relative) in appearance or character: *He takes after his father*. **take against** *chiefly Brit* to come to dislike (somebody or something). **take it** to understand or assume (something): *I take it she's not coming*. **take it upon oneself** to agree or presume (to do something). **take somebody or something apart 1** to dismantle (e.g. a piece of machinery); to separate (something) into its component parts. **2** to analyse or dissect (something, e.g. a proposal). **3** *informal* to deal with (somebody) roughly or angrily, *esp* because of a failure or misdemeanour. **take that!** said when hitting or attempting to hit somebody. **take to 1** to form a liking for (somebody or something): *I really took to the new member of staff.* **2** to adapt to or fit in with (something). **3** to go to or into (something), *esp* for escape or refuge. **4** to begin to do (something). **what it takes** the qualities or resources needed for success or for the attainment of some goal: *When it comes to bravery, she's got what it takes.* ➤➤ **takable** *adj*, **takeable** *adj*, **taker** *noun*. [Old English *tacan* from Old Norse *taka*]

take² *noun* **1** the act or an instance of taking (something). **2a** the killing, capturing, or catching of something, e.g. game or fish. **b** the number or quantity, e.g. of animals, fish, or pelts, taken at one time; a catch or haul. **3a** the uninterrupted recording, filming, or televising of something, e.g. a gramophone record or film sequence. **b** the recording or scene produced by one take. **4a** the amount of money received, e.g. from a business venture, sales, or admission charges; proceeds or takings. **b** a share or cut. **5** *chiefly NAmer, informal* interpretation or slant. **6** the act or an instance of seizing bait. **7** a catch: *That was a good take by the wicketkeeper.* **8a** a local or general bodily reaction indicative of successful vaccination. **b** a successful union, e.g. of a stem graft. ✳ **on the take** *informal* taking bribes.

takeaway¹ *adj* **1** *Brit* said of a meal, etc: taken away from its place of sale rather than eaten on the premises. **2** said of a shop or restaurant: that sells such food.

takeaway² *noun Brit* **1** a cooked meal that is eaten away from the premises from which it was bought: *She had a Chinese takeaway for supper.* **2** a shop or restaurant that sells takeaways.

take away¹ *verb trans* **1** to remove (something) or deprive somebody of (something): *Take away hatred from some people, and you have men without faith* — Eric Hoffer. **2** to subtract (an amount or number). **3** (*often* + from) to put an end to (pain, etc). **4** to buy (food) for eating elsewhere. ➤ *verb intrans* (+ from) to detract from or spoil (something): *Nothing should take away from the happiness of the day.*

take away² *prep* subtracting: *Thirteen take away four is nine.*

take back *verb trans* **1** to lead or accompany (somebody or something) to a former place. **2** to return (unsatisfactory goods) to the place where they were bought. **3** to accept (somebody or something) again into one's possession or affections. **4** to retract (an accusation, etc). **5** (*often* + to) to remind (somebody) of the past. **6** in printing, to move (text) to the previous line.

take down *verb trans* **1** to remove or dismantle (a fitting). **2** to write (something) on paper, etc. **3** to lower (clothing) without removing it.

take-home pay *noun* the part of gross salary or wages remaining after deductions, e.g. for income tax, insurance, pension contributions, etc.

take in *verb trans* **1** to offer accommodation or shelter to (somebody). **2** to include (something). **3** *informal* to deceive or trick (somebody). **4** to perceive or understand (something). **5** to make (a garment) smaller, e.g. by altering the positions of the seams or making tucks. **6** to accept (paid work) into one's house. **7** to furl (a flag).

taken /'tayk(ə)n/ *verb past part.* of TAKE¹.

takeoff *noun* **1** an imitation, *esp* a caricature or impersonation. **2** the act of leaving or a rise from a surface, e.g. in making a jump, dive, or flight or in the launching of an aircraft or rocket. **3** a starting point; a point at which something starts or takes off.

take off *verb trans* **1** to remove (something, *esp* an item of clothing). **2** to release (e.g. a brake). **3** to discontinue or withdraw (a service, etc). **4** to deduct (an amount). **5** to take or spend (a period of time) as a holiday, rest, etc. **6** to mimic or ridicule (a person's manner or actions, etc). ➤ *verb intrans* **1** said of an aircraft, etc: to become airborne. **2** to begin a leap or spring. **3** *informal* to leave abruptly. **4** *informal* to be suddenly successful.

take on *verb trans* **1** to agree to (a task or undertaking). **2** to contend with or challenge (an opponent or rival). **3** to engage or hire (somebody as staff, etc). **4** to assume or acquire (e.g. an appearance or quality): *The city takes on a carnival air at New Year.* ➤ *verb intrans informal* to become emotional or distraught: *They cried and took on something terrible* — Bob Hope.

takeout *noun* **1** the action or act or an instance of taking out; *esp* a bid made in bridge that takes a partner out of a bid, DOUBLE² (5) or REDOUBLE² (bids that increase the value of tricks won and lost). **2** *NAmer* = TAKEAWAY².

take out *verb trans* **1** to extract or remove (something). **2** to escort or accompany (somebody) for recreation. **3a** to obtain (an official document or authorization): *to take out a warrant.* **b** to acquire (insurance) by making the necessary payment. **4** (+ on) to give vent to (feelings): *Let them take out their frustrations on one another.* **5** *informal* to kill or disable (somebody) or destroy or disable (something). **6** to overcall (a bridge partner) in a different suit. ✳ **take it out of** to fatigue or exhaust (somebody). **take it out on** to vent one's anger or frustration on (somebody or something). **take somebody out of himself/herself** to provide somebody with a needed distraction or diversion.

takeover *noun* the action or act or an instance of taking over, *esp* the act of gaining control of a business company by buying a majority of the shares.

take over *verb trans* **1** to assume control or possession of (something). **2** in printing, to move (text) to the following line. ➤ *verb intrans* **1** to assume control or possession. **2** to become dominant.

take up *verb trans* **1a** to pick up or lift up (something). **b** to remove (something) by lifting or pulling up. **2** to receive or absorb (something): *Plants take up nutrients from the soil.* **3a** to begin to engage in or study (something). **b** to raise (a matter) for consideration. **4** to occupy (e.g. space or time) entirely or exclusively. **5** to shorten (e.g. a garment). **6** (+ on) to respond favourably to a challenge or offer: *I'll take you up on that.* **7** to resume or continue (something): *She took up the story where her mother had left off.* **8a** to discuss (a matter) further. **b** (+ on) to argue with (somebody) about something they have said. ⟩ *verb intrans* to resume or continue. ✻ **take up with** to begin to associate with (somebody).

take-up *noun* **1a** the action of taking something up, by gathering, contraction, absorption, adjustment, etc. **b** any of various devices for tightening or drawing in something, e.g. slack or lost motion. **2** the act of claiming something, such as a grant or benefit.

takin /'tahkeen/ *noun* a large heavily built hoofed mammal with a shaggy coat and backward-pointing horns. It lives in the mountains of China, the Himalayas, and Myanmar (formerly Burma) and is related to the goats: *Budorcas taxicolor.* [Mishmi (Tibeto-Burman language of NE India)]

taking *adj dated* attractive; captivating.

takings *pl noun* money, *esp* the amount earned by a business during a specified period.

tala[1] /'tahlə/ *noun* any of the traditional rhythmic patterns of Indian music. [Sanskrit *tāla*, literally 'hand-clapping']

tala[2] *noun* the basic monetary unit of Western Samoa, divided into 100 sene. [Samoan *tala*, from DOLLAR]

talapoin /'taləpoyn/ *noun* **1** in Thailand and Myanmar, a Buddhist monk or priest. **2** a small West African monkey with a long tail and a greenish tinge to its fur: *Miopithecus talapoin* and *Cercopithecus talapoin.* [French *talapoin* Buddhist monk, from Portuguese *talapão* from Mon (language related to Khmer and Vietnamese) *tala poi* our lord]

talaria /tə'leəri·ə/ *pl noun* in Greek and Roman mythology, winged sandals worn by certain deities, *esp* Hermes or Mercury. [Latin *talaria*, neuter pl of *talaris* of the ankles, from *talus* ankle]

talc[1] /talk/ *noun* **1** = TALCUM POWDER. **2** a soft usu greenish or greyish mineral with a greasy feel, consisting of a magnesium silicate. ⟩⟩ **talcose** /'talkohs/ *adj,* **talcous** /'talkəs/ *adj.* [early French *talc* mica, via medieval Latin *talk* from Arabic *ṭalq*]

talc[2] *verb trans* (**talced** *or* **talcked, talcing** *or* **talcking**) to treat (something) with talc; to apply talc to (it).

talcum[1] /'talkəm/ *noun* = TALCUM POWDER. [medieval Latin *talcum* mica, alteration of *talk:* see TALC[1]]

talcum[2] *verb trans* (**talcumed, talcuming**) to put talcum powder on (something).

talcum powder *noun* a preparation made from finely powdered talc, often perfumed, used for dusting the body to give it a pleasant smell or to absorb moisture.

tale /tayl/ *noun* **1** a series of events or facts told or presented; an account. **2a** a usu fictitious narrative; a story: *Life is as tedious as a twice-told tale* — Shakespeare. **b** a lie; a falsehood: *I don't believe you. That's just a tale.* **c** a malicious report or piece of gossip: *Don't you go telling tales, now.* [Old English *talu*]

talebearer *noun dated* a person who spreads rumours or reveals secrets, *esp* maliciously. ⟩⟩ **talebearing** *adj and noun.*

talent /'talənt/ *noun* **1a** a special often creative or artistic aptitude. **b** general ability or intelligence. **c** a person or people of talent in a field or activity. **2** *informal* (*treated as sing. or pl*) people considered in terms of their sexual attractiveness or as potential romantic or sexual partners: *He sat outside the pub eyeing up the local talent.* **3a** any of several ancient units of weight. **b** a unit of money equal to the value of a talent of gold or silver. ⟩⟩ **talented** *adj,* **talentless** *adj.*

Word history
Old English *talente* from Latin *talenta,* pl of *talentum* unit of weight or money, from Greek *talanton.* The meaning was influenced by the parable of the talents in Matthew 25:14–30.

talent scout *noun* a person engaged in discovering and recruiting people with talent in a specialized field of activity, *esp* in sport or entertainment.

talent show *noun* a show consisting of a series of individual performances by amateurs who may be selected for training or professional engagements if talented.

tales /'tayleez, taylz/ *noun* (*pl* **tales**) **1** (*in pl*) a number of people summoned or selected to make up a deficiency in the available number of jurors. **2** a writ summoning people as tales. [Middle English *tales* talesmen, from medieval Latin *tales de circumstantibus*

such (persons) of the bystanders; from the wording of the writ summoning them]

talesman /'tayleezmən, 'taylzmən/ *noun* (*pl* **talesmen**) a person added to a jury, usu from among bystanders, to make up a deficiency in the available number of jurors; a member of a group of TALES.

tali /'taylie/ *noun* pl of TALUS[2].

talipes /'talipeez/ *noun technical* = CLUB FOOT. [scientific Latin, from Latin *talus* ankle + *pes* foot]

talipot /'talipot/ *noun* a tall showy palm, found in India, Sri Lanka, and the Philippines, which has huge fan-shaped leaves used as umbrellas, fans, etc: *Corypha umbraculifera.* [Bengali *tālipōt* palm leaf, from Sanskrit *tālī palm* + *tāla* leaf]

talisman /'talizmən, 'talismən/ *noun* (*pl* **talismans**) **1** an engraved object believed to act as a charm to avert evil and bring good fortune. **2** something believed to produce magical or miraculous effects. ⟩⟩ **talismanic** /-'manik/ *adj,* **talismanically** /-'manikli/ *adv.* [French *talisman,* Spanish *talismán* or Italian *talismano,* all from Arabic *ṭilsam,* ultimately from Greek *telein* to initiate into the mysteries]

talk[1] /tawk/ *verb intrans* **1a** to produce speech; to speak: *Is the baby talking yet?* **b** to imitate human speech: *He taught his budgie to talk.* **2a** (*often* + about) to express or exchange ideas by means of spoken words. **b** (*often* + to/with) to have discussions; to confer: *I need to talk to you about tomorrow's meeting.* **3** to convey information or communicate in any way, e.g. with signs or sounds: *He can make his trumpet talk.* **4a** to speak idly; to chatter or gossip: *You know how people talk.* **b** to reveal secret or confidential information: *You'll never make me talk.* **5** to give a talk or lecture. **6** to have influence or the power to persuade: *Money talks.* ⟩ *verb trans* **1a** to express (something) in speech: *He's talking nonsense.* **b** to make (something) the subject of conversation or discourse; to discuss (it): *OK, let's talk business.* **c** *informal* to discuss (something): *We're talking serious money here.* **2** to use (a language) for conversing or communicating; to be able to communicate in (a language). **3** (*usu* + into/out of) to bring (somebody) to a specified state by talking: *She talked them into going; I couldn't talk him out of it.* ✻ **now you're talking** *informal* now at last you are saying something interesting, sensible, etc. **talk about** *informal* used to introduce a comment, often a wry or ironic comment, about something: *Talk about bad luck. She won the lottery and couldn't find her ticket!* **you can talk 1** it is easy for you to say that as you are not involved, have nothing to fear, etc. **2** (*also* **you can't talk**) you are just as bad yourself; you are in no position to comment or criticize. ⟩⟩ **talker** *noun.* [Middle English *talken,* of Germanic origin]

talk[2] *noun* **1** a verbal exchange of thoughts or opinions; a conversation: *When two Englishmen meet, their first talk is of the weather* — Dr Johnson. **2a** meaningless speech; bluster or empty threats: *It's all talk. He'll not actually do anything.* **b** rumour; gossip: *It's just talk. I don't believe a word of it.* **3** (*also in pl*) a formal discussion or exchange of views. **4** the topic of interested comment or gossip: *The scandal is the talk of the town.* **5** an address or lecture, often a relatively informal one. **6** communicative sounds or signs functioning as talk: *baby talk.*

talkative /'tawkətiv/ *adj* given to talking a lot. ⟩⟩ **talkatively** *adv,* **talkativeness** *noun.*

talkback *noun* **1** in radio and television broadcasting, a communication system that allows staff to talk to each other without what they are saying being broadcast. **2** *Aus, NZ* = PHONE-IN.

talk back *verb intrans* to answer impertinently.

talk down *verb trans* **1** to defeat or silence (somebody) by argument or by loud talking. **2** to give radio instructions to (a pilot) to assist the landing of a plane when conditions are difficult. ⟩ *verb intrans* (+ to) to speak in a condescending or oversimplified fashion to.

talkie /'tawki/ *noun* a cinema film with a synchronized sound track, *esp* as distinct from a silent one. [TALK[1] + MOVIE]

talking book *noun* a recording of somebody reading a book or magazine aloud, produced *esp* for the benefit of the blind.

talking head *noun* somebody talking directly to the audience on television, e.g. reading the news, being interviewed, or giving an opinion, unsupported by film or other illustrative material: *Labour's final party election broadcast last night consisted largely of* *three dozen talking heads – some famous, others unknown – telling the viewers why it was time for a change* — Daily Telegraph.

talking picture *noun* = TALKIE.

talking point *noun* a subject of conversation or argument.

talking shop *noun* **1** a place where matters are discussed, often with no useful outcome. **2** the people involved in this.

talking-to *noun* (*pl* **talking-tos**) *informal* a reprimand or scolding.

talk out *verb trans* **1** to clarify or settle (e.g. a problem) by discussion: *They tried to talk out their differences.* **2** to prevent (a bill) from being passed by a legislative assembly by continuing discussion beyond the time allotted for it.

talk over *verb trans* to review or consider (something) in conversation.

talk radio *noun* **1** a radio broadcast in which topical issues are discussed, often with the audience having a chance to phone in with their views. **2** radio or a radio station that concentrates on this type of broadcasting.

talk round *verb trans* to persuade or convince (somebody) at some length: *They didn't agree at first, but we talked them round.*

talk show *noun* = CHAT SHOW.

tall /tawl/ *adj* **1a** of above average height: *a tall woman; tall trees.* **b** of a specified height: *five feet tall.* **2** said of a plant: of a higher growing variety or species. **3** highly exaggerated; incredible: *a tall story.* ✳ **a tall order** a task that will be difficult to complete or a requirement that is difficult to fulfil, often unreasonably difficult. ➤➤ **tallish** *adj*, **tallness** *noun*. [Middle English, in the senses 'active', 'handsome, elegant', and 'bold, strong', prob from Old English *getæl* quick, ready]

tallage /'talij/ *noun* **1** a tax levied in the Middle Ages on royal towns and crown lands. **2** in feudal times, a tax levied by a lord on his tenants. [Middle English *taillage, tallage* from Old French *taillage*, from *taillier*: see TAILOR¹]

tallboy *noun* **1** a tall chest of drawers supported on a low legged base. **2** a double chest of drawers usu with the upper section slightly smaller than the lower.

tallith /'talith, 'tahlith, 'talis, 'tahlis (*Hebrew* ta'liːt)/ *or* **tallis** /'talis, 'tahlis/ *noun* (*pl* **talliths** *or* **tallithim** /tahli'theem, -'seem, -'teem/ *or* **tallisim** /-'seem/) a shawl with fringed corners traditionally worn over the head or shoulders by Jewish men during morning prayers and at certain other services. [Hebrew *ṭallīth* cover, cloak]

tallow /'taloh/ *noun* the solid white rendered fat of cattle and sheep, used chiefly in soap, candles, and lubricants. ➤➤ **tallowy** *adj*. [Middle English *talgh, talow*, of Germanic origin]

tall poppy *noun Aus, informal* a wealthy or eminent person, *esp* one who is thought to need cutting down to size.

tall poppy syndrome *noun Aus, informal* the tendency to disparage the achievements of wealthy or eminent people.

tall ship *noun* a sailing ship with tall masts and square rig.

tally¹ /'tali/ *noun* (*pl* **tallies**) **1a** a record or account, e.g. of items or charges: *Is anyone keeping a tally of the phone calls we've had?* **b** a record of the score, e.g. in a game. **2** a part or person that corresponds to an opposite or companion object or member; a counterpart. **3a** a device for visibly recording or accounting *esp* business transactions; *specif* a wooden stick notched with marks representing numbers and split lengthways through the notches so that each of two parties may have a record of a transaction. **b** a notch on a tally stick, or any mark recording a number counted. [Middle English *talye* from medieval Latin *talea, tallia* from Latin *talea* twig, cutting]

tally² *verb* (**tallies, tallied, tallying**) ➤ *verb trans* **1** to make a count of (something). **2a** to mark (something) on a tally or tabulate (it) as if on a tally. **b** to list or check off (e.g. a cargo) by items. **3** to put a tag on (something) to identify it. ➤ *verb intrans* **1** to correspond or match: *Their stories tally.* **2a** to make a tally or tabulation. **b** to register a point in a contest.

tally-ho¹ /,tali 'hoh/ *noun* (*pl* **tally-hos**) a call given by a huntsman to the hounds on sighting a fox. [prob from French *taïaut*, a cry used to urge hounds in deer hunting]

tally-ho² *verb intrans* (**tally-hos, tally-hoed, tally-hoing**) to shout tally-ho.

tallyman *or* **tallywoman** *noun* (*pl* **tallymen** *or* **tallywomen**) **1** a man or woman who checks or keeps an account or record, e.g. of the receipt of goods. **2** *Brit*. **a** a man or woman who sells goods on credit, *esp* from door to door. **b** a man or woman who calls to collect hire-purchase payments.

Talmud /'talmood, 'tahlmood/ *noun* the authoritative body of Jewish tradition comprising the MISHNAH and GEMARA. ➤➤ **Talmudic** /tal'moohdik, tahl-/ *adj*, **Talmudical** /tal'moohdikl, tahl-/ *adj*. [late Hebrew *talmūdh* instruction]

Talmudist *noun* a specialist in Talmudic studies. ➤➤ **Talmudism** *noun*.

talon /'talən/ *noun* **1** a claw, *esp* of a bird of prey. **2a** an object or part of something shaped like or suggestive of a claw. **b** the shoulder of the bolt of a lock on which the key acts to shoot the bolt. **c** in architecture = OGEE. **3** in the Stock Exchange, a printed slip of paper attached to some bonds to allow the person holding the bonds to apply for new coupons (detachable parts of bonds that are presented when payment of interest is due; see COUPON). **4** in various card games, the pile of cards that remain undealt. ➤➤ **taloned** *adj*. [Middle English via French from Latin *talus* ankle, anklebone]

talus¹ /'taylas/ *noun* (*pl* **taluses**) a slope, *esp* one of rock debris at the base of a cliff or in a fortification. [French *talus* from Latin *talutium* slope indicating presence of gold under the soil]

talus² *noun* (*pl* **tali** /'taylie/) *technical* the large bone in the ankle that articulates with the tibia above it, the fibula to the outer side of it, and the calcaneus below it; the anklebone. [Latin *talus* ankle, anklebone]

TAM *abbr* television audience measurement.

tam /tam/ *noun* = TAM-O'-SHANTER.

tamale /tə'mahli/ *noun* (*pl* **tamales**) a Mexican dish of minced meat seasoned usu with chilli, rolled in maize flour, wrapped in maize husks, and steamed. [Mexican Spanish *tamales*, pl of *tamal*, from Nahuatl *tamalli*]

tamandua /taman'dooə, tə'mandooə/ *noun* either of two species of tree-dwelling anteater of tropical America: genus *Tamandua*. [Portuguese *tamanduá* from Tupi]

tamarack /'tamarak/ *noun* **1** a N American larch: *Larix laricina*. **2** the wood of this tree. [Canadian French *tamarac*, perhaps of Algonquian origin]

tamari /tə'mahri/ *noun* a rich soy sauce made in Japan from fermented soya beans with wild rice, used as a flavouring in oriental cooking. [Japanese *tamari*]

tamarillo /tamə'riloh/ *noun* (*pl* **tamarillos**) = TREE TOMATO. [modification of Spanish *tomatillo*, dimin. of *tomate*: see TOMATO]

tamarin /'tamərin/ *noun* any of several species of small, long-tailed, highly vocal S American monkeys that have silky fur and are closely related to the marmosets: genera *Saguinus* and *Leontopithecus*. [French *tamarin*, from Galibi]

tamarind /'tamərind/ *noun* **1a** a pod-like fruit eaten fresh or made into chutney. **b** the acidic sticky brown pulp of this fruit used as a flavouring, *esp* in oriental cookery, and medicinally as a laxative. **2** the tropical leguminous tree that bears this fruit: *Tamarindus indica*. **3** the wood of this tree. [Spanish and Portuguese *tamarindo*, from Arabic *tamr hindī* Indian date]

tamarisk /'tamərisk/ *noun* any of various tropical or Mediterranean shrubs and trees that have tiny narrow leaves and masses of minute flowers: genus *Tamarix*. [Middle English *tamarisc* via late Latin *tamariscus* from Latin *tamaric-, tamarix*]

tambala /tam'bahlə/ *noun* (*pl* **tambala** *or* **tambalas**) a unit of currency in Malawi, worth 100th of a kwacha. [Nyanja *tambala*, literally 'cockerel']

tambour¹ /'tambooə/ *noun* **1** a small drum. **2a** in embroidery, a frame consisting of a set of two interlocking hoops between which cloth is stretched during stitching. **b** embroidery made on such a frame. **3** a rolling top or front, e.g. of a rolltop desk, consisting of narrow strips of wood glued on canvas. **4** a circular wall, *esp* one supporting a dome. **5** an angled projection on the side wall of a real-tennis court. [French *tambour* drum, from Arabic *ṭanbūr*, modification of Persian *tabīr*]

tambour² *verb trans* to embroider (e.g. cloth) using a tambour. ➤➤ **tambourer** *noun*.

tamboura *or* **tambura** /tam'booərə/ *noun* an Asian stringed musical instrument used to produce a drone accompaniment to singing. [Persian *ṭambūra*]

tambourin /'tamboorin/ *noun* **1** a small drum. **2** a folk dance of Provence or music for it. [French *tambourin* small drum, dimin. of *tambour*: see TAMBOUR[1]]

tambourine /tambə'reen/ *noun* a percussion instrument resembling a shallow one-headed drum with loose metallic discs at the sides. It is held in the hand and played by shaking, striking with the hand, or rubbing with the thumb. ➤➤ **tambourinist** *noun*. [early French *tambourin*: see TAMBOURIN]

tambura /tam'boorə/ *noun* see TAMBOURA.

tame[1] /taym/ *adj* **1** changed from or not having a state of native wildness, *esp* so as to be trainable and useful to human beings. **2** said of an animal: not afraid of human beings. **3** made docile and submissive. **4** lacking spirit, zest, or interest: *a tame adaptation of the play*. ➤➤ **tamely** *adv*, **tameness** *noun*. [Old English *tam*]

tame[2] *verb trans* **1a** to make (an animal) tame; to domesticate (it). **b** to subject (land) to cultivation. **2** to deprive (somebody) of spirit; to subdue (them). **3** to soften (something) or tone (it) down: *You'll need to tame your language a little.* ➤ *verb intrans* to become tame. ➤➤ **tamable** *or* **tameable** *adj*, **tamer** *noun*.

Tamil /'tamil/ *noun* (*pl* **Tamils** *or collectively* **Tamil**) **1** a member of an indigenous people inhabiting parts of southern India and Sri Lanka. **2** the Dravidian language of this people. ➤➤ **Tamil** *adj*.

Word history
the Tamil name for the language and people. Tamil words that have passed into English include *catamaran, cheroot, corundum, mango, mulligatawny,* and *pariah*.

tammy /'tami/ *noun* (*pl* **tammies**) = TAM-O'-SHANTER. [by shortening and alteration]

tam-o'-shanter /,tam ə 'shantə/ *noun* a round flat woollen or cloth cap of Scottish origin, with a tight headband, a full crown, and usu a pom-pom on top. [named after *Tam o' Shanter*, hero of the poem of that name by Robert Burns d.1796, Scottish poet]

tamoxifen /tə'moksifen/ *noun* a drug used to treat breast cancer and female infertility. [TRANS- + AMINE + OXY-[2] + PHENOL]

tamp /tamp/ *verb trans* **1** (*often* + down) to pack (something) in or down by a succession of light or medium blows. **2** to fill up (a drill hole above a blasting charge) with material, e.g. clay, to confine the force of the explosion. ➤➤ **tamper** *noun*. [prob back-formation from *tampin*, variant of TAMPION, taken to be *tamping*]

tamper /'tampə/ *verb intrans* (**tampered, tampering**) **1** (+ with) to interfere or meddle without permission: *The car lock had been tampered with.* **2** (+ with) to carry on underhand or improper negotiations or exert improper influence, e.g. by bribery. ➤➤ **tamperer** *noun*, **tamperproof** *adj*. [prob from early French *temprer*: see TEMPER[1]]

tampion /'tampi-ən/ *or* **tompion** /'tom-/ *noun* a plug inserted into the muzzle of a gun when it is not in use. [Middle English from early French *tampon*, of Germanic origin]

tampon[1] /'tampon/ *noun* an absorbent plug put into a cavity, e.g. a wound or the vagina, to absorb secretions, arrest bleeding, etc. [early French *tampon* plug: see TAMPION]

tampon[2] *verb trans* (**tamponed, tamponing**) to plug (a wound, the vagina, etc) with a tampon.

tam-tam /'tam tam/ *noun* = GONG[1]. [Hindi *ṭamṭam*]

tan[1] /tan/ *verb* (**tanned, tanning**) ➤ *verb trans* **1** to convert (animal skin) into leather by treatment with e.g. an infusion of tannin-rich bark, chromium salts, or fish oil. **2** to make (skin) take on a light-brown colour, *esp* by exposure to the sun. **3** *informal* to thrash or beat (somebody). ➤ *verb intrans* to get or become tanned. ✳ **tan somebody's hide/tan the hide off somebody** *informal* to beat somebody severely; to thrash them. ➤➤ **tannable** *adj*, **tanner** *noun*, **tanning** *noun*. [Middle English *tannen* via early French *tanner* from medieval Latin *tannare*, from *tanum, tannum* tanbark]

tan[2] *noun* **1** a brown colour given to the skin by exposure to sun. **2** a light yellowish brown. **3** = TANBARK. ➤➤ **tannish** *adj*. [French *tan* tanbark, from medieval Latin *tanum*]

tan[3] *adj* **1** of the colour tan. **2** *NAmer* said of a person, body part, or skin: having a brown colour after exposure to the sun; tanned.

tan[4] *abbr* tangent.

tanager /'tanəjə/ *noun* any of numerous chiefly woodland American birds the males of which are usu brightly coloured: subfamily Thraupidae. [scientific Latin *tanagra* from Portuguese *tangará*, from Tupi]

tanbark *noun* a bark, e.g. of an oak, rich in tannin, bruised or cut into small pieces, and used in tanning hides.

tandem[1] /'tandəm/ *noun* **1** a bicycle or tricycle having two or more seats one behind the other. **2a** a carriage drawn by two horses harnessed one before the other. **b** the horses themselves. **3** any arrangement of two people or things one behind the other. ✳ **in tandem 1** in partnership or conjunction; together. **2** arranged or harnessed one behind the other. ➤➤ **tandem** *adj*. [Latin *tandem* at last, at length, taken to mean 'lengthwise']

tandem[2] *adv* one behind the other.

tandoori /tan'dooəri/ *noun* **1** a N Indian method of cooking meat, usu on a long spit, using a large clay oven. **2a** meat, or a meat dish, cooked in this way. **b** (*used before a noun*) relating to or denoting meat or a dish cooked in this way: *tandoori chicken*. [Urdu *tānduri* from *tāndur* oven, from Arabic *tannūr*]

tang /tang/ *noun* **1a** a sharp distinctive flavour. **b** a pungent or distinctive smell. **c** something stimulating to the senses: *treated murder as a joke with a tang to it* — Graham Greene. **2** a faint suggestion; a trace. **3** a projecting shank or tongue, e.g. on a knife, file, or sword, that connects with and is enclosed by a handle. ➤➤ **tanged** *adj*. [Middle English, in the sense 'insect's sting', also 'snake's tongue' (believed to sting), from Old Norse *tangi* point, tang of a knife]

tanga /'tanggə/ *noun* (*pl* **tangas**) a very brief undergarment or swimsuit for the lower part of the body in the form of two tiny triangles of material, one at the front and one at the back, held together by strings at the sides. [via Portuguese denoting a triangular loincloth worn by some indigenous American peoples; ultimately from Bantu]

tangelo /'tanjiloh/ *noun* (*pl* **tangelos**) **1** a citrus fruit that is a cross between a tangerine and a grapefruit. **2** the tree that bears this fruit. [blend of TANGERINE and POMELO]

tangent[1] /'tanjənt/ *noun* **1** in mathematics, the trigonometric function that, for an acute angle in a right-angled triangle, is the ratio between the shorter sides opposite and adjacent to the angle: compare SINE, COSINE. **2** a straight line touching a curve or surface at only one point. **3** an upright flat-ended metal pin at the inner end of a clavichord key that strikes the string to produce the note. ✳ **fly/go off at/on a tangent** to change suddenly from one subject, course of action, etc, to another. [medieval Latin *tangent-, tangens*, from *linea tangens* tangent line, from *tangere* to touch]

tangent[2] *adj* **1** touching a curve or surface at only one point: *Draw a straight line tangent to the curve.* **2** having a common tangent at a point: *tangent curves*. ➤➤ **tangency** *noun*.

tangential /tan'jensh(ə)l/ *adj* **1** of or like a tangent. **2** acting along or lying in a tangent: *tangential forces*. **3a** divergent; digressive. **b** incidental; peripheral; barely relevant. ➤➤ **tangentiality** /-shi'al-iti/ *noun*, **tangentially** *adv*.

tangerine /tanjə'reen/ *noun* **1a** a small loose-skinned citrus fruit, related to the mandarin, with deep orange skin and pulp. **b** the tree that bears this fruit: *Citrus reticulata*. **2** a bright reddish orange colour. [from *Tanger*, former name of Tangier, city and port in Morocco, from where the fruit was exported]

tangible[1] /'tanjəbl/ *adj* **1a** capable of being perceived, *esp* by the sense of touch. **b** substantially real; material. **2** capable of being appraised at an actual or approximate value: *tangible assets*. ➤➤ **tangibility** /-'biliti/ *noun*, **tangibleness** *noun*, **tangibly** *adv*. [late Latin *tangibilis* from Latin *tangere* to touch]

tangible[2] *noun* something tangible, *esp* a tangible asset.

tangle[1] /'tanggl/ *verb trans* **1** to bring (something) together or intertwine (things) in disordered confusion. **2** to involve (somebody or something) so as to be trapped or hampered. ➤ *verb intrans* **1** to become tangled. **2** *informal* (*often* + with) to engage in conflict or argument. ➤➤ **tangled** *adj*. [Middle English *tangilen*, prob of Scandinavian origin]

tangle[2] *noun* **1** a confused twisted mass. **2** a complicated or confused state. **3** *informal* a fight or disagreement. ➤➤ **tangly** *adj*.

tango[1] /'tanggoh/ *noun* (*pl* **tangos**) **1** a ballroom dance of Latin-American origin in four time, characterized by long pauses and stylized body positions. **2** music for this dance. [American Spanish *tango*, perhaps of African origin]

tango[2] *verb* (**tangoes, tangoed, tangoing**) ➤ *verb intrans* to dance the tango. ➤ *verb trans* to make (one's way) by tangoing.

tangram /'tanggrəm, 'tanggram/ *noun* a Chinese puzzle made by cutting a square into five triangles, a square, and a rhomboid which can be recombined in many different ways to form different figures. [perhaps from Chinese *tang* Chinese + -GRAM]

tangy *adj* (**tangier, tangiest**) having a sharp pungent taste or smell. ➤ **tanginess** *noun*.

tanh /than, tansh, ˌtan 'aych/ *abbr* hyperbolic tangent. [shortening of TANGENT¹ + *h* for HYPERBOLIC²]

tank¹ /tangk/ *noun* **1a** a large receptacle for holding, transporting, or storing liquids or gas. **b** a container for fuel in a motor vehicle. **c** the amount of fuel contained in this or that it can contain: *a full tank of petrol.* **2a** *dialect* a pond or pool. **b** *Aus, India* a reservoir. **3** a clear-sided container in which to keep fish, etc. **4** an enclosed heavily armed and armoured combat vehicle that moves on caterpillar tracks. **5** *NAmer* a cell or jail. ➤ **tankful** (*pl* **tankfuls**) *noun*. [Gujarati *tānkū* or Merathi *tānke* pond, cistern, from Sanskrit *tadāga* pond, prob influenced by Portuguese *tanque* pond, ultimately from Latin *stagnum*]

tank² *verb trans* **1** to place, store, or treat (something) in a tank. **2** *informal* to inflict a heavy defeat on (an opponent or an opposing team, etc). ➤ *verb intrans informal* to move very fast; to run: *She tanked up the road to catch the bus.*

tanka /ˈtangkə/ *noun* (*pl* **tanka** or **tankas**) **1** an unrhymed Japanese verse form of five lines containing five, seven, five, seven, and seven syllables respectively. **2** a poem in this form: compare HAIKU. [Japanese *tanka*, literally 'short song']

tankage /ˈtangkij/ *noun* **1** the capacity or contents of a tank. **2** storage in tanks or a fee charged for this. **3** dried residues from tanks in which animal carcasses have been rendered used as fertilizer and feedstuff.

tankard /ˈtangkəd/ *noun* a tall one-handled drinking vessel, *esp* a silver or pewter beer mug sometimes with a hinged lid. [Middle English, orig in the sense 'large tub', of Germanic origin]

tanked *adj informal* drunk.

tanked-up *adj* = TANKED.

tank engine *noun* a steam locomotive that carries its own water and coal and does not have a tender.

tanker *noun* a ship, aircraft, or road or rail vehicle designed to carry fluid, *esp* liquid, in bulk.

tank farming *noun* = HYDROPONICS.

tank top *noun* a sleeveless pullover with a U-shaped neckline, usu worn over a shirt or jumper.

tank up *verb intrans* **1** to fill the tank of a vehicle with fuel. **2** to drink a large amount of alcohol: *He'd tanked up a good deal at luncheon* — F Scott Fitzgerald. ➤ *verb trans* to fill the tank of (a vehicle) with fuel.

tanner¹ *noun* a person who tans animal hides.

tanner² *noun Brit, informal* a coin worth six old pence. [origin unknown]

tannery *noun* (*pl* **tanneries**) a place where tanning is carried out.

tannic /ˈtanik/ *adj* of, resembling, or derived from tanbark or a tannin. [French *tannique*, from *tan*: see TANNIN]

tannic acid *noun* = TANNIN.

tannin /ˈtanin/ *noun* any of various soluble astringent complex phenolic substances of plant origin used *esp* in tanning, dyeing, and making ink. [French *tanin, tannin* from *tan*: see TAN²]

Tannoy /ˈtanoy/ *noun trademark* a public address system, *esp* one that can broadcast throughout a large building. [shortening of *tantalum* alloy, used as a rectifier]

tansy /ˈtanzi/ *noun* (*pl* **tansies**) any of several species of aromatic composite plants with finely divided leaves and button-shaped yellow flowers that are common weeds: genus *Tanacetum*. [Middle English *tanesey* via Old French *tanesie* from medieval Latin *athanasia* immortality, from Greek; perhaps because of its long-lasting flowers]

tantalise /ˈtantəliez/ *verb trans* see TANTALIZE.

tantalite /ˈtantəliet/ *noun* a heavy dark lustrous mineral consisting mainly of iron and tantalum oxide. [Swedish *tantalit*, from TANTALUM + -ITE¹]

tantalize or **tantalise** /ˈtantəliez/ *verb trans* to tease or frustrate (somebody) by presenting something desirable that is just out of reach or promising something and then withholding it. ➤➤ **tantalization** /-ˈzaysh(ə)n/ *noun*, **tantalizer** *noun*, **tantalizing** *adj*, **tantalizingly** *adv*. [from *Tantalus*: see TANTALUS]

tantalum /ˈtantələm/ *noun* a white metallic chemical element that is hard and acid-resistant, occurs naturally in tantalite, and is used in surgical equipment: symbol Ta, atomic number 73. [scientific Latin, from Latin *Tantalus* (see TANTALUS); from its resistance to acids, which created tantalizing problems]

tantalus /ˈtantələs/ *noun* (*pl* **tantaluses**) a locked container for holding bottles or decanters of wine, spirits, etc in which the contents are visible but not obtainable without a key. [named after *Tantalus*, in Greek mythology a king of Phrygia condemned to stand in Hades up to his chin in water and under branches of fruit, but to be unable to eat or drink because the water and fruit drew back when he tried to reach them]

tantamount /ˈtantəmownt/ *adj* (+ to) equivalent in value, significance, or effect to; virtually the same as. [obsolete *tantamount* to amount to as much, from early French dialect *tant amunter* or Italian *tanto montare*]

tantara /ˈtantərə, tanˈtahrə/ *noun* the blare of a trumpet or horn. [Latin *taratantara*, of imitative origin]

tantivy¹ /tanˈtivi/ *noun* (*pl* **tantivies**) a fast gallop or a ride at full speed. [prob imitative of the sound of fast galloping hooves]

tantivy² *adj* moving, galloping, or riding fast or at full speed.

tantivy³ *interj* a hunting call given *esp* when riding at a fast gallop.

tant mieux *adv* so much the better. [French *tant mieux*]

tanto /ˈtantoh/ *adv* used, *esp* with a negative, as an instruction in music: so much or too much. [Italian *tanto*]

tant pis /ˌtonh 'pee/ *adv* too bad; so much the worse. [French *tant pis*]

tantra /ˈtantrə/ *noun* **1** any of a body of later Hindu and Buddhist scriptures marked by mysticism and magic. **2** the doctrine and cult deriving from the tantras, including the practice of Shaktism.

Editorial note

Tantra means a handbook or manual and, by extension, the teachings contained therein. In both Hinduism and Buddhism, tantra often refers to practices found outside earlier canons, especially magical techniques that may derive their potency from the violation of social conventions. The equation of tantra with 'the yoga of sex', however, misrepresents the diversity of tantric practice and its pervasiveness even in what are considered orthodox traditions — Professor Donald Lopez.

➤➤ **tantric** *adj*, **tantrism** *noun*, **tantrist** *noun*. [Sanskrit *tantra* warp, doctrine, from *tanoti* he weaves]

tantrum /ˈtantrəm/ *noun* (*pl* **tantrums**) a fit of childish bad temper. [origin unknown]

Tanzanian /tanzəˈnee-ən/ *noun* a native or inhabitant of Tanzania in E Africa. ➤➤ **Tanzanian** *adj*.

Tao /tow, dow/ *noun* **1** the principle of creative harmony which, in Taoism, is believed to underlie and govern the natural order of the universe. **2** (*often* **tao**) the path of virtuous conduct of Confucian doctrine. [Chinese *tao* way]

Taoiseach /ˈteeshəkh/ *noun* the prime minister of the Republic of Ireland. [Irish Gaelic *taoiseach* leader]

Taoism *noun* a Chinese philosophy traditionally founded by Lao-tzu in the sixth cent. BC that teaches action in conformity with nature rather than striving against it, or a religion developed from this philosophy together with folk and Buddhist religion and concerned with obtaining long life and good fortune, often by magical means. ➤➤ **Taoist** *adj and noun*, **Taoistic** /tow'istik, dow-/ *adj*. [TAO]

tap¹ /tap/ *noun* **1a** a device consisting of a spout and valve attached to a pipe, bowl, etc to control the flow of a fluid. **b** a plug designed to fit an opening, *esp* in a barrel. **2** a removal of fluid from a body cavity. **3** a tool for forming an internal screw thread. **4a** a device that can be attached to a telephone to allow somebody to listen secretly to conversations. **b** the act or an instance of using such a device. **5a** = TAPROOM. **b** a quality of alcoholic drink. **6** an issue of a government security released slowly onto the market when its market price reaches a particular predetermined level. **7** *Brit, informal.* **a** the act or an instance of asking for or getting money from somebody. **b** the amount of money involved in this. ✳ **on tap 1** said of beer, etc: on draught. **2** readily available. [Old English *tæppa*]

tap² *verb trans* (**tapped, tapping**) **1** to let (liquid) out or cause (it) to flow by piercing or by drawing a plug from the containing vessel. **2a** to pierce (a container, body cavity, tree, etc) so as to let out or draw off a fluid. **b** to draw from or upon (a source or supply). **c** to fit a tap to (something). **d** to connect an electronic listening device to (a telephone or telegraph wire), *esp* in order to acquire secret information. **3** to form an internal screw thread in (e.g. a nut) by means of a special tool. **4** *informal* (*usu* + for) to ask for or get money from (somebody) as a loan or gift. ⮞ **tapper** *noun.*

tap³ *noun* **1** a light blow, or the sound it makes. **2** any of several usu rapid drumbeats on a snare drum. **3a** a small piece of metal attached to the sole or heel of a tap-dancing shoe. **b** tap-dancing.

tap⁴ *verb* (**tapped, tapping**) ⮞ *verb trans* **1a** to strike (somebody or something) lightly, *esp* with a slight sound. **b** (*often* + out) to produce (a sound, rhythm, etc) by striking in this manner. **2** to give a light blow with (something): *She tapped her pencil on the table.* **3** to fit taps (small pieces of metal; see TAP³) to (tap-dancing shoes). ⮞ *verb intrans* to strike a light audible blow; to make a slight sound or a series of sounds in this way. ⮞⮞ **tapper** *noun* [Middle English *tappen* from early French *taper* to strike with the flat of the hand, of Germanic origin]

tapa /'tahpə/ *noun* the bark of the paper mulberry or cloth made from it. [Marquesan (a Polynesian language) and Tahitian]

tapas /'tapəs/ *pl noun* **1** light savoury snacks or appetizers, eaten *esp* with an alcoholic drink. **2** (*used before a noun*) relating to, denoting, or serving such food: *a tapas bar.* [Spanish *tapas*, from *tapar* to cover; tapas are traditionally served on a dish on top of the glass the drink is in]

tap dance *noun* a step dance tapped out audibly by means of shoes with hard soles or soles and heels to which small pieces of metal have been fitted.

tap-dance *verb intrans* to perform a tap dance. ⮞⮞ **tap-dancer** *noun,* **tap-dancing** *noun.*

tape¹ /tayp/ *noun* **1** a narrow band of woven fabric. **2** the string stretched above the finishing line of a race. **3** a narrow flexible strip or band: e.g. **a** = MAGNETIC TAPE. **b** = TAPE MEASURE: *How few things can a man measure with the tape of his understanding!* — Henry David Thoreau. **c** adhesive tape, INSULATING TAPE, MASKING TAPE, etc. **4a** = TAPE RECORDING. **b** = CASSETTE (1). **c** = VIDEOTAPE¹. [Old English *tæppe*]

tape² *verb trans* **1** to fasten, tie, or bind (something) with tape. **2** to record (something, e.g. music, a television programme, etc) on tape, *esp* magnetic tape: *You don't mind if I tape this interview, do you?* ⮞ *verb intrans* to record something on *esp* magnetic tape. ✳ **have something taped** to have the measure of something; to be in command or control of it: *We'll soon have the problem taped.*

tape deck *noun* a mechanism or self-contained unit, e.g. a tape recorder, that causes magnetic tape to move past the heads of a magnetic recording device in order to generate electrical signals or to make a recording.

tape machine *noun* **1** a telegraphic receiving instrument that automatically prints out information, e.g. share prices, on paper tape. **2** a machine that functions as a TAPE RECORDER.

tape measure *noun* a narrow strip, e.g. of a limp cloth or steel tape, marked off in units, e.g. inches or centimetres, for measuring.

tapenade /tapə'nahd/ *noun* a paste or dip made from capers, black olives, anchovies, olive oil, and lemon juice. [Provençal *tapenade*, from *tapeno* capers]

taper¹ /'taypə/ *noun* **1a** a slender candle. **b** a long waxed wick used *esp* for lighting candles, fires, etc. **2** a gradual narrowing in thickness, diameter, or width. [Old English *tapor, taper*]

taper² *verb* (**tapered, tapering**) ⮞ *verb intrans* **1** to decrease gradually in thickness, diameter, or width towards one end. **2** (*often* + off) to diminish gradually: *His voice tapered off.* ⮞ *verb trans* to cause (something) to taper. ⮞⮞ **taperer** *noun,* **tapering** *adj.*

tape-record /,tayp ri'kawd/ *verb trans* to make a tape recording of (somebody or something). [back-formation from *tape recording*]

tape recorder *noun* a device for recording signals, *esp* sounds, on magnetic tape and for subsequently reproducing them.

tape recording *noun* a recording, usu on magnetic tape, of sounds, a television programme, etc, that can be reproduced on a tape recorder or video recorder.

tape streamer *noun* in computing, a device for copying data from a hard disk onto magnetic tape.

tapestry /'tapəstri/ *noun* (*pl* **tapestries**) **1a** a heavy handwoven textile used for hangings, curtains, and upholstery and characterized by complicated pictorial designs. **b** a machine-made imitation of tapestry used chiefly for upholstery. **2** embroidery on canvas that resembles woven tapestry. **3** something that has great complexity or variety: *It's all part of life's rich tapestry.* ⮞⮞ **tapestried**

/-strid/ *adj.* [Middle English *tapistry* from early French *tapisserie*, from Old French *tapis* carpet, from Greek *tapēs* rug, carpet]

tapeworm *noun* any of numerous species of parasitic worms that have long, ribbon-like, segmented bodies and live in the intestine of human beings or other vertebrates: class Cestoda. [from its shape]

tapioca /tapi'ohkə/ *noun* **1** a usu granular preparation of cassava starch used *esp* in puddings and as a thickening in liquid food. **2** a milk pudding made with this. [Spanish and Portuguese *tapioca* from Tupi *tipióca*, from *tipi* residue + *oca* to squeeze out, remove]

tapir /'taypə/ *noun* (*pl* **tapirs** *or collectively* **tapir**) any of a genus of hoofed mammals that have elongated flexible snouts, are found in tropical America and Asia and are related to the horses and rhinoceroses: genus *Tapirus*. [Tupi *tapiíra*]

tapis /'tapee, 'tapi (*French* tapi)/ *noun* (*pl* **tapis**) *archaic* tapestry or similar material used for wall hangings and floor and table coverings. [Old French *tapis*: see TAPESTRY]

tappet /'tapit/ *noun* a lever or projection moved by or moving some other piece, such as a cam. [from TAP⁴]

taproom *noun* a room in a hotel or pub where alcoholic drinks are available, *esp* one serving draught beers. [TAP¹]

taproot *noun* a main root of a plant that grows vertically downwards and gives off small side roots. [TAP¹]

taps *pl noun* (*treated as sing. or pl*) **1** *chiefly NAmer.* **a** the last bugle call at night, blown as a signal that lights are to be put out. **b** a similar call blown at military funerals and memorial services. **2** *Brit* in the Guide movement, a song sung at the close of a meeting, etc. [prob alteration of *taptoo*, earlier form of TATTOO³]

tapster /'tapstə/ *noun archaic* a person employed to serve drinks in a tavern or public house: *The oath of a lover is no stronger than the word of a tapster; they are both the confirmer of false reckonings* — Shakespeare.

tap stock *noun* = TAP¹ (6).

tar¹ /tah/ *noun* **1** a dark bituminous usu strong-smelling viscous liquid obtained by heating and distilling wood, coal, peat, etc. **2** a residue present in smoke from burning tobacco that contains resins, acids, phenols, etc. [Old English *teoru*]

tar² *verb trans* (**tarred, tarring**) to cover or smear (somebody or something) with tar. ✳ **tar and feather** to smear (a person) with tar and cover (them) with feathers as a punishment or humiliation. **tarred with the same brush** said of two or more people: having the same faults or assumed to have.

tar³ *noun informal, dated* a sailor. [short for TARPAULIN]

taradiddle *or* **tarradiddle** /'tarədidəl/ *noun chiefly Brit, informal* **1** a lie, *esp* one of little consequence. **2** pretentious talk; nonsense. [origin unknown]

tarakihi /'tarəkeehee/ *or* **terakihi** /'te-/ *noun* a silver marine food fish that has a black band behind its head and lives in the waters around New Zealand: *Nemadactylus macropterus*. [Maori *tarakihi*]

taramasalata /,tarəməsə'lahtə/ *noun* a pinkish paste made from fish roe, e.g. that of grey mullet or smoked cod, olive oil, and seasoning, usu eaten as a starter. [modern Greek *taramosalata*, from *taramas* preserved roe + *salata* salad]

tarantass /tarən'tas/ *noun* a four-wheeled, horse-drawn Russian carriage mounted on a flexible wooden chassis without any springs. [Russian *tarantas*]

tarantella /tarən'telə/ *noun* **1** a vivacious folk dance of southern Italy in 6/8 time. **2** music for or in the style of this dance. [Italian *tarantella*, named after *Taranto*: see TARANTISM; so called because it was thought that dancing the tarantella until exhausted was a cure for tarantism]

tarantism /'tarəntiz(ə)m/ *noun* a psychological disorder characterized by uncontrollable dancing movements. It was prevalent in medieval Italy and was popularly attributed to the bite of the tarantula. [scientific Latin *tarantismus*, from *Taranto*, city and port in Italy]

tarantula /tə'ranchoolə/ *noun* (*pl* **tarantulas** *or* **tarantulae** /-lee/) **1** any of various large hairy spiders of tropical and subtropical America that can bite sharply but are not significantly poisonous to human beings: family Theraphosidae. **2** a European wolf spider of southern Europe formerly held to be the cause of tarantism: *Lycosa tarentula*. [medieval Latin *tarantula* from Old Italian *tarantola*, from *Taranto*: see TARANTELLA]

taraxacum /tə'raksəkəm/ *noun* **1** any of a genus of plants, such as the dandelion, that have flowerheads made up of tiny florets and whose wind-dispersed seeds are attached by slender stalks to a canopy of fine hairs: genus *Taraxacum*. **2** an extract of dandelion roots or leaves, used as a laxative, diuretic, and liver tonic. [Latin genus name, from medieval Latin *altaraxacon*, from Arabic and Persian *tarakhshaqūn* dandelion, from Persian *talk* bitter + *cakūk* purslane]

tarboosh or **tarbush** /tah'boohsh/ *noun* a usu red hat similar to the fez worn *esp* by Muslim men. [Arabic *ṭarbūsh* via Turkish from Persian *sarpūš*, from *sar* head + *puš* cover]

Tardenoisian /tahdə'noyzi-ən/ *adj* relating to, or dating from a late Mesolithic culture of western and central Europe lasting from about 6000 BC to 4000 BC, and marked by the use of flint tools. [French *Tardenoisien*, from *Fère-en-Tardenois* in northeastern France where tools and other objects belonging to the culture were discovered]

tardigrade /'tahdigrayd/ *noun* any of a phylum of microscopic arthropods, such as the water bears, that live usu in water or damp moss: phylum Tardigrada. ➤➤ **tardigrade** *adj*. [Latin *tardigradus* slow-moving, from *tardus* slow + *gradi* to step, go]

tardy /'tahdi/ *adj* (**tardier, tardiest**) **1** delayed beyond the expected or proper time; late: *See nations slowly wise, and meanly just, to buried merit raise the tardy bust* — Dr Johnson. **2** moving or progressing slowly; sluggish. ➤➤ **tardily** *adv*, **tardiness** *noun*. [alteration of *tardif*, from early French, ultimately from Latin *tardus* slow]

tare[1] /teə/ *noun* **1** any of several vetches. **2** (*in pl*) in some translations of the Bible, a weed found in cornfields, usu held to be darnel: Matthew 13:24-30. [Middle English; earlier history unknown]

tare[2] *noun* **1a** the weight of the wrapping material or container in which goods are packed. **b** a deduction from the gross weight of a substance and its container made in allowance for the weight of the container. **2** the weight of an unloaded goods vehicle without its fuel. **3** a container used as a counterweight in calculating the net weight of goods. [Middle English from early French *tare* wastage, deficiency, ultimately from Arabic *ṭarḥa*, literally 'that which is removed', from *taraha* to reject, deduct]

tare[3] *verb trans* to weigh (something) in order to determine the tare.

targe /tahj/ *noun archaic* a light shield. [Middle English from Old French *targe*, of Germanic origin]

target[1] /'tahgit/ *noun* **1a** an object to fire at in practice or competition, *esp* one consisting of a series of concentric circles with a bull's-eye at the centre. **b** a person or object that is selected to be fired at or attacked. **2a** somebody or something that is the object of ridicule, criticism, etc. **b** a goal or objective. **3a** a body, surface, or material bombarded with nuclear particles or electrons, *esp* to produce X-rays. **b** in a television camera tube, the PHOTOMOSAIC (array of light-sensitive cells scanned by electron beam to create signal). **4** formerly, a small round shield. ✳ **on/off target 1** likely or unlikely to hit or achieve whatever has been set as a target or objective. **2** succeeding or not succeeding in this. [Middle English from early French *targette*, dimin. of *targe*: see TARGE]

target[2] *verb trans* (**targeted, targeting**) **1** to make (somebody or something) a target. **2** to set (something) as a goal. **3** (*often* + *on*) to aim (a weapon) at a target: *Missiles were said to have been targeted on London and other major cities.*

target practice *noun* the procedure of repeatedly shooting or firing arrows at a target to improve one's aim.

tariff[1] /'tarif/ *noun* **1a** a schedule of duties imposed by a government on imported, or in some countries exported, goods. **b** a duty or rate of duty imposed in such a schedule. **2a** the rates or charges of a business, e.g. a hotel, or public service, e.g. an electricity board, or a schedule of these rates. **b** *chiefly Brit* a menu. **3** a schedule of the sentences and damages that apply to different crimes, varying in severity according to the gravity of the crime. [Italian *tariffa* from Arabic *ta'rif* notification]

tariff[2] *verb trans* **1** to set a tariff on (something). **2** to price (something) according to a tariff.

tarlatan /'tahlətən/ *noun* a sheer cotton fabric in open plain weave usu heavily sized to give stiffness to garments, *esp* ball gowns. [French *tarlatane*]

tarmac[1] /'tahmak/ *noun* **1** = TARMACADAM. **2** a runway, apron, or road made of tarmac.

tarmac[2] *verb trans* (**tarmacked, tarmacking**) to apply tarmac to (a road, path, etc).

tarmacadam /tahmə'kadəm/ *noun* a mixture of tar and aggregates used for surfacing roads: compare MACADAM. [TAR[1] + MACADAM]

tarn /tahn/ *noun* a small mountain lake. [Middle English *tarne* from Old Norse *tjorn*]

tarnation /tah'naysh(ə)n/ *noun chiefly NAmer, euphem* = DAMNATION[1]. [alteration, influenced by *tarnal*, a dialect form of ETERNAL[1], of *darnation*, alteration of DAMNATION[1]]

tarnish[1] /'tahnish/ *verb trans* **1** to dull the lustre of (something) by, or as if by, dirt, air, etc. **2a** to mar or spoil (something). **b** to bring discredit on (e.g. a person's reputation). ➤ *verb intrans* to become tarnished. ➤➤ **tarnishable** *adj*. [Middle English from early French *ternir*, from *terne* dark, dull, of Germanic origin]

tarnish[2] *noun* a film of chemically altered material on the surface of a metal, mineral, etc.

taro /'tahroh/ *noun* (*pl* **taros**) **1** a tropical plant of the arum family cultivated for its edible starchy tuberous rootstock: *Colocasia esculenta*. **2** the rootstock of this plant, used as a vegetable. [Tahitian and Maori *taro*]

tarot /'tahroh/ *noun* **1a** any of a set of 22 pictorial playing cards formerly used in card games but now usu used for fortune-telling. **b** (**the Tarot**) the 22 cards collectively. **2** fortune-telling with these cards. [early French *tarot* from Italian *tarocchi* tarots]

tarp /tahp/ *noun informal* a tarpaulin, *esp* one used for covering something.

tarpan /'tahpan/ *noun* an extinct wild greyish brown horse of Eastern Europe and Western Asia: *Equus caballus gomelini*. [Russian *tarpan*, of Turkic origin]

tarpaulin /tah'pawlin/ *noun* **1a** heavy waterproof usu tarred canvas material used for protecting objects or ground exposed to the elements. **b** a piece or sheet of this. **2** *esp* formerly, a sailor's hat made of tarpaulin or something similar. [prob from TAR[1] + *-palling, -pauling*, from PALL[1]]

tarpon /'tahpən, 'tahpon/ *noun* (*pl* **tarpons** or *collectively* **tarpon**) **1** a large silvery elongated edible marine fish that is common off the coast of Florida: *Tarpon atlanticus*. **2** a related fish of the Indo-Pacific: *Megalops cyprinoides*. [origin unknown]

tarradiddle /'tarədid(ə)l/ *noun* see TARADIDDLE.

tarragon /'tarəgən/ *noun* **1** a European plant of the daisy family, grown for its pungent aromatic leaves: *Artemisia dracunculus*. **2** the leaves of this plant, which are used as a flavouring, e.g. in making chicken dishes and vinegar. [early French *targon* via medieval Latin from Arabic *ṭarkhūn*]

tarry[1] /'tari/ *verb intrans* (**tarries, tarried, tarrying**) *archaic or literary* **1** to stay in or at a place; to wait for a while. **2** to delay or be slow in acting. ➤➤ **tarrier** *noun*. [Middle English *tarien*; earlier history unknown]

tarry[2] /'tahri/ *adj* (**tarrier, tarriest**) of, like, or covered with tar. ➤➤ **tarriness** *noun*.

tarsal[1] /'tahs(ə)l/ *adj* relating to or in the region of the tarsus.

tarsal[2] *noun* a bone or cartilage of the tarsus: compare TARSUS.

tarsi /'tahsie/ *noun* pl of TARSUS.

tarsia /'tahsi-ə/ *noun* = INTARSIA. [Italian *tarsia* from Arabic *tarṣī']

tarsier /'tahsi-ə/ *noun* any of a genus of small nocturnal tree-dwelling SE Asian mammals related to the lemurs, with thick fur, large eyes, and adhesive pads at the ends of their digits: genus *Tarsius*. [French *tarsier* from *tarse* tarsus, from its long tarsal bones]

tarsus /'tahsəs/ *noun* (*pl* **tarsi** /'tahsie/) **1a** the part of the vertebrate foot between the leg and the metatarsus, *esp* the human ankle, heel, and upper part of the foot: compare TARSAL[2]. **b** any of the bones in this part of a vertebrate foot, *esp* the seven small ones of the human foot. **2** the part of the limb of an arthropod furthest from the body. **3** the plate of dense connective tissue that forms the stiffened outer edge of the eyelid. [scientific Latin from Greek *tarsos* wickerwork mat, flat of the foot, ankle, edge of the eyelid]

tart[1] /taht/ *adj* **1** sharp or acid to the taste. **2** sarcastic, bitter, or hurtful: *A tart temper never mellows with age* — Washington Irving. ➤➤ **tartly** *adv*, **tartness** *noun*. [Old English *teart* sharp, severe]

tart[2] *noun* a pastry shell or shallow pie containing a sweet or savoury filling. [Middle English *tarte* from early French]

tart[3] *noun informal* **1** a female prostitute. **2** a girl or woman who is or appears to be, e.g. by the clothes she wears, sexually promiscuous. [prob short for SWEETHEART]

tartan /'taht(ə)n/ *noun* **1a** any of a large number of textile designs of Scottish origin consisting of checks and stripes of varying width and colour, usu patterned to designate a particular clan. **b** (*used before a noun*) having a design of this kind: *tartan ribbons*. **2** a fabric, *esp* a twilled woollen cloth, with a tartan design. **3** clothing of tartan. [prob from early French *tiretaine* linsey-woolsey, ultimately from medieval Latin *tyrius* cloth from *Tyre*, port in Lebanon, formerly a centre of Phoenician trade]

Tartar /'tahtə/ *noun* **1** a member of a group of peoples of central Asia, including the Turks and the Mongols. **2** (**tartar**) a formidable, irascible, or exacting person. ➤➤ **Tartar** *adj*, **Tartarian** /tah'tarian/ *adj*, **Tartaric** /tah'tarik/ *adj*. [Middle English *Tartre* via early French *Tartare*: see TATAR]

tartar *noun* **1** a substance consisting essentially of CREAM OF TARTAR (potassium hydrogen tartrate) that is formed during the fermentation of grapes and is deposited in wine casks as a reddish crust or sediment. **2** an incrustation on the teeth consisting *esp* of calcium salts: compare PLAQUE. [Middle English via medieval Latin *tartarum* from medieval Greek *tartaron*]

tartare /tah'tah/ *adj* said of fish or meat: served raw, usu minced, seasoned, and formed into a round patty. See also STEAK TARTARE.

Tartarean /tah'tehri·ən/ *adj* **1** in Greek mythology, relating to or denoting the part of the underworld where sinners were punished. **2** *informal* hellish; infernal. [Greek *Tartarus* the abyss in Hades where the wicked were imprisoned and punished, from *Tartaros*, of unknown origin]

tartar emetic *noun* a complex tartrate of antimony and potassium used in dyeing as a mordant and in medicine.

tartare sauce /'tahtə/ *noun* see TARTAR SAUCE.

tartaric acid /tah'tarik/ *noun* a strong carboxylic acid that is usu obtained from tartar and is used *esp* in food and medicines: formula $C_4H_6O_6$. [French *tartarique* from medieval Latin *tartarum*: see TARTAR]

tartar sauce /'tahtə/ *or* **tartare sauce** /'tahtə, 'tahtah/ *noun* mayonnaise with chopped pickles, olives, capers, and parsley, served *esp* with fish. [French *sauce tartare*]

tartlet /'tahtlit/ *noun* a small tart with a sweet or savoury filling.

tartrate /'tahtrayt/ *noun* any of various chemical salts or esters formed by combination between tartaric acid and a metal atom, an alcohol, or another chemical group. [TARTARIC ACID + -ATE[1]]

tartrazine /'tahtrəzeen, -zin/ *noun* a yellow dye, $C_{16}H_9N_4Na_3O_9S_2$, used in foods, drugs, *esp* as an additive, and dyeing. [TARTRATE + AZINE]

tart up *verb trans* **1** to dress (oneself) up, put on make-up, etc: *Daisy would so like to have got tarted up, but at least her hair was newly washed that morning and her teeth were clean* — Jilly Cooper. **2** to do up or redecorate (a place) *esp* somewhat cheaply or gaudily; generally, to embellish (something): *a nice old-fashioned bar, not the tarted-up variety*; *I suppose I should think about tarting up my thesis for publication.*

tarty *adj* (**tartier, tartiest**) *informal* of or like a prostitute or a tarted-up woman. ➤➤ **tartily** *adv*, **tartiness** *noun*.

tarwhine /'tahwien/ *noun* (*pl* **tarwhine**) a yellowish food and game fish that lives in the warm inshore waters of the Indian and Pacific Oceans and is related to the sea breams: *Rhabdosargus globiceps*. [Dharuk (an extinct native Australian language) *darawayn* a fish]

Tarzan /'tahz(ə)n, 'tahzan/ *noun* a strong, well-built man who is also very agile. [named after *Tarzan*, hero of adventure stories by Edgar Rice Burroughs d.1950, US author]

Tas. *abbr* Tasmania.

task[1] /tahsk/ *noun* **1** an assigned piece of work; a duty: *The long day's task is done, and we must sleep* — Shakespeare. **2** something hard or unpleasant that has to be done; a chore. ✳ **take somebody to task** to rebuke or scold somebody for a failure or mistake. [Middle English *taske* from Old French dialect *tasque*, from medieval Latin *tasca* tax or service imposed by a feudal superior, from *taxare*: see TAX[1]]

task[2] *verb trans* **1** to assign a task to (somebody). **2** to burden (somebody or something) with great labour; to subject (them or it) to severe exertion: *Don't task his mind with petty details.*

task force *noun* **1** a temporary military grouping under one leader for the purpose of accomplishing a definite objective. **2** a group of people or an organization that has been assigned a specific task, often with ongoing duties connected to it.

taskmaster *or* **taskmistress** *noun* a man or woman who assigns tasks: *He's a hard taskmaster.*

taskwork *noun* hard, difficult, or unpleasant work.

Tasmanian /taz'mayni·ən/ *noun* a native or inhabitant of Tasmania, an island off the SE coast of Australia, or of the state of Tasmania, which is made up of Tasmania and several other smaller islands. ➤➤ **Tasmanian** *adj*.

Tasmanian devil *noun* a powerful flesh-eating burrowing Tasmanian marsupial that is about the size of a badger and has a black coat marked with white: *Sarcophilus harrisii*.

Tasmanian tiger *noun* = TASMANIAN WOLF.

Tasmanian wolf *noun* a flesh-eating Tasmanian marsupial that somewhat resembles a dog and was formerly common in Australia, but is now confined to Tasmania: *Thylacinus cynocephalus*. Also called THYLACINE.

tass /tas/ *noun* see TASSIE.

tassel[1] /'tasl/ *noun* **1** a dangling ornament, e.g. on a curtain, bedspread, etc or on a garment, *esp* a hat, consisting of a bunch of cords or threads usu of even length fastened at one end. **2** the tassel-like flower clusters of some plants, *esp* maize. [Middle English from Old French, ultimately from Latin *taxillus* small die]

tassel[2] *verb* (**tasselled, tasselling,** *NAmer* **tasseled, tasseling**) ➤ *verb trans* to decorate (something) with tassels. ➤ *verb intrans* to form tassel flower clusters.

tassie /'tasi/ *or* **tass** /tas/ *noun Scot, archaic* a goblet or cup. [early French *tasse* cup, via Arabic from Persian *tast* bowl]

taste[1] /tayst/ *verb trans* **1** to test the flavour of (food, drink, etc) by taking a little into the mouth. **2** to perceive or recognize (a substance, flavour, etc) by, or as if by, the sense of taste: *She could taste the salt on his lips.* **3** to eat or drink (something), *esp* in small quantities: *That's the first food she has tasted in two days.* **4** to experience or undergo (something): *We have never tasted defeat.* ➤ *verb intrans* **1** to test the flavour of something by taking a little into the mouth. **2** (*often* + of) to have a specified flavour: *The milk tastes sour*; *This drink tastes of aniseed.* **3** *archaic or literary* (+ of) to experience or enjoy something: *Cowards die many times before their deaths; the valiant never taste of death but once* — Shakespeare. [Middle English *tasten* to touch, test, taste, from Old French *taster*]

taste[2] *noun* **1a** the one of the five basic physical senses by which the qualities of substances in contact with taste buds on the tongue are interpreted by the brain as one or a combination of the four basic taste sensations, sweet, bitter, sour, or salt. **b** the quality of a substance as perceived by this sense.

Editorial note
One of the five senses, taste is the sense by which we are made aware of the flavours of foodstuffs and, equally important in evolutionary terms, are protected from harmful substances. Taste buds are located in the walls of structures known as papillae on the upper surface of the tongue and are divided into four groups, which give the four sensations of taste — Dr John Cormack.

2a the act or an instance of tasting. **b** a small amount tasted. **c** the act or an instance of experiencing or undergoing something: *This was her first taste of success.* **3** an individual preference; an inclination. **4** critical judgment or discernment *esp* in aesthetic or social matters, or a manner or quality indicative of this: *I thought his remarks were in rather bad taste*; *His choice in furnishing showed taste.*

taste bud *noun* any of the small organs, *esp* on the surface of the tongue, that receive and transmit the sensation of taste.

tasteful /'taystf(ə)l/ *adj* showing or conforming to good judgment or acceptable behaviour. ➤➤ **tastefully** *adv*, **tastefulness** *noun*.

tasteless *adj* **1** lacking flavour; insipid. **2** not showing or conforming to good judgment or acceptable behaviour: *the 1930s, surely the most determinedly tasteless of all our decades* — J B Priestley. ➤➤ **tastelessly** *adv*, **tastelessness** *noun*.

taster *noun* **1** somebody who tests food or drink by tasting, *esp* in order to assess quality or, formerly, to check for poison in it. **2** a sample or specimen of something, *esp* one intended to stimulate interest or demand. **3** a device used for tasting or sampling something.

tasty *adj* (**tastier, tastiest**) **1** having an appetizing flavour. **2** *informal* arousing interest: *I've just heard some tasty gossip.* **3** *Brit, informal* attractive; sexually appealing: *She's a tasty bit of stuff.* ➤➤ **tastily** *adv*, **tastiness** *noun*.

tat[1] /tat/ *noun* **1** *Brit, informal* low-quality or tasteless material or goods. **2** a tangled mass. [back-formation from TATTY]

tat[2] *verb* (**tatted, tatting**) ➤ *verb intrans* to work at tatting. ➤ *verb trans* to make (something) by tatting. [back-formation from TATTING]

ta-ta /ˌtah'tah, ta'tah/ *interj chiefly Brit, informal* goodbye. [orig baby talk]

Tatar /'tahtə/ *noun* **1** a member of an indigenous people inhabiting parts of European Russia, *esp* around the central part of the river Volga, the N Caucasus, Crimea, and parts of Siberia. **2** the Turkic language spoken by this people. ➤➤ **Tatar** *adj*, **Tatarian** /tə'tari·ən/ *adj*, **Tataric** /tə'tarik/ *adj*. [Middle English *Tartre* from early French *Tartare*, ultimately from Persian *Tātār*, of Turkic origin]

tater /'taytə/ *or* **tatie** /'tayti/ *noun dialect* = POTATO. [by shortening and alteration]

tatter /'tatə/ *noun* **1** an irregular torn shred, *esp* of material. **2** (*in pl*) tattered clothing; rags. ✳ **in tatters 1** torn or worn to pieces; ragged. **2** in a state of ruin or disarray; useless or hopeless: *Her hopes and dreams were in tatters.* [Middle English, from Old Norse *tǫtrar* rags]

tatterdemalion /ˌtatədi'malyən/ *noun* a person dressed in ragged clothing; a ragamuffin. [TATTER + *-demalion* of unknown origin]

tattered *adj* **1** said *esp* of clothes, books, etc: old and torn. **2** dressed in tattered clothes. **3** run-down; dilapidated.

tattersall /'tatəsawl/ *noun* **1** a pattern of coloured lines forming squares on a light background. **2** a fabric woven or printed in this pattern. [from the pattern of the horse-blankets orig used at *Tattersall's* horse market, formerly held in London]

tattie /'tati/ *noun dialect* = POTATO. [by shortening and alteration]

tatting /'tating/ *noun* **1** a delicate handmade lace formed usu by making loops and knots using a single cotton thread and a small shuttle. **2** the act, process, or art of making such lace. [origin unknown]

tattle[1] /'tatl/ *verb intrans* to chatter or gossip. ➤ *verb trans* to disclose (e.g. secrets) by gossiping. ➤➤ **tattler** *noun*. [early Dutch *tatelen*, of imitative origin]

tattle[2] *noun* **1** chatter; gossip. **2** a tattler.

tattletale *noun chiefly NAmer* a tattler; a TELLTALE.

tattoo[1] /ta'tooh/ *noun* (*pl* **tattoos**) **1** an indelible mark or design on the skin made by tattooing. **2** the act of tattooing or having oneself tattooed. [Tahitian *tatau*]

tattoo[2] *verb trans* (**tattooed, tattooing**) **1** to mark (the body) by inserting pigments under the skin. **2** to mark (a design) on the body by tattooing. ➤➤ **tattooer** *noun*, **tattooist** *noun*.

tattoo[3] *noun* (*pl* **tattoos**) **1a** an evening drum or bugle call sounded as a call to soldiers to return to quarters. **b** an outdoor military display of marching, music, gymnastic exercises, etc given by troops as a usu evening entertainment. **2** a rapid rhythmic beating or tapping. [alteration of earlier *taptoo*, from Dutch *taptoe*, from the phrase *tap toe!* taps shut! (i.e. the taps on beer barrels)]

tatty /'tati/ *adj* (**tattier, tattiest**) *chiefly Brit, informal* shabby; dilapidated. ➤➤ **tattily** *adv*, **tattiness** *noun*. [orig Scots; perhaps ultimately from Old English *tætteca* rag]

tau /taw, tow/ *noun* the 19th letter of the Greek alphabet (Τ, τ), equivalent to and transliterated as roman t. [Greek *tau*, of Semitic origin; related to Hebrew *tāw*, 23rd letter of the Hebrew alphabet]

tau cross *noun* a T-shaped cross.

taught /tawt/ *verb* past tense and past part. of TEACH.

tau neutrino *noun* = TAU PARTICLE.

taunt[1] /tawnt/ *verb trans* to provoke (somebody) in a mocking way; to jeer at (them). ➤➤ **taunter** *noun*, **tauntingly** *adv*.

taunt[2] *noun* a sarcastic provocation or insult. [French *tant* in *tant pour tant* so much for so much, tit for tat, from Latin *tantus* so much]

tau particle *noun* a subatomic particle, one variety of lepton.

taupe /tohp/ *adj* of a brownish grey colour. ➤➤ **taupe** *noun*. [French *taupe*, literally 'mole', from Latin *talpa*]

taurine /'tawrien/ *adj* of or resembling a bull. [Latin *taurinus*, from *taurus* bull]

tauromachy /taw'roməki/ *noun* (*pl* **tauromachies**) **1** bullfighting. **2** a bullfight. [Greek *tauromachiā*, from *tauros* bull + *machē* fight]

Taurus /'tawrəs/ *noun* **1** in astronomy, a constellation (the Bull) depicted as the bull tamed by Jason. **2a** in astrology, the second sign of the zodiac. **b** a person born under this sign. ➤➤ **Taurean** /'tawri·ən/ *adj and noun*. [Latin *taurus* bull]

taut /tawt/ *adj* **1a** tightly drawn; tensely stretched. **b** showing anxiety; tense; stressed. **2** said *esp* of a ship: kept in good order. ➤➤ **tautly** *adv*, **tautness** *noun*. [Middle English *tought*; earlier history unknown]

taut- *or* **tauto-** *comb. form* forming words, with the meaning: same: *tautomerism*. [Greek *tauto*, contraction of *to auto* the same]

tauten /'tawtən/ *verb* (**tautened, tautening**) ➤ *verb trans* to make (something) taut or more taut. ➤ *verb intrans* to become taut or more taut.

tauto- *comb. form* see TAUT-.

tautog /'tawtog/ *noun* a dark-coloured N American food fish of the wrasse family, found along the Atlantic coast: *Tautoga onitis*. [Narraganset *tautauog*, pl of *taut*]

tautology /taw'toləji/ *noun* (*pl* **tautologies**) **1a** the needless repetition of an idea, statement, or word. **b** an instance of this. **2** in logic, a statement that is true by virtue of its logical form; an analytic proposition. ➤➤ **tautological** /-'lojikl/ *adj*, **tautologically** /-'lojikli/ *adv*, **tautologous** /-gəs/ *adj*, **tautologously** /-əsli/ *adv*. [via late Latin from Greek *tautologia*, from *tautologos* repeating what has been said, from TAUTO- + *legein* to say]

tautomer /'tawtəmə/ *noun* any of the forms of a tautomeric compound. [from *tautomeric* (see TAUTOMERISM)]

tautomerism /taw'toməriz(ə)m/ *noun* isomerism in which the isomers change into one another with great ease so that they ordinarily exist together in equilibrium. ➤➤ **tautomeric** /-'merik/ *adj*. [TAUTO- + ISOMERISM]

tautonym /'tawtənim/ *noun* in biology, a taxonomic name in which the generic name and the specific name is the same, for example *Buteo buteo*, the buzzard, *Phoxinus phoxinus*, the minnow, and *Dama dama*, the fallow deer. ➤➤ **tautonymous** /taw'toniməs/ *adj*. [TAUT- + -ONYM]

tavern /'tavən/ *noun* **1** *Brit, humorous or archaic* a pub or inn. **2** *NAmer and NZ* a place where alcoholic drinks are sold and served. [Middle English *taverne* via French from Latin *taberna* shed, hut, shop]

taverna /tə'vuhnə/ *noun* a Greek inn or restaurant. [modern Greek from Latin *taberna* shed, hut, TAVERN]

TAVR *abbr* Territorial Army and Volunteer Reserve.

taw[1] /taw/ *verb trans* to dress (skins), usu by a dry process, e.g. with alum or salt, as opposed to using tannin. [Old English *tawian*]

taw[2] *noun* **1** a large marble. **2** the game of marbles. **3** the line which players shoot in marbles. [origin unknown]

tawa /'tahwə/ *noun* a New Zealand tree of the laurel family, with edible purple fruit: *Beilschmiedia tawa*. [Maori *tawa*]

tawdry /'tawdri/ *adj* (**tawdrier, tawdriest**) **1** cheap and tastelessly ornate in appearance. **2** sordid or sleazy. ➤➤ **tawdrily** *adv*, **tawdriness** *noun*.

Word history
obsolete *tawdry lace*, a silk ribbon worn around the neck in the 16th cent., alteration of *St Audrey's Lace*, named after *St Audrey* (Etheldreda) d.679, Queen of Northumbria. Tawdry laces and cheap imitations of them were sold at a fair commemorating St Audrey at Ely in E England.

tawny /'tawni/ *adj* (**tawnier, tawniest**) of a warm sandy or brownish orange colour, like that of well-tanned skin. ➤➤ **tawniness** *noun*, **tawny** *noun*. [Middle English from early French *tanné*, past part. of *tanner*: see TAN[1]]

tawny owl *noun* a common brown European owl: *Strix aluco*.

tawse /tawz/ *noun chiefly Scot esp* formerly in schools, a leather strap slit into strips at the end, used for beating children. [prob from *taws*, pl of obsolete *taw* tawed leather]

tax[1] /taks/ *verb trans* **1** to levy a tax on (income, a person, etc). **2** to make strenuous demands on (somebody, a person's patience, etc). **3** (+ with) to charge (somebody) with a fault, or blame them for it: *Shakespeare has been sometimes taxed with the barbarism of profuseness and exaggeration* — J R Lowell. **4** to assess (the legal costs of a case). ➤➤ **taxable** *adj*, **taxer** *noun*. [Middle English *taxen* to estimate, assess, tax, via French from Latin *taxare* to feel, estimate, censure, frequentative of *tangere* to touch]

tax² *noun* **1** a charge, usu of money, imposed by a government on individuals, organizations, or property, *esp* to raise revenue: *In this world nothing can be said to be certain, except death and taxes* — Benjamin Franklin. **2** a heavy demand or strain. ✷ **after tax** net. **before tax** gross.

tax- *or* **taxi-** *or* **taxo-** *comb. form* forming words, denoting: arrangement: *taxidermy*. [Greek *taxi-*, from *taxis*: see TAXIS]

taxa /'taksə/ *noun* pl of TAXON.

taxation /tak'saysh(ə)n/ *noun* **1** the action of taxing, *esp* the imposition of taxes. **2** revenue obtained from taxes. **3** a rate of tax or the amount assessed as a tax. ⟫⟫ **taxational** *adj*.

tax avoidance *noun* the legal avoiding of paying taxes, by minimizing activities that make one liable for tax or by claiming for properly allowable deductions from income before tax: compare TAX EVASION.

tax-deductible *adj* legally permitted to be deducted from taxable income or capital: *tax-deductible expenses*.

tax disc *noun* a circle of paper that must be displayed on the windscreen of a motor vehicle to show that its road tax has been paid.

taxes *noun* **1** /'taksiz/ pl of TAX². **2** /'takseez/ pl of TAXIS.

tax evasion *noun* deliberate failure to pay taxes, usu by falsely reporting taxable income or property: compare TAX AVOIDANCE.

tax exile *noun* a person who lives abroad in order to avoid paying high taxes in their home country.

tax-free *adj* exempted from tax.

tax haven *noun* a country with a relatively low level of taxation, *esp* on incomes.

tax holiday *noun* a period of time during which a person or company is exempt from taxation for some reason.

taxi¹ /'taksi/ *noun* (*pl* **taxis** *or* **taxies**) = TAXICAB.

taxi² *verb* (**taxis** *or* **taxies, taxied, taxiing** *or* **taxying**) ⟫ *verb intrans* **1** to travel by taxi. **2** said of an aircraft: to move at low speed along a runway before take-off or after landing. ⟫ *verb trans* **1** to transport (somebody or something) by taxi. **2** to cause (an aircraft) to taxi.

taxi- *comb. form* see TAX-.

-taxic *comb. form* see -TAXIS.

taxicab *noun* a motor car that may be hired, together with its driver, to carry passengers, the fare usu being calculated by a taximeter. [short for *taximeter cab*]

taxidermy /'taksiduhmi/ *noun* the art of preparing, stuffing, and mounting the skins of animals to give a lifelike appearance. ⟫⟫ **taxidermal** /-'duhmal/ *adj*, **taxidermic** /-'duhmik/ *adj*, **taxidermist** *noun*. [TAXI- + DERM- + -Y³]

taximeter *noun* a meter fitted in a taxi to calculate the charge for each journey, usu determined by the distance travelled. [French *taximètre*, modification of German *Taxameter*, from medieval Latin *taxa* tax, charge + -METER²]

taxing *adj* onerous; wearing; physically, mentally, or emotionally demanding. ⟫⟫ **taxingly** *adv*. [from TAX¹]

tax inspector *noun* an official who assesses tax liabilities, checks tax returns, collects taxes, and provides advice on taxation matters.

taxi rank *noun* a place where taxicabs park, usu to wait for customers.

taxis /'taksis/ *noun* (*pl* **taxes** /'takseez/) **1** the manual restoration of a displaced body part, *esp* a hernia, by pressure. **2** movement, or a reflex reaction involving movement, by a freely motile usu simple organism such as a bacterium towards or away from a source of stimulation, e.g. a light, or a temperature or chemical gradient: compare TROPISM. [Greek *taxis* arrangement, order, from *tassein* to arrange]

-taxis *comb. form* (*pl* **-taxes**) forming nouns, denoting: **1** arrangement or order: *phyllotaxis*. **2** orientation or movement towards or in relation to a specified force or agent: *thermotaxis*. ⟫⟫ **-tactic** *comb. form*, **-taxic** *comb. form*. [scientific Latin from Greek, from *taxis*: see TAXIS]

taxi stand *noun* = STAND² (11).

taxiway *noun* a usu paved strip for aircraft taxiing, e.g. from the terminal to a runway, at an airport.

tax loss *noun* an actual or nominal loss that can be offset against tax liabilities.

taxman *noun* (*pl* **taxmen**) **1** *informal* an official who assesses and collects taxes, etc; = TAX INSPECTOR. **2** (**the taxman**) *Brit, informal* the Inland Revenue personified.

taxo- *comb. form* see TAX-.

taxon /'takson/ *noun* (*pl* **taxa** /'taksə/) a taxonomic group or entity, or the name of such a group or entity. [scientific Latin, back-formation from TAXONOMY]

taxonomy /tak'sonəmi/ *noun* (*pl* **taxonomies**) **1** classification, *esp* of plants and animals according to their presumed natural relationships. **2** the scientific study of the principles of classification. ⟫⟫ **taxonomic** /-'nomik/ *adj*, **taxonomical** /-'nomikl/ *adj*, **taxonomically** /-'nomikli/ *adv*, **taxonomist** *noun*. [French *taxonomie*, from TAXO- + -*nomie* -NOMY]

taxpayer *noun* somebody who pays or is liable for a tax. ⟫⟫ **taxpaying** *adj*.

tax relief *noun* a reduction in income tax that must be paid, e.g. for tax-deductible expenses.

tax return *noun* a formal statement, made to the Inland Revenue, of income and allowable deductions for tax assessment purposes.

tax shelter *noun* a strategy or system under which the payment of tax can be minimized or avoided. ⟫⟫ **tax-sheltered** *adj*.

-taxy *comb. form* = -TAXIS. [Greek *-taxia*, from *tassein* to arrange]

tax year *noun* the year that is taken as the basis for calculations of tax. In Britain, the tax year generally runs from 6 April of one year to 5 April of the following year.

tayberry /'tayberi/ *noun* (*pl* **tayberries**) **1** a sweet dark red edible berry. **2** the shrub that bears this fruit, a hybrid of the blackberry and raspberry. [named after the River *Tay* in central Scotland where it was introduced]

Tay-Sachs disease /,tay 'saks/ *noun* a rare hereditary metabolic disorder involving an enzyme deficiency that causes a build-up of lipids (fatty substances; see LIPID) in brain and nerve tissue, resulting in mental retardation, paralysis, epileptic seizures, blindness, and, ultimately, death. Tay-Sachs disease mostly affects very young children, *esp* of eastern European Jewish descent. [named after Warren *Tay* d.1927, British physician, and Bernard *Sachs* d.1944, American neurologist, who each independently described it]

tazza /'tatsə/ *noun* (*pl* **tazzas** *or* **tazze** /'tatsay/) a shallow cup or vase on a pedestal. [Italian *tazza* cup, via Arabic from Persian *tast* bowl]

TB *noun* = TUBERCULOSIS. [short for TUBERCLE BACILLUS]

Tb *abbr* the chemical symbol for terbium.

T-bar *noun* **1** a metal bar or beam having a cross-section in the form of the letter T. **2a** a T-shaped bar on a ski lift by which skiers are pulled up a slope. **b** a T-shaped wrench. **c** a T-shaped strap on a shoe, *esp* a child's sandal.

T-bone *or* **T-bone steak** *noun* a thick steak from the thin end of a beef sirloin containing a T-shaped bone.

tbs *or* **tbsp** *abbr* (*pl* **tbs** *or* **tbsp** *or* **tbsps**) **1** tablespoon. **2** tablespoonful.

Tc *abbr* the chemical symbol for technetium.

Tce *abbr Brit* in street names, terrace.

T-cell /'teesel/ *noun* (*pl* **T-cells**) a type of lymphocyte cell that is produced or processed in the thymus gland and is involved in the destruction of cells infected by a virus and is important in the maintenance of the body's immune response. Also called T LYMPHOCYTE. [the T stands for *thymus-derived*]

TCH *abbr* Tchad (international vehicle registration for Chad).

TCP/IP *abbr* in computing, a protocol for communications between computers and the one that has become the standard for transmitting data over networks, including the Internet. [an acronym based on *transmission control protocol/Internet protocol*]

TD *abbr* member of the Dáil. [Irish Gaelic *Teachta Dála*]

t distribution *noun* = STUDENT'S T TEST.

Te *abbr* the chemical symbol for tellurium.

te *or* **ti** /tee/ *noun* in music, the seventh note of a major scale in the tonic sol-fa system, or the note B in the fixed-doh system. [see GAMUT]

tea /tee/ *noun* **1a** a shrub of the camellia family that is cultivated, *esp* in tropical and subtropical Asia, for its leaves that are a source of a refreshing drink: *Camellia sinensis*. **b** the leaves and leaf buds of the tea plant, prepared and cured. Tea is classed according to the method of manufacture, e.g. green tea, black tea, or oolong, and graded according to leaf size, e.g. orange pekoe, pekoe, or souchong. **c** an aromatic refreshing drink prepared from tea leaves by steeping them in boiling water. **d** a cup or pot of tea: *Two teas, please*. **2a** any of various plants somewhat resembling tea in appearance or properties: *Maté is sometimes known as Paraguay tea*. **b** their leaves prepared for use medicinally or to make a drink. **c** the leaves, flowers, fruit, etc of various other plants prepared for using to make a drink: *camomile tea*. **d** a cup or pot of such a drink. **3a** refreshments, usu including tea with sandwiches, cakes, or biscuits, served in the late afternoon. **b** a late-afternoon or early-evening meal. **c** the food prepared for a late-afternoon or early-evening meal: *Your tea's on the table*. [Chinese (Amoy) *t'e*]

tea bag *noun* a cloth or paper bag holding enough tea for an individual serving when infused.

tea ball *noun* a perforated metal ball-shaped container that holds tea leaves and is used in brewing tea, *esp* in a cup.

tea boy *noun Brit* a young man whose job is to make tea for the other employees in an office or factory.

tea bread *noun* any of various light often sweet breads or plain cakes.

tea break *noun Brit* a short pause during the working day, usu in the middle of the morning or afternoon, for refreshment, e.g. tea or coffee.

tea cake *noun* a round yeast-leavened sweet bread bun that often contains currants and is usu eaten toasted with butter.

teach /teech/ *verb* (*past tense and past part.* **taught** /tawt/) ➤ *verb trans* **1a** to cause (somebody or something) to know something or how to do something, *esp* by showing or instruction: *My wife is teaching me to drive*. **b** to guide the studies of (somebody). **c** to impart the knowledge of (a subject, skill, etc): *I teach maths and RE*. **2a** to instruct (somebody) by precept, example, or experience. **b** to advocate (something): *He teaches the way of peace*. **3** *informal* to cause (somebody) to suffer the disagreeable consequences of something: *I'll teach you to come home late*. ➤ *verb intrans* to provide instruction: *He who can, does. He who cannot, teaches* — George Bernard Shaw. [Old English *tæcan*]

teachable *adj* **1** capable of being taught. **2** apt and willing to learn. ➤➤ **teachability** /-'biliti/ *noun*, **teachableness** *noun*, **teachably** *adv*.

teacher *noun* **1** a person whose occupation is teaching, *esp* in a school. **2** a person who instructs another in a subject, skill, etc.

teacher's pet *noun* a person who ingratiates himself or herself with an authority, *esp* a teacher.

tea chest *noun* a large square box used for exporting tea and also for storage, removals, etc: *She stored her books in a tea chest*.

teach-in *noun* **1** an informally structured conference on a usu topical issue. **2** an extended meeting for lectures, demonstrations, and discussions on a topic.

teaching *noun* **1** the profession of a teacher, *esp* in a school. **2** something taught, *esp* a doctrine: *the teachings of Confucius*.

teaching aid *noun* a device, e.g. a record player, map, or picture, used in teaching.

teaching assistant *noun* a person, often a recent graduate doing a post-graduate degree, who is paid to take university tutorials, but who usu does not lecture.

teaching fellow *noun* = TEACHING ASSISTANT.

teaching hospital *noun* a hospital that is affiliated to a medical school and provides medical students with the opportunity of gaining practical experience under supervision.

teaching machine *noun* any of various mechanical devices for presenting instructional material, *esp* one that gives the user the opportunity to answer questions on the material, assess their responses, and so gives an indication of progress.

tea cloth *noun* **1** a small cloth for a table or trolley on which tea is to be served. **2** = TEA TOWEL.

tea cosy *noun* a thick or padded covering for a teapot, used to keep the tea warm.

teacup *noun* **1** a small cup, usu larger than a coffee cup and smaller than a mug, used for hot beverages, *esp* tea. **2** the quantity contained in a teacup; TEACUPFUL.

teacupful /'teekupf(ə)l/ *noun* (*pl* **teacupfuls**) as much as a teacup will hold.

tea dance *noun* a dance held in the late afternoon.

tea garden *noun* a public garden where tea and light refreshments are served.

teahouse /'teehows/ *noun* a restaurant, *esp* in China or Japan, where tea and light refreshments are served.

teak /teek/ *noun* **1** a tall tree of the vervain family that is native to India and SE Asia: *Tectona grandis*. **2** the hard yellowish brown wood of this tree, used for furniture and shipbuilding. [Portuguese *teca* from Malayalam *tēkka*]

teal /teel/ *noun* (*pl* **teals** *or collectively* **teal**) **1** any of various small freshwater dabbling ducks, the males of which often have distinctive bright patches of plumage: genus *Anas*, several species, *esp Anas crecca*, the common green-winged teal. **2** (*also* **teal blue**). **a** a greenish blue colour. **b** (*used before a noun*) of a greenish blue colour. [Middle English *tele*, of Germanic origin]

tea lady *noun chiefly Brit* a woman who makes and/or serves tea, coffee, etc in a factory or office.

tea leaf *noun* **1** (*usu in pl*) a fragment of a leaf of the tea plant, *esp* for or after infusion or soaking. **2** *Brit, informal* a thief. [(sense 2) *tea leaf* rhyming slang]

tealight *noun* a small round candle, typically about 4 cm (1.5 in) in diameter and 1.5 cm (0.75 in) tall, usually in a metal or plastic container.

team[1] /teem/ *noun* **1** (*treated as sing. or pl*). **a** a group of players forming on one side in a sporting contest, debate, etc. **b** a group of two or more people who work together. **2a** two or more draught animals harnessed together, *esp* for ploughing. **b** a vehicle together with its harness and the animal or animals pulling it. [Old English *tēam* offspring, lineage, group of draught animals]

team[2] *verb intrans* **1** (*often* + up) to come together as a team or as if in a team: *Let's team up with them for a night out*. **2** (*usu* + up) to form a harmonizing combination. ➤ *verb trans* **1** to yoke or join (people, animals, etc) in a team. **2** (+ with) to combine (e.g. items of clothing) so as to form a harmonizing arrangement: *You can't team those shoes with that dress*.

tea-maker *noun* **1** an electrical device for heating water and making tea, sometimes with a timer that allows it to come into operation at a preset time, e.g. early morning. **2** a device, such as a tea ball, that can be used to make tea in a cup or mug.

teammate *noun* a fellow member of a team.

team player *noun* **1** a sportsperson who is good at playing as part of a team, *esp* somebody who acts as an inspiration to the other players and who makes an effort not to monopolize the play. **2** a person who is good at working as part of a team, *esp* somebody who has respect for and gets on well with their colleagues.

team spirit *noun* willingness to work as part of a team and subordinate personal aims to group objectives.

teamster /'teemstə/ *noun* **1** somebody who drives a team of horses. **2** *NAmer* a lorry driver.

team teaching *noun* a method of teaching, *esp* in schools, in which two or more teachers with different specialisms combine to teach as a team.

teamwork *noun* mutual cooperation in a group enterprise.

teapot *noun* a usu round pot with a lid, spout, and handle in which tea is brewed and from which it is served.

teapoy /'teepoy/ *noun* a three-legged ornamental stand or table. [Hindi *tipāī*, from Sanskrit *tri* three + *pāda* foot]

tear[1] /tiə/ *noun* **1** a drop of clear salty fluid secreted by the lachrymal gland that lubricates the eye and eyelids and is often released as a result of grief or other emotion: *Sometimes she scolded herself so severely as to bring tears to her eyes* — Lewis Carroll. **2** a transparent drop of fluid or hardened fluid, e.g. resin. * **in tears** crying; weeping. **to tears** to a great extent: *I was bored to tears*. ➤➤ **tearless** *adj*. [Old English *tæhher*, *tēar*]

tear[2] /teə/ *verb* (*past tense* **tore** /taw/, *past part.* **torn** /tawn/) ➤ *verb trans* **1a** to pull (something) apart by force; to damage (something) in this way. **b** to wound (e.g. a part of the body) by tearing. **2** to cause division or distress to (e.g. a person's mind). **3** (*often* + from) to remove (somebody or something) by force. **4** to make (a hole, pattern, etc) by tearing. ➤ *verb intrans* **1** to separate on being pulled: *This cloth tears easily*. **2** to move or act with violence, haste, or force: *The children went tearing down the street*. * **tear a strip off**

informal to rebuke (somebody) angrily. **tear at** to cause distress or pain to (somebody). **tear into** to attack (somebody) physically or verbally without restraint or caution. **tear one's hair** to experience or express grief, rage, desperation, or anxiety. ⟫ **tearable** *adj*, **tearer** *noun*. [Old English *teran*]

tear³ /teə/ *noun* a hole, rip, or flaw made by tearing.

tearaway /'teərəway/ *noun Brit, informal* an unruly and reckless young person.

tear away /teə/ *verb trans* to remove (oneself or another) reluctantly: *They could hardly tear themselves away from the television.*

tear down /teə/ *verb trans* to demolish (something).

teardrop /'tiədrop/ *noun* = TEAR¹ (1).

tear duct /tiə/ *noun* a tube which carries tears from the tear gland to the eye or from the eye to the nose.

tearful /'tiəf(ə)l/ *adj* **1** accompanied by tears: *He ignored her tearful entreaties to stay.* **2** causing tears. **3a** crying or weeping. **b** inclined or about to cry; sad or depressed: *I was feeling a bit tearful this morning.* ⟫ **tearfully** *adv*, **tearfulness** *noun*.

tear gas /tiə/ *noun* a solid, liquid, or gaseous substance that on dispersion in the atmosphere blinds the eyes with tears and is used chiefly in dispelling crowds.

tear gland /tiə/ *noun* a gland above the outer side of the eye where tears are formed.

tearing /'teəring/ *adj informal* said of a hurry: very great: *Why are you in such a tearing hurry?*

tearjerker /'tiəjuhkə/ *noun informal* an excessively sentimental play, film, etc designed to provoke tears. ⟫ **tear-jerking** *adj.*

tear off /teə/ *verb trans* **1** to remove (something) by tearing. **2** to remove (e.g. an item of clothing) quickly. **3** to compose (e.g. a letter) rapidly. ⟫ *verb intrans* to leave or go rapidly. ✳ **tear somebody off a strip** *informal* to rebuke somebody angrily.

tearoom *noun* a restaurant where light refreshments are served.

tea rose *noun* any of numerous hybrid garden roses with abundant large pinkish or yellowish blossoms with a scent resembling that of tea: *Rosa odorata.*

tear sheet /teə/ *noun* a perforated sheet that can be torn from a publication, e.g. so that it can be sent somewhere or kept for future reference.

tear up /teə/ *verb trans* **1** to tear (something) into pieces. **2** to cancel or annul (e.g. an agreement or treaty), usu unilaterally.

teary /'tiəri/ *adj* (**tearier, teariest**) **1** = TEARFUL. **2** resembling a tear or tears. ⟫ **tearily** *adv*, **teariness** *noun*.

tease¹ /teez/ *verb trans* **1a** to persistently and usu playfully irritate or make fun of (somebody). **b** to pretend to offer (somebody) something and then withhold it as a means of provoking anger or frustration. **c** to arouse (somebody) sexually with no intention of permitting sexual fulfilment. **2a** to persuade (somebody) to agree to something, *esp* by persistent small efforts; to coax (them). **b** to obtain (something) by repeated coaxing: *She managed to tease the money out of her father.* **3a** to disentangle and straighten (wool) by combing it. **b** to teasel (cloth). **4** to tear (something) into pieces; *esp* to shred (a tissue or specimen) for microscopic examination. **5** *chiefly NAmer* to backcomb (the hair). ⟫ *verb intrans* to tease someone or something. ⟫ **teasingly** *adv*. [Old English *tǣsan*]

tease² *noun informal* **1** somebody or something that teases. **2** the act or an instance of teasing.

teasel¹ *or* **teazel** *or* **teazle** /'teezl/ *noun* **1a** any of several species of tall European and N African plants of the scabious family with flower heads that are covered with stiff hooked bracts: genus *Dipsacus.* **b** a flower head of any of these plants, formerly used when dried to raise a nap on woollen cloth. **2** a wire substitute for this flower head. [Old English *tǣsel*]

teasel² *verb trans* (**teaselled, teaselling**, *NAmer* **teaseled, teaseling**) to raise a nap on (cloth) with teasels. ⟫ **teaseller** *noun*.

tease out *verb trans* **1** to remove (tangles and knots) from hair, etc by careful combing or brushing. **2** to gain (information, the truth, etc) with difficulty, e.g. by working through a mass of data or by persuading somebody to speak.

teaser *noun* **1** *informal* a frustratingly difficult question or problem. **2** somebody who derives malicious pleasure from teasing. **3** an advertisement, *esp* for a new product, that does not refer to the

product explicitly or that only refers to it cryptically, in order to capture consumer interest and curiosity.

tea service *noun* = TEA SET.

tea set *noun* a matching set of usu china dishes, e.g. teapot, jug, cups and saucers, and plates, for serving tea.

tea shop *noun chiefly Brit* = TEAROOM.

teaspoon *noun* **1** a small spoon used *esp* for eating soft foods and for adding sugar, etc to hot drinks and stirring them. **2** = TEASPOONFUL.

teaspoonful /'teespoohnf(ə)l/ *noun* (*pl* **teaspoonfuls**) **1** as much as a teaspoon will hold. **2** a unit of measure equal to about 5ml (about 0.12fl oz).

teat /teet/ *noun* **1** a nipple of the mammary gland of a female animal. **2** a rubber or plastic mouthpiece with one or more holes in it, attached to the top of a baby's feeding bottle. ⟫ **teated** *adj.* [Middle English from Old French *tete*, of Germanic origin; related to Old English *tit* TIT²]

teatime *noun* the customary time for tea; late afternoon or early evening.

tea towel *noun* a cloth for drying dishes after they have been washed.

tea tray *noun* a tray on which a tea set, food, etc is carried, e.g. when afternoon tea is served.

tea tree *noun* any of several species of shrubs or trees of the myrtle family found in Australia and New Zealand, whose leaves can be used as a substitute for tea and which yield an antiseptic oil used e.g. in cosmetics: genus *Leptospermum.*

tea trolley *noun* a small trolley used in serving tea or light refreshments.

tea wagon *noun NAmer* = TEA TROLLEY.

teazel *or* **teazle** /'teezl/ *noun* = TEASEL¹.

TEC /tek/ *abbr Brit* Training and Enterprise Council.

tech /tek/ *noun Brit, informal* a technical school or college.

tech. *abbr* **1** technical. **2** technically. **3** technician. **4** technological. **5** technology.

techie /'teki/ *noun informal* somebody who is an expert in or an enthusiast for new technology, *esp* anything to do with electronic gadgetry, computing, the Internet, etc. [from TECHNICAL, TECHNICIAN, etc]

technetium /tek'neeshi·əm/ *noun* a radioactive metallic chemical element, that is artificially produced as a product of fission in nuclear reactors, and is used e.g. in radiotherapy: symbol Tc, atomic number 43. [scientific Latin, from Greek *technētos* artificial, from *technē* art, craft, skill, + -IUM]

technic /'teknik/ *noun* **1** *chiefly NAmer* = TECHNIQUE. **2** = TECHNICS. [Greek *technikos*: see TECHNICAL]

technical *adj* **1a** involving special and usu practical knowledge, *esp* of mechanical, industrial, or scientific subjects: *My brother went to a school that specialized in technical education.* **b** skilled in practical and scientific subjects. **2a** marked by or characteristic of specialization. **b** relating to or used in a particular subject: *I'll try to use as few technical terms as possible.* **c** complicated or difficult to understand: *I'm sorry if my explanation was too technical for you to follow.* **3** marked by a strict legal interpretation or rigid application of the rules: *He had technical responsibility for all his subordinates.* **4** relating to technique. **5** of or produced by ordinary commercial processes without being subjected to special purification. **6** resulting chiefly from internal market factors rather than external influences: *This was a technical reaction of the stock market.* ⟫ **technicalness** *noun.* [Greek *technikos* of art, skilful, from *technē* art, craft, skill]

technical college *noun* a further education college that offers courses in practical subjects, e.g. hairdressing, secretarial skills, computing, applied sciences, etc, usu up to HND level and with the aim of providing vocational training.

technical drawing *noun* **1** the technique or practice of draughtsmanship, e.g. as taught in schools. **2** an accurate drawing or plan of e.g. machinery or a building as produced by a draughtsman.

technicality /tekni'kaliti/ *noun* (*pl* **technicalities**) **1** the quality or state of being technical. **2a** a detail meaningful only to a specialist. **b** a detail arising from a strict or literal interpretation of a rule or law: *Everyone knew he was guilty but he got off on a technicality.*

technical knockout *noun* the termination of a boxing match when a boxer is declared by the referee to be unable to continue the fight, e.g. because of injuries.

technically *adv* **1** in a technical manner. **2** according to a strict interpretation: *Technically that was a foul, but we'll let it pass.*

technician /tek'nish(ə)n/ *noun* **1a** a specialist in the technical details of a subject or occupation. **b** somebody who has acquired the technique of an area of specialization, e.g. an art: *She was a superb technician and an artist of ingenuity.* **2** somebody employed to do practical work, e.g. in a laboratory: *a lab technician; a medical technician.*

Technicolor /'teknikulə/ *noun trademark* a process of colour photography in the cinema in which the three primary colours are recorded on separate films and then combined in a single print. [blend of TECHNICAL + COLOR]

technicolour *noun* vivid and often garish colour. ➤➤ **technicolour** *adj,* **technicoloured** *adj.*

technics *pl noun* **1** (*treated as sing.*) = TECHNOLOGY. **2** (*treated as sing. or pl*) rules, procedures, technique, or technical details.

technique /tek'neek/ *noun* **1** the manner in which an artist, performer, or athlete displays or manages the formal aspect of his or her skill. **2a** a body of technical methods, e.g. in a craft or in scientific research. **b** a method of accomplishing a desired aim; a knack. [French *technique* technical, from Greek *technikos:* see TECHNICAL]

techno /'teknoh/ *noun* a form of fast electronically produced modern dance music with few, simple vocals. [short for *technological*]

techno- *comb. form* forming words, with the meaning: technical or technological: *technocracy.* [Greek, from *technē* skill, art, craft]

technobabble /'teknoh,babl/ *noun informal* language that is full of complicated technical terms, often pretentiously or needlessly so, and is difficult for the ordinary person to understand.

technocracy /tek'nokrəsi/ *noun* (*pl* **technocracies**) *chiefly derog* **1** a body of technical experts, *esp* one that exerts influence in the running of a country, etc. **2a** management of society by a body of technical experts. **b** a society managed by such people. ➤➤ **technocrat** /'teknəkrat/ *noun,* **technocratic** /teknə'kratik/ *adj,* **technocratically** /-'kratikli/ *adv.*

technol. *abbr* **1** technological. **2** technology.

technology /tek'noləji/ *noun* (*pl* **technologies**) **1** the theory and practice of applied science as used in commerce and industry. **2** applied scientific methods. **3** the totality of the means and knowledge used to provide objects necessary for human sustenance and comfort. ➤➤ **technological** /-'lojikl/ *adj,* **technologically** /-'lojikli/ *adv,* **technologist** *noun.* [Greek *technologia* systematic treatment of an art, from TECHNO- + *-logia* -LOGY]

technophilia /teknə'fili·ə/ *noun* enthusiasm for new technology, such as computers. ➤➤ **technophile** /'teknəfiel/ *noun,* **technophilic** /-'filik/ *adj.*

technophobia /teknə'fohbi·ə/ *noun* fear or distrust of new technology, *esp* of computers. ➤➤ **technophobe** /'teknəfohb/ *noun,* **technophobic** /-bik/ *adj.*

technospeak /'teknoh,speek/ *noun informal* = TECHNOBABBLE.

techy[1] /'techi/ *adj* (**techier, techiest**) = TETCHY.

techy[2] *noun* = TECHIE.

tectonic /tek'tonik/ *adj* **1** relating to or resulting from the deformation of the earth's crust, the forces involved in this, or the structures formed by it. **2** relating to or involved in building or construction. ➤➤ **tectonically** *adv.* [via late Latin from Greek *tektonikos* of a builder, from *tektōn* builder]

tectonics *pl noun* **1** (*treated as sing. or pl*) the science or art of construction and building. **2a** (*treated as sing. or pl*) in geology, structural features, *esp* those connected with folding and faulting. **b** (*treated as sing.*) the scientific study of such structural features.

tectrix /'tektriks/ *noun* (*pl* **tectrices** /-seez/) one of the coverts (feathers covering bases of main feathers; see COVERT[2]) of a bird's wing. [Latin *tectrix,* feminine of *tector* plasterer, from *tegere* to cover]

Ted /ted/ *noun informal* = TEDDY BOY.

ted *verb trans* (**tedded, tedding**) to turn over and spread (e.g. new-mown grass) for drying. ➤➤ **tedder** *noun.* [Old Norse *tethja* to spread manure]

teddy[1] /'tedi/ *noun* (*pl* **teddies**) = TEDDY BEAR.

teddy[2] *noun* (*pl* **teddies**) a woman's one-piece undergarment that combines a camisole and French knickers. [origin unknown]

teddy bear *noun* a stuffed toy bear. [*Teddy,* nickname of *Theodore* Roosevelt d.1919, US president; from a cartoon depicting the president sparing the life of a bear cub while hunting]

Teddy boy *noun* a member of a cult of British youths, *esp* in the 1950s, who adopted the dress of the early 20th cent., wore their hair in swept-up quiffs, were rock 'n' roll enthusiasts, and sometimes had a reputation for unruly behaviour. [*Teddy,* nickname for *Edward,* i.e. King Edward VII d.1910; from the Edwardian style of dress]

Te Deum /,tay 'dayəm, ,tee 'dee·əm/ *noun* (*pl* **Te Deums**) **1a** a liturgical Christian hymn of praise to God. **b** a musical setting for this. **2** a service in which this prayer is recited. [Middle English, from late Latin *Te Deum Laudamus* Thee, God, we praise; the opening words of the hymn]

tedious /'teedi·əs/ *adj* **1** said of a task, homily, etc: tiresome through being both dull and interminable. **2** said of people: boring; tiresome; dull: *Don't squander the gold of your days listening to the tedious* — Oscar Wilde. ➤➤ **tediously** *adv,* **tediousness** *noun.* [Middle English from late Latin *taediosus,* from Latin *taedium:* see TEDIUM]

tedium /'teedi·əm/ *noun* **1** the state or quality of being tedious. **2** boredom. [Latin *taedium* disgust, irksomeness, from *taedēre* to disgust, weary]

tee[1] /tee/ *noun* **1** something shaped like a capital T, such as a T-shaped pipe fitting. **2** a mark aimed at in various games, e.g. curling.

tee[2] *noun* **1** in golf, a peg or a small mound used to raise a golf ball into position for striking at the beginning of play on a hole. **2** the area from which a golf ball is struck at the beginning of play on a hole. [back-formation from obsolete *teaz* (taken as pl), of unknown origin]

tee[3] *verb trans* (*often* + up) to place (a golf ball) on a tee.

tee[4] *noun* (*pl* **tees**) *informal* a T-shirt.

tee-hee[1] *or* **te-hee** /,tee 'hee/ *interj* used to express amusement or derision. [Middle English *te he,* of imitative origin]

tee-hee[2] *or* **te-hee** *noun* a chuckle, suppressed giggle, or mocking laugh.

tee-hee[3] *or* **te-hee** *verb intrans* (**tee-hees,** *or* **te-hees, tee-heeing** *or* **te-heeing, tee-heed** *or* **te-heed**) to give a chuckle, suppressed giggle, or mocking laugh.

teem[1] /teem/ *verb intrans* **1** (+ with) to abound: *I can remember when these rivers teemed with salmon.* **2** to be present in large quantities. **3** *archaic* to be or become pregnant: *Chaste to her husband, frank to all beside, a teeming mistress, but a barren bride*— Pope. ➤➤ **teeming** *adj.* [Old English *tīman, tǣman;* related to Old English *tēam* TEAM[1]]

teem[2] *verb intrans Brit* (*also* + down) to rain hard. [Middle English *temen* to empty, pour out, from Old Norse *tœma*]

teen[1] /teen/ *adj informal* = TEENAGE.

teen[2] *noun informal* = TEENAGER.

-teen *comb. form* forming words for the numbers between 13 and 19: *sixteen.* [Old English *-tīne, from* tien ten]

teenage /'teenayj/ *adj* relating to, denoting, or suitable for a teenager or people in their teens: *teenage boys, goaded by their surging hormones* — Camille Paglia.

teenaged /'teenayjd/ *adj* = TEENAGE.

teenager /'teenayjə/ *noun* a person who is aged between 13 and 19.

teens *pl noun* the numbers 13 to 19 inclusive; *specif* the years 13 to 19 in a lifetime. [from -TEEN]

teensy-weensy /,teenzi 'weenzi/ *adj* see TEENY-WEENY.

teeny /'teeni/ *or* **teensy** /'teenzi/ *adj* (**teenier** *or* **teensier, teeniest** *or* **teensiest**) *informal* tiny. [*teeny* by alteration of TINY[1]; *teensy* from *teeny*]

teenybopper /'teenibopə/ *noun informal* a young teenage girl who zealously follows the latest trends in clothes, pop music, etc. [TEEN[1] + -Y[4] + *bopper:* see BOP[2]]

teeny-weeny /,teeni 'weeni/ *or* **teensy-weensy** /,teenzi 'weenzi/ *adj informal* tiny.

tee off *verb intrans* **1** to drive a golf ball from a tee. **2** *informal* to make a start.

teepee /'teepee/ *noun* see TEPEE.

tee shirt *noun* see T-SHIRT.

teeter /'teetə/ *verb intrans* (**teetered, teetering**) **1** to wobble or move unsteadily. **2** to waver or be unable to make up one's mind. [Middle English *titeren* to totter, reel, from Old Norse *titra* to shake]

teeth /teeth/ *noun* pl of TOOTH[1].

teethe /teedh/ *verb intrans* to cut one's milk teeth; to grow teeth. ➤➤ **teething** *noun*. [earliest as *teething*, from TEETH]

teething ring /'teedhing/ *noun* a usu plastic ring for a teething infant to bite on.

teething troubles /'teedhing/ *pl noun* temporary problems occurring with new machinery or during the initial stages of an activity.

teetotal /tee'tohtl/ *adj* practising complete abstinence from alcoholic drinks. ➤➤ **teetotalism** *noun*. [*total* + *total* abstinence; said to have been coined in 1833 by Richard Turner d.1846, advocate of total abstinence]

teetotaller (*NAmer* **teetotaler**) *noun* somebody who is teetotal.

teetotum /tee'tohtəm/ *noun* (*pl* **teetotums**) **1** a small top, usu inscribed with letters and used in games of chance. **2** any small top spun with the fingers.

Word history

TEE[1] + Latin *totum* all, neuter of *totus* whole; from the letter *T* inscribed on one side as an abbr of *totum* all, i.e. 'take all'. The other letters were *A* for *auferre* 'to take away', *D* for *deponere* 'to put down', and *N* for *nihil* 'nothing'.

---

teff /tef/ *noun* an African cereal grass grown for its grain which yields a white flour: *Eragrostis tef*. [Amharic *ṭēf*]

TEFL /,tee ee ef 'el, 'tefl/ *abbr* teaching English as a foreign language.

Teflon /'teflon/ *noun trademark* polytetrafluoroethylene. [TETRA- + FLUORO- + *-on* as in NYLON]

teg /teg/ *noun chiefly Brit* a sheep in its second year. [prob of Scandinavian origin]

tegmen /'tegmən/ *noun* (*pl* **tegmina** /'tegmənə/) **1** either of the leathery front wings of a grasshopper, cricket, cockroach, etc that cover and protect the hind wings. **2** the thin inner covering of a seed. **3** any similar covering structure such as the thin plate of bone covering the middle ear. ➤➤ **tegmental** /teg'mentl/ *adj*. [Latin *tegmin-, tegmen* covering, from *tegere* to cover]

tegmentum /teg'mentəm/ *noun* (*pl* **tegmenta** /-tə/) a region of the midbrain containing the nuclei of several cranial nerves and nerve pathways that connect the forebrain and the spinal cord. ➤➤ **tegmental** *adj*. [Latin *tegumentum, tegmentum* covering, from *tegere* to cover]

tegmina /'tegmənə/ *noun* pl of TEGMEN.

tegument /'tegyoomənt/ *noun* = INTEGUMENT. ➤➤ **tegumental** /-'mentl/ *adj*, **tegumentary** /-'ment(ə)ri/ *adj*. [Middle English from Latin *tegumentum*: see TEGMENTUM]

te-hee[1] /,tee 'hee/ *interj* see TEE-HEE[1].

te-hee[2] *noun* see TEE-HEE[2].

te-hee[3] *verb intrans* see TEE-HEE[3].

tein /'tay·in/ *noun* (*pl* **teins** or **tein**) a unit of currency in Kazakhstan, worth 100th of a tenge.

tektite /'tektiet/ *noun* a rounded dark glassy object believed to have been formed as a result of meteorite impact. ➤➤ **tektitic** /tek'titik/ *adj*. [Greek *tēktos* molten, from *tēkein* to melt]

tel. *abbr* **1** telegram. **2** telegraph. **3** telegraphic. **4** telephone.

tel-[1] *or* **telo-** *comb. form* forming words, denoting: end: *telophase*. [Greek *telos* end]

tel-[2] *comb. form* see TELE-.

telaesthesia (*NAmer* **telesthesia**) /teləs'theezyə, -zh(y)ə/ *noun* perception, e.g. of an object, at a distance without the use of the sense organs. ➤➤ **telaesthetic** /-'thetik/ *adj*. [TELE- + AESTHESIA]

telamon /'teləmon/ *noun* (*pl* **telamons** or **telamones** /-'mohneez/) in classical architecture, a pillar in the shape of a man, *esp* one supporting an entablature; ATLAS. [via Latin from Greek *telamōn* bearer, from *tlēnai* to bear]

telangiectasia /te,lanji·ek'tayzi·ə, -zhə/ *or* **telangiectasis** /-'ektəsis, -'taysis/ *noun* (*pl* **telangiectasias** *or* **telangiectases** /-seez/) an abnormal dilation of small blood vessels that often forms an ANGIOMA (small reddish or purplish benign tumour).

➤➤ **telangiectatic** /-'tatik/ *adj*. [scientific Latin from TEL-[1] + ANGI- + *ectasia, ectasis* dilation, from Greek *ekteinein* to stretch out]

tele- *or* **tel-** *comb. form* forming words, with the meanings: **1** distant; at a distance; over a distance: *telegram; telepathy*. **2a** telegraph: *teleprinter*. **b** television: *telecast; telecamera*. [Greek *tēle-, tēl-*, from *tēle* far off]

telecast[1] /'telikahst/ *verb trans and intrans* to televise (something). ➤➤ **telecaster** *noun*. [TELE- + BROADCAST[1]]

telecast[2] *noun* a televised broadcast.

telecom /'telikom/ *noun* = TELECOMMUNICATION.

telecommunication /,telikəmyoohni'kaysh(ə)n/ *noun* **1** communication at a distance, e.g. by telegraph, telephone, television, etc. **2** (*usu in pl*) the science and technology of telecommunication.

telecommute /,telikə'myooht/ *verb intrans* to work from home, using a personal computer, a modem, electronic mail, etc to communicate with clients and a central office. ➤➤ **telecommuter** /'tel-/ *noun*.

telecoms *or* **telecomms** /'telicomz/ *pl noun* telecommunications (see TELECOMMUNICATION).

teleconferencing /'telikonf(ə)rənsing/ *noun* the process of holding a meeting involving people in different places who are linked by a telecommunication system, e.g. telephone or television. ➤➤ **teleconference** *noun*.

teledu /'telədooh/ *noun* a flesh-eating mammal of Java and Sumatra that is related to the skunk, resembles the badger, and secretes an offensive-smelling liquid: *Mydaus javanensis*. [Malay *tēledu*]

telegenic /teli'jenik/ *adj* looking attractive or having a pleasant manner on television. [TELE- + *-genic* as in PHOTOGENIC]

telegnosis /teli'nohsis, telig-/ *noun* knowledge of things that are happening far away, not obtained through any of the normal senses. [TELE- + -GNOSIS]

telegony /ti'legəni/ *noun* the supposed carrying over of the influence of a male animal to the offspring resulting from subsequent matings of the female with other males. ➤➤ **telegonic** /teli'gonik/ *adj*, **telegonous** /-nəs/ *adj*. [TELE- + -GONY]

telegram /'teligram/ *noun* a message sent by telegraph and delivered as a written or typed note and, since 1981 in Britain, only used internationally: compare TELEMESSAGE.

telegraph[1] /'teligrahf, -graf/ *noun* an apparatus or system for communicating at a distance, *esp* by making and breaking an electric circuit. [French *télégraphe*, from *télé-* TELE- + *-graphe* -GRAPH]

telegraph[2] *verb trans* **1a** to send or communicate (a message) by telegraph: *He telegraphed to me from London that he had arrived all safe* — Conan Doyle. **b** to send a message to (somebody) by telegraph: *He telegraphed his Aunt Pratt: Have seen awful news in the papers ... Shall start by packet today* — Mark Twain. **2** to make (something) known by signs, *esp* unknowingly and in advance: *telegraph a punch*. ➤➤ **telegrapher** /tə'legrəfə/ *noun*, **telegraphist** /tə'legrəfist/ *noun*.

telegraphese /,teligrah'feez, -grafeez/ *noun* the terse and abbreviated language characteristic of telegrams.

telegraphic /teli'grafik/ *adj* **1** of the telegraph. **2** concise; terse. ➤➤ **telegraphically** *adv*.

telegraph plant *noun* a tropical Asian leguminous shrub whose leaves have small leaflets that make jerky movements in sunshine: *Codariocalyx motorius*.

telegraph pole *noun* a pole erected to hold telephone or telegraph wires.

telegraphy /tə'legrəfi/ *noun* the use or operation of a telegraphic apparatus or system.

Telegu /'teligooh/ *noun* see TELUGU.

telekinesis /,teliki'neesis/ *noun* **1** the supposed ability to move distant objects without physically touching them, *esp* just by concentrating the mind on them. **2** the movement of something that results from this. ➤➤ **telekinetic** /-'netik/ *adj*.

telemark /'telimahk/ *noun* a turn in skiing in which the outside ski is advanced ahead of the other ski and then turned inwards at a steadily widening angle. [Norwegian, named after *Telemark*, region in Norway where it originated]

telemarketing /'telimahkiting/ *noun* the practice of telephoning companies or individuals to try to sell them something; telephone selling. ➤➤ **telemarketer** *noun*.

telemedicine /teli'med(ə)sin/ *noun* the use of the telephone, email, video, etc for medical purposes, e.g. for consultations between doctors and patients.

Telemessage /'telimesij/ *noun trademark* a message sent by telephone or telex and printed out for the recipient. It has replaced the telegram for inland messages in Britain: compare TELEGRAM.

telemeter[1] /tə'lemitə/ *noun* **1** an instrument for measuring the distance of an object from an observer: compare TELLUROMETER. **2** an electrical apparatus for measuring a quantity, e.g. pressure, speed, or temperature, and transmitting the result, e.g. by radio, to a distant place at which it is indicated or recorded. ⟩⟩ **telemetric** /teli'metrik/ *adj*, **telemetrically** /teli'metrikli/ *adv*, **telemetry** /-tri/ *noun*.

telemeter[2] *verb* (**telemetered, telemetering**) to obtain and transmit (a reading, e.g. the measurement of a quantity) by telemeter.

telencephalon /telən'sefəlon/ *noun* the front part of the forebrain comprising the cerebral hemispheres and associated structures. ⟩⟩ **telencephalic** /-'falik/ *adj*. [TEL-[1] + ENCEPHALON]

teleology /teli'oləji, tee-/ *noun* **1** a doctrine explaining phenomena by reference to goals or purposes. **2** the character attributed to nature or natural processes of being directed towards an end or designed according to a purpose. ⟩⟩ **teleological** /-'lojikl/ *adj*, **teleologist** *noun*. [TELE- + -LOGY]

teleost /'teliost, 'tee-/ *noun* any of a large group of fish including salmon, herring, etc; BONY FISH: suborder Teleostei. ⟩⟩ **teleostean** /-'osti-ən/ *adj and noun*. [Greek *teleios* complete, perfect + *osteon* bone]

telepathize or **telepathise** *verb intrans* to communicate or connect with somebody using telepathy.

telepathy /tə'lepəthi/ *noun* communication that supposedly occurs directly from one mind to another without use of the known senses. ⟩⟩ **telepathic** /teli'pathik/ *adj*, **telepathically** /teli'pathikli/ *adv*, **telepathist** *noun*.

telephone[1] /'telifohn/ *noun* **1** a device for reproducing sounds at a distance; *specif* one for converting sounds into electrical impulses for transmission to a particular receiver. **2** the system of communications that uses telephones: *We can get in touch by telephone.* ⟩⟩ **telephonic** /-'fonik/ *adj*, **telephony** /tə'lefəni/ *noun*.

telephone[2] *verb intrans* to make a telephone call. ⟩ *verb trans* **1** to send (a message) by telephone. **2a** to speak or attempt to speak to (somebody) by telephone. **b** to dial (a telephone number, service, helpline, etc). ⟩⟩ **telephoner** *noun*.

telephone banking *noun* the carrying out of banking operations by means of a telephone link.

telephone book *noun* = TELEPHONE DIRECTORY.

telephone booth *noun NAmer* = TELEPHONE BOX.

telephone box *noun* a booth containing a public telephone.

telephone directory *noun* a book giving the telephone numbers of subscribers.

telephone number *noun* **1** a number assigned to a particular telephone and used to call that telephone. **2** (*in pl*) large numbers or huge amounts of money: *Sales are huge. We're talking telephone numbers here.*

telephone selling *noun* = TELESALES.

telephonist /tə'lefənist/ *noun Brit* a telephone switchboard operator.

telephoto /'telifohtoh/ *adj* relating to or used in telephotography. [short for *telephotographic*]

telephotography /,telifə'togrəfi/ *noun* photography of distant objects, e.g. by a camera that has a telephoto lens. ⟩⟩ **telephotographic** /-fohtə'grafik/ *adj*.

telephoto lens *noun* a compound camera lens that has a longer focal length than a simple standard lens, to give a narrow field of vision and a magnified image.

teleport /'telipawt/ *verb trans* in science fiction, to transport (something, somebody, or oneself) across a considerable distance instantaneously, often with the use of machinery that causes dematerializing at the point of origin and rematerializing at the destination. ⟩ *verb intrans* to be transported in this way. ⟩⟩ **teleportation** /-'taysh(ə)n/ *noun*. [TELE- + -*port* as in TRANSPORT[1]]

teleprinter /'teliprintə/ *noun* a typewriter keyboard that transmits telegraphic signals, a typewriting device activated by telegraphic signals, or a machine that combines both these functions, or any similar machine, e.g. one attached to a computer.

Teleprompter /'telipromptə/ *noun NAmer, trademark* a device for unrolling a magnified version of a script in front of a speaker on television.

Teleran /'telərən/ *noun trademark* a system of navigation in which the results of a scan by ground-based radar are televised to the pilot of an aircraft so that he or she can see the positions of all aircraft in the vicinity. [contraction of *television radar navigation*]

telesales /'telisaylz/ *pl noun* (*treated as sing.*) a means of selling or promoting goods and services that involves unsolicited telephone calls to potential customers, either individuals or businesses.

telescope[1] /'teliskohp/ *noun* **1** a usu tubular optical instrument for viewing distant objects by means of the refraction of light rays through a lens or the reflection of light rays by a concave mirror. **2** a RADIO TELESCOPE or any similar device. [Greek *tēleskopos* far-seeing, from *tēle-* TELE- + *skopein* to look]

telescope[2] *verb intrans* **1** to slide one part within another like the cylindrical sections of a hand telescope. **2** to become compressed under impact. **3** to become condensed or shortened. ⟩ *verb trans* **1** to cause (something) to telescope. **2** to condense or shorten (something).

telescopic /teli'skopik/ *adj* **1a** of or performed with a telescope. **b** suitable for seeing or magnifying distant objects. **c** only able to be seen by means of a telescope: *telescopic stars*. **2** able to discern objects at a distance. **3** having parts that telescope; collapsible: *a telescopic umbrella*. ⟩⟩ **telescopically** *adv*.

telescopic sight *noun* a telescope used as a sight on a rifle, etc.

telescopy /tə'leskəpi/ *noun* the design and use of telescopes.

teleshopping /'telishoping/ *noun* the ordering of goods, e.g. those advertised on television, by means of a telephone or computer link.

telespectroscope /teli'spektrəskohp/ *noun* an apparatus combining a telescope and a stereoscope, used for observing and analysing the radiation given off by stars and other celestial bodies.

telestereoscope /teli'steri-əskohp, -'stiəri-əskohp/ *noun* a binocular telescope that allows distant objects to be viewed in three dimensions.

telesthesia /teləs'theezyə, -zh(y)ə/ *noun* see TELAESTHESIA.

teletex /'teliteks/ *noun* an advanced form of telex in which documents are scanned and then reproduced by the receiver. [prob blend of TELEX[1] and TEXT[1]]

Teletext /'telitekst/ *noun trademark* an information service provided by a television network broadcasting special pages of news, sports results, games, etc at the same time as ordinary programmes: compare ORACLE, VIDEOTEX, VIEWDATA.

telethon /'telithon/ *noun* a long television programme, usu involving celebrity guests, designed to raise money for charity by getting viewers to phone in and pledge donations. [TELE- + MARATHON]

Teletype[1] /'telitiep/ *noun* **1** *trademark* a teleprinter. **2** (*often* **teletype**) a message printed on a Teletype. **3** (*often* **teletype**) a network of Teletypes.

Teletype[2] *or* **teletype** *verb trans trademark* to send (a message) by Teletype.

teletypewriter /teli'tieprietə/ *noun chiefly NAmer* = TELEPRINTER.

televangelist /teli'vanjəlist/ *noun* a Christian evangelist, *esp* in the USA, who hosts television shows in which the church's message is preached and appeals are made to viewers for donations. ⟩⟩ **televangelism** *noun*. [TELE- + EVANGELIST]

televise /'teliviez/ *verb trans* to broadcast (a programme, event, or film) by television. [back-formation from TELEVISION]

television /'telivizh(ə)n/ *noun* **1** an electronic system of transmitting changing images together with sound along a wire or through space by converting the images and sounds into electrical signals and then reconverting the received signals into images and sound: *Television was not invented to make human beings vacuous, but is an emanation of their vacuity* — Malcolm Muggeridge. **2** a device with a screen and sound system for receiving and displaying television signals. **3** the television broadcasting industry. **4a** a television broadcasting organization or station: *Scottish Television*. **b** the medium of television communication. **c** the programmes broadcast on television.

television set *noun* = TELEVISION (2).

television tube *noun* a cathode-ray tube for producing pictures in a television set.

televisual /teli'vizhyooəl/ *adj chiefly Brit* of or suitable for broadcast by television. ➤➤ **televisually** *adv*.

teleworking /'teliwuhking/ *noun* = telecommuting (working from home by computer; see TELECOMMUTE). ➤➤ **teleworker** *noun*.

telex¹ /'teleks/ *noun* **1** a communications service involving teleprinters connected by wire through automatic exchanges. **2** a message by telex. [blend of TELEPRINTER + EXCHANGE¹]

telex² *verb trans* to send (a message) by telex.

tell¹ /tel/ *verb* (*past tense and past part.* **told** /tohld/) ➤ *verb trans* **1a** to relate (facts, a story, etc) in detail. **b** to give information to (somebody). **2** to order (somebody) to do something: *I told them to wait*. **3** to discern or ascertain (something): *You can tell a lot about a fellow's character by his way of eating jelly beans* — Ronald Reagan. **4a** to perceive (a difference). **b** (+ from) to distinguish or discriminate (something or somebody): *It's hard to tell one from the other*. ➤ *verb intrans* **1** (*usu* + of) to give an account of something. **2** to make a positive assertion; to decide definitely: *You can never tell for certain*. **3** (*often* + on) to act as an informer. **4** (*usu* + on) to have an effect: *The worry began to tell on her nerves*. **5a** (+ of) to indicate something. **b** to play a part in or have an effect on a process: *That will tell against you in court*. ✳ **tell a tale** to hold or reveal significant information. **tell tales 1** to be untruthful. **2** to reveal secrets or spread gossip. **tell the time** to read the information on a clock or watch. **you're telling me!** *informal* expressing agreement or prior knowledge. [Old English *tellan* to count, recite a list, give an account of; related to Old English *talu* TALE]

tell² *noun* in the Middle East, a mound formed by the accumulated debris, e.g. the mud brick walls of collapsed buildings, of successive ancient settlements. [Arabic *tall* hill, mound]

teller *noun* **1** somebody who relates or communicates: *a teller of stories*. **2a** somebody appointed to count votes. **b** a member of a bank's staff who deals directly with customers' transactions, paying out and taking in money, cheques, etc over a counter.

telling *adj* carrying great weight and producing a marked effect; revealing; significant: *That was a telling slip of the tongue*. ➤➤ **tellingly** *adv*.

telling-off *noun* (*pl* **tellings-off** *or* **telling-offs**) *informal* a harsh or severe reprimand.

tell off *verb trans* **1** to choose (a group of people) for special duty. **2** *informal* to scold or reprimand (somebody).

telltale *noun* **1** somebody who spreads gossip or rumours; an informer. **2** a device for indicating or recording something, e.g. the position of a vessel's rudder. **3** (*used before a noun*) revealing, betraying, or indicating something: *A rash is often the first telltale sign of the disease*.

tellur- *or* **telluro-** *comb. form* forming words, denoting: **1** earth: *tellurian*. **2** tellurium: *telluride*. [Latin *tellur-, tellus* earth]

tellurian /tə'l(y)ooəri·ən/ *noun* **1** *esp* in science fiction, an inhabitant of the earth. **2** = TELLURION. ➤➤ **tellurian** *adj*.

telluric /tə'l(y)ooərik/ *adj* **1** of or containing tellurium in its higher valency. **2** *formal* of the planet earth or soil.

telluride /'telyooried/ *noun* a compound of tellurium, usu with a more electropositive element or radical.

tellurion /tə'l(y)ooəri·ən/ *noun* an instrument that shows how day and night, the seasons, etc result from the earth's rotation on its axis and its orbit around the sun.

tellurium /tə'l(y)ooəri·əm/ *noun* a silver-white semimetallic chemical element chemically related to selenium and sulphur, that occurs naturally in silver and gold ores, and is used in alloys: symbol Te, atomic number 52. [scientific Latin, from Latin *tellur-, tellus* earth + -IUM]

telluro- *comb. form* see TELLUR-.

tellurometer /telyoo'romitə/ *noun* an electronic surveying device that measures distance by means of radio waves: compare TELEMETER¹.

tellurous /'telyooərəs/ *adj* of or containing tellurium in its lower valency.

telly /'teli/ *noun* (*pl* **tellies**) *chiefly Brit, informal* = TELEVISION. [by shortening and alteration]

telo- *comb. form* see TEL-¹.

telophase /'teləfayz, 'tee-/ *noun* the final stage of cell division in which the mitotic spindle disappears and two new nuclei appear, each with a set of chromosomes. [TELO- + PHASE¹]

telpher /'telfə/ *noun* a container or light passenger car suspended from and running on aerial cables or rails and working by electricity. ➤➤ **telpherage** /-rij/ *noun*. [TELE- + Greek *pherein* to bear]

telson /'telsən/ *noun* the last segment of the body of an arthropod, *esp* a crustacean, or of a segmented worm. [Greek *telson* end of a ploughed field]

Telugu *or* **Telegu** /'teləgooh/ *noun* (*pl* **Telugus** *or* **Telegus** *or collectively* **Telugu** *or* **Telegu**) **1** a member of the predominant indigenous people of Andhra Pradesh in India. **2** the Dravidian language spoken by this people. ➤➤ **Telegu** *adj*, **Telugu** *adj*. [Telugu *telungu*]

temazepam /tə'mazipam/ *noun* a tranquillizing drug, used e.g. to treat insomnia and as a sedative. [*tem-*, of unknown origin, + *azepam* as in DIAZEPAM]

temblor /'temblə, 'temblaw/ *noun* (*pl* **temblors** *or* **temblores** /tem'blawrayz/) *chiefly NAmer* an earthquake. [Spanish *temblor*, literally 'trembling', from *temblar* to tremble, from medieval Latin *tremulare*, from Latin *tremulus*: see TREMULOUS]

temerarious /temə'reəri·əs/ *adj formal or literary* rashly or presumptuously daring. ➤➤ **temerariously** *adv*, **temerariousness** *noun*. [Latin *temerarius*, from *temere* rashly]

temerity /tə'meriti/ *noun* unreasonable disregard for danger or opposition; *broadly* cheek, nerve, or excessive boldness. [Middle English *temeryte* from Latin *temeritas*, from *temere* at random, rashly]

temp¹ /temp/ *noun informal* a person, e.g. a typist, secretary, or other office worker, employed temporarily, usu through an agency. [short for TEMPORARY²]

temp² *verb intrans informal* to work as a temp.

temp. *abbr* **1** temperature. **2** temporary. **3** in the time of. [(senses 2, 3) Latin *tempore*, from *tempor-, tempus* time]

temper¹ /'tempə/ *noun* **1a** an uncontrolled and often disproportionate rage: *He is in a terrible temper*. **b** proneness to displays of such rages: *He has a terrible temper*. **2** a characteristic cast of mind or state of feeling: *Scrooge resumed his labours with an improved opinion of himself, and in a more facetious temper than usual with him* — Dickens. **3** characteristic tone: *You could put that down to the temper of the times*. **4** the state of a substance with respect to certain desired qualities, e.g. the degree of hardness or resilience given to steel by tempering. ✳ **keep one's temper** to keep one's anger under control; to avoid getting into a rage. **lose one's temper** to show one's anger; to get into a rage: *Madame was not best pleased at being contradicted on a professional matter, and when Madame lost her temper you usually found it afterwards in the bill* — Saki. **out of temper** *dated* in a bad mood: *He ... appeared to be perfectly resigned, was seldom fretful or out of temper* — James Boswell.

Word history

from TEMPER². The orig sense was 'the proper mixture or combination of elements or qualities'; (senses 1, 2) from the belief that temperament was governed or influenced by the combination of the four bodily humours.

temper² *verb trans* (**tempered, tempering**) **1** (+ with) to moderate (something harsh) with the addition of something less severe: *We must temper justice with mercy*. **2** to bring (something) to a suitable state, *esp* by mixing in or adding a liquid ingredient, *esp* to mix (clay) with water or a modifier and knead to a uniform texture. **3** to bring (*esp* steel) to the right degree of hardness by reheating and cooling it. **4** to strengthen the character of (somebody) through hardship: *All his troops had been tempered in battle*. **5** to adjust the pitch of (a note, chord, or instrument) to a temperament. ➤➤ **temperable** *adj*, **temperer** *noun*. [Old English *temprian* and Old French *temprer*, both from Latin *temperare* to moderate, mix, temper]

tempera /'tempərə/ *noun* **1a** a method of painting using pigment ground and mixed with an emulsion, e.g. of egg yolk and water. **b** the emulsion used in this painting. **2** a painting produced in this way. [Italian *tempera* temper, from *temperare* to temper, from Latin *temperare*]

temperament /'temprəmənt/ *noun* **1a** a person's own particular mental and emotional character, *esp* with regard to its effect on behaviour. **b** excessive sensitivity or irritability: *This display of* *temperament did not go down well with the judges.* **2** the modification of the musical intervals of the scale to produce a set of twelve fixed notes to the octave, thus enabling a keyboard instrument to play in more than one key. [Middle English from Latin *temperamentum*, from *temperare* to mix, TEMPER²]

temperamental /temprə'mentl/ *adj* **1a** easily upset or irritated; liable to sudden changes of mood. **b** unpredictable in behaviour or operation; unreliable: *Watch that coffee machine, it's a bit temperamental.* **2** relating to or arising from individual character or constitution: *temperamental peculiarities.* >>> **temperamentally** *adv.*

temperance /'tempərəns/ *noun* **1** moderation or self-restraint, *esp* in the indulgence of appetites or desires or the display of emotion. **2** abstinence from alcohol. [Middle English from Latin *temperantia*, from *temperant-, temperans*, present part. of *temperare* to moderate, be moderate]

temperate /'tempərət/ *adj* **1** not extreme or excessive: *a temperate climate; a temperate speech.* **2** moderate in the indulgence of appetites or desires; *esp* abstemious in the consumption of alcohol. **3a** having a moderate climate. **b** found in or associated with a temperate climate. >>> **temperately** *adv*, **temperateness** *noun.* [Middle English *temperat* from Latin *temperatus*, past part. of *temperare* to moderate, be moderate]

temperate zone *noun* either of the two regions between a polar circle and the nearest tropic.

temperature /'temprəchə/ *noun* **1** degree of hotness or coldness as measured on a scale, e.g. in degrees Celsius. **2a** the degree of heat present in the body of a person or animal: *Have you taken her temperature?* **b** *informal* an abnormally high body heat, usu indicative of illness: *I think I'm running a temperature.* [Latin *temperatura* mixture, moderation, from *temperare* to mix, moderate]

temperature inversion *noun* = INVERSION (7).

tempered *adj* **1a** qualified, moderated, or diluted by the mixture or influence of an additional ingredient. **b** said of a musical instrument: adjusted in accordance with a system of temperament. **2** (*used in combinations*) having a temper of a specified kind: *short-tempered.*

tempest /'tempist/ *noun* **1** a violent storm. **2** a tumult or uproar. [Middle English via Old French *tempeste* from Latin *tempestas* season, weather, storm, from *tempus* time]

tempestuous /tem'peschoo-əs/ *adj* **1** characterized by passion, violence, and emotional turbulence: *a tempestuous relationship.* **2** characterized by storms and bad weather. >>> **tempestuously** *adv*, **tempestuousness** *noun.*

tempi /'tempee/ *noun* pl of TEMPO.

Templar /'templə/ *noun* a knight of a religious military order, the Knights of the Temple of Solomon, founded in Jerusalem in the early 12th cent. for the protection of pilgrims and suppressed in the 14th cent. [Middle English *templer* via Old French from medieval Latin *templarius*, from Latin *templum* TEMPLE¹]

template /'templayt, 'templət/ *or* **templet** /'templit/ *noun* **1a** a pattern, mould, or stencil used as a guide to the shape of something that is being made or drawn. **b** a thing that serves as a model for other things. **2** a molecule in a biological system carrying information that codes or acts as a pattern for the structure of another molecule, e.g. a protein. **3** a short piece or block placed horizontally in a wall under a beam to distribute its weight or pressure, e.g. over a door. [*template* alteration (influenced by *plate*) of *templet*, prob from French *templet*, dimin. of *temple*: see TEMPLE³]

temple¹ /'templ/ *noun* **1a** a building dedicated to religious worship among any of various ancient civilizations (e.g. the Egyptians, the Greeks, and the Romans) and present-day non-Christian religions (e.g. Hinduism and Buddhism). **b** (*often* **Temple**) any of three successive national sanctuaries for the Jews in ancient Jerusalem. **2** a place devoted or dedicated to a specified purpose. **3** *chiefly NAmer* a synagogue of Reform Judaism or Conservative Judaism. [Old English *tempel* and early French *temple*, both from Latin *templum* space marked out for observation of auguries, temple]

temple² *noun* the flattened space on either side of the forehead. [Middle English from early French *temple*, ultimately from Latin *tempora* (pl) temples, prob from Latin *tempor-, tempus* time]

temple³ *noun* a device in a loom for keeping the cloth stretched. [Middle English *tempylle* from early French *temple*, prob from Latin *templum* small timber, TEMPLE¹]

templet /'templit/ *noun* see TEMPLATE.

tempo /'tempoh/ *noun* (*pl* **tempi** /'tempee/ *or* **tempos**) **1** the speed of a musical piece or passage indicated by any of a series of directions and often by an exact metronome marking. **2** the speed or rate of motion or activity. [Italian *tempo* time, from Latin *tempus*]

temporal¹ /'temp(ə)rəl/ *adj* **1a** relating to time as opposed to eternity or space; *esp* transitory. **b** relating to or characteristic of earthly life. **2** relating to, dealing with, or having authority over lay or secular matters. **3** relating to grammatical tense or the expression of time in language: *'When' is a temporal conjunction.* >>> **temporally** *adv.* [Middle English from Latin *temporalis*, from *tempor-, tempus* time]

temporal² *adj* relating to the temple or the equivalent part of the side of the skull. [early French *temporal* from late Latin *temporalis*, from Latin *tempora*: see TEMPLE²]

temporal bone *noun* either of two large bones, each of which forms a side and base of the human skull, is composed of four fused parts, and encloses the middle ear.

temporality /tempə'raliti/ *noun* (*pl* **temporalities**) **1** civil or political power as distinguished from spiritual or ecclesiastical authority. **2** (*also in pl*) an ecclesiastical property or revenue.

temporal lobe *noun* a large lobe at the side of each cerebral hemisphere that contains a sensory area associated with hearing and speech.

temporary¹ /'temp(ə)rəri, 'tempəreri/ *adj* lasting, or intended to last, only for a limited time. >>> **temporarily** /'tempərəli, tempə'rerəli/ *adv*, **temporariness** *noun.* [Latin *temporarius*, from *tempor-, tempus* time]

temporary² *noun* (*pl* **temporaries**) = TEMP¹.

temporize *or* **temporise** /'tempəriez/ *verb intrans* **1** to avoid making a decision or commitment or to draw out negotiations so as to gain time. **2** to comply temporarily with the demands of the time or occasion. >>> **temporization** /-'zaysh(ə)n/ *noun*, **temporizer** *noun.* [early French *temporiser* from medieval Latin *temporizare* to pass the time, from Latin *tempor-, tempus* time]

Tempranillo /ttemprəneeyoh, -neelyoh/ *noun* **1** a variety of grape used in the production of Rioja wine. **2** a Rioja wine produced from this grape. [named after a village in N Spain]

tempt /tempt/ *verb trans* **1a** to make (somebody) feel strongly inclined to do something: *He was tempted to call it quits.* **b** to attract or appeal to (somebody): *The idea tempts me.* **2** to try to persuade (somebody) to do something, *esp* something wicked, immoral, or unwise, by the promise of pleasure or gain. **3** to risk provoking harm or retribution from (somebody or something): *You shouldn't tempt fate.* >>> **temptable** *adj.* [Middle English *tempten* via Old French from Latin *temptare, tentare* to feel, try, tempt]

temptation /temp'taysh(ə)n/ *noun* **1a** an urge to do, take, or enjoy something, *esp* something forbidden or unwise. **b** the state of being tempted, *esp* to do something evil or forbidden. **2** something tempting.

tempter *noun* **1** somebody who tempts or entices other people. **2** (*usu* **the Tempter**) the Devil.

tempting *adj* **1** arousing temptation; enticing. **2** attractive or appealing. >>> **temptingly** *adv.*

temptress /'temptris/ *noun* a woman who tempts or entices; *specif* a woman who has very strong and obvious sex appeal.

tempura /tem'pooərə, 'tempərə/ *noun* a Japanese dish of seafood or vegetables dipped in batter and fried. [Japanese *tenpura*]

ten /ten/ *noun* **1** the number 10, or the quantity represented by it. **2** something having ten parts or members. **3a** the age of 10 years. **b** the hour two hours before midday or midnight. **4** (*usu in pl*) the number occupying the position two to the left of the decimal point in Arabic notation, or this position in a number or sum. **5** a note, bill, or coin worth ten units of currency, e.g. a ten-pound note or ten-pence piece. >>> **ten** *adj*, **tenfold** *adj and adv.* [Old English *tiene*, from *tien* (adj) ten]

ten. *abbr* tenuto.

tenable /'tenəbl/ *adj* **1a** capable of being defended or justified by rational argument or evidence. **b** capable of being held or defended against military attack. **2** (*usu* + for) said of a position, award, etc: to be held for a specified period. >>> **tenability** /-'biliti/ *noun*, **tenableness** *noun*, **tenably** *adv.* [French *tenable* from *tenir* to hold, from Latin *tenēre*]

tenace /'tenays/ *noun* in bridge or whist, a combination of two cards of the same suit, one ranking two degrees below the other, in one hand. [modification of Spanish *tenaza*, literally 'forceps', prob from Latin *tenacia*, neut pl of *tenax*: see TENACIOUS]

tenacious /tə'nayshəs/ *adj* **1a** holding on very firmly: *a tenacious grip.* **b** tending to stick or cling, *esp* to another substance. **2a** unwilling to desist or to give up on something; stubborn or persistent. **b** able to recall things clearly for a long time; retentive: *a tenacious memory.* >>> **tenaciously** *adv,* **tenaciousness** *noun,* **tenacity** /tə'nasiti/ *noun.* [Latin *tenac-, tenax* tending to hold fast, from *tenēre* to hold]

tenaculum /tə'nakyooləm/ *noun* (*pl* **tenacula** /-lə/ *or* **tenaculums**) a slender sharp-pointed hook used mainly in surgery for picking up and holding parts, e.g. arteries. [scientific Latin *tenaculum* instrument for holding, from Latin *tenēre* to hold]

tenancy /'tenənsi/ *noun* (*pl* **tenancies**) **1a** temporary occupancy of land, a house, etc under a lease or rental agreement. **b** the period for which somebody occupies a property. **2** *formal* the holding of a particular office or position, or the period for which it is held.

tenant[1] /'tenənt/ *noun* **1** an occupant of land or property belonging to somebody else; *specif* somebody who rents or leases a house or flat from a landlord. **2** in law, a holder of property or land by any kind of right. >>> **tenantable** *adj,* **tenantless** *adj.* [Middle English from early French *tenant*, present part. of *tenir* to hold, from Latin *tenēre*]

tenant[2] *verb trans* to live in or have the use of (a property) as a tenant. >>> **tenantable** *adj.*

tenant farmer *noun* a farmer who works land owned by somebody else and pays rent.

tenantry /'tenəntri/ *noun* (*pl* **tenantries**) **1** (*treated as sing. or pl*) tenants collectively. **2** *dated* = TENANCY.

tench /tench/ *noun* (*pl* **tenches** *or collectively* **tench**) a Eurasian freshwater fish of the carp family with a greenish or blackish skin, noted for its ability to survive outside water: *Tinca tinca.* [Middle English via early French *tenche* from late Latin *tinca*]

Ten Commandments *pl noun* the commandments given by God to Moses on Mount Sinai, recorded in Exodus 20:1–17.

tend[1] /tend/ *verb intrans* **1a** to be likely or inclined to do something, or to have the habit of doing something: *She tends to exaggerate; The weather tends to be stormy during October and November.* **b** (+ to/towards) to be likely or inclined to have or acquire a particular characteristic: *His style is plain and direct, tending sometimes to terseness.* **2** to move or direct one's course in a specified direction. [Middle English *tenden* via French from Latin *tendere* to stretch]

tend[2] *verb trans* **1a** to be in charge of and look after (somebody or something): *Her job was to tend her father's sheep.* **b** to provide care and treatment for (somebody or something). **2** *chiefly NAmer* to oversee the operations or running of (something); to manage or mind (something): *I was tending the store while Mr Lafferty was on vacation.* > *verb intrans chiefly NAmer* (*usu* + to) to pay attention or to apply oneself: *You'd do better to tend to your own affairs.* [Middle English *tenden*, short for *attenden*: see ATTEND]

tendencious /ten'denshəs/ *adj* see TENDENTIOUS.

tendency /'tendənsi/ *noun* (*pl* **tendencies**) **1a** (*usu* + to) an inclination or predisposition to do something, or to have a particular characteristic: *His books show a tendency to drop into sentimentality.* **b** a general trend or movement: *There is a growing tendency for prices to rise faster than wages.* **2** a usu radical group working within a political party, etc: *the militant tendency.* [medieval Latin *tendentia*, from Latin *tendent-, tendens*, present part. of *tendere* to stretch]

tendentious *or* **tendencious** /ten'denshəs/ *adj chiefly derog* presenting a biased view, *esp* so as to promote a particular stance, ideology, etc: *He sounded to himself like some tendentious student with balloon words coming out of his mouth* — Penelope Gilliatt; *tendentious readings of history.* >>> **tendentiously** *adv,* **tendentiousness** *noun.* [from TENDENCY]

tender[1] /'tendə/ *adj* (**tenderer, tenderest**) **1** showing or characterized by great gentleness and kindness: *tender care.* **2** showing or characterized by warmth of feeling, love, or affection: *a tender glance.* **3a** having a soft or yielding texture; easily broken, cut, or damaged. **b** said of meat: easy to cut and chew. **4** sensitive or sore: *The area around the wound was inflamed and tender.* **5** young and vulnerable: *She was left in charge of the family at the tender age of nine.* **6** delicate or soft in quality or tone. **7** demanding careful and sensitive handling; tricky. **8** *formal* (+ of) adopting a protective or defensive attitude towards something: *He was more than usually tender of his wife's reputation.* **9** said of a ship: inclined to heel over

easily under sail. ✳ **tender mercies** ungentle, unkind, or positively brutal treatment. >>> **tenderly** *adv,* **tenderness** *noun.* [Middle English via Old French *tendre* from Latin *tener* soft, young]

tender[2] *noun* **1** a boat or ship that carries supplies, passengers, etc to and from other ships. **2** a vehicle attached to a steam locomotive for carrying a supply of fuel and water. **3** a road vehicle that carries tools, equipment, or personnel, *esp* for use in an emergency. **4** somebody who is in charge of and tends something. [TEND[2] + -ER[2]]

tender[3] *verb* (**tendered, tendering**) > *verb trans* **1** to present (something) formally for acceptance: *He tendered his resignation.* **2** to offer (money) in payment. > *verb intrans* (*often* + for) to present a bid in the hope of gaining a contract. >>> **tenderer** *noun.* [early French *tendre* to stretch, stretch out, offer, from Latin *tendere*]

tender[4] *noun* **1a** a formal *esp* written offer or bid for a contract to carry out work, supply goods, etc. **b** a public expression of willingness to buy not less than a specified number of shares at a fixed price from shareholders. **2** something that may be offered in payment; *specif* money: *legal tender.* **3** in law, an unconditional offer of money or service towards paying off a debt or obligation, made to avoid a penalty for non-payment or non-performance. ✳ **put something out to tender** to invite people or companies to tender for a contract to carry out work, supply goods, etc.

tenderfoot *noun* (*pl* **tenderfeet** *or* **tenderfoots**) *chiefly NAmer* an inexperienced beginner: *Oh, maybe you think I've been to nowheres – maybe you think I'm a tenderfoot?* — Stephen Crane. [TENDER[1] + FOOT[1]; orig in the sense of somebody who was not hardened to frontier or outdoor life in the American West]

tenderhearted *adj* easily moved to love, pity, or sorrow. >>> **tenderheartedly** *adv.*

tenderize *or* **tenderise** *verb trans* to make (meat or meat products) tender by beating or using a substance that breaks down fibrous tissue. >>> **tenderization** /-'zaysh(ə)n/ *noun,* **tenderizer** *noun.*

tenderloin *noun* **1** a pork or beef fillet cut from between the sirloin and the ribs. **2** *NAmer, informal* a district of a city noted for its vice and corruption.

tendinitis *or* **tendonitis** /,tendə'nietəs/ *noun* inflammation of a tendon. [scientific Latin, from *tendin-, tendo* tendon]

tendon /'tendən/ *noun* a tough cord or band of dense white fibrous tissue that connects a muscle with a bone or other part and transmits the force exerted by the muscle. >>> **tendinous** /'tendənəs/ *adj.* [Middle English via early French *tendon* or medieval Latin *tendon-, tendo,* from Latin *tendere* to stretch]

tendonitis /,tendə'nietəs/ *noun* see TENDINITIS.

tendril /'tendrəl/ *noun* a slender spirally coiling outgrowth that attaches a climbing plant to its support. [prob dimin. of early French *tendron,* alteration of *tendon*: see TENDON]

Tenebrae /'tenəbray/ *noun* in the Roman Catholic Church, the service of matins and lauds for the last three days of Holy Week, commemorating the sufferings and death of Christ. [medieval Latin, from Latin *tenebrae* darkness]

tenebrism /'tenəbriz(ə)m/ *noun* a style of painting, *esp* in 17th-cent. Naples and Spain, in which large areas of the canvas are covered in dark shadowy tones, often pierced by dramatic shafts of light. [Italian *tenebroso* dark, from Latin *tenebrosus*: see TENEBROUS]

tenebrous /'tenəbrəs/ *adj literary* **1** in shadow or shut off from the light; dark; murky. **2** hard to understand; obscure. [Middle English via early French *tenebreus* from Latin *tenebrosus,* from *tenebrae* darkness]

tenement /'tenəmənt/ *noun* **1a** a large building constructed as or divided up into separate dwellings, *esp* one meeting only minimum standards and typically found in the poorer parts of a large city in Scotland or the USA. **b** a flat in a tenement building. **2** in law, land or other property held by one person from another. [Middle English via French from medieval Latin *tenementum,* from Latin *tenēre* to hold]

tenesmus /tə'nezməs/ *noun* a painful and ineffectual urge to defecate or urinate. [via Latin from Greek *teinesmos,* from *teinein* to stretch, strain]

tenet /'tenət/ *noun* a principle, belief, or doctrine, *esp* one held in common by the members of an organization or group. [Latin *tenet* he holds, from *tenēre* to hold]

ten-gallon hat *noun* a large hat with a broad brim and a very high crown, traditionally worn by cowboys. [from its great size]

tenge /'tengay/ *noun* (*pl* **tenge** *or* **tenges**) **1** the basic monetary unit of Kazakhstan, divided into 100 teins. **2** a unit of currency in Turkmenistan, worth 100th of a manat.

tenia /'teeni-ə/ *noun NAmer* see TAENIA.

teniasis /tee'nie-əsis/ *noun NAmer* see TAENIASIS.

ten minute rule *noun* a rule under which an MP may briefly introduce a private member's bill in the British House of Commons.

Tenn. *abbr* Tennessee.

tenner /'tenə/ *noun Brit, informal* a £10 note, or the sum of £10.

tennis /'tenis/ *noun* **1** a game for two or four players that is played with rackets and a light elastic ball on a flat court divided by a low net. **2** = REAL TENNIS. [Middle English *tenetz, tenys*, prob from Anglo-French *tenetz* take, receive, imperative of *tenir* to hold, take (called by server to opponent), from Latin *tenēre*]

tennis elbow *noun* inflammation and pain of the elbow, usu resulting from excessive twisting movements of the hand and forearm.

tennis shoe *noun* a light shoe with a canvas or soft leather upper and a rubber sole, worn when playing tennis or for general recreational and leisure use.

tenon[1] /'tenən/ *noun* a projecting part of a piece of material, *esp* wood, specially shaped for insertion into a MORTISE[1] (matching slot). [Middle English from Old French *tenon*, from *tenir*: see TENABLE]

tenon[2] *verb trans* (**tenoned, tenoning**) **1** to join (two pieces of wood) by a tenon. **2** to cut (something) in the shape of a tenon for insertion in a mortise.

tenon saw *noun* a woodworking saw that has a reinforced blade and is used for making fine cuts.

tenor /'tenə/ *noun* **1** a high adult male singing voice, or a singer with this voice. **2** (*used before a noun*) denoting a musical instrument having a range below that of the alto instrument. **3** the next to lowest singing part in conventional four-part harmony. **4** the general meaning or implication of something spoken or written. **5** a continuance in a course or activity: *Along the cool sequestered vale of life they kept the noiseless tenor of their way* — Gray. ➤➤ **tenor** *adj*. [Middle English via Old French from Latin *tenor* uninterrupted course, from *tenēre* to hold; (sense 2) from the fact that the *tenor*, a continuous part or melodic line in medieval polyphony, was assigned to this voice]

tenor clef *noun* a C clef placed so as to designate the fourth line of the stave as middle C.

tenorist *noun* a person who plays a tenor instrument.

tenosynovitis /,tenohsinoh'vietəs, ,tee-/ *noun* inflammation of the sheath covering a tendon. [scientific Latin, from Greek *tenōn* tendon + SYNOVITIS] .

tenotomy /tə'notəmi/ *noun* (*pl* **tenotomies**) a surgical operation to cut a tendon, *esp* to cure a club foot. [Greek *tenōn* tendon + -TOMY]

tenpin *noun* a bottle-shaped pin used in tenpin bowling. [back-formation from *tenpins* tenpin bowling, from *ten pins*]

tenpin bowling *noun* an indoor bowling game using ten bottle-shaped pins and a large ball in which each player is allowed to bowl two balls in each of ten frames.

tenrec /'tenrek/ *noun* any of a family of small, often spiny, insect-eating mammals of Madagascar: family Tenrecidae. [French *tenrec* from Malagasy *tàndraka*]

TENS *abbr* transcutaneous electrical nerve stimulation.

tense[1] /tens/ *adj* **1a** feeling or showing nervousness and anxiety. **b** marked by strain or suspense. **2** stretched tight; taut. **3** said of a speech sound, *esp* a vowel: articulated with relatively tense muscles: compare LAX. ➤➤ **tensely** *adv*, **tenseness** *noun*. [Latin *tensus*, past part. of *tendere* to stretch]

tense[2] *verb intrans and trans* (*often* + up) to become or make (somebody or something) tense.

tense[3] *noun* a set of inflectional forms of a verb that express action taking place at a particular time. [Middle English *tens* time, tense, via French from Latin *tempus* time]

tensile /'tensiel/ *adj* **1** able to be stretched or drawn out; ductile. **2** relating to or involving tension. ➤➤➤ **tensility** /ten'siliti/ *noun*. [medieval Latin *tensilis* from Latin *tendere* to stretch]

tensile strength *noun* the greatest tension a substance can bear without breaking.

tensimeter /ten'simitə/ *noun* an instrument for measuring differences of vapour pressure. [TENSION[1] + -METER[2]]

tensiometer /tensi'omitə/ *noun* **1a** a device for measuring tension, e.g. of a fabric, yarn, or structural material. **b** a device for measuring tensile strength. **2** an instrument for measuring the moisture content of soil. **3** an instrument for measuring the surface tension of liquids. ➤➤ **tensiometric** /-'metrik/ *adj*, **tensiometry** *noun*. [TENSION[1] + -METER[2]]

tension[1] /'tensh(ə)n/ *noun* **1** the act or action of stretching or the condition or degree of being stretched tight; tautness: *muscular tension*. **2a** mental or emotional unease often accompanied by an inability to relax, increased heart rate, etc; stress. **b** a feeling or state of nervous and excited anticipation or suspense: *The tension becomes almost unbearable during the last act*. **3** a state of latent hostility or opposition between individuals or groups: *World War II was followed by a period of East-West tension known as the Cold War*. **4a** the strain caused by two forces pulling in opposite directions. **b** a balance maintained in an artistic work between opposing forces or elements. **5** voltage or electrical potential, *esp* of a specified kind: *high tension*. **6** the degree of tightness or looseness of the stitches in knitting or sewing. ➤➤ **tensional** *adj*, **tensionless** *adj*. [early French *tension* from Latin *tension-, tensio*, from *tendere* to stretch]

tension[2] *verb trans* to tighten (something) to a desired or appropriate degree. ➤➤➤ **tensioner** *noun*.

tensor /'tensə, 'tensaw/ *noun* **1** a muscle that stretches a body part. **2** in mathematics, a generalized form of a VECTOR[1] (a quantity with magnitude and direction) that enables it to be transformed from its original system of coordinates into others. [scientific Latin *tensor*, from Latin *tendere* to stretch]

tent[1] /tent/ *noun* **1** a collapsible shelter made of canvas or similar material stretched and supported by poles. **2** a canopy or enclosure placed over the head and shoulders to retain vapours or oxygen during medical treatment. ➤➤ **tented** *adj*, **tentless** *adj*. [Middle English *tente* via Old French from Latin *tenta*, fem past part. of *tendere* to stretch]

tent[2] *verb intrans* to live in a tent. ➤ *verb trans* to cover (somebody or something) with or as if with a tent.

tent[3] *noun* a cone-shaped plug inserted into a wound or incision during surgery to keep it open. [Middle English in the sense 'probe', from Old French *tente*, from *tenter* to probe, from Latin *tentare* to feel, touch, try]

tentacle /'tentəkl/ *noun* **1** an elongated flexible animal part, usu on the head or around the mouth, used for feeling, grasping, etc. **2** something resembling a tentacle in form or function; *esp* something that reaches out or spreads insidiously to grasp or control. **3** a sensitive hair-like growth on a plant such as the sundew that can curve by growing asymmetrically. ➤➤ **tentacled** *adj*, **tentacular** /ten'takyoolə/ *adj*. [scientific Latin *tentaculum*, from Latin *tentare* to feel, touch, try]

tentage /'tentij/ *noun* a collection of tents, or tent equipment.

tentative /'tentətiv/ *adj* **1** not fully worked out or developed; provisional: *tentative plans*. **2** hesitant or uncertain: *a tentative smile*. ➤➤ **tentatively** *adv*, **tentativeness** *noun*. [medieval Latin *tentativus*, from Latin *tentare* to feel, touch, try]

tent dress *noun* a long, large, and very loose-fitting dress for a woman.

tenter *noun* an apparatus used for drying and stretching cloth. [Middle English *teyntur, tentowre*, from medieval Latin *tentorium*, from Latin *tendere* to stretch]

tenterhook *noun* a sharp hooked nail used *esp* for fastening cloth on a tenter. ✳ **on tenterhooks** in a state of suspense or nervous anticipation.

tenth *adj and noun* **1** denoting a person or thing having the position in a sequence corresponding to the number ten. **2** one of ten equal parts of something. **3** in music, an interval of ten degrees of a diatonic scale, or the combination of two notes at such an interval. ➤➤ **tenthly** *adv*.

tenth-rate *adj* of the lowest character or quality.

tent stitch *noun* a short diagonal stitch used in embroidery and canvas work to form a solid background of even lines of parallel stitches.

tenuous /'tenyoo-əs/ *adj* **1** having little substance or strength; weak or flimsy: *He seemed to have only a tenuous hold on reality.* **2** not thick; fine. **3** not dense in consistency: *a tenuous fluid.* ⮞⮞ **tenuity** /tə'nyooh·iti/ *noun,* **tenuously** *adv,* **tenuousness** *noun.* [Latin *tenuis* thin, slight, tenuous]

tenure /'tenyə/ *noun* **1** the holding of a position or an office, or the period of time for which it is held. **2** *chiefly NAmer* an enhanced and more secure employment status giving freedom from summary dismissal until retirement, *esp* in a teaching post. **3** the conditions under which a property is held or occupied. ⮞⮞ **tenurial** /tə'nyoori·əl/ *adj.* [Middle English via Old French *teneüre, tenure* from medieval Latin *tenitura*, ultimately from Latin *tenēre* to hold]

tenured *adj chiefly NAmer* having or offering more secure employment status: *a tenured post.*

tenure-track *adj NAmer* said of a teaching post: offering eligibility for tenure.

tenuto /te'nyoohtoh/ *adj and adv* said of a note or chord in music: to be held or sustained. [Italian *tenuto*, past part. of *tenere* to hold, from Latin *tenēre*]

teocalli /teeoh'kali/ *noun* (*pl* **teocallis**) an ancient temple in Mexico or Central America usu built on the flat summit of a pyramid-like mound, or the mound on which the temple is built. [Nahuatl *teocalli*, from *teotl* god + *calli* house]

teosinte /teeoh'sinti/ *noun* a tall grass native to Mexico and Central America that resembles and is closely related to maize and is grown *esp* for fodder: *Euchlaena mexicana.* [Mexican Spanish *teosinte* from Nahuatl *teocentli*, from *teotl* god + *centli* ear of corn]

tepee *or* **teepee** /'teepee/ *noun* a Native American conical tent, usu made of skins. [Dakota *tipi*, from *ti* to dwell + *pi* to use for]

tephra /'tefrə/ *noun chiefly NAmer* solid material such as volcanic ash and cinders, ejected during the eruption of a volcano. [Greek *tephra* ashes]

tepid /'tepid/ *adj* **1** moderately warm: *a tepid bath.* **2** not enthusiastic: *a tepid interest.* ⮞⮞ **tepidity** /te'piditi/ *noun,* **tepidly** *adv,* **tepidness** *noun.* [Latin *tepidus*, from *tepēre* to be moderately warm]

tepidarium /tepi'deəri·əm, -'dahri·əm/ *noun* (*pl* **tepidaria** /-ri·ə/) the room in a Roman bathhouse containing the warm bath. [Latin *tepidarium*, from *tepidus* (see TEPID) + -ARIUM]

tequila /tə'keelə/ *noun* **1** a strong Mexican alcoholic drink made by redistilling MESCAL (spirit distilled from agave sap). **2** a Mexican agave plant cultivated as a source of mescal. [named after *Tequila*, district of Mexico where the drink was orig made]

tequila sunrise *noun* a cocktail in which orange juice and grenadine are mixed with tequila.

ter- *comb. form* forming words, with the meaning: three times, threefold, or three: *tercentenary.* [Latin *ter* three times]

tera- *comb. form* forming words, denoting: **1** a factor of one million million (10^{12}): *teraton; terahertz.* **2** in computing, a factor of 2^{40}: *terabyte.* [Greek *terat-, teras* marvel, monster]

terabyte /'terəbiet/ *noun* in computing, a unit of data or storage equal to one million million bytes or (more accurately) 2^{40} bytes.

teraflop /'terəflop/ *noun* a unit of computer processing speed equal to one million million floating-point operations per second. [TERA- + *flop* (see FLOPS)]

terai /tə'rie/ *noun* a wide-brimmed felt sun hat worn *esp* in subtropical regions. [named after *Tarai*, a region in NE India]

terakihi *noun* see TARAKIHI.

terat- *or* **terato-** *comb. form* forming words, denoting: monster or monstrosity: *teratology.* [Greek *terat-, teras* marvel, monster]

teratogen /tə'ratəjən/ *noun* something that causes developmental malformations in foetuses. ⮞⮞ **teratogenesis** /,terətə'jenəsis/ *noun,* **teratogenic** /,terətə'jenik/ *adj,* **teratogenicity** /,terətəjə'nisiti/ *noun.*

teratology /terə'toləji/ *noun* **1** the study of malformations in foetuses. **2** a collection of stories about mythical creatures and monsters. ⮞⮞ **teratological** /,terətə'lojikl/ *adj,* **teratologist** *noun.*

teratoma /terə'tohmə/ *noun* (*pl* **teratomas** *or* **teratomata** /-mətə/) a tumour derived from embryonic tissues and made up of a mixture of several types of tissue. ⮞⮞ **teratomatous** *adj.*

terbium /'tuhbi·əm/ *noun* a silvery metallic chemical element of the rare-earth group: symbol Tb, atomic number 65. [scientific

Latin, named after *Ytterby*, a town in Sweden where it was discovered]

terce *or* **Terce** /tuhs/ *noun* the third of the canonical hours, observed at 9 a.m. [Middle English, in the senses 'third, terce': see TIERCE]

tercel /'tuhsl/ *noun* a male hawk, *esp* the male of the peregrine or goshawk, *esp* when used in falconry: compare FALCON (2). [Middle English *tercel* from early French, ultimately from Latin *tertius* third; perhaps from the belief that the third egg of a clutch produced a male bird]

tercentenary /tuhsən'teenəri, -'tenəri/ *noun* (*pl* **tercentenaries**) a 300th anniversary or its celebration. ⮞⮞ **tercentenary** *adj.*

tercentennial /tuhsən'teni·əl/ *noun* a tercentenary. ⮞⮞ **tercentennial** *adj.*

tercet /'tuhsit/ *noun* a unit or group of three lines of verse. [Italian *terzetto*, dimin. of *terzo* third, from Latin *tertius* third]

terebene /'terəbeen/ *noun* a mixture of terpenes from oil of turpentine. [French *térébène*, from early French *térébinthe*: see TEREBINTH]

terebinth /'terəbinth/ *noun* a small European tree of the sumach family that was formerly a source of turpentine: *Pistacia terebinthus.* [Middle English *terebynt* via early French *terebinthe* from Latin *terebinthus*]

terebinthine /terə'binthien/ *adj* consisting of or resembling turpentine. [Latin *terebinthinus* of the terebinth, from *terebinthus* TEREBINTH]

teredo /tə'raydoh/ *noun* (*pl* **teredos** *or* **teredines** /tə'redineez/) = SHIPWORM. [via Latin from Greek *terēdōn*; related to Greek *tetrainein* to bore]

terete /tə'reet/ *adj* said of a plant or animal part: approximately cylindrical with a smooth surface. [Latin *teret-, teres* well turned, rounded]

terga /'tuhgə/ *noun* pl of TERGUM.

tergiversate /'tuhjivəsayt, 'tuhgi-/ *verb intrans formal* **1** to change sides or loyalties; to become a renegade. **2** to act evasively or equivocally: *Wyatt was examined again and again, and wavered and tergiversated a good deal* — Charlotte M Yonge. ⮞⮞ **tergiversation** /-'saysh(ə)n/ *noun,* **tergiversator** *noun.* [Latin *tergiversatus*, past part. of *tergiversari* to turn the back, shuffle, from *tergum* back + *versare*: see VERSATILE]

tergum /'tuhgəm/ *noun* (*pl* **terga** /'tuhgə/) the plate forming the back surface of a segment of an insect, spider, crab, etc. ⮞⮞ **tergal** *adj.* [Latin *tergum* back]

-teria *suffix* forming nouns, denoting: a self-service establishment: *washeteria.* [from CAFETERIA]

teriyaki /teri'yahki/ *noun* a Japanese dish consisting of pieces of meat or fish marinated in a mixture of soy sauce, sugar, and rice wine and grilled. [Japanese *teriyaki*, literally 'glaze grill']

term¹ /tuhm/ *noun* **1a** a word or expression with a precise meaning, *esp* one used mainly in a particular field: *legal terms.* **b** (*in pl*) words or a mode of expression of a specified kind: *She spoke in flattering terms of my previous achievements.* **2** (*in pl*) provisions relating to an agreement: *terms of sale.* **3** a limited or definite extent of time; *esp* the time for which something lasts: *There is a risk of environmental damage in the long term.* **4a** any of the usu three periods of instruction into which an academic year is divided. **b** any one of the periods of the year during which the courts are in session. **5a** an end or termination, *esp* a time fixed as the end of something or on which something falls due. **b** the time at which a pregnancy of normal length ends: *She had her baby at full term.* **6a** a mathematical expression connected to another by a plus or minus sign. **b** an expression that forms part of a fraction or proportion or of a series or sequence. **7** a concept, word, or phrase appearing as subject or predicate in a logical proposition. **8** an estate or interest held for a limited period of time. **9** = TERMINUS (3). ✳ **be on good/bad terms with** to have a friendly/unfriendly relationship with (somebody). **come to terms 1** (+ with) to accept or resign oneself to something sad or unpleasant. **2** to reach an agreement. **in terms of** as expressed by; in relation to. **on terms** on an equal footing, *esp* having the same or nearly the same score in a game. [Middle English *terme* boundary, end, via Old French from Latin *terminus*]

term² *verb trans* to apply a particular term to (somebody or something); to call: *I wouldn't term it difficult.*

termagant /'tuhməgənt/ *noun* **1** an overbearing or nagging woman: *the ill treatment which he had received from a clergyman's wife, who was a noted termagant* — James Boswell. **2** (**Termagant**) a violent character in English miracle plays representing an Islamic deity. [Middle English *Termagant*]

terminable /'tuhminəbl/ *adj* capable of being terminated. ➤➤ **terminableness** *noun*. [Middle English, from *terminen* to terminate, via Old French *terminer* from Latin *terminare*: see TERMINATE]

terminal¹ /'tuhminl/ *adj* **1a** forming an end, extremity, boundary, or terminus. **b** growing at the end of a branch or stem: *a terminal bud*. **2** occurring during a term or each term in a school, college, etc. **3a** occurring at or causing the end of life: *terminal cancer*. **b** relating to or suffering from a disease that is certain to cause death. **4** *informal* extreme or irreversible: *terminal lethargy*. ➤➤ **terminally** *adv*. [Latin *terminalis*, from *terminus* boundary, end]

terminal² *noun* **1a** the end of a transport route, with its associated buildings and facilities. **b** a building at an airport with facilities for arriving and departing passengers. **2** a device attached to the end of a wire or cable or to an electrical apparatus for convenience in making connections. **3** a device through which a user can communicate with a computer. **4** an industrial installation where raw materials are stored and processed, *esp* an onshore installation receiving oil or gas through a pipeline. **5** = TERMINUS (3).

terminal velocity *noun* the constant maximum velocity attained by an object falling through a fluid under gravity when resistance prevents any further acceleration.

terminate /'tuhminayt/ *verb trans* **1a** to bring (something) to an end. **b** to take action to end (a pregnancy) prematurely. **2** to serve as an ending, limit, or boundary of (something). **3** *NAmer, euphem* to kill or assassinate (somebody). **4** *NAmer* to dismiss (somebody) from employment. ➤ *verb intrans* **1** to go or extend only as far as a particular point and then stop; *esp* to reach a terminus: *This train terminates at Glasgow*. **2** (*often* + in) to come to an end, *esp* in time: *The coalition terminated with the election*. ➤➤ **termination** /-'naysh(ə)n/ *noun*. [Latin *terminatus*, past part. of *terminare* to end, from *terminus* end, boundary]

terminator *noun* **1** somebody or something that terminates something or somebody. **2** the dividing line between the illuminated and the unilluminated part of the moon or other celestial body.

terminator technology *noun* = GENETIC USE RESTRICTION TECHNOLOGY.

termini /'tuhminie, -nee/ *noun* pl of TERMINUS.

terminology /tuhmi'nolǝji/ *noun* (*pl* **terminologies**) the technical terms used in a particular subject. ➤➤ **terminological** /-'lojikl/ *adj*, **terminologically** /-'lojikli/ *adv*. [medieval Latin *terminus* term, expression (from Latin, boundary, limit) + -O- + -LOGY]

term insurance *noun* **1** insurance for a specified period. **2** *chiefly Brit* life insurance under which payment is made only if the insured dies within a specified period.

terminus /'tuhminəs/ *noun* (*pl* **termini** /-nie, -nee/ *or* **terminuses**) **1** the end of a transport line or travel route, or the station or town at which it ends. **2** a finishing point; an end. **3** in architecture, a square post whose top is carved into an armless human bust or an animal figure. [Latin *terminus* boundary, end]

terminus ad quem /,tuhminəs ad 'kwem/ *noun* **1** a finishing point in time. **2** a goal, objective, or destination. [Latin *terminus ad quem*, literally 'limit to which']

terminus ante quem /,tuhminəs ,anti 'kwem/ *noun* the latest possible date. [Latin *terminus ante quem*, literally 'limit before which']

terminus a quo /,tuhminəs ah 'kwoh/ *noun* **1** a starting point in time. **2** a point of departure or origin. [Latin *terminus a quo*, literally 'limit from which']

terminus post quem /,tuhminəs ,pohst 'kwem/ *noun* the earliest possible date. [Latin *terminus post quem*, literally 'limit after which']

termitarium /tuhmi'teari·əm, tuhmie-/ *noun* (*pl* **termitaria** /-ri·ə/) a termites' nest. [scientific Latin, from Latin *termit-, termes*: see TERMITE]

termite /'tuhmiet/ *noun* any of numerous species of often destructive insects with pale-coloured soft bodies that live in colonies and feed on wood: order Isoptera. [late Latin *termit-, termes* a worm that eats wood, alteration of Latin *tarmes* + -ARIUM]

termless *adj* **1** having no term or end; boundless, unending. **2** unconditioned or unconditional.

terms of reference *pl noun* the precise definition of the scope allowed to an individual or a body such as a committee.

terms of trade *pl noun* the ratio of an index of export prices to the index of import prices.

tern /tuhn/ *noun* any of numerous water birds that are smaller than the related gulls and have a black cap, a white body, and often forked tails: genus *Sterna* and other genera. [prob ultimately from Old Norse *therna*]

ternary /'tuhnəri/ *adj* **1** made up of three parts. **2** using three as the base: *a ternary logarithm*. **3** third in order or rank. [Middle English from Latin *ternarius*, from *terni* three each, from *ter* three times]

ternary form *noun* a common musical structure, e.g. for a movement in a sonata or symphony, in which a first section is followed by a related second section that is followed in turn by a repetition of the first.

ternate /'tuhnayt/ *adj* **1** arranged in threes. **2** composed of three leaflets or subdivisions. ➤➤ **ternately** *adv*. [scientific Latin *ternatus*, past part. of *ternare* to treble, from Latin *terni*: see TERNARY]

terne /tuhn/ *noun* **1** an alloy consisting of about four parts lead to one part tin. **2** = TERNEPLATE. [prob from French *terne* dull, of Germanic origin]

terneplate /'tuhnplayt/ *noun* sheet iron or steel plated with terne.

terotechnology /,terohtek'nolǝji/ *noun* a branch of technology that deals with the efficient installation and operation of equipment. [Greek *tērein* to watch over + -O- + TECHNOLOGY]

terpene /'tuhpeen/ *noun* any of various hydrocarbons present in essential oils, e.g. from conifers, and used *esp* as solvents and in organic synthesis. ➤➤ **terpenic** /tuh'peenik, tuh'penik/ *adj*, **terpenoid** /'tuhpənoyd, tuh'peenoyd/ *adj and noun*. [*terp-* from German *terpentin* turpentine (ultimately from Latin *terebinthina resina* resin of the terebinth) + -ENE]

terpsichorean /,tuhpsikə'ree·ən, -'kawri·ən/ *adj* relating to dancing. [from *Terpsichore*, the muse of dancing and choral song in Greek and Latin mythology]

Terr. *abbr* **1** in street names, terrace. **2** territory.

terra /'terə/ *noun* land, earth, or territory. [Latin *terra* earth]

terra alba /'albə/ *noun* any of several earthy white mineral substances, such as gypsum or kaolin. [scientific Latin, literally 'white earth']

terrace¹ /'terəs/ *noun* **1** a relatively level paved or planted area adjoining a building. **2** a horizontal ridge cut, usu as one of a series, into a hillside and used for farming. **3** a level usu narrow and steep-fronted area bordering a river, sea, etc. **4** *chiefly Brit* a row of similar houses joined by common dividing walls, or a street lined by a row of houses of this type. **b** a row of houses or flats on raised ground or a sloping site. **5** *Brit* a series of shallow steps providing standing accommodation for spectators, *esp* formerly at a football ground. [early French *terrasse* pile of earth, platform, terrace, from Old Provençal *terrassa*, from Latin *terra* earth, land]

terrace² *verb trans* **1** to cut terraces in (a slope). **2** to make (an area of ground) into a terrace.

terraced house *noun Brit* a house in a continuous row of dwellings connected by common dividing walls.

terracotta /terə'kotə/ *noun* **1** an unglazed brownish red fired clay used *esp* for statuettes and vases and as a building material. **2** a brownish orange colour. [Italian *terra cotta*, literally 'baked earth']

terra firma /'fuhmə/ *noun* dry land; solid ground. [Latin *terra firma*, literally 'solid land']

terrain /tə'rayn/ *noun* **1** an area of land, *esp* with respect to its physical features. **2** an environment or milieu. [French *terrain* land, ground, from Latin *terrenum*, neuter of *terrenus* of earth, from *terra* earth]

terra incognita /inkog'neetə, in'kognitə/ *noun* (*pl* **terrae incognitae** /,teree inkog'neetee, in'kognitee/) an unexplored country or field of knowledge. [Latin *terra incognita*, literally 'unknown land']

terrane /tə'rayn/ *noun* the area or surface over which a particular rock or group of rocks is prevalent. [alteration of *terrain*]

terrapin /'terəpin/ *noun* any of several species of small edible freshwater reptiles that are related and similar to tortoises but adapted for swimming: family Emydidae and other families. [of Algonquian origin]

terrarium /təˈreəri·əm/ *noun* (*pl* **terraria** /-ri·ə/ *or* **terrariums**) **1** an enclosure, *esp* a glass-fronted case, for small land-dwelling animals. **2** a transparent often globe-shaped container in which plants are grown indoors. [Latin *terra* earth + -ARIUM]

terra sigillata /siji'lahtə/ *noun* **1** a reddish brown clay found on the Greek islands of Lemnos or Samos that is used to make pottery and, formerly, as an astringent. **2** pottery made with this clay. [Middle English from medieval Latin *terra sigillata*, literally 'sealed earth']

terrazzo /teˈrahtsoh/ *noun* a mosaic flooring made by embedding and polishing small pieces of marble or granite in mortar. [Italian *terrazzo* terrace, ultimately from Latin *terra* earth]

terrene /teˈreen, təˈreen/ *adj* **1** relating to or living on dry land. **2** *formal* mundane or earthly. [Middle English from Latin *terrenus* of earth, from *terra* earth]

terreplein /ˈteəplayn/ *noun* the level space behind the parapet of a rampart where guns are mounted. [early French *terreplein* via Old Italian from medieval Latin *terraplenum*, neuter of *terra plenus* filled with earth]

terrestrial /təˈrestri·əl/ *adj* **1** relating to the planet earth or its inhabitants. **2a** relating to land as distinct from air or water. **b** said of organisms: living on or in land or soil. **3** said of a planet: like the earth in density, composition, etc. **4** said of a television system or service: not transmitting programmes via a satellite. **5** mundane or prosaic. ➤➤ **terrestrial** *noun,* **terrestrially** *adv.* [Middle English in the sense 'worldly, temporal', from Latin *terrestris*, from *terra* earth]

terrestrial telescope *noun* a telescope used for viewing objects on earth rather than in space, with an extra lens or a prism to produce an uninverted image.

terret /ˈterit/ *noun* either of the rings on the top of a driving saddle through which the reins pass. [Middle English *teret*, alteration of Old French *toret*, dimin. of *tour* ring: see TOUR[1]]

terre verte /teə ˈveət/ *noun* a greyish green pigment used in paints, made from the mineral glauconite. [French *terre verte*, literally 'green earth']

terrible /ˈterəbl/ *adj* **1** *informal.* **a** of very poor quality; awful: *a terrible performance.* **b** highly unpleasant: *We had a terrible journey.* **2** *informal* extreme or very great: *They went to a terrible amount of trouble arranging all this.* **3** *informal.* **a** very unwell. **b** very upset or guilty: *I felt terrible about leaving her to cope on her own.* **4a** causing intense fear; terrifying. **b** formidable, intimidating, or awesome in nature: *a terrible responsibility.* ➤➤ **terribleness** *noun.* [Middle English via French from Latin *terribilis*, from *terrēre* to frighten]

terribly *adv informal* very: *terribly lucky.*

terricolous /teˈrikələs, tə-/ *adj* living on or in the ground. [Latin *terricola* earth-dweller, from *terra* earth + *colere* to inhabit]

terrier[1] /ˈteri·ə/ *noun* **1** a usu small dog belonging to any of various breeds, orig used by hunters to drive out small furred game from underground. **2** (*usu* **Terrier**) *Brit* a member of the Territorial Army. [(sense 1) French (*chien*) *terrier* earth dog, from *terrier* of earth, from medieval Latin *terrarius*, from Latin *terra* earth; (sense 2) by shortening and alteration]

terrier[2] *noun* in former times, a register of land ownership. [Old French *terrier* via medieval Latin from Latin *terra* earth]

terrific /təˈrifik/ *adj* **1** *informal* extraordinarily large or intense. **2** *informal.* **a** excellent, wonderful, or highly enjoyable. **b** in very good health or spirits. **3** arousing fear or awe. ➤➤ **terrifically** *adv.* [Latin *terrificus*, from *terrēre* to frighten]

terrify /ˈterifie/ *verb trans* (**terrifies, terrified, terrifying**) **1** to fill (somebody) with terror or great apprehension. **2** (*usu* + into) to drive or impel (somebody) to do something through threats or fear. ➤➤ **terrifyingly** *adv.* [Latin *terrificare*, from *terrificus*: see TERRIFIC]

terrigenous /təˈrijənəs/ *adj* **1** denoting or relating to sediment on the sea floor derived directly from erosion of the land surface. **2** denoting or relating to sedimentary inorganic deposits laid down on a land surface, e.g. blown sand. [Latin *terrigena* earthborn, from *terra* earth + *gignere* to beget]

terrine /təˈreen/ *noun* **1** an earthenware baking dish. **2** a food, *esp* pâté, cooked in a terrine. [French *terrine* large earthenware pot, fem of *terrin* of earth, from Latin *terra* earth]

territorial[1] /teriˈtawri·əl/ *adj* **1a** relating to territory or land. **b** relating to the ownership of territory or land. **2a** restricted to a particular area or district. **b** relating to the natural instinct of an animal or bird to mark out and defend its own territory: *territorial behaviour; Cats are territorial animals.* ➤➤ **territorially** *adv.*

territorial[2] *or* **Territorial** *noun* a member of a territorial army, *esp* the Territorial Army and Volunteer Reserve.

territorial army *noun* a voluntary force organized by a country or locality to provide a trained army reserve that can be mobilized in an emergency.

Territorial Army and Volunteer Reserve *noun* the present-day British territorial army.

territoriality /ˌteritawriˈaliti/ *noun* the pattern of behaviour in animals and birds associated with the defence of a territory.

territorial waters *pl noun* the waters under the sovereign jurisdiction of a nation.

territory /ˈterit(ə)ri/ *noun* (*pl* **territories**) **1a** a geographical area under the jurisdiction of a government. **b** an administrative subdivision of a country, *esp* a part of the USA not included within any state but with a separate legislature. **2a** an indeterminate geographical area, *esp* one having a specific characteristic. **b** a field of knowledge or interest. **3a** an assigned area; *esp* one in which an agent, sales representative, or distributor operates. **b** an area, often including a nesting site or den, occupied and defended by an animal or group of animals. [Middle English from Latin *territorium* land round a town, from *terra* land + -*torium* as in *dormitorium* DORMITORY]

terror /ˈterə/ *noun* **1** a state of intense fear. **2** somebody or something that inspires fear. **3** = REIGN OF TERROR. **4** acts of terrorism, e.g. the planting of bombs. **5** *informal* an appalling person or thing; *esp* a naughty child. [Middle English via French from Latin *terror*, from *terrēre* to frighten]

terrorise *verb trans* see TERRORIZE.

terrorism *noun* the systematic use of terror, violence, and intimidation for political ends: *the subtle terrorism of words* — Hugh Gaitskell. ➤➤ **terrorist** *adj and noun,* **terroristic** /-ˈristik/ *adj.*

terrorize *or* **terrorise** *verb trans* **1** to fill (somebody) with terror or anxiety. **2** (*often* + into) to coerce (somebody) by threats or violence. ➤➤ **terrorization** /-ˈzaysh(ə)n/ *noun.*

terror-stricken *adj* overcome by uncontrollable terror.

terror-struck *adj* = TERROR-STRICKEN.

terry /ˈteri/ *noun* (*pl* **terries**) **1** an absorbent fabric with uncut loops on both faces, used *esp* for towels. **2** a baby's nappy made of this. ➤➤ **terry** *adj.* [perhaps modification of French *tiré*, past part. of *tirer* to draw]

terse /tuhs/ *adj* **1** using few words; concise. **2** brusque or curt. ➤➤ **tersely** *adv,* **terseness** *noun.*

Word history
Latin *tersus* clean, neat, past part. of *tergēre* to wipe off. Orig in the senses 'trim, neat', of language 'polished, polite', hence 'to the point, concise, brusque'.

tertian /ˈtuhsh(ə)n/ *adj* said of malarial fever: recurring at approximately 48-hour intervals. [Middle English *tercian* from Latin *tertianus* of the third, from *tertius* third, the fever recurring roughly every third day]

tertiary[1] /ˈtuhshəri/ *adj* **1** of third rank, importance, or value. **2a** *Brit* relating to higher education. **b** denoting or relating to service industries: compare PRIMARY[1], SECONDARY[1]. **3** (**Tertiary**) relating to or dating from a geological period, the first period of the Cenozoic era, lasting from about 65 million to about 1.6 million years ago, and marked by the dominance of mammals and the evolution of modern plants. **4** occurring in or being a third stage. ➤➤ **Tertiary** *noun.* [Latin *tertiarius* of or containing a third, from *tertius* third]

tertiary[2] *noun* (*pl* **tertiaries**) somebody belonging to a monastic third order.

tertiary consumer *noun* a carnivore that eats another carnivore: compare PRIMARY CONSUMER, SECONDARY CONSUMER.

tertiary syphilis *noun* the third stage of syphilis, marked by ulcers and tumours of the skin and usu skeletal, cardiovascular, and nervous disorders, e.g. locomotor ataxia: compare PRIMARY SYPHILIS, SECONDARY SYPHILIS, SYPHILIS.

tertium quid /ˌtuhshi·əm ˈkwid, ˌtuhti·əm/ *noun* an unknown factor distinct from, but related to, two known ones, often a middle course or intermediate element. [late Latin *tertium quid*, literally 'third something']

tervalent /tuh'vaylənt/ *adj* = TRIVALENT.

Terylene /'terəleen/ *noun trademark* a synthetic polyester textile fibre. [from syllables of its chemical name, *polyethylene terephthalate*]

terza rima /,tuhtsə 'reemə/ *noun* a verse form consisting of three-line stanzas, usu in iambic pentameter, in which the first and third lines of each stanza rhyme together and the second line rhymes with the first and third lines of the following stanza. [Italian *terza rima*, literally 'third rhyme']

TES *abbr* Times Educational Supplement.

TESL *abbr* teaching English as a second language.

tesla /'teslə/ *noun* the SI unit of magnetic flux density. [named after Nikola *Tesla* d.1943, US electrician and inventor]

TESOL /,tee ee es oh 'el, 'teesol/ *abbr* **1** Teachers of English to Speakers of Other Languages. **2** teaching English to speakers of other languages.

TESSA /'tesə/ *abbr Brit* Tax-Exempt Special Savings Account, a former interest-earning account in a bank or building society that was free from tax subject to certain conditions.

tessellate /'tesəlayt/ *verb trans* **1** to construct, pave, or decorate (something) with mosaic. **2** to cover (a surface) with shapes that tessellate. ➤ *verb intrans* said of geometric shapes: to fit together exactly leaving no spaces. ➤➤ **tessellated** *adj*, **tessellation** /-'laysh(ə)n/ *noun*. [late Latin *tessellatus*, past part. of *tessellare* to pave with tesserae, from Latin *tessella*, dimin. of *tessera*: see TESSERA]

tessera /'tesərə/ *noun* (*pl* **tesserae** /-ree/) **1** a small square piece of marble, glass, etc used in mosaic: compare MOSAIC[1]. **2** a piece of bone or wood used as a dice, ticket, or token in ancient Greece and Rome. [Latin *tessera*, prob from Greek *tessares* four, because it has four corners]

tessitura /tesə't(y)ooərə/ *noun* the part of the register in which most of the notes of a melody or voice part lie, or in which a voice or instrument naturally sounds its best. [Italian *tessitura* texture, from Latin *textura*: see TEXTURE[1]]

Test. *abbr* Testament.

test[1] /test/ *noun* **1** a means of assessing the quality, capabilities, reliability, or endurance of somebody or something; a trial. **2** a series of questions or exercises for measuring the knowledge, intelligence, ability, etc of an individual or group. **3** a real-life situation that reveals the worth or quality of something or somebody by subjecting them to stress, difficulties, etc. **4a** a chemical or physical procedure or reaction, or a chemical reagent, used to identify or test for the presence of a substance or constituent. **b** a procedure used to diagnose a medical disorder. **5** a basis for assessment; a criterion. **6** = TEST MATCH. **7** *chiefly Brit* = CUPEL[1]. ✳ **put to the test** to take action to determine whether (somebody or something) has the required qualities. [Middle English in the sense 'cupel', via French from Latin *testum* earthen vessel, variant of *testa* jug, shell: compare TEST[3]]

test[2] *verb trans* **1** to subject (something or somebody) to a test in order to ascertain quality, capabilities, etc, to measure knowledge or intelligence, or for medical purposes. **2** (*usu* + for) to use a chemical procedure to ascertain whether or not a substance or constituent is present in (something). **3** to subject (something) to severe strain: *His obtuseness tested my patience to the limit.* ➤ *verb intrans* **1** (*usu* + for) to apply a test as a means of analysis, assessment, or diagnosis: *We use this exercise to test for mechanical aptitude.* **2** (*usu* + for) to produce a specified result, usu positive or negative, in a medical or chemical test: *She tested negative for HIV.* ✳ **test the water** to find out what people's opinions or feelings about a matter are. ➤➤ **testable** *adj*.

test[3] *noun* an external hard or firm covering of an invertebrate, e.g. the shell of a mollusc. [Latin *testa* shell, earthenware pot: compare TEST[1]]

testa /'testə/ *noun* (*pl* **testae** /'testee/) the hard external coat of a seed. [Latin *testa*: see TEST[3]]

testaceous /te'stayshəs/ *adj* **1** having a shell or testa. **2** reddish brown in colour. [Latin *testaceus*, from *testa*: see TEST[3]]

testament /'testəmənt/ *noun* **1** (**Testament**). **a** either of the two main divisions of the Bible. **b** a copy of the Bible or of the Old or New Testament. **2** (*usu* + to) a tangible proof of or tribute to something: *The project is a testament to our belief in the future of this company.* **3** a will. **4** *archaic* a covenant between God and humanity. ➤➤ **testamentary** /-'ment(ə)ri/ *adj*. [Middle English from Latin *testamentum* last will, from *testari* to be a witness, call to witness, make a will, from *testis* witness, TESTIS]

testate[1] /'testayt/ *adj* having made a valid will. [Middle English from Latin *testatus*, past part. of *testari*: see TESTAMENT]

testate[2] *noun* a person who dies testate.

testator /te'staytə/ *noun* a person who makes a will or leaves a valid will after his or her death. [Middle English *testatour* via Anglo-French from late Latin *testator*, from *testari*: see TESTAMENT]

testatrix /te'staytriks/ *noun* (*pl* **testatrices** /-seez/ *or* **testatrixes**) *dated* a female testator.

test ban *noun* a self-imposed ban on the testing of nuclear weapons.

test bed *noun* a piece of equipment for testing a component separately from its intended working environment.

test card *noun* a geometric pattern or fixed picture broadcast by a television transmitting station to facilitate the testing or adjustment of receivers.

test case *noun* in law, a representative case whose outcome is likely to serve as a precedent.

test-drive *verb trans* (*past tense* **test-drove**, *past part.* **test-driven**) to drive (a motor vehicle) before buying it in order to evaluate its suitability. ➤➤ **test drive** *noun*.

tested *adj* (*usu used in combinations*) subjected to or qualified through testing: *time-tested principles*.

tester[1] *noun* **1** a person or device that carries out tests. **2** a sample of a product, such as a cosmetic, for a prospective customer to try.

tester[2] *noun* the canopy over a bed, pulpit, or altar. [Middle English from early French *testiere* headpiece, head covering, from *teste* head]

testes /'testeez/ *noun* pl of TESTIS.

testicle /'testikl/ *noun* a testis, *esp* either of the two oval sperm-producing organs of a male mammal, usu with its enclosing structures, e.g. the scrotum. ➤➤ **testicular** /te'stikyoolə/ *adj*. [Middle English *testicule* from Latin *testiculus*, dimin. of *testis* TESTIS]

testiculate /te'stikyoolət/ *adj* said *esp* of the tubers of some orchids: oval in shape.

testify /'testifie/ *verb* (**testifies, testified, testifying**) ➤ *verb intrans* **1** to give evidence under oath as a witness in a court. **2** (*usu* + to) to serve as evidence or proof. **3** to make a statement based on personal knowledge or belief. ➤ *verb trans* **1a** to affirm the truth of (something). **b** to serve as evidence of (something). **2** to make known (a personal conviction). **3** to declare (something) under oath. ➤➤ **testifier** *noun*. [Middle English *testifien* from Latin *testificari*, from *testis* witness, TESTIS]

testimonial[1] /testi'mohni-əl/ *noun* **1** a letter of recommendation. **2** an expression of appreciation or esteem, e.g. in the form of a gift. **3** a sports match arranged in honour of and to raise money for a particular player.

testimonial[2] *adj* **1** of or constituting testimony. **2** expressive of appreciation, gratitude, or esteem: *a testimonial dinner*.

testimony /'testiməni/ *noun* (*pl* **testimonies**) **1** a sworn statement or the evidence given by a witness in a court. **2** (*often* + of/to) an outward sign; evidence: *His success is testimony of his abilities.* **3** first-hand authentication of a fact. [Middle English, ultimately from Latin *testimonium* evidence, witness, from *testis* witness, TESTIS]

testis /'testis/ *noun* (*pl* **testes** /'testeez/) a male reproductive gland that produces sperm. [Latin *testis* witness, testis; perhaps from its being evidence of virility]

test match *noun* any of a series of international matches, *esp* cricket matches.

testosterone /tes'tostərohn/ *noun* a male steroid hormone, produced by the testes or made synthetically, that induces and maintains male secondary sex characteristics. [TESTIS + -*sterone*, blend of STEROL + KETONE]

test pilot *noun* a pilot who specializes in putting new or experimental aircraft through manoeuvres designed to test their strength, performance, etc, *esp* in abnormal conditions.

test tube *noun* a thin glass tube closed at one end and used in chemistry, biology, etc.

test-tube baby *noun* a baby conceived by fertilization of an ovum outside the mother's body.

testudo /te'styoodoh/ *noun* (*pl* **testudines** /-dineez/ *or* **testudos**) an overhead cover of overlapping shields or a movable roofed shelter used by the ancient Romans to protect an attacking force. [Latin *testudin-*, *testudo*, literally 'tortoise, tortoise shell', from *testa* shell]

testy /'testi/ *adj* (**testier, testiest**) impatient or ill-humoured. ➤➤ **testily** *adv*, **testiness** *noun*. [Middle English in the sense 'headstrong', from Anglo-French *testif*, from Old French *teste* head]

tetanic /te'tanik/ *adj* relating to or tending to produce tetanus or tetany. ➤➤ **tetanically** *adv*.

tetanus /'tet(ə)nəs/ *noun* **1** an infectious disease characterized by spasms of voluntary muscles, *esp* of the jaw, or the bacterium that produces this. **2** prolonged contraction of a muscle resulting from rapidly repeated motor impulses. ➤➤ **tetanize** *verb trans*. [Middle English via Latin *tetanus* from Greek *tetanos* muscular spasm, from *teinein* to stretch]

tetany /'tet(ə)ni/ *noun* muscle spasm usu associated with deficient secretion of parathyroid hormones. [from Latin *tetanus*: see TETANUS]

tetchy or **techy** /'techi/ *adj* (**tetchier, tetchiest**) irritably or peevishly sensitive. ➤➤ **tetchily** *adv*, **tetchiness** *noun*. [prob from Middle English *tecche, tache* fault, bad habit, from early French *teche, tache* stain, spot, of Germanic origin]

tête-à-tête[1] /,tet ah 'tet, ,tayt ah 'tayt/ *adv and adj* in private; private and intimate. [French *tête-à-tête*, literally 'head to head']

tête-à-tête[2] *noun* **1** a private conversation between two people. **2** an S-shaped sofa, designed for two people to sit facing each other.

tête-bêche /tet 'besh/ *adj and adv* said of a pair of stamps: inverted in relation to one another. [French *tête-bêche* pair of inverted stamps, from *tête* head + *-bêche*, alteration of early French *bechevet* double bedhead]

tether[1] /'tedhə/ *noun* a rope, chain, etc by which an animal is fastened so that it can move only within a set radius. ✱ **at the end of one's tether** having come to the end of one's patience, resources, or ability to cope. [Middle English *tethir* from Old Norse *tjōthr*]

tether[2] *verb trans* (**tethered, tethering**) to fasten or restrain (an animal or person) by or as if by a tether.

tetr- *comb. form* see TETRA-.

tetra /'tetrə/ *noun* any of numerous small brightly coloured S American fishes often kept in tropical aquariums: family Characidae. [by shortening from scientific Latin *Tetragonopterus* former genus name, from late Latin *tetragonum* quadrangle + Greek *pteron* wing]

tetra- or **tetr-** *comb. form* forming nouns and their derivatives, with the meanings: **1** four or having four parts: *tetragonal*. **2** containing four atoms, groups, or chemical equivalents in the molecular structure: *tetroxide*. [Middle English via Latin from Greek *tetra-*, from *tettares* four]

tetrabasic /tetrə'baysik/ *adj* **1** said of an acid: having four hydrogen atoms capable of reacting as acids in each molecule. **2** said of a chemical compound: containing four atoms of a metal with a valency of one, or their equivalent.

tetrachord /'tetrəkawd/ *noun* a diatonic series of four notes with an interval of a perfect fourth between the first and last. [Greek *tetrachordon*, neuter of *tetrachordos* of four strings, from TETRA- + *chordē* string]

tetracycline /tetrə'siekleen/ *noun* any of several broad-spectrum antibiotics obtained *esp* from a soil bacterium. [TETRA- + CYCLIC + -INE[2]]

tetrad /'tetrad/ *noun* a group or arrangement of four cells, atoms, etc. ➤➤ **tetradic** /te'tradik/ *adj*. [Greek *tetrad-, tetras* group of four]

tetraethyl lead /,tetraethəl 'led/ *noun* a poisonous liquid formerly used as a petrol additive to prevent knocking in internal-combustion engines.

tetrafluoroethylene /tetrəflooəroh'ethəleen/ *noun* a colourless gas that is polymerized (chemically combined with itself; see POLYMERIZE) in the production of the plastic polytetrafluoroethylene: formula C_2F_4.

tetragonal /te'tragənl/ *adj* denoting or relating to a crystal system characterized by three axes at right angles of which only two axes are equal. ➤➤ **tetragonally** *adv*. [late Latin *tetragonalis* having four angles and four sides, ultimately from Greek *tetragōnon* quadrangle, from TETRA- + *gōnia* angle]

tetragram /'tetrəgram/ *noun* a word made up of four letters or characters.

Tetragrammaton /tetrə'gramətən/ *noun* the four Hebrew letters, usu transliterated YHWH or JHVH, used to refer to God in the Old Testament: compare YAHWEH. [Middle English from Greek *tetragrammaton*, neuter of *tetragrammatos* having four letters, from TETRA- + *grammat-, gramma* letter]

tetrahedron /tetrə'heedrən/ *noun* (*pl* **tetrahedrons** or **tetrahedra** /-drə/) a polyhedron with four faces. ➤➤ **tetrahedral** *adj*. [via Latin from late Greek *tetraedron*, neuter of *tetraedros* having four faces, from Greek TETRA- + *hedra* seat, face]

tetrahydrocannabinol /,tetrəhiedrohkə'nabinol/ *noun* a hallucinogenic drug that is the main active constituent of marijuana. [*tetrahydro-* combined with four atoms of hydrogen + CANNABIN + -OL[1]]

tetralogy /te'traləji/ *noun* (*pl* **tetralogies**) a series of four closely related literary, cinematic, or musical works. [Greek *tetralogia*, from TETRA- + *-logia* -LOGY]

tetramerous /te'tramərəs/ *adj* having four parts, or having parts arranged in groups of four: *tetramerous flowers*. [scientific Latin *tetramerus* from Greek *tetramerēs*, from TETRA- + *meros* part]

tetrameter /te'tramitə/ *noun* a line of verse consisting of four metrical feet. [Greek *tetrametron*, neuter of *tetrametros* having four measures, from TETRA- + *metron* measure]

tetraplegia /tetrə'pleejə/ *noun* = QUADRIPLEGIA. ➤➤ **tetraplegic** *adj and noun*.

tetraploid[1] /'tetrəployd/ *adj* having four times the basic number of chromosomes arranged in homologous pairs. ➤➤ **tetraploidy** *noun*.

tetraploid[2] *noun* a tetraploid cell or organism.

tetrapod /'tetrəpod/ *noun* **1** a vertebrate animal with two pairs of limbs. **2** an object with four legs or supports. [scientific Latin *tetrapodus* from Greek *tetrapod-, tetrapous* four-footed, from TETRA- + *-pod-, pous* foot]

tetrapterous /ti'traptərəs/ *adj* having four wings. [scientific Latin from Greek *tetrapteros*, from TETRA- + *pteron* wing]

tetrarch /'tetrahk/ *noun* **1a** one of four joint rulers. **b** in the Roman Empire, the governor of a quarter of a province or country. **2** a subordinate ruler. ➤➤ **tetrarchic** /te'trahkik/ *adj*. [Middle English via Latin from Greek *tetrarchēs*, from TETRA- + *-archēs* -arch]

tetrastich /'tetrəstik/ *noun* a poem or stanza made up of four lines of verse. [via Latin from Greek *tetrastichon* having four rows, from TETRA- + *stikhos* row]

tetratomic /tetrə'tomik/ *adj* having four atoms in its molecular structure.

tetravalent /tetrə'vaylənt/ *adj* in chemistry, having a valency of four.

tetri /'tetri/ *noun* (*pl* **tetri**) a unit of currency in Georgia, worth 100th of a lari.

tetryl /'tetril/ *noun* a pale yellow explosive used *esp* as a detonator: formula $(NO_2)_3C_6H_2N(NO_2)CH_3$. [TETRA- + -YL]

tetter /'tetə/ *noun archaic* any of various pustular skin diseases, such as eczema or herpes. [Old English *teter*]

Teuton /'tyoohtən/ *noun* **1** a member of an ancient Germanic people who lived in Jutland in the fourth cent. BC and had migrated to southern France by the second cent. BC. **2** a German. [Latin *Teutoni* (pl)]

Teutonic /tyooh'tonik/ *adj* **1** supposedly characteristic of the Germans: *Teutonic efficiency*. **2** relating to or characteristic of the Teutons.

Tewa /'taywə/ *noun* (*pl* **Tewas** or collectively **Tewa**) **1** a member of a Native American people orig of New Mexico. **2** the language of this people. ➤➤ **Tewa** *adj*. [Tewa *téwa*, literally 'moccasins']

Tex. *abbr* Texas.

Texan /'teks(ə)n/ *noun* a native or inhabitant of the US state of Texas. ➤➤ **Texan** *adj*.

Tex-Mex /teks'meks/ *adj* said of food, music, clothing, etc: having a mixture of Mexican and Texan elements.

text[1] /tekst/ *noun* **1a** printed or written words. **b** the main body of printed or written matter on a page or in a book, as opposed to illustrations, notes, etc. **2** the original written or printed words and form of a literary composition, as opposed to a revision or translation. **3a** a literary or other work selected for special study. **b** = TEXTBOOK. **4a** a passage of Scripture chosen *esp* for the subject of a sermon or in authoritative support of a doctrine: *What damnéd* *error, but some sober brow will bless it and approve it with a text?* — Shakespeare. **b** a passage from an authoritative source providing a theme, e.g. for a speech. **5** a theme or topic. **6** = TEXT MESSAGE. [Middle English via French from Latin *textus* texture, context, past part. of *texere* to weave]

text² *verb trans* to send a text message to (somebody or their mobile phone). ➤➤ **texting** *noun*.

Usage note
New means of communication sometimes bring in new ways – especially new space-and-money-saving ways – of writing English. The electric telegraph produced telegraphese (ARRIVED CREWE STOP DEPARTING STOCKPORT FRIDAY AM), and now email and the text-message facility on mobile phones have engendered other abbreviated forms of expression. Formulas such as *4 sale* (= for sale) and *Y R U w8ing* (= why are you waiting?) have a practical space-saving value in the world of tiny hand-held devices, but they should not be used in place of ordinary full-length prose in normal writing.

textbook *noun* **1** a book used in the study of a subject; *specif* one containing a presentation of the principles of a subject and used by students. **2** (*used before a noun*) conforming to the principles or descriptions in textbooks; exemplary or typical: *This is a textbook case of insider dealing.*

textile /ˈtekstiel/ *noun* **1** cloth, *esp* a woven or knitted cloth; fabric. **2** a fibre, filament, or yarn used in making cloth. **3** (*used before a noun*) relating to fabrics or their production: *the textile industry.* [Latin *textile*, neuter of *textilis* woven, from *texere* to weave]

text message *noun* an alphanumeric message sent from one mobile phone to another. ➤➤ **text-messaging** *noun*.

textual /ˈtekstyooəl/ *adj* of or based on a text. ➤➤ **textually** *adv*. [Middle English from medieval Latin *textualis*, from Latin *textus*: see TEXT¹]

textual criticism *noun* **1** study of a literary work that aims to establish the original text. **2** criticism of literature emphasizing a close reading and analysis of the text.

textualist *noun* somebody who studies or adheres to the text of a work closely, *esp* the text of the Bible. ➤➤ **textualism** *noun*.

texture¹ /ˈtekschə/ *noun* **1a** the visual or tactile surface characteristics of something, *esp* fabric. **b** the structure formed by the threads of a fabric. **2a** the distinctive or identifying part or quality; character: *the rich texture of his prose.* **b** a pattern of musical sound created by notes or lines played or sung together. **3** the size or organization of the constituent particles of a body or substance: *a soil that is coarse in texture.* ➤➤ **textural** *adj*. [Latin *textura*, from *texere* to weave]

texture² *verb trans* to give a particular texture to (something). ➤➤ **textured** *adj*.

textured vegetable protein *noun* a vegetable substance made from high-protein soya beans that is used as a meat substitute.

TFT *abbr* thin-film transistor, used in making thin flat computer monitors and television screens.

TG *abbr* **1** Togo (international vehicle registration). **2** transformational grammar.

TGV *abbr train grande vitesse* (a high-speed train in France).

TGWU *abbr Brit* Transport and General Workers' Union.

Th *abbr* the chemical symbol for thorium.

Th. *abbr* Thursday.

-th¹ *or* **-eth** *suffix* **1** forming ordinal numbers: *hundredth; fortieth.* **2** forming nouns, denoting: fractions: *a fortieth; two hundredths of an inch.* [Middle English *-the, -te* from Old English *-tha, -ta*]

-th² *suffix* forming nouns, denoting: **1** an act or process: *growth; birth.* **2** a state or condition: *dearth; filth.* [Old English]

-th³ *suffix* see -ETH¹.

Thai /tie/ *noun* **1** a native or inhabitant of Thailand in SE Asia. **2** a Tai language, the national language of Thailand. ➤➤ **Thai** *adj*. [Thai, literally 'free']

thalamus /ˈthaləməs/ *noun* (*pl* **thalami** /-mie/) either of two eggshaped masses in the base of the brain that together form a coordinating centre through which different nerve impulses are directed to appropriate parts of the brain. ➤➤ **thalamic** /thəˈlamik/ *adj*. [scientific Latin, from Greek *thalamos* inner chamber]

thalassaemia /thaləˈseemi·ə/ *noun* a hereditary anaemia common in Mediterranean regions and characterized by abnormally small red blood cells. [scientific Latin, from Greek *thalassa* sea + -AEMIA]

thalassic /thəˈlasik/ *adj* **1** living or growing in the sea: *thalassic fishes.* **2** relating to a sea, *esp* to a small or inland sea: *thalassic civilizations.* [French *thalassique*, from Greek *thalassa* sea]

thalassotherapy /thəlasohˈtherəpi/ *noun* a system of therapy involving seawater baths, seaweed skin packs, and seaside exercise. [Greek *thalassa* sea]

thalidomide /thəˈlidəmied/ *noun* a sedative and hypnotic drug found to cause foetal malformation when used during pregnancy. [PHTHALIC ACID + *imido* (comb. form of IMIDE) + IMIDE]

thalli /ˈthalie, ˈthalee/ *noun* pl of THALLUS.

thallium /ˈthali·əm/ *noun* a white soft metallic chemical element chemically resembling lead that occurs naturally in some ores and is used as a poison and in glass: symbol Tl, atomic number 81. ➤➤ **thallic** /ˈthalik/ *adj*, **thallous** /ˈthaləs/ *adj*. [scientific Latin, from Greek *thallos* green shoot (see THALLUS) + -IUM; from the bright green line in its spectrum]

thallophyte /ˈthaləfiet/ *noun* any of a primary group of living things with a body consisting of a thallus that includes the algae, fungi, and lichens. ➤➤ **thallophytic** /-ˈfitik/ *adj*. [Greek *thallos* (see THALLUS) + *phyton* plant]

thallus /ˈthaləs/ *noun* (*pl* **thalli** /ˈthalie, ˈthalee/ *or* **thalluses**) a body of a plant, alga, or fungus that is not differentiated into distinct tissues or parts, such as a stem or leaves. ➤➤ **thalloid** /ˈthaloyd/ *adj*. [scientific Latin from Greek *thallos* green shot, from *thallein* to sprout]

thalweg /ˈtahlvayg, ˈthahlwayg/ *noun* in geology, a line connecting the lowest points in a series of cross-sections across a valley. [German *Thalweg*, from obsolete *Thal* valley + *Weg* way]

than¹ /dhən; *strong* dhan/ *conj* **1** used with comparatives to introduce the second element in a comparison: *She is older than I am; That is easier said than done.* **2** used to introduce an alternative or a contrast: *They would starve rather than beg.* **3** used after expressions such as *no sooner* to introduce what happened next: *No sooner had I sat down than the doorbell rang again.* [Old English *thanne, thonne, thaenne* than, THEN¹]

Usage note
My sister can run faster than I. This is the grammatically correct form – *than I*, as traditionalists frequently point out, is short for *than I can*. However, the form that is considered correct by traditionalists sometimes sounds rather pedantic in speech: *My sister can run faster than I can* is correct, but *My sister can run faster than me* is more frequently used. Filling in the missing verb is often a good way of preserving grammar and avoiding awkwardness: *She spent far less time on it than he did.*

than² *prep* in comparison with (something or somebody): *You're older than me; The bill came to less than £1000.*

thanatology /thanəˈtoləji/ *noun* the study of medical, sociological, and psychological aspects and effects of death. ➤➤ **thanatological** /-ˈlojikl/ *adj*, **thanatologist** *noun*. [Greek *thanatos* death + -LOGY]

Thanatos /ˈthanatos/ *noun* a desire for death that in Freudian theory is one of the two primal instincts: compare EROS. [Greek *thanatos* death]

thane /thayn/ *noun* **1** a free retainer of an Anglo-Saxon lord, *esp* one holding lands in exchange for military service. **2** a Scottish feudal lord. ➤➤ **thaneship** *noun*. [Old English *thegn*]

thank /thangk/ *verb trans* **1** to express gratitude to (somebody). **2** (*usu* + for) to hold (somebody) responsible; to blame: *He had only himself to thank for his loss.* **3** used ironically as a way of phrasing a sharp request or rebuff: *I'll thank you to mind your own business!* ✳ **thank God/goodness/heaven** used to express gratitude or relief for something. **thank one's lucky stars** to consider oneself very fortunate. **thank you** used as a conventional and polite formula for expressing gratitude. ➤➤ **thanker** *noun*. [Old English *thancian*]

thankful /ˈthangkf(ə)l/ *adj* **1** conscious of having received a benefit; grateful. **2** feeling or expressing thanks. **3** pleased or glad: *He was thankful that the room was dark.* ➤➤ **thankfulness** *noun*.

thankfully *adv* **1** in a thankful manner. **2** it is a relief that: *But thankfully things have changed.*

Usage note
Thankfully has now, like *hopefully*, been widely accepted in normal usage as an adverb that can relate to a whole sentence as well as to a single verb: *Thankfully, no damage was done.* It is usually easy to distinguish between this sense, meaning 'fortunately', and the other sense 'in a thankful way': *He sank down thankfully into the soft warm bed.* In writing, care should be taken to make sure that it is clear which sense is intended.

thankless *adj* **1a** bringing neither profit nor appreciation: *Alas, what boots it with uncessant care to tend the homely, slighted shepherd's trade and strictly meditate the thankless Muse?* — Milton. **b** futile: *It's a thankless task trying to grow tomatoes out of doors in England.* **2** not expressing or feeling gratitude. >>> **thanklessly** *adv*, **thanklessness** *noun*.

thanks *pl noun* **1** gratitude or appreciation. **2** an expression of gratitude. **3** (*often* + for) used as a somewhat informal but nonetheless courteous expression of gratitude: *Thanks for all your help.* ✳ **no thanks to** not as a result of any help from or goodwill on the part of (somebody or something): *He feels better now, no thanks to you.* **thanks a bunch/lot/million** *informal* used ironically as a reproach. **thanks to 1** with the help of (something or somebody): *Thanks to modern medicine, life expectancy is increasing year by year.* **2** because of or owing to (something or somebody): *Our arrival was delayed, thanks to the fog.* [pl of Middle English *thank*, from Old English *thanc* thought, gratitude]

thanksgiving /thangks'giving, 'thangks-/ *noun* **1** an expression of gratefulness, *esp* to God. **2** a prayer of gratitude. **3** (**Thanksgiving**) = THANKSGIVING DAY.

Thanksgiving Day *noun* **1** the fourth Thursday in November observed as a public holiday in the USA. **2** the second Monday in October observed as a public holiday in Canada.

thank-you *noun* a polite expression of one's gratitude. [from the phrase (*I*) *thank you*]

thar /thah/ *or* **tahr** /tah/ *noun* a Himalayan beardless wild goat: genus *Hermitragus*. [Nepali *thār*]

that[1] /dhat/ *pronoun* (*pl* **those** /dhohz/) **1** the thing or idea just mentioned: *After that he went to bed; That is a lie!* **2** a relatively distant person or thing introduced for observation or discussion: *Those are chestnuts and these are elms; Who is that?* **3** the kind or thing specified as follows: *The purest water is that produced by distillation; We only picked those ripe enough to eat.* **4** (*in pl*) people: *There are those who think the time has already come.* **5** used to indicate emphatic agreement with or confirmation of an idea previously presented: *Is he a good worker? He is that.* ✳ **and (all) that** *informal* and everything connected with it; and so on. **like that 1** *informal* at once and without any apparent effort or difficulty. **2** *informal* apt to do that sort of thing or behave in that way. **that is (to say)** used to introduce an explanation or clarification of what has just been said; in other words. **that's that** that concludes the matter; there is nothing more to say. [Old English *thæt*, neuter nominative and accusative sing. of *sē*: see THE[1]]

that[2] /dhat/ *adj* (*pl* **those**) **1** denoting the person, thing, or idea specified, mentioned, or understood: *That painting he sold me was a fake.* **2** denoting the one farther away or less immediately under consideration: *This chair or that one?*

that[3] /dhat; *strong* dhat/ *conj* **1** used to introduce a noun clause, e.g. as subject, object, or complement of a verb: *He said that he was afraid; It is unlikely that he'll be in.* **2** used to introduce a subordinate clause expressing purpose, reason, or result: *They died that we might live; She walked so fast that we couldn't keep up.* **3** used to introduce an exclamation, or to express a wish: *That it should come to this!; Oh, that he would come!*

that[4] /dhat; *strong* dhat/ *pronoun* **1** used to introduce a restrictive relative clause identifying or characterizing a particular person, thing, or group: *It was George that told me; The book that you want is on the table.* **2** at, in, on, by, with, for, or to which: *the reason that he came; the way that he spoke.*

Usage note

that, which, *and* who. The general rule is that either *that* or *which* can be used to introduce clauses attached to nouns that add crucial identifying pieces of information: *The briefcase that* (or *which*) *I left on the train contained important papers* (my other briefcase didn't); *This is the book that* (or *which*) *you need.* There is an increasing tendency for *that* to be preferred to *which* in such sentences, and whichever is used the clause is not separated from the noun by commas. *Which*, on the other hand, must be used in clauses that give purely incidental information: *The weather, which was sunny that day, contributed greatly to the success of the event.* Such clauses must be enclosed by commas and – the crucial test for distinguishing between the two kinds – can be wholly removed from the sentence without making it unclear what is being referred to. Though *who* is the usual pronoun used for people, it is perfectly acceptable to use *that* in place of it: *I've been sent a letter by someone that I met on holiday; You are the only person that knows the whole truth.*

that[5] /dhat/ *adv* **1** to the extent indicated or understood: *a nail about that long.* **2** (*usu with the negative*) very; extremely: *It's not that*

expensive. **3** *Brit, informal* to such an extreme degree: *I'm that hungry I could eat a horse.*

thataway /'dhataway/ *adv informal* in that direction or manner. [alteration of the phrase *that way*]

thatch[1] /thach/ *verb trans* to roof (a building) with thatch. >>> **thatcher** *noun.* [Old English *theccan* to cover]

thatch[2] *noun* **1** plant material such as straw or reeds used as a roof covering. **2** anything resembling the thatch of a house, *esp* the hair on somebody's head.

Thatcherism /'thacheriz(ə)m/ *noun* the political and economic policies associated with Margaret Thatcher, Conservative prime minister of Britain 1979–90. These policies include monetarism, strict control of public spending, and the promotion of free-market capitalism and individual enterprise.

thaumatrope /'thawmatrohp/ *noun* a 19th-cent. toy consisting of a disc of card with a picture on either side of it. When the card is rotated rapidly, the two pictures appear to merge. [Greek *thauma* miracle + *tropos* turning]

thaumaturge /'thawmatuhj/ *noun* a performer of miracles, *esp* a magician.

thaumaturgy /'thawmatuhji/ *noun* the performance of miracles; *specif* magic. >>> **thaumaturgic** /-'tuhjik/ *adj,* **thaumaturgist** *noun.* [Greek *thaumatourgia*, from *thaumatourgos* working miracles, from *thaumat-, thauma* miracle + *ergon* work]

thaw[1] /thaw/ *verb intrans* **1a** to go from a frozen to a liquid state. **b** (*often* + out) to become less numb or stiff from cold as a result of exposure to warmth. **2** said of the weather: to be warm enough to melt ice and snow. **3** to become less hostile: *Relations with Iran have thawed.* **4** to become less aloof, cold, or reserved. > *verb trans* (*often* + out) to cause (something) to thaw: *A largess unsearching like the sun, his liberal eye doth give to every one, thawing cold fear* — Shakespeare. [Old English *thawian*]

thaw[2] *noun* **1** the action, fact, or process of thawing. **2** a period of weather warm enough to thaw ice.

THC *noun* tetrahydrocannabinol.

ThD *abbr* Doctor of Theology. [Latin *theologiae doctor*]

the[1] /dhə *before consonants,* dhi, dhee *strong and before vowels/* *definite article* **1a** used before nouns when the object or person in question has been previously referred to or is obvious from the circumstances: *Put the cat out; She ordered bread and cheese, but didn't eat the cheese.* **b** used to indicate that the noun that follows it refers to somebody or something unique or universally recognized: *the pope; the south; the future.* **2** used to limit the application of a noun to that specified by what follows: *the University of London; the man on my right; I didn't have the time to write.* **3** used before the name of a familiar feature of daily life: *We talked on the telephone; I turned off the gas; The postman is late today.* **4** used before a noun denoting a period of time to indicate the present one or the one under consideration: *book of the month; We left on the Monday.* **5** used before a singular noun to indicate generic use: *a history of the novel.* **6a** used before certain proper names: *the Mayflower; the Rhine.* **b** used in the distinguishing titles given to some people, *esp* monarchs: *George the Fourth; Ethelred the Unready; Brueghel the Elder.* **7a** used before the names of parts of the body, clothing, etc instead of a possessive adjective: *inflammation of the bladder; She took him by the sleeve.* **b** *informal* used before a noun denoting a member of one's family instead of a possessive adjective: *The wife's been a bit poorly recently.* **8** used emphatically to designate one of a class as the best, most famous, etc: *This is the life; You can't be the Elvis Presley!* **9** used in prepositional phrases to indicate that the following noun serves as a basis for computation: *Eggs are sold by the dozen.* **10** used to transform an adjective or participle into a noun: *I can't stand the waiting; the British.* [Old English *thē,* masc demonstrative pronoun and definite article, dialect alteration of *sē*]

the[2] *adv* **1** (*used with comparatives*) than before; than otherwise: *I was none the wiser for attending; so much the worse.* **2** used with a pair of comparatives to indicate a relative relationship between them: *the sooner the better; The more you put into an activity, the more you'll get out of it.* **3** used with superlatives: beyond all others: *I like this the best; with the greatest difficulty.* [Old English *thȳ* by that, from *thæt* THAT[1]]

the[3] *prep* = PER (1).

the- *or* **theo-** *comb. form* forming words, denoting: god; God: *theism; theocentric.* [Middle English *theo-* via Latin from Greek *the-, theo-,* from *theos* god]

theanthropic /theeən'thropik/ *adj* ascribing human characteristics to a god, or representing a god or the divine in human form. **>> theanthropism** /thi'anthrəpiz(ə)m/ *noun*. [ecclesiastical Greek *theanthrōpos* god-man, from *theos* god + *anthrōpos* man]

thearchy /'theeahki/ *noun* (*pl* **thearchies**) rule by a god or the gods. **>> thearchic** /thi'ahkik/ *adj*.

theatre (*NAmer* **theater**) /'thiətə/ *noun* **1** a building specially constructed for the presentation of dramatic performances. **2** *chiefly NAmer* a cinema. **3a** dramatic literature or performances. **b** dramatic effectiveness or quality: *The effect is pure theatre*. **4** (**the theatre**) the world of actors, acting, and drama generally. **5** the place where significant events or actions take place: *the theatre of public life; the theatre of war*. **6a** a room with rising tiers of seats: *a lecture theatre*. **b** *Brit* = OPERATING THEATRE. **7** (*used before a noun*) in warfare, confined or appropriate to a limited sphere of operations. [Middle English *theatre* via French and Latin from Greek *theatron*, from *theasthai* to see, view, from *thea* act of seeing]

theatre-in-the-round *noun* **1** the performance of plays on a stage surrounded by an audience. **2** a theatre arranged for this type of performance.

theatre of the absurd *noun* theatre that seeks to represent the absurdity of human beings' existence in a meaningless universe by bizarre or fantastic means.

theatrical /thi'atrikl/ *adj* **1** relating to the theatre or the presentation of plays: *a theatrical costume*. **2a** marked by exhibitionism; histrionic: *a theatrical gesture*. **b** marked by artificiality, e.g. of emotion. **>> theatricalism** *noun*, **theatricality** /-'kaliti/ *noun*, **theatrically** *adv*.

theatricals *pl noun* **1** the performance of plays: *amateur theatricals*. **2** theatrical behaviour.

theatrics /thi'atriks/ *pl noun* **1** the art of performing plays; theatrical technique. **2** showy or extravagant gestures, or theatrical behaviour.

thebaine /'theebayeen/ *noun* a poisonous white alkaloid obtained from opium: formula $C_{19}H_{21}NO_3$. [Latin *thebia* opium of Thebes, ancient city of Egypt]

Theban /'theebən/ *noun* a native or inhabitant of Thebes, either the ancient city of S Egypt on the Nile or the ancient city of Greece, NW of Athens. **>> Theban** *adj*.

thebe /'tebay/ *noun* (*pl* **thebe**) a unit of currency in Botswana, worth 100th of a pula. [Tswana *thebe*, literally 'shield']

theca /'theekə/ *noun* (*pl* **thecae** /'theesee, 'theekee/) **1** an urn-shaped spore receptacle of a moss. **2** an enveloping sheath or case of an animal, or part of an animal's body. **>> thecal** *adj*, **thecate** /'theekayt/ *adj*. [scientific Latin from Greek *thēkē* case]

thecodont[1] /'theekədont/ *adj* having teeth that are inserted in sockets. [scientific Latin, from *theca* (see THECA) + -ODONT]

thecodont[2] *noun* a thecodont animal, *esp* any of an order of thecodont reptiles of the Triassic period believed to be ancestors of the dinosaurs, birds, and crocodiles.

thé dansant /,tay 'donhsonh/ *noun* (*pl* **thés dansants** /,tay 'donhsonh/) an afternoon dance during which tea is served. [French *thé dansant*, literally 'tea dancing']

thee /dhee/ *pronoun* **1** *archaic or dialect* the objective case of THOU[1]. **2** used by Quakers, *esp* among themselves: thou: *Thee must wait*. [Old English *thē*, accusative and dative of *thū* THOU[1]: see YOU]

theft /theft/ *noun* the act or crime of stealing. [Old English *thīefth*; related to *thēof* THIEF]

thegn /thayn/ *noun* = THANE (1).

theine /'thee·in/ *noun* caffeine, *esp* when found in tea. [Latin *theina* from *thea* tea, from Chinese (Amoy) *t'e*]

their /dhə; *strong* dheə/ *adj* **1a** belonging to or associated with them: *their house; their children; their being late; their acquittal*. **b** belonging to or associated with an indefinite singular person: *Has anybody lost their car keys?* **2** used in titles: *Their Royal Highnesses*. [Middle English from Old Norse *theirra*]

Usage note ____
their, there, or they're? These three words, which are pronounced the same, are sometimes confused. *Their* is the possessive form of *they* (*It's their fault; They'll bring their own tools*). *There* is an adverb of place (*You'll find it over there*) and is used with the verb *to be* (*There is nothing I can do about it; Are there any more questions?*). *They're* is the shortened form of *they are*: *They're not quite ready yet*.

theirs /dheəz/ *pronoun* the one or ones that belong to them or are associated with them: *Is this house theirs?; Theirs are on the table; children younger than theirs*. *** of theirs** belonging to or associated with them: *friends of theirs*.

theism /'theeiz(ə)m/ *noun* belief in the existence of a creator god who is present in the universe and yet transcends it.

Editorial note ____
Theism is the belief that God exists (monotheism is the belief that there is one and only one god). As generally held, it combines biblical concepts of a loving, judging, personal creator, the object of worship, with Greek philosophical concepts of God as a reality that is both within everything (immanent) and yet also transcendent, giving value and coherence to an overall understanding of the cosmos — Dr Mel Thompson.

>> theist *noun and adj*, **theistic** /thee'istik/ *adj*, **theistical** /thee'istikl/ *adj*. [Greek *theos* god + -ISM]

-theism *comb. form* forming nouns, denoting: belief in a god or gods of the kind specified: *pantheism; monotheism*.

them[1] /dhəm; *strong* dhem/ *pronoun* used as the objective case: they: *I hate them; I moved towards them; Somebody's responsible, and when I find them, I'll make them pay*. [Middle English *thǣm, thām*, from Old Norse *theim* to these, to them]

them[2] /dhem/ *adj non-standard* those: *them blokes*.

them-and-us *adj* characterized by tension or resentment between those who exercise authority and the people over whom they exercise it.

thematic /thi'matik/ *adj* **1** relating to or constituting a theme. **2a** said of a vowel: being the last part of a word stem before an inflectional ending. **b** said of a verb form: containing a thematic vowel. **>> thematically** *adv*. [Greek *thematikos*, from *themat-*, *thema*: see THEME[1]]

thematic apperception test *noun* in psychology, a test involving a depiction of an ambiguous situation or relationship between people that the subject is asked to interpret as a way of bringing to light his or her attitudes or needs.

theme[1] /theem/ *noun* **1** a subject or topic dealt with in a discursive or artistic work and usu forming a unifying thread running through it. **2a** a unifying concept in the planning or design of something. **b** (*used before a noun*) planned or designed around a single unifying concept. **3** a group of notes or melody forming the basis of a musical composition; a subject. **4** *chiefly NAmer* a written exercise; a composition. **5a** in linguistics, the STEM[1] (part that remains unchanged) of a word. **b** the part of an utterance that contributes the least amount of new information to the evolving overall meaning. [Middle English *teme, theme* via Old French and Latin from Greek *thema*, literally 'something laid down', from *tithenai* to place]

theme[2] *verb trans* to design, create, organize, or arrange (something) in accordance with a theme: *themed amusements such as the Mystic East and CircusWorld* — The Guardian.

theme park *noun* an amusement park in which the structures and settings are all based on a specific theme, e.g. space travel.

theme song *noun* **1** a recurring melody in a musical play or in a film that characterizes the production or one of its characters. **2** a signature tune.

themself /dhəm'self/ *pronoun* = THEMSELVES (1B).

themselves /dhəm'selvz/ *pronoun* **1a** used reflexively to refer to the people, animals, or things that are the subject of the clause: *They were looking very pleased with themselves*. **b** used reflexively to refer to an indefinite singular person that is the subject of the clause: *We just prayed that nobody would hurt themselves*. **2** used for emphasis: *They designed the kitchen themselves*. *** be themselves** to be fit or healthy as normal: *They aren't quite themselves today*.

Usage note ____
themselves and themself. *Themselves* is the standard reflexive form of *they*: *I hope the children enjoyed themselves*. *Themself* is a 14th to 16th cent. form that has recently been revived for use as an equivalent to *they* meaning 'a person of either sex': *No one should blame themself for this tragedy*. There is a certain logic to this if they is given a singular meaning, but the form *themselves* is also used in this context: *Everyone ought to try it for themselves*. '*We are looking for a Producer/Director who, when necessary, can use a camera themselves, and who has …*' — BBC advertisement. This is a very controversial area of English usage where, in formal writing, it is often best to abide by what is universally approved or to take avoiding action: *Everyone ought to try it for himself or herself* or *Everyone ought to try it personally*. See also note at THEY.

then[1] /dhen/ *adv* **1** at that time: *Only then did I realize what she had meant.* **2a** soon after that; next: *He walked to the door, then turned.* **b** besides or in addition: *Then there is the interest to be paid.* **3a** in that case: *Take it, then, if you want it so much.* **b** as may be inferred: *Your mind is made up, then?* **4** as a necessary consequence: *If the angles are equal, then the complements are equal.* **5** used after *but*: in fact; on the other hand: *He lost the race, but then he never expected to win.* ✳ **then and there** at once; straight away. [Old English *thonne, thænne, thanne* then, THAN[1]]

then[2] *noun* that time: *Since then, he's been more cautious.*

then[3] *adj* existing, in office, or in operation at that time: *the then secretary of state.*

thenar /'theenah, 'theenə/ *noun* **1** the ball of the thumb. **2** the palm of the hand. ⋙ **thenar** *adj*. [Greek *thenar* palm of the hand]

thence /dhens/ *adv* **1** from there: *We flew first to London and thence to Paris.* **2** *formal* from that preceding fact or premise: *It thence transpired that the two cases were indeed related.* [Middle English *thennes* from Old English *thanon* + genitive suffix *-es*]

thenceforth /dhens'fawth/ *adv chiefly formal* from that time or point on.

thenceforward *adv* = THENCEFORTH.

theo- *prefix* see THE-.

theobromine /thee-ə'brohmeen/ *noun* an alkaloid that is closely related to caffeine, occurs *esp* in cacao beans and tea, and is used as a diuretic and heart stimulant: formula $C_7H_8N_4O_2$. [scientific Latin *Theobroma*, genus name of the cacao tree, from THEO- + Greek *brōma* food, from *bibrōskein* to devour]

theocentric /thee-ə'sentrik/ *adj* having God as the central interest and ultimate concern: *a theocentric culture.* ⋙ **theocentricity** /-'trisiti/ *noun*.

theocracy /thi'okrəsi/ *noun* (*pl* **theocracies**) government by immediate divine guidance or by officials regarded as divinely guided, or a state with this type of government. ⋙ **theocrat** /'thee-əkrat/ *noun*, **theocratic** /-'kratik/ *adj*, **theocratical** /-'kratikl/ *adj*. [Greek *theokratia*, from THEO- + *-kratia* -cracy]

theodicy /thi'odəsi/ *noun* (*pl* **theodicies**) a defence of the doctrines of God's goodness and omnipotence against arguments derived from the existence of evil, or a branch of theology devoted to this. [modification of French *théodicée*, from *théo-* THEO- + Greek *dikē* judgment, right]

theodolite /thi'od(ə)liet/ *noun* a surveyor's instrument for measuring horizontal and usu also vertical angles. ⋙ **theodolitic** /-'li-tik/ *adj*. [scientific Latin *theodelitus*, of unknown origin]

theogony /thi'ogəni/ *noun* (*pl* **theogonies**) an account of the origin and genealogy of the gods. ⋙ **theogonic** /thee-ə'gonik/ *adj*. [Greek *theogonia*, from THEO- + *-gonia* -GONY]

theol. *abbr* **1** theologian. **2** theological. **3** theology.

theologian /thee-ə'lohjən/ *noun* a specialist in theology.

theological college /thee-ə'lojikl/ *noun* a college for the training of candidates for the clergy.

theological virtue *noun* any of the three spiritual graces, faith, hope, and charity, which, according to medieval theology, draw the soul to God: compare NATURAL VIRTUE.

theology /thi'oləji/ *noun* (*pl* **theologies**) **1** the study of God, *esp* by analysis of the origins and teachings of an organized religion.

Editorial note
Traditionally an intellectual activity studying beliefs about God and reflecting systematically in the light of philosophy and knowledge about the world, theology has broadened its scope to include practical concerns and those of interest groups. This is seen in titles such as liberation theology, feminist theology, and ecotheology — Professor John Rogerson.

2 a theological theory, system, or body of opinion: *Catholic theology.* ⋙ **theological** /thee-ə'lojikl/ *adj*. [Middle English *theologie* from Latin from Greek *theologia*, from THEO- + *-logia* -LOGY]

theomachy /thi'oməki/ *noun* (*pl* **theomachies**) a war between gods, or a war against God. [Greek *theomakhia*, from THEO- + *makhia* battle]

theomania /thee-ə'mayni-ə/ *noun* religious madness, *esp* the belief that one is a god.

theophany /thi'ofani/ *noun* (*pl* **theophanies**) a visible manifestation of God or a god. ⋙ **theophanic** /thee-ə'fanik/ *adj*. [medieval Latin *theophania* from late Greek *theophaneia*, from THEO- + Greek *-phaneia* as in *epiphaneia* appearance: see EPIPHANY]

theophylline /thi'ofilin/ *noun* an alkaloid similar to theobromine, occurring in plants such as tea, used *esp* to treat some types of heart failure and respiratory disorders: formula $C_7H_8N_4O_2$. [Latin *thea* tea (see THEINE) + PHYLL- + -INE[2]]

theorbo /thi'awboh/ *noun* (*pl* **theorbos**) a 17th-cent. musical instrument resembling a large lute but having an extra set of bass strings. [modification of Italian *tiorba, teorba*]

theorem /'thiərəm, 'thee-ərəm/ *noun* **1** a proposition in mathematics or logic deducible from other more basic propositions. **2** a rule or statement in algebra, geometry, etc expressed as a formula or equation: *binomial theorem.* ⋙ **theorematic** /-'matik/ *adj*. [via late Latin from Greek *theōrēma*, from *theōrein* to look at, from *theōros* spectator, from *thea* act of seeing]

theoretic /thee-ə'retik/ *adj* = THEORETICAL.

theoretical /thee-ə'retikl/ *adj* **1a** relating to or having the character of theory; abstract. **b** confined to theory or speculation: *theoretical mechanics.* **2** existing only in theory; hypothetical. ⋙ **theoretically** *adv*. [via late Latin from Greek *theōrētikos*, from *theōrein*: see THEOREM]

theoretician /thee-ərə'tish(ə)n/ *noun* somebody who specializes in the theoretical aspects of a subject.

theoretics *pl noun* (*treated as sing. or pl*) the theoretical part of a subject.

theorise /'thiəriez, 'thee-əriez/ *verb intrans* see THEORIZE.

theorist /'thiərist, 'thee-ərist/ *noun* = THEORETICIAN.

theorize *or* **theorise** /'thiəriez, 'thee-əriez/ *verb intrans* to form a theory; to speculate. ⋙ **theorizer** *noun*.

theory /'thiəri, 'thee-əri/ *noun* (*pl* **theories**) **1** a belief, policy, or procedure forming the basis for action: *Her method is based on the theory that children want to learn.* **2a** the general or abstract principles of a subject: *music theory.* **b** a body of theorems presenting a concise systematic view of a subject: *the theory of equations.* **3** a scientifically acceptable body of principles offered to explain a phenomenon: *the wave theory of light.* **4a** a hypothesis assumed for the sake of argument or investigation. **b** an unproved assumption; a conjecture. ✳ **in theory** on the basis of abstract principles or under ideal circumstances, but not necessarily in practice or reality. [via late Latin from Greek *theōria*, from *theōrein*: see THEOREM]

theory of games *noun* = GAME THEORY.

theory of numbers *noun* = NUMBER THEORY.

theosophy /thi'osəfi/ *noun* (*pl* **theosophies**) **1** a religious or philosophical system stressing the validity of mystical insight. **2** (*usu* **Theosophy**) the teachings of a modern movement originating in the USA in 1875 and following chiefly Buddhist and Brahmanic theories, *esp* of pantheistic evolution and reincarnation. ⋙ **theosophical** /thee-ə'sofikl/ *adj*, **theosophist** *noun*. [via medieval Latin from late Greek *theosophia*, from THEO- + Greek *sophia* -SOPHY]

therapeutic /therə'pyoohtik/ *adj* **1** relating to the treatment of disease or disorders by remedial agents or methods. **2** having a beneficial effect on a person's health. ⋙ **therapeutically** *adv*. [Greek *therapeutikos*, from *therapeuein* to attend, treat, from *theraps* attendant]

therapeutic index *noun* a measure of the effectiveness of a drug that indicates how good the drug is at producing the desired therapeutic effects without causing toxic side effects.

therapeutics *pl noun* (*treated as sing.*) a branch of medicine dealing with the application of remedies to diseases.

therapist /'therəpist/ *noun* somebody trained in methods of treatment and rehabilitation other than the use of drugs or surgery: *a speech therapist.*

therapsid /thə'rapsid/ *noun* any of an order of reptiles of the Permian and Triassic periods that are believed to be ancestors of the mammals: order Therapsida. ⋙ **therapsid** *adj*. [scientific Latin *Therapsida* group name, perhaps from Greek *theraps* attendant]

therapy /'therəpi/ *noun* (*pl* **therapies**) therapeutic treatment of physical or mental disorders, or a specific type of treatment. [scientific Latin from Greek *therapeia*, from *therapeuein*: see THERAPEUTIC]

Theravada /therə'vaydə/ *noun* a conservative and non-theistic branch of Buddhism comprising sects chiefly in Sri Lanka and Indochina and viewing the original Pali scriptures alone as canonical: compare MAHAYANA. [Pali *theravāda*, literally 'doctrine of the elders']

there[1] /dheə/ *adv* **1** in, at, or to that place: *Stand over there.* **2** on that point or in that particular respect: *I disagree with you there.* **3** used to draw attention to something: *There goes John; Hello there!* **4** used as an interjection to express satisfaction, approval, encouragement, or defiance: *There, it's finished; There, it didn't hurt much, did it?* ✳ **be there for somebody** to give somebody support, advice, and love or friendship. **have been there before** *informal* to know about or have experienced something already. **so there** used to express defiance and emphasize a refusal: *I won't go, so there!* **there** used when trying to comfort somebody. **there and then** at once. **there and back** for a round trip. **there it is** such is the unfortunate fact. **there's a …** used when urging a course of action: *Don't sulk, there's a dear!* **there you are 1** used when handing or presenting something to somebody. **2** I told you so. [Old English *thǣr*]

Usage note

there, their, *or* they're? See note at THEIR.

there[2] *pronoun* used to introduce a sentence or clause that expresses the idea of existence: *What is there to eat?; There won't be another opportunity.*

there[3] *noun* that place or point.

there[4] *adj non-standard* used for emphasis between a demonstrative and the following noun: *that there cow.*

thereabouts (*NAmer also* **thereabout**) *adv* **1** in that vicinity. **2** near that time, number, degree, or quantity: *a boy of 18 or thereabouts.*

thereafter *adv* after that.

thereat *adv formal* **1** at that place. **2** because of or after that.

thereby *adv* **1** by that means; as a result of which. **2** in which connection: *And thereby hangs a tale* — Shakespeare.

there'd /dheəd/ *contraction* **1** there had. **2** there would.

therefor *adv formal* for that, or in return for that.

therefore /'dhuhfə/ *adv* **1** because of that; consequently: *The baby was tired and therefore irritable.* **2** as this proves: *I think, therefore I exist.*

therefrom *adv formal* from that or it.

therein *adv formal* in that; *esp* in that respect: *Therein lies the problem.*

thereinafter /dheərin'ahftə/ *adv formal* in the following part of that document, speech, etc.

thereinto *adv archaic* into that or it.

there'll /dheərəl/ *contraction* **1** there will. **2** there shall.

thereof *adv formal* **1** of that or it. **2** from that or it.

thereon *adv formal* on or onto that or it: *a text with a commentary thereon.*

there's /dheəz/ *contraction* **1** there is. **2** there has.

thereto *adv formal* **1a** to that place. **b** to that matter or document: *conditions attaching thereto.* **2** *archaic* in addition.

theretofore /dheətə'faw, dheətooh'faw/ *adv formal* up to that time.

thereunder *adv formal* under that or it: *the heading and the items listed thereunder.*

thereupon *adv formal* **1** on that matter. **2** immediately after that.

therewith *adv* **1** *formal* with that or it: *a letter enclosed therewith.* **2** *archaic* thereupon, forthwith.

therewithal /'dheəwidhawl/ *adv* **1** *formal* therewith. **2** *archaic* besides.

therianthropic /,thiərian'thropik/ *adj* said of mythical creatures: combining human and animal form. [Greek *thērion* beast + *anthropos* man]

theriomorphic /,thiərioh'mawfik/ *adj* said *esp* of a god: having an animal form. [Greek *thēriomorphos*, from *thērion* beast + *morphē* form]

therm /thuhm/ *noun* a quantity of heat equal to 100,000Btu (about 105,506MJ). [Greek *thermē* heat]

therm- *or* **thermo-** *comb. form* forming words, denoting: heat: *thermion; thermostat.* [Greek, from *thermē* heat]

-therm *comb. form* forming nouns, denoting: an animal having a particular body temperature: *ectotherm.* [Greek *thermē* heat]

thermae /'thuhmee/ *noun* public baths, *esp* in ancient Greece or Rome. [via Latin from Greek *thermai*, pl of *thermē* heat]

thermal[1] /'thuhml/ *adj* **1** relating to or caused by heat: *thermal stress; thermal insulation.* **2** designed to prevent the dissipation of body heat: *thermal underwear.* ➤➤ **thermally** *adv.* [Greek *thermē* heat]

thermal[2] *noun* **1** a rising body of warm air. **2** (*in pl*) thermal underwear or clothing.

thermal barrier *noun* a limit to increase in aircraft or rocket speeds imposed by aerodynamic heating.

thermal capacity *noun* = HEAT CAPACITY.

thermal efficiency *noun* the ratio of the amount of work done by a heat engine to the amount of energy supplied to it.

thermal imaging *noun* a technique for detecting and producing a picture of a heat source, *esp* a hidden one, used e.g. to find missing people or locate a target. ➤➤ **thermal imager** *noun.*

thermalize *or* **thermalise** *verb trans* to cause (neutrons) to lose energy in a reactor and become thermal neutrons.

thermal neutron *noun* a neutron in thermal equilibrium with its surroundings.

thermal printer *noun* a printer that uses a heated printing device to produce an image on heat-sensitive paper.

thermal reactor *noun* a nuclear reactor in which fission is mainly caused by thermal neutrons.

thermal spring *noun* = HOT SPRING.

thermic /'thuhmik/ *adj* = THERMAL[1] (1): *thermic energy.* ➤➤ **thermically** *adv.*

thermion /'thuhmi·ən, -on/ *noun* an electrically charged particle, *specif* an electron, emitted by an incandescent substance. [THERM- + ION]

thermionic /,thuhmi'onik/ *adj* **1** relating to the emission of thermions. **2** denoting or relating to a device, e.g. a valve, that uses thermionic electrons as charge carriers.

thermionic tube *noun* = THERMIONIC VALVE.

thermionic valve *noun* an electron tube in which a regulated flow of electrons is produced by thermionic emission from a heated CATHODE (a conducting structure with a negative electric charge), used *esp* for controlling the flow of current in an electric circuit.

thermistor /thuh'mistə/ *noun* a semiconducting electrical resistor whose resistance varies significantly with temperature. [contraction of *thermal resistor*]

Thermit /'thuhmiet, 'thuhmət/ *noun trademark* = THERMITE.

thermite /'thuhmiet/ *noun* a mixture of aluminium powder and iron oxide that produces a great deal of heat when ignited and is used in welding and in incendiary bombs.

thermo- *comb. form* see THERM-.

thermobaric weapon /,thuhmoh'barik/ *noun* a weapon that destroys buildings and kills people by means of a massive wave of heat and pressure.

thermochemistry /thuhmoh'kemistri/ *noun* the branch of chemistry dealing with heat changes in chemical reactions. ➤➤ **thermochemical** *adj*, **thermochemist** *noun.*

thermochromic /thuhmoh'krohmik/ *adj* able to change colour, reversibly, when heated or cooled, or involving a colour-changing process of this kind.

thermocline /'thuhmohklien/ *noun* a layer of water in a lake, sea, etc that separates an upper warmer zone from a lower colder zone; *specif* a stratum in which temperature declines at least 1°C with each metre increase in depth.

thermocouple /'thuhmohkupl/ *noun* a combination of two conductors for producing a thermoelectric effect used in measuring temperature differences.

thermodynamics /,thuhmohdie'namiks, -di'namiks/ *pl noun* (*treated as sing. or pl*) the mechanical action of, or relations between, heat and other forms of energy, or the branch of physics that deals with this.

Editorial note

Thermodynamics is used to assess the efficiency of thermal processes and to discuss the equilibrium composition of chemical reactions. There are three laws of thermodynamics. The first law expresses the conservation of energy and the equivalence of heat and work. The second law introduces the concept of increasing entropy as the signpost of spontaneous change.

The third law expresses the unattainability of absolute zero — Professor Peter Atkins.

➤➤ **thermodynamic** *adj,* **thermodynamically** *adv,* **thermodynamicist** /-'naməsist/ *noun.*

thermoelectric /,thuhmohi'lektrik/ *adj* **1** relating to or dependent on the relationship between temperature and the electrical properties of materials. **2** producing electricity by means of differences in temperature. ➤➤ **thermoelectricity** /-'trisiti, -elik'trisiti/ *noun.*

thermoform /'thuhməfawm/ *verb trans* to give a final shape to (e.g. a plastic) with the aid of heat and usu pressure. ➤➤ **thermoformable** /-'fawməbl/ *adj.*

thermogenesis /thuhmoh'jenəsis/ *noun* the production of heat by metabolic processes in the body. ➤➤ **thermogenic** *adj.*

thermogram /'thuhməgram/ *noun* the record made by a thermograph.

thermograph /'thuhməgrahf, -graf/ *noun* a device that measures and keeps a record of variations in temperature over a period or area.

thermography /thuh'mografi/ *noun* **1** a process of writing or printing involving heat. **2** a technique for photographically recording variations in the heat emitted by various regions, *esp* of the body, e.g. for the detection of tumours. ➤➤ **thermographic** /-'grafik/ *adj.*

thermolabile /thuhmoh'laybiel/ *adj* unstable, *specif* losing characteristic properties, when heated above a moderate temperature. ➤➤ **thermolability** /-lə'biliti/ *noun.*

thermoluminescence /,thuhmohloohmi'nes(ə)ns/ *noun* phosphorescence developed in a previously irradiated substance when it is subsequently heated. ➤➤ **thermoluminescent** *adj.*

thermolysis /thuh'molasis/ *noun* **1** the dissipation of heat from the living body. **2** the breakdown of a substance by means of heat. ➤➤ **thermolytic** /-'litik/ *adj.*

thermometer /thə'momitə/ *noun* an instrument that measures and indicates temperature, *esp* a glass bulb attached to a fine graduated tube of glass and containing a liquid, e.g. mercury, that rises and falls with changes of temperature. ➤➤ **thermometric** /thuhmə'metrik/ *adj,* **thermometry** *noun.* [French *thermomètre,* from Greek *thermē* heat + French *-o-* + *-mètre* -METER²]

thermonuclear /thuhmoh'nyoohkli·ə/ *adj* relating to or making use of transformations occurring in the nuclei of atoms of low atomic weight, e.g. hydrogen, at very high temperatures: *a thermonuclear reaction; thermonuclear bombs.*

thermophile /'thuhməfiel/ *noun* a living organism thriving at relatively high temperatures. ➤➤ **thermophilic** /-'filik/ *adj.*

thermopile /'thuhməpiel/ *noun* a device that consists of a number of thermoelectric units combined so as to multiply their effect, used e.g. for measuring intensity of radiation or generating thermoelectric current.

thermoplastic /thuhmə'plastik/ *adj* capable of softening or melting when heated and of hardening again when cooled: compare THERMOSETTING. ➤➤ **thermoplastic** *noun.*

thermoregulation /,thuhmohregyoo'laysh(ə)n/ *noun* the natural maintenance of the living body at a constant temperature. ➤➤ **thermoregulatory** /-'regyoolət(ə)ri/ *adj.*

Thermos /'thuhməs/ *noun trademark* a Thermos flask.

thermosetting /'thuhmohseting/ *adj* capable of becoming permanently rigid when heated: compare THERMOPLASTIC.

Thermos flask *noun trademark* a vacuum flask. [Greek *thermos* hot]

thermosphere /'thuhməsfiə/ *noun* the part of the earth's atmosphere, above the MESOSPHERE, that begins at about 85km (50mi) above the earth's surface, extends to outer space, and is characterized by steadily increasing temperature as altitude increases.

thermostable /thuhmoh'staybl/ *adj* stable, *specif* retaining characteristic properties, when heated above a moderate temperature. ➤➤ **thermostability** /-stə'biliti/ *noun.*

thermostat /'thuhməstat/ *noun* an automatic device for regulating temperature. ➤➤ **thermostatic** /-'statik/ *adj,* **thermostatically** /-'statikli/ *adv.*

thermotaxis /thuhmoh'taksis/ *noun* the movement of an organism towards or away from a source of heat. ➤➤ **thermotactic** *adj.*

thermotropism /thuhmo'trohpiz(ə)m/ *noun* growth in a plant towards or away from a source of heat. ➤➤ **thermotropic** /-'tropik/ *adj.*

-thermy *comb. form* forming nouns, denoting: the state of having a particular body temperature: *poikilothermy.* [scientific Latin *-thermia* from Greek *thermē* heat]

THES *abbr* Times Higher Educational Supplement.

thesaurus /thi'sawrəs, 'thesərəs/ *noun* (*pl* **thesauri** /-rie, -ree/ *or* **thesauruses**) **1** a book listing words and their synonyms. **2** a book of words or of information about a particular field or set of concepts. [Latin *thesaurus* treasure, collection, from Greek *thēsauros*]

these /dheez/ *pronoun* pl of THIS¹. [Old English *thās,* pl of *thes* THIS]

thesis /'theesis/ *noun* (*pl* **theses** /'theeseez/) **1a** a proposition that a person offers to support and substantiate by argument. **b** a proposition to be proved or one advanced without proof; a hypothesis. **2** in philosophy, the first stage of a reasoned argument presenting the case: compare ANTITHESIS, SYNTHESIS. **3** a dissertation embodying the results of original research; *specif* one submitted for a doctorate in Britain. **4** the unstressed part of a metrical foot: compare ARSIS. [via Latin from Greek *thesis* act of laying down, from *tithenai* to put, lay down]

thespian¹ /'thespi·ən/ *adj* relating to acting, drama, or the theatre. [named after *Thespis* fl.534 BC, poet, reputed founder of Greek drama]

thespian² *noun chiefly formal or humorous* an actor.

Thess. *abbr* Thessalonians (books of the Bible).

theta /'theetə, 'thaytə/ *noun* the eighth letter of the Greek alphabet (Θ, θ), equivalent to and transliterated as roman th. [Greek *thēta,* of Semitic origin; related to Hebrew *ṭēth,* ninth letter of the Hebrew alphabet]

theurgy /'theeuhji/ *noun* (*pl* **theurgies**) **1** the intervention of a supernatural force in human affairs, or the effect produced by such an intervention. **2** the art or technique of evoking the aid of divine or kindly spirits. ➤➤ **theurgic** /thi'uhjik/, **theurgical** /thi'uhjikl/ *adj,* **theurgist** *noun.* [via late Latin from late Greek *theourgia,* from *theourgos* miracle worker, from Greek THEO- + *ergon* work]

thew /thyooh/ *noun* **1** (*usu in pl*) muscle or sinew. **2** *literary.* **a** muscular power or development. **b** strength or vitality: *the naked thew and sinew of the English language* — G M Hopkins. [Old English *thēaw*]

they /dhay/ *pronoun* **1a** used to refer to a previously mentioned group of people or things, not including the speaker or hearer, when the subject of a verb: *They taste better with sugar.* **b** used to refer to an indefinite singular person previously mentioned, when the subject of a verb: *If anyone knows, they will tell you.* **2a** used to refer to people in general: *They say we'll have a hard winter.* **b** used to refer to the authorities: *They took my licence away.* [Middle English from Old Norse *their*]

Usage note

The use of *they* as a singular pronoun meaning 'a person of either sex' has a very long history. It is no less controversial for all that. It is no longer appropriate to use *he, him, his,* or *himself* after words like *everyone* or *no one.* A sentence such as *Everyone should do his best* would rightly be seen as sexist except where all the people referred to were male. The forms *he or she, his or her* etc are undoubtedly often awkward to use. The use of *they, them* and *their* presents itself as an obvious and convenient solution – except that, traditionally, *they* is plural. A blanket objection to a singular *they* seems unreasonable. It is best perhaps to avoid it in formal writing and where the clash between singular and plural is very marked. *Everyone should do their best* is acceptable inasmuch as *everyone* is a plural concept if not a plural word. *A lawyer must respect their clients' confidence* is far less acceptable and could so easily be recast in unexceptionable form: *Lawyers must respect their clients' confidence.* In this dictionary the gender-neutral *they* is generally used.

they'd /dhayd/ *contraction* **1** they had. **2** they would.

they'll /dhayl/ *contraction* **1** they will. **2** they shall.

they're /dheə/ *contraction* they are.

Usage note

they're, their, *or* there? See note at THEIR.

they've /dhayv/ *contraction* they have.

thi- *or* **thio-** *comb. form* forming words, with the meaning: containing sulphur in the molecular structure: *thiamine.* [Greek *thei-, theio-,* from *theion* sulphur]

thiamine or **thiamin** /'thie-əmin/ noun a vitamin of the vitamin B complex, found esp in cereals and beans, that is essential to normal metabolism and nerve function and is widespread in plants and animals; vitamin B_1. [THI- + AMINE]

thiazide /'thie-əzied/ noun any of several synthetic drugs used as oral diuretics, esp in the treatment of high blood pressure and oedema. [THI- + AZINE + OXIDE]

thiazine /'thie-əzeen/ noun any of various compounds that are characterized by a ring structure composed of four carbon atoms, one sulphur atom, and one nitrogen atom and include some important dyes and tranquillizers. [THI- + AZINE]

thiazole /'thie-əzohl/ noun 1 a colourless liquid consisting of atoms arranged in a five-membered ring and having a pungent smell like pyridine: formula C_3H_3NS. 2 any of various thiazole derivatives including some used in the treatment of inflammation and others important as chemical accelerators (substances that speed up reactions; see ACCELERATOR).

thick[1] /thik/ adj 1a having or being of relatively great depth or extent between opposite surfaces: a thick plank. b of comparatively large diameter in relation to length: a thick rod. c having the specified thickness: twelve centimetres thick. 2a containing closely-packed objects or material; dense: The air was thick with snow; a thick forest. b great in number. 3a not flowing or pouring easily; viscous: thick syrup. b not easy to see through, esp because foggy or misty: The air was thick with smoke. 4a imperfectly articulated: thick speech. b plainly apparent; marked: a thick French accent. 5a sluggish or dull: My head feels thick after so little sleep. b informal obtuse or stupid. 6 informal on close terms; intimate: He was quite thick with his boss. ✳ **a bit thick** Brit, informal unreasonable or unfair. **be as thick as a plank/two short planks** informal to be very stupid or unintelligent. **be as thick as thieves** informal to be very friendly or intimate with each other. **be thick on the ground** to be numerous or common. **give somebody/get a thick ear** Brit, informal to give somebody/receive a blow on the ear as punishment. **have a thick skin** to be insensitive or not easy to provoke. **lay it on thick** 1 to overstate or exaggerate something. 2 to flatter somebody excessively. **thick and fast** in very quick succession. >> **thick** adv, **thickish** adj, **thickly** adv. [Old English thicce]

thick[2] noun 1 the most crowded or active part: in the thick of the battle. 2 the part of greatest thickness: the thick of the thumb. ✳ **through thick and thin** in good times and bad times; in spite of every difficulty and obstacle.

thicken verb (**thickened, thickening**) >> verb trans 1 to make (something) thick, compact, dense, or viscous: We thicken the gravy with flour. 2 to make (something) inarticulate; to blur: Alcohol thickened his speech. >> verb intrans 1 to become thick or thicker: The mist thickened. 2 to grow blurred or obscure. 3 to grow more complicated or intense: The plot thickens. >> **thickener** noun.

thickening noun 1 the act of making or becoming thick. 2 something used to thicken something else, esp in cookery. 3 a thickened part or place.

thicket /'thikit/ noun 1 a dense growth of shrubbery or small trees. 2 something like a thicket in density or impenetrability. [Old English thiccet, from thicce THICK[1]]

thickhead /'thikhed/ noun informal a stupid person. >> **thickheaded** /'hedid/ adj.

thick-knee noun = STONE CURLEW.

thickness noun 1 the smallest of the three dimensions of a solid object, the distance through it as opposed to its length or height. 2 the thick part of something. 3 a layer or ply: a single thickness of canvas.

thicko /'thikoh/ noun (pl **thickos**) informal a stupid person.

thickset adj 1 heavily built; burly. 2 placed close together, or growing thickly.

thick-skinned adj 1 callous or insensitive. 2 not easily provoked or upset.

thick-witted adj dull or stupid.

thief /theef/ noun (pl **thieves** /theevz/) somebody who steals, esp secretly and without violence. >> **thievery** /'theevəri/ noun, **thievish** /'theevish/ adj, **thievishness** /'theevishnis/ noun. [Old English theof]

thieve /theev/ verb intrans to steal; to be a thief. >> verb trans informal to steal (something). [from THIEF, by analogy with grief: grieve]

thieves /theevz/ noun pl of THIEF.

thigh /thie/ noun the segment of the vertebrate hind limb nearest the body that extends from the hip to the knee and is supported by a single large bone. >> **thighed** adj. [Old English theoh]

thighbone noun the femur.

thimble /'thimbl/ noun 1 a pitted metal or plastic cap worn to protect the finger and to push the needle in sewing. 2a a thin metal grooved ring used to fit in a spliced loop in a rope as protection from chafing. b a movable ring, tube, or lining in a hole. [Middle English thymbyl, prob alteration of Old English thymel thumbstall, from thuma THUMB[1]]

thimbleful noun (pl **thimblefuls**) as much as a thimble will hold; a very small quantity.

thimblerig noun a swindling trick in which a small object, e.g. a pea, is placed under one of three small cups that are quickly moved around, the object being secretly shifted from one cup to another to fool the spectator trying to guess its location. >> **thimblerigger** noun. [THIMBLE + RIG[3] to swindle]

thin[1] /thin/ adj (**thinner, thinnest**) 1a having little depth between opposite surfaces: a thin book. b measuring little in cross-section: thin rope. 2 without much flesh or fat on the body. 3 not dense or closely-packed: thin hair. 4a more rarefied than normal: thin air. b few in number. 5a lacking substance or strength: thin broth; a thin plot. b flimsy or unconvincing: a thin disguise. 6a somewhat feeble and lacking in resonance: a thin voice. b lacking in intensity or brilliance: thin colour. 7 informal disappointingly poor or hard: We've had a thin time of it recently. ✳ **be thin on the ground** to be relatively few in number or uncommon. **vanish/disappear into thin air** to cease to be visible, present, or existent; to disappear completely. >> **thin** adv, **thinly** adv, **thinness** noun, **thinnish** adj. [Old English thynne]

thin[2] verb (**thinned, thinning**) >> verb trans 1 to reduce (something) in thickness or depth. 2 to reduce (something) in strength or density. 3 to reduce (something) in number or bulk. >> verb intrans 1 to become thin or thinner. 2 to diminish in strength, density, or number.

thine[1] /dhien/ adj archaic used esp before a vowel or h: thy. [Old English thīn: see THY]

thine[2] pronoun (pl **thine**) chiefly archaic the one or ones that belong to thee or are associated with thee. [Old English thīn: see THY]

thing /thing/ noun 1 an inanimate object as distinguished from a living being. 2a a matter, affair, or concern: Things are not improving. b an event or circumstance: That shooting was a terrible thing. 3a an activity or action: Abusive moralizing … is about the least productive thing to do — Nation Review (Melbourne). b the aim of effort or activity: The main thing is to get well. 4a an object or entity not able to be precisely named: What's that thing on the table? b (in pl) imaginary objects or entities: I must be seeing things. 5a (in pl) possessions or personal effects: Pack your things and go. b (in pl) equipment or utensils, esp for a particular purpose: Bring the tea things. 6 a detail or point: She checks every little thing. 7a a spoken or written observation or point. b an idea or notion. 8 used with an adjective expressing pity, envy, etc: a person or animal: Poor thing!; You lucky thing! 9 (usu **the thing**) the proper or fashionable way of behaving, talking, or dressing: It's the latest thing. 10 informal. a a preoccupation, e.g. a mild obsession or phobia, of a specified type: He has a thing about driving. b a sexual or romantic relationship: She had a thing going with her boss. 11 informal something, e.g. an activity, that offers special interest and satisfaction to the individual: letting students do their own thing — Newsweek. 12a in philosophy, a separate and distinct object of thought, e.g. a quality, fact, idea, etc. b the concrete entity as distinguished from its appearances. ✳ **a close/near thing** a situation that almost ended in disaster, defeat, or some other unpleasant outcome. **be on to a good thing** informal to be able to take advantage of a very favourable situation. **of all things** used to show surprise: She wants a xylophone of all things. **there's only one thing for it** there is only one possible course of action. [Old English thing, assembly]

thingamabob /'thing-əməbob/ noun informal = THINGAMAJIG. [alteration of thingum (see THINGUMMY) + arbitrary suffix]

thingamajig or **thingumajig** /'thing-əməjig/ noun informal something or somebody that is hard to classify or whose name is unknown or forgotten. [alteration of thingum (see THINGUMMY) + arbitrary suffix]

thingie /'thing-i/ noun Brit, informal = THINGAMAJIG: those pyramid-shaped thingies — Punch.

thingumajig /'thing·əməjig/ *noun* see THINGAMAJIG.

thingummy /'thing·əmi/ *noun* (*pl* **thingummies**) *informal* = THINGAMAJIG. [alteration of *thingum*, from THING]

think[1] /thingk/ *verb* (*past tense and past part.* **thought** /thawt/) ➤ *verb intrans* **1** to use mental powers; to produce or work on ideas in the mind. **2** (+ of/about) to have in one's mind as the object of consideration or reflection: *I was thinking about you; He thinks of himself as a poet.* **3** (+ of) to remember or call to mind; to have consideration for: *You must think first of your family.* **4** to expect or suspect: *Things turned out better than we thought possible.* **5** (+ to) to remember or have the presence of mind (to do something): *I didn't think to ask his name.* ➤ *verb trans* to form or have (an idea, fact, etc) in the mind as information, an opinion, expectation, etc. ❧ **think better of** to decide on reflection to abandon (a plan). **think much of** to have a high opinion of. **think nothing of 1** to be entirely unconcerned about. **2** to disregard. **think on one's feet** to be able to react quickly to rapidly changing circumstances. **think twice** to consider very carefully. ➤➤ **thinkable** *adj*, **thinker** *noun*. [Old English *thencan*]

think[2] *noun informal* an act of thinking ❋ **have another think coming** *informal* used to suggest that somebody is mistaken.

thinking[1] *noun* **1** the action of using one's mind to produce thoughts. **2** opinion that is characteristic, e.g. of a period, group, or individual: *the current thinking on immigration.* ❋ **put/have on one's thinking cap** to ponder or reflect on something [from the cap formerly worn by judges while considering and announcing the sentence].

thinking[2] *adj* likely or able to give serious consideration to matters; intelligent or reflective.

think out *verb trans* to consider all the implications of (something) before acting.

think over *verb trans* to consider (something) carefully.

think tank *noun* (*treated as sing. or pl*) a group of people formed as a consultative body to evolve new ideas and offer expert advice.

think through *verb trans* = THINK OUT.

think up *verb trans* to devise or invent (something) by thinking.

thin-layer chromatography *noun* chromatography in which the absorbent medium is a thin layer, e.g. of KIESELGUHR (silica-containing substance), on a glass plate or other support. ➤➤ **thin-layer chromatographic** *adj*.

thinner *noun* a solvent such as turpentine, *esp* one added to paint or varnish to thin it.

thin-skinned *adj* unduly susceptible to criticism or insult.

thio- *comb. form* see THI-.

thiol /'thieol, 'thieohl/ *noun* an organic compound similar to an alcohol but with a sulphur atom replacing the oxygen atom. ➤➤ **thiolic** /thie'olik, thie'ohlik/ *adj*. [THI- + -OL[1]]

thiopental /thieoh'pental/ *noun NAmer* thiopentone. [THIO- + contraction of *pentobarbital*, from PENTOBARBITONE]

thiopentone /thieoh'pentohn/ *noun* a barbiturate used *esp* intravenously as a general anaesthetic and in psychotherapy. [THIO- + *pentobarbital* (from PENTOBARBITONE) + -ONE]

thiosulphate (*NAmer* **thiosulfate**) /thieoh'sulfayt/ *noun* a salt or ester containing the group S_2O_3.

thiourea /ˌthieohyoo(ə)'ree·ə, -'yooəri·ə/ *noun* a bitter compound used *esp* in photography and organic chemistry: formula $CS(NH_2)_2$. [scientific Latin, from THIO- + UREA]

third /thuhd/ *adj and noun* **1** denoting a person or thing having the position in a sequence corresponding to the number three. **2** one of three equal parts of something. **3** the third forward gear of a motor vehicle. **4a** in music, an interval of three degrees of a diatonic scale, or the combination of two notes at such an interval. **b** = MEDIANT. **5** in Britain, a third-class honours degree. ➤➤ **thirdly** *adv*. [Old English *thridda, thirdda*]

third age *noun Brit* the later stages of human life, after middle age; old age.

third class *noun* **1** the third group in a classification. **2** the least expensive class of accommodation, e.g. on a ship.

third-class *adj* of a class or grade next below the second. ➤➤ **third-class** *adv*.

third degree *noun* the subjection of a prisoner to torture to obtain information.

third-degree burn *noun* a burn characterized by destruction of the skin and possibly the underlying tissues, loss of fluid, and sometimes shock: compare FIRST-DEGREE BURN, SECOND-DEGREE BURN.

third dimension *noun* the dimension of thickness or depth. ➤➤ **third-dimensional** *adj*. [from its being the third dimension, in addition to length and breadth, of a solid body]

third estate *noun* the third of the traditional political orders; *specif* the Commons.

third eyelid *noun* = NICTITATING MEMBRANE.

thirdhand *adj* **1** received from a second intermediary: *thirdhand information*. **2** acquired after use by two previous owners. ➤➤ **thirdhand** *adv*.

third man *noun* a fielding position in cricket lying near the boundary on the off side behind the slips.

Third Order *noun* an organization of lay people under a religious rule, directed by a religious order but living in secular society. [translation of medieval Latin *tertius ordo*; from the partial resemblance to an order of monks or nuns]

third party *noun* **1** somebody other than the people principally involved in an action: *a third party to a divorce proceeding*. **2a** a major political party in addition to two others in a state normally characterized by a two-party system. **b** a political party whose electoral strength is so small that it can rarely gain control of a government.

third-party *adj* of a third party; *specif* of insurance covering loss or damage sustained by somebody other than the insured.

third person *noun* in grammar, any of the verb forms or pronouns that refer to somebody or something other than the speaker or writer or the person or thing addressed: compare FIRST PERSON, PERSON, SECOND PERSON.

third rail *noun* = CONDUCTOR RAIL. [from its being third in addition to the two rails on which the wheels of a locomotive run]

third-rate *adj* of extremely poor quality; mediocre. ➤➤ **third-rater** *noun*.

third reading *noun* **1** in the British parliament, the discussion of the committee's report on a bill. **2** the final stage of the consideration of a legislative bill before a vote.

third way *noun* a policy or course of action between two extremes, *esp* a political programme that is neither of the right nor of the left, but aimed at reaching a consensus in the centre.

Third World *noun* **1** (*treated as sing. or pl*) a group of nations, *esp* in Africa, Asia, and Latin America, that were not formerly aligned with either the communist or the capitalist blocs: compare FIRST WORLD, SECOND WORLD. **2** the less industrialized nations of the world: compare FOURTH WORLD.

thirst[1] /thuhst/ *noun* **1** a desire or need to drink, or the sensation of dryness in the mouth and throat associated with this. **2** an ardent desire; a craving. [Old English *thurst*]

thirst[2] *verb intrans* **1** to feel thirsty. **2** (*often* + for/after) to crave eagerly.

thirsty *adj* (**thirstier, thirstiest**) **1a** feeling thirst. **b** causing thirst: *thirsty work*. **2** deficient in moisture; parched: *thirsty land*. **3** said of a machine or engine: consuming large quantities of liquid fuel. **4** having a strong desire; avid. ➤➤ **thirstily** *adv*, **thirstiness** *noun*.

thirteen /thuh'teen/ *adj and noun* the number 13 or the quantity represented by it. ➤➤ **thirteenth** *adj and noun*. [Old English *thrēotīne*, from *thrēo* THREE + *tīne* -TEEN]

thirty /'thuhti/ *adj and noun* (*pl* **thirties**) **1** the number 30, or the quantity represented by it. **2** (*in pl*) the numbers 30 to 39; *specif* a range of temperatures, ages, or dates within a century characterized by these numbers. ➤➤ **thirtieth** *adj and noun*. [Old English *thrītig*, group of 30, from *thrīe* THREE + *-tig* group of ten]

thirty-eight *noun* a 0.38in (9.65mm) calibre revolver. ➤➤ **thirty-eight** *adj*.

thirty-second note *noun NAmer* a demisemiquaver.

thirty-twomo /'thuhti'toohmoh/ *noun* (*pl* **thirty-twomos**) the size of a piece of paper cut 32 from a sheet, or a book, a page, or paper of this size. [from *thirty-two* + *-mo* as in DUODECIMO]

this[1] /dhis/ *pronoun* (*pl* **these** /dheez/) **1a** the thing or idea that has just been mentioned: *Who told you this?* **b** what is to be shown or stated: *Do it like this*. **2** a nearby person or thing introduced for observation or discussion: *This is iron and that is tin; Hello! This is*

Anne Fry speaking. ✳ **this and that** various unspecified and relatively unimportant things. [Old English *thes* (masc), *this* (neuter)]

this² *adj* (*pl* **these**) **1a** denoting the person, thing, or idea that is present or near in time or thought: *early this morning; Who's this Mrs Fogg anyway?* **b** denoting the one nearer at hand or more immediately under consideration: *This book is cheaper than that one.* **2a** constituting or belonging to the immediate past or future period: *They have lived here these ten years.* **b** constituting what is to be shown or stated: *Have you heard this one?* **3** a certain: *There was this Irishman ....*

this³ *adv* **1** to the extent indicated or specified: *I've known her since she was this high.* **2** to this extreme degree: *We didn't expect to wait this long.*

thistle /'thisl/ *noun* any of various prickly composite plants with dense heads of mostly tubular flowers, usu purple in colour: genera *Carlina* and *Caroluus* and other genera. ➤➤ **thistly** *adj*. [Old English *thistel*]

thistledown *noun* the fluffy hairs from the ripe flower head of a thistle.

thither /'dhidhə/ *adv formal* to or towards that place. [Old English *thider*]

thixotropy /thik'sotrəpi/ *noun* the property of various gels of becoming fluid when disturbed, e.g. by shaking. ➤➤ **thixotropic** /thiksə'trohpik, -'tropik/ *adj.* [*thixo-* (from Greek *thixis* act of touching, from *thinganein* to touch) + *-tropy* from Greek *-tropē* turning from *trepein* to turn]

tho' *or* **tho** /dhoh/ *adv or conj chiefly informal or literary* though.

thole¹ /thohl/ *or* **tholepin** /'thohlpin/ *noun* a peg or pin; *esp* either of a pair of wooden pegs serving as rowlocks on a boat. [Old English *thol*]

thole² *verb trans and intrans dial* to endure or tolerate (something). [Old English *tholian*]

tholos /'thohlos/ *noun* (*pl* **tholoi** /'thohloy/) an ancient Greek tomb or other building with a domed shape, *esp* one dating from the Mycenaean period.

Thomism /'tohmiz(ə)m/ *noun* the scholastic, philosophical, and theological system of St Thomas Aquinas. ➤➤ **Thomist** *noun and adj*, **Thomistic** /toh'mistik/ *adj.* [St *Thomas* Aquinas d.1274, Italian theologian]

Thompson submachine gun /'tom(p)sən/ *noun* a submachine gun with a calibre of 0.45in (11.43mm), a box or drum magazine, and a hand grip like that on a pistol. [named after John T *Thompson* d.1940, US army officer who designed it]

Thomson's gazelle *noun* a small light brown gazelle of E Africa which has a broad dark stripe along each flank: *Gazella thomsonii*. [named after Joseph *Thomson* d.1894, Scottish explorer]

-thon *comb. form* see -ATHON.

thong /thong/ *noun* **1** a narrow strip, *esp* of leather. **2** a skimpy bathing costume or piece of underwear resembling a G-string. **3** *NAmer* = FLIP-FLOP¹ (4). ➤➤ **thonged** *adj.* [Old English *thwong*]

thoraces /'thawrəseez/ *noun* pl of THORAX.

thoracic /thə'rasik/ *adj* relating to, located in, or involving the thorax. ➤➤ **thoracically** *adv*.

thoracotomy /thawrə'kotəmi/ *noun* (*pl* **thoracotomies**) surgical cutting of the chest wall. [Latin *thorac-, thorax* breastplate, thorax + -TOMY]

thorax /'thawraks/ *noun* (*pl* **thoraxes** *or* **thoraces** /'thawrəseez/) **1** the part of the mammalian body between the neck and the abdomen, or the cavity inside it in which the heart and lungs lie. **2** the division of the body of an insect, spider, etc corresponding to this. [Middle English via Latin from Greek *thōrak-, thōrax* breastplate, thorax]

thoria /'thawri·ə/ *noun* a powdery white oxide of thorium used *esp* as a catalyst and in heat-resisting material and optical glass: formula ThO₂. [scientific Latin, from *thorium*: see THORIUM]

thorium /'thawri·əm/ *noun* a silver-white radioactive metallic chemical element that occurs naturally in various ores and is used in alloys and as a source of nuclear energy: symbol Th, atomic number 90. [scientific Latin, named after Thor, Norse god of thunder, weather, and crops]

thorn /thawn/ *noun* **1** a short hard plant part with a sharp point, usu projecting from a stem. **2** a woody plant, shrub, or tree whose branches are covered in thorns. **3** an orig runic letter þ used in Old and Middle English for either of the sounds /th/ or /dh/: compare ETH. ✳ **a thorn in somebody's flesh/side** a cause of great irritation. ➤➤ **thorned** *adj*, **thornless** *adj*. [Old English]

thorn apple *noun* a tall very poisonous annual plant of the nightshade family with spherical prickly fruits: *Datura stramonium.*

thornbill *noun* **1** any of various S American hummingbirds with thorn-like bills: genus *Chalcostigma* and other genera. **2** any of various Australian songbirds with short sharp bills: genus *Acanthiza* and other genera.

thornbush *noun* any of various thorny shrubs or small trees.

thorny *adj* (**thornier, thorniest**) **1** full of or covered in thorns. **2** full of difficulties or controversial points: *a thorny problem.* ➤➤ **thorniness** *noun*.

thoron /'thawron/ *noun* a gaseous radioactive isotope of radon formed by the radioactive decay of thorium. [scientific Latin, from *thorium*: see THORIUM]

thorough¹ /'thurə/ *adj* **1** carried out with or showing great care, attention to detail, and a desire to leave nothing undone; painstaking: *a thorough search.* **2** fully and without qualification as specified: *a thorough rogue.* ➤➤ **thoroughly** *adv*, **thoroughness** *noun*. [Old English *thurh, thuruh* THROUGH¹]

thorough² *prep and adv archaic* through.

thoroughbass *noun* a continuo.

thoroughbred¹ *adj* **1** bred from the best members of the same breed, strain, etc over many generations; purebred. **2** (**Thoroughbred**) relating to or being a Thoroughbred. **3** having the characteristics associated with good breeding or pedigree.

thoroughbred² *noun* **1** (**Thoroughbred**) any of an English breed of horses kept chiefly for racing that originated from crosses between English mares of uncertain ancestry and Arabian stallions. **2** a purebred or pedigree animal. **3** somebody or something with the characteristics associated with good breeding.

thoroughfare /'thurəfeə/ *noun* **1** a public way, e.g. a road, street, or path; *esp* a main road. **2** passage or transit: *no thoroughfare.*

thoroughgoing *adj* **1** extremely thorough or zealous. **2** absolute or utter: *a thoroughgoing villain.*

thorough-paced *adj* **1a** said of a horse: trained and able to perform well at all paces. **b** thoroughly trained; accomplished. **2** = THOROUGHGOING.

thorp *or* **thorpe** /thawp/ *noun archaic* a village or hamlet. [Old English *thorp*]

those /dhohz/ *pronoun and adj* pl of THAT¹ and THAT². [Old English *thās*, pl of *thes* THIS¹, THIS², later used, orig in northern England, as the plural of THAT¹]

thou¹ /dhow/ *pronoun archaic or dialect* the one being addressed; you. [Old English *thū*: see YOU]

thou² /thow/ *noun* (*pl* **thou** *or* **thous**) **1** *informal* a thousand of something, *esp* of a money unit. **2** a unit of length equal to one thousandth of an inch (about 0.0254mm). [short for THOUSAND]

though¹ /dhoh/ *adv* however; nevertheless: *It's hard work. I enjoy it though.* [Old English *thēah* and Old Norse *thó, thau*]

though² *conj* **1** in spite of the fact that; while: *Though it's hard work, I enjoy it.* **2** and yet; but: *It works, though not as well as we hoped.* **3** *archaic* in spite of the possibility that; even if: *though the whole world turn to coal* — George Herbert.

thought¹ /thawt/ *verb* past tense and past part. of THINK¹.

thought² *noun* **1a** the act or process of thinking: *lost in thought.* **b** serious consideration: *She gave no thought to the danger.* **2** an idea, opinion, concept, or intention. **3a** reasoning or conceptual power. **b** the intellectual product or the organized views of a period, place, group, or individual. **4** hope or expectation: *They gave up all thought of winning.* ✳ **a thought** *dated* a slight amount: *There's a thought too much seasoning in the stew.* [Old English *thōht*]

thoughtful /'thawtf(ə)l/ *adj* **1a** having thoughts; absorbed in thought. **b** showing careful reasoned thinking: *a thoughtful analysis of the problem.* **2** showing concern for others. ➤➤ **thoughtfully** *adv*, **thoughtfulness** *noun*.

thoughtless *adj* **1** lacking forethought; rash. **2** lacking concern for others. ➤➤ **thoughtlessly** *adv*, **thoughtlessness** *noun*.

thought-out *adj* arrived at or produced by careful or deliberate consideration.

thought transference *noun* the apparent power to read another person's thoughts or transfer an idea into another person's mind directly; telepathy.

thousand /'thowz(ə)nd/ *noun* (*pl* **thousands** *or* **thousand**) **1** the number 1000, or the quantity represented by it. **2** (*usu in pl*) the number occupying the position four to the left of the decimal point in Arabic notation, or this position in a number or sum. **3** an indefinitely large number: *thousands of ants.* ➤➤ **thousand** *adj,* **thousandth** *adj and noun.* [Old English *thūsend*]

Thousand Island dressing *noun* a usu pink mayonnaise-based salad dressing flavoured with tomatoes, green peppers, pimientos, etc. [prob from *Thousand Islands,* the islands in the St Lawrence river between the USA and Canada]

Thracian /'thraysh(ə)n/ *noun* **1** a native or inhabitant of Thrace, an ancient country in SE Europe. **2** the extinct language of Thrace. ➤➤ **Thracian** *adj.* [via Latin from Greek *Thraikios* Thracian, from *Thraikē* Thrace]

thrall[1] /thrawl/ *noun* **1** a state of complete absorption or enslavement: *Her beauty held him in thrall.* **2a** somebody in a state of total absorption or enslavement. **b** a slave or serf. ➤➤ **thraldom** (*NAmer* **thralldom**) *noun.* [Old English *thrǣl*]

thrall[2] *verb trans archaic* to enslave (somebody).

thrash[1] /thrash/ *verb trans* **1a** to beat (somebody) soundly, *esp* with a stick or whip. **b** to defeat (somebody) heavily or decisively. **2a** to beat or strike (something) wildly or violently. **b** to move or wave (e.g. one's arms or legs) about wildly or violently. **3** = THRESH (1). **4** to sail (a ship) to windward. ➤ *verb intrans* **1** (+ around/about) to move or toss about violently: *He was thrashing around in bed with a fever.* **2** to deal repeated blows with or as if with a flail or whip. **3** = THRESH (1). ➤➤ **thrashing** *noun.* [Old English, alteration of THRESH]

thrash[2] *noun* **1** an act of thrashing. **2** *informal* a wild party. **3** = THRASH METAL.

thrasher[1] *noun* any of several species of long-tailed American songbirds of the mockingbird family similar to thrushes: genus *Toxostoma* and other genera. [prob alteration of THRUSH[1]]

thrasher[2] *noun* = THRESHER.

thrash metal *noun* a type of very loud, fast, and discordant rock music that combines features of punk and heavy metal.

thrash out *verb trans* **1** to discuss (e.g. a problem) exhaustively with a view to finding a solution. **2** to arrive at (e.g. a decision) in this way.

thrawn /thrawn/ *adj* **1** *chiefly Scot* perverse and recalcitrant. **2** crooked and misshapen. ➤➤ **thrawnly** *adv.* [Middle English (Scots) *thrawin,* past part. of *thrawen:* see THROW[1]]

thread[1] /thred/ *noun* **1a** a filament, group of filaments twisted together, or continuous strand formed by spinning and twisting together short textile fibres. **b** any of various natural filaments: *the threads of a spider's web.* **2a** something, e.g. a thin stream of liquid, that resembles a thread in length and narrowness. **b** a projecting spiral ridge, e.g. on a bolt or pipe, by which parts can be screwed together. **3** something continuous or drawn out, e.g.: **a** a train of thought: *I've lost the thread of this argument.* **b** a pervasive recurring element: *a thread of melancholy marked all his writing.* **4** a precarious or weak support: *to hang by a thread.* **5** a series of linked messages replying to or commenting on each other on the Internet. **6** *chiefly NAmer, informal* (*in pl*) clothes. ➤➤ **threadless** *adj,* **threadlike** *adj,* **thready** *adj.* [Old English *thrǣd*]

thread[2] *verb trans* **1a** to pass a thread through the eye of (a needle). **b** to arrange a thread or lead-in piece in working position for use in (a machine). **2** to pass something through the entire length of (something): *The electrician now had to thread the pipe with wire.* **3a** to pass (e.g. tape or rope) into or through something: *I threaded elastic into the waistband.* **b** to make (one's way) cautiously along, through, or between something. **4** to string (things) together on a thread: *thread beads.* **5** to intermingle (something) with threads or threadlike elements of something else: *dark hair threaded with silver.* **6** to form a screw thread on (e.g. a bolt) or in (e.g. a hole). ➤ *verb intrans* **1** to make one's way cautiously. **2** to form a thread when poured from a spoon. ➤➤ **threader** *noun.*

threadbare *adj* **1** having the nap worn off so that the woven threads show; worn or shabby. **2** hackneyed: *threadbare phrases.* ➤➤ **threadbareness** *noun.*

thread mark *noun* a fine line of silk fibre put into a bank note to prevent counterfeiting.

threadworm *noun* any of various small usu parasitic nematode worms that infest the intestines, *esp* the caecum, of vertebrates.

thready *adj* (**threadier, threadiest**) **1a** of threadlike appearance or substance; fibrous. **b** said *esp* of a liquid: tending to form strands; viscid or stringy. **2** lacking in strength or vigour: *a thready voice; a thready pulse.* ➤➤ **threadiness** *noun.*

threat /thret/ *noun* **1** an indication of something unpleasant to come. **2** an expression of an intention to inflict punishment, injury, or damage. **3** something that is a source of imminent danger or harm. [Old English *thrēat* coercion, danger]

threaten *verb* (**threatened, threatening**) ➤ *verb trans* **1** to utter threats against (somebody): *He threatened his employees with the sack.* **2a** to give ominous signs of (something): *The clouds threaten rain.* **b** to be a potential source of harm or danger to (somebody or something): *a scandal that threatened his career.* **3** to announce (something unpleasant or undesirable) as intended or possible: *The workers threatened a strike.* ➤ *verb intrans* **1** to utter threats. **2** to appear menacing: *The sky threatened.* ➤➤ **threatener** *noun,* **threateningly** *adv.*

three /three/ *noun* **1** the number 3, or the quantity represented by it. **2** something having three parts or members. **3a** the age of 3 years. **b** the hour three hours after midday or midnight. ➤➤ **three** *adj,* **threefold** *adj and adv.* [Old English *thrīe* (masc), *thrēo* (fem and neuter)]

three-card trick *noun* a card game in which players place bets on which of three cards lying face downwards is the queen.

three-colour *adj* denoting or relating to a printing or photographic process in which three primary colours are used to reproduce all the other colours.

three-D *or* **3-D** *noun* three-dimensional form. ➤➤ **3-D** *adj,* **three-D** *adj.* [abbr of *dimensional*]

three-day event *noun* an equestrian contest involving dressage, cross-country, and showjumping and continuing over three days.

three-decker *noun* something with three tiers, layers, etc; *esp* a sandwich with three slices of bread and two fillings.

three-dimensional *adj* **1** having three dimensions, or giving the illusion of having three dimensions. **2** describing or being described in great depth; *esp* lifelike: *a story with three-dimensional characters.* ➤➤ **three-dimensionality** *noun.*

three-handed *adj* played by three players: *three-handed bridge.*

three-legged race *noun* a race between pairs in which each contestant has one leg tied to one of his or her partner's legs.

three-line whip *noun* an instruction from a party to its Members of Parliament that they must attend a debate and vote in the specified way: compare FREE VOTE. [from the triple underlining of words in the written instruction]

three of a kind *noun* three cards of the same rank in one hand.

threepence /'thrupəns, 'threpəns/ *noun* **1** the sum of three pence, *esp* three old pence (1.25p) in Britain before decimalization. **2** = THREEPENNY BIT.

threepenny bit *noun* a small twelve-sided British coin in use until early 1971 and worth three old pence.

three-phase *adj* of or operating by means of a combination of three circuits energized by alternating electromotive forces that differ in phase by one third of a cycle.

three-piece *adj* comprising or made in three, usu matching, pieces; *esp* denoting a suit of clothes consisting of a matching jacket, waistcoat, and trousers, or a set of furniture consisting of a sofa and two armchairs of the same design. ➤➤ **three-piece** *noun.*

three-ply *adj* **1** having three layers. **2** said of knitting wool: three-stranded.

three-point landing *noun* an aircraft landing in which the main wheels of the undercarriage touch the ground simultaneously with the tail wheel, skid, or nose wheel.

three-point turn *noun* a method of turning a vehicle round in a narrow road by first turning obliquely forwards, then reversing, and finally turning forwards again.

three-quarter[1] *adj* **1** consisting of three fourths of the whole. **2** said *esp* of a view of a rectangular object: including one side and one end: *a three-quarter view of a vehicle.*

three-quarter[2] *noun* = THREE-QUARTER BACK.

three-quarter back *noun* a player in rugby, positioned between the halfbacks and the fullback. ➤➤ **three-quarter-back** *adj.*

three quarters *pl noun* a part or collection consisting of about three fourths of some larger whole or group: *Cut off three quarters of the new growth to leave a stem about a foot long; Three quarters of the new class are girls.*

three-ring circus *noun* **1** a circus with simultaneous performances in three rings. **2** something confusing, engrossing, or spectacular.

three R's *pl noun* the fundamentals taught in primary school; *esp* reading, writing, and arithmetic. [from the facetious phrase *reading, 'riting, and 'rithmetic*]

threescore *noun and adj* sixty.

threesome /'threes(ə)m/ *noun* a group of three people or things.

three-spined stickleback *noun* a stickleback of fresh and brackish waters that typically has three spines on its back.

three strikes *pl noun* a policy of imposing a mandatory heavy punishment on any offender convicted three times of an offence. [from the baseball phrase *three strikes and you're out*]

three-wheeler *noun* a vehicle, *esp* a small car, with three wheels.

thremmatology /thremə'toləji/ *noun* the science of breeding animals and plants in domestication. [Greek *thremmat-, thremma* nursling + -O- + -LOGY]

threnode /'threnohd, 'threenohd/ *noun* = THRENODY. ⟫ **threnodic** /thri'nodik/ *adj,* **threnodist** *noun.*

threnody /'threnədi, 'three-/ *noun* (*pl* **threnodies**) a song of lamentation, *esp* for the dead. [Greek *thrēnōidia,* from *thrēnos* dirge + *aeidein* to sing]

threonine /'three-əneen, -nin/ *noun* an amino acid found in most proteins and an essential constituent of the human diet. [from *threose,* a sugar with a similar molecular structure + -INE²]

thresh /thresh/ *verb trans* **1** to separate the seeds from (a harvested plant) by beating it with a machine or flail. **2** to strike (something) repeatedly. ⟩ *verb intrans* **1** to thresh grain. **2** = THRASH¹ (1), (2). [Old English *threscan*]

thresher *noun* **1** a person or machine that threshes. **2** a large shark reputed to thresh the water, using the greatly elongated curved upper lobe of its tail, to round up fish on which it feeds: *Alopias vulpinus.*

threshold /'threshohld, 'threshhohld/ *noun* **1** the plank, stone, etc that lies under a door. **2a** the doorway or entrance to a building. **b** the point of entering or beginning: *You're on the threshold of a new career.* **3** the point at which a physiological or psychological effect begins to be produced by a stimulus of increasing strength. **4** a level, point, or value above which something is true or will take place. [Old English *threscwald*]

threw /throoh/ *verb* past tense of THROW¹.

thrice /thries/ *adv archaic or literary* **1** three times. **2a** in a threefold manner or degree. **b** (*usu in combination*) to a high degree: *thrice-blessed.* [Middle English *thrie, thries,* from Old English *thrīe* THREE + -S¹]

thrift /thrift/ *noun* **1** careful management, *esp* of money; frugality: *Thrift, thrift, Horatio! The funeral baked meats did coldly furnish forth the marriage tables* — Shakespeare. **2** any of various tufted herbaceous plants, a sea-pink: *Armeria maritima.* ⟫ **thriftless** *adj.* [Middle English from Old Norse *thrift* prosperity, from *thrīfask:* see THRIVE]

thrifty *adj* (**thriftier, thriftiest**) **1** showing careful management, *esp* of money. **2** *archaic* thriving. ⟫ **thriftily** *adv,* **thriftiness** *noun.*

thrill¹ /thril/ *noun* **1** a sudden feeling of pleasurable excitement. **2** something that causes such a feeling. **3** a sudden tremor of fear, nervousness, or emotion. **4** *archaic* a tingle or throb. ✳ **thrills and spills** excitement mixed with surprise. [Middle English alteration of Old English *thyrlian* to pierce, penetrate, from *thyrel* hole, from *thurh* THROUGH¹]

thrill² *verb trans* **1a** to cause (somebody) to experience a sudden feeling of excitement. **b** to cause (somebody) to have a shivering or tingling sensation. **2** to cause (an object) to vibrate or tremble perceptibly. ⟩ *verb intrans* **1** (*often* + at/to) to experience a sudden tremor of excitement or emotion: *She thrilled at his touch.* **2** to tingle or throb. ⟫ **thrilling** *adj,* **thrillingly** *adv.*

thriller *noun* a work of fiction or a film or drama characterized by a high degree of intrigue or suspense: *Thrillers are like life – more like life than you are. It's what we've all made of the world* — Graham Greene.

thrips /thrips/ *noun* (*pl* **thrips**) any of numerous species of small sucking insects that feed on and damage plants: order Thysanoptera. [Latin *thrips* woodworm, from Greek]

thrive /thriev/ *verb intrans* (*past tense* **throve** /throhv/ *or* **thrived,** *past part.* **thriven** /'thriv(ə)n/ *or* **thrived**) **1** to grow vigorously. **2** to gain in wealth or possessions. **3** (+ on) to enjoy or be stimulated by something: *She thrives on being busy.* ⟫ **thriver** *noun,* **thriving** *adj.* [Middle English *thriven* from Old Norse *thrīfask,* prob reflexive of *thrīfa* to grasp]

thro *or* **thro'** /throoh/ *prep, adv, and adj informal or literary* see THROUGH¹, THROUGH², and THROUGH³.

throat /throht/ *noun* **1a** the passage through the neck to the stomach and lungs. **b** the part of the neck in front of the spinal column. **2** something throatlike, *esp* in being a constricted passageway. **3** the upper forward corner of a fore-and-aft four-cornered sail. ✳ **at each other's throats** quarrelling violently. ⟫ **throated** *adj.* [Old English *throte*]

throaty *adj* (**throatier, throatiest**) **1** uttered or produced low in the throat; hoarse or guttural. **2** *informal* suffering from a sore throat: *I'm feeling a bit throaty today.* ⟫ **throatily** *adv,* **throatiness** *noun.*

throb¹ /throb/ *verb intrans* (**throbbed, throbbing**) **1** to pulsate with unusual force or rapidity. **2** said of a pain: to come in waves that seem to beat or vibrate rhythmically. **3** said of machinery: to operate with a strong, audible, rhythmic beat or vibration. ⟫ **throbbing** *adj.* [Middle English *throbben,* prob of imitative origin]

throb² *noun* a beat or pulse.

throe /throh/ *noun* **1** (*usu in pl*) a pang or spasm: *death throes; the throes of childbirth.* **2** (*in pl*) a hard or painful struggle: *The country is in the throes of revolutionary change.* [Middle English *thrawe, throwe, thrahe,* of Germanic origin]

thromb- *or* **thrombo-** *comb. form* forming words, denoting: blood clot; clotting of blood: *thrombosis.* [Greek *thrombos* clot]

thrombi /'thrombie/ *noun* pl of THROMBUS.

thrombin /'thrombin/ *noun* an enzyme formed from PROTHROMBIN (protein in blood) that acts in the process of blood clotting by catalysing the conversion of FIBRINOGEN (protein in blood) to FIBRIN (fibrous protein).

thrombo- *comb. form* see THROMB-.

thrombocyte /'thrombəsiet/ *noun* a blood platelet. ⟫ **thrombocytic** /-'sitik/ *adj.*

thromboembolism /thromboh'embəliz(ə)m/ *noun* the blocking of a blood vessel by a piece of blood clot that has formed elsewhere in the body and broken away from its site of formation. ⟫ **thromboembolic** /-'bolik/ *adj.*

thrombose /throm'bohz/ *verb intrans* to develop thrombosis. ⟩ *verb trans* to develop thrombosis in (a part of the circulatory system).

thrombosis /throm'bohsis/ *noun* (*pl* **thromboses** /-seez/) the formation or presence of a blood clot within a blood vessel. ⟫ **thrombotic** /throm'botik/ *adj.* [scientific Latin from Greek *thrombōsis* clotting, from *thrombos* clot]

thrombus /'thrombəs/ *noun* (*pl* **thrombi** /'thrombie/) a blood clot formed within a blood vessel and remaining attached to its place of origin. [scientific Latin from Greek *thrombos* clot]

throne¹ /throhn/ *noun* **1** the chair of state of a sovereign or bishop. **2** (**the throne**) sovereignty. **3** *informal* a lavatory or WC. [Middle English *trone, throne* via French and Latin from Greek *thronos* raised seat]

throne² *verb trans literary* to seat (somebody) on a throne; = ENTHRONE.

throng¹ /throng/ *noun* **1** a multitude of assembled people, *esp* when crowded together. **2** a large number. [Old English *thrang, gethrang*]

throng² *verb trans* **1** to crowd in on (a person). **2** to crowd into (a place): *Shoppers thronged the streets.* ⟩ *verb intrans* to crowd together in great numbers.

throstle /'throsl/ *noun* **1** *Brit, archaic* = SONG THRUSH. **2** formerly, a frame for spinning cotton, wool, etc. [Old English]

throttle¹ /'throtl/ *noun* **1** a valve for regulating the supply of a fluid, e.g. fuel, to an engine. **2** *archaic.* **a** = THROAT. **b** = TRACHEA.

throttle² *verb trans* **1a** to compress the throat of (somebody); to choke (them). **b** to kill (somebody) by such action. **2** to prevent or check expression or activity of (something or somebody); to suppress (it or them). **3a** to control the flow of (steam or fuel to an engine) by means of a valve. **b** (*usu* + back/down) to regulate, *esp* reduce the speed of (an engine), by such means. ⨠ **throttler** *noun*. [Middle English *throtlen* from *throte* THROAT]

through¹ *or* **thro** *or* **thro'** (*NAmer* **thru**) /throoh/ *prep* **1** into at one side or point and out at the other: *I drove a nail through the board*; *We took a path through the woods.* **2a** past a deceptive aspect of: *She saw through their deception.* **b** used to indicate passage into and out of during a treatment, handling, or process: *A thought flashed through my mind.* **3a** used to indicate means, agency, or intermediacy; by means of; by the agency of. **b** because of: *The plan failed through lack of preparation.* **4a** over or among the whole surface or extent of: *There are little farms scattered through the valley*; *They searched through my papers.* **b** used to indicate movement within a large expanse: *The ball flew through the air.* **c** used to indicate exposure to a set of conditions: *He put her through hell.* **5** (*usu* + all) during the entire period of; throughout: *She suffered from depression all through her life.* **6a** used to indicate completion, exhaustion, or accomplishment: *He went through a fortune in a year.* **b** used to indicate acceptance or approval: *She got the bill through Parliament.* **7** *chiefly NAmer* up till and including: *We'll be here Monday through Friday.* [Old English *thurh*]

through² *or* **thro** *or* **thro'** (*NAmer* **thru**) *adv* **1** from one end or side to the other: *He squeezed through.* **2a** all the way from beginning to end: *The train goes right through to London.* **b** to a favourable or successful conclusion: *I failed the exam, but he got through.* **3** to the core; completely: *We got wet through.* **4** *chiefly Brit* in or into connection by telephone: *Put me through to the manager.* ✱ **through and through** thoroughly; completely.

through³ *or* **thro** *or* **thro'** (*NAmer* **thru**) *adj* **1a** allowing a continuous journey from point of origin to destination without change or further payment: *a through train.* **b** starting at and destined for points outside a local zone: *through traffic.* **2** direct: *a through road.* **3** arrived at completion, cessation, or dismissal; finished: *I'm through with women.*

through-composed *adj* **1** said of a song: having different music for each stanza. **2** in opera, having continuous music as opposed to separate numbers. [translation of German *durchkomponiert*]

throughout¹ *adv* **1** in or to every part; everywhere: *Oddly, the house had been painted one colour throughout.* **2** during the whole time or action; from beginning to end: *His wife remained loyal throughout.*

throughout² *prep* **1** in or to every part of: *This is happening in cities throughout Europe.* **2** during the entire period of: *Backache troubled him throughout his life.*

throughput *noun* the amount of material put through a process: *There are various ways of increasing the throughput of a computer.*

throughway *or* **thruway** *noun NAmer* a main road or motorway.

throve /throhv/ *verb* past tense of THRIVE.

throw¹ /throh/ *verb* (*past tense* **threw** /throoh/, *past part.* **thrown** /throhn/) ⨠ *verb trans* **1** to send (something) with force through the air, *esp* by a forward motion of the hand and arm. **2** to cause (something or somebody) to move violently into or against something: *The ship was thrown against the rocks.* **3a** to force (somebody) to fall to the ground: *The boxer threw his opponent.* **b** said of a horse: to unseat (its rider). **4** to put (somebody) in a specified position or condition, *esp* suddenly: *The news threw him into confusion.* **5a** (+ on/off) to put (clothing) on or off hurriedly. **b** to exert or apply (energy, effort, etc) to something: *He threw all his weight behind the proposal.* **6** to shape (a pot, etc) by hand on a potter's wheel. **7** to deliver (a punch). **8** to twist two or more filaments (of silk, etc) into a thread or yarn. **9** to make a cast of (dice or a specified number on dice). **10** to direct (light, a look, etc) in a certain direction: *He threw me a glance.* **11** to commit (oneself) for help, support, or protection: *He threw himself on the mercy of the court.* **12** said of an animal: to bring forth or produce (young): *The sow threw large litters.* **13** to move (a lever or switch) so as to connect or disconnect parts of a mechanism. **14** to project (the voice) so that it seems to come from another source. **15** to give (a party). **16** to have (a tantrum or fit). **17** *informal* to confuse or disconcert (somebody). **18** *chiefly NAmer, informal* to lose (a game) intentionally, especially in return for payment. ⨠ *verb intrans* to perform a movement to throw something: *your turn to throw.* ✱ **be thrown back on** to have to rely on

(something) when no other resources are available. **throw oneself into** to devote one's energy to (an activity). **throw one's weight about/around** *informal* to behave in a bullying or domineering manner. ⨠⨠ **thrower** *noun*. [Middle English *thrawen*, *throwen* to cause to twist, throw, from Old English *thrawan* to cause to twist or turn]

throw² *noun* **1a** the act or an instance of throwing. **b** a method of throwing an opponent in wrestling or judo, or the act or an instance of doing so. **2** the distance something may be thrown: *We lived within a stone's throw from school.* **3** the amount of vertical displacement produced by a geological fault. **4** the extent of movement of a cam, crank, or other pivoted or reciprocating piece. **5** a light cover, e.g. for a bed. **6** *informal* a chance, try, turn, etc: *Admission is £5 a throw.*

throwaway¹ *adj* **1** designed to be discarded after use; disposable: *throwaway containers.* **2** said of a remark: written or spoken with deliberate casualness.

throwaway² *noun* **1** something intended to be thrown away after use. **2** *chiefly NAmer* a free handbill or circular.

throw away *verb trans* **1** to get rid of (something) as worthless or unwanted. **2a** to use (something) in a foolish or wasteful manner. **b** to fail to take advantage of (an opportunity, etc). **3** to make (a line in a play, etc) unemphatic by casual delivery.

throwback *noun* **1** reversion to an earlier genetic type or phase. **2** an individual exhibiting this.

throw down *verb trans* to demolish (a building).

throw in *verb trans* **1** to add (something) as a free item with other goods or services. **2** to introduce or interject (a remark, etc). ✱ **throw in the sponge/towel** to abandon a struggle or contest; to acknowledge defeat.

throw-in *noun* in football, a throw made from the touchline to put the ball back in play after it has gone over the touchline.

thrown /throhn/ *verb* past tense of THROW¹.

throw off *verb trans* **1a** to be rid of (something): *I'm trying to throw off a cold.* **b** to divert or distract (a person or animal). **2** to produce or execute (a piece of writing, etc) in an offhand manner. ⨠ *verb intrans* to begin hunting with a pack of hounds.

throw out *verb trans* **1** to get rid of (something) as worthless or unwanted. **2** to expel (somebody) abruptly from a room or building. **3** to express (a remark, etc) casually. **4** to dismiss or reject (a plan, proposal, etc). **5** said of a plant or tree: to give forth (shoots) from within.

throw over *verb trans* to forsake or abandon (a lover, etc).

throwster /'throhstə/ *noun* somebody who throws textile filaments.

throw together *verb trans* **1** to make or assemble (something) hurriedly or in a makeshift way. **2** to cause (people) to meet casually or by chance.

throw up *verb trans* **1** to abandon or discontinue (an activity): *the urge to throw up all intellectual work* — Norman Mailer. **2** to build or assemble hurriedly. **3** to cause or produce (something): *Science … will continue to throw up discoveries which threaten … society* — Times Literary Supplement. **4** *informal* to vomit (food, one's dinner, etc). ⨠ *verb intrans informal* to vomit.

thru /throoh/ *prep, adv, and adj NAmer, informal* see THROUGH¹, THROUGH², and THROUGH³.

thrum¹ /thrum/ *verb* (**thrummed, thrumming**) ⨠ *verb intrans* **1** to make a monotonous hum. **2** to play or pluck a stringed instrument idly. **3** to drum or tap idly. ⨠ *verb trans* to play (a stringed instrument, etc) in an idle or relaxed manner. [imitative]

thrum² *noun* a thrumming sound.

thrum³ *noun* a fringe of threads, e.g. a fringe of warp threads left on a loom after the cloth has been removed, or any of these threads. [Old English *-thrum*, as in *tungethrum* ligament of the tongue]

thrum⁴ *verb trans* (**thrummed, thrumming**) to furnish (something) with thrums; to fringe (it).

thrush¹ /thrush/ *noun* **1** any of a family of small or medium-sized light-brown birds with spotted breasts, noted for their singing ability, e.g. a song thrush or mistle thrush: genus *Turdus.* **2** any of a family of birds, such as the blackbird and fieldfare, belonging to the thrush genus or family: family Turdidae. [Old English *thrysce*]

thrush² *noun* **1** a whitish irritating fungal growth occurring on mucous membranes, *esp* in the mouth or vagina. **2** a suppurative disorder of the feet in various animals, *esp* horses. [origin unknown; possibly two different words]

thrust¹ /thrust/ *verb* (*past tense and past part.* **thrust**) ➤ *verb trans* **1** to push or drive (something or somebody) with force. **2** (+ on/upon) to press, force, or impose the acceptance of (something or somebody) on or upon somebody. **3** to put (an unwilling person) into a course of action or position: *He was thrust into power against his will.* **4** (+ through) to stab or pierce (somebody). **5** to produce (something): *The plants will soon thrust out roots.* ➤ *verb intrans* **1** (*often* + into/through) to force an entrance or passage. **2** to make a thrust, stab, or lunge with or as if with a pointed weapon. [Middle English *thrusten, thristen*, from Old Norse *thrysta*]

thrust² *noun* **1a** a push or lunge with a pointed weapon. **b** a verbal attack. **c** a concerted military attack. **2** the salient or essential meaning: *The thrust of her argument was that all war was evil.* **3** a strong continued pressure, e.g.: **a** the force exerted by a propeller, jet engine, etc to give forward motion. **b** the sideways force of one part of a structure against another. **4** a forward or upward push.

thruster *noun* **1** somebody or something that thrusts. **2** a rocket engine used *esp* to control the altitude of a spacecraft.

thrust fault *noun* a FAULT¹ (fracture in the earth's crust) caused by compression in which the upper older layers of rock are thrust over the lower younger ones at a very low angle.

thrusting *adj* aggressive or pushy.

thrust stage *noun* a stage that extends out into the auditorium.

thud¹ /thud/ *noun* **1** a dull thump. **2** a blow.

thud² *verb* (**thudded, thudding**) ➤ *verb intrans* to move or fall with a thud. ➤ *verb trans* to strike (something or somebody) with a thud. [Middle English *thudden*, prob from Old English *thyddan* to thrust]

thug /thug/ *noun* **1** a violent person, *esp* a violent criminal. **2** (**Thug**) a member of a former religious sect in India given to robbery and murder in honour of Kali, the Hindu goddess of destruction. ➤➤ **thuggery** *noun*, **thuggish** *adj*. [Hindi *thag*, literally 'thief', from Sanskrit *sthaga* rogue, from *sthagati* he covers or conceals]

thuggee /thu'gee, 'thugee/ *noun* formerly, murder and robbery as practised by the Thugs of India. [Hindi *thagī* robbery, from *thag*: see THUG]

thuja *or* **thuya** /'thooh·yə/ *noun* any of a genus of coniferous trees of N America and E Asia with small cones and aromatic wood: genus *Thuja*. [Latin genus name, from Greek *thuia* an African tree formerly included in the genus]

thulium /'thyoohli·əm/ *noun* a silver-grey metallic chemical element of the rare-earth group that occurs naturally in apatite, and is used in portable X-ray machines: symbol Tm, atomic number 69. [scientific Latin *thulium*, named after Thule, legendary land at the northernmost point of the world, prob because its atomic number falls between that of erbium and ytterbium, both of which were discovered in Sweden]

thumb¹ /thum/ *noun* **1a** the short thick digit of the human hand that is next to the forefinger and is opposable to the other fingers. **b** the corresponding digit in animals. **2** the part of a glove or mitten that covers the thumb. ✳ **all thumbs** extremely awkward or clumsy: *I'm all thumbs today. I keep dropping things.* **under somebody's thumb** under somebody's control; in a state of subservience to somebody: *Her father had her completely under his thumb.* ➤➤ **thumbless** *adj*. [Middle English *thoume, thoumbe* from Old English *thūma*]

thumb² *verb trans* **1a** to leaf through (pages) with the thumb. **b** to soil or wear (something) by or as if by repeated thumbing. **2** to request or obtain (a lift) in a passing vehicle by signalling with the thumb. ➤ *verb intrans* **1** (+ through) to turn over the pages of a book, magazine, etc. **2** to travel by thumbing lifts; to hitchhike. ✳ **thumb one's nose at** *informal* to behave defiantly or contemptuously towards (somebody). ➤➤ **thumbed** *adj*.

thumb index *noun* a series of notches cut in the unbound edge of a book for ease of reference.

thumb-index *verb trans* to provide (a book) with a thumb index.

thumbnail *noun* **1** the nail of the thumb. **2** (*used before a noun*) brief; concise: *a thumbnail sketch.*

thumb piano *noun* = MBIRA.

thumbscrew *noun* **1** an instrument of torture for squeezing the thumb. **2** a screw with a flat-sided or ridged head so that it may be turned by the thumb and forefinger.

thumbs-down *noun informal* rejection, disapproval, or condemnation.

thumbstall *noun* a protective covering or sheath for the thumb.

thumbs-up *noun informal* approval; affirmation.

thumbtack *noun NAmer* = DRAWING PIN.

thump¹ /thump/ *verb trans* **1** to thrash or beat (somebody). **2** to strike or knock (something) with a thump. **3** (+ out) to produce (music) mechanically or in a mechanical manner: *He thumped out a tune on the piano.* ➤ *verb intrans* **1a** to beat rapidly: *His heart thumped.* **b** to make a thumping sound. **2** to come together or hit something with a thump. ➤➤ **thumper** *noun*. [imitative]

thump² *noun* a blow or knock with or as if with something blunt or heavy, or the sound of this.

thumping *adj* **1** *Brit, informal* impressively large, great, or excellent: *a thumping majority.* **2** very bad: *a thumping headache.* [present part. of THUMP¹]

thunder¹ /'thundə/ *noun* **1** the low loud sound that follows a flash of lightning and is caused by sudden expansion of the air in the path of the electrical discharge. **2** a loud reverberating noise: *He could hear the thunder of big guns.* ➤➤ **thundery** *adj*. [Middle English *thoner, thunder*, from Old English *thunor*]

thunder² *verb* (**thundered, thundering**) ➤ *verb intrans* **1a** (*usu impersonally*) to give forth thunder: *It's thundering.* **b** to make a sound like thunder: *Horses thundered down the road.* **2** to roar or shout. ➤ *verb trans* to utter (something) in a loud threatening tone. ➤➤ **thunderer** *noun*.

thunderbolt *noun* **1a** a single discharge of lightning with the accompanying thunder. **b** an imaginary bolt or missile cast to earth in a flash of lightning. **2** something like lightning in suddenness, effectiveness, or destructive power.

thunderclap *noun* **1** a clap of thunder. **2** something like thunder in loudness or suddenness.

thundercloud *noun* a cloud charged with electricity and producing lightning and thunder.

thunderhead *noun* a rounded mass of cumulonimbus cloud often appearing before a thunderstorm.

thundering *adj informal* very great, remarkable, or unusual: *a thundering bore.* ➤➤ **thunderingly** *adv*. [present part. of THUNDER²]

thunderous /'thundərəs/ *adj* **1** producing thunder. **2** making or accompanied by a noise like thunder: *thunderous applause.* ➤➤ **thunderously** *adv*.

thunderstorm *noun* a storm accompanied by lightning and thunder.

thunderstruck *adj* extremely surprised; astonished.

Thur. *abbr* Thursday.

thurible /'thyooəribl/ *noun* a censer. [Middle English *turrible* via French from Latin *thuribulum*, from *thur-, thus* incense, from Greek *thyos* incense, sacrifice, from *thyein* to sacrifice]

Thurs. *abbr* Thursday.

Thursday /'thuhzday, 'thuhzdi/ *noun* the fifth day of the week, following Wednesday. [Old English *thursdæg* day of thunder, named after Thor, the Norse god of thunder, translation of Latin *Jovis dies* day of Jupiter, the supreme god in Roman mythology, who was also associated with thunder]

thus /dhus/ *adv literary, formal* **1** because of this preceding fact or premise; consequently: *The unleashed power of the atom has changed everything save our modes of thinking and we thus drift toward unparalleled catastrophe* — Albert Einstein. **2** in the manner indicated; in this way. **3** to this degree or extent; so: *thus far.* [Old English]

thuya /'thooh·yə/ *noun* see THUJA.

thwack¹ /thwak/ *verb trans and intrans* to whack (somebody or something). [imitative]

thwack² *noun* a sharp blow; a whack.

thwart¹ /thwawt/ *verb trans* **1** to defeat the hopes or aspirations of (somebody). **2** to defeat (somebody's plans). [Middle English *thwerten, thwarten*, from *thwert, thwart*: see THWART³]

thwart² *noun* a seat extending across a boat.

thwart[3] *adv and prep archaic or literary* = ATHWART[1], ATHWART[2]. [Middle English *thwert, thwart*, from Old Norse *thvert*, neuter of *thverr* transverse, oblique]

thy /dhie/ *adj archaic or dialect* of thee or thyself: *Thy books should, like thy friends, not many be, yet such wherein men may thy judgment see* — William Wycherley. [Middle English *thin, thy*, from Old English *thīn*, genitive of *thū* THOU[1]]

thylacine /'thieləseen/ *noun* = TASMANIAN WOLF. [from the Latin genus name *Thylacinus*, from Greek *thylakos* sack, pouch]

thyme /tiem/ *noun* any of a genus of plants of the mint family with small pungent aromatic leaves, *esp* a garden plant used in cooking as a seasoning and formerly in medicine: genus *Thymus*. ▶ **thymy** *adj*. [Middle English via French from Latin *thymum* from Greek *thymon*, from *thyein* to make a burned offering, sacrifice]

thymi /'thiemie/ *noun* pl of THYMUS.

-thymia *comb. form* forming nouns, denoting: state of mental health: *schizothymia*. [scientific Latin from Greek, from *thymos* mind]

thymidine /'thiemideen/ *noun* a nucleoside containing thymine.

thymine /'thiemeen/ *noun* a pyrimidine base that is one of the four bases whose order in the DNA chain codes genetic information: compare ADENINE, CYTOSINE, GUANINE, URACIL. [German *Thymin* from scientific Latin *thymus*: see THYMUS]

thymol /'thiemol/ *noun* an antiseptic phenol made from thyme oil and used chiefly as a fungicide. [Latin *thymum* (see THYME) + -OL[1]]

thymus /'thieməs/ *noun* (*pl* **thymi** /'thiemie/) a gland in the lower neck region that functions in the development of the body's immune system and in humans tends to atrophy after sexual maturity. ▶ **thymic** /'thiemik/ *adj*. [scientific Latin from Greek *thymos* warty excrescence, thymus]

thyr- *or* **thyro-** *comb. form* forming words, denoting: thyroid: *thyrotoxicosis; thyroxine*. [THYROID[2]]

thyristor /'thie'ristə/ *noun* a semiconductor device that acts as a switch or rectifier. [blend of *thyratron* a kind of thermionic valve (from Greek *thyra* gate) + TRANSISTOR]

thyro- *comb. form* see THYR-.

thyroid[1] /'thieroyd/ *noun* **1** (*also* **thyroid gland**) a large endocrine gland that lies at the base of the neck and produces hormones, e.g. thyroxine, that increase the metabolic rate and influence growth and development. **2** a preparation of mammalian thyroid gland used in treating conditions in which the thyroid gland produces insufficient quantities of hormones. [scientific Latin from Greek *thyreoeidēs* shield-shaped, thyroid, from *thyreos* shield shaped like a door, from *thyra* door]

thyroid[2] *adj* **1** of or relating to the thyroid gland. **2** of or relating to the chief cartilage of the larynx.

thyroid-stimulating hormone *noun* a hormone secreted by the front lobe of the pituitary gland that regulates the formation and secretion of thyroid hormones.

thyrotoxicosis /,thierohtoksi'kohsis/ *noun* = HYPERTHYROIDISM.

thyrotrophin /thieroh'trohfin/ *or* **thyrotropin** /-pin/ *noun* = THYROID-STIMULATING HORMONE.

thyroxine /thie'rokseen, -sin/ *or* **thyroxin** /-sin/ *noun* the major hormone produced by the thyroid gland that is used to treat conditions in which the thyroid gland produces insufficient quantities of hormones.

thyrsus /'thuhsəs/ *noun* (*pl* **thyrsi** /'thuhsie/) **1** in ancient Greece and Rome, a staff, usu surmounted by a pine cone, that was carried by Bacchus and his followers. **2** (*also* **thyrse** /thuhs/) a flower cluster, e.g. in the lilac and horse chestnut, with a long main axis bearing short branches which in turn bear the flowers. [via Latin from Greek *thyrsos*; (sense 2) because the flower cluster resembles a pine cone in appearance]

thyself /dhie'self/ *pronoun archaic or dialect* that identical person that is thou; yourself: *The only gift is a portion of thyself* — Ralph Waldo Emerson.

Ti *abbr* the chemical symbol for titanium.

ti /tee/ *noun NAmer* see TE. [alteration of SI: see GAMUT]

TIA *abbr* transient ischaemic attack, a mild stroke.

tiara /ti'ahrə/ *noun* (*pl* **tiaras**) **1** a decorative jewelled band worn on the head by women on formal occasions. **2** the three-tiered crown worn by the pope. **3** a tall headdress formerly worn by Persians and differing in style according to the wearer's status. [Latin *tiara* royal Persian headdress, from Greek]

Tibetan /ti'bet(ə)n/ *noun* **1** a native or inhabitant of Tibet. **2** the Sino-Tibetan language of Tibet. ▶ **Tibetan** *adj*.

Word history
Tibetan words which have passed into English include *yak* and *yeti*. *Polo* derives from the closely related Balti language.

Tibeto-Burman /tibetoh'buhmən/ *noun* a branch of the Sino-Tibetan family of languages that includes Tibetan, Burmese and some languages of N India and China. ▶ **Tibeto-Burman** *adj*.

tibia /'tibi-ə/ *noun* (*pl* **tibiae** /'tibi-ee/ *or* **tibias**) **1** the inner and usu larger of the two bones of the hind limb of higher vertebrates between the knee and ankle; the shinbone: compare FIBULA. **2** the fourth joint of the leg of an insect between the femur and the tarsus. ▶ **tibial** *adj*. [Latin *tibia* shinbone]

tic /tik/ *noun* a habitual spasmodic motion of particular muscles, *esp* of the face; a twitch. [French *tic* from Italian *ticchio*]

tic douloureux /,tik doohlə'ruh/ *noun* = TRIGEMINAL NEURALGIA. [French *tic douloureux* painful twitch]

tick[1] /tik/ *noun* **1** a small spot or mark, typically (√); *esp* one used to mark something as correct, to check an item on a list, etc: compare CROSS[1] (1B). **2** a light rhythmic audible tap or beat, or a series of such sounds. **3** *Brit, informal* a moment or second. **4** on the stock market, the smallest amount by which the price of a stock, etc can fluctuate. [Middle English *tek*, prob of Germanic origin]

tick[2] *verb trans* **1** to mark (something) with a written tick. **2** (*often* + off) to mark or count (something) by ticks or as if by ticks: *I eat in the taxi watching the meter ticking off the fare.* ▶ *verb intrans* **1** to make the sound of a tick. **2** *informal* to function or behave characteristically: *I'd like to know what makes him tick.*

tick[3] *noun* **1** a bloodsucking arachnid that feeds on warm-blooded animals and often transmits infectious diseases. **2** *informal* a wingless bloodsucking insect, e.g. one that is parasitic on sheep. [Old English *ticia*]

tick[4] *noun informal* credit; trust: *I bought it on tick.* [short for TICKET[1] in the obsolete sense 'IOU']

tick[5] *noun* **1** a strong coarse fabric case of a mattress, pillow, or bolster. **2** = TICKING. [Middle English *tike*, prob via a prehistoric Germanic word from Latin *theca* case, from Greek *thēkē*]

tickbird *noun* = OXPECKER.

ticker *noun* **1** *informal*. **a** a watch. **b** the heart. **2** *NAmer* = TAPE MACHINE.

ticker tape *noun* a paper tape on which a certain type of telegraphic receiving instrument prints out its information.

ticket[1] /'tikit/ *noun* **1** a printed card or piece of paper entitling its holder to the use of certain services, e.g. a library, showing that a fare or admission has been paid, etc. **2a** a document that serves as a certificate, licence, or permit, *esp* a mariner's or pilot's certificate. **b** a tag or label. **3** an official notification issued to somebody who has violated a traffic regulation. **4** *chiefly NAmer*. **a** a list of candidates for nomination or election. **b** a declaration of political principles and policies; = PLATFORM. **5** (**the ticket**) *informal* the correct, proper, or desirable thing [from the tickets exchangeable for food and clothing which were formerly given by charities to paupers]. **6** *Brit, informal* a certificate of discharge from the armed forces. [obsolete French *etiquet* (now *étiquette*) notice attached to something, from early French *estiquet*, from *estiquier* to attach, from Middle Dutch *steken* to stick]

ticket[2] *verb trans* (**ticketed, ticketing**) **1** to furnish or serve (somebody) with a ticket: *He was ticketed for illegal parking.* **2** *NAmer* to set (funds, etc.) aside for a particular purpose; to designate (them).

ticket inspector *noun* = INSPECTOR (1B).

ticket-of-leave *noun* (*pl* **tickets-of-leave**) formerly, a permit by which a convict who had served part of a sentence was released on certain conditions.

tickety-boo /,tikiti'booh/ *adj Brit, informal, dated* fine; perfect; great. [perhaps from Hindi *ṭhīk hai* all right]

tick fever *noun* any disease transmitted by the bites of ticks.

ticking *noun* a strong linen or cotton fabric used *esp* for a case for a mattress or pillow. [TICK[5]]

tickle[1] /'tikl/ *verb trans* **1** to touch (a person or a body part) lightly and repeatedly so as to excite the surface nerves and cause uneasiness, laughter, or spasmodic movements. **2a** to excite (somebody) or stir (them) up agreeably. **b** to provoke (somebody) to laughter. **3** to catch (a trout) in one's hands. ➤ *verb intrans* to have or cause a tingling or prickling sensation. ✳ **tickle pink/to death** *informal* to amuse or delight (somebody). ➤➤ **tickler** *noun*. [Middle English *tikelen* to be delighted or thrilled, prob from TICK² in the obsolete sense 'to touch lightly']

tickle² *noun* **1** a tickling sensation. **2** the act or an instance of tickling.

ticklish *adj* **1** sensitive to tickling. **2** said of a cough: causing irritation in the throat. **3** requiring delicate handling. **4** easily upset. ➤➤ **ticklishly** *adv*, **ticklishness** *noun*.

tick off *verb trans Brit, informal* to scold or rebuke (somebody): *His father ticked him off for his impudence.* ➤➤ **ticking-off** *noun*. [TICK²]

tick over *verb intrans* **1** said of an engine: to be turned on and running but with the transmission disengaged so that motion is impossible; to idle. **2** to continue to operate smoothly but quietly or at a minimum level: *The firm is still ticking over but profits will be well down on last year.*

ticktacktoe *or* **tic-tac-toe** /tiktak'toh/ *noun NAmer* = NOUGHTS AND CROSSES. [*tic-tac-toe*, former game in which players with eyes shut brought a pencil down on a slate marked with numbers and scored the number hit]

ticktock¹ /'tiktok/ *noun* the rhythmic ticking of a clock. [imitative]

ticktock² /'tik'tok/ *verb intrans* said of a clock: to make a rhythmic ticking sound.

tic tac man /'tik tak man/ *noun* in Britain, a bookmaker's assistant who signals changing odds at a race meeting by means of special hand signals. [*ticktack, tictac* ticking or tapping sound, of imitative origin]

tic-tac-toe /tiktak'toh/ *noun* see TICKTACKTOE.

tidal /'tiedl/ *adj* of, caused by, or having tides. ➤➤ **tidally** *adv*.

tidal basin *noun* a basin that only fills at high tide.

tidal bore *noun* = BORE⁵.

tidal wave *noun* **1** an unusually high sea wave that sometimes follows an earthquake. **2** an unexpected, intense, and often widespread reaction, e.g. a sweeping majority vote or an overwhelming impulse.

tidbit /'tidbit/ *noun NAmer* see TITBIT.

tiddler /'tidlə/ *noun Brit, informal* somebody or something small in comparison to others of the same kind, *esp* a minnow, stickleback, or other small fish. [prob from TIDDLY]

tiddly /'tidli/ *adj* (**tiddlier, tiddliest**) *informal* **1** *chiefly Brit* slightly drunk. **2** *Brit* very small: *a tiddly bit of food.* [alteration of LITTLE¹]

tiddlywink /'tidliwingk/ *noun* **1** (*in pl, but treated as sing.*) a game in which the object is to flick small discs from a flat surface into a small container. **2** any of the small discs used in this game. [prob from TIDDLY]

tide¹ /'tied/ *noun* **1a** the periodic rise and fall of the surface of a body of water, *specif* the sea, that occurs twice a day and is caused by the gravitational attraction of the sun and moon. **b** a current of water resulting from this. **2a** the level or position of water on a shore with respect to the tide. **b** the water at its highest level. **3** something that fluctuates like the tides: *the tide of public opinion.* **4** (*in combination*). **a** a space of time; a period: *noontide.* **b** the season of an ecclesiastical anniversary or festival: *Whitsuntide.* **5** *archaic* a suitable or opportune time; an opportunity. ➤➤ **tideless** *adj*.

Word history ━━━━━━━━━
Old English *tīd* time, period. Senses relating to the sea first appear in the 14th cent., orig referring to the time of high or low water.

tide² *verb intrans archaic* to drift with the tide, *esp* in navigating a ship into or out of an anchorage, harbour, or river.

tideland *noun NAmer* (*also in pl*) land in the zone between low and high water marks.

tideline *noun* = TIDEMARK (1).

tidemark *noun* **1** a mark left by or indicating the highest position of the tide. **2** *Brit.* **a** a mark left on a bath that shows the level reached by the water. **b** *informal* a mark left on the body showing the limit of washing.

tide over *verb trans* to enable (somebody) to surmount or withstand a difficulty, *esp* by giving them money. [TIDE²]

tide rip *noun* an area of rough sea caused *esp* by the meeting of opposing tides or currents.

tidewaiter *noun* formerly, a customs inspector working on the docks or aboard ships.

tidewater *noun* **1a** water overflowing land at flood tide. **b** water affected by the ebb and flow of the tide. **2** *NAmer* low-lying coastal land.

tideway *noun* a channel in which the tide runs.

tidings /'tiedingz/ *pl noun* a piece of news: *good tidings.* [Old English *tīdung*, from *tīdan* to betide]

tidy¹ /'tiedi/ *adj* (**tidier, tidiest**) **1a** neat and orderly in appearance or habits; well ordered and cared for. **b** methodical; precise: *The country is laid out in a haphazard, sloppy fashion, offensive to the tidy, organized mind* — Alan Brien. **2** *informal* large or substantial: *She got a tidy sum for her car.* ➤➤ **tidily** *adv*, **tidiness** *noun*. [Middle English *tidi* timely, in good condition, from TIDE¹ in the sense 'time']

tidy² *verb* (**tidies, tidied, tidying**) to put (things) in order; to make (things) neat or tidy.

tidy³ *noun* (*pl* **tidies**) **1** the act or an instance of tidying: *This room could do with a tidy.* **2a** a receptacle for odds and ends, e.g. sewing materials or pens and pencils. **b** a small receptacle for rubbish in a sink. **3** *chiefly NAmer* a decorative cover used to protect the back, arms, or headrest of a chair or sofa from wear or dirt.

tidy away *verb trans* to put (something) away for the sake of tidiness: *Tidy away all those papers before you go out.*

tidy up *verb trans and intrans* to make (something) tidy or tidier. ➤➤ **tidy-up** *noun*.

tie¹ /'tie/ *verb* (**ties, tied, tying**) ➤ *verb trans* **1a** to fasten or attach (something) with cord or string, etc. **b** to form a knot or bow in (something). **2** to make (something) by tying the constituent elements: *He tied a fishing fly.* **3** to make a bond or connection between (things or people). **4** (*often + down*) to restrict or limit the place or range of activity of (somebody). **5a** to even (the score) in a game or contest. **b** to even the score of (a game). **6** to unite (people) in marriage. **7** to link (musical notes) with a tie. ➤ *verb intrans* to achieve an equal score in a game or contest. [Old English *tigan*]

tie² *noun* **1** something that serves as a connecting link, e.g.: **a** a moral or legal obligation to somebody or something that restricts freedom of action. **b** a bond of kinship or affection. **2** a narrow length of material designed to be worn round the neck and tied in a knot in the front. **3a** a line, ribbon, or cord used for fastening or drawing something together. **b** a structural element, e.g. a rod or angle iron, holding two pieces together. **4** *NAmer* a railway sleeper. **5** a curved line that joins two musical notes of the same pitch to denote a single sustained note with the time value of the two. **6a** *Brit* a match or game between two teams, players, etc: *a cup tie.* **b** a draw or dead heat in a contest. ➤➤ **tieless** *adj*. [Old English *tēag*]

tie-back *noun* a decorative loop of fabric or cord used for draping a curtain to the side of a window.

tie-beam *noun* a beam joining the lower ends of rafters to prevent them from spreading apart.

tie break *noun* a contest or game used to select a winner from among contestants with tied scores at the end of a previous contest or phase of a contest.

tie breaker *noun* = TIE BREAK.

tie clip *noun* a pin or clasp used to hold a tie in place.

tied *adj* **1** *Brit* said of a house: owned by an employer and reserved for occupancy by an employee. **2** said of a public house: bound to sell only the products of the brewery that owns it or rents it out: compare FREE HOUSE; *a tied house.* **3** said of aid or a loan: given on condition that it is spent on goods or services from the donor or lender.

tie-dye¹ *noun* a hand method of producing patterns in textiles by tying portions of the fabric or yarn so that they will not absorb the dye.

tie-dye² *verb trans* to dye (fabric) using the tie-dye method. ➤➤ **tie-dyed** *adj*, **tie-dyeing** *noun*.

tie in *verb trans* to bring (a thing) into harmony with another: *The illustrations are well tied in with the text.* ➤ *verb intrans* to be closely connected; to correspond: *That ties in with what I know already.*

tie-in *noun* **1** something that ties in, relates, or connects. **2** a book published to coincide with a film or television production to which it is related in some way. **3** *chiefly NAmer* (*used before a noun*) denoting the sale of an item that is conditional on the purchaser buying an additional item.

tiepin *noun* a decorative pin used to hold a tie in place.

tier[1] /tiə/ *noun* **1** a row, rank, or layer of articles, *esp* any of two or more rows or ranks arranged one above another. **2** any of a series of levels, e.g. in an administration: *the top tier of local government.* [early French *tire* order, rank, from *tirer* to draw out]

tier[2] *verb trans* to place or arrange (things) in tiers. ➤ *verb intrans* to rise in tiers. ➤➤ **tiered** *adj.*

tierce /tiəs/ *noun* **1** = TERCE. **2** a sequence of three playing cards of the same suit. **3** in fencing, the third of eight parrying positions. **4** a formerly used unit of liquid capacity equal to about 159l (one third of a pipe). [Middle English *terce, tierce* third part, via French from Latin *tertius* third]

tiercel /'tiəsl/ *noun* = TERCEL.

tie up *verb trans* **1a** to attach or fasten (somebody or something) securely. **b** to wrap (something) up and fasten it. **2** to conclude (a matter) satisfactorily. **3** to connect or link (things or people) closely. **4** to invest (capital) in a way that leaves it unavailable for immediate use. **5** *informal* to keep (somebody) busy. **6** to restrain (something) from operation or progress. ➤ *verb intrans* **1** said of a vessel: to dock. **2** (+ with) to relate or correspond to something.

tie-up *noun* **1** a connection or association: *He was elected to Congress in spite of his known tie-up with gangsters.* **2** *NAmer* a traffic jam.

TIFF *abbr* tagged image file format.

tiff[1] /tif/ *noun informal* a petty quarrel. [origin unknown]

tiff[2] *verb intrans* to have a tiff.

tiffany /'tifəni/ *noun* a sheer silk gauze. [prob from obsolete French *tiphanie* Epiphany, via Latin from Greek *theophaneia*, from *theos* god + *phainein* to show]

tiffin /'tifin/ *noun* a meal or snack taken at midday or in the middle of the morning, *esp* by the British in India. [prob alteration of *tiffing*, verbal noun from obsolete *tiff* to eat or drink between meals, of unknown origin]

tig[1] /tig/ *noun chiefly Brit* = TAG[3].

tig[2] *verb trans* (**tigged, tigging**) *chiefly Brit* = TAG[4].

tiger /'tiegə/ *noun* **1** a very large Asian cat having a tawny coat transversely striped with black: *Panthera tigris.* **2** a fierce or aggressive person. **3a** a country, *esp* in E Asia, with a dynamic economy. **b** (*used before a noun*) denoting such a dynamic economy. ➤➤ **tigerish** *adj,* **tigerishly** *adv.* [Middle English *tigre* via French and Latin from Greek *tigris,* of Iranian origin]

tiger beetle *noun* any of various active flesh-eating beetles, the larvae of which tunnel in the soil: genus *Cicindela* and other genera.

tiger cat *noun* a serval, ocelot, or other wildcat of moderate size and variegated coloration.

tigereye *noun* = TIGER'S-EYE.

tiger lily *noun* an Asian lily commonly grown for its drooping orange-coloured flowers densely spotted with black: *Lilium lancifolium.*

tiger moth *noun* any of numerous species of stout-bodied moths with broad striped or spotted wings: family Arctiidae.

tiger prawn *noun* a large edible prawn of the Pacific and Indian oceans: genus *Penaeus.*

tiger's-eye *noun* a yellowish brown ornamental gemstone consisting mainly of silicates of sodium and iron.

tiger shark *noun* a large grey or brown shark that is dangerous to humans and is found in most parts of the world, *esp* in warm seas: genus *Galeocerdo.*

tiger shrimp *noun* = TIGER PRAWN.

tiger snake *noun* either of two species of Australian snakes with dark stripes on the back, *esp* one with brown and yellow markings and a fatal bite: genus *Notechis.*

tight[1] /tiet/ *adj* **1a** fixed very firmly in place. **b** firmly stretched, drawn, or set. **c** said of clothing: fitting closely or too closely. **2** (*often in combination*) so close or solid in structure as to prevent passage, e.g. of a liquid or gas: *a tight seal; an airtight compartment.* **3** firm in control, or characterized by such firmness. **4** packed, compressed, or condensed to the limit or near the limit: *a tight literary style; a tight schedule.* **5** set close together: *The team plays a tight defensive formation.* **6** difficult to get through or out of: *We're in a tight spot.* **7** evenly contested: *a tight match.* **8a** scarce in proportion to demand: *tight money.* **b** characterized by such scarcity: *a tight labour market.* **9** playing in unison: *His three-week-old band was*

surprisingly tight — The Age (Melbourne). **10** *informal* stingy or miserly. **11** *informal* intoxicated; drunk. **12** *informal* tense. **13** secretive. ✳ **run a tight ship** to keep strict control over an organization, etc. ➤➤ **tightly** *adv,* **tightness** *noun.* [Middle English, alteration of *thight,* of Germanic origin]

tight[2] *adv* **1** fast; tightly: *The door was shut tight.* **2** in a sound manner: *Sleep tight.*

tightass *noun chiefly NAmer, slang* a very inhibited or restrained person. ➤➤ **tight-assed** *adj.*

tighten /'tiet(ə)n/ *verb* (**tightened, tightening**) ➤ *verb trans* to make (something) tight or tighter. ➤ *verb intrans* to become tight or tighter.

tighten up *verb intrans* (*usu* + on) to become firmer or more severe: *The government is tightening up on tax dodgers.* ➤ *verb trans* to make (something) firmer or stricter.

tightfisted *adj informal* reluctant to part with money.

tight head *noun* in rugby, the prop forward to the right of the hooker in the scrum.

tight-knit *adj* said of a group of people: closely linked because of shared interests or affection.

tight-lipped *adj* **1** having the lips compressed, e.g. in determination. **2** reluctant to speak; taciturn.

tightrope *noun* a rope or wire stretched taut for acrobats to perform on. ✳ **walk a tightrope** to deal with a dangerously precarious situation.

tights *pl noun* a skintight garment covering each leg and foot and reaching to the waist.

tightwad /'tietwod/ *noun chiefly NAmer, informal* a mean or miserly person.

tiglon /'tiglon/ *noun* = TIGON.

tigon /'tiegon/ *noun* a hybrid produced by a mating between a tiger and a lioness.

Tigré /'teegray/ *noun* a Semitic language of NE Ethiopia. ➤➤ **Tigré** *adj.* [the Tigré name]

tigress /'tiegris/ *noun* **1** a female tiger. **2** an aggressive or passionate woman.

tike /tiek/ *noun* see TYKE.

tiki /'teekee/ *noun* a Polynesian, *esp* Maori, image of an ancestor, either large and made of wood, or small and made of greenstone, often in the form of a pendant. [Maori and Marquesan *tiki,* named after *Tiki,* first man or creator of first man in Polynesian mythology]

tikka /'teekə/ *noun* an Indian dish of pieces of meat or vegetables marinated in spices and roasted on skewers. [Punjabi *tikkā*]

tilak /'tilak/ *noun* in Hinduism, a mark, generally made on the forehead, that indicates sectarian affiliation, caste, or in the case of a woman, marital status. [Sanskrit *tilaka* mark]

tilapia /ti'lapi·ə/ *noun* (*pl* **tilapias** or *collectively* **tilapia**) any of several species of African freshwater fishes used as food: genus *Tilapia* and other genera. [Latin genus name, of unknown origin]

tilbury /'tilb(ə)ri/ *noun* (*pl* **tilburies**) formerly, a light two-wheeled horse-drawn carriage. [named after *Tilbury,* 19th-cent. English coach builder who invented it]

tilde /'tildə/ *noun* **1** a mark (˜) placed over the letter *n,* e.g. in Spanish *señor,* to denote the sound /ny/, or over vowels, e.g. in Portuguese *irmã,* to indicate nasality. **2** a swung dash, *esp* as used in mathematics to indicate similarity or equivalence. [Spanish *tilde* from medieval Latin *titulus:* see TITLE[1]]

tile[1] /tiel/ *noun* **1** a thin slab of fired clay, stone, or concrete shaped according to use, e.g.: **a** a flat or curved slab for use on roofs. **b** a flat slab for floors, walls, or surrounds. **c** a tube-shaped or semicircular and open slab for constructing drains. **2** a thin piece of resilient material, e.g. cork or linoleum, used for covering floors or walls. **3** a square or rectangular piece of plastic or other material, usu bearing special markings or figures, and used in mah-jong, Scrabble, etc. ✳ **on the tiles** *chiefly Brit* enjoying oneself socially, *esp* in an intemperate or wild manner: *He looks terrible this morning after his night out on the tiles.* [Old English *tigele* from Latin *tegula,* from *tegere* to cover]

tile[2] *verb trans* **1** to cover (a surface) with tiles. **2** to arrange (windows) on a computer screen without overlapping. ➤➤ **tiler** *noun.*

till[1] /til, tl/ *prep and conj* until. [Old English *til*]

till² *noun* **1** = CASH REGISTER. **2** a receptacle, e.g. a drawer or tray, in which money is kept in a shop or bank. [Middle English from Anglo-French *tylle* drawer for valuables]

till³ /til/ *verb trans* to work (land) by ploughing, sowing, and raising crops. ➤➤ **tillable** *adj*, **tillage** /'tilij/ *noun*, **tiller** *noun*. [Old English *tilian*]

till⁴ *noun* glacial drift consisting of clay, sand, gravel, and boulders not deposited in distinct layers. [origin unknown]

tiller¹ *noun* a lever used to turn the rudder of a boat from side to side. [Middle English *tiler* stock of a crossbow, via Anglo-French *telier* beam of a loom, from Latin *tela*: see TOIL³]

tiller² *noun* a sprout or stalk that grows from the base of a plant in response to injury of the main stem, e.g. in grasses after grazing and in hazel after coppicing. [Old English *telgor, telgra* twig, shoot]

tiller³ *verb intrans* (**tillered, tillering**) said of a plant: to produce tillers.

tilley lamp or **tilly lamp** /'tili/ *noun trademark* a type of oil- or paraffin-burning lamp. [from the name of the manufacturers]

tilt¹ /tilt/ *verb trans* **1** to cause (something) to slope or sit at an angle: *Don't tilt the boat.* **2** formerly, to point or thrust (a lance) in a joust. ➤ *verb intrans* **1** to shift so as to lean or incline. **2a** *archaic* (+ with) to engage in combat with somebody using lances. **b** (+ at) to make an impetuous attack on something or somebody: *She's always tilting at wrongs.* ➤➤ **tilter** *noun*. [Middle English *tulten, tilten* to topple, of Germanic origin]

tilt² *noun* **1** the act or an instance of tilting, or the state of being tilted. **2** a sloping position or surface. **3a** formerly, a contest on horseback in which two combatants charging with lances or similar weapons try to unhorse each other, or an exercise or contest in which a mounted person charges at a mark. **b** formerly, a thrust or charge with a lance or similar weapon. **4a** (+ at) a written or verbal attack: *She produced a tilt at her critics.* **b** (+ with) a dispute or altercation: *She had a tilt with her boss.* ✳ **full tilt/at full tilt** with maximum speed.

tilth /tilth/ *noun* **1** the state of being tilled. **2** the condition of tilled land: *The land is certainly in good tilth.* [Old English, from *tilian* TILL³]

tilt hammer *noun* a heavy pivoted hammer used to forge metal.

tiltyard *noun* formerly, a place for tilting contests.

Tim. *abbr* Timothy (books of the Bible).

timbal /'timbl/ *noun archaic* a kettledrum. [French *timbale* via early Spanish from Arabic *at-tabl* the drum]

timbale /tam'bahl/ *noun* **1** a creamy mixture of meat, vegetables, etc baked in a cup-shaped mould. **2** the cup-shaped mould in which a timbale is baked. [French *timbale*: see TIMBAL]

timber¹ /'timbə/ *noun* **1** wood suitable for carpentry or woodwork. **2a** growing trees or their wood. **b** used interjectionally to warn of a falling tree. **3a** a large squared or dressed piece of wood ready for use or forming part of a structure. **b** (*used before a noun*) made of timber: *a timber building.* **4** *chiefly NAmer, informal* material, stuff, *esp* personal character or quality. [Old English *timber* building, wood]

timber² *verb trans* (**timbered, timbering**) to frame, cover, or support (something) with timbers. ➤➤ **timbered** *adj*, **timbering** *noun*.

timber hitch *noun* a knot used to secure a line to a log or spar.

timberline *noun NAmer* = TREE LINE.

timberman *noun* (*pl* **timbermen**) a man who works with timber.

timber wolf *noun* a wolf formerly common over much of eastern N America: *Canis lupus lycaon.*

timberyard *noun Brit* a place where prepared timber is stored and sold to the public.

timbre /'tambə/ *noun* **1** the quality of tone distinctive of a particular singing voice or musical instrument. **2** the resonance by which the ear recognizes a voiced speech sound. [French *timbre*, ultimately from Greek *tympanon* drum]

timbrel /'timbrəl/ *noun archaic* a small hand drum or tambourine. [dimin. of Middle English *timbre* tambourine, via Old French from Greek *tympanon* drum]

time¹ /tiem/ *noun* **1a** the measurable period during which an action, process, or condition exists or continues. **b** a continuum in which events succeed one another: *Will this band stand the test of time?* **2a** the point or period when something occurs: *What time is it?; At the time of writing no revolution seems likely.* **b** the period required or taken for an action: *The winner's time was under four minutes.* **c** leisure: *I never have enough time for reading.* **d** (**a time**) an indefinite period of time: *I was for a time a teacher.* **3a** a period set aside or suitable for an activity or event: *This is a time for celebration.* **b** an appointed, fixed, or customary moment for something to happen, begin, or end: *It's time we were going.* **c** *Brit* closing time in a public house as fixed by law: *Hurry up please, it's time* — T S Eliot. **d** a schedule or timetable: *We finished the project ahead of time.* **4a** (*also in pl*) a historical period: *modern times.* **b** (*usu in pl*) conditions or circumstances prevalent during a period: *Times are hard.* **c** (**the time**) the present time: *These are the issues of the time.* **d** the expected moment of giving birth or dying: *Her time is near.* **e** the end or course of a future period: *It will happen in time.* **5a** a period of apprenticeship: *He's served his time as a joiner.* **b** *informal* a term of imprisonment: *He's doing time for armed robbery.* **6** a season: *It's very hot for this time of year.* **7a** in music, a tempo. **b** in music, the grouping of the beats; the metre. **8a** a moment, hour, day, or year as measured or indicated by a clock or calendar. **b** any of various systems, e.g. sidereal or solar, of reckoning time. **9a** any of a series of recurring instances or repeated actions: *You've been told many times.* **b** (*in pl*) multiplied instances or fractional parts: *Our losses might have been five times greater; Yield was seven times smaller than usual.* **10** a person's specified experience, *esp* on a particular occasion: *I had a good time at the zoo.* **11a** the hours or days occupied by one's work: *You have to make up time if you come in late.* **b** an hourly rate of pay: *We're on double time at weekends.* **12** (*often used as an interjection*) the end of the playing time of a game or section of a game. **13** (*used before a noun*) set or able to be set to function at a specific moment: *a time bomb.* ✳ **at times** at intervals; occasionally. **behind the times** old-fashioned. **for the time being** for the present. **from time to time** at irregular intervals. **have no time for** to be unable or reluctant to spend time on (something or somebody); to dislike (them). **have the time of one's life** to enjoy oneself very much. **in no time** very soon; very quickly. **in time 1** sufficiently early. **2** eventually. **3** in correct tempo: *You must learn to play in time.* **make time** to find enough time to do something. **on time** at the appointed time. **take one's time** to be leisurely about doing something: *A burglar who respects his art takes his time before taking anything else* — O Henry. **take somebody all their time** *Brit* to be the most somebody can manage to do: *Don't come asking me for money for fancy boots. It takes me all my time to afford shoes for you all.* **time and again** frequently; repeatedly. **time out of mind** from time immemorial. [Old English *tima*]

time² *verb trans* **1** to determine or record the time, duration, or speed of (something or somebody): *He timed the journey to the airport.* **2** to arrange or set the time of (something). **3** to regulate the moment, speed, or duration of (something), *esp* to achieve the desired effect: *that was a rather ill-timed remark.*

time and a half *noun* payment of a worker, *esp* for overtime, at 1½ times the regular wage rate.

time and motion *adj* of or concerned with studying the efficiency of working methods, *esp* in industry: *a time and motion study.*

time bomb *noun* **1** a bomb equipped with a timing device so that it will explode at a predetermined time. **2** something likely to have dangerous or catastrophic effects in the future. **3** a computer virus designed to become active at a predetermined time.

time capsule *noun* a capsule that has contemporary articles sealed in it and is then buried with the intention that those who open it in future years may gain an impression of what life was like when it was buried.

time charter *noun* the chartering of a ship or aircraft for a specified period of time: compare VOYAGE CHARTER.

time clock *noun* a clock that stamps an employee's starting and finishing times on a card.

time-consuming *adj* using or taking up much time: *time-consuming chores.*

time exposure *noun* **1** exposure of a photographic film for a relatively long time, usu more than 0.5 seconds. **2** a photograph taken by time exposure.

time-honoured *adj* sanctioned by custom or tradition.

time immemorial *noun* time beyond living memory or historical record.

timekeeper *noun* **1** somebody who records the time worked by employees, elapsed in a race, etc. **2a** an employee considered with regard to their record of conforming to the correct working hours: *She's a poor timekeeper.* **b** a clock or watch considered in terms of its ability to keep time. ⋙ **timekeeping** *noun.*

time lag *noun* an interval of time between two related phenomena.

time-lapse *adj* of or constituting a method of cinema photography in which a slow action is filmed in successive stages so as to appear speeded up on the screen.

timeless *adj* **1** not affected by time; ageless. **2** unending; eternal. ⋙ **timelessly** *adv,* **timelessness** *noun.*

time lock *noun* a lock on a safe, etc with a timing mechanism that prevents it being opened before a certain time.

timely *adj* at an appropriate time. ⋙ **timeliness** *noun.*

time machine *noun* in science fiction, a machine that enables people to travel through time.

timeous /'tiemǝs, 'timi·ǝs/ *adj chiefly Scot* = TIMELY. ⋙ **timeously** *adv.*

time out *verb trans* said of a computer or a program: to interrupt (an operation) automatically because a predetermined interval of time has elapsed.

time-out *noun* **1** *chiefly NAmer* a brief suspension of activity. **2** *chiefly NAmer* a suspension of play in any of several sports, e.g. basketball. **3** in computing, the automatic interruption of an operation after a predetermined interval of time has elapsed.

timepiece *noun* a clock, watch, etc that measures or shows progress of time.

time policy *noun* a marine insurance policy covering property for a specified period: compare VOYAGE POLICY.

time porn *noun informal* the portrayal in the media, *esp* in television drama and advertising, of people who appear to have large amounts of leisure time.

timer[1] *noun* somebody or something that times, e.g.: **a** a device that can be set to give an indication, e.g. a sound when an interval of time has passed, or that starts or stops a device at predetermined times. **b** a timepiece, *esp* a stopwatch for timing races.

timer[2] *noun* (*used in combinations*) somebody or something involved in something for the first, second, etc time: *I'm not sure what to do. I'm a first-timer here.*

times *prep* multiplied by: *Two times two is four.*

time scale *noun* the amount of time allotted for the completion of something.

timeserver *noun* **1** somebody who fits behaviour and ideas to prevailing opinions or to their superiors' views. **2** somebody who makes little effort at work because they are just passing the time until they retire or leave.

timeshare *noun* **1** = TIME-SHARING. **2** a share in a property under a time-sharing scheme.

time-sharing *noun* a method of sharing holiday accommodation whereby each of a number of people buys a share of a lease on a property, entitling them to spend a proportionate amount of time there each year.

time sheet *noun* **1** a sheet for recording an employee's starting and finishing times each day or on each job. **2** a sheet for summarizing hours worked by each worker during a pay period.

time signature *noun* a sign placed on a musical staff or stave, being a fraction with the denominator indicating the kind of note taken as the unit for the beat and the numerator indicating the number of units per bar.

time switch *noun* an electrical switch that operates automatically at a set time.

timetable[1] *noun* **1** a schedule showing a planned order or sequence of events, *esp* of classes, e.g. in a school. **2** a table of departure and arrival times of public transport.

timetable[2] *verb trans* to arrange or provide for (something) in a timetable.

time travel *noun* in science fiction, travel to another time, either in the past or in the future.

time trial *noun* a race against the clock, *esp* in bicycle racing, in which competitors are successively timed over a set distance or in which distance travelled is measured for a set time.

time value *noun* in music, the duration of a note in comparison with other notes: *A minim has half the time value of a semibreve.*

time warp *noun* an imaginary distortion of time in which the usual rules governing its progression do not apply.

timeworn *adj* **1** worn or impaired by time. **2** ancient; age-old.

time zone *noun* a geographical region within which the same standard time is used.

timid /'timid/ *adj* (**timider, timidest**) lacking in courage, boldness, or self-confidence. ⋙ **timidity** /ti'miditi/ *noun,* **timidly** *adv,* **timidness** *noun.* [Latin *timidus,* from *timēre* to fear]

timing *noun* selection for maximum effect of the precise moment for doing something.

timocracy /tie'mokrǝsi/ *noun* (*pl* **timocracies**) **1** government in which a certain amount of property is necessary for office. **2** government in which love of honour is the ruling principle. ⋙ **timocratic** /·'kratik/ *adj.* [early French *tymocracie* via Latin from Greek *timokratia,* from *timē* price, value, honour + *-kratia* -CRACY]

Timorese /tiǝ'reez/ *noun* (*pl* **Timorese**) a native or inhabitant of the island of Timor in the Malay Archipelago. ⋙ **Timorese** *adj.*

timorous /'tim(ǝ)rǝs/ *adj* timid or nervous. ⋙ **timorously** *adv,* **timorousness** *noun.* [Middle English via French, ultimately from Latin *timor* fear]

timothy *noun* a European grass widely grown for hay: *Phleum pratense.* [prob named after *Timothy* Hanson, 18th-cent. US farmer said to have introduced it from New England to the southern states of the USA]

timpani *or* **tympani** /'timpǝni/ *pl noun* a set of two or three kettledrums played by one performer, e.g. in an orchestra. ⋙ **timpanist** *noun.* [Italian *timpani,* pl of *timpano* kettledrum, from Latin *tympanum* drum, from Greek *tympanon*]

tin[1] /tin/ *noun* **1** a silvery lustrous metallic element that is malleable and ductile at ordinary temperatures, occurs naturally in various ores, and is used for plating and in alloys: symbol Sn, atomic number 50. **2** *chiefly Brit.* **a** a hermetically sealed tinplate or aluminium container for preserving foods. **b** the contents of a tin or the quantity contained in a tin. **3** a tinplate or aluminium container in which food is cooked, *esp* in an oven: *a loaf tin.* **4** (*used before a noun*). **a** made of tin or metal coated with tin. **b** made of corrugated iron: *a tin roof.* **c** made of lead or other metal: *a tin soldier.* ⋙ **tinful** (*pl* **tinfuls**) *noun.* [Old English *tin*]

tin[2] *verb trans* (**tinned, tinning**) **1** *chiefly Brit* to can (food). **2** to cover or plate (something) with tin or a tin alloy. ⋙ **tinned** *adj.*

tinamou /'tinǝmooh/ *noun* (*pl* **tinamous** *or collectively* **tinamou**) any of various small to medium-sized game birds of Central and S America: family Tinamidae. [French *tinamou* from Galibi *tinamu*]

tinctorial /tingk'tawri·ǝl/ *adj* of colours, dyeing, or staining. [Latin *tinctorius,* from *tingere* TINGE[1]]

tincture[1] /'ting(k)chǝ/ *noun* **1** a solution of a substance in alcohol for medicinal use: *tincture of iodine.* **2** a slight addition; a trace. **3** a heraldic metal, colour, or fur. **4a** a substance that colours or stains. **b** a colour or hue. [Middle English from Latin *tinctura* act of dyeing, from *tingere* TINGE[1]]

tincture[2] *verb trans* (*usu in passive*) to tint or stain (something) with a colour.

tinder /'tindǝ/ *noun* any combustible substance suitable for use as kindling. ⋙ **tindery** *adj.* [Old English *tynder*]

tinderbox *noun* **1** formerly, a metal box for holding tinder and usu a flint and steel for striking a spark. **2** a potentially unstable place, situation, or person.

tine /tien/ *noun* **1** a prong, e.g. of a fork. **2** a pointed branch of an antler. ⋙ **tined** *adj.* [Old English *tind*]

tinea /'tini·ǝ/ *noun* a fungal disease of the skin, *esp* ringworm. ⋙ **tineal** *adj.* [Middle English from Latin *tinea* worm, moth]

tinfoil *noun* a thin metal sheeting of tin, aluminium, or a tin alloy.

ting[1] /ting/ *verb intrans* to make a high-pitched sound like that made by a light tap on a crystal goblet. [Middle English *tingen,* of imitative origin]

ting[2] *noun* a tinging sound.

ting-a-ling /'tingə'ling/ *noun* a light ringing sound, as of a small bell.

tinge[1] /'tinj/ *verb trans* (**tingeing** *or* **tinging**) **1** to colour (something) with a slight shade. **2** to impart a slight smell, taste, or other quality to (something). [Middle English *tingen* from Latin *tingere* to dip, moisten, tinge]

tinge[2] *noun* **1** a slight modifying quality; a trace. **2** a slight staining or suffusing colour.

tin glaze *noun* an opaque ceramic glaze containing tin oxide.

tingle[1] /'tinggl/ *verb intrans* to feel or cause a stinging, prickling, or thrilling sensation. ➤➤ **tingly** *adj*. [Middle English *tinglen*, alteration of *tinklen*: see TINKLE[1]]

tingle[2] *noun* a tingling sensation.

tin god *noun* **1** a pompous and self-important person. **2** somebody who is unjustifiably esteemed or venerated.

tin hat *noun chiefly Brit, informal* a metal military helmet.

tinker[1] /'tingkə/ *noun* **1** an itinerant mender of household utensils. **2** *Brit, usu derog* a gypsy. **3** *Brit, informal* a mischievous child, dog, etc. [Middle English *tinkere*, first recorded as a surname; earlier history unknown]

tinker[2] *verb intrans* (**tinkered, tinkering**) (+ with) to repair, adjust, or work with something in an unskilled or experimental manner: *He's tinkering with the engine.* ➤➤ **tinkerer** *noun*.

tinker's cuss *or* **tinker's damn** ✳ **not give a tinker's cuss/damn** *informal* not to care at all. [prob from the tinkers' reputation for swearing]

tinkle[1] /'tingkl/ *verb intrans* **1** to make a tinkle. **2** *informal* to urinate. ➤ *verb trans* **1** to cause (something) to tinkle. **2** *said of a clock:* to make (the time) known by a tinkle. ➤➤ **tinkly** *adj*. [Middle English *tinklen* to tinkle, tingle, frequentative of *tinken* to tinkle, of imitative origin]

tinkle[2] *noun* **1** a series of short light ringing or clinking sounds. **2** *Brit, informal* a telephone call. **3** *informal* the act or an instance of urinating.

tin Lizzie *noun chiefly NAmer, informal, dated* an old or dilapidated car.

tinner *noun* a tin miner or tinsmith.

tinnitus /'tinitəs, ti'nietəs/ *noun* a ringing or roaring sensation in the ears that has no external cause. [Latin *tinnitus* ringing, tinnitus, past part. of *tinnire* to ring, of imitative origin]

tinny[1] *adj* (**tinnier, tinniest**) **1** of, containing, or yielding tin. **2** having a thin metallic sound. **3a** not solid or durable; shoddy: *a tinny car.* **b** having the taste, smell, or appearance of tin. **4** *Aus, NZ, informal* lucky. ➤➤ **tinnily** *adv*, **tinniness** *noun*.

tinny[2] *noun* (*pl* **tinnies**) *Aus, NZ, informal* a can of beer.

tin opener *noun Brit* a tool for opening tins.

Tin Pan Alley *noun* **1** a district that is a centre for composers and publishers of popular music. **2** the body of such composers and publishers. **3** the type of songs purveyed by such publishers.

Word history

orig applied to a district in New York, later to Denmark Street in Central London, both then centres of popular music publishing. The term prob derives from jazz musicians' slang *tin pan* an inferior, tinny piano.

tinplate *noun* thin sheet iron or steel coated with tin.

tin-plate *verb trans* to plate or coat (e.g. a metal sheet) with tin.

tin-pot *adj informal* paltry or inferior: *a tin-pot little organization.*

tinsel[1] /'tins(ə)l/ *noun* **1** a thread, strip, or sheet of metal, plastic, or paper used to produce a glittering and sparkling effect, e.g. in decorations. **2** something superficial, showy, or glamorous: *Strip away the phony tinsel of Hollywood and you find the real tinsel underneath* — Oscar Levant. ➤➤ **tinselled** *adj*. [Middle English from early French *estincelle* spark, glitter, spangle, from Latin *scintilla* spark]

tinsel[2] *adj* cheaply gaudy; tawdry.

Tinseltown *noun derog* Hollywood.

tinsmith *noun* somebody who works with sheet metal, e.g. tinplate.

tin soldier *noun* a toy soldier made of lead or some other metal.

tinstone *noun* = CASSITERITE.

tint[1] /tint/ *noun* **1a** any of various lighter or darker shades of a colour, *esp* one produced by adding white. **b** a usu slight or pale coloration; a hue. **2** hair dye. **3** a panel of light colour serving as background for printing on. **4** a shaded effect in engraving produced by fine parallel lines close together. **5** a small quantity or degree; a drop. [alteration of earlier *tinct*, from Latin *tinctus* act of dyeing, from *tingere* TINGE[1]]

tint[2] *verb trans* to apply a tint to (something); to colour (it). ➤➤ **tinter** *noun*.

tintinnabulation /,tintinabyoo'laysh(ə)n/ *noun formal* **1** the ringing of bells. **2** a sound resembling that of bells. [Latin *tintinnabulum* bell, from *tintinnare* to ring, jingle, of imitative origin]

tin whistle *noun* = PENNY WHISTLE.

tiny[1] /'tieni/ *adj* (**tinier, tiniest**) very small or diminutive: *Sometimes you can tell a large story with a tiny subject* — Eliot Porter. ➤➤ **tinily** *adv*, **tininess** *noun*. [alteration of Middle English *tine*, of unknown origin]

tiny[2] *noun* (*pl* **tinies**) *informal* a very young child.

tip[1] /tip/ *noun* **1** the pointed end of something. **2** a small piece or part serving as an end, cap, or point: *a filter tip.* ✳ **on the tip of one's tongue 1** about to be uttered: *It was on the tip of my tongue to tell him exactly what I thought.* **2** not quite remembered: *Her name's on the tip of my tongue.* [Middle English from Old Norse *typpi*]

tip[2] *verb trans* (**tipped, tipping**) **1a** to supply (something) with a tip. **b** to cover or adorn the tip of (something). **2** (+ in) to attach (an insert) in a book. ➤➤ **tipped** *adj*.

tip[3] *verb* (**tipped, tipping**) ➤ *verb trans* **1** (*often* + over) to overturn or upset (something). **2** to cant or tilt (something). **3** *Brit* to deposit or transfer (rubbish, coal, etc) by tilting. ➤ *verb intrans* **1** (*often* + over) to topple. **2** to lean or slant. ➤➤ **tipper** *noun*. [Middle English *tipen*; earlier history unknown]

tip[4] *noun* **1** *Brit* a place for tipping something, e.g. rubbish or coal; a dump. **2** *informal* a messy place.

tip[5] *noun* a sum of money given in appreciation of a service performed. [prob from TIP[9]]

tip[6] *verb trans* (**tipped, tipping**) to give (somebody) a tip: *She tipped the waiter a pound.* ➤➤ **tipper** *noun*.

tip[7] *noun* **1** a piece of useful or expert information. **2** a piece of inside information which, acted upon, may bring financial gain, e.g. by betting or investment. [prob from TIP[5]]

tip[8] *verb trans* (**tipped, tipping**) *Brit* to mention (somebody or something) as a prospective winner, success, or profitable investment.

tip[9] *verb trans* (**tipped, tipping**) to strike (somebody) lightly. [Middle English *tippe* light blow, tap]

tip off *verb trans* to give a tip-off to (somebody): *The police were tipped off about the raid.*

tip-off *noun informal* a tip given usu as a warning.

tipper *noun* a lorry, trailer, etc whose body can be tipped on its chassis to empty the contents.

tippet /'tipit/ *noun* **1** a shoulder cape of fur or cloth often with hanging ends. **2** a long black scarf worn over the surplice by Anglican clergymen during morning and evening prayer. **3** a long hanging end of cloth attached to a sleeve, cap, or hood, *esp* in the 16th cent. [Middle English *tipet*; prob from TIP[1]]

Tipp-Ex[1] /'tipeks/ *noun Brit, trademark* correction fluid. [German, from *tippen* to type + Latin *ex* out]

Tipp-Ex[2] *verb trans* (*often* + out) to blot out (something typed or written) with correction fluid.

tipple[1] /'tipl/ *verb intrans* to drink alcohol, *esp* continuously in small amounts. ➤➤ **tippler** *noun*. [orig as *tippler*, in the obsolete sense 'seller of drink', perhaps of Scandinavian origin]

tipple[2] *noun informal* an alcoholic drink.

tipstaff *noun* an officer in certain law courts. [orig in the sense 'staff tipped with metal' (carried by a bailiff), contraction of *tipped staff*]

tipster /'tipstə/ *noun* somebody who gives or sells tips, *esp* for gambling or speculation.

tipsy /'tipsi/ *adj* (**tipsier, tipsiest**) **1** slightly drunk. **2** askew: *The gate was leaning at a tipsy angle.* ➤➤ **tipsily** *adv*, **tipsiness** *noun*. [from TIP[3]]

tipsy cake *noun Brit* a sponge cake soaked in wine or sherry and decorated with fruit and nuts.

tiptoe[1] *verb intrans* **1** to stand or walk on tiptoe. **2** to walk silently or stealthily with one's heels off the ground.

tiptoe[2] *noun* the tip of a toe, or the ends of the toes: *She was walking on tiptoe.*

tiptoe[3] *adv* on tiptoe.

tiptoe[4] *adj* standing or walking on tiptoe.

tip-top[1] *adj* excellent or first-rate: *in tip-top condition.*

tip-top[2] *adv* in a first-rate manner.

tip-top[3] *noun* the highest point or degree.

tip-up *adj* denoting a seat that can be tipped up when not in use.

TIR *abbr* International Road Transport. [French *Transports Internationaux Routiers*]

tirade /tie'rayd/ *noun* a long vehement speech or denunciation. [French *tirade* shot, tirade, from Old Italian *tirata*, from *tirare* to draw or shoot]

tiramisu /ˌtirəmi'sooh/ *noun* an Italian dessert made from layers of sponge cake soaked in coffee and Marsala, with mascarpone cheese and powdered chocolate. [Italian *tiramisu*, from *tira mi sù* pick me up]

tire[1] /tie·ə/ *verb trans* **1** to fatigue (somebody). **2** to wear out the patience of (somebody) ⟫ *verb intrans* **1** to become tired. **2** (+ of) to become bored or wearied: *Death will find me long before I tire of watching you* — Rupert Brooke. [Old English *tēorian, tȳrian*]

tire[2] *noun NAmer* see TYRE.

tired *adj* **1** weary; fatigued. **2** (+ of) exasperated; FED UP: *I'm tired of listening to your complaints.* **3a** trite; hackneyed: *the same old tired themes.* **b** lacking freshness: *a tired skin.* ⟫ **tiredly** *adv,* **tiredness** *noun.*

tireless *adj* indefatigable; untiring. ⟫ **tirelessly** *adv,* **tirelessness** *noun.*

tiresome /'tie·əs(ə)m/ *adj* wearisome; tedious. ⟫ **tiresomely** *adv,* **tiresomeness** *noun.*

tirewoman /'tie·əwoomən/ *noun archaic* a lady's maid. [Old English *tire* attire]

tiro /'tieroh/ *noun* (*pl* **tiros**) see TYRO.

'tis /tiz/ *contraction* it is: *'Tis strange what a man may do, and a woman yet think him an angel* — Thackeray.

tisane /ti'zan/ *noun* an infusion of dried herbs used as a beverage or for medicinal effects. [Middle English via French and Latin from Greek *ptisanē*, literally 'crushed barley']

tissue /'tishooh, 'tisyooh/ *noun* **1** a cluster of cells, usu of a particular kind, together with their intercellular substance that form any of the structural materials of a plant or animal. **2** = TISSUE PAPER. **3** a paper handkerchief. **4a** a fine gauzy sheer fabric. **b** a web or network: *a tissue of lies.* ⟫ **tissuey** *adj.* [Middle English *tissu* a rich fabric, from early French *tissu* woven, ultimately from Latin *texere* to weave]

tissue culture *noun* **1** the process or technique of growing fragments of body tissue in a sterile nourishing medium outside the organism. **2** the product of such a process.

tissue paper *noun* a thin gauzy paper used *esp* for wrapping delicate objects.

tissue type *noun* the particular set of histocompatibility antigens displayed by an individual.

tissue-type *verb trans* to identify the tissue type of (an individual) in order to assess its compatibility with tissue from another source, *esp* in preparation for an organ transplant.

Tit. *abbr* Titus (book of the Bible).

tit[1] /tit/ *noun* any of numerous species of small tree-dwelling birds that live on insects: family Paridae. [short for TITMOUSE]

tit[2] *noun* **1** *coarse slang* a woman's breast. **2** a teat or nipple. **3** *Brit, informal* a stupid or despicable person. [Old English *tit*]

titan /'tiet(ə)n/ *noun* **1** somebody or something that is very large or strong. **2** somebody who is notable for outstanding achievement. [named after the *Titans*, a family of giants in Greek mythology who once ruled the earth]

titaness /'tiet(ə)nes/ *noun* a female titan.

titanic[1] /tie'tanik/ *adj* colossal or gigantic. ⟫ **titanically** *adv.* [Greek *titanikos* of the Titans: see TITAN]

titanic[2] *adj* of or containing titanium, *esp* when tetravalent. [scientific Latin *titanium*]

titanium /ti'tayni·əm/ *noun* a grey metallic chemical element that is light and strong, and is used in alloys and in aircraft manufacture etc: symbol Ti, atomic number 22. [scientific Latin *titanium* from Greek *Titan*: see TITAN]

titanium dioxide *or* **titanium oxide** *noun* a white oxide of titanium that is widely used as a pigment.

titanous /'tie'tanəs/ *adj* of or containing titanium, *esp* when trivalent.

titbit /'titbit/ (*NAmer* **tidbit** /'tidbit/) *noun* a choice or pleasing piece, e.g. of food or news. [dialect *tit, tid* tender + BIT[1]]

titchy /'tichi/ *adj* (**titchier, titchiest**) *Brit, informal* small or short.

Word history ───────────────
tich, titch small person or thing, from *Little Tich,* stage-name of Harry Ralph d.1928, English comedian, who was very small. Ralph got his nickname from his resemblance to Arthur Orton, known as *the Tichborne claimant,* who in 1866 claimed to be Roger Tichborne, heir to an English baronetcy, believed to have been lost at sea. Orton lost his case and was imprisoned for perjury.
─────────────────────────

titer /'tietə, 'teetə/ *noun NAmer* see TITRE.

titfer /'titfə/ *noun Brit, informal* a hat. [rhyming slang *tit for* (*tat*)]

tit for tat /tat/ *noun* an equivalent given in retaliation, e.g. for an injury or insult. [alteration of earlier *tip for tap,* from *tip* a light blow + FOR[1] + TAP[1]]

tithe[1] /tiedh/ *noun* **1** a tax or contribution of a tenth part of something, e.g. income, for the support of a religious establishment or other charitable work, *esp* such a tax formerly due in an English parish to support its church. **2** *archaic* a tenth. [Old English *teogotha* tenth]

tithe[2] *verb trans* **1** to levy a tithe on (somebody or something). **2** to give a tithe of (one's income, etc). ⟫ *verb intrans* to tithe income, etc. ⟫ **tithable** *adj.*

tithe barn *noun* formerly, a barn used to hold produce given in tithes.

tithing *noun* a former small administrative division of England apparently orig consisting of ten men with their families. [Old English *tēothung,* from *teogothan, tēothian* to tithe, take one tenth, from *teogotha* tenth, TITHE[1]]

titi /'teetee/ *noun* (*pl* **titis** *or collectively* **titi**) any of several species of small S American monkeys with long soft fur: genus *Callicebus.* [Spanish *tití* from Aymara *titi,* literally 'little cat']

titian /'tish(ə)n/ *adj* (*also* **Titian**) said *esp* of hair: reddish brown. [named after *Titian* (Tiziano Vecelli) d.1576, Italian painter, because he often portrayed auburn-haired people]

titillate /'titilayt/ *verb trans* **1** to excite (somebody) pleasurably; to arouse (them) by stimulation. **2** *archaic* to tickle or caress (somebody). ⟫ **titillating** *adj,* **titillatingly** *adv,* **titillation** /-'laysh(ə)n/ *noun.* [Latin *titillatus,* past part. of *titillare* to tickle]

titivate *or* **tittivate** /'titivayt/ *verb intrans or trans informal* to smarten up (oneself or another). ⟫ **titivation** /-'vaysh(ə)n/ *noun.* [perhaps from TIDY[1] + -*vate* as in RENOVATE]

titlark /'titlahk/ *noun* a pipit, *esp* a meadow pipit. [TIT[1] + LARK[1]]

title[1] /'tietl/ *noun* **1** the distinguishing name of a work of art, e.g. a book, film, or musical composition. **2a** (*usu in pl*) written material introduced into a film or television programme to represent credits, dialogue, or fragments of narrative. **b** a descriptive or general heading, e.g. of a chapter in a book. **c** a title page and the printed matter on it. **3** a literary work as distinguished from a particular copy: *The firm published 25 titles last year.* **4** a descriptive name. **5** a hereditary or acquired appellation given to a person or family as a mark of rank, office, or attainment. **6** designation as champion: *the world heavyweight title.* **7** legal ownership, or a document giving proof of this. **8a** something that justifies or substantiates a claim. **b** an alleged or recognized right. **9a** in the Roman Catholic Church, a titular parish. **b** in the Church of England, a sphere of work or other source of income required before ordination, or a certificate attesting this. [Middle English via early French *title* from Latin *titulus* inscription, title]

title[2] *verb trans* (*usu in passive*) **1** to provide a title for (something). **2** to designate or call (somebody) by a title. ⟫ **titled** *adj.*

title deed *noun* the deed constituting evidence of ownership of property.

titleholder *noun* somebody who holds a title; *specif* a champion in a sporting competition.

title page *noun* a page of a book giving the title, author, publisher, and publication details.

title role *noun* the role in a film, play, etc that has the same name as the title of the production.

titmouse *noun* (*pl* **titmice** /'titmies/) = TIT[1]. [Middle English *titmose*, from *tit* any small object or creature + *mose* titmouse, from Old English *māse*]

titrate /tie'trayt/ *verb trans and intrans* to subject (a substance) to titration. ➤ **titratable** *adj*. [French *titrer*, from *titre*: see TITRE]

titration /tie'traysh(ə)n/ *noun* a method or the process of determining the strength of, or the concentration of a substance in, a solution by finding the amount of test liquid needed to bring about a complete reaction with a liquid of known concentration.

titre (*NAmer* **titer**) /'tietə, 'teetə/ *noun* the strength of a solution or the concentration of a substance in solution as determined by titration. [French *titre* title, proportion of gold or silver in a coin, from Old French *title*: see TITLE[1]]

titter[1] /'titə/ *verb intrans* (**tittered, tittering**) to giggle or snigger. ➤ **titterer** *noun*, **tittering** *adj and noun*. [imitative]

titter[2] *noun* a giggle or snigger.

tittivate /'titivayt/ *verb trans and intrans* see TITIVATE.

tittle /'titl/ *noun* **1** a very small part. **2** a point or small sign used as a diacritical mark in writing or printing. [Middle English *titel* from a medieval Latin sense 'accent, small mark', of Latin TITLE[1]]

tittle-tattle[1] /'titltatl/ *noun* gossip. [reduplication of TATTLE[2]]

tittle-tattle[2] /'tatl/ *verb intrans* to gossip or prattle.

tittup[1] /'titəp/ *verb intrans* (**tittuped, tittuping**) *chiefly Brit* to move in a lively prancing manner. [imitative of the sound of a horse's hooves]

tittup[2] *noun chiefly Brit* a lively or spirited movement; a prance or caper.

titty /'titi/ *noun* (*pl* **titties**) *informal* = TIT[2].

titubate /'tityoobayt/ *verb intrans technical* to reel or totter as if drunk. ➤ **titubation** /-'baysh(ə)n/ *noun*. [Latin *titubatus*, past part. of *titubare* to totter]

titular[1] /'tityoolə/ *adj* **1** of or constituting a title: *the titular hero of the play*. **2** in title only; nominal: *He was the titular head of the party but without power*. **3** denoting any of the churches in Rome to which cardinals or bishops are attached. ➤ **titularly** *adv*. [Latin *titulus* TITLE[1]]

titular[2] *noun* somebody holding a title or titular position.

tiyin /'tee'yin/ *noun* (*pl* **tiyin** *or* **tiyins**) a unit of currency in Uzbekistan and Kyrgystan, worth 100th of a som.

tizzy /'tizi/ *or* **tizz** /'tiz/ *noun* (*pl* **tizzies** *or* **tizzes**) *informal* a highly excited and confused state of mind. [origin unknown]

TJ *abbr* Tajikistan (international vehicle registration).

T junction *or* **T-junction** *noun* a junction formed by one road joining another at right angles.

TKO *abbr* technical knockout.

Tl *abbr* the chemical symbol for thallium.

TLC *abbr informal* tender loving care.

Tlingit /'tlinggit, 'klingkit/ *noun* (*pl* **Tlingits** *or collectively* **Tlingit**) **1** a member of a Native American people of SE Alaska. **2** the Na-Dené language of this people. ➤ **Tlingit** *adj*. [Tlingit, literally 'person']

T lymphocyte *noun* = T-CELL.

TM *abbr* **1** transcendental meditation. **2** Turkmenistan (international vehicle registration).

Tm *abbr* the chemical symbol for thulium.

tmesis /'tmeesis/ *noun* (*pl* **tmeses** /'tmeeseez/) separation of parts of a word, usu a grammatical compound, by another word or words, e.g. in *every-bloody-where* or *abso-blooming-lutely*. [via late Latin from Greek *tmēsis* act of cutting, from *temnein* to cut]

TN *abbr* **1** Tennessee (US postal abbreviation). **2** Tunisia (international vehicle registration).

TNT *noun* trinitrotoluene. [*trinitrotoluene*]

to[1] /tooh; *unstressed preceding vowels* too, *unstressed preceding consonants* tə/ *prep* **1** used to indicate a terminal point or destination, e.g.: **a** a place where a physical movement or an action or condition suggestive of movement ends: *a drive to the city*. **b** a direction: *the road to London*. **c** a terminal point in measuring or reckoning or in a statement of extent or limits: *It's ten miles to the nearest town; I'm wet to the skin*. **d** a point in time before which a period is reckoned:

five minutes to five. **e** a point of contact or proximity: *I pinned the brooch to my coat*. **f** a purpose, result, or end: *It just came to pieces in my hand; much to my surprise*. **g** the one to or for which something exists or is done or directed: *She's always kind to animals; I said so in my letter to John*. **2** used to indicate: **a** addition, connection, or possession: *Add 17 to 20; I've lost the key to the door*. **b** accompaniment or response: *We danced to live music*. **3** used to indicate relationship or conformity, e.g.: **a** relative position: *next door to me*. **b** proportion or composition: *She won by 17 points to 11*. **c** correspondence to a standard: *true to type*. **4a** used to introduce or stand for an infinitive form of a verb: *I have work to do; She knows more than she used to*. **b** used to denote purpose: *He did it to annoy them*. [Old English *tō*]

Usage note

to, too, *or* **two?** Being pronounced the same, these three words are sometimes confused. *To* is mainly used as a preposition (*to the top of the hill*) and in forming the infinitive of a verb (*to make*). *Too* is the adverb that means 'overmuch' and usually precedes an adjective (*too difficult for me*). It also means 'as well', in which case it often comes at the end of a sentence (*Can Jenny come too?*). *Two* is the number between one and three (*Two and two make four*).

to[2] *adv* **1** said of a door or window: into contact, *esp* with the frame; shut: *The door slammed to*. **2a** used to indicate direction towards. **b** close to the wind. **3** back into consciousness or awareness: *He brought her to with smelling salts*. ✳ **to and fro** from one place to another; back and forth.

toad /tohd/ *noun* **1** a tailless leaping amphibian that differs from the related frogs by living more on land and in having a shorter squatter body with a rough, dry, and warty skin: order Anura. **2** a loathsome and contemptible person. ➤ **toadish** *adj*. [Middle English *tode* from Old English *tāde, tādige*]

toadfish *noun* (*pl* **toadfishes** *or collectively* **toadfish**) any of various fishes with a large thick head and a wide mouth: family Batrachoididae.

toadflax *noun* any of several species of common Eurasian perennial plants of the figwort family typically having showy yellow and orange flowers: genus *Linaria* and other genera.

toad-in-the-hole *noun Brit* a dish of sausages baked in batter.

toadstone *noun* an object, e.g. a stone, supposed to have been formed in the body of a toad and formerly worn as a charm or as an antidote to poison.

toadstool *noun* a poisonous or inedible umbrella-shaped fungus: compare MUSHROOM[1]. [Middle English *todestool* from *tode*: see TOAD + STOOL[1]]

toady[1] *noun* (*pl* **toadies**) a sycophant. ➤ **toadyish** *adj*, **toadyism** *noun*. [from earlier *toadeater* mountebank's assistant who pretended to eat poisonous toads to prove the value of his master's antidote, hence a servile dependant, a sycophant]

toady[2] *verb intrans* (**toadies, toadied, toadying**) to behave as a toady; to be obsequious: *He toadies to his superiors*.

to-and-fro[1] *noun* activity involving alternating movement forward and backward.

to-and-fro[2] *adj* involving alternating movement forward and backward: *a to-and-fro motion*.

to-and-fro[3] *verb intrans* (**toing-and-froing**) to move to and fro; to come and go: *She watched the crowds of shoppers toing-and-froing in the street below*.

toast[1] /tohst/ *noun* **1** sliced bread browned on both sides by heat. **2a** the act or an instance of drinking in honour of somebody or something. **b** something in honour of which people drink. **c** a highly popular or admired person: *She's the toast of London*. [TOAST[2]; (sense 2) from the use of pieces of spiced toast to flavour drinks]

toast[2] *verb trans* **1** to make (bread, etc) crisp, hot, and brown by heat. **2** to warm (oneself, one's feet, etc) thoroughly, e.g. at a fire. ➤ *verb intrans* to become toasted, *esp* to become thoroughly warm. [Middle English *tosten* to burn, parch, via Old French from Latin *tostus*, past part. of *torrēre* to dry or parch]

toast[3] *verb trans* to drink to (somebody or something) as a toast. [TOAST[1]]

toast[4] *verb intrans* said of a DJ: to provide rap vocals over a pre-recorded music track, *esp* a reggae track. [perhaps from TOAST[2]]

toaster *noun* **1** an electrical appliance for toasting *esp* bread. **2** a DJ who toasts.

toastie /'tohsti/ *noun Brit, informal* a toasted sandwich.

toasting fork *noun* a long-handled fork on which bread is held for toasting in front of a fire.

toastmaster *noun* somebody who presides at a banquet, proposes toasts, and introduces after-dinner speakers.

toastmistress *noun* a female toastmaster.

Tob. *abbr* Tobit (book of the Apocrypha).

tobacco /tə'bakoh/ *noun* (*pl* **tobaccos** *or collectively* **tobacco**) **1** any of a number of chiefly American plants of the nightshade family, *esp* a tall erect annual S American herb cultivated for its leaves: genus *Nicotiana*. **2** the leaves of cultivated tobacco prepared for use in smoking or chewing or as snuff. [Spanish *tabaco*, prob from a Taino word for a roll of tobacco leaves smoked by the Indians of the Antilles at the time of Columbus]

tobacco mosaic *noun* any of several mosaic virus diseases of plants of the nightshade family, *esp* tobacco.

tobacconist /tə'bakənist/ *noun chiefly Brit* somebody who sells tobacco, *esp* in a shop. [irreg from TOBACCO + -IST[1]]

Tobagan /tə'baygən/ *noun* a native or inhabitant of the island of Tobago. ⪢ **Tobagan** *noun*.

to-be *adj* (*used after a noun, in combination*) future: *the bride-to-be.*

toboggan[1] /tə'bogən/ *noun* a long light sledge, usu curved up at the front and used for gliding downhill over snow or ice. [Canadian French *tobogan*, of Algonquian origin]

toboggan[2] *verb intrans* (**tobogganed, tobogganing**) to ride on a toboggan. ⪢ **tobogganist** *noun.*

toby /'tohbi/ *noun* (*pl* **tobies**) a small jug or mug generally used for beer and shaped like a stout man with a cocked hat for the brim. [*Toby*, nickname for *Tobias*; said to come from an 18th-cent. poem about one *Toby* Philpott, who enjoyed tippling]

toby jug *noun* = TOBY.

toccata /tə'kahtə/ *noun* (*pl* **toccatas**) a musical composition in a free idiomatic style and characterized by rapid runs, usu for a keyboard instrument. [Italian *toccata*, fem past part. of *toccare* to touch]

Toc H /,tok 'aych/ *noun* a Christian society for fellowship and charitable work, founded in Ypres in 1915 by Rev. P. T. B. Clayton. [*toc* (signallers' former code word for the letter *t*) + *h*, initials of *Talbot House*, name of club from which the society developed]

Tocharian *or* **Tokharian** /to'kahri-ən/ *noun* **1** a member of a people possibly of European origin inhabiting central Asia during the first millennium AD. **2** an extinct Indo-European language of central Asia. ⪢ **Tocharian** *adj*, **Tokharian** *adj*. [Latin *Tochari* (pl) from Greek *Tocharoi*, the name of a Scythian tribe]

tocopherol /to'kofərol/ *noun* any of several fat-soluble compounds found *esp* in leaves and oils made from seeds, whose lack leads to infertility and the degeneration of muscle in many vertebrate animals; vitamin E. [Greek *tokos* childbirth, offspring + *pherein* to carry or bear + -OL[1]]

tocsin /'toksin/ *noun archaic* an alarm bell rung as a warning. [early French *toquassen* from Old Provençal *tocasenh*, from *tocar* to touch + *senh* signal bell]

tod /tod/ ✱ **on one's tod** *Brit, informal* alone. [rhyming slang *Tod (Sloan)* own, alone, prob from the nickname of James Forman (*Tod*) *Sloan* d.1933, US jockey]

today[1] /tə'day/ *adv* **1** on this day. **2** at the present time or age. [Old English *tōdæge, tōdæg*, from *tō* TO[1], at + *dæge*, dative of *dæg* DAY]

today[2] *noun* **1** this day. **2** the present time or age: *the youth of today.*

toddle[1] /'todl/ *verb intrans* **1** said of a very young child: to walk unsteadily. **2** *informal*. **a** to take a stroll; to saunter. **b** (+ off) to depart: *I'll just toddle off home.* [origin unknown]

toddle[2] *noun* the act or an instance of toddling.

toddler *noun* a very young child who is just learning to walk.

toddy /'todi/ *noun* (*pl* **toddies**) **1** a hot drink consisting of whisky or other spirits mixed with water, sugar, and spices. **2** the sap of certain palm trees, fermented into an alcoholic drink. [Hindi *tāṛī* juice of the palmyra palm, from *tāṛ* palmyra palm, from Sanskrit *tāla*]

todger /'tojə/ *noun Brit, slang* see TADGER.

to-do *noun* (*pl* **to-dos**) *informal* bustle or fuss.

toe[1] /toh/ *noun* **1** any of the digits at the end of a human's or animal's foot. **2a** the fore end of a foot or hoof. **b** the front of

something worn on the foot. **3** a part like a toe in position or form: *the toe of Italy.* ✱ **on one's toes** alert; ready to act. [Old English *tā*]

toe[2] *verb* ⪢ *verb trans* **1** to provide (a shoe) with a toe, *esp* to renew the toe of (it). **2** to touch, reach, or drive (somebody or something) with the toe. ⪢ *verb intrans* (+ in/out) to walk with the toes pointed in or out. ✱ **toe the line** to conform rigorously to a rule or standard.

toea /'toh·ə/ *noun* (*pl* **toea**) a unit of currency in Papua New Guinea, worth 100th of a kina. [Motu *toea*, literally 'cone-shaped shell']

toe cap *noun* a piece of steel or leather attached to the toe of a shoe or boot to reinforce or decorate it.

toed *adj* (*used in combinations*) having a toe or toes, *esp* of a specified kind or number: *five-toed; square-toed shoes.*

toehold *noun* **1a** a hold or place of support for the toes, e.g. in climbing. **b** a slight footing: *The firm had a toehold in the export market.* **2** a wrestling hold in which the aggressor bends or twists their opponent's foot.

toe-in *noun* adjustment of the front wheels of a motor vehicle so that they are closer together at the front than at the back.

toenail *noun* the nail of a toe.

toerag *noun Brit, informal* a despicable person. [from the rags wrapped round a tramp's feet in place of socks]

toff /tof/ *noun chiefly Brit, derog* a rich or upper-class person. [prob alteration of TUFT[1], in the sense 'a titled undergraduate', from the gold tassel on the caps formerly worn by titled undergraduates at Oxford and Cambridge]

toffee *or* **toffy** /'tofi/ *noun* (*pl* **toffees** *or* **toffies**) a sweet with a texture ranging from chewy to brittle, made by boiling sugar, water, and often butter. ✱ **not for toffee** *informal* not at all well: *She can't play the piano for toffee.* [alteration of TAFFY]

toffee-apple *noun* a toffee-covered apple held on a stick.

toffee-nosed *adj chiefly Brit, informal* stuck-up.

toffy /'tofi/ *noun* (*pl* **toffies**) see TOFFEE.

toft /toft/ *noun archaic* an entire holding comprising a homestead and additional land. [Old English, from Old Norse *topt*]

tofu /'tohfooh/ *noun* = BEAN CURD. [Japanese *tōfu*]

tog[1] /tog/ *verb trans* (**togged, togging**) *informal* (+ up/out) to dress (somebody), *esp* in fine clothing: *She was all togged up for the office party.* [TOGS]

tog[2] *noun* **1** *Brit* a unit of thermal resistance used to measure the insulating properties of a quilt, a garment, etc. **2** (*used before a noun*) of or relating to togs: *tog rating.* [from TOGS, one tog being roughly equivalent to the insulating properties of a single layer of clothing]

toga /'tohgə/ *noun* (*pl* **togas**) a loose outer garment worn in public by citizens of ancient Rome. ⪢ **togaed** /'tohgəd/ *adj.* [Latin *toga*]

together[1] /tə'gedhə/ *adv* **1a** in or into one place, mass, collection, or group: *The men get together every Thursday for poker.* **b** in joint agreement or cooperation; as a group: *Students and staff together presented the petition.* **2a** in or into contact, e.g. connection, collision, or union: *Mix these ingredients together; Tie the ends together.* **b** in or into association, relationship, or harmony: *We need to choose colours that go well together.* **3a** at one time; simultaneously: *Everything happened together.* **b** in succession; without intermission: *She was depressed for days together.* **4a** to or with each other: *His eyes are too close together.* **b** used as an intensive after certain verbs: *Add these numbers together; You can confer together.* **c** considered as a unit; collectively: *These arguments taken together make a convincing case.* ✱ **together with** with the addition of. [Old English *togædere*, from *tō* TO[1] + *gædere* together]

together[2] *adj informal* self-possessed and emotionally stable: *She's a very together person.*

togetherness *noun* **1** the feeling of belonging together. **2** the state of being together.

toggery /'togəri/ *noun informal* clothing.

toggle[1] /'tog(ə)l/ *noun* **1** a piece or device for holding or securing, *esp* a crosspiece attached to a loop in a chain, rope, line, etc, to prevent slipping, to serve as a fastening, or as a grip for tightening. **2a** a toggle joint. **b** a device with a toggle joint. **3** in computing, a key or command for automatically alternating between operations. [origin unknown]

toggle² *verb trans* to provide or fasten (something) with or as if with a toggle. ➤ *verb intrans* (+ between) in computing, to alternate automatically between operations using a toggle.

toggle joint *noun* a device having two bars joined end to end so that when a force is exerted by a screw at the joint, a pressure is exerted along the two bars.

toggle switch *noun* an electric switch that opens or closes a circuit by means of a projecting lever.

Togolese /tohgoh'leez/ *noun* (*pl* **Togolese**) a native or inhabitant of Togo, in W Africa. ➤➤ **Togolese** *adj*.

togs /togz/ *pl noun informal* clothes. [pl of slang *tog* coat, short for obsolete *togeman, togman*, ultimately from Latin *toga* TOGA]

toil¹ /toyl/ *noun* fatiguing labour: *I have nothing to offer but blood, toil, tears and sweat* — Winston Churchill. [Middle English *toile* from Old French *toeil* battle, confusion, from *toeillier* to stir, disturb, dispute, from Latin *tudiculare*: see TOIL²]

toil² *verb intrans* **1** to work hard and long. **2** to proceed with laborious effort: *They were toiling wearily up the hill.* ➤➤ **toiler** *noun*. [Middle English *toilen* to argue or struggle, via Old French from Latin *tudiculare* to crush, grind, from *tudicula* machine for crushing olives, dimin. of *tudes* hammer]

toil³ *noun* (*usu in pl*) something by or with which one is held fast or inextricably involved: *He was caught in the toils of the law.* [early French *toile* cloth, net, from Latin *tela* web, from *texere* to weave or construct]

toile /twahl/ *noun* **1** a muslin model of a garment. **2** a plain or simple twill weave fabric, *esp* linen. [French *toile*: see TOIL³]

toilet /'toylit/ *noun* **1a** a fixture for receiving and disposing of faeces and urine. **b** a room or compartment containing a toilet and sometimes a washbasin. **2** *archaic or literary* the act or process of dressing and grooming oneself: *After making a quick toilet she felt much revived* — Hardy; *a railed shelf, containing combs, brushes, and other implements of the toilet* — Herman Melville. **3** cleansing in association with a medical or surgical procedure. **4** *archaic or literary* a person's attire: *He had not been … half an hour on English soil before he perceived that he was dressed like a rustic, and he had immediately reformed his toilet* — Henry James. [early French *toilette* cloth put over the shoulders while dressing the hair or shaving, dimin. of *toile*: see TOIL³]

toilet paper *noun* a thin absorbent paper for sanitary use after defecation or urination.

toiletry /'toylitri/ *noun* (*pl* **toiletries**) (*usu in pl*) an article or preparation used in washing, grooming, etc.

toilet set *noun* a matching set of items such as a comb, a brush, and a mirror, that are used for keeping one's hair tidy.

toilette /twah'let/ *noun dated* = TOILET (2). [French *toilette* from early French: see TOILET]

toilet tissue *noun* = TOILET PAPER.

toilet-train *verb trans* to give (a young child) toilet training.

toilet training *noun* the process of training a young child to control their bladder and bowel movements and to learn to use the toilet.

toilet water *noun* liquid containing a high percentage of alcohol, used as a light perfume.

toilsome /'toyls(ə)m/ *adj archaic or literary* involving fatiguing labour.

to-ing and fro-ing /ˌtooh·ing ənd 'froh·ing/ *noun* (*pl* **to-ings and fro-ings**) bustling unproductive activity. [TO-AND-FRO¹]

tokamak /'tokəmak/ *noun* an experimental nuclear fusion reactor that consists of a ring-shaped tube through which circulates a plasma of atoms controlled by an electromagnetic field. [Russian *tokamak*, contraction of *toroidal'naya kamera s aksial'nym magnitnym polem* toroidal chamber with axial magnetic field]

Tokay /toh'kay/ *noun* a sweet dark gold wine made near Tokaj in Hungary.

toke¹ /tohk/ *noun informal* a puff on a cigarette or pipe containing marijuana. [possibly from Spanish *tocar* to touch]

toke² *verb trans and intrans informal* to take a puff on (a cigarette or pipe containing marijuana).

token¹ /'tohk(ə)n/ *noun* **1** an outward sign or expression, e.g. of an emotion: *Please accept this book as a token of my gratitude.* **2a** *archaic* something given or shown as a guarantee, e.g. of authority, right, or identity. **b** a souvenir or keepsake. **3** a coinlike piece issued: **a**

for use in place of money, e.g. for a bus fare. **b** as money by anyone other than a government. **4** a certified statement redeemable for a specified form of merchandise to the amount stated thereon: *a book token.* **5** a characteristic mark or feature: *A white flag is a token of surrender.* **6** an instance of a linguistic expression: compare TYPE¹ (5). ✳ **by the same token** furthermore and for the same reason. [Old English *tācen*, *tācn* sign, token]

token² *adj* **1** done or given as a token, *esp* in partial fulfilment of an obligation or engagement: *a token payment.* **2** done or given merely for show: *token resistance.*

tokenism *noun* the making of only a token effort.

token money *noun* money of regular government issue having a greater face value than intrinsic value.

Tokharian /to'kahri·ən/ *noun and adj* see TOCHARIAN.

tokoloshe /tokə'loshi/ *noun* a mischievous or evil spirit in Southern African folklore, usu having the form of a hairy dwarfish man. [Xhosa *utikoloshe*]

Tok Pisin /tok 'pisin/ *noun* = NEO-MELANESIAN. [alteration of *talk pidgin*]

tolar /'tolah/ *noun* the basic monetary unit of Slovenia, divided into 100 stotins. [Slovene *tolar* from German *Taler*: see DOLLAR]

tolbooth /'tolboohth, 'tohlboohth/ *noun* **1** see TOLLBOOTH. **2** *Scot, archaic* a town hall. **3** *Scot, archaic* a jail.

told /tohld/ *verb* past tense and past part. of TELL¹.

tole /tohl/ *noun* brightly painted lacquered or enamelled metal used for decorative objects. [French *tôle* sheet iron]

tolerable /'tol(ə)rəbl/ *adj* **1** capable of being borne or endured: *tolerable pain.* **2** moderately good or agreeable: *a tolerable singing voice.* ➤➤ **tolerability** /-'biliti/ *noun*, **tolerably** *adv*.

tolerance /'tolərəns/ *noun* **1a** the act or fact of allowing something; toleration. **b** indulgence for beliefs or practices differing from one's own. **2** the ability to endure or adapt physiologically to the effects of a drug, virus, radiation, etc. **3** an allowable variation from a standard dimension.

tolerance zone *noun* an area of a city in which prostitution and some forms of drug-taking are tolerated.

tolerant /'tolərənt/ *adj* **1** inclined to tolerate, *esp* marked by forbearance or endurance. **2** exhibiting tolerance, e.g. to a drug or environmental condition. ➤➤ **tolerantly** *adv*.

tolerate /'tolərayt/ *verb trans* **1** to endure or resist the action of (a drug, etc) without grave or lasting injury. **2** to allow or endure (something or somebody) without prohibition, hindrance, or contradiction. ➤➤ **tolerator** *noun*. [Latin *toleratus*, past part. of *tolerare* to endure, put up with]

toleration /tolə'raysh(ə)n/ *noun* **1** the act or practice or an instance of tolerating. **2** a government policy of permitting forms of religious belief and worship not officially established.

toll¹ /tohl/ *noun* **1** a fee paid for some right or privilege, e.g. of passing over a highway or bridge, or for services rendered. **2** a grievous or ruinous price, *esp* cost in life or health: *Her job was very stressful, which took its toll on her health.* [Old English *toll* charge, tax, via Latin from Greek *telōnion* tollhouse, from *telos* tax]

toll² *verb trans* **1** to sound (a bell) by pulling the rope. **2** to signal or announce (something) by or as if by means of a tolled bell. ➤ *verb intrans* said of a bell: to sound with slow measured strokes. [Middle English *tollen*, perhaps from *tollen* to attract, entice]

toll³ *noun* the sound of a tolling bell.

tollbooth *or* **tolbooth** /'tolboohth, 'tohlboohth/ *noun* a booth, e.g. on a bridge, where tolls are paid. [Middle English *tolbothe, tollbothe* tollbooth, town hall, jail, from *tol, toll* TOLL¹ + *bothe* BOOTH]

tollgate *noun* a barrier across a road to prevent passage until a toll is paid.

tollhouse /'tohlhows/ *noun* a house or booth where tolls are paid.

tollie /'toli/ *noun SAfr* a castrated calf. [Afrikaans *tollie* from Zulu *ithole* calf]

Toltec /'toltek/ *noun* a member of a Nahuatlan people of central and S Mexico. ➤➤ **Toltecan** *adj*. [Spanish *tolteca* from Nahuatl *toltecatl* a person from *Tula*, the ancient Toltec capital in central Mexico]

tolu /tə'looh/ *noun* a balsam obtained from a tropical American tree of the pea family and used in making perfumes. [Spanish *tolú*, named after Santiago de *Tolú*, town in Colombia from which it was exported]

toluene /'tolyooeen/ *noun* a toxic inflammable hydrocarbon that is used as a solvent and in organic synthesis. [from TOLU + -ENE]

Tom, Dick, and Harry *or* **Tom, Dick, or Harry** /,tom dik ənd 'hari/ *noun* people taken at random: *Not every Tom, Dick, and Harry can join this club.*

tom /tom/ *noun* **1** the male of various animals, *esp* a tomcat. **2** *Brit* a female prostitute. [*Tom*, nickname for *Thomas*]

tomahawk /'toməhawk/ *noun* a light axe used by Native Americans as a throwing or hand weapon. [*tomahak* (in some Algonquian language of Virginia)]

tomatillo /tohmə'teeoh, tom-, -'teelyoh/ *noun* (*pl* **tomatillos**) **1** an edible, sticky, yellow to purple fruit used e.g. in Mexican cooking. **2** the plant on which this fruit grows; *Physalis ixocarpa*. [Spanish *tomatillo*, dimin. of *tomate* tomato]

tomato /tə'mahtoh/ *noun* (*pl* **tomatoes**) **1** a rounded red, yellow, or green pulpy fruit, used as a vegetable, *esp* in salads. **2** the orig S American plant of the nightshade family that bears this fruit: *Lycopersicon esculentum*. [alteration of *tomate*, via Spanish, French, or Portuguese from Nahuatl *tomatl*]

tomb /toohm/ *noun* **1a** a chamber or vault for the dead, built either above or below ground and usu serving as a memorial. **b** an excavation in which a corpse is buried. **2** (**the tomb**) *literary* the state of being dead. [Middle English *tombe* via Old French and Latin from Greek *tymbos*]

tombola /tom'bohlə/ *noun* *Brit* a lottery in which people buy tickets which may entitle them to a prize. [Italian *tombola* from *tombolare* to tumble, from *tombare* to fall, from vulgar Latin *tumbare* to tumble, fall]

tomboy /'tomboy/ *noun* a girl who behaves in a manner conventionally thought of as typical of a boy. ➤➤ **tomboyish** *adj*, **tomboyishly** *adv*, **tomboyishness** *noun*.

tombstone *noun* = GRAVESTONE.

tomcat *noun* a male cat.

Tom Collins /'kolinz/ *noun* a tall iced drink consisting of a gin base with lime, lemon juice, or soda and sugar. [from the name *Tom Collins*, possibly named after a 19th-cent. London barman]

tome /tohm/ *noun* *formal* a book, *esp* a large scholarly one. [early French *tome* via Latin from Greek *tomos* section, roll of papyrus, tome, from *temnein* to cut]

-tome *comb. form* forming nouns, denoting: cutting instrument: *microtome*. [Greek *tomos*: see TOME]

tomentum /tə'mentəm/ *noun* (*pl* **tomenta** /-tə/) *technical* a covering of densely matted woolly hairs on the leaf or stem of a plant. ➤➤ **tomentose** /-tohs/ *adj*. [scientific Latin from Latin *tomenta* cushion stuffing]

tomfool /tom'foohl/ *noun* *dated* an extremely foolish or stupid person.

tomfoolery *noun* foolish trifling; nonsense.

Tommy /'tomi/ *noun* (*pl* **Tommies**) *informal* a British private soldier. [named after *Thomas* Atkins, name used as model in official army forms in the 19th cent.]

Tommy Atkins /'tomi 'atkinz/ *noun* = TOMMY.

tommy gun *noun* *informal* = THOMPSON SUBMACHINE GUN. [by shortening and alteration]

tommyrot /'tomirot/ *noun* *informal*, *dated* utter foolishness or nonsense. [English dialect *tommy* fool + ROT²]

tomography /tə'mogrəfi/ *noun* a diagnostic technique using X-ray photographs in which the shadows of structures in front of and behind the section under scrutiny do not show. ➤➤ **tomogram** /'toməgram/ *noun*. [Greek *tomos* (see TOME) + -GRAPHY]

tomorrow¹ /tə'moroh/ *adv* **1** on the day after today. **2** in the future: *the world of tomorrow.* [Old English *tō morgen*, from *tō* TO¹ + *morgen* morrow, morning]

tomorrow² *noun* **1** the day after today. **2** the future: *Europe and the U.K. are yesterday's world. Tomorrow is in the United States* — R W 'Tiny' Rowland.

tompion /'tompi-ən/ *noun* = TAMPION.

Tom Thumb *noun* a dwarf type, race, or individual. [named after *Tom Thumb*, English folktale character who was no bigger than his father's thumb]

tomtit /'tomtit/ *noun* **1** any of various small active birds. **2** *Brit* a blue tit. [prob short for *tomtitmouse*, from the name *Tom* + TITMOUSE]

tom-tom /'tom tom/ *noun* a long narrow drum commonly beaten with the hands. [Hindi *ţamţam*, of imitative origin]

-tomy *comb. form* forming nouns, denoting: incision; cutting: *laparotomy*. [scientific Latin *-tomia* from Greek, from *-tomos* that cuts, from *temnein* to cut]

ton¹ /tun/ *noun* **1a** = LONG TON. **b** = SHORT TON. **c** = TONNE. **2a** = NET TON. **b** = DISPLACEMENT TON. **c** = GROSS TON. **3** *informal*. **a** (*also in pl*) a great quantity: *There's tons of room on the back seat.* **b** a great weight: *This bag weighs a ton.* **4** *chiefly Brit*, *informal* a group, score, or speed of 100.

Word history
Middle English *tunne* variant of TUN¹. Both forms were used interchangeably for units of weight and capacity, and for the cask, until the 17th cent., when the current divisions began to emerge.

ton² /tonh/ *noun* **1** the prevailing fashion: *A clergyman cannot be high in state or fashion. He must not … set the ton in dress* — Jane Austen. **2** the quality or state of being fashionable. [French *ton*, literally 'tone', from Latin *tonus*: see TONE¹]

tonal /'tohn(ə)l/ *adj* **1** of tone, tonality, or tonicity. **2** having tonality. ➤➤ **tonally** *adv*.

tonality /toh'naliti/ *noun* (*pl* **tonalities**) **1** the organization of a musical composition in relation to its tonic key. **2** the arrangement or interrelation of the colours or shades of a picture.

tondo /'tondoh/ *noun* (*pl* **tondi** /'tondee/) a circular painting or relief. [Italian *tondo*, literally 'round', short for *rotondo*, from Latin *rotundus*: see ROTUND]

tone¹ /tohn/ *noun* **1** a vocal or musical sound, *esp* one of a specified quality: *He spoke in low tones.* **2** an accent or inflection of the voice expressive of a mood or emotion. **3** style or manner of verbal expression: *It seemed wise to adopt a conciliatory tone.* **4** in some languages, e.g. Chinese, any of a set of different pitches which together with vowels and consonants form different words. **5a** a sound of a definite pitch. **b** = WHOLE TONE. **6a** colour quality or value. **b** the colour that appreciably modifies a hue or white or black. **7** the general effect of light, shade, and colour in a picture. **8a** normal tension or responsiveness to stimuli. **b** the state of a living body in which the functions are healthy and performed with due vigour. **9** prevailing character, quality, or trend, e.g. of morals: *He lowered the tone of the discussion.* ➤➤ **toneless** *adj*, **tonelessly** *adv*. [Middle English *tone* from Latin *tonus* from Greek *tonos* tone, tension, from *teinein* to stretch]

tone² *verb trans* (*often* + up) to impart tone to (something or somebody): *I need some sort of medicine to tone up my system.* ➤ *verb intrans* (+ with) to blend or harmonize in colour with something.

tone arm *noun* the movable arm of a record player or deck that carries the pickup and permits tracking.

toned *adj* **1** (*used in combinations*) having the tone specified; characterized or distinguished by a tone: *shrill-toned*. **2** said of paper: having a slight tint.

tone-deaf *adj* relatively insensitive to musical pitch. ➤➤ **tone-deafness** *noun*.

tone down *verb trans* to soften or reduce (something) in colour, intensity, violence, loudness, or force: *He was told to tone down his views.*

tone group *noun* a unit of speech consisting of a strongly stressed syllable with or without other stressed and unstressed syllables.

tone language *noun* a language, e.g. Chinese, in which variations in tone distinguish words of different meaning.

toneme /'tohneem/ *noun* a tone phoneme in a tone language such as Chinese. ➤➤ **tonemic** /toh'neemik/ *adj*.

tone poem *noun* = SYMPHONIC POEM.

toner *noun* **1** somebody or something that tones or is a source of tones. **2** a cosmetic preparation applied to the skin to reduce oiliness. **3** a solution used to impart colour to a silver photographic image. **4** a substance used to develop a xerographic (dry-photocopied; see XEROGRAPHY) image.

tone-row /roh/ *noun* a series of chromatic notes within an octave placed in a fixed order that form the basis of a serial musical composition.

tong /tong/ *noun* a Chinese secret society or fraternal organization formerly notorious for gang warfare. [Chinese (Cantonese) *tohng* hall]

tonga /'tonggə/ *noun* a light one-horse vehicle for two or four people in common use in India. [Hindi *tāṅgā*]

Tongan /'tonggən/ *noun* **1** a native or inhabitant of the Tonga Islands in the S Pacific. **2** the Polynesian language of the Tongans. ⟫ **Tongan** *adj.*

tongs /tongz/ *pl noun* any of various grasping devices consisting commonly of two pieces joined at one end by a pivot or hinged like scissors. [Middle English *tonges*, pl of *tonge* pair of tongs, from Old English *tang*]

tongue¹ /tung/ *noun* **1a** a fleshy muscular movable organ of the floor of the mouth of a human being or other vertebrate animal that bears sensory end organs and small glands and functions in tasting and swallowing food and, in human beings, as a speech organ. **b** a similar organ in invertebrate animals. **2** the tongue of an ox, sheep, etc used as food. **3a** manner or quality of utterance: *a sharp tongue*. **b** a language. **c** the ability to speak: *Have you lost your tongue?* **d** (*usu in pl*) ecstatic utterance, *esp* in Christian worship, of unintelligible sounds or of a language that the speaker does not know: *Many Christians practise speaking and praying in tongues*. **4** a long narrow strip of land projecting into a body of water. **5** something elongated and fastened at one end only, e.g.: **a** the flap under the lacing or buckles on the front of a shoe or boot. **b** a piece of metal suspended inside a bell so as to strike against the sides as the bell is swung. **c** the reed of a musical instrument or organ pipe. **6** the rib on one edge of a board that fits into a corresponding groove in an edge of another board to make a flush joint. **7** a tapering or flickering strip or cone: *a tongue of flame*. ✳ **hold one's tongue** to keep quiet; to say nothing. **with one's tongue hanging out** showing eagerness. **with one's tongue in one's cheek** in a tongue-in-cheek manner. ⟫ **tongueless** *adj*, **tonguelike** *adj*. [Old English *tunge*]

tongue² *verb* (**tongues, tongued, tonguing**) ⟩ *verb trans* **1** to articulate (notes) on a wind instrument by tonguing. **2** to touch or lick (something) with or as if with the tongue. ⟩ *verb intrans* to articulate notes on a wind instrument by successively interrupting the stream of wind with the action of the tongue.

tongue and groove *noun* a joint made by a projecting rib on one edge of a board fitting into a corresponding groove on the edge of another board. ⟫ **tongued and grooved** *adj*.

tongued *adj* (*used in combinations*) having a tongue of the kind specified: *sharp-tongued*.

tongue-in-cheek *adj* characterized by irony or whimsical exaggeration: *Madonna ... comes across now like a modern day Mae West, with tongue-in-cheek and wise-ass lines* — The Face. ⟫ **tongue in cheek** *adv*.

tongue-lashing *noun* a scolding or rebuke.

tongue-tie *noun* limited mobility of the tongue due to shortness of its FRAENUM (connecting membrane).

tongue-tied *adj* **1** unable to speak freely, e.g. because of shyness. **2** affected with tongue-tie.

tongue twister *noun* a word or phrase difficult to articulate because of several similar consonant sounds, e.g. 'She sells seashells on the seashore'.

tonic¹ /'tonik/ *noun* **1a** something, e.g. a medicine, that increases body tone. **b** something that invigorates, refreshes, or stimulates: *A day in the country was a tonic for him; a skin tonic*. **c** = TONIC WATER. **2** in music, the first note of a diatonic scale.

tonic² *adj* **1** of or based on the first note of a scale. **2** said of a syllable: bearing a principal stress or accent. **3** increasing or restoring physical or mental tone. **4** marked by prolonged muscular contraction: *tonic convulsions*. ⟫ **tonically** *adv*. [Greek *tonikos* from *tonos*: see TONE¹]

tonic accent *noun* accentuation of a syllable by means of higher pitch as opposed to stress.

tonicity /toh'nisiti/ *noun* the property of possessing tone; *esp* healthy vigour of body or mind.

tonic sol-fa *noun* a system of solmization that replaces the normal notation with sol-fa syllables.

tonic water *noun* a carbonated slightly bitter-tasting mineral water flavoured with a small amount of quinine, lemon, and lime.

tonight¹ /tə'niet/ *adv* on this night or the night following today. [Old English *tō niht*, from *tō* TO¹, at + *niht* NIGHT]

tonight² *noun* this night or the night following today: *I wonder if the story will be on tonight's news*.

tonka bean /'tongkə/ *noun* **1** the coumarin-containing seed of a leguminous tree. **2** a tree bearing tonka beans: *Dipteryx odorata*. [prob from Tupi *tonka*]

tonnage /'tunij/ *noun* **1** total weight in tons shipped, carried, or produced. **2** the carrying capacity of a merchant ship in gross tons. **3** ships considered in terms of the total number of tons registered or carried or of their carrying capacity. **4** a duty or tax on vessels based on cargo capacity. [Middle English from Old French *tonne*: see TUNNEL¹]

tonne /tun/ *noun* a metric unit of weight equal to 1000kg. [French *tonne* from Old French: see TUNNEL¹]

tonneau /'tonoh/ *noun* (*pl* **tonneaus**) **1** the rear seating compartment of a motor car. **2** a cover used to protect the seats in an open-topped vehicle.

Word history
French *tonneau*, literally 'tun', from Old French *tonel*: see TUNNEL¹. The word orig denoted a unit of capacity for wine (equal to 900l); in the early 20th cent. it was applied to the rounded rear part of a car, thought to resemble a barrel, hence the rear compartment, whatever its shape. Sense 2 is short for *tonneau cover*.

tonometer /toh'nomitə/ *noun* **1** an instrument, e.g. a tuning fork, for determining the exact pitch of tones. **2** an instrument for measuring pressure, e.g. in the eyeball, or of the blood or a gas. ⟫ **tonometric** /tonə'metrik/ *adj*. [Greek *tonos* (see TONE¹) + -METER²]

tons /tunz/ *adv Brit, informal* a great deal: *This album is tons better than their last one*.

tonsil /'tons(ə)l/ *noun* either of a pair of small oval masses of lymphoid tissue that lie one on each side of the throat at the back of the mouth. ⟫ **tonsillar** *adj*. [Latin *tonsillae* (pl) tonsils]

tonsillectomy /tonsi'lektəmi/ *noun* (*pl* **tonsillectomies**) the surgical removal of the tonsils.

tonsillitis /tonsi'lietəs/ *noun* inflammation of the tonsils.

tonsorial /ton'sawri·əl/ *adj formal* of hairdressers or hairdressing. [Latin *tonsorius*, from *tondēre* to shear]

tonsure¹ /'tonshə/ *noun* **1** the shaved patch on a monk's or other cleric's head. **2a** the Roman Catholic Eastern or Celtic Christian rite of admission to the clerical state by the shaving of a portion of the head. **b** any similar rite, e.g. in Buddhism, Hinduism, or Jainism. [Middle English from medieval Latin *tonsura*, literally 'act of shearing', from *tondēre* to shear]

tonsure² *verb trans* to shave the head of (a monk or other cleric), *esp* to confer the tonsure on them. ⟫ **tonsured** *adj*.

tontine /'tonteen, ton'teen/ *noun* a financial arrangement whereby a group of participants share various advantages on such terms that on the death or default of any member their advantages are distributed among the remaining members until one member remains or an agreed period has elapsed. [French *tontine*, named after Lorenzo *Tonti* d.1695, Italian banker, who started such a scheme in France as a way of raising government loans]

ton-up /tun/ *adj Brit, informal* denoting a person who has achieved a score or speed of 100: *He hates the local motorcycle ton-up boys*.

Tony /'tohni/ *noun* (*pl* **Tonys** *or* **Tonies**) in the USA, any of a number of awards given for notable achievement in the theatre. [*Tony*, nickname of Antoinette Perry d.1946, US actress and producer]

tony /'tohni/ *adj* (**tonier, toniest**) *NAmer, informal* marked by an aristocratic or fashionable manner or style.

too /tooh/ *adv* **1a** to a regrettable degree; excessively: *It's too large a house for us.* **b** to a higher degree than meets a standard: *She's too pretty for words.* **c** *informal* very: *You're too kind.* **2** also; in addition: *They sold the house and the furniture too.* **3** *NAmer, informal* used to counter a negative claim: indeed; so: '*I didn't do it.' 'You did too'.* [Old English *tō* TO¹, too]

Usage note
too, to, *or* two? See note at TO¹.

toodle-oo /'toohdl ooh/ *interj informal, dated* good-bye. [possibly from French *à toute à l'heure* see you later]

took /took/ *verb* past tense of TAKE¹.

tool[1] /toohl/ *noun* **1a** an implement that is used, *esp* by hand, to carry out work of a mechanical nature, e.g. cutting, levering, or digging. **b** a machine tool. **c** a hand implement used to letter or ornament (leather, etc). **2** something, e.g. an instrument or apparatus, used in performing an operation, or necessary for the practice of a vocation or profession: *Books are the tools of a scholar's trade.* **3** somebody who is used or manipulated by another. **4** *coarse slang* a penis. [Old English *tōl*]

tool[2] *verb trans* **1** (*usu in passive*) to work, shape, or finish (something) with a tool, *esp* to letter or ornament (leather, etc) by means of hand tools. **2** (*often + up*) to equip (a plant or industry) with tools, machines, and instruments for production. ➤ *verb intrans* **1** (+ up) to get tooled up for production. **2** *informal* to drive or ride: *He tooled round the neighbourhood in a small car.* ➤➤ **tooler** *noun*, **tooling** *noun*.

toolbar *noun* a row or block of icons on a computer screen which can be clicked on to perform certain functions.

toolmaker *noun* a skilled worker who makes, repairs, maintains, and calibrates the tools and instruments of a machine shop. ➤➤ **toolmaking** *noun*.

tool pusher *noun* a person who supervises the drilling work on an oil rig.

toolroom *noun* a room where tools are kept, *esp* a room in a machine shop in which tools are made, stored, and issued for use.

toon /toohn/ *noun informal* an animated cartoon or a cartoon character.

toot[1] /tooht/ *verb intrans* said of a horn, etc: to produce a short blast or similar sound. ➤ *verb trans* to cause (an instrument, etc) to produce a short blast: *He stopped the car outside her house and tooted his horn.* ➤➤ **tooter** *noun*. [prob imitative]

toot[2] *noun* **1** a tooting sound. **2** *slang* cocaine.

tooth[1] /toohth/ *noun* (*pl* **teeth** /teeth/) **1a** any of the hard bony structures in the jaws of vertebrates that are used for biting and chewing food. **b** any of various hard and sharp projecting parts about the mouth of an invertebrate. **2** a taste or liking: *a sweet tooth.* **3a** a projection like the tooth of an animal, e.g. in shape, arrangement, or action: *a saw tooth.* **b** any of the regular projections on the rim of a cogwheel. **4** (*in pl*) effective means of enforcement: *This law has no teeth.* ✳ **get one's teeth into something** *informal* to begin to understand and derive satisfaction from something. **in the teeth of** in direct opposition to: *Rule had ... been imposed by conquest in the teeth of obstinate resistance* — A J Toynbee. **set somebody's teeth on edge** to cause a jarringly unpleasant physical reaction in somebody, as, for example, when hearing a harsh squeaking sound. **sink one's teeth into something** *informal* to do something energetically and enthusiastically; to become completely absorbed or involved in something. **tooth and nail** with every available means: *She would fight tooth and nail to protect her child.* **to the teeth** *informal* to a great or the greatest extent: *Her bodyguards were armed to the teeth.* ➤➤ **toothless** *adj*, **toothlike** *adj*. [Old English *tōth*]

tooth[2] *verb trans* to provide (a saw, etc) with teeth, *esp* by cutting notches. ➤ *verb intrans* said of cogwheels: to interlock.

toothache *noun* pain in or about a tooth.

toothbrush *noun* a brush for cleaning the teeth.

toothcomb ✳ **with a fine toothcomb** *Brit* thoroughly: *I went through the accounts with a fine toothcomb.* [prob by incorrect division of *fine-tooth comb*]

toothed *adj* (*used in combinations*) having teeth, *esp* of the kind or number specified: *sharp-toothed.*

toothed whale *noun* a whale with numerous simple conical teeth: suborder Odontoceti.

tooth fairy *noun* (**the tooth fairy**) a fairy said to remove a child's milk tooth from under their pillow and leave money in its place.

toothpaste *noun* a paste for cleaning the teeth.

toothpick *noun* a pointed instrument for removing food particles lodged between the teeth.

tooth powder *noun* a powder for cleaning the teeth.

tooth shell *noun* any of various burrowing marine molluscs with a tapering tubular shell: class Scaphopoda.

toothsome /toohths(ə)m/ *adj* **1** said of food: delicious. **2** *informal* sexually attractive. ➤➤ **toothsomely** *adv*, **toothsomeness** *noun*.

toothwort *noun* a parasitic European plant of the figwort family with a rootstock covered with tooth-shaped scales: *Lathraea squamaria.*

toothy *adj* (**toothier**, **toothiest**) having or showing prominent teeth: *a toothy grin.* ➤➤ **toothily** *adv*.

tootle[1] /toohtl/ *verb intrans* **1** to toot gently or continuously. **2** *informal* to drive or move along in a leisurely manner. [frequentative of TOOT[1]]

tootle[2] *noun* a tootling or hooting sound.

tootsy *or* **tootsie** /tootsi/ *noun* (*pl* **tootsies**) **1** used chiefly to children: a foot or toe. **2** *chiefly NAmer, informal.* **a** a young woman, *esp* a sexually attractive or available one. **b** used as a familiar or patronizing form of address to a woman. [baby-talk alteration of FOOT[1]]

top[1] /top/ *noun* **1a** the highest point, level, or part of something; the summit or crown. **b** the upper end, edge, or surface. **2** a garment worn on the upper body. **3** a fitted or attached part serving as an upper piece, lid, or covering. **4** the head of a plant, *esp* one with edible roots: *beet tops.* **5a** the highest position, e.g. in rank or achievement. **b** somebody or something in the highest position. **6** (**the top**) the highest degree or pitch conceivable or attained; the acme or pinnacle. **7** the part that is nearest in space or time to the source or beginning. **8a** a platform surrounding the head of a lower mast that serves to spread the topmast rigging, strengthen the mast, and provide a standing place for people aloft. **b** a comparable part on a ship without masts. **9** = TOPSPIN. **10** = TOP GEAR. ✳ **from top to bottom** throughout or very thoroughly. **off the top of one's head** without taking time to think about or research the matter; impromptu: *I can't give you the figures off the top of my head.* **on top 1a** resting on the highest point or surface of something. **b** uppermost. **2** in a dominant position. **on top of 1** placed on or above the highest part of something. **2** in control of: *I'm trying to keep on top of my job.* **3** informed about. **4** in sudden and unexpected proximity to: *The situation was on top of me before I knew it.* **5** in addition to: *On top of everything else, he managed to break his arm.* **on top of the world** in high spirits; in a state of exhilaration and well-being. **over the top** exaggerated; *esp* excessively dramatic. [Old English *topp*]

top[2] *verb trans* (**topped, topping**) **1a** to be or become higher than (something). **b** to exceed or surpass (something): *This tops the previous record.* **c** to be superior to (something): *This book tops everything of its kind in print.* **d** to gain ascendancy over (somebody). **2a** to cover (something) with a top or on the top; to provide, form, or serve as a top for (it). **b** to supply (something) with a decorative or protective finish or final touch. **3a** to cut the top off (something). **b** to shorten or remove the top of (a plant). **c** to remove the calyx of (e.g. a strawberry): compare TAIL[2] (2B). **4a** to rise to, reach, or be at the top of (something). **b** to go over the top of (something); to clear or surmount (it). **5** to strike (a ball) above the centre, thereby imparting topspin. **6** *informal* to kill (somebody), *esp* by hanging: *They discovered he'd topped himself.* ✳ **top and tail 1** *Brit* to cut the ends off (a fruit or vegetable). **2** *Brit* to wash a baby's face and bottom.

top[3] *adj* **1** of or at the top. **2** foremost or leading: *one of the world's top journalists.* **3** of the highest quality, amount, or degree: *top form.*

top[4] *noun* a child's toy that has a tapering point on which it is made to spin. [Old English]

topaz[1] /tohpaz/ *noun* **1** a mineral that is predominantly a silicate of aluminium, usu occurs in variously coloured translucent or transparent crystals, and is used as a gem. **2a** a yellow sapphire. **b** a yellow quartz, e.g. cairngorm or citrine. [Middle English *topace* via Old French and Latin from Greek *topazos*]

topaz[2] *adj* of a yellowish brown colour. ➤➤ **topaz** *noun*.

top boot *noun* a high boot, often with an upper part of a different material or colour.

top brass *noun* (*treated as sing. or pl*) military officers or other officials of high rank.

topcoat *noun* **1** a lightweight overcoat. **2** a final coat of paint.

top dog *noun informal* a person in a position of authority, *esp* through victory in a hard-fought competition.

top dollar *noun NAmer, informal* a very large amount of money: *We had to pay top dollar for it.*

top-down *adj* **1** controlled or initiated by the most senior people. **2** starting from general principles and proceeding from there to deal with specific details: compare BOTTOM-UP.

top drawer *noun informal* the highest level, *esp* of society. ➤➤ **top-drawer** *adj*.

top-dress *verb trans* to scatter fertilizer over (land) without working it in. ➤➤ **top-dressing** *noun*.

tope[1] /'tohp/ *verb intrans archaic or literary* to drink alcohol to excess. ➤➤ **toper** *noun*. [obsolete *tope*, an interjection used to wish good health before drinking]

tope[2] *noun* a small shark with a liver very rich in vitamin A: *Galeorhinus galeus*. [origin unknown]

topee /'tohpi/ *noun* see TOPI[1].

top-flight *adj* of the highest rank or quality; best.

topgallant /top'galənt, tə'galənt/ *noun* **1** the part of a ship's mast next above the topmast. **2** a sail set on a topgallant mast. [TOP[1] + GALLANT[1]]

top gear *noun* **1** the transmission gear of a motor vehicle giving the highest ratio of propeller-shaft to engine-shaft speed and hence the highest speed of travel. **2** a state of intense or maximum activity.

top hat *noun* a man's tall-crowned hat with a flat top and vertical sides, usu made of silk and worn on formal occasions.

top-heavy *adj* **1** having the top part too heavy for, or disproportionate to, the lower part. **2** in finance, capitalized beyond what is prudent.

Tophet /'tohfet/ *noun* a place or state of misery; hell. [Middle English from Hebrew *tōpheth*, a shrine south of ancient Jerusalem where human sacrifices were performed (Jeremiah 7:31)]

top-hole *adj Brit, informal, dated* excellent.

tophus /'tohfəs/ *noun* (*pl* **tophi** /'tohfie/) a hard chalky deposit in tissues, e.g. cartilage, characteristic of gout. [Latin *tophus* tufa]

topi[1] *or* **topee** /'tohpi/ *noun* (*pl* **topis** *or* **topees**) a lightweight helmet-shaped hat made of pith or cork and worn in the tropics. [Hindi *ṭopī* hat]

topi[2] *noun* (*pl* **topis** *or collectively* **topi**) a brown African antelope with dark markings: *Damaliscus lunatus*. [Mende *topi*]

topiary /'tohpi·əri/ *noun* (*pl* **topiaries**) **1** the practice or art of training, cutting, and trimming trees or shrubs into odd or ornamental shapes. **2** a tree or shrub cut in this way. **3** a garden containing topiaries. ➤➤ **topiarist** *noun*. [Latin *topiarius* of ornamental gardening, from *topia* ornamental gardening, irreg from Greek *topos* place]

topic /'topik/ *noun* a subject for discussion or consideration in writing or conversation. [Latin *Topica* Topics (a work by Aristotle), from Greek *ta Topika*, literally 'matters concerning commonplaces', from *topos* place, commonplace]

topical *adj* **1** concerned with events and matters of current interest: *a topical quiz show*. **2** of or arranged by topics: *set down in topical form*. **3** said of medical drugs or treatments: designed to be applied externally to the affected part of the body: *a topical remedy*. **4** *formal* of a place; local. ➤➤ **topicality** /-'kaliti/ *noun*, **topically** *adv*.

topknot *noun* **1** an arrangement or growth of hair or feathers on top of the head. **2** an ornament, e.g. of ribbons, worn as a headdress or as part of a hairstyle.

topless *adj and adv* **1a** nude above the waist; *esp* having the breasts exposed: *topless dancers*. **b** said of a garment: leaving the breasts exposed: *topless dresses*. **2** having no top; so high that the top is out of sight: *the topless towers of Ilium* — Marlowe.

top-level *adj* **1** at the highest level of authority or importance: *top-level management*. **2** made by or involving the most senior or important people.

top-line *adj* = TOP-LEVEL.

toplofty *adj NAmer, informal* haughty or condescending.

topmast /'topmahst, 'topməst/ *noun* a mast fixed on top of the section of mast that rises from the deck.

topmost /'topmohst/ *adj* highest of all.

top-notch *adj informal* of the highest quality. ➤➤ **top-notcher** *noun*.

top off *verb trans* to finish (something): *We topped off the evening with a meal at a restaurant*.

topographic /topə'grafik/ *adj* = TOPOGRAPHICAL.

topographical /topə'grafikl/ *adj* **1** of or concerned with topography. **2** of or concerned with the artistic representation of a particular locality: *a topographical poem*; *topographical painting*. ➤➤ **topographically** *adv*.

topography /to'pografi/ *noun* **1a** the configuration of a land surface, including its relief and the position of its natural and man-made features. **b** the art or practice of making detailed maps or charts of a region. **2** the physical or natural features of an object or entity and their structural relationships. ➤➤ **topographer** *noun*. [Middle English *topographie* via late Latin from Greek *topographia*, from *topographein* to describe a place, from *topos* place + *graphein* to write]

topology /to'poləji/ *noun* **1** a branch of mathematics that deals with geometric properties which are unaltered by elastic deformation, e.g. stretching or twisting. **2** the way in which the various parts or features of something are interrelated; configuration: *the topology of a molecule*; *the topology of a magnetic field*. ➤➤ **topological** /-'lojikl/ *adj*, **topologically** /-'lojikli/ *adv*, **topologist** *noun*. [Greek *topos* place + -LOGY]

toponym /'topənim, 'toh-/ *noun* a place name, or a name or word derived from a place name. [back-formation from TOPONYMY]

toponymic /topə'nimik/ *adj* of toponyms or toponymy.

toponymy /to'ponəmi, toh-/ *noun* the study of place names. [Greek *topos* place + *onyma, onoma* name]

top out *verb trans* to complete the basic structure of (a building) by putting on a cap or uppermost section. ➤ *verb intrans* to reach a peak or its highest level: *The business-investment boom has topped out*.

topper *noun* **1** *informal* = TOP HAT. **2** *Brit, informal, dated* a very agreeable person.

topping[1] *noun* something that forms a top; *esp* a garnish or edible decoration on top of a food: *pizza toppings*.

topping[2] *adj Brit, informal, dated* excellent or very enjoyable.

topple /'topl/ *verb intrans* **1** to fall down or over, *esp* through being top-heavy. **2** to be or seem unsteady. ➤ *verb trans* **1** to cause (something) to topple. **2** to overthrow (e.g. a government). [frequentative of TOP[2]]

tops[1] *noun* (*usu* **the tops**) *informal* somebody or something excellent, important, or popular: *She's the tops*.

tops[2] *adv informal* at the most: *We were doing 40 tops when we skidded*.

topsail /'topsayl, 'topsl/ *noun* **1** the sail next above the lowest sail on a mast in a square-rigged ship. **2** the sail set above and sometimes on the gaff in a fore-and-aft rigged ship.

top secret *adj* **1** demanding the greatest secrecy. **2** containing information whose unauthorized disclosure could result in exceptionally grave danger to the nation.

topside[1] *noun* **1** *Brit* a lean boneless cut of beef from the inner part of a round. **2** (*in pl*) the sides of a ship above the waterline.

topside[2] *adv and adj* on deck.

topsoil *noun* surface soil, usu including the organic layer in which plants form roots and which is turned over in ploughing.

topspin *noun* a rotary motion imparted to a ball that causes it to rotate forwards in the direction of its travel: compare BACKSPIN.

topstitch *verb trans* to make a line of stitching on the outside of (a garment) close to a seam or finished edge. ➤➤ **topstitching** *noun*.

topsy-turvy /,topsi 'tuhvi/ *adj and adv* **1** upside down. **2** in utter confusion or disorder. ➤➤ **topsy-turvily** *adv*, **topsy-turviness** *noun*. [prob derivative of *tops* (pl of TOP[1]) + obsolete *terve* to turn upside down, from Middle English *terven*]

top up *verb trans* **1** to make (something) up to the full quantity, capacity, or amount; to replenish (it). **2** to increase (a money sum set aside for a specific purpose): *topping up your pension*. **3** to replenish (a drink) or the drink of (somebody): *I offered to top him up*.

top-up *noun* **1** an amount added to make something up to the full quantity, capacity, or amount: *Can I give you a top-up?* **2** (*used before a noun*) used to increase a sum of money set aside for a specific purpose: *a top-up loan*.

toque /tohk/ *noun* **1** a woman's small soft brimless hat. **2** a tall white hat worn by a chef. [early French *toque* soft hat with a narrow brim worn in the 16th cent., from Old Spanish *toca* headdress]

tor /taw/ *noun* a high rock or rocky mound. [Old English *torr*]

Torah /'tawrə/ *noun* **1a** the Pentateuch. **b** Jewish Scripture and other sacred Jewish literature and oral tradition. **2** a leather or parchment scroll of the Pentateuch used in a synagogue. [Hebrew *tōrāh* instruction, law]

torc *or* **torque** /tawk/ *noun* a twisted collar or neck chain, usu made of metal, worn by the ancient Gauls, Germans, and Britons. [French *torque* from Latin *torques*, from *torquēre* to twist]

torch[1] /tawch/ *noun* **1** *Brit* a small portable electric lamp powered by batteries. **2** *esp* formerly, a burning stick of resinous wood or twist of tow used to give light. **3** a gas-burning implement providing a hot flame, *esp* for welding. **4** something, e.g. wisdom or knowledge, that gives enlightenment or guidance. ✳ **carry a torch for** to be in love with (somebody who does not return one's love), put to the torch/nut a torch to to destroy (something) by burning it. [Middle English from Old French *torche* twist of material for burning, ultimately from Latin *torques*: see TORC]

torch[2] *verb trans informal* to set fire to (something), *esp* as an act of arson.

torchbearer *noun* somebody in the forefront of a campaign or movement.

torchere /taw'sheə/ *noun* a tall stand for a candlestick or candelabrum. [French *torchère* from *torche* torch]

torch song *noun* a popular song of unrequited love. ➤➤ **torch singer** *noun*.

tore /taw/ *verb* past tense of TEAR[1].

toreador /'tori-ədaw/ *noun* a bullfighter, *esp* one on horseback. [Spanish *toreador* from *torear* to fight bulls, from *toro* bull, from Latin *taurus*]

torero /to'reəroh/ *noun* (*pl* **toreros**) a bullfighter, *esp* one on foot. [Spanish *torero* from *toro*: see TOREADOR]

toreutics /tə'roohtiks/ *pl noun* (*treated as sing.*) the art of working in metal, *esp* by embossing or chasing. ➤➤ **toreutic** *adj*. [*toreutic* (adj) from Greek *toreutikos*, from *toreuein* to bore through, chase, from *toreus* boring tool]

tori /'tawrie/ *noun* pl of TORUS.

toric /'torik/ *adj* shaped like a torus or part of a torus: *a toric lens*.

torii /'tawri-ee/ *noun* (*pl* **torii**) a Japanese gateway, commonly built at the approach to a Shinto shrine. [Japanese *torii*, literally 'a perch for birds']

torment[1] /'tawment/ *noun* **1** extreme pain or anguish of body or mind. **2** a source of vexation or pain. [Middle English via Old French from Latin *tormentum* torture, from *torquēre* to twist]

torment[2] /taw'ment/ *verb trans* **1** to cause severe usu persistent distress of body or mind to (somebody). **2** to tease (somebody) unkindly. ➤➤ **tormented** *adj*, **tormentor** *noun*.

tormentil /'tawməntil/ *noun* a common Eurasian plant of the rose family with yellow flowers and a root used in tanning and dyeing: *Potentilla erecta*. [Middle English *turmentill* from medieval Latin *tormentilla*, prob from Latin *tormentum* (see TORMENT[1]) from its use in allaying pain]

torn /tawn/ *verb* past part. of TEAR[1].

tornado /taw'naydoh/ *noun* (*pl* **tornadoes** *or* **tornados**) a violent or destructive whirlwind, usu progressing in a narrow path over the land and accompanied by a funnel-shaped cloud. ➤➤ **tornadic** /taw'nadik/ *adj*. [modification of Spanish *tronada* thunderstorm, from *tronar* to thunder, from Latin *tonāre*]

toroid /'tawroyd/ *noun* a doughnut-shaped figure; *specif* a surface or solid generated by a plane closed curve, e.g. an ellipse or circle, rotated about a line that lies in the same plane as the curve but does not intersect it. [Latin *torus* TORUS + -OID]

toroidal /to'roydl/ *adj* of or shaped like a torus or toroid; ring-shaped: *a toroidal resistance coil*. ➤➤ **toroidally** *adv*.

torpedo[1] /taw'peedoh/ *noun* (*pl* **torpedoes**) **1** a self-propelling cigar-shaped underwater explosive projectile used by submarines, aircraft, etc for attacking ships. **2** *NAmer* a small firework that explodes when thrown against a hard object. **3** a charge of explosive enclosed in a container or case. **4** an electric ray. ➤➤ **torpedo-like** *adj*. [Latin *torpedo*, literally 'stiffness, numbness', from *torpēre* to be stiff or numb; from the paralysing effect of the electric ray's sting]

torpedo[2] *verb trans* (**torpedoes**, **torpedoed**, **torpedoing**) **1** to hit or destroy (e.g. a ship) by torpedo. **2** to destroy or nullify (e.g. a plan).

torpedo boat *noun* a small fast warship armed primarily with torpedoes.

torpedo tube *noun* a tube in a submarine or ship from which torpedoes are fired.

torpid /'tawpid/ *adj* **1** lacking energy or vigour, and slow and heavy when moving or functioning; sluggish. **2** said of a hibernating animal: = DORMANT. **3** having temporarily lost the power of movement or feeling; numb. ➤➤ **torpidity** /taw'piditi/ *noun*, **torpidly** *adv*. [Latin *torpidus* from *torpēre* to be stiff or numb]

torpor /'tawpə/ *noun* **1** a state of sleepy inactivity or slow, heavy functioning; sluggishness; apathy. **2** a state of mental and motor inactivity with partial or total insensibility. [Latin *torpor* from *torpēre* to be stiff or numb]

torque[1] /tawk/ *noun* **1** a force that produces or tends to produce rotation or torsion: *A car engine delivers torque to the drive shaft*. **2** a measure of the effectiveness of such a force. [Latin *torquēre* to twist]

torque[2] *noun* see TORC.

torque converter *noun* a device for transmitting and amplifying torque, *esp* by hydraulic means.

torque wrench *noun* a wrench with a gauge attached that shows when adequate torque is reached.

torr /taw/ *noun* (*pl* **torr**) a unit of pressure equal to 133.32 pascals. [named after Evangelista *Torricelli* d.1647, Italian mathematician and physicist, who invented the barometer and defined atmospheric pressure]

torrent /'torənt/ *noun* **1** a violent stream of water, lava, etc. **2** a raging tumultuous flow: *The stranger attempted, once or twice, to stem the torrent of words, but in vain, so he bowed his head and suffered it flow on* — Washington Irving. [French *torrent* from Latin *torrent-*, *torrens* burning, seething, rushing, present part. of *torrēre* to parch, burn]

torrential /tə'rensh(ə)l/ *adj* of, caused by, or resembling a torrent: *torrential rains*. ➤➤ **torrentially** *adv*.

torrid /'torid/ *adj* **1a** parched with heat, *esp* the heat of the sun: *torrid sands*. **b** giving off intense heat. **2** ardent or passionate: *torrid love letters*. **3** very uncomfortable or unpleasant: *The examiners gave her a rather torrid time*. ➤➤ **torridity** /tə'riditi/ *noun*, **torridly** *adv*, **torridness** *noun*. [Latin *torridus* from *torrēre* to parch, burn]

torrid zone *noun* the belt of the earth between the tropics.

torsi /'tawsee/ *noun* pl of TORSO.

torsion /'tawsh(ə)n/ *noun* **1a** the act or process of twisting or turning something, *esp* by forces exerted on one end while the other is fixed or twisted in the opposite direction. **b** the state of being twisted. **2** the equal and opposite torque that an elastic solid exerts by reason of being under torsion. **3** the twisting of a body organ on its own axis. ➤➤ **torsional** *adj*, **torsionally** *adv*. [Middle English via French from late Latin *torsion-*, *tortio* twisting, from Latin *torquēre* to twist]

torsion balance *noun* an instrument used to measure minute forces, e.g. magnetic attraction and repulsion, by the torsion of a wire or filament.

torsion bar *noun* a steel bar that is part of the suspension of a vehicle and that acts as a torsional spring.

torsk /tawsk/ *noun* a large edible marine fish of the N Atlantic related to the cod: *Brosme brosme*. [Norwegian *torsk* from Old Norse *thorskr*]

torso /'tawsoh/ *noun* (*pl* **torsos** *or* **torsi** /'tawsee/) **1a** the human trunk. **b** a sculptured representation of the trunk. **2** something, e.g. a piece of writing, that is mutilated or left unfinished. [Italian *torso*, literally 'stalk', from Latin *thyrsus*]

tort /tawt/ *noun* in law, a wrongful act, other than breach of contract, for which a civil action for damages may be brought. [Middle English via French and late Latin from Latin *tortum* wrong, injustice, neuter past part. of *torquēre* to twist]

torte /'tawtə/ *noun* (*pl* **torten** /'tawtən/ *or* **tortes** /'tawtəz/) a gateau, *esp* a flat one topped with fruit, cream, etc. [German *Torte*, prob via Italian *torta* cake, from late Latin *torta* round loaf of bread]

tortellini /tawtə'leeni/ *pl noun* (*treated as sing. or pl*) pasta cut into small rounds, folded over a savoury filling, and boiled. [Italian *tortellini*, pl of *tortellino*, dimin. of *tortello* small cake, fritter, dimin. of *torta*: see TORTE]

tortfeasor /'tawtfeezə/ *noun* in law, somebody who commits a tort. [French *tortfaiseur*, from *tort* wrong (from Latin *tortum*: see TORT) + *faiseur* doer, maker]

torticollis /tawti'kolis/ *noun* a permanent twisting of the neck resulting in an abnormal position of the head. [Latin *torticollis*, from Latin *tortus* (see TORTURE¹) + *collum* neck]

tortilla /taw'teeyə/ *noun* a round thin maize pancake, usu eaten hot with a filling of meat or cheese. [American Spanish *tortilla*, dimin. of Spanish *torta* cake, from late Latin *torta* round loaf of bread]

tortious /'tawchəs/ *adj* in law, implying or involving a tort. ➤➤ **tortiously** *adv.*

tortoise /'tawtəs, 'tawtoys/ *noun* **1** any of numerous species of land, freshwater, and marine reptiles with a toothless horny beak and a bony shell which encloses the trunk and into which the head, limbs, and tail may be withdrawn: family Testudinidae. **2** = TESTUDO. **3** somebody or something that moves very slowly or lags behind. [Middle English *tortu, tortuce* from early French *tortue* and Spanish *tortuga*, both from medieval Latin *tortuca*]

tortoiseshell /'tawtəshel/ *noun* **1** the mottled horny substance of the shell of some marine turtles used in inlaying and in making various ornamental articles. **2** any of several species of butterflies with striking orange, yellow, brown, and black coloration: family Nymphalidae. **3** a breed of cat with black, brown, and yellow markings.

tortricid /'tawtrisid/ *noun* any of a family of small stout-bodied moths many of whose larvae live in nests formed by rolling up plant leaves: family Tortricidae. ➤➤ **tortricid** *adj.* [Latin family name, from *Tortric-, Tortrix*: see TORTRIX]

tortrix /'tawtriks/ *noun* (*pl* **tortrices** /-seez/) a tortricid moth. [Latin *Tortric-, Tortrix*, genus of moths, from *torquēre* to twist; from its habit of twisting or rolling leaves to make a nest]

tortuous /'tawtyoo·əs/ *adj* **1** marked by repeated twists, bends, or turns. **2a** marked by devious or indirect tactics. **b** circuitous or involved. ➤➤ **tortuosity** /-'ositi/ *noun*, **tortuously** *adv*, **tortuousness** *noun.* [Middle English via French from Latin *tortuosus*, from *tortus* twist, from *torquēre* to twist]

torture¹ /'tawchə/ *noun* **1** the infliction of intense physical or mental suffering as a means of punishment, coercion, or sadistic gratification. **2** anguish of body or mind, or something causing this. [Middle English via French from late Latin *tortura* twisting, torment, from Latin *tortus*, past part. of *torquēre* to twist]

torture² *verb trans* **1** to subject (a person or animal) to torture. **2** to cause intense suffering to (a person or animal). **3** to twist or wrench (something) out of shape. ➤➤ **torturer** *noun.*

torturous /'tawchərəs/ *adj* of or involving torture: *We spent several torturous hours looking at his holiday snaps.* ➤➤ **torturously** *adv.*

torula /'toryoolə, 'tawyələ/ *noun* (*pl* **torulae** /-lee/ *or* **torulas**) any of various fungi, *esp* yeasts, that lack sexual spores and do not produce alcoholic fermentations. [Latin *torula* from *torus* protuberance]

torus /'tawrəs/ *noun* (*pl* **tori** /'tawrie/ *or* **toruses**) **1** in geometry, a ring-shaped surface generated by a surface rotated about an axis in its plane that does not intersect the circle. **2** in architecture, a large convex semicircular moulding, *esp* on the base of a column, pedestal, etc. **3** = RECEPTACLE (2). [Latin *torus* protuberance, bulge]

Tory /'tawri/ *noun* (*pl* **Tories**) **1a** a supporter of a Conservative party, *esp* the British Conservative Party. **b** a member of a major British political group of the 18th and early 19th cents favouring at first the Stuarts and later royal authority and the established Church and seeking to preserve the traditional political structure and defeat parliamentary reform: compare WHIG. **2** an American upholding the cause of the crown during the American Revolution. ➤➤ **Tory** *adj*, **Toryism** *noun.*

Word history
Irish Gaelic *tóraidhe* pursuer, robber, from early Irish *tóir* pursuit. The word was orig applied to dispossessed Irish Royalists in the 17th cent., then to those who upheld James II's claim to the throne, later to supporters of the Established Church: compare WHIG.

tosa /'tohsa/ *noun* a breed of dog that is a cross between a mastiff and a Great Dane, orig developed for dogfighting. [named after *Tosa*, a former Japanese province]

tosh¹ /tosh/ *noun Brit, informal* sheer nonsense. [origin unknown]

tosh² *noun Brit, informal* used as a familiar term of address: a man, a chap. [origin unknown]

toss¹ /tos/ *verb trans* **1a** to throw (something) with a quick, light, or careless motion: *They were just tossing a ball around for catching practice.* **b** to throw (something or somebody) up in the air. **2** to move (something) violently and repeatedly to and fro or up and down: *a ship tossed by waves.* **3** to shake or lift (one's head, hair, mane, etc) with a sudden jerking motion: *She tossed her head angrily.* **4** to mix (food) lightly with a tossing motion; *esp* to mix (a salad) lightly until well coated with a dressing. **5a** to flip (a coin) to decide an issue according to which face lands uppermost. **b** to toss a coin to decide an issue with (somebody): *I'll toss you for who goes first.* ➤ *verb intrans* **1** to move restlessly or turbulently; *esp* to twist and turn repeatedly: *I tossed sleeplessly all night.* **2** to decide an issue by flipping a coin: *Let's toss for it.* [prob from Scandinavian origin]

toss² *noun* **1** an act or instance of tossing, e.g.: **a** an abrupt upward or sideways movement. **b** a throw or pitch. **2** an act of tossing a coin to decide something: *We won the toss and chose to field first.* ✳ **not give/care a toss** *Brit, informal* not to care at all; to be totally indifferent. **take a toss** to fall off a horse.

tosser *noun Brit, coarse slang* an ineffective or despicable person. [from TOSS OFF in the sense 'to masturbate']

toss off *verb trans* **1** to accomplish, produce, or write (something) readily or easily: *She tossed off a few chapters before breakfast.* **2** to consume (a drink) quickly; *esp* to drink (it) in a single draught. **3** *Brit, coarse slang* to masturbate (somebody). ➤ *verb intrans Brit, coarse slang* to masturbate.

tosspot *noun informal* used as a general term of abuse: a drunkard or sot.

toss-up *noun* **1** the tossing of a coin. **2** *informal* an even chance or choice: *It was an absolute toss-up whether that book [Das Kapital] caught on or not* — Independent.

tot¹ /tot/ *noun* **1** a small child; a toddler. **2** a small amount or allowance of alcoholic drink: *a tot of rum.* [origin unknown]

tot² *verb* (**totted, totting**) ➤ *verb trans chiefly Brit* (*usu* + up) to add (figures or amounts) together; to total (them): *She totted up the score.* ➤ *verb intrans chiefly Brit* (+ up) to increase by additions; to mount: *The money soon tots up.* [short for TOTAL³]

total¹ /'tohtl/ *adj* **1** comprising or constituting a whole; entire. **2** complete or absolute: *a total success.* ➤➤ **totally** *adv.* [Middle English via French and late Latin from Latin *totus* whole, entire]

total² *noun* **1** an amount that is the end product of adding two or more smaller amounts together. **2** an entire quantity.

total³ *verb trans* (**totalled, totalling,** *NAmer* **totaled, totaling**) **1** to amount to (a figure): *The bill totalled £200.* **2** to add (something) up: *He totalled their scores.* **3** *informal* to demolish (something) completely. **4** *chiefly NAmer, slang* to maim or kill (somebody).

total eclipse *noun* an eclipse in which one celestial body is completely obscured by another.

total internal reflection *noun* in physics, the inability of a light ray to pass from one medium, e.g. glass, into another less dense medium, e.g. air, if it meets the interface between the two media at an angle greater than the critical angle, and the reflection of all its light back into the denser medium.

totalisator /'tohtəliesaytə/ *noun* see TOTALIZATOR.

totalise *verb trans* see TOTALIZE.

totaliser *noun* see TOTALIZER.

totalitarian /toh,tali'teəri·ən/ *adj* **1** of or constituting a political regime based on subordination of the individual to the state and strict control over all aspects of the life and productive capacity of the nation. **2** authoritarian or dictatorial. ➤➤ **totalitarianism** *noun.*

totality /toh'taliti/ *noun* **1** an entire amount; a whole. **2** the quality or state of being total; wholeness. **3** a period during which one body is completely obscured by another during an eclipse.

totalizator *or* **totalisator** /'tohtəliezaytə/ *noun* **1** a machine for registering bets and calculating winnings in the tote betting system. **2** = TOTE².

totalize *or* **totalise** *verb trans* **1** to add (something) up. **2** to express (something) as a whole; to summarize (it).

totalizer *or* **totaliser** *noun* something that totalizes, *esp* a totalizator.

total quality management *noun* a management approach based on the continuous improvement of standards and the reduction of costs.

tote[1] /toht/ *verb trans informal* to carry (something) by hand or on the person. [origin unknown]

tote[2] *noun* (*also* **the tote**) *informal* a betting system in which winners are paid a proportion of the total amount staked, less tax, based on the size of their stake, using a totalizator to calculate payouts.

tote bag *noun* a large bag for carrying articles, e.g. shopping or personal possessions.

totem /'tohtəm/ *noun* **1a** a natural object serving as the emblem of a family or clan. **b** a carved or painted representation of this. **2** something that serves as an emblem or revered symbol. ⟩⟩ **totemic** /toh'temik/ *adj.* [Ojibwa *ototeman* his totem]

totemism *noun* the belief in a mystical relationship between a group or individual and a totem. ⟩⟩ **totemist** *noun*.

totem pole *noun* **1** a pole carved and painted with a series of totemic symbols erected by some Native American peoples. **2** *chiefly NAmer* an order of rank; a hierarchy.

t'other *or* **tother** /'tudhə/ *pronoun and adj chiefly dialect* the other. [Middle English *tother*, alteration, by incorrect division, of *thet other* the other]

totter[1] /'totə/ *verb intrans* (**tottered, tottering**) **1a** to tremble or rock as if about to fall. **b** to become unstable; to threaten to collapse. **2** to move unsteadily; to stagger. ⟩⟩ **totterer** *noun.* [Middle English *toteren* to swing, from early Dutch *touteren*]

totter[2] *noun* an unsteady gait. ⟩⟩ **tottery** *adj.*

totting /'toting/ *noun Brit, informal* the occupation of scavenging refuse for saleable goods, *esp* illicitly. ⟩⟩ **totter** *noun.* [obsolete *tot* bone, something salvaged from refuse, of unknown origin]

totting-up *noun Brit, informal* a legal procedure whereby accumulating a certain number of penalty points from convictions for traffic offences within a particular period disqualifies one from driving.

totty /'toti/ *noun* (*pl* **totties**) *Brit, informal, offensive* **1** a girl or woman, *esp* one who is attractive or sexually available. **2** women collectively, *esp* when viewed as sexual objects. [TOT[1]]

toucan /'toohkən/ *noun* any of several species of fruit-eating birds of tropical America with brilliant colouring and a very large but light beak: genera *Ramphastos* and *Andigera*. [French *toucan* via Portuguese from Tupi *tucan*]

touch[1] /tuch/ *verb trans* **1** to bring the hand or other part of the body in contact with (something). **2** to tap or push (somebody or something) lightly. **3** to grasp or move (something) in any way or degree: *Don't touch anything.* **4** (*usu in negative contexts*) to harm (somebody): *He swears he never touched the child.* **5** to cause (something) to be briefly in contact with something else: *She touched a match to the wick.* **6** to meet or adjoin (something) without overlapping or penetrating. **7** to reach (e.g. a certain level): *The speedometer needle touched 80.* **8** (*usu in negative contexts*) to use or accept (something): *He never touches alcohol; I wouldn't touch any job they offered me.* **9** to concern or affect (somebody). **10a** to leave a mark or impression on (something): *Few reagents will touch gold.* **b** to harm (something) slightly by contact: *fruit touched by frost.* **11** to give a delicate tint or expression to (something): *A smile touched her lips.* **12** to move (somebody) to sympathetic feeling: *He was touched by the loyalty of his friends.* **13** *informal* (*usu in negative contexts*) to rival (something or somebody) in ability or value: *When it comes to dancing, nobody can touch her.* **14** *informal* to induce (somebody) to give or lend money. ⟩ *verb intrans* **1** to be in contact. **2** to come close; to verge. **3** (+ on/upon) to have a bearing; to relate. **4** (+ on/upon) to treat a topic in a brief or casual manner: *He touched upon many points.* **5** (+ at) said of a ship: to make a brief or incidental stop at a port, etc. ✳ **touch wood** with luck [from the superstition that certain trees, *usu* the ash and oak, could give protection against evil]. ⟩⟩ **touchable** *adj,* **toucher** *noun.* [Middle English *touchen* via Old French *tochier* from (assumed) vulgar Latin *toccare* to knock, strike a bell, touch, of imitative origin]

touch[2] *noun* **1** a light stroke, tap, or push. **2** the act or fact of touching. **3** the sense of feeling, *esp* as exercised deliberately with the hands, feet, or lips.

Editorial note
One of the five senses, touch is the sense by which we are made aware of the solids, liquids, and gases that surround us when they come into contact with receptors in the skin and mucous membranes. A certain minimum level of stimulation is required to produce the sensation of touch and this level varies in different areas of the body. Most sensitive are the tongue, lips, genitalia, and fingertips. Hairs present on the skin increase the level of sensitivity, owing to sensory receptors located at the base of the follicle — Dr John Cormack.

4 a specified sensation produced by touching something; a feel: *I felt the soft touch of her hand.* **5** mental or moral sensitivity, responsiveness, or tact: *He has a wonderful touch in dealing with children.* **6** the testing of gold or silver on a touchstone. **7a** a light attack: *a touch of fever.* **b** a small amount; a trace or dash: *a touch of spring in the air.* **c** (**a touch**) a bit; a little: *I aimed a touch too low and missed.* **8a** a manner or method of touching or striking something, *esp* the keys of a keyboard instrument. **b** the relative resistance to pressure of the keys of a keyboard: *a piano with a stiff touch.* **9** an effective and appropriate detail; *esp* one used in creating or improving an artistic composition: *He applied the finishing touches to his story.* **10** a distinctive or characteristic manner, trait, or quality: *a woman's touch; service with a personal touch.* **11** the state or fact of being in contact or communication: *She had lost touch with her cousin; He is out of touch with modern times.* **12a** in football and hockey, the area outside the touchlines. **b** in rugby, the area outside and including the touchlines. **13** a set of changes in bell-ringing that is shorter than a peal. **14** the testing of gold or silver on a touchstone.

touch-and-go *adj* highly uncertain or precarious: *It was touch-and-go whether they would survive.*

touchdown *noun* **1** the moment when an aircraft or spacecraft makes contact with the ground in landing. **2** in rugby, the act of touching down a ball. **3** in American football, the act of receiving or having possession of the ball across the opponents' goal line, or the six-point score awarded for this.

touch down *verb trans* in rugby, to score by placing (the ball) on the ground over an opponent's goal line. ⟩ *verb intrans* said of an aircraft or spacecraft: to reach the ground in landing.

touché /tooh'shay/ *interj* used to acknowledge a hit in fencing or the success of an argument, accusation, or witty point. [French *touché*, past part. of *toucher* to touch, from Old French *tochier*: see TOUCH[1]]

touched *adj* **1** emotionally moved, e.g. with gratitude. **2** *informal* slightly unbalanced mentally.

touchhole *noun* the hole in early cannon or firearms through which the charge was ignited.

touching[1] *adj* capable of arousing tenderness or compassion. ⟩⟩ **touchingly** *adv.*

touching[2] *prep formal* in reference to; concerning.

touch judge *noun* in rugby, = LINESMAN.

touchline *noun* in rugby and football, either of the lines that bound the sides of the field of play.

touchmark *noun* an identifying maker's mark impressed on pewter.

touch-me-not *noun* a Eurasian balsam plant with spotted bright yellow flowers and seedpods that, when ripe, burst open on being touched: *Impatiens noli-tangere.*

touch off *verb trans* **1** to cause (something) to explode by touching it with a naked flame. **2** to release (something) with sudden intensity: *The incident touched off a storm of protest.*

touch pad *noun* in computing, an input device used instead of a keyboard or to control a program; consisting of a plastic pad on which the user touches the area required.

touchpaper *noun* paper impregnated with a substance, e.g. potassium nitrate, that burns slowly and is used for the ignition of fireworks or for firing gunpowder.

touch screen *noun* in computing, a system which enables the operator to touch part of the screen physically instead of using a mouse to select menu items.

touchstone *noun* **1** a black flintlike siliceous stone that when rubbed by gold or silver shows a streak of colour, formerly used to test the purity of these metals. **2** a test or criterion for determining the genuineness of something.

touch-tone *adj* having or using dialling buttons that generate a particular pitch when pressed: *a touch-tone phone.*

touch-type *verb intrans* to type without looking at the keyboard, using a system that assigns a particular finger to each key. ⟩⟩ **touch-typist** *noun.*

touch up *verb trans* **1** to improve or perfect (something) by small alterations. **2** *Brit, informal* to make unwelcome physical or sexual contact with (somebody).

touchwood *noun archaic* wood so decayed as to be dry, crumbly, and useful for tinder.

touchy *adj* (**touchier, touchiest**) **1** ready to take offence on slight provocation. **2** calling for tact, care, or caution: *a touchy subject.* ⮞⮞ **touchily** *adv*, **touchiness** *noun*.

touchy-feely /'feeli/ *adj informal* **1** showing emotion openly and readily, *esp* through physical contact or gestures and often in a way considered excessive; demonstrative. **2** encouraging or character-istic of this type of behaviour.

tough[1] /tuf/ *adj* **1a** strong and flexible; not brittle or liable to cut, break, or tear easily. **b** said of food: not easily chewed. **2** character-ized by severity or uncompromising determination: *a tough and inflexible foreign policy* — New Statesman. **3** capable of enduring great hardship or exertion; hardy. **4** very hard to influence; stub-born. **5** extremely difficult or testing: *a tough question to answer.* **6** stubbornly fought: *a tough contest.* **7** aggressive or threatening in behaviour; unruly or rowdy. **8** without softness or sentimentality. **9** *informal* unfortunate or unpleasant: *That's tough.* ⮞⮞ **toughly** *adv*, **toughness** *noun*. [Old English *tōh*]

tough[2] *noun informal* a tough person, *esp* somebody aggressively violent.

tough[3] *adv* in a tough manner: *He likes to talk tough.*

tough[4] *verb trans informal* (+ out) to endure (a difficult situation) without weakening: *The Prime Minister is still toughing it out.*

toughen *verb trans and intrans* (**toughened, toughening**) to become, or make something, tough.

tough love *noun* a policy of helping a friend or family member with a serious problem, e.g. drug addiction, by being strict rather than indulgent.

tough-minded *adj* unsentimental or realistic in disposition or outlook. ⮞⮞ **tough-mindedness** *noun*.

toupee /'toohpay/ *noun* a wig or hairpiece worn to cover a bald spot. [French *toupet* forelock, dimin. of Old French *top, toup* tuft, of Germanic origin]

tour[1] /tooə/ *noun* **1a** a journey, e.g. for business or pleasure, in which one returns to the starting point. **b** a visit, e.g. to a historic site or factory, for pleasure or information: *a guided tour of the castle.* **c** a series of professional engagements involving travel: *a theatrical company on tour.* **2** (*also* **tour of duty**) a period during which an individual or unit is engaged on a specific duty, *esp* in one place: *His regiment did a tour in Northern Ireland.* [Middle English from Old French *tourn, tour* lathe, circuit, turn, from Latin *tornus*: see TURN[1]]

tour[2] *verb intrans* to make a tour. ⮞ *verb trans* **1** to make a tour of (e.g. a building or place). **2** to present (e.g. a theatrical production or concert) on a tour.

touraco /'tooərəkoh/ *noun* see TURACO.

tour de force /ˌtooə də ˈfaws (*French* tuːr də fɔrs)/ *noun* (*pl* **tours de force** /ˌtooə (*French* tuːr)/) an extremely impressive feat, performance, piece of work, etc. [French *tour de force*, literally 'feat of strength']

tourer *noun* **1** a car suitable for touring. **2** a bicycle for touring.

Tourette's syndrome /too'rets/ *noun* a neurological disorder that causes the sufferer to make sudden involuntary movements and often obscene exclamations. [named after Gilles de la *Tourette* d.1904, French neurologist, who identified it]

tourism *noun* **1** the activity of visiting places, *esp* in foreign coun-tries, for pleasure. **2** the organizing by commercial companies of travel, accommodation, etc for tourists.

tourist *noun* **1** somebody who goes on a tour for pleasure, *esp* somebody who takes a holiday abroad. **2** a member of a sports team that is visiting another country to play usu international matches. ⮞⮞ **touristic** /tooə'ristik/ *adj*.

tourist class *noun* the lowest class of accommodation, e.g. on a ship.

touristy *adj informal, derog* frequented by or appealing to tourists.

tourmaline /'tooəmaleen/ *noun* a variously coloured mineral consisting of a complex silicate of boron and aluminium, used in electrical and optical equipment and as a gem when transparent. [Sinhalese *toramalli* carnelian]

tournament /'tooənəmənt, 'taw-/ *noun* **1** a series of games or contests for a championship. **2** a contest between two parties of mounted medieval knights armed with usu blunted lances or swords. [Middle English *tornement* from Old French *torneiement*, from *torneier*: see TOURNEY[2]]

tournedos /'tooənədoh/ *noun* (*pl* **tournedos** /-doh(z)/) a small steak cut from the centre of a beef fillet and usu larded, tied, and held in shape with a skewer. [French *tournedos* from *tourner* to turn, from Old French *torner* (see TURN[1]) + *dos* back, from Latin *dorsum*]

tourney[1] *noun* (*pl* **tourneys**) a tournament, *esp* in the Middle Ages.

tourney[2] /'tooəni, 'tawni/ *verb intrans* (**tourneys, tourneyed, tourneying**) to take part in a tournament, *esp* in the Middle Ages. [Middle English *tourneyen* from Old French *torneier*, from *torn, tourn* lathe, circuit, from Latin *tornus*: see TURN[1]]

tourniquet /'tooənikay, 'taw-/ *noun* a bandage or other device for applying pressure to check bleeding or blood flow. [French *tourni-quet* turnstile, tourniquet, from *tourner* to turn, from Old French *torner*: see TURN[1]]

tousle /'towzl/ *verb trans* (*usu in passive*) **1** to make (something, *esp* somebody's hair) untidy: *running his fingers through his tousled locks.* **2** to make (a person) untidy or dishevelled: *He got up himself, laugh-ing and glowing, and tousled* — Frances Hodgson Burnett. [Middle English *touselen*, frequentative of dialect *touse* to pull roughly]

tout[1] /towt/ *verb intrans* to solicit for customers. ⮞ *verb trans* **1** to praise or publicize (something) loudly or extravagantly: *It was touted as the most elaborate suburban shopping development in all Shropshire.* **2a** to try to sell (something) by a very direct or insistent approach to potential customers. **b** *Brit* to sell (tickets in great demand) at exploitative prices. **3a** *Brit* to spy out information about (e.g. a racing stable or horse). **b** *NAmer* to give a tip or solicit bets on (a racehorse). ⮞⮞ **touter** *noun*. [Old English *tyten* to peer, look out]

tout[2] *noun* **1** (*also* **ticket tout**) *Brit* somebody who offers tickets for an event, e.g. a concert or football match, at vastly inflated prices. **2** somebody who touts.

tout de suite /ˌtooh də ˈsweet (*French* tu d(ə) sɥit)/ *adv* immedi-ately; at once. [French *tout de suite*]

tovarish *or* **tovarich** /təˈvahrish/ *noun* a comrade, used *esp* as a general, egalitarian form of address in the former Soviet Union. [Russian *tovarishch* comrade]

tow[1] /toh/ *verb trans* to draw or pull (something) along behind, *esp* by a rope or chain. ⮞⮞ **towable** *adj*. [Old English *togian*]

tow[2] *noun* **1** the act of towing or the state of being towed. **2** some-thing towed, e.g. a boat or car. * **in tow 1** being towed: *a break-down lorry with a car in tow.* **2** under guidance or protection: *I was taken in tow by a friendly neighbour.* **3** in the position of a companion or follower: *A young man passed with a good-looking girl in tow.*

tow[3] *noun* short or broken fibre, e.g. of flax or hemp, prepared for spinning. ⮞⮞ **towy** *adj*. [Old English *tow-*, recorded in *towcraeft* spinning]

towage /'toh·ij/ *noun* the price paid for towing.

toward[1] /tə'wawd/ *prep chiefly NAmer* towards.

toward[2] *adj archaic* happening at the moment; afoot. [Old English *tōweard* facing, imminent, from *tō* TO[1] + *-weard* -WARD]

towards *prep* **1** moving or situated in the direction of: *driving towards town.* **2a** along a course leading to: *a long stride towards dis-armament.* **b** in relation to: *an attitude towards life.* **3** turned in the direction of: *His back was towards me.* **4** not long before: *towards the end of the afternoon.* **5** for the partial financing of: *I put the extra money towards a holiday.* [Old English *tōweardes*, alteration of *tōweard*: see TOWARD[2]]

tow bar *noun* a bar attached to the back of a vehicle so that a caravan or trailer can be towed.

tow-coloured *adj* said of hair: pale yellow; blonde.

towel[1] /'towəl/ *noun* **1** an absorbent cloth for wiping or drying something, e.g. crockery or the body, after washing. **2** a piece of absorbent paper used for drying the hands. **3** = SANITARY TOWEL. [Middle English *towaille* from Old French *toaille*, of Germanic origin]

towel[2] *verb trans* (**towelled, towelling**, *NAmer* **toweled, towel-ing**) **1** to rub or dry (e.g. the body) with a towel. **2** *Aus, NZ, informal* to beat (somebody).

towelling (*NAmer* **toweling**) *noun* a cotton or linen fabric often used for making towels.

tower[1] /'towə/ *noun* **1** a typically tall and narrow building or structure that may stand alone or be attached to a larger structure and that may be fully walled in or have a skeleton framework. **2** a citadel or fortress. **3** a tall unit for storage: *a CD tower*. ➤➤ **towered** *adj.* [Old English *torr* and Old French *tur*, via Latin from Greek *turris, tyrsis*]

tower[2] *verb intrans* (**towered, towering**) to reach or rise to a great height.

tower block *noun Brit* a tall multi-storey building, usu containing flats or offices.

towering *adj* **1** impressively high or great: *towering pines*. **2** reaching a high point of intensity: *a towering rage*. **3** going beyond proper bounds: *towering ambitions*.

tower of strength *noun* somebody who can be relied on as a source of sympathy and support.

towhead *noun* **1** somebody with a head of hair resembling tow, *esp* in being flaxen or tousled. **2** such a head of hair. ➤➤ **towheaded** *adj.*

towhee /'tohhee, 'towhee/ *noun* any of several species of large brown N American songbirds with a long tail: genus *Pipilo*. [of imitative origin]

to wit *adv* that is to say. [archaic *wit* to know, from Old English *witan*]

towline *noun* = TOWROPE.

town /town/ *noun* **1a** a compactly settled area as distinguished from surrounding rural territory; *esp* one larger than a village but smaller than a city. **b** a large densely populated urban area; a city. **2** a neighbouring city, capital city, or metropolis: *He travels into town daily*. **3** the business centre of a large town or city. **4** the city or urban life as contrasted with the country or rural life. **5** the townspeople: *It was the talk of the town*. **6** *NAmer* = TOWNSHIP. **✳ go to town** to deal with or exploit something enthusiastically, thoroughly, or ostentatiously: *The papers went to town on the hidden life of Leroy* — Sunday Times. **on the town** in usu carefree pursuit of entertainment or amusement, e.g. city nightlife. [Old English *tūn* enclosure, village, town]

town clerk *noun* **1** in the USA, a public officer charged with recording the official proceedings and statistics of a town. **2** in Britain until 1974, an official appointed to administer municipal affairs and to act as secretary to the town council.

town crier *noun* somebody employed to make public proclamations.

townee /'towni, tow'nee/ *noun* see TOWNIE.

town gas *noun Brit* = COAL GAS.

town hall *noun* the chief administrative building of a town.

town house /hows/ *noun* **1** a terrace house typically of three storeys. **2** the city residence of somebody who has a country seat.

townie *or* **townee** /'towni, tow'nee/ *noun informal* a townsman, *esp* as distinguished from a country dweller or from a member of the academic community in a university town.

town planning *noun* the study of the function of the various components of the urban environment and the planning of their arrangement and interrelationship for best results. ➤➤ **town planner** *noun.*

townscape /'townskayp/ *noun* the overall visual aspect of a town.

townsfolk *pl noun* = TOWNSPEOPLE.

township *noun* **1** an urban area inhabited by non-white citizens in S Africa; *esp* one formerly designated as a black settlement. **2** in the USA and Canada: **a** a subdivision of a county, often with some powers of local government. **b** an area of surveyed land six miles square. **3** an ancient unit of administration in England identical in area with or being a division of a parish. **4** a small town or settlement in Australia or New Zealand.

townsman *or* **townswoman** *noun* (*pl* **townsmen** *or* **townswomen**) **1** a man or woman who is a native or resident of a town or city. **2** a fellow citizen of a town.

townspeople *pl noun* the inhabitants of a town or city.

townswoman *noun* see TOWNSMAN.

towpath *noun* a path, e.g. along a canal, for use in towing boats.

towrope *noun* a line used in towing a boat, car, etc.

tox- *or* **toxi-** *or* **toxic-** *or* **toxico-** *or* **toxo-** *comb. form* forming words, denoting: poison: *toxaemia; toxicology*. [late Latin *tox-* from Latin *toxicum* poison]

toxaemia (*NAmer* **toxemia**) /tok'seemi·ə/ *noun* **1** an abnormal condition associated with the presence of toxic substances in the blood. **2** = PREECLAMPSIA. ➤➤ **toxaemic** /-mik/ *adj.* [Latin *toxaemia*, from TOX- + -AEMIA]

toxi- *comb. form* see TOX-.

toxic /'toksik/ *adj* **1** = POISONOUS. **2** relating to or caused by a poison or toxin. ➤➤ **toxically** *adv*, **toxicity** /tok'sisiti/ *noun*. [late Latin *toxicus* from Latin *toxicum* poison, from Greek *toxikon* arrow poison, neuter of *toxikos* of a bow, from *toxon* bow, arrow]

toxic- *comb. form* see TOX-.

toxicant /'toksikənt/ *noun* a toxic substance; *esp* one used for insect control that kills rather than repels. [medieval Latin *toxicant-, toxicans*, present part. of *toxicare* to poison, from Latin *toxicum* poison]

toxico- *comb. form* see TOX-.

toxicological /ˌtoksikə'lojikl/ *adj* relating to toxicology or toxins. ➤➤ **toxicologically** *adv.*

toxicology /ˌtoksi'koləji/ *noun* a branch of biology that deals with poisons and their effects and with medical, industrial, legal, or other problems arising from them. ➤➤ **toxicologist** *noun.*

toxic shock syndrome *noun* acute septicaemia that may be caused by toxins produced by certain bacteria and that has been linked with the use of tampons during menstruation.

toxigenic /ˌtoksi'jenik/ *adj* producing toxin: *toxigenic bacteria*. ➤➤ **toxigenicity** /-'nisiti/ *noun.*

toxin /'toksin/ *noun* an often extremely poisonous protein produced by a living organism, e.g. a bacterium, *esp* in the body of a host. [TOX- + -IN[1]]

toxo- *comb. form* see TOX-.

toxocariasis /ˌtoksəkə'rie·əsis/ *noun* an infection in humans transmitted via domestic pets or soil contaminated by the larvae of a genus of roundworms. [Latin genus name *Toxocara*, from TOXO- + Greek *kara* head + -IASIS]

toxoid /'toksoyd/ *noun* a toxin of a disease-causing organism treated so as to destroy its toxicity but leave it capable of inducing the formation of antibodies on injection.

toxophilite /tok'sofiliet/ *noun formal* a lover of or expert at archery. ➤➤ **toxophily** /-li/ *noun*. [Greek *toxon* bow, arrow + *philos* dear, loving]

toxoplasmosis /ˌtoksohplaz'mohsis/ *noun* a disease caused by a genus of parasitic protozoans that is transmitted to humans, other mammals, and birds via infected soil or animal faeces. [Latin genus name *Toxoplasma* + -OSIS]

toy[1] /toy/ *noun* **1a** something for a child to play with. **b** something designed for amusement or diversion rather than practical use: *an executive toy*. **2** (*used before a noun*) something tiny; *esp* an animal of a breed or variety of exceptionally small size: *a toy poodle*. ➤➤ **toylike** *adj.* [Middle English *toye* joke, prank; earlier history unknown]

toy[2] *verb intrans* **1** (+ with) to touch or handle something in an absent-minded or nonchalant way; to play or fiddle with it. **2** (+ with) to consider something as a possibility but without committing oneself at all: *I'm toying with the idea of going freelance*. **3** (+ with) to flirt.

toy boy *noun Brit, informal* a young man taken as lover or companion by an older woman.

TQM *abbr* total quality management.

TR *abbr* Turkey (international vehicle registration).

tr. *abbr* **1** transitive. **2** translated. **3** translator. **4** trill. **5** trustee.

trabeate /'traybiət, -ayt/ *adj* = TRABEATED.

trabeated /'traybiaytid/ *adj* designed or constructed with vertical posts and horizontal beams. ➤➤ **trabeation** /-'aysh(ə)n/ *noun.* [Latin *trabes* beam]

trabecula /trə'bekyoolə/ *noun* (*pl* **trabeculae** /-lee/) **1** in anatomy, a small bar, rod, bundle of fibres, or dividing membrane in the framework of a body organ or part. **2** in botany, a fold, ridge, or bar projecting into or extending from a plant part. ➤➤ **trabecular** *adj*, **trabeculate** /-lət/ *adj*. [Latin *trabecula* little beam, dimin. of *trabs, trabes* beam]

trace[1] /trays/ *noun* **1a** a mark or line left by something that has passed. **b** = FOOTPRINT. **2** something traced or drawn; *esp* the graphic record made by a seismograph or other recording _instrument. **3a** a minute and often barely detectable amount or indication: *a trace of a smile.* **b** an amount of a chemical constituent not quantitatively determined because of minuteness: *The product contained a trace of impurity.* **4** a sign or evidence of some past thing; a vestige; *specif* an ENGRAM (physical change in brain tissue involved in creating a memory). **5** an attempt to find something or somebody. **6** the intersection of a line or plane with a plane. **7** in mathematics, the sum of the elements of the principal diagonal of a matrix. **8** *chiefly NAmer* = TRACK[1] (1). [Middle English from French, from *tracier*: see TRACE[2]]

trace[2] *verb trans* **1a** to find (something or somebody) by using signs, evidence, or remains: *She is trying to trace her real father.* **b** to follow back or study (something) in detail or step by step: *The book traces the history of the labour movement.* **c** to follow the course or trail of (something). **2a** to copy (e.g. a drawing) by following the lines or letters as seen through a semitransparent superimposed sheet. **b** to delineate or sketch (something). **c** to write (e.g. letters or figures) painstakingly. **d** to record a tracing of (something), usu in the form of a curved, wavy, or broken line. **e** to adorn (something) with ornamental lines, e.g. architectural tracery. ➤ *verb intrans* to be traceable historically. ➤ **traceability** /-'biliti/ *noun*, **traceable** *adj*, **traceless** *adj*. [Middle English *tracen* from early French *tracier*, ultimately from Latin *tractus*, past part. of *trahere* to pull, draw]

trace[3] *noun* either of two straps, chains, or lines of a harness for attaching a vehicle to a horse. [Middle English *trais* traces, from early French *trais*, pl of *trait* pull, draught trace, from Latin *tractus*: see TRACE[2]]

trace element *noun* a chemical element present in minute quantities; *esp* one essential to a living organism for proper growth and development.

trace fossil *noun* a fossil of a trace left by an animal, e.g. a footprint.

tracer *noun* **1** ammunition containing a chemical composition to mark the flight of projectiles by a trail of smoke or fire. **2** a substance, *esp* a labelled element or atom, used to trace the course of a chemical or biological process. **3** somebody or something that traces.

tracery *noun* (*pl* **traceries**) **1** ornamental stone openwork in architecture, *esp* in the head of a Gothic window. **2** a decorative interlacing of lines, e.g. in a frost pattern or insect's wing. ➤ **traceried** *adj*.

trache- *or* **tracheo-** *comb. form* forming words, denoting: the trachea: *tracheotomy.* [Latin *trache-* from late Latin *trachea*]

trachea /trə'kee-ə/ *noun* (*pl* **tracheae** /trə'kee-ee/ *or* **tracheas**) **1** the main trunk of the system of tubes by which air passes to and from the lungs in vertebrates; the windpipe. **2** any of the small tubes carrying air through the bodies of most insects and many other arthropods. **3** a vessel in a plant conveying water and nutrients. ➤ **tracheal** /'trayki-əl, trə'kee-əl/ *adj*, **tracheate** /'trayki-ət, -ayt, 'trak-/ *adj*. [Middle English via late Latin from Greek *tracheia* (*artēria*) rough (artery), from fem of *trachys* rough]

tracheo- *comb. form* see TRACHE-.

tracheotomy /traki'otəmi/ *noun* (*pl* **tracheotomies**) the surgical operation of cutting into the trachea, *esp* through the skin, usu to relieve suffocation by inhaled matter.

trachoma /trə'kohmə/ *noun* a chronic contagious eye disease that is caused by a minute organism and commonly results in blindness if left untreated. ➤ **trachomatous** /trə'komətəs, trə'koh-/ *adj*. [via Latin from Greek *trachōma* roughness, from *trachys* rough]

trachyte /'trakiet, 'traykiet/ *noun* a usu light-coloured volcanic rock consisting chiefly of potash feldspar. [French *trachyte* from Greek *trachys* rough]

trachytic /trə'kitik/ *adj* said of the texture of igneous rock: having lath-shaped feldspar crystals arranged in almost parallel lines.

tracing *noun* **1** a copy, e.g. of a design or map, made on a superimposed semitransparent sheet. **2** a graphic record made by an instrument that monitors some movement.

tracing paper *noun* a semitransparent paper for tracing drawings.

track[1] /trak/ *noun* **1a** a path beaten by feet, or as if by feet; a trail. **b** a roughly made path or road. **2a** detectable evidence, e.g. a line of footprints or a wheel rut, that something has passed. **b** a recent or fossil footprint: *the huge track of a dinosaur.* **3** a specially laid-out course, *esp* for racing. **4a** the parallel rails of a railway. **b** a rail or length of railing along which something, *esp* a curtain, moves or is pulled. **5a** the course along which something moves: *the track of a bullet.* **b** the projection on the earth's surface of the path along which something, e.g. a missile or an aircraft, has flown. **6** a course of action or line of thought. **7a** either of two continuous usu metal belts on which a tracklaying vehicle travels. **b** the width of a wheeled vehicle from wheel to wheel, usu measured from the outside of the rims. **8a** any of a series of parallel elongated regions on a magnetic tape on which a recording is made. **b** a more or less independent sequence of recording, e.g. a single movement or song, on a compact disc, record, or cassette. ✳ **in one's tracks** where one stands or is at the moment: *He was stopped in his tracks.* **keep/lose track of** to remain aware/no longer be aware of the development or whereabouts of something or somebody. **make tracks** *informal* to leave. **off track** not following the correct course; inaccurate or unlikely to succeed. **on the right/wrong track** likely/unlikely to achieve something by continuing one's present course of action. **on track** following the correct course or taking the correct action to achieve something. ➤➤ **trackless** *adj*. [Middle English *trak* from early French *trac*, perhaps of Germanic origin]

track[2] *verb trans* **1** to follow the tracks or traces of (somebody or something); to trail (them): *tracking game.* **2** to follow the progress of (somebody or something): *We tracked the company's performance.* **3** to observe or plot the course of (e.g. a spacecraft or missile) instrumentally. **4** *chiefly NAmer* to carry (something) on the feet and deposit it: *Don't track mud into the house.* **5** to travel through (an area): *tracking a desert.* ➤ *verb intrans* **1a** to move a film or television camera towards, beside, or away from a subject while shooting a scene. **b** said of a camera: to undergo tracking. **2a** said of a gramophone needle: to follow the groove of a record. **b** said of a pair of wheels: to fit a track or rails. **c** said of a rear wheel of a vehicle: to follow accurately the corresponding front wheel on a straight track. ➤➤ **tracker** *noun*.

trackball *noun* in computing, a type of mouse consisting of a ball mounted in a box; the ball being rotated by the fingers or palm to control the cursor.

track down *verb trans* to search for (somebody or something) until found: *Police tracked the criminal down; I tracked down their new telephone number.*

tracked *adj* = TRACKLAYING.

tracker ball *noun* = TRACKBALL.

track event *noun* an athletic event that is a race: compare FIELD EVENT.

tracking *noun* **1** the act or process of following the trail of a person or animal. **2** the alignment of a vehicle's wheels. **3** the process of finding the best quality video picture by aligning the heads with the tape: *digital tracking.* **4** in electrical engineering, the leaking of current between two insulated points because of moisture or dirt.

tracking shot *noun* a camera shot in which the camera follows the action.

tracking station *noun* a place from which satellites, missiles, etc are tracked with radar or radio signals.

tracklaying *adj* said of a vehicle: travelling on two or more endless usu metal belts.

track record *noun* a record of the past achievements or performance of an individual in some capacity, or of an organization, team, etc: *Each professor has a right to money and manpower resources depending only on his level of seniority and not on his track record in research* — New Scientist.

track rod *noun* a rod that connects the steering column of a motor vehicle to the front wheels.

track shoe *noun* a lightweight usu leather shoe with metal spikes protruding from the sole, worn by runners.

tracksuit *noun* a warm loose-fitting suit worn by athletes when training, or as casual wear.

tract[1] /trakt/ *noun* a short practical treatise; *esp* a pamphlet of religious propaganda. [Middle English, modification of Latin *tractatus* treatise, past part. of *tractare* to draw out, handle, treat, frequentative of *trahere* to pull, draw]

tract[2] *noun* **1** a region or area of land of indefinite extent. **2** a system of body parts or organs that collectively serve some often specified purpose: *the digestive tract.* **3** *archaic* an extent or lapse of time. [Latin *tractus* action of drawing, extension, past part. of *trahere* to pull, draw]

tractable /'traktəbl/ *adj* **1** said of a person or animal: easily taught or controlled: *a tractable horse.* **2a** said of a material: easily handled, shaped, or worked with. **b** said of a problem or situation: easy to deal with. ➤➤ **tractability** /-'biliti/ *noun,* **tractably** *adv.* [Latin *tractabilis* from *tractare*: see TRACT¹]

Tractarianism /trak'teəri·əniz(ə)m/ *noun* a system of High Church principles set forth in a series of tracts at Oxford (1833–41); the doctrines of the early Oxford Movement. ➤➤ **Tractarian** *adj.*

tractate /'traktayt/ *noun* a treatise or dissertation. [Latin *tractatus,* past part. of *tractare*: see TRACT¹]

traction /'traksh(ə)n/ *noun* **1a** pulling, being pulled, or the force exerted in pulling. **b** the use of motive power to pull a vehicle, or the motive power employed. **2** in medicine, a pulling force exerted on part of the body by means of a special device to treat fractures, cure deformities, etc. **3** the adhesive friction of a body on a surface on which it moves, e.g. a tyre on a road surface; grip. ➤➤ **tractional** *adj,* **tractive** /'traktiv/ *adj.* [late Latin *traction-, tractio,* from Latin *trahere* to pull, draw]

traction engine *noun* a large steam- or diesel-powered vehicle used to draw other vehicles or equipment over roads or fields and sometimes to provide power, e.g. for sawing or ploughing.

tractor /'traktə/ *noun* **1** a four-wheeled or tracklaying vehicle used for pulling or using farm machinery. **2** a truck with a short chassis and no body except a driver's cab, used to haul a large trailer or trailers. [Latin *tractor* from *trahere* to pull, draw]

trad¹ /trad/ *adj informal* = TRADITIONAL.

trad² *noun informal* traditional jazz.

trade¹ /trayd/ *noun* **1** the business of buying and selling or bartering commodities: *Trade was brisk.* **2a** (*treated as sing. or pl*) the people or group of firms engaged in a particular business or industry: *the shoe trade.* **b** (*treated as sing. or pl*) a firm's customers; a clientele. **3a** the business or work in which one engages regularly; an occupation. **b** an occupation requiring manual or mechanical skill; a craft. **c** *dated, derog* commerce as opposed to the liberal professions or landed property. **d** *dated, derog* the social group deriving its income from commerce. **4** = TRADE WIND. **5** *chiefly NAmer* a transaction, or an exchange of property usu without the involvement of money.

Word history
Middle English from early Low German, literally 'track'. The orig senses in English were 'course', 'track', 'way'; hence 'way of life or of making a living'.

trade² *verb intrans* **1** to engage in the exchange, purchase, or sale of goods. **2** to give one thing in exchange for another. **3** *NAmer* to make one's purchases; to shop. **4** (+ on) to exploit or take advantage of (something): *They traded on his good nature.* ➤ *verb trans* **1** to give (something) in exchange for another commodity; to barter (something). **2** to engage in frequent buying and selling of (e.g. shares or commodities) usu in search of quick profits. ➤➤ **tradable** *adj,* **tradeable** *adj.*

trade cycle *noun* the regularly recurrent fluctuation in the level of economic activity.

trade deficit *noun* = TRADE GAP.

trade discount *noun* a discount price at which goods are sold to people in the same trade or by a manufacturer or wholesaler to a retailer.

traded option *noun* an option to buy or sell securities or commodities that can itself be bought or sold.

trade down *verb intrans* to trade something in for something of the same kind but less expensive or valuable.

trade edition *noun* an edition of a book in a standard format intended for general distribution.

trade gap *noun* the amount by which the value of a country's imports exceeds that of its exports.

trade in *verb trans* to give (a used item) as payment or part payment for a new item.

trade-in *noun* an item of merchandise, e.g. a car or refrigerator, that is traded in.

trademark¹ *noun* **1** a name or distinctive symbol or device attached to goods produced by a particular firm or individual and legally reserved to the exclusive use of the owner of the mark as

maker or seller. **2** a distinguishing feature firmly associated with somebody or something.

trademark² *verb trans* to secure trademark rights for (something); to register the trademark of (it).

trade name *noun* **1a** the name used for an article by the trade. **b** a name given by a manufacturer or seller to an article or service to distinguish it and protect it as a trademark. **2** the name under which a concern does business.

trade off *verb trans* to give (something) up in return for something else.

trade-off *noun* a giving up of one thing in return for another, *esp* as a compromise.

trade plates *pl noun Brit* temporary number plates used on a vehicle before it is registered.

trade price *noun* the price at which goods are sold to other people in the same trade or by a manufacturer or wholesaler to a retailer.

trader *noun* **1** a retail or wholesale dealer. **2** somebody who buys and sells shares, commodities, etc in search of short-term profits. **3** a ship engaged in trade.

tradescantia /traydə'skanshi·ə, tradə'skanti·ə/ *noun* a commonly grown houseplant with usu blue or violet flowers and striped leaves: genus *Tradescantia.* [Latin genus name, named after John *Tradescant* d.1638, English traveller and gardener]

tradesman *noun* (*pl* **tradesmen**) **1** a shopkeeper. **2** a worker in a skilled trade.

trades union *noun* = TRADE UNION.

trade surplus *noun* the amount by which the value of a country's exports exceeds that of its imports.

trade union *noun* an organization of workers formed for the purpose of advancing its members' interests. ➤➤ **trade unionism** *noun,* **trade unionist** *noun.*

trade up *verb intrans* to trade something in for something of the same kind but more expensive or valuable.

trade wind *noun* a mainly sea wind blowing almost continually towards the equator from the NE in the northern hemisphere and from the SE in the southern hemisphere roughly between latitudes 0 and 30. [obsolete *trade* in a regular course or direction, from TRADE¹]

trading estate *noun Brit* an industrial estate.

trading post *noun* a station of a trader or trading company established in a sparsely settled region where trade, *esp* in products of local origin, e.g. furs, is carried on.

trading stamp *noun* a printed stamp of a certain value given by a retailer to a customer, to be accumulated and redeemed in merchandise or cash.

tradition /trə'dish(ə)n/ *noun* **1** the handing down of information, beliefs, and customs by word of mouth or by example from one generation to another. **2a** an inherited pattern of thought or action, e.g. a religious practice or a social custom. **b** a convention or set of conventions associated with or representative of an individual, group, or period: *The title poem represents a complete break with nineteenth-century tradition* — F R Leavis. **3** cultural continuity in social attitudes and institutions. **4a** in Christianity, doctrine deriving from oral tradition rather than the Bible. **b** in Judaism, laws regarded as having been given by God to Moses. **c** in Islam, beliefs and customs not in the Koran, e.g. the words of Muhammad. ➤➤ **traditionless** *adj.* [Middle English *tradicioun* via French from Latin *tradition-, traditio* action of handing over, tradition, from *tradere* to hand over, deliver, betray, from TRANS- + *dare* to give]

traditional *adj* **1** of or handed down by tradition. **2** of or being a style of jazz orig played in New Orleans in the early 1900s. ➤➤ **traditionally** *adv.*

traditionalism *noun* **1** the doctrines or practices of those who follow or accept tradition. **2** the beliefs of those opposed to modernism, liberalism, or radicalism, e.g. in religious matters. ➤➤ **traditionalist** *noun and adj,* **traditionalistic** /-'listik/ *adj.*

traduce /trə'dyoohs/ *verb trans formal* to attempt to damage the reputation or standing of (somebody), *esp* by misrepresentation; to defame (them). ➤➤ **traducement** *noun,* **traducer** *noun.* [Latin *traducere* to lead across, transfer, degrade, from TRANS- + *ducere* to lead]

traffic¹ /'trafik/ *noun* **1a** the movement, e.g. of vehicles or pedestrians, through an area or along a route. **b** the vehicles, pedestrians, ships, or aircraft moving along a route. **c** the information or signals transmitted over a communications system. **2a** the passengers or cargo carried by a transport system. **b** the business of transporting passengers or freight. **3a** trade, *esp* in illegal or disreputable merchandise: *drug traffic*. **b** exchange or interchange: *a lively traffic in ideas*. **4** *formal* dealings between individuals or groups. [early French *trafique* from Old Italian *traffico*, from *trafficare* to trade]

traffic² *verb intrans* (**trafficked, trafficking**) to trade, *esp* in something illegal or disreputable. >> **trafficker** *noun.*

trafficator /'trafikaytə/ *noun Brit* a hinged retractable illuminated arm on the side of an old motor car. [blend of TRAFFIC¹ and INDICATOR]

traffic calming *noun* the use of deterrents to speed, e.g. the narrowing of a road or the installation of humps in it, in order to slow vehicles in an area.

traffic circle *noun NAmer* = ROUNDABOUT¹ (1).

traffic island *noun* a paved or planted island in a road designed to guide the flow of traffic and provide refuge for pedestrians.

traffic jam *noun* a line of vehicles that cannot move normally because of an obstruction.

traffic light *noun* (*usu in pl*) an automatically operated signal with coloured lights for controlling traffic.

traffic pattern *noun* a pattern of routes to be followed by aircraft approaching or leaving an airport.

traffic signal *noun* a signal, e.g. traffic lights, for controlling traffic.

traffic warden *noun Brit* an official who enforces car-parking regulations and helps in maintaining the traffic flow in urban areas.

tragacanth /'tragəkanth/ *noun* a gum obtained from various Asiatic or E European leguminous plants, used in manufacturing and in pharmacy. [early French *tragacanthe* via Latin from Greek *tragakantha*, from *tragos* goat + *akantha* thorn]

tragedian /trə'jeedi·ən/ *noun* **1** an actor who plays tragic roles. **2** a writer of tragedies.

tragedienne /trəjeedi'en/ *noun* a female tragedian.

tragedy /'trajədi/ *noun* (*pl* **tragedies**) **1** a disastrous event; a calamity. **2** a serious drama in which destructive circumstances result in adversity for, and usu the deaths of, the main characters: compare COMEDY.

𝔚ord history
Middle English *tragedie* via French and Latin from Greek *tragōidia*, prob from *tragos* goat + *aeidein* to sing. It has been suggested that the origin of the word is linked with the goat-satyrs which appeared in some Peloponnesian plays, but there is no evidence to prove or disprove this.

tragi /'trayjee, -jie, -gee/ *noun* pl of TRAGUS.

tragic /'trajik/ *adj* **1a** deplorable or lamentable: *a tragic waste of young talent.* **b** relating to sombre or disastrous events: *the tragic significance of the atomic bomb* — Harry S Truman. **2** of, appropriate to, dealing with, or treated in literary tragedy: *the tragic hero; tragic delivery.* **3** expressive of woe: *in a tragic voice; with a tragic expression.* >> **tragical** *adj,* **tragically** *adv.* [Latin *tragicus* from Greek *tragikos,* irreg from *tragōidia:* see TRAGEDY]

tragic flaw *noun* a character flaw that brings about the downfall of the hero of a tragedy.

tragic irony *noun* = IRONY¹ (2C).

tragicomedy /traji'komədi/ *noun* (*pl* **tragicomedies**) a literary work in which tragic and comic elements are mixed in a usu ironic way. >> **tragicomic** /-mik/ *adj,* **tragicomical** /-mikl/ *adj,* **tragicomically** /-mikli/ *adv.* [early French *tragicomedie* via Old Italian and Old Spanish from Latin *tragicomoedia,* from *tragicus* (see TRAGIC) + *comoedia* from Greek *kōmōidia:* see COMEDY]

tragopan /'tragəpan/ *noun* any of a genus of brilliantly coloured Asiatic pheasants: genus *Tragopan.* [Latin genus name, from Latin *Tragopan* an Ethiopian bird, from Greek, from *tragos* goat + *Pan* Pan, the horned god of woods and shepherds: so called from the fleshy 'horns' of some species]

tragus /'traygəs/ *noun* (*pl* **tragi** /'trayjee, -jie, -gee/) the prominence in front of the external opening of the ear. [via Latin from Greek *tragos* a part of the ear, literally 'goat']

trail¹ /trayl/ *noun* **1a** a trace or mark left by somebody or something that has passed; a scent or track: *a trail of blood; on the trail of the killer.* **b** a track made by the passage of people or animals, *esp* through a wilderness. **c** a marked path through a forest or mountainous region. **d** a route followed or to be followed for a particular purpose: *a campaign trail.* **2a** something that follows or moves along as if being drawn behind; a train: *a trail of admirers.* **b** the streak of light produced by a meteor. **c** a continuous line produced photographically by permitting the image of a celestial body, e.g. a star, to move over the plate. **d** a chain of consequences; an aftermath: *She left a trail of broken hearts behind her.* **3** the part of a gun carriage that rests on the ground when the gun is detached and ready for action. >> **trailless** *adj.*

trail² *verb intrans* **1a** to hang down so as to sweep the ground: *His coat trailed in the dust.* **b** to extend over a surface in a loose or straggling manner: *The vine trails over the ground.* **c** said of a plant, branch, etc: to grow to such a length as to droop over towards the ground: *the trailing branches of a weeping willow.* **2a** (*usu* + along) to walk or proceed draggingly, heavily, or wearily; to plod or trudge. **b** to lag behind; to do poorly in relation to others. **3** (*usu* + off/away) to become quieter or weaker; to dwindle: *Her voice trailed off uncertainly.* > *verb trans* **1a** to drag (something) loosely along a surface; to allow (it) to sweep the ground. **b** to drag (e.g. a limb or the body) heavily or wearily. **c** to carry or bring (something) along as an addition, burden, or encumbrance. **d** to draw (something) along in one's wake: *trailing clouds of glory do we come* — Wordsworth. **2a** to follow the scent or trace of (e.g. an animal); to track (it). **b** to follow behind or in the footsteps of (somebody). **c** to lag behind (e.g. a competitor). **3** to advertise (e.g. a film) with a trailer. ＊ **trail arms** to carry a weapon horizontally. [Middle English *trailen* from early French *trailler* to tow, ultimately from Latin *tragula* sledge, dragnet]

trail bike *noun* a light motorcycle for cross-country or off-road riding.

trailblazer *noun* **1** somebody who finds and marks a new route through wild country. **2** a pioneer; an innovator: *a trailblazer in astrophysics.* >> **trailblazing** *adj.*

trailer *noun* **1a** a wheeled vehicle designed to be towed, e.g. by a lorry or car. **b** *NAmer* = CARAVAN¹. **c** the rear part of an articulated lorry. **2** a set of short excerpts from a film shown in advance for publicity purposes. **3** a trailing plant.

trailer park *noun NAmer* a caravan or mobile home site.

trailing edge *noun* the rearmost edge of an aerofoil, e.g. a wing or propeller blade.

train¹ /trayn/ *noun* **1** a connected line of railway carriages or wagons with or without a locomotive. **2** a moving file of people, vehicles, or animals. **3** = RETINUE. **4** the vehicles, men, and sometimes animals that accompany an army with baggage, supplies, ammunition, or siege artillery. **5** a connected series of ideas, actions, or events. **6** a part of a gown that trails behind the wearer. **7** a series of connected moving mechanical parts, e.g. gears. **8** a line of gunpowder laid to lead fire to a charge. [Middle English from Old French *train,* from *trahiner* to draw, drag, from Latin *trahere*]

train² *verb trans* **1** to teach (a person or animal) to do something; to make (them) fit, qualified, or proficient. **2** to prepare (somebody), e.g. by exercise, for a test of skill. **3** to direct the growth of (a plant), usu by bending, pruning, and tying. **4** to aim (something) at an object or objective; to direct (it): *He trained his rifle on the target.* > *verb intrans* **1** to undergo training. **2** *dated* to go by train. >> **trainable** *adj.* [Middle English *trainen* from Old French *trahiner:* see TRAIN¹]

trainband *noun* a 17th-cent. or 18th-cent. English militia company. [alteration of *trained band*]

trainbearer *noun* an attendant who holds the train of a robe or gown, e.g. on a ceremonial occasion.

trainee /tray'nee/ *noun* somebody who is being trained for a job.

trainer *noun* **1a** a person who trains the members of an athletic team, e.g. footballers. **b** a person who trains and prepares horses for racing. **c** an aircraft or piece of equipment for training aircrew. **2** *Brit* a sports shoe designed for running, jogging, etc.

training *noun* **1** the bringing of a person or animal to a desired degree of proficiency in some activity or skill. **2** the condition of being trained, *esp* for a contest: *an athlete out of training.*

training college *noun Brit* a school offering specialized instruction.

training shoe *noun* = TRAINER (2).

train oil *noun* oil from a whale or other marine animal. [obsolete *train* train oil, from early Dutch *trane* or early Low German *trān*, literally 'tear', because it was extracted in small drops]

trainspotter *noun* **1** *Brit* somebody whose hobby is to observe locomotives and trains and collect information about them. **2** *Brit, informal* somebody who is obsessed with any specialized hobby or interest, *esp* one that is regarded as boring. ➤➤ **trainspotting** *noun*.

traipse[1] /trayps/ *verb intrans* to walk or trudge about, often to little purpose. [origin unknown]

traipse[2] *noun* a long or unpleasant walk.

trait /trayt, tray/ *noun* a distinguishing quality or characteristic. [early French *trait*, literally 'act of pulling', from Latin *trahere* to draw, pull]

traitor /'traytə/ *noun* **1** somebody who betrays another's trust. **2** somebody who commits treason. ➤➤ **traitorous** /-rəs/ *adj*, **traitorously** /-rəsli/ *adv*. [Middle English *traitre* via Old French from Latin *traditor*, from *tradere*: see TRADITION]

trajectory /trə'jektəri/ *noun* (*pl* **trajectories**) **1** the curve that a planet, projectile, etc follows as it moves through space. **2** in geometry, a curve or surface that intersects a family of curves or surfaces at a constant angle. [Latin *trajectoria*, fem of *trajectorius* of passing, from *traicere* to cause to cross, cross]

tram /tram/ *noun* **1** *chiefly Brit* a passenger vehicle running on rails and typically operating on urban streets. **2** a boxlike wagon running on rails, e.g. in a mine. [English dialect *tram* shaft of a wheelbarrow, prob from Low German *traam* beam, shaft]

tramcar /'tramkah/ *noun* = TRAM.

tramline *noun* **1** *Brit* a track on which trams run. **2** (*in pl*) either of the two pairs of sidelines on a tennis or badminton court that mark off the area used in doubles play.

trammel[1] /'traml/ *noun* **1** a net for catching birds or fish; *esp* one having three layers with the middle one finer-meshed and slack so that fish passing through with carry some of the centre net through the coarser opposite net and are trapped. **2** *literary* (*in pl*) something that impedes freedom of action: *the trammels of convention*. **3a** an instrument for drawing ellipses. **b** (*also in pl*) a compass for drawing large circles that consists of a beam with two sliding parts. **4** *NAmer* an adjustable hook for pots over a fireplace. [Middle English *tramayle*, a kind of net, via French from late Latin *tremaculum*, from Latin *tres* three + *macula* mesh, spot]

trammel[2] *verb trans* (**trammelled, trammelling,** *NAmer* **trammeled, trammeling**) to restrain or confine (somebody or something).

tramontana /tramon'tahnə/ *noun* a cold dry northerly wind blowing down the west coast of Italy. [Italian *tramontana*, fem of *tramontano*: see TRAMONTANE[1]]

tramontane[1] /trə'montayn/ *adj* lying on or coming from the other side of a mountain range, *esp* the Alps as seen from Italy. [Italian *tramontano* from Latin *transmontanus*, from TRANS- + *mont-, mons* MOUNTAIN]

tramontane[2] *noun* **1** = TRAMONTANA. **2** somebody who lives in a tramontane region.

tramp[1] /tramp/ *verb intrans* **1** to walk or tread, *esp* heavily. **2a** to travel about on foot. **b** to journey as a tramp. ➤ *verb trans* **1** to travel or wander through (an area) on foot. **2** to trample (something). ➤➤ **tramper** *noun*. [Middle English *trampen*, prob of Germanic origin]

tramp[2] *noun* **1** a wandering homeless person who survives by taking the occasional job or by begging money and food. **2** a usu long and tiring walk. **3** the heavy rhythmic tread of feet. **4** *chiefly NAmer, informal* a promiscuous woman. **5** a merchant vessel that does not work a regular route but carries general cargo to any port as required. **6** an iron plate to protect the sole of a shoe. ➤➤ **trampish** *adj*.

trample[1] /'trampl/ *verb trans* to press down, crush, or injure (something) by treading, or as if by treading. ➤ *verb intrans* **1** to tread heavily so as to bruise, crush, or injure something: *Don't trample on the flower beds*. **2** (*usu* + on/over/upon) to inflict injury with ruthlessness or contempt: *trampling on the rights of others*. ➤➤ **trampler** *noun*. [Middle English *tramplen*, frequentative of *trampen*: see TRAMP[1]]

trample[2] *noun* an act or sound of trampling.

trampoline[1] /'trampəleen/ *noun* a resilient sheet or web supported by springs in a frame and used for bouncing up and down on and performing gymnastic tricks in the air. ➤➤ **trampolining** *noun*. [Spanish *trampolín* from Italian *trampolino*, of Germanic origin]

trampoline[2] *verb intrans* to jump on a trampoline. ➤➤ **trampoliner** *noun*, **trampolinist** *noun*.

tramroad *noun* a track for hauling trams in a mine.

tramway *noun* **1** *Brit* a system of tracks, e.g. laid in the surface of urban streets, for trams. **2** = TRAMROAD.

trance /trahns/ *noun* **1** a state of semiconsciousness or unconsciousness with reduced or absent sensitivity to external stimulation. **2** a usu self-induced state of altered consciousness or ecstasy in which religious or mystical visions may be experienced. **3** a state of profound abstraction or absorption. **4** a type of electronic dance music with a hypnotic beat. ➤➤ **trancelike** *adj*. [Middle English from Old French *transir* to fall into a trance, from Latin *transire* to pass, pass away]

tranche /trahnch (*French* trãʃ)/ *noun* **1** a block of shares usu supplementary to an already existing issue. **2** any of a series of sets, portions, etc of something made available at a particular time: *The discs are to be issued in alphabetical order of composer: the first tranche includes some Bartok, the nine Beethoven symphonies, the Brahms symphonies and works by Bernstein himself* — Daily Telegraph. [French *tranche* slice, from Old French *trenchier, trancher* to cut, from Latin *truncare* to lop off, maim]

tranny *or* **trannie** /'trani/ *noun* (*pl* **trannies**) **1** *chiefly Brit, informal* a transistor radio. **2** *informal* = TRANSVESTITE. **3** = TRANSPARENCY (2).

tranquil /'trangkwil/ *adj* free from mental agitation or from disturbance or commotion; quiet or peaceful. ➤➤ **tranquillity** /tran-g'k-wiliti/ *noun*, **tranquilly** *adv*. [Middle English from Latin *tranquillus*]

tranquillize *or* **tranquillise** (*NAmer* **tranquilize**) *verb trans* to make (a person or animal) tranquil or calm; *esp* to relieve (them) of mental tension and anxiety with drugs.

tranquillizer *or* **tranquilliser** (*NAmer* **tranquilizer**) *noun* a drug, e.g. diazepam, used to tranquillize.

trans. *abbr* **1** transitive. **2** translated. **3** translator.

trans- *prefix* forming words, with the meanings: **1** on or to the other side of, across, or beyond: *transatlantic; transcontinental*. **2** through: *transcutaneous*. **3** so or such as to change or transfer: *transliterate; translocation; transship*. **4** (*usu printed in italic*) characterized by having identical atoms or chemical groups on opposite sides of a chemical double bond in a molecule: *trans-dichlorethylene*. [Latin *trans-, tra-* across, beyond, through, so as to change, from *trans* across, beyond]

transact /tran'zakt/ *verb trans* to perform (something); *esp* to conduct (business). ➤➤ **transactor** *noun*. [Latin *transactus*, past part. of *transigere* to drive through, complete, transact, from TRANS- + *agere* to drive, do]

transaction /tran'zaksh(ə)n/ *noun* **1a** something transacted, *esp* an instance of buying and selling or a business deal. **b** the act of carrying out or conducting *esp* business. **2** (*in pl*) the published record of the meeting of a society or association. ➤➤ **transactional** *adj*.

transalpine /tran'zalpien/ *adj* **1** situated on the north side of the Alps: *transalpine Gaul*. **2** crossing the Alps. [Latin *transalpinus*, from TRANS- + *Alpes* the Alps]

transatlantic /tranzət'lantik/ *adj* **1** crossing or extending across the Atlantic Ocean: *a transatlantic cable*. **2** situated beyond the Atlantic Ocean. **3** relating to or characteristic of people or places situated beyond the Atlantic Ocean: *a transatlantic accent*.

transceiver /tran'seevə/ *noun* a combined radio transmitter and receiver. [blend of TRANSMITTER + RECEIVER]

transcend /tran'send/ *verb trans* **1** to go beyond the limits of (something). **2** to surpass (somebody or something). [Latin *transcendere* to climb across, transcend, from TRANS- + *scandere* to climb]

transcendent /tran'send(ə)nt/ *adj* **1a** exceeding usual limits; surpassing. **b** beyond the limits of ordinary experience. **c** in the philosophy of Kant, beyond the limits of possible experience and knowledge. **2** transcending the universe or material existence: compare IMMANENT. ➤➤ **transcendence** *noun*, **transcendency**

/-si/ *noun,* **transcendently** *adv.* [Latin *transcendent-, transcendens,* present part. of *transcendere:* see TRANSCEND]

transcendental /transen'dentl/ *adj* **1** beyond the limits of ordinary experience; transcendent. **2** = SUPERNATURAL[1]. **3** of or employing the basic categories, e.g. space and time, presupposed by knowledge and experience: *a transcendental proof.* **4** in the philosophy of Kant, transcending direct experience but not rational knowledge. **5a** being or relating to a transcendental number. **b** being, involving, or representing a function that cannot be expressed by a finite number of algebraic operations: *transcendental curves.* ⋙ **transcendentally** *adv.*

transcendentalism *noun* **1** a philosophical system associated with Kant that emphasizes that analysis of the basic categories of knowledge and experience is a precondition for an understanding of reality. **2** a philosophy that asserts the primacy of the spiritual over the material or that fundamental reality is transcendent. **3** a transcendental outlook or attitude, *esp* visionary idealism. ⋙ **transcendentalist** *adj and noun.*

transcendental meditation *noun* a method, derived from Hinduism, of relaxing and refreshing oneself by silently repeating a sacred word or sound.

transcendental number *noun* a number, e.g. e or π, that cannot be the root of an algebraic equation with rational coefficients.

transcontinental /ˌtranzkonti'nentl/ *adj* crossing or extending across a continent. ⋙ **transcontinentally** *adv.*

transcribe /tran'skrieb/ *verb trans* **1a** to make a written copy or version of (e.g. something written or printed). **b** to write (something) in a different medium; to transliterate (it): *transcribe a word in phonetics; transcribe shorthand.* **c** to write down or record (something). **2** to transfer (data) from one recording form to another. **3** to make a musical transcription of (something). **4** to cause (e.g. DNA) to undergo genetic transcription. ⋙ **transcriber** *noun.* [Latin *transcribere,* from TRANS- + *scribere* to write]

transcript /'transkript, 'trahn-/ *noun* **1a** a written, printed, or typed copy; *esp* a usu typewritten copy of dictated or recorded material or shorthand notes. **b** an official or legal and often published copy: *a court reporter's transcript.* **c** *NAmer* an official copy of a student's educational record. **2** a length of nucleic acid, e.g. messenger RNA, produced by transcription. [Middle English from late Latin *transcriptum,* neuter past part. of *transcribere:* see TRANSCRIBE]

transcriptase /'transkriptayz, 'trahn-/ *noun* an enzyme that catalyses the synthesis of RNA from DNA.

transcription /tran'skripsh(ə)n/ *noun* **1** the act or an instance of transcribing. **2** a copy or transcript, e.g.: **a** an often free arrangement of a musical composition for some instrument or voice other than the original. **b** a sound recording suitable for broadcasting and thus usu of high quality. **3** a written form of a sound or word, e.g. using phonetic symbols. **4** the naturally occurring process of constructing a molecule of nucleic acid, e.g. messenger RNA, using a DNA molecule as a template, with resulting transfer of genetic information to the newly formed molecule. ⋙ **transcriptional** *adj,* **transcriptive** /-tiv/ *adj.*

transcutaneous /tranzkyooh'tayni·əs/ *adj* passing or entering through the skin.

transducer /tranz'dyoohsə/ *noun* a device that transfers energy from one system to another; *esp* one that converts nonelectrical energy into electrical energy or vice versa. [Latin *transducere* to lead across, from TRANS- + *ducere* to lead]

transect[1] /tran'sekt/ *verb trans* to cut (something) transversely. ⋙ **transection** /-sh(ə)n/ *noun.* [TRANS- + -SECT]

transect[2] /'transekt, 'trahn-/ *noun* a sample area, e.g. of vegetation, usu in the form of a long continuous strip, that is used to study the composition of plant species, animal populations, etc.

transept /'transept/ *noun* either of the projecting arms of the part of a cross-shaped church that crosses the E end of the nave at right angles. ⋙ **transeptal** /tran'septl/ *adj.* [Latin *transeptum,* from TRANS- + *septum, saeptum* enclosure, wall]

transexual /tran'seksyooəl, -sh(ə)l/ *noun* see TRANSSEXUAL.

transfer[1] /'trans'fuh, trahns'fuh/ *verb* (**transferred, transferring**) ⋙ *verb trans* **1a** to carry or take (something) from one person, place, or situation to another; to transport (it). **b** to move or send (something) to another location: *He transferred his business to another bank.* **c** to move (a professional football player) to another football club. **d** to cause (something) to pass from one person or

thing to another; to transmit (it): *Power is transferred from the engine to the wheels.* **2** to make over the possession or control of (e.g. property); to convey (it): *He transferred the title to his son.* **3** to copy (e.g. a design) from one surface to another by contact. ⋙ *verb intrans* **1** to move to a different place, region, or situation; *esp* to withdraw from one educational institution to enrol at another. **2** to change from one vehicle or transport system to another. ⋙ **transferable** *adj,* **transferral** *noun,* **transferrer** *noun.* [Middle English *transferren* from Latin *transferre,* from TRANS- + *ferre* to carry]

transfer[2] /'transfuh, 'trahnsfuh/ *noun* **1** an act, process, or instance of transferring. **2** somebody or something that transfers or is transferred. **3** *Brit* a graphic image transferred by contact from one surface, e.g. specially prepared paper, to another. **4** *NAmer* a ticket entitling a passenger to continue a journey on another route.

transferable vote *noun* a vote which in balloting by proportional representation may be transferred to a candidate other than the first choice.

transferase /'transfərayz, -rays/ *noun* an enzyme that promotes transfer of a chemical group from one molecule to another.

transferee /transfə'ree, trahns-/ *noun* **1** a person to whom a property is transferred. **2** somebody who is transferred.

transference /'transf(ə)rəns, 'trahns-/ *noun* **1** the redirection of feelings and desires, *esp* those unconsciously retained from childhood, towards a new object, e.g. towards a psychoanalyst conducting therapy. **2** the action or process of transferring. ⋙ **transferential** /transfə'rensh(ə)l, trahns-/ *adj.*

transfer fee *noun* the fee paid by one professional football club to another for the transfer of a player.

transferrin /trans'fuhrin, trahns-/ *noun* a protein in blood that is capable of combining with electrically charged atoms of iron and transporting iron in the body. [TRANS- + Latin *ferrum* iron + -IN[1]]

transfer RNA *noun* a relatively small RNA that transfers a particular amino acid to a growing polypeptide chain at the ribosome site for protein synthesis: compare MESSENGER RNA.

transfiguration /transˌfigə'raysh(ə)n, trahns-/ *noun* **1a** a change in form or appearance; a metamorphosis. **b** an exalting, glorifying, or spiritual change. **2** (**Transfiguration**) a festival of the Christian Church celebrated on 6 August commemorating the transfiguration of Christ (Matthew 17:2 and Mark 9:2–3).

transfigure /trans'figə, trahns-/ *verb trans* to give a new appearance to (something); to transform (it) outwardly and usu for the better. [Middle English *transfiguren* from Latin *transfigurare,* from TRANS- + *figurare* to shape, fashion, from *figura:* see FIGURE[1]]

transfinite /trans'fieniet, trahns-/ *adj* of or being a number that can be shown to be greater than the number of positive integers: *The number of real numbers is a transfinite quantity.* [German *transfinit,* from TRANS- + *finit* finite, from Latin *finitus,* past part. of *finire:* see FINISH[1]]

transfix /trans'fiks/ *verb trans* **1** to hold (a person or animal) motionless, *esp* with horror or shock. **2** to pierce (something) through, e.g. with a pointed weapon. ⋙ **transfixion** /-sh(ə)n/ *noun.* [Latin *transfixus,* past part. of *transfigere,* from TRANS- + *figere* to fasten, pierce]

transform[1] /trans'fawm, trahns-/ *verb trans* **1** to change (something) radically, e.g. in structure, appearance, or character. **2** to subject (e.g. a configuration) to mathematical transformation. **3** to change (a current) in potential, e.g. from high voltage to low, or in type, e.g. from alternating to direct. **4** to cause (a cell) to undergo transformation. ⋙ *verb intrans* to become transformed. ⋙ **transformable** *adj,* **transformative** /-tiv/ *adj.* [Middle English *transformen* from Latin *transformare,* from TRANS- + *formare* to form, from *forma* FORM[1]]

transform[2] /'transfawm, 'trahnsfawm/ *noun* a mathematical element or linguistic structure producible by a transformation.

transformation /transfə'maysh(ə)n, trahns-/ *noun* **1** the act or an instance of transforming or being transformed. **2** in mathematics, the operation of changing, e.g. by rotation or mapping, one configuration or expression into another in accordance with a mathematical rule, *esp* a change of variables or coordinates. **3** in linguistics, any of a set of rules for transforming the supposed underlying structures of a language into actual sentences. **4** in biology, the modification of plant or animal cell culture, e.g. by a cancer-producing virus, resulting in unlimited cell growth and division. **5** in genetics, the modification of a cell, *esp* by a bacterium, by introduction of DNA from a genetically different source. ➤➤ **transformational** *adj.*

transformational grammar /transfə'maysh(ə)nl, trahns-/ *noun* in linguistics, a grammar that attempts to find a set of transformations for generating an infinite number of possible sentences.

transformer /trans'fawmə, trahns-/ *noun* an electrical device making use of the principle of mutual induction to convert variations of current in a primary circuit into variations of voltage and current in a secondary circuit.

transfuse /trans'fyoohz, trahns'fyoohz/ *verb trans* **1a** to transfer (e.g. blood) into a vein or artery. **b** to subject (somebody) to transfusion. **2a** to diffuse into or through (something); to permeate (it). **b** to transmit or instil (something). [Middle English *transfusen* from Latin *transfusus*, past part. of *transfundere* to transfer by pouring, from TRANS- + *fundere* to pour]

transfusion /trans'fyoohzh(ə)n, trahns-/ *noun* an act, process, or instance of transfusing; *esp* the act or process of transfusing liquid, *esp* blood, into a vein or artery.

transgender /tranz'jendə/ *adj* transsexual.

transgendered /tranz'jendəd/ *adj* = TRANSGENDER.

transgenic /tranz'jenik/ *adj* having a gene or genes from another individual transplanted into the normal genetic material, e.g. to improve the qualities of the breed or confer disease resistance: *The transgenic tomato will provide commercial growers with a more reliable crop* — New Scientist.

transgress /trans'gres, trahns'gres/ *verb trans* **1** to go beyond limits set or prescribed by (e.g. a principle): *transgress the divine law.* **2** to pass beyond or go over (a boundary). ➤ *verb intrans* to violate a command or law. ➤➤ **transgressive** /-siv/ *adj,* **transgressor** *noun.* [French *transgresser* from Latin *transgressus*, past part. of *transgredi* to step beyond or across, from TRANS- + *gradi* to step]

transgression /trans'gresh(ə)n, trahns-/ *noun* infringement or violation of a law, command, or duty.

tranship /tranz'ship/ *verb trans* see TRANSSHIP.

transhumance /trans'hyoohməns, trahns-/ *noun* the seasonal movement of livestock, *esp* sheep, between mountain and lowland pastures. ➤➤ **transhumant** *adj.* [French *transhumance* from *transhumer* to practise transhumance, from Spanish *trashumar*, from *tras-* TRANS- + Latin *humus* earth]

transient[1] /'tranzi-ənt/ *adj* **1** passing quickly away; transitory. **2** making only a brief stay: *a transient summer migrant.* ➤➤ **transience** *noun,* **transiency** /-si/ *noun,* **transiently** *adv.* [Latin *transient-, transiens*, present part. of *transire* to go across, pass, from TRANS- + *ire* to go]

transient[2] *noun* **1** a transient guest or worker. **2a** a temporary oscillation that occurs in a circuit because of a sudden change of voltage or load. **b** a transient current or voltage.

transilluminate /tranzi'l(y)oohminayt/ *verb trans* to cause light to pass through (something); *esp* to pass light through (a body part) for medical examination. ➤➤ **transillumination** /-'naysh(ə)n/ *noun.*

transistor /tran'zistə/ *noun* **1** any of several semiconductor devices that have usu three electrodes and make use of a small current to control a larger one. **2** = TRANSISTOR RADIO. [blend of TRANSFER[1] + RESISTOR; because it transfers an electrical signal across a resistor]

transistorize *or* **transistorise** *verb trans* to equip (a device) with transistors. ➤➤ **transistorization** /-'zaysh(ə)n/ *noun.*

transistor radio *noun* a radio using transistorized circuitry.

transit[1] /'transit, 'tranzit/ *noun* **1** the act or an instance of passing or conveying through or over; passage: *goods lost in transit.* **2** *NAmer* the conveyance of people or things from one place to another; transport. **3** a change or transition. **4a** the passage of a celestial body, e.g. a planet, over the MERIDIAN (imaginary circle passing through both poles) of a place or through the field of view of a telescope. **b** the passage of a smaller body, e.g. Venus, across the disc of a larger, e.g. the sun: compare ECLIPSE[1], OCCULTATION. [Latin *transitus*, past part. of *transire*: see TRANSIENT[1]]

transit[2] *verb trans* (**transited, transiting**) **1** to pass over or through (something); to traverse (it). **2** said of a celestial body: to pass across (a meridian, a celestial body, or the field of view of a telescope).

transit camp *noun* a temporary camp set up for people, e.g. refugees, who are travelling through a region.

transit instrument *noun* a telescope for observing the time of transit of a celestial body over a MERIDIAN (imaginary circle passing through both poles).

transition /tran'zish(ə)n/ *noun* **1a** the process of passing or developing from one state, stage, or form to another: *Her form, voice, and manner belonged to the period of transition from girlhood* — Lew Wallace; *Every orbit is in a state of transition, either from circle to ellipse, or from ellipse to circle* — Poe. **b** a change or transfer, e.g. from one point to the next, from one topic to another, etc: *The young Englishmen ... talked together, as they usually talked, with many odd silences, lapses of logic, and incongruities of transition* — Henry James. **2a** a musical modulation. **b** a musical passage leading from one section of a piece to another. **3** an abrupt change in energy state or level, e.g. of an atomic nucleus or a molecule, usu accompanied by loss or gain of a single quantum of energy. ➤➤ **transitional** *adj,* **transitionally** *adv.* [Latin *transition-, transitio*, from *transire*: see TRANSIENT[1]]

transition element *noun* = TRANSITION METAL.

transition metal *noun* any of various metallic elements, e.g. chromium, iron, or platinum, that have valency electrons in two shells instead of only one.

transitive /'transitiv, 'tranzitiv/ *adj* **1** in grammar, having or containing a direct object: *a transitive verb; a transitive construction.* **2** in logic or mathematics, of or being a relation such that if the relation holds between a first element and a second and between the second element and a third, it holds between the first and third elements. **3** of or characterized by transition. ➤➤ **transitively** *adv,* **transitiveness** *noun,* **transitivity** /-'tiviti/ *noun.* [late Latin *transitivus*, from Latin *transire*: see TRANSIENT[1]]

transitory /'transit(ə)ri, 'tranzit(ə)ri/ *adj* **1** tending to pass away. **2** of brief duration. ➤➤ **transitorily** *adv,* **transitoriness** *noun.* [Middle English *transitorie* via French from late Latin *transitorius* of or allowing passage, from *transire*: see TRANSIENT[1]]

transl. *abbr* **1** translated. **2** translator.

translate /trans'layt, trahns'layt/ *verb trans* **1** to turn (text) into another language. **2** to express (something) in different or more comprehensible terms; to explain or interpret (it). **3** to subject (e.g. a figure) to mathematical translation. **4** to subject (genetic information, *esp* messenger RNA) to translation. **5** to bear, remove, or change (somebody or something) from one place or condition to another; to transfer or transform (them): *She is good at translating ideas into action; a country boy translated to the city.* **6** to transfer (a bishop) from one bishopric to another. **7** to convey (somebody) to heaven or to an eternal condition, *esp* while alive. ➤ *verb intrans* **1a** to practise translation or make a translation. **b** to be capable of or adaptable to translation: *a word that doesn't translate easily.* **2** to undergo a translation. ➤➤ **translatability** /-'biliti/ *noun,* **translatable** *adj.* [Latin *translatus*, past part. of *transferre* to transfer, translate, from TRANS- + *ferre* to carry]

translation /trans'laysh(ə)n, trahns-/ *noun* **1a** the act of rendering from one language into another. **b** a version thus produced. **2** a transformation of mathematical coordinates in which the new axes are parallel to the old ones. **3** uniform motion of a body in a straight line, usu parallel to one of its sides or axes. **4** the process of forming a protein molecule inside a living cell from information contained usu in messenger RNA. **5** a change to a different condition, place, substance, or form. ➤➤ **translational** *adj.*

translator /trans'laytə, trahns-/ *noun* **1** somebody who translates from one language into another. **2** a computer program used to convert from one computer language into another.

transliterate /tranz'litərayt/ *verb trans* to represent or spell (a letter or word) in the characters of another alphabet. ➤➤ **transliteration** /-'raysh(ə)n/ *noun,* **transliterator** *noun.* [TRANS- + Latin *littera* LETTER[1]]

translocate /tranzloh'kayt/ *verb trans and intrans* to move (something) to another place.

translocation /tranzloh'kaysh(ə)n/ *noun* a change of location; *esp* the conduction of soluble material from one part of a plant to another.

translucent /tranz'loohs(ə)nt, trahnz-/ *adj* transmitting and diffusing light so that objects beyond cannot be seen clearly; semitransparent: *a translucent window of frosted glass; translucent porcelain.* ➤➤ **translucence** *noun,* **translucency** /-si/ *noun,*

translucently *adv.* [Latin *translucent-, translucens*, present part. of *translucēre* to shine through, from TRANS- + *lucēre* to shine]

transmarine /tranzmə'reen/ *adj* being, coming from, or extending across the sea; overseas: *a transmarine people.* [Latin *transmarinus*, from TRANS- + *mare* sea]

transmigrate /tranzmie'grayt/ *verb intrans* **1** said of a soul: to pass at death from one body or being to another. **2** = MIGRATE. ▶▶ **transmigration** /-sh(ə)n/ *noun*, **transmigrator** *noun*, **transmigratory** /tranz'miegrət(ə)ri/ *adj.* [Latin *transmigratus*, past part. of *transmigrare* to migrate to another place, from TRANS- + *migrare* to migrate]

transmissible /trans'misəbl/ *adj* capable of being transmitted.

transmission /trans'mish(ə)n, trahns-/ *noun* **1** the act or an instance of transmitting. **2** something, e.g. a message or television programme, that is transmitted. **3a** the passage of radio waves between transmitting and receiving stations. **b** the act or process of transmitting by radio or television. **4a** an assembly of parts including the clutch, speed-changing gears, and the propeller shaft by which the power is transmitted from a motor vehicle engine to an axle. **b** an assembly transmitting moving power on a bicycle. ▶▶ **transmissive** /-siv/ *adj*, **transmissivity** /-'siviti/ *noun*. [Latin *transmission-, transmissio*, from *transmittere*: see TRANSMIT]

transmission line *noun* a conductor, e.g. a coaxial cable, that carries electrical signals from one place to another.

transmit /trans'mit, tranz'mit/ *verb* (**transmitted, transmitting**) ▶ *verb trans* **1** to send or transfer (something) from one person or place to another. **2a** to pass on (infection). **b** to convey (something) by inheritance or heredity; to hand (it) down. **3** to cause (e.g. force) to pass or be conveyed through a medium. **4a** to allow the passage of (e.g. energy); to conduct (it). **b** to send out (a signal) either by radio waves or over a wire. ▶ *verb intrans* to send out a signal either by radio waves or over a wire. ▶▶ **transmittable** *adj*, **transmittal** *noun*. [Middle English *transmitten* from Latin *transmittere*, from TRANS- + *mittere* to send]

transmittance /trans'mit(ə)ns, tranz-/ *noun* **1** = TRANSMISSION. **2** a measure of the ability of a body or substance to transmit electromagnetic radiation, e.g. light.

transmitter /trans'mitə, tranz-/ *noun* **1** the portion of a telegraphic or telephonic instrument that sends the signals. **2** a radio or television transmitting station or set. **3** = NEUROTRANSMITTER.

transmogrify /tranz'mogrifie/ *verb trans* (**transmogrifies, transmogrified, transmogrifying**) to transform (something), often with grotesque or humorous effect. ▶▶ **transmogrification** /-fi'kaysh(ə)n/ *noun*. [perhaps alteration of TRANSMIGRATE]

transmontane /tranzmon'tayn/ *adj* = TRAMONTANE[1]. [Latin *transmontanus*, from TRANS- + *mont-, mons* MOUNTAIN]

transmutation /tranzmyoo(h)'taysh(ə)n/ *noun* **1** the act or an instance of transmuting or being transmuted. **2a** the conversion of one chemical element into NUCLIDE (type of atom) into another, either naturally or artificially. **b** the conversion of base metals, e.g. iron and copper, into gold or silver. ▶▶ **transmutational** *adj*, **transmutative** /tranz'myoohtətiv/ *adj*.

transmute /tranz'myooht/ *verb trans* **1** to change (something) in form, substance, or characteristics. **2** to subject (e.g. an element) to transmutation. ▶ *verb intrans* to undergo transmutation. ▶▶ **transmutability** /-'biliti/ *adj*, **transmutable** *adj*. [Middle English *transmuten* from Latin *transmutare*, from TRANS- + *mutare* to change]

transnational /tranz'nash(ə)nl/ *adj* extending beyond national boundaries.

transoceanic /,tranzohshi'anik/ *adj* **1** situated beyond the ocean. **2** crossing or extending across the ocean: *a transoceanic telephone cable.*

transom /'transəm/ *noun* **1a** any of several crosswise timbers or beams secured to the sternpost of a boat. **b** the planking forming the stern of a square-ended boat. **c** = LINTEL. **d** a horizontal crossbar in a window, over a door, or between a door and a window above it: compare MULLION[1]. **e** the horizontal bar or member of a cross or gallows. **2** *NAmer* a window above a door or other window, built on and commonly hinged to a transom; a fanlight. ▶▶ **transomed** *adj*. [Middle English *traunsom*, alteration of *traversayn*, from Old French *traversia*, from *traverser*: see TRAVERSE[1]]

transonic /tran'sonik/ *or* **trans-sonic** /,tranz 'sonik/ *adj* **1** of or being a speed near the speed of sound in air. **2** moving, capable of

moving, or using air currents moving, at a transonic speed. [TRANS- + -*sonic* as in SUPERSONIC]

transparency /tran'sparənsi, trahn-/ *noun* (*pl* **transparencies**) **1** being transparent. **2** a picture or design on glass, film, etc viewed by a light shining through it from behind; *esp* a photographic slide.

transparent /tran'sparənt, trahn-/ *adj* **1a** transmitting light without appreciable scattering so that bodies lying beyond are entirely visible. **b** fine or sheer enough to be seen through. **2a** free from pretence or deceit: *transparent sincerity.* **b** easily detected or seen through: *a transparent lie.* **c** readily understood: *The meaning of this word is transparent.* **d** open to public scrutiny; not clandestine: *To make sure sponsorship is transparent to viewers ... sponsors should be given far more prominence* — Independent. **3** penetrable by a specified form of radiation, e.g. X-rays or ultraviolet. ▶▶ **transparently** *adv*. [Middle English from late Latin *transparent-, transparens*, present part. of *transparēre* to show through, from TRANS- + Latin *parēre* to show oneself]

transpire /tran'spie·ə, trahn'spie·ə/ *verb intrans* **1** to become known; to come to light. **2** to occur; to take place. **3a** to give off a vapour; *specif* to give off or exude water vapour, *esp* from the surfaces of leaves. **b** to pass in the form of a vapour, *esp* from a living body. ▶ *verb trans* to pass off or give passage to (a gas or liquid) through pores or interstices; *esp* to excrete (e.g. water vapour) through a skin or other living membrane. ▶▶ **transpiration** /transpi'raysh(ə)n, trahnspi-/ *noun.* [early French *transpirer*, from TRANS- + Latin *spirare* to breathe]

Usage note

Transpire has two common non-technical meanings – 'to become known' (*It eventually transpired that the documents had been lost*) and 'to happen' (*A most unfortunate incident transpired as the guests were leaving the hotel*). The use of the word in the second meaning is objected to by some traditionalists. There are no historical grounds for this, but it is argued, first, that *transpire* is simply a pompous alternative for *happen* or *occur* and, second, that in phrases such as *what transpired at the meeting* it is impossible to know which sense is intended. On these grounds, *transpire* is better avoided in the second sense.

transplant[1] /trans'plahnt, trahns-/ *verb trans* **1** to lift and reset (a plant) in another soil or place. **2** to remove (something) from one place and settle or introduce it elsewhere. **3** to transfer (an organ or tissue) from one part or individual to another. ▶▶ **transplantable** /trans'plahntəbl, trahns-/ *adj*, **transplantation** /-'taysh(ə)n/ *noun*, **transplanter** *noun*. [Middle English *transplaunten* from late Latin *transplantare*, from TRANS- + Latin *plantare* to plant]

transplant[2] /'transplahnt, 'trahnsplahnt/ *noun* **1** the act or an instance of transplanting, *esp* a surgical operation to transplant an organ: *a heart transplant.* **2** something transplanted.

transponder /tran'spondə/ *noun* a radio or radar set that responds to a designated signal by emitting a radio signal of its own. [blend of TRANSMITTER + *responder* (see RESPOND[1])]

transpontine /tranz'pontien, trahnz-, trans-, trahns-/ *adj* **1** situated on the farther side of a bridge. **2** *Brit* situated on the south side of the Thames. [TRANS- + Latin *pont-, pons* bridge]

transport[1] /tran'spawt/ *verb trans* **1** to transfer or convey (somebody or something) from one place to another: *It is a mechanism for transporting ions across a living membrane.* **2** to carry (somebody) away with strong and often pleasurable emotion. **3** to send (a convict) to a penal colony overseas. ▶▶ **transportable** *adj*. [Middle English *transporten* via French from Latin *transportare*, from TRANS- + *portare* to carry]

transport[2] /'transpawt, 'trahnspawt/ *noun* **1** the conveying of goods or people from one place to another. **2a** a ship or aircraft for carrying soldiers or military equipment. **b** a lorry, aeroplane, etc used to transport people or goods. **3** a burst or experience of strong and usu pleasurable emotion: *transports of joy.*

transportation /transpaw'taysh(ə)n, trahn-/ *noun* **1** the act of transporting. **2** banishment to a penal colony. **3** *NAmer* a means of conveyance or travel from one place to another.

transport café /'transpawt, 'trahnspawt/ *noun Brit* an inexpensive roadside restaurant catering mainly for long-distance lorry drivers.

transporter /tran'spawtə, trahn-/ *noun* a vehicle for transporting large or heavy loads: *a tank transporter.*

transposable element *noun* = TRANSPOSON.

transpose[1] /tran'spohz/ *verb trans* **1** to change the relative position of (two or more things); to alter the sequence of (them).

2 to transfer (something) from one place or period to another. **3** to write or perform (music) in a different key. **4** in mathematics, to bring (a term) from one side of an algebraic equation to the other with a change of sign. ➤ *verb intrans* to transpose music. ➤➤ **transposable** *adj*, **transposal** *noun*, **transposer** *noun*. [Middle English *transposen* via French from Latin *transponere* to change the position of, from TRANS- + *ponere* to put, place]

transpose² /'transpohz/ *noun* in mathematics, a matrix formed by interchanging the rows of a given matrix with its corresponding columns.

transposing instrument /tran'spohzing, trahn-/ *noun* a musical instrument, e.g. a trumpet or saxophone, that sounds notes at a fixed interval higher or lower than those written.

transposition /tranzpǝ'zish(ǝ)n/ *noun* **1** the act or an instance of transposing or being transposed. **2a** the transfer of a term of an equation from one side to the other with a change of sign. **b** a mathematical permutation that is the interchange of two elements. ➤➤ **transpositional** *adj*. [late Latin *transposition-, transpositio*, from Latin *transponere*: see TRANSPOSE¹]

transposon /tran'spohzon/ *noun* any of a wide variety of genetic elements or DNA sequences that possess the property of inserting themselves by transposition at various regions on the chromosomes or other DNA in the bacterial cell or eukaryotic nucleus.

transputer /tran'spjoohtǝ/ *noun* a powerful microprocessor chip capable of handling very large amounts of information very fast, which was developed as the building block for supercomputers. [blend of TRANSISTOR + COMPUTER]

transsexual *or* **transexual** /tranz'seksyoo(ǝ)l, -sh(ǝ)l/ *noun* somebody physically of one sex with an urge to belong to or resemble the opposite sex. ➤➤ **transsexual** *adj*, **transsexualism** *noun*.

transship *or* **tranship** /tranz'ship/ *verb trans* (**transshipped, transshipping**) to transfer (something) from one ship or conveyance to another for further transportation. ➤➤ **transshipment** *noun*.

trans-sonic /,tranz 'sonik/ *adj* see TRANSONIC.

transubstantiate /transǝb'stanshiayt, trahn-, -siayt/ *verb trans* **1** to change (something) into another substance; to transmute (it). **2** to bring about transubstantiation in (the bread and wine used at communion). [late Latin *transubstantiatus*, past part. of *transubstantiare*, from TRANS- + Latin *substantia*: see SUBSTANCE]

transubstantiation /,transǝbstanshi'aysh(ǝ)n, trahn-, -si'aysh(ǝ)n/ *noun* the miraculous change by which, according to Roman Catholic and Eastern Orthodox dogma, bread and wine used at communion become the body and blood of Christ when they are consecrated, although their appearance remains unchanged.

transude /tran'syoohd/ *verb intrans* said of a fluid: to pass through a membrane or permeable substance. ➤ *verb trans archaic* to permit passage of (a fluid). ➤➤ **transudation** /-'daysh(ǝ)n/ *noun*. [Latin *transudare*, from TRANS- + *sudare* to sweat]

transuranic /tranzyoo'ranik/ *noun* said of an element: having an atomic number greater than that of uranium.

transversal¹ /tranz'vuhsl, trans-/ *adj* = TRANSVERSE: *transversal lines*.

transversal² *noun* a line that intersects a system of lines.

transverse /tranz'vuhs, trans-/ *adj* lying or being across; set or made crosswise. ➤➤ **transversely** *adv*. [Latin *transversus*, past part. of *transvertere* to turn across, from TRANS- + *vertere* to turn]

transverse wave *noun* in physics, a wave, e.g. a wave on a string or an electromagnetic wave in free space, in which the displacements of the medium or the vectors, e.g. of the electric and magnetic fields, describing the wave are perpendicular to the direction of propagation of the wave: compare LONGITUDINAL WAVE.

transvestism /tranz'vestiz(ǝ)m/ *noun* the adoption of the dress and often the behaviour of the opposite sex. [German *Transvestismus*, from TRANS- + Latin *vestire*: see VEST²]

transvestite /tranz'vesteit/ *noun* somebody who adopts the dress of the opposite sex.

transvestitism /tranz'vestitiz(ǝm)/ *noun* = TRANSVESTISM.

trap¹ /trap/ *noun* **1** a device for catching animals; *esp* one that holds them by springing shut suddenly. **2a** a plan or trick designed to catch a person unawares and put them at a disadvantage: *Police laid a trap for the criminal*. **b** a situation from which it is difficult or impossible to escape: *caught in a poverty trap*. **3** any of various devices for preventing passage of something, often while allowing other matter to proceed; *esp* a device for drains or sewers consisting of a bend or partitioned chamber in which the liquid forms a seal to prevent the passage of sewer gas. **4a** a device from which a greyhound is released at the start of a race. **b** a device for hurling clay pigeons into the air. **5** a golf bunker. **6** a light carriage with springs, pulled by a horse or pony. **7** *informal* the mouth. **8** *informal* (*in pl*) a group of percussion instruments, e.g. a bass drum, snare drums, and cymbals, used *esp* in a dance or jazz band. ➤➤ **trap-like** *adj*. [Old English *treppe*]

trap² *verb* (**trapped, trapping**) ➤ *verb trans* **1a** to catch or take (an animal) in a trap. **b** to place (something or somebody) in a restricted position; to confine (them): *They were trapped in the burning wreck*. **2** to provide or set (a place) with traps. **3** to stop or retain (something): *These mountains trap the rain*. ➤ *verb intrans* to engage in trapping animals, e.g. for furs.

trap³ *noun* any of various dark-coloured fine-grained igneous rocks, e.g. basalt, used *esp* in road making. [Swedish *trapp* from *trappa* stair, from early Low German *trappe*; because it often appears in stepped outcrops]

trapdoor *noun* a lifting or sliding door covering an opening in a floor, ceiling, etc.

trapdoor spider *noun* a large burrowing spider that constructs a nest topped with a hinged lid: family Ctenizidae.

trapes /trayps/ *verb intrans and noun archaic* = TRAIPSE¹, TRAIPSE².

trapeze /trǝ'peez/ *noun* a gymnastic or acrobatic apparatus consisting of a short horizontal bar suspended by two parallel ropes. [French *trapèze* from Latin *trapezium*: see TRAPEZIUM]

trapezium /trǝ'peezi-ǝm/ *noun* (*pl* **trapeziums** *or* **trapezia** /-zi-ǝ/) **1** *Brit* a quadrilateral that has only two sides parallel. **2** *NAmer* a quadrilateral that has no sides parallel. [Latin *trapezium* from Greek *trapezion* small table, dimin. of *trapeza* table]

trapezius /trǝ'peezi-ǝs/ *noun* (*pl* **trapezii**) either of two large flat triangular muscles, one on each side of the upper part of the back, that serve chiefly to raise and rotate the shoulder blades. [Latin *trapezius* from *trapezium*: see TRAPEZIUM; from the trapezium shape formed by the pair of muscles]

trapezoid /trǝ'peezoyd, 'trapizoyd/ *noun* **1** *Brit* a quadrilateral that has no sides parallel. **2** *NAmer* a quadrilateral that has only two sides parallel. ➤➤ **trapezoidal** /trapi'zoydl/ *adj*. [via Latin from Greek *trapezoeidēs* trapezium-shaped, from *trapeza* table]

trapper *noun* a person who traps wild animals for their skin or fur.

trappings *noun* **1a** outward decoration or dress; ornamental equipment. **b** outward signs and accessories: *These but the trappings and the suits of woe* — Shakespeare. **2** ornamental coverings and harness for a horse. [Middle English, from *trappen* to adorn, from *trappe* cloth, from Old French *drap*: see DRAB¹]

Trappist /'trapist/ *noun* a member of a reformed branch of the Cistercian Order established in 1664 and noted for its vow of silence. ➤➤ **Trappist** *adj*. [French *trappiste*, from La *Trappe*, the monastery in Normandy where the order was established]

traprock *noun* = TRAP³.

traps *noun informal* personal belongings; luggage. [Middle English *trappe*: see TRAPPINGS]

trapshooting *noun* shooting at clay pigeons sprung into the air from a trap so as to simulate the angles of flight of birds. ➤➤ **trapshooter** *noun*.

trash¹ /trash/ *noun chiefly NAmer* **1a** junk or rubbish. **b** inferior or worthless literary or artistic work. **2a** a worthless person. **b** (*treated as sing. or pl*) such people as a group. **3** something in a crumbled or broken condition or mass; *esp* debris from pruning or processing plant material. [prob of Scandinavian origin]

trash² *verb trans* **1** *chiefly NAmer, informal* to destroy (something) wilfully or maliciously; to vandalize (it). **2** *chiefly NAmer, informal* to reject (something); to throw (it) away. **3** *chiefly NAmer, informal* to criticize (somebody or something). **4** to free (something) from trash or refuse; *specif* to strip outer leaves from (young sugar cane).

trash can *noun NAmer* = DUSTBIN.

trashed *adj informal* highly intoxicated by alcohol or drugs.

trashy *adj* (**trashier, trashiest**) of inferior quality or worth: *a trashy novel*. ➤➤ **trashiness** *noun*.

trass /tras/ *noun* a light-coloured tuff rock sometimes ground for use in a hydraulic cement. [Dutch *trass* from early French *terrasse*: see TERRACE¹]

trattoria /tratə'ree-ə/ *noun* (*pl* **trattorias** *or* **trattorie** /-'reeay/) an Italian restaurant. [Italian *trattoria* from *trattore* innkeeper, restaurateur, ultimately from Old French *traitier*: see TREAT[1]]

trauma /'trawmə/ *noun* (*pl* **traumata** /-tə/ *or* **traumas**) **1a** a disordered mental or behavioural state resulting from mental or emotional stress or shock. **b** an injury, e.g. a wound, to living tissue caused by an outside agent. **2** an agent, force, or mechanism that causes trauma. ➤➤ **traumatic** /traw'matik/ *adj*, **traumatically** /traw'matikli/ *adv*. [Greek *traumat-, trauma* wound]

traumatise /'trawmətiez/ *verb trans* see TRAUMATIZE.

traumatism /'trawmətiz(ə)m/ *noun* the development or occurrence of trauma.

traumatize *or* **traumatise** /'trawmətiez/ *verb trans* to inflict a trauma on (somebody). ➤➤ **traumatization** /-'zaysh(ə)n/ *noun*.

travail[1] /'travayl, trə'vayl/ *noun* **1** *literary* (*also in pl*) physical or mental exertion, *esp* of a painful or laborious nature. **2** *archaic* labour pains.

travail[2] *verb intrans* **1** *literary* to labour hard. **2** *archaic* to suffer labour pains. [Middle English *travailen* from Old French *travaillier* to harass, afflict, labour, from medieval Latin *tripalium* instrument of torture, from Latin *tripalis* having three stakes, from TRI- + *palus* stake]

travel[1] /'travl/ *verb* (**travelled, travelling,** *NAmer* **traveled, traveling**) ➤ *verb intrans* **1a** to go on a trip or tour; to journey. **b** to go as if by travelling; to pass: *The news travelled fast; My mind travelled back to our last meeting.* **2** to move or be transmitted from one place to another: *The sound travelled in the still air; Wine travels badly.* **3** *informal* to move at high speed: *a car that can really travel.* **4** *said esp* of machinery: to move along a specified direction or path: *The stylus travels in a groove.* **5** in basketball, to walk or run more than one pace with a ball, in violation of the rules. ➤ *verb trans* **1** to journey through or over (an area): *She wanted to travel the world.* **2** to follow (a course or path) as if by travelling. * **travel light** to travel with a minimum of equipment or baggage. [Middle English *travailen* to travail, journey, from Old French *travaillier*: see TRAVAIL[2]]

travel[2] *noun* **1a** the act of travelling; passage. **b** (*in pl*) journeys, *esp* to distant or unfamiliar places: *He set off on his travels.* **2** (*used before a noun*) suitable for use when travelling, *esp* in being small and light: *a travel iron.* **3** the motion of a piece of machinery; *esp* alternate forward and backward motion.

travel agency *noun* an agency that gives information on and arranges travel.

travel agent *noun* somebody who sells and arranges personal transport, tours, or trips for travellers.

travel bureau *noun* = TRAVEL AGENCY.

traveled *adj NAmer* = TRAVELLED.

traveler *noun NAmer* = TRAVELLER.

traveler's check *noun NAmer* = TRAVELLER'S CHEQUE.

travelled (*NAmer* **traveled**) *adj* **1** experienced in travel: *a widely travelled journalist.* **2** used by travellers: *a well-travelled route.*

traveller (*NAmer* **traveler**) *noun* **1** somebody who goes on a trip or journey; *esp* somebody who travels frequently. **2a** somebody who lives an alternative lifestyle, moving around from place to place in a van or other vehicle. **b** = GYPSY. **c** *Aus* an itinerant worker; a swagman. **3** any of various devices for handling something that is being moved sideways.

traveller's cheque (*NAmer* **traveler's check**) *noun* a cheque that is purchased from a bank or travel agency and that may be exchanged abroad for foreign currency.

traveller's joy *noun* a wild clematis of Europe and N Africa with white flowers and whitish grey feathery flower-parts: *Clematis vitalba.*

travelling salesman *noun* somebody who travels for a company, selling goods or gaining orders.

travelling wave *noun* in physics, a wave that carries energy continuously away from its source.

travelogue (*NAmer* **travelog**) /'travəlog/ *noun* **1** a film or illustrated talk or lecture on some usu exotic or remote place. **2** a narrated documentary film about travel. [TRAVEL[1] + *-ogue* as in MONOLOGUE]

traverse[1] /trə'vuhs, 'travuhs/ *verb trans* **1** to pass or travel across, over, or through (something): *traverse a terrain; light rays traversing a crystal.* **2a** to move to and fro over or along (something). **b** to ski across (a slope) rather than down. **c** to move sideways across (a rock face). **d** to move (a gun) to right or left on a pivot. **3** to lie or extend across (something); to cross (it): *The bridge traverses a brook.* **4** to work through (a subject) carefully; to examine (it). **5a** in law, to deny (e.g. an allegation of fact or an indictment) formally. **b** *archaic* to go against or act in opposition to (e.g. a plan); to obstruct or thwart (it). ➤ *verb intrans* **1** to move back and forth or from side to side. **2** to climb or ski across rather than straight up or down a hill. ➤➤ **traversable** /trə'vuhs-/ *adj*, **traversal** /trə'vuhsl/ *noun*, **traverser** /trə'vuhsə/ *noun*. [Middle English via Old French *traverser* from late Latin *traversare* from Latin *transversus*: see TRANSVERSE]

traverse[2] /'travuhs, trə'vuhs/ *noun* **1** the act or an instance of traversing; crossing. **2** a route or way across or over, e.g.: **a** a curving or zigzag way up a steep slope. **b** the course followed in traversing. **3** in mountaineering, a horizontal movement across a rock face. **4a** a sideways movement, e.g. of the sliding part containing the cutter on a lathe. **b** a device for imparting such movement. **c** the sideways movement of a gun on a pivot or carriage to change direction of fire. **5** something that crosses or lies across. **6** a transverse gallery in a large building, e.g. a church. **7** in surveying, a survey consisting of a series of measured lines whose bearings are known. **8** in law, a formal denial of a matter of fact alleged by the opposite party in a legal pleading.

traverse[3] /'travuhs/ *adj* lying across.

travertine /'travətin/ *noun* a mineral consisting of a limestone that has no clear crystalline form, is usu layered, and is formed as a deposit from spring waters or hot springs. [French *travertin* from Italian *travertino, tivertino* from Latin *Tiburtinus* of *Tibur*, former name of Tivoli near Rome, where it is quarried]

travesty[1] /'travəsti/ *noun* (*pl* **travesties**) **1** a crude or grotesque literary or artistic parody. **2** a debased, distorted, or grossly inferior imitation: *a travesty of justice.* [obsolete *travesty* disguised, parodied, from French *travesti*, past part. of *travestir* to disguise, ultimately via Italian from Latin TRANS- from *tra-* across + *vestire*: see VEST[1]]

travesty[2] *verb trans* (**travesties, travestied, travestying**) to make a travesty of (something or somebody); to parody or caricature (them).

travois /trə'voy/ *noun* (*pl* **travois** /trə'voyz/) a primitive vehicle formerly used by Native Americans of the Great Plains region, consisting of two trailing poles serving as shafts for a dog or horse and bearing a platform or net for the load. [Canadian French *travois*, alteration of French *travail* shaft of a vehicle, from Latin *trabs* beam]

trawl[1] /trawl/ *verb intrans* **1** to fish with a trawl. **2** to search through a large number of things: *She trawled through the files to find his address.* ➤ *verb trans* **1** to catch (fish) with a trawl. **2** to fish (an area) with a trawl. [prob from obsolete Dutch *tragelen*, from early Dutch *tragel* dragnet, prob from Latin *tragula*]

trawl[2] *noun* **1** a large conical net dragged along the sea bottom to catch fish or other marine life. **2** *NAmer* a long heavy fishing line; a setline. **3** an act of trawling. **4** a search through a large number of things or sources: *an unsuccessful trawl through the job adverts.*

trawler *noun* a boat used in trawling.

tray /tray/ *noun* an open receptacle with a flat bottom and a low rim for holding, carrying, or exhibiting articles. ➤➤ **trayful** *noun*. [Old English *trig, trēg*]

treacherous /'trech(ə)rəs/ *adj* **1** characterized by treachery; perfidious. **2a** of uncertain reliability. **b** providing insecure footing or support: *a treacherous surface of black ice.* **c** marked by hidden dangers or hazards: *the treacherous waters round the coast.* ➤➤ **treacherously** *adv*, **treacherousness** *noun*.

treachery /'trech(ə)ri/ *noun* (*pl* **treacheries**) **1** violation of allegiance; betrayal of trust. **2** an act of betrayal or treason. [Middle English from Old French *trecherie*, from *trechier, trichier* to deceive, TRICK[1]]

treacle /'treekl/ *noun* **1** *chiefly Brit* any of the edible grades of molasses that are obtained in the early stages of sugar refining. **2** = GOLDEN SYRUP. ➤➤ **treacly** *adj*.

Word history
Middle English *triacle* a medicinal compound used as an antidote to poison, via French and Latin from Greek *thēriakē* antidote against a poisonous bite, fem of *thēriakos* of a wild animal, from *thērion* wild animal. The current sense, which dates from the 17th cent., comes from the practice of giving medicine in sugar syrup to disguise its taste.

tread[1] /tred/ *verb* (*past tense* **trod** /trod/, *past part.* **trodden** /'trod(ə)n/ *or* **trod**) ➤ *verb trans* **1a** to step or walk on or over (something). **b** to walk along (e.g. a road); to follow (it): *treading the long road home.* **2** to beat or press (something) with the feet; to trample or crush (it): *They had trodden mud into the carpet.* **3a** to form (e.g. a path) by treading; to beat (it). **b** to execute (e.g. a dance) by stepping or dancing: *tread a measure.* ➤ *verb intrans* **1** to move on foot; to walk: *Tread lightly, she is near* — Oscar Wilde. **2a** to set foot. **b** to put one's foot; to step: *He trod on a stone.* ✳ **tread on somebody's toes/corns** to give offence to or hurt somebody's feelings, *esp* by encroaching on their rights. **tread water 1** to keep the body nearly upright in the water and the head above water by a treading motion of the feet, usu aided by the hands. **2** to stay in the same position without making progress: *She was just treading water in that company, so she decided to leave.* ➤➤ **treader** *noun*. [Old English *tredan*]

tread[2] *noun* **1a** the action of treading. **b** an act of treading; a step. **c** the sound or manner of stepping or treading: *the heavy tread of feet.* **2** the upper horizontal part of a step. **3a** the part of a wheel or tyre that makes contact with a road or rail. **b** the pattern of ridges or grooves made or cut in the face of a tyre. **c** the part of a sole that touches the ground.

treadle[1] /'tredl/ *noun* a lever pressed by the foot to drive a machine, e.g. a sewing machine. [Old English *tredel* step of a stair, from *tredan* TREAD[1]]

treadle[2] *verb trans* to operate (a machine) using a treadle.

treadmill *noun* **1a** a mill, used formerly to employ or punish prisoners, worked by people treading on steps inside a wide wheel with a horizontal axis. **b** a mill worked by an animal treading an endless belt. **2** an exercise machine that has a continuous moving belt on which to run or walk. **3** a wearisome or monotonous routine.

treadwheel *noun* = TREADMILL (1).

treason /'treez(ə)n/ *noun* **1** (*also* **high treason**) the offence of violating the duty of allegiance owed to one's crown or government. **2** the betrayal of a trust. ➤➤ **treasonous** /-nəs/ *adj.* [Middle English *tresoun* via Old French from Latin *tradition-*, *traditio*: see TRADITION]

treasonable *adj* constituting treason. ➤➤ **treasonably** *adv.*

treasure[1] /'trezhə/ *noun* **1** wealth, *esp* in a form which can be accumulated or hoarded: *buried treasure.* **2a** something of great worth or value. **b** *informal* somebody highly valued or prized. [Middle English from Old French *tresor*, via Latin from Greek *thēsauros*]

treasure[2] *verb trans* **1** to hold or preserve (something) as precious; to cherish or prize (it): *They treasured those memories.* **2** to collect and store up (something valuable); to hoard (it).

treasure hunt *noun* a game in which each player or team tries to be first to find whatever has been hidden.

treasurer *noun* the financial officer of an organization, e.g. a society. ➤➤ **treasurership** *noun.*

treasure trove *noun* **1** under English law until 1996, hidden valuables, such as coins, articles of gold or silver, or jewellery, that are of unknown ownership and become the property of the Crown when found. **2** a valuable or productive discovery or source. [from Anglo-French *tresor trové* found treasure, from Old French *tresor* (see TREASURE[1]) + *trové*, past part. of *trover* to find]

treasury *noun* (*pl* **treasuries**) **1a** a depository where the collected funds or revenues of a state, organization, or individual are kept. **b** the funds or revenues in such a depository. **2** (*often* **Treasury**) **a** in certain countries, the government department in charge of finance and the economy. **b** the building housing such a department. **3** a place where treasure is kept. **4** a source or collection of valuable or pleasing things: *a treasury of poems.* [Middle English from Old French *tresorie*, from *tresor*: see TREASURE[1]]

Treasury bench *noun* in Britain, the first row of seats on the right of the speaker in the House of Commons, traditionally reserved for senior government ministers.

Treasury bill *noun* a bill of exchange issued by the treasury. It yields no interest, but a profit can usually be made on its redemption value.

Treasury note *noun* in the USA and formerly in Britain and other countries, a note issued by the government treasury and used in place of currency.

treat[1] /treet/ *verb trans* **1a** to behave towards (a person or animal) in a certain way: *He always treats us with respect.* **b** to regard and deal with (something) in a specified manner: *I treated the remark as*

a joke. **2** to present and discuss (a subject). **3** to care for or deal with (somebody or something) medically or surgically: *The cancer can be treated if caught early; I was treating a patient for pneumonia.* **4** to apply a process or substance to (something): *The wood is treated with a preservative.* **5a** (+ to) to provide (somebody) with food, drink, or entertainment at one's own expense. **b** (+ to) to provide (oneself) with enjoyment or gratification. ➤ *verb intrans formal* (*usu* + with/for) to discuss terms with somebody; to negotiate: *Specially trained officers were treating with the enemy.* ➤➤ **treatable** *adj*, **treater** *noun.* [early French *traitier*, from Latin *tractare* to handle, from *trahere* to draw or haul]

treat[2] *noun* **1** something that gives great pleasure. **2** (**one's treat**) an act of providing something for somebody else at one's own expense: *Let's go out for dinner. It'll be my treat.* ✳ **a treat** *Brit, informal* very well, successfully, or pleasurably: *The speech went down a treat; The work's coming on an absolute treat.* **look a treat** *Brit, informal* to look particularly attractive: *Angus looked a treat in his kilt.*

treatise /'treetiz/ *noun* a formal written report on a subject, *esp* a systematic or technical one: *a treatise on higher education.* [Middle English *tretis* from Anglo-French *tretiz*, from Old French *traitier*: see TREAT[1]]

treatment *noun* **1** the act, manner, or process of handling somebody or something. **2** the discussion or presentation of a subject, theme, etc, *esp* in the arts: *His treatment of issues of class is particularly well done.* **3a** the medicine, therapy, surgery, etc involved in caring for or dealing with a patient or an injury or illness. **b** the application or administration of such remedies. **4** the use of a substance, etc to achieve a particular effect or to eliminate a specific condition: *treatment for woodworm.* **5** (*usu* **the full treatment**) *informal* the techniques or actions customarily applied in a particular situation: *The winners were given the full VIP treatment.*

treaty /'treeti/ *noun* (*pl* **treaties**) **1** a formal agreement made by negotiation, *esp* between two or more states, governing the end of hostilities, outlining an alliance, setting down trade arrangements, etc. **2** a document giving the terms and conditions of such an agreement and signed by the parties involved. [early French *traité* from Latin *tractatus* handling or management, from *tractare*: see TREAT[1]]

treaty port *noun* in China, Japan, and Korea during the 19th cent. and early 20th cent., a port or other city that was bound by a treaty to allow foreign, *esp* Western, traders to operate.

Trebbiano /trebi'ahnoh/ *noun* **1** a variety of grape cultivated mainly in Italy and used in the production of white wine. **2** a wine produced from this grape. [named after the River *Trebbia* in northern Italy, where it was first developed]

treble[1] /'trebl/ *adj* **1** having three parts or uses; threefold. **2** being three times as great in number or as much in amount. **3a** relating to or having the range or part of a treble. **b** high-pitched or shrill. [Middle English via French from Latin *triplus*: see TRIPLE[1]]

treble[2] *noun* **1** a high-pitched singing voice, *esp* a boy's, or a singer with this voice. **2** (*used before a noun*) denoting a musical instrument having a relatively high range. **3** the higher portion of the audio frequency range considered *esp* in relation to its electronic reproduction. **4a** in darts, the middle narrow ring on the board, scoring three times the number shown on any sector. **b** a throw that lands in this ring. **5** *Brit* a bet, *esp* in horseracing, involving three selections in different events. If the first selection is successful, the stake and winnings are bet on the second, and so on. **6** *Brit* in sport, three wins by a player or team.

treble[3] *verb trans and intrans* to increase, or cause (something) to increase, to three times as much or as many.

treble chance *noun Brit* a football pool that involves forecasting three possible results, draws, away wins, and home wins, for a set number of matches.

treble clef *noun* in musical notation, a clef placing the G above middle C on the second lowest line of the stave.

trebly[1] *adj* said of sound: having too much treble.

trebly[2] *adv* three times as much.

trebuchet /'treb(y)ooshet/ *or* **trebucket** /'treebukit/ *noun* a military device used in medieval siege warfare for hurling large missiles at castle walls, etc. [early French *trebuchet* from *trebucher* to overthrow or stumble]

trecento /tray'chentoh/ *noun* (*often* **Trecento**) the 14th cent., *esp* in Italian art. [Italian, literally 'three hundred', a shortened form of *mille trecento* one thousand three hundred]

tree¹ /tree/ *noun* **1a** a woody plant having a single tall and erect main stem, generally with few or no branches on its lower part. **b** a shrub or herbaceous plant that looks similar to a tree. **2** a diagram or graph with a branching structure that shows the relationships or processes connecting the various elements plotted on it: *a genealogical tree.* **3** a branched system, *esp* of veins, nerves, etc in an animal or plant body: *the vascular tree.* **4** a piece of wood or a wooden structure. **5a** *archaic or literary* the cross on which Jesus was crucified. **b** *archaic* a gallows. **✳ be barking up the wrong tree** *informal* to be taking useless action or acting misguidedly [from racoon-hunting at night: hounds were trained to bark when they had treed their prey, but sometimes mistook the tree in the dark]. **out of one's tree** *chiefly NAmer, informal* crazy. **up a tree** *chiefly NAmer, informal* caught in a difficult situation with no apparent means of escape. **➤➤ treeless** *adj,* **treelessness** *noun,* **tree-like** *adj.* [Old English *trēow*]

tree² *verb trans* (**trees, treed, treeing**) **1** *NAmer* to drive (an animal being hunted) to or up a tree. **2** *chiefly NAmer, informal* to put (somebody) into a position of extreme difficulty or disadvantage.

treecreeper *noun* any of various small songbirds with slender curved beaks that they use for pulling insects out of the bark of trees: genera *Certhia* and *Climacteris*.

tree fern *noun* any of various tree-like ferns with woody stems: genera *Cyathea, Dicksonia,* and other genera.

tree frog *noun* any of numerous species of usu brightly coloured tropical or subtropical frogs with long toes ending in adhesive pads that enable them to climb trees: genus *Hyla* and other genera.

tree fruit *noun* edible fruit that grows on trees, e.g. apples, pears, plums, and peaches.

treehopper *noun* any of various species of tropical and subtropical jumping insects that live in trees and have sucking mouthparts: family Membracidae.

tree house /hows/ *noun* a structure built in the branches of a tree for children to play in.

tree-hugger *noun informal* a person who campaigns about environmental issues, *esp* against the development of the countryside for industrial, residential, or transport uses. **➤➤ tree-hugging** *noun.* [so called because of the habit some protesters have of wrapping their arms round tree trunks to prevent the trees being felled by developers]

tree kangaroo *noun* any of several species of tree-dwelling kangaroos of Australia and New Guinea that have front and hind limbs of similar lengths: genus *Dendrolagus*.

tree line *noun* the upper limit of tree growth on a mountain or at a high northern or southern latitude.

treen /'treen/ *noun* (*treated as pl*) small domestic articles, *esp* antique tableware, made of wood. [Old English *trēowen* wooden, from *trēow* TREE¹ + -EN¹]

treenail *or* **trenail** /'treenayl, 'trenl/ *noun* a hard wooden peg used for joining planks or other pieces of wood together.

tree of heaven *noun* a tropical Asian tree that is widely grown for shade and as an ornamental tree: *Ailanthus altissima*.

tree of knowledge *noun* according to the Bible, the tree in the Garden of Eden of which Adam and Eve ate the fruit, thereby disobeying God (Genesis 3:22–4).

tree of life *noun* **1** (**Tree of Life**) according to the Bible, a tree in the Garden of Eden bearing fruit that gave anyone eating it eternal life (Genesis 2:9; 3:22). **2** = ARBOR VITAE.

tree ring *noun* = ANNUAL RING.

tree shrew *noun* any of various small tree-dwelling insectivorous mammals of SE Asia that resemble squirrels, with large eyes and pointed snouts: genus *Tupaia* and other genera.

tree sparrow *noun* **1** a Eurasian sparrow related to the house sparrow but with a dark chestnut head: *Passer montanus*. **2** a N American sparrow with a reddish chestnut head and a dark patch on its breast: *Spizella arborea*.

tree surgeon *noun* a person who specializes in treating and preserving diseased, damaged, and decaying trees by pruning them, filling in cavities, and applying braces to support weakened parts. **➤➤ tree surgery** *noun.*

tree toad *noun* = TREE FROG.

tree tomato *noun* **1** an oval red edible fruit. **2** the S American tree-like shrub that bears this fruit: *Cyphomandra betaceae*. Also called TAMARILLO.

treetop *noun* **1** the topmost part of a tree. **2** (*in pl*) the height or line marked by the tops of a group of trees.

tref /trayf/ *adj* said of food: unfit to eat because its preparation does not satisfy Jewish dietary laws. [Yiddish *treyf,* from Hebrew *terēpāh* torn, with reference to flesh just torn from an animal's body]

trefoil /'trefoyl, 'treefoyl/ *noun* **1** any of several species of wild plants with three-lobed leaves or leaves divided into five leaflets with the bottom two bent back: genera *Trifolium* and *Lotus*. **2** a leaf divided into three leaflets. **3** a stylized figure or ornament, *esp* in architectural tracery, in the form of a three-lobed leaf or flower. **➤➤ trefoiled** *adj.* [French *trifoil* from Latin *trifolium,* from *tri-* three + *folium* leaf]

trek¹ /trek/ *noun* **1** a journey; *esp* a long or arduous one made on foot. **2** *SAfr.* **a** a journey by ox wagon or one stage of such a journey. **b** an organized migration by a group of settlers. [via Afrikaans from South African Dutch *trek* a haul, from *trekken* to travel, from Dutch *trekken* to pull]

trek² *verb intrans* (**trekked, trekking**) **1** to travel, *esp* by going on a long or arduous walk. **2a** *chiefly SAfr* to travel or migrate by ox wagon. **b** *SAfr* said of an ox: to pull a vehicle or load. **➤➤ trekker** *noun.*

Trekkie /'treki/ *noun* (*pl* **Trekkies**) *informal* an ardent fan of *Star Trek,* a US television science-fiction series.

trellis¹ /'trelis/ *noun* a frame of latticework used as a screen or as a support for climbing plants. **➤➤ trellised** *adj.* [Middle English *trelis* from early French *treliz* fabric of coarse weave, from Latin *tri-* three + *licium* thread]

trellis² *verb trans* (**trellised, trellising**) to provide or support (something) with a trellis.

trematode /'tremətohd, 'tree-/ *noun* any of a class of parasitic flatworms including the flukes: class Trematoda. [Greek *trēmatōdēs* pierced with holes, from *tetrainein* to bore; because some species have skin perforated by pores]

tremble¹ /'trembl/ *verb intrans* **1** to shake involuntarily, *esp* with fear or cold; to shiver. **2** to be affected by a quivering or vibratory motion: *The building trembled from the blast; His voice trembled with emotion.* **3** to be affected with fear or apprehension: *We trembled for their safety.* **➤➤ trembling** *adj,* **tremblingly** *adv.* [Middle English from early French *trembler,* from Latin *tremere* to tremble]

tremble² *noun* **1** a fit or spell of involuntary shaking or quivering. **2** (*in pl, but treated as sing.*) a condition characterized by trembling; *specif* a severe disorder of livestock, *esp* cattle, characterized by muscular tremors, weakness, and constipation. **✳ all of a tremble** trembling with fear, anxiety, or excitement.

trembler *noun Brit* a vibrating device that automatically makes or breaks an electric circuit.

trembling poplar *noun* = ASPEN.

trembly *adj* (**tremblier, trembliest**) *informal* shaking or quivering.

tremendous /trə'mendəs/ *adj* **1** very great in size, degree, amount, intensity, etc: *That fire gives off a tremendous heat.* **2** *informal.* **a** highly impressive, unusual, or exciting: *We saw a tremendous film last night.* **b** great or extreme: *You've been a tremendous comfort to me.* **3** *archaic* such as to arouse awe or fear: *Probably its regular visitants, like the initiates of freemasonry, wished there were something a little more tremendous to keep to themselves about it* — George Eliot. **➤➤ tremendously** *adv,* **tremendousness** *noun.* [Latin *tremendus,* from *tremere* to tremble + -OUS]

tremolite /'tremǝliet/ *noun* a white or grey mineral consisting of a calcium magnesium silicate in the form of long slender crystals. [French *trémolite,* named after *Tremola,* a valley in Switzerland where it was discovered]

tremolo /'tremoloh/ *noun* (*pl* **tremolos**) **1** in music, a very rapid repetition of a note or notes to produce a trembling effect. **2a** a mechanical device in an organ that produces a trembling effect. **b** a device on an electric guitar that produces a similar effect. [Italian *tremolo,* literally 'tremulous', from Latin *tremulus:* see TREMULOUS]

tremolo arm *noun* = TREMOLO (2B).

tremor¹ /'tremǝ/ *noun* **1** an involuntary trembling or shaking, e.g. because of a nervous disorder. **2** a slight quivering or vibratory motion; *esp* a distinct small movement of the earth that precedes or follows a major earthquake. **3** a sudden thrill or quiver of fear or excitement. [Latin *tremor,* from *tremere* to tremble]

tremor[2] *verb intrans* (**tremored, tremoring**) to undergo or experience a tremor or tremors.

tremulous /'tremyoolǝs/ *adj* **1** characterized by or affected with trembling or tremors; shaking or quivering: *a tremulous voice; tremulous handwriting.* **2** uncertain, timid, or fearful. ➤➤ **tremulously** *adv*, **tremulousness** *noun*. [Latin *tremulus* trembling, from *tremere* to tremble]

trenail /'treenayl, 'trenl/ *noun* see TREENAIL.

trench[1] /trench/ *noun* **1** a long narrow excavation in the ground, *esp* one dug for drainage or to allow underground pipes, cables, etc to be laid. **2** a deep ditch, often one of a series, used for military defence, usu with the excavated earth banked up in front for protection. **3** a long, narrow, and usu steep-sided depression in the ocean floor. [early French *trenche* an act of cutting or something cut off, from *trenchier* to cut, cut off, from Latin *truncare* to lop off, maim]

trench[2] *verb trans* **1** to dig a trench or trenches in (a piece of ground). **2** to protect (a military position or its troops) by digging a trench or trenches. **3** to dig or plough (a field) deeply; *esp* to turn over (soil) three or more times the depth of a spade. ➤ *verb intrans archaic* (+ on/upon) to encroach on something or come close to it: *trenching on other domains which were more vital* — Winston Churchill.

trenchant /'trenchǝnt/ *adj* **1** incisive and penetrating: *trenchant criticism.* **2** vigorously effective and articulate: *a trenchant analysis of the situation.* **3** clear-cut, obvious, or distinct: *the trenchant divisions between right and wrong* — Edith Wharton. **4** *archaic or literary* said of a weapon or tool: sharp-edged. ➤➤ **trenchancy** *noun*, **trenchantly** *adv*. [French *trenchant*, literally 'cutting', present part. of *trenchier*: see TRENCH[1]]

trench coat *noun* **1** a double-breasted raincoat with deep pockets, a belt, and epaulettes. **2** a waterproof overcoat with a removable lining, designed to be worn by soldiers, *esp* in trenches.

trencher *noun* **1** a wooden platter formerly used for serving food. **2** *dated* = MORTARBOARD (2). [Middle English from early French *trencheoir*, from *trenchier*: see TRENCH[1]]

trencherman *noun* (*pl* **trenchermen**) a hearty eater or a person who enjoys good food.

trench fever *noun* an infectious disease caused by a RICKETTSIA (parasitic micro-organism resembling a bacterium) that is transmitted by the body louse, resulting in fever and severe pains in the muscles, bones, and joints. [so called because of its prevalence among soldiers in the trenches during World War I]

trench foot *noun* a painful disorder of the foot, resembling frostbite, caused by prolonged immersion in cold water or mud.

trench mortar *noun* a light portable mortar used in trench warfare for propelling a bomb at a high trajectory over a relatively short distance.

trench warfare *noun* a type of warfare in which the opposing forces fight from systems of trenches that face each other.

trend[1] /trend/ *noun* **1** a general or prevailing direction, tendency, or inclination. **2** a general movement or change: *There seems to be a trend away from the city and towards suburban living.* **3** a current style, fashion, or taste. **4** the general movement in the course of time of a statistically detectable change, or a statistical curve reflecting such a change.

trend[2] *verb intrans* **1** said *esp* of a geographical feature: to extend or bend in a specified direction. **2** *chiefly NAmer* to shift towards or go in a specified direction: *Public opinion is trending more to the political right again.* [Old English *trendan* to revolve]

trendify /'trendifie/ *verb trans* (**trendifies, trendified, trendifying**) *informal* to make (something) more fashionable: *The town council proposes developing and trendifying the area round the old docks.*

trendsetter *noun* somebody who starts a new trend in fashion or popularizes an idea, theory, etc. ➤➤ **trendsetting** *adj*.

trendy[1] *adj* (**trendier, trendiest**) *informal* **1** very fashionable or up-to-date. **2** characterized by unthinking adherence to the latest fashions or progressive ideas: *His concern for good composition … prevents the up-to-date from dwindling into the merely trendy* — The Listener. ➤➤ **trendily** *adv*, **trendiness** *noun*.

trendy[2] *noun* (*pl* **trendies**) *informal* a person who follows the latest fashions or who accepts the most up-to-date ideas, etc, often without considering their value: *The wine bar caters for young trendies.*

trente et quarante /,trohnt ay ka'ronht/ *noun* a gambling game that involves playing cards being laid on either of two diamonds, a red one or a black one, with players betting on which colour will have cards with a total closest to 31. [French *trente et quarante*, literally 'thirty and forty']

trepan[1] /tri'pan/ *noun* **1** a primitive type of TREPHINE[1] (surgical instrument for removing circular pieces of tissue or bone), *esp* one used to penetrate the skull. **2** a heavy tool used in boring mine shafts. [Middle English via Latin from Greek *trupanon* auger, from *trupan* to bore, from *trupa* a hole]

trepan[2] *verb trans* (**trepanned, trepanning**) **1** to remove a circular piece of bone from (a person's skull) using a trepan. **2a** to remove a disc or cylindrical core from (metal) with a machine tool. **b** to cut (a hole or groove) in something using a trepan. ➤➤ **trepanation** /trepǝ'naysh(ǝ)n/ *noun*.

trepang /tri'pang/ *noun* any of several large sea cucumbers that are used, *esp* in Chinese, Japanese, and Indonesian cookery, for making soup: genus *Holothuria*. Also called BÊCHE-DE-MER. [Malay *tĕripang*]

trephine[1] /tri'teen/ *noun* a surgical instrument for cutting out circular sections, *esp* of bone or the cornea of the eye. [probably from Latin *tres fines* three ends]

trephine[2] *verb trans* **1** to operate on (somebody's skull) using a trephine. **2** to extract (a section of bone or tissue) with a trephine. ➤➤ **trephination** /trifi'naysh(ǝ)n/ *noun*.

trepidation /trepi'daysh(ǝ)n/ *noun* **1** a feeling of nervous agitation or fear, *esp* at the thought of something that is about to happen. **2** *archaic* a quivering or trembling motion. [Latin *trepidatio(n-)*, from *trepidare* to tremble, from *trepidus* alarmed]

treponema /trepǝ'neemǝ/ *or* **treponeme** /-'neem/ *noun* (*pl* **treponemata** /-tǝ/ *or* **treponemes**) any of a genus of spirally coiled parasitic bacteria, some of which cause diseases such as syphilis and yaws: genus *Treponema*. ➤➤ **treponemal** *adj*. [Latin genus name, from Greek *trepein* to turn + *nēma* thread]

trespass[1] /'trespǝs/ *verb intrans* **1** to enter somebody's land or property unlawfully or without permission. **2** (+ on/upon) to make an unwarranted or uninvited intrusion on or take unfair advantage of something: *She didn't want to trespass on his time.* **3** *archaic or literary* (+ against) to commit an offence against a person or break a rule or law. ➤➤ **trespasser** *noun*. [Middle English from early French *trespasser* to pass or go across, from Latin *transpassare* to pass through, from TRANS- + *passare* to pass]

trespass[2] *noun* **1** entry to somebody's land or property that is unlawful or done without permission. **2** *archaic or literary* a moral violation; a sin.

tress[1] /tres/ *noun* **1** (*also in pl*) a long lock of hair, *esp* the long unbound hair of a woman. **2** *archaic* a plait of hair. ➤➤ **tressy** *adj*. [Middle English from early French *tresse* a braid of hair, perhaps from Greek *trikha* triple]

tress[2] *verb trans archaic* to arrange (a person's hair) into long locks or plaits.

tressed *adj* (*used in combinations*) having tresses of a specified kind: *golden-tressed.*

tressure /'treshǝ, 'tresyooǝ/ *noun* **1** in heraldry, a narrow band set within the edge of a shield, usu an ornamented one and usu one of a pair. **2** a similar ornamentation formerly found on the edge of coins. [Middle English *tressour* a band or ribbon for the hair, from early French, from *tresse*: see TRESS[1]]

trestle /'tresl/ *noun* **1** a framework consisting typically of a horizontal bar held at each end by two pairs of sloping legs, *esp* one designed to support something such as a table top. **2a** a braced framework of timbers, piles, or girders for carrying a road or railway over a depression. **b** a bridge that is constructed from this type of framework. **3** = TRESTLETREE. [early French *trestel*, probably related to Latin *transtrum* a beam]

trestle table *noun* a table consisting of a board or boards supported on trestles.

trestletree *noun* on a sailing ship, either of a pair of timber crosspieces fixed fore and aft on the masthead to support the crosstrees and topmast.

trestlework *noun* = TRESTLE (2A).

trevally /trǝ'vali/ *noun* (*pl* **trevallies**) any of several species of spiny-finned edible marine fishes that live in the waters around Australia and New Zealand, some of which are prized as sporting fish: genus *Caranx* and other genera. [probably an alteration of *cavally* a horse mackerel, from Spanish *caballo* a horse, from Latin *caballus*]

trews /troohz/ *pl noun* **1** *chiefly Brit* trousers, *esp* close-fitting tartan trousers. **2** tartan trousers cut on the cross and extending over the top of the feet, worn in Highland dress and formerly by soldiers in some Highland regiments. [Scottish Gaelic *triubhas* (sing.) trousers]

trey /tray/ *noun* (*pl* **treys**) **1** a card, dice, or domino that has three spots on it. **2** in basketball, a shot that scores three points. [early French *trei* three, from Latin *tres*]

tri- *comb. form* forming words, with the meanings: **1** three: *tripartite*. **2** having three elements or parts: *trigraph*. **3** into three: *trisect*. **4a** thrice: *triweekly*. **b** every third: *trimonthly*. [from Latin *tres*, Greek *treis* three]

triable /'trie·əbl/ *adj* said of a criminal offence or a court case: liable or subject to trial.

triac /'trieak/ *noun* a semiconductor device with three layers that acts as a high-speed electronic switch for alternating current power supplies. [TRI- + *ac*, abbr of ALTERNATING CURRENT]

triacetate /trie'asitayt/ *noun* **1** a chemical compound containing three acetate groups in the molecular structure. **2** an artificial textile fibre made from a triacetate of cellulose.

triad /'triead/ *noun* **1a** a union or group of three related or associated people or things. **b** in music, a chord made up of a given note plus the two notes a third and fifth above it. **c** a form of Welsh literary composition in which the subjects or statements are arranged in groups of three. **2** (*often* **Triad**). **a** any of various Chinese secret societies, *esp* one engaged in organized crime, such as drug trafficking, extortion, and prostitution. **b** a member of such a society. ➤➤ **triadic** /trie'adik/ *adj*, **triadism** *noun*. [probably from French *triade*, via Latin from Greek *triad-*, *trias*, from *treis* three]

triage /'tree'ahzh/ *noun* **1** the act or an instance of sorting or grouping things according to need or potential benefit. **2a** the process of prioritizing or allocating treatment to patients, *esp* accident, battle, or disaster victims, according to an initial assessment of the urgency of their medical needs. **b** the area of an accident and emergency department where such assessment takes place. [French *triage*, literally 'sorting', from *trier* to sort, sift, TRY¹]

trial¹ /'trie·əl/ *noun* **1** a formal examination of the evidence in a court case in order to determine an accused person's guilt or innocence. **2a** the act or process of testing something, *esp* in order to assess its quality, durability, suitability, performance, etc: *The new drug is undergoing clinical trials before being put on the market*. **b** (*used before a noun*) involving or used as a test; experimental: *They decided on a trial separation*. **3a** a sports match in which the comparative skills of players are evaluated, *esp* in order to select team members. **b** (*in pl*) a competition in which the individual skills of a person or an animal are tested. **c** a motorcycling competition over rough terrain: *sheepdog trials*. **4a** a test of faith, patience, or stamina, *esp* one that involves suffering or temptation. **b** somebody or something that is a source of worry, trouble, or annoyance: *Their son has always been a great trial to them*. **5** an attempt or effort. ✳ **on trial 1** said of an accused person: undergoing trial in a court of law. **2** said of a new product: undergoing testing. **3** said of something that might be purchased: on loan for assessment: *We have the car on trial for a week*. [Anglo-French *trial*, from *trier* TRY¹]

trial² *verb* (**trialled, trialling**, *NAmer* **trialed, trialing**) ➤ *verb trans* to test (something) in order to assess its quality, durability, suitability, performance, etc. ➤ *verb intrans* said of a sheepdog, horse, motorcyclist, or sports player: to take part in a trial or trials.

trial and error *noun* a process of trying out a number of methods in order to find the best way to achieve a desired result.

trial balance *noun* a statement of the debit and credit balances of accounts in a double-entry ledger at a given date, prepared primarily to check that they agree.

trial balloon *noun* a tentatively suggested project, scheme, idea, etc put forward to test public opinion or reaction. [orig a balloon sent up to test air currents and wind speed]

trial court *noun* *chiefly NAmer* a court of law where initial trials are heard, as distinct from a court of appeal.

trialist (*Brit* **triallist**) *noun* **1** a person who takes part in a sports trial, e.g. in motorcycling or for team selection. **2** a person who takes part in the trial of a new product.

trial lawyer *noun* *NAmer* a lawyer engaged chiefly in cases before trial courts.

triallist *noun Brit* see TRIALIST.

trial run *noun* an exercise to test the performance of something, *esp* a new system or product.

triangle /'trieanggl/ *noun* **1** a polygon with three angles and three sides. **2** something shaped like a triangle. **3** a percussion instrument consisting of a steel rod bent into the form of a triangle and sounded by striking with a small metal rod. **4** *NAmer* = SET SQUARE. **5a** a romantic or sexual relationship involving three people. **b** any situation where three people, things, opinions, etc are involved. [Middle English from Latin *triangulum*, neuter of *triangulus* triangular, from *tri-* three + *angulus* ANGLE¹]

triangle of forces *noun* in physics, a triangle with sides that represent the magnitudes and directions of three forces in equilibrium.

triangular /trie'anggyoolə/ *adj* **1a** relating to or having the form of a triangle: *a triangular plot of land*. **b** having a triangular base or principal surface: *a triangular pyramid*. **2** between or involving three elements, things, or people: *a triangular love affair*. ➤➤ **triangularity** /trie,anggyoo'lariti/ *noun*, **triangularly** *adv*.

triangulate /trie'anggyoolayt/ *verb trans* **1a** to divide (something, *esp* land) into triangles. **b** to survey or map (an area) by triangulation. **c** to calculate (a height, distance, etc) by triangulation. **2** to give triangular form to (something).

triangulation /trie,anggyoo'laysh(ə)n/ *noun* the measurement of the angles and one side of a triangle to find an unknown position, distance, etc, *esp* in determining the network of triangles into which any part of the earth's surface is divided in surveying.

triangulation point *noun* = TRIG POINT.

triangulation station *noun* = TRIG POINT.

Triassic /trie'asik/ *adj* relating to or dating from a geological period, the first period of the Mesozoic era, lasting from about 245 million to about 208 million years ago, and marked by an abundance of reptiles and the first appearance of dinosaurs. [Latin *trias* TRIAD, so called because of the three subdivisions of the European Triassic]

triathlon /trie'athlon/ *noun* an athletic contest in which all contestants compete in three events, typically long-distance running, swimming, and cycling. ➤➤ **triathlete** /-leet/ *noun*. [TRI- + Greek *athlon* contest]

triatomic /trie-ə'tomik/ *adj* having three atoms in the molecule: *Ozone is triatomic oxygen*.

triaxial /trie'aksi·əl/ *adj* having or involving three axes.

tribade /'tribəd/ *noun* a lesbian, *esp* one who practises tribadism. [French *tribade* from Latin *tribad-*, *tribas*, from Greek *tribein* to rub]

tribadism /'tribədiz(ə)m/ *noun* a lesbian sexual practice involving genital contact, with one partner lying on top of the other.

tribal¹ /'triebl/ *adj* **1** relating to or characteristic of a tribe or tribes: *tribal customs*. **2** characterized by a tendency to form insular groups or by feelings of strong or excessive group loyalty. ➤➤ **tribally** *adv*.

tribal² *noun* a member of a tribal group, *esp* in the Indian subcontinent.

tribalism *noun* **1** the state of belonging to a tribe. **2** tribal consciousness and loyalty, *esp* exaltation of the tribe above other groups: *The ANC ... purports to eschew tribalism in favour of an all-embracing black nationalism* — Independent. **3** strong loyalty or attachment to a group, often to an excessive degree: *this nostalgic aspect of skinhead culture ... the exaggerated tribalism, the bullheaded racism of an Alf Garnett, the dogged male chauvinism of an Andy Capp* — Nick Knight. ➤➤ **tribalist** *noun*, **tribalistic** /-'listik/ *adj*.

tribasic /trie'baysik/ *adj* said of an acid: having three replaceable hydrogen atoms in each molecule.

tribe /trieb/ *noun* **1a** a group of people, families, or clans with shared economic and social ties and usu a common culture, dialect, religion, and ancestry. **b** such a group living in a non-industrialized society. **2** in ancient Rome, one of several (orig three) political divisions of the Roman people. **3** *derog* a group of people sharing a common occupation or interest, *esp* an insular social or political group: *attempts to portray the whole tribe of parliamentarians as either stupid or vicious* — The Listener. **4** *informal* (*also in pl*) a large number of people or things: *The streets were packed with tribes of tourists*. **5a** a category in biological taxonomy ranking above a genus and below a family. **b** a group of related animals or plants. [Middle English from Latin *tribus*, a division of the Roman people, tribe, prob from *tres* three, referring to the three ethnic groups of ancient Rome]

tribesman or **tribeswoman** noun (pl **tribesmen** or **tribeswomen**) a man or woman who is a member of a tribe, esp one living in a non-industrialized society.

tribo- comb. form forming words, denoting: friction: triboluminescence. [Greek tribein to rub]

triboelectricity /ˌtrieboh·ilek'trisiti, -elik'trisiti/ noun a charge of electricity generated by friction, e.g. by rubbing glass with silk.

tribology /trie'boləji/ noun the scientific study of the design, friction, wear, and lubrication of interacting surfaces in relative motion, e.g. in bearings or gears. ⟫ **tribological** /-'lojikl/ adj, **tribologist** noun.

triboluminescence /ˌtriebohloohmi'nes(ə)ns/ noun the emission of light from a substance when it is rubbed or scraped. ⟫ **triboluminescent** adj.

tribrach /'triebrak, 'tribrak/ noun in prosody, a metrical foot consisting of three short or unstressed syllables. ⟫ **tribrachic** /trie'-brakik, tri'brakik/ adj. [Greek tribrakhus, from TRI- + brachus short]

tribulation /ˌtribyoo'laysh(ə)n/ noun **1** a state of great distress or suffering. **2** a source or cause of this. [via French from Latin tribulation-, tribulatio, from tribulare to press or oppress, from tribulum board used in threshing, ultimately from terere to rub]

tribunal /trie'byoohnl/ noun **1** Brit a board appointed to decide disputes of a specified kind: an industrial tribunal. **2** a court or forum of justice. **3** a bench or platform on which a judge sits. [via French from Latin tribunal platform for magistrates, from tribunus: see TRIBUNE[1]]

tribune[1] /'tribyoohn/ noun **1a** (also **tribune of the people**) an official of ancient Rome elected by and from the common people to protect their interests. **b** (also **military tribune**) a senior officer in the army of ancient Rome. **2** a person who defends the rights of the people. ⟫ **tribunate** /-nayt/ noun, **tribuneship** noun. [Middle English from Latin tribunus, literally 'leader of a tribe', from tribus: see TRIBE]

tribune[2] noun **1a** an apse in a basilica where the bishop's throne is placed. **b** the throne itself. **2** a dais or platform, esp one from which a congregation is addressed in a church. [French tribune from Italian tribuna the main room in a mansion, from Latin tribunal: see TRIBUNAL]

tributary[1] /'tribyoot(ə)ri/ noun (pl **tributaries**) **1** a stream or river feeding a larger river or a lake. **2** formerly, a ruler or state paying tribute to a conqueror. [Latin tributarius, from tributum: see TRIBUTE]

tributary[2] adj **1** said of a stream or river: feeding a larger river or a lake. **2a** said of a ruler or state: paying tribute to another to acknowledge submission, obtain protection, or secure peace. **b** said of a payment: given or owed as tribute.

tribute /'tribyooht/ noun **1** something, esp a gift or a formal statement, given or made as a demonstration of respect, gratitude, or affection: Floral tributes were left at the gates of the palace. **2** evidence of the worth or effectiveness of something specified: The vote was a tribute to their good sense. **3a** a payment formerly made by one ruler or nation to another, in acknowledgment of submission or as the price of protection. **b** the tax levied for such a payment. **4** in feudal society, a payment in money or kind made by a vassal to his lord as a sign of allegiance or homage. **5** any charge levied by a person or group that has power over another or others. [Latin tributum from tribuere to allot, bestow, or grant, orig 'to distribute between tribes', from tribus: see TRIBE]

tribute band noun a group of musicians, singers, or both who perform the music or songs of a more famous group or band and attempt to replicate their appearance, stage behaviour, etc.

trice /tries/ noun a brief space of time; an instant. ✳ **in a trice** very soon or immediately: I'll be back in a trice. [Middle English trise a tug or pull, from Dutch trisen to haul, to hoist a sail]

tricentenary /triesen'teenəri, -'tenəri/ noun (pl **tricentenaries**) = TERCENTENARY. ⟫ **tricentennial** /-'teni·əl/ adj and noun.

triceps /'trieseps/ noun (pl **tricepses** /-seez/ or **triceps**) a muscle with three points of attachment, esp the large muscle along the back of the upper arm that extends the forearm from the elbow. [Latin triceps, literally 'three-headed', from TRI- + caput head]

triceratops /trie'serətops/ noun a large plant-eating dinosaur of the Cretaceous period with three horns, a bony neck frill, and hoofed toes. [Latin genus name Triceratops, from Greek trikeratos three-horned + ōps face]

trich- comb. form see TRICHO-.

trichiasis /tri'kie·əsis/ noun an ingrowing of the eyelashes that leads to irritation of the CONJUNCTIVA (membrane lining the inner surface of the eyelids). [via Latin from Greek trikhiasis, from trikh-, thrix a hair]

trichina /tri'kienə/ noun (pl **trichinae** /-nee/) a small slender nematode worm that in the larval state is parasitic in the muscles of flesh-eating mammals, e.g. human beings and pigs: genus Trichinella. [via Latin from Greek trikhinos made of hair, from trikhos hair]

trichinosis /triki'nohsis/ noun infestation with or disease caused by trichinae and marked esp by muscular pain, fever, and oedema.

trichloride /trie'klawried/ noun a compound or a chemical element or radical with three atoms of chlorine.

tricho- or **trich-** comb. form forming words, denoting: the hair, or something resembling hair: trichology. [Greek trikhos hair]

trichology /tri'koləji/ noun the scientific study of hair, hair growth, and disorders of the hair and scalp. ⟫ **trichological** /-'lojikl/ adj, **trichologist** noun.

trichome /'triekohm, 'trikohm/ noun a hair or hair-like outgrowth, esp a structure on the surface tissue of a plant. [from Greek trikhōma, from trikhoun to cover with hair, from trikhos hair]

trichomonad /trikə'mohnad/ noun a parasitic protozoan that moves by means of beating flagella and infests the reproductive, urinary, and digestive tracts of many animals, including human beings: order Trichomonadida. ⟫ **trichomonal** adj. [Latin genus name Trichomonad-, Trichomonas, from TRICHO- + Latin monas a unit]

trichomoniasis /ˌtrikəmə'nie·əsis/ noun infection with or disease caused by trichomonads.

trichopteran /tri'koptərən/ noun any of an order of insects consisting of the caddis flies: order Trichoptera. ⟫ **trichopteran** adj. [Latin Trichoptera, literally 'hairy winged', from TRICHO- + Greek pteron wing]

trichotomy /tri'kotəmi/ noun (pl **trichotomies**) division into three parts, elements, or classes. ⟫ **trichotomous** adj. [Greek trikha threefold, from treis three, + -otomy as in DICHOTOMY]

trichroic /trie'kroh·ik/ adj said of a crystal: showing varying colours when viewed along three different axes under white light. ⟫ **trichroism** noun. [Greek trikhroos three-coloured, from TRI- + khrōma colour]

trichromatic /triekrə'matik/ adj **1** relating to, consisting of, or using three colours, esp the three primary colours. **2** relating to or having normal colour vision, in which the eye is sensitive to all three primary colours. [TRI- + Greek khrōma colour]

trichromatism /trie'krohmətiz(ə)m/ noun vision in which all three primary colours are perceived, though not necessarily with equal facility.

trick[1] /trik/ noun **1a** a crafty action or plan, esp one intended to deceive, defraud, or outwit somebody. **b** a mischievous act; a prank. **c** a deceptive, dexterous, or ingenious feat designed to puzzle or amuse: a conjuring trick. **2a** a deceptive appearance; an illusion: I thought I saw somebody, but it must have been a trick of the light. **b** (used before a noun) relating to, denoting, or involving trickery or illusion: trick photography; a trick question. **3a** a quick or effective way of getting a result; a knack. **b** a special technique or piece of technical knowledge. **c** a habitual peculiarity of behaviour or manner; a mannerism: He fell down a great deal during this period, because of a trick he had of walking into himself — James Thurber. **4** the cards played in one round of a card game, often used as a scoring unit. **5** informal. **a** a prostitute's client. **b** a session with a prostitute. **6** a sailor's turn of duty at the helm of a ship. **7** NAmer (used before a noun) injured, damaged, or defective: a trick knee. ✳ **do the trick** informal to produce the desired result: Just that little extra second did the trick — H Rider Haggard. **how's tricks?** informal how are you?; how are things going? **tricks of the trade** the techniques that are used by experts in a particular profession or craft. **turn a trick** informal said of a prostitute: to have a session with a client. **up to one's (old) tricks (again)** informal behaving in a characteristic, often undesirable, way. [Middle English from early French triche, from trichier to deceive or cheat]

trick[2] verb trans (often + into/out of) to deceive, defraud, cheat, or outwit (somebody): She tricked me into telling her my middle name; Several people had been tricked out of their savings by the gang.

trick cyclist *noun* **1** *Brit, humorous* a psychiatrist. **2** somebody who performs tricks on a cycle.

trickery *noun* (*pl* **trickeries**) **1** the use of tricks. **2** the act or an instance of using a trick or tricks.

trickle[1] /'trikl/ *verb intrans* **1** to flow in drops or a thin slow stream: *Tears trickled down her cheeks.* **2a** to move or go gradually or one by one: *The audience trickled out of the hall.* **b** to dissipate slowly: *Time trickles away.* **3** (+ down) said of the wealth of large businesses and the rich: to benefit small businesses and poorer people after a period of time. ➤ *verb trans* to cause (something) to flow in drops or a thin slow stream: *He trickled butterscotch sauce over the ice cream.* [Middle English, of imitative origin]

trickle[2] *noun* a thin slow stream or movement.

trickle charger *noun* an apparatus for charging a battery, e.g. a car battery, at a steady slow rate, using mains electricity.

trick or treat *interj chiefly NAmer* used as a cry by children trick-or-treating.

trick-or-treat *verb intrans chiefly NAmer* said of a child: to take part in a Halloween custom that involves dressing up and going from door to door to ask for treats, e.g. sweets and money, and threatening to play tricks on any householders who refuse.

trick out *verb trans* to dress or decorate (somebody or something), *esp* in a fancy way or a way intended to deceive: *He tricked himself out as a lieutenant* — Evelyn Waugh.

trickster /'trikstə/ *noun* **1** a person who defrauds others by trickery. **2** a person, e.g. a stage magician, who is skilled in the performance of tricks.

tricksy /'triksi/ *adj* (**tricksier, tricksiest**) **1** full of tricks; mischievous or playful. **2** difficult to follow or make out; intricate or complicated. **3** excessively elaborate. ➤➤ **tricksiness** *noun*.

trick up *verb trans* = TRICK OUT.

tricky *adj* (**trickier, trickiest**) **1** said of a task, problem, situation, etc: requiring great skill, care, or tact. **2** full of difficulties, hazards, or problems. **3** inclined to be sly, wily, or deceitful: *He's a bit of a tricky customer.* ➤➤ **trickily** *adv,* **trickiness** *noun.*

triclinia /trie'klini·ə/ *noun* pl of TRICLINIUM.

triclinic /trie'klinik/ *adj* said *esp* of a crystal: having three unequal axes intersecting at oblique angles. [TRI- + -*clinic* as in MONO-CLINIC]

triclinium /trie'klini·əm/ *noun* (*pl* **triclinia** /-i·ə/) **1** in ancient Rome, a couch that extended round three sides of a table and was large enough to allow people to eat in reclining positions. **2** a dining room with a couch or couches of this kind. [via Latin from Greek *triklinion,* from TRI- + *klinein* to lean or recline]

tricolour[1] (*NAmer* **tricolor**) /'trikələ, 'triekulə/ *noun* a flag with three bands or blocks of different colours, *esp* the French national flag with its vertical bands of blue, white, and red. [French *tricolore* three-coloured, from TRI- + Latin *color* COLOUR[1]]

tricolour[2] /'triekulə/ *or* **tricoloured** (*NAmer* **tricolor** *or* **tricolored**) *adj* having or using three colours.

tricorn[1] *or* **tricorne** /'triekawn/ *adj* said of a hat: having three horns or corners. [Latin *tricornis* three-horned, from TRI- + *cornu* horn]

tricorn[2] *or* **tricorne** *noun* a type of three-cornered hat with an upturned brim worn by men. [French *tricorne,* literally 'three-horned', from Latin *tricornis:* see TRICORN[1]]

tricot /'trikoh, 'treekoh/ *noun* a fine plain knitted fabric used in clothing, *esp* formerly for underwear: compare RASCHEL. [French *tricot,* literally 'knitting', from *tricoter* to knit]

tricuspid /trie'kuspid/ *adj* **1** said of a tooth: having three cusps or points: *a tricuspid molar.* **2** said of an anatomical valve: having three segments or cusps. ➤➤ **tricuspid** *noun.* [Latin *tricuspis,* from TRI- + *cuspis* a point]

tricuspid valve *noun* a heart valve whose function is to channel blood from the right atrium to the right ventricle and, with its three cusps, prevent any backflow of blood.

tricycle[1] /'triesikl/ *noun* **1** a three-wheeled pedal-driven vehicle. **2** a light three-wheeled motor-driven vehicle used by a physically disabled person. [French *tricycle,* orig referring to a three-wheeled horse-drawn coach, from TRI- + Greek *kyklos* a wheel]

tricycle[2] *verb intrans* to ride or drive a tricycle. ➤➤ **tricyclist** *noun.*

tridactyl /trie'daktil/ *adj* said of an animal: having three digits or claws on each limb. [TRI- + Greek *daktulos* finger]

trident /'tried(ə)nt/ *noun* **1** a three-pronged spear carried by and symbolizing the authority of Neptune (Poseidon) and Britannia. **2** a three-pronged spear used for fishing or as a weapon. [Latin *trident-, tridens* having three teeth, from TRI- + *dens* tooth]

tridental /trie'dentl/ *adj* having three prongs or points.

tridentate /trie'dentayt/ *adj* = TRIDENTAL.

Tridentine[1] /tri'dentien/ *adj* relating to, resulting from, or in accordance with the Council of Trent, held between 1545 and 1563 to deliberate on Roman Catholic doctrine: *the Tridentine mass.* [Latin *Tridentinus,* from *Tridentum* Trento (English name, Trent), the town in NE Italy where the council was held]

Tridentine[2] *noun* an orthodox Roman Catholic.

tried /tried/ *verb* past tense and past part. of TRY[1].

triennia /trie'eni·ə/ *noun* pl of TRIENNIUM.

triennial[1] /trie'eni·əl/ *adj* **1** lasting for three years. **2** occurring every three years. ➤➤ **triennially** *adv.* [late Latin *triennis,* from TRI- + Latin *annus* year, + -AL[1]]

triennial[2] *noun* **1** a third anniversary. **2** something that happens once every three years; *esp* a ceremony or celebration, e.g. in the Anglican Church.

triennium /trie'eni·əm/ *noun* (*pl* **trienniums** *or* **triennia** /-ni·ə/) a period of three years. [Latin *triennium,* from TRI- + *annum* year]

trier /'trie·ə/ *noun* **1** somebody who perseveres with something, *esp* something that they have little aptitude for or that they have already failed to do. **2** a person who examines a judicial case. **3** an implement, e.g. a tapered hollow tube, used in obtaining samples of foodstuffs or wine for examination and testing.

trifacial nerves /trie'fayshəl/ *pl noun* = TRIGEMINAL NERVES.

trifecta /trie'fektə/ *noun NAmer, Aus, NZ* a bet, e.g. on a horse or dog race, that involves forecasting the first three finishers in correct order. [from TRI- + PERFECTA]

trifid /'triefid/ *adj* said *esp* of a plant part or body part: deeply and narrowly cleft into three teeth, parts, or points. [Latin *trifidus* split into three, from TRI- + *findere* to split]

trifle[1] /'triefl/ *noun* **1** *Brit* a type of cold dessert made from sponge cake usu soaked in sherry, fruit, jelly, and custard and topped with whipped cream. **2** something of little value or importance: *You know my method. It is founded upon the observance of trifles* — Conan Doyle. **3** an insignificant amount of something. ✱ **a trifle** to some small degree; slightly: *He seems a trifle upset.* [early French *trufle,* from *trufe* mockery]

trifle[2] *verb intrans* **1** (*often* + with) to behave frivolously, thoughtlessly, or disrespectfully towards somebody or something: *He was just trifling with your affections.* **2** to talk in a jesting or mocking manner or with intent to delude or mislead: *I fear he did but trifle and meant to wreck thee* — Shakespeare. ➤➤ **trifler** *noun.*

trifling *adj* unimportant, trivial, or frivolous. ➤➤ **triflingly** *adv.*

trifocal[1] /trie'fohkl/ *adj* said of spectacles or lenses: having three focal lengths.

trifocal[2] *noun* **1** (*in pl*) spectacles with three focal lengths. **2** a trifocal lens.

trifoliate /trie'fohli·ət, -ayt/ *adj* **1** said of a compound leaf: having three leaflets. **2** said of a plant: having three leaves.

triforium /trie'fawri·əm/ *noun* (*pl* **triforia** /-ri·ə/) a gallery forming an upper storey of a church, typically an arcaded storey above the arches of the nave and below the clerestory. [origin unknown]

triform /'triefawm/ *adj technical* having three parts.

trifurcate[1] /'triefuhkat, -kayt/ *verb intrans* to divide into three branches or forks. ➤➤ **trifurcation** /-'kaysh(ə)n/ *noun.* [from Latin *trifurcus,* from TRI- + *furca* FORK[1] + -ATE[4]]

trifurcate[2] *adj* divided into three branches or forks.

trig[1] /trig/ *noun informal* trigonometry.

trig[2] *adj NAmer or archaic* smart, neat, or jauntily trim: *The district ... is thickly peopled with sugar-planters, whose showy houses, gray piazzas, trig gardens ... gave an exceedingly thriving air to the river scenery* — Basil Hall. [Middle English, in the sense 'faithful, trusty', from Norse *tryggr*]

trig[3] *verb trans* (**trigged, trigging**) (*often* + up) to make (somebody or something) smart or trig.

trigamous /'trigəməs/ *adj* having three husbands or wives at the same time. ➤➤ **trigamist** *noun,* **trigamy** *noun.* [TRI- + -*gamous* as in *bigamous:* see BIGAMY]

trigeminal /trie'jeminl/ *adj* relating to or in the region of the trigeminal nerves. [Latin *trigeminus* triplet, from TRI- + *geminus* twin]

trigeminal nerves *pl noun* the fifth and largest pair of cranial nerves, each of which splits into three divisions and carries both motor and sensory fibres to the eyes, the upper and lower jaws, and the skin around the eyes, nose, brow, and mouth.

trigeminal neuralgia *noun* an intense neuralgia involving one or more branches of the trigeminal nerves and characterized by intense pain in the face.

trigger[1] /'trigə/ *noun* **1** a device that can be moved to release a catch or spring, activating a mechanism, *esp* the part of a gun that makes it fire. **2** something that causes an event or reaction. ≫ **triggered** *adj*. [alteration of *tricker*, from Dutch *trekker*, from *trekken* to pull]

trigger[2] *verb trans* (**triggered, triggering**) **1** to activate (a mechanism, *esp* that of a gun) by means of a trigger. **2** (*often* + off) to initiate, bring about, or set off (something, *esp* something unpleasant or unwanted): *Food shortages triggered riots.*

triggerfish *noun* (*pl* **triggerfishes** *or collectively* **triggerfish**) any of numerous species of deep-bodied bony tropical fishes with erectile spines on the dorsal fins: family Balistidae.

trigger-happy *adj* **1** inclined to resort to violence or guns too quickly or in an irresponsible way. **2** inclined to act or speak rashly, without considering the potential consequences.

triglyceride /trie'glisəried/ *noun* an ESTER (chemical compound) that is formed by the combination of one molecule of the alcohol glycerol and three organic acid molecules.

triglyph /'trieglif/ *noun* in Doric architecture, a projecting rectangular tablet with three vertical grooves, used on ornamental friezes. ≫ **triglyphic** /trie'glifik/ *adj*. [via Latin from Greek *trigluphos*, from TRI- + *gluphe* a carving]

trigon /'triegon/ *noun* **1** a triangular harp or lyre used in ancient Greece and Rome. **2** a triangular cutting surface formed by the three cusps on an upper molar tooth. **3** *archaic* a triangle. [via Latin from Greek *trigōnon*, neuter of *trigōnos* triangular, from TRI- + *gōnos* angle]

trigonal /'trigənl/ *adj* **1** triangular. **2** said of a plant or animal part: triangular in cross section. **3** relating to or denoting a crystal system that has a vertical axis of threefold symmetry. ≫ **trigonally** *adv*.

trigonometric /,trigənə'metrik/ *adj* of or relating to trigonometry. ≫ **trigonometrical** *adj*.

trigonometric function *noun* a function of an arc or angle most simply expressed in terms of the ratios of pairs of sides of a right-angled triangle; a sine, cosine, tangent, cotangent, secant, or cosecant.

trigonometry /trigə'nomətri/ *noun* the branch of mathematics concerned with the properties of triangles and trigonometric functions and their applications. [scientific Latin *trigonometria*, from TRIGON + -O- + -METRY]

trig point *noun Brit* a hilltop reference point, usu marked by a small tower, used by surveyors.

trigram /'triegram/ *noun* **1** in the Chinese system of divination, I Ching, any one of eight symbols composed of various combinations of three broken and unbroken lines, which, when paired, form the 64 hexagrams that are used as the basis for interpretations. **2** = TRIGRAPH.

trigraph /'triegrahf, 'triegraf/ *noun* a combination of three letters representing a single speech sound, e.g. *eau* in *beau*.

trihedron /trie'heedrən/ *noun* (*pl* **trihedra** /-drə/ *or* **trihedrons**) a geometrical figure with three faces formed by the intersection of three planes. ≫ **trihedral** *adj and noun*.

trihydric /trie'hiedrik/ *adj* said of an alcohol such as glycerine: containing three hydroxyl groups attached to three different carbon atoms.

trike /triek/ *noun informal* a tricycle.

trilateral[1] /trie'lat(ə)rəl/ *adj* **1** said of talks, an agreement, etc: involving three parties, states, etc. **2** said of a geometric figure: having three sides.

trilateral[2] *noun* a triangle.

trilby /'trilbi/ *noun* (*pl* **trilbies**) *chiefly Brit* a soft felt hat with an indented crown. [so called because this type of hat was worn in the

London stage version of *Trilby*, a novel by George Du Maurier d.1896, English artist and writer]

trilinear /trie'lini-ə/ *adj* relating to, having, or involving three lines.

trilingual /trie'linggwəl/ *adj* **1** using or able to use three languages fluently. **2** involving, relating to, or expressed in three languages: *a trilingual phrase book.* ≫ **trilingualism** *noun*. [TRI- + *lingual* as in BILINGUAL]

trilith /'trielith/ *noun* = TRILITHON.

trilithon /'trielithon, 'trie-/ *noun* an ancient stone structure consisting of two large upright stones with a third resting across the top, a feature of Stonehenge and other stone circle sites. [via Latin from Greek *trilithon*, from TRI- + *lithos* a stone]

trill[1] /tril/ *noun* **1** in music, a rapid alternation of a main note and one above it. **2** a sound resembling a musical trill, e.g. one made by a bird; a warble. **3a** a rapid vibration of one speech organ against another, e.g. of the tip of the tongue against the ridge of flesh behind the front teeth, or of the UVULA (fleshy projection at the back of the mouth) against the back of the tongue. **b** a speech sound, *esp* /r/, produced by this type of vibration. [Italian *trillo*, from *trillare* to trill, of imitative origin]

trill[2] *verb intrans* to produce a warbling sound. ≫ *verb trans* **1** to utter (a speech sound, *esp* /r/) as a trill or with a trill. **2** to play or sing (something) with a trill. ≫ **triller** *noun*.

trillion /'trilyən/ *noun* (*pl* **trillions** *or* **trillion**) **1a** a million million (10^{12}), or the quantity represented by it. **b** *Brit, dated* a million million million (10^{18}). **2** *informal* (*in pl*) an indefinitely large number, often an exaggeration: *I've got trillions of things to do today.* ≫ **trillion** *adj*, **trillionth** *adj and noun*. [French *trillion*, from TRI- + -*illion* as in MILLION]

trillium /'trili·əm/ *noun* a wild plant that produces a solitary pink, red, white, or yellow flower and that has leaves, petals, and sepals arranged in threes: genus *Trillium*. [prob an alteration of Swedish *trilling* a triplet]

trilobite /'trieləbiet/ *noun* any of numerous extinct Palaeozoic marine arthropods that had a three-lobed body. [Greek *trilobos* three-lobed, from TRI- + *lobos* LOBE]

trilogy /'trilə ji/ *noun* (*pl* **trilogies**) **1** a group of three closely related literary, cinematic, or musical works. **2** in classical Greek theatre, a series of three tragedies performed consecutively. [Greek *trilogia* a group of three related tragedies, from TRI- + -LOGY]

trim[1] /trim/ *verb* (**trimmed, trimming**) ≫ *verb trans* **1a** to make (something) neater, shorter, or smaller by cutting or clipping: *He trimmed the hedge.* **b** (*often* + off/from) to remove (a specified length or part) from something by cutting or clipping. **2a** to reduce the size of (something, *esp* expenditure) by eliminating any unnecessary or superfluous things. **b** to remove (a specified amount of money) from something, *esp* by making financial cuts: *This could trim thousands from the running costs.* **3** to decorate (something) with ribbons, lace, ornaments, etc. **4a** to adjust (a sail on a boat) to take advantage of the wind. **b** to adjust the balance and position in the water of (a ship), *esp* by rearranging the ballast, cargo, or passengers. **c** to adjust (an aircraft or submarine) for horizontal movement or for motion upwards or downwards. **5** *informal, dated.* **a** to defeat (somebody) resoundingly, *esp* at a gambling game. **b** to cheat or swindle (somebody). **c** to beat or rebuke (somebody) severely. ≫ *verb intrans* to change one's views, *esp* to come into line with current political thinking in the hope of achieving personal advancement. ✳ **trim one's sails (to the wind)** to alter one's way of life, *esp* in response to changed circumstances. [Old English *trymian, trymman* to strengthen, make firm, arrange]

trim[2] *noun* **1** the act or an instance of trimming: *Your beard needs a trim.* **2** a haircut that tidies up an existing style, rather than creating a new one. **3a** material used for decoration or trimming. **b** the upholstery, interior, and decorative accessories of a motor vehicle. **4a** the position of a ship or boat, *esp* with reference to the horizontal. **b** the difference between the depth in water of a vessel at the front and at the back. **c** the relation between the position of a sail and the direction of the vessel. **d** the inclination of an aircraft or spacecraft in flight with reference to a fixed point such as the horizon, *esp* with the controls in a neutral position. ✳ **in trim 1** fit and healthy: *He goes jogging to keep in trim.* **2** well-maintained: *It's an old house, but it's in trim.*

trim[3] *adj* (**trimmer, trimmest**) in good order; neat and smart: *a trim figure.* ≫ **trimly** *adv*, **trimness** *noun*.

trimaran /'triemərən/ *noun* a yacht with three parallel hulls. [TRI- + *-maran* as in CATAMARAN]

trimer /'triemə/ *noun* a large chemical molecule composed of three small identical molecules. ➤➤ **trimeric** /trie'merik/ *adj*.

trimerous /'trimərəs, 'trie-/ *adj* **1** said of an animal or plant: having parts arranged or grouped in threes. **2** said of an animal or plant organ or part: consisting of three joints, lobes, etc.

trimester /'triemestə/ *noun* **1** a period of three months, *esp* any of the three periods of about three months into which human pregnancy may be divided. **2** *NAmer* any of the three divisions of the academic year. ➤➤ **trimestral** /trie'mestrəl/ *adj*, **trimestrial** /trie'mestri·əl/ *adj*. [French *trimestre*, from Latin *trimestris* relating to a period of three months, from TRI- + *mensis* a month]

trimeter /'trimitə/ *noun* in prosody, a line of verse consisting of three metrical feet. ➤➤ **trimetric** /tri'metrik/ *adj*, **trimetrical** /tri-'metrikl/ *adj*.

trimmer *noun* **1a** an instrument or machine for trimming: *a hedge trimmer*. **b** somebody who trims something: *a sail trimmer*. **2** a capacitor or other element in an electrical circuit used to tune the circuit to a desired frequency. **3** a short beam or rafter fitted at one side of an opening to support the free ends of floor joists or rafters. **4** a person who changes his or her views, *esp* in a way that brings them into line with current political thinking in the hope of achieving personal advancement.

trimming *noun* **1** (*in pl*) pieces cut off in trimming something. **2** ribbon, lace, or other decoration added to clothing, upholstery, linen, etc: *cushions with velvet trimming*. **3** *informal* (*in pl*) the traditional garnishes accompanying a dish or meal: *a boiled leg of mutton with the usual trimmings* — Dickens.

trimonthly /trie'munthli/ *adj* occurring every three months. ➤➤ **trimonthly** *adv*.

trimorphic /trie'mawfik/ *or* **trimorphous** /-fəs/ *adj* **1** said of some species: occurring in or having three distinct forms. **2** said of a mineral: existing in three crystalline forms. ➤➤ **trimorph** /'trie-mawf/ *noun*, **trimorphism** *noun*. [Greek *trimorphos* having three forms, from TRI- + *morphē* form]

trinary /'trienəri/ *adj* = TERNARY. [Latin *trinarius*, from *trini*: see TRINE[1]]

trine[1] /trien/ *noun* **1** a group of three. **2** in astrology, an aspect between two bodies that are 120°, or one third of the celestial sphere, apart. ➤➤ **trinal** *adj*. [early French *trin* from Latin *trini* three each, from *tres* three]

trine[2] *adj* **1** triple or threefold. **2** relating to or being an astrological trine.

Trinidadian /trini'dadi·ən/ *noun* a native or inhabitant of Trinidad, an island in the Caribbean. ➤➤ **Trinidadian** *adj*.

Trinitarian /trini'teəri·ən/ *noun* an adherent of the doctrine of the Trinity. ➤➤ **Trinitarian** *adj*, **Trinitarianism** *noun*.

trinitrotoluene /,trienietroh'tolyooeen/ *noun* an inflammable derivative of toluene used as a high explosive and in chemical synthesis: formula $C_6H_2(CH_3)(NO_2)_3$. [TRI- + NITRO[1] + TOLUENE]

trinity /'triniti/ *noun* (*pl* **trinities**) **1** (**the Trinity**) according to Christian theology, the unity of Father, Son, and Holy Spirit as three persons in one Godhead. **2** a group of three closely related people or things: *Inside the rose-tinted, air-conditioned, environment-proof bulk reigned the modern architectural trinity, cleanliness, spaciousness and luminosity* — Richard G Stern. [from early French *trinité*, from Latin *trinitas* the state of being threefold, from *trinus* threefold, from *tres* three]

Trinity Brethren *pl noun* the members of Trinity House.

Trinity House /hows/ *noun* the British organization that is responsible for licensing maritime pilots and constructing and maintaining navigational markers, such as buoys and lighthouses.

Trinity Sunday *noun* the Sunday after Pentecost observed as a festival in honour of the Trinity.

Trinity term *noun Brit* the name given at some universities to the term that begins after Easter.

trinket /'tringkit/ *noun* a small ornament or piece of jewellery, *esp* one of little material value: *A cross is the last thing I would wear as a trinket* — Geoge Eliot. ➤➤ **trinketry** *noun*. [origin unknown]

trinomial[1] /trie'nohmi·əl/ *adj* **1** said of an algebraic expression: consisting of three terms. **2** said of a biological taxonomic classification: having three terms, the first designating the genus, the second the species, and the third the subspecies or variety. [from TRI-, modelled on BINOMIAL[1]]

trinomial[2] *noun* a trinomial algebraic expression or taxonomic classification.

trio /'treeoh/ *noun* (*pl* **trios**) **1** a group or set of three people or things. **2** a group of three musicians or singers. **3a** a musical composition for three players, singers, or instruments. **b** the name given to the middle section of a minuet, scherzo, or march. **4** in some card games, *esp* piquet: a set of three aces, kings, queens, jacks, or tens in a hand, or a hand of this type. [French *trio*, from Italian, from Latin *tres* three]

triode /'trieohd/ *noun* **1** a thermionic valve with three electrodes used *esp* in amplification circuits. **2** a semiconductor rectifier with three connections.

triolet /'trie·əlit, 'tree-/ *noun* a poem or stanza of eight lines in which the first line is repeated as the fourth and seventh and the second line as the eighth, giving a rhyme scheme of *abaaabab*. [French *triolet*, dimin. of *trio*: see TRIO]

triose /'trieohz, 'trieohs/ *noun* any of various monosaccharides (simple carbohydrates; see MONOSACCHARIDE) having three carbon atoms in the molecule. [from TRI- + -OSE[2]]

trioxide /trie'oksied/ *noun* an oxide containing three atoms of oxygen per molecule.

trip[1] /trip/ *verb* (**tripped, tripping**) ➤ *verb intrans* **1** (*also* + on/up/over) to catch the foot on or against something and stumble or fall. **2** (*often* + up) to make a mistake. **3** (*often* + along/down) to dance, skip, or walk with light quick steps. **4** (*often* + off) to proceed smoothly, lightly, and easily; to flow: *words that trip off the tongue*. **5** (*often* + over) to stumble or hesitate in speaking. **6** said of machinery: **a** to become operative or activated, *esp* through the release of a catch. **b** to stop working, often as a result of an automatic safety mechanism being activated. **7** to go on a journey. **8** *informal* to experience the effects of a psychedelic drug, *esp* LSD. ➤ *verb trans* **1** (*often* + up) to cause (somebody or something) to stumble or fall over. **2** (*often* + up) to cause (somebody) to make a mistake. **3** (*usu* + up) to detect (somebody) in a fault or blunder; to catch out. **4** to cause (a device or mechanism) to start or stop operating, *esp* by releasing a catch or producing an electrical signal. **5** to raise (an anchor) from the seabed. **6** to pull (the spar supporting a sail) into a perpendicular position for lowering. ✳ **trip the light fantastic** to dance. [Middle English via early French *tripper* from early Dutch *trippen* to skip, hop]

trip[2] *noun* **1a** a journey or outing, *esp* a short one taken for pleasure. **b** a period spent away from home, *esp* one related to work: *a business trip; a fact-finding trip*. **2** the act or an instance of catching the foot and stumbling or falling. **3** the act or an instance of making a mistake, or of stumbling or hesitating when speaking. **4** *informal*. **a** a hallucinogenic experience induced by a psychedelic drug, *esp* LSD. **b** any highly charged, often distressing, emotional experience. **5** *informal* an obsessive, self-indulgent, or self-serving course of action or frame of mind: *We got out our old school photos and went on a nostalgia trip*. **6** *informal* a sphere of activity or lifestyle: *She gave up the whole superstar trip to become a wife and mother*. **7a** the act or an instance of releasing a catch or other device in order to activate, operate, or stop machinery or a mechanism. **b** a catch or other device used for this. **8** *archaic* a quick light step.

tripartite /trie'pahtiet/ *adj* **1** divided into or composed of three parts. **2** made between or involving three parties: *a tripartite treaty*. ➤➤ **tripartitely** *adv*, **tripartition** /-'tish(ə)n/ *noun*.

tripe /triep/ *noun* **1** the stomach tissue of a cow or similar animal used as food. **2** *informal* something inferior, worthless, or offensive; rubbish or nonsense. [Middle English from early French, of unknown origin]

trip-hammer *noun* a large hammer raised by machinery and then dropped on work below, used *esp* in forging metals.

triphibious /trie'fibi·əs/ *adj* said *esp* of a military operation: employing or involving land, naval, and air forces. [TRI- + *-phibious* as in AMPHIBIOUS]

trip hop *noun* music that combines hip-hop rhythms with psychedelic and dub effects to produce a type of mainly instrumental dance music with more mellow sounds. [from TRIP[2] (4A) + the second element of HIP HOP]

triphthong /'trifthong/ *noun* **1** a vowel sound, e.g. /ie·ə/ in *fire*, composed of three elements. **2** = TRIGRAPH. ➤➤ **triphthongal**

/trif'thong·gl/ *adj.* [French *triphtongue* via Latin from Greek *triph-thongos*, from TRI- + *thongos* sound]

Tripitaka /tri'pitəkə/ *noun* a collection of writings sacred to the Theravada Buddhists and composed of three sections covering monastic discipline, the discourses of Buddha, and the analysis of Buddhist doctrine. [Sanskrit *tripitaka*, literally 'three baskets']

triplane /'trieplayn/ *noun* an aeroplane with three main pairs of wings arranged one above the other.

triple[1] /'tripl/ *adj* **1** having three units or members. **2** three times as much or as many. **3** repeated three times. **4** marked by three beats per bar of music. ➤➤ **triply** *adv.* [Middle English from Latin *triplus* three times, from Greek *triplous*]

triple[2] *noun* **1** a triple sum, quantity, or number. **2** a combination, group, or series of three. **3** in baseball, a hit that enables the batter to reach third base.

triple[3] *verb trans and intrans* to become or make (something) three times as much or as many.

triple bond *noun* a chemical bond consisting of three pairs of electrons that are shared between two atoms in a molecule.

triple crown *noun* **1** (*often* **Triple Crown**). **a** the winning of three important sporting matches or horse races in a single season. **b** a title, often unofficial, that acknowledges this. **c** *NAmer* in major league baseball, an unofficial title awarded to the player whose batting average is the highest of the season. **2** the pope's tiara.

triple harp *noun* a large harp with three rows of strings and no pedals.

triple jump *noun* an athletic field event in which a competitor takes a running start and then performs a hop, a step, and a jump in succession, in an attempt to jump the longest distance.

triple-jump *verb intrans* to perform a triple jump. ➤➤ **triple jumper** *noun.*

triple point *noun* the condition of temperature and pressure under which the gaseous, liquid, and solid phases of a substance can exist in equilibrium.

triplet /'triplit/ *noun* **1** one of three children or animals born at one birth. **2** a combination, set, or group of three similar things. **3** a group of three musical notes performed in the time of two or four of the same value. **4** a unit of three lines of verse, *esp* lines that share the same end rhyme. [from TRIPLE[2], modelled on DOUBLET]

triplet code *noun* the genetic code in which the sequence of three successive nucleotides in a molecule of DNA or RNA forms the basis or code for a specific amino acid.

triple time *noun* musical time with three beats to the bar.

triple-tongue *verb intrans* to use tongue movements to produce a very fast succession of detached notes on a wind instrument. ➤➤ **triple tonguing** *noun.*

Triplex /'tripleks/ *noun trademark* laminated or toughened safety glass, used *esp* for car windows and windscreens. [Latin *triplex* threefold, because it is made of a layer of celluloid between two layers of glass]

triplex[1] *adj* threefold or triple. [Latin *triplex* threefold, from TRI- + *plicare* to fold]

triplex[2] *noun* **1** *NAmer.* **a** a residential building that is divided into three separate apartments or that has several separate apartments, each of which has rooms on three floors. **b** an apartment in such a building. **2** a three-stranded polynucleotide molecule.

triplex[3] *verb trans* to provide or fit (electrical equipment, computer systems, etc) in triplicate so that there will be backups in the event of any failures.

triplicate[1] /'triplikət/ *adj* **1** consisting of or existing in three corresponding or identical parts or copies: *triplicate invoices.* **2** relating to or denoting the third of three things that are exactly alike: *You should file the triplicate copy.* ➤➤ **triplicity** /tri'plisiti/ *noun.* [Middle English from Latin *triplicatus*, past part. of *triplicare* to triple, from *triplic-, triplex*: see TRIPLEX[1]]

triplicate[2] /'triplikayt/ *verb trans* **1** to make three copies of (something, *esp* a document). **2** to multiply (something) by three. ➤➤ **triplication** /-'kaysh(ə)n/ *noun.*

triplicate[3] /'triplikət/ *noun archaic* any of three things that are exactly alike or that form a set with corresponding parts. ✱ **in triplicate** in the form of three exact copies: *Your application must be submitted in triplicate.*

triploid /'triployd/ *adj* said of a cell, nucleus, or organism: having or containing three times the basic number of chromosomes. ➤➤ **triploidy** *noun.*

tripmeter *noun* a device in a motor vehicle that measures distance, usu one that can be reset to record the mileage of individual journeys.

tripod /'triepod/ *noun* **1** a three-legged stand, *esp* one for supporting a camera or other piece of equipment. **2** *archaic* a stool, table, or vessel, e.g. a cauldron, with three legs. **3** in ancient Greece, an altar resting on three legs, *esp* the bronze one at Delphi where the priestess sat and delivered oracular messages. ➤➤ **tripodal** /'tripəd(ə)l/ *adj.* [Latin *tripod-, tripus* from Greek *tripous*, from TRI- + *pous* foot]

tripoli /'tripəli/ *noun* = ROTTENSTONE. [French *tripoli*, named after *Tripoli*, either the city in Libya or the one in Lebanon]

tripos /'triepos/ *noun* an honours examination for a BA degree at Cambridge University. [modification of Latin *tripus* (see TRIPOD), so called because of the three-legged stool formerly occupied by a graduate appointed to dispute satirically with candidates at the degree ceremonies]

trippant /'tripənt/ *adj* in heraldry, said of a representation of a stag or deer: walking. [Old French *trippant*, present part. of *tripper*: see TRIP[1]]

tripper *noun* **1** *Brit, informal* somebody who goes on a journey or outing, *esp* a short one taken for pleasure: *The streets were crammed with day trippers.* **2** = TRIP[2] (7B).

trippy *adj* (**trippier, trippiest**) *informal* said of music, visual effects, etc: resembling or producing a hallucinogenic or psychedelic experience similar to that induced by a drug such as LSD.

triptane /'triptayn/ *noun* a liquid hydrocarbon compound used in aviation fuel: formula C_7H_{16}. [alteration of *trimethylbutane*, its scientific name]

triptych /'triptik/ *noun* **1** a picture or carving covering three panels side by side, *esp* an altarpiece consisting of a central panel with two hinged flanking panels that can be folded inwards to cover it completely. **2** a group of three related literary, cinematic, or musical works; a trilogy. [Greek *triptukhos*, from TRI- + *ptux* a plate]

triptyque /'trip'teek/ *noun dated* a customs permit allowing a vehicle to be temporarily imported into a country. [from TRIPTYCH, so called because the document was in three sections]

trip wire *noun* a concealed wire placed near the ground that is used to trip up an intruder or to activate an explosive or warning device when pulled.

triquetral /trie'kweetrəl, trie'kwetrəl/ *noun* (*also* **triquetral bone**) a bone of the CARPUS (wrist) on the side of the little finger, which articulates with the ULNA (bone of the lower arm) and with three other bones of the carpus. [Latin *triquetrus* three-cornered]

trireme /'triereem/ *noun* a galley with three banks of oars, *esp* one used by the ancient Greeks and Romans as a warship. [Latin *triremis*, from TRI- + *remus* oar]

trisaccharide /trie'sakəried/ *noun* a sugar that yields on complete breakdown three sugar molecules that cannot be broken down into simpler sugars.

trisect /trie'sekt/ *verb trans* to divide (something) into three parts; *specif* to divide (an angle or line segment) into three equal parts. ➤➤ **trisection** *noun,* **trisector** *noun.*

trishaw /'trieshaw/ *noun* a passenger vehicle consisting of a tricycle with a rickshaw body over the rear wheels, used *esp* in Asian cities. [from TRI- + the second element of RICKSHAW]

triskaidekaphobia /ˌtriskiedekə'fohbi·ə/ *noun* an extreme fear or dislike of the number thirteen, *esp* an exaggerated feeling of superstition relating to it. [Greek *treiskaideka* thirteen + -PHOBIA]

triskelion /tris'keli·ən/ *noun* (*pl* **triskelia** /-i·ə/) a figure or symbol in the shape of three bent legs or lines radiating from a common centre, e.g. the emblem of the Isle of Man. [Greek *triskelēs* three-legged, from TRI- + *skelos* leg]

trismus /'trizməs/ *noun* a condition in which the muscles of the jaw go into spasm, so that the mouth remains firmly closed. It is a symptom of tetanus, but it can also be caused by sensitivity to certain drugs. [via Latin from Greek *trismos* a grinding (of teeth)]

trisomy /'triesohmi/ *noun* a condition in which there is one extra chromosome, in addition to the normal diploid chromosome set, in all or a high proportion of cells. This leads to chromosomal disorders such as Down's syndrome. ➤➤ **trisomic** /trie'sohmik/ *adj*. [TRI- + -SOME³ + -Y²]

trisomy-21 *noun* the most common cause of Down's syndrome, in which an extra copy of chromosome 21 is present in all or a high proportion of cells.

triste /treest/ *adj archaic* sad or melancholy: *He looked rather triste, like his mother, a woman of little spirit* — Rose Macaulay. [Middle English via French from Latin *tristis* sad]

tristesse /tri'stes/ *adj literary* sadness or a feeling of wistful melancholy. [French *tristesse* sadness, from Latin *tristitia*, from *tristis* sad]

trisyllable /'triesiləbl/ *noun* a word or metrical foot of three syllables. ➤➤ **trisyllabic** /-'labik/ *adj*.

tritanope /'tritənohp/ *noun* a person who is affected by tritanopia.

tritanopia /tritə'nohpi·ə/ *noun* a form of colour blindness in which insensitivity to blue light causes an inability to distinguish between blue and green: compare DEUTERANOPIA, PROTANOPIA. [Greek *tritos* third (with reference to blue being the third colour of the spectrum) + -AN¹, + -OPIA]

trite /triet/ *adj* said of a word, phrase, remark, idea, etc: lacking originality; hackneyed from overuse: *For England expects – I forbear to proceed: 'tis a maxim tremendous, but trite* — Lewis Carroll. ➤➤ **tritely** *adv*, **triteness** *noun*. [Latin *tritus*, past part. of *terere* to rub, wear away]

tritheism /'trietheeiz(ə)m/ *noun* in Christian theology, the unorthodox doctrine that the Father, Son, and Holy Spirit are three distinct gods. ➤➤ **tritheist** *noun and adj*.

tritiated /'trishiaytid, 'triti-/ *adj* said of a molecule: containing tritium in place of the ordinary isotope of hydrogen. ➤➤ **tritiation** /-'ayshən/ *noun*.

triticale /tritə'kayli/ *noun* a cereal grass, a hybrid between wheat and rye, that has a high yield and rich protein content, used as animal fodder. [scientific Latin, blend of *Triticum* genus of wheat + *Secale* genus of rye]

tritium /'trishi·əm, 'triti·əm/ *noun* a radioactive isotope of hydrogen with atoms of three times the mass of ordinary hydrogen atoms: symbol T: compare DEUTERIUM, HYDROGEN, PROTIUM. [scientific Latin *tritium* from Greek *tritos* third]

triton¹ /'triet(ə)n/ *noun* **1** (**Triton**) in Greek mythology, a minor sea god, the son of Poseidon, usu represented as having a man's head and trunk and a fish's tail, and carrying a trident and a shell used as a trumpet. **2a** any of various large marine invertebrates, related to the snails and whelks, with a heavy elongated conical shell: genus *Charonia*. **b** the shell itself.

triton² *noun* the nucleus of a tritium atom, containing one proton and two neutrons.

tritone /'trietohn/ *noun* in music, an interval of three whole tones between notes.

triturate¹ /'trityoorayt/ *verb trans technical* **1** to crush or grind (a substance) into a fine powder. **2** to chew (food) thoroughly before swallowing. ➤➤ **trituration** /-'raysh(ə)n/ *noun*, **triturator** *noun*. [Latin *trituratus*, past part. of *triturare* to thresh, from *terere* to rub]

triturate² /'trityoorət/ *noun* a chemical substance that has been ground to a powder.

triumph¹ /'trie·umf/ *noun* **1a** a notable success, victory, or achievement. **b** the feeling of happiness, exultation, or satisfaction that such success, etc brings. **c** a highly successful or spectacular example of something: *Her achievement was a triumph of will and an inspiration to all*. **2** in ancient Rome, a ceremonial procession that accompanied a general as he returned to the city after a decisive victory over a foreign enemy. ➤➤ **triumphal** /trie'umf(ə)l/ *adj*. [Middle English via French from Latin *triumphus* a triumph, perhaps related to Greek *triambos* a hymn to Bacchus, the god of wine and religious celebrations]

triumph² *verb intrans* **1** (*often* + over) to obtain victory: *She triumphed over her illness to make a successful career*. **2** to celebrate victory or success, *esp* boastfully or with too much exultation. **3** said of a victorious general in ancient Rome: to return to the city and receive the honour of a triumph.

triumphalism /trie'umfəliz(ə)m/ *noun* excessive or boastful exultation following a success, victory, or achievement. ➤➤ **triumphalist** *adj and noun*.

triumphant /trie'umfənt/ *adj* **1** having won a battle, sports match, or contest; victorious. **2** rejoicing in or celebrating victory; jubilant. ➤➤ **triumphantly** *adv*.

triumvir /trie'umvə/ *noun* (*pl* **triumvirs** *or* **triumviri** /-rie/) **1** in ancient Rome, each of the three public officials who shared the responsibility of running any of the city's administrative departments. **2** a member of a commission or ruling body composed of three people with joint authority. ➤➤ **triumviral** *adj*. [Latin *triumvir*, back-formation from *triumviri* board of three men, from *trium virorum* of three men, from *tres* three + *viri* men]

triumvirate /trie'umvirət/ *noun* **1** a group of three, *esp* a group of three powerful people or three notable things. **2a** in ancient Rome, a group of three men jointly holding a public office. **b** the office or term of office of a triumvir. **c** government by triumvirs. [Latin *triumviratus*, from *triumviri*: see TRIUMVIR]

triumviri *noun* pl of TRIUMVIR.

triune /'trieyoohn/ *adj* three in one, *esp* in reference to or denoting the Trinity: *the triune God*. ➤➤ **triunity** /trie'yoohniti/ *noun*. [from TRI- + Latin *unus* one]

trivalent /trie'vaylənt, 'trivələnt/ *adj* in chemistry, having a valency of three.

trivet /'trivit/ *noun* **1a** a three-legged usu iron stand placed over an open fire to support a cooking pot or kettle. **b** a bracket that hooks onto a grate to support a pot or kettle. **2** a stand, usu metal with three feet, for putting a hot dish on at the table or on a worktop. [Old English *trefet*, prob from Latin *triped-*, *tripes* three-footed, from TRI- + *pes* foot]

trivia¹ /'trivi·ə/ *pl noun* **1** (*treated as sing. or pl*) unimportant matters or details; trifles. **2** inessential or little known information or facts: *a book of pop music trivia*. [Latin *trivia*, pl of *trivium* (see TRIVIUM); influenced in meaning by TRIVIAL]

trivia² /'trivi·ə/ *noun* pl of TRIVIUM.

trivial *adj* **1** of little worth or importance; insignificant. **2** commonplace or ordinary. **3** in mathematics, relating to or denoting the simplest case, *esp* in having all variables equal to zero. ➤➤ **triviality** /-'aliti/ *noun*, **trivially** *adv*, **trivialness** *noun*. [Latin *trivialis* found everywhere, commonplace, from *trivium*: see TRIVIUM]

trivialize *or* **trivialise** *verb trans* to treat (something) as being unimportant or less important than it is: *He was accused of trivializing her concerns*. ➤➤ **trivialization** /-'zaysh(ə)n/ *noun*.

trivial name *noun* **1** the second part of a two-word Latin name of an animal, plant, etc, which follows the genus name and with it denotes the species. **2** a common or non-technical name of an organism or chemical.

trivium /'trivi·əm/ *noun* (*pl* **trivia** /'trivi·ə/) grammar, rhetoric, and logic, forming the lower division of the seven liberal arts studied in medieval universities: compare QUADRIVIUM. [Latin *trivium*, literally 'meeting of three ways, crossroads', from TRI- + *via* way]

triweekly /trie'weekli/ *adj* **1** occurring or appearing three times a week. **2** occurring or appearing every three weeks. ➤➤ **triweekly** *adv*.

-trix *suffix* (*pl* **-trices** *or* **-trixes**) forming nouns, with the meaning: a female agent, usu corresponding to masculine nouns ending in -*tor*, and now only current in legal contexts: *aviatrix*; *executrix*. [from Latin]

tRNA *noun* = TRANSFER RNA.

trocar /'trohkah/ *noun* a sharp-pointed instrument used *esp* to insert a fine tube into a body cavity as a drainage outlet. [French *trocart*, from *trois* three + *carre* side of a sword blade or other instrument]

trochaic /troh'kayik/ *adj* said of a poem, verse, or a line of poetry: featuring trochees or composed mainly of trochees.

trochaics *pl noun* trochaic verse.

trochal /'trohkl/ *adj* said *esp* of animal or plant parts: resembling a wheel. [Greek *trochos* wheel]

trochanter /tro'kantə/ *noun* **1** in many vertebrates, any of various bony processes at the upper part of the thighbone to which muscles are attached. **2** the second segment of an insect's leg, between the COXA (basal segment) and the femur. [Greek *trokhantēr*, from *trekhein* to run]

trochee /'trohkee/ *noun* in prosody, a metrical foot consisting of one long or stressed syllable followed by one short or unstressed syllable, as in *apple*: compare IAMB. [via Latin from Greek *trokhaios pous* running foot, from *trekhein* to run]

trochlea /'trokli·ə/ *noun* (*pl* **trochleae** /'trokli·ee/) an anatomical structure resembling a pulley, *esp* a surface of a bone over which a tendon passes. ➤➤ **trochlear** *adj.* [Latin *trochlea*, literally 'block of pulleys']

trochlear nerve *noun* either of a pair of cranial nerves that supply the superior oblique muscle of the eyeballs, one of the muscles responsible for movement of the eyeball in its socket.

trochoid¹ /'trohkoyd/ *adj* **1** said of an anatomical joint: having one part that moves round a central axis to allow rotational movement, e.g. the joint between the vertebrae at the top of the neck. **2** said of a curve in geometry: following a path generated by a point on the radius of a circle as the circle rolls on a fixed straight line. **3** said of the shell of certain molluscs: conical with a flat base. ➤➤ **trochoidal** /-troh'koydl/ *adj.* [Greek *trokhoeidēs* like a wheel, from *trokhos* a wheel]

trochoid² *noun* **1** a trochoid curve. **2** a trochoid joint.

trod /trod/ *verb* past tense and past part. of TREAD¹.

trodden /'trod(ə)n/ *verb* past part. of TREAD¹.

troglodyte /'troglədiet/ *noun* **1** a person who lives in a cave, *esp* a prehistoric cave-dweller. **2** a person who deliberately shuns other people and the outside world and who is therefore considered rather eccentric, out of touch, or unsophisticated. ➤➤ **troglodytic** /-'ditik/ *adj*, **troglodytism** *noun*. [via Latin from Greek *trōoglodytēs*, from *trōglē* a hole or cave + *dyein* to enter]

trogon /'trohgon/ *noun* any of numerous Central American birds, such as the quetzal, that have brightly coloured feathers and long tails: genus *Trogon* and other genera. [via Latin from Greek *trōgōn*, from *trōgein* to gnaw]

troika /'troyka/ *noun* **1a** a Russian vehicle pulled by three horses abreast. **b** the team of three horses pulling such a vehicle. **2** a group of three people, *esp* three managers, administrators, etc who work as a team. [Russian *troika* from *troe* set of three]

troilism /'troyliz(ə)m/ *noun* any form of sexual activity that involves three people simultaneously. [perhaps from French *trois* three]

Trojan /'trohj(ə)n/ *noun* **1** a native or inhabitant of ancient Troy, a city in Asia Minor. **2** somebody who shows the qualities, e.g. pluck or endurance, attributed to the defenders of ancient Troy: *They worked like Trojans to get the job finished.* ➤➤ **Trojan** *adj.* [Middle English from Latin *Troian*, from *Troie* Troy]

Trojan Horse *noun* **1** somebody or something that undermines an organization from within it. **2** in computing, a program whose function is to cause some kind of damage to a system or to allow an unauthorized user to bypass a system's security, *esp* one that is disguised as ordinary software.

Word history ────
so called because of the large hollow wooden horse which, in Greek mythology, was left by the Greeks outside Troy, which they were besieging. The Trojans took the wooden horse into the city, whereupon soldiers hidden inside it let the Greek army in.

troll¹ /trohl, trol/ *noun* in Germanic and Scandinavian folklore, an ugly dwarf or giant that lives in caves or hills. [from Norwegian *troll* and Danish *trold* a giant or demon]

troll² *verb* (**trolled, trolling**) ➤ *verb trans* **1a** to try to catch (fish) with a hook and line drawn through the water behind a moving boat. **b** to try to catch fish in (a river, lake, etc) using this method. **2** to search (a place) for something. **3** *informal.* **a** to send (an email) with a contentious or offensive message intended to provoke outrage. **b** to post (a contentious message) on an Internet newsgroup notice board or other public forum in the hope of starting a heated debate. **4** to sing (something) loudly or happily. ➤ *verb intrans* chiefly *Brit* to stroll or wander from place to place: *travel writers ... trolling around from free hotel to free hotel* — The Bookseller. ➤➤ **troller** *noun*. [Middle English *trollen* to move about, perhaps related to French *troller* to go about looking for game, prob of Germanic origin]

troll³ *noun* **1** the action of trolling. **2** the bait or line used in trolling. **3** *informal* an email or Internet posting designed to provoke a response.

trolley /'troli/ *noun* (*pl* **trolleys**) **1** *Brit.* **a** a large basket or a small cart on wheels, used for carrying things, e.g. supermarket shopping, luggage at an airport or railway station, etc. **b** a shelved stand on wheels used for conveying something, *esp* food or drinks: *a tea*

trolley. **c** a hospital stretcher on wheels used for transporting patients. **2a** a device attached to a pole on the roof of an electrically powered vehicle, *esp* a tram, for collecting the current from an overhead wire: compare PANTOGRAPH. **b** = TROLLEYBUS. **c** *NAmer* = TROLLEY CAR. **3a** a small wagon that runs on rails, e.g. one for transporting things in a mine, quarry, or factory. **b** a cage, basket, or truck with a similar function, but suspended from and running on an overhead track. ✳ **off one's trolley** *Brit, informal* crazy or stupid. [orig an English dialect word, prob from TROLL²]

trolleybus *noun* an electrically propelled bus running on a road and drawing power from overhead wires via a trolley.

trolley car *noun NAmer* a tram that is powered by electricity collected from overhead wires.

trolley wheel *noun* = TROLLEY (2A).

trollius /'troli·əs/ *noun* (*pl* **trollius**) = GLOBEFLOWER. [prob from German *Trollblume* globeflower]

trollop /'troləp/ *noun dated* a slovenly, immoral, or sexually promiscuous woman. [prob from German *Trulle* prostitute, TRULL]

trombone /trom'bohn/ *noun* a brass musical instrument consisting of a long cylindrical metal tube that expands into a bell, with a movable slide to extend its length and thus vary the pitch. ➤➤ **trombonist** *noun*. [Italian *tromba* trumpet]

trommel /'troməl/ *noun* in mining, a usu cylindrical revolving sieve, used *esp* for screening or sizing pieces of coal or ore. [German *Trommel* drum]

tromp /tromp/ *verb intrans NAmer, informal* **1** to walk with heavy or noisy footsteps; to trudge. **2** (*often* + on) to step heavily on something. ➤ *verb trans NAmer, informal* **1** to trample (something). **2** to defeat (an opponent) convincingly; to trounce. [alteration of TRAMP¹]

trompe l'oeil /,tromp 'luh·i (*French* trɔ̃p lœːj)/ *noun* (*pl* **trompe l'oeils** /,tromp 'luh·i (*French* trɔ̃p lœːj)/) **1** a style of painting or decorating in which objects are depicted with three-dimensional realism. **2** a trompe l'oeil painting or effect. [French *trompe-l'oeil*, literally 'deceives the eye']

-tron *suffix* forming nouns, denoting: **1** a device for the manipulation of subatomic particles: *cyclotron*. **2** a subatomic particle: *positron*. **3** a thermionic valve or an electron or vacuum tube: *magnetron*. [Greek *-tron*, suffix denoting an instrument, or from ELECTRON]

tronc /tronk/ *noun* a pool for tips and service charges received by staff in a hotel or restaurant, which is divided among all the employees, including those who do not have direct contact with customers, e.g. the kitchen staff. [French *tronc* collecting box]

troop¹ /troohp/ *noun* **1** (*in pl*) soldiers or the army: *The government sent the troops in to deal with the riot.* **2a** a subdivision of a cavalry or tank regiment corresponding to an infantry platoon. **b** an artillery unit smaller than a battery. **3** a group of similar people, animals, etc. **4** a unit of at least three patrols of Scouts and their leader. **5** (*in pl*) a large number: *Troops of football supporters got on the train.* [French *troupe* a company, from *troupeau* a flock, prob of Germanic origin]

Usage note
troop or **troupe?** These two words are sometimes confused. A *troop* is a group of soldiers or Scouts, and the word is sometimes extended to mean simply any 'large group': *The visitors were beginning to arrive in troops.* A *troupe* is a group of actors or circus performers.

troop² *verb intrans* **1** said of a group of people: to move together, *esp* in a way that suggests regimentation: *Everyone trooped into the meeting.* **2** said of a group of people: to move in large numbers: *The children and their friends have been trooping in and out all day.* ✳ **troop the colour** to parade a regiment's flag along the ranks of its soldiers ceremonially.

troop carrier *noun* a large aircraft or armoured vehicle for transporting military personnel.

trooper *noun* **1a** a cavalry soldier, *esp* a private in a cavalry or tank regiment. **b** a cavalry soldier's horse. **2a** *NAmer, Aus* a mounted police officer. **b** *NAmer* a state police officer, *esp* one on a motorcycle or in a car. **3** *chiefly Brit* a troopship. ✳ **swear like a trooper** to be in the habit of using bad language.

troopship *noun* a ship for transporting military personnel.

trop- *or* **tropo-** *comb. form* forming words, denoting: turn, turning, or change: *troposphere; tropism.* [from Greek *tropos*: see TROPE]

tropaeolum /troh'pee-ələm/ *noun* (*pl* **tropaeolums** *or* **tropaeola**) any of a genus of trailing or climbing plants, orig of Central and S America, including some popular garden plants such as the nasturtium: genus *Tropaeolum*. [Latin *tropaeum* a trophy, so called because the flowers are shaped like a helmet and the leaves are like shields]

trope /trohp/ *noun* a figurative use of a word or expression. [via Latin from Greek *tropos* turn, way, manner, style, trope, from *trepein* to turn]

troph- *or* **tropho-** *comb. form* forming words, with the meaning: nutritive: *trophoblast*. [from Greek *trophē*: see TROPHIC]

trophic /'trofik, 'trohfik/ *adj* **1** relating to or denoting nutrition or growth: *trophic disorders of muscle*. **2** said of a hormone or its effect: influencing the activity of a gland. [Greek *trophikos*, from *trophē* nourishment, from *trephein* to nourish]

-trophic *comb. form* **1** forming adjectives, denoting: a specified mode of feeding: *oligotrophic*. **2** forming adjectives, with the meaning: attracted to, acting upon, or stimulating the bodily function or organ specified: *corticotrophic*. [Greek *trophik* from *trophē*: see TROPHIC]

tropho- *comb. form* see TROPH-.

trophoblast /'trofəblast, 'troh-/ *noun* a layer of cells that forms the outside of the early embryo of many placental mammals, initially nourishes the embryo, and subsequently forms a major part of the placenta. ▶▶ **trophoblastic** /-'blastik/ *adj*.

trophy /'trohfi/ *noun* (*pl* **trophies**) **1a** a silver cup, an engraved medal, a decorative plate, etc awarded to a person or team as a symbol of victory or success in a sports match or other contest. **b** (*often* **Trophy**) a competition played for such a prize: *the NatWest Bank Trophy*. **2** something, such as a stuffed and mounted animal, that is a memento of a successful achievement, e.g. in hunting. **3a** a memorial of an ancient Greek or Roman victory, often formed using the weapons of the defeated army, raised on or near the site of the battle. **b** a representation of such a memorial, e.g. on a medal or as an architectural ornament. [French *trophée* via Latin from Greek *tropaion*, from *tropē*: see TROPIC¹]

-trophy *comb. form* forming nouns, denoting: nutrition or growth: *hypertrophy*.

trophy wife *noun informal* a young and attractive woman married to a much older man and regarded as a status symbol.

tropic¹ /'tropik/ *noun* **1a** a parallel of latitude at about 23½° north of the equator. Also called TROPIC OF CANCER. **b** a parallel of latitude at about 23½° south of the equator. Also called TROPIC OF CAPRICORN. **c** (**the tropics**) the region between these two parallels. **2** in astronomy, either of the two corresponding parallel celestial latitudes that are the apparent northern and southern limits of the passage of the sun. [Middle English, via Latin from Greek *tropikos*, from *tropē* a route, a turning, from *trepein* to turn]

tropic² /'tropik/ *adj* tropical.

tropic³ /'trohpik/ *adj* **1** of, relating to, or exhibiting tropism. **2** = TROPHIC (2).

-tropic *comb. form* **1** forming adjectives, with the meaning: turning, changing, or tending to turn or change in a specified manner or in response to the specified stimulus: *geotropic*. **2** = -TROPHIC (2). [Greek *tropē*: see TROPIC¹]

tropical /'tropikl/ *adj* **1a** relating to, denoting, occurring in, or characteristic of the tropics. **b** said of the weather or a climate: very hot and usu humid. **2** *archaic* relating to a trope; metaphorical or figurative. ▶▶ **tropically** *adv*.

tropical cyclone *noun* a tropical storm.

tropical storm *noun* a low-pressure weather system that originates over tropical oceans, bringing heavy rains and winds that can reach hurricane force.

tropical year *noun* = SOLAR YEAR.

tropic bird /'tropik/ *noun* any of several species of web-footed birds, related to the gannets, that are found chiefly in tropical seas, often far from land: genus *Phaethon*.

tropic of Cancer /,tropik əv 'kansə/ *noun* = TROPIC¹ (IA).

tropic of Capricorn /,tropik əv 'kaprikawn/ *noun* = TROPIC¹ (IB).

tropism /'trohpiz(ə)m/ *noun* the turning or growing of all or part of an organism, *esp* a plant part, towards or away from an external stimulus, such as light, gravity, or heat: compare TAXIS. [from Greek *tropos* (see TROPE) + -ISM]

-tropism *comb. form* forming words, denoting: a tendency to turn in response to a specified external stimulus: *phototropism*; *geotropism*.

tropo- *comb. form* see TROP-.

tropology /tro'poləji/ *noun* **1** the figurative use of words. **2** a way of interpreting the Bible as moral teaching conveyed through metaphor. ▶▶ **tropological** /-'lojikl/ *adj*. [via Latin from Greek *tropos* (see TROPE) + -LOGY]

tropopause /'tropəpawz/ *noun* the region where the troposphere meets the stratosphere.

troposphere /'tropəsfiə/ *noun* the lowest part of the earth's atmosphere, extending from the surface of the planet to the stratosphere. Its depth varies from about 18km (11mi) at the equator to about 6km (4mi) at the poles. ▶▶ **tropospheric** /-'sferik/ *adj*.

troppo¹ /'tropoh/ *adj Aus, NZ, informal* behaving in an eccentric or crazy way; mad. [from TROPIC¹ + -O¹, so called because extended exposure to heat or the sun can have this effect]

troppo² *adv* in music, too much; excessively: *non troppo*. [Italian *troppo*, literally 'too much']

-tropy *comb. form* the state of turning in a specified way or from a specified stimulus. [Greek *-tropia*, from *trope* turn, turning]

Trot /trot/ *noun informal, derog* a Trotskyist or a person who holds extremely left-wing political views.

trot¹ *verb* (**trotted, trotting**) ▶ *verb intrans* **1** to progress or ride at a trot. **2** to run at a moderately fast pace. **3** *informal* to proceed briskly; to hurry. ▶ *verb trans* to cause (a horse) to trot. [Middle English via French *troter* from medieval Latin *trottare*, of Germanic origin]

trot² /trot/ *noun* **1a** a moderately fast pace of a horse or other four-legged animal in which the legs move in diagonal pairs. **b** a ride at this speed. **2** an act or period of trotting: *They set off at a trot*. **3** (**the trots**) *informal* diarrhoea. ✳ **on the trot 1** *Brit, informal* in succession: *They had been kept awake for three nights on the trot*. **2** *informal* busy, *esp* kept on one's feet for a long time.

troth /trohth/ *noun* **1** *archaic or formal*. **a** faith or loyalty. **b** a pledge to be faithful or loyal. **2** *archaic* truth. ✳ **pledge/plight one's troth** to make a solemn promise to be faithful or loyal, *esp* in marriage. [Old English *trēowth*: see TRUTH]

trot out *verb trans informal* to produce or utter (something) habitually, repeatedly, or predictably: *He trots out the same old complaints every time I see him*.

Trotskyism /'trotskiiz(ə)m/ *noun* the political, economic, and social principles advocated by the Russian revolutionary Leon Trotsky (d.1940), *esp* the belief that continuing worldwide revolution is the only way to achieve a world where socialism is dominant. ▶▶ **Trotskyist** *noun and adj*, **Trotskyite** /-iet/ *noun and adj*.

trotter *noun* **1** a horse trained for trotting races. **2** the foot of a pig, used as food.

trotting *noun* racing at trotting speed with horses harnessed to sulkies (two-wheeled carriages; see SULKY²) carrying drivers.

troubadour /'troohbədaw/ *noun* **1** one of the original group of medieval poet musicians of S France whose works were on the theme of courtly love and inspired the trouvères (medieval poet musicians of N France; see TROUVÈRE) and MINNESINGER (German lyric poets and musicians). **2** any poet or musician whose main theme is love. [French *troubador* from Provençal *trobador*, from *trobar* to find or compose]

trouble¹ /'trubl/ *noun* **1a** difficulty, problems, or danger: *His gambling debts got him into all sorts of trouble*. **b** a state of distress, anxiety, or concern. **c** an instance, cause, or source of this. **2a** a problem, snag, or drawback: *The trouble with computers is that they become outdated so quickly*. **b** a weakness or character flaw: *His trouble is that he's too gullible*. **3a** disease or disorder of a specified part or organ of the body: *She's been having heart trouble*. **b** malfunction of a machine, mechanism, etc: *We've got engine trouble*. **4** (*also in pl*) public unrest or demonstrations of dissatisfaction: *The years were marred by labour troubles*. **5** effort or exertion taken over something: *She went to a lot of trouble to make them feel welcome*. ✳ **ask for trouble** *informal* to do or say something that may lead to personal difficulty, problems, or danger. **in trouble 1** liable to be punished or suffer something unpleasant: *I'm in trouble with the authorities for tax evasion*. **2** *dated* said of an unmarried girl or woman: pregnant. **look for trouble** *informal* to do or say something that is deliberately provocative, *esp* in order to start a fight or argument.

[Middle English from early French *trouble*, prob from Latin *turbidus*: see TURBID]

trouble² *verb trans* **1a** to cause distress, anxiety, or concern to (somebody): *Nothing puzzles me more than time and space; and yet nothing troubles me less, as I never think about them* — Charles Lamb. **b** to cause pain or discomfort to (somebody): *His back has troubled him for years.* **2** to put (somebody) to some exertion or inconvenience: *Could I trouble you to close the door?* **3** to make (e.g. the surface of water) turbulent or ruffled. ⟩ *verb intrans* **1** (*often* + to) to make an effort or take the time to do or say something: *She didn't even trouble to phone and say she wasn't coming.* **2** (+ about/over/with) to worry about somebody or something: *She was troubling over her application form.* ⟩⟩ **troubler** *noun*.

trouble and strife *noun Brit, slang* a wife. [rhyming slang]

troubled *adj* **1** worried or anxious. **2** characterized by or experiencing difficulty or problems: *He had a troubled childhood.*

troublemaker *noun* somebody who deliberately and habitually causes trouble, *esp* by making others discontented. ⟩⟩ **troublemaking** *noun and adj.*

troubleshoot *verb intrans* **1** to identify the causes of problems or disputes, e.g. in business or politics, and try to resolve them. **2** to locate faults and make repairs in machinery and technical equipment. ⟩⟩ **troubleshooter** *noun*, **troubleshooting** *noun and adj.*

troublesome /ˈtrʌbl(ə)m/ *adj* **1** causing difficulty or problems: *a troublesome cough.* **2** turbulent or violent: *We are living in troublesome times.* ⟩⟩ **troublesomely** *adv*, **troublesomeness** *noun.*

trouble spot *noun* a place where unrest, rioting, or conflict frequently occur.

troublous /ˈtrʌbləs/ *adj archaic or literary* **1** full of trouble. **2** agitated or uneasy. ⟩⟩ **troublously** *adv.*

trough /trof/ *noun* **1a** a long shallow receptacle for the food or drinking water of domestic animals. **b** any of various similar containers used for domestic or industrial purposes. **2a** a drain or channel for water; *esp* a gutter along the eaves of a building. **b** a long narrow or shallow trench, e.g. between waves or ridges. **c** a long shallow depression in the bed of the sea. **3** in meteorology, an elongated area of low atmospheric pressure: compare RIDGE¹. **4** in physics, a minimum point in a wave or an alternating signal. **5** any notably low point in activity or achievement, e.g. in a trade cycle or on a statistical graph. [Old English *trog*]

trounce /trowns/ *verb trans* **1** to defeat (a person, team, army, etc) decisively in a competition, contest, or battle: *the unknown who trounced a field of top-class sprinters.* **2** to rebuke or punish (somebody or something) severely. ⟩⟩ **trouncer** *noun*. [origin unknown]

troupe¹ /troohp/ *noun* a group of actors, dancers, or other performers, *esp* a touring company. [French *troupe*: see TROOP¹]

Usage note
troupe *or* troop? See note at TROOP¹.

troupe² *verb intrans* said of a troupe or a member of a troupe: to travel from venue to venue, putting on performances: *a time when Helen Keller earned her living by trouping up and down the land in vaudeville* — Saturday Review. ⟩ *verb trans* to put on (performances) in different venues: *They trouped their plays to camps in the area* — Theatre Arts.

trouper *noun* **1** a member of a troupe, *esp* a veteran actor or entertainer. **2** a loyal or dependable person.

trouser¹ /ˈtrowzə/ *noun* (*used before a noun*) relating to or designed for trousers: *a trouser pocket.*

trouser² *verb trans* (**trousered, trousering**) *Brit, informal* **1** to put (something) in one's trouser pocket: *He trousered his change.* **2** to take (something) for oneself, *esp* dishonestly, illegally, or without permission: *She had trousered the money that had been collected for charity.*

trousers *pl noun* an outer garment extending from the waist to the ankles, with tube-like parts that cover each leg separately. ✳ **wear the trousers** *informal* to have the controlling authority in a household or be the dominant person in a relationship. ⟩⟩ **trousered** *adj.* [alteration of *trouse*, from Scottish Gaelic *triubhas* TREWS, and influenced by *drawers* (see DRAWER)]

trouser suit *noun Brit* a woman's suit consisting of a matching jacket and trousers.

trousseau /ˈtroohsoh/ *noun* (*pl* **trousseaux** *or* **trousseaus** /ˈtroohsohz/) the clothes, linen, and other items that a woman collects for her marriage. [French *trousseau*, literally 'a little bundle', from *trousse* a bundle, from early French *trousser*: see TRUSS²]

trout /trowt/ *noun* (*pl* **trouts** *or collectively* **trout**) any of several species of food and sport fish that are related to but mostly smaller than the salmon. Many species have distinctive spotted markings: genera *Salmo* and *Salvelinus*. ✳ **old trout** *informal* an irritating, interfering, or bad-tempered person, *esp* an old woman. [Old English *trūht* from Latin *tructa* a fish with sharp teeth, from Greek *trōgein* to gnaw]

trouvaille /troohˈvie/ *noun* a chance or unexpected find. [French *trouvaille* from early French *trover* to find]

trouvère /troohˈvea/ *noun* one of a group of medieval poet musicians of N France whose works were on the theme of courtly love. [French *trouvère* from early French *trovere*, from *trover* to find or compose]

trove /trohv/ *noun* a store of valuable things that have been discovered; a treasure trove.

trover /ˈtrohvə/ *noun* in common law, action to recover the value of goods wrongfully taken or kept by another. [early French *trover* to find]

trow /troh/ *verb trans archaic* to think or believe (something). [Old English *trēowan* to trust, from *trēow* trust, fidelity]

trowel¹ /ˈtrowəl, trowl/ *noun* **1** a small hand tool with a flat tapering blade used to apply, mix, and spread plaster, cement, etc. **2** a small hand tool with a scoop-shaped blade used for lifting small plants, turning earth, etc. [Middle English via French from Latin *truella*, alteration of *trulla* a scoop]

trowel² *verb trans* (**trowelled, trowelling**, *NAmer* **troweled, troweling**) to smooth, mix, and apply (plaster, etc) with or as if with a trowel.

troy /troy/ *noun* a system of weights, used mainly for precious metals and gemstones, in which there are 12oz or 5760 grains to the pound: compare AVOIRDUPOIS. [Middle English, so called because of a weight used at fairs in the French city of *Troyes*]

troy weight *noun* = TROY.

truancy /ˈtrooh·ənsi/ *noun* (*pl* **truancies**) the act or an instance of staying away from school without good reason or permission.

truant¹ /ˈtrooh·ənt/ *noun* a pupil who stays away from school without good reason or permission. ✳ **play truant** to truant. [Middle English, orig referring to a person who chooses a life of begging, from early French, prob of Celtic origin]

truant² *verb intrans* to stay away from school without good reason or permission.

truant³ *adj* relating to or denoting a truant; straying or wandering: *a truant disposition* — Shakespeare.

truce /troohs/ *noun* **1** an agreement between enemies to stop fighting, often for a set period of time; a ceasefire. **2** a period of respite from something unpleasant. [Old English *trēow* trust, fidelity]

truck¹ /truk/ *noun* **1a** a large road vehicle for moving heavy loads; a lorry. **b** *Brit* a wagon for carrying goods by rail. **2** a frame with two or more pairs of wheels attached below a railway carriage; a bogie. **3** a wheeled cart for carrying heavy things, e.g. luggage at railway stations. **4** a type of steerable axle, usu one of a pair, attached to a skateboard. **5** a small wooden cap at the top of a flagstaff or masthead, usu with holes for the ropes used for hoisting a flag or signal. ⟩⟩ **truckage** /ˈtrukij/ *noun*, **truckload** *noun*. [Middle English, denoting a solid wooden wheel, prob related to TRUCKLE¹]

truck² *verb trans chiefly NAmer* to transport (goods) in a truck. ⟩ *verb intrans* **1** *chiefly NAmer* to work as a truck driver. **2** *informal* to walk or proceed at a leisurely pace.

truck³ *noun* **1** *archaic*. **a** commercial dealings, *esp* bartering. **b** commodities for sale or barter, *esp* small household goods. **2** *archaic* payment for services in kind or with vouchers, as distinct from money. **3** *NAmer* fruit or vegetables grown for sale in a market garden. **4** *informal* miscellaneous bits and pieces. ✳ **have/want no truck with** to refuse to have anything to do with (somebody or something).

truck⁴ *verb trans archaic* to exchange or barter (goods). [Middle English, prob from early French *troquer* to barter, perhaps from Latin *trocare* to exchange]

trucker *noun* a person who drives a truck, *esp* over long distances.

truck farm *noun chiefly NAmer* a small farm where fruit and vegetables are grown commercially; a market garden. ➤➤ **truck farmer** *noun*, **truck farming** *noun*.

truckie /'truki/ *noun Aus, NZ, informal* a truck driver.

trucking *noun chiefly NAmer* the business or process of transporting goods by truck; road haulage.

truckle[1] /'trukl/ *noun* a small drum-shaped cheese, *esp* Cheddar, often with a wax coating. [Middle English, in the sense 'wheel, pulley', via Anglo-French from Latin *trochlea* block of pulleys]

truckle[2] *verb intrans* (*usu* + to) to act in a subservient or obsequious manner; to submit weakly. ➤➤ **truckler** *noun*. [a figurative use that came about because of the low position of a TRUCKLE BED]

truckle bed *noun chiefly Brit* a low bed on castors that can be stored under a higher bed and slid out when needed.

truck stop *noun NAmer* a transport café.

truculent /'trukyoolənt/ *adj* aggressively defiant, sullen, or antagonistic. ➤➤ **truculence** *noun*, **truculency** *noun*, **truculently** *adv*. [Latin *truculentus* from *trux* fierce]

trudge[1] /truj/ *verb intrans* to walk with slow, weary, or laborious steps; to plod: *We trudged through the deep snow.* ➤➤ **trudger** *noun*. [origin unknown]

trudge[2] *noun* a long tiring walk.

trudgen /'truj(ə)n/ *noun* a type of swimming stroke using the same arm action as the crawl, but with a scissors leg movement. [named after John *Trudgen* d.1902, the English swimmer who introduced it]

true[1] /trooh/ *adj* (**truer, truest**) **1a** in accordance with fact or reality; not false, wrong, or made-up: *a true story.* **b** genuine or real: *She says that this time it really is true love.* **c** properly or strictly so called: *Spiders aren't true insects.* **d** basic or essential: *This is the true nature of socialist economics.* **2a** accurate: *a true copy.* **b** said of a musical note: properly in tune. **c** said of a compass bearing: determined or measured according to the earth's geographical poles, as distinct from its magnetic poles. **d** correctly or accurately fitted, adjusted, or aligned. **e** upright or level. **3a** steadfast, loyal, or trusted: *a true friend.* **b** (*usu* + to) consistent or conforming, e.g. to a standard or to expectations. **c** honest and trustworthy; truthful: *twelve good men and true; speak, sad brow and true maid* — Shakespeare. ✳ **true to form/type** behaving as expected. **true to life 1** accurately reflecting what goes on in real life: *The storyline is very true to life.* **2** realistic or lifelike: *The portrait is so true to life.* ➤➤ **trueness** *noun*. [Old English *trēowe* steadfast or faithful]

true[2] *noun* correct alignment. ✳ **in/out of (the) true** correctly, or incorrectly, aligned, *esp* in terms of being upright or level.

true[3] *verb trans* (**trues, trued, truing** *or* **trueing**) to adjust or restore (e.g. a mechanical part) to the correct level, shape, or degree of accuracy.

true[4] *adv* **1** in accordance with fact or reality: *Her story rings true.* **2** without deviation: *The bullet flew straight and true.* **3** in genetics, without variation from type: *a species that breeds true.* **4** certainly; admittedly. ✳ **come true** to happen; to become real: *His wish came true.*

true bill *noun* under US law, a bill of indictment that a grand jury endorses when it has found that there is sufficient evidence for a criminal case to be heard.

true-blue *adj* **1** *Brit* staunchly loyal to the Conservative Party or strongly in favour of the monarchy. **2** *NAmer* loyal or faithful. ➤➤ **true blue** *noun*. [from the traditional association of blue with fidelity and its adoption as a party colour by various conservative groups]

true-born *adj* of a specified type through birth; genuine: *his prejudices as a 'true-born Englishman' not only against foreign countries, but against Ireland and Scotland* — James Boswell.

true horizon *noun* = HORIZON (1E).

truelove *noun literary* a sweetheart.

truelove knot *noun* a complicated ornamental knot that is difficult to undo, symbolizing the ties of mutual love.

true lover's knot *noun* = TRUELOVE KNOT.

true north *noun* north as determined by the earth's axis, as distinct from magnetic north.

true rib *noun* a rib, e.g. any of the upper seven pairs in human beings, that is joined directly to the breastbone: compare FALSE RIB, FLOATING RIB.

truffle[1] /'trufl/ *noun* **1** any of various dark rough-skinned European fungi that grow underground and are considered a great delicacy: *Tuber melansporum* and others. **2** a rich chocolate sweet, often flavoured with alcohol, made into a rough ball shape and dusted with cocoa powder. [obsolete French *truffle*, prob from Latin *tubera*, pl of *tuber* a hump or swelling]

truffle[2] *verb intrans* to hunt for and dig up truffles.

trug /trug/ *noun Brit* a shallow rectangular wooden basket used *esp* for carrying fruit, flowers, and vegetables. [perhaps a dialectal alteration of TROUGH]

truism /'trooh·iz(ə)m/ *noun* **1** an undoubted or self-evident truth, *esp* one too obvious or unimportant to be mentioned. **2** in logic, a statement or proposition that implies nothing other than what is stated within its own terms. ➤➤ **truistic** *adj*.

trull /trul/ *noun archaic* a prostitute. [German *Trulle*]

truly /'troohli/ *adv* **1** in agreement with fact or reality; truthfully, accurately, or exactly. **2** to a great or the greatest extent; absolutely or completely: *It was a truly dreadful film.* **3** genuinely; sincerely: *He was truly sorry.* **4** used to express astonishment or doubt: *Truly, you amaze me!* **5** *archaic* loyally or faithfully. ✳ **well and truly** totally; completely: *Our team was well and truly beaten.* **yours truly 1** (**Yours truly**) used as a formula to end a letter. **2** *humorous* used to refer to oneself: *And who had to do the washing up yet again? Yours truly!*

trumeau /trooh'moh/ *noun* (*pl* **trumeaux** /trooh'mohz/) a section of wall or a pillar between two openings, e.g. between two large doors forming a single doorway in a church. [French *trumeau*, literally 'the calf of the leg']

trump[1] /trump/ *noun* **1a** (*in pl*) in various card games, *esp* bridge and whist, the suit of cards that has been chosen, usu for the duration of a single hand, to have a higher value than the other three suits. **b** a card of the suit that is trumps, which beats any card of another suit. **2** something that can be used to gain an advantage. **3** *informal, dated* a very worthy, admirable, or dependable person. ✳ **come/turn up trumps** *chiefly Brit, informal* to do what is right, needed, or desirable, *esp* unexpectedly and at the last moment. [alteration of TRIUMPH[1]]

trump[2] *verb trans* **1** to play a trump on (a card or cards of another suit). **2** to beat or surpass (somebody) by doing or saying something better.

trump[3] *noun archaic* a trumpet or a call made on one. [early French *trompe*, of Germanic origin, prob imitative]

trump card *noun* = TRUMP[1] (1B). ✳ **play one's trump card** to use a resource or advantage, *esp* one held in reserve until the most opportune moment, to produce a decisive effect or make a crucial difference.

trumpery[1] *noun* (*pl* **trumperies**) something showy but useless or worthless. [Middle English *tromperie* deceit, from early French *tromper* to deceive]

trumpery[2] *adj* **1** worthless or useless. **2** cheap or tawdry.

trumpet[1] /'trumpit/ *noun* **1a** the highest-pitched of the brass musical instruments, with a cylindrical body that widens into a flared bell, and three valves to vary the pitch. **b** a musical instrument, e.g. a cornet, that resembles this. **c** an organ stop that gives a sound quality similar to that of the trumpet. **2** = EAR TRUMPET. **3** something that resembles the flared shape of a trumpet, e.g. a daffodil's CORONA[1] (part of flower). **4** a loud sound, *esp* the loud penetrating cry of an elephant. ✳ **blow one's (own) trumpet** to boast about one's own abilities, achievements, virtues, etc. [Middle English, from early French *trompette*, dimin. of *trompe*: see TRUMP[3]]

trumpet[2] *verb* (**trumpeted, trumpeting**) ➤ *verb intrans* **1** to play a trumpet. **2** to make the characteristic sound of an elephant. ➤ *verb trans* to proclaim (something) loudly or widely: *my head filled with China's trumpeted agricultural renaissance* — Colin Thubron.

trumpet climber *noun* = TRUMPET VINE.

trumpet creeper *noun* = TRUMPET VINE.

trumpeter *noun* **1** a trumpet player; *esp* somebody using a trumpet to give a fanfare, signal, etc. **2** any of several species of large birds related to the cranes, living in the jungles of S America, that have mainly dark plumage, long legs and neck, and a characteristic hunched posture: genus *Psophia*. **3** any of various domestic pigeons with a rounded crest and heavily feathered feet, noted for their trumpet-like call.

trumpeter swan *noun* a large white N American swan with a distinctive black and yellow bill, noted for its loud honking call: *Cygnus buccinator*.

trumpet major *noun* the chief trumpet player of a cavalry regiment, often the regiment's principal musician.

trumpet vine *noun* a climbing plant with reddish orange trumpet-shaped flowers: *Campsis radicans* (the N American species) and *Campsis grandiflora* (the Chinese species). Also called TRUMPET CLIMBER, TRUMPET CREEPER.

trump up *verb trans* to make up (a false charge, accusation, or excuse).

truncal /'trungk(ə)l/ *adj* **1** relating to or in the region of the trunk of the body. **2** relating to or in the region of a tubular body part, *esp* a nerve.

truncate[1] /'trungkayt, trung'kayt/ *verb trans* to shorten (something) by cutting off a part, *esp* by removing a top or end part. ➤➤ **truncation** /trung'kaysh(ə)n/ *noun*. [Latin *truncare* to lop off, to maim]

truncate[2] /'trungkayt/ *adj* **1** said of a leaf, feather, etc: having a blunt end. **2** cut short.

truncated /trung'kaytid/ *adj* **1** said of a cone, pyramid, etc: having the apex replaced by a plane section, *esp* one parallel to the base. **2** shortened.

truncheon /'trunchən/ *noun* **1** *chiefly Brit* a short thick stick carried and used as a weapon by police officers: compare NIGHTSTICK. **2** a staff or baton carried as a symbol of office or authority. [Middle English *tronchoun* broken spear or a cudgel, from early French *tronchon* stump, from Latin *truncus* TRUNK]

trundle[1] /'trundl/ *verb intrans* **1** to move on or as if on wheels: *Trams trundled up and down the street.* **2** to move heavily or laboriously; to lumber: *His horse trundled in last.* ➤ *verb trans* **1** to propel (something) by rotating: *We trundled the boulder down the hill.* **2** to move (something) on or as if on wheels: *He trundled the potatoes home in the trolley.*

trundle[2] *noun* **1** an act of trundling. **2** a small wheel or roller. [alteration of *trendle* wheel, from Old English *trendel* circle, ring]

trundle bed *noun chiefly NAmer* = TRUCKLE BED.

trunk /trungk/ *noun* **1** the main stem of a tree, as distinguished from branches and roots. **2** a person's or animal's body apart from the head, limbs, and other appendages; a torso. **3** the main or central part of something, *esp* a blood vessel or nerve. **4** the long flexible muscular nose of an elephant. **5** a large rigid box with a hinged lid, used for storing or transporting clothing and personal articles. **6** *NAmer* the boot of a motor vehicle. **7** (*used before a noun*) relating to or denoting a main transport or communication route. ➤➤ **trunkful** (*pl* **trunkfuls**) *noun*, **trunkless** *adj*. [Middle English via French from Latin *truncus* tree trunk, torso. (Sense 5) (17th cent.) comes from a Middle English sense 'box, chest', orig one made from a tree trunk, hence sense 6; (sense 4) (16th cent.) comes from a more general sense 'pipe, cylinder', from the shape of a tree trunk]

trunk call *noun chiefly Brit, dated* a telephone call made from long-distance within a country.

trunkfish *noun* (*pl* **trunkfishes** or *collectively* **trunkfish**) any of numerous species of small brightly coloured tropical fishes with the body and head enclosed in a rigid box-like cover formed from thickened scales: *Tetrosomus gibbosus* and other species.

trunking *noun* **1** a system of shafts housing cables, wires, ventilation ducts, etc. **2** the main cables used in linking trunk lines at a telephone exchange, or the way these are arranged or used.

trunk line *noun chiefly Brit* **1** *dated* a direct telephone line connecting two exchanges or switchboards that are far away from each other, e.g. in different cities. **2** a main railway line.

trunk road *noun Brit* a road of primary importance.

trunks *pl noun* men's tight-fitting shorts worn for sports, *esp* swimming and boxing.

trunnel /'trun(ə)l/ *noun NAmer* = TREENAIL.

trunnion /'trunyən/ *noun* a pin or pivot on which something can be rotated or tilted, *esp* either of two opposite projections on which a gun barrel can be tilted vertically. [from French *trognon* core, stump]

truss[1] /trus/ *noun* **1** an arrangement of beams, rafters, girders, etc forming a rigid framework, e.g. in a roof or bridge. **2** a surgical appliance, often in the form of a padded belt tightly strapped to the body, used as a support for a hernia. **3** a large CORBEL[1] (stone or timber projection from a wall), *esp* one supporting a cornice. **4a** a bundle or package. **b** *chiefly Brit* a bundle of hay or straw, *esp* formerly, one with a fixed weight of 56lb (25.4kg) for old hay, 60lb (27.2kg) for new hay, and 36lb (16.3kg) for straw. **5** a compact cluster of flowers or fruit growing on a single stalk, e.g. of a tomato plant. **6** in sailing, a heavy metal ring securing a yard to a mast.

truss[2] *verb trans* **1** to tie up the wings or legs of (a chicken, turkey, etc) in preparation for cooking. **2** (*often* + up) to secure or bind (something or somebody) tightly. **3** to support, strengthen, or stiffen (something, *esp* a hernia) with a truss. ➤➤ **trusser** *noun*. [Middle English from early French *trousser* to bind, ultimately from Latin *torquere* to twist]

trust[1] /trust/ *noun* **1a** confident belief in or reliance on the character, ability, strength, honesty, etc of somebody or something: *Put your trust in God, my boys, and keep your powder dry* — Valentine Blacker. **b** acceptance of the truth of something, *esp* without proof: *He took nothing on trust.* **2a** a charge or duty imposed in faith or as a condition of some relationship: *A public office is a public trust* — Grover Cleveland. **b** responsible charge or office: *I am putting you in a position of trust.* **c** care or custody: *The child was committed to his trust.* **3** an arrangement whereby money or other property is held by one person for the benefit of another. **4a** a body of trustees. **b** something managed by trustees: *a hospital trust; a charitable trust.* **c** *NAmer, dated* a combination of companies formed by a legal agreement; *esp* one that reduces or threatens to reduce competition. **5** *W Ind or archaic* financial credit. **6** *literary* a hope. ✳ **in trust** in the care or possession of a trustee. ➤➤ **trustful** *adj*, **trustfully** *adv*, **trustfulness** *noun*. [Middle English from Old Norse *traust*, from *traustr* strong]

trust[2] *verb trans* **1a** to rely on or believe in the truthfulness, accuracy, ability, etc of (somebody or something): *You can't always trust the description in the brochure.* **b** to place one's confidence in or rely on (somebody or something). **2** to expect (something) with confidence; to assume: *I trust you are well; We'll see you soon, I trust.* **3a** to place (somebody or something) in somebody's care or keeping; to entrust. **b** to be confident about allowing (somebody to do, have, or look after something): *Mum doesn't trust me with her car.* ➤ *verb intrans* (*often* + to/in) to place one's confidence in or rely on somebody or something: *She trusts in God; We'll have to trust to luck.* ✳ **trust somebody to ...** used ironically to comment on the reliability of somebody: *Trust him to arrive late!* ➤➤ **trustable** *adj*, **trusted** *adj*, **truster** *noun*.

trust company *noun* a company that functions as a trustee for individuals or for companies and institutions and usu also engages in the normal activities of a commercial bank.

trustee /trus'tee/ *noun* **1** a person appointed to administer money or other property for a beneficiary, e.g. another person or a charitable organization. **2** any member of a board of people appointed to administer the affairs of a company, organization, or institution. **3** a state appointed by the United Nations to supervise a trust territory. ➤➤ **trusteeship** *noun*.

trustee in bankruptcy *noun* a person who has the legal responsibility for administering the financial affairs of somebody declared bankrupt, *esp* in trying to realize assets to pay off creditors.

trust fund *noun* property, money, shares, or other assets held in trust.

trusting *adj* having or showing great trust, often to the extent of risking being exploited or hurt. ➤➤ **trustingly** *adv*, **trustingness** *noun*.

trust territory *noun* a dependent territory placed under an administrative authority by the United Nations.

trustworthy *adj* known to be honest, truthful, and reliable. ➤➤ **trustworthily** *adv*, **trustworthiness** *noun*.

trusty[1] *adj* (**trustier, trustiest**) *archaic or humorous* reliable; trustworthy: *I don't need a car – I go everywhere on my trusty bicycle.* ➤➤ **trustily** *adv*, **trustiness** *noun*.

trusty[2] *noun* (*pl* **trusties**) a trusted person, *esp* a convict who, because of good behaviour, has been given special privileges or responsibilities.

truth /troohth/ *noun* (*pl* **truths** /troohdhz, troohths/) **1** the state or quality of being true or factual: *There's a lot of truth in what she says.*

Editorial note ━━━━━━━━━━━━━
Truth is what is or what was: the actualité. Usually it is revealed as a conclusion, reliably evidenced by observation or documentation, or as an inference from primary facts. Historical truth is more elusive, since history,

as Richard Nixon pointed out, depends on who writes it. A jury delivers a 'true' verdict, but only in respect of the evidence presented to it, which may lead to false conclusions — Geoffrey Robertson.

2a something that is true or is believed to be true, as distinct from a lie: *With a child or two in the house, there is an unconscious check upon too free an indulgence in the truth* — Saki. **b** a statement, proposition, theory, etc that has been proved to be fact or that is generally accepted as true: *Her research is based on fundamental scientific truths.* **3** real life: *Truth is often stranger than fiction.* **4** sincerity in action, character, and speech; honesty: *He's known to be a man of truth.* **5** *archaic* loyalty, fidelity, or constancy: *what should I say since faith is dead and truth away from you is fled* — Thomas Wyatt. **✴ in truth** in fact; really. **to tell the truth/if truth be told/truth to tell** to speak openly and honestly: *To tell the truth, I've never liked these curtains.* [Old English *trēowth* fidelity, from *trēowe* faithful, TRUE[1]]

truth condition *noun* **1** the condition under which a specific logical proposition is true. **2** a statement of this condition.

truth drug *noun* a substance believed to have properties that will induce a person to whom it is administered to tell the truth or talk freely.

truthful /'troohthf(ə)l/ *adj* **1a** telling or expressing the truth. **b** inclined to tell the truth or be honest. **2** said *esp* of a portrait, sculpture, etc: realistic. **≫ truthfully** *adv*, **truthfulness** *noun*.

truth function *noun* a logical function whose own truth value depends on the truth values of its component statements without reference to their meanings.

truth table *noun* **1** in logic, a table that shows whether a compound statement is true or false for each combination of truth values of its component statements. **2** a similar table, e.g. for a computer logic circuit, showing the value of the output for each value of each input.

truth value *noun* the truth or falsity of a statement, *esp* in logic.

try[1] /trie/ *verb* (**tries, tried, trying**) ▷ *verb intrans* to make an attempt to do something. ▷ *verb trans* **1a** to make an attempt at (something). **b** to test or operate (a device, etc) to see if it is working: *Try the light again now.* **c** to investigate or approach (something or somebody) to determine suitability or effectiveness: *Try the shop next door.* **2a** to conduct the trial of (an accused person). **b** to investigate (a case or issue) judicially. **3** to make severe demands on (somebody's patience, endurance, etc). **4** to melt (fat, lard, etc) in order to separate out any impurities. **✴ tried and tested/true** known to be reliable. **try and** *informal* to try to do something: *I'll try and finish the work today.* **try for size** to test (something) for its suitability. **try it on** *Brit, informal* to test somebody's credulity or patience. **try one's hand at** to attempt (something new). [Middle English from early French *trier* to sift, sort]

try[2] *noun* (*pl* **tries**) **1** an attempt: *That wasn't bad for a first try.* **2** an experimental trial. **3a** in rugby, a score made by touching down the ball behind the opponent's goal line, entitling the scoring side to attempt a kick at the goal for additional points. **b** in American football, an attempt to score an extra point following the scoring of a touchdown.

trying *adj* **1** annoying or irritating. **2** uncomfortable, unpleasant, tiring, or enervating: *Boston in this weather would be very trying* — Henry James. **≫ tryingly** *adv*.

trying plane *noun* a long heavy plane used for smoothing rough edges on long planks of wood.

try on *verb trans* to put on (a piece of clothing) to test the fit and suitability.

try-on *noun Brit, informal* a test of somebody's credulity or patience.

tryout *noun* the act or an instance of trying out; a trial.

try out *verb trans* to test or investigate (something new) to determine suitability. ▷ *verb intrans* to compete for a position in a sports team or for a part as an actor.

trypanosome /tri'panəsohm, 'tripə-/ *noun* any of a genus of parasitic protozoans (minute single-celled animals; see PROTOZOAN) that move by means of whiplike structures. Usu transmitted through insect bites, they can infest the blood of various vertebrate animals, including human beings, causing serious diseases: genus *Trypanosoma*. **≫ trypanosomal** /-'sohməl/ *adj*, **trypanosomic** /-'sohmik/ *adj*. [scientific Latin, from Greek *trypanon* auger + -SOME[3]]

trypanosomiasis /tri,panəsə'mie-əsis/ *noun* a disease caused by trypanosomes, *esp* sleeping sickness or Chagas' disease.

trypsin /'tripsin/ *noun* a digestive enzyme formed from trypsinogen that breaks down proteins in the small intestine. **≫ tryptic** /'triptik/ *adj*. [from Greek *tripsis* friction, from *tribien* to rub or wear down (because it was first obtained by rubbing the pancreas with glycerine) + -IN[1]]

trypsinogen /trip'sinəjin/ *noun* an inactive substance secreted by the pancreas that, when converted by an enzyme in the duodenum, forms the digestive enzyme trypsin.

tryptamine /'triptəmeen/ *noun* any of various hallucinogenic substances derived from a derivative of tryptophan. [blend of TRYPTOPHAN + AMINE]

tryptophan /'triptəfan/ *noun* an essential amino acid, present in most proteins, that is necessary to vertebrates for growth and for synthesis of the vitamin niacin. [from *tryptic* (see TRYPSIN) + Greek *phainien* to appear]

trysail /'triesayl, 'tries(ə)l/ *noun* a small fore-and-aft sail used *esp* in rough weather to help keep a sailing vessel's head to the wind.

try square *noun* an L-shaped instrument used for marking and checking right angles, e.g. in brickwork or carpentry.

tryst[1] /trist/ *noun literary* **1** an agreement to meet, *esp* a secret agreement for a romantic meeting. **2** an appointed meeting or meeting place. [Middle English from early French *triste* a prearranged meeting place (orig a hunting term)]

tryst[2] *verb intrans literary* to make or keep a tryst. **≫ tryster** *noun*.

tsar *or* **czar** *or* **tzar** /zah, tsah/ *noun* **1** an emperor of Russia before 1917. **2** any of various Slavic rulers, *esp* of Serbia during the 14th cent. **3** a tyrant or somebody who keeps strict control, e.g. of their staff. **4** a person with great power or authority, *esp* somebody with overall responsibility for something: *The government has appointed a homelessness tsar.* **≫ tsardom** *noun*, **tsarism** *noun*, **tsarist** *noun and adj*. [Russian *tsar'*, via Gothic *kaisar* emperor, from Latin *Caesar*: see CAESAR]

tsarevich *or* **tsarevitch** *or* **czarevich** *or* **tzarevich** /'zahrəvich/ *noun* a son of a Russian tsar, *esp* the eldest son. [Russian *tsar'* (see TSAR) + -*evich* a patronymic suffix]

tsarina *or* **czarina** *or* **tzarina** /zah'reenə/ *noun* a Russian empress before 1917. [Spanish and Italian *tsarina*, from German *Zarin*, fem of *Zar* tsar]

tsetse /'tetsi, 'tsetsi/ *noun* a two-winged blood-sucking African fly that transmits diseases, *esp* sleeping sickness: genus *Glossina*. [via Afrikaans from Tswana *tsêtsê*, the name for this type of fly]

TSH *abbr* thyroid-stimulating hormone.

T-shirt *or* **tee shirt** *noun* a collarless short-sleeved casual top, usu made from knitted cotton. [so called because, when laid out flat, it resembles an uppercase letter T]

tsimmes *or* **tzimmes** /'tsiməs/ *noun* (*pl* **tsimmes** *or* **tzimmes**) **1** a dish of stewed fruit or vegetables, cooked for a long time over a very low heat. **2** a state of confusion; a muddle. [Yiddish *tsimmes*, prob from early High German *enbizzan* to eat]

Tsimshian /'tshimshi-ən/ *noun* (*pl* **Tsimshian**) **1** a member of an indigenous N American people inhabiting the Pacific coast of Alaska and British Columbia. **2** the language spoken by this people. **≫ Tsimshian** *adj*. [Tsimshian *čamsián*, literally 'inside the Skeena River']

tsk tsk /,t(ə)sk 't(ə)sk/ *interj* used to express disapproval, irritation, disappointment, or sympathy. [imitative]

Tsonga /'tsongə/ *noun* (*pl* **Tsongas** *or collectively* **Tsonga**) **1** a member of an indigenous people living in southern Africa, mainly in Mozambique, Swaziland, and S Africa. **2** the Bantu language of this people. **≫ Tsonga** *adj*. [the local name for this people in various Bantu languages]

tsotsi /'tsotsi/ *noun* (*pl* **tsotsis**) *SAfr* a young black street criminal or urban gang member. [perhaps a corruption of *tsotsa*, a local word meaning 'to dress in a flamboyant way', or of ZOOT SUIT, with reference to the flashy clothes they wear]

tsp *abbr* **1** teaspoon. **2** teaspoonful.

T square *noun* a ruler with a crosspiece or head at one end used in making and testing parallel lines.

TSR *abbr* terminate-and-stay-resident, denoting a computer program that remains loaded in a computer's memory even when it is not running, so that it can quickly be invoked, often by using a HOT KEY (key or keys programmed to carry out commands).

TSS *abbr* toxic shock syndrome.

tsunami /tsoo'nahmi/ *noun* (*pl* **tsunami** or **tsunamis**) a huge sea wave that is produced by underwater earth movement or volcanic eruption, causing severe devastation if it reaches land. [Japanese *tsunami*, from *tsu* a harbour + *nami* a wave]

tsutsugamushi disease /,tsutsugə'mooshi/ *noun* = SCRUB TYPHUS. [Japanese *tsutsugamushi*, from *tsutsuga* disease + *mushi* mite]

Tswana /'tswahnə/ *noun* (*pl* **Tswanas** or *collectively* **Tswana**) **1** a member of a people inhabiting Botswana, S Africa and other parts of southern Africa. **2** the Bantu language spoken by this people. Also called SETSWANA. ➤➤ **Tswana** *adj.* [from the local name for this people in various Bantu languages]

TT *abbr* **1** teetotal or teetotaller. **2** Tourist Trophy. **3** Trinidad and Tobago (international vehicle registration). **4** tuberculin-tested.

TTL *abbr* **1** transistor transistor logic, denoting a widely used system of constructing integrated circuits. **2** through-the-lens, denoting a type of camera in which the same lens is used to form both the exposed image and the viewfinder image.

TU *abbr* Trade Union or Trades Union.

Tu. *abbr* Tuesday.

Tuareg /'twahreg/ *noun* (*pl* **Tuaregs** or *collectively* **Tuareg**) **1** a member of a nomadic people inhabiting the western and central parts of the Sahara Desert. **2** the Berber language spoken by this people. ➤➤ **Tuareg** *adj.* [the local name for this people in various Berber languages]

tuatara /tooh-ə'tahrə/ *noun* a large nocturnal burrowing reptile resembling a lizard with soft spines along its neck and back, now found only on certain islands off the coast of New Zealand: *Sphenodon punctatum*. [Maori *tuatara*, literally 'with spines on its back', from *tua* back + *tara* a spine]

tub¹ /tub/ *noun* **1a** a low wide lidless container used for holding water, growing plants, etc. **b** a small plastic or cardboard container for food, *esp* semiliquid food such as cream, ice cream, margarine, etc. **c** the amount that one of these containers will hold. **2** *chiefly NAmer, informal* a bath: *I had a long relaxing soak in the tub.* **3** *informal* an old or slow boat, *esp* one that is awkward to sail. **4** in mining, a low open truck that runs on rails and is used for carrying coal, ore, etc from where it is excavated to the surface. ➤➤ **tubful** (*pl* **tubfuls**) *noun.* [Middle English, prob of Low German or Dutch origin]

tub² *verb trans* (**tubbed, tubbing**) **1** to plant, put, or store (something) in a tub. **2** to wash (somebody or something) in a tub. ➤ *verb intrans Brit, informal* to have a bath. ➤➤ **tubbable** *adj.*

tuba /'tyoohbə/ *noun* the largest and lowest-pitched of the brass musical instruments, with a cylindrical body that widens into a flared upward-pointing bell, and usu four or five valves to vary the pitch. [via Italian from Latin *tuba*, literally 'trumpet']

tubal /'tyoohbl/ *adj* relating to, denoting, or occurring in a tube, *esp* one in the body such as a Fallopian tube.

tubby *adj* (**tubbier, tubbiest**) **1** *informal* podgy or fat. **2** said of a sound, *esp* a musical one, or a musical instrument: lacking resonance: *a tubby violin.* ➤➤ **tubbiness** *noun.* [from TUB¹ + -Y¹]

tube¹ /tyoohb/ *noun* **1** a hollow elongated flexible or rigid cylinder, *esp* one that conveys liquids or gases. **2a** a slender channel within a plant or animal body; a duct: *the bronchial tubes.* **b** *informal* (*in pl*) the Fallopian tubes. **3** a small cylindrical container of soft metal or plastic sealed at one end and fitted with a cap at the other, from which a paste or other semisolid substance is dispensed by squeezing: *a tube of toothpaste.* **4** *Brit, informal.* **a** (**the tube**) an underground railway running through deep tunnels, *esp* the one in London. **b** a train running on an underground railway. **5a** an electron tube. **b** *chiefly NAmer* a thermionic valve. **c** a cathode-ray tube, e.g. of a television set. **d** (**the tube**) *NAmer, informal* television. **6** in surfing, a rounded hollow formed under the crest of a large breaking wave. **7** *informal* a cigarette. **8** *Aus, informal* a can of beer. ✱ **go down the tube/tubes** *informal* said of a business, project, etc: to fail or be completely lost or wasted. ➤➤ **tubeless** *adj.* [French *tube*, from Latin *tubus*]

tube² *verb trans* **1** to provide (something) with a tube or a system of tubes. **2** to convey (liquid or gas) in a tube or through a system of tubes. ➤➤ **tubed** *adj.*

tube foot *noun* any of the small flexible tubular parts of starfish and similar marine animals that are used *esp* in locomotion, grasping, or collecting food.

tubeless tyre *noun* a pneumatic tyre with a casing that forms an airtight seal with the wheel rim, making an inner tube unnecessary.

tuber /'tyoohbə/ *noun* **1a** a short fleshy usu underground stem, e.g. of a potato, bearing buds that may develop into new plants and serving as a food store for the plant: compare BULB, CORM. **b** a fleshy root resembling this, e.g. that of the ginger plant. **2** a swelling on an organ or other body part. [Latin *tuber*, literally 'lump or swelling']

tubercle /'tyoohbəkl/ *noun* **1** a small rounded outgrowth or prominence, *esp* on a bone or on an outer part of a plant or animal; a nodule. **2** a small abnormal lump in an organ or in the skin, *esp* a lesion in the lungs or other tissue that is characteristic of tuberculosis. ➤➤ **tuberculate** /tyoo'buhkyoolayt/ *adj*, **tuberculated** /tyoo'buhkyoolaytid/ *adj.* [Latin *tuberculum*, dimin. of *tuber* lump, swelling, TUBER]

tubercle bacillus *noun* the bacterium that causes tuberculosis: *Mycobacterium tuberculosis.*

tubercular¹ /tyoo'buhkyoolə/ *adj* **1** relating to, characteristic of, or affected with tuberculosis: *Who would think from the urbanity of this week's column that I am sitting at my keyboard shivering, sniffing, coughing and streaming like a tubercular poet of the 1890s?* — New Statesman. **2a** relating to, denoting, or resembling a tubercle. **b** said of an animal or plant part: covered with tubercles.

tubercular² *noun* a person who has tuberculosis.

tuberculation /tyoo,buhkyoo'laysh(ə)n/ *noun* the formation or presence of tubercles.

tuberculin /tyoo'buhkyoolin/ *noun* a sterile liquid extracted from the tubercle bacillus and used in the diagnosis of tuberculosis, *esp* in human beings and cattle.

tuberculin test *noun* a test for hypersensitivity to tuberculin as an indication of past or present tubercular infection.

tuberculin-tested *adj* said of milk: from cows that have been tested for tuberculosis and certified as being free from the disease.

tuberculoid /tyoo'buhkyooloyd/ *adj* **1** said of certain diseases, *esp* a mild form of leprosy: characterized by the presence of lesions similar to those of tuberculosis. **2** resembling tuberculosis.

tuberculosis /tyoo,buhkyoo'lohsis, tə-/ *noun* a serious infectious disease of human beings and other vertebrates caused by the tubercle bacillus and characterized by fever and the formation of abnormal lumps in the body, *esp* in the lungs. [from Latin *tuberculum* (see TUBERCLE) + -OSIS]

tuberculous /tyoo'buhkyooləs/ *adj* = TUBERCULAR¹.

tuberose¹ /'tyoohbərohz/ *noun* a perennial Mexican plant cultivated for its fragrant white flowers and, formerly, for use as a flavouring, *esp* in making chocolate: *Polianthes tuberosa.* [Latin *tuberosa*, fem of *tuberosus* covered in tubercles, from *tuber* lump, TUBER; so called because of the many nodules on its roots]

tuberose² *adj* = TUBEROUS.

tuberous /'tyoob(ə)rəs/ *adj* **1** in botany, relating to, forming, or having a tuber or tubers. **2** in medicine, characterized by or affected with rounded swellings. ➤➤ **tuberosity** /-'rositi/ *noun.*

tube worm *noun* any of various worms that make and live in tube-like structures built from sand, grit, etc held together with a substance that they secrete.

tubicolous /tyoo'bikələs/ *adj* said of various worms: living in a tube.

tubifex /'tyoohbifeks/ *noun* (*pl* **tubifexes** or *collectively* **tubifex**) a slender reddish segmented worm that lives partly buried in tubes in fresh or slightly salt water and is widely used as food for aquarium fish: genus *Tubifex.* [Latin *tubus* TUBE¹ + *-fex*, from *facere* to make]

tubing /'tyoohbing/ *noun* **1** a length or lengths of material in the form of a tube. **2** a series or system of tubes. **3** *NAmer* the sport or pastime of floating down rivers or skimming down snow-covered slopes on inflated inner tubes.

tubocurarine /tyoohbohkyoo'rahrin, -reen/ *noun* an alkaloid that is obtained chiefly from the bark and stems of a S American climbing plant. It constitutes the chief active constituent of curare: formula $C_{38}H_{44}Cl_2N_2O_6 \cdot 5H_2O.$ [*tubo-* (from Latin *tubus* tube) + CURARE + -INE²; from its being shipped in sections of hollow bamboo]

tub-thumping *adj informal* said of a person, speech, etc: expressing opinions in an impassioned, ranting, or overzealous way. ➤➤ **tub-thumper** *noun*, **tub-thumping** *noun.*

tubular /'tyoohbyoolə/ *adj* **1a** cylindrical and hollow, like a tube. **b** made of or fitted with tubes or tube-shaped pieces. **2** said *esp* of an animal or plant part: having the form of or consisting of a tube or tubule: *a tubular calyx*.

tubular bells *pl noun* a musical instrument consisting of a set of metal tubes tuned to different notes and suspended from a frame, played by striking the tubes with a mallet.

tubule /'tyoohbyoohl/ *noun* **1** a small tube, *esp* a minute anatomical structure. **2** a slender convoluted tubule in the vertebrate kidney through which water and certain dissolved substances are reabsorbed into the blood. [Latin *tubulus*, dimin. of *tubus* TUBE¹]

TUC *abbr* Brit Trades Union Congress.

tuck¹ /tuk/ *verb trans* **1a** to push or fold (something) into a confined or hidden place or between two surfaces: *He tucked the letter under the book*. **b** to push (something or the loose or stray parts of something) into a more secure or tidy position or state: *She tucked her hair under her hat*. **2** (+ in/up) to settle (somebody or oneself) in a comfortable position *esp* in bed and usu by securing bedclothes under the mattress. **3** to draw or gather (something, *esp* one's legs) into a folded position. **4** to stitch a flattened fold in (fabric or a garment), *esp* as a decorative finish or to improve the fit. **>** *verb intrans* to fit snugly: *The stool tucks neatly under the table*. **✲ tuck into** to start eating (food) with enjoyment.

Word history
Old English *tūcian* to ill-treat, in Middle English to pluck or pull, hence to pull or gather cloth into folds (15th cent.). This gave rise from the 16th cent. onwards to various senses expressing the idea of folding or putting away.

tuck² *noun* **1a** a narrow flattened fold, stitched into fabric or a garment, *esp* as a decorative finish or to improve the fit. **b** *informal* a cosmetic surgical operation to remove fat or tighten the skin: *a tummy tuck*. **2** in diving, gymnastics, downhill skiing, etc, a body position in which the knees are bent, the thighs drawn tightly to the chest, and the hands clasped round the shins. **3** Brit, *informal* food, e.g. sweets or crisps, eaten as a snack, *esp* by schoolchildren.

tuckahoe /'tukəhoh/ *noun* **1** any of various plants with edible roots or underground stems formerly eaten by indigenous N American peoples: *Peltandra virginica, Orantium aquaticum* and others. **2** a root or stem of one of these plants. [Virginian Algonquian *tock-awhoughe*]

tuck away *verb trans* **1** *informal* to eat (a large amount of food): *He tucks away a good dinner every day*. **2** to store or hide (something or somebody) in a place that is difficult to find: *They tucked themselves away in a cottage in the country*.

tucker¹ *noun* **1** Aus, NZ, *informal* food. **2** a piece of lace or cloth formerly worn in the neckline of a low-cut dress.

tucker² *verb trans* (**tuckered, tuckering**) NAmer, *informal* (often + out) to exhaust (somebody or something): *I'm tuckered out after all that dancing*.

tucket /'tukit/ *noun* archaic a fanfare on a trumpet. [prob from obsolete *tuck* to beat the drum, from early French dialect *toquer*, variant of Old French *tochier*: see TOUCH¹]

tuck in *verb intrans* informal to eat heartily: *Come on, tuck in – it's getting cold*.

tuck-in *noun* Brit, *informal* a hearty meal.

tuck-point *verb trans* to finish (the mortar joints between bricks or stones) with a narrow ridge of putty or fine lime mortar.

tuck position *noun* = TUCK² (2).

'tude /toohd/ *noun* NAmer, *informal* swaggering, arrogant, or defiant behaviour, outlook, or style: *They're a band whose live sets always ooze 'tude*. [contraction of *attitude*; see ATTITUDE (4)]

-tude *suffix* forming nouns, denoting: a state or condition: *plenitude; altitude*. [via French from Latin *-tudo*]

Tudor¹ /'tyoohdə/ *adj* **1** relating to or characteristic of the English royal house that ruled from the accession of Henry VII in 1485 until the death of Elizabeth I in 1603. **2** denoting styles of art and architecture associated with this period, *esp* half-timbered houses. [from the name of the Welsh squire, Owen *Tudor* d.1461, from whom the family is descended]

Tudor² *noun* a member of the Tudor royal house.

Tudor rose *noun* a stylized figure of a rose, combining the red rose of the House of Lancaster and the white rose of the House of York, that Henry VII adopted as the emblem of the royal House of Tudor. It was used as a decorative feature in architecture, heraldry, etc.

Tue. *or* **Tues.** *abbr* Tuesday.

Tuesday /'tyoohzday, 'tyoohzdi/ *noun* the third day of the week, following Monday. [Old English *tiwesdæg* day of *Tiw*, the Norse god of war; translation of Latin *Martis dies* day of Mars, the Roman god of war]

tufa /'tyoohfə/ *noun* a porous rock composed of calcium carbonate and formed as a deposit by mineral springs. **>>> tufaceous** /tyooh'fayshəs/ *adj*. [Italian *tufa, tufo*, from Latin *tophus* a type of porous rock]

tuff /tuf/ *noun* a light porous rock consisting of consolidated volcanic ash. **>>> tuffaceous** /tu'fayshəs/ *adj*. [French *tuff* from Italian *tufo*: see TUFA]

tuffet /'tufit/ *noun* **1** a tuft or clump, *esp* of grass. **2** a low seat or footstool. [alteration of TUFT¹]

tuft¹ /tuft/ *noun* **1a** a small cluster of hairs, feathers, threads, grasses, etc attached or close together at the base. **b** a bunch of soft fluffy threads cut off short and used for decoration. **2** a clump or cluster, e.g. of trees or bushes. **>>> tufty** *adj*. [Middle English, modification of early French *tufe*, of unknown origin]

tuft² *verb trans* **1** to decorate (something) with a tuft or tufts. **2** to make (a carpet) by fastening tufts of pile into a backing material. **3** to make (e.g. a mattress) firm by stitching with tufts to form a pattern of regular depressions. **>>> tufted** *adj*.

tufted duck *noun* a European freshwater diving duck, the male of which has a black tufted head and white flanks: *Aythya fuligula*.

tug¹ /tug/ *verb* (**tugged, tugging**) **>** *verb trans* **1** to pull (something) hard or suddenly. **2** to tow (a ship), *esp* by means of a tugboat. **>** *verb intrans* to pull hard. **>>> tugger** *noun*. [Middle English; related to Old English *togian* TOW¹]

tug² *noun* **1** a hard sudden pull or jerk: *She felt the tug of the current; the tug of nostalgia*. **2a** a strongly built powerful boat used for towing larger boats and ships, *esp* in a harbour. **b** an aircraft that tows a glider. **3** a struggle or fight.

tugboat *noun* = TUG² (2A).

tug-of-love *noun* a situation involving conflict over the custody of a child, e.g. between the child's divorced or separated parents, or between natural parents and foster or adoptive parents.

tug-of-war *noun* (*pl* **tugs-of-war**) **1** a contest in which teams pulling at opposite ends of a rope attempt to pull each other across a line marked between them. **2** a struggle for supremacy.

tugrik /'toohgrik/ *noun* (*pl* **tugrik** *or* **tugriks**) the basic monetary unit of Mongolia, divided into 100 mongos. [Mongolian *dughurik*, literally 'a wheel']

tui /'tooh·i/ *noun* a New Zealand songbird, a type of honey-eater, that has glossy black plumage with tufts of white feathers at its throat: *Prosthemadura novaeseelandiae*. [Maori *tui*]

tuition /tyooh'ish(ə)n/ *noun* **1** teaching or instruction, *esp* of small groups or individuals: *piano tuition; tuition fees for university students*. **2** NAmer a fee for this, *esp* at a college or private school. **>>> tuitional** *adj*. [Middle English *tuicioun* care or protection, via French from Latin *tuition-, tuitio*, from *tueri* to guard or look after]

tularaemia (NAmer **tularemia**) /toohlə'reemi·ə/ *noun* an infectious disease of rodents and rabbits that can be transmitted to humans by insects. The symptoms include ulceration at the site of the insect bite, fever, and severe weight loss. **>>> tularaemic** *adj*. [scientific Latin, named after *Tulare* County, the district of California where it was first observed]

tule /'tooli/ *noun* NAmer either of two species of bulrushes that grow in low-lying marshy areas of California: *Scirpus acutus* and *Scirpus validus*. [Spanish *tule* from Nahuatl *tollin* reed]

tulip /'tyoohlip/ *noun* **1** a Eurasian bulbous plant of the lily family, widely grown for its showy cup-shaped flowers: genus *Tulipa*. **2** a flower of this plant. **3** (*used before a noun*) having the shape of a tulip: *a tulip wine glass*. [Turkish *tülbend* (see TURBAN); from the shape of the flower]

tulip tree *noun* **1** a tall N American deciduous tree with large greenish yellow cup-shaped flowers: *Liriodendron tulipifera*. **2** *informal* a magnolia.

tulipwood *noun* **1** the wood of the N American tulip tree. **2** any of various distinctive striped or variegated woods used by cabinet-makers, *esp* for inlaying.

tulle /t(y)oohl/ *noun* a sheer, often silk, net fabric used chiefly for veils and dresses. [French *tulle*, named after *Tulle*, the city in France where it was first produced]

tum /tum/ *noun informal* a person's stomach or the area around it. [contraction of TUMMY]

tumble¹ /'tumbl/ *verb intrans* **1** to fall suddenly, helplessly, or awkwardly: *He tumbled down the stairs.* **2** to perform acrobatic moves such as handstands, somersaults, back flips, etc. **3a** to roll over and over or to and fro: *The puppies tumbled around the garden.* **b** to move hurriedly and confusedly: *The children tumbled out of school.* **4** said of prices, etc: to decline suddenly and sharply. **5** *informal* (+ to) to realize, understand, or become aware of something suddenly: *She eventually tumbled to the fact that he'd been lying to her.* ➤ *verb trans* **1** to cause (somebody or something) to tumble; to push or topple. **2a** to throw (things) together in a confused mass. **b** to rumple or disarrange (something, *esp* hair or clothes). **3** to dry (laundry) in a tumble-dryer. **4** to polish or clean (gemstones, etc) in a rotating drum. **5** *informal* to have sexual intercourse with (somebody): *Quoth she, 'Before you tumbled me, you promised me to wed.' —* Shakespeare. [Middle English *tumblen* to dance in a contorted way, from early Low German *tummelen*, prob influenced by French *tomber* to fall down]

tumble² *noun* **1** an unexpected fall or drop. **2** a confused heap or an untidy state. **3** an acrobatic move such as a handstand, somersault, back flip, etc. **4** an act or spell of tumbling.

tumbledown *adj* said of a building, etc: in a state of disrepair; dilapidated or ramshackle.

tumble-drier *noun* see TUMBLE-DRYER.

tumble-dry *verb trans* (**tumble-dries, tumble-dried, tumble-drying**) to use a tumble-dryer to dry (laundry).

tumble-dryer *or* **tumble-drier** *noun* an electric machine that dries laundry by rotating it in hot air inside a metal drum.

tumbler *noun* **1** a large drinking glass without a handle, orig with a convex base but now flat-bottomed. **2** an acrobat or gymnast. **3** = TUMBLE-DRYER. **4a** a movable part of a lock, e.g. a lever, wheel, or pin, that must be adjusted to a particular position before the lock can be opened. **b** a spring-operated lever that forces the hammer of a firearm forwards when released by the trigger. **5** the movable part of a reversing or speed-changing gear. **6** = TUMBLING BARREL. **7** any of various domestic pigeons that tumble or somersault backwards in flight or on the ground.

tumbleweed *noun* any of various plants that grow in arid regions, *esp* in N America and Australia, which become so light and dried out after the heat of the summer months that they break off from their roots and are blown about in the wind: genera *Salsola* and *Amaranthus*.

tumbling barrel *noun* a revolving device in which objects or materials, such as gemstones, are whirled about for cleaning, polishing, etc.

tumbrel *or* **tumbril** /'tumbr(ə)l/ *noun* **1** an open-ended farm cart that can be tipped up in order to empty out its contents. **2** a cart of this kind used for carrying political prisoners during the French Revolution to a place of execution. [Middle English *tombrel* a ducking stool, from early French *tumberel*, from *tomber* to fall]

tumefacient /,tyoohmi'fayshənt/ *adj* said *esp* of a drug: capable of producing swelling. [Latin *tumefacere* to cause to swell, from *tumere* to swell]

tumefy /'tyoomifie/ *verb intrans* (**tumefies, tumefied, tumefying**) to become swollen. ➤➤ **tumefaction** /-'faksh(ə)n/ *noun*. [French *tuméfier* from Latin *tumefactus*, from *tumefacere*: see TUMEFACIENT]

tumescent /tyooh'mes(ə)nt/ *adj* swollen or distended, or in the process of becoming so. ➤➤ **tumescence** *noun*, **tumescently** *adv*. [Latin *tumescent-*, *tumescens*, present part. of *tumescere* to begin to swell, from *tumere* to swell]

tumid /'tyoohmid/ *adj* **1** said *esp* of a body part or tissue: marked by swelling or distension; bulging. **2** said of a speech, writing, etc: pompous, bombastic, or inflated. ➤➤ **tumidity** /tyooh'miditi/ *noun*, **tumidly** *adv*, **tumidness** *noun*. [Latin *tumidus*, from *tumere* to swell]

tummy /'tumi/ *noun* (*pl* **tummies**) *informal* a person's stomach or the area around it. [reflecting a child's pronunciation of STOMACH¹]

tummy button *noun informal* a person's navel.

tumor /'tyoohmə/ *noun NAmer* see TUMOUR.

tumorigenesis /,tyoohməri'jenisis/ *noun* the formation of a tumour or tumours.

tumorigenic /,tyoohməri'jenik/ *adj* producing or tending to produce tumours. ➤➤ **tumorigenicity** /-'nisiti/ *noun*.

tumour (*NAmer* **tumor**) /'tyoohmə/ *noun* a swelling on or in a part of the body, *esp* one involving an abnormal growth of tissue that may be benign or malignant. ➤➤ **tumorous** *adj*. [Latin *tumor*, from *tumere* to swell]

tump /tump/ *noun chiefly English dialect* a small clump or a low rounded hill. [origin unknown]

tumpline *noun NAmer* a strap or band fixed across the forehead or chest to help to support a load carried on the back. [from *tump*, contraction of Algonquian *mattump* a strap for a pack + LINE¹]

tumuli /'tyoohmyoolie, -lee/ *noun* pl of TUMULUS.

tumult /'tyoohmult, 'tyoohməlt/ *noun* **1** a loud confused noise caused by a large number of people behaving boisterously; a commotion: *The bugles blew madly for more pickets with officers to control the tumult —* Kipling. **2** a state of violent mental or emotional agitation: *He walked away with a tumult of thoughts in his head —* Somerset Maugham. **3** a confusion or disordered medley, e.g. of sounds or colours. [Middle English via French from Latin *tumultus*, from *tumere* to swell]

tumultuous /tyooh'multyoo-əs/ *adj* **1** characterized by noise, disorder, commotion, or uproar: *tumultuous applause.* **2** marked by violent turbulence or upheaval: *a tumultuous love affair.* ➤➤ **tumultuously** *adv*, **tumultuousness** *noun*.

tumulus /'tyoohmyoolə s/ *noun* (*pl* **tumuli** /-lie, -lee/) an artificial mound, *esp* one over a grave. [Middle English from Latin *tumulus*, prob ultimately from *tumere* to swell]

tun¹ /tun/ *noun* **1** a large cask, *esp* for beer or wine. **2** any of various units of capacity, *esp* a measure for wine equal to four hogsheads or about 252 gall (about 953l). [Old English *tunne* from medieval Latin *tunna*: see TUNNEL¹]

tun² *verb trans* (**tunned, tunning**) *archaic* to put or store (wine, beer, etc) in a tun.

tuna¹ /'tyoohnə/ *noun* (*pl* **tunas** *or collectively* **tuna**) **1** any of several species of large marine food fishes of warm waters that are related to the mackerel: genus *Thunnus* and other genera. **2** the flesh of a tuna used as food. [American Spanish *tuna*, alteration of Spanish *atún* tunny]

tuna² *noun* any of several species of prickly pears with flattened jointed stems, widely cultivated in tropical America, *esp* Mexico: *Opuntia tuna* and other species. [Spanish *tuna*, from Taino]

tunable *or* **tuneable** /'tyoohnəbl/ *adj* capable of being tuned.

tuna fish *noun* = TUNA¹ (2).

tundish /'tundish/ *noun Brit* **1** a reservoir in the top part of a mould into which molten metal is poured. **2** *dated* a funnel. [Middle English, denoting a wide shallow funnel for filling a tun, from TUN¹ + DISH¹]

tundra /'tundrə/ *noun* a vast level or undulating treeless plain characteristic of arctic and subarctic regions, that consists of a thin layer of black marshy soil overlying a permanently frozen subsoil. [Russian *tundra* from Lappish *tundar*]

tune¹ /tyoohn/ *noun* a succession of musical notes; a melody. ✳ **call the tune** see CALL¹. **change one's tune** *informal* to adopt a noticeably different attitude or point of view. **in/out of tune 1** said of a musician, singer, musical instrument, etc: having or not having the correct or required musical pitch or intonation. **2** said of a motor vehicle's engine: correctly or incorrectly adjusted to give the best performance. **3** said of people: in or not in harmony or agreement. **to the tune of** *informal* to the amount or extent of (a specified quantity, number, etc, often a sum of money): *a repair bill to the tune of £1000.* [Middle English, alteration of TONE¹]

tune² *verb trans* **1** to adjust the musical pitch of (an instrument), *esp* to the correct or required pitch. **2** (*often* + up) to adjust (the engine of a motor vehicle) for optimum performance. **3** to adjust (e.g. an electronic circuit or a laser) so that resonance occurs at the desired frequency; *esp* to adjust (a radio or television receiver) to respond to waves of a particular frequency. **4** (+ out) to adjust a radio, television, etc to avoid the reception of (unwanted signals or effects): *You need to tune out the interference.* ➤ *verb intrans* **1** (+ to) to become attuned to something. **2** (+ into) to become aware of something or somebody. **3** *informal* (+ out) to stop listening or paying attention. ➤➤ **tuning** *noun*.

tuneable *adj* see TUNABLE.

tuneful /'tyoohnf(ə)l/ *adj* having a pleasant tune; melodious. ➤➤ **tunefully** *adv*, **tunefulness** *noun*.

tune in *verb intrans* to switch on and listen to or watch radio or television, or a particular radio or television programme or channel.

tuneless *adj* not pleasant to listen to; unmelodious: *tuneless whistling*. ➤➤ **tunelessly** *adv*, **tunelessness** *noun*.

tuner *noun* **1** a person who tunes musical instruments, *esp* pianos. **2** an electronic device for tuning something, e.g. a circuit that acts as a filter for radio and television broadcast signals, amplifying those required and converting them into audio or visual signals.

tunesmith /'tyoohnsmith/ *noun informal* a composer of popular songs.

tune up *verb intrans* said of a musician, orchestra, etc: to bring a musical instrument or instruments to the correct or required pitch. ➤ *verb trans* to tune (a musical instrument).

tune-up *noun* a general adjustment to an engine to ensure operation at peak efficiency.

tung oil /tung/ *noun* a yellow or brownish oil obtained from the seeds of various trees, *esp* Asian trees of the genus *Aleurites*, and added to paints, inks, and varnishes as a drying agent. [Chinese (Pekingese) *tongyou* oil of the tung tree]

tungsten /'tungstən/ *noun* a grey–white metallic chemical element that is hard and heavy, has a high melting point, and is used for electrical purposes, *esp* as filaments in light bulbs, and in hardening and increasing the strength of alloys, e.g. steel: symbol W, atomic number 74. [Swedish *tungsten*, from *tung* heavy + *sten* stone]

tungstite /'tungstiet/ *noun* a mineral consisting of an oxide of tungsten and occurring in a yellow or yellowish green crumbly coating on ores of tungsten: formula WO_3.

Tungus /'toong·goohz, 'tungoohz/ *noun* (*pl* **Tunguses** *or* **Tungus**) **1** a member of a people widely spread over E Siberia. **2** the Tungusic language spoken by this people. [via Russian from Yakut]

Tungusic /tung'goohzik/ *noun* a branch of the Altaic language family spoken in Manchuria and eastern parts of Asiatic Russia. ➤➤ **Tungusic** *adj*.

tunic /'tyoohnik/ *noun* **1a** a simple loose usu sleeveless thigh-length or knee-length garment, sometimes belted at the waist. **b** a garment of this kind worn in ancient Greece and Rome or medieval Europe. **2** a close-fitting hip-length jacket worn as part of a uniform: *a policeman's tunic*. **3a** a membrane that encloses or lines a part of an animal or plant: *the tunic of a seed*. **b** any of the fleshy layers that form the bulb of an onion or other plant, or the thin membranous covering of one of these segments. **4** a short smock-like garment worn by a subdeacon or bishop, *esp* at celebrations of the Eucharist. [Old English via Old French *tunique* from Latin *tunica*]

tunica /'tyoohnikə/ *noun* (*pl* **tunicae** /-kie/) **1** an enveloping membrane or layer of body tissue. **2** the outermost group of cells at the tip of a growing shoot. [Latin *tunica* TUNIC]

tunicate[1] /'tyoohnikət, -kayt/ *noun* a marine animal, such as the sea squirt, that has an unsegmented body protected by a tough or rubbery membranous outer layer. They are free-floating or live attached to rocks and feed by filtering particles from the water: subphylum Urochordata.

tunicate[2] *adj* said of a bulb: having, arranged in, or made up of concentric fleshy layers. [Latin *tunicātus* wearing a tunic, from *tunica* TUNIC]

tunicated /'tyoohnikaytid/ *adj* = TUNICATE[2].

tunicle /'tyoohnikl/ *noun* = TUNIC (4). [Middle English from Latin *tunicula*, dimin. of *tunica* TUNIC]

tuning fork *noun* a two-pronged metal implement that gives a fixed tone when struck and is used for tuning musical instruments and setting pitches for singing.

tuning peg *noun* any of the small pegs at the end of the neck of a stringed musical instrument used for adjusting the tension of the strings in order to tune the instrument.

Tunisian /tyoo'nizi·ən/ *noun* a native or inhabitant of Tunisia in N Africa. ➤➤ **Tunisian** *adj*.

tunnel[1] /'tunl/ *noun* **1** an underground passage, *esp* one that allows people, vehicles, etc to have access through or under an obstruction such as a hill, river, or building. **2** a small underground passage, often one of many forming an interconnected system, excavated by a burrowing animal, e.g. a mole. [Middle English *tonel*

a tube-shaped net, from Old French dimin. of *tunne* cask, tun, from Latin *tunna*, prob of Celtic origin]

tunnel[2] *verb* (**tunnelled, tunnelling**, *NAmer* **tunneled, tunneling**) ➤ *verb trans* to make (one's way) by digging: *He tunnelled his way under the prison walls.* ➤ *verb intrans* **1** (*often* + under/through) to construct an underground passage under or through an obstruction. **2** said of a particle: to pass through a potential energy barrier. ➤➤ **tunneller** *noun*.

tunnel diode *noun* a semiconductor diode in which tunnelling electrons are used for performing high-speed switching operations.

tunnel vision *noun* **1** an eye condition in which objects at the edges of the visual field are lost or can only be seen indistinctly. **2** *informal* extreme narrowness of viewpoint; narrow-mindedness.

tunny /'tuni/ *noun* (*pl* **tunnies** *or collectively* **tunny**) a tuna. [early French *thon* via Latin from Greek *thunnus*]

tup[1] /tup/ *noun* **1** *chiefly Brit* a ram. **2** the heavy metal head of a steam hammer, pile driver, etc. [origin unknown]

tup[2] *verb trans* (**tupped, tupping**) *chiefly Brit* said of a ram: to copulate with (a ewe).

tupelo /'tyoohpəloh/ *noun* (*pl* **tupelos**) **1** any of several species of N American and Asian trees that grow in damp or marshy conditions: *Nyssa sylvatica* and other species. **2** the soft light-coloured wood of this tree. [Creek *ito* tree + *opilwa* swamp]

Tupi /tooh'pee/ *noun* (*pl* **Tupis** *or collectively* **Tupi**) **1** a member of a group of indigenous peoples of Brazil. **2** any of the languages spoken by these peoples. ➤➤ **Tupi** *adj*, **Tupian** /'toohpee·ən, tooh'pee·ən/ *adj*.

Word history

Tupi words that have passed into English, by way of Portuguese, French, or Spanish, include *cashew, cayenne, cougar, jaguar, petunia, tapioca*, and *toucan*.

Tupi-Guarani /tooh,pee gwahrə'nee/ *noun* a group of S American languages spoken in parts of Brazil, Peru, and Paraguay, including Tupi and Guarani. ➤➤ **Tupi-Guarani** *adj*, **Tupi-Guaranian** *adj*.

tuppence /'tup(ə)ns/ *noun Brit* see TWOPENCE.

tuppenny /'tup(ə)ni/ *adj Brit* see TWOPENNY.

Tupperware /'tupəweə/ *noun trademark* a range of kitchenware, *esp* sealable plastic containers for storing food. [from the name of its American inventor, Earl W *Tupper* + WARE[1]]

tuque /'toohk/ *noun Can* a close-fitting knitted hat in the form of a tube, usu with one or two long tapering ends, sometimes with a tassel or bobble attached. [Canadian French *tuque* from French *toque*: see TOQUE]

turaco *or* **touraco** /'tooərəkoh/ *noun* (*pl* **turacos** *or* **touracos**) any of several species of brightly coloured birds with a prominent crest and a long tail, which live in densely forested areas of Africa: genus *Tauraco* and other genera. [French *touraco*, from a W African language]

turban /'tuhbən/ *noun* **1** a headdress worn *esp* by Muslim and Sikh men, consisting of a long cloth wound either round a cap or directly round the head. **2** a woman's hat or a headdress that resembles this: *Anne Mitchell had tried to put on a turban like mine ... but made wretched work of it* — Jane Austen. ➤➤ **turbaned** *adj*, **turbanned** *adj*. [early French *turbant* via Italian from Turkish *tülbend*, from Persian *dulband*]

turbary /'tuhb(ə)ri/ *noun* (*pl* **turbaries**) *Brit* **1** land where peat or turf is dug or cut. **2** the right to dig or cut peat or turf from common land or from land belonging to somebody else. [Middle English via French from Latin *turbāria*, from *turba* a turf]

turbellarian /tuhbi'leəri·ən/ *noun* any of a class of mostly aquatic and non-parasitic flatworms: class Turbellaria. ➤➤ **turbellarian** *adj*. [Latin class name, from *turba* confusion, crowd; with reference to the tiny eddies created in water by the cilia (the vibrating hair-like parts covering its body that are used for propulsion; see CILIUM)]

turbid /'tuhbid/ *adj* **1a** said of a liquid: cloudy, thick, or opaque, e.g. because of disturbed sediment. **b** said of air: thick with smoke or mist. **2** characterized by or producing confusion, *esp* of the mind or emotions. ➤➤ **turbidity** /tuh'biditi/ *noun*, **turbidly** *adv*, **turbidness** *noun*. [Middle English from Latin *turbidus* confused, from *turba* a crowd]

turbinal /'tuhbinl/ *noun* any of the thin folded or spirally coiled plates of bone, covered by mucous membranes, on the walls of the cavities of the nose. [Latin *turbin-, turbo* spinning top + -AL[1]]

turbinate[1] /'tuhbinət/ *adj* **1** shaped like a spinning top or an inverted cone: *a turbinate shell*. **2** relating to or in the region of the turbinals. [Latin *turbinatus*, from *turbin-*, *turbo* spinning top]

turbinate[2] *noun* **1** a turbinate structure, *esp* a shell. **2** = TURBINAL.

turbine /'tuhbien/ *noun* a power-generating machine with a wheel or rotor, often fitted with vanes, that is driven by the pressure of water, steam, exhaust gases, etc. [French *turbine* from Latin *turbin-*, *turbo* spinning top]

turbit /'tuhbit/ *noun* a domestic pigeon with a short beak, frilled breast, and mostly white plumage. [Latin *turbo* a spinning top, so called because its rather squat body resembles the shape of a spinning top]

turbo /'tuhboh/ *noun* (*pl* **turbos**) **1** a turbine. **2** a turbocharger.

turbo- *comb. form* forming words, with the meaning: consisting of, incorporating, or driven by a turbine: *turbojet*; *turbocharger*. [from TURBINE]

turbocharge *verb trans* to fit (an internal-combustion engine) with a turbocharger in order to give an increase in power.

turbocharger *noun* a compressor device, usu powered by a turbine driven by exhaust gases, that is used to supercharge an internal-combustion engine.

turbofan *noun* **1a** a fan that is directly connected to and driven by a turbine and is used to supply air for cooling, ventilation, or combustion. **b** an extra large fan of this kind in front of the main compressor of a jet engine. **2** a jet engine with a turbofan.

turbojet *noun* **1** a jet engine in which a compressor, driven by power from a turbine, supplies compressed air to the combustion chamber and in which thrust is derived from the rearward expulsion of hot gases. **2** an aircraft powered by engines of this kind.

turboprop *noun* **1** a jet engine with a turbine-driven propeller. **2** an aircraft powered by a propeller of this kind.

turboshaft *noun* a gas turbine engine in which the power is used to drive a shaft other than a propeller shaft, used *esp* in helicopter rotors and pumps.

turbot /'tuhbət/ *noun* (*pl* **turbots** or collectively **turbot**) **1** a large European flatfish that has a brownish upper surface scattered with knobbly tubercles instead of scales. It is a highly valued food fish: *Scophthalmus maximus*. **2** any of various similar flatfish. [Middle English via early French *tourbot* from Latin *turbo* a spinning top, because it was thought to resemble the shape of a top]

turbulence /'tuhbyoolǝns/ *noun* **1** a commotion or a confused state; disorderliness. **2** irregular atmospheric motion, *esp* when characterized by strong currents of rising and falling air. **3** departure from a smooth flow in a gas or liquid.

turbulent /'tuhbyoolǝnt/ *adj* **1** characterized by agitation or tumult; stormy: *the turbulent years of the revolution*. **2** *archaic* said of a person: fomenting unrest or disorder: *Will no one rid me of this turbulent priest?* — Henry II. **3** relating to or denoting irregular atmospheric motion. **4** *technical* relating to or denoting departure from a smooth flow. >>> **turbulently** *adv*. [Latin *turbulentus*, from *turba* confusion, crowd]

Turco- or **Turko-** *comb. form* forming words, with the meaning: Turkey or Turkish people, culture, etc.

Turcoman /'tuhkǝmǝn/ *noun* see TURKOMAN.

turd /tuhd/ *noun coarse slang* **1** a piece of excrement. **2** a contemptuous term for an obnoxious person. [Old English *tord*]

tureen /tyoo'reen, tǝ'reen/ *noun* a deep bowl, often with a lid, from which food such as soup is served. [French *terrine*: see TERRINE]

turf[1] /tuhf/ *noun* (*pl* **turfs** or **turves** /tuhvz/) **1a** grass and the soil that is bound to its roots, forming a thick mat. **b** a piece of this that has been cut from the ground. **2** (**the turf**). **a** the sport or business of horse racing. **b** racecourses in general. **3** *informal*. **a** an area regarded as the domain of a particular person or group, e.g. a part of a city in which a gang conducts illegal activities. **b** a person's sphere of interest, knowledge, or control. >>> **turfy** *adj*. [Old English]

turf[2] *verb trans* to cover (an area) with turf.

turf accountant *noun Brit, formal* a bookmaker.

turfman *noun* (*pl* **turfmen**) *chiefly NAmer* a devotee of horse racing.

turf out *verb trans chiefly Brit, informal* **1** to force (somebody) to leave: *The bouncers turfed the drunks out of the club*. **2** to dismiss, reject, or discard (something): *They turfed out our proposal*.

turgescent /tuh'jes(ǝ)nt/ *adj technical* becoming or appearing to be swollen or distended. >>> **turgescence** *noun*. [Latin *turgescent-*, *turgescens*, present part. of *turgescere* to begin to swell, from *turgēre* to swell]

turgid /'tuhjid/ *adj* **1a** swollen or distended. **b** said of a cell: exhibiting turgor. **2** said of language, a speech, a piece of writing, etc: pompous or bombastic and lacking any liveliness of style. >>> **turgidity** /tuh'jiditi/ *noun*, **turgidly** *adv*, **turgidness** *noun*. [Latin *turgidus*, from *turgēre* to swell]

turgor /'tuhgǝ/ *noun* the normal state of firmness and tension of a living cell, *esp* the normal rigid condition of a plant cell in which the cell wall is distended by the pressure of the liquid contents. [scientific Latin, from Latin *turgēre* to swell]

Turing machine /'tooǝring/ *noun* a hypothetical computing machine that performs according to a prescribed set of logical rules and is a concept used in theories of computability and automata. [named after Alan *Turing* d.1954, British mathematician, who invented the concept of a computing machine and investigated artificial intelligence]

Turing test *noun* a test for artificial intelligence, e.g. of a computer, that involves replacing one person by the machine under test, e.g. in a situation where two or more people are communicating with each other through computer terminals. If the machine is intelligent, the other person or people will be unaware of the change. [named after Alan *Turing*: see TURING MACHINE]

turion /'t(y)oori·ǝn/ *noun* a scaly shoot that detaches from an aquatic plant and sinks to the bottom of the river, lake, etc, where it remains dormant until the spring, when it may produce a new plant. [French *turion* from Latin *turion-*, *turio* a shoot]

Turk /tuhk/ *noun* **1** a native or inhabitant of Turkey. **2** a person who speaks any of the Turkic languages. **3** a member of any of various ancient peoples who lived around the eastern Mediterranean. **4** a member, *esp* a Muslim, of the Ottoman Empire. **5** *archaic* a tyrannical or violent person. [Middle English via French from Latin *Turcus*, from Persian *turk*, perhaps from early Turkish *türk* strong]

turkey[1] /'tuhki/ *noun* (*pl* **turkeys** or collectively **turkey**) **1a** a large often domesticated game bird, orig native to N America, that has a heavy rounded body, lustrous black or bronze plumage, a bald head, and, in the male, distinctive red wattles: *Meleagris gallopavo*. **b** the flesh of a turkey used as food. **2** *chiefly NAmer, informal* something, *esp* a film or play, that is considered to be an utter failure. **3** an ineffectual or stupid person. ✳ **talk turkey** *NAmer, informal* to have a frank and open discussion, *esp* one that relates to business. [shortened from TURKEY-COCK or *turkeyhen*, a name applied to a type of African guinea fowl imported via Turkey and later erroneously also applied to the American bird]

turkey[2] *verb trans and intrans* (**turkeys**, **turkeyed**, **turkeying**) *slang* to withdraw, or cause (somebody) to withdraw, from an addictive drug, *esp* heroin: see also COLD TURKEY.

turkey buzzard *noun NAmer* = TURKEY VULTURE.

turkey-cock *noun* a male turkey.

turkey oak *noun* (*pl* **turkey oaks** or collectively **turkey oak**) an oak tree of southern Europe that has leaves with deeply jagged lobes and almost stalkless acorn cups that are covered by long green curling scales: *Quercus cerris*.

Turkey red *noun* a bright red dye obtained from madder or alizarin, used for colouring fabric.

turkey trot *noun* a ragtime dance, popular during the 1920s, characterized by bouncy walking steps with the feet well apart and shuddering up and down shoulder movements.

turkey vulture *noun* an American vulture with blackish brown plumage and a bald red wrinkly head and neck: *Cathartes aura*.

Turki /'tuhki/ *noun* (*pl* **Turkis** or collectively **Turki**) **1** any of the Turkic languages, particularly those of the eastern group. **2** a speaker of any of these languages. >>> **Turki** *adj*. [Persian *turkī* (adj) from *turk*: see TURK]

Turkic /'tuhkik/ *noun* the branch of the Altaic family of languages that includes Turkish, Azerbaijani, and Tatar. >>> **Turkic** *adj*. [TURK + -IC[2]]

Turkish /'tuhkish/ *noun* the national language of the people of Turkey, belonging to the Turkic branch of Altaic languages and written in the Roman alphabet. ➤➤ **Turkish** *adj.*

Word history
Words of Turkish origin that have passed into English include *bosh, janissary, kebab, shagreen,* and *yogurt.* In addition, Turkish has been the medium through which a number of Arabic and Persian words have spread to Europe and eventually into English; these include *coffee, dervish, divan, kiosk, sherbet,* and *turban.*

Turkish bath *noun* **1** a type of therapeutic or relaxing treatment that involves sitting in hot steam followed by a rubdown, massage, and cold shower. **2** (*also in pl*) a room or building where this is available.

Turkish coffee *noun* a strong usu sweetened coffee made from very finely ground beans.

Turkish delight *noun* a jellylike confection, usu flavoured with flower essences, cut in cubes, and dusted with icing sugar.

Turkish towel *noun* a towel made of cotton cloth with a rough pile of uncut loops.

Turkish Van *noun* a cat of a long-haired breed having white fur with ginger markings on the head and tail, and distinctive pale reddish brown eyes. [named after *Van,* a town in Turkey]

Turkmen /'tuhkmen/ *noun* (*pl* **Turkmens** *or collectively* **Turkmen**) **1** a member of a group of peoples inhabiting parts of Turkmenistan and Afghanistan. **2** the Turkic language spoken by these peoples. [Persian *Turkmāen,* from *Tūkmen,* the Turkish name for these peoples]

Turko- *comb. form* see TURCO-.

Turkoman *or* **Turcoman** /'tuhkəmən/ *noun* (*pl* **Turkomans** *or* **Turcomans**) = TURKMEN.

Turk's cap lily *noun* = MARTAGON LILY.

Turk's head *noun* an ornamental turban-shaped knot used *esp* at the end of a rope to prevent it slipping through an eyelet, etc.

turmeric /'tuhmərik/ *noun* **1** an Asian plant of the ginger family with a large rhizome: *Curcuma longa.* **2** a bright yellow aromatic powder obtained from the rhizome of this plant, used for flavouring and as a colouring agent, *esp* in Asian cookery. **3** a yellow dye made from this powder, formerly used for colouring fabrics. [prob via early French *terre mérite* from Latin *terra merita,* literally 'deserving earth']

turmoil /'tuhmoyl/ *noun* an extremely confused or agitated state. [origin unknown]

turn[1] /tuhn/ *verb trans* **1** to make (something) move round an axis or face the opposite direction. **2** to make (something) change course, position, or direction. **3a** to go past round (a point, *esp* a corner). **b** to reach or go beyond (something, *esp* an age or time): *It's just turned midnight.* **4** to perform (an acrobatic manoeuvre) by rotating. **5** to make or form (something) using a lathe. **6** (*often* + into/to) to make (something, somebody, or oneself) into a different form, type, shape, etc. **7** (*often* + to/towards) to direct (the mind, attention, thoughts, etc) to a specified topic, etc. **8** to cause something or somebody to change form, position, or condition*esp:* **a** to cause (milk, etc) to become sour. **b** to cause (leaves) to change colour. **c** to give (words, etc) an elegant form. **d** to cause (the stomach) to be affected with nausea or revulsion. **9** to bring (soil) from a lower position to the surface. **10** in cricket, to give (a bowled ball) spin. **11** to sprain (an ankle). **12** to make (a specified profit). ➤ *verb intrans* **1** to move round on an axis or so as to face an opposite direction. **2a** to move into or take a different position, condition, etc: *The weather has turned cold.* **b** said of leaves: to change colour. **c** said of milk, etc: to become sour. **3** (+ to) to consult or seek support from (somebody or something): *I always turn to you for advice.* **4** to become giddy or dizzy; to reel. **5** said of a person's stomach: to feel nauseated. ✳ **turn against** to become hostile towards (somebody or something). **turn colour** to change colour; *esp* to grow pale or red. **turn loose** to release (somebody or something) from constraint or captivity. ➤➤ **turnable** *adj.* [Old English *tyrnian* via Old French *torner* from Latin *tornare* to turn on a lathe, from *tornus* a lathe, from Greek *tornos*]

turn[2] *noun* **1** an act of turning. **2a** a bend or curve in a path, road, river, etc. **b** a place where a road divides; turning. **c** in cricket, deviation of the ball after a bounce. **d** a single coil, e.g. of rope or wire wound round an object. **e** something that revolves round a centre, *esp* a lathe. **3a** a point at which events or circumstances change: *a turn for the better.* **b** a point at the beginning or end of a

century or other period. **4** an opportunity or obligation to do something occurring in succession or rotation: *It's your turn to go.* **5a** *informal* a shock: *It gave me a turn.* **b** a spell or attack of illness, faintness, dizziness, etc. **6a** a complete transaction involving a purchase and sale of securities. **b** a profit from such a transaction. **7** a musical ornament based on a note and consisting of the note itself and the notes above and below. **8** a short act or performance, e.g. in a variety show. **9** a short walk or drive taken for pleasure. ✳ **at every turn** on every occasion; constantly or continually. **by turns** alternately or successively: *We are all rovers and all fixtures by turns —* Ralph Waldo Emerson. **do somebody a good turn** to do a favour for somebody. **in turn** in the correct order of succession. **on the turn** at the point of turning. **out of turn 1** not in the correct order of succession. **2** at a wrong time or place; imprudently or unwisely. **take turns/take it in turns** to do something alternatively or successively. **to a turn** perfectly; to the required degree. **turn and turn about** *chiefly Brit* one after another.

turnabout *noun* a change or reversal of direction, trend, etc.

turnaround *noun* **1a** the act or process of unloading cargo or passengers from an aircraft, ship, lorry, etc at the end of a journey, reloading it and making it ready for its next trip. **b** the time this takes. **2** the act or process of completing something, or the time this takes. **3** = TURNABOUT. **4** *chiefly NAmer* a place where vehicles can turn.

turn around *verb trans* = TURN ROUND.

turn away *verb trans* **1** to change the direction of (something): *He turned his face away.* **2a** to reject, dismiss, or send (somebody or something) away. **b** to refuse to allow (somebody) entrance to a place. ➤ *verb intrans* **1** to start to go away; to depart. **2** to change direction.

turn back *verb intrans* to go in the reverse direction; to return. ➤ *verb trans* **1** to drive (somebody or something) back or away. **2** to prevent (somebody or something) from going any further. **3** to fold (something, e.g. a collar, page of a book, etc) back.

turnbuckle *noun* a device that connects and pulls together the ends of a wire, stay, etc to make it taut.

turncoat *noun* a person who switches from one party, cause, etc to an opposing one.

turndown *adj* worn, or designed to be worn, folded down: *a turndown collar.*

turn down *verb trans* **1** to reduce the intensity of (a volume level, etc) by adjusting a control. **2** to decline to accept (an offer, etc). **3** to fold (bedclothes, etc) over. ➤ *verb intrans* to be capable of being folded down.

turned-on *adj informal* keenly aware of and responsive to what is new and fashionable.

turner *noun* a person who forms articles on a lathe. ➤➤ **turnery** *noun.*

Turner's syndrome /'tuhnəz/ *noun* a genetically determined condition in women that is associated with the presence of only one X chromosome. It is characterized by a stocky physique and underdevelopment of the sex organs. [named after Henry Hubert Turner d.1970, US physician, who first described it]

turn in *verb trans* **1** to hand (somebody or something) over to the authorities. **2** to provide or produce (work, etc). ➤ *verb intrans informal* to go to bed for the night.

turning *noun* **1a** a road, path, river, etc, that branches off another road, etc. **b** a place on a road, etc where it branches; a junction. **2a** the act, process, or skill of using a lathe. **b** (*in pl*) waste parts formed in the process of using a lathe.

turning circle *noun* the smallest circle in which a vehicle or vessel can turn without having to reverse.

turning point *noun* a point at which a significant change occurs.

turnip /'tuhnip/ *noun* **1** a plant of the cabbage family widely cultivated for its large yellowish or white edible root: *Brassica rapa.* **2** the root of this plant, used as a vegetable and livestock fodder. ➤➤ **turnipy** *adj.* [from NEEP + a first element of unknown origin]

turnkey[1] *noun* (*pl* **turnkeys**) *archaic* a jailer; a prison warder.

turnkey[2] *adj* **1** said of a product, service, etc: supplied, installed, built, etc complete and ready for immediate use. **2** said of a contract: involving no subcontractors.

turn off *verb trans* **1** to stop (something) from working or flowing by means of a switch, tap, etc. **2** *informal.* **a** to bore or disconcert (somebody). **b** to cause (somebody) to lose sexual interest. ➤ *verb* *intrans* **1** to leave a straight course or depart from a main road. **2** *informal* to lose interest or stop paying attention.

turn-off *noun* **1a** a road, path, etc that branches off another road, etc. **b** a place on a road, etc where it branches; a junction. **2** *informal* somebody or something that a person finds repulsive or boring: *Hairy backs are such a turn-off.*

turn on *verb trans* **1** to cause (something) to start working or flowing by means of a switch, tap, etc. **2** to produce (an agreeable aspect) as required. **3** *informal*. **a** to cause (somebody) to become excited or stimulated, *esp* sexually. **b** to cause (somebody) to experience the effects of a drug, *esp* a hallucinogenic one. ➤ *verb intrans* *informal* to become excited or stimulated, *esp* sexually.

turn-on *noun informal* somebody or something that a person finds attractive, exciting, interesting, or sexually stimulating: *The way the lead singer struts across the stage is a real turn-on.*

turnout *noun* **1** the number of people attending or taking part in an event: *There was a good turnout at the meeting.* **2** *NAmer* a widened place on a road where vehicles can overtake or park. **3** *NAmer* a junction. **4** *dated* a carriage, the horse or horses pulling it, and all its equipment.

turn out *verb trans* **1** to cause (an electric light) to stop working by operating a switch. **2** to expel or evict (somebody). **3a** to empty (something, *esp* a pocket). **b** to clean (a room) thoroughly, *esp* by removing its contents. **4** to produce (something), *esp* mechanically or in large quantities. **5** to equip, dress, or finish (somebody or something) in a specified way: *He was nicely turned out in a suit and tie.* **6** to transfer (something) from a receptacle, *esp* by inverting. **7** to call (a guard or a company) out from rest or shelter and into formation. ➤ *verb intrans* **1** to leave one's home for a special purpose. **2** to prove ultimately to be in a specified condition, etc: *Everything turned out happily.*

turnover *noun* **1a** the amount of money taken by a business in a particular period. **b** the amount of business transacted in a particular period. **c** the rate at which a business loses and replaces its staff. **d** the rate at which a business, *esp* a shop, sells and replaces stock. **2** the act or result of turning over, *esp* an unexpected upset. **3** an individual pie made by folding a circle of pastry in half and sealing it to enclose a filling: *an apple turnover.* **4** *chiefly NAmer* in sports, *esp* American football and basketball, the loss of possession of the ball.

turn over *verb trans* **1** to rotate or invert (something). **2** to cause (an internal-combustion engine) to revolve and fire. **3a** to search through (e.g. clothes or papers) by moving them one by one. **b** *informal* to ransack (a room, house, etc), *esp* when looking for something. **c** to think over (a matter, problem, etc). **4** to deliver or pass (somebody or something) to the proper authority. **5** said of a business: **a** to receive and dispose of (stock or merchandise). **b** to do business to the amount of (a specified sum). ➤ *verb intrans* **1** to be rotated or inverted; to go the other way up. **2** said of an internal-combustion engine: to run at low speed. **3a** said of the stomach: to heave with nausea. **b** said of the heart: to seem to leap or lurch convulsively with sudden fright.

turnpike *noun* **1** *NAmer* a road on which a toll is payable, *esp* an expressway or other major road. **2a** formerly, a toll gate. **b** formerly, a road on which a toll was payable. **c** a spiked obstruction formerly placed across a road to prevent attacks, or a similar obstruction that could be lifted to allow passage when a toll had been paid. [TURN¹ + PIKE²]

turnround *noun* = TURNAROUND.

turn round *verb trans* **1** to complete the processing of (goods or work) in a specified time. **2** to reform (a failing concern, *esp* a commercial business) so that it becomes profitable.

turnsole /'tuhnsohl/ *noun* **1a** a Mediterranean plant with flowers that are said to keep facing the sun as it crosses the sky: *Chrozophora tinctoria.* **b** a purple dye formerly obtained from this plant. **2** any of various other plants, e.g. the heliotrope, with flowers that follow the direction of the sun. [Middle English from early French *tournesol*, ultimately from Latin *tornare* (see TURN¹) + *sole* sun]

turnspit *noun* **1** formerly, a small dog that turned a spit by running on a treadmill. **2** formerly, a servant whose job was to turn a spit by hand.

turnstile *noun* a gate with arms pivoted on the top that turns to admit one person at a time, used e.g. at sports grounds.

turnstone *noun* either of two species of wading birds of the sandpiper family with a stubby wedge-shaped bill that they use for

turning over pebbles on the shore to find small crustaceans, insects, etc: genus *Arenaria*.

turntable *noun* **1** the platform on which a gramophone record is rotated while being played. **2** a circular platform for turning wheeled vehicles, *esp* railway engines.

turntable ladder *noun* a large power-operated ladder mounted on a revolving platform, *esp* on a fire engine.

turn to *verb intrans* to apply oneself to work; to act vigorously: *We must turn to and get the job done.*

turn up *verb trans* **1** to find or discover (somebody or something). **2** to increase the intensity of (a volume level) by adjusting a control. **3** to fold and attach (a strip of material, etc). ➤ *verb intrans* **1** to be found unexpectedly or after being lost. **2** to appear or become known. **3** to happen or occur unexpectedly, *esp* to one's advantage: *Something may turn up.*

turn-up *noun Brit* **1** a hem, *esp* on a pair of trousers, that is folded up over itself on the outside. **2** (*in pl*) a pair of trousers with such hems. **3** *informal* an unexpected or surprising event or outcome.

turpentine¹ /'tuhpentien/ *noun* **1a** a thick sticky yellow or brown OLEORESIN (natural oily secretion) obtained from certain conifer trees and distilled to make rosin and oil of turpentine. Also called GUM TURPENTINE. **b** any of various colourless volatile oils distilled from this, used as solvents for paints and varnishes and as medicinal liniments. Also called OIL OF TURPENTINE, SPIRITS OF TURPENTINE. **2** a name loosely applied to any of various paint and varnish thinners derived from other sources; white spirit. [Middle English from early French *ter(e)bentine*, from Latin *ter(e)binthina resina* resin of the TEREBINTH tree]

turpentine² *verb trans* to apply turpentine to (something).

turpentine tree *noun* **1** any of various trees, *esp* the terebinth, that yield a resin from which oil of turpentine was formerly distilled. **2** any of various Australian trees, e.g. some eucalyptuses, that yield an oily resinous liquid: *Syncarpia laurifolia* and others.

turpitude /'tuhpityoohd/ *noun formal* baseness, depravity, or wickedness: *moral turpitude.* [early French *turpitude* from Latin *turpitudo*, from *turpis* vile, base]

turps /tuhps/ *noun informal* turpentine. [contraction of TURPENTINE¹]

turquoise /'tuhkwoyz/ *noun* **1** a blue, bluish green, or greenish grey mineral consisting of a hydrated phosphate of copper and aluminium, which takes a high polish and is valued as a semi-precious gemstone. **2** a light greenish blue colour. ➤➤ **turquoise** *adj.* [Middle English from early French *turqueise* Turkish (stone)]

turret /'turit/ *noun* **1** a little tower, often at the corner of a larger building, *esp* a castle. **2** an armoured structure, typically revolving, on warships, forts, tanks, aircraft, etc in which guns are mounted. **3** a rotatable holder, e.g. for a tool or die, in a lathe, milling machine, etc. ➤➤ **turreted** *adj.* [Middle English from early French *torete*, dimin. of *tour, tur*: see TOWER¹]

turret lathe *noun* = CAPSTAN LATHE.

turtle¹ /'tuht(ə)l/ *noun* **1** any of several species of marine and freshwater reptiles that resemble the related tortoises, having a bony or leathery shell but with limbs adapted for swimming: families Cheloniidae and Dermmochelyidae. **b** the flesh of a sea turtle used as food. **2** in computer graphics, a small on-screen shape used as a drawing tool that is easily manipulated, *esp* by children learning basic computing skills. ✳ **turn turtle** said *esp* of a boat: to capsize or overturn. [prob an alteration of French *tortue*: see TORTOISE]

turtle² *noun archaic* a turtledove. [Old English *turtla* from Latin *turtur*, an imitation of the bird's soft call]

turtledove *noun* any of several species of small wild doves with a distinctive soft cooing call. They are noted for being particularly affectionate towards their mates: genus *Streptopelia*.

turtleneck *noun* **1** *Brit*. **a** a high close-fitting neck on a garment. **b** a jumper, T-shirt, etc with a neck of this kind. **2** *NAmer* = POLO NECK.

turves /tuhvz/ *noun* pl of TURF¹.

Tuscan /'tuskən/ *noun* **1** a native or inhabitant of Tuscany in N Italy. **2a** the dialect of the Italian language spoken in Tuscany. **b** the standard Italian language, regarded as based on the dialect of Florence and Tuscany. **3** an order of classical architecture that is a modification of the Greek Doric but plainer in style. ➤➤ **Tuscan**

adj. [Middle English from Latin *tuscanus* of Etruria, from *Tusci* Etruscans]

Tuscarora /tuskə'rawrə/ *noun* (*pl* **Tuscaroras** or collectively **Tuscarora**) **1** a member of an indigenous N American people orig inhabiting North Carolina, and later New York State and Ontario. **2** the extinct Iroquois language of this people. [from the name in various Iroquois languages for this people, literally 'hemp gatherers']

tush[1] /tush/ *interj* archaic or humorous used to express disapproval, irritation, contempt, etc: *'Tush! Foolery!' interposed the beadle* — Dickens.

tush[2] /tush/ *noun* a long pointed tooth, *esp* a canine tooth of a male horse. [Old English *tūsc*: see TUSK]

tush[3] /toosh/ *noun* chiefly NAmer, informal a person's buttocks. [Yiddish *tokhes* from Hebrew *tahat* below]

tushy or **tushie** /'tooshi/ *noun* (*pl* **tushies**) chiefly NAmer, informal a person's buttocks. [from TUSH[3]]

tusk[1] /tusk/ *noun* **1** a very long tapering tooth, *esp* one of a pair belonging to an elephant, walrus, boar, etc, that is visible when the animal's mouth is closed. It is used for digging for food or as a weapon. **2** something resembling a tusk, e.g. a pointed projection. ▶▶ **tusked** *adj.* [Old English *tūsc*, prob from early Frisian *tusk* a tooth]

tusk[2] *verb trans* to gash, gore, or wound (a person or animal) with a tusk.

tusker *noun* an animal, *esp* a male elephant or wild boar, with two prominent tusks.

tusk shell *noun* = TOOTH SHELL.

tussah /'tusə/ *noun* = TUSSORE.

tussie-mussie /'tusimusi/ *noun* a small bouquet of flowers or bunch of aromatic herbs. [origin unknown]

tussive /'tusiv/ *adj* technical relating to or involved in coughing. [Latin *tussis* cough + -IVE[1]]

tussle[1] /'tusl/ *verb intrans* to struggle or fight roughly. [Middle English, prob from dialect *touse* to handle roughly]

tussle[2] *noun* **1** a physical contest or rough fight. **2** a struggle, controversy, or argument.

tussock /'tusək/ *noun* a compact tuft of grass, sedge, etc. ▶▶ **tussocky** *adj.* [origin unknown]

tussock grass *noun* any of various grasses or sedges that typically grow in tussocks: *Deschampsia cespitosa* and other species.

tussock moth *noun* any of various mainly grey or brown woodland moths whose caterpillars are covered in prominent clumps of bristly hairs, which can sometimes cause severe irritation if handled: family Lymantriidae.

tussore /'tusaw/ *noun* a type of coarse silk produced by the larvae of various moths, *esp* the tussore moth, or a fabric made from this. [Hindi *tasar* from Sanskrit *tasara* a shuttle]

tussore moth *noun* any of various moths whose larvae produce a strong coarse brown or yellowish silk: *Antheraea paphia* and other species.

tut[1] /tut; or clicked t/ *interj* used to express disapproval or impatience.

tut[2] *verb intrans* (**tutted, tutting**) to express disapproval or impatience by uttering 'tut' or 'tut-tut'.

tutee /tyooh'tee/ *noun* somebody who is being tutored. [TUTOR[2] + EE[1]]

tutelage /'tyoohtilij/ *noun* **1** guardianship. **2** the state or period of being under a guardian or tutor. **3** instruction; tuition. [Latin *tutela* protection, guardian, from *tueri* to look at, guard, + -AGE]

tutelary[1] /'tyoohtiləri/ *adj* **1** having the guardianship of somebody or something: *a tutelary deity.* **2** relating to or denoting a guardian. [Latin *tutelarius*, from *tutela*: see TUTELAGE]

tutelary[2] *noun* (*pl* **tutelaries**) a tutelary power, e.g. a deity.

tutor[1] /'tyoohtə/ *noun* **1** a person employed as a private teacher, *esp* one who teaches individuals or small groups, often giving extra instruction or remedial help. **2a** *Brit* a university or college teacher who teaches a small group, often also having responsibility for students' welfare. **b** *NAmer* a junior university or college teacher, *esp* one without TENURE (secure employment status). **3** *Brit* an instruction book. ▶▶ **tutorage** /-rij/ *noun*, **tutorship** *noun*. [Middle English via French from Latin *tutor*, from Latin *tueri* to look at or guard]

tutor[2] *verb* (**tutored, tutoring**) ▶ *verb trans* to act as a tutor to (a person or group). ▶ *verb intrans* to work as a tutor.

tutorial[1] /tyooh'tawri-əl/ *noun* **1** a session of tuition given by a university or college tutor. **2** in computing, a teaching aid, often a series of on-screen interactive exercises, designed to familiarize a new user with a particular piece of software, equipment, etc.

tutorial[2] *adj* **1** relating to or denoting a tutor or the work of a tutor. **2** relating to or involving special or private tuition.

tutsan /'tutsən/ *noun* a Eurasian woodland plant with yellow flowers and red berries that turn black when ripe. Its large stalkless leaves have antiseptic properties and were formerly used in treating wounds: *Hypericum androsaemum.* [Anglo-French *toute-saine*, literally 'all healthy']

Tutsi /'toohtsi/ *noun* (*pl* **Tutsis** or collectively **Tutsi**) a member of a Bantu-speaking people inhabiting Rwanda and Burundi where they are one of the minority ethnic groups: compare HUTU. [the local name for this people in several Bantu languages]

tutti /'tooti/ *adj and adv* said of a piece of music: to be performed by all the instruments of the orchestra or all the voices of the choir. [Italian *tutti*, pl of *tutto* all, from Latin *totus*]

tutti-frutti /,toohti 'froohti/ *noun* (*pl* **tutti-fruttis**) a type of ice cream or confectionery containing a mixture of chopped, dried, or candied fruits. [Italian *tutti-frutti*, literally 'all fruits']

tut-tut[1] /,tut 'tut/ *interj* = TUT[1].

tut-tut[2] *verb intrans* (**tut-tutted, tut-tutting**) = TUT[2].

tutu[1] /'toohtooh/ *noun* a very short projecting stiff skirt worn by a ballerina. [French *cucu* backside, a children's alteration of *cul* buttocks, from Latin *culus*]

tutu[2] *noun* a New Zealand shrub with poisonous black berries: *Coriaria arborea.* [Maori *tutu*]

Tuvaluan /toovə'looh-ən/ *noun* **1** a native or inhabitant of Tuvalu, a country in the southwest Pacific comprising several coral islands. **2** the Austronesian language of the people of Tuvalu. ▶▶ **Tuvaluan** *adj.*

tu-whit tu-whoo /tə ,wit tə 'wooh/ *noun* the conventional representation of an owl's cry. [imitative]

tux /tuks/ *noun* chiefly NAmer, informal a tuxedo.

tuxedo /tuk'seedoh/ *noun* (*pl* **tuxedos** or **tuxedoes**) chiefly NAmer **1** a man's formal tailless dinner jacket. **2** a formal evening suit with this type of jacket. ▶▶ **tuxedoed** *adj.* [named after the country club, *Tuxedo* Park, in New York State, USA, where it was first worn]

tuyère /'tweeyeə (French tyijɛːr)/ *noun* a nozzle through which a blast of air is delivered to a forge or furnace. [French *tuyère*, from early French *tuyau* pipe]

TV *noun* television.

TV dinner *noun* a pre-packaged meal that only needs to be heated, in a conventional oven or microwave oven, before serving.

TVEI *abbr Brit* Training and Vocational Education Initiative.

TVP *abbr trademark* textured vegetable protein.

Twa /twah/ *noun* (*pl* **Twas** or collectively **Twa**) a member of an indigenous pygmy people inhabiting Rwanda, Burundi, and Zaire. ▶▶ **Twa** *adj.* [the local name for this people, literally 'foreigner']

twaddle[1] /'twodl/ *noun informal* trivial or nonsensical speech or writing; drivel. [alteration of English dialect *twattle*, of unknown origin]

twaddle[2] *verb intrans* archaic to speak or write twaddle. ▶▶ **twaddler** *noun*.

twain /twayn/ *noun* archaic two: *There is an old England and a new, and ye stand perplexed between the twain* — George Bernard Shaw. ✲ **in twain** archaic into two parts: *O Hamlet, thou hast cleft my heart in twain* — Shakespeare. [Old English *twēgen*: see TWO]

twang[1] /twang/ *noun* **1** a strong quick ringing sound like that of the string of a musical instrument being plucked or of a bowstring being released. **2** a distinctive nasal quality in the speech of a person or region: *a Glasgow twang.* ▶▶ **twangy** *adj.* [imitative]

twang[2] *verb intrans* **1** to make the sound of a twang. **2** to speak with a nasal twang. ▶ *verb trans* **1** to cause (*esp* a musical instrument or its strings) to make a twang. **2** to utter or pronounce (something) with a nasal twang.

'twas /twəz, strong twoz/ *contraction* archaic or literary it was.

twat /twat, twot/ *noun* coarse slang **1** a woman's genitals. **2** a stupid, obnoxious, or contemptible person. [origin unknown]

twayblade /'twayblayd/ *noun* any of various orchids that have a single pair of opposite leaves and a spike of small greenish or yellowish brown flowers: *Listera ovata* and related species. [English dialect *tway*, variant of TWAIN + BLADE]

tweak[1] /tweek/ *verb trans* **1** to pinch and pull (something) with a sudden strong jerking or twisting movement: *She tweaked his ear.* **2** *informal* to make fine adjustments to (something, *esp* a mechanical or electronic device). [prob ultimately from Old English *twiccian* to pluck, TWITCH[1]]

tweak[2] *noun* **1** an act of tweaking. **2** *informal* a fine adjustment.

twee /twee/ *adj* (**tweer, tweest**) *Brit* excessively or affectedly sentimental, pretty, cute, or coy. ➤➤ **tweely** *adv*, **tweeness** *noun*. [representation of a childish pronunciation of *sweet*]

tweed /tweed/ *noun* **1** a rough woollen fabric, orig produced in Scotland, often of a brownish or greenish colour flecked with other colours, and used *esp* for suits and coats. **2** (*in pl*) tweed clothing, *esp* a tweed suit. [alteration of Scottish *tweel*, variant of TWILL, prob influenced by the name of the River *Tweed* in Scotland]

Tweedledum and Tweedledee /tweedl,dum ən tweedl'dee/ *noun* two individuals or groups that are practically indistinguishable.

Word history
with reference to the two identical quarrelling characters in Lewis Carroll's *Through the Looking Glass* (1872). The names, however, were in common use for almost 150 years before Carroll adopted them. They originated in a satirical poem by John Byrom (1692–1763) on the rivalry between the musicians G F Handel and G B Bononcini: 'Strange! That such high dispute should be twixt Tweedledum and Tweedledee'. Here, Tweedledum and Tweedledee are imitations of piffling musical notes, used to suggest that the two composers are negligibly different and indifferently negligible.

tweedy *adj* (**tweedier, tweediest**) **1** made of tweed. **2** *informal* said of a person or group: enjoying country pursuits or holding staunchly conservative views. ➤➤ **tweedily** *adv*, **tweediness** *noun*.

tween *noun* = TWEENAGER.

'tween /tween/ *contraction archaic or literary* between.

tweenager /'tweenayjə/ *noun* a child who is not yet a teenager, *esp* one between the ages of eight and twelve.

'tween deck *or* **'tween decks** *noun* the space between the decks of a ship.

tweeny /'tweeni/ *noun* (*pl* **tweenies**) **1** *informal, archaic* a young female domestic servant. **2** (*also* **tweenie**) = TWEENAGER. [(1) a shortened form of *between maid*, so called because her duties involved assisting both the cook and the housemaid]

tweet[1] /tweet/ *verb intrans* to make the characteristic chirping sound of a small bird. [imitative]

tweet[2] *noun* a tweeting sound.

tweeter *noun* a small loudspeaker that mainly reproduces higher frequencies: compare WOOFER.

tweet tweet *verb intrans and noun* = TWEET[1], TWEET[2].

tweeze /tweez/ *verb trans* to pluck, remove, or handle (something) with or as if with tweezers. [back-formation from TWEEZERS]

tweezers *pl noun* (*also* **pair of tweezers**) a small pincer-like device used for plucking out hairs and handling small or delicate objects. [extended form of obsolete *tweeze* a case of small surgical instruments, from *etweese*, an anglicized plural of ETUI]

twelfth /twelfth/ *adj and noun* **1** denoting a person or thing having the position in a sequence corresponding to the number twelve. **2** one of twelve equal parts of something. **3** in music, an interval of twelve degrees of a diatonic scale, or the combination of two notes at such an interval. **4** (**the (Glorious) Twelfth**) in Britain, 12 August, the day on which the grouse-shooting season begins. [Old English *twelfta*, from *twelf* TWELVE + *ta* -TH[1]]

Twelfth Day *noun* 6 January, the feast of the Epiphany and the twelfth day after Christmas Day.

twelfth man *noun* the reserve member of a cricket team.

Twelfth Night *noun* **1** the evening of 5 January, traditionally the end of Christmas festivities. **2** = TWELFTH DAY.

twelve /twelv/ *noun* **1** the number 12, or the quantity represented by it. **2** something having twelve parts or members. **3a** the age of 12 years. **b** the hour of midday or midnight. **c** in Britain, a classification of cinema films only suitable for people of 12 years or over. **4** (**the Twelve**) the twelve Apostles. ➤➤ **twelve** *adj*, **twelvefold** *adj and adv*. [Old English *twelf(e)*]

twelvemo /'twelvmoh/ *noun* (*pl* **twelvemos**) = DUODECIMO. [TWELVE + *-mo* as in DUODECIMO]

twelvemonth *noun archaic* a year.

twelve-note *adj* relating to or denoting a system of composing music that treats the twelve chromatic notes of the octave equally, with no group of notes predominant as they are in the system of major and minor keys.

twelve-step[1] *adj* relating to or denoting a programme of twelve progressive stages designed to aid the recovery of addicts, people with eating disorders, etc, orig the system introduced by Alcoholics Anonymous for alcoholics.

twelve-step[2] *verb intrans* (**twelve-stepped, twelve-stepping**) said of an addict: to take part in a twelve-step programme of recovery. ➤➤ **twelve-stepper** *noun*, **twelve-stepping** *noun*.

twelve-tone *adj* = TWELVE-NOTE.

twenty /'twenti/ *adj and noun* (*pl* **twenties**) **1** the number 20, or the quantity represented by it. **2** (*in pl*) the numbers 20 to 29; *specif* a range of temperatures, ages, or dates within a century characterized by these numbers. ➤➤ **twentieth** *adj and noun*. [Old English *twēntig* group of 20, from *twēgen* two + *tig* group of 10]

twenty-four-hour clock *noun* a system of measuring time in which the hours of the day are numbered from one to 24, rather than in two sets of twelve.

twenty-four-seven *or* **24–7** *or* **24/7** *adv chiefly NAmer, informal* 24 hours a day, seven days a week; constantly: *You can't watch your teenage kids twenty-four-seven.*

twenty-one *noun* the card game pontoon.

twenty-twenty *or* **20/20** *adj* said of a person's sight: of normal acuity; perfect. [so called because of the practice of testing the vision of each eye separately to assess its capacity to distinguish characters on a chart 20ft (about 6m) away]

'twere /twə, *strong* twuh/ *contraction archaic or literary* it were.

twerp *or* **twirp** /twuhp/ *noun informal* an absurd, stupid, or contemptible person. [origin unknown]

Twi /twee, chee/ *noun* (*pl* **Twis** *or collectively* **Twi**) **1** a member of an indigenous people inhabiting southern parts of Ghana. **2** the dialect of Akan spoken by this people. ➤➤ **Twi** *adj*. [the Akan name for this people]

twibill /'twibil/ *noun archaic* a battle-axe with two blades. [Old English *twibile*, from *twi-* double + BILL[5]]

twice /twies/ *adv* **1** on two occasions: *I visit him twice a week.* **2** in doubled quantity or degree: *Twice two is four; I should have made twice as much.* [Middle English *twiges*, from Old English *twi* two + *-s*[1]]

twiddle[1] /'twidl/ *verb intrans* **1** (*often* + with) to play absentmindedly with something; to fiddle with it. **2** *archaic* to turn or twirl lightly. ➤ *verb trans* to rotate or twist (something) lightly or idly: *He twiddled the knob on the radio.* * **twiddle one's thumbs** to have nothing to do; to be bored or idle. ➤➤ **twiddler** *noun*. [prob imitative, perhaps a blend of TWIRL[1] or TWIST[1] + FIDDLE[2]]

twiddle[2] *noun* **1** an act or an instance of twiddling. **2** in music, a rapid or intricate series of notes. ➤➤ **twiddly** *adj*.

twig[1] /twig/ *noun* **1** a small woody shoot or branch of a tree or bush, usu without its leaves. **2** something that resembles this, *esp* a slender branch of an anatomical structure such as a blood vessel or nerve. ➤➤ **twigged** *adj*, **twiggy** *adj*. [Old English *twigge*]

twig[2] *verb* (**twigged, twigging**) ➤ *verb intrans Brit, informal* **1** to notice or observe something. **2** to grasp or understand something; to catch on. ➤ *verb trans archaic* to perceive or observe (something). [perhaps from Scottish Gaelic *tuig* I understand]

twilight /'twieliet/ *noun* **1a** the soft shadowy or glowing light between sunset and the full darkness of the night. **b** the period between sunset and full night. **2a** a period or state of obscurity or decline: *Her best work was actually produced in the twilight of her career.* **b** any intermediate or undefined state. [Middle English, from Old English *twi* two, half + LIGHT[1]]

twilighted /'twielietid/ *adj* twilit.

twilight sleep *noun* a condition of semiconsciousness, usu lasting a few hours and induced by drugs, alcohol, epilepsy, or severe shock or trauma, in which some degree of awareness is retained, but memory of the period is often non-existent or distorted.

twilight zone *noun* **1** any state or area characterized by ambiguity, despair, or decline: *that vast number of people caught in* *the twilight zone between middle-class comfort and the lumpen-proletariat* — Peter Stead. **2** a decaying urban area. **3** the lowest level of the ocean where light can still be seen to penetrate.

twilit /'twielit/ *adj* lit by or as if by twilight.

twill /twil/ *noun* **1** a weave that produces fabric with slightly raised parallel diagonal lines. **2** a fabric with this type of weave. ➤ **twilled** *adj.* [Old English *twilic* having a double thread]

'twill /twil/ *contraction archaic or literary* it will.

twin[1] /twin/ *noun* **1a** either of two offspring born to the same mother at the same birth: see FRATERNAL (2), IDENTICAL (3). **b** (*used before a noun*) relating to or denoting a person or animal that is a twin: *a twin sister.* **2a** either of two people or things corresponding to or resembling each other. **b** (*used before a noun*) relating to or denoting two people or things of this kind: *twin engines.* **3** a compound crystal composed of two or more parts of the same kind that have a definite orientation to each other. [Old English *twinn* double, twofold, from *twi* two]

twin[2] *verb* (**twinned, twinning**) ➤ *verb trans* **1** (+ with) to link or pair (one thing) with another. **2** *Brit* (+ with) to associate (a town in one country) officially with a town in another, *esp* in order to promote cultural, commercial, etc exchange. ➤ *verb intrans* **1** to become paired or closely associated. **2** said of a crystal: to grow as or become a twin. ➤➤ **twinned** *adj,* **twinning** *noun.*

twin bed *noun* either of a pair of matching single beds. ➤➤ **twin-bedded** *adj.*

twine[1] /twien/ *noun* **1** strong string, *esp* of a kind made from two or more strands twisted together. **2** a twisted, coiled, or interlaced part or object. [Old English *twīn* thread, from *twi* two, referring to the two strands]

twine[2] *verb trans* **1** to twist (two or more things) together. **2** to form (something) by twisting or weaving. ➤ *verb intrans* **1** (*usu* + round/around) to coil round or encircle something: *Ivy had twined around the tree trunk.* **2** to follow a winding course; to meander: *The river twines through the valley.* ➤➤ **twiner** *noun.*

twin-engine *adj* said of an aircraft: powered by two engines.

twinflower *noun* a low-growing creeping evergreen shrub with fragrant, pendulous, bell-shaped flowers arranged in pairs: *Linnaea borealis* and *Linnaea americana.*

twinge[1] /twinj/ *noun* **1** a sudden sharp stab of pain. **2** a moral or emotional pang: *I had a twinge of conscience.* [Old English *twengan* to tweak or squeeze]

twinge[2] *verb intrans* (**twingeing** *or* **twinging**) said of a part of the body: to suffer or be affected by a twinge.

twinkle[1] /'twingkl/ *verb intrans* **1** said of a star, light, precious stone, etc: to shine with a flickering or sparkling effect. **2** said of a person's eyes: to have a bright sparkle, *esp* as a sign of amusement, mischief, etc. **3** to move lightly and rapidly: *He danced with twinkling feet.* ➤➤ **twinkler** *noun.* [Old English *twinclian* to flicker]

twinkle[2] *noun* **1** a flickering or sparkling effect. **2** a flash or gleam, *esp* in a person's eye: *'Wait and see,' she said with a twinkle in her eye.* ➤➤ **twinkly** *adj.*

twinkletoed *adj informal* said of a person, *esp* a dancer: very quick, nimble, and graceful. ➤➤ **twinkletoes** *noun.*

twinkling *noun* an instant: *The kettle will boil in a twinkling* — Punch. ✳ **in a/the twinkling of an eye** immediately or very quickly.

twin-lens reflex *noun* (*used before a noun*) denoting a camera having two identical lenses that either work together to produce stereoscopic images or work independently, one producing the viewfinder image and the other producing the image that will form the photograph.

Twins *noun* (**the Twins**) the constellation and sign of the zodiac Gemini.

twin-screw *adj* said of a ship: fitted with two propellers, *esp* on separate shafts with their spirals going in opposite directions.

twin set *noun chiefly Brit* a woman's jumper and cardigan designed to be worn together.

twin-tub *noun* a type of washing machine with two separate top-loading drums, one for washing the laundry and the other for spinning it dry.

twirl[1] /twuhl/ *verb trans and intrans* to revolve, or cause (something) to revolve, rapidly. ➤➤ **twirler** *noun.* [perhaps a blend of TWIST[1] and WHIRL[1], influenced by obsolete *trill* a spin]

twirl[2] *noun* **1** an act of twirling. **2** a coiled or spiralling shape, *esp* a decorative one, e.g. an embellishment on a written letter or character. ➤➤ **twirly** *adj.*

twirp /twuhp/ *noun* see TWERP.

twist[1] /twist/ *verb trans* **1a** to join (two or more things or parts) together by winding: *Twist the strands of wool together.* **b** to combine (things or parts) by interlacing; to interweave. **2** to twine or coil (something). **3** to cause (something or somebody) to move with a rotating motion. **4** to bend (something) in a specified way: *The officers twisted the man's arms behind his back.* **5** to form (something) into a spiral shape. **6** to pull off, turn, or break (something) by twisting. **7** to wring or wrench (a joint) painfully; *esp* to sprain. **8** to distort the meaning of (e.g. facts). **9** to contort (something): *He twisted his face into an ugly grin.* **10** to make (somebody or something) abnormal; to debase: *a twisted and embittered society.* **11** *Brit, informal* to cheat (somebody). ➤ *verb intrans* **1** to follow a winding course. **2** to assume a spiral shape. **3** to turn or change shape under bending or wrenching. **4** to squirm or writhe: *The boy managed to twist himself free.* **5** to dance the twist. **6** to turn round: *I twisted round to see who was coming.* **7** in the card game pontoon, to request another card from the dealer. ✳ **twist somebody round one's little finger** see FINGER[1]. **twist somebody's arm** *informal* to persuade or force a person to do something. [Old English]

twist[2] *noun* **1** an act or an instance of twisting. **2a** something with a spiral shape. **b** a strong sewing thread with tightly twisted strands. **c** tobacco twisted into a thick roll. **d** a strip of citrus peel used to flavour a drink: *gin and tonic with a twist of lemon.* **e** *Brit* a piece of paper twisted to form a small sachet, e.g. to hold salt. **f** a type of carpet with a tightly curled pile. **3** (**the twist**) a dance, first popular in the 1960s, featuring exaggerated twisting movements of the body, *esp* the hips and legs. **4a** force causing twisting or turning applied to a body, e.g. a rod or shaft. **b** the angle through which a thing is twisted. **5** a turn, curve, or bend: *a twist in the path.* **6a** an unexpected turn or development: *a twist of fate; a short story with a twist at the end.* **b** a different approach or method: *a modern twist on an old theme.* **7** *Brit, informal* a swindle. ✳ **get one's knickers in a twist** see KNICKERS. **round the twist** *Brit, informal* completely mad. ➤➤ **twisty** *adj.*

twist drill *noun* a drill bit having deep spiral grooves extending from the cutting edges to the smooth portion of the shank.

twister *noun* **1** *Brit, informal* a dishonest person; a cheat or swindler: *Young master Harold's turned out to be the little twister he always was* — Angus Wilson. **2** *chiefly NAmer* a tornado. **3** somebody or something that twists.

twit[1] /twit/ *noun chiefly Brit, informal* a silly or stupid person. ➤➤ **twittish** *adj.* [from TWIT[2], orig in the sense 'censure, teasing', later 'a person given to teasing or telling tales']

twit[2] *verb trans* (**twitted, twitting**) *informal* to tease or ridicule (somebody), *esp* light-heartedly. [Old English *ætwītan* to reproach, from *æt* with or against + *wītan* to blame, from *witan* to know]

twitch[1] /twich/ *verb trans* **1** to move (something) with a sudden jerky motion. **2** to pull or tug (something). ➤ *verb intrans* to move jerkily or involuntarily: *A muscle below his eye twitched.* [Old English *twiccian* to pluck]

twitch[2] *noun* **1** a twitching movement. **2** a physical or emotional pang; a twinge. **3** a loop of rope or a strap that is tightened over a horse's upper lip as a restraining device.

twitcher *noun Brit, informal* a birdwatcher, *esp* one dedicated to finding rare birds and logging their sightings.

twitch grass *noun* = COUCH GRASS. [alteration of QUITCH]

twitchy *adj* (**twitchier, twitchiest**) **1** *informal* nervous or anxious. **2** said of a muscle, eye, etc: inclined to twitch.

twite /twiet/ *noun* a northern European moorland finch with yellowish brown plumage streaked with darker brown and black: *Acanthis flavirostris.* [imitative of its call]

twitter[1] /'twita/ *verb intrans* (**twittered, twittering**) **1** said of a bird: to make a series of quick tremulous or chirping sounds. **2** to talk quickly, *esp* in a nervous or giggling way or about trivial things. ➤➤ **twitterer** *noun.* [imitative]

twitter[2] *noun* **1** a twittering sound. **2** nervous, giggling, or trivial chatter. ✳ **all of/in a twitter** *informal* in a state of nervous agitation; quivering. ➤➤ **twitterer** *noun,* **twittery** *adj.*

'twixt /twikst, 'twixt/ *contraction* betwixt.

twizzle[1] /'twizl/ *verb trans and intrans informal or dialect* to spin, or cause (something) to spin, round and round. [imitative, prob influenced by TWIST[1]]

twizzle[2] *noun* a twizzling movement.

two /tooh/ *noun* **1** the number 2, or the quantity represented by it. **2** something having two parts or members. **3a** the age of 2 years. **b** the hour two hours after midday or midnight. **4** an unspecified small number: *It'll just take a minute or two.* ✳ **put two and two together** to use the available evidence, or separate pieces of information, to draw a conclusion, *esp* an obvious one. **that makes two of us** *informal* we are both of the same opinion or in the same situation; the same is also true for me. **two by/and two** in pairs, *esp* side by side. **two can play at that game** *informal* used to state forcibly that the speaker will resort to the same unfair tactics, etc. ⟫⟫ **two** *adj,* **twofold** *adj and adv.* [Old English *twā,* fem and neuter of *twēgen*]

Usage note ─────────

two, too, *or* to? See note at TO[1].

two-bit *adj NAmer, informal* worthless, insignificant, or contemptible. [from TWO BITS]

two bits *pl noun chiefly NAmer, informal* **1** a quarter of a dollar or a coin of this value. **2** any small unspecified sum.

two-by-four *noun* **1** a length of trimmed timber that measures two inches by four inches in cross-section. **2** *NAmer, W Ind* a small, petty, or worthless thing.

twoc /twok/ *verb trans* (**twocced, twoccing**) *Brit, slang* to steal (a car), *esp* for joyriding. ⟫⟫ **twoccer** *noun.* [acronym, orig police slang, from *taken without owner's consent,* the legal offence that a suspected car thief is charged with]

two-dimensional *adj* **1** having two dimensions, *esp* having, or appearing to have, length and breadth but no depth. **2** said of a person, fictional character, etc: lacking depth; superficial. ⟫⟫ **two-dimensionality** *noun,* **two-dimensionally** *adv.*

two-edged *adj* = DOUBLE-EDGED.

two-faced *adj* insincere, double-dealing, or hypocritical.

two-fisted *adj NAmer, informal* characterized by vigorous energy or great enthusiasm; aggressive.

two-handed *adj* **1** designed to be used with both hands: *a two-handed sword.* **2** requiring two people: *a two-handed saw.* **3** ambidextrous.

two-hander *noun* a play with only two actors.

two-horse *adj* said of a race, contest, etc: in which there are only two likely winners.

twoness *noun* the state or fact of being a pair.

twopence *or* **tuppence** /'tup(ə)ns/ *noun Brit* **1** the sum of two pence, *esp* before decimalization in 1971. **2** *informal* (used with negatives) a small amount; anything at all: *He said he didn't care twopence what I thought.*

twopenn'orth /tooh'penəth/ *noun* **1** an amount worth or costing two pence. **2** any small amount or value. ✳ **add/put in one's twopenn'orth** *informal* to have one's say; to make one's contribution to a discussion, etc. [contraction of *twopenny worth*]

twopenny *or* **tuppenny** /'tup(ə)ni/ *adj Brit* costing or worth two pence, *esp* before decimalization in 1971.

twopenny-halfpenny /,tup(ə)ni 'haypni/ *adj Brit, informal* worthless or insignificant.

two-phase *adj* said of an electricity supply: generating or using two alternating currents with voltages that are 90° out of phase with one another.

two-piece[1] *adj* said of clothing: having two matching or suitably contrasting parts, usu one top part and one bottom part, that are designed to be worn together: *a two-piece suit.*

two-piece[2] *noun* a two-piece garment, e.g. a swimming costume or suit.

two-ply *adj* consisting of two strands, layers, or thicknesses: *two-ply wool.*

twosome /'toohs(ə)m/ *noun* **1** a group of two people or things. **2** a sports match, *esp* in golf, played between two people.

two-step *noun* a fast ballroom dance in duple time characterized by sliding steps.

two-stroke *adj* relating to or denoting an internal-combustion engine with a power cycle that is completed in a single up-and-down movement of a piston.

two-time *verb trans informal* **1** to be unfaithful to (a partner or lover) by having a relationship with somebody else: *His brief relationship with a page three girl ... hit the skids when the press revealed that the bold Frank was two-timing her for another model* — Stuart Cosgrove. **2** to cheat or double-cross (somebody). ⟫⟫ **two-timer** *noun.*

two-tone *adj* **1** having two colours or two shades of one colour: *two-tone shoes.* **2** having two sounds or tones: *a two-tone siren.*

two-toned *adj* = TWO-TONE.

'twould /twɪd, *strong* twood/ *contraction archaic* it would.

two-up *noun Aus, NZ* a game in which players bet on the fall of tossed coins.

two-up two-down *noun Brit, informal* a house with two rooms, usu bedrooms, upstairs, and two rooms, usu a living room and a dining room, downstairs.

two-way *adj* **1** relating to, denoting, or involving movement, communication, etc that goes in two opposite directions: *a two-way bridge.* **2** involving two participants. ✳ **a two-way street** a situation that involves mutual responsibility or a reciprocal relationship.

two-way mirror *noun* a piece of glass that reflects an image from one side and can be seen through from the other.

two-way switch *noun* either of two electrical switches, e.g. at the top and bottom of a stairway, controlling a single device, *esp* a light.

two-wheeler *noun* a vehicle with two wheels, e.g. a bicycle or motorcycle.

TX *abbr* Texas (US postal abbreviation).

-ty[1] *suffix* forming words, denoting: the group of ten specified: *twenty; fifty.* [Old English *-tig* a group of ten]

-ty[2] *suffix* forming nouns, denoting: a state, quality, or condition: *cruelty.* [via French, from Latin *-tat-, -tas*]

tychism /'tiekiz(ə)m/ *noun* in philosophy, the theory that chance must be accepted as an objective reality. [Greek *tukhē* chance]

tycoon /tie'koohn/ *noun* **1** a person in business or industry who has exceptional wealth and power; a magnate. **2** a title given by foreigners to the shogun of Japan who ruled between 1857 and 1868. [Japanese *taikun* a great ruler, from Chinese (Pekingese) *da* great + *jun* ruler]

tying /'tieing/ *verb* present part. of TIE[1].

tyke *or* **tike** /tiek/ *noun* **1** *informal* a small child, *esp* a cheeky or mischievous one. **2** *chiefly Brit, dated* a boorish, coarse, or churlish person, *esp* a man. **3** a dog, *esp* a scruffy mongrel. **4** *Brit, informal* a person from Yorkshire. **5** *Aus, NZ, informal, derog* a Roman Catholic. [Middle English from Old Norse *tík* bitch]

tympan /'timpən/ *noun* **1** in letterpress printing, a layer of paper or packing material placed between the impression surface of a press and the paper to be printed in order to give equal pressure over the whole FORME (frame containing printing type). **2** = TYMPANUM. [Middle English via French from Latin *tympanum*: see TYMPANUM]

tympana /'timpənə/ *noun* pl of TYMPANUM.

tympani /'timpəni/ *noun* see TIMPANI.

tympanic /tim'panik/ *adj* **1** relating to or in the region of the tympanum. **2** resembling a drumhead in form or function.

tympanic bone *noun* a bone enclosing part of the middle ear and supporting the tympanic membrane.

tympanic membrane *noun* a thin membrane separating the outer ear from the middle ear; the eardrum. It receives sound waves and transmits them to the site of sensory reception.

tympanites /timpə'nieteez/ *noun* a distension of the abdomen caused by accumulation of gas in the intestinal tract or peritoneal cavity. ⟫⟫ **tympanitic** /-'nitik/ *adj.* [Middle English via Latin from Greek *tympanitēs,* from *tympanon* a drum]

tympanum /'timpənəm/ *noun* (*pl* **tympana** /-nə/ *or* **tympanums**) **1a** the cavity of the middle ear. **b** = TYMPANIC MEMBRANE. **2** in architecture: **a** the recessed triangular face of a pediment. **b** the space within an arch and above a lintel, e.g. in a medieval doorway. [via Latin from Greek *tympanon* a drum]

tympany /'timpəni/ *noun* = TYMPANITES. [via Latin from Greek *tympanon* a drum]

Tynwald /'tinwəld/ *noun* the Parliament of the Isle of Man. [Old Norse *thingvollr* place of assembly, from *thing* assembly, parliament + *vollr* field]

type[1] /tiep/ *noun* **1a** a class or group of people, animals, or things that share similar characteristics; a kind or variety. **b** a person or thing that is considered to be representative of such a class or group. **c** *informal* a person who has a specified characteristic, nature, etc: *He's the quiet type.* **2a** a category of living organisms that is selected as a reference for a higher category, usu the subgroup most perfectly exemplifying the higher category: *a type species.* **b** = TYPE SPECIMEN. **3a** a small metal block with a raised letter or other character on its upper surface, used in printing. **b** a set of such blocks. **c** printed characters, words, etc: *This section is in italic type.* **4** a figure or device on either side of a coin or medal. **5** the form common to all instances of a word or other linguistic form: compare TOKEN[1] (6). **6** in theology, a person or event, e.g. in the Old Testament, regarded as foreshadowing another, e.g. in the New Testament. **7** (*used in combinations*) resembling: *Cheddar-type cheese.* >> **typal** *adj.* [French *type* via Latin *typus* from Greek *typos* an impression, model, or figure, from *typtein* to strike]
Usage note
type, kind, *and* sort. See note at KIND[1].

type[2] *verb trans* **1** to write (something) using a typewriter or computer. **2** to determine the class of (something, *esp* blood or tissue). >> **typing** *noun.*

typecast *verb trans* (*past tense and past part.* **typecast**) **1** to cast (an actor) repeatedly in the same kind of role, *esp* because of previous successes in such roles. **2** to stereotype (somebody or something).

typeface *noun* in printing, a particular style or design of type.

typefounder *noun* a person who designs and produces metal printing type for hand composition. >> **typefoundry** *noun.*

type metal *noun* an alloy of lead, antimony, and tin, used in making printing type.

typescript *noun* a typed copy of a text.

typeset *verb trans* (**typesetting,** *past tense and past part.* **typeset**) to arrange the printing type for (a text). >> **typesetter** *noun,* **typesetting** *noun.*

type specimen *noun* a single specimen or individual that is designated as the reference for a species or lesser group in the biological classification of living organisms, and whose characteristics are used for the description of members of that group.

typewrite /'tiepriet/ *verb trans* (*past tense* **typewrote** /'tieproht/, *past part.* **typewritten** /'tiepritn/) to write (something) using a typewriter. [back-formation from TYPEWRITER]

typewriter *noun* a machine with a keyboard for writing in characters resembling printed type.

typewritten /'tiepritn/ *verb* past part. of TYPEWRITE.

typewrote /'tieproht/ *verb* past tense of TYPEWRITE.

typhlitis /ti'flietəs/ *noun* inflammation of the CAECUM (pouch connected to large intestine). >> **typhlitic** /ti'flitik/ *adj.* [scientific Latin, from Greek *typhlon* caecum + -ITIS]

typhoid /'tiefoyd/ *noun* a serious infectious bacterial disease characterized by fever, spots, diarrhoea, headache, and intestinal inflammation. >> **typhoidal** *adj.* [from TYPHUS + -OID]

typhoid fever *noun* = TYPHOID.

typhoon /tie'foohn/ *noun* a violent tropical storm, *esp* one occurring in the Indian or W Pacific oceans. >> **typhonic** /tie'fonik/ *adj.* [partly from Chinese (Pekingese) *tai feng* great wind, partly via Portuguese and Arabic from Greek *typhōn* whirlwind]

typhus /'tiefəs/ *noun* an infectious disease marked by high fever, stupor alternating with delirium, intense headache, and a dark red rash. It is caused by rickettsiae (micro-organisms resembling bacteria; see RICKETTSIA) and transmitted *esp* by body lice. >> **typhous** /'tiefəs/ *adj.* [via Latin from Greek *typhos* smoke, stupor, from *typhein* to smoke]

typical /'tipikl/ *adj* **1a** combining or exhibiting the essential characteristics of a type: *These are typical suburban houses.* **b** characteristic of somebody or something, *esp* showing the usual unfavourable trait: *It's just typical of him to complain.* **2** conforming to a

biological type, *esp* having all or most of the essential characteristics of a particular biological category. **3** constituting or having the nature of a type; symbolic. >> **typicality** /-'kaliti/ *noun,* **typically** *adv.*

typify /'tipifie/ *verb trans* (**typifies, typified, typifying**) to be typical of (somebody or something). >> **typification** /-fi'kaysh(ə)n/ *noun,* **typifier** *noun.*

typist /'tiepist/ *noun* a person who uses a typewriter, *esp* somebody employed to type letters, etc.

typo /'tiepoh/ *noun* (*pl* **typos**) *informal* a printing error. [short for *typographical error*]

typographer /tie'pogrəfə/ *noun* **1** somebody who sets type; a compositor. **2** a specialist in the design and arrangement of printed matter.

typography /tie'pogrəfi/ *noun* the style, arrangement, or appearance of printed matter. >> **typographic** /-'grafik/ *adj,* **typographical** /-'grafikl/ *adj,* **typographically** /-'grafikli/ *adv.* [from Latin *typographia,* from *typus* (see TYPE[1]) + -graphia -GRAPHY]

typology /tie'poləji/ *noun* (*pl* **typologies**) **1** a classification according to general type, *esp* in the fields of archaeology, psychology, biology, and social science. **2** the study or analysis and classification of types, *esp* in theology. >> **typological** /-'lojikl/ *adj,* **typologist** *noun.*

tyramine /'tierəmin/ *noun* a chemical compound found in cheese and various other foods that can cause some types of high blood pressure: formula $C_8H_{11}NO$. [blend of TYROSINE + AMINE]

tyrannical /ti'ranikl/ *adj* **1** relating to, denoting, or characteristic of a tyrant or tyranny: *tyrannical rule.* **2** characterized by oppressive, unjust, or arbitrary behaviour or control. >> **tyrannic** *adj,* **tyrannically** *adv.*

tyrannicide /ti'ranisied/ *noun* **1** the act of killing a tyrant. **2** a person who kills a tyrant. >> **tyrannicidal** /-'siedl/ *adj.* [French *tyrannicide* from Latin *tyrannicida* a killer of a tyrant, from *tyrannus* (see TYRANT) + -cida -CIDE]

tyrannize *or* **tyrannise** /'tirəniez/ *verb trans* to treat (a person, people, etc) cruelly or oppressively. >> *verb intrans* (*usu* + over) to rule with cruel or oppressive power. >> **tyrannizer** *noun.*

tyrannosaur /ti'ranəsaw/ *or* **tyrannosaurus** /-'sawrəs/ *noun* a very large flesh-eating dinosaur of the Cretaceous period that had small forelegs and walked on its hind legs. [Latin genus name *Tyrannosaurus,* from Greek *tyrannos* TYRANT + *sauros* lizard]

tyranny /'tirəni/ *noun* (*pl* **tyrannies**) **1a** rule or government that is cruel or oppressive. **b** a state under such rule. **2a** any form of cruel or oppressive treatment. **b** a cruel or oppressive act. **3** rule by a tyrant, *esp* in ancient Greece. >> **tyrannous** *adj,* **tyrannously** *adv.* [Middle English via French from Latin *tyrannia,* from *tyrannus:* see TYRANT]

tyrant /'tierənt/ *noun* **1** a cruel or oppressive ruler. **2** any person who exerts cruel or oppressive power or control. **3** a ruler who takes absolute power without any legal right, *esp* in ancient Greece. [Middle English via French from Latin *tyrannus,* from Greek *tyrannos* an illegal or oppressive ruler]

tyrant flycatcher *noun* any of numerous species of large American flycatchers that have a flattened bill, often hooked at the tip: family Tyrannidae. [so called because of the aggressive behaviour it exhibits towards other birds]

tyre (*NAmer* **tire**) /tie-ə/ *noun* **1a** a solid or inflated hollow rubber cushion fitted round a wheel to absorb shock and improve traction. **b** the external covering of a pneumatic tyre that has an inner tube. **2** a metal hoop that forms a strengthening band around a wheel, *esp* of a horse-drawn wagon or a railway carriage. [Middle English, perhaps a shortened form of ATTIRE[2], because it formed the covering of a wheel]

Tyrian /'tiri-ən/ *noun* a native or inhabitant of Tyre, an ancient Phoenician city and port in present-day Lebanon. >> **Tyrian** *adj.*

Tyrian purple *noun* a crimson or purple dye related to indigo, obtained by the ancient Greeks and Romans from gastropod molluscs, and now made synthetically. [named after *Tyre:* see TYRIAN]

tyro *or* **tiro** /'tieroh/ *noun* (*pl* **tyros** *or* **tiros**) a beginner or novice: *It is a strange sight to the tyro to see with what wondrous habitude of unconscious skill the whaleman will maintain an erect posture in his boat* — Herman Melville. [Latin *tiro* young soldier, novice]

Tyrolean /tirə'lee·ən/ *noun* a native or inhabitant of the Alpine district of Tyrol, a region lying partly in W Austria and partly in N Italy. ▶▶ **Tyrolean** *adj.*

Tyrolese /tirə'leez/ *noun* = TYROLEAN.

tyrosine /'tierəseen/ *noun* an amino acid found in most proteins and important in the synthesis of certain hormones. [Greek *tyros* cheese + -INE²]

Tyrrhenian /ti'reeni·ən/ *noun* a native or inhabitant of Tyrrhene, an ancient name for the Italian region of Etruria. ▶▶ **Tyrrhenian** *adj.*

tzar /zah, tsah/ *noun* see TSAR.

tzarevich /'zahrəvich/ *noun* see TSAREVICH.

tzarina /zah'reenə/ *noun* see TSARINA.

tzatziki /tsat'seeki/ *noun* a dip or side dish that originated in Greece, made from yoghurt, cucumber, and garlic, often flavoured with mint. [Greek *tzatziki*]

tzedakah /tse'dahka/ *noun* the donation of money or gifts to charity, regarded as a moral obligation in Jewish communities. [Hebrew *sedāqāh* righteousness]

Tzeltal /(t)sel'tahl, '(t)seltahl/ *noun* (*pl* **Tzeltals** or *collectively* **Tzeltal**) **1** a member of an indigenous people inhabiting parts of S Mexico. **2** the Mayan language spoken by this people. ▶▶ **Tzeltal** *adj.* [the Spanish name for one of the three regions that form the Mexican state of *Chiapas*]

tzigane /(t)si'gahn/ *noun* (*pl* **tziganes** or *collectively* **tzigane**) a Hungarian gypsy. ▶▶ **tzigane** *adj.* [French *tzigane* from Hungarian *c(z)igány*]

tzimmes /'tsiməs/ *noun* see TSIMMES.

Tzotzil /(t)soh'tzil, '(t)sohtzil/ *noun* (*pl* **Tzotzils** or *collectively* **Tzotzil**) **1** a member of an indigenous people inhabiting parts of S Mexico. **2** the Mayan language spoken by this people. ▶▶ **Tzotzil** *adj.* [the Tzotzil name for this people]

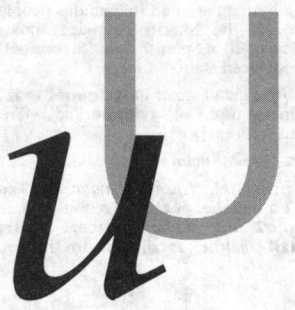

U¹ *or* **u** *noun* (*pl* **U's** *or* **Us** *or* **u's**) **1a** the 21st letter of the English alphabet. **b** a written character or design denoting this letter. **c** the sound represented by this letter, one of the English vowels. **2** an item designated as U, *esp* the 21st in a series.

U² *abbr* **1** Unionist. **2** United. **3** university. **4** Uruguay (international vehicle registration).

U³ *abbr* the chemical symbol for uranium.

U⁴ *noun* **1** in Britain, a classification of cinema films suitable for all age groups. **2** (*used before a noun*) of or being such a film. [short for UNIVERSAL¹]

U⁵ *adj chiefly Brit, informal* said of an accent, or language or behaviour, etc: characteristic of the upper classes.

Word history ────────────
short for UPPER-CLASS. The terms U and NON-U were invented by Prof. Alan Ross in 1954, in an article entitled *Linguistic class indicators in present-day English*, published in a Finnish philological journal; they were popularized by Nancy Mitford d.1973, English writer and editor, who quoted them in a popular magazine in 1955 and later published a condensed version of Prof. Ross's article.

u *abbr* **1** unit. **2** upper.

UA *abbr* Ukraine (international vehicle registration).

UAE *abbr* United Arab Emirates.

UAR *abbr* United Arab Republic.

UB40 /'yooh bee 'fawti/ *noun* (*pl* **UB40's** *or* **UB40s**) **1** in Britain, a card issued to somebody registered as unemployed. **2** *informal* somebody registered as unemployed.

U-bend *noun* a U-shaped bend in a pipe, *esp* one in the waste pipe of a sink that prevents bad smells escaping.

Übermensch /'oobəmensh/ *noun* (*pl* **Übermenschen** /-shən/) in Nietzschean philosophy, an ideal human being who, in the future, would be able to use their passions creatively, instead of having to suppress them in order to follow Christian teachings, and, by doing this, would be able to formulate their own moral code. [German *Übermensch*, literally 'over man', from *über* super + *Mensch* man, a back-formation from *übermenschlich* superhuman; from *Thus Spake Zarathustra*, a book by Friedrich Nietzsche (d.1900), German philosopher]

ubiety /yooh'bieiti/ *noun literary* the state of being in a definite place. [Latin *ubi* where + *-ety* as in SOCIETY]

ubiquitarian /yoo,bikwi'teəri·ən/ *noun* a Christian, *esp* a member of the Lutheran Church, who believes that Christ is present in all places at all times. ➤ **ubiquitarian** *adj*, **ubiquitarianism** *noun*. [Latin *ubique* everywhere, from *ubi* where + -ARIAN]

ubiquitous /yoo'bikwitəs/ *adj* existing or seeming to be everywhere at the same time; frequently encountered.

➤➤ **ubiquitously** *adv*, **ubiquitousness** *noun*, **ubiquity** *noun*. [Latin *ubique* everywhere, from *ubi* where + -OUS]

U-boat *noun* a German submarine, *esp* as used in World Wars I and II. [translation of German *U-Boot*, short for *Unterseeboot*, from *unter* under + *See* sea + *Boot* boat]

UBR *abbr* uniform business rate.

UC *abbr* University College.

u.c. *abbr* upper case.

UCAS /'yoohkas/ *abbr Brit* Universities and Colleges Admissions Service.

UCATT /'yoohkat/ *abbr* Union of Construction, Allied Trades, and Technicians.

UDA *abbr* Ulster Defence Association.

udal /'yoohdl/ *noun* in law, *esp* in Orkney and Shetland, freehold possession of land passed on by inheritance. [Old Norse *othal*]

UDC *abbr Brit* **1** Urban Development Corporation. **2** formerly, Urban District Council.

udder /'udə/ *noun* a large bag-like organ, e.g. of a cow, consisting of two or more mammary glands enclosed in a common structure and each having a single nipple. [Old English *ūder*]

UDI *abbr* unilateral declaration of independence.

UDM *abbr* Union of Democratic Mineworkers.

UDR *abbr* Ulster Defence Regiment.

UEFA /yooh'eefə, yooh'ayfə/ *abbr* Union of European Football Associations.

UFO /'yoohfoh, ,yooh ef 'oh/ *noun* (*pl* **UFO's** *or* **UFOs**) an unidentified flying object, *esp* one popularly believed to be of extraterrestrial origin. [short for *unidentified flying object*]

ufology /yooh'foləji/ *noun* the study of unidentified flying objects. ➤ **ufologist** *noun*.

Ugandan /yoo'gandən/ *noun* a native or inhabitant of Uganda in E Africa. ➤➤ **Ugandan** *adj*.

Ugaritic /oohgə'ritik/ *noun* an ancient extinct Semitic language formerly spoken by the people of Ugarit, a port in N Syria. ➤ **Ugaritic** *adj*.

UGC *abbr Brit* University Grants Committee.

ugh /ookh, ukh/ *interj informal* used to express disgust or horror.

Ugli /'ugli/ *noun* (*pl* **Uglis** *or* **Uglies**) *trademark* a large citrus fruit that is a cross between a grapefruit and a tangerine. [prob alteration of UGLY; from its unattractive wrinkled skin]

Ugli fruit *noun* = UGLI.

uglify /'uglifie/ *verb* (**uglifies, uglified, uglifying**) ➤ *verb trans* to make (something or somebody) ugly or uglier. ➤ *verb intrans* to become ugly or uglier. ➤➤ **uglification** /-fi'kaysh(ə)n/ *noun*.

ugly /'ugli/ *adj* (**uglier, ugliest**) **1** offensive or displeasing to any of the senses, *esp* to the sight. **2** morally offensive or objectionable. **3a** ominous; threatening: *an ugly customer; ugly weather.* **b** surly; quarrelsome: *an ugly disposition.* **c** frightful; horrible: *an ugly wound.* >> **uglily** *adv,* **ugliness** *noun.* [Middle English from Old Norse *uggligr* frightful, terrifying, from *uggr* fear]

ugly duckling *noun* somebody or something that appears unattractive or unpromising but turns out to be admirable or successful. [from *The Ugly Duckling,* story by Hans Christian Andersen d.1875, Danish writer, in which an ugly young bird thought to be a duckling grows into a beautiful swan]

Ugrian /'oohgri-ən, 'yooh-/ *noun* **1** a member of a group of indigenous peoples inhabiting Hungary and western parts of Siberia. **2** = UGRIC. >> **Ugrian** *adj.* [Old Russian *Ugre* Hungarians]

Ugric /'oohgrik, 'yoohgrik/ *noun* a group of languages, forming a branch of the Finno-Ugric family, spoken by the Ugrians, including Hungarian and two languages of Siberia. >> **Ugric** *adj.*

UHF *abbr* ultrahigh frequency.

uh-huh /,u 'hu/ *interj* used to indicate affirmation or agreement.

uhlan /'oohlahn, 'yoohlahn/ *noun* any of a body of European light cavalry, orig modelled on Tartar lancers. [German *Uhlan* from Polish *ulan,* from Turkish *oglan* boy, servant]

UHT *abbr* said of milk or cream: ultraheat-treated.

Uighur *or* **Uigur** /'weegə/ *noun* (*pl* **Uighurs** *or* **Uigurs,** *or collectively* **Uighur** *or* **Uigur**) **1** a member of an indigenous people inhabiting northwest China. **2** the Turkic language spoken by this people. >> **Uighurian** *adj,* **Uighuric** *adj.*

uillean pipes /'ilin, 'oohli-ən/ *pl noun* Irish bagpipes played by working bellows under the arm. [Irish *píob uilleann,* from *píob* pipe + *uilleann* of the elbow, from *uille* elbow]

uitlander /'aytlandə, owt-/ *noun* (*also* **Uitlander**) *SAfr* a foreigner, *esp* a British resident in the former republics of the Transvaal and Orange Free State. [via Afrikaans from Dutch *Uitlander,* from *uit* out + *land* land]

UK *abbr* United Kingdom.

UKAEA *abbr* United Kingdom Atomic Energy Authority.

ukase /yooh'kayz/ *noun* **1** a proclamation by a Russian emperor or government having the force of law. **2** an edict. [French *ukase* from Russian *ukaz,* from *ukazat'* to show, order]

Ukrainian /yoo'krayni-ən/ *noun* **1** a native or inhabitant of Ukraine. **2** the Slavonic language of the people of Ukraine. >> **Ukrainian** *adj.*

ukulele /yoohkə'layli/ *noun* a small usu four-stringed guitar of Portuguese origin, popularized in light music and often conveying a Hawaiian atmosphere. [Hawaiian *'ukulele,* from *'uku* small person, flea + *lele* jumping]

ulama *noun* see ULEMA.

-ular *suffix* forming adjectives, with the meaning: of or resembling: *angular.* [Latin *-ularis,* from *-ulus, -ula, -ulum* -ULE + *-aris* -AR[1]]

ulcer /'ulsə/ *noun* **1** an open sore on the skin or a mucous membrane, often one that discharges pus and is slow to heal. **2** something that festers and corrupts: *This jail was a Noah's ark of the city's crime – there were murderers, 'hold-up men', burglars ... They were the drainage of the great festering ulcer of society* — Upton Sinclair. >> **ulcerous** /-rəs/ *adj.* [Middle English from Latin *ulcer-, ulcus*]

ulcerate /'ulsərayt/ *verb intrans* **1** to develop into an ulcer. **2** to become affected with or as if with an ulcer. >> *verb trans* to cause (something) to do this. >> **ulceration** /-'raysh(ə)n/ *noun,* **ulcerative** /-tiv/ *adj.*

-ule *suffix* forming nouns, denoting: a small kind of a specified thing: *granule.* [via French from Latin *-ulus, -ula, -ulum,* dimin. suffixes]

ulema *or* **ulama** /'oohlimə/ *noun* **1** (*treated as sing. or pl*) a body of theologians and scholars who are experts in Islamic theology and sacred law. **2** a member of such a body. [Turkish and Persian *'ulemā,* from Arabic *'ulamā,* plural of *'ālim* learned, from *'āhma* to know]

-ulent *suffix* forming adjectives, with the meaning: full of the thing specified: *succulent; corpulent.* [Latin *-ulentus*]

ullage /'ulij/ *noun* **1** the amount by which a container is less than full. **2a** loss of a liquid through evaporation, leakage, etc. **b** the amount of liquid lost through this. [Middle English *ulage* from early French *eullage* act of filling a cask, from *eullier* to fill a cask, from Old French *ouil* eye, bunghole, from Latin *oculus* eye]

ulna /'ulnə/ *noun* (*pl* **ulnae** /'ulnee/ *or* **ulnas**) **1** the bone of the human forearm on the side of the little finger: compare RADIUS[1] (4). **2** a corresponding part of the forelimb of other mammals, birds, reptiles, and amphibians. >> **ulnar** *adj.* [Latin *ulna* elbow]

ulster /'ulstə/ *noun* a long loose overcoat made of heavy material, often with a belt or half belt and usu worn by men: *A man passed him in the mist, walking very fast, and with the collar of his grey ulster turned up* — Oscar Wilde. [named after *Ulster,* ancient kingdom and former province of Ireland, where it was first produced]

Ulsterman *or* **Ulsterwoman** *noun* (*pl* **Ulstermen** *or* **Ulsterwomen**) a native or inhabitant of Northern Ireland or Ulster.

ult. *abbr* **1** ultimate. **2** ultimo.

ulterior /ul'tiəri-ə/ *adj* **1** underlying or going beyond what is openly said or shown; intentionally concealed: *ulterior motives.* **2a** further or future. **b** more distant or remote. >> **ulteriorly** *adv.* [Latin *ulterior* farther, further, compar of (assumed) Latin *ulter:* see ULTIMATE[1]]

ultima /'ultimə/ *noun* the last syllable of a word. [Latin *ultima,* fem of *ultimus:* see ULTIMATE[1]]

ultimata /ulti'maytə/ *noun* pl of ULTIMATUM.

ultimate[1] /'ultimət/ *adj* **1a** last in a progression or series: *Their ultimate destination was Paris.* **b** eventual: *ultimate success.* **2a** fundamental; basic: *ultimate reality.* **b** incapable of further analysis, division, or separation. **3** maximum; greatest: *the ultimate sacrifice.* >> **ultimately** *adv,* **ultimateness** *noun.* [late Latin *ultimatus* last, final, past part. of *ultimare* to come to an end, be last, from Latin *ultimus* farthest, last, final, superl of (assumed) Latin *ulter* situated beyond, from *uls* beyond]

ultimate[2] *noun* **1** (*usu* **the ultimate**) the most extreme, significant, important, etc of its kind: *the ultimate in stupidity.* **2** a basic fact or principle.

ultimate fighting *noun* a combat sport combining the moves of boxing, wrestling, and kickboxing, and of martial arts such as judo and karate.

ultima Thule /,ultimə 'th(y)oohli/ *noun* a remote and unknown region. [Latin *ultima Thule* farthest Thule, from Greek *Thoulē* land at the northernmost point of the world]

ultimatum /ulti'maytəm/ *noun* (*pl* **ultimatums** *or* **ultimata** /-tə/) a final proposition, condition, or demand, *esp* one whose rejection will end negotiations and cause a resort to direct action or retaliation. [late Latin *ultimatum,* neuter of *ultimatus:* see ULTIMATE[1]]

ultimo /'ultimoh/ *adj formal, dated* used in business correspondence: of or occurring in the previous month: compare INSTANT[1], PROXIMO. [Latin *ultimo mense* in the last month]

ultra[1] /'ultrə/ *adj* going beyond others or beyond due limits; extreme. [from ULTRA-]

ultra[2] *noun* an extremist.

ultra- *prefix* forming words, with the meanings: **1** beyond in space; on the other side of: *ultramontane; ultraplanetary.* **2** beyond the range or limits of; transcending: *ultramicroscopic; ultrasound.* **3** excessively; extremely: *ultramodern.* [Latin *ultra-* from *ultra* (adv and prep) beyond, from (assumed) Latin *ulter:* see ULTIMATE[1]]

ultracentrifuge /ultrə'sentrifyoohj/ *noun* a high-speed centrifuge that causes colloidal and other small particles to separate from and settle at the bottom of a liquid and is used *esp* in determining the size of such particles.

ultrafiche /'ultrəfeesh/ *noun* (*pl* **ultrafiche** *or* **ultrafiches**) a form of microfiche with many more compressed images on it than the normal microfiche.

ultrahigh frequency /ultrə'hie/ *noun* (*also* **UHF**) a radio frequency in the range between 300 megahertz and 3000 megahertz.

ultraism /'ultraiz(ə)m/ *noun* the principles of those who advocate extreme measures; extremism. >> **ultraist** *adj and noun.*

ultramarine[1] /,ultramə'reen/ *noun* **1** a vivid deep blue pigment formerly made by powdering lapis lazuli. **2** the vivid deep blue colour of this. [late Latin *ultramarinus* coming from beyond the sea, from ULTRA- + Latin *mare* sea. The pigment was formerly made from lapis lazuli imported from Asia]

ultramarine[2] *adj* **1** of a vivid deep blue colour. **2** *archaic* situated or coming from beyond the sea.

ultramicroscope /ultrə'miekrəskohp/ *noun* an apparatus using scattered light to make visible particles that are too small to be perceived by the ordinary microscope. [back-formation from ULTRAMICROSCOPIC]

ultramicroscopic /ˌʌltrəmiekrəˈskopik/ *adj* **1** too small to be seen with an ordinary microscope. **2** of an ultramicroscope.

ultramodern /ˌʌltrəˈmodən/ *adj* having the very latest ideas, styles, etc. ⟫⟫ **ultramodernist** *noun*.

ultramontane[1] /ˌʌltrəmonˈtayn/ *adj* **1** of countries or peoples beyond the Alps or other mountains. **2** favouring greater or absolute supremacy of papal authority over national or diocesan authority in the Roman Catholic Church. ⟫⟫ **ultramontanism** /-ˈmontəniz(ə)m/ *noun*. [late Latin *ultramontanus*, from ULTRA- + Latin *mont-, mons* MOUNTAIN]

ultramontane[2] *noun* **1** (*also* **Ultramontane**) somebody from beyond the Alps or other mountains. **2** a supporter or advocate of supreme papal authority.

ultramundane /ˌʌltrəmunˈdayn/ *adj chiefly literary* situated or existing beyond the earth or the solar system. [Latin *ultramundanus*, from *ultra* beyond + *mundus* world]

ultrasonic[1] /ʌltrəˈsonik/ *adj* **1** said of waves and vibrations: having a frequency above the range of the human ear, e.g. above about 20,000Hz. **2** using or produced by ultrasonic waves or vibrations: *an ultrasonic dog whistle.* ⟫⟫ **ultrasonically** *adv*.

ultrasonic[2] *noun* an ultrasonic wave or frequency.

ultrasonics *pl noun* (*treated as sing.*) the scientific study or technology of ultrasonic waves or vibrations.

ultrasound /ˈʌltrəsownd/ *noun* **1** ultrasonic waves or vibrations. **2a** the use of ultrasonic waves or vibrations in therapy or diagnostics, e.g. to examine internal bodily structures. **b** a medical examination using this technique.

ultrastructure /ˈʌltrəstrukchə/ *noun* the minute structure of biological material as revealed by a microscope, *esp* an electron microscope.

ultraviolet[1] /ʌltrəˈvie·ələt/ *noun* electromagnetic radiation having a wavelength between the violet end of the visible spectrum and X-rays.

ultraviolet[2] *adj* relating to, producing, or employing ultraviolet: *an ultraviolet lamp.*

ultraviolet light *noun* = ULTRAVIOLET[1].

ultra vires /ˈviereez/ *adv and adj* beyond the legal power or authority of a person or body. [Latin *ultra vires*, literally 'beyond the powers']

ululate /ˈyoohlyoolayt/ *verb intrans* to howl or wail, *esp* as an expression of grief. ⟫⟫ **ululant** *adj*, **ululation** /-ˈlaysh(ə)n/ *noun*. [Latin *ululatus*, past part. of *ululare* to howl, of imitative origin]

umbel /ˈumb(ə)l/ *noun* a flower cluster typical of plants of the carrot family in which the flower stalks arise from a central point to form a flat or rounded surface of small flowers. ⟫⟫ **umbellate** *adj*. [Latin *umbella* sunshade, dimin. of *umbra* shade]

umbellifer /umˈbelifə/ *noun* any of a family of plants, such as the carrot, parsley, fennel, and parsnip, that have hollow stems, flower heads made up of simple or compound umbels, and fruits that split into two one-seeded portions: family Umbelliferae. ⟫⟫ **umbelliferous** /-ˈlifərəs/ *adj*. [scientific Latin *umbellifer* bearing umbels, from Latin *umbel*: see UMBEL]

umber /ˈumbə/ *noun* **1** an earthy substance, rich in oxides of iron and manganese, that is greenish brown when raw and dark brown when burned and is used to colour paint, ink, etc. **2** the dark brown or yellowish brown colour of burnt umber. ⟫⟫ **umber** *adj*. [French *terre d'ombre* or Italian *terra di ombra*, literally 'earth of shadow', from Latin *umbra* shade, shadow]

umbilical /umˈbilikl, -ˈliekl/ *adj* **1** relating to or in the region of the navel. **2** relating to or in the region of the umbilical cord. **3** of or being a tethering or supply line. [scientific Latin *umbilicalis*, from Latin *umbilicus* navel]

umbilical cord *noun* **1** a ropelike tube that connects a foetus with the placenta and is detached at the navel after birth. **2a** a cable conveying power to a rocket or spacecraft before takeoff. **b** a tethering or supply line, e.g. for an astronaut outside a spacecraft or a diver underwater.

umbilicate /umˈbilikət, -kayt/ *adj* **1a** shaped like a navel. **b** having a central depression. **2** having an umbilicus. ⟫⟫ **umbilication** /-ˈkaysh(ə)n/ *noun*.

umbilicus /umˈbilikəs, -ˈliekəs/ *noun* (*pl* **umbilici** /-sie/ *or* **umbilicuses**) **1** *technical* a small depression on the surface of the abdomen at the point where the umbilical cord was attached; the navel. **2** any of several depressions comparable to an umbilicus, e.g. one at the base of some gastropod shells. [Latin *umbilicus* navel]

umbles /ˈumb(ə)lz/ *pl noun archaic* the entrails of an animal, *esp* a deer, formerly used as food. [Middle English, alteration of *nombles* the back and loins, later also the entrails, of a deer, from early French *nomble* fillet of beef, pork loin, modification of Latin *lumbulus*, dimin. of *lumbus* loin]

umbo /ˈumboh/ *noun* (*pl* **umbones** /umˈbohneez/ *or* **umbos**) **1** the BOSS[4] (raised central ornament) of a shield. **2** a rounded anatomical elevation. ⟫⟫ **umbonal** /umˈbohnl, ˈumbənl/ *adj*, **umbonate** /umˈbohnət, ˈumbənayt/ *adj*. [Latin *umbo* shield boss]

umbra /ˈumbrə/ *noun* (*pl* **umbras** *or* **umbrae** /ˈumbree/) **1** a region of total shadow, e.g. in an eclipse. **2** the central dark region of a sunspot. ⟫⟫ **umbral** *adj*. [Latin *umbra* shade, shadow]

umbrage /ˈumbrij/ *noun* **1** a feeling of pique or resentment: *She took umbrage at the chairman's comment.* **2** *archaic*. **a** shade or shadow, *esp* when cast by trees. **b** shady branches; foliage.

Word history ——————
Middle English via French from Latin *umbraticum*, neuter of *umbraticus* of shade, from *umbrare* to shade, from *umbra* shade, shadow. Orig in sense 2a, later (17th cent.) 'shadowy appearance, a suspicion or glimmering of something', hence 'grounds for suspicion', giving rise to sense 1.

umbrageous /umˈbrayjəs/ *adj* **1** inclined to take offence easily. **2** *archaic* shadowy or shady.

umbrella /umˈbrelə/ *noun* **1** a collapsible circular shade for protection against rain, consisting of fabric stretched over hinged ribs radiating from a central rod. **2** the bell-shaped or saucer-shaped largely gelatinous structure that forms the chief part of the body of most jellyfishes. **3** something that provides protection or cover: *the umbrella of the welfare state.* **4** something that covers or embraces a broad range of elements or factors: *the Electricity Council: umbrella of the area electricity boards* — The Economist. **5** a protective screen, *esp* of aircraft artillery or gunfire. [Italian *ombrella*, modification of Latin *umbella*, dimin. of *umbra* shade]

umbrella pine *noun* = STONE PINE.

umbrella tree *noun* **1** an American magnolia having large leaves clustered at the ends of the branches: *Magnolia tripetala*. Also called SCHEFFLERA. **2** any of various trees or shrubs resembling an umbrella in the arrangement of leaves: genus *Schefflera*.

Umbrian /ˈumbri·ən/ *noun* **1a** a native or inhabitant of the Italian province of Umbria. **b** a member of an indigenous people of ancient Italy that inhabited Umbria. **2** the extinct Italic language of the people of ancient Umbria. ⟫⟫ **Umbrian** *adj*.

umiak /ˈoohmiak/ *noun* an open boat made of a wooden frame covered with hide, traditionally paddled by Inuit women. [Inuit *umiaq*]

umlaut /ˈoomlowt/ *noun* **1** a mark (¨) placed over a vowel, *esp* to show a change of quality caused e.g. by the influence of a vowel in the following syllable. **2** the change indicated by such a mark or the result of this change. [German *Umlaut*, from *um-* round, transformation + *Laut* sound]

umpire[1] /ˈumpie·ə/ *noun* **1** a referee in any of several sports, e.g. cricket and table tennis. **2** a person who has the authority to settle a controversy or question between parties. [Middle English *oumpere*, alteration (by incorrect division) of *noumpere*, from early French *nomper* not equal, not paired, from NON- + *per* equal, from Latin *par*]

umpire[2] *verb trans* to act as umpire in (a match or dispute). ⟫ *verb intrans* to act as an umpire.

umpteen /umpˈteen/ *adj and noun informal* very many; an indefinitely large number. ⟫⟫ **umpteenth** *adj*. [blend of *umpty* so many + -TEEN]

UN *abbr* United Nations.

un *or* **'un** /ən/ *pronoun dialect* one; a person or thing of a specified type: *He's a strange 'un.* [by alteration]

un-[1] *prefix* forming adjectives, nouns, and adverbs, with the meanings: **1** not; lack of something: *unskilled; unbelief.* **2** opposite of or contrary to something: *ungrateful; unrest.* [Old English]

Usage note ——————
un- *and* non-. Both these prefixes are used to produce negative forms of words. In cases where they can both be attached to the same root, the resulting *un-* word is generally stronger than the *non-* word. A *non-*

professional tutor is one who is not qualified; *unprofessional* behaviour contravenes professional ethics. If somebody's methods are described as *unscientific*, a criticism is usually implied (the methods do not come up to the standards required by science); if they are described as *non-scientific*, the effect is usually more neutral (the methods come from some other field than science).

---

un-² *prefix* forming verbs, with the meanings: **1** the opposite or reversal of the action specified: *unbend; undress; unfold.* **2a** deprivation or removal of something: *unfrock; unsex; unnerve.* **b** release from something: *unhand; untie.* **c** extraction from something: *unearth; unsheathe.* **d** removal or dislodgment from something: *unhorse; unseat.* **3** completeness: *unloose.* [Old English *un-, on-*, alteration of *and-* against]

UNA *abbr* United Nations Association.

unabashed *adj* not embarrassed, ashamed, or humbled.

unabated *adj* at full strength or force; undiminished. ⟫⟫ **unabatedly** *adv.*

unable /un'aybl/ *adj* not able; incapable, unqualified, or powerless: *unable to help.*

unabridged *adj* not abridged; complete: *the unabridged version of the story.*

unaccented /unak'sentid/ *adj* **1** without stress or emphasis, e.g. in pronunciation: *unaccented notes of the bar.* **2** not marked with an accent: *unaccented letters.*

unacceptable *adj* **1** not satisfactory; not good enough. **2** not tolerable or permissible: *an unacceptable state of affairs.* ⟫⟫ **unacceptability** /-'biliti/ *noun,* **unacceptably** *adv.*

unaccompanied *adj* **1** alone, *esp* having no companion or escort; not accompanied, *esp* by an adult: *unaccompanied children.* **2** without piano or other instrumental accompaniment: *an unaccompanied violin sonata.*

unaccountable *adj* **1** inexplicable; strange. **2** not to be called to account; not responsible. ⟫⟫ **unaccountability** /-'biliti/ *noun,* **unaccountably** *adv.*

unaccounted *adj* (+ for) not explained or taken into account.

unaccustomed *adj* **1** not customary; not usual or common. **2** (+ to) not used to (something). ⟫⟫ **unaccustomedly** *adv.*

unacknowledged *adj* **1** in existence or having taken place but lacking acceptance or acknowledgment. **2** lacking the appropriate or deserved level of recognition.

una corda /,oohnə 'kawdə/ *adv and adj* said of piano music: to be performed with the soft pedal depressed. [Italian *una corda*, literally 'one string'; the soft pedal on a grand piano shifts the hammers so that they strike only one string for each note]

unacquainted *adj* **1** (+ with) lacking experience of or familiarity with (somebody or something). **2** never having met.

unadjusted *adj* said of information, *esp* statistical data: without any adjustments having been made or taken into account.

unadopted *adj Brit* said of a road: not maintained by a local authority.

unadulterated *adj* **1** unmixed, *esp* with anything inferior; pure. **2** complete; utter.

unadventurous *adj* **1** lacking the inclination to do or try new or different things. **2** not offering any challenges. ⟫⟫ **unadventurously** *adv.*

unadvised *adj* not prudent; indiscreet or rash: compare ADVISED, ILL-ADVISED, WELL-ADVISED. ⟫⟫ **unadvisedly** /-zidli/ *adv.*

unaffected *adj* **1** not influenced or changed by something. **2** free from affectation; genuine. ⟫⟫ **unaffectedly** *adv,* **unaffectedness** *noun.*

unaffiliated *adj* said of a person or group: not belonging or connected to an organization, *esp* a trade union or political party; independent.

unaffordable *adj* too expensive, *esp* for the average person.

unaided *adj* not requiring any help or done without assistance: *her own unaided work.*

unalienable *adj* = INALIENABLE.

unaligned *adj* **1** said of two or more things: not arranged in such a way as to be in a straight line or in the correct place relative to each other. **2** = NON-ALIGNED.

unalterable *adj* not capable of being altered or changed: *an unalterable resolve.* ⟫⟫ **unalterableness** *noun,* **unalterably** *adv.*

unambiguous *adj* not ambiguous; clear or precise. ⟫⟫ **unambiguously** *adv.*

un-American *adj* **1** not consistent with US customs, principles, or traditions; *broadly* radical or subversive. **2** acting against the interests of the USA, *esp* formerly by sympathizing with Communism or being a member of the Communist Party. ⟫⟫ **un-Americanism** *noun.*

unanimous /yoo'nanimas/ *adj* **1** being of one mind; all agreeing. **2** characterized by or having the agreement and consent of all: *a unanimous decision.* ⟫⟫ **unanimity** /yoohnə'nimiti/ *noun,* **unanimously** *adv.* [Latin *unanimus,* from *unus* one + *animus* mind]

unannounced *adj* **1** happening without warning; sudden and unexpected: *his unannounced arrival.* **2** not publicized.

unanswerable *adj* **1** said of a question: having no answer. **2** incapable of being argued against; irrefutable. ⟫⟫ **unanswerably** *adv.*

unappealing *adj* not appealing; unattractive or uninviting. ⟫⟫ **unappealingly** *adv.*

unappetizing or **unappetising** *adj* not appetizing; insipid or unattractive. ⟫⟫ **unappetizingly** *adv.*

unapproachable *adj* **1** aloof or unfriendly. **2** physically inaccessible. ⟫⟫ **unapproachability** /-'biliti/ *noun,* **unapproachably** *adv.*

unapt *adj* **1** unsuitable; inappropriate. **2** not accustomed and not likely: *a man unapt to tolerate carelessness.* **3** slow to learn; unintelligent: *unapt scholars.* ⟫⟫ **unaptly** *adv,* **unaptness** *noun.*

unarmed *adj* **1** without weapons; not armed or armoured: *unarmed combat.* **2** said of a plant or animal: having no spines, spurs, claws, etc.

unashamed *adj* without guilt or embarrassment. ⟫⟫ **unashamedly** /-midli/ *adv.*

unasked *adj* **1** not asked or invited. **2** not sought or asked for: *unasked advice.*

unassailable *adj* **1** not open to doubt or question. **2** not able to be attacked. **3** not able to be challenged or overtaken: *an unassailable lead.* ⟫⟫ **unassailability** /-'biliti/ *noun,* **unassailably** *adv.*

unassisted *adj* not assisted; acting or done without help.

unassuming *adj* not arrogant or presumptuous; modest. ⟫⟫ **unassumingly** *adv,* **unassumingness** *noun.*

unattached *adj* **1** not assigned, committed, or connected, e.g. to a particular task or organization. **2** not involved in a serious or established romantic or sexual relationship. **3** not joined or united: *unattached buildings.*

unattended *adj* **1** not cared for or looked after. **2** not dealt with.

unattractive *adj* not attractive, pleasing, or inviting. ⟫⟫ **unattractively** *adv,* **unattractiveness** *noun.*

unauthorized or **unauthorised** *adj* without official approval or permission: *an unauthorized biography.*

unavailable *adj* not available; not capable of being obtained, contacted, etc. ⟫⟫ **unavailability** /-'biliti/ *noun.*

unavailing *adj* futile; useless. ⟫⟫ **unavailingly** *adv.*

unavoidable *adj* not avoidable; inevitable. ⟫⟫ **unavoidability** /-'biliti/ *noun,* **unavoidably** *adv.*

unaware¹ *adj* (*often* + of) not aware; ignorant or lacking knowledge. ⟫⟫ **unawareness** *noun.*

unaware² *adv* = UNAWARES.

unawares /unə'weəz/ *adv* **1** without noticing or intending. **2** suddenly; unexpectedly. [UN-¹ + AWARE + -s, adv suffix, from Middle English -s, genitive sing. ending of nouns]

unbacked *adj* **1** lacking support or aid. **2** said of a horse: having no backers in betting. **3** having no back or backing: *an unbacked chair.*

unbalance¹ *verb trans* **1** to put (something or somebody) out of balance. **2** to derange (somebody) mentally.

unbalance² *noun* lack of balance; imbalance or instability.

unbalanced *adj* **1** not in equilibrium. **2** mentally disordered or deranged. **3** not adjusted so as to make credits equal to debits: *an unbalanced account.* **4** not giving equal treatment to both sides or aspects; biased or partial: *an unbalanced report.*

unbar *verb trans* (**unbarred, unbarring**) to remove a bar from (e.g. a door); to unlock or open (it).

unbearable *adj* not endurable; intolerable. ➤➤ **unbearably** *adv.*

unbeatable *adj* **1** not able to be defeated or surpassed. **2** outstandingly good of its kind. ➤➤ **unbeatably** *adv.*

unbeaten *adj* not defeated or surpassed: *an unbeaten record.*

unbecoming *adj* **1** not attractive or flattering: *an unbecoming dress.* **2** improper; unseemly: *unbecoming conduct.* ➤➤ **unbecomingly** *adv,* **unbecomingness** *noun.*

unbeknown /unbi'nohn/ *adj* (+ to) happening without the knowledge of (somebody). [UN-¹ + obsolete *beknown* known]

unbeknownst /unbi'nohnst/ *adj* = UNBEKNOWN.

unbelief *noun* incredulity or scepticism, *esp* in matters of religious faith.

unbelievable *adj* **1** too improbable for belief; incredible. **2** extraordinary, *esp* exceptionally good or bad. ➤➤ **unbelievably** *adv.*

unbeliever *noun* somebody who does not believe, *esp* in a particular religion.

unbelieving *adj* marked by unbelief; sceptical. ➤➤ **unbelievingly** *adv.*

unbend *verb* (*past tense and past part.* **unbent** /un'bent/) ➤ *verb trans* **1** to return (something) to a straight position: *She unbent her cramped fingers.* **2a** to unfasten (e.g. a sail) from a spar or stay. **b** to cast loose or untie (e.g. a rope). ➤ *verb intrans* **1** to become more relaxed, informal, or outgoing in manner: *Then the great man unbent. His face beamed* — Samuel Butler; *Mrs Saunders so far unbent as to remark to Mrs Crick that the evening had been a fine one* — Saki. **2** to become straight.

unbending *adj* **1** unyielding; inflexible: *his unbending will; an unbending rule.* **2** aloof or unsociable in manner: *Never ... had she seen him so desirous to please, so free from self-consequence or unbending reserve* — Jane Austen. ➤➤ **unbendingly** *adv,* **unbendingness** *noun.*

unbent /un'bent/ *verb* past tense and past part. of UNBEND.

unbiased *or* **unbiassed** *adj* free from all prejudice and partiality.

unbidden *adj* **1** unasked or uninvited. **2** voluntary or spontaneous.

unbind *verb trans* (*past tense and past part.* **unbound** /un'bownd/) **1** to untie or unfasten (something or somebody). **2** to set (somebody or something) free.

unbirthday *noun humorous* any day that is not a person's birthday. [coined by Lewis Carroll d.1898, English novelist, in *Through the Looking Glass*]

unblemished *adj* not having or marred by flaws, faults, errors, etc: *an unblemished record.*

unblinking *adj* showing no signs of emotion. ➤➤ **unblinkingly** *adv.*

unblushing *adj* showing no shame or embarrassment. ➤➤ **unblushingly** *adv.*

unbolt *verb trans* to open or unfasten (e.g. a door) by withdrawing a bolt.

unborn *adj* **1** not yet born: *her unborn child.* **2** still to appear; future: *unborn ages.*

unbosom *verb trans* **1** to disclose the thoughts or feelings of (oneself). **2** to give expression to (thoughts, feelings, etc).

unbound¹ *adj* **1** not fastened or confined. **2a** not having the leaves fastened together: *an unbound book.* **b** having no binding or case: *unbound periodicals.* [UN-¹ + BOUND⁴]

unbound² *verb* past tense and past part. of UNBIND.

unbounded *adj* having no limits or constraints. ➤➤ **unboundedly** *adv,* **unboundedness** *noun.*

unbowed /un'bowd/ *adj* not bowed down, *esp* not subdued.

unbranded *adj* **1** said of livestock: without an owner's brand mark. **2** said of consumer goods: without a brand name.

unbreakable *adj* not capable of being broken.

unbridgeable *adj* **1** said of a gap: too wide to be bridged. **2** said of a difference in opinions, outlooks, etc: extreme and unlikely to be resolved.

unbridled *adj* **1** unrestrained; uncontrolled: *unbridled joy.* **2** said of a horse: not confined by a bridle.

unbroken *adj* **1** whole; intact. **2** not beaten or surpassed: *an unbroken record.* **3** said of an animal, *esp* a horse: not subdued or

tamed, *esp* not trained for riding or draught: *unbroken colts.* **4** uninterrupted. **5** not disorganized or in disarray: *The troops advanced in unbroken ranks.* ➤➤ **unbrokenly** *adv,* **unbrokenness** *noun.*

unbuckle *verb trans* to undo the buckle of (e.g. a belt).

unbundle *verb trans* to divide (something composite) into its constituent parts, *esp* to split up (a conglomerate company) with a view to selling some of the subsidiaries. ➤➤ **unbundler** *noun,* **unbundling** *noun.*

unburden *verb trans* (**unburdened, unburdening**) **1** to free or relieve (somebody) from or as if from a burden. **2** to relieve (oneself, one's conscience, etc) of cares, fears, worries, etc, *esp* by relating them to somebody else.

unbutton *verb* (**unbuttoned, unbuttoning**) ➤ *verb trans* to undo the buttons of (a garment). ➤ *verb intrans informal* to become free from constraint, tension, etc; to relax. ➤➤ **unbuttoned** *adj.*

uncalled-for *adj* **1** not needed; unnecessary. **2** offered without provocation or justification; gratuitous: *an uncalled-for display of temper.*

uncanny /un'kani/ *adj* (**uncannier, uncanniest**) **1** eerie; mysterious. **2** beyond what is normal or expected: *an uncanny sense of direction.* ➤➤ **uncannily** *adv,* **uncanniness** *noun.*

uncap *verb trans* (**uncapped, uncapping**) **1** to remove a cap or covering from (e.g. a bottle); to open (it). **2** to remove a previously set upper limit on (something, *esp* a cost).

uncapped *adj* said of a sports player: never having been selected to play for the national side.

uncared-for *adj* not looked after; neglected.

uncaring /un'keəring/ *adj* not solicitous, sympathetic, or concerned: *uncaring parents.*

unceasing *adj* never ceasing; continuous or incessant. ➤➤ **unceasingly** *adv.*

unceremonious *adj* **1** not ceremonious; informal. **2** abrupt or rude: *an unceremonious dismissal.* ➤➤ **unceremoniously** *adv,* **unceremoniousness** *noun.*

uncertain *adj* **1a** not definitely known; undecided or unpredictable: *The outcome is uncertain.* **b** not confident or sure; doubtful: *uncertain of the truth.* **2** not reliable or trustworthy. **3** variable; changeable: *uncertain weather.* ✱ **in no uncertain terms** forcefully and without ambiguity. ➤➤ **uncertainly** *adv,* **uncertainness** *noun.*

uncertainty *noun* (*pl* **uncertainties**) **1** the state of being uncertain; doubt. **2** something uncertain.

uncertainty principle *noun* a principle in quantum mechanics stating that it is impossible to determine both the momentum and the position of a particle, e.g. a photon, at the same time.

unchangeable *adj* not changing or able to be changed; immutable. ➤➤ **unchangeability** /-'biliti/ *noun,* **unchangeableness** *noun,* **unchangeably** *adv.*

unchanging *adj* constant; invariable. ➤➤ **unchangingly** *adv.*

uncharacteristic *adj* not characteristic; not typical or distinctive: *It was uncharacteristic of him to refuse.* ➤➤ **uncharacteristically** *adv.*

uncharitable *adj* severe in judging others; harsh or unkind. ➤➤ **uncharitableness** *noun,* **uncharitably** *adv.*

uncharted *adj* said of an area of land or sea: not recorded or plotted on a map, chart, or plan; *broadly* unknown or unexplored.

unchartered *adj* **1** not authorized or regulated. **2** without a charter.

unchecked *adj* said *esp* of something undesirable: allowed to progress or develop without control or restraint.

unchivalrous *adj* not chivalrous; lacking in courtesy or consideration. ➤➤ **unchivalrously** *adv.*

unchristian *adj* **1** contrary to the teachings or spirit of Christianity. **2** barbarous, uncivilized, or pagan. ➤➤ **unchristianly** *adv.*

unchurch *verb trans* **1** to excommunicate (somebody). **2** to deprive (a building) of church status.

uncial¹ /'unsi·əl/ *adj* written in a style of handwriting formed of somewhat large rounded usu separated letters and used *esp* in Greek and Latin manuscripts. ➤➤ **uncially** *adv.* [Latin *uncialis* inch-high, from *uncia* twelfth part, ounce, inch]

uncial² *noun* **1** an uncial letter or manuscript. **2** the uncial style of handwriting.

unciform /'unsifawm/ *adj* hook-shaped. [Latin *uncinus* hook + -FORM]

uncinate /'unsinayt/ *adj* said of a plant or animal part: having a hook-shaped tip. [Latin *uncinatus*, from *uncinus* hook]

uncircumcised *adj* **1** not circumcised. **2** spiritually impure; heathen. ⫸ **uncircumcision** /-'sizh(ə)n/ *noun*.

uncivil *adj* lacking in courtesy; ill-mannered or impolite. ⫸ **uncivilly** *adv*.

uncivilized *or* **uncivilised** *adj* **1** said of a people: not civilized, *esp* in not having a written language. **2** rude, bad-mannered, or unsophisticated.

unclad *adj* not clothed; naked.

unclasp *verb trans* **1** to open the clasp of (something). **2** to release (something) from a grip: *He unclasped my hand.*

unclassified *adj* **1** not divided into classes or placed in a class. **2** said *esp* of information: not subject to a security classification. **3** *Brit* said of a minor road: not part of the classified system of motorways, A-roads, and B-roads.

uncle /'ungkl/ *noun* **1** the brother of one's father or mother, or the husband of one's aunt. **2** used by a child as a term of affection for an adult male friend. **3** *dated slang* a pawnbroker. [Middle English via Old French from Latin *avunculus* mother's brother: see AVUNCULAR]

unclean *adj* **1** dirty; filthy. **2** morally or spiritually impure. **3a** ritually prohibited as food. **b** ceremonially unfit or defiled. ⫸ **uncleanness** *noun*.

uncleanly[1] /un'klenli/ *adj* morally or physically unclean. ⫸ **uncleanliness** /un'klenlinəs/ *noun*.

uncleanly[2] /un'kleenli/ *adv* in an unclean manner.

unclear *adj* not clear, obvious, or easy to understand. ⫸ **unclearly** *adv*, **unclearness** *noun*.

uncleared *adj* **1** said of a cheque: not having gone through a clearing house and so with the funds yet to go into the payee's account. **2** said of a tract of land: under natural vegetation.

Uncle Sam /sam/ *noun* the US nation, people, or government. [prob jocular expansion of *US*, abbr of *United States*]

Uncle Tom /tom/ *noun chiefly derog* a black American eager to win the approval of white people and willing to cooperate with them. [named after *Uncle Tom*, faithful black slave in the novel *Uncle Tom's Cabin* by Harriet Beecher Stowe d.1896, US author]

unclothe *verb trans* **1** to take the clothes off (somebody). **2** to uncover (something).

unclothed *adj* not clothed; naked.

unco[1] /'ungkoh/ *adj chiefly Scot* **1** strange; unknown. **2** extraordinary; remarkable. [Middle English (Scots) *unkow*, alteration of UNCOUTH]

unco[2] *adv chiefly Scot* extremely; remarkably.

uncoil *verb trans* to release (something) from a coiled state; to unwind (it). ⫸ *verb intrans* to become uncoiled.

uncomfortable *adj* **1** causing discomfort: *an uncomfortable chair*; *an uncomfortable silence*. **2** feeling discomfort; ill at ease. ⫸ **uncomfortableness** *noun*, **uncomfortably** *adv*.

uncommercial *adj* **1** not engaged in or related to commerce. **2** not based on commercial principles. **3** not commercially viable.

uncommitted *adj* not pledged to a particular belief, allegiance, or course of action.

uncommon[1] *adj* **1** not normally encountered; unusual. **2** remarkable; exceptional. ⫸ **uncommonly** *adv*, **uncommonness** *noun*.

uncommon[2] *adv archaic or dialect* unusually; exceedingly: *I feel uncommon nervous about the ceremony, Colonel* — George Bernard Shaw.

uncommunicative *adj* not disposed to talk or impart information; reserved. ⫸ **uncommunicatively** *adv*, **uncommunicativeness** *noun*.

uncomplaining *adj* not complaining; patient or stoical. ⫸ **uncomplainingly** *adv*.

uncomplicated *adj* not complex; straightforward.

uncomprehending *adj* having or showing a lack of comprehension or understanding. ⫸ **uncomprehendingly** *adv*.

uncompromising *adj* not making or accepting a compromise; unyielding or inflexible. ⫸ **uncompromisingly** *adv*.

unconcern *noun* **1** lack of interest; indifference. **2** freedom from anxiety.

unconcerned *adj* **1** not involved or interested. **2** not anxious or upset. ⫸ **unconcernedly** /-'nidli/ *adv*.

unconditional *adj* absolute; unqualified; without any conditions attached: *an unconditional offer*. ⫸ **unconditionally** *adv*.

unconditioned *adj* **1** said of behaviour, instinctive reflexes, etc: not dependent on, established by, or subjected to conditioning or learning. **2** = UNCONDITIONAL.

unconfined *adj* **1** without limit. **2** said of an emotional response: without restraint.

unconfirmed *adj* not confirmed as true: *unconfirmed reports of a riot*.

unconformable *adj* **1** not conforming. **2** said of rock strata: exhibiting geological unconformity. ⫸ **unconformably** *adv*.

unconformity *noun* **1** lack of conformity. **2a** a break in the sequence of rock strata corresponding to a period of erosion or non-deposition. **b** the surface of contact between rocks of different ages marking such a break.

uncongenial *adj* **1** not sympathetic or compatible: *uncongenial roommates*. **2** disagreeable; unpleasant: *an uncongenial task*. **3** not fitted; unsuitable: *a soil uncongenial to most crops*.

unconnected *adj* **1** not linked or associated: *The crimes are unconnected*. **2** not connected or joined.

unconquerable *adj* **1** indomitable; unyielding. **2** incapable of being surmounted. ⫸ **unconquerably** *adv*.

unconscionable *adj* **1** unscrupulous; unprincipled. **2** excessive; unreasonable. ⫸ **unconscionably** *adv*. [UN-[1] + obsolete *conscionable* having or guided by a conscience, from CONSCIENCE, incorrectly interpreted as pl]

unconscious[1] *adj* **1** not knowing or perceiving: *unconscious of the danger*. **2a** not possessing or having lost consciousness: *unconscious matter*; *unconscious for three days*. **b** not marked by or resulting from conscious thought, sensation, or feeling: *unconscious motivation*. **3** not intentional or deliberate: *unconscious bias*. ⫸ **unconsciously** *adv*, **unconsciousness** *noun*.

unconscious[2] *noun* the part of the mind that does not ordinarily enter a person's awareness but nevertheless is held to influence behaviour and may be manifested in dreams or slips of the tongue.

unconsidered *adj* **1** disregarded. **2** not carefully thought out: *unconsidered opinions*.

unconstitutional *adj* not in accordance with the constitution of a nation, organization, etc. ⫸ **unconstitutionality** /-'naliti/ *noun*, **unconstitutionally** *adv*.

uncontrollable *adj* incapable of being controlled; ungovernable. ⫸ **uncontrollably** *adv*.

unconventional *adj* not bound by or conforming with generally accepted standards or practices; different from the norm. ⫸ **unconventionality** /-'naliti/ *noun*, **unconventionally** *adv*.

unconvincing *adj* not convincing; implausible or unimpressive. ⫸ **unconvincingly** *adv*.

uncool *adj informal* not fashionable or sophisticated: *People knew raisins were good for them. They liked them, but they were regarded as wimpy and very uncool. Eating raisins just wasn't the neat thing to do* — Good Food.

uncoordinated *adj* **1** lacking in coordination, *esp* in bodily movements. **2** said *esp* of a joint venture: badly planned or organized.

uncork *verb trans* **1** to draw a cork from (a bottle). **2** to release (e.g. emotions) from a pent-up state.

uncountable *adj* incapable of being counted; too numerous to count. ⫸ **uncountability** /-'biliti/ *noun*, **uncountably** *adv*.

uncountable noun *noun* = MASS NOUN.

uncounted *adj* **1** not counted. **2** innumerable.

uncouple *verb trans* **1** to detach or disconnect (e.g. railway wagons). **2** to release (dogs) from being fastened together in a couple.

uncouth /un'koohth/ *adj* rude, awkward, or uncultivated in speech or behaviour; lacking in good manners or refinement. ⫸ **uncouthly** *adv*, **uncouthness** *noun*. [Old English *uncūth*, from UN-[1] + *cūth* familiar, known, past part. of *cunnan* to know]

uncover *verb* (**uncovered, uncovering**) ➤ *verb trans* **1** to remove the cover from (something). **2** to reveal or discover (something): *uncover the truth.* **3** to remove the hat from (one's head). ➤ *verb intrans* to take off one's hat as a token of respect.

uncovered *adj* **1** not supplied with or protected by a cover. **2** not covered by insurance, security, etc.

uncritical *adj* **1** showing no discrimination. **2** showing a lack or improper use of critical standards or procedures. ➤➤ **uncritically** *adv.*

uncrowned *adj* **1** not having yet been crowned. **2** having a specified status in fact but not in name: *the uncrowned champion.*

UNCSTD *abbr* United Nations Conference on Science and Technology for Development.

UNCTAD /'ungktad/ *abbr* United Nations Conference on Trade and Development.

unction /'ungksh(ə)n/ *noun* **1** the act or an instance of anointing, *esp* as a rite of consecration. **2** something used for anointing; an ointment or unguent. **3** exaggerated, assumed, or superficial earnestness of language or manner; unctuousness. [Middle English *unctioun* from Latin *unction-, unctio*, from *unguere* to anoint]

unctuous /'ungktyooəs/ *adj* **1** fatty, oily, or greasy in texture or appearance. **2** marked by ingratiating smoothness and false sincerity. ➤➤ **unctuously** *adv,* **unctuousness** *noun.* [Middle English via French from late Latin *unctuosus,* irreg from Latin *unctum* ointment, from *unguere* to anoint]

uncultivated *adj* **1** said of land: not under cultivation; not planted with crops. **2** said of a person: not refined or educated.

uncurl *verb intrans* to straighten out from a curled or coiled position. ➤ *verb trans* to cause (something) to uncurl.

uncut *adj* **1** not cut down or into. **2** not shaped by cutting: *an uncut diamond.* **3** said of a book: not having the folds of the leaves trimmed off. **4** said of a book, film, etc: not abridged or edited, *esp* left as the author, director, etc intended. **5** said of alcohol or drugs: undiluted or unadulterated.

undaunted *adj* not discouraged by danger, difficulty, or setbacks, etc. ➤➤ **undauntedly** *adv,* **undauntedness** *noun.*

undead¹ /un'ded/ *adj* said of a character in a horror book or film or of a vampire, etc: having died or been killed but still able to maintain a physical presence.

undead² *noun* (**the undead**) people, animals, vampires, etc that have died or been killed but are still able to maintain a physical presence.

undecagon /un'dekəgon/ *noun* a two-dimensional geometrical figure having eleven sides. [Latin *undecim* eleven (from *unus* one + *decem* ten) + -GON]

undeceive *verb trans* to free (somebody) from deception, illusion, or error: *Her unhappy father is … under the impression that she is attending a … lecture by the University Extension Scheme on the influence of a permanent income on Thought. I do not propose to undeceive him. Indeed I have never undeceived him on any question —* Oscar Wilde.

undecidable *adj* in logic or mathematics, incapable of being formally proved or disproved. ➤➤ **undecidability** /-'biliti/ *noun.*

undecided *adj* **1** in doubt. **2** without a result: *The match was left undecided.* ➤➤ **undecidedly** *adv,* **undecidedness** *noun.*

undemocratic *adj* not following democratic practices, principles, or ideals. ➤➤ **undemocratically** *adv.*

undemonstrative *adj* not showing one's feelings, *esp* of affection; reserved. ➤➤ **undemonstratively** *adv,* **undemonstrativeness** *noun.*

undeniable *adj* plainly true; incontestable: *undeniable evidence.* ➤➤ **undeniably** *adv.*

under¹ /'undə/ *adv* **1** in or to a position below or beneath something. **2** in or to a lower rank, number, or quantity: *£10 or under.* **3** in or into a condition of subjection, subordination, or unconsciousness. **4** lower on the same or a following page. [Old English]

under² *prep* **1a** below or beneath (something). **b** covered, protected, or hidden by (something): *under cover of darkness.* **c** using (a name) as a pseudonym or alias. **2a** subject to the authority, control, guidance, or instruction of (somebody): *serving under the general.* **b** during the rule or control of (somebody): *India under the Raj.* **c** inferior in rank to (somebody). **3a** receiving or undergoing the action or effect of (something): *under pressure; under discussion.*

b bearing (something) as a crop: *three fields under corn.* **4** within the group or designation of (something): *under this heading.* **5a** less than (a number or quantity): *under an hour.* **b** falling short of (a standard or required degree): *under par.*

under- *comb. form* forming words, with the meanings: **1** lying or placed below, beneath, or on the lower side: *underground.* **2** lower in rank or authority; subordinate: *undersecretary.* **3** less than usual, proper, or desired in amount or degree: *undernourished.*

underachieve *verb intrans* to fail to realize one's full potential, *esp* at school. ➤➤ **underachievement** *noun,* **underachiever** *noun.*

underact *verb trans* **1** to perform (a dramatic part) without adequate force or skill. **2** to perform (a part or role) with restraint for greater dramatic impact. ➤ *verb intrans* to perform feebly or with restraint.

under-age *adj* **1** being below the legal age: *under-age drinkers.* **2** done by somebody below the legal age: *under-age sex.*

underarm¹ *adj* **1** under or along the underside of the arm: *underarm seams.* **2** said e.g. of a throw or hit: made with the hand brought forward and up from below shoulder level.

underarm² *adv* with an underarm motion: *bowl underarm.*

underarm³ *noun* **1** the armpit. **2** the part of a garment that covers the underside of the arm.

underbelly *noun* (*pl* **underbellies**) **1** the underside of an animal, object, etc. **2** a vulnerable area: *the soft underbelly of capitalism.*

underbid *verb* (**underbidding,** *past tense and past part.* **underbid**) ➤ *verb trans* **1** to bid less than (a competing bidder). **2** to make a lower bid (on a hand of cards) than the strength of the hand warrants. ➤ *verb intrans* to bid too low. ➤➤ **underbidder** *noun.*

underbite *noun* the projection of the teeth of the lower jaw beyond the teeth of the upper jaw, a condition that sometimes requires corrective surgery.

underbody *noun* (*pl* **underbodies**) **1** the underside of an animal's body. **2** the lower surface of the body of a vehicle.

underbred *adj* **1** of inferior or mixed breed: *an underbred dog.* **2** dated ill-bred; rude or vulgar.

underbrush *noun NAmer* undergrowth in a wood or forest.

undercapitalize *or* **undercapitalise** *verb trans* to provide (e.g. a company) with too little capital for efficient operation.

undercarriage *noun* **1** the part of an aircraft's structure that supports it on the ground and assists in takeoff and landing. **2** a supporting framework, e.g. of a motor vehicle.

undercharge *verb trans* to charge (somebody) too little. ➤ *verb intrans* to charge too little.

underclass *noun* a class of people considered as being below all other social classes, *esp* people with little chance of employment, an adequate income, or a stable way of life: *an underclass of people outside the commercial system —* Anthony Sampson.

underclothes *pl noun* = UNDERWEAR.

underclothing *noun* = UNDERWEAR.

undercoat¹ *noun* **1** a coat, e.g. of paint, applied as a base for another coat. **2** a growth of short hair or fur partly concealed by a longer growth: *a dog's undercoat.*

undercoat² *verb trans* to apply an undercoat of paint to (something).

undercover *adj and adv* acting or done in secret; *specif* employed or involved in spying.

undercroft /'undəkroft/ *noun* a crypt. [Middle English, from UNDER¹ + *crofte* crypt, via early Dutch from Latin *crypta*: see CRYPT]

undercurrent *noun* **1** a current below the surface or beneath another current. **2** a hidden or underlying opinion, feeling, or tendency.

undercut¹ /undə'kut/ *verb trans* (**undercutting,** *past tense and past part.* **undercut**) **1** to charge less than (a competitor) for goods or services. **2** to cut away the lower part of (something). **3** to cut or wear away material from the underside of (something) so as to leave a portion overhanging. **4** to strike (a ball) with a downward glancing blow so as to give backspin or elevation to the shot.

undercut² /'undəkut/ *noun* **1** the action or result of undercutting. **2** Brit the underside of a sirloin of beef. **3** NAmer a notch cut in a tree before felling to determine the direction in which it will fall.

underdeveloped *adj* **1** not normally or adequately developed: *underdeveloped muscles; an underdeveloped film.* **2** said of a country or region: without modern industries or the means of financing them. ➤➤ **underdevelopment** *noun.*

underdog *noun* **1** a competitor who is expected to lose in a struggle or contest. **2** a victim of injustice, persecution, poverty, etc.

underdone *adj* said of food, *esp* meat: not thoroughly cooked.

underdress *verb intrans* to dress less formally than is appropriate. ➤➤ **underdressed** *adj.*

underemployed *adj* **1** having less than full-time or adequate employment. **2** employed in work that does not make full use of a person's talents, capabilities, etc.

underemployment *noun* **1** less than full employment of the work force in an economy. **2a** the state of being underemployed. **b** partial or inadequate employment.

underestimate[1] /undər'estimayt/ *verb trans* **1** to estimate (something) as being less than the actual size, quantity, etc. **2** to regard (somebody) as less capable, powerful, etc than they actually are. ➤➤ **underestimation** /-'maysh(ə)n/ *noun.*

underestimate[2] /undə'restimat/ *noun* an estimate that is too low.

underexpose /ˌundərik'spohz/ *verb trans* to expose (e.g. photographic film) insufficiently. ➤➤ **underexposure** /-zhə/ *noun.*

underfeed *verb trans* (*past tense and past part.* **underfed** /-'fed/) to feed (somebody or something) insufficiently.

underfelt *noun* thick felt placed under a carpet for insulation, protection, comfort, etc.

underfoot *adv* **1** under the feet, *esp* against the ground: *trampled underfoot.* **2** in the way: *children always getting underfoot.*

underfur *noun* the thick soft undercoat of fur lying beneath the longer and coarser hair of a mammal.

undergarment *noun* an item of underwear.

undergird *verb trans* **1** to support (something) from underneath, e.g. with a rope or chain. **2** *formal* to strengthen, support, or bolster (something): *Faith undergirds morals.*

underglaze *noun* **1** colour, decorations, etc applied or suitable for applying to pottery before the glaze is put on. **2** (*used before a noun*) applied or suitable for applying before the glaze: *underglaze pigments.*

undergo *verb trans* (**undergoes**, *past tense* **underwent** /-'went/, *past part.* **undergone** /-'gon/, **undergoing**) **1** to go through or experience (something): *undergo a period of training.* **2** to be subjected to (something unpleasant).

undergrad *noun informal* an undergraduate.

undergraduate *noun* somebody studying at a college or university for a first degree.

underground[1] /undə'grownd/ *adv* **1** beneath the surface of the earth. **2** in or into hiding or secret operation.

underground[2] /'undəgrownd/ *adj* **1** growing, operating, or situated below the surface of the ground. **2a** conducted in hiding or in secret. **b** existing, produced, or operating outside the establishment; experimental or avant-garde.

underground[3] /'undəgrownd/ *noun* **1** the region beneath the ground surface. **2** *treated as sing. or pl.* **a** a secret movement or group, *esp* in an occupied country, formed for concerted resistance. **b** a secret conspiratorial organization dedicated to disruption of civil order. **c** an unofficial usu avant-garde group or movement that functions outside the establishment. **d** (*used before a noun*) relating to or denoting a secret or avant-garde group: *an underground resistance movement.* **3** *Brit* an underground urban railway.

undergrowth *noun* vegetation, e.g. saplings, bushes, and ferns, growing on the floor of a wood or forest.

underhand[1] /'undəhand/ *adj* **1** marked by subterfuge, trickery, and deception; sly. **2** done secretly; clandestine. **3** = UNDERARM[1] (2). ➤➤ **underhandedly** *adv.*

underhand[2] /'undəhand, -'hand/ *adv* **1** in an underhand manner. **2** = UNDERARM[2].

underhanded /-'handid/ *adj* = UNDERHAND[1].

underhung *adj* said of a lower jaw: projecting beyond the upper jaw: compare PROGNATHOUS.

underinsured *adj* insured for less than the amount needed to cover possible loss or damage. ➤➤ **underinsurance** *noun.*

underlaid *verb* past tense and past part. of UNDERLAY[1].

underlain *verb* past part. of UNDERLIE.

underlay[1] /undə'lay/ *verb trans* (*past tense and past part.* **underlaid** /-'layd/) to raise or support (something) by laying something underneath.

underlay[2] /'undəlay/ *noun* something designed to be laid under something else, *esp* thick foam, felt, or other material laid under a carpet for insulation, protection, comfort, etc.

underlie *verb trans* (**underlying**, *past tense* **underlay** /-'lay/, *past part.* **underlain** /-'layn/) **1** to lie or be situated under (usu an overlying layer). **2** to be hidden beneath (e.g. a facade or superficial behaviour): *Rowland saw that an intense agitation, hitherto successfully repressed, underlay her calmness* — Henry James. **3** to be the basis, foundation, or cause of (something).

underline[1] /undə'lien/ *verb trans* **1** to mark (a word, phrase, or passage) with a line underneath. **2** to emphasize or stress (something).

underline[2] /'undəlien/ *noun* a line marked underneath a word, phrase, or passage.

underlinen *noun archaic* = UNDERWEAR.

underling /'undəling/ *noun* a subordinate or inferior.

underlip *noun* the lower lip.

underlying *adj* **1** lying beneath or below: *the underlying rock.* **2** hidden beneath the surface: *underlying hostility.* **3** basic; fundamental: *the underlying issues.* **4** anterior and prior in claim: *an underlying mortgage.*

undermanned *adj* = UNDERSTAFFED.

undermentioned *adj Brit* referred to at a later point in the text.

undermine *verb trans* **1** to excavate the earth beneath (e.g. a fortification). **2** to wear away the base or foundations of (e.g. a rock formation). **3** to subvert, weaken, or destroy (something) gradually or insidiously: *undermining her confidence.*

undermost *adj* lowest in relative position.

underneath[1] /undə'neeth/ *prep* **1** directly below (something). **2** close under (something), *esp* so as to be hidden. [Old English *underneothan*, from UNDER[1] + *neothan* below]

underneath[2] *adv* **1** under or below an object or a surface; beneath. **2** on the lower side.

underneath[3] *noun* the bottom part or surface: *the underneath of the bowl.*

undernourished *adj* supplied with less than the minimum amount of the foods essential for sound health and growth. ➤➤ **undernourishment** *noun.*

underpaid *verb* past tense and past part. of UNDERPAY.

underpants *pl noun* an undergarment for men or boys that covers the hips, crotch, and sometimes the upper thighs.

underpart *noun* a part lying on the lower side, *esp* of a bird or mammal.

underpass *noun* a tunnel or passage taking a road or footpath under another road or a railway.

underpay *verb trans* (*past tense and past part.* **underpaid** /-'payd/) **1** to give less than adequate or normal payment to (e.g. a worker). **2** to pay too little for (e.g. a job). ➤➤ **underpayment** *noun.*

underpin *verb trans* (**underpinned, underpinning**) **1** to form part of, strengthen, or replace the foundation of (a building or other structure). **2** to support or substantiate (something): *the evidence underpinning her thesis.*

underpinning *noun* **1** the material and construction used for support of a structure. **2** (*also in pl*) a basis, support, or foundation.

underplay *verb trans* **1** to underact (a part or role). **2** to play down or underemphasize the importance of (something).

underprice *verb trans* to price (something) too low.

underprivileged *adj* deprived, usu through social or economic conditions, of some of the fundamental rights and opportunities of a civilized society: *underprivileged children.*

underproduction *noun* the production of less than enough or of less than is usual or possible. ➤➤ **underproductive** /-'duktiv/ *adj.*

underproof *adj* containing less alcohol than proof spirit.

underquote *verb trans* **1** to quote a lower price than (another person). **2** to quote a price for (e.g. goods or services) that is lower than another's or the market price.

underrate *verb trans* to rate (somebody or something) too low; to undervalue or underestimate (them).

underscore[1] /undə'skaw/ *verb trans* = UNDERLINE[1].

underscore[2] /'undəskaw/ *noun* = UNDERLINE[2].

undersea[1] *adj* **1** being or carried on under the sea or under the surface of the sea: *undersea oil deposits; undersea warfare*. **2** designed for use under the surface of the sea.

undersea[2] *adv* under the sea or under the surface of the sea.

underseal[1] *noun* a protective corrosion-proof substance, e.g. bitumen, used *esp* to coat vehicle undersurfaces.

underseal[2] *verb trans* to apply underseal to (something).

underseas *adv* = UNDERSEA[2].

undersecretary *noun* (*pl* **undersecretaries**) a secretary immediately subordinate to a principal secretary, *esp* a secretary of state.

undersell *verb trans* (*past tense and past part.* **undersold** /-'sohld/) **1** to sell something at a lower price than (a competitor). **2** to be sold cheaper than (another similar item): *imported cars that undersell domestic ones*. **3a** to make little of the merits of (somebody or something): *He undersold himself*. **b** to promote or publicize (something) in a deliberately restrained or low-key manner.

undersexed *adj* lacking or having an unusually low sexual drive or interest.

undershirt *noun chiefly NAmer* = VEST[1] (1).

undershoot *verb trans* (*past tense and past part.* **undershot** /-'shot/) **1** to shoot short of (a target). **2** said of an aircraft: to land short of (a runway).

undershorts *pl noun chiefly NAmer* = UNDERPANTS.

undershot[1] /undə'shot/ *adj* **1** = UNDERHUNG. **2** said of a waterwheel: moved by water passing beneath.

undershot[2] *verb* past tense and past part. of UNDERSHOOT.

underside *noun* the side or surface lying underneath.

undersigned[1] *adj* having signed one's name at the end of a document.

undersigned[2] *noun* (**the undersigned**) (*treated as sing. or pl*) somebody who signs their name at the end of a document.

undersize *adj* = UNDERSIZED.

undersized *adj* of less than average or normal size.

underskirt *noun* an undergarment that hangs loosely from the waist and is worn under a skirt or dress.

underslung *adj* **1** suspended from the underside of something. **2** said of a vehicle frame: suspended below the axles.

undersold *verb* past tense and past part. of UNDERSELL.

understaffed *adj* inadequately staffed.

understand /undə'stand/ *verb* (*past tense and past part.* **understood** /-'stood/) ➤ *verb trans* **1a** to grasp the meaning of (e.g. words or a speaker). **b** to have a thorough knowledge of or expertise in (a specified subject, etc): *understand finance*. **2** to assume, infer, or suppose (something): *We understand that he is abroad*. **3** to interpret (something) in one of a number of possible ways: *as I understand it*. **4** to supply mentally (something implied though not expressed). ➤ *verb intrans* **1** to have a grasp or understanding of something. **2** to believe or infer something to be the case. **3** to show a sympathetic or tolerant attitude: *If he loves her he'll understand*. [Old English *understandan*, from UNDER[1] + *standan* to STAND[1]]

understandable *adj* **1** normal and reasonable, *esp* in a particular situation. **2** capable of being understood. ➤➤ **understandability** /-'biliti/ *noun*, **understandably** *adv*.

understanding[1] *noun* **1** a mental grasp; comprehension. **2** the power of comprehending; intelligence, *esp* the power to make experience intelligible by applying concepts: *Bathsheba, though she had too much understanding to be entirely governed by her womanliness, had too much womanliness to use her understanding to the best advantage* — Hardy. **3a** a friendly or harmonious relationship. **b** an informal mutual agreement. **4** meaning or interpretation. **5** tolerance or sympathy.

understanding[2] *adj* **1** tolerant or sympathetic. **2** *archaic* having intelligence or insight. ➤➤ **understandingly** *adv*.

understate *verb trans* **1** to state or represent (something) as being less than is the case. **2** to present (something) with restraint, *esp* for greater effect. ➤➤ **understatement** *noun*.

understeer[1] /undə'stiə/ *verb intrans* said of a motor vehicle: to turn less sharply than expected in response to movements of the steering wheel.

understeer[2] /'undəstiə/ *noun* the act or an instance of understeering or a tendency to understeer.

understood /undə'stood/ *verb* past tense and past part. of UNDERSTAND.

understudy[1] *verb* (**understudies, understudied, understudying**) ➤ *verb intrans* to study another actor's part in order to be able to take it over in an emergency. ➤ *verb trans* **1** to prepare (a part) as understudy. **2** to prepare a part as understudy to (another actor).

understudy[2] *noun* (*pl* **understudies**) somebody who is prepared to act another's part or take over another's duties.

undersubscribed *adj* **1** said of a share issue, etc: having fewer applicants than there are shares, etc on offer. **2** said of a course of study, event, etc: having fewer applicants than there are places, tickets, etc on offer.

undertake *verb trans* (*past tense* **undertook** /-'took/, *past part.* **undertaken** /-'taykən/) **1** to take (something) upon oneself as a task or responsibility. **2** to put oneself under obligation to do (something). **3** to guarantee or promise (something).

undertaker *noun* somebody whose business is preparing the dead for burial and arranging and managing funerals.

undertaking *noun* **1** an enterprise. **2** a pledge or guarantee. **3** the business of an undertaker.

undertenant *noun* = SUBTENANT.

under-the-counter *adj informal* said *esp* of goods: sold or obtained illegally, illicitly, or surreptitiously. [from the practice of hiding illicit wares under the counter of shops where they are sold]

underthings *pl noun informal* = UNDERWEAR.

underthrust *noun* in geology, a fault in which one body of rock moves beneath another.

undertone *noun* **1** a low or subdued utterance or tone of voice. **2** a quality or feeling underlying an utterance or action. **3** a subdued colour; *specif* one seen through and modifying another colour.

undertook *verb* past tense of UNDERTAKE.

undertow /'undətoh/ *noun* **1** an undercurrent that flows in a different direction from the surface current, *esp* out to sea. **2** a hidden tendency often contrary to the one that is publicly apparent.

undertrick *noun* in bridge, a trick by which a player or partnership falls short of fulfilling their contract: compare OVERTRICK.

undervalue *verb trans* (**undervalues, undervalued, undervaluing**) to value, rate, or estimate (something or somebody) below the real worth: *undervalue stock; She was undervalued as a poet*. ➤➤ **undervaluation** /-'aysh(ə)n/ *noun*.

undervest *noun chiefly Brit* = VEST[1] (1).

underwater[1] *adj* **1** situated or used below the surface of the water. **2** below the waterline of a ship.

underwater[2] *adv* below the surface of the water.

under way *adv* **1** in or into motion. **2** in progress. **3** said of a vessel: moving or beginning to move through the water. [prob from Dutch *onderweg*, from *onder* under, in the course of, + *weg* way]

underwear *noun* clothing, e.g. knickers, pants, vests, bras, etc, worn under other clothing, *esp* next to the skin.

underweight[1] /undə'wayt/ *adj* weighing less than the normal, average, or requisite weight.

underweight[2] /'undəwayt/ *noun* a weight that is below the normal, average, or requisite weight.

underwent *verb* past tense of UNDERGO.

underwhelm /undə'welm/ *verb trans humorous* to fail to impress (somebody): *'From now on, it's healthy eating,' she announces to her underwhelmed offspring and insists that they and their father go jogging and serves up watercress soup for tea* — Guardian. [UNDER[1] + *-whelm* as in OVERWHELM]

underwing *noun* **1** either of the hind wings of an insect. **2** any of various moths that have drab brown or black forewings and colourful hind wings: *Noctua pronuba* (the large yellow underwing) and others.

underwired *adj* said of a bra: with a semicircular wire stitched into the underside of each cup for greater uplift.

underwood *noun* undergrowth, *esp* small trees and shrubs.

underworld *noun* **1** in mythology, the abode of the souls of the dead, regarded as being below the surface of the earth. **2** the world of organized crime.

underwrite *verb* (*past tense* **underwrote** /-'roht/, *past part.* **underwritten** /-'ritn/) ➤ *verb trans* **1a** to put one's signature on (an insurance policy) thereby assuming liability in case of specified loss or damage. **b** to assume (a sum or risk) by way of insurance. **2a** to agree to purchase (a security issue) usu on a fixed date at a fixed price. **b** to guarantee financial support of (an enterprise). **3** to subscribe or agree to (something). **4** to write (something) under or at the end of something else. ➤ *verb intrans* to carry on the business of an underwriter.

underwriter *noun* **1** somebody who underwrites something *esp* an insurance policy. **2** an employee of an insurance company who rates the acceptability of risks solicited and determines appropriate premiums.

underwritten *verb* past part. of UNDERWRITE.

underwrote *verb* past tense of UNDERWRITE.

undescended *adj* said of a testicle: retained within the abdomen rather than descending into the scrotum at the normal age.

undesirable[1] *adj* unwanted or objectionable: *undesirable elements in society.* ➤➤ **undesirability** /-'biliti/ *noun,* **undesirably** *adv.*

undesirable[2] *noun* an undesirable person or thing, *esp* somebody considered socially unacceptable.

undetermined *adj* not resolved, decided, or settled.

undeterred *adj* not deterred by setbacks, warnings, etc from pursuing a particular course of action.

undid *verb* past tense of UNDO.

undies /'undiz/ *pl noun informal* underwear, *esp* women's underwear. [by shortening and alteration]

undignified *adj* lacking in dignity: *She made a rather undignified exit.*

undiminished *adj* not diminished; as great as before.

undine /'undeen/ *noun* in the theory of Paracelsus, any of a group of female elemental beings that inhabit water. [scientific Latin *undina,* term coined by Paracelsus d.1541, Swiss physician, from Latin *unda* wave]

undischarged *adj* **1** said of a bankrupt person: having debts or liabilities that are still to be discharged. **2** said of a debt: unpaid.

undisclosed *adj* not revealed or made known: *sold for an undisclosed sum.*

undisguised *adj* not concealed; frank or open: *undisguised admiration.* ➤➤ **undisguisedly** /-zidli/ *adv.*

undisputed *adj* not questioned, challenged, or disputed; universally accepted.

undistinguished *adj* lacking in distinction; not exceptional: *an undistinguished career.*

undistributed *adj* **1** not distributed or shared out: *undistributed profits.* **2** said of a term in logic: not referring to all members of a class, e.g. *sheep* in *Some sheep have horns.*

undivided *adj* **1** complete; total: *his undivided attention.* **2** not split into separate parts.

undo *verb* (*past tense* **undid** /un'did/, *past part.* **undone** /un'dun/) ➤ *verb trans* **1** to open or loosen (something) by releasing a fastening. **2** to reverse or cancel out the effects of (something). **3** to destroy the standing, reputation, hopes, etc of (somebody). ➤ *verb intrans* to come open, unfastened, etc.

undoing *noun* **1** ruin. **2** a cause of ruin or downfall: *The Captain keeps too good company ever to grow rich … and the chocolate houses are his undoing* — John Gay.

undone[1] *verb* past part. of UNDO.

undone[2] *adj* **1** not performed or finished. **2** unfastened or untied. **3** ruined or destroyed.

undoubted *adj* not disputed; certain or genuine. ➤➤ **undoubtedly** *adv.*

UNDP *abbr* United Nations Development Programme.

undreamed /un'dreemd/ *or* **undreamt** /un'dremt/ *adj* (*usu* + of) not conceived of; unimagined: *They found undreamed-of happiness.*

undress[1] *verb trans* to remove the clothes from (somebody). ➤ *verb intrans* to take off one's clothes.

undress[2] *noun* **1** a state of having little or no clothing on. **2** informal or ordinary clothing or uniform, as opposed to that worn on formal or ceremonial occasions.

undressed *adj* **1** partially or completely unclothed. **2** not fully processed or finished: *undressed hides.* **3** not cared for or tended: *an undressed wound.* **4** said of food: served without a dressing.

undrinkable *adj* not safe or pleasant to drink.

UNDRO *abbr* United Nations Disaster Relief Office.

undue *adj* **1** excessive; immoderate. **2** not yet payable.

undulant /'undyoolənt/ *adj* rising and falling in waves; rolling.

undulant fever *noun* the disease brucellosis occurring in human beings and contracted by contact with infected domestic animals or consumption of their products, e.g. milk. [from the intermittent fever that is a symptom of the disease]

undulate[1] /'undyoolət, -layt/ *adj* having a wavy surface, edge, or markings: *the undulate margin of a leaf.* [late Latin *undulatus,* from *undula:* see UNDULATE[2]]

undulate[2] /'undyoolayt/ *verb intrans* **1** to rise and fall in waves; to fluctuate. **2** to have a wavy form or appearance. ➤➤ **undulating** *adj,* **undulatory** /-lət(ə)ri/ *adj.* [late Latin *undula* small wave, dimin. of Latin *unda* wave]

undulation /undyoo'laysh(ə)n/ *noun* **1a** a gentle rising and falling in or as if in waves. **b** a single wave or gentle rise and fall. **2** a wavy appearance, outline, or form.

unduly *adv* excessively: *not unduly concerned.*

undying *adj* eternal; perpetual: *undying love.*

unearned *adj* not gained by work, service, skill, or merit.

unearned income *noun* income derived from investments, rents, etc rather than employment.

unearned increment *noun* an increase in the value of property, e.g. land, due to increased demand rather than the owner's labour or investment.

unearth /un'uhth/ *verb trans* **1** to dig (something) up out of the ground. **2** to find or discover (something), *esp* after searching: *unearth an old photograph.* **3** to force (an animal, *esp* a fox) from a hole, burrow, etc.

unearthly *adj* **1** not terrestrial: *unearthly radio sources.* **2** exceeding what is normal or natural; supernatural: *an unearthly light.* **3** weird; eerie: *unearthly howls.* **4** *informal* unreasonable; preposterous: *getting up at an unearthly hour.* ➤➤ **unearthliness** *noun.*

unease *noun* a feeling of disquiet or awkwardness.

uneasy *adj* (**uneasier, uneasiest**) **1** marked by lack of *esp* mental ease; uncomfortable or awkward. **2** apprehensive or worried. **3** precarious or unstable: *an uneasy truce.* ➤➤ **uneasily** *adv,* **uneasiness** *noun.*

uneatable *adj* not fit or safe to be eaten; inedible.

uneconomic *adj* not profitable or economically practicable.

uneconomical *adj* not economical; wasteful.

uneducated *adj* having or showing a lack of education; ignorant.

unemployable *adj* not acceptable or fitted for any form of employment. ➤➤ **unemployability** *noun.*

unemployed[1] *adj* **1** not engaged in a job. **2** not invested. **3** not being used.

unemployed[2] *pl noun* (**the unemployed**) people who are not employed.

unemployment *noun* **1** the state of being unemployed; lack of available employment. **2** the number or percentage of people out of work in a country, region, etc.

unemployment benefit *noun* a sum of money paid, e.g. by the state, at regular intervals to an unemployed person.

unending *adj* never ending; seemingly endless. ➤➤ **unendingly** *adv,* **unendingness** *noun.*

unenforceable *adj* said e.g. of a law: incapable of being enforced.

unenterprising *adj* having or showing a lack of enterprise or initiative.

unenthusiastic *adj* not enthusiastic or excited. ➤➤ **unenthusiastically** *adv.*

unenviable *adj* not arousing envy; highly undesirable: *the unenviable task of informing the next-of-kin.* ➤➤ **unenviably** *adv.*

UNEP *abbr* United Nations Environment Programme.

unequal adj **1a** not of the same measurement, quantity, or number as another. **b** not alike in quality, nature, or status. **c** not the same for every member of a group, class, or society: *unequal rights.* **2** badly balanced or matched: *an unequal contest.* **3** not uniform. **4** (+ to) incapable of meeting the requirements of (something, e.g. a task). ➤➤ **unequally** adv.

unequalled (*NAmer* **unequaled**) adj not equalled; unparalleled or unrivalled.

unequivocal adj clear and unambiguous. ➤➤ **unequivocally** adv, **unequivocalness** noun.

unerring adj faultless or unfailing: *unerring judgment.* ➤➤ **unerringly** adv, **unerringness** noun.

UNESCO /yooh'neskoh/ abbr United Nations Educational, Scientific, and Cultural Organization.

unethical adj not conforming to accepted, *esp* professional, standards of conduct or morality. ➤➤ **unethically** adv.

uneven adj **1a** not level, smooth, or uniform. **b** varying from the straight or parallel. **c** irregular; inconsistent. **d** varying in quality: *an uneven performance.* **2** badly balanced or matched: *an uneven contest.* ➤➤ **unevenly** adv, **unevenness** noun.

uneventful adj without any noteworthy or untoward incidents: *an uneventful journey.* ➤➤ **uneventfully** adv, **uneventfulness** noun.

unexampled adj having no example or parallel; unprecedented.

unexceptionable adj beyond reproach or criticism; unimpeachable. ➤➤ **unexceptionableness** noun, **unexceptionably** adv. [UN-¹ + obsolete *exception* to take exception, object]

Usage note ─────────
unexceptionable *or* unexceptional? See note at UNEXCEPTIONAL.

unexceptional adj commonplace, ordinary, or normal. ➤➤ **unexceptionally** adv.

Usage note ─────────
unexceptional *or* unexceptionable? These two words are quite close together in meaning and could be confused. *Unexceptional* means 'not outstanding', therefore 'ordinary' or 'rather dull' (*an unexceptional year for wine*). If a thing is *unexceptionable* it causes no offence or controversy: *It was just that one remark – the rest of the speech was totally unexceptionable.* See also note at EXCEPTIONAL.

unexpected adj not expected or foreseen. ➤➤ **unexpectedly** adv, **unexpectedness** noun.

unexplained adj **1** not explained or made clear. **2** not understandable or accounted for.

unexpurgated adj unabridged or uncensored; complete: *the unexpurgated text.*

unfailing adj **1** able to be relied on; constant or sure: *a subject of unfailing interest.* **2** continuous. ➤➤ **unfailingly** adv, **unfailingness** noun.

unfair adj **1** unjust or unequal. **2** not honest or ethical, *esp* in business dealings: *unfair competition.* ➤➤ **unfairly** adv, **unfairness** noun.

unfaithful adj **1** not adhering to vows, allegiance, or duty; disloyal or faithless. **2** not faithful to a marriage partner, lover, etc, *esp* in having sexual relations with another person. **3** inaccurate or untrustworthy. ➤➤ **unfaithfully** adv, **unfaithfulness** noun.

unfaltering adj not wavering or hesitating; firm. ➤➤ **unfalteringly** adv.

unfamiliar adj **1** not well-known; strange: *an unfamiliar place.* **2** (+ with) not acquainted with or lacking an understanding of (a subject, etc): *unfamiliar with his writings.* ➤➤ **unfamiliarity** /-li'ar-iti/ noun, **unfamiliarly** adv.

unfancied adj said of a competitor: considered unlikely to win or attracting few bets.

unfasten verb trans (**unfastened, unfastening**) **1** to loosen or undo (something). **2** to untie or detach (something).

unfathomable adj **1** impossible to comprehend: *like a ripple on an unfathomable enigma* — Joseph Conrad. **2** immeasurable: *unfathomable seas.* ➤➤ **unfathomableness** noun, **unfathomably** adv.

unfavourable (*NAmer* **unfavorable**) adj **1** expressing disapproval or lack of support; negative. **2** disadvantageous; adverse: *an unfavourable economic climate.* ➤➤ **unfavourably** adv.

unfazed adj informal not disconcerted or daunted: *Private Boyd walked through, unfazed by the half-clothed bodies scrabbling for cover* — Mike Ripley.

unfeeling adj **1** not kind or sympathetic; hardhearted. **2** devoid of physical feeling or sensation. ➤➤ **unfeelingly** adv, **unfeelingness** noun.

unfetter verb trans (**unfettered, unfettering**) **1** to release (somebody) from fetters: *unfetter a prisoner.* **2** to free (something) from restraint; to liberate (it): *unfettered trade.*

unfinished adj **1** not brought to an end or to the desired final state; incomplete. **2a** not having been given a finish: *unfinished woodwork.* **b** said of fabric: subjected to no other processes, e.g. bleaching or dyeing, after coming from the loom.

unfit¹ adj **1** unsuitable or inappropriate. **2** incapable or incompetent: *unfit for duty.* **3** physically or mentally unsound. ➤➤ **unfitly** adv, **unfitness** noun.

unfit² verb trans (**unfitted, unfitting**) to make (somebody) unfit; to disqualify (them): *unfitted by temperament for the scholastic life.*

unfix verb trans to detach or loosen (something) from a fastening.

unfixed adj unstable, unsettled, or uncertain.

unflagging adj never flagging; tireless. ➤➤ **unflaggingly** adv.

unflappable adj informal remaining calm and composed; imperturbable. ➤➤ **unflappability** /-'biliti/ noun, **unflappably** adv.

unflattering adj not flattering, *esp* unfavourable: *unflattering comments.* ➤➤ **unflatteringly** adv.

unfledged adj **1** said of a young bird: having not yet developed the feathers necessary for flight. **2** not fully developed; immature: *an unfledged writer.*

unflinching adj not flinching or shrinking; steadfast. ➤➤ **unflinchingly** adv.

unfocused *or* **unfocussed** adj **1** lacking direction or a specific aim: *an unfocused approach to the problems.* **2** not focused or out of focus.

unfold verb trans **1** to open the folds of (e.g. a map or blanket); to spread or straighten (it) out. **2** to disclose or reveal (something) gradually. ➤ verb intrans **1** to open from a folded state. **2** to be disclosed or revealed gradually: *as the story unfolded.*

unforeseeable adj incapable of being foreseen or predicted.

unforeseen adj not predicted or expected.

unforgettable adj incapable of being forgotten; memorable. ➤➤ **unforgettably** adv.

unforgivable adj too bad, cruel, etc to be forgiven or excused. ➤➤ **unforgivably** adv.

unformed adj **1** not shaped. **2** immature or undeveloped.

unfortunate¹ adj **1a** unsuccessful or unlucky. **b** accompanied by or resulting in misfortune: *an unfortunate decision.* **2** unsuitable; inappropriate: *an unfortunate choice of words.* ➤➤ **unfortunately** adv.

unfortunate² noun an unlucky person.

unfounded adj lacking a sound basis; groundless: *unfounded accusations.* ➤➤ **unfoundedly** adv, **unfoundedness** noun.

UNFPA abbr United Nations Fund for Population Activities.

unfreeze verb (*past tense* **unfroze** /un'frohz/, *past part.* **unfrozen** /un'frohz(ə)n/) ➤ verb trans **1** to cause (something) to thaw. **2** to free (e.g. prices or assets) from restrictions. ➤ verb intrans to thaw.

unfrequented adj not often visited or travelled over.

unfriendly adj (**unfriendlier, unfriendliest**) **1** not friendly; hostile or unsympathetic. **2** inhospitable or unfavourable: *an unfriendly climate.* **3** not user-friendly. ➤➤ **unfriendliness** noun.

unfrock verb trans to deprive (somebody, *esp* a priest) of the right to exercise the functions of office.

unfroze verb past tense of UNFREEZE.

unfrozen verb past part. of UNFREEZE.

unfunded adj **1** said of a debt: not funded; floating. **2** not provided with funds: *The school remains unfunded by the state.*

unfurl verb intrans to open out from a furled state; to unroll. ➤ verb trans to cause (something) to unfurl.

unfurnished adj said *esp* of a rented property: not equipped with furniture.

ungainly /un'gaynli/ adj (**ungainlier, ungainliest**) **1** lacking in grace or dexterity; clumsy. **2** unwieldy or awkward. ➤➤ **ungainliness** noun. [UN-¹ + Middle English *gainly* suitable, graceful, from Old English *gēn* straight, handy, from Old Norse *gegn*]

ungenerous *adj* **1** petty or uncharitable. **2** showing a lack of generosity; mean. ➤➤ **ungenerously** *adv*.

ungetatable /unget'atǝbl/ *adj informal* inaccessible; unapproachable.

ungodly *adj* (**ungodlier, ungodliest**) **1a** denying God or disobedient to him; irreligious or impious. **b** sinful, wicked, or immoral. **2** *informal* unreasonable, inconvenient, or outrageous: *getting up at an ungodly hour.* ➤➤ **ungodliness** *noun*.

ungovernable *adj* not capable of being controlled or restrained. ➤➤ **ungovernably** *adv*.

ungraceful *adj* lacking in grace; awkward or inelegant. ➤➤ **ungracefully** *adv*, **ungracefulness** *noun*.

ungracious *adj* **1** rude, impolite. **2** not pleasing, disagreeable. ➤➤ **ungraciously** *adv*, **ungraciousness** *noun*.

ungrateful *adj* **1** showing no gratitude. **2** disagreeable; unpleasant. ➤➤ **ungratefully** *adv*, **ungratefulness** *noun*.

ungual *adj* of, bearing, or resembling a nail, claw, or hoof. [Latin *unguis* nail, claw, hoof]

unguarded *adj* **1** vulnerable to attack. **2** showing poor judgment or lack of forethought, *esp* in speech; imprudent or careless. **3** without a guard or screen: *an unguarded fire.* ➤➤ **unguardedly** *adv*, **unguardedness** *noun*.

unguent /'unggwǝnt/ *noun* a soothing or healing salve; an ointment. [Middle English from Latin *unguentum*, from *unguere* to annoint]

ungues /'unggweez/ *noun* pl of UNGUIS.

unguiculate /ung'gwikyoolǝt, -layt/ *adj* **1** said of an animal: having nails or claws. **2** said of a petal: having an unguis. [Latin *unguiculus* fingernail, dimin. of *unguis* nail, claw]

unguis /'unggwis/ *noun* (*pl* **ungues** /'unggweez/) **1** a nail, claw, or hoof, *esp* on a digit of a vertebrate animal. **2** a narrow pointed clawlike or stalk-like base of a petal. [Latin *unguis* nail, claw, hoof]

ungulate /'ungyoolǝt, -layt/ *noun* any of the hoofed mammals, e.g. cattle, pigs, horses, and deer, most of which are plant-eating and many of which have horns: order Ungulata. [Latin group name, neuter pl of late Latin *ungulatus* hoofed, from Latin *ungula* hoof, from *unguis* nail, hoof]

unhand *verb trans archaic, literary, humorous* to remove one's hands from (somebody or something); to release (them) from one's grasp.

unhappy *adj* (**unhappier, unhappiest**) **1** sad; miserable. **2** not fortunate; unlucky. **3** unsuitable; inappropriate: *an unhappy remark.* ➤➤ **unhappily** *adv*, **unhappiness** *noun*.

unharmed *adj* not damaged or injured.

UNHCR *abbr* United Nations High Commissioner for Refugees.

unhealthy *adj* (**unhealthier, unhealthiest**) **1a** not in good health. **b** not characteristic of or conducive to good health. **2** unnatural, indecent, or morbid: *an unhealthy interest in death.* ➤➤ **unhealthily** *adv*, **unhealthiness** *noun*.

unheard *adj* **1** not perceived by the ear. **2** not given a hearing; disregarded.

unheard-of *adj* previously unknown; unprecedented.

unheeded *adj* not heeded; ignored or disregarded.

unhelpful *adj* not helpful; uncooperative. ➤➤ **unhelpfully** *adv*.

unheralded *adj* not previously announced: *unheralded changes to the system.*

unhinge *verb trans* **1** to remove (e.g. a door) from hinges. **2** to disturb the balance of (a person or their mind): *The psychologist, to show that he was not unhinged, helped himself to a cigar and tried to light it uncut* — H G Wells; *Her mind was unhinged by grief.*

unholy *adj* (**unholier, unholiest**) **1** wicked, immoral, or unnatural: *an unholy alliance.* **2** *informal* terrible; awful: *making an unholy racket.* ➤➤ **unholiness** *noun*.

unhook *verb trans* **1** to remove (something) from a hook. **2** to unfasten the hooks of (something).

unhorse *verb trans* **1** to cause (somebody) to fall from a horse. **2** to dislodge (somebody) from a position of power.

unhurried *adj* not hurried; leisurely. ➤➤ **unhurriedly** *adv*.

unhurt *adj* not injured or harmed.

unhygienic *adj* not in accordance with the rules of hygiene.

uni /'yoohni/ *noun* (*pl* **unis**) *informal* = UNIVERSITY.

uni- *prefix* forming words, with the meaning: one; single: *unicellular; unicameral; unicorn.* [Middle English via French from Latin *unus* one]

Uniate[1] /'yoohniit, -ayt/ *or* **Uniat** /-at/ *adj* belonging or relating to or denoting a Christian Church that adheres to Eastern rites but submits to papal authority. [Russian *uniyat* from Polish *uniat*, from *unja* union, from late Latin *union-, unio*: see UNION]

Uniate[2] *or* **Uniat** *noun* a member of a Uniate Church.

uniaxial /yoohni'aksi·ǝl/ *adj* of or having only one axis. ➤➤ **uniaxially** *adv*.

unicameral /yoohni'kamǝrǝl/ *adj* of or having a single legislative chamber. ➤➤ **unicamerally** *adv*. [UNI- + *-cameral* as in BICAMERAL]

UNICEF /'yoohnisef/ *abbr* United Nations Children's Fund (formerly United Nations International Children's Emergency Fund).

unicellular /yoohni'selyoolǝ/ *adj* consisting of a single cell. ➤➤ **unicellularity** /-'lariti/ *noun*.

unicorn /'yoohnikawn/ *noun* **1** a mythical animal usu depicted as a white horse with a single straight horn in the middle of the forehead. **2** a heraldic representation of this often depicted as having a spiral horn, a stag's legs, and a lion's tail. [Middle English *unicorne* via Old French from Latin *unicornis* having one horn, from UNI- + *cornu* horn]

unicycle /'yoohnisiekl/ *noun* any of various vehicles that have a single wheel, are usu propelled by pedals, and are used *esp* by acrobats. ➤➤ **unicyclist** *noun*.

unidentified *adj* not known, recognized, or identified.

unidirectional /,yoohnidi'reksh(ǝ)nl, -die'reksh(ǝ)nl/ *adj* involving, functioning in, or moving in a single direction. ➤➤ **unidirectionally** *adv*.

UNIDO /yooh'needoh/ *abbr* United Nations Industrial Development Organization.

unification /,yoohnifi'kaysh(ǝ)n/ *noun* the act, process, or result of unifying; the state of being unified.

Unification Church *noun* the Church of the Moonies (members of a religious sect founded in South Korea; see MOONIE).

unified field theory /'yoohnified/ *noun* in physics, a theory describing the properties of gravitational and electromagnetic fields and strong and weak interactions in the same set of equations.

uniform[1] /'yoohnifawm/ *adj* not varying in character, appearance, quantity, etc: *at a uniform speed.* ➤➤ **uniformly** *adv*, **uniformness** *noun*. [early French *uniforme* from Latin *uniformis*, from UNI- + *-formis* -FORM]

uniform[2] *noun* **1a** clothing of a distinctive design, colour, etc worn by members of a particular group, e.g. soldiers, and serving as a means of identification. **b** the prescribed clothes that must be worn by the pupils of a particular school. **2** *chiefly NAmer, informal* a police officer wearing a uniform, *esp* as distinct from a plainclothes detective, etc.

uniform[3] *verb trans* **1** to clothe (somebody) in a uniform: *a uniformed officer.* **2** to make (something) uniform.

uniformitarianism /,yoohnifawmi'teǝri·ǝniz(ǝ)m/ *noun* the theory that all geological changes can be accounted for by gradual continuing processes, e.g. faulting and erosion. ➤➤ **uniformitarian** *adj and noun*.

uniformity /yoohni'fawmiti/ *noun* (*pl* **uniformities**) **1** lack of variation or diversity. **2** an instance of uniformity.

unify /'yoohnifie/ *verb* (**unifies, unified, unifying**) ➤ *verb trans* to make (a group of people or things) into a unit or a coherent whole; to unite (them): *In short Australia – which used to have one unifying rite, cricket – has now become pluralist* — Thomas Kenneally. ➤ *verb intrans* to become unified. ➤➤ **unifiable** *adj*, **unifier** *noun*. [late Latin *unificare*, from UNI- + Latin *-ficare* -FY]

unilateral /yoohni'lat(ǝ)rǝl/ *adj* **1** done or undertaken by only one person or group: *unilateral disarmament.* **2** of or affecting only one side: *unilateral paralysis.* **3** situated on or directed towards one side: *a stem bearing unilateral flowers.* ➤➤ **unilateralism** *noun*, **unilaterally** *adv*.

unimaginative *adj* **1** not given to creative thought. **2** not interesting, unusual, or innovative. ➤➤ **unimaginatively** *adv*.

unimpeachable *adj* **1** not to be doubted; beyond question. **2** irreproachable; blameless. ➤➤ **unimpeachably** *adv*.

unimportant *adj* having little or no importance. ≫ **unimportance** *noun*.

unimproved *adj* **1** not improved for use, e.g. by being cleared or cultivated: *unimproved land*. **2** not used or employed advantageously. **3** not improved or better.

unincorporated *adj* **1** not part of a whole or a corporate body. **2** said of a business: privately owned and not legally registered as a company.

uninformed *adj* **1** lacking awareness, knowledge, or understanding of something. **2** said of a decision, etc: made without being aware of, knowing, or understanding all the relevant facts.

uninhabited *adj* having no inhabitants.

uninhibited *adj* acting or speaking spontaneously without constraint or regard for what others might think. ≫ **uninhibitedly** *adv*, **uninhibitedness** *noun*.

uninitiated *adj* lacking special knowledge or experience of something.

uninspiring *adj* not arousing interest, excitement, or enthusiasm. ≫ **uninspiringly** *adv*.

unintelligible *adj* not capable of being understood; obscure. ≫ **unintelligibility** /-'biliti/ *noun*, **unintelligibly** *adv*.

unintentional *adj* not done deliberately; accidental. ≫ **unintentionally** *adv*.

uninterested *adj* not having the interest aroused or attention engaged; unconcerned. ≫ **uninterestedly** *adv*, **uninterestedness** *noun*.

Usage note ─────
uninterested or disinterested? See note at DISINTERESTED.

uninteresting *adj* not arousing interest or engaging the attention; boring. ≫ **uninterestingly** *adv*, **uninterestingness** *noun*.

uninterrupted *adj* **1** not interrupted; continuous. **2** not obstructed: *an uninterrupted view*. ≫ **uninterruptedly** *adv*.

uninvited *adj* not having been asked for or invited: *uninvited guests; uninvited opinions*.

union /'yoohnyən/ *noun* **1a** the act or an instance of uniting or joining two or more things into one. **b** a unified condition; combination or junction. **2a** a uniting in marriage. **b** sexual intercourse. **3a** something that is made one; something formed by a combining or coalition of parts or members. **b** an association of independent individuals or groups for some common purpose. **c** an organization run by the students of an educational institution. **d** = TRADE UNION. **e** (*used before a noun*) of or belonging to a union, *esp* a trade union. **4** in mathematics, the set of all elements belonging to one or both of two given sets. **5a** (*often* **the Union**) a political unit made up from previously independent units that have surrendered their principal powers to the government of the whole, e.g. England and Scotland in 1707, or to a newly created government, e.g. the USA in 1789. **b** (*often* **Union**) the formation of such a political unit. **6a** an emblem of the union of two or more sovereignties borne on a national flag. **b** the upper inner corner of a flag. **7** any of various devices for connecting parts, e.g. of a machine, *esp* a coupling for pipes or pipes and fittings. **8** any of various cloths having the warp and the weft of different fibres. **9** any of various groups of English parishes that joined together in the 19th cent. in order to make administering the Poor Laws easier and more efficient. [Middle English via French from late Latin *union-*, *unio* oneness, union, from Latin *unus* one]

union catalogue *noun* a catalogue that lists all the books, periodicals, etc held at a group of libraries.

union cloth *noun* = UNION (8).

Union Flag *noun* = UNION JACK.

unionise *verb trans and intrans* see UNIONIZE.

unionism *noun* **1** the principles of trade unions or the adherence to these principles. **2** (**Unionism**) the policy of union between the states of the USA, *esp* during the Civil War or the adherence to this policy. **3** (**Unionism**) before 1920, the policy of union between Great Britain and Ireland. **4** (**Unionism**) the principles and policies of the Unionist party of N Ireland.

unionist¹ *adj* **1** (**Unionist**) of or being a political party of N Ireland that supports the union with Britain and draws support generally from the Protestant community. **2** (*also* **Unionist**) of or supporting union, unionism, or Unionism.

unionist² *noun* **1** (*also* **Unionist**) an advocate or supporter of union, unionism, or Unionism. **2** a member of a trade union.

unionize *or* **unionise** *verb trans* **1** to cause (a worker or workers) to become a member or members of a trade union. **2** to subject (something) to the rules of a trade union. ≫ *verb intrans* to become a member or members of a trade union. ≫ **unionization** /-'za-ysh(ə)n/ *noun*.

Union Jack *noun* the national flag of Britain combining the crosses of St George, St Andrew, and St Patrick.

Word history ─────
properly called the *Union Flag*, a *jack* (from the name *Jack*) being a small flag flown on a ship to indicate its nationality. However, *Union Jack* has been used at least since the early 19th cent. for any size or adaptation of the Union Flag.

union suit *noun* NAmer, dated a one-piece undergarment; combinations.

uniparous /yoo'nipərəs/ *adj* producing only one egg or offspring at a time.

unipolar /'yoohni'pohlə/ *adj* **1** having or produced by a single magnetic or electrical pole. **2** said of a nerve cell: having a single projecting structure along which nerve impulses are conducted. **3** said of a transistor: using charge carriers of a single polarity, either negative or positive. ≫ **unipolarity** /-'lariti/ *noun*.

unique /yooh'neek, yoo'neek/ *adj* **1** being the only one; sole: *his unique concern*. **2a** without a like or equal. **b** (+ to) belonging to or occurring in only one (person, place, etc). **3** producing only one result: *the unique factorization of a number into prime factors*. ≫ **uniquely** *adv*, **uniqueness** *noun*. [French *unique* from Latin *unicus*, from *unus* one]

Usage note ─────
If something is *unique* it is the only one of its kind. It is consequently illogical to speak of one thing being *more* or *less unique* than another or of something as being *rather*, *very*, *comparatively* or *somewhat unique*. It is correct to talk of, for example, a *unique opportunity* or to describe something as *almost unique* or *nearly unique*, but, where any kind of comparison is implied, it is better to choose another adjective such as *unusual* or *rare*.

unisex /'yoohniseks/ *adj* **1** suitable or designed for either sex: *a unisex jacket*. **2** dealing in unisex products or styles: *a unisex hairdresser's*.

unisexual /yoohni'seksyooəl, -shooəl/ *adj* **1** of or restricted to one sex. **2** said of an animal or plant: male or female but not both; having either male or female reproductive organs. ≫ **unisexuality** /-'aliti/ *noun*, **unisexually** *adv*.

UNISON /'yoohnis(ə)n/ *noun* in Britain, a trade union for employees in local government, the health service, and other parts of the public sector.

unison /'yoohnis(ə)n/ *noun* **1** harmonious agreement or union. **2a** identity in musical pitch. **b** the writing, playing, or singing of parts in a musical passage at the same pitch or one or more octaves apart. **c** (*used before a noun*) played or sung in unison. ✳ **in unison 1** in perfect agreement or harmony. **2** saying or doing the same thing at the same time: *But when all the arts journalists in London start fluffing up their tail feathers in unison, the effect is not so much of natural compulsion as of chummy conspiracy* — Independent. ≫ **unisonous** *adj*. [Middle English via French from late Latin *unisonus* having the same sound, from Latin UNI- + *sonus* sound]

unit /'yoohnit/ *noun* **1a** a single thing, person, or group that is a constituent of a whole. **b** a part of an organization, e.g. a military establishment, that has a specific function. **c** a piece of apparatus or part of a device serving to perform one particular function. **2** a determinate quantity, e.g. of length, time, heat or value, adopted as a standard of measurement: *Kilograms and ounces are units of weight*. **3a** a single quantity regarded as a whole in calculation. **b** the number occupying the position immediately to the left of the decimal point. **4a** the first and lowest natural number; one. **b** (*used before a noun*) of or having a value of one. **5** a single manufactured article. **6** a group of buildings, a single building, or a distinct part of a building, usu with a specified purpose: *the intensive care unit*. **7a** a standard measure of the alcohol content of a drink, used *esp* as a way of monitoring alcohol intake and advising on recommended drinking levels. **b** a measure of a drug, vaccine, etc that is needed for a particular effect. **c** a quantity of blood for transfusion: *two units of O negative*. **8** a distinct section of academic work, usu part of a larger course or module. ≫ **unitive** /-tiv/ *adj*. [back-formation from UNITY]

UNITAR *abbr* United Nations Institute for Training and Research.

unitarian /yoohni'teəri·ən/ *noun* **1a** a Christian who rejects the doctrine of the Trinity and believes that God is a single being. **b** (**Unitarian**) a member of a Christian denomination that stresses individual freedom of belief, the free use of reason in religion, a united world community, and liberal social action. **2** an advocate of unity or a unitary system. ⧭ **Unitarian** *adj*, **unitarian** *adj*, **Unitarianism** *noun*, **unitarianism** *noun*. [Latin *unitarius*, from *unitas*: see UNITY]

unitary /'yoohnit(ə)ri/ *adj* **1a** of or relating to a unit or units. **b** based on or characterized by unity. **2** undivided; whole. ⧭ **unitarily** *adv*.

unitary authority *noun* in Britain, a district with a single-tier system of local government.

unit character *noun* a genetically determined characteristic that is inherited either as a whole or not at all, *esp* one dependent on the presence or absence of a single gene.

unite /yoo'niet/ *verb trans* **1** to join (people or things) together to form a single unit. **2** to cause (people) to form an alliance or association: *The minister united them in marriage.* **3** to cause (things) to adhere or fuse. ⧭ *verb intrans* **1** to become a single unit. **2** to act together for a common purpose. **3** to adhere or fuse. ⧭ **unitive** /-tiv/ *adj*. [Middle English *uniten* from late Latin *unitus*, past part. of *unire*, from Latin *unus* one]

united *adj* **1** combined; joined. **2** relating to or produced by joint action: *a united effort.* **3** in agreement; harmonious. ⧭ **unitedly** *adv*.

unitize *or* **unitise** /'yoohnitiez/ *verb trans* **1** to form (something) into a unit. **2** to divide (something) into units: *the added cost of unitizing bulk products.* **3** to convert (an investment trust) into a unit trust. ⧭ **unitization** /-'zaysh(ə)n/ *noun*.

unit trust *noun* an investment company that minimizes the risk to investors by collective purchase of shares in many different enterprises: compare INVESTMENT TRUST.

unity /'yoohniti/ *noun* (*pl* **unities**) **1** the state of being one or united: *Strength lies in unity.* **2a** concord; harmony. **b** continuity and agreement, e.g. in aims or interests: *unity of purpose.* **3** singleness of effect or symmetry in a literary or artistic work. **4** a whole made up of related parts. **5a** the number one or a definite amount taken as one for the purpose of calculation. **b** a number by which any element of an arithmetical or mathematical system can be multiplied without change in the resultant value. **6** any of the three principles of dramatic structure, observed in classical drama, which require a play to have a single plot (unity of action) occurring in one place (unity of place) within one day (unity of time). [Middle English *unite* via Old French from Latin *unitat-*, *unitas*, from *unus* one]

univ. *abbr* **1** universal. **2** university.

univalent[1] /yoohni'vaylənt/ *adj* **1** in chemistry, having a valency of one; monovalent. **2** said of a chromosome: remaining unpaired during cell division in which chromosomes from each parent associate in pairs.

univalent[2] *noun* a univalent chromosome.

univalve[1] /'yoohnivalv/ *adj* having or being a shell consisting of one valve.

univalve[2] *noun* a snail, whelk, or similar invertebrate animal with a univalve shell.

universal[1] /yoohni'vuhs(ə)l/ *adj* **1** including or covering all without limit or exception. **2** present or occurring everywhere or under all conditions. **3** including a major part or the greatest portion of a whole: *universal practices.* **4** said of a proposition in logic: affirming or denying something about every member of a class: compare PARTICULAR[1] (5): *'No man knows everything' is a universal negative.* **5** adapted or adjustable to meet varied requirements, e.g. of use, shape, or size. ⧭ **universality** /-'saliti/ *noun*, **universally** *adv*. [Middle English via French from Latin *universalis*, from *universum*: see UNIVERSE]

universal[2] *noun* **1** a universal proposition in logic. **2a** a general concept or term. **b** something to which a general term corresponds; essence. **3** a characteristic that exists in all cultures or among all normal adult members of a particular society.

universal coupling *noun* = UNIVERSAL JOINT.

universalise *verb trans* see UNIVERSALIZE.

universalism *noun* **1** (*often* **Universalism**) a theological doctrine that everyone will eventually be saved. **2** the state of being universal; universality. **3** something that is universal. ⧭ **universalist** *noun and adj*.

universalize *or* **universalise** *verb trans* to make (something) universal. ⧭ **universalization** /-'zaysh(ə)n/ *noun*.

universal joint *noun* a joint uniting two shafts and capable of transmitting rotation from one shaft to the other at an angle.

Universal Time *noun* = GREENWICH MEAN TIME.

universe /'yoohnivuhs/ *noun* **1** all things that exist; the cosmos. **2** the whole world; everybody. **3** a set that contains all elements relevant to a particular discussion or problem. **4** a sphere of activity. [Latin *universum*, neuter of *universus* entire, whole, from UNI- + *versus* turned towards, past part. of *vertere* to turn]

university /yoohni'vuhsiti/ *noun* (*pl* **universities**) **1** an institution of higher learning that provides facilities for full-time teaching and research and is authorized to grant academic degrees. **2** the premises, staff, students, or campus of such an institution. [Middle English *universite* via Old French from late Latin *universitat-*, *universitas*, from Latin *universus*: see UNIVERSE]

univocal /yoohni'vohkl, yooh'nivəkl/ *adj* having one meaning only; unambiguous. ⧭ **univocally** *adv*. [late Latin *univocus*, from UNI- + Latin *voc-*, *vox* voice]

unjust *adj* characterized by injustice; unfair. ⧭ **unjustly** *adv*, **unjustness** *noun*.

unkempt /un'kempt/ *adj* **1** not combed; dishevelled: *unkempt hair.* **2** not neat or tidy. ⧭ **unkemptly** *adv*, **unkemptness** *noun*. [UN-[1] + Middle English *kempt* combed, neat, past part. of *kemben* to comb, from Old English *cemban*]

unkind /un'kiend/ *adj* lacking in kindness or sympathy; harsh or cruel. ⧭ **unkindly** *adv*, **unkindness** *noun*.

unknowable *adj* not knowable, *esp* lying beyond the limits of human experience or understanding.

unknowing *adj* not knowing; unaware. ⧭ **unknowingly** *adv*.

unknown[1] *adj* **1** not known. **2** having an unknown value: *an unknown quantity.* **3** not famous or familiar.

unknown[2] *noun* **1** somebody who is little known, e.g. to the public. **2** something that requires to be discovered, identified, or clarified. **3** a symbol in a mathematical equation representing an unknown quantity.

Unknown Soldier *noun* an unidentified soldier whose body is entombed in a national memorial as a representative of all the members of the armed forces of the same nation who died in a war, *esp* either of the World Wars.

Unknown Warrior *noun* = UNKNOWN SOLDIER.

unlace *verb trans* to undo the lacing of (e.g. a shoe).

unlaid *verb* past tense and past part. of UNLAY.

unlatch *verb trans* to open (e.g. a door) by lifting a latch. ⧭ *verb intrans* to become unlatched.

unlawful *adj* **1** against the law or contrary to the rules; illegal. **2** not morally right or conventional. ⧭ **unlawfully** *adv*, **unlawfulness** *noun*.

unlay *verb trans* (*past tense and past part.* **unlaid** /-'layd/) to untwist the strands of (e.g. a rope).

unleaded /un'ledid/ *adj* **1** said *esp* of petrol: not treated or mixed with lead or lead compounds. **2** in printing, not having leads between the lines for spacing.

unlearn *verb trans* (*past tense and past part.* **unlearned** /un'luhnd, un'luhnt/ *or* **unlearnt** /un'luhnt/) **1** to put (something) out of one's knowledge or memory. **2** to discard the habit of (something).

unlearned /un'luhnid/ *adj* not educated; ignorant. ⧭ **unlearnedly** *adv*.

unlearnt *or* **unlearned** *adj* not gained by study, training, or experience.

unleash *verb trans* to free (something or somebody) from or as if from a leash; to loose (them) from restraint or control.

unleavened *adj* made from or denoting dough that contains no yeast or other raising agent.

unless /ən'les/ *conj* **1** except on the condition that: *I won't go unless you want me to.* **2** except when: *We swim every day unless it's very cold.* [Middle English *unlesse*, alteration of *onlesse*, from *on* ON[1] + *lesse* LESS[1]]

unlettered *adj* uneducated or illiterate.

unlicensed *adj* not having a licence, *esp* one permitting the sale of alcoholic drinks.

unlike[1] *prep* **1** different from (another person or thing). **2** not characteristic of (somebody or something): *It's unlike him to be late.* **3** in a different manner from (another person or thing).

unlike[2] *adj* **1** marked by dissimilarity; different. **2** unequal. >> **unlikeness** *noun*.

unlikely *adj* (**unlikelier, unlikeliest**) **1** having a low probability of being or occurring. **2** not believable; incredible: *an unlikely story.* **3** likely to fail; unpromising. >> **unlikelihood** *noun*, **unlikeliness** *noun*.

unlimber *verb trans* (**unlimbered, unlimbering**) **1** to detach (a gun) from its LIMBER[2] (part of gun carriage) and so make it ready for use. **2** to prepare (something) for action or use.

unlimited *adj* **1** lacking any controls or restrictions. **2** boundless; infinite. >> **unlimitedly** *adv*, **unlimitedness** *noun*.

unlined[1] *adj* not marked with lines, creases, wrinkles, etc: *unlined paper; a youthful unlined face.*

unlined[2] *adj* without a lining: *unlined curtains.*

unlisted *adj* **1** not appearing on a list. **2** *chiefly NAmer* = EX-DIRECTORY.

Unlisted Securities Market *noun* a market for trading in shares, e.g. of small or new companies, that are not traded on the Stock Exchange.

unlit *adj* **1** without any lighting: *a dark unlit cellar.* **2** not lit: *an unlit cigarette.*

unload *verb trans* **1a** to remove or discharge (e.g. cargo). **b** to take the cargo from (e.g. a lorry or ship). **2** to relieve (a person or animal) of something burdensome. **3** to give vent to (e.g. feelings). **4a** to remove the cartridge or projectile from (e.g. a gun). **b** to take (the cartridge or projectile) from a gun, etc. **5a** to remove the film from (a camera). **b** to take (the film) from a camera. **6a** to get rid of (something unwanted or surplus). **b** to sell (merchandise), *esp* in large quantities; to dump (it). >> *verb intrans* to unload something. >> **unloader** *noun*.

unlock *verb trans* **1** to unfasten the lock of (something). **2** to release (something): *unlock a flood of tears.* **3** to provide a key to (something mysterious): *unlock the secrets of nature.* >> *verb intrans* to become unlocked.

unlooked-for *adj* not foreseen or expected.

unloose *verb trans* **1** to relax the strain of (e.g. a grip). **2** to release (something or somebody) from or as if from restraints; to set (them) free. **3** to loosen or undo the ties of (something).

unloosen *verb trans* = UNLOOSE.

unloved *adj* not loved by anybody.

unlovely *adj* disagreeable; unpleasant. >> **unloveliness** *noun*.

unlucky *adj* (**unluckier, unluckiest**) **1** marked by adversity or failure: *an unlucky year.* **2** likely to bring misfortune: *an unlucky omen.* **3** having or meeting with bad luck: *unlucky people.* >> **unluckily** *adv*, **unluckiness** *noun*.

unmade *adj* **1** said of a bed: not put in order ready for sleeping. **2** *Brit* said of a road: not having a hard smooth surface; not metalled.

unmake *verb trans* (*past tense and past part.* **unmade** /un'mayd/) **1** to undo or destroy (somebody or something). **2** to deprive (somebody) of rank or office; to depose (them). **3** to change the nature of (something).

unman /un'man/ *verb trans* (**unmanned, unmanning**) *literary, humorous* to deprive (a man) of vigour, fortitude, courage, resolve, etc: *Indeed, it was his very mildness, chiefly, which not only disarmed me but unmanned me, as it were* — Herman Melville.

unmanageable *adj* difficult or impossible to handle or control. >> **unmanageably** *adv*.

unmanly *adj* **1** lacking in manly virtues; weak or cowardly. **2** effeminate. >> **unmanliness** *noun*.

unmanned *adj* not having or needing a human crew: *an unmanned spaceflight.*

unmannerly *adj* discourteous; rude. >> **unmannerliness** *noun*.

unmask *verb trans* **1** to remove a mask or disguise from (somebody). **2** to reveal the true character or nature of (somebody or something); to expose (them).

unmatched *adj* not equalled; beyond compare.

unmentionable *adj* not fit to be mentioned; unspeakable. >> **unmentionableness** *noun*, **unmentionably** *adv*.

unmentionables *pl noun euphem, humorous* underwear.

unmerciful *adj* **1** showing no mercy; merciless. **2** excessive or extreme. >> **unmercifully** *adv*, **unmercifulness** *noun*.

unmindful *adj* (+ of) not taking (something) into account; forgetful of (it). >> **unmindfully** *adv*, **unmindfulness** *noun*.

unmissable *adj* **1** impossible not to hit or notice. **2** said e.g. of a television programme: too good to miss.

unmistakeable *or* **unmistakeable** *adj* not capable of being mistaken or misunderstood; clear or obvious. >> **unmistakably** *adv*.

unmitigated *adj* **1** not diminished in severity, intensity, etc. **2** out-and-out; downright: *The evening was an unmitigated disaster.* >> **unmitigatedly** *adv*.

unmoral *adj* having no moral quality or significance. >> **unmorality** /-'raliti/ *noun*.

unmoved *adj* not affected by emotion. >> **unmovable** *adj*, **unmoveable** *adj*.

unmurmuring *adj* uncomplaining. >> **unmurmuringly** *adv*.

unmuzzle *verb trans* **1** to remove a muzzle from (an animal). **2** to free (somebody or something) as if from a muzzle, *esp* by restoring freedom of expression.

unnatural *adj* **1** not in accordance with nature or a normal course of events. **2** not in accordance with normal feelings or behaviour. **3** artificial or contrived in manner. **4** *archaic* wicked; monstrous: *Revenge his foul and most unnatural murther* — Shakespeare. >> **unnaturally** *adv*, **unnaturalness** *noun*.

unnecessary *adj* not necessary. >> **unnecessarily** *adv*, **unnecessariness** *noun*.

unnerve *verb trans* **1** to deprive (somebody) of courage, strength, confidence, etc. **2** to make (somebody) nervous. >> **unnerving** *adj*, **unnervingly** *adv*.

unnumbered *adj* **1** innumerable. **2** without an identifying number: *unnumbered pages.*

UNO /,yooh en 'oh, 'yoohnoh/ *abbr* United Nations Organization.

unobserved *adj* not seen or noticed.

unobtainable *adj* impossible to acquire or attain.

unobtrusive *adj* not easily seen or noticed; inconspicuous. >> **unobtrusively** *adv*, **unobtrusiveness** *noun*.

unoccupied *adj* **1** not occupied, *esp* not lived in. **2** not busy; unemployed.

unofficial *adj* not authorized or official. >> **unofficially** *adv*.

unorganized *or* **unorganised** *adj* **1** not organized into a coherent or well-ordered whole. **2** not belonging to a trade union. **3** not having the characteristics of a living organism.

unorthodox *adj* not conventional in behaviour, beliefs, etc. >> **unorthodoxly** *adv*, **unorthodoxy** *noun*.

unowned *adj* **1** having no owner. **2** not acknowledged.

unpack *verb trans* **1** to remove the contents of (e.g. a suitcase). **2** to remove (something) from packing or from a container. **3** in computing, to restore (compressed data, files, etc) to the original form. >> *verb intrans* to unpack something. >> **unpacker** *noun*.

unpaid *adj* **1** not paid or not yet paid: *unpaid debts.* **2a** not paying a salary, wage, or fee: *an unpaid job.* **b** not receiving payment: *unpaid assistants.*

unpaired *adj* not paired, *esp* not matched or mated.

unpalatable *adj* **1** not pleasing to the taste. **2** unpleasant; disagreeable. >> **unpalatability** /-'biliti/ *noun*, **unpalatably** *adv*.

unparalleled *adj* having no equal or match; unique.

unpardonable *adj* incapable of being forgiven: *an unpardonable offence.* >> **unpardonably** *adv*.

unparliamentary *adj* not in accordance with parliamentary practice.

unpeg *verb trans* (**unpegged, unpegging**) **1** to remove a peg or pegs from (something); to unfasten (it). **2** to cease to hold (e.g. prices or exchange rates) at a predetermined level.

unpeople *verb trans* to empty (a place) of inhabitants.

unperson *noun* (*pl* **unpersons**) a person whose existence is officially denied or unrecognized, *usu* for political or ideological reasons; a non-person.

unperturbed /unpə'tuhbd/ *adj* not disturbed or concerned. ➤➤ **unperturbedly** /-'tuhbidli/ *adv.*

unpick *verb trans* **1** to undo (e.g. sewing) by taking out stitches. **2** to take (something, *esp* an argument, theory, etc) apart in order to examine or analyse the underlying elements.

unpin *verb trans* (**unpinned, unpinning**) **1** to remove a pin or pins from (something). **2** to loosen or unfasten (something) by removing a pin or pins.

unplaced *adj* **1** *chiefly Brit* having failed to finish in a leading place in a competition, *esp* a horse race. **2** having no assigned or recognized place.

unpleasant *adj* not pleasant or agreeable; displeasing. ➤➤ **unpleasantly** *adv.*

unpleasantness *noun* **1** the quality or state of being unpleasant. **2** an unpleasant situation, experience, etc, *esp* bad feeling between people.

unplug *verb trans* (**unplugged, unplugging**) **1** to disconnect (e.g. an electrical appliance) by removing a plug from a socket. **2a** to take a plug out of (something). **b** to remove an obstruction from (something).

unplugged *adj* said *esp* of rock music or musicians: performed or performing on acoustic rather than electric instruments.

unplumbed *adj* **1** not thoroughly explored. **2** of unknown depth. **3** not supplied with plumbing.

unpolled *adj* **1** not having voted at an election. **2** not questioned or canvassed in an opinion poll.

unpopular *adj* **1** viewed or received unfavourably by the general public or a specified group of people. **2** said of a person: having few friends. ➤➤ **unpopularity** /-'lariti/ *noun.*

unpractical *adj* **1** incapable of dealing with practical matters; impractical. **2** incapable of being put to use; not practical.

unpractised (*NAmer* **unpracticed**) *adj* **1** not skilled or experienced. **2** not done repeatedly to develop proficiency.

unprecedented *adj* having no precedent; novel or unparalleled. ➤➤ **unprecedentedly** *adv.*

unpredictable *adj* not predictable; changeable or erratic. ➤➤ **unpredictability** /-'biliti/ *noun,* **unpredictably** *adv.*

unprejudiced *adj* impartial; fair.

unpremeditated *adj* not showing or resulting from premeditation, forethought, or planning. ➤➤ **unpremeditatedly** *adv.*

unprepared *adj* not ready or made ready. ➤➤ **unpreparedness** *noun.*

unprepossessing *adj* not attractive or pleasing: *The countenance of the priest was remarkably unprepossessing* — E Bulwer-Lytton.

unpretentious *adj* not seeking to impress others by means of wealth, standing, etc; not affected or ostentatious. ➤➤ **unpretentiously** *adv,* **unpretentiousness** *noun.*

unprincipled *adj* without moral principles; unscrupulous. ➤➤ **unprincipledness** *noun.*

unprintable *adj* incapable of being printed without causing offence; unfit for publication.

unprofessional *adj* not conforming to the technical or ethical standards of a profession. ➤➤ **unprofessionally** *adv.*

unprofitable *adj* **1** not yielding profit. **2** useless; vain. ➤➤ **unprofitability** /-'biliti/ *noun,* **unprofitably** *adv.*

unpromising *adj* seeming unlikely to prove worthwhile or have a favourable result. ➤➤ **unpromisingly** *adv.*

unpronounceable *adj* very difficult or impossible to pronounce.

unprotected *adj* **1** said of sexual intercourse: performed without contraception or protection against the transmission of disease, *esp* without using a condom. **2** not kept or made safe.

unprovoked *adj* done or happening without provocation: *an unprovoked attack.*

unputdownable /unpoot'downəbl/ *adj chiefly Brit, informal* said of a book or story: very interesting or exciting; compulsively readable.

unqualified *adj* **1** not having the necessary qualifications. **2** not modified or restricted by reservations: *unqualified approval.* ➤➤ **unqualifiedly** *adv.*

unquestionable *adj* not able to be doubted or challenged; indisputable: *unquestionable evidence.* ➤➤ **unquestionability** /-'biliti/ *noun,* **unquestionably** *adv.*

unquestioned *adj* **1** not doubted or challenged; undisputed. **2** accepted without question. **3** not subjected to questioning or interrogation.

unquestioning *adj* without doubt or hesitation: *unquestioning obedience.* ➤➤ **unquestioningly** *adv.*

unquiet *adj* **1** agitated; turbulent. **2** physically or mentally restless; uneasy. ➤➤ **unquietly** *adv,* **unquietness** *noun.*

unquote *noun* used in speech to indicate the end of a direct quotation.

unravel *verb* (**unravelled, unravelling,** *NAmer* **unraveled, unraveling**) ➤ *verb trans* **1** to disengage or separate the threads of (something knitted, woven, or tangled). **2** to clear up or solve (something intricate, complex, or obscure). ➤ *verb intrans* to become unravelled.

unread /un'red/ *adj* **1** not read: *unread letters.* **2** not familiar with or knowledgeable in a specified field: *unread in political science.*

unreadable /un'reedəbl/ *adj* **1** incapable of being read; not legible. **2** too difficult, boring, badly composed, etc to read. ➤➤ **unreadability** /-'biliti/ *noun.*

unready /un'redi/ *adj* **1** unprepared. **2** slow to act. ➤➤ **unreadiness** *noun.*

unreal *adj* **1** lacking in reality, substance, or genuineness; artificial or illusory. **2** *chiefly NAmer, informal* excellent; amazing. ➤➤ **unreality** /-'aliti/ *noun,* **unreally** *adv.*

unrealistic *adj* inappropriate to reality, fact, practicality, or good sense. ➤➤ **unrealistically** *adv.*

unreason *noun* the absence of reason or sanity; irrationality or madness.

unreasonable *adj* **1a** not governed by or acting according to reason: *unreasonable people.* **b** not complying with or based on reason: *unreasonable beliefs.* **2** excessive or immoderate: *unreasonable demands.* ➤➤ **unreasonableness** *noun,* **unreasonably** *adv.*

unreasoning *adj* not moderated or controlled by reason: *unreasoning fear.* ➤➤ **unreasoningly** *adv.*

unregenerate /unri'jenərət/ *adj* **1** not repentant or reformed. **2** obstinate; stubborn: *struggling against unregenerate impulses.* ➤➤ **unregeneracy** *noun,* **unregenerately** *adv.*

unrelenting *adj* **1** not weakening in determination; hard or stern. **2** not letting up in vigour, pace, etc. ➤➤ **unrelentingly** *adv,* **unrelentingness** *noun.*

unreliable *adj* incapable of being relied on; likely to fail. ➤➤ **unreliability** /-'biliti/ *noun,* **unreliably** *adv.*

unremitting *adj* constant; incessant; never lessening or letting up. ➤➤ **unremittingly** *adv,* **unremittingness** *noun.*

unremunerative *adj* providing inadequate or no remuneration; unprofitable. ➤➤ **unremuneratively** *adv.*

unrepeatable *adj* **1** incapable of being repeated: *an unrepeatable offer.* **2** unfit for repetition; too shocking, offensive, rude, etc to be repeated: *Her reply was unrepeatable.*

unrepresentative *adj* not typical or characteristic, *esp* as a sample or example.

unrequited *adj* said *esp* of love: not returned: *Love, unrequited, robs me of my rest* — W S Gilbert. ➤➤ **unrequitedly** *adv,* **unrequitedness** *noun.*

unreserved *adj* **1** entire and unqualified; without reservation: *unreserved enthusiasm.* **2** frank and open in manner; without reserve. **3** not booked or set aside; not reserved. ➤➤ **unreservedly** /-vidli/ *adv,* **unreservedness** *noun.*

unresponsive *adj* not reacting or answering. ➤➤ **unresponsively** *adv,* **unresponsiveness** *noun.*

unrest *noun* agitation or turmoil, *esp* caused by rebellion or dissatisfaction: *political unrest.*

unrestrained *adj* not held in check; uncontrolled. ➤➤ **unrestrainedly** /-nidli/ *adv,* **unrestrainedness** /-nidnis/ *noun.*

unrewarding *adj* **1** not yielding a reward. **2** not personally satisfying.

unripe *adj* **1** not ripe; immature. **2** unready; unprepared. ➤➤ **unripeness** *noun.*

unrivalled (*NAmer* **unrivaled**) *adj* unequalled; unparalleled.

unroll *verb trans* to open out (something rolled); to uncoil or unwind (it). ➤ *verb intrans* to be or become unrolled.

unruffled *adj* **1** poised and serene, *esp* in the face of setbacks or confusion. **2** smooth; calm: *unruffled water.*

unruly /un'roohli/ *adj* (**unrulier, unruliest**) difficult to discipline or manage. ➤➤ **unruliness** *noun.* [Middle English *unreuly*, from UN-¹ + *reuly* disciplined, from *reule* RULE¹]

UNRWA /'unrǝ/ *abbr* United Nations Relief and Works Agency.

unsaddle *verb trans* **1** to take the saddle from (a horse). **2** to throw (a rider) from the saddle. ➤ *verb intrans* to remove the saddle from a horse.

unsafe *adj* **1** not safe to do, use, etc; dangerous. **2** said of a legal verdict or conviction: based on false, unreliable, or inadequate evidence. **3** said of a sexual activity: exposing the participants to the possibility of contracting a sexually transmitted disease, *esp* through not using a condom.

unsaid¹ *adj* not said, *esp* not spoken aloud.

unsaid² *verb* past tense and past part. of UNSAY.

unsatisfactory *adj* not acceptable or adequate. ➤➤ **unsatisfactorily** *adv.*

unsaturated *adj* **1** not saturated; capable of absorbing or dissolving more of something: *an unsaturated solution.* **2** able to form products by chemical addition, *esp* containing double or triple bonds between carbon atoms. **3** said of a fat, *esp* vegetable fat: containing a relatively high proportion of fatty acids that have double bonds and so are less likely to result in higher cholesterol levels.

unsavoury (*NAmer* **unsavory**) *adj* **1** disagreeable or distasteful, *esp* morally offensive. **2** unpleasant to taste or smell. ➤➤ **unsavourily** *adv,* **unsavouriness** *noun.*

unsay *verb trans* (*past tense and past part.* **unsaid** /un'sed/) to retract or withdraw (e.g. a statement, opinion, etc).

unscathed /un'skaydhd/ *adj* entirely unharmed or uninjured.

unschooled *adj* **1** untaught; untrained. **2** not artificial; natural: *unschooled talent.*

unscientific *adj* **1** not in accordance with the principles and methods of science. **2** without scientific knowledge. ➤➤ **unscientifically** *adv.*

unscramble *verb trans* **1** to restore (scrambled communication) to intelligible form; to decode (it). **2** to restore (something) to order; to disentangle or clarify (it). ➤➤ **unscrambler** *noun.*

unscrew *verb trans* **1** to remove the screws from (something). **2** to loosen or withdraw (a screw, lid, threaded part, etc) by turning. ➤ *verb intrans* to be or become unscrewed.

unscripted *adj* said of a speech, play, etc: not following a prepared script.

unscrupulous *adj* without moral scruples; unprincipled. ➤➤ **unscrupulously** *adv,* **unscrupulousness** *noun.*

unseal *verb trans* to break or remove the seal of (something); to open (it).

unsealed *adj* **1** not sealed. **2** *chiefly Aus, NZ* said of a road: not surfaced with bitumen or a similar sealant.

unseasonable *adj* **1** untimely; inopportune. **2** not normal for the season of the year: *unseasonable weather.* ➤➤ **unseasonableness** *noun,* **unseasonably** *adv.*

unseasonal *adj* = UNSEASONABLE (2).

unseat *verb trans* **1** to dislodge (somebody) from a seat, *esp* on horseback. **2** to remove (somebody) from a position of power, authority, etc.

unseeded *adj* said of a sports player: not seeded; not ranked amongst the best in a tournament.

unseeing *adj* not noticing or perceiving anything.

unseemly *adj* **1** not conforming to established standards of good behaviour or taste. **2** *archaic* not attractive or becoming. ➤➤ **unseemliness** *noun.*

unseen¹ *adj* **1** not observed or perceived. **2** *chiefly Brit* said of an examination passage: presented to candidates who have not seen it before: *an unseen translation.*

unseen² *noun chiefly Brit* an unseen passage for translation: *a Latin unseen.*

unselfish *adj* not selfish; generous. ➤➤ **unselfishly** *adv,* **unselfishness** *noun.*

unsentimental *adj* not affected or influenced by sentiment: *an unsentimental decision.* ➤➤ **unsentimentally** *adv.*

unserviceable *adj* not fit for use. ➤➤ **unserviceability** /-'biliti/ *noun.*

unsettle *verb trans* **1** to move (something or somebody) from a settled state or condition. **2** to perturb or agitate (somebody or something). ➤ *verb intrans* to become unsettled. ➤➤ **unsettlement** *noun,* **unsettling** *adj,* **unsettlingly** *adv.*

unsettled *adj* **1a** not calm or tranquil; disturbed: *unsettled political conditions.* **b** variable; changeable: *unsettled weather.* **c** anxious or uneasy. **d** lacking in stability. **2** not resolved or worked out; undecided. **3** not inhabited or populated: *unsettled land.* **4** not paid or discharged: *unsettled debts.* ➤➤ **unsettledness** *noun.*

unsex *verb trans* to deprive (somebody) of sexual power or the typical qualities of their sex.

unshackle *verb trans* to free (somebody or something) from shackles or restraints.

unshakable *or* **unshakeable** *adj* incapable of being changed or destroyed; firm and unwavering: *unshakable faith.* ➤➤ **unshakably** *adv.*

unshaven *adj* not having shaved or been shaved.

unsheathe *verb trans* to draw (something, *esp* a weapon such as a knife or sword) from a sheath or scabbard.

unship *verb* (**unshipped, unshipping**) ➤ *verb trans* **1** to unload or disembark (something or somebody) from a ship. **2** to remove (e.g. an oar or tiller) from position. ➤ *verb intrans* to be unshipped.

unsighted *adj* **1** not having the power of sight. **2** prevented from seeing or from having a clear view: *The goalkeeper was unsighted and missed the ball.*

unsightly /un'sietli/ *adj* (**unsightlier, unsightliest**) not pleasing to the eye; ugly. ➤➤ **unsightliness** *noun.*

unsinkable *adj* said of a boat or ship: incapable of sinking or being sunk. ➤➤ **unsinkability** /-'biliti/ *noun.*

unskilful (*NAmer* **unskillful**) *adj* lacking in skill or proficiency. ➤➤ **unskilfully** *adv,* **unskilfulness** *noun.*

unskilled *adj* **1** not having or requiring special skill in any particular branch of work: *an unskilled labourer.* **2** showing a lack of skill.

unskillful *adj NAmer* see UNSKILFUL.

unsling *verb trans* (*past tense and past part.* **unslung** /un'slung/) **1** to remove (something) from being slung. **2** to release (something) from slings.

unsnap *verb trans* (**unsnapped, unsnapping**) to open or free (something) by undoing a catch or fastener, *esp* one that opens with a snap.

unsociable *adj* **1** not liking social activity; reserved or solitary. **2** not conducive to sociability. ➤➤ **unsociability** /-'biliti/ *noun,* **unsociableness** *noun,* **unsociably** *adv.*

Usage note

unsociable, antisocial, asocial, non-social, *or* unsocial? See note at ANTISOCIAL.

unsocial *adj* **1** marked by or showing a dislike for social interaction. **2** *Brit* said of working hours: falling outside the normal working day and preventing participation in social activities. ➤➤ **unsocially** *adv.*

Usage note

unsocial, antisocial, asocial, non-social, *or* unsociable. See note at ANTISOCIAL.

unsolicited *adj* **1** sent or received but not requested or ordered: *unsolicited mail.* **2** done or given voluntarily.

unsophisticated *adj* **1** not socially or culturally sophisticated. **2** simple and straightforward; not complex or complicated. **3** pure; unadulterated. ➤➤ **unsophisticatedly** *adv,* **unsophisticatedness** *noun,* **unsophistication** /-'kaysh(ǝ)n/ *noun.*

unsound *adj* **1** not healthy or whole. **2** ill, injured, or diseased: *of unsound mind.* **3** not firmly made, placed, or fixed. **4** not valid or true; fallacious or unreliable: *an unsound premise.* ➤➤ **unsoundly** *adv,* **unsoundness** *noun.*

unsparing *adj* **1** not merciful; hard or ruthless. **2** liberal; generous. ➤➤ **unsparingly** *adv,* **unsparingness** *noun.*

unspeakable /un'speekəbl/ *adj* **1** incapable of being expressed in words. **2** too bad or shocking to be uttered. ≫ **unspeakableness** *noun*, **unspeakably** *adv*.

unspecified *adj* not named or stated explicitly.

unspoiled /un'spoyld/ *adj* = UNSPOILT.

unspoilt /un'spoylt, un'spoyld/ *adj* not spoilt; not changed for the worse, e.g. by modern developments: *an unspoilt fishing village.*

unspoken *adj* not expressed in words.

unstable *adj* **1a** not stable; not firm, fixed, or constant. **b** unsteady or irregular. **c** apt to move, sway, or fall. **2** characterized by or given to sudden changes of mood or an inability to control the emotions. **3a** readily changing in chemical composition or physical properties: *unstable compounds; an unstable emulsion.* **b** said of an atom or atomic particle: existing only for a short time. **c** said of an atom or chemical element: undergoing spontaneous radioactive decay or decomposition. ≫ **unstableness** *noun*, **unstably** *adv*.

unsteady *adj* (**unsteadier, unsteadiest**) **1a** not firm or stable; likely to fall. **b** walking in an erratic or staggering manner. **2** changeable; fluctuating. **3** not uniform or even; irregular. ≫ **unsteadily** *adv*, **unsteadiness** *noun*.

unstep *verb trans* (**unstepped, unstepping**) to remove (a mast) from its STEP¹ (supporting socket or frame).

unstick *verb trans* (*past tense and past part.* **unstuck**) to release (something) from being stuck or fixed.

unstinting *adj* not sparing or frugal; generous; done or given without restraint: *unstinting efforts to find a solution.*

unstop *verb trans* (**unstopped, unstopping**) **1** to free (something) from an obstruction. **2** to remove a stopper from (e.g. a bottle).

unstoppable *adj* incapable of being stopped, *esp* determined or forceful. ≫ **unstoppably** *adv*.

unstressed *adj* **1** not bearing a stress or accent: *unstressed syllables.* **2** not subjected to stress.

unstring *verb trans* (*past tense and past part.* **unstrung** /un'strung/) **1** to loosen or remove the strings of (e.g. a violin). **2** to remove (e.g. beads) from a string. **3** to make (somebody) emotionally upset or mentally disordered: *unstrung by the news.*

unstructured *adj* **1** not formally or systematically structured or organized. **2** said of a garment: loose-fitting or untailored.

unstrung *verb* past tense and past part. of UNSTRING.

unstuck¹ *adj* no longer fastened by glue or other adhesive. **✳ come unstuck** to go wrong; to be unsuccessful: *The government came unstuck over food prices.*

unstuck² *verb* past tense and past part. of UNSTICK.

unstudied *adj* not done or planned for effect; spontaneous or natural.

unsubstantial *adj* lacking substance, firmness, strength, or solidity: *deep but unsubstantial meditations* — Edward Gibbon. ≫ **unsubstantiality** /-shi'aliti/ *noun*, **unsubstantially** *adv*.

unsubstantiated *adj* not verified or established by proof or evidence.

unsuccessful *adj* not meeting with or producing success. ≫ **unsuccessfully** *adv*, **unsuccessfulness** *noun*.

unsuitable *adj* not suitable or fitting; inappropriate. ≫ **unsuitability** /-'biliti/ *noun*, **unsuitably** *adv*.

unsung *adj* not celebrated or praised: *The wretch … shall go down to the vile dust, from whence he sprung, unwept, unhonoured, and unsung* — Scott.

unsure *adj* **1** not fixed or certain. **2** lacking self-assurance or confidence: *She's always been a bit unsure of herself.* ≫ **unsurely** *adv*, **unsureness** *noun*.

unsuspected *adj* **1** not imagined to exist or to be possible. **2** not distrusted or regarded with suspicion. ≫ **unsuspectedly** *adv*.

unsuspecting *adj* **1** not suspicious; unaware of something, *esp* something dangerous or undesirable. ≫ **unsuspectingly** *adv*.

unswerving *adj* not turning aside; constant: *unswerving loyalty.*

untangle *verb trans* **1** to free (something) from tangles or entanglement; to unravel (it). **2** to make (something) intelligible; to clear (it) up.

untapped *adj* **1** not yet drawn from: *an untapped keg.* **2** said of a resource, etc: not yet drawn on or exploited: *untapped markets.*

untarnished *adj* **1** not sullied or disgraced: *an untarnished reputation.* **2** not affected by tarnishing: *untarnished silver.* **3** not spoilt or destroyed: *untarnished dreams.*

untaught *adj* **1** not educated; ignorant. **2** not acquired by teaching; natural or spontaneous: *untaught kindness.*

untenable *adj* **1** said of an argument, theory, etc: not able to be defended: *an untenable opinion.* **2** said of a person's position, standing, etc: no longer able to be maintained. ≫ **untenability** /-'biliti/ *noun*, **untenably** *adv*.

untenured *adj* said of a college or university teacher or teaching post: not permanent or not yet permanent.

unthinkable /un'thingkəbl/ *adj* contrary to what is acceptable or probable; out of the question. ≫ **unthinkability** /-'biliti/ *noun*, **unthinkably** *adv*.

unthinking *adj* **1** without thinking; heedless or unmindful. **2** lacking concern for others; inconsiderate. ≫ **unthinkingly** *adv*.

unthought of *adj* not thought of or imagined.

unthread *verb trans* **1** to draw out or remove a thread from (something, e.g. a needle): *unthread a string of beads.* **2** to disentangle (something): *trying to unthread her confused thoughts.*

untidy *adj* (**untidier, untidiest**) not neat; slovenly or disorderly. ≫ **untidily** *adv*, **untidiness** *noun*.

untie *verb* (**unties, untied, untying**) ≫ *verb trans* **1a** to undo (a knot). **b** to unfasten (something tied). **2** to disentangle or resolve (something). **3** to free (something) from restraint, limitation, or constriction. ≫ *verb intrans* to become untied.

until¹ /un'til, ən'til/ *prep* **1** up to as late as (a specified time or event): *not available until tomorrow.* **2** up to as far as (a specified place): *stay on the train until Birmingham.* [Middle English, from Old Norse *und* until + TILL¹]

Usage note _____
until *or* till? See note at TILL¹.

until² *conj* up to the time that: *Wait until he arrives.*

untimely¹ *adj* **1** occurring before the natural or proper time; premature: *her untimely death.* **2** inopportune; unseasonable: *untimely frost.* ≫ **untimeliness** *noun*.

untimely² *adv chiefly formal* **1** at an inopportune time; unseasonably. **2** before the natural or proper time; prematurely.

untitled *adj* **1** said e.g. of a book: not having a title. **2** not called by a title: *untitled nobility.*

unto /'untoo, 'untə/ *prep archaic* = TO¹ (indicating destination, relationship, etc). [Middle English, from UNTIL¹ + TO¹]

untold *adj* **1a** incalculable: *fans arriving in untold numbers.* **b** indescribably great: *untold pain and suffering.* **2** not told or revealed.

untouchable¹ *adj* **1** not able or permitted to be touched. **2** lying beyond reach: *untouchable mineral resources.* **3** exempt from criticism or control. **4** unable to be equalled; unparalleled. ≫ **untouchability** /-'biliti/ *noun*.

untouchable² *noun* a member of a large formerly segregated CASTE (hereditary group) who in traditional Hindu belief can defile a member of a higher caste by contact or proximity: compare DALIT, SCHEDULED CASTE.

untouched *adj* **1** not touched or handled. **2** said of a subject: not described, discussed, or dealt with. **3** said of food or drink: not tasted. **4** in the original state or condition; not altered. **5** not influenced; unaffected.

untoward /untə'wawd/ *adj* **1** not favourable; adverse or unfortunate. **2** unseemly or improper. **3** unexpected or unusual: *They didn't notice anything untoward.* ≫ **untowardly** *adv*, **untowardness** *noun*. [UN-¹ + TOWARD² in an obsolete sense 'promising, propitious']

untried *adj* **1** not tested or proved by experience. **2** not tried in court.

untrodden *adj* **1** not walked on: *untrodden snow.* **2** unexplored.

untroubled *adj* **1** not troubled; not made uneasy. **2** calm; tranquil.

untrue *adj* **1** false or inaccurate. **2** not faithful; disloyal. **3** not level or exactly aligned: *The doors are untrue.* ≫ **untruly** *adv*.

untrustworthy *adj* **1** incapable of being trusted. **2** not dependable or reliable. ≫ **untrustworthiness** *noun*.

untruth *noun* **1** lack of truthfulness. **2** something untrue; a lie or falsehood.

untruthful *adj* not telling the truth; false or lying. ➤ **untruthfully** *adv*, **untruthfulness** *noun*.

untuck *verb trans* to release (e.g. bedding) from being tucked in or up. ➤ *verb intrans* to become untucked.

untutored *adj* **1** having no formal learning or education. **2** not produced by instruction; natural: *untutored shrewdness*.

unusable *adj* not fit, suitable, or convenient for use.

unused *adj* **1** /un'yoohzd/. **a** not used; fresh or new. **b** not used up: *unused sick leave*. **c** not put to use: *unused land*. **2** /un'yoohst/ (+ to) unaccustomed to (something).

unusual *adj* **1** uncommon; rare. **2** different, exceptional, or remarkable: *an unusual painting*. ➤ **unusually** *adv*, **unusualness** *noun*.

unutterable *adj* **1** beyond the powers of description; inexpressible: *He was silent, and I guessed at his unutterable depression* — F Scott Fitzgerald. **2** out-and-out; downright: *an unutterable fool*. ➤ **unutterably** *adv*.

unvarnished *adj* **1** not adorned or glossed; plain: *the unvarnished truth*. **2** said of wood, a surface, etc: not varnished.

unveil *verb trans* **1** to remove a veil or covering from (something): *unveil a statue*. **2** to make (something) public; to divulge (it): *a document unveiling their plans*. ➤ *verb intrans* to remove a veil or protective cloak.

unvoiced *adj* **1** not expressed in words; unspoken. **2** said of a speech sound, *esp* a consonant: pronounced without vibration of the vocal cords.

unwaged[1] /un'wayjd/ *adj* not in paid employment.

unwaged[2] *pl noun* (**the unwaged**) people currently not in paid employment, e.g. the unemployed, students, the retired: *The unwaged get in to the exhibition for free.*

unwanted *adj* not wanted or needed.

unwarrantable *adj* not justifiable; inexcusable. ➤ **unwarrantably** *adv*.

unwarranted *adj* not justified; said or done without good reason.

unwary *adj* not alert or cautious; easily fooled or surprised. ➤ **unwarily** *adv*, **unwariness** *noun*.

unwashed[1] *adj* not cleaned with or as if with soap and water.

unwashed[2] ✳ **the great unwashed** *derog* the common people; the rabble.

unwavering *adj* fixed; steadfast. ➤ **unwaveringly** *adv*.

unwearied *adj* not tired or jaded; fresh. ➤ **unweariedly** *adv*.

unwelcome *adj* **1** not welcome: *unwelcome guests*. **2** not gladly received; unwanted: *unwelcome news*.

unwell *adj* in poor health; ill.

unwholesome *adj* **1** having a harmful or detrimental effect on physical or mental health. **2** having a corrupting effect on morality. **3** unhealthy, *esp* in appearance: *Her face has an unwholesome pallor*.

unwieldy /un'weeldi/ *adj* (**unwieldier, unwieldiest**) difficult to move or handle; cumbersome. ➤ **unwieldily** *adv*, **unwieldiness** *noun*. [UN-[1] + *wieldy* easily wielded or handled, from WIELD + -Y[1]]

unwilling *adj* **1** loath; reluctant: *unwilling to learn*. **2** done or given reluctantly: *his unwilling approval*. ➤ **unwillingly** *adv*, **unwillingness** *noun*.

unwind /un'wiend/ *verb* (*past tense and past part.* **unwound** /un'-wownd/) ➤ *verb trans* **1** to cause (something) to uncoil; to unroll (it). **2** to cause or help (somebody) to become less tense; to relax (them). ➤ *verb intrans* **1** to become unwound. **2** to become less tense; to relax.

unwise *adj* foolish; imprudent. ➤ **unwisdom** /un'wizd(ə)m/ *noun*, **unwisely** *adv*.

unwitting *adj* **1** not intended; inadvertent: *Darwin's unwitting contribution to twentieth-century racism*. **2** ignorant or unaware: *an unwitting accomplice; I had been the unwitting cause of his dismissal*. ➤ **unwittingly** *adv*, **unwittingness** *noun*. [UN-[1] + *witting*, present part. of archaic *wit* to know, from Old English *witan*]

unwonted *adj* **1** uncharacteristic: *'How do you do, Arthur?' asked Jasper, with unwonted affability, for he did not care for children* — Horatio Alger. **2** novel; unaccustomed: *There was a long pause, and every man at the table meditated in ways unwonted and profound* — Jack London. ➤ **unwontedly** *adv*, **unwontedness** *noun*.

unworkable *adj* **1** not practicable or feasible. **2** incapable of being worked: *unworkable materials*.

unworldly *adj* **1** naive; unsophisticated. **2** not swayed by material considerations, e.g. of wealth or personal gain. **3** not of this world; *specif* spiritual. ➤ **unworldliness** *noun*.

unworn *adj* **1** not impaired by use; not worn away. **2** never worn; new.

unworthy *adj* (**unworthier, unworthiest**) **1a** lacking in excellence or quality; poor. **b** base; dishonourable. **2** not befitting somebody's position in life: *behaviour unworthy of an ambassador*. **3** not deserving: *unworthy of attention*. ➤ **unworthily** *adv*, **unworthiness** *noun*.

unwound *verb* past tense and past part. of UNWIND.

unwrap *verb trans* (**unwrapped, unwrapping**) to remove the wrapping from (e.g. a parcel).

unwritten *adj* **1** not written down. **2** said of a law, rule, etc: established and obeyed on the basis of custom and precedent.

unyielding *adj* **1** lacking in softness or flexibility. **2** firm or stubborn. ➤ **unyieldingly** *adv*.

unyoke *verb trans* **1** to release (a draught animal) from a yoke or harness. **2** to set (somebody or something) free.

unzip *verb trans* (**unzipped, unzipping**) **1** to undo the zip of (a garment). **2** in computing, to decompress (a zipped file).

up[1] /up/ *adv* **1a** at or towards a relatively high level or a plane perceived as higher: *live up in the mountains*. **b** from beneath the ground or water to the surface. **c** above the horizon. **d** upstream. **e** in or to a raised or upright position: *sit up*. **f** out of bed: *You'll soon be up and about again*. **g** off or out of the ground or a surface: *lift the piano up*. **h** so as to expose a particular surface: *The coin landed tails up*. **i** to the top, *esp* so as to be full: *top up the radiator*. **j** in a direction conventionally the opposite of down. **k** in or towards the north. **l** *chiefly Brit* to or in the capital of a country or a more important place: *up in London*. **m** so as to arrive or approach: *He walked up to her*. **n** *chiefly Brit* to or at university: *up at Oxford*. **2a** into a state of greater intensity or activity: *speak up*. **b** into a faster pace or higher gear. **3a** in or into a relatively high or more advanced position or status: *go up in the world*. **b** above a normal or former level: *sales are up*. **c** towards a higher number, degree, or rate: *Prices are going up*. **d** higher in price: *Petrol is up*. **e** ahead of an opponent: *We're three points up*. **4** in or into existence, evidence, prominence, or prevalence: *set up a business*. **5a** under consideration or attention: *The licence is up for renewal*. **b** before a court: *up for robbery*. **6** so as to be together: *add up the figures*. **7a** entirely; completely: *eat up your spinach*. **b** so as to be firmly closed, joined, or fastened: *nail up the door*. **c** so as to be fully inflated: *blow up the tyre*. **8** in or into storage: *lay up supplies*. **9** to the direction from which the wind is blowing; to windward. **10** in or into parts: *chop up*. **11** to a stop: *pull up*. ✳ **up against 1** touching. **2** faced with; confronting. **up against it** in great difficulties. **up and down 1** to and fro. **2** here and there. **up for 1** being considered for (e.g. election or appointment). **2** *informal* keen or ready (to do something). **3** available. **up to 1** used to indicate an upward limit or boundary: *up to his knees in mud; up to 50,000 copies a month*. **2** as far as; until. **3a** equal to (something): *I didn't feel up to driving*. **b** good enough for (something): *My German isn't up to reading Schiller*. **4** engaged in (a suspect activity): *What's he up to?* **5** being the responsibility or choice of (somebody): *It's up to you*. **up top** *informal* in the head: *He hasn't got much up top*. **up with** used to express enthusiastic approval or support: *Up with the republic!* **up yours** *Brit, coarse slang* used to express contemptuous defiance and dismissal. [Old English *ūp* upwards or *uppe* on high]

up[2] *adj* **1a** moving, inclining, or directed upwards: *the up escalator*. **b** heading in a direction regarded as up: *the up train*. **2** ready; prepared: *Dinner's up!* **3** going on or taking place, *esp* being the matter: *What's up?* **4a** at an end: *Time's up*. **b** hopeless: *It's all up with him now*. **5a** well informed. **b** abreast; up-to-date. **6** said of a computer system: functioning normally. **7** said of a road: being repaired; having a broken surface. **8** ahead of an opponent: *two strokes up after nine holes*.

up[3] *verb* (**upped, upping**) ➤ *verb intrans informal* used with *and* to indicate that the action of the following verb is either surprisingly or abruptly initiated: *He upped and left*. ➤ *verb trans informal* to increase or raise (something): *They upped the price of milk*.

up[4] *prep* **1a** up along, through, towards, into, on, etc: *walk up the hill; water up my nose*. **b** at the top of: *The office is up those stairs*. **2** *Brit, informal* to: *going up the West End*.

up[5] *noun* **1** a high position or an upward slope. **2** a period or state of prosperity or success. **3** the part of a ball's trajectory in which it is still rising after having bounced: *hit the ball on the up.* **✳ on the up** on an upward trend. **on the up and up** increasingly successful. **ups and downs** alternating rises and falls, *esp* in fortune.

up- *comb. form* forming words, with the meanings: **1** upwards: *uphill.* **2** at or to a higher or more advanced position: *upland; upgrade.* **3** up: *uphold; uptake.*

up-anchor *verb intrans* (**up-anchored, up-anchoring**) said of a ship: to weigh anchor.

up-and-coming *adj* likely to succeed.

up-and-down *adj* **1** marked by alternate upward and downward movement. **2** perpendicular. **3** hilly.

up-and-over *adj* said e.g. of a garage door: opening upwards and sliding into a horizontal position above the doorway.

up-and-under *noun* a rugby move consisting of a high kick upwards followed by a charge by the forward players to the place where the ball lands.

Upanishad /ooh'panishad/ *noun* any of a collection of philosophical treatises on the nature of the universe, the deity, and humankind, which form part of Hindu scriptures. [Sanskrit *upaniṣad*, literally 'act of sitting down near', from *upa* near to + *ni* down + *sīdati* he sits, from the idea of sitting at the feet of a master]

upas /'yoohpəs/ *noun* **1** a tall Asiatic and E Indian evergreen tree of the fig family with a poisonous milky juice that acts on the heart and is used as an arrow poison: *Antiaris toxicaria.* **2** a poisonous concentrate of the juice of a upas tree. [Malay *pohon upas* poison tree]

upbeat[1] *noun* an unaccented beat in a musical bar, *esp* the last beat of the bar.

upbeat[2] *adj* *informal* optimistic, cheerful.

upbraid /up'brayd/ *verb trans* to scold or reproach (somebody) severely. **➤➤ upbraider** *noun.* [Old English *ūpbregdan*]

upbringing *noun* early training, *esp* a particular way of bringing up a child: *He had a strict Calvinist upbringing.*

upcast[1] *noun* **1** something cast up, e.g. by digging. **2** a shaft or passage through which air returns to the surface from a mine: compare DOWNCAST[2].

upcast[2] *verb trans* (*past tense and past part.* **upcast**) to throw or cast (something) upwards.

upchuck *verb intrans* *informal* to vomit.

upcoming *adj* *chiefly NAmer* about to happen; forthcoming.

upcountry[1] *adj* **1** of or characteristic of an inland, upland, or outlying region. **2** *chiefly derog* not socially or culturally sophisticated.

upcountry[2] *adv* to or towards an upcountry region, *esp* inland.

update[1] /up'dayt, 'updayt/ *verb trans* to bring (somebody or something) up-to-date. **➤➤ updatable** *adj.*

update[2] /'updayt/ *noun* **1** an act of updating. **2** something that has been updated.

updraught (*NAmer* **updraft**) *noun* an upward movement of air or other gas.

upend *verb trans* **1** to cause (something) to stand on end. **2** *informal* to affect (somebody) to the point of being very upset.

upfield *adv and adj* = DOWNFIELD.

up-front[1] *adj* **1** paid or done in advance or at the beginning. **2** *chiefly NAmer* uninhibitedly honest; candid.

up-front[2] *adv* in advance or at the beginning.

upgrade[1] /up'grayd, 'upgrayd/ *verb trans* **1** to raise or improve the grade, standard, value, performance, etc of (something). **2** to advance (somebody) to a job requiring a higher level of skill or greater responsibility. **➤➤ upgradable** *adj,* **upgradeable** *adj.*

upgrade[2] /'upgrayd/ *noun* **1a** the act or process or an instance of upgrading something or somebody. **b** an upgraded version, e.g. of computer software. **2** *NAmer* an upward gradient or slope. **✳ on the upgrade** improving, *esp* in health, status, profitability, etc.

upgrowth *noun* the process or result of growing upwards.

upheaval /up'heevl/ *noun* **1** an instance of great disturbance or radical change. **2** an upward displacement of something, *esp* part of the earth's crust.

upheave /up'heev/ *verb trans* to heave or thrust (something) upwards. **➤** *verb intrans* to move upwards, *esp* with power.

upheld *verb* past tense and past part. of UPHOLD.

uphill[1] /up'hil/ *adv* upwards on a hill or incline.

uphill[2] /'uphil/ *adj* **1** situated on high or higher ground. **2** going up; ascending. **3** difficult; laborious: *an uphill struggle.*

uphill[3] /'uphil/ *noun* rising ground; an upward incline.

uphold *verb trans* (*past tense and past part.* **upheld** /-'held/) **1** to give support to or maintain (something): *uphold standards.* **2** to support or defend (something) against opposition or challenge: *uphold the ruling of the lower court.* **➤➤ upholder** *noun.*

upholster /up'hohlstə/ *verb trans* (**upholstered, upholstering**) to fit or provide (e.g. a chair or sofa) with upholstery. [back-formation from UPHOLSTERER]

upholsterer *noun* somebody who upholsters furniture as an occupation. [Middle English *upholdester* dealer in small articles, upholsterer, from UPHOLD in the obsolete sense 'to keep something in repair']

upholstery *noun* **1** materials, e.g. fabric, padding, and springs, used to make a soft covering, *esp* for a seat. **2** the art, work, or occupation of upholstering furniture.

upkeep *noun* **1** the act or process of maintaining something in good condition. **2** the cost of such maintenance.

upland *noun* **1** (*also in pl*) an area of high land, *esp* when inland or some distance from the sea. **2** (*used before a noun*) of, being, or found in such an area.

uplift[1] /up'lift/ *verb trans* **1a** to raise or elevate (something). **b** to cause (a part of the earth's surface) to be raised above adjacent areas. **2** to improve the spiritual, social, moral, or intellectual condition of (something or somebody). **➤➤ uplifter** *noun,* **uplifting** *adj.*

uplift[2] /'uplift/ *noun* **1a** the act or result of uplifting something: *a bra that gives uplift.* **b** the uplifting of part of the earth's surface, or an uplifted mass of land. **c** support and lifting for the breasts provided by a bra, etc. **2** a spiritual, social, moral, or intellectual improvement, or something causing this.

uplighter *noun* a source of light, e.g. a wall light, designed or positioned to throw its light upwards.

upload[1] *verb trans* in computing, to transfer (a program or data) from a smaller to a larger or more central computer.

upload[2] *noun* **1** in computing, the act or process or an instance of transferring a program or data from a smaller computer to a larger or more central one. **2** in computing, a copy of the program or data that has been transferred by doing this.

up-market[1] *adj* denoting, relating to, producing, or dealing in goods designed to appeal to the more prosperous or higher-status section of a market.

up-market[2] *adv* to or towards the more prosperous or higher-status section of a market: *The shop has moved up-market.*

upmost *adj* = UPPERMOST.

upon /ə'pon/ *prep chiefly formal* = ON[1].

upper[1] /'upə/ *adj* **1a** higher in physical position, rank, or order. **b** farther inland: *the upper Thames.* **2** (**Upper**) relating to or denoting a later division of the specified geological period, system of rocks, etc: *Upper Carboniferous.* **✳ have/get the upper hand** to have or gain a position of superiority, control, advantage, etc. [Middle English, from *uppe* up + -ER[1]]

upper[2] *noun* the parts of a shoe or boot above the sole. **✳ on one's uppers** at the end of one's resources, *esp* penniless.

upper[3] *noun informal* a stimulant drug, *esp* an amphetamine. [UP[3] + -ER[2]]

upper case *noun* **1** capital letters. **2** a printer's tray holding the type for capitals and usu small capitals, fractions, symbols, and accents. [from the compositor's practice of keeping capital letters in the upper of a pair of type cases]

upper-case *adj* said of a letter: capital.

upper chamber *noun* = UPPER HOUSE.

upper class *noun* the class occupying the highest position in a society, *esp* the aristocracy.

upper-class *adj* of or characteristic of the upper class.

upper crust *pl noun* (**the upper crust**) *informal* (*treated as sing. or pl*) the highest social class.

uppercut¹ *noun* a swinging blow directed upwards with a bent arm.

uppercut² *verb* (**uppercutting,** *past tense and past part.* **uppercut**) ➤ *verb trans* to hit (somebody) with an uppercut. ➤ *verb intrans* to deliver an uppercut.

upper house *noun* in a legislature consisting of two houses or chambers, the branch that is usu more restricted in membership, possesses greater traditional prestige, and is often less powerful.

uppermost *adj and adv* in or into the highest or most prominent position.

upper regions *pl noun literary* the sky; the heavens.

upper works *pl noun* the parts of a fully laden ship or boat that are above the waterline.

uppish /'upish/ *adj informal* = UPPITY. ➤➤ **uppishly** *adv,* **uppishness** *noun.*

uppity /'upiti/ *adj informal* **1** putting on airs of superiority; supercilious. **2** excessively self-assertive. [prob from UP² + -*ity* (arbitrary suffix)]

upraise *verb trans* to raise or lift (something) up; to elevate (it).

uprate *verb trans* to raise (something or somebody) in rank, status, size, power, etc.

upright /'upriet/ *adj* **1a** perpendicular; vertical. **b** erect in carriage or posture. **c** having the vertical dimension or dimensions greater than the horizontal: *an upright freezer.* **d** having the main part perpendicular. **2** characterized by strong moral correctness; honest or honourable. ➤➤ **uprightly** *adv,* **uprightness** *noun.*

upright² *adv* in an upright position.

upright³ *noun* **1** something that stands upright, *esp* a vertical support. **2** *informal* an upright piano.

upright piano *noun* a piano with a vertical frame and strings.

uprise /up'riez/ *verb intrans* (*past tense* **uprose** /up'rohz/, *past part.* **uprisen** /up'riz(ə)n/) *archaic, literary* to rise up or to a higher position: *Whisper of gongs and trumpets uprose* — James Hilton.

uprising /'upriezing/ *noun* a usu localized rebellion, *esp* against an established government.

upriver *adv and adj* towards or at a point nearer the source of a river.

uproar /'upraw/ *noun* **1** a noisy commotion or violent disturbance: *He moves from point to point with as little uproar as a jellyfish* — P G Wodehouse. **2** a noisy or violent protest. [by folk etymology from Dutch *oproer,* from early Dutch *op* up + *roer* motion]

uproarious /up'rawri·əs/ *adj* **1** characterized by noise and disorder. **2** extremely funny: *an uproarious comedy.* ➤➤ **uproariously** *adv,* **uproariousness** *noun.*

uproot *verb trans* **1a** to pull (something) up by the roots. **b** to remove (something) as if by uprooting it. **2** to displace (somebody) from their home, country, or habitual environment. **3** to destroy or eradicate (something). ➤➤ **uprooter** *noun.*

uprose *verb* past tense of UPRISE.

uprush *noun* **1** an upward rush of gas, liquid, etc. **2** an upward rush of feeling or emotion from the unconscious or subconscious.

upsadaisy /'upsədayzi/ *interj* = UPSYDAISY.

upscale *adj and adv chiefly NAmer* = UP-MARKET¹, UP-MARKET².

upsell *verb intrans* to make an additional sale of a product or service to a client or customer who has already purchased a form of it: compare CROSS-SELL.

upset¹ /up'set/ *verb* (**upsetting,** *past tense and past part.* **upset**) ➤ *verb trans* **1** to knock (something) over; to overturn (it). **2** to trouble (somebody) mentally or emotionally; to make (them) sad, disappointed, anxious, etc. **3** to throw (something) into disorder; to disrupt (it). **4** to make (somebody or something) physically unwell or somewhat ill: *Cheese upsets her stomach.* **5** to thicken and shorten (e.g. a heated iron bar) by hammering on the end. ➤ *verb intrans* to become overturned. ➤➤ **upsetter** *noun,* **upsetting** *adj,* **upsettingly** *adv.*

upset² /'upset/ *noun* **1** a minor physical disorder: *a stomach upset.* **2** an emotional disturbance. **3** an unexpected defeat, e.g. in politics, a sporting competition, etc.

upset³ /up'set/ *adj* **1** /up'set/ mentally or emotionally troubled; sad, disappointed, anxious, etc. **2** /'upset/ physically disturbed or disordered: *an upset stomach.*

upset price /'upset/ *noun chiefly NAmer* = RESERVE PRICE.

upshot /'upshot/ *noun* the final result; the outcome. [UP² + SHOT¹, orig referring to the final shot in an archery contest]

upside *noun* **1** an upward trend, *esp* in economics. **2** the favourable or advantageous aspect of something. **3** the upper side, surface, or part.

upside down *adv and adj* **1** with the upper and the lower parts reversed; inverted. **2** in or into great disorder or confusion: *She turned the room upside down, looking for her glasses.* [alteration of Middle English *up so doun,* from UP¹ + SO¹ + *doun* down]

upside-down cake *noun* a cake inverted after baking so that fruit etc cooked at the base of the mixture becomes the topping of the cake.

upsides *adv Brit, informal* (+ with) so as to be even or equal with (somebody or something).

upsilon /'upsilon, up'sielən, 'yoohp-/ *noun* the 20th letter of the Greek alphabet (Υ, υ), equivalent to and transliterated as roman u. [Middle Greek *y psilon,* literally 'simple *y*' from the desire to distinguish it from the diphthong *oi,* which was pronounced the same in later Greek]

upstage¹ *adv* **1** at or towards the rear of a theatrical stage. **2** away from a film or television camera.

upstage² *adj* **1** of or at the rear of a stage. **2** *informal* haughty; aloof.

upstage³ *verb trans* **1** said of an actor: to force (another actor) to face away from the audience by moving to or speaking from an upstage position. **2** to steal attention from (somebody).

upstage⁴ *noun* the part of a stage that is farthest from the audience or camera.

upstair *adj* = UPSTAIRS².

upstairs¹ /up'steəz/ *adv* **1** up the stairs; to or on a higher floor. **2** *informal* to or at a higher position, usu with less responsibility.

upstairs² /'upsteəz, up'steəz/ *adj* situated on an upper floor.

upstairs³ /'upsteəz, up'steəz/ *noun* the part of a building above the ground floor.

upstanding *adj* **1** erect; upright. **2** characterized by integrity; honest and respectable. ✳ **be upstanding** used to ask or order all present, e.g. in a court of law or at a formal occasion such as a dinner or wedding, etc, to rise to their feet.

upstart /'upstaht/ *noun* **1** somebody who has risen suddenly, e.g. from a low position to wealth or power, *esp* somebody who behaves with unwarranted arrogance or self-importance. **2** (*used before a noun*) denoting, relating to, or characteristic of such a person: *a little upstart, vulgar being, with her Mr. E., and her caro sposo ... and all her airs of pert pretension and underbred finery* — Jane Austen.

upstate¹ /up'stayt/ *adv and adj* to or in the usu northerly part of a US state that is away from metropolitan areas.

upstate² /'upstayt/ *noun* the upstate part of a US state. ➤➤ **upstater** *noun.*

upstream *adv and adj* in the direction opposite to the flow of a stream.

upstroke *noun* an upward stroke.

upsurge *noun* a rapid or sudden rise.

upswept *adj* swept, curved, or brushed upwards.

upswing *noun* **1** an upward swing, trend, or movement. **2** a marked increase or rise.

upsydaisy /'upsidayzi/ *interj* used to express comfort and reassurance, *esp* to a small child after a fall or while lifting a child up. [alteration of *up-a-day,* literally 'up to the day', expressing surprise]

uptake *noun* **1a** the act, process, or extent of accepting or taking up something. **b** the act or process of physically absorbing and incorporating something, *esp* the uptake of food, nutrients, oxygen, etc by a living organism. **2** a ventilating shaft leading upwards. ✳ **quick/slow on the uptake** *informal* quick or slow to understand or learn.

up-tempo *adj and adv* said of a piece of music, *esp* jazz: to be performed at a fast-moving tempo.

upthrow *noun* an upward displacement, *esp* of a body of rock on one side of a fault.

upthrust *noun* an upward thrust, *esp* an upheaval of part of the earth's surface.

uptight /up'tiet/ *adj informal* **1** tense or nervous. **2** angry or indignant.

uptime *noun* the time during which a piece of equipment, *esp* a computer, is functioning or able to function.

up-to-date *adj* **1** extending up to the present time; including the latest information. **2** abreast of the times; modern. **3** fully informed of the latest developments. ➤➤ **up-to-dateness** *noun*.

up-to-the-minute *adj* completely up-to-date.

uptown[1] /up'town/ *adj chiefly NAmer* **1** to or in the residential part of a town or city. **2** denoting or characteristic of the more affluent neighbourhoods of a town or city or of the people who live there. ➤➤ **uptown** *adv*.

uptown[2] /'uptown/ *noun chiefly NAmer* the upper part of a town or city, *esp* the residential district. ➤➤ **uptowner** *noun*.

upturn[1] /up'tuhn/ *verb trans* **1** to turn (something) up or over. **2** to direct (something) upwards: *with upturned faces*. ➤ *verb intrans* **1** to turn upwards. **2** to turn upside down.

upturn[2] /'uptuhn/ *noun* an upward turn, *esp* towards better conditions or higher prices.

UPU *abbr* Universal Postal Union.

UPVC *abbr* unplasticized polyvinyl chloride.

upward[1] /'upwəd/ *adj* moving or extending upwards; ascending: *an upward movement*. ➤➤ **upwardly** *adv*.

upward[2] *adv* = UPWARDS.

upwardly mobile *adj* moving to or having the ambition to move to a higher social status or a better economic class.

upward mobility *noun* movement towards a higher social standing or a better economic class.

upwards *adv* **1a** from a lower to a higher place, condition, or level; in the opposite direction from down. **b** so as to expose a particular surface: *Hold out your hand, palm upwards*. **2a** to an indefinitely greater amount, price, age, rank, etc: *from £5 upwards*. **b** towards a higher number, degree, or rate. ✳ **upwards/upward of** more than; in excess of: *They cost upwards of £25*.

upwind /up'wind/ *adv and adj* in the direction from which the wind is blowing.

Ur- *prefix* forming words, with the meaning: original; primitive: *Urtext*; *Ursprache*. [German *Ur-*, from Old High German *ir-*, *ur-* thoroughly]

ur- *or* **uro-** *comb. form* forming words, with the meanings: **1** urine: *uric*. **2** urinary tract: *urology*. **3** urinary and: *urogenital*. [via Latin from Greek *our-*, *ouro-*, from *ouron* urine]

uracil /'yooərəsil/ *noun* a chemical compound that is one of the four bases whose order in the molecular chain of RNA codes genetic information: compare ADENINE, CYTOSINE, GUANINE, THYMINE. [UR- + ACETIC + -IL]

uraei /yoo'reeie/ *pl noun* pl of URAEUS.

uraemia (*NAmer* **uremia**) /yoo'reemi-ə/ *noun* the accumulation in the blood of poisonous substances normally excreted in the urine. ➤➤➤ **uraemic** /-mik/ *adj*.

uraeus /yoo'ree-əs/ *noun* (*pl* **uraei** /yoo'reeie/ *or* **uraeuses**) a representation of a small cobra on the headdress of ancient Egyptian rulers, symbolizing absolute sovereignty. [via Latin from late Greek *ouraios* a snake]

Ural-Altaic /,yooərəl al'tayik/ *noun* a hypothetical superfamily of languages formerly thought of as comprising the Uralic and Altaic language families. ➤➤ **Ural-Altaic** *adj*.

Uralian /yoo'rayli-ən/ *adj* = URALIC. ➤➤ **Uralian** *adj*.

Uralic /yoo'ralik/ *noun* a language family comprising the Finno-Ugric and Samoyedic branches. ➤➤ **Uralic** *adj*. [named after the *Ural* mountains in NW Asia]

uran-[1] *or* **urano-** *comb. form* forming words, denoting: sky; heaven: *uranography*. [via Latin from Greek *ouran-*, *ourano-*, from *ouranos* sky, heaven]

uran-[2] *or* **urano-** *comb. form* forming words, denoting: uranium: *uraninite*.

uraninite /yoo'raniniet/ *noun* a brownish black radioactive mineral that is the chief source of uranium, consisting mainly of uranium dioxide. [URANIUM + -ITE[1]]

uranium /yoo'rayni-əm/ *noun* a silvery radioactive metallic chemical element that occurs naturally in several minerals, *esp* pitchblende and uraninite, and is used as fuel in nuclear reactors: symbol U, atomic number 92. [named after the planet Uranus,

which was discovered just before the element: compare NEPTUNIUM, PLUTONIUM]

urano-[1] *comb. form* see URAN-[1].

urano-[2] *comb. form* see URAN-[2].

uranography /yooərə'nogrəfi/ *noun dated* the branch of astronomy that deals with the description and mapping of the heavens and celestial bodies. ➤➤ **uranographer** *noun*, **uranographic** /-'grafik/ *adj*. [Greek *ouranographia* description of the heavens, from URANO-[1] + -GRAPHY]

urate /'yooərayt/ *noun* any of various chemical salts formed by the combination of uric acid and a metal atom or other chemical group. ➤➤ **uratic** /yoo'ratik/ *adj*.

urban /'uhbən/ *adj* of or constituting a city or town: compare RURAL. [Latin *urbanus* urban, elegant, sophisticated, from *urbs* city]

urban district *noun* in Britain in former times, any of various divisions of counties that had urban communities at their centres and that elected their own councils for administering housing and environmental services.

urbane /uh'bayn/ *adj* **1** notably polite or smooth in manner; suave. **2** elegant or sophisticated. ➤➤ **urbanely** *adv*. [Latin *urbanus*: see URBAN]

urban guerrilla *noun* a terrorist who operates in towns and cities.

urbanise *verb trans* see URBANIZE.

urbanite /'uhbəniet/ *noun* a person who lives in a town or city.

urbanity /uh'baniti/ *noun* (*pl* **urbanities**) **1** the state or quality of being urbane. **2** (*in pl*) urbane acts or conduct; civilities.

urbanize *or* **urbanise** *verb trans* **1a** to cause (something) to take on urban characteristics. **b** to make (e.g. a rural area) more built-up, industrialized, developed, etc. **2a** to impart an urban way of life to (somebody). **b** to cause (e.g. rural dwellers) to migrate to towns and cities. ➤➤ **urbanization** /-'zaysh(ə)n/ *noun*.

urban legend *noun* = URBAN MYTH.

urban myth *noun* a usu amusing, bizarre, or horrific tale in general circulation that is alleged to be the personal experience of somebody indirectly related to or acquainted with the teller.

urban renewal *noun* the planned replacement of substandard urban buildings or redevelopment of dilapidated urban areas.

URC *abbr* United Reformed Church.

urceolate /'uhsi-ələt, -layt/ *adj* said of a plant or animal part: shaped like an urn. [scientific Latin *urceolatus* from Latin *urceolus*, dimin. of *urceus* pitcher]

urchin /'uhchin/ *noun* **1** a mischievous or impudent child, *esp* one who is small and scruffy. **2** = SEA URCHIN. **3** *archaic, dialect* a hedgehog. [Middle English in the sense 'hedgehog', via French *herichon* from Latin *ericius*]

Urdu /'ooədooh, 'uhdooh/ *noun* the Indic language of the people of Pakistan, closely related to Hindi and also spoken in Bangladesh and parts of India. [Persian *urdū-zabān*, literally 'camp language', because it developed as a means of communication between the Mogul invaders and the local people around Delhi]

-ure *suffix* forming nouns from verbs, denoting: **1** an act or process: *exposure*; *closure*. **2** an office or function, or the body performing it: *legislature*. [Middle English via Old French from Latin *-ura*]

urea /yoo'ree-ə, 'yooəri-ə/ *noun* a nitrogen-containing chemical compound formed as the final product of protein breakdown and present in the urine of mammals and some other animals, a synthetic form of which is used in the manufacture of plastics, in fertilizers, and in animal feeds: formula $CO(NH_2)_2$. [scientific Latin from French *urée*, from Greek *ouron* urine]

uremia /yoo'reemi-ə/ *noun NAmer* see URAEMIA.

ureter /yoo'reetə/ *noun* a duct that carries urine away from a kidney to the bladder or cloaca. ➤➤ **ureteral** *adj*, **ureteric** /yooəri'terik/ *adj*. [via Latin from Greek *ourētēr*, from *ourein* to urinate]

urethane /'yooərithayn/ *or* **urethan** /-than/ *noun* **1** a chemical compound that is used *esp* as a solvent, as an anaesthetic for small animals, and medicinally in the treatment of some tumours. **2** = POLYURETHANE. [French *uréthane*, from UR- + ETH- + -ANE]

urethr- *or* **urethro-** *comb. form* forming words, denoting: urethra: *urethritis*; *urethroscope*.

urethra /yoo'reethrə/ *noun* (*pl* **urethras** *or* **urethrae** /-ree/) the canal that in most mammals carries urine from the bladder out of the body, and in the male also serves to convey semen.

➤ **urethral** adj. [via late Latin from Greek *ourēthra*, from *ourein* to urinate]

urethritis /yooəri'thrietəs/ noun inflammation of the urethra.

urethro- comb. form see URETHR-.

urethroscope /yoo'reethrəskohp/ noun a medical instrument for examining the urethra.

urge[1] /uhj/ verb trans **1** to strongly encourage or try to persuade (somebody): *He urged her to stay.* **2** to advocate or demand (something) earnestly or pressingly: *urging greater cooperation.* **3** to serve as a motive or reason for (something). **4** to force or impel (somebody or something) in a specified direction or to greater speed. [Latin *urgēre* to press or drive on]

urge[2] noun a strong impulse or desire: *an urge to laugh.*

urgent /'uhjənt/ adj **1a** calling for immediate attention; pressing: *urgent appeals.* **b** conveying a sense of urgency. **2** urging insistently; persistent or demanding. ➤ **urgency** /-si/ noun, **urgently** adv. [Middle English via French, from Latin *urgent-, urgens*, present part. of *urgēre* URGE[1]]

-urgy comb. form forming nouns, denoting: technology; art; technique: *metallurgy; dramaturgy.* [scientific Latin *-urgia* from Greek *-ourgia*, from *-ourgos* working, from *ergon* work]

-uria comb. form forming nouns, denoting: the usu abnormal presence or excess of (the substance specified) in urine: *albuminuria; pyuria.* [via Latin from Greek *-ouria*, from *ouron* urine]

uric /'yooərik/ adj of or found in urine. [French *urique* from *urine*: see URINE]

uric acid noun a white odourless tasteless chemical compound that is present in small quantities in the urine of some mammals and is the chief excretory product of birds, most reptiles, and some insects: formula $C_5H_4N_4O_3$.

uridine /'yooərideen/ noun a nucleoside that forms part of RNA, contains URACIL, and is important in the form of its phosphates in the synthesis and breakdown of carbohydrates in living cells.

urin- or **urino-** comb. form = UR-: *urinogenital; urinary.* [Middle English via Old French from Latin *urina* URINE]

urinal /yoo'rienl/ noun **1** a fixture, usu attached to a wall, for men to urinate into. **2** a room, building, etc containing a urinal or urinals. [Middle English via Old French and late Latin from Latin *urina* urine]

urinalysis /yooəri'naləsis/ noun (pl **urinalyses** /-seez/) chemical analysis of the urine, usu for diagnostic purposes. [URIN- + ANALYSIS]

urinary /'yooərin(ə)ri/ adj **1** of, occurring in, or being the organs concerned with the formation and discharge of urine. **2** of or for urine. **3** excreted as or in urine.

urinate /'yooərinayt/ verb intrans to discharge urine. ➤ **urination** /-'naysh(ə)n/ noun.

urine /'yooərin/ noun the waste material that is secreted by the kidney in vertebrate animals, contains the end products of protein and nucleic acid breakdown, and forms a usu slightly acid pale yellow to amber liquid in mammals but is semisolid in birds and reptiles. [Middle English via French *urine* from Latin *urina*]

urino- comb. form see URIN-.

urinogenital /ˌyooərinoh'jenitl/ adj = GENITOURINARY.

URL abbr uniform resource locator: the address of a page on the World Wide Web.

urn /uhn/ noun **1** an ornamental vase used for storing the ashes of a dead person: *So may some gentle Muse with lucky words favour my destined urn* — Milton. **2** a large closed container, usu with a tap at its base, for making, storing, and serving large quantities of tea, coffee, etc. [Middle English *urne* from Latin *urna*]

uro- comb. form see UR-.

urochordate /ˌyooərə'kawdayt/ noun any of a group of marine animals comprising the tunicates: subphylum Urochordata. [from the Latin name, from *uro-* (from Greek *oura* tail) + *chordatus* CHORDATE[1]]

urochrome /'yooərəkrohm/ noun the yellow pigment that gives urine its colour.

urodele /'yooərədeel/ noun any of an order of amphibians, e.g. the newts and salamanders, that have a tail throughout life: order Urodela. ➤ **urodele** adj. [French *urodèle*, from Greek *oura* tail + *dēlos* evident, showing]

urogenital /ˌyooəroh'jenitl/ adj = GENITOURINARY.

urology /yoo'roləji/ noun the branch of medicine dealing with the urinary tract. ➤ **urologic** /ˌyooərə'lojik/ adj, **urological** /ˌyooərə'lojikl/ adj, **urologist** noun.

uropygial gland /ˌyooəroh'piji-əl/ noun a large gland at the base of the tail feathers in most birds that secretes an oily fluid used by the bird in preening its feathers.

uropygium /ˌyooəroh'piji-əm/ noun the prominence at the rear end of a bird's body that supports the tail feathers. ➤ **uropygial** adj. [via Latin from Greek *ouropygion*, from *oura* tail + *pygē* rump]

uroscopy /yoo'roskəpi/ noun examination of the urine, usu for diagnostic purposes.

Ursa Major /'uhsə/ noun a constellation that contains the seven stars forming the Plough. [Latin *ursa major*, literally 'greater bear']

Ursa Minor noun a constellation that includes the N pole of the heavens and seven stars resembling the Plough with the Pole Star at the tip of the handle. [Latin *ursa minor*, literally 'lesser bear']

ursine /'uhsin, 'uhsien/ adj of or resembling a bear or the bear family. [Latin *ursinus*, from *ursus* bear]

Ursprache /'ooəshprahkhə/ noun a parent language, esp a hypothetical one reconstructed from the evidence of later languages. [German *Ursprache*, from Ur- + *Sprache* language]

Ursuline /'uhsyoolien/ noun a member of any of several Roman Catholic teaching orders of nuns, esp a member of a teaching order founded by St Angela Merici in Brescia, a city in northern Italy, in 1535. [Latin *Ursulina*, named after St *Ursula*, the founder's patron saint]

Urtext /'ooətekst/ noun the original or earliest version of a text.

urticaria /ˌuhti'keəri-ə/ noun an allergic condition marked by raised itchy red or white patches on the skin and caused by a specific factor, e.g. a food or drug. Also called HIVES. ➤ **urticarial** adj. [scientific Latin *urticaria* from Latin *urtica* nettle]

urticate /'uhtikayt/ verb intrans to produce weals, itching, or a burning or stinging sensation. ➤ **urtication** /-'kaysh(ə)n/ noun. [late Latin *urticatus*, past part. of *urticare* to sting, from Latin *urtica* nettle]

Uruguayan /ˌyooərə'gwie-ən/ noun a native or inhabitant of Uruguay in S America. ➤ **Uruguayan** adj.

urus /'yooərəs/ noun = AUROCHS. [via Latin from Greek *ouros*]

US abbr United States.

us /əs/ strong us/ pronoun **1** objective case of WE: *Tell us what to do.* **2** chiefly Brit, informal me: *Give us a kiss.* [Old English *ūs*]

USA abbr **1** United States of America. **2** United States Army.

usable or **useable** /'yoohzəbl/ adj **1** capable of being used. **2** convenient for use. ➤ **usability** /-'biliti/ noun.

USAF abbr United States Air Force.

usage /'yoohsij, 'yoohzij/ noun **1a** established and generally accepted practice or procedure or an instance of this. **b** the way in which words and phrases are actually used in a language or an instance of this. **2a** the action, amount, or manner of using: *roads subject to frequent usage.* **b** manner of treating: *They suffered ill usage at the hands of their captors.*

usance /'yoohz(ə)ns/ noun **1** the time allowed by custom for payment of a bill of exchange in foreign commerce. **2** archaic use or usage. [Middle English *usaunce* usage, from late Latin *usantia*, from *usant-, usans*, present part. of *usare* to use, from Latin *usus*: see USE[1]]

USDAW /'uzdaw/ abbr Union of Shop, Distributive, and Allied Workers.

use[1] /yoohs/ noun **1a** the action of using or the state of being used: *in daily use.* **b** a way of using something: *a machine with many different uses.* **c** habitual or customary usage. **2a** the right or benefit of using something: *She gave him the use of her car.* **b** the ability or power to use something, e.g. a limb. **c** the legal enjoyment of property. **3a** a purpose or end: *put learning to practical use.* **b** practical worth or application: *things that might be of use.* **4** a form or observance of public worship, esp one with modifications peculiar to a local church or religious order. ✳ **have no use for 1** to have no occasion or need to use (something). **2** to view (something) with dislike, contempt, or disfavour: *I have no use for modern art.* **make use of** to use or take advantage of (something): *It has been asserted that man alone … makes use of tools or fire* — Darwin.

[Middle English *us* via Old French from Latin *usus*, past part. of *uti* to use]

use² /yoohz/ *verb trans* **1** to put (something or somebody) into action or service. **2** to employ (something) for a specified purpose: *use flattery to persuade them.* **3a** to expend or consume (something). **b** to consume or take (e.g. drugs) regularly. **4** to exploit (somebody) as a means to one's own ends: *I feel I am being used.* **5** to treat (somebody or something) in a specified manner: *They used the prisoners cruelly.* ✳ **used to** used to express a former habitual action or state: *She used to play tennis; He used not to mind.*

Usage note

used to. The strictly correct negative form of *used to* is *used not to*, which can be shortened to *usedn't to*: *You used not to* (or *usedn't to*) *mind if we came in a little late.* This often sounds rather formal, so that *did not use to* or *didn't use to* (but not *didn't used to*) are generally acceptable in informal speech or writing. Likewise, the traditionally correct negative question form *used you not to …?* or *usedn't you to …?* is often replaced, more informally, by *didn't you use to …?* If neither of these options seems acceptable, *you used to …, didn't you?* can be used.

useable /'yoohzəbl/ *adj* see USABLE.

use-by date /yoohz/ *noun* a date marked on the packaging of a perishable product by which the product should be used or consumed: compare SELL-BY DATE.

used /yoohzd/ *adj* **1** employed in accomplishing something. **2** that has endured use; *specif* secondhand. **3** /yoohst/ accustomed; habituated: *I'm not used to drinking.*

useful /'yoohsf(ə)l/ *adj* **1** having a practical worth or applicability. **2** *informal* highly satisfactory in quality; commendable: *The team's new player looks a useful striker.* ⟩⟩⟩ **usefully** *adv*, **usefulness** *noun*.

useless /'yoohslis/ *adj* **1** having or being of no use. **2** *informal* inept; lacking skill or aptitude; stupid: *I'm useless at singing.* ⟩⟩⟩ **uselessly** *adv*, **uselessness** *noun*.

user /'yoohzə/ *noun* **1** (*also used in combinations*) somebody who uses something. **2** *informal* a drug addict. **3** the legal enjoyment of property.

user-friendly *adj* easy to operate or understand: *a user-friendly machine; The textbook explains everything in user-friendly terms.* ⟩⟩⟩ **user-friendliness** *noun*.

use up /yoohz/ *verb trans* **1** to consume (something) completely. **2** to deprive (somebody or something) wholly of strength or useful properties; to exhaust (them).

usher¹ /'ushə/ *noun* **1** somebody who shows people to their seats, e.g. in a theatre or at a wedding. **2** an officer or servant who acts as a doorkeeper, e.g. in a court of law. **3** an officer who walks before a person of rank. **4** *archaic* an assistant teacher. [Middle English *ussher* doorkeeper, via French from medieval Latin *ustiarius*, from Latin *ostium, ustium* door, mouth of a river]

usher² *verb trans* (**ushered, ushering**) **1** to guide or escort (somebody) to a place. **2** (*usu* + in) to inaugurate or introduce (something): *usher in a new era.*

usherette /ushə'ret/ *noun dated* a woman who shows people to their seats in a theatre or cinema.

USM *abbr* unlisted securities market.

USN *abbr* United States Navy.

USP *abbr* unique selling proposition, used in advertising and marketing to refer to a characteristic of a commercial product that makes it different from others on the market.

usquebaugh /'uskwibaw/ *noun Irish, Scot* whisky. [Irish Gaelic *uisce beathadh* and Scottish Gaelic *uisge beatha* water of life]

USS *abbr* United States ship.

USSR *abbr* formerly, Union of Soviet Socialist Republics.

usual¹ /'yoohzhooəl, 'yoohzhəl/ *adj* **1** in accordance with usage, custom, or habit; normal. **2** commonly or ordinarily used. ✳ **as usual** in the accustomed or habitual way: *as usual he was late.* ⟩⟩⟩ **usually** *adv*, **usualness** *noun*. [late Latin *usualis*, from Latin *usus*: see USE¹]

usual² *noun* **1** (*often* **the usual**) something that is habitually done or that normally happens; the ordinary. **2** (**the/one's usual**) *informal* somebody's usual or preferred drink.

usufruct /'yoohzyoofrukt, 'yoohsyoofrukt/ *noun* the legal right of using and enjoying something belonging to another, on condition that the property, etc remains intact and its value is undiminished. ⟩⟩⟩ **usufructuary** /-'fruktyoo(ə)ri/ *noun and adj.* [Latin *ususfructus*, from *usus et fructus* use and enjoyment]

usurer /'yoohzhərə/ *noun* somebody who lends money, *esp* at an exorbitant rate of interest. [Middle English from medieval Latin *usurarius*, from Latin *usura*: see USURY]

usurp /yooh'suhp, yooh'zuhp/ *verb trans* to seize and possess (something) by force or without right: *usurp a throne.* ⟩⟩⟩ *verb intrans* to seize possession or exercise authority wrongfully. ⟩⟩⟩ **usurpation** /-'paysh(ə)n/ *noun*, **usurper** *noun*. [Middle English *usurpen* via French from Latin *usurpare*, literally 'to take possession of by use', from *usu* (ablative of *usus*: see USE¹) + *rapere* to seize]

usury /'yoohzhəri/ *noun* **1** the lending of money at interest, *esp* at an exorbitant or illegal rate of interest. **2** an exorbitant or illegal rate or amount of interest. ⟩⟩⟩ **usurious** /yooh'zhooəri-əs/ *adj*, **usuriously** /yooh'zhooəri-əsli/ *adv.* [Middle English from late Latin *usuria*, alteration of Latin *usura*, from *usus*: see USE¹]

UT *abbr* **1** Universal Time. **2** Utah (US postal abbreviation).

Ut *abbr* Utah.

ut /ut, ooht/ *noun* in music, used in fixed-doh solmization to refer to the note C in any scale or context. [Middle English, from medieval Latin *ut*: see GAMUT]

UTC *abbr* Universal Time Coordinated.

Utd *abbr* United, used in the names of sports teams, *esp* football teams.

ute /yooht/ *noun Aus, NZ, informal* = UTILITY VEHICLE. [by shortening and alteration]

utensil /yooh'tens(i)l/ *noun* **1** a piece of portable equipment, *esp* a tool or container, used in the household: *kitchen utensils.* **2** any useful tool or implement: *writing utensils.* [Middle English in the sense 'vessels for domestic use', via French from Latin *utensilia*, neuter pl of *utensilis* useful, from *uti* to use]

uteri /'yoohtərie/ *noun* pl of UTERUS.

uterine /'yoohtərin, -rien/ *adj* **1** relating to or in the region of the uterus. **2a** said of two or more offspring: born of the same mother but having a different father. **b** related through the female line. [Middle English from late Latin *uterinus*, from Latin *uterus* womb]

uterus /'yoohtərəs/ *noun* (*pl* **uteri** /-rie/) **1** a thick-walled hollow organ of the female mammal that contains and usu nourishes the young during development before birth; the womb. **2** a structure in some lower animals analogous to the uterus, in which eggs or young develop. [Latin *uterus* womb]

utilise /'yoohtiliez/ *verb trans* see UTILIZE.

utilitarian¹ /yooh,tili'teəri-ən/ *noun* an advocate of utilitarianism.

utilitarian² *adj* **1** designed for practical use rather than beautiful appearance. **2** relating to or characteristic of utilitarianism: *I shall … attempt to contribute something towards the understanding and appreciation of the Utilitarian or Happiness theory, and towards such proof as it is susceptible of* — John Stuart Mill.

utilitarianism *noun* **1** the doctrine that the criterion for right conduct should be the overall value of its consequences; *specif* the theory that the aim of action or social policy should be the greatest happiness of the greatest number. **2** utilitarian character, spirit, or quality.

utility¹ /yooh'tiliti/ *noun* (*pl* **utilities**) **1** fitness for some purpose; ability to be used advantageously. **2** something useful or designed for use. **3** an organization performing a public service, e.g. by providing gas or electricity, and operated privately, by local government, or by the state. **4** in computing, a program or piece of software that carries out a routine task. **5** *Aus, NZ* = UTILITY VEHICLE. [Middle English *utilite* via French from Latin *utilitat-, utilitas*, from *utilis* useful, from *uti* to use]

utility² *adj* **1** serving primarily for utility rather than beauty; utilitarian: *utility furniture.* **2** designed or adapted for general use. **3** capable of serving as a substitute in various roles or positions: *a utility player.*

utility room *noun* a room in a private house typically having a sink and storage space and often containing large items of household equipment, e.g. a freezer or washing machine.

utility truck *noun* = UTILITY VEHICLE.

utility vehicle *noun Aus, NZ* a van or truck with an open-topped or fabric-covered rear compartment.

utilize *or* **utilise** /'yoohtiliez/ *verb trans* to make use of (something); to turn (it) to practical use or account. ⟩⟩⟩ **utilizable** *adj*, **utilization** /-'zaysh(ə)n/ *noun*, **utilizer** *noun*. [French *utiliser*, from *utile* useful, from Latin *utilis*: see UTILITY¹]

utmost¹ /'utmohst/ *adj* **1** situated at the farthest or most distant point; extreme: *the utmost point of the earth* — John Hunt. **2** of the greatest or highest degree or amount: *a matter of the utmost concern*. [Old English *ūtmest*, from *ūt* OUT¹ + *-mest* -MOST]

utmost² *noun* **1** the highest point or degree; the extreme limit. **2** the best of one's abilities, powers, etc: *He did his utmost to help*.

utopia *or* **Utopia** /yooh'tohpi·ə/ *noun* **1** an imagined place or state of perfection, *esp* with regard to laws, government, and social conditions: compare DYSTOPIA. **2** an impractical scheme for social or political improvement. [named after *Utopia*, title of book about an imaginary ideal country, by Sir Thomas More d.1535, English statesman and writer, from Greek *ou* not, no + *topos* place]

utopian¹ *or* **Utopian** *adj* **1** impossibly ideal, *esp* with regard to social and political organization. **2** advocating impractically ideal social and political schemes. ➤➤ **utopianism** *noun*.

utopian² *or* **Utopian** *noun* **1** a believer in the possibility of creating a utopia. **2** an advocate of utopian schemes.

utricle /'yoohtrikl/ *noun* **1** any of various small pouches or pouched parts of an animal or plant body. **2** the larger of the two connected chambers of the sensory structures of the inner ear into which the semicircular canals open: compare SACCULE. **3** a small dry usu one-seeded fruit. ➤➤ **utricular** /yooh'trikyoolə/ *adj*. [Latin *utriculus*, dimin. of *uter* leather bag]

utter¹ /'utə/ *adj* absolute; total: *utter desolation*. ➤➤ **utterly** *adv*. [Middle English in the senses 'remote, extreme', from Old English *ūtera* outer, from *ūt* OUT¹]

utter² *verb trans* (**uttered, uttering**) **1a** to emit (something) as a sound: *utter a sigh*. **b** to give *esp* verbal expression to (something): *utter an opinion*. **2** to put (e.g. currency) into circulation; *specif* to circulate (forged or counterfeit money) as if legal or genuine. ➤➤ **utterable** *adj*, **utterer** *noun*. [Middle English *uttren* from early Dutch *ūteren*]

utterance /'ut(ə)rəns/ *noun* **1** something uttered, *esp* an oral statement. **2** vocal expression; speech: *give utterance to opinions*.

uttermost /'utəmohst/ *adj and noun* = UTMOST¹, UTMOST². [Middle English, alteration of *uttermest*, from UTTER¹ + *-mest* -MOST]

U-turn *noun* **1** the turning of a vehicle to face the opposite direction without reversing. **2** a total reversal of policy: *a U-turn on wage controls*.

UV *abbr* ultraviolet.

UVA *abbr* ultraviolet radiation with a range between 320 and 380 nanometres.

UVB *abbr* ultraviolet radiation with a range between 280 and 320 nanometres.

uvea /yooh'vi·ə/ *noun* the pigment-containing layer of the eye that includes the iris, ciliary body, and choroid. ➤➤ **uveal** *adj*. [late Latin *uvea* from Latin *uva* grape]

UVF *abbr* Ulster Volunteer Force.

uvula /'yoohvyoolə/ *noun* (*pl* **uvulas** *or* **uvulae** /-lee/) the fleshy lobe hanging in the middle of the back of the soft palate. [medieval Latin *uvula*, dimin. of Latin *uva* grape, uvula]

uvular¹ *adj* **1** relating to or in the region of the uvula: *uvular glands*. **2** said of a consonant: articulated with the back of the tongue and the uvula: *a French uvular /r/*.

uvular² *noun* a uvular consonant.

uxorial /uk'sawri·əl/ *adj formal* relating to or characteristic of a wife. [Latin *uxor* wife]

uxoricide /uk'sawrisied/ *noun* **1** the act or an instance of killing one's own wife. **2** a man who kills his own wife. ➤➤ **uxoricidal** /-'siedl/ *adj*. [Latin *uxor* wife + -CIDE]

uxorious /uk'sawri·əs/ *adj formal* excessively fond of or submissive to one's wife: *Passion in a lover's glorious, but in a husband is pronounced uxorious* — Byron. ➤➤ **uxoriously** *adv*, **uxoriousness** *noun*. [Latin *uxorius*, from *uxor* wife]

Uzbek /'oozbek, 'uzbek/ *noun* **1** (*pl* **Uzbeks** *or collectively* **Uzbek**) a member of an indigenous Turkic people inhabiting Uzbekistan. **2** (*pl* **Uzbeks**) a native or inhabitant of Uzbekistan. **3** the Turkic language of the people of Uzbekistan.

V¹ *or* **v** *noun* (*pl* **V's** *or* **Vs** *or* **v's**) **1a** the 22nd letter of the English alphabet. **b** a written character or design denoting this letter. **c** the sound represented by this letter, one of the English consonants. **2** an item designated as V, *esp* the 22nd in a series. **3** the Roman numeral for five.

V² *abbr* **1** Vatican City (international vehicle registration). **2** venerable. **3** verb. **4** very. **5** vice-. **6** victory. **7** viscount. **8** volt. **9** voltage. **10** volume.

V³ *abbr* the chemical symbol for vanadium.

v *abbr* **1** specific volume. **2** vector. **3** velocity. **4** ventral. **5** verb. **6** verse. **7** verso. **8** versus. **9** very. **10** vice. **11** vide. **12** used in German personal names: von.

V-1 *noun* a flying bomb used by the Germans in World War II. [German *Vergeltungswaffe*, from *Vergeltung* reprisal + *Waffe* weapon]

V-2 *noun* a long-range rocket used by the Germans in World War II.

V6 *noun* (*pl* **V6's**) **1** an internal-combustion engine with two banks of three cylinders each, the banks being at an angle to each other: compare V8, V-TYPE ENGINE. **2** a vehicle with such an engine.

V8 *noun* (*pl* **V8's**) **1** an internal-combustion engine with two banks of four cylinders each, the banks being at an angle to each other: compare V6, V-TYPE ENGINE. **2** a vehicle with such an engine.

VA *abbr* **1** *Brit* Order of Victoria and Albert. **2** *NAmer* Veterans' Administration. **3** Vicar Apostolic. **4** Vice-Admiral. **5** Virginia (US postal abbreviation). **6** volt-ampere.

Va *abbr* Virginia.

vac /vak/ *noun Brit, informal* **1** a vacation, *esp* from college or university. **2** = VACUUM CLEANER.

vac. *abbr* vacant.

vacancy /'vayk(ə)nsi/ *noun* (*pl* **vacancies**) **1a** a place, e.g. a room in a hotel, or property that is not being occupied or used. **b** an unfilled position in a factory, office, etc: *We have a vacancy for an assistant accounts clerk.* **c** the time that an office, post, or property is vacant between occupants. **2a** the state of being vacant; emptiness. **b** empty space, or an empty space. **c** emptiness of mind; vacuity; inanity.

vacant /'vayk(ə)nt/ *adj* **1** not occupied by an incumbent or officer: *The office of Treasurer is vacant at the moment.* **2a** without an occupant: *The room next door is vacant.* **b** not lived in; empty: *We passed through depressing villages with streets full of vacant houses.* **3** free from activity or work: *vacant hours.* **4a** stupid or foolish: *I've spent a lifetime trying to drum elementary mathematics into classfuls of vacant minds.* **b** expressionless: *a vacant look.* **c** being or during a respite from thought or care: *when on my couch I lie in vacant or in pensive mood* — Wordsworth. ➤➤ **vacantly** *adv*, **vacantness** *noun*. [Middle English via French from Latin *vacant-, vacans*, present part. of *vacare* to be empty, be free]

vacant possession *noun* ownership of property from which the previous owner or tenant has departed and which is therefore available for immediate occupation.

vacate /vay'kayt/ *verb trans* **1** to give up the possession or occupancy of (a room, building, etc). **2** to make (something) vacant; to leave (it) empty: *The police gave instructions for everybody to vacate the cinema.* **3** in law, to annul or cancel (something). ➤➤ **verb intrans** to vacate premises, a job, etc. ➤➤ **vacatable** *adj*. [Latin *vacatus*, past part. of *vacare* to be empty, be free]

vacation¹ /vay'kaysh(ə)n, və-/ *noun* **1** a scheduled period during which activity, e.g. of a university or the law courts, is suspended. **2** the act or an instance of vacating. **3** *chiefly NAmer* a holiday: *We had a restful vacation at the beach.* [Middle English *vacacioun* via French from Latin *vacation-, vacatio* freedom, exemption, from *vacare* to be empty, be free]

vacation² *verb intrans chiefly NAmer* to take or spend a holiday. ➤➤ **vacationer** *noun*, **vacationist** *noun*.

vaccinate /'vaksinayt/ *verb trans* **1** to administer a vaccine to (somebody), usu by injection. **2** to inoculate (somebody) with cowpox virus in order to produce immunity to smallpox. ➤➤ **verb intrans** to perform or practise the administration of vaccine. ➤➤ **vaccination** /-'naysh(ə)n/ *noun*, **vaccinator** *noun*.

vaccine¹ /'vakseen/ *noun* **1a** a preparation of killed microorganisms, e.g. viruses or bacteria, living inactivated organisms, or living fully infectious organisms, that is administered usu by injection to produce or artificially increase immunity to a particular disease. **b** a preparation containing the virus of cowpox in a form used for vaccination. **2** a piece of computer software designed to counteract electronic viruses. ➤➤ **vaccinal** /'vaksin(ə)l/ *adj*. [Latin *vaccinus* of or from cows, from *vacca* cow; from the use of vaccinia (cowpox) virus as the first vaccine]

vaccine² *adj* of cowpox or vaccination: *a vaccine pustule.*

vaccinia /vak'sini-ə/ *noun* = COWPOX. ➤➤ **vaccinial** *adj*. [scientific Latin, from *vaccinus* of or from cows, from *vacca* cow]

vacherin /vashə'ranh (*French* vaʃrɛ̃)/ *noun* a cake or dessert typically consisting of layers or a shell of meringue sandwiched or filled with whipped cream and often fruit. [French *vacherin*, orig denoting a type of cheese, from *vache* cow, from Latin *vacca*]

vacillate /'vasilayt/ *verb intrans* **1** to hesitate or waver in choosing between opinions or courses of action. **2a** to sway through imperfect balance. **b** to fluctuate or oscillate. ➤➤ **vacillatingly** *adv*, **vacillation** /-'laysh(ə)n/ *noun*, **vacillator** *noun*. [Latin *vacillatus*, past part. of *vacillare* to sway, waver]

vacua /'vakyooə/ *noun pl of* VACUUM¹.

vacuity /və'kyooh-iti/ *noun* (*pl* **vacuities**) **1** an empty space. **2** vacuousness or meaninglessness. **3** something, e.g. an idea, that is stupid or inane. **4** a lack of something. [Latin *vacuitas*, from *vacuus* empty]

vacuolate /'vakyoo(ə)layt, -lət/ *adj* containing one or more vacuoles.

vacuolated /'vakyoo(ə)laytid/ *adj* = VACUOLATE.

vacuolation /ˌvakyoo·ə'laysh(ə)n/ *noun* the development or formation of vacuoles.

vacuole /'vakyoo·ohl/ *noun* a small cavity or space containing air or fluid in the tissues of an organism or in the protoplasm of an individual cell. ➤➤ **vacuolar** /'vakyoo·ələ, -'ohlə/ *adj*. [French *vacuole* small vacuum, from Latin *vacuum*: see VACUUM¹]

vacuous /'vakyoo·əs/ *adj* **1** stupid; inane: *a vacuous expression.* **2** idle; aimless. **3** *archaic* empty. ➤➤ **vacuously** *adv*, **vacuousness** *noun*. [Latin *vacuus* empty]

vacuum¹ /'vakyoohm, 'vakyoom/ *noun* (*pl* **vacuums** or **vacua** /'va-kyooə/) **1a** a space absolutely devoid of matter: compare PLENUM (2). **b** a space from which as much air or other substance as possible has been removed, e.g. by an air pump. **c** an air pressure below atmospheric pressure. **d** (*used before a noun*) of, containing, producing, or using a partial vacuum: *a vacuum chamber*. **2a** a vacant space; a void. **b** a state of isolation from outside influences: *people who live in a vacuum … so that the world outside them is of no moment* — Somerset Maugham. **3** *informal* a vacuum cleaner. [Latin *vacuum*, neuter of *vacuus* empty]

vacuum² *verb trans and intrans informal* to clean (a carpet, etc) using a vacuum cleaner.

vacuum brake *noun* a continuous brake system worked by vacuum and used *esp* on trains.

vacuum-clean *verb trans and intrans* = VACUUM². ➤➤ **vacuum-cleaning** *noun*.

vacuum cleaner *noun* an electrical appliance for removing dust and dirt, *esp* from carpets or upholstery, by suction.

vacuum flask *noun chiefly Brit* a cylindrical container with a vacuum between an inner and an outer wall, usu of silvered glass, used to keep material, *esp* liquids, either hot or cold for considerable periods.

vacuum gauge *noun* a gauge indicating the degree to which a vacuum has been created in an enclosed space.

vacuum-packed *adj* packed in a wrapping from which most of the air has been removed. ➤➤ **vacuum pack** *noun*.

vacuum pump *noun* a pump for producing a vacuum.

vacuum tube *noun* an ELECTRON TUBE (electronic device that generates and controls a beam of electrons) in which there is a vacuum.

vade mecum /ˌvahday 'maykəm, ˌvaydi 'meekəm/ *noun* (*pl* **vade mecums**) **1** a book for ready reference; a handbook or manual. **2** something regularly carried about by a person. [Latin *vade mecum*, literally 'go with me']

V Adm. *abbr* Vice Admiral.

vadose /'vaydohs/ *adj* of or being water or solutions in the earth's crust above the water table. [Latin *vadosus* shallow, from *vadum* shallows, ford]

vagabond¹ /'vagəbond/ *noun* a wanderer; a tramp; a person with no settled home. ➤➤ **vagabondage** /-dij/ *noun*, **vagabondism** *noun*. [Middle English via French from Latin *vagabundus*, from *vagari* to wander]

vagabond² *adj* **1** of or characteristic of a wanderer. **2** leading an unsettled, irresponsible, or disreputable life. ➤➤ **vagabondish** *adj*.

vagal /'vaygəl/ *adj* of or affected or controlled by the vagus nerve. ➤➤ **vagally** *adv*.

vagary /'vaygəri/ *noun* (*pl* **vagaries**) an erratic, unpredictable, or extravagant motion, action, etc. ➤➤ **vagarious** /və'geəri·əs/ *adj*. [prob from Latin *vagari* to wander]

vagi /'vayjie, 'vaygie/ *noun* pl of VAGUS.

vagina /və'jienə/ *noun* (*pl* **vaginas** or **vaginae** /-nee/) **1** a canal in a female mammal that leads from the uterus to the external orifice of the genital canal. **2** a sheath or sheath-like structure, *esp* a leaf base that forms a sheath, usu round the main stem of a plant. ➤➤ **vaginal** /və'jienl, 'vajinl/ *adj*, **vaginate** /'vajinayt/ *adj*. [Latin *vagina* sheath]

vaginectomy /vaji'nektəmi/ *noun* (*pl* **vaginectomies**) **1** surgical removal of all or part of the vagina. **2** surgical removal of all or part

of the membrane surrounding the testis and epididymis. [VAGINA + -ECTOMY]

vaginismus /vaji'nizməs/ *noun* a painful spasmodic contraction of the vagina. [scientific Latin, from Latin *vagina* + -*ismus* -ISM]

vaginitis /vaji'nietəs/ *noun* inflammation of the vagina or of a covering structure such as a tendon sheath.

vagotomy /və'gotəmi/ *noun* (*pl* **vagotomies**) surgical cutting of the vagus, e.g. to reduce the flow of digestive juices in the treatment of a stomach ulcer. [VAGUS + -TOMY]

vagotonia /vaygə'tohni·ə/ *noun* overactivity of the vagus. [VAGUS + -*tonia* from Greek *tonos* TONE¹]

vagrant¹ /'vaygrənt/ *noun* **1** a person who has no established residence or lawful means of support. **2** *archaic* a wanderer or vagabond. [Middle English *vagraunt*, prob from Anglo-French *vagrant* walking about, from Old French *waucrer, wacrer* to roll, wander, of Germanic origin; influenced by Latin *vagari* to wander]

vagrant² *adj* **1** wandering about from place to place, usu with no means of support. **2** of or characteristic of a vagrant or vagabond; *specif* idle and disorderly. **3** having no fixed course; random; erratic. **4** said of a plant: growing in a straggling fashion. ➤➤ **vagrancy** /-si/ *noun*, **vagrantly** *adv*.

vague /vayg/ *adj* **1a** not having a precise meaning: *Vague terms like 'sort of' have no place in scientific reports.* **b** not clearly expressed; stated in indefinite terms: *All this amounts to is a few vague accusations of impropriety.* **c** not thinking, or expressing one's thoughts, clearly or precisely. **2a** not clearly defined, known, grasped, or understood; indistinct: *She has only a vague idea of what happened.* **b** not clearly felt or sensed: *He felt a vague longing for a baked potato.* **c** not sharply outlined; hazy: *He could make out a vague shape in the mist, which he assumed to be a sheep.* **3a** not alert; absentminded. **b** lacking expression; vacant: *That vague look on his face drives me mad!* ➤➤ **vaguely** *adv*, **vagueness** *noun*. [French *vague* from Latin *vagus*, literally 'wandering']

vagus /'vaygəs/ *noun* (*pl* **vagi** /'vayjie, 'vaygie/) either of a pair of cranial nerves that supply chiefly the heart and viscera. [scientific Latin *vagus nervus* wandering nerve]

vagus nerve *noun* = VAGUS.

vail /vayl/ *verb trans archaic or literary* to lower (something, e.g. a flag), often as a sign of respect or submission: *France must vail her lofty-plumed crest* — Shakespeare. ➤➤ *verb intrans archaic or literary* **1** to remove one's hat as a sign of respect. **2** to submit or yield: *and Greek itself vail to our English voice* — George Chapman. [Middle English *valen* short for obsolete *avalen* to let fall, from early French *avaler*, from Old French *aval*: see VALANCE]

vain /vayn/ *adj* **1** having or showing excessive pride in one's appearance, abilities, etc; conceited. **2** unsuccessful; ineffectual: *in a vain attempt to be amusing.* **3** idle; worthless: *vain talk.* * **in vain** to no end; without success or result. **take somebody's name in vain 1** to use a name, *esp* the name of God, profanely or without proper respect. **2** to mention a person by name. ➤➤ **vainly** *adv*, **vainness** *noun*. [Middle English via French from Latin *vanus* empty, vain]

vainglorious *adj literary* boastful. ➤➤ **vaingloriously** *adv*, **vaingloriousness** *noun*.

vainglory *noun literary* **1** excessive or ostentatious pride. **2** vanity or boastfulness. [Middle English via Old French from Latin *vana gloria* empty glory]

vair /veə/ *noun* **1** the bluish grey and white fur of a squirrel prized for ornamental use in medieval times. **2** one of the principal furs in heraldry, represented on a heraldic shield by horizontal rows of alternate blue and silver bells. [Middle English *veir* from Old French *vair* variegated, from Latin *varius* variegated, VARIOUS]

Vaishnava /viesh'nahvə/ *noun* a member of a major Hindu sect devoted to the cult of the god Vishnu: compare SHAKTISM. ➤➤ **Vaishnavism** *noun*. [Sanskrit *vaiṣṇava* of Vishnu, from *Viṣṇu* Vishnu]

Vaisya /'viesyə, 'vieshyə/ or **Vaishya** /'vieshyə/ *noun* a Hindu of an upper caste traditionally following commercial and agricultural occupations: compare BRAHMAN, KSHATRIYA, SUDRA. [Sanskrit *vaiśya* peasant, from *viś* settlement]

valance or **valence** /'valəns, 'vayləns/ *noun* **1** a piece of drapery hung as a border, *esp* along the edge of a bed, canopy, or shelf. **2** a pelmet. ➤➤ **valanced** *adj*. [Middle English *vallance*, prob ultimately from Old French *aval* downward, from *a* in, to (from AD-) + *val*: see VALLEY]

vale¹ /vayl/ *noun esp literary* a valley. [Middle English from Old French *val*: see VALLEY]

vale² /'vahlay/ *interj archaic* an exclamation of farewell. [Latin *vale* farewell, literally 'be healthy', from *valere* to be strong, be well]

valediction /valə'diksh(ə)n/ *noun formal* **1** an act of bidding farewell. **2** an address or statement of farewell or leave-taking. [Latin *valediction-*, *valedictio*, from *valedicere* to say farewell, from *vale* VALE² + *dicere* to say]

valedictorian /,valədik'tawri-ən/ *noun NAmer* a student who has attained the highest grades in their class in the final year at a school, and who delivers the farewell address at the commencement ceremony.

valedictory¹ /valə'dikt(ə)ri/ *adj formal* expressing or containing a farewell.

valedictory² *noun* (*pl* **valedictories**) *formal* a valedictory speech.

valence¹ /'vayləns/ *noun NAmer* see VALENCY.

valence² /'valəns/ *noun* see VALANCE.

Valenciennes /,valənsi'en, va,lensi'en(z)/ *noun* a fine pillow lace. [named after *Valenciennes*, town in N France formerly noted for its handmade lace]

valency /'vaylənsi/ (*NAmer* **valence** /'vayləns/) *noun* (*pl* **valencies** *or NAmer* **valences**) **1** the degree of combining power of an element or radical as shown by the number of atomic weights of a univalent element, e.g. hydrogen, with which the atomic weight of the element will combine or for which it can be substituted or with which it can be compared. **2** a unit of valency: *Carbon has four valencies.* **3** the ability to form chemical bonds. [late Latin *valentia* power, capacity, from Latin *valent-*, *valens*, present part. of *valere* to be strong]

valency electron *noun* any of the electrons in the outermost shell of an atom that are involved in the formation of chemical bonds.

-valent *comb. form* forming adjectives, with the meanings: **1** having the valency specified: *bivalent*; *multivalent*. **2** having the number of chromosomal strands or homologous chromosomes specified: *univalent*.

valentine /'valəntien/ *noun* **1** a sweetheart chosen on St Valentine's Day, 14 February. **2** a greeting card sent or given, often anonymously, *esp* to a sweetheart, on St Valentine's Day.

Word history
St Valentine's Day is the feast day of two saints named Valentine; one martyred in Rome c.270, the other the Bishop of Terni, martyred soon afterwards. The custom of sending cards to one's sweetheart on this day has nothing to do with the saints; it is probably a remnant of the Roman festival Lupercalia, held on 15 February, which included fertility rites, influenced by the belief that birds choose their mates at this time.

valerian /və'liəri-ən, və'leə-/ *noun* **1** any of several species of usu perennial plants, many of which possess medicinal properties: family Valerianaceae. **2** a drug prepared from the roots of valerian, used as a sedative and CARMINATIVE² (drug given to relieve flatulence). [Middle English from medieval Latin *valeriana*, prob named after *Valeria*, Roman province in SE Europe]

valeric acid /və'liərik, və'lerik/ *noun* = PENTANOIC ACID. [from VALERIAN; from its occurrence in the plant's root]

valet¹ /'valay, 'valit/ *noun* **1** a man's male servant who performs personal services, e.g. taking care of clothing, or an employee of a hotel, etc who performs similar services for patrons. **2** an employee of a hotel, restaurant, etc who provides valet parking for customers. [early French *vaslet*, *varlet*, *valet* young nobleman, page, domestic servant, from assumed medieval Latin *vassellittus*, dimin. of *vassallus*: see VASSAL¹]

valet² *verb* (**valeted**, **valeting**) ➤ *verb trans* **1** to serve (somebody) as a valet. **2** to clean (a car) as a service. ➤ *verb intrans* to work as a valet.

valeta /və'leetə/ *noun* see VELETA.

valet de chambre /,valay də 'shombr/ *noun* (*pl* **valets de chambre** /,valay/) = VALET¹ (1). [French *valet de chambre* room valet]

valet parking /'valay/ *noun* a service providing attendants who take a customer's car from the door of a hotel, restaurant, etc, park it, and return it when required.

valetudinarian¹ /,valityoohdi'neəri-ən/ *noun formal* a person of a weak or sickly constitution, *esp* a hypochondriac. ➤➤ **valetudinarianism** *noun*. [Latin *valetudinarius* sickly, infirm, from

valetudin-, *valetudo* state of health, sickness, from *valere* to be strong, be well]

valetudinarian² *adj formal* weak; sickly.

valetudinary¹ /vali'tyoohdin(ə)ri/ *noun* (*pl* **valetudinaries**) *formal* = VALETUDINARIAN¹. [Latin *valetudinarius*: see VALETUDINARIAN¹]

valetudinary² *adj formal* = VALETUDINARIAN².

valgus /'valgəs/ *noun* the position of a bone or part that is turned outward to an abnormal degree at its joint: compare VARUS. [Latin *valgus* bowlegged]

Valhalla *or* **Walhalla** /val'halə/ *noun* in Norse mythology, one of the most beautiful halls of Asgard, where the souls of heroes slain in battle were taken to spend eternity in joy and feasting. [Old Norse *Valhöll*, from *valr* the slain + *höll* hall]

valiant /'vali-ənt/ *adj* characterized by or showing valour; courageous. ➤➤ **valiance** *noun*, **valiantly** *adv*, **valiantness** *noun*. [Middle English *valiaunt* from early French *vaillant*, present part. of *valoir* to be of worth, from Latin *valere* to be strong]

valid /'valid/ *adj* **1a** well-grounded or justifiable; relevant and meaningful. **b** logically sound. **2a** having legal efficacy, *esp* executed according to the proper formalities: *a valid contract.* **b** (*often* + for) able to be used lawfully, *esp* for a stated period or under certain conditions; legally acceptable: *This ticket is valid for three months.* ➤➤ **validity** /və'liditi/ *noun*, **validly** *adv*, **validness** *noun*. [early French *valide* from Latin *validus* strong, from *valere* to be strong]

validate /'validayt/ *verb trans* **1** to make (something) legally valid. **2** to corroborate or authenticate (something): *Further experiments validated his hypothesis.* ➤➤ **validation** /-'daysh(ə)n/ *noun*.

valine /'vayleen, 'valeen/ *noun* an essential amino acid found in most proteins. [VALERIC ACID + -INE²]

valise /və'leez, və'lees/ *noun dated* a small piece of luggage; a travelling bag. [French *valise* from Italian *valigia*]

Valium /'vali-əm/ *noun trademark* a tranquillizer; = DIAZEPAM.

Valkyrie /'valkiri, val'kiəri/ *noun* in Norse mythology, any of the maidens, usu twelve in number, who were servants of the god Odin and who chose heroes killed in battle and conducted them to an afterlife of feasting and heroic deeds in Valhalla. [Old Norse *valkyrja*, literally 'chooser of the slain', from *valr* those slain in battle + *kjósa* to choose]

valla /'valə/ *noun* pl of VALLUM.

vallecula /və'lekyoolə/ *noun* (*pl* **valleculae** /-lee/) an anatomical groove, channel, or depression, *esp* one between the base of the tongue and the epiglottis. ➤➤ **vallecular** *adj*. [late Latin *vallecula* little valley, dimin. of Latin *valles* VALLEY]

valley /'vali/ *noun* (*pl* **valleys**) **1a** an elongated depression of the earth's surface, usu between hills or mountains. **b** an area drained by a river and its tributaries. **2a** a hollow or depression. **b** the internal angle formed at the meeting of two roof surfaces. [Middle English *valey* from Old French *valee*, from *val* vale, valley, from Latin *vall-*, *valles*]

vallum /'valəm/ *noun* (*pl* **vallums** *or* **valla** /'valə/) an ancient Roman defensive embankment. [Latin *vallum*, from *vallus* palisade, stake]

valonia /və'lohni-ə/ *noun* dried acorn cups, *esp* from a Eurasian evergreen oak, used in tanning or dressing leather. [Italian *vallonia* from late Greek *balanidia*, pl of *balanidion*, dimin. of Greek *balanos* acorn]

valor /'valə/ *noun NAmer* see VALOUR.

valorize *or* **valorise** /'valəriez/ *verb trans* to enhance, or try to enhance, the price, value, or status of (a commodity) by organized action, *esp* by a government. ➤➤ **valorization** /-'zaysh(ə)n/ *noun*. [Portuguese *valorizare*, from *valor* value, price, from medieval Latin: see VALOUR]

valorous /'valərəs/ *adj* valiant; courageous. ➤➤ **valorously** *adv*.

valour (*NAmer* **valor**) /'valə/ *noun* strength of mind or spirit that enables somebody to encounter danger with firmness; personal bravery. [Middle English via French from medieval Latin *valor* value, valour, from Latin *valere* to be strong, be worth]

Valpolicella /,valpoli'chelə/ *noun* a light red wine produced in NE Italy in the region of Verona. [named after *Valpolicella*, valley in N Italy]

valse /vals/ *noun* (*pl* **valses** /vals, 'valsiz/) = WALTZ[1]. [French *valse* from German *Walzer*]

valuable[1] /'valyoo(ə)bl/ *adj* **1** having high money value. **2** of great use or worth: *That was valuable advice.* **3** /'valyoo·əbl/ able to be valued. ⨠ **valuableness** *noun*, **valuably** *adv.*

valuable[2] *noun* (*usu in pl*) a personal possession of relatively great monetary value.

valuation /valyoo'aysh(ə)n/ *noun* **1** the act or an instance of valuing something, *esp* property. **2** the estimated or determined value, *esp* market value, of a thing. **3** judgment or appraisal of worth or character. ⨠ **valuational** *adj*, **valuationally** *adv*, **valuator** /'va-lyooaytə/ *noun.*

value[1] /'valyooh/ *noun* **1** a fair return or equivalent for something exchanged: *I like to get value for money when I buy clothes.* **2** the worth in money or commodities of something. **3** relative worth, utility, or importance: *Nowadays people know the price of everything and the value of nothing* — Oscar Wilde. **4** (*usu in pl*) a moral principle or standard of behaviour: *traditional family values.* **5a** a numerical quantity assigned or computed. **b** the magnitude of a physical quantity. **c** precise meaning or significance, e.g. of a word. **6** the denomination of a note or coin. **7** the relative duration of a musical note. **8a** relative lightness or darkness of a colour. **b** the relation of one part in a picture to another with respect to lightness and darkness. **9** in phonetics, the quality of a sound that a letter represents. [Middle English from early French, fem past part. of *valoir* to be worth, from Latin *valēre* to be worth, be strong]

value[2] *verb trans* (**values, valued, valuing**) **1a** (*often* + at) to estimate the worth of (something) in terms of money: *The property was valued at £85,000.* **b** to rate (somebody or something) in terms of usefulness, importance, etc. **2** to consider or rate (something) highly: *I really value your advice.* ⨠ **valued** *adj*, **valuer** *noun.*

value-added[1] *noun* **1** the amount by which the value of an article is increased at each stage of its manufacturing progress: *the application of advanced information technology to increase value-added* — The Economist. **2** the difference between the revenues and the costs of a firm or industry; profits.

value-added[2] *adj* with value added, e.g. by additional processing or special features: *We have been producing value-added products from lamb and beef.*

value-added tax *noun* a tax levied at each stage of the production and distribution of a commodity and passed on to the consumer as a form of purchase tax.

valued policy *noun* an insurance policy in which the amount to be paid in the event of a loss is set at the outset and is not dependent on the size of the loss.

value judgment *noun* a judgment attributing a value, e.g. good, evil, or desirable, to a particular action or thing, usu contrasted with a tolerant, factual, or objective assessment.

valueless *adj* worthless. ⨠ **valuelessness** *noun.*

valuta /və'l(y)oohtə/ *noun* the agreed exchange value of a currency. [Italian *valuta* value, ultimately from Latin *valēre* to be worth, be strong]

valvate /'valvayt/ *adj* **1** having valves or parts resembling a valve. **2** opening by or as if by valves. **3** said of petals or sepals: meeting at the edges without overlapping in the bud: compare IMBRICATE[1] (1). [Latin *valvatus* having folding doors, from *valva* one leaf of a folding door]

valve /valv/ *noun* **1** a structure, *esp* in the heart or a vein, that closes temporarily to obstruct passage of material or permits movement of fluid in one direction only. **2a** any of numerous mechanical devices by which the flow of liquid, gas, or loose material in bulk may be controlled, usu to allow movement in one direction only. **b** a device in a brass musical instrument for varying the tube length in order to change the fundamental tone by a definite interval. **3** any of the separate joined pieces that make up the shell of an invertebrate animal; *specif* either of the two halves of the shell of a bivalve mollusc. **4** any of the segments or pieces into which a ripe seed capsule or pod separates. **5** *chiefly Brit* a vacuum- or gas-filled device for the regulation of electric current by the control of free electrons or ions. ⨠ **valved** *adj*, **valveless** *adj.* [Latin *valva* a leaf of a folding door]

valvular /'valvyoolə/ *adj* **1a** resembling or functioning as a valve. **b** opening by valves. **2** of a valve, *esp* of the heart.

valvulitis /valvyoo'lietəs/ *noun* inflammation of a body valve, *esp* of the heart.

vamoose /va'moohs/ *verb intrans informal* to depart quickly. [Spanish *vamos* let us go, from Latin *vadere* to go]

vamp[1] /vamp/ *noun informal* a woman who uses her charm to seduce and exploit men. [short for VAMPIRE]

vamp[2] *verb trans informal* said of a woman: to practise seductive wiles on (a man); to entice (him). ⨠ *verb intrans informal* to act as a vamp.

vamp[3] *noun* **1** the part of a shoe or boot covering the front of the foot. **2** a simple improvised musical accompaniment. **3** something patched up to look new. **4** a reworking of an old story, sermon, etc. [Middle English *vampe* sock, from Old French *avantpié*, from *avant-* fore- + *pié* foot, from Latin *ped-*, *pes*]

vamp[4] *verb trans* **1** to provide (a shoe) with a new vamp. **2** *informal* (+ up) to rework (something old, e.g. a story or sermon) with new material or in a new way. **3** to play an improvised musical accompaniment to (a tune). ⨠ *verb intrans* to play a musical vamp. ⨠ **vamper** *noun.*

vampire /'vampie·ə/ *noun* **1** a dead person believed to come from the grave at night and suck the blood of sleeping people. **2a** any of several species of S American bats that feed on blood and are dangerous to human beings and domestic animals, *esp* as transmitters of diseases such as rabies: family Desmodontidae. **b** any of several other bats that do not feed on blood but are sometimes reputed to do so: family Megadermatidae and others. **3** a person who lives by preying on and exploiting others. ⨠ **vampiric** /vam'pirik/ *adj.* [French *vampire* or German *Vampir*, from Hungarian *vampir*]

vampire bat *noun* = VAMPIRE (2A).

vampirism /'vampiriz(ə)m/ *noun* **1** belief in vampires. **2** the actions of a vampire.

van[1] /van/ *noun* **1** an enclosed motor vehicle used for transport of goods, animals, furniture, etc. **2** *Brit* an enclosed railway goods wagon. **3** *Brit* = CARAVAN[1] (1). [short for CARAVAN[1]]

van[2] *noun* = VANGUARD. [by shortening]

van[3] *noun Brit, informal* = ADVANTAGE (4). [by shortening]

van[4] *noun* **1** *archaic* a winnowing device, e.g. a fan. **2** *archaic or literary* a bird's wing. [Middle English via French from Latin *vannus*]

vanadium /və'naydi·əm/ *noun* a grey metallic chemical element that is hard and malleable, occurs naturally in minerals, and is used *esp* in alloys: symbol V, atomic number 23. ⨠ **vanadate** /'vanədayt/ *noun*, **vanadic** /və'naydik, və'nadik/ *adj*, **vanadous** /'vanədəs/ *adj.* [scientific Latin, from Old Norse *Vanadīs* Freya, Norse goddess of love and beauty; because of the beautiful colours of vanadium's compounds in solution]

Van Allen belt /van 'alən/ *noun* either of two belts of intense ionizing radiation in the earth's outer atmosphere. [named after James A *Van Allen* b.1914, US physicist who discovered the belts]

V and A *abbr* Victoria and Albert Museum.

vandal /'vandl/ *noun* **1** a person who wilfully or ignorantly destroys or defaces property. **2** (**Vandal**) a member of a Germanic people who overran Gaul, Spain, and N Africa in the fourth and fifth cents and in 455 sacked Rome. ⨠ **Vandalic** /van'dalik/ *adj.* [Latin *Vandalus*]

vandalise /'vandəliez/ *verb trans* see VANDALIZE.

vandalism *noun* wilful destruction or defacement of property. ⨠ **vandalistic** /-'listik/ *adj*, **vandalistically** /-'listikli/ *adv.*

vandalize *or* **vandalise** /'vandəliez/ *verb trans* to destroy or damage (property), *esp* ignorantly or maliciously.

Van de Graaff generator /van də 'grahf/ *noun* an apparatus for the production of electrical discharges at high voltage, typically consisting of an insulated hollow conducting sphere that accumulates in its interior the charge continuously conveyed from a source of direct current by a belt of flexible non-conducting material. [named after Robert J *Van de Graaff* d.1967, US physicist who devised it]

van der Waals forces /van də 'wahlz, 'vahlz/ *pl noun* the relatively weak attractive forces that are operative between neutral atoms and molecules and that arise because of differences in electric potential. [named after Johannes *van der Waals* d.1923, Dutch physicist]

Vandyke /van'diek/ *noun* **1a** a wide collar with a deeply indented edge. **b** a series of V-shaped points forming a decorative edging, or any of the points themselves. **2** a trim pointed beard. [Sir Anthony

Vandyke (orig Van Dyck) d.1641, Flemish painter, who depicted such styles in his works]

Vandyke beard *noun* = VANDYKE (2).

Vandyke brown *noun* a dark brown pigment. [from its use by the painter Sir Anthony *Vandyke*: see VANDYKE]

Vandyke cape *noun* = VANDYKE (1A).

Vandyke collar *noun* = VANDYKE (1A).

vane /vayn/ *noun* **1** = WEATHER VANE. **2a** a thin flat or curved object that is rotated about an axis by wind or water: *the vanes of a windmill.* **b** a device revolving in a similar manner and moving in water or air: *the vanes of a propeller.* **3** the flat expanded part of a feather. **4** a stabilizing fin or similar part on a projectile, such as any of the feathers fastened to the shaft of an arrow. **5a** the target of a levelling staff. **b** any of the sights of a compass or quadrant. ➤➤ **vaned** *adj.* [Old English *fana* banner]

vanguard /'van·gahd/ *noun* **1** the troops moving at the head of an army. **2** the forefront of an action or movement. [Middle English *vantgard* from early French *avant-garde*, from *avant-* fore- + *garde* guard]

vanilla[1] /və'nilə/ *noun* **1a** any of a genus of tropical American climbing orchids with long capsular fruits that yield an important flavouring: genus *Vanilla*. **b** the fruit of this plant. **2a** a commercially important extract of the vanilla pod that is used *esp* as a flavouring. **b** the flavour of vanilla. [Spanish *vainilla*, dimin. of *vaina* sheath, from Latin *vagina* sheath, vagina]

vanilla[2] *adj* **1** flavoured with vanilla: *vanilla ice cream.* **2** *informal* ordinary or plain; standard: *a vanilla modem.*

vanilla pod *noun* = VANILLA[1] (1B).

vanillin /və'nilin/ *noun* the chief fragrant component of vanilla.

vanish /'vanish/ *verb intrans* **1a** to pass quickly from sight; to disappear. **b** to cease to exist. **2** to assume the value zero. ➤➤ **vanisher** *noun*. [Middle English *vanisshen* from early French *evanir*, ultimately from Latin *evanescere* to dissipate like vapour, vanish, from E-[1] + *vanescere* to vanish]

vanishing cream *noun* a light cosmetic cream used chiefly as a foundation for face powder.

vanishing point *noun* **1** a point at which receding parallel lines seem to meet when represented in linear perspective. **2** a point at which something disappears or ceases to exist.

Vanitory unit /'vanit(ə)ri/ *noun trademark* a vanity unit. [blend of VANITY + LAVATORY]

vanity /'vaniti/ *noun* (*pl* **vanities**) **1** something vain, empty, or worthless. **2** the quality of being vain or futile; worthlessness: *No place affords a more striking conviction of the vanity of human hopes than a public library* — Dr Johnson. **3** excessive pride in oneself; conceit. **4** an instance or a display of being vain, or a cause of this. [Middle English *vanite* via Old French from Latin *vanitat-, vanitas* quality of being empty or vain, from *vanus* empty, VAIN]

vanity bag *noun* = VANITY CASE.

vanity case *noun* a small case used by women for carrying toilet articles and cosmetics.

vanity publisher *noun* a publishing house that publishes books at the author's expense. ➤➤ **vanity publishing** *noun*.

vanity unit *noun* a piece of furniture consisting of a small fitted, sometimes shelved, cupboard with a washbasin set into its upper surface.

vanquish /'vangkwish/ *verb trans literary* **1** to overcome or conquer (somebody or something); to beat (them): *He vanquished all his foes.* **2** to gain mastery over (an emotion, passion, etc): *There are many ways of vanquishing your fears.* ➤➤ **vanquishable** *adj,* **vanquisher** *noun.* [Middle English *venquissen* from early French *venquis,* past tense of *veintre* to conquer, from Latin *vincere*]

vantage /'vahntij/ *noun* **1** a position giving a strategic advantage or commanding perspective, or the advantage gained from this. **2** *Brit* = ADVANTAGE (4). **3** = VANTAGE POINT. [Middle English from early French *avantage*: see ADVANTAGE]

vantage point *noun* a place or position that affords one a clear view over an area or a clear perspective on a situation.

Vanuatuan /vanoo'ahtooh·ən/ *noun* a native or inhabitant of Vanuatu in the SW Pacific. ➤➤ **Vanuatuan** *adj.*

vapid /'vapid/ *adj* lacking liveliness, interest, or force; insipid. ➤➤ **vapidity** /və'piditi/ *noun,* **vapidly** *adv,* **vapidness** *noun.* [Latin *vapidus* flat-tasting]

vapor[1] /'vaypə/ *noun NAmer* see VAPOUR[1].

vapor[2] *verb trans and intrans NAmer* see VAPOUR[2].

vaporescence /vaypə'res(ə)ns/ *noun* the formation or creation of vapour. ➤➤ **vaporescent** *adj.*

vaporetto /vapə'retoh/ *noun* (*pl* **vaporettos** or **vaporetti** /-tee/) a passenger boat used on the canals of Venice. [Italian *vaporetto,* dimin. of *vapore* steam, steamboat, from Latin *vapor* steam, VAPOUR[1]]

vaporific /vaypə'rifik/ *adj* **1** of or like vapour. **2** producing vapour. **3** readily turning into a vapour.

vaporing *noun NAmer* see VAPOURING.

vaporise *verb trans and intrans* see VAPORIZE.

vaporiser *noun* see VAPORIZER.

vaporize or **vaporise** *verb trans* **1** to convert (liquid) into vapour, e.g. by the application of heat. **2** to destroy (somebody or something) by converting them into vapour. ➤ *verb intrans* to become vaporized. ➤➤ **vaporizable** *adj,* **vaporization** /-'zaysh(ə)n/ *noun.*

vaporizer or **vaporiser** *noun* **1** = ATOMIZER. **2** a device for converting water or a medicated liquid into a vapour for inhalation.

vaporous /'vayp(ə)rəs/ *adj* **1** resembling, consisting of, or characteristic of vapour. **2** producing vapours; volatile. **3** containing or obscured by vapours; misty. **4** lacking solidness. **5** fanciful or foolish. ➤➤ **vaporously** *adv,* **vaporousness** *noun.*

vapour[1] (*NAmer* **vapor**) /'vaypə/ *noun* **1** smoke, fog, etc suspended floating in the air and impairing its transparency. **2** a substance in the gaseous state, *esp* such a substance that is liquid under normal conditions. **3** (**the vapours**) *dated* a depressed or hysterical condition. **4** *archaic* a foolish or fanciful idea: *What amazing vapours a lonely man may get into his head* — H G Wells. ➤➤ **vapourish** *adj,* **vapoury** *adj.* [Middle English *vapour* via French from Latin *vapor* steam, vapour]

vapour[2] (*NAmer* **vapor**) *verb intrans* **1** to rise or pass off in vapour. **2** to emit vapour. **3** to indulge in bragging, blustering, or foolish talk. ➤ *verb trans* to cause (something) to pass off as vapour. ➤➤ **vapourer** *noun.*

vapour density *noun* the density of a vapour or gas relative to the density of hydrogen at the same temperature and pressure.

vapouring (*NAmer* **vaporing**) *noun* (*usu in pl*) foolish, extravagant, or boastful talk.

vapour lock *noun* a partial or complete stopping of the flow of fuel in an internal-combustion engine due to the formation of bubbles of vapour or gas, e.g. because the engine has become overheated.

vapour pressure *noun* the pressure exerted by a vapour that is in equilibrium with its solid or liquid form.

vapour trail *noun* a trail of condensed water vapour created in the air by an aircraft flying at high altitude.

vaquero /və'keəroh/ *noun* (*pl* **vaqueros**) in the SW USA, a herdsman or cowboy. [Spanish *vaquero,* from *vaca* cow, from Latin *vacca*]

var. *abbr* **1** variable. **2** variant. **3** variation. **4** variety. **5** various.

varactor /və'raktə/ *noun* a semiconductor device that is a component of an electronic circuit, e.g. a switch, and whose capacitance depends on the applied voltage: compare VARISTOR. [contraction of *variable reactor*]

varec /'varek/ *noun* **1** a seaweed such as kelp. **2** ash obtained from burning kelp, a source of iodine and potash. [French *varech,* of Scandinavian origin]

vari- or **vario-** *comb. form* forming words, with the meaning: varied; diverse: *variform.* [Latin *varius* VARIOUS]

variable[1] /'veəri·əbl/ *adj* **1a** able or apt to vary; subject to variation or changes. **b** said of the wind: liable to change in strength and direction. **2** said of behaviour, etc: fickle or inconstant. **3** said of a quantity: able to assume any of a range of values. **4** said of a biological group or character: deviating or liable to deviate from its true type; aberrant. **5** said of an electrical device, etc: allowing some property to be varied. ➤➤ **variability** /-'biliti/ *noun,* **variableness** *noun,* **variably** *adv.*

variable[2] *noun* **1** something that varies or that can be varied. **2a** a quantity that may assume any of a set of values. **b** a symbol representing a variable quantity or entity. **3** = VARIABLE STAR. **4a** a variable wind. **b** (*in pl*) a region where variable winds occur.

variable cost *noun* a cost, e.g. for labour or materials, that varies directly with the level of production: compare FIXED COSTS, OVERHEAD³.

variable-geometry *adj* said of an aeroplane: having wings whose angle can be varied for best performance at high and low speeds; = SWING-WING.

variable star *noun* a star with regularly or irregularly varying brightness.

variable-sweep *adj* = VARIABLE-GEOMETRY.

variance /'veəri·əns/ *noun* 1 the fact, quality, or state of being variable or variant; difference or variation: *Researchers are working to find the cause of the variance in the crop yields.* 2 the fact or state of being in disagreement; dissension or dispute. 3 a discrepancy. 4 in law, an inconsistency, *esp* between two pieces of evidence that are intended to support one another. 5 in statistics, the square of the standard deviation. ✻ **at variance with** not in harmony or agreement with (something): *Such conclusions would be at variance with the available evidence.*

variant¹ /'veəri·ənt/ *noun* 1 any of two or more people or things displaying usu slight differences. 2a something that shows variation from a type or norm. b any of two or more different spellings, pronunciations, or forms of the same word.

variant² *adj* 1 varying, *esp* only slightly, from the standard form: *There are variant readings for this verse.* 2 varying or liable to vary.

variate /'veəri·ət/ *noun* a statistical variable that can take on a defined range of values which are governed by a probability distribution: *The number of spots showing if two dice are thrown is a variate.*

variation /veəri'aysh(ə)n/ *noun* 1a the act or an instance of varying. b the extent to which or the range in which a thing varies. c something showing variation. 2 = DECLINATION (2). 3 a change in the mean motion or orbit of a celestial body. 4 a varied version of a musical idea. 5a divergence in characteristics of an organism or genotype from those typical or usual of its group. b an individual or group exhibiting such divergence. 6 a solo dance in ballet. ►► **variational** *adj*, **variationally** *adv*.

varic- or **varico-** *comb. form* forming words, denoting: a varix or varicose vein: *varicotomy.*

varicella /vari'selə/ *noun technical* = CHICKENPOX. ►► **varicellar** *adj.* [scientific Latin, dimin. of VARIOLA]

varices /'variseez/ *noun* pl of VARIX.

varico- *comb. form* see VARIC-.

varicocele /'varikohseel/ *noun* a varicose enlargement of the veins of the spermatic cord. [VARICO- + -CELE]

varicoloured (*NAmer* **varicolored**) /'veərikuləd/ *adj* having various colours.

varicose /'varikəs, -kohs/ *adj* 1 abnormally swollen or dilated: *varicose veins.* 2 relating to varicose veins. ►► **varicosity** /-'kositi/ *noun.* [Latin *varicosus* full of dilated veins, from *varic-, varix* dilated vein]

varicosed /'varikohst/ *adj* = VARICOSE.

varicosis /vari'kohsis/ *noun* (*pl* **varicoses** /-seez/) abnormal swelling or dilation of a vein.

varicotomy /vari'kotəmi/ *noun* (*pl* **varicotomies**) surgical removal of a varicose vein.

varied /'veərid/ *adj* 1 having numerous forms or types; diverse. 2 having a variety of contents or parts. 3 = VARIEGATED. ►► **variedly** *adv.*

variegate /'veərigayt/ *verb trans* to alter (something) in appearance, *esp* with patches of different colours; to dapple (it). ►► **variegation** /-'gaysh(ə)n/ *noun,* **variegator** *noun.* [Latin *variegatus,* past part. of *variegare,* from *varius* VARIOUS + *agere* to drive]

variegated /'veərigaytid/ *adj* marked with patches of different colours: *variegated leaves.*

varietal¹ /və'rie·ətl/ *adj* of a particular variety of animal or plant. ►► **varietally** *adv.*

varietal² *noun* 1 a particular variety of grape. 2 a wine classified and known by the name of the variety of grape it was made from, rather than by its place of origin.

variety /və'rieiti/ *noun* (*pl* **varieties**) 1 the state of having different forms or types; diversity. 2 an assortment of different things, *esp* of a particular class. 3a something differing from others of the same general kind; a sort. b any of various groups of plants or animals ranking below a species, sometimes one produced by artificial breeding. 4 theatrical entertainment consisting of separate performances of songs, sketches, acrobatics, etc. [early French *variété* from Latin *varietat-, varietas,* from *varius* VARIOUS]

varifocal /'veərifohkl/ *adj* said of a lens, e.g. of a pair of spectacles: formed so as to allow focusing on close, middle-distance, and faraway objects.

varifocals *pl noun* spectacles with varifocal lenses.

variform /'veərifawm/ *adj* varied in form. ►► **variformly** *adv.*

vario- *comb. form* see VARI-.

variola /və'rie·ələ/ *noun technical* smallpox, cowpox, or any of various other virus diseases marked by a rash of pustular spots. ►► **variolous** /-ləs/ *adj.* [medieval Latin *variola* pustule, pox, from Latin *varius* VARIOUS]

variometer /veəri'omitə/ *noun* 1 an instrument for measuring magnetic VARIATION (the angle between magnetic north and true north). 2 an aeronautical instrument for indicating rate of climb.

variorum¹ /veəri'awrəm, va-/ *noun* 1 an edition or text with notes by different people. 2 an edition of a publication containing variant readings of the text. [Latin *variorum* of various persons, in the phrase *cum notis variorum* with the notes of various persons]

variorum² *adj* 1 said of an edition or text: having notes by different people. 2 said of an edition of a publication: containing variant readings of the text.

various /'veəri·əs/ *adj* 1a of differing kinds; diverse: *There are various remedies for itching.* b dissimilar in nature or form; unlike. 2 more than one; several: *We made short stops at various towns along the way.* 3 archaic having a number of different aspects or characteristics: *one whose conversation was so various and delightful —* Thackeray. ►► **variousness** *noun.* [Latin *varius*]

variously *adv* 1 in various ways. 2 at various times. 3 by various designations: *Head teachers are known variously as principals, headmasters or headmistresses, or rectors.*

varistor /və'ristə/ *noun* a semiconductor device that is a component of an electronic circuit and whose electrical resistance depends on the applied voltage: compare VARACTOR. [contraction of *varying resistor*]

varix /'variks/ *noun* (*pl* **varices** /-seez/) 1 an abnormally dilated and lengthened vein, artery, or lymph vessel, *esp* a varicose vein. 2 any of the prominent ridges across each whorl of a gastropod shell. [Latin *varic-, varix*]

varlet /'vahlit/ *noun* 1 archaic a base unprincipled person. 2 formerly, a knight's page. 3 formerly, a menial servant. ►► **varletry** /-tri/ *noun.* [Middle English from early French *vaslet, varlet*: see VALET¹]

varmint /'vahmint/ *noun NAmer, informal* or *Brit, dialect* 1 an animal or bird considered a pest. 2 a rascal. [alteration of VERMIN]

varna /'vahnə/ *noun* any of the four major Hindu castes: see BRAHMAN, KSHATRIYA, VAISYA, SUDRA. [Sanskrit *varna* class, literally 'colour']

varnish¹ /'vahnish/ *noun* 1a a liquid preparation that forms a hard shiny transparent coating on drying. b the covering or glaze given by the application of varnish. c resin or sap used to make varnish. 2 archaic outside show; = VENEER¹ (3): *Once you remove the varnish of respectability, you see the man in his true colours.* ►► **varnishy** *adj.* [Middle English *vernisch* via French *vernis* and Old Italian *vernice,* from medieval Latin *veronic-, veronix* sandarac resin]

varnish² *verb trans* 1 to apply varnish to (a floor, fingernails, etc.). 2 to cover (something unpleasant) with a fair appearance; to gloss (it) over. ►► **varnisher** *noun.*

varnish tree *noun* any of various trees from which varnish or lacquer can be prepared; *specif* a Japanese tree: *Rhus verniciflua.*

varsity /'vahsiti/ *noun* (*pl* **varsities**) *Brit, SAfr, NZ, dated* = UNIVERSITY. [by shortening and alteration]

varus /'veərəs/ *noun* the position of a bone or part that is turned inward at its joint to an abnormal degree: compare VALGUS. [Latin *varus* bent, knock-kneed]

varve /vahv/ *noun* a band of sediment composed of two distinct layers of silt or clay believed to comprise an annual cycle of deposition in a body of still water. ►► **varved** *adj.* [Swedish *varv* turn, layer]

vary /'veəri/ *verb* (**varies, varied, varying**) ➤ *verb trans* **1** to make a change in (something). **2** to ensure variety in (something): *To be healthy, you must vary your diet.* ➤ *verb intrans* **1** to exhibit or undergo change. **2** (*usu* + from) to deviate. **3** (*usu* + with) to take on values: *Y varies inversely with x.* **4** to exhibit biological variation. ➤➤ **varyingly** *adv.* [Middle English *varien* via French from Latin *variare*, from *varius* VARIOUS]

vas /vas, vaz, vahs/ *noun* (*pl* **vasa** /'vaysə, 'vahsə/) an anatomical vessel; a duct. ➤➤ **vasal** *adj.* [Latin *vas* VESSEL]

vas- or **vaso-** *comb. form* forming words, denoting: vessel; blood vessel: *vasodilator.* [Latin *vas* VESSEL]

vasa /'vaysə, 'vahsə/ *noun* pl of VAS.

vasa deferentia /defə'renshi·ə, -shə/ *noun* pl of VAS DEFERENS.

vascular /'vaskyoolə/ *adj* **1** of or being a channel or system of channels conducting blood, sap, etc in a plant or animal. **2** supplied with or made up of such channels, *esp* blood vessels: *a vascular tumour.* ➤➤ **vascularity** /-'lariti/ *noun.* [scientific Latin *vascularis* from Latin *vasculum* small vessel, dimin. of *vas* VESSEL]

vascular bundle *noun* a single strand of the vascular system of a plant consisting usu of XYLEM (water-conducting tissue) and PHLOEM (food-conducting tissue) together with PARENCHYMA (soft thin-walled plant tissue).

vascularize or **vascularise** *verb intrans* to become vascular. ➤ *verb trans* to make (something) vascular. ➤➤ **vascularization** /-'zaysh(ə)n/ *noun.*

vascular plant *noun* a plant having a specialized system for conducting liquid that includes XYLEM (water-conducting tissue) and PHLOEM (food-conducting tissue).

vascular tissue *noun* plant tissue concerned mainly with conducting liquids, *esp* the specialized tissue of higher plants consisting essentially of XYLEM (water-conducting tissue) and PHLOEM (food-conducting tissue) and forming a continuous conducting system throughout the plant body.

vas deferens /,vaz 'defərenz, ,vas/ *noun* (*pl* **vasa deferentia** /,vaysə defə'renshi·ə, -shə, ,vahsə, ,vayzə/) a duct, *esp* of a higher vertebrate animal, that carries sperm from the testis towards the penis. [scientific Latin, literally 'deferent vessel']

vase /vahz/ *noun* an ornamental vessel usu of greater depth than width, used *esp* for holding flowers. ➤➤ **vaselike** *adj.* [Middle English via French from Latin *vas* VESSEL]

vasectomize or **vasectomise** *verb trans* to perform a vasectomy on (somebody).

vasectomy /və'sektəmi, va-/ *noun* (*pl* **-ies**, *pl* **vasectomies**) surgical cutting out of a section of the vas deferens, usu to induce sterility.

Vaseline /vas(ə)'leen/ *noun trademark* petroleum jelly. [German *Wasser* water + Greek *elaion* oil + -INE²]

vasiform /'vasifawm/ *adj* having the form of a hollow tube. [VAS- + -IFORM]

vaso- *comb. form* see VAS-.

vasoactive /vayzoh'aktiv/ *adj* affecting, *esp* in relaxing or contracting, the blood vessels. ➤➤ **vasoactivity** /-'tiviti/ *noun.*

vasoconstriction /,vayzohkən'striksh(ə)n/ *noun* narrowing of the diameter of blood vessels. ➤➤ **vasoconstrictive** /-tiv/ *adj.*

vasoconstrictor /,vayzohkən'striktə/ *noun* a nerve fibre, drug, etc that induces or initiates vasoconstriction.

vasodilation /,vayzohdie'laysh(ə)n/ *noun* widening of the blood vessels, *esp* as a result of nerve action.

vasodilator /,vayzohdie'laytə/ *noun* a nerve fibre, drug, etc that induces or initiates vasodilation.

vasoinhibitor /,vayzoh·in'hibitə/ *noun* a drug or other agent that inhibits the action of the vasomotor nerves.

vasomotor /vayzoh'mohtə/ *adj* of nerves or centres controlling the size of blood vessels.

vasopressin /vayzoh'presin/ *noun* a pituitary hormone that increases blood pressure and decreases urine flow. Also called ANTI-DIURETIC HORMONE. [VASOPRESSOR² + -IN¹]

vasopressor¹ /vayzoh'presə/ *noun* a substance that causes a rise in blood pressure by constricting the blood vessels.

vasopressor² *adj* acting as a vasopressor.

vassal¹ /'vas(ə)l/ *noun* **1** formerly, a man, or sometimes a woman, in a feudal society who vowed homage and loyalty to another as their feudal lord in return for protection and often a source of income, *esp* land: *How much more safe the vassal than the lord* — Dr Johnson. **2** a person, nation, etc in a subservient or subordinate position. ➤➤ **vassalage** /-lij/ *noun.* [Middle English via French from medieval Latin *vassallus*, from *vassus* servant, vassal, of Celtic origin]

vassal² *adj* of or being a vassal; subservient or subordinate.

vast¹ /vahst/ *adj* very great in amount, degree, intensity, or *esp* in extent or range: *America is a vast conspiracy to make you happy* — John Updike. ➤➤ **vastly** *adv,* **vastness** *noun.* [Latin *vastus*]

vast² *noun archaic or literary* a boundless space; an immensity: *the vast of heaven* — Milton.

VAT /,vee ay 'tee, vat/ *noun Brit* VALUE ADDED TAX.

Vat. *abbr* Vatican.

vat¹ /vat/ *noun* **1** a tub, barrel, or other large vessel, *esp* for holding liquids undergoing chemical change or preparations for dyeing or tanning. **2** a liquid containing a dye in a soluble form, that, on textile material being steeped in the liquor and then exposed to the air, is converted to the original insoluble dye by oxidation and is precipitated in the fibre. [Old English *fæt*]

vat² *verb trans* (**vatted, vatting**) to put (liquid) into a vat or treat it in a vat.

vat dye *noun* a water-insoluble generally fast dye used in the form of a vat liquor: see VAT¹. ➤➤ **vat-dyed** *adj.*

vatic /'vatik/ *adj literary* prophetic or oracular: *Her poetry is filled with wild and doom-laden vatic imagery.* [Latin *vates* seer, prophet]

Vatican /'vatikən/ *noun* (**the Vatican**) the official residence of the pope and the administrative centre of Roman Catholicism. [Latin *Vaticanus* Vatican Hill in Rome]

vaudeville /'vawdəvil/ *noun* **1** *NAmer* = VARIETY (4). **2** a light, often comic, theatrical piece frequently combining pantomime, dialogue, dancing, and song. [early French *vaudeville* popular satirical song, alteration of *vaudevire*, from *vau-de-Vire* valley of Vire in NW France, where such songs were composed]

vault¹ /vawlt, volt/ *noun* **1a** an arched structure of masonry, usu forming a ceiling or roof. **b** a room with an arched ceiling that comes down to the floor, *esp* a cellar. **c** something, e.g. the sky, resembling a vault. **d** an arched or dome-shaped anatomical structure. **2a** an underground passage, room, or storage compartment. **b** a room or compartment for the safekeeping of valuables. **3a** a burial chamber, *esp* beneath a church or in a cemetery. **b** a prefabricated container, usu of metal or concrete, into which a coffin is placed at burial. ➤➤ **vaulted** *adj,* **vaulty** *adj.* [Middle English from early French *voute*, ultimately from Latin *volvere* to roll]

vault² *verb trans* to form or cover (something) with or as if with a vault. ➤ *verb intrans* to be in the shape of a vault.

vault³ *verb trans* to bound vigorously over (something), *esp* to execute a leap over it using the hands or a pole. ➤ *verb intrans* **1** to leap over something using the hands or a pole. **2** to jump to a high or higher position, status, etc. ➤➤ **vaulter** *noun.* [early French *volter* from Old Italian *voltare*, ultimately from Latin *volvere* to roll]

vault⁴ *noun* the act or an instance of vaulting.

vaulting¹ *noun* vaults; a vaulted construction.

vaulting² *adj* **1** very confident, or over-confident; reaching for the heights: *Nothing could lessen her vaulting ambition.* **2** designed for use in vaulting.

vaulting horse *noun* a padded wooden block without pommels that is used for vaulting in gymnastics.

vaunt¹ /vawnt/ *verb trans* to call attention to (something, e.g. one's achievements), proudly and often boastfully. ➤ *verb intrans archaic* to boast or brag. ➤➤ **vaunted** *adj,* **vaunter** *noun,* **vauntingly** *adv.* [Middle English *vaunten* via French from late Latin *vanitare*, from Latin *vanitas*: see VANITY]

vaunt² *noun archaic or literary* **1** a bragging assertive statement; a boast. **2** a boastful display.

vavasour /'vavəsooə/ or **vavasor** /'vavəsaw/ *noun* a feudal tenant ranking directly below a baron. [Middle English from Old French *vavasour*, prob from medieval Latin *vassus vassorum* vassal of vassals]

vb *abbr* **1** verb. **2** verbal.

VC *abbr* **1** vice-chairman. **2** vice-chancellor. **3** vice-consul. **4** Victoria Cross.

V-chip *noun* a computer chip that can be installed in a television set and that can be programmed to block material that has been classified as violent, sexually explicit, or obscene.

VCR *abbr* videocassette recorder.

VD *abbr* venereal disease.

VDQS *abbr* vin délimité de qualité supérieure, a classification of French wine that guarantees that a particular wine comes from an approved region and meets its standard of quality.

VDU *noun* = VISUAL DISPLAY UNIT.

've *contraction* have: *We've been there.*

veal /veel/ *noun* the flesh of a calf used as food. ➤➤ **vealy** *adj.* [Middle English via French *veel* from Latin *vitellus* small calf, dimin. of *vitulus* calf]

vector[1] /'vektə/ *noun* **1a** a quantity, e.g. velocity or force, that has magnitude and direction and that is commonly represented by a directed line segment whose length represents the magnitude and whose orientation in space represents the direction: compare PHASOR, SCALAR[2] (2). **b** an element of a VECTOR SPACE (set consisting of generalized vectors). **2a** an organism, e.g. an insect, that transmits a disease-causing agent. **b** a pollinator (see POLLINATE). **c** in genetic engineering, something such as a PLASMID (strand of genetic material) that is used to introduce foreign DNA into a cell. **3** a course or compass direction, *esp* of an aircraft. ➤➤ **vectorial** /vek'tawri-əl/ *adj*, **vectorially** /vek'tawri-əli/ *adv*. [Latin *vector* carrier, from *vehere* to carry]

vector[2] *verb trans* (**vectored, vectoring**) **1** to change the direction of (the thrust of a jet engine) for steering. **2** to guide (an aircraft, its pilot, or a missile in flight) by means of a vector transmitted by radio.

vector field *noun* a region of space in which a vector function is determined.

vector product *noun* a vector *c* whose length is the product of the lengths of two vectors *a* and *b* and the sine of their included angle, whose direction is perpendicular to their plane, and whose sense for the vector product *ab* is that of a right-handed screw with axis *c* when *a* is rotated into *b*.

vector space *noun* in mathematics, a set whose elements are generalized vectors and which is a commutative group under addition that is also closed under an operation of multiplication by elements of a given field having the properties that $c(A + B) = cA + cB$ and $(c + d)A = cA + dA$, $(cd)A = c(dA)$, and $1A = A$ where *A, B* are vectors, *c, d* are elements of the field, and 1 is the identity element of the field under multiplication.

vector sum *noun* the sum of vectors that for two vectors is geometrically represented by the diagonal of a non-parallel parallelogram whose sides represent the two vectors being added.

VED *abbr* Vehicle Excise Duty.

Veda /'veedə, 'vaydə/ *noun* any or all of four canonical collections of hymns, prayers, and liturgical formulas that comprise the earliest Hindu sacred writings.
> **Editorial note**
> The four Vedas are the Rig-Veda (the Veda of Hymns), the Yajur-Veda (the Veda of Prayers), the Sama-Veda (the Veda of Charms), and the Atharva-Veda (the Veda of the Atharvans or magician-priests).

[Sanskrit *veda*, literally 'knowledge']

vedalia /vi'dayli-ə/ *noun* (*pl* **vedalias**) an Australian ladybird introduced into many countries to control scale insects which are pests on a wide variety of plants: *Rodolia cardinalis*. [Latin *Vedalia*, the former name of the genus]

Vedanta /və'dahntə, və'dantə/ *noun* an orthodox system of Hindu philosophy developing the speculations of the Upanishads on ultimate reality and the liberation of the soul. ➤➤ **Vedantism** *noun*, **Vedantist** *noun*. [Sanskrit *Vedānta* end of the Veda, from VEDA + *anta* end]

Vedantic /və'dantik/ *adj* **1** of the Vedanta philosophy. **2** = VEDIC[1].

V-E Day *noun* the day on which hostilities in Europe in World War II ended, 8 May 1945, or any anniversary of that day. [short for *Victory in Europe*]

Vedda *or* **Veddah** /'vedə/ *noun* (*pl* **Veddas** *or* **Veddahs** *or collectively* **Vedda** *or* **Veddah**) a member of an aboriginal people of Sri Lanka. [Sinhalese *vaddā* hunter]

vedette /vi'det/ *noun* **1** a mounted sentinel stationed forward of pickets. **2** a small naval launch used as a patrol vessel. [French

vedette from Italian *vedetta*, alteration of *veletta*, prob from Spanish *velar* to keep watch, from Latin *vigilare*: see VIGILANT]

Vedic[1] /'veedik, 'vaydik/ *adj* of the Vedas, the language in which they are written, or Hindu history and culture between 1500 BC and 500 BC.

Vedic[2] *noun* the form of Sanskrit in which the Vedas are written.

veena /'veenə/ *noun* see VINA.

veer[1] /viə/ *verb intrans* **1** to change direction, position, opinion, or inclination. **2** said of the wind: to shift in a clockwise direction: compare BACK[4] (2). **3** to WEAR[3] a ship (change tack of ship). ➤ *verb trans* to direct (a ship) to a different course; *specif* to WEAR[3] a ship (change its tack). ➤➤ **veeringly** *adv.* [early French *virer*, prob of Celtic origin]

veer[2] *noun* a change in direction, position, opinion, or inclination.

veer[3] *verb trans* to let out or pay out (a rope or cable). [Middle English *veren* from early Dutch *vieren*]

veg /vej/ *noun* (*pl* **veg**) *Brit, informal* a vegetable: *meat and two veg.*

vegan[1] /'veegən/ *noun* a strict vegetarian who avoids food or other products derived from animals. ➤➤ **veganism** *noun.* [by contraction from VEGETARIAN[1]]

vegan[2] *adj* of vegans or veganism.

Vegeburger /'vejibuhgə/ *noun trademark* a veggieburger.

Vegemite /'vejimiet/ *noun Aus, trademark* a savoury yeast extract used as a spread. [from VEGETABLE[1], on the pattern of *Marmite*]

vegetable[1] /'vej(i)təbl/ *noun* **1a** a plant, e.g. the cabbage, bean, or potato, grown for an edible part which is usu eaten with the principal course of a meal. **b** the edible part of the plant. **2** *derog.* **a** a person with a dull undemanding existence. **b** a person whose physical and *esp* mental capacities are severely impaired by illness or injury. **3** any member of the plant kingdom.

vegetable[2] *adj* **1a** of, constituting, or growing like plants. **b** consisting of plants. **2** made or obtained from plants or plant products. [Middle English from medieval Latin *vegetabilis* growing, from *vegetare* to grow, 'to animate', from *vegetus* lively, from *vegēre* to rouse, excite]

vegetable ivory *noun* **1** the hard white opaque endosperm of the seed of a S American palm that is used as a substitute for ivory. It is used to make buttons and billiard balls. **2** the seed itself; = IVORY NUT.

vegetable marrow *noun* = MARROW (1).

vegetable oil *noun* an oil of plant origin, e.g. olive oil or sunflower oil.

vegetable oyster *noun* = SALSIFY. [from the oyster-like flavour of its roots]

vegetable silk *noun* a cottony fibrous material obtained from the coating of the seeds of certain plants and used *esp* for stuffing cushions.

vegetable wax *noun* a wax of plant origin commonly secreted in thin flakes by the walls of the cells of the outer layer of plant stems or leaves, and obtained *esp* from certain palm trees.

vegetal /'vejitl/ *adj* **1** = VEGETABLE[2]. **2** = VEGETATIVE. [medieval Latin *vegetare*: see VEGETABLE[1]]

vegetarian[1] /veji'teəri-ən/ *noun* a person who practises vegetarianism. [VEGETABLE[1] + -ARIAN]

vegetarian[2] *adj* **1** of vegetarians or vegetarianism. **2** said of food, cooking, etc: consisting wholly of vegetables, or of vegetables, fruit, nuts, etc and milk, cheese, and eggs; excluding meat and fish.

vegetarianism *noun* the theory or practice of living on a diet that excludes the flesh of animals and often other animal products and that is made up of vegetables, fruits, cereals, and nuts: compare LACTO-VEGETARIAN.

vegetate /'vejitayt/ *verb intrans* **1** to lead a passive monotonous inactive existence. **2** *dated.* **a** to grow in the manner of a plant. **b** to produce vegetation. [medieval Latin *vegetatus*, past part. of *vegetare*: see VEGETABLE[1]]

vegetation /veji'taysh(ə)n/ *noun* **1** plant life, or the total plant cover of an area. **2** the act or an instance of vegetating. **3** an abnormal outgrowth on a body part, e.g. a heart valve. ➤➤ **vegetational** *adj*, **vegetationally** *adv*.

vegetative /'vejitətiv/ *adj* **1a** of or functioning as part of nutrition and growth as contrasted with reproductive functions. **b** of or involving propagation by non-sexual processes or methods. **2** relating to, composed of, or suggesting vegetation. **3** affecting, arising from, or relating to involuntary bodily functions. **4** inactive. ➤➤ **vegetatively** *adv*, **vegetativeness** *noun*.

veggie[1] /'veji/ *noun informal* = VEGETARIAN[1]. [by shortening and alteration]

veggie[2] *adj informal* = VEGETARIAN[2].

veggieburger /'vejibuhgə/ *noun* a burger made with vegetable ingredients, e.g. soya beans, rather than meat. [VEGETABLE[1] + BURGER]

veg out *verb intrans* (**vegges, vegged, vegging**) *informal* to spend time idly and inactively; = VEGETATE (1): *veg out in front of the telly.* [short for VEGETATE]

vehement /'vee-əmənt/ *adj* **1** intensely felt; impassioned. **2** forcibly expressed. ➤➤ **vehemence** *noun*, **vehemently** *adv*. [early French *vehement* from Latin *vehement-, vehemens*]

vehicle /'veeik(ə)l/ *noun* **1** a car, bus, lorry, etc; = MOTOR VEHICLE. **2** a means of transmission; a carrier. **3** a medium through which something is expressed or communicated. **4** a work created to display the talents of a particular performer. **5** any of various usu liquid media acting *esp* as solvents, carriers, or binders for active ingredients, e.g. drugs, or pigments. [French *véhicule* from Latin *vehiculum* carriage, conveyance, from *vehere* to carry]

vehicle excise duty *noun* a tax paid on road vehicles either yearly or half-yearly.

vehicle excise licence *noun* = TAX DISC.

vehicular /vee'ikyoolə/ *adj* of or designed for vehicles, *esp* motor vehicles.

veil[1] /vayl/ *noun* **1a** a length of cloth worn by women as a covering for the head and shoulders and often, *esp* in eastern countries, the face. **b** a length of sheer fabric or netting worn over the head or face or attached for protection or ornament to a hat or headdress. **2** a concealing curtain or cover of cloth. **3a** something that hides or obscures like a veil: *A veil of smoke hung over the houses.* **b** a disguise or pretext: *Under the veil of national defence, preparations for war began.* **4a** the outer covering of a nun's headdress. **b** (**the veil**) the cloistered life of a nun. **5** a covering body part or membrane, e.g.: **a** = VELUM (1). **b** a layer of protective tissue enclosing the developing fruiting body of fungi. **6** any of various cloths used in religious ceremonies, *esp* a cloth used to cover the chalice containing the consecrated wine used at Communion. ✳ **draw a veil over something** to avoid mentioning something unpleasant or undesirable: *That whole shopping trip was something I'd rather draw a veil over … because my street cred would be severely dented if the saga got out* — Mike Ripley. **take the veil** to become a nun. [Middle English *veile* via Anglo-French from Latin *vela*, pl of *velum* sail, awning, curtain, cloth]

veil[2] *verb trans* to cover, provide, or conceal (somebody or something) with a veil, or as if with a veil. ➤ *verb intrans* to put on or wear a veil. ➤➤ **veiler** *noun*.

veiled *adj* **1** indistinct or muffled. **2** thinly disguised: *After a few veiled threats, she stalked out.* ➤➤ **veiledly** /'vaylidli/ *adv*.

veiling *noun* **1** a veil. **2** any of various light sheer fabrics.

vein[1] /vayn/ *noun* **1a** any of the tubular converging vessels that carry blood from the capillaries towards the heart: compare ARTERY, CAPILLARY[1]. **b** = BLOOD VESSEL. **2** a distinctive element or quality; a strain. **3** a frame of mind; a mood. **4** a streak or marking suggesting a vein, e.g. in marble. **5a** any of the vascular bundles forming the framework of a leaf. **b** any of the thickened ribs that stiffen the wings of an insect. **6** a deposit of ore, coal, etc, *esp* in a rock fissure. ➤➤ **veinal** *adj*, **veinlet** /'vaynlit/ *noun*, **vein-like** *adj*, **veiny** *adj*. [Middle English *veine* via Old French from Latin *vena*]

vein[2] *verb trans* to pattern (something) with veins or vein-like markings.

veining *noun* a pattern of veins.

vel. *abbr* velocity.

vela /'veelə/ *noun* pl of VELUM.

velamen /və'laymən/ *noun* (pl **velamina** /və'layminə/) **1** the thick corky outer layer of the aerial roots of an epiphytic orchid (one that grows on another plant but is not parasitic on it; see EPIPHYTE) that absorbs water from the atmosphere. **2** = VELUM (1). [Latin *velamen* covering, from *velare* to cover, from *velum* veil]

velar[1] /'veelə/ *adj* **1** of or forming a velum, *esp* the soft palate. **2** said of a speech sound: formed with the back of the tongue touching or near the soft palate, e.g. /k/ or /g/. [scientific Latin *velaris*, from *velum* VELUM]

velar[2] *noun* a velar consonant.

velarize *or* **velarise** *verb trans* to modify (a speech sound) by velar articulation.

Velcro /'velkroh/ *noun trademark* a fastening device consisting of two pieces, *esp* strips, of fabric that stick to each other by means of very small hooks on one piece that cling to loops on the other. [shortening of French *velours croché* hooked velvet]

veld *or* **veldt** /velt, felt/ *noun* grassland, *esp* in southern Africa. [Afrikaans *veld* from Dutch *veldt* field]

veldskoen /'veltskoohn, 'feltskoohn/ *or* **velskoen** /'velskoohn, 'felskoohn/ *noun* (pl **veldskoen** *or* **velskoen**) *SAfr* a strong heavy shoe, *esp* of rawhide. [Afrikaans *velskoen*, from *vel* skin + *skoen* shoe: the *d* was inserted from an association with *veld* field]

veldt /velt, felt/ *noun* see VELD.

veleta *or* **valeta** /və'leetə/ *noun* a ballroom dance of English origin in waltz time. [Spanish *veleta* weather vane, from *vela* cloth, veil, from Latin *vela*, pl of *velum* veil]

veliger /'veelijə/ *noun* a free-swimming larva of certain marine molluscs, e.g. oysters, whelks, or limpets, that has developed a VELUM (swimming organ). [scientific Latin, from VELUM + Latin *-ger* -GEROUS]

vellum /'veləm/ *noun* **1a** a fine-grained parchment prepared *esp* for writing on or binding books. **b** something written or printed on vellum. **2** a strong cream-coloured paper. [Middle English *velim* from early French *veelin* of a calf, from *veel*: see VEAL]

veloce /vay'lohchay/ *adj and adv* said of a piece of music: to be performed in a rapid manner. [Italian *veloce* from Latin *veloc-, velox* swift]

velocipede /və'losipeed/ *noun* **1** an early type of bicycle propelled by the rider's feet in contact with the ground, or a later form propelled by pedalling cranks on the front axle. **2** *NAmer* a child's tricycle. ➤➤ **velocipedist** *noun*. [French *vélocipède*, from Latin *veloc-, velox* quick + *ped-, pes* foot]

velocity /və'lositi/ *noun* (pl **velocities**) **1** speed, *esp* of inanimate things; rapidity. **2** speed in a given direction. [early French *velocité* from Latin *velocitat-, velocitas*, from *veloc-, velox* quick]

velocity of circulation *noun* the average rate at which money is used. Velocity of circulation for a given period, e.g. a year, is calculated by dividing the amount of money spent in that time by the amount of money in circulation at that time.

velodrome /'velədrohm/ *noun* a stadium or arena for bicycle racing, *esp* in France. [French *vélodrome*, from *vélo* cycle, short for *vélocipède*, + -DROME]

velour *or* **velours** /və'looə/ *noun* (pl **velours** /və'looəz/) **1** any of various fabrics with a pile or napped surface resembling velvet. **2** a fur felt finished with a long velvety nap, used *esp* for hats. [French *velours* velvet, velour, from Old French *velour*, from Latin *villosus* shaggy, from *villus* shaggy hair]

velouté /və'loohtay/ *noun* a basic white sauce made with a roux and chicken, veal, or fish stock: compare BÉCHAMEL. [French *velouté*, literally 'velvety', from *velours*: see VELOUR]

velskoen /'velskoohn, 'felskoohn/ *noun* see VELDSKOEN.

velum /'veeləm/ *noun* (pl **vela** /'veelə/) **1** a curtainlike membrane or anatomical partition. **2** = SOFT PALATE. **3** a swimming organ that is well developed in the later larval stages of certain marine molluscs, e.g. oysters, whelks, or limpets. [Latin *velum* curtain, veil]

velure /və'l(y)ooə/ *noun archaic* velvet, or a fabric resembling velvet. [modification of Old French *velour*: see VELOUR]

velvet /'velvit/ *noun* **1** any of various clothing or upholstery fabrics of e.g. silk, rayon, or cotton with a short soft dense pile. **2a** something suggesting velvet, e.g. in softness or smoothness. **b** softness or smoothness. **c** (*used before a noun*) resembling or suggesting velvet, *esp* in smoothness or softness; velvety: *the velvet voice of Nat King Cole.* **3** the soft downy skin containing blood vessels that envelops and nourishes the developing antlers of deer. **4** *chiefly NAmer, slang.* **a** a profit or gain beyond ordinary expectation: *If one of them is real lucky … and finally gets to be well known and makes some money, well, it's so much velvet then* — Louis Armstrong. **b** a gambler's winnings. [Middle English *veluet, velvet* from early French *velu* shaggy, ultimately from Latin *villus* shaggy hair]

velveteen /'velviteen, -'teen/ *noun* a fabric made with a short close pile in imitation of velvet.

velvet glove *noun* outward affability concealing ruthless inflexibility: compare IRON HAND.

velvety *adj* soft and smooth like velvet.

Ven. *abbr* Venerable.

ven- *or* **vene-** *or* **veni-** *or* **veno-** *comb. form* forming words, denoting: vein: *venation; venepuncture.* [Latin *vena*]

vena /'veenə/ *noun* (*pl* **venae** /'veenee/) = VEIN[1] (1). [Latin *vena*]

vena cava /'kayvə/ *noun* (*pl* **venae cavae** /,veenee 'kayvee/) either of the two large veins by which, in humans and other air-breathing vertebrates, the blood is returned to the right atrium of the heart. ➤➤ **vena caval** *adj.* [scientific Latin *vena cava* hollow vein]

venae /'veenee/ *noun* pl of VENA.

venae cavae /'kayvee/ *noun* pl of VENA CAVA.

venal /'veenl/ *adj* **1** open to corrupt influence, *esp* bribery. **2** characterized by corruption, *esp* corrupt bargaining and bribery. ➤➤ **venality** /vi'naliti/ *noun*, **venally** *adv.* [orig in the sense 'for sale': Latin *venalis*, from *venum* something for sale]

venation /vi'naysh(ə)n/ *noun* an arrangement or system of veins in a leaf, insect wing, etc, or the veins themselves. ➤➤ **venational** *adj.* [Latin *vena* VEIN[1] + -ATION]

vend /vend/ *verb intrans* *formal* **1** to sell things; to engage in selling. **2** to be sold. ➤ *verb trans* **1** to sell (goods), *esp* in a small way. **2** to sell (food, drinks, etc) by means of a vending machine. ➤➤ **vendee** /ven'dee/ *noun*, **vendible** *adj.* [via French *vendre* from Latin *vendere* to sell, from *venum* something for sale + *dare* to give]

vendace /'vendis, 'vendays/ *noun* (*pl* **vendaces** *or collectively* **vendace**) a whitefish of various European lakes: *Coregonus albula.* [early French *vandoise*, of Celtic origin]

vender *noun* see VENDOR.

vendetta /ven'detə/ *noun* **1** a blood feud arising from the murder or injury of a member of one family by a member of another. **2** a prolonged bitter feud. ➤➤ **vendettist** *noun.* [Italian *vendetta* revenge, from Latin *vindicta*, from *vindicare*: see VINDICATE]

vending machine *noun* a coin-operated machine for selling merchandise.

vendor *or* **vender** *noun* **1a** a seller. **b** in law, the seller of a house. **2** = VENDING MACHINE. [VEND + -OR[1], -ER[2]]

vene- *comb. form* see VEN-.

veneer[1] /və'niə/ *noun* **1** a thin layer of wood, plastic, etc of superior appearance, quality, or hardness, used *esp* to give a decorative finish to cheaper material. **2** a protective or ornamental facing, e.g. of brick or stone. **3** a superficial or deceptively attractive appearance. [German *Furnier* from *furnieren* to veneer, from French *fournir*: see FURNISH]

veneer[2] *verb trans* **1a** to overlay (a cheap wood, etc) with veneer. **b** to face (material) with a material giving a superior surface. **2** to conceal (something) under a superficial and deceptive attractiveness. ➤➤ **veneerer** *noun.*

veneering *noun* **1** material used as veneer. **2** a veneered surface.

venepuncture *or* **venipuncture** /'venipungkchə/ *noun* surgical puncture of a vein, *esp* for the withdrawal of blood or for intravenous medication.

venerable /'ven(ə)rəbl/ *adj* **1a** commanding respect through age, character, and attainments: *Tea! Thou soft, ... sober, sage, and venerable liquid* — Colley Cibber. **b** impressive by reason of age: *The cottage was surrounded by venerable pines.* **2** made sacred, *esp* by religious or historical association. **3a** a title for an Anglican archdeacon. **b** a title given to a Roman Catholic who has been accorded the lowest of three degrees of recognition for sainthood. ➤➤ **venerability** /-'biliti/ *noun*, **venerableness** *noun*, **venerably** *adv.* [Latin *venerabilis* from *venerari*: see VENERATE]

venerate /'venərayt/ *verb trans* to regard (somebody or something) with reverence or admiring deference; to honour or respect (them). ➤➤ **venerator** *noun.* [Latin *veneratus*, past part. of *venerari*, from *vener-, venus* love, charm]

veneration /venə'raysh(ə)n/ *noun* **1** reverential respect, deference, or honour. **2** the act or an instance of venerating.

venereal /və'niəri·əl/ *adj* **1** of sexual desire or sexual intercourse. **2a** resulting from or contracted during sexual intercourse: *venereal infections.* **b** of or affected with venereal disease: *a high venereal rate.* [Middle English *venerealle* from Latin *venereus*, from *vener-, venus* love, sexual desire]

venereal disease *noun* = SEXUALLY TRANSMITTED DISEASE.

venereology /və,niəri'oləji/ *noun* the branch of medicine dealing with venereal diseases. ➤➤ **venereological** /-'lojikl/ *adj*, **venereologist** *noun.*

venery[1] /'venəri/ *noun* *archaic* the art, act, or practice of hunting. [Middle English from early French *venerie*, from *vener* to hunt, from Latin *venari*]

venery[2] *noun* *archaic* the pursuit of sexual pleasure. [Middle English *venerie* from medieval Latin *veneria*, from Latin *vener-, venus* love, sexual desire]

venesection *or* **venisection** /'veniseksh(ə)n/ *noun* the operation of opening a vein for letting blood. [scientific Latin *venae section-, venae sectio*, literally 'cutting of a vein']

Venetian /və'neesh(ə)n/ *noun* a native or inhabitant of Venice, a city in Italy. ➤➤ **Venetian** *adj.* [Latin *Venetia* Venice]

venetian blind *noun* a window blind made of horizontal slats that may be adjusted so as to vary the amount of light admitted.

Venetian glass *noun* coloured and elaborately decorated glassware made at Murano, near Venice.

Venetian red *noun* **1a** an earthy HAEMATITE (iron oxide mineral) used as a pigment. **b** a synthetic iron oxide pigment. **2** the reddish brown colour of these pigments.

Venezuelan /veni'zwaylən/ *noun* a native or inhabitant of Venezuela. ➤➤ **Venezuelan** *adj.*

vengeance /'venj(ə)ns/ *noun* punishment inflicted on somebody in retaliation for an injury received or offence felt: *Something of vengeance I had tasted for the first time* — Charlotte Brontë. ✳ **with a vengeance 1** with great force or vehemence. **2** to an extreme or excessive degree. [Middle English from Old French, from *vengier* to avenge, from Latin *vindicare*: see VINDICATE]

vengeful /'venjf(ə)l/ *adj* **1** desiring or seeking revenge. **2** serving to gain revenge; taking revenge. ➤➤ **vengefully** *adv*, **vengefulness** *noun.* [obsolete *venge* revenge, from Old French *vengier*: see VENGEANCE]

veni- *comb. form* see VEN-.

venial /'veeni·əl/ *adj* forgivable; pardonable. ➤➤ **veniality** /-'aliti/ *noun*, **venially** *adv*, **venialness** *noun.* [Middle English via French from late Latin *venialis*, from Latin *venia* favour, indulgence, pardon]

venial sin *noun* in Christian theology, a sin that does not deprive the soul of divine grace: compare MORTAL SIN.

venin /'venin/ *noun* any of various toxic substances in snake venom. [VENOM + -IN[1]]

venipuncture /'venipungkchə/ *noun* see VENEPUNCTURE.

venisection /'veniseksh(ə)n/ *noun* see VENESECTION.

venison /'venis(ə)n/ *noun* the flesh of a deer used as food. [Middle English *venison* flesh of a wild animal taken by hunting, from Old French *veneison* hunting, game, from Latin *venation-, venatio*, from *venari* to hunt, pursue]

Venite /vi'nieti/ *noun* a liturgical chant composed of parts of Psalms 95 and 96, or a musical setting of this. [Latin *venite* O come, from *venire* to come; from the opening word of Psalms 95:1]

Venn diagram /ven/ *noun* a graph that uses plane shapes, *esp* circles, to represent sets and terms of propositions, the logical relations between and operations on the sets and terms being shown by the inclusion, exclusion, or intersection of the shapes. [named after John *Venn* d.1923, English logician, who devised it]

veno- *comb. form* see VEN-.

venom /'venəm/ *noun* **1** poisonous matter normally secreted by snakes, scorpions, etc and transmitted chiefly by biting or stinging. **2** ill will; malevolence. [Middle English *venim, venom* from Old French *venim*, ultimately from Latin *venenum* magic charm, drug, poison]

venomous /'venəməs/ *adj* **1a** poisonous. **b** spiteful or malevolent. **2** able to inflict a poisoned wound. ➤➤ **venomously** *adv*, **venomousness** *noun.*

venose /'veenohs/ *adj* said of a wing, a leaf, etc: veined, *esp* having many branching veins. [Latin *venosus*: see VENOUS]

venosity /vi'nositi/ *noun* **1** the state of having veins, *esp* many branching veins. **2** the state of having an abnormally large number of veins or blood vessels. **3** the condition of venous blood. **4** the condition of having an abnormally high amount of blood in the veins or elsewhere.

venous /'veenəs/ *adj* **1** of veins. **2** having or consisting of veins: *the venous system of the body*. **3** said of blood: circulating in the veins. [Latin *venosus* from *vena* VEIN[1]]

vent[1] /vent/ *noun* **1** an opening for the escape of a gas or liquid or for the relief of pressure, e.g.: **a** the anus, *esp* of the cloaca of a bird or reptile. **b** an outlet of a volcano; = FUMAROLE. **c** formerly, a hole at the breech of a gun through which the powder was ignited. **2** a means of escape or release; an outlet. * **give vent to something** to give strong expression to one's feelings, etc. >> **ventless** *adj*. [Middle English *venten*, prob from early French *esventer* to expose to the air, from *es*- EX-[1] + *vent* wind, from Latin *ventus*]

vent[2] *verb trans* **1** to provide (something) with a vent. **2** to release (gas, etc) through a vent. **3** (*often* + on) to give vigorous expression to (one's feelings): *He vented his anger on his wife*.

vent[3] *noun* a slit in a garment; *specif* an opening in the lower part of a seam, e.g. of a jacket. [Middle English *vente* from early French *fente* slit, fissure, from *fendre* to split, from Latin *findere*]

vent[4] *verb trans* to put a vent in (a jacket, etc).

ventage /'ventij/ *noun* a small hole, e.g. a flute stop.

venter /'ventə/ *noun* **1** a rounded or swollen, often hollow, anatomical structure, e.g.: **a** the abdomen or belly of a vertebrate animal. **b** the enlarged thick or fleshy part of a muscle. **c** a broad smooth shallow inward-curving surface, *esp* of a bone. **d** the swollen base of an ARCHEGONIUM (female sex organ in a moss, fern, etc) in which the egg cell develops. **2** in law, a wife or mother considered as a source of offspring. [Latin *venter* belly, womb]

ventilate /'ventilayt/ *verb trans* **1a** to cause fresh air to circulate through (a room, etc). **b** said of a current of air: to pass or circulate through (a room, etc) so as to freshen it. **2a** to expose (something, e.g. stored grain) to air, *esp* a current of fresh air, to purify, cure, or refresh it. **b** *archaic* to increase the oxygen content of (blood). **3** to examine (a matter) freely and openly; to expose (it) to the public. >> **ventilable** /-ləbl/ *adj*, **ventilative** /-laytiv/ *adj*. [late Latin *ventilatus*, past part. of *ventilare* to fan, winnow, from *ventulus*, dimin. of *ventus* wind]

ventilation /venti'laysh(ə)n/ *noun* **1** the act or an instance of ventilating. **2** a system or means of providing fresh air.

ventilator *noun* **1** an apparatus or aperture for introducing fresh air or expelling stagnant air. **2** an apparatus for providing artificial respiration for a patient who cannot breathe normally; = RESPIRATOR (2).

Ventolin /'ventəlin/ *noun trademark* = SALBUTAMOL.

ventral /'ventrəl/ *adj* **1a** abdominal. **b** relating to or situated near or on the front or lower surface of an animal or aircraft opposite the back: compare DORSAL, HAEMAL, NEURAL. **2** being or located on the lower or inner surface of a plant structure. >> **ventrally** *adv*. [French *ventral* from Latin *ventralis*, from *ventr*-, *venter* belly, womb]

ventricle /'ventrikl/ *noun* **1** a chamber of the heart that receives blood from a corresponding atrium and from which blood is pumped into the arteries. **2** any of the system of communicating cavities in the brain that are continuous with the central canal of the spinal cord. >> **ventricular** /ven'trikyoolə/ *adj*. [Middle English from Latin *ventriculus*: see VENTRICULUS]

ventricose /'ventrikohs/ *adj* in biology, markedly swollen, distended, or inflated, *esp* on one side: *ventricose shells*. [scientific Latin *ventricosus* from Latin *ventr*-, *venter* belly, womb]

ventriculus /ven'trikyoolə/ *noun* (*pl* **ventriculi** /-lie/) **1** the stomach. **2** the gizzard of a bird. **3** the middle part of an insect's digestive tract, where digestion of food occurs. [Latin *ventriculus*, dimin. of *venter* belly, womb]

ventriloquise /ven'triləkwiez/ *verb intrans* see VENTRILOQUIZE.

ventriloquism /ven'triləkw(ə)m/ *noun* the production of the voice in such a manner that the sound appears to come from a source other than the vocal organs of the speaker and *esp* from a dummy manipulated by the producer of the sound. >> **ventriloquial** /-'lohkwi·əl/ *adj*, **ventriloquially** /-'lohkwi·əli/ *adv*, **ventriloquist** *noun*, **ventriloquy** /-kwi/ *noun*. [late Latin *ventriloquus* ventriloquist, from *ventr*-, *venter* belly + *loqui* to speak; from the belief that the voice is produced from the ventriloquist's stomach]

ventriloquize *or* **ventriloquise** /ven'triləkwiez/ *verb intrans* to use ventriloquism.

venture[1] /'venchə/ *verb trans* **1** to expose (one's life, etc) to hazard; to risk or gamble (it). **2** to face the risks and dangers of (something); to brave (it). **3a** to offer (an opinion, etc) at the risk of opposition or censure. **b** to say (something) tentatively or as a guess. > *verb intrans* (*often* + out/forth) to proceed despite danger; to dare to go or do. [Middle English *venteren*, by shortening and alteration from *aventuren*, from *aventure*: see ADVENTURE[1]]

venture[2] *noun* **1** an undertaking involving chance, risk, or danger, e.g. in business. **2** something, e.g. money or property, at risk in a speculative venture.

venture capital *noun* capital invested or available to be invested in a new or fresh enterprise. >> **venture capitalist** *noun*.

Venture Scout *noun* a senior member of the British Scout movement, aged from 16 to 20.

venturesome /'venchəs(ə)m/ *adj* **1** ready to take risks; daring. **2** involving risk; hazardous. >> **venturesomely** *adv*, **venturesomeness** *noun*.

venturi /ven'tyooəri/ *noun* (*pl* **venturis**) a short tube that is inserted in a wider pipeline and is used for measuring flow rate of a fluid or for providing suction. [named after Giovanni B *Venturi* d.1822, Italian physicist, who studied the properties of moving fluids]

venturous /'venchərəs/ *adj* = VENTURESOME. >> **venturously** *adv*, **venturousness** *noun*.

venue /'venyooh/ *noun* **1** the place where a gathering or event takes place; a meeting place. **2** in law, the place in which a legal case is to be tried and from which the jury is drawn. [Middle English *venyw* action of coming, from early French *venue*, from *venir* to come, from Latin *venire*]

venule /'venyoohl/ *noun* a small vein. [Latin *venula*, dimin. of *vena* VEIN[1]]

Venus flytrap /'veenus/ *or* **Venus'-flytrap** *or* **Venus's-flytrap** *noun* an insect-eating plant of the sundew family that has modified leaves consisting of two hinged spiky-edged lobes that snap together to trap insects, which are then digested by the plant: *Dionaea muscipula*.

Venus'-flytrap /'veenusiz/ *noun* see VENUS FLYTRAP.

Venusian /vi'nyoohzh(ə)n/ *noun* a hypothetical native or inhabitant of the planet Venus. >> **Venusian** *adj*.

Venus's looking-glass *noun* a European annual plant with small five-petalled blue or white flowers: *Legousia hybrida*.

ver. *abbr* verse.

veracious /və'rayshəs/ *adj formal* **1** reliable in testimony; truthful; honest. **2** true or accurate. >> **veraciously** *adv*, **veraciousness** *noun*, **veracity** /və'rasiti/ *noun*. [Latin *verac*-, *verax* truthful, from *verus* true]

veranda *or* **verandah** /və'randə/ *noun* a roofed open gallery or portico attached to the outside of a building. [Hindi *varaṇḍā* from Portuguese *varanda* railing, balustrade]

veratrine /'verətreen/ *or* **veratrin** /-trin/ *noun* a poisonous mixture of alkaloids obtained from sabadilla seed and used *esp* to reduce inflammation and as an insecticide. [scientific Latin *veratrina*, from *Veratrum*, genus of hellebores which also contain veratrine, + -INE[2]]

verb /vuhb/ *noun* a word that characteristically is the grammatical centre of a predicate and expresses an act, occurrence, or mode of being, e.g. *run*, *give*, *be*, *have*. [Middle English *verbe* via French from Latin *verbum* word, verb]

verbal[1] *adj* **1** of, involving, or expressed in words. **2** of or formed from a verb. **3** spoken rather than written; oral: *a verbal contract*. **4** verbatim; word-for-word. >> **verbally** *adv*. [early French from late Latin *verbalis* from Latin *verbum* word, VERB]

verbal[2] *noun* **1** a word that combines characteristics of a verb with those of a noun or adjective. **2** *Brit, slang*. **a** (*also in pl*) a spoken statement. **b** (*also in pl*) a statement made to the police admitting or implying guilt and used in evidence.

verbal[3] *verb trans* (**verballed**, **verballing**, *NAmer* **verbaled**, **verbaling**) *Brit, slang* to implicate (somebody) in a crime by making false statements or by introducing an admission of guilt.

verbalise *verb trans and intrans* see VERBALIZE.

verbalism *noun* **1** a verbal expression. **2** an excessive emphasis on words as opposed to the ideas or realities they represent. **3** meaningless or empty words.

verbalize or **verbalise** verb intrans **1** to speak or write verbosely. **2** to express something in words. ➤ verb trans **1** to name or describe (something) in words. **2** to convert (a word) into a verb. ➤➤ **verbalization** /-'zaysh(ə)n/ noun, **verbalizer** noun.

verbal noun noun a noun derived from, and having some of the constructions of, a verb, esp a gerund.

verbatim /vuh'baytim, və-/ adv and adj in the exact words used; word for word. [Middle English from medieval Latin, from Latin verbum word, VERB]

verbena /və'beenə/ noun **1** any of a genus of chiefly N and S American plants and small shrubs of the teak family that are often cultivated for their heads or spikes of showy white, pink, red, blue, or purplish flowers: genus Verbena. **2** any of a number of similar plants, e.g. lemon verbena. [Latin verbena: see VERVAIN]

verbiage /'vuhbiij/ noun wordiness; verbosity; unnecessary words. [French verbiage from early French verbier to chatter, from verbe speech, from Latin verbum word, VERB]

verbose /və'bohs/ adj **1** containing more words than necessary: What he had to say was confused, halting, and verbose — Somerset Maugham. **2** given to wordiness: like the conveyances of a verbose attorney — Adam Smith. ➤➤ **verbosely** adv, **verboseness** noun, **verbosity** /və'bositi/ noun.

verboten /feə'bohtn, vuh-/ adj prohibited, esp by authority. [German verboten, past part. of verbieten to forbid]

verb phrase noun a part of a sentence containing one or more verbs and other sentence elements other than the subject of the sentence.

verdant /'vuhd(ə)nt/ adj **1a** said of plants: green in tint or colour. **b** green with growing plants: verdant fields. **2** immature; unsophisticated. ➤➤ **verdancy** /-si/ noun, **verdantly** adv. [modification of early French verdoyant, present part. of verdoyer to be green, from Old French verd, vert green, from Latin viridis]

verd antique or **verde antique** /,vuhd an'teek/ noun **1** a decorative green mottled or veined SERPENTINE³ (variety of stone). **2** a dark green PORPHYRY (variety of stone). [Italian verde antico, literally 'ancient green']

verderer or **verderor** /'vuhdərə/ noun a former English judicial officer of the royal forests. [Anglo-French verderer from Old French verdier, from verd, vert: see VERDANT]

verdict /'vuhdikt/ noun **1** the decision of a jury on the matter submitted to them. **2** an opinion or judgment. [alteration of Middle English verdit, from Old French ver true (from Latin verus) + dit saying, dictum, from Latin dictum]

verdigris /'vuhdigree(s)/ noun **1** a green or bluish deposit formed on copper, brass, or bronze surfaces. **2** a green or greenish blue poisonous pigment resulting from the action of acetic acid on copper; copper acetate. [Middle English vertegrez from Old French vert de Grice, literally 'green of Greece']

verdure /'vuhdyə, 'vuhjə/ noun **1** growing vegetation, or its greenness. **2** health, freshness, and vigour. ➤➤ **verdured** adj, **verdureless** adj, **verdurous** /-rəs/ adj, **verdurousness** /-rəsnis/ noun. [Middle English from early French, from Old French verd, vert: see VERDANT]

verge[1] /vuhj/ noun **1** something that borders, limits, or bounds, e.g.: **a** an outer margin of an object or structural part. **b** the edge of a roof projecting over the gable. **2** the brink or threshold of something. **3** Brit a surfaced or planted strip of land at the side of a road. **4** a rod or staff carried as an emblem of authority or symbol of office. **5** formerly, the area forming the royal court and under the jurisdiction of the Lord High Steward. [Middle English verge penis, rod, via French from Latin virga rod, stripe; senses 1, 2, 3 developed from senses 4, 5 via the obsolete phrase within the verge meaning within the area subject to the authority of a verge-bearer]

verge[2] verb trans to edge or border (something): A narrow strip of grass verges the road. ✳ **verge on/upon something** to be close to something: Their familiarity verged on insolence.

verge[3] verb intrans **1** (+ into) to gradually change into something: His eccentricity finally verged into madness. **2** (+ towards) to move gradually towards something: There was a track that verged towards the cliff edge and disappeared. **3** said of the sun: to incline towards the horizon; to sink. [Latin vergere to bend, incline]

verger noun **1** a church official who keeps order during services or serves as an usher or sacristan and caretaker. **2** an attendant who carries a VERGE¹ (rod or staff), e.g. in front of a bishop.

Vergilian /vuh'jili·ən/ adj see VIRGILIAN.

verglas /'veəglah/ noun a thin layer of ice, e.g. on rock. [French verglas from Old French verre-glaz, from verre glass (from Latin vitrum) + glas, glace ice, from Latin glacies]

veridical /vi'ridikl/ adj formal **1** truthful; veracious. **2** not illusory; genuine. **3** said of a vision or dream: matching something that has happened or manifesting something that subsequently does happen. ➤➤ **veridicality** /-'kaliti/ noun, **veridically** adv. [Latin veridicus, from verus true + dicere to say]

verification /,verifi'kaysh(ə)n/ noun **1** the act or an instance of verifying. **2** evidence; proof.

verify /'verifie/ verb trans (**verifies, verified, verifying**) **1** to ascertain the truth, accuracy, or reality of (something). **2** to bear out, confirm, or fulfil (something): You see how this House of Commons has begun to verify all the ill prophecies that were made of it — Coleridge. **3** to substantiate (something) in law, esp formally or on oath. ➤➤ **verifiable** adj, **verifier** noun. [Middle English verifien via French from medieval Latin verificare, from Latin verus true]

verily /'verəli/ adv archaic **1** indeed; certainly. **2** truly; confidently. [Middle English verraily, from verray: see VERY¹]

verisimilar /veri'similə/ adj formal appearing to be true; probable. ➤➤ **verisimilarly** adv. [Latin verisimilis, from veri similis like the truth]

verisimilitude /,verisi'milityoohd/ noun formal **1** the quality or state of appearing to be true. **2** a statement that has the appearance of truth. ➤➤ **verisimilitudinous** /-'tyoohdinəs/ adj. [Latin verisimilitudo from verisimilis: see VERISIMILAR]

verism /'viəriz(ə)m/ noun artistic use of contemporary everyday material in preference to the heroic or legendary. ➤➤ **verist** noun and adj, **veristic** /viə'ristik/ adj. [Italian verismo from vero true, from Latin verus]

verismo /ve'rizmoh/ noun verism, esp in grand opera.

Editorial note ——————
Verismo is a term taken over from Italian literature to describe a style in late 19th-cent. opera which exchanged the former historical and mythological subjects for the everyday life of the lower classes (a parallel can be made with 1950s kitchen-sink drama). The recitatives and arias of earlier opera were abandoned in favour of a freer musical style in which extremes of human behaviour were portrayed with both passion and sentimentality — Amanda Holden.

[Italian verismo: see VERISM]

veritable /'veritəbl/ adj (often used to stress the aptness of a metaphor) being in fact the thing named; not false or imaginary: She produced a veritable mountain of references. ➤➤ **veritableness** noun, **veritably** adv. [Middle English from early French, from verité: see VERITY]

verity /'veriti/ noun (pl **verities**) **1** the quality or state of being true or real. **2** something, e.g. a statement, that is true, esp a permanently true value or principle. [Middle English verite via French verité from Latin veritat-, veritas, from verus true]

verjuice /'vuhjoohs/ noun **1** the sour juice of crab apples or unripe fruit formerly used in cooking. **2** sharpness or sourness of tone, manner, or behaviour. [Middle English from early French verjus from vert jus green juice]

verkramp /fə'krump/ adj = VERKRAMPTE².

verkrampte[1] /fə'krramptə/ noun SAfr a person holding ultraconservative or bigoted views, esp on social, political, or religious matters: compare VERLIGTE¹. [Afrikaans verkramp, verkrampte narrow]

verkrampte[2] /fə'krump/ adj SAfr of or characteristic of a verkrampte: compare VERLIGTE².

verlig /fə'likh/ adj = VERLIGTE².

verligte[1] /fə'likhtə/ noun SAfr an advocate of liberal policies: compare VERKRAMPTE¹. [Afrikaans verlig, verligte enlightened]

verligte[2] /fə'likh/ adj SAfr of or characteristic of a verligte: compare VERKRAMPTE².

vermeil /'vuhmayl/ noun **1** gilded silver, bronze, or copper. **2** literary = VERMILION. [early French vermeil: see VERMILION]

vermes /'vuhmeez/ noun pl of VERMIS.

vermi- comb. form forming words, denoting: worm: vermiform. [Latin vermis worm]

vermicelli /vuhmi'cheli/ pl noun (treated as sing. or pl) **1** pasta in the form of long thin solid threads smaller in diameter than spaghetti. **2** small thin strands of sugar or chocolate that are used as a decoration, e.g. on iced cakes. [Italian *vermicelli*, pl of *vermicello*, dimin. of *verme* worm, from Latin *vermis*]

vermicide /'vuhmisied/ *noun* something, e.g. a drug, that destroys worms, *esp* parasitic worms.

vermicular /vuh'mikyoolə/ *adj* **1a** resembling a worm in form or motion. **b** = VERMICULATE. **2** of or caused by worms. [Latin *vermiculus*: see VERMILION]

vermiculate /vuh'mikyoolət/ *adj* **1** marked with irregular or wavy lines: *a vermiculate nut.* **2** *archaic* full of worms; worm-eaten. **3** *formal* tortuous or intricate. ➤➤ **vermiculation** /-'laysh(ə)n/ *noun.* [Latin *vermiculatus*, from *vermiculus*: see VERMILION]

vermiculated /vuh'mikyoolaytid/ *adj* = VERMICULATE.

vermiculite /vuh'mikyooliet/ *noun* any of various minerals of hydrous silicates derived from mica that expand on heating to form a lightweight highly water-absorbent material. [Latin *vermiculus*: see VERMILION; from the worm-like projections produced when it is rapidly heated]

vermiform /'vuhmifawm/ *adj* resembling a worm in shape.

vermiform appendix *noun* a narrow short blind tube that extends from the caecum in the lower right-hand part of the abdomen.

vermifuge[1] /'vuhmifyoohj/ *adj* used to destroy or expel parasitic worms; = ANTHELMINTIC[1]. [Latin *vermis* worm + *fugare* to put to flight]

vermifuge[2] *noun* something, *esp* a drug, used to destroy or expel parasitic worms.

vermilion *or* **vermillion** /və'milyən/ *noun* **1** mercuric sulphide used as a pigment. **2** the brilliant red colour of this pigment. ➤➤ **vermilion** *adj.* [Middle English *vermilioun* from Old French *vermeillon*, from *vermeil* bright red, vermilion, from late Latin *vermiculus* kermes, earlier 'little worm', dimin. of Latin *vermis* worm]

vermin /'vuhmin/ *noun* (*pl* **vermin**) **1** (*in pl*). **a** lice, rats, or other common harmful or objectionable animals. **b** birds and mammals that prey on game. **2** an offensive person. ➤➤ **verminous** /-nəs/ *adj*, **verminously** /-nəsli/ *adv.* [Middle English, orig denoting creatures, such as reptiles and snakes, considered nasty or harmful, from early French, ultimately from Latin *vermis* worm]

vermis /'vuhmis/ *noun* (*pl* **vermes** /'vuhmeez/) a wormlike structure, *esp* the middle lobe of the cerebellum. [Latin *vermis* worm]

vermouth /'vuhmэth/ *noun* a dry or sweet alcoholic drink that has a white wine base and is flavoured with aromatic herbs. [French *vermout* from German *Wermut* wormwood]

vernacle /'vuhnəkl/ *noun* see VERNICLE.

vernacular[1] /və'nakyoolə/ *adj* **1a** expressed or written in a language or dialect native to a region or country, rather than a literary, learned, or foreign language. **b** of or being the normal spoken form of a language. **c** of or being the name applied to an animal or plant in common everyday language, as opposed to the technical Latin name. **2** of or being the common building style of a period or place. ➤➤ **vernacularly** *adv.* [Latin *vernaculus* native, from *verna* slave born in a master's house, native]

vernacular[2] *noun* **1a** the local vernacular language. **b** *informal* the mode of expression of a group or class. **2** the vernacular name of an animal or plant. **3** a vernacular building style. ➤➤ **vernacularism** *noun.*

vernal /'vuhnl/ *adj* **1** of or occurring in the spring. **2a** fresh or youthful. **b** of or characteristic of youth. ➤➤ **vernally** *adv.* [Latin *vernalis*, alteration of *vernus*, from *ver* spring]

vernal equinox *noun* the time in March when the sun crosses the equator and day and night are everywhere of equal length.

vernal grass *noun* a slender fragrant Eurasian grass: *Anthoxanthum odoratum.*

vernalize *or* **vernalise** *verb trans* to hasten the flowering and fruiting of (plants), *esp* by chilling seeds, bulbs, or seedlings. ➤➤ **vernalization** /-'zaysh(ə)n/ *noun.*

vernation /vuh'naysh(ə)n/ *noun* the arrangement of foliage leaves within the bud: compare AESTIVATION. [scientific Latin *vernation-, vernatio*, from Latin *vernare* to behave as in spring, from *vernus*: see VERNAL]

vernicle /'vuhnikl/ *or* **vernacle** /'vuhnəkl/ *noun* = VERONICA[2]. [Middle English, from Middle French *veronique, vernicle* from medieval Latin *veronica*]

vernier /'vuhni·ə/ *noun* **1** a short, specially graduated scale that slides along another graduated scale allowing fine measurements of parts of graduations to be made. **2a** a small auxiliary device used with a main device to obtain fine adjustment. **b** any of two or more small supplementary rocket engines or gas nozzles on a rocket vehicle for making fine adjustments in the velocity or attitude. **3** (*used before a noun*) having or comprising a vernier: *a vernier rocket.* [named after Pierre *Vernier* d.1637, French mathematician, inventor of a measuring device with a vernier]

vernissage /vuhni'sahzh/ *noun* a private showing of an art exhibition held before the official opening. [French *vernissage* varnishing, from *vernis*: see VARNISH[1]; orig the vernissage was the time before the official opening of an exhibition, used by artists for varnishing their paintings]

Veronal /və'rohnl/ *noun trademark* = BARBITONE. [named after *Verona*, city in N Italy]

veronica[1] /və'ronikə/ *noun* = SPEEDWELL. [Latin genus name, perhaps named after St Veronica (see VERONICA[2])]

veronica[2] *noun* **1** a copy in cloth or metal, e.g. a small badge, of the legendary cloth of St Veronica which was said to be imprinted with an image of Christ's face. **2** a cloth believed to be the cloth of St Veronica. [named after St *Veronica*, a woman of Jerusalem who, according to tradition, wiped Christ's face with a cloth when he was on his way to Calvary; when she did so, the cloth was imprinted with the image of his face]

veronica[3] *noun* a movement in bullfighting in which the cape is swung slowly away from the charging bull while the matador's feet are kept in the same position. [Spanish *verónica*, named after St *Veronica* (see VERONICA[2]); from the supposed resemblance between the movement of the matador and the movement made by St Veronica in wiping Christ's face]

veronique /vayro'neek/ *adj* (*used after a noun*) said of a fish or chicken dish: prepared or served with grapes: *sole veronique.* [from the French woman's name *Véronique* Veronica]

verruca /və'roohkə/ *noun* (*pl* **verrucas** *or* **verrucae** /-kee, -see/) **1** a wart or warty skin growth, *esp* on the underside of the foot. **2** a warty prominence on a plant or animal. ➤➤ **verrucose** /'verookohs, və'roohkəs/ *adj*, **verrucous** /'verookəs, və'roohkəs/ *adj.* [Latin *verucca* wart]

versant /'vuhsant/ *noun* **1** the slope of a mountain or mountain chain. **2** the general slope of land. [French *versant*, present part. of *verser* to turn, pour, from Latin *versare* to turn; because it sheds water]

versatile /'vuhsətiel/ *adj* **1a** said of a person: turning with ease from one thing to another. **b** embracing or competent in a variety of subjects, fields, or skills. **c** having many uses or applications: *a versatile building material.* **2a** capable of turning forward or backward: *a bird's versatile toe.* **b** capable of moving sideways and up and down: *an insect's versatile antennae.* **c** said of a flower's ANTHER (pollen-containing structure): attached at or near the middle and swinging freely in the wind. **3** *archaic* changing or fluctuating readily; variable: *a versatile disposition.* ➤➤ **versatilely** *adv*, **versatileness** *noun*, **versatility** /-'tiliti/ *noun.* [French *versatile* from Latin *versatilis* turning easily, from *versare* to keep turning, from *vertere* to turn]

verse[1] /vuhs/ *noun* **1** one section of a poem, song, or hymn, marked off by a particular set of rhymes or assonances and, when printed, generally separated from the preceding and following sections by a space; = STANZA. **2** *archaic* a line of metrical writing. **3a** poetry, or the writing of poetry. **b** a poem: *After her death, they found a notebook containing her verses and short stories.* **c** a body of poetry, e.g. of a period or country: *Elizabethan verse.* **d** metrical language or writing distinguished from poetry, e.g. by its lower level of intensity, or an example of this: *I'm not really a poet, just a writer of comic verse.* **4** any of the short divisions into which a chapter of the Bible is traditionally divided. [Middle English *vers* via French from Latin *versus* turning of a plough, furrow, line of verse, from *vertere* to turn]

verse[2] *verb trans archaic* to change (text) from prose into verse.

versed *adj* (+ in) possessing a thorough knowledge of or skill in something: *She's well versed in astrology.* [French *versé* from Latin *versatus*, past part. of *versari* to be active, be occupied in, passive of *versare*: see VERSATILE]

versed sine *noun* in mathematics, 1 minus the cosine of an angle. [Latin *versus*, past part. of *vertere* to turn]

versicle /'vuhsikl/ *noun* a short verse or sentence, e.g. one from a psalm, said or sung by a leader in public worship and followed by a response from the congregation. [Middle English from Latin *versiculus*, dimin. of *versus*: see VERSE[1]]

versicolour /'vuhsikulə/ (*NAmer* **versicolor**) *adj* **1** having various colours; variegated. **2** changeable in colour; iridescent: *versicolour silk*. [Latin *versicolor*, from *versus*, past part. of *vertere* to turn, change, + *color* COLOUR[1]]

versicoloured /'vuhsikuləd/ (*NAmer* **versicolored**) *adj* = VERSICOLOUR.

versify /'vuhsifie/ *verb* (**versifies, versified, versifying**) ➤ *verb intrans* to compose verses. ➤ *verb trans* to turn (something) into verse. ➤➤ **versification** /-fi'kaysh(ə)n/ *noun*, **versifier** *noun*.

versine /'vuhsien/ *noun* = VERSED SINE.

version /'vuhsh(ə)n, 'vuhzh(ə)n/ *noun* **1a** an account or description of something from a particular point of view, *esp* as contrasted with another account or description: *A book is a version of the world —* Salman Rushdie. **b** an adaptation of a work of art into another medium: *They're making a film version of the novel*. **c** an arrangement of a musical composition. **d** a form or variant of a type or original: *This is just an experimental version of the plane*. **e** a translation from another language. **f** (*often* **Version**) a translation of the Bible or a part of it: *the Authorized Version*. **2** manual turning of a foetus in the uterus to aid delivery. ➤➤ **versional** *adj*. [early French *version* from medieval Latin *version-, versio* act of turning or changing, from Latin *vertere* to turn, change]

vers libre /,veə 'leebrə/ *noun* (*pl* **vers libres** /,veə 'leebrə/) = FREE VERSE. ➤➤ **vers-librist** *noun*. [French *vers libre*]

verso /'vuhsoh/ *noun* (*pl* **versos**) **1** the side of a leaf, e.g. of a manuscript, that is to be read second, or in printing, a left-hand page or the page on the opposite side of a right-hand page: compare RECTO. **2** the reverse side of a coin. [Latin *verso folio* the page having been turned, from *folium* page + *versus*, past part. of *vertere* to turn]

verst /veəst, vuhst/ *noun* a Russian unit of distance equal to about 1.1km (0.7mi). [French *verste* or German *Werst* from Russian *versta* line]

versus /'vuhsəs/ *prep* **1** *esp* in sport and other competitive activities: against. **2** in contrast to or as the alternative of: *The question is one of free trade versus protection*. [medieval Latin *versus* towards, against, from Latin *versus* turned so as to face, past part. of *vertere* to turn]

vert. *abbr* vertical.

vertebra /'vuhtibrə/ *noun* (*pl* **vertebrae** /-bree/ *or* **vertebras**) any of the bony or cartilaginous segments composing the spinal column. ➤➤ **vertebral** *adj*, **vertebrally** *adv*. [Latin *vertebra* joint, vertebra, from *vertere* to turn]

vertebrate[1] /'vuhtibrət, -brayt/ *adj* **1** having a spinal column. **2** of the vertebrates. [scientific Latin *vertebratus*, from Latin *vertebra*: see VERTEBRA]

vertebrate[2] *noun* any of a large subphylum of animals including the mammals, birds, reptiles, amphibians, and fishes, with a segmented backbone, together with a few primitive forms, e.g. lampreys, in which the backbone is represented by a NOTOCHORD (flexible rod of cells): subphylum Vertebrata.

vertebration /vuhti'braysh(ə)n/ *noun* **1** the formation of, or division of something into, vertebrae or parts resembling vertebrae. **2** vertebral structure.

vertex /'vuhteks/ *noun* (*pl* **vertices** /'vuhtiseez/ *or* **vertexes**) **1** the highest point; the summit. **2a** in mathematics, the point opposite to and farthest from the base in a figure. **b** in mathematics, the termination or intersection of lines or curves: *the vertex of an angle*. **c** in mathematics, a point where a main axis of an ellipse, parabola, or hyperbola intersects the curve. **3** = ZENITH (1). **4** in anatomy, the top of the head. [Latin *vertic-, vertex* whirl, whirlpool, top of the head, summit, from *vertere* to turn]

vertical[1] /'vuhtikl/ *adj* **1** perpendicular to the plane of the horizon or to a primary axis. **2** of, involving, or integrating discrete elements, e.g. from lowest to highest: *a vertical business organization*. **3** of or concerning the relationships between people of different rank in a hierarchy: compare HORIZONTAL[1]. **4** situated at the highest point; directly overhead or in the zenith. **5** relating to a mathematical vertex. **6** in anatomy, relating to the top of the head. ➤➤ **verticality** /-'kaliti/ *noun*, **vertically** *adv*, **verticalness**

noun. [early French *vertical* from late Latin *verticalis*, from Latin *vertic-, vertex*: see VERTEX]

vertical[2] *noun* **1** verticality. **2** something that is vertical.

vertical angles *pl noun* the two opposite and equal angles formed by the intersection of two lines.

vertical mobility *noun* the movement of people to higher or lower positions in society, etc.

vertices /'vuhtiseez/ *noun* pl of VERTEX.

verticil /'vuhtisil/ *noun* a circular arrangement of similar parts, e.g. leaves, about a point on an axis; = WHORL (1). [scientific Latin *verticillus*, dimin. of Latin *vertex*: see VERTEX]

verticillate /vuh'tisilət, -layt, vuhti'silayt/ *adj* whorled, *esp* arranged in a transverse whorl like the spokes of a wheel: *a verticillate shell*.

vertiginous /və'tijinəs/ *adj* **1** characterized by or suffering from vertigo. **2** inclined to frequent and often pointless change; inconstant. **3** causing or tending to cause dizziness: *vertiginous heights*. **4** marked by turning; rotary. ➤➤ **vertiginously** *adv*. [Latin *vertiginosus*, from *vertigin-, vertigo*: see VERTIGO]

vertigo /'vuhtigoh/ *noun* a disordered state in which one loses balance and the surroundings seem to whirl dizzily. [Latin *vertigin-, vertigo*, from *vertere* to turn]

vertu /vuh'tooh/ *noun* see VIRTU.

vervain /'vuhvayn/ *noun* a plant that bears heads or spikes of blue, purple, pink, or white flowers: *Verbena officinalis*. [Middle English *verveine* via French from Latin *verbena*, sing. of *verbenae* sacred boughs, applied to certain medicinal plants]

verve /vuhv/ *noun* **1** energy or vitality. **2** the spirit and enthusiasm animating artistic work. [French *verve* fantasy, caprice, animation, from Latin *verba*, pl of *verbum* word, VERB]

vervet monkey /'vuhvit/ *noun* a S and E African tree-dwelling monkey with soft dense fur that has a greenish tinge, pale yellow to white underparts, and a black face: *Cercopithecus aethiops*. [French *vervet*, of unknown origin]

very[1] /'veri/ *adv* **1** to a high degree; exceedingly. **2** used for emphasis: *She makes the very best cakes in town*. ✳ **very well** **1** used to express often reluctant consent or agreement: *Very well, we'll go tomorrow*. **2** with certainty; unquestionably: *You know very well what you should do*. [Middle English *verray, verry* from Old French *verai*, from Latin *verac-, verax* truthful, from *verus* true]

very[2] *adj* **1** actual; genuine: *My father was the very man you met that day*. **2** exact; right: *I have the very thing you need*. **3** being no more than; mere: *The very thought of speaking in public terrified me*. **4** (**veriest**) the most absolute possible: *the veriest fool alive —* Milton; *It was by the veriest chance that I was there at all*.

very high frequency *noun* a radio frequency in the range between 30MHz and 300MHz.

Very light /'viəri, 'veəri/ *noun* a white or coloured ball of fire that is fired from a Very pistol and that is used as a signal flare. [named after Edward W Very d.1910, US naval officer]

very low frequency /'veri/ *noun* a radio frequency or band of frequencies in the range between 3kHz and 30kHz.

Very pistol /'viəri, 'veəri/ *noun* a pistol for firing Very lights.

Very Reverend /'veri/ *noun* a title for various ecclesiastical officials, e.g. cathedral deans and canons, rectors of Roman Catholic colleges, and superiors of some religious houses.

Vesak /'vesak/ *or* **Wesak** /'wesak/ *noun* a Buddhist festival commemorating the birth, enlightenment, and death of the Buddha, celebrated in May. [Sinhalese *vesak*]

vesica /'vesikə/ *noun* (*pl* **vesicae** /-see/ *or* **vesicas**) **1** a bladder or bladder-like structure, *esp* the urinary bladder. **2** a decorative form, e.g. in architecture, in the shape of a two-pointed oval. ➤➤ **vesical** *adj*. [Latin *vesica* bladder, blister]

vesicant[1] /'vesikənt/ *noun* a drug, war gas, etc that induces blistering. [Latin *vesicant-, vesicans*, present part. of *vesicare* to cause blisters, from *vesica* bladder, blister]

vesicant[2] *adj* causing blisters.

vesicate /'vesikayt/ *verb trans* to cause blisters in (something). ➤ *verb intrans* to form blisters. ➤➤ **vesication** /-'kaysh(ə)n/ *noun*. [Latin *vesicatus*, past part. of *vesicare*: see VESICANT[1]]

vesicle /'vesikl/ *noun* **1a** a membranous pouch, e.g. a cyst, vacuole, or cell, in a plant or animal, *esp* one filled with fluid or air. **b** a blister. **c** a pocket of embryonic tissue that is the beginning of an organ. **2** a small cavity in a mineral or rock. ➤➤ **vesicular**

/vi'sikyoolə/ *adj,* **vesicularity** /vi,sikyoo'lariti/ *noun,* **vesiculate** /vi'sikyoolət, -layt/ *adj.* [early French *vesicule* from Latin *vesicula* small bladder, blister, dimin. of *vesica* blister]

vesper[1] /'vespə/ *noun* **1** (**Vesper**) *literary* = EVENING STAR. **2** *archaic* evening or eventide. [Middle English from Latin *vesper* evening, evening star]

vesper[2] *adj* **1** of vespers. **2** *archaic* of the evening.

vespers *noun* **1** the sixth of the canonical hours, said or sung in the late afternoon. **2** a service of evening worship; = EVENSONG. [French *vespres* from medieval Latin *vesperas,* accusative pl of Latin *vesper* evening]

vespertine /'vespətien/ *adj* **1** active or flourishing in the evening, e.g.. a said of an animal: feeding or flying in early evening. **b** said of a flower: opening in the evening. **2a** *literary* of or occurring in the evening: *vespertine shadows.* **b** said of a star: setting in the evening. [Latin *vespertinus* from *vesper* evening]

vespiary /'vespi·əri/ *noun* (*pl* **vespiaries**) a nest of a wasp that lives in organized colonies, or the colony inhabiting it. [Latin *vespa* + English *-iary* as in APIARY]

vespid[1] /'vespid/ *noun* a member of a widely distributed family of insects comprising the wasps that live together in organized colonies like bees: family Vespidae. [derivative of Latin *vespa* wasp]

vespid[2] *adj* of or relating to vespids.

vessel /'vesl/ *noun* **1** a hollow utensil, e.g. a jug, cup, or bowl, for holding liquid, etc. **2** a large hollow structure designed to float on and move through water carrying a crew, passengers, or cargo; a ship. **3a** a tube or canal, e.g. an artery, in which a body fluid is contained and conveyed or circulated. **b** a conducting tube in a plant. **4** *esp* in biblical use, a person into whom some quality, e.g. grace, is infused. [Middle English via Old French from late Latin *vascellum,* dimin. of Latin *vas* vase, vessel]

vest[1] /vest/ *noun* **1** *chiefly Brit* a usu sleeveless undergarment for the upper body. **2** *chiefly NAmer* = WAISTCOAT. ➤➤ **vested** *adj,* **vestlike** *adj.* [French *veste* via Italian from Latin *vestis* garment]

vest[2] *verb trans* **1a** (*usu* + in) to give (property, power, a title, etc) into the possession or discretion of another, *esp* to give to a person an immediate and legally fixed right to a present or future enjoyment of (an estate, etc), **b** (*usu* + with) to give (somebody) a particular authority, right, or property. **2a** to robe (somebody) in ecclesiastical vestments. **b** *literary* to clothe (somebody) with or as if with a garment. ➤ *verb intrans* **1** (*usu* + in) to become granted or legally vested. **2** *literary* to robe in ecclesiastical vestments. ➤➤ **vested** *adj.* [Middle English *vesten* from early French *vestir* to clothe, invest, from Latin *vestire* to clothe, from *vestis* clothing, garment]

vestal[1] /'vestl/ *adj* **1** of a vestal virgin. **2** *literary* chaste; virgin. ➤➤ **vestally** *adv.* [Middle English *vestalle* from Latin *vestalis* of *Vesta,* Roman goddess of the hearth and household]

vestal[2] *noun* **1** a priestess of the Roman goddess Vesta, responsible for tending the sacred fire perpetually kept burning on her altar. **2** *literary* a chaste woman, *esp* a nun.

vestal virgin *noun* = VESTAL[2] (I).

vested interest *noun* **1** an interest, e.g. in an existing political or social arrangement, in which the holder has a strong personal commitment, *esp* because of a potential financial benefit: *It is ideas, not vested interests, which are dangerous for good or evil* — John Maynard Keynes. **2** somebody or something having a vested interest in something; *specif* a group enjoying benefits from an existing privilege. **3** an interest carrying a legal right.

vestiary /'vesti·əri/ *noun* (*pl* **vestiaries**) a room where clothing is kept; a vestry. [Middle English from Old French *vestiarie:* see VESTRY]

vestibule /'vestibyoohl/ *noun* **1** a lobby or chamber between the outer door and the interior of a building. **2** any of various bodily cavities, *esp* when serving as or resembling an entrance to some other cavity or space, e.g.: **a** the central cavity of the bony labyrinth of the ear. **b** the part of the mouth cavity outside the teeth and gums. ➤➤ **vestibular** /ve'stib-/ *adj,* **vestibuled** *adj.* [Latin *vestibulum* entrance, courtyard]

vestige /'vestij/ *noun* **1a** a trace or visible sign left by something that has vanished or been lost; a minute remaining amount. **b** a minute amount. **2** a small or imperfectly formed body part or organ that remains from one more fully developed in an earlier stage of the individual, in a past generation, or in closely related forms.

➤➤ **vestigial** /ve'stij(y)əl/ *adj,* **vestigially** /və'stij(y)əli/ *adv.* [French *vestige* from Latin *vestigium* footstep, footprint, track]

vestment /'vestmənt/ *noun* **1** *archaic* an outer garment, *esp* a robe of ceremony or office. **2** any of the ceremonial garments and insignia worn by ecclesiastical officiants and assistants as appropriate to their rank and to the rite being celebrated. ➤➤ **vestmental** /vest'mentl/ *adj.* [Middle English *vestement* via French from Latin *vestimentum,* from *vestire:* see VEST[2]]

vest-pocket *adj NAmer* **1** adapted to fit into the waistcoat pocket: *a vest-pocket edition of a book.* **2** very small.

vestry /'vestri/ *noun* (*pl* **vestries**) **1a** a room where vestments are kept and clergy dress, often used as the church office for the clergy; ~ SACRISTY. **b** a room used for church meetings and classes. **2a** the business meeting of an English parish. **b** an elective administrative body in an Episcopal parish in the USA and Scotland. ➤➤ **vestral** *adj.* [Middle English *vestrie,* prob modification of early French *vestiarie* from medieval Latin *vestiarium,* from Latin *vestire:* see VEST[2]; from its use as a robing room for the clergy]

vestryman *or* **vestrywoman** *noun* (*pl* **vestrymen** *or* **vestrywomen**) a man or woman who is a member of a vestry.

vesture[1] /'veschə/ *noun* **1** *formal* clothing or apparel. **2** *literary* something that covers like clothing: *The hills were clothed in a vesture of mist.* [Middle English from early French, from *vestir* to clothe, from Latin *vestire:* see VEST[2]]

vesture[2] *verb trans formal or literary* to clothe or cover (somebody or something).

vet[1] /vet/ *noun* = VETERINARY SURGEON.

vet[2] *verb trans* (**vetted, vetting**) **1** *chiefly Brit* to subject (somebody or something) to careful and thorough appraisal: *The book was carefully vetted for possible libels.* **2** to subject (a person or animal) to a physical examination or checkup.

vet[3] *noun NAmer, informal* = VETERAN (2).

vet. *abbr* **1** veteran. **2** veterinarian. **3** veterinary.

vetch /vech/ *noun* any of several species of climbing or twining plants of the pea family, including some valuable fodder and soil-improving plants: genus *Vicia.* [Middle English *vecche* via Anglo-French from Latin *vicia*]

vetchling /'vechling/ *noun* a small scrambling plant of the pea family, usu with yellow or red flowers: genus *Lathyrus.*

veteran /'vet(ə)rən/ *noun* **1** a person who has had long experience of an occupation, skill, or service, e.g. in the armed forces. **2** *NAmer* a former member of the armed forces. **3** *Brit* = VETERAN CAR. [French *vétéran* from *veteranus* old, of long experience, from *veter-, vetus* old]

veteran car *noun Brit* an old motor car; *specif* one built before 1905: compare EDWARDIAN CAR, VINTAGE CAR.

Veterans Day *noun* a day set aside in the USA and Canada in commemoration of the end of hostilities in 1918 and 1945, *esp* 11 November, observed as a public holiday in Canada and some states of the USA: compare REMEMBRANCE SUNDAY.

veterinarian /vet(ə)ri'neəri·ən/ *noun chiefly NAmer* a veterinary surgeon.

veterinary[1] /'vet(ə)rinəri/ *adj* of the medical care of animals, *esp* domestic animals: *veterinary medicine.* [Latin *veterinarius* of beasts of burden, from *veterinae* beasts of burden]

veterinary[2] *noun* (*pl* **veterinaries**) = VETERINARY SURGEON.

veterinary surgeon *noun* a person who is qualified and authorized to treat diseases and injuries of animals.

veto[1] /'veetoh/ *noun* (*pl* **vetoes**) **1a** the forbidding or banning of something by somebody in authority. **b** the right to forbid or ban something, e.g. a proposal. **2a** a right formally vested in a person or constitutional body to declare decisions made by others to be inoperative, *esp* a power vested in a chief executive, e.g. the president of the USA, to prevent permanently or temporarily the enactment of measures passed by a law-making body, e.g. Congress. **b** the exercise of such authority. **c** a message communicating the reasons for vetoing a proposed law. [Latin *veto* I forbid]

veto[2] *verb trans* (**vetoes, vetoed, vetoing**) to subject (a proposal, etc) to a veto; to ban or forbid (it). ➤➤ **vetoer** *noun.*

vex /veks/ *verb trans* **1a** to bring distress, discomfort, or agitation to (somebody). **b** to irritate or annoy (somebody) by petty provocations; to harass (them). **2** to puzzle or baffle (somebody): *This is a problem to vex the keenest brains in the Government.* ➤➤ **vexed** *adj,*

vexedly /'veksidli/ *adv,* **vexer** *noun,* **vexingly** *adv.* [Middle English *vexen* via French from Latin *vexare* to agitate, trouble]

vexation /vek'saysh(ə)n/ *noun* a cause of trouble; an affliction.

vexatious /vek'sayshəs/ *adj* **1** causing vexation; distressing: *It is always so pleasant to be generous, though very vexatious to pay debts —* Ralph Waldo Emerson. **2** said of an action in law: brought without sufficient grounds, and simply intended to annoy and harass the defendant. ➤➤ **vexatiously** *adv,* **vexatiousness** *noun.*

vexed question *noun* a question that has been discussed at length, usu without a satisfactory solution being reached.

vexilla /vek'silə/ *noun* pl of VEXILLUM.

vexillology /veksi'loləji/ *noun* the study of flags. ➤➤ **vexillological** /-'lojikl/ *adj,* **vexillologist** *noun.* [Latin *vexillum* flag + -LOGY]

vexillum /vek'siləm/ *noun* (*pl* **vexilla** /-lə/) **1** = STANDARD[1] (10). **2** = VANE (3). [Latin *vexillum* flag, standard]

VF *abbr* video frequency.

VG *abbr* **1** very good. **2** Vicar-General.

VGA *abbr* video graphics array.

VHF *abbr* very high frequency.

VHS *abbr trademark* video home system.

v.i. *abbr* see below. [Latin *vide infra*]

via /'vie·ə, 'vee·ə/ *prep* **1** passing through or calling at (a place) on the way. **2** through the medium of; by means of. [Latin *via* by way of, ablative of *via* way]

viable /'vie·əbl/ *adj* **1** capable of working; practicable: *viable alternatives.* **2** said of a foetus: born alive and developed enough to be capable of living. **3** said of seeds, eggs, etc: capable of growing or developing. ➤➤ **viability** /-'biliti/ *noun,* **viably** *adv.* [French *viable* from *vie* life, from Latin *vita*]

viaduct /'vie·ədukt/ *noun* a long bridge, *esp* on a series of arches, that carries a road, railway, canal, etc over a deep valley. [Latin *via* way, road + -*duct* as in AQUEDUCT]

Viagra /vie'agrə, vi-/ *noun trademark* a drug used to treat impotence in men.

vial /'vie·əl/ *noun* = PHIAL. [Middle English *fiole, viole* via French and Provençal from Latin *phiala:* see PHIAL]

via media /,vie·ə 'meedi·ə/ *noun formal* a middle way; a compromise. [Latin]

viand /'vie·ənd/ *noun archaic* **1** an item of food, *esp* a choice or tasty one. **2** (*in pl*) provisions; food. [Middle English from early French *viande,* from medieval Latin *vivanda* food, alteration of Latin *vivenda* things needed for living, from *vivere* to live]

viatica /vie'atikə/ *noun* pl of VIATICUM.

viatical settlement *noun* an arrangement by which a terminally ill person sells their life insurance policy to a third party, e.g. a charitable organization or an investment company, for a sum less than its face value. The seller then lives on the proceeds of the sale until their death and the purchaser collects the full sum insured after the person has died.

viaticum /vie'atikəm/ *noun* (*pl* **viaticums** *or* **viatica** /-kə/) **1** the Christian Eucharist given to a person in danger of death. **2** *archaic* an allowance, e.g. of food or travelling expenses, for a journey. [Latin *viaticum* money for a journey, from *via* way]

vibes /viebz/ *pl noun informal* **1** (*treated as sing. or pl*) = VIBRAPHONE. **2** vibrations (emotional atmosphere; see VIBRATION): *The tension and excitement built gradually all day and the ... audience caught the vibes and responded, making every artist want to give more —* Marti Caine. [by shortening and alteration]

vibist /'viebist/ *noun* a person who plays the vibes; a vibraphonist.

vibrant /'viebrənt/ *adj* **1a** oscillating or pulsating rapidly. **b** pulsating with life, vigour, or activity: *a vibrant personality.* **2** sounding as a result of vibration; resonant: *a vibrant voice.* ➤➤ **vibrancy** /-si/ *noun,* **vibrantly** *adv.* [Latin *vibrant-, vibrans,* present part. of *vibrare* to shake, VIBRATE]

vibraphone /'viebrəfohn/ *noun* a percussion instrument resembling the xylophone but having metal bars and motor-driven resonators for sustaining its sound and producing a vibrato. ➤➤ **vibraphonist** *noun.* [Latin *vibrare* to VIBRATE + -PHONE]

vibrate /vie'brayt/ *verb intrans* **1a** to move to and fro rapidly. **b** to be in a state of vibration; to quiver. **c** to oscillate. **2** said of a sound: to resonate or resound. **3** to move or have an effect like vibration:

Evil thoughts were vibrating in her mind. ➤ *verb trans* **1** to cause (something) to vibrate; to set (it) in vibration. **2** to emit (sound) with or as if with a vibratory motion. **3** to mark or measure (something) by oscillations. ➤➤➤ **vibrative** /'viebrətiv/ *adj,* **vibratory** /vie'brayt(ə)ri, 'viebrə-/ *adj.* [Latin *vibratus,* past part. of *vibrare* to shake]

vibratile /'viebrətiel/ *adj* **1** characterized by vibration. **2** used in vibratory motion: *the vibratile organs of insects.* ➤➤ **vibratility** /-'tiliti/ *noun.*

vibration /vie'braysh(ə)n/ *noun* **1** the action of vibrating, the state of being vibrated or in vibratory motion, or an instance of vibrating or of vibration, e.g.: **a** a quivering or trembling motion; a quiver. **b** an oscillation. **c** a periodic motion of the particles of an elastic body, e.g. a stretched string of a musical instrument, or of a physical medium, e.g. air or water, in alternately opposite directions from the position of equilibrium when that equilibrium has been disturbed, e.g. when a string is plucked or a wave of sound, water, etc is created. **d** a single cycle of movement of a particle undergoing vibration. **2** *informal.* **a** (*usu in pl*) a characteristic aura or spirit felt to emanate from somebody or something and instinctively sensed or experienced. **b** (*usu in pl*) a distinctive, usu emotional, atmosphere capable of being sensed. ➤➤ **vibrational** *adj,* **vibrationless** *adj.*

vibrato /vi'brahtoh/ *noun* (*pl* **vibratos**) an effect adding colour and expressiveness to musical tone, by tiny rapid imperceptible variations in pitch. [Italian *vibrato,* past part. of *vibrare* to vibrate, from Latin]

vibrator *noun* a vibrating electrical apparatus used in massage or to provide sexual stimulation.

vibrissa /vie'brisə/ *noun* (*pl* **vibrissae** /-see/) any of the stiff hairs on a mammal's face, e.g. round the nostrils, often organs of touch, or any of the similar bristles round the beaks of some birds. [Latin *vibrissa,* ultimately from *vibrare* to shake, VIBRATE]

viburnum /vie'buhnəm, vi-/ *noun* any of a genus of shrubs or trees of the honeysuckle family with white or pink flowers: genus *Viburnum.* [Latin *viburnum* the wayfaring tree, which belongs to this genus]

Vic. *abbr* **1** vicar. **2** Victoria.

vicar /'vikə/ *noun* **1a** a member of the clergy of the Church of England in charge of a parish in which the incumbent was formerly paid a stipend, as opposed to receiving tithes: compare RECTOR. **b** in the USA, a member of the clergy or a lay person in charge of a mission or chapel of the Episcopal Church. **c** a member of the clergy of the Anglican or Roman Catholic Churches exercising a broad pastoral responsibility as the representative of a bishop or other high-ranking churchman. **2** in the Church of England, a member of a choir who sings particular parts of a cathedral service. ➤➤ **vicarship** *noun.* [Middle English, orig denoting a person regarded as Christ's representative, or a clergyman deputizing for the rectors of a parish, from Latin *vicarius* substitute, from *vic-, vicis* change, alternation, stead]

vicarage /'vikərij/ *noun* **1** the house of a vicar. **2** formerly, the BENEFICE (position with income) of a vicar.

vicar apostolic /apə'stolik/ *noun* (*pl* **vicars apostolic**) a Roman Catholic titular bishop who governs a territory not organized as a diocese.

vicar general *noun* (*pl* **vicars general**) an administrative deputy of a Roman Catholic or Anglican bishop or of the head of a religious order.

vicarial /vie'keəri·əl, vi-/ *adj archaic* of a vicar.

vicariate /vie'keəri·ət, vi-/ *noun* the office, jurisdiction, or tenure of a vicar. [medieval Latin *vicariatus,* from Latin *vicarius:* see VICAR]

vicarious /vie'keəri·əs, vi-/ *adj* **1** performed or suffered by one person as a substitute for, or to the benefit of, another: *a vicarious sacrifice.* **2** experienced through imaginative participation in the experience of another: *vicarious pleasure.* **3a** serving instead of another. **b** delegated: *vicarious authority.* ➤➤ **vicariously** *adv,* **vicariousness** *noun.* [Latin *vicarius:* see VICAR]

Vicar of Christ *noun* in the Roman Catholic Church, the pope.

vice[1] /vies/ *noun* **1a** moral depravity or corruption, or an example of this; wickedness: *A new philosophy generally means ... the praise of some old vice —* G K Chesterton. **b** sexual immorality, *esp* prostitution. **c** a grave moral fault. **2** a habitual and usu minor fault, shortcoming, or character failing. **3** habitual abnormal behaviour in a domestic animal that is detrimental to its health or usefulness. [Middle English via French from Latin *vitium* fault, vice]

vice² (*NAmer* **vise**) *noun* any of various tools, usu attached to a workbench, that have two jaws that close by operation of a screw, lever, or cam and hold an object tightly so that it can be worked. ➤➤ **vicelike** *adj*. [Middle English *vis*, *vice* screw, from early French *vis*, *viz* something winding, from Latin *vitis* vine]

vice³ (*NAmer* **vise**) *verb trans* to hold, force, or squeeze (something) in or with a vice, or as if in a vice.

vice⁴ /'viesee/ *prep* in the place of; succeeding. [Latin *vice*, ablative of *vicis* change, alternation, stead]

vice- *comb. form* forming words, denoting: **1** person next in rank below or qualified to act in place of; deputy: *vice-president*; *viceroy*. **2** office next in rank below: *vice-admiral*. [Middle English *vis-*, *vice-* via French from late Latin *vice-*, from Latin *vice*, ablative of *vicis* change, alternation, stead]

vice admiral /vies/ *noun* an officer in the Royal Navy and US Navy ranking below an admiral.

vice-chairman /vies/ *noun* (*pl* **vice-chairmen**) a person who acts as a deputy to a chairman. ➤➤ **vice-chairmanship** *noun*.

vice-chancellor /vies/ *noun* an officer ranking next below a chancellor, *esp* the administrative head of a British university. ➤➤ **vice-chancellorship** *noun*.

vice-consul /vies/ *noun* a consular officer subordinate to a consul or consul general.

vicegerent /vies'jerənt/ *noun formal* an administrative deputy of a king or magistrate. ➤➤ **vicegerency** /-si/ *noun*. [medieval Latin *vicegerent-*, *vicegerens*, from VICE- + Latin *gerent-*, *gerens*, present part. of *gerere* to carry, carry on]

vicennial /vi'seni·əl/ *adj* **1** occurring once every 20 years. **2** lasting 20 years. [late Latin *vicennium* period of 20 years, from Latin *vicies* 20 times + *annus* year]

vice-president /vies/ *noun* an officer next in rank to a president and usu empowered to serve as president in the president's absence, death, or disability. ➤➤ **vice-presidency** /-si/ *noun*, **vice-presidential** /-'densh(ə)l/ *adj*.

viceregal /vies'reegl/ *adj* of a viceroy. ➤➤ **viceregally** *adv*.

vicereine /'viesrayn/ *noun* **1** the wife of a viceroy. **2** a female governor of a country or province who rules as the representative of her sovereign. [French *vicereine*, from VICE- + *reine* queen, from Latin *regina* queen]

viceroy /'viesroy/ *noun* a male governor of a country or province who rules as the representative of his sovereign. ➤➤ **viceroyalty** /vies'royəlti/ *noun*, **viceroyship** *noun*. [early French *vice-roi*, from VICE- + *roi* king, from Latin *reg-*, *rex*]

vice squad /vies/ *noun* a police department enforcing laws concerning gambling, pornography, and prostitution.

vice versa /,vies 'vuhsə, ,viesi/ *adv* with the order changed or relations reversed; conversely; the other way round: *Ann hates Jane and vice versa*. [Latin *vice versa* the position being reversed]

vichyssoise /veeshee'swahz/ *noun* a thick soup made of pureed leeks and potatoes, cream, and chicken stock and usu served cold. [French *vichyssoise*, from fem of *vichyssois* of Vichy, town in France]

vichy water /'veeshi/ *noun* a natural sparkling mineral water from Vichy in France, or any similar water.

vicinage /'visinij/ *noun chiefly NAmer, formal* **1** = VICINITY. **2** the residents of a neighbourhood. [Middle English *vesinage* from early French, from *vesin* neighbouring, from Latin *vicinus*: see VICINITY]

vicinal /'visinl/ *adj formal* **1** of a limited district; local. **2** adjacent; neighbouring. [Latin *vicinalis* from *vicinus* neighbour, from *vicinus*: see VICINITY]

vicinity /vi'siniti/ *noun* (*pl* **vicinities**) **1** a surrounding area or district; a neighbourhood. **2** *formal* being near; proximity. [early French *vicinité* from Latin *vicinitat-*, *vicinitas*, from *vicinus* neighbouring, from *vicus* row of houses, village]

vicious /'vishəs/ *adj* **1a** given to or showing cruelty or violence: *His bodyguards were vicious thugs*. **b** showing great ferocity. **c** unpleasantly fierce, malignant, or severe: *a vicious form of flu*. **d** dangerous; refractory: *a vicious horse*. **2** malicious; spiteful: *vicious gossip*. **3** worsened by internal causes that reciprocally augment each other: *These factors were the cause of a vicious wage-price spiral*. **4** having the nature or quality of vice; depraved: *a man of vicious habits*. **5** said *esp* of language or reasoning: defective; faulty.

➤➤ **viciously** *adv*, **viciousness** *noun*. [Middle English via French from Latin *vitiosus* full of faults, corrupt, from *vitium* blemish, VICE¹]

vicious circle *noun* **1** a chain of events in which the apparent solution of one difficulty creates a new problem that makes the original difficulty worse. **2** the logical fallacy of using one argument or definition to prove or define a second on which the first depends.

vicissitude /vi'sisityoohd/ *noun* **1** a change or alteration, e.g. in nature or human affairs. **2** (*usu in pl*) an accident of fortune: *the vicissitudes of daily life*. **3** *formal* the quality of being changeable; mutability. ➤➤ **vicissitudinous** /-'tyoohdinəs/ *adj*. [early French *vicissitude* from Latin *vicissitudo*, from *vicissim* in turn, from *vicis* change, alternation]

victim /'viktim/ *noun* **1** somebody or something that is adversely affected by a force or agent, e.g.: **a** somebody or something that is injured, destroyed, or subjected to oppression or mistreatment: *She was a victim of frequent political attacks*. **b** a person who is tricked or cheated; a dupe. **2** a living animal or person offered as a sacrifice in a religious rite. ➤➤ **victimless** *adj*. [Latin *victima* sacrificial victim]

victimize or **victimise** *verb trans* **1** to punish (somebody) selectively, e.g. by unfair dismissal. **2** to make a victim of (somebody or something): *It pains me physically to see a woman victimized … by fashion* — Yves Saint Laurent. ➤➤ **victimization** /-'zaysh(ə)n/ *noun*, **victimizer** *noun*.

victimology /vikti'moləji/ *noun* the study of people who have been victims of criminal acts, e.g. to investigate their role in the commission of the crimes and the psychological effect the crimes have on them. ➤➤ **victimologist** *noun*.

victor /'viktə/ *noun* a person, country, etc that defeats an enemy or opponent; a winner. [Middle English from Latin *victor*, from *vincere* to conquer, win]

victoria /vik'tawri·ə/ *noun* **1** *Brit* a large red sweet type of plum. **2** either of two species of S American water lilies with large spreading leaves and immense bright white flowers: genus *Victoria*. **3** a low four-wheeled carriage for two with a folding hood. [named after *Victoria* d.1901, Queen of Great Britain]

Victoria Cross *noun* a bronze Maltese cross that is the highest British and Commonwealth military decoration for conspicuous bravery in the face of the enemy. [instituted in 1856 by Queen *Victoria*]

Victoria Day *noun* the Monday preceding 24 May, observed in Canada as a legal holiday. [orig commemorating Queen Victoria's birthday, 24 May]

Victoria lily *noun* = VICTORIA (2).

Victorian¹ *adj* **1a** relating to or characteristic of the reign of Queen Victoria of Great Britain (1837–1901). **b** denoting styles of art, literature, and taste associated with this period. **2** typical of the moral standards or conduct associated with the age of Queen Victoria, *esp* in being prudish or hypocritical. **3** of a place called Victoria, such as the State in Australia or the capital of British Columbia.

Victorian² *noun* a person living during Queen Victoria's reign.

Victoriana /vik,tawri'ahnə/ *pl noun* articles, *esp* ornaments, from the Victorian period. [*Victoria* + -ANA]

victoria plum *noun Brit* = VICTORIA (1).

Victoria sandwich *noun Brit* a sponge cake made from a creamed mixture containing equal weights of fat, flour, sugar, and egg and sandwiched with a layer of jam or cream.

victorious /vik'tawri·əs/ *adj* **1a** having won a victory. **b** of or characteristic of victory. **2** successful; triumphant. ➤➤ **victoriously** *adv*, **victoriousness** *noun*.

victory /'vikt(ə)ri/ *noun* (*pl* **victories**) **1** the act or an instance of overcoming an enemy or antagonist. **2** achievement of mastery or success in a struggle or endeavour. [Middle English via French from Latin *victoria*, ultimately from Latin *vincere* to conquer]

victory roll *noun* a rolling manoeuvre made by an aeroplane as a sign of victory, success, or celebration.

victory sign *noun* a gesture of victory, approval, etc made by forming a V with the first and middle fingers; = V SIGN.

victual /'vitl/ *verb* (**victualled**, **victualling**, *NAmer* **victualed**, **victualing**) ➤ *verb trans dated* to supply (a ship, etc) with food.

➤ *verb intrans dated* to lay in food. [early French *vitaillier* from *vitaille*: see VICTUALS]

victualler (*NAmer* **victualer**) *noun* **1** *Brit* a person who sells provisions, *esp* alcoholic drink. **2** *dated*. **a** somebody or something that provisions an army, a navy, or a ship with food. **b** a provisioning ship.

victuals *pl noun dated* food; provisions: *Up at the service counter there was a pleasant clank of stout crockery as occasional customers came in and ordered their victuals* — Christopher Morley.

Word history
Middle English *vitaille* from early French, from late Latin *victualia* provisions, victuals, ultimately from Latin *victus* livelihood, food, past part. of *vivere* to live. The spelling was changed in the 17th cent. to conform with Latin *victualia*, but the word is still pronounced *vittles*.

vicuña /vi'koohnyə/ *or* **vicuna** /vi'kyoohnə, vi'koohnyə/ *noun* **1** a wild ruminant mammal of the Andes, related to the domesticated llama and alpaca, that has long fine light-brown to pale-whitish hair: *Vicugna vicugna*. **2a** the wool from the fine undercoat of the vicuña. **b** a fabric made of vicuña wool, or a sheep's-wool imitation of this. [Spanish *vicuña* from Quechua *wikúña*]

vid /vid/ *noun informal* a video film. [short for VIDEO¹]

vide /'viedi/ *verb imperative* used to direct a reader to another item: see. [Latin *vide*, from *vidēre* to see]

videlicet /vi'deliset/ *adv* used to introduce one or more examples: that is to say; namely. [Middle English from Latin, from *vidēre* to see + *licet* it is permitted]

video¹ /'vidioh/ *noun* (*pl* **videos**) **1a** material, e.g. a film or television programme, recorded on videotape, a videodisc, etc: *We spent the evening watching videos.* **b** the making or transmission of such material. **c** a videotape or videocassette. **2** a videotape recorder or a machine for playing information recorded on videodisc. **3** the visual part of television broadcasts, as opposed to the sound. **4** *chiefly NAmer, informal* television. [Latin *vidēre* to see + *-o* on the model of AUDIO¹]

video² *adj* **1** of reproduction of a television image, or used in its transmission or reception: compare AUDIO¹. **2** of a form of magnetic recording for reproduction on a television screen.

video³ *verb trans and intrans* (**videoes**, **videoed**, **videoing**) to record (something) on videotape, a videodisc, etc.

videocassette /,vidioh-kə'set/ *noun* a cassette containing videotape.

videocassette recorder *noun* a videotape recorder using videocassettes.

videoconference /,vidioh'konf(ə)rəns/ *noun* a conference involving people in different places who communicate with each other by electronic means using television, telephone, or satellite. ➤ **videoconferencing** *noun*.

videodisc /'vidiohdisk/ *noun* a disc on which information is stored in digital form and is used to play back prerecorded video material on a television screen, as a computer memory unit, etc.

video frequency *noun* a frequency that is in the range required for the transmission of video information by a television system.

video game *noun* a game played by manipulating elements of a picture on the screen of a visual display unit.

video jockey *noun* a person who introduces videos of music, *esp* pop music, on television.

video-link *noun* a combination of television and telephone that enables people to see each other while they talk.

video nasty *noun* a video film including scenes of explicit sex, violence, and horror.

videophone /'vidiohfohn/ *noun* an electronic device for transmitting both sounds and pictures down a telephone line.

videorecorder /'vidiohrikawdə/ *noun* = VIDEOTAPE RECORDER.

videotape¹ /'vidiohtayp/ *noun* **1** magnetic tape used for recording visual images. **2** a length of such tape, e.g. a videocassette.

videotape² *verb trans* to make a recording of (something that is televised) on magnetic tape.

videotape recorder *noun* a tape recorder for recording television pictures on videotape and playing back video recordings; *esp* a videocassette recorder.

videotex /'vidiohteks/ *noun* any computerized information service that transmits data by telephone or cable link from a central database to subscribers' terminals: compare ORACLE, TELETEXT, VIEWDATA.

videotext *noun* = VIDEOTEX.

vidicon /'vidikon/ *noun* a television camera TUBE¹ (part of camera where images are converted into electrical impulses) in which light is focused onto a photoconductive material (material that becomes electrically charged according to the amount of light falling on it; see PHOTOCONDUCTIVITY) lining the tube, producing a pattern of electrical charge. [VIDEO² + ICON + -SCOPE]

vie /vie/ *verb intrans* (**vies**, **vied**, **vying**) (+ for/with) to strive for superiority; to contend with somebody for something: *They vied with each other for the prize.* ➤ **vier** *noun*. [modification of early French *envier* to invite, challenge, wager, from Latin *invitare* to INVITE¹]

Viennese /vee-ə'neez/ *noun* (*pl* **Viennese**) a native or inhabitant of Vienna, city in Austria. ➤ **Viennese** *adj*.

Vietcong /vee-et'kong/ *noun* (*pl* **Vietcong**) an adherent of the Vietnamese communist movement supported by N Vietnam and engaged in warfare against the S Vietnamese regime during the Vietnam War. [Vietnamese *Viêt NAm công-san* Vietnam communists]

Vietnamese /vee-etnə'meez/ *noun* (*pl* **Vietnamese**) **1** a native or inhabitant of Vietnam. **2** the official language of Vietnam, belonging to the Austroasiatic family. ➤ **Vietnamese** *adj*.

vieux jeu /,vyuh 'zhuh/ *adj* out-of-date; = OLD HAT. [French *vieux jeu*, literally 'old game']

view¹ /vyooh/ *noun* **1** a scene or prospect: *There's a lovely view from the balcony.* **2** an aspect: *the rear view of the house.* **3** extent or range of vision; sight: *They tried to keep the ship in view.* **4** a pictorial or photographic representation. **5** a way of regarding something; an opinion: *No work of art ever puts forward views. Views belong to people who are not artists* — Oscar Wilde. **6a** an intention or object: *He bought a gun with a view to murdering his mother.* **b** a hope. **7** the foreseeable future: *There's no hope in view.* **8** the act or an instance of seeing or examining; inspection. **9** a survey: *a view of English literature.* ✳ **in my view** in my opinion. **in view of 1** taking the specified feature into consideration: *In view of his age, the police have decided not to prosecute.* **2** able to be seen by or from: *He punched the goalkeeper in full view of the spectators.* **on view** open to public inspection. [Middle English *vewe* from early French *veue, vue*, from *veeir, voir* to see, from Latin *vidēre*]

view² *verb trans* **1a** to see or watch (somebody or something). **b** (*often* + as) to look on (somebody or something) in a specified way: *He doesn't view himself as a rebel.* **2** to look at (something) attentively; to inspect (it): *They viewed the house but decided not to buy it.* **3** to survey or examine (something) mentally; to consider (it): *I like to view all sides of a question.* **4** to see (a hunted animal) break cover. ➤ *verb intrans* to watch television. ➤ **viewable** *adj*, **viewing** *noun*.

Viewdata *noun trademark* information held in a computer and accessible to users via a telephone link to a television set: compare ORACLE, TELETEXT, VIDEOTEX.

viewer *noun* **1** a person who watches television. **2** an optical device used in viewing.

viewfinder *noun* a device on a camera for showing what will be included in the photograph.

view halloo /ha'looh/ *noun* (*pl* **view halloos**) a shout given by a hunter on seeing a fox break cover.

viewless *adj* **1** affording no view. **2** holding no opinions. ➤ **viewlessly** *adv*.

viewphone *noun* a telephone allowing its user to see the person with whom they are in contact on a small screen.

viewpoint *noun* **1** a standpoint; = POINT OF VIEW. **2** a place from which something, *esp* a panorama or picturesque scene, can be viewed.

vigesimal /vie'jesiməl/ *adj* based on the number 20. [Latin *vicesimus, vigesimus* twentieth, from *viginti* twenty]

vigia /vi'jee-ə/ *noun* something that is marked on a chart as a possible hazard to shipping, although its existence, position, and nature have not been confirmed. [Portuguese *vigia* lookout, from Latin *vigilia*: see VIGIL]

vigil /'vij(ə)l/ *noun* **1** the act or a period of watching or surveillance; a watch. **2** the act of keeping awake at times when sleep is customary; a period of wakefulness. **3a** a devotional watch formerly kept on the night before a religious festival. **b** the day before a religious festival, observed as a day of spiritual preparation. [Middle English *vigile* via French from late Latin *vigilia* watch on the eve of a feast, from Latin *vigilia* wakefulness, watch, from *vigil* awake, watchful]

vigilance committee /'vij(ə)ləns/ *noun NAmer* an unauthorized self-appointed committee of citizens organized to suppress and punish crime or immorality without recourse to the established legal processes, e.g. when the processes of law appear inadequate.

vigilant /'vij(ə)lənt/ *adj* alert and watchful, *esp* to avoid trouble or danger. ➤➤ **vigilance** *noun*, **vigilantly** *adv*. [Middle English via French from Latin *vigilant-*, *vigilans*, present part. of *vigilare* to keep watch, stay awake, from *vigil* awake]

vigilante /vij'lanti/ *noun* a member of a vigilance committee or any similar self-appointed guardian of law and order. ➤➤ **vigilantism** *noun*. [Spanish *vigilante* watchman, guard, from *vigilante* vigilant, from Latin *vigilant-*, *vigilans*: see VIGILANT]

vigil light *noun* a candle lighted devotionally, e.g. in a Roman Catholic church, before a shrine or image.

vigneron /'vccnyəronh (*French* vipr5)/ *noun* a winegrower. [Middle English *vigneroun* from early French *vigneron*, from Old French *vine*, *vigne*: see VINE]

vignette[1] /vi'nyet, vee'nyet/ *noun* **1** a decorative design or illustration on a title page or at the beginning or end of a chapter. **2** a picture, e.g. an engraving or photograph, that shades off gradually into the surrounding background. **3a** a short descriptive literary sketch. **b** a brief incident or scene, e.g. in a play or film, *esp* a charming one. ➤➤ **vignettist** *noun*. [early French *vignete*, dimin. of *vigne*: see VINE; vine leaves, tendrils, and grapes were commonly used as book decorations]

vignette[2] *verb trans* **1** to finish (a photograph, etc) in the manner of a vignette. **2** to portray (somebody or something) in a vignette or anything similar. ➤ *verb intrans* said of a camera lens: to allow more light through to the centre of a photographic plate than to the edges or corners.

vigor /'vigə/ *noun NAmer* see VIGOUR.

vigoro /'vigəroh/ *noun* an Australian team game that combines elements of cricket and baseball. It is played by women in teams of twelve players. [prob from VIGOROUS]

vigorous /'vigərəs/ *adj* **1** possessing or showing vigour; full of active strength. **2** done with vigour; carried out forcefully and energetically: *vigorous exercises*. ➤➤ **vigorously** *adv*, **vigorousness** *noun*. [Middle English via Old French from medieval Latin *vigorosus*, from Latin *vigor*: see VIGOUR]

vigour (*NAmer* **vigor**) /'vigə/ *noun* **1** active physical or mental strength or force. **2** intensity of action or effect; force. **3** active healthy well-balanced growth, *esp* of plants, or the capacity for this. **4** the most active stage in life or development. [Middle English via French from Latin *vigor*, from *vigēre* to flourish]

Viking /'vieking/ *noun* a Norse trader and warrior of the eighth to tenth cents. [Old Norse *vīkingr*, from *vik* creek or Old English *wic* camp]

vile /viel/ *adj* **1a** morally despicable or abhorrent. **b** physically repulsive; foul. **2** tending to degrade or humiliate: *vile employments*. **3** disgustingly or utterly bad; contemptible: *A man who could make so vile a pun would not scruple to pick a pocket* — John Dennis. **4** very unpleasant: *The weather is vile these days*. ➤➤ **vilely** *adv*, **vileness** *noun*. [Middle English in the sense 'base, common, worthless', from Old French *vil*, from Latin *vilis* of small worth]

vilify /'vilifie/ *verb trans* (**vilifies**, **vilified**, **vilifying**) to utter slanderous or abusive statements against (somebody or something), or defame them: *It has now been fashionable, for near half a century, to defame and vilify the house of Stuart, and to exalt and magnify the reign of Elizabeth* — Dr Johnson. ➤➤ **vilification** /-fi'kaysh(ə)n/ *noun*, **vilifier** *noun*. [Middle English *vilifien* to make less valuable, from late Latin *vilificare*, from Latin *vilis* of little worth + *facere* to make, do]

vilipend /'vilipend/ *verb trans* **1** *formal* to express a low opinion of (somebody); to disparage (them). **2** *archaic* to hold or treat (somebody) as contemptible. [Middle English *vilipenden* via French from Latin *vilis* of small worth + *pendere* to weigh, estimate]

villa /'vilə/ *noun* **1** *Brit* a detached or semidetached suburban house, usu having a garden. **2** a country mansion. **3** an ancient Roman mansion and the surrounding agricultural estate. [via Italian from Latin *villa* country house or estate]

village /'vilij/ *noun* **1** a group of houses in the country, larger than a hamlet and smaller than a town. **2** (*treated as sing. or pl*) the residents of a village. **3** something, e.g. a group of burrows or nests, suggesting a village. **4** *NAmer* a legally constituted municipality smaller than a town. [Middle English from Old French, from *ville* farm, village, from Latin *villa* country estate]

villager *noun* an inhabitant of a village.

villain /'vilən/ *noun* **1a** a scoundrel or rascal. **b** a criminal. **2** a character in a story or play whose evil actions affect the plot: *In 'Vanity Fair' Becky Sharp is both heroine and villain*. **3** *informal* somebody or something that is the cause of or is blamed for a particular evil or difficulty: *This plug must be the villain*. [Middle English *vilain*, *vilein* peasant, churl, via French from medieval Latin *villanus*, from Latin *villa* country estate]

villainess /'vilənes/ *noun* a female villain, *esp* a female character in a story or play whose evil actions affect the plot.

villainous /'vilənəs/ *adj* **1** being, befitting, or characteristic of a villain; evil: *a villainous attack*. **2** highly objectionable: *villainous weather*. ➤➤ **villainously** *adv*, **villainousness** *noun*.

villainy /'viləni/ *noun* (*pl* **villainies**) **1** villainous conduct, or a villainous act. **2** depravity.

villanelle /vilə'nel/ *noun* a chiefly French verse form consisting of five tercets (three-line stanza; see TERCET) and a QUATRAIN (four-line stanza) using two rhymes, or a poem in this form. The rhyme scheme is *aba aba aba aba aba abaa*; the first and third lines are repeated alternately in the following tercets and together in the quatrain. [French *villanello* from Italian *villanella*, from *villano* peasant, from medieval Latin *villanus*: see VILLAIN]

-ville *suffix informal* forming nouns from adjectives and nouns, denoting: place or thing of the nature or character specified: *dullsville*. [-ville, suffix occurring in names of towns, from French *ville* town, from Latin *villa* country estate]

villein /'vilən/ *noun* **1** formerly, a peasant standing as the slave of his feudal lord. **2** formerly, a free village peasant. [Middle English *vilain*, *vilein*: see VILLAIN]

villeinage *or* **villenage** /'vilənij/ *noun* formerly, the tenure or status of a villein.

villi /'vilie/ *noun* pl of VILLUS.

villiform /'vilifawm/ *adj* **1** having the form or appearance of a villus or a number of villi: *a fish with villiform teeth*. **2** resembling bristles or the pile of velvet.

villous /'viləs/ *adj* said of a leaf: having villi or soft long hairs. ➤➤ **villosity** /vi'lositi/ *noun*, **villously** *adv*.

villus /'viləs/ *noun* (*pl* **villi** /'vilie/) **1** any of the many minute projections from the membrane of the small intestine that provide a large area for the absorption of digested food. **2** any of the branching parts on the surface of the CHORION (outer membrane) of the developing embryo of most mammals that help to form the placenta. [Latin *villus* tuft of shaggy hair]

vim /vim/ *noun informal* robust energy and enthusiasm. [Latin *vim*, accusative of *vis* strength]

vin- *or* **vini-** *comb. form* forming words, denoting: wine: *vinaceous*; *viniculture*. [Latin *vinum* WINE[1]]

vina *or* **veena** /'veenə/ *noun* an Indian stringed musical instrument with usu four strings on a long bamboo fingerboard and a gourd resonator at each end. [Sanskrit *vīṇā*]

vinaceous /vie'nayshəs/ *adj* **1** of the colour of red wine. **2** of wine. [Latin *vinaceus* of wine, from *vinum* WINE[1]]

vinaigrette /vini'gret/ *noun* **1a** a sharp sauce of oil and vinegar flavoured with salt, pepper, mustard, herbs, etc and used as a salad dressing. **b** a dish made with this. **2** a small ornamental box or bottle with a perforated top, formerly used for holding an aromatic preparation, e.g. smelling salts. [French *vinaigrette*, from *vinaigre*: see VINEGAR]

vinblastine /vin'blasteen/ *noun* a chemical compound obtained from the Madagascar periwinkle and used as an anticancer drug, *esp* in the treatment of leukaemias and lymphomas. [contraction of *vincaleukoblastine*, from scientific Latin *Vinca*, genus name of the periwinkle + *leukoblast* developing leukocyte + -INE[2]]

vinca /'vingkə/ *noun* a periwinkle plant. [scientific Latin, short for Latin *pervinca* periwinkle]

vincible /'vinsəbl/ *adj literary* capable of being overcome or subdued. ➤➤ **vincibility** /-'biliti/ *noun*, **vincibleness** *noun*. [Latin *vincibilis*, from *vincere* to conquer]

vincristine /vin'kristeen/ *noun* a chemical compound obtained from the Madagascar periwinkle and used as an anticancer drug. [VINCA + CRISTA + -INE²]

vinculum /'vingkyoolǝm/ *noun* (*pl* **vinculums** *or* **vincula** /-lǝ/) **1** a straight horizontal mark placed over two or more members of a compound mathematical expression and equivalent to brackets round them. **2** in anatomy, a band of connective tissue. [Latin *vinculum* bond, from *vincire* to bind]

vindaloo /vindǝ'looh/ *noun* a very hot Indian curry. [possibly from Portuguese *vin d'alho* wine and garlic sauce, from *vinho* wine (from Latin *vinum*) + *alho* garlic, from Latin *allium*]

vin de pays /,vanh dǝ pay'ee (*French* vɛ̃ dǝ pei)/ *noun* (*pl* **vins de pays** /,vanh dǝ pay'ee (*French* vɛ̃ dǝ pei)/) a table wine that is produced in a particular locality and is usu relatively unsophisticated and inexpensive. [French *vin de pays*, literally 'wine of the locality']

vindicable /'vindikǝbl/ *adj* capable of being vindicated. ➤➤ **vindicability** /-'biliti/ *noun*.

vindicate /'vindikayt/ *verb trans* **1a** to exonerate or absolve (somebody). **b** to provide justification for (something, e.g. an opinion); to justify (it). **2** to maintain the existence of (something); to uphold (it): *He sought a means to vindicate his honour.* ➤➤ **vindicator** *noun*. [Latin *vindicatus*, past part. of *vindicare* to lay claim to, avenge, from *vindic-, vindex* claimant, avenger]

vindication /vindi'kaysh(ǝ)n/ *noun* **1** the act or an instance of vindicating. **2** justification against denial or censure; defence.

vindicatory /'vindikaytǝri, -kǝt(ǝ)ri/ *adj* **1** providing vindication; justificatory. **2** punitive; retributive.

vindictive /vin'diktiv/ *adj* **1a** disposed to seek revenge; vengeful. **b** intended as revenge: *vindictive punishments.* **2** intended to cause anguish; spiteful. **3** in law, said of damages: set higher than is necessary for compensation in order to punish the guilty party. ➤➤ **vindictively** *adv*, **vindictiveness** *noun*. [Latin *vindicta* revenge, vindication, from *vindicare*: see VINDICATE]

vin du pays /,vanh dooh pay'ee (*French* vɛ̃ dy pei)/ *noun* (*pl* **vins du pays** /,vanh dooh pay'ee (*French* vɛ̃ dy pei)/) = VIN DE PAYS.

vine /vien/ *noun* **1** the climbing plant that bears grapes, or its stem. **2** a plant with a stem that requires support and that climbs by tendrils or twining, or its stem. ➤➤ **viny** *adj*. [Middle English via Old French *vigne* from Latin *vinea* vine, vineyard, fem of *vineus* of wine, from *vinum* WINE¹]

vinedresser *noun* a person who cultivates and prunes grapevines, *esp* as an occupation.

vinegar /'vinigǝ/ *noun* **1** a sour liquid obtained *esp* by acetic fermentation of wine, cider, etc and used as a condiment or preservative. **2** ill humour; peevishness. [Middle English *vinegre* from Old French *vinaigre*, from *vin* wine (from Latin *vinum*) + *aigre* keen, sour (from Latin *acer* sharp)]

vinegarish *adj* = VINEGARY.

vinegary *adj* **1** containing or resembling vinegar; sour. **2** bitter or irascible in character or manner.

vinery /'vienǝri/ *noun* (*pl* **vineries**) an area or greenhouse in which vines are grown.

vineyard /'vinyahd, 'vinyǝd/ *noun* a plantation of grapevines.

vingt-et-un /,vant ay 'uhn (*French* vɛ̃t e œ̃)/ *noun* = PONTOON². [French *vingt-et-un* twenty-one]

vinho verde /,veenyoh 'verdi/ *noun* a light dry wine from northern Portugal. [Portuguese *vinho verde*, literally 'green wine'; from the immaturity of the wine]

vini- *comb. form* see VIN-.

viniculture /'vinikulchǝ/ *noun* = VITICULTURE. ➤➤ **vinicultural** *adj*, **viniculturist** *noun*. [Latin *vinum* WINE¹ + CULTURE¹]

vinification /,vinifi'kaysh(ǝ)n/ *noun* the conversion of a sugar-containing solution, e.g. a fruit juice, into wine by fermentation. [French *vinification*, from VINI- + -FICATION]

vino /'veenoh/ *noun* (*pl* **vinos**) *informal* wine. [Italian and Spanish *vino* from Latin *vinum*]

vin ordinaire /,vanh awdi'neǝ/ *noun* table wine that is undistinguished and sufficiently inexpensive for everyday drinking. [French *vin ordinaire*, literally 'ordinary wine']

vinous /'vienǝs/ *adj* **1** of wine. **2** made with wine: *vinous medications.* **3** addicted to wine, or showing the effects of such

addiction. ➤➤ **vinosity** /vie'nositi, vi'nositi/ *noun*, **vinously** *adv*. [Latin *vinosus*, from *vinum* WINE¹]

vins de pays /,vanh dǝ pay'ee/ *noun* pl of VIN DE PAYS.

vins du pays /,vanh dooh pay'ee/ *noun* pl of VIN DU PAYS.

vintage¹ /'vintij/ *noun* **1** a season's yield of grapes or wine from a vineyard. **2a** a wine; *specif* one of a particular type, region, and year and usu of superior quality that is dated and allowed to mature: *Happiness is a wine of the rarest vintage* — Logan Pearsall Smith. **b** a collection of contemporaneous and similar people or things; a crop. **3** the act or time of harvesting grapes or making wine. **4** a period of origin or manufacture: *a piano of 1845 vintage.* [Middle English, alteration of *vendage*, via French *vendenge* from Latin *vindemia*, from *vinum* WINE¹, grapes + *demere* to take off]

vintage² *adj* **1** of a vintage, *esp* being a high-quality wine of one particular year rather than a blend of wines from different years. **2** of enduring interest or quality; classic. **3** of the best and most characteristic: *The book contains a vintage collection of British comic writing.* **4** old-fashioned; dated; outmoded.

vintage car *noun* an old motor car; *specif* one built between 1919 and 1930: compare EDWARDIAN CAR, VETERAN CAR.

vintager *noun* a person who is concerned with the production of grapes and wine.

vintner /'vintnǝ/ *noun* a wine merchant. [Middle English *vineter* via Old French from medieval Latin *vinetarius*, from Latin *vinetum* vineyard, from *vinum* WINE¹]

vinyl /'vienl/ *noun* **1** a univalent radical CH_2=CH derived from ethylene by removal of one hydrogen atom. **2** a plastic that is a polymer of a derivative of this radical. **3** *informal* traditional gramophone records, as opposed to CDs, DVDs, or tapes. ➤➤ **vinylic** /vie'nilik/ *adj*. [Latin *vinum* WINE¹ + -YL]

vinyl acetate *noun* a colourless liquid that polymerizes in light and that is used to make polyvinyl acetate.

vinyl chloride *noun* a colourless flammable gaseous compound used to make PVC and as a refrigerant.

vinyl polymer *noun* = VINYL RESIN.

vinyl resin *noun* any of a group of plastic materials, e.g. PVC, made from chemical compounds containing the vinyl group.

viol /'vie·ǝl/ *noun* any member of a family of bowed stringed musical instruments chiefly of the 16th and 17th cents made in various sizes, usu with six strings and a fretted fingerboard, played resting on or between the player's knees; precursors of the modern violin family. [early French *viole* viol, viola, from Old Provençal *viola* viol]

viola¹ /vi'ohlǝ/ *noun* a stringed musical instrument of the violin family that is intermediate in size and range between the violin and cello and is tuned a fifth below the violin. ➤➤ **violist** *noun*. [Italian and Spanish *viola* viol, viola, from Old Provençal *viola* VIOL]

viola² /'vie·ǝlǝ, vie'ohlǝ/ *noun* a violet, *esp* any of various cultivated violets with flowers resembling but smaller than those of pansies: genus *Viola*. [Latin *viola*]

viola clef /vi'ohlǝ/ *noun* = ALTO CLEF.

viola da braccio /vi,ohlǝ dǝ 'brachioh/ *noun* (*pl* **viole da braccio** /vi,ohlay/) a member of the early violin family, *esp* a viola. [Italian *viola da braccio*, literally 'arm viol']

viola da gamba /'gambǝ/ *noun* (*pl* **viole da gamba**) a bass member of the viol family having a range like that of the cello. [Italian *viola da gamba*, literally 'leg viol']

viola d'amore /da'mawri/ *noun* (*pl* **viole d'amore**) a bowed stringed musical instrument which is related to the viol family but has no frets and is played under the chin. [Italian *viola d'amore*, literally 'viol of love']

violate /'vie·ǝlayt/ *verb trans* **1** to fail to comply with (a law, etc); to infringe (it): *The Government was accused of violating the agreement with the Opposition.* **2** to do harm to (somebody); *specif* to sexually assault or rape (them). **3** to fail to respect (something sacred); to desecrate (it): *He would never violate a shrine.* **4** to interrupt or disturb (something): *The press have no scruples about violating one's privacy.* ➤➤ **violable** *adj*, **violater** *noun*, **violation** /-'laysh(ǝ)n/ *noun*, **violative** /-tiv/ *adj*, **violator** *noun*. [Middle English *violaten* from Latin *violatus*, past part. of *violare* to treat with violence]

viole da braccio /vi'ohlay/ *noun* pl of VIOLA DA BRACCIO.

viole da gamba *noun* pl of VIOLA DA GAMBA.

viole d'amore *noun* pl of VIOLA D'AMORE.

violence /'vie·ələns/ *noun* **1a** exertion of physical force so as to injure or abuse, *esp* unnecessary or unlawful force: *An unjust law is itself a species of violence* — Mohandas K Gandhi. **b** an instance of violent treatment or procedure. **2a** intense or turbulent action or force: *They tried to shelter from the violence of the storm.* **b** vehement feeling or expression, or an instance of such feeling or expression; fervour or forcefulness. **3** the quality of being abrupt or discordant: *I don't like the violence of the contrast in the colours.* ✳ **do violence to something 1** to outrage or insult somebody's feelings, etc: *His over-familiar behaviour did violence to her sensibilities.* **2** to distort or misinterpret the meaning of something: *The editors have certainly done violence to the original text.* [Middle English via French from Latin *violentia*, from *violentus* VIOLENT]

violent /'vie·ələnt/ *adj* **1a** marked by extreme force or sudden intense activity: *a violent attack.* **b** said of a person: prone to using physical force and causing injury to others. **c** excited or mentally disordered to the point of loss of self-control: *The patient became violent and had to be restrained.* **2** caused by force or violence; not natural: *He died a violent death.* **3a** powerfully intense or furious: *a violent denunciation.* **b** extreme or intense: *She was suffering violent pains in her stomach.* ➤➤ **violently** *adv.* [Middle English via French from Latin *violentus* forceful, vehement]

violent storm *noun* a storm with winds having speeds of 103 to 117km/h (64 to 72mph). Such storms cause great damage to property, etc.

violet /'vie·ələt/ *noun* **1** any of a genus of plants with often sweet-scented flowers, usu of all one colour, *esp* as distinguished from the usu larger-flowered violas and pansies: genus *Viola*. **2a** the bluish purple colour at the end of the spectrum next to indigo. **b** a violet dye or pigment. **c** violet material or clothes. ➤➤ **violet** *adj.* [Middle English from early French *violete*, dimin. of *viole* violet, from Latin *viola*]

violin /vie·ə'lin/ *noun* a bowed stringed musical instrument of a family of instruments having a fingerboard with no frets, four strings, and a usual range from G below middle C upwards for more than 4.5 octaves. ➤➤ **violinist** *noun.* [Italian *violino*, dimin. of *viola*: see VIOLA[1]]

violoncello /ˌvie·ələn'cheloh/ *noun* (*pl* **violoncellos**) *formal* = CELLO. ➤➤ **violoncellist** *noun.* [Italian *violoncello*, dimin. of *violone*, augmentative of *viola*: see VIOLA[1]]

VIP *noun* **1** a person of great influence or prestige. **2** (*used before a noun*) for VIPs: *a VIP lounge.* [short for *very important person*]

viper /'viepə/ *noun* **1a** the adder, or any of a family of Old World snakes related to it: family VIPERIDAE. **b** = PIT VIPER. **2** a malignant or treacherous person: *O villains, vipers, damn'd without redemption!* — Shakespeare. [early French *vipere* from Latin *vipera*, from *vivus* alive + *parere* to bring forth; because many species of Old World vipers bear live young]

viperine /'viepərien/ *adj* of or resembling a viper; venomous.

viperish *adj* spitefully abusive.

viperous *adj* **1** of or like a viper; venomous. **2** = VIPERISH. ➤➤ **viperously** *adv.*

viper's bugloss *noun* a coarse bristly Old World plant of the borage family with showy blue tubular flowers: *Echium vulgare.* [because it was long believed to be an antidote to snake venom]

viraemia (*NAmer* **viremia**) /vie·ə'reemi·ə/ *noun* the presence of a particular virus in the blood. [scientific Latin, from VIRUS + -AEMIA]

virago /vi'rahgoh/ *noun* (*pl* **viragoes** or **viragos**) **1** a loud overbearing woman; a termagant. **2** *archaic* a woman of great stature, strength, and courage. ➤➤ **viraginous** /vi'rajinəs/ *adj.* [Latin *viragin-, virago* a man-like woman, female warrior, from *vir* man]

viral /'vie·ərəl/ *adj* see VIRUS.

viral marketing *noun* a marketing technique that induces a firm's customers to pass on a marketing message to other potential customers, thereby greatly increasing its effect.

viremia /vie·ə'reemi·ə/ *noun* *NAmer* see VIRAEMIA.

vireo /'virioh/ *noun* (*pl* **vireos**) any of several species of small insect-eating American birds with greenish or greyish upper parts: family Vireonidae. [Latin *vireo* a small green bird, from *virēre* to be green]

virescent /vi'res(ə)nt/ *adj* **1** *literary* greenish. **2** said *esp* of plant organs such as petals that are not normally green: becoming green. ➤➤ **virescence** *noun.* [Latin *virescent-, virescens*, present part. of *virescere* to become green, from *viridis* green, from *virēre* to be green]

virgate /'vuhgət, 'vuhgayt/ *noun Brit* formerly, any of various units of land area; *esp* a unit equal to 30 acres (about 0.12km²). [medieval Latin *virgata*, from Latin *virga* rod, later a unit of land measurement]

Virgilian *or* **Vergilian** /vuh'jili·ən/ *adj* of or relating to the Roman poet Virgil (Publius Vergilius Maro) (d.19 BC).

virgin[1] /'vuhjin/ *noun* **1** a person, *esp* a girl or woman, who has not had sexual intercourse. **2** an unmarried virgin or girl, *esp* one who has taken a vow of chastity. **3** (**the Virgin**) the Virgin Mary, or a statue or picture of her. **4** (**the Virgin**) the constellation and sign of the zodiac Virgo. **5** a female animal that has never copulated. **6** a female insect that produces offspring without the aid of a male. ➤➤ **virginity** /və'jiniti/ *noun.* [Middle English via Old French from Latin *virgin-, virgo* young woman, virgin]

virgin[2] *adj* **1** free of impurity or stain; unsullied. **2** being a virgin. **3** characteristic of or befitting a virgin; modest. **4** untouched or unexploited; *specif* not altered by human activity: *virgin forest.* **5** initial; maiden. **6** said of metal: produced directly from ore; not scrap. **7** occurring naturally in a pure or free form: *virgin sulphur.*

virginal[1] *adj* **1** of a virgin or virginity, *esp* pure; chaste. **2** fresh; untouched; uncorrupted. ➤➤ **virginally** *adv.*

virginal[2] *noun* (*also in pl*) a small rectangular harpsichord popular in the 16th and 17th cents. ➤➤ **virginalist** *noun.* [prob from Latin *virginalis* of a virgin, from *virgin-, virgo* virgin, young woman; prob because played mainly by young women]

virgin birth *noun* **1** in zoology, birth from a virgin. **2** (**the Virgin Birth**) the doctrine that Jesus Christ was born of a virgin mother.

Virginia /və'jinyə/ *noun* a usu mild-flavoured flue-cured tobacco grown orig in N America and used *esp* in cigarettes. [named after *Virginia*, state of the USA, where it is produced]

Virginia creeper *noun* any of several species of plants of the grape family that climb by means of tendrils and have dark berries and leaves that turn red in autumn: genus *Parthenocissus.*

Virginian /və'jinyən/ *noun* a native or inhabitant of the US state of Virginia. ➤➤ **Virginian** *adj.*

Virginia reel *noun* an American country dance danced by couples, the partners standing facing each other in a double line and participating in turn in a series of figures.

Virginia stock *noun* an annual plant of the mustard family with small pink, white, red, or lilac flowers: *Malcolmia maritima.*

Virgin Mary /'meəri/ *noun* the mother of Jesus Christ.

virgin soil *noun* **1** ground that has never been cultivated. **2** somebody or something that has never been tried, investigated, exploited, etc.

virgin wool *noun* new wool not yet processed.

Virgo /'vuhgoh/ *noun* **1** in astronomy, a constellation (the Virgin) depicted as a young woman. **2a** in astrology, the sixth sign of the zodiac. **b** a person born under this sign. ➤➤ **Virgoan** *adj and noun.* [Latin *virgin-, virgo* young woman, virgin]

virgo intacta /ˌvuhgoh in'taktə/ *noun esp* in law, a girl or woman with an unbroken hymen. [Latin *virgo intacta*, literally 'untouched virgin']

virgule /'vuhgyoohl/ *noun* = SOLIDUS (1). [French *virgule* from Latin *virgula* small stripe, obelus, dimin. of *virga* rod]

viricide *or* **virucide** /'vie·ərəsied/ *noun* something that destroys viruses or inhibits the growth of viruses. ➤➤ **viricidal** *adj*, **viricidally** *adv.*

viridescent /viri'des(ə)nt/ *adj* slightly green, or becoming so. ➤➤ **viridescence** *noun.* [Latin *viridescent-, viridescens*, present part. of *viridescere*: see VIRESCENT]

viridian /vi'ridi·ən/ *noun* a chrome oxide pigment having a strong bluish green colour. [Latin *viridis*: see VIRESCENT]

viridity /vi'riditi/ *noun formal* **1** being green. **2** naive innocence. [Middle English *viridite* greenness, via French from Latin *viriditat-, viriditas*, from *viridis*: see VIRESCENT]

virile /'viriel/ *adj* **1** having the nature, properties, or qualities typical of, or often thought of as typical of, a man. **2** characteristic of or associated with adult males; masculine. **3a** capable of functioning as a male in copulation. **b** having a great appetite and capacity for intercourse. **4** vigorous; forceful. ➤➤ **virility** /və'riliti/ *noun.* [early French *viril* from Latin *virilis*, from *vir* man, male]

virilism /'viriliz(ə)m/ *noun* the abnormal appearance of male secondary sex characteristics, either precociously in the male or in the female.

virology /vie'roləji/ *noun* a branch of science that deals with viruses. ⟩⟩ **virologic** /-'lojik/ *adj*, **virological** /-'lojikl/ *adj*, **virologically** /-'lojikli/ *adv*, **virologist** *noun*.

virtu *or* **vertu** /vuh'tooh/ *noun* **1a** a taste for or knowledge of curios or objets d'art. **b** excellence, e.g. artistic worth, rarity, or antiquity, in such objects: *Regency snuffboxes and other objects of virtu.* **2** curios, objets d'art, or antiques collectively. [Italian *virtù* virtue, from Latin *virtut-, virtus*: see VIRTUE]

virtual /'vuhchooəl/ *adj* **1** being such in essence or effect though not formally recognized or admitted as such: *Although called Consul, he was a virtual dictator; I looked on that as a virtual promise.* **2a** in computing, relating to a storage capacity that appears greater to the user than the physical amount available as a result of the rapid movement of data between different storage areas. **b** relating to a technique by which a person wearing a special headset, and using articles such as specially equipped gloves or a joystick, has the illusion of being in a computer-simulated environment and is able to interact with it: compare VIRTUAL REALITY. **c** operating or linked by means of computer links to the Internet. **3** said of an image, etc: formed by the apparent rather than the actual convergence of light rays at a point: compare REAL[1]. **4** in physics, of a particle that is considered to exist for a very brief time in an interaction between other particles. [Middle English in the sense 'possessing certain physical virtues', from medieval Latin *virtualis*, from Latin *virtus*: see VIRTUE]

virtually /'vuhchəli, 'vuhchooəli/ *adv* almost entirely; for all practical purposes: *She became virtually a prisoner in her own home.*

virtual memory *noun* = VIRTUAL STORAGE.

virtual reality *noun* a computer-simulated environment with which a person can interact almost as if it were part of the real world, or the technique of producing such a simulation: compare VIRTUAL (2B).

Editorial note
While immersing yourself in a computer-simulated world certainly enhances the experience of playing a computer game, the underlying technology of virtual reality is no toy. Because it can provide three-dimensional models of highly complex data, scientists, economists, architects, and doctors can manipulate more information than ever before — David Blatner.

virtual storage *noun* a means of increasing the apparent size of a computer memory by moving data back and forward between the memory and an external storage device such as a floppy disk as required.

virtue /'vuhtyooh, 'vuhchooh/ *noun* **1a** conformity to a standard of right; morality. **b** a particular moral excellence: *Truthfulness is a virtue.* **2** a beneficial or commendable quality: *The wardrobe has the virtue of being easily assembled.* **3** *archaic* chastity, *esp* in a woman. **4** *archaic* a capacity to act; potency. ✳ **by virtue of 1** through the force of; having as a right. **2** as a result of; because of. **make a virtue of necessity** to do something one does not want to do with a show of goodwill because one is going to have to do it whether one likes it or not. ⟩⟩ **virtueless** *adj*. [Middle English *virtu* via French from Latin *virtut-, virtus* strength, manliness, virtue, from *vir* man]

virtuosi /vuhtyooh'ohsee, -zee/ *noun* pl of VIRTUOSO[1].

virtuosity /vuhtyooh'ositi/ *noun* great technical skill, *esp* in the practice of a fine art. [from VIRTUOSO[1]]

virtuoso[1] /vuhtyooh'ohsoh, -zoh/ *noun* (*pl* **virtuosos** *or* **virtuosi** /-see, -zee/) **1** a person who excels in the technique of an art, *esp* in musical performance. **2** a person who is skilled in or who has a taste for the fine arts. ⟩⟩ **virtuosic** /-sik, -zik/ *adj*. [Italian *virtuoso* virtuous, skilled, from late Latin *virtuosus* virtuous, from Latin *virtus*: see VIRTUE]

virtuoso[2] *adj* characteristic of a virtuoso; having the manner or style of a virtuoso; highly skilled: *a virtuoso performance.*

virtuous /'vuhchoo·əs/ *adj* **1** having or exhibiting virtue, *esp* morally excellent; righteous: *There are nine hundred and ninety-nine patrons of virtue to one virtuous man* — Henry David Thoreau. **2** *archaic* said of a woman: chaste. ⟩⟩⟩ **virtuously** *adv*, **virtuousness** *noun*.

virucide /'vie·ərəsied/ *noun* see VIRICIDE. [VIRUS + -CIDE]

virulence /'viryooləns, 'virələns/ *noun* **1** extreme bitterness or malignity of temper; rancour. **2** malignancy; venomousness. **3** the relative capacity of a pathogen to overcome body defences.

virulency /'viryoolənsi, 'virə-/ *noun* = VIRULENCE.

virulent /'viryoolənt, 'virələnt/ *adj* **1a** said of a disease: severe and developing rapidly. **b** able to overcome bodily defensive mechanisms: *a virulent strain of bacterium.* **2** extremely poisonous or venomous. **3** full of malice; malignant. **4** objectionably harsh or strong: *a virulent purple.* ⟩⟩ **virulently** *adv*. [Middle English from Latin *virulentus*, from *virus* poison]

virus /'vierəs/ *noun* **1a** any of a large group of minute parasitic entities that are regarded either as the simplest micro-organisms or as extremely complex molecules, typically consist of a protein coat surrounding a core of DNA or RNA, are capable of growth and multiplication only in living cells, and that cause various common diseases in animals and plants. **b** *informal* a disease caused by a virus. **2** a small program or short code that is deliberately and maliciously inserted into a computer program or system to attack the software by destroying data files, erasing disks, etc. **3** something that poisons the mind or soul: *The Government will take all necessary steps to combat the virus of racism.* ⟩⟩ **viral** *adj*, **virally** *adv*. [Middle English in the sense 'venom, poison', from Latin *virus* slimy liquid, poison, stench]

Vis. *abbr* **1** Viscount. **2** Viscountess.

visa /'veezə, 'veesə/ *noun* an endorsement made on a passport by the proper authorities of a country denoting that the bearer may enter or leave the country, a region, etc. [French *visa* from Latin, neuter pl of *visus*: see VISAGE]

visage /'vizij/ *noun formal or literary* **1** a face or countenance: *On the sand, half sunk, a shattered visage lies, whose frown, and wrinkled lip, and sneer of cold command, tell that its sculptor well those passions read which yet survive* — Shelley. **2** an aspect or appearance: *She was tired of the grimy visage of the little mining town.* ⟩⟩ **visaged** *adj*. [Middle English from Old French, from *vis* face, from Latin *visus*, past part. of *vidēre* to see]

vis-à-vis[1] /,vee zah 'vee/ *prep* **1** face to face with; opposite. **2** in relation to. [French *vis-à-vis*, literally 'face to face']

vis-à-vis[2] *noun* (*pl* **vis-à-vis** /'vee, 'veez/) **1** a person or thing that is face to face with another. **2** a counterpart. **3** a private conversation; a tête-à-tête.

vis-à-vis[3] *adv archaic* face to face.

viscacha /vis'kachə/ *or* **vizcacha** /viz-/ *noun* any of several species of S American burrowing rodents related to the chinchilla: genera *Lagidium* and *Lagostomus.* [Spanish *vizcacha* from Quechua *wiskácha*]

viscera /'visərə/ *noun* pl of VISCUS.

visceral *adj* **1** of or located on or among the viscera. **2a** instinctive; unreasoning: *a visceral conviction.* **b** deeply or intensely felt: *a visceral sensation.* ⟩⟩ **viscerally** *adv*.

viscid /'visid/ *adj* **1a** adhesive; sticky. **b** glutinous; viscous. **2** said *esp* of a leaf: covered with a sticky layer. ⟩⟩ **viscidity** /vi'siditi/ *noun*, **viscidly** *adv*. [late Latin *viscidus* from Latin *viscum* birdlime, mistletoe]

viscose /'viskohs, 'viskohz/ *noun* **1** a viscous solution made by treating cellulose with caustic alkali solution and carbon disulphide and used in making rayon and cellulose films. **2** viscose rayon. [late Latin *viscosus*: see VISCOUS]

viscosity /vis'kositi/ *noun* (*pl* **viscosities**) **1** being viscous. **2** the property of a liquid, gas, or semifluid that enables it to offer resistance to flow, or a measure of the force needed to overcome this.

viscount /'viekownt/ *noun* **1** a member of the peerage in Britain ranking below an earl and above a baron. **2** in some European countries, a nobleman of a similar rank. ⟩⟩ **viscountcy** /-si/ *noun*, **viscounty** /-ti/ *noun*. [Middle English *viscounte* via French from medieval Latin *vicecomit-, vicecomes*, from VICE- + *comit-, comes*: see COUNT[3]]

viscountess /viekown'tes, 'viekowntis/ *noun* **1** the wife or widow of a viscount. **2** a woman having the same rank as a viscount.

viscous /'viskəs/ *adj* **1** sticky; glutinous. **2** having or characterized by viscosity, *esp* high viscosity: *viscous flow.* ⟩⟩ **viscously** *adv*, **viscousness** *noun*. [Middle English *viscouse* from late Latin *viscosus* full of birdlime, viscous, from Latin *viscum* mistletoe, birdlime]

viscus /'viskəs/ *noun* (*pl* **viscera** /'visərə/) **1** (*usu in pl*) the heart, liver, intestines, or other internal body organs located *esp* in the great cavity of the trunk. **2** (*in pl*) the intestines. [Latin *viscus*]

vise[1] /vies/ *noun NAmer* see VICE[2].

vise[2] *verb trans NAmer* see VICE[3].

Vishnu /'vishnooh/ *noun* the preserver god of the Hindu sacred triad: compare BRAHMA, SIVA. [Sanskrit *Viṣṇu*]

visibility /vizə'biliti/ *noun* **1** being visible. **2a** the clearness of the atmosphere as revealed by the greatest distance at which prominent objects can be identified visually with the naked eye. **b** this distance: *Visibility is down to 20 yards*. **3** capability of affording an unobstructed view: *The car has excellent rear visibility*.

visible /'vizəbl/ *adj* **1** (*also* + to) capable of being seen: *Only the nearest stars are visible to the naked eye*. **2a** exposed to view: *the visible horizon*. **b** in the public eye; prominent: *a panel of highly visible people*. **3** capable of being perceived; noticeable: *She has no visible means of support*. **4** tangibly or implicitly present. **5** said of exports, etc: of or being trade in goods rather than services: compare INVISIBLE¹. ➤ **visibleness** *noun*, **visibly** *adv*. [Middle English via French from Latin *visibilis*, from *vidēre* to see]

visible balance *noun* = BALANCE OF TRADE.

visible horizon *noun* = HORIZON (1A).

visible radiation *noun* the radiation that permits sight; light.

visible spectrum *noun* = SPECTRUM (1).

Visigoth /'vizigoth/ *noun* a member of the western division of the Goths. ➤ **Visigothic** /-'gothik/ *adj*. [late Latin *Visigothus*; the name possibly means 'western Goth']

vision /'vizh(ə)n/ *noun* **1a** the act or power of seeing; sight. **b** the special sense by which the qualities of an object, e.g. colour, luminosity, shape, and size, constituting its appearance are perceived via the eye. **2a** something seen. **b** a lovely or charming sight: *She looked a vision in that dress*. **3** the degree of clarity with which something appears on a television screen, or the control for this: *You'll need to adjust the vision*. **4a** something seen in a dream, trance, or ecstasy; *specif* a supernatural appearance that conveys a revelation. **b** any supernatural apparition. **5a** the power of imagination. **b** the manner of perceiving mental images: *an artist's vision*. **6a** discernment; foresight; imagination: *His main problem is that he lacks vision*. **b** (*also in pl*) a mental image of something; a thought or fear: *Sitting in the traffic jam, I had visions of missing the train*. ➤ **visional** *adj*, **visionally** *adv*, **visionless** *adj*. [Middle English via French from Latin *vision-, visio*, from *vidēre* to see]

visionary¹ /'vizh(ə)nri, -nəri/ *adj* **1** showing discernment, foresight, or imagination. **2a** able or likely to see visions. **b** disposed to daydreaming or imagining; dreamy. **3a** of the nature of a vision; illusory. **b** impracticable; utopian: *a visionary scheme*. **4** of or characterized by visions or the power of vision. ➤ **visionariness** *noun*.

visionary² *noun* (*pl* **visionaries**) **1** a person who shows discernment, foresight, or imagination. **2** a person whose ideas or projects are impractical; a dreamer. **3** a person who sees visions; a seer.

vision mixer *noun* **1** a person who mixes the pictures from different cameras during the making of a television programme or cinema film. **2** the apparatus used for this purpose.

visit¹ /'vizit/ *verb* (**visited, visiting**) ➤ *verb trans* **1a** to pay a call on (somebody) for reasons of kindness, friendship, ceremony, or business. **b** to reside with (somebody) temporarily as a guest. **c** to go or come to look at or stay at (a place), e.g. for business or sightseeing. **d** to go or come officially to inspect or oversee (a place): *The bishop regularly visits the parishes of his diocese*. **2a** (*usu passive*) to afflict (something unpleasant) on a person or place: *The city was frequently visited by the plague*. **b** *archaic* (+ on/upon) to inflict punishment on somebody for (something): *He will visit the sins of the fathers upon the children*. **c** *archaic* said of God: to comfort (somebody): *Visit us with thy salvation* — Charles Wesley. ➤ *verb intrans* **1** to make a visit or visits. **2** *NAmer, informal* (*often* + with) to chat with somebody. ➤ **visitable** *adj*. [Middle English *visiten* via French from Latin *visitare*, frequentative of *visere* to go to see, from *vidēre* to see]

visit² *noun* **1a** the act or an instance of visiting; a call. **b** a temporary residence as a guest. **c** a journey to a place for an extended but temporary stay: *I make annual visits to France*. **2** an official or professional call; a visitation. **3** the act of boarding a merchant ship in time of war to ascertain its nationality and cargo. **4** *NAmer, informal* a chat.

visitant *noun* **1** *archaic* = VISITOR (1). **2** a supernatural apparition. **3** = VISITOR (2).

visitation /vizi'taysh(ə)n/ *noun* **1a** the act or an instance of visiting, *esp* an official visit, e.g. for inspection. **b** an appearance by a supernatural being, seen or unseen. **c** *informal* a long, *esp* over-long, social visit. **2a** a special dispensation of divine favour or wrath. **b** a severe trial; an affliction. **3** (**the Visitation**) the visit of the Virgin Mary to Elizabeth celebrated as a festival in the Christian Church on 2 July (Luke 1:39–56). ➤ **visitational** *adj*.

visitatorial /,vizitə'tawri-əl/ *adj* of a visitation or an official visitor.

visiting card *noun Brit* a small card of introduction bearing the name and sometimes the address and profession of the owner.

visiting professor *noun* a professor invited to join the academic staff of an institution other than their own for a limited time.

visitor *noun* **1a** a person who is paying a visit. **b** a person who makes formal visits of inspection. **2** a migratory bird that visits a locality for a short time at regular intervals.

visitor centre *noun* a building, e.g. at a historical or archaeological site or a nature reserve, often containing a shop and exhibition area, where visitors can obtain information and other services.

visitors' book *noun* a book in which visitors, e.g. to a place of interest or hotel, write their names and addresses and sometimes comments.

visor *or* **vizor** /'vieze/ *noun* **1** a movable part of a helmet that covers the face. **2** a flat sunshade attached at the top of a vehicle windscreen. **3** *NAmer* a peak on a cap. ➤ **visored** *adj*, **visorless** *adj*. [Middle English *viser* via Anglo-French from Old French *visiere*, from *vis*: see VISAGE]

vista /'vistə/ *noun* **1** a distant view, *esp* through or along an avenue or opening; a prospect. **2** an extensive mental view, e.g. over a stretch of time or a series of events. ➤ **vistaed** *adj*, **vistaless** *adj*. [Italian *vista* sight, from *visto*, past part. of *vedere* to see, from Latin *vidēre*]

visual¹ /'vizhyooəl, 'vizyooəl/ *adj* **1a** of, used in, or produced by vision: *The eyes are our visual organs; visual impressions*. **b** optical: *the visual focus of a lens*. **2** visible: *The tic is a visual indication of his feelings*. **3** producing mental images; vivid. **4** done or executed by sight only: *visual navigation*. **5** of interest to the eye; colourful: *The dancers were very visual in their bright costumes*. ➤ **visually** *adv*. [Middle English from late Latin *visualis*, from Latin *visus* sight, from *vidēre* to see]

visual² *noun* **1** (*usu in pl*) a photograph, graph, chart, etc used for illustration, information, advertising, etc; = VISUAL AID. **2** (*in pl*) visual effects: *balancing the impact of the words with the impact of the visuals* — Sunday Times. **3** a rough sketch of the layout of an advertisement.

visual aid *noun* an instructional device, e.g. a chart, model, photograph, or film, that is used to illustrate a talk, clarify an explanation, etc.

visual arts *pl noun* artistic activities such as painting, sculpture, cinematography, etc, as opposed to music, literature, etc.

visual display unit *noun chiefly Brit* a device that has a cathode ray tube on which information held in a computer may be displayed or updated.

visual field *noun* the entire expanse of space visible at a given instant without moving the eyes.

visualize *or* **visualise** *verb trans* **1** to see or form a mental image of (somebody or something). **2** to make (something) visible, e.g. by surgery or X-ray photography. ➤ *verb intrans* to see or form a mental image of somebody or something. ➤ **visualization** /-'zaysh(ə)n/ *noun*.

visually impaired *adj* having poor eyesight.

visual purple *noun* a light-sensitive red or purple pigment in the rods (light-sensitive cells; see ROD) of the retina of the eye; = RHODOPSIN.

visual violet *noun* a light-sensitive pigment in the cones (light-sensitive cells; see CONE¹) of the retina of the eye; = IODOPSIN.

visual yellow *noun* a yellowish to orange compound that forms pigments in the rods (see ROD) and cones (light-sensitive cells; see CONE¹) of the retina of the eye; = RETINAL. It is a derivative of vitamin A.

vital /'vietl/ *adj* **1** of the utmost importance; essential. **2** concerned with or necessary to the maintenance of life: *Luckily the knife missed all the vital organs*. **3** full of life and vigour; animated. **4** concerned with, affecting, or being a manifestation of life or living beings. **5** tending to renew or refresh the living; invigorating. ➤ **vitally** *adv*. [Middle English via French from Latin *vitalis* of life, from *vita* life]

vital capacity *noun* the breathing capacity of the lungs expressed as the maximum volume of air that can be forcibly exhaled.

vital force *noun* the creative urge, *esp* for improved and superior evolutionary development, held by the philosopher Henri Bergson to be inherent in all living organisms.

vitalise *verb trans* see VITALIZE.

vitalism *noun* a doctrine that the functions of a living organism are due to a special life force or principle and are not wholly explicable by the laws of physics and chemistry. ➤➤ **vitalist** *noun and adj*, **vitalistic** /-'listik/ *adj*.

vitality /vie'taliti/ *noun* **1** physical or mental liveliness. **2** power of enduring: *the vitality of an idiom*. **3a** the quality that distinguishes the living from the dead or inanimate. **b** capacity to live and develop.

vitalize *or* **vitalise** *verb trans* to endow (somebody or something) with vitality; to animate (them). ➤➤ **vitalization** /-'zaysh(ə)n/ *noun*.

vitals *pl noun* **1** the vital organs, e.g. the heart, liver, or brain. **2** essential parts.

vital signs *pl noun* **1** the functioning or rate of the heartbeat and breathing, the level of body temperature, and other measurable indicators of body activity and functioning. **2** any signs that indicate the presence of life or level of activity: *The Council has been checking the city's vital signs.*

vital staining *noun* the staining of cells and tissue with dyes that do not harm them, so that they can be observed under a microscope.

vital statistics *pl noun* **1** statistics relating to births, deaths, health, etc. **2a** facts considered to be interesting or important. **b** *informal* a woman's bust, waist, and hip measurements.

vitamin /'vitəmin, 'vie-/ *noun* any of various organic chemical substances naturally present in foods, that are essential in minute quantities in the diet of most animals for the maintenance of health and growth and the proper functioning of life-supporting chemical processes, but that do not directly provide energy or serve as building units. [Latin *vita* life + AMINE; from the former belief that vitamins contained an amino acid]

vitamin A *noun* = RETINOL.

vitamin B *noun* (*pl* **B vitamins**) **1** = VITAMIN B COMPLEX. **2** = VITAMIN B_1. **3** = VITAMIN B_2. **4** = VITAMIN B_6. **5** = VITAMIN B_{12}.

vitamin B_1 *noun* = THIAMINE.

vitamin B_2 *noun* = RIBOFLAVIN.

vitamin B_3 *noun* = PYRIDOXINE.

vitamin B_{12} /,bee 'twelv/ *noun* = CYANOCOBALAMIN.

vitamin B complex *noun* a group of water-soluble vitamins that are found in most foods and include biotin, choline, folic acid, nicotinic acid, and pantothenic acid.

vitamin C *noun* = ASCORBIC ACID.

vitamin D *noun* (*pl* **D vitamins**) any of several fat-soluble vitamins chemically related to the steroids and found *esp* in animal products, e.g. fish liver oils, or milk, and that are essential for normal bone and tooth structure, e.g. VITAMIN D_2, VITAMIN D_3.

vitamin D_2 *noun* = CALCIFEROL.

vitamin D_3 *noun* = CHOLECALCIFEROL.

vitamin E *noun* = TOCOPHEROL.

vitamin G *noun chiefly NAmer* = RIBOFLAVIN.

vitamin H *noun chiefly NAmer* = BIOTIN.

vitaminize *or* **vitaminise** *verb trans* to provide or supplement (something, e.g. food) with vitamins. ➤➤ **vitaminization** /-'zaysh(ə)n/ *noun*.

vitamin K *noun* (*pl* **K vitamins**) any of several chemically related naturally occurring or synthetic fat-soluble vitamins essential for the clotting of blood, e.g. VITAMIN K_1, VITAMIN K_2. [*K* short for Danish *koagulation* coagulation]

vitamin K_1 *noun* = PHYLLOQUINONE.

vitamin K_2 *noun* = MENAQUINONE.

vitamin M *noun chiefly NAmer* = FOLIC ACID.

vitamin P *noun* = BIOFLAVONOID. [*P* short for *paprika* and *permeability*; because it is obtained from some peppers and it regulates the permeability of the blood capillaries]

vitelli /vi'telie/ *noun* pl of VITELLUS.

vitellin /vi'telin/ *noun* a phosphorus-containing protein that is the main protein of egg yolk. [VITELLUS + -IN¹]

vitelline membrane /vi'telin, -lien/ *noun* the membrane that encloses the developing embryo in an egg and that in many invertebrates acts to prevent other spermatozoa from entering.

vitellus /vi'teləs/ *noun* (*pl* **vitelluses** *or* **vitelli** /-lie/) in embryology, the yolk of an egg. ➤➤ **vitelline** /-lin, -lien/ *adj*. [Latin *vitellus*]

vitiate /'vishiayt/ *verb trans* **1** to make (something) faulty or defective; to debase (it). **2** to invalidate (a legal document, etc). ➤➤ **vitiation** /-'aysh(ə)n/ *noun*, **vitiator** *noun*. [Latin *vitiatus*, past part. of *vitiare*, from *vitium* fault, VICE¹]

viticulture /'vitikulchə/ *noun* the science or process of cultivating grapevines; the study of grapes and grapevines. ➤➤ **viticultural** /-'kulchərəl/ *adj*, **viticulturist** *noun*. [Latin *vitis* vine + CULTURE¹]

vitreous /'vitri-əs/ *adj* **1** of or consisting of glass. **2a** resembling glass in colour, composition, brittleness, etc: *vitreous rocks*. **b** characterized by low porosity and usu translucence: *vitreous china*. **3** of the vitreous humour. ➤➤ **vitreously** *adv*, **vitreousness** *noun*. [Latin *vitreus* from *vitrum* glass]

vitreous body *noun* = VITREOUS HUMOUR.

vitreous humour *noun* the colourless transparent jelly that fills the eyeball behind the lens.

vitrify /'vitrifie/ *verb* (**vitrifies, vitrified, vitrifying**) ➤ *verb trans* to convert (something) into glass or a glassy substance, e.g. by heat and fusion. ➤ *verb intrans* to become glass or a glassy substance in this way. ➤➤ **vitrifiable** *adj*, **vitrification** /-fi'kaysh(ə)n/ *noun*. [Middle English from French *vitrifier* from Latin *vitrum* glass]

vitrine /'veetreen, 'vitreen/ *noun* a glass-sided showcase for delicate articles, works of art, specimens, etc. [French *vitrine* shop window, ultimately from Latin *vitrum* glass]

vitriol /'vitri-əl/ *noun* **1a** a sulphate of iron, copper, zinc, etc, *esp* if hydrated (combined with water; see HYDRATE²). **b** concentrated sulphuric acid. **2** virulent speech, expression, feeling, etc: *This introduction, with its mixture of genius, shrewdness, and vitriol, is a piece of prose not to be missed* — Literary World. ➤➤ **vitriolic** /-'olik/ *adj*. [Middle English via French from medieval Latin *vitriolum*, alteration of late Latin *vitreolum*, neuter of *vitreolus* glassy, from Latin *vitreus*: see VITREOUS]

vittles /'vitlz/ *pl noun archaic* food. [alteration of VICTUALS]

vituperate /vi'tyoohpərayt/ *verb trans* to subject (somebody or something) to severe or abusive censure; to berate (them). ➤ *verb intrans* to use harsh condemnatory language. ➤➤ **vituperation** /-'raysh(ə)n/ *noun*, **vituperative** /-rətiv/ *adj*, **vituperator** *noun*. [Latin *vituperatus*, past part. of *vituperare*, from *vitium* fault, VICE¹ + *parare* to make, prepare]

viva¹ /'veevə/ *interj* used to express goodwill towards or approval of a person or thing: *Viva Mandela!* [Italian and Spanish *viva* long live, may he/she/it live, from Latin *vivat*, from *vivere* to live]

viva² /'vievə/ *noun* an examination for an academic degree conducted by word of mouth rather than in writing. [shortening of VIVA VOCE¹]

viva³ /'vievə/ *verb trans* (**vivas, vivaed, vivaing**) to subject (somebody) to a viva.

vivace /vi'vahchi/ *adj and adv* said of a piece of music: to be performed in a brisk spirited manner. [Italian *vivace* vivacious, from Latin *vivac-*, *vivax*: see VIVACIOUS]

vivacious /vi'vayshəs/ *adj* attractively lively in temper or conduct. ➤➤ **vivaciously** *adv*, **vivaciousness** *noun*, **vivacity** /vi'vasiti/ *noun*. [Latin *vivac-*, *vivax*, literally 'long-lived', from *vivere* to live]

vivarium /vie'veəri-əm/ *noun* (*pl* **vivaria** /-ri-ə/ *or* **vivariums**) an enclosure for keeping and observing plants or animals indoors. [Latin *vivarium* park, preserve, from *vivus* (see VIVI-) + -ARIUM]

viva voce¹ /,vievə 'vohchi/ *adj and adv* by word of mouth. [medieval Latin *viva voce* with the living voice]

viva voce² *noun* (*pl* **viva voces**) = VIVA².

vive /veev/ *interj* used to express acclamation of a specified person or thing: *Vive la France!* [French *vive* long live, may he/she/it live, from Latin *vivat*: see VIVA¹]

viverrid /vie'verid/ *noun* any of a family of slender weasel-like flesh-eating mammals, including the civets, genets, and mongooses, with usu retractable claws: family Viverridae.

[scientific Latin *Viverridae* group name, from *Viverra* genus, from Latin *viverra* ferret]

vivi- *comb. form* forming words, with the meaning: alive; living: *vivisection*. [Latin *vivus* alive, from *vivere* to live]

vivid /'vivid/ *adj* **1a** said of a light or colour: bright, glaring, or intense. **b** having bright colouring. **2a** producing a strong or clear impression on the senses. **b** producing strong clear mental pictures; having exciting, realistic, true-to-life, etc descriptions: *The book contains a vivid description of the Battle of Waterloo*. **c** said of the mind: able to create vivid pictures or imaginative stories: *Your daughter has a very vivid imagination*. **d** very clear and distinct: *I have a vivid memory of that holiday*. **3a** having vigour, life, or freshness; lively: *a vivid personality*. **b** doing something, or done, with vigour. ▶▶ **vividly** *adv*, **vividness** *noun*. [Latin *vividus* animated from *vivere* to live]

vivify /'vivifie/ *verb trans* (**vivifies, vivified, vivifying**) **1** to give life, *esp* renewed life to (something); to animate (it). **2** to impart vitality or vividness to (something). ▶▶ **vivification** /-fi'kaysh(ə)n/ *noun*, **vivifier** *noun*. [early French *vivifier* from late Latin *vivificare*, from Latin *vivificus* enlivening, from *vivus*: see VIVI-]

viviparous /vi'vipərəs, vie-/ *adj* **1** producing living young rather than eggs from within the body in the manner of nearly all mammals, many reptiles, and a few fishes: compare OVIPAROUS. **2a** said of a seed: germinating while still attached to the parent plant: *the viviparous seed of the mangrove*. **b** said of a plant: having viviparous seeds. **3** said of a plant: multiplying by means of shoots, buds, bulbils (small bulbs; see BULBIL), etc rather than seeds. ▶▶ **viviparity** /vivi'pariti/ *noun*, **viviparously** *adv*, **viviparousness** *noun*. [Latin *viviparus*, from VIVI- + -PAROUS]

vivisect /'vivisekt, -'sekt/ *verb trans and intrans* to perform vivisection on (an animal). ▶▶ **vivisector** *noun*. [back-formation from *vivisection*]

vivisection /vivi'seksh(ə)n/ *noun* **1a** operation or physical experimentation on a living animal, usu for scientific investigation. **b** any animal experimentation, e.g. for testing cosmetics, *esp* if causing distress to the subject. **2** minute examination or relentless criticism. ▶▶ **vivisectional** *adj*, **vivisectionally** *adv*, **vivisectionist** *noun*, **vivisector** *noun*.

vivo /'veevoh/ *adj and adv* said of a piece of music: to be performed in a lively manner. [Italian *vivo* alive, lively, from Latin *vivus*: see VIVI-]

vixen /'viks(ə)n/ *noun* **1** a female fox. **2** a scolding ill-tempered woman. ▶▶ **vixenish** *adj*, **vixenishly** *adv*. [alteration of Middle English *fixen*, from Old English *fyxe*, fem of FOX¹]

viz. *abbr* videlicet.

vizard /'vizəd/ *noun archaic or literary* a mask for disguise or protection. [alteration of Middle English *viser* mask, visor: see VISOR]

vizcacha /viz'kachə/ *noun* see VISCACHA.

vizier /vi'ziə/ *noun* a high executive officer of various Muslim countries, *esp* of the former Ottoman Empire. ▶▶ **vizierate** /-rət, -rayt/ *noun*, **vizierial** /-ri·əl/ *adj*, **viziership** *noun*. [Turkish *vezir* from Arabic *wazīr*]

vizor /'vieze/ *noun* see VISOR.

VJ *abbr* video jockey.

V-J Day *noun* the day at the end of World War II when Japan surrendered to the Allied forces, 15 August 1945, or any anniversary of that day. [short for *Victory in Japan*]

VLF *abbr* very low frequency.

VLSI *abbr* very large-scale integration.

VN *abbr* Vietnam (international vehicle registration).

V neck *noun* a V-shaped neck on a garment, or a garment with such a neck. ▶▶ **V-necked** *adj*.

voc. *abbr* vocative.

vocab /'vohkab/ *noun informal* = VOCABULARY (2).

vocab. *abbr* vocabulary.

vocable /'vohkəbl/ *noun* a word considered as a combination of sounds or letters without regard to its meaning. [early French *vocable* word, name, from Latin *vocabulum* name, from *vocare* to call]

vocabulary /və'kabyooləri/ *noun* (*pl* **vocabularies**) **1a** the words employed by a language, group, or individual, or in a field of work or knowledge: *She has a very limited vocabulary*. **b** a list or collection of terms or codes available for use, e.g. in an indexing system. **2** a list of words, and sometimes phrases, usu arranged alphabetically and defined or translated: *There's a vocabulary at the back of the book*. **3** a supply of expressive techniques or devices, e.g. of an art form. [early French *vocabulaire* from medieval Latin *vocabularius* verbal, from Latin *vocabulum*: see VOCABLE]

vocal¹ /'vohkl/ *adj* **1** uttered by the voice; oral. **2** of, composed or arranged for, or sung by the human voice. **3** having or exercising the power of producing voice, speech, or sound. **4a** given to strident or insistent expression; outspoken: *She was very vocal in her opposition to the new regulations*. **b** full of the sound of voices. **5** relating to the voice, speech sounds, voiced speech sounds, or vowels. ▶▶ **vocality** /voh'kaliti/ *noun*, **vocally** *adv*. [Middle English from Latin *vocalis*, from *voc-*, *vox* VOICE¹]

vocal² *noun* **1** (usu in pl) a song part in a piece of music, esp popular or jazz music, or the performance of this part: *On this track, we have Paul McCartney on vocals*. **2** a vocal sound.

vocal cords *pl noun* either of a pair of mucous membrane folds in the cavity of the larynx whose free edges vibrate to produce sound.

vocalic /voh'kalik/ *adj* containing, consisting of, being, functioning as, or associated with a vowel or voiced speech segment. ▶▶ **vocalically** *adv*. [Latin *vocalis* vowel, from *vocalis*: see VOCAL¹]

vocalise¹ *verb trans and intrans* see VOCALIZE.

vocalise² /vohkə'leez, 'voh-/ *noun* **1** an exercise for singers, commonly using vowels or special syllables designed to develop vocal beauty or agility. **2** a vocalized melody or passage without words. [French *vocalise*, from *vocaliser* to vocalize]

vocalism *noun* vocal art or technique in singing.

vocalist *noun* a singer, *esp* with a rock or jazz band or pop group.

vocalize *or* **vocalise** *verb trans* **1** to give voice to (thoughts, etc); to utter (them). **2** to sing (something). **3a** to utter (a sound) while vibrating the vocal cords; to voice (it). **b** to convert (a sound) into a vowel. **c** to convert (a sound) into a separate syllable. **4** to provide (a Hebrew or Arabic text consisting of consonants) with vowels or vowel points. ▶ *verb intrans* **1a** to sing. **b** to sing without words. **2** to utter vocal sounds: *In the distance they could hear a gorilla vocalizing*. ▶▶ **vocalization** /-'zaysh(ə)n/ *noun*, **vocalizer** *noun*.

vocal score *noun* a score of a musical work, *esp* an opera, in which the voice parts are given in full and the orchestral parts are given in the form of a transcription for piano.

vocat. *abbr* vocative.

vocation /voh'kaysh(ə)n, və-/ *noun* **1a** a summons or strong inclination to a particular state or course of action, *esp* a divine call to the religious life: *The test of a vocation is the love of the drudgery it involves* — Logan Pearsall Smith. **b** an entry into the priesthood or a religious order. **2** the work in which a person is regularly employed; a career. **3** the special function of an individual or group. [Middle English *vocacioun* a divine call to do certain work, from Latin *vocation-*, *vocatio* summons, from *vocare* to call]

vocational *adj* **1** of or being training in a skill or trade to be pursued as a career: *vocational courses*. **2** relating to a vocation. ▶▶ **vocationally** *adv*.

vocational guidance *noun* guidance given to a person on what sort of career would be suitable for them to follow, based on an analysis of their skills, aptitudes, personality, etc.

vocative¹ /'vokətiv/ *adj* denoting a grammatical case expressing the person or thing addressed. ▶▶ **vocatively** *adv*. [Middle English *vocatif* via French from Latin *vocativus*, from *vocare* to call]

vocative² *noun* the vocative case or a word in this case.

vociferate /və'sifərayt/ *verb trans* to cry out about (something); to utter (it) loudly. ▶ *verb intrans* to clamour or shout. ▶▶ **vociferant** *noun*, **vociferation** /-'raysh(ə)n/ *noun*, **vociferator** *noun*. [Latin *vociferatus*, past part. of *vociferari*, from *voc-*, *vox* VOICE¹ + *ferre* to bear]

vociferous /və'sif(ə)rəs/ *adj* marked by or given to vehement insistent outcry. ▶▶ **vociferously** *adv*, **vociferousness** *noun*.

vocoder /'vohkohdə/ *noun* **1** an electronic mechanism that reduces speech signals to low-frequency signals which can be transmitted over a communications system of limited bandwidth. **2** an electronic mechanism that separates speech signals into their component frequencies for transformation by a synthesizer into musical notes that retain the characteristics of speech. [contraction of *voice coder*]

vodka /'vodkə/ *noun* **1** a colourless neutral spirit made by distilling a mash, e.g. of rye or wheat. **2** a glass or measure of vodka. [Russian *vodka*, dimin. of *voda* water]

voe /voh/ *noun* an inlet or narrow bay of the Orkney or Shetland Islands. [Norwegian *våg* from Old Norse *vágr*]

vogue¹ /vohg/ *noun* **1** the prevailing, *esp* temporary, fashion: *Long skirts were in vogue then.* **2** popular acceptance or favour; popularity: *The book enjoyed a great vogue about 1960.* ➤➤ **voguish** *adj.* [early French *vogue* action of rowing, course, fashion, from Old Italian *voga*, from *vogare* to row]

vogue² *adj* fashionable; in vogue: *a vogue word.*

voice¹ /voys/ *noun* **1a** sound produced by animals and birds by forcing air from the lungs through the larynx or, in birds, the syrinx. **b** sound produced in this way by human beings, *esp* in speaking: *Miriam takes nine in voices* — Saki. **c** sound produced in this way by a particular human being: *I knew it was him. I recognized his voice.* **d** a person speaking: *I could hear voices in the street.* **e** a person's voice expressing or indicative of a given emotion, etc: *'Oh, do go away,' she said in a weary voice.* **f** a sound suggesting vocal utterance: *Through the mist she could hear the voice of a foghorn.* **g** something that seems to speak as a voice: *Conscience is the inner voice that warns us somebody may be looking* — H L Mencken. **2a** musical sound produced by the vocal cords and resonated by the cavities of the head and throat. **b** the power or ability to sing or produce musical tones: *She has a beautiful voice.* **c** the condition of the vocal organs for singing: *You were in good voice tonight.* **d** a singer: *a male-voice choir.* **e** any of the melodic parts in a vocal or instrumental piece of music. **3** the use of the voice, e.g. in singing or acting: *One of the things we had to do was study voice.* **4a** an instrument or medium of expression: *The party became the voice of the workers.* **b** the expressed wish or opinion: *He claimed to be following the voice of the people.* **c** right of expression; say: *I have no voice in this matter.* **5** a willingness to speak, express opinions, etc: *So you've found your voice at last, then.* **6** the ability to speak: *I had a sore throat last week and lost my voice for a couple of days.* **7** distinction of form or a particular system of inflections of a verb to indicate the relation of the subject of the verb to the action which the verb expresses. **8** in phonetics, breathing out of air with the vocal cords drawn close so as to vibrate audibly, e.g. in uttering consonant sounds such as /v/ or/z/ or any vowel. ✴ **give voice to** to express (feelings, etc). **with one voice** without dissent; unanimously. [Middle English via Old French *vois* from Latin *voc-, vox*]

voice² *verb trans* **1** to express (a feeling or opinion) in words; to utter (it). **2** to adjust (an organ pipe, etc) in manufacture, for producing the proper musical sounds. **3** to pronounce (a sound) with vibrations of the vocal cords. ➤➤ **voicer** *noun.*

voice box *noun* **1** = LARYNX. **2** an electronic device that allows a guitarist to modulate the sound produced by means of their voice.

voiced *adj* **1** (*used in combinations*) having a voice of the kind specified: *soft-voiced.* **2** in phonetics, uttered with vocal cord vibration. ➤➤ **voicedness** *noun.*

voice input *noun* the control of a computer system by means of the operator's voice.

voiceless *adj* **1** not having a voice. **2** unexpressed; unspoken. **3** silent; unspeaking. **4** in phonetics, not voiced. ➤➤ **voicelessly** *adv,* **voicelessness** *noun.*

voice mail *noun* a system for storing telephone messages in digitalized form so that they can be retrieved at a later time at the user's convenience.

voice-over *noun* **1** the voice of an unseen narrator in a film or television programme. **2** the voice of a visible character in a film or television programme indicating their thoughts.

voice part *noun* = VOICE¹ (2E).

voiceprint *noun* a graph of sound frequencies and amplitudes in the voice that is hypothetically distinctive for each person. [VOICE¹ + -*print* as in FINGERPRINT¹]

void¹ /voyd/ *adj* **1** containing nothing; unoccupied. **2** vain; useless. **3** of no legal effect. **4a** (+ of) devoid: *a nature void of all malice.* **b** having no members or examples. **c** said of a suit of cards: having no cards represented in a particular hand. **d** said of a card-player: having no cards of a particular suit. **5** *formal* having no holder or occupant; vacant: *a void bishopric.* ➤➤ **voidness** *noun.* [Middle English *voide* from Old French, ultimately from Latin *vacuus* empty, void]

void² *noun* **1a** empty space; vacuum. **b** an opening or gap. **2** a feeling of lack, want, or emptiness. **3** (+ in) a lack of cards of a particular suit: *a void in clubs.* **4** the act or an instance of voiding.

void³ *verb trans* **1a** to make (something) empty or vacant; to clear (it). **b** to remove (something) from a container, etc. **2** to nullify or annul (a contract, transaction, etc). **3** to discharge or emit (urine, excrement, etc). ➤ *verb intrans* to void something. ➤➤ **voidable** *adj,* **voidance** *noun,* **voider** *noun.* [Middle English *voiden* from early French *vuidier*, ultimately from Latin *vacuus* empty, void]

voile /voyl/ *noun* a fine soft sheer fabric used *esp* for women's summer clothing or curtains. [French *voile* veil, from Latin *vela:* see VEIL¹]

vol. *abbr* **1** volcano. **2** volume. **3** volunteer.

volant /'vohlənt/ *adj* **1** capable of flying or gliding. **2** in heraldry, having the wings extended as if in flight. [early French from Latin *volant-, volans*, present part. of *volare* to fly]

volar /'vohlə/ *adj* of the palm of the hand or the sole of the foot. [Latin *vola* palm of the hand, sole of the foot]

volatile¹ /'volətiel/ *adj* **1** capable of being readily vaporized at a relatively low temperature: *Alcohol is a volatile liquid.* **2a** dangerously unstable; explosive: *a volatile social situation.* **b** characterized by rapid change. **3a** said of a person: frivolously changeable; fickle. **b** light-hearted; lively. **4** lasting only a short time: *the volatile joys of love.* **5** said of a computer memory: not retaining stored data when the power supply is cut off. ➤➤ **volatility** /-'tiliti/ *noun.* [Middle English via Old French from Latin *volatilis* winged, flying, from *volare* to fly]

volatile² *noun* a volatile substance.

volatilize *or* **volatilise** /və'latiliez/ *verb intrans* to evaporate as vapour. ➤ *verb trans* to cause (something) to evaporate as vapour. ➤➤ **volatilizable** *adj,* **volatilization** /-'zaysh(ə)n/ *noun.*

vol-au-vent /'vol oh vonh/ *noun* a round case of puff pastry filled with meat, vegetables, etc in a thick sauce. [French *vol-au-vent*, literally 'flight in the wind']

volcanic /vol'kanik/ *adj* **1a** of or produced by a volcano. **b** characterized by volcanoes. **2** explosively violent; volatile: *volcanic emotions.* ➤➤ **volcanically** *adv.*

volcanic bomb *noun* a rounded mass of lava exploded from a volcano.

volcanic glass *noun* natural glass produced by the rapid cooling of molten lava.

volcanicity /volkə'nisiti/ *noun* volcanic power or action.

volcanism /'volkəniz(ə)m/ *noun* = VOLCANICITY.

volcano /vol'kaynoh/ *noun* (*pl* **volcanoes** *or* **volcanos**) **1** an outlet in a planet's crust from which molten or hot rock and steam issue, or a hill or mountain surrounding it. **2a** a dynamic or violently creative person. **b** a situation liable to become violent: *All civilization has from time to time become a thin crust over a volcano of revolution* — Havelock Ellis. [Italian *vulcano* from Latin *Volcanus, Vulcanus* Vulcan, Roman god of fire and metalworking]

volcanology /volkə'noləji/ *or* **vulcanology** /vulkə'noləji/ *noun* a branch of science that deals with volcanoes and volcanic phenomena. ➤➤ **volcanologic** /-'lojik/ *adj,* **volcanological** /-'lojikl/ *adj,* **volcanologist** *noun.*

vole /vohl/ *noun* any of numerous species of small plant-eating rodents usu with a stout body, blunt nose, and short ears: genus *Microtus* and other genera. [earlier *vole-mouse*, from Norwegian *vollmus* field mouse]

volitant /'volitənt/ *adj* flying, or able to fly. [Latin *volitant-, volitans*, present part. of *volitare*, frequentative of *volare* to fly]

volition /və'lish(ə)n/ *noun* **1** a free choice or decision, or the act of making such a choice or decision: *I went of my own volition.* **2** the power of choosing or determining; will. ➤➤ **volitional** *adj.* [French *volition* from medieval Latin *volition-, volitio*, from Latin *vol-, velle* to will, wish]

volitive /'volətiv/ *adj formal* of the will.

volk /folk/ *noun SAfr* the Afrikaner people. [Afrikaans *volk* people]

volley¹ /'voli/ *noun* (*pl* **volleys**) **1a** a flight of arrows, bullets, or other missiles. **b** simultaneous discharge of a number of missile weapons. **c** a burst or emission of many things at once or in rapid succession: *a volley of oaths.* **2a** the course or flight of a ball, shuttle, etc before striking the ground. **b** a return or succession of returns made by hitting a ball, shuttle, etc before it touches the ground:

compare GROUND STROKE. **c** a kick of the ball in football before it touches the ground. [early French *volee* flight, from *voler* to fly, from Latin *volare*]

volley[2] *verb* (**volleys, volleyed, volleying**) ➤ *verb trans* **1** to discharge (something) in a volley, or as if in a volley. **2a** to propel (an object, e.g. a ball, that has not yet hit the ground) with an implement or the hand or foot. **b** in tennis, to play a volley against (an opponent). **3** to say (something) vehemently. ➤ *verb intrans* **1** to be discharged in or as if in a volley. **2** to make a volley. ➤➤ **volleyer** *noun*.

volleyball *noun* a game between two teams of usu six players who volley a ball over a high net in the centre of a court using only their hands and arms.

volplane[1] /'volplayn/ *verb intrans* **1** to glide to earth in an aero plane with the engine shut down. **2** to glide to earth. [French *vol plané* gliding flight]

volplane[2] *noun* the act or an instance of volplaning; a glide without power.

vols *abbr* volumes.

volt[1] /vohlt, volt/ *noun* the SI unit of electrical potential difference and electromotive force equal to the difference of potential between two points in a conducting wire carrying a constant current of one ampere when the power dissipated between these two points is equal to one watt. [named after Alessandro *Volta* d.1827, Italian physicist, who invented the voltaic pile]

volt[2] /volt/ *noun* see VOLTE.

voltage /'vohltij, 'voltij/ *noun* an electric potential difference; electromotive force measured in volts.

voltaic /vol'tayik/ *adj* relating to the production of a direct current of electricity by chemical action, e.g. in a battery; = GALVANIC. [named after Alessandro *Volta*: see VOLT[1]]

voltaic cell *noun* = PRIMARY CELL.

voltaic couple *noun* two dissimilar metals immersed in an electrolyte, with a POTENTIAL DIFFERENCE (difference in voltage between two points) between them created by chemical action.

voltaic pile *noun* = PILE[1] (5).

voltameter /vohl'tamitə, vol-/ *noun* an apparatus for measuring the quantity of electricity passed through a conductor by the amount of electrolysis produced. ➤➤ **voltametric** /voltə'metrik/ *adj*. [VOLTAIC + -METER[2]]

voltammeter /vohl'tamitə/ *noun* an apparatus that can measure both POTENTIAL DIFFERENCE (difference in voltage between two points) in volts and electric current in amps. [VOLT[1] + AMMETER]

volt-ampere *noun* a unit of electrical power in a circuit using alternating current, equal to the power required for one amp of current to flow in a circuit driven by a potential difference of one volt: compare WATT.

volte *or* **volt** /volt/ *noun* **1** in fencing, a leaping movement to avoid a thrust. **2a** a movement in dressage in which a horse going sideways traces a complete circle. **b** a circle traced by a horse in this movement. [French *volte* from Italian *volta* turn, from *voltare* to turn, ultimately from Latin *volvere* to roll]

volte-face /,volt 'fas/ *noun* (*pl* **volte-face** *or* **volte-faces** /'fas(iz)/) **1** a sudden reversal of attitude or policy; = ABOUT-TURN[1] (2). **2** a turn so as to be facing in the opposite direction. [French *volte-face* from Italian *voltafaccia*, from *voltare* to turn + *faccia* face]

voltmeter /'vohltmeetə, 'volt-/ *noun* an instrument for measuring in volts the differences of potential between different points of an electrical circuit.

voluble /'volyoobl/ *adj* **1** talking a great deal. **2** spoken at great length. ➤➤ **volubility** /-'biliti/ *noun*, **volubleness** *noun*, **volubly** *adv*. [early French *voluble* variable, rotating, from Latin *volubilis*, from *volvere* to roll]

volume /'volyoom/ *noun* **1a** a book, *esp* one of a set or one forming one part of a large work: *Anybody can write a three-volume novel. It merely requires a complete ignorance of both life and literature* — Oscar Wilde. **b** a series of printed sheets bound typically in book form. **c** a series of issues of a periodical for a given period of time, *esp* one year. **d** formerly, a roll of parchment or papyrus. **2a** space occupied as measured in cubic units; cubic capacity. **b** the amount of a substance occupying a particular volume. **3a** an amount. **b** a bulk or large mass. **c** (*also in pl*) a considerable quantity; a great deal. **4a** the degree of loudness or the intensity of a sound. **b** a control on a radio, etc by means of which the loudness of the sound can be

adjusted. **5** mass in art or architecture, or the representation of it. ➤➤ **volumed** *adj*. [Middle English via French from Latin *volumen* roll, scroll, from *volvere* to roll: senses 2–5 from sense 1, via an absolute sense 'size or extent of a book']

volumetric /volyoo'metrik/ *adj* **1** of or involving the measurement of volume. **2** relating to volumetric analysis. ➤➤ **volumetrically** *adv*.

volumetric analysis *noun* **1** the determination of the amount of a substance present in a liquid by measuring the amount of the liquid required to react with a solution of known volume and concentration. **2** analysis of gases by volume.

voluminous /və'l(y)oohminəs/ *adj* **1** having or containing a large volume or quantity; very large. **b** said of a piece of clothing: very full, having a lot of material: *a voluminous ball gown*. **2a** consisting of, filling, or being enough to fill, a large volume or several volumes: *It took ten years to publish her voluminous correspondence*. **b** writing much or at great length. ➤➤ **voluminosity** /-'nositi/ *noun*, **voluminously** *adv*, **voluminousness** *noun*. [late Latin *voluminosus*, from Latin *volumin-, volumen*: see VOLUME]

voluntarism /'voləntəriz(ə)m/ *noun* **1a** the principle of relying on voluntary action rather than on compulsion. **b** the principle of relying on voluntary support for churches, schools, etc rather than relying on state aid. **2** a philosophical theory that conceives the human will to be the dominant or most basic element in experience or in the world. ➤➤ **voluntarist** *noun*, **voluntaristic** /-'ristik/ *adj*.

voluntary[1] /'volənt(ə)ri/ *adj* **1** proceeding from free choice or consent; done without compulsion and without payment; spontaneous. **2a** acting without compulsion and without payment: *voluntary workers*. **b** comprising or made up of people acting without payment: *voluntary organizations*. **c** provided or supported by voluntary action: *a voluntary hospital*. **3** intentional: *voluntary manslaughter*. **4** of, subject to, or controlled by the will: *voluntary behaviour; voluntary muscles*. **5** having power of free choice: *People are voluntary agents*. **6** in law, acting or done of one's own free will without legal obligation or regard to the financial consequences: *a voluntary legal transaction*. ➤➤ **voluntarily** /-t(ə)rəli, -'terəli/ *adv*, **voluntariness** *noun*. [Middle English from Latin *voluntarius*, from *voluntas* will, from *vol-, velle* to will, wish]

voluntary[2] *noun* (*pl* **voluntaries**) **1** an organ piece played before or after a religious service. **2** a musical piece, often improvised, coming before the main work.

voluntary arrangement *noun* a procedure, often carried out after a court order, by which an insolvent company makes arrangements with its creditors to resolve its financial difficulties.

voluntaryism *noun* = VOLUNTARISM (1). ➤➤ **voluntaryist** *noun*.

voluntary muscle *noun* muscle, e.g. most striated muscle, under voluntary control.

voluntary school *noun* in Britain, a school built by an independent, usu religious, body but maintained wholly or largely by a local education authority.

volunteer[1] /volən'tiə/ *noun* **1** a person who undertakes a service of their own free will, e.g.: **a** a person who does something without being under any legal or moral obligation to do so. **b** a person who enters into military service voluntarily. **2** (*used before a noun*) being a volunteer; consisting of or engaged in by volunteers: *a volunteer army; volunteer activities to help the homeless*. **3a** (*used before a noun*) said of a plant or crop: growing spontaneously without direct human control, cultivation, or supervision, *esp* from seeds dropped from a previous crop. **b** a volunteer plant or crop. [obsolete French *voluntaire*, from Latin *voluntarius*: see VOLUNTARY[1]]

volunteer[2] *verb trans* **1a** to offer (help, etc) voluntarily: *Is anyone going to volunteer their services?* **b** to say that (somebody else) will be willing to do something: *My wife volunteered me to be Santa Claus at a kids' Christmas party*. **2** to communicate (something) voluntarily: *Tell them if you have to, but don't volunteer the information*. ➤ *verb intrans* to offer oneself as a volunteer.

voluptuary[1] /və'luptyoo(ə)ri, -chəri/ *noun* (*pl* **voluptuaries**) a person whose chief interest is luxury and sensual pleasure: *the voluptuary who disguises sheer sensuality under a sentimental veil* — Mary Wollstonecraft. [Latin *voluptuarius*, from *voluptas* pleasure]

voluptuary[2] *adj* of or providing luxury and sensual pleasure.

voluptuous /və'luptyooəs, -chooəs/ *adj* **1** causing delight or pleasure to the senses; conducive to, occupied with, or arising from luxury and sensual gratification: *a voluptuous dance*. **2** suggestive of sensual pleasure: *a voluptuous mouth*. **3** sexually attractive, *esp* owing to shapeliness. ➤➤ **voluptuously** *adv*, **voluptuousness** *noun*. [Middle English from Latin *voluptuosus*, from *voluptas* pleasure]

volute[1] /vəˈl(y)ooht, volˈyoot/ *noun* **1** a form that is shaped like a spiral or curled over on itself like a scroll. **2** an ornament characteristic of classical architecture that is shaped like a roll of material or a scroll. **3a** any of various marine gastropod molluscs: family Volutidae. **b** the short-spined thick shell of any of these molluscs. ➤➤ **voluted** *adj*. [Latin *voluta*, fem past part. of *volvere* to roll]

volute[2] *adj* voluted; spiral.

volution /vəˈl(y)oohsh(ə)n/ *noun* **1** *literary* a rolling or revolving motion. **2** a spiral turn; a twist. [Latin *volution-, volutio*, from *volvere* to roll]

vomer /ˈvohmə/ *noun* a bone of the skull of most vertebrate animals that in human beings forms part of the division between the nostrils. [Latin *vomer* ploughshare; from its shape]

vomit[1] /ˈvomit/ *verb trans and intrans* (**vomited, vomiting**) **1** to disgorge (the contents of the stomach) through the mouth. **2** to eject (something) violently or abundantly. ➤➤ **vomiter** *noun*. [Middle English via French from Latin *vomitus*, past part. of *vomere* to vomit]

vomit[2] *noun* **1a** the act or an instance of vomiting. **b** vomited matter: *To write a diary … is like returning to one's own vomit* — Enoch Powell. **2** *archaic* an emetic.

vomitive /ˈvomitiv/ *adj* causing vomiting.

vomitorium /vomiˈtawri-əm/ *noun* (*pl* **vomitoria** /-ˈtawri-ə/) = VOMITORY[2] (2). [late Latin *vomitorium*, see VOMITORY[2]]

vomitory[1] /ˈvomit(ə)ri/ *adj* causing vomiting.

vomitory[2] *noun* (*pl* **vomitories**) **1** something that causes vomiting. **2** an entrance in the middle of a bank of seats in an ancient Roman amphitheatre, stadium, etc. [late Latin *vomitorium*, from Latin *vomitus*, past part. of *vomere* to vomit; from its disgorging the spectators]

voodoo[1] /ˈvoohdooh/ *noun* (*pl* **voodoos**) **1** a set of beliefs and practices, mainly of W African origin, practised chiefly in Haiti and characterized by communication by trance with deities. **2a** a person who practises voodoo; a person who is skilled in voodoo spells and necromancy. **b** a voodoo spell or charm. ➤➤ **voodooism** *noun*, **voodooist** *noun*. [Louisiana French *voudou* from Kwa *vodu* tutelary deity, demon]

voodoo[2] *verb trans* (**voodoos, voodooed, voodooing**) to bewitch (somebody) by or as if by means of voodoo.

Voortrekker /ˈfawtrekə, ˈfooə-/ *noun* **1** a S African pioneer of Dutch descent who moved north from the Cape of Good Hope in 1838 to evade British rule. **2** a member of an Afrikaner youth movement. [Afrikaans *Voortrekker*, from *voor* before, in front + *trekker* emigrant, from *trek* to pull, move, emigrate, from Dutch]

voracious /vəˈrayshəs/ *adj* **1** having a huge appetite; ravenous. **2** excessively eager; insatiable: *a voracious reader*. ➤➤ **voraciously** *adv*, **voraciousness** *noun*, **voracity** /vəˈrasiti/ *noun*. [Latin *vorac-, vorax*, from *vorare* to devour]

-vore *comb. form* forming nouns, with the meaning: an individual eating or feeding on: *carnivore*. [Latin *-vorus*: see -VOROUS]

-vorous *comb. form* forming adjectives, with the meaning: eating; feeding on: *herbivorous*. [Latin *-vorus*, from *vorare* to devour]

vortex /ˈvawteks/ *noun* (*pl* **vortices** /ˈvawtiseez/ *or* **vortexes**) **1a** a mass of whirling water, air, etc that tends to form a cavity or vacuum in the centre of the circle, into which material is drawn, *esp* a whirlpool or whirlwind. **b** a region within a body of fluid in which the fluid is rotating. **2** something that resembles a whirlpool in violent activity or in engulfing or overwhelming. ➤➤ **vortical** /ˈvawtikl/ *adj*, **vorticity** /vawˈtisiti/ *noun*. [Latin *vertex, vortex* whirlpool]

vorticella /vawtiˈselə/ *noun* (*pl* **vorticellas** *or* **vorticellae** /-lee/) a freshwater bell-shaped single-celled organism that has a ring of cilia (small hairlike structures; see CILIUM) round the mouth and a long elastic stalk by which it is attached to rocks: genus *Vorticella*. [scientific Latin, from Latin *vortic-, vortex* whirlpool]

vortices /ˈvawtiseez/ *noun* pl of VORTEX.

vorticism /ˈvawtisiz(ə)m/ *noun* an English art movement active from about 1912 and related to cubism and futurism. ➤➤ **vorticist** *noun and adj*. [Latin *vortic-, vortex* whirlpool; from the characteristic use of forms arranged in arcs or whirls around a central point]

vostro account /ˈvostroh/ *noun* a bank account that a foreign bank holds with a British bank, usu in sterling: compare NOSTRO ACCOUNT. [Italian *vostro* your]

votary /ˈvohtəri/ *noun* (*pl* **votaries**) **1** a staunch admirer, worshipper, or advocate; a devotee. **2** a person, e.g. a monk or nun, who has taken vows to dedicate themselves to religion. ➤➤ **votarist** *noun*. [Latin *votum*: see VOW[1]]

vote[1] /voht/ *noun* **1a** the usu formal act or process of expressing one's opinion or will in response to a proposed decision, e.g. by raising a hand or marking a special card or paper, *esp* one given as an indication of approval or disapproval of a proposal, motion, or candidate for election: *Let's put it to a vote*. **b** a means of voting, such as a ballot. **c** a method of voting: *Voting will be by the single transferable vote system*. **d** an expression of opinion or preference that resembles a vote. **2a** an individual person's or group's response in such a process: *There were no votes against the proposal*. **b** the way in which such a response is indicated, e.g. a piece of paper: *Please put your votes in this box*. **c** the total number of such expressions of opinion made known at a single time, e.g. at an election. **3** the collective opinion or verdict of a body of people expressed by voting. **4** (*usu* **the vote**) the right to cast a vote, *esp* the right of voting in parliamentary and other elections. **5** a group of voters with some common and identifying characteristics: *There may be some difficulty getting the Labour vote out to the polls*. **6** *informal* support for a proposal or plan: *Going to the pub certainly gets my vote*. **7** *chiefly Brit*. **a** a proposition to be voted on, *esp* a legislative money item. **b** a sum of money voted for a special use. ✳ **vote of confidence/no confidence** a vote expressing continuing support for, or loss of faith in, a leader or controlling body. ➤➤ **voteless** *adj*. [Middle English (Scots) from Latin *votum*: see VOW[1]]

vote[2] *verb intrans* **1a** (*often* + for/against) to express one's views by means of a vote, e.g. by raising one's hand or marking a special card or paper: *I never vote for anyone. I always vote against* — W C Fields. **b** to exercise a political franchise: *old enough to vote*. **c** (*often* + for) to give one's support to a political party, candidate, etc in an election: *I wouldn't vote for him if you paid me!; I voted Green last time*. **2** to express an opinion: *People are voting with their feet and looking for new jobs in other companies*. ➤➤ *verb trans* **1a** to choose, endorse, or defeat (somebody) by vote; to cause something to happen to (them) by voting for it: *After the financial scandal broke, he was voted out of office*. **b** to authorize or award (something) by vote: *The first thing they did was vote themselves a pay increase*. **2** to adjudge or declare (somebody or something) to be something by general agreement: *The concert was voted a flop*. **3** *informal* to offer (something) as a suggestion; to propose (it): *I vote we all go home*. ➤➤ **votable** *adj*, **voteable** *adj*.

vote down *verb trans* to defeat (a proposal or a person making a proposal) by voting against them.

voter *noun* a person who votes or has the legal right to vote, *esp* in a political election.

voting machine *noun* a mechanical device for recording votes.

votive /ˈvohtiv/ *adj* **1** offered or performed in fulfilment of a vow and often in gratitude or devotion. **2** consisting of or expressing a religious vow, wish, or desire. ➤➤ **votively** *adv*, **votiveness** *noun*. [Latin *votivus*, from *votum*: see VOW[1]]

votive mass *noun* in the Roman Catholic Church, a mass celebrated for a special intention, e.g. for a wedding or funeral, in place of the mass of the day.

vouch /vowch/ *verb intrans* **1** (+ for) to give or act as a guarantee for somebody or something. **2** (+ for) to supply supporting evidence or personal assurance for somebody or something. ➤➤ *verb trans* **1** to testify the truth of (something); to substantiate (it). **2** to verify (a business transaction, etc) by examining documentary evidence. [Middle English *vochen, vouchen* to assert, call to witness, via French *vocher* from Latin *vocare* to call, summon]

voucher *noun* **1a** a documentary record of a business transaction. **b** a written certificate or authorization. **2** *Brit* a ticket that can be exchanged for specific goods or services. **3** a person who vouches. [early French *vocher, voucher*: see VOUCH]

vouchsafe /vowchˈsayf/ *verb trans* **1** to grant (something) as a special privilege or in a gracious or condescending manner. **2** to condescend or deign (to do something). ➤➤ **vouchsafement** *noun*. [orig in the construction *to vouch something safe on somebody* 'to vouch for the certain granting of something to somebody']

voussoir /vooh'swah/ *noun* in architecture, any of the wedge-shaped blocks forming an arch or vault. [French, ultimately from *volsus*, past part. of Latin *volvere* to roll]

vow[1] /vow/ *noun* a solemn and often religiously binding promise or assertion; *specif* one by which somebody binds themselves to an act, service, or condition. [Middle English *vowe* via Old French from Latin *votum* vow, wish, neuter past part. of *vovēre* to vow]

vow[2] *verb trans* **1** to promise (something) solemnly; to swear (it). **2** *archaic* to dedicate or consecrate (something) by a vow. **3** to resolve to bring (something) about: *She vowed revenge.* ➤ *verb intrans* to make a vow. ➤➤ **vower** *noun.*

vow[3] *verb trans archaic* to avow or declare (something). [Middle English *vowen*, short for *avowen*: see AVOW]

vowel /vowl/ *noun* **1** any of a class of speech sounds, e.g. /ee/ or /i/, characterized by lack of closure in the breath channel or lack of audible friction. **2** a letter or character representing such a sound. [Middle English via French *vouel* from Latin *vocalis*: see VOCAL[1]]

vowel gradation *noun* systematic vowel variation in the forms of a root word that conveys grammatical information, e.g. *sing, sang, sung*; = ABLAUT.

vowel harmony *noun* a restriction in certain languages, e.g. Turkish, as to the permissible combinations of vowels in the successive syllables of a word, e.g. all the vowels of a word must be either front vowels or back vowels.

vowelize *or* **vowelise** /'vowaliez/ *verb trans* = VOCALIZE (4).

vowel mutation *noun* change of a vowel sound caused by a following vowel sound; = UMLAUT.

vowel point *noun* a mark that is placed below or above a consonant in some languages, e.g. Hebrew, and represents the vowel sound that precedes or follows the consonant.

vow of stability *noun* = STABILITY (6).

vox angelica /voks an'jelika/ *noun* any of various organ stops having a delicate refined trembling tone. [scientific Latin *vox angelica*, literally 'angelic voice']

vox humana /hyooh'mahna/ *noun* an organ stop of reed pipes that imitates the human voice. [scientific Latin *vox humana*, literally 'human voice']

vox pop /'pop/ *noun informal* **1** = VOX POPULI. **2** an interview with one or more members of the public, e.g. in the street, to determine public opinion.

vox populi /'popyoolie, -lee/ *noun* the opinion of the general public. [Latin *vox populi* voice of the people]

voyage[1] /'voyij/ *noun* a considerable course or period of travelling by other than land routes; a journey, *esp* by sea or air. [Middle English from Old French *voiage* from Latin *viaticum* provisions for a journey, later 'journey', neuter of *viaticus* of a journey, from *via* way]

voyage[2] *verb intrans* to make a voyage. ➤ *verb trans* to make a voyage over (the sea, etc): *We voyaged the Seven Seas.* ➤➤ **voyager** *noun.* [French *voyager* from Old French *voiage*: see VOYAGE[1]]

voyage charter *noun* the chartering of a ship or aircraft for a specified voyage or number of voyages: compare TIME CHARTER.

voyage policy *noun* a marine insurance policy that covers only a specified voyage: compare TIME POLICY.

voyageur /vwah·yah'zhuh, 'voyizha/ *noun* in NW Canada, formerly, a guide or boatman employed, *esp* by a fur company, to take goods and passengers to and from remote trading stations. [Canadian French from French *voyageur* traveller, from *voyager*: see VOYAGE[2]]

voyeur /vwah'yuh/ *noun* **1** a person who obtains sexual gratification by looking at other people's sexual organs, sexual acts, etc. **2** a prying observer who gets excitement from witnessing other people's suffering or distress: *There are some disasters that are so ghastly that even the voyeur averts the eyes* — Guardian. ➤➤ **voyeurism** /'vwahyariz(a)m/ *noun,* **voyeuristic** /-'ristik/ *adj,* **voyeuristically** /-'ristikli/ *adv.* [French *voyeur*, literally 'one who sees', from *voir* to see, from Latin *vidēre*]

VP *abbr* **1** verb phrase. **2** vice-president.

VPL *abbr* visible panty line.

VPRC *abbr* Video Packaging Review Committee.

VR *abbr* **1** Queen Victoria. **2** variant reading. **3** virtual reality. **4** Volunteer Reserve. [(sense 1) Latin *Victoria Regina*]

vroom /vroom, vroohm/ *noun informal* a noise of an engine revving up or of a high-speed vehicle. [imitative]

vrou /froh/ *noun SAfr* an Afrikaner woman. [Afrikaans *vrou* from Dutch *vrouw* from early Dutch *vrouwe* lady, woman]

VS *abbr* veterinary surgeon.

vs. *abbr* **1** verse. **2** versus.

v.s. *abbr* see above. [Latin *vide supra*]

V sign *noun* a gesture made by raising the index and middle fingers in a V. With the palm outward it signifies victory; with the palm inward it signifies insult or contempt.

VSO *abbr* **1** Very Special Old (brandy). **2** Voluntary Service Overseas.

VSOP *abbr* Very Special Old Pale (brandy).

VT *abbr* Vermont (US postal abbreviation).

Vt *abbr* Vermont.

VTOL /'veetol/ *abbr* vertical takeoff and landing.

VTR *abbr* videotape recorder.

V-type engine *noun* an internal-combustion engine with two cylinder blocks which form a V: compare V8, V6.

vug *or* **vugg** *or* **vugh** /vug/ *noun* a small cavity in an ore seam or in rock, usu lined with crystals. ➤➤ **vuggy** *adj.* [Cornish *vooga* underground chamber, from Latin *fovea* small pit]

vulcanian /vul'kayni·an/ *adj* **1** volcanic. **2** of a highly explosive volcanic eruption in which blocks of extremely viscous or already solidified lava are thrown out, together with a usu large cloud of dust, ash, and gas.

vulcanicity /vulka'nisiti/ *noun* = VOLCANICITY.

vulcanise /'vulkaniez/ *verb trans* see VULCANIZE.

vulcanism /'vulkaniz(a)m/ *noun* = VOLCANICITY.

vulcanite /'vulkaniet/ *noun* a hard vulcanized rubber. Also called EBONITE.

vulcanize *or* **vulcanise** /'vulkaniez/ *verb trans* to treat (rubber or similar material) chemically in order to give it elasticity, strength, stability, etc. ➤➤ **vulcanization** /-'zaysh(a)n/ *noun.* [Latin *Vulcanus* Vulcan, Roman god of fire; from the high temperature used in the process]

vulcanology /vulka'nolaji/ *noun* see VOLCANOLOGY.

Vulg. *abbr* Vulgate.

vulg. *abbr* **1** vulgar. **2** vulgarly.

vulgar /'vulga/ *adj* **1a** lacking in cultivation, breeding, or taste; coarse. **b** ostentatious or excessive in expenditure or display; pretentious. **2** lewdly or profanely indecent; obscene. **3a** generally current; public: *vulgar opinion.* **b** generally used, applied, or accepted. **c** *dated* of or being the common people; plebeian. ➤➤ **vulgarity** /vul'gariti/ *noun,* **vulgarly** *adv.* [Middle English from Latin *vulgaris* of the mob, vulgar, from *volgus, vulgus* mob, common people]

vulgar fraction *noun Brit* a fraction in which both the denominator and numerator are explicitly present and are separated by a horizontal or slanted line.

vulgarian /vul'geari·an/ *noun* a vulgar person, *esp* one who is rich.

vulgarise *verb trans* see VULGARIZE.

vulgarism *noun* **1** a word or expression originated or used chiefly by illiterate people. **2** vulgarity.

vulgarize *or* **vulgarise** *verb trans* **1** to make (something) vulgar, coarse, or less refined. **2** to present or diffuse (information) in a way that can be generally understood by the average person; to popularize (it). ➤➤ **vulgarization** /-'zaysh(a)n/ *noun,* **vulgarizer** *noun.*

Vulgar Latin *noun* the informal Latin of ancient Rome, the source of the Romance languages.

vulgate /'vulgayt, 'vulgat/ *noun* **1** (**the Vulgate**) the Latin version of the Bible authorized and used by the Roman Catholic Church. **2** *formal* a commonly accepted text or reading. [medieval Latin *vulgata*, from late Latin *vulgata editio* edition in general circulation]

vulnerable /'vuln(a)rabl/ *adj* **1** capable of being physically or mentally hurt. **2** open to criticism or censure. **3** liable to temptation. **4** (*often* + to) open to attack or damage; assailable. **5** in contract bridge, liable to increased penalties but entitled to increased bonuses after winning a game. ➤➤ **vulnerability** /-'biliti/

noun, **vulnerableness** *noun,* **vulnerably** *adv.* [late Latin *vulnerabilis* from Latin *vulnerare* to wound, from *vulner-, vulnus* wound]

vulnerary[1] /'vulnərəri/ *adj* used for or useful in healing wounds. [Latin *vulnerarius,* from *vulner-, vulnus* wound]

vulnerary[2] *noun* (*pl* **vulneraries**) an ointment or other remedy used for treating wounds.

vulpine /'vulpien/ *adj* **1** of or resembling a fox. **2** foxy; crafty. [Latin *vulpinus* from *vulpes* fox]

vulture /'vulchə/ *noun* **1** any of several species of large bald-headed birds of prey that are related to the hawks, eagles, and falcons and feed on carrion: families Cathartidae and Accipitridae. **2** a rapacious or predatory person. ➤➤ **vulturine** /-rien/ *adj,* **vulturous** /-rəs/ *adj.* [Middle English via Anglo-French from Latin *vulturius*]

vulva /'vulvə/ *noun* (*pl* **vulvas** *or* **vulvae** /'vulvee/) the external parts of the female genital organs, or the opening between them. ➤➤ **vulval** *adj,* **vulvar** *adj.* [scientific Latin from Latin *volva, vulva* integument, womb]

vulvitis /vul'vietəs/ *noun* inflammation of the vulva.

vv *abbr* **1** verses. **2** vice versa. **3** volumes.

vying /'vieing/ *verb* present part. of VIE.

W¹ *or* **w** *noun* (*pl* **W's** *or* **Ws** *or* **w's**) **1a** the 23rd letter of the English alphabet. **b** a written character or design denoting this letter. **c** the sound represented by this letter, one of the English consonants. **2** an item designated as W, *esp* the 23rd in a series.

W² *abbr* **1** watt(s). **2** West. **3** Western. **4** West (London postcode). **5** in cricket, wicket(s). **6** on clothing, women's, used to denote a size suitable for an average woman.

W³ *abbr* the chemical symbol for tungsten. [see WOLFRAM]

w *abbr* **1** week. **2** weight. **3** in cricket, wicket. **4** wide. **5** width. **6** wife. **7** with.

WA *abbr* **1** Washington (US postal abbreviation). **2** Western Australia.

WAAC *abbr Brit* Women's Army Auxiliary Corps, the women's component of the British army between 1914 and 1918.

Waac /wak/ *noun* formerly, a member of the Women's Army Auxiliary Corps. [from WAAC]

WAAF *abbr Brit* Women's Auxiliary Air Force, the women's component of the RAF from 1942 to 1948.

Waaf /waf/ *noun* formerly, a member of the Women's Auxiliary Air Force. [from WAAF]

WAC *abbr NAmer* Women's Army Corps, the women's component of the US army between 1942 and 1978.

Wac /wak/ *noun* formerly, a member of the Women's Army Corps.

wack /wak/ *noun Brit, dialect, informal* used to address somebody, *esp* a man. [perhaps from *whacker* heavy blow, something large, from WHACK¹ + -ER²]

wacke /ˈwakə/ *noun* any of various soft rocks that are forms of sandstone. [German *Wacke* rock, gravel, from Old High German *wacko* pebble]

wacked /wakt/ *adj* see WHACKED.

wacko¹ *or* **whacko** /ˈwakoh/ *adj chiefly NAmer, informal* mad or eccentric. [back-formation from WACKY]

wacko² *or* **whacko** *noun* (*pl* **wackos** *or* **wackoes** *or* **whackos** *or* **whackoes**) *chiefly NAmer, informal* somebody who is crazy or eccentric.

wacky *or* **whacky** /ˈwaki/ *adj* (**wackier** *or* **whackier**, **wackiest** *or* **whackiest**) *informal* absurdly or amusingly eccentric or irrational; crazy. ▶▶ **wackily** *adv*, **wackiness** *noun*. [orig dialect; prob from WHACK¹]

wad¹ /wod/ *noun* **1** a soft mass of a loose fibrous material used in various ways, e.g. to stop an aperture, pad a garment, or hold grease round an axle. **2** a soft plug used to retain a powder charge or to fill the gap between the projectile and the bore of a cannon or gun that is loaded at the discharging end. **3** a felt, paper, or plastic disc that separates the powder from the shot in a shotgun cartridge. **4**

NAmer a small mass of a chewing substance: *a wad of gum.* **5** a roll of paper, *esp* paper money. **6** *informal* a large supply of money. **7** *informal* (*also in pl*) a considerable amount: *They were getting wads of publicity.* [origin unknown]

wad² *verb trans* (**wadded, wadding**) **1** to form (material) into a wad or wadding. **2** to stuff, pad, or line (something) with some soft substance. **3** to roll or crush (something) tightly: *He wadded his shirt up into a ball.* **4a** to insert a wad into (a gun). **b** to hold (e.g. a bullet) in by a wad.

wadding *noun* stuffing or padding in the form of a soft mass or sheet of short loose fibres.

waddle¹ /ˈwodl/ *verb intrans* to walk with short steps, swinging the body from side to side. ▶▶ **waddler** *noun*. [frequentative of WADE¹]

waddle² *noun* an awkward clumsy swaying gait.

waddy /ˈwodi/ *noun* (*pl* **waddies**) *Aus* a club or stick, *esp* one used as a weapon by Australian Aboriginals. [Dharuk *wadi* tree, stick]

wade¹ /wayd/ *verb intrans* **1** to walk through a medium, e.g. water, that offers more resistance than air. **2** to proceed with difficulty or effort: *She was wading through a dull book.* **3** *informal* (+ in/into) to attack with determination or vigour: *He waded into the task.* ▶ *verb trans* to cross (a stream, etc) by walking through the water. ▶▶ **wadable** *adj*, **wadeable** *adj*. [Old English *wadan*]

wade² *noun* the act or an instance of wading.

wader *noun* **1** (*usu in pl*) a high waterproof boot used for wading. **2** any of numerous long-legged birds, e.g. sandpipers and snipes, that wade in water in search of food.

wadge /woj/ *noun Brit, informal* a thick bundle; a wad. [alteration of WEDGE¹]

wadi *or* **wady** /ˈwodi/ *noun* (*pl* **wadis** *or* **wadies**) the bed of a stream in regions of SW Asia and N Africa that is dry except during the rainy season. [Arabic *wādiy*]

WAF *abbr NAmer* Women in the Air Force, formerly a separate women's component of the US Air Force.

Waf /waf/ *noun NAmer* a member of the Women in the Air Force.

wafer /ˈwayfə/ *noun* **1a** a thin crisp biscuit. **b** a biscuit consisting of layers of wafers sometimes sandwiched with a filling. **2** a round thin piece of unleavened bread used in the Eucharist. **3** an adhesive disc of dried paste used, *esp* formerly, as a seal. **4** a thin disc or ring resembling a wafer and used in various ways, e.g. for a valve or diaphragm. **5** a thin slice of silicon or other material that can be cut into many separate sections for the production of integrated circuits, microprocessors, etc. ▶▶ **wafery** *adj*. [Middle English from Anglo-French *waufre*, from Old French *gaufre*: see GOFFER¹]

waffle¹ /ˈwofl/ *noun* a cake of batter that is baked in a waffle iron and has a crisp dimpled surface. [early Dutch *wafel*]

waffle² *verb intrans chiefly Brit, informal* to talk or write foolishly, inconsequentially, and usu at length; to blather. ➤➤ **waffler** *noun*. [frequentative of obsolete *waff* to yelp, of imitative origin]

waffle³ *noun chiefly Brit, informal* empty or pretentious words. ➤➤ **waffly** *adj.*

waffle iron *noun* a cooking utensil with two hinged metal parts that shut on each other and impress surface projections on the waffle being cooked.

waft¹ /woft/ *verb intrans* to be conveyed lightly by the impulse of wind or waves, or as if by wind or waves. ➤ *verb trans* to convey (something) in this way.

Word history
from obsolete *wafter* ship guarding a convoy, from early Dutch or early Low German *wachter*, from *wachten* to watch, guard. The earliest sense was 'to escort a convoy'; the current sense arose in the 17th cent. from the 16th-cent. senses 'to sail' and 'to convey by water'.

waft² *noun* **1** a slight breeze; a puff. **2** something, e.g. a smell, that is wafted; a whiff. **3** formerly, a pennant or flag flown on a ship and used to signal or to show wind direction.

WAG *abbr* West Africa Gambia (international vehicle registration for Gambia).

wag¹ /wag/ *verb* (**wagged, wagging**) ➤ *verb intrans* **1** to move to and fro, *esp* with quick jerky motions. **2** said of the tongue: to move in chatter or gossip. ➤ *verb trans* **1** to cause (something) to swing to and fro, *esp* with quick jerky motions. **2** (*often* + at) to nod (the head) in disagreement, reproof, etc. **3** (*often* + at) to shake (a finger) in mock or mild reproof. **4** to move (e.g. the tongue) animatedly in conversation. [Middle English *waggen*, of Germanic origin]

wag² *noun* the act or an instance of wagging; a shake.

wag³ *noun informal* a wit or joker. [prob short for obsolete *waghalter* gallows bird, from WAG¹ + HALTER¹]

wage¹ /wayj/ *noun* **1** (*usu in pl*) a payment for work or services, *esp* of a manual kind, usu according to contract and on an hourly, daily, weekly, or piecework basis: compare SALARY¹. **2** (*in pl*) in economics, the share of the national product attributable to labour as a factor of production. **3** (*in pl, but treated as sing. or pl*) recompense or reward: *The wages of sin is death* — Bible. ➤➤ **waged** *adj*, **wageless** *adj*. [Middle English, in the senses 'pledge', 'wage', from Anglo-French and Old Northern French *wage*, of Germanic origin]

wage² *verb trans* to engage in or carry on (a war, conflict, etc). [Middle English *wagen* to pledge, give as security, from Anglo-French and Old Northern French *wagier* to pledge, of Germanic origin]

wage-earner *noun* **1** somebody who earns a wage by working. **2** somebody who brings in money to a household by working.

wager¹ /wayjə/ *noun* **1** something, e.g. a sum of money, risked on an uncertain event; a stake. **2** something on which bets are laid; the act or an instance of gambling or betting: *He did the stunt as a wager*. [Middle English, in the senses 'pledge', 'bet', from Anglo-French *wageure* from Old Northern French *wagier*: see WAGE²]

wager² *verb* (**wagered, wagering**) ➤ *verb trans* **1** (*often* + on) to risk or venture (e.g. a sum of money) on an uncertain final outcome; *specif* to lay (it) as a bet: *He wagered £5 on a horse*. **2** to state (something) with assurance; to bet (it): *I'll wager they won't come*. ➤ *verb intrans* to make a bet. ➤➤ **wagerer** *noun*.

wager of battle *noun* trial by combat, formerly used to determine guilt or innocence.

wager of law *noun* in law, formerly, the joint swearing by several witnesses to a defendant's innocence.

wage slave *noun informal* somebody dependent on wages or a salary for his or her livelihood. ➤➤ **wage slavery** *noun*.

waggish *adj informal* befitting or characteristic of a wag; humorous: *a waggish disposition*. ➤➤ **waggishly** *adv*, **waggishness** *noun*.

waggle¹ /'wagl/ *verb intrans* to reel, sway, or move repeatedly from side to side; to wag or wiggle. ➤ *verb trans* to cause (something) to move repeatedly one way and the other; to wag (it). ➤➤ **waggly** *adj*. [frequentative of WAG¹]

waggle² *noun* **1** the act or an instance of waggling. **2** in golf, a movement of the head of a club back and forth over the ball before the swing.

waggon /'wagən/ *noun chiefly Brit* see WAGON.

waggoner *noun chiefly Brit* see WAGONER.

waggonette /wagə'net/ *noun chiefly Brit* see WAGONETTE.

Wagnerian¹ /vahg'niəri·ən/ *adj* characteristic of the music of Richard Wagner (d.1883), *esp* in being on a grandiose scale or exhibiting dramatic intensity.

Wagnerian² *noun* an admirer of the musical theories and style of Richard Wagner.

Wagner tuba /'vahgnə/ *noun* a brass instrument of mid to low range that somewhat resembles the true tuba but is more closely related to the French horn, having the horn's funnel-shaped mouthpiece and smooth tone. [named after Richard *Wagner*: see WAGNERIAN¹; the instrument was first used in Wagner's *Der Ring des Nibelungen*]

wagon *or* **waggon** /'wagən/ *noun* **1** a usu four-wheeled vehicle for transporting bulky or heavy loads, often having a removable canopy, and drawn orig by animals. **2** a low cart with a long handle, used as a child's toy. **3** *chiefly NAmer* a cart with wheels, used as a food stall. **4** *Brit* a railway goods vehicle. **5** *Brit, informal* a lorry. ✳ **off the wagon** *informal* no longer abstaining from alcoholic drink. **on the wagon** *informal* abstaining from alcoholic drink. ➤➤ **wagonload** *noun*. [early Dutch *wagen*]

wagoner *or* **waggoner** *noun* the driver of a wagon.

wagonette *or* **waggonette** /wagə'net/ *noun* a light horse-drawn wagon with two inward-facing seats along the sides behind a forward-facing front seat.

wagon-lit /,vagonh 'lee/ *noun* (*pl* **wagons-lits** /,vagonh 'lee/) a sleeping car on a continental train. [French *wagon-lit*, from *wagon* railway carriage + *lit* bed]

wagon train *noun* a convoy of wagons, e.g. carrying a group of settlers, travelling overland in N America.

wagon vault *noun* = BARREL VAULT.

wagtail *noun* any of several species of birds with trim slender bodies and very long tails that they habitually jerk up and down: family Motacillidae.

Wahhabi *or* **Wahabi** /wə'hahbi/ *noun* (*pl* **Wahhabis** *or* **Wahabis**) a member of a strict Muslim sect founded in Arabia in the 18th cent. by Muhammad ibn Abd al-Wahhab and revived by ibn-Saud in the 20th cent. ➤➤ **Wahhabism** *noun*. [Arabic *wahhābīy*, named after Muḥammad ibn Abd al-*Wahhāb* d.1792, Arabian religious reformer]

wahine /wah'heeni/ *noun* a Maori or Polynesian woman. [Maori and Hawaiian *wahine*]

wahoo¹ /wah'hooh/ *noun* (*pl* **wahoos**) a large tropical fish of the mackerel family: *Acanthocybium solanderi*. [origin unknown]

wahoo² *noun* (*pl* **wahoos**) **1** either of two species of N American shrubs or small shrubby trees of the spindle tree family with purple capsules that split open to expose the scarlet-covered seeds: genus *Euonymus*. **2a** a N American elm tree: *Ulmus alata*. **b** any of several similar trees. [(sense 1) Dakota *wāhu* arrow-wood; (sense 2) possibly from Creek *ahá·hura* walnut]

wahoo³ *interj NAmer* used to express exuberance or enthusiasm or to attract attention.

wah-wah *or* **wa-wa** /'wah wah/ *noun* **1** in music, a fluctuating muted effect produced by an electronic device connected to an amplifier and operated by a foot pedal; used with an electric guitar. **2** a pedal used to produce such an effect. **3** a similar sound made by a brass instrument, which is produced by alternately covering and uncovering the bell.

waif /wayf/ *noun* **1a** a stray helpless person or animal, *esp* a homeless child. **b** a young woman of appealingly childlike appearance and slenderness, *esp* a fashion model: *the sought-after waifs of the catwalk*. **2** a piece of property found but unclaimed. ➤➤ **waifish** *adj*, **waiflike** *adj*. [Middle English from Old Northern French *waif* lost, unclaimed, prob of Scandinavian origin]

wail¹ /wayl/ *verb intrans* **1** to make a sound suggestive of a mournful cry. **2** *literary* to express sorrow by uttering mournful cries; to lament. ➤ *verb trans archaic* to bewail (something). ➤➤ **wailer** *noun*, **wailing** *noun*. [Middle English *wailen*, of Scandinavian origin]

wail² *noun* **1** a usu loud prolonged high-pitched cry expressing grief or pain. **2** a sound suggestive of wailing: *the wail of an air-raid siren*.

wailful /'waylf(ə)l/ *adj literary* sorrowful or mournful.

wain /wayn/ *noun archaic* a usu large and heavy wagon for farm use. [Old English *wægn*]

wainscot[1] /'waynskət, 'waynskot/ *noun* **1** a usu panelled wooden lining of an interior wall or lower part of a wall: *The smoking-room ... was ... papered from top to bottom with an imitation of oak wainscot* — Stevenson. **2** *Brit* a fine grade of oak formerly imported for woodwork. [Middle English from early Dutch *wagenschot*, literally 'wagon-boarding']

wainscot[2] *verb trans* (**wainscoted** *or* **wainscotted, wainscoting** *or* **wainscotting**) to line (a wall or room) with boards or panelling.

wainscoting *or* **wainscotting** /'waynskəting, 'waynskoting/ *noun* a wainscot, or material used for a wainscot.

wainwright /'waynriet/ *noun* somebody who makes and repairs wagons.

waist /wayst/ *noun* **1a** the part of the body between the chest and hips, in the greatly constricted part of the abdomen of a wasp, fly, etc. **2** the part of a garment covering the body at the waist or waistline. **3** the part of something corresponding to or resembling the human waist. **4a** the middle part of a sailing ship between foremast and mainmast. **b** the middle section of the fuselage of an aircraft. ➤➤ **waistless** *adj*. [Middle English *wast*, of Germanic origin; related to Old English *weaxan* to grow, WAX[3]]

waistband *noun* a band, e.g. on trousers or a skirt, fitting round the waist.

waistcoat *noun Brit* a sleeveless upper garment that fastens down the centre front and usu has a V-neck, *esp* such a garment worn under a jacket as part of a man's suit. ➤➤ **waistcoated** *adj*.

waisted *adj* (*usu used in combinations*) having a waist, *esp* a specified kind: *high-waisted*.

waistline *noun* **1a** an imaginary line encircling the narrowest part of the waist. **b** the part of a garment corresponding to this line or to the place where fashion dictates this should be. **2** the body circumference at the waist.

wait[1] /wayt/ *verb intrans* **1** to remain stationary in readiness or expectation: *We waited for the train.* **2** to pause for somebody to catch up. **3** to look forward expectantly: *She was just waiting to see her rival lose.* **4** to hold back expectantly: *You'll have to wait till Thursday.* **5** to serve at meals; to act as a waiter. **6** to be ready and available: *His slippers were waiting by the bed.* **7** to remain temporarily neglected or unrealized. **8** *Brit* to park a vehicle for a short period at the edge of a road: *No waiting.* ➤ *verb trans* **1** to stay in place in expectation of (something); to await (it): *Wait your turn.* **2** to delay serving (a meal) while waiting for somebody to arrive: *Shall we wait supper for her?* **3** *chiefly NAmer* to serve as waiter for (a table). ✳ **wait on/upon 1** to act as an attendant to (somebody). **2** *chiefly NAmer* to wait for (somebody or something): *We were waiting on his answer.* **3** *archaic* to make a formal call on (somebody). [Middle English *waiten* to watch, watch for, lie in wait for, from Old Northern French *waitier* to watch, of Germanic origin]

wait[2] *noun* **1** the act or a period of waiting: *We had a long wait for the bus.* **2** *Brit, archaic* (*in pl*) a group who serenade for gratuities, *esp* at Christmas. ✳ **in wait** in a hidden position, *esp* in readiness to attack. [Middle English (sense 1) from WAIT[1]; (sense 2) from *waite* watchman, public musician, wait, from Old Northern French *wait* watchman, watch, from *waitier*: see WAIT[1]]

wait-a-bit *noun* any of various tropical or subtropical plants or shrubs with hooked thorns that catch on clothing.

waiter *noun* **1** somebody who waits at table, e.g. in a restaurant, *esp* as a regular job. **2** somebody who waits. **3** a salver or tray.

waiting game *noun* a postponement of action in the hope of a more favourable opportunity later.

waiting list (*NAmer* **wait list**) *noun* a list of those waiting, e.g. for a vacancy or for something to become available, arranged usu in order of application.

waiting room *noun* a room for the use of people who are waiting, e.g. for a train or to see a doctor.

wait list *noun NAmer* see WAITING LIST.

wait out *verb trans* to delay in hope of a favourable change in (something): *We usually waited out her strange moods.*

waitress /'waytrəs, 'waytris/ *noun* a female person who waits at tables, e.g. in a restaurant, *esp* as a regular job.

wait up *verb intrans* **1** to delay going to bed, *esp* in expectation of somebody's arrival or return. **2** *NAmer* (*usu in imperative*) to wait for somebody.

waive /wayv/ *verb trans* to refrain from demanding or enforcing (e.g. a right); to relinquish or forgo (it). [Middle English *weiven* from

Old Northern French *weyver* to abandon, waive, from *waif*: see WAIF]

waiver *noun* **1** the relinquishing of a right. **2** a document giving proof of this. [Anglo-French *weyver* from Old Northern French *weyver*: see WAIVE]

Usage note
---
waiver *or* waver? See note at WAVER[1].

wakame /wa'kahmi/ *noun* an edible seaweed used in Japanese cooking, *esp* in soups: *Undaria pinnatifida.* [Japanese *wakame*]

Wakashan /wah'kashən, wahkə'shan, waw-/ *noun* a family of Native American languages spoken by the Nootka, Kwakiutl, and other peoples of the coastal areas of British Columbia and Washington. ➤➤ **Wakashan** *adj*. [from Nootka *wawhaaak* brave]

wake[1] /wayk/ *verb* (*past tense* **woke** /wohk/, *NAmer or dialect or archaic* **waked**, *past part.* **woken** /'wohk(ə)n/, *NAmer or dialect or archaic* **waked**) ➤ *verb intrans* **1** (*often* + up) to stop sleeping; to awake. **2** to be or remain awake: *The fears never came on her during waking hours, only in her dreams.* **3** (+ up) to pay more attention to what is happening or what one is doing. **4** (+ up) to realize or become aware of a problem, an unpalatable truth, etc. ➤ *verb trans* **1** (*often* + up) to rouse (somebody) from sleep. **2a** (+ to) to arouse conscious interest in (something). **b** (+ to) to alert (somebody) to something: *It woke him to the fact of her existence.* **3** (+ up) to make (somebody) pay more attention to what is happening or what they are doing. **4** to hold a wake over (e.g. a dead person). ➤➤ **waker** *noun*. [partly from Old English *wacan* to awake, and partly from Old English *wacian* to be awake]

wake[2] *noun* **1** a watch held over the body of a dead person prior to burial and sometimes accompanied by festivity. **2** (*in pl, but treated as sing. or pl*) the festivities originally connected with the annual fair or festival of an English parish church and now marked by an annual holiday, typically in the industrial north of England: *We all go off to Blackpool during wakes week.* [partly from assumed Old English *wacu* wakefulness, partly from Old English *wacian* (see WAKE[1]); (sense 2) prob from Old Norse *vaka* vigil on the eve of a festival]

wake[3] *noun* **1** the track left by a moving body, e.g. a ship, in a fluid, e.g. water. **2** a track or path left behind after something has passed: *The hurricane left thousands of dollars' worth of damage in its wake.* [prob of Scandinavian origin]

wakeful /'waykf(ə)l/ *adj* **1** not sleeping or able to sleep. **2** spent without sleep: *a wakeful night.* ➤➤ **wakefully** *adv*, **wakefulness** *noun*.

waken /'wayk(ə)n/ *verb intrans and trans* (**wakened, wakening**) (*often* + up) = WAKE[1]. [Old English *wæcnian*]

wake-robin *noun* **1** *Brit* = CUCKOOPINT. **2** *NAmer* = TRILLIUM. [prob from WAKE[1] + ROBIN]

wake-up call *noun* **1** a telephone call made to wake a person at an agreed time. **2** an unexpected event that acts as a warning and a call to action to remedy a problem or deal with a danger.

WAL *abbr* West Africa Leone (international vehicle registration for Sierra Leone).

Waldenses /wol'denseez/ *pl noun* a Christian sect arising in S France in the 12th cent., adopting Calvinist doctrines in the 16th cent., and later living chiefly in Piedmont. ➤➤ **Waldensian** /-si·ən/ *adj and noun*. [Middle English *Waldensis* from late Latin *Waldenses, Valdenses*, named after Peter *Waldo* (or *Valdo*) d.1205, French merchant, who founded it]

waldo /'wawldoh/ *noun* (*pl* **waldos** *or* **waldoes**) a device by means of which objects can be manipulated by remote control. [named after *Waldo* F Jones, eponymous hero of a story by Robert Heinlein d.1988, American writer]

Waldorf salad /'wawldawf/ *noun* a salad consisting typically of apples, celery, and walnuts dressed with mayonnaise. [named after the *Waldorf*-Astoria Hotel in New York City, where it was first made]

wale /wayl/ *noun* **1** any of a series of even ribs in a fabric, e.g. corduroy. **2** any of a number of extra thick and strong planks in the sides of a wooden ship. **3** = WEAL[1]. [Old English *walu* stripe, weal]

Walhalla /val'halə/ *noun* see VALHALLA.

walk[1] /wawk/ *verb intrans* **1** to move along on foot; to advance by steps in such a way that at least one foot is always in contact with the ground. **2** to go on foot for exercise or pleasure. **3** said of an animal: to go at a walk. **4** said of a spirit: to move about in visible form; to appear. **5** *chiefly NAmer, informal* to be found innocent or be released from prison. **6** *chiefly NAmer, informal* to leave a job, *esp* to go on strike. **7** said of an inanimate object: to disappear or be taken. **8** in cricket, to leave the field before being given out by the umpire. **9** in baseball, to go to first base after four balls have been pitched. **10** in basketball, to move while holding the ball. **11** *archaic* to pursue a course of action or way of life; to conduct oneself. ➤ *verb trans* **1** to pass on foot through, along, over, or upon (e.g. a route): *I spent hours walking the streets looking for a hotel.* **2** to take (an animal) for a walk: *They have somebody walk the dog while they're out at work.* **3** to cause (an animal) to go at a walk: *Walk the horse round the paddock so that I can see its limp.* **4** to cause (an inanimate object) to move in a manner suggestive of walking. **5** to accompany (somebody) on foot; to walk with (them): *I walked her home.* **6** to bring (somebody) to a specified condition by walking: *He walked us off our feet.* **7** to go through, round, or over (something that will be performed at a faster pace) at a walk, e.g. to walk round a show jumping course for the purposes of examining, measuring, etc. **8** to take charge of (a hound puppy) at a walk. ✳ **walk into** to place oneself or find oneself in (a trap, etc). **walk it** *informal* to win easily. **walk on eggshells** to act or speak cautiously, *esp* to avoid being tactless. **walk over/all over 1a** to treat (somebody) thoughtlessly or with disrespect: *He lets his children walk all over him.* **b** to beat (somebody) easily and decisively. **2** said of a racehorse: to win a walkover. **walk tall** to bear oneself proudly. **walk through** to have a walk-through of (a play, etc). ➤➤ **walkable** *adj.* [Old English *wealcan* to roll, toss, wander]

walk² *noun* **1** the act or an instance of going on foot, *esp* for exercise or pleasure: *We went for a walk.* **2** a journey undertaken on foot along a usu agreed route to earn money promised by sponsors for charity: *a sponsored walk.* **3** a ceremonial procession; a march. **4** a manner of walking: *His walk is just like his father's.* **5** a route for walking: *There are many delightful walks in the neighbourhood.* **6** a path specially arranged or surfaced for walking; a footpath: *gravelled garden walks.* **7** a distance to be walked: *The house is a quarter of a mile's walk from here; a minute's walk.* **8a** the gait of a two-legged animal in which the feet are lifted alternately with one foot not clear of the ground before the other touches. **b** the gait of a four-legged animal in which there are always at least two feet on the ground; *specif* a four-beat gait of a horse in which the feet strike the ground in the sequence left hind, left front, right hind, right front. **9** a low rate of speed: *The shortage of raw materials slowed production to a walk.* **10** a route regularly covered by a person, e.g. a postman or policeman, in the performance of a particular activity. **11** a place where animals, e.g. sheep, are kept with minimal restraint. **12** a forest area under one keeper. **13** *chiefly Brit* a place, e.g. a farm, to which a hound puppy is sent to develop. ✳ **walk of life 1** an occupation or calling. **2** a range or sphere of action; a field or province.

walkabout *noun* **1** a short period of wandering bush life engaged in by an Australian Aborigine for ceremonial reasons as an occasional interruption of normal life. **2** an informal walk among the crowds by a public figure: *My mother met the Queen on her Jubilee walkabout.* ✳ **go walkabout** *Aus* to go on a walkabout.

walk away *verb intrans* to leave, *esp* to run away from a difficult situation. ✳ **walk away with 1** *informal* to win or gain (something), *esp* by outdoing one's competitors without difficulty: *She walked away with first prize.* **2** *informal* to steal (something).

walker *noun* **1** somebody who walks. **2a** a framework designed to support a baby learning to walk. **b** a frame used by an adult learning to walk again, e.g. after an injury, or to enable a disabled person to walk.

walkies /'wawkiz/ *pl noun informal* used *esp* to children or animals: *a walk.*

walkie-talkie /ˌwawki 'tawki/ *noun* a compact battery-operated radio transmitting and receiving set.

walk-in *adj* large enough for a person to enter and move around in: *a walk-in safe.*

walking *adj* **1** that walks, e.g.: **a** animate, *esp* human: *She's a walking encyclopedia, that one!* **b** able to walk: *The seriously injured were dealt with first, the walking wounded afterwards.* **2a** used for or in walking: *walking shoes.* **b** characterized by or consisting of walking: *a walking tour.* **3** that moves or appears to move in a manner suggestive of walking: *a walking toy.* **4** guided or operated by a walker: *a walking plough.*

walking papers *pl noun chiefly NAmer, informal* notice of dismissal; marching orders.

walking stick *noun* a stick used as an aid to walking.

Walkman *noun* (*pl* **Walkmen** *or* **Walkmans**) *trademark* a small portable cassette player or CD player with earphones: compare PERSONAL STEREO.

walk off *verb intrans* to leave suddenly or abruptly. ➤ *verb trans* to get rid of (e.g. an ailment or mood) by walking: *walking off a hangover.* ✳ **walk off with 1** *informal* to steal and take (something) away. **2** *informal* to take (something) away unintentionally. **3** *informal* to win or gain (something), *esp* by outdoing one's competitors without difficulty: *Our team walked off with the trophy every year.*

walk-on *noun* **1** a small usu nonspeaking part in a dramatic production. **2** somebody who has such a part.

walkout *noun* **1** a strike by workers. **2** the action of leaving a meeting or organization as an expression of protest.

walk out *verb intrans* **1** to go on strike. **2** to depart suddenly, often as an expression of protest. **3** *chiefly Brit, dated* (*often* + with) to court. ✳ **walk out on** to leave (somebody) in the lurch; to abandon (them).

walkover *noun* **1** an easily won contest. **2** an advance from one round of a competition to the next without contest, due to the withdrawal or absence of other entrants. [from the practice of walking a racehorse round the course in order to claim victory for a race for which there are no other entrants]

walk-through *noun* a perfunctory performance of a play or acting part, e.g. in an early stage of rehearsal.

walk-up¹ *adj NAmer* **1** said of a building: having no lift. **2** not accessible by lift: *I'm in a walk-up office on the third floor.*

walk-up² *noun NAmer* a building or office that has no lift.

walkway *noun* a passage, path, or platform for walking.

wall¹ /wawl/ *noun* **1** a usu upright and solid structure, *esp* of stone, brick, or concrete, having considerable height and length in relation to width and serving to divide, enclose, retain, or support. **2** (*also in pl*) a high thick masonry structure forming a long rampart or an enclosure, chiefly for defence: *the city walls.* **3** a structure bounding a garden, park, or estate. **4** any of the upright enclosing structures of a room or house. **5** the surface of a wall: *The wall was painted cream.* **6** an upright structure serving to hold back pressure, e.g. of water or sliding earth. **7** a material layer enclosing space: *the wall of a container.* **8** in anatomy, a lining or membrane enclosing a cavity or structure: *heart walls.* **9** an almost vertical rock surface. **10** something that acts as a barrier or defence: *a wall of silence.* ✳ **off the wall 1** *chiefly NAmer, informal* unconventional; unusual [prob from games such as squash, when a ball can rebound off the wall at an unexpected angle]. **2** *chiefly NAmer, informal* ridiculous or foolish: *That plan is totally off the wall.* **to the wall** *informal* into a hopeless position; out of existence: *During the recession several small firms went to the wall.* **up the wall** into a state of exasperation or unreasoning fury: *I don't know what he's got against roses, but if you use even one in a bouquet he goes up the wall* — Eleanor Rees. ➤➤ **walled** *adj.* [Old English *weall*]

wall² *verb trans* **1** (*usu* + in) to protect or surround (something) with a wall: *The lake is walled in by mountains.* **2** (+ off) to separate or shut out (something) by a wall: *They walled off half the house.* **3** (+ in/up) to immure (somebody). **4** (+ up) to close (an opening) with a wall. ➤➤ **walling** *noun.*

Wallaby /'woləbi/ *noun* (*pl* **Wallabies**) a member of the Australian international rugby union team.

wallaby *noun* (*pl* **wallabies** *or collectively* **wallaby**) any of numerous species of small or medium-sized mammals closely related to the kangaroos: family Macropodidae. [Dharuk *wolabā*]

Wallace's line /'wolisiz/ *noun* a hypothetical boundary separating the characteristic Asiatic flora and fauna from that of Australasia. [named after Alfred Russel *Wallace* d.1913, English naturalist, who proposed it]

wallah /'wolə/ *noun informal* (*usu in combinations*) a person who does a specified type of work or performs a specified duty: *The book wallah was an itinerant peddler* — George Orwell. [Hindi -*wālā* man, one in charge, from Sanskrit *pāla* protector]

wallaroo /woləˈrooh/ *noun* (*pl* **wallaroos**) a large reddish grey kangaroo: *Macropus robustus.* [Dharuk *wolarū*]

wall bars *pl noun* horizontal parallel bars that are attached to a wall and used for gymnastic exercises.

wallboard *noun chiefly NAmer* a structural boarding of any of various materials, e.g. wood pulp, gypsum, or plastic, used for sheathing interior walls and ceilings.

wallcreeper *noun* a small S European and Asian bird with grey upper parts and blackish wings with crimson patches, inhabiting cliffs and rocky areas, usu in mountainous regions: *Tichodroma muraria*.

wallet /'wolit/ *noun* **1** a holder for paper money, usu with compartments for other items, e.g. credit cards and stamps. **2** a flat case or folder. **3** *archaic* a travelling bag. [Middle English *walet* travelling bag, prob of Germanic origin]

walleye *noun* **1** an eye that turns outwards, showing more than a normal amount of white. **2** an eye with a whitish iris. **3** an eye in which the normally transparent cornea is white and opaque. **4** a N American pikeperch that has opaque eyes: *Stizostedion vitreum*. [back-formation from WALLEYED]

walleyed *adj* having walleyes. [by folk etymology from Middle English *wawil-eghed*, part translation of Old Norse *vagl-eygr*, from *vagl* of uncertain meaning + *eygr* eyed]

wallflower *noun* **1** a hardy plant widely cultivated for its spikelike clusters of typically golden to brown sweet-scented flowers: *Cheiranthus cheiri*. **2** *informal* a person who from shyness or unpopularity remains on the sidelines of a social activity, *esp* a woman who fails to get partners at a dance.

wall of death *noun* a fairground attraction consisting of a large cylinder around the inside of which a motorcyclist rides.

Walloon /wo'loohn/ *noun* **1** a member of the French-speaking people of S Belgium and adjacent parts of France: compare FLEMING. **2** the French dialect spoken by the Walloons. ➤➤ **Walloon** *adj.* [early French *Wallon* (adj and noun), of Germanic origin]

wallop¹ /'woləp/ *verb trans* (**walloped, walloping**) *informal* **1** to hit (somebody or something) with force. **2** to beat (an opponent) by a wide margin; to trounce (them). ➤➤ **walloping** *noun*. [Middle English *walopen* to gallop, from Old Northern French *waloper*, prob of Germanic origin]

wallop² *noun informal* **1** a powerful body blow; a punch. **2** the ability, e.g. of a boxer, to hit hard. **3** emotional or psychological force; impact. **4** *Brit* beer.

walloper *noun* **1** somebody or something that wallops. **2** *Aus, informal* a policeman.

walloping *adj informal* large or whopping.

wallow¹ /'woloh/ *verb intrans* **1** to roll or lie around lazily or luxuriously: *I love watching pigs wallowing in mud.* **2** (+ in) to indulge oneself immoderately; to revel: *I can't stand all this wallowing in sentiment.* **3** said of a ship: to struggle laboriously in or through rough water; to pitch or lurch: *The ship wallowed down the coast.* ➤➤ **wallower** *noun.* [Old English *wealwian* to roll]

wallow² *noun* **1** the act or an instance of wallowing. **2a** a muddy or dusty area used by animals for wallowing. **b** a depression formed by the wallowing of animals.

wallpaper¹ *noun* **1** decorative paper for the walls of a room. **2** something that serves as a bland decorative background: *Popular television is merely wallpaper.* **3** in computing, a decorative background on a monitor.

wallpaper² *verb trans* (**wallpapered, wallpapering**) to apply wallpaper to (a room or the walls of a room).

wall pepper *noun* a wild Eurasian fleshy-leaved plant that grows amongst rocks and on walls: genus *Sedum*.

wall plate *noun* a horizontal structural member, e.g. a timber, that provides bearing and anchorage, *esp* for the beams of a roof or the rafters.

wall rocket *noun* a yellow-flowered European plant of the cabbage family, which is a weed of cultivated land: *Diplotaxis muralis*.

wall rue *noun* a small delicate spleenwort found *esp* on walls or cliffs: *Asplenium ruta-muraria*.

Wall Street *noun* the influential financial interests of the US economy. [*Wall Street* in New York City, site of the New York Stock Exchange]

wall-to-wall *adj* **1** said of carpeting: covering the whole floor of a room. **2** continuous or uninterrupted: *a film with wall-to-wall commentary*.

wally /'woli/ *noun* (*pl* **wallies**) *Brit, informal* a silly or useless person. [perhaps from English dialect *wally* pickled cucumber, or from the name *Walter*]

walnut /'wawlnut/ *noun* **1** an edible two-lobed nut with a wrinkled shell. **2** any of several species of trees that bear this nut: genus *Juglans*. **3** the richly grained wood of any of these trees, often used for cabinetmaking and veneers. **4** a light yellowish brown colour.

Word history

Old English *wealhhnutu* literally 'foreign nut', from *Wealh* Welshman, foreigner + *hnutu* nut. The walnut was introduced to Britain from overseas, prob by the Romans, hence the connection with the Old English word for foreigner.

Walpurgis Night /val'pooəgis/ *noun* the eve of May Day on which, according to Germanic legend, witches gather in an annual ceremony. [part translation of German *Walpurgisnacht*, from *Walpurgis* St Walburga d.777, English saint whose feast day falls on May Day + German *Nacht* night]

walrus /'wawlrəs/ *noun* (*pl* **walruses** *or collectively* **walrus**) either of two large sea mammals of northern seas, related to the seals, and hunted for their tough heavy hide, ivory tusks, and the oil yielded by the blubber: genus *Odobenus*. [Dutch *walrus*, of Scandinavian origin]

walrus moustache *noun* a thick moustache that droops down at each side.

waltz¹ /wawlts/ *noun* a ballroom dance in triple time with strong accent on the first beat, or a piece of music for or in the tempo of this.

Editorial note

The waltz is the essence of the ballroom, with a characteristic strong beat followed by two lighter ones. A heady mixture of whirling and swaying that originated in the Austrian peasant Ländler, from the 18th cent. onwards inspired countless compositions and is still popular in Vienna, the city of The Blue Danube. This was the first dance in which couples embraced each other, which naturally rendered it both popular and scandalous — Amanda Holden.

[German *Walzer*, from *walzen* to roll, dance, from Old High German *walzan* to turn, roll]

waltz² *verb intrans* **1** to dance a waltz. **2** to move in a lively or confident manner. **3** to proceed easily or boldly; to breeze: *He waltzed through his finals; We can't just waltz up and introduce ourselves.* ➤ *verb trans* **1** to dance a waltz with (somebody): *I waltzed her round the room.* **2** (+ off) to grab and lead (e.g. a person) unceremoniously; to march (them).

waltzer *noun* **1** somebody who waltzes. **2** a fairground roundabout that moves up and down as well as round and round.

wampum /'wompəm/ *noun* beads of polished shells strung together, formerly used by Native Americans as money and ornaments. [short for *wampumpeag* from Narraganset *wampompeag*, from *wampan* white + *api* string + *-ag* (pl suffix)]

WAN /wan/ *abbr* **1** wide area network. **2** West Africa Nigeria (international vehicle registration for Nigeria).

wan /won/ *adj* (**wanner, wannest**) **1a** suggestive of poor health; pallid. **b** lacking vitality; feeble. **2** said of light: dim or faint. ➤➤ **wanly** *adv*, **wanness** *noun*. [Old English *wan* dark, livid]

wand /wond/ *noun* **1** a slender rod used by conjurers and magicians. **2** a slender staff carried as a sign of office. **3** *informal* a conductor's baton. **4** an electronic device used to read bar codes. **5** in archery, a long narrow vertical strip used as a target. **6** *literary* a plant shoot. [Middle English in the sense 'slender stick', from Old Norse *vöndr*]

wander¹ /'wondə/ *verb* (**wandered, wandering**) ➤ *verb intrans* **1** to go or travel idly or aimlessly: *She wandered across the room.* **2** to follow or extend along a winding course; to meander: *The road wanders across the plain.* **3a** to deviate from a course, or as if from a course; to stray: *My eyes wandered from the page.* **b** to lose concentration; to stray in thought: *As the lecturer droned on, her mind began to wander.* **c** to think or speak incoherently or illogically: *As the fever worsened, he began to wander.* ➤ *verb trans* to roam over (an area): *We wandered the hillside in search of shelter.* [Old English *wandrian*]

wander² *noun* an idle or aimless walk or journey.

Wandering Jew *noun* **1** a Jew of medieval legend condemned by Christ to wander over the earth till Christ's second coming. **2** (**wandering Jew**) either of two trailing or creeping plants with showy often white-striped foliage: genus *Tradescantia*.

wanderlust *noun* eager longing for or impulse towards travelling. [German *Wanderlust*, from *wandern* to wander + *Lust* desire, pleasure]

wanderoo /wondə'rooh/ *noun* (*pl* **wanderoos**) **1** a purple-faced langur of Sri Lanka: *Presbytis vetulus*. **2** a macaque of the Indian subcontinent: *Presbytis entellus*. [Sinhalese *vanduru*, pl of *vandurā*, from Sanskrit *vānara* monkey, from *vanar-, vana* forest]

wane¹ /wayn/ *verb intrans* **1** said of the moon: to diminish in apparent size or intensity. **2** said of light or colour: to become less brilliant; to dim. **3** to fall gradually from power, prosperity, or influence; to decline. [Old English *wanian*]

wane² *noun* **1a** the act or process of waning. **b** a time of waning; *specif* the period from full phase of the moon to the new moon. **2** a defect in prepared timber characterized by bark or lack of wood at a corner or edge. **✳ on the wane** in a state of decline; waning. **⋙ waney** *adj*, **wany** *adj*.

wangle¹ /'wanggl/ *verb trans* **1** to bring about or get (something) by devious means: *We wangled an invitation to the party.* **2** to adjust or manipulate (something) for personal or fraudulent ends: *She wangled it so that she got an extra day off.* **⋙ wangler** *noun*. [perhaps alteration of WAGGLE¹]

wangle² *noun* a devious way of doing or getting something.

wank¹ /wangk/ *verb intrans* *Brit, coarse slang* to masturbate. [origin unknown]

wank² *noun* *Brit, coarse slang* the act or an instance of masturbating.

Wankel engine /'wangkl/ *noun* a rotary internal-combustion engine that has an eccentrically mounted rounded triangular rotor functioning as a piston and rotating in a space in the engine, and only two major moving parts. [named after its inventor Felix Wankel d.1988, German engineer]

wanker *noun* *Brit, coarse slang* **1** somebody who masturbates. **2** a foolish, incompetent, or unpleasant person.

wanna /'wonə/ *contraction* often used in writing to represent casual or American speech: want to: *Do you wanna come?* [by alteration]

wannabe /'wonəbee/ *noun* *informal* a person who wishes to be like something or somebody else: *a Madonna wannabe.* [alteration of *want to be*]

want¹ /wont/ *verb trans* **1** to have a desire for (something). **2** to wish or demand the presence of (somebody): *The boss wants you.* **3** to desire (somebody): *She wanted him.* **4** to hunt or seek (somebody) in order to apprehend them: *He is wanted for murder.* **5** *chiefly Brit, informal* to require or have need of (something): *This room wants decorating.* **6** *chiefly Brit, informal* ought: *You want to see a doctor about that toe.* **7** to suffer from the lack of (something); to need (it): *Thousands still want food and shelter.* **➤** *verb intrans* **1** to be needy or destitute. **2** (*usu* + for) to have need; to be lacking in the specified respect: *He never wants for friends.* **3** *chiefly NAmer* to desire to come or go: *I wanted out of the syndicate.* [Middle English *wanten* from Old Norse *vanta* to be lacking]

want² *noun* **1** the quality or state of lacking something required or usual; lack: *This whole proposal shows a want of good sense.* **2** grave and extreme poverty that deprives one of the necessities of life. **3** something wanted; a need or desire: *We can satisfy all your wants.*

wanting *adj* **1** not present or in evidence; absent. **2a** not up to the required standard or expectation: *The candidate was tested and found wanting.* **b** lacking in the specified ability or capacity; deficient: *He was wanting in gratitude.*

wanton¹ /'wont(ə)n/ *adj* **1** sexually unbridled; promiscuous. **2** having no just foundation or provocation; malicious: *wanton indifference to the needs of others.* **3** gratuitously brutal or violent: *As flies to wanton boys are we to the gods. They kill us for their sport* — Shakespeare. **4** uncontrolled or unbridled: *wanton inflation.* **5** *literary* luxuriant or lavish. **6** *archaic* hard to control; undisciplined or unruly. **⋙ wantonly** *adv*, **wantonness** *noun*. [Middle English, from *wan-* mis-, badly + Old English *togen*, past part. of *teōn* to draw, train, discipline]

wanton² *noun archaic* a wanton person, *esp* a lewd or lascivious woman: *Sleep, pretty wantons, do not cry* — Thomas Dekker.

wanton³ *verb intrans archaic or literary* to behave in a wanton manner, *esp* to act promiscuously.

WAP /wap/ *abbr* Wireless Application Protocol, technology that allows mobile phone users to send e-mails, get information from the Internet, etc via their mobile phone.

wapentake /'wopəntayk, 'wap-/ *noun* a former subdivision of some English shires, *esp* northern ones, corresponding to a hundred in other shires. [Old English *wǣpentæc* from Old Norse *vápnatak* act of grasping weapons, from *vápn* weapon + *tak* act of grasping, from *taka* to take; prob from the brandishing of weapons as an expression of approval when the chief of the wapentake entered upon his office]

wapiti /'wopiti/ *noun* (*pl* **wapitis** or *collectively* **wapiti**) an American deer similar to the European red deer but larger: *Cervus canadensis.* *NAmer* Also called ELK. [Shawnee *wapiti*, literally 'white rump']

War. *abbr* Warwickshire.

war¹ /waw/ *noun* **1** a state or period of usu open and declared armed hostile conflict between states or nations. **2** a struggle between opposing forces or for a particular end: *a war against disease.* **✳ in the wars** *informal* suffering several injuries at once. [Middle English *werre* from Anglo-French, of Germanic origin]

war² *verb intrans* (**warred, warring**) **1** to engage in warfare. **2a** to be in active or vigorous conflict. **b** to be opposed or inconsistent: *warring principles.*

waratah /'worətah/ *noun* any of several species of Australasian shrubs that have clusters of crimson or scarlet flowers: genus *Telopea.* [Dharuk *waratah*]

warble¹ /'wawbl/ *verb intrans* to sing or sound in a trilling manner or with many turns and variations. **➤** *verb trans* to render (something) musically, *esp* in an ornamented or trilling manner. [Old Northern French *werbler* from *werble* tune, modulation, of Germanic origin]

warble² *noun* **1** a musical trill. **2** a warbled song or tune. **3** the act or an instance of warbling.

warble³ *noun* **1** a swelling under the hide of cattle, horses, etc caused by the maggot of a warble fly. **2** the maggot causing this. [Middle English, prob of Scandinavian origin]

warble fly *noun* any of several species of two-winged flies whose larvae live under the skin of various mammals and cause swellings: genus *Hypoderma.*

warbler *noun* **1** any of numerous small active insect-eating birds, many of which are noted singers: families Sylviidae and Parulidae. **2** *informal* somebody who warbles; a singer.

war chest *noun* a fund accumulated to finance a war, or one used to finance any campaign.

war correspondent *noun* a newspaper, television, or radio journalist employed to report news concerning the conduct of a war, *esp* events at the scene of a battle.

war crime *noun* a crime, e.g. genocide or maltreatment of prisoners, committed during or in connection with war. **⋙ war criminal** *noun.*

war cry *noun* **1** a cry used during charging or rallying by a body of fighters in war. **2** a slogan used to rally people to a cause.

ward¹ /wawd/ *noun* **1a** a division of a hospital, *esp* a large room where a number of patients are accommodated. **b** a division of a prison, e.g. a cell or block. **2** a division of a city, town, or other area for electoral or administrative purposes. **3** a person under guard, protection, or surveillance, *esp* somebody under the care or control of a legal guardian: *a ward of court.* **4a** a projecting ridge of metal in a lock casing or keyhole allowing only a key with a corresponding notch to operate. **b** a corresponding notch on a key. **5** the inner court of a castle or fortress: compare BAILEY. **6** *archaic* the action or process of guarding. **7** the state of being under guard; custody. [Old English *weard* act of watching or guarding]

ward² *verb trans* **1** to assign (somebody) to or confine (them) in a hospital ward. **2** *archaic* to keep watch over (somebody or something); to guard (them). [Old English *weardian*]

-ward *or* **-wards** *suffix* forming words, with the meanings: **1** facing or tending in the direction specified: *homeward; earthwards.* **2** in the spatial or temporal direction specified: *upward; afterwards.* [*-ward* from Old English *-weard; -wards* from Old English *-weardes*]

war dance *noun* a dance performed as preparation for battle or in celebration of victory.

warden /'wawd(ə)n/ *noun* **1** somebody who has care or charge of something; a guardian. **2** an official charged with special supervisory duties or with the enforcement of specified laws or regulations: *an air-raid warden; a traffic warden.* **3** *Brit* any of various college or school officials. **4** *NAmer* a prison governor. ➤➤ **wardenship** *noun.* [Middle English *wardein* from Old Northern French *wardein* from *warder* to guard, variant of Old French *garder*: see GUARD¹]

warder *noun chiefly Brit* a prison guard. [Middle English in the sense 'somebody who guards a gate', from Anglo-French *wardere* from Old Northern French *warder*: see WARDEN]

ward heeler /'heelə/ *noun NAmer* a worker for a political boss in a local area, e.g. a ward.

ward off *verb trans* to deflect or avert (somebody or something). [*ward* to guard, via Middle English *warden* from Old English *weardian*]

wardress /'wawdris/ *noun* a female prison guard.

wardrobe /'wawdrohb/ *noun* **1** a large cupboard, *esp* one fitted with shelves and a rail, where clothes are kept. **2a** a collection of clothes, e.g. belonging to one person. **b** a collection of stage costumes and accessories. **3** the department of a royal or noble household entrusted with the care of clothes, jewels, and personal articles. [Middle English *warderobe* from Old North French, from *warder* to guard (see WARDEN) + *robe* ROBE¹: compare GARDEROBE]

wardrobe trunk *noun chiefly NAmer* a large trunk with a rail and compartments for clothes.

wardroom /'wawdroohm, 'wawdroom/ *noun* the space in a warship allotted to the commissioned officers, except the captain.

-wards *suffix* see -WARD.

wardship *noun* **1** care and protection of a ward; tutelage. **2** the state of being under a guardian.

ware¹ /weə/ *noun* **1** (*often in combination*) manufactured articles or products of art or craft; goods: *tinware.* **2** (*in pl*) goods for sale. **3** articles of fired clay, *esp* a specified make of pottery or china: *Samian ware.* [Old English *waru*]

ware² *verb trans* used chiefly as a command to hunting animals or other hunters: to beware of (something). [Old English *warian*]

warehouse¹ /'weəhows/ *noun* **1** a building or room for the storage of merchandise or commodities. **2** *chiefly Brit* a large retail outlet.

warehouse² /'weəhowz/ *verb trans* to deposit, store, or stock (goods) in a warehouse. ➤➤ **warehousing** *noun.*

warehouseman /'weəhowsmən/ *noun* (*pl* **warehousemen**) somebody who controls or works in a warehouse.

warehouse party /'weəhows/ *noun Brit* a large-scale commercial dance party held in a warehouse, hangar, or similar building and usu featuring acid house music.

warfare /'wawfeə/ *noun* **1** hostilities or war. **2** struggle or conflict. [Middle English, in the sense 'the action of going to war', from WAR¹ + FARE¹ in the sense 'journey']

warfarin /'wawfərin/ *noun* a synthetic compound that is used in medicine to prevent the blood clotting, e.g. in the treatment of thrombosis, and is also used as a rodent poison: formula $C_{19}H_{16}O_4$. [acronym from *Wisconsin Alumni Research Foundation* (its patentee) + *-arin* as in COUMARIN]

war game *noun* **1** an exercise or simulated battle to test military ability. **2** an enactment of a conflict in miniature using counters or models to represent the combatants. ➤➤ **war gaming** *noun.*

warhead *noun* the section of a missile containing the explosive, chemical, or incendiary charge.

war-horse *noun* **1** a powerful horse used in war. **2** *informal* a veteran soldier or public figure.

warlike *adj* **1** fond of war. **2** of or useful in war. **3** threatening war; hostile.

warlock /'wawlok/ *noun* a man practising black magic; a sorcerer.
Word history
Old English *wǣrloga* traitor, scoundrel, the Devil, from *wǣr* faith, troth + *-loga* from *lēogan* to lie. The sense 'the Devil' probably comes from the idea of the Devil as a traitor to God; this led in Middle English to the sense 'one in league with the Devil', having or using occult powers. From the 15th cent. the word was mainly Scots, until popularized by Sir Walter Scott in the 19th cent.

warlord *noun* a supreme military leader.

warm¹ /wawm/ *adj* **1a** having or giving out heat to a moderate or adequate degree: *a warm bath.* **b** experiencing heat to this degree: *Are you warm enough?* **2** serving to maintain or preserve heat, *esp* to a satisfactory degree: *a warm sweater.* **3** feeling or causing sensations of heat brought about by strenuous exertion: *a warm climb.* **4** marked by enthusiasm; ardent or cordial: *a warm welcome.* **5** affectionate and outgoing in temperament: *a warm personality.* **6** suggestive of warmth in colour or tone; *specif* of a hue in the range yellow through orange to red. **7** marked by excitement, disagreement, or anger. **8** dangerous or hostile: *The minister got a warm reception from a group of angry demonstrators.* **9** newly made; fresh: *a warm scent.* **10** used chiefly in children's games: near to a goal, object, or solution sought. ➤➤ **warmish** *adj*, **warmly** *adv*, **warmness** *noun.* [Old English *wearm*]

warm² *verb trans* **1** to make (somebody or something) warm. **2** to infuse (somebody) with a feeling of love, friendship, well-being, or pleasure. **3** (*often + up/through/over*) to reheat (cooked food) for eating. **4** (*often + up*) to bring (something) to the necessary temperature for comfort or efficient working: *The fire soon warmed the room; I'll just warm up the engine.* ➤ *verb intrans* **1** to become warm. **2** (*usu + up*) to become ardent, interested, or lively: *The party began to warm up.* **3** to experience feelings of pleasure; to bask. ✳ **warm to/towards** **1** to begin to like (somebody or something): *You do not warm to this lady, who delivers her lines to camera as if waiting for the canned laughter* — Daily Telegraph. **2** to begin to take interest in (a subject). **warm the cockles of one's heart** see COCKLE². ➤➤ **warmer** *noun.*

warm³ *noun* **1** (**the warm**) a warm place or state: *Sit here in the warm.* **2** the act or an instance of getting or making warm: *Come to the fire for a warm.*

warm-blooded *adj* **1** having a relatively high and constant body temperature more or less independent of the environment: compare COLD-BLOODED. **2** fervent or ardent in spirit. ➤➤ **warm-bloodedness** *noun.*

warm down *verb intrans* to do gentle exercises after more strenuous physical activity.

warm front *noun* an advancing edge of a warm air mass.

warmhearted *adj* marked by ready affection, cordiality, generosity, or sympathy. ➤➤ **warmheartedly** *adv*, **warmheartedness** *noun.*

warming pan *noun* a usu long-handled flat covered pan, e.g. of brass, filled with hot coals, formerly used to warm a bed.

warmonger /'wawmunggə/ *noun* somebody who attempts to stir up war. ➤➤ **warmongering** *noun and adj.*

warmth /wawmth/ *noun* the quality or state of being warm in temperature or in feeling: *A child needs human warmth.*

warm up *verb intrans* **1** to do gentle exercises before more strenuous physical activity. **2** to practise before a game or contest; to get ready. **3** said of an engine or machine: to come to the necessary temperature for comfort or efficient working. **4** to become more lively or exciting. **5** to approach a state of violence, conflict, or danger. ➤ *verb trans* **1** to put (an audience) into a receptive mood, e.g. before a comedy show. **2** to warm (food).

warm-up *noun* **1** the act or an instance of warming up. **2** a procedure, e.g. a set of exercises, used in warming up.

warn /wawn/ *verb trans* **1a** to give notice to (somebody) beforehand, *esp* of danger or evil: *There was nothing to warn them of the danger of flooding.* **b** to give admonishing advice to (somebody); to counsel (them): *I warned them not to open the door.* **c** to notify or inform (somebody): *I did warn them of my intentions.* **2** (*often + off/away*) to order (somebody) to go or stay away. ➤ *verb intrans* to give a warning: *She had warned against getting too friendly with him.* ➤➤ **warner** *noun.* [Old English *warnian*]

warning *noun* **1** the act or an instance of warning, or the state of being warned: *He had some warning of his illness.* **2** something that warns or serves to warn. **3** a notice of termination of an agreement, employment, etc. ➤➤ **warningly** *adv.*

warning coloration *noun* an animal's conspicuous colouring that warns off potential enemies.

warp¹ /wawp/ *verb trans* **1** to turn or twist (something) out of shape, *esp* out of flatness or straightness. **2** to falsify or distort (something): *You've got a warped sense of humour.* **3** to cause (somebody) to judge, choose, or act wrongly or crookedly; to pervert (them). **4** to manoeuvre (a ship) by hauling on a line attached to a fixed object. **5** to arrange (yarns) so as to form a warp. **6** to flood (land) with water containing sediment. ➤ *verb intrans* **1** to become warped. **2** to move a ship by warping. ➤➤ **warper** *noun.* [Old English *weorpan* to throw]

warp² *noun* **1** a twist or curve that has developed in something originally flat or straight: *There's a warp in that door panel.* **2** a series of yarns extended lengthways in a loom and crossed by the weft. **3a** a rope for warping a ship. **b** a rope used to secure a vessel alongside a quay. **4** *archaic* sediment deposited by water, e.g. in an estuary. ➤➤ **warpage** *noun.* [Old English *wearp*]

war paint *noun* **1** paint put on the body by Native Americans as a sign of going to war. **2** *informal* make-up.

war party *noun* a group of Native Americans going on a warlike expedition.

warpath *noun* the route taken by a war party of Native Americans. ✳ **on the warpath** pursuing an angry or hostile course; taking or starting to take action in a struggle or conflict.

warplane *noun* an armed military aircraft.

warrant¹ /'worənt/ *noun* **1a** a sanction or authorization. **b** evidence for or a token of authorization. **2** a commission or document giving authority, e.g.: **a** a document authorizing somebody to receive money or other consideration: *a travel warrant.* **b** a document authorizing an officer to make an arrest, a search, etc. **c** an official certificate of appointment, e.g. one issued to a warrant officer. **d** a short-term obligation of a governmental body, e.g. a municipality, issued in anticipation of revenue. **e** a document issued by a company giving to the holder the right to purchase the capital stock of the company at a stated price either prior to a stipulated date or at any future time. **3** a ground or justification; proof: *His assertion was totally without warrant.* [Middle English in the senses 'protector', 'safety, security', from Old Northern French *warant*, of Germanic origin]

warrant² *verb trans* **1** to serve as or give adequate ground or reason for (something): *Nothing could warrant such behaviour; The situation warrants dramatic action.* **2** to give warrant or sanction to (something); to authorize (it): *The law warrants this procedure.* **3** to assure (somebody) of the truth of what is said. **4** to guarantee to a person good title to and undisturbed possession of (e.g. an estate). **5a** to guarantee (e.g. a fact or statement of fact) to be as represented. **b** to guarantee (something), *esp* to guarantee (e.g. goods sold) in respect of the quality or quantity specified: *The roof is warranted against faulty workmanship.* **6** to declare or maintain (something) with certainty; to state (it) as being true: *I'll warrant he'll be here by noon.*

warrantee /worən'tee/ *noun* somebody to whom a warranty is made.

warrant officer *noun* an officer in the armed forces holding a rank below commissioned officers but above non-commissioned officers.

warrantor /'worəntə, -'taw/ *noun* a person or company that gives a warranty.

warranty /'worənti/ *noun* (*pl* **warranties**) **1** a usu written guarantee of the soundness of a product and of the maker's responsibility for repair or replacement. **2** a collateral undertaking that a fact regarding the subject of a contract is or will be as declared. **3** something that authorizes, supports, or justifies; a warrant. [Middle English *warantie* from Anglo-French, variant of early French *garantie*: see GUARANTY]

warren /'worən/ *noun* **1a** an area of ground where rabbits breed. **b** (*treated as sing. or pl*) the rabbits of a warren. **2a** a crowded tenement or district. **b** a maze of narrow passageways or cubbyholes. **c** anything intricate or confused. **3** *chiefly Brit* a place for keeping small game animals. [Middle English *warenne* land reserved for breeding game, *esp* rabbits, from Old Northern French, of Germanic origin]

warrigal¹ /'worigl/ *noun Aus* **1** a dingo. **2** a wild horse. [Dharuk *warrigal*]

warrigal² *adj Aus* wild.

warrior /'wori·ə/ *noun* a person engaged or experienced in warfare, *esp* tribal or medieval warfare. [Middle English *werriour* from Old Northern French *werreieur* from *werreier* to make war, from *werre* war, of Germanic origin]

warship *noun* an armed ship for use in warfare.

wart /wawt/ *noun* **1** a lumpy projection on the skin, usu of the hands or feet, caused by a virus. **2** a protuberance, *esp* on a plant, resembling this. ✳ **warts and all** *informal* in an imperfect state; showing any blemishes. ➤➤ **warty** *adj.* [Old English *wearte*]

warthog *noun* an African wild pig with two pairs of rough warty lumps on the face and large protruding tusks: *Phacochoerus aethiopicus.*

wartime *noun* a period during which a war is in progress.

wary /'weəri/ *adj* (**warier, wariest**) marked by caution and watchful prudence in detecting and escaping danger. ➤➤ **warily** *adv,* **wariness** *noun.* [archaic *ware* conscious, cautious, from Old English *wær*]

was /wəz, *strong* woz/ *verb* first person and third person sing. past tense of BE.

wasabi /wə'sahbi/ *noun* **1** a thick plant root that is grated or made into a pungent paste and served with sushi or sashimi. **2** the Japanese plant from which this root is taken: *Eutrema wasabi.* [Japanese *wasabi*]

Wash. *abbr* Washington.

wash¹ /wosh/ *verb trans* **1** to make (something) clean by using water or other liquid and soap or detergent. **2** to remove (dirt, a stain, etc) by rubbing or drenching with liquid. **3** to bathe or moisten (a part of the body) with a liquid. **4** said of an animal: to clean (its fur or other body covering) by licking. **5** to wet (something) thoroughly. **6** to send water over or through (something), *esp* to carry off material from the surface or interior. **7** to flow along or dash or overflow against (something): *Waves were washing the shore.* **8** to carry or deposit (something) by or as if by the force of water in motion: *Houses were washed away by the flood.* **9a** to agitate (earth, gravel, or crushed ore) in order to separate valuable material. **b** to separate (particles of gold) from an ore, gravel, etc by agitation with or in water. **c** to pass (a substance) through a vessel containing a liquid in order to remove impurities or soluble components. **d** to pass (a gas or gaseous mixture) through or over a liquid to purify it, *esp* by removing soluble components. **10a** to cover or daub (something) lightly with an application of a thin liquid, e.g. whitewash or varnish. **b** (*often* + in) to depict or paint (something) by a broad sweep of thin colour with a brush. **11** to cause (a liquid) to swirl. **12** to suffuse (something) with light. ➤ *verb intrans* **1** to wash oneself. **2** to wash articles; to do the washing. **3** to be capable of being washed without damage. **4a** to drift along on water. **b** to pour or flow in a stream or current. **5** *informal* (*in negative contexts*) to be convincing: *The story didn't wash with me.* ✳ **wash one's dirty linen in public** *informal* to discuss one's private affairs in public: *The amount of women in London who flirt with their own husbands is perfectly scandalous … It is simply washing one's clean linen in public* — Oscar Wilde. **wash one's hands of** to disclaim interest in or responsibility for (somebody or something). [Old English *wascan*]

wash² *noun* **1** the act or an instance of washing or being washed. **2** articles, *esp* clothes, that have been or are to be washed. **3** the surging action of waves. **4a** a thin coat of paint, e.g. watercolour. **b** a drawing done mainly in washes of ink or watercolour. **5** a thin liquid used for coating a surface, e.g. a wall. **6** an antiseptic or soothing lotion. **7a** a piece of ground habitually washed by the sea or river. **b** a shallow body of water. **8** loose or eroded surface material of the earth, e.g. rock debris, transported and deposited by running water. **9a** a backwash, e.g. behind a boat. **b** a disturbance in the air produced by the passage of an aircraft. **10** the liquor that comes from fermenting malt. **11a** worthless liquid waste. **b** swill. ✳ **come out in the wash 1** *informal* to become known in the course of time. **2** *informal* to reach a satisfactory conclusion.

washable *adj* capable of being washed without damage. ➤➤ **washability** /-'biliti/ *noun.*

wash bag *noun Brit* a small waterproof bag for carrying toiletries when travelling.

washbasin *noun* a basin or sink usu connected to a water supply for washing the hands and face.

washboard *noun* **1a** a board that consists typically of a corrugated rectangular metal surface set into a wooden frame, used for scrubbing clothes when washing. **b** a board like this played as a musical instrument. **2** a broad plank fastened to and projecting above the side or foredeck of a small craft to keep out spray.

washcloth *noun NAmer* a flannel or facecloth.

wash down *verb trans* **1** to wash (something) completely. **2** to facilitate the swallowing of (food, a pill, etc) by drinking liquid.

wash drawing *noun* watercolour painting done mainly in washes, *esp* in black, white, and grey tones only.

washed-out *adj* **1** faded in colour. **2** listless or exhausted.

washed-up *adj informal* no longer successful or useful; finished: *He was all washed up as a footballer at the age of 28.*

washer *noun* **1** somebody or something that washes. **2** a washing machine. **3** *Aus* a flannel or facecloth. **4** a thin flat ring or perforated plate used in various mechanical joints and assemblies.

washer-dryer *noun* a combined washing machine and tumble-dryer.

washerwoman *or* **washerman** *noun* (*pl* **washerwomen** *or* **washermen**) somebody who washes clothes for a living.

wash-hand basin *noun Brit* a washbasin.

washhouse *noun* a building used or equipped for washing clothes.

washing *noun* **1** articles, *esp* clothes, that have been or are to be washed. **2** material, e.g. metal ore, obtained by washing. **3** a thin covering or coat.

washing liquid *noun* detergent in liquid form for use in a washing machine.

washing machine *noun* a machine for washing clothes and household linen.

washing powder *noun* powdered detergent for use in a washing machine.

washing soda *noun* a transparent crystalline hydrated sodium carbonate used as a household cleaning agent: formula $Na_2CO_3.10H_2O$.

washing-up *noun Brit* **1** the act or process of washing dishes and kitchen utensils. **2** the dishes and utensils to be washed.

washing-up liquid *noun* liquid detergent or soap used for washing dirty dishes.

wash leather *noun* a soft leather similar to chamois, prepared usu from sheepskin, or a piece of this, used for washing things, e.g. windows.

wash off *verb trans and intrans* to disappear or cause (e.g. dirt) to disappear as the result of washing.

washout *noun* **1** *informal* a failure or fiasco. **2a** the washing out or away of a road, railway line, etc by a large amount of water. **b** a place where this has occurred.

wash out *verb trans* **1a** to wash (something) free of a usu unwanted substance, e.g. dirt. **b** to remove (dirt, a stain, etc) by washing. **2a** to cause (e.g. clothes) to fade by laundering. **b** to deplete the strength or vitality of (somebody): *She was feeling quite washed out.* **3** to cancel (e.g. an event) because of rain. ➤ *verb intrans* to become depleted of colour or vitality; to fade.

washroom *noun NAmer, euphem* a toilet.

washstand *noun* a piece of furniture used, *esp* formerly, to hold a basin, jug, etc needed for washing one's face and hands.

washtub *noun* a tub in which clothes, etc are washed or soaked.

wash up *verb trans* **1** *Brit* to wash the dishes and utensils after a meal. **2** *NAmer* to wash one's face and hands. ➤ *verb trans* **1** *Brit* to wash (dishes and utensils) after a meal. **2** to bring (something) into the shore from the sea or a lake.

washy *adj* (**washier**, **washiest**) **1** weak or watery: *washy tea.* **2** deficient in colour; pallid. **3** lacking in vigour, individuality, or definite form. ➤➤ **washiness** *noun*.

wasn't /'woznt/ *contraction* was not.

WASP *or* **Wasp** /wosp/ *noun* an American of N European, *esp* British, stock and of Protestant background, *esp* somebody considered to be a member of the dominant and most privileged class. ➤➤ **Waspish** *adj*, **Waspy** *adj*. [acronym from *white Anglo-Saxon Protestant*]

wasp /wosp/ *noun* **1** any of numerous largely flesh-eating slender narrow-waisted insects, many of which have an extremely painful sting: order Hymenoptera. **2** *esp* a very common social wasp with black and yellow stripes: *Vespula vulgaris.* ➤➤ **wasplike** *adj*. [Old English *wæps*, *wæsp*]

waspish *adj* resembling a wasp in behaviour, *esp* snappish. ➤➤ **waspishly** *adv*, **waspishness** *noun*.

wasp waist *noun* a woman's very slender waist, *esp* one created by a tight corset. ➤➤ **wasp-waisted** *adj*.

wassail¹ /'wosayl/ *noun archaic* **1** a liquor made of spiced ale or wine, often with baked apples, and served in a large bowl, *esp* formerly, at Christmas and other festive occasions. **2** revelry;

carousing: *The King doth wake tonight and ... keeps wassail* — Shakespeare. **3** a toast to somebody's health made in former times. [Middle English *wæs hæil* from Old Norse *ves heill* be well, from *ves* imperative sing. of *vera* to be + *heill* healthy]

wassail² *verb intrans* **1** *archaic* to hold a wassail; to carouse. **2** *Brit, dialect or archaic* to sing carols from house to house at Christmas. ➤ *verb trans archaic* to drink to the health or prosperity of (somebody). ➤➤ **wassailer** *noun*.

wassail bowl *noun* wassail, or a bowl or cup from which wassail is served.

wassail cup *noun* = WASSAIL BOWL.

Wassermann test /'vasəmən, 'was-/ *noun* a test for the presence of a specific antibody in blood serum, used in the detection of syphilis. [named after August von *Wassermann* d.1925, German bacteriologist]

wast /wəst, *strong* wost/ *verb archaic* second person sing. past tense of BE.

wastage /'waystij/ *noun* **1a** loss, decrease, or destruction of something, e.g. by use, decay, or leakage, *esp* wasteful or avoidable loss of something valuable. **b** waste or refuse. **2** reduction or loss in numbers, e.g. of employees or students, usu caused by individuals leaving or retiring voluntarily: *The job cuts can be made by natural wastage.*

waste¹ /wayst/ *noun* **1** the act or an instance of wasting or being wasted. **2** damaged, defective, or superfluous material. **3** human or animal refuse. **4a** gradual loss or decrease by use, wear, or decay. **b** in law, damage to an estate, *esp* as caused by a tenant. **5a** a sparsely settled, barren, or devastated region; a desert. **b** uncultivated land. **c** a broad and empty expanse, e.g. of water. ✳ **go to waste** to be squandered or wasted. **lay waste to** to destroy (something, *esp* a place) completely. [Middle English *waste*, *wast* from Old Northern French, from Latin *vastus* desolate, WASTE²]

waste² *verb trans* **1** to spend or use (something) carelessly or inefficiently; to squander (it). **2** to fail to use (an opportunity). **3** to dispose of (something unwanted) as waste. **4** *literary* to lay waste to (a place); to devastate (it): *The land has been wasted by stripmining.* **5** *NAmer, slang* to murder (somebody). ➤ *verb intrans* (*often* + away) to lose weight, strength, substance, or vitality. ✳ **waste one's breath** to accomplish nothing by speaking. [Middle English *wasten* via Old Northern French *waster* from Latin *vastare*, from *vastus* desolate, waste]

waste³ *adj* **1** discarded as refuse: *waste material.* **2a** uninhabited or desolate. **b** not cultivated or used; not productive: *waste land.*

wasted *adj* **1** unprofitably used, made, or expended: *wasted effort.* **2** impaired in strength or health; emaciated. **3** *informal* drunk or affected by illegal drugs.

waste-disposal unit *noun* an electrical device that grinds up waste food so that it can be disposed of down a waste pipe.

waste disposer *noun* = WASTE-DISPOSAL UNIT.

wasteful /'waystf(ə)l/ *adj* given to or marked by waste; prodigal. ➤➤ **wastefully** *adv*, **wastefulness** *noun*.

wasteland *noun* **1** an area of barren or uncultivated land: *a desert wasteland.* **2** a desolate or barely inhabitable place or area. **3** something, e.g. a way of life, that is spiritually and emotionally arid and unsatisfying.

wastepaper *noun* paper discarded as used or unwanted.

wastepaper basket *noun* a receptacle for refuse, *esp* wastepaper.

waste pipe *noun* a pipe for carrying off waste fluid.

waster *noun* **1** somebody who spends or consumes extravagantly without thought for the future. **2** *informal* a good-for-nothing; an idler.

wasting *adj* undergoing or causing decay or loss of strength: *He had made a study of wasting diseases such as tuberculosis.* ➤➤ **wastingly** *adv*.

wastrel /'waystrəl/ *noun* **1** somebody who spends or consumes extravagantly without thought for the future; a waster. **2** a vagabond or waif. [irreg from WASTE²]

watch¹ /woch/ *verb trans* **1** to keep one's eyes fixed on (something or somebody). **2** to look at (an event or moving scene). **3** to take an interest in the progress of (something or somebody): *She watched his rise to stardom with amazement.* **4** to keep (somebody) under surveillance or protective guard. **5** to be careful or cautious about (something): *You need to watch your speed here.* ➤ *verb intrans* **1** to be closely observant of an event or action; to look attentively. **2** (*also* + over) to protect or take charge. **3** (+ for) to be attentive or vigilant: *Police surrounded the house, watching for any movement.* **4** *archaic* to keep vigil as an act of devotion: *And he cometh unto his disciples, and findeth them asleep, and saith unto Peter, 'What, could ye not watch with me one hour?'* — Bible. ✳ **watch it** (*usu in imperative*) to be careful. **watch one's step** to proceed with care; to act or talk warily. ⟫⟫ **watcher** *noun.* [Old English *wæccan*]

watch[2] *noun* **1** a small timepiece worn on the wrist or carried in the pocket. **2** the act or an instance of keeping awake or alert to guard, protect, or attend. **3** close observation; surveillance: *He kept careful watch on the prisoner.* **4** a state of alert and continuous attention; a lookout: *They were always on the watch.* **5** a period of keeping guard. **6a** a period of time during which a part of a ship's company is on duty while another part rests. **b** the part of a ship's company on duty during a particular watch. **c** a period of duty. **7** somebody who watches; a lookout or watchman. **8** a body of sentinels or watchmen; *specif* those formerly assigned to patrol the streets of a town at night, announce the hours, and act as police. **9** (*usu in pl*) a wakeful interval during the night. ✳ **on the watch** keeping watch; on the alert.

watchable *adj* worth watching.

watch chain *noun* a chain attached to a pocket watch.

watch committee *noun* (*often* **Watch Committee**) a British local government committee formerly responsible for supervising police discipline and public order.

watchdog *noun* **1** a dog kept to guard property. **2** a person or group, e.g. a committee, that guards against inefficiency, undesirable practices, etc.

watch fire *noun* a fire lit, *esp* at night, as a signal or for the use of a guard.

watchful /'wochf(ə)l/ *adj* **1** carefully observant or attentive: *She kept a watchful eye on the proceedings.* **2** *archaic* wakeful. ⟫⟫ **watchfully** *adv*, **watchfulness** *noun.*

watchglass *noun* **1** a transparent cover protecting the face of a watch. **2** a shallow glass dish used in a laboratory.

watching brief *noun* **1** *Brit* in law, instructions to a barrister to follow a case on behalf of somebody not directly involved. **2** observation of proceedings on behalf of another.

watchmaker *noun* somebody who makes and repairs clocks and watches. ⟫⟫ **watchmaking** *noun.*

watchman *noun* (*pl* **watchmen**) **1** somebody who keeps watch; a guard: *a night watchman.* **2** a member of a body formerly assigned to patrol the streets at night.

watch night *noun* a devotional service lasting until after midnight, *esp* on Christmas Eve or New Year's Eve.

watch out *verb intrans* **1** to be vigilant. **2** (*usu in imperative*) to be careful; to take care.

watchtower *noun* a tower from which a lookout can keep watch.

watchword *noun* **1** a motto that embodies a guiding principle; a slogan. **2** a word or phrase used as a sign of recognition among members of the same group.

water[1] /'wawtə/ *noun* **1a** the colourless odourless tasteless liquid that falls from the clouds as rain, forms streams, lakes, and seas, and is a major constituent of all living matter. It is an oxide of hydrogen, H_2O, that freezes at 0°C and boils at very nearly 100°C, is at its densest at 4°C, and is a poor conductor of electricity and a good solvent. **b** one of the four elements of the alchemists, the others being earth, air, and fire. **2** (*in pl*). **a** the water occupying or flowing in a particular bed: *the waters of the Nile.* **b** a stretch of sea abutting on the land of a specified sovereignty and under the control of that sovereignty: *in British waters.* **c** the sea of a specified part of the earth: *in tropical waters.* **3** (**the waters**) a natural mineral water: *He had been to Bath to take the waters.* **4** *chiefly Brit* often used in place names: a body of water; a lake or river: *Derwent Water.* **5** a depth of water: *She stood in half a metre of water.* **6** a water supply: *They threatened to turn off the water.* **7** travel or transport on water: *We went by water.* **8** the level of water at a specified state of the tide: compare HIGH WATER, LOW WATER. **9** the surface of the water: *He swam under water.* **10** a medicinal or cosmetic preparation made with water: *rose water.* **11** a solution of a gaseous or readily vaporized substance in water: *ammonia water.* **12** a watery liquid, e.g. tears, urine, or sap, formed in and secreted from, or circulating in a living body. **13** (*usu in pl*) the AMNIOTIC FLUID (watery liquid) surrounding a foetus in the womb. **14a** the clarity and lustre of a

precious stone, *esp* a diamond. **b** degree of excellence: *She's a pianist of the first water.* **15** a wavy lustrous pattern, e.g. of a textile. ✳ **hold water** to stand up under criticism or analysis. **make water** *euphem* to urinate. **pass water** *euphem* to urinate. **water under the bridge** past events that it is futile to try to alter. ⟫⟫ **waterless** *adj.* [Old English *wæter*]

water[2] *verb* (**watered, watering**) ⟫ *verb trans* **1** to moisten, sprinkle, or soak (something) with water, *esp* to provide (seeds or growing plants) with water. **2** to supply (e.g. a horse) with water for drink. **3** to supply water to (e.g. a ship). **4** to be a source of water for (an area): *This land is watered by the Thames.* **5** to treat (something) with water, or as if with water; *specif* to impart a lustrous appearance and wavy pattern to (cloth) by pressing between rollers or plates: *watered silk.* **6** (*often* + down) to dilute (something) by or as if by the addition of water: *The public outcry had forced the government to water down the proposals.* **7** in finance, to add to the aggregate PAR[1] value (monetary value assigned to each share of stock) of (securities of a company) by the issue of more stock without a corresponding addition to the assets represented by this stock. ⟫ *verb intrans* **1** to form or secrete water or watery matter, e.g. tears or saliva. **2** to take on a supply of water. **3** said of an animal: to drink water. ⟫⟫ **waterer** *noun.*

water bailiff *noun Brit* an official employed to enforce bylaws relating to angling.

water bear *noun* a microscopic invertebrate animal with a flattened body and four pairs of clawed legs, living in water or damp moss: phylum Tardigrada.

water bed *noun* a bed with a water-filled plastic or rubber mattress.

water beetle *noun* **1** any of numerous oval flattened aquatic beetles that swim by means of their fringed hind legs which act together as oars: family Dytiscidae. **2** any of numerous similar aquatic insects: order Coleoptera.

water bird *noun* a bird that frequents or lives on or near water, e.g. a swimming or wading bird.

water biscuit *noun* an unsweetened biscuit made with flour and water.

water blister *noun* a blister with a clear watery content that does not contain pus or blood.

water bloom *noun* an accumulation of algae at or near the surface of a body of water.

water boatman *noun* **1** any of various aquatic bugs that swim on their backs: family Notonectidae. **2** any of various aquatic bugs of a related family that swim on their fronts: family Corixidae.

waterborne *adj* supported or carried by water: *waterborne commerce; waterborne infection.*

waterbuck *noun* (*pl* **waterbucks** *or collectively* **waterbuck**) any of various African antelopes that commonly frequent streams or wet areas; *specif* either of two shaggy-haired antelopes found near rivers and lakes: genus *Kobus.*

water buffalo *noun* an often domesticated Asiatic buffalo with large horns: *Bubalus bubalis.*

water caltrop *noun* = WATER CHESTNUT (2A).

water cannon *noun* a device for shooting out a jet of water with great force, e.g. to disperse a crowd.

water carrier *noun* (**the Water Carrier**) the constellation and sign of the zodiac Aquarius.

water chestnut *noun* **1a** a SE Asian sedge cultivated for its edible enlarged tubers: *Eleocharis tuberosa.* **b** a tuber of this plant, commonly used in Chinese cookery. **2a** an aquatic plant with white flowers, floating leaves arranged in a rosette and narrow rootlike submerged leaves: *Trapa natans.* Also called CALTROP. **b** the edible nutlike spiny-angled fruit of this plant. Also called CALTROP.

water clock *noun* an instrument designed to measure time by the fall or flow of water.

water closet *noun dated* a toilet with a bowl that can be flushed with water: *I am happy to learn it has that useful English comfort, a water-closet* — Scott.

watercolour (*NAmer* **watercolor**) *noun* **1** a paint made from pigment mixed with water rather than oil. **2** a picture or design painted with watercolours. **3** the art of painting with watercolours. ⟫⟫ **watercolourist** *noun.*

water-cool *verb trans* to cool (e.g. an engine) by means of *esp* circulating water.

water cooler *noun* a machine that dispenses cooled water for drinking.

watercourse *noun* **1** a natural or artificial channel through which water flows or may flow. **2** a stream of water, e.g. a river, brook, or underground stream.

watercraft *noun* (*pl* **watercraft**) **1** skill in handling boats, sailing, etc. **2** a vessel for water transport.

watercress *noun* any of several cresses that grow in wet places, *esp* either of two cresses widely grown for their peppery-flavoured dark green leaves used in salads: genus *Rorippa*.

water-diviner *noun Brit* somebody who searches for water using a divining rod; a dowser.

watered-down *adj* modified or reduced in force or effectiveness. *a watered-down version of the original.*

waterfall *noun* a vertical or steep descent of the water of a river or stream.

water flea *noun* a small aquatic crustacean: genus *Daphnia*.

waterfowl *noun* (*pl* **waterfowls** *or collectively* **waterfowl**) **1** a bird, *esp* a duck, that frequents water. **2** swimming game birds collectively, e.g. duck, as distinguished from upland game birds, e.g. grouse.

waterfront *noun* land or a section of a town fronting or bordering on a body of water.

water gas *noun* a poisonous inflammable gaseous mixture that consists chiefly of carbon monoxide and hydrogen, is usu made by blowing air and then steam over red-hot coke or coal, and is used *esp* as a fuel.

water gate *noun* **1** a gate giving access to a body of water. **2** a floodgate.

water gauge *noun* an instrument that indicates the height of water, *esp* in a steam boiler.

water glass *noun* **1** a solution of sodium or potassium silicate used as a cement, as a protective coating and fireproofing agent, and in preserving eggs. **2** an open box or tube with a glass bottom used for examining objects under water.

water hammer *noun* the sound of a violent shaking or agitation of a moving liquid or gas, e.g. water or steam, against the sides of a containing pipe or vessel.

water hemlock *noun* = COWBANE.

water hen *noun* any of various waterside birds, e.g. a coot or moorhen, related to the rails.

water hole *noun* a natural hollow in which water collects, used *esp* by animals as a drinking place.

water hyacinth *noun* a showy S American floating aquatic plant that often clogs waterways in warm regions: *Eichhornia crassipes*.

water ice *noun* a frozen dessert of water, sugar, and flavouring.

watering can *noun* a vessel with a handle and a long spout often fitted with a rose, used for watering plants.

watering hole *noun* **1** a pool or water-filled depression where animals come to drink. **2** *informal* a pub, hotel, or other place used, *esp* habitually, for convivial drinking.

watering place *noun* **1** a place where water may be obtained, *esp* one where animals come to drink. **2** a health or recreational resort featuring mineral springs or bathing, *esp* a spa.

water jacket *noun* an outer casing which holds water or through which water circulates, *esp* for cooling.

water jump *noun* an obstacle, e.g. in a steeplechase, consisting of a pool or ditch of water.

water level *noun* **1** the level reached by the surface of a body of water. **2** = WATER TABLE.

water lily *noun* any of numerous species of aquatic plants with floating leaves and usu showy colourful flowers: family Nymphaeaceae.

waterline *noun* **1a** the level on the hull of a vessel to which the surface of the water comes when it is afloat. **b** any of several lines marked on the hull to correspond with this level. **2** a line marking the level that a river or the sea has reached.

waterlogged /ˈwawtəlogd/ *adj* **1** filled or soaked with water: *waterlogged soil.* **2** said of a ship: so filled with water as to be unable to float or almost unable to float. [WATER¹ + LOG² in the obsolete sense 'to cause to become like a log']

waterloo /wawtəˈlooh/ *noun* (*pl* **waterloos**) (*often* **Waterloo**) a decisive defeat. [named after *Waterloo*, a town in Belgium, scene of Napoleon's defeat by British and Prussian armies in 1815]

water main *noun* a major pipe for conveying water.

waterman *noun* (*pl* **watermen**) a man who works on or near water or who engages in water recreations, *esp* a boatman whose boat and services are available for hire.

watermark¹ *noun* **1** a marking in paper visible when the paper is held up to the light. **2** a mark indicating the height to which water has risen; a waterline.

watermark² *verb trans* to mark (paper) with a watermark.

water meadow *noun* a meadow kept fertile by a regular influx of water, e.g. from the flooding of a bordering river.

watermelon *noun* **1** a large melon with a hard green or white often striped or variegated rind, a sweet watery pink, yellowish, or red pulp, and many seeds. **2** the widely cultivated African climbing plant that bears this fruit: *Citrullus lanatus*.

water meter *noun* a meter for measuring the rate of flow of water through a pipe or the quantity of water that flows through it.

water milfoil *noun* = MILFOIL (2).

water mill *noun* a mill whose machinery is moved by water.

water moccasin *noun* a venomous semiaquatic snake of the pit viper family, found in marshes and swamps in the southern USA: *Agkistrodon piscivorus*.

water nymph *noun* a nymph, e.g. a naiad, associated with a body of water.

water of crystallization *noun* water of hydration present in many crystallized substances that is usu essential for maintenance of a particular crystal structure.

water of hydration *noun* water that is chemically combined with a substance to form a hydrate and can be expelled, e.g. by heating, without essentially altering the composition of the substance.

water ouzel *noun* = DIPPER (2).

water pepper *noun* an annual plant of wet places with extremely acrid peppery juice: *Polygonum hydropiper*.

water pipe *noun* **1** a pipe for conveying water. **2** a large chiefly oriental smoking apparatus consisting of a bowl containing tobacco or other smoking material mounted on a vessel of water through which smoke is drawn and cooled before reaching the mouth.

water pistol *noun* a toy pistol designed to shoot a jet of liquid.

water plantain *noun* a marsh or aquatic plant with acrid juice: genus *Alisma*.

water polo *noun* a game played in water by teams of seven swimmers who try to get an inflated ball into the opposing side's goal.

waterpower *noun* the power derived from movement of a body of water.

waterproof¹ *adj* impervious to water, *esp* covered or treated with a material to prevent passage of water. ➤➤ **waterproofness** *noun*.

waterproof² *noun Brit* a garment made of waterproof fabric.

waterproof³ *verb trans* to make (something) waterproof. ➤➤ **waterproofer** *noun*, **waterproofing** *noun*.

water purslane *noun* a trailing fleshy-leaved plant found in wet places: *Lythrum portula*.

water rail *noun* a Eurasian rail with olive brown upper parts, conspicuous black and white bars on the flanks, and a long red bill: *Rallus aquaticus*.

water rat *noun* a rodent that frequents water, *esp* a water vole.

water rate *noun* in Britain, the charge made to a householder for the use of the public water supply.

water-repellent *adj* treated with a finish that is resistant but not impervious to penetration by water.

water-resistant *adj* = WATER-REPELLENT.

water scorpion *noun* any of several species of aquatic bugs with the abdomen extended into a long breathing tube: family Nepidae.

watershed *noun* **1** a dividing ridge between two drainage areas. **2** a crucial turning point: *Suez was the watershed between our imperial past and our offshore island future* — General William Jackson. **3** *Brit* the time of day before which material considered unsuitable for children should not be shown on television: *the nine o'clock watershed.* [WATER[1] + *shed* a ridge of high ground, from Old English *scead* separation]

waterside *noun* the margin of a body of water.

watersider *noun Aus, NZ* a docker.

water sign *noun* in astrology, any of the three signs of the Zodiac Cancer, Scorpio, and Pisces: compare AIR SIGN, EARTH SIGN, FIRE SIGN.

water ski *noun* a board used singly or in pairs for standing on and planing over water while being towed at speed.

water-ski *verb intrans* (**water-skis, water-skied** *or* **water-ski'd, water-skiing**) to use water skis. ➤ **water-skier** *noun,* **water-skiing** *noun.*

water-softener *noun* a substance or device for softening hard water.

water spaniel *noun* a spaniel of a large breed, having a heavy curly coat, and used *esp* for retrieving waterfowl.

watersplash *noun Brit* a stretch of road submerged by water.

watersports *pl noun* sports that take place on or in water.

waterspout *noun* **1** a funnel-shaped column of rotating wind usu extending from the underside of a cumulus or cumulonimbus cloud down to a cloud of spray torn up from the surface of a sea, lake, etc. **2** a pipe, duct, or orifice from which water is spouted or through which it is carried.

water table *noun* the level below which the ground is wholly saturated with water.

watertight *adj* **1** of such tight construction or fit as to be impermeable to water. **2** said of an argument: impossible to disprove; without loopholes. **3** isolated from other ideas, influences, etc; discrete: *Experiences cannot be divided into watertight compartments.*

water tower *noun* a tower supporting a raised water tank to provide the necessary steady pressure to distribute water.

water vapour *noun* water in a vaporous form, *esp* when below boiling temperature and diffused, e.g. in the atmosphere.

water vole *noun* a common large vole of W Europe that inhabits river banks and often digs extensive tunnels: *Arvicola terrestris.*

waterway *noun* **1** a navigable route or body of water. **2** a groove at the edge of a ship's deck for draining the deck.

waterweed *noun* any of various aquatic plants, e.g. a pondweed, with inconspicuous flowers.

waterwheel *noun* **1** a wheel made to rotate by direct action of water, and used *esp* to drive machinery. **2** a wheel for raising water.

water wings *pl noun* a pair of usu air-filled floats worn to give support to the body of somebody learning to swim.

water witch *noun NAmer* a dowser.

waterworks *noun* (*pl* **waterworks**) **1** (*treated as sing.*) the reservoirs, mains, building, and pumping and purifying equipment by which a water supply is obtained and distributed, e.g. to a city. **2** *Brit, euphem or humorous* the urinary system. **3** *informal* the shedding of tears: *She turns on the waterworks whenever she wants her own way.*

waterworn *adj* worn or smoothed by the action of water.

watery *adj* **1a** consisting of or filled with water. **b** containing, sodden with, or yielding water or a thin liquid: *a watery solution; watery vesicles.* **c** containing too much water: *watery soup.* **d** secreting water, *esp* tears: *watery eyes.* **2a** pale or faint: *a watery sun.* **b** vapid or wishy-washy: *a watery writing style.* ➤ **wateriness** *noun.*

watt /wot/ *noun* the SI unit of power equal to the expenditure of one joule of energy in one second or to the electrical power required for one amp of current to flow across a potential difference of one volt: compare VOLT-AMPERE. [named after James *Watt* d.1819, Scottish engineer]

wattage /'wotij/ *noun* an amount of power expressed in watts, *esp* the amount of electrical power required by an appliance.

watt-hour *noun* a unit of work or energy equivalent to the power of one watt operating for one hour.

wattle[1] /'wotl/ *noun* **1a** a framework of poles interwoven with slender branches or reeds and used, *esp* formerly, in building. **b** material for such a construction. **2** a fleshy protuberance usu near or on the head or neck, *esp* of a bird. **3** an Australian acacia with spikes of brightly coloured flowers: *Acacia pycnatha* and related

species. ➤➤ **wattled** *adj.* [Old English *watel;* (sense 2) may be of different origin]

wattle[2] *verb trans* **1** to form or build (something) of or with wattle. **2** to interlace (e.g. branches) to form wattle.

wattle and daub *noun* a framework of wattle or infill of wattle covered and plastered with clay and used in building construction.

wattmeter *noun* an instrument for measuring electrical power in watts.

waul /wawl/ *verb intrans* to howl, wail, or cry like a cat or newborn baby. [imitative]

Wave /wayv/ *noun NAmer* formerly, a member of WAVES.

wave[1] /wayv/ *verb intrans* **1** to give a signal or salute by moving the hand or fingers or something held in the hand. **2** to flutter loosely to and fro: *Flags were waving in the breeze.* **3** to be flourished or brandished to and fro: *Their swords waved and flashed.* **4** to sway in the wind with a wavelike motion: *a field of waving grain.* **5** to follow a curving line or take a wavy form; to undulate. ➤ *verb trans* **1** to cause (something) to swing to and fro. **2** to direct (somebody) by waving; to flag or signal (them): *The man waved us on; She waved the car to a halt.* **3** to gesture with (the hand or an object) in greeting, farewell, or homage. **4** to convey (something) by waving: *We went to the station to wave farewell.* **5** to brandish or flourish (something): *The gangster waved a pistol menacingly.* **6** to give a curving or undulating shape to (e.g. hair). ✳ **wave something aside** to dismiss or put something out of mind; to disregard it. [Old English *wafian* to wave with the hands]

wave[2] *noun* **1** a moving ridge or swell on the surface of a liquid, e.g. the sea. **2** (**the waves**) *literary* open water. **3a** a shape or outline that has successive curves. **b** one of the crests of such a form or a crest together with its adjacent trough. **4** a waviness of the hair. **5** an undulating line or streak, or a pattern formed by such lines. **6** a surge of sensation or emotion: *A wave of anger swept over her.* **7** a movement involving large numbers of people in a common activity: *waves of protest.* **8** an *esp* artistic trend, tendency, or movement: *the new wave of French film directors.* **9** a sudden increase or wide occurrence of a specified activity: *a wave of house-buying.* **10** a sweep of the hand or arm, or of some object held in the hand, used as a signal or greeting. **11** a rolling or undulatory movement, or any one of a series of such movements, passing along a surface or through the air. **12a** a surging movement of a group: *a sudden wave of new arrivals.* **b** any of a succession of influxes of people migrating into a region. **c** (*treated as sing. or pl*) a line of attacking or advancing troops, aircraft, etc. **13a** a periodic disturbance or variation of a physical quantity, e.g. electric or magnetic intensity or air pressure, by which energy is transferred progressively from point to point either through space or through a physical medium, e.g. water or air, by transient local displacement of the particles of the medium but without its permanent movement: *a sound wave; a radio wave.* **b** one complete cycle of such a disturbance. **14** a graphical representation of a wave; a waveform: *a sine wave.* **15** a marked change in temperature; a period of hot or cold weather. **16** an undulating or jagged line constituting a graphical representation of an action, e.g. the beating of the heart. ✳ **make waves 1** *informal* to cause trouble or make a fuss. **2** *informal* to create a considerable, usu good, impression. ➤➤ **waveless** *adj.*

wave band *noun* a band of radio frequency waves.

wave equation *noun* in mathematics, a partial differential equation of the second order whose solutions describe wave phenomena.

waveform *noun* in physics, the graphic representation of the variation of a quantity, e.g. voltage, with respect to some other factor, e.g. time or distance.

wave front *noun* in physics, a surface composed at any instant of all the points just reached by a wave in its propagation through a medium.

wave function *noun* in physics, a quantum mechanical function representing the probability of finding a specified elementary particle within a specified volume of space.

waveguide *noun* a metal tube or similar structure of such dimensions that it will guide electromagnetic waves, *esp* microwaves, along its length.

wavelength *noun* the distance in the line of advance of a wave from any one point to the next point of corresponding phase, e.g. from one peak to the next. ✳ **be on somebody's/the same wavelength** to have the same outlook, views, etc as somebody else: *I've* *seen her with kids once or twice and she seems to get on with them instinctively. To be on the same wavelength* — Julian Barnes.

wavelet /'wayvlit/ *noun* a little wave; a ripple.

wave mechanics *pl noun* (*treated as sing.*) in physics, a theory of matter that gives a mathematical interpretation of the structure of matter based on the concept that elementary particles, e.g. electrons, protons, or neutrons, possess wave properties.

wave number *noun* in physics, the number of waves per unit distance of radiant energy; the reciprocal of the wavelength.

waver[1] /'wayvə/ *verb intrans* (**wavered, wavering**) **1** to vacillate between choices; to fluctuate. **2a** to sway unsteadily to and fro; to reel. **b** to quiver or flicker: *wavering flames.* **c** to hesitate as if about to give way; to falter. **3** to make a tremulous sound; to quaver. ➤➤ **waverer** *noun*, **wavering** *noun and adj*, **waveringly** *adv*, **wavery** *adj*. [Middle English *waveren* from Old Norse *vafra* to flicker]

Usage note _____

waver or waiver? These two words are easily confused. To *waver* is a verb meaning 'to be unable to decide', 'to show signs of indecision', or 'to totter': *A week ago she was firmly on our side, but now she's starting to waver. Waiver* is a noun from the verb *to waive* and means 'a statement or document renouncing a right or claim': *We had to sign a waiver giving up our right to compensation in case of injury.*

waver[2] *noun* the act or an instance of wavering.

WAVES *abbr* NAmer Women Accepted for Volunteer Emergency Service, the women's reserve of the US Navy, organized during World War II, but now no longer a separate branch.

wave theory *noun* in physics, the theory that light and other electromagnetic radiation consists of waves.

wave train *noun* a succession of similar waves at equal intervals.

wavy *adj* (**wavier, waviest**) **1** having waves: *wavy hair.* **2** having a wavelike form or outline: *a wavy line.* ➤➤ **wavily** *adv*, **waviness** *noun*.

wa-wa /'wah wah/ *noun* see WAH-WAH.

wax[1] /waks/ *noun* **1** = BEESWAX. **2a** any of numerous plant or animal substances that are harder, more brittle, and less greasy than fats. **b** a solid substance, e.g. ozocerite or paraffin wax, of mineral origin consisting usu of higher hydrocarbons. **c** a pliable or liquid composition used *esp* for sealing, taking impressions, or polishing. **d** a resinous preparation used by shoemakers for rubbing thread. **3** a waxy secretion, *esp* cerumen. [Old English *weax*]

wax[2] *verb trans* **1** to treat or rub (something) with wax, usu for polishing or stiffening. **2** to remove hair from (a part of the body) using melted wax.

wax[3] *verb intrans* **1** said of the moon, a satellite, etc: to have an increasing area of the illuminated surface visible. **2** to assume a specified characteristic, quality, or state; *specif* to become, *esp* in speaking or describing: *She waxed indignant; He waxed lyrical about the joys of Greece.* **3** *formal or literary* to increase in size, numbers, strength, prosperity, intensity, or duration; to grow. [Old English *weaxan*]

wax[4] *noun* Brit, informal, dated a fit of temper. [perhaps from WAX[3]]

waxberry /'waksb(ə)ri/ *noun* (*pl* **waxberries**) **1** the wax-coated berry of the wax myrtle. **2** the snowberry.

waxbill *noun* any of several species of African or Asian birds with white, pink, or reddish bills of a waxy appearance: family Estrildidae.

waxcloth *noun* = OILCLOTH.

waxed cloth *noun* = OILCLOTH.

waxed paper *noun* paper coated or impregnated with wax to make it resistant to water and grease, used *esp* as a wrapping for food.

waxen *adj* **1** resembling wax, *esp* in being pliable, smooth, or pallid: *For men have marble, women waxen, minds* — Shakespeare. **2** made of or covered with wax: *The doll flew out of Menie's hand, fell on the hearthstone, and broke its waxen face* — Scott.

wax myrtle *noun* any of several species of trees or shrubs with aromatic evergreen leaves; *esp* a N American shrub with small hard berries that have a thick coating of white wax: genus *Myrica.* Also called CANDLEBERRY.

wax palm *noun* **1** an Andean palm with a stem that yields a resinous wax used in candles: *Ceroxylon andicolum.* **2** = CARNAUBA (I).

wax paper *noun* = WAXED PAPER.

wax resist *noun* a method of decorating paper, pottery, etc by using wax to mark out a pattern which will resist paint and glaze.

waxwing *noun* a Eurasian bird with a pinkish chestnut crest, a short yellow-tipped tail, and red waxlike tips to the secondary wing feathers: *Bombycilla garrulus* and related species.

waxwork *noun* **1** an effigy in wax, usu of a person. **2** (*in pl, but treated as sing.*) an exhibition of wax effigies.

waxy[1] *adj* (**waxier, waxiest**) **1** resembling wax, *esp* in smooth whiteness or pliability. **2** made of, full of, or covered with wax. ➤➤ **waxiness** *noun*.

waxy[2] *adj* Brit, informal, dated highly irritated; angry. [WAX[4]]

way[1] /way/ *noun* **1** a method of doing or accomplishing; a means: *What's the best way to make coffee?* **2** the manner in which something is done or happens: *the British way of life; I don't like the way he's breathing.* **3** a characteristic, regular, or habitual manner or mode of being, behaving, or happening: *He knows nothing of the ways of women; She was old and set in her ways.* **4** a feature or respect: *The book was useful in more ways than one.* **5** a course leading in a direction or towards an objective: *She took the easy way out.* **6** the course of one's life: *He put opportunities in my way.* **7** what one desires, or wants to do: *She always manages to get her own way.* **8** a usu specified degree of participation in an activity or enterprise: *She's also a painter in a small way.* **9** a category or kind: *She hasn't got much in the way of brains; Porridge is all right in its way.* **10a** a thoroughfare for travel or transport from place to place; a road or path: *I live across the way; This year I'm going to walk the West Highland Way; He lives somewhere in Bradfield Way.* **b** an opening for passage: *This door is the only way out.* **c** space or room, *esp* for forward movement: *Move that chair please, it's in my way; Get out of the way!* **11** the course to be travelled from one place to another; a route: *I asked the way to the station; She lost her way.* **12** the length of a course; a distance: *a long way from home; The company has gone a long way towards becoming profitable.* **13** an advance accompanied by or achieved through a specific action: *He's working his way through college; People coughed their way through the concert.* **14** (*often in combination*) a direction or side: *It is coming this way; Stand it the other way up; a three-way junction; a one-way street.* **15** (*in pl*) used adverbially to denote a specified number of participants: *They split the money four ways.* **16** *informal* the area in which one lives, or the direction of this: *Do drop in if you're ever down my way.* **17** a state of affairs; a condition or state: *That's the way things are.* **18** (*in pl*). **a** an inclined structure on which a ship is built or supported in launching. **b** the guiding surfaces on the bed of a machine along which a table or carriage moves. **19** motion or speed of a ship or boat through the water. * **by the way** usu used to introduce or to comment on the introduction of a new subject; incidentally. **by way of 1** to be considered as; as a sort of: *by way of light relief.* **2** by the route through; via. **3** in the form of: *money received by way of grants.* **get/have one's own way** to get what one wants. **have a way with** to be good at dealing with (people, animals, etc): *She has a way with children.* **have a way with one** to be charming, *esp* persuasively charming. **in a way** from one point of view; to some extent. **in the way of** in the form of: *What have we got in the way of food?* **no way** *informal* under no circumstances. **one way and another** taking everything into consideration; on balance. **one way or the other** somehow; by any possible means. **on the way out** *informal* about to disappear, go out of fashion, be dismissed, etc. **on the way 1** while moving along a course; in the course of travelling. **2** coming or approaching. **3** *informal* said of a child: conceived but not yet born: *She's got two kids and another on the way.* **out of the way 1** unusual or remarkable. **2** in or to a secluded or remote place. **3** done or completed: *I always liked to get my homework out of the way before tea.* **under way** in progress; started. **way to go** *chiefly* NAmer an exclamation of approval or encouragement. [Old English *weg*]

way[2] *adv* **1** *informal* considerably; far: *She is way ahead of the class.* **2** *chiefly* NAmer, *informal* all the way: *Pull the switch way back.* * **way back** long ago: *They were friends from way back.*

waybill *noun* a document showing the number of passengers or parcels carried on a vehicle and the fares charged.

wayfarer /'wayfeərə/ *noun* literary a traveller, *esp* on foot. ➤➤ **wayfaring** *noun*. [Middle English *weyfarere*, from *wey, way* WAY[1] + *-farere* traveller, from *faren* FARE[2]]

wayfaring tree /'wayfeəring/ *noun* a European and W Asian shrub of the honeysuckle family with white flowers in dense flat-topped clusters and large oval leaves: *Viburnum lantana.*

waylay *verb trans* (*past tense and past part.* **waylaid** /way'layd/) **1** to ambush and attack (somebody). **2** to accost (somebody): *She waylaid me after the lesson and asked where I'd been the week before.* ▶▶ **waylayer** *noun*.

wayleave *noun* a right of way over private property, e.g. as granted to an electricity company laying cables.

waymark *noun* a signpost marking out a route, e.g. along a footpath.

waymarker *noun* = WAYMARK.

way-out *adj informal* out of the ordinary, *esp* in being daring or experimental: *a film too way-out for mainstream audiences.*

waypoint *noun* a point on a route, e.g. a point at which one's position can be checked or where one can stop or change one's course.

-ways *suffix* forming adverbs, with the meaning: in a stated way, direction, or manner: *sideways*; *lengthways*. [Middle English, from *ways, wayes*, genitive of WAY[1]]

ways and means *pl noun* **1** methods and resources for accomplishing something, *esp* for paying expenses. **2** methods and resources for raising revenue for the use of government.

wayside *noun* **1** the side of a road, or land adjacent to a road. **2** (*used before a noun*) adjacent to a road: *a wayside chapel.*

way station *noun NAmer* an intermediate stopping place.

wayward /'waywəd/ *adj* **1** following one's own capricious or wanton inclinations; ungovernable. **2** following no clear principle or law; unpredictable. ▶▶ **waywardly** *adv*, **waywardness** *noun*. [Middle English, short for *awayward* turned away, from AWAY[1] + -WARD]

wazzock /'wazək/ *noun Brit, informal* a fool. [of unknown origin]

Wb *abbr* weber.

WBA *abbr* World Boxing Association.

WBC *abbr* World Boxing Council.

WC *abbr* **1** *Brit* water closet. **2** West Central (London postcode).

WCC *abbr* World Council of Churches.

WD *abbr* Windward Islands Dominica (international vehicle registration for Dominican Republic).

we /wee/ *pronoun* **1** I and you and/or one or more other people: *Shall we dance, Mary?*; *May we go, Sir?* **2a** used in place of *I* by sovereigns, and occasionally others, in making public pronouncements: *We are no tyrant, but a Christian king* — Shakespeare; *We have become a grandmother* — Margaret Thatcher. **b** used in place of *I* by writers and editors to preserve an impersonal character. **3** used patronizingly in place of *you*, e.g. to children or the sick: *How do we find ourselves today, Mr Jones?* [Old English *wē*]

WEA *abbr Brit* Workers' Educational Association.

weak /week/ *adj* **1a** deficient in physical vigour; feeble or debilitated. **b** not able to sustain or exert much weight, pressure, or strain. **c** not able to resist external force or withstand attack. **2a** lacking a particular mental or intellectual quality, e.g. decisiveness, judgment, or discernment. **b** not firmly decided; vacillating. **c** unable to withstand temptation or persuasion. **3** not factually grounded or logically presented: *a weak argument.* **4a** unable to function properly: *weak eyes.* **b** lacking skill or proficiency: *Weaker students will need extra tutoring.* **c** indicative of a lack of skill or aptitude: *Maths was his weakest subject.* **5** without vigour of expression or effect: *a weak retort; a weak joke.* **6** deficient in strength or flavour; dilute: *weak coffee.* **7a** deficient in the required quality or ingredient: *My hand was weak in trumps.* **b** lacking normal intensity or potency: *a weak strain of virus.* **8** not having or exerting authority or political power: *weak government.* **9** tending towards a lower price: *a weak market.* **10** in grammar, of or being an English verb or verb conjugation that forms the past tense and past participle by adding the suffix *-ed* or *-d* or *-t*, or a similar verb or verb conjugation in other Germanic languages: compare STRONG. **11** said of a syllable: unstressed. **12** in chemistry, forming ions only slightly in solution: *weak acids and bases.* ▶▶ **weakish** *adj*. [Middle English *weike* from Old Norse *veikr*]

weaken *verb* (**weakened, weakening**) ▶ *verb trans* to make (somebody or something) weak or weaker. ▶ *verb intrans* to become weak or weaker.

weak force *noun* = WEAK INTERACTION.

weak interaction *noun* in physics, an interaction between elementary particles that is responsible for some particle decay processes, for beta decay, and for emission and absorption of neutrinos: compare STRONG INTERACTION.

weak-kneed *adj* **1** feeling faint and weak. **2** lacking in resolution; easily intimidated.

weakling /'weekling/ *noun* a person or animal weak in body, character, or mind.

weakly *adj* (**weaklier, weakliest**) feeble or poorly. ▶▶ **weakliness** *noun*, **weakly** *adv*.

weak-minded *adj* **1** lacking willpower or resolution. **2** feebleminded. ▶▶ **weak-mindedness** *noun*.

weakness *noun* **1a** the quality or state of being weak. **b** an instance or period of being weak: *In a moment of weakness, I agreed to go.* **2** a fault or defect. **3a** a special desire or fondness: *a weakness for chocolates.* **b** an object of special desire or fondness.

weak sister *noun NAmer, informal* a member of a group who is weak and needs aid.

weal[1] *or* **wheal** /weel, wiəl/ *noun* a raised mark on the surface of the body; a welt. [alteration of WALE]

weal[2] *noun archaic or formal* a sound, healthy, or prosperous state; well-being. [Old English *wela*]

Weald /weeld, wiəld/ *noun* (**the Weald**) an area of open grassland, once wooded, covering parts of Sussex, Kent, and Surrey. [Old English *weald* forest]

wealth /welth/ *noun* **1** abundance of money and valuable material possessions. **2** the state of being rich: *There is no road to wealth so easy and respectable as that of matrimony* — Trollope. **3** an abundant supply; a profusion: *a wealth of detail.* [Middle English *welthe*, from WEAL[2] or WELL[2]]

wealth tax *noun* a tax on the value of assets owned by persons and private institutions.

wealthy *adj* (**wealthier, wealthiest**) **1** having wealth; extremely affluent. **2** characterized by abundance: *a country wealthy in oil.* ▶▶ **wealthily** *adv*.

wean[1] /ween/ *verb trans* **1** to accustom (a child or other young mammal) to take food other than the mother's milk. **2** (*usu* + off/from) to cause (somebody) to abandon a state of usu unwholesome dependence or preoccupation. **3** (+ on) to cause (somebody) to become acquainted with an idea, writer, etc at an early age. [Old English *wenian* to accustom, wean]

wean[2] /wayn/ *noun Scot, N Eng* a small child. [contraction of *wee ane* wee one]

weaner *noun* a young animal recently weaned.

weanling /'weenling/ *noun* an animal newly weaned.

weapon /'wepən/ *noun* **1** an instrument of offensive or defensive combat. **2** a means used to further one's cause in conflict: *His caustic wit was his best weapon.* ▶▶ **weaponed** *adj*, **weaponless** *adj*. [Old English *wǽpen*]

weaponize *verb trans* **1** to make (something) suitable for use as a weapon. **2** to deploy weapons in (a place).

weaponry /'wepənri/ *noun* weapons.

wear[1] /weə/ *verb* (*past tense* **wore**, *past part.* **worn**) ▶ *verb trans* **1a** to have or carry (a garment) on the body as clothing or adornment. **b** to use (a type or style of clothing) habitually: *She wears dark colours at work.* **c** to have (the hair) in a specified style. **2** to have or show (a specified expression) on the face: *She wore a happy smile.* **3** to damage or diminish (something) by use. **4** to produce (damage) gradually by use or friction: *They had worn a hole in the rug.* **5** *Brit, informal* (*usu in negative contexts*) to find (a claim or proposal) acceptable: *I don't think the boss will wear it.* **6** to show or fly (a flag or colours) on a ship. **7** to exhaust or lessen the strength of (somebody); to weary or fatigue (somebody). ▶ *verb intrans* **1** to endure use; to last to a specified extent under use or the passage of time: *The curtains have worn well.* **2a** to diminish or decay through use: *The heels of his shoes had begun to wear.* **b** to go by slowly or tediously: *The day wore into afternoon.* **c** to assume a specified quality by use or the passage of time: *His hair is wearing thin.* ✻ **wear the trousers** to have the controlling authority in a household. **wear thin** to become weakened or exhausted: *His patience was wearing thin.* ▶▶ **wearability** /weərə'biliti/ *noun*, **wearable** *adj*, **wearer** *noun*. [Old English *werian*]

wear[2] *noun* **1** wearing or being worn: *We sell mainly clothes for everyday wear.* **2** (*often in combinations*) clothing, usu of a specified kind or for a specified occasion: *men's wear; swimwear.* **3** capacity to withstand use; durability: *There was plenty of wear left in it.* **4** minor damage or deterioration through use.

wear³ *verb* (*past tense* **wore** /waw/, *past part.* **worn** /wawn/) ➤ *verb trans* in sailing, to bring (a vessel) onto another tack by turning the bows away from the wind until the wind is on its stern and then bringing the bows up towards the wind on the other side: *Stand by to wear ship.* ➤ *verb intrans* said of a ship: to change to an opposite tack by turning the stern to the wind. [origin unknown]

wear and tear *noun* the normal deterioration or depreciation which something suffers in the course of use.

wear down *verb trans* to weary and overcome (somebody) by persistent resistance or pressure.

wearing *adj* causing fatigue; tiring. ➤➤ **wearingly** *adv.*

wearisome /'wiəris(ə)m/ *adj* causing weariness; tiresome. ➤➤ **wearisomely** *adv*, **wearisomeness** *noun.*

wear off *verb intrans* to decrease or lose effectiveness gradually.

wear out *verb trans* **1** to make (something) useless by long or excessive wear or use. **2** to tire or exhaust (somebody). ➤ *verb intrans* to become useless from long or excessive wear or use.

weary¹ /'wiəri/ *adj* (**wearier, weariest**) **1** exhausted or tired. **2** expressing or characteristic of weariness: *a weary smile.* **3** (+ of) having one's patience, tolerance, or pleasure exhausted. ➤➤ **weariless** *adj*, **wearily** *adv*, **weariness** *noun.* [Old English *wērig*]

weary² *verb* (**wearies, wearied, wearying**) ➤ *verb intrans* **1** to become weary. **2** *chiefly Scot* (*usu* + on/for) to feel a desire; to long. ➤ *verb trans* to make (somebody) weary: *Age shall not weary them, nor the years condemn* — Laurence Binyon. ➤➤ **wearying** *adj*, **wearyingly** *adv.*

weasel¹ /'weezl/ *noun* (*pl* **weasels** or collectively **weasel**) **1** any of several species of small slender active flesh-eating mammals that feeds on small birds and mammals, are mostly reddish brown with white or yellowish underparts, and, in northern forms, turn white in winter: genus *Mustela*. **2** *informal* somebody who is treacherous. ➤➤ **weaselly** *adj.* [Old English *weosule*]

weasel² *verb intrans* (**weaselled, weaselling,** NAmer **weaseled, weaseling**) **1** (*often* + out) to escape from or evade a situation or obligation. **2** *chiefly NAmer* to use weasel words; to equivocate.

weasel words *pl noun* words used in order to evade or retreat from a direct or forthright statement or position; an equivocation. [from the weasel's reputed habit of sucking the contents out of an egg while leaving the shell superficially intact]

weather¹ /'wedhə/ *noun* **1** the prevailing atmospheric conditions, *esp* with regard to heat or cold, wetness or dryness, calm or storm, and clearness or cloudiness. **2** (*used before a noun*) windward. ✳ **make heavy weather 1** said of a ship: to pitch and roll because of rough seas. **2** *informal* (+ of) to have difficulty in doing or completing (something). **under the weather** *informal* mildly ill or depressed; not fully well. [Old English *weder*]

weather² *verb* (**weathered, weathering**) ➤ *verb trans* **1** to expose or subject (something) to atmospheric conditions. **2** to bear up against and come safely through (something): *We had to weather a storm.* **3** to sail or pass to the windward of (a piece of land). **4** to make (a surface) slope so that it will shed water. ➤ *verb intrans* to undergo or be resistant to change by weathering: *Wood weathers better if creosoted.*

weather-beaten *adj* **1** worn or damaged by exposure to weather. **2** toughened or tanned by the weather.

weatherboard *noun* **1** a board fixed horizontally and usu overlapping the board below to form a protective outdoor wall covering that will throw off water. **2** a sloping board fixed to the bottom of a door for excluding rain, snow, etc. ➤➤ **weatherboarding** *noun.*

weather-bound *adj* unable to proceed or take place because of bad weather.

weathercock *noun* a weather vane, *esp* one in the figure of a cockerel.

weathered *adj* **1** seasoned by exposure to the weather. **2a** altered in form by weathering. **b** altered by artificial means, *esp* staining, to produce a similar effect: *weathered oak.* **3** made sloping so as to shed water: *a weathered windowsill.*

weather eye *noun* **1** an eye quick to observe coming changes in the weather. **2** a constant and shrewd alertness: *He had … promised me a silver fourpenny on the first of every month if I would only keep my 'weather-eye open for a seafaring man with one leg'* — Stevenson.

weatherglass *noun dated* a barometer.

weather house *noun* a model house containing two figures, one of which emerges in fine weather, the other when it rains.

weathering *noun* **1** the action of wind, rain, frost, etc in altering the colour, texture, composition, or form of exposed objects; *specif* the physical disintegration and chemical decomposition of rock at or near the earth's surface. **2** a slope given to a surface so that it will shed water.

weatherly *adj* said of a ship: able to sail close to the wind with little leeway. ➤➤ **weatherliness** *noun.*

weatherman *noun* (*pl* **weathermen**) a man, *esp* a meteorologist, who reports and forecasts the weather, usu on the radio or television.

weather map *noun* a map or chart showing meteorological conditions at a given time and over an extended region.

weatherproof¹ *adj* able to withstand exposure to weather without damage or loss of function.

weatherproof² *verb trans* to make (something) weatherproof.

weather station *noun* a station for taking, recording, and reporting meteorological observations.

weather strip *noun* a strip of material used to exclude rain, snow, and cold air from the joints of a door or window.

weather-strip *verb trans* (**weather-stripped, weather-stripping**) to apply a weather strip to (a door or window). ➤➤ **weather-stripping** *noun.*

weather vane *noun* a movable device attached to an elevated structure, e.g. a spire, in order to show the direction of the wind.

weather-wise *adj* **1** skilful in forecasting the weather. **2** skilful in forecasting changes in opinion or feeling: *a weather-wise politician.*

weatherwoman *noun* (*pl* **weatherwomen**) a woman, *esp* a meteorologist, who reports and forecasts the weather, usu on the radio or television.

weatherworn *adj* weather-beaten.

weave¹ /weev/ *verb* (*past tense* **wove** /wohv/, *past part.* **wove** or **woven** /'wohv(ə)n/) ➤ *verb trans* **1a** to form (cloth) by interlacing strands, e.g. of yarn; *specif* to make (cloth) on a loom by interlacing warp and weft threads. **b** to interlace (e.g. threads) to form cloth. **c** to make (e.g. a basket) by intertwining. **2** said of a spider or an insect: to spin (a web, cocoon, etc). **3** to interlace (things), *esp* to form a texture, fabric, or design. **4a** to produce (something) by elaborately combining elements into a coherent whole. **b** (*usu* + in/into) to introduce (something) as an appropriate element. ➤ *verb intrans* to work at weaving; to make cloth by weaving. [Old English *wefan*]

weave² *noun* a pattern or method for interlacing the threads of woven fabrics.

weave³ *verb trans* to direct (e.g. the body or one's way) in a winding or zigzag course, *esp* to avoid obstacles. ➤ *verb intrans* to move by weaving. [prob from Old Norse *veifa* to wave]

weaver *noun* **1** somebody who weaves, *esp* as an occupation. **2** any of numerous species of African and Asian birds that resemble finches and usu construct elaborate nests of interlaced vegetation: family Ploceidae.

weaverbird *noun* = WEAVER (2).

web¹ /web/ *noun* **1a** the silken structure spun by most spiders and used as a resting place and a trap for small prey, e.g. insects. **b** a similar network spun by an insect or insect larva. **2** an intricate structure suggestive of something woven; a network. **3** (**the Web**) the World Wide Web. **4** a tissue or membrane of an animal or plant, *esp* that uniting fingers or toes either at their bases, e.g. in human beings, or along most of their length, e.g. in ducks and many other water birds. **5** a thin metal sheet, plate, or strip, *esp* the plate connecting the upper and lower flanges of a girder or rail. **6a** a continuous sheet of paper manufactured or undergoing manufacture on a paper machine. **b** a roll of such paper for use in a rotary printing press. **7** a woven fabric, *esp* a length of fabric while still being woven on a loom or in the process of being removed from a loom. **8** a snare or entanglement: *They were caught in a web of intrigue.* [Old English *webb* woven fabric]

web² *verb* (**webbed, webbing**) ➤ *verb trans* to cover (something) with a web or network. ➤ *verb intrans* to construct or form a web.

webbed *adj* having or being toes or fingers joined by a web.

webbing *noun* a strong narrow closely woven tape used for straps, upholstery, or harnesses.

web browser *noun* = BROWSER (3).

webcam /'webkam/ *noun* **1** a web page that displays images or videos produced by a digital camera connected to a computer. **2** a camera that produces such images. [WEB¹ (3) + CAMERA]

webcast /'webkast/ *noun* a live broadcast that goes out on the Internet, usu with images as well as sound. ➤➤ **webcasting** *noun*.

weber /'vaybə/ *noun* the SI unit of magnetic flux. [named after Wilhelm *Weber* d.1891, German physicist]

webfoot *noun* a foot with webbed toes. ➤➤ **web-footed** *adj*.

weblog /'weblog/ *noun* a website on which visitors can record points of interest or information about themselves or other sites. ➤➤ **weblogger** *noun*, **weblogging** *noun*.

web offset *noun* offset printing by a web press.

web page *noun* a hypertext document that can be accessed via the World Wide Web.

web press *noun* a press that prints a continuous roll of paper.

website *noun* a group of related web pages giving information about a particular subject, company, institution, etc.

web wheel *noun* **1** a wheel with a plate or web instead of spokes. **2** a wheel formed from one piece.

wed /wed/ *verb* (**wedding, past tense and past part. wedded** *or* **wed**) ➤ *verb trans* **1a** said *esp* of a minister, priest, etc: to marry (two people). **b** to get married to (somebody): *He wedded his childhood sweetheart.* **2** to unite (two things) as if by marriage. ➤ *verb intrans* to get married. [Old English *weddian*]

we'd /wid, *strong* weed/ *contraction* **1** we had. **2** we would. **3** we should.

wedded *adj* **1** joined in marriage. **2** relating to marriage; conjugal or connubial: *wedded bliss*. **3** (+ to) strongly attached or committed to something: *He is firmly wedded to this view.*

wedding *noun* **1** a marriage ceremony, usu with its accompanying festivities; nuptials. **2** a joining in close association. **3** (*usu in combination*) a wedding anniversary or its celebration: *a golden wedding*.

wedding breakfast *noun* a celebratory meal that follows a marriage ceremony.

wedding cake *noun* a rich cake, often a fruit cake with marzipan and royal icing and typically in two or more tiers, served at a wedding reception.

wedding ring *noun* a ring, usu a plain band of gold, given by one marriage partner to the other during the wedding ceremony and worn thereafter to signify marital status.

wedge¹ /wej/ *noun* **1** a piece of wood, metal, etc that tapers to a thin edge and is used *esp* for splitting wood or for raising or securing heavy objects. **2** something wedge-shaped: *a wedge of pie*. **3** a shoe with a wedge-shaped sole raised at the heel and tapering towards the toe. **4** an iron golf club with a broad face angled for maximum loft, used *esp* for bunker shots and short pitches to the green. **5** something causing a breach or separation: *The affair drove a wedge between us*. ✱ **thin end of the wedge** something apparently insignificant that is the forerunner of a more important development. [Old English *wecg*]

wedge² *verb trans* **1** to secure (something) by driving in a wedge. **2** (+ in/into) to force or press (somebody or something) into a narrow space. **3** to split or force (something) apart with or as if with a wedge.

Wedgwood /'wejwood/ *noun trademark* a type of fine ceramic ware made orig by Josiah Wedgwood and typically decorated with a classical cameo-like design in white relief on a coloured ground. [named after Josiah *Wedgwood* d.1795, English potter]

Wedgwood blue *adj* of a light blue colour typically used in Wedgwood ware. ➤➤ **Wedgwood blue** *noun*.

wedlock /'wedlok/ *noun* the state of being married; marriage. ✱ **out of wedlock** *dated* with the natural parents not legally married to each other: *born out of wedlock*. [Old English *wedlāc* marriage bond, from *wedd* pledge + *-lāc* (suffix denoting activity)]

Wednesday /'wenzday, 'wenzdi, 'wednzday/ *noun* the fourth day of the week, following Tuesday.

Word history
Old English *wōdnesdæg* day of *Wōden*, Odin, the chief god in Norse mythology, a translation of Latin *Mercurii dies* day of Mercury, messenger of the

gods. Odin was often associated with Mercury because of his eloquence and his wide-ranging and swift travels.

Weds *abbr* Wednesday.

wee¹ /wee/ *adj* (**weer, weest**) *chiefly Scot* very small; diminutive. [Middle English *we* from *we* (noun) little bit, from Old English *wǣge* a unit of weight]

wee² *noun chiefly Brit, informal* urine or an act of passing urine. [short for WEE-WEE¹]

wee³ *verb intrans* (**wees, weed, weeing**) *chiefly Brit, informal* to urinate.

weed¹ /weed/ *noun* **1** a wild plant that grows where it is not wanted and spreads over or chokes out cultivated plants. **2** *informal* a weak or unattractively thin person. **3** *informal*. **a** (**the weed**) tobacco. **b** cannabis. **4** a weak, poorly built or lanky horse. ➤➤ **weedless** *adj*. [Old English *wēod*]

weed² *verb intrans and trans* to remove weeds or clear (an area) of weeds: *weed a garden*. ➤➤ **weeder** *noun*.

weedkiller *noun* any of various substances used for killing weeds.

weed out *verb trans* to remove or get rid of (somebody or something harmful or unwanted): *They weeded out the weaker applicants.*

weeds *pl noun* = WIDOW'S WEEDS. [Middle English *wede* garment, from Old English *wǣd, gewǣde*]

weedy *adj* (**weedier, weediest**) **1** covered with or consisting of weeds: *weedy pastures*. **2** *informal* noticeably weak, thin, and ineffectual. ➤➤ **weediness** *noun*.

week¹ /week/ *noun* **1a** a period of seven consecutive days considered as a unit of time: *six weeks later*. **b** the working days during each seven-day period: *She stays in London during the week*. **c** a weekly period of work: *He works a 40-hour week*. **2** a week beginning with a specified day or containing a specified event: *Easter week*. ✱ **week in, week out** for an indefinite or seemingly endless number of weeks. [Old English *wicu, wucu*]

week² *adv chiefly Brit* at a time that is seven days before or after a specified day: *The next meeting is Tuesday week.*

weekday *noun* any day of the week except Saturday and Sunday.

weekend¹ *noun* the period from Friday night to Sunday night.

weekend² *verb intrans informal* to spend the weekend, e.g. at a place away from home. ➤➤ **weekender** *noun*.

weekly¹ *adv* **1** every week. **2** once a week. **3** by the week.

weekly² *adj* **1** occurring, appearing, or done weekly. **2** calculated by the week.

weekly³ *noun* (*pl* **weeklies**) a weekly newspaper or periodical.

weeknight *noun* a night of any day of the week except Saturday and Sunday.

weeny /'weeni/ *adj* (**weenier, weeniest**) *informal* exceptionally small; tiny. [blend of WEE¹ + TINY¹]

weenybopper /'weenibopə/ *noun* a child, *esp* one aged between 8 and 12, who has a keen interest in pop music and follows the latest fashions. [WEENY + -*bopper* as in TEENYBOPPER]

weep¹ /weep/ *verb* (*past tense and past part.* **wept** /wept/) ➤ *verb intrans* **1** to express an emotion, *esp* grief, by shedding tears. **2** to give off or leak liquid slowly; to ooze: *The infected wound was weeping*. **3** said of a tree: to droop over; to bend. ➤ *verb trans* **1** to shed (tears) from the eyes. **2** *archaic* to mourn (somebody). **3** said *esp* of a wound: to exude (a liquid, pus, etc) slowly. [Old English *wēpan*]

weep² *noun* a period or an act of weeping.

weeper *noun* **1** a person who weeps, *esp* a professional mourner. **2** a small statue of a mourning figure on a funeral monument. **3** (*in pl*) something, e.g. a black veil or hatband, worn as a sign of mourning.

weepie *or* **weepy** /'weepi/ *noun* (*pl* **weepies**) *informal* a sad or sentimental film, play, or book.

weeping *adj* said of a tree or shrub: having slender drooping branches.

weeping willow *noun* an Asian willow tree with long drooping branches that is widely grown for ornament: *Salix babylonica*.

weepy¹ *adj* (**weepier, weepiest**) *informal* inclined to weep; tearful. ➤➤ **weepily** *adv*, **weepiness** *noun*.

weepy² *noun* = WEEPIE.

weever /'weevə/ *noun* any of several species of edible marine fishes with a broad spiny head and venomous spines on the dorsal fin: family Trachinidae. [early French *wivre* viper, modification of Latin *vipera*]

weevil /'weevl/ *noun* any of numerous usu small beetles with a long snout bearing jaws at the tip, many of which are harmful, *esp* as larvae, to grain, fruit, and plants: family Curculionidae. ⟫ **weevily** *adj*. [Old English *wifel*]

wee-wee[1] /'wee wee/ *noun informal* urine or an act of urinating, used *esp* by a child or when addressing a child. [baby talk, of imitative origin]

wee-wee[2] *verb intrans* (**wee-wees, wee-weed, wee-weeing**) *informal* to urinate, used *esp* by a child or when addressing a child

w.e.f. *abbr* with effect from.

weft /weft/ *noun* the crosswise yarn that interlaces the warp in a fabric. [Old English *wefta*]

Wehrmacht /'veəmakht/ *noun* the German armed forces just before and during World War II. [German *Wehrmacht*, from *Wehr* defence + *Macht* force, might]

weigela /wie'jeelə, wie'geelə/ *noun* any of various ornamental Asian shrubs with attractive clusters of pink or red flowers: genus *Weigela* and others. [Latin genus name, named after Christian Weigel d.1831, German physician and botanist]

weigh /way/ *verb trans* **1** to ascertain the heaviness of (something), *esp* by using scales. **2** (*often* + out) to measure (a definite quantity of something) on or as if on scales. **3** (*often* + up) to consider (something) carefully, *esp* by balancing opposing factors, in order to reach a conclusion; to evaluate: *weighing the pros and cons*; *She weighed up the advantages of the scheme*. **4a** (*often* + down) to make (something) heavy; to weight. **b** (+ down) to be a burden to (somebody). ⟫ *verb intrans* **1a** to have weight or a specified weight. **b** (+ in/out) to register a weight, e.g. on scales. **2** to be considered important; to count: *The evidence will weigh heavily against him*. **3** (*often* + on/upon) to press down with or as if with a heavy weight: *Her responsibilities weighed upon her*. ✳ **weigh anchor** to pull up an anchor preparatory to sailing. ⟫ **weighable** *adj*, **weigher** *noun*. [Old English *wegan* to move, carry, weigh]

weighbridge *noun* a large scale used for weighing vehicles, usu consisting of a plate level with the surface of a road onto which the vehicles are driven.

weigh in *verb intrans* **1** to have oneself or one's possessions, e.g. luggage, weighed; *esp* to be weighed before or after a horse race or a boxing or wrestling match. **2** *informal* to make a contribution; to join in: *It was a decision they quickly came to regret when the … cousins all weighed in with suggestions of what should go into the window —* A N Wilson.

weigh-in *noun* (*pl* **weigh-ins**) the act or an instance of officially weighing a jockey, boxer, etc before or after a race or match and recording the weight.

weigh out *verb intrans* said of a jockey: to be weighed before a horse race.

weight[1] /wayt/ *noun* **1** the heaviness of a quantity or body; the amount that a quantity or body weighs. **2** the force with which a body is attracted towards the earth or another celestial body by gravitation, equal to the mass of the body multiplied by the local gravitational acceleration. **3a** a system of units of weight or mass: *troy weight*. **b** any of the units of weight used in such a system. **c** a piece of material, e.g. metal, of known weight for use in weighing articles. **4a** something heavy; a load. **b** a heavy object used to hold or press something down or as a counterbalance: *the weights of the clock*. **5** a heavy object thrown or lifted as an athletic exercise or contest. **6** any of the classes into which contestants in certain sports, e.g. boxing and wrestling, are divided according to body weight. **7a** (*often in combination*) the quality of a fabric, e.g. lightness or closeness of weave, that makes it suitable for a particular use or season. **b** (*used before a noun*) denoting a garment made from such a fabric: *a summer-weight suit*. **8** a burden or pressure: *That is a weight off my mind*. **9** excessive body fat: *I'm putting on weight*. **10** relative importance, authority, or influence: *His views don't carry much weight*. **11** in mathematics and statistics, a number assigned to an item to express its relative importance in a frequency distribution or in the set of items to which it belongs. ✳ **worth one's/its weight in gold** very useful, desirable, or valuable. [Old English *wiht*; the spelling has been influenced by WEIGH]

weight[2] *verb trans* **1** to make (something) heavy with or as if with a weight. **2** to oppress (somebody) with a burden: *He's weighted down with cares*. **3** to assign a statistical weight to (something). **4** to arrange (something) in such a way as to create a bias: *This wage structure is weighted in favour of employees with long service*. **5** to increase the heaviness of (e.g. a fabric) by adding an ingredient, e.g. size.

weighted *adj* **1a** said of data, quantities, etc: having a statistical weight assigned. **b** compiled from weighted statistical data: *a weighted average*. **2** said of a racehorse: carrying or handicapped with a particular weight: *He was badly weighted compared to the favourite*.

weighting *noun* **1a** an allowance made to compensate for something that has a distorting effect. **b** the amount of such an allowance. **2** *Brit* an additional sum paid on top of wages or salary, *esp* one paid to offset the higher cost of living in a particular area: *a London weighting of £5000*.

weightless *adj* said of a body or object in a spacecraft or in space: not apparently acted on by gravity or not experiencing the effects of gravity. ⟫ **weightlessly** *adv*, **weightlessness** *noun*.

weightlifting *noun* a sport that involves competitors lifting progressively heavier barbells or other weights, according to prescribed rules. ⟫ **weightlifter** *noun*.

weight training *noun* physical training involving the lifting of usu heavy weights, *esp* barbells.

weight-watcher *noun* somebody who is dieting to lose weight. ⟫ **weight-watching** *noun and adj*.

weighty *adj* (**weightier, weightiest**) **1** having importance, influence, or consequence; momentous. **2** heavy, *esp* in proportion to bulk: *weighty metal*. **3** burdensome or onerous: *the weighty cares of state*. ⟫ **weightily** *adv*, **weightiness** *noun*.

Weil's disease /vielz/ *noun* a form of LEPTOSPIROSIS (a bacterial infection) transmitted by rats. [named after Adolf *Weil* d.1916, German physician, who first described it]

Weimaraner /'viemərahnə/ *noun* a dog of a breed originating in Germany, having a thin short-haired grey coat, and often used as a gundog. [German *Weimaraner* from *Weimar*, a city in Germany where the breed originated]

weir /wiə/ *noun* **1** a dam in a stream to raise the water level or control its flow. **2** a fence or enclosure set in a waterway for trapping fish. [Old English *wer*]

weird[1] /wiəd/ *adj* **1** suggestive of or caused by the supernatural. **2** *informal* very strange or bizarre. ⟫ **weirdly** *adv*, **weirdness** *noun*. [Middle English (Scots) *werd* fateful, from Old English *wyrd* fate, destiny]

weird[2] *noun chiefly Scot, archaic* fate or destiny.

weirdie /'wiədi/ *noun informal* a weirdo.

weirdo /'wiədoh/ *noun* (*pl* **weirdos**) *informal* somebody who is very strange or eccentric.

weka /'wekə/ *noun* a large flightless bird found in New Zealand: *Gallirallus australis*. [Maori *weka*]

welch /welch/ *verb intrans* see WELSH.

welcome[1] /'welkəm/ *interj* used to greet a guest or newcomer on his or her arrival.

welcome[2] *noun* **1** a greeting or reception on arrival or first appearance. **2** the hospitable treatment that a guest may expect: *They had outstayed their welcome*. [alteration, influenced by WELL[1], of Old English *wilcuma* desirable guest, from *wil* desire, pleasure + *cuman* to come]

welcome[3] *adj* **1** received gladly into one's presence or companionship: *I was always welcome in their home*. **2** giving pleasure; received with gladness, *esp* because fulfilling a need: *a welcome relief*. **3** (+ to) willingly permitted or given the right to do or have something: *You're welcome to read it*; *He's welcome to my share*. ✳ **you're welcome** used as a reply to an expression of thanks. ⟫ **welcomely** *adv*, **welcomeness** *noun*.

welcome[4] *verb trans* **1** to greet (somebody) hospitably and with courtesy. **2** to greet or receive (somebody) in the specified, *esp* unpleasant, way: *They welcomed the intruder with a hail of bullets*. **3** to receive or accept (something) with pleasure: *He welcomes danger*. ✳ **welcome with open arms** to greet or accept (somebody or something) with great cordiality or pleasure. ⟫ **welcomer** *noun*, **welcoming** *noun and adj*.

weld[1] /weld/ *verb trans* **1a** to fuse (metallic parts) together by heating and allowing the metals to flow together or by hammering or compressing with or without heating. **b** to unite (plastics) in a similar manner by heating or by using a chemical solvent. **c** to repair, produce, or create (something) by or as if by such a process. **2** to unite (things) closely or inseparably. ➤ *verb intrans* to become or be capable of being welded. ➤➤ **weldability** /-'biliti/ *noun*, **weldable** *adj*, **welder** *noun*. [alteration of obsolete *well* to weld, from Old English *waellan* to boil]

weld[2] *noun* a welded joint.

weld[3] *noun* **1** a European plant with spikes of small yellowish green flowers, formerly widely grown for the yellow dye it yields: *Reseda luteola*. **2** the yellow dye obtained from this plant.

welfare /'welfeə/ *noun* **1** well-being: *She was concerned for her child's welfare*. **2** aid in the form of money or necessities for those not able to provide for themselves, e.g. through poverty, age, or handicap. **3** = WELFARE WORK. ✳ **on welfare** *chiefly NAmer* receiving financial help from the state. [Middle English, from the phrase *wel faren* to fare well]

welfare state *noun* a social system based on the assumption by the state of responsibility for the individual and social welfare of its citizens, e.g. through the provision of unemployment, sickness, etc benefits, old age pensions, free or subsidized health care, etc.

welfare work *noun* organized efforts to improve the living conditions of the poor, elderly, etc. ➤➤ **welfare worker** *noun*.

welkin /'welkin/ *noun literary* **1a** the sky: *The starry welkin cover thou anon with drooping fog* — Shakespeare. **b** heaven. **2** the upper atmosphere. [Old English *wolcen* cloud, sky]

well[1] /wel/ *adv* (**better** /'betə/, **best** /best/) **1a** in a good or proper manner; rightly or satisfactorily: *I did well in maths*. **b** with good effect: *He carries himself well*. **c** with skill or aptitude; expertly: *Well caught!* **d** with prudence; sensibly: *You would do well to ask*. **2** in a kind or friendly manner; favourably: *She spoke well of your idea*. **3** in a prosperous or affluent manner: *He lives well*. **4** to an extent approaching completeness; thoroughly: *The house was well hidden from the road*. **5** easily or fully: *It was well worth the price*. **6** much or considerably: *She's well ahead of her rivals*. **7** in all likelihood; indeed: *That may well be true*. **8** *Brit, informal* very: *a well wicked bike*. ✳ **well and truly** see TRULY. **well away 1** *informal* making good progress. **2** *informal* drunk. **well out of** lucky to be free from or not involved in (something). **well up on** having a good knowledge of (something). [Old English *wel*]

Usage note

Adjectives such as *well-mannered* and *well-known* should always be spelt with a hyphen when used before a noun: *a well-mannered young man; a well-known story*. The hyphen is not usually necessary when the adjective is used after a verb: *She seemed so well mannered*; *As is probably well known to most of you....* The correct way of forming the comparative and superlative of most such adjectives is with *better* and *best*: *the best-equipped research department; You would be better advised to wait*.

well[2] *adj* (**better** /'betə/, **best** /best/) **1** healthy, *esp* cured or recovered. **2** satisfactory or pleasing: *All's well that ends well*. **3** advisable or desirable: *She thought it would be well to leave*. **4** giving cause for thankfulness; fortunate: *It is well that this has happened*. ➤➤ **wellness** *noun*.

well[3] *interj* **1** used to express surprise, indignation, or resignation. **2** used to indicate a pause in talking or to introduce a remark.

well[4] *noun* **1** a pit or hole sunk in the earth to reach a supply of water. **2** a shaft or hole sunk in the earth to reach a natural deposit, e.g. oil or gas. **3** a vessel, space, or hole that contains or holds liquid. **4** a source from which something springs; a fountainhead. **5** an open space extending vertically through the floors of a structure: *a stair well*. **6** *Brit* the open space in front of the judge in a law court. **7** *archaic* a spring of water. **8** in physics, a range of values in which a variable is at a minimum. [Old English (northern and Midland) *wella*]

well[5] *verb intrans* **1** to rise to the surface and usu flow forth: *Tears welled from her eyes*. **2** to rise to the surface like a flood of liquid: *Longing welled up in his breast*. [Old English (northern and Midland) *wellan* to cause to well]

we'll /wiel, weel/ *contraction* **1** we will. **2** we shall.

well-advised *adj* **1** acting with wisdom; prudent: *You would be well advised to consult a solicitor*. **2** resulting from or showing wisdom: compare ADVISED, ILL-ADVISED, UNADVISED: *well-advised plans*.

well-appointed *adj* having good and complete facilities, furniture, etc: *a well-appointed house*.

well-behaved *adj* showing proper manners or conduct.

well-being *noun* the state of being happy, healthy, or prosperous.

well-bred *adj* **1** having or indicating good breeding; refined. **2** of good pedigree.

well-connected *adj* having useful social or family contacts.

well-disposed *adj* having a favourable or sympathetic disposition: *He was well disposed towards his workmates*.

well-done *adj* **1** said of food, *esp* meat: cooked thoroughly. **2** completed, performed, or done properly or satisfactorily.

well dressing *noun* the decorating of village wells with intricate designs or scenes made with flowers, an annual tradition in parts of Britain.

well-favoured (*NAmer* **well-favored**) *adj* good-looking; handsome.

well-found *adj* properly equipped: *a well-found ship*.

well-founded *adj* based on good grounds or reasoning: *a well-founded argument*.

well-groomed *adj* clean and smart.

well-grounded *adj* **1** having a good basic knowledge: *well grounded in Latin and Greek*. **2** well-founded.

wellhead *noun* **1** the source of a spring or stream. **2** the top of a well or a structure built over a well.

well-heeled *adj* *informal* having a great deal of money; wealthy.

well-hung *adj* **1** *informal* said of a man: having a large penis or large genitals. **2** said of game: having been hung for a relatively long time.

wellie /'weli/ *noun* see WELLY.

wellies /'weliz/ *pl noun informal* wellington boots. [by shortening and alteration]

well-informed *adj* **1** having a good knowledge of a wide variety of subjects. **2** having reliable information on a usu specified topic, event, etc.

wellington /'welingtən/ *noun* = WELLINGTON BOOT.

wellington boot *noun chiefly Brit* a waterproof rubber boot that usu reaches the knee.

Word history

named after Arthur Wellesley, first Duke of *Wellington* d.1852, British general and statesman. Orig denoting a kind of knee-length leather boot worn by Wellington.

wellingtonia /weling'tohni-ə/ *noun* = REDWOOD (1). [named after the first Duke of *Wellington*: see WELLINGTON BOOT]

well-intentioned *adj* well-meaning.

well-knit *adj* having a compact usu muscular physique: *a well-knit athlete*.

well-known *adj* fully or widely known; famous.

well-meaning *adj* having or based on good intentions though often failing: *well-meaning but misguided idealists*.

well-meant *adj* based on good intentions.

well-nigh *adv archaic or literary* almost or nearly.

well-off *adj* **1** prosperous or rich. **2** in a favourable or fortunate situation: *You don't know when you're well off*. **3** well provided: *He's not very well off for sheets*.

well-oiled *adj informal* drunk.

well-preserved *adj* said of an older person: retaining a youthful appearance.

well-read /red/ *adj* having read a lot either on a particular subject or on a wide range of subjects.

well-rounded *adj* **1** having a pleasantly curved or rounded shape: *a well-rounded figure*. **2** having or denoting a background of broad experience or education. **3** agreeably complete and well constructed.

well-set *adj* **1** well or firmly established. **2** strongly built: *a short but well-set young man*.

well-spoken *adj* **1** speaking clearly, courteously, and usu with a refined accent. **2** spoken in a pleasing or fitting manner: *well-spoken words*.

wellspring *noun* **1** a source of continual supply. **2** a spring that is the source of a stream.

well-stacked *adj informal* said of a woman: having large breasts.

well-thought-of *adj* of good repute; respected.

well-thumbed *adj* said of a book: showing signs of having been read many times.

well-to-do *adj* rich; prosperous.

well-tried *adj* thoroughly tested and found reliable.

well-turned *adj* **1** pleasingly formed; shapely: *a well-turned ankle.* **2** concisely and appropriately expressed: *a well-turned compliment.*

well-upholstered *adj informal* said of a person: plump.

well-wisher *noun* somebody who feels or expresses goodwill towards a person, cause, etc. ➤ **well-wishing** *adj and noun.*

well-worn *adj* **1** having been much used or worn: *well-worn shoes.* **2** said of a phrase, joke, idea, etc: made trite by overuse; hackneyed.

welly *or* **wellie** /'weli/ *noun Brit, informal* **1** see WELLIES. **2** concentration, power, or effort: *Give it some welly!*

wels /welz/ *noun* a large freshwater catfish that lives in deep slow-flowing waters from central Europe to central Asia: *Silurus glanis.* [German *Wels*]

Welsh /welsh/ *noun* **1** (**the Welsh**) (*treated as plural*) the people of Wales. **2** the Celtic language spoken by this people. ➤ **Welsh** *adj,* **Welshman** *noun,* **Welshness** *noun,* **Welshwoman** *noun.*

Word history
Old English *Wealh* Celtic, Welshman, foreigner, via a prehistoric Germanic word from Latin *Volcae,* the name of a Celtic people. Welsh words that have passed into English include *coracle, corgi, cwm, eisteddfod,* and *flummery.*

welsh /welsh/ *or* **welch** /welch/ *verb intrans* (*usu* + on) to evade an obligation, *esp* payment of a debt. ➤ **welsher** *noun.* [origin unknown]

Welsh corgi *noun* = CORGI.

Welsh dresser *noun* a dresser that has open shelves above a flat surface with drawers and small cupboards below.

Welsh harp *noun* a harp with the strings arranged in three rows.

Welsh poppy *noun* a widely cultivated European poppy with large yellow flowers: *Meconopsis cambrica.*

Welsh rabbit *noun* = WELSH RAREBIT.

Welsh rarebit /'reəbit/ *noun* a snack of melted cheese, mixed with seasonings, on toast.

Word history
alteration of *Welsh rabbit,* prob because the earlier term was too obscure or demeaning. *Welsh rabbit* probably comes from the association of Wales with cheese, and the idea of dairy products being a poor substitute for meat.

Welsh terrier *noun* a terrier of a breed originating in Wales, having a rough wiry black-and-tan coat and a stocky build.

welt[1] /welt/ *noun* **1** a strip, usu of leather, between a shoe sole and upper through which they are fastened together. **2** a doubled edge, ribbed strip, insert, or seam, e.g. on a garment, for ornament or reinforcement. **3** a ridge or lump raised on the body, usu by a heavy blow; a weal. **4** a heavy blow. [Middle English *welte;* earlier history unknown]

welt[2] *verb trans* **1** to provide (e.g. a garment) with a welt. **2a** to raise a welt on the body of (somebody). **b** to hit (somebody) hard.

Weltanschauung /'veltahnshow-oong/ *noun* (*pl* **Weltanschauungen** /-ən/) a particular conception of the nature and purpose of the world; a philosophy of life. [German *Weltanschauung,* from *Welt* world + *Anschauung* view]

welter[1] /'weltə/ *noun* **1** a state of wild disorder; a turmoil. **2** a chaotic mass or jumble: *a bewildering welter of data.*

welter[2] *verb intrans* (**weltered, weltering**) **1a** to writhe or toss. **b** to wallow. **2** to become soaked in something, e.g. blood. **3** to be in turmoil: *The Revolution had weltered into a more squalid chaos —* Colin Thubron. [Middle English *welteren,* from early Dutch or early Low German]

welterweight *noun* **1** a weight in boxing of 63.5–66.5kg (140–147lb) if professional or 63.5–67kg (140–148lb) if amateur. **2** a weight in wrestling of 71–75kg (155–165lb) if professional or 69–74kg (151–161lb) if amateur. [prob from WELT[2]]

Weltschmerz /'veltshmeəts/ *noun* a feeling of melancholy caused by contemplating the state of the world. [German *Weltschmerz,* from *Welt* world + *Schmerz* pain]

Wemba-wemba /'wembə,wembə/ *noun* an Aboriginal language of SE Australia, now extinct. ➤ **Wemba-wemba** *adj.* [the name in Wemba-wemba]

wen[1] /wen/ *noun* **1** a cyst formed by obstruction of a sebaceous gland and filled with fatty material. **2** *archaic* a large overcrowded city, *esp* London: *But what is to be the fate of the great wen ... the monster, called ... 'the metropolis of the empire'? —* William Cobbett. [Old English *wenn*]

wen[2] /wen/ *or* **wyn** /win/ *noun* a letter used in Old English with the value of Modern English *w.* [Old English *wen, wyn*]

wench[1] /wench/ *noun* **1** *archaic or humorous* a young woman; a girl. **2** *archaic* a promiscuous woman; a prostitute. **3** *archaic* a female servant or worker: *a serving wench.* [Middle English *wenche,* short for *wenchel* child, young woman, from Old English *wencel* child, servant, prostitute]

wench[2] *verb intrans archaic* said of a man: to have sexual relations habitually with prostitutes or promiscuous women. ➤ **wencher** *noun.*

Wend /wend/ *noun* a member of an indigenous Slavonic people who inhabited parts of northeastern Germany during the Middle Ages. Also called SORB. ➤ **Wendish** *adj and noun.* [German *Wende* from Old High German *Winida*]

wend *verb trans* to proceed on (one's way), often at a leisurely pace: *wending their way home.* [Old English *wendan*]

wendigo /'wendigoh/ *noun* see WINDIGO.

wendy house /'wendi/ *noun* (*often* **Wendy house**) *chiefly Brit* a toy house for children to play in. [named after *Wendy,* a character in *Peter Pan,* a children's book by J M Barrie d.1937, Scottish writer]

Wensleydale /'wenzlidayl/ *noun* **1** a crumbly mild-flavoured English cheese. **2** a sheep of a breed with long wool. [named after *Wensleydale,* a district in Yorkshire]

went /went/ *verb* past tense of GO[1].

wentletrap /'wentltrap/ *noun* any of numerous species of marine snails with spiral usu white shells: family Epitoniidae. [Dutch *wenteltrap* winding stair, from early Dutch *wendel* turning + *trappe* stairs]

wept /wept/ *verb* past tense and past part. of WEEP[1].

were /wə, *strong* wuh/ *verb* second person sing. past, plural past, and past subjunctive of BE.

we're /wiə/ *contraction* we are.

weren't /wuhnt/ *contraction* were not.

werewolf /'weəwoolf, 'wiəwoolf/ *noun* (*pl* **werewolves** /'weəwoolvz, 'wiəwoolvz/) in folklore, a person who periodically transforms into a wolf or is capable of assuming a wolf's form at will. [Old English *werwulf,* from *wer* man + *wulf* WOLF[1]]

wert /wuht/ *verb* archaic second person sing. past of BE.

Wesak /'wesak/ *noun* see VESAK.

Wesleyanism /'wezli-əniz(ə)m/ *noun* the system of Methodism taught by John Wesley. ➤ **Wesleyan** *adj and noun.* [named after John *Wesley* d.1791, English preacher, co-founder of Methodism]

west[1] /west/ *noun* **1** the direction 180° from east that is the general direction of sunset. **2a** (*often* **West**) regions or countries lying to the west of a specified or implied point of orientation. **b** (*usu* **the West**) the western part of the world, including much or all of Europe and N America, historically and culturally contrasted with the East. [Old English]

west[2] *adj and adv* **1** at, towards, or coming from the west. **2** said of the wind: blowing from the west. ✳ **west by north** in a position or direction between west and west-northwest. **west by south** in a position or direction between west and west-southwest.

westbound *adj and adv* going or moving west: *the westbound carriageway.*

West Country *noun* (**the West Country**) the West of England, *esp* the counties of Cornwall, Devon, and Somerset.

West End *noun* (**the West End**) the western part of central London where the main shopping streets, theatres, etc are located.

wester /'westə/ *verb intrans* (**westered, westering**) to turn or decline westwards: *The half moon westers low —* A E Housman. [Middle English *westren* from WEST[1]]

westerly[1] *adj and adv* **1** in a western position or direction. **2** said of a wind: blowing from the west.

westerly[2] *noun* (*pl* **westerlies**) a wind blowing from the west.

western[1] /'westən/ *adj* **1** in or towards the west; inhabiting the west. **2** (*often* **Western**). **a** relating to any region conventionally designated West. **b** steeped in or stemming from the traditions of Europe or N America. ➤➤ **westernmost** *adj*.

western[2] *noun* (*often* **Western**) a novel, film, etc dealing with cowboys, frontier life, etc in the western USA, *esp* during the latter half of the 19th cent.

Western Church *noun* the Roman Catholic or Protestant branches of Christianity as opposed to the Eastern or Eastern Orthodox Churches.

Westerner *noun* a native or inhabitant of the west of a country or of a region conventionally designated West, *esp* Europe or N America.

westernize *or* **westernise** *verb trans* to cause (somebody or something) to adopt or be influenced by the culture, economics, politics, etc of N America or Europe. ➤ *verb intrans* to become westernized. ➤➤ **westernization** /-'zaysh(ə)n/ *noun*.

western saddle *or* **Western saddle** *noun* = STOCK SADDLE.

West Germanic *noun* the group of Germanic languages that includes English, Frisian, Dutch, and German. ➤➤ **West Germanic** *adj*.

West Indian *noun* a native or inhabitant of the West Indies, or a person descended from West Indians. ➤➤ **West Indian** *adj*.

Word history
West Indies (formerly *West India*), a group of islands in the Caribbean Sea. They were so named by Christopher Columbus d.1506, Spanish explorer, who believed they were islands off the coast of India.

westing *noun* **1** distance due west in longitude from the preceding point of measurement. **2** westerly progress.

Westminster /'westminstə, west'minstə/ *noun* the British Parliament. [named after *Westminster*, the district of London in which the Houses of Parliament are situated]

west-northwest[1] *noun* the direction midway between west and northwest.

west-northwest[2] *adj and adv* at, towards, or coming from the west-northwest.

Westphalian /west'fayli·ən/ *noun* a native or inhabitant of Westphalia, a former region in NW Germany. ➤➤ **Westphalian** *adj*.

west-southwest[1] *noun* the direction midway between west and southwest.

west-southwest[2] *adj and adv* at, towards, or coming from the west-southwest.

westward /'westwəd/ *adv and adj* towards the west; in a direction going west.

westwards *adv* towards the west; westward.

wet[1] /wet/ *adj* (**wetter, wettest**) **1** consisting of, containing, or covered or soaked with liquid, e.g. water. **2** said of weather: rainy. **3a** still moist enough to smudge or smear: *wet paint*. **b** not yet set: *wet cement*. **4** involving the use or presence of liquid. **5** *Brit, informal* said of a person: feeble, ineffectual, or dull. **6** *informal* said of a state or region: permitting the sale or consumption of alcoholic drink. ✳ **wet behind the ears** *informal* immature or inexperienced [referring to the small dent behind the ears of a new-born animal, which is the last part to dry]. ➤➤ **wetly** *adv*, **wetness** *noun*, **wettish** *adj*. [Old English *wǣt*]

wet[2] *noun* **1** moisture or wetness. **2** (**the wet**) rainy weather. **3** *Brit, informal* a feeble, ineffectual, or dull person; a drip. **4** *Brit* a moderate Conservative politician. **5** *Brit, informal* a drink. **6** *NAmer* an advocate of a policy permitting the sale of alcoholic drink.

wet[3] *verb trans* (**wetting**, past tense and past part. **wet** *or* **wetted**) **1** to make (somebody or something) wet. **2a** to urinate in or on (something, e.g. one's clothing or bed). **b** to urinate on (oneself). **3** *dialect* to infuse (tea) with boiling water. ✳ **wet one's whistle** *informal* to have a drink, *esp* an alcoholic one. ➤➤ **wettable** *adj*. [Old English *wǣtan* from *wǣt* WET[1]]

weta /'waytə/ *noun* any of various large wingless long-horned insects of New Zealand that resemble grasshoppers: family Stenopelmatidae. [Maori *weta*]

wetback *noun* *NAmer, informal* a Mexican who enters the USA illegally. [WET[1] + BACK[1]; from a person having to swim or wade across the Rio Grande in order to cross from Mexico into Texas]

wet blanket *noun* *informal* a person who spoils other people's fun or whose lack of enthusiasm makes it difficult for others to enjoy themselves.

wet bulb *noun* a thermometer in a PSYCHROMETER (device for measuring atmospheric humidity) with a bulb that is kept moistened and that registers a temperature lower than that of the surrounding air.

wet cell *noun* a battery cell that contains a free-flowing electrolyte: compare DRY CELL.

wet dream *noun* an erotic dream that results in the involuntary ejaculation of semen.

wet fish *noun* fresh uncooked fish, *esp* as opposed to dried, cured, or cooked fish.

wet fly *noun* an artificial angling fly designed to be used under water.

wether /'wedhə/ *noun* a male sheep castrated before sexual maturity. [Old English]

wetland *noun* land or areas, e.g. tidal flats or swamps, covered with soil that is more or less permanently saturated.

wetlands *pl noun* = WETLAND.

wet look *noun* a glossy sheen that suggests surface wetness, e.g. on leather or plastic. ➤➤ **wet-look** *adj*.

wet nurse *noun* a woman who cares for and breastfeeds a child or children she did not give birth to.

wet-nurse *verb trans* **1** to act as wet nurse to (a child). **2** *informal* to give constant and often excessive care to (somebody).

wet pack *noun* **1** a therapeutic treatment that involves wrapping the body in wet cloth. **2** a hot or cold wet cloth used for this.

wet rot *noun* **1** any of various fungi that attack moist wood and cause it to decay: *Coniophora puteana* and others. **2** the state of decay caused by any of these fungi.

wet suit *noun* a close-fitting suit made of rubber or other material that admits water but retains body heat so as to insulate its wearer, e.g. a skin diver, *esp* in cold water: compare DRYSUIT.

wetter *noun* **1** a worker who wets material in any of several manufacturing processes. **2** a wetting agent.

wetting agent *noun* a substance added to a liquid to make surfaces less repellent to it.

wetware /'wetweə/ *noun informal* people or their brains, *esp* when contrasted with computers, software, etc.

WEU *abbr* Western European Union.

we've /wiv, *strong* weev/ *contraction* we have.

w.f. *abbr* in printing, wrong fount.

WFTU *abbr* World Federation of Trade Unions.

WG *abbr* Windward Islands Grenada (international vehicle registration for Grenada).

Wg Cdr *abbr* Wing Commander.

whack[1] /wak/ *verb trans informal* **1** to strike (something or somebody) with a smart or resounding blow. **2** to defeat or get the better of (somebody). **3** to place or insert (something) roughly, casually, or quickly: *I'll just whack the washing in the machine before we go*. **4** *chiefly NAmer* to murder (somebody): *He got whacked in a drive-by*. ➤➤ **whacker** *noun*. [prob imitative]

whack[2] *noun informal* **1** a smart resounding blow, or the sound it makes. **2** *Brit* a portion or share: *I've paid my whack*. **3** an attempt or go. ✳ **out of whack** not functioning properly; not working at all. **top/full whack** *chiefly Brit* the maximum amount: *They're paying her top whack*.

whacked *or* **wacked** *adj* **1** *chiefly Brit, informal* (*often* + out) completely exhausted. **2** *chiefly NAmer, informal* (*often* + out) intoxicated by drugs.

whacking *adj Brit, informal* extremely big; whopping.

whacko[1] /wak'oh/ *interj Brit, informal, dated* used to express delight.

whacko[2] /'wakoh/ *adj* see WACKO[1].

whacko[3] /'wakoh/ *noun* see WACKO[2].

whacky /'waki/ *adj* see WACKY.

whale[1] /wayl/ *noun* (*pl* **whales** *or collectively* **whale**) any of various often enormous aquatic mammals that superficially resemble large fish, have tails modified as paddles, and are frequently hunted for oil, flesh, or whalebone: order Cetacea. ✳ **a whale of a** *informal* an exceptionally good or large example of (something). **have a whale of a time** to have an exceptionally enjoyable time. [Old English *hwæl*]

whale² *verb trans chiefly NAmer, informal* to hit or defeat (somebody) soundly. [from WALE]

whaleback *noun* something shaped like the back of a whale, e.g. an arched structure on a ship.

whaleboat *noun* a long narrow rowing boat with pointed ends, formerly used for hunting whales.

whalebone *noun* a horny substance found in two rows of plates attached along the upper jaw of whalebone whales and formerly used in strips for stiffening corsets, etc.

whalebone whale *noun* = BALEEN WHALE.

whale oil *noun* = TRAIN OIL.

whaler *noun* **1** a person or ship engaged in whaling. **2** any of various slender-bodied aggressive sharks inhabiting inshore waters, e.g. of Australia: *Carcharhinus brachyurus* and others.

whaler shark *noun* = WHALER (2).

whale shark *noun* a large tropical shark found in warm waters that feeds on plankton: *Rhincodon typus*.

whaling *noun* the occupation of catching and processing whales for oil, food, etc.

wham¹ /wam/ *noun informal* a forceful blow, or the sound made by a blow. [imitative]

wham² *interj informal* used to express the noise of a forceful blow or impact.

wham³ *verb* (**whammed, whamming**) ➤ *verb trans informal* to throw or strike (something) with a loud impact. ➤ *verb intrans informal* to crash or explode with a loud impact.

whammy /'wami/ *noun* (*pl* **whammies**) *informal* **1** something that has a bad effect. **2** *chiefly NAmer* a hypothetical power or force bringing bad luck; a jinx. [prob from WHAM¹]

whang¹ /wang/ *verb trans informal* to throw, strike, or work at (something) with force. [*whang* thong, lash, alteration of Middle English *thwong* THONG]

whang² *noun informal* a loud sharp vibrant sound. [imitative]

whangee /wang'ee/ *noun* **1** a Chinese bamboo plant: genus *Phyllostachys*. **2** a walking stick or riding crop made from the stem of a whangee. [prob from Chinese (Pekingese) *huangli*, from *huang* yellow and *li* bamboo cane]

whap¹ /wop/ *verb trans NAmer* see WHOP¹.

whap² *noun NAmer* see WHOP².

whare /'wori/ *noun* **1** a Maori house of traditional design. **2** *NZ* a hut or shack. [Maori *whare*]

wharf /wawf/ *noun* (*pl* **wharves** /wawvz/ *or* **wharfs**) a structure built along or out from the shore of navigable water so that ships may load and unload. [Old English *hwearf* embankment, wharf]

wharfage /'wawfij/ *noun* **1a** the use of a wharf. **b** a charge for this. **2** a system of wharves.

wharfie /'wawfi/ *noun Aus, NZ, informal* a docker.

wharfinger /'wawfinjə/ *noun* the owner or manager of a commercial wharf. [irreg from WHARFAGE]

wharves /'wawvz/ *noun* pl of WHARF.

what¹ /wot/ *pron* (*pl* **what**) **1** used as an interrogative expressing enquiry about the identity, nature, purpose, or value of something: *What are these?*; *I wonder what he meant.* **2** used rhetorically with the effect of a negative statement: *What is wealth without friends?* **3** used to ask for repetition of something not properly heard or understood: *He bought what?* **4** used as an interrogative expressing enquiry about the character, occupation, position, or role of a person: *What is she like?* **5** used as an exclamation expressing surprise or excitement and frequently introducing a question: *What, no breakfast?* **6** used to direct attention to a statement that the speaker is about to make: *Guess what.* **7** *chiefly Brit, informal, dated* used like a question-tag demanding assent: *A clever play, what?* **8** *non-standard* that, which, or who: *He has no income but what he gets from his writing.* **10** whatever: *Say what you will.* **11** used in exclamations: how much: *What it must cost!* ✻ **or what** used at the end of a question to express enquiry about additional possibilities: *Is it raining, snowing, or what?* **what 1** what news or plans do you have concerning (somebody or something). **2** used to make a suggestion. **what d'you call him/her/it** used to replace a forgotten name. **what for 1** for what purpose or

reason; why. **2** *informal* punishment, *esp* by blows or by a sharp reprimand: *She gave the other driver what for.* **what have you** any of various other things that might also be mentioned: *paper clips, pins, and what have you.* **what if 1** what will or would be the result if. **2** what does it matter if. **what it takes** the qualities or resources needed for success. **what not** what have you. **what of 1** what is the situation with respect to (somebody or something). **2** what importance can be assigned to (something). **what of it** what does it matter. **what's his/her/its name** used to replace a forgotten name. **what's what** the true state of things: *He knows what's what when it comes to fashion.* **what's yours** what would you like to drink. **what with** having as a contributory circumstance: *I'm very busy what with all these guests to feed.* [Old English *hwæt*, neuter of *hwā* WHO]

what² *adv* in what respect?; how much?: *What does he care?*

what³ *adj* **1a** used with a following noun as an adjective equivalent in meaning to the interrogative pronoun *what*: *What minerals do we export?* **b** which: *What size do you take?* **c** how remarkable or striking: *What a suggestion!* **2** the … that; as much or as many … as: *I told him what little I knew.*

whatever¹ *pronoun* **1a** anything or everything that: *Take whatever you want.* **b** no matter what. **2** *informal* used for emphasis in place of the interrogative pronoun *what*: *Whatever do you mean?* ✻ **or whatever** *informal* or anything else at all: *chips or mash or whatever.*

whatever² *adj* **1a** any … that; all … that: *buy peace on whatever terms could be obtained* — C S Forester. **b** no matter what. **2** of any kind at all: *We had no food whatever.*

whatnot *noun* **1** *informal* other usu related goods, objects, etc: *carrying all his bags and whatnot.* **2** *informal* a whatsit. **3** a lightweight open set of shelves for ornaments, potted plants, etc. [*what not?*]

whatsit /'wotsit/ *noun informal* somebody or something that is of unspecified, nondescript, or unknown character, or whose name has been forgotten. [*what's it?*]

whatsoever *pronoun and adj* whatever.

whaup /wawp/ *noun* (*pl* **whaups** *or collectively* **whaup**) *chiefly Scot* a curlew. [imitative]

wheal /weel/ *noun* see WEAL¹.

wheat /weet/ *noun* any of several species of cereal grasses cultivated in temperate areas for a grain that yields a fine white flour used for making bread, pasta, etc: genus *Triticum*. ✻ **separate the wheat from the chaff** to separate or distinguish what is useful from what is worthless: *An editor is someone who separates the wheat from the chaff and then prints the chaff* — Adlai Stevenson. [Old English *hwæte*]

wheatear *noun* any of several species of small usu white-rumped Eurasian birds related to the thrushes: *Oenanthe oenanthe* and others. [back-formation from earlier *wheatears*, prob by folk etymology or euphemism from WHITE¹ + ARSE]

wheaten *adj* made of wheat.

wheat germ *noun* the embryo of the wheat kernel separated in milling and used *esp* as a source of vitamins.

wheatmeal *noun* brown flour made from wheat with some bran and germ taken out.

Wheatstone bridge /'weetstohn, 'wetstohn/ *noun* an electrical device used to measure the resistance of an electrical component, consisting of a four-sided circuit made up of the component together with three others whose resistances are known. A current is applied across two diagonals and the known resistances are adjusted until no current flows between the other two diagonals, at which point the unknown resistance can be calculated. [named after Sir Charles *Wheatstone* d.1875, English physicist and inventor]

whee /wee/ *interj* used to express delight or exuberance.

wheedle /'weedl/ *verb intrans* to use soft words or flattery. ➤ *verb trans* **1** to influence, persuade, or entice (somebody) by soft words or flattery. **2** (+ out of) to cause somebody to part with (something) by wheedling: *He wheedled her last £5 out of her.* ➤➤ **wheedler** *noun*, **wheedling** *adj*, **wheedlingly** *adv*. [perhaps from German *wedeln* to cringe, fawn]

wheel¹ /weel/ *noun* **1** a circular disc of hard material, or a circular frame joined to a central hub by spokes, that is attached to and capable of turning on an axle. **2a** = POTTER'S WHEEL. **b** = SPINNING WHEEL. **c** = STEERING WHEEL. **d** = FERRIS WHEEL. **3** a wheel that controls the steering gear of a ship. **4** a revolving disc or drum that helps to produce an arbitrary value on which to gamble: *a roulette wheel.* **5** (*also* **the wheel of fortune**) an imaginary turning wheel symbolizing the inconstancy of fortune. **6** (**the wheel**) a medieval instrument of torture consisting of a round wooden revolving frame to which the victim was tied while their limbs were broken by a metal bar. **7** a curving or circular movement. **8** a rotation or turn usu about an axis or centre; *specif* a turning movement of troops or ships in line. **9** (*in pl*) the moving or controlling parts of something compared to a machine: *the wheels of government.* **10** *informal* (*in pl*) a motor vehicle, *esp* a car. **11** *NAmer, informal* a bicycle. **✴ wheels within wheels** a series of hidden and interrelated circumstances, influences, etc, often causing complications. ➤➤ **wheelless** *adj.* [Old English *hweogol, hwēol*]

wheel² *verb intrans* **1** to turn as if on an axis; to revolve. **2** to change direction as if revolving on a pivot: *She wheeled round and walked away.* **3** (*often* + about/round) to alter or reverse one's procedure or opinion. **4** to move or extend in a circle or curve: *birds in wheeling flight.* ➤ *verb trans* **1** to cause (somebody or something) to turn as if on an axis; to rotate. **2** to convey or move (somebody or something) on wheels or in a wheeled vehicle; *esp* to push (a wheeled vehicle or its occupant): *Wheel the baby into the shade.* **3** to cause (somebody or something) to change direction as if revolving on a pivot. **4** *informal* (+ in/on/out) to produce (somebody or something that is tediously familiar): *They wheel out the same old experts every time.* **✴ wheel and deal** to pursue one's own usu commercial interests, *esp* in a shrewd or unscrupulous manner.

wheelbarrow *noun* a load-carrying device that consists of a shallow box supported at one end by a wheel and at the other by a stand when at rest or by handles when being pushed.

wheelbase *noun* the distance between the front and rear axles of a vehicle.

wheelchair *noun* a chair mounted on wheels for disabled people or invalids.

wheel clamp *noun* a clamp that is locked on to a wheel of an illegally parked vehicle and is removed only on payment of a fine by the driver of the vehicle.

wheel-clamp *verb trans* to put a wheel clamp on (a vehicle).

wheeled *adj* (*usu used in combinations*) equipped with or moving on wheels: *wheeled vehicles; two-wheeled.*

wheeler *noun* **1** (*esp in combination*) something, e.g. a vehicle, that has wheels: *a three-wheeler.* **2** a maker of wheels. **3** a draught animal, e.g. a horse, pulling in the position nearest the front wheels of a wagon.

wheeler and dealer *noun* = WHEELER-DEALER.

wheeler-dealer *noun* a shrewd operator, *esp* in business or politics. ➤➤ **wheeler-dealing** *noun.* [from the phrase *wheel and deal*: see WHEEL²]

wheelhorse *noun* = WHEELER (3).

wheelhouse /'weelhows/ *noun* a cabin or shelter for a vessel's helmsman.

wheelie /'weeli/ *noun informal* a manoeuvre in which a motorcycle or bicycle is momentarily balanced or ridden for a short distance on its rear wheel.

wheelie bin *or* **wheely bin** *noun* a large wheeled dustbin with a hinged lid and a horizontal bar at the back, which is lifted and emptied by a mechanism attached to the dustcart.

wheel lock *noun* **1** a gunlock in which sparks are struck from a flint or a piece of iron pyrites by a revolving wheel. **2** a gun having this kind of gunlock.

wheelsman *noun* (*pl* **wheelsmen**) *NAmer* a helmsman.

wheelspin *noun* the usu rapid turning of a vehicle's wheels without getting any grip and therefore skidding on the surface.

wheelwright /'weelriet/ *noun* somebody who makes or repairs wheels, *esp* wooden ones for carts.

wheely bin *noun* see WHEELIE BIN.

wheen /ween/ *noun Scot* a considerable number or amount. [Old English *hwǣne, hwēne* (adv) somewhat]

wheesht /wisht/ *interj* see WHISHT.

wheeze¹ /weez/ *verb intrans* **1** to breathe with difficulty, usu with a whistling sound. **2** to make a sound like that of wheezing. ➤ *verb trans* to utter (something) wheezily. ➤➤ **wheezer** *noun.* [Middle English *whesen*, prob of Scandinavian origin]

wheeze² *noun* **1** a sound of wheezing. **2** *Brit, informal* a cunning trick or a clever scheme. ➤➤ **wheezily** *adv*, **wheeziness** *noun*, **wheezy** *adj.*

whelk¹ /welk/ *noun* any of numerous large marine snails, *esp* the European edible one: *Buccinum undatum* and others. [Old English *weoloc*]

whelk² *noun archaic* a pustule or pimple. [Old English *hwylca* from *hwelian* to suppurate]

whelm /welm/ *verb trans* **1** *archaic* to cover or engulf (something) completely and usu disastrously. **2** to overcome (somebody) in thought or feeling; to overwhelm. [Middle English *whelmen*, of Germanic origin]

whelp¹ /welp/ *noun* **1** any of the young of various flesh-eating mammals, *esp* a dog. **2** a disagreeable or impudent child or youth. **3** a ridge on the drum of a capstan or windlass. [Old English *hwelp*]

whelp² *verb trans and intrans* to give birth to (e.g. a puppy).

when¹ /wen/ *adv* **1** at what time? **2a** at or during which time: *the day when we met.* **b** and then; whereupon. [Old English *hwanne, hwenne*]

when² *conj* **1a** at or during the time that: *He went fishing when he was a boy.* **b** as soon as: *Stop writing when the bell goes.* **c** whenever: *When he listens to music, he falls asleep.* **2** in the event that; if. **3a** considering that: *Why smoke when you know it's bad for you?* **b** in spite of the fact that; although: *He gave up politics when he might have done well.*

when³ *pronoun* what or which time: *Since when have you known that?*

when⁴ *noun* a date or time: *She was worried about the wheres and whens.*

whence /wens/ *adv and conj formal or archaic* **1** from which place, source, or cause. **2** to the place from which: *They returned whence they came.* [Middle English *whennes* from *whenne* whence, from Old English *hwanon*, + genitive suffix *-s*]

whencesoever *conj formal or archaic* from whatever place or source.

whenever¹ *conj* **1** at every or whatever time: *The roof leaks whenever it rains.* **2** in any circumstance: *Whenever possible, he tries to help.* **✴ or whenever** *informal* or at any similar time: *in 1922 or whenever.*

whenever² *adv informal* used for emphasis in place of the interrogative adverb *when*: *Whenever did you find the time?*

whensoever¹ *conj formal* whenever.

whensoever² *adv formal* at any time whatever.

where¹ /weə/ *adv* **1a** at, in, or to what place?: *Where is the house?* **b** at, in, or to what situation, direction, circumstances, or respect?: *Where does this plan lead?* **2** at, in, or to which place: *the town where she lives.* [Old English *hwǣr*]

where² *conj* **1a** at, in, or to the place at which: *Stay where you are.* **b** wherever: *He goes where he likes.* **c** in a case, situation, or respect in which: *She is careful where money is concerned.* **2** whereas or while: *He wants a house, where I would prefer a flat.* **✴ where it's at** *informal* the scene of the most interesting or exciting action; the most fashionable place to be.

where³ *noun* a place or point: *I'm not interested in the wheres and whens.*

whereabouts¹ /weərə'bowts/ *adv and conj* in what vicinity: *Do you know whereabouts he lives?*

whereabouts² /'weərəbowts/ *pl noun* (*treated as sing. or pl*) the place or general locality where a person or thing is: *His present whereabouts are a secret.*

whereas *conj* **1** while on the contrary. **2** used to introduce a preamble: in view of the fact that; since.

whereat *conj* **1** in consequence of which; whereupon. **2** *formal or archaic* at or towards which.

whereby *conj* **1** in accordance with which: *a law whereby children receive cheap milk.* **2** *formal* by which means.

wherefore¹ /'weəfaw, weə'faw, 'wuhfə/ *adv formal* **1** for what reason; why. **2** for that reason; therefore.

wherefore² *noun* a reason or cause: *He wants to know all the whys and wherefores.*

wherefrom *conj archaic* from which.

wherein *adv formal* **1** in what respect; how: *They showed him wherein he was wrong.* **2** in which; where: *the city wherein he lived.*

whereof *conj, pronoun, and adv formal* of what, which, or whom.

whereon *adv and conj archaic* on which or what: *the base whereon it rests.*

wheresoever *conj formal* wherever.

whereto *adv and conj formal or archaic* to which or what; whither.

whereupon *adv and conj* **1** closely following and in consequence of which: *He saw me coming, whereupon he offered me his seat.* **2** *formal* on which; whereon.

wherever¹ *adv* used for emphasis in place of the interrogative adverb *where*: *Wherever have you been?* ✳ **or wherever** *informal* or anywhere else at all: *Bring me back a present if you go to China or wherever.*

wherever² *conj* at, in, or to every or whatever place: *He can sleep wherever he likes.*

wherewith *adv formal or archaic* with or by means of which.

wherewithal /'weəwidhawl/ *noun* means or resources; *specif* money. *We didn't have the wherewithal for an expensive dinner.*

wherry /'weri/ *noun* (*pl* **wherries**) **1** a long light rowing boat used to transport passengers on rivers and about harbours. **2** *Brit* a large light barge, lighter, or fishing boat. ➤➤ **wherryman** *noun*. [Middle English *whery*; earlier history unknown]

whet¹ /wet/ *verb trans* (**whetted, whetting**) **1** to sharpen (a blade) by rubbing on or with something, e.g. a stone. **2** to make (something) keen or more acute; to stimulate: *The film had whetted her appetite for travel.* [Old English *hwettan*]

whet² *noun archaic* **1** a goad or incitement. **2** an appetizer.

whether /'wedhə/ *conj* **1** used to indicate an indirect question involving alternatives: *He couldn't decide whether he should agree or protest.* **2** used to indicate a choice between two alternatives: *I wonder whether he heard.* **3** used to indicate indifference between alternatives: *whether by accident or design.* [Old English *hwæther, hwether*]

Usage note

whether *and* **if.** See note at IF¹.

whetstone /'wetstohn/ *noun* a stone for sharpening an edge, e.g. of a chisel.

whew /fyooh/ *interj* used to express amazement, discomfort, or relief. [imitative]

whey /way/ *noun* the watery part of milk separated from the curd, *esp* in cheese-making, and rich in lactose, minerals, and vitamins. [Old English *hwæg*]

whey-faced *adj* having a pale face, e.g. from illness, shock, or fear.

which¹ /wich/ *adj* **1** used to ask for identification of one or ones out of a known or limited group: *Which tie should I wear?* **2** whichever: *It will not fit, turn it which way you like.* **3** used to introduce a non-restrictive relative clause by modifying a noun referring to a preceding word, phrase, or clause: *He may come, in which case I'll ask him.* [Old English *hwilc*]

which² *pron* (*pl* **which**) **1** which thing, person, etc: *Which is the cheapest?* **2** whichever: *Take which you like.* **3** used to introduce a non-restrictive clause: **a** in reference to an animal, thing, or idea: *a large dog, which bit me.* **b** in reference to a human group, *esp* when a singular verb follows: *this people, which has aroused much interest among anthropologists.* **c** in reference to a preceding clause or sentence in its entirety: *She can sing, which is an advantage.* **4** used in place of *that* to introduce a restrictive clause.

Usage note

which, that, *and* **who.** See note at THAT⁴.

whichever¹ *pronoun* (*pl* **whichever**) **1** any one or ones out of a group: *Take two of the four optional papers, whichever you prefer.* **2** no matter which. **3** *informal* used for emphasis in place of the interrogative pronoun *which*: *Whichever did you choose?*

whichever² *adj* any one or ones out of a group; no matter which: *She won't eat the sandwiches whichever way you make them.*

whichsoever *pronoun and adj archaic* whichever.

whicker¹ /'wikə/ *verb intrans* (**whickered, whickering**) to neigh or whinny.

whicker² *noun* a whinnying sound. [imitative]

whidah /'widə/ *noun archaic* a whydah.

whiff¹ /wif/ *noun* **1** a brief inhalation of odour, gas, etc; a smell or sniff. **2** a quick puff or slight gust. **3** a slight trace: *a whiff of scandal.* [imitative]

whiff² *verb intrans* **1** to inhale an odour; to sniff. **2** *Brit, informal* to smell unpleasant. **3** to emit whiffs; to puff. ➤ *verb trans* **1** to sniff or smell (something). **2** to blow, emit, or convey (something) in whiffs.

whiffle /'wifl/ *verb intrans* **1** to blow with or emit a light whistling sound: *The wind whiffled in the leaves.* **2** to be undecided; to vacillate. ➤➤ **whiffler** *noun*. [prob frequentative of WHIFF²]

whiffletree *noun NAmer* = SWINGLETREE. [alteration of WHIPPLE-TREE]

Whig /wig/ *noun* **1** a member or supporter of a major British political group of the 18th cent. and early 19th cent. seeking to limit royal authority and increase parliamentary power: compare TORY. **2** an American favouring independence from Britain during the American Revolution. **3** a member or supporter of an American political party formed about 1834 in opposition to the Democrats, associated chiefly with manufacturing, commercial, and financial interests, and succeeded about 1854 by the Republican party. ➤➤ **Whiggery** *noun*, **Whiggish** *adj*, **Whiggism** *noun*.

Word history

short for *Whiggamore*, a member of a largely Presbyterian Scottish group that marched to Edinburgh in 1648 to oppose the court party, prob from Scottish *whig* to drive + *more* MARE¹. Both *Whig* and *Tory* were introduced as derogatory nicknames for political groups in England during the controversy about the succession to the throne in 1679–80. A *Whig*, or *Exclusioner*, was originally a member of a group petitioning Charles II to call a parliament with the aim of passing a Bill to exclude his Roman Catholic brother, James, from succession. The nickname denoted nonconformity and anti-royalism, from its earlier application to Scottish Presbyterians. It soon lost its derogatory sense, and was adopted as the name of one of the two major British political groups until it was superseded by *Liberal* in the mid-19th cent: compare TORY.

while¹ /wiel/ *noun* **1** a period of time, *esp* when short and marked by the occurrence of an action or condition; a time: *Stay here for a while.* **2** the time and effort used; trouble: *It's worth your while.* [Old English *hwil*]

while² *conj* **1a** during the time that. **b** providing that; as long as: *While there's life there's hope.* **2a** when on the other hand; whereas. **b** in spite of the fact that; although: *While respected, he is not liked.*

while³ *prep archaic or dialect* until.

while away *verb trans* to pass (time) in a leisurely, often pleasant, manner: *while away the afternoon.*

whiles¹ *adv chiefly Scot* sometimes. [Old English *hwile* formerly]

whiles² *conj archaic* while.

whilom¹ /'wieləm/ *adv archaic* formerly; once: *Whilom my sire was king of this city* — Richard Burton. [Old English *hwilum* at times, dative pl of *hwil* time, WHILE¹]

whilom² *adj archaic* former; one-time: *the tombstone of Robert Preston, whilom drawer at the tavern* — Washington Irving.

whilst /wielst/ *conj chiefly Brit* while. [Middle English *whilest*, alteration of *whiles*, from WHILE² + -*s* (adv suffix)]

whim /wim/ *noun* **1** a sudden, capricious, or eccentric idea or impulse; a fancy. **2** *archaic* a large capstan formerly used in mines for raising ore or water. [short for *whim-wham* trifle, trinket, of unknown origin]

whimbrel /'wimbrəl/ *noun* a small Eurasian curlew: *Numenius phaeopus.* [prob from WHIMPER¹, imitative of the bird's call]

whimper¹ /'wimpə/ *verb intrans* (**whimpered, whimpering**) **1** to make a low plaintive whining sound. **2** to make a petulant complaint or protest. ➤➤ **whimperer** *noun*, **whimpering** *adj*, **whimperingly** *adv*. [imitative]

whimper² *noun* **1** a whimpering cry or sound. **2** a petulant complaint or protest.

whimsey /'wimzi/ *noun* see WHIMSY.

whimsical /'wimzikl/ *adj* **1** resulting from or suggesting whimsy; quizzical or playful: *a whimsical smile.* **2** full of whims; capricious. ➤➤ **whimsicality** /-'kaliti/ *noun*, **whimsically** *adv*. [WHIMSY]

whimsy *or* **whimsey** /'wimzi/ *noun* (*pl* **whimsies** *or* **whimseys**) **1** an affected or fanciful device, creation, or style, *esp* in writing or art. **2** a whim or caprice. [irreg from *whim-wham* trifle, trinket, of unknown origin]

whin[1] /win/ *noun* = GORSE. [Middle English *whynne*, of Scandinavian origin]

whin[2] *noun* any of various dark fine-grained rocks, e.g. basalt, formed by the cooling and solidification of molten rock material. [alteration of Middle English (northern) *quin* very hard rock, of unknown origin]

whinchat /'winchat/ *noun* a small brown and buff Eurasian songbird: *Saxicola rubetra*. [WHIN[1] + CHAT[2]]

whine[1] *verb intrans* **1** to utter a prolonged high-pitched cry, usu expressive of distress or pain, or make a sound resembling such a cry. **2** to complain querulously or peevishly. ➤ *verb trans* to utter or express (something) with a whining sound, querulously or peevishly. ➤ **whiner** *noun*, **whining** *adj*, **whiningly** *adv*. [Old English *hwīnan* to whiz]

whine[2] /wien/ *noun* **1** a whining sound. **2** a querulous or peevish complaint. ➤➤ **whiny** *adj*.

whinge[1] /winj/ *verb intrans* (**whinges, whingeing, whinged**) *Brit, informal* to complain or moan. ➤➤ **whinger** *noun*. [Old English *hwinsian*]

whinge[2] *noun Brit, informal* a complaint. ➤➤ **whingy** *adj*.

whinny[1] *verb intrans* (**whinnies, whinnied, whinnying**) to utter a low gentle neigh or similar sound. [prob imitative]

whinny[2] /'wini/ *noun* (*pl* **whinnies**) a whinnying sound.

whinstone /'winstohn/ *noun* = WHIN[2].

whip[1] /wip/ *verb* (**whipped, whipping**) ➤ *verb trans* **1** to beat (e.g. eggs or cream) into a froth with a utensil, e.g. a whisk or fork. **2** to take, pull, jerk, or move (something) very quickly and forcefully: *He whipped out a gun*. **3a** to strike (a person or animal) with a slender flexible implement, e.g. a lash or rod, *esp* as a punishment. **b** to drive or urge (an animal) on with a whip. **4** to strike (something) as if with a lash: *rain whipping the pavement*. **5** to wind or wrap cord round (e.g. a rope or rod) for protection and strength or to bind parts together. **6** to oversew (an edge, hem, or seam) with shallow overcasting stitches. **7** *informal* to defeat or overcome (somebody or something) decisively. **8** *Brit, informal* to snatch (something) suddenly; *esp* to steal (something). ➤ *verb intrans* **1** to move, go, or come quickly or violently: *She whipped out of the turning at top speed*. **2** to thrash about flexibly like a whiplash: *flags whipping in the wind*. ✳ **whip into shape** to bring (somebody or something) into a desired state, *esp* by hard work or practice. ➤➤ **whipper** *noun*. [Middle English *wippen, whippen*, of Germanic origin]

whip[2] *noun* **1** an instrument consisting usu of a flexible leather strip or cord attached to a handle, used for driving and controlling animals and for punishment. **2a** somebody appointed by a political party to enforce party discipline and to secure the attendance and votes of party members at important sessions. **b** (*often* **Whip**) *Brit* an instruction to each member of a political party in Parliament to be in attendance for voting. **c** (**the Whip**) *Brit* membership of the group of MPs that constitutes the official parliamentary representation of a political party, together with the privileges and duties of that membership: *He was deprived of the Labour Whip*. **3** a dessert made by whipping some of the ingredients: *prune whip*. **4** a whipping or thrashing motion. **5** a whipper-in. **6** a hoisting apparatus, *esp* one consisting of a single block and a small rope for lifting light articles. ✳ **the whip hand** the advantage. ➤➤ **whiplike** *adj*.

whip bird *noun* either of two species of Australian birds that have a call sounding like the crack of a whip: genus *Psophodes*.

whipcord *noun* **1** a thin tough cord made of tightly braided or twisted hemp or catgut. **2** a usu cotton or worsted cloth with fine diagonal cords or ribs. [from its use in making whips]

whip graft *noun* in horticulture, a graft made by putting a tongue cut on the scion into a slit cut diagonally in the stock.

whip in *verb trans* to keep (hounds in a pack) from scattering by use of a whip.

whiplash *noun* **1** the flexible part of a whip. **2** injury to the neck resulting from a sudden sharp whipping movement of the neck and head, e.g. in a car collision.

whiplash injury *noun* = WHIPLASH (2).

whipper-in *noun* (*pl* **whippers-in**) a huntsman's assistant who keeps the hounds from scattering by use of a whip.

whippersnapper /'wipəsnapə/ *noun informal* an insignificant but impudent person, *esp* a child. [prob alteration of earlier *snippersnapper*, prob from SNIP[2] + SNAP[1]]

whippet /'wipit/ *noun* a dog of a breed related to the greyhound, having a short coat and a small slender body. [prob from WHIP[1] in the sense 'to move quickly']

whipping *noun* **1** a severe beating or chastisement. **2a** stitching with whipstitch. **b** material used to whip or bind something, e.g. rope.

whipping boy *noun* a person who is blamed or punished for the mistakes, incompetence, etc of another or others; a scapegoat. [orig a boy who was educated alongside a prince and who was punished for any mistakes the prince made]

whippletree /'wipltree/ *noun archaic* = SWINGLETREE. [prob from WHIP[2] + TREE[1]]

whippoorwill /'wipəwil/ *noun* a N American nightjar that lives in woodland close to open country and feeds on insects: *Caprimulgus vociferus*. [imitative]

whip-round *noun Brit, informal* a collection of money made usu for a benevolent purpose: *We had a whip-round to buy him a leaving present.*

whipsaw[1] *noun* any of various types of saw with a long flexible blade. [WHIP[2]]

whipsaw[2] *verb trans* (*past tense* **whipsawed**, *past part.* **whipsawn** /'wipsawn/ *or* **whipsawed**) *NAmer* **1** to saw (something) with a whipsaw. **2** *informal*. **a** to defeat or victimize (somebody) in two different ways at once. **b** to subject (somebody) to two difficult or unwelcome situations simultaneously.

whip scorpion *noun* an arachnid with a long slender tail but no sting: order Uropygi.

whip snake *noun* any of various slender fast-moving snakes with whiplike tails: *Coluber viridiflavus*, of Europe and Asia, *Desmansia psammophis*, of Australia, and others.

whipstitch *noun* a small overcasting stitch.

whip up *verb trans* **1** to stir (somebody or something) up; to stimulate: *He whipped up the emotions of the crowd*. **2** to produce (something) in a hurry: *I'll whip a meal up in no time.*

whir[1] /wuh/ *verb intrans* see WHIRR[1].

whir[2] *noun* see WHIRR[2].

whirl[1] /wuhl/ *verb intrans* **1** to move along a curving or circling course, *esp* with force or speed: *planets whirling in their orbits*. **2** to turn abruptly or rapidly round on an axis; to rotate or wheel: *He whirled round to face me*. **3** to pass, move, or go quickly: *She whirled down the hallway*. **4** to become giddy or dizzy; to reel: *My head's whirling*. ➤ *verb trans* **1** to convey (somebody or something) rapidly; to whisk: *The ambulance whirled him away*. **2** to cause (somebody or something) to turn usu rapidly round on an axis; to rotate. ➤➤ **whirler** *noun*, **whirling** *adj*, **whirlingly** *adv*. [Middle English *whirlen*, prob of Scandinavian origin]

whirl[2] *noun* **1** a rapid rotating or circling movement. **2a** a confused tumult; a bustle: *the social whirl*. **b** a confused or disturbed mental state; a turmoil: *My mind is in a whirl all the time* — Arnold Bennett. **3** *informal* an experimental or brief attempt; a try: *I'll give it a whirl*.

whirligig /'wuhligig/ *noun* **1** a child's toy, e.g. a top, that whirls. **2** a merry-go-round. **3** a whirligig beetle. [Middle English *whirlegigg*, from *whirlen* WHIRL[1] + obsolete *gigg* spinning top]

whirligig beetle *noun* any of various beetles that live mostly on the surface of water where they move swiftly about in curves: family Gyrinidae.

whirlpool *noun* **1** a circular eddy of rapidly moving water with a central depression into which floating objects may be drawn. **2** a bath equipped with a device to produce whirling currents of hot water, used *esp* in hydrotherapy.

whirlpool bath *noun* = WHIRLPOOL (2).

whirlwind /'wuhlwind/ *noun* **1** a small rapidly rotating windstorm marked by an inward and upward spiral motion round a core of low pressure. **2** a confused rush; a whirl. **3** (*used before a noun*) happening with great speed or suddenness: *a whirlwind romance*.

whirlybird /'wuhlibuhd/ *noun chiefly NAmer, informal* a helicopter.

whirr[1] *or* **whir** /wuh/ *verb intrans* (**whirred, whirring**) to revolve or move with a continuous buzzing or vibrating sound. [Middle English (Scottish) *quirren*, prob of Scandinavian origin]

whirr[2] *or* **whir** *noun* a whirring sound.

whisht *or* **wheesht** /wisht, weesht/ *or* **whist** /wist/ *interj dialect* hush. [imitative]

whisk¹ /wisk/ *noun* **1** any of various small usu hand-held kitchen utensils used for whisking food. **2** a small bunch of flexible strands, e.g. twigs or feathers, attached to a handle for use as a brush. **3** a quick light brushing or whipping motion. [Middle English *wisk*, prob of Scandinavian origin]

whisk² *verb trans* **1** to convey (somebody or something) briskly: *He whisked the children off to bed.* **2** to mix or beat (something, e.g. egg whites) into a light froth with a whisk. **3** to brush or wipe off (e.g. crumbs) lightly. **4** to brandish (something) lightly; to flick: *The horse whisked its tail.* ➤ *verb intrans* to move lightly and swiftly.

whisker /'wiskə/ *noun* **1** any of the long projecting hairs or bristles growing near the mouth of an animal, e.g. a cat. **2** (*in pl*) the hair of a man's beard or moustache. **3** *informal* a very small amount or narrow margin: *She lost the race by a whisker.* **4** a thin hairlike crystal, e.g. of sapphire or a metal, of exceptional mechanical strength. ➤➤ **whiskered** *adj*, **whiskery** *adj*. [orig denoting something used as a whisk; from WHISK² + -ER²]

whiskey /'wiski/ *noun* (*pl* **whiskeys**) whisky produced in Ireland or the USA.

whisky /'wiski/ *noun* (*pl* **whiskies**) **1** a spirit made by distilling fermented mash of barley or other grain, e.g. rye, corn, or wheat. **2** a glass or measure of whisky. [Irish Gaelic *uisce beathadh* and Scottish Gaelic *uisge beatha*, literally 'water of life']

whisky mac *noun* a drink of whisky mixed with ginger wine, usu in equal measures.

whisky sour *noun* a drink of whisky mixed with lemon or lime juice, often sweetened and served with ice.

whisper¹ /'wispə/ *verb* (**whispered, whispering**) ➤ *verb intrans* **1** to speak softly with little or no vibration of the vocal cords. **2** to make a hissing or rustling sound like whispered speech. ➤ *verb trans* **1** to utter (something) in a whisper. **2** to report or suggest (something) confidentially: *It is whispered that he will soon resign.* ➤➤ **whisperer** *noun*. [Old English *hwisprian*]

whisper² *noun* **1a** the act or an instance of whispering; *esp* speech without vibration of the vocal cords: *It is impossible that the whisper of a faction should prevail against the voice of a nation* — Lord John Russell. **b** a hissing or rustling sound like whispered speech. **2a** a rumour: *whispers of scandal.* **b** a hint or trace. ➤➤ **whispery** *adj*.

whispering campaign *noun* the systematic dissemination by word of mouth of derogatory rumours or charges, *esp* against a candidate for public office.

whispering gallery *noun* a gallery or dome in which sounds carry a long way because of its acoustic properties.

whist¹ /wist/ *noun* a card game, usu for four players in two partnerships, in which tricks are won and points scored. [alteration of *whisk*, prob from WHISK²; from whisking up the tricks]

whist² /wist/ *interj* see WHISHT. [imitative]

whist drive *noun Brit* a social event at which whist is played with a periodic change of partners, usu with prizes at the finish.

whistle¹ /'wisl/ *noun* **1** a device in which the forcible passage of air, steam, the breath, etc through a slit or against a thin edge in a short tube produces a loud sound. **2** a shrill clear sound produced by or as if by whistling: *the whistle of the wind.* ✷ **blow the whistle on** *informal* to report (a person acting wrongly or a wrong act) to an authority or person with responsibility. **clean as a whistle** absolutely clean or perfectly clear. [Old English *hwistle*]

whistle² *verb intrans* **1** to make a shrill clear sound by blowing or drawing air through the puckered lips. **2a** to make a whistling sound by rapid movement. **b** to move rapidly with or as if with such a sound: *The train whistled by.* **3** to blow or sound a whistle. ➤ *verb trans* **1** to send, bring, call, or signal to (somebody) by whistling. **2** to produce, utter, or express (something) by whistling: *He whistled a tune.* ✷ **whistle for** *informal* to demand or request (something) in vain: *The plumber did a sloppy job so he can whistle for his money.* **whistle in the dark** to keep one's courage by or as if by whistling; to pretend to be brave despite being afraid. ➤➤ **whistler** *noun*.

whistle-blower *noun informal* somebody who reveals something secret or informs against another person. ➤➤ **whistle-blowing** *noun and adj*.

whistle-stop *noun* **1** *NAmer.* **a** a small station at which trains stop only on signal. **b** a small unimportant town. **2** *NAmer* a brief personal appearance, *esp* by a political candidate, during the course of a tour. **3** (*used before a noun*) consisting of brief stops in several places: *a whistle-stop tour of Europe.*

Whit /wit/ *noun* Whitsuntide.

whit *noun* the smallest part imaginable; a bit: *She was not a whit abashed.* [Old English *wiht*]

white¹ /wiet/ *adj* **1** of the colour of new snow or milk, the lightest colour from its reflection of all visible rays of light. **2** free from colour. **3** light or pallid in colour: *Their faces were white with fear.* **4** lustrous pale grey; silvery: *a white alloy.* **5** said of wine: made from green grapes, or dark grapes with the skins removed, and having a light yellow or amber colour. **6** *Brit* said of coffee: containing milk or cream. **7** said of flour, sugar, etc: refined and white in colour. **8** (*often* **White**). **a** relating to or denoting a member of a group of people characterized by reduced skin pigmentation. **b** of, intended for, or consisting of white people: *white schools.* **9** free from moral impurity; innocent. **10** said of a wedding: in which the bride wears white clothes as a symbol of purity. **11** said of a lie: not intended to cause harm. **12** snowy: *a white Christmas.* **13** (*also* **White**) ultra-conservative or reactionary in political outlook and action: compare RED¹ (7). **14** said of electromagnetic radiation, sound, etc: consisting of a wide range of frequencies. **15** said of light: containing all the wavelengths in the visible range at approximately equal intensities. ✷ **bleed somebody or something white** to deprive somebody of all their money or use up all the resources of something, *esp* unreasonably or unfairly. ➤➤ **whitely** *adv*, **whiteness** *noun*, **whitish** *adj*. [Old English *hwīt*]

Usage note

When describing people of a particular skin colour, *white*, like *black*, should generally be used without an initial capital letter. Although *white* is an acceptable term in most contexts, American usage often prefers to refer to peoples in terms of geographical origin, thus preferring *European* or *Caucasian* to *white*. Neither of these terms, however, is particularly common in British English.

white² *noun* **1** the colour of new snow or milk, the lightest colour. **2** the mass of albumin-containing material surrounding the yolk of an egg. **3** the white part of the ball of the eye. **4a** the light-coloured pieces in a board game, e.g. chess or draughts, for two players. **b** the player who uses these pieces. **5** (*also in pl*) white clothing, worn *esp* when playing summer sports. **6** a white animal, e.g. a butterfly or pig. **7** (*often* **White**) a person belonging to a light-skinned people. **8** (*also* **White**) a member of an ultraconservative or reactionary political group.

white admiral *noun* any of several species of Eurasian butterflies that have brown wings with white markings: *Ladoga camilla* and other species.

white ant *noun* a termite.

whitebait *noun* the young of any of several European herrings, e.g. the common herring or the sprat, eaten whole. [WHITE¹ + BAIT¹; because they were formerly used as bait]

whitebeam *noun* a European tree of the rose family with leaves covered in fine white hairs on the undersurface, white flowers, and scarlet berries: *Sorbus aria.* [WHITE¹ + *-beam*, from Old English *bēam* tree]

white belt *noun* **1** a white belt worn by a beginner in certain martial arts, *esp* judo and karate. **2** a person who is a beginner in such a sport.

white blood cell *noun* any of the white or colourless blood cells that have nuclei, do not contain haemoglobin, and are primarily concerned with body defence mechanisms and repair: compare RED BLOOD CELL. Also called LEUCOCYTE.

whiteboard *noun* a smooth white wipeable surface used, *esp* in classrooms, presentations, etc for writing or drawing on with special pens.

whitecap *noun* a wave crest breaking into white foam far from land.

white cell *noun* = WHITE BLOOD CELL.

white clover *noun* a Eurasian clover with round heads of white flowers that often grows among grass: *Trifolium repens.*

white-collar *adj* belonging or relating to the class of non-manual employees whose duties do not call for the wearing of work clothes or protective clothing, *esp* those who work in offices: compare BLUE-COLLAR.

white currant *noun* a variety of redcurrant with pale berries.

whited sepulchre *noun literary* a hypocrite. [from the simile applied by Jesus to the scribes and Pharisees, Matthew 23:27]

white dwarf *noun* a small whitish star of high surface temperature, low brightness, and high density.

white elephant *noun* **1** a possession, usu something valuable or rare, that requires a large amount of time or money to be spent on maintaining it. **2** something that is no longer of value to its owner. [from the story that the kings of Siam made a gift of a white elephant to any courtier they disliked, the cost of maintaining one being ruinous]

white ensign *noun* a white flag flown by the Royal Navy and the Royal Yacht Squadron, having a red cross on a white background and a Union Jack at the top next to the flagstaff.

white-eye *noun* any of various small usu greenish songbirds of Africa, Asia, Australia, and New Zealand that have a distinctive white ring of feathers around the eye: family Zosteropidae.

white feather *noun* a mark or symbol of cowardice: *You can get along perfectly … if you only keep your courage up, and don't show the white feather* — Harold Frederic. [from the superstition that a white feather in the plumage of a gamecock is a mark of a poor fighter]

whitefish *noun* (*pl* **whitefishes** *or collectively* **whitefish**) any of various freshwater food fishes related to the salmons and trouts: genus *Coregonus* and others.

white fish *noun Brit* any of various edible marine fish with white flesh, e.g. haddock, cod, whiting, etc, *esp* as contrasted with oily fish such as mackerel.

white flag *noun* **1** a flag of plain white used to signal a request for a truce or as a token of surrender. **2** a token of weakness or yielding.

whitefly *noun* (*pl* **whiteflies** *or collectively* **whitefly**) **1** any of numerous species of small insects that are harmful plant pests and are related to the scale insects: family Aleyrodidae. **2** an infestation of these insects.

white friar *or* **White Friar** *noun* a Carmelite friar. [from their white habits]

white gold *noun* a pale silvery alloy of gold, *esp* with nickel or palladium, resembling platinum in appearance.

white goods *pl noun* **1** major articles of household equipment, e.g. cookers and refrigerators, that are typically finished in white enamel: compare BROWN GOODS. **2** household linen, e.g. sheets, pillow cases, towels, etc.

Whitehall *noun* the British government. [named after *Whitehall*, a thoroughfare of London containing the chief offices of British government]

whitehead *noun informal* a small whitish lump in the skin due to blockage of an oil gland duct.

white heat *noun* **1** a temperature higher than red heat, at which a body emits white light. **2** *informal* a state of intense mental or physical activity or strain.

white hole *noun* a hypothetical region in space that emits radiation of all wavelengths and is thought to be the converse of a BLACK HOLE.

white hope *noun* (*also* **great white hope**) a person expected to bring fame and glory to his or her group, country, team, etc.

white horse *noun* **1** a usu prehistoric figure of a horse made by cutting away the turf from a chalk hillside. **2** (*in pl*) waves with crests breaking into white foam.

white-hot *adj* **1** at or radiating white heat. **2** *informal* ardently zealous; fervid.

White House /hows/ *noun* (*usu* **the White House**) the executive branch of the US government. [named after the *White House, a* mansion in Washington DC, assigned to the president of the USA]

white knight *noun* somebody who comes to the rescue of a person or organization, *esp* a person or company that finances a company to save it from an unwelcome takeover.

white-knuckle *adj* causing tension, anxiety, or excitement: *a white-knuckle ride.*

white lead /led/ *noun* any of several white lead-containing pigments, *esp* a heavy poisonous carbonate of lead used formerly in exterior paints.

white lie *noun* a harmless or unimportant lie, *esp* one that is told to avoid hurting somebody's feelings or as a way of being tactful.

white magic *noun* magic used for good purposes, e.g. to cure disease.

white matter *noun* whitish nerve tissue that consists largely of myelinated nerve fibres and underlies the grey matter of the brain and spinal cord or is gathered into nerves.

white meat *noun* light-coloured meat, e.g. poultry breast or veal: compare RED MEAT.

white metal *noun* any of several alloys based on tin or sometimes lead used *esp* for bearings, type metal, and domestic utensils.

whiten *verb intrans and trans* (**whitened, whitening**) to become or make (something) white or whiter; to bleach or blanch. ➤➤ **whitener** *noun*, **whitening** *noun*.

white noise *noun* sound or electrical noise that has many continuous frequencies of equal intensity.

whiteout *noun* **1** a weather condition in a snowy area in which the horizon cannot be seen and only dark objects are discernible. **2** white correction fluid.

white out *verb trans* **1** said *esp* of snow: to cause (something) to turn white. **2** to cover (a mistake in writing, typing, etc) with correction fluid. ➤ *verb intrans* to lose colour vision prior to losing consciousness.

White Paper *noun* a British government report containing information about or proposals on a particular issue.

white pepper *noun* a condiment prepared from the husked dried berries of an E Indian plant used either whole or ground: compare BLACK PEPPER.

white poplar *noun* a Eurasian poplar with smooth whitish bark and leaves that are densely covered with white hairs on the undersurface: *Populus alba.*

white pudding *noun* a sausage made from minced pork meat, oatmeal, and fat: compare BLACK PUDDING.

white rose *noun* the emblem of Yorkshire and the House of York.

White Russian *noun* **1** a Belorussian. **2** an opponent of the Bolsheviks during the Russian Civil War.

white sauce *noun* a sauce made with milk, cream, or a chicken, veal, or fish stock: compare BROWN SAUCE.

white slave *noun* a woman or girl held unwillingly, *esp* abroad, and forced to be a prostitute. ➤➤ **white slaver** *noun*, **white slavery** *noun*.

whitesmith /'wietsmith/ *noun* **1** a tinsmith. **2** somebody who finishes or polishes newly made metal goods.

white spirit *noun* a flammable liquid distilled from petroleum and used *esp* as a solvent and thinner for paints.

white supremacy *noun* the doctrine of the inherent superiority of the white race over others. ➤➤ **white supremacist** *noun*.

whitethorn *noun* = HAWTHORN.

whitethroat *noun* a Eurasian and African warbler with a white throat, reddish brown wings, and buff underparts tinged with pink: *Sylvia communis* and others.

white tie *noun* formal evening dress for men; *specif* a tail coat and a white bow tie.

white trash *noun NAmer, derog* poor white people.

white van man *noun* a male van driver, *esp* a driver of a white delivery van, who drives in an aggressive or reckless manner.

whitewall *noun* a car tyre with a white band on the sidewall.

whitewash[1] *noun* **1** a liquid mixture, e.g. of lime and water or whiting, size, and water, for whitening exterior walls or similar surfaces. **2** the act or an instance of whitewashing. **3** a deliberate concealment of a mistake or fault.

whitewash[2] *verb trans* **1** to apply whitewash to (e.g. a wall). **2a** to gloss over or cover up (e.g. a mistake or fault). **b** to exonerate (somebody) by concealment or through biased presentation of data. **3** *informal* to defeat (somebody) overwhelmingly in a contest or game. ➤➤ **whitewashed** *adj*, **whitewasher** *noun*.

white water *noun* fast-moving choppy water, e.g. in breakers or rapids.

white whale *noun* = BELUGA (2).

whitewood *noun* the pale or white wood of any of various trees, e.g. the lime, *esp* when used for furniture.

whitey[1] *noun* (*pl* **whiteys**) *informal, derog* a white person.

whitey[2] *adj* see WHITY.

whither /'widhə/ *adv and conj formal, archaic, or literary* **1** to or towards what place?: *Whither democracy?* **2** to the place at, in, or to which: *Go whither you wish.* **3** to which place. [Old English *hwider*]

whithersoever *conj archaic* to whatever place: *I will go whithersoever you lead.*

whiting[1] /'wieting/ *noun* (*pl* **whiting**) any of various marine food fishes, *esp* one related to the cod: *Merlangus merlangus* and others. [Middle English from early Dutch *witinc*, from *wit* white]

whiting[2] *noun* washed and ground chalk used *esp* as a pigment and in paper coating. [Middle English, verbal noun from *whiten* to make white]

whitlow /'witloh/ *noun* a deep usu pus-producing inflammation of the finger or toe, *esp* round the nail. [Middle English *whitflawe, whitflowe, whitlowe*, prob from *whit* WHITE[1] + *flawe* break, fissure, FLAW[1]]

Whitsun /'wits(ə)n/ *noun* Whitsuntide. [Middle English *Whitson* from *Whitsonday*: see WHIT SUNDAY]

Whit Sunday /'wit'sunday, -di/ *noun* a festival celebrated in the Christian Church commemorating the descent of the Holy Spirit at Pentecost, observed on the seventh Sunday after Easter. [Middle English *Whitsonday* from Old English *hwīta sunnandæg*, literally 'white Sunday'; prob from the custom of wearing white robes by the newly baptized, who were numerous at this season]

Whitsuntide /'wits(ə)ntied/ *noun* the week beginning with Whit Sunday.

whittle /'witl/ *verb trans and intrans* **1a** to pare or cut off chips from the surface of (wood) with a knife. **b** to shape or form (something) by doing this. **2** (+ down/away) to reduce, remove, or destroy (something) gradually as if by cutting off bits with a knife: *Try to whittle down your expenses; They are whittling away at our rights.* [Middle English *whittel*, alteration of *thwitel* a paring knife, from Old English *thwītan* to cut down, whittle]

whity or **whitey** /'wieti/ *adj* somewhat white; whitish: *whity grey.*

whiz[1] /wiz/ *verb* see WHIZZ[1].

whiz[2] *noun* see WHIZZ[2].

whiz-bang *noun* see WHIZZ-BANG.

whiz kid *noun* see WHIZZ KID.

whizz[1] or **whiz** /wiz/ *verb intrans* **1** to speed through the air with a buzzing, whirring, or hissing sound, or to make such a sound: *The arrow whizzed past his ear.* **2** *informal* to fly or move swiftly. ➤ *verb trans* to cause (something) to whizz. [imitative]

whizz[2] or **whiz** *noun* **1** a whizzing sound. **2** *informal* a swift movement or passage: *a 72-hour whizz round twenty hotels — Punch.* **3** (*also* **wiz**) *informal* somebody who is clever or skilful, *esp* in a specified field: *a whizz at maths.* **4** *informal* the act or an instance of urinating. **5** *Brit, informal* amphetamines.

whizz-bang or **whiz-bang** *noun* **1** a high-explosive shell, *esp* one used in World War I, with an explosion that is heard directly after the noise of its flight. **2** a firework that is suggestive of a whizz-bang. **3** *chiefly NAmer* a person or thing that is conspicuous for noise, speed, or startling effect.

whizz kid or **whiz kid** *noun* a person who is unusually intelligent, clever, or successful, *esp* at an early age.

WHO *abbr* World Health Organization.

who /hooh/ *pron* (*pl* **who**) **1** used as an interrogative: what or which person?: *Who was elected President?* **2** used to introduce a restrictive or non-restrictive clause in reference to a person or animal: *my father, who was a lawyer.* **3** used to introduce a human group, *esp* when a plural verb follows: *an orchestra who play the wartime hits —* The Observer. **4** *archaic* the person that; whoever. [Old English *hwā*]

Usage note

who *or* whom? Grammatically, *who* and *whom* are the subject and object forms respectively of the same word. *Who* corresponds to *I, he, she* or *they; whom* corresponds to *me, him, her* or *them: They saw whom? –They saw him.* Whom, however, is being increasingly relegated to very formal use in modern English, especially in questions: *Whom have I the honour of addressing?,* but *Who were you speaking to just then?* or *Who did you see at the meeting?* The same is largely true for the use of *whom* as a relative pronoun. Many people would argue that if *the man who I saw yesterday* is grammatically incorrect, *the man whom I saw yesterday* sounds pedantic, and it is therefore better to say *the man that I saw yesterday* or, simply, *the man I saw yesterday.* See also note at THAT[4].

whoa /'woh-ə, woh/ *interj* used as a command, e.g. to a draught animal, to stand still. [Middle English *whoo, who*]

who'd /hood, *strong* hoohd/ *contraction* **1** who would. **2** who had.

whodunit or **whodunnit** /hooh'dunit/ *noun* a play, film, or story dealing with the detection of crime or criminals. [substandard or facetious *who done it?* who did it?]

whoever *pronoun* **1** whatever person. **2** no matter who. **3** *informal* used for emphasis in place of the interrogative pronoun *who: Whoever can it be?*

whole[1] /hohl/ *adj* **1** each or all of; total or entire: *It took three whole weeks; She made the whole class stay in.* **2** having all its proper constituents; unmodified: *whole milk.* **3** not divided or broken; intact. **4a** free of wounds or injury; unhurt. **b** physically sound and healthy; free of disease or deformity. **c** free of defect or impairment. **5** used for emphasis: *The whole idea is to help, not hinder.* ➤➤ **wholeness** *noun.* [Old English *hāl*]

whole[2] *noun* **1** a complete amount or sum; a number or totality lacking no part, member, or element: *the whole of society.* **2** something constituting a complex unity; a coherent system or organization of parts. ✱ *as a whole* considered all together as a body rather than as individuals. **on the whole 1** in view of all the circumstances or conditions; all things considered. **2** in most instances; typically.

whole[3] *adv* **1** in an undivided piece or state: *The snake swallowed the rabbit whole.* **2** *informal* used for emphasis: *I feel a whole lot better now; a whole new ball game.*

wholefood or **wholefoods** *noun* food, e.g. pulses and grains, in a simple and natural form that has undergone minimal processing and refining: compare HEALTH FOOD, JUNK FOOD.

wholehearted *adj* earnestly committed or devoted; free from all reserve or hesitation. ➤➤ **wholeheartedly** *adv.*

whole-life *adj* said of life insurance: for which premiums are payable as long as the insured person lives.

wholemeal *adj* said of bread or flour: produced from ground entire wheat kernels.

whole note *noun chiefly NAmer* = SEMIBREVE.

whole number *noun* an integer.

wholesale[1] *noun* the sale of commodities in large quantities usu for resale by a retailer: compare RETAIL[2].

wholesale[2] *adj* **1** relating to or denoting the sale of commodities in large quantities. **2** performed on a large scale, *esp* without discrimination: *wholesale slaughter.*

wholesale[3] *adv* **1** being sold at wholesale. **2** on a large scale.

wholesale[4] *verb trans* to sell (commodities) at wholesale.

wholesaler *noun* somebody who sells commodities chiefly to retailers, merchants, or industrial, institutional, and commercial users, mainly for resale or business use.

wholesome /'hohls(ə)m/ *adj* **1** promoting health of body: *a light wholesome diet.* **2** healthy: *wholesome-looking children.* **3** promoting the well-being of mind or spirit: *wholesome literature.* **4** based on well-grounded fear; prudent: *a wholesome respect for the law.* ➤➤ **wholesomely** *adv,* **wholesomeness** *noun.* [Middle English *holsom, hoolsom,* from *hol, hool* healthy, WHOLE[1] + *-som* -SOME[1]]

whole tone *noun* a musical interval, e.g. C-D or G-A, comprising two semitones.

whole-wheat *adj* = WHOLEMEAL.

wholly /'hohli/ *adv* **1** to the full or entire extent; completely: *wholly incompetent.* **2** to the exclusion of other things; solely: *a book dealing wholly with herbs.* [Middle English *hoolly,* from *hool* WHOLE[1]]

whom /hoohm/ *pron* used in place of *who,* as the object of a preceding preposition, or less frequently as the object of a verb or of a following preposition: *And therefore never send to know for whom the bell tolls —* John Donne; *Whom are you addressing?* [Old English *hwām,* dative of *hwā* WHO]

Usage note

whom *or* who? See note at WHO.

whomever *pron formal* used in place of *whoever* as the object of a preposition or verb: *He reserved a special kind of behaviour or language for whomever he was with —* Peter Ackroyd.

whomso *pron archaic* whoso.

whomsoever *pronoun formal* used in place of *whosoever* as the object of a preposition or verb.

whoop[1] /woohp/ *noun* **1** a loud yell expressive of eagerness, exuberance, or jubilation. **2** the hoot of an owl, crane, etc. **3** /hoohp/ the crowing intake of breath following a paroxysm in whooping cough. [Middle English, of imitative origin]

whoop[2] *verb intrans* to utter or make a whoop. ➤ *verb trans* **1** to utter or express (something) with a whoop. **2** to urge or cheer (somebody) on with a whoop. ✳ **whoop it up** *informal* to celebrate riotously; to carouse.

whoopee[1] /woo'pee/ *interj informal* used to express exuberance. [from WHOOP[1]]

whoopee[2] /'woopi/ *noun informal* boisterous convivial fun. ✳ **make whoopee 1** *informal* to have great fun; to celebrate noisily. **2** *informal* to have sexual intercourse.

whoopee cushion /'woopi/ *noun* an inflatable trick cushion that produces the noise of breaking wind when sat on.

whooper swan /'hoohpə/ *noun* a large white yellow-billed European swan with a loud ringing call: *Cygnus cygnus*.

whooping cough /'hoohping/ *noun* an infectious bacterial disease, *esp* of children, marked by a convulsive spasmodic cough sometimes followed by a crowing intake of breath.

whooping crane /'hoohping/ *noun* a large white nearly extinct N American crane noted for its loud mournful ringing call: *Grus americana*.

whoops /woops, woohps/ *interj* used to express dismay or an apology, *esp* on being clumsy or making a silly mistake.

whoops-a-daisy *interj* = WHOOPS.

whoosh[1] *or* **woosh** /woosh, woohsh/ *verb intrans* to move quickly with a swift or explosive rushing sound: *cars whooshing along the motorway.* ➤➤ **whooshing** *adj.* [imitative]

whoosh[2] *or* **woosh** *noun* a swift or explosive rush or spurt: *The fire suddenly gave a whoosh.*

whop[1] /wop/ (*NAmer* **whap**) *verb trans* (**whopped, whopping**) *informal* **1** to beat or strike (somebody or something). **2** to defeat (somebody) totally. [Middle English *whappen*, alteration of *wappen* to throw violently, of unknown origin]

whop[2] (*NAmer* **whap**) *noun informal* a heavy blow; a thump.

whopper /'wopə/ *noun informal* **1** something unusually large or otherwise extreme of its kind. **2** an extravagant or monstrous lie.

whopping /'woping/ *adj informal* extremely big: *They won by a whopping majority.*

whore[1] /haw/ *noun* a prostitute or a woman who has many casual sexual relationships. ➤➤ **whorish** *adj.* [Old English *hōre*]

whore[2] *verb intrans* **1** to have sexual intercourse, *esp* with a prostitute or with many casual partners. **2** to be or work as a prostitute. **3** (+ after) to pursue an unworthy or idolatrous desire: *Growth was a false god which had been whored after for too long* — The Guardian.

whoredom *noun* the practice of prostitution.

whorehouse /'hawhows/ *noun informal* a brothel.

whoremaster *noun archaic* a man who consorts with prostitutes or is given to lechery.

whoremonger /'hawmunggə/ *noun archaic* a whoremaster.

whoreson /'haws(ə)n/ *noun archaic* a contemptible person; a scoundrel.

whorl /wuhl, wawl/ *noun* **1** an arrangement of similar parts, e.g. leaves, in a circle round a point on an axis, e.g. a stem. **2** something spiral in form or movement: *whorls of smoke.* **3** a single turn of a spiral, *esp* on a shell. **4** a fingerprint in which the central ridges turn through at least one complete circle. ➤➤ **whorled** *adj.* [Middle English *wharle, whorle* small pulley in a spinning machine, prob alteration of *whirle*, from *whirlen* WHIRL[1]]

whortleberry /'wuhtlb(ə)ri, -beri/ *noun* (*pl* **whortleberries**) = BILBERRY. [alteration of *hurtleberry*, from Old English *horte* whortleberry + BERRY[1]]

who's /hoohz/ *contraction* **1** who is. **2** who has.

Usage note

who's *or* **whose**? These two words are pronounced the same, but it is important to distinguish between them in writing, especially in questions. *Who's* is the shortened form of *who is* or *who has*: *Who's that? – It's only me; Who's done the washing-up? Whose* is the possessive form of *who*: *Whose that?* ('Who owns that?'); *Whose turn is it to do the washing-up?*

whose[1] /hoohz/ *adj* of whom or which, *esp* as possessor or possessors, agent or agents, or object or objects of an action: *Whose hat is this?; the factory in whose construction they were involved.* [Old English *hwaes*, genitive of *hwā* WHO, *hwaet* WHAT[1]]

Usage note

whose *or* **who's**? See note at WHO'S.

whose[2] *pronoun* (*pl* **whose**) used without a following noun as a pronoun equivalent in meaning to the adjective *whose*: *Tell me whose it was.*

whosesoever *adj formal* of whomsoever.

whoso *pronoun archaic* whoever.

whosoever *pronoun formal* whoever.

who's who *noun* a collection of short biographical sketches of prominent people, usu in a specified field: *a who's who of sports figures.*

whump[1] /wump/ *noun* a thump or thud. [imitative]

whump[2] *verb* to bang or thump (somebody or something).

whup /wup/ *verb trans* (**whupped, whupping**) *chiefly NAmer, informal* to beat or thrash (somebody or something). [variant of WHIP[1]]

why[1] /wie/ *adv* for what cause, reason, or purpose? ✳ **why not** used in making a suggestion: *Why not boil them?* [Old English *hwī, hwy* instrumental case of *hwæt* WHAT[1]]

why[2] *conj* **1** the cause, reason, or purpose for which: *That's why I'm so tired.* **2** on which grounds: *That's the reason why I left.*

why[3] *noun* (*pl* **whys**) a reason or cause: *He wants to know all the whys and wherefores.*

why[4] *interj* used to express mild surprise, hesitation, approval, disapproval, or anger: *Why, here's what I was looking for.*

whydah *or* **whyda** /'widə/ *noun* any of several species of mostly black and white African weaverbirds: genus *Vidua*. [alteration (influenced by *Whydah*, a town in Dahomey) of *widow bird*; from its dark plumage suggesting a widow's dress]

WI *abbr* **1** West Indies. **2** Wisconsin (US postal abbreviation). **3** *Brit* Women's Institute.

Wicca /'wikə/ *noun* an ancient religion of the Celtic people, revived as modern witchcraft. ➤➤➤ **Wiccan** *noun and adj.* [Old English *wicca* WITCH[1]]

Wick. *abbr* Wicklow.

wick[1] /wik/ *noun* a cord, strip, or cylinder of loosely woven material through which a liquid, e.g. paraffin, oil, or melted wax, is drawn by capillary action to the top for burning in a candle, lamp, oil stove, etc. ✳ **dip one's wick** *coarse slang* said of a man: to have sexual intercourse. **get on somebody's wick** *Brit, informal* to annoy or irritate somebody. [Old English *wēoce*]

wick[2] *noun* used in place names: a village or hamlet. [Old English *wīc*]

wicked /'wikid/ *adj* **1** morally bad; evil. **2** disposed to mischief; roguish: *a wicked grin.* **3** very unpleasant, vicious, or dangerous: *a wicked waste.* **4** *informal* extremely stylish, skilful, or good: *We had a wicked night out.* ➤➤➤ **wickedly** *adv,* **wickedness** *noun.* [Middle English, alteration of *wicke*, perhaps from Old English *wicca* wizard]

wicker /'wikə/ *noun* interlaced osiers, twigs, canes, or rods: *a wicker basket.* [Middle English *wiker*, of Scandinavian origin]

wickerwork *noun* work consisting of wicker.

wicket /'wikit/ *noun* **1a** in cricket, either of the two sets of stumps set 20.12m (22yd) apart, at which the ball is bowled and which the batsman defends. **b** the area 3.66m (12ft) wide bounded by these wickets. **c** a terminated innings of a batsman. **d** a partnership between two batsmen who are in at the same time. **2** a small gate or door, *esp* one forming part of or placed near a larger one. **3** *chiefly NAmer* an opening like a window, *esp* a grilled or grated window through which business is transacted, e.g. at a bank. **4** a small gate for emptying the chamber of a canal lock or regulating the amount of water passing through a channel. **5** *NAmer* a croquet hoop. ✳ **a sticky wicket** *informal* a difficult or awkward situation. [Middle English *wiket* a small gate or grille, from early French, of Germanic origin]

wicketkeeper *noun* in cricket, the fielder who is stationed behind the wicket to catch balls missed by the batsman or hit with the edge of the bat. ➤➤➤ **wicketkeeping** *noun.*

wickiup /'wikiup/ *noun* a Native American hut made of reeds, grass, or brushwood. [Fox *wikiyap* dwelling]

widdershins /'widəshinz/ *or* **withershins** /'widh-/ *adv* in a left-handed, wrong, or contrary direction; in the direction that is apparently contrary to the path of the sun; anticlockwise. [early Low German *weddersinnes* from early High German *widersinnes*, from *widersinnen* to go back, from *wider* back, against, again + *sinnen* to go]

widdle¹ /'widl/ *verb intrans informal* to urinate. [prob from WEE-WEE² + PIDDLE¹]

widdle² *noun informal* **1** an act of passing urine. **2** urine.

wide¹ /wied/ *adj* **1** having great horizontal extent; vast: *a wide area.* **2** having a specified width: *63 metres wide.* **3** having much extent between the sides; broad: *a wide doorway.* **4** fully opened: *wide eyes.* **5** embracing much; comprehensive: *wide experience.* **6** extending or fluctuating over a considerable range: *a wide variation.* **7** distant or deviating from a target or from something specified: *His remark was wide of the truth.* ➤➤ **widely** *adv,* **wideness** *noun,* **widish** *adj.* [Old English *wīd*]

wide² *adv* **1** over a great horizontal distance or extent; widely: *They searched far and wide.* **2** so as to leave much space or distance between: *legs wide apart.* **3** so as to miss or clear a point by a considerable distance: *The bullet went wide.* **4** to the fullest extent; completely or fully: *wide awake.*

wide³ *noun* in cricket, a bowled ball that is out of reach of the batsman in the normal position and counts as one run.

-wide *comb. form* forming adjectives from nouns, with the meaning: over (the distance, area, or extent specified); throughout (the area or scope specified): *nationwide.*

wide-angle *adj* said of a lens: having an angle of view wider than a standard lens.

wide area network *noun* a communications system where the various computer terminals are far apart and linked by radio, satellite, etc.

wideawake /'wiedəwayk/ *noun* a wide-brimmed, soft felt hat with a low crown.

wide-awake *adj* **1** fully awake. **2** alert and watchful, *esp* for advantages or opportunities.

wide ball *noun* = WIDE³.

wide-body *adj* said of an aircraft: having a wide fuselage.

wide boy *noun Brit, informal* a man who is involved in petty crime or who uses unscrupulous methods to earn a living.

wide-eyed *adj* **1** amazed or astonished. **2** marked by uncritical acceptance or admiration; naive: *wide-eyed innocence.*

widen *verb intrans and trans* (**widened, widening**) to become or make (something) wider. ➤➤ **widener** *noun.*

wide receiver *noun* in American football, a player positioned to the side of the offensive formation to catch passes from the quarterback.

wide-screen *adj* **1** said of a format of cinema film: having a projected picture that is substantially wider than the standard one. **2a** said of a television broadcast: transmitted in a format that fills the width of a standard television screen, but leaves a gap at the top and bottom of it. **b** said of a television set: having a screen that is wider than a standard screen.

widespread *adj* **1** widely extended or spread out. **2** widely diffused or prevalent: *In view of the silliness of the majority of mankind, a widespread belief is more likely to be foolish than sensible* — Bertrand Russell.

widgeon *noun* see WIGEON.

widget /'wijit/ *noun informal* any small usu mechanical device whose name is unknown or irrelevant. [alteration of GADGET]

widow¹ /'widoh/ *noun* **1a** a woman whose husband has died and who has not remarried. **b** *informal* a woman whose husband spends much time away from her, pursuing a specified activity: *a golf widow.* **2** an extra hand of cards dealt face down and usu placed at the disposal of the highest bidder. **3** a single usu short last line, e.g. of a paragraph, at the top of a printed page or column. [Old English *wuduwe*]

widow² *verb trans* to cause (a woman) to become a widow. ➤➤ **widowed** *adj.*

widow bird *noun* = WHYDAH.

widower *noun* a man whose wife has died and who has not remarried. [Old English *wuduwa* widower]

widowhood *noun* the state or period of being a widow.

widow's cruse *noun* a small source or supply of something that, despite being used, is never exhausted. [from the widow whose cruse of oil was made unfailing (Kings 17:14–16)]

widow's mite *noun* a small gift, *esp* of money, ungrudgingly given by somebody who can little afford it. [from the widow who cast two mites (a farthing) into the temple treasury (Mark 12:42)]

widow's peak *noun* a point formed by the downward growth of the hairline in the middle of the forehead. [from the belief that a woman with such a hairline would be widowed]

widow's weeds *pl noun* black mourning clothes worn by a widow.

width /witth, width/ *noun* **1a** the measurement taken at right angles to the length. **b** the lesser of two dimensions or the least of three dimensions. **2** largeness of extent or scope. **3** a measured and cut piece of material.

Word history
WIDE¹ + *-th* as in BREADTH. In his *Dictionary* (1755), Samuel Johnson labels *width* 'a low word'. His objection was etymological: *width* was a word formed artificially in the 17th cent. on the model of the much earlier *breadth* and *length*. Even by Johnson's time, however, it was in reputable use, replacing the more natural form *wideness.*

widthways /'witthwayz, 'widthwayz/ *adv* in the direction of the width; crosswise.

widthwise /'witthwiez, 'widthwiez/ *adv* = WIDTHWAYS.

wield /weeld/ *verb trans* **1** to handle (a tool or weapon) effectively: *wielding a sword.* **2** to exert or exercise (power or influence). ➤➤ **wielder** *noun.* [Old English *wieldan*]

wieldy *adj* (**wieldier, wieldiest**) easy to use or wield. [*wieldy* easily wielded or handled, from WIELD + -Y¹; in recent use back-formation from UNWIELDY]

wiener /'weenə/ *noun NAmer* **1** a frankfurter. **2** *coarse slang* a man's penis. [short for German *Wienerwurst*, from *Wiener* of Vienna + *Wurst* sausage]

Wiener schnitzel /'veenə shnitsəl/ *noun* a thin slice of veal coated in breadcrumbs and fried. [German *Wiener Schnitzel*, from *Wiener* of Vienna + *Schnitzel* cutlet]

wife /wief/ *noun* (*pl* **wives** /wievz/) **1** a married woman, *esp* in relation to her husband: *What man thinks of changing himself to suit his wife?* — Trollope. **2** (*in combinations*) a woman acting or working in a specified capacity: *a fishwife.* **3** *archaic or dialect* a woman: *an old wives' tale.* ➤➤ **wifehood** *noun,* **wifeless** *adj.* [Old English *wīf* woman]

wifely *adj* of or befitting a good wife. ➤➤ **wifeliness** *noun.*

wife-swapping *noun informal* the temporary exchange of sexual partners by two or more married couples.

wig¹ /wig/ *noun* a manufactured covering of natural or synthetic hair for the head, worn e.g. to cover baldness, by a judge, lawyer, etc as part of professional dress, or as a disguise. ➤➤ **wigged** *adj,* **wigless** *adj.* [short for PERIWIG]

wig² *verb trans* (**wigged, wigging**) *Brit, informal, dated* to chastise or rebuke (somebody) severely. [perhaps from WIG¹ and influenced by BIGWIG, with the idea of being rebuked by somebody in authority]

wigeon *or* **widgeon** /'wijin/ *noun* (*pl* **wigeons** *or collectively* **wigeon**) any of several species of freshwater dabbling ducks, the males of which have a chestnut head: genus *Anas.* [origin unknown]

wigging /'wiging/ *noun Brit, informal, dated* a severe scolding.

wiggle¹ /'wigl/ *verb intrans and trans* to move or cause (something) to move from side to side, up and down, or round and round with short smooth or jerky movements: *He wiggled his toes.* ➤➤ **wiggler** *noun.* [Middle English *wiglen*, from early Dutch or early Low German *wiggelen* to totter]

wiggle² *noun* **1** a wiggling movement. **2** a wavy line; a squiggle. ➤➤ **wiggly** *adj.*

wight /wiet/ *noun archaic or dialect* a person, usu of a specified kind: *an unfortunate wight.* [Old English *wiht* a thing or creature]

wigwag /'wigwag/ *verb* (**wigwagged, wigwagging**) ➤ *verb intrans NAmer, informal* to send a signal by waving a flag or light according to a code. ➤ *verb trans NAmer, informal* **1** to signal (something) by wigwagging. **2** to wave (a flag or light) as a signal. [English dialect *wig* to move + WAG¹]

wigwam /'wigwam/ *noun* a dwelling made from a conical or dome-shaped framework of poles covered with bark, rush mats, or hides, *esp* as used formerly by Native Americans. [Abnaki and Massachuset *wīkwām*]

wilco /'wilkoh/ *interj* used *esp* in radio and signalling to indicate that a received message will be complied with. [short for *will comply*]

wild[1] /wield/ *adj* **1** living in a natural state; not tame or domesticated: *a wild duck*. **2** growing or produced without the aid and care of humans: *wild honey*. **3** related to or resembling a corresponding cultivated or domesticated organism: *wild strawberries*. **4** said of land: not inhabited or cultivated. **5** said of scenery: desolate. **6** free from restraint or regulation; uncontrolled or unruly: *a wild mob*. **7** *informal* passionately eager or enthusiastic: *He was wild about jazz*. **8** *informal* very angry; infuriated: *She drove me wild with her whining*. **9** emotionally overcome: *wild with grief*. **10** marked by turbulent agitation: *a wild frenzy*. **11** stormy: *a wild night*. **12** going beyond reasonable or conventional bounds; fantastic: *a wild scheme; beyond my wildest dreams*. **13** indicative of strong passion, desire, or emotion: *a wild gleam of delight in his eyes*. **14** uncivilized or barbaric. **15** haphazard: *a wild guess*. **16** *informal* fashionably outrageous: *That shirt is really wild*. ✳ **wild and woolly 1** lacking refinement; uncivilized: *a wild and woolly town*. **2** impractical or not properly thought out: *wild and woolly ideas*. ➤➤ **wildish** *adj*, **wildly** *adv*, **wildness** *noun*. [Old English *wilde*]

wild[2] *noun* **1** a sparsely inhabited or uncultivated region; a wilderness. **2** (**the wild**) a wild, free, or natural state or existence: *living in the wild*. **3** (**the wilds**) remote country: *the wilds of Norfolk*.

wild[3] *adv* in a wild manner: *rhododendrons growing wild*.

wild boar *noun* a Eurasian wild pig, having a bristly greyish coat and prominent tusks: *Sus scrofa*.

wild card *noun* **1** a playing card able to represent any card designated by the holder. **2** a person or team selected to take part in a tournament despite not having qualified to participate through previous performances. **3** something or somebody irregular or unpredictable. **4** in computing, a character that can be used, e.g. in searching for files, to represent any character or string of characters.

wild carrot *noun* an Eurasian plant of the carrot family that is probably the ancestor of the cultivated carrot and has an acrid unpleasant-tasting root: *Daucus carota*. Also called QUEEN ANNE'S LACE.

wildcat[1] *noun* (*pl* **wildcats** *or collectively* **wildcat**) **1a** either of two cats that resemble but are heavier in build than the domestic cat and are usu held to be among its ancestors: *Felis sylvestris* and *Felis ocreata*. **b** any of various small or medium-sized cats, e.g. the lynx or ocelot. **2** a savage quick-tempered person. **3** a wildcat oil or gas well.

wildcat[2] *adj* **1** operating, produced, or carried on outside the bounds of standard or legitimate business practices: *a wildcat insurance scheme*. **2** relating to or denoting an oil or gas well drilled in territory not known to be productive. **3** initiated by a group of workers without formal union approval or in violation of a contract: *a wildcat strike*.

wildcat[3] *verb intrans* (**wildcatted, wildcatting**) *NAmer* to prospect for oil or gas, usu by drilling an experimental well. ➤➤ **wildcatter** *noun*.

wild cherry *noun* = GEAN.

wild dog *noun* a wild member of the dog family, *esp* a dingo.

wildebeest /'wildəbeest, 'vil-/ *noun* (*pl* **wildebeests** *or collectively* **wildebeest**) = GNU. [Afrikaans *wildebees* (*pl* **wildebeeste**), from *wilde* wild + *bees* ox, beast]

wilder /'wieldə/ *verb* (**wildered, wildering**) ➤ *verb trans archaic* **1** to lead (somebody) astray. **2** to bewilder or perplex (somebody). ➤ *verb intrans archaic* to move at random; to wander. [prob irreg from WILDERNESS]

wilderness /'wildənis/ *noun* **1a** a region or area that is uncultivated and uninhabited by human beings. **b** an empty or pathless area or region: *the remote wildernesses of space*. **c** a part of a garden or nature reserve devoted to wild growth. **2** a confusing multitude or mass. **3** the state of exclusion from office or power. ✳ **a voice in the wilderness 1** a plea for something, *esp* reform, that is ignored. **2** the person or group making such a plea. [Old English *wildēoren* of wild beasts, from *wilde* WILD[1] + *dēor* wild animal, DEER + -NESS]

wild-eyed *adj* glaring wildly.

wildfire *noun* **1** in former times, an incendiary substance used in warfare, e.g. Greek fire. **2** a phosphorescent glow, e.g. will-o'-the-wisp. ✳ **spread like wildfire** to spread very rapidly.

wildfowl *noun* (*pl* **wildfowl**) a wild duck, goose, or other game bird, *esp* a waterfowl. ➤➤ **wildfowler** *noun*, **wildfowling** *noun*.

wild-goose chase *noun* a hopeless pursuit after something unattainable.

wild hyacinth *noun* a common European woodland plant of the hyacinth family with spikes of blue drooping flowers; a bluebell: *Hyacinthoides nonscripta*.

wilding /'wielding/ *noun* **1** a plant, *esp* a wild apple or crab apple, growing uncultivated in the wild, either as a native plant or as a cultivated plant that has run wild. **2** the fruit of such a plant. [WILD[1] + -*ing* one belonging to or descended from such a kind, from Old English]

wildlife *noun* the wild animals and plants of a region collectively, *esp* wild animals.

wildling /'wieldling/ *noun* = WILDING.

wild oat *noun* a wild grass that is common in meadows and grows as a weed on arable land: *Avena fatua*. ✳ **sow one's wild oats** see SOW[2].

wild rice *noun* a tall aquatic N American grass that yields an edible purplish black grain: *Zizania aquatica*.

wild silk *noun* silk produced by wild silkworms that is coarser and stronger than cultivated silk.

wild type *noun* in genetics, the typical form of an organism as ordinarily encountered in nature, in contrast to atypical individuals resulting from a change in the chromosomes or genes in the cells.

Wild West *noun* the western USA in its frontier period.

wile[1] /wiel/ *noun* (*usu in pl*) a deceitful or beguiling trick or stratagem. [Middle English *wil*, prob of Scandinavian origin]

wile[2] *verb trans archaic* to lure (somebody), as if by a magic spell; to entice (them).

wilful (*NAmer* **willful**) /'wilf(ə)l/ *adj* **1** done deliberately; intentional. **2** obstinately and often perversely self-willed. ➤➤ **wilfully** *adv*, **wilfulness** *noun*. [WILL[2] + -FUL[1]]

will[1] /wil/ *verb* (*third person sing. present tense* **will**, *past tense* **would** /wəd/) ➤ *verb aux* **1** used to express an action or state in the future: *Tomorrow morning I will wake up in this first-class hotel suite* — Tennessee Williams. **2** used to express intention or determination: *I will go, whatever they do; You will do as I say.* **3** used to express willingness or consent: *Is there no one who will help us?* **4** used to express a request or invitation: *Will you please stop talking; Will you have some tea?* **5** used to express likelihood or probability: *Accidents will happen; That will be the postman.* **6** used with emphatic stress to express annoyance: *He will call the radio the 'wireless'.* **7** used to express capability: *The back seat will hold three passengers.* ➤ *verb intrans* **1** *formal, literary* to wish or desire: *We shall do it whether they will or no.* **2** *archaic* to be about to go: *Thither will I then* — Scott. [Old English *wyllan* to wish, intend, or be going to do]

Usage note

will *or* shall? See note at SHALL.

will[2] *noun* **1a** a mental power by which one controls one's wishes, choices, intentions, etc or initiates action: *He has a will of his own; As men's prayers are a disease of the will, so are their creeds a disease of the intellect* — Ralph Waldo Emerson. **b** an inclination to act according to principles or ends: *the will to believe*. **c** a specified attitude towards others: *I bear him no ill will*. **2** a desire or wish, e.g.: **a** a resolute intention: *Where there's a will there's a way*. **b** an inclination: *I did it against my will*. **c** a choice or wish: *the will of the people*. **3** what is wished or ordained by the specified person, body, etc: *God's will be done*. **4** willpower; self-control: *She has an iron will*. **5** a legal declaration of the manner in which somebody wishes to have their property disposed of after their death. ✳ **at will** as one wishes; as or when it pleases or suits oneself. **with a will** enthusiastically and energetically. **with the best will in the world** no matter how good one's intentions are. [Old English *willa* will, desire]

will[3] *verb trans* **1** (+ to) to bequeath (property) to somebody: *He willed all his worldly goods to his daughter*. **2a** to determine (something) deliberately. **b** to decree or ordain (something): *Providence wills it*. **c** to cause or attempt to cause (something) by exercise of the will: *I willed her to go away*. ➤ *verb intrans* **1** to exercise the will. **2** to choose. ➤➤ **willer** *noun*.

willed *adj* (*used in combinations*) having a will of a specified kind: *strong-willed*.

willet /'wilət/ *noun* (*pl* **willets** *or collectively* **willet**) a large N American sandpiper with greyish plumage: *Catoptrophorus semipalmatus*. [imitative of its call, *pill-will-willet*]

willful *adj NAmer* see WILFUL.

willie /'wili/ *noun* see WILLY.

willies /'wiliz/ *pl noun* (**the willies**) *informal* a feeling of nervousness or fear: *Walking home through the cemetery gives me the willies.* [origin unknown]

willie wagtail *noun* see WILLY WAGTAIL.

willing /'wiling/ *adj* **1** inclined or favourably disposed in mind; ready: *willing to work.* **2** done, borne, or given without reluctance: *willing help.* **3** prompt to act or respond: *a willing horse.* ➤➤ **willingly** *adv* **willingness** *noun*

williwaw /'wiliwaw/ *noun* **1** a sudden strong gust of cold air blowing offshore along a mountainous coast. **2** *NAmer* a violent commotion; a tumult. [origin unknown]

will-o'-the-wisp /,wil ə dhə 'wisp/ *noun* **1** a phosphorescent light sometimes seen at night over marshy ground and often caused by the combustion of gas from decomposed organic matter. **2** an enticing but elusive goal. **3** an unreliable or elusive person. [*Will*, nickname for *William* + OF + THE[1] + WISP in the sense 'bundle of straw etc burnt as a torch']

willow /'wiloh/ *noun* **1** any of numerous species of trees or shrubs bearing catkins or flowers with no petals, including some grown for their pliant branches used in basketry: genus *Salix.* **2** the whitish wood of this tree. **3** *informal* an object made of willow wood, *esp* a cricket bat. [Middle English *wilghe, wilowe* from Old English *welig*]

willowherb *noun* any of numerous species of plants of the evening primrose family, *esp* ROSEBAY WILLOWHERB: genus *Epilobium* and other genera.

willow pattern *noun* china tableware decorated with a blue-and-white design of oriental style that usu tells a story. [from the large willow tree in the design]

willow warbler *noun* any of several species of small warblers of Europe, Asia, and Africa with dull greenish plumage: genus *Phylloscopus.*

willowy *adj* **1** full of or shaded by willows. **2a** said of a person: gracefully tall and slender. **b** supple or pliant.

willpower *noun* self-control or resoluteness.

willy *or* **willie** /'wili/ *noun* (*pl* **willies**) *Brit, informal* a penis. [*Willy*, nickname for *William*]

willy-nilly /,wili 'nili/ *adv* **1** by compulsion; without choice. **2** in a haphazard or random manner: *She distributed the gifts willy-nilly among the crowd.* [alteration of *will I nill I*, literally 'I am willing, I am not willing', or *will ye nill ye* or *will he nill he*]

willy wagtail *or* **willie wagtail** *noun* a common flycatcher of Australia and Asia with black-and-white plumage: *Rhipidura leucophrys.*

willy-willy /'wili wili/ *noun* (*pl* **willy-willies**) *Aus* a whirlwind. [from Yindjibarndi, an Aboriginal language of W Australia]

wilt[1] /wilt/ *verb intrans* **1** said of a plant: to lose freshness and become limp; to droop. **2** said of a person: to grow weak, tired, or faint; to languish. ➤ *verb trans* to cause (a plant or person) to wilt.

Word history
alteration of dialect *welk* to become stale, of Low German origin. Although *wilt* was in use in British dialect at least as long ago as the 17th cent., it did not gain general currency in British English until the second half of the 19th cent.; it was then reintroduced from American English, where it had long been widespread.

wilt[2] *noun* a disease of plants marked by wilting.

wilt[3] *verb* archaic second person sing. present tense of WILL[1]: *Do what thou wilt shall be the whole of the law* — Aleister Crowley.

Wilton /'wilt(ə)n/ *noun* **1** a carpet weave in which a pattern is woven into a carpet in loops of cut or uncut pile, rather than being inserted in a backing: compare AXMINSTER. **2** a carpet woven in this way. [named after *Wilton*, town in Wiltshire, England, where such carpets were made]

Wilts /wilts/ *abbr* Wiltshire.

wily /'wieli/ *adj* (**wilier, wiliest**) full of wiles; crafty. ➤➤ **wilily** *adv*, **wiliness** *noun*.

WIMP /wimp/ *abbr* **1** in physics, weakly interacting massive particle. **2** in computing, window, icon, mouse, pointer; denoting software and hardware devices designed for ease of use.

wimp /wimp/ *noun informal* a weak, ineffectual, or cowardly person: *Lunch is for wimps* — Oliver Stone. ➤➤ **wimpish** *adj*, **wimpishly** *adv*, **wimpy** *adj*. [perhaps from WHIMPER[1]]

wimple[1] /'wimpl/ *noun* a cloth covering worn over the head and round the neck and chin by women in the late medieval period and by some nuns. [Old English *wimpel*]

wimple[2] *verb trans* **1** to cover (the head) with a wimple. **2** to cause (e.g. a veil) to fall or lie in folds. ➤ *verb intrans* **1** to ripple. **2** to fall or lie in folds.

wimp out *verb intrans informal* to withdraw or refuse to take part because of lack of nerve.

win[1] /win/ *verb* (**winning**, *past tense and past part.* **won** /wun/) ➤ *verb intrans* **1a** to gain the victory in a battle or contest; to defeat opponents or rivals: *My father always wins at chess.* **b** to be right in an argument, dispute, etc. **c** to have one's way: *OK, you win, we'll go to the theatre.* **2** *archaic* to succeed in arriving at a place or state: *They eventually won free.* ➤ *verb trans* **1a** to get possession of (something) by personal qualities, good fortune, etc: *She wants to win their approval; I won £10 in the National Lottery.* **b** to obtain (something) by effort; to earn (it): *They are striving to win a living from the soil.* **2a** to gain (a victory or prize) in or as if in a battle or contest. **b** to defeat opponents or rivals in (a war, competition, etc): *You can no more win a war than you can win an earthquake* — Jeannette Rankin. **3a** (+ over/round) to gain the favour of or persuade (somebody): *His argument soon won them over.* **b** to induce (a woman) to accept oneself in marriage. **4** *archaic* to reach (a place) by expenditure of effort: *We finally won the summit.* **5** to obtain (ore, coal, etc) by mining. ➤➤ **winnable** *adj*. [Old English *winnan* to struggle]

win[2] *noun* a victory or success, *esp* in a game or sporting contest.

wince[1] /wins/ *verb intrans* to shrink back or grimace involuntarily, e.g. in pain; to flinch. ➤➤ **wincer** *noun*, **wincingly** *adv*. [Middle English *wenchen* to kick from pain or restlessness, from early French *wenchier* to turn aside, of Germanic origin]

wince[2] *noun* an act of wincing.

wince[3] *noun Brit* a roller used to move fabric through a dyeing vat. [variant of WINCH[1]]

wincey /'winsi/ *noun Brit* a plain or twilled fabric, usu made of cotton or linen woven with wool. [alteration and contraction of LINSEY-WOOLSEY]

winceyette /winsi'et/ *noun Brit* a lightweight cotton fabric with a nap on one or both sides.

winch[1] /winch/ *noun* **1** a machine or instrument for hoisting or pulling by means of a rope or chain wound round a rotating drum. **2** a crank or handle for giving motion to a machine, e.g. a grindstone. [Old English *wince* roller, pulley]

winch[2] *verb trans* (*often* + up) to hoist or pull (something or somebody) with a winch: *The children were winched to safety.* ➤➤ **wincher** *noun*.

Winchester /'winchistə/ *noun trademark* a breech-loading repeating rifle. [named after Oliver F *Winchester* d.1880, US gun manufacturer, who developed it]

wind[1] /wind/ *noun* **1** a natural movement of air, *esp* horizontally: *The older you get the stronger the wind gets – and it's always in your face* — Jack Nicklaus. **2** a force or agency that carries along or influences; a trend: *the winds of change.* **3** breath or the ability to breathe: *The fall knocked the wind out of him; He soon recovered his wind.* **4** *Brit* gas generated in the stomach or the intestines. **5** mere talk; idle words. **6** air carrying a scent, e.g. of a hunter or game. **7a** musical wind instruments collectively, *esp* as distinguished from string and percussion instruments. **b** (*treated as sing. or pl*) the group of players of such instruments, e.g. in an orchestra. **8** *literary* a direction from which the wind may blow, *esp* a point of the compass. ✱ **before the wind** in sailing, in the same direction as the main force of the wind. **get/have wind of** to hear a rumour of (something); to become aware of (it). **have the wind up** *Brit, informal* to be scared or frightened. **in the wind** about to happen; astir or afoot. **off the wind** in sailing, away from the direction from which the wind is blowing. **on the wind** in sailing, towards the direction from which the wind is blowing. **put the wind up somebody** *Brit, informal* to scare or frighten somebody: *That letter really put the wind up me.* **sail close to the wind 1** to sail as nearly as possible against the main force of the wind. **2** *informal* to come close to a point of danger; to get near the permissible limits. **take the wind out of somebody's sails 1** to frustrate somebody, or take away their advantage, by anticipating or forestalling them. **2** to make somebody less confident or self-important. ➤➤ **windless** *adj*. [Old English]

wind² /wind/ *verb trans* **1** to make (somebody) short of breath. **2** *Brit* to help (a baby) to bring up wind after feeding. **3** to detect or follow (an animal) by scent.

wind³ /wiend/ *verb* (*past tense and past part.* **wound** /wownd/) ➤ *verb intrans* **1** to have a curving, spiralling, or twisting course; to extend or proceed in a series of curves: *The path winds down the hill.* **2** to pass round something so as to encircle it, *esp* repeatedly; to coil or twine: *ivy winding round the pillar.* **3** to bend or warp. ➤ *verb trans* **1** to pass (something) round an object or central core, *esp* repeatedly; to coil (it): *Wind the wool into a ball.* **2** to surround or wrap (something or somebody) with something pliable: *Wind the baby in a shawl.* **3** to hoist or haul (something) by means of a rope or chain and a winch or windlass. **4a** to tighten the spring of (a clock, watch, or similar mechanism), e.g. by turning a key, to make it operate. **b** to turn (e.g. a crank or handle) repeatedly. **5** to put (something) into the specified state or position by winding it: *Wind the video back to the beginning; I wound the window down.* ➤➤ **winding** *adj*. [Old English *windan* to twist, to move with speed or force, to brandish]

wind⁴ /wiend/ *noun* **1** a coil or turn made by winding. **2** a curve or bend, e.g. in a river.

wind⁵ /wiend/ *verb trans* (*past tense and past part.* **winded** *or* **wound** /wownd/) to sound (e.g. a call or note) on a horn, bugle, etc. [WIND¹]

windage /'windij/ *noun* **1a** the influence of the wind in deflecting the course of something, *esp* a bullet or other projectile. **b** the amount of this deflection, or the compensation that must be made for it in aiming a gun. **2** the difference between the diameter of the bore of a gun and that of the projectile. **3** the surface exposed by something, e.g. a ship, to the wind. [WIND¹]

windbag /'windbag/ *noun informal* an excessively talkative person.

windblown /'windblohn/ *adj* blown by the wind, *esp* shaped or deformed by the prevailing winds: *windblown trees.*

windbound /'windbownd/ *adj* said of a ship: unable to sail because of contrary or excessive winds.

windbreak /'windbrayk/ *noun* something that breaks the force of the wind, e.g. a line of trees, a fence, or a screen.

windburn /'windbuhn/ *noun* irritation of the skin caused by the wind. ➤➤ **windburned** *adj*, **windburnt** /'windbuhnt/ *adj*.

windcheater /'windcheetə/ *noun chiefly Brit* a weatherproof or windproof coat or jacket, *esp* one fitting closely at the neck, waist, and cuffs.

windchill /'windchil/ *noun* the effect of cold winds on living beings, which can lead to a lowering of body temperature and possible hypothermia.

wind chimes /wind/ *pl noun* an arrangement of small pieces of glass or metal hung loosely so that they tinkle musically in the wind.

wind-cone /wind/ *noun* = WIND-SOCK.

wind down /wiend/ *verb intrans* **1** *informal* to become gradually more relaxed; to unwind. **2** said of a clockwork mechanism: to become slower because of decreasing tension in the spring. ➤ *verb trans* to bring (something) to an end gradually; to cause (it) to cease: *They are winding down their operations in France.*

winder /'wiendə/ *noun* **1** a device for winding something, e.g. a clock. **2** a step in a spiral staircase: compare FLYER (6).

windfall /'windfawl/ *noun* **1** something, *esp* a fruit, blown down by the wind. **2** an unexpected gain or advantage, e.g. a legacy or a large dividend.

windfall tax *noun* a tax on a company considered to have made excessive profits.

wind farm /wind/ *noun* an array of wind turbines or windmills for generating electric power.

windflower /'windflowə/ *noun* an anemone, *esp* the WOOD ANEMONE.

wind gauge /wind/ *noun* = ANEMOMETER.

windhover /'windhovə/ *noun dialect* a kestrel.

windigo /'windigoh/ *or* **wendigo** /'wen-/ *noun* (*pl* **windigos** *or* **windigoes** *or* **wendigos** *or* **wendigoes**) in Native American folklore, a person who changes into a monster after eating human flesh. [Ojibwa *wintiko*]

winding /'wiending/ *noun* **1** a curved or sinuous course, line, or progress: *the windings of the path.* **2** material wound or coiled about an object, e.g. wire around a metal core in an electric motor, or a single turn of the wound material. **3** the act or manner of winding something.

winding-sheet /'wiending/ *noun* a sheet in which a corpse is wrapped for burial.

wind instrument /wind/ *noun* a musical instrument, e.g. a trumpet or clarinet, sounded by air, *esp* by the player's breath.

windjammer /'windjamə/ *noun* in former times, a large fast square-rigged sailing vessel. [WIND¹ + JAM¹ + -ER²; because of its large amount of sail]

windlass¹ /'windləs/ *noun* **1** a machine for hoisting or hauling, *esp* one consisting of a horizontal drum supported on vertical posts and turned by a crank so that the rope or chain is wound round the drum. **2** a steam or electric winch with a horizontal or vertical shaft and two drums, used to raise a ship's anchor. [Middle English *wyndlas*, alteration of *wyndas*, from Old Norse *vindāss*, from *vinda* to wind + *āss* pole]

windlass² *verb trans* to hoist or haul (something) with a windlass.

windlestraw /'windlstraw/ *noun Scot, N Eng* a dry thin stalk of grass. [Old English *windelstrēaw*, from *windel* basket (from *windan* WIND³) + *strēaw* STRAW]

wind machine /wind/ *noun* a machine used *esp* in the theatre for producing a gust of wind or the sound of wind.

windmill¹ /'windmil/ *noun* **1a** a mill operated by vanes that are turned by the wind. **b** a similar structure using wind power to generate electricity, pump water, etc. **2** *Brit* a toy consisting of lightweight vanes at the end of a stick that revolve in the wind.

windmill² *verb intrans* to move like the vanes of a windmill. ➤ *verb trans* to cause (something) to move in this way.

window /'windoh/ *noun* **1** an opening in the wall of a building, side of a vehicle, etc to let in light and air, usu fitted with a frame containing glass and capable of being opened and shut. **2** a pane of glass in a window. **3** a display area behind the window of a shop. **4** a transparent panel in an envelope, through which the address on the enclosure is visible. **5** in computing, a rectangular area of the display on a VDU or monitor within which part of an image or file can be displayed. **6** a brief time available for something: *a window of opportunity.* **7** something that functions like a window, e.g. in allowing people to see what is normally hidden: *a window on the Western world.* **8** a range of wavelengths in the electromagnetic spectrum that can pass through a planet's atmosphere. **9** an interval of time within which a rocket or spacecraft must be launched to accomplish a particular mission. **10** an area at the limits of the earth's atmosphere through which a spacecraft must pass for successful re-entry. ✳ **go out of the window** *informal* to die out or come to an end. ➤➤ **windowed** *adj*, **windowless** *adj*. [Middle English *windowe* from Old Norse *vindauga*, from *vindr* wind + *auga* eye]

window box *noun* a box for growing plants on the outside sill of a window.

window dressing *noun* **1** the act or art of arranging a display of merchandise in a shop window. **2** the act or an instance of making something appear more attractive or favourable. ➤➤ **window dresser** *noun*.

window pane *noun* a panel of transparent material, *esp* glass, forming part of a window.

window seat *noun* **1** a seat under a window, *esp* a bay window. **2** a seat beside the window in an aircraft, train, or bus.

window-shop *verb intrans* to look at the displays in shop windows without intending to buy anything. ➤➤ **window-shopper** *noun*, **window-shopping** *noun*.

windowsill *noun* the shelf or horizontal member at the bottom of a window opening; the sill of a window.

windpipe /'windpiep/ *noun* = TRACHEA.

wind rose /wind/ *noun* a diagram showing for a given place the relative frequency and strength of winds from different directions. [German *Windrose* compass card]

windrow /'windroh/ *noun* **1** a row of hay, grain, etc raked up to dry: *In the first mead they were already loading hay, the women raking it into cocks and windrows, and the men tossing it upon the waggon* — Hardy. **2** *NAmer* a row of anything, e.g. leaves or snow, heaped up by or as if by the wind.

windscreen /'windskreen/ *noun Brit* a transparent screen, *esp* of glass, at the front of a motor vehicle.

windscreen wiper *noun* a mechanically operated metal arm with a rubber blade for clearing rain from windscreens.

windshield /'windsheeld/ *noun NAmer* = WINDSCREEN.

wind-sock /wind/ *noun* a cloth cone open at both ends that is mounted on a pole and is used to indicate the direction of the wind, *esp* at an airfield.

Windsor chair /'winzə/ *noun* a wooden chair with a back of turned rods or rails, legs that slant outward, and a slightly concave seat. [named after *Windsor*, town in England]

Windsor knot *noun* a wide bulky knot for tying a tie.

windstorm /'windstawm/ *noun* a storm with high winds but little or no rain, snow, etc.

wind-surfing /wind/ *noun* the sport of riding across water on a sailboard. ➤➤ **wind-surfer** *noun*.

windswept /'windswept/ *adj* **1** swept by strong winds: *a windswept beach.* **2** dishevelled from being exposed to the wind: *a windswept appearance.*

wind tunnel /wind/ *noun* a tunnel-like apparatus through which air is blown at a known velocity to determine the effects of wind pressure on or the aerodynamic properties of an object placed inside it.

windup /'wiendup/ *noun* **1** *Brit, informal* an act of teasing or tricking somebody as a joke. **2** a conclusion or finish. **3** a preliminary swing of the arms, e.g. before throwing or bowling a ball.

wind up /wiend/ *verb trans* **1** to bring (something) to a conclusion; *specif* to bring (a business) to an end by liquidation. **2** to put (something) in order; to settle (it). **3** to wind (a watch, clock, etc) completely or tightly. **4** *Brit, informal* to deceive (somebody) playfully; to tease (them). **5** to raise (somebody) to a high level of excitement, tension, etc: *He wound himself up into a frenzy.* ➤ *verb intrans* **1** to come to a conclusion. **2** *informal* to arrive in a place, situation, or condition at the end of or because of a course of action: *He wound up a millionaire.*

windward[1] /'windwəd/ *adj and adv* in or facing the direction from which the wind is blowing: compare LEEWARD[1].

windward[2] *noun* the side or direction from which the wind is blowing: compare LEEWARD[2]. ✳ **to windward of** *dated* having the advantage over (somebody or something).

windy /'windi/ *adj* (**windier, windiest**) **1a** marked by strong or stormy wind. **b** exposed to the wind; windswept. **2** *Brit* suffering from or causing flatulence. **3** *informal* verbose or bombastic. **4** *Brit, informal* frightened or nervous. ➤➤ **windily** *adv*, **windiness** *noun*.

wine[1] /wien/ *noun* **1a** an alcoholic drink made from fermented grape juice: *It is a maudlin and indecent verity that comes out through the strength of wine* — Joseph Conrad. **b** an alcoholic drink made from the fermented juice of another plant or fruit: *rice wine.* **2** something that invigorates or intoxicates. **3** the dark or purplish red colour of red wine. [Old English *win* via a prehistoric Germanic word from Latin *vinum*]

wine[2] ✳ **wine and dine 1** to entertain (somebody) with good food and wine. **2** to be entertained in this way.

wine bar *noun* an establishment serving wine and usu food for consumption on the premises.

winebibber /'wienbibə/ *noun formal or humorous* a drunkard. [*bibber* from archaic *bib* to drink, tipple, prob from Latin *bibere* to drink]

wine box *noun* a carton of wine with a tap for dispensing it.

wine cellar *noun* **1** a room for storing wines. **2** a stock of wines.

wine cooler *noun* **1** a bucket containing ice for cooling wine. **2** = COOLER (3).

wineglass *noun* a drinking glass for wine, having usu a rounded bowl and mounted on a stem and foot. ➤➤ **wineglassful** (*pl* **wineglassfuls**) *noun*.

winegrower *noun* a person who cultivates a vineyard and makes wine. ➤➤ **wine growing** *noun*.

wine gum *noun* a firm jelly-like fruit-flavoured sweet.

winery *noun* (*pl* **wineries**) a wine-making establishment.

wineskin *noun* a bag that is made from the skin of an animal and is used for holding wine.

wine taster *noun* a person who evaluates wine by tasting.

wine tasting *noun* an occasion for evaluating wine by tasting, *esp* a promotional event at which wine sellers offer potential customers a chance to sample their products before buying them.

wine vinegar *noun* vinegar made from wine.

winey *adj* see WINY.

wing[1] /wing/ *noun* **1a** any of the movable feathered or membranous paired appendages by means of which a bird, bat, or insect flies. **b** any of various body parts, e.g. of a flying fish or flying lemur, providing means of limited flight. **2a** either of the horizontal structures projecting from the sides of an aircraft, which provide lift and stability. **b** (*in pl*) a pilot's badge, *esp* in the British armed forces. **3** an appendage or part resembling a wing in shape, function, or position, e.g.: **a** *Brit* an integral part of the body of a motor vehicle above the wheels. **b** any of various projecting anatomical parts. **c** a membranous, leaflike, or woody growth in a plant, e.g. on a sycamore fruit. **d** a sidepiece at the top of a high-backed armchair. **4** a part of a building projecting from the main or central part. **5** (*treated as sing. or pl*) a group or faction holding distinct opinions or policies within an organized body, e.g. a political party: compare LEFT WING, RIGHT WING. **6** (*in pl*) the area at the sides of a theatre stage out of sight of the audience. **7a** the left or right section of a playing field that is near the sidelines. **b** any of the attacking positions or players in these sections. **8** a left or right flank of an army or fleet. **9** a unit of the Royal Air Force higher than a squadron. ✳ **in the wings** in the background; in readiness to act. **on the wing** said of a bird: in flight; flying. **spread/stretch one's wings** to venture out into the world; to break away from one's background. **take wing** to fly away. **under one's wing** under one's protection; in one's care. ➤➤ **winged** *adj*, **wingless** *adj*, **winglet** /'winglit/ *noun*, **winglike** *adj*. [Middle English *winge* from Old Norse *vaengr*]

wing[2] *verb trans* **1a** to wound (a bird) in the wing. **b** to wound (somebody), e.g. with a bullet, without killing them: *He was winged by a sniper.* **2a** to enable (something or somebody) to fly or move swiftly. **b** to fit (something or somebody) with wings. **3** to make (one's way) by or as if by flying. ➤ *verb intrans* to go with or as if with wings; to fly. ✳ **wing it** *informal* to perform or speak without rehearsal; to improvise. ➤➤ **winged** *adj*.

wingbeat *noun* a single complete movement of a wing in flying.

wing case *noun* = ELYTRON.

wing chair *noun* an upholstered armchair with a high solid back and sidepieces that provide a rest for the head.

Wing Co. *abbr* Wing Commander.

wing collar *noun* a man's stand-up collar with the upper corners turned down, now worn only for formal evening dress.

wing commander *noun* an officer in the Royal Air Force ranking above a squadron leader and below a group captain.

wingding /'wingding/ *noun chiefly NAmer, informal* **1** a wild, lively, or lavish party. **2** a usu pretended fit or seizure. [origin unknown]

winge[1] /winj/ *verb intrans Aus* = WHINGE[1].

winge[2] *noun Aus* = WHINGE[2].

winger /'wingə/ *noun* a player positioned on the wing in football, hockey, etc.

wing forward *noun* = FLANKER (1).

wingman *noun* (*pl* **wingmen**) a pilot who flies behind and outside the leader of a flying formation.

wing mirror *noun* a mirror on the outside of a motor vehicle, usu projecting from the lower front corner of the window on the driver's and passenger's doors, giving the driver a view of vehicles behind and to either side.

wing nut *noun* a nut that has projecting wings or flanges so that it may be turned by finger and thumb.

wingspan *noun* the distance from the tip of one of a pair of wings to that of the other.

wingspread *noun* = WINGSPAN.

wink[1] /wingk/ *verb intrans* **1a** to shut one eye briefly as a signal or in teasing. **b** said of an eye: to shut briefly. **2** to gleam or flash intermittently; to twinkle. **3** (+ at) to avoid seeing or noting something; to disregard or condone it: *They wink at his absence.* ➤ *verb* *trans* to shut (one's eye) briefly. ➤➤ **winker** *noun*. [Old English *wincian*]

wink² *noun* **1** an act of winking. **2** a brief period, *esp* of sleep: *I didn't get a wink of sleep all night*. **3** the time of a wink; an instant: *I'll be there in a wink*. ✻ **tip somebody the wink** *informal* to give them a useful piece of information, *esp* covertly: *The bloke … tipped him the wink* — Richard Llewellyn.

winkle /'wingkl/ *noun* = PERIWINKLE².

winkle out *verb trans chiefly Brit* **1** to displace or extract (something or somebody) from a position, *esp* with difficulty. **2** to discover (information) with difficulty: *winkling out the facts about the country's stocks of coal* — The Observer. [WINKLE, from the process of extracting a winkle from its shell]

winkle-picker *noun Brit, informal* a shoe with a very pointed toe.

winner *noun* **1** somebody or something that wins. **2** *informal* something that is or is expected to be successful: *This new scheme is a real winner.*

winning *adj* **1** tending to please or delight; endearing: *a winning smile*. **2a** that wins or has won: *the winning ticket; the winning team*. **b** that results in victory: *the winning goal*. ➤➤ **winningly** *adv*.

winning post *noun* a post marking the finishing line on a race-course.

winnings *pl noun* money won by success in a game or competition, *esp* in gambling.

winnow /'winoh/ *verb trans* **1a** to remove waste matter from (grain) by exposure to a current of air. **b** to remove (waste matter) from grain in this way. **2a** (*often* + out) to separate or select (the most valuable things or people) from a mass or group. **b** (*often* + out) to get rid of (something undesirable or unwanted); to remove (it). **3** *literary* said of the wind: to blow on (something); to fan (it): *the wind winnowing his thin white hair* — Time. ➤ *verb intrans* **1** to separate chaff from grain by exposure to a current of air. **2** to separate desirable and undesirable elements. ➤➤ **winnower** *noun*. [Middle English *winewen* from Old English *windwian* to fan or winnow, from WIND¹]

wino /'wienoh/ *noun* (*pl* **winos**) *informal* an alcoholic, *esp* one who drinks cheap wine.

win out *verb intrans* = WIN THROUGH.

winsome /'wins(ə)m/ *adj* pleasing and engaging: *a winsome smile*. ➤➤ **winsomely** *adv*, **winsomeness** *noun*. [Old English *wynsum*, from *wynn* joy]

winter¹ /'wintə/ *noun* **1a** the season between autumn and spring, the coldest part of the year, in the N hemisphere the months December, January, and February; = WINTERTIME: *Let no man boast … that he has got through the perils of winter till at least the seventh of May* — Trollope. **b** in astronomy, the period in the N hemisphere extending from the December SOLSTICE (shortest day of the year) to the March EQUINOX (time when day and night are of equal length). **2** a period of inactivity or decay. **3** *literary* (*usu in pl*) a year: *It happened many winters ago*. ➤➤ **winterless** *adj*. [Old English]

winter² *adj* said of crops: sown in the autumn and harvested the following spring or summer: compare SUMMER².

winter³ *verb* (**wintered, wintering**) ➤ *verb intrans* to pass or survive the winter: *They wintered in Chamonix*. ➤ *verb trans* to keep or feed (livestock) during the winter. ➤➤ **winterer** *noun*.

winter aconite *noun* any of several species of small Eurasian and African plants of the buttercup family with bright yellow flowers that bloom in early spring: genus *Eranthis*.

winter garden *noun* **1** a garden containing plants, e.g. evergreens, that flourish in winter. **2** a conservatory in which plants, *esp* flowering plants, are grown during the winter.

wintergreen *noun* **1** any of various perennial evergreen plants related to the heathers: genus *Pyrola* and other genera. **2a** a low American evergreen plant of the heather family with white flowers and red berries: *Gaultheria procumbens*. **b** an essential oil from this plant, or a similar oil produced synthetically, used medicinally and as a flavouring.

winterize or **winterise** *verb trans chiefly NAmer* (*usu in passive*) to make (something) ready for or proof against winter weather. ➤➤ **winterization** /-'zaysh(ə)n/ *noun*.

winter jasmine *noun* a variety of jasmine with yellow flowers that appear during the winter: *Jasminum nudiflorum*.

winter sport *noun* (*usu in pl*) a sport on snow or ice, e.g. skiing or tobogganing.

wintertime *noun* the season of winter.

wintery *adj* see WINTRY.

win through *verb intrans* to reach a desired or satisfactory end, *esp* after overcoming difficulties.

wintry /'wintri/ or **wintery** *adj* (**wintrier, wintriest**) **1** said of the weather: characteristic of winter; cold. **2** chilling or cheerless: *a bitter wintry smile*. ➤➤ **wintrily** *adv*, **wintriness** *noun*.

winy or **winey** /'wieni/ *adj* (**winier, winiest**) having the taste, smell, or other qualities of wine.

wipe¹ /wiep/ *verb trans* **1a** to clean or dry (something) by rubbing it lightly or quickly, *esp* with or on something soft: *She wiped the counter*. **b** to draw or pass (something) over a surface to clean or dry it: *I wiped a cloth over the table*. **c** to remove (something) by wiping: *He wiped the sweat from his brow*. **2a** to remove (something) as if by rubbing: *Wipe that smile off your face!* **b** to erase (something) completely; to obliterate (it): *She wiped the recording from the tape; He tried to wipe the scene from his memory*. **3** to spread (something) by or as if by wiping: *I wiped grease on my skates*. **4** *Aus, NZ, informal* to reject (somebody). ✻ **wipe the floor with** *informal* to defeat (somebody) decisively. [Old English *wīpian*]

wipe² *noun* **1** the act or an instance of wiping. **2** a disposable moist cloth.

wipeout *noun* **1** complete or utter destruction. **2** *informal* a fall from a surfboard caused usu by loss of control. **3** the obliteration of one radio signal by another.

wipe out *verb trans informal* **1** to destroy (people or things) completely; to annihilate (them). **2** to obliterate or cancel (something). ➤ *verb intrans informal* to fall from a surfboard.

wiper *noun* **1a** a mechanically operated metal arm with a rubber blade for clearing rain or spray from windscreens, headlights, etc. **b** something, e.g. a towel or sponge, used for wiping. **2** a moving contact for making connections with the terminals of an electrical device, e.g. a rheostat. **3** a cam or tappet.

WIPO *abbr* World Intellectual Property Organization (a branch of the United Nations).

Wiradhuri /wi'rajəri/ *noun* an Aboriginal language of SE Australia, now extinct. ➤➤ **Wiradhuri** *adj*. [the Wiradhuri name]

wire¹ /wie·ə/ *noun* **1** metal in the form of a flexible thread or slender rod. **2a** a line of wire, usu insulated, for conducting electrical current. **b** a telephone or telegraph wire or system. **c** *informal, dated* a telegram or cablegram. **3** a barrier or fence of barbed wire. **4** (*used before a noun*) made of wire: *a wire fence*. ✻ **pull the wires** *NAmer, informal* to control a situation; to have great influence: *the woman behind the president pulling the wires*. **to the wire** *chiefly NAmer, informal* to the last possible moment, *esp* neck and neck until the very end of a contest. **under the wire** *chiefly NAmer, informal* only just in time. ➤➤ **wirelike** *adj*. [Old English *wīr*]

wire² *verb trans* **1** to provide or connect (something) with wire or wiring. **2** *chiefly NAmer, informal, dated*. **a** to send a message to (somebody) by telegraph. **b** to send (money, news, etc) by telegraph. **3** to catch (e.g. a rabbit) in a wire snare. ➤ *verb intrans chiefly NAmer, informal, dated* to send a message by telegraph. ➤➤ **wirer** *noun*.

wire brush *noun* **1** a brush with short tough wire bristles. **2** a brush with long wire strands used on cymbals.

wired *adj* **1** provided with wires, e.g. for electric connections. **2** reinforced or bound with wire. **3** *informal*. **a** tense or nervous. **b** intoxicated, *esp* by a drug.

wiredraw *verb trans* (*past tense* **wiredrew**, *past part.* **wiredrawn**) **1** to draw (metal) into wire. **2** *archaic* (*usu in passive*) to spin (something) out to excessive subtlety: *wiredrawn comparisons*.

wire gauge *noun* **1** a gauge for measuring the diameter of wire. **2** a system of standard sizes used in describing the diameter of wire or the thickness of sheet metal.

wire gauze *noun* a thin fabric of fine wire mesh.

wire grass *noun NAmer, Aus* a coarse grass with wiry stems.

wirehaired *adj* said of a dog: having stiff wiry hair.

wireless¹ *noun chiefly Brit, dated* a radio.

wireless² *adj* **1** *chiefly Brit, dated* relating to radiotelegraphy, radiotelephony, or radio. **2** not having or requiring wires.

wireman *noun* (*pl* **wiremen**) *chiefly NAmer* a maker of or worker with wire, *esp* somebody who wires electric or electronic circuitry.

wire netting *noun* a network of woven or twisted wire used *esp* for fencing.

wire-puller *noun* *NAmer, informal* a person who controls a situation or has great influence, *esp* behind the scenes. ➤ **wire-pulling** *noun*.

wire rope *noun* a rope formed of wires twisted together or round a core.

wire service *noun* *NAmer* a news agency that sends out syndicated news copy to subscribers telegraphically or electronically.

wiretap *noun* an electrical connection for wiretapping.

wiretapping *noun* the act or an instance of tapping a telephone or telegraph wire, e.g. to monitor conversations to obtain information. ➤ **wiretapper** *noun*.

wire wheel *noun* a wheel on a motor vehicle, *esp* a sports car, that has thin metal spokes.

wire wool *noun* *Brit* an abrasive material consisting of fine wire strands woven into a mass and used for scouring *esp* kitchen utensils.

wireworm *noun* any of the slender larvae of various click beetles that cause damage to plant roots.

wiring /'wie-əring/ *noun* a system of wires, *esp* one that carries electric currents in a device, building, etc.

wiry /'wie-əri/ *adj* (**wirier**, **wiriest**) **1** resembling wire, *esp* in form and flexibility. **2** lean and vigorous; sinewy. ➤ **wirily** *adv*, **wiriness** *noun*.

Wis. *abbr* Wisconsin.

wis /wis/ *verb trans and intrans* (**wissed**, **wissing**) *archaic* to know (something). [by incorrect division of Middle English *iwis* certainly (from Old English *gewis*), understood as *I wis*, with *wis* taken to be the first person sing. pres indicative of WIT[2]]

wisdom /'wizd(ə)m/ *noun* **1** good sense; judgment: *Nine-tenths of wisdom consists in being wise in time* — Theodore Roosevelt. **2** the thoughtful application of learning; insight. **3** accumulated learning; knowledge. [Old English *wīsdōm*, from *wīs* WISE[1]]

wisdom tooth *noun* any of the four molar teeth in human beings that are the last to erupt on each side at the back of each jaw. [from its being cut usu at an age when one may have acquired some wisdom]

wise[1] /wiez/ *adj* **1a** characterized by or showing wisdom; marked by deep understanding, keen discernment, and sound judgment. **b** judicious or prudent: *Some say it is not wise to eat oysters.* **2** well-informed: *I'm none the wiser.* **3** *informal* (+ to) possessing inside knowledge or shrewd awareness of something: *He was wise to what was happening.* **4** *archaic* skilled in magic or divination. **＊ put somebody wise** to inform or enlighten somebody. ➤ **wisely** *adv*, **wiseness** *noun*. [Old English *wīs*]

wise[2] *noun* *archaic* manner or way: *in no wise.* [Old English *wīse*]

-wise *comb. form* forming adverbs and adjectives from nouns, with the meanings: **1a** in the specified manner: *He entered the room crabwise.* **b** in the specified position or direction: *a clockwise movement*; *They laid it out lengthwise.* **2** with regard to or in respect of the specified thing: *Careerwise, it seems like a good move.* [Middle English from Old English *-wīsan*, from *wīse* WISE[2]]

Usage note

Sentences such as *How are things going workwise?* and *Careerwise, it seems like a good move* are very commonly used. The use of *-wise* added to the end of a noun, disliked by some traditionalists, is often a neat way of conveying the idea 'as far as something is concerned'. It is not, however, recommended in formal writing, and if *-wise* words are overused, or if *-wise* is attached to a long word or phrase (*research-and-development-wise*; *cost-effectivenesswise*), the results sound like jargon or can be unintentionally comic.

wiseacre /'wiezaykə/ *noun* a person who claims or pretends to be clever or knowledgeable. [Middle Dutch *wijssegger* soothsayer, modification of Old High German *wīzzago*]

wisecrack[1] *noun* *informal* a flippant remark or witticism: *An epigram is only a wisecrack that's played at Carnegie Hall* — Oscar Levant.

wisecrack[2] *verb intrans* *informal* to make wisecracks. ➤ **wisecracker** *noun*.

wise guy *noun informal* **1** a conceited and self-assertive person, *esp* one who claims to know all about something: *OK, wise guy, you try and fix it.* **2** *NAmer* a member of the Mafia.

wisent /'weezent/ *noun* the European bison. [German *Wisent* from Old High German *wisant*, *wisunt* bison]

wise up *verb intrans* *informal* to become informed or aware.

wish[1] /wish/ *verb trans* **1a** to give form to (a wish): *I wish I had more leisure time.* **b** to feel or express a wish for (something); to want (it): *I wish to be alone.* **c** to request (something) in the form of a wish; to order (it): *He wishes us to leave.* **2a** to express the hope that somebody will have or attain (something): *I wish them success.* **b** to bid (somebody) the specified greeting: *I wished him good night.* ➤ *verb intrans* **1** (+ for) to have a desire for something. **2** to make a wish. **＊ wish on/upon 1** to hope that (somebody) will suffer (e.g. an unpleasant situation): *I wouldn't wish that on my worst enemy.* **2** to confer or foist (something or somebody unwanted) on (somebody else). ➤ **wisher** *noun*. [Old English *wýscan*]

wish[2] *noun* **1a** the act or an instance of wanting or hoping for something; a desire: *her wish to become a doctor.* **b** an object of desire; a goal: *You got your wish.* **2** a ritual act of wishing: *She made a wish as she blew out the candles.* **3a** an expressed will or desire: *He obeyed their wishes.* **b** (*usu in pl*) a conventional greeting: *Give your mother my best wishes.*

wishbone *noun* **1** a forked bone in front of the breastbone of a bird consisting chiefly of the two clavicles (equivalents of collarbone; see CLAVICLE) joined at their lower ends; = FURCULA. **2** something shaped like a wishbone, e.g. part of the suspension of a motor vehicle. [from the superstition that when two people pull the bone apart the one getting the longer piece will have a wish granted]

wishful /'wishf(ə)l/ *adj* **1a** expressive of a wish. **b** having a wish; desirous. **2** in accordance with wishes rather than reality: *wishful thinking.* ➤ **wishfully** *adv*, **wishfulness** *noun*.

wish fulfilment *noun* the satisfaction of desires, *esp* symbolically through dreams and fantasies.

wishy-washy /'wishi woshi/ *adj informal* **1** said e.g. of a drink: lacking in strength or flavour. **2** lacking in character or determination; ineffectual. **3** lacking in intensity, *esp* of colour: *a wishy-washy pink rug.* [reduplication of WASHY]

wisp /wisp/ *noun* **1a** a thin insubstantial strand, streak, or fragment: *a wisp of smoke; a wisp of hair.* **b** something frail, slight, or fleeting: *a wisp of a girl; a wisp of a smile.* **2** a small handful, *esp* a wad of hay or straw for grooming an animal. **3** a flock of birds, e.g. snipe. ➤ **wispily** *adv*, **wispiness** *noun*, **wisplike** *adj*, **wispy** *adj*. [Middle English; earlier history unknown]

wist /wist/ *verb* past tense of WIT[2].

wisteria /wi'stiəri·ə/ *or* **wistaria** /wi'steəri·ə/ *noun* any of a genus of Asiatic and N American climbing plants with showy blue, white, purple, or rose flowers like those of the pea: genus *Wisteria*. [from the Latin genus name, named after Caspar *Wistar* d.1818, US physician]

wistful /'wistf(ə)l/ *adj* **1** full of unfulfilled desire; yearning. **2** musingly sad; pensive. ➤ **wistfully** *adv*, **wistfulness** *noun*. [blend of WISHFUL and obsolete *wistly* intently, prob from WHIST[2] + -LY[1]]

wit[1] /wit/ *noun* **1a** (*also in pl*) reasoning power; intelligence: *Man forgives women anything save the wit to outwit him* — Minna Antrim; *slow wits.* **b** (*also in pl*) sanity: *out of their wits.* **2a** the ability to relate seemingly disparate words or ideas so as to create a humorous effect. **b** a talent for making quick clever amusing replies. **c** written or spoken examples of this ability or talent: *the wit of Oscar Wilde.* **3** a witty person. **4** *archaic.* **a** the five mental faculties of common sense, imagination, fancy, estimation, and memory: *In our last conflict four of his five wits went halting off and now is the whole man governed with one* — Shakespeare. **b** more loosely, the five bodily senses of sight, hearing, taste, touch, and smell. **5** *archaic* a person of superior intellect; a thinker. **＊ be at one's wits' end** to be so harassed or worried that one does not know what to do. **frighten/scare somebody out of their wits** to frighten somebody very much; to terrify them. **have/keep one's wits about one** to be alert. **live by one's wits** to make one's living by clever or cunning methods rather than regular or honest work. [Old English]

wit[2] *verb trans and intrans* (first and third person sing. present tense **wot** /wot/, past tense **wist** /wist/) *archaic* **1** to know (something). **2** to come to know (something); to learn (it). **＊ to wit** that is to say; namely. [Old English *witan*]

witan /'witən/ *noun* = WITENAGEMOT.

witch[1] /wich/ *noun* **1** a person who is credited with supernatural powers, *esp* a woman practising magic: *In the past, men created witches; now they create mental patients* — Thomas Szasz. **2** *informal* an ugly old woman; a hag. **3** a charming or alluring woman. **4** a N Atlantic flatfish related to the plaice and flounder: *Glyptocephalus cynoglossus*. ➤➤ **witchlike** *adj*, **witchy** *adj*. [Middle English *wicche* from Old English *wicca* (masc) wizard and *wicce* (fem) witch]

witch[2] *verb trans* **1** to harm (somebody or something) by means of witchcraft. **2** *archaic* to fascinate or charm (somebody).

witchcraft *noun* **1** the use of sorcery or magic. **2** an irresistible influence or fascination; enchantment.

witch doctor *noun* a professional sorcerer, *esp* in a primitive tribal society, who is credited with healing and other powers.

witch elm *noun* see WYCH ELM.

witchery *noun* **1** witchcraft or sorcery. **2** an irresistible fascination; charm.

witches'-broom *noun* an abnormal tufted growth of small branches on a tree or shrub caused *esp* by fungi or viruses.

witches' sabbath *noun* = SABBATH (3).

witchetty /'wichəti/ *noun* (*pl* **witchetties**) a large white grub, the larva of an Australian moth, that is eaten *esp* by some Aborigines: family Cossidae. [Adnyamathanha *wityu* stick for extracting grubs + *varti* grub (Adnyamathanha is an Aboriginal language of S Australia)]

witchetty grub *noun* = WITCHETTY.

witch hazel *noun* **1** any of several species of shrubs with yellow flowers borne in late autumn or early spring: genus *Hamamelis*. **2** a soothing astringent lotion made from the bark and leaves of this shrub. [*witch, wych*: see WYCH ELM]

witch-hunt *noun* **1** the searching out and harassment of those with unpopular or unorthodox views, usu on the basis that they pose a threat to others. **2** in former times, a campaign of persecution of those accused of witchcraft: *the Salem witch-hunts of 1692*. ➤➤ **witch-hunting** *noun*.

witching *adj* of or suitable for witchcraft: *the very witching time of night* — Shakespeare.

witching hour *noun* the critical or significant time when something is to happen.

witenagemot /'wit(ə)nəgimoht/ *noun* an Anglo-Saxon council convened from time to time to advise the king. [Old English *witena gemōt* assembly of advisers, from *wita* sage, adviser + *gemōt* assembly, from *mōt* MOOT[1]]

with /widh/ *prep* **1a** used to indicate accompaniment or association: *She ran off to live with the gypsies*. **b** used to indicate reciprocal action or communication: *talking with a friend*. **c** used to express agreement or sympathy: *I must conclude, with him, that the painting is a forgery*. **d** able to follow the reasoning of (somebody): *Are you with me?* **2a** in opposition to (somebody); against (them): *He had a fight with his brother*. **b** so as to be separated or detached from (somebody or something): *She broke with her family*. **3a** in relation to (something): *the Italian frontier with Switzerland*. **b** used to indicate the object of attention, behaviour, or feeling: *He is in love with her*. **c** in respect to (something); as concerns (it): *the trouble with this machine*. **d** used to indicate the object of an adverbial expression of imperative force: *Off with his head*. **4a** on the side of (a person or group); for (them): *She voted with the government*. **b** employed by (a company, institution, etc): *He's a salesman with ICI*. **5a** used to indicate the object of a statement of comparison, equality, or harmony: *level with the street; Her dress doesn't go with her shoes*. **b** as well as (somebody or something): *He can ride with the best of them*. **c** in addition to (something): *His money, with his wife's, comes to a million pounds*. **d** inclusive of (something): *It costs £5 with tax*. **6a** by means of (something); using (it): *Dab at the stain with a damp cloth*. **b** through the effect of (something): *pale with anger*. **7a** used to indicate manner of action: *She ran with effort*. **b** used to indicate an attendant or contributory circumstance: *He stood there with his hat on*. **c** in possession of (something); having or bearing (it): *She came with good news*. **d** in the possession or care of (somebody): *The decision rests with you*. **8a** used to indicate a close association in time: *With the outbreak of war they went home*. **b** in proportion to (something): *The pressure varies with the depth*. **9a** notwithstanding (something); in spite of (it): *I love her with all her faults*. **b** except for (something): *They are very similar, with one important difference*. **10** in the direction of (something): *travelling with the wind*. [Old English *with* against, from, with]

withal[1] /wi'dhawl/ *adv archaic* **1** together with this; besides. **2** on the other hand; nevertheless. [Middle English, from WITH + ALL[1]]

withal[2] *prep archaic* (*used after its object*) with (somebody or something): *I'll tell you who Time ambles withal, who Time trots withal, who Time gallops withal, and who he stands still withal* — Shakespeare.

withdraw /widh'draw/ *verb* (*past tense* **withdrew** /widh'drooh/, *past part.* **withdrawn** /widh'drawn/) ➤ *verb trans* **1a** to draw (something) back, away, or aside; to remove (it): *withdraw one's hand*. **b** to remove (money) from a place of deposit, e.g. a bank account. **2** to take (something) back; to retract (it): *I withdrew my offer*. ➤ *verb intrans* **1a** to go back or away; to retire from participation. **b** to leave a place, *esp* to retreat. **2** to become socially or emotionally detached: *He had withdrawn into himself*. **3** to retract a statement. [Middle English, from WITH in the sense 'from' + *drawen* DRAW[1]]

withdrawal /widh'drawəl/ *noun* **1** the act or an instance of withdrawing, e.g.: **a** removal of money or other assets from a place of deposit or investment. **b** social or emotional detachment. **2** the discontinuance of use of a drug, often accompanied by unpleasant side effects.

withdrawalist *noun* someone who advocates withdrawal, *esp* a person advocating withdrawal from the European Union. ➤➤ **withdrawalist** *adj*.

withdrawing room *noun archaic* = DRAWING ROOM.

withdrawn[1] /widh'drawn/ *adj* **1** socially detached and unresponsive; shy. **2** secluded or isolated.

withdrawn[2] *verb* past part. of WITHDRAW.

withdrew /widh'drooh/ *verb* past tense of WITHDRAW.

withe /with/ *noun* a slender flexible branch or twig used for binding things together. [Old English *withthe*]

wither /'widhə/ *verb* (**withered, withering**) ➤ *verb intrans* **1** to become dry and shrivelled, e.g. from loss of moisture, age, or disease. **2** to lose vitality, force, or freshness. ➤ *verb trans* **1** to cause (something) to wither. **2** to make (somebody) speechless or incapable of action, *esp* with a scornful look or remark: *She withered him with a look* — Dorothy Sayers. ➤➤ **withering** *adj*, **witheringly** *adv*. [Middle English, alteration of WEATHER[2]]

withers /'widhəz/ *pl noun* the ridge between the shoulder bones of a horse. [prob from obsolete *wither* against (because the collar lies against it), from Old English]

withershins /'widhəshinz/ *adv* see WIDDERSHINS. [by alteration]

withhold /widh'hohld/ *verb* (*past tense and past part.* **withheld** /widh'held/) ➤ *verb trans* **1** to refrain from granting or giving (something): *They withheld permission*. **2** to hold (somebody or something) back; to check or restrain (them). ➤ *verb intrans* (*usu + from*) to forbear or refrain from doing something. ➤➤ **withholder** *noun*. [Middle English *withholden*, from WITH in the sense 'from' + *holden* to HOLD[1]]

within[1] /wi'dhin/ *prep* **1** used to indicate enclosure or containment, *esp* in something large; inside (something): *within the castle walls*. **2** to the inside of (something); into (it). **3a** in or into the range of (something): *within reach*. **b** not beyond the quantity or limitations of (something): *He lives within his income*. **c** not further than a specified distance: *within a mile of the town*. **d** in or into the scope of (something): *He is well within his rights*. **e** since the beginning of (a period of time): *She must have been there within the last week*. **f** before the end of (a period of time): *He was gone within a week*. [Old English *withinnan*, from WITH + *innan* inwardly, within]

within[2] *adv* **1** in or into the interior; inside: *Please enquire within*. **2** in one's inner thought, mood, or character.

with-it *or* **with it** *adj informal* **1** *dated* up-to-date; fashionable. **2** (*usu in negative contexts*) mentally quick or alert: *I'm not very with it this morning*.

without[1] /wi'dhowt/ *prep* **1a** used to indicate the absence or lack of something: *A day without an argument is like an egg without salt* — Angela Carter. **b** used to indicate that something does not happen: *He poured out the drinks without spilling a drop*. **2** *literary* outside (something). [Old English *withūtan*, from WITH + *ūtan* outside, from *ūt* OUT[1]]

without[2] *adv* **1** *literary* on or to the exterior; outside. **2** with something lacking or absent: *She has learned to do without*.

without[3] *conj dialect* unless: *Without you have a stunt, what is there?* — Punch.

withstand /widh'stand/ *verb trans* (*past tense and past part.* **withstood** /widh'stood/) **1** to be proof against (something); to be unharmed by (it): *plants that can withstand arid conditions.* **2** to resist (something) with determination, *esp* to stand up against it successfully. ➤➤ **withstander** *noun.* [Middle English *withstanden* from Old English *withstandan*, from WITH + *standan* to STAND¹]

withy /'widhi/ *noun* (*pl* **withies**) **1** = WITHE. **2** = OSIER (1). [Old English *wīthig*]

witless *adj* lacking wit or understanding; foolish. ➤➤ **witlessly** *adv*, **witlessness** *noun.*

witling /'witling/ *noun archaic* a would-be wit.

witness¹ /'witnis/ *noun* **1** a person who sees or hears an event take place. **2** a person who gives evidence, *esp* in a court of law. **3a** a person asked to be present, e.g. at a marriage, so as to be able to testify to its having taken place. **b** a person who watches another sign a document and adds their own signature as an indication of authenticity. **4a** the act of certifying that a fact is true or an event has happened; testimony. **b** something that serves as evidence; proof. **5** public affirmation by word or example of religious faith or conviction. [Old English *witnes* knowledge, testimony, witness, from WIT¹ + -NESS]

witness² *verb trans* **1** to observe (an event) personally or directly; to see (it) for oneself. **2** to be the scene or time of (something): *structures which this striking Dorset hilltop once witnessed* — Times Literary Supplement. **3** to give proof of (something); to betoken (it): *His appearance witnesses what he has suffered.* **4** to act as legal witness of (a marriage, the signature of a document, etc). ➤ *verb intrans* **1** (+ to) to testify to something. **2** to affirm one's religious convictions in public: *an opportunity to witness for Christ* — Billy Graham.

witness-box *noun* an enclosure in which a witness testifies in court.

witness stand *noun NAmer* = WITNESS-BOX.

witted *adj* (*used in combinations*) having wit or understanding of the kind specified: *dull-witted.*

witter /'witə/ *verb intrans* (**wittered**, **wittering**) *Brit, informal* to talk in a long-winded rambling fashion, *esp* about inconsequential matters. [prob imitative]

witticism /'witisiz(ə)m/ *noun* a witty remark. [WITTY + -*cism* as in CRITICISM]

witting /'witing/ *adj* **1** deliberate; intentional. **2** fully aware. [present part. of WIT²]

wittingly /'witingli/ *adv* deliberately; intentionally: *She wouldn't wittingly have shown that she knew his secret.*

witty /'witi/ *adj* (**wittier**, **wittiest**) **1** having or showing wit; cleverly humorous: *a witty speaker; a witty remark.* **2** amusingly or ingeniously clever in conception or execution: *a witty musical theme.* **3** *archaic* intelligent. ➤➤ **wittily** *adv*, **wittiness** *noun.*

wive /wiev/ *verb intrans* to marry a woman. ➤ *verb trans* **1** to provide a wife for (somebody). **2** to take (a woman) for a wife. [Old English *wīfian*, from *wīf* woman, wife]

wivern /'wievən/ *noun* = WYVERN.

wives /wievz/ *noun* pl of WIFE.

wiz /wiz/ *noun* see WHIZZ² (3).

wizard¹ /'wizəd/ *noun* **1** somebody skilled in magic, *esp* a man with supernatural powers; a sorcerer. **2** a person who is very clever or skilful, *esp* in a specified field: *a wizard at maths.* **3** a computer program providing a step-by-step guide to a particular task. ➤➤ **wizardly** *adj.* [Middle English *wysard* wise man, from *wis, wys* WISE¹]

wizard² *adj Brit, informal, dated* outstanding or excellent.

wizardry /'wizədri/ *noun* **1** the art or practices of a wizard; sorcery. **2** great cleverness or skill, *esp* in a specified field, or the product of this: *technical wizardry.*

wizen /'wiz(ə)n/ *verb trans* (**wizened**, **wizening**) (*usu in passive*) to cause (somebody) to become dry, shrunken, and wrinkled, often as a result of ageing. ➤ **wizened** *adj.* [Old English *wisnian*]

wk *abbr* **1** week. **2** work.

wkly *abbr* weekly.

WL *abbr* Windward Islands St Lucia (international vehicle registration for St Lucia).

Wlk *abbr* in street names, walk.

WLTM *abbr* used in personal advertisements: would like to meet.

WMD *abbr* weapon, or weapons, of mass destruction.

WMO *abbr* World Meteorological Organization.

WNW *abbr* west-northwest.

WO *abbr* Warrant Officer.

wo /woh/ *interj* = WHOA.

woad /wohd/ *noun* **1** a European plant of the mustard family formerly grown for the blue dyestuff obtained from its leaves: *Isatis tinctoria.* **2** the blue dyestuff obtained from the leaves of this plant. [Old English *wād*]

wobbegong /'wobigong/ *noun Aus* = CARPET SHARK. [native name in Australia]

wobble¹ /'wobl/ *verb intrans* **1a** to rock unsteadily from side to side. **b** to proceed with an irregular swerving or staggering motion: *He wobbled down the road on his bicycle.* **c** said of the voice: to tremble or quaver. **2** to waver or vacillate. ➤ *verb trans* to cause (something or somebody) to wobble. [prob from Low German *wabbeln*]

wobble² *noun* **1** a wobbling movement or sound. **2** the act or an instance of wobbling.

wobble-board *noun Aus* a musical instrument consisting of a piece of fibreboard that is flexed repeatedly to produce a low rhythmic sound.

wobbler *noun* **1** somebody or something that wobbles. **2** *Brit, informal* = WOBBLY².

wobbly¹ *adj* (**wobblier**, **wobbliest**) tending to wobble; unsteady.

wobbly² ✲ **throw a wobbly** *Brit, informal* to have a fit of temper, irrational behaviour, or great agitation.

wodge /woj/ *noun Brit, informal* a bulky mass or chunk: *a wodge of papers; a wodge of ice.* [alteration of WEDGE¹]

woe¹ /woh/ *noun* **1** *literary* great sorrow or suffering caused by misfortune, grief, etc: *Life protracted is protracted woe* — Dr Johnson. **2** (*usu in pl*) a trouble or affliction: *I could observe a melancholy sweetness in the countenance, that seemed to speak of woes endured* — Scott. ✲ **woe betide somebody** somebody will suffer or be punished if they do the specified thing: *Woe betide you if you forget!* **woe is me!** an exclamation of distress. [from WOE²]

woe² *interj literary* used to express grief, regret, or distress. [Old English *wā*]

woebegone /'wohbigon/ *adj* expressive of great sorrow or misery: *a woebegone look.* [Middle English *wo begon* from *wo* WOE¹ + *begon*, past part. of *bego* to go about or beset, from Old English *begān*, from BE- + *gān* GO¹]

woeful /'wohf(ə)l/ *adj* **1** feeling or expressing woe: *woeful prophecies.* **2** inspiring woe; grievous: *It was woeful to see him spoiling it* — Henry James. ➤➤ **woefully** *adv*, **woefulness** *noun.*

wog¹ /wog/ *noun Brit, offensive* a non-white person. [sometimes said to be an acronym from *westernized oriental gentleman*, but prob short for GOLLIWOG]

wog² *noun Aus, informal* a minor ailment. [origin unknown]

woggle /'wogl/ *noun* a ring, usu of leather, used to secure a Scout's neckerchief at the throat. [origin unknown]

wok /wok/ *noun* a large bowl-shaped cooking utensil used *esp* for stir-frying in Chinese cookery. [Chinese (Cantonese) *wohk*]

woke /wohk/ *verb* past tense of WAKE¹.

woken /'wohk(ə)n/ *verb* past part. of WAKE¹.

wold /wohld/ *noun* **1** an upland area of open country. **2** (**the Wolds**) a region of chalk downlands: *the Yorkshire Wolds.* [Old English *weald, wald* forest]

wolf¹ /woolf/ *noun* (*pl* **wolves** /woolvz/ *or collectively* **wolf**) **1a** a large predatory flesh-eating mammal that is related to and resembles the dog and hunts in packs: *Canis lupus.* **b** any of several similar or related animals, e.g. the coyote. **c** the fur of a wolf. **2** a fiercely rapacious person. **3** *informal* a man who pursues women in an aggressive way. **4a** dissonance in some chords produced on musical instruments with fixed notes tuned by unequal temperament, e.g. organs and pianos. **b** a harshness due to faulty vibration in various notes in a bowed instrument. ✲ **cry wolf** to raise a false alarm and risk the possibility that a future real need will not be taken seriously [from the fable of the shepherd boy who repeatedly called for help against a non-existent wolf; when a wolf did attack, nobody believed him]. **have/hold a wolf by the ears** to be in a precarious situation. **keep the wolf from the door** to have enough money to avoid or prevent starvation or want. **wolf in sheep's clothing** a person who hides hostile intentions behind a friendly manner. ➤➤ **wolfish** *adj*, **wolfishly** *adv*, **wolflike** *adj*. [Old English *wulf*; (sense 4) from German *Wolf*, from the howling sound]

wolf² *verb trans* (*often* + *down*) to eat (food) greedily.

Wolf Cub *noun chiefly Brit* a former name for CUB SCOUT.

wolffish *noun* (*pl* **wolffishes** *or collectively* **wolffish**) any of several species of large ferocious sea blennies (fish with elongated body; see BLENNY) with strong sharp teeth: family Anarhichadidae.

wolfhound *noun* a large dog of a breed used, *esp* formerly, in hunting large animals, e.g. wolves.

wolfram /'woolfrəm/ *noun* **1** = TUNGSTEN. **2** = WOLFRAMITE. [German *Wolfram*, prob from *Wolf* wolf + dialect *Rahm* soot, dirt]

wolframite /'woolfrəmiet/ *noun* a brownish black mineral containing tungsten, iron, and manganese. [German *Wolframit*, from WOLFRAM]

wolfsbane /'woolfsbayn/ *noun* any of several species of yellow-flowered Eurasian aconites: genus *Aconitum*. [so called because it was once used to poison wolves]

wolf spider *noun* a spider that lives on the ground and chases its prey: family Lycosidae.

wolf whistle *noun* a distinctive whistle sounded to express sexual admiration, *esp* by a man for a woman.

wolf-whistle *verb trans and intrans* to sound a wolf whistle at (somebody).

Wolof /'wohlof/ *noun* (*pl* **Wolof** *or* **Wolofs**) **1** a member of a people of Senegal and the Gambia. **2** a major Niger-Congo language of Senegal and the Gambia. ➤➤ **Wolof** *adj*. [the Wolof name]

wolverine /'woolvəreen/ *noun* a flesh-eating mammal of northern forests that is related to the weasel, has blackish fur, and is noted for its strength and ferocity: *Gulo gulo*. *NAmer* Also called CARCAJOU. [prob irreg from *wolv-* as in WOLVES]

wolves /woolvz/ *noun* pl of WOLF¹.

woman /'woomən/ *noun* (*pl* **women** /'wimin/) **1a** an adult human female: *A woman is like a teabag – only in hot water do you realize how strong she is* — Nancy Reagan. **b** (*usu used in combinations*) a woman belonging to a usu specified category, e.g. by birth, residence, membership, or occupation: *a councilwoman; an Englishwoman*. **2** women as a whole; womankind: *I expect that Woman will be the last thing civilised by Man* — George Meredith. **3** distinctively feminine nature; womanliness: *There's something of the woman in him*. **4a** a charwoman: *the daily woman*. **b** a personal maid, *esp* in former times. **5a** a female sexual partner, *esp* a mistress. **b** a girlfriend. **c** a wife. ✳ **woman of the streets** *euphem, dated* a prostitute. **woman to woman** frankly, as one woman to another. ➤➤ **womanless** *adj*, **womanlike** *adj*.

Word history
Old English *wīfman*, from *wīf* woman, WIFE + MAN¹. The oldest English words for man and woman were *wer* (related to *virile*) and *wīf* (the source of *wife*). *Woman* derives from *wīfman*, a compound of *wīf* and *man* (in the sense 'human being') first recorded in the 9th cent.; the male equivalent was *wǣpman*, from *wǣpen* 'weapon' (probably referring to the penis) and *man*. As *man* was increasingly applied to males only, by the 13th cent. the contrasting pair *man/woman* was generally established.

womanhood *noun* **1** the condition of being an adult female as distinguished from a child or male. **2** *literary* the adult females of a country, etc collectively: *The true worth of a race must be measured by the character of its womanhood* — Mary McLeod Bethune. **3** the distinguishing character or qualities of a woman or of womankind.

womanise *verb intrans* see WOMANIZE.

womanish *adj derog* unsuitable to a man or to a strong character of either sex; effeminate: *womanish fears*. ➤➤ **womanishly** *adv*, **womanishness** *noun*.

womanize *or* **womanise** *verb intrans* said of a man: to associate with many women habitually, *esp* for sexual relations. ➤➤ **womanizer** *noun*.

womankind *noun* female human beings; women as a whole, *esp* as distinguished from men.

womanly *adj* having or showing the good qualities traditionally thought to befit or be typical of a woman, e.g. gentleness or grace. ➤➤ **womanliness** *noun*.

womb /woohm/ *noun* **1** = UTERUS: *But if God had wanted us to think just with our wombs, why did He give us a brain?* — Clare Boothe Luce. **2a** a hollow enveloping cavity or space. **b** a place where something is generated. ➤➤ **wombed** *adj*. [Old English]

wombat /'wombat/ *noun* any of several species of stocky plant-eating Australian marsupial mammals that resemble a small bear: family Vombatidae. [from Dharuk]

women /'wimin/ *noun* pl of WOMAN.

womenfolk /'wiminfohk/ *pl noun* women in general, *esp* the women of a family or community.

Women's Institute *noun* in Britain, an organization of women who meet regularly and engage in various social and cultural activities.

women's lib /lib/ *noun informal* = WOMEN'S LIBERATION: *I owe nothing to Women's Lib* — Margaret Thatcher.

women's liberation *noun* a modern feminist movement stressing the social and psychological emancipation of women as well as the improvement of their civil and legal status.

women's movement *noun* a movement working for the improvement of the social and political position of women.

women's rights *pl noun* legal, political, and social rights for women equal to those of men.

women's studies *pl noun* (*treated as sing.*) academic studies, e.g. history, literature, sociology, and psychology, relating to the changing role of women in society.

won¹ /wun/ *verb* past tense and past part. of WIN¹.

won² /won/ *noun* (*pl* **won**) the basic monetary unit of North and South Korea, divided into 100 jun in North Korea and 100 jeon in South Korea. [Korean *wǒn*]

wonder¹ /'wundə/ *noun* **1** rapt attention, admiration, or astonishment at something unexpected, strange, beautiful, etc: *The children gazed in wonder at the snow*. **2** a cause of astonishment or admiration; a marvel: *It's a wonder he wasn't killed*. **3** (*used before a noun*) noted for outstanding success or achievement: *a wonder drug*. ✳ **no/little/small wonder** it is no surprise: *No wonder you're tired after staying up so late last night*. **work/do wonders** to have a positive effect: *A good night's sleep can work wonders*. [Old English *wundor*]

wonder² *verb* (**wondered, wondering**) ➤ *verb intrans* **1** to feel curiosity or doubt; to speculate: *I wondered about his motives*. **2a** (*often* + *at*) to be in a state of wonder; to marvel. **b** *informal* to feel surprise: *I shouldn't wonder if he's late*. ➤ *verb trans* to be curious or in doubt about (something): *I wonder who she is*. ➤➤ **wonderer** *noun*.

wonderful /'wundəf(ə)l/ *adj* **1** unusually good; admirable or excellent. **2** exciting wonder: *a sight wonderful to behold*. ➤➤ **wonderfully** *adv*, **wonderfulness** *noun*.

wonderland *noun* **1** a place that excites wonder. **2** an imaginary place where strange or magical things happen.

wonderment *noun* **1** the state of wonder; awe or astonishment. **2** curiosity about something. **3** a cause of or occasion for wonder.

wonder-worker *noun* a performer of wonders or miracles. ➤➤ **wonder-working** *adj*.

wondrous¹ /'wundrəs/ *adj literary* wonderful. ➤➤ **wondrously** *adv*, **wondrousness** *noun*. [alteration of Middle English *wonders*, genitive of WONDER¹]

wondrous² *adv archaic* wonderfully: *wondrous strange*.

wonk /wongk/ *noun chiefly NAmer informal, derog* **1** somebody who studies excessively; a swot. **2** an expert or enthusiast in some specialized field or topic. [origin unknown]

wonky /'wongki/ *adj* (**wonkier, wonkiest**) *informal* **1** awry or crooked. **2** shaky or unsteady: *He's still a bit wonky after the flu*. [alteration of English dialect *wankle*, from Old English *wancol*]

wont¹ /wohnt/ *adj archaic* accustomed or used: *places where people are wont to meet*. [Middle English *woned, wont*, past part. of *wonen* to dwell, be used to, from Old English *wunian*]

wont² *noun archaic* customary practice: *as was his wont*.

wont³ *verb* (*past tense and past part.* **wont** *or* **wonted**) ➤ *verb intrans archaic* to be or become accustomed. ➤ *verb trans* to make (somebody) accustomed.

won't /wohnt/ *contraction* will not.

wonted *adj archaic* customary or habitual: *He spoke with his wonted slowness*.

wonton /'wonton/ *noun* **1** in Chinese cookery, a case of thin dough with a savoury filling that is boiled, steamed, or fried and eaten *esp* in soup. **2** soup containing wontons. [Chinese (Cantonese) *wahn tan*]

woo /wooh/ *verb* (**woos, wooed, wooing**) ⊳ *verb trans* **1** to try to win the affection of and a commitment of marriage from (somebody, *esp* a woman); to court (them). **2** to solicit or entreat (somebody, e.g. a potential customer or voter), *esp* with importunity. ⊳ *verb intrans* to court somebody, *esp* a woman: *Men are April when they woo, December when they wed* — Shakespeare. ⊳⊳ **wooer** *noun*. [Old English *wōgian*]

wood[1] /wood/ *noun* **1a** a hard fibrous plant tissue that makes up the greater part of the stems and branches of trees or shrubs beneath the bark. **b** wood suitable or prepared for some use, e.g. burning or building. **2** something typically made of wood, e.g.: a (**the wood**) wooden casks: *wine from the wood*. **b** a golf club with a wooden head. **c** a wooden bowling ball. **3** (*also in pl*) a dense growth of trees, usu smaller than a forest. ✳ **not see the wood for the trees** to fail to have overall understanding of a subject, situation, etc as a result of concentration on details. **out of the wood/woods** (*usu in negative contexts*) escaped from danger or difficulty: *We're not out of the woods yet.* [Old English *widu, wudu*]

wood[2] *adj* **1** made of wood. **2** (*used before a noun*) suitable for cutting, storing, or carrying wood: *a wood saw*. **3** (*used before a noun*) living or growing in woods or woodland: *a wood nymph*.

wood alcohol *noun* = METHANOL.

wood anemone *noun* a common Eurasian anemone that grows in woodland and has white or pinkish flowers: *Anemone nemorosa*.

wood avens *noun* a Eurasian plant with yellow flowers that grows in damp dark places: *Geum urbanum*.

woodbine /'woodbien/ *noun* **1** = HONEYSUCKLE. **2** *NAmer* = VIRGINIA CREEPER. [Old English *wudubinde*, from *wudu* WOOD[1] + *bindan* BIND[1]]

woodblock *noun* a block of wood used to produce a woodcut.

woodchip *noun chiefly Brit* a textured wallpaper with small fragments of wood embedded in it.

woodchip paper *noun* = WOODCHIP.

woodchuck *noun* a thickset N American MARMOT (burrowing rodent) with reddish brown fur: *Marmota monax*. [by folk etymology from Ojibwa *otchig* fisher, marten, or Cree *otcheck*]

woodcock *noun* (*pl* **woodcocks** *or collectively* **woodcock**) a long-billed wading bird of wooded regions that is related to the sandpipers: *Scolopax rusticola*.

woodcraft *noun chiefly NAmer* **1** skill in making things from wood. **2** skill and practice in anything relating to woods or forests, *esp* in surviving, travelling, and hunting.

woodcut *noun* a print taken from the surface of a wooden block with a design cut in relief in the direction of the grain: compare WOOD ENGRAVING.

woodcutter *noun* **1** a person who cuts down trees or chops wood. **2** a person who makes woodcuts. ⊳⊳ **woodcutting** *noun*.

wooded *adj* said of land: covered with growing trees.

wooden *adj* **1** made of wood. **2** lacking ease or flexibility; awkwardly stiff: *a wooden performance*. ⊳⊳ **woodenly** *adv*, **woodenness** *noun*.

wood engraving *noun* **1** a print taken from the surface of a wooden block with a design cut into the end grain: compare WOODCUT. **2** the art of making such prints. ⊳⊳ **wood engraver** *noun*.

woodenhead *noun informal* a stupid person. ⊳⊳ **woodenheaded** *adj*, **woodenheadedness** *noun*.

wooden spoon *noun chiefly Brit* a consolation or booby prize. [from the wooden spoon formerly presented to the lowest graduand in the mathematical tripos at Cambridge]

woodland *noun* **1** (*also in pl*) land covered with trees, scrub, etc. **2** (*used before a noun*) living or growing in woodland: *woodland fauna*. ⊳⊳ **woodlander** *noun*.

woodlark *noun* a small European lark with a melodious song: *Lullula arborea*.

woodlouse *noun* (*pl* **woodlice** /'woodlies/) a small ground-living invertebrate animal with a flattened elliptical body often capable of rolling into a ball in defence: suborder Oniscoidea.

woodman *noun* (*pl* **woodmen**) *dated* a forester or woodcutter.

woodnote *noun* a musical note or song that is natural and artless: *or sweetest Shakespeare, Fancy's child, warble his native wood-notes wild* — Milton. [from its likeness to the call of a bird in the woods]

wood nymph *noun* a DRYAD or HAMADRYAD.

woodpecker *noun* any of numerous species of usu multicoloured birds with a stiff tail and a very hard bill used to drill holes in the bark or wood of trees to find insects for food or to form nesting cavities: family Picidae.

woodpigeon *noun* a large grey-and-white wild pigeon: *Columba palumbus*.

woodpile *noun* a pile of wood, e.g. firewood. ✳ **in the woodpile** doing or responsible for secret mischief: *the No 1 villain in the woodpile* — Howard Whitman.

wood pulp *noun* pulp from wood used in making cellulose derivatives, e.g. paper or rayon.

wood rat *noun* = PACK RAT.

woodruff *noun* a small sweet-scented plant with white flowers used in perfumery and for flavouring drinks: *Galium odoratum*. [Old English *wudurofu*, from *wudu* WOOD[1] | *rofu* of unknown meaning, perhaps related to Old High German *rāba* turnip]

wood screw *noun* a pointed screw that has an external screw thread and a slotted head to receive the blade of a screwdriver.

woodshed *noun* a shed for storing wood, *esp* firewood.

woodsman *noun* (*pl* **woodsmen**) a man who lives in, frequents, or works in the woods.

wood sorrel *noun* a plant of shady places with pink or white flowers and leaves made up of three leaflets: *Oxalis acetosella*.

wood spirit *noun* = METHANOL.

woodturning *noun* the art of producing wooden articles, e.g. bowls or chair legs, on a lathe. ⊳⊳ **woodturner** *noun*.

wood warbler *noun* **1** a European songbird with yellowish plumage that is found in woodland: *Phylloscopus sibilatrix*. **2** a small N American songbird with brightly coloured plumage or markings: family Parulidae.

wood wasp *noun* any of several species of wasplike insects related to the sawflies with larvae that burrow in woody plants and a stout hornlike egg-laying organ: family Siricidae.

woodwind *noun* **1a** any of a group of orchestral wind instruments, including the clarinet, flute, oboe, and bassoon, that has a cylindrical or conical tube of wood or metal, usu with finger holes or keys, producing notes by the passing of air over a mouth hole or through a reed. **b** (*used before a noun*) denoting or relating to such an instrument or instruments. **2a** (*treated as sing. or pl*) the woodwind section of an orchestra. **b** (*usu in pl*) a member of the woodwind section.

woodwork *noun* **1** parts or items made of wood, *esp* wooden interior fittings. **2** *Brit* the craft of constructing things from wood. ⊳⊳ **woodworker** *noun*, **woodworking** *noun and adj*.

woodworm *noun* **1** any of various insect larvae, *esp* that of the furniture beetle, that bore in dead wood. **2** an infestation of such larvae.

woody *adj* (**woodier, woodiest**) **1** covered with trees or having many woods. **2a** of or containing wood or wood fibres. **b** said of a plant: having woody parts; rich in XYLEM (water-conducting tissue) and associated structures. **c** said of a plant stem: tough and fibrous. **3** characteristic of or suggestive of wood: *wine with a woody flavour*. ⊳⊳ **woodiness** *noun*.

woodyard *noun* a yard where timber is chopped or stored.

woody nightshade *noun* a rambling poisonous plant of the potato family with purple flowers and red berries: *Solanum dulcamara*. Also called BITTERSWEET[2].

woof[1] /woof/ *noun* the low gruff sound characteristic of a dog; a bark. [imitative]

woof[2] *verb intrans* to utter a woof; to bark.

woof[3] /woohf/ *noun* = WEFT. [alteration of Middle English *oof* from Old English *ōwef*, from *ō*- (from ON[1]) + *wefan* WEAVE[1]]

woofer /'woohfə/ *noun* a loudspeaker that responds mainly to low frequencies: compare TWEETER.

woofter /'woohftə/ *noun Brit, derog* a male homosexual. [alteration of *poofter*, irreg from POOF[1]]

wool /wool/ *noun* **1** the soft wavy coat of various hairy mammals, *esp* the sheep, that is made up of fibres of KERATIN (strong fibrous protein) covered with minute scales. **2** yarn made from wool by spinning. **3** articles, *esp* knitted garments or woven fabrics, made of wool: *I always wear wool in the winter.* **4a** a dense hairy covering, e.g. on a plant. **b** (*usu in combination*) a wiry or fibrous mass, e.g. of steel or glass. **✳ pull the wool over somebody's eyes** to blind somebody to the true situation; to hoodwink somebody. **➤ woolled** *adj*, **wool-like** *adj*. [Old English *wull*]

woolen¹ /'woolən/ *adj NAmer* see WOOLLEN¹.

woolen² *noun NAmer* see WOOLLEN².

woolgathering *noun* indulging in idle daydreaming.

wool grower *noun* a person who breeds sheep for their wool.

woollen¹ (*NAmer* **woolen**) /'woolən/ *adj* **1** made of wool. **2** of or for the manufacture or sale of woollen products: *the woollen industry.*

woollen² (*NAmer* **woolen**) *noun* **1** (*in pl*) woollen garments. **2** a fabric made of wool.

woolly¹ (*NAmer* **wooly**) /'wooli/ *adj* (**woollier, woolliest,** *NAmer* **woolier, woolliest**) **1a** made of or resembling wool. **b** said of an animal or plant: covered with wool or with soft hairs resembling wool. **2a** marked by mental vagueness or confusion: *woolly thinking.* **b** lacking in clearness or sharpness: *a woolly TV picture.* **➤ woollily** *adv*, **woolliness** *noun*.

woolly² (*NAmer* **wooly**) *noun* (*pl* **woollies,** *NAmer* **woolies**) *chiefly Brit* a woollen jumper or cardigan.

woolly bear *noun* a large hairy caterpillar, *esp* the larva of a tiger moth.

woolpack *noun* in former times, a bale of wool.

Woolsack *noun* in Britain, the official seat of the Lord Chancellor in the House of Lords.

woolshed *noun* in Australia and New Zealand, a building or range of buildings in which sheep are sheared and wool is prepared for market.

woolsorter's disease *noun* anthrax affecting the lungs that results from inhalation of bacterial spores from contaminated wool or hair.

wool stapler *noun archaic* a person who grades raw wool before selling it to a manufacturer.

wooly¹ /'wooli/ *adj NAmer* see WOOLLY¹.

wooly² *noun NAmer* see WOOLLY².

woomera /'woomərə/ *noun Aus* a wooden rod with a hooked end that is used by Aborigines for throwing a spear. [Dharuk *wamara*]

Woop Woop /'woop woop/ *noun Aus, informal* a remote provincial district or settlement. [imaginary place name]

woosh¹ /woosh, woohsh/ *verb intrans* see WHOOSH¹. [imitative]

woosh² *noun* see WHOOSH².

woozy /'woohzi/ *adj* (**woozier, wooziest**) *informal* **1** dizzy or slightly nauseous. **2** mentally unclear or hazy. **➤ woozily** *adv*, **wooziness** *noun*. [perhaps a blend of WOOLLY¹ + DIZZY¹]

wop /wop/ *noun offensive* an Italian. [Italian dialect *guappo* blusterer, swaggerer, bully]

Worcester sauce /'woostə/ *noun* a pungent sauce containing soy sauce, vinegar, and spices. [named after *Worcester*, county town of *Worcestershire*, England, where it was orig made]

Worcestershire sauce /'woostəshə/ *noun* = WORCESTER SAUCE.

Worcs *abbr* Worcestershire.

word¹ /wuhd/ *noun* **1a** a meaningful unit of spoken language that can stand alone as an utterance and is not divisible into similar units. **b** a written or printed representation of a spoken word that is usu set off by spaces on either side: *the number of words to a line.* **c** in computing, a string of bits (smallest units of computer information; see BIT²) that is typically longer than a BYTE (eight bits) and is processed by a computer as a unit: *a 16-bit word.* **2** something that is said, e.g.: **a** a short remark, statement, or conversation: *I would like to have a word with you.* **b** (*in pl*) talk or discourse: *putting one's feelings into words.* **c** (*in pl*) the text of a vocal musical composition. **3** (*in pl*) a quarrelsome utterance or conversation: *I've been having words with my wife.* **4** (**the word**) an order, command, or verbal signal: *Don't move till I give the word.* **5** the act of speaking or of making verbal communication: *in word and deed.* **6** (**one's word**) a promise: *She kept her word.* **7** news or information: *He sent word that he would be late.* **8** (**the Word**). **a** = GOSPEL (1A). **b** the divine wisdom manifest in the creation and redemption of the world, and identified in Christian thought with the second person of the

Trinity; Jesus Christ. **✳ at a word** at once. **be as good as one's word** to keep a promise. **from the word go** from the beginning. **in a word** in short. **in other words** expressing the same thing in a different and usu more straightforward way. **in so many words** in exactly those terms: *He implied that such actions were criminal but did not say so in so many words.* **my word!** used to express surprise or astonishment. **of one's word** who can be relied on to keep a promise: *He is a man of his word.* **take somebody at their word** to believe somebody literally. **take the words out of somebody's mouth** to say the very thing that somebody else was about to say. **➤ wordless** *adj*, **wordlessly** *adv*. [Old English]

word² *verb trans* to express (something) in words; to phrase (it).

wordage /'wuhdij/ *noun* **1** the length in words of an article, story, etc. **2** wordiness; verbiage.

word association *noun* in psychology, the act of responding to a given word with the first word that comes into one's mind.

word-blindness *noun* **1** = ALEXIA. **2** = DYSLEXIA.

wordbook *noun* a book listing words with or without definitions.

word class *noun* a group of grammatically similar linguistic items consisting of words; a part of speech.

word deafness *noun* an inability to understand ordinary spoken words as a result of a brain defect.

word-for-word *adj* said e.g. of a report or translation: in or following the exact words; verbatim. **➤ word for word** *adv*.

wording *noun* the act or manner of expressing something in words or the words so used: *the exact wording of the will.*

word of honour *noun* a promise pledging one's honour.

word of mouth *noun* oral communication.

word-perfect *adj* said of an actor or speaker: having memorized something perfectly.

wordplay *noun* verbal wit.

word processor *noun* a computer or program that stores text for subsequent manipulation, e.g. by deleting, moving, or inserting new material, and that produces printed or typewritten text on paper. **➤ word processing** *noun*.

wordsearch *noun* a puzzle consisting of a grid filled with letters including a number of concealed words that have been entered forward or backward in a horizontal, vertical, or diagonal line.

word square *noun* a series of words of equal length arranged in a square pattern to read the same horizontally and vertically.

wordy *adj* (**wordier, wordiest**) using or containing too many words. **➤ wordily** *adv*, **wordiness** *noun*.

wore /waw/ *verb* past tense of WEAR¹.

work¹ /wuhk/ *noun* **1a** activity in which one exerts physical strength or mental faculties to do or produce something: *I like work; it fascinates me. I can sit and look at it for hours* — Jerome K Jerome. **b** sustained physical or mental effort to achieve a result. **c** the activities that provide one's accustomed means of livelihood. **d** a specific task, duty, function, or assignment. **2a** something produced in a specified way or by a specified person, thing, etc: *the work of a craftsman; clever camera work.* **b** (*often used in combinations*) something made from a specified material: *ironwork.* **c** (*usu in pl*) something produced by the exercise of creative talent or effort; an artistic production or creation: *the works of Shakespeare.* **3a** a fortified structure, e.g. a fort, earthen barricade, or trench. **b** (*in pl*) structures in engineering, e.g. docks, bridges, or embankments, or in mining, e.g. shafts or tunnels. **4** (*in pl, but treated as sing. or pl; often used in combinations*) a place where industrial activity is carried out; a factory: *the brickworks.* **5** (*in pl*) the working or moving parts of a mechanism: *the works of a clock.* **6** something being worked on; a workpiece. **7** (*in pl*) performance of moral or religious acts: *salvation by works.* **8a** effective operation; an effect or result: *We must wait for time to do its healing work.* **b** activity, behaviour, or experience of the specified kind: *Dancing reels is thirsty work.* **9a** in physics, the amount of energy that is transferred to a body by a force in producing movement, measured by multiplying the force by the distance it moves while causing motion. **b** the transference of energy in this way. **10** (**the works**). **a** *informal* everything possessed, available, or belonging: *The whole works – rod, reel, tackle box – went overboard.* **b** *informal* subjection to all possible physical violence: *They gave him the works.* **11a** (*used before a noun*) suitable for wear while working: *work clothes.* **b** (*used before a noun*) used for work: *a work elephant.* **✳ at work 1** engaged in works, *esp* working at one's regular occupation. **2** at one's place of work. **have one's**

work cut out to have a difficult task: *She'll have her work cut out to keep all those children under control.* **in the works** chiefly NAmer in process of preparation, development, or completion. **out of work** without regular employment; unemployed. ➤➤ **workless** *adj.* [Old English *werc, weorc*]

work² *verb* (*past tense and past part.* **worked** or archaic **wrought** /rawt/) ➤ *verb intrans* **1a** to do work to achieve a purpose. **b** to perform work or fulfil duties regularly for a living. **2** to operate or function: *The lifts don't work at night.* **3** to produce a desired effect; to succeed: *I hope your plan will work.* **4** to exert an influence or have a tendency: *Events have worked in our favour.* **5** (+ in) to produce artefacts by shaping or fashioning a specified material: *She works in copper.* **6a** to get into a specified condition by slow or imperceptible movements: *The knot began to work loose.* **b** to be in agitation or restless motion: *Her mouth worked nervously.* **7** (+ on) to strive to influence or persuade somebody. **8** to sail to windward. ➤ *verb trans* **1** to cause (a person or animal) to do work. **2** to carry on an operation in (a place or area). **3** to finance (something) by working. **4** to operate (something): *The pump is worked by hand.* **5** to manoeuvre (oneself or an object) gradually or with difficulty into or out of a specified condition or position: *The screw worked itself loose.* **6** to contrive or arrange (something): *We can work it so that you can take your holiday early.* **7** to bring about (an effect or result): *I cannot work miracles.* **8a** to fashion or create (something) by expending labour on it; to forge or shape (something). **b** to make or decorate (something) with needlework: *She was working a sampler.* **9** to prepare or form (something) into a desired state for use by kneading, hammering, etc. **10** (+ out) to solve (a problem) by reasoning or calculation. **11** to excite or provoke (somebody): *He worked himself into a rage.* * **work to rule** chiefly Brit to obey the rules of one's work precisely and so reduce efficiency, *esp* as a form of industrial action. [Middle English *werken, worken*, from Old English *wyrcan*]

workable *adj* **1** capable of being worked: *a workable vein of coal.* **2** said of a plan: practicable or feasible. ➤➤ **workability** /-'biliti/ *noun*, **workableness** *noun.*

workaday /'wuhkəday/ *adj* **1** prosaic or ordinary: *Let us escape from this weary workaday world by the side door of music* — Conan Doyle. **2** of or suitable for working days. [alteration of *workyday* workday]

workaholic¹ /wuhkə'holik/ *noun* a person with an excessive need to work; a compulsive worker. [blend of WORK¹ + ALCOHOLIC²]

workaholic² *adj* having an excessive or compulsive need to work.

workbench *noun* a bench on which work, *esp* of mechanics or carpenters, is performed.

workbook *noun* an exercise book of problems to be solved or questions to be answered directly on the pages.

work camp *noun* a camp where volunteers do community work.

worked *adj* that has been subjected to work, *esp* embroidery.

worked up *adj* emotionally aroused; angry or upset.

worker *noun* **1a** a person who works, often in a specified place: *an office worker.* **b** a member of the working class. **c** a member of the main body of employees of a company, as distinguished from the management. **d** a person who works in a specified way: *a hard worker.* **2** any of the sexually underdeveloped usu sterile members of a colony of ants, bees, etc that perform most of the labour and protective duties of the colony.

worker-priest *noun* a priest who spends part of each weekday as a worker in a secular job.

work ethic *noun* = PROTESTANT ETHIC.

work experience *noun* a short spell of unpaid employment experience arranged by schools for senior pupils.

workfare /'wuhkfeə/ *noun* a scheme under which certain people receiving state welfare benefits are required to undergo training or do unpaid work on behalf of the community. [WORK¹ + -fare as in WELFARE]

workforce *noun* **1** (*treated as sing. or pl*) the workers employed by a particular company or engaged in a specific activity. **2** (*treated as sing. or pl*) the people potentially available for work: *the nation's workforce.*

work-harden *verb trans* to harden and strengthen (metal) by hammering, rolling, etc.

workhorse *noun* **1** a willing worker, *esp* for a voluntary cause. **2** a markedly useful or durable vehicle, craft, or machine. **3** a horse used chiefly for labour rather than riding or racing.

workhouse /'wuhk·hows/ *noun* **1** in Britain in former times, an institution maintained at public expense to house needy or dependent people. **2** in the USA, a prison for minor offenders.

work in *verb trans* **1a** to insinuate (something) unobtrusively: *He worked in a few topical jokes.* **b** to find room for (something). **2** to cause (something) to penetrate by persistent effort: *Work the ointment in thoroughly.*

work-in *noun* a continuous occupation of a place of employment by employees continuing to work normally as a protest, usu against the threat of factory closure or redundancy.

working¹ *adj* **1a** that functions or performs work: *a working model.* **b** said of a domestic animal: trained or bred for useful work: *a working dog.* **c** engaged in paid work: *working mothers.* **2** adequate to permit effective work to be done: *a working majority.* **3** serving as a basis for further work: *a working draft.* **4a** during which one works: *working hours.* **b** during which one discusses business or policy: *a working lunch.* **5** suitable for or used in work: *working clothes.*

working² *noun* **1** (*usu in pl*) a part of a mine, quarry, or similar excavation. **2** (*usu in pl*) the act or manner of functioning or operating: *the workings of his mind.* **3** a record of the steps taken to solve a mathematical problem.

working capital *noun* capital actively turned over or available for use in the course of business activity.

working class *noun* (*treated as sing. or pl*) the class of people who work, *esp* manually, for wages: compare PROLETARIAT. ➤➤ **working-class** *adj.*

working day *noun* **1** a day on which work is done or business transacted: *Allow five working days for your payment to be processed.* **2** the period of time in a day during which work is performed: *At the end of the working day he cycles home.*

working drawing *noun* a scale drawing of an object to be made or a structure to be built that is used as a guide.

working girl *noun euphem* a prostitute.

working party *noun* **1** Brit a committee set up to investigate and report on a particular problem. **2** a group of prisoners, soldiers, etc assigned to a manual task.

work load *noun* the amount of work that somebody has to do.

workman *noun* (*pl* **workmen**) **1** a manual worker, *esp* one employed on a casual basis. **2** a person skilled at their trade to the specified degree: *a poor workman.*

workmanlike *adj* skilful or competent.

workmanly *adj* = WORKMANLIKE.

workmanship *noun* **1** the relative art or skill of a workman; craftsmanship. **2** the quality or finish exhibited by a product: *a vase of exquisite workmanship.*

workmate *noun chiefly Brit* a companion at work.

work of art *noun* **1** a product of any of the fine arts, *esp* a painting or sculpture of high artistic quality. **2** a human creation that gives high aesthetic satisfaction: *The wedding cake was a work of art.*

work off *verb trans* to dispose of or get rid of (a commitment, emotion, etc) by work or activity: *I've worked off my debt; He went for a walk to work off his anger.*

workout *noun* a period of usu vigorous physical exercise.

work out *verb trans* **1a** to determine or resolve (a question) by calculation or reasoning: *I couldn't work out how they kept the prices so low.* **b** to devise (something) by resolving difficulties: *The parties worked out an agreement.* **c** to elaborate (a plan, etc) in detail. **2** to discharge (a debt) by labour. **3** to exhaust (a mine) by working it. ➤ *verb intrans* **1a** to prove effective or successful: *The marriage didn't work out.* **b** (*often* + at/to) to amount to (a total or calculated figure). **c** said of a sum: to yield a result. **2** to engage in physical exercise.

work over *verb trans informal* to beat (somebody) up.

workpeople *pl noun* Brit workers or employees.

work permit *noun* a document authorizing a foreigner to do paid work in a country.

workpiece *noun* something being worked on.

workplace *noun* a place, e.g. an office or factory, where paid work is done.

workroom *noun* a room used for work, *esp* manual work.

works council *noun chiefly Brit* a representative group of employees taking part in talks with their employers.

work sheet *noun* **1** a document on which work done and in progress is recorded. **2** = WORKBOOK.

workshop *noun* **1** a room or place, e.g. in a factory, in which manufacture or repair work is carried out. **2** a brief intensive session of study, training, or discussion for a relatively small group of people with an emphasis on active participation: *a drama workshop*.

workshy *adj* disliking work; lazy.

workstation *noun* **1** a self-contained unit that is equipped with facilities for computing activities, e.g. a VDU and keyboard linked to a computer network in an office. **2** a desk suitable for housing a computer terminal. **3** a place in a factory where a particular task is carried out.

worktable *noun* a table at which work is done, often with drawers for holding materials and implements, *esp* one used for sewing.

worktop *noun Brit* a flat surface on a kitchen unit that is suitable for working on.

work-to-rule *noun chiefly Brit* a form of industrial action designed to reduce output or efficiency by deliberately keeping very rigidly to rules and regulations.

work up *verb trans* **1** to rouse or stir (somebody or something): *I can't work up much interest.* **2** to produce (something) by mental or physical work. **3** to improve (something), *esp* by mental work. ➤ *verb intrans* (+ to) to rise gradually in intensity or emotional tone towards something.

world /wuhld/ *noun* **1** (**the world**) the earth with everybody and everything on it: *He's travelling round the world.* **2** (**the world**) the course of human affairs: *knowledge of the world.* **3** (**the world**) the human race. **4a** (**the world**) secular affairs as distinguished from religious and ecclesiastical matters. **b** existence during life or after death: *in this world and the next.* **5a** a division, section, or generation of the inhabitants of the earth distinguished by living together at the same place or at the same time: *the medieval world.* **b** a distinctive class of people or their sphere of interest: *the academic world.* **6** (**the world**) human society or social interaction: *All the world knows that; He withdrew from the world.* **7** a part or section of the world considered as a separate independent unit. **8** one's personal environment in the sphere of one's life or work: *the world of Van Gogh.* **9** an indefinite or very great number or amount: *That makes a world of difference.* **10** a planet, *esp* one that is inhabited. **11a** (*used before a noun*) of the whole world: *the world championship.* **b** (*used before a noun*) extending or found throughout the world; worldwide: *world peace.* ❉ **best of both worlds** the advantages of two alternatives, *esp* without their disadvantages. **bring into the world** to deliver or give birth to (a baby). **come into the world** to be born. **for all the world** in every way; exactly: *copies which look for all the world like the original.* **for the world** in any circumstances; for anything: *I wouldn't hurt her feelings for the world.* **in the world** among innumerable possibilities; ever: *What in the world is it?* **out of this world** *informal* of extraordinary excellence; superb. **set the world on fire** see FIRE[1]. **think the world of** to have great love or admiration for (somebody or something). [Old English *woruld* human existence, this world, age]

world-beater *noun* somebody or something that excels all others; a champion.

world-class *adj* of the highest quality in the world: *a world-class polo player.*

World Cup *noun* an international sporting tournament held at regular intervals, *esp* in football.

world fair *noun* an international exhibition featuring exhibits and participants from all over the world.

world-famous *adj* universally known.

worldling /'wuhldling/ *noun* a worldly person; a person who is not interested in spiritual affairs.

worldly *adj* (**worldlier, worldliest**) **1** of or devoted to this world and its pursuits rather than to religion or spiritual affairs: *my worldly goods.* **2** = WORLDLY-WISE. ➤➤ **worldliness** *noun.*

worldly-wise *adj* possessing a shrewd understanding of human affairs; sophisticated.

world music *noun* a type of popular music that incorporates elements of traditional music from various countries.

world power *noun* a political unit, e.g. a nation or state, powerful enough to affect the entire world by its influence or actions.

world-shaking *adj* having tremendous importance.

world view *noun* = WELTANSCHAUUNG.

world war *noun* **1** a war engaged in by most of the principal nations of the world. **2** (**World War**) either of two such wars of the first half of the 20th cent.

world-weary *adj* bored with life and the material pleasures of the world. ➤➤ **world-weariness** *noun.*

worldwide[1] *adj* extending throughout or involving the entire world.

worldwide[2] *adv* throughout the entire world.

World Wide Web *noun* in computing, a vast information system composed of interconnected sites and files to which individuals have access through the Internet.

WORM /wuhm/ *noun* in computing, a large-capacity optical disk that allows the user to store but not alter data. [short for *write once read many times*]

worm[1] /wuhm/ *noun* **1** any of numerous relatively small elongated invertebrate animals with soft or cuticle-covered bodies, e.g. an earthworm or a tapeworm. **2** any of various invertebrate animals that resemble worms, e.g. a silkworm, woodworm, or other insect larva. **3** (*in pl*) infestation with or disease caused by parasitic worms. **4** *informal* a person who is an object of contempt, loathing, or pity; a wretch. **5a** the thread of a screw. **b** a short revolving cylindrical screw whose threads engage with a worm wheel in a worm gear. **c** a spiral condensing tube used in distilling. **6** a computer program that replicates itself many times in a network, often having a destructive effect. ➤➤ **wormlike** *adj.* [Old English *wyrm* serpent, worm]

worm[2] *verb intrans* to proceed windingly or insidiously. ➤ *verb trans* **1a** to cause (somebody or something) to move or proceed windingly or insidiously. **b** to insinuate or introduce (oneself) by devious or subtle means. **c** to make (one's way) insidiously or deviously: *She tried to worm her way out of the situation.* **2** (+ out of) to obtain or extract (information) from somebody by artful or persistent questioning or by pleading, asking, or persuading: *He wormed the secret out of her.* **3** to rid (an animal) of parasitic worms. ➤➤ **wormer** *noun.*

wormcast *noun* a small heap of earth or sand excreted by a worm on the surface.

worm-eaten *adj* **1** said of timber, wooden furniture, etc: eaten or burrowed into by or as if by worms. **2** worn-out; antiquated: *worm-eaten regulations.*

worm gear *noun* **1** = WORM WHEEL. **2** a gear consisting of a WORM[1] (revolving screw) and a worm wheel working together.

wormhole *noun* **1** a hole or passage burrowed by a worm. **2** in physics, a hypothetical connection between different parts of the space-time continuum.

worm's-eye view *noun* a view from a low or humble position.

worm wheel *noun* a toothed wheel that engages with the thread of a WORM[1] (revolving screw).

wormwood *noun* **1** any of several species of European composite plants that yield a bitter aromatic oil used in absinthe: genus *Artemisia.* Also called ABSINTHE. **2a** something bitter or mortifying. **b** bitterness: *That the step-mother had joy, or indeed anything but gall and wormwood, out of all this is not to be pretended* — Harold Frederic. [Middle English *wormwode*, alteration, by association with WORM[1] and WOOD[1], of Old English *wermōd*]

wormy *adj* (**wormier, wormiest**) **1** containing, infested with, or damaged by worms. **2** *informal* contemptible or wretched. ➤➤ **worminess** *noun.*

worn /wawn/ *verb* past part. of WEAR[1].

worn-out *adj* **1** exhausted. **2** made useless or destroyed by or as if by wear.

worriment /'wurimənt/ *noun chiefly NAmer, archaic or humorous* **1** worrying. **2** trouble or anxiety.

worrisome /'wuris(ə)m/ *adj chiefly NAmer* **1** causing distress or worry. **2** inclined to worry or fret. ➤➤ **worrisomely** *adv.*

worrit /'wurit/ *verb trans* (**worrited, worriting**) *Brit, archaic* to worry (somebody). [by alteration]

worry[1] /'wuri/ *verb* (**worries, worried, worrying**) ➤ *verb intrans* **1** to feel or experience concern or anxiety; to fret. **2** to work at something difficult: *He worried away at the problem till he found a solution.* ➤ *verb trans* **1** to afflict (somebody) with mental distress or agitation; to make (them) anxious. **2a** to subject (somebody) to persistent or nagging attention. **b** to bother or disturb (somebody). **3** said of an animal, *esp* a dog: to harass (e.g. a sheep or rabbit) by biting, shaking, chasing, etc. **4** to touch or fiddle with (something) repeatedly. ✳ **not to worry** *informal* do not worry; do not feel anxious or troubled. ➤➤ **worried** *adj*, **worriedly** *adv*, **worrier** *noun*, **worrying** *adj*, **worryingly** *adv*. [Middle English *worien* to seize by the throat, harass, devour, from Old English *wyrgan* to strangle]

worry² *noun* (*pl* **worries**) **1** mental distress or agitation resulting from concern; anxiety. **2** a cause of worry; a trouble or difficulty.

worry beads *pl noun* a string of beads fingered so as to calm oneself.

worryguts *noun informal* (*treated as sing.*) a person who is inclined to worry unduly.

worse¹ /wuhs/ *adj* **1** of a lower quality. **2** in poorer health. **3** more serious or severe. ✳ **the worse for** harmed by (something): *He was none the worse for his fall; The carpet is none the worse for wear.* **worse off** suffering worse circumstances, *esp* financially. [Old English *wiersa, wyrsa*]

worse² *adv* **1** in a worse manner. **2** to a worse extent or degree: *It's ruining worse than ever.*

worse³ *noun* **1** something worse. **2** (**the worse**) what is inferior or less desirable: *a change for the worse.*

worsen *verb* (**worsened, worsening**) ➤ *verb intrans* to become worse. ➤ *verb trans* to make (something) worse.

worship¹ /'wuhship/ *noun* **1** reverence offered to a divine being or supernatural power: *Worship is transcendent wonder* — Thomas Carlyle. **2** a form of religious practice with its set of beliefs and rituals. **3** extravagant admiration for or devotion to an object of esteem: *worship of the dollar.* **4** (**Your/His/Her Worship**) *chiefly Brit* used as a title for various officials, e.g. magistrates and mayors. [Old English *weorthscipe* worthiness, repute, respect, homage, from *weorth* worthy, WORTH¹ + -*scipe* -SHIP]

worship² *verb* (**worshipped, worshipping**, *NAmer* **worshiped, worshiping**) ➤ *verb trans* **1** to honour or offer reverence to (a deity). **2** to regard (somebody or something) with great or excessive respect, admiration, or devotion. ➤ *verb intrans* to perform or take part in worship: *It is only when men begin to worship that they begin to grow* — Calvin Coolidge. ➤➤ **worshipper** *noun*.

worshipful /'wuhship(ə)l/ *adj* **1** rendering worship or veneration. **2** (**Worshipful**) *chiefly Brit* used as a title for various people or groups of rank or distinction. ➤➤ **worshipfully** *adv*, **worshipfulness** *noun*.

worst¹ /wuhst/ *adj* **1** of the lowest quality: *the worst student.* **2** least appropriate or advisable: *the worst thing you could have done.* **3** most severe or serious. [Old English *wierresta, wyrsta*, superl from the root of Old English *wiersa, wyrsa* WORSE¹]

worst² *adv* **1** in the worst manner. **2** to the worst extent or degree: *the worst-dressed woman.*

worst³ *noun* (*pl* **worst**) **1** the worst state or part: *The worst of the storm was over.* **2** (**the worst**) what is least desirable: *To fear the worst oft cures the worse* — Shakespeare. ✳ **at one's worst** in one's worst mood, health, state of awareness, etc: *I'm always at my worst before breakfast.* **at worst/at the worst** under the worst circumstances; seen in the worst light. **do one's worst** to do the utmost harm of which one is capable. **if the worst comes to the worst** if the very worst thing happens.

worst⁴ *verb trans* (*usu in passive*) to get the better of (somebody); to defeat (them).

worsted /'woostid/ *noun* **1** a smooth compact yarn spun from long wool fibres. **2** a fabric made from worsted yarn, having a firm texture and no nap. **3** (*used before a noun*) made of worsted: *a worsted suit.* [Middle English, named after WORSTEAD (now *Worstead*), village in Norfolk, England, where it was first made]

wort¹ /wuht/ *noun* (*usu used in combinations*) a herbaceous plant, *esp* one used medicinally in former times: *stinkwort; Saint John's wort.* [Old English *wyrt* root, herb, plant]

wort² *noun* a dilute solution containing sugars obtained typically from malt by soaking and fermented to form beer. [Old English *wyrt*]

worth¹ /wuhth/ *adj and prep* **1a** equal in value to (something). **b** having money or property equal to (a sum): *He's worth £1,000,000.* **2** deserving of (something): *The castle is well worth a visit.* ✳ **for all one is worth** *informal* with all one's energy or enthusiasm. **for what it is worth** without guarantee of wisdom or accuracy. **worth**

it worth the time or effort spent. [Old English *weorth* worthy, of a specified value]

worth² *noun* **1a** value, *esp* financial value. **b** the equivalent of a specified amount or figure: *twenty pounds' worth of petrol.* **2** moral or personal merit, *esp* high merit: *He has proved his worth in the job.*

worthless *adj* **1a** lacking worth; valueless: *worthless currency.* **b** useless: *It would be worthless to continue searching.* **2** contemptible or despicable. ➤➤ **worthlessly** *adv*, **worthlessness** *noun*.

worthwhile *adj* worth the time or effort spent.

Usage note

In front of a noun, *worthwhile* is usually written as one word: *a worthwhile effort.* After a verb it may be written either as one or two words: *The effort was not worthwhile* (or *worth while*). The two parts of the word are separated in the phrase *to be worth one's while. It wouldn't be worth your while to spend too much time on the job.*

worthy¹ /'wuhdhi/ *adj* (**worthier, worthiest**) **1** good or important enough; deserving: *a suggestion that is worthy of consideration; a worthy opponent.* **2a** having moral worth or value: *a worthy cause.* **b** honourable or meritorious: *They were all worthy men.* ➤➤ **worthily** *adv*, **worthiness** *noun*.

worthy² *noun* (*pl* **worthies**) *often humorous* a worthy or prominent person.

-worthy *comb. form* forming adjectives from nouns, with the meanings: **1** deserving of the specified thing: *praiseworthy.* **2** fit or safe for the specified thing: *a seaworthy vessel.*

wot /wot/ *verb* first and third person sing. present tense of WIT².

wotcher *or* **wotcha** /'wochə/ *interj Brit, informal* used as a greeting. [alteration of *what cheer*]

would /wəd, *strong* wood/ *verb aux* the past tense of WILL¹, used: **1** to introduce a possibility or presumption: *He would have won if he hadn't tripped.* **2** after a verb expressing a wish or request: *I wish he would go away.* **3** in negative constructions to express doubt: *He would not hurt a fly.* **4** to express a polite request or invitation: *Would you please help me?; Would you like some tea?* **5** in reported speech to express an action or state in the future: *He said he would come.* **6** to express a preference: *I would rather go to the cinema.* **7** to express habitual action in the past: *We would meet often for lunch.* **8** with emphatic stress to express annoyance: *She would keep complaining.* **9** *literary* to express a wish or desire: *Men would be angels, angels would be gods* — Pope. [Old English *wolde*, past part. of *wyllan* WILL¹]

Usage note

would or *should*? See note at SHOULD.

would-be *adj often derog* desiring or intended to be: *a would-be film star.*

wouldn't /'woodnt/ *contraction* would not.

wouldst /woodst/ *verb archaic* second person sing. past tense of WILL¹.

Woulfe bottle /woolf/ *noun* in chemistry, a glass bottle with more than one neck used to pass gases through liquids. [named after P *Woulfe* d.1803, British chemist]

wound¹ /woohnd/ *noun* **1** an injury, e.g. from violence, accident, or surgery, that involves tearing, cutting, or breaking of a membrane, *esp* the skin, and damage to underlying tissues. **2** a mental or emotional hurt or blow. [Old English *wund*]

wound² *verb trans* to inflict a wound on (somebody or something). ➤ *verb intrans* to inflict a wound. ➤➤ **wounding** *adj*, **woundingly** *adv*.

wound³ /wownd/ *verb* past tense and past part. of WIND¹.

wounded /'woohndid/ *adj* hurt by or suffering from a wound: *a wounded soldier; wounded pride.*

woundwort /'woohndwuht/ *noun* any of several species of plants of the mint family with spikes of purple, pink, yellow, or white flowers, and soft downy leaves formerly used in dressing wounds: genus *Stachys.*

wove¹ /wohv/ *verb* past tense of WEAVE¹.

wove² *noun* paper made in such a way that no fine lines run across the grain: compare LAID PAPER.

woven *verb* past part. of WEAVE¹.

wow¹ /wow/ *interj informal* used to express pleasure, admiration, or surprise.

wow² *noun informal* a striking success; a hit. [WOW¹]

wow³ *verb trans informal* to excite (e.g. an audience) to enthusiastic admiration or approval.

wow⁴ *noun* a distortion in reproduced sound that is heard as a slow rise and fall in the pitch of the sound and is caused by variations in the speed of the reproducing system: compare FLUTTER² (3). [imitative]

wowser /'wowzə/ *noun Aus, NZ, informal* **1** an oppressively puritanical person; a killjoy. **2** a teetotaller. [origin unknown]

WP *abbr* **1** word processing. **2** word processor.

WPB *abbr* wastepaper basket.

WPC *abbr Brit* Woman Police Constable.

wpm *abbr* words per minute.

WRAC *abbr* in Britain, formerly, Women's Royal Army Corps.

wrack¹ /rak/ *verb trans* = RACK² (I), (2).

wrack² *noun* **1** see RACK⁶. **2** see RACK⁸.

wrack³ *noun* **1** *archaic.* **a** a wrecked ship. **b** a shipwreck. **2** any of numerous brown seaweeds, *esp* kelp: genus *Fucus* and other genera. [Middle English *wrak* from early Dutch or early Low German *wrak*; (sense 2) orig applied to seaweed washed up on the shore, hence to species that grow in the intertidal zone]

WRAF *abbr* in Britain, formerly, Women's Royal Air Force.

wraith /rayth/ *noun* **1** an apparition of a living person in their exact likeness seen shortly before or after death. **2** *literary* an insubstantial replica or shadow. ➤➤ **wraith-like** *adj.* [perhaps alteration of obsolete Scots *warth* guardian angel, from Old Norse *vörthr* guardian]

wrangle¹ /'ranggl/ *noun* an angry or prolonged dispute or quarrel.

wrangle² *verb intrans* **1** to dispute angrily or peevishly; to bicker. **2** to engage in argument or controversy. ➤ *verb trans NAmer* to herd and care for (livestock, *esp* horses) on the range. [Middle English *wranglen*, perhaps of Low German origin]

wrangler *noun* **1** *NAmer* a ranch hand who takes care of the horses and other livestock. **2** a person who is in charge of the welfare, training, and handling of animals used in a film. **3** a person who engages in a wrangle. **4** *Brit* the holder of a first-class Cambridge honours degree in mathematics.

wrap¹ /rap/ *verb* (**wrapped, wrapping**) ➤ *verb trans* **1a** to cover, pack, or enfold (something or somebody) in something flexible, e.g. paper or fabric. **b** to fold or wind (something flexible) round somebody or something: *He wrapped a blanket round her.* **2** to obscure or surround (something) with the specified covering: *The castle was wrapped in mist; The affair was wrapped in scandal.* **3** in computing, to cause (text) to be automatically carried over to the next line. **4** *informal* to finish filming or recording (something). ➤ *verb intrans* **1** to curl round something; to be a wraparound: *a skirt that wraps over.* **2** in computing, said of text: to be automatically carried over to the next line. ✳ **wrap in cotton wool** to pamper (somebody); to keep (them) in a comfortable environment. [Middle English *wrappen*; earlier history unknown]

wrap² *noun* **1** an article of clothing that may be wrapped round a person, *esp* a shawl. **2** *chiefly NAmer* a wrapping; *specif* a waterproof wrapping placed round food to be frozen, *esp* in a domestic freezer. **3** *informal* the end of a filming or recording session. **4** *informal* a small packet containing an illegal drug. **5** a sandwich filling wrapped in a tortilla, eaten as a cold snack. ✳ **under wraps** secret.

wraparound¹ *adj* **1** said of a garment, *esp* a skirt: made to be wrapped round the body with the edges overlapping. **2** shaped to follow a contour, *esp* made to curve from the front round to the side: *a wraparound windscreen.*

wraparound² *noun* a wraparound garment or object.

wrapped *adj Aus, informal* extremely pleased; delighted. [prob from *wrapped up* in absorbed in, influenced by RAPT]

wrapper *noun* **1** something in which an article is wrapped. **2** = DUST JACKET. **3** *chiefly NAmer* a fine quality tobacco leaf used for the covering of a cigar. **4** *chiefly NAmer* a loose dressing gown.

wrapping *noun* paper or other material used to wrap an object.

wrap up *verb trans* **1** to bring (something) to a successful conclusion; to end (it). **2** (*usu in passive*) to involve (somebody) completely; to engross (them): *He was totally wrapped up in his family.* ➤ *verb intrans* **1** to protect oneself with outer garments: *Wrap up warm before you go out.* **2** *Brit, informal* to stop talking; to shut up.

wrasse /ras/ *noun* (*pl* **wrasses** *or collectively* **wrasse**) any of numerous brilliantly coloured marine food fishes with spiny fins, thick lips, and strong teeth: family Labridae. [Cornish *gwragh, wragh*]

wrath /roth/ *noun* **1** strong vengeful anger or indignation. **2** divine retribution or punishment. [Old English *wræththu*, from *wrāth* WROTH]

wrathful /'rothf(ə)l/ *adj literary* filled with wrath; irate. ➤➤ **wrathfully** *adv,* **wrathfulness** *noun.*

wreak /reek/ *verb trans* **1** to give free play to (malevolent feeling); to inflict (it): *He wreaked his wrath on her; She wreaked her revenge.* **2** to cause or create (havoc or destruction). **3** *archaic* (*often in passive, with reflexive sense*) to avenge (usu oneself): *Be wreaked on him ... 'Tis he, foul creature, that hath done thee wrong* — Shakespeare. ➤➤ **wreaker** *noun.* [Old English *wrecan* to drive, punish, avenge]

wreath /reeth/ *noun* (*pl* **wreaths** /reedhz, reeths/) **1** something intertwined into a circular shape, *esp* a garland: *He laid a wreath on the coffin.* **2** a representation of a wreath, e.g. in heraldry. **3** a curl, ring, or coil: *wreaths of smoke.* [Old English *writha*]

wreathe /reedh/ *verb trans* **1** to shape (flowers, leaves, etc) into a wreath. **2** to encircle (something) with or as if with a wreath: *a bust wreathed with laurel.* **3** to coil about (something). ➤ *verb intrans* to twist or move in coils: *Smoke wreathed from the chimney.* ✳ **wreathed in smiles** with a happy joyful expression. [partly from WREATH, partly a back-formation from *wrethen* twisted, archaic past part. of WRITHE¹]

wreck¹ /rek/ *noun* **1a** a shipwreck. **b** something cast up on the land by the sea, *esp* after a shipwreck. **2** wrecking or being wrecked; destruction: *the wreck of our hopes.* **3a** the broken remains of something, e.g. a building or vehicle, wrecked or ruined. **b** a person of broken constitution, health, or spirits: *Since the burglary she has been a nervous wreck.* [Middle English *wrek* from Anglo-French *wrec*, of Scandinavian origin]

wreck² *verb trans* **1** (*usu in passive*) to cause (a vessel) to sink, break up, or be destroyed. **2** to reduce (something) to a state of ruin or destruction by violent action or accident: *The train was wrecked.* **3** to involve (something) in disaster or ruin: *He has wrecked his marriage with his womanizing.* ➤ *verb intrans archaic* to become wrecked.

wreckage /'rekij/ *noun* **1** broken and disordered parts or material from a wrecked structure. **2** wrecking or being wrecked.

wrecked *adj informal* drunk or exhausted.

wrecker *noun* **1** somebody or something that wrecks something. **2** in former times, a person who wrecked ships for plunder. **3a** *chiefly NAmer* a person whose work is the demolition of buildings. **b** *NAmer* a person who deals in parts and material salvaged from scrapped motor vehicles. **4** *NAmer* a breakdown lorry.

Wren /ren/ *noun* in Britain, a woman serving in the Women's Royal Naval Service. [from the spoken form of WRNS]

wren *noun* **1** a very small European bird that has a short erect tail and is noted for its loud song: *Troglodytes troglodytes.* **2** any of various similar or related birds. [Old English *wrenna*]

wrench¹ /rench/ *verb trans* **1** to pull or twist (something) violently: *He wrenched the door open.* **2** to injure (a part of the body) by a violent twisting or straining. **3** to snatch (something) forcibly; to wrest (it): *I wrenched the knife from her hand.* **4** *archaic* to distort or twist (something from its original meaning). ➤ *verb intrans* **1** (*usu + at*) to pull or strain at something with violent twisting: *He wrenched at the handle.* **2** to make a violent twisting movement. [Old English *wrencan*]

wrench² *noun* **1a** a violent twisting or a sideways pull. **b** a sharp twist or sudden jerk causing a strain to a muscle, ligament, etc. **c** acute emotional distress or something causing this, e.g. a parting. **2** a spanner or similar tool, *esp* one with jaws adjustable for holding nuts of different sizes.

wrest¹ /rest/ *verb trans* **1** to take (something) by violent pulling or twisting. **2** to obtain (something) with difficulty by force or determined labour: *They wrested a living from the stony soil.* **3** *archaic* = WRENCH¹ (4). [Old English *wræstan*]

wrest² *noun* **1** the act or an instance of wresting; a wrench. **2** *archaic* a key used to tune a harp or piano.

wrestle¹ /'resl/ *verb intrans* **1** to contend with an opponent in wrestling. **2** to engage in a violent or determined struggle; to grapple: *He was wrestling with some cumbersome luggage; I'm wrestling with a difficult problem.* ➤ *verb trans* **1** to wrestle with (somebody). **2** to push, pull, or manhandle (somebody or something) by force: *The bouncers wrestled the drunk out of the door.* ➤➤ **wrestler** *noun.* [Old English *wræstlian*, frequentative of *wræstan* WREST¹]

wrestle² *noun* the act or an instance of wrestling, *esp* a wrestling bout.

wrestling *noun* a sport or contest in which two unarmed people struggle hand to hand according to agreed rules, each attempting to subdue or unbalance their opponent without hitting with the closed fist.

wrest pin *noun* any of the pins to which the strings of a piano, harpsichord, etc are attached and that can be turned to tune the instrument.

wrest plank *noun* a plank or block in which the wrest pins of a musical instrument are embedded.

wretch /rech/ *noun* **1** a profoundly unhappy or unfortunate person. **2** *informal* a base, despicable, or vile person. [Old English *wrecca* outcast, exile]

wretched /'rechid/ *adj* **1** deeply afflicted, dejected, or unfortunate. **2** deplorably bad: *She was in wretched health; wretched workmanship.* **3** mean, squalid, or contemptible: *He was dressed in wretched old clothes.* **4** used as a general expression of annoyance: *I've lost my wretched socks.* ➤➤ **wretchedly** *adv.* **wretchedness** *noun.* [irreg from WRETCH]

wrick /rik/ *verb trans* = RICK³. ➤➤ **wrick** *noun.*

wriggle¹ /'rigl/ *verb intrans* **1** to move to and fro with short writhing motions; to squirm. **2** to move or advance by twisting and turning. **3** to extricate or insinuate oneself by manoeuvring, equivocation, or ingratiation: *The minister managed to wriggle out of a difficult question.* ➤ *verb trans* to cause (a body part) to wriggle: *She wriggled her hips.* ➤➤ **wriggler** *noun.* [Middle English *wrigglen* from early Low German *wriggeln*]

wriggle² *noun* a wriggling movement. ➤➤ **wriggly** *adj.*

wright /riet/ *noun* (*usu used in combinations*) a person who makes or creates a specified thing: *a shipwright; a playwright.* [Old English *wyrhta, wryhta* worker, maker]

wring¹ /ring/ *verb trans* (*past tense and past part.* **wrung** /rung/) **1** to twist or compress (something), *esp* so as to extract liquid: *He wrung the towel dry.* **2a** to expel or obtain (liquid) by twisting and compressing something: *She wrung the water from the towel.* **b** (*often + from/out of*) to exact or extort (something) by coercion or with difficulty: *They tried to wring a confession from the suspect.* **3a** to twist (an animal's neck), *esp* so as to break it. **b** to twist together (one's clasped hands) as a sign of anguish. **4** to shake (somebody's hand) vigorously in greeting. **5** to distress or torment (a person or their heart): *a tragedy that wrings the heart.* [Old English *wringan*]

wring² *noun* an act of wringing.

wringer *noun* = MANGLE² (1).

wringing *adj* said e.g. of clothes: so wet that liquid is dripping out.

wringing wet *adj* = WRINGING.

wrinkle¹ /'ringkl/ *noun* **1** a small ridge, crease, or furrow formed in the skin or on a previously smooth surface. **2** *informal* a valuable trick or hint for bringing about a result. [Middle English, back-formation from *wrinkled* twisted, winding, prob from Old English *gewrinclod*, past part. of *gewrinclian* to wind]

wrinkle² *verb trans* (*usu in passive*) to contract (something) into wrinkles; to pucker or crease (it). ➤ *verb intrans* to become marked with or contracted into wrinkles.

wrinkly¹ /'ringkli/ *adj* (**wrinklier, wrinkliest**) having many wrinkles.

wrinkly² *noun* (*pl* **wrinklies**) *Brit, derog* an elderly person.

wrist /rist/ *noun* **1a** the joint between the human hand and the arm. **b** a part of a lower animal corresponding to this. **2** the part of a garment or glove covering the wrist. **3** = WRIST PIN. [Old English]

wristband *noun* **1** a band on the sleeve of a garment encircling the wrist. **2** the strap of a wristwatch. **3** a band worn around the wrist, e.g. for identity purposes or to absorb sweat.

wristlet /'ristlit/ *noun* **1** a band encircling the wrist, *esp* a closely fitting knitted band attached to the top of a glove or the end of a sleeve. **2** a bracelet.

wrist pin *noun* a stud or pin that forms a bearing for a connecting rod in a machine.

wristwatch *noun* a watch attached to a strap or bracelet and worn round the wrist.

wristy *adj* (**wristier, wristiest**) said of a cricket or tennis stroke: characterized by a lot of wrist movement.

writ /rit/ *noun* **1** a formal document issued in the name of the sovereign or of a court commanding or forbidding an act specified in it: *a writ of execution.* **2** *archaic* something written; writing: *holy writ.* [Old English]

write /riet/ *verb* (*past tense* **wrote** /roht/, *past part.* **written** /'ritn/) ➤ *verb trans* **1a** to form (legible characters, symbols, or words) on a surface, *esp* with an instrument. **b** to put (a word) in writing. **c** to complete or fill in (something) by writing: *I wrote a cheque.* **2** to set down in writing, e.g.: **a** to be the author or composer of (a piece of writing, music, etc): *Alas, Sir ... what a mass of confusion we should have, if every bishop, and every judge, every lawyer, physician, and divine, were to write books* — Dr Johnson. **b** to use (a specific script or language) in writing. **3** to describe (something) in or as if in writing: *His words are written on my heart.* **4** *informal* (*usu in passive*) to make (a quality or condition) evident: *Guilt was written all over his face.* **5** to introduce or transfer (information) into or from a computer memory. **6** *chiefly NAmer* to communicate with (somebody) in writing: *He wrote his parents on his arrival.* ➤ *verb intrans* **1** to make significant written characters, inscriptions, words, or sentences: *My son is learning to write at school.* **2** to compose and send a letter: *Please write soon.* **3** to produce or compose a written work, *esp* professionally, for publication or entertainment: *She writes for a national newspaper.* ➤➤ **writable** *adj.* [Old English *wrītan* to scratch, draw, inscribe]

write down *verb trans* **1** to record (information) in written form. **2** to disparage, injure, or minimize (somebody) by writing. **3** to reduce the BOOK VALUE (value in accounting) of (an asset). ➤ *verb intrans* (+ to) to write so as to appeal to a lower level of taste, comprehension, or intelligence.

write-down *noun* a deliberate reduction in the book value of an asset.

write in *verb intrans* to write and send a letter to an organization or institution. ➤ *verb trans chiefly NAmer* to insert (a name not listed on a ballot or voting machine) in an appropriate space and vote for that candidate.

write-in *noun NAmer* a vote cast by writing in the name of a candidate.

write off *verb trans* **1** to concede (something or somebody) to be irreparably lost, useless, or dead: *This two square miles isn't being written off as a ghetto* — Colin MacInnes. **2** to cancel the record of (bad debt). ➤ *verb intrans* to write and send a letter.

write-off *noun* **1** something or somebody written off as a total loss: *He survived the crash, but the car was a write-off.* **2** an elimination of an item from accounts.

write out *verb trans* to put (information) in writing; *esp* to put the whole of something into a written form.

writer *noun* **1** a person who writes books, articles, etc as an occupation; an author: *I am the kind of writer that people think other people are reading* — V S Naipaul. **2** a person who has written a particular text or document. **3** *Brit* formerly, a scribe. **4** *Scot* = WRITER TO THE SIGNET.

writer's cramp *noun* a painful spasmodic cramp of the hand or finger muscles brought on by excessive writing.

Writer to the Signet *noun Scot* a member of a body of senior solicitors who prepare Crown writs. [orig a clerk who prepared State documents for the royal signature or seal]

write up *verb trans* **1a** to write an account of (something). **b** to put (something) into finished written form: *I'm going to write up my notes.* **2** to bring up to date the writing of (a diary, etc). **3** to praise or maximize (somebody or something) in writing.

write-up *noun* a written account or review.

writhe¹ /riedh/ *verb intrans* **1** to twist in or as if in pain or struggling. **2** to proceed with twists and turns. **3** to suffer keenly: *She was writhing under his insult.* ➤ *verb trans* to twist (the body or a bodily part) in pain. [Old English *wrīthan* to twist]

writhe² *noun* an instance of writhing.

writing /'rieting/ *noun* **1** the act, practice, or occupation of literary composition. **2a** written letters or words, *esp* handwriting: *I can't read your writing.* **b** (*usu in pl*) a written composition: *the writings of Marx.* **c** a written or printed letter, notice, document, or inscription. ✳ **the writing on the wall** an omen of impending disaster or ruin.

writing desk *noun* a desk for writing on, *esp* one with a sloping top.

writing paper *noun* paper that can be written on with ink, *esp* notepaper.

written /'ritn/ *verb* past part. of WRITE.

WRNS /renz/ *abbr* in Britain, formerly, Women's Royal Naval Service.

wrong[1] /rong/ *adj* **1** not according to truth or facts; incorrect: *That fellow seems to me to possess one idea, and that is a wrong one* — Dr Johnson. **2** in error; mistaken: *You're quite wrong about that.* **3** against moral standards; evil: *She thought that war was wrong.* **4** not right or proper according to a code, standard, or convention: *It was wrong not to thank your host.* **5** not satisfactory, e.g. in condition, health, or temper: *There's something wrong with my toe.* **6** being the side of fabric that is not intended to be seen, e.g. on a finished garment: *She put her jumper on wrong side out.* **7** not in accordance with one's needs, intentions, or expectations: *He took the wrong bus.* ✳ **get (hold of) the wrong end of the stick** to misunderstand. **on the wrong side of 1** out of favour with: *I wouldn't like to get on the wrong side of her.* **2** more than the specified age: *He's on the wrong side of forty.* ➤➤ **wrongly** *adv*, **wrongness** *noun*. [Old English *wrang* from Old Norse *rangr* amiss, unjust, askew]

wrong[2] *adv* **1** without accuracy; incorrectly: *They spelt my surname wrong.* **2** without regard for what is right or proper: *You acted wrong.* **3** out of proper working order: *The washing machine has gone wrong.*

wrong[3] *noun* **1** an injurious, unfair, or unjust act: *You did him a great wrong.* **2** what is wrong, immoral, or unethical: *She knows the difference between right and wrong.* **3a** the state of being mistaken or incorrect: *My guess was hopelessly in the wrong.* **b** the state of being or appearing to be guilty: *I admit I was in the wrong.*

wrong[4] *verb trans* **1** to do wrong to (somebody); to treat (them) unjustly or unfairly. **2** to mistakenly ascribe an unworthy motive to (somebody); to misrepresent (them). ➤➤ **wronger** *noun*.

wrongdoer /'rongdooh·ə/ *noun* a person who behaves immorally or illegally. ➤➤ **wrongdoing** *noun*.

wrong-foot *verb trans* **1** *Brit* to make (an opponent) move in the wrong direction by deception, e.g. in tennis or football. **2** to put (somebody) at a disadvantage by a sudden change of approach.

wrongful /'rongf(ə)l/ *adj* wrong, unjust, or unlawful. ➤➤ **wrongfully** *adv*, **wrongfulness** *noun*.

wrongheaded *adj* stubborn in adherence to wrong opinion or principles; perverse. ➤➤ **wrongheadedly** *adv*, **wrongheadedness** *noun*.

wrote /roht/ *verb* past tense of WRITE.

wroth /roth/ *adj archaic* wrathful. [Old English *wrāth*]

wrought /rawt/ *adj* **1** said of metals: beaten into shape by tools: compare WROUGHT IRON. **2** worked or formed by artistry or effort: *carefully wrought essays.* **3** (+ up) deeply stirred; excited: *He gets wrought up over nothing.* [past part. of WORK[2]]

wrought iron *noun* a tough pure form of iron that is easily worked and contains very little carbon: compare WROUGHT.

wrung /rung/ *verb* past tense and past part. of WRING[1].

WRVS *abbr* in Britain, Women's Royal Voluntary Service.

wry /rie/ *adj* (**wryer** or **wrier, wryest** or **wriest**) **1** ironically or grimly humorous: *wry wit.* **2a** bent or twisted, *esp* to one side: *a wry smile.* **b** contorted into an expression of distaste, disapproval, etc: *She made a wry face.* ➤➤ **wryly** *adv*, **wryness** *noun*. [Middle English *wrien* to twist, writhe, from Old English *wrigian* to strive, go forward]

wrybill *noun* a New Zealand bird related to the plovers that has a beak curved sharply to the right: *Anarhynchus frontalis.*

wryneck *noun* **1** a grey-brown bird that is related to the woodpeckers and can twist its head sideways over its shoulder: *Jynx torquilla.* **2** = TORTICOLLIS.

WS *abbr* Western Samoa (international vehicle registration).

WSW *abbr* west-southwest.

wt *abbr* weight.

WTO *abbr* World Trade Organization.

wunderkind /'voondəkint/ *noun* (*pl* **wunderkinds** or **wunderkinder** /-kində/) **1** a child prodigy. **2** a person who succeeds in a competitive field at an early age. [German *Wunderkind*, from *Wunder* wonder + *Kind* child]

wurst /vuhst, vooəst, wuhst, wooəst/ *noun* (*usu used in combinations*) a sausage typical of those made in Germany and Austria: *liverwurst.* [German *Wurst* sausage]

wuss /woos/ *noun chiefly NAmer, Aus, informal* a weak or ineffectual person; a wimp. ➤➤ **wussy** *adj.* [origin unknown]

wussy /'woosi/ *noun chiefly NAmer, Aus, informal* = WUSS.

WV *abbr* **1** West Virginia (US postal abbreviation). **2** Windward Islands St Vincent (international vehicle registration).

W. Va. *abbr* West Virginia.

WWF *abbr* **1** World Wide Fund for Nature. **2** World Wrestling Federation.

WWI *abbr* World War I.

WWII *abbr* World War II.

WWW *abbr* World Wide Web.

WY *abbr* Wyoming (US postal abbreviation).

wych elm or **witch elm** /wich/ *noun* **1** a hardy elm that grows in N Europe and Asia: *Ulmus glabra.* **2** the wood of the wych elm. [*wych, witch* a tree with pliant branches, from Old English *wice, wic*]

wyn /win/ *noun* see WEN[2].

wynd /wiend/ *noun Scot, N Eng* usu in place names: a very narrow street: *Church Wynd.* [Middle English (Scots) *wynde*, prob from Old English *windan* WIND[3]]

Wyo. *abbr* Wyoming.

WYSIWYG /'wiziwig/ *adj* denoting a computer system in which all text, typefaces, underlinings, and graphics displayed on screen can be faithfully reproduced on printout. [short for *what you see is what you get*]

wyvern /'wievən/ *noun* a mythical and heraldic animal usu represented as a two-legged winged creature with a long tail that resembles a dragon. [Middle English *wiverne* viper, via early French *wivre* from Latin *vipera*: see VIPER]

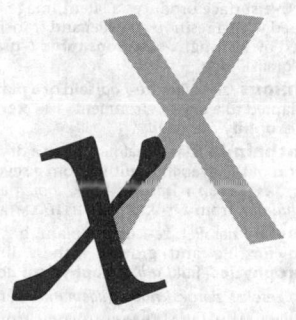

X¹ *or* **x** *noun* (*pl* **X's** *or* **Xs** *or* **x's**) **1a** the 24th letter of the English alphabet. **b** a written character or design denoting this letter. **c** the sound represented by this letter, one of the English consonants. **2** an item designated as X, *esp* the 24th in a series. **3** the Roman numeral for ten. **4** used to represent the first unknown quantity in an algebraic equation or expression. **5** used to designate the horizontal axis in a plane coordinate system. **6** somebody or something whose identity is unknown or withheld. **7** used in place of a signature by somebody who cannot write. **8** used to indicate a choice on a ballot paper. **9** used to symbolize a kiss on a letter or card. **10** used to indicate a mistake, e.g. when marking written work.

X² *adj* said of a film: certified in Britain, formerly, as suitable only for people over 18. ⟫ **X** *noun*.

X³ *abbr* Christ. [Greek χ (chi), initial letter of *Christos* Christ]

x *abbr* **1** ex. **2** extra.

Xanadu /'zanədooh/ *noun* an imaginary place of idyllic beauty. [from *Xanadu*, alteration of *Shang-tu*, a city in Mongolia, used in the poem *Kubla Khan* by S T Coleridge d.1834, English poet]

xanth- *or* **xantho-** *comb. form* forming words, with the meaning: yellow: *xanthophyll*. [Greek *xanthos* yellow]

xanthic /'zanthik/ *adj* **1** of or tending towards a yellow colour. **2** denoting or relating to any of various unstable oily acids. [French *xanthique*, from Greek *xanthos* yellow]

xanthine /'zanthien, 'zantheen/ *noun* a yellow crystalline compound that occurs in blood and urine and in plant tissue: formula $C_5H_4N_4O_2$.

xantho- *comb. form* see XANTH-.

xanthoma /zan'thohmə/ *noun* (*pl* **xanthomas** *or* **xanthomata** /-tə/) a skin condition characterized by raised yellowish patches, e.g. on the eyelids, neck, or back.

xanthophyll /'zanthohfil, 'zanthəfil/ *noun* any of several yellow to orange pigments that are derivatives of carotenes and occur in plants, e.g. nettles and yellow flower petals, algae, and animal tissues, *esp* lutein. ⟫ **xanthophyllous** /-'filəs/ *adj*. [French *xanthophylle*, from XANTHO- + *-phylle* -PHYLL]

x-axis *noun* **1** the horizontal axis in a Cartesian coordinate system having two axes at right angles. **2** one of the three axes in a three-dimensional rectangular coordinate system, usu the horizontal one.

X chromosome *noun* a SEX CHROMOSOME (strand of gene-carrying material concerned with the inheritance of sex) that usu occurs paired with an identical chromosome in one sex, and with a dissimilar chromosome in the other sex. In many animals, including human beings, the inheritance of two X chromosomes determines that the sex of the animal is female and the inheritance of an X chromosome and a Y chromosome determines that the sex is male: compare Y CHROMOSOME.

XD *abbr* ex dividend.

Xe *abbr* the chemical symbol for xenon.

xebec *or* **zebec** /'zeebek/ *noun* a usu three-masted Mediterranean sailing ship with mixed lateen and square rig. [prob modification of French *chebec*, from Arabic *shabbāk*]

xen- *or* **xeno-** *comb. form* forming nouns and their derivatives, with the meanings: **1** of or relating to foreigners: *xenophobia*. **2** different, strange, or foreign: *xenolith*. [from Greek *xenos* stranger, guest, host]

xenobiotic¹ /,zenohbie'otik/ *adj* denoting or involving a substance, usu a chemical compound, that is foreign to the body or to a particular ecological system.

xenobiotic² *noun* a xenobiotic substance.

xenogamy /ze'nogəmi/ *noun* = CROSS-FERTILIZATION. ⟫ **xenogamous** *adj*. [XEN- + -GAMY]

xenogeneic /,zenohjə'nayik, -'nee·ik/ *adj* derived from or originating in a member of another species; heterologous: *a xenogeneic antibody*. [XEN- + GENE + -IC¹]

xenograft /'zenəgrahft/ *noun* a tissue graft carried out between members of different species.

xenolith /'zenəlith/ *noun* a fragment of rock embedded in a rock of a different type. ⟫ **xenolithic** /-'lithik/ *adj*.

xenon /'zenon, 'zeenon/ *noun* a heavy colourless, odourless, gaseous chemical element of the noble gas group, used *esp* in specialized lamps and electronic tubes: symbol Xe, atomic number 54. [Greek *xenon*, neuter of *xenos* strange]

xenophile /'zenəfiel/ *noun* somebody who is attracted to foreign things, e.g. foreign manners, styles, or people. ⟫ **xenophilous** /ze'nofiləs/ *adj*.

xenophobia /zenə'fohbi·ə/ *noun* an intense fear or dislike of foreigners or strangers. ⟫ **xenophobe** /'zenəfohb/ *noun*, **xenophobic** *adj*.

xenotransplantation /,zenohtransplahn'taysh(ə)n, -trahnsplahn'taysh(ə)n/ *noun* transplantation of cells or organs from one species into a member of another species, e.g. the transplanting of pig cells and organs into human beings for medical purposes. ⟫ **xenotransplant** /'zenohtransplahnt, -trahnsplahnt/ *noun*.

xer- *or* **xero-** *comb. form* forming words, with the meaning: dry: *xerophyte*; *xerography*. [Greek *xēr-, xĕro-*, from *xēros* dry]

xeric /'zeerik/ *adj* relating to or adapted to living in dry conditions: compare HYDRIC, MESIC¹: *a xeric habitat*; *a xeric plant*.

xero- *comb. form* see XER-.

xeroderma /ziəroh'duhmə/ *noun* a condition characterized by abnormally dry skin resulting from the malfunctioning of sweat

glands. ➤➤ **xerodermatous** /-təs/ *adj.* [scientific Latin, from
XERO- + -DERMA]

xerography /ziə'rogrəfi, ze-/ *noun* a photocopying process in
which the action of light on an electrically charged photoconductive surface produces a latent image of the original that is
developed with a resinous powder and transferred to paper, where
it is fixed by heating. ➤➤ **xerographic** /-'grafik/ *adj,* **xerographi-
cally** /-'grafikli/ *adv.*

xerophilous /ziə'rofiləs, ze-/ *adj* said of a plant or animal: thriving
in or adapted to a dry environment. ➤➤ **xerophile** /'ziərəfiel, 'ze-/
noun, **xerophily** /-li/ *noun.*

xerophthalmia /ziərof'thalmi·ə/ *noun* a dry, thickened, lustreless
condition of the eyeball resulting from a severe deficiency of Vitamin A. ➤➤ **xerophthalmic** /-mik/ *adj.* [late Latin from Greek
xērophthalmia, from *xēr-* XER- + OPHTHALMIA]

xerophyte /'ziərəfiet, ze-/ *noun* a plant, e.g. a cactus, structurally
adapted for life and growth with a limited water supply.
➤➤ **xerophytic** /-'fitik/ *adj,* **xerophytism** *noun.*

Xerox /'zeroks, 'ziəroks/ *noun trademark* a xerographic copier.

xerox *verb trans (also* **Xerox)** to copy (something) on a Xerox
machine.

x height *noun* the height of a lower-case x used to represent the
relative height of small to capital letters in a complete set of type.

Xhosa /'khohsə, 'khawsə/ *noun (pl* **Xhosas** *or collectively* **Xhosa) 1**
a member of a people chiefly inhabiting the Cape Province of
South Africa, related to the Zulus. **2** the Bantu language spoken by
this people. ➤➤ **Xhosa** *adj.* [Xhosa *umXhosa*]

xi /sie, zie/ *noun* the 14th letter of the Greek alphabet (Ξ, ξ),
equivalent to and transliterated as roman x. [Greek *xeî*]

xiphisternum /ziefi'stuhnəm, zi-/ *noun (pl* **xiphisterna** /-nə/) the
lowest segment of the sternum, a cartilaginous plate not connected
to any of the ribs. [scientific Latin, from Greek *xiphos* sword + Latin
sternum STERNUM]

xiphoid /'ziefoyd, 'zifoyd/ *adj* **1** sword-shaped. **2** denoting or relating to the xiphisternum. [via Latin from Greek *xiphoeidēs,* from
xiphos sword]

xiphoid cartilage *noun* = XIPHISTERNUM.

xiphoid process *noun* = XIPHISTERNUM.

XL *abbr* extra large.

Xmas /'eksməs/ *noun informal* Christmas. [*X* symbol for *Christ* (see
X³) + -*mas* in CHRISTMAS]

X-rated *adj* **1** involving pornography, indecency, or extreme
violence. **2** formerly, said of a film: given an X classification;
suitable only for adults.

X-ray¹ *noun* **1a** an electromagnetic radiation of extremely short
wavelength that has the properties of ionizing a gas when passing
through it, of penetrating various thicknesses of all solids, and of
acting like light to expose photographic films and plates. **b** *informal
(used before a noun)* involving the use of X-rays or having the ability
to penetrate or see through solid substances: *X-ray vision.* **2** an
examination or photograph made by means of X-rays.

Word history

translation of German *X-Strahlen* X-rays, from X + *Strahl* ray. X was used
because when the rays were discovered their nature was not known.

X-ray² *verb trans (also* **x-ray)** to examine, treat, or photograph
(somebody or something) with X-rays.

X-ray astronomy *noun* the branch of astronomy concerned
with the detection and investigation of objects in outer space by
means of the X-rays they emit.

X-ray crystallography *noun* the investigation of the structure
of crystals using the characteristic patterns produced by the scattering of an X-ray beam that is passed through them.

X-ray tube *noun* an evacuated tube in which a concentrated
stream of electrons strikes a metal target and produces X-rays.

xu /sooh/ *noun (pl* **xu)** a unit of currency in Vietnam, worth 100th
of a dong. [Vietnamese *xu* from French *sou*: see SOU]

xyl- *or* **xylo-** *comb. form* forming words, denoting: **1** wood: *xylophone.* **2** xylene: *xylidine.* [Latin from Greek, from *xylon* wood]

xylem /'ziləm, 'zieləm/ *noun* a complex vascular tissue found in
higher plants that forms the woody supporting part of their stems
and conveys water and nutrients upward from their roots: compare
PHLOEM. [German *Xylem* from Greek *xylon* wood]

xylene /'zieleen/ *noun* a toxic inflammable oily hydrocarbon
obtained from wood tar, coal tar, etc used in fuels and solvents:
formula C_8H_{10}.

xylidine /'zielideen, -dien, 'zili-/ *noun* any of a mixture of six
poisonous chemical compounds derived from xylene that are used
chiefly in the manufacture of dyes: formula $(CH_3)_2C_6H_3NH_2$.

xylo- *comb. form* see XYL-.

xylography /zie'logrəfi/ *noun* the art of making wood engravings.
➤➤ **xylograph** /'zieləgrahf, -graf/ *noun.* [French *xylographie,* from
XYLO- + -*graphie* -GRAPHY]

xylophagous /zie'lofəgəs/ *adj* feeding on or in wood: *xylophagous
insect larvae.* [Greek *xylophagos,* from XYLO- + -*phagos* -phagous (see
-PHAGY)]

xylophone /'zieləfohn/ *noun* a percussion instrument that has a
series of wooden bars graduated in length to produce the musical
scale. It is sounded by striking with two small wooden hammers.
➤➤ **xylophonic** /-'fonik/ *adj,* **xylophonist** /'zie-, zie'lofənist/ *noun.*

xylose /'zielohz, 'zielohs/ *noun* a sugar that occurs *esp* in woody
plant tissue and is used in dyes, in tanning, and in foods for
diabetics: formula $C_5H_{10}O_5$.

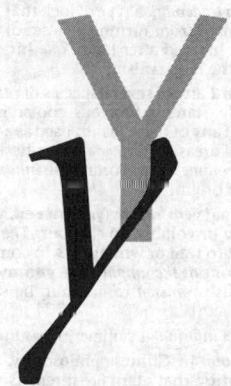

Y¹ *or* **y** *noun* (*pl* **Y's** *or* **Ys** *or* **y's**) **1a** the 25th letter of the English alphabet. **b** a written character or design denoting this letter. **c** the sound represented by this letter, one of the English consonants, also functioning as a vowel. **2** an item designated as Y, *esp* the 25th in a series. **3** used to represent the second unknown quantity in an algebraic equation or expression. **4** used to designate the vertical axis in a plane coordinate system. **5** somebody or something whose identity is unknown or withheld.

Y² *abbr* the chemical symbol for yttrium.

Y³ *abbr NAmer, informal* a YMCA or YWCA hostel.

y *abbr* year.

-y¹ *or* **-ey** *suffix* forming adjectives from nouns and verbs, with the meanings: **1a** covered with or full of: *blossomy*; *dirty*; *hairy*. **b** having the quality of: *waxy*; *icy*; *cheery*. **2** tending or inclined to: *sleepy*; *sticky*; *curly*. **3** slightly or rather: *chilly*. **4** addicted to or enthusiastic about: *horsey*. [Old English *-ig*]

-y² *suffix* forming nouns, denoting: **1** a state, condition, or quality: *beggary*; *jealousy*. **2** a whole body or group sharing a specified class or state: *soldiery*. [Middle English *-ie* via Old French from Latin *-ia*, from Greek *-ia*, *-eia*]

-y³ *suffix* forming nouns, denoting: an instance of the action specified: *entreaty*; *enquiry*. [Middle English *-ie* via Anglo-French from Latin *-ium*]

-y⁴ *or* **-ie** *suffix* forming nouns, with the meanings: **1** somebody or something little or dear: *doggy*; *grannie*. **2** somebody associated with, enthusiastic about, or addicted to something specified: *a foodie*; *a towny*; *a junkie*. **3** a person or thing of a specified kind or quality: *a biggie*; *a hippy*. [Middle English (Scots)]

Y2K *abbr* the year 2000, *esp* in connection with the so-called millennium bug.

yabby *or* **yabbie** /'yabi/ *noun* (*pl* **yabbies**) *Aus* a small Australian freshwater crayfish: *Charax destructor* and related species. [Wembawemba *yabij*]

yacht¹ /yot/ *noun* a relatively small sailing or powered vessel that characteristically has a sharp prow and graceful lines and is used for pleasure cruising or racing. [obsolete Dutch *jaght* from early Low German *jacht*, short for *jachtschiff*, literally 'hunting ship']

yacht² *verb intrans* to race or cruise in a yacht. ➤➤ **yachting** *noun*.

yachtie /'yoti/ *noun informal* a yachting enthusiast.

yachtsman *or* **yachtswoman** *noun* (*pl* **yachtsmen** *or* **yachtswomen**) a man or woman who owns or sails a yacht.

yack¹ /yak/ *noun informal* see YAK².

yack² *verb intrans* see YAK³.

yacker /'yakə/ *noun* see YAKKA.

yackety-yack¹ /,yakiti 'yak/ *noun informal* = YAK². [reduplication of YAK²]

yackety-yack² *verb intrans informal* = YAK³.

Yagi aerial /'yahgi, 'yagi/ *noun* an aerial, e.g. for a television, that picks up radio waves from a very small number of directions only. It consists of an array of horizontal closely spaced parallel elements, the direction of maximum signal reception being along the line of the centres. [named after Hidetsugu *Yagi* d.1976, Japanese engineer]

Yagi antenna *noun* = YAGI AERIAL.

yah¹ /yah/ *interj* used to express disgust, defiance, or derision. [prob imitative of the sound of retching]

yah² *interj* used to represent the affected drawl of some members of the British upper classes: yes.

yahoo¹ /'yah·hooh, yə'hooh/ *noun* (*pl* **yahoos**) *informal* an uncouth, rowdy, or degraded person. [from *Yahoo*, one of a race of human brutes in *Gulliver's Travels* by Jonathan Swift d.1745, Irish satirist]

yahoo² /yah'hooh, ya'hooh/ *interj* used to express wild excitement or delight.

Yahweh /'yahway/ *or* **Yahveh** /'yahvay/ *noun* the God of the Hebrews: compare TETRAGRAMMATON. [Hebrew *YHWH*, with the addition of the vowels thought most likely to represent the pronunciation: compare JEHOVAH]

Yahwism /'yahwiz(ə)m, 'yahviz(ə)m/ *noun* the worship of Yahweh among the ancient Hebrews. ➤➤ **Yahwistic** /-'wistik, -'vistik/ *adj*.

Yajur-Veda /yujooə' veedə, -'vaydə/ *noun* the second of the four sacred books of the Veda, consisting of a collection of mantras, verses, and sacrificial prayers.

yak¹ /yak/ *noun* (*pl* **yaks** *or collectively* **yak**) a large long-haired wild or domesticated ox of Tibet and nearby mountainous regions: *Bos grunniens*. [Tibetan *gyak*]

yak² *or* **yack** *noun informal* persistent, voluble, and usu trivial or irritating talk. [prob imitative]

yak³ *or* **yack** *verb intrans* (**yakked** *or* **yacked**, **yakking** *or* **yacking**) *informal* to talk persistently; to chatter.

yakitori /yaki'tawri/ *noun* a kebab consisting of small pieces of marinated chicken. [Japanese *yakitori*, from *yaki* roasting + *tori* bird, chicken]

yakka *or* **yacker** /'yakə/ *noun Aus, NZ, informal* work. [Jagara (an Aboriginal language), in the sense 'to work']

Yakut /ya'kooht/ *noun* (*pl* **Yakuts** *or collectively* **Yakut**) **1** a member of an indigenous people of NE Siberia. **2** the Turkic language of this people. ➤➤ **Yakut** *adj*. [via Russian from Yakut]

yakuza /yə'koohzə/ *noun* (*pl* **yakuza**) **1** (**the Yakuza**) an organized body of Japanese criminals. **2** a criminal belonging to this organization. [Japanese *yakuza*, from *ya* eight + *ku* nine + *za* three, alluding to the worst possible hand in a particular card game]

Yale /yayl/ *noun trademark* a type of lock that has a revolving barrel which is prevented from turning by a set of pins until the correct key is inserted. [named after Linus *Yale* Jnr d.1868, US locksmith who invented the mechanism]

yam /yam/ *noun* **1** any of several species of plants widely cultivated for their edible starchy tuberous roots: genus *Dioscorea*. **2** a tuberous root of any of these plants, used as a vegetable and a staple food in tropical areas. **3** *NAmer* a moist-fleshed usu orange sweet potato. [earlier *iname*, from Portuguese *inhame* and Spanish *ñame*, of West African origin]

yammer[1] /'yamə/ *verb intrans* (**yammered, yammering**) *informal* **1** to talk loudly or volubly; to clamour: *The purists are yammering for censorship.* **2** to wail or whimper. **3** to complain or grumble: *It's no good yammering at the umpire.* >> **yammerer** *noun*. [alteration of Middle English *yomeren* to murmur, be sad, from Old English *gēomrian*]

yammer[2] *noun informal* a yammering sound.

yang /yang/ *noun* in Chinese philosophy, the masculine active principle in nature that eternally interacts with its opposite and complementary principle, yin. Yang is expressed in positive forces and qualities, e.g. light, heat, and dryness. [Chinese (Pekingese) *yáng* the sun, male genitals, positive]

Yank /yangk/ *noun* **1** *informal, often derog* an American. **2** *NAmer, informal* somebody from New England or the northern USA; a Yankee. [short for YANKEE]

yank[1] *verb trans informal* to pull or extract (something) with a quick vigorous movement: *It won't take him long to yank that tooth out.* [origin unknown]

yank[2] *noun* a vigorous pull or jerk.

Yankee /'yangki/ *noun* **1** *informal* an American. **2** *NAmer, informal* somebody from New England or the northern USA. **3** *NAmer, informal* a Federal soldier in the Civil War. **4** *informal* a combination of bets, e.g. on horse races, covering four selections in different events in their eleven possible permutations of doubles, trebles, and a fourfold accumulator. >> **Yankee** *adj*. [perhaps from the Dutch names *Jantje* (dimin. of *Jan* John) or *Jan Kees* (John Cornelius), allegedly used as nicknames by early Dutch settlers in America]

yap[1] /yap/ *verb intrans* (**yapped, yapping**) **1** to bark in a high-pitched or snappish way; to yelp. **2** *informal* to talk in a shrill insistent querulous way; to scold. >> **yapper** *noun*, **yappy** *adj*. [imitative]

yap[2] *noun* **1** a quick sharp bark; a yelp. **2** *informal* foolish chatter.

yapok *or* **yapock** /yə'pok/ *noun* a grey and white S American aquatic opossum with webbed hind feet and a long tail: *Chironectes minimus*. [named after the *Oyapok*, a river in northern Brazil]

YAR *abbr* Yemen Arab Republic (international vehicle registration).

yarborough /'yahb(ə)rə/ *noun* a hand in bridge or whist containing no card higher than a nine. [named after Charles Anderson Worsley, second Earl of *Yarborough* d.1897, an English nobleman who allegedly bet 1000 to 1 against the dealing of such a hand]

yard[1] /yahd/ *noun* **1a** a unit of length equal to three feet (about 0.914m). **b** a unit of volume equal to one cubic yard (about 0.765m[3]). **2** a long spar tapered towards the ends to support and spread a sail. [Old English *gierd* spar]

yard[2] *noun* **1** *chiefly Brit.* **a** a small usu walled and often paved area open to the sky and adjacent to a building; a courtyard. **b** (*used in combinations*) the grounds of a specified building or group of buildings: *a farmyard; a churchyard.* **c** (*usu used in combinations*) an area with its buildings and facilities set aside for a usu specified business or activity: *a brickyard.* **2** *NAmer* a garden of a house: *Jem and I had always enjoyed the free run of Miss Maudie's yard if we kept out of her azaleas* — Harper Lee. **3** a system of tracks for the storage and maintenance of railway carriages and wagons and the making up of trains. **4** (**the Yard**) *Brit, informal* Scotland Yard. [Old English *geard* enclosure, yard]

yard[3] *verb trans* to drive (animals) into a restricted area; to herd or pen (them).

yardage[1] /'yahdij/ *noun* the length, extent, or volume of something as measured in yards.

yardage[2] *noun archaic* the use of a livestock enclosure at a railway station, or the charge for this. [YARD[2]]

yardarm *noun* either end of the yard of a square-rigged ship.

yardbird *noun* *NAmer, slang* **1** a military recruit. **2** a serviceman punished by being confined or assigned to menial tasks. **3** a convict.

Yardie /'yahdi/ *noun informal* a member of a West Indian criminal gang originating in Jamaica, *esp* one involved in drug dealing. [from YARD[2] in the West Indian sense 'house, home', used by expatriate Jamaicans as a term for Jamaica]

yardman *noun* (*pl* **yardmen**) **1** a person who works in a timber yard or a railway yard. **2** *NAmer* a handyman who does outdoor jobs.

yardmaster *noun* a person in charge of operations in a railway yard.

yard of ale *noun Brit* the amount of beer or ale, usu 1 or 2l (2 or 3pt), contained in a slender horn-shaped glass about 1m (3ft) tall, or the glass itself.

yard sale *noun chiefly NAmer* a sale of goods, usu household effects, held outdoors at a private house.

yardstick *noun* **1** a graduated measuring stick one yard (about 0.9m) long. **2** a standard basis of calculation or judgment; a criterion.

yarmulke *or* **yarmulka** /'yahmulkə/ *noun* a skullcap worn by *esp* Orthodox and Conservative Jewish males, in the synagogue and the home. [Yiddish *yarmolke* from Polish *jarmulka* skullcap]

yarn[1] /yahn/ *noun* **1** thread, *esp* a spun thread, e.g. of wool, cotton, or hemp, as prepared and used for weaving, knitting, and ropemaking. **2a** *informal* a narrative of adventures, *esp* a tall tale: *And all I ask is a merry yarn from a laughing fellow-rover* — John Masefield. **b** *Aus, NZ, informal* a conversation or chat. [Old English *gearn*; (sense 2) from the phrase *to spin a yarn* to tell a long story]

yarn[2] *verb intrans informal* **1** to tell a yarn. **2** *Aus, NZ* to chat.

yarn-dye *verb trans* to dye (yarn) before weaving or knitting.

yarran /'yarən/ *noun* a small Australian tree of the acacia family with hard, scented wood: *Acacia omalophylla*. [Kamilaroi *yarraan*]

yarrow /'yaroh/ *noun* a strong-scented Eurasian plant with dense heads of small usu white flowers: *Achillea millefolium*. [Old English *gearwe*]

yashmak /'yashmak/ *noun* a veil worn over the face by Muslim women, so that only the eyes remain exposed. [Turkish *yaşmak*]

yataghan /'yatəgan, -gən/ *noun* a sword without a guard used formerly by Muslims and typically having a long blade with a double curved edge. [Turkish *yatagan*]

yatter[1] /'yatə/ *verb intrans* (**yattered, yattering**) *informal* to chatter or prattle. [perhaps blend of YAP[1] and CHATTER[1]]

yatter[2] *noun informal* chatter or prattle.

yaup[1] /yawp/ *verb intrans* see YAWP[1].

yaup[2] *noun* see YAWP[2].

yaw[1] /yaw/ *verb intrans* **1** said of a ship: to deviate erratically from a straight course, e.g. when sailing with a following wind or sea. **2** said of an aircraft, spacecraft, or projectile: to deviate from a straight course, *esp* by side-to-side movement, the nose going to the left while the tail goes to the right and vice versa. [origin unknown]

yaw[2] *noun* the action of yawing; *esp* a side-to-side movement, e.g. of an aircraft, ship, or missile.

yawl /yawl/ *noun* **1** a two-masted, fore-and-aft rigged sailing vessel with sails set from a mainmast and a mizzenmast that is situated aft of the rudder. **2** a small boat carried on a ship. [Low German *jolle*]

yawn[1] /yawn/ *verb intrans* **1** to open the mouth wide and inhale, usu in reaction to fatigue or boredom. **2** to be menacingly wide, deep, and open; to gape: *a yawning chasm.* > *verb trans* to utter (something) with a yawn. >> **yawner** *noun*, **yawning** *adj*, **yawningly** *adv*. [Old English *geonian*]

yawn[2] *noun* **1** a deep usu involuntary intake of breath through the wide open mouth. **2** *informal* a boring thing or person: *She has even formed her own film and video group because she finds most training films 'a yawn a minute'* — David Oates, Derek Ezra.

yawp¹ or **yaup** /yawp/ *verb intrans* **1** to make a raucous noise; to squawk. **2** *NAmer* to clamour or complain. ➤➤➤ **yawper** *noun*. [Middle English *yolpen*, of imitative origin]

yawp² or **yaup** *noun* **1** a raucous noise; a squawk. **2** *NAmer* a clamour or complaint: *I sound my barbaric yawp over the roofs of the world* — Walt Whitman.

yaws /yawz/ *pl noun* (*treated as sing. or pl*) an infectious tropical disease marked by ulcerating sores. It is caused by a bacterium that enters via abrasions in the skin. [prob from Carib *yáya*]

y-axis *noun* **1** the vertical axis that intersects the horizontal x-axis in a Cartesian coordinate system having two axes at right angles. **2** that one of the three axes in a three-dimensional rectangular coordinate system that is not the x-axis or z-axis.

Yb *abbr* the chemical symbol for ytterbium.

Y chromosome *noun* a SEX CHROMOSOME (strand of gene-carrying material concerned with the inheritance of sex) that usu occurs paired with a dissimilar chromosome in one sex and does not occur in the other sex. In many animals, including human beings, the inheritance of a Y chromosome and an X chromosome determines that the sex of the animal is male: compare X CHROMOSOME.

yclept or **ycleped** /i'klept/ *adj archaic* called or named. [Old English *geclipod*, past part. of *clipian* to cry out, name]

yd *abbr* yard.

ye¹ /yee/ *pronoun archaic* or *dialect* the ones being addressed; you: *O ye of little faith* — Bible. [Old English *gē*, pl of *thu* THOU¹: compare YOU]

ye² /dhee, yee/ *definite article* used as an archaism: the: *Ye Olde Gifte Shoppe.*

Word history
alteration of Old English *þe* THE¹; from the use by early printers of the letter *y* to represent the *þ* in manuscripts. The runic character *þ* was used in English to represent the sound /th/ until the 15th cent., but in many manuscripts from the 14th cent. onwards it was increasingly represented by a character indistinguishable from *y*. After the runic character had fallen out of use, *y* continued in use as an abbreviation for *th* in some early printed books and in manuscript throughout the 17th cent. and probably later. Usually, however, it was written with the following character in a superior position to show that it was an abbreviation rather than a word. *Ye* was never pronounced /yee/ until it was revived in modern times as a largely jocular archaism, usually to suggest picturesque quaintness.

yea¹ /yay/ *adv* **1** *archaic* or *formal* more than this; indeed: *Yea, even unto the second and third generation.* **2** *archaic* yes: *In russet yeas and honest kersey noes* — Shakespeare. [Old English *gēa*]

yea² *noun* **1** an affirmation or assent. **2** an affirmative vote in the US congress, or a person casting such a vote.

yeah /yeə/ *adv informal* yes. [by alteration]

yean /yeen/ *verb trans archaic* said of a sheep or goat: to produce (young). [Middle English *yenen* from Old English *ēanian*]

yeanling /'yeenling/ *noun* a lamb or kid.

year /yiə/ *noun* **1** the period of about 365¼ solar days required for one revolution of the earth round the sun. **2a** a cycle in the Gregorian calendar of 365 or 366 days divided into twelve months beginning with January and ending with December; a calendar year or civil year. **b** a period of time equal to one year of the Gregorian calendar but beginning at a different time. **3** a calendar year, specified usu by a number. **4** a period of time, e.g. that in which a school is in session, other than a calendar year. **5** (*treated as sing. or pl*) the body of students who enter a school, university, etc in one academic year. **6** *informal* (*in pl*) a very long time. **7** (*in pl*). **a** age: *He was a man in years but a child in understanding.* **b** old age: *He was beginning to show his years.* ❋ **the year dot** *informal* a time as long ago as anyone can remember. **year in, year out** for an indefinite or seemingly endless number of successive years. [Old English *gēar*]

yearbook *noun* **1** a book published yearly as a report or summary of statistics or facts. **2** a school publication in the USA, compiled by students in their final year to serve as a record of the year's activities.

yearling /'yiəling/ *noun* **1** an animal one year old or in its second year. **2** a racehorse between 1 January of the year following its birth and the next 1 January. ➤➤➤ **yearling** *adj*.

yearling bond *noun* a BOND¹ (certificate of debt repayable at a fixed time) with a life of one year.

yearly *adj* **1** done or occurring once every year; annual. **2** reckoned by the year. ➤➤➤ **yearly** *adv*.

yearn /yuhn/ *verb intrans* **1** to long persistently, wistfully, or sadly: *Give me your tired, your poor, your huddled masses yearning to breathe free* — Emma Lazarus. **2** *archaic* to feel tenderness or compassion: *Her heart yearned towards the child.* ➤➤➤ **yearner** *noun*, **yearning** *adj*, **yearningly** *adv*. [Old English *giernan*]

year of grace *noun* a year of the Christian era: *the year of grace 1982.*

year-on-year *adj* said of figures, etc: compared with corresponding figures, etc from the previous year.

year-round *adj* effective, employed, or operating for the full year; not seasonal: *a year-round resort.*

yeast /yeest/ *noun* **1** a minute fungus that is able to ferment sugars and other carbohydrates and reproduces by budding: genus *Saccharomyces*. **2a** a commercial product that is used for the fermentation of alcohol or for raising bread and that contains yeast plants in a moist or dry medium. **b** a yellowish surface froth or sediment that consists largely of yeast cells also used *esp* in the making of alcoholic drinks and as a raising agent in baking. **3** a medicinal preparation containing yeast, usu in the form of tablets, used to treat vitamin B deficiency. **4** something that causes ferment or activity. [Old English *gist*]

yeasty *adj* (**yeastier, yeastiest**) **1** of, resembling, or relating to yeast. **2a** frothing and foaming. **b** churning with growth and change; turbulent. **3** trivial or frivolous. ➤➤➤ **yeastily** *adv*, **yeastiness** *noun*.

yegg /yeg, yayg/ *noun chiefly NAmer, slang* a safecracker or burglar. [origin unknown]

yell¹ /yel/ *verb intrans* to utter a sharp loud cry, scream, or shout: *We all yelled for help.* ➤ *verb trans* to utter or declare (something) in a scream; to shout (it): *He was yelling curses at someone in the street.* ➤➤➤ **yeller** *noun*. [Old English *giellan*]

yell² *noun* **1** a sharp loud scream or shout. **2** *NAmer* an organized rhythmic chant or shout, *esp* one used to support a sports team.

yellow¹ /'yeloh/ *adj* **1** of the colour of egg yolk or lemons, between orange and green in the spectrum. **2** *offensive* said of people originating from the Far East: having a yellow or light brown complexion or skin. **3** yellowish through age, disease, or discoloration; sallow. **4** said of writing: featuring sensational or scandalous items or ordinary news sensationally distorted. **5** *informal* dishonourable or cowardly: *You're too yellow to fight.* ➤➤➤ **yellowness** *noun*. [Old English *geolu*]

yellow² *noun* **1** the colour of egg yolk or lemons, between orange and green in the spectrum. **2** the yolk of an egg. **3** (*in pl, but treated as sing.*) any of several plant diseases caused *esp* by viruses and marked by yellowing of the foliage and stunting. ➤➤➤ **yellowy** *adj*.

yellow³ *verb intrans* to become yellow. ➤ *verb trans* to make (something) yellow.

yellow archangel *noun* = ARCHANGEL (2).

yellow-belly *noun* (*pl* **yellow-bellies**) *informal* a coward. ➤➤➤ **yellow-bellied** *adj*.

yellow bile *noun* in medieval physiology, the one of the four humours that was believed to be secreted by the liver and to cause irascibility.

yellow card *noun* a yellow card held up by a football referee to indicate the taking of a player's name for committing an offence: compare RED CARD.

yellow-card *verb trans* to show a yellow card to (a player).

yellow fever *noun* an often fatal infectious disease of warm regions caused by a virus transmitted by mosquitoes and marked by fever, jaundice, and often bleeding.

yellowfin *noun* = YELLOWFIN TUNA.

yellowfin tuna *noun* a rather small, widely distributed tuna with yellow-tipped fins and delicate light flesh: *Thunnus albacares*.

yellow flag *noun* **1** a yellow Eurasian iris that grows in damp places: *Iris pseudacorus*. **2** a ship's quarantine flag, usu indicating disease on board. **3** a flag used in motor racing to warn drivers of a hazard ahead.

yellowhammer *noun* a common Eurasian bunting, the male of which is largely yellow with a reddish brown back: *Emberiza citrinella*. [alteration of *yelambre*, from YELLOW¹ + a second element which may be from Old English *amore*, a kind of bird, or Old English *hama* covering, feathers, or from German *Ammer* bunting]

yellow jack *noun* **1** *archaic* = YELLOW FEVER. **2** a flag raised on ships in quarantine.

yellow jasmine *noun* a climbing plant originating from the southeastern USA, with sweet-smelling, trumpet-shaped yellow flowers: *Gelsemium sempervirens.*

yellow jersey *noun* in cycle racing, a yellow jersey awarded to the winner of a particular stage in a race such as the Tour de France, or to the eventual winner.

yellow metal *noun* a type of brass consisting of 60% copper and 40% zinc.

yellow ochre *adj* of an orange-yellow colour. ➤➤ **yellow ochre** *noun.*

Yellow Pages *pl noun trademark* a telephone directory that lists organizations and services alphabetically within sections classified according to the nature of their business.

yellow peril *noun* (**the yellow peril**) *offensive* a danger to Western civilization held to arise from expansion of the power and influence of the peoples of China or SE Asia.

yellow underwing *noun* a common European moth with pale or brownish front wings and yellow hind wings: *Noctua pronuba.*

yelp[1] /yelp/ *verb intrans* to utter a sharp quick shrill cry: *The dog yelped when I stepped on its tail.* ➤➤ **yelper** *noun.* [Old English *gielpan* to boast, exult]

yelp[2] *noun* a sharp shrill cry or bark.

Yemeni /'yeməni/ *noun* a native or inhabitant of Yemen in SW Arabia. ➤➤ **Yemeni** *adj.*

yen[1] /yen/ *noun* (*pl* **yen**) the basic monetary unit of Japan, divided into 100 sen. [Japanese *en*, literally 'round']

yen[2] *noun informal* a strong desire or inclination; a longing. [obsolete English slang *yen-yen* craving for opium, from Chinese (Cantonese) *yin-yahn*, from *yin* opium + *yahn* craving]

yen[3] *verb intrans* (**yenned, yenning**) to yearn.

yeo. *abbr* yeomanry.

yeoman /'yohmən/ *noun* (*pl* **yeomen**) **1** formerly, a small farmer who cultivated his own land; *specif* one belonging to a class of English freeholders below the gentry. **2** formerly, a servant or minor official in a royal or noble household. **3** *Brit* a member of the yeomanry. **4a** in the British navy, a petty officer who carries out visual signalling. **b** in the US navy, a petty officer who performs clerical duties. [Middle English *yoman* attendant in a noble household, freeholder, prob contraction of *yong man* young man]

yeomanly *adj* **1** relating to a yeoman. **2** having the qualities attributed to a yeoman; sturdy and loyal. ➤➤ **yeomanly** *adv.*

yeoman of signals *noun* = YEOMAN (4A).

Yeoman of the Guard *noun* a member of a military corps attached to the British Royal Household who serve as ceremonial attendants of the sovereign and as warders of the Tower of London.

yeomanry /'yohmənri/ *noun* **1** (*treated as sing. or pl*) small landed proprietors considered as a group or class. **2** a British volunteer cavalry force created from yeomen in 1761 as a home defence force and reorganized in 1907 as part of the territorial force.

yep /yep/ *adv informal* yes. [by alteration]

yer /yə/ *adj nonstandard* your. [by alteration]

-yer *suffix* = -ER[2].

yerba /'yuhbə, 'yeəbə/ *noun* = MATÉ.

yerba maté /'mahtay/ *noun* = MATÉ. [American Spanish *yerba mate*, from *yerba* herb + *mate* maté]

yes[1] /yes/ *interj* **1** used in answers expressing affirmation, agreement, or willingness; contrasted with no: *Are you ready? Yes, I am.* **2** used in answers correcting or contradicting a negative assertion: *Don't say that! Yes, I will.* **3** used to indicate uncertainty or polite interest or attentiveness: *Yes? What do you want?* **4** used to express great satisfaction or delight. [Old English *gēse*]

yes[2] *noun* (*pl* **yeses** *or* **yesses**) an affirmative reply or vote.

yeshiva *or* **yeshivah** /yə'sheevə/ *noun* (*pl* **yeshivas** *or* **yeshivahs** *or* **yeshivoth** /-voht, -vohth/) **1** a school for Talmudic study. **2** an Orthodox Jewish rabbinic seminary. **3** a Jewish day school providing secular and religious instruction. [late Hebrew *yĕshībhāh*]

yes-man *noun* (*pl* **yes-men**) *informal* somebody who agrees with or supports everything said by a superior; a sycophant.

yester- *comb. form literary or archaic* forming words, denoting: a period of time before the present one: *yesteryear.* [Old English *giestra* yesterday]

yesterday[1] /'yestəday, -di/ *adv* **1** on the day before today: *I saw him yesterday.* **2** in the recent past. [Old English *glestran dæg*, from *giestran* yesterday + *dæg* DAY]

yesterday[2] *noun* **1** the day before today. **2** recent time; time not long past: *the fashions of yesterday.*

yesteryear /'yestəyiə/ *noun literary* **1** the years of the fairly recent past. **2** last year. ➤➤ **yesteryear** *adv.* [*yester* as in YESTERDAY[1] + YEAR]

yet[1] /yet/ *adv* **1a** up to this or that time; so far: *She hasn't had breakfast yet.* **b** only having done so much or got so far; now: *Carry on, you can't stop yet.* **2a** as of now; still: *We have yet to learn the truth.* **b** at some future time and despite present appearances: *We may win yet.* **3a** used to indicate an addition to an existing number or series of things; in addition: *This is yet another reason for treating the offer with caution.* **b** used to indicate a still greater degree; even: *They were travelling at a yet higher speed.* **4** nevertheless: *It is strange and yet true.* ✳ **yet again** one more time; as often before: *The experiment failed yet again.* [Old English *gīet*]

yet[2] *conj* but nevertheless: *I don't want to go, yet I can't think of a good excuse not to.*

yeti /'yeti/ *noun* = ABOMINABLE SNOWMAN. [Tibetan *yeh-teh* small manlike animal]

yettie /'yeti/ *noun chiefly NAmer, informal* a young person making his or her fortune in the Internet-based economy. [*young, entrepreneurial, technology-based* + -IE]

yew /yooh/ *noun* **1** any of several species of evergreen coniferous trees and shrubs with stiff straight leaves and red fruits: genus *Taxus.* **2** the fine-grained and springy wood of any of these trees. [Old English *īw*]

Y-fronts *pl noun Brit, trademark* men's closely fitting underpants in which the front seams take the form of an inverted Y: *I know I ought to plunge headlong into the Y-fronts versus boxer shorts debate — She.*

YHA *abbr Brit* Youth Hostels Association.

YHWH *noun* Yahweh: compare TETRAGRAMMATON.

yid /yid/ *noun* (*also* **Yid**) *offensive* a Jew. [Yiddish *yid* from early High German *Jude, Jüde*, from Old High German *Judo, Judeo*, from Latin *Judaeus*: see JEW]

Yiddish *noun* a language closely related to High German containing elements of Hebrew and Slavonic that is usu written in Hebrew characters and is spoken by Jews chiefly in or from E Europe. ➤➤ **Yiddish** *adj.*

Word history

Yiddish *yidish*, short for *yidish daytsh* Jewish German. Yiddish words that have passed into English include *bagel, chutzpah, goy, kosher, nosh, pogrom, schlep,* and *schmaltz.* Most have entered American English as a consequence of the immigration of almost three million Yiddish-speaking Ashkenazi Jews into the USA between 1880 and 1910, although a few words of Yiddish origin (such as *shtum*) are found only in British English.

Yiddisher[1] *adj* **1** Yiddish. **2** Jewish. [Yiddish *Yiddisher*]

Yiddisher[2] *noun* **1** a speaker of Yiddish. **2** a Jew.

yield[1] /yeeld, yiəld/ *verb trans* **1a** to bear or bring forth (something) as a natural product: *The tree yields good fruit.* **b** to produce (something) as a result of expended effort: *Properly handled this soil should yield good crops.* **2** to produce (money or its equivalent) as revenue: *The tax is expected to yield millions; This bond yields 12%.* **3a** (*often* + up) to give up possession of (e.g. a position of advantage or point of superiority); to relinquish (it). **b** to grant or concede (a point in dispute). **4a** (*often* + up) to surrender or submit (oneself) to somebody. **b** to give (oneself) up to an inclination, temptation, or habit. ➤ *verb intrans* **1a** (*often* + to) to give way to pressure or influence; to submit to urging, persuasion, or entreaty. **b** to give way under physical force, e.g. bending, stretching, or breaking. **2** to give up and cease resistance or contention; to surrender or submit. **3a** (*often* + to) to give place or precedence; to acknowledge the superiority of somebody or something: *I yield to your greater experience in these matters.* **b** to give way to another speaker in a parliament. **4** to be fruitful or productive. **5** to give way to other traffic. ➤➤ **yielder** *noun.* [Old English *gieldan*]

yield[2] *noun* **1** something yielded or produced, or the amount of it: *New plant varieties have enabled us to increase the yield of wheat per acre.* **2** the capacity for yielding produce: *a high-yield strain of wheat.*

yielding *adj* **1** lacking rigidity or firmness; flexible. **2** tending to give way in disputes; compliant. ⟫⟫ **yieldingly** *adv*.

yield point *noun* the degree of stress under which an elastic material ceases to behave elastically.

yin /yin/ *noun* in Chinese philosophy, the feminine passive principle in nature that eternally interacts with its opposite and complementary principle, yang. Yin is expressed in qualities of darkness, cold, wetness, etc. [Chinese (Pekingese) *yin* the moon, negative, feminine]

yip¹ /yip/ *verb intrans* (**yipped, yipping**) to utter a short sharp cry. [imitative]

yip² *noun* a short sharp cry; a yelp.

yippee /yi'pee/ *interj* used to express exuberant delight or triumph.

yippie *or* **yippy** /'yipi/ *noun* (*pl* **yippies**) a politically active hippie, *esp* in the USA in the 1960s. [blend of the initials of *Youth International Party*, an organization founded in the US in 1968 which opposed the Vietnam War and criticized the American economic and political system, and HIPPIE]

yips /'yips/ *pl noun* (**the yips**) *informal* acute nervousness or trembling when about to play a stroke or perform some other action in sport: *The yips once again destroyed the German's putting action* — The Guardian.

-yl *suffix* forming nouns, denoting: a chemical radical: *ethyl*; *carbonyl*; *phenyl*. [Greek *hylē* matter, material, literally 'wood']

ylang-ylang *or* **ilang-ilang** /,eelang 'eelang/ *noun* **1** an essential oil distilled from the fragrant yellow flowers of a Malayan tree and used in perfumery and aromatherapy. **2** the tree of the custard-apple family from which this oil is obtained: *Cananga odorata*. [Tagalog *ilang-ilang*]

ylem /'ieləm/ *noun* according to the big bang theory, the primordial matter from which the chemical elements are said to have been formed in the original explosion that brought the universe into being. [Latin *hylem*, accusative of *hyle* matter, from Greek *hylē* wood]

YMCA *abbr* Young Men's Christian Association.

-yne *suffix* forming nouns, denoting: an unsaturated compound containing a triple bond: *alkyne*.

yo /yoh/ *interj informal* used as a greeting or as a way of attracting somebody's attention.

yob /yob/ *noun Brit, slang* a loutish young man, *esp* a hooligan. ⟫⟫ **yobbery** *noun*, **yobbish** *adj*, **yobbishly** *adv*, **yobbishness** *noun*, **yobby** *adj*. [back slang for BOY¹]

yobbo /'yoboh/ *noun* (*pl* **yobbos** *or* **yobboes**) *Brit, slang* = YOB.

yodel¹ /'yohdl/ *verb* (**yodelled, yodelling,** *NAmer* **yodeled, yodeling**) ➤ *verb intrans* to sing, shout, or call by suddenly changing from a natural voice to a falsetto and back. ➤ *verb trans* to sing, shout, or call (something) by yodelling. ⟫⟫ **yodeller** *noun*. [German *jodeln*]

yodel² *noun* a yodelled song, shout, or cry.

yoga /'yohgə/ *noun* **1** (**Yoga**) a Hindu philosophy teaching the control or suppression of all activity of body, mind, and will so that the self may attain liberation. **2** a system of exercises for attaining bodily or mental control and well-being. ⟫⟫ **yogic** *adj*. [Sanskrit *yoga*, literally 'yoking', from *yunakti* he yokes]

yogh /yohk, yohg, yohkh/ *noun* a letter (ȝ) which in Old and Middle English represented a velar or palatal fricative. The sound is not used in modern English but traces of it survive in the spellings *w*, e.g. in *own*, and *gh*, e.g. in *bough*. [Middle English *yogh, zogh*, of unknown origin]

yoghourt *or* **yoghurt** /'yogət/ *noun* see YOGURT.

yogi /'yohgi/ *noun* (*pl* **yogis** *or* **yogin** /'yohgin/) **1** somebody who practises or is a master of yoga. **2** (**Yogi**) an adherent of Yoga philosophy. [Sanskrit *yogin*, from *yoga*: see YOGA]

yogurt *or* **yoghurt** *or* **yoghourt** /'yogət/ *noun* a slightly acid semisolid food made of milk fermented by bacteria. [Turkish *yogurt*]

yo-heave-ho *interj* = HEAVE-HO¹.

yohimbine /yoh'himbeen, -bin/ *noun* a drug obtained from an African tree, used as a tranquillizer and also as an aphrodisiac: formula $C_{21}H_{26}N_2O_3$. [from *yohimbe* (the tree whose bark yields the drug), of Bantu origin]

yo-ho-ho *interj* **1** *dated* used to attract attention. **2** *archaic* used by seamen as a chant while hauling ropes.

yoicks /yoyks/ *interj* used as a cry of encouragement to foxhounds.

yoke¹ /yohk/ *noun* **1** a bar or frame by which two draught animals, e.g. oxen, are joined at the heads or necks for working together. **2** a frame fitted to somebody's shoulders to carry a load, e.g. two buckets, in two equal portions. **3** an arched device formerly laid on the neck of a defeated person to symbolize defeat, *esp* in a triumphal procession. **4** a fitted or shaped piece at the top of a garment from which the rest hangs. **5** a crosspiece on a rudder to which steering lines are attached. **6a** something that is felt to be oppressive or burdensome. **b** a tie or link; *esp* marriage. **7** (*treated as sing. or pl*) two animals yoked or worked together. [Old English *geoc*]

yoke² *verb trans* **1** to put a yoke on (e.g. a pair of oxen). **2** to connect (two things) as if by a yoke; to couple (them).

yokel /'yohkl/ *noun* a naive or gullible rustic; a country bumpkin. [perhaps from English dialect *yokel* green woodpecker, of imitative origin]

yolk /yohk/ *noun* **1** the usu yellow spheroidal mass of stored food that forms the inner portion of the egg of a bird or reptile and is surrounded by the white. **2** a mass of protein, lecithin, cholesterol, etc that is stored in an ovum as food for the developing embryo. ⟫⟫ **yolked** *adj*, **yolky** *adj*. [Old English *geoloca*, from *geolu* YELLOW¹]

yolk sac *noun* a membranous sac attached to an embryo and containing yolk which passes to the intestine through a narrow tubular stalk. It serves as food for the developing embryo of some animals, e.g. fishes, amphibians, and reptiles, but is much reduced and nonfunctional in mammals with placentas.

Yom Kippur /,yom ki'pooə, 'kipə/ *noun* a Jewish festival observed with fasting and prayer on the tenth day of the Jewish year; the Day of Atonement. [Hebrew *yōm kippūr*, from *yōm* day + *kippūr* atonement]

yomp¹ /yomp/ *verb intrans Brit, slang* said of a soldier: to march or trek over difficult terrain. [Brit military slang, of unknown origin]

yomp² *noun Brit, informal* a difficult march or trek.

yon /yon/ *adj and adv literary or dialect* = YONDER. [Old English *geon*]

yonder /'yondə/ *adj and adv archaic or dialect* over there. [Middle English, from *yond* (from Old English *geond*) + *-er* as in HITHER¹]

yoni /'yohni/ *noun* (*pl* **yonis**) a stylized representation of the female genitals used in Hindu temples to symbolize the feminine cosmic principle: compare LINGA. [Sanskrit *yoni* vulva]

yonks /yongks/ *noun Brit, informal* a long time; ages: *We haven't seen her for yonks*. [origin unknown]

yoo-hoo /'yooh hooh/ *interj* used to attract attention.

yore /yaw/ ✳ **of yore** *literary* long ago. [Old English *geāra* long ago, from *gēar* YEAR]

york /yawk/ *verb trans* in cricket, to bowl (a batsman) out with a yorker. [back-formation from YORKER]

yorker *noun* in cricket, a ball bowled to bounce on the popping crease and so pass under the bat. [prob from *Yorkshire*, where it was allegedly introduced]

yorkie /'yawki/ *noun informal* = YORKSHIRE TERRIER.

Yorkist /'yawkist/ *adj* relating to the English royal house of York that ruled from 1461 to 1485. ⟫⟫ **Yorkist** *noun*. [named after Edward, Duke of *York* (Edward IV of England) d.1483]

Yorks /yawks/ *abbr* Yorkshire.

Yorkshire fog /'yawkshə/ *noun* a perennial grass with a velvety stem: *Holcus lanatus*. [*Yorkshire*, county in N England + FOG³]

Yorkshireman *noun* (*pl* **Yorkshiremen**) a man who was born or brought up in Yorkshire.

Yorkshire pudding *noun* a savoury baked pudding made from a batter and usu eaten before or with roast beef.

Yorkshire terrier *noun* a compact toy terrier of a breed with long straight silky hair mostly bluish grey but tan on the head and chest.

Yorkshire tyke *noun Brit, informal* = TYKE (4).

Yorkshirewoman *noun* (*pl* **Yorkshirewomen**) a woman who was born or brought up in Yorkshire.

Yoruba /'yoroobə/ *noun* (*pl* **Yorubas** *or collectively* **Yoruba**) **1** a member of an African people of Benin and SW Nigeria. **2** the Kwa language of the Yoruba, one of the national languages of Nigeria. ⟫⟫ **Yoruba** *adj*. [the Yoruba name]

you /yə, yoo, *strong* yooh/ *pronoun* (*pl* **you**) **1** used as subject or object: the person being addressed: *Can I pour you a cup of tea?* **2** used as an exclamation with vocatives: *You angel; You scoundrels.* **3** a person; one: *It's funny, when you come to think of it.* ✳ **you and yours** you and your family.

Word history

Old English *ēow*, dative and accusative of *gē* YE¹. In the 14th cent. *you* began to be used also for the nominative plural YE¹, and during the 15th cent. for the singular forms THOU¹ and THEE, orig to show respect when addressing a superior, but later also to an equal, although *thou* and *thee* were still used when addressing a child or one lower in the social scale and, paradoxically, God. By 1700 *you* was the usual form for the nominative, accusative, and dative cases, singular and plural, *thou* and the other singular forms being used mainly in dialect, as archaisms, and by the Society of Friends (Quakers) as a sign of their disregard of social distinctions.

you-all /yawl/ *pronoun NAmer* used *esp* in the southern USA in addressing two or more people or sometimes one person as representing also another or others; you.

you'd /yəd, yood, *strong* yoohd/ *contraction* **1** you had. **2** you would.

you-know-where *noun* a place understood but unspecified.

you-know-who *noun* somebody understood but unspecified.

you'll /yəl, yool, *strong* yoohl/ *contraction* **1** you will. **2** you shall.

young¹ /yung/ *adj* (**younger** /'yunggə/, **youngest** /'yunggist/) **1** in the first or an early stage of life, growth, or development. **2** recently come into being or not yet far advanced; new: *a young industry; The night is young.* **3** of an early or tender age for eating or drinking: *fresh young lamb.* **4** suitable for or having the characteristics, e.g. vigour or gaiety, of young people: *That young style of dress just makes her look silly.* ➤➤ **youngish** /'yunggish, yungish/ *adj.* [Old English *geong*]

young² *pl noun* **1** (*treated as pl*) immature offspring, *esp* of an animal. **2** (**the young**) young people; youth. ✳ **with young** said of a female animal: pregnant.

young blood *noun* freshness, vigour, etc brought by new people joining an organization.

youngling /'yungling/ *noun literary* a young person or animal.

young offender *noun Brit* a person under the age of 18 who has been convicted of a criminal offence.

Young's modulus *noun* a measure of elasticity equal to the ratio of the applied load per unit area of cross section to the increase in length per unit length. [named after Thomas *Young* d.1829, English physicist]

youngster /'yungstə/ *noun* a young person or creature.

Young Turk *noun* **1** a member of a revolutionary party in Turkey in the early 20th cent. **2** a young person who agitates for radical change.

younker /'yungkə/ *noun dated* **1** a young man. **2** a child or youngster. [Dutch *jonker* young nobleman, from early Dutch *jonchere*, from *jonc* young + *here* lord, master]

your /yə, *strong* yaw/ *adj* **1a** belonging to or associated with you: *your house; your children; your being chosen; your acquittal.* **b** belonging to or associated with an indefinitely indicated person or people in general: *When you face north, east is on your right.* **2** used in titles: *Your Majesty.* **3** *informal* used to indicate something or somebody well-known and characteristic: *He's not your typical commuter.* [Old English *ēower*, genitive of *gē* YE¹]

Usage note

your or **you're**? *Your* is the possessive form of *you* (*It's your turn now; May I borrow your pen?*) and should not be confused with *you're*, which is pronounced the same, but is the shortened form of *you are*: *You're not as young as you were; I hope you're not getting bored.*

you're /yə, yaw, *strong* yooə/ *contraction* you are.

Usage note

you're or **your**? See note at YOUR.

yours /yawz/ *pronoun* (*pl* **yours**) the one or ones that belong to you or are associated with you: *Is this car yours?; Yours are on the table; children younger than yours.* ✳ **of yours** belonging to or associated with you: *friends of yours.*

yourself /yə'self, yaw'self/ *pronoun* (*pl* **yourselves** /yə'selvz, yaw'selvz/) **1** used reflexively to refer to the person or people addressed: *Did you hurt yourselves?* **2** used for emphasis: *Carry it yourself.* **3** = ONESELF. ✳ **be yourself** to be fit or healthy or as normal: *You'll soon be yourself again.*

youth /yoohth/ *noun* (*pl* **youths** /yoohdhz/) **1** the time of life when one is young, *esp* adolescence: *He lived there in his youth.* **2a** a young male adolescent. **b** (*treated as sing. or pl*) young people: *An author ought to write for the youth of his own generation, the critics of the next, and the schoolmasters of ever afterwards* — F Scott Fitzgerald. **3** the quality or state of being youthful: *My youth may wear and waste, but it shall never rust in my possession* — Congreve. [Old English *geoguth*; related to Old English *geong* YOUNG¹]

youth club *noun* a local organization providing leisure activities for young people, or the premises where such a club meets.

youthful /'yoohthf(ə)l/ *adj* **1** relating to or characteristic of youth: *A youthful passion for abstracted devotion should not be encouraged* — Dr Johnson. **2** not yet mature or old; young. ➤➤ **youthfully** *adv,* **youthfulness** *noun.*

youth hostel *noun* a lodging providing inexpensive bed and breakfast accommodation, *esp* for young travellers or hikers. ➤➤ **youth-hosteller** *noun,* **youth-hostelling** *noun.*

Youth Training Scheme *noun* a government scheme in Britain that formerly provided training and temporary work for school leavers.

you've /yəv, yoov, *strong* yoohv/ *contraction* you have.

yowl¹ /yowl/ *verb intrans* to utter the loud long wail of a cat or dog in pain or distress. [Middle English *yowlen*, of imitative origin]

yowl² *noun* a yowling cry.

yo-yo¹ /'yohyoh/ *noun* (*pl* **yo-yos**) **1** *trademark* a toy that consists of two discs separated by a deep groove in which a string is attached and wound and that is made to fall and rise when held by the string. **2** *chiefly NAmer, informal* a fool. [native name in Philippines]

yo-yo² *verb intrans* (**yo-yoes** or **yo-yos, yo-yoed, yo-yoing**) to fluctuate.

yr *abbr* **1** year. **2** younger. **3** your.

yrs *abbr* **1** years. **2** used as the closing formula of a letter: yours.

YTS *abbr Brit* Youth Training Scheme.

ytterbium /i'tuhbi·əm/ *noun* a silver-white metallic chemical element of the rare-earth group that resembles and occurs with yttrium: symbol Yb, atomic number 70. [scientific Latin, named after *Ytterby*, a town in Sweden where the first rare-earth mineral was found]

yttrium /'itri·əm/ *noun* a greyish white metallic chemical element that occurs naturally in various minerals, and is used as a compound to provide the red phosphor in colour television: symbol Y, atomic number 39. [scientific Latin, from *yttria* yttrium oxide, irreg from *Ytterby*: see YTTERBIUM]

YU *abbr* Yugoslavia (international vehicle registration).

yuan /'yooh·ən, yooh'ahn/ *noun* (*pl* **yuan**) the basic monetary unit of China, divided into 10 jiao or 100 fen. [Chinese (Pekingese) *yuan*, literally 'round']

yucca /'yukə/ *noun* any of a genus of sometimes treelike plants of the agave family with long often rigid leaves and a large cluster of white flowers: genus *Yucca*. [Latin genus name, from Spanish *yuca*, from Taino]

yuck or **yuk** /yuk/ *interj informal* used to express a sense of disgust and revulsion *esp* at something filthy, gooey, or messy. ➤➤ **yucky** *adj,* **yukky** *adj.* [imitative]

Yugoslav /'yoohgəslahv/ *noun* a native or inhabitant of Yugoslavia. ➤➤ **Yugoslav** *adj,* **Yugoslavian** *noun and adj.*

yuk /yuk/ *interj* see YUCK.

yule /yoohl/ *noun* (*also* **Yule**) *archaic* Christmas. [Old English *gēol*]

yule log *noun* **1** a large log formerly put on the hearth on Christmas Eve as the foundation of the fire. **2** a chocolate cake in the shape of a log, traditionally eaten at Christmas.

yuletide /'yoohltied/ *noun* (*also* **Yuletide**) *archaic* Christmas.

yummy /'yumi/ *adj* (**yummier, yummiest**) *informal* highly attractive or pleasing, *esp* to the taste; delicious. [from YUM-YUM]

yum-yum /,yum 'yum/ *interj informal* used to express pleasurable satisfaction, *esp* in the taste of food. [imitative of the sound of smacking the lips]

Yupik /'yoopik/ *noun* (*pl* **Yupiks** or *collectively* **Yupik**) **1** a member of an Eskimo people of Alaska, the Aleutian Islands, and Siberia. **2** any of the Eskimo languages of the Yupik. ➤➤ **Yupik** *adj.* [Alaskan Yupik *Yup'ik*, literally 'real person']

yuppie *or* **yuppy** /'yupi/ *noun* (*pl* **yuppies**) *informal, derog* a young person in a professional job with a high income and a fashionable lifestyle. ➤➤ **yuppiedom** *noun.* [from the initials of *young urban professional* + -IE]

yuppie flu *noun informal, derog* = CHRONIC FATIGUE SYNDROME.

yuppify /'yupifie/ *verb trans* (**yuppifies, yuppified, yuppifying**) *informal, derog* to change (e.g. an area) to make it more attractive to yuppies or more in keeping with their lifestyle. ➤➤ **yuppification** /-fi'kayshən/ *noun.*

yuppy /'yupi/ *noun* (*pl* **yuppies**) see YUPPIE.

yurt /yooət/ *noun* a collapsible domed tent of skins or felt used by nomads of Mongolia, Siberia, and Turkey. [Russian *yurta* from Turkic *yurt* dwelling]

Yuwaalaraay /yoo'wahlərie/ *noun* an Aboriginal language of New South Wales. [local name]

YV *abbr* Venezuela (international vehicle registration).

YWCA *abbr* Young Women's Christian Association.

Z¹ *or* **z** *noun* (*pl* **Z's** *or* **Zs** *or* **z's**) **1a** the 26th letter of the English alphabet. **b** a written character or design denoting this letter. **c** the sound represented by this letter, one of the English consonants. **2** an item designated as Z, *esp* the 26th in a series. ✳ **catch some/a few Zs** *chiefly NAmer, informal* to have a sleep.

Z² *abbr* Zambia (international vehicle registration).

ZA *abbr* Zuid Afrika (international vehicle registration for South Africa).

zabaglione /zabə'lyohni/ *noun* a thick creamy dessert made by whipping eggs, sugar, and Marsala wine over hot water. [Italian *zabaglione*]

zaffre *or* **zaffer** /'zafə/ *noun* an impure oxide of cobalt used *esp* as a blue ceramic colouring. [Italian *zaffera* from French *safre*]

zaibatsu /zie'batsooh/ *noun* (*pl* **zaibatsu**) a cartel or family group that controls a Japanese business or industry. [Japanese *zaibatsu*, from *zai* wealth + *batsu* clique]

zaïre /zie'iə, zah'iə/ *noun* (*pl* **zaïre**) the basic monetary unit of the Democratic Republic of Congo (formerly Zaire). [French *zaïre* from *Zaïre*, a local name for the River Congo in central Africa]

Zairean *or* **Zairian** /zie'iəri·ən, zah-/ *noun* a native or inhabitant of Zaire, known since 1997 as the Democratic Republic of Congo. ➤➤ **Zairean** *adj*.

Zambian /'zambi·ən/ *noun* a native or inhabitant of Zambia. ➤➤ **Zambian** *adj*.

ZANU /'zahnooh/ *abbr* Zimbabwe African National Union.

zany¹ /'zayni/ *adj* (**zanier, zaniest**) fantastically or absurdly comical. ➤➤ **zanily** *adv*, **zaniness** *noun*.

zany² *noun* (*pl* **zanies**) **1** a zany person. **2** formerly, an assistant to a clown who mimicked the clown's actions: *He's like a zany to a tumbler, that tries tricks after him to make men laugh* — Ben Jonson. [Italian *zanni* a traditional masked clown, from Italian dialect *Zanni*, nickname for *Giovanni* John]

zap¹ /zap/ *interj informal* used to indicate a sudden or instantaneous occurrence. [imitative]

zap² *verb* (**zapped, zapping**) ➤ *verb trans informal* **1** to destroy or kill (somebody or something). **2** to cause (somebody or something) to move with speed or force. ➤ *verb intrans informal* **1** to move with speed or force. **2** to switch swiftly from channel to channel on a television set by means of a remote control.

zap³ *noun informal* vitality or force; energy.

zapateado /,zahpətay'ahdoh/ *noun* (*pl* **zapateados**) a Spanish and Latin American dance marked by rhythmic stamping or tapping of the feet. [Spanish *zapateado* from *zapatear* to strike or tap with the shoe, from *zapato* shoe]

zapper *noun informal* a remote control used to operate a television set or other piece of electronic equipment.

zappy *adj* (**zappier, zappiest**) *informal* **1** energetic or dynamic: *Perhaps you could make your presentation a bit more zappy*. **2** fast-moving: *a zappy little car*.

ZAPU /'zahpooh/ *abbr* Zimbabwe African People's Union.

zareba *or* **zariba** /zə'reebə/ *noun* an improvised stockade constructed, *esp* of thorny bushes, in parts of Africa. [Arabic *zarībah* enclosure]

zarzuela /zah'zwaylə/ *noun* **1** a traditional Spanish comic opera. **2** a Spanish seafood stew. [Spanish *zarzuela*]

zax *or* **sax** /zaks/ *noun* a tool with a blade and a spike for chopping and making holes in slates. [Old English *seax* knife]

z-axis *noun* the axis in a three-dimensional rectangular coordinate system that is not the x-axis or y-axis.

zeal /zeel, ziəl/ *noun* eagerness and ardent interest in pursuit of something; keenness. [Middle English *zele* via medieval Latin from Greek *zēlos*]

zealot /'zelət/ *noun* **1** (**Zealot**) a member of a fanatical sect arising in Judea during the first cent. AD who militantly opposed the Roman domination of Palestine. **2** a zealous person; *esp* a fanatical partisan of a religious or political movement. ➤➤ **zealotry** /-tri/ *noun*. [late Latin *zelotes* from Greek *zēlōtēs*, from *zēlos* ZEAL]

zealous /'zeləs/ *adj* filled with or characterized by zeal. ➤➤ **zealously** *adv*, **zealousness** *noun*.

zebec /'zeebek/ *noun* see XEBEC.

zebra /'zebrə, 'zeebrə/ *noun* (*pl* **zebras** *or collectively* **zebra**) any of several species of black and white striped fast-running African mammals related to the horse: genus *Equus*. [Italian *zebra* from Spanish *cebra* wild ass]

zebra crossing *noun Brit* a crossing marked by a series of broad white stripes to indicate that pedestrians have the right of way across a road: compare CROSSWALK.

zebra finch *noun* a small largely grey and white Australian weaver bird: *Poephila guttata*.

zebu /'zeeb(y)ooh/ *noun* an Asiatic ox of any of several domesticated breeds with a large fleshy hump over the shoulders, used in Asia as a draught animal. [French *zébu*]

Zech. *abbr* Zechariah (book of the Bible).

zed /zed/ *noun chiefly Brit* the letter z. [Middle English via French and late Latin *zeta* from Greek *zēta* ZETA]

zedoary /'zedoh·əri/ *noun* (*pl* **zedoaries**) **1** an Asian plant related to turmeric, with an aromatic root: *Curcuma zedoaria*. **2** the dried root of this plant, used in medicine, perfumery, etc. [medieval Latin *zedoarium* from Arabic *zadwār*, from Persian]

zee /zee/ *noun NAmer* = ZED.

Zeeman effect /'zaymən, 'zeemən/ *noun* the dividing of spectral lines of a substance into two or more parts when the substance is placed in a magnetic field. [named after Pieter *Zeeman* d.1943, Dutch physicist]

zein /'zeein/ *noun* a protein in maize used *esp* in making textile fibres, printing inks, coatings, etc. [Latin *Zea*, genus of grasses including Indian corn, from Greek *zeia* wheat]

zeitgeist /'tsietgiest/ *noun* the general intellectual and moral character or cultural climate of an era. [German *Zeitgeist*, from *Zeit* time + *Geist* spirit]

Zen /zen/ *noun* a Japanese sect of Mahayana Buddhism that aims at enlightenment by direct intuition through meditation.

Editorial note
Zen is the Japanese word for 'meditation' and is a name for a school of East Asian Buddhism (known as Chan in China) that traces itself back to 'a special transmission outside the teachings', brought to China from India by the possibly mythical 6th-cent. figure Bodhidharma. Known for its antinomian style in the West, Zen monks have traditionally undergone some of the strictest training in East Asian Buddhism — Professor Donald Lopez.

[Japanese *zen* religious meditation, via Chinese (Pekingese) *chan* and Pali *jhāna* from Sanskrit *dhyāna*, from *dhyāyati* he thinks]

zenana /ze'nahnə/ *noun* in India and Iran, the women's quarters in a house. [Urdu *zanāna*, from Persian, from *zan* woman]

Zend-Avesta /,zend ə'vestə/ *noun* = AVESTA. [early Persian *Avastāk va Zand* Avesta and commentary]

Zener diode /'zenə, 'zeenə/ *noun* a silicon semiconductor device that is used to provide a stable voltage for reference or voltage regulation. [named after C M *Zener* d.1993, US physicist]

zenith /'zenith/ *noun* **1** the point of the celestial sphere that is directly opposite the nadir and vertically above the observer. **2** the highest point reached in the heavens by a celestial body. **3** the culminating point or stage: *He was at the zenith of his powers.* ➤➤ **zenithal** *adj*. [Middle English *senith* via French and medieval Latin from Old Spanish *zenit*, modification of Arabic *samt ar-ra's* path (above the head)]

zenithal projection *noun* a type of map projection in which a part of the earth's surface is projected onto a plane at a tangent to it, in such a way that all directions are shown correctly from the centre.

zeolite /'zee-əliet/ *noun* **1** any of various minerals that are hydrous aluminium silicates analogous in composition to the feldspars and can act as ion-exchangers. **2** a water softening. **2** a synthetic silicate resembling this. ➤➤ **zeolitic** /-'litik/ *adj*. [Swedish *zeolit*, from Greek *zein* to boil + *-o-* + Swedish *-lit* -lite]

Zeph. *abbr* Zephaniah (book of the Bible).

zephyr /'zefə/ *noun* **1** *literary* a gentle breeze, *esp* from the west: *Parting they seemed to tread upon air, twin roses by the zephyr blown apart* — Keats. **2** any of various lightweight fabrics or articles of clothing. [Middle English *Zephirus*, the west wind personified, via Latin from Greek *Zephyros*, *zephyros* west wind, zephyr]

zeppelin /'zep(ə)lin/ *noun* (*also* **Zeppelin**) a large rigid cigar-shaped airship of a type built in Germany in the early 20th cent. [named after Count Ferdinand von *Zeppelin* d.1917, German general and aeronaut, who developed it]

zero¹ /'ziəroh/ *noun* (*pl* **zeros** *or* **zeroes**) **1** the arithmetical symbol 0 denoting the absence of all magnitude or quantity; nought. **2** the point of departure in reckoning; *specif* the point from which the graduation of a scale, e.g. of a thermometer, begins. **3** the temperature represented by the zero mark on a thermometer. **4a** nothing; nil. **b** the lowest point or degree. **5** *informal* a completely worthless or insignificant person or thing. [French *zéro* via Italian from medieval Latin *zephirum*, from Arabic *sifr* zero, CIPHER¹]

zero² *adj* **1** having no magnitude or quantity: *There has been zero growth.* **2a** said of a cloud ceiling: limiting vision to 15m (about 50ft) or less. **b** said of horizontal visibility: limited to 50m (about 165ft) or less.

zero³ *verb trans* (**zeroes** *or* **zeros**, **zeroed**, **zeroing**) **1** to return (a counter) to zero. **2** to adjust the sights of (e.g. a gun).

zero hour *noun* the time at which an event, *esp* a military attack, is scheduled to begin. [because it is marked by the count of zero in a countdown]

zero in *verb intrans* **1** (+ on) to move near to a target; to close in on it: *Reporters zeroed in on the young princess.* **2** (+ on) to focus attention on something, e.g. a problem.

zero option *noun* a proposal for the reduction of nuclear weapons which envisages the withdrawal of all short-range nuclear missiles from a particular region: compare ZERO-ZERO OPTION.

zero-rated *adj Brit* exempt from value-added tax.

zero-sum *adj* denoting or relating to a situation, e.g. a game or relationship, in which a gain for one side entails a corresponding loss for the other side.

zeroth /'ziərohth/ *adj* in mathematics and physics, denoting the item in a series that immediately precedes the first. [ZERO¹ + -TH¹]

zero tolerance *noun* a policy of total strictness in law enforcement in which not even the most minor offences are overlooked.

zero-zero option *noun* a proposal for the reduction of nuclear weapons which envisages the withdrawal of all short-range and all intermediate-range nuclear missiles from a particular region: compare ZERO OPTION.

zest /zest/ *noun* **1** the outer peel of a citrus fruit used as flavouring. **2** piquancy or spice: *Danger added zest to the proceedings.* **3** keen enjoyment; gusto: *They envied her zest for living.* ➤➤ **zestful** *adj*, **zestfully** *adv*, **zestfulness** *noun*, **zesty** *adj*. [obsolete French *zest* (now *zeste*) orange or lemon peel]

zester *noun* a small kitchen tool for removing the peel of a citrus fruit in thin strips.

zeta /'zeetə/ *noun* the sixth letter of the Greek alphabet (Ζ, ζ), equivalent to and transliterated as roman z. [Greek *zēta*]

zeugma /'zyoohgmə/ *noun* the use of a word to modify or govern two or more words, usu in such a manner that it applies to each in a different sense, e.g. in *She opened the door and her heart to him.* ➤➤ **zeugmatic** /zyoohg'matik/ *adj*. [Greek *zeugma* joining, from *zeugnynai* to join]

zho /zoh/ *noun* (*pl* **zhos** *or collectively* **zho**) see DZO.

zibet /'zibit/ *noun* a common Asian civet that has tawny fur with black spots: *Viverra zibetha*. [Italian *zibetto* or medieval Latin *zibethum*, from Arabic *zabād* civet perfume]

zidovudine /zi'dovyoodeen/ *noun* an antiviral drug used in the treatment of Aids. [prob based on *azido-* (comb. form of AZIDE) + THYMIDINE]

ziggurat /'zigərat/ *noun* a temple tower of ancient Mesopotamia in the form of a stepped pyramid. [Akkadian *ziqqurratu* pinnacle]

zigzag¹ /'zigzag/ *noun* **1** a line, course, or pattern consisting of a series of alternate sharp turns or angles, first in one direction then in the opposite one. **2** a turn that is part of such a course or pattern. [French *zigzag* from German *Zickzack*]

zigzag² *adj* forming or going in a zigzag; consisting of zigzags: *a zigzag path.* ➤➤ **zigzag** *adv*.

zigzag³ *verb intrans* (**zigzagged**, **zigzagging**) to proceed along, or consist of, a zigzag course.

zilch /zilch/ *noun chiefly NAmer, informal* zero: *a reflective, needy relationship ... made all the more poignant by the airman's total lack of English and Jones's zilch German* — Today. ➤➤ **zilch** *adj*. [origin unknown]

zillion /'zilyən/ *noun* (*pl* **zillions** *or* **zillion**) *informal* (*also in pl*) an indefinitely large number: *There were zillions of mosquitoes.* ➤➤ **zillionth** *adj and noun*. [z + *-illion* as in MILLION]

Zimbabwean /zim'bahbwi·ən, zim'bab-/ *noun* a native or inhabitant of Zimbabwe in southern Africa. ➤➤ **Zimbabwean** *adj*.

Zimmer /'zimə/ *noun trademark* an orthopaedic walking frame. [named after its manufacturer, *Zimmer* Orthopaedic Limited, London]

Zimmer frame *noun* = ZIMMER.

zinc¹ /zingk/ *noun* **1** a bluish white metallic chemical element that occurs abundantly in minerals, and is used *esp* as a protective coating for iron and steel: symbol Zn, atomic number 30. **2** zinc-coated corrugated iron. [German *Zink*]

zinc² *verb trans* (**zinced** *or* **zincked**, **zincing** *or* **zincking**) to treat or coat (something) with zinc.

zinc blende /blend/ *noun* = SPHALERITE.

zinc ointment *noun* a soothing ointment that contains about 20% zinc oxide and is used in treating skin disorders.

zinc oxide *noun* a white solid used *esp* as a pigment and in medicinal and cosmetic preparations: formula ZnO.

zinc white *noun* zinc oxide used as a pigment.

zine /zeen/ *noun informal* **1** a usu noncommercial magazine containing specialized material appealing to a limited number of readers. **2** a fanzine. [shortening of MAGAZINE]

Zinfandel /'zinfəndel/ *noun* **1** a variety of grape used, *esp* in California, in the production of medium-quality red wine. **2** a wine produced from this grape. [origin unknown]

zing[1] /zing/ *noun informal* **1** energy or vim. **2** a shrill humming noise. [*zing* a shrill humming noise, of imitative origin]

zing[2] *verb intrans informal* to move briskly or with a humming sound.

zingy *adj* (**zingier, zingiest**) *informal* strikingly exciting or attractive: *a zingy musical; a zingy new outfit.*

zinnia /'zini·ə/ *noun* a tropical American composite plant with large colourful flower heads and long-lasting ray flowers: genus *Zinnia.* [Latin genus name, named after Johann Zinn d.1759, German botanist]

Zion or **Sion** /'zieon, 'zie·ən/ *noun* **1a** the Jewish people; Israel. **b** the Jewish homeland that is symbolic of Judaism or Jewish national aspiration. **2** in Christianity, heaven regarded as the city of God. [named after *Zion*, a citadel in Palestine which was the nucleus of Jerusalem, from Hebrew *Siyōn*]

Zionism /'zie·əniz(ə)m/ *noun* a movement initially for setting up a Jewish homeland in Palestine, now for protecting, developing, and furthering the interests of the state of Israel. ➤➤ **Zionist** *adj and noun.*

zip[1] /zip/ *noun* **1** *chiefly Brit* a fastener that joins two edges of fabric by means of two flexible spirals or rows of teeth brought together by a sliding clip. **2** *informal* energy or liveliness. **3** a light sharp hissing sound. **4** *NAmer, informal* nothing; nil; zero.

zip[2] *verb* (**zipped, zipping**) ➤ *verb trans* **1** to close or open (something) with a zip. **2** (+ into) to enclose (somebody or something) in something by means of a zip: *It took two of us to zip him into his wet suit.* **3** to cause (a zip) to open or shut. **4** in computing, to compress (a file). ➤ *verb intrans* **1** *informal* to move with speed and vigour: *Waitresses zipped by.* **2** to become open, closed, or attached by means of a zip. **3** to travel with a sharp hissing or humming sound. [imitative of the sound of a speeding object]

zip code *noun* (*also* **ZIP code**) a number that is used in the postal address of a place in the USA to assist sorting: compare POSTCODE. [acronym from *zone improvement plan*]

zip gun *noun NAmer, informal* a crude home-made gun, e.g. one operated by a rubber band or a spring.

zipper *noun chiefly NAmer* a zip.

zippy *adj* (**zippier, zippiest**) *informal* lively or energetic. ➤➤ **zippily** *adv,* **zippiness** *noun.*

zip-up *adj chiefly Brit* fastened by means of a zip.

zircon /'zuhkon/ *noun* a variously coloured mineral consisting of a zirconium silicate and used as a gem when transparent. [German *Zirkon,* modification of French *jargon,* from Italian *giargone*]

zirconium /zuh'kohni·əm/ *noun* a steel-grey metallic chemical element that occurs widely in combined form, e.g. in zircon, and is used *esp* in alloys and in heat-resisting ceramic materials: symbol Zr, atomic number 40. [scientific Latin, from ZIRCON]

zit /zit/ *noun chiefly NAmer, informal* a pimple on the skin, *esp* of the face. [origin unknown]

zither /'zidhə/ *noun* a stringed musical instrument having usu 30 to 40 strings over a shallow horizontal soundboard and played with plectrum and fingers. ➤➤ **zitherist** *noun.* [German *Zither* via Latin from Greek *kithara* CITHARA]

zizz[1] /ziz/ *verb intrans Brit, informal* **1** to nap or doze. **2** to make a whizzing sound. [imitative of the sound of a sleeper's breathing]

zizz[2] *noun Brit, informal* **1** a nap. **2** a whizzing sound.

zloty /'zloti/ *noun* (*pl* **zlotys** or **zloties** or **zloty**) the basic monetary unit of Poland, divided into 100 groszy. [Polish *zloty,* literally 'golden']

Zn *abbr* the chemical symbol for zinc.

zo /zoh/ *noun* (*pl* **zos** or *collectively* **zo**) see DZO.

zo- or **zoo-** *comb. form* forming words, denoting: animals or animal life: *zooid; zoology.* [Greek *zōi-, zōo-,* from *zōion* animal]

-zoa *comb. form* forming plural nouns, denoting: classes of animals: *protozoa.* [scientific Latin, from Greek *zōia,* pl of *zōion* animal]

zodiac /'zohdiak/ *noun* an imaginary belt in the heavens that encompasses the apparent paths of all the principal planets except Pluto, has the ECLIPTIC[1] (apparent annual path of the sun) as its central line, and is divided into twelve constellations or signs each taken for astrological purposes to extend 30° of longitude. ➤➤ **zodiacal** /zoh'die·əkl, zə-/ *adj.* [Middle English via early French and Latin *zodiacus,* from Greek *zōidiakos,* from *zōidion* carved figure, sign of the zodiac, dimin. of *zōion* living being, figure]

zodiacal light /zoh'die·əkl, zə-/ *noun* a diffuse glow seen in the west after twilight and in the east before dawn.

zoetrope /'zoh·itrohp/ *noun* a mechanical toy with pictures on the inside of a drum, which seem to move when the drum is turned. [from Greek *zōē* life + *-tropos* turning]

-zoic[1] *comb. form* forming adjectives, with the meaning: being an animal that has the mode of existence specified: *holozoic.* [Greek *zōikos* of animals, from *zōion* animal]

-zoic[2] *comb. form* forming adjectives, with the meaning: denoting or relating to a particular geological era: *Mesozoic.* [Greek *zōē* life]

zombie /'zombi/ *noun* **1** a human in the W Indies capable only of automatic movement who is held, *esp* in Haitian voodooism, to have died and been reanimated. **2** *informal* a person resembling the walking dead; *esp* a shambling automaton. [of Niger–Congo origin; related to Kongo *zambi* god]

zonal /'zohnl/ *adj* of, affecting, or being a zone: *a zonal boundary.* ➤➤ **zonally** *adv.*

zonate /'zohnayt/ *adj* marked with or arranged in zones. ➤➤ **zonated** *adj.*

zonation /zoh'naysh(ə)n/ *noun* **1** zonate structure or arrangement. **2** the distribution of living organisms in biogeographic zones.

zone[1] /zohn/ *noun* **1a** an area distinct from adjoining parts: *an erogenous zone.* **b** any of the sections into which an area is divided for a particular purpose: *a smokeless zone.* **2a** any of five great divisions of the earth's surface with respect to latitude and temperature. **b** in mathematics, a portion of the surface of a sphere included between two parallel planes. **3a** a subdivision of a biogeographic region that supports a similar fauna and flora throughout its extent. **b** a distinctive layer of rock or other earth materials. **c** an encircling anatomical structure. **4** *archaic* a girdle or belt. [Latin *zona* belt, zone, from Greek *zōnē*]

zone[2] *verb trans* **1** to arrange in, mark off, or partition (something) into zones. **2** to assign (an area) to a zone: *This neighbourhood has been zoned as residential.* **3** *archaic* to surround (something) with a zone; to encircle (it).

zone melting *noun* the purification of a crystalline material, *esp* a metal, by allowing a molten section to travel the length of a bar of the material to pick up impurities.

zone refining *noun* the production or refining of a material by zone melting.

zone therapy *noun* a form of therapy in alternative medicine that involves massaging nerve endings; *esp* reflexology. ➤➤ **zone therapist** *noun.*

zonk /zongk/ *verb trans informal* to strike (somebody or something) hard. [imitative]

zonked *adj* **1** *slang* (*often* + out) highly intoxicated by alcohol, LSD, etc. **2** *informal* completely exhausted.

zonk out *verb intrans slang* to lose consciousness or fall asleep, *esp* when intoxicated with drugs or alcohol.

zoo /zooh/ *noun* (*pl* **zoos**) a place where a collection of living animals is kept and usu exhibited to the public. [short for ZOOLOGICAL GARDEN]

zoo- *comb. form* see ZO-.

zoogeography /ˌzoh·əji'ogrəfi/ *noun* the branch of zoology dealing with the geographical distribution of animals. ➤➤ **zoogeographer** *noun,* **zoogeographic** /-jee·ə'grafik/ *adj,* **zoogeographical** /-jee·ə'grafikl/ *adj,* **zoogeographically** /-jee·ə'grafikli/ *adv.*

zooid /'zoh·oyd/ *noun* an entity that resembles but is not wholly the same as a separate individual organism; *esp* a more or less independent animal produced by fission, proliferation, or other methods that do not directly involve sex. Several animal colonies are formed of zooids. ➤➤ **zooidal** /zoh'oydl/ *adj.*

zoolatry /zoh'olətri/ *noun* animal worship. [Latin *zoolatria,* from ZOO- + *-latria* -LATRY]

zoological garden /zooh·ə'lojikl/ *noun dated* a zoo.

zoology /zooh'oləji/ *noun* (*pl* **zoologies**) **1** the branch of biology that deals with animals and animal life, usu excluding human beings. **2** the animals found in a particular area or geological era. ⋙ **zoological** /-'lojikl/ *adj*, **zoologically** /-'lojikli/ *adv*, **zoologist** *noun*. [scientific Latin *zoologia*, from ZOO- + -*logia* -LOGY]

zoom[1] /zoohm/ *verb intrans* **1a** to move quickly: *We'll just have time to zoom through the exhibition; The bikers zoomed off down the road.* **b** to move with a loud low hum or buzz. **2** said of an aircraft: to climb for a short time at a steep angle and high speed. **3** to focus a camera or microscope using a zoom lens that permits the apparent distance of the object to be varied. **4** to increase sharply: *Inflation zoomed.* ⋙ *verb trans* **1** to cause (something) to zoom. **2** to operate the zoom lens of (e.g. a camera). [imitative]

zoom[2] *noun* **1** the action of zooming. **2** a zoom lens.

zoom in *verb intrans* (*often* + on) to use a zoom lens to change from long shot to close-up: *I zoomed in to focus on the butterfly's wing; The camera zoomed in on the child's face.*

zoom lens *noun* a lens, e.g. in a camera, in which the image size can be varied continuously so that the image remains in focus at all times: *Recently, photographers have discovered, via the zoom lens, the aesthetic possibilities of putting a distant object into hard focus while the foreground is fuzzy — Krome Barratt.*

zoomorphic /zoh·ə'mawfik/ *adj* **1** resembling the form of an animal or part of an animal: *a zoomorphic orchid.* **2** said of a god: conceived of in animal form, or having the attributes of an animal. ⋙ **zoomorphism** *noun*.

zoom out *verb intrans* to use a zoom lens to change from close-up to long shot.

-zoon *comb. form* forming nouns, denoting: an animal: *spermatozoon.* [scientific Latin, from Greek *zōion* animal]

zoonosis /zoh'onəsis, zoh·ə'nohsis/ *noun* (*pl* **zoonoses** /-seez/) any disease, e.g. rabies or anthrax, communicable from lower animals to human beings. ⋙ **zoonotic** /zoh·ə'notik/ *adj*. [scientific Latin, from ZOO- + Greek *nosos* disease]

zoophilia /zoh·ə'fili·ə/ *noun* sexual attraction to animals; bestiality. [scientific Latin, from ZOO- + -PHILIA]

zoophilous /zoh'ofiləs/ *adj* **1** having a particular affection for and devotion to animals and to preserving them from human interference. **2a** adapted for pollination by animals other than insects: compare ENTOMOPHILOUS. **b** said of a blood-sucking insect: preferring lower animals to human beings as a source of food.

zoophobia /zoh·ə'fohbi·ə/ *noun* an abnormal fear or hatred of animals. [scientific Latin, from ZOO- + -PHOBIA]

zoophyte /'zoh·əfiet/ *noun* a coral, sponge, or other branching or treelike invertebrate animal superficially resembling a plant. ⋙ **zoophytic** /-'fitik/ *adj*. [Greek *zōiophyton*, from *zōi-*, *zō-* ZO- + *phyton* plant]

zooplankton /zoh·ə'plangktən, -ton/ *noun* planktonic animal life: compare PHYTOPLANKTON. ⋙ **zooplanktonic** /-'tonik/ *adj*.

zoospore /'zoh·əspaw/ *noun* a spore from an alga or fungus capable of independent movement by means of a FLAGELLUM (thread-like projection).

zoot suit /zooht/ *noun* a flamboyant suit worn by men, typically consisting of a thigh-length jacket with wide padded shoulders and trousers tapering to narrow turn-ups. [*zoot* prob arbitrary rhyme on *suit*]

zorilla /zo'rilə/ *noun* a S African animal that is a member of the weasel family and has black and white fur like a skunk: *Ictonyx striatus.* [French *zorille* from Spanish *zorilla*, *zorillo*, dimin. of *zorra*, *zorro* fox]

Zoroastrianism /zoroh'astri·əniz(ə)m/ *noun* a Persian dualistic religion founded in the sixth cent. BC by the prophet Zoroaster, promulgated in the Avesta, and characterized by worship of a supreme god Ahura Mazda who is engaged in a constant cosmic struggle against the evil spirit Ahriman. ⋙ **Zoroastrian** *adj and noun*.

Zouave /zooh'ahv, zwahv/ *noun* a member of a French infantry unit, orig composed of Algerians, noted for its brilliantly coloured uniform. [French *Zouave* from Berber *Zwāwa*, an Algerian tribe]

zouk /zoohk/ *noun* a style of popular music for guitars and synthesizers with a strong beat, originating in the Caribbean. [via French from Creole *zouk* to party]

zounds /zoohnz, zownz/ *interj archaic* used as a mild oath. [euphemism for *God's wounds*]

Zr *abbr* the chemical symbol for zirconium.

zucchetto /tsooh'ketoh, sooh-, zooh-/ *noun* (*pl* **zucchettos**) a skullcap worn by Roman Catholic ecclesiastics, coloured according to the rank of the wearer. [Italian *zucchetto* from *zucca* gourd, head, from late Latin *cucutia* gourd]

zucchini /zoo'keeni/ *noun* (*pl* **zucchinis** or collectively **zucchini**) chiefly NAmer a courgette. [Italian *zucchini*, pl of *zucchino*, dimin. of *zucca*: see ZUCCHETTO]

zugzwang /'tsoohgtsvang, 'zoohgzwang/ *noun* in chess, a situation in which a player has to make a move, although any move made would be disadvantageous. [German *Zugzwang*, from *Zug* move + *Zwang* force, compulsion]

Zulu /'zoohlooh/ *noun* (*pl* **Zulus** or collectively **Zulu**) **1** a member of a Bantu-speaking people living mainly in Kwazulu/Natal province in South Africa. **2** the Bantu language spoken by this people. ⋙ **Zulu** *adj*. [Zulu *umZulu*]

Zuni or **Zuñi** /'zoohni, 'zoohnyi/ *noun* (*pl* **Zunis** or **Zuñis** or collectively **Zuni** or **Zuñi**) **1** a member of a Native American people of NE Arizona. **2** the language spoken by this people. ⋙ **Zunian** *adj*, **Zuñian** *adj*. [American Spanish *Zuñi*]

ZW *abbr* Zimbabwe (international vehicle registration).

zwieback /'sweebak, 'zweebak/ *noun* a usu sweetened rich bread that is baked and then sliced and toasted until dry and crisp. [German *Zwieback*, literally 'twice baked', from *zwie-* twice + *backen* to bake]

Zwinglian /'zwinggli·ən, 'tsving-/ *adj* relating to the Swiss Reformation theologian Ulrich Zwingli (d.1531) or his teachings, *esp* the doctrine that Christ's presence in the Eucharist is symbolic. ⋙ **Zwinglian** *noun*.

zwitterion /'tsvitərie·ən/ *noun* an ion with both a positive and a negative charge. ⋙ **zwitterionic** /-'onik/ *adj*. [German *Zwitterion*, from *Zwitter* hybrid + ION]

zydeco /'ziedəkoh/ *noun* a style of dance music originating in southern Louisiana that combines French and Caribbean elements and blues and is usu played by a small group featuring a guitar and accordion. [Louisiana Creole *zydeco*, perhaps an alteration of French *les haricots* in the title of a popular dance tune *Les haricots sont pas salé*, literally 'the beans are not salted']

zyg- or **zygo-** *comb. form* forming words, denoting: a pair: *zygodactyl.* [scientific Latin from Greek, from *zygon* yoke]

zygodactyl /ziegə'daktil/ *adj* said of a bird: having two toes pointing forwards and two backwards. ⋙ **zygodactyl** *noun*, **zygodactylous** /-ləs/ *adj*. [ZYG- + Greek *daktylos* toe]

zygoma /zie'gohmə, zi-/ *noun* (*pl* **zygomata** /-tə/) = ZYGOMATIC ARCH. ⋙ **zygomatic** /-'matik/ *adj*. [scientific Latin from Greek *zygōmat-*, *zygōma*, from *zygoun* to join together, from *zygon* yoke]

zygomatic arch /ziegə'matik, zi-/ *noun* the arch of bone that extends along the front or side of the skull beneath the eye socket.

zygomatic bone *noun* a bone of the side of the face below the eye that in mammals forms part of the zygomatic arch and part of the eye socket; a cheekbone.

zygomorphic /ziegoh'mawfik, ziegə-, zig-/ *adj* said of a flower: symmetrical only along a vertical axis. ⋙ **zygomorphy** /'ziegohmawfi, 'zig-/ *noun*.

zygospore /'ziegohspaw, 'ziegə-, 'zig-/ *noun* a plant spore, e.g. in some algae, formed by the union of two similar sexual cells, that grows to produce the phase of the plant that produces asexual spores: compare OOSPORE.

zygote /'ziegoht, 'zigoht/ *noun* **1** a cell formed by the union of two gametes (reproductive cells; see GAMETE). **2** the developing organism produced from such a cell. ⋙ **zygotic** /zie'gotik/ *adj*. [Greek *zygōtos* yoked, from *zygoun*: see ZYGOMA]

zygotene /'ziegəteen/ *noun* the stage in meiotic cell division in which homologous chromosomes pair.

-zygous *comb. form* forming adjectives, with the meaning: having a particular zygotic constitution: *heterozygous.* [Greek *-zygos* yoked, from *zygon* yoke]

zym- or **zymo-** *comb. form* forming words, denoting: **1** fermentation: *zymurgy.* **2** enzymes: *zymogen.* [scientific Latin from Greek *zymē* leaven]

zymase /'ziemayz, 'ziemays/ *noun* an enzyme or complex of enzymes that promotes the breakdown of glucose.

zymo- *comb. form* see ZYM-.

zymogen /'ziemajen, -jan/ *noun* an inactive protein secreted by living cells and activated by a catalyst, e.g. an acid, to form an enzyme.

zymology /zie'molaji/ *noun* the science of fermentation. [scientific Latin *zymologia*, from ZYMO- + *-logia* -LOGY]

zymotic /zie'motik/ *adj* **1** relating to, causing, or caused by fermentation. **2** relating to, being, or causing an infectious or contagious disease. ➤➤ **zymotically** *adv.* [Greek *zymōtikos*, from *zymōtos* fermented, from *zymoun* to ferment, from *zymē* leaven]

zymurgy /'ziemuhji/ *noun* the branch of chemistry that deals with fermentation processes.

zzz /z/ *interj* used as a visual representation of sleep or snoring, *esp* in cartoons. [imitative of snoring]